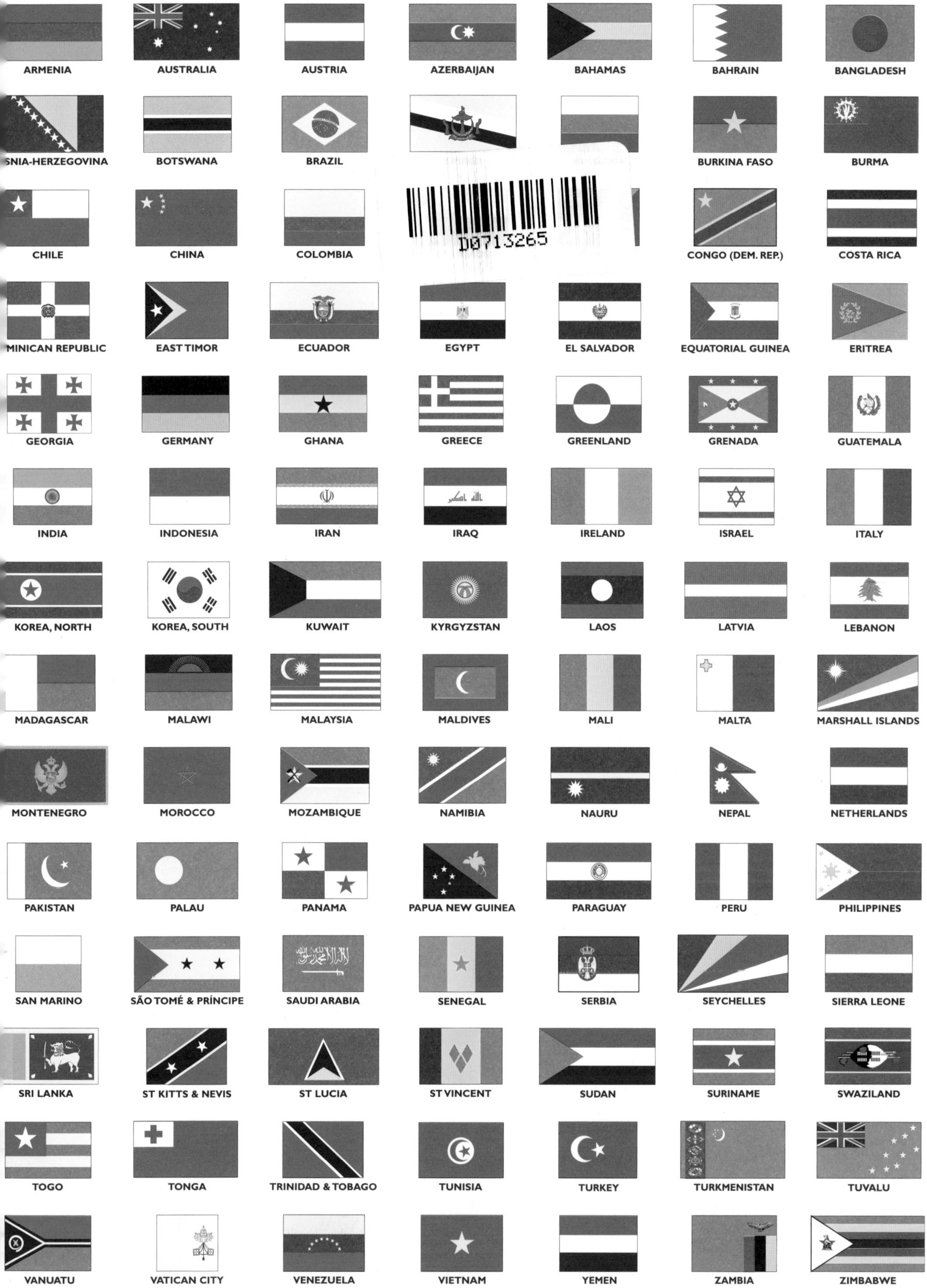

ARMENIA AUSTRALIA AUSTRIA AZERBAIJAN BAHAMAS BAHRAIN BANGLADESH

SNIA-HERZEGOVINA BOTSWANA BRAZIL BURKINA FASO BURMA

CHILE CHINA COLOMBIA CONGO (DEM. REP.) COSTA RICA

MINICAN REPUBLIC EAST TIMOR ECUADOR EGYPT EL SALVADOR EQUATORIAL GUINEA ERITREA

GEORGIA GERMANY GHANA GREECE GREENLAND GRENADA GUATEMALA

INDIA INDONESIA IRAN IRAQ IRELAND ISRAEL ITALY

KOREA, NORTH KOREA, SOUTH KUWAIT KYRGYZSTAN LAOS LATVIA LEBANON

 MADAGASCAR MALAWI MALAYSIA MALDIVES MALI MALTA MARSHALL ISLANDS

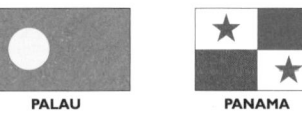      MONTENEGRO MOROCCO MOZAMBIQUE NAMIBIA NAURU NEPAL NETHERLANDS

      PAKISTAN PALAU PANAMA PAPUA NEW GUINEA PARAGUAY PERU PHILIPPINES

   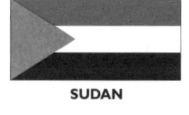   SAN MARINO SÃO TOMÉ & PRÍNCIPE SAUDI ARABIA SENEGAL SERBIA SEYCHELLES SIERRA LEONE

      SRI LANKA ST KITTS & NEVIS ST LUCIA ST VINCENT SUDAN SURINAME SWAZILAND

     TOGO TONGA TRINIDAD & TOBAGO TUNISIA TURKEY TURKMENISTAN TUVALU

VANUATU VATICAN CITY VENEZUELA VIETNAM YEMEN ZAMBIA ZIMBABWE

PHILIP'S

ENCYCLOPEDIA

Published in Great Britain in 2008
by Philip's,
a division of Octopus Publishing Group Limited
www.octopusbooks.co.uk
2–4 Heron Quays, London E14 4JP
An Hachette Livre UK Company
www.hachettelivre.co.uk

Copyright © 2008 Philip's

Cartography by Philip's

ISBN 978–0–540–09451–6

EDITOR   Lester Hawksby
ART EDITOR   Mike Brown
PRODUCTION   Aggeliki Rabaouni

The editors have made every effort to ensure
the quality, suitability and legality of material to
be found on the internet and websites referred
to in this book. However, Philip's has no control
over the content of such sites, which can change
without notice, and so cannot be held responsible
for any material that may be found there.

A catalogue record for this book is available
from the British Library

Printed in Hong Kong

Details of other Philip's titles and services
can be found on our website at
www.philips-maps.co.uk

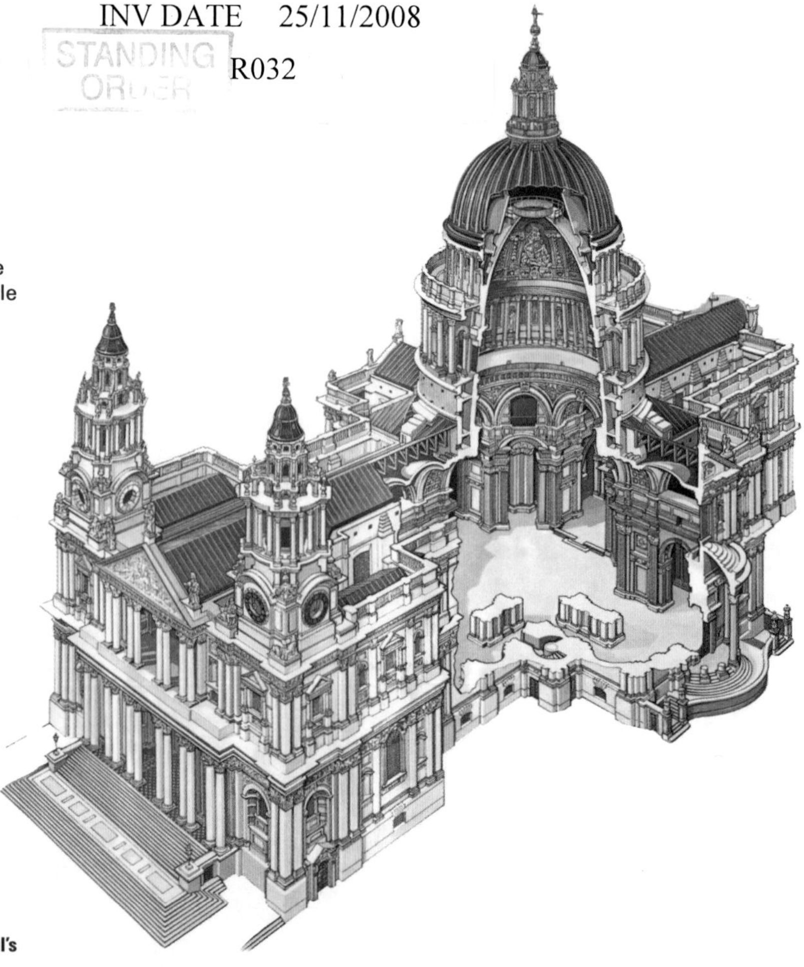

▶ St Paul's

PREFACE

Philip's Encyclopedia has been created as an authoritative and stimulating reference source for everyday family use – as a study aid for secondary school students, a first stop for general enquiries and puzzle answers, and a treasure-trove for browsers. The 13,000 clear and concise A-Z entries provide essential information on a vast variety of subjects, from world affairs to science and the arts. The wealth of colour illustrations, including maps, photographs, technical 'cutaways' and artworks, convey visual information far beyond the descriptive power of many thousands of words.

When choosing a single-volume encyclopedia, the most important consideration for the user is the criteria by which the articles have been selected. *Philip's Encyclopedia* has been created with secondary school students particularly in mind. Core subjects (science and technology, English, history, maths, geography, art and music) have been given the greatest attention. The articles, compatible with and complementary to what is taught in the classroom, are written with exceptional clarity so that even complex concepts can be understood by readers as young as 13 or 14.

Equally full in their treatment are the articles that cover leisure interests, such as sports and popular music, animals and plants, cinema and current affairs, making this encyclopedia ideal for home reference as well as an important resource at school or college.

Identification Guide
The Identification Guide is a treasure-trove of more than 1000 illustrations commissioned from leading artists in each field. The guide is invaluable for the identification of trees, mammals, birds, and butterflies. The section also includes easy-to-use astronomical charts and superb anatomical artworks of the human body.

History of the World
Organized by region and subject, the specially commissioned History of the World section found at the back of *Philip's Encyclopedia* details more than 5000 significant historical events from 15,000 BC to the present day. Fully international in its coverage, the History of the World provides a fascinating cross-section of events around the globe at any given moment in history.

Ready Reference
Supplementing the main body of the Encyclopedia, the Ready Reference section collates the kind of information best presented in tables and lists. Along with standard items such as conversion units and lists of international leaders, the section provides rapid access to many areas of interest, from the results of the Olympic Games to how a chess board is set up.

Cross-references
Philip's Encyclopedia has more than 35,000 cross-references, indicated by SMALL CAPITALS, which take the reader from one article to other articles that provide useful related information. For example, the 'pancreas' article cross-refers to small intestine, amylase, trypsin, insulin, and diabetes.

Alphabetical order
The order of articles is strictly alphabetical, except that Mc is treated as if it were spelt Mac, and abbreviations as if spelt out in full, thus St is treated as Saint. Articles that have more than one word in the heading, such 'Panama Canal', are ordered as if there were no space between the words. Foreign place names have been anglicized, with the local spelling (or its transliteration) in brackets, for example, Florence (Firenze).

Alternative spellings
For Chinese spellings the Pinyin system of transliteration is generally preferred, with cross-references to the Wade-Giles system where appropriate, for example, Peking *See* Beijing. Wade-Giles transliterations have also been retained where they remain in common use, for example, Chiang Kai-shek.

Alternative spellings and names of headwords follow in parenthesis, for example, Dalai Lama (Grand Lama).

International coverage
The importance of cultures beyond the English-speaking world is deliberately emphasized. In an age when international barriers are being steadily removed, *Philip's Encyclopedia* provides a greater number of entries on peoples, cultures, and beliefs than any other single-volume encyclopedia.

Science
In keeping with the methods taught in schools and colleges, modern scientific names have been used. For example information on 'acetaldehyde' will be found under 'ethanal'. Where less well-known modern names are used, cross-references from the old names will take the reader to the new headings.

Metric units have been used throughout with corresponding imperial measurements following in brackets.

Internet
The grey boxes at the sides of the pages give references to internet sites for selected articles on that page. When you are entering an address in a web browser, it should be prefixed by "http://" (though in most browsers this is automatic if the address begins "www").

▲ cormorant

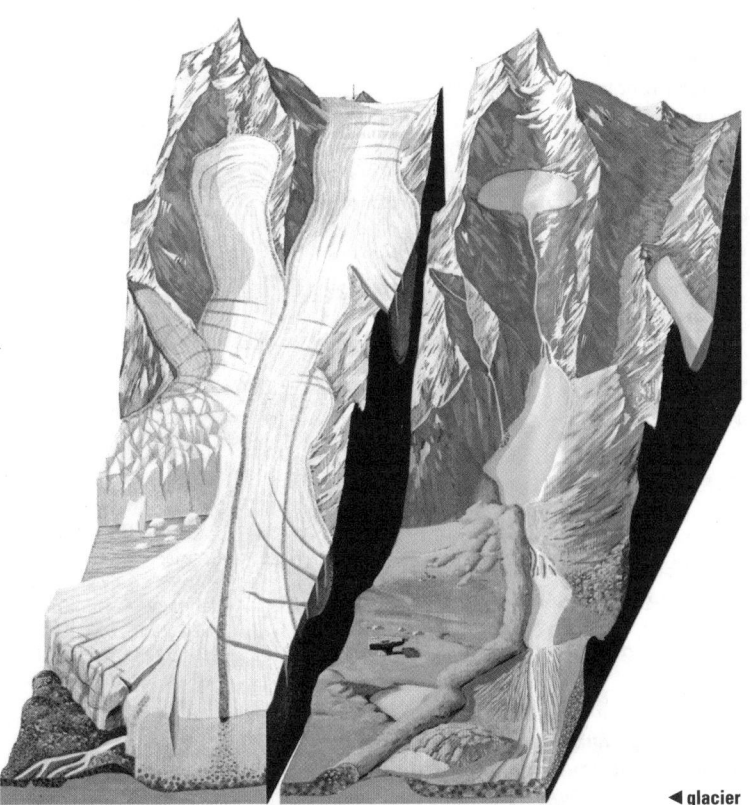

◀ glacier

CONSULTANTS

Anatomy
Prof. A.E. Walsby *University of Bristol*
Animals and Agriculture
Prof. K. Simkiss *University of Reading*
Archaeology
David Miles *Director of The Oxford Archaeological Unit*
Art
Prof. Martin Pitts *Middlesex University*
Aviation
Dr I. Hall *Victoria University of Manchester*
Biology
Prof. T. Halliday *Open University*
Botany
Prof. A.E. Walsby *University of Bristol*
Chemistry
Dr A.S. Bailey *University of Oxford*
Earth Sciences/ Atmospheric Sciences/ Geology
Prof. Michael Tooley *University of St Andrews*
Economics
Prof. A. Thirlwall
University of Kent at Canterbury
Education
Dr Charles Beresford *(Institute of Education) University College London*
History (to 1300)
Dr P.J. Heather *University College London*
History (1301 to present)
Dr Rick Halpern *University College London*
Dr Jonathan Morris *University College London*
Language
Prof. Richard Coates *University of Sussex*
Literature/ Drama
Dr Mary Peace
Roehampton Institute, London
Mathematics
Dr Jan Brandts *University of Bristol*
Medicine
Prof. S.L. Lightman *University of Bristol*
Motion Pictures/ Media and Publishing/ Television and Radio/ Communications
Uma Dinsmore *Goldsmiths College, London*
Music
Dr Derrick Puffett *University of Cambridge*
Mythology
Dr Allan Griffiths *University College London*
Philosophy/ Computing
Prof. Ron Chrisley *University of Sussex*
Physics
Prof. John Gribbin *University of Sussex*
Politics
Prof. Brian Barry *London School of Economics and Political Science*
Psychology/ Psychiatry
Prof. Margaret Boden *University of Sussex*
Religion
Prof. Colin Gunton *Kings College London*
Sport
Bob Peach *The Sports Council*
Technology and Industrial Processes/ Engineering/ Material Science
Dr P.L. Domone *University College London*

EDITORIAL CREDITS

Jane Alden
Peter Astley
Ralph Aytoun
Jill Bailey
John Bailie
Richard Bird
Richard Brzezinski
Frances Button
Ian Chilvers
Roy Carr
John O.E. Clark
Sean Connolly
Peter Cowie
Mike Darton
Stephanie Driver
Harry Drost
Roger Few
William Gould
Neil Grant
Miles Gregory
Clare Haworth-Maden
Bill Hemsley
Tony Holmes
William Houston
Christian Humphries
Elisabeth Ingles
Caroline Juler
Louise B. Lang
Jacqueline Lewis
Steven Luck
Keith Lye
Angela Mackworth-Young
Judith Millidge
Eddie Mizzi
Joanna Potts
Paulette Pratt
Jenny Roberts
A.T.H. Rowland-Entwistle
Tom Ruppel
Jennifer Story
Clint Twist
Cecily Webster
Neil Wenborn
Keith Wicks
Richard Widdows
John D. Wright
Richard Wright
Iain Zaczek
Curriculum consultants
Duncan Hawley
David J. McHugh
Silvia Newton
Brian Speed
Jane Wheatley

PICTURE CREDITS

Bridgeman Art Library /Belvoir Castle, Leicestershire 315, /British Museum, London 513 top right, /Christie's, London 699 bottom, /Crown Estate, Institute of Directors, London 216 bottom right, /Fitzwilliam Museum, University of Cambridge 643, 715 top, /Giraudon /Louvre, Paris 156 top, /Glasgow Art Gallery and Museum 201, /Guildhall Art Gallery, Corporation of London 472 bottom right, /Guildhall Library, Corporation of London 468, /Historisches Museum der Stadt, Vienna 75, /Index /Prado, Madrid 96 bottom right, 219 /Index /Private Collection / © Demart Pro Arte BV/DACS 1997, 196 bottom right, /Kunsthistorisches Museum,Vienna 125, /Art Institute of Chicago, USA 21, /Philip Mould, Historical Portraits Ltd, London 231 bottom right, 651 top right, /Musee d'Orsay, Paris 565 right, /Musee de la Tapisserie, Bayeux, with special authorisation of the city of Bayeux /Giraudon 72, /Nasjonalgalleriet, Oslo/The Munch Museum/The Munch-Ellingsen Group/DACS 1997 463 bottom, /National Museum of Wales, Cardiff 142, /National Palace, Mexico City 571 bottom right, /Novosti 393 top right, /Palazzo Medici-Riccardi, Florence 437, /Private Collection/ARS, NY and DACS, London 1997 2, 306, 452 top left, /Rafael Valls Gallery, London 531 right, /Schloss Immendorf, Austria 375, /Solomon R Guggenheim Museum, New York/ADAGP, Paris and DACS, London 1997 367, /Tate Gallery, London 577, /The Trustees of the Weston Park Foundation 321, /Vatican Museums and Galleries, Rome 443, /Wilhelm Lehmbruck Museum, Duisburg 484 bottom left.
Hulton Getty Picture Collection 79, 89, 92, 130, 144,145 bottom right, 158, 180 bottom right, 193 top right, 203 top left, 211 top right, 220 top left, 227 top right, 234, 238, 249 top right, 269, 275, 293 top right, 301 top right, 314 top left, 328 top left, 334 bottom left, 364, 369, 373 bottom right, 382, 383, 400 left of centre, 431 top right, 439 top right, 440 top left, 457 bottom right, 480 top left, 495 bottom right, 502 top left, 509 top right, 514, 542 left, 548 top left, 550 top left, 552 top left, 582, 587 bottom right, 591, 598 top left, 608, 641 bottom, 673 top right, 724, 725, 730, 735 top, 744.
Picture Bank 4, 16 bottom, 26 bottom, 256 bottom left, 460, 479 bottom right, 503 bottom left, 552 bottom left, 638 top left, 641 top, 655 top right, 675.
Rex Features 24, 26 top right, 73, 80, 154, 168 right of centre, 181, 184 top left, 203 bottom right, 207, 247, 255 bottom right, 263 bottom, 273 right of centre, 277, 284 top left, 291, 307, 311 bottom, 311 top right, 312 top left, 314 bottom, 319, 320 bottom, 355 right of centre, 360, 370, 385 top left, 390, 395 bottom, 419 bottom right, 420 left of centre, 433, 456, 522 top right, 527 left, 562 top right, 569 bottom right, 573 top right, 579 bottom right, 601, 605, 609 top right, 613 bottom right, 634 top left, 638 bottom, 648 bottom left, 659 bottom right, 663 bottom right, 700, 714 bottom, 735 bottom, 892, /Action Press 519 top right, /Stephen Barker 18, /Michel Boudin 112 top, /Mark Brewer 305 top right, /Peter Brooker 261 bottom left, /Paul Brown 322 top, /Julian Calder 666, /David Cole 200, /Frederick de Klerk 425 right of centre, /Delahaye 138, /Demulder 34, /Doc Pele 392 top left, /Farnood 557 bottom right, /Fotex /Zone 5 199 top right, /Richard Gardner 217, /Gilson 489, /Grande 276 top left, /Chris Harris 685 bottom right, /David Hartley 164 top, /Percy Hatchman 719, /Peter Heimsath 39 bottom right, /Nils Jorgensen 88 bottom, /Robert Judges 895 /JSU/Sutton-Hibert 543, /Charles Knight 621 bottom right, /Dave Lewis 297, 479 centre right, /Miladinovic 310 left of centre, /NASA 327, /Rangefinders 350, /Larry Reider 135 bottom right, /Lehtikuva Oy 629/Tim Rooke 292 above centre, 588, /Setboun 330 top left, /Sichov 374 bottom, 623, /Sipa Press 57 top right, 143, 157 top, 170, 177 bottom right, 203 top right, 222 top left, 259 bottom, 330 bottom left, 344, 409, 469 bottom right, 491, 570 bottom left, 890, 891, 893, /Stills 406, /SUU/Joffet 103 top, /Today 386, /Trippett 556, 561 bottom right, /Scott Wachter 362, /Gerry Whitmont 245, /Geoff Wilkinson 596, /Richard Young 417, 696 bottom.
Science Photo Library 732, /CERN, P. Loiex 110.
Corbis 547 top right
US Federal Government 185, www.whitehouse.gov

CONTENTS

Northern polar chart

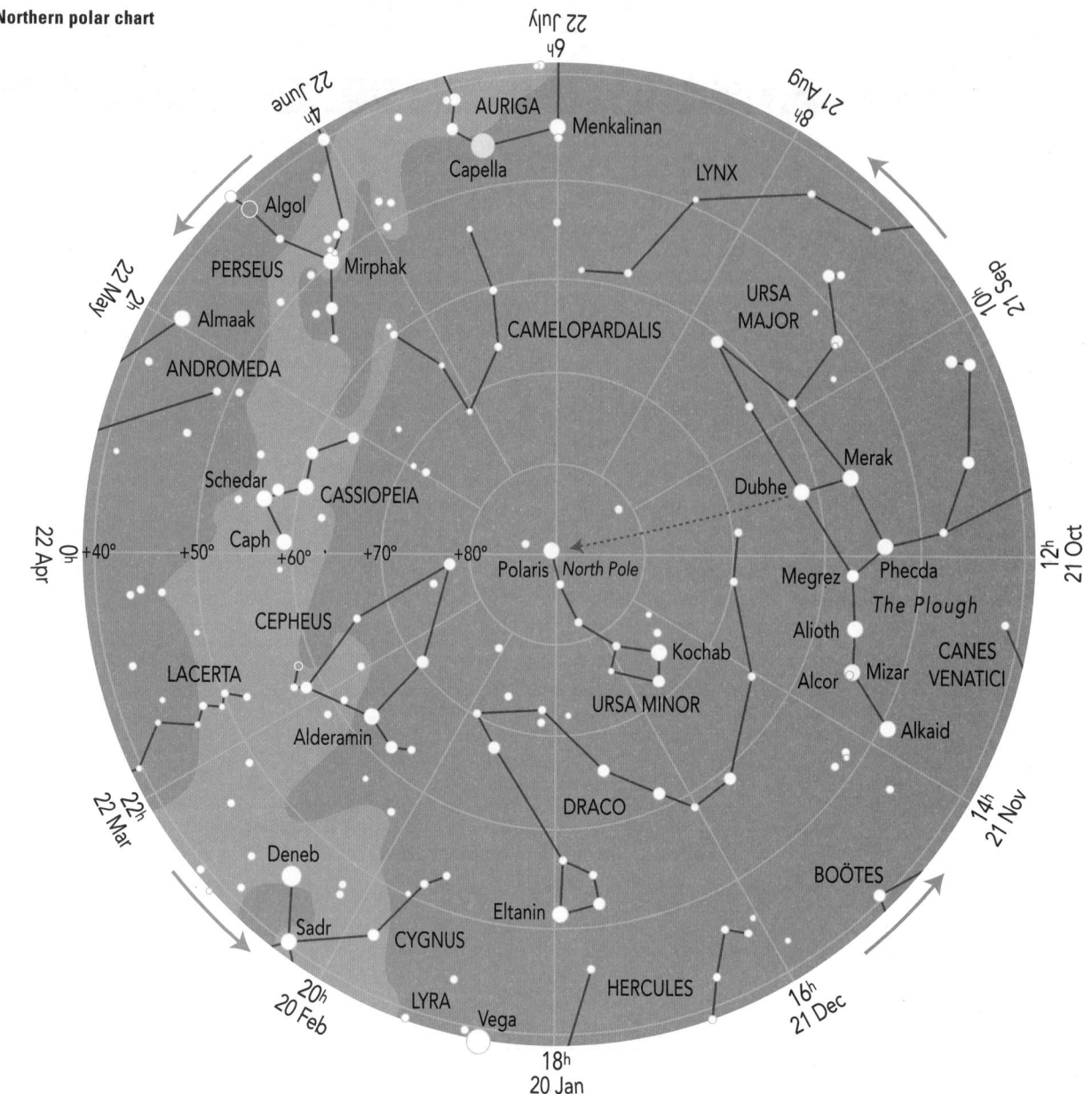

POLAR STAR CHARTS

For the purposes of star charts, the easiest way to conceive of the night sky is as a vast hollow sphere with the Earth at its centre. From wherever we stand on the surface of the Earth, one half of this sphere is visible at any one time, while the other half is invisible. This imaginary sphere is known as the celestial sphere. All the stars, though they are at different distances from the Earth, may then be depicted as if they occupied fixed positions on this sphere. We imagine that the celestial sphere, with the stars fixed upon it, rotates once a day around the Earth, though we know that this is not so. The sphere must then be drawn on a flat surface using a 'projection' that attempts to minimize distortion, in much the same way as when drawing maps of the Earth.

The star charts on this page and on pages 7, 8 and 9 cover the whole of the sky, with some

overlap between them. The polar star charts show the regions around the north and south celestial poles; the equatorial star charts show a broad strip of the sky either side of the celestial equator. They fit together rather like the parts of a food can. The polar charts are the top and bottom of the can, and the equatorial charts join together to form the cylindrical side.

All 88 constellations are shown. Constellation names appear in capital letters, while star names are in lower case with an initial capital. Prominent groupings of stars, such as The Plough, are in italic. The Milky Way is shown in a lighter blue than the rest of the sky. The brightest stars are shown in their true colours.

In the **polar charts**, the dates round the outside indicate when the lines that make up the radial spokes of the coordinate grid are aligned

with the north point of the horizon at 10pm. For instance, on April 22 the 0h line is to the north; Cassiopeia is quite low in the north, while on the other side of Polaris the stars of The Plough are high in the sky.

The lines marked with hours and dates are lines of 'right ascension', the equivalent of longitude, but measured in hours. The arrows indicate the apparent motion of the stars. Two hours of right ascension correspond to two hours of time.

Polaris, marking the north celestial pole, is easily located from the stars at the end of The Plough, as indicated. The south celestial pole is not marked by a prominent star. It can be located using the stars of the constellation Crux (Southern Cross), which point towards it. Also, the pole lies about halfway between the bright stars Achernar, in Eridanus, and Hadar, in Centaurus.

THE EIGHTY-EIGHT CONSTELLATIONS

Andromeda
Antlia (Air Pump)
Apus (Bird of Paradise)
Aquarius (Water Carrier)
Aquila (Eagle)
Ara (Altar)
Aries (Ram)
Auriga (Charioteer)
Boötes (Herdsman)
Caelum (Chisel)
Camelopardalis (Camel)
Cancer (Crab)
Canes Venatici (Hunting Dogs)
Canis Major (Great Dog)
Canis Minor (Little dog)
Capricornus (Goat)
Carina (Keel)
Cassiopeia

Centaurus (Centaur)
Cepheus
Cetus (Whale)
Chamaeleon (Chameleon)
Circinus (Compasses)
Columba (Dove)
Coma Berenices (Berenice's Hair)
Corona Australis (Southern Crown)
Corona Borealis (Northern Crown)
Corvus (Crow)
Crater (Cup)
Crux (Southern Cross)
Cygnus (Swan)
Delphinus (Dolphin)
Dorado (Swordfish)
Draco (Dragon)
Equuleus (Little Horse)
Eridanus

Fornax (Furnace)
Gemini (Twins)
Grus (Crane)
Hercules
Horologium (Clock)
Hydra (Water Snake)
Hydrus (Sea Serpent)
Indus (Indian)
Lacerta (Lizard)
Leo (Lion)
Leo Minor (Little Lion)
Lepus (Hare)
Libra (Scales)
Lupus (Wolf)
Lynx
Lyra (Lyre)
Mensa (Table)
Microscopium (Microscope)

Monoceros (Unicorn)
Musca (Fly)
Norma (Level)
Octans (Octant)
Ophiuchus (Serpent Bearer)
Orion
Pavo (Peacock)
Pegasus (Winged Horse)
Perseus
Phoenix
Pictor (Easel)
Pisces (Fishes)
Piscis Austrinus (Southern Fish)
Puppis (Ship's Stern)
Pyxis (Mariner's Compass)
Reticulum (Net)
Sagitta (Arrow)
Sagittarius (Archer)

Scorpius (Scorpion)
Sculptor
Scutum (Shield)
Serpens (Serpent)
Sextans (Sextant)
Taurus (Bull)
Telescopium (Telescope)
Triangulum (Traingle)
Triangulum Australae
  (Southern Triangle)
Tucana (Toucan)
Ursa Major (Great Bear)
Ursa Minor (Little Bear)
Vela (Sails)
Virgo (Virgin)
Volans (Flying Fish)
Vulpecula (Fox)

Southern polar chart

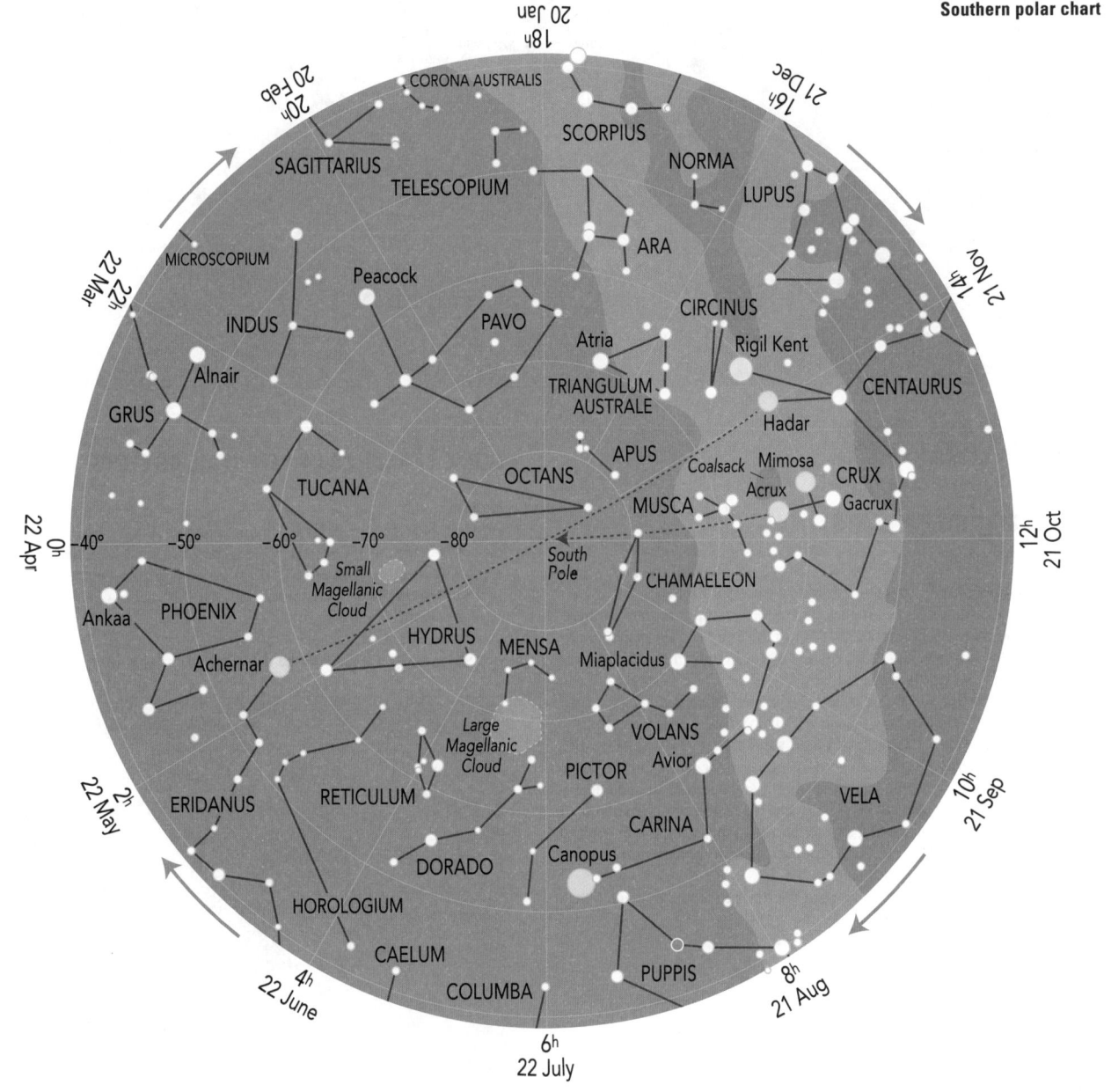

7

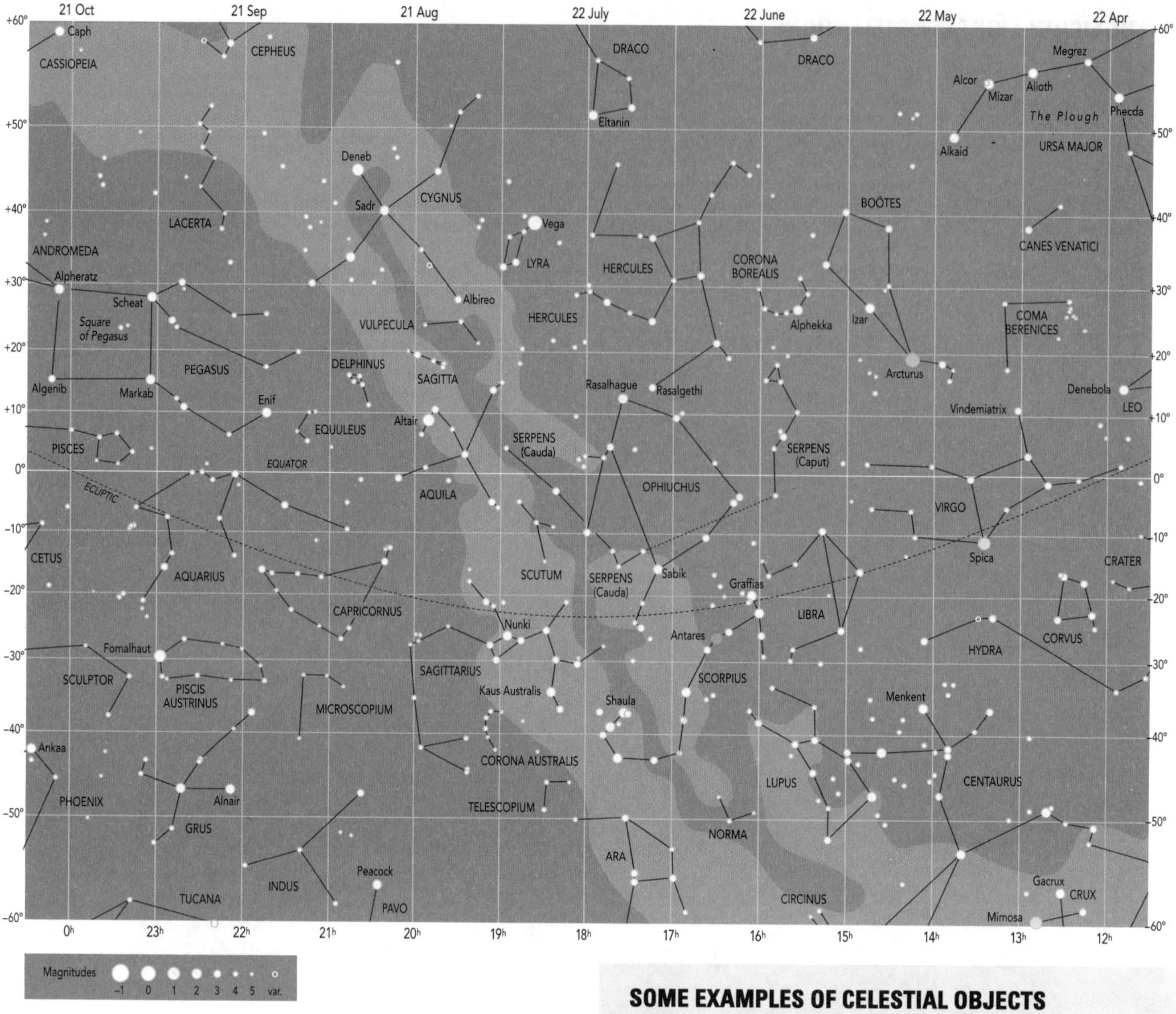

The star chart with dates along the top:

21 Oct · 21 Sep · 21 Aug · 22 July · 22 June · 22 May · 22 Apr

Right ascension along bottom: 0h, 23h, 22h, 21h, 20h, 19h, 18h, 17h, 16h, 15h, 14h, 13h, 12h

Declination scale: +60°, +50°, +40°, +30°, +20°, +10°, 0°, −10°, −20°, −30°, −40°, −50°, −60°

Constellations and stars labelled: Caph, CASSIOPEIA, CEPHEUS, DRACO, DRACO, Megrez, Alcor, Mizar, Alioth, The Plough, Phecda, Eltanin, Deneb, CYGNUS, Vega, Alkaid, URSA MAJOR, Sadr, LACERTA, LYRA, HERCULES, BOÖTES, CANES VENATICI, ANDROMEDA, Alpheratz, Albireo, HERCULES, CORONA BOREALIS, COMA BERENICES, Scheat, VULPECULA, Alphekka, Izar, Square of Pegasus, DELPHINUS, SAGITTA, Arcturus, Denebola, PEGASUS, Algenib, Markab, Enif, Rasalhague, Rasalgethi, Vindemiatrix, LEO, EQUULEUS, Altair, SERPENS (Cauda), SERPENS (Caput), PISCES, EQUATOR, AQUILA, OPHIUCHUS, VIRGO, ECLIPTIC, CETUS, SCUTUM, SERPENS (Cauda), Sabik, Graffias, Spica, CRATER, AQUARIUS, Nunki, Antares, LIBRA, CORVUS, CAPRICORNUS, SCORPIUS, HYDRA, Fomalhaut, SAGITTARIUS, Kaus Australis, Shaula, Menkent, SCULPTOR, PISCIS AUSTRINUS, MICROSCOPIUM, CORONA AUSTRALIS, LUPUS, CENTAURUS, Ankaa, Alnair, TELESCOPIUM, NORMA, PHOENIX, GRUS, ARA, Peacock, CIRCINUS, Gacrux, CRUX, INDUS, TUCANA, PAVO, Mimosa

Magnitudes: −1, 0, 1, 2, 3, 4, 5, var.

EQUATORIAL STAR CHARTS

The equatorial star charts show the stars near to the celestial equator, which is the projection of the Earth's equator onto the celestial sphere.

The dates at which stars are highest in the sky at 10pm in the Northern Hemisphere and lowest in the sky at 10pm in the Southern Hemisphere are given at the top of the charts. So, for example, in July the constellation Draco will be at its highest in the northern sky.

The dashed red line shows the ecliptic – the Sun's path against the background stars. The Moon and the planets are always found near the ecliptic.

Unavoidably, the projections used on all star charts introduce some distortions. This is more of a problem with the equatorial charts than the polar charts. To depict the constellations at the north and south of the equatorial charts in their correct shapes, the scale has been stretched at the top and bottom. This has the effect of making constellations on these parts of the charts look rather larger in relation to the constellations near the celestial equator when compared with how they appear in the sky.

For further information about these star charts, see the text on page 6 that accompanies the polar star charts.

SOME EXAMPLES OF CELESTIAL OBJECTS

Nebula

As well as stars, our galaxy contains nebulae, huge clouds of gas and dust – the raw materials from which stars are made. In some nebulae stars are actually in the process of being born. This is happening in the **Orion Nebula**, in the constellation Orion. The nebula is in the middle of the 'sword' hanging from Orion's 'belt' and is 1500 light years away. The light of the new stars forming within it illuminates the nebula, making it visible to the naked eye as a faint misty patch.

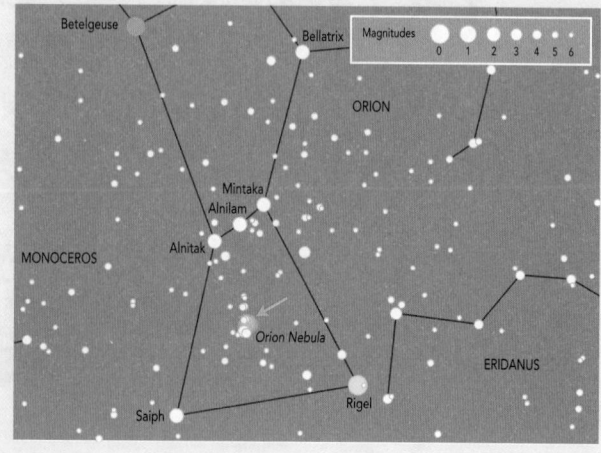

Betelgeuse, Bellatrix, Magnitudes 0 1 2 3 4 5 6, ORION, Mintaka, Alnilam, Alnitak, MONOCEROS, Orion Nebula, ERIDANUS, Saiph, Rigel

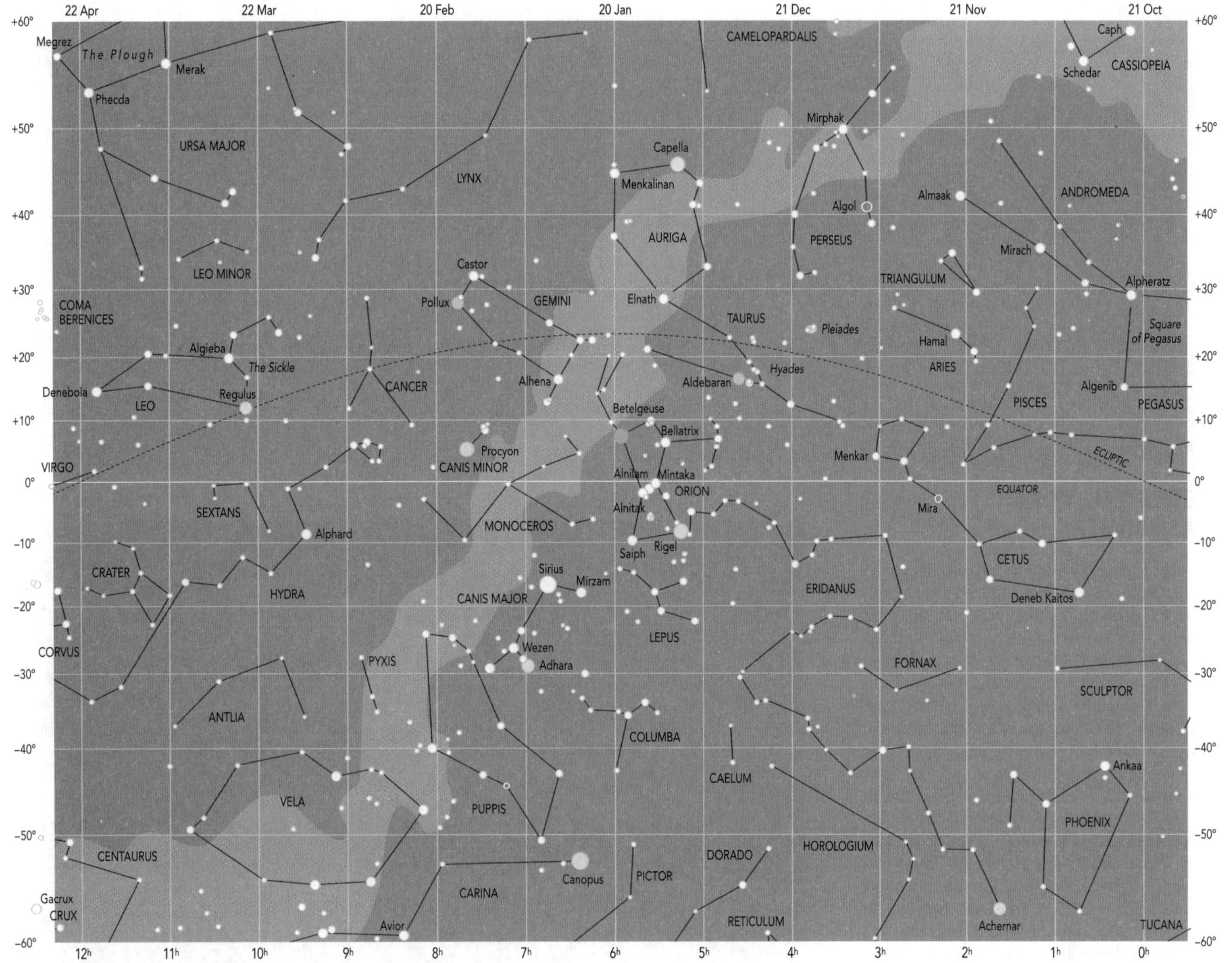

Galaxy

Our own galaxy, which we see on a clear night as the Milky Way, is just one of countless millions in the universe. Only a handful are visible to the naked eye, the nearest being two dwarf galaxies known as the Magellanic Clouds. The Large Magellanic Cloud lies in the constellations Dorada and Mensa, and the Small Magellanic Cloud lies in the constellation Tucana. The only other large galaxy visible to the naked eye is the **Andromeda Galaxy,** a spiral galaxy 2.4 million light years away. It can be seen in the constellation Andromeda as an elongated blur on a clear night. It is the most distant object visible to the naked eye.

Star cluster

Some stars reside not alone or in pairs, but in clusters, groups with anything from a dozen to a million members. Most striking to the naked eye are two in the constellation Taurus. The **Pleiades** are also known as the Seven Sisters, seven being the number many people can see. In fact, there are more than a thousand stars in the cluster. The Pleiades looks something like a miniature version of The Plough. To the east of the Pleiades, but still in Taurus, are the **Hyades,** a much less compact group of stars. The brightest members form a V-shape near the bright orange star Aldebaran (which is not a member of the cluster).

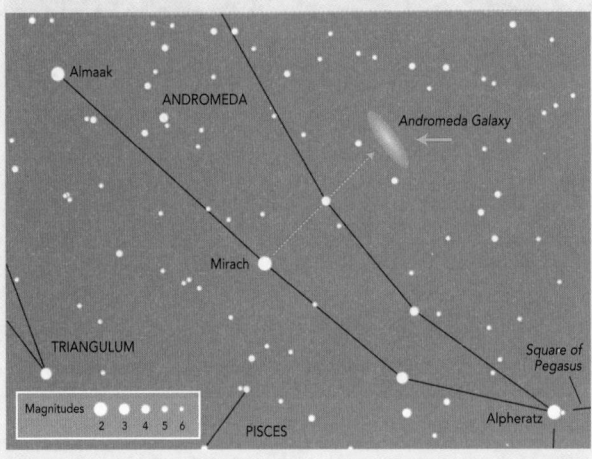

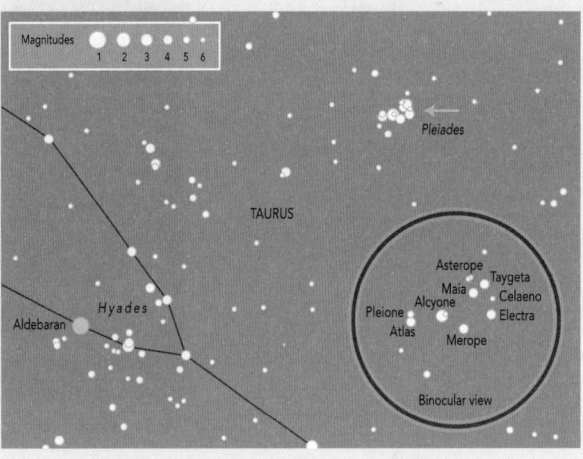

Orion

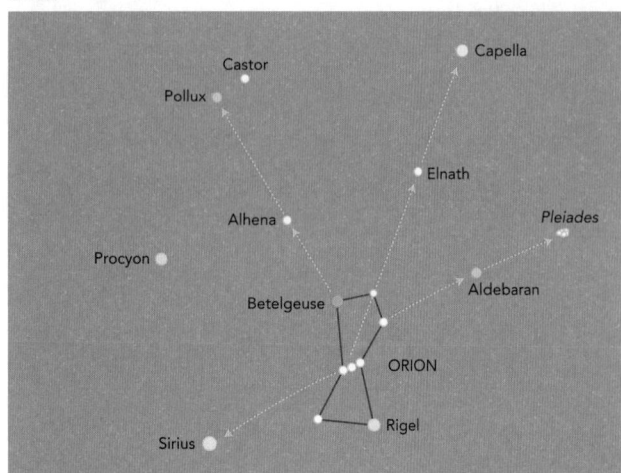

Cygnus

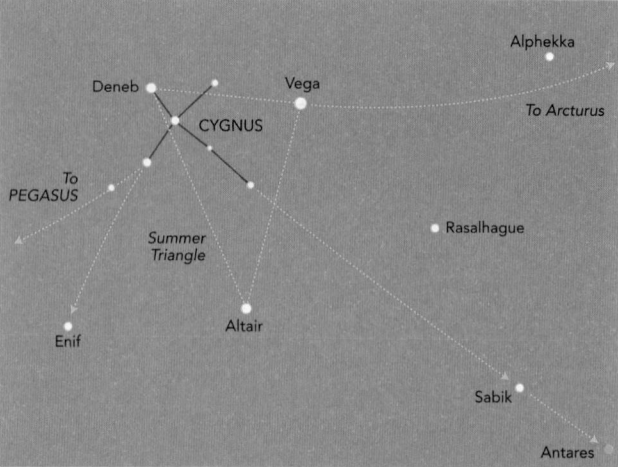

CONSTELLATIONS AS POINTERS

Some of the most prominent constellations are excellent celestial signposts and are invaluable for learning to find your way about the night sky. Four particularly useful examples are given here. (Note that the examples are not drawn to the same scale as each other.)

It is helpful to study how the charts link together when the same star can be found from more than one constellation. For example, the most famous instance of stars used as pointers is the two stars of The Plough (Leo) that point to Polaris, the marker for the north celestial pole. However, Polaris can also be found using Andromeda and Cassiopeia. The Plough also points to Capella, Arcturus, and Castor and Pollux, which can be found, in turn, from Andromeda, Cygnus and Orion.

As you become familiar with the night sky, you will find many more useful examples of celestial pointers.

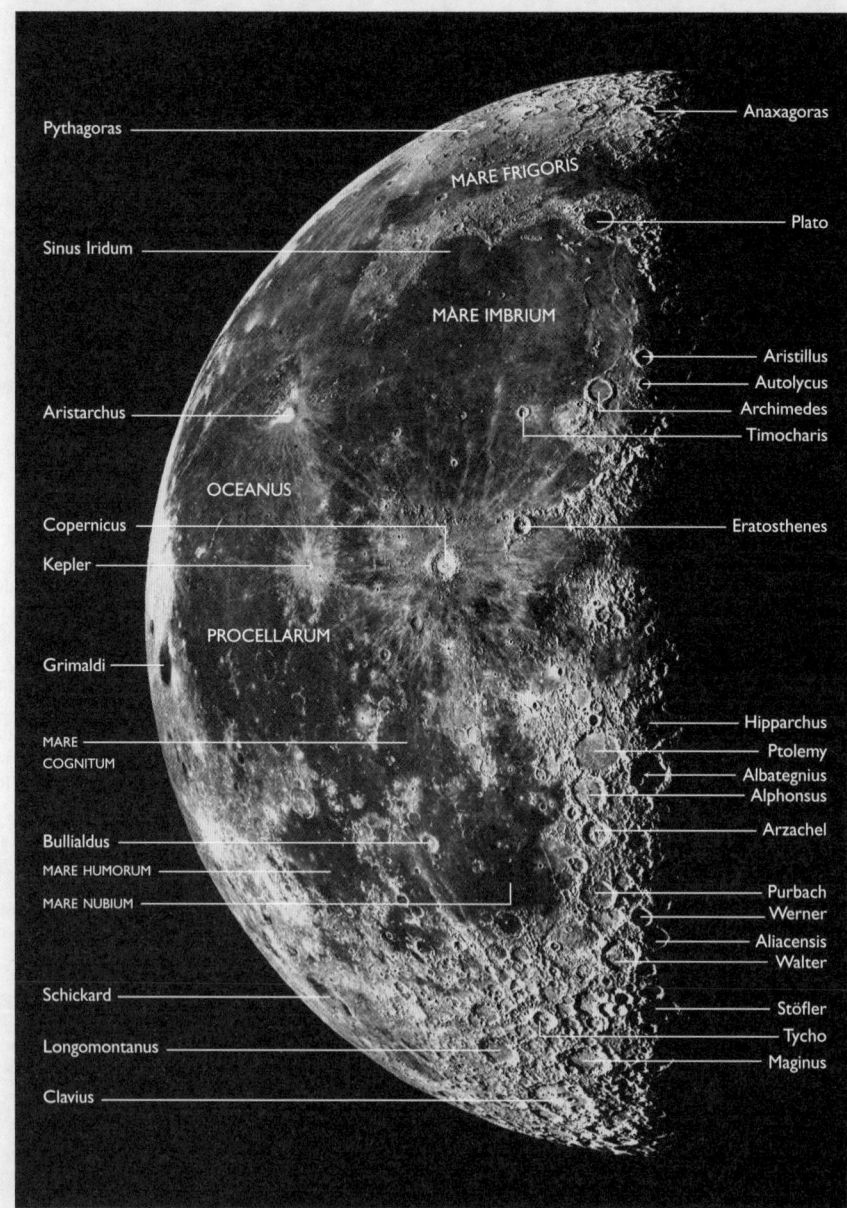

Moon at last quarter, one week after full Moon

Leo

Andromeda and Cassiopeia

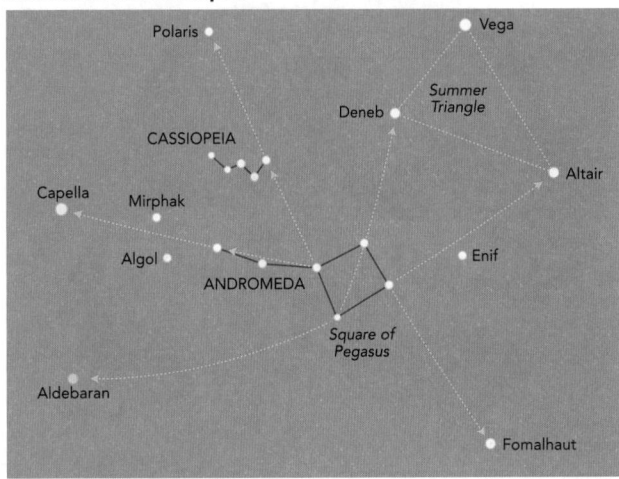

THE MOON

A pair of photographs showing the Moon at first and last quarter. Some of the largest features are labelled, and many of these can be identified with the naked eye. Binoculars or a small telescope will show many more.

The word *mare* means 'sea' in Latin. Astronomers once thought that the Moon was Earth-like, but these dark areas are in fact solidified lava which flooded into giant impact craters, formed when the Moon was young. The *maria* have rather fanciful names: Oceanus Procellarum means 'Ocean of Storms', while Mare Serenitatis is the 'Sea of Serenity'. The craters are named mostly after famous astronomers of the past.

The visibility of lunar features depends on the phase of the Moon. At full Moon, for example, the surface appears very bright and some features are hard to see. When the Moon is less bright and the angle of light from the Sun causes features that face the Earth to cast shadows (as in these photographs), many more features can be seen.

Moon at first quarter, one week before full Moon

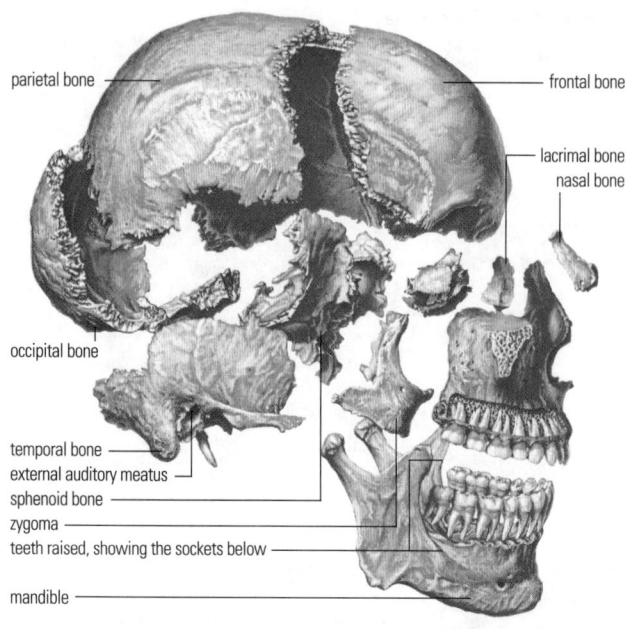

parietal bone

frontal bone

lacrimal bone
nasal bone

occipital bone

temporal bone
external auditory meatus
sphenoid bone
zygoma
teeth raised, showing the sockets below

mandible

◀ **skull** Composed of the facial and cranial bones, the skull supports and protects the brain as well as the chief sensory organs: eyes, ears, nose, and mouth.

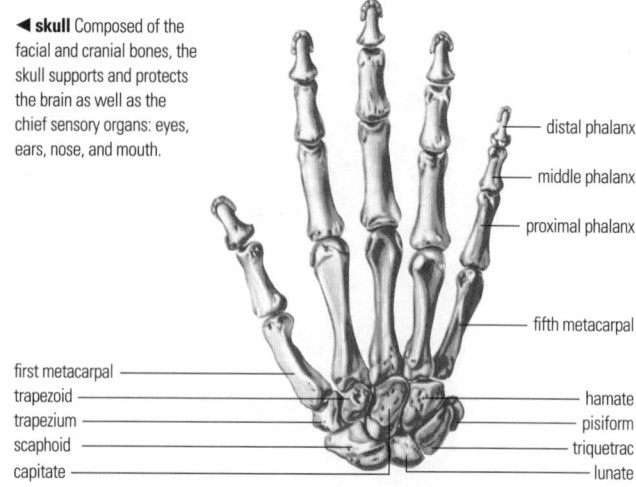

distal phalanx

middle phalanx

proximal phalanx

fifth metacarpal

first metacarpal
trapezoid
trapezium
scaphoid
capitate

hamate
pisiform
triquetrac
lunate

▲ **hand** The hand consists of 27 bones interconnected by ligaments. A wrist, palm, four fingers, and an opposable thumb enable precise movement and grip.

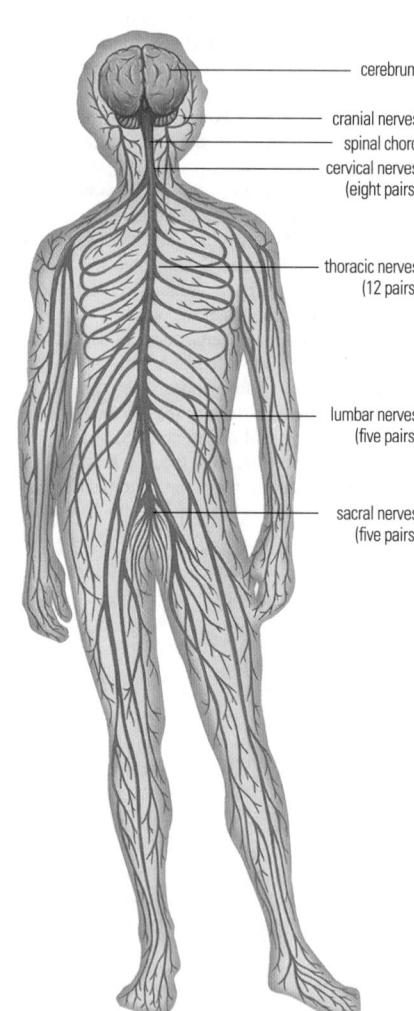

cerebrum

cranial nerves
spinal chord
cervical nerves
(eight pairs)

thoracic nerves
(12 pairs)

lumbar nerves
(five pairs)

sacral nerves
(five pairs)

▼ **spine** The spinal column consists of 24 vertebrae. This protects the spinal cord, which occupies the vertebral canal, and connects the brain to nerves throughout the body.

spinal chord

sensory route
spinal nerve
vertebra

motor root

▲ **nervous system**
Coordinates all actions and responses through

interconnected neurons that receive and transmit impulses from the brain.

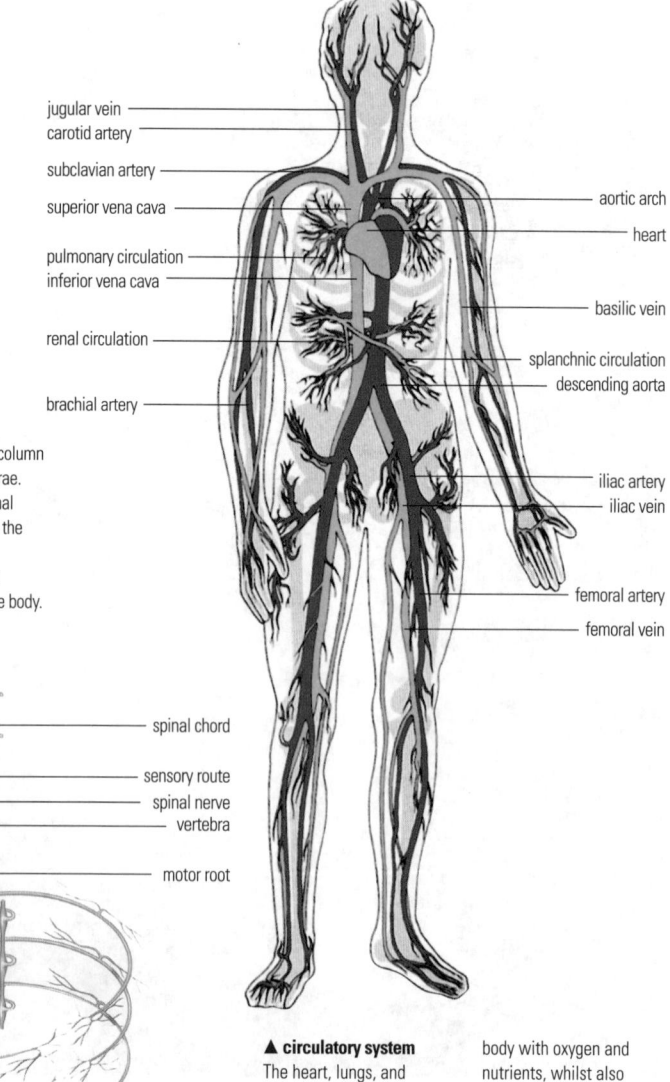

jugular vein
carotid artery

subclavian artery

superior vena cava

pulmonary circulation
inferior vena cava

renal circulation

brachial artery

aortic arch

heart

basilic vein

splanchnic circulation
descending aorta

iliac artery
iliac vein

femoral artery

femoral vein

▲ **circulatory system**
The heart, lungs, and blood vessels work together to provide the

body with oxygen and nutrients, whilst also removing wastes and carbon dioxide from cells.

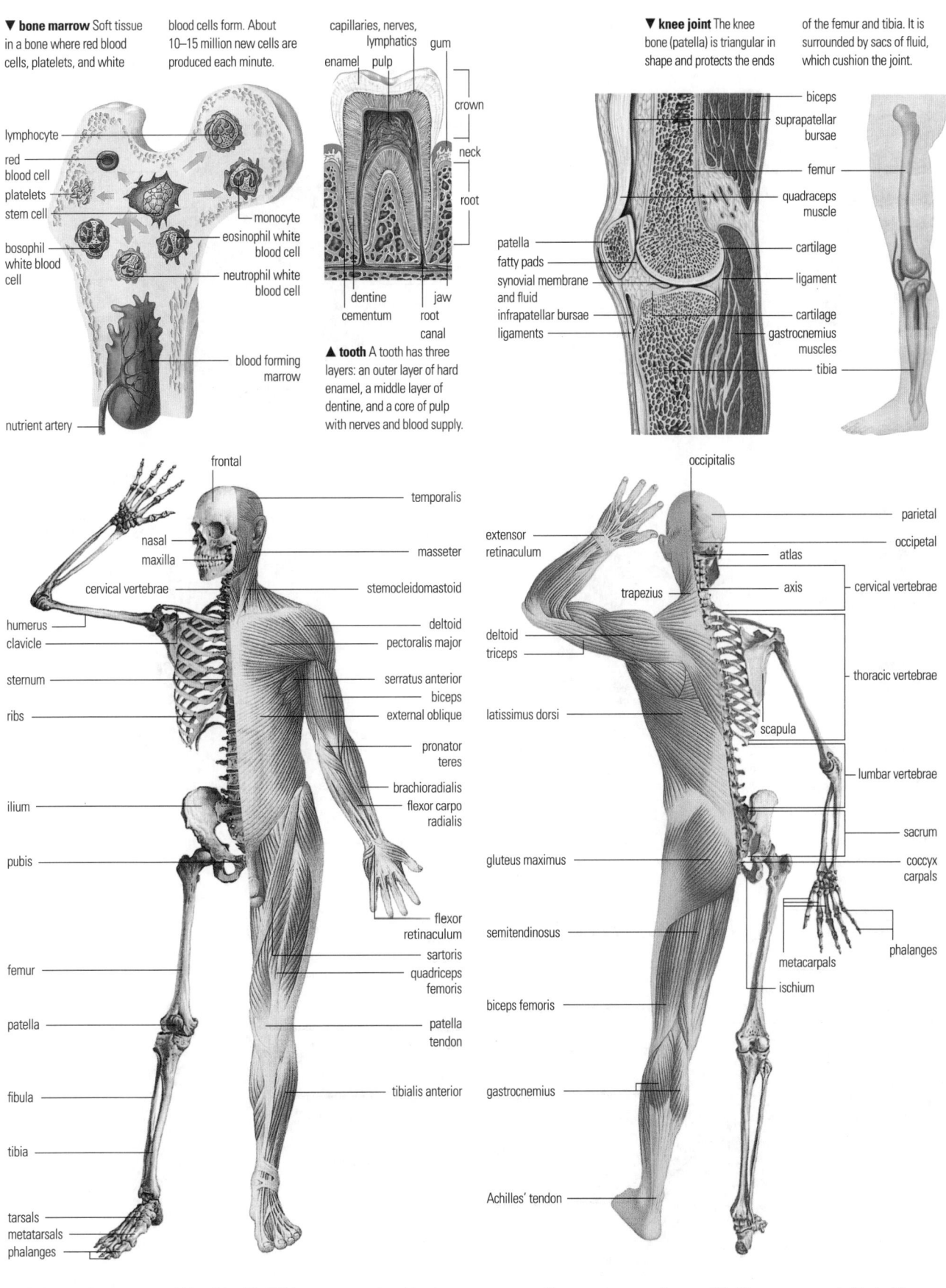

▼ **bone marrow** Soft tissue in a bone where red blood cells, platelets, and white blood cells form. About 10–15 million new cells are produced each minute.

lymphocyte
red blood cell
platelets
stem cell
bosophil white blood cell
monocyte
eosinophil white blood cell
neutrophil white blood cell
blood forming marrow
nutrient artery

capillaries, nerves, lymphatics
enamel
pulp
gum
crown
neck
root
dentine
cementum
jaw
root canal

▲ **tooth** A tooth has three layers: an outer layer of hard enamel, a middle layer of dentine, and a core of pulp with nerves and blood supply.

▼ **knee joint** The knee bone (patella) is triangular in shape and protects the ends of the femur and tibia. It is surrounded by sacs of fluid, which cushion the joint.

biceps
suprapatellar bursae
femur
quadraceps muscle
patella
fatty pads
synovial membrane and fluid
infrapatellar bursae
ligaments
cartilage
ligament
cartilage
gastrocnemius muscles
tibia

frontal
temporalis
nasal
maxilla
masseter
cervical vertebrae
sternocleidomastoid
humerus
clavicle
deltoid
pectoralis major
sternum
serratus anterior
biceps
ribs
external oblique
pronator teres
brachioradialis
flexor carpo radialis
ilium
pubis
flexor retinaculum
sartoris
quadriceps femoris
femur
patella
patella tendon
fibula
tibialis anterior
tibia
tarsals
metatarsals
phalanges

occipitalis
parietal
extensor retinaculum
occipetal
atlas
trapezius
axis
cervical vertebrae
deltoid
triceps
latissimus dorsi
thoracic vertebrae
scapula
lumbar vertebrae
gluteus maximus
sacrum
coccyx
carpals
semitendinosus
phalanges
metacarpals
ischium
biceps femoris
gastrocnemius
Achilles' tendon

▲ **skeleton and muscles** The human skeleton has 206 bones which weigh c.10kg (22lb). It provides a framework that supports and protects organs and provides sites for the attachment of muscles used in movement. There are more than 650 skeletal (striated) muscles in the human body making up c.40% of its weight. Striated muscle gives the body form, makes up most of the body's muscle tissue, and is under conscious control.

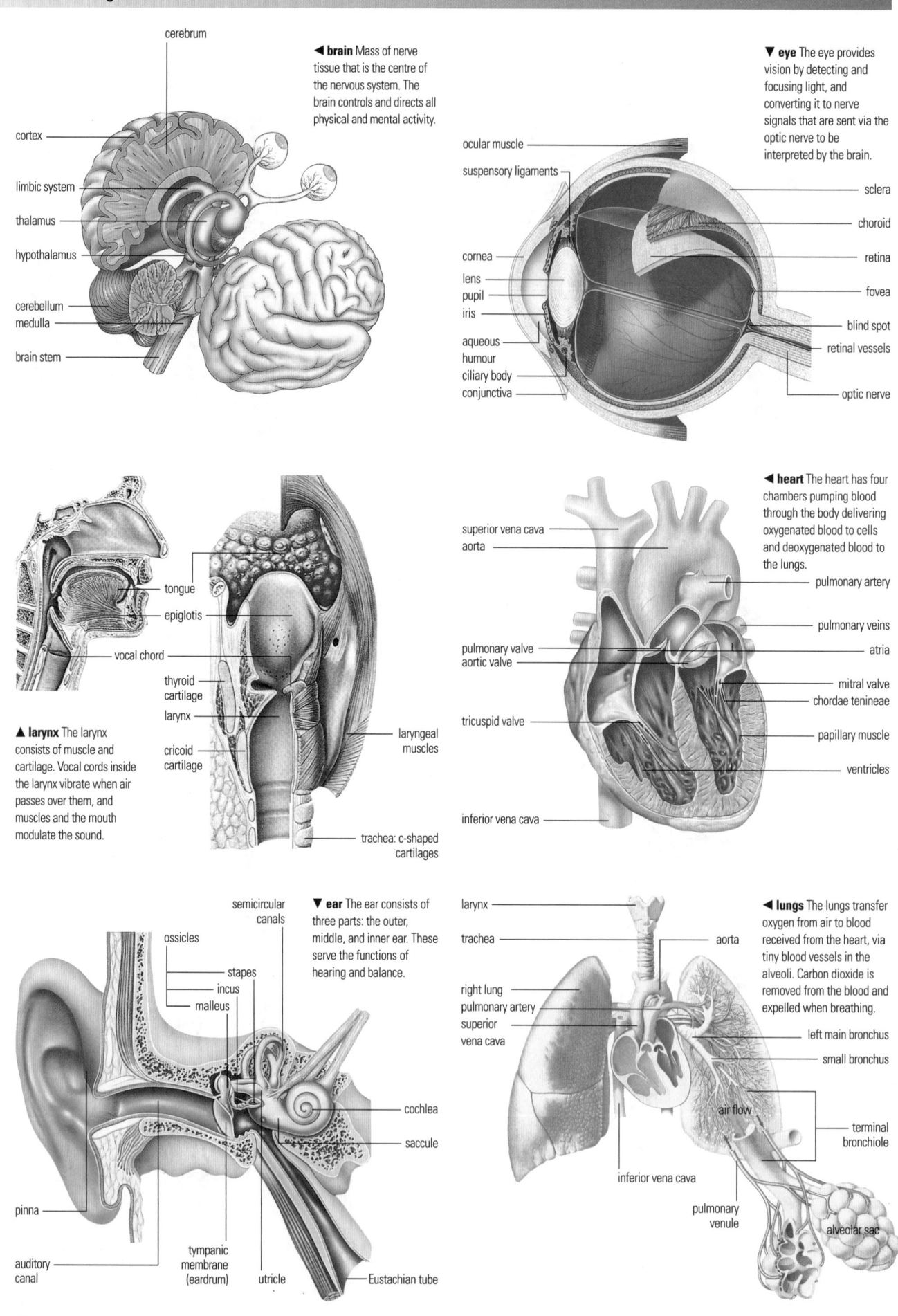

brain Mass of nerve tissue that is the centre of the nervous system. The brain controls and directs all physical and mental activity.

cerebrum
cortex
limbic system
thalamus
hypothalamus
cerebellum
medulla
brain stem

eye The eye provides vision by detecting and focusing light, and converting it to nerve signals that are sent via the optic nerve to be interpreted by the brain.

ocular muscle
suspensory ligaments
cornea
lens
pupil
iris
aqueous humour
ciliary body
conjunctiva
sclera
choroid
retina
fovea
blind spot
retinal vessels
optic nerve

tongue
epiglotis
vocal chord
thyroid cartilage
larynx
cricoid cartilage
laryngeal muscles
trachea: c-shaped cartilages

larynx The larynx consists of muscle and cartilage. Vocal cords inside the larynx vibrate when air passes over them, and muscles and the mouth modulate the sound.

heart The heart has four chambers pumping blood through the body delivering oxygenated blood to cells and deoxygenated blood to the lungs.

superior vena cava
aorta
pulmonary valve
aortic valve
tricuspid valve
inferior vena cava
pulmonary artery
pulmonary veins
atria
mitral valve
chordae tenineae
papillary muscle
ventricles

semicircular canals
ossicles
stapes
incus
malleus
cochlea
saccule
pinna
auditory canal
tympanic membrane (eardrum)
utricle
Eustachian tube

ear The ear consists of three parts: the outer, middle, and inner ear. These serve the functions of hearing and balance.

larynx
trachea
right lung
pulmonary artery
superior vena cava
aorta
left main bronchus
small bronchus
air flow
terminal bronchiole
inferior vena cava
pulmonary venule
alveolar sac

lungs The lungs transfer oxygen from air to blood received from the heart, via tiny blood vessels in the alveoli. Carbon dioxide is removed from the blood and expelled when breathing.

▶ **stomach** Stomach muscles work to mix food with enzymes secreted by the stomach. Sphincter muscles ensure food does not enter the duodenum until this stage of digestion is complete.

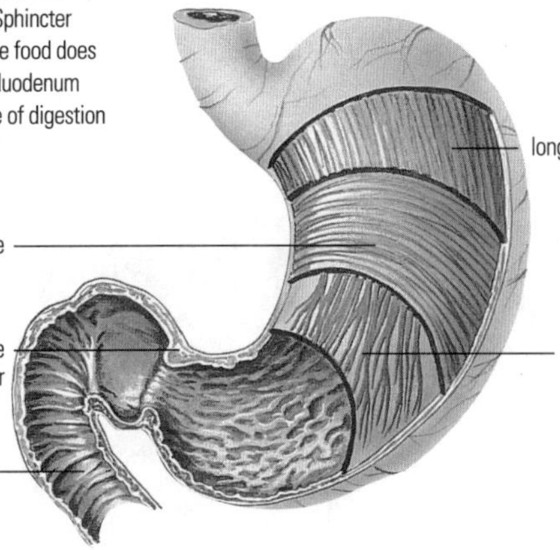

longitudinal muscle

circular muscle

circular muscle valve sphincter

oblique muscle

duodenum

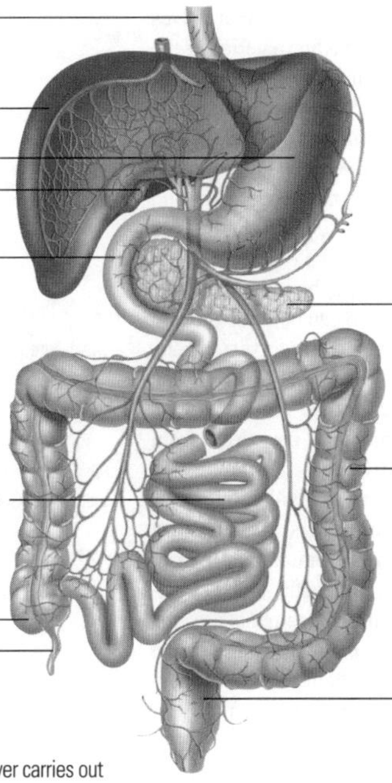

oesophagus

liver

stomach

gall bladder

duodenum

◀ **digestive system** The digestive system breaks down food into smaller molecules that can be easily absorbed by the body and used to keep cells functioning.

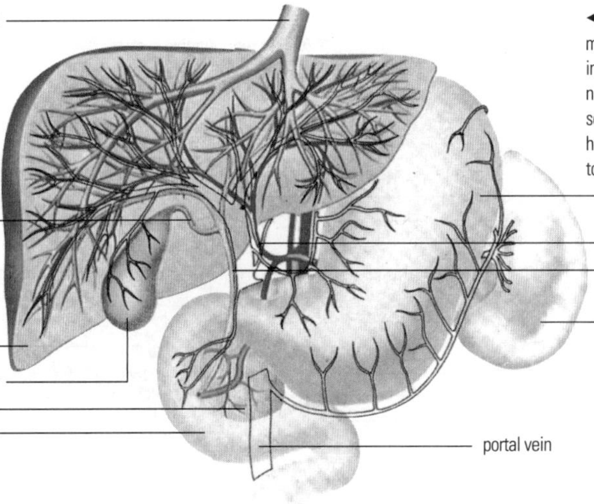

pancreas

small intestine

colon

caecum

appendix

rectum

hepatic vein

◀ **liver** The liver carries out many essential functions including processing nutrients, aiding digestion by secreting bile, maintaining homeostasis and removing toxins from the blood.

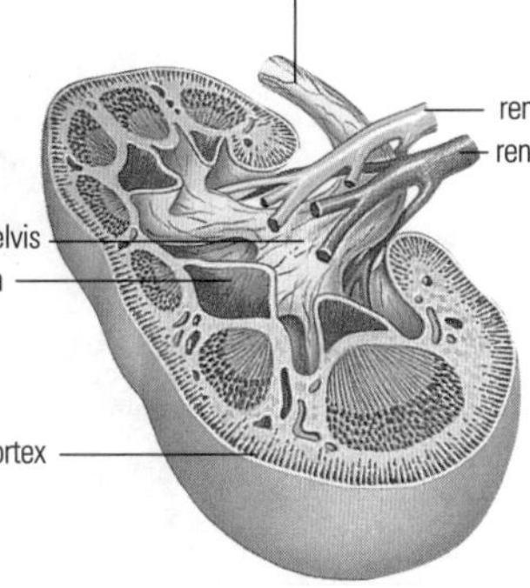

stomach

cystic duct

hepatic artery

common bile duct

spleen

liver

gall bladder

pancreas

duodenum

portal vein

ureter

renal vein

renal artery

inner pelvis

medulla

outer cortex

▲ **kidney** The kidneys act as the body's filter. Blood enters the kidneys via the renal artery, where it is filtered by nephrons in the medulla. Wastes, including urea and excess water, excrete in urine and exit the kidney via the ureter, which leads to the bladder. Filtered blood returns to the rest of the body via the renal vein.

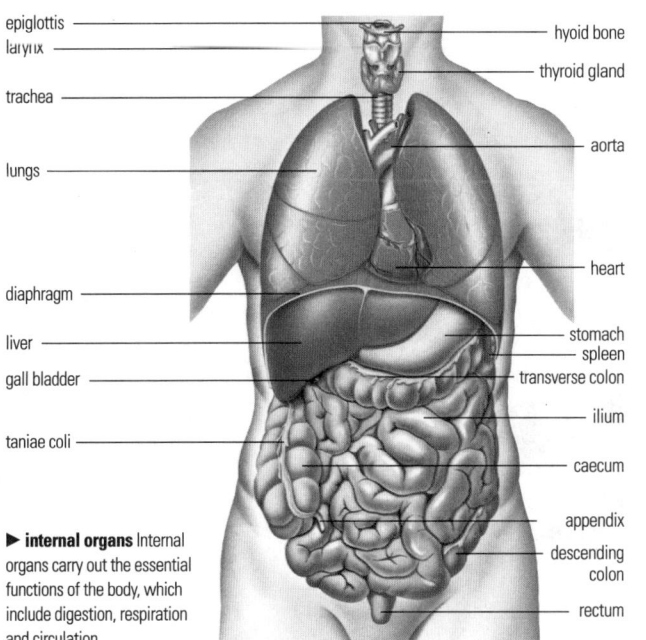

epiglottis

larynx

hyoid bone

thyroid gland

trachea

lungs

aorta

heart

diaphragm

liver

stomach

spleen

gall bladder

transverse colon

ilium

taniae coli

caecum

appendix

descending colon

rectum

▶ **internal organs** Internal organs carry out the essential functions of the body, which include digestion, respiration and circulation.

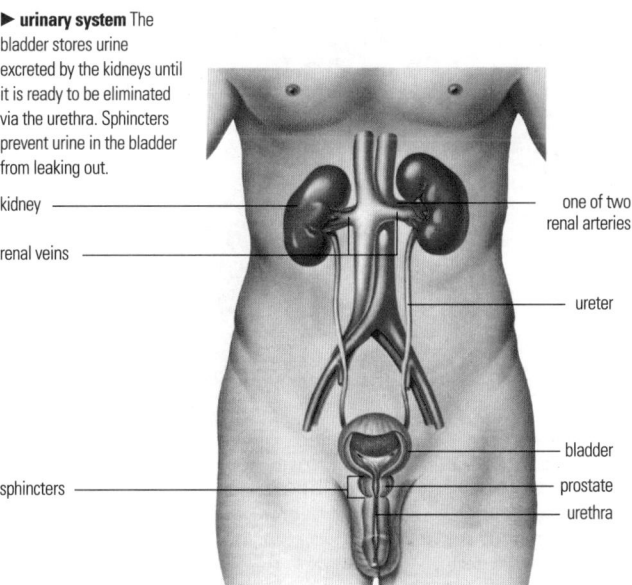

▶ **urinary system** The bladder stores urine excreted by the kidneys until it is ready to be eliminated via the urethra. Sphincters prevent urine in the bladder from leaking out.

kidney

renal veins

one of two renal arteries

ureter

bladder

sphincters

prostate

urethra

Humans reproduce sexually, which involves the combination of genetic material in the form of sex cells (gametes) from two parents; male and female. The male gametes (sperm) are produced in the seminiferous vesicles and stored in the epididymus in the testis. During intercourse, the sperm pass through the vas deferens and ejaculate in semen through the urethra. Female gametes (ova) are produced in the ovaries. During ovulation an ovum releases into the Fallopian tube. If sperm are present, the ovum can be fertilized and the nuclei of the two gametes fuse to form a zygote. The zygote cell divides and develops into an embryo which is nourished by the mother via the placenta as it grows. Pregnancy is the period from fertilization until birth, in humans normally *c*.40 weeks (280 days). It is generally divided into three 3-month periods called trimesters. In the **first trimester**, the embryo grows from a small ball of cells to a fetus *c*.7.6cm (3in) in length. At the beginning of the **second trimester**, movements are first felt and the fetus grows to *c*.36cm (14in). In the **third trimester**, the fetus attains its full bodyweight. Birth is the act of bearing live, partly or fully formed, offspring.

▼ **male reproductive system**

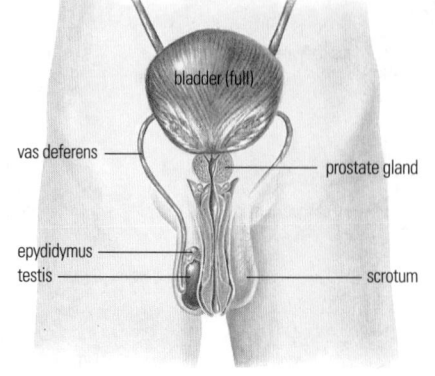

▼ **female reproductive system**

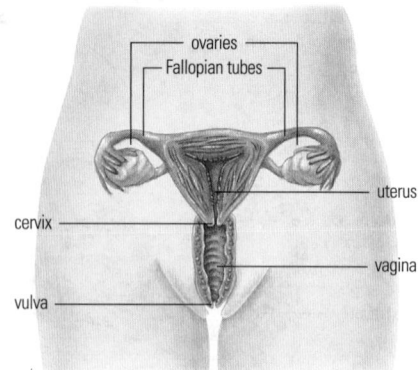

▼ **male reproductive system**

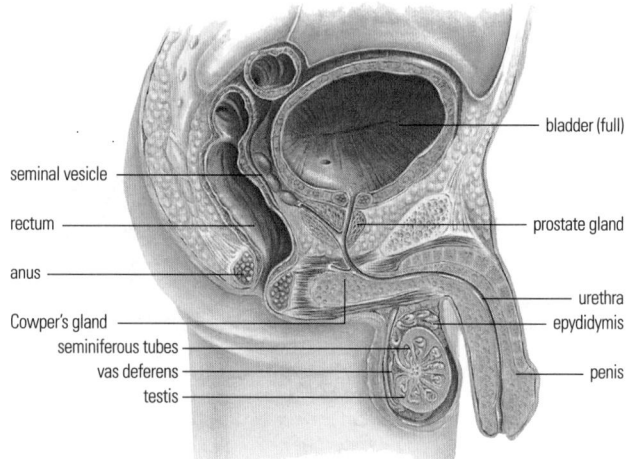

▼ **female reproductive system**

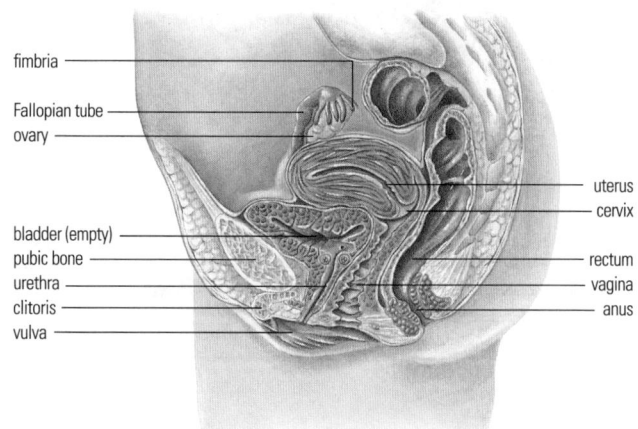

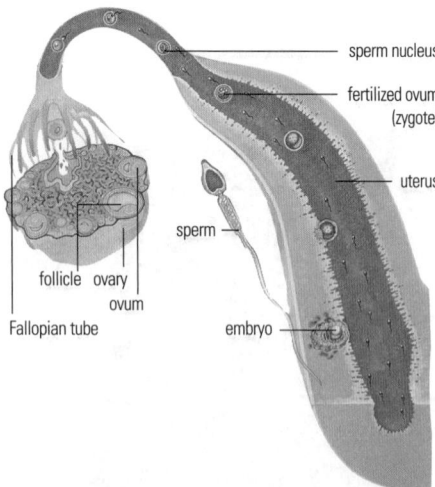

▲ **fertilization** During ovulation an ovum releases into the Fallopian tube. Sperm ejaculated during copulation swim up the uterus, and the first sperm to penetrate the ovum releases enzymes making the ovum impenetrable to other sperm. The sperm fuses its nucleus with that of the ovum to produce a zygote.

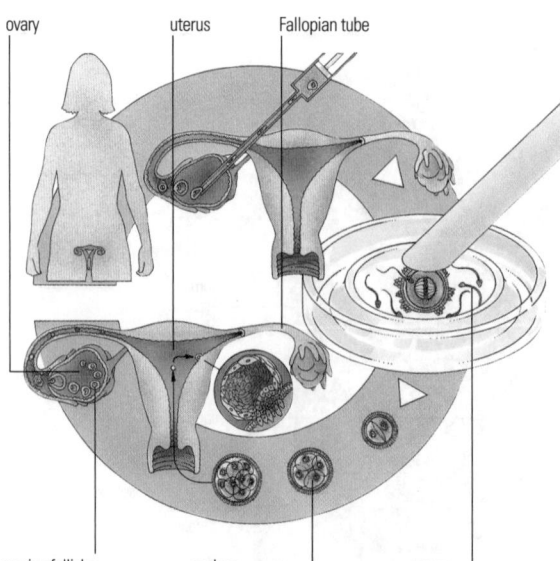

◄ **in vitro fertilization** Process of conceiving an embryo in an artificial environment outside the mother's body. IVF is used to assist infertile couples to have children of their own. Ova are removed from the mother's ovaries and placed in a special culture in a petri dish. Sperm are added and, if fertilization occurs, the zygote divides to form an embryo. It is then transferred to the mother's (or surrogate mother's) body where the embryo hopefully develops normally in the uterus. The embryo(s) can also be frozen and implanted at a later time.

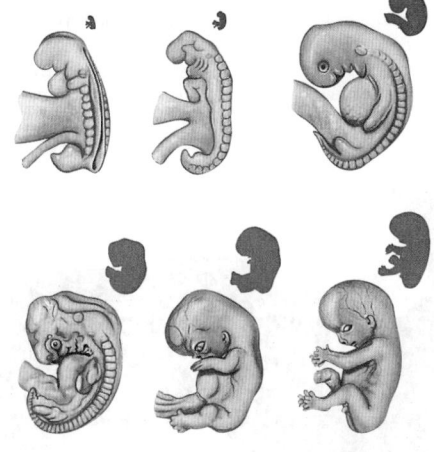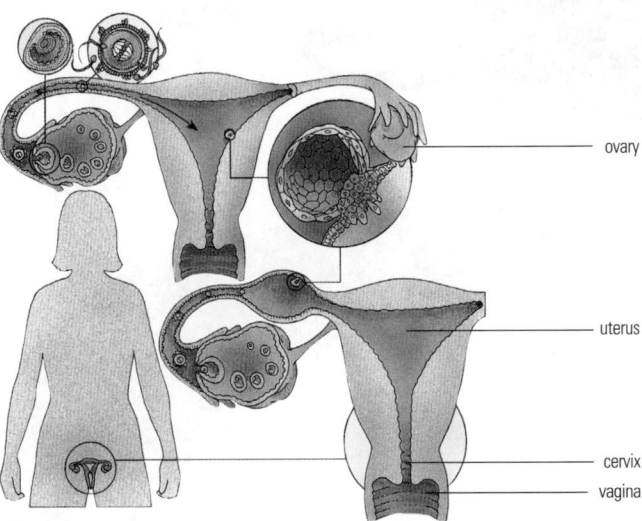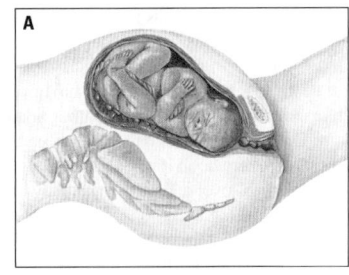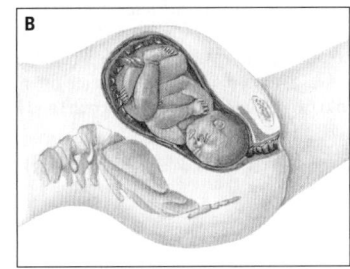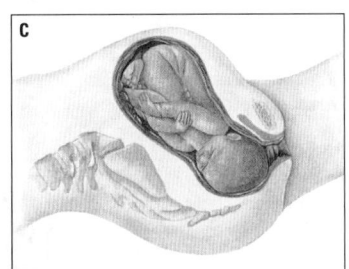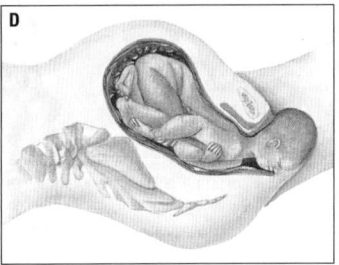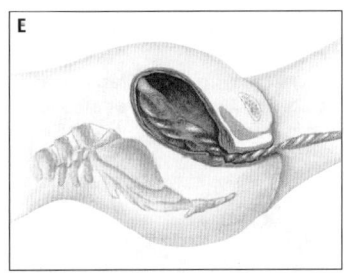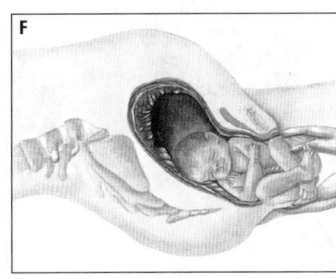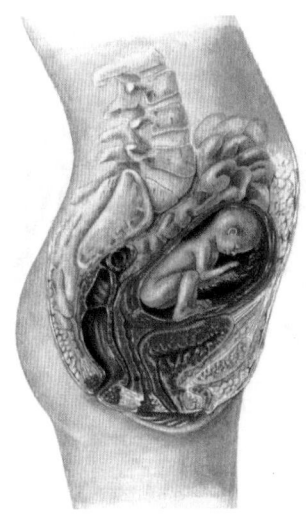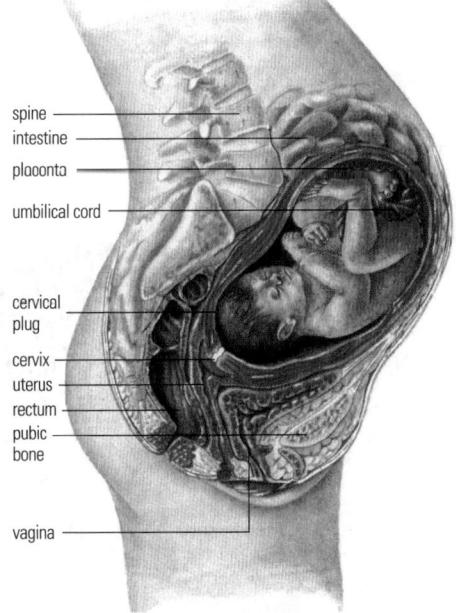

► **embryo** At four weeks, an embryo is just 4mm (0.1in) long. Primitive eyes and nose grow in the fifth week. Arms then legs begin to develop in the sixth week. The embryo, now almost 1.5cm (0.6in) long, has a beating heart and tiny ears. By the seventh week the embryo has a clearly defined head with facial features. By the eighth week the embryo is about 2.5cm (0.98in) long. It has eyelids, fingers and toes.

ovary

uterus

cervix

vagina

▲ **ectopic pregnancy** This occurs when an embryo implants outside the uterus, most commonly in the Fallopian tube, and begins to develop there. Normal development cannot occur and surgery is urgently required to prevent rupturing, which can result in severe haemorrhaging and even death.

spine
intestine
placenta
umbilical cord
cervical plug
cervix
uterus
rectum
pubic bone
vagina

► **Sequence of normal birth** In the 32–34 weeks of pregnancy, the fetus' head engages in its mother's pelvis (**A**). The first stage of labour occurs as the fetus' head moves deeper into the pelvis and turns sideways (**B**). The mother feels contractions in her uterus about every two minutes and lasting for 30–40 seconds. The cervix stretches until it is wide enough (fully dilated) for the head to pass into the vagina (**C**). The vulva expands and the head is pushed out (**D**). The baby takes its first breath and cries. The baby can now be delivered with the mother's next contraction. Ten to 20 minutes later, the placenta separates from the uterus (**E**).

Breech birth is when the fetus' feet and buttocks engage in the mother's pelvis instead of the head (**F**). This complicates delivery because the largest part of the baby, its head, emerges last. Breathing cannot start until the placenta begins to separate.

A
B
C
D
E
F

▲ **After four months** in its mother's womb, the fetus weighs c.125g (4.4oz) and is c.12.5cm long (5in). The genitals develop and tissue areas appear from which bone is formed. In the fifth month (left), the mother may feel the fetus moving in its surrounding (amniotic) fluid. In the sixth month, fine hair covers the fetus' head and body. At 28 weeks, the fetus weighs c.500g (17½oz).

Cats are carnivorous mammals of the family Felidae. Cats cannot chew their food, and their teeth are adapted to stab, anchor, and cut flesh. All cats (except the cheetah) have strong, sharp, retractile claws. They are not adapted for long chases but prowl their prey on padded feet and try to overwhelm it in a short dash or pounce. Big cats roam over a large area, usually alone but sometimes in family groups, for example a pride of lions can contain as many as 37 individuals. Cats generally are nocturnal animals, the retina of their eyes made extra-sensitive to light by a layer of guanine, which causes the eyes to shine in the dark. Cats' sense of smell is so keen that they may completely lose their appetite when their nasal passages become blocked. Cats are often divided into two groups: Felis (cats that purr) and Panthera (cats that growl).

▼ **leopard** or panther (*Panthera pardus*) Solitary animals of the bush and forests of sub-Saharan Africa and s Asia. The black panther (left), is actually a member of the same species but with different colouration and is more common in Asia than in other parts of the range of the leopard. Body length: 210cm (84in); tail: 90cm (35in); height (at shoulder): up to 70cm (28in); weight: to 90kg (200lbs).

▶ **cheetah** or hunting leopard (*Acinoyx jubatus*) Fastest land animal. The cheetah reaches speeds of 100km/h (60mph). They mainly live on the plains of central and s Africa, but also inhabit areas of the Middle East and India. The cheetah has well-developed eyesight and is the only cat with non-retractile claws. Unlike other cats, it hunts in the morning or late afternoon. Its preferred prey is small antelopes. Body length: *c.*140cm (55in); tail: 75–80 cm (30–31in); height (at shoulder): 80cm (31in); weight: 50–60kg (110–130lbs).

▲ **puma** or cougar or mountain lion (*Felis concolor*) Second largest cat species in the Americas (after jaguars). They live in remote wilderness areas from British Columbia to Patagonia. Body length: up to 2m (6ft); tail: 1m (3ft); height (at shoulder): up to 75cm (30in); weight: up to 100kg (220lbs).

▼ **lion** (*Panthera leo*) Second largest of the big cats (after tigers). They live in sub-Saharan Africa and NW India. The male lion (shown standing) is larger than the lioness, and often has a splendid mane. Lions are unique among cats in that they live in a group called a pride which can consist of between four and 37 individuals.

The lioness does most of the hunting, preying on wildebeest, zebra, impala and other mammals. If prey is plentiful, they typically spend 20 hours a day at rest and are often seen lazing in the shade of a tree. Body length: up to 2.1m (7m); tail 1m (3ft); height (at shoulder): up to 1.2m (4ft); weight: 230kg (500lbs).

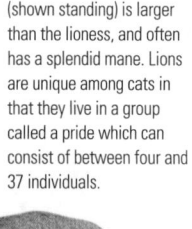

▲ **tiger** (*Panthera tigris*) Largest of the cats. They are identified by their characteristic striped coat. They inhabit forests and grasslands in Asia where populations have suffered from hunting, deforestation, and demand for tiger parts in traditional medicine. Only four races of tiger survive (Chinese, Bengal, Siberian, and Sumatran) and these are all endangered species. Body length: *c.*2.2m (7m); tail: 1m (3ft); height (at shoulder): 1m (3ft); weight: up to 290kg (640lbs).

▶ **lynx** (*Felis lynx*) Medium sized cat that lives in W Europe, Siberia, Canada, and N USA. The male is larger than the female. It hunts very small mammals, fishes and birds in a variety of habitats, often in forest or dense vegetation and will sometimes hunt from trees. The lynx is threatened by destruction and overuse of its habitat, the diminishment of its prey species, and the hunting for its fur. Its coat colour varies from grey-brown to reddish, sometimes with dark spots. The lynx is distinguished by its short tail and by its ear tufts tipped with black. Body length: 67–110cm (26–43in); tail: 5–17cm (2–7in); height (at shoulder): 18–33cm (7–13in); weight: 5–18kg (11–40lbs).

▲ **clouded leopard** (*Neofelis nebulosa*) Big cat with distinctive patterns of dark stripes, spots and patches on a coat that varies from dark brown to yellow. It inhabits dense, high-altitude forests in India and SE Asia. An excellent climber, it hunts pigs and deer on the ground, and squirrels and monkeys in the trees. It is heavily built with short legs. Body length: 60–110cm (24–43in); tail: 60–90cm (24–35in); weight: 16–20kg (20-40lbs); height (at shoulder): 54cm (21in).

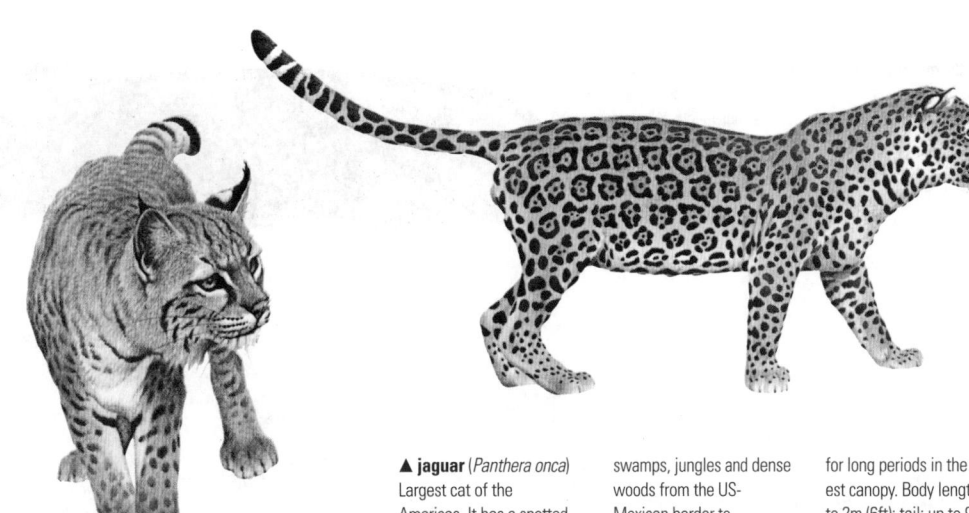

▶ **bob-cat** (*Felis rufus*) Most common wildcat in North America. It lives in rough, rocky, forested areas from S Canada through the USA to Mexico. It spends less time in trees than the lynx and is active at twilight, when it hunts rodents, small mammals and large ground birds. The bob-cat has slightly tufted ears and gets its name from its short bobbed tail. It has become increasingly threatened following the introduction of hunting restrictions on other types of lynx. Body length: 62–76cm (24–30in); tail: 10–20cm (4–8in); height (at shoulder): 13–24cm (5–9in); weight 6–13kg (14-29 lbs).

▲ **jaguar** (*Panthera onca*) Largest cat of the Americas. It has a spotted yellow coat with black rings that distinguish it from the leopard. It inhabits swamps, jungles and dense woods from the US-Mexican border to Patagonia. During the wet season when the jungle floor is flooded, it can live for long periods in the forest canopy. Body length: up to 2m (6ft); tail: up to 90cm (35in); height (at shoulder): 80cm (31in); weight: up to 160kg (350lbs).

▼ **snow leopard** (*Panthera uncia*) Mountain-dwelling cat that lives high in the Altai, Hindu Kush and Himalayas. It follows the seasonal migrations of the ibex, wild sheep, marmots and ground-dwelling birds on which it preys. The pads of its feet are thickly furred to act as 'snow shoes'. The snow leopard's coat is covered in grey rosettes and it has a dark stripe down its spine. Once hunted for its long fur, it is now an endangered species. Length: 120–150cm (47–59in); tail: 90cm (35in); height (at shoulder): 60cm (23in); weight: up to 55kg (121lbs).

▲ **ocelot** (*Felis pardalis*) Small to medium cat that lives in S USA, Central and South America. Its valuable fur is yellowish with dark spots, rings and stripes. The ocelot lives mainly in forests and is nocturnal, resting in dense scrub during the day and hunting usually at night. It feeds on small birds, mammals and reptiles. It is an endangered species and is very rare in the N of its range due to habitat destruction. Length: 92–137cm (36in–54in); tail: 27–40cm (11–16in); height (at shoulder): 41cm (16in); weight: 9–18kg (20–40lb).

Whales are members of the Cetacoa order of mammals. They are unique among mammals in that spend their entire life underwater, surfacing regularly for air. Characteristics shared by all species include a large streamlined body, paddle-shaped forelimbs, a tail flattened horizontally into flukes for locomotion, and at least one blowhole. Two sub-orders exist: baleen whales and toothed whales. **Baleen** (Mysticeti) whales are very large and carry comb-like plates of horny material (baleen or whalebone) in the roof of the mouth which are used to strain krill and plankton on which they feed. **Toothed** (Odontoceti) whales are more numerous, diverse, and smaller in size. They have teeth and eat a variety of food that includes fish, squid, crustaceans, and invertebrates. They are more social than baleen whales and use echolocation to hunt and navigate. In the past, whales were hunted intensively for their oil and flesh, leading some species to the brink of extinction. Protective measures allowed numbers to increase, however some species are still very rare and remain endangered.

▲ **killer whale** (*Orcinus orca*) Found in cool coastal waters worldwide. It is the largest member of the dolphin family and is strikingly marked with black above, a white underside and white spots behind the eyes. The male's dorsal fin is the tallest in the animal kingdom and can measure up to 2m (6.6ft). The female's dorsal fin is shorter and curved in a more typical dolphin shape. They live in pods of five to 50 individuals and hunt cooperatively for fish, squid, sea birds and other marine mammals. Length: 5–8m (23–32ft); weight: 3–5 tonnes.

▶ **northern bottlenose whale** (*Hyperoodon ampullatus*) Protected species that inhabits cold-temperate to Arctic waters. They are black to brown with a white underside, bulbous melon, and a small beak and dorsal fin. They live in small groups of one to four individuals. Whalers exploited their refusal to leave a wounded companion. Length: 6–9m (20–30ft); weight: 6–8 tonnes.

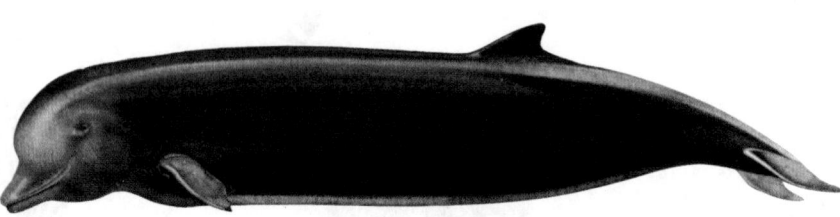

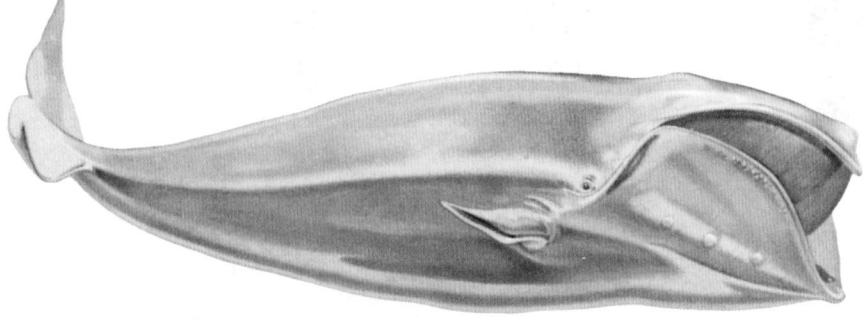

◀ **right whale** (*Balaena glacialis*) So called because they were considered the 'right' whale to catch, they suffered greatly at the hands of the whaling industry and, despite years of protection, they are still an endangered species. Their bodies are black or grey with white patchy undersides and are usually covered in barnacles and other parasites. They have no dorsal fin. They live in small groups in temperate waters and feed by skimming through plankton and straining off crustaceans with 2.5m (8ft)-long baleen plates. Length: 15–18m (16–59 ft); weight: 30–80 tonnes.

▶ **beluga whale** (*Delphinapterus leucas*) They have no dorsal fin and unlike other whales, can turn their heads from side to side. Calves are grey at birth and get lighter with age. They earned the nickname 'sea canaries' from their social behaviour and the wide variety of sounds they make. They inhabit Arctic waters and catch their prey using echolocation and by working together to herd fish into shallow waters. Length: 3–5m (10–16ft); weight: 500–1500kg.

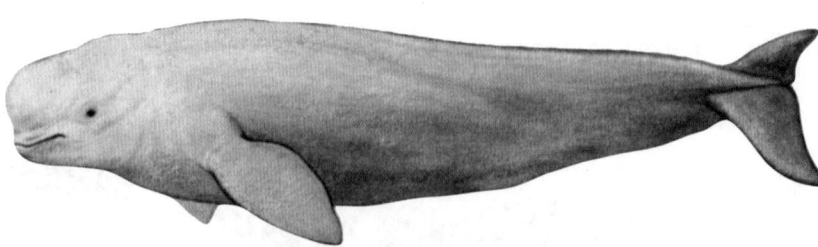

◀ **pilot whale** (*Globicephala melas*) Found in coastal waters of tropical and temperate oceans, they are mainly black, with a white patch on the underside between their long, narrow, front flippers. They have the bulging forehead common to other members of the dolphin family. They live in small groups with strong social bonds and because of this groups often strand themselves on beaches. They communicate using a wide range of sounds and employ echolocation to hunt squid and fish. Length: 4.8–8.5m (16–28ft); weight: 2–3.5 tonnes.

▼ baleen whale's skeleton Whales are thought to have descended from a land animal, and through time the skeleton evolved to suit the marine environment. The vestigial pelvic bones (1) show where hind limbs once protruded. In baleen whales, the jawbones (2) are greatly enlarged and curved to accommodate the huge sieve-like plates of baleen.

◄ baleen whale's mouth Baleen plates hanging from each side of the mouth strain krill and plankton. When the whale closes its mouth, water is forced out and food is trapped in the fringe.

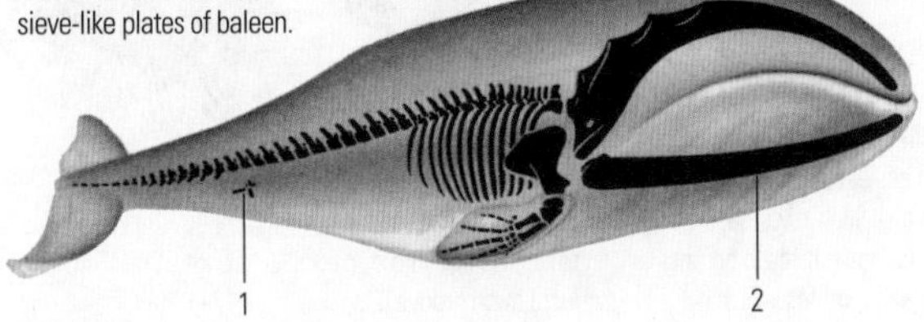

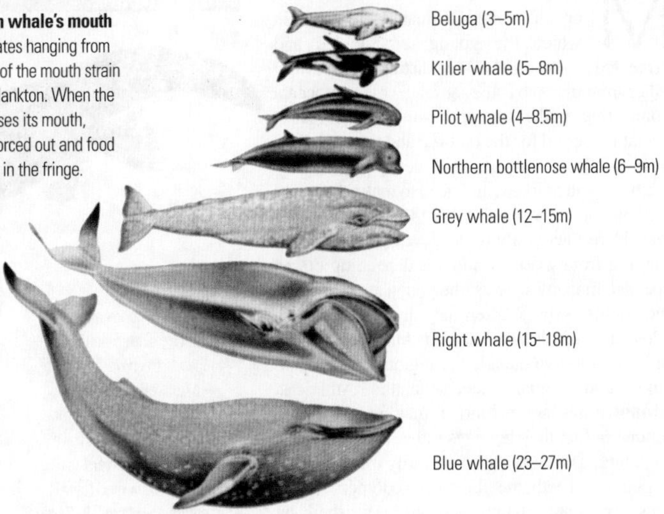

Beluga (3–5m)

Killer whale (5–8m)

Pilot whale (4–8.5m)

Northern bottlenose whale (6–9m)

Grey whale (12–15m)

Right whale (15–18m)

Blue whale (23–27m)

▼ sperm whale (*Physeter macrocephalus*) Largest of the toothed whales, its huge head takes up one-third of its length. The head contains an oil-like wax called spermaceti, thought to control buoyancy when diving to 3000m (9000ft) or more to hunt for squid. They have a series of humps on their backs, large tail flukes and short flippers. Length: 11–20m (36–66ft); weight: 40–50 tonnes.

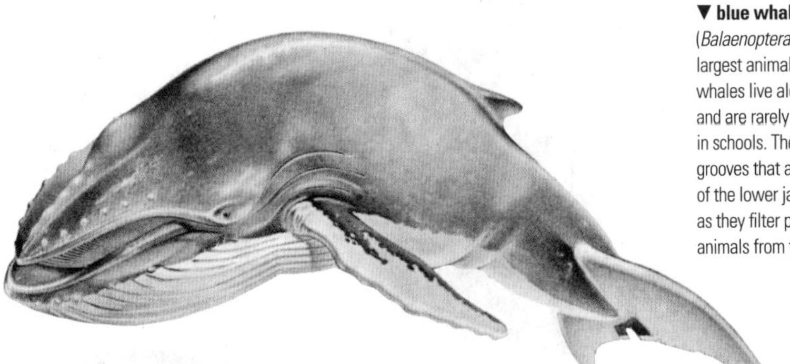

▲ grey whale (*Eschrichtius robustus*) Inhabiting the waters of the N Pacific Ocean, they migrate thousands of kilometres S to breed in winter. Their mottled grey skin is covered with barnacles and they have a row of humps along the back instead of a dorsal fin. They feed at the bottom of the sea stirring sediment and filtering shellfish through baleen plates hanging from the upper jaw. Length: 12–15m (40–50ft); weight: 27–36 tonnes.

▼ blue whale (*Balaenoptera musculus*) The largest animal on Earth, blue whales live alone or in pairs and are rarely encountered in schools. They have throat grooves that allow the skin of the lower jaw to expand as they filter planktonic animals from the water. In summer, while in polar seas, they eat more than four tonnes of food a day. In winter, they migrate to the Equator where they fast, give birth, and mate. Although protected they are still in danger of extinction. Length: 23–27m (75–88ft); weight: 100–120 tonnes.

▲ humpback whale (*Megaptera novaeangliae*) Black or grey filter feeder distinguished by long flippers, a short body, and a small dorsal fin on a hump. They are famous for their acrobatic behaviour and complex vocalizations ('songs'). They migrate from polar regions to tropical breeding grounds in winter. Length: 14.5–19m (48–62ft); weight: 25–30 tonnes.

Mammal of which the female usually has a pouch, called a marsupium, within which the young are suckled and protected. Marsupials are distinguished from other mammals by the absence of a placenta connecting mother and embryo. There is a short gestation period for the embryo and the young are born at a very early stage of development; they are blind and hairless, and need to make their way to their mother's pouch where they attach to her teat. Here they continue to develop for a period ranging from weeks to months depending on the species. In many species, the young are carried on the mother's back after they leave the pouch. Most marsupials are found in Australasia – the only ones to live outside the region are the opossums and similar species in the Americas. **Monotremes** are primitive mammals that are unique in that they lay eggs rather than give birth to young. The eggs are temporarily transferred to a pouch beneath the female's abdomen, where they eventually hatch and are nourished by rudimentary mammary glands.

Monotremes

▲ **platypus**
(*Ornithorhynchus anatinus*) Elusive monotreme that inhabits freshwater streams in E Australia. They have dense water-repellent fur and webbed feet. Males have venomous backward-facing spurs on their hind feet (1). Length: 45–60cm (18–24in).

▶ **echidna** (*Tachyglossus aculeatus*) Solitary animal that lives in various habitats. It feeds on ants and termites which it catches with its long, sticky tongue. When it lays an egg, it uses its hind limbs to roll the egg into a special incubation groove (2). Length: 30–45cm (12–18in).

▼ **grey kangaroo**
(*Macropus*) Either of two species (*M. giganteus* and *M. fuliginosus*). They graze on vegetation and are regarded as pests when abundant. The joey lives in the mother's pouch for 320 days. Head-tail length: up to 240cm (94in).

▼ **ring-tailed wallaby** or yellow-footed rock wallaby (*Petrogale xanthopus*) Adept at climbing they are the largest of the rock wallabies. They are fawn-grey with a brown dorsal stripe and have long orange-brown tails and orange-yellow legs, feet and ears. Length: 29–80cm (11–31in); tail: 25–70cm (10–28in).

▼ **pretty-faced wallaby**
(*Macropus parryi*) Also known as the whiptail wallaby, after its long tail which often exceeds the length of its body. It is identified by distinctive white markings on its cheeks and can be found in the hills and woodlands of E Australia in 'mobs' of up to 80 individuals. Length: 90cm (35in); tail: 95cm (37in).

◀ **red kangaroo**
(*Macropus rufus*) Largest living marsupial, it lives on the grazing plains and grasslands of central Australia. Red kangaroos are most active at dawn and dusk, and can survive long periods without water. They travel in 'mobs' and at full speed can cover 8m (26ft) in one leap. The males ('boomers') often fight for supremacy in the mob, some reaching more than 2m (6ft) tall in fighting stance. The females ('flyers') are smaller and blue-grey in colour. They can mate after giving birth, however the embryo will not develop until the joey leaves the pouch. Head-tail length: up to 280cm (110in).

▲ **koala** (*Phascolarctos cinereus*) Territorial tree-dwellers native to E and S Australia. Their diet is mostly eucalyptus leaves. After leaving the pouch, joeys travel on the mother's back for several months. Length: 60–85cm (23–34in).

▼ **common wombat**
(*Vombatus ursinus*) One of three species of wombats that occupy SE Australian forests and grasslands. Short-legged and bear-shaped, they have long claws and a backward-opening pouch adapted for digging large burrows where they sleep during the day. Length: 80–100cm (31–39in).

▼ **numbat** (*Myrmecobius fasciatus*) Endangered species that inhabits forests in sw Australia. It feeds almost exclusively on termites, using its sticky tongue which can be as much as half the length of its body. Unlike most marsupials it is pouchless. Its young must cling to their mother's fur for the first six months whilst suckling. Length: 35–45cm (14–18in).

◄ **Tasmanian devil** (*Sarcophilus harrisii*) Found only in Tasmania it has dark fur with some white patches and is renowned for its frightening screams. It preys by night on a variety of animals. Very strong for its size, its prey is sometimes much larger than itself. Length: 75–110cm (29–43in).

▼ **sugar glider** (*Petaurus breviceps*) Small and agile, they have a thin membrane stretched between their fore and hind limbs and can glide 50–100m (164–328ft) between trees. They inhabit forests along the E coast of Australia where they shelter in tree hollows and feed on eucalyptus sap and gum. Length: 20cm (8in); weight: up to 160g (6oz).

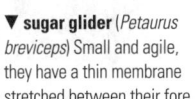

► **kultarr** (*Antechinomys laniger*) Carnivorous marsupial mouse from central Australia. It has large ears and a long tail, with dark patches present around the eyes, in the middle of the forehead and at the tip of the tail. It inhabits dry desert and grassland regions, nesting in logs and vegetation. Length: 8–11cm (3–4in); tail: 10–14cm (4–6in).

► **ringtail possum** (*Pseudocheirus peregrinus*) Highly specialized, tree-climbing, leaf and flower-eating possum found in Australia and New Guinea. It has a long prehensile tail with a white hairless tip, which acts as a fifth limb. It is arboreal and makes spherical nests called 'dreys'. Length: 16–46cm (6–18in); tail: 17–40cm (7–16in).

▼ **Leadbetter's possum** (*Gymnobelideus leadbeateri*) Thought to be extinct but now found in a pocket of mountainous forest in SE Australia. It is arboreal and highly agile and has paws adapted to this, with wide tips and strong short claws. Its fur ranges from grey to brown with a prominent dorsal stripe. Head-tail length: 30cm (12in).

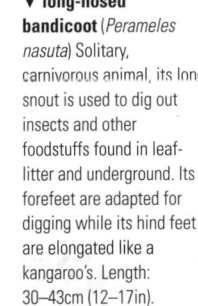

◄ **quokka** (*Setonix brachyurus*) Small wallaby about the size of a hare, with small round ears and a wide flat face. Found in sw Australia, their preferred habitat is in thick scrub near streams and swamps. They can survive without freshwater for long periods by getting moisture from plant life. They live in shared territories which they rarely leave. Head-tail length: 73–95cm (29–38in).

▲ **monito del monte** (*Dromiciops australis*) Small, grey-brown, arboreal marsupial with a thick tail and round ears. It inhabits humid forests of central Chile where it constructs spherical nests in which to hibernate. Length: 8–13cm (3–5in); tail: 9–13cm (4–5in).

▼ **marsupial cat** (*Dasyurus albopunctatus*) Nocturnal hunters found in rocky, forested areas of Australia and New Guinea. They are aggressive predators which prey on small mammals, reptiles, and birds. They are mainly terrestrial but are adept at climbing rocks and trees. Head-tail length: 45–130cm (18–51in).

▼ **greater bilby** (*Macrotis lagotis*) Endangered species found in remote areas of the Australian desert. They have long ears with a plentiful blood supply which helps reduce body heat. During the day they shelter in burrows. They can rear two to three young in a backward-opening pouch. Length: 40–75cm (16–29in).

▲ **cuscus** (*Phalanger maculatus*) Large, tree-dwelling and nocturnal, they inhabit rainforests and woodland in Australia and New Guinea. They have a long, prehensile tail and sharp claws for climbing. They eat leaves, fruit, insects and will also take eggs. Head-tail length: 64–120cm (25–47in).

▼ **long-nosed bandicoot** (*Perameles nasuta*) Solitary, carnivorous animal, its long snout is used to dig out insects and other foodstuffs found in leaf-litter and underground. Its forefeet are adapted for digging while its hind feet are elongated like a kangaroo's. Length: 30–43cm (12–17in).

African mammals include some of the largest and most endangered animals on the planet. Changing conditions and the destruction of natural habitats led to a depletion in numbers of many African species, but perhaps the biggest threat has been the human hunter. Demand for animal skins, ivory and game meat brought some species close to extinction. Only one family of elephants, the Elephantidae, exists today where once there were six. African mammals include species such as the hyena – a scavenger and hunter that can rival many of the big cats in terms of strength. Mammals like the hyrax need moisture from grasses and leaves in their diet. Small mammals from the order Rodentia are either burrowers or small enough to live in natural crevices away from the heat of the sun, others are noctural, conserving their energy during the day in order to hunt or forage at night. African mammals also include those unique to the island of Madagascar, such as the lemur and the aye-aye. There are many species of primate in Africa, all show various degrees of adaptation to life in trees.

▼ **hippopotamus**
(*Hippopotamidae*) Inhabits areas with adequate water and grazing. It has a grey or brown body and a large head and snout. It has the largest mouth of any mammal, with long incisor and canine teeth. Its skin dehydrates easily and it spends the day in the water, emerging at night to graze. Length: 3m (11ft); weight: up to 3 tonnes.

▲ **white rhinoceros**
(*Ceratotherium simum*) Grazing animal of the savannas of Uganda and Zimbabwe. Its long head has two horns, the larger front horn measuring up to 150cm (59in). They tend to live in same-sex groups. Length: 3.5–5m (12–16ft); height (at shoulder): 1.5–2m (5–7ft); weight: c.1.5–3.5 tonnes.

▶ **giraffe** (*Giraffe camelopardalis*) The tallest mammal, they live in dense forest or open plains with trees. The reticulated giraffe (pictured) is recognizable by its large tan to dark brown patches outlined in cream. Giraffes have small, hair-covered knobs on their heads to protect them from collision. Their extremely long necks allow them to reach the best leaves and they have elasticated blood vessels to prevent them from fainting. Height: up to 6m (18ft); weight: 700–1814kg (1540–4000lbs).

◀ **elephant** (*Loxodonta Africana*) Largest land animal, the only surviving member of the Proboscidea order, which included the mammoth. They live in the savannahs and forests of Africa. The ivory tusks are used for digging up roots. The trunk, used for drinking and picking up food, is an elongated nose and upper lip. The African elephant is bigger than the Indian and has larger ears. The female is about half the size of the male. Elephants are herbivores and move in herds. They live for 60–70 years. Length (with trunk): 6–7m (20–23ft); height (at shoulder): 3–4m (10–13 ft); weight: 5–8 tonnes.

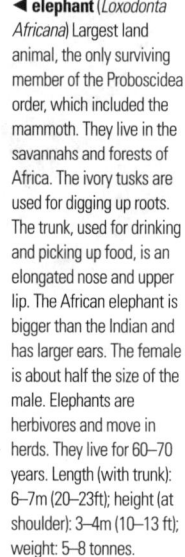

▼ **Burchell's zebra**
(*Equus burchelli*) The most common of the zebra species, it inhabits the savannahs and woodlands of Africa. The Burchell's stripes are wide and extend over the belly. The stripes act as camouflage, distorting distance and size. It is shorter and lighter than the Grevy's zebra. Height: 1–1.5m (3–5ft); weight: c.220–300kg (485–661lbs).

▼ **brindled gnu** or blue wildebeest (*Connochaetes taurinus*) It lives on the savannahs of s and e Africa. It has a beard and a horse-like tail. There are both migratory and sedentary herds. Length: up to 2.4m (7.8ft); height: up to 1.5m (5ft); weight: up to 275kg (600lbs).

▲ **African buffalo**
(*Syncerus caffer*) Found in the clearings and floodplains of Africa's rainforests. The adults are dark brown to black and have characteristic curved horns that measure up to 1m (3ft). They are primarily nocturnal but can be seen during the day. Length: 2–3.5m (7–11ft); height: 135–165cm (54–66in); weight: 576–870kg (1270–1918lbs).

▲ common eland (*Taurotragus oryx*) Cow-like antelope native to E Africa. It is fawn to grey coloured with a tuft of hair growing from the dewlap and white lateral stripes on its back. Length: 2–3.5m (7–12ft); height: up to 1.8m (6ft); weight: up to 680kg (1500lbs).

▼ giant eland (*Taurotragus derbianus*) Endangered plains-dwelling antelope in W and central Africa. It is reddish brown with white stripes extending over its torso and black and white markings on its legs and hooves. Their large twisted horns grow to 64cm (25in) in females and 127cm (50in) in males. Length: up to 3m (10ft); height: up to 1.8m (6ft); weight: up to 1 tonne.

◄ impala (*Aepyceros melampus*) It Inhabits savannas and wooded areas. It is reddish brown with white underparts, chin, eye area and hindquarters. Black lines extend from its hindlegs to its tail. Height: 75–95cm (30–37in); weight: 41–68kg (90–150lbs).

► Thomson's gazelle (*Gazella thomsoni*) It grazes on the grass plains of Africa. It has a fawn coloured coat with a black stripe defining white underparts. Height: 58–64cm (23-35in); weight: 13kg–27kg (29–60lbs).

▲ spotted hyena or laughing hyena (*Crocuta crocuta*) The most common hyena, it lives in a variety of habitats and is known for its distinctive vocalizations which sound vaguely like laughter. It has a slightly sloping back, large ears, and spots that cover most of its body. A hunter and a scavenger, its large teeth are designed to crush bones. Height: 71–89cm (28–35in); weight: 40–55kg (88–121lbs).

► brown hyena (*Hyaena brunnea*) Inhabits dry, rocky areas of S Africa. It has a dark brown long haired coat, with a whitish collar and horizontal, dark stripes on the legs. It scavenges for food but will also hunt small vertebrates and eat fruit in the dry season. It is shyer and rarer than the spotted hyena. All hyenas live in territorial clans dominated by females. Height: 65–88cm (25–35in); weight: 37–47kg (82–104lbs).

◄ striped hyena (*Hyaena hyaena*) It lives in the mountains and bushlands of N and E Africa and can also be found in the Middle East and India. It is greyish-brown with long hair all over its body. It gains its name from its striped back and legs. The striped hyena is a scavenger and will only hunt very small prey such as rabbits. It also eats fruit and insects. Height: 60–94cm (23–37in); weight: 25–55kg (55–121lbs).

▲ gorilla (*Gorilla gorilla*) Powerfully built great ape native to the forests of equatorial Africa. The largest primate, it is brown or black, with long arms and short legs and walks on all fours. Gorillas are shy and will only attack if they feel threatened. Populations have suffered from destruction of habitat and trophy hunting. Height: up to 1.8m (6ft); weight: 136–193kg (300–425lbs).

▼ mandrill (*Mandrillus sphinx*) Relative of the baboon, it has a furry brown to grey body and an amazing brightly coloured face and rump. The colours are especially strong on the male and intensify when it becomes angry or excited. Mandrills have pouches in their cheeks enabling them to store food as they travel, or free the use of their hands. Height: 56–109cm (22–43in); weight: 11–34kg (25–75lbs).

▲ chimpanzee (*Pan troglodytes*) Primate with long arms and human-like hands capable of grasping and using tools which, for example, can be used to extract termites. They live in rainforests and wet savannahs. They have dark hair covering most of their bodies apart from their faces, ears, fingers and toes. There are four subspecies of chimpanzee. Height: 91–122cm (36–48in); weight: 45–59kg (100–130lbs).

▼ **white-collared mangabey** (*Cercocebus torquatus*) Native to the swamps and forests of Africa. It has cream to white markings extending from the side of its face to

its chest. Mangabeys have long, agile bodies with strong tails adapted for living in trees. They move on all fours and communicate with calls and by flickering their striking white eyelids. Length: 38–88 cm (15–35in); tail: 43–76cm (17–30in); weight: 7–14kg (15–31lbs).

▶ **Verreaux's sifaka** (*Propithecus verreauxi*) Critically endangered species found only in certain forests on Madagascar. Sifakas vary from white through to dark brown but all have a black hairless face. Length: 39–48cm (15–19in); tail: 50–60cm (20–24in).

◀ **black and white colobus monkey** (*Colobus guereza*) Found in E Africa, the colobus lives in the treetops of forests. Its black body is trimmed with a white mantle that runs to its lower back. It has a tufted tail. Length: 45–72cm (18–28in); tail: 52–100cm (21–39in).

▲ **black and white ruffed lemur** (*Varecia variegata*) Subspecies of lemur found in the rainforests of Madagascar. It is black with large white areas on the lower parts of the body and a white ruff surrounding the face. Length: 51–60cm (20–24in); tail: 56–65cm (22–26in).

▲ **ring-tailed lemur** (*Lemur catta*) Found in the deciduous forests of Madagascar. It has a grey back with white underparts and distinctive black marks on the top of its head, around its eyes and on its

nose. Its tail, which is often held in the air, has black and white bands. The ring-tailed lemur is unusual in that it travels both along the ground and through trees. Length: 39–46cm (15–18in); tail: 56–63cm (22–25in).

▼ **vervet monkey** (*Cercopithecus aethiops*) It inhabits trees along the watercourses of the River Senegal to Somalia and South Africa. Coat colours

vary from olive green to silver, although all types have black faces framed by a white band. Length: 46–80cm (18–31in); tail: 50–70cm (20–28in).

▼ **aye-aye** (*Daubentonia madagascariensis*) Endangered species that is the largest nocturnal primate. It inhabits forests of Madagascar and has coarse dark hair, a bushy tail, and large naked ears. The aye-aye taps on dead wood to find insect larvae and uses its elongated middle finger to draw out food. Length: 40cm (16in); tail: 42cm (16½in).

◀ **desert jerboa** (*Jaculus jaculus*) Rodent found in the deserts of N Africa and central Asia. The jerboa is nocturnal and lives in a burrow to protect itself both from the heat and from predators like the desert fox. It has a satiny, sand coloured

body, long hind legs, and a long tail. It moves around on its hind legs making jumps of up to 3m (9.5ft) and uses its tail as a prop when stationary. It has furry feet to stop it from slipping on the sand. Length: 15cm (6in); tail: up to 25cm (10in).

▶ **rock hyrax** (*Procavia capensis*) Small, herbivorous, hoofed mammal. Rock hyraxes live in the deserts and hills of E Africa. A hyrax is about the same size as a rabbit and has a yellowish brown coat. They do not burrow but live in the natural

crevices of rocks in colonies of as many as 50 hyraxes. They feed on bird and lizard eggs, insects, grasses and leaves and can go a long time without water. Tree hyraxes look very similar to the rock hyrax but live in trees and are nocturnal. Length: to 50cm (20in).

▶ **Grant's desert mole** or Grant's golden mole (*Eremitalpa granti*) Solitary species that inhabits the coastal dunes of South Africa. It is heavily clawed to assist with burrowing in the sand and has pale grey to yellow fur. It is blind, its eyes being covered in skin and fur. Length: 7–9cm (3–4in).

▶ **banded mongoose** (*Mungos mungo*) Mongoose found from Gambia to Ethiopia and in South Africa. It is brownish-grey with yellow or white stripes across its back. It lives in communal burrows and forages in groups. Length: 30–45cm (12–18in); tail: 23–30cm (9–12in).

◀ **striped field mouse** (*Rhabdomys pumilio*) Medium-sized mouse with a dark greyish-brown coat and yellowish and black dorsal stripes. It usually lives in a nest of moss, leaves and grass and eats mainly grasses, seeds and insects. Length: 9–14cm (4–6in); tail: 8–14cm (3–6in).

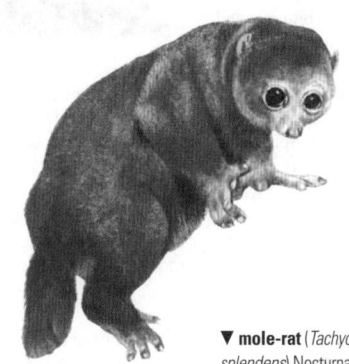

◀ **common potto** (*Perodicticus potto*) Slow-moving primate found in the forests of w Africa. It has sturdy limbs, a short tail, and grey-red woolly fur. It is omnivorous, eating seeds, fruit, insects and insect larvae, as well as tree gum. Length (excluding the tail): 37cm (25in).

▼ **forest elephant shrew** (*Petrodromus tetradactylus*) Named after its long, mobile trunk-like nose, it is found in the forests and thickets of Africa. It has soft grey to sandy fur, sometimes with a black stripe down its back and white rings around its eyes. It does not build a nest but instead sleeps under vegetation or in empty holes. Its diet consists largely of termites. It makes a noise like a cricket and beats its tail on the ground or raps its hind legs together to signal danger. Length: 10–39cm (4–15in); tail: 13–26cm (5–10in).

▼ **Guinea gerbil** (*Tatera guineae*) Nocturnal rodent native to arid regions of Africa. It has powerful hind legs with which it can make long, swift leaps to escape from predators. Using its tail as a rudder, a gerbil can alter course in mid-air. It is also protected by its sensitive hearing. It digs burrows and eats seeds and roots. Gerbils are very popular pets. Length: 15–18cm (6–7in).

▼ **mole-rat** (*Tachyoryctes splendens*) Nocturnal rodent found in E and w Africa. It has very small ears and eyes. It uses its long incisor teeth and sharp claws to dig burrows and tunnels underground. Mole-rats have short, dumpy bodies and short but strong limbs. Their coats are short and thick and colours range from black to brown. Some mole-rats have white markings. The naked mole-rat (*Heterocephalus glaber*) is completely hairless except for its inside mouth and lives entirely underground. Length: 9–27cm (4–11in); tail: 1–3cm (¼–1in).

▲ **common genet** (*Genetta genetta*) Arboreal carnivore found in wooded areas of Africa. A cat-like creature, the common genet has a long body, short legs, and rounded ears. It is grey coloured with dark spots on its sides and a black stripe running down its back. It has dark rings running down its tail and white patches under its eyes. It is mainly nocturnal spending the day in rock crevices or hollow trees, and hunting small mammals and birds on the ground at night. Length: 40–50cm (16–20in); tail: 37–46cm (15–18in).

▼ **fennec fox** or desert fox (*Vulpes zerda*) Tiny canine found in N Africa. The fennec fox is sandy coloured in order to blend in with its desert surroundings. It has very large ears, a small head and bushy tail and is extremely agile. It is nocturnal, spending the day sheltering from the sun in its burrow. It feeds on large insects, small rodents, lizards, and birds. Length: 24–40cm (9–16in); tail: 25cm (10in); ears: 15cm (6in).

▶ **tree pangolin** or scaly anteater (*Manis tricuspis*) The pangolin lives in the forests of Uganda, Kenya, and Tanzania. It is covered with horny, overlapping brown scales and has short, powerful forelegs with which it climbs trees. It has a long broad powerful tail which also assists in climbing. It feeds on termites which it collects with its long, sticky tongue. Length: to 175cm (70in).

Divers and grebes are aquatic birds. As a result they are awkward on land and only come ashore to nest. They have long, slender, pointed bills, which are ideal for dealing with slippery fish. **Shearwaters** and **petrels** are also weak-legged marine birds that come ashore to nest. They are excellent fliers and travel vast distances. Gannets and cormorants look very different but share several structural features including webbed toes. **Gannets** are large birds that are superb fliers and feed by diving into water. **Cormorants** are adapted for swimming underwater and are less skilful fliers. **Herons**, bitterns, and egrets are long legged waterside birds. They have slender bodies to allow them to move through vegetation. Cranes are large birds resembling herons, but they are heavier bodied and have smaller bills. Storks travel great distances by gliding. Spoonbills and ibises are closely related to the storks. Spoonbills are adapted for feeding in shallow water. **Pelicans** are actually related to the gannets and cormorants. They have large throat pouches for scooping fish from the water.

▲ black-necked grebe
or eared grebe (*Podiceps nigricollis*) Tailless grebe with a steep forehead and peaked crown. The breeding adult (bottom) has a black head with a fan of coppery-gold or yellow feathers. Its flanks are coppery-red. In winter (top), the black-necked grebe is dusky grey, black and white. It dives frequently, feeding on insects and tiny fish. Length: 28–34cm (11–14in).

◄ Cory's shearwater
(*Calonectris diomedea*) Bigger and longer winged than a fulmar, for which it is often mistaken. It has a silvery white underside, except for the wingtips, and is dull grey-brown above. It has a yellowish bill. Its head lacks the dark cap of the great shearwater. It is a languid flier, lazily flapping its bowed wings in gentle winds, but rising steeply in strong winds. Cory's shearwater feeds at night on fish and squid, and often scavenges from trawlers. It has a mournful, rasping *kaa-ough* cry. It breeds on rocky islands. Length: 45–55cm (18–22in).

► great shearwater
(*Puffinus gravis*) Large, exclusively marine bird from the Southern Hemisphere. It is more slender than Cory's shearwater, and has a dark cap. It has a white crescent on its rump and a white underside with a dusky belly and wingpit smudges. The great shearwater covers vast distances, soaring on high winds. It is rarer in Europe than the sooty shearwater. It breeds on the island of Tristan da Cunha in the South Atlantic, while the sooty shearwater breeds in the Falklands. They feed on small fish and squid. Length: 43–51cm (17–20in).

▼ great cormorant
(*Phalacrocorax carbo*) Large bird with a slender, hooked-tip bill, which it uses to grasp slippery, muscular fish. After feeding, they often stand with their wings half outspread. Length: 80–100cm (32–39in).

▲ red-necked grebe
(*Podiceps grisegena*) Grebe with a black and white face. It is a good diver, feeding mainly on crustacea and insects, but is a poor flier. In summer, the breeding adult (left) has a deep rusty-red neck. It breeds on ponds and lakes. In winter (right), it has a grey foreneck. It migrates to the coast or larger lakes in the winter. Length: 40–50cm (16–20in).

► northern gannet
(*Morus bassanus*) It dives from a great height and plunges into the sea with a great splash, feeding on fish such as mackerel and herring. The adult has a white body and pointed tail, and black wingtips. Its yellow head fades in winter. Length: 90–100cm (35–39in).

▼ black-throated diver or Arctic loon (*Gavia arctica*) Diver with delicate plumage pattern. The breeding adult (top) has white chequers in two ovals on each side of its back, a black throat, and grey parallel stripes on its neck. The non-breeding adult (bottom) has duller plumage and a paler neck. It emits a howling call in summer, and a deep, short *kwok* in flight. In North America, it is found only in w Alaska. Length: 60–70cm (24–28in).

▼ great northern diver
or common loon (*Gavia immer*) Large, heavy diving bird. It feeds on fish and crab caught in long dives up to 60m (200ft) underwater. It has a huge, dagger shaped bill. The breeding adult (bottom) has an evenly chequered black-and-white back with a black head and black-and-white striped necklace. The non-breeding adult's (top) crown, hindneck, and upperparts are a dull grey, and its throat and underparts are white. In summer, they have a loud, mournful half-wailing, half-laughing call. Length: 70–80cm (28–32in).

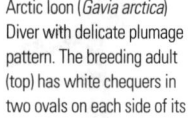

▲ red-throated diver or red-throated loon (*Gavia stellata*) Smallest of the divers, the red-throated diver tilts its slender bill upwards. The breeding adult (top) has a grey head, dark red throat, and fine stripes on its hindneck. In winter (bottom), it has speckled black and white plumage with a white face. In summer, it makes loud quacking notes in flight, and syncopated wailing and rattling sounds in courtship. It builds simple scrape nests on lake shores. It feeds on small fish. Length: 55–69cm (22–27in).

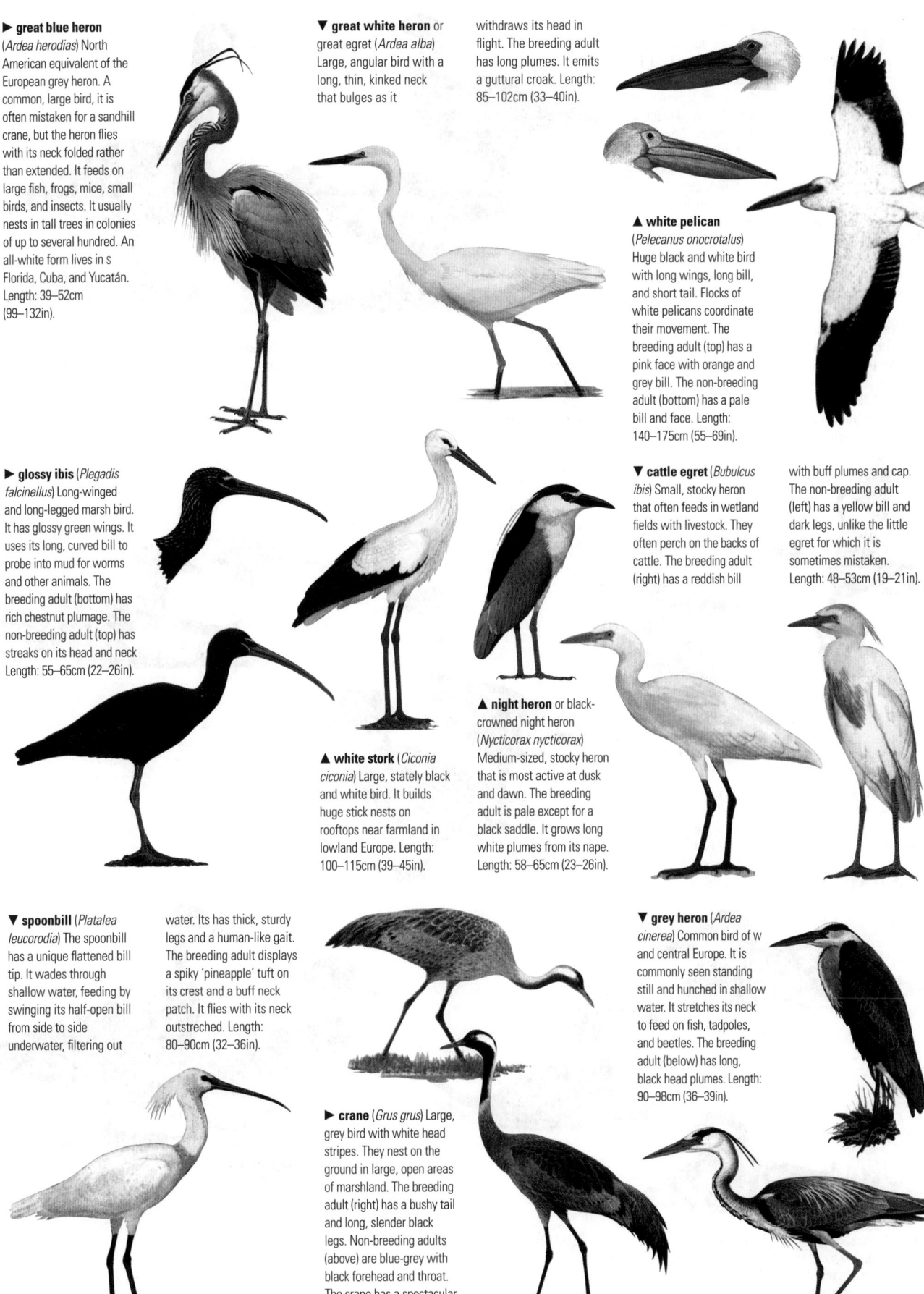

► **great blue heron** (*Ardea herodias*) North American equivalent of the European grey heron. A common, large bird, it is often mistaken for a sandhill crane, but the heron flies with its neck folded rather than extended. It feeds on large fish, frogs, mice, small birds, and insects. It usually nests in tall trees in colonies of up to several hundred. An all-white form lives in s Florida, Cuba, and Yucatán. Length: 39–52cm (99–132in).

▼ **great white heron** or great egret (*Ardea alba*) Large, angular bird with a long, thin, kinked neck that bulges as it withdraws its head in flight. The breeding adult has long plumes. It emits a guttural croak. Length: 85–102cm (33–40in).

▲ **white pelican** (*Pelecanus onocrotalus*) Huge black and white bird with long wings, long bill, and short tail. Flocks of white pelicans coordinate their movement. The breeding adult (top) has a pink face with orange and grey bill. The non-breeding adult (bottom) has a pale bill and face. Length: 140–175cm (55–69in).

► **glossy ibis** (*Plegadis falcinellus*) Long-winged and long-legged marsh bird. It has glossy green wings. It uses its long, curved bill to probe into mud for worms and other animals. The breeding adult (bottom) has rich chestnut plumage. The non-breeding adult (top) has streaks on its head and neck Length: 55–65cm (22–26in).

▲ **white stork** (*Ciconia ciconia*) Large, stately black and white bird. It builds huge stick nests on rooftops near farmland in lowland Europe. Length: 100–115cm (39–45in).

▼ **cattle egret** (*Bubulcus ibis*) Small, stocky heron that often feeds in wetland fields with livestock. They often perch on the backs of cattle. The breeding adult (right) has a reddish bill with buff plumes and cap. The non-breeding adult (left) has a yellow bill and dark legs, unlike the little egret for which it is sometimes mistaken. Length: 48–53cm (19–21in).

▲ **night heron** or black-crowned night heron (*Nycticorax nycticorax*) Medium-sized, stocky heron that is most active at dusk and dawn. The breeding adult is pale except for a black saddle. It grows long white plumes from its nape. Length: 58–65cm (23–26in).

▼ **spoonbill** (*Platalea leucorodia*) The spoonbill has a unique flattened bill tip. It wades through shallow water, feeding by swinging its half-open bill from side to side underwater, filtering out water. Its has thick, sturdy legs and a human-like gait. The breeding adult displays a spiky 'pineapple' tuft on its crest and a buff neck patch. It flies with its neck outstreched. Length: 80–90cm (32–36in).

► **crane** (*Grus grus*) Large, grey bird with white head stripes. They nest on the ground in large, open areas of marshland. The breeding adult (right) has a bushy tail and long, slender black legs. Non-breeding adults (above) are blue-grey with black forehead and throat. The crane has a spectacular courtship dance. Length: 115–130cm (45–51in).

▼ **grey heron** (*Ardea cinerea*) Common bird of w and central Europe. It is commonly seen standing still and hunched in shallow water. It stretches its neck to feed on fish, tadpoles, and beetles. The breeding adult (below) has long, black head plumes. Length: 90–98cm (36–39in).

Wildfowl includes all the swans, geese, and ducks. **Swans** are large, short-legged, long-necked birds that feed in water or on land. **Geese** are stockier than swans but larger than most ducks, with longer legs which make them more mobile on land. They feed in large flocks and fly in wonderful V-formations, lines, and chevrons. They form two basic groups, the 'grey geese' (grey-brown and white with variously coloured legs and bills) and the 'black geese' (grey or dark brown with a lot of black, and black legs and bills). Dabbling or surface-feeding **ducks** feed by filtering water through fine 'combs' in their bills to extract food; they also feed underwater by 'up-ending' but rarely diving, and graze or pick on grain on land. They have short legs but walk moderately well, and long wings which, despite their heavy bodies, allow fast and powerful flight. Diving ducks feed underwater, diving from the surface. Some species live at sea, others mostly freshwater or both. Finally, the sawbills are fish-catching species whose bills have toothed edges for gripping slippery prey. Shown here are some wildfowl common to North America and Europe.

▲ **brent goose** or brant goose (*Branta bernicla*) Small, chunky, dark goose with a dark head and small neck patches. The pale-bellied form (bottom) winters in Ireland and central Britain. The black brant (top) is native to North America. Length: 56–61cm (22–24in).

▲ **Canada goose** (*Branta canadensis*) One of the most common birds in North America. It was introduced into Britain as an ornamental species. Canada geese emit a deep *ah-honk* call. They feed on grassland close to water. Length: 90–110cm (35–43in).

▼ **pintail** (*Anas acuta*) Common bird in North America but rare in Western Europe. The male (bottom) has elegant plumage and a whistling call. The female (top) is akin to a mallard but has a more refined shape. Length: 51–76cm (20–30in).

▲ **goldeneye** (*Bucephala clangula*) Solitary bird that is a fast flier as well as a fine diver and feeds on molluscs and crustacea. The male (left) has a glossy green head with a distinct, large, white spot under the eye. The female (right) has a darker head with dark grey-brown plumage. Length: 42–50cm (16–20in).

▲ **red-breasted merganser** (*Mergus serrator*) Large, long duck with a sawbill, which it uses to catch fish. The male (left) has a pied body with black lines across the inner wing, and a dark green-black head. The female (right) is drabber and browner. The red-breasted merganser has a slimmer beak and more spiky plumage than the common merganser or goosander. The female lacks the white chin patch of the female goosander. They nest on the ground in tall grass close to the shore. Length: 51–62cm (20–24in).

▲ **ruddy duck** (*Oxyura jamaicensis*) Duck native to North America, but which established itself in Europe after some escaped in Britain in the 1950s. In winter, the male ruddy duck has a white face and dark brown body (top). The female (middle) has a darker face crossed with a brown bar. In spring, the male acquires a splendid reddish body (bottom) and blue bill. They swim with their tails pointing up. Ruddy ducks build platform nests in reeds. Length: 35–43cm (14–17in).

▲ **mallard** (*Anas platyrhynchos*) Common wild and domesticated duck in North America and Europe. From autumn to spring, the adult male or drake (left) has a glossy green head, white neck ring, chocolate breast, and purple-blue patches on each wing. In summer, the drake moults to resemble the female (right). Length: 51–62cm (20–24in).

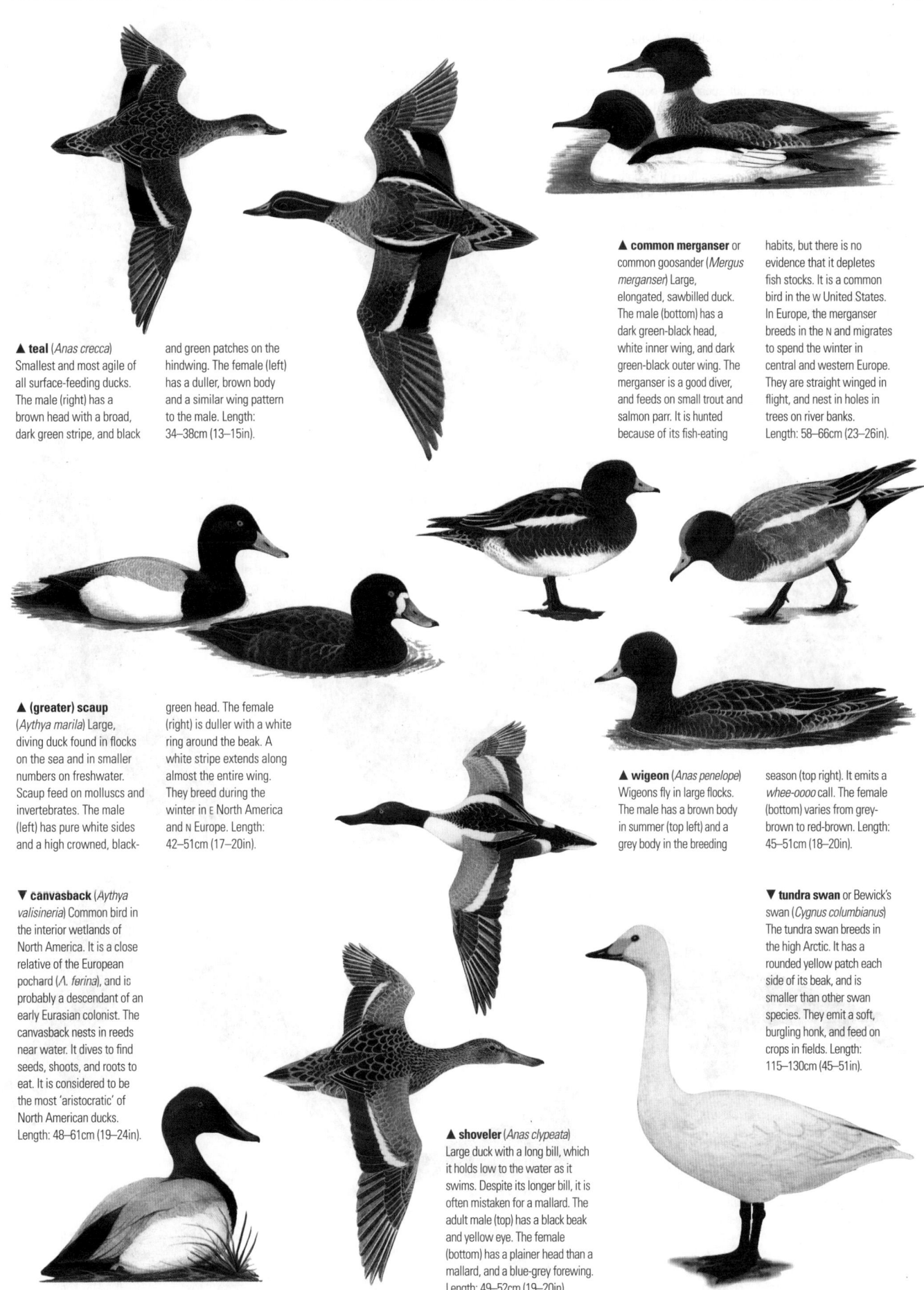

▲ **teal** (*Anas crecca*) Smallest and most agile of all surface-feeding ducks. The male (right) has a brown head with a broad, dark green stripe, and black and green patches on the hindwing. The female (left) has a duller, brown body and a similar wing pattern to the male. Length: 34–38cm (13–15in).

▲ **common merganser** or common goosander (*Mergus merganser*) Large, elongated, sawbilled duck. The male (bottom) has a dark green-black head, white inner wing, and dark green-black outer wing. The merganser is a good diver, and feeds on small trout and salmon parr. It is hunted because of its fish-eating habits, but there is no evidence that it depletes fish stocks. It is a common bird in the w United States. In Europe, the merganser breeds in the N and migrates to spend the winter in central and western Europe. They are straight winged in flight, and nest in holes in trees on river banks. Length: 58–66cm (23–26in).

▲ **(greater) scaup** (*Aythya marila*) Large, diving duck found in flocks on the sea and in smaller numbers on freshwater. Scaup feed on molluscs and invertebrates. The male (left) has pure white sides and a high crowned, black-green head. The female (right) is duller with a white ring around the beak. A white stripe extends along almost the entire wing. They breed during the winter in E North America and N Europe. Length: 42–51cm (17–20in).

▼ **canvasback** (*Aythya valisineria*) Common bird in the interior wetlands of North America. It is a close relative of the European pochard (*A. ferina*), and is probably a descendant of an early Eurasian colonist. The canvasback nests in reeds near water. It dives to find seeds, shoots, and roots to eat. It is considered to be the most 'aristocratic' of North American ducks. Length: 48–61cm (19–24in).

▲ **wigeon** (*Anas penelope*) Wigeons fly in large flocks. The male has a brown body in summer (top left) and a grey body in the breeding season (top right). It emits a *whee-oooo* call. The female (bottom) varies from grey-brown to red-brown. Length: 45–51cm (18–20in).

▲ **shoveler** (*Anas clypeata*) Large duck with a long bill, which it holds low to the water as it swims. Despite its longer bill, it is often mistaken for a mallard. The adult male (top) has a black beak and yellow eye. The female (bottom) has a plainer head than a mallard, and a blue-grey forewing. Length: 49–52cm (19–20in).

▼ **tundra swan** or Bewick's swan (*Cygnus columbianus*) The tundra swan breeds in the high Arctic. It has a rounded yellow patch each side of its beak, and is smaller than other swan species. They emit a soft, burgling honk, and feed on crops in fields. Length: 115–130cm (45–51in).

Birds of prey have hooked bills and sharp, carved claws to catch live food or forage for dead animals (carrion) or refuse. Most birds of prey are superb fliers, but spend long periods inactive on perches. Vultures, kites, harriers, hawks, buzzards, and eagles all belong to the same family, the Accipitridae. **Vultures** are carrion-eaters that exploit air currents to glide as they search the ground for food. **Kites** are elegant fliers that both kill live prey and eat carrion and refuse. **Harriers** are long-winged birds with sharp claws and a long reach, adapted for snatching prey while hunting low over grassy or reed-covered areas and open moors. Bird-eating **hawks** also have a long reach, with long needle-sharp claws; they are short winged, long tailed, fast, agile hunters in woods and gardens. **Buzzards** soar and hover. They catch live food and eat a lot of carrion. **Eagles** are the largest birds of prey. They are powerful hunters and expert fliers that kill much of their food, but often scavenge meat from dead animals. **Falcons** belong to a different family; long-winged and long-tailed, their prey ranges from insects to large birds.

▼ **osprey** (*Pandion haliaetus*) The osprey has a spectacular fishing method. Hovering until they spy their prey, they dive headlong, wings swept back, towards the water, then swing back before entering the water to grasp their prey. They are brown above and white below. Length: 55–65cm (22–26in).

▲ **gyr falcon** (*Falco rusticolus*) Large, heavy, and powerful bird. The gyr falcon is often spotted perched on a rock, watching for prey such as big birds and small mammals. The species has many plumage variations. Length: 55–60cm (22–24in).

▼ **hen harrier** or northern harrier (*Circus cyaneus*) Bird with a disc-shaped face like an owl. The adult male (left) is pale grey with a white underwing and dark trailing edge. The adult female (right) is brown with a white rump and barred tail. They fly close to the ground, hunting rodents and small birds. Length: 43–50cm (17–20in).

▼ **sparrowhawk** (*Accipiter nisus*) Quick, broad-winged, long-tailed hawk, which usually flies low to the ground in woodland, hunting small birds such as tits and finches. The adult female (below) is larger than the male, has darker grey upperparts, and is white rather than rufous below, with dark bars. Length: 28–38cm (11–15in).

▲ **red kite** (*Milvus milvus*) Most elegant of the large raptors. The red kite has long, angled wings and a forked tail, which makes it a supreme flier. The adult bird has a grey-white head with neat fine streaks. It is a symbol of the success of bird conservation efforts in Britain. The red kite searches for its prey, chiefly worms and small birds, on the wing. They emit loud, wavering squeals. Length: 60–65cm (24–26in).

▶ **peregrine** (*Falco peregrinus*) Peregrines are fast and wide-ranging flyers that hunt birds. They have bold head patterns. Length: 39–50cm (15–20in).

▶ **California condor** (*Gymnogyps californianus*) Largest bird of prey in North America. It is an endangered species, and none are currently breeding in the wild. It is susceptible to poisoning from lead in its prey of large mammals. Length: 110–140cm (45–55in).

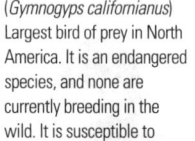

▲ **merlin** (*Falco columbarius*) Small, agile, and fast-flying falcon, commonly seen over moorland hunting for small birds and large moths. The merlin watches its prey from a low perch. It has broad wings and short, tapering wingtips. The adult male (right) is bluish-grey above and orange-buff below. The adult female is earthy-brown. Merlins are solitary birds. Length: 25–30cm (10–12in).

▶ **bald eagle** (*Haliaeetus leucocephalus*) National bird of the United States. It has a black body and wings, a white head and tail, and a heavy yellow bill. They eat fish, which they snatch from the surface with their talons or steal from osprey. Once abundant in the flat pinelands of Florida, it has become an endangered species due to the presence of pesticides in the Everglades food chain. Alaska is the only state where the bald eagle is not threatened by extinction. The name bald does not imply a lack of feathers, but derives from an redundant word meaning marked with white, as in piebald. Length: 76–79cm (30–31in).

▲ **kestrel** (*Falco tinnunculus*) Most common of the European falcons. It is often spotted perched or hovering beside a road, watching for small mammals, especially voles, to eat. The adult female (right) has beautifully barred plumage over its back and tail. The adult male (centre) has a grey head, with weak moustache, spotted back, and blue-black tail. Both sexes have a distinctive pale inner wing and underwing and dark outer wing. Length: 33–39cm (13–15in) .

▼ **rough-legged buzzard** (*Buteo lagopus*) Large, long-winged bird. It is more accomplished at hovering than other buzzards. Length: 50–60cm (20–24in).

▲ **golden eagle** (*Aquila chrysaetos*) Majestic and powerful raptor. It soars on broad, long, outstretched wings. Its new feathers are black-brown, while the older feathers bleach to a golden, buff, or greyish colour. The base of the tail is often pale grey with dark bars. Golden eagles feed mainly on dead sheep and deer, but also eat medium-sized live animals. Length: 76–89cm (30–35in).

▲ **swallow-tailed kite** (*Elanoides forficatus*) Most aerial of all birds of prey in North America, as it not only captures its food (mainly insects) on the wing but also drinks while flying. It breeds in the Gulf of Florida area. Length: 56–61cm (22–24in).

◀ **common buzzard** (*Buteo buteo*) Most frequently sighted bird of prey in w Britain. A stocky bird, the buzzard is often spotted perched on poles, trees, or fences, or soaring with wings held in a V-shape. It feeds on small mammals and insects. They typically have dark plumage that pales towards the tail. The plumage on the inner wing is barred with a distinct pale patch towards the tip. Length: 51–57cm (20–23in).

▲ **turkey vulture** (*Cathartes aura*) Most widespread vultures of the Americas, nesting everywhere in the United States, except N New England. It is ungainly on land but a majestic flyer. They are often spotted soaring on thermals, searching for carrion. Length: 64–81cm (25–32in).

▲ **goshawk** (*Accipiter gentilis*) Essentially a much larger version of the sparrowhawk, it is far less common than its relative. The goshawk is a powerful woodland predator, catching much larger prey than the sparrowhawk. They usually hunt low over the ground. The female goshawk is larger and stockier than the male. Length: 48–61 cm (19–24in).

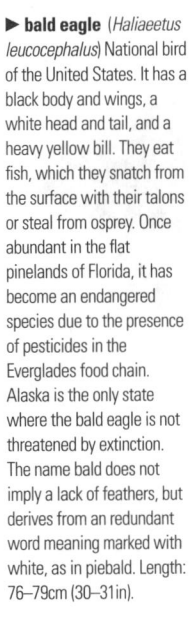

Game birds are a small but diverse group of seed-eating birds with short, curved bills, longish legs with sharp 'spurs', and a low fast, whirring flight. Game birds include grouse, partridges, pheasants, and quails. **Grouse** are mainly upland birds adapted to harsh climates. **Partridges** are squat, short-tailed birds, while **pheasants** are larger and have longer tails. **Quails** are tiny, secretive birds that usually live in fields of dense crops. **Crakes** and **rails** are waterside birds with long toes, sometimes lobed, that allow them to walk over waterlogged ground and floating weed. From the side they appear to have round bodies, but in fact their bodies are extremely slim, enabling them to slip through dense vertical stems of reedbeds. Some are common and obvious, often spotted on open water, while others are rare and secretive, living in dense vegetation.

▲ **spruce grouse** (*Dendragapus canadensis*) Most common grouse of the coniferous forests in Canada and the N United States. Each male defends a separate territory. They eat insects, berries, and conifer needles. Length: 38–43cm (15–17in).

▲ **coot** (*Fulica atra*) Common water bird in Europe, often seen swimming in flocks. Coots graze on grass, but also eat aquatic plants, seeds, insects, snails, and tadpoles, diving regularly and bobbing up again like a cork. In their breeding season they are aggressive and territorial, and males often fight noisily. Coots build large nests at the water's edge. Length: 36–38cm (14–15in).

▲ **(rock) ptarmigan** (*Lagopus mutus*) The ptarmigan lives in the tundra of North America and Europe. In winter, it is white except for a black tail and black line through the eye. Its winter plumage provides good protection against the cold because white feathers have empty cells filled with air that help insulation, whereas coloured feathers contain pigment. In summer, the male (left) has wing feathers flecked with dark grey-brown. The female (right) is paler, with yellowish brown feathers. Length: 34–36cm (13–14in).

◄ **quail** (*Coturnix coturnix*) Small, plump game bird. the quail is elusive, rarely seen but frequently heard in cereal fields. It projects its territorial song of *whit, whit-it* over long distances. Its natural habitat is grassland and steppe. The quail is a stocky bird with sharp wings and a very short tail. The male (top) is striped above with a boldly marked head and black throat. The female (bottom) has a weaker version of the male's face pattern. Length: 16–18cm (6½–7in).

▲ **Gambel's quail** (*Callipepla gambelii*) Quail that lives in the SW deserts of the United States. The barking call of the male is one of the most familiar sounds in the desert. A stocky, mainly grey bird, it has a distinctive, curved black head plume and rusty sides with diagonal stripes. Gambel's quail are often seen, in coveys of up to 40 birds, drinking at cattle troughs. Length: 25–29cm (10–11½in).

▲ **chukar** (*Alectoris chukar*) It was introduced to North America and Britain from the SE Mediterranean region. It has widely interbred with the red-legged partridge (*Alectoris rufa*). The chukar has a cream face, bordered by a neat black bib, and bold chestnut and black diagonal stripes on its flanks. It has a fast, loud song of *chuk chuk chuk-ke-cher*. Length: 32–34cm (13–13½in).

▼ **moorhen** (*Gallinula chloropus*) Familiar yet shy water bird. It has distinctive white flank stripes and patches under the tail. The male (top) has richer, more glossy brown upperparts than the female (bottom). Length: 32–35cm (12½–14in).

▼ **wild turkey** (*Meleagris gallopavo*) Common wild bird in North America and a familiar domestic species in Europe. The male is larger (120cm/48in) than the female (91cm/36in) and has a long 'beard' on its breast.

▲ **willow grouse** or willow ptarmigan (*Lagopus lagopus*) Thick-set game bird of northern forests and tundra. It is entirely white in winter. The female (top) is slightly larger than the (rock) ptarmigan and is less grey in summer. The male (bottom) is more rufous and less barred than its (rock) ptarmigan counterpart. Length: 37–42cm (14.5–16½in).

▲ **greater prairie chicken** (*Tympanuchus cupido*) Chicken found in 11 Midwestern and Plains states of the United States. It is threatened by the shrinking of the prairies. During courtship display, male prairie chickens inflate orange air sacs along their throats, and erect the long black feathers on their necks. Length: 41–46cm (16–18in).

▼ **grey partridge** (*Perdix perdix*) Britain's only native partridge, it was introduced in North America. It is a small, stocky, largely grey bird, which flies with bowed wings. It has a deep brown flank and dark horsehoe marking on its lower breast. Some birds have very rufous back feathers. Males have a loud cry of *kee-err-ik*. Like many farmland birds, it declined dramatically in the late 20th century. Length: 42–51cm (16½–20in).

 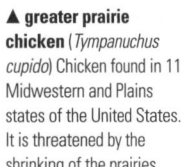

▲ **corncrake** (*Crex crex*) Secretive bird, it is rarely seen but often heard in its mating grounds in the dense grasslands of Europe. Early hay-cutting has led to a drastic decline in the corncrake population. The male (left) looks dark and grey with barred flanks and has a loud, harsh cry of *crek-crek*. The female (right) is more orange. In autumn, they migrate from Europe to Africa. They eat small insects and seeds. Length: 27–30cm (10½–12in).

▲ **sora rail** (*Porzana carolina*) Common but very secretive bird in the marshlands of North America. Its whinnying call of piping, rapidly descending notes is a familiar sound in marsh areas. It is closely related to the spotted crake of Eurasia. In winter, they migrate south. Length: 20–25cm (8–10in).

▼ **spotted crake** (*Porzana porzana*) Secretive, shuffling bird of European marshland. It is rare in Britain. The spotted crake has richly barred and spotted plumage, a short orange-red bill, and green legs. The juvenile (bottom) and the female are browner with whiter belly markings than the male (top). It eats insects, worms, seeds, and berries, which it picks from the mud beneath reeds. It has a *whit-whit-whit* call. Length: 22–24cm (9–9½in).

▼ **pheasant** or ring-necked pheasant (*Phasianus colchicus*) Long-tailed, heavy-bodied game bird that is native to Asia. It is often tame where released for shooting. The male (bottom) has richly varied plumage with coppery flanks and redder back. The female (top) is duller and paler. Length: 52–90cm (21–35in).

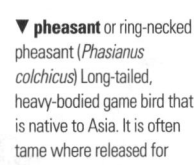

▲ **water rail** (*Rallus aquaticus*) Usually seen in reedbeds and freshwater marshes, water rails are elusive birds. The adult is blue-grey below with white bars on the flank and long red-pink toes. The tail (top) pattern is individually unique. Length: 22–28cm (9–11in).

Waders form a very large and complex group of bird families. Many live far from any shore and rarely wade; some breed in dry areas but spend the winter on shorelines. All families, however, have long legs and thin bills. The **avocets** are true wading birds that exploit shallow water and sweep their curved bills through muddy water to catch tiny shrimps and other small animals. **Oystercatchers** eat shellfish when they can, smashing or prising them open with their strong, red bills. They are noisy, eye-catching birds that nest in pairs, probably for life. The **plovers** include the widespread but declining **lapwing** that breeds and spends the winter on arable land and marshes, and the **dotterel** that breeds on mountain grasslands and the northern tundra. The **sandpipers** include some very numerous and gregarious species such as the **knot**, which flies in huge, highly coordinated flocks often migrating impressive distances. The **dunlin** is one of the most widespread and familiar of the sandpipers, and a 'standard' by which others are judged and identified.

▲ **avocet** (*Recurvirostra avosetta*) Round-bodied, small-headed wader with stark black and white patterning and an upcurved, black bill. It feeds by sweeping its bill sideways through water or mud to capture tiny invertebrates. Length: 42–45cm (16–18in).

▲ **oystercatcher** (*Haematopus ostralegus*) The summer adult (right) has an orange bill, red eyes, black upperside and white underparts. The winter adult (left) has a white collar. White tail and wing markings visible in flight. Length: 40–45cm (16–18in).

▼ **dotterel** (*Charadrius morinellus*) Short-billed bird with a striking V on the head and a white band around the breast. The breeding female (below) is dark underneath, the winter female (top right) is similar to the male (bottom right). Length: 20–22cm (8–9in).

▲ **American avocet** (*Recurvirostra americana*) It has a slender, upturned bill like the European avocet. Its head and neck are rust coloured, but white in winter, and its upperparts and wings are black and white. It has a white body and blue-grey legs. It lives in freshwater marshes and shallow lakes across most of central and w USA. Length: 41–51cm (16–20in).

▲ **Kentish plover** or snowy plover (*Charadrius alexandrinus*) It has pale grey-brown upperparts and a white belly and face. The breeding male (bottom) has black marks on its head and sides of breast. The female (top) is a paler sandy colour and has no black markings. It eats molluscs and crustacea. Length: 13–18cm (5–7in).

▲ **killdeer** (*Charadrius vociferus*) Common in North America and also found in South America. It will feign injury to lure predators away from its young and then fly off. It has a brown back, white underparts and face, and two black bands across the breast. Length: 23–28cm (9–11in).

▲ **sanderling** (*Calidris alba*) The breeding adult (top) is mottled black and rust-red in spring, the non-breeding adult (bottom) is grey and white. Its blackish wings have a broad white stripe. It is often seen running along the water's edge on sandy beaches. Flocks twitter when feeding. Length: 20–21cm (8in).

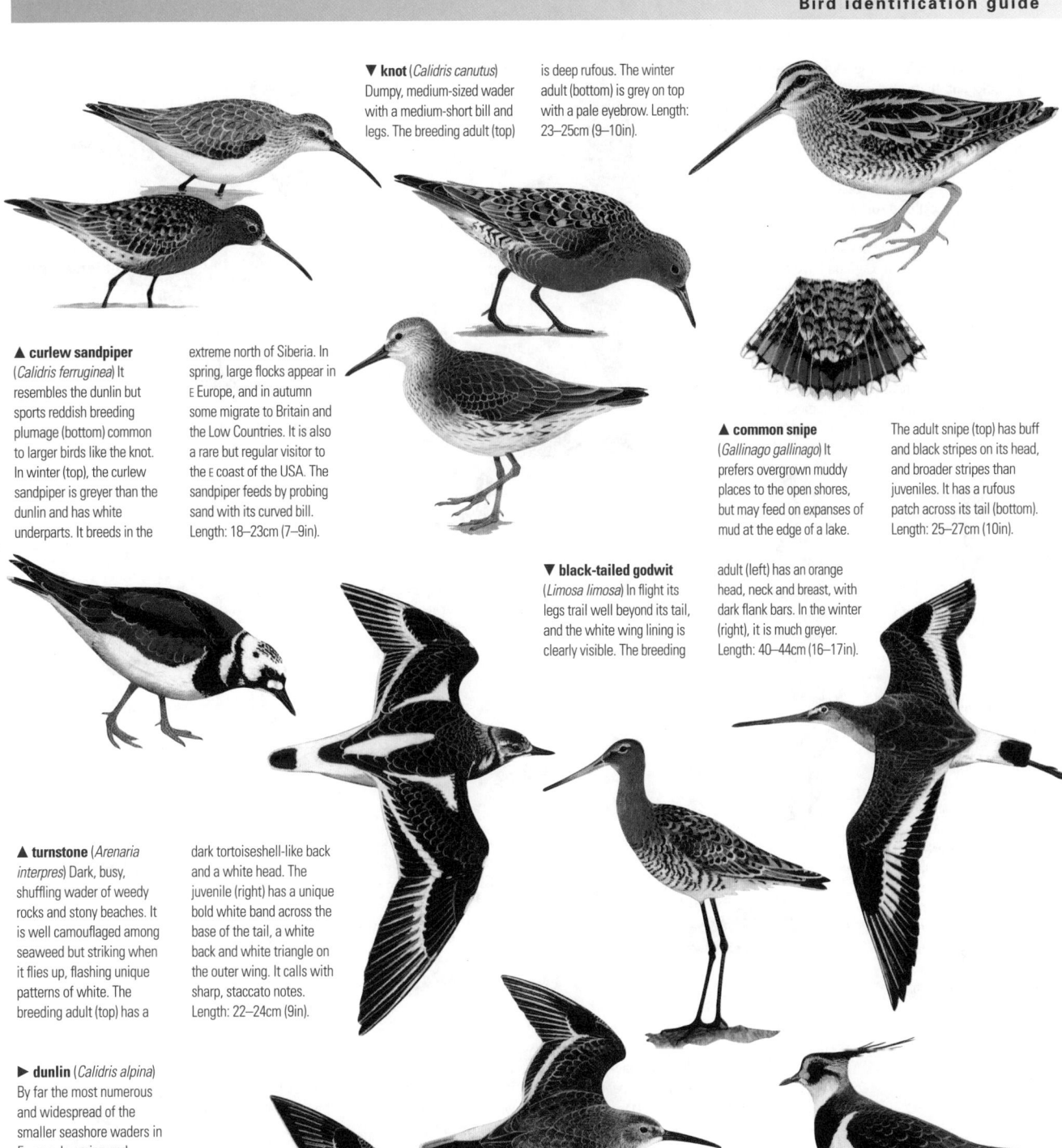

▲ **curlew sandpiper** (*Calidris ferruginea*) It resembles the dunlin but sports reddish breeding plumage (bottom) common to larger birds like the knot. In winter (top), the curlew sandpiper is greyer than the dunlin and has white underparts. It breeds in the extreme north of Siberia. In spring, large flocks appear in E Europe, and in autumn some migrate to Britain and the Low Countries. It is also a rare but regular visitor to the E coast of the USA. The sandpiper feeds by probing sand with its curved bill. Length: 18–23cm (7–9in).

▼ **knot** (*Calidris canutus*) Dumpy, medium-sized wader with a medium-short bill and legs. The breeding adult (top) is deep rufous. The winter adult (bottom) is grey on top with a pale eyebrow. Length: 23–25cm (9–10in).

▲ **common snipe** (*Gallinago gallinago*) It prefers overgrown muddy places to the open shores, but may feed on expanses of mud at the edge of a lake. The adult snipe (top) has buff and black stripes on its head, and broader stripes than juveniles. It has a rufous patch across its tail (bottom). Length: 25–27cm (10in).

▲ **turnstone** (*Arenaria interpres*) Dark, busy, shuffling wader of weedy rocks and stony beaches. It is well camouflaged among seaweed but striking when it flies up, flashing unique patterns of white. The breeding adult (top) has a dark tortoiseshell-like back and a white head. The juvenile (right) has a unique bold white band across the base of the tail, a white back and white triangle on the outer wing. It calls with sharp, staccato notes. Length: 22–24cm (9in).

▼ **black-tailed godwit** (*Limosa limosa*) In flight its legs trail well beyond its tail, and the white wing lining is clearly visible. The breeding adult (left) has an orange head, neck and breast, with dark flank bars. In the winter (right), it is much greyer. Length: 40–44cm (16–17in).

▶ **dunlin** (*Calidris alpina*) By far the most numerous and widespread of the smaller seashore waders in Europe. In spring and autumn they are often seen inland, close to lakes and reservoirs. The winter adult (right) has a grey-brown upper with dark streaks. The transitional autumn coat (left) shows scattered dark-chestnut summer feathers among grey. In spring, dunlin flocks separate into pairs, and the males advertise their territories in flight displays. These begin with a fast steep rise, followed by a hovering or switchback flight into the wind, with a prolonged, whinnying trill. Length: 16–20cm (6–8in).

◀ **lapwing** (*Vanellus vanellus*) Short-billed bird with a wispy crest. A black breastband contrasts with white belly and underwing. The breeding male (left) has a black throat, the non-breeding male and female (top) have white throats. It has an unmistakable broad-winged, jerky flight. Length: 28–31cm (11–12in).

This group includes the **skuas**: long-winged, elegant fliers that are both predatory and piratical, stealing much of their food from other species. The more abundant and widespread **gulls** range from small and neat to very large and aggressive, with several 'generalist' and opportunist species such as the black-headed gull and some very specialized ones. The rather similar **terns** include pale-plumaged 'sea terns' that plunge-dive for fish, and 'marsh terns' that dip the surface for food while flying and have a great deal of black plumage in summer. **Auks** are a small group of sea birds that spend most of their life at sea, coming inland usually only to nest, rather like the shearwaters (*see* page 28). Unlike the shearwaters, however, auks spend their time swimming rather than flying, since they are heavy bodied and short winged. They can ride out most storms so long as they are not driven too close to shore.

▼ **kittiwake** (*Rissa tridactyla*) Small gull of the open ocean, named after its call. The breeding adult (left) is matt grey across the back with a long white head, white tail, black wingtips, black eyes, and yellow bill. In winter, the kittiwake (below) has a dusky ear patch and smoky grey nape. It eats mostly fish. Length: 38–40cm (15–16in).

▲ **black-headed gull** (*Larus ridibundus*) Very familiar bird, spotted inland as often as by the coast. It is small, pale, and noisy. The non-breeding adult (top) has a white head with grey crown. The breeding adult (bottom) has a black head. Length: 34–37cm (13–14in).

▶ **common gull** or mew gull (*Larus canus*) Confusingly not the most common gull in most of Europe and North America. It has similar patterns to a herring gull, but is smaller and neater. The breeding adult has black wingtips with two large white spots. It eats mainly earthworms, insect larvae, and other invetebrates. It is typically spotted foraging in flocks on fields or beaches. Length: 40–43cm (16–17in).

▼ **herring gull** (*Larus argentatus*) The quintessential 'seagull'. A big, bold, noisy bird, the herring gull is white-headed in winter (right) but streaked in autumn and winter (left). It has a grey back and black and white wingtips. It is often spotted eating food leftover by humans. Length: 55–64cm (22–25in).

▲ **glaucous gull** (*Larus hyperboreus*) Large, powerful bird. The adult is white below and pearl grey above. Its broad primary and secondary tips extend beyond the tail to form a bold white triangle. In summer, the adult (right) has a white head. The rest of the year, it is streaked (left). Length: 63–68cm (25–27in).

▶ **fulmar** or northern fulmar (*Fulmarus glacialis*) Stocky petrel whose grey tail and stiff, almost straight-winged, gliding flight distinguishes it from the gulls. The fulmar has a large white head. It is rarely seen from the shore since they eat at sea, feeding largely on dead fish and offal thrown overboard from fishing boats. The expansion of commercial fishing in the 20th century greatly increased the fulmar population. Length: 45–50cm (18–20in).

▼ **great black-backed gull** (*Larus marinus*) Largest of the gulls. It is a stocky, heavy billed bird. Its plumage is heavily contrasted, with a dark black back and bright white head and body in summer (bottom). In winter, the head (top) is mottled but whiter than the lesser black-backed gull. Length: 64–78cm (25–31in).

▲ **ring-billed gull** (*Larus delawarensis*) Common bird of North America and a rare visitor to NW Europe. It is larger and paler than the common gull. In summer, the adult (right) has black wingtips with smaller white spots than the common gull. In winter (above), it has a streaked head. Length: 43–47cm (17–18.5in).

◄ **great skua** (*Stercorarius skua*) Largest and heaviest of the skuas. It is a powerful, gull-like bird with long wings and a short, squarish tail. The great skua is a mottled grey-brown colour with large white patches on its outer wing. It is a pirate of the air, stealing fish from other birds. It can kill gulls and auks with hammer blows of its thick, hooded, dark bill. Length: 53–58cm (21–23in).

◄ **guillemot** or common murre (*Uria aalge*) Sleek, elegant auk. It is brown above with a white front. It stands upright, resting on the full length of its leg. The entire head and neck of the breeding adult (top) is dark brown. The non-breeding adult (middle and bottom) has a white face with a dark stripe through the eye and a dark crescent on the side of its chest. Guillemots use their wings to make deep dives for fish. They breed in large colonies on open ledges of sheer cliffs. Length: 38–41cm (15–16in).

► **puffin** (*Fratercula arctica*) Small auk with sharply contrasting black and white plumage and a colourful red and yellow triangular bill in summer. In winter, the bill is smaller and duller (top). For most of the year, puffins live far out at sea, feeding mainly on fish and small crustaceans. Puffins have a clumsy, waddling walk that is faintly comical, but they are excellent swimmers and divers. Length: 26–29cm (10–11in).

▼ **razorbill** (*Alca torda*) Penguin-like on land, with a white line in front of the eye in the breeding season (right). The non-breeding adult (left) has a black crescent on its neck. Length: 37–39cm (14¾–15½in).

▲ **Caspian tern** (*Sterna caspia*) Largest tern. It is a rare migrant to N and W Europe. It has a stout, deep-red bill, black legs and long wings with black under the wingtips. The

breeding adult (top) has a flat, bushy crest and black forehead until midsummer. The winter adult (bottom) has a pale streaked cap. Length: 47–54cm (18½–21in).

▼ **Arctic tern** (*Sterna paradisaea*) Most slender and elegant of the terns (right and bottom). Compared with the common tern, it has a shorter head and legs, shorter and deeper red bill, longer tail, more rounded cap, and more uniformly grey wings. Length: 33–35cm (13–14in).

▲ **common tern** (*Sterna hirundo*) Pale grey bird with a flat, black cap and black-tipped red bill in summer. The common tern has a longer head and bill, shorter tail, and duskier outer primary feathers than the Arctic tern. It has grey wings above (left) and paler grey below (right). Length: 31–35cm (12–14in).

◄ **gull-billed tern** (*Gelochelidon nilotica*) Stocky, long-winged, short-billed, and long-legged bird. Unlike most other terns, it feeds mainly over pastures and moorlands. In the summer breeding season, it has a distinctive black cap and all-black bill (top and bottom). Unlike the Sandwich tern, it has an all-grey upperside. In winter, it looks very pale despite its grey rump and grey or black eye patch. It eats insects, lizards, and voles. Length: 35–38cm (14–15in).

The **swifts** are almost exclusively aerial birds; unable to perch or walk they spend most of their lives in the air. They are rapid fliers, catching and feeding on flying insects and landing only to nest. Swifts are long-range, migratory birds with many species found worldwide, particularly in tropical regions. **Woodpeckers** are members of the family *Picidae*. They excavate holes in trees for nesting using their stout bills for pecking, sharp claws for climbing and their stiff tails as a prop. Some woodpeckers extract prey from tree bark and wood using their strong beaks. They have loud calls and can be heard 'drumming' on resonant, dead wood in spring. One North American group of woodpeckers are the **flickers**. This group feed from the ground and eat mostly ants. The **sapsucker** group of woodpeckers are also North American and use their strong bills to drill into the sap of trees. There are more than 90 species of **kingfishers** throughout the world. Strikingly coloured they are related to the conspicuous **hoopoe**, which is the only species in the hoopoe family.

► **swift** (*Apus apus*) Superb fliers that spend most of their time in the air. Swifts eat insects, mate, and even sleep on the wing. They are slim, dark birds with a whitish chin. They are usually seen in noisy flocks around buildings. They cannot perch and never land on the ground. They are common throughout Europe in the summer. Length: 16–17cm (6–7in).

▲ **white-throated swift** (*Aeronautes saxatalis*) The white-throated swift lives in arid mountain ranges of SW USA. Often seen and heard chattering in groups around high cliffs, their nests are difficult to see from a distance. The nest consist of a shallow cup of twigs, feathers and grass, glued together with saliva and attached to the rockface. White-throated swifts fly far in search of food and can be seen over desert lowlands, miles from their colonies. Length: 15–18cm (6–7in).

► **Alpine swift** (*Apus melba*) The Alpine swift is a large swift. Its broad wings provide powerful flight. It has brown plumage and a white belly and chin. A vagrant to Britain in the spring, when the occasional bird overshoots its path, they are common in S European mountain ranges and gorges. In autumn, they migrate to Africa. Length: 20–22cm (8–9in).

▲ **little swift** or house swift (*Apus affinis*) Typically seen in the skies of towns and cities. They are easy to distinguish from the similar white-rumped swift by their short, square tails, large pale chins, and broad rump. They make a high, screeching trill. Little swifts live in Africa and the Middle East, but are occasionally spotted in Europe. Pairs of little swifts make globular nests of straw feathers and saliva on buildings. Length: 14cm (6in).

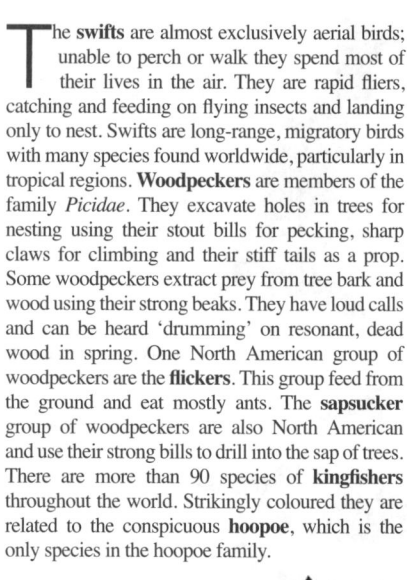

◄ **great spotted woodpecker** (*Dendrocopos major*) The most common of the 'spotted' woodpeckers in Europe, it inhabits most parts except the far N. The great spotted woodpecker breeds and winters in woodland. It is easily located by its loud drumming from late winter onwards and by its frequent sharp call (*tchik*). It has white shoulder patches, buff underside, a red undertail, and a black bar across its cheek that extends from the beak around the shoulder and nape. The male (near left) has a red spot on its nape. The female (far left) has no red on its head. Length: 22–23cm (8½–9in).

▲ **Arizona woodpecker** (*Picoides arizonae*) Shy bird inhabiting oak forests in SW USA. It has a white breast with dark spotting. The male has a red nape patch. Length: 18cm (7in).

▲ **Gila woodpecker** (*Melanerpes uropygialis*) The Gila woodpecker lives in the hot deserts of SW USA, excavating nest cavities in the soft flesh of cacti, and occasionally willow or cottonwood. It has a buff underside, neck, and head. It is black and white above with white wing patches that are prominent in flight. The male has a small red cap. It emits a rolling *churrr*. It eats eggs and nestlings, seeds, fruits, nuts and insects. Length: 20–25cm (8–10in).

◀ **green woodpecker**
(*Picus viridis*) It has a loud, laughing call, a yellow rump, and green wings that age to brown. The female (left) has an all black moustache, while the male (below) has a red centre to its moustache. Length: 31–33cm (12–13in).

▲ **roller** (*Coracias garrulus*)
A large bird with a pale blue head and breast, it has vivid blue and turquoise wing colours. In autumn, the roller is much duller. In spring, they migrate from Africa to E and S Europe. Length: 30–32cm (12–12½ in).

▼ **acorn woodpecker**
(*Melanerpes formicivorus*) Bird from the Americas that stores acorns in holes drilled in trees. The female has a black band between the red crown and forehead. Length: 20–24cm (8–9½ in).

▶ **lesser-spotted woodpecker** (*Dendrocopos minor*) Very small, sparrow-sized woodpecker, found throughout most of Europe. The lesser-spotted woodpecker is elusive, tending to stay in the tops of trees. They have blurred black-and-white barred markings on the upper and a creamy underside. They are distinguished from other black and white woodpeckers by the lack of a red patch under the tail. The male (bottom) has a red cap. The female (top) has no red cap although it may have some red spots. Length: 31–33cm (12–13in).

▲ **red-headed woodpecker** (*Melanerpes erythrocephalus*) Striking woodpecker from the Americas with an entirely red head, neck, and upper breast. The juvenile has a brown head. The upperside

is bluish-black with white patches on the wings and a white rump. They are often seen in open agricultural land, especially orchards. They nest in dead trees and catch insects on the wing. Length: 21–25cm (8–10in).

▲ **yellow-bellied sapsucker** (*Sphyrapicus varius*) American woodpecker that laps up oozing sap from trees. The male (shown) has a red crown and throat. The female has only a red crown. Length: 22cm (8¾ in).

▼ **northern flicker**
(*Colaptes auratus*) Large brownish woodpecker, the northern flicker lives throughout North America. It has two colour forms: yellow-shafted and red-shafted (shown here). The yellow-shafted male has a black moustache. Length: 30–35cm (12–14in).

▲ **kingfisher** (*Alcedo atthis*) The kingfisher is common throughout Europe. It has a large head and long bill. It is usually seen flying or hovering over water, looking for fish and aquatic insects to eat. It has a unique green-blue

and orange plumage with white cheeks. The vivid blue rump is most clearly seen when in flight. The male (left) has a black lower mandible, while the female (right) has an orange-red lower mandible. Length: 16–17cm (6½ in).

◀ **hoopoe** (*Upupa epops*)
The hoopoe lives in N Europe and is rare in Britain. It has the black and white wing markings of a spotted woodpecker but its wings are uniquely broad and floppy. It also has an unmistakeable thin, slightly curved bill. Its black-tipped crest fans upwards and forwards when excited. The pink-buff coloured body fades to a dull grey-brown in autumn. It feeds on insects, frogs and lizards, extracting them from tree bark with its long bill. Length: 26–28cm (10–11in).

Larks are short-billed birds that perform their extended song flights in the breeding season. They have long hind claws for walking through short vegetation, and indistinctive streaky brown plumages that make some species difficult to tell apart. **Swallows** and **martins** are long winged, fork tailed, swift-like birds that catch insects in flight with their wide-open mouths. They have tiny feet, but unlike the swifts they are able to perch. They are often seen in groups on overhead wires before undertaking their long-distance migrations. The **pipits** and **wagtails** are ground-feeding birds with long legs, long hind claws, and short bills. Wagtails have striking plumage patterns or colours, while most pipits are duller, streaky, and brown. They have an undulating flight and launch themselves from trees or from the ground into flights of song.

▲ **poorwill** (*Phalaenoptilus nuttallii*) Small nightjar found in arid regions of North America. It gets its name from its mournful call. By day, they sleep on the ground. At night, they forage. Uniquely for birds, they sometimes hibernate. Length: 18–22cm (7–8½ in).

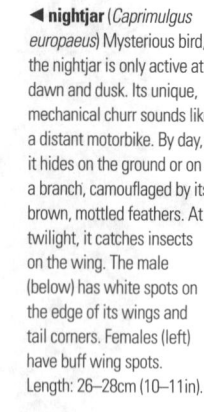

◄ **nightjar** (*Caprimulgus europaeus*) Mysterious bird, the nightjar is only active at dawn and dusk. Its unique, mechanical churr sounds like a distant motorbike. By day, it hides on the ground or on a branch, camouflaged by its brown, mottled feathers. At twilight, it catches insects on the wing. The male (below) has white spots on the edge of its wings and tail corners. Females (left) have buff wing spots. Length: 26–28cm (10–11in).

▲ **whip-poor-will** (*Caprimulgus vociferus*) Named after its repetitive call of *whip-poor-will*, they are leaf-brown birds with a black throat. The male has broad white markings on the outer tips of its tail. They are rarely seen during the day, lying asleep and camouflaged on the ground. They feed on insects that swarm over livestock at dusk. Length: 25cm (10in).

▲ **red-throated pipit** (*Anthus cervinus*) It breeds in the Arctic, migrating s to marshes, beaches, meadows, and fields. The male (middle) has a black and yellow bill. Its face, throat, and often entire breast are brick-red. In autumn, its red markings become subtler (top). The breeding female has a pale head and breast (bottom). Length: 15cm (6in).

▲ **yellow wagtail** (*Motacilla flava*) Small, slender legged, slim tailed bird of open grassy areas, often seen near water or livestock. There are many different races. Shown here is the female (left) and male (right) of the race *flavissima*. Length: 17cm (6¾ in).

▼ **skylark** (*Alauda arvensis*) The male skylark's trilling song flight lasts from one to five minutes. In song flight, it appears as if suspended on a string. Slightly bigger than a sparrow, the skylark (below and right) is a light-brown, earthy colour. It has a short, stubby crest and angular wings that are nearly white on the trailing edge. In North America, it is found only on Vancouver Island, w Canada. Skylarks often pair for life. Length: 18–19cm (7–7½ in).

▲ **house martin** (*Delichon urbica*) Small, black and white bird with triangular wings and a forked tail. It has black upperparts and a broad white rump. It flies high, often in flocks, feeding on the wing. The male (bottom) has a longer tail and narrower wings than the female (top right). Length: 12½ cm (5in).

▲ cliff swallow
(*Petrochelidon pyrrhonota*)
Common swallow of the
mountains of w North
America, nesting on the
vertical faces of cliffs and
the walls of canyons. It is
also found in E North
America, where it nests in
buildings. It faces stiff
competition from the non-
native house sparrow,
which usurps its nests and
often cause the cliff
swallows to abandon a
colony. The cliff swallow is
square-tailed with a pale
buff rump. Its upperparts
are a dull steel-blue.
Length: 13–15cm (5–6in).

▼ white wagtail
(*Motacilla alba*) It spends
most of its time on the
ground looking for insects.
The male (right) has a grey
rump that contrasts with
the dark tail. In winter, the
female (left) has a white
throat and black bib. They
are regular migrants in
Britain in the spring.
Length: 18cm (7in).

▲ swallow (*Hirundo
rustica*) The swallow lives in
rural areas, typically nesting
in barns. It has deeply forked
tail streamers. The breeding
adult has gleaming steel-
blue upperparts, a deep-red
forehead and throat, and
blue breastband. Swift and
graceful fliers, they migrate
to Africa in autumn and
return to Britain in April.
Length: 17–19cm (7–7½in).

▼ shore lark (*Eremophila
alpestris*) Long, slim-winged
lark often seen shuffling
along salt marshes or
beaches. It has yellow and
black head markings. The
non-breeding male (top) has
tiny black 'horns'. The
breeding female (bottom)
has bright yellow forehead
and throat. Length:
14–17cm (5½–7in).

▼ cactus wren
(*Campylorhynchus
brunneicapillus*) It lives in
the deserts of SW USA. It
has a dark crown, white
eyebrow and throat, and
densely spotted upper
breast and underparts. It
builds many decoy 'nests'
that it uses for roosting. It
has a *chug-chug* call.
Length: 18–21cm (7–8in).

**▲ long-billed marsh
wren** (*Cistothorus palustris*)
The long-billed marsh wren
lives in North America. They
are territorial, secretive
birds, often glimpsed among
cattails. They build decoy
nests. In summer, they
spend much time singing
and displaying. They are
brown above, buff below
with a bold white eyebrow.
Length: 10–14cm (4–5½in).

▲ water pipit (*Anthus
spinoletta*) In summer, the
male water pipit (top) has
a peachy-pink flush and
grey streaks. In winter
(bottom), the male has a
dark U marking around a
pale bib. The female
(middle) has a brown back
and a whiter underside
with stripes. Length:
16.5–17cm (6½–7in).

▼ wren (*Troglodytes
troglodytes*) The wren is a
warm brown colour with
darker bars across the wing
and flanks, and a pale stripe
over the eye. The tail is
often cocked and it has a
loud, fast trill. When
breeding, the male builds
several nests and lines the
one chosen by the female.
Length: 9–10cm (3½–4in).

▲ dipper (*Cinclus cinclus*)
Uniquely, for a songbird, it
feeds in and under water,
and is invariably seen close
to a stream. The dipper has a
distinctive white bib. The
British race has a broad
ginger-brown breastband. It
has strong legs and toes in
order to grip onto stones in
fast-flowing water. It bobs up
and down as if on a string.
Length: 18cm (7in).

▼ dunnock (*Prunella
modularis*) Streaky, dark
brown and grey bird of many
habitats. In autumn (bottom),
the adult has a brown cap
and ear coverts within blue-
grey. In spring (top), the
white spots on the wing
soon wear off. Length:
13–14cm (5–5½in).

▲ waxwing (*Bombycilla
garrulus*) Often a very tame
bird, the waxwing's
splendid crest, black bib,
grey rump, and red
undertail make it quite
unmistakable. The male's
crest (right) is longer than
the female's (left). The
waxwing has yellow tips on
the ends of its tail feathers
and white markings on its
wings. It feeds on
hawthorn and cottoneaster
berries. In winter, if berries
are in short supply, large
flocks migrate from the
tundra of N Europe and can
occasionally be seen in the
UK. Length: 18cm (7in).

andgrouse are terrestrial, seed eating birds. They resemble game birds but are actually close relatives of the **pigeons** and doves. Small-billed and round-headed with long tails and soft dense plumage, they are successful inhabitants of woods, farmland, and suburbs. They have familiar cooing songs but no obvious flight calls. The **cuckoos** are superficially hawk-like birds with slender bodies, long tails, and short legs. They are celebrated for their simple, unmistakable two-note song. Species of the European cuckoos are famous for their parasitism; placing their eggs in the nests of other birds, who then rear the cuckoo chicks as their own. **Owls** are round-headed with large forward-facing eyes and ears. Most are specialized nocturnal predators with eyes that are adapted to seeing in partial darkness. Most have soft plumage that is silent in flight. The larger species prey on mammals and birds, while the smaller ones eat mostly insects. Some species are opportunistic breeders that rear large families when food is abundant, but raise few or no chicks in leaner years.

▶ **rock dove** (*Columba livia*) Common wild pigeon (right and below) of many European and American cities (introduced from Europe). Over the centuries, many varieties developed through interbreeding with domestic breeds. It is typically bluish-grey with two narrow black wing bands, broad black tail, and white rump. Length: 31–34cm (12–13in).

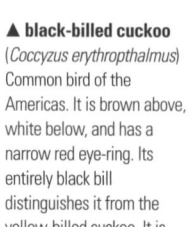

▲ **black-billed cuckoo** (*Coccyzus erythropthalmus*) Common bird of the Americas. It is brown above, white below, and has a narrow red eye-ring. Its entirely black bill distinguishes it from the yellow-billed cuckoo. It is more commonly heard than seen, with distinctive soft *cu-cu-cu-cu* notes often repeated in groups of two to five, all on the same pitch. It lives in damp thickets in low, overgrown pastures and orchards. It mainly eats hairy caterpillars, which destroy farm crops. Length: 30cm (12in).

▼ **roadrunner** (*Geococcyx californianus*) Fast-running ground cuckoo of the deserts of North America. It prefers running to flying. The roadrunner preys on rodents, small birds, insects, small snakes, and lizards. Unlike European cuckoos, it builds its own nest. It raises its bushy crest when excited. Length: 61cm (24in).

▼ **mourning dove** (*Zenaida macroura*) Most common bird in North America. It gains its name from its mounful cry of *cooah, coo*. Length: 30cm (12in).

▲ **wood pigeon** (*Columba palumbus*) Plump pigeon with boldly contrasted wings. The wood pigeon is smooth, glossy and colourful, with a bright bill and eyes, and rich pink breast. When alarmed, it flies up with a loud clatter of wings. Woodpigeons eat seeds, grain, leaves and berries, and are considered a pest by farmers. Length: 40–42cm (16–16½in).

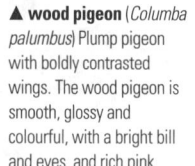

▲ **turtle dove** (*Streptopelia turtur*) Scarce, delicate dove with chequered upperparts, white belly and tail band, pink breast, and striped neck patch. It flies with occasional sideways rolls. the turtle dove eats mainly shoots and leaves. Length: 26–28cm (10–11in).

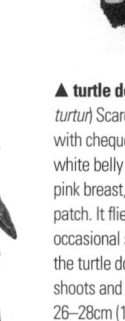

▼ **great grey owl** (*Strix nebulosa*) Giant, rare, and elusive owl of coniferous forests in Scandinavia and N North America. It can detect (by sound) rodents moving under deep snow. It attacks humans who threaten its nest. Length: 64–70cm (25–28in).

◀ **cuckoo** (*Cuculus canorus*) Named after its distinctive *cuc-coo* song, cuckoos are often seen perching on wire or twigs. In flight, they resemble a small bird of prey. The male (top) has a clean grey chest, while the female's (bottom) chest has a tinge of tawny brown. They usurp other birds' nests and eat hairy caterpillars. Length: 32–34cm (12½–13½in).

▲ **collared dove** (*Streptopelia decaocto*) One of the most widespread bird species in Britain and it is also common throughout mainland Europe. It has a long tail, pale head and breast, pink-buff plumage and adults have a white-edged collar. The female (top) has a more buff face but is difficult to tell apart from the male (bottom). Its song is a familiar *coo-coo-cuk*, with emphasis on the second note. Length: 31–33cm (12–13in).

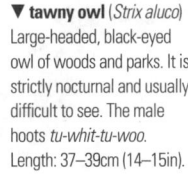

▼ **tawny owl** (*Strix aluco*) Large-headed, black-eyed owl of woods and parks. It is strictly nocturnal and usually difficult to see. The male hoots *tu-whit-tu-woo*. Length: 37–39cm (14–15in).

▲ **elf owl** (*Micrathene whitneyi*) Tiny owl that inhabits arid regions of Mexico and sw USA. Elf owls have a short tail and are brown-grey with a white underside. They feign death in order to escape capture. They feed largely on insects. Length: 14–16cm (5½–6in).

▲ **hawk owl** (*Surnia ulula*) It inhabits coniferous forests in Scandinavia and N North America. The hawk owl behaves much like a bird of prey, flying and hunting by day. It has a barred breast, fierce expression and a long tail (shorter in the female). Length: 36–39cm (14–15in).

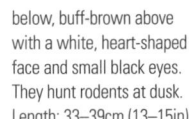

▲ **barn owl** (*Tyto alba*) The barn owl lives on every continent except Antarctica. Markings vary but they are usually white below, buff-brown above with a white, heart-shaped face and small black eyes. They hunt rodents at dusk. Length: 33–39cm (13–15in).

◄ **long-eared owl** (*Asio otus*) Richly coloured and elusive owl with a chestnut face and distinctive long ear tufts (if raised). It has a longer tail than the short-eared owl, and the tail lacks a white tip. The long-eared owl is strictly nocturnal. Normally silent, except during the breeding season, parliaments of up to a dozen owls can go undetected, roosting together in thickets and tree tops. They are widespread in North America, Europe, and Asia. Length: 35–37cm (14–14½in).

▲ **northern saw-whet owl** (*Aegolius acadicus*) Small, earless owl of coniferous woods in North America. Hunting by night, during the day they roost in trees, camouflaged by their chocolate-brown plumage. Length: 18–20cm (7–8in).

▲ **burrowing owl** (*Athene cunicularia*) Small, ground-dwelling owl of North America. Often seen close to its burrow, it bobs up and down before finally diving into its hole. Length: 23–28cm (9–11in).

▲ **short-eared owl** (*Asio flammeus*) Large, long winged owl with a fierce expression. On summer afternoons, the short-eared owl can be seen hovering over marshes. It is tawny brown with black patches around the eyes and small ear tufts. It has a very short tail. Length: 34–42cm (13⅓–16½in).

▼ **Tengmalm's owl** or boreal owl (*Aegolius funereus*) Large-headed owl with warm brown coloured plumage and a spotted crown. It is a strictly nocturnal owl of coniferous forests in Eurasia and N North America. Length: 24–26cm (9¾–10in).

► **great horned owl** (*Bubo virginianus*) Largest and best known of the common North American owls, the great horned owl lives in forests throughout North America south of the tree line. It varies in colour from nearly white to brown and grey. The underside is mottled with a white throat. It has yellow eyes and prominent raised tufts that resemble horns. The great horned owl preys on a large variety of animals but prefers small mammals like rabbits, mice, or squirrels. It hunts at night when it has better vision. Soft feathers enable it to dive silently and snatch prey in its powerful talons. It is one of the earliest birds to nest. Length: 50cm (20in).

▲ **snowy owl** (*Nyctea scandiaca*) Huge, rounded, white or heavily barred owl of wild, open country in N regions of Eurasia and America. The male snowy owl (top) is smaller than the female (bottom). They are highly nomadic, moving wherever there is a plentiful supply of lemmings and rodents. They lay eggs on raised hummocks or rocks. Length: 55–65cm (22–26in).

Thrushes and chats belong to the *Turdidae* family. They live in most parts of the world. **Thrushes** are usually larger than chats, with stout bills and legs, and many are known for their beautiful song. They feed on fruit and berries or specialize in catching earthworms or snails. Some have become familiar garden birds, a habitat that provides a reasonable replacement for a glade or edge of a wood, although the food supply is usually poorer. **Chats** are a single, large and varied group of small birds found in the open country of America, Europe, Africa, and Asia. They include familiar species like the robin as well as much rarer ones such as the striking wheatears of more open habitats. They are named after their call which sounds like a loud *chat*. Mainly insectivores, they are commonly seen on the gound or in low bushes. Chats have a characteristic upright stance, with a flicking tail.

▼ sage thrasher
(*Oreoscoptes montanus*) The sage thrasher lives in sagebrush plains and other arid regions of North America. It is brown-grey above with a buff underside that has distinctive black

markings. Its general appearance and flicking of its tail is akin to a mockingbird. Yet it has the terrestrial habits of a thrasher, including darting out of sight when disturbed. Length: 22cm (8½in).

▲ robin (*Erithacus rubecula*) The adult robin has unmistakable plumage. Its red-orange breast is bright when fresh but fades during summer. The sides of the neck, face and chest are blue-grey, while the upperside is warm brown. Juveniles have a blotchy brown plumage but still

have the same alert stance and plump shape. Both sexes are notoriously aggressive and territorial, and use their breast patch in threatening displays. They are found throughout Europe, inhabiting parks, woodlands, or gardens. They avoid open spaces. Length: 14cm (5½in).

▼ black redstart
(*Phoenicurus ochruros*) The black redstart is common around old towns, industrial sites, and cliffs in Europe. The male (top) is grey-black with a long red tail. Females (below) are sooty brown-grey. Length: 14.5cm (6in).

▲ mockingbird (*Mimus polyglottos*) The mockingbird of North America mimics other birdsong. It is grey with white patches on its wings and long tail. It is very territorial, sometimes attacking its own reflection. Length: 23–28cm (9–11in).

▲ bluethroat (*Luscinia svecica*) As its name suggests, the breeding male bluethroat (left) has a blue bib. In N Europe, males have a red patch inside the blue, while elsewhere this is normally white. Breeding

females (right) have a white throat and some have small spots of blue on the edges. They migrate from Africa in the spring and breed in E Europe, N Scandinavia, and across central Europe. Length: 14cm (5½in).

◄ whinchat (*Saxicola rubetra*) The whinchat is slimmer than the stonechat, and has a white line over its eye and a white patch on its tail. They are often seen perched on posts or conifer branches in grassy places. The male (above right) has an apricot breast that fades by late summer (above left). The female (below) is paler but still has the distinct head pattern. Length: 12.5cm (5in).

► wheatear (*Oenanthe oenanthe*) In spring, males (below right) are grey, buff-pink below with a white rump. The grey bloom of the spring female (below left) wears off to brown by June. The autumn male (right) is warm brown with

a distinct white stripe above the eye and lighter wings than the female. They are often seen outside their summer breeding areas and migrate from North America and Europe to winter in Africa. Length: 14.5–15cm (6–6½in).

▲ **stonechat** (*Saxicola torquata*) Often mistaken for a whinchat, the stonechat is stockier with shorter wings, longer tail, and no white markings on its face. The male (right) has a black head and body, apricot underside, and white patches on the shoulders and wings. The female (left) has a brown body and paler markings. Stonechats live throughout w Europe. They are often seen perched on bushes or overhead wires, scolding intruders with agitated notes. Length: 12.5cm (5in).

▼ **nightingale** (*Luscinia megarhynchos*) The nightingale is best known for its beautiful song, which is a unique blend of slow piping notes, high warbles, and sudden deep phrases. It is discernible from a thrush nightingale by its warmer, brighter olive-brown upperparts and a rufous tail. They often skulk in dense bushes, feeding on berries, ants, beetles and worms picked from the ground. They live throughout w Europe and winter in Africa. Length: 16.5cm (6½ in).

▲ **songthrush** (*Turdus philomelos*) The songthrush is a small, neat, spotted thrush with a plain head pattern and neat V-shaped spots underneath a yellow-cream breast. The sexes are alike with an olive upperside and a soft orange-buff underwing. They often feed with their wings drooped. They live in gardens, farmland and woods, building nests, lined with dung or mud, in trees and shrubs. Length: 23cm (9in).

▼ **wrentit** (*Chamaea fasciata*) The wrentit has the head, beak and eyes of a tit, and the tail of a wren. It is brown with a light-streaked underside. It is very secretive and inhabits shrubs and brush in sw North America. Length: 15cm (6in)

▲ **blackbird** (*Turdus merula*) The blackbird is a common garden, woodland, and farmland thrush. It has a beautiful song. The male (left) is all black with a yellow bill and eye-ring. The female (right) is dark brown and has a yellow bill in the summer. Blackbirds raise their tail when landing and feed with a characteristic series of hops and shuffles, bending forwards to pick up earthworms. Never seen in flocks, they are widespread throughout Europe. Length: 24cm (9½ in).

▼ **American robin** (*Turdus migratorius*) The American robin is not a true robin but a large thrush, nearly twice as big as its European namesake. It is grey above with a red underside. Males have a black head and tail, which are dull grey in the females. It lives in town gardens, forests, and farms throughout North America. It feeds on earthworms. Length: 23–28cm (9–11in).

▶ **ring ouzel** (*Turdus torquatus*) The ring ouzel is a shy, wild and dark thrush of uplands, rocks, and coastal scrub. In spring, the male (top) resembles a blackbird, except for a white crescent across its breast. In winter, the male (middle) acquires a paler breastband and broader, paler scales on its body. The female (middle) is brown with a duller breast band. Both sexes have grey edges on their feathers. Length: 23cm (9in).

▼ **redstart** (*Phoenicurus phoenicurus*) Elegant chat with a light red tail and rump. The female (right) has a mostly buff body. In spring, the male (bottom right) has a white forehead and black face and bib. In autumn (bottom left), pale feathers hide its black and white marks. Length: 14cm (5½ in)

Shrikes, starlings, and crows are members of the Passeriformes family, or the perching songbirds. The corvids are the largest songbirds in the order, including species of **crows** such as ravens, jays, magpies, nutcrackers, and choughs. Crows are recognizable by their size and dark colouring. Some crows, like the raven, are predators and kill small animals or feed on carrion. They are bold and inquisitive birds that venture into many urban areas. Of the corvids, the raven is the most common species. **Starlings** are part of the separate family Starnidae, and before their recent decline could be seen in huge flocks, drifting across the sky, sometimes numbering tens or hundreds of thousands. Such concentrations are rarer now due to changes in agricultural practice. **Shrikes**, from the Laniidae family are medium sized migratory songbirds found across Europe and North America. They have a characteristic habit of dashing across open spaces and swooping to new vantage points. They feed mainly on large insects and have a distinctive hooked bill.

▲ pinyon jay (*Gymnorhinus cyanocephalus*) The pinyon jay lives in pine and oak forests and in pinyon juniper. Their range extends from the central to the sw states of the USA. They are short-tailed with grey-blue plumage, a darker head, and white markings on the throat. Pinyon jays have long bills and feed mainly on pine nuts, with some insects and fruit. Length: 23–30cm (9–11in).

▼ Steller's jay (*Cyanocitta stelleri*) Steller's jay lives in the coniferous forests of North and Central America. It has a striking, dark-blue body, with a black crest and head, and dark bars on its wings and tail. It is the only western jay to have a crest. It has darker underparts than the similarly coloured and crested blue jay. Length: 28–34cm (11–13in).

▼ great grey shrike or northern shrike (*Lanius excubitor*) Large, long-tailed, short-winged bird with a stout, hooked bill. It is grey, black and white with a pale belly and white wing patches. The great grey shrike is commonly seen perched on a tree in heathland, open woodland or marshes. Length: 24–25cm (9½–10in).

▲ jackdaw (*Corvus monedula*) Bold, noisy crow. The adult has a shiny black cap and a pale bluish-grey nape. It is duller in the summer and as a juvenile. It breeds in most of Europe, avoiding excessively hot or cold temperatures. Murders of jackdaws are often found in urban and suburban areas where there are plenty of sheltered ledges for nesting and roosting. It eats a variety of foods from caterpillars to acorns. It feeds from the ground and can usually be seen on open lawns or in fields. Length: 33–34cm (13in).

▼ Clark's nutcracker (*Nucifraga columbiana*) It is a pale grey bird with a white face, black wings with white stripes, a black tail with white outer tail feathers, and white underparts. It has a long, pointed bill and can store nuts and seeds in a cheek pouch below its tongue. It is found in coniferous forests on mountain ranges from British Columbia to California and Colorado. Length: 28–34cm (11–13in).

◄ magpie (*Pica pica*) Bold, attractive crow that thrives in modern suburbia. From a distance, it looks largely black and white, but a better view reveals the plumage to be a complex mix of iridescent colours. The wings are largely glossed blue, the tail green with purple towards the tip. Juveniles have a short tail. It is found throughout Europe. The Spanish magpie may have a blue spot beneath its eye. It eats insects, berries, seeds and scraps, and lives in roofed, mud-lined nests in trees or hedges. The magpie is vilified for its reputation for killing songbirds. Length: 44–46cm (17–18in).

◄ chough (*Pyrrhocorax pyrrhocorax*) Crow found mainly around coastal regions or inland cliffs and mountains of Britain and Ireland, and parts of w Europe. The adult female (top) has wingtips that meet the end of the tail, while the adult male (bottom) has wingtips beyond the tail and shaggy underneath coverts. Both sexes have dark feathers and distinctive bright red bills and feet. The chough feeds on ants and other insects found in or under animal dung or seaweed. It is the most energetic and graceful member of the crow family. It has a loud, yelping call of *pch-oow!* or *keyaaa*. Length: 39–40cm (15in).

▶ **jay** (*Garrulus glandarius*) Colourful and elusive crow native to most of Europe, although some birds from the N and E move south in the winter. The jay has a speckled crown, bold black moustache, and a white chin. It has a broad black tail, a white rump, and a bright blue wing patch. They are darker in W Europe, greyer in the N, and pinker in the S. Juveniles have less intense colouring. They eat nuts, seeds and berries, and occasionally small mammals or birds and their eggs. Length: 35cm (14in).

▲ **starling** (*Sturnus vulgaris*) The boisterous starling is the most common bird sighted in Britain. It has a sharp face and a square tail. The winter female (left) has bold spots of buff and cream, merging into a silvery face and throat, with orange-buff feather edges on its wings. The male (right) has smaller spots and a darker bill in winter. Male and female are darker in summer – the female with bright wing feather edges, the male with a green and purple gloss. The dark bill turns yellow in summer. The male starling (top) has a blue bill base while the female (bottom) has a pink bill base. Length: 21cm (8in).

▲ **western scrub jay** (*Aphelocoma californica*) It lives in high scrub and woodlands in W and SW USA. The western scrub jay has a blue head, rump, wings and tail, with a dull brown back. It has dark cheeks, a grey-white throat with a dark lower border. It is very similar in appearance to the island scrub jay which is native to Santa Cruz island off the coast of California. The Florida scrub jay has a more dusky appearance. Length: 28–33cm (11–13in).

▶ **rook** (*Corvus frugilegus*) Big, black crow with a strong, purplish-blue gloss. It has a steep forehead, a pointed bill, and hanging underpart feathers. The adult female (top) has wings that reach the tip of the tail, unlike the male (bottom) which has a protruding tail as well as a steeper forehead. The juvenile rook has a black face and bill with a dull head and neck but a glossy body. Rooks are found throughout Britain and Ireland and in much of central and SE Europe. Their staple diet consists of earthworms and large insects such as beetles. They will also eat seeds. Length: 44–46cm (17–18in).

▲ **carrion crow** (*Corvus corone*) Common resident in the British Isles and W Europe. It can be distinguished from the rook by its less scruffy forehead, shorter bill, and lack of a pale face patch. It has slow, steady wingbeats and is not as acrobatic as the rook or raven. Length: 45cm (18in).

▼ **raven** (*Corvus corax*) The raven is the largest of the crows. Compared to other crows, it is more likely to kill small animals such as rabbits, and eats more dead meat. It breeds in most of Europe, but is generally absent from large lowland regions. The adult has a powerful, arched bill, and neat black plumage with long wingtips and a wedge- or diamond-shaped tail. It has longer, more shapely wings than the carrion crow. Breeding pairs are territorial. Length: 64cm (25in).

▼ **blue jay** (*Cyanocitta cristata*) It has a bright blue upperside with strong white and black markings on the wings. The underside is grey-white and it has a long blue tail with black bars and white corners. It is found in oak woods and parks S from Canada through central and E USA to the Gulf of Mexico. Length: 28–33cm (11–13in).

▲ **red-backed shrike** (*Lanius collurio*) The small, upright and colourful red-backed shrike is the most common shrike in W and central Europe. The male (far right and centre) is distinguished by a bold combination of black, grey, pink, and chestnut. The males pictured here have a blue-grey cap and broad black mask with a pale, pink-washed underside. The female (far left) is more difficult to identify but shares the same hook-bill and square tail. It is most easily distinguished by its prominent scaly underparts. The juvenile is browner with a barred back, uppertail coverts, and flanks. Length: 17cm (6½in).

Warblers and flycatchers, tits, treecreepers, and nuthatches are representatives of some of the smallest songbirds. The small, slim, but varied **warblers** include some wide-spread and easily-identified birds, as well as a few rare local and visitor birds that are hard to identify, many are best located by their distinctive voice. 'Crests' such as the goldcrest are minute warblers with striped crowns and needle-sharp calls that test our high-frequency hearing. The **flycatchers** are a family of upright, short-legged, insect-eaters. The striking vermilion flycatcher is unusual in that it is the only flycatcher with colour differentiation between the sexes. Stout, with strong feet and short, thick bills, the **tits** are acrobatic birds well equipped for foraging in trees; they are also familiar visitors to garden bird-feeders. The tit is sometimes called the titmouse in North America. The **treecreepers** and **nuthatches** are mostly specialized for picking food from tree bark: the treecreepers use their tails for support as they creep over bark, while nuthatches use their strong feet. The wallcreeper is an excep-tion, living on cliffs and crags in mountain regions.

▲ grasshopper warbler
(*Locustella naevia*) Slim, round-tailed warbler, commonly seen creeping in long grass. The grasshopper warbler has a slender bill and a distinctive high, reeling song that makes it relatively easy to spot. It is usually olive in colour, although some are more grey or yellow. It has a pale throat. It eats insects from low vegetation or takes them from the ground. It is found throughout Europe. Length: 12–13.5cm (5in).

▼ Arctic warbler
(*Phylloscopus borealis*) The Arctic warbler breeds in the birch woods and thickets of Alaska but can also be found in N Europe. A stocky, thick-billed warbler marked by a thin wingbar and a long, striking stripe over the eye. It has an olive green back, a whitish throat and underparts. The female (top) has a shorter tail and the male (bottom) has a long wingtip. Length: 10.5cm (4½ in).

► goldcrest
(*Regulus regulus*) Minute woodland bird combining some features of warblers and tits. The adult male (top) has a bright orange crown with a black cap, the female (bottom) has a yellow crown stripe. It is widespread across Europe. Length: 9cm (3½ in).

▲ reed warbler
(*Acrocephalus scirpaceus*) One of the most common Acrocephalus warblers, it is mostly restricted to reeds and willow. The most rufous of the plain brown warblers, it has an unstreaked back and a very slight pale line over the eye with a brighter eye-ring. It breeds across Europe moving S to Africa in the autumn. Length: 13cm (5in).

▼ chiffchaff
(*Phylloscopus collybita*) Common, slim warbler, characterized by its dull olive-green colours and lack of strong pattern. The winter adult (top) is dull and brownish, the W and S European adult (bottom) may show yellow feathers from the underwing. Length: 10–11cm (4–4¼ in)

▼ sedge warbler
(*Acrocephalus schoenobaenus*) Small, dark, rusty warbler of waterside scrubs and thickets. It has a noisy, springtime song and a striking pale stripe over the eye. It breeds in Europe and migrates to Africa. Length: 13cm (5in).

▲ magnolia warbler
(*Dendroica magnolia*) The magnolia warbler lives in N and NE USA and S Canada, The male has bright yellow underparts with black streaks, a black facial patch and large white wing patch. The wings are grey and it has a broken white band on the tail. It has a white stripe over the eye and a broken eye-ring. The female is similar in appearance but duller. Length: 13cm (5in).

▲ black-throated blue warbler (*Dendroica caerulescens*) Bird found throughout North America. The male (shown) is blueish, with a black face and sides. The female is duller with cream underparts. It has a white wing patch. Length: 13cm (5in).

▼ blackpoll warbler
(*Dendroica striata*) One of the most common warblers in E USA, it is found in coniferous forests and high trees and migrates to South America. The adult male has a striking black cap with white cheeks, a black body with white underparts and black and white streaks. The juvenile and female blackpoll warbler are greenish with thin black streaking and yellowish green underparts. Length: 14cm (5½ in).

▲ vermilion flycatcher (*Pyrocephalus rubinus*) Bird with a fiery scarlet crown and underparts, and brown back, wings and tail. The female is greyish brown with a pink-yellow belly. It lives in s and sw USA. Length: 15cm (6in).

► scissor-tailed flycatcher (*Tyrannus forficatus*) The scissor-tailed flycatcher lives on the s plains of North America. The adult has bright salmon-pink sides and belly and a pale greyish-white head, upper back and breast. The long and deeply forked black and white tail accounts for more than half of its length. The scissor-like tail adds to the splendour of its courtship display. It erects its crest, emits harsh cries, and attacks large birds that invade its nest. The scissor-tailed flycatcher diet consists of insects, largely captured on the wing. Length: 36cm (14in).

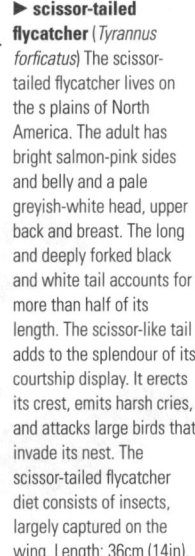
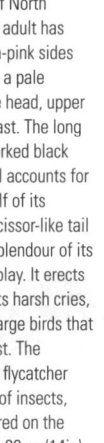

▲ spotted flycatcher (*Muscicapa striata*) The adult female (shown) has fine streaks on the crown and broad, soft streaking on the chest. It is olive-brown with a pale underside. The male has a longer tail. Length: 14cm (5½in).

▼ willow warbler (*Phylloscopus trochilus*) Breeds in Europe and migrates to Africa in the winter. The spring male (shown) may be dark olive above with a whitish underside and lemon-yellow wash. It has pale brown legs. The female's tail is shorter then the male's and shares the juvenile's more yellow belly and yellow stripe over the eye. Both sexes have a distinctive song. Length: 11cm (4in).

▼ chestnut-backed chickadee (*Poecile rufescens*) Bird that lives on the w coast of USA. It has a black cap and bib, chestnut flanks and back, and grey wings and tail. Length: 11–13cm (4½–5in).

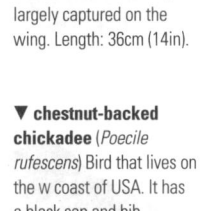

▲ great tit (*Parus major*) Largest of the tits, with white cheeks on a black head, and a long black stripe running down the yellow chest. Length: 14cm (5½in).

▲ coal tit (*Parus ater*) Miniature, acrobatic bird with boldly patterned plumage. It lives in conifer trees, its feet and slim bill perfectly adapted to search the long needles for insects. It has a black head with a white nape patch, white cheeks, and a black bib. The Irish variety has a yellow nape. Length: 11.5cm (4½in)

▼ nuthatch (*Sitta europaea*) Dumpy, large-headed bird with a square tail, grey upperside, and a black mask. The N and E European varieties have much whiter underparts. The pictured nuthatch is from Sweden. The British race has pale orange underparts and richer flanks. It wedges large insects and tough seeds in crevices so it can break into them with its sharp, strong beak and its song is loud and ringing. Length: 14cm (5½in).

▼ blue tit (*Parus caeruleus*) Bright, tiny bird that is a garden favourite. It looks blue, pale green, or light yellow according to the angle of view or light. At his brightest, the male has a vivid blue cap, wings and tail, and a white ring around the top of his head. Blue tits have white cheeks and a blue-black chin. The juvenile is duller with a yellow face and greenish cap. They eat insects, seeds, and human offerings such as peanuts. Blue tits are highly acrobatic when feeding, especially from garden feeders. They are common throughout Europe. Length: 11.5 cm (4½in).

▲ tufted titmouse or black-crested titmouse (*Baeolophus bicolor*) The tufted and black-crested titmouse were considered separate species until recently. It has a short bill, a grey back, and pale underparts. The variety shown has a black crest and pale forehead. It is a social species and is found in sw Oklahoma and Texas. Length: 15cm (6in).

▲ treecreeper (*Certhia familiaris*) Mouse-like bird that creeps up trees, probing with its fine, curved bill. The Scandinavian race (right) has a brighter stripe over the eye and whiter underparts than the British race (left). Both have mottled brown backs, with spots and degrees of orange on the rump which provide good camouflage. Length: 12.5cm (5in).

Mainly belonging to the families of Fringillidae, Ploceidae and Passeridae, **sparrows** are a large group of small, reddish-brown streaked birds with short legs and stout bills for seed eating. They are drab brown at a glance but actually strong patterned, some with marked differences between the sexes. The sparrows of Europe, Asia and Africa are often gregarious and nest in large colonies, while those of the Americas are more solitary. The **finches** are quite varied, ranging from cross-billed pine-cone specialists to stout-billed seed crackers. The males are brightly coloured, while the females tend to be duller and similar to sparrows. Finches have a characteristically undulating or dancing flight. Some breed semi-colonially, sharing sources of abundant food, while others are territorial and defend scarcer, more dispersed food supplies. The **buntings** are smaller and plumper and have slightly differently shaped bills, longer tails, and live in a variety of open places from moors and fields to marshland.

▲ **house sparrow** (*Passer domesticus*) Common in Europe, Asia and Africa, the house sparrow has been introduced to most other parts of the world. In many areas they have become a pest, competing for food with native species. They are streaky above and plain beneath. The female (left) is paler and has a broad band above the eye. The male (right) has a grey cap, chestnut nape and black bib that is more prominent in summer. Length: 14–17cm (5½–6½ in).

▼ **tree sparrow** (*Passer montanus*) The tree sparrow is smaller and brighter in colour than the house sparrow. It has a chestnut-brown cap and black spot on its white cheek. The sexes are alike. The male (bottom) has a slightly longer tail than the female (top) but otherwise they are difficult to tell apart. Like the house sparrow, tree sparrows live in parks, farmland, and urban areas. Length: 14cm (5½ in).

▶ **hawfinch** (*Coccothraustes coccothraustes*) One of the larger and heavier finches, the hawfinch has a large head, big bill, and short tail. It feeds on the ground or perches in treetops. They are very secretive and the least disturbance causes them to fly up into the trees or foliage. They are richly coloured with an orange-brown crown against a pale grey neck. The sexes are difficult to tell apart except for the grey secondaries behind the white wing patch on the female (bottom). The male has black secondaries. In winter (middle), the bill is all-pale. Length: 18cm (7in).

▶ **brambling** (*Fringilla montifringilla*) The breeding male (top right) has a solid black head and back, while the breeding female (middle) is a blotchy grey-brown. In winter (bottom), the female has a dark cheek-surround and an orange patch above the bend of its wing. The winter male (top left) has a yellow bill and more intense orange markings. Length: 15cm (6in).

▶ **chaffinch** (*Fringilla coelebs*) Common finch showing much white above and beneath the wings when it flies but which is hidden when standing. The brighter spring colours of pink and blue on the male (top) are obscured by buff feather tips in the winter (middle). The female (bottom) is an olive-brown colour that becomes greyer during the summer. They have a lively, energetic song that can be heard from late winter. Length: 14.5cm (6in).

▲ **pine siskin** (*Carduelis pinus*) Its small size and bright colours are helpful in identifying a siskin. The male (top) has a distinct black cap and chin, and lime-green to yellow neck and chest. The female (bottom) has heavy streaks on a white underside. They eat seeds, often hanging upside down to pluck them from pods and cones. Length: 12cm (5in).

▼ **common redpoll** (*Carduelis flammea*) Small, streaky finch, identified by a red spot on the forehead which may be indistinct in the females (bottom) and juveniles. The male (top) has a pink breast. They are found throughout Europe, Asia, and North America. Their usually make their nests in small willows, poplars, birches, or alders. They can be nomadic birds, moving to different areas where food supplies are more abundant. Length: 13–15cm (5–6in).

▼ **goldfinch** (*Carduelis carduelis*) Goldfinches have unique bold red, white and black head patterns and black wings with bright yellow bands above. They live in overgrown areas where seeds are abundant. They build nests in the outer twigs of tall leafy trees. Length: 12cm (5in).

▲ **Cassin's finch** (*Carpodacus cassinii*) Finch that lives at high altitudes, nesting in conifers. It is common in the w mountains of North America. It has a pale pink breast, cap and rump, and a brown-streaked upperside. In cold winters, it descends to lower altitudes to feed. It has a high *pwee-de-lip* call. Length: 15–17cm (6–6½ in).

▼ **pine grosbeak** (*Pinicola enucleator*) The pine grosbeak is distinguished by its black wings with white feather edges. The male (top) has a red head and breast while the female's (bottom) is bronze-yellow. Length: 18cm (7in).

▶ **greenfinch** (*Carduelis chloris*) Large, sociable finch, with yellow streaks along the wings and tail, and a distinctive large, pale orange-pink bill. The male (right) has wider yellow wing markings and is a brighter green than the female (above). They breed in gardens, parks and hedges, and are present all year in Europe. Length: 15cm (6in).

▼ **yellowhammer** (*Emberiza citrinella*) Slender bunting with a long body, white-edged tail, and sharp face. Females (below) are less yellow than males (left). Length: 16cm (6in).

▲ **western meadowlark** (*Sturnella neglecta*) Bird that has a bright yellow breast with a bold black V. It is almost identical to *S. magna* and the two can only be distinguished by their songs. Length: 22–28cm (8½–11in).

▼ **Lapland bunting** (*Calcarius lapponicus*) Inconspicuous bird in most plumages. Spring males (top) are obvious with their black face and breast, rufous nape and white cheek edges. Females (bottom) and winter males (left) are more difficult and have blackish ear-covert corners, mottled breast sides, and a rufous panel on the midwing. They breed in far N Scandanavia and winter around coastal fringes of the North sea. Length: 15cm (6in).

▼ **crossbill** (*Loxia curvirostra*) The males (bottom) are red with dark wings, some with white wingbars, while the females (above) are grey-green. All have remarkable bills with crossed tips. The juvenile bill is not crossed (or only weakly) at first. They feed on seeds, using their curved bills to extract them from cones. Length: 16.5cm (6½ in).

▼ **red-winged blackbird** (*Agelaius phoeniceus*) Bird that nests in moist habitats such as marshes and swamps throughout North America. The male is black with bright shoulder patches while the female is brown and with streaks. Length: 18–24cm (7–9½ in).

▲ **brown-headed cowbird** (*Molothrus ater*) The male (above) has a black body and brown head while the female (right) is grey-brown all over. They are parasitic, and are known to have laid their eggs in the nests of no less than 205 different species. Without the burden of nest building, they are highly social birds. Length: 18cm (7in).

Butterflies are part of the order Lepidoptera; a large group of insects found throughout the world. Their wings are covered in scales, which form a colour and pattern important in identification and survival. Some colours warn predators they are poisonous or taste bad. Butterflies flash the eye-spots on their wings at predators to mimic the eyes of a larger animal. When at rest, they show their undersides which are usually more dull and aid camouflage. Butterflies are active by day and most feed on flower nectar, assisting pollination in the process. The female lays eggs on specific food sources which they detect through specialized sense organs, such as compound eyes sensitive to wavelengths beyond human vision. The larvae (caterpillars) emerge within days or hours and, while feeding, are capable of doing great damage to plants and crops. They then enter the pupa stage, forming a chrysalis in which metamorphosis occurs and an adult is formed. The larvae and pupa are both attractive food sources for animals and very few adult butterflies emerge from a large number of eggs.

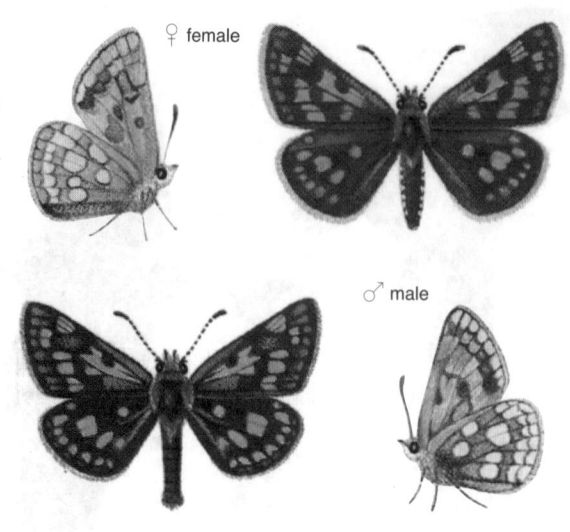

♀ female

♂ male

◄ **chequered skipper** or Arctic skipper (*Carterocephalus palaemon*) Thought to be extinct in England, the chequered skipper survives in Scotland and is common throughout Canada, Alaska, and N USA. It is found in open woodland, along banks of streams and in sub-alpine meadows. The upper wings have dark brown cheques with deep yellow patches which may vary in size. The underside wing is brown with tinged yellow to pale yellow spots. The female (top) is slightly larger than the male (bottom) but usually has less distinct markings. Wingspan: 28–29mm; Flight: June–July.

▼ **black swallowtail** (*Papilio polyxenes*) One of 15 swallowtail species found in North and Central America. The upper wing is blue-black with cream-yellow and blue spots and orange eyespots on the hindwing. The innermost band of yellow spots is more common on the male. It inhabits farms, meadows, and open areas. Wingspan: 67–89mm; Flight: Feb–Nov.

▲ **silver-spotted skipper** (*Hesperia comma*) Found throughout North America, numbers have declined in Britain. It inhabits sub-alpine meadows and foothills. The female is larger and darker with more extensive spots. Wingspan: 28–30mm; Flight: July–Aug.

▲ **large white** (*Pieris brassicae*) The forewing has a black apex and the female (top) has markings on the upper side. The male (bottom) upper is unmarked but has two spots on the underside. Caterpillars can be a garden pest. Wingspan: 57–66mm; Flight: Apr–Oct.

▼ **clouded yellow** (*Colias crocea*) Found throughout Europe in temperate climates. It is strongly migratory. They prefer open spaces and are attracted to fields of clover or lucerne. The female has wider black margins enclosing yellow spots. Wingspan: 45–54mm; Flight: Apr–Sept.

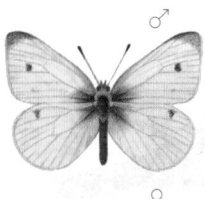

▲ **small white** or cabbage white (*Pieris rapae*) Found in a variety of habitats, the caterpillar is a common pest on cabbage plants. Milk-white to pale yellow, the female's charcoal spots are more defined. Wingspan: 46–55mm; Flight: Mar–Sept.

▲ **green-veined white** or mustard white (*Pieris napi*) Although it can be mistaken for the small white, it is not a garden pest and prefers to inhabit damp meadows and cooler regions of the Northern Hemisphere where it is better able to compete. It has rounded white wings that are more yellow-cream below. The veins beneath are lined in a characteristic green, making it easy to identify from the small white. The female (top) markings are better-defined. Wingspan: 36–50mm; Flight: May–Sept.

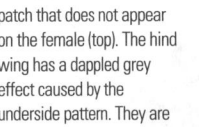

▼ **orange tip** (*Anthocharis cardamines*) Distinguished by a dappled-green underside, the male (bottom) forewing has a large orange patch that does not appear on the female (top). The hind wing has a dappled grey effect caused by the underside pattern. They are common in meadows, woodland edges and country lanes throughout most of Europe. Wingspan: 39–48mm; Flight: Mar–May.

▲ **Bath white** (*Pieris daplidice*) Distributed throughout central and s Europe, it is a rare migrant to Britain and other N European countries. The underwings are distinguished by a green apex. The female has more extensive black markings on the upperside. It has a rapid flight and may be seen bobbing around in clover fields. Wingspan: 42–48mm; Flight: Feb–Sept.

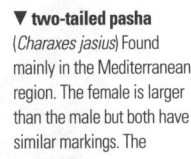

▼ **two-tailed pasha** (*Charaxes jasius*) Found mainly in the Mediterranean region. The female is larger than the male but both have similar markings. The underside is marked with black spots and streaks outlined in white and set against a brown background. Wingspan: 76–83mm; Flight: May–Sept.

▲ **brimstone** (*Gonepteryx rhamni*) Commonly seen feeding on meadow flowers in Europe, it is named after its deep yellow colouration, close to that of brimstone. The female is paler and can be mistaken for a white butterfly except for the leaf-like shape of the wings that distinguish her. Wingspan: 52–60mm; Flight: July–Sept.

▲ **monarch** (*Danaus plexippus*) Large, migratory butterfly found throughout Australasia and the Americas. It has orange wings with black veins, and black borders. Its caterpillars feed on milkweed which gives their bodies a taste disliked by birds. The unrelated viceroy mimics its colouration to avoid being eaten by birds. Wingspan: 75–100mm; Flight: all year.

▼ **small tortoiseshell** (*Aglais urticae*) Native to Europe and temperate regions of Asia. Their wings have tortoise-shell-like markings of orange, black brown and yellow with distinctive blue spots bordering both wings. Wingspan: 44–50mm. Flight: June–Oct.

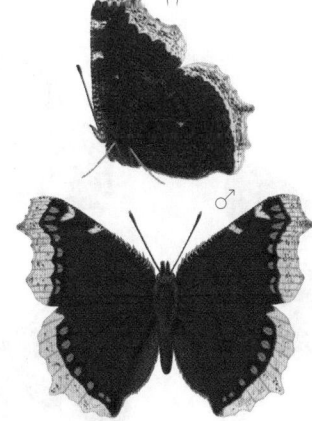

▲ **white admiral** (*Limenitis populi*) Found in s Britain and central Europe. They tend to occur singly and are commonly seen in woodland where they feed on blackberry blossom. The female is larger and slightly paler but otherwise similar in colouration. Wingspan: 52–60mm; Flight: June–July.

▲ **Camberwell beauty** or mourning cloak (*Nymphalis antiopa*) Large, striking butterfly found in Europe, North America and Asia. It is a regular migrant with a powerful flight. It is brown with violet-blue spots and a strip of yellow on the wing margins. The larvae feed on various host trees including elms, poplars and willows. Wingspan: 60–65mm; Flight: June–Sept.

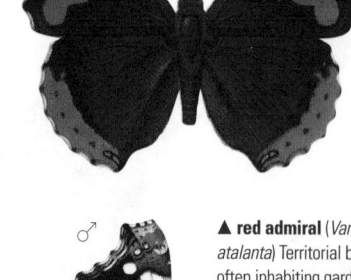

▲ painted lady (*Vanessa cardui*) Strongly migratory, it has many food sources in a variety of habitats around the world. The forewing has clear white spots on a black apex whilst the underside is paler with five eyespots on the hindwings. Wingspan: 54–58mm.

▲ red admiral (*Vanessa atalanta*) Territorial butterfly often inhabiting gardens, it is also a strong migrant. The uppers have scarlet bands and a bright blue spot on each lower hind wing. There is a pink bar on the forewing underside. Wingspan: 56–63mm.

▲ peacock butterfly (*Inachis io*) Camouflaged by its dark underside when at rest, if disturbed the large peacock eyespots on the uppers can startle predators. Although not migratory, it is common in many habitats throughout Europe. Wingspan: 54–60mm.

► Queen of Spain fritillary (*Issoria lathonia*) Common on rough, dry slopes, this species is found throughout the year in s Europe, nw Africa, and temperate regions throughout Asia. It is a strong migrant but rarely reaches as far n as Britain. It is identified by a spotty upperside with conspicuous large silver spots on the hindwing underside. It is also distinguished by the shape of its wings which are more pointed than other fritillaries. Wingspan: 38–46mm; Flight: Mar–Oct.

▲ spotted fritillary (*Melitaea didyma*) Variable in size and pattern, they are best distinguished by their features on the underside. These include round black spots in the pale yellow margin and the unbroken orange basal band. The male is more orange than the female. Wingspan: 30–44mm; Flight: May–Sept.

▼ marsh fritillary (*Euphydryas aurinia*) As well as having a liking for wet, boggy areas, it also inhabits dry mountain slopes. It can be found throughout most of Europe and w Britain. It is a variable species with differences occurring between indivduals. Spots vary in size and the female is larger than the male. The pale underside contrasts with the dark uppers. Wingspan: 30–46mm.

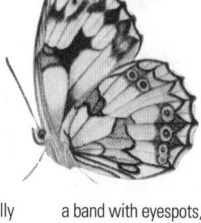

▲ marbled white (*Melanargia galathea*) Widespread in grassy areas up to 1800m (5905ft). They can be seen in central and s areas of Britain, especially around chalk downs. The female lays her eggs in flight so they fall at random. The hindwing underside has a band with eyespots, broken in the middle. The female is usually larger with an ochre-yellow underside. Wingspan: 46–56mm.

▲ speckled wood
(*Pararge aegeria*) Often found in areas with dappled light, such as woodland edges and forest clearings, where its spotted pattern blends in well with the surroundings. The species *P. aegeria aegeria* (top) occurs in S Europe. Further N *P. aegeria tircis* (bottom), identified by creamy-white spots instead of orange, replaces it. Wingspan: 38–44mm; Flight: Mar–Oct.

▶ wall brown
(*Lasiommata megera*) A widespread species found in a variety of habitats including rough open ground and along hedgerows. Fluttery in flight, they settle on bare soil to bask in the sun. Like other brown butterflies, they have brown bodies and eyespots towards the edges of their wings. The uppers are orange-yellow with brown criss-cross patterns. The underside hindwing is grey with intricate markings. The female is larger and paler. They inhabit Europe except N Scotland and Scandinavia. Wingspan: 36–50mm; Flight: Mar–Sept.

▲ Duke of Burgundy fritillary (*Hamearis lucina*) Resembling the fritillary superficially, it is the only member of the Riodinidae to occur in Europe. The female has wider orange markings. Wingspan: 28–34mm.

▼ small copper or American copper (*Lycaena phlaeas*) Widespread in Europe, North America, and Asia. The hind-wing is mostly dark grey and the underside has prominent red-orange marginal marks. Wingspan: 24–30mm.

▲ sloe hairstreak or Acadian hairstreak (*Satyrium acaciae*) Inhabits S Europe and North America. Grey-brown above with an orange spot on each hindwing. Silver-grey below with charcoal markings. Wingspan: 28–32mm.

▼ common blue
(*Polyommatus icarus*) Very common throughout Europe, it is found in open grassy places. The male has bright blue uppers with a black marginal line and white fringes. The female is more brown with orange lunules on the uppers and across both underside wings. Wingspan: 28–36mm.

▲ purple-shot copper
(*Lycaena alciphron*) Widespread species found in warm, flowery meadows throughout most of Europe. The male's uppers are copper, obscured by purple scales on the forewing. The female's wings are dark brown and broader with darker spots. Both sexes have well-defined spots on the underside. Wingspan: 32–36mm; Flight: June–July.

The first step in the identification of a tree is to establish whether it is a conifer or a broadleaf. Conifers bear cones, and have needle-like leaves which contrast with the wider foliage of the broadleaf trees. When identifying trees, bear in mind a few general points. Leaf character varies even on a single tree, the leaves at the top generally being shorter. Remember that shoots of a tree that has been pruned will grow with greater vigour, giving rise to untypical proportions. As a rule you will find more typical features on short shoots. Examine the foliage, noting its colour and whether it is hanging. Inspect the leaves, note their shape and how they are set upon the shoot. Pay special attention to the shape of a leaf's base and tip, its veins, and its petiole or stalk. Also look at the shoots and buds, noting their colour, shape, and whether they are hairy or not. The size, colour, and the breaking pattern of bark on the bole or trunk can also be useful identification features. The bole or trunk of a tree increases in diameter every year. The average increase in the girth of a tree growing in the open is 2.5cm (1in) a year. The best way to estimate the age of a tree is to measure its girth about 1.5m (5ft) above the ground.

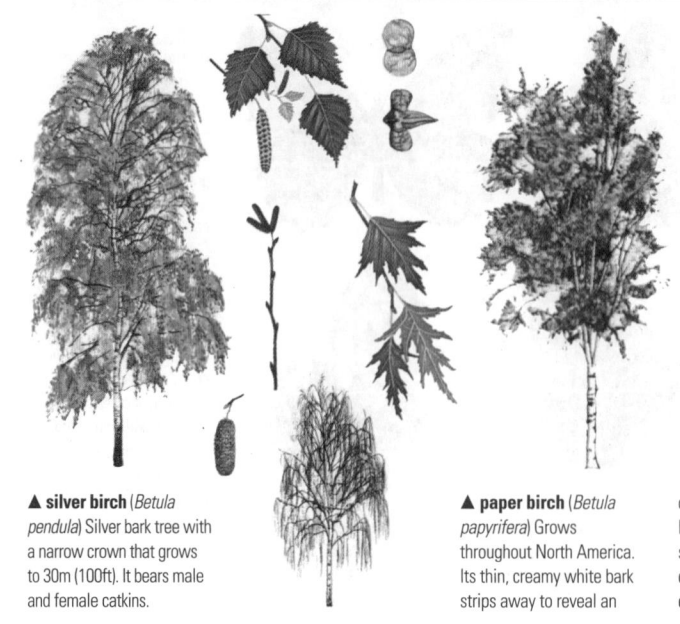

▲ **silver birch** (*Betula pendula*) Silver bark tree with a narrow crown that grows to 30m (100ft). It bears male and female catkins.

▲ **paper birch** (*Betula papyrifera*) Grows throughout North America. Its thin, creamy white bark strips away to reveal an orange inner bark. Native Indians once used the stripped bark to cover their canoes. The stiff, narrow crown grows to 20m (65ft).

▲ **yellow birch** (*Betula alleghaniensis*) Notable for its yellow autumn foliage and the long hairs of its leaves and young shoots. It is native to eastern North America where it can grow to 30m (100ft). The bark is bronze, yellowish or grey and is very inflammable.

▼ **white willow** (*Salix alba*) European native that grows to 25m (82ft). It can be identified from crack willow by its less fragile twigs and less deeply fissured bark. Its leaves grow to 8cm (3in) with white silky hairs above and dense tomentum beneath.

▶ **hazel** (*Corylus avellana*) Shrubby, European native that grows up to 10m (30ft). Its nuts ripen brown in clusters of one to four in papery, toothed bracts.

▲ **sallow willow** or goat willow (*Salix caprea*) Belongs to a group of related species collectively known as pussy willows. The sallow willow grows to 10m (33ft). Its leaves grow to 10cm (4in). The flowering shoots decorate churches on Palm Sunday.

▼ **alder** (*Alnus glutinosa*) Typically seen by streams, it is tolerant of water-logged conditions and its deep roots help limit erosion on river banks. The fruit releases buoyant seeds that are distributed by water. Native to Britain and most of Europe, it grows up to 20m (66ft) and can live up to 150 years.

▲ **weeping willow** (*Salix x sepulcralis*) Hybrid of the white willow (*S. alba*) and the rarer Chinese weeping willow (*S. babylonica*). They are commonly grown as ornamentals and are found beside water towards which the foliage tends to bend. The broad crown grows to 20m (66ft).

▶ **black walnut** (*Juglans nigra*) North American tree with dark, cross-furrowed bark. It grows up to 30m (100ft) tall and has a narrower crown than the walnut (*J. regia*). Its leaves are serrated and *c*.50cm (20in) long. The fruit is either pickled while still fleshy, or left to harden and form an edible nut.

▲ **beech** (*Fagus sylvatica*) Grows to 40m (130ft) tall and flourishes on chalky, high ground. The dark glossy leaves grow to 10cm (4in), and turn russet in autumn. The green, prickly fruit ripens to golden brown and bursts into four. The nuts are three-sided and 1cm (½ in) long.

▶ **black cottonwood** or balsam poplar (*Populus trichocarpa*) Recognized by the balsamiferous odour from the resinous buds. They have large leaves and grow to 35m (115ft).

▼ **red oak** (*Quercus rubra*) From E USA, it has matt leaves, smoothish bark and 2.5cm (1in) acorns. It grows vigorously to 35m (115ft).

▲ **English oak** (*Quercus robur* or *Q. pedunculata*) Grows to 35m (115ft) tall. The leaves grow to 12cm (4½ in). Acorns ripen over one or two years. Oaks have separate male and female flowers on the same tree; the female flowers are erect but inconspicuous, while the male catkins are long and pendulous. The heavy, heartwood of the oak was once widely used in English shipbuilding.

▼ **aspen** (*Populus tremula*) Hardy species that grows well on high ground or wet lowland. It has a distinct 6cm (2in) petiole and its open crown grows to 20m (66ft).

▲ **black poplar** (*Populus nigra*) Common in Britain is *P. nigra betulifolia* (left), which grows to 30m (100ft). The *P. nigra 'Italica'* (right) has erect branches and grows to 35m (115ft). The leaves of both trees are 8cm (3in) and yellow in autumn. They are often attacked by aphids that produce spiralled galls on their leaf stalks.

▲ **hornbeam** (*Carpinus betulus*) Often mistaken for beech, it is distinguished by its serrated leaves with deep veins, and smaller buds set closely against the shoots. The catkins expand in March. The male catkin is 3cm (1in) and the female is 5cm (2in) and pendent. It grows to 30m (100ft) and was once valued for its hard, smooth timber.

► **bay laurel** (*Laurus nobilis*) Mediterranean native with elliptic, pointed leaves that are strongly aromatic, especially when crushed. They are dark green and leathery and typically 5–13cm (2–5in) long. Its broad crown grows to 20m (66ft). An infusion of the leaves is toxic, but in small quantities may be used with impunity to flavour food. The ancient Greeks and Romans used the foliage to crown conquering generals and favoured poets. This practice lives on in the awarding of a bachelor's degree, derived from the French *baccalaureate*, and in the title of poet laureate.

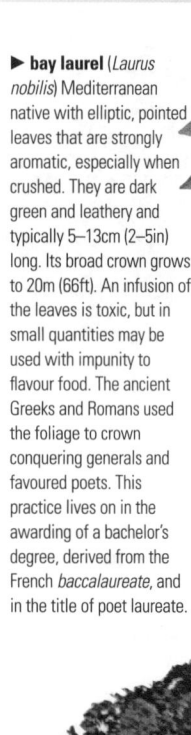

▼ **sassafras** (*Sassafras albidum*) Freely suckering tree native to E USA that grows to 25m (82ft) with an open flat-topped crown. Its three-veined leaves are typically 15cm (6in) long. The dark blue drupe fruit grows on a red pedicel. The aromatic twigs, bark, and roots of the sassafras produce a fragrant oil or tea.

▲ **wych elm** (*Ulmus glabra*) Native to Britain, its botanical name derives from the smoothness of its young bark. It has a majestic, spreading crown, which reaches up to 40m (130ft). The leaves (right) are 18cm (7in) long.

▼ **laburnum** (*Laburnum anagyroides*) Small garden tree with a colourful display of pendulous, yellow flowers on racemes up to 50cm (20in). The flowers have five petals. Its crown, spreading on arching, ascending branches, reaches to 8m (26ft) high. Its flat winged seeds are toxic. The bark is smoothish, and the leaves are trifoliate.

▲ **black mulberry** (*Morus nigra*) Thought to be of Chinese origin, it is grown for its tangy, raspberry-like fruit, which turns from red to black in late summer. The low, rounded crown grows to 10m (33ft). The short bole often leans, and the branches are twisted. The leaves, 15cm (6in) long, are rough, glossy, and hairy.

▼ **tulip tree** (*Liriodendron tulipifera*) Native to E USA that produces yellow-green tulip-shaped flowers in early summer. It has regular spaced branches and a dense crown that grows to 35m (115ft) high. Its 15cm (6in) long leaves are usually four-lobed and shiny and smooth above and glaucous beneath.

▲ **hawthorn** (*Crataegus monogyna*) Grows to 15m (50ft) tall. It also known as a May tree, after the month in which it flowers, or a quickthorn tree because of the rapidity of its growth. It is ideal for hedge planting.

▲ **cockspur thorn** (*Crataegus crus-galli*) Native to E USA. It is a low, rounded tree that grows to 7m (23ft) tall. In autumn, it assumes a rich orange colour.

▶ **rowan** or mountain ash (*Sorbus aucuparia*) Produces large, dome-shaped clusters of strongly scented, white flowers in late spring. These develop into scarlet berries in late summer. The rowan tree is small, growing up to 15m (49ft), with an ovoid crown. Its branches ascend or arch, and its leaves, 20cm (8in) long, are pinnate. The rowan dislikes shade, and grows in the open or in sparse woodland. The 'Beissneri' clone is a popular tree in residential streets. It has shiny and smooth, orange or pinkish brown bark, and deeply serrated, yellowish green leaflets.

▼ **holly** (*Ilex aquifolium*) It has prickly leaves on the lower boughs that are often spineless higher up. It grows to 25m (82ft) high.

▲ **black cherry** (*Prunus serotina*) One of the largest members of the cherry family, growing up to 25m (82ft) high. It has an irregularly domed crown carried on a few stems. Its branches are arched, and its bark is aromatic. The leaves have a hairy midrib below.

▲ **honey locust** (*Gleditsia triacanthos*) Distinguished from *Robinia pseudoacacia* by its spiny bark, greenish flowers, and larger pods. It often has bipinnate leaves on slender shoots. Livestock and wildlife consume the sweet pulp of its pods. It grows to 24m (80ft).

▼ **southern magnolia** (*Magnolia grandiflora*) Small, evergreen tree from s USA. It grows to 24m (80ft) high and bears very large, very fragrant white flowers from July to November. The southern magnolia has leathery, thick, shiny leaves, up to 20cm (8in) long.

▲ **sweet chestnut** (*Castanea sativa*) Large tree, up to 30m (100ft). It is unusual in that both male and females flowers are on the same stalk and pollination is by insects. The spiky fruit husks contain the chestnuts, which drop in September.

▼ **London plane** (*Platanus* x *orientalis*) Hardy tree, widely planted in the streets of London. It is a hybrid of the American plane (*P. occidentalis*) and *P. orientalis*. The crown grows to 45m (148ft), with mostly ascending branches. The glossy leaves grow to 20cm (8in). The bark flakes to give a dappled effect.

▲ **box** (*Buxus sempervirens*) Native to s England, it grows to 10m (33ft) often with a leaning aspect. The bark cracks into square plates. Its hard, heavy wood is a popular material for engraving.

▲ **crab apple** (*Malus sylvestris*) British native that has white flowers with a hint of pink, and which produces a hard and sour fruit that is yellow-green, ripening with a reddish flush. Its leaves grow to 6cm (2in). It is a parent of orchard apple (*M. domestica*), which has pinker flowers and sweeter, softer and larger fruit. It can grow up to 10m (30ft).

▲ Norway maple (*Acer platanoides*) European native and introduced in North America. It grows to 25m (82ft), and is most attractive in autumn when its leaves turn yellow. The leaves have a long stalk with milky white sap. Yellow-green flowers open in early spring. The winged fruit hangs on a long stalk and matures in summer.

▲ sycamore (*Acer psuedoplatanus*) Member of the maple family. It has a broad crown and scaly, light grey-brown bark and winged fruit to enable wide dispersal. It grows to 35m (115ft) tall.

► sugar maple (*Acer saccharum*) North American native that grows to 30m (100ft) and has an open dense crown. The leaves are dark green above and paler below, and are similar to the Norway maple except that they have a water sap. The foliage turns a striking gold and scarlet in autumn. The sap of the sugar maple is the source of maple syrup. Around 114–190 litres (25–42 gallons) of sap needs to be boiled to make four litres (one gallon) of maple syrup. A sugar maple is about 40 years old before it can be tapped for sap. Tapping is in February to April each year and one tree can yield up to 230 litres (50 gallons) of sap per season.

▲ red maple (*Acer rubrum*) North American native with red flowers, fruits, shoots and autumn foliage. The leaf undersides and bark are silver. It has a tall, domed crown that grows to 30m (100ft).

▲ ash-leaf maple or box elder (*Acer negundo*) Medium-sized tree that grows to 18m (30ft). It is identified by its pinnately, bright green leaves that have no autumn colour. Its samaras ripen early and remain in winter.

▼ striped maple or moosewood (*Acer pensylvanicum*) Found in E North America. Its distinctive bark, which is eaten by moose and other mammals, is bright green with white stripes and is the only snake-bark not indigenous to Asia. The fruit is abundant, measuring 5cm (2in) across. The leaves turn red in autumn. It grows to 9m (30ft).

▼ American lime or linden (*Tilia americana*) It grows up to 38m (125ft) tall with a diameter of up to 1.5m (5ft). Its leaves are up to 30cm (12in) long.

▲ horse chestnut (*Aesculus hippocastanum*) Native to SE Europe and introduced across North America. Named after the resemblance of its fruit to a chestnut. The horse chestnut's fruit, which can be toxic, provides the ammunition for the game of 'conkers'. The tree grows to 21m (70ft) tall.

► **black tupelo** (*Nyssa sylvatica*) It has many slender branches and its grey-brown bark is rough and fissured. The leaves turn bright red and gold in autumn. Its conical crown grows to 25m (82ft).

▲ **common persimmon** (*Diospyros virginiana*) Native to SE USA. It grows up to 20m (66ft) as a tree. It is sometimes grown as a shrub. It is identified by its glossy leaves that turn yellow in autumn, its urn-shaped flowers that open in July, and its sweet orange fruit that is highly astringent before ripening in autumn. The grey-black bark is cracked into squares.

▼ **northern catalpa** (*Catalpa speciosa*) From central USA, it grows up to 40m (131ft), although it reaches half this height in Europe. It has large bell-shaped flowers and ovate, leathery leaves. The northern catulpa is also called a cigar tree because of its long, distinctive, hanging fruit pods that mature in autumn and measure 40cm (16in).

◄ **Pacific flowering dogwood** (*Cornus nuttallii*) Native of the w coast of North America. It grows to 30m (100ft) and is most attractive in May when the creamy flowers bloom. The cluster of fruit resembles a flower and the hairy leaves turn red below in autumn.

◄ **yellow buckeye** (Aesculus flava) It has a rounded crown that grows to 20m (66ft), and bright, upright flowers that are sometimes pink. The leaves have five to seven leaflets that can be downy below and turn yellow and orange-red in autumn. The shiny seeds are poisonous.

► **white ash** (*Fraxinus americana*) Member of the olive family found in North America. Its dark leaves are whitish beneath. It reaches 24m (80ft) tall and its wood is used for baseball bats.

▲ **ash** (*Fraxinus excelsior*) Large, forest tree, native throughout Europe and Asia Minor. It can grow up to 45m (148ft), and has distinct, smooth black twigs and bark which becomes thick and grey in older trees. Distinct clusters of black buds can be seen in the winter. Flowers open in April before the leaves. Male flowers (top) have stamens set more densely than the female's (bottom), and whilst they normally appear on separate trees, one tree can carry both sexes.

63

Found throughout the world, **conifers** thrive in cool, mountainous areas of temperate regions. The group includes pines, spruces, and firs. They are mostly evergreen trees, although some (such as the larch) are deciduous and shed their leaves in autumn. Conifers have narrow, needle-like leaves and the seeds are not protected within an ovary. They produce neither flowers nor fruit but bear seeds in cones. A central stem supports upward growth, and some conifers are among the largest and oldest living things in the world. **Broadleaf** trees have more varied foliage than conifers and reproduce by fruits and seeds. The leaves are flat, broad and thin with networked veins that allow for a variety of leaf shapes. The central stem divides into numerous branches which form a broad, rounded, dense crown. Some broadleaves, such as holly, are evergreen, while many are deciduous and shed their leaves annually. Some deciduous broadleaves, such as maples, have characteristic foliage that turns to vibrant shades of reds or yellows before falling.

▲ **ginkgo** (*Ginkgo biloba*) Chinese native with primitive ancestry. It grows to 30m (100ft) and its leaves are 6–12cm (2–5in) and turn golden in autumn.

▲ **yew** (*Taxus baccata*) European native known for its longevity, living for more than 1000 years. Its dense crown can grow to 25m (82ft) tall. Its red berry-like fruit are poisonous. It is common in churchyards where it is planted as an ornamental tree.

▼ **Monterey cypress** (*Cupressus macrocarpa*) Found wild on the coast of California, it is also planted widely as a hedge tree. On the coast, trees are often distorted in shape from wind and salt blasting. The foliage is salt-resistant with slender, scale-like leaves that are lemon-scented when crushed. The cone is 4cm (1.5in) and has eight or 10 peltate scales. It can grow up to 24m (80ft) tall.

▲ **monkey puzzle** (*Araucaria araucana*) Its name alludes to the problems its sharply tipped, leathery leaves pose to potential climbers. It has a straight bole and domed crown that grows to 25m (82ft). The cone is green at first then ripens to brown.

▼ **western red cedar** (*Thuja plicata*) Native to the w coast of North America. It has aromatic, flattened, overlapping foliage. The crown grows to 40m (131ft).

▲ **Leyland cypress** (*Cupressus x leylandii*) Vigorous and durable hybrid with a dense, columnar crown that leans slightly and grows to 40m (131ft) tall.

▲ **Lawson cypress** (*Chamaecyparis lawsoniana*) Common, hardy, ornamental conifer that has been easily propagated into more than 250 varieties. It grows to 20–35m (66–115ft), 50m (164ft) in the wild. Foliage is flat and the crown is regular in young trees while it is more spaced in older ones.

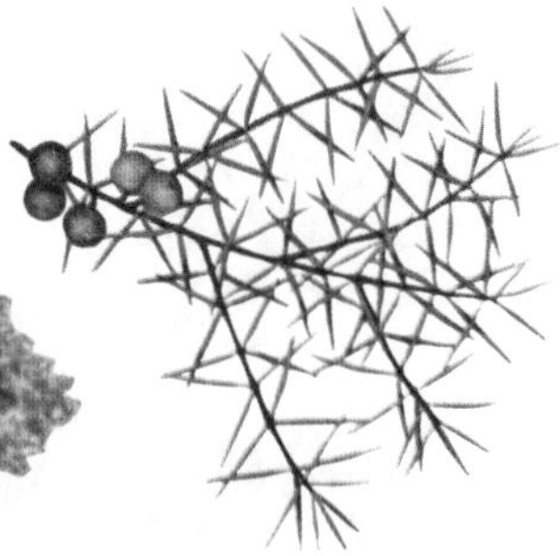

▲ **juniper** (*Juniperus communis*) Thriving in acid or alkaline soil, the juniper grows widely throughout the Northern Hemisphere. Its slender leaves are white on the inner surface and set in whorls of three. The cone is 1cm (0.4in) and green for 2–3 years and blue-black when ripe. It grows to 8m (26ft), usually as a shrub.

▶ **Wellingtonia** or giant sequoia (*Sequoiadendron giganteum*) Californian native that is the largest (but not tallest) living thing. It can weigh up to 1000 tonnes, have a trunk diameter of 10m (33ft) and live up to 4000 years, although the average age is around 1000 years. The bark is up to 30cm (12in) thick, and is soft and resilient to fire. The average height is 50m (164ft) although the largest, 'General Sherman', is 83m (272ft) tall. Branches have upswept tips with shiny, dark green foliage. The leaves are up to 7mm (0.3in) long. Deep roots enable the Wellingtonia to withstand long, dry periods.

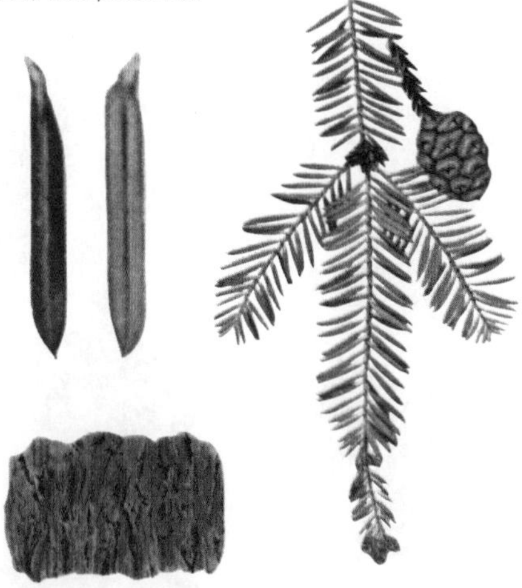

▲ **(California) redwood** (*Sequoia sempervirens*) Tallest tree in the world, reaching 112m (368ft). The crown is on average 50m tall (164ft). The thick, fibrous bark is bright red-brown on young trees and darker on old ones. The 3cm (1in) cone ripens in its first season.

▼ **swamp cypress** or bald cypress (*Taxodium distichum*) Native to s USA, it grows well in moist areas but prefers swamps and wetland areas where it develops aerial roots ('knees'). Its yellow-green foliage resembles that of other conifers except it is deciduous. It reaches heights of 30m (100ft) or more.

▲ **Douglas fir** (*Pseudotsuga menziesii*) False hemlock, native to the American Rockies. It has a powerful, sweet aroma and the leaves have blunt apexes. It is widely planted for its vigorous growth and excellent timber. The blue Douglas fir (*ssp. glavea*) is smaller and has blue-grey foliage with little scent.

▶ **cedar of Lebanon** (*Cedrus libani*) Ornamental native of Asia Minor. It has horizontal layers of dense, dark green foliage on branches that arch before becoming level. Cones measure 8–14cm (3–5.5in) and are usually conspicuous on lower branches. It grows to 40m (131ft) tall.

► **larch** (*Larix decidua*)
Native to central and N
Europe and introduced to
North America, the larch is
the only deciduous European
conifer. Its light green leaves
turn yellow before falling in
autumn. It has a straight
trunk and open crown that
grows to 45m (148ft). The
cones are reddish, and grow
to 4cm (2in) . They have
narrow, blunt and erect
scales. The hybrid larch (*L. x
marschlinsii*) is a natural
cross between a Japanese
and European tree. It is more
widely planted for its better
form, vigorous growth, and
resistance to disease. It can
be identified by cone scales
that are slightly reflexed like
rose petals.

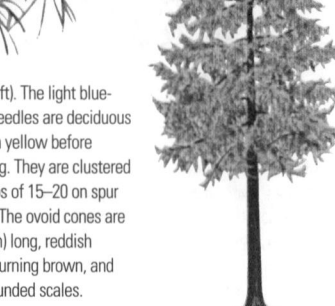

▲ **tamarack** (*Larix laricina*)
One of the most widely
distributed conifers in North
America, it grows in any
habitat – from swamps to
sub-Arctic conditions. It has
a long, straight trunk with
reddish-brown bark, and a
slender crown that grows to

20m (66ft). The light blue-
green needles are deciduous
and turn yellow before
shedding. They are clustered
in groups of 15–20 on spur
shoots. The ovoid cones are
2cm (1in) long, reddish
before turning brown, and
have rounded scales.

▲ **Norway spruce** (*Picea
abies*) The familiar
'Christmas tree' of N Europe,
where it grows in temperate
regions at high altitudes
with moist soils. The

pendulous cones grow to
18cm (7in) long, making
them the largest cones of
the spruces. Its needles are
four-sided, and 2cm (1in)
long. It grows to 24m (80ft).

▼ **Sitka spruce** (*Picea
sitchensis*) Native to the W
coast of North America. the
Sitka spruce has horizontal
branches with bright green
needles that are 3cm (1in)
long. The cones are
cyclindrical, measuring 8cm

(3in) long with papery thin
scales that ripen to yellow-
brown. It is widely planted
for its high-grade timber. It
is the tallest spruce,
growing up to 80m (262ft),
although the average
height is 50m (164ft).

▲ **blue spruce** (*Picea
pungens*) Its dense blue-
green foliage on horizontal
branches forms a conical
crown that grows to 25–30m
(82–98ft). The needles are
four-sided and 2cm (1in) long
with sharp tips. The
cylindrical cone is 12cm (5in).

▲ **white spruce** (*Picea
glauca*) Found widely across
Canada and N USA. It is an
important commercial tree,
harvested primarily for
pulpwood. The twigs are

orange-brown with blue-
grey needles that are 1.5cm
(.5in) long and have a strong
odour when crushed. The
cones are 6cm (2in) and it
can grow to 30m (100ft).

► **western hemlock**
(*Tsuga heterophylla*) Native
to the Pacific NW of North
America. It is a fast-
growing tree, tolerant of
shade and dry, acid
conditions. The young tree
has a leading shoot that
arches over. An older tree
has dense foliage and a

broad conic crown that
grows to 50m (164ft).
Needles measure up to 2cm
(1in) and are flat, rounded
and white beneath.

▶ **eastern hemlock** (*Tsuga canadensis*) Native to the E half of North America. It has a conical crown of long horizontal branches that usually droop to the ground. It grows to 21m (70ft) although some individulas have been measured at more than 30m (100ft). Needles grow on grey-brown twigs and are flat, rounded at the tip with two broad silvery-white bands below. The cones are ovoid-conic in shape with rounded scales and always grow at the end of branches, initially green and becoming brown in the second year. The bark is grey-brown and was once used as a source of tannin for leather production.

▲ **Scots pine** (*Pinus sylvestris*) The only native British pine, it grows to 40m (131ft) and lives 150 years on average. The bark is orange in the upper crown, becoming grey and heavily fissured at the base. The leaves are 8cm (3in) long and 15cm (6in) on young trees.

▼ **Lodgepole pine** (*Pinus contorta*) The only pine native to both Alaska and Mexico. Its name refers to the native Americans' use of the trunk as poles for their tents. Its dense crown grows to 24m (80ft). The bark is finely scaled and the foliage splayed and twisted with 10cm (4in) long leaves. Flowers shed pollen in April.

▲ **Ponderosa pine** (*Pinus ponderosa*) It thrives at varying altitudes and on dry sites throughout w North America. Its grows to 40m (131ft) and the foliage is variable, even on the same tree. Leaves are 15–20cm (6–8in) long, usually in bundles of two or three.

▲ **western white pine** (*Pinus monticola*) Native to w North America. It has a dense crown and grows to 50m (164ft), although it can reach heights of 70m (230ft). The bark is grey-green and is often attacked by blister rust, a fungal disease affecting white pines. There are numerous cones measuring 35cm (14in) long.

▼ **Weymouth pine** (*Pinus strobus*) Large conifer with a straight trunk and a crown that is conical when young and becomes irregular as it matures. It differs from the western white pine by its stiffer leaves and shorter cones, 15cm (6in) -long. It grows up to 33m (100ft).

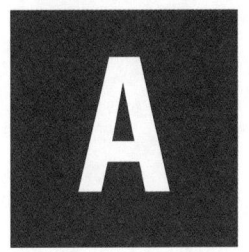

Aachen (Aix-la-Chapelle) City in sw North Rhine-Westphalia, w Germany. The city is noted for its sulphur baths, used by the Romans, which are the hottest in N Europe. It was the site of medieval imperial diets and the coronations of the monarchs of the Holy Roman Empire from 1349 to 1531. The local economy is dominated by manufacturing. Industries: iron and steel, machinery, textiles. Pop. (1999) 243,600.

Aalto, Alvar (1898–1976) Finnish architect and furniture designer, famous for his imaginative handling of floor levels and use of natural materials and irregular forms. Aalto's work includes the Sanatorium at Paimio (1931), the Finnish Pavilion at the New York International Exhibition (1939), Baker House at the Massachusetts Institute of Technology (1947–49), and Finlandia House, Helsinki (1967–71). *See also* MODERNISM

aardvark Nocturnal, bristly haired mammal of central and s Africa. It feeds on termites and ants, which it scoops up with its sticky 30cm (12in) tongue. Length: up to 1.5m (5ft); weight: up to 70kg (155lb). It is the only representative of the order *Tubulidentata*.

Aaron In the Old Testament, brother of Moses and the founder of the Jewish priesthood. According to the book of Exodus, he led the Israelite tribe of Levi out of slavery in Egypt. Aaron's magic brought the first three of ten plagues upon Egypt. He lapsed into idolatry and made a golden calf for the people to worship, but was later restored to divine favour.

abacus Mathematical tool used since ancient times in the Middle and Far East for addition, subtraction, multiplication, and division. One form consists of beads strung on wires and arranged in columns.

abalone (ormer) Gastropod MOLLUSC with a single, flattened, spiral shell perforated by a row of respiratory holes. They are found in the shallows of rocky shores. Abalones are eaten and their shells used as ornaments. Length: to 30cm (12in). Family Haliotidae; species include *Haliotis rufescens*.

Abbado, Claudio (1933–) Italian conductor. He was musical director at La Scala, Milan (1972–86), the London Symphony Orchestra (1983–88), Vienna State Opera (1986–91), and the Berlin Philharmonic (1989–2002). Abbado is noted for his interpretations of 20th-century music.

Abbas I (the Great) (1571–1629) Shah of Persia (1588–1629). The outstanding ruler of the Safavid dynasty, Abbas restored Persia as a great power, waging war successfully against the invading Uzbeks and Ottoman Turks and recapturing Hormuz from the Portuguese. Tolerant in religion, he encouraged Dutch and English merchants and admitted Christian missionaries. He made Isfahan his capital and turned it into one of the world's most beautiful cities.

Abbasid Muslim CALIPH dynasty (750–1258). They traced their descent from al-Abbas, the uncle of Muhammad, and came to power by defeating the Umayyads. In 862 the Abbasids moved the caliphate from Damascus to Baghdad, where it achieved great splendour. From the 10th century Abbasid caliphs ceased to exercise political power, becoming religious figureheads. After the family's downfall in 1258, following the fall of Baghdad to the Mongols, one member was invited by the Mamluk sultan to Cairo where the dynasty was recognized until the 16th century.

Abbey Theatre Theatre erected on Abbey Street, Dublin (1904), by Annie E.F. Horniman to house the Irish National Theatre Society. In 1925 the Abbey became the National Theatre of Ireland. Works by W.B. Yeats, Lady Gregory, J.M. Synge and Sean O'Casey have been introduced here, and the Theatre is renowned for its support of new writers.

Abd al-Kadir (1808–83) Algerian leader. He displaced (1832–39) the French and Turks from N Algeria, and then launched a holy war against the French. In 1843 he was forced to retreat to Morocco, where he enlisted the support of the sultan. Abd al-Kadir and his Moroccan forces were defeated at Isly (1844). He was imprisoned in France (1847–52).

Abdul Hamid II (1842–1918) Last Ottoman sultan (1876–1909). On his accession, Abdul Hamid suspended Parliament and the new constitution. At the Treaty of San Stefano (1878), he concluded the Russo-Turkish Wars by ceding vast lands to Russia. Abdul Hamid is known as the 'Great Assassin' for his part in the Armenian massacres (1894–96) – it is estimated

that more than 200,000 Armenians were killed in 1896 alone. In 1908 the Young Turks forced him to reimplement the 1876 constitution, and he was deposed shortly after.

Abdullah ibn Hussein (1882–1951) King of Jordan (1946–51), son of Hussein ibn Ali of the Hashemite family. In 1921, after aiding Britain in World War 1, he became Emir of Trans-Jordan. Abdullah lost control of Hejaz to Ibn Saud. In World War 2, he resisted the Axis. Abdullah fought against the creation of Israel, annexed Palestinian land, and signed an armistice (1949). He was assassinated in Jerusalem.

Abel In the Old Testament (Genesis), the second son of Adam and Eve. Abel, a shepherd, was killed by his brother Cain, a farmer, who was jealous that God had rejected his offering but accepted Abel's.

Abélard, Pierre (1079–1142) French philosopher noted for his application of LOGIC in approaching theological questions. In *Sic et Non*, he attempted to reconcile differences between the Fathers of the Church by using the method of DIALECTICS. In 1140, the Council of Sens condemned his views. Abélard is best known for his tragic love for his pupil Héloise. The affair scandalized his contemporaries. He was castrated and became a monk, and Héloise was forced to enter a convent. The events inspired Abélard's *Historia Calamitatum Mearum*.

Aberdeen Third-largest city in Scotland (after Glasgow and Edinburgh), situated between the rivers Dee (S) and Don (N). Aberdeen is the main port on the NE coast of Scotland. Chartered by William the Lion in 1179, it is known as the 'Granite City' for its grey granite architecture such as St Machar's Cathedral (1131). Since the 1970s, the city has become a major centre of the British oil industry. Pop. (2001) 211,910.

Aberdeen, George Hamilton Gordon, 4th Earl of (1784–1860) British statesman, prime minister (1852–55). As foreign secretary (1841–46) to Sir Robert Peel, he negotiated the Webster-Ashburton and the Oregon Boundary treaties with the United States. He and Peel resigned over the issue of the Corn Laws. Aberdeen emerged to form the 'Aberdeen coalition' Ministry. He was swayed into entering the Crimean War by Viscount Palmerston, but was blamed for the mismanagement of the war and was forced to resign.

aberration In astronomy, apparent slight change of position of a star due to the effect of the Earth's orbital motion and the finite velocity of light. A telescope must be inclined by an angle of up to 20° to compensate for aberration. The effect was first described by James Bradley in 1729 and was used to prove that the Earth orbits the Sun.

aberration In physics, defect in lens and mirror images arising when incoming light falls on the periphery of the lens or mirror. **Spherical** aberration occurs when these rays of a lens or mirror are not brought to the same focus as rays falling at the centre; the image is blurred. **Chromatic** aberration occurs when the wavelengths of dispersed light are not brought to the same focus; the image is falsely coloured.

Abidjan Former capital of the Ivory Coast, situated on Ebrie Lagoon, inland from the Gulf of Guinea. A port and commercial centre, Abidjan was founded by French colonists at the end of the 19th century. Although Yamoussoukro replaced it as the capital in 1983, Abidjan remains a cultural and economic centre. Industries: textiles, sawmilling. Pop. (2005) 3,516,000.

A/a, first letter of the Roman alphabet. It evolved from the ancient Egyptian hieroglyph representing the head of an ox through the Hebrew word **aleph***, meaning ox, to the Greek* **alpha***.*

INTERNET

Aachen
▶ www.aachen.de

Aberdeen, George Hamilton Gordon, 4th Earl of
▶ www.number-10.gov.uk

◄ **aardvark** Found throughout much of Africa, the termite-eating aardvark (*Orycteropus afer*) is a shy, nocturnal animal. Its presence may be detected by the large burrows it digs using the hoof-like claws on its front feet.

Abkhazia Autonomous republic on the Black Sea coast of GEORGIA; the capital is Sukhumi. The area was conquered by Romans, Byzantines, Arabs and Turks before becoming a Russian protectorate in 1910. It was made a Soviet republic in 1921, and an autonomous republic within Georgia in 1930. In 1992, after the establishment of an independent Georgia, the Abkhazian parliament declared independence. The following year, Abkhazian forces seized the capital from the Georgian army. In 1995, its independent status was confirmed by a new Georgian constitution. Tobacco, tea, and grapes are the main crops. Area: 8600sq km (3320sq mi). Pop. (1993 est.) 516,600.

abolitionist Person who sought to end SLAVERY. In the UK, William WILBERFORCE headed the Clapham Sect that led to the end of Britain's role in the slave trade in 1807. In 1831, William Lloyd Garrison published *The Liberator*, an antislavery journal. The American Anti-Slavery Society was formed in 1833, and within five years such societies had over 250,000 members. Harriet Beecher STOWE's abolitionist novel *Uncle Tom's Cabin* (1852) sold more than 300,000 copies in its first year. The militant actions of abolitionists culminated in John BROWN's raid on the US arsenal at Harper's Ferry, Virginia, and the antagonism between North and South over slavery was a major cause of the American CIVIL WAR.

aborigines Strictly, the indigenous inhabitants of a country. The term is usually applied to NATIVE AUSTRALIANS.

abortion Termination of pregnancy before a FETUS is sufficiently advanced to survive outside the mother's UTERUS. **Spontaneous** abortion (miscarriage) occurs in *c*.20% of apparently normal pregnancies. Miscarriages in the first three months of pregnancy are usually caused by fetal abnormalities. Miscarriages later in pregnancy may be caused by defects in the maternal environment, such as reproductive system disorders. **Induced** or **therapeutic** abortion is the termination of pregnancy by drugs or surgery. The rights of the fetus and the mother's right to choose provoke much political and ethical debate. Currently, the legal time-limit in the UK for an induced abortion is up to 24 weeks after conception.

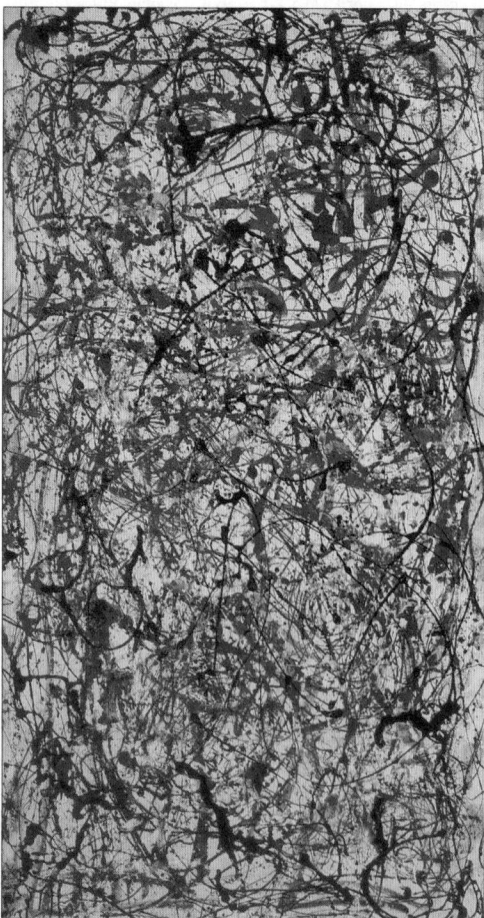

▶ **abstract expressionism**
Black and White (1948) by Jackson Pollock. Pollock's "action painting" is often regarded as the quintessential form of abstract expressionism. It was the first US art movement to influence European trends.

Abraham In the Old Testament, progenitor of the Hebrews and founder of JUDAISM. In Judaeo-Christian tradition God tested Abraham's loyalty by demanding the sacrifice of his son ISAAC (in Muslim tradition, ISHMAEL). Abraham is esteemed by Muslims who regard him as the ancestor, through Ishmael, of the Arabs.

abrasive Hard and rough substances used to grind and polish surfaces. Some abrasives are used as fine powders, others in larger fragments with cutting edges. Most natural abrasives are minerals, such as DIAMOND, CORUNDUM, PUMICE and FLINT.

Absalom In the Old Testament, third and favourite son of King DAVID. A youth of uncontrollable arrogance, he murdered his brother Amnon, and led a failed rebellion against David. Trapped in flight when his hair became entangled in the branches of an oak, he was killed by David's general Joab.

abscess Collection of pus anywhere in the body, contained in a cavity of inflamed tissue. It is caused by bacterial infection.

absolute zero Temperature at which all parts of a system are at the lowest energy permitted by the laws of QUANTUM MECHANICS; zero on the Kelvin temperature scale, which is $-273.16°C$ $(-459.67°F)$. At this temperature the system's ENTROPY, its energy available for useful work, is also zero.

absolutism Government with unlimited power vested in one individual or group. Absolutism is used primarily to describe 18th-century European monarchies that claimed a divine hereditary right to rule.

absorption Taking up chemically or physically of molecules of one substance into another. This includes a gas taken in by a liquid and a liquid or gas absorbed by a solid. The process is often utilized commercially, such as the purification of natural gas by the absorption of hydrogen sulphide in aqueous ethanolamine. Absorption is also the term used when light and other electromagnetic waves lose some energy as they pass through a medium. *See also* ADSORPTION

abstract art Art in which recognizable objects are reduced to schematic marks. Although abstraction was evident in the impressionist, neo- and post-impressionist movements of the late 19th century, a separate identity did not become established until the early 20th century. Its most radical form is called **non-objective** or non-iconic art. In this, the artist creates marks, signs or three-dimensional constructions that have no connection with images or objects in the visible world. There are two main types of non-objective art: **expressionist,** which is fundamentally emotional, spontaneous and personal; and **geometrical**, which works from the premise that geometry is the only discipline precise and universal enough to express our intellectual and emotional longings. Art historians often credit Wassily KANDINSKY with being the first to explore expressionist abstraction in *c*.1910. Kandinsky inspired the BLAUE REITER group and helped to pave the way towards ABSTRACT EXPRESSIONISM, ACTION PAINTING, and Tachism. Geometrical abstraction found (*c*.1913) its most adept, early exponents in Russia. The pioneers included Kasimir MALEVICH, who invented SUPREMATISM, and El LISSITZKY, a leading proponent of CONSTRUCTIVISM. Others who provided landmarks in geometrical abstraction include Piet MONDRIAN, Naum GABO, and Ben NICHOLSON; influential movements include De STIJL and concrete art. *See also* EXPRESSIONISM; KUPKA

abstract expressionism Mainly US art movement in which the creative process itself is examined and explored. It is neither wholly abstract nor wholly expressionist. The term originally applied to paintings created (1945–55) by about 15 artists from the New York School. Although very different in temperament and style, these individuals shared a fascination with SURREALISM as well as other progressive European styles. Towards the early 1950s, two distinct groups emerged with Willem DE KOONING and Jackson POLLOCK heading the most aggressive trend (loosely known as ACTION PAINTING), which involved dripping or throwing paint on the canvas. Barnett NEWMAN, AD Reinhardt and Mark ROTHKO were more contemplative.

Absurd, Theatre of the Dramatic and literary critical term developed from the philosophy of Albert CAMUS to describe discordant human experience in an inhuman world. It was first applied (*c.*1961) to drama that depicted the irrationality of life in an unconventional style. Exponents include Samuel BECKETT, Eugène IONESCO, Jean GENET, and Edward ALBEE; the style flourished between the late 1940s and the 1960s. The connection between language and meaning is fractured and characters appear dislocated from their surroundings. Beckett's play *Waiting for Godot* (1952) is a classic of the genre.

Abu Bakr (*c.*573–634) First Muslim CALIPH (632–34). One of the earliest converts to ISLAM, Abu Bakr was chief adviser to the Prophet MUHAMMAD. After Muhammad's death he was elected leader of the Muslim community. During his short reign, he defeated the tribes that revolted against Muslim rule in Medina and restored them to Islam. By invading the Byzantine Christian provinces of Syria and Palestine and the Persian province of Iraq, he launched the Holy Wars through which the first major expansion of the Islamic world was accomplished.

Abu Dhabi (Abu Zaby) Largest and wealthiest of the seven UNITED ARAB EMIRATES, lying on the s coast of the Persian Gulf. Also the name of its capital city (1995 pop. 398,695), federal capital of the UAE. It has been ruled since the 18th century by the Al-bu-Falah clan of the Bani Yas tribe. There are long-standing frontier disputes with Saudi Arabia and Oman. Since the discovery of oil in the late 1950s, Abu Dhabi's economy has been based almost entirely on crude oil production. It has an international airport and a modern container port. Area: 67,340sq km (26,000sq mi). Pop. (2005) 928,000.

Abuja Nigeria's administrative capital since 1991. The new city was designed by the Japanese architect Kenzo Tange, and work began in 1976. Pop. (1996 est.) 350,000.

Abu Simbel Ancient Egyptian village on the w bank of the River Nile, near the border with Sudan. It is the location of two rock-cut sandstone temples built by RAMSES II (*c.*1292–1225BC). In a huge operation (1963–66), the temples and statuary were moved further inland. This was to prevent their disappearance under the waters of Lake Nasser, created by the construction of the new High Dam at ASWAN.

abyssal Term to describe oceanic features occurring at great depths, usually more than *c.*3,000m (10,000ft) below sea level. Abyssal **plains** cover *c.*30% of the Atlantic and nearly 75% of the Pacific ocean floors. They are covered by deposits of biogenic oozes formed by the remains of microscopic plankton and nonbiogenic sediments. The gradient is less than 1:1,000, except for the occasional low hill. The abyssal **zone** is the deepest area of the ocean. It receives no sunlight, so there are no seasons and no plants, but there are many forms of life, such as sponges, crinoids (sea lilies) and BRACHIOPODA (lampshells).

acacia (mimosa, wattle) Evergreen shrubs and trees widely distributed in tropical and subtropical regions. They have compound leaves and yellow or white flowers. Height: 1.2–18m (4–59ft). Family Leguminosae; genus *Acacia*.

Académie Française Official French literary society, now part of the *Institut de France*. Originating as a private discussion group whose members were persuaded by Cardinal RICHELIEU to become an official body in 1635, the society is the guardian of the French language and of literary conventions. Past members have included many of the giants of French literature, such as RACINE, VOLTAIRE, and HUGO.

Academy School of PHILOSOPHY founded (*c.*387BC) by PLATO. He met his pupils in a garden outside Athens, said to have belonged to a Greek hero called Academus. Much of the history of the Academy is uncertain, though we know its students included ARISTOTLE, EPICURUS and ZENO OF CITIUM. In AD 529, it was closed by Emperor Justinian. *See also* NEOPLATONISM; SCEPTICISM; UNIVERSITY

Academy Award *See* OSCAR

acanthus Perennial plant with thistle-like leaves, found in Africa, the Mediterranean region, India and Malaysia. It has lobed, often spiny leaves and white or coloured flower spikes. Family Acanthaceae.

Acapulco (Acapulco de Juárez) City on the sw coast of Mexico. Founded in 1550, it was for 250 years an important port on the galleon route linking Spain and the Philippines. Now the country's most famous Pacific resort, it is noted for beautiful scenery, deep-sea fishing, and luxurious hotels. Exports: cotton, fruit, hides, tobacco. Pop. (2000) 722,499.

◄ **accordion** Invented in the 1820s, the accordion is a reed organ working along the same principle as the mouth organ – separate reeds are provided for each note. Air is forced through the reeds by bellows that form the centre of the instrument. The right hand plays the melody on the keyboard, while the left hand operates the buttons for accompanying chords.

acceleration Amount by which the VELOCITY (speed in a particular direction) of an object changes in a given time. Acceleration can change both speed and direction. It is often measured in metres per second per second (m/s^2). For example, if an object accelerates from 20m/s to 30m/s in one second, it has accelerated by 10m/s^2. The earth's gravity causes falling objects to accelerate downwards by 9.8m (32.2ft) per second per second unless slowed by air resistance. The acceleration can be found by applying the equation: acceleration = (change in velocity)/(time taken). A decrease in velocity, or negative acceleration, is known as a deceleration. *See also* GRAVITATION

accelerator, particle In PARTICLE PHYSICS, machine for increasing the energy of charged particles by using alternating electric fields to increase the particles' speed. Accelerators are used in experiments to force high-energy particles to collide with other particles. The way the fragments of particles behave after the collision provides information on the forces within atoms. This is used for research purposes and to generate high-energy X-rays and gamma rays. In a **linear** accelerator, particles travel in a straight line, usually accelerated by an electric field. In a **cyclotron**, particles are accelerated in a spiral path between pairs of D-shaped magnets with an alternating voltage between them. In a **synchrocyclotron**, the accelerating voltage is synchronized with the time it takes the particles to make one revolution. A **synchrotron** consists of a large circular tube with magnets to deflect the particles in a curve and radio-frequency fields to accelerate them. The most advanced accelerators are **colliders**, in which beams of particles moving in opposite directions collide, thus achieving higher energy of interaction. *See also* BUBBLE CHAMBER

accessory In law, person associated with a criminal act. An accessory before the fact consults, encourages and advises the criminal. An accessory after the fact is one who, with knowledge of a crime, receives or assists the criminal.

accomplice In law, person associated with another or others in the commission of a crime. Unlike an ACCESSORY, an accomplice generally takes an active part in the crime.

accordion Musical instrument of the reed organ type. It has an organ-like tone produced by air from the bellows vibrating reeds. It is played by keys or buttons, usually one set of each. The accordion evolved in the early 19th century, and is now used in folk music around the world.

Accra Capital and largest city of Ghana, on the Gulf of Guinea. Occupied by the Ga people since the 15th century, it became capital of Britain's Gold Coast colony in 1875. Today it is a major port and economic centre and is increasingly popular with tourists. Industries: engineering, timber, textiles, chemicals. The principal export is cacao. Pop. (2005) 1,970,000.

acetaldehyde *See* ETHANAL

acetate *See* ETHANOATE

acetone *See* PROPANONE

acetylene *See* ETHYNE

Achaemenid Ruling dynasty of the first Persian empire, which stretched from the River Nile as far E as modern Afghanistan. The dynasty was founded by CYRUS THE GREAT (r.559–529BC) and named after his ancestor Achaemenes. DARIUS I (r.521–486BC) decentralized government administration. The last Achaemenid ruler, DARIUS III (r.336–330BC), was defeated by ALEXANDER THE GREAT. The dynasty was responsible for the spread of ZOROASTRIANISM through Asia, and the remains at PERSEPOLIS are testimony to the splendour of PERSIAN ART and architecture at this time.

Achebe, (Albert) Chinua (Chinualumogu) (1930–) Nigerian novelist. His work explores the effects of cultural change in modern Africa. Achebe's highly acclaimed debut novel, *Things Fall Apart* (1958), depicts life in an African village before and after the arrival of missionaries. Other works include *Arrow of God* (1964) and *Anthills of the Savannah* (1987). He received the Nobel Prize in literature in 1989.

Acheson, Dean Gooderham (1893–1971) US statesman, secretary of state (1949–53) under Harry S TRUMAN. Acheson's desire to restrict the growth of communism was fundamental to the establishment of the North Atlantic Treaty Organization (NATO), the ANZUS Pact, and the Marshall Plan.

Achilles In the Greek epic tradition, a formidable warrior, the most fearless Greek fighter of the Trojan War and the hero of Homer's *Iliad*. Legend held him invulnerable from weapons because he had been dipped by his mother, Thetis, in the River Styx at birth, except for the heel by which he was held. Achilles sought glory fighting at TROY, but an arrow shot by PARIS struck his heel and killed him.

Achilles tendon Strong band of elastic connective tissue at the back of the ankle. One of the largest tendons in the human body, it connects the calf muscles to the heel bone. The spring it provides is very important in walking, running and jumping.

acid Chemical compound containing hydrogen that can be replaced by a metal or other positive ION to form a SALT. Acids dissociate in water to yield aqueous hydrogen ions (H^+), and thus are sometimes described as "proton donors". The solutions are corrosive and have a pH below 7. Strong acids, such as SULPHURIC ACID, are fully dissociated into ions, making good ELECTROLYTES. Weak acids, such as ETHANOIC ACID, only partially dissociate. *See also* BASE

acid rain Rain that is highly acidic because of sulphur oxides, nitrogen oxides, hydrocarbons, and other air pollutants dissolved in it. Acid rain can severely damage both plant and animal life; certain forests have died and lakes have lost all fish and plant life because of acid rain. It also damages buildings and statues. The major causes of acid rain are motor vehicle emissions, industrial processes, and the burning of fossil fuels in power-stations.

acne Inflammatory disorder of the sebaceous (oil-producing) glands of the SKIN resulting in skin eruptions such as blackheads and infected spots; it is seen mostly on the face, neck and back. Acne is common in both sexes at PUBERTY. It does not usually persist beyond early adulthood.

Aconcagua Mountain in the Andes on the border between Argentina and Chile. An extinct volcano, it is the highest peak outside Asia, at 6962m (22,841ft). The W slopes are in Chile, but the summit lies in Argentina. The River Aconcagua rises at its NW foot and enters the Pacific N of Valparaiso.

acorn Fruit of an OAK tree

acoustics Study of SOUND, especially the behaviour of sound waves. Experts apply acoustics to the design of concert and lecture halls, microphones, loudspeakers, and musical instruments. *See also* ANECHOIC CHAMBER

Acquired Immune Deficiency Syndrome (AIDS) Fatal disease caused by a RETROVIRUS, called Human Immunodeficiency Virus (HIV), that mainly attacks T-4 cells (which help

the production of ANTIBODIES) and renders the body's IMMUNE SYSTEM incapable of resisting infection. The first diagnosis was made in New York in 1979. In 1983, scientists at the Pasteur Institute in France and the National Cancer Institute in the USA isolated HIV as the cause of the disease. The virus can remain dormant in infected cells for up to 10 years. Initial AIDS-related complex (ARC) symptoms include severe weight loss and fatigue. It may develop into the AIDS syndrome, characterized by secondary infections, neurological damage and cancers. AIDS is transmitted only by a direct exchange of body fluids. Transmission is most commonly through sexual intercourse, the sharing of contaminated needles by intravenous drug users, and the uterus of infected mothers to their babies. In the USA and Europe the earlier victims were predominantly homosexual or bisexual men, but heterosexual transmission is now more common. 90% of reported cases are in the developing world, and AIDS is now the leading cause of death in sub-Saharan Africa. Recent combinations of drugs have met with some success in controlling symptoms. By 2007, more than 25 million people had died from AIDS.

acropolis Hilltop fortress of an ancient Greek city. The earliest known examples were fortified castles built for the Mycenaean kings, and it was only later that they became the symbolic homes of the gods. The most famous acropolis, in Athens, acquired walls by the 13th century BC but the Persians destroyed the complex. The surviving buildings, including the PARTHENON, the Erechtheion, the Propylaea, and the Temple of Athena Nike, date from the late 5th century BC.

acrylic Type of plastic, one of a group of synthetic, short-chain, unsaturated CARBOXYLIC ACID derivatives. Variation in the reagents and the method of formation yields either hard and transparent, soft and resilient, or liquid products. Their toughness and dimensional stability make acrylics useful for moulded structural parts, lenses, adhesives and paints.

actinide series Group of radioactive elements with similar chemical properties. Their atomic numbers range from 89 to 103. Each element is analogous to the corresponding LANTHANIDE SERIES (rare earth metals). Those having atomic numbers greater than 92 (uranium) are the TRANSURANIC ELEMENTS.

actinium (symbol Ac) Radioactive, metallic element, the first of the ACTINIDE SERIES, discovered (1899) by French chemist André Debierne. It is found associated with uranium ores. Ac^{227}, a decay product of U^{235}, emits beta particles during disintegration. Properties: at.no.89; r.d.10.07; m.p. 1100°C (1900°F); b.p. 3200°C (5800°F); most stable isotope Ac^{227} (half-life 21.8 yr).

action painting Act and result of applying paint spontaneously. It gained momentum in 1952 when painters such as Willem DE KOONING and Jackson POLLOCK moved away from ABSTRACT EXPRESSIONISM to make pictures with spontaneous gestures, such as dripping and pouring paint onto their canvases. It aimed to stimulate vision and to record emotions. Other practitioners include Robert MOTHERWELL and Alan Davie.

action potential Change that occurs in the electrical potential between the outside and the inside of a nerve fibre or muscle fibre when stimulated by the transmission of a nerve impulse. At rest, the fibre is electrically negative inside and positive outside. When the nerve or muscle is stimulated, the charges are momentarily reversed.

Actium, Battle of (31BC) Naval battle in which the fleet of Octavian (later Emperor AUGUSTUS), commanded by Marcus Vipsanius AGRIPPA, defeated the fleets of Mark ANTONY and CLEOPATRA. Mark Antony's army surrendered a week later, and Octavian became sole ruler of the Roman Empire.

active transport Energy-requiring process by which molecules or ions are transported across the membranes of living cells against a concentration gradient. The energy is supplied by RESPIRATION. It is particularly important in the uptake of food across the gut lining, in the reabsorption of water and salts from the urine in the kidney before excretion, and in the uptake of minerals by the plant root. Active transport enables cells to maintain an internal chemical environment of a different composition from that of their surroundings. Active transport is different from DIFFUSION which requires no energy.

INTERNET

acropolis
► www.culture.gr

► **acropolis** The fortified high point of many Greek cities, the most famous acropolis is that of Athens. It is dominated by the Parthenon, one of the world's most impressive structures. Built as an expression of Athens' supremacy, it housed a vast ivory and gold statue of Athena, the Greek goddess of war, wisdom, and the arts.

Act of Congress Statute adopted by the CONGRESS of the United States. It overrides conflicting legislation from any other source, although the SUPREME COURT may rule that an act of Congress is unconstitutional.

Act of Parliament Statute created in Britain when a bill, having passed through various stages in both the HOUSE OF COMMONS and HOUSE OF LORDS, receives the royal assent. Embodying the supreme force of British law, an act remains in force until it is repealed by Parliament.

Act of Union Any of several acts of Parliament which created a unified British state. *See* UNION, ACTS OF

Actors' Studio Theatre workshop founded (1947) in New York by Elia KAZAN, Cheryl Crawford, and Robert Lewis. It became noted for the 'method' approach to acting, particularly under Lee STRASBERG. Its eminent members include Marlon BRANDO, Dustin HOFFMAN and Robert DE NIRO.

Acts of the Apostles Book of the New Testament describing the spread of the Gospel of Christ immediately after his death and resurrection. It mainly focuses on Saint PETER and Saint PAUL. The book was probably written (*c*.AD 65) by the author of the gospel of St Luke.

acupuncture Practice in traditional Chinese medicine in which needles are inserted into the body to assist healing or relieve pain. No scientific evidence has been produced for acupuncture's effectiveness in treating disease, but there is limited evidence that it may help to control pain.

Adam In the Old Testament, first man, progenitor of mankind, created from dust by God in his own image. He and his wife EVE were cast out of the Garden of EDEN to become mortal after they ate forbidden fruit from the Tree of the Knowledge of Good and Evil. Their sons were Seth, CAIN, and ABEL.

Adam, Robert (1728–92) Scottish architect, best known of four brothers who were all architects. Adam was the greatest British architect of the late-18th century and his refined neoclassical style was highly influential. He was also a brilliant interior decorator and furniture designer. The Adelphi complex, London (begun 1768), was his most ambitious project. His interior designs include Kenwood House, London (1767).

Adams, Ansel (1902–84) US photographer. Concentrating on the scenic grandeur of the West, Adams produced magnificent prints which are widely exhibited. A co-founder of Group f/64, he was instrumental in forming museum and university photographic departments and was a celebrated teacher. He wrote the *Basic Photo-Books* series of manuals (1968).

Adams, Gerry (1948–) Northern Irish politician, president of SINN FÉIN (1983–). He was interned (1972–78) by the British for his involvement in the IRISH REPUBLICAN ARMY (IRA), before becoming vice president (1978–83) of Sinn Féin. Adams served (1983–92, 1997–) as a member of parliament for Belfast West, but never took his seat at Westminster. Adams' negotiations with John HUME led to an IRA ceasefire in 1994. He headed the Sinn Féin delegation in the 1997 peace talks, and became the first Republican leader since 1921 to meet a British prime minister. Following the GOOD FRIDAY AGREEMENT, Adams continued to play a pivotal rule in the peace talks and negotiations on the decommissioning of arms.

Adams, Henry Brooks (1838–1918) US historian and writer. A direct descendant of John ADAMS and John Quincy ADAMS, his best-known work is *The Education of Henry Adams* (1907), an ironic analysis of a technological society.

Adams, John Couch (1819–92) British astronomer. Noting that Uranus' observed path was not in agreement with its calculated orbit, Adams believed that the discrepancies could be accounted for by the gravitational influence of an undiscovered planet. NEPTUNE, as it was subsequently called, was discovered near a position predicted by Urbain LEVERRIER.

Adams, John Quincy (1767–1848) Sixth US president (1825–29), son of the second president John ADAMS. He served in his father's administration, before acting (1803–08) as a FEDERALIST PARTY member in the US Senate. Adams was secretary of state (1817–24) for James MONROE. He was largely responsible for formulating the MONROE DOCTRINE and negotiating the ADAMS-ONÍS TREATY (1819). Adams became president without a majority, his appointment confirmed by the House of Representatives. His lack of a mandate and non-parti-

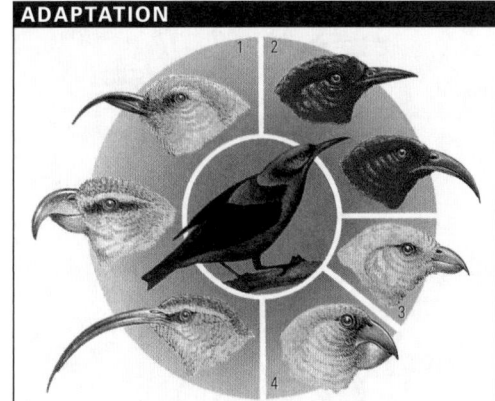

ADAPTATION

The various honeycreepers of Hawaii evolved from one species of bird now long extinct (centre). Over millions of years the honeycreepers evolved different methods of feeding. This ensured the island's various habitat niches could be exploited, resulting in less competition among the birds and allowing more to survive. The main adaptation was the dramatic change in the shape of the beaks. A few species evolved beaks best suited to feed on nectar (1), others feed purely on insects (2), while some feed on fruit (3) or seeds (4).

san approach led to his electoral defeat by Andrew JACKSON. He served in the House of Representatives (1830–48).

Adams, John (1735–1826) Second US president (1797–1801). Influenced by his radical cousin Samuel ADAMS, he helped draft the DECLARATION OF INDEPENDENCE (1776) and the Treaty of Paris (1783) ending the AMERICAN REVOLUTION. Adams was George WASHINGTON's vice president (1789–97). His presidency was marked by conflict between the FEDERALIST PARTY, led by Alexander HAMILTON, and Thomas JEFFERSON's DEMOCRATIC REPUBLICAN PARTY. Adams' moderate stance enabled a negotiated settlement of the XYZ Affair (1797–98), a diplomatic dispute with France. He reluctantly endorsed the ALIEN AND SEDITION ACTS (1798). Adams was succeeded by Thomas Jefferson.

Adams, John (1947–) US composer. Influenced by composers such as John CAGE and Morton FELDMAN, Adams' work is a fusion of electronics, jazz, and MINIMALISM. He won a Grammy Award (1989) for his opera *Nixon in China* (1987).

Adams, Samuel (1722–1803) American revolutionary leader. As a member (1765–74) of the Massachusetts legislature, he was the chief spokesman for revolution. Adams helped form several radical organizations, led the STAMP ACT protest in 1765, helped plan the BOSTON TEA PARTY of 1773, and was a signatory of the DECLARATION OF INDEPENDENCE (1776). He was a delegate to the CONTINENTAL CONGRESS until 1781.

Adams-Onís Treaty (February 22, 1819) Agreement between the USA and Spain. Negotiated by secretary of state John Quincy ADAMS and Spanish minister Luis de Onís, Spain gave up its land E of the Mississippi River and claims to the Oregon Territory; the US assumed debts of US$5 million and gave up claims to Texas.

adaptation In biology, a trait of an organism that increases its chances of success in its environment. Animals and plants adapt to changes in their environment through variations in structure, reproduction or organisation within communities. These variations are the result of the individual organism's DNA, so are more prevalent in the next generation if they increase its chances of survival and reproductive success. This is the process which drives EVOLUTION. Adaptation takes place over generations and should not be confused with acclimatisation to new conditions within a single organism's lifetime.

adaptive radiation In biology, the EVOLUTION of different forms of living organisms from a common ancestral stock, as different populations adapt to different environmental conditions or modes of life. Eventually, the populations may become so different that they constitute separate

A

► **adrenal gland** Located just above the kidneys (1), the two adrenal glands (2) are well supplied with blood entering from the aorta (3), and from the tributaries of the renal arteries (4). Each gland consists of an outer layer (the cortex) and a central medulla. The cortex produces steroid hormones, and hormones involved in maintaining water-balance, and small quantities of sex hormones. The medulla produces adrenaline and noradrenaline, both of which prepare the body for an emergency or stressful situation.

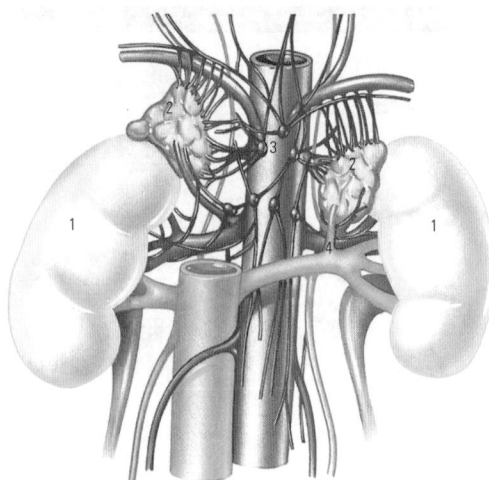

species. Examples are the many different kinds of finches found on the GALÁPAGOS ISLANDS, which diversified to specialize in different kinds of food, feeding methods, and HABITATS. *See also* ADAPTATION

Addams, Jane (1860–1935) US social reformer. In 1931, she became the first US woman to receive the Nobel Peace Prize, sharing the prize with Nicholas M. Butler. In 1889, she founded Hull House, Chicago, an early social settlement house. Addams pioneered labour, housing, health, and legal reforms, and campaigned for female suffrage and pacifism.

adder Any of several snakes in various parts of the world, some poisonous and others harmless. The European viper (*Vipera berus*) is called an adder in Britain. The puff adder (*Bitis arietans*) is a large African viper, and the death adder (*Acanthophis antarcticus*) is a dangerous Australian elapid.

addiction Inability to control the use of a particular substance, resulting in physiological or psychological dependence. It is most frequently associated with DRUG ADDICTION. In a medical context, addiction requires a physical dependence. When the dose of a drug is reduced or withdrawn, the addict experiences withdrawal syndromes. Psychological dependence on activities such as gambling or exercise are difficult to distinguish from a disorder or MANIA.

Addis Ababa (Amharic, "new flower") Capital and largest city in Ethiopia, located on a plateau at *c.*2440m (8000ft) in the highlands of Shewa province. Addis Ababa was made capital of Ethiopia in 1889. It is the headquarters of the AFRICAN UNION (AU). It is the main centre for the country's vital coffee trade. Industries: food, tanning, textiles, wood products. Pop. (2005) 2,899,000.

Addison, Joseph (1672–1719) English essayist, poet, and politician. Addison's poetic celebration of Marlborough's victory at the Battle of Blenheim, *The Campaign* (1704), led to a government appointment. He is remembered as a brilliant essayist and his stylish articles were a major reason for the success of the newly established *Tatler* and *Spectator* periodicals. He was secretary of state (1717–18) and an MP (1708–19).

addition reaction CHEMICAL REACTION in which two substances combine to form a third substance, with no other substance being produced. Addition reactions are most commonly used in organic CHEMISTRY, particularly by adding a simple molecule across a carbon-carbon double bond in an UNSATURATED COMPOUND. *See also* SUBSTITUTION

Adelaide State capital of SOUTH AUSTRALIA, located at the mouth of the River Torrens on the Gulf of St Vincent. Founded in 1836 by Colonel William Light and named after the wife of William IV, Adelaide is noted for its fine cathedrals, large parks, and cultural festivals. It is home to the largest fresh produce market in the Southern Hemisphere. Exports: wool, wheat. Industries: food and wine manufacture, motor vehicle assembly, pharmaceutical products, aerospace. Pop. (2005) 1,137,000.

Aden Commercial capital and largest city of Yemen, historic capital of the Aden Protectorate (1937–67) and the former People's Democratic Republic of Yemen (1967–90). A seaport city

on the Gulf of Aden, 160km (100 mi) E of the Red Sea, Aden was an important Roman trading port. With the opening of the SUEZ CANAL in 1869, its importance increased. It was made a crown colony in 1937 and the surrounding territory became the Aden Protectorate. When the (northern) Yemen Arab Republic and the (southern) People's Democratic Republic of Yemen combined to form the united Republic of Yemen in 1990, SANA' became the official capital. Industries: cigarette manufacture, oil and salt refining. Pop. (1995) 562,000.

Adenauer, Konrad (1876–1967) German statesman, first chancellor of the Federal Republic of Germany (1949–63). He was Lord Mayor of Cologne (1917–33) and was twice imprisoned by the Nazis. He helped to create the Christian Democratic Union (CDU), West Germany's dominant post-war party, and was its leader (1946–66). Adenauer led West Germany into NATO (1955) and campaigned for the establishment of the European Economic Community.

adenoids Masses of LYMPH tissue in the upper part of the PHARYNX (throat) behind the NOSE; part of a child's defences against disease, they often enlarge after infections in the area. Adenoids normally disappear by the age of ten.

adhesion In medicine, fibrous band of connective tissue developing at a site of inflammation or damage; it may bind together adjacent tissues, such as loops of intestine, occasionally causing obstruction. Most adhesions result from inflammation or surgery.

Adi Granth (Hindi, 'First Book') Principal sacred text of SIKHISM. The preachings of the first five Sikh Gurus were collected by Guru Arjan (1536–1606), the fifth Guru, and the text was expanded by the tenth Guru, GOBIND SINGH. Gobind Singh declared that he was the last Guru, and the book retitled **Granth Sahib** (Hindi, 'Revered Book').

adipose tissue (fatty tissue) Connective tissue made up of body cells which store large globules of fat.

Adirondack Mountains Circular mountain group located in NE New York, USA, reaching from Mohawk valley in the s to the St Lawrence River in the N. There are many gorges, waterfalls, and lakes. Much of the area makes up the Adirondack Forest Preserve. Noted for its resorts (including Lake Placid) its highest point is Mount Marcy, at 1629m (5344ft).

adjutant stork Large scavenging bird found in Africa, India and SE Asia, named for its military gait. It has white, black and grey plumage and throat pouches; it feeds on carrion. Length: up to 152cm (60in). Species *Leptoptilos crumeniferus*.

Adler, Alfred (1870–1937) Austrian psychiatrist. After working with Sigmund FREUD (1902–11), Adler established his own school of "individual psychology". He believed that striving for success and power was fundamental to human motivation. According to his theory, individuals develop problems and maladjustments when they cannot surmount feelings of inferiority acquired in childhood. This inferiority complex is often compensated for by assertive or aggressive behaviour.

Adler, Felix (1851–1933) US ethical philosopher, b. Germany. Like KANT he stressed the importance of the individual, and believed that ETHICS need not be founded on religious or philosophical beliefs nor assume the existence of a supreme being. In 1876 he founded the Society for Ethical Culture. Among its aims were the economic, social and intellectual development of disadvantaged people. Adler also supported social reforms, such as improved housing and the abolition of child labour. His books include *Creed and Deed* (1877), *The Moral Instruction of Children* (1892) and *An Ethical Philosophy of Life* (1918).

Admiral's Cup International yachting competition, established in 1957 and held biennially at Cowes, Isle of Wight. Teams of three yachts from each participating country compete in four events.

Adonis In Phoenician and Greek myth, a youth of remarkable beauty. He was loved by the goddesses PERSEPHONE and APHRODITE. Adonis was gored to death by a boar and, during his afterlife, Zeus decreed that Adonis should spend part of the year with Persephone, queen of the underworld, and part with Aphrodite.

adoption Act of a person legally taking as a child one who is not his/her own by birth or law. In Britain, anyone over 21

INTERNET

Adenauer, Konrad
► www1.kas.de/stiftung/ adenauer/lang-en.html

Adirondack Mountains
► www.adirondacks.com

years of age can adopt a child. Usually the child's natural parent/s must consent to the adoption. Once adopted, the child assumes the rights and responsibilities of a natural offspring.

adrenal gland One of a pair of small endocrine glands situated on top of the KIDNEYS. They produce many STEROIDS that regulate the blood's salt and water balance and are concerned with the METABOLISM of carbohydrates, proteins, and fats, and the secretion of the HORMONES ADRENALINE and NORADRENALINE. *See also* ENDOCRINE SYSTEM

adrenaline HORMONE secreted by the ADRENAL GLANDS, important in preparing the body's response to stress. It has widespread effects in the body, increasing the strength and rate of heartbeat and the rate and depth of BREATHING, diverting blood from the SKIN and DIGESTIVE SYSTEM to the heart and muscles, and stimulating the release of GLUCOSE from the LIVER to increase energy supply by promoting increased RESPIRATION. Synthetic adrenaline is used medicinally in the resuscitation of patients in shock or following cardiac arrest.

Adrian IV (*c.*1100–59) Pope (1154–59), b. Nicholas Breakspear. The only English pope, Adrian crowned Emperor FREDERICK I (BARBAROSSA) in 1155.

Adriatic Sea Shallow arm of the Mediterranean Sea, separated from the Ionian Sea by the Strait of Otranto. Lobsters and sardines are the chief catches. Length: *c.*800km (500mi). Max. depth: 1230m (4035ft).

adsorption Attraction of a gas or liquid to the surface of a solid or liquid. It involves attraction of molecules at the surface, unlike ABSORPTION which implies incorporation. The amounts adsorbed and the rate of adsorption depend on the structure exposed, the chemical identities and concentrations of the substances involved, and the temperature. Corrosion on the surface of a metal involves a chemical adsorption.

Advaita (Sanskrit, 'non-duality') Most influential school of VEDANTA Hinduism, based on the thought of Shankara (AD 788–820). Shankara systematized the teachings of the UPANISHADS, stressing the indivisibility of BRAHMAN and ATMAN.

Advent (Lat. coming) Liturgical season preceding Christmas. It begins on the Sunday nearest November 30 (St Andrew's Day). In many countries, observances during Advent include the lighting of candles. Advent refers both to Christ's birth and his coming in glory as judge at the end of history.

Adventists Christians belonging to any of a group of churches who believe in the imminent Second Coming of Christ. William Miller (1782–1849) formed the first organized Adventist movement in the USA in 1831. Christ's failure to return on dates forecast by Miller led to splits in the movement. The largest group to emerge was the SEVENTH-DAY ADVENTISTS.

Aegean civilization (*c.*3000–1100BC) Bronze Age cultures, chiefly MINOAN and MYCENAEAN, of Greece and the Aegean islands.

Aegean Sea Part of the Mediterranean Sea between Greece and Turkey, bounded by Crete to the s and connected to the Black Sea and the Sea of Marmara by the Dardanelles to the NE. The principal income is derived from tourism, fishing, and crops such as citrus fruits, olives, and grapes.

Aeneas In Greek mythology, the son of Anchises and APHRODITE. Active in the defence of TROY, he led the Trojans to Italy. The Romans acknowledged Aeneas and his Trojan company as their ancestors. The exploits of Aeneas form the basis of the *Aeneid*, a 12–volume book of poetry written (30–19BC) by the Roman poet VIRGIL.

aerial (antenna) Conductor component of radio and television systems for the reception and transmission of signals. An aerial's design usually depends on the wavelength of the signal.

aerobic Connected with, or dependent on, the presence of free oxygen or air. An aerobic organism, including all animals and plants, can only survive in the presence of oxygen and depends on it for breaking down GLUCOSE into CARBON DIOXIDE and water to release energy. This process is called aerobic respiration. It differs from ANAEROBIC respiration, in which an organism releases energy in the absence of oxygen.

aerodynamics Science of gases in motion and the forces acting on objects, such as aircraft, in motion through the air. An aircraft designer must consider four main factors and their interrelationships: **weight** of the aircraft and the load it will

carry; **lift** to overcome the pull of gravity; **drag**, or the forces that retard motion; and **thrust**, the driving force. Air resistance (drag) increases as the square of an object's speed and is minimized by streamlining. Engineers use the wind tunnel and computer systems to predict aerodynamic performance.

aerofoil Any shape or surface, such as a wing, tail or propeller blade on an aircraft, that has as its major function the deflection of airflow to produce a pressure differential or LIFT. A typical aerofoil has a leading and trailing edge, and an upper and lower camber.

aeronautics Study of flight and the control of AIRCRAFT, involving AERODYNAMICS, aircraft structures and methods of propulsion. Aeronautics started with the study of the BALLOON, which mainly concerned the raising of a load by means of BUOYANCY. It later included the heavier-than-air flight of gliders, planes, helicopters and rockets. A HELICOPTER utilizes LIFT provided by a rotor. Gliders and planes use wings to provide lift, which requires a minimum forward speed to be maintained. A plane is pulled forward by propeller, or is pushed by the reaction forces of expanding gases from one or more jet or ROCKET engines. The development of aircraft capable of supersonic speeds (in excess of that of sound, *c.*1200km/h or 750mph) has required radical changes in wing and fuselage designs to improve streamlining and cope with the shock waves produced. At speeds in excess of mach 5, known as hypersonic speeds, the forces involved and design requirements again change fundamentally.

aeroplane *See* AIRCRAFT

aerosol Suspension of liquid or solid particles in a gas. Fog – millions of tiny water droplets suspended in air – is a liquid-based example; airborne dust or smoke is a solid-based equivalent. Manufactured aerosols are used in products such as deodorants, cosmetics, paints and household sprays. CHLOROFLUOROCARBONS (CFCs) are being phased out as aerosol propellants because they damage the OZONE LAYER.

Aeschylus (525?-456 BC) Earliest of the great Greek dramatists. Aeschylus is said to have been responsible for the development of TRAGEDY as a dramatic form through his addition of a second actor and reduction of the role of the chorus. He was also the first to introduce scenery. His best-known work is the trilogy *Oresteia*, which comprises *Agamemnon*, *The Choephori*, and *The Eumenides*.

Aesir Primary group of Nordic gods who lived in Asgard. Woden (Odin), Thor (Donar) and Tyr (Tiw), and others, were the object of a cult that extended throughout the Germanic lands. Secondary to the Aesir were gods known as the Vanir.

INTERNET

Aeschylus
▶ classics.mit.edu/Browse/
browse-Aeschylus.html

AEROFOIL

As air passing over the top edge of an aerofoil (1) has to travel further than the air flowing beneath it (2), an area of low pressure forms above the wing that generates lift (3). In modern, high-lift aerofoils (A) the centre of pressure is further towards the rear of the wing (4). By moving the point of maximum lift backwards, the aerofoil has a more even distribution of lift, allowing a plane to fly more slowly without stalling.

Aesop Legendary Greek fabulist. He was the reputed creator of numerous short tales about animals, all illustrating human virtues and failings. In fact, the stories are almost certainly written by several people.

aesthetic movement Late 19th-century English cult of beauty. It grew out of aestheticism, a philosophy which spread across Europe in reaction to industrialization and UTILITARIANISM. The principal figures of the movement were Aubrey BEARDSLEY, Walter Pater, J.M. WHISTLER, and Oscar WILDE.

aesthetics (Gk. *aisthesis*, perception) Specialized branch of philosophy concerned with the arts. PLATO's classical formulation of art as a mirror of nature was developed by ARISTOTLE in his *Poetics*. As a distinct discipline, aesthetics dates from Alexander Baumgarten's *Reflections on Poetry* (1735). Common problems in aesthetics include a definition of beauty and the ascribing of artistic value. For Plato and Aristotle beauty is objective, it resides in the object. While Plato argued that art represented the form of particular objects, Aristotle believed that art imitated a universal essence through a particular form. David HUME argued that the value of art was dependent on subjective perception. In *Critique of Judgement* (1790), Immanuel KANT mediated between the two, arguing that artistic value may be subjective, but it has universal validity in the form of pleasure. Later philosophers, such as George SANTAYANA and Benedetto CROCE, focused on art as a socially symbolic act.

affidavit Formal written statement testifying on oath that a specified fact or account is true. Countersigned (usually with an official seal) by a witness of juridical authority, affidavits may be used as evidence in court and tribunal proceedings, or to guarantee the identity of a person claiming legal rights.

Afghanistan Landlocked republic in s central Asia. *See* country feature.

Africa Second-largest continent (after Asia), straddling the equator and lying largely within the tropics. **Land** Africa forms a plateau between the Atlantic and Indian Oceans. Its highest features include the ATLAS and Ahaggar mountains in the NW, the Ethiopian Highlands in the E, the Drakensberg Mountains in the s, and Mount KILIMANJARO. Lake Assal in the Afar Depression of Djibouti is the lowest point at −153m (−502ft). The huge sunken strip in the E is the African section of the Great RIFT VALLEY. The SAHARA

AFGHANISTAN

The Islamic Republic of Afghanistan is a landlocked country bordered by Turkmenistan, Uzbekistan, Tajikistan, China, Pakistan and Iran. The main regions are the N plains, highlands in the centre of the country, and the sw lowlands.

The central highlands, comprising most of the HINDU KUSH and its foothills, with peaks rising to more than 6,400m [21,000ft], cover nearly three-quarters of the land. Many Afghans live in the deep valleys of the highlands. The River Kabul flows east to the KHYBER PASS border with Pakistan.

Much of the sw is desert, while the N plains contain most of the country's limited agricultural land. Grasslands cover much of the N, while the vegetation in the dry s is sparse.

Trees are rare in both regions, but forests of such coniferous trees as pine and fir grow on the higher mountain slopes, with cedars lower down. Alder, ash, juniper, oak and walnut grow in the mountain valleys.

CLIMATE

The height of the land and the country's remote position have a great effect on the climate. In winter, northerly winds bring cold, snowy weather in the mountains, but summers are hot and dry. The rainfall decreases to the s with temperatures higher throughout the year.

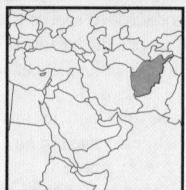

HISTORY

Afghanistan's location on the overland routes between Iran, the Indian subcontinent and Central Asia has invited numerous invasions. Its rugged terrain, however, helped to repulse many of these attacks. In ancient times, Afghanistan was invaded successively by Aryans, Persians, Greeks, Macedonians and armies from central Asia. Buddhism was introduced in the 2nd century BC, while Arab armies brought Islam in the late 7th century. Shah NADIR extended Persian rule to encompass most of Afghanistan. His successor, AHMAD DURRANI, founded the Durrani dynasty and established the first unified state in 1747.

In 1818 the dynasty died out, and a civil war was fought between 1819 and 1835. Factions struggled for power as Russia and Britain competed for control. Russia wanted an outlet to the Indian Ocean, while Britain sought to protect its Indian territories. The first Afghan War (1838–42) was inconclusive; the second Afghan War (1878–80) ended with the accession of Abd ar-Rahman as Emir. The Anglo-Russian Agreement (1907) recognized the dominance of British interests. In 1919, after the Third Afghan War, Afghanistan regained its independence.

POLITICS

In 1964 Afghanistan adopted a democratic constitution, but the legislature and the country's ruler King Zahir failed to agree on reforms. Muhammad Daoud Khan, the king's cousin, seized power in 1973 and abolished the monarchy. He ruled as president until 1978, when he was killed during a left-wing coup. The new regime's socialist policies conflicted with Islam and provoked a rebellion.

On 25 December 1987, Soviet troops invaded Afghanistan to support the left-wing regime. The Soviet occupation led to a protracted civil war. Various Muslim groups united behind the banner of the MUJAHEDDIN to wage a guerrilla campaign, financed by the United States and aided by Pakistan. Soviet forces withdrew in 1989. By 1992, the Mujaheddin had overthrown the government. The

AREA 652,090sq km [251,772sq mi]
POPULATION 31,890,000
CAPITAL (POPULATION) Kabul (3,288,000)
GOVERNMENT Transitional regime
ETHNIC GROUPS Pashtun (Pathan) 44%, Tajik 25%, Hazara 10%, Uzbek 8%, others 8%
LANGUAGES Pashtu, Dari/Persian (both official), Uzbek
RELIGIONS Islam (Sunni Muslim 84%, Shiite Muslim 15%), others
CURRENCY Afghani = 100 puls

fundamentalist Muslim TALIBAN became dominant and, by 2000, their regime controlled 90% of the country.

In October 2001, the Taliban regime refused to hand over OSAMA BIN LADEN, the man suspected of masterminding the attacks on New York City and Washington D.C. on 11 September 2001, to US authorities. An American-led coalition and US airstrikes backed local Northern Alliance troops to depose the Taliban and attack al-QAEDA. In November the Taliban regime collapsed and a coalition government led by HAMID KARZAI was set up.

A draft constitution was approved in January 2004. The first democratic elections for president were held in October 2004 and won by Hamid Karzai, but the government's power outside Kabul and surrounding regions is limited. Much of the country is ruled by local warlords, who have encouraged the drug trade, and Taliban insurgents remain in the s. In 2005 NATO took command of the US-led peacekeeping force, and in 2006 fighting intensified between the Taliban cand NATO and Afghan troops. In 2007 the insurgency spread into the rest of the country.

ECONOMY

Afghanistan is one of the world's poorest countries. About 60% of the people are farmers or semi-nomadic herders. The largest economic activity, c. 30% of GDP, is the illegal farming of opium poppies to manufacture over 90% of the world's HEROIN. Rich mineral and natural gas resources remain underexploited.

MAP SCALE
0   100   200   300   400 km
0   100   200 miles

stretches across the N, while the KALAHARI and NAMIB are smaller deserts in the s and sw. MADAGASCAR lies off the SE coast. **Structure and geology** Africa is composed largely of ancient metamorphic rocks overlain with Tertiary, Mesozoic and Palaeozoic sediments. The mountains of the NW are folded sedimentary material, roughly contemporaneous with the Alps. The Great Rift Valley, formed by the progressive movement of the Arabian Peninsula away from Africa, is mainly igneous in the N and older Precambrian in the s. **Lakes and rivers** The Rift Valley contains Lakes ALBERT, MALAWI, and TANGANYIKA. VICTORIA to the E is Africa's largest lake; Lake CHAD which shrinks to a salt pan in dry periods, lies in the s Sahara. Rivers include the NILE, NIGER, CONGO, and ZAMBEZI. **Climate and vegetation** Much of the continent is hot and (outside the desert areas) humid. The belt along the Equator receives more than 250cm (100in) of precipitation a year and is covered by rainforest. The forest gives way both in the N and s to areas of acacia and brush, and then through savanna to

desert. The N strip of the continent and the area around the Cape have a Mediterranean climate. **Peoples** Africa is home to more than 13% of the world's population, divided into more than 700 distinct tribes and groups. North of the Sahara Arabs and Berbers predominate, while to the s tribes include the FULANI, GALLA, HAUSA, HOTTENTOTS, IGBO, MASAI, MOSSI, SAN, YORUBA, and ZULU. Indians and Europeans also form significant minorities. Africa is relatively thinly populated and *c.*75% of the population is rural. **Economy** Agriculture is restricted in central Africa by the large expanse of rainforest, although cash crops such as cocoa, rubber, and peanuts are grown on plantations. Along the N coast, crops such as citrus fruits, olives, and cereals are grown. The Sahara is largely unproductive, supporting only a nomadic herding community. East and s Africa are the richest agricultural areas. Apart from South Africa, the continent is industrially underdeveloped. Mining is the most important industry. Zambia has the world's largest deposits of copper ore. Bauxite is extracted in w Africa,

INTERNET

Afghanistan
▶ www.afghangovernment.com

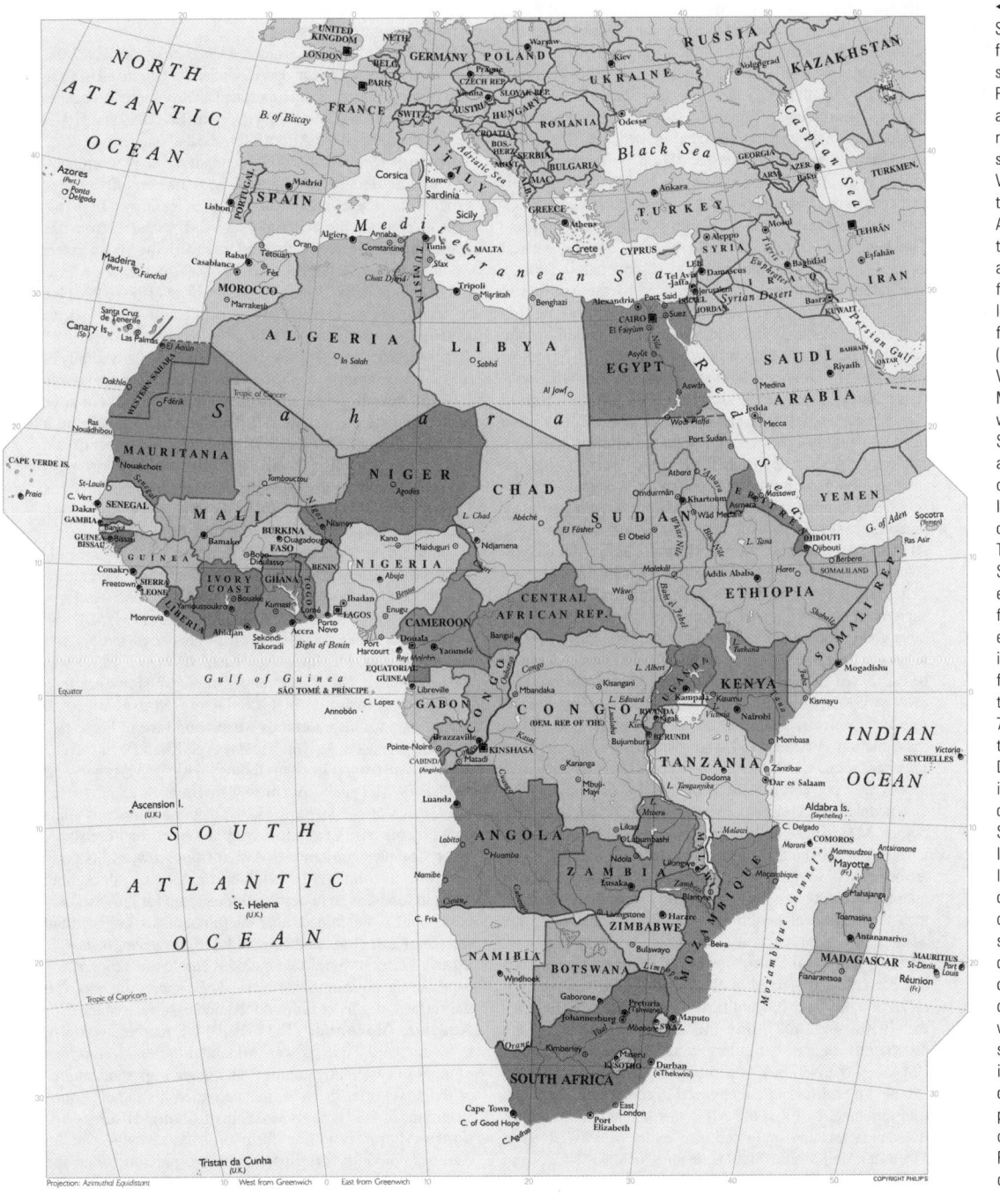

◀ **Africa** Africa and South America once formed a vast supercontinent, known as Pangaea. Plate tectonics are also thought to be responsible for the spectacular Great Rift Valley, which dominates the landscape of E Africa. Africa's highest mountain, the volcanic Kilimanjaro, is associated with the rift formation. The world's longest river, the Nile, flows more than 6,600km (4,100mi) from Lake Victoria to the Mediterranean Sea. The world's largest desert, the Sahara, forms an ethnic and cultural divide. North of the Sahara, Arabs and Islam predominate in coastal areas, Berbers and Tuareg in the interior. Sub-Saharan Africa is more ethnically diverse. Africa's first great civilization emerged in ancient Egypt in *c.*3400 BC. Carthago was founded by Phoenicians in the 9th century BC. In the 7th century, Islam spread throughout North Africa. Due to the oral nature of its culture, the pre-16th-century history of Sub-Saharan Africa is unclear. In 1498, Vasco da Gama landed in E Africa and centuries of European domination followed. The slave trade increased dramatically in the 17th century. The 19th century discovery of mineral wealth in Africa's interior spurred European imperialism and colonization as European powers scrambled to divide up the continent. Post-1945, the process of decolonization was rapid.

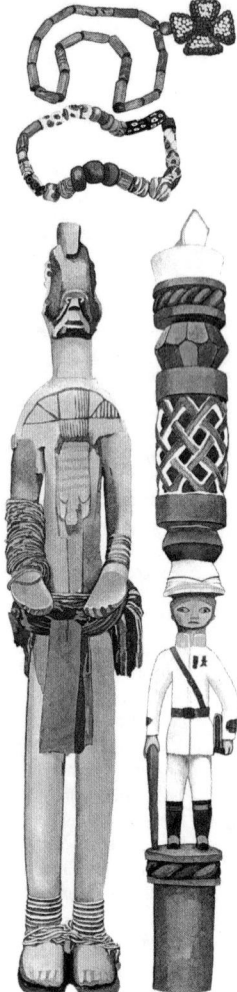

▲ **African art** Sculpture and the decorative arts are among the most varied and finest throughout Africa. The illustration shows beads, a large carved ancestral figure from Nigeria, and a colonial carving.

and oil is produced in Nigeria, Libya, and Algeria. South Africa is rich in minerals: gold, diamonds, and coal being the most important. **Recent History** Before the 1880s, Europeans were, except in South Africa, largely confined to the coastal regions. By the end of the 19th century, the whole continent, except for Liberia and Ethiopia, was under foreign domination either by European powers, or (in the N) by the Ottoman Empire. Starting in the 1950s the colonies rapidly secured their independence, but this process brought unrest and instability to much of Africa. A major cause of unrest was, and continues to be, the artificial boundaries created by COLONIALISM. Lasting democracy proved difficult to achieve in many countries and military rule is prevalent. Area: *c.*30 million sq km (11.7 million sq mi) *Highest mountain* Kilimanjaro (Tanzania) 5895m (19,340ft) *Longest river* Nile 6670km (4140mi) *Population* 812 million *Largest cities* LAGOS (8,029,200); CAIRO (7,764,700); KINSHASA (6,301,100); ALEXANDRIA (3,328,196); CASABLANCA (3,595,100); ALGIERS (2,562,428) *See also* articles on individual countries.

African art Naturalistic rock paintings and engravings from pre-4000 BC are found in the Sahara Desert. They are similar to European PALAEOLITHIC ART. Later African tribal art is inseparable from the ritual life of the community. Examples include: body painting and dance; music and musical instruments (especially the drum); ceremonial masks and small SCULPTURES used in ANCESTOR WORSHIP; weapons and everyday utensils. Wood is the most commonly used material. Artists were usually professionals and received great respect and status. Except EGYPTIAN ART, the most fertile artistic region is sub-Saharan Africa. The Nok terracotta heads from Nigeria are the earliest examples of African sculpture yet discovered (*c.*500BC). The naturalistic bronze heads produced by the YORUBA at Ife, SW Nigeria, reveal an early (12th-15th century) mastery of the CIRE PERDUE process. This skill passed to the ASHANTI of Ghana, who produced exaggerated figurative sculpture. The Dogon of Mali are renowned for their wooden sculpture, especially stylized wooden masks featuring recessed rectangles. The stonework of GREAT ZIMBABWE reveals a highly advanced grasp of architectural design. Interest in African art flourished in the West through its influence on early modern European art, especially PICASSO's development of CUBISM and MODIGLIANI's figurative paintings. *See also* ISLAMIC ART AND ARCHITECTURE

African mythology North Africans are predominantly Islamic, but the many peoples in sub-Saharan Africa have a rich collection of traditional beliefs. Almost all recognize a supreme being who created the universe. There are also many other gods, whose cults flourish in W Africa. Many Africans believe in the power of the spirit world. Spirits are thought to be capable of exerting a friendly or malignant influence (*see* ANIMISM). Many of these spirits are associated with agriculture and receive special offerings at harvest time. Belief in reincarnation is widespread, and ANCESTOR WORSHIP is an important social ritual. The dead are feared because they possess greater powers than the living. Many Africans believe that people are reborn in living animals or in inanimate objects. MAGIC plays an important part in everyday life. Medicine men make amulets, necklaces, and other charms which are believed to ward off evil. Other objects are used to protect houses or to bring rain. Belief in magic proves more enduring than the traditional mythologies, which declined with the advance of CHRISTIANITY and ISLAM.

African National Congress (ANC) South African political party. It was formed in 1912 with the aim of securing racial equality and full political rights for non-whites. By the 1950s, the ANC was the main opposition to the APARTHEID regime. A military wing, *Umkhonte We Sizwe* ('Spear of the Nation'), was set up in the aftermath of the SHARPEVILLE MASSACRE. It engaged in economic and industrial sabotage. In 1961, the ANC was banned and many of its leaders arrested or forced into exile. In 1964, Nelson MANDELA and Walter SISULU, leaders of the ANC, began their long sentences as political prisoners. In 1990, the ANC

was legalized, Mandela was released from Robben Island, and many of the legislative pillars of apartheid dismantled. In the first multiracial elections in 1994, the ANC gained more than 60% of the vote. Nelson Mandela became the first post-apartheid president of South Africa. In 1997 he was succeeded as leader of the ANC by Thabo MBEKI.

African Union (AU) Intergovernmental organization. Previously known as the Organization of African Unity (OAU). Founded in 1963 and renamed in 2001, it aims to safeguard the interests and independence of all African states, encourage the continent's development, and settle disputes among member states. Its headquarters are in Addis Ababa, Ethiopia. In 2003, the AU elected its first president, Alpha Oumar Konaré.

Afrikaans One of 11 official languages of the Republic of South Africa. Derived from the language spoken by the original Dutch settlers of the 17th century, it quickly evolved its own forms to become a distinct language. Afrikaans is regarded as a cultural focal point by South Africans of Dutch origin. It is the everyday means of communication for some three million speakers of European, African, and mixed descent.

Afrika Korps German armoured force in World War 2 that operated in the N African desert. Under the command of General Erwin ROMMEL, it had spectacular early successes against the British. MONTGOMERY's victory at EL ALAMEIN (1942) turned the tide and the Afrika Korps beat a long retreat.

Afrikaner (*Boer*, farmer) Descendant of the predominantly Dutch settlers in SOUTH AFRICA. Afrikaners first settled around the Cape region in the 17th century. To avoid British control, the Afrikaners spread N and E from the Cape in the GREAT TREK and founded the independent South African Republic (TRANSVAAL) and Orange Free State. Defeat in the SOUTH AFRICAN WAR (1899–1902) led to the republics merging in the Union of South Africa (1910). *See also* CAPE PROVINCE

Afro-Asiatic languages (Hamito-Semitic) Only family of languages common to both Asia and Africa. They are spoken by *c.*130 million people in N Africa, the Sahara, parts of E, W, and central Africa, and W Asia. On the African continent, it includes such languages as Berber and the now extinct Coptic and ancient Egyptian. It also includes the SEMITIC LANGUAGES, notably Arabic and Hebrew, that originated in Syria, Mesopotamia, Arabia, and Palestine. With a few exceptions, the family uses scripts that are read from right to left.

Agadir Atlantic seaport, SW Morocco. In 1960, Agadir suffered a disastrous earthquake. It was rebuilt as a tourist centre and is now a popular European tourist destination. Fishing is the other main economic activity. Pop. (1994) 524,564.

Aga Khan Since 1818, title of the leader of the ISMAILI sect of SHI'ITE Muslims. Aga Khan III (1877–1957) was the best known. He headed the All-India Muslim League in support of British rule in 1906. He moved to Europe and was known for his enormous wealth and love of horse racing. His grandson, Karim, became Aga Khan IV in 1957.

Agamemnon In Greek mythology, king of Mycenae, and brother of Menelaus. According to Homer's *Iliad*, he led the Greeks at the siege of TROY. Agamemnon was murdered by his wife CLYTEMNESTRA and her lover Aegisthus.

agar Complex substance extracted from seaweed; its powder forms a 'solid' gel in solution. It is used as a thickening agent in foods; as an adhesive; as a medium for growing bacteria, MOULD, YEAST and other microorganisms; as a medium for TISSUE CULTURE; and as a gel for ELECTROPHORESIS.

agaric Order of fungi that includes edible mushrooms, ink caps and the poisonous AMANITA. Their spores are borne on the surface of gills or pores on the under-surface of the cap.

Agassiz, Alexander (1835–1910) US marine zoologist, b. Switzerland. Agassiz was influential in the development of modern systematic zoology, and made important studies of the SEAFLOOR. In 1874, he succeeded his father, Louis, as curator of the Harvard Museum of Natural History.

agate Microcrystalline form of QUARTZ with parallel bands of colour. It is regarded as a semi-precious stone and is used for making jewellery. Hardness *c.*6.5; r.d. *c.*2.6.

agave Succulent, flowering plant found in tropical, subtropical and temperate regions. Agaves have narrow, lance-shaped leaves clustered at the base of the plant, and many have large flower clusters. The flower of the well-known century plant (*Agave americana*) of sw North America grows up to 7.6m (25ft) in one season. The century plant was thought to flower only once in 100 years, but in fact it flowers every 20 to 30 years. Other species are sisal (*A. sisalana*) and mescal (*Lophophora williamsii*), whose fermented sap forms the basis of the alcoholic drink tequila. Family Agavaceae.

Agee, James (1909–55) US writer. A novelist, poet, influential film critic and screenwriter for films such as *The African Queen* (1951, co-scripted with John HUSTON) and *The Night of the Hunter* (1955). He is perhaps best known for his study of rural poverty, *Let Us Now Praise Famous Men* (1941). His novel *A Death in the Family* (1957) won a Pulitzer Prize.

agglutination Clumping of BACTERIA or ERYTHROCYTES by ANTIBODIES that react with ANTIGENS on the cell surface.

Agincourt, Battle of (October 25, 1415) Engagement between England and France during the Hundred Years' War. The battle took place in modern Azincourt, Pas de Calais, NE France. Poor French tactics and the superior rate of fire of the English longbow over the French crossbow contributed to the English victory against a much larger French force. Some 6000 French soldiers died in the battle. Henry V of England's succcess, later celebrated by Shakespeare, gained him France and the French princess Catherine de Valois as his wife.

Agnew, Spiro Theodore (1918–96) US statesman, vice president (1969–73) to Richard M. NIXON. Agnew served as governor of his native Maryland (1967–69). He was a staunch advocate of US involvement in the VIETNAM WAR. Re-elected as vice president in 1972, he was forced to resign after the discovery of political bribery and corruption in Maryland. He did not contest further charges of tax evasion and was given a three-year probationary sentence and fined US$10,000.

Agni Fire god in Vedic mythology, revered as god of the home and appearing in lightning and the Sun as a nature deity.

Agnon, Shmuel Yosef (1888–1970) Hebrew writer, b. Poland as Samuel Josef Czaczkes. A key figure in Hebrew literature, he shared the 1966 Nobel Prize in literature with Nelly SACHS. Agnon wrote an epic trilogy of novels on the plight of East European Jewry: *The Bridal Canopy* (1919), *A Guest for the Night* (1938), and *The Day Before Yesterday* (1945).

agnosticism Philosophical viewpoint according to which it is impossible either to demonstrate or refute the existence of a supreme being or ultimate cause on the basis of available evidence. It was particularly associated with the rationalism of Thomas HUXLEY and is used as a reasoned basis for the rejection of both Christianity and ATHEISM.

Agra City in Uttar Pradesh, site of the TAJ MAHAL, N central India. It was founded (1566) by AKBAR I. Agra's importance declined after 1658 when the Mogul capital moved to DELHI. It was annexed to the British Empire in 1803, and later became the capital of North-West Province (1835–62). Agra's fine Mogul architecture make it a major tourist destination. It is an important rail junction and a commercial and administrative centre. Industries: glass, shoes, textiles. Pop. (2005) 1,526,000.

Agricultural Revolution Series of changes in farming practice in the 18th and early 19th centuries. The main changes comprised crop rotation, new machinery, increased capital investment, scientific breeding, land reclamation and ENCLOSURE of common lands. Originating in Britain, these advances led to greatly increased agricultural productivity in Europe.

agriculture Practice of cultivating crops and raising livestock. Early humans were hunters and gatherers, but development of husbandry and crop farming skills enabled them to produce food on a small scale. Modern archaeological dating techniques suggest that the production of CEREALS and the domestication of animals were widespread throughout E Mediterranean countries by c.7000 BC. The Egyptians and Mesopotamians (c.3000BC) were the earliest peoples to organize agriculture on a large scale, using irrigation techniques and manure as fertilizer. Farming formed the foundations of later societies in China, India, Europe, Mexico and Peru. By Roman times (200BC–AD 400), crop farming and the domestication of animals were commonplace in w Europe. In 17th- and 18th-century Europe, selective breeding improved milk and meat yields. The use of the four-field system of crop rotation meant that fields could be used continuously for production with no deterioration in yield or quality of the crops. The greatest changes in agriculture came with the INDUSTRIAL REVOLUTION. Many items of farm machinery were introduced in the 19th century. In Western Europe and North America, mechanization advanced rapidly and a large proportion of agricultural production is now carried out by FACTORY FARMING methods. In much of the underdeveloped world, agriculture (especially RICE production) is still labour intensive. More than 40% the world's workforce is engaged in farming.

Agrippa, Marcus Vipsanius (b.63BC) Roman general, adviser to Octavian (later AUGUSTUS). He helped Octavian to power by winning naval battles against Sextus Pompeius (36BC) and Mark ANTONY at the Battle of ACTIUM (31BC).

agronomy Science of soil management and improvement in the interests of AGRICULTURE. It includes the studies of particular plants and soils and their interrelationships. Agronomy involves disease-resistant plants, selective breeding, and the development of chemical fertilizers.

Ahern, Bertie (1951–) Irish statesman, taoiseach (1997–2008). Ahern was first elected to the Dáil Éireann in 1977. He served as vice president (1983–94) of FIANNA FÁIL, before becoming leader. He succeeded John BRUTON as taoiseach. Re-elected in 2002, Ahern resigned in 2008.

ahimsa Non-violence or non-injury to both people and animals. It is a central concept of JAINISM and BUDDHISM, and is also important in HINDUISM. This belief inspired the passive resistance of 'Mahatma' GANDHI.

Ahmadabad (Ahmedabad) City on the Sabarmati River, Gujarat, w India. Founded in 1411 by Ahmad Shah, the Muslim ruler of Gujurat, it is the cultural and commercial centre of Gujarat, with many magnificent mosques, temples and tombs. Ahmadabad is the headquarters of the Indian CONGRESS PARTY. Industries: cotton. Pop. (2005) 5,171,000.

Ahmad Durrani (1722–73) Emir of Afghanistan (1747–73) and founder of the Durrani dynasty. He united the Afghan tribes and is sometimes known as the founder of Afghanistan.

Ahriman (Angra Mainyu) Supreme evil spirit in ZOROASTRIANISM. Ahriman is the equivalent of Satan in Christian theology, and is permanently at war with AHURA MAZDAH. He heads an army of demons who embody envy and other evil qualities.

Ahura Mazdah (Ormazd, Ormuzd) In ZOROASTRIANISM, the supreme deity and god of light and wisdom. Ahura Mazdah created the universe and the twin spirits of good and evil. He later became identified with the good spirit, who was in constant conflict with AHRIMAN, the evil spirit and god of darkness.

aid, development Funds, goods, equipment, and expertise donated or loaned by the world's richer countries to poorer countries and used to promote development. The largest amount of development aid is paid out by the WORLD BANK, specifically through its International Development Association (IDA). All industrialized member states of the UNITED NATIONS (UN) allocate a specific proportion of their own GROSS NATIONAL PRODUCT (GNP) for development projects.

Aidan, Saint (d.651) Irish monk from Iona who brought Christianity to NE England. He became the first Bishop of Lindisfarne, where he established a monastery and sent out missionaries all over N England. His feast day is August 31.

AIDS *See* ACQUIRED IMMUNE DEFICIENCY SYNDROME

Aiken, Conrad Potter (1889–1973) US poet, novelist and critic. Aiken's *Selected Poems* (1929) won him a Pulitzer Prize. His interest in psychoanalysis and musical form are evident in *Collected Poems* (1953). His also wrote five novels and an autobiography, *Ushant* (1952).

aikido Martial art based on an ancient Japanese system of self-defence. Unlike some other martial art forms, in which force is met with counter-force, aikido employs the technique of avoiding action by making use of an opponent's forward impetus, causing the attacker to suffer a temporary loss of balance. Some forms of aikido, such as tomiki, are also sports.

AIR-CUSHION VEHICLE (ACV)

A

Air-cushion vehicles, or hovercraft, float on a bed of air allowing them to operate on both land and water. A turbine (1) powers a propeller (2) for forward motion. Two main fans (3) provide lift by pulling air into the skirt (4) beneath the vehicle. Two smaller fans (5) blow air through directable nozzles on top of the craft providing manouevrability. The skirt is divided into cells (6) that seal the air cushion and act as a giant shock absorber.

ALABAMA
Statehood
December 14, 1819
Nickname
The Heart of Dixie
State bird
Yellowhammer
State flower
Camellia
State tree
Southern pine
State motto
We dare defend our rights

aileron Hinged control surface on the outer trailing edge of each wing of an AIRCRAFT. By moving down or up in opposite directions, ailerons cause the aeroplane to roll, or bank.

Ailey, Alvin (1931–89) US modern dancer and choreographer. Ailey studied dance with Martha GRAHAM. In 1958 he formed the American Dance Theater and acted as its artistic director (1958–89). The company introduced many leading African-American and Asian dancers to worldwide audiences. His works, such as *Roots of the Blues* (1961), incorporate elements of jazz, African and MODERN DANCE.

Ainu Aboriginal people of Hokkaido (N Japan), Sakhalin and the Kuril Islands. Traditionally hunters, fishermen and trappers, they practise ANIMISM and are famed for their bear cult.

air Gases above the Earth's surface. *See* ATMOSPHERE

aircraft Any vehicle capable of travelling in the Earth's atmosphere. By far the most common aircraft is the airplane (aeroplane or plane). The airplane is a heavier-than-air flying machine that depends upon fixed wings for LIFT in the air, as it moves under the THRUST of its engines. This thrust may be provided by an airscrew (propeller) turned by a piston or turbine engine, or by the exhaust gases of a JET ENGINE or rocket motor. Gliders differ from planes only in their sole dependence upon air currents to keep them airborne. The main body of a plane is the fuselage, to which are attached the wings and tail assembly. Engines may be incorporated into (or slung below) the wings, but are sometimes mounted on the fuselage towards the tail or, as in some fighter aircraft, built into the fuselage near the wings. The landing gear (undercarriage), with its heavy wheels and stout shock absorbers, is usually completely retractable into the wings or fuselage. High-speed fighters have slim, often swept-back or adjustable wings that minimize air resistance (drag) at high speeds. Heavy air freighters need broader wings in order to achieve the necessary lift at take-off. A delta wing is a broad wing, or fuselage extension, that is aerodynamically suited for both large and small high-speed

planes. A plane is steered by flaps and AILERONS on the wings, and rudder and elevators on the tail assembly. This deflects the pressure of air on the aerofoil surfaces, causing the plane to rise or descend, to bank (tilt) or swing and turn in the air. RADAR systems aid NAVIGATION and an AUTOPILOT keeps the aircraft on a steady, fixed course. Pressurized cabins allow passenger planes to fly at heights exceeding 10,000m (33,000ft). *See also* AIRSHIP; AERODYNAMICS; AEROFOIL; BALLOON; GLIDING; HELICOPTER

aircraft carrier Military vessel with a wide open deck that serves as a runway for the launching and landing of aircraft. A modern nuclear-powered carrier may have a flight deck *c.*300m (1,000ft) long, a displacement of *c.*75,000 tonnes, a 4,000–man crew, and carry 90 aircraft of various types. Some carriers have large, angled decks to permit launching and landing simultaneously.

air-cushion vehicle (ACV) Vehicle that is lifted from the ground by air as it is forced out from under the craft. The best-known example is a HOVERCRAFT.

air force Military air power, first used in World War 1. In 1918 the British government formed the Royal AIR FORCE (RAF), the world's first separate air force. The United States AIR FORCE (USAF) was created in 1947.

Air Force, Royal (RAF) Youngest of the British armed services, formed in 1918 by the amalgamation of the Royal Naval Air Service and the Royal Flying Corps. It was controlled by the Air Ministry from 1919–64, when it was merged into the Ministry of Defence. Total personnel (1998): 56,064.

Air Force, US (USAF) One of the three major US military services established under the Department of Defense in the National Security Act of 1947. It began as the Aeronautical Division of the Army in 1907, became the Aviation Section of the Signal Corps in 1914, the Air Service in 1918, the Army Air Corps in 1926, and the Army Air Forces in 1941. It is the world's largest air force. Total personnel (1998): 382,200.

airship (dirigible) Powered lighter-than-air craft able to control its direction of motion. A gas that is less dense than air, nowadays helium, provides LIFT. A rigid airship, or Zeppelin, maintains its form with a framework of girders covered by fabric or aluminium alloy. Non-rigid airships, or blimps, have no internal structure. They rely on the pressure of the contained gas to maintain the shape.

Aix-en-Provence City in SE France. Founded (123BC) by the Romans, Aix-en-Provence is a cultural centre with a university (1409) and an 11th-13th-century cathedral. Industries: winemaking equipment, electrical apparatus. Agricultural products include olives and almonds. Pop. (1999) 134,222.

Aix-la-Chapelle, Treaty of (1748) Diplomatic agreement, principally between France and Britain, that ended the War of the AUSTRIAN SUCCESSION (1740–48). The treaty, which contributed to the rise of PRUSSIA, provided for the restitution of conquests made during the war and confirmed British control of the American slave trade. An earlier treaty signed at Aix-la-Chapelle ended the War of Devolution (1668).

Ajax In Greek mythology, name given to two heroes who fought for Greece against TROY. The 'Greater' Ajax is depicted in Homer's *Iliad* as a courageous warrior who led the troops of Salamis against Troy. The 'Lesser' Ajax was shipwrecked by ATHENA for raping CASSANDRA.

Akbar I (the Great) (1542–1605) Emperor of India (1556–1605). Generally regarded as the greatest ruler of the MOGUL EMPIRE, he assumed personal control in 1560 and set out to establish Mogul control of the whole of India, extending his authority as far s as Ahmadnagar. Akbar built a new capital at Fatehpur Sikri and endeavoured to unify his empire by conciliation with Hindus. He also tolerated Christian missionaries.

Akhmatova, Anna (1889–1966) Russian poet. Akhmatova's simple, intense lyrics and personal themes appear in *The Rosary* (1914) and *The Willow Tree* (1940). Her longest work, *Poem Without a Hero* (trans. 1971), is her masterpiece. Although officially ostracized for "bourgeois decadence", she remained popular in the Soviet Union. Her poems, published in full in 1990, confirmed her as one of Russia's greatest poets.

Akhnaten (d. *c.*1362BC) Ancient Egyptian king of the 18th dynasty (r. *c.*1379–1362BC). He succeeded his father,

AMENHOTEP III, as Amenhotep IV. In an attempt to overthrow the influence of the priests of the Temple of AMUN at LUXOR, he renounced the old gods and introduced an almost monotheistic worship of the sun god, ATEN. He adopted the name Akhnaten and established a new capital at Akhetaten (modern Tell el-Amarna). After his death TUTANKHAMEN reinstated Amun as national god, and the capital reverted to Luxor.

Akiba Ben Joseph (AD 50–135) Jewish rabbi and martyr in Palestine. He developed a new method of interpreting the Halakah, Hebrew oral laws, and supported a revolt (132) against the Roman Emperor HADRIAN. He was imprisoned by the Romans and tortured to death.

Akihito (1933–) Emperor of Japan (1989–). In 1959 Akihito married a commoner, Michiko Shoda, the first such marriage in the history of the imperial dynasty. Akihito succeeded his father, HIROHITO, and was formally enthroned in 1990.

Akron City on the River Cuyahoga, NE Ohio, USA. The Ohio and Erie Canal (1827) spurred Akron's growth. Once "the rubber capital of the world", the first tyre factory opened here in 1871, and it remains the headquarters of Goodyear. Other industries: plastics, chemicals. Pop. (2000) 217,074.

Alabama State in SE USA in the chief cotton-growing region; the state capital is MONTGOMERY. BIRMINGHAM is the largest city and a leading iron and steel centre. Settled by the French in 1702, the region was acquired by Britain in 1763. Most of it was ceded to the USA after the American Revolution in 1783, and Alabama was admitted as the 22nd state of the Union in 1819. It seceded in 1861 as one of the original six states of the Confederacy, and was readmitted to the Union in 1868. It was a centre of the civil rights movement in the 1960s. The N of the state lies in the Appalachian Highlands, which have coal, iron ore, and other mineral deposits, and the rest consists of the Gulf coastal plain, crossed by a wide strip of fertile agricultural land. The Mobile river and its tributaries form the chief river system. The principal crops are peanuts, soya beans, and maize, with cotton decreasing important. Industries: chemicals, textiles, electronics, metal and paper products. Area: 133,915sq km (51,705sq mi). Pop. (2000) 4,447,100.

ALBANIA

The Republic of Albania lies in the Balkan Peninsula. It faces the Adriatic Sea in the W and is bordered by Serbia, Montenegro, Macedonia and Greece. About 70% of the land is mountainous, with the highest point, Korab, reaching 2,764m [9,068ft] on the Macedonian border. Most Albanians live in the W on the coastal lowlands – the main farming region. Albania lies in an earthquake zone and severe earthquakes occur occasionally.

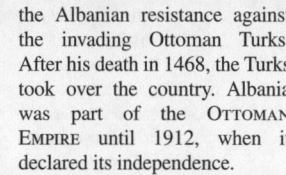

CLIMATE

The coastal areas of Albania have a typical Mediterranean climate, with fairly dry, sunny summers and cool, moist winters. The mountains have a severe climate, with heavy winter snow.

HISTORY

Albania was originally part of a region called ILLYRIA. In 167 BC, it became part of the ROMAN EMPIRE. When the Roman Empire broke up in AD 395, much of Albania became part of the BYZANTINE EMPIRE. The country was subsequently conquered by Goths, Bulgarians, Slavs and Normans, although S Albania remained part of the Byzantine Empire until 1204.

Much of Albania became part of the Serbian Empire in the 14th century. In the 15th century a leader named Skanderbeg, now regarded as a national hero, successfully led the Albanian resistance against the invading Ottoman Turks. After his death in 1468, the Turks took over the country. Albania was part of the OTTOMAN EMPIRE until 1912, when it declared its independence.

Italy invaded Albania in 1939, but German forces took over the country in 1943. At the end of World War 2, an Albanian People's Republic was formed under the Communist leaders who had led the partisans against the Germans. Pursuing a modernization programme on rigid Stalinist lines, the regime of Enver HOXHA at various times associated politically and economically with Yugoslavia (to 1948), the Soviet Union (1948–61) and China (1961–77), before following a fiercely independent policy. After Hoxha died in 1985, his successor, Ramiz Alia, continued the dictator's austere policies, but by the end of the decade, even Albania was affected by the sweeping changes in E Europe.

POLITICS

In 1990 the more progressive wing of the COMMUNIST PARTY, led by Ramiz Alia, won the struggle for power. The new government instituted a wide programme of reforms including the legalization of religion, the encouragement of foreign investment, the introduction of a free market for peasants' produce and the establishment of pluralist democracy. The Communists comfortably retained their majority in 1991 elections, but the government was brought down two months later by a general strike. An interim coalition "national salvation" committee took over, but collapsed within six months. Elections in 1992 finally brought to an end the last Communist regime in Europe when the non-Communist Democratic Party won power.

In 1997, amid a financial crisis caused by the inevitable collapse of fraudulent "pyramid" schemes, fresh elections took place. The socialist-led government that took power was re-elected in 2001. The stability of the region was threatened when Albanian-speaking Kosovars and Macedonians, many favouring the creation of a Greater Albania, fought with government forces in NW Macedonia.

ECONOMY

Albania is Europe's poorest country. Agriculture employs 62% of the population. Major crops include fruit, maize, olives, potatoes, sugar beet, vegetables and wheat. Livestock farming and the fishing industry are also important.

Private ownership has been encouraged since 1991, but change has been slow. Albania has some minerals, and chromite, copper and nickel are exported. There is also some oil, brown coal and hydroelectricity.

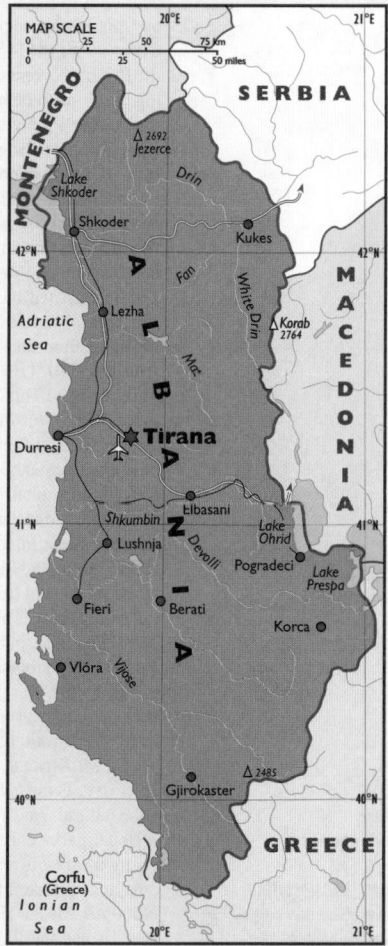

AREA 28,748sq km [11,100sq mi]
POPULATION 3,600,000
CAPITAL (POPULATION) Tirana (300,000)
GOVERNMENT Multiparty republic
ETHNIC GROUPS Albanian 95%, Greek 3%, Macedonian, Vlachs, Gypsy
LANGUAGES Albanian (official)
RELIGIONS A majority of Albania's people claim no religious belief; of the believers, 70% follow Islam and 30% follow Christianity (Orthodox 20%, Roman Catholic 10%)
CURRENCY Lek = 100 qindars

A

ALASKA
Statehood
January 3, 1959
Nickname
The Last Frontier
State bird
Willow ptarmigan
State flower
Forget-me-not
State tree
Sitka spruce
State motto
North to the future

INTERNET

Alberta
► www.gov.ab.ca

Alberti, Leon Battista
► www.mega.it/eng/egui/
pers/lbalber.htm

ALBINO

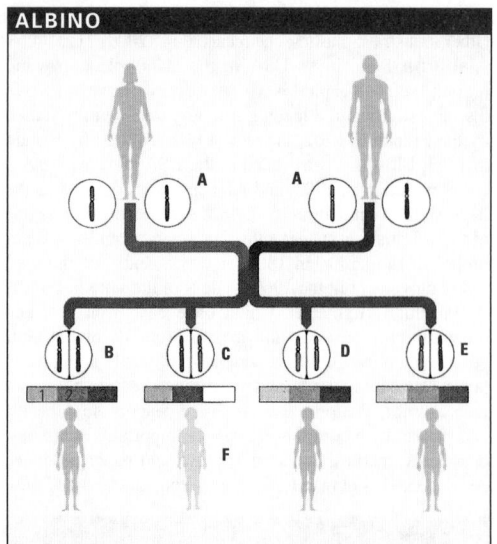

A male and female both carrying a recessive gene (green) for albinism (A) will have three normally pigmented children (B, D, and E) to every one albino (C). The corresponding normal gene (orange or purple) in both produces normal skin colour. This is due to an amino acid, phenyl-alanine (1), which has been converted to tyrosine (2) and then to the pigment melanin (3). However, a recessive gene in double quantity only allows the conversion of phenyl-alanine to tyrosine (F) resulting in an albino with a lack of pigment in the skin, hair and eyes.

Alabama claims (1872) Award of US$155 million compensation to the USA against the UK for damage inflicted by Confederate ships built in England during the American CIVIL WAR (1861–65). An international tribunal ruled that the British government had violated its neutrality by allowing the ships to be built on British territory.

alabaster Fine-grained, massive variety of GYPSUM (calcium sulphate), snow-white and translucent in its natural form. It can be dyed or made opaque by heating and is used for making statues and other ornaments.

Alamein, El *See* EL ALAMEIN

Alamo Mission in San Antonio, Texas, scene of a battle between Mexico and the Republic of Texas (1836). About 180 Texans, led by William Travis, Davy CROCKETT, and Jim BOWIE, were overwhelmed by Mexican forces numbering in the thousands following a siege that lasted 11 days.

Alaric I (370–410) King of the VISIGOTHS (395–410). His forces ravaged Thrace, Macedonia, and Greece, and occupied Epirus (395–96). In 401 Alaric invaded Italy. Defeated by Roman General Stilicho, he formed a pact with him. Emperor Honorius executed Stilicho for treason and Alaric besieged (408) and captured Rome (410). He planned an invasion of Sicily and Africa, but his fleet was destroyed in a storm.

Alaska State in NW North America, separated from the rest of continental USA by the province of British Columbia, Canada, and from Russia by the Bering Strait. The capital is JUNEAU. The largest city is ANCHORAGE on the S coast. The USA purchased Alaska for US$7.2 million from Russia (1867). Fishing drew settlers and, after the gold rush of the 1890s, the population doubled within a decade. It became the 49th state of the Union in 1959. About 25% lies inside the Arctic Circle. The main Alaska Range includes Mount McKINLEY, the highest peak in North America. The chief river is the YUKON. The Alaskan economy is based on fish, natural gas, timber, quartz and, primarily, oil. The national parks encourage tourism. Because of its strategic position and oil reserves, Alaska developed as a military area and is linked to the rest of the USA by the 2450km (1500mi) Alaska Highway. Although by far the largest US state, it has the third smallest population (after Wyoming and Vermont). Of the total state population (2000), 98,043

are Native Americans (mainly Inuit-Aleut). Area: 1,530,700sq km (591,004sq mi). Pop. (2000) 626,932.

Albania *see* country feature, p. 81.

Albany State capital of New York, on the HUDSON River. Settled by the Dutch in 1614 and British from 1664, it replaced New York as state capital in 1797. It has many fine old buildings. Albany developed in the 1820s with the building of the Erie Canal, linking it to the Great Lakes, and it remains an important river port. Industries: paper, brewing, machine tools, metal products, textiles. Pop. (2000) 95,658.

Albany Congress (1754) North American colonial conference to discuss Native American relations. Representatives from seven northern and middle colonies met Iroquois leaders and negotiated an alliance against the French. At this meeting Benjamin FRANKLIN proposed a plan for union of the colonies, which was rejected by the colonial governments.

albatross Large, migratory oceanic bird of the Southern Hemisphere famed for its effortless, gliding flight. There are 13 species. The wandering albatross has a long, hooked bill, short tail, webbed toes and the greatest wing span of any living bird – 3.5m (11.5ft) or more. Length: 0.7–1.4m (2.3–4.4ft). Family Diomedeidae.

albedo Fraction of light or other radiation that is reflected from a surface. An ideal reflector has an albedo of 1; those of real reflectors are less; that of the Earth, viewed from satellites, is 0.35.

Albee, Edward Franklin (1928–) US playwright. Albee's debut play *The Zoo Story* (1959) is a classic text of the Theatre of the ABSURD. His best-known play *Who's Afraid of Virginia Woolf?* (1962) is an intense portrait of a destructive marriage. Other works include *The Ballad of the Sad Cafe* (1963). *A Delicate Balance* (1966) and *Seascape* (1975) won Pulitzer Prizes.

Albert, Lake Lake on the border between Democratic Republic of Congo and Uganda, in the Rift Valley of E central Africa. Albert is fed by the River Semliki and the Victoria Nile and drained by the Albert Nile (*Bahr el-Jebel*). Ugandans call it Lake Nyanza and the Zaïrians named it Lake Mobuto Sese Seko. Length: 160km (100mi). Average width: 35km (22mi). Max. depth: 51m (168ft). Area: 5350sq km (2050sq mi).

Albert, Prince (1819–61) Consort of Queen VICTORIA. Prince of Saxe-Coburg-Gotha and first cousin of Victoria, he married her in 1840. Albert took an active role in diplomatic affairs and called for moderation in the TRENT AFFAIR (1861).

Alberta Province of W Canada bounded on the W mainly by the Rocky Mountains and in the S by the USA; the capital is EDMONTON. Other major cities include CALGARY. Most of Alberta is prairie land. The principal rivers are the Athabasca, Peace, and North and South Saskatchewan. Lesser Slave Lake is the largest of the many lakes. The area was part of a huge territory granted (1670) by Charles II to the HUDSON'S BAY COMPANY, and in 1870 the government of Canada bought the region from the company. In 1882, Northwest Territories was divided into four districts and Alberta was created. It was admitted to the confederation as a province in 1905. The fertile plains support wheat farming and livestock. Major resources are coal, minerals, and wood from the forests in the N. Oil and natural gas fields in central Alberta have been a major stimulus to the post-1945 economy. Industries: petroleum products, metals, chemicals, food, wood products. Area: 661,188sq km (255,285sq mi). Pop. (2001) 2,974,807.

Alberti, Leon Battista (1404–72) Italian architect, humanist and writer. The first major art theorist of the RENAISSANCE, Alberti's treatise *On Painting* (1435) was highly influential. His buildings include the Rucellai Palace, Florence, Tempio Malatestiano, Rimini, and the Church of San Andrea, Mantua.

Albigenses (Cathars) Members of a heretical religious sect that existed in southern France from the 11th to the early 14th centuries and took its name from the French city of Albi. In 1200, Pope Innocent III ordered a crusade against them, which caused much death and damage in Languedoc and Provence.

albino Person or animal with a rare hereditary absence of pigment from the skin, hair, and eyes. The hair is white and the skin and eyes are pink because, in the absence of pigment, the blood vessels are visible. The eyes are abnormally sensitive to light and vision is often poor.

Albinoni, Tomaso (1671–1750) Italian violinist and composer. He worked mainly in Venice, where he was a friend of Vivaldi. He was one of the first composers of CONCERTOS for a solo instrument; he also wrote nearly 50 operas.

albumin (albumen) Type of water-soluble PROTEIN occurring in animal tissues and fluids. Principal forms are egg albumin (egg white), milk albumin and blood albumin. In a healthy human, it constitutes about 5% of the body's total weight. It is composed of a colourless, transparent fluid called plasma in which are suspended microscopic ERYTHROCYTES (red blood cells), LEUCOCYTES (white blood cells) and PLATELETS.

Albuquerque City in W central New Mexico, USA, on the Upper Río Grande, the state's largest city. Traditionally a centre for rail workshops and the livestock trade, it is now a centre for high-technology industries and is home to the Atomic Energy Commission. A popular health resort, its population increased by nearly 20% between 1980 and 1992. Pop. (2000) 448,607.

Alcatraz (Sp. *álcatraces*, pelican) Island in San Francisco Bay. Discovered by the Spanish in 1769, it served as a fort and then US federal prison (1933–63).

alchemy A system in European PHILOSOPHY in the MIDDLE AGES and RENAISSANCE. It contained elements such as GNOSTICISM and ASTROLOGY, now regarded as MYSTICISM, alongside early scientific ideas. By the medieval period alchemy was interwoven with many other aspects of thought. It later helped inspire the origins of science, and alchemists pioneered the techniques of CHEMISTRY. However, alchemy hid ideas in complex symbolism and became widely misunderstood. Its reputation declined as it was abused by hoaxers claiming to be able to create material, rather than spiritual, wealth.

Alcock, Sir John William (1892–1919) Pioneer British airman who, together with Arthur Whitten-Brown, was the first to fly non-stop across the Atlantic Ocean. Their transatlantic flight began in St John's, Newfoundland on June 14, 1919, and landed 16.5 hours later near Clifden, Ireland.

alcohol Organic compound having a hydroxyl (-OH) group bound to a carbon atom. ETHANOL (C_2H_5OH) is the alcohol found in alcoholic drinks. Some other members include ETHANOL, PROPANOL, and butanol. Alcohols are used to make dyes and perfumes and as SOLVENTS in lacquers and varnishes.

Alcott, Louisa May (1832–88) US writer, daughter of Amos Bronson Alcott. Her first book, *Flower Fables* (1854), helped ease the family's finances. *Hospital Sketches* (1863) is an account of her experiences as a nurse in the Civil War. *Little Women* (1868), one of the most successful children's books ever written, was the first of a semi-autobiographical series.

Aldrin, "Buzz" (Edwin) (1930–) US astronaut. Aldrin piloted the Gemini XII orbital-rendezvous space flight (November 1966) and the lunar module for the first Moon landing (July 20, 1969). He followed Neil ARMSTRONG to become the second man on the Moon.

Aleichem, Sholem (1859–1916) Yiddish novelist, dramatist, and short story writer, b. Sholem Yakov Rabinowitz. He portrayed the oppression of Russian Jews with humour and compassion. Aleichem's numerous works include *Tevye the Dairyman* (c.1949), which was later adapted as the musical *Fiddler on the Roof* (1964), and *The Old Country* (1954).

Alembert, Jean le Rond d' (1717–83) French mathematician and philosopher. D'Alembert was a leading figure in the ENLIGHTENMENT. DIDEROT's co-editor on the first edition of the *Encyclopedie* (1751), he contributed the "Preliminary Discourse". His systematic *Treatise on Dynamics* (1743) provided a solution, D'Alembert's principle, which enables Newton's third law of motion to be applied to moving objects.

Aleppo (Halab) City in NW Syria; Syria's second-largest city (after the capital DAMASCUS. Like Damascus, it has claims to be the oldest continually inhabited city in the world. A part of Syria since 1924, Aleppo has a 12th-century citadel, the Great Mosque (715), and a covered bazaar more than 800m (2625ft) long. Industries: cotton products, silk weaving, dried nuts and fruit. Pop. (2005) 2,505,000.

Aleut Branch of the ESKIMO people who occupy the ALEUTIAN ISLANDS and Alaska Peninsula. They are divided into two major language groups, the Unalaska and Atka. About 4000 Aleuts live in scattered villages throughout SW Alaska.

Aleutian Islands Volcanic island chain, separating the Bering Sea from the Pacific Ocean. They were purchased with Alaska by the USA in 1867. The islands have several US military bases and wildlife reserves. Industries: fishing and furs. Area: 17,666sq km (6821sq mi). Pop. (1996) 7951.

Alexander the Great (356–323 BC) King of Macedonia (336–323BC), considered the greatest conqueror of classical times. Son of PHILIP II of Macedonia and tutored by ARISTOTLE, Alexander rapidly consolidated Macedonian power in Greece. In 334 BC he began his destruction of the vast Achaemenid Persian Empire, conquering W Asia Minor and storming Tyre in 332 BC. He subdued Egypt and occupied Babylon, marching N in 330 BC to Media, and then conquering central Asia in 328 BC. In 327 BC Alexander invaded India but the threat of mutiny prevented him from advancing beyond the Punjab. He died in Babylon, planning new conquests in Arabia. Although his empire did not outlive him, for he left no heir, he was chiefly responsible for the spread of Greek civilization in the Mediterranean and W Asia.

Alexander I (1777–1825) Russian tsar (1801–25). After repulsing Napoleon's attempt to conquer Russia (1812), he led his troops across Europe and into Paris (1814). He helped form the Holy Alliance with other European powers. He was named constitutional monarch of Poland in 1815, and also annexed Finland, Georgia, and Bessarabia to Russia.

Alexander I (1888–1934) King of the Serbs, Croats, and Slovenes (1921–29) and king of Yugoslavia (1929–34). In his efforts to forge a united country from the rival national groups and ethnically divided political parties, he created an autocratic police state. He was assassinated by a Croatian terrorist.

Alexander II (1818–81) Russian tsar (1855–81), known as the 'Tsar Liberator' for his emancipation of the serfs in 1861. He warred with Turkey (1877–78) and gained much influence in the Balkans. He sold Alaska (1867), but expanded the eastern part of the empire. Alexander brutally suppressed a revolt in Poland (1863). He was assassinated by revolutionaries.

Alexander III (c.1105–81) Pope (1159–81), b. Orlando Bandinelli. Emperor FREDERICK I opposed his election to the papacy and had an antipope, Victor IV, appointed. The ensuing schism ended 17 years later with the victory of the LOMBARD LEAGUE over Frederick at the Battle of Legnano.

Alexander III (1845–94) Russian tsar (1881–94). He introduced reactionary measures limiting local government; censorship of the press was enforced and arbitrary arrest and exile

INTERNET

Alcatraz
▶ www.nps.gov/alcatraz

Aldrin, "Buzz" (Edwin)
▶ www.buzzaldrin.com

Alexander the Great
▶ wso.williams.edu/
~junterek

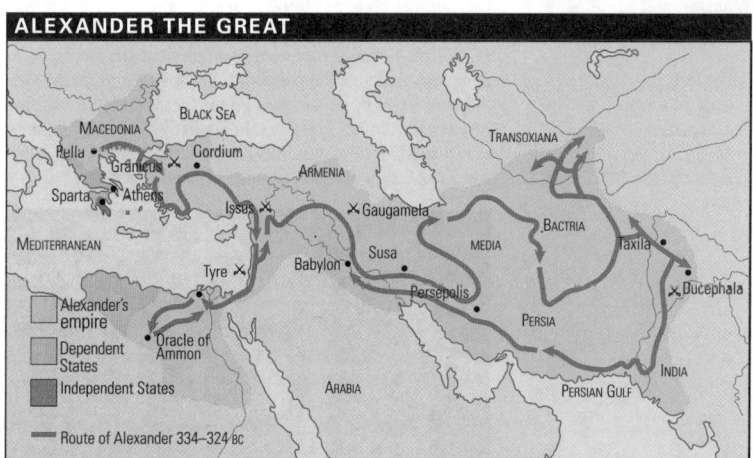

ALEXANDER THE GREAT

In the spring of 334 BC, Alexander's army of 32,000 infantry, 5,000 cavalry and 160 ships crossed the Hellespont and defeated the Persians at the Battle of Granicus. In 333 BC, he won another victory against the Persians at Issus. He then marched on and besieged Tyre, before advancing into Egypt where he founded the city of Alexandria. In 331 BC, he left Egypt and again defeated the Persians at Gaugamela, before capturing Babylon and the Persian cities of Susa and Persepolis. In pursuit of Darius he penetrated the heart of Asia, overcoming the Iranians. At the foot of the Himalayas, his army refused to cross the daunting barrier and Alexander turned south, following the Indus River to the Indian Ocean, before marching west through Gedrosia. Alexander returned to Babylon where he died at the age of 32.

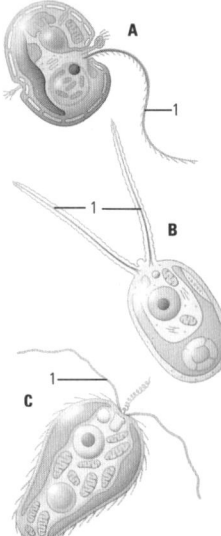

▲ **algae** Many unicellular (single-celled) algae are said to be motile, that is they move in response to changes in their environment, in particular to light. This is achieved with tail-like flagella (1) which propel them through the water. The illustration shows three types of algae. (A) *Gonyaulax tamarensis*, (B) *Chlamydomonas* and (C) *Prymnesium parvum*. Algae have been found in rocks more than 2,700 million years old. They are a vital source of oxygen.

▶ **Alhambra** Built in the 13th–14th centuries, the Alhambra complex in Granada, s Spain, is considered a masterpiece of Moorish architecture. The Court of the Lions (shown) is surrounded by delicate columns and features a marble fountain supported by a circle of stone-carved lions, and is believed to represent the Muslim idea of paradise.

became common. Ethnic minorities were persecuted. Toward the end of his reign, he formed an alliance with France.

Alexander Nevski, Saint (1220–63) Russian ruler, Grand Duke of Novgorod and of Vladimir. He pragmatically submitted to Mongol rule following their invasion of Russia, and was appointed Grand Duke of Kiev by the Great Khan. He defeated the Swedes on the River Neva in 1240 (hence the name 'Nevski') and the Teutonic Knights on frozen Lake Peipus in 1242. He was canonized by the Russian Orthodox Church in 1547.

Alexandria Chief port and second largest city of Egypt, situated on the w extremity of the Nile delta. Founded by ALEXANDER THE GREAT in 332 BC it became a great centre of Greek (and Jewish) culture. An offshore island housed the 3rd-century BC Pharos lighthouse, one of the SEVEN WONDERS OF THE WORLD, and the city contained a great library (founded by Ptolemy I, and said to contain 700,000 volumes). Today, it is a deep-water port handling more than 75% of Egypt's trade. Alexandria is the Middle East headquarters for the WORLD HEALTH ORGANIZATION (WHO). Industries: oil refining, cotton textiles, plastics, paper. Pop. (2005) 3,760,000.

Alexandrian school Group of Greek poets including Aratus, Apollonius Rhodius, and THEOCRITUS who worked in Alexandria between the 3rd and 1st centuries BC.

Alexius I (1048–1118) Byzantine Emperor (1081–1118), founder of the Comnenian dynasty. He held off the Normans, who threatened Constantinople and turned the Western armies of the First Crusade to his own advantage by using them to reconquer parts of Anatolia.

alfalfa (lucerne) Leguminous, perennial plant with spiral pods and purple, clover-like flowers. Like other legumes, it has the ability to enrich the soil with nitrogen and is often grown by farmers and then ploughed under. It is a valuable fodder plant. Height: 0.5–1.2m (1.5–4ft). Species *Medicago sativa*. Family Leguminosae. *See also* NITROGEN FIXATION

Alfonso V (the Magnanimous) (1394–1458) King of Aragón and Sicily (1416–58) and of Naples (1443–58). During his reign the Catalan-Aragónese empire reached its greatest extent. In 1442 Alfonso captured Naples and in 1443 he transferred his court there.

Alfonso VIII (the Noble) (1155–1214) King of Castile (1158–1214), son of Sancho III. He took personal control of his kingdom in 1166. In 1212 Alfonso forged a coalition with the Christian kings and won an important victory against the ALMOHADS at Las Navas de Tolosa. He married Eleanor, daughter of HENRY I of England.

Alfonso X (the Wise) (1221–84) King of Castile and León (1252–84), son and successor of Ferdinand III. He failed to complete his father's reconquest of s Spain from the Moors. Alfonso was a noted scholar and his *Sieste Partidas* codified Spanish law. In 1275 civil war in Spain thwarted his ambition to become Holy Roman Emperor. In 1282 the rebellion of his son, later Sancho IV, left Alfonso isolated in Seville.

Alfonso XIII (1886–1941) King of Spain (1886–1931). He was born after the death of his father, Alfonso XII, and his mother Maria Christina (1858–1929) acted as regent until 1902. Civil unrest marked Alfonso's reign, and he survived several assassination attempts. He suppressed republicans and Catalan and Basque nationalists. In 1923 Alfonso supported the founding of a military dictatorship under General Miguel PRIMO DE RIVERA. In 1930 the collapse of the dictatorship left Alfonso discredited and he was forced into exile (1931).

Alfred the Great (849–99) King of WESSEX (871–99). A warrior and scholar, Alfred saved Wessex from the Danes and laid the foundations of a united English kingdom. After the Danish invasion of 878, he escaped to Athelney in Somerset, returning to defeat the Danes at Edington and recover the kingdom. In a pact with the Danish leader, Guthrum (who accepted Christian baptism), England was roughly divided in two; the DANELAW occupying the NE. Although he controlled only Wessex and part of Mercia, Alfred's leadership was widely recognized throughout England after his capture of London (886). To strengthen Wessex against future attack he built a fleet of ships, constructed forts, and reorganized the army.

algae Large group of essentially aquatic photosynthetic organisms found in salt and freshwater worldwide. Algae are a primary source of food for molluscs, fish, and other aquatic animals. Algae are directly important to humans as food and FERTILIZERS. They range in size from unicellular microscopic organisms, such as those that form green pond scum, to huge brown SEAWEEDS more than 45m (150ft) long. Algae belong to the kingdom PROTOCTISTA. *See also* GREEN ALGAE; PHOTOSYNTHESIS; RED ALGAE

Algarve Southernmost province of Portugal, and the country's most popular tourist area; the capital is Faro. Irrigated orchards produce almonds, oranges, figs and olives, and the main fish catches are tuna and sardines. Area: 4986sq km (1925sq mi). Pop. (2001) 424,208.

algebra (Arabic, *al-jabr* 'to find the unknown') Branch of MATHEMATICS dealing with the study of equations that are written using numbers and alphabetic symbols, which themselves represent quantities to be determined. An algebraic equation may be thought of as a constraint on the possible values of the alphabetic symbols. For example, $y + x = 8$ is an algebraic equation involving the variables x and y. Given any value of x the value of y may be determined, and vice-versa. *See also* BOOLE, GEORGE

Algeria Republic in NW Africa. *See* country feature

Algiers Capital and largest city of Algeria, N Africa's chief port on the Mediterranean. Founded by the Phoenicians, it has been ruled by Romans, Berber Arabs, Turks and Muslim Barbary pirates. In 1830 the French made Algiers the capital of the colony of Algeria. In World War 2 it was the headquarters of the Allies and seat of the French provisional government. During the 1950s and 1960s it was a focus for the violent struggle for independence. The old city is based round a 16th-century Turkish citadel. The 11th-century Sidi Abderrahman Mosque is a major destination for pilgrims. Industries: oil refining, phosphates, wine, metallurgy, tobacco. Pop. (2005) 3,260,000.

Algonquin (Algonkin) Group of Canadian Native American tribes that gave their name to the Algonquian languages of North America. The Algonquin people occupied the Ottawa River area in *c.*AD 1600. Driven from their home by the IROQUOIS in the 17th century, they were eventually absorbed into other related tribes in Canada.

algorithm Step-by-step set of instructions needed to obtain some result from given starting data. The term is also used in computer science for the method of a COMPUTER in following an established series of steps in the solution of a problem. An algorithm can be represented visually by a flow chart.

Alhambra Spanish citadel of the sultans of GRANADA; a world heritage site and major tourist attraction. Standing on a plateau overlooking the city of Granada, s Spain, it is one of the most beautiful and well-preserved examples of medieval ISLAMIC ART AND ARCHITECTURE. Most of the complex dates from the period of the Nasrid dynasty (1238–1358).

Ali (*c*.600–61) Fourth Muslim CALIPH (656–61), cousin and son-in-law of the Prophet MUHAMMAD. Ali was married to FATIMA. He is regarded by the SHI'ITES as the first Imam and rightful heir of Muhammad. Ali succeeded OTHMAN as caliph, despite opposition from Aishah and Muawiya, but was soon assassinated. His first son, Hasan, abdicated in favour of Muawiya, who founded the UMAYYAD dynasty. His second son, Husayn, led the insurrection against the Umayyads, but was defeated and killed at the Battle of Karbala (680). These conflicts over the Caliphate were the origin of the division between the SUNNI and Shi'ite branches of Islam.

Ali, Muhammad (1942–) US boxer, b. Cassius Marcellus Clay. He defeated Sonny Liston to gain the world heavyweight championship in 1964. He converted to Islam and joined the BLACK MUSLIMS. Ali successfully defended the title nine times. In 1967 he refused to fight in the Vietnam War and the World Boxing Association (WBA) took away his title. In 1971 the US Supreme Court upheld Ali's appeal against the ban, but he was defeated in the ring by Joe FRAZIER. He regained the title from George Foreman in the 1974 'rumble in the jungle' fight. In 1978 Ali was defeated by Leon Spinks, but won the rematch, becoming the first heavyweight to win the title three times.

ALGERIA

The People's Democratic Republic of Algeria is Africa's second largest country after Sudan. Most Algerians live in the N, on the fertile coastal plains and hill country. S of this region lie high plateaux and ranges of the ATLAS Mountains. Four-fifths of Algeria is in the SAHARA, the world's largest desert.

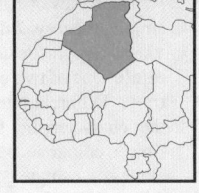

CLIMATE
The coast has a Mediterranean climate, with warm and dry summers and mild and moist winters. The N highlands have warmer summers and colder winters. The arid Sahara is hot by day and cool by night. Annual rainfall is less than 200mm [8in].

HISTORY
By 2000 BC, Berbers had established village communities. In the 9th century BC, coastal Algeria (Numidia) formed part of CARTHAGE's trading empire. By the end of the 2nd century BC, Rome had gained control of the coast and parts of the immediate interior. As Numidia, it became an integral part of the Roman Empire. Saint AUGUSTINE of Hippo (now Annaba) was a casualty of the 5th-century invasion of the VANDALS.

In the late 7th century, Arabs conquered Algeria and converted the people to Islam. Arabic became the main language; Intermarriage has made it difficult to distinguish Arabs from Berbers by ancestry, though Berber dialects are still spoken. In the early 10th century, the FATIMIDS rapidly built an empire from their base in NE Algeria. In the late 15th century, as part of the reconquest of S Spain, the Spanish gained control of coastal Algeria. The Spanish were ousted by the Ottomans and Algeria's coast became a haven for pirates and slave traders. In 1830, France invaded Algeria and rapidly began

AREA 2,381,741sq km [919,590sq mi]
POPULATION 33,333,000
CAPITAL (POPULATION) Algiers (Alger, 3,260,000)
GOVERNMENT Socialist republic
ETHNIC GROUPS Arab-Berber 99%
LANGUAGES Arabic and Berber (both official), French
RELIGIONS Sunni Muslim 99%
CURRENCY Algerian dinar = 100 centimes

the process of colonization. ABD AL-KADIR led Algerian resistance until 1847.

The European domination of the economy exacerbated discontent among the Muslim population. During World War 2, Algiers served as Allied headquarters in North Africa. At the end of the war, nationalist demands intensified.

POLITICS
Algeria experienced French colonial rule and colonization by settlers, finally achieving independence in 1962 following years of bitter warfare between nationalist guerrillas and French armed forces. After independence, the socialist FLN (National Liberation Party) formed a one-party government. Opposition parties were permitted in 1989.

In 1991, a Muslim party, the FIS (Islamic Salvation Front) won an election. The FLN cancelled the election results and declared a state of emergency. Terrorist activities mounted and, between 1991 and 1999, about 100,000 people were killed. A proposal to ban political parties based on religion was approved in a referendum in 1996. In 1999, Abdelaziz Boutflika, a candidate favoured by the army, was elected president. In 2005 the government agreed to some demands of the Berber community, including official recognition of the Berber language. An amnesty for Islamist guerrillas was approved in a referendum, and terrorism greatly reduced, but violence soon returned and remains ongoing.

ECONOMY
Algeria is a developing country whose main income is from its two main natural resources, oil and natural gas. Its natural gas reserves are among the world's largest. Oil and gas account for around two-thirds of the country's total revenues and more than 90% of the exports. Algeria's crude oil refining capacity is the biggest in Africa. Agriculture employs about 16% of the population.

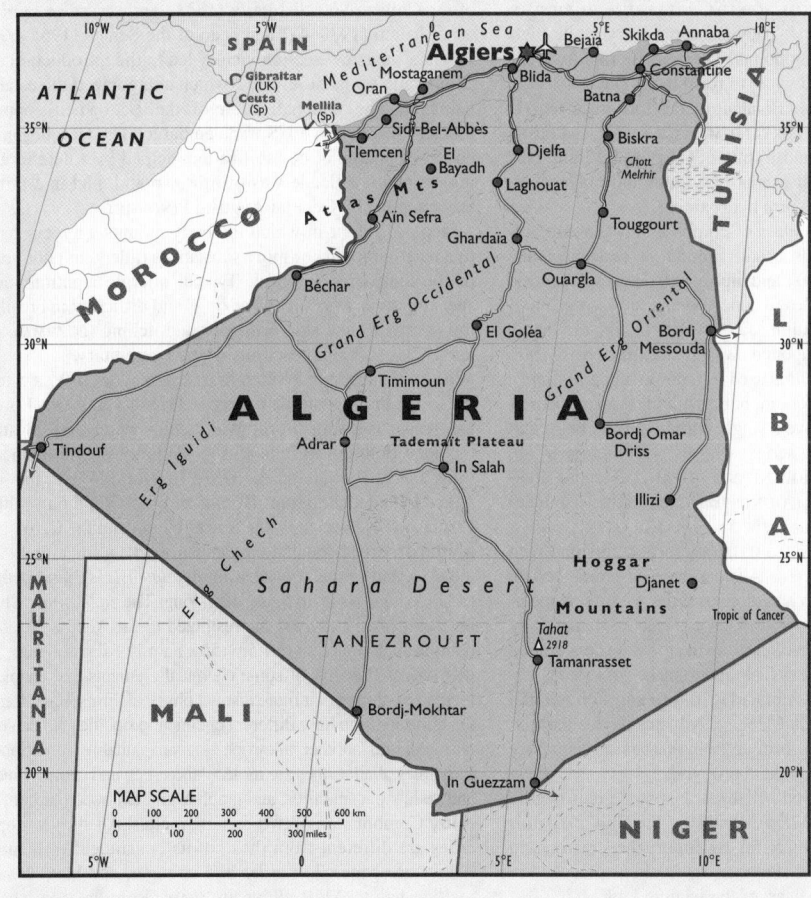

▲ **Ali** Perhaps the greatest heavyweight boxer of all time, Muhammad Ali's skilful footwork and stylish boxing were matched by his quick-fire wit. In 1984, Ali revealed he was suffering from Parkinson's disease, probably caused and certainly exacerbated by the punches he received in a long boxing career.

Alice Springs Town on the River Todd, s Northern Territory, central Australia. Founded in 1860, it is a crucial railhead, livestock shipping centre and supply source for a vast area that includes AYERS ROCK. It is the headquarters of the Flying Doctor Service and the School of the Air (radio-linked classes for children living in the 'outback'). It is the state's second largest town (after Darwin). Pop. (1996) 22,488.

Alien and Sedition Acts (1798) Four US acts designed to curb criticism of the government at a time when war with France seemed imminent. Many of the severest critics were refugees from Europe who were regarded as disloyal. The acts imposed stringent rules on residency before naturalization, and gave the president unprecedented powers to deport undesirable foreigners or imprison them in time of war.

alienation Term used in PSYCHOLOGY to mean a feeling of estrangement and separation from other people. In existential psychology this meaning is extended to include the perception that one is alienated or estranged from one's 'real self' because of being forced to conform to society's expectations. The sociological definition of alienation derives from the work of Hegel and Marx. In *The Economic and Philosophical Manuscripts of 1844* (1930), Marx outlined four types of alienation caused by industrial capitalism: the commodification of labour, dissociation from the products of one's labour, social detachment, and estrangement from one's own human essence.

alimentary canal Digestive tract of an animal that begins with the MOUTH, continues through the OESOPHAGUS to the STOMACH and INTESTINES, and ends at the anus. It is about 9m (30ft) long in humans. *See also* DIGESTIVE SYSTEM

aliphatic compound Any organic chemical compound whose carbon atoms are linked in straight chains, not closed rings. They include the ALKANES, ALKENES, and ALKYNES.

alkali Soluble BASE that reacts with an ACID to form a SALT and water. A solution of an alkali has a pH greater than 7. Alkali solutions are used as cleaning materials. Strong alkalis include the hydroxides of the ALKALI METALS and ammonium hydroxide. The carbonates of these metals are weak alkalis.

alkali metals Univalent metals forming Group I of the PERIODIC TABLE: LITHIUM, SODIUM, POTASSIUM, RUBIDIUM, CAESIUM, and FRANCIUM. They are soft silvery-white metals that have low melting points. They tarnish rapidly in air and react violently with water to form hydroxides.

alkaline-earth metals Bivalent metals forming Group II of the PERIODIC TABLE: BERYLLIUM, MAGNESIUM, CALCIUM, STRONTIUM, BARIUM, and RADIUM. They are all light, soft and highly reactive. All except beryllium and magnesium can react with water to form hydroxides.

alkaloid Member of a class of complex nitrogen-containing organic compounds usually found in certain plants. They are sometimes bitter and highly poisonous substances, used as DRUGS. Examples include codeine, morphine, nicotine, and quinine. Epibatidine, a new class of alkaloid that is an organochlorine compound, was first extracted in 1992 from the skin of a frog. It is used as a powerful painkiller.

alkane HYDROCARBON compound with the general formula C_nH_{2n+2}. Alkanes have a single carbon-carbon bond and form an homologous series whose first members are METHANE, ETHANE, PROPANE and BUTANE. Because alkanes are SATURATED COMPOUNDS they are relatively unreactive. Alkanes are used as fuels. *See also* PARAFFIN

alkene (olefin) Unsaturated HYDROCARBON compound with the general formula C_nH_{2n}. Alkenes have a carbon-carbon double bond and form an homologous series whose first members are ETHENE and PROPENE. They are reactive, particularly in ADDITION REACTIONS. Alkenes are made by the dehydration of alcohols, and are used as fuels and to make POLYMERS.

alkyne (acetylene) Unsaturated HYDROCARBON compound with the general formula C_nH_{2n-2}. Alkynes have a carbon-carbon triple bond and form an homologous series whose first members are ETHYNE and propyne.

Allah One and only God of ISLAM. His name is probably derived from Arabic *al-Illah*, meaning "the God". Allah is the omnipresent and merciful rewarder, the creator and judge of all. Unreserved surrender to Allah, as preached in the KORAN, is the very heart of the Islamic faith.

Allahabad City at the confluence of the Ganges and Yamuna rivers, Uttar Pradesh, N central India. Allahabad is a pilgrimage centre for Hindus because of the belief that the goddess SARASVATI joined the two rivers at this point. The Kumbh Mela fair, a religious celebration, takes place here every 12 years. It has one of the oldest universities in India (1887) and is also an agricultural trade centre. Pop. (2005) 1,153,000

All Blacks National RUGBY union team of New Zealand. The first New Zealand touring side visited the British Isles and France in 1905–06, establishing the All Blacks as the world's leading rugby team. The All Blacks won the inaugural World Cup (1987). The team is famous for the 'haka', a ceremonial Maori war dance performed before each match.

allegory Literary work in either prose or verse in which more than one level of meaning is expressed simultaneously. The fables of AESOP and LA FONTAINE are examples of simple allegory. *Pilgrim's Progress* (1684) by John BUNYAN is a sophisticated religious allegory.

allele One of two or more alternative forms of a particular GENE. Different alleles may give rise to different forms of the characteristic for which the gene codes. Different flower colour in peas is due to the presence of different alleles of a single gene. *See also* MENDEL, GREGOR

Allen, Woody (1935–) US film director, actor and screenwriter, b. Allen Stewart Konigsberg. Allen made his debut as actor and screenwriter in *What's New Pussycat?* (1965). His directorial debut was *Take the Money and Run* (1969). During the 1970s, he established his trademark style of urbane, angst-ridden New York-based comedies. Allen won Academy Awards for Best Picture, Best Screenplay, and Best Director for *Annie Hall* (1977). He gained an Oscar nomination for his first serious drama, the BERGMAN-like *Interiors* (1978). His next film, *Manhattan* (1979), returned to a semi-autobiographical format. *Hannah and Her Sisters* (1986) won Allen an Oscar for Best Screenplay. Other films include *Zelig* (1983), *The Purple Rose of Cairo* (1985), and *Mighty Aphrodite* (1996).

Allende Gossens, Salvador (1908–73) Chilean statesman, president (1970–73). Allende was one of the founders of the Chilean Socialist Party (1933), and served as minister of health (1939–42) and head of the Senate (1965–69). Allende's narrow election victory led to the introduction of democratic socialist reforms, which antagonized the establishment. The nationalization of the US-owned copper industry resulted in a US trade embargo. The CIA began a covert campaign of destabilization, helped by a deteriorating economy. Allende was overthrown and died in a military coup led by General Augusto PINOCHET.

allergy Disorder in which the body mounts a hypersensitive reaction to one or more substances (allergens) not normally considered harmful. Typical allergic reactions are sneezing (HAY FEVER), "wheezing" and difficulty in breathing (ASTHMA) and skin eruptions and itching (ECZEMA). A tendency to allergic reactions is often hereditary.

Allies Term used in WORLD WAR I and WORLD WAR 2 for the forces that fought the CENTRAL POWERS and AXIS POWERS respectively. In World War 1, they numbered 23 and included Belgium, Britain and its Commonwealth, France, Italy, Japan, Russia and the USA. In World War 2, the 49 Allies included Belgium, Britain and the Commonwealth, France, the Netherlands, the Soviet Union and the USA.

alligator Broad-snouted crocodilian REPTILE found only in the USA and China. *Alligator mississippiensis* is found in the SE USA; it grows up to 5.8m (19ft) long. The endangered Chinese alligator, *A. sinensis*, is restricted to the Yangtze-Kiang river basin. Length: up to 1.5m (5ft). Family Alligatoridea.

allotropy Property of some chemical elements that enables them to exist in two or more distinct physical forms. Each form (an allotrope) can have different chemical properties but can be changed into another allotrope – given suitable conditions. Examples of allotropes are molecular oxygen and ozone, white and yellow phosphorous, and graphite and diamond (carbon).

alloy Combination of two or more metals. An alloy's properties are different from those of its constituent elements. Alloys are generally harder and stronger, and have lower melting points. Most alloys are prepared by mixing when molten. Some mixtures that combine a metal with a non-metal, such as STEEL, are also referred to as alloys.

All Saints' Day In the Christian liturgical calendar, the day on which all the saints are commemorated. The feast is observed on November 1 in the West, and on the first Sunday after Pentecost (Whitsun) in the East. The eve of the day is celebrated in some western countries as HALLOWE'EN.

All Souls' Day Day of remembrance and prayer for all the departed souls. Observed by Roman Catholics and High Church Anglicans on November 2 or November 3.

allspice (pimento) Aromatic tree native to the West Indies and Central America. The fruits are used as a spice, in perfume and in medicine. Height: up to 12m (40ft). Family Myrtaceae; species *Pimenta officinalis*

Allston, Washington (1779–1843) US Romantic painter. A pupil of Benjamin WEST at London's Royal Academy, Allston was the pioneer of romantic LANDSCAPE PAINTING in the US and a precursor of the HUDSON RIVER SCHOOL. His work in England includes a portrait of Coleridge (1814). In 1818 he returned to the USA. Allston's most famous work is the lyrical *Moonlit Landscape* (1819). He spent 20 years working on the disappointing, unfinished *Belshazzar's Feast*.

alluvial fan Fan-shaped area of ALLUVIUM (water-borne sediment) deposited by a river when the stream reaches a plain on lower ground, and the water velocity is abruptly reduced. Organic matter is also transported, making the soil highly fertile. Valuable minerals such as cassiterite (tin ore, SnO_2), diamonds, gold, and platinum are often found in alluvial fans.

alluvium General term that describes the sediments (sand, silt, and mud) deposited by flowing water along the banks, delta, or flood-plain of a river or stream. Fine textured sediments that contain organic matter form soil.

Almaty (formerly Alma-Ata) Largest city and, until 2000, capital of Kazakhstan, near the SE border with Kyrgyzstan. In 1991 it hosted the meeting of 11 former Soviet republics that led to the Alma-Ata Declaration, which created the COMMONWEALTH OF INDEPENDENT STATES (CIS). In 1995 the government decided to move the capital to Aqmola (now ASTANA). Industries: foodstuffs, tobacco, timber, printing, film-making, leather, machinery. Pop. (2005) 1,103,000.

Almodóvar, Pedro (1951–) Spanish film director and screenwriter. His debut film was *Dos Putas* (1974). A master of kitsch, black comedies, Almodóvar achieved international fame with *Women on the Verge of a Nervous Breakdown* (1988) and *Tie Me Up! Tie Me Down!* (1990). Other films include *Kika* (1993) and *All About My Mother* (1999).

Almohad BERBER Muslim dynasty (1145–1269) in North Africa and Spain, the followers of a reform movement within ISLAM. It was founded by Muhammad ibn Tumart, who set out from the Atlas Mountains to purify Islam and oust the ALMORAVIDS from Morocco and eventually Spain. In 1212 Alfonso VIII of Castile routed the Almohads, and in 1269 their capital, MARRAKECH, fell to the Marinids.

almond Small tree native to the E Mediterranean region and SW Asia; also the seed of its nut-like fruit. Family Rosaceae; species *Prunus dulcis*.

Almoravid BERBER Muslim dynasty (1054–1145) in Morocco and Spain. They rose to power under Abdullah ibn Yasin who converted Saharan tribes in a religious revival. Abu Bakr founded Marrakesh as their capital in 1070; his brother Yusuf ibn Tashufin defeated Alfonso VI of Castile in 1086. Almoravid rule was ended by the rise of the ALMOHADS.

aloe Genus of plants native to S Africa, with spiny-edged, fleshy leaves. Aloe grows in dense rosettes and has drooping red, orange or yellow flower clusters. Family Liliaceae.

alpaca *See* LLAMA

alphabet System of letters representing the sounds of speech. The word alphabet is derived from the first two letters of the Greek alphabet, *alpha* and *beta*. The most important alphabets in use today are Roman, CYRILLIC, GREEK, ARABIC, HEBREW, and Devanagari. The Latin alphabet, which grew out of the Greek by way of the Etruscan, was perfected around AD 100, and is the foundation on which Western alphabets are based. In some alphabets, such as the Devanagari of India, each character represents a syllable.

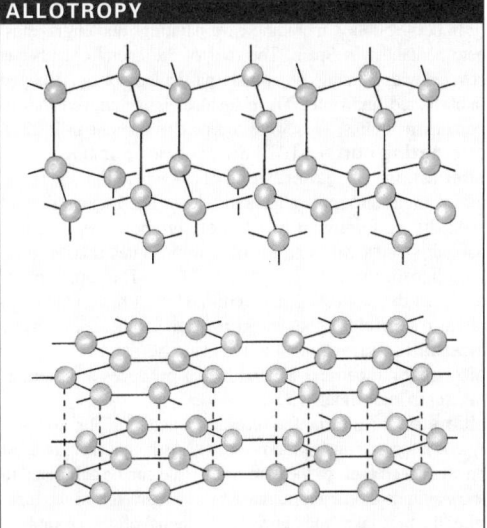

ALLOTROPY

Carbon can exist in three forms, diamond, graphite and buckminsterfullerene, known as allotropes of carbon. The top diagram shows the atomic structure of diamond, revealing its sharp, angular structure. The bottom diagram depicts graphite, which shows its regular, layered structure. The carbon atoms bond strongly in sheets but the forces between layers are weak, making graphite slippery and an effective lubricant. The structure of buckminsterfullarenes (not shown) consists of pentagons and hexagons: they are shaped like footballs.

Alpha Centauri Brightest star in the constellation Centaurus, and the third-brightest star in the sky. It is a visual BINARY.

alpha particle (alpha rays) Stable, positively charged particle emitted spontaneously from the nuclei of certain radioactive isotopes undergoing alpha decay. They consist of two PROTONS and two NEUTRONS and are identical to the nuclei of helium atoms. Their penetrating power is low compared with that of beta particles (electrons) but they cause intense ionization along their track. This ionization is used to detect them. *See also* RADIOACTIVITY; RUTHERFORD, ERNEST

Alps Mountain system in S central Europe, extending *c.*1,200km (750mi) in a broad arc from near the Gulf of Genoa on the Mediterranean Sea through France, Italy, Switzerland, Liechtenstein, Austria, Germany, and Slovenia. The system was formed by the collision of the European and African tectonic plates. Glaciers form the headwaters of many major European rivers, including the Rhine, Rhône, and Po. The highest peak is MONT BLANC, at 4807m (15,771ft).

al-Qaeda *See* QAEDA, AL-

Alsace Region in E France, comprising the departments of Bas-Rhin and Haut-Rhin. STRASBOURG is the leading city, Mulhouse and Colmar are the main industrial centres. Separated from Germany by the River RHINE, the Alsace-LORRAINE region has often caused friction between France and Germany. There are rich deposits of iron ore and potash. Most of the region is fertile and productive, with riesling wine the major agricultural product. Industries: steel, textiles, chemicals. Area: 8280sq km (3200sq mi). Pop. (1999) 1,734,145.

Altai Mountain system in central Asia, stretching from Kazakhstan into N China and W Mongolia, and from S Siberia to the Gobi Desert. A densely forested area, it is the source of the Irtys and Ob rivers. The average height is 2000–3000m (6500–10,000ft), and the highest peak is Mount Belukha, on the Kazakhstan-Russia border, at 4506m (14,783ft).

Altaic languages Family of languages spoken by *c.*80 million people in parts of Turkey, Iran, Mongolia, the former Soviet Union and China. It has three branches: Turkic, Mongolian, and Tungusic. They are named after the ALTAI Mountains.

Altair (Alpha Aquilae) Star whose luminosity is ten times that of the Sun. Characteristics: apparent mag. 0.77; spectral type A7; distance 16 light-years.

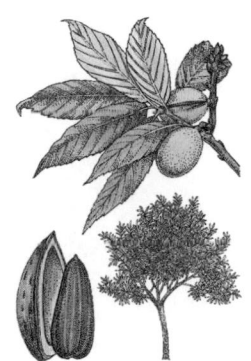

▲ **almond** Bitter and sweet almonds are related to stone fruits such as the peach, and are cultivated in temperate climates. Sweet almonds are edible, but the kernel of the bitter variety is inedible and used only for the extraction of its oil. The almond tree is native to SW Asia and almonds are one of the earliest foods cultivated by humans. California, USA, produces 80% of the world's crop.

Altamira World heritage site of notable PALAEOLITHIC ART (c.14,000–9500BC), including cave paintings and engravings, near Santander, N Spain. The roof of the lateral chamber is covered with paintings of animals, particularly bison, depicted in black, red, and violet. There are also eight engraved anthropomorphic figures. They were accepted as genuine in 1902.

alternating current (AC) *See* ELECTRIC CURRENT

alternation of generations Two-generation cycle by which plants and some algae reproduce. The asexual diploid SPOROPHYTE form with two sets of chromosomes produces haploid SPORES with one set of chromosomes that, in turn, grow into the sexual (GAMETOPHYTE) form. The gametophyte produces the egg cell that is fertilized by a male gamete to produce a diploid zygote that grows into another sporophyte.

alternative energy *See* RENEWABLE ENERGY

alternator Electrical generator that produces an alternating ELECTRIC CURRENT.

altimeter Instrument for measuring altitude. The simplest type is a form of aneroid BAROMETER. As height increases, air pressure decreases, so the barometer scale can be calibrated to show altitude. Some aircraft have a radar altimeter, which measures the time taken to bounce a radar signal off the ground.

Altiplano High plain in the South American Andes of Peru and Bolivia. It has an average elevation of c.3650m (12,000ft).

altitude In astronomy, angular distance of a celestial body above the observer's horizon. It is measured in degrees from 0 (on the horizon) to 90 (at the zenith) along the great circle passing through the body and the zenith. If the object is below the horizon, the altitude is negative.

Altman, Robert (1925–2006) US film director. Altman gained an Oscar nomination for *M*A*S*H* (1970). A second nomination followed for *Nashville* (1975). *The Player* (1992) enhanced his iconoclastic reputation. *Short Cuts* (1993), an adaptation of Raymond Carver's short stories, earned him a third nomination. Other films include *McCabe and Mrs Miller* (1971), *The Long Goodbye* (1973), *Kansas City* (1996), and *Gosford Park* (2001).

alto In singing, the highest male voice, also called COUNTERTENOR; or the lowest female voice, also called CONTRALTO. It is also used to describe that member of a family of instruments with a range that corresponds to the alto voice; for example, an alto FLUTE is a fourth lower than a standard one.

alumina (aluminium oxide, Al_2O_3) Mineral used as an abrasive, electrical insulator and furnace lining. Other forms of alumina include corundum, two impure varieties of which are the gemstones SAPPHIRE and RUBY.

aluminium (symbol Al) Metallic silvery white element of group III of the periodic table. It is the most common metal in the Earth's crust; the chief ore is BAUXITE from which the metal is extracted by electrolysis. Alloyed with other metals, it is used extensively in machined and moulded articles, particularly where lightness is important, such as aircraft. It is protected from oxidation (corrosion) by a natural layer of oxide. Properties: at.no. 13; r.a.m. 26.98; r.d. 2.69; m.p. 660.2°C (1220.38°F); b.p. 1800°C (3272°F); most common isotope Al^{27}. Aluminium was first isolated in 1825 in an impure form by Danish physicist Hans Christian OERSTED. *See also* ANODIZING

Alvarez, Luis Walter (1911–88) US physicist who received the 1968 Nobel Prize in physics for developing the liquid-hydrogen BUBBLE CHAMBER. Alvarez used it to identify many 'resonances' (very short-lived particles). He also helped construct the first proton linear ACCELERATOR. Alvarez worked on the MANHATTAN PROJECT to develop the atom bomb, and invented a RADAR guidance system for aircraft.

alveolus (pl. alveoli) One of a cluster of microscopic tiny air-sacs that open out from the alveolar ducts at the far end of each bronchiole in the LUNGS. The alveolus is the site for the exchange of gases between the air and the bloodstream, and is covered in a network of CAPILLARY blood vessels. *See also* GAS EXCHANGE; RESPIRATORY SYSTEM

Alzheimer's disease Degenerative condition characterized by memory loss and progressive mental impairment; it is the commonest cause of DEMENTIA. Sometimes seen in the middle years, Alzheimer's becomes increasingly common with advancing age. Many factors have been implicated, but the precise cause is unknown.

AM Abbreviation of AMPLITUDE MODULATION

Amado, Jorge (1912–2001) Brazilian novelist. Amado's early novels, such as *Sweat* (1934) and *The Violent Land* (1942) are powerful, bleak realist novels on poverty in Brazil. His later works, such as *Dona Flor and Her Two Husbands* (1966), are more lyrical, using folklore and humour to examine Brazilian society. Other works include *The War of the Saints* (1993).

Amal (Arabic 'hope', in full *Afwaj al-Muqawama al-Lubnaniyya* 'Masses of the Lebanese Resistance') Lebanese SHI'ITE political movement. Amal was established (1974) by Musa Sadr to press for greater Shiite political representation in Lebanon. In 1982, it split into extremist and moderate groups. Backed variously by Syria and the Palestinian Liberation Organization (PLO), its members have perpetrated a number of terrorist acts, such as the kidnappings in Lebanon during the 1980s. In 1991, the Lebanese National Assembly decreed the dissolution of all militias and the Amal moderated their stance.

amalgam Solid or liquid alloy of mercury with other metals. Dentists used to fill teeth with amalgams usually containing copper and zinc. Most metals dissolve in mercury, although iron and platinum are exceptions.

amanita Large, widely distributed genus of fungi. Amanitas usually have distinct stalks and the prominent remains of a veil in a fleshy ring under the cap and at the bulbous base. They include some of the most poisonous fungi known, such as the DEATH CAP and destroying angel.

amaryllis Genus consisting of a single species of bulbous plant, *Amaryllis belladonna*, the belladonna lily, which has several trumpet-shaped pink or white flowers. Amaryllis is also the common name for *Hippeastrum*, a bulbous houseplant.

Amaterasu Sun goddess of the SHINTO pantheon, considered to be the ancestor of the Japanese imperial clan.

Amati Family of Italian violinmakers in Cremona in the 16th and 17th centuries. They included Andrea (c.1520–78), the founder of the Cremona school of violinmaking; his two sons Antonio (c.1550–1638) and Girolamo (1551–1635); and Girolamo's son Nicolò (1596–1684) and grandson Girolamo (1649–1740). The Amati family are credited with establishing the design of the modern violin.

Amazon World's second-longest river (after the NILE), draining the vast RAINFOREST basin of N South America. The Amazon carries by far the greatest volume of water of any river in the world: the average rate of discharge is c.95,000m³ (3,355,000ft³) every second, nearly three times as much as its nearest rival, the CONGO. The flow is so great that its silt discolours the water up to 200km (125mi) into the Atlantic. At c.7 million sq km (2.7 million sq mi), the Amazon River basin comprises nearly 40% of the continent of South America. Its tributaries include the XINGU. Length: c.6430km (3990mi).

Amazon In Greek mythology, a race of female warriors who formed a totally matriarchal society. HERACLES, THESEUS, and other Greek heroes challenged the Amazons. As allies of the Trojans, they took part in the defence of TROY, where their queen Penthesilea was slain by ACHILLES.

amber Hard, yellow or brown, translucent fossil resin, mainly from pine trees. Amber is most often found in alluvial soils, in lignite beds or around seashores, especially the BALTIC SEA. The resin sometimes occurs with embedded fossil insects or plants. Amber can be polished to a high degree, and is used to make necklaces and other items of jewellery.

ambergris Musky, waxy solid formed in the intestine of a SPERM WHALE. It is used in perfumes as a fixative for the scent.

Ambrose, Saint (c.339–97) Roman cleric who, as Bishop of Milan from 374, resisted demands to surrender Milan's churches to the Arians and refused to compromise his orthodox position. He was the author of works on theology and ethics that greatly influenced the thought of the Western Church. His feast day is December 7. *See also* ARIANISM

Amenhotep III (c.1417–c.1379 BC) King of ancient Egypt. He succeeded his father, Thutmose IV. The 18th dynasty was at its height during his reign. Amenhotep maintained peace throughout the empire and undertook extensive building works. His wife, Queen Tiy, played a vital role in state affairs. He was succeeded by his son, who took the name AKHNATEN.

Amenhotep IV *See* AKHNATEN

America Western hemisphere, consisting of the continents of NORTH AMERICA and SOUTH AMERICA, joined by the isthmus of CENTRAL AMERICA. It extends from N of the Arctic Circle to 56°S, separating the Atlantic Ocean from the Pacific. NATIVE AMERICANS settled the entire continent by 8000 BC. Norsemen were probably the first Europeans to explore America in the 8th century, but Christopher COLUMBUS is popularly credited with the first European discovery in 1492. The name 'America' was first applied to the lands in 1507, and derives from Amerigo Vespucci, a Florentine navigator falsely believed to be the first European to set foot on the mainland.

American Academy and Institute of Arts and Letters US association formed by the merger (1977) of the National Institute of Arts and Letters and the American Academy of Arts and Letters. The academy's membership is limited to 250 individuals of literary, musical, or artistic achievement. Awards are given annually for distinguished and creative work in painting, sculpture, literature, and drama.

American art During the colonial era, American art reflected the taste of European settlers. In Spanish territories, the main demand was for religious art; while in Dutch and English areas, there was a greater emphasis on portraiture. In the 18th century, America produced its first artists of international standing, John Singleton COPLEY and Benjamin WEST. Both spent much of their career in England, where they became leading exponents of history painting. After independence, there was a movement away from European traditions. This was most evident in the field of LANDSCAPE PAINTING, where artists from the HUDSON RIVER SCHOOL and the Rocky Mountain School recorded the beauty of the wilderness. Thomas EAKINS and Winslow HOMER also celebrated American life, although in a more realistic vein. Realism was the cornerstone of the ASHCAN SCHOOL. In the 20th century, the key event was the ARMORY SHOW of 1913, which encouraged the spread of modern art. Alfred STIEGLITZ was a seminal figure in the development of modern art in the US. Georgia O'KEEFFE and Edward HOPPER were arguably its two greatest stylists. With the development of ABSTRACT EXPRESSIONISM in the 1940s, US artists became the standard-bearers of the avant-garde, a role they have never relinquished. *See also* LUMINISM; NATIVE NORTH AMERICAN ART

American Bar Association (ABA) US organization whose members are attorneys admitted to the bar of any state. Founded in 1878, the association attempts to ensure parity of law nationwide, improve the efficiency of the legal system, and maintain high standards. The association comprises over 25 committees, each responsible for specialized areas of law. By the mid-1990s the association boasted over 400,000 members.

American Colonization Society Group founded in 1817 by Robert Finley to return free African-Americans to Africa for settlement. More than 11,000 African-Americans were transported to Sierra Leone and, after 1821, MONROVIA. Leading members of the society included James MONROE, James MADISON, and John Marshall.

American Federation of Labor and Congress of Industrial Organizations (AFL-CIO) US labour organization, the largest union in North America. It is a federation of individual trade unions from the USA, Canada, Mexico, Panama, and some US dependencies. It was formed in 1955 by the merger of the American Federation of Labor (AFL) and Congress of Industrial Organizations (CIO). Although each union within the federation is fully autonomous, the ultimate governing body of the AFL-CIO is an executive council made up of president, vice presidents and secretary-treasurer. In recent years, the reduction of union membership (c.15% of US workers in 1995) has seen the AFL-CIO concentrate on recruiting public sector workers.

American Fur Company First US business monopoly, owned by John Jacob ASTOR. John Jay's Treaty of 1794 permitted US fur trading in the Pacific Northwest to compete with Montreal interests and the North West Company. Fort Astoria was set up in Oregon in 1805. During the WAR OF 1812 the USA was unable to defend Astoria, and Astor was forced to sell out to the North West Company. As the fur trade declined in the 1840s, Fort Astoria reverted to US control.

American Indians Old term for NATIVE AMERICANS

American Legion Association of US military veterans. Founded in Paris in 1919, its US headquarters are at Indianapolis, Indiana. Qualifications for membership are honourable service or honourable discharge. It sponsors many social causes, notably education and sports for young people, and care of sick and disabled veterans.

American literature English explorers and early colonists produced literary accounts of North America. The first English language work published in New England was the *Bay Psalm Book* (1640). Early colonial literature was often an expression of Puritan piety, designed as a moral framework for a religious colony. Many of the leading figures in the AMERICAN REVOLUTION, such as Thomas PAINE and Benjamin FRANKLIN, produced important literary works. Early 19th-century writers, such as Washington IRVING and James Fenimore COOPER were influenced by European romanticism. The preeminent US romantic poet was Henry Wadsworth LONGFELLOW. TRANSCENDENTALISM was the first truly distinctive national literary movement. Leading writers included the essayists Henry David THOREAU, Ralph Waldo EMERSON, Oliver Wendell HOLMES and Louisa May ALCOTT. Walt WHITMAN's free-verse epic *Leaves of Grass* (1855–92) is perhaps the most fully realized poetic expression of transcendentalism. The 1840s and 1850s produced many American fiction classics, such as Herman MELVILLE's *Moby Dick* (1851), and Nathaniel HAWTHORNE's *The Scarlet Letter* (1850). Harriet Beecher STOWE's anti-slavery story *Uncle Tom's Cabin* (1852) was the best-selling novel of the 19th century. Literature of the immediate post-Civil War period is characterized by parochialism. The two great exceptions to the trend (and precursors of a new realism) were Henry JAMES and Mark TWAIN. While James emigrated to Europe and embraced psychological realism in novels such as *Portrait of a Lady* (1881), Twain used distinctive national dialects in humorous classics such as *Huckleberry Finn* (1885). Realism fed into NATURALISM, producing writers who either focused on the development of cities (Theodore DRIESER and Edith WHARTON), or those who concentrated on a hostile wilderness, such as Jack LONDON. Stephen CRANE's *Red Badge of Courage* (1895) was ground-breaking in its naturalistic treatment of the American Civil War. Emily DICKINSON was finally published posthumously in 1890. In the early 20th century many US writers settled

◀ **American art** *The Artist's Studio* (c.1865) by James Abbot McNeil Whistler (1834–1903). Like many 19th-century American artists, Whistler was heavily influenced by European art. He spent much of his life in London. His assertion that art should be independent of moral and social concerns influenced the development of abstract art, but also led to a fierce debate with John Ruskin which ended in a bitter libel trial.

abroad. In Paris, Gertrude STEIN held court over the 'Lost Generation', a large group of emigrés that included Ernest HEMINGWAY and Henry MILLER. T.S. ELIOT and Ezra POUND led the search for experimental poetic forms. Eliot's bleak and fragmentary poem *The Wasteland* (1922) is often viewed as the archetype of high MODERNISM. Wallace STEVENS and William Carlos WILLIAMS developed the new poetry, while William FAULKNER is regarded as one of the leading modernist novelists. The HARLEM RENAISSANCE witnessed the emergence of African-American writers, such as Langston HUGHES. The style and decadence of the 'jazz age' in 1920s New York was captured by F. Scott FITZGERALD in *The Great Gatsby* (1925). The 1920s also witnessed the debut of the first great American dramatist, Eugene O'NEILL. Writers such as John STEINBECK, Carson MCCULLERS, and Eudora WELTY emerged in the 1930s. Post-war literature and drama can be characterized by a sense of despair and the meaningless absurdity of artistic expression when confronted by the violence of the 20th century. In the 1950s, major dramatists such as Arthur MILLER, Edward ALBEE, and Sam SHEPARD developed the American theatre. African-American writers, such as Richard WRIGHT, Ralph Ellison and James BALDWIN, dealt with racial inequality and violence in contemporary US society. Maya ANGELOU and Toni MORRISON focused on the 20th century history of African-American women. During the 1960s, novelists such as Saul BELLOW, Philip ROTH and Joseph HELLER examined the Jewish urban intellectual approach to American society, often adopting a deeply ironic tone. Humour was also a major outlet for writers such as John UPDIKE, Kurt VONNEGUT, and Thomas PYNCHON. Norman MAILER used a more muscular, controversialist approach. The BEAT MOVEMENT (including Jack KEROUAC and Allen GINSBERG) urged the rejection of the established order and embraced alternative values. A major trend in American poetry was the 'confessional' style of personal revelation by poets such as Robert LOWELL and Sylvia PLATH. POST-MODERNISM informed the work of writers such as Kathy Acker and Bret Easton Ellis.

American Medical Association (AMA) US federation of 54 state and territorial medical associations, founded in 1847. The AMA develops programmes to provide scientific information for the profession and health-education materials for the public. By the mid-1990s, there were *c.*300,000 members.

American Revolution (1775–83, American War of Independence) Successful revolt by the THIRTEEN COLONIES in North America against British rule. A number of issues provoked the conflict including restrictions on trade and manufacturing imposed by the NAVIGATION ACTS, restrictions on land settlement in the West, and attempts to raise revenue in America by such means as the STAMP ACT (1765) and the Tea Act (1773) that led to the BOSTON TEA PARTY. "No taxation without representation" became the colonial radicals' rallying cry. The intellectual battle for independence was led by Thomas PAINE, Thomas JEFFERSON, and Benjamin FRANKLIN. A CONTINENTAL CONGRESS was summoned in 1774, and in April 1775 the first shots were fired at LEXINGTON AND CONCORD, Massachusetts. The following month, the second Continental Congress met at Philadelphia and assumed the role of a revolutionary government. George WASHINGTON established an army. On July 4, 1776, the DECLARATION OF INDEPENDENCE made the break with Britain decisive. Initially the Americans suffered a series of military defeats, which saw Washington retreat from New York to Pennsylvania. Crossing the River Delaware, he surprised and captured the British at TRENTON (December 26, 1776). On January 3, 1777, he defeated the British at PRINCETON, further strengthening American morale. The British attempted a three-pronged attack, focusing on New York. The strategy failed with the first decisive colonial victory at SARATOGA (October 17, 1777), and the entry of France into the war against Britain. During the winter of 1777, Washington's forces reorganized in Pennsylvania. In 1778 the British forces concentrated on the South, taking SAVANNAH in December 1778. Following the defeat at

King's Mountain in 1780, the British, under General Charles CORNWALLIS, were forced to withdraw N to YORKTOWN, Virginia. In 1781, surrounded by American forces and the French navy, Cornwallis was forced to surrender. Fighting ceased and the Treaty of Paris (1783) recognized the independence of the USA.

American Samoa US-administered group of five volcanic islands and two coral atolls of the SAMOA island chain in the S Pacific, *c.*1050km (650mi) NE of Fiji. The principal islands are Tutuila, the Manu'a group (Ta'u, Ofu and Olosega) and Aun'u. In 1899, a treaty between the USA, Germany, and the UK granted the USA rights to the islands E of 171° longitude, and Germany the rights to the W sector. American Samoa remained under the jurisdiction of the US Navy until 1951. Administration was transferred to the Department of the Interior. In 1978 the first gubernatorial elections took place. The population is largely Polynesian, who are considered US nationals. The US government and the tuna fish canning industry are the main sources of employment. Pop. (2000) 40,000.

America's Cup International competition for racing yachts. A trophy was established in 1857 by the New York Yacht Club. Several countries compete in a series of eliminators, before challenging the previous winners. The USA has won the best-of-seven series on almost every occasion, and traditionally hosts the contest off Newport, Rhode Island.

americium (symbol Am) Radioactive metallic element of the ACTINIDE SERIES, first made (1944) by US nuclear chemist Glenn Seaborg (1912–99) and others by neutron bombardment of plutonium. It is used in smoke detectors, and Am^{241} is a source of gamma rays. Properties: at.no. 95; r.a.m. 243.13; r.d. 13.67; m.p. 995°C (1821°F); b.p. unknown; most stable isotope Am^{243} (half-life 7650 yr).

amethyst Transparent, violet variety of crystallized QUARTZ, containing more iron oxide than other varieties. It is found mainly in Brazil, Uruguay, Ontario, Canada, and North Carolina, USA. Amethyst is valued as a semi-precious gem.

Amin, Idi (1925–2003) President of Uganda (1971–79). He gained power by a military coup in 1971, overthrowing Milton OBOTE. Amin established a dictatorship marked by atrocities and expelled *c.*80,000 Asian Ugandans in 1972. Amin fled to Libya after Tanzanian forces joined rebel Ugandans in a march on Kampala. He was forced to leave Libya in 1979, and eventually settled in Saudi Arabia.

amine Any of a group of organic compounds derived from AMMONIA by replacing hydrogen atoms with alkyl groups. Methylamine (CH_3NH_2) has one hydrogen replaced. Replacement of two hydrogens gives a secondary amine and of three hydrogens, a tertiary amine. Amines are produced in the putrefaction of organic matter and are weakly basic. *See also* ALKALOID

amino acid Organic acid containing at least one carboxyl group (COOH) and at least one amino group (NH_2). Amino acids are of great biological importance because they combine together to form PROTEIN. Amino acids form PEPTIDES by the reaction of adjacent amino and carboxyl groups. Proteins are polypeptide chains consisting of hundreds of amino acids. About 20 amino acids occur in proteins; not all organisms are able to synthesize all of them. **Essential** amino acids are those that an organism has to obtain ready-made from its environment. There are ten essential amino acids for humans: arginine, histidine, isoleucine, leucine, lysine, methionine, phenylalanine, threonine, tryptophan and valine.

Amis, Kingsley (1922–95) English novelist, father of Martin AMIS. Amis' debut novel *Lucky Jim* (1954) is a classic of post-1945 British fiction. A satire on academia, it established Amis as one of the ANGRY YOUNG MEN. Other novels include *That Uncertain Feeling* (1955), *Take a Girl Like You* (1960), *One Fat Englishman* (1963), *Girl, 20* (1971), and *Stanley and the Women* (1984). Amis wrote a James Bond novel, *Colonel Sun* (1968), under the pseudonym Robert Markham. His tragicomedy *The Old Devils* (1986) won the Booker Prize.

Amis, Martin (1949–) British novelist and journalist, son of Kingsley AMIS. Amis' debut novel, *The Rachel Papers* (1974), won the Somerset Maugham Award. *Money* (1984) is a stylish critique of the dehumanizing tendencies of capitalism;

AMMONITE

Ammonites had a soft anatomy, similar to that of the modern nautilus which lives in the open end of its shell. As the animal grew it secreted more shell and moved forward into the new part, walling off the old section with a septum (1). The walled-off chambers were used for buoyancy, being supplied with air from a tissue filament or siphuncle (2) connecting them all. The septa met the shell wall in suture lines that had identifiable patterns for each species and became more complex as the group advanced.

Einstein's Monsters (1987) a set of short stories on nuclear war. *Time's Arrow* (1991) is a complex work on the holocaust. Other novels include *Success* (1978) and *Night Train* (1997). In 2000 he published *Experience*, an autobiography.

Amish Highly conservative Protestant sect of North America, whose members form an offshoot of the ANABAPTIST MENNONITE Church. The strict Old Order Amish Mennonite Church, to which most sect members belong, was founded (1693) in Switzerland by Jakob Ammann (*c.*1645–*c.*1730). In 1720 the Amish began migrating to North America, and they eventually died out in Europe. In the USA and Canada, they established small closed agricultural communities. After 1850, tensions between traditionalist 'old order' Amish and more liberal 'new order' communities split the sect. Today, a few groups of traditionalist Amish still work the land, practice non-cooperation with the state, wear plain, homemade clothes and shun modern conveniences such as telephones and cars.

Amman Capital and largest city of Jordan, 80km (50 mi) ENE of Jerusalem. Known as Rabbath-Ammon, it was the chief city of the Ammonites in biblical times. Ptolemy II Philadelphus renamed it Philadelphia. A new city was built on seven hills from 1875, and it became the capital of Trans-Jordan in 1921. From 1948 it grew rapidly, partly as a result of the influx of Palestinian refugees. Industries: cement, textiles, tobacco, leather. Pop. (2005) 1,292,000.

ammeter Instrument for measuring ELECTRIC CURRENT in AMPERES. An ammeter is connected in series in a circuit. In the moving-coil type for direct current (DC), the current to be measured passes through a coil suspended in a magnetic field and deflects a needle attached to the coil. In the moving-iron type for both direct and alternating current (AC), current through a fixed coil magnetizes two pieces of soft iron that repel each other and deflect the needle. Digital ammeters are now also used.

ammonia Colourless, nonflammable, pungent gas (NH_3) manufactured by the HABER PROCESS. It is used to make nitrogenous fertilisers. Ammonia solutions are used in cleaning and bleaching. The gas is extremely soluble in water, forming an alkaline solution of ammonium hydroxide (NH_4OH) that can give rise to ammonium salts containing the ion NH_{4+}. Chief properties: r.d. 0.59; m.p. $-77.7°C$ ($-107.9°F$); b.p. $-33.4°C$ ($-28.1°F$).

ammonite Any of an extinct group of shelled cephalopod MOLLUSCS. Most ammonites had a spiral shell, and they are believed to be related to the nautiloids, whose only surviving form is the pearly NAUTILUS. They are common as FOSSILS in marine rocks.

Amnesty International Human rights organization, founded in 1961 by Peter Benenson. It campaigns on behalf of prisoners of conscience. Based in the UK, and funded entirely by private donations, it champions the rights of individuals detained for political or religious reasons. Advocating non-violence, and politically impartial, it opposes the use of torture and the death penalty. Today, Amnesty has more than one million members and offices in more than 40 countries. In 1977 it received the Nobel Peace Prize.

amnion Membrane or sac that encloses the EMBRYO of a reptile, bird, or mammal. The embryo floats in the amniotic fluid within the sac. This sac usually ruptures shortly before birth to discharge the fluid, commonly referred to as 'the waters breaking'. *See also* UTERUS

amoeba Microscopic, almost transparent, single-celled protozoan animal that has a constantly changing, irregular shape. Found in ponds, damp soil and animal intestines, it consists of a thin outer cell membrane, a large nucleus, food and contractile vacuoles and fat globules. It reproduces by binary fission. Length: up to 3mm (0.1in). Class Sarcodina; species include the common *Amoeba proteus* and *Entamoeba histolytica*, which causes amoebic DYSENTERY.

Amos (active *c.*750BC) Old Testament prophet. He was named as the author of the Book of Amos, the third of the 12 books of the Minor Prophets.

ampere (symbol A) SI unit of ELECTRIC CURRENT. It is defined as the current in a pair of straight, parallel conductors of infinite length and 1m (39in) apart in a vacuum that produces a force of 2×10^{-7} newton per metre in their length. This force may be measured on a current balance instrument, the standard against which current meters, such as an AMMETER, are calibrated.

Ampère, André Marie (1775–1836) French physicist and mathematician. He founded electrodynamics (now called ELECTROMAGNETISM) and performed numerous experiments to investigate the magnetic effects of ELECTRIC CURRENTS. He devised techniques for detecting and measuring currents, and constructed an early type of galvanometer. Ampère's law (proposed by him) is a mathematical description of the magnetic force between two electric currents. His name is also commemorated in the fundamental unit of current, the AMPERE (A).

amphetamine DRUG that stimulates the central NERVOUS SYSTEM. These drugs (also known as 'pep pills' or 'speed') can lead to drug abuse and dependence. They can induce a temporary sense of well-being, often followed by fatigue and depression. An example is the synthetic drug methamphetamine, a methyl derivative of amphetamine. *See also* ADDICTION

amphibian Class of egg-laying VERTEBRATES, whose larval stages (tadpoles) are usually spent in water but whose adult life is normally spent on land. Amphibians have smooth, moist skin and are cold-blooded. Larvae breathe through gills; adults usually have lungs. All adults are carnivorous but larvae are frequently herbivorous. There are three living orders: Urodela (NEWTS and SALAMANDERS); Anura (FROGS and TOADS) and Apoda or CAECILIANS.

amphibole Any of a large group of complex rock-forming minerals characterized by a double-chain silicate structure (Si_4O_{11}). They all contain water as OH ions and usually calcium, magnesium, iron. Found in IGNEOUS and METAMORPHIC rocks, they form wedge-shaped fragments on cleavage. Crystals are orthorhombic or monoclinic.

amphitheatre In ancient Rome and the Roman Empire, a large circular or oval building with the performance space surrounded by tiered seating. It was used as a theatre for gladiatorial contests, wild-animal shows and similar events. Many ruined amphitheatres remain; the best-known being the COLOSSEUM in Rome. The term is now used generically to refer to any open, banked arena.

amplifier Device for changing the magnitude (size) of a signal, such as voltage or current, but not the way it varies. Amplifiers are used in radio and television transmitters and receivers, and in audio equipment. *See also* THERMIONICS

amplitude modulation (AM) Form of RADIO transmission. Broadcasts on the short-, medium- and long-wave bands are

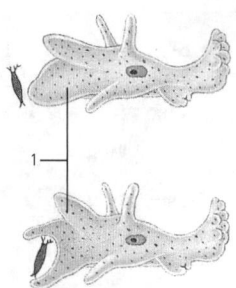
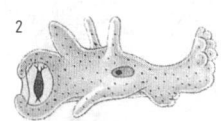
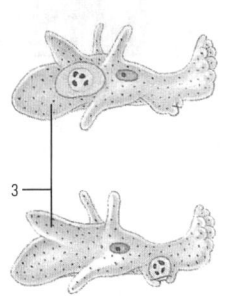
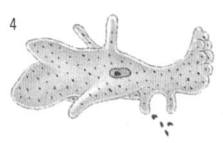

▲ **amoeba** In order to move, an amoeba pushes out projections called *pseudopods* (lit. fake foot) from its body. Cytoplasm – the fluid content of the cell – flows into the pseudopod, constantly enlarging it until all the cytoplasm has entered and the amoeba as a whole has moved. Pseudopods are also used in feeding: they move out to engulf a food particle (1), which then becomes enclosed in a membrane-bound food vacuole (2). Digestive enzymes enter the vacuole, which gradually shrinks as the food is broken down (3). Undigested material is discharged by the vacuole and left behind as the amoeba moves on (4).

INTERNET

Amnesty International
► www.amnesty.org

▲ **Amritsar** The Golden Temple (*Harmandir Sahib*) in Amritsar, Punjab, NW India, is the spiritual centre of Sikhism. Arjan (1563–1606), the fifth guru, laid the foundation of the temple in 1589. It was rebuilt by the Sikh ruler, Ranjit Singh (1780–1839), in 1803. In 1984, armed Sikh extremists, demanding greater autonomy in the Punjab, sought refuge in the Temple, and c.400 Sikhs died when Indian security forces stormed the Temple complex. In a act of revenge, a Sikh bodyguard assassinated the Indian Prime Minister Indira Gandhi.

transmitted by amplitude modulation. The sound signals to be transmitted are superimposed on a constant-amplitude radio signal called the carrier or carrier wave. The resulting modulated radio signal varies in amplitude according to the strength of the sound signal. *See also* FREQUENCY MODULATION (FM)

Amritsar City in Punjab state, NW India. Founded in 1577, Amritsar is the religious centre of SIKHISM, and site of its holiest shrine, the Golden Temple. It was the scene of the Amritsar Massacre (1919), when hundreds of Indian nationalists were killed by British troops. Amritsar is noted for its handicrafts. Industries: textiles, silk weaving. Pop. (2005) 1,162,000.

Amsterdam Capital and largest city in the Netherlands, on the River Amstel and linked to the North Sea by the North Sea Canal. Amsterdam was chartered in c.1300 and joined the Hanseatic League in 1369. The Dutch East India Company (1602) brought great prosperity to the city. It became a notable centre of learning and book printing during the 17th century. It declined when captured by the French in 1795 and blockaded by the British during the Napoleonic Wars. Amsterdam was badly damaged during the German occupation during World War 2 (1939–45). A major port and one of Europe's leading financial and cultural centres, it has an important stock exchange and diamond-cutting industry. Sights include the Old Church (c.1300), the house of Rembrandt, the Royal Palace, the Rijksmuseum, the Van Gogh Museum, and the Anne Frank House. Industries: iron and steel, oil refining, rolling stock, chemicals, glass, shipbuilding. Pop. (2005) 1,157,000.

Amun (Amon) Ancient Egyptian deity of reproduction or the animating force. The 'invisible one', Amun is commonly represented as a human being wearing ram's horns and a twin-feathered crown. He gradually assimilated other Egyptian gods, becoming Amun-Ra (the supreme creator). During the dynasties of the New Kingdom, Amun was worshipped as a victorious national god. His cult temple was at Weset (LUXOR).

Amundsen, Roald (1872–1928) Norwegian explorer and the first man to reach the SOUTH POLE. In 1903–06, Amundsen became the first man to sail through the NORTHWEST PASSAGE and determined the exact position of the magnetic NORTH POLE. He was beaten by Robert PEARY in the race to the North Pole and he turned to ANTARCTICA. Amundsen reached the South Pole on December 14, 1911 (35 days before SCOTT). In 1918, he sailed for the Northeast Passage. In 1926, Amundsen and Umberto Nobile made the first flight across the North Pole. He died in a plane crash while searching for Nobile.

amylase Digestive enzyme secreted by the SALIVARY GLANDS (salivary amylase) and the PANCREAS (pancreatic amylase. It aids digestion by breaking down starch into MALTOSE (a disaccharide) and then GLUCOSE (a monosaccharide).

Anabaptists Radical Protestant sects in the REFORMATION who shared the belief that infant baptism is not authorized by

Scripture, and that it was necessary to be baptized as an adult. The first such baptisms were conducted by the Swiss Brethren sect in Zürich (1525). The sect were the first to completely separate Church from State, when they rejected Ulrich ZWINGLI's Reformed Church. Aided by social upheavals (such as the PEASANTS' WAR) and the theological arguments of Martin LUTHER and Thomas Münzer, Anabaptism spread rapidly to Germany and the Netherlands. It stressed the community of believers. The communal theocracy established by John of Leiden at Münster was brutally suppressed (1535).

anabolic steroid Any of a group of hormones that stimulate the growth of tissue. Synthetic versions are used in medicine to treat OSTEOPOROSIS and some types of ANAEMIA; they may also be prescribed to aid weight gain in severely ill or elderly patients. These drugs are associated with a number of side effects, including acne, fluid retention, liver damage and masculinization in women. Some athletes have been known to abuse anabolic steroids in order to increase muscle bulk.

anabolism *See* METABOLISM

anaconda Large, constricting BOA of South America, the longest (up to 9m/30ft) and heaviest (up to 500kg/1100lb) snake in the world. Anacondas are mainly aquatic. They feed on birds and small mammals. Females give birth to up to 75 live young. Species *Eunectes murinus*. *See also* PYTHON

anaemia Condition in which there is a shortage of HAEMOGLOBIN, the oxygen-carrying pigment contained in ERYTHROCYTES (red blood cells). Symptoms include weakness, pallor, breathlessness, faintness, palpitations, and lowered resistance to infection. It may be due to a decrease in the production of haemoglobin or red blood cells, excessive destruction of red blood cells, or blood loss. Worldwide, iron deficiency is the commonest cause of anaemia.

anaerobic Connected with the absence of oxygen or air, or not dependent on oxygen or air for survival. An anaerobic organism (anaerobe), such as a bacterium and yeast, is a microorganism that can survive by releasing energy from GLUCOSE and other foods in the absence of oxygen. The process by which it does so is called anaerobic respiration. It differs from aerobic respiration, in which an organism must have oxygen to release energy. Most anaerobes can survive in oxygen but do not need it for RESPIRATION.

anaesthesia State of insensibility or loss of sensation produced by disease or by various anaesthetic drugs used during surgical procedures. During general, or total, anaesthesia the entire body becomes insensible and the individual sleeps; in local anaesthesia only a specific part of the body is rendered insensible and the patient remains conscious. A general anaesthetic may be either an injected drug, such as the barbiturate thiopentone, used to induce unconsciousness, or an inhalation agent such as halothane, which is used to maintain anaesthesia for surgery. Local anaesthetics, such as lignocaine, numb the relevant part of the body by blocking the transmission of impulses through the sensory nerves which supply it.

analgesic DRUG that relieves or prevents pain without causing loss of consciousness. It does not cure the cause of the pain, but helps to deaden the sensation. Some analgesics are also NARCOTICS, and many have valuable anti-inflammatory properties. Common analgesics include aspirin, codeine and morphine. *See also* ANAESTHESIA

analogue signal In telecommunications and electronics, transmission of information by means of variation in a continuous waveform. An analogue signal varies (usually in AMPLITUDE or FREQUENCY) in proportion to the value of the information in the signal. *See also* DIGITAL SIGNAL

anarchism (Gk. "no government") Political theory that regards the abolition of the state as a prerequisite for equality and social justice. In place of government, anarchy is a social form based upon voluntary cooperation between individuals. ZENO OF CITIUM, leader of the STOICS, is regarded as the architect of anarchism. Millenarian movements of the Reformation, such as the ANABAPTISTS, espoused a form of anarchism. As a modern political philosophy, anarchism dates from mid-19th century, and writers such as P.J. PROUDHON. Often in conflict with emerging COMMUNISM, Mikhail BAKUNIN's brand of violent, revolutionary anarchism led to his expulsion from the First International (1872). Anarchism has been a popular political force only in conjunction with SYNDICALISM. Its support of civil disobedience and sometimes political violence has led to its marginalization.

Anatolia *See* ASIA MINOR

anatomy Branch of biological science that studies the structure of an organism. The study of anatomy can be divided in several ways. On the basis of size, there is **gross** anatomy, which is studying structures with the naked eye; **microscopic** anatomy, studying finer detail with a light microscope; **submicroscopic** anatomy, studying even finer structural detail with an electron microscope; and **molecular** anatomy, studying with sophisticated instruments the molecular make-up of an organism. Microscopic and submicroscopic anatomy involve two closely related sciences: HISTOLOGY (tissues and structures) and CYTOLOGY (cells). Anatomy can also be classified according to the type of organism studied, plant, invertebrate, vertebrate, or human anatomy. Comparative anatomy compares the structures of organisms. *See also* PHYSIOLOGY

Anaximander (611–*c*.547 BC) Greek philosopher, student of THALES. Anaximander's lasting reputation is based on his notion of *apeiron* (Gr. infinite), a non-perceivable substance which he regarded as the primary source material of the natural world. His ideas are regarded as the precursor of a modern conception of the indestructibility of matter. He also anticipated the theory of evolution and is said to have made the first map of the Earth, which he conceived of as a self-supporting immobile cylindrical object at the centre of the universe.

ancestor worship Term used in ANTHROPOLOGY and ARCHAEOLOGY to describe an aspect of religious belief found in a wide range of societies. Cultures practising ancestor worship believe that the spirits of the dead remain in the world and can influence the fate of their living descendants for good or ill. Attempts to maintain ancestors' favour or avoid their anger usually involve prayer, sacrifice, or adherence to specific standards of behaviour.

Anchorage City in s central Alaska. By far the state's largest city, Anchorage was founded as a railway town in 1914 and became the supply centre for the gold- and coal-mining regions of N Alaska. It suffered a severe earthquake in 1964. Industries: tourism, oil, and natural gas. Pop. (2000) 260,283.

anchovy Commercially valuable food fish found worldwide in shoals in temperate and tropical seas. There are more than 100 species, including the European anchovy *Engraulis encrasicolus*. Length: 10–25cm (4–10in). Family Engraulidae.

ancien régime Term used to describe the political, legal, and social system in France before the FRENCH REVOLUTION of 1789. It was characterized by a rigid social order, a fiscal system weighted in favour of the rich, and an absolutist monarchy.

Andalusia (Andalucía) Largest, most populous and southernmost region of Spain, crossed by the River Guadalquivir, and comprising eight provinces. The capital is SEVILLE, other major cities include MÁLAGA, GRANADA, and CÓRDOBA. In the N are the Sierra Morena mountains, which are rich in minerals. In the s are the Sierra Nevada, rising to Mulhacén (Spain's highest point), at 3378m (11,411ft). Farms in the low-lying sw raise horses and cattle (including fighting bulls) and grow most of the country's cereals; other important crops are citrus fruits, olives, sugar, and grapes. Sherry is made from grapes grown in the environs of Jerez de la Frontera, near Cádiz. The region has many fine buildings (such as the ALHAMBRA) dating from between 711 and 1492, when it was ruled by the Moors. Area: 87,268sq km (33,707sq mi). Pop. (2001) 7,357,558.

Andaman and Nicobar Islands Territory of India comprising two chains of islands in the Bay of Bengal. The capital is Port Blair (on South Andaman). It's main exports are timber, coffee, coconuts, and copra. Area: 8300sq km (3200sq mi). Pop. (2001) 356,265.

Andean Indians *See* NATIVE AMERICANS

Andersen, Hans Christian (1805–75) Danish writer of some of the world's best-loved fairy tales. He gained a reputation as a poet and novelist before his talent found its true expression. His humorous, delicate but frequently melancholic stories, were first published in 1835. They include "The Ugly Duckling", "The Little Mermaid", "The Little Match Girl" and "The Emperor's New Clothes".

Anderson, Carl David (1905–91) US physicist who shared the 1936 Nobel Prize in physics with Victor HESS. In 1932 he discovered the first known particle of antimatter, the POSITRON or anti-electron. He later helped to discover the muon, an elementary particle.

Anderson, Elizabeth Garrett (1836–1917) English physician and pioneer of women's rights. She had to overcome intense prejudice against women doctors to become one of the first women to practise medicine. Later she became England's first woman mayor.

Anderson, Marian (1902–93) US contralto. She secured her reputation as a singer by touring America and Europe in recitals (1925–35). In 1955, she made her debut with the METROPOLITAN OPERA COMPANY (as Ulrica in Verdi's *Un Ballo in Maschera*) – the first appearance of a black singer in a leading role at the Metropolitan Opera.

Andes Chain of mountains in South America, extending along the whole length of the w coast. The longest mountain range in the world, they stretch for 8900km (5500mi). At their widest they are *c*.800km (500mi) across. There are more than 50 peaks over 6700m (22,000ft) high. They contain many active volcanoes, including COTOPAXI in Ecuador. Earthquakes are common, and cities such as LIMA, VALPARAÍSO, and Callao have been severely damaged. The highest peak is ACONCAGUA, rising 6960m (22,834ft) in Argentina. Lake TITICACA, the world's highest lake at 3810m (12,500ft), lies in the Andes on the Peru-Bolivia border.

Andhra Pradesh State in SE India on the Bay of Bengal; the capital is HYDERABAD. It was created in 1953 from part of MADRAS, and in 1956 it incorporated the state of Hyderabad. A flat coastal plain rises to mountains in the NE. Products include rice and groundnuts; coal, chrome and manganese are mined. The principal language is Teluga. Area: 276,814sq km (106,878sq mi). Pop. (2001) 75,727,541.

Andorra Small, independent state situated high in the E Pyrenees between France and Spain. Andorra consists mainly of six valleys that drain to the River Valira. These deep glaciated valleys lie at altitudes of 1,000–2,900m (3,300–9,500ft). In the N, a lofty watershed forms the frontier with France, and to the s the land falls away to the Segre Valley in Spain. It is a rare surviving example of a medieval principality. In 1993 a new democratic constitution was adopted. The main sources of income include livestock rearing and agriculture, especially tobacco; the sale of water and hydroelectricity to Catalonia; tourism, particularly skiing; and the sale of duty-free goods. Area: 468sq km (181sq mi). Pop. (1999) 69,000.

Andrea del Sarto (1486–1531) (Andrea d'Agnolo di Francesco) Florentine artist. A contemporary of MICHELANGELO and RAPHAEL, he was one of the outstanding painters and draughtsmen of the High RENAISSANCE. He was an excellent portraitist, a master of composition, and he produced many frescos and altarpieces. His frescos include the cycles in the cloister of SS. Annunziata (1514–24) and the terra verde grisailles in the Chiostro dello Scalzo (1511–26), Florence.

Andrew, Saint In the New Testament, brother of Simon Peter and one of the original 12 disciples of Jesus. According to tradition he was crucified on an x-shaped cross. He is patron saint of Scotland and Russia; his feast day is November 30.

Androcles In Roman legend, a Roman slave who ran away from his master and hid in a cave. Androcles removed a thorn from the paw of a suffering lion. When he later faced the same lion in the Roman Arena, the lion refused to harm him. He was immortalized in George Bernard Shaw's play *Androcles and the Lion* (1912).

androgen General name for male sex HORMONES, such as TESTOSTERONE.

◄ **anchovy** A member of the herring family, the European anchovy (*Engraulis encrasicolus*) is a popular food fish. They are found throughout the Mediterranean and in the Eastern Atlantic. The species found in the Northeast Pacific is the Californian or northern anchovy (*Engraulis mordax*).

INTERNET

Andorra
► www.andorra.ad
► www.turisme.ad

▲ **anemone** The wood anemone (*Anemone nemorosa*) is found in woodlands in Europe and Asia. It is one of the earliest spring flowers. Like all anemones, what appear to be petals are actually sepals. In Greek mythology, anemones grew from the blood of Adonis. In Chinese mythology, they represent death. Anemones contain the poison anemonin.

INTERNET

Andropov, Yuri Vladimirovich
▶ www.coldwar.org

Angelico, Fra
▶ mv.vatican.va/3_EN/pages/ PIN/PIN_Sala03.html
▶ www.christusrex.org/ www2/art/san_marco.htm
▶ www.nationalgallery.org. uk/collection/default.htm

Angkor
▶ www.angkorwat.org

Andromeda Large constellation of the Northern Hemisphere, adjoining the Square of Pegasus. The main stars lie in a line leading away from Pegasus, and the star Alpha Andromedae actually forms one corner of the Square. The most famous object in the constellation is the ANDROMEDA GALAXY.

Andromeda In Greek mythology, daughter of Cepheus and Cassiopea, king and queen of Ethiopia. When her country was under threat from a sea dragon, Andromeda was offered as a sacrifice and chained to a rock by the sea. She was saved by PERSEUS.

Andromeda Galaxy Spiral GALAXY 2.2 million light-years away in the constellation ANDROMEDA, the most distant object visible to the naked eye. The Andromeda Galaxy has a mass of more than 300,000 million Suns. Its diameter is *c.*150,000 light-years, somewhat larger than our own Galaxy.

Andropov, Yuri Vladimirovich (1914–84) Soviet statesman, president of the Soviet Union (1983–84), general secretary of the Communist Party (1982–84). Andropov first gained attention for his role in the suppression of the Hungarian Uprising (1956). As head of the KGB (1967–82), Andropov took a hardline stance against political dissidence, supporting Soviet intervention in Czechoslovakia (1968) and Poland (1981). He joined the Politburo in 1973. Andropov succeeded Leonid BREZHNEV as leader. His term in office was the shortest in Soviet history. Perhaps his most significant decision was the promotion of Mikhail GORBACHEV. He was succeeded by Konstantin Chernenko.

anechoic chamber (dead room) Room designed to be echo-free and used in ACOUSTIC laboratories to measure sound reflection and transmission, and to test audio equipment. The walls, floor, and ceiling are insulated and covered with an absorbent material, often over pyramid shapes to reduce reflection. The room is usually asymmetrical to reduce stationary waves, which are waves reflected back over their own paths.

anemometer Instrument using pressure tubes or rotating vanes to measure the speed or force of the wind. Also, an instrument for measuring the flow of any liquid or gas.

anemone (windflower) Perennial plant found worldwide. Anemones have sepals resembling petals, and numerous stamens and pistils covering a central knob; two or three deeply toothed leaves appear in a whorl midway up the stem. Many are wild flowers, such as the wood anemone (*Anemone nemorosa*), common in Britain and Europe. There are 120 species. Family Ranunculaceae. *See also* BUTTERCUP; SEA ANEMONE

angel (Gk. messenger) Spiritual being superior to man but inferior to God. In the Bible, angels appear as messengers and servants of God. Angels form an integral part of Judaism and Islam. Christian tradition gives a hierarchy of nine orders of angel: seraphim, cherubim, thrones, dominions (or dominations), virtues, powers, principalities, archangels, and angels.

Angel Falls World's highest uninterrupted waterfall, in La Gran Sabrana, E Venezuela. Part of the River Caroni, it was discovered in 1935 and named after its discoverer Jimmy Angel, a US aviator who crashed there. Total drop: 980m (3212ft).

angelfish Tropical fish found in the Atlantic and Indo-Pacific oceans, popular as an aquarium fish because of its graceful, trailing fins and beautiful markings. Length: 2–10cm (1–4in). Family Cichlidae.

Angelico, Fra (*c.*1400–55) (Guido di Pietro) Florentine painter and Dominican friar. Angelico and his assistants

▶ **Angel Falls** The spectacular Angel Falls in E Venezuela, S America, is the world's highest waterfall. The longest single drop is 807m (2648ft).

▲ **Angelou, Maya** Angelou's varied and often tragic life is evoked in her influential volumes of autobiography. She was a singer and actor before taking an active role in the US civil rights movement.

painted a cycle of some 50 devotional frescos in the friary of San Marco, Florence (*c.*1438–45). These pictures show great technical skill and are the key to Angelico's reputation as an artist of extraordinary sweetness and serenity. Despite being part of a strict order, Angelico stayed in touch with developments in contemporary Florentine art and later travelled widely on commissions. International Gothic influenced his early work but he also found great inspiration in representations of architectural perspective by MASACCIO. His style showed a marked change towards narrative detail in frescos carried out for Pope Nicholas V's Vatican chapel (1447–50).

Angelou, Maya (1928–) US writer, editor, and entertainer. She is best known for six volumes of autobiography, starting with *I Know Why the Caged Bird Sings* (1970). Evoking her childhood in 1930s Arkansas, it relates the rape that left Angelou mute for the next five years. The fourth volume, *The Heart of a Woman*, deals with her involvement in the 1960s CIVIL RIGHTS movement as the Northern Coordinator for Martin Luther KING, Jr.

Angevins English royal dynasty named after King Henry II, son of the Count of Anjou (and grandson of Henry I), who ascended the throne in 1154. The Angevins, who later became the PLANTAGENET royal line, retained the crown until 1485.

angina Pain in the chest due to an insufficient blood supply to the heart, usually associated with diseased coronary arteries. Generally induced by exertion or stress, it is treated with drugs, such as glyceryl trinitrate, or surgery.

angiosperm Plants with true flowers, as distinct from GYMNOSPERM and other non-flowering plants. They include most trees, bushes, and non-woody herbs. There are two main groups: MONOCOTYLEDONS (which have one seed leaf) such as grasses and daffodils, and DICOTYLEDONS (which have two seed leaves) such as peas and oak.

Angkor Ancient KHMER capital and temple complex, NW Cambodia. The site contains the ruins of several stone temples erected by Khmer rulers, many of which lie within the walled enclosure of Angkor Thom, the capital built (1181–95) by Jayavarman VII (*c.*1120–1215). **Angkor Wat**, the greatest structure in terms of its size and the quality of its carving, lies outside the main complex. Thai invaders destroyed the Angkor complex in 1431, and it remained virtually neglected until French travellers rediscovered it in 1858. Conservationists restored Angkor Wat piece by piece until the followers of POL POT ravaged Cambodia in the civil war (1970–75).

angle Measure of the inclination of two straight lines or planes to each other. One complete revolution is divided into 360 degrees or 2π radians. One degree may be subdivided into 60 minutes, and one minute into 60 seconds.

Angles Germanic tribe from a district of Schleswig-Holstein now called Angeln. In the 5th century they invaded England with neighbouring tribes, JUTES, SAXONS, and others. They settled mainly in Northumbria and East Anglia. The name England (Angle-land) derives from them.

Anglesey (Ynys Môn) Island off the NW coast of Wales, separated from the mainland by the narrow Menai Strait. Formerly a Welsh county, it became part of GWYNEDD in 1974.

The chief town is Beaumaris, famous for a moated castle built by Edward I (1295). Holyhead is a major ferry terminus for Ireland. Area: 718sq km (276sq mi). Pop. (2001) 66,829.

Anglican Communion Fellowship of 37 independent national or provincial worldwide churches, many of which are in Commonwealth nations and originated from missionary work by the CHURCH OF ENGLAND. An exception is the EPISCOPAL CHURCH in the USA, founded by the Scottish Episcopal Church. There is no single governing authority, but all recognize the leadership of the Archbishop of CANTERBURY. Worship is liturgical, based on the Book of COMMON PRAYER. Once a decade, the bishops of the Communion meet at the Lambeth Conference. The 1968 Conference established a Consultative Council to discuss issues that arise between conferences. In 1982 diplomatic ties with the Roman Catholic Church were restored. In 1988 the Conference passed a resolution in support of the ordination of women as priests. Today, there are *c*.70 million Anglicans organized into *c*.30,000 parishes.

angling Popular freshwater or marine sport. The two basic types of freshwater FISHING are game fishing and coarse fishing. **Game** fishing uses artificial bait, such as spinning lures

and flies (imitation insects), and is undertaken in fast-moving water where salmon and trout can be found. **Coarse** fishing takes place in slow-moving water and uses either live bait, such as maggots and worms, or cereal bait, such as sweetcorn. **Saltwater** fishing requires heavier rods and reels, and includes trolling and big-game fishing. Flatfish, mackerel, and sea bass are among the more common seafish caught, while tuna, swordfish, marlin, and shark are landed in big-game fishing.

Anglo-Irish Agreement (Hillsborough Agreement) Treaty aiming to clarify the status of Northern IRELAND, signed (1985) by Margaret THATCHER and Garret Fitzgerald. It gave the Republic of Ireland the right of consultation; it asserted that any future changes would have to be ratified by a majority of the people of Northern Ireland; and it set up the Anglo-Irish Intergovernmental Conference to promote cooperation. It was denounced by the Ulster Unionists. *See also* DOWNING STREET DECLARATION

Anglo-Saxon art and architecture Art and architecture produced in Britain from the 5th to the 11th centuries, following the invasions by the ANGLO-SAXONS. The most famous archaeological find is the pagan ship-burial at SUTTON HOO. Anglo-Saxon art is predominantly Christian, consisting of

ANGOLA

The Republic of Angola is a large country, more than twice the size of France, on the sw coast of Africa. The majority of the country is part of the plateau that forms most of s Africa, with a narrow coastal plain in the w.

Angola has many rivers. In the NE, several rivers flow N to become tributaries of the River CONGO, while in the s some rivers, including the Cubango (Okavango) and the Cuanda, flow SE into inland drainage basins in the interior of Africa.

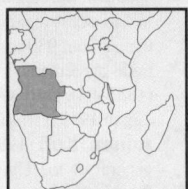

CLIMATE
Angola has a tropical climate, with temperatures of over 20°C [68°F] all year round, though upland areas are cooler. The coastal regions are dry, increasingly so to the s of LUANDA, but the rainfall increases to the N and E. The rainy season is between November and April. Tropical forests flourish in the N, but the vegetation along the coast is sparse, with semi-desert in the s.

HISTORY
Bantu-speaking people from the N settled in Angola *c*.2,000 years ago. In the later part of

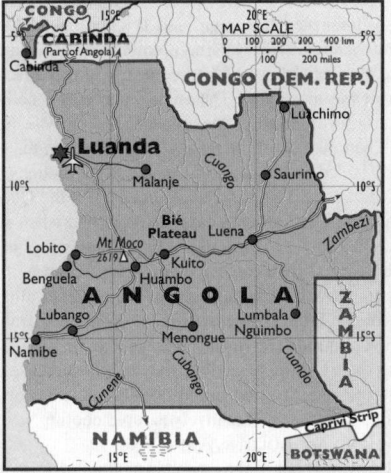

the 15th century, Portuguese navigators, seeking a route to Asia round Africa, explored the coast and, in the early 17th century, the Portuguese set up supply bases. Angola became important as a source of slaves for the Portuguese colony of Brazil. After the decline of the slave trade, Portuguese settlers began to develop the land, and the Portuguese population increased rapidly in the first half of the 20th century.

In the 1950s, nationalists began to demand independence. In 1956, the Popular Movement for the Liberation of Angola (MPLA) was founded, drawing support from the Mbundu tribe and *mestizos* (people of African and European descent). In 1961 the MPLA led a revolt in Luanda, but it was put down by Portuguese troops. Other opposition movements developed among different ethnic groups. In the N, the Kongo set up the FNLA (Front for the Liberation of Angola), and in 1966 southern peoples, including many Ovimbundu, formed the National Union for the Total Independence of Angola (UNITA).

POLITICS
The Portuguese agreed to grant Angola independence in 1975, after which rival nationalist forces began a struggle for power. A long-running civil war developed between government forces and the FNLA in the N and UNITA in the s. The government received aid from the Soviet Union and Cuba and, as the war developed, both the FNLA and UNITA turned to the West for support. UNITA also received support from South Africa. FNLA guerrilla activity ended in 1984, but UNITA took control of large areas. Economic progress was hampered not only by the vast spending on defence and security, but also by the MPLA government's austere Marxist policies.

In 1991, a peace accord was agreed and multiparty elections were held. The MPLA, which had renounced Marxism, won a majority. Jose Eduardo DOS SANTOS, president since 1979, retainined power. UNITA's leaders rejected the

AREA 1,246,700sq km [481,351sq mi]
POPULATION 12,263,000
CAPITAL Luanda (2,839,000)
GOVERNMENT Multiparty republic
ETHNIC GROUPS Ovimbundu 37%, Kimbundu 25%, Bakongo 13%, others 25%
LANGUAGES Portuguese (official), many others
RELIGIONS Traditional beliefs 47%, Roman Catholic 38%, Protestant 15%
CURRENCY Kwanza = 100 lwei

election results and civil war resumed in 1994. In 1997, the government invited UNITA leader Jonas SAVIMBI to join a coalition but he refused. Savimbi was killed in action in February 2002, raising hopes of peace, and the army and rebels signed a ceasefire to end conflict.

Angola then started the lengthy process of rebuilding its devastated infrastructure. Millions of refugees have begun to resettle, but landmine clearance work proceeds slowly and is a major obstacle to redevelopment.

ECONOMY
Angola is a developing country, where 70% of the people are poor farmers, although agriculture contributes only about 9% of the gross domestic product. The main food crops include cassava, maize, sweet potatoes and beans, while cattle are the leading livestock, with sheep and goats raised in drier areas. The widespread use of landmines in the civil war has made much land impossible to farm, and many Angolans are dependent on food aid.

Despite widespread poverty and a low per capita GNP, Angola has much economic potential. It has oil reserves near Luanda and in Cabinda, an enclave separated from the rest of Angola by a strip of the Democratic Republic of Congo. Oil and mineral fuels are the leading exports.

Other resources include diamonds (the second most important export), copper and manganese. Angola also has a growing industrial sector. Manufactures include cement, chemicals, processed food and textiles.

stone crosses, ivory carvings and illuminated manuscripts (the most important are the LINDISFARNE GOSPELS). Anglo-Saxon churches are characterized by square apses, aisles or side chambers (*porticus*), pilaster strips and distinctive timber work.

Anglo-Saxons People of Germanic origin comprising ANGLES, SAXONS, and other tribes who began to invade England from the mid-5th century, when Roman power was in decline. By AD 600 they were well established in most of England. They were converted to Christianity in the 7th century. Early tribal groups were led by warrior lords whose thegns (nobles) provided military service in exchange for rewards and protection. The tribal groups eventually developed into kingdoms, such as Northumbria and WESSEX. The term Anglo-Saxon was first used in the late 8th century to distinguish the Saxon settlers in England from the 'Old Saxons' of N Germany, and became synonymous with 'English'. The Anglo-Saxon period ended with the NORMAN CONQUEST (1066).

Angola Republic in SW Africa. *See* country feature, page 95

Angora *See* ANKARA

Angry Young Men Loose literary and dramatic term, applied to an anti-establishment group of British writers in the 1950s. Taken from Leslie Allen Paul's autobiography *Angry Young Man* (1951), it was popularized through John OSBORNE's play *Look Back in Anger* (1956). The group included Kingsley AMIS, Arnold WESKER and Alan SILLITOE.

angstrom (angstrom unit) (symbol Å) Obsolete unit of length, equal to 10^{-10} m or 0.1nm (nanometre). It was used to express the wavelength of light and ultraviolet radiation, and to measure distances between atoms and between molecules. The angstrom was replaced by the nanometre.

Anguilla Island in the West Indies, most northerly of the Leeward Islands; the capital is The Valley. Settled in the 17th century by English colonists, it eventually became part of the St Kitts-Nevis-Anguilla group. Declared independent in 1967, it re-adopted British colonial status in 1980, and is now a self-governing dependency. The economy of the flat, coral island is based on fishing and tourism. Area: 96sq km (37sq mi). Pop. (2000) 13,000. *See* WEST INDIES map

aniline (phenylamine) Highly poisonous, colourless oily liquid ($C_6H_5NH_2$) made by the reduction of nitrobenzene. It is an important starting material for making organic compounds such as drugs, explosives, and dyes. Properties: r.d. 1.02; m.p. −6.2°C (20.8°F); b.p. 184.1°C (363.4°F). *See also* AMINE

animal Living organism of the animal kingdom, usually distinguishable from members of the PLANT kingdom by its power of locomotion (at least during some stage of its existence); a well-defined body shape; limited growth; its feeding exclusively on organic matter; the production of two different kinds of sex cells; and the formation of an embryo or larva during the developmental stage. Higher animals, such as the VERTEBRATES, are easily distinguishable from plants, but the distinction becomes blurred with the lower forms. Some one-celled organisms could easily be assigned to either category. Scientists have classified about a million different kinds of animals in more than twenty phyla. The simplest (least highly evolved) animals include the PROTOZOA, SPONGES, JELLYFISH, and WORMS. Other invertebrate phyla include ARTHROPODS (arachnids, crustaceans, and insects), MOLLUSCS (shellfish, octopus, and squid) and ECHINODERMS (sea urchins and starfish). Vertebrates belong to the CHORDATA phylum, which includes fish, amphibians, reptiles, birds, and mammals.

animal rights Campaign for more humane treatment of animals, aiming to reduce the infliction of pain and distress, Activists' efforts have particularly focused on the use of animals in scientific experiments, but have also drawn attention to the practices of the meat industry. *See also* VIVISECTION

animation Illusion of motion created by projecting successive images of still drawings or objects. Drawn cartoons are the most common form. Each of a series of drawings is photographed singly. The illusion of motion is created when the photographs are displayed in rapid succession. Computer animation programs have advanced to a point where the drawings themselves are no longer a necessity.

animism Belief that within every animal, plant, or inanimate object dwells an individual spirit capable of governing

its existence and influencing human affairs. Natural objects and phenomena are regarded as possessing life, consciousness, and a spirit. In animism, the spirits of dead animals live on, and can inflict harm if the animals have been killed improperly. These beliefs are widespread among tribal peoples, and anthropologists formerly believed that they represented the beginnings of organized religion.

anion Negative ION attracted to the ANODE (positive electrode) during electrolysis.

Anjou Region and former province in W France, straddling the lower Loire valley. It was ruled by Henry II of England after his marriage to Eleanor of Aquitaine, and Louis XI annexed it to the French crown in 1480. It ceased to be a province in 1790.

Ankara Capital of Turkey, at the confluence of the Cubuk and Ankara rivers. In ancient times it was known as Ancyra, and was an important commercial centre as early as the 8th century BC. It was a Roman provincial capital and flourished under Augustus. Tamerlane took the city in 1402. In the late 19th century it declined in importance, until Kemal ATATÜRK set up a provisional government here in 1920. It replaced Istanbul as the capital in 1923, changing its name to Ankara in 1930. It is noted for its angora wool (a mixture of sheep's wool and rabbit hair) and mohair. Pop. (2000) 3,203,000.

Annam Former kingdom on E coast of INDOCHINA, now in Vietnam; the capital was Hué. The ancient empire fell to China in 214 BC. It regained self-government but was again ruled by China from 939 to 1428. The French obtained missionary and trade agreements in 1787, and a protectorate was established (1883–84). During World War 2 it was occupied by the Japanese; in 1949 it was incorporated into the Republic of VIETNAM.

Annan, Kofi (1938–) Ghanaian diplomat, seventh secretary-general of the United Nations (1997–2006). Annan was the first black African secretary-general. In 1993 he became under-secretary-general for peacekeeping, handling the withdrawal of UN troops from Bosnia. His diplomacy helped secure a peaceful resolution (1998) to the weapons' inspection crisis in Iraq. Annan and the UN received the 2001 Nobel Peace Prize.

Annapolis State capital of Maryland, USA, on the s bank of the Severn River on Chesapeake Bay. Founded in 1649 by Puritans from Virginia, it was laid out as the state capital in 1694. The site of the signing of the peace treaty ending the AMERICAN REVOLUTION, it has many buildings dating from colonial times. It is the seat of the US Naval Academy (1845). Industries: boatyards, seafood packing. Pop. (2000) 35,838.

Annapurna Mountain massif in the HIMALAYAS, N central Nepal, notoriously dangerous to climbers. It has two of the world's highest peaks: Annapurna 1 in the W rises to 8078m (26,504ft); Annapurna 2 in the E rises to 7937m (26,041ft).

Anne (1665–1714) Queen of Great Britain and Ireland (1702–14). The second daughter of JAMES II, Anne succeeded WILLIAM III as the last STUART sovereign and, after the Act of UNION (1707), the first monarch of the United Kingdom of England and Scotland. Brought up a Protestant, she married Prince George of Denmark (1683). Despite 18 pregnancies, no child survived her. The War of the SPANISH SUCCESSION (1701–14) dominated her reign, and is often called Queen Anne's War. Anne was the last English monarch to exercise the royal veto over legislation (1707), but the rise of parliamentary government was inexorable. The military success of the Duke of MARLBOROUGH increased the influence that his wife, Sarah Churchill, had over domestic policy. Tory victory in the elections of 1710 led to the dismissal of the Marlboroughs, and Abigail Masham and Robert Harley emerged as the Queen's new favourites. The JACOBITE cause was crushed when Anne was succeeded by GEORGE I. The most lasting aspect of her reign was the strength of contemporary arts and culture.

annealing Slow heating and cooling of a metal, alloy or glass to relieve internal stresses and make up dislocations or vacancies introduced during mechanical shaping, such as rolling or extruding (ejection). Annealing increases the material's workability and durability. TEMPERING, on the other hand, is a process that involves rapid cooling.

Anne Boleyn *See* BOLEYN, ANNE

annelid Any member of the Annelida phylum of segmented WORMS. All have encircling grooves usually corresponding to internal partitions of the body. A digestive tube, nerves, and blood vessels run through the entire body, but each segment has its own set of internal organs. The three main classes are: Polychaeta (marine worms), Oligochaeta (freshwater or terrestrial worms), and Hirudinea (LEECHES).

Anne of Austria (1601–66) Daughter of Philip III of Spain, wife of LOUIS XIII of France, and mother of LOUIS XIV. Her husband died in 1643, and she ruled France as regent in close alliance with Cardinal MAZARIN until her death. The era was immortalized by Alexandre DUMAS in his novels, *The Three Musketeers* (1844) and *Twenty Years After* (1845).

Anne of Cleves (1515–57) Fourth wife of HENRY VIII of England. Her marriage (1540) was a political alliance joining Henry with the German Protestants, and was never consummated, being declared null after only six months. Anne received a pension, and remained in England until her death.

annual Plant that completes its life cycle in one growing season, such as the sweet pea, sunflower, and wheat. Annual plants overwinter as seeds. *See also* BIENNIAL; PERENNIAL

annual ring (growth ring) Concentric circles visible in cross-sections of woody stems or trunks. Each year the CAMBIUM layer produces a layer of XYLEM, the vessels of which are large and thin-walled in the spring and smaller and thick-walled in the summer, creating a contrast between the rings. Used to determine the age of trees, the thickness of these rings also reveals environmental conditions during a tree's lifetime.

Annunciation Announcement made to the Virgin Mary by the angel Gabriel that she was to be the mother of Christ (Luke 1). In many Christian Churches, the Feast of the Annunciation is kept on March 25, a date often called 'Lady Day'. The Annunciation was a common subject for painters during medieval and Renaissance times.

anode Positive electrode of an electrolytic CELL that attracts ANIONS (negative ions) during ELECTROLYSIS.

anodizing Electrolytic process to coat ALUMINIUM or MAGNESIUM with a thin layer of oxide to help prevent corrosion. The process makes the metal the ANODE (positive electrode) in an acid solution. The protective coating is insoluble, a good insulator, and can be colourfully dyed.

anorexia nervosa Abnormal loss of the desire to eat. A pathological condition, it is seen mainly in young women anxious to lose weight. It can result in severe emaciation and in rare cases may be life-threatening. *See also* BULIMIA NERVOSA

Anouilh, Jean (1910–87) French playwright and screenwriter. A major dramatist of the mid-20th century, influenced by NEO-CLASSICISM. Often reinterpreting Greek myth as a means of exploring oppression, *Antigone* (1944) is perhaps his most celebrated play. Other works include *Becket* (1959).

Anschluss Unification of Austria and Germany. Prohibited by treaty after World War 1 (1914–18) expressly to limit the strength of Germany, Anschluss was nevertheless favoured by many Germans and Austrians. It was achieved by force by Adolf HITLER (1938) but dissolved by the Allies in 1945.

Anselm of Canterbury, Saint (1033–1109) English theologian, b. Italy. He was an early scholastic philosopher and became Archbishop of CANTERBURY in 1093. His belief in the rational character of Christian belief led him to propose an ontological argument for the existence of God. His feast day is April 21. *See also* ONTOLOGY

ant Social insect belonging to a family that also includes the BEE and WASP. A typical ant colony consists of one or more queens (fertile females), workers (sterile females), and winged males. Some species also have a caste of soldier ants which guard the colony. Ants range in length from two to 25mm (0.08–1.0in) and are found worldwide except in Antarctica. They feed on plants, nectar, and other insects. Most ants are wingless except at times of dispersal. Family Formicidae.

Antakya (formerly Antioch, now also Hatay) City in s Turkey on the River Orontes; capital of Hatay province. Founded in *c.*300 BC by SELEUCUS I, it was taken for Rome by Pompey (64BC), and earned the title 'queen of the east'. Saint Paul preached here, and the city was a centre of early Christianity. Part of the Ottoman Empire from 1516 to 1919, it passed from Syrian to Turkish control. in 1939. Products include olives, tobacco, cotton, and cereals. Pop. (1994) 137,200.

Antananarivo (Tananarive) Capital and largest city of Madagascar. Founded in *c.*1625, the city became the capital and residence for Imerina rulers in 1794. Antananarivo was taken by the French in 1895, and became part of a French protectorate. It is the seat of the University of Madagascar (1961). A trade centre for a rice-producing region, it has textile, tobacco, and leather industries. Pop. (2005) 1,808,000.

Antarctica Fifth-largest continent (larger than Europe or Australasia), covering almost 10% of the world's total land area. Surrounding the SOUTH POLE, it is bordered by the Antarctic Ocean and the s sections of the Atlantic, Pacific, and Indian Oceans. Almost entirely within the Antarctic Circle, it is of great strategic and scientific interest. No people live here permanently, though scientists frequently stay for short periods to conduct research and exploration. Seven

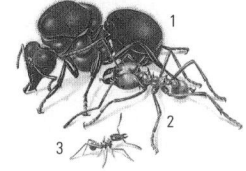

▲ **ant** Most ant societies are made up of different types of ant known as castes. Shown here are the queen (1), soldier (2), and small worker (3) of the leaf-cutter species *Atta caphalotes*. Females develop from fertilized and males from unfertilized eggs. Nutrition determines whether a female becomes a queen or worker. First generation larvae are fed entirely by the queen's saliva. Mating takes place in flight, after which the male dies. The queen proceeds to lay eggs for the remainder of her life (up to 15 years).

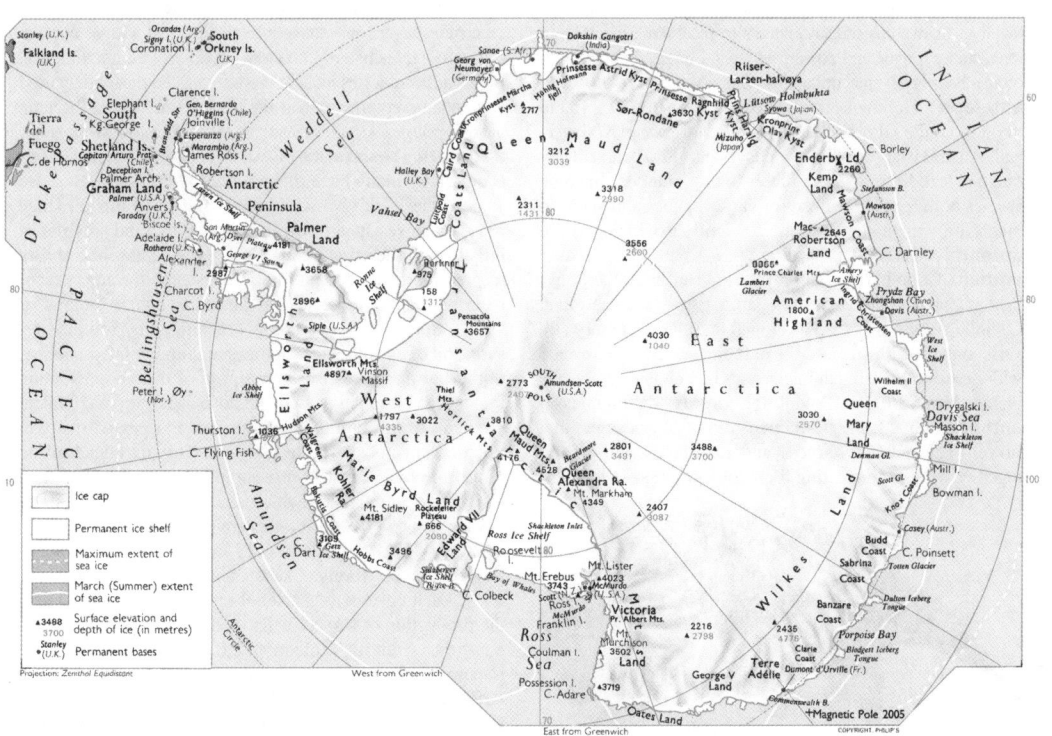

◀ **Antarctica** The mountainous archipelago of w Antarctica is joined to the continental shield of E Antarctica by a vast ice sheet. More than 95% of Antarctica remains covered in ice throughout the year. Ross Sea and Weddell Sea form the two major coastlines. Its interior is the coldest place on Earth, with temperatures as low as −90°C (−130°F). The severity of its climate makes it inhospitable to almost all life, except for nematode worms, and some mosses and plants. The krill-rich waters of the Antarctic Ocean attract whales, seals, and penguins. Captain Cook was the first to cross the Antarctic Circle (1772–75). In the early 19th century, humans were attracted by the commercial value of seal fur. In the 1890s, Antarctica became the centre of the whaling industry and the focus of many scientific studies. In 1911 Roald Amundsen beat Captain Scott in the race to become the first man to reach the South Pole.

nations lay claim to sectors of it. Covered by an ice-sheet with an average thickness of *c*.1800m (5900ft), it contains *c*.90% of the world's ice and more than 70% of its freshwater. **Land** Resembling an open fan, with the Antarctic Peninsula as a handle, the continent is a snowy desert covering *c*.14.2 million sq km (5.5 million sq mi). The land is a high plateau, having an average elevation of 1800m (6000ft) and rising to 5140m (16,863ft) in the Vinson Massif. Mountain ranges occur near the coasts. The interior, or South Polar Plateau, lies beneath *c*.2000m (6500ft) of snow, accumulated over tens of thousands of years. Mineral deposits exist in the mountains, but their recovery has not become practicable. Coal may be plentiful, but the value of known deposits of copper, nickel, gold, and iron will not repay the expenses of extracting and exporting them. **Seas and glaciers** Antarctic rivers are frozen, inching towards the sea, and instead of lakes there are large bodies of ice along the coasts. The great Beardmore Glacier creeps down from the South Polar Plateau, and eventually becomes part of the Ross Ice Shelf. The southernmost part of the Atlantic is the portion of the Antarctic Ocean known as the Weddell Sea. **Climate and vegetation** Antarctica remains cold all year, with only a few coastal areas being free from snow or ice in summer (December to February). On most of the continent the temperature remains below freezing, and in August it has been recorded at nearly −90°C (−130°F). Precipitation generally amounts to 18–38cm (7–15in) of snow a year, but melting is less than that, allowing a build-up over the centuries. Nevertheless, mosses manage to survive on rocks along the outer rim of the continent. Certain algae grow on the snow, and others appear in pools of freshwater when melting occurs. **History** Antarctic islands were sighted first in the 18th century, and in 1820 Nathaniel Palmer reached the Antarctic Peninsula. Between 1838 and 1840, US explorer Charles Wilkes discovered enough of the coast to prove that a continent existed, and the English explorer James Clark Ross made coastal maps. Towards the end of the 19th century, exploration of the interior developed into a race for the SOUTH POLE. Roald AMUNDSEN reached the Pole on December 14, 1911, a month before Captain Robert SCOTT. The aeroplane brought a new era of exploration, and Richard E. BYRD became the best-known of the airborne polar explorers. The Antarctic Treaty (1959), which pledged international scientific co-operation, was renewed and extended in 1991, banning commercial exploitation of the continent.

anteater Toothless, mainly nocturnal, insect-eating mammal that lives in swamps and savannas of tropical America. It has a long, sticky tongue and powerful claws. Length: up to 152cm (60in). Family Myrmecophagidae. *See also* EDENTATE

antelope Hollow-horned, speedy RUMINANT found throughout the Old World except in Madagascar, Malaysia and Australasia; most antelopes occur in Africa. They range in size from that of a rabbit to that of an ox. In some species both sexes bear horns of varied shapes and sizes; in others, only the males are horned. Family Bovidae.

antenna *See* AERIAL

anthem Choral composition in Anglican and other English-language church services, analogous to the Roman Catholic MOTET in Latin. Developed in the 16th century as a verse anthem with soloists, the anthem was later performed with orchestral accompaniment and by a choir. Composers include Henry PURCELL and Ralph VAUGHAN WILLIAMS.

anther In botany, the fertile part of a male sex organ in a flower. The anther produces and distributes pollen, and together with its connecting filament forms a STAMEN.

Anthony, Saint (*c*.250–*c*.355) Egyptian saint and first Christian monk. He withdrew into complete solitude at the age of 20 to practise ascetic devotion. The monastic ideal, outlined by Saint ATHANASIUS in the *Life of St Anthony*, attracted many devotees. By the time of Saint Anthony's death, Christian MONASTICISM was well established. His feast day is January 17.

Anthony, Susan Brownell (1820–1906) US reformer and woman suffragist. She established the first woman's TEMPERANCE association and, with Elizabeth Cady Stanton, she co-organized the National Woman Suffrage Association (1869). It later became the National American Woman Suffrage Association (1890), and she acted as president (1892–1900). *See also* SUFFRAGETTE MOVEMENT

anthracite Form of COAL consisting of more than 90% CARBON, relatively hard, black, and with a metallic lustre. It burns with the hot pale-blue flame of complete combustion. It is the final form in the series of fuels: PEAT, lignite, bituminous coal, and black coal.

anthrax Contagious disease, chiefly of livestock, caused by the microbe *Bacillus anthracis*. Human beings can catch anthrax from contact with infected animals or their hides. In 2001, five US citizens died after contact with mail contaminated by anthrax spores, provoking worries of bio-terrorism.

Anthropoidea Suborder of primates including monkeys, apes and humans. Anthropoids have flatter faces, larger brains and are larger in size than prosimian PRIMATES.

anthropology Scientific study of human development and how different societies are interrelated. It is concerned with the chronological and geographical range of human societies. Modern anthropology stems from the first half of the 19th century. Public interest in cultural EVOLUTION followed the publication of *On the Origin of Species* by Charles DARWIN (1859). **Physical** anthropologists are concerned with the history of human evolution in its biological sense. **Social** anthropologists study living societies in order to learn about cultural and social evolution. **Applied** anthropology is the specific study of a particular community and its collective and individual relationships. *See also* ETHNOGRAPHY; ETHNOLOGY

antibiotic Substance that is capable of stopping the growth of, or destroying, BACTERIA and other microorganisms. Antibiotics are germicides that are safe enough to be eaten or injected into the body. The post-1945 introduction of antibiotics has revolutionized medical science, making possible the virtual elimination of once widespread and often fatal diseases, including TYPHOID FEVER, PLAGUE and CHOLERA. Some antibiotics are selective – that is, effective against specific microorganisms; those effective against a large number of microorganisms are known as broad-spectrum antibiotics. Important antibiotics include PENICILLIN, the first widely used antibiotic, streptomycin and the tetracyclines. Some bacteria have developed ANTIBIOTIC RESISTANCE. *See also* ANTISEPTIC

antibiotic resistance Resistance to antibiotic drugs acquired by many bacteria and other PATHOGENS. Because some bacteria survive while non-resistant strains die, they pass their resistance to their progeny and resistance increases in the population. Some bacteria have the ability to pass the genes for antibiotic resistance to other organisms of different species on plasmids (small lengths of DNA). Spread of resistance is accelerated by routine prescription of antibiotics to humans and unregulated application to farm animals for the purpose of disease prevention rather than cure. An inadequate dose or failure to complete a course of antibiotics increases the chances of resistant microorganisms surviving to breed. This may lead to the return of epidemics of untreatable infectious disease, and can create a cycle in which the development of more advanced, powerful antibiotics are constantly needed.

antibody PROTEIN synthesized in the BLOOD in response to the entry of "foreign" substances or organisms into the body. Each episode of bacterial or viral infection prompts the production of a specific antibody to fight the disease in question. After the infection has cleared, the antibody remains in the blood to fight off any future invasion.

Antichrist Term loosely referring to the supreme enemy of Christ. It is used in the letters of Saint JOHN to refer to a

▶ **anteater** The giant anteater (*Myrmecophaga tridactyla*) is found in South America, particularly in the swampy regions of the Chaco in Argentina. It uses its claws to rip open termite mounds before scooping up the termites with its long tongue.

force that will appear at the end of time. Martin LUTHER and other leaders of the REFORMATION applied it to the papacy.

anticline Arch-shaped fold in rock strata. Unless the formation has been overturned, the oldest rocks are found in the centre with younger rocks symmetrically on each side of it.

Anti-Corn Law League Organization formed (1839) in Manchester, England, to agitate for the removal of import duties on grain. It was led by the Radical members of Parliament, Richard COBDEN and John BRIGHT. By holding mass meetings, distributing pamphlets, and contesting elections it helped bring about the repeal of the CORN LAWS in 1846.

anticyclone Area of high atmospheric pressure around which air circulates. The direction of circulation is clockwise in the Northern Hemisphere and anticlockwise in the Southern Hemisphere. Anticyclones are associated with settled weather conditions. In middle latitudes, they bring periods of hot, dry weather in summer, and cold, often foggy, weather in winter.

Antietam, Battle of (September 17, 1862) Fought around Sharpsburg, Maryland, during the American CIVIL WAR. General George McClellan's Army of the Potomac made a series of assaults on the Confederates of General Robert E. LEE. Casualties were very heavy. McClellan's losses, c.12,000, were slightly greater, but Lee was forced to abandon his Maryland campaign and retreat to Virginia.

Anti-Federalist Party Organized in 1792 to oppose the proposed Constitution of the United States, mainly on the grounds that it gave the central government power. Anti-Federalist leaders included Richard Henry Lee and Patrick Henry of Virginia, and George Clinton of New York. Their support came mostly from the back country and agricultural sections.

antifreeze Substance dissolved in a liquid to lower its freezing point. Ethylene glycol (ethane diol, HOC_2H_4OH) is commonly used in car radiators.

antigen Substance or organism that induces the production of an ANTIBODY, part of the body's defence mechanism against disease. An antibody reacts specifically with the antigen. Antigen tissue proteins can cause problems in organ transplants by causing the body to reject the new organ.

Antigonus I (the One-eyed) (382?-301 BC) General of ALEXANDER THE GREAT. He became governor of Phrygia (333BC) and defeated challengers to gain control of Mesopotamia, Syria, and Asia Minor. In 306 BC he defeated his former ally, Ptolemy I, at Salamis. He was killed at Ipsus.

Antigua and Barbuda Caribbean islands in the LEEWARD ISLANDS group, part of the Lesser ANTILLES. The capital is St John's (on Antigua). **Antigua** is atypical of the Leeward Islands in that, despite its height – rising to 405m (1328ft) – it has no rivers or forests; **Barbuda**, in contrast, is a wooded, low coral atoll. Only 1400 people live on the game reserve island of Barbuda, where lobster fishing is the main occupation, and none on the rocky island of Redondo. Antigua and Barbuda were linked by Britain after 1860, gained internal self-government in 1967, and independence in 1981. The islands are dependent on tourism, though some attempts at diversification (notably Sea Island cotton) have been successful. Other industries: livestock rearing, market gardening, fishing. Area: 442sq km (171sq mi). Pop. (2000) 68,000. *See* WEST INDIES map

antihistamine Any one of certain drugs that counteracts or otherwise prevents the effects of histamine, a natural substance released by the body in response to injury, or more often as part of an allergic reaction. Histamine can produce symptoms such as sneezing, running nose, and sore eyes. *See also* HAY FEVER

Antilles Collective name for the two major island groups in the West Indies archipelago, between the Atlantic Ocean and the Caribbean Sea, stretching in an arc from Puerto Rico to the N coast of Venezuela. The Greater Antilles (larger of the two groups) includes CUBA, HISPANIOLA, JAMAICA, PUERTO RICO, and the CAYMAN ISLANDS. The Lesser Antilles comprises the British VIRGIN ISLANDS, the US VIRGIN ISLANDS, the LEEWARD ISLANDS, and WINDWARD ISLANDS, plus small islands off Venezeula. *See* WEST INDIES map

antimatter Matter made up of antiparticles, identical to ordinary particles in every way except the charge, SPIN and magnetic moment are reversed. Its existence is predicted by the QUANTUM MECHANICS. When an antiparticle, such as a positron (anti-electron), antiproton, or antineutron meets its respective particle, both are annihilated. The possibility exists that there are stars or galaxies composed entirely of antimatter. *See also* SUBATOMIC PARTICLES

antimony (symbol Sb) Toxic semimetallic element of group V of the PERIODIC TABLE. Stibnite (a sulphide) is its commonest ore. It is used in some alloys, particularly in hardening lead for batteries and type metal, and in semiconductors. The element has two allotropes: a silvery white metallic and an amorphous grey form. Properties: at.no. 51; r.a.m. 121.75; r.d. 6.68; m.p. 630.5°C (1166.9°F); b.p. 1750°C (3182°F); most common isotope Sb^{121} (57.25%).

Antioch *See* ANTAKYA

Antiochus III (242–187 BC) King of Syria (223–187BC), son of Seleucus II. After his defeat at Rafa (217BC) by Ptolemy IV, he invaded Egypt (212–202BC), seizing land from Ptolemy V with the help of Philip V of Macedon. He recaptured Palestine, Asia Minor, and the Thracian Cheronese. The Romans overwhelmed him at Thermopylae (191BC) and at Magnesia (190BC). The rebuilt SELEUCID Empire shrank when he gave up all possessions W of the Taurus. Seleucus IV succeeded him.

antiphon Alternate short verses or phrases (usually of a psalm or canticle) sung by two spatially separated halves of a choir (designated *decani* and *cantoris*). More generally, antiphon refers to a short piece of PLAINSONG during the recitation of divine office. The text of the antiphon usually serves to reinforce a psalm's Christian significance. The music and text of antiphons is contained in an antiphonal or antiphonary.

antipope Name given to rivals of legitimately elected popes, generally appointed by religious factions. The first was HIPPOLYTUS (217–35), a Trinitarian heretic and rival of Calixtus I. The most famous were the AVIGNON popes, who rivalled those of ROME during the GREAT SCHISM (1378–1417).

antiseptic Chemicals that destroy or stop the growth of many microorganisms. Antiseptics are weak germicides that can be used on the skin. The English surgeon Joseph Lister pioneered the use of antiseptics in 1867. Those commonly used include ALCOHOL, iodine, and hydrogen peroxide. *See also* ANTIBIOTIC

antitoxin ANTIBODY produced by the body in response to a TOXIN. It is specific in action and neutralizes the toxin. Antitoxin sera are used to treat and prevent bacterial diseases such as TETANUS and DIPHTHERIA.

antler Bony outgrowth on the skulls of male DEER (and female reindeer). In temperate-zone species, antlers begin to grow in early summer. They are soft, well supplied with blood, and covered with thin, velvety skin. Later, the blood recedes and the dried skin is rubbed off. Antlers then serve as sexual ornaments and weapons until they are shed the following spring. First-year males grow short spikes. More branches (points) are added each year until maturity is reached.

ant lion Larva of the neuropteran family Myrmeleontidea, found in most parts of the world. Carnivorous, with large, sickle-shaped jaws, it digs a pit in dry sand where it lies waiting for ants and other insects to fall in. *See also* LACEWING

Antofagasta Seaport and rail centre on the coast of N Chile and capital of Antofagasta province. Built in 1870 to provide port facilities for the nitrate and copper deposits in the ATACAMA DESERT, it has both ore refining and concentration plants. The Chuquicamata open-cast copper mine, 220km (135mi) to the NE, is the world's largest. Pop. (2000) 257,976.

Antonello da Messina (1430–79) Sicilian artist. A pioneer of oil painting in Italy, he spent much of his working life in Milan, Naples, Venice, and Rome. He probably learned the oil technique in Naples, a centre for Dutch artists. His work married Netherlandish taste for detail with Italian clarity. Apart from religious paintings, such as *Salvator Mundi* (1465) and *Ecce Homo* (1470), he produced some remarkable male portraits. His knowledge of oil glazes had a great influence on Venetian painters, notably Giovanni BELLINI.

Antonescu, Ion (1882–1946) Romanian general and fascist dictator. In 1938 he was imprisoned by King CAROL II for leading an unsuccessful fascist coup. In September 1940, in the face of German aggression, Carol appointed Antonescu premier. Carol was forced to abdicate in favour of his son

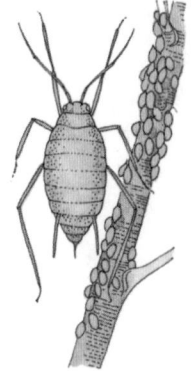

▲ **aphid** The greenfly (*Aphis* sp) occurs in enormous numbers, and the 2000 or species probably inflict more damage on crops than any other insect pest. Their remarkable power of reproduction is because the females are parthenogenetic, that is they can produce young without fertilization by a male.

MICHAEL, and Antonescu assumed dictatorial powers. Romania joined the Axis Powers and helped in the fated invasion of the Soviet Union. At home, Antonescu unleashed pogroms against Romanian Jews. The Red Army invasion of Romania led to his arrest. Antonescu was executed for war crimes.

Antony, Mark (82–30 BC) (Marcus Antonius) Roman general and statesman. Antony fought with distinction in Julius CAESAR's campaign in Gaul (54–50BC). In 49 BC Antony became tribune. Civil war broke out between POMPEY and Caesar, and after the decisive Battle of Pharsalus, Antony was made consul. After Caesar's assassination (44BC), Antony inspired the mob to drive the conspirators, BRUTUS and CASSIUS, from Rome. Octavian (later AUGUSTUS) emerged as Antony's main rival. Octavian and Brutus joined forces and Antony retreated to Transalpine Gaul. Antony sued for peace. Antony, Octavian and Lepidus formed the Second Triumverate, which divided up the ROMAN EMPIRE: Antony received Asia. He and CLEOPATRA, queen of Egypt, became lovers. CICERO, Antony's great rival, was killed. In 40 BC Antony married Octavian's sister Octavia, but Antony continued to live with Cleopatra in Alexandria and became isolated from Rome. In 32 BC the senate deprived Antony of his posts. He was defeated at the Battle of ACTIUM (31BC). Antony and Cleopatra committed suicide.

Antrim County in Northern Ireland, bounded N by the Atlantic Ocean and E by the North Channel. The capital is BELFAST. Other notable centres are Ballymena, Antrim (on the N shore of Lough Neagh), and the ferry port of Larne. Mainly a low basalt plateau, it is noted for the GIANT'S CAUSEWAY. It is chiefly an agricultural region, cereals and livestock being most important. Industries: linen and shipbuilding, concentrated in Belfast. Area: 3043sq km (1175sq mi). Pop. (2001 est.) 48,761.

Antwerp (Flemish *Antwerpen*, Fr. *Anvers*) City-port on the River Scheldt, capital of Antwerp province and Belgium's second-largest city (after BRUSSELS). Antwerp rose to prominence in the 15th century and became a centre for English mercantile interests. It was the site of Europe's first stock exchange (1460). Sites include the State University Centre (1965), the Royal Museum of Fine Arts (1880–90), and the 14th-century Cathedral of Notre Dame. Though heavily bombed during World War 2, it retains many attractive old, narrow streets and fine buildings. Industries: oil refining, food processing, tobacco, diamond cutting. Pop. (2000) 446,525.

Anubis In Egyptian mythology, a jackal-headed god. Son of Nephthys and OSIRIS, he conducted the souls of the dead to the underworld and presided over mummification and funerals. Anubis accompanied Osiris on his world conquest and buried him after his murder.

ANZAC (acronym for Australian and New Zealand Army Corps) Volunteer force of 30,000 men which spearheaded the disastrous GALLIPOLI CAMPAIGN in World War 1. Troops landed at GALLIPOLI on April 25, 1915. Anzac Day (April 25) is a public holiday in Australia and New Zealand. About 8500 Anzac troops were killed during World War 1.

ANZUS Pact (Australia-New Zealand-United States Treaty Organization) Military alliance organized by the US in 1951. ANZUS was set up in response to waning British power, the Korean War (1950–53), and alarm at increasing Soviet influence in the Pacific. The treaty stated that an attack on any one of the three countries would be considered as an attack on them all. It was replaced in 1954 by the SOUTHEAST ASIA TREATY ORGANIZATION (SEATO).

aorta Principal ARTERY in the body. Carrying freshly oxygenated blood, the aorta leaves the left ventricle of the heart and descends the length of the trunk, finally dividing to form the two main arteries that serve the legs. *See also* CIRCULATORY SYSTEM; HEART

Apache Athabascan-speaking tribe of Native North Americans that live in Arizona, New Mexico and Colorado. Divided culturally into Eastern Apache (including Mescalero and Kiowa) and Western Apache (including Coyotero and Tonto), they migrated from the NW with the NAVAJO in about AD 1,000 but separated to form a distinct tribal group. They retained their earlier nomadic raiding customs, which brought them into military conflict with Mexico and the USA during the 19th century. The total population is now c.11,000.

Apache Wars Series of battles in Arizona, New Mexico, Texas, and Oklahoma between the Apache and white settlers. One Apache chief, COCHISE, made peace in 1872, but GERONIMO fought on until 1886. Atrocities occurred on both sides.

apartheid Policy of racial segregation practised by the South African government from 1948 to 1990. Racial inequality and restricted rights for non-whites were institutionalized when the AFRIKANER-dominated National Party came to power in 1948. Officially a framework for "separate development" of races, in practice apartheid enforced white-minority rule. It was based on segregation in all aspects of life including residence, land ownership, and education. Non-whites, c.80% of the population, were also given separate political structures and quasi-autonomous homelands or bantustans. The system was underpinned by extensive repression, and measures such as pass laws which severely restricted the movements of non-whites. In 1990 the South African government, increasingly isolated internationally and beset by economic difficulties and domestic unrest, pledged to dismantle the system. Elections in April 1994 completed the transition to a nonracial democracy. *See also* AFRICAN NATIONAL CONGRESS (ANC)

apatosaur *See* BRONTOSAURUS

ape Term usually applied to the anthropoid apes (PRIMATES) that are the closest relatives of humans. There are three great apes – CHIMPANZEE, GORILLA and ORANG-UTAN – and one lesser, the GIBBON. An ape differs from a MONKEY in being larger, having no visible tail, and in possessing a more complex brain. Two monkeys are also called 'apes' – the BARBARY APE of N Africa and Gibraltar, and the black ape of Celebes.

Apennines (Appennino) Mountain range extending the length of Italy, a continuation of the Pennine Alps. The 'backbone' of Italy, it stretches c.1350km (840mi) from the Genoese Riviera to the tip of the country's 'toe'. Deforestation caused deep erosion and landslides. The Apennines are the location of numerous hydroelectric plants. Sheep and goats graze on its slopes. The highest point is Mount Corno, at 2914m (9560ft).

aperture In photography, a hole that allows light to pass through the lens onto the film. Modern cameras usually have a diaphragm aperture which works like the iris of a human eye. The photographer can widen or narrow the diaphragm according to a series of points on the lens dial called 'f-numbers' or 'f-stops'. The individual f-numbers represent the focal length of the lens divided by the diameter of the aperture. As the aperture narrows, it gives a longer depth of field.

aphasia Group of disorders of language arising from disease of or damage to the brain. In aphasia, a person has problems formulating or comprehending speech and difficulty in reading and writing. *See also* BRAIN DISORDERS

aphid (plant louse) Winged or wingless, soft-bodied insect found worldwide. It transmits virus diseases of plants when sucking plant juices. Females reproduce with or without mating, producing one to several generations annually. Common species are also known as blackfly and greenfly. Length: to 5mm (0.2in). Family Aphididae.

Aphrodite Greek goddess of love, beauty, and fruitfulness, identified by the Romans as VENUS. She was the daughter of ZEUS and Dione. Her husband was HEPHAESTUS (in Roman mythology, VULCAN). Among her many lovers were ARES, ADONIS (whose death left her broken-hearted) and Anchises, the father of AENEAS. Statues of her include the Venus de Milo (Paris) and Aphrodite of Cnidus (Rome).

Apocrypha Certain books included in the Bible as an appendix to the OLD TESTAMENT in the SEPTUAGINT and in Saint Jerome's Vulgate translation but not forming part of the Hebrew canon. Nine books are accepted as canonical by the Roman Catholic Church. They are: Tobit, Judith, Wisdom, Ecclesiasticus, Baruch (including the Letter to Jeremiah), 1 and 2 Maccabees, and parts of Esther and Daniel. Other books are found in Eastern Orthodox bibles and in the appendix to the Roman Catholic Old Testament. Anglican and Protestant translations of the Bible have, since the 16th century, placed books of the Apocrypha between the Old and New Testaments.

Apollinaire, Guillaume (1880–1918) (Wilhelm Apollinaris de Kostrowitzky) French experimental poet, essayist, and playwright. One of the most extraordinary artists of early 20th-century Paris, his *Peintres Cubistes* (1913) was the first attempt to define CUBISM. He also experimented with typography in his poetry collection *Calligrammes* (1918). His masterpiece was the wholly unpunctuated *Alcools* (1913), in which he relived the wild romances of his youth.

Apollo In Greek mythology, god of the Sun, archery, and prophecy; patron of musicians, poets, and physicians; founder of cities and giver of laws. He was the son of ZEUS and Leto, twin to ARTEMIS. In the Trojan War he sided with Troy, sending a plague against the Greeks.

Apollonius of Perga (*c.*262–190 BC) Greek mathematician and astronomer. He built on the foundations laid by EUCLID. In *Conics,* he showed that an ELLIPSE, a PARABOLA, and a HYPERBOLA can be obtained by taking plane sections at different angles through a cone. In astronomy, he described the motion of the planets in terms of epicycles, which remained the basis of the system used until the time of COPERNICUS.

Apollo program US SPACE EXPLORATION project to land men on the MOON. Initiated in May 1961 by President John Kennedy, it achieved its objective on July 20, 1969, when Neil ARMSTRONG set foot on the Moon. The project terminated with the successful **Apollo-Soyuz** linkup in space during July 1975. It placed more than 30 astronauts in space and 12 on the Moon.

Apostle Missionary sent out and empowered by divine authority to preach the gospel and heal the sick. Jesus commissioned his 12 original DISCIPLES to carry out the purpose of God for man's salvation (Mark 3, Matthew 10, Luke 6). The first qualification for being an apostle was to have "seen the Lord". The 12 disciples thus became the first and original Apostles. The term is also applied in the New Testament to St Paul. In modern usage, it is sometimes given to the leader of the first Christian mission to a country. For example, Saint Patrick is described as the "Apostle of Ireland".

Apostles' Creed Statement of Christian faith. The last section affirms the tradition of the "holy Catholic Church; the communion of saints; the forgiveness of sins; the resurrection of the body; and the life everlasting". The text evolved gradually, and its present form was fixed by the early 7th century. It is used widely in private and public worship in all the major Churches in the West. *See also* NICENE CREED

Appalachians Mountain system stretching 2570km (1600mi) from E Canada to Alabama, USA. A series of parallel ridges divided by valleys, the mountains restricted early European settlers to the E coast. The Appalachians includes the White Mountains, Green Mountains, Catskills, Alleghenies, Blue Ridge, and Cumberland Mountains; the highest point is Mount Mitchell in North Carolina at 2037m (6684ft). Rich in timber and coal, the ranges are home to many national parks.

appeasement Policy in which one government grants unilateral concessions to another to forestall a political, economic or military threat. The 1938 MUNICH AGREEMENT is considered a classic example of appeasement.

Appel, Karel (1921–2006) Dutch painter, sculptor and muralist. In the 1940s, he was one of several painters who reacted against the strict formalism of De STIJL, and invented a wildly expressionist language of his own, similar to ABSTRACT EXPRESSIONISM. His most powerful work, often portraying fantastic, aggressive and tragic figures, anticipated *Art Informel*. Appel is one of the most important post-1945 Dutch artists.

appendicitis Inflammation of the APPENDIX caused by obstruction and infection. Symptoms include severe pain in the central abdomen, nausea, and vomiting. Acute appendicitis is generally treated by surgery. A ruptured appendix can cause peritonitis and even death.

appendix In some mammals, finger-shaped organ, *c.*10cm (4in) long, located near the junction of the small and large intestines, usually in the lower right part of the abdomen. It has no known function in humans but can become inflamed or infected (APPENDICITIS).

apple Common name for the most widely cultivated fruit tree of temperate climates. Developed from a tree native to Europe and SW Asia, apple trees are propagated by budding or grafting. From the flowers, which require cross-pollination, the fleshy fruit grows in a variety of sizes, shapes and acidities; it

is generally roundish, 5–10cm (2–4in) in diameter, and a shade of yellow, green, or red. A mature tree may yield up to one cubic metre (30 bushels) of fruit in a single growing season. Europe produces 50–60% of the world's annual crop, and the USA accounts for 16–20%. Cider is made from fermented apple juice. Family Rosaceae; genus *Malus*.

apricot Tree cultivated throughout temperate regions, believed to have originated in China. The large, spreading tree with dark green leaves and white blossoms bears yellow or yellowish-orange edible fruit, with a large stone. Family Rosaceae; species *Prunus armeniaca.*

apsis (pl. apsides) Either of two points in an object's orbit. The closest point to the primary body is known as the **periapsis**, and the furthest the **apapsis**. The apsides of the Earth's orbit are its perihelion and aphelion; in the Moon's orbit they are its perigee and apogee. The line of apsides connect these points.

aptitude test Test used to measure potential for educational achievement. Some (such as 'intelligence tests') purport to measure general capacity. Others are designed to measure potential for a specific aptitude.

Aqaba, Gulf of Northeast arm of the Red Sea between the Sinai Peninsula and Saudi Arabia. AQABA and ELAT lie at the N end of the Gulf. The gulf has played an important role in ARAB-ISRAELI WARS. It was blockaded by the Arabs between 1949 and 1956, and again in 1967, when Israel held strategic points along the Strait of Tiran to guarantee open passage for ships. The Gulf has excellent coral beds and rich marine life.

aqualung *See* SCUBA DIVING

aquamarine *See* BERYL

Aquarius (water-bearer) Eleventh constellation of the zodiac, represented by a figure pouring water from a jar.

aquatint Method of engraving on metal plates. Aquatint was invented in the mid-18th century to imitate the effect of brush drawing or watercolour. It involves sprinkling a plate with fine grains of acid-resistant resin, fusing the resin to the metal (modern enamel spray makes this unnecessary), and letting acid bite around and through some of the grains. Printmakers can achieve extremely varied effects depending on the thickness of the resin and the immersion time. Aquatint enables line engraving or drawing on the resin with an acid-resistant varnish. GOYA and PICASSO were masters of the process.

aqueduct Artificial channel for conducting water from its source to its distribution point. While the ancient Romans were not the first to build these conduits, their aqueducts are the most famous because of their graceful architectural structures. One of their most extensive water systems, which served Rome itself, consisted of 11 aqueducts and took 500 years to complete. California has the world's largest conduit system: it carries water across a distance of more than 800km (500mi).

aquifer Rock, often sandstone or limestone, which is capable of both storing and transmitting water owing to its porosity and permeability. Much of the world's human population depends on aquifers for its water supply. They may be directly exploited by sinking wells.

Aquinas, Saint Thomas (1225–74) Italian theologian and philosopher, Doctor of the Church. St Thomas is the greatest figure of SCHOLASTICISM. His *Summa Theologiae* (*Theological Digest,* 1267–73) was declared (1879) by Pope Leo XIII to be the basis of official Catholic philosophy. Thomas joined the Dominican Order in 1244, and studied under the Aristotelian philosopher Albertus Magnus. In 1252 he became a professor of theology in Paris, and rapidly distinguished himself as a major authority on ARISTOTLE. Aquinas disagreed with the Averroist and Augustinian schools by arguing that faith and reason are two complementary realms; both are gifts of God, but reason is autonomous. His four hymns for the feast of Corpus Christi are among the greatest devotional pieces. Thomas was canonized in 1323. Thomist METAPHYSICS, a moderate form of REALISM, was the dominant world view until the mid-17th century. Other writings include *Commentary in the Sentences* (1254–56), and *Summa Contra Gentiles* (*Against the Errors of the Infidels,* 1259–64). His feast day is March 7.

Aquino, (Maria) Cory (Corazon) (1933–) Philippine stateswoman, president (1986–92), b. Maria Corazon. In

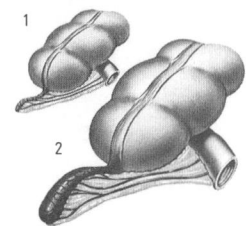

▲ **appendicitis** In appendicitis, the tissues lining the appendix become infected and inflamed, which causes the organ to swell (1) and its vascularization to increase (2). Prompt surgical removal is usually carried out to prevent the appendix bursting and causing peritonitis by the spread of its infection.

▲ **apple** Grown predominantly in temperate regions since prehistoric times, the apple is thought to be native to the Caucasus. China and the United States (particularly Washington state) are the world's largest producers. Its juice is fully fermented to make cider vinegar. The apple is often believed to be the forbidden fruit in the Garden of Eden.

INTERNET

Apollo program
▶ www.nasm.si.edu/ exhibitions/attm/attm.html
▶ nssdc.gsfc.nasa.gov/ planetary/lunar

Aquinas, St Thomas
▶ www.newadvent.org/ summa

1954 she married Benigno Aquino (1932–83), an outspoken opponent of the MARCOS regime. While he was in prison (1973–81), Cory campaigned tirelessly for his release. Benigno was assassinated by Marcos' agents. Cory claimed to have defeated Marcos in the 1986 presidential election and accused the government of vote-rigging. A bloodless 'people's revolution' forced Marcos into exile. Aquino's administration was beset by economic obstacles and she survived a coup attempt only with US help (1989). Aquino declined to run for re-election in 1992, but supported the campaign of her successor Fidel Ramos.

Arab Peoples of many nationalities, found predominantly in the Middle East and North Africa, who share a common heritage in the religion of ISLAM and their language (ARABIC). The patriarchal family is the basic social unit in a strongly traditional culture that has been little affected by external influences. Wealth from oil has brought rapid modernization in some Arab countries, but a great deal of economic inequality exists.

Arabia Peninsular region of sw Asia bordered by the Persian Gulf (E), the Arabian Sea (S), the Syrian Desert (N), and the Red Sea (W). The original homeland of the ARABS, it is the world's largest peninsula, consisting largely of a plateau of crystalline rock. It is mostly desert, including the vast, barren Rub al-Khali (Empty Quarter) in the s and the An Nafud in the N. Muslims unified Arabia in the 7th century, and Ottoman Turks dominated it after 1517. In 1916, Hussein ibn Ali led a successful revolt against the Turks and founded an independent state in the Hejaz region, but he was subsequently defeated by the Saud family, who founded SAUDI ARABIA in 1925. After World War 2 independent Arab states emerged, many of them exploiting the peninsula's vast reserves of oil. Area: c.2.6 million sq km (1 million sq mi).

Arabic Language originating in the Arabian Peninsula and now spoken in a variety of dialects throughout North Africa and the Middle East. It is a Semitic language, belonging to a major subfamily of AFRO-ASIATIC LANGUAGES. Classical Arabic is the language of the KORAN. It began to spread during the Islamic expansion of the 7th and 8th centuries. It is estimated that more than 100 million people are native speakers. Arabic uses a script written from right to left. Other languages, such as URDU, borrowed the script.

Arab-Israeli Wars (1948–49, 1956, 1967, 1973–74) Conflicts between Israel and the Arab states. After the creation of the state of Israel (May 14, 1948), troops from Egypt, Iraq, Lebanon, Syria, and Transjordan (now Jordan) invaded the new nation. Initial Arab gains were halted and armistices arranged at Rhodes (January-July 1949). UN security forces

upheld the truce until October 1956, when Israeli forces under Moshe DAYAN attacked the SINAI peninsula with support from France and Britain, alarmed at Egypt's nationalization of the SUEZ CANAL. International opinion forced a ceasefire in November. In 1967 guerrilla raids led to Israeli mobilization, and in the ensuing SIX-DAY WAR, Israel captured Sinai, the GOLAN HEIGHTS on the Syrian border, and the Old City of JERUSALEM. In the October War of 1973 (after intermittent hostilities), Egypt and Syria invaded on the Jewish holiday of YOM KIPPUR (October 6), Israel pushed back their advance after severe losses. Fighting lasted 18 days. The UN supervised subsequent disengagement agreements. In 1979 Israel signed a peace treaty with Egypt, but relations with other Arab states remained hostile. In 1982, Israeli forces invaded Lebanon under the pretext of destroying bases of the PALESTINE LIBERATION ORGANIZATION (PLO). In 1984, after widespread international criticism, Israeli forces withdrew to s Lebanon. After 1988 the PLO renounced terrorism and gained concessions, including limited autonomy in parts of the occupied territories. *See also* ISRAELI-PALESTINIAN ACCORD

Arab League Organization formed in 1945 to give a collective political voice to Arab nations. Its members include Syria, Lebanon, Iraq, Jordan, Sudan, Algeria, Kuwait, Saudi Arabia, Libya, Morocco, Tunisia, Yemen, Qatar, and the United Arab Emirates. It has often been divided, notably by the Egyptian peace treaty with Israel (1979) and over the GULF WAR (1991), and politically less effective than its founders hoped.

arachnid Arthropod of the class Arachnida, which includes the SPIDER, TICK, MITE, SCORPION, and HARVESTMAN. Arachnids have four pairs of jointed legs, two distinct body segments (cephalothorax and abdomen), and chelicerate jaws (consisting of clawed pincers). They lack antennae and wings.

Arafat, Yasir (1929–2004) Palestinian statesman, first president of Palestine (1996–2004), leader of the PALESTINE LIBERATION ORGANIZATION (PLO), b. Egypt. From a base in Lebanon, Arafat led the anti-ISRAEL guerrilla organization, Fatah. He sought the abolition of Israel and the creation of a secular Palestinian state. The INTIFADA in Israel's occupied territories (GAZA and the WEST BANK) prompted secret talks between Israel and the PLO. In 1993, Arafat and Yitzhak RABIN signed an agreement in which Arafat renounced terrorism and recognized the state of Israel. In return, Rabin recognized the PLO as the legitimate representative of Palestinians and agreed to a withdrawal of Israeli troops from parts of the occupied territories. In 1994 the Palestinian National Authority, headed by Arafat, assumed limited self-rule in the territories relinquished by the Israeli army. Arafat became president in 1996 elections. Following the failure of the Oslo peace process in 2000, Arafat was involved in a new Intifada. This lead to Israel blockading him into his West Bank headquarters in 2001. He was unable to leave until 2004, when he was allowed to travel to Paris for hospital treatment.

Aragón Region in NE Spain. In 1479 the Kingdom of Aragón became part of Spain, but retained its own government, currency and military forces until the early 18th century. It is now an autonomous region, comprising the provinces of Huesca, Teruel, and Zaragoza. It produces grapes, wheat, and sugar-beet. Industries: textiles, chemicals, iron ore, marble, and limestone. Area: 47,670sq km (18,500sq mi). Pop. (2001) 1,204,215.

Aral Sea (Aralskoye More) Inland sea in central Asia, sw Kazakhstan and NW Uzbekistan. Once the world's fourth largest inland body of water, it has no outlet, contains many small islands and is fed by the rivers Syrdarya in the NE and Amudarya (Oxus) in the s. It is generally shallow and only slightly saline. The diversion of the rivers for irrigation by the Soviet government led to its area shrinking by more than a third between 1960 and 1995. Many fishing communities were left stranded. Area (1993): 33,642sq km (12,989sq mi).

Aramaic Ancient Semitic language used in Palestine and other parts of the Middle East at the time of Christ. Originally the language of nomadic groups who established small states in MESOPOTAMIA during the late 2nd millennium BC it became the common spoken and written language of the Middle East under the Persian Empire until replaced by ARABIC. Parts of the

INTERNET

Arab League
▶ www.arableagueonline.org

▶ **Arafat** Following a 30-year struggle with Israel, Palestine Liberation Organization (PLO) leader Yasir Arafat returned to Jericho on July 1, 1994, as head of the Palestinian National Authority. He shared the 1994 Nobel Peace Prize with Shimon Peres. In 1996 Arafat became president of the Palestinian National Authority. His career remained controversial, with some Palestinians criticizing him for relinquishing too much to Israel, while some Israelis accused him of harbouring violent extremists.

Old Testament were originally written in Aramaic, and it was the language that Jesus spoke. Minor dialects still persist today in small Christian communities of the Near and Middle East.

Ararat, Mount (Agri Dagi) Two extinct volcanic peaks in the E extremity of Turkey. The highest peaks in Turkey, they are just N of where Noah's Ark is said to have come to rest (Genesis 8). There are two peaks: Great Ararat, 5165m (16,945ft, last eruption in 1840), and Little Ararat, 3925m (12,877ft).

Araucanian Independent language family of South American Indians who live in Chile and Argentina. A loose confederation of Araucanian-speaking sub-tribes (including the Picunche, Mapuche, and Huilliche) offered strong resistance to the Spanish invasion under Diego de Almagro in 1536. They drove the Spaniards back to the River Bio-Bio in 1598, and retained possession of interior portions of Chile to the present time. Their descendants prefer the name *Mapuche* (land people). The population has declined from c.1 million in the 16th century to c.300,000 today.

Arawak Largest and most widely spread Native South American language family, at one time spoken from the Caribbean to the GRAN CHACO. Today, some 40 Arawak tribes remain in Brazil.

arbor vitae Common name for five species of trees or shrubs of the genus *Thuja*, resinous, evergreen conifers of the cypress family native to North America and E Asia. They have thin outer bark, fibrous inner bark, and characteristically flattened branches. Family Cupressaceae.

arc Portion of a curve. For a circle, the length (*s*) of an arc is found either by $2\pi r \times \theta/360$ or the product of the radius (*r*) and the angle (θ), measured in RADIANS, that it subtends at the centre: that is, $s = r\theta$.

Arc de Triomphe TRIUMPHAL ARCH in the Place Charles de Gaulle, Paris. The Arc de Triomphe de l'Etoile is a generalized copy of the triumphal arches erected in ancient Rome to commemorate the victories of individual emperors. Napoleon I commissioned J.F. Chalgrin to design this version, completed in 1836. It is one of the city's most celebrated landmarks.

arch Upward-pointing or curving arrangement of masonry blocks or other load-bearing materials, also used in architectural decoration. The ancient Romans invented traditional masonry arches but later cultures extended their repertoire to include many different and elaborate shapes. The basic structure of a masonry arch consists of wedge-shaped blocks (*voussoirs*) placed on top of each other and a central keystone which holds them together at the top. Modern materials, such as steel and reinforced concrete, are strong and flexible enough to stand on their own and can also stretch across much wider areas. The form of an arch helps to date a building. *See also* VAULT

Archaean Sub-division of PRECAMBRIAN geological time. It ended c.2.5 billion years ago.

Archaebacteria Sub-kingdom of the kingdom PROKARY-OTE, which, on the basis of both RNA and DNA composition and biochemistry, differs significantly from other BACTERIA. They are thought to resemble ancient bacteria that first arose in extreme environments such as sulphur-rich, deep-sea vents. Archaebacteria have unique protein-like cell walls and cell membrane chemistry, and distinctive RIBOSOMES. They include methane-producing bacteria, which use simple organic compounds such as methanol and acetate as food, combining them with carbon dioxide and hydrogen gas from the air, and releasing methane as a by-product. The bacteria of hot springs and saline areas have a variety of ways of obtaining food and energy, including the use of minerals instead of organic compounds. They include both AEROBIC and ANAEROBIC bacteria. Some hot springs bacteria can tolerate temperatures up to 88°C (190°F) and acidities as low as pH 0.9. One species, *Thermoplasma*, may be related to the ancestor of the nucleus and cytoplasm of the more advanced EUKARYOTE cells. Some taxonomists consider archaebacteria to be so different from other living organisms that they constitute a higher grouping called a DOMAIN. *See also* TAXONOMY

archaeology Scientific study of former human life and activities through material remains such as artefacts and

◀ **archaeopteryx** The earliest known recognizable bird, archaeopteryx dates from the upper Jurassic period. The presence of wings and feathers define it as a bird, but the skeleton is quite reptilian. The wings, instead of being the specialized flying limbs of modern birds, were really elongated forelimbs, complete with claws. The tail resembles a lizard's and the skull had teeth. The small breastbone shows it was a poor flyer.

buildings. An archaeologist excavates and retrieves remains from the ground or seabed; recording and interpreting the circumstances in which objects were found, such as their level in the soil and association with other objects. This information can then be used to build a picture of the culture that produced the objects.

archaeopteryx First known bird. About the size of a crow and fully feathered, its fossilized skeleton is more like that of a reptile than a modern bird, and its beak had pronounced jaws with teeth. It was capable probably only of weak flight.

Archangel (Archangel'sk) City and major port on the North Dvina delta, NW Russia. Archangel was opened to European trade in c.1600 and prospered as Russia's only port until 1703. The monastery of Archangel Michael was built here (1685–99). The port received supplies from Allied convoys during World War 2. In the winter, icebreakers keep the large harbour clear, but the port remains ice-free for about six months – a crucial factor for commerce in N European Russia. Timber and wood products are the main exports. Industries: building, paper. Pop. (1994) 407,000.

archbishop Chief or highest-ranking bishop who is head of an ecclesiastical province or archdiocese. The main function of an archbishop is to supervise the work of BISHOPS.

archery Target sport that makes use of a bow and arrow or a crossbow and bolt. Commonly, archers use a longbow to shoot arrows at a target that consists of concentric scoring rings of five colours. The three other divisions of archery are field, flight and crossbow. The sport's world authority is the *Fédération Internationale de Tir à l'Arc (FITA)*, based in Milan, Italy. Archery returned to the Olympic Games in 1972.

Archimedes (287–212 BC) Greek mathematician and engineer. He developed a method for expressing large numbers and made outstanding discoveries about the determination of areas and volumes, which led to an accurate method of measuring π (pi). In his work *On Floating Bodies* he stated ARCHIMEDES' PRINCIPLE. He also invented the ARCHIMEDES' SCREW.

Archimedes' principle Observation by ARCHIMEDES that a body immersed in a FLUID is pushed up by a force equal to the weight of the displaced fluid. He supposedly formulated this principle after stepping into a bath and watching it overflow.

Archimedes' screw Machine used for raising water, thought to have been invented by Archimedes in the 3rd century BC. The most common form of the machine is a cylindrical pipe enclosing a helix, inclined at a 45° angle to the horizontal with its lower end in the water. When the machine rotates, water rises through the pipe.

Archipenko, Alexander (1887–1964) Russian-US modernist sculptor, one of the most radical innovators of his day. Largely self-taught, Archipenko helped to introduce the idea of making space an integral element of sculpture, as in the cubist *Walking Woman* (1912). He also developed a form of sculpture using light. He took part in the ARMORY SHOW (1913) and opened a sculpture school in New York in the late 1930s. His work influenced GABO and Henry MOORE.

architecture Art and science of designing permanent buildings for human use. Architecture can express aesthetic ideas from the most restrained UTILITARIANISM to extravagantly ornate decoration. The difference between 'architecture' and 'building' is a subject that has exercised theorists since the discipline was invented. In reality, architecture is usually a compromise between aesthetic creation and the demands of practicality. There are many different areas of architecture and, apart from the stylistic and historical periods (*see* individual articles), it comes under such broad categories as civic, commercial, religious, recreational, and domestic. In the 20th century, traditional barriers between artistic disciplines have gradually dissolved, so that it is possible to see architecture as a type of sculpture. Key figures in the development of western architectural theory include VITRUVIUS, who believed that architecture was merely a form of applied mathematics, and ALBERTI whose pioneering treatise *De re Aedificatoria* (1485) introduced the idea that architecture was an art form in it's own right. After the 18th century, European architects tended to regard 'building' as a cheap substitute for their profession and something that engineers carried out. Architects began to swing back in the other direction with the arrival of the ARTS AND CRAFTS MOVEMENT, and the introduction of efficient, mass-produced materials. The 20th-century modernists, such as Walter GROPIUS, believed that the form of a building should follow its function.

INTERNET

Argentina
▶ www.turismo.gov.ar
▶ arg.org.nz

ARGENTINA

The Argentine Republic is the largest of South America's Spanish-speaking countries. Its w boundary lies in the Andes, with basins, ridges and peaks of more than 6,000m [19,685ft] in the north. s of latitude 27°S, the ridges merge into a single cordillera, with ACONCAGUA, at 6,962m [22,849ft], the tallest mountain in the w hemisphere.

In the s, the Andes are lower, with glaciers and volcanoes. E Argentina is a series of alluvial plains, from the Andean foothills to the sea. The GRAN CHACO in the N slopes down to the PARANÁ River, from the high desert of the Andean foothills to lowland swamp forest. Between the Paraná and Uruguay rivers is Mesopotamia, a fertile region. Further s are the damp and fertile pampa grasslands. Thereafter, the pampa gives way to the dry, windswept plateaux of PATAGONIA towards Tierra del Fuego.

CLIMATE
The climate varies from subtropical in the N to temperate in the s. Rainfall is abundant in the NE, but is lower to the w and s. Patagonia is a dry region, crossed by rivers that rise in the Andes mountains.

HISTORY
Spanish explorers first reached the coast in 1516, landing on the shores of the Rio de la Plata. They were soon followed by others in search of gold and silver Spanish rule lasted until revolutionaries, led by General Belgrano, took power in 1810. In 1816 Argentina declared independence. A long civil war ensued between centralizers and federalists.

Following General Juan Manuel de Rosas' dictatorship (1835–52), Argentina adopted a federal constitution (1853). Early prosperity, based on stock raising and farming combined with stable government, was boosted from 1870 by a massive influx of European immigrants, particularly Italians and Spaniards, for whom Argentina was a viable alternative to the United States. They settled lands recently cleared of Native Americans, often organised by huge land companies.

Development of a good railway network to the ports, plus steamship services to Europe and, from 1877, refrigerated vessels, helped to create the strong meat, wool and wheat economy that carried Argentina into the 20th century.The presidency of General Julio Roca (1880–86, 1898–1904) saw the triumph of federalism and the development of Argentina's trading economy, and until the Great Depression in the 1930s Argentina was one of the world's more prosperous nations.

The collapse in the economy during the Great Depression led to a military coup in 1930. This started a long period of military intervention in the politics of the country. For much of World War 2, Argentina was a pro-Axis 'neutral' power, but in 1944 Ramón Castillo was overthrown in a military coup led by Juan PERÓN and Argentina switched to the Allies. With the aid of his wife Eva, Perón established a popular dictatorship. In 1955, a military junta overthrew Perón. Political instability dominated the 1960s, with the military seeking to dampen Perónist support. In 1973 an ailing Perón returned from exile to head a civilian government. He was succeeded in 1974 by his third wife, Isabel Martinez Perón, who was in turn deposed by a military coup in 1976.

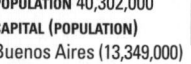

AREA 2,780,400sq km [1,073,512sq mi]
POPULATION 40,302,000
CAPITAL (POPULATION) Buenos Aires (13,349,000)
GOVERNMENT Federal republic
ETHNIC GROUPS European 97%, Mestizo, Amerindian
LANGUAGES Spanish (official)
RELIGIONS Roman Catholic 92%, Protestant 2%, Jewish 2%, others
CURRENCY Peso = 10,000 australs

POLITICS
From 1976, the 'dirty war' saw the torture, wrongful imprisonment and murder of up to 15,000 people by the military, and 2 million people fled the country. In 1982 the government, blamed for the poor state of the economy, launched an invasion of the FALKLAND ISLANDS (Islas Malvinas) which they had claimed since 1820. Britain regained the islands by sending an expeditionary force. After losing the conflict, Argentina's President Galtieri resigned. Constitutional government was restored in 1983, though the army remained influential.

In 1999, Argentina and Britain signed an agreement concerning the Falkland Islands, the first since 1982. Argentines were allowed to visit the Falkland Islands and erect a memorial to their war dead, and Argentina agreed to allow flights from the Falkland Islands to Chile.

In December 2001, violent protests broke out when the peso devalued and the government introduced severe austerity measures aimed at restoring the failing economy. 2003 and 2004 saw a slow return to economic growth. In 2007, during a dispute with the UK over oil rights, Argentina renewed its claims to the Falkland Islands.

ECONOMY
Argentina is an 'upper-middle-income' developing country and one of the richest in South America in terms of natural resources, especially its fertile farmland. The economic base is mainly agricultural. The chief products are beef, maize and wheat. Sheep are raised in drier parts of the country, while other crops include citrus fruits, cotton, flax, grapes, potatoes, sorghum, sugar cane, sunflower seeds and tea.

Oilfields in Patagonia and the Piedmont make Argentina almost self-sufficient in oil and natural gas. These are a valuable export.

Arctic Vast region of icy seas and cold lands around the NORTH POLE, often defined as extending from the Pole to the Arctic Circle. In areas N of latitude 66° 30'N, the sun does not set during the height of summer, nor rise during the depths of winter. Many place the s limit of the Arctic proper at the northern boundary of forest growth, others make the limit the summer isotherm of 18°C (50°F). The more southerly areas are frequently referred to as the subarctic. At the centre of the Arctic is the ARCTIC OCEAN. In the region around the North Pole, the waters of the Arctic are permanently covered with sheet ice or a floating mass of ice debris called the ice pack, but some parts of the ocean are frozen only in winter. When the ice starts to melt in spring, it breaks into floes and drifting pack ice. Icebergs have their origins in freshwater glaciers flowing into the ocean from the surrounding lands. **Lands and climate** Bordering the Arctic Ocean are the most northerly lands of Asia, Europe, and North America. The greater part of the huge frozen island of GREENLAND lies N of the Arctic Circle. Five-sixths of Greenland's surface is always hidden by a thick ice-cap. Arctic lands generally have a summer without ice and snow. Most of the Arctic tundra is flat and marshy in summer but the subsoil is PERMAFROST. For most of the year Arctic temperatures are below freezing point. In spring the sun appears, and some Arctic lands have sunshine every day from March to September. **People** Despite the severity of the climate and the restricted food resources, many peoples live in the Arctic. The most scattered are the *c.*60,000 ESKIMOS spread across polar North America, Greenland, and NE Siberia. Several culturally separate groups of people live in N Siberia. In the European part of Russia there are the Zyryans, and in LAPLAND the LAPPS. Most of these peoples follow ancient, traditional patterns of life, but the discovery of great mineral wealth, especially in Alaska and Russia, brought huge change. **History** The region was first explored by Norsemen as early as the 9th century. The search for the NORTHWEST PASSAGE gave impetus to further explorations in the 16th and 17th centuries, though a route was not found until the early 1900s. In 1909 the US explorer Robert PEARY reached the North Pole, and in 1959 the first crossing of the Arctic Ocean under the polar ice-cap was completed.

Arctic Ocean Ocean N of the Arctic Circle, between North America and Eurasia. Almost totally landlocked and the Earth's smallest ocean, it is bordered by Greenland, Canada, Alaska, Russia, and Norway. Connected to the Pacific Ocean by the Bering Strait, and to the Atlantic Ocean by the Davis Strait and Greenland Sea, it includes the Barents, Beaufort, Chukchi, Greenland, and Norwegian seas. There is animal life (plankton) in all Arctic water. Polar bears, seals, and gulls live up to *c.*88°N. Area: 14 million sq km (5.4 million sq mi).

Arctic tern Sea bird whose migrations are the longest of any bird – from summer breeding areas in the far N to wintering areas in Antarctica, a round trip of *c.*35,500km (22,000mi). It has grey, black, and white feathers and a reddish bill and feet. It nests in colonies and lays one to four eggs in a sandy scrape nest. Length: 38cm (15in). Species *Sterna paradisaea*.

Ardashir I (d.AD 240) King of Persia (*c.*224–41). Ardashir overthrew the last Parthian king, Artabanus V, and reunited Persia. He founded the Sassanian empire, establishing its capital at Ctesiphon. He established ZOROASTRIANISM as the state religion. Ardashir strengthened Persia by going to war against the Roman Emperor Alexander Severus. He was succeeded by Shapur I. *See also* SASSANID

Ardennes Sparsely populated wooded plateau in SE Belgium, N Luxembourg, and the Ardennes department of N France. The capital is Charleville-Mézières. It was the scene of heavy fighting in both World Wars; notably in the Battle of the Bulge (1944). In the well-preserved forest regions wild game is abundant and cleared areas support arable and dairy farming.

area Two-dimensional measurement of a plane figure or body (such as this page) given in square units, such as cm^2 or m^2. The area of a rectangle of sides a and b is ab; the areas of triangles and other polygons can be determined using TRIGONOMETRY. Areas of curved figures and surfaces can be determined by integral CALCULUS.

Arequipa Second-largest city of Peru and capital of Arequipa department. It was established in 1540 by Francisco Pizarro on the site of an INCA settlement. Located at the foot of the extinct volcano El Misti (5822m/19,100ft), it is known as the 'White City' because many of its buildings are made of white volcanic stone. A regional trade centre, its main industries are wool processing, textiles and leather. Pop. (2000) 762,000.

Ares In Greek mythology, the god of war, identified with the Roman MARS. Son of Zeus and HERA and lover of APHRODITE. In the Trojan War he sided with the Trojans. Among his offspring was the cruel Cycnus, who was slain by Heracles.

Argentina Republic in s South America. *See* country feature

argon (symbol Ar) Monatomic (single-atom), colourless and odourless gaseous element that is the most abundant NOBLE GAS (inert gas). English physicist Lord Rayleigh and Scottish chemist Sir William Ramsay discovered argon in 1894. It makes up 0.93% of the atmosphere by volume. Obtained commercially by the fractionation of liquid air, it is used in electric light bulbs, fluorescent tubes, argon lasers, arc welding, and semiconductor production. The element has no known true compounds. Properties: at.no. 18; r.a.m. 39.948; r.d. 0.0017837g cm^3; m.p. −189.4 °C (−308.9°F); b.p. −185.9°C (−302.6°F).

Argonauts In Greek legend, 50 heroes, including HERACLES, ORPHEUS, and CASTOR AND POLLUX, who sailed the ship *Argo* to Colchis, a kingdom to the E of the Black Sea, in search of the Golden Fleece. Their leader was JASON, husband of MEDEA.

aria Solo song with instrumental accompaniment, or a lyrical instrumental piece. An important element of operas, cantatas and oratorios, the aria form originated in the 17th century.

Ariadne In Greek mythology, Cretan princess (daughter of MINOS) who fell in love with THESEUS but was abandoned by him after saving him from the Minotaur. She was consoled by the god DIONYSUS whom she later married.

Arianism Theological school based on the teachings of Arius (*c.*AD 250–336), considered heretical by orthodox Christianity. Arius taught that Christ was a created being, and that the Son, though divine, was neither equal nor co-eternal with the Father. Arianism was condemned by the first Council of NICAEA (325).

Aries (Ram) First constellation of the zodiac. In mythology, it represents the lamb with the golden fleece.

Aristarchus of Samos (active *c.*310–*c.*230 BC) Greek mathematician and astronomer. He calculated the distances of the Sun and Moon from Earth, as well as their sizes. Though his method was sound, the results were inaccurate. He was the first to propose that the Sun is the centre of the Universe (heliocentric theory); the idea was not taken up because it did not seem to make the calculation of planetary positions any easier.

Aristophanes (*c.*448–*c.*380 BC) Greek writer of comedies. Of his more than 40 plays, only 11 survive, the only extant comedies from the period. All follow the same basic plan: caricatures of contemporary Athenians in absurd situations. Graceful, choral lyrics frame caustic personal attacks. A conservative, Aristophanes parodied EURIPIDES' innovations in drama, and satirized the philosophical radicalism of SOCRATES and Athens' expansionist policies. The importance of the chorus in the early works is reflected in titles such as *The Wasps* (422BC), *The Birds* (414BC), and *The Frogs* (405BC). Other notable plays include *The Clouds* (423BC) and *Lysistrata* (411BC).

Aristotle (384–322 BC) Greek philosopher, founder of the science of LOGIC and one of the greatest figures in Western philosophy, b. Macedonia. Aristotle studied (367–347BC) under PLATO at the ACADEMY in Athens. After Plato's death he tutored the young ALEXANDER THE GREAT, before founding the Lyceum (335BC). Anti-Macedonian disturbances forced Aristotle to flee (323BC) to Chalcis on the island of Euboea, where he died. In direct opposition to Plato's IDEALISM, Aristotle's METAPHYSICS is based on the principle that all knowledge proceeds directly from observation of the particular. Aristotle argued that a particular object can only be explained through an understanding of causality. He outlined four causes: the **material** cause (an object's substance); **formal** cause (design); **efficient** cause (maker) and the **final** cause (function). For Aristotle this final cause was the primary one. Form was inherent in matter. His ethical philosophy

ARIZONA
Statehood
February 14, 1912
Nickname
The Grand Canyon State
State bird
Cactus wren
State flower
Saguaro (giant cactus)
State tree
Paloverde
State motto
God enriches

stressed the exercise of rationality in political and intellectual life. Aristotle's writings cover nearly every branch of human knowledge, from statecraft to astronomy. His principal works are the *Organon* (six treatises on logic and SYLLOGISM); *Politics* (the conduct of the state); *Poetics* (analysis of poetry and TRAGEDY) and *Rhetoric*. After the decline of the Roman Empire, Aristotle was forgotten by the West. But he had a profound effect on the development of Islamic philosophy, and it was through Arab scholarship that his thought filtered into medieval Christian SCHOLASTICISM and in particular the work of Saint Thomas AQUINAS.

arithmetic Calculations and reckoning using numbers and operations such as addition, subtraction, multiplication and division. The study of arithmetic traditionally involves procedures for operations such as long division and extractiing square roots. The procedures of arithmetic were put on a formal axiomatic basis (see AXIOM) by Guiseppe Peano in the late 19th century. Using such statements (including that there is a unique natural number, 1) one can give formal definitions of the set of natural numbers and the arithmetical operations.

arithmetic progression Sequence of numbers in which each term is produced by adding a constant term (the common difference d) to the preceding one. It has the form $a, a + d, a + 2d$, and so on. An example is the sequence 1, 3, 5, ... The sum of such a progression, $a + (a + d) + (a + 2d) + ...$ is an arithmetic series. For n terms, it has a value $\frac{1}{2}n [2a + 0.5(n - 1) d]$.

Arizona State in the SW USA, bordering on Mexico; the capital is PHOENIX, other cities include Tucson and Mesa. After the end of the MEXICAN WAR (1848), Mexico ceded most of the present state to the USA, and it became the 48th state of the Union in 1912. The Colorado Plateau occupies the N part of the state, and is cut by many steep canyons, notably the GRAND CANYON, through which the COLORADO RIVER flows. Arizona's mineral resources, grazing and farmland have long been mainstays of the economy. Mining and agriculture are still important, but since the 1950s manufacturing has been the most profitable sector. The state has many scenic attractions (including the Petrified Forest, Fort Apache, and the reconstructed London Bridge at Lake Havasu). Tourism is now a major source of income. It also has the largest Native American population of any US state (255,879 in 2000), with Indian reservations comprising 28% of the land area. Between 1950 and 1970 Arizona's population more than doubled; in

---

ARMENIA

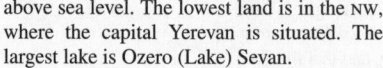

The Republic of Armenia is a landlocked country in SW Asia, mostly consisting of a rugged plateau, criss-crossed by long faults. Movements along the faults cause earth tremors and occasionally major earthquakes. Armenia's highest point is Mount Aragats, at 4,090m [13,149ft] above sea level. The lowest land is in the NW, where the capital Yerevan is situated. The largest lake is Ozero (Lake) Sevan.

The vegetation in Armenia ranges from semi-desert to grassy steppe, forest, mountain pastures and treeless tundra at the highest levels. Oak forests are found in the SE, with beech being the most common tree in the forests of the NE. Originally it was a much larger kingdom centred on Mount Ararat, incorporating present-day NE Turkey and parts of NW Iran.

CLIMATE

The height of the land, which averages 1,500m [4,920ft] gives rise to severe winters and cool summers. The highest peaks are snow-capped, but the total yearly rainfall is low, at between and 200 and 800mm [8 and 31in].

HISTORY

Armenia was an advanced ancient kingdom, considered to be one of the original sites of iron and bronze smelting. A nation was established in the 6th century BC, and Alexander the Great expelled the Persians in 330 BC.

In 69 BC, Armenia was incorporated into the ROMAN EMPIRE. In AD 303, Armenia became the first country to adopt Christianity as its state religion. From 886 to 1046 Armenia was an independent kingdom. From the 11th to 15th centuries, the Mongols were the greatest power in the region. By the 16th century, Armenia was controlled by the Ottoman Empire. Despite religious discrimination, the Armenians generally prospered under Turkish rule. E Armenia was the battleground between the rival Ottoman and Persian Empires. In 1828 Russia acquired Persian Armenia, and – drawn by promises of religious tolerance – many Armenians moved into the Russian-controlled area. In Turkish Armenia, British promises of protection encouraged nationalist movements. The Turkish response was uncompromising, killing c.200,000 Armenians in 1896 alone. In the Russian sector, a process of Russification was enforced. During World War 1, Armenia was the battleground for the Turkish and Russian armies. Armenians were accused of aiding the Russians, and Turkish atrocities intensified. More than 600,000 Armenians were killed by Turkish troops, and 1.75 million were deported to Syria and Palestine. In 1918, Russian Armenia became the Armenian Autonomous Republic, the w part remained part of Turkey, and the NW became part of Iran. In 1920, Armenia became a Communist republic. In 1922, Armenia, Azerbaijan and Georgia federated to form the Transcaucasian Soviet Socialist Republic (one of the four original republics in the Soviet Union), but in 1936 the three territories divided into separate Soviet Socialist Republics. Earthquakes in 1984 and 1988 killed more than 80,000 people and destroyed many cities. In 1990 Armenia voted to break from the Soviet

AREA 29,800sq km [11,506sq mi]
POPULATION 2,971,000
CAPITAL (POPULATION) Yerevan (1,066,000)
GOVERNMENT Multiparty republic
ETHNIC GROUPS Armenian 93%, Russian 2%, Azeri 1%, others (mostly Kurds) 4%
LANGUAGES Armenian (official)
RELIGIONS Armenian Apostolic 94%
CURRENCY Dram = 100 couma

Union, and in 1991 joined the COMMONWEALTH OF INDEPENDENT STATES (CIS).

POLITICS

Armenia has long disputed the status of NAGORNO-KARABAKH, an Armenian-majority enclave in Azerbaijan. In 1992, Armenia occupied the territory between its E border and Nagorno-Karabakh. A ceasefire in 1994 left Armenia in control of about 20% of Azerbaijan's land area. Azerbaijan and its ally Turkey blockaded the borders, making Armenia dependent on Iran and Georgia for access to the outside world.

In 1998 Robert Kocharian, former leader of Nagorno-Karabakh, became president. Elections are frequently held, most recently in 2007, but are marked by alleged fraud by the ruling party.

ECONOMY

Earthquakes and the conflict with Azerbaijan in the early 1990s have damaged the economy, and it is rated lower-middle-income' by the World Bank. Since 1992 the government has encouraged free enterprise.

Poverty, corruption and political unrest led 20% of the population to emigrate in the 1990s. The country is highly industrial, with production dominated by mining and chemicals. Copper is the chief metal, but gold, lead and zinc are also mined. Agriculture is the second-largest sector, with cotton, tobacco, fruit and rice the main products. Disputes with Russia over fuel subsidies have raised energy costs.

the 1970s its annual growth rate was more than 35%, and it grew a further 41% between 1980 and 1982. Area: 295,025sq km (113,909sq mi). Pop. (2000) 5,130,632.

ark According to Genesis 6, the floating house Noah was ordered to build and live in with his family and one pair of each living creature during the flood. As the flood waters receded, it came to rest on a mountain top, believed to be Mount ARARAT.

Arkansas State in s central USA, bounded on the E by the Mississippi River. The capital (and only large city) is LITTLE ROCK. It was acquired by the LOUISIANA PURCHASE (1803) and was admitted to the Union as the 25th state in 1836. Arkansas was one of the 11 Confederate states during the American Civil War, and noted for its resistance to black equality in the 1960s. Former US President Bill CLINTON was governor of Arkansas (1978–80, 1983–92). In the E and s the land is low, providing excellent farmland for cotton, rice, and soya beans. The principal waterway is the ARKANSAS river which (like all the state's rivers) drains into the Mississippi. The NW of the state, including part of the Ozarks, is higher land. Little Rock is located on the Arkansas, where the hills meet the plains. Forests are extensive and economically important. Bauxite processing, timber, and chemicals are the main industries. Area: 137,539sq km (53,104sq mi). Pop. (2000) 2,673,400.

Arkansas River with its source high up in the Rockies of central Colorado, USA, and flowing 2335km (1450mi) to the Mississippi River in SE Arkansas. Fourth-longest river in the US, it flows E through Kansas, SE across the NE corner of Oklahoma, and then SE to Arkansas.

Ark of the Covenant In Jewish tradition, a gold-covered chest of acacia that contained the stone tablets on which the TEN COMMANDMENTS were inscribed. It rested in the Holy of Holies within the tabernacle. Only the high priest could look upon the Ark and no one could touch it. In Palestine, the Israelites set up a permanent resting place for the ark in Shiloh. In the 10th century BC the Ark was moved to the temple built by King SOLOMON in Jerusalem. After the destruction of Solomon's temple in 586 BC there is no further record of the Ark's location. In today's synagogues, the Ark of the Covenant is a closet or recess in which the sacred scrolls of the congregation are kept.

Arkwright, Sir Richard (1732–92) British inventor and industrialist. He introduced powered machinery to the textile industry with his water-driven frame for spinning; he started work on the machine in 1764 and patented his invention in 1769. He opened textile factories in Nottingham.

Arlington County in N Virginia, across the Potomac River from Washington, D.C. Since 1943 it has been the location of the PENTAGON. The 200–ha (500–acre) Arlington National Cemetery was built (1864) on the former estate of Robert E. LEE. It contains the Tomb of the Unknown Soldier, a memorial amphitheatre and the graves of many servicemen and prominent Americans. Originally a part of the District of Columbia, it became a county of Virginia in 1847. Pop. (2000) 189,453.

Armada, Spanish (1588) Fleet launched by the Catholic Philip II of Spain against England to overthrow the Protestant Elizabeth I. English support for the rebels in the Spanish Netherlands and pirate attacks on Spanish possessions convinced Philip that England must be conquered. The 130 ships of the Armada were supposed to collect troops from the Netherlands but, hampered by English attacks and poor planning, it proved impossible. After an indecisive engagement with the English off Gravelines, the Spanish ships ran out of ammunition. Their commander, the Duke of Medina Sidonia, withdrew around N Scotland, suffering severe losses through shipwreck and disease. Though a blow to Spanish prestige, the defeat had little effect on the balance of naval power.

armadillo Nocturnal, burrowing mammal found from Texas to Argentina, noted for the armour of bony plates that protect its back and sides. When attacked, some species roll into a defensive ball. It eats insects, carrion and plants. Length: 130–150cm (50–59in). Family Dasypodidae.

Armagh City and county in SE Northern Ireland, between Lough Neagh and the border with the Republic. Armagh became an ecclesiastical centre in the 5th century (founded, in legend, by St Patrick) and is now the seat of Roman Catholic and Protestant archbishops. It was settled by Protestants in the 16th century. The county is low-lying in the N and hilly in the s. Much of the land is used for farming and the town acts as a market for agricultural produce. Lurgan and Portadown are centres for textiles and various light industries. Area: 676sq km (261sq mi). Pop. (county, 2001) 54,263; (town, 1991) 14,625.

Armenia *see* country feature.

Arminius, Jacobus (1560–1609) Dutch theologian whose system of beliefs, especially concerning salvation, became widespread and was later known as Arminianism. He rejected the notion of PREDESTINATION developed by John CALVIN, in favour of a more liberal concept of conditional election and universal redemption. Arminianism, though at first bitterly rejected, finally achieved official recognition in the Netherlands in 1795. It was a major influence on METHODISM.

Armistice Day Day of remembrance for the dead of the two world wars, held on November 11, the day World War 1 ended in 1918. In the USA, it was renamed Veterans' Day in 1954 in honour of the dead in all wars.

Armory Show (1913) Landmark exhibition of contemporary American and European art held in New York, USA. The European section of the exhibition caused great controversy. It looked back to IMPRESSIONISM, tracing the history of modernism through NEO-IMPRESSIONISM and POST-IMPRESSIONISM with examples of work by GAUGUIN, VAN GOGH, and the Nabis, but came right up to date with examples of CUBISM, ORPHISM, and DADA and was the first time a large US audience encountered modernist works. Many were scandalized by them, but the exhibition succeeded in bringing the revolution in European art to the US. It travelled successfully to Chicago and Boston, attracting *c.*500,000 visitors.

arms control Activity undertaken by powerful nations to prevent mutual destruction in warfare, especially with nuclear weapons. The nations attempt to maintain a balance of power by regulating each other's stockpile of weapons. *See also* DISARMAMENT; STRATEGIC ARMS LIMITATION TALKS (SALT)

arms race Rivalry between states or blocs of states to achieve supremacy in military strength. The first modern instance was the race between Germany and Britain to build up their navies before World War 1. The term refers principally to the race in nuclear weapons between the Soviet Union in the COLD WAR, though arms races also occur at regional levels.

Armstrong, (Daniel) Louis (1900–71) US jazz trumpeter, singer and bandleader, nicknamed 'Satchmo'. Armstrong was one of the most distinctive sounds in 20th-century music. He learned to play in New Orleans, and in 1922 joined the King Oliver band. The Hot Fives and Hot Sevens recordings (1925–29) are some of the most influential in the history of jazz. In the 1930s he became a successful bandleader, his deep, bluesy voice featured on tunes like "Mack the Knife". He also appeared in films such as *Pennies from Heaven* (1936), *New Orleans* (1947), and *High Society* (1956).

Armstrong, Neil Alden (1930–) US astronaut. He was chosen as a NASA astronaut in 1962, and was the command pilot for the Gemini 8 orbital flight in 1966. On July 20, 1969, he became the first man to walk on the Moon, remarking that it was "one small step for man, one giant leap for mankind".

army Body of men organized to fight on land. Armies are probably as old as urban civilisation, and the first written evidence of an army comes from third millennium BC Sumer.

◀ **Armstrong, Neil**
Armstrong (second from the left), commander of Apollo 11, will forever be remembered as the first man to walk on the Moon (July 20, 1969). After retiring as an astronaut, he remained an influential figure in the world of aerospace and aeronautics.

▲ **arrowroot** The island of St Vincent in the West Indies is the main source of arrowroot (*Maranta arundinacea*). It has rhizomes that produce a light starch used in food preparation.

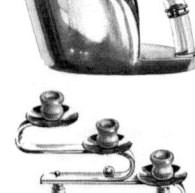

▲ **art deco** Examples of art deco-style goods, fashionable during the 1920s and 1930s.

Early armies were rarely composed of professional soldiers, instead being recruited primarily by short-term CONSCRIPTION, and warfare between ancient states was often formally structured by unspoken social conventions. From the BRONZE AGE onwards armies began to need different types of soldier, with different arms and training, to be effective. In the IRON AGE this specialisation continued as technology advanced, and armies became increasingly professional. The campaigns of ALEXANDER THE GREAT and of the ROMAN EMPIRE relied on full-time professional soldiers and broke with earlier social structures of war, but earlier conventions returned after each fell. At the start of the MIDDLE AGES the FEUDAL SYSTEM provided effective but inflexible armies, but as Europe became richer these were supplemented and eventually replaced by hired professional mercenaries. By the RENAISSANCE paid mercenaries predominated, but began to acquire a reputation for unreliability. The rise of GUNPOWDER weapons, particularly the MUSKET, allowed 17th century states to replace mercenary forces with permanent standing armies – the ancestors of all modern European forces. The IMPERIALISM of European powers overwhelmed other military cultures and spread European military technology and organisation to the entire world. The INDUSTRIAL REVOLUTION changed the nature of war, as mass production allowed ever larger armies to be equipped, and from the 19th century mass CONSCRIPTION was needed to supplement professional armies. Armies were slow to adjust to the impact of changed technology, leading to terrible casualties in the CRIMEAN WAR, American CIVIL WAR and ultimately WORLD WAR I. The deadlock of industrial warfare was only broken at the end of that war by the invention of the TANK and air power. WORLD WAR 2 saw highly mechanized and mobile armies whose logistics of supply and support demanded an integration of the land, sea and air forces.

Army, British Ground service of the UK armed forces. Regular Army personnel number *c*.110,000, including *c*.7200 women and *c*.30,000 personnel overseas. Since 1945 it has formed part of NORTH ATLANTIC TREATY ORGANIZATION (NATO) forces and maintained overseas garrisons in such areas as the Falklands, Cyprus and Gibraltar. The monarch is the official head of the British Army. Control of all British armed forces is exercised by the Ministry of DEFENCE, headed by the secretary of state for defence. General supervision of the army is conducted by the chief of the general staff, who heads an army council. In addition to the Regular Army there is a reserve force of *c*.230,000, more than 80,000 of which is in the Territorial Army (TA) and the remainder in the Regular Army Reserve. The end of the Cold War and financial pressures produced major reductions in conventional forces.

Army, US Ground service of the US armed forces. Active Army personnel number *c*.500,000, *c*.30% stationed overseas. Army personnel are under the general supervision of the secretary of the army and his adviser, the army chief of staff, who is the army's highest ranking officer and a member of the Joint Chiefs of Staff (JCS). The president is commander-in-chief of the armed forces. The department of the Army is charged with the organization, training, and equipping of these forces, but not their military deployment. The army also provides assistance in disaster relief, conducts weapons research and administers the US Military Academy at West Point. The army has 16 active divisions and helps to maintain 8 National Guard and 12 reserve divisions; major overseas commands are the Seventh Army in Europe and the Eighth Army in South Korea. The Continental Army existed from 1775, but the first regular standing army was authorized by Congress in 1785. The war department was established in 1789, became the department of the Army in 1947, became a part of the Department of DEFENSE in 1949. A draft was occasionally employed and was used in peacetime after World War 2. In 1973 Congress established an all-volunteer army, though draft registration was resumed in 1980 and conscription could be reinstated.

Arnhem City in E central Netherlands. An important trading centre since medieval times, Arnhem was almost destroyed by

an abortive Allied strike in 1944. Industries: metallurgy, textiles, electrical equipment, chemicals. Pop. (2001) 139,360.

Arnold, Benedict (1741–1801) American colonial soldier. During the American Revolution, Arnold commanded Philadelphia (1778) after being wounded at the Battle of SARATOGA. In 1780 he became commander of West Point, a fort he planned to betray to the British for money. After the plot was discovered, Arnold fled to the British. His name has become proverbial in modern US usage for treachery.

Arnold, Sir Malcolm (1921–2006) English composer. He started his career as principal trumpet with the London Philharmonic Orchestra but won acclaim for his accessible compositions. His output includes symphonies, concertos, overtures, ballets, and film scores (*The Bridge on the River Kwai*, 1957).

Arnold, Matthew (1822–88) English poet and critic. Arnold held the Oxford chair in poetry (1857–67). A school inspector (1851–86), his writings include literary criticism, such as *Essays in Criticism* (series 1, 1865; series 2, 1888), and social studies, such as *Culture and Anarchy* (1869), as well as classic Victorian poems, such as "Dover Beach" and "The Scholar Gypsy". His theories about the social and moral benefits of culture were largely responsible for the establishment of English literature as a "core" subject in schools and universities.

Aroostook War (1838–39) Dispute over the Maine-New Brunswick boundary. The Aroostook Valley was claimed by both Canada and the USA, and a conflict arose over Canadian lumber operations in the area. In 1839 a contingent of 50 Maine militia men also moved into the valley. War loomed, but General Winfield Scott negotiated a truce. It was settled by the Webster-Ashburton Treaty (1842).

Arp, Jean (Hans) (1887–1966) Alsatian sculptor, painter and poet. During World War 1, he founded the Zurich DADA movement with the Romanian artists Tristan Tzara, Marcel Janco, and others. He worked briefly with the BLAUE REITER group, and in the 1920s joined the SURREALISM movement. His sculpture spans the divide between Dada humour and the purity of non-iconic ABSTRACT ART. *Navel Shirt and Head* (1926) and *Human Concretion* (1935) are typical.

arrowroot Tropical and subtropical perennial plant found in wet habitats of North and South America, and some islands of the West Indies. Its leaves are lance-shaped and the flowers are usually white. The dried and ground roots are used in cooking. Family Marantaceae; species *Maranta arundinaceae*.

arsenic (symbol As) Semimetallic element of group V of the periodic table, probably obtained in 1250 by German chemist Albertus Magnus. Arsenic compounds are used as a poison, to harden lead, and to make semiconductors. Three allotropes are known: white arsenic, black arsenic, and a yellow nonmetallic form. Properties: at.no. 33; r.a.m. 74.9216; r.d. 5.7; m.p. 986°C (1806°F); sublimes 613°C (1135°F); most common isotope As^{75} (100%).

Artaud, Antonin (1896–1948) French drama theorist and director. In 1927 he co-founded the *Théâtre Alfred Jarry*, which produced surreal, symbolist plays. His most significant contribution to 20th-century drama was his concept of the theatre of CRUELTY. Influenced by the psychoanalytical theories of Carl JUNG, he proposed a physical theatre based on unconscious myth and symbol, rather than on narrative and psychological realism. His most important work was the volume of essays *The Theatre and its Double* (1938).

art deco Fashionable style of design and interior decoration in the 1920s and 1930s. It took its name from the *Exposition Internationale des Arts Décoratifs et Industriels Modernes* held in Paris in 1925. The art deco style is characterized by sleek forms, simplified lines, and geometric patterns. It began as a luxury style, an example of modern design fashioned from expensive, hand-crafted materials. After the Depression, art deco shifted towards mass production and low-cost materials.

Artemis In Greek mythology, the goddess of hunting and light, identified as DIANA by the Romans. She was the daughter of Zeus and Leto, and twin sister of APOLLO. Associated with the Moon, she was a virgin who assisted in childbirth and protected infants and animals.

arteriosclerosis Blanket term for degenerative diseases of the arteries, in particular atherosclerosis (hardening of the arteries). It is caused by deposits of fatty materials and scar tissue on the ARTERY walls, which narrow the channel and restrict blood flow, causing an increased risk of heart disease, stroke, or gangrene. Evidence suggests that predisposition to the disease is hereditary. Risk factors include cigarette smoking, inactivity, obesity, and a diet rich in animal fats and refined sugar. Treatment is by drugs and, in some cases, surgery to replace a diseased length of artery.

artery One of the BLOOD VESSELS that carry BLOOD away from the HEART. The **pulmonary** artery carries deoxygenated blood from the heart to the lungs, but all other arteries, such as the AORTA, carry oxygenated blood to the body's tissues. An artery's walls are thick, elastic, and muscular, and pulsate as they carry the blood. A severed artery causes major HAEMORRHAGE. A general term for degenerative diseases of the arteries is ARTERIOSCLEROSIS.

artesian well Well from which water is forced out naturally under pressure. Artesian wells are bored where water in a layer of porous rock is sandwiched between two layers of impervious rock. The water-filled layer is called an AQUIFER. Water flows up to the surface because distant parts of the aquifer are higher than the well-head.

arthritis Inflammation of the joints, with pain and restricted mobility. The most common forms are osteoarthritis and rheumatoid arthritis. **Osteoarthritis**, common among the elderly, occurs with erosion of joint cartilage and degenerative changes in the underlying bone. It is treated with analgesics and anti-inflammatories and, in some cases (especially a diseased hip), by joint replacement surgery. **Rheumatoid arthritis**, more common in women, is generally more disabling. It is an autoimmune disease which may disappear of its own accord but is usually slowly progressive. Treatment includes analgesics to relieve pain. The severest cases may need to be treated with CORTISONE injections, drugs to suppress immune activity or joint replacement surgery. *See also* RHEUMATISM

arthropod Member of the largest animal phylum, Arthropoda. Living forms include CRUSTACEA, ARACHNID, CENTIPEDE, MILLIPEDE, and INSECT. The species (numbering well over 1 million) are thought to have evolved from ANNELIDS. All have a hard outer skin of CHITIN that is attached to the muscular system on the inside. The body is divided into segments, modified among different groups, with each segment originally carrying a pair of jointed legs. In some animals, legs have evolved into jaws, sucking organs or weapons. Arthropods have well-developed digestive, circulatory and nervous systems. Land forms use tracheae for respiration.

Arthur Legendary British king who was said to rule the Knights of the Round Table. Two medieval chroniclers, Gildas and Nennius, tell of Arthur's fighting against the invading West Saxons and his final defeat of them at Mount Badon (possibly Badbury Hill, Dorset) in the early 6th century. However, some consider these sources unreliable and a modern view is that Arthur was a professional soldier in service to the British kings after the Roman occupation. GEOFFREY OF MONMOUTH's 12th century *Historia Regum Brittaniae*, based on Nennius and Welsh folklore, gave the legend – with the Round Table, Camelot, Lancelot, Guinevere, and the Holy Grail – the form in which it was transmitted through the Middle Ages. MALORY's *Morte D'Arthur* (1470) was based on Monmouth's version.

Arthur, Chester Alan (1830–86) 21st US president (1881–85). In 1880 Arthur was nominated by the Republican Party as vice president. He became president after the assassination of James GARFIELD and tried to reform the spoils system, in which incoming presidents replaced government staff with their own appointees. A Civil Service Commission was created, but his reforms were often frustrated by Congress. Gentlemanly but uninspiring, he was not renominated (1884). He was succeeded by Grover CLEVELAND.

artichoke (globe artichoke) Tall, thistle-like perennial plant with large, edible, immature flower heads, native to the Mediterranean region. It has spiny leaves and blue flowers. Height: 0.9–1.5m (3–5ft). Family Asteraceae/Compositae; species *Cynara scolymus*. A different plant, the Jerusalem artichoke, is grown for its edible tubers. Family Asteraceae/Compositae; species *Helianthus tuberosus*.

ARTHRITIS

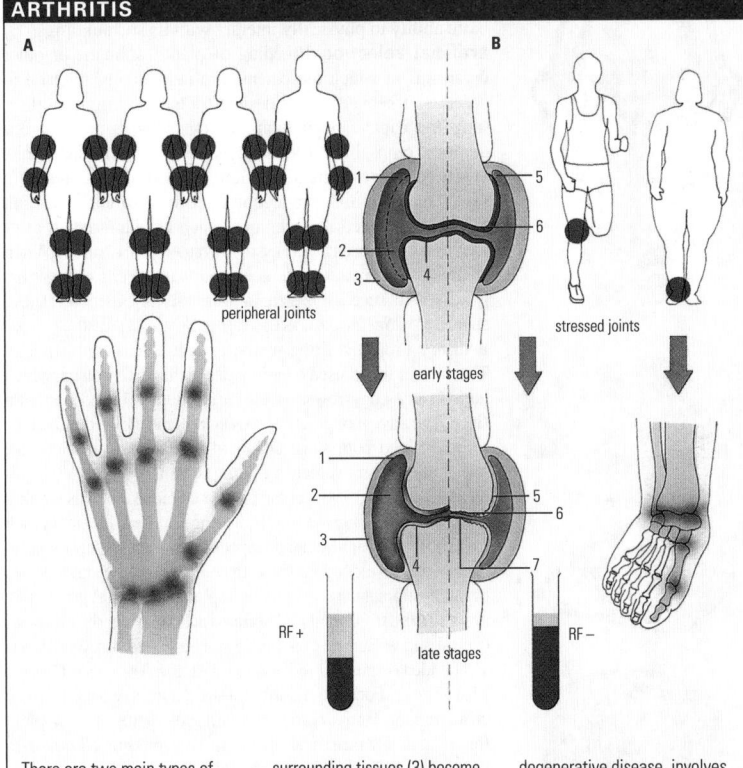

There are two main types of arthritis. In rheumatoid arthritis (A) the synovial membrane (1) becomes inflamed and thickened and produces increased synovial fluid within the joint (2). The capsule and surrounding tissues (3) become inflamed, while joint cartilage is damaged (4). Peripheral joints, such as hands and feet, are most commonly affected. Blood tests show rheumatoid factor. Osteoarthritis (B), a degenerative disease, involves thinning of cartilage (5), loss of joint space (6) and bone damage (7). Heavily used or weight-bearing joints, such as knees and feet, are affected. Blood tests are normal.

Articles of Confederation (1781) First Federal constitution of the USA, drafted by the CONTINENTAL CONGRESS in 1777. Distrust of central authority and state rivalries produced a weak central government, with Congress dependent on the states and unable to enforce its own legislation. Alexander HAMILTON and James MADISON analysed the weakness of the Articles in *The Federalist*, and the CONSTITUTIONAL CONVENTION met in 1787 to draft the CONSTITUTION OF THE UNITED STATES.

artificial insemination Method of inducing PREGNANCY without sexual intercourse by injecting SPERM into the female genital tract. It was first used in livestock farming, where artificial insemination allows proven sires to breed with a great many females at low cost. It has more recently been developed to help infertile humans have children, as in the techniques of IN VITRO FERTILIZATION (IVF).

artificial intelligence (AI) Science concerned with developing COMPUTERS and computer programs that model human intelligence. The most common form of AI involves programming a computer to answer questions on a specialized subject. Such 'expert systems' are said to display the human ability to perform expert analytical tasks. A similar system in a WORD PROCESSOR may highlight incorrect spellings, and be 'taught' new words. A closely related science, sometimes known as 'artificial life', is concerned with more low-level intelligence. For example, a ROBOT may be

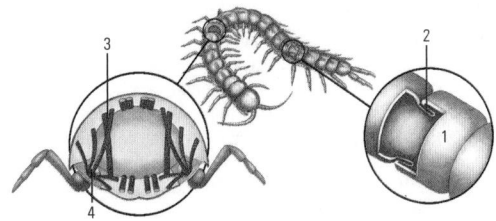

INTERNET

Arp, Jean (Hans)
▸ hirshhorn.si.edu/collection

art deco
▸ www.discoverfrance.net/
  France/Art/deco.shtml

Arthur, Chester Alan
▸ www.whitehouse.gov/
  history/presidents

Articles of Confederation
▸ www.usconstitution.net/
  articles.html

◀ **arthropod** The most numerous invertebrates (animals without a backbone) are the arthropods (joint-legged animals), such as the centipede. They owe their success to the exoskeleton that covers their bodies and allows the development of jointed limbs. A rigid protein cuticle encases the body segments (1), and an overlapping membrane (2) permits flexibility. The strength of the exoskeleton allows muscles (3) to be anchored to the inside. Groups of muscles (4) are used to move the legs.

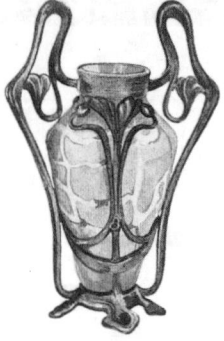

▲ **art nouveau** A decorative style from the turn of the 19th century, examples of art nouveau are mainly found in architecture and the applied arts, such as jewellery and glass design.

▼ **ash** The white ash (*Fraxinus americana*) of E North America grows to 40m (135ft). Part of the olive family, the leaves of the ash are distinctive in being split into many small leaflets, giving the impression of very fine foliage. The wood is used for baseball bats.

programmed to find its way around a maze, displaying the basic ability to physically interact with its surroundings.

artificial selection Breeding of plants, animals, or other organisms in which the parents are individually selected in order to perpetuate certain desired traits and eliminate others from the captive population. By this means, most of our domestic crops, livestock, and pets have arisen. Desired traits produced by artificial selection include disease-resistant plants and high milk production in cows. Artificial selection can be accelerated by techniques such as plant TISSUE CULTURE and the ARTIFICIAL INSEMINATION of livestock. When an organism in nature undergoes an advantageous change that is passed to successive generations, this is called NATURAL SELECTION. *See also* CLONE; GENETIC ENGINEERING

artillery Projectile-firing weapons with a carriage or mount. The ancient world used a variety of mechanical artillery which hurled stones or arrows, usually immobile and used only in a siege. The advent of practical CANNON in the early Renaissance revolutionized both siege and field warfare, as wheeled carriages allowed movement in battle. Cannon improved incrementally until the 19th century, when advances such as smokeless powder, elongated shells, rifling, and rapid-fire breach loading led to rapid change. Specialized types such as howitzers were developed. In the 20th century, rockets and missiles began to supplant and eventually replace traditional guns.

art nouveau Ornamental style which flourished in most of central and w Europe and the USA from *c.*1890 to World War 1. The idea originated in England with the ARTS AND CRAFTS MOVEMENT. Focusing mainly on the decorative arts, its most characteristic forms come from sinuous distortions of plant forms and asymmetrical lines. It is sometimes known in France by its English name, the 'Modern Style'. Outstanding art nouveau graphic artists include BEARDSLEY, TIFFANY, and Mucha. Charles Rennie MACKINTOSH, Antonio GAUDI, and Victor Horta were among its most gifted architects.

Arts and Crafts Movement Late 19th- and early 20th-century British movement, led by artists who wanted to revitalize the decorative arts by returning to the ideals of medieval craftsmanship. Inspired by William MORRIS, the movement contributed to European ART NOUVEAU, but was eventually transformed by the acceptance of modern industrial methods.

Aruba Dutch island in the Caribbean, off the coast of NW Venezuela; the capital is Oranjestad. It was part of the Netherlands Antilles until 1986. Independence was revoked in 1990, at Aruba's request, and it is now an autonomous part of the Netherlands. Industries: oil refining, phosphates, tourism. Area: 193sq km (75sq mi). Pop. (2000) 71,000.

arum *See* CUCKOOPINT

Arunachal Pradesh State of the eastern Himalayas in the far NE of India; the capital is Itanagar. Once a district of ASSAM, it was invaded by the Chinese in 1962, but returned to India the following year. It became a union territory in 1972, and the 24th state of India in 1986. Most of the state is mountainous forest and jungle. Its main products are coffee, rubber, fruit, spices, and rice. It is India's least densely populated state. Area: 81,426sq km (31,438sq mi). Pop. (2001) 1,091,117.

Aryan Language of an ancient people in the region between the Caspian Sea and Hindu Kush mountains. About 1500 BC one branch entered India, introducing the SANSKRIT language; another branch migrated to Europe. In their racist propaganda of the 1930s, the Nazis traced German descent from Aryans.

asbestos Group of fibrous, naturally occurring, silicate minerals used in insulation and fireproofing. "White" asbestos is the most common of several types. Many countries have banned its use, as it causes respiratory diseases including lung cancer.

Ascension Island in the s Atlantic Ocean; a UK dependency administered from the colony of ST HELENA. Discovered by the Portuguese in 1501, it was occupied by Britain in the early 19th century. It now serves as a telecommunications centre, and was an important base for British forces and supplies during the FALKLANDS WAR. Area: 88sq km (34sq mi). Pop. (1993) 1117.

Ascension Day Christian feast day that commemorates Christ's ascension into heaven, 40 days after his resurrection. It falls on a Thursday, the 40th day after EASTER. It used to be called Holy Thursday.

ascorbic acid *See* VITAMIN

asexual reproduction Type of reproduction in organisms that does not involve the union of male and female reproductive cells (GAMETES). It occurs in several forms: FISSION (division), BUDDING and VEGETATIVE REPRODUCTION. *See also* CLONE; SEXUAL REPRODUCTION

ash Group of mainly deciduous trees of the genus *Fraxinus* growing in temperate regions, usually having leaves made up of many small leaflets, and winged fruits. The wood is elastic, strong and shock-resistant, and is widely used for furniture. Species include manna ash, *F. ornus*, the flowering ash of s Europe and Asia Minor; the European ash, *F. excelsior*, which grows to 45m (148ft) tall; and *F. floribunda*, a native of the Himalayas. Family Oleaceae. The mountain ash of Europe and Asia (*Sorbus aucuparia*) comes from a different family.

Ashanti Administrative region and ethnic group of central GHANA, W Africa; the capital is KUMASI. The Ashanti people (a matrilineal society) established a powerful empire based on the slave trade with the British and Dutch. In the 18th century their influence extended into Togo and the Ivory Coast. Conflicts with the British throughout the 19th century were finally resolved in 1902, when the Ashanti territories (a British protectorate since 1896) were declared a crown colony. The society is traditionally agricultural. The region is the main area of Ghana's vital cocoa production. The Ashanti are renowned for their crafts, including high-quality goldwork (a gold-encrusted stool was a symbol of their sovereignty) and weaving. Today, Ashanti is the most populous of Ghana's ten regions. Area: 24,390sq km (9414sq mi). Pop. (2000) 3,187,601.

Ashcan school Nickname given to a group of late 19th- and early 20th-century US artists, including George BELLOWS, Robert HENRI, and Edward HOPPER, who rejected academic and traditional artistic subjects for the seamier aspects of urban life. The inspiration for the group's interest in everyday life came from four core members William Glackens, John Sloan, George Luks, and Everett Shinn, all of whom worked as artist-reporters in Philadelphia before joining Henri's circle.

Ashdown, Paddy (Jeremy John Durham) (1941–) British politician, first leader of the Social and LIBERAL DEMOCRATS (1988–99), b. India. Ashdown was a commander in the Royal Marines (1960–72), before becoming a diplomat. In 1983 he was elected to Parliament for the LIBERAL PARTY and quickly became a leading spokesman for the party. He succeeded David STEEL, who stood down as Liberal leader when the merger with the SOCIAL DEMOCRATIC PARTY (SDP) was formalized. He was succeeded by Charles Kennedy.

Ashes, The Cricket trophy, consisting of an urn containing the ashes of stumps and bails, nominally held by the winner of the test series between England and Australia. The urn was presented to the English captain in 1883, after Australia's victory in the 1882 Oval test match had prompted a mock obituary to English cricket in the *Sporting Times*.

Ashgabat (formerly Ashkhabad) Capital of the central Asian republic of Turkmenistan, located 40km (25mi) from the Iranian border. Founded in 1881 as a Russian fortress between the Kara-Kum Desert and the Kopet Dagh Mountains, it was largely rebuilt after a severe earthquake in 1948. The city was known as Poltaratsk from 1919 to 1927. Its present name was adopted after the republic attained independence from the former Soviet Union in 1992. Industries: textiles, carpets, silk, metalware, glass, light machinery. Pop. (1995) 604,700.

Ashkenazim JEWS who originally settled in NW Europe, as opposed to the SEPHARDIM, who settled in Spain and Portugal.

Ashkenazy, Vladimir (1937–) Icelandic pianist and conductor, b. Russia. His interpretations of Russian piano music earned international praise, and he shared first prize in the Tchaikovsky Piano Competition (1962). Ashkenazy was musical director of the Philharmonia Orchestra (1981–86) and the Royal Philharmonic Orchestra (1987– 96).

Ashoka (*c.*271–238 BC) Indian emperor (r.264–238BC). The greatest emperor of the MAURYA EMPIRE, he at first fought to expand his Empire. He was revolted by the bloodshed of war and, renouncing conquest by force, embraced BUDDHISM. He became one of its most fervent supporters and spread its ideas through missionaries to neighbouring countries and through edicts engraved on pillars. His empire encompassed most of India and large areas of Afghanistan.

Ashton, Sir Frederick (1904–88) British choreographer and ballet director. In 1935 he joined Sadler's Wells Ballet, London, and was its chief choreographer until 1963, then its director (1963–70). His work for dancers such as Margot FONTEYN and Ninette de VALOIS earned him a reputation as Britain's greatest choreographer. Major pieces include *Cinderella* (1948), *Ondine* (1958), *Marguèrite*, and *Armand* (both 1963).

Ashurbanipal (d. *c.*626BC) (Assurbanipal) Last great king of ASSYRIA (669–633BC). During his reign, Assyria reached its largest extent, encompassing Upper Egypt, before a rapid decline. Excavations at NINEVEH after 1850 revealed an advanced civilization.

Ash Wednesday First day of LENT

Asia World's largest continent. Entirely in the Eastern Hemisphere, it extends from N of the Arctic Circle in Russia to S of the Equator in Indonesia. **Land** On the W, Asia's boundary with Europe follows a line through the Ural Mountains, W of the CASPIAN SEA and along the Caucasus. Geographically, Europe and Asia are one enormous continent (Eurasia) but historically they have always been regarded as separate. Asia has six regions, each largely defined by mountain ranges. Northern Asia includes the massive inhospitable region of SIBERIA. A large part lies within the Arctic Circle forming a vast cold, treeless plain (tundra) where the soil, except on the surface, is permanently frozen to depths exceeding 700m (2000ft). Southern Siberia includes great coniferous forests (taiga) and the Russian steppes. Its S boundary runs through the TIAN SHAN and Yablonovy

mountains and Lake BAIKAL, the world's deepest lake. The high plateau area of Central Asia extends S to the HIMALAYAS and includes the W Chinese provinces of TIBET and XINJIANG as well as MONGOLIA. This is a region of low rainfall and very low winter temperatures. Much of the area is desert, the largest being the GOBI and Takla Makan. The Tibetan plateau is mostly barren. Eastern Asia lies between the plateaux of Central Asia and the Pacific. It is a region of highlands and plains, watered by broad rivers. Off the E coast there are many islands, the most important being the Japanese islands of HOKKAIDO, HONSHU, and KYUSHU, and the Chinese island of TAIWAN. Southeast Asia includes the INDOCHINA peninsula, part of which forms the MALAY PENINSULA, BURMA and a large number of islands, among which the PHILIPPINES and INDONESIA are the most important. The N of this region is mountainous and the S mainly low-lying. Southern Asia consists of the Indian subcontinent and the island of SRI LANKA. In the N it is bounded by the HINDU KUSH, Pamir, KARAKORAM, and Himalayan mountains. In the Himalayas is Mount EVEREST, the world's highest mountain. To the S of the mountains lie wide plains, crossed by rivers flowing from the Himalayas. Farther S is the DECCAN plateau that rises on its E and W edges culminating in the E and W GHATS. South-west Asia includes most of the region known as the MIDDLE EAST. It is made up largely of two peninsulas; Anatolia (ASIA MINOR) and the vast Arabian Peninsula. It is also a region of large inland seas: the Aral, Caspian, Dead and Black seas. **Structure and geology** The most striking feature of the continent is the massive range of Himalayan fold mountains that were formed when the Indo-Australian and Eurasian tectonic plates collided in

▼ **Asia** Geographically, Asia and Europe form one vast continent (Eurasia). Asia is home to 60% of Earth's total population. Its climate and topography determine settlement, economic and cultural patterns. North, Central and NW Asia witnessed dramatic political upheavals in the 20th century, with the rise and fall of the Soviet Union. Northern Asia is dominated by the wastelands of Siberia. East Asia is the most industrialized region, and its history has been determined largely by the civilizations along the Yangtze and Huang He rivers. The dominant religion of E Asia is Buddhism. The monsoon region of Southeast Asia is a fusion of Indian and Chinese cultures. South Asia is isolated from the rest of the continent by huge mountain ranges. The arid deserts of Southwest Asia are a strategic crossroads between Africa, Asia and Europe. Here, Islam is the principal religion and the economy is dominated by the petroleum industry.

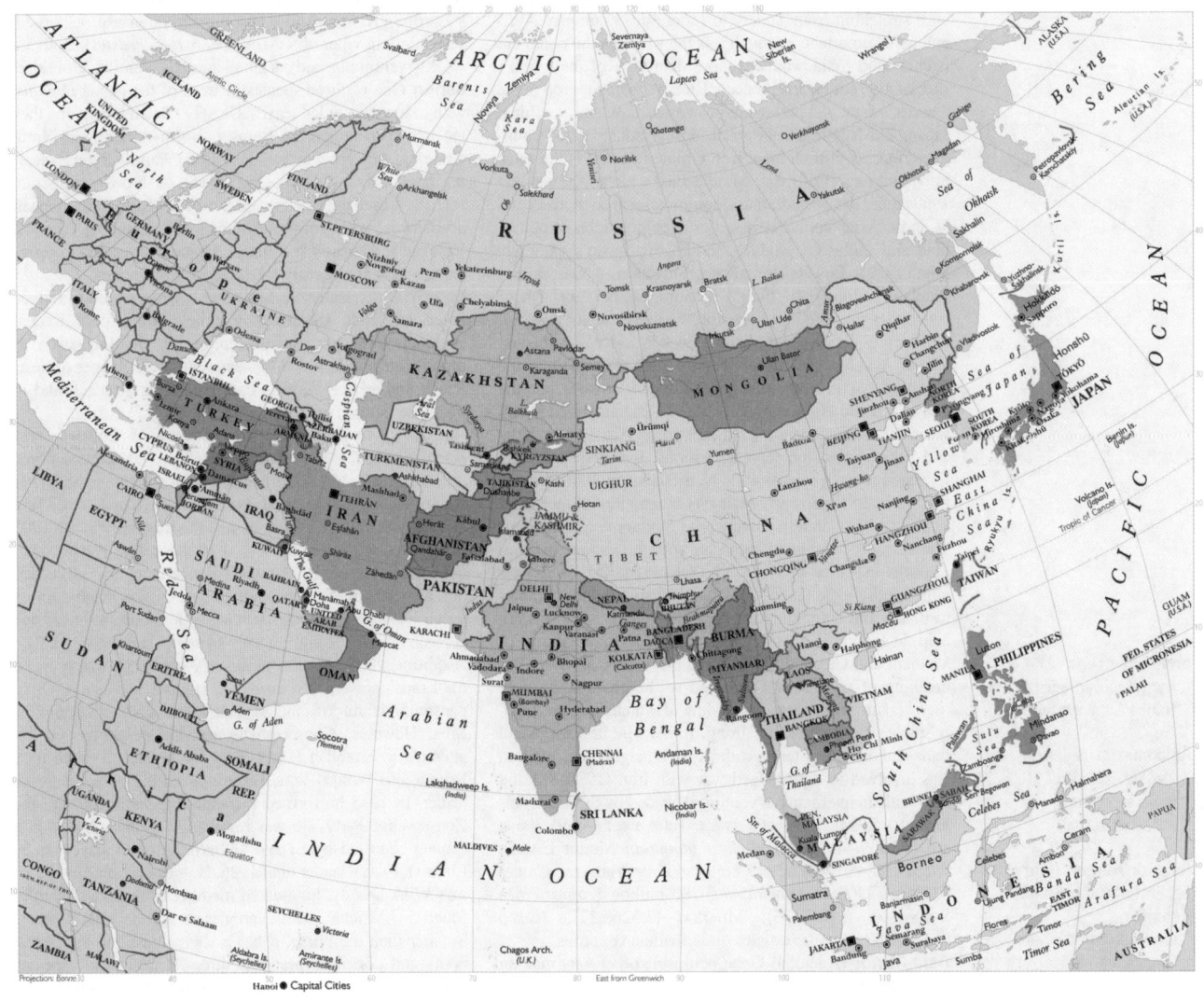

Hanoi ● Capital Cities

the Mesozoic era. Most of China and s central Asia is composed of folded Palaeozoic and Mesozoic sediments, and large expanses of central Siberia consist of flat-lying sediments of the same age. The Indian subcontinent is largely Precambrian except for the Deccan Plateau which is a complex series of lava flows. **Lakes and rivers** Most of the major Asian lakes are found in the centre of the continent, and include the Caspian Sea, the ARAL SEA, and Lake BALKHASH. The River YANGTZE in China, is Asia's longest. The River HUANG HE is China's other major river and, until control measures were taken, it flooded regularly, drowning thousands of people. Like these rivers, the three principal waterways of SE Asia (IRRAWADDY, SALWEEN, MEKONG) rise on the Tibetan plateau but flow s instead of E. The INDUS, BRAHMAPUTRA and GANGES are the largest rivers of the Indian subcontinent, and the OB, YENISEI and LENA are the continent's major N-flowing rivers, emptying into the Arctic Ocean. **Climate and vegetation** Except for the w temperate seaboards, all the world's major climatic divisions (with local variations) are represented in the continent. The monsoon climates of India and Southeast Asia are peculiar to these regions and, apart from extremes of heat and cold, typify the continent. Large expanses are covered by desert and semi-arid grassland, with belts of coniferous forest to the N and tropical forest to the s. **People** Asians constitute 60% of the world's population. The main language groups are Indo-Aryan, Sino-Tibetan, Ural-Altaic, Malayan, and Semitic. Mandarin Chinese is the most numerous (if not the most widespread) language. HINDUISM is the religion with the most adherents, although it is confined to India and SE Asia. ISLAM, CONFUCIANISM, BUDDHISM, SHINTO, CHRISTIANITY, TAOISM, and JUDAISM are also important, with Islamic influence stretching from Turkey to Indonesia. **Economy** Agriculture is important, although less than 10% of the continent is cultivated. Asia produces more than 90% of the world's rice, rubber, cotton and tobacco. Rice is the major crop in the E and S, wheat and barley are grown in the w and N. China, Japan, and Russia are the most highly industrialized countries in terms of traditional heavy materials. Oil is the most important export of many Middle East countries. Since the 1960s there has been dramatic commercial growth in several SE and E Asian countries based on a combination of household and high-tech products. Following Japan's example, South Korea, Taiwan, Hong Kong, Singapore, Malaysia, and Thailand form the 'tiger' economies. In 1997 these economies plunged into recession, fuelling fears of a worldwide depression. **Recent history** Since World War 2, the history of Asia has been dominated by three main themes: the legacy of COLONIALISM, the growth of COMMUNISM, and the rise of Islamic FUNDAMENTALISM. The Indian subcontinent gained its independence from Britain in 1947, when India and Pakistan became separate nations. Indonesia achieved formal independence from the Netherlands in 1949. During the 1950s, Indochina and Malaysia won independence from France and Britain respectively after military confrontations. The spread of communism began with the victory of MAO ZEDONG in China in 1949. North Korea failed, in its war with South Korea (1950–53), to establish a united communist state and communism was also repulsed with Western help, in Indonesia. Communism did finally gain control of Vietnam and Cambodia, following the VIETNAM WAR. The break-up of the Soviet Union led to the creation of eight 'new' countries in central Asia, few of which were politically stable or economically strong. In the Middle East, Israel remained on uneasy terms with its Arab neighbours, and Iraq was involved in a prolonged war with Iran (1980–88) and later with an international coalition, headed by the USA, following Iraq's invasion of Kuwait. Total area: 44,391,206sq km (17,139,445sq mi) *Highest mountain* Mount Everest (Nepal) 8848m (29,029ft) *Longest river* Yangtze (China) 6300km (3900mi) *Population* 3,780 million *Largest cities* SHANGHAI (8,937,175); MUMBAI (3,326,837); TOKYO (8,130,408); *See also* articles on individual countries

Asia Minor (Anatolia) Great peninsula of w Asia making up most of modern Turkey. The BOSPORUS, the Sea of Mar-

mara, and the DARDANELLES divide both Turkey and Europe from Asia. Apart from a very narrow coastal plain, the area is a high, arid plateau. In the SE, the Taurus Range rises to more than 3750m (12,000ft). The area has been inhabited since the Bronze Age, with civilizations such as Troy. The HITTITES established a kingdom here in c.1800 BC. From the 8th century BC the Greeks established colonies in the area; the Persians invaded in the 6th century BC and the PERSIAN WARS followed. ALEXANDER THE GREAT's empire included this region, although it split into several states after his death. The Romans unified the area in the 2nd century AD. By the 6th century it had become part of the Byzantine empire. In the 13th-15th centuries it was conquered by the Ottoman Turks and remained part of the Ottoman Empire until the establishment of the Republic of Turkey in 1923.

Asimov, Isaac (1920–92) US writer and scientist, b. Russia. Though he published several serious scientific works, he is best known for his science fiction stories. His prolific output contains some of the finest novels in the genre, including *I, Robot* (1950) and *The Foundation Trilogy* (1951–53).

Asmara (Asmera) Capital of Eritrea, NE Africa. Occupied by Italy in 1889, it was their colonial capital and the main base for the invasion of Ethiopia (1935–36). It was captured by the British in 1941 and, in the 1950s, the US built Africa's biggest military communications centre here. The city was absorbed by Ethiopia in 1952, and was the main garrison in the fight against Eritrean rebels seeking independence. In 1993 Asmara became the capital of independent ERITREA. Though ravaged by drought, famine and war, it began a strong recovery based on numerous light industries, including ceramics, footwear, and textiles. Pop. (1995) 431,000.

asp Popular name for two species of VIPER, the asp viper of s Europe (*Vipera aspis*), and the Egyptian asp, a horned, side-winding viper of N Africa (*Cerastes cerastes*). Both are weakly venomous and eat small animals. Family: Viperidae.

aspen One of three species of trees of the genus *Populus*, with toothed, rounded leaves. Closely related to poplars, they are native to temperate Eurasia, North Africa, and North America, they grow up to 30m (100ft). Family Salicaceae.

asphalt Naturally occurring black or brown semi-solid BITUMEN, used mainly for road covering and roofing. Asphalt deposits occur in many parts of the world, including Trinidad, Venezuela, Alabama and Texas. Asphalt also occurs in petroleum, and is now mostly extracted in oil refineries.

aspirin (acetylsalicylic acid) DRUG widely used to reduce fever, and as an ANALGESIC to relieve minor pain. Recent evidence indicates aspirin can inhibit the formation of blood clots and in low doses can reduce the danger of heart attack and stroke. Aspirin can irritate the stomach and in overdose is toxic and can cause death.

Asquith, Herbert Henry, 1st Earl of Oxford and Asquith (1852–1928) British statesman, last Liberal prime minister (1908–16). Asquith entered Parliament in 1886, later serving as home secretary to William GLADSTONE (1892–95). His support of FREE TRADE helped the Liberals win the 1905 general election. Asquith served as chancellor of the exchequer under Sir Henry Campbell-Bannerman, and succeeded him as prime minister. His administration was notable for its social welfare legislation, such as the introduction of old age pensions (1908) and unemployment insurance (1911). Asquith also passed the Parliament Act (1911), which ended the Lords' power of veto over Commons legislation. Other constitutional reforms included the introduction of salaries for MPs. However, Conservatives and Unionists rejected his attempts to establish Home Rule for Ireland. Asquith took Britain into WORLD WAR I, but was an ineffective wartime leader. In 1915 he formed a coalition government with the Conservative Party. He was replaced as prime minister in a cabinet coup led by LLOYD GEORGE. Asquith stayed on as LIBERAL PARTY leader until 1926. He was ennobled in 1925.

ass Wild, speedy, long-eared member of the HORSE family found in African and Asian desert and mountain areas. Smaller than the horse, it has a short mane and tail, small hoofs and dorsal stripes. The three African races (species *Equus africanus*) are the Nubian, North African and the rare

INTERNET

art nouveau (page 110)
▶ www.discoverfrance.net/
France/Art/nouveau.shtml

Ashkenazim (page 110)
▶ www.us-israel.org/
jsource/Judaism/
Ashkenazim.html

**Asquith, Herbert Henry,
1st Earl of Oxford and
Asquith**
▶ www.number-10.gov.uk/
output/Page140.asp

Somali. Height: 90–150cm (3–5ft) at shoulder. Asian races are the kiang and the ONAGER. A further strain has long been domesticated as the DONKEY, *Equus asinus*. Family Equidae.

Assad, Hafez al- (1928–2000) Syrian statesman, president (1970–2000). Assad served as minister of defence (1965–70), before seizing power in a military coup. He was elected president in 1971. Assad took a hardline stance against Israel and Syrian troops participated in the 1973 ARAB-ISRAELI WAR. He was accused of harbouring terrorists. In 1976 Syrian troops were deployed in the Lebanese civil war. In 1987 the Syrian army moved into Beirut to restore order. In the mid-1990s, Assad's stance towards Israel softened and he played a vital role in the Israeli-Palestinian peace negotiations. Syria supported the coalition forces arrayed against Iraq in the GULF WAR. He was succeeded as president by his son, Bashar al-Assad.

Assam State in NE India, almost separated from the rest of the country by Bangladesh. The capital is Dispur and the largest city is Guwahati. It became a state in 1950, but its people have resented, and forcibly resisted, immigration from West Bengal and Bangladesh. The Bodo minority continue to push for a separate state N of the River BRAHMAPUTRA. Industries: tea, jute, timber, oil. Area: 78,438sq km (30,277sq mi). Pop. (2001) 26,638,407.

assassin (Arabic, users of hashish) Name given to a Muslim sect of ISMAILIS, founded in *c*.1090 by Hasan ibn al-Sabbah. They fought against orthodox Muslims and Christian Crusaders and committed many political murders, until their eventual defeat in the 13th century.

assay Test to determine the amount of a metal present in a sample of material such as ores and alloys. The term is normally reserved for finding the proportion of gold, silver or platinum present. *See also* HALLMARK

Assemblies of God Largest PENTECOSTAL religious sect in the US. Founded in 1914 by preachers of the Church of God in Hot Springs, Arkansas, in 1916 it was incorporated and titled General Council of Assemblies of God. Today, the Church has *c*.600,000 members.

asset Anything owned by a person or a company that has a money value. **Current** assets can be easily liquidated to produce their cash value. **Fixed** assets include buildings and land. Goodwill and PATENTS are **intangible** assets because they have potential, rather than actual, money value. Asset stripping is the practice of taking over a business and selling off its assets.

assimilation Process by which an organism uses substances taken in from its surroundings to make new living tissue or to provide energy. It includes the incorporation of the products of food digestion into living tissues in animals, and the synthesis of new organic material by a plant during photosynthesis.

Assiniboine Nomadic tribe of Native North Americans. Their language is Siouan, and they are related to the Dakotas, although they migrated W from Minnesota to Saskatchewan and the Lake Winnipeg area. Their culture is that of the Plains Indians. They were trading partners of the English HUDSON'S BAY COMPANY, and their trade helped to destroy the French monopoly among tribes of the region. Today they number *c*.5,000; 4,000 on reservations in Montana and 1,000 in Canada.

Association of Southeast Asian Nations (ASEAN) Regional alliance formed in 1967 to promote economic cooperation. Its members are Indonesia, Malaysia, Philippines, Singapore, Thailand, Brunei, Vietnam, Laos, and Burma. Based in Jakarta, Indonesia, it took over the nonmilitary aspects of SOUTHEAST ASIA TREATY ORGANIZATION (SEATO) in 1975.

associative law Rule of combination in mathematics, in which the result of two or more operations on terms does not depend on the way in which the numbers and symbols are grouped. Thus, normal addition and multiplication of numbers follows the associative law, since $a + (b + c) = (a + b) + c$, and $a \times (b \times c) = (a \times b) \times c$.

Assumption In the Roman Catholic Church, principal feast of the Blessed Virgin Mary. It is celebrated on August 15, and marks the occasion when she was taken up into heaven at the end of her life on Earth.

Assyria Ancient empire of the Middle East. It took its name from the city of Ashur (Assur) on the River Tigris,

near modern Mosul, Iraq. The Assyrian Empire was established in the 3rd millennium BC and reached its zenith between the 9th and 7th centuries BC when it extended from the Nile to the Persian Gulf and N into Anatolia. Thereafter it declined and was absorbed by the Persian Empire. Under ASHURBANIPAL, art (especially bas-relief sculpture) and learning reached their peak. The luxuriance of Ashurbanipal's court at NINEVEH was legendary and, combined with the cost of maintaining his huge armies, fatally weakened the Empire. The capture of Nineveh in 612 BC marked the terminal decline of Assyria.

Assyro-Babylonian mythology Early mythology of Mesopotamia. It described a cosmic order of heaven, Earth, and an underworld. Some 4000 deities and demons directed the physical and spiritual activities of the world.

Astaire, Fred (1899–1987) US dancer, actor, and choreographer. Astaire's sparkling, improvised solo dances redefined the musical. In 1933 cinema's greatest partnership was formed, when he starred opposite Ginger ROGERS in *Flying Down to Rio*. Fred and Ginger made ten films together. Their first major MGM musical was *The Gay Divorcee* (1934). Classics include *Top Hat* (1935) and *Swing Time* (1936). Other dance partners included: Audrey HEPBURN in *Funny Face* (1957), Rita Hayworth in *You Were Never Lovelier* (1942), and Judy GARLAND, *Easter Parade* (1948). In 1949 he received a special Academy Award for his contribution to film.

Astana (formerly Aqmola) Capital-designate of Kazakhstan, on the River Ishim in the steppes of N central Kazakhstan. Under Soviet rule, Aqmola functioned as capital of the Virgin Lands. From 1961 to 1993 it was known as Tselinograd; from 1993 to 1998 as Aqmola. Pop. (1999) 313,000.

astatine (symbol At) Semimetallic radioactive element that is one of the HALOGENS (group VII of the PERIODIC TABLE). It is rare in nature, and is found in radioactive decay. At^{211} will collect in the thyroid gland and is used in medicine as a radioactive tracer. Properties: at.no. 85; r.a.m. 211; m.p. 302°C (575.6°F); b.p. 377°C (710.6°F); most stable isotope At^{210} (half-life 8.3hr).

aster Genus of mostly perennial, leafy stemmed plants native to the Americas and Eurasia. Asters are popular garden plants and most bear daisy-like flowers. Family Asteraceae/Compositae.

asteroid Small body in an independent orbit around the Sun. The majority move between the orbits of Mars and Jupiter, in the main asteroid belt. The largest asteroid (and the first to be discovered) was CERES, with a diameter of 913km (567mi). There are thought to be a million asteroids with a diameter greater than 1km (0.6mi); below this, they decrease in size to dust particles. Some very small objects find their way to Earth as METEORITES. Today, nearly 6000 asteroids have been catalogued and have had their orbits calculated. This figure is increasing by several hundred a year. At least 10,000 more have been observed, but not often enough for an orbit to be calculated. Some of the larger asteroids are spherical, but most are irregularly shaped, and a wide variety of compositional types have been identified. Asteroids almost certainly originate from the time of the formation of the SOLAR SYSTEM and are not remnants of a large planet that disintegrated, as was once thought.

asthma Disorder of the respiratory system in which the bronchi (air passages) of the lungs go into spasm, making

▲ **Assyria** The relief (*c*.650 BC), now bare stone but originally painted, shows King Ashurbanipal's lion hunt. This is part of a series of narrative wall reliefs, found in the Northern Palace, Nineveh, and representing the highest achievement of Assyrian art.

INTERNET

Association of Southeast Asian Nations (ASEAN)
▶ www.aseansec.org

asteroid
▶ seds.lpl.arizona.edu/ nineplanets/nineplanets/ asteroids.html
▶ neat.jpl.nasa.gov

ASTRONAUT

Astronauts on NASA's shuttle use spacesuits (1) that allow the crew members to work in space for up to seven hours. The suit is multi-layered with eight materials combined. The outside is treated nylon to stop damage from tiny meteorites. Four layers of aluminium material provide a heat shield from solar radiation backed by a fire- and tear-resistant layer. The astronaut is protected from the vacuum of space by a pressure suit of nylon coated with polyurethane and is kept comfortable in extremes of heat and cold by water pumped through a network of tubes in a nylon chiffon undergarment. (2) The manned manoeuvring unit (MMU) allows an astronaut to move away from the shuttle. Power comes from 24 thrusters arranged at the corners of the MMU. By releasing pressurized nitrogen from two tanks (3) through nozzles the astronaut can propel himself/herself through the vacuum. The hand controllers regulate rotation (4) and speed (5). A video camera (6) sends pictures to the shuttle and records the work carried out.

breathing difficult. It can be triggered by infection, air pollution, allergy, certain drugs, exertion or emotional stress. Allergic asthma may be treated by injections aimed at lessening sensitivity to specific allergens. Otherwise treatment is with bronchodilators to relax the bronchial muscles and ease breathing; in severe asthma, inhaled steroids may be given. Children often outgrow asthma, while some people suddenly acquire the disease in middle age. Air pollution is increasing the number of asthma sufferers. *See also* BRONCHITIS; EMPHYSEMA; LUNGS

astigmatism Defect of vision in which the curvature of the lens differs from one perpendicular plane to another. It can be compensated for by use of corrective lenses.

Aston, Francis William (1877–1945) British physicist awarded the 1922 Nobel Prize in chemistry for his work on ISOTOPES. He developed the MASS SPECTROGRAPH, which he used it to identify 212 naturally occurring isotopes.

Astor, John Jacob (1763–1848) US financier, b. Germany. Astor founded the AMERICAN FUR COMPANY in 1808 and, after 1812, acquired a virtual monopoly of the US fur trade. In the 1830s he concentrated on land investment and became the wealthiest man in the USA. His great-great-grandson, Viscount William Waldorf Astor (1879–1952), was married to Nancy ASTOR. Viscount Astor was owner of the *Observer* newspaper and his brother, John Jacob (1886–1971), 1st Baron Astor of Hever, was owner (1922–66) of *The Times*.

Astor, Nancy Witcher (Langhorne), Viscountess (1879–1964) British politician, b. USA, the first woman elected to the House of Commons (1919–45). A Conservative, she

advocated temperance, educational reform, and women's and children's welfare. In the 1930s she and her husband Viscount William Waldorf Astor headed a group of influential proponents of APPEASEMENT toward Nazi Germany.

Astrakhan (Astrachan) City in s Russia, a port on the Caspian Sea, s Russia. It was developed by the Mongols in the 13th century. In the Russian Civil War (1917–20) the city remained in 'White Russian' hands, becoming a base for the Caspian Sea conquest of 1920. It possesses a walled kremlin (1587–89) and cathedral (1700–10). A railway, airline and oil shipping terminal, it is also an important trade centre. Industries: fishing, shipbuilding, engineering, oil-refining. Pop. (1994) 481,171.

astrolabe Early astronomical instrument for showing the appearance of the celestial sphere at a given moment and for determining the altitude of celestial bodies. The basic form consisted of two concentric disks, one with a star map and one with a scale of angles around its rim, joined and pivoted at their centres (rather like a modern planisphere), with a sighting device attached. Astrolabes were used from the time of the ancient Greeks until the 17th century for navigation, measuring time, and terrestrial measurement of height and angles.

astrology Belief in influences supposedly exerted by stars and planets on the natures and lives of human beings. Many cultures throughout the world have developed some form of astrology. The oldest known originated in ancient Babylon and Persia *c.*4000 years ago. European astrology developed in the middle ages, despite church disapproval, and draws on the movements of the Sun, Moon and major planets of the Solar System in relation to the stars that make up the 12 constellations known as the ZODIAC. Belief in astrology remains widespread, and HOROSCOPES continue to be published in popular newspapers.

astronaut (Rus. *cosmonaut*) Person who navigates or rides in a space vehicle. The first man to orbit the Earth was the Russian Yuri GAGARIN in 1961. The first man to walk on the Moon was the American Neil ARMSTRONG in 1969. The first woman in space was the Russian Valentina Tereshkova in 1963.

astronomical unit (AU) Mean distance between the Earth and the Sun, used as a fundamental unit of distance, particularly for distances in the Solar System. It is equal to 149.598 million km (92.956 million mi).

astronomy Branch of science studied since ancient times and concerned with the universe and its components in terms of the relative motions of celestial bodies, their positions on the celestial sphere, physical and chemical structure, evolution and the phenomena occurring on them. It includes celestial mechanics, ASTROPHYSICS, COSMOLOGY, and astrometry. Waves in all regions of the ELECTROMAGNETIC spectrum can now be studied either with ground-based instruments or by observations and measurements made from satellites, space probes and rockets. **History** Astronomy was first used practically to develop a calendar, the units of which were determined by observing the heavens. The Chinese had a calendar in the 14th century BC. The Greeks developed the science between 600 BC and AD 200. THALES introduced geometrical ideas and PYTHAGORAS saw the universe as a series of concentric spheres. ARISTOTLE believed the EARTH to be stationary but he explained lunar eclipses correctly. ARISTARCHUS put forward a heliocentric theory. HIPPARCHUS used trigonometry to determine astronomical distances. The system devised by PTOLEMY was a geometrical representation of the SOLAR SYSTEM that predicted the motions of the planets with great accuracy. From then on astronomy remained dormant until the scientific revolution of the 16th and 17th centuries, when COPERNICUS stated his theory that the Earth rotates on its axis and, with all the other planets, revolves round the SUN. This had a profound effect upon contemporary religion and philosophy. KEPLER and his laws of planetary motion refined the theory of heliocentric motion, and his contemporary, GALILEO, made use of the TELESCOPE and discovered the moons of JUPITER. Isaac NEWTON combined the sciences of astronomy and physics. His laws of motion and universal theory of GRAVITATION provided a physical basis for Kepler's laws and enabled the later prediction of HALLEY'S COMET and the discovery of the planets URANUS, NEPTUNE, and PLUTO. By the early 19th century the science of celestial mechanics (the study of the motions of bodies in space as they move under the influence of their mutual gravitation) had become highly advanced and new mathematical techniques permitted the solution of the remaining problems of classical gravitation theory as applied to the Solar System. In the second half of the 19th century astronomy was revolutionized by the introduction of techniques based on photography and SPECTROSCOPY. These encouraged investigation into the physical composition of stars. Ejnar HERTZSPRUNG and H.N. Russell studied the relationship between the colour of a star and its luminosity. By this time larger telescopes were being constructed, which extended the limits of the universe known to man. Harlow SHAPLEY determined the shape and size of our galaxy and E.P. HUBBLE's study of distant galaxies led to his theory of an expanding universe. The BIG BANG and STEADY-STATE THEORY of the origins of the universe were formulated. In recent years, space exploration and observation in different parts of the electromagnetic spectrum have contributed to the discovery and postulation of such phenomena as the QUASAR, PULSAR, and BLACK HOLE. There are various branches of modern astronomy. **Optical** astronomy studies sources of light in space. Light rays can penetrate the atmosphere but, because of disturbances, many observations are now made from above the atmosphere. **Gamma-ray**, **infrared**, **ultraviolet**, and **X-ray** astronomy study the emission of radiation (at all wavelengths) from astronomical objects. Higher wavelengths can be studied from the ground, while lower wavelengths require the use of satellites and balloons. Other branches within astronomy include RADAR ASTRONOMY and RADIO ASTRONOMY.

astrophysics Branch of ASTRONOMY that studies the physical and chemical nature of celestial bodies and their evolution. Many branches of physics, including nuclear physics, plasma physics, relativity, and SPECTROSCOPY, are used to predict properties of stars, planets, and other celestial bodies. Astrophysicists also interpret the information obtained from astronomical studies of the electromagnetic spectrum, including light, X-rays, and radio waves.

Asturias Region in NW Spain, bordering the Bay of Biscay and traversed by the Cantabrian Mountains. The capital is Oviedo. Asturias was named by the Iberians in the 2nd century BC and is famous for its cider. Its coal mines are the richest in Spain. Industries: coal, manganese, mining, steel and nonferrous metal production, fishing, fruit. Pop. (2001) 1,062,998.

Asunción Capital, chief port, and largest city of Paraguay, located on the E bank of the Paraguay River near its junction with the River Pilcomayo. Founded by the Spanish *c.*1536 as a trading post, Asunción was the scene of the Communeros rebellion against Spanish rule in 1721 and was later occupied by Brazil (1868–76). City sites include the Pantéon Nacional (a tomb for national heroes), Encarnación Church, National University (1889) and the Catholic University (1960). It is an administrative, industrial and cultural centre. Industries: vegetable oil, textiles. Pop. (2005) 1,750,000.

Aswan City on the E bank of the River NILE just above Lake Nasser, SE Egypt. Aswan was of strategic importance in ancient times because it controlled all shipping and communications above the first cataract of the Nile. The modern city is a commercial and winter resort centre and has benefited greatly from the construction of the Aswan High Dam. The dam, built with Soviet aid between 1960 and 1970, has a generating capacity of 10,000 million kilowatt-hours and supersedes the first Aswan Dam completed in 1902 to establish flood control on the Nile. Many Nubians displaced by the dam's construction have moved to Aswan. The AGA KHAN's tomb overlooks the city from the W bank of the Nile. The rock terrain surrounding Lake Nasser abounds in Egyptian and Greek temples and, though some sites submerged, the temples of ABU SIMBEL remain. Industries: copper, steel, textiles. Pop. (1996) 219,017.

Atacama Desert Desert of N Chile, stretching *c.*1,000km (600mi) s from the Peru border. Despite its proximity to the Pacific Ocean it is considered to be the most arid in the world; some areas had no recorded rainfall in 400 years.

Except where it is artificially irrigated, it is devoid of vegetation. Until the advent of synthetic fertilizers, the desert was extensively mined for sodium nitrate. Large deposits of copper and other minerals remain. Nitrates and iodine are extracted from the salt basins.

Atahualpa (1502–33) (Atabalipa) Last INCA ruler of Peru. The son of Huayna Capac, upon his father's death he inherited Quito, while his half-brother Huáscar controlled the rest of the Inca kingdom. In 1532 Atahualpa defeated Huáscar, but in November of the same year Spanish conquistador Francisco PIZARRO captured Atahualpa. He was later executed.

Atatürk, (Mustafa) Kemal (1881–1938) Turkish general and statesman, first president (1923–38) of the Turkish republic. As a young soldier he joined the YOUNG TURKS and was chief of staff to ENVER PASHA in the successful revolution (1908). He fought against the Italians in Tripoli (1911) and defended Gallipoli in the BALKAN WARS. During World War 1 he led resistance to the Allies' GALLIPOLI CAMPAIGN. The defeat of the OTTOMAN EMPIRE and the capitulation of the sultan persuaded Mustafa Kemal to organize the Turkish Nationalist Party (1919) and set up a rival government in ANKARA. The Treaty of SÈVRES (1920) forced him on the offensive. His expulsion of the Greeks from ASIA MINOR (1921–22) led the sultan to flee Istanbul. The Treaty of Lausanne (1923) saw the creation of a independent republic. His dictatorship undertook sweeping reforms, which transformed Turkey into a secular, industrial nation. In 1934 he adopted the title Atatürk (Turkish, father of the Turks). He was succeeded by Ismet INÖNÜ.

ataxia In medicine, condition where muscles are uncoordinated. It results in clumsiness, irregular and uncontrolled movements, and difficulties with speech. It may be caused by physical injury to the brain or nervous system, by a STROKE, or by disease.

Aten Ancient Egyptian god. Originally referring to the disc of the Sun, Aten entered into the Egyptian pantheon as the sun god. AKHNATEN elevated his status and virtually established the first monotheistic religion. After Akhnaten's death, the worship of AMUN was restored.

Athabasca Lake in W central Canada, on the border of NE Alberta and NW Saskatchewan. The fourth-largest lake in Canada, it is fed by the Athabasca River from the s and drained by the Slave River to the N. Fort Chipewyan (1788) is preserved at the W end of the lake. There are gold and uranium deposits nearby. Area: 8080sq km (3120sq mi).

Athabascan (Athapascan or Slave Indians) Tribe and language group of Native North Americans, inhabiting NW Canada. They were forced N to the Great Slave Lake and Fort Nelson by the Cree. The term Slave Indian derives from the domination and forced labour exacted by the Cree. The Athabascan tribe has always been closely linked to the Chipewyan people, and some regard them as one group. The Athabascan language is a subgroup of the Na-Dené linguistic phylum. It covers the largest geographical area of all Native North American groups, including Alaska, Yukon, N and W Canada, Oregon, California, New Mexico, and W Arizona. By the mid-1980s, the number of Athabascan speakers was believed to exceed 160,000, including the APACHE (with more than 13,000) and NAVAJO.

Athanasian Creed Christian profession of faith, probably written in the 6th century, that explains the teachings of the Church on the Trinity and the incarnation. The Roman Catholic and some Protestant churches accept its authority.

Athanasius, Saint (d.373) Early Christian leader. As patriarch of Alexandria he confuted ARIANISM, and in various writings defended the teaching that the Son and the Holy Spirit were of equal divinity with God the Father and so shared a three-fold being. He is no longer considered the author of the ATHANASIAN CREED, but he did write the *Life of St Anthony*. His feast day is May 2.

atheism Philosophical position rejecting the idea of the existence of a god or gods. Early Christians were called atheists because they denied Roman religions, but the term now usually indicates a rejection of Christian theism. During the 18th-century ENLIGHTENMENT, David HUME, Immanuel

KANT, and the Encyclopedists laid the foundations for atheism. In the 19th century, Karl MARX, Friedrich NIETZSCHE, and Sigmund FREUD all accommodated some form of atheism into their respective philosophies. Today many individuals and groups advocate atheism. *See also* AGNOSTICISM

Athena In Greek mythology, the goddess of war, wisdom and patroness of the arts and industry, identified with MINERVA. Athena emerged from the head of Zeus fully grown and armed; thereafter, she was her father's most reliable supporter, and the sponsor of heroes such as Heracles, Perseus, and Odysseus. In the Trojan War she sided with the Greeks. She helped Argus build the ship *Argo* for JASON and the ARGONAUTS. She received special worship at Athens, where her main temples were the PARTHENON and the Erechtheum.

Athens (Athínai) Capital and largest city of Greece, situated on the Saronic Gulf. The ancient city was built around the Acropolis, a fortified citadel, and was the greatest artistic and cultural centre in ancient Greece, gaining importance after the PERSIAN WARS (500–449BC). Athens prospered under Cimon and PERICLES during the 5th century BC and provided a climate in which the great classical works of philosophy and drama were created. The most noted artistic treasures are the PARTHENON (438BC), Athena Parthenos (a Doric statue), the Erechtheum (406BC), and the Theatre of Dionysus (c.500 BC the oldest of the Greek theatres). Modern Athens and its port of PIRAEUS form a major Mediterranean transport and economic centre. Overcrowding and severe air pollution are damaging the ancient sites and the tourist industry. Other industries: shipbuilding, paper, steel machinery, textiles, pottery, brewing, chemicals and glass. Pop. (2005) 3,238,000.

athletics (track and field) Composite sport that includes running and hurdling events on the track, jumping and throwing field events, cross-country and long-distance road running and walking. The first ancient Greek OLYMPIC GAMES (held in 775BC) featured many athletics events. The first

INTERNET

Atlantic, Battle of the
▶ www.iwm.org.uk/upload/
package/8/atlantic/
campaign.htm

Atlantic Charter
▶ usinfo.state.gov/usa/
infousa/facts/democrac/
53.htm

modern Olympic Games were held at Athens in 1896. The world's governing body, the International Amateur Athletic Federation (IAAF), was established in 1912, and the sport maintained its amateur status. In the late 20th century, commercial sponsorship and media coverage ended top flight amateurism and introduced professional grand prix events.

Atlanta Capital of Georgia, USA, in the NW centre of the state. The land was ceded to Georgia in 1821 by the CREEK and was settled in 1833. The city was founded in 1837 at the E end of the Western and Atlantic Railroad. Originally called Terminus, it became Marthasville (1843) and Atlanta in 1845. It served as a Confederate supply depot and communications centre during the American CIVIL WAR. On September 2, 1864, it fell to General Sherman, whose army razed the city. Atlanta rapidly rebuilt and soon recovered its importance as a transport and cotton manufacturing centre. It became the permanent state capital in 1887. In the late 20th century, Atlanta became a major US city. It is the headquarters of Coca Cola. It contains the High Museum of Art and Emory University (founded 1836). Atlanta hosted the 1996 Summer Olympic Games. Despite a bomb and complaints about public transport provisions, the Games were a success. Industries: textiles, chemicals, iron and steel, electronics. Pop. (2000) 3,500,000.

Atlantic, Battle of the (1939–43) Campaign for control of the Atlantic sea routes waged by air and naval forces during WORLD WAR 2. The Germans hoped to starve Britain into submission by U-boat attacks on merchant shipping, and later to prevent US reinforcements reaching the Mediterranean and Europe. More than 14 million tonnes of shipping were destroyed.

Atlantic Charter Joint declaration of peace aims issued in August 1941 by US President Franklin ROOSEVELT and British Prime Minister Winston CHURCHILL. It affirmed the right of all nations to choose their own form of government, promised to restore sovereignty to all nations, and advocated the disarmament of aggressor nations.

Atlantic City Resort city in SE New Jersey, built on a 16km (10mi) sandbar in the Atlantic Ocean and settled as a fishing village in 1790. Famous for its 6km (4mi) boardwalk (1896) and its annual Miss America pageant (started in 1921), it is a centre for political and business conventions. In 1976 gambling was legalized and, since the first casinos were opened in 1978, Atlantic City has become a major tourist centre and stage for sporting events (especially boxing). Pop. (2000) 40,517.

Atlantic Ocean World's second-largest ocean stretching from the Arctic Circle in the N to the Antarctic Ocean in the S. Its name derives from the ATLAS Mountains, which, for the ancient Greeks, marked the western boundary between the known and the unknown world. Its most striking feature is the MID-ATLANTIC RIDGE, which runs N-S for its entire length. At the crest, the ridge is cleft by a deep rift valley which is frequently offset by E-W transform faults. The age of the crust increases with distance from the central rift, and so there is little doubt that the rift has evolved by seafloor spreading and is associated with the movement of the Americas away from Europe and Africa at a yearly rate of 2–4cm (0.8–1.6in). The average depth of the Atlantic is 3,700m (12,100ft). The greatest known depth is the Milwaukee Deep in the Puerto Rico Trench, at 8,650m (28,370ft). The N clockwise gyre is dominated by the fast-flowing GULF STREAM, travelling at speeds of up to 130km (80mi) a day, and forming the W boundary current of the gyre. The S anti-clockwise gyre is atypical in having a weak western boundary current, the Brazil Current. Apart from oil (found mainly in the Gulf of Guinea), sand and gravel are the most important minerals from the Atlantic. The world's largest single offshore mining operation is located at Ocean Cay on the Grand Bahamas bank, where calcium carbonate is extracted in the form of aragonite. Valuable diamond deposits occur off the coast of Namibia. Area: 82 million sq km (32 million sq mi).

Atlantis Mythical island in the Atlantic Ocean from which, according to Plato, a great empire tried to subdue the Mediterranean countries. It has been identified by some with the Greek island of Thera, destroyed by an earthquake c.1450 BC.

Atlas Mountain system in NW Africa, comprising several folded and roughly parallel chains extending 2,400km

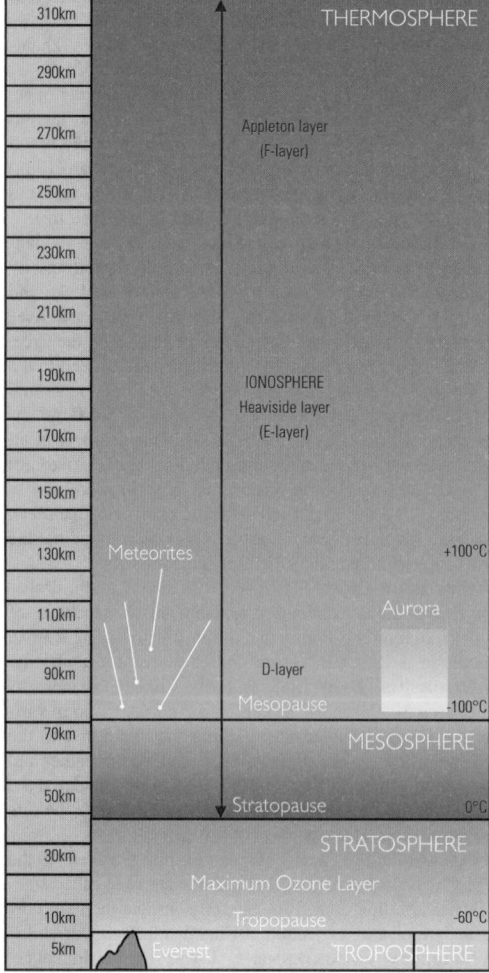

▶ **atmosphere** The Earth's atmosphere is formed of various layers. It is believed that the atmosphere has changed three times during the Earth's history. The present atmosphere consists mainly of nitrogen and oxygen.

310km
290km
270km   Appleton layer
         (F-layer)
250km
230km
210km
190km   IONOSPHERE
         Heaviside layer
170km   (E-layer)
150km
130km   Meteorites   +100°C
110km   Aurora
90km   D-layer
70km   Mesopause   -100°C
         MESOSPHERE
50km
         Stratopause   0°C
30km   STRATOSPHERE
         Maximum Ozone Layer
10km   Tropopause   -60°C
5km   Everest
         TROPOSPHERE

THERMOSPHERE

(1500mi) from the coast of sw Morocco to the coast of N Tunisia. North Africa's highest peak, Djebel Toubkal, 4170m (13,671ft), is found in the Grand Atlas range in W Morocco.

Atlas In Greek mythology, one of the TITANS, brother of PROMETHEUS. Having fought against Zeus, he was condemned to hold up the heavens.

atman Human soul or self in Hindu religion. *See* BRAHMAN

atmosphere Envelope of gases surrounding the Earth and shielding it from the harsh environment of space. The gases it contains are vital to life. About 95% by weight of the Earth's atmosphere lies below the 25km (15mi) altitude; the mixture of gases in the lower atmosphere is commonly called air. The atmosphere's composition by weight is: nitrogen 78.09%, oxygen 20.9%, argon 0.93%, 0.03% of carbon dioxide, plus 0.05% of hydrogen, the inert gases and varying amounts of water vapour. The force of gravity creates an atmospheric pressure. The atmosphere can be conceived as concentric shells; the innermost is the **troposphere**, in which dust and water vapour create clouds and weather. The **stratosphere** extends from 10–55km (8–36mi) and is cooler and clearer and contains ozone. Above, to a height of 70km (43mi), is the **mesosphere** in which chemical reactions occur, powered by sunlight. The temperature climbs steadily in the thermosphere, which gives way to the **exosphere** at *c.*400km (250mi), where helium and hydrogen may be lost into space. The IONOSPHERE ranges from *c.*50km (30mi) out into the VAN ALLEN RADIATION BELTS.

atmospheric pressure Pressure exerted by the ATMOSPHERE because of its gravitational attraction to the Earth (or other body), measured by barometers and usually expressed in units of mercury. Standard atmospheric pressure at sea level is 760mm (29.92in) of mercury or 101,325 pascals. The column of air above each cm^2 of Earth's surface weighs *c.*1kg (or 14.7lb above each in^2).

atoll Ring-shaped REEF of CORAL enclosing a shallow LAGOON. An atoll begins as a reef surrounding a slowly subsiding island, usually volcanic. As the island sinks, the coral continues to grow upwards until eventually the island is below sea level and only a ring of coral is left at the surface.

atom Smallest particle of matter that can take part in a chemical reaction, every element having its own characteristic atoms. The atom, once thought indivisible, consists of a central, positively charged NUCLEUS orbited by negatively charged ELECTRONS, a balance that makes the atom neutral. The nucleus (identified in 1911 by Ernest RUTHERFORD) is composed of tightly packed protons and neutrons. It occupies a small fraction of the atomic space but accounts for almost all of the mass of the atom. In 1913 Niels BOHR suggested that electrons moved in fixed orbits. The study of QUANTUM MECHANICS modified the concept of orbits: the Heisenberg UNCERTAINTY PRINCIPLE states that it is impossible to know the exact position and MOMENTUM of a subatomic particle. The number of electrons in an atom and their configuration determine its chemical properties. Adding or removing one or more electrons produces an ION. *See also* SUBATOMIC PARTICLES

atomic bomb *See* NUCLEAR WEAPON

atomic clock Most accurate of terrestrial CLOCKS. It is an electric clock regulated by such natural periodic phenomena as emitted radiation or atomic vibration; the atoms of CAESIUM are most commonly used. Clocks that run on radiation from hydrogen atoms lose one second in 1.7 million years.

atomic energy *See* NUCLEAR ENERGY

atomic mass number (nucleon number) Number of nucleons (protons and neutrons) in the nucleus of an atom. It is represented by the symbol A. In nuclear notation, such as $^7_3$ Li, the mass number is the upper number and the ATOMIC NUMBER (the number of protons) is the lower one. ISOTOPES of an element have different mass numbers but identical atomic numbers.

atomic mass unit (amu) Unit of mass used to compare relative atomic masses, defined as 1/12th the mass of the most abundant isotope of carbon, carbon-12 (6 electrons, 6 protons, and 6 neutrons). One amu is equal to 1.66033×10^{-27} kg.

atomic number (proton number) Number of protons in the nucleus of an atom of an element, which is equal to the number of electrons moving around that nucleus. It is abbreviated to

ATOM

model of an atom

uranium

hydrogen

nucleus — neutron

proton

electron

The mass of an atom depends on the size of the nucleus. The nucleus makes up the very great majority of the atom's mass, as the mass of an electron is tiny compared to that of a proton. A uranium atom, for example, has the greatest mass of all naturally occurring atoms. It has 146 neutrons, 92 protons and 92 electrons. A hydrogen atom on the other hand, has the least mass. It has only 1 proton and 1 electron. However, while a uranium atom has a mass 230 times greater than that of a hydrogen atom, it is only 3 times larger.

'at.no.' and represented by the symbol Z. The atomic number determines the chemical properties of an element and its position in the PERIODIC TABLE. ISOTOPES of an element all have the same atomic number but a different ATOMIC MASS NUMBER.

atomism (Gk. *atmos* uncuttable) Philosophical theory originated in Greece by Leucippus and elaborated by DEMOCRITUS during the 5th and 4th centuries BC. It held that everything is made of immutable and indivisible particles called atoms. The theory was an attempt to reconcile the single immutable substance theory of being, espoused by Parmenides and other Eleatic philosophers, with HERACLITUS' view that all things are subject to change.

atonality Musical composition without reference to traditional KEYS and HARMONY. Examples include *Pierrot Lunaire* (1912) by Arnold SCHOENBERG.

atonement In religion, the process by which a sinner seeks forgiveness from and reconciliation with God, through an act of expiation such as prayer, fasting or good works. In Christian theology, Jesus Christ atoned for the sins of the world by his sacrifice on the cross. Jews observe YOM KIPPUR, their most sacred feast, as a day of repentance.

atrophy In medicine, shrinking or wastage of tissues or organs. It may be associated with disease, malnutrition, or, in the case of muscle atrophy, with disuse.

atropine Poisonous ALKALOID drug ($C_{17}H_{23}NO_3N$) obtained from certain plants such as *Atropa belladonna* (DEADLY NIGHTSHADE). Atropine is used medicinally to regularize the heartbeat during anaesthesia, to dilate the pupil of the eye and to treat motion sickness.

attar of roses (otto) Essential oil obtained from rose petals, and used as a perfume and perfumery agent. Attar is any fragrant oil derived from plants, although attar of roses (produced by crushing and distilling petals from the damask rose cultivated in the Balkans) is by far the best known.

Attenborough, Sir David Frederick (1926–) English naturalist and broadcaster; brother of Richard ATTENBOROUGH. He was controller of BBC2 television (1965–68). From 1954 he travelled on zoological and ethnographical filming expeditions, which formed the basis of such landmark natural history series as *Life on Earth* (1979), *The Living Planet* (1984), *The Trials of Life* (1990), and *The Private Life of Plants* (1995). He was knighted in 1985.

Attenborough, Sir Richard (1923–) English film actor and director. His career has spanned more than 50 years, beginning with *In Which We Serve* (1942). He delivered a menacing

▲ **aubergine** Grown widely in tropical Asia, the aubergine or eggplant (*Solanum melongena*), although commonly thought of as a vegetable, is in fact a fruit.

performance in *Brighton Rock* (1947). His directorial debut was the World War 1 satire *Oh! What a Lovely War* (1971). His directorial style suited biographical films. *Gandhi* (1982) won Oscars for Best Film and Best Director. *Cry Freedom* (1987) was the story of Steve Biko, while *Shadowlands* (1993), his biopic of C.S. Lewis, brought further critical praise.

Attila (406–453) King of the HUNS (*c*.439–53), co-ruler with his elder brother until 445. Attila defeated the Eastern Roman Emperor THEODOSIUS II, extorting land and tribute, and invaded Gaul in 451. Although his army suffered heavy losses, he invaded Italy in 452, but disease forced his withdrawal. Attila has a reputation as a fierce warrior, but was fair to his subjects and encouraged learning. On his death the empire fell apart.

Attlee, Clement Richard, 1st Earl (1883–1967) British statesman, prime minister (1945–51). Attlee became a Labour member of Parliament in 1922. He joined the Labour government in 1930, but resigned when Ramsay MACDONALD formed a National Coalition (1931). Attlee became leader of the LABOUR PARTY in 1935. During World War 2, he served in Winston CHURCHILL's wartime cabinet, first as Dominions Secretary (1942–43) and then as deputy prime minister (1942–45). Attlee won a landslide victory in the 1945 general election. His administration was notable for the introduction of important social reforms, such as the NATIONAL HEALTH SERVICE (NHS) and the nationalization of the power industries, the railways and the BANK OF ENGLAND. He also granted independence to India (1947) and Burma (1948).

attorney general Principal law officer. In the USA, the attorney general is the highest law officer of the government and head of the department of justice, and advises the president and heads of the executive department. In the UK, it is the chief law officer of the crown and head of the English bar, and also legal adviser to the House of Commons and the government.

Atwood, Margaret Eleanor (1939–) Canadian novelist, poet, and critic. Best known outside Canada for her novels, she also published numerous volumes of poetry. Her debut novel, *The Edible Woman* (1969), received immediate acclaim for its stylish and articulate treatment of complex gender relationships. In 2000, Atwood won the Booker Prize with the novel *The Blind Assassin*.

Auber, Daniel-François-Esprit (1782–1871) French composer. He studied under Cherubini and wrote more than 40 operas, often collaborating with the librettist Scribe. His operas include *La Muette de Portici* (or *Masaniello*) and *Fra Diavolo*. He is regarded as the founder of French grand opera.

aubergine (eggplant) Tropical member of the potato (and nightshade) family. The fruit may be eaten as a vegetable. A bushy perennial with violet flowers native to the New World, it is now widely cultivated in temperate regions. Family Solanaceae; species *Solanum melongena*.

Auckland Largest city, chief port, and region of New Zealand, lying on an isthmus on NW North Island. The port, built on land purchased from the Maoris in 1840, handles around 60% of New Zealand's trade. The first immigrants arrived from Scotland in 1842 and in 1854 the first New Zealand parliament opened here. It remained the capital until 1865. Within the city there are many volcanic cones. Industries: vehicle assembly, boatbuilding, footwear, food canning, chemicals. Auckland has the largest Polynesian population (*c*.65,000) of any city in the world. Pop. (2005) 1,152,000.

Auden, W.H. (Wystan Hugh) (1907–73) Anglo-American poet, b. England, one of the major poets of the 20th century. Auden's first volume of poetry, *Poems* (1930), established him as the leading voice in a group of left-wing writers, which included Stephen SPENDER, Louis MACNEICE, Cecil DAY-LEWIS, and Christopher ISHERWOOD. Auden and Isherwood collaborated on a series of plays, such as *The Ascent of F6* (1936). Auden joined the Republican cause in the Spanish Civil War and wrote *Spain* (1937). In 1939 he emigrated to New York, becoming a US citizen in 1946. His volume *The Age of Anxiety* (1947) won a Pulitzer Prize. From 1956 to 1961, Auden was professor of poetry at Oxford University. His poetry adopts many tones, often using colloquial and everyday language. His later poetry reflected his conversion to Anglicanism. Auden's *Collected Poems* was published in 1976.

auditory canal Tube leading from the outer EAR to the eardrum. It is about 2.5cm (1in) long. The auditory canal and the **auricle** (visible part of the ear) form the outer ear.

Audubon, John James (1785–1851) US ornithologist and artist. His remarkable series of some 400 watercolours of birds, often in action, were published in *Birds of America* (1827–38).

Augsburg Historic city on the River Lech, Bavaria, Germany. Founded by the Romans (*c*.15BC) and named after the Emperor Augustus, it became a free imperial city in 1276 and was a prosperous banking and commercial centre in the 15th and 16th centuries. The AUGSBURG CONFESSION was presented and the Peace of Augsburg (1555) was signed here. The cathedral (started 994) claims the oldest stained-glass windows in Europe (11th century). Industries: textiles, engineering, motor vehicles. Pop. (1997) 262,110.

Augsburg, League of (1686) Alliance of the enemies of the French King LOUIS XIV. Composed of Spain, Sweden, the Holy Roman Empire, and lesser states, its formation under Emperor Leopold I was a reaction to French encroachment on the land bordering the Holy Roman Empire. Following the French attack on the PALATINATE in 1688 a new coalition against the French, the Grand Alliance, was formed in 1689.

Augsburg, Peace of (1555) Agreement, reached by the Diet of the Holy Roman Empire in Augsburg, ending the conflict between Roman Catholics and Lutherans in Germany. It established the right of each Prince to decide on the nature of religions practice in his lands, *cuius regio, cuius religio*. Dissenters were allowed to sell their lands and move. Free cities and imperial cities were open to both Catholics and Lutherans. The exclusion of other Protestant sects such as Calvinism proved to be a source of future conflict.

Augsburg Confession (1530) Summation of the Lutheran faith, presented to Emperor Charles V at the Diet of Augsburg. Its 28 articles were formulated from earlier Lutheran statements principally by Philip MELANCHTHON. It was denounced by the Roman Catholic Church, but became a model for later Protestant creeds.

Augusta State capital of Maine, USA, on the Kennebec River, 72km (45mi) from the Atlantic Ocean. Founded by settlers from Plymouth as a trading post in 1628, it was incorporated in 1797. A dam built across the Kennebec River in 1837 led to Augusta's industry changing from shipping to manufacturing textiles, paper and steel. The city also benefits from tourism. Pop. (2000) 18,560.

Augustine, Saint (354–430) Christian theologian and philosopher. Augustine's *Confessions* provide a psychological self-portrait of a spirit in search of ultimate purpose. This he found in his conversion to Christianity in 386. As Bishop of Hippo, N Africa (395–430), he defended Christian orthodoxy against Manichaeism, Donatism and Pelagianism. In *Enchiridion* (421) he emphasized the corruption of human will and the freedom of the divine gift of grace. *The City of God* (426) is a model of Christian apologetic literature. Of the Four Fathers of the Latin Church, AMBROSE, JEROME and GREGORY I, Augustine is considered the greatest. His feast day is August 28.

Augustine of Canterbury, Saint (d.604) First Archbishop of CANTERBURY. He was sent from Rome in 596 by Pope GREGORY I, at the head of a 40–strong mission. Arriving in Kent in 597, Augustine converted King ETHELBERT and introduced Roman ecclesiastical practices into England. This brought him into conflict with the Celtic monks of Britain and Ireland whose traditions had developed in isolation from the continent. The Synod of Whitby (663) settled disputes in favour of Rome. His feast day is May 28 (May 26 in England and Wales).

Augustinian Name of two distinct and long-established Christian orders. The order of Augustinian Canons was founded in the 11th century. Based on the recommendations of Saint AUGUSTINE, its discipline was milder than those of full monastic orders. The mendicant order of Augustinian Hermits or Friars was founded in the 13th century and modelled on the DOMINICANS.

Augustus (63 BC–AD 14) (Gaius Julius Caesar Octavianus) First Roman Emperor (29BC–AD 14), also called **Octavian**. Nephew and adopted heir of Julius CAESAR, he formed the Second Triumvirate with Mark ANTONY and Lepidus after

INTERNET

Attlee, Clement Richard 1st Earl
▶ www.number-10.gov.uk

Audubon, John James
▶ www.audubon.org/nas/jja. html

Caesar's assassination. They defeated BRUTUS and CASSIUS at Philippi in 42 BC and divided the empire between them. Rivalry between Antony and Octavian was resolved by the defeat of Antony at Actium in 31 BC. While preserving the form of the republic, Octavian held supreme power. He introduced peace and prosperity after years of civil war. He built up the power and prestige of Rome, encouraging patriotic literature and rebuilding much of the city in marble. He extended the frontiers and fostered colonization, took general censuses, and attempted to make taxation more equitable. He tried to arrange the succession to avoid future conflicts, though had to acknowledge an unloved stepson, TIBERIUS, as his successor.

Augustus II (the Strong) (1670–1733) King of Poland (1697–1704, 1709–33) and, as Frederick Augustus I, Elector of Saxony (1694–1733). He was elected by the Polish nobles in order to secure an alliance with Saxony, but the result was to draw Poland into the Great NORTHERN WAR on the side of Russia. In 1704 Augustus surrendered his crown to Stanislas I Leszcynski. Civil war (1704–09) and invasion by CHARLES XII of Sweden weakened the Polish state. Augustus regained the throne after Tsar PETER I (THE GREAT) defeated Sweden at the Battle of Poltava in 1709, but at the cost of growing Russian dominance in Polish affairs

auk Squat-bodied sea bird of colder Northern Hemisphere coastlines. The flightless great auk (*Pinguinus impennis*), or the Atlantic penguin, became extinct in the 1840s; height: 76cm (30in). The razorbill auk (*Alca torda*) is the largest of living species. Family Alcidae.

Aung San (1914–47) Burmese politician who opposed British rule, father of AUNG SAN SUU KYI. Initially collaborating with the Japanese (1942), he later helped expel the invaders. He was assassinated shortly after his appointment as deputy chairman of the executive council.

Aung San Suu Kyi (1945–) Burmese politician, daughter of AUNG SAN. She was under house arrest (1989–95) for leading the National League for Democracy, a coalition opposed to Burma's oppressive military junta. Dedicated to peaceful resistance, she received the Nobel Peace Prize in 1991. Aung San Suu Kyi won 2000 elections, but the junta ignored the result and again placed her under house arrest. She was released in 2002 after UN pressure, but rearrested in 2003. Further UN demands for her release have been refused.

Aurangzeb (1619–1707) Emperor of India (1659–1707). The last of the great emperors of the MOGUL Empire, Aurangzeb seized the throne from his enfeebled father, SHAH JAHAN. He reigned over an even greater area, and spent most of his reign defending it. Aurangzeb was a devout Muslim, whose intolerance of Hinduism provoked long wars with the MARATHA. The empire was already breaking up before his death.

Aurelian (*c*.215–75) Roman Emperor. Having risen through the army ranks, he succeeded Claudius II in 270. His victories against the Goths, reconquest of Palmyra and recovery of Gaul and Britain earned him the title 'Restorer of the World'. He built the Aurelian Wall to protect Rome and was assassinated in a complex military plot.

Aurelius, Marcus *See* MARCUS AURELIUS ANTONINUS

aurochs (urus) Extinct European wild ox, the long-horned ancestor of modern domesticated cattle. Once found throughout the forests of Europe and central and SE Asia, it became extinct in 1627. A dark, shaggy animal, it stood up to 2m (7ft) tall at the shoulder. Family Bovidae; species *Bos primigenius*.

Aurora In Roman mythology, the goddess of dawn, equivalent to the Greek goddess EOS.

aurora Sporadic, radiant display of coloured light in the night sky, caused by charged particles from the Sun interacting with air molecules in the Earth's magnetic field. Auroras occur in polar regions and are known as **aurora borealis** in the N, and **aurora australis** in the S.

Auschwitz (Pol. *Oświęcim*) Town in S Poland. It was the site of a German concentration camp during World War 2. A group of three main camps, with 39 smaller camps nearby, Auschwitz was Hitler's most "efficient" extermination centre. Between June 1940 and January 1945 more than 4 million people were executed here, mostly Jews, and comprising

about 40 different nationalities, principally Polish. The vast majority were gassed in its chambers, but many others were shot, starved or tortured to death. Pop. (1999) 43,700.

Austen, Jane (1775–1817) English novelist. She completed six novels of great art, insight and wit, casting an ironic but sympathetic light on the society of upper-middle-class England. In order of composition they are: *Northanger Abbey* (1818), a parody on the contemporary Gothic novel; *Sense and Sensibility* (1811); *Pride and Prejudice* (1813); *Mansfield Park* (1814); *Emma* (1816) and *Persuasion* (1818). Not particularly successful in their time, they have since established their place among the most popular and well-crafted works in English literature. Her work has recently undergone an enthusiastic revival in the public imagination, following several film adaptations, most notably *Sense and Sensibility* (1995).

Austerlitz, Battle of (December 2, 1805) French victory, led by NAPOLEON I, over the Austrians and Russians under Mikhail Kutuzov in Bohemia. One of Napoleon's greatest victories, it was also called the Battle of the Three Emperors.

Austin Capital of Texas, on the Colorado River, USA. Originally called Waterloo, it was first settled in 1835 and renamed after Stephen AUSTIN in 1839. The market centre for a farming and ranching area, Austin hosts national conventions. Industries: high-tech electronics, furniture, machinery, building materials, food processing. Pop. (2000) 902,000.

Austin, Stephen (1793–1836) US pioneer. On his father's death in 1821, he acquired a grant in the Spanish territory that was to become Texas. He settled the first English-speaking colony here, and was followed by many other colonists.

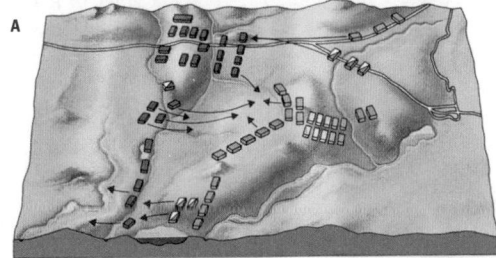

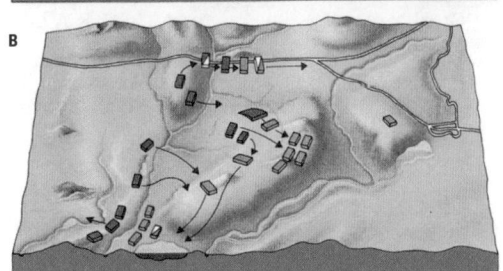

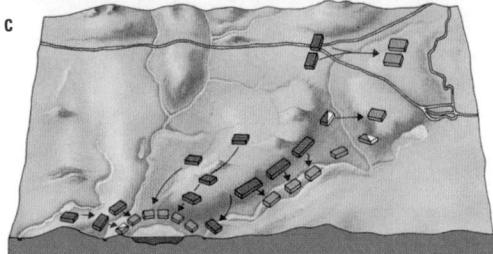

◀ **Austerlitz, Battle of**
Napoleon's defeat of the Allied forces at the Battle of Austerlitz was one of his greatest triumphs. By evacuating Austerlitz and the Pratzen Heights, Napoleon feigned weakness. The Allied forces camped on the heights (A). Their plan was to overwhelm the (deliberately) weak French right flank, before heading north to envelop the French as they headed for Brünn. Beneath the cover of mist, elements of the French forces manoeuvred beneath the Pratzen Heights. The Allies attacked the French right flank. While the Allies were engaged in battle to the south, French forces marched up and occupied the Pratzen Heights (B). Additional support was provided by other French forces that had initially engaged the Allies to the north. Together the French forces dispersed the Allies, driving them on to the frozen lakes near Telnitz, where many drowned as Napoleon ordered his artillery to open fire, breaking the ice (C).

Australia is the world's sixth-largest country. The huge Western Plateau makes up 66% of its land area, and is mainly flat and dry. Off the coast of NE Queensland lies the GREAT BARRIER REEF. The GREAT DIVIDING RANGE extends down the entire E coast and into VICTORIA. The mountains of TASMANIA are a southern extension of the range. The highlands separate the E coastal plains from the Central Lowlands and include Australia's highest peak, Mount KOSCIUSZKO, in NEW SOUTH WALES. The capital, CANBERRA, lies in the foothills. The SE lowlands are drained by the MURRAY and Darling, Australia's two longest rivers. Lake EYRE is the continent's largest lake. It lies on the edge of the Simpson Desert and is a dry salt flat for most of the year. ALICE SPRINGS lies in the heart of the continent, close to AYERS ROCK (Uluru).

Much of the W plateau is desert, although areas of grass and low shrubs are found on its margins. The grasslands of the Central Lowlands are used to raise livestock. The N has

areas of savanna and rainforest. In dry areas, acacias are common. Eucalyptus grows in wetter regions.

CLIMATE

Only 10% of Australia has an average annual rainfall greater than 1,000mm [39in]. These areas include some of the tropical NORTH (where DARWIN is situated), the NE coast, and the SE. The coasts are usually warm and many parts of the S and SW, including PERTH, enjoy a Mediterranean climate of dry summers and moist winters. The interior is dry and many rivers are only seasonal.

HISTORY

NATIVE AUSTRALIANS (Aborigines) entered the continent from SE Asia more than 50,000 years ago. They settled throughout the country and remained isolated from the rest of the world until the first European explorers, the Dutch, arrived in the 17th century. The Dutch did not settle. In 1770 British explorer Captain James Cook reached BOTANY BAY and

AREA 7,741,229sq km [2,988,885sq mi]
POPULATION 20,434,000
CAPITAL (POPULATION) Canberra (309,000)
GOVERNMENT Federal constitutional monarchy
ETHNIC GROUPS Caucasian 92%, Asian 7%, Aboriginal 1%
LANGUAGES English (official)
RELIGIONS Roman Catholic 26%, Anglican 26%, other Christian 24%, non-Christian 24%
CURRENCY Australian dollar = 100 cents

National flag

Native Australian flag

claimed the E coast for Great Britain. In 1788 Britain built its first settlement, for convicts, on the site of present-day SYDNEY. The first free settlers arrived three years later.

In the 19th century, the economy developed rapidly, based on mining and sheep-rearing. The continent was divided into colonies, which later became states. In 1901 the six states of QUEENSLAND, Victoria, Tasmania, New South Wales, SOUTH AUSTRALIA and

AUSTRALIA

WESTERN AUSTRALIA federated to create the Commonwealth of Australia. In 1911, the NORTHERN TERRITORY joined the federation. A range of progressive social welfare policies were adopted, such as old-age pensions (1909). The federal capital was established (1927) at Canberra, AUSTRALIAN CAPITAL TERRITORY. Australia fought as a member of the Allies in both world wars. The Battle of the Coral Sea (1942) prevented a full-scale attack on the continent.

POLITICS

After 1945 Australia steadily realigned itself with its Asian neighbours. Robert MENZIES, Australia's longest-serving prime minister, oversaw many economic and social reforms and dispatched Australian troops to the Vietnam War. In 1977 Prime Minister Gough WHITLAM was removed from office by the British governor-general. He was succeeded by Malcolm FRASER. In 1983 elections, the LABOR PARTY defeated Fraser, and Bob HAWKE became prime minister. His shrewd handling of industrial disputes and economic recession

helped him win a record four terms in office. In 1991, Hawke was forced to resign as leader and was succeeded by Paul KEATING, who proposed that Australia should become a republic. Keating won the 1993 general election and persevered with his free market reforms.

In 1996 elections, Keating was defeated by a coalition led by John HOWARD, who secured a second term in 1998. In a referendum of 1999 Australia voted against becoming a republic. In 2000 Sydney hosted the 28th Summer Olympic Games.

The historic maltreatment of Native Australians remains a contentious political issue. In 1993 the government passed the Native Title Act which restored to Native Australians land rights over their traditional hunting and sacred areas. Native peoples still suffer poverty and low life expectancy.

Howard secured a fourth term in 2004 elections. His government attempted to delay action on global warming, despite rising temperatures which are already causing increased bush fires and severe drought. In 2007 elections Kevin Rudd of the Labor Party became

Prime Minister. He committed the country to the KYOTO PROTOCOL and made the government's first formal apology for the past treatment of native Australians.

ECONOMY

Australia is a prosperous country. Originally it was an agrarian economy, although crops grow on only 6% of the land. The country remains a major producer and exporter of farm products, particularly cattle, wheat and wool. Grapes grown for winemaking, and the wine produced from them, are also important. Australia is rich in natural resources and is a major producer of minerals, such as bauxite, coal, copper, diamonds, gold, iron ore, manganese, nickel, silver, tin, tungsten and zinc. Some oil and natural gas is also produced.

The majority of Australia's imports are manufactured products. They include machinery and other capital goods required by factories. The country has a highly developed manufacturing sector; the major products include consumer goods, notably foodstuffs and household articles. Tourism is a vital industry.

Mexico opposed this colonization, and Austin went to Mexico City to argue his case, but was arrested. On his return in 1835, he became a leader in the fight for Texan independence.

Australasia Region that includes Australia, New Zealand and Papua New Guinea. The term Australasia is inexact. It is sometimes used to include various Asian countries (usually Indonesia and Malaysia), or extended to include Pacific island groups and the Australian and New Zealand territories in Antarctica. Many botanists and zoologists use the term to mean the lands and seas to the E and s of Wallace's Line. The native flora and fauna on one side of the line differ from those on the other.

Australia Earth's smallest continent, between the Pacific and Indian Oceans. Combined with the island of TASMANIA, it forms the independent Commonwealth country of Australia. *See* country feature

Australia Day Annual national holiday in Australia, celebrated on the Monday following January 26. It commemorates the arrival of the First Fleet (carrying the first colonists) at Port Jackson, Sydney, on January 26, 1788.

Australian art Term applied to art produced by Native Australians and also that produced by descendants of European settlers. The art of Native Australians dates back to prehistoric times. They painted on a variety of surfaces, including rock, bark and shells. The most remarkable examples are the so-called X-ray paintings in Arnhem Land, in which hunters depicted the internal anatomy of the beasts they killed, and the *wondjina* figures, which were found near water holes in the NW. European influence on the continent dates from 1788, when the first penal colony was established. The Australian landscape attracted a significant number of foreign painters, such as John Glover (1767–1849) and Conrad Martens (1801–78); however, Australian artists still felt the need to train in Europe. The late 19th-century Heidelberg School, based in Heidelberg, Victoria, represented the first truly national movement in Australian art. It was led by Tom Roberts, whose impressionist-inspired landscapes influenced Australian art for many decades. In the 20th century, the Melbourne journal *Angry Penguins* (1940–46) proved a seminal influence, fostering the talents of many avant-garde painters. Among these were the two most celebrated names in Australian art, Sir Sidney Nolan and Arthur Boyd.

Australian Capital Territory (ACT) (Commonwealth Territory) District within NEW SOUTH WALES but administratively independent of it. It contains the Australian capital,

CANBERRA. The area was first settled in 1824 and was set aside as the capital territory in 1908. In 1915 an additional 72sq km (28sq mi) were added, making a total of 2432sq km (939sq mi). Pop. (2001 est.) 322,638.

Australopithecus *See* HUMAN EVOLUTION

Austria Landlocked republic in the heart of Europe. *See* country feature, page 122

Austrian Succession, War of the (1740–48) Conflict between Austria and Prussia for control of the German states, prompted by the succession (1740) of MARIA THERESA to the Habsburg lands of her father, CHARLES VI. Maria Theresa was faced with counterclaims to her succession from PHILIP V of Spain, Augustus III of Poland and Charles Albert, Elector of Bavaria. The war began with FREDERICK II of Prussia's invasion of the Habsburg province of SILESIA. In 1741, with French aid, Charles Albert captured Prague. In 1742, with British and Hungarian support, Maria Theresa launched a counter-offensive that overrran Bavaria. This first phase (First Silesian War) was concluded by the Treaty of Berlin (1742) in which Prussia gained most of Silesia. The French army was forced to retreat from Prague and was defeated at Dettingen (1743) by GEORGE III of Britain. In 1744 Frederick II launched a second invasion of Silesia, but was repulsed. In 1745 the French won a major victory over the British at Fontenoy. George III and Frederick II signed the Convention of Hanover in which Britain recognized Prussia's claims to Silesia in return for Frederick's support of the candidacy of the husband of Maria Theresa as Emperor FRANCIS I. War was formally ended by the Treaty of Aix-La-Chapelle (1748). *See also* FRENCH AND INDIAN WARS

Austro-Hungarian Empire (1867–1918) Organization of the old Austrian Empire into the Kingdom of Hungary and the Empire of Austria, also known as the "Dual Empire". The Emperor of Austria and the King of Hungary were the same person, but each nation had its own parliament and controlled its internal affairs. This arrangement ignored other nationalist minorities and pleased neither the Hungarians, who wanted greater autonomy, nor the Austrians, many of whom wanted a realignment with other German states. After World War 1 Hungary and Czechoslovakia declared their independence, the Emperor Charles abdicated and Austria became a republic.

Austronesian languages (Malayo-Polynesian) Family that includes Malay, Indonesian, Tagalog, Malagasy, and numerous other languages spoken in Indonesia, the Philippines, and the islands of the Pacific Ocean. There are four branches: Indonesian, Melanesian (which includes Fijian), Micronesian (which includes Chamorro, spoken on Guam), and the Polynesian languages, which include Maori, Tongan, Tahitian, and Samoan. There are *c.*175 million speakers in all.

Austro-Prussian War (1866) Conflict between Prussia and Austria, also known as the Seven Weeks' War. Otto von BISMARCK engineered the war to further Prussia's supremacy in Germany and reduce Austrian influence. Defeat at Sadowa forced Austria out of the German Confederation (a federation of 39 German principalities set up by the Congress of Vienna to replace the HOLY ROMAN EMPIRE).

auteur In film theory, the notion that the director is the prime creator, or 'author' of a film. Developed by François TRUFFAUT in 1954, the theory focuses on directorial style and use of recur-

ring motifs to develop a canon of auteurs. Its popularity has waned because it minimizes the importance of collaboration.

authoritarianism System of government that concentrates power in the hands of one person or small group of people not responsible to the population as a whole. Freedom of the press and of political organization are suppressed. Many authoritarian regimes arise from military takeovers.

autism Disorder, usually first appearing in early childhood, characterized by a withdrawal from social behaviour, communication difficulties and ritualistic behaviour. Autistic people have difficulty understanding themselves or others as agents with varying beliefs and desires. The causes of autism may originate in genetics, brain damage or psychology.

autobiography Narrative account of a person's life, written by the subject. The modern autobiography has become a distinctive literary form. The first important example of the genre

AUSTRIA

The Republic of Austria is a landlocked country in the heart of Europe. About three-quarters of the land is mountainous. N Austria contains the valley of the River DANUBE, and the VIENNA Basin. This is Austria's main farming region.

Southern Austria contains ranges of the ALPS, which rise to their highest point of 3,797m [12,457ft] at Gross Glockner.

CLIMATE
The climate is influenced both by westerly and easterly winds. The moist westerly winds bring rain and snow. They also moderate the temperatures. Dry easterly winds bring very cold weather during the winter, and hot weather during the summer.

HISTORY
Following the collapse of the ROMAN EMPIRE, of which Austria s of the Danube formed a part, the area was invaded and settled by waves of Asian, Germanic and Slav peoples. In the late 8th century, Austria came under the rule of CHARLEMAGNE, but in the 10th century the area was overrun by MAGYARS.

In 955, the German king OTTO I brought Austria under his rule, and in 962 it became part of what later became known as the HOLY

ROMAN EMPIRE. In 1526 it was united with BOHEMIA and Hungary, and under HABSBURG rule it became the most important state in the empire. The succession of MARIA THERESA (1740) prompted the War of the AUSTRIAN SUCCESSION. JOSEPH II's reforms encountered fierce resistance. The FRENCH REVOLUTIONARY WARS and the NAPOLEONIC WARS, culminating in defeat at AUSTERLITZ, led to the dissolution of the Holy Roman Empire (1806); however, through the auspices of Prince METTERNICH, Austria continued to dominate European politics. The REVOLUTIONS OF 1848 forced the succession of FRANZ JOSEPH. Austrian power further declined after the AUSTRO-PRUSSIAN WAR (1866). In 1867 Austria and Hungary set up the AUSTRO-HUNGARIAN EMPIRE, whose disregard for individual nationalities later precipitated WORLD WAR I. The defeated empire collapsed in 1918. and Austria's present boundaries derive from the 1919 VERSAILLES TREATY, in which ANSCHLUSS (union) with Germany was forbidden. In 1933, the Christian Socialist Chancellor Engelbert DOLLFUSS ended parliamentary democracy and ruled as a dictator. He was assassinated in 1934 because of his opposition to the Austrian Nazi Party's aim of uniting Austria and Germany in Anschluss, which was

AREA 83,859sq km [32,378sq mi]
POPULATION 8,199,000
CAPITAL (POPULATION) Vienna (2,190,000)
GOVERNMENT Federal republic
ETHNIC GROUPS Austrian 90%, Croatian, Slovene, others
LANGUAGES German (official)
RELIGIONS Roman Catholic 78%, Protestant 5%, Islam and others 17%
CURRENCY Euro = 100 cents

achieved by the German invasion in March 1938. Austria became a province of the Third Reich, called Ostmark, until the defeat of the Axis powers in 1945, when the Allies partitioned and occupied Austria.

POLITICS
After World War 2, Austria was occupied by the Allies, Britain, France and the United States and it paid reparations for a ten-year period. After agreeing to be permanently neutral, Austria became an independent federal republic in 1955.

In 1994, two-thirds of the people voted in favour of joining the European Union. EU membership followed in 1995. Austria became a centre of controversy in 1999 when the extreme right-wing Freedom Party, whose leader Jörg Haider had described Nazi Germany's employment policies as 'sound', came second in national elections. A coalition government was formed, divided equally between the conservative People's Party and the Freedom Party. Elections in 2002 halved the Freedom Party's share of the vote, but the coalition continued. In 2006 elections it was replaced by a coalition between the People's Party and the Social Democrat party.

ECONOMY
Austria is a prosperous country with plenty of hydroelectric power, some oil and gas, and reserves of brown coal. The country's leading economic activity is manufacturing metals and metal products, including iron and steel, vehicles, machinery, machine tools and ships. Craft industries, making such things as fine glassware, jewellery and porcelain are also important. Dairy and livestock farming are the leading agricultural activities. Major crops include barley, potatoes, rye, sugar beet and wheat.

AUTOMOBILE

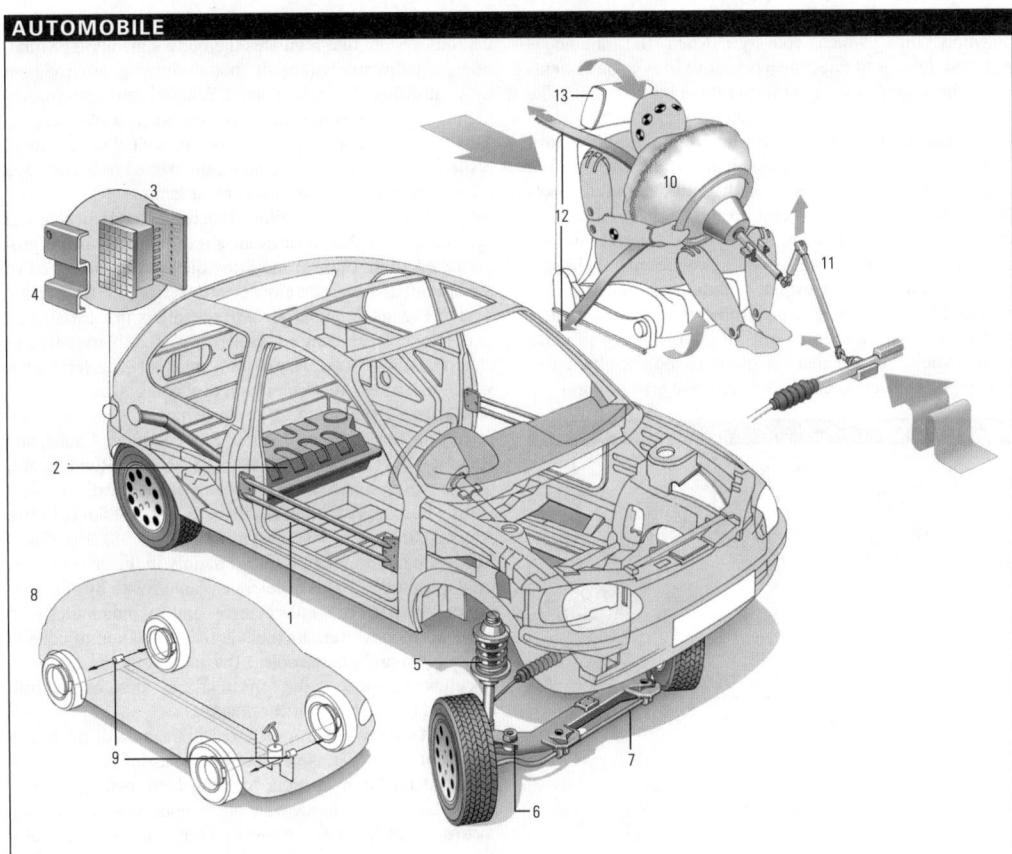

A modern car is designed with crumple zones at the front and rear to absorb the energy of a crash and protect the car's passengers. Side-impact protection bars (1) give strength to the side of the vehicle and spread energy to either side of the passenger cell. Fuel tanks (2) are situated in front of the rear axle to protect the tank if the car is hit from behind. Some manufacturers have replaced the traditional rear brake lights with LEDs (3) which light more quickly. The cover is stepped (4) to prevent the light being obscured by dirt. The suspension, a MacPherson strut (5) system, allows vertical movement through the spring (5) while the wishbone (6) and anti-roll bar (7) keep the wheels in position and stop excessive roll respectively. Anti-skid braking systems (ABS) (8) prevent the wheels locking under heavy braking or in poor weather. Sensors (9) detect when a wheel is about to lock and release the brake pads for a fraction of a second. An explosive charge inflates the air bag (10), which prevents the driver or passenger from hitting the steering wheel or dashboard. The steering column (11) is designed to collapse so the driver is not impaled. Seat belt tensioners use the impact to pull the belt tight (12) holding the passenger in place. The headrest (13) helps stop whiplash injuries when heads snap back in the aftermath of the impact.

was the 4th-century *Confessions* of Saint AUGUSTINE. The modern, introspective autobiography, dealing frankly with all aspects of life, is usually dated from the remarkable *Confessions* of ROUSSEAU (1765–72; published 1782). *See also* BIOGRAPHY

autochrome Method developed by the LUMIÈRE brothers for colour PHOTOGRAPHY. Marketed in 1907, it was the first simple, commercially successful colour process and saw widespread use for more than 30 years. Glass plates were coated with a layer of translucent grains of starch, dyed red, blue and green, which filtered the light passing through a monochrome photographic emulsion. The resulting colour image had a speckled quality reminiscent of POINTILLISM in painting. The Lumières' process was highly secret, and is now lost; no modern researcher has succeeded in replicating it.

autocracy System of government in which a single person or small group of people wields absolute power. It is imposed and generally aimed at furthering the interests of specific individuals or groups. The term is applied usually to those regimes which came before the development of modern technology and state institutions which made TOTALITARIANISM possible.

autoimmune disease Any one of a group of disorders caused by the body's production of antibodies which attack the body's own tissues. One example of such an autoimmune disease is systemic LUPUS erythematosus, an inflammation of the connective tissue occurring most often in young women. The occasional presence of so-called auto-antibodies in an individual does not necessarily indicate autoimmune disease.

Autolycus In Greek mythology, son of Hermes and the mortal Chione. He received from his father the gift of making whatever he touched invisible. In this way, he was able to commit numerous thefts until one day he was caught by SISYPHUS, whose oxen he had stolen.

automation Use of self-governing machines to carry out manufacturing, distribution and other processes automatically. By using FEEDBACK, sensors check a system's operations and send signals to a computer that automatically regulates the process. *See also* MASS PRODUCTION; ROBOT

automobile Road vehicle that first appeared in the 19th century. The first cars were propelled by steam, but were not a success. The age of the motor car really dates from the introduction (1885–86) of the petrol-driven carriages of Gottlieb DAIMLER and Karl BENZ. The INTERNAL COMBUSTION ENGINE for these cars had been developed earlier by several engineers (most notably Nikolaus Otto in 1876). The main components of a motor car remain unchanged. A body (**chassis**) to which are attached all other parts including: an **engine** or power plant; a **transmission** system for transferring the drive to the wheels, and steering, braking and suspension for guiding, stopping and supporting the car. Early cars were assembled by a few experts, but modern mass-production began in the early 1900s with Henry FORD and R.E. Olds in the USA. In most modern motor factories, component parts are put together on assembly lines. Each worker has a specific task (such as fitting doors or crankshafts). Bodies and engines are made on separate assembly lines which converge when the engine is installed. Overhead rail conveyors move heavy components along the assembly lines, lowering them into position. The final stages of assembly include the fitting of items such as lamps and paint spraying. Electrical, braking and control systems are checked. The assembled car is tested before sale. Recent technology has seen the introduction of robots (properly, robotic arms secured to the workshop floor) on the assembly line. They are usually used for welding and painting. Increasing concern over the environmental impact of the car (such as congestion, pollution, and energy consumption) has encouraged governments to examine alternative forms of mass transport, oil companies to produce cleaner fuels, and car manufacturers to look at alternative power plants (such as electric- or gas-powered motors).

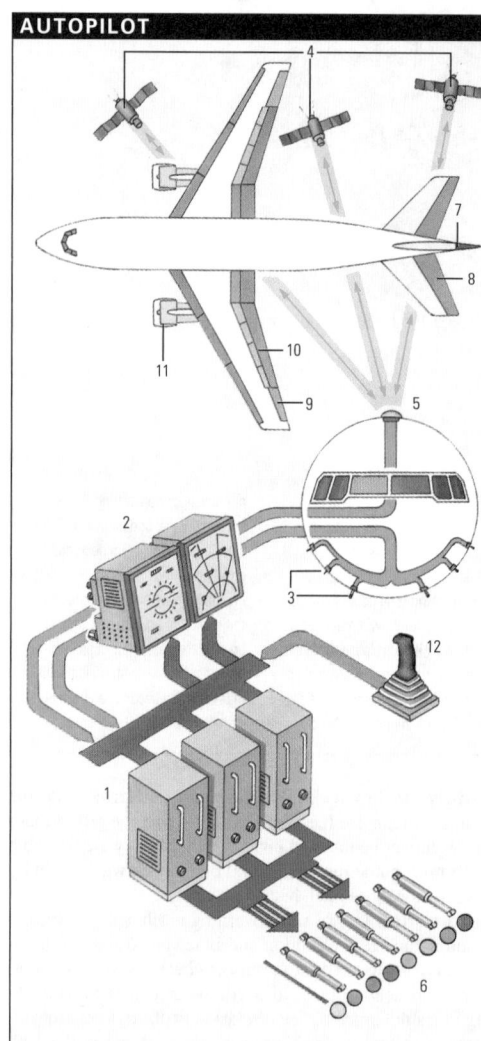

AUTOPILOT

The diagram shows how a typical autopilot system works. A pre-programmed flight plan is loaded into the aircraft's computers (1). After take-off the autopilot is engaged. Two visual display units (2) show the aircraft's position, its intended route and its attitude. The change in movement of small vanes (3) on the outside of the aircraft alert the computers to any change in the aircraft's orientation. The aircraft uses a Global Positioning System (GPS) to determine its position (4). The receiver is located on top of the aircraft (5). The computers track the aircraft's route and automatically make any adjustments via servos (6), which control the rudder (7), elevators (8), ailerons (9), flaps (10), and throttle settings on the engines (11). The pilots can override the automatic system at anytime and revert to manual controls (12).

▲ **avocado** A member of the laurel family, the fruit of the avocado tree (*Persea americana*) contains a single large seed surrounded by pale green flesh. When the skin of an avocado is soft, it is ripe to eat. It was probably first cultivated by the Aztecs. Mexico is the world's largest producer.

autonomic nervous system (ANS) Part of the body's nervous system that regulates the body's involuntary functions. It helps to regulate the body's internal environment by controlling the rate of heart beat, PERISTALSIS (movements of food through the digestive tract) and sweating. This system is also part of an individual's emotional response, such as blushing and a quickened heartbeat. *See also* HOMEOSTASIS; INVOLUNTARY MUSCLE

autopilot (automatic pilot) Electronic and mechanical control system that ensures an aircraft follows a pre-programmed flight plan. It monitors the course and speed of the aircraft and corrects any deviations from the flight plan. Systems range from simple wing-levellers in light aircraft to computer-operated units consisting of: a GYROSCOPE; an electric SERVOMECHANISM unit and an accelerometer, which measures the acceleration of the aircraft.

Auvergne Region and former province of s France, comprising the departments of Allier, Puy-de-Dôme, Cantal, and Haute-Loire. The capital is Clermont-Ferrand. Running N-S are the Auvergne Mountains, a scenic chain of extinct volcanoes, whose highest peak is Puy de Sancy, 1886m (6188ft). Area: 26,013sq km (10,047sq mi). Pop. (1999) 1,308,878.

auxin Plant hormone produced mainly in the growing tips of plant stems. Auxins accelerate plant growth by stimulating cell division and enlargement, and by interacting with other hormones. Actions include the elongation of cells in geotropism and phototropism (by increasing the elasticity of cell walls, allowing the cells to take up more water), fruit drop and leaf fall. *See also* GIBBERELLIN

Avalokitesvara In BUDDHISM, one of the most distinguished of the BODHISATTVAS. Noted for his compassion and mercy, he remained on Earth in order to bring help to the suffering. DALAI LAMAS are considered reincarnations of Avalokitesvara.

avatar In HINDUISM, an incarnation of a god (especially VISHNU) in human or animal form that appears on Earth to combat evil and restore virtue. In Hindu tradition, there have been nine incarnations of VISHNU and a tenth is yet to come: these include BUDDHA, KRISHNA, and RAMA.

average In statistics, the one score that most typifies an entire set of scores. It is the arithmetic MEAN of the scores. Other calculations that are also used to express what is typical in a set of scores are the mode (the one score that occurs most often), and the median (the middle score in a range which thus divides the set of scores into upper and lower halves).

Averroës (Abu al-Walid ibn Rushd) (1126–98) Leading Islamic philosopher in Spain. He became physician to the caliph of Marrakesh in 1182, but was banished to Spain in 1195 for advocating reason over religion. His major work, *Incoherence of the Incoherence*, defends Neoplatonism and ARISTOTLE. He exercised a powerful influence on Christian thought that persisted into the Renaissance. *See also* AQUINAS, SAINT THOMAS; SCHOLASTICISM

Avesta (Zend-Avesta) Sacred book of ZOROASTRIANISM. Most of the original was apparently lost when ALEXANDER THE GREAT burned Persepolis, the capital of ancient Persia, in 331 BC. The Gathas, forming the oldest part, originated with Zoroaster. The other remaining parts are the Yashts, Yasna, and Vendidad and prayers. Together they contain the world-view, law, and liturgy of Zoroastrianism. The writings were systematized under the Sassanid kings of Persia between the 3rd and 7th centuries AD.

Avicenna (980–1037) (Abu Ali al-Husayn ibn abd Allah ibn Sina) Persian physician and philosopher whose work, through his *Canon Medicinae*, influenced the science of medicine for many centuries. He was a great philosopher and scientist of the golden age of Islamic learning. He also made enduring contributions in the field of Aristotelian philosophy.

Avignon City at the confluence of the Rhône and Durance rivers, Vaucluse department, Provence, SE France. A thriving city under Roman rule, it was the seat of the Popes during their exile from Rome in the 14th century. There is a Papal Palace begun in 1316 and a Romanesque cathedral. The papacy held Avignon until 1791, when it was annexed to France by the Revolutionary authorities. Industries: tourism. soap, wine, grain, leather. Pop. (1999) 88,312 (metropolitan, 253,580).

avocado Evergreen, broad-leafed tree native to the tropical New World. The name is extended to its green to dark purple, pear-shaped fruit. Avocados have a high oil content and a nutty flavour. Weight: 200g (7oz) but exceptionally up to 2kg (4.4lb). Family Lauraceae; species *Persea americana*.

Avogadro, Amedeo, Conte di Quaregna (1776–1856) Italian physicist and chemist. His hypothesis, **Avogadro's law** (1811), states that equal volumes of gases at the same pressure and temperature contain an equal number of molecules. This led later physicists to determine that the number of molecules in one gram molecule (the relative molecular mass expressed in grams) is constant for all gases. This number, called Avogadro's number, equals 6.02257×10^{23}. It is both the ratio of the universal gas constant to Boltzmann's constant and of Faraday's constant to the charge of the electron.

Avon Name of four British rivers. The **Bristol** (Lower) Avon rises in the Cotswold Hills in Gloucestershire and flows s and then w through Bristol, entering the Severn estuary at Avonmouth. Length: 121km (75mi). The **Warwickshire** (Upper) Avon rises in Northamptonshire, and flows sw through Stratford-on-Avon to join the River Severn at Tewkesbury. Length: 155km (96mi). The **Wiltshire** (East) Avon rises near Devizes and flows s into the English Channel. Length: 77km (48mi). The **Scottish** Avon flows E into the Firth of Forth. Length: 29km (18mi).

axiom Assumption used as a basis for deductive reasoning. The axiomatic method is fundamental to the philosophy of modern mathematics. It was used by the Ancient Greeks and formalized early in the 20th century by David HILBERT. In an axiomatic system, certain undefined entities (**terms**) are taken and described by a set of axioms. Other, often unsuspected, relationships (**theorems**) are then deduced by logical reasoning. For example, the points, lines and angles of Euclidean (traditional) geometry are connected by postulates (assumptions); theorems, such as Pythagoras' theorem, can be deduced.

axis Imaginary straight line about which a body rotates. In mechanics, an axis runs longitudinally through the centre of an axle or rotating shaft. In geography and astronomy, it is a line through the centre of a planet or star, about which the planet or star rotates. Earth's axis between the North and South geographic poles is 12,700km (7900mi) long and is inclined at an angle of 66.5° to the plane in which the Earth orbits the Sun. A mathematical axis is a fixed line, such as the x, y or z axis, chosen for reference.

Axis Powers Term applied to Germany and Italy after they signed the Rome-Berlin Axis in October 1936. It included Japan after it joined them in the Tripartite Pact (September 1940). Other states that joined the Axis were Hungary and Romania (1940) and Bulgaria (1941).

axolotl Larval form of certain species of SALAMANDER native to w USA and Mexico. Axolotls are aquatic amphibians that normally mature and reproduce without developing into adult salamanders. Length: *c.*25cm (10in). Family Ambystomidae.

ayatollah (Arabic, reflection of God) Honorific title bestowed upon a Muslim leader who has attained significant distinction and, often, political influence. *See also* KHOMEINI, RUHOLLAH

aye-aye (aare) Primitive, squirrel-like LEMUR of Madagascar. Nocturnal and tree-dwelling, it has dark shaggy fur and an elongated third finger with which it scrapes insects and pulp from bamboo canes. Length: 40cm (16in) excluding tail. Species *Daubentonia madagascariensis*.

Ayer, Sir A.J. (Alfred Jules) (1910–89) English philosopher. Building on the ideas of the Vienna Circle of positivists and of George BERKELEY, David HUME, Bertrand RUSSELL, and Ludwig WITTGENSTEIN, he introduced LOGICAL POSITIVISM into British and US philosophy. His works include *Language, Truth and Logic* (1936) and *Philosophy and Language* (1960).

Ayers Rock (*Uluru*) Outcrop of rock, 448km (280mi) sw of Alice Springs, Northern Territory, Australia. Named after the South Australian politician Sir Henry Ayers (1821–97), it remained undiscovered by Europeans until 1872. It stands 348m (1142ft) high, and is the second largest single rock in the world – the distance around its base is *c.*10km (6mi). The rock, caves of which are decorated with ancient paintings, is of great religious significance to Native Australians.

Aymara Major tribe of Native South Americans who live in the highlands of Bolivia and Peru. By 1500 they had been brought into the INCA Empire, which was subsequently conquered by the Spanish. Today, the Aymara number *c.*1,360,000. The Ayamara language is spoken by *c.*1 million people in Bolivia and 3 million people in Peru.

Ayub Khan, Muhammad (1907–74) Pakistani general and statesman, president (1958–69). After the partition of British India, Ayub Khan assumed control of the army in East Pakistan (now Bangladesh). In 1951 he became commander-in-chief of the army and served as defence minister (1954–56). In 1958 Ayub Khan led the military coup that overthrew Iskander Mirza. He was confirmed as president in a 1960 referendum. His administration was notable for its economic modernization and reforms to the political system. The failure of his regime to deal with poverty and social inequality forced him to resign.

Ayurveda System of medicine practised by the ancient Hindus and derived from the VEDAS. It is still practised in India.

azalea Name given to certain shrubs and small trees of the genus *Rhododendron*, from temperate regions of Asia and North America. Mostly deciduous, they have leathery leaves and funnel-shaped red, pink, magenta, orange, yellow or white flowers, sometimes variegated. Family Ericaceae.

Azazel A fallen angel in Hebrew mythology, he was one of the fathers of the Nephilim. According to the apocryphal Book of Enoch, he taught men to make weapons and women to wear cosmetics. This lead to the corruption of human society and God's decision to destroy the world in the great FLOOD. Cursed for his actions, he became the spirit of the wilderness to whom sins were sent via a scapegoat, according to the book of LEVITICUS. He thus became the Lord of Goats and earned the title the Eternal Scapegoat himself. Azazel also appears as Hell's standard-bearer in MILTON's *Paradise Lost*.

Azerbaijan Republic in sw Asia. *See* country feature, p.126

azimuth Angle between the vertical plane through a celestial body and the N-S direction. Astronomers measure the angle eastwards from the N point of the observer's horizon. Navigators and surveyors measure it westwards from the s point. Altitude and azimuth form an astronomical co-ordinate system for defining position.

Aznar, Jose Maria (1953–) Spanish statesman, prime minister (1996–2004). In 1990 Aznar became president of the centre-right Popular Party. In 1995 he survived a bomb attack by ETA. In 1996 elections, his centrist agenda ended the 13–year rule of socialist Prime Minister Felipe Gonzalez, and Aznar formed a minority government. In 2000 elections, Aznar gained an outright majority – the first time the Spanish right held majority power since democracy was restored in 1977.

Azores Portuguese island group in the N Atlantic Ocean, 1290km (800mi) w of Portugal. The capital and chief port is Ponta Delgada (on São Miguel). Although they were known to early explorers, such as the Phoenicians and the Norsemen,

▲ **Ayers Rock** The site of many ancient cave paintings, Ayers Rock is now officially known by its Native Australian name, *Uluru*. Lying in Northern Territory, Australia, it is the second largest outcrop of free-standing rock in the world, the largest is Mount Augustus, or *Burringurrah*, in Western Australia.

INTERNET

Ayers Rock
▶ www.heritage.gov.au

Azerbaijan
▶ www.azer.com
▶ www.mys.azeri.com

Aztec (page 126)
▶ www.indians.org/welker/aztec.htm

they were first settled by the Portuguese in the 15th century. The Azores served as military bases in both World Wars. Volcanic in origin, they consist of nine main islands, divided into three groups. They export a variety of fruits, vegetables, and fish. The islands' economy, dependent on small-scale farming and fishing, improved with the development of tourism. Since 1976, the islands form an autonomous region of Portugal. Pico Alto at 2351m (7713ft) is Portugal's highest mountain. Area: 2247sq km (868sq mi). Pop. (2000) 243,895.

Azov, Sea of (Azovskoye More) Northern arm of the Black Sea. A shallow sea with only slight salinity, Azov has fishing ports on its E and S coasts. The marshes and lagoons at the W (Crimean peninsula) end were so noxious the sea was known as *Sivash* (putrid lake). Area: 37,607sq km (14,520sq mi).

Aztec (Tenochca) Native American civilization that rose to a position of dominance in the central valley of MEXICO in c.AD 1450. A warlike group, the Aztec settled near Lake Texcoco in about 1325, where they founded their capital Tenochtitlan on an artificial island. Tenochtitlan grew to a great size but was heavily damaged by the Spanish and their allies in 1521; Mexico City now covers its remains. They established an empire that included most of modern Mexico and extended s as far as Guatemala. The state was a THEOCRACY in which the rulers were also the highest priests, serving a number of deities whose worship included the human sacrifice of prisoners of war. The Aztec built temples, pyramids and palaces adorned with stone images and symbolic carvings. At the time of the Spanish conquest, the Aztec economy was based on the exploitation of their neighbours, from whom Hernan CORTÉS recruited allies to defeat the Aztec in 1521. *See also* CENTRAL AND SOUTH AMERICAN MYTHOLOGY

AZERBAIJAN

The Republic of Azerbaijan lies in E Transcaucasia, bordering the CASPIAN SEA to the E. The CAUCASUS Mountains are in the north and include Azerbaijan's highest peak, Mount Bazar-Dyuzi, at 4,480m [14,698ft]. Another highland region, including the Little Caucasus Mountains and part of the rugged Armenian plateau, lies in the sw.

Between these regions lies a broad plain drained by the River Kura. Its E part, s of the capital BAKU, lies below sea level. Azerbaijan also includes the NAKHICHEVAN Autonomous Republic on the Iran frontier, an area cut off from the rest of Azerbaijan by Armenian territory. Forests grow on the mountains, while the lowlands comprise grassy steppe or semi-desert.

CLIMATE
Azerbaijan has hot summers and cool winters. The plains have low rainfall ranging from c.130 to 380mm [5 to 15in] a year. The

uplands have much higher rainfall as does the subtropical SE coast.

HISTORY
In ancient times, the area now called Azerbaijan was invaded many times. Arab armies introduced Islam in 642, but most modern Azerbaijanis are descendants of Persians and Turkic peoples who migrated to the area from the east by the 9th century.

Azerbaijan was ruled by the MONGOLS between the 13th and 15th centuries and then by the Persian SAFAVID dynasty. By the early 19th century it was under Russian control.

After the Russian Revolution of 1917, attempts were made to form a Transcaucasian Federation made up of Armenia, Azerbaijan and Georgia. When this failed, Azerbaijanis set up an independent state. But Russian forces occupied the area in 1920. In 1922, the Communists set up a Republic of TRANSCAUCASIA consisting of Armenia, Azerbaijan and Georgia, and placed it under Russian control. In 1936, the areas became separate Soviet Socialist Republics within the SOVIET UNION.

POLITICS
Following the break-up of the Soviet Union in 1991, Azerbaijan became independent. In 1992, Abulfaz Elchibey became president in Azerbaijan's first contested election. In 1993 Elchibey fled and Heydar Aliev, former head of the Communist Party and the KGB in Azerbaijan, assumed the presidency. He was elected later that year and Azerbaijan joined the COMMONWEALTH OF INDEPENDENT STATES (CIS).

In 1992 conflict with Armenia arose over NAGORNO-KARABAKH, an enclave in Azerbaijan where the majority of people are Christian

AREA 86,600sq km [33,436sq mi]
POPULATION 8,120,000
CAPITAL (POPULATION) Baku (1,830,000)
GOVERNMENT Federal multiparty republic
ETHNIC GROUPS Azeri 90%, Dagestani 3%, Russian, Armenian, others
LANGUAGES Azerbaijani (official), Russian, Armenian
RELIGIONS Islam 93%, Russian Orthodox 2%, Armenian Orthodox
CURRENCY Azerbaijani manat = 100 gopik

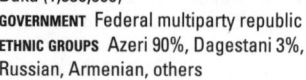

Armenians. A ceasefire in 1994 left Armenia in control of about 20% of Azerbaijan's land area, but negotiations remain inconclusive and neither side has been able to safely re-settle.

In 1998 Aliev was re-elected. In 2003 his son Ilham became president, and was re-elected in 2005 despite charges of fraud. In 2006-7 disputes with Russia over gas prices led Azerbaijan to redirect its oil exports, opening new pipelines to Turkey to allow direct access to European markets.

ECONOMY
In the mid-1990s the World Bank classified Azerbaijan as a 'lower-middle-income' economy. By the late 1990s, oil reserves in the Caspian Sea and the Baku area allowed an economic boom. Oil extraction and refining made Azerbaijan one of the world's fastest growing economies by the mid-2000s. Chemicals, machinery and textiles are also valuable sources of revenue.

Large areas of land are irrigated and crops include cotton, fruit, grains, tea, tobacco and vegetables. Fishing is still important, although the Caspian Sea is becoming increasingly polluted. Private enterprise is now encouraged.

Baade, Walter (1893–1960) US astronomer, b. Germany. From Mount Wilson Observatory, in the 1943 wartime blackout, he observed individual stars in the Andromeda Galaxy and distinguished the younger, bluer Population I stars from the older, redder Population II stars. He went on to improve the use of CEPHEID VARIABLE stars as distance indicators, and showed that the universe was older and larger than had been thought.

Baalbek Town in the Bekaa Valley, E Lebanon. An early Phoenician settlement, the Greeks occupied the site in 323 BC and renamed it Heliopolis. The Romans colonized it in the 1st century BC. Baalbek is noted for its Greek and Roman remains, especially the Temple of Jupiter. Pop. (2002 est.) 29,000.

Ba'ath Party Arab political party, founded in 1943. Its major objectives are socialism and Arab unity. It is strongest in Iraq and Syria, and militaristic elements of the Ba'ath Party seized power in those countries in 1968 and 1970 respectively. *See also* ASSAD, HAFEZ AL-; HUSSEIN, SADDAM

Babbage, Charles (1791–1871) British mathematician. Babbage compiled the first actuarial tables and planned a mechanical calculating machine, the forerunner of the modern COMPUTER. He failed to complete the construction of the machine because the financial support recommended by the Royal Society was refused by the British government.

Babbitt, Milton (1916–) US composer, musicologist, and teacher. Babbitt studied with Roger SESSIONS and his mathematical background influenced his music. He systematized the analysis of TWELVE-TONE MUSIC. His compositions include vocal, piano and chamber music, as well as electronic music.

Babel, Isaac Emmanuelovich (1894–1941) Russian short-story writer. Babel's works, many of which are informed by his military service and experience of persecution, include *Tales of Odessa* (1924) and *Red Cavalry* (1926). He died in a Siberian concentration camp, a victim of Stalin's purges.

Babel, Tower of Tower begun on the plain of Shinar, in Babylonia, by the descendants of NOAH as a means of reaching heaven (Genesis 11). God prevented its completion by confusing the speech of the people and scattering them throughout the world. The Genesis story was probably inspired by a ZIGGURAT or staged temple-tower in Babylon, seven storeys high and with a shrine to the god Marduk on its top.

Babi faith (Babism) Muslim religious sect founded (1844) in Persia (Iran) by Sayyid Ali Muhammad, the self-proclaimed prophet Bab (Arabic, 'gate'). Drawing on the teachings of existing branches of ISLAM, Babists believed in the imminent coming of the Promised One. In 1848 they declared secession from Islam, but their rebellion against the new Shah of Iran was crushed and their founder executed in 1850. *See also* BAHA'I

baboon Large, African MONKEY with a dog-like face, which walks on all fours. Its buttocks have callus-like pads surrounded by brilliantly coloured skin. Baboons are ground dwellers and active by day, travelling in families and larger troops led by old males, usually in open, rocky country. Their diet consists of plants, insects, and small animals. They can carry food in their cheek pouches. The males have large canine teeth up to 5cm (2in) long. Weight: 14–41kg (30–90lb). Genus *Chaeropithecus* (or *Papio*).

Babur (1483–1530) First Mogul Emperor of India (1526–30), b. Zahir ud-Din Muhammad. Babur (Turk. 'tiger') became ruler of Fergana in 1495, and engaged in a long conflict for control of SAMARKAND, but ultimately lost both territories. Raising an army, he captured KABUL and carved out a new kingdom for himself in Afghanistan. From here he invaded India, gaining Delhi (1526) and Agra (his future capital) (1527), and conquering N India as far as Bengal.

Babylon Ancient city on the River Euphrates in MESOPOTAMIA, capital of the empire BABYLONIA. It was rebuilt after being destroyed by ASSYRIA *c*.689 BC and its new buildings included the HANGING GARDENS, one of the SEVEN WONDERS OF THE WORLD. This was the period, under NEBUCHADNEZZAR, of the BABYLONIAN CAPTIVITY of the Jews. Babylon declined after 275 BC as Seleucia ascended.

Babylonia Ancient region and empire of MESOPOTAMIA, based on the city of BABYLON. The Babylonian Empire was first established in the early 18th century BC by HAMMURABI the Great, but declined under the impact of HITTITES and Kassites in *c*.1595 BC. After a long period of weakness and confusion, the Empire eventually fell to ASSYRIA in the 8th century BC. In *c*.625 BC Babylon regained its independence and former glory, when Nabopolassar captured the Assyrian capital of NINEVEH. In 586 BC the New Babylonian (Chaldaean) Empire defeated Egypt and took the Jews to captivity in Babylon. In 538 BC the Empire fell to the Persians.

Babylonian Captivity Deportation of the Jews to BABYLON, between the capture of Jerusalem in 586 BC by NEBUCHADNEZZAR and the reformation of a Palestinian Jewish state (*c*.538BC) by CYRUS THE GREAT. Many Jewish religious institutions, such as SYNAGOGUES, were founded in the period of exile and parts of the Hebrew Bible also date from this time. The term was later applied to the exile of the popes at AVIGNON (1309–77). *See also* DIASPORA; GREAT SCHISM

Bacall, Lauren (1924–) US film actress. Following her screen debut opposite Humphrey BOGART, in *To Have and Have Not* (1944), Bacall and Bogart married in 1945. They starred together in a further three films: *The Big Sleep* (1946) *Dark Passage* (1947), and *Key Largo* (1948).

Bacchus In Roman mythology, the god of wine and fertility, identified with the Greek god DIONYSUS.

Bach, Carl Philipp Emanuel (1714–88) German composer, second surviving son of J.S. BACH. The most prolific and famous of Bach's sons, he wrote more than 150 keyboard sonatas, 20 symphonies, *c*.50 harpsichord concertos, many chamber works and sacred music, and *c*.300 songs. He was a fine keyboard player and became a leading theorist with his *Essay on the True Art of Keyboard Playing* (1753–62).

Bach, Johann Christian (1735–82) German composer, youngest son of J.S. BACH. He was organist at Milan Cathedral, composed operas that were staged in Turin and Naples, but soon moved to London where his operas were better received. In 1763 he became music-master to Queen Charlotte. Besides 11 operas, he wrote many instrumental and vocal works. He was much admired by Mozart.

Bach, Johann Sebastian (1685–1750) Prolific German BAROQUE composer. He held a series of successive court positions as organist and music director and had 20 children, four of whom were also composers. Bach brought contrapuntal forms to their highest expression and is unrivaled in his ability to interweave melodies within the exacting rules of baroque harmony and counterpoint. While at the court in Weimar (1708–17), he wrote many of his great organ works (preludes, fugues, toccatas), such as the Fugue in C minor. At Köthen (1717–23), he wrote instrumental works for keyboard, such as Book I of the *The Well-Tempered Clavier,* and the six *Brandenburg Concertos* for chamber orchestra. As musical director of St Thomas, Leipzig (1723–50), Bach wrote his celebrated church music, including *St Matthew Passion* (1729) and Mass in B Minor. Other works included the *Goldberg Variations* (1742). *The Art of Fugue* remained incomplete at his death.

B/b, second letter of the alphabet. It is probably derived from an Egyptian hieroglyph for a house (c.3000 BC), which entered the Semitic alphabet 1,500 years later as the letter beth. From there it was taken to Greece to become beta, which was a similar shape to the modern B.

INTERNET

Bach, Johann Sebastian
▶ www.jsbach.org

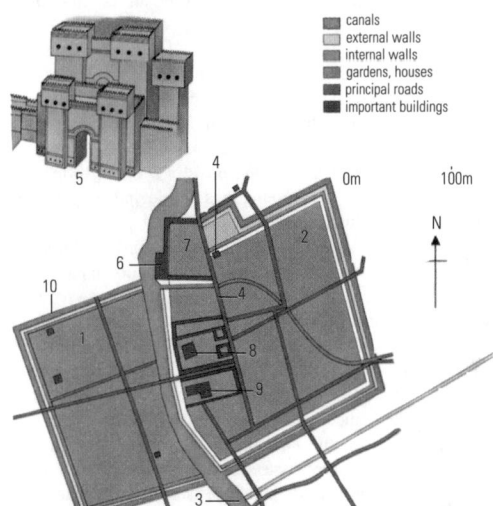

◀ **Babylon** Early Babylon was often rebuilt. The excavated, sophisticated layout we see today was created mainly by Nebuchadnezzar II (c.604–561 BC). Old city (1) and new (2) are separated by the River Euphrates (3), and contained within two fortification walls, reinforced by a moat (10) and accessible through fortified gateways connected to the major streets. A SE outer wall gave additional protection. The ritual Processional Way (4) enters the new city through the Ishtar Gate (5), passing a fortress (6) and the main citadel complex (7) of administration and garrison buildings, palaces and vaulted Hanging Gardens. Skirting Etemenanki enclosure with its ziggurat (8) – possibly that of Babel – it turns W past the temple of Marduk (9) and crosses the five-pier bridge to the old city. Navigable canals irrigated the dry soil and helped prevent flooding of the Euphrates.

canals
external walls
internal walls
gardens, houses
principal roads
important buildings

0m   100m

N

BACTERIA

Bacteria occur in three basic shapes: spherical forms called cocci (A), rod-like bacilli (B), and spiral spirilla (C). Cocci can occur in clumps known as staphylococci (1), groups of two called diplococci (2) or chains called streptococci (3). Unlike cocci, which do not move, bacilli are freely mobile; some are termed peritrichous and use many flagellae (4) to swim about, while other monotrichous forms use a single flagellum (5). Bacilli can also form spores (6) to survive unfavourable conditions. Spirilla may be either cork-screw-shaped spirochaetes like Leptospira (7), or less coiled and flagellated, such as Spirillum (8) – magnification x 5000.

▶ **badger** Eurasian badgers (*Meles meles*) of s China live in large family groups in large burrows known as setts. Setts have a complex network of tunnels and chambers, each serving a particular function.

bacillus Genus of rod-like BACTERIA present everywhere in the air and soil. One example of a species that is pathogenic in man is *Bacillus anthracis*, which causes ANTHRAX.

background radiation Radiation that is normally present in an environment. Such radiation must be taken into account when measuring radiation from a particular source. On Earth, background radiation is caused by the decay of naturally occurring radioactive substances in surface rocks. In space, the so-called 'microwave background' is attributed to the BIG BANG explosion that supposedly created the Universe.

Bacon, Francis (1561–1626) English philosopher, statesman and early advocate of the scientific method. Bacon was also an important essayist. Successively attorney general, lord keeper and lord chancellor, he was forced to resign his offices when found guilty of corruption in 1621. None of this interrupted his efforts to break the hold of Aristotelian LOGIC and establish an inductive EMPIRICISM. Bacon entertained the idea of cataloguing all useful knowledge in his *Advancement of Learning* (1605) and *Novum Organum* (1620). *The New Atlantis* (1627) discusses his philosophy as practised in an imaginary nation.

Bacon, Francis (1909–92) English painter, one of the most controversial artists of his generation. In 1945 he changed the face of British painting when he exhibited his TRIPTYCH, *Three Studies for Figures at the Base of a Crucifixion*. The shock of the distorted representations of grieving people in his work stems from his violent handling of paint as much as from the subjects themselves. Precedents for Bacon's nightmarish scenes lie in the vengeful images of medieval doom paintings. The religious focus of his work continued in a savage series of portraits of Roman Catholic popes. The protagonists of his pictures are usually set against a blank background. For much of his life Bacon was shunned by the critical establishment.

bacteria Simple, unicellular, microscopic organisms. They lack a clearly defined nucleus and most are without CHLOROPHYLL. Many are motile, swimming by means of whip-like flagella. Most multiply by FISSION. In adverse conditions, many can remain dormant inside highly resistant SPORES with thick protective coverings. Bacteria may be AEROBIC or ANAEROBIC.

Although pathogenic bacteria are a major cause of human disease, many bacteria are harmless or even beneficial to humans by providing an important link in FOOD CHAINS, by decomposing plant and animal tissue, or converting free nitrogen and sulphur into AMINO ACIDS and other compounds that plants and animals can use. Some contain a form of chlorophyll and carry out PHOTOSYNTHESIS. Bacteria belong to the kingdom Prokaryotae. *See also* ARCHAEBACTERIA; EUBACTERIA

bacteriology Scientific study of BACTERIA. Bacteria were first observed in the 17th century by Anton van LEEUWENHOEK, but it was not until the researches of Louis PASTEUR and Robert Koch in the mid-19th century that bacteriology was established as a scientific discipline.

bacteriophage VIRUS that lives on and infects BACTERIA. It has a protein head containing a core of DNA and a protein tail. Discovered in 1915, it is important in the study of GENETICS.

Baden-Powell, Robert Stephenson Smyth, Baron of Gilwell (1857–1941) British soldier and founder of the BOY SCOUT movement. He held Mafeking against the Boers (1899–1900). His sister **Agnes** (1858–1945) founded the GIRL GUIDES (1910).

Baden-Württemberg State in sw Germany, formed in 1952 by the merger of Baden, Württemberg-Baden, and Württemberg-Hohenzollern; the capital is STUTTGART. A forested and fertile region drained by the Rhine and Danube rivers, agriculture and livestock-rearing are important, but industry is the main economic activity. Chief products include electrical goods, machinery, and vehicle-assembly at the industrial centres of Stuttgart, MANNHEIM, and Karlsruhe. There are famous universities at HEIDELBERG and Freiburg im Breisgau. A popular tourist region, visitors are drawn to the spa at Baden-Baden and the beauty of the Neckar Valley and the Black Forest. Area: 35,750sq km (13,803sq mi). Pop. (2001) 10,600,906.

badger Burrowing, nocturnal mammal that lives in Eurasia, North America, and Africa. It has a stocky body with short legs and tail. Eurasian badgers (*Meles meles*) have grey bodies with black-and-white striped heads. American badgers (*Taxidea taxus*) are smaller and have grey-reddish fur with a white head stripe. The honey badger lives in Africa. Body length: 42–90cm (17–35in); weight: 10–20kg (22–44lb). Family Mustelidae.

badlands Eroded, barren plateau in an arid or semi-arid area characterized by steep gullies and ravines. Because of the lack of adequate vegetation (due to climate or human intervention), the rainwater runs off very quickly and erodes soft and exposed rock. The best-known examples are the badlands of sw South Dakota and NW Nebraska, USA.

badminton Court game for two or four players, popular since the 1870s. The object is to use a light racket to volley a shuttlecock over a net until missed or hit out of bounds by an opponent. Traditionally, only the player serving can score a point; in 2006, tournament games adopted a new system in which both can score.

Baffin, William (1584–1622) English navigator and explorer. Baffin took part in several expeditions (1612–16) in search of the NORTHWEST PASSAGE. He discovered the Canadian Arctic seaways, the island now named after him, and Lancaster Sound. An outstanding navigator, he published a method of determining longitude by the stars, using nautical tables, and was possibly the first to make lunar observations at sea.

Baffin Island Largest and most easterly island of the Canadian Arctic Archipelago, separated from QUÉBEC province by the Hudson Strait. It is the fifth-largest island in the world, with largely mountainous terrain and an almost entirely Inuit population. Area: 507,451sq km (195,928sq mi).

Bagehot, Walter (1826–77) English economist and writer. Editor of *The Economist* (1860–77), he is chiefly remembered for his influential treatise *The English Constitution* (1867).

Baghdad Capital of Iraq, on the River Tigris. Established in 762 as capital of the ABBASID caliphate, it became a centre of Islamic civilization and focus of caravan routes between Asia and Europe. It was almost destroyed by the Mongols in 1258. In 1921 Baghdad became the capital of newly independent Iraq. It was badly damaged during the Gulf War (1991). Notable sites include the 13th-century Abbasid Palace. In 2003 Baghdad was badly damaged by bombing during the US invasion of Iraq. It became a battleground for warring factions during the subsequent occupation. Industries: building materials, textiles, tanning, petrochemicals. Pop. (2005) 5,910,000.

bagpipes Musical instrument with reed pipes connected to a windbag held under the arm and filled by mouth or bellows. The chanter pipe has finger-holes for melody, while drone pipes produce monotone accompaniment.

Baha'i Religion founded in the 1860s by as an outgrowth of the BABI FAITH. Its headquarters are in Haifa, Israel. It regards Baha'i global THEOCRACY as the path to world peace and claims its founder Bahaullah as the latest prophet of God.

Bahamas Small independent state in the West Indies, in the w Atlantic, SE of Florida. It consists of *c.*700 islands, 2000 cays and numerous coral reefs. The largest island is Grand Bahama and the capital is NASSAU (on New Providence). The islands consist mainly of limestone and coral, and the rocky terrain provides little chance for agricultural development. Most of the islands are low, flat, and riverless with mangrove swamps. The climate is subtropical with temperatures averaging 21–32°C (70–90°F). The population is 90% African or African-European, and the majority live on New Providence. Anglicanism is the predominant religion, and English the official language. Before the arrival of the Europeans, the islands were inhabited by the Lucayos, later exterminated by the Spanish. San Salvador island is traditionally believed to have

▼ **bagpipes** Although associated with Celtic music, the bagpipes probably originated in Asia. The drone usually has a single reed.

BAHRAIN

The Kingdom of Bahrain, a former Emirate and now a constitutional hereditary monarchy, is an archipelago consisting of more than 30 islands in the Persian Gulf. The largest of the islands, also called Bahrain, makes up seven-eighths of the country. Causeways link the island of Bahrain to the second largest island, Al Muharraq, to the NE and also to the Arabian peninsula.

Sandy, desert plains make up most of this small, low-lying island country. In the N coastal areas of Bahrain, freshwater springs provide water for drinking and also for irrigation.

CLIMATE

Bahrain has a humid climate. Winters are mild, with temperatures ranging from about 10°C [50°F] to 27°C [80°F]. Summers are hot and humid, with temperatures often soaring to more than 38°C [100°F]. The average annual rainfall is low. N Bahrain is the wettest area, with about 80mm [3in] a year. The rain occurs mainly in winter and rainfall is almost non-existent in summer months.

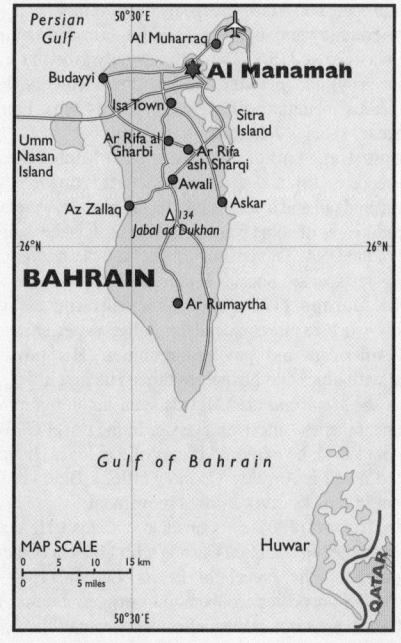

HISTORY

Bahrain was part of a trading civilization called Dilmun, which prospered between about 2000 and 1800 BC. This civilization was linked to the Sumerian, Babylonian and Assyrian civilizations to the N, and with the Indus Valley civilization in what is now Pakistan. Bahrain later came under Islamic Arab influence from the 7th century.

Portugal seized the archipelago from its Arab rulers in 1521, but the Persians conquered the islands in 1603, holding against attacks by the Portuguese and Omanis. However, in 1782, the Al Khalifah Arabs from Saudi Arabia took over the islands and they have ruled ever since.

In the early 19th century, Britain helped Bahrain to prevent annexation by Saudi Arabian invaders. As a result, Bahrain agreed to let Britain take control of its foreign affairs. Bahrain effectively became a British protectorate, although it was not called one. In the 1920s and 1930s the Bahrainis established welfare systems, later funded by revenue from oil, which was discovered in 1932.

Political reforms began in the 1950s and, in 1970, the Emir turned over some of his power to a Council of State, which became a Cabinet. Britain withdrew from the Persian Gulf region in 1971 and Bahrain became fully independent.

POLITICS

Bahrain adopted a new constitution in 1973. This created a National Assembly with 30 elected members. However, relations between the National Assembly and the ruling Al Khalifa family were difficult and the National Assembly was dissolved in 1975. The country was then ruled by the Emir and his cabinet, headed by the prime minister, the Emir's appointee.

In February 2002, a new constitution changed the country from an Emirate into a constitutional hereditary monarchy and the ruler Sheikh Hamad bin Isa Al-Khalifa became king. Elections for a new directly elected House of Deputies took place later that year, with women allowed to vote for the first time. The 40-member House of Deputies – together with a second chamber, a *Shura Council,* consisting of experts appointed by

AREA 694sq km [268sq mi]

POPULATION 709,000

CAPITAL (POPULATION) Manama (140,000)

GOVERNMENT Constitutional hereditary monarchy

ETHNIC GROUPS Bahraini 62%, others

LANGUAGES Arabic, English, Farsi, Urdu

RELIGIONS Muslim (Shi'a and Sunni) 81%, Christian 9%, other

CURRENCY Bahraini dinar = 1000 fils

the king – made up the National Assembly, Bahrain's first parliament since 1975.

Political problems in recent years have included tensions between ruling SUNNI Muslims and the SHIITE majority. During the IRAN-IRAQ WAR, Bahrain supported Iraq against Iran, but in the Gulf War it joined the coalition against its former ally.

Since 1991, the US Navy has used Bahrain as its permanent headquarters in the Persian Gulf. This has provoked terrorist incidents. Although the people have more freedom than others in the region, opposition groups continue to press for further progress, including greater powers for the elected House of Deputies. The opposition Shiite Al-Wefaq party won over 40% of parliamentary seats in November 2006 elections.

ECONOMY

The people of Bahrain enjoy one of the highest standards of living in the Persian Gulf region. The average life expectancy at birth (2005 estimate) is 74 years and free medical services are available. The adult literacy rate is 89%.

Bahrain's prosperity is based on oil, although the country lacks major reserves. Petroleum and petroleum products accounted for 68% of the exports in 2002. Its aluminium smelting plant is the Persian Gulf's largest non-oil industrial complex and aluminium, in all forms, accounted for 15% of the exports in 2002. Textiles and clothing accounted for another 8%.

Bahrain is a major banking and financial centre, and it is home to numerous multinational companies that operate in the Persian Gulf region. It is a popular tourist destination.

been the first stop of Christopher Columbus in his exploration of the New World (1492). The islands were partially settled by England's Eleutherian Adventurers (1648). Charles II granted the islands to six lord proprietors of Carolina in 1670, but development was continually hindered by pirates. Britain assumed direct control by 1729. Held briefly by Spain (1782) during the American Revolution, the islands were given back to England by the Treaty of Versailles (1783) in exchange for E Florida. In 1834, slavery was abolished. During World War 2, the Bahamas were used by US and British forces for training and air bases. In 1963 a new constitution provided for parliamentary government. In 1973 the Bahamas became an independent nation. Industries: tourism, commercial fishing, salt, rum, handicrafts. Area: 13,878sq km (5358sq mi). Pop. (2000 est.) 297,000. *See* WEST INDIES map

Bahia Coastal state in E Brazil; the capital is SALVADOR. Portuguese explorers reached Bahia in 1501. Declared a province in 1823, it achieved statehood in 1889. Products: cacao, tobacco, hardwood, natural gas, lead, asbestos, hydroelectricity. Area: 561,026sq km (216,612sq mi). Pop. (2000) 13,066,764.

Bahrain Emirate archipelago in the Persian (Arabian) Gulf, SW Asia; the capital is MANAMA. *see* country feature, p. 129.

Baikal, Lake (Baykal) World's deepest lake in S Siberia, Russia; the largest freshwater feature in Asia. Fed by numerous small rivers, its outlet is the River Angara. Framed by mountains, Baikal has rich fish stocks and the world's only freshwater seal species. Its ecology is threatened by pollutants from lakeside factories, and government schemes have been introduced to protect the environment. Irkutsk lies on its N shore and the Trans-Siberian Railway runs along its S edge. Area: 31,494sq km (12,160sq mi). Max. depth: 1743m (5714ft).

Baird, John Logie (1888–1946) Scottish electrical engineer, inventor of TELEVISION. In 1926 he demonstrated the first working television to members of the Royal Institution, London. In 1928 he transmitted to a ship at sea, and in 1929 was granted experimental broadcasting facilities by the BRITISH BROADCASTING CORPORATION (BBC). In 1936 his 240–line, part-mechanical, television system was used for the world's first public television service by the BBC. In 1937 it was superseded by MARCONI's fully electronic scanning.

Baja California (Lower California) Peninsula of NW Mexico, extending SSE for 1220km (760mi) between the Gulf of California and the Pacific Ocean. The peninsula consists of two states, Baja California (capital: Mexicali) and Baja California Sur (capital: La Paz). The chief product of the region is long-staple cotton and the main industry is tourism. Area: *c.*141,500sq km (54,500sq mi). Pop. (2000) 2,911,216.

Bakelite Trade name, coined by its inventor US chemist Leo Baekeland, for a thermosetting plastic used for insulating purposes and in making paint. It was the first PLASTIC made by the process of condensation, in which many molecules of two chemicals (in this case phenol and formaldehyde) are joined together to form large polymer molecules, by splitting off water molecules.

Baker, Dame Janet Abbott (1933–) English mezzo-soprano. She was renowned as a singer of *Lieder*, oratorio and opera. Well known at the ROYAL OPERA HOUSE (Covent Garden), Sadler's Wells and GLYNDEBOURNE, she is particularly admired for her interpretations of Mahler's song cycles.

Baker, Josephine (1906–75) US dancer and singer. After a sensational 1925 Paris debut in *La Revue Nègre*, she became internationally famous for her jazz singing and dancing. Her outrageous art deco costumes and regal stage act made her one of the most photographed stars of the era. She took French citizenship in 1937, and was made a member of the French Legion of Honour for her work in the resistance.

Baku Capital of Azerbaijan, a port on the W coast of the Caspian Sea. A trade and craft centre in the Middle Ages, Baku prospered under the Shirvan shahs in the 15th century. Commercial oil production began in the 1870s. At the beginning of the 20th century, Baku lay at the centre of the world's largest oilfield. Industries: oil processing and equipment, shipbuilding, electrical machinery, chemicals. Pop. (2005) 1,830,500.

Bakunin, Mikhail Alexandrovich (1814–76) Russian political philosopher. He became a believer in violent revolution while in Paris in 1848, and was active in the first Communist International until expelled by Karl MARX in 1872. His approach, known as revolutionary ANARCHISM, repudiated all forms of governmental authority as fundamentally at variance with human freedom and dignity. In *God and the State* (1882), Bakunin argued that only natural law is consistent with liberty.

Balaclava (Balaklava) Town in the Crimea, site of an inconclusive battle (1854) during the CRIMEAN WAR. The British, French and Turks held off a Russian attack on their supply port of Balaclava. The battle is famous for a disastrous charge by Lord Cardigan's Light Brigade to capture Russian guns.

Balakirev, Mili Alexeievich (1837–1910) Russian composer. He was one of the RUSSIAN FIVE dedicated to promoting Russian nationalism in 19th-century music. To this end, he incorporated Russian folk idioms into his compositional style. His best-known compositions are two symphonies, *Islamey* (1869) and incidental music to *King Lear* (1858–61). He founded the St Petersburg Free School of Music in 1862.

balalaika Triangular musical instrument popular in Russia. Strings (usually three) are fingered on a fretted neck and may be picked, or plucked with the fingers. It sounds similar to the MANDOLIN.

balance of payments Overall surplus or deficit that occurs as a result of the exchange of all goods and services between one nation and the rest of the world. A country with a balance of payments deficit must finance it by borrowing from other countries or the INTERNATIONAL MONETARY FUND (IMF), or by using foreign currency reserves. Such deficits, if frequent, can pose a serious problem, because they cause a reduction in the reserves. This in turn leads to economic pressure for DEVALUATION in order to correct the imbalance. A country with a surplus is in a favourable position, but may come under international pressure to revalue its currency.

Balanchine, George (1904–83) US choreographer and ballet dancer. One of the greatest artists in 20th-century ballet, in 1924 Balanchine defected from Russia to work as principal dancer and choreographer for DIAGHILEV and the BALLETS RUSSES. He moved to the USA in 1933. Ballet pieces include *The Nutcracker* (1954) and *Don Quixote* (1965).

Balaton Largest lake in central Europe, SW of Budapest, in central Hungary. Rich in fish, many holiday resorts and vineyards line its shores. Area: 600sq km (232sq mi).

Balboa, Vasco Núñez de (1475–1519) Spanish conquistador, the first European to see the Pacific Ocean. He went to Hispaniola in 1500, and to Darién (Panama) ten years later. In September 1513, accompanied by a group of locals, he crossed the isthmus and saw the Pacific, which he called the South Sea. He was later executed on a false charge by the governor.

bald cypress (swamp cypress) Deciduous tree growing in shallow water in SE USA. They have woody growth on the roots that grow above water and lose their feathery, light green needles in autumn. Height: to 15ft (4.6m). Family Taxodiaceae; species *Taxodium distichum*.

bald eagle Large bird of prey that lives in North America, where it feeds on fish and small mammals. It is brown with a white head and tail and a yellow bill. Its tail feathers were used in the headdresses of some Native Americans. It is the national emblem of the USA. Though now protected by law, it remains an endangered species. Species *Haliaeetus leucocephalus*.

Baldwin, James (1924–87) US novelist and essayist. Baldwin's work explores social prejudice experienced by African-American and gay communities. His prose is inflected with blues and gospel rhythms. His first novel, *Go Tell It on the Mountain* (1953), was semi-autobiographical and has become an American classic. In the novel *Giovanni's Room* (1956), he explored issues of gay love. His most celebrated novel is *Another Country* (1962). Baldwin was prominent in the US CIVIL RIGHTS movement.

Baldwin, Robert (1804–58) Canadian statesman. He shared the first premiership of united Canada with Louis la Fontaine, who represented the French of Lower Canada (1841–43, 1847–51). He advocated cooperation between French and British Canadians, organized an effective system of municipal government for Ontario and reorganized the courts.

Baldwin, Stanley, 1st Earl of Bewdley (1867–1947) British Conservative statesman and prime minister (1923–24, 1924–29, 1935–37). He entered Parliament in 1908, and was chancellor of the exchequer (1922–23). As prime minister Baldwin responded to the General Strike (1926) by passing the Trades Disputes Acts (1927), which made general strikes illegal. Baldwin opposed EDWARD VIII's marriage to Wallis Simpson and secured the King's abdication (1936). Baldwin's APPEASEMENT of European fascism is often cited as a cause of Britain's lack of preparedness at the start of World War 2.

Balearic Islands Group of Spanish islands in the W Mediterranean, off the E coast of Spain; the capital is PALMA. The Balearics were successively occupied by all the great Mediterranean civilizations of antiquity. A Moorish kingdom used them as a base for piracy in the 11th century. The chief islands are MAJORCA, Minorca, and IBIZA. Industries: tourism, silverworking, olive oil, wine, fruit. Area: 5014sq km (1936sq mi). Pop. (2001) 878,627.

Balfour, Arthur James Balfour, 1st Earl of (1848–1930) British statesman, prime minister (1902–05), b. Scotland. Balfour succeeded his uncle, the Marquess of SALISBURY, as prime minister. His government introduced educational reforms (1902), but the CONSERVATIVE PARTY fractured over the tariff reform proposed by Joseph CHAMBERLAIN. Balfour resigned and the Conservatives lost the ensuing general election. Balfour returned to the cabinet in the coalition governments of Herbert ASQUITH and David LLOYD GEORGE. As foreign secretary, he issued the BALFOUR DECLARATION (1917).

Balfour Declaration (1917) Letter written by British foreign minister Arthur BALFOUR to the British Zionist Federation pledging support for the settlement of Jews in PALESTINE. Jews were admitted to the area when it became a British mandated territory after World War 1. *See also* ZIONISM

Bali Island province off the E tip of Java, between the Bali Sea and the Indian Ocean, INDONESIA. The main town is Denpasar. Under Javanese control from the 10th century, Bali was a Dutch possession from 1908 to 1949, apart from Japanese occupation during World War 2. It is the centre of Majaphit Hinduism. Its scenic beauty and native culture make it a popular tourist resort. The island is fertile and densely populated. Industries: rice, sweet potatoes, cassava, copra, meat processing. Area: 5561sq km (2147sq mi). Pop. (2001) 3,124,674.

Balkan mountains Major mountain range of the Balkan Peninsula, extending from E Serbia through central Bulgaria to the Black Sea. The range is a continuation of the CARPATHIAN MOUNTAINS. It is rich in minerals and forms a climatic barrier for the interior. The highest pass is Shipka Pass, *c.*1270m (4166ft), and the highest peak is Botev, 2375m (7793ft).

Balkan Wars (1912–13) Two wars involving the Balkan states and the OTTOMAN EMPIRE. In the first, the Balkan League (Serbia, Bulgaria, Greece, and Montenegro) conquered most of the European territory of the Ottoman Empire. The second war (mainly between Serbia and Bulgaria) arose out of dissatisfaction with the distribution of these lands. Serbia's victory added to the regional tension before World War 1.

Balkhash (Balchas) Lake in SE Kazakhstan extending from the Kazak Hills (NE) to the desert steppes (SW). It has no outlet. The chief inlet is the freshwater River Ili, therefore the W half of the lake is freshwater, with salinity increasing towards the E. Area: 18,428sq km (7115sq mi). Max. depth: 26m (85ft).

Balla, Giacomo (1871–1958) Italian artist. Influenced by the poet MARINETTI, founder of FUTURISM, Balla adopted the movement's philosophical outlook and urged artists to use art as a means to change Italy's culture through the acceptance of science and technology. His works, which emphasize movement and abstraction, include *The Street Light – Study of Light* (1909), and *Dynamism of Dog on a Leash* (1912).

Ballard, J.G. (James Graham) (1930–) British novelist and short-story writer, b. China. Ballard is best known for his highly stylized science fiction. Novels such as *The Wind from Nowhere* (1962), *The Drought* (1965), *The Crystal World* (1966), and *Crash* (1973, filmed 1999) explore psychological reactions to catastrophic situations. *Empire of the Sun* (1984, filmed 1987) explores his childhood experiences in a Japanese prisoner-of-war camp.

ballet Theatrical dance form set to music. The first formal ballet, *Ballet comique de la Reine*, was performed at the court of Catherine de' Medici (1581). In 1661 LOUIS XIV founded the Royal Academy of Dance. Exclusively performed by male dancers, ballet was confined to the French court. *The Triumph of Love* (1681) was the first ballet to use trained female dancers. The first public performance of a ballet was in 1708. Choreographic notation developed, and Pierre Beauchamp (1631–1719) established the five classical positions. Jean-Georges Noverre (1727–1810), the most influential choreographer of the 18th century, argued for a greater naturalism. In 1820 Carlo Blasis (1797–1878) codified the turn out technique, which facilitated the freer movement of the dancer. The 1832 performance of *Les Sylphides* set the choreographic model for 19th-century Romantic ballets, stressing the role of the prima ballerina. Dancing on the toes (*sur les pointes*) was introduced. At the end of the 19th century, Russian ballet emphasized technique and virtuosity. Subsequently, Sergei DIAGHILEV and his BALLETS RUSSES revolutionized ballet with dynamic choreography and dancing. Today, the preeminence of Russian ballet is maintained by the KIROV and BOLSHOI companies. In 1930 Dame Marie RAMBERT founded the first English ballet school, and in 1931 Dame Ninette de VALOIS established the Sadler's Wells Ballet (now the Royal Ballet). Rudolf NUREYEV's influential work for the Royal Ballet enlarged the role and dramatic range of the male dancer. In 1934 the first major US ballet school was instituted under the direction of George BALANCHINE. The New York City Ballet was established in 1948, and is now one of the world's principal ballet companies. American ballet introduced a more abstract style and eclectic approach, fusing elements of classical ballet, jazz, popular and MODERN DANCE. *See also* FOKINE, MICHEL; MASSINE, LEONIDE; MASQUE; NIJINSKY, VASLAV

Ballets Russes Dance company founded (1909) in Paris by Sergei DIAGHILEV, with Michel FOKINE as chief choreographer. It revitalized and reshaped ballet by bringing together great dancers (PAVLOVA and NIJINSKY) and choreographers (MASSINE, Nijinsky, and BALANCHINE). Leading composers, such as STRAVINSKY, DEBUSSY, and Richard STRAUSS composed music for the company, and top artists such as PICASSO, CHAGALL and MATISSE designed sets and costumes. It disbanded soon after Diaghilev's death in 1929.

balloon Unsteerable, lighter-than-air craft, usually made of nylon. Balloons are used for recreation, scientific, and military purposes. Ballooning was the first means of human 'flight'. Generally credited with the achievement are the French brothers Jacques and Joseph MONTGOLFIER, who devised a hot-air balloon in which Jean François Pilâtre de Rozier and the Marquis d'Arlandes made the first ascent (November 21, 1783).

◀ **balloon** Man's first balloon flight took place on November 21, 1783, when a balloon designed by the Montgolfier brothers, and carrying Jean-François Pilâtre de Rozier and the Marquis d'Arlandes, flew *c.*8km (5mi) across Paris. The flight is believed to have lasted 23 minutes, during which time the balloon is thought to have reached a height of 900m (3,000ft). Made of paper-lined linen and coated with alum to reduce the fire risk, the balloon was 15m (50ft) high, and weighed 785kg (1,730lb). The air inside was heated by a large mass of burning straw resting on a wire grid in the centre of the gallery.

▶ **bamboo** Woody members of the grass family, bamboos can vary in height from a few centimetres to several metres. While most bamboo grows in dense clumps in tropical regions, some bamboo such as *Arundinaria alpina* (shown here) grows on mountainsides and can withstand cold conditions. Though hollow, bamboo is surprisingly strong for its weight, and is used sometimes for building houses and making furniture.

Unmanned military, meteorological or other scientific balloons are usually filled with hydrogen, which is the least dense of all gases but dangerously flammable. Manned balloons are generally filled with safer helium gas or hot air. In the hot-air method, burning propane gas is used to heat the air through an opening in the bottom of the balloon, which is usually made of nylon fabric. On March 20, 1999, Bertran Piccard and Brian Jones competed the first non-stop flight around the world.

ballot Object used to cast a vote, or process of voting in an election. The word derives from the Italian *ballotta* (little ball) and since 5th-century BC Athens, balls have been used to cast votes. Today, the ballot is a sheet (or sheets) of paper, although in some countries voting machines are used to register votes.

balm Resin from a BALSAM plant and the name of various aromatic plants, particularly those of the genera *Melissa* and *Melittis*, both family Lamiaceae/Labiatae. Also, an old name for any soothing ointment.

Balmoral Private residence of the British monarch, in the Scottish Highlands, 85km (53mi) W of Aberdeen. Built in the reign of Queen Victoria, it was left to her by Prince Albert on his death in 1861.

balsa Lightweight wood obtained from a South American tree, used for modelling and for building rafts. Family Bombacaceae; species *Ochroma lagopus*.

balsam Aromatic RESIN obtained from plants; or healing preparations, especially those with benzoic and cinnamic acid added to the resin; or balsam-yielding trees, such as the balsam fir and balsam poplar. The name is also given to numerous species of the family Balsaminaceae that are plants of moist areas, with pendent flowers. *See also* IMPATIENS

Baltic Sea Part of the Atlantic extending past Denmark, along the N coasts of Germany and Poland, and the E coasts of the BALTIC STATES, and separating Sweden from Russia and Finland. The sea extends N-S with an arm reaching out to the E. The N part is the Gulf of Bothnia, the E part is the Gulf of Finland. The Baltic is the largest body of brackish water in the world. Its low salinity (due to its large catchment area, about four times the area of the sea) accounts for the ease with which the Gulf of Bothnia freezes in the winter. The tidal range is low and currents are weak. During the Middle Ages there was an important herring fishing industry. Its decline at the end of the 15th century is thought to be a contributory factor in the demise of the HANSEATIC LEAGUE. Area: 414,400sq km (160,000sq mi).

Baltic states Countries of ESTONIA, LATVIA, and LITHUANIA, on the E coast of the BALTIC SEA. Settled by various tribes in the 7th century, it remained mostly under Danish, Russian or Polish rule until the 20th century. Following the Russian Revolution (1917), each state became independent, but were submerged into the Soviet Union in 1940. They regained independence following the break-up of the Soviet Union in 1991.

Baltimore City and port in N Maryland, USA, at the mouth of the Patapsco River, on Chesapeake Bay. Founded

by the Irish baronial family of Baltimore as a tobacco port in 1729. During the 19th century it became an important shipbuilding centre. It is a notable centre of commerce and education, with three universities, and a major port. Industries: steelworks, oil refineries, shipbuilding, aerospace equipment. Pop. (2000) 2,076,000.

Baltimore oriole American songbird. The male has black head, neck, back, and wings and orange breast, rump and outer tail feathers. Females (olive upper and yellow lower body) build long, slender weed-and-bark nests in high trees. Length: to 20cm (8in). Species *Icterus galbula*.

Baluchistan Region and province in central and SW Pakistan, bordered by Iran (W), Afghanistan (N) and the Arabian Sea (S). Quetta is the capital. The boundaries with Iran and Afghanistan were settled in 1885–96. The region became part of Pakistan in 1947. The terrain is mostly hilly desert and is inhabited by nomadic tribes such as the Baluchi. Much of the population is employed in sheep raising. Some cotton is grown, and fishing is the chief occupation on the coast. Natural gas is extracted and exported, along with salt and fish. Area: 347,190sq km (134,102sq mi). Pop. (1998) 6,511,000.

Balzac, Honoré de (1799–1850) French novelist. One of the greatest novelists of the 19th century, Balzac's first success was *Les Chouans* (1829). More than 90 novels and short stories followed during a lifetime of extraordinary creative effort. He organized these works into a grand fictional scheme, intended as a detailed, realistic study of the whole of contemporary French society, which he called *La Comédie Humaine* (*The Human Comedy*). Among his best-known novels are *Eugénie Grandet* (1833), *Le Pére Goriot* (1834–35), and *La Cousine Bette* (1846).

Bamako Capital of Mali, on the River Niger, 145km (90mi) NE of the border with Guinea, W Africa. Once a centre of Muslim learning (11th-15th centuries), it was occupied by the French in 1883 and became capital of the French Sudan (1908). Industries: shipping, groundnuts, meat, metal products. Pop. (2005) 1,379,000.

bamboo Tall, tree-like GRASS native to tropical and subtropical regions. The hollow, woody stems grow in branching clusters from a thick rhizome and the leaves are stalked blades. It is used in house construction and for household implements. Some bamboo shoots are eaten. The pulp and fibre may form a basis for paper production. Height: to 40m (131ft). There are *c.*1,000 species. Family Poaceae/Gramineae; genus *Bambusa*.

banana Long, curved, yellow or reddish fruit of the tree of the same name. It has soft, creamy flesh. A spike of yellow, clustered flowers grows from the centre of the crown of the tree and bends downwards and develops into bunches of 50–150 fruits in 'hands' of 10–20. More than 100 varieties are cultivated. Fruits used for cooking are called plantains. Height: 3–9m (10–30ft). Family Musaceae; genus *Musa*.

band Instrumental ensemble, usually consisting of wind and percussion instruments. A **big** band performs swing music and has about 16 musicians in four sections: trumpets, trombones, saxophones and a rhythm section. A **brass** band contains only brass and percussion instruments. A **dance** band has a rhythm section to provide the strict beat and melody instruments such as saxophone and violin to play the tunes. A **jazz** band varies according to the style of jazz: a traditional jazz band usually has a clarinet, trumpet, trombone and a rhythm section; a modern jazz quartet may feature saxophone, piano, drums and bass. A **military** (marching) band contains brass and woodwind instruments with percussion. A **rock** band has a core of electric guitar, bass guitar and drums to which singers and other instruments may be added.

Banda, Hastings Kamuzu (1902–97) Malawian statesman, the country's first president (1966–94). He guided Nyasaland to independence as MALAWI (1964) establishing an autocratic regime. In 1971 Banda became president-for-life. He was the only African leader to maintain friendly relations with the South African apartheid regime. In 1994, after two years of political unrest and economic crisis, he was forced to allow multi-party elections, which he lost.

Bandaranaike, Sirimavo Ratwatte Dias (1916–2000) Sri Lankan stateswoman, prime minister (1960–65, 1970–77, 1994–2000). Following the assassination (1959) of her husband Solomon BANDARANAIKE, she assumed control of the Sri Lanka Freedom Party and became the world's first woman prime minister. Her daughter, Kumaratunga (1945–), was president from 1994–2005.

Bandaranaike, Solomon West Ridgeway Dias (1899–1959) Ceylonese statesman, prime minister (1956–59). He made Sinhalese the official language and founded the Sri Lanka Freedom Party to unite nationalists and socialists. He was assassinated by a dissident Buddhist monk, and his wife, Sirimavo BANDARANAIKE, succeeded him.

Bandar Seri Begawan (formerly Brunei Town) Capital of BRUNEI, Borneo, SE Asia. The town port was superseded in 1972 by a new deepwater harbour at Maura. The capital includes the Sultan Omar Ali Saifuddin Masjid, SE Asia's largest mosque. Pop. (2001 est.) 46,000.

bandicoot Australian MARSUPIAL about the size of a rabbit, and with similarly long ears, hopping gait, and burrowing habits. It eats insects rather than vegetation, and its long pointed snout is probably adapted for its diet. Genus *Perameles*.

Bandung Capital of West Java province, Indonesia. Founded in 1810, Bandung was the administrative centre of the Dutch East Indies, and is now the third largest city in Indonesia. A centre for Sundanese culture, the non-aligned movement of LESS-DEVELOPED COUNTRIES met here in 1955. Industries: canning, chemicals, quinine and textiles. Pop. (2005) 4,020,000.

Bandung Conference (1955) International meeting in Bandung, Indonesia. Representatives of 29 non-aligned countries of Asia and Africa, including China, met to express their united opposition to colonialism and to gain recognition for less developed nations.

Bangalore (Bangalur) Capital of Karnataka state, s central India. Established in 1537 by the Mysore dynasty, Britian retained the city as a military headquarters until 1947. Bangalore is the sixth largest city in India, and an important industrial and communications centre. Main products include aircraft and machine tools. Pop. (2005) 6,532,000.

Bangkok Capital and chief port of Thailand, on the E bank of the River Menam (Chao Phraya). Bangkok became the capital in 1782, when King Rama I built a royal palace here. It quickly became Thailand's largest city. The Grand Palace (including the sacred Emerald Buddha) and more than 400 Buddhist temples (*wats*) are notable examples of Thai culture. It has a large Chinese minority. During World War 2 it was occupied by the Japanese. Today, Bangkok is a busy market centre, much of the city's commerce taking place on the numerous canals. The port handles most of Thailand's imports and exports. Industries: tourism, building materials, rice processing, textiles, jewellery. Pop. (2005) 6,604,000.

Bangladesh Republic in s Asia. *See* country feature, p.134

Bangui Capital of the Central African Republic, on the River Ubangi, near the Zaïre border. Founded in 1889 by the French, it is the nation's chief port for international trade. Industries: textiles, food processing, beer, soap. Pop. (2002 est.) 652,900.

banjo Musical instrument with four to nine strings, a body of stretched parchment on a metal hoop, and a long, fretted neck. It is played with a plectrum or the fingers. Probably of African origin, it was taken to the USA by slaves. It is most often used in Dixieland jazz and folk-music.

Banjul (Bathurst) Capital of The Gambia, w Africa, on St Mary's Island, where the River Gambia enters the Atlantic Ocean. Founded as a trading post by the British in 1816, it is Gambia's chief port and commercial centre. The main industry is groundnut processing, though tourism is growing rapidly. Pop. (2002 est.) 57,800.

banking Commercial process providing a wide range of financial services, such as holding and transferring money, providing loans, and giving stability to the financial sector of the economy. There are a variety of sectors in the banking industry. **Clearing** banks in the UK and **commercial** banks in the USA deal with the public, as well as with small and medium-sized businesses and corporations; MER-CHANT BANKS or investment banks provide services to

business and industry, such as investment loans or share flotations. In many countries there are other providers of banking services, such as insurance companies and credit card firms, as well as BUILDING SOCIETIES in the UK and savings and loan associations in the USA. A country's CEN-TRAL BANK, sometimes under government control, is the bankers' bank and can be used to regulate an economy.

Bank of England Britain's central banking institution, founded in 1694 by a group of London merchants. Nationalized in 1946, it regulates foreign exchange, issues bank notes, advises the government on monetary matters and acts as the government's financial agent. It is situated in Threadneedle Street, City of London. The governor of the Bank of England is appointed by the government. Since 1997, following legislation put forward by Gordon BROWN, the Bank has operational responsibility for setting national interest rates.

Bank of the United States Two US national banks. The first was established in 1791 and aimed to provide the USA with a solid economic basis. Although it was soundly operated, autonomous state banking interests defeated its rechartering in 1811. Following the War of 1812, a second national bank was chartered by Congress in 1816. There was much opposition to its power to establish local branches that could compete with state-chartered banks, and many in western states believed the bank favoured eastern business interests. President Andrew JACKSON supported the bank's opponents, and vetoed its rechartering. The bank became obsolete in 1836. It was not until the creation of the FEDERAL RESERVE SYSTEM (1913) that the USA achieved a central banking system.

bankruptcy Legally determined status of a person or company, usually when debts greatly exceed income and assets. A person or company may ask to be declared bankrupt by the court, or else the creditors may do so. A court-appointed receiver takes charge of the bankrupt's property with the aim of meeting, as far as possible, the bankrupt's financial obligations to his or her creditors.

Banks, Sir Joseph (1743–1820) English botanist. He was the senior scientist of the group who sailed to Tahiti with Captain James COOK aboard *HMS Endeavour* in 1768. At Botany Bay, Australia, Banks collected (1770) examples of plants hitherto unknown in Europe, including the shrub BANKSIA named in his honour. Upon his return, he helped establish the Royal Botanic Gardens at Kew, w London, and financed several international plant-collecting expeditions. In 1778 he became president of the Royal Society.

banksia Any of *c.*70 species of flowering shrubs and small trees found in Australia and New Guinea that belong to the genus *Banksia*. Their evergreen leaves are long and leathery, and they bear tube-shaped heads of yellowish or reddish flowers. Sir Joseph BANKS discovered the genus in 1770. Most banksias are pollinated by birds, but some are pollinated by the honey possum, a small, mouse-like marsupial that feeds on their nectar and pollen. Family Proteaceae.

Bannister, Sir Roger Gilbert (1929–) English track and field athlete. On May 6, 1954, Bannister became the first man to run a mile in less than four minutes (3min. 59.4sec). He was knighted in 1975, and in 1995 was appointed chair of a government scheme to introduce sports scholarships.

Bannockburn Town and moor in central Scotland, scene of a Scottish victory over the English in 1314. The English army of EDWARD II, advancing on Stirling, was intercepted by Scottish troops under ROBERT I (THE BRUCE). The Scots held a dominant position above the Bannock burn, while the more heavily armed English floundered in swampy ground. Fighting began at dawn, and before noon the English survivors fled. Although conflict continued for many years, the victory secured Scottish independence from the English, who made no serious effort to regain territory in Scotland.

Banting, Sir Frederick Grant (1891–1941) Canadian physician. He shared, with J.J.R. Macleod, the 1923 Nobel Prize in physiology or medicine for his work in extracting the hormone INSULIN from the PANCREAS. This made possible the effective treatment of DIABETES.

Bantu Group of African languages generally considered as forming part of the Benue-Congo branch of the Niger-Congo

▲ **banjo** Originating in the 18th century, the banjo is popularly supposed to have been brought by slaves from Africa to the USA. By the middle of the 19th century it had become the traditional instrument of African-Americans. It has four or more strings, which are plucked, and a resonating body consisting of parchment stretched over a metal hoop.

family. SWAHILI, XHOSA, and ZULU are among the most widely spoken of the several hundred Bantu languages spoken from the Congo Basin to South Africa, and almost all are tone languages. There are more than 70 million speakers of Bantu.

banyan Evergreen tree of E India. The branches send down aerial shoots that take root, forming new trunks. Such trunks from a single tree may form a circle up to 100m (330ft) across. Height: to 30m (100ft). Family Moraceae; species *Ficus benghalensis*.

baobab Tropical tree native to Africa. It has a stout trunk containing water storage tissue, and short, stubby branches with sparse foliage. Fibre from its bark is used for rope. Its gourd-like fruit is edible. Height: to 18m (60ft); trunk diameter: to 12m (40ft). Family Bombacaceae; species *Adansonia digitata*.

baptism Pouring of water on a person's forehead or the immersion of the body in water, used as a rite of initiation into the Christian Church to which it is one of the SACRA-MENTS. The water symbolizes regeneration. Total immersion is practised by the BAPTISTS. In churches that practise infant baptism, the rite is usually referred to as christening.

Baptist Member of various Protestant and Evangelical sects who practise BAPTISM of believers and regard immersion as the only legitimate form sanctioned by the New Testament. Like the ANABAPTISTS, to whom they have an affinity but no formal links, they generally reject the practice of infant baptism, insisting that initiates must have freedom of thought and expression and must already be believers. Baptists originated among English dissenters of the 17th century, but have spread worldwide through emigration and missionary work. They uphold the principle of religious liberty. There is no official creed nor hierarchy and individual churches are autonomous. Baptists traditionally advocate the separation of Church and State. The Baptist World Alliance (founded 1905) holds regular international congresses. Today, the number of Baptists worldwide is estimated at more than 50 million.

bar Unit of pressure, the pressure created by a column of mercury 75.007cm high. It is equal to 10^5 pascals. Standard atmospheric pressure (at sea level) is 1.01325 bars, or 1013.25 millibars.

BANGLADESH

The People's Republic of Bangladesh is one of the world's most densely populated countries. Apart from the hilly regions in the far NE and SE, most of the land is flat and covered by fertile alluvium spread over the land by the GANGES, BRAHMAPUTRA and Meghna rivers. These rivers overflow when they are swollen by the annual monsoon rains. Floods also occur along the coast, 575km [357mi] long, when tropical cyclones (the name for hurricanes in this region) drive seawater inland. These periodic storms cause great human suffering.

The world's most devastating tropical cyclone ever recorded occurred in Bangladesh in 1970, when an estimated 1 million people were killed. Most of Bangladesh is cultivated, but forests cover about 16% of the land. They include bamboo forests in the NE and mangrove forests in the swampy Sundarbans

region in the SW, which is a sanctuary for the Royal Bengal tiger.

CLIMATE
Bangladesh has a tropical monsoon climate. Dry northerly winds blow during the winter, but in summer moist winds from the S bring monsoon rains. In 1998 around two-thirds of the entire country was submerged by the monsoon, causing extensive damage. In December 2004 Bangladesh escaped the tsunami in the Indian Ocean with relatively little damage.

HISTORY
The early history of Bangladesh is synonymous with that of BENGAL. For 300 years after the mid-8th century AD, Buddhist rulers governed eastern Bengal, the area that now makes up Bangladesh. In the 13th century, Muslims from the N extended their rule into Bengal and, in 1576, the area became part of the Muslim Mughal Empire which was ruled by the emperor AKBAR I. This empire, which also included India, Pakistan and Afghanistan, began to break up in the early 18th century. Europeans, who had first made contact with the area in the 16th century, began to gain influence.

The EAST INDIA COMPANY, chartered by the English government in 1600 to develop trade in Asia, became the leading trading power in Bengal by the mid-18th century. In 1757, following the defeat of the Nawab of Bengal in the Battle of Plassey, the East India Company effectively ruled Bengal. Discontent with the company led to the Sepoy Rebellion in 1857. In 1858, the British government took over the East India Company and its territory became known as British India.

POLITICS
In 1947, British India was partitioned between the mainly Hindu India and the Muslim Pakistan. Pakistan consisted of two parts, W and E Pakistan, separated by about 1,600km [1,000mi] of Indian territory. Differences developed between the two sides as people in the E felt themselves victims of ethnic and economic discrimination by the Urdu and

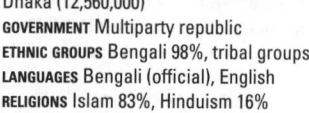

AREA 143,998sq km [55,598sq mi]
POPULATION 150,448,000
CAPITAL (POPULATION) Dhaka (12,560,000)
GOVERNMENT Multiparty republic
ETHNIC GROUPS Bengali 98%, tribal groups
LANGUAGES Bengali (official), English
RELIGIONS Islam 83%, Hinduism 16%
CURRENCY Taka =100 paisas

Punjabi-speaking peoples of the W. In 1971 resentment turned to war when Bengali irregulars, aided by Indian troops, established the independent nation of 'Free Bengal' with Sheikh Mujibur Rahman as head of state.

Rahman's assassination in 1975 led to a takeover by General Zia Rahman, who created an Islamic state before he, too, was assassinated in 1981. General Ershad took over in a coup in 1982. He resigned as army chief in 1986 to become a civilian president.

In 1990 protests toppled Ershad from power and, after the first free parliamentary elections since independence, a coalition government was formed in 1991. Many problems arose in the 1990s, including increasing Muslim fundamentalism and severe cyclone damage. In 1996, Sheikh Hasina Wajed of the Awami League became prime minister, but in 2001 she was defeated by Khaleda Zia, leader of the Nationalist Party. Elections scheduled for January 2007 were postponed after disputes over their fairness led to rioting. An army-backed administration took control, claiming it intended to clean up politics before holding elections in 2008.

ECONOMY
Bangladesh is one of the world's poorest countries. Agriculture employs more than half of the workforce. Rice is the chief crop, and Bangladesh is the world's fourth largest producer. Other important crops include jute, sugar cane, tobacco and wheat.

Clothing manufacture is the largest industry and dominant export. Shipbreaking is also important. The country has some gas reserves which may allow future economic expansion.

MAP SCALE
0   50   100 km
0   50 miles

Barabbas In the New Testament, convicted criminal or terrorist who was in prison at the time of Jesus Christ's trial before PONTIUS PILATE. In accordance with a PASSOVER custom, Pilate offered to release a prisoner. The Jerusalem mob, given the choice of which prisoner should be allowed to go free, nominated Barabbas and called for Christ to be crucified (Matthew 27, Mark 15, Luke 23, John 18).

Barak, Ehud (1942–) Israeli statesman, prime minister (1999–2001). Barak was chief of staff (1991–94) of the Israeli Defence Forces before joining the cabinet of Yitzhak RABIN. He succeeded Shimon PERES as leader of the Labour Party. Despite the optimism that greeted Barak's landslide victory over Binyamin NETANYAHU in the 1999 elections, there was little progress towards peace with the Palestinians. In May 2000, he withdrew Israeli troops from s Lebanon. Escalating violent clashes with the Palestinians dented Barak's popularity, and Ariel SHARON, leader of Likud, defeated him in elections.

Barbados Island state in the Windward Islands, West Indies; the capital is BRIDGETOWN. Barbados' warm climate encouraged the growth of its two largest industries – sugar cane and tourism. It was settled by the British in 1627, and dominated by British plantation owners (using African slave labour until the abolition of slavery) for the next 300 years. It gained independence in 1966. Area: 430sq km (166sq mi). Pop. (2000) 277,000. *See* WEST INDIES map

Barbarossa (1466–1546) (Redbeard) Name given by Christians to two Muslim privateers in the Mediterranean, **Aruj** (d.1518) and Khizr or **Khayr ad-Din** (d.1546). Aruj was killed in battle against the Spanish, but Khayr seized Algiers from Spain (1533), took Tunis (1534), raided Christian coasts and shipping and gained control of the Barbary States. He acknowledged the Ottoman sultan as his overlord, and was commander (1533–44) of the fleet of SULEIMAN I (THE MAGNIFICENT), which controlled the E Mediterranean. His forces were defeated by Spain and Italy in the Battle of LEPANTO.

Barbary ape Tailless, yellowish-brown ape-like MONKEY native to Algeria and Morocco, and introduced into Gibraltar. It is the size of a small dog. The Gibraltar Barbary apes are the only wild monkeys in Europe. Species *Macaca sylvana*. *See also* MACAQUE; PRIMATE

barbel (barb) CARP-like freshwater fish of W Asia and S central Europe. A game and food fish, it has an elongated body, flattened underside, and two pairs of fleshy mouth whiskers (barbels). Length: 50–90cm (20–35in); weight: 16kg (35lb). Family Cyprinidae; species *Barbus barbus*.

Barber, Samuel (1910–81) US composer. He composed chamber music, notably *Dover Beach* (1931) for voice and string quartet, two symphonies, a piano concerto (1962), and three operas including *Vanessa* (1958) and *Antony and Cleopatra* (1966). His style, initially quite romantic, became increasingly dissonant. He won two Pulitzer Prizes for music.

Barbie, Klaus (1913–91) Nazi chief of the German Gestapo in France during World War 2. He was known as the 'Butcher of Lyon' for his persecution and murder of French Resistance fighters and Jews. Barbie sent thousands of people to AUSCHWITZ. After the war, he worked for US counter-intelligence before escaping to Bolivia in 1951. He was captured in 1987, brought to Lyon, and sentenced to life imprisonment.

Barbirolli, Sir John (1899–1970) English conductor who won international acclaim for his sensitive interpretations. He conducted the New York Philharmonic (1937–42), and was then resident with the Hallé Orchestra, Manchester (1943–68), which he transformed into a world-class ensemble.

barbiturate DRUG used as a sedative or to induce sleep. Highly addictive and dangerous in high doses, or in combination with other drugs such as alcohol or tranquillizers, most barbiturates are no longer prescribed. Short-acting barbiturates are used in surgery to induce general anaesthesia; long-acting formulations are prescribed for epilepsy.

Barbizon School French school of landscape painting in the 19th century. Led by Théodore ROUSSEAU in the late 1840s, the group worked near Barbizon, N France. Artists included Charles Daubigny, Diaz de la Peña, Jules Dupré, and Constant Troyon. They embraced a longing for the

BAR CODE

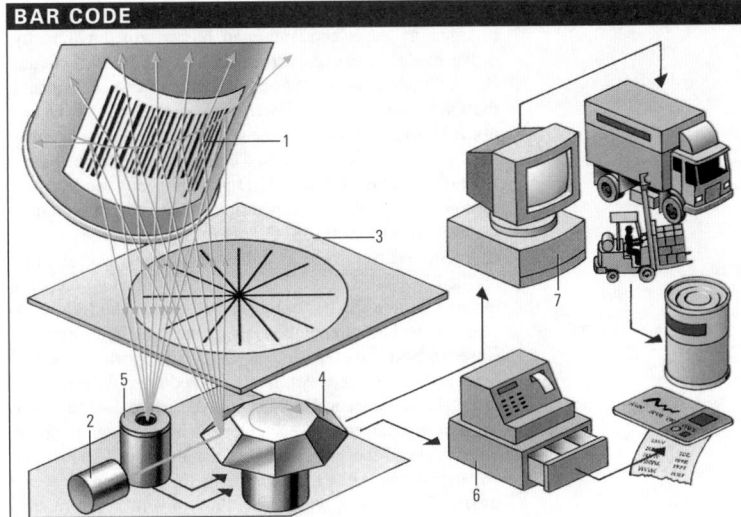

Bar codes represent information concerning a product and its manufacturer in a series of thick and thin black and white lines (1). A laser (2) is reflected through a glass screen (3) onto the bar code by a rotating multi-faceted mirror (4). The laser light is scattered by the white lines and absorbed by the black lines. A sensor (5) detects the reflected laser light and compares the relative width of the lines. Because the relative widths are compared, the bar code does not have to be on a flat surface. The sensor passes the bar code information to the till (6) for billing the customer, and a central store computer (7) monitors stock levels and order supplies of goods.

freedom of nature, escaping the restraints of Parisian art. Inspired by CONSTABLE and 17th-century Dutch landscapists, they were forerunners of IMPRESSIONISM.

Barcelona City and Mediterranean port in NE Spain, capital of CATALONIA and Spain's second-largest city. Reputedly founded by the Carthaginian Barca family, it was ruled by Romans, Visigoths, and Moors and by the late Middle Ages had become a major trading centre. It is the focus of radical political and Catalan separatist movements. The autonomous Catalan government based here (1932–39) was swept away by the Spanish CIVIL WAR. Modern Barcelona is the cosmopolitan, cultural capital of Spain. The 1992 summer Olympic Games were held here. Historic buildings include the gothic Cathedral of Santa Eulalia (13th-15th century), the Church of the Sagrada Familia designed by Antonio GAUDÍ (begun 1882), and the Monument to Christopher Columbus. There are two universities, a Museum of Modern Art, and the Picasso Museum. Barcelona is an important shipping, banking and financial centre. Industries: vehicles, textiles, machinery, petrochemicals, electrical goods. Pop. (2000) 1,527,000.

bar code (Universal Product Code) Coded information consisting of thick and thin lines, and designed for computer recognition. At checkouts, a laser beam scans the bar code and a light-sensitive detector picks up the reflected signal, which consists of a pattern of pulses. The store's computer translates this into product information.

Bardeen, John (1908–91) US physicist known for his research into SEMICONDUCTORS. He worked (1945–51) with the Bell Telephone Laboratories, and was professor of physics (1951–75) at the University of Illinois. He was the first person to win the Nobel Prize twice in the same field, physics: in 1956 he shared it with William SHOCKLEY and Walter BRATTAIN, for their invention of the TRANSISTOR, and in 1972 with Leon Cooper and John Schrieffer, for the theory of SUPERCONDUCTIVITY.

Barebone's Parliament (Parliament of the Saints, July-December 1653) Last Parliament of the English COMMONWEALTH. Successor to the RUMP PARLIAMENT, it was named after a prominent member, 'Praise-God Barebone'. Members were selected by CROMWELL and the Puritan army leaders. Religious disputes ruined its effectiveness. It voted its own dissolution and made Cromwell Lord Protector.

B

Barenboim, Daniel (1942–) Israeli pianist and conductor, b. Argentina. An eclectic musician, he performed with many of the world's great orchestras, such as the New York and Berlin Philharmonics, the London Symphony Orchestra, and the Orchestre de Paris. Barenboim succeeded Sir Georg SOLTI as artistic director of the Chicago Symphony Orchestra (1992–). In 1967 he married cellist Jacqueline DU PRÉ.

Barents, Willem (d.1597) Dutch navigator and Arctic explorer. He made three expeditions (1594–97) in search of the NORTHEAST PASSAGE. On his third voyage, he discovered SVALBARD and, crossing the sea now named after him, reached Novaya Zemlya. His ship was trapped by ice, and the crew built a shelter – most survived until the following year's thaw, but Barents died before they reached safety.

Barents Sea Part of the ARCTIC OCEAN lying between SVALBARD and Novaya Zemlya, it was named after Willem BARENTS. The seafloor consists of an uneven surface distribution of Quaternary sediments. Deeper, older sediments bear evidence of long periods above sea level. The fishing-grounds are rich in cod and herring. Area: 1,370,360sq km (529,096sq mi).

barite Translucent, white or yellow mineral, barium sulphate ($BaSO_4$), found in SEDIMENTARY ROCKS and in ore veins in limestone. Radiating clusters of crystals are called 'barite roses'. It occurs as a gangue mineral with ores of lead, copper and zinc, and as a replacement for limestone. It is used as a weighting agent in oil-rig drilling, and in the chemical industry for paper-making, rubber manufacture, high-quality paints and X-rays. Hardness: 3–3.5; r.d. 4.5.

baritone Name for the register of the human voice that falls between that of TENOR and BASS. It has been much used in operas since the 18th century; Mozart, Verdi, and Wagner, among others, have written major roles for the baritone voice.

barium (symbol Ba) Metallic element of the alkaline-earth group, discovered in 1808 by the English chemist Sir Humphry DAVY. It is a soft, silvery-white metal whose chief sources are heavy spar (barium sulphate) and witherite (barium carbonate). Barium compounds are used as rodent poison, pigments for paints and as drying agents. Barium sulphate ($BaSO_4$) is swallowed to allow X-ray examination of the stomach and intestines because barium atoms are opaque to X-rays. Properties: at.no. 56; r.a.m. 137.34; r.d. 3.51; m.p. 725°C (1,337°F); b.p. 1,640°C (2984°F); most common isotope Ba^{138} (71.66%).

bark Outer protective covering of a woody plant stem. It is made up of several layers. The CORK layer, waxy and waterproof, is the thickest and hardens into the tough, fissured outer covering. Lenticels (pores) in the bark allow GAS EXCHANGE between the stem and the atmosphere. *See also* CAMBIUM

Barker, Pat (1943–) English novelist. Barker's novels often focus on the plight of women, usually in the N of England. Her debut novel was *Union Street* (1982). *Regeneration* (1991) and *The Eye in the Door* (1993) began a World War 1 trilogy; the final part, *The Ghost Road*, won the 1995 Booker Prize.

Barlach, Ernst (1870–1938) German sculptor, graphic artist, writer and dramatist. He was a pioneer of the German EXPRESSIONISM movement. His distinctive style was influenced by medieval German woodcarving and art nouveau. Barlach's sculptures, such as the bronze angel in Güstrow Cathedral, northern Germany, have a raw, emotional quality and vigour.

barley Cereal GRASS native to Asia and Ethiopia, cultivated perhaps since 5000 BC. Three cultivated species are: *Hordeum distichum*, commonly grown in Europe; *H. vulgare*, favoured in the USA; and *H. irregulare*, grown in Ethiopia. Barley is eaten by humans and animals, and is used to make malt beverages. Family Poaceae/Gramineae.

bar mitzvah Jewish ceremony in which a young male is initiated into the religious community. At the ceremony, which traditionally takes place when he is aged 13 years and a day, he reads a portion of the TORAH in a synagogue. The religious rite is followed by a social celebration. Some non-orthodox communities also celebrate a bas (or bat) mitzvah for girls.

barn (symbol *b*) Scientific unit of area used in nuclear physics to measure the cross-sections in interactions of particles. A barn equals $10^{-24}cm^2$ per nucleus. This area is a measure of the probability that FISSION, the splitting of a heavy atomic nucleus, will occur when a neutron moves towards a heavy nucleus.

Barnabas, Saint Early Christian apostle, originally named Joseph, who was a companion of St PAUL. He travelled with Paul on two proselytizing missions to Cyprus and the European mainland. His feast day is June 11.

barnacle Crustacean that lives mostly on rocks and floating timber. Some barnacles live on whales, turtles and fish without being parasitic, although there are also parasitic species. The larvae swim freely until ready to become adults, when they settle permanently on their heads; their bodies become covered with calcareous plates. The adult uses its feathery appendages to scoop food into its mouth. Two main types are those with stalks (**goose** barnacles) and those without (**acorn** barnacles). Subclass Cirripedia.

Barnard, Christiaan (1922–2001) South African surgeon. Barnard was the first to perform a human heart transplant (December 3, 1967). In 1974 Barnard performed the first 'piggy-back' transplant, implanting a second heart in a patient and linking it to the existing heart to assist the healing.

Barnardo, Thomas John (1845–1905) British philanthropist who founded the Dr Barnardo homes for destitute children, b. Ireland. In 1867, he founded the East End Mission for orphan children, the first of his famous homes. These homes spread rapidly throughout the UK and still flourish today.

Barnard's Star Red dwarf star six light years away in the constellation Ophiuchus. It is the closest star to the Sun after the ALPHA CENTAURI system, and was discovered in 1916 by the US astronomer Edward Barnard (1857–1923).

barn owl Generally nocturnal bird of prey, living mainly in the Eastern Hemisphere. The widely distributed common barn owl (*Tyto alba*) has a heart-shaped face. It sometimes lives in buildings, and acute hearing enables it to locate rodents and other prey in almost total darkness. Family Tytonidae.

Barnum, Phineas Taylor (1810–91) US showman. He established the American Museum in New York City (1842), where he presented the "dwarf" Tom Thumb, the Fijian mermaid and other "freaks". In 1847 he introduced Swedish soprano Jenny LIND to US audiences. In 1871 he opened his circus, billed as "The Greatest Show on Earth". In 1881 he merged with rival James Bailey to form Barnum and Bailey's Circus.

barometer Instrument for measuring atmospheric pressure. There are two basic types. A **mercury** barometer has a vertical column of mercury, whose length alters with changes in atmospheric pressure. An **aneroid** barometer has a chamber containing a partial vacuum, and the chamber changes shape with shifts in pressure. Barometers are used in WEATHER FORECASTING to predict local weather changes: a rising barometer (increasing pressure) indicates dry weather; a falling barometer indicates wet weather. In a **barograph**, the pointer of an aneroid barometer is replaced by a pen that traces variations in pressure on a revolving cylindrical chart. A barometer can also be used in an ALTIMETER to measure altitude by indicating changes in atmospheric pressure. *See also* BAR

Barons' War (1263–67) In English history, conflict between HENRY III and his barons, led by Simon de MONTFORT. In 1261 Henry renounced the Provisions of Oxford (1258) and Westminster (1259) that had proposed he rule through a council of barons rather than rely on favourites. The barons decided to force the king to submit and defeated Henry's army in the battle of Lewes (1264). Henry's son, the future EDWARD I, formed an army which defeated the barons, and Montfort was killed at the battle of Evesham (1265).

baroque Term (perhaps derived from the Portuguese *barroca*, a misshapen pearl) applied to the style of art and architecture prevalent in Europe in the 17th and early 18th centuries. Baroque was at its height in the Rome of BERNINI, BORROMINI, and Pietro de Cortona (*c.*1630–80), and in s Germany with Balthazar Neumann and Fischer von Erlach (*c.*1700–50). At its best, high baroque was a blend of light, colour and movement calculated to overwhelm the spectator by a direct emotional appeal. Paintings contained visual illusions, and sculpture exploited the effect of light on surface and contour. Buildings were heavily decorated with stucco ornament and free-standing sculpture. Baroque was closely linked to the COUNTER-REFORMATION and was therefore strongest in Roman Catholic countries. Baroque became increasingly florid before merging with the lighter style of ROCOCO. The term is often used to describe the period as well as the style. In music, the period is notable for several stylistic developments. Musical textures became increasingly contrapuntal, culminating in the masterpieces of J.S. BACH and HANDEL. Many purely instrumental forms of increasing virtuosity, such as the fugue, sonata, concerto, suite, toccata, passacaglia, and chaconne, emerged and became popular.

barracuda Marine fish found in tropical Atlantic and Pacific waters. Known to attack people, it has a large mouth with many large, razor-sharp teeth. It is long, slender and olive-green. Length: usually 1.2–1.8m (4–6ft); weight: 1.4–22.7kg (3–50lb). The great barracuda of the Florida coast grows to 2.5m (8ft). Family Sphyraenidae; there are 20 species.

Barrie, Sir James Matthew (1860–1937) Scottish dramatist and novelist. He is chiefly remembered as the writer of *Peter Pan* (1904), about a boy who refuses to grow up. Although criticized for sentimentality, his best works are clever, romantic fantasies. Other plays include *The Admirable Crichton* (1902) and *What Every Woman Knows* (1908).

barrier reef Long, narrow CORAL REEF lying some distance from, and roughly parallel to, the shore, and separated by a lagoon. Australia's GREAT BARRIER REEF is the most famous.

Barrow Village in Alaska; the northernmost US community. The US Navy operates a research station nearby. Whaling is the chief industry. Pop. (2000) 4581.

barrow In archaeology, a prehistoric burial mound. Various types of barrow are found, but in Europe they are usually either long or round. **Long** barrows were built in the NEOLITHIC period, and consisted of a long vault built of huge stones, roofed with stone slabs and covered with soil or chalk. Many long barrows were used for multiple burials. **Round** barrows primarily date to the early BRONZE AGE, but some in England were built as late as Roman and Saxon times. Usually containing a single body, round barrows vary in diameter from 1.5–50m (4.5–160ft) and are often surrounded by banks and ditches.

Barry, Sir Charles (1795–1860) English architect. He redesigned the HOUSES OF PARLIAMENT at Westminster, London, in a Gothic style after the original building burned down. He worked on the project with Augustus PUGIN, who was responsible for much of the exterior and interior decoration. Barry's preference for Italian Renaissance architecture shows in the classical ground plan for the parliament building.

Barrymore US family of actors. **Maurice** (1847–1905) made his stage debut in London in 1872. In 1875 he emigrated to the USA, where he married the actress Georgiana Drew. They had three children. **Lionel** (1878–1954), a fine character actor, made many films, including *Dinner at Eight* (1933) and *A Free Soul* (1931), for which he won an Oscar for Best Actor. **Ethel** (1879–1959) was best known for her stage performances in *A Doll's House* (1905) and *The Corn is Green* (1942). She won an Oscar for Best Supporting Actress in *None but the Lonely Heart* (1944). **John** (1882–1942) was a matinee idol. His many films include *Beau Brummel* (1924), *Don Juan* (1926), and *Grand Hotel* (1932). **Drew** Barrymore (1975–) became a childhood star in *E.T. The Extra-Terrestrial* (1982). As an adult, her films include *The Wedding Singer* (1998).

Barth, John Simmons (1930–) US writer and founder of post-modern literary pastiche. His best known novels include *The End of the Road* (1958), *The Sot-Weed Factor* (1960), and *Giles Goat-Boy* (1966). In 1973 he won the US National Book Award for three novellas, collectively entitled *Chimera* (1972).

Barth, Karl (1886–1968) Swiss theologian. Barth was a leading thinker of 20th-century PROTESTANTISM, and tried to lead theology back to principles of the REFORMATION. He emphasized the revelation of God through Jesus Christ. His school has been called dialectical theology or theology of the word. In 1935 he was suspended from his position at the University of Bonn for his anti-Nazi stance, and he returned to Switzerland. His works include *Epistle to the Romans* (1919).

Barthes, Roland (1915–80) French academic, writer and cultural critic. A leading proponent of STRUCTURALISM and SEMIOTICS, his notion of the literary text as a "system of signs" was informed by Ferdinand de SAUSSURE. Perhaps his best-known contribution to literary theory was the notion of the

"death of the author", in which the meaning of a text is generated by the reader, rather than by reference to biographical detail. His diverse works include *Writing Degree Zero* (1953), *Mythologies* (1957), *S/Z* (1970) and *Camera Lucida* (1980).

Bartholdi, Frédéric Auguste (1834–1904) French sculptor His most famous piece is *Liberty Enlightening the World* (The Statue of Liberty) in New York harbour, dedicated in 1886.

Bartók, Béla (1881–1945) Hungarian composer and pianist. With Zoltán KODALY, Bartók amassed a definitive collection of Hungarian folk music. His orchestral works include *Music for Strings, Percussion and Celesta* (1936), two violin concertos (1908 and 1938) and the Concerto for Orchestra (1943). He wrote one opera, *Bluebeard's Castle* (1911). He also composed piano concertos and six five-string quartets. His style combines folk music idioms with dissonance and great rhythmic energy.

Bartolommeo, Fra (1457–1517) (Bartolommeo della Porta) Florentine draughtsman and Dominican friar. In parallel with RAPHAEL, he contributed to the development of a new type of Madonna with Saints, specific to the High RENAISSANCE, in which the Madonna acts as a central point for the whole composition. Bartolommeo's characteristic style is one of restraint combined with monumentality, exemplified by *The Mystical Marriage of St Catherine* (1511).

baryon Any elementary particle affected by the strong interaction of nuclear force. A baryon consists of three QUARKS. Baryons are subclasses of the HADRON group of subatomic particles. The only stable baryons are the PROTON and (provided it is inside a nucleus) the NEUTRON. Heavier baryons are hyperons. *See also* LEPTON; MESON

Baryshnikov, Mikhail (1948–) US ballet dancer, b. Russia. A leading member (1969–74) of the KIROV BALLET, his defection to the West received much publicity. He was with the American Ballet Theater as principal dancer (1974–78) and artistic director (1980–89). He starred in several films and set up the White Oak Dance Project.

basal metabolic rate (BMR) Amount of energy required to sustain basic life processes, including breathing and circulation. It is calculated by measuring oxygen consumption. Metabolic rate increases above BMR during physical activity or fever, or under the influence of some drugs. It falls below BMR during sleep, general ANAESTHESIA or starvation. BMR is highest in children and decreases with age. *See also* METABOLISM

basalt Hard, fine-grained, basic IGNEOUS ROCK, which may be intrusive or extrusive. Its colour can be dark green, brown, dark grey or black. It can have a glassy appearance. There are many types of basalt with different proportions of elements. It may be compact or vesicular (porous) because of gas bubbles contained in the lava while it was cooling. If the vesicles are subsequently filled with secondary minerals, such as quartz or calcite, it is called amygdaloidal basalt. Basalts are the main rocks of ocean floors, and form the world's major lava flows, such as the Deccan Trap, India.

base Chemical compound that accepts hydrogen ions (H+), sometimes described as a "proton acceptor". A base will neutralise an ACID to form a SALT and water. Most are oxides or hydroxides of metals; others, such as ammonia, are compounds that yield hydroxide IONS in water. Soluble bases are called ALKALIS. Strong bases fully dissociate into ions; weak bases partially dissociate in solution. *See also* NEUTRALIZATION

base In mathematics, the number of units in a number system that is equivalent to one unit in the next higher counting place. Thus 10 is the base of the decimal system: only the ten digits 0–9 can be used in the units, tens, hundreds, and so on. Each number system has a number of symbols equal to its base. In the BINARY SYSTEM (base 2) there are two symbols, 0 and 1.

baseball National summer sport of the USA and Canada, also popular in the Japan, Korea, Taiwan, Latin America, Australia, and Europe. A baseball field comprises an inner diamond 27m (90ft) on each side, and an outfield. The diamond has a central pitcher's mound with bases at three corners. The batter stands at the fourth, home plate. Each team has nine players: pitcher, catcher, four infielders, and three outfielders. One run is scored every time a batter runs around all three bases and reaches home plate. To get back to home base with a single strike is a **home run**. A game is divided

▲ **Baryshnikov** One of the world's leading ballet dancers, Baryshnikov is known for the brilliance of his technique and the strength of his character interpretations. As well as performing in all the standard ballets, Baryshnikov has starred in several films, including *The Turning Point* (1977), *White Nights* (1985), and *The Cabinet of Dr Ramirez* (1991).

INTERNET

barrier reef
► www.reef.crc.org.au/ discover

Bartók, Béla
► www.classical.net

▲ **bat** The large mouse-eared bat (*Myotis myotis*) is the biggest of all European bats. It has a wingspan of up to 38cm (15in) and migrates up to 200km (125mi) from its summer habitat in s Europe to the Middle East where it spends the winter months. Though it prefers open farmland and woodland, the large mouse-eared bat is sometimes known to live in cellars or the attics of houses. A nocturnal animal, it lives on insects, particularly moths.

into nine innings (during which each team bats once): a team's innings ends when a third batter or runner is out, either by missing three consecutive valid pitches (**strikes**), by a field catch, or by not making it to the next base before a fielder throws the ball to the player on that base. Games tied at the end of nine innings are played until there is a winner. Every autumn the top teams of the two major leagues (American and National), including Canadian teams, compete in a best-of-seven 'World Series'. The basic rules of baseball were compiled by Alexander J. Cartwright in 1845.

Basel (Bâle or Basle) City and river port on the River Rhine; capital of Basel-Stadt canton, NW Switzerland. Basel joined the Swiss Confederation in 1501. It is an economic, financial, and cultural centre. There is a cathedral, a 15th-century university, and a 16th-century town hall. It is the centre of the Swiss pharmaceutical industries. Other industries: publishing, silk, electrical engineering, metal goods. Pop. (2000) 166,009.

Basel, Council of Ecumenical council convoked at BASEL in 1431. It instituted church reforms and conciliated the HUSSITES in Bohemia. Conflict with Pope Eugene IV over conciliar authority led the pope to denounce the council in 1437. In 1439, the council declared Eugene deposed and chose an anti-pope, Amadeus of Savoy, as Pope Felix V. In 1449, Felix resigned and the council was dissolved.

Basie, Count (William) (1904–84) US jazz band leader, pianist and composer. In 1935 Basie formed his own band in Kansas City. It was centred around a rhythm section of himself, Freddie Green, Walter Page, and Jo Jones. The Count Basie Orchestra recordings (1937–39) are among the most powerful works of the swing era. In 1952 Basie formed a new orchestra, which made the explosive *The Atomic Mr. Basie* (1957).

basil Tropical plant of the MINT family, whose leaves are used for flavouring food. It has white or purple flowers. Family Lamiaceae/Labiatae; species *Ocimum basilicum*.

Basil I (*c*.813–86) Byzantine Emperor (r.867–86) and founder of the Macedonian dynasty. Emperor Michael III assisted Basil in his rise to power. After Michael designated him co-emperor, Basil had his former patron murdered and assumed sole power in Byzantium. Basil's most effective policies include: the conversion of the Bulgars to Orthodox Christianity, military campaigns against the Paulician religious sect in Asia Minor, and a revision of Roman legal codes.

Basil II (*c*.958–1025) Byzantine Emperor (976–1025), nicknamed '*Bulgaroctonus*' ('Bulgar-slayer'). One of Byzantium's ablest rulers, Basil reigned during the heyday of the empire. He is best known for his military victory over the Bulgarian Tsar Samuel in 1014, which brought the entire Balkan peninsula under Byzantine control. During Basil's reign, Byzantium's sphere of influence was extended by the conversion of Kievan Russia to Orthodox Christianity.

basilica Roman colonnaded hall used for public business; also an early Christian church based on this design. The main characteristics of a basilica church, established by the 4th century AD were: a rectangular plan with a longitudinal axis, a wooden roof and an E end, which was either rectangular or contained a semicircular apse. The body of the church usually had a central nave and two flanking aisles.

basilisk Semi-aquatic LIZARD found in trees near streams of tropical America. It has a compressed greenish body, whip-like tail, a crest along its back and an inflatable pouch on its head. It can run over water for short distances on its hindlegs, and eats plants and insects. Length: up to 61cm (2ft). Family Iguanidae; genus *Basiliscus*. The basilisk is also a legendary serpent with the body of a cockerel.

Basil the Great, Saint (329–79) Doctor of the Church and one of the four Fathers of the Greek Church. He founded a monastic community, and in 370 was ordained bishop of Caesarea, Cappadocia. Basil established the dominance of the NICENE CREED, and was a fierce opponent of ARIANISM. He is thought to have composed the *Liturgy of St Basil*, which is still used in the Eastern Orthodox Church. His feast day is January 2 in the West; January 1 in the East.

basketball Game that originated in the USA, and is now played worldwide. Devised in 1891 by Dr James Naismith, it has been an Olympic sport since 1936. It is played by two

teams of five (plus substitutes), usually indoors. The court is up to 27.8m (91ft) long and 15m (49ft) wide. At each end is a backboard on which a bottomless netting basket hangs from a hoop 3m (10ft) above the floor. The object is to put the ball down through the opposing team's basket, scoring points. In normal play, two points are scored when the ball is thrown from within a ZONE close to the basket, and three points from farther away; a free throw (for a foul) counts one point. Players may move with the ball when dribbling it one-handed. With growing commercialization and the worldwide transmission of National Basketball Association (NBA) games, basketball is one of the most popular spectator sports.

Basov, Nikolai Gennadievich (1922–2001) Soviet physicist who developed the MASER, which amplifies microwaves, and the LASER, which amplifies light. For these contributions, Basov and his co-worker Aleksandr PROKHOROV shared the 1964 Nobel Prize in physics with the US physicist Charles Townes (who had made similar discoveries independently).

Basque Country Region of the W Pyrenees in both Spain and France, consisting of the provinces of Alava, Guipúzcoa, and parts of Navarra and Vizcaya in Spain, and Basse-Navarre, Labourd and Soule in France. The main towns are BILBAO and San Sebastian. The region is populated by the BASQUES. It lost its autonomy in the late 18th and early 19th centuries and separatist movements were formed in response.

Basques Indigenous people of the W Pyrenees in N Spain and SW France, numbering *c*.3,900,000. Their language is not related to any other European tongue. Throughout history they have tenaciously maintained their cultural identity. The kingdom of NAVARRE, which existed for 350 years, was home to most of the Basques. After its dissolution in 1512, most Spanish Basques enjoyed a degree of political autonomy. This autonomy was revoked in 1873, and Basque unrest followed. Some local autonomy was restored in 1978–79, but Basque separatists (ETA) continued to agitate for an independent state. In 1998 ETA announced a ceasefire and opened negotiations with the Spanish government.

Basra (Al-Basrah) City and chief port on Shatt al-Arab channel, S Iraq; capital of Basra province. An ancient centre of Arabic learning, it was captured by the Turks in 1668. In the early 20th century, large oilfields were discovered nearby, resulting in Basra's revival as a commercial and industrial centre. It suffered serious damage during the Iran-Iraq War and Gulf Wars. Industries: oil refining, flour, wool. Pop. (2005) 1,187,000.

bass Any of several bony fishes, both freshwater and marine, and not all closely related. Together they make up a valuable commercial and game fish. They include the white, black, striped, rock and calico basses. The two main bass families are Serranidae and Centrarchidae.

bass Term denoting low or deep pitch. It is used of the lowest-pitched part of a composition, or the lowest-pitched member of a family of instruments. It applies to the deepest male singing voice. The bass line in a composition is the bottom note of a chord or the lowest line in polyphony.

basset Short-legged hunting hound, originally bred in France to flush out game. After the BLOODHOUND, it has the most highly developed sense of smell among dogs. Bassets have long bodies and long floppy ears. Standard size: 30–38cm (12–15in) at the shoulder; weight: 11.3–22.7kg (25–50lb).

Basseterre Capital and chief port of the federated state of ST KITTS-NEVIS, on the SW coast of St Kitts, Leeward Islands, E Caribbean. Founded in 1627, it is an important commercial centre. Industries: sugar-refining. Pop. (1994 est.) 12,220.

bassoon Bass WOODWIND instrument with a range of three octaves, corresponding to that of the CELLO. It has a double-reed mouthpiece and a conical bore, the tube bending back on itself to reduce the instrument's length. Bassoons are used in symphonic and chamber music. The double bassoon or contrabassoon is the lowest-pitched woodwind instrument, sounding an octave below the bassoon.

Bastille Fortress and prison in Paris, built in the late 14th century and destroyed during the FRENCH REVOLUTION. Political prisoners were incarcerated here, and it became a symbol of royal oppression. On July 14, 1789, now a national holiday in France, a revolutionary mob stormed it, captured the ammunition store and released its seven prisoners. The Bastille was pulled down soon afterwards.

bat Only MAMMAL that has true flight (although a few mammals can glide). Bats are nocturnal and found in all tropical and temperate regions. Most are brown, grey, or black. A bat's wing is formed by a sheet of skin stretched over a frame of greatly elongated bones. Bats are able to navigate in complete darkness by means of a kind of SONAR, which uses echoes of the bat's own supersonic squeaks to locate obstacles and prey. Many bats live largely on insects, some are carnivorous, some drink blood, some live on nectar and pollen, and one group – flying foxes – subsist on fruit. Most are small, although they range in wingspan from 25cm-147cm (10–58in). The 178 genera of bats make up the order Chiroptera.

Bates, H.E. (Herbert Ernest) (1905–74) English novelist, playwright, and short story writer. His novels include *Fair Stood the Wind for France* (1944), *The Jacaranda Tree* (1949), and a popular series featuring the Larkin family – including *The Darling Buds of May* (1958), *Oh! To Be in England* (1963), and *A Little of What You Fancy* (1970).

Bath Spa city on the River Avon, sw England. Bath has been designated a world heritage site. Its hot springs were discovered in the 1st century AD by the Romans, who named the city *Aquae Sulis* (waters of the sun). The bathing complex and temple are the finest Roman remains in Britain. Bath flourished as a centre of the cloth and wool industries. The 15th-century Roman bath museum is adjacent to the ornate, gothic Bath Abbey. In the 18th century (under the direction of Beau Nash), the city became a fashionable resort. John Wood transformed the city into a showcase for Georgian architecture: the Royal Crescent, Queen Square, and the Circus are among his notable achievements. The University of Bath was established in 1966. Industries: tourism, printing, bookbinding, engineering, clothing. Pop. (1991) 79,900.

batholith Huge mass of igneous rock at the Earth's surface that has an exposed surface of more than 100sq km (40sq mi). It may have originated as an intrusive igneous structure that was gradually eroded and became surface material. Most batholiths consist of granite rock types, and are associated with the mountain-building phases of PLATE TECTONICS.

batik Method of decorating textiles, practised for centuries in Indonesia and introduced into Europe by Dutch traders. Molten wax is applied to the parts of a fabric that are to remain undyed, before the fabric is dipped into cool vegetable dye. The fabric is then dipped in hot water to remove the wax from the undyed areas. The process may be repeated, using different coloured dyes to form intricate patterns.

Batista y Zaldívar, Fulgencio (1901–73) Cuban political leader. A sergeant in the army, he led a successful coup in 1933, and then ruled through a succession of puppet presidents. In 1940 he became president. In 1944 Batista retired and moved to Florida, but in 1952 a military coup returned him to power. In 1959 he was overthrown by Fidel CASTRO.

Baton Rouge Capital of Louisiana, USA, on the Mississippi River. Founded in 1719 by French colonists, it was ceded to Britain by France in 1763, and to the USA with the Louisiana Purchase (1803). It became the state capital in 1849. The city contains both Louisiana State University and Southern University, and is the site of a large petrochemical complex. Industries: natural gas, chemicals, plastics, wood products. Pop. (2000) 227,818.

battery Collection of voltaic cells that convert chemical energy into direct current (DC) electricity. The term is also commonly used for a single cell, particularly the dry, electrochemical CELL used in electronic equipment. Most primary cell batteries are not rechargeable; some types of primary cell – such as nickel-cadmium (Nicad) batteries – and all accumulators (storage batteries) can be recharged when a current passed through them in the reverse direction restores the original chemical state. A battery's capacity is normally measured in ampere-hours; one ampere-hour is equal to 3600 coulombs.

battleship Most powerful type of naval warship in use during the late 19th and early 20th centuries. The largest battleships, the *Musachi* and the *Yamato*, displaced more than 72,000 tonnes and were built by the Japanese. Both were sunk in World War 2. Battleships combined the thickest armour and the most powerful naval guns. Modern battleships also carry a variety of missile systems. *See also* AIRCRAFT CARRIER

baud Unit for measuring the speed at which a digital communications device carries information. One baud is equal to one BIT per second. The word was coined in the 1930s by the French engineer Jean M E Baudot. Although the term **baud rate** is still used, the data-transfer speed of modern equipment is more often described in kilobits or megabits per second. See also MODEM

Baudelaire, Charles Pierre (1821–67) French poet and critic. His collection of poems, *Les Fleurs du Mal* (1857), represents one of the highest achievements of 19th century French poetry. Baudelaire explores the poetic theory of correspondences (scent, sound, and colour), and the aesthetic creed of the inseparability of beauty and corruption. The poems were condemned by the censor, and six of them were subsequently suppressed. Baudelaire was much influenced by the Edgar Allan POE, whose poetry he translated and whose works figure prominently in his major pieces of criticism, *Curiosités Esthetiques* and *L'Art Romantique* (both 1869).

Bauhaus German school for architecture and the applied arts, which played an important role in developing links between design and industry. Founded by Walter GROPIUS in 1919, it aimed to combine great craftsmanship with an ideal of an all-embracing modern art. Though Bauhaus specialized in architecture and design, several progressive painters, including KANDINSKY and KLEE, taught there. The studios focused on designing products for manufacturing industry. Typical Bauhaus design was severe and impersonal. In 1928 Hannes Meyer succeeded Gropius as director. MIES VAN DER ROHE took Meyer's place in 1930 but in 1933, after it moved to Berlin, the Nazis closed the school. Many students and staff emigrated, taking Bauhaus style and ethos with them. MOHOLY-NAGY, a Hungarian designer who taught at the Bauhaus in the 1920s, founded the New Bauhaus in Chicago in 1937. This later became the Institute of Design. *See also* BREUER, MARCEL

bauxite Rock from which most ALUMINIUM is extracted. Bauxite is a mixture of several minerals, such as diaspore, gibbsite, boehmite and IRON. It is formed by prolonged weathering and leaching of rocks containing aluminium silicates.

Bavaria (Bayern) Largest state in Germany; the capital is MUNICH. Other major cities include NUREMBERG. Part of the Roman Empire until the 6th century, taken by CHARLEMAGNE in 788, it formed part of the Holy Roman Empire until the 10th century. Incorporated into Germany in 1871, it remained a kingdom until 1918, becoming a state of the German Federal Republic in 1946. Industries: glass, porcelain, brewing. Area: 70,553sq km (27,256sq mi). Pop. (2001) 12,329,714.

bay Tree or shrub of the LAUREL family, the leaves of some varieties are used as to flavour food. In the classical tradition, head wreaths of bay leaves were awarded as tokens to conquerors and bards. Family Lauraceae; species *Laurus nobilis*.

Bayeux Tapestry (*c.*1080) Strip of linen embroidered in wool, measuring 70m × 48cm (231ft × 19in), which depicts the life of HAROLD II of England and the NORMAN CONQUEST in more than 70 scenes. An unfounded tradition attributes its design to Matilda, wife of WILLIAM I (THE CONQUEROR), but it was probably commissioned by William's half-brother Odo,

INTERNET

Bauhaus
▶ www.bauhaus.de/english

▼ **Bayeux Tapestry** The tapestry (strictly an embroidery) depicts the history of the Norman Conquest of England. It begins with Harold's visit to France, and ends with his defeat by the forces of William the Conqueror. This section of the tapestry depicts Breton cavalry forces floundering in marshy ground having failed to break the English line of foot soldiers located on the top of a small hill. The English soldiers are always shown with large moustaches.

Bishop of Bayeux, to glorify William and legitimate his rule.. It is now in a museum in Bayeux, N France.

Bay of Pigs (April 17, 1961) Unsuccessful effort by Cuban exiles (aided by the USA) to overthrow Fidel CASTRO by invading Cuba near the Bay of Pigs. About 1500 Cubans, trained, equipped and transported by the US government, were involved. The invasion was badly planned and the Cuban army defeated the exiles within three days. US President John F. KENNEDY initially denied US involvement and was later subject to criticism for its failure. *See also* CUBAN MISSILE CRISIS

Bayreuth City in Bavaria, Germany, where an annual festival is held, staging exclusively the work of composer Richard WAGNER. The festivals are held in the *Festspielhaus*, built to Wagner's specifications for the performance of great German theatre. The first festival was held in 1876. Pop. (1997) 73,669.

BBC *See* BRITISH BROADCASTING CORPORATION (BBC)

BCG (**B**acille **C**almette **G**uérin) Vaccine against tuberculosis. It was discovered by the French bacteriologists Albert Calmette (1863–1933) and Camille **G**uérin (1872–1961).

beach Sloping zone of the shore, covered by sediment, sand, or pebbles, that extends from the low-water line to the limit of the highest storm waves. The sediment is derived from coastal erosion or river ALLUVIUM.

Beadle, George Wells (1903–89) US geneticist. During his study of MUTATIONS in bread mould (*Neurospora crassa*), Beadle and Edward Tatum found that GENES are responsible for the synthesis of ENZYMES, and that these enzymes control each step of all biochemical reactions occurring in an organism. For this discovery they shared, with J. Lederberg, the 1958 Nobel Prize in physiology or medicine.

beagle Hunting dog, used to chase and follow small game. Of ancient origin, the modern breed was developed in England in the mid-1800s. It has a long, slightly domed head with a square-cut muzzle, long, hanging ears and widely set, large, eyes. Average size: (two varieties) not exceeding 38cm (15in) at the shoulder; weight: 8–14kg (18–31lb).

Beagle, HMS British survey ship that carried Charles DARWIN as ship's naturalist. The *Beagle* left England in December 1831, and for five years explored parts of South America and the Pacific islands. Darwin's observations formed the basis for his theory of EVOLUTION by NATURAL SELECTION.

Beaker culture Distinctive Neolithic culture that spread throughout Europe in the late 3rd millennium BC. Beaker culture is characterized by single-grave burials in round BARROWS, and by a common type of decorated, beaker-shaped pot that accompanied the burial. It is likely that the diffusion of this culture represented a gradual spread of new ideas to existing groups, rather than the migration of large numbers of people.

bean Plant grown for its edible seeds and seed pods. The broad bean (*Vicia faba*) is native to N Africa. The string bean (*Phaseolus vulgaris*) is native to tropical South America, and is common in the USA; several varieties are cultivated. The runner (*P. coccineus*) has scarlet, rather than white or lilac flowers, and shorter, broader seeds. *See also* SOYA BEAN

bear Large, omnivorous mammal with a stocky body, thick coarse fur and a short tail. Bears are native to the Americas and Eurasia. The sun bear is the smallest species, the Kodiak brown bear the largest. Bears have poor sight and only fair hearing, but an excellent sense of smell. They kill prey with a blow from their powerful forepaws. In cold regions, most bears become dormant or hibernate in winter. Length: 1.3–3m (4–10ft); weight: 45–725kg (100–1600lb). Order Carnivora; family Ursidae; there are approximately nine species.

Beardsley, Aubrey (1872–98) English illustrator. His highly wrought, stylized, black-and-white drawings epitomize the English ART NOUVEAU style. Associated with the Decadent writers of the 1890s and the AESTHETIC MOVEMENT, Beardsley illustrated the first four volumes of the *Yellow Book* (1894–95) and Oscar Wilde's play *Salome*. His mainstream work, such as *Isolde* (1895), enabled him to produce more outrageous, erotic 'Japonesque' illustrations.

beatitudes Blessings spoken by Jesus at the opening of his SERMON ON THE MOUNT upon those worthy of admission to the Kingdom of God. (Luke 6, Matthew 5).

Beatles, The British rock group. Perhaps the most influential band in the history of 20th-century popular music. Formed in Liverpool in 1960, The Beatles initially consisted of John LENNON (1940–80), Paul McCARTNEY (1942–), George Harrison (1943–2001), and Pete Best (1941–). In 1962 Best was replaced by Ringo Starr (Richard Starkey, 1940–). The Beatles' early style was US-derivative rhythm and blues blended with Lennon and McCartney's song-writing talent and attractive harmonies. Between 1964 and 1970, they dominated pop music with 18 albums, including *Revolver* (1966) and *Sgt. Pepper's Lonely Hearts Club Band* (1967). After 1966 they never publicly performed live. The group made four feature films: *A Hard Day's Night* (1964), *Help!* (1965), *Magical Mystery Tour* (1968), and *Let It Be* (1970). They also supplied the soundtrack for the cartoon *Yellow Submarine* (1968). In 1970 the Beatles disbanded to pursue individual careers.

beat movement Term derived from John Clellon Holmes' novel *Go* (1952) and applied to a group of US writers in the 1950s who rejected middle-class values and commercialism. Seen as the first modern subculture, they also experimented with different states of perception through drugs and meditation and had a strong influence on the cultural transformations of the 1960s. The group included the poets Allen GINSBERG, Gregory Corso and Lawrence FERLINGHETTI, and the novelists Jack KEROUAC and William BURROUGHS.

Beaton, Sir Cecil Walter Hardy (1904–80) British photographer, costume and stage designer, and writer. He began his career as a fashion photographer in the 1920s, and took up stage design in the 1930s. His film and stage designs include *Gigi* (1951), *My Fair Lady* (stage, 1956; film, 1964), and *Coco* (1969). Beaton's books include *The Wandering Years* (1962).

Beaufort, Henry (1374–1447) English statesman and prelate, illegitimate son of John of Gaunt. As chancellor to Henry IV and Henry V, Beaufort considerably influenced English domestic and foreign policy. Guardian of Henry VI (1422), he controlled England in the 1430s.

Beaufort wind scale Range of numbers from 0–17 representing the force of winds, together with descriptions of the corresponding land or sea effects. Beaufort 0 means calm wind less than 1km/h (0.6mph), with smoke rising vertically. Beaufort 3 means light breeze, 12–19km/h (8–12mph), with leaves in constant motion. Beaufort 11 is a storm, 103–116km/h (64–72mph). Beaufort 12–17 is a hurricane, 117.5–219+km/h (73–136+mph), with devastation. The scale is named after its inventor, Admiral Sir Francis Beaufort (1774–1857).

Beauharnais, Josephine de *See* JOSÉPHINE

Beaumarchais, Pierre Augustin Caron de (1732–99) French dramatist. Beaumarchais' principal plays were the related court satires, *The Barber of Seville* (1775) and *The Marriage of Figaro*, which were transformed into operas by ROSSINI and MOZART respectively. He was also employed as a secret agent by the French to supply arms to the Americans during the American Revolution.

Beaumont, Sir Francis (1584–1616) English dramatist closely associated with John FLETCHER. Between 1607 and 1613 they produced at least ten plays, including *Philaster*, *The Maid's Tragedy* and *A King and No King*. Beaumont is usually credited with sole authorship of two plays, *The Woman Hater* (1607) and *The Knight of the Burning Pestle* (c.1607).

Beauregard, Pierre Gustave Toutant de (1818–93) Confederate general in the American CIVIL WAR. He served in the Mexican War and was superintendent of West Point when Civil War broke out in 1861. On April 13, 1861, he forced the Union surrender of Fort Sumter in the first action of the war.

Beauvoir, Simone de (1908–86) French novelist, essayist, and critic. Her novels *She Came to Stay* (1943) and *The Mandarins* (1954) are portraits of the existentialist intellectual circle of which she and her lifelong companion, Jean-Paul SARTRE, were members. Her best-known work is the feminist treatise *The Second Sex* (1949). Other significant works include *The Prime of Life* (1960), *A Very Easy Death* (1964), and *Old Age* (1970). *See also* EXISTENTIALISM

beaver Large RODENT with brown to black fur, webbed hind feet, and a broad tail; it lives in streams and lakes of Europe, North America and Asia. Beavers build 'lodges' of trees and branches above water level and dam streams and rivers with

INTERNET

Bayreuth
▶ www.bayreuther-
festspiele.de

Beagle, HMS
▶ www.aboutdarwin.com

stones, sticks and mud. Length: to 1.2m (4ft); weight: up to 32kg (70lb). Family Castoridae; species *Castor fiber*.

Beaverbrook, William Maxwell Aitken, 1st Baron (1879–1964) British newspaper proprietor and politician, b. Canada. He entered Parliament in 1910 and became a peer in 1917. He was chancellor of the Duchy of Lancaster (1918–22) and one of Winston CHURCHILL's war cabinet (1940–45). He bought a majority interest in the *Daily Express* (1916), and later founded the *Sunday Express* and the *Evening Standard*.

be-bop (bop) Form of JAZZ with subtle harmonies and shifting rhythms. It arose in the late 1940s as a development from the simpler SWING style. Complex and dynamic, involving the extensive use of improvisation, the movement was pioneered by musicians such as Charlie PARKER and Dizzy GILLESPIE.

Beckenbauer, Franz (1945–) German footballe, captain of the West German squad that won the 1974 World Cup. In 1990, as coach of the German national team, he became the only person to both captain and manage a World Cup-winning team.

Becker, Boris (1967–) German tennis player. Becker rose from obscurity to win the 1985 Wimbledon singles title. His booming serve and athleticism gained him two more Wimbledon titles (1986, 1989). He won the US Open (1989) and the Australian Open (1991, 1996). He retired in 1997.

Becket, Saint Thomas à (1118–70) English Church leader. He was appointed chancellor of England (1155), and became a friend of HENRY II. In 1162 Henry made him archbishop of Canterbury, hoping for his support in asserting royal control, but Becket devoted his loyalty to the Church. His defence of clerical privileges against the monarchy, which sought independence from civil law, led to fierce conflict. Becket spent six years in exile. Reconciliation was short-lived; Becket turned on those who had violated his rights during exile, including the king. Four of Henry's knights, misinterpreting the king's words and falsely assuming they would gain the his gratitude, killed Becket in Canterbury Cathedral. Henry did penance and Becket was acclaimed a martyr. He was canonized in 1173.

Beckett, Samuel (1906–89) Irish playwright and novelist. One of the most influential writers of the 20th-century, Beckett wrote in both French and English. He emigrated to Paris in the 1920s and became an assistant to James JOYCE. His first published work was a volume of verse *Whoroscope* (1930). His first novel was *Murphy* (1938). Beckett's reputation is based largely on three full-length plays – *Waiting for Godot* (1952), *Endgame* (1957), and *Happy Days* (1961) – which explore notions of suffering, paralysis and endurance. His work is often linked to the Theatre of the ABSURD with its repetitive, inventive language and obsession with futility and meaninglessness. His short plays include *Krapp's Last Tape* (1958), *Not I* (1973), and *Footfalls* (1975). Other novels include the French trilogy *Molloy* (1951), *Malone Dies* (1951), and *The Unnameable* (1953). He was awarded the 1969 Nobel Prize in literature.

Beckham, David (1975–) English midfield footballer who played for Manchester United in the 1990s, Real Madrid from 2003–7, and LA Galaxy. He was England captain 2000–2006 and is widely known through the use of his image in marketing.

Beckmann, Max (1884–1950) German expressionist painter. He was disturbed by his experiences as a medical orderly in World War 1, and changed his painting style to reflect this awareness of human brutality. His EXPRESSIONISM often took the form of allegory and he drew inspiration from German gothic art. In 1933, after being dismissed from teaching by the Nazis, he started work on *Departure*, the first of nine TRIPTYCHS that express the sense of dislocation he felt in the modern world. As a result of Nazi harassment, which included condemning his work as "degenerate", he moved to Amsterdam and then to the USA. He came to regard art as a matter of ethical necessity rather than aesthetics.

Becquerel, Antoine Henri (1852–1908) French physicist. He was professor of physics at the Paris Museum of Natural History, and later at the Ecole Polytechnique. In 1896 he discovered RADIOACTIVITY in uranium salts, for which he shared the 1903 Nobel Prize in physics with Pierre and Marie CURIE. The becquerel standard unit for measuring radioactivity, which has replaced the CURIE, was named after him. *See also* BETA PARTICLE

bed In geology, a layer of sedimentary rock, internally consistent and distinguishable from adjacent layers. Usually deposited in a broadly horizontal sheet, it underlies the surface material (regolith) except where regolith has been removed by EROSION.

bedbug Broad, flat, wingless insect found worldwide. It feeds by sucking blood from mammals, including human beings. Bedbugs usually gorge themselves at night and remain hidden during the day. Length: to 6mm (0.25in). Family Cimicidae; species *Cimex lectularius*.

Bede, Saint (673?-735) (Venerable Bede) An English monk and scholar and the most learned Briton of his day, Bede's works were profoundly influential across early medieval Europe. His most important work is the *Ecclesiastical History of the English People*, a vital source for early English history (54BC–AD 697). His combination of his own work with that of earlier chroniclers is made particularly valuable by his care in mentioning his sources, rare in Mediaeval scholarship. Bede's other works covered biblical commentary, science, music and chronology, and he also pioneered an early form of Anno Domini dates. He he spent his life in the Northumbrian monastery of Jarrow, and is buried in Durham cathedral.

Bedfordshire County in central s England; the county town is Bedford. The land is mostly flat with low chalk hills, the Chilterns, in the s. The region (drained by the River Ouse) is fertile, and agriculture includes the growing of cereal crops, cattle raising and market gardening. Industries: motor-vehicle manufacture, electrical equipment, precision instruments. Area: 1235sq km (477sq mi). Pop. (2001) 381,571.

Bedouin Nomadic, desert-dwelling ARAB peoples of the Middle East and followers of ISLAM. Traditionally they live in tents, moving with their herds across vast areas of arid land in search of grazing areas. Bedouin society is patrilineal. They are renowned for their hospitality, honesty and fierce independence. In the 20th century, many Bedouin have been forced to abandon their nomadic way of life, and now work in towns.

bee Insect distinguished from other members of the order Hymenoptera, such as ants and wasps, by the presence of specially adapted hairs, with which they collect POLLEN; all bees feed their young NECTAR and pollen. The body is usually quite hairy, and the hairs are multi-branched (plumose). Although the honeybee and BUMBLEBEE are social insects living in well-organized colonies, many other bees are solitary, and some species even live in the colonies of other bees. Found worldwide, except in polar regions, they are important pollinators of flowers. Entomologists recognize *c.*12,000 species, but only the honeybee provides the HONEY that we eat. It builds combs of six-sided cells with wax from glands on its abdomen. A honeybee colony may have up to 60,000 individuals, consisting mainly of infertile female workers, with a few male drones and one egg-laying queen.

INTERNET

Beckett, Samuel
▶ beckett.english.ucsb.edu

▼ **The Beatles** Their clean-cut image, and the songwriting talents of Paul McCartney and John Lennon, ensured that 'Beatlemania' was a transatlantic phenomenon. The Beatles dominated the pop charts in the 1960s. Their later albums such as *Sgt Pepper's Lonely Hearts Club Band* (1967) and the *White Album* (1968) were more experimental.

A

B

C

▲ **beech** Beech trees flourish on chalky high ground. The northern beech (A, *Fagus sylvatica*) reaches 40m (130ft) in height. The dark green and glossy leaves grow to 10cm (4in), and turn russet in autumn. The green, prickly fruit ripens to golden brown and bursts into four. The oriental beech (B, *F. orientalis*) is similar to *F. sylvatica*, but may have furrowed bark and is usually found in more sheltered areas. The Antarctic beech (C, *Nothofagus antarctica*) grows to 30m (100ft) and is found in the Andes, SE Australia, and New Zealand. Unlike its (deciduous) northern cousin, it is an evergreen.

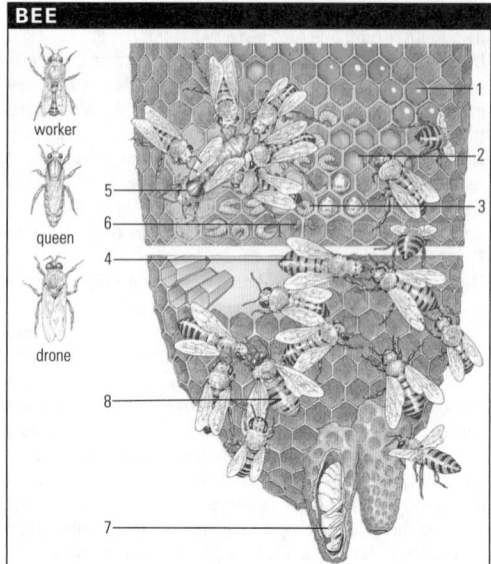

BEE

worker

queen

drone

The nest of the honeybee consists of a number of wax combs suspended in a shelter, such as a hollowed-out tree. The cells of the outer edges of the comb (1) contain nectar mixed with saliva, which the workers fan with their wings to evaporate excess water before the cell is capped with wax; this mixture eventually turns into honey. Other cells are used to contain reserves of pollen (2). Developing larvae (3) in open cells are kept clean by worker bees to prevent fungal infestations. They are fed by young workers with regurgitated food, and with honey and pollen from the storage cells. When a newly formed worker emerges from its cell it is fed regurgitated pollen and nectar from another worker (4). Its vacated cell is thoroughly cleaned and re-used. The queen (5), surrounded by a retinue of workers, rests on a group of capped cells, each of which contains a worker pupa. Eggs (6) are laid by the queen in the centre of the comb. When new queens are needed, the workers construct extra large cells at the edge of the comb (7) in order to accommodate them. Drones (8) do not perform 'housekeeping' duties and are driven away in times of food scarcity.

beech Deciduous tree native to the Northern Hemisphere. Beeches have wide-spreading branches, smooth grey bark and alternate, coarse-toothed leaves. Male flowers hang from thin stems; pairs of female flowers hang on hairy stems and develop into triangular, edible nuts enclosed by burs. The American beech (*Fagus grandifolia*) and the European beech (*F. sylvatica*) are important timber trees used for furniture and tool handles. Height: to 36m (117ft). Family Fagaceae; there are 10 species. All belong to the genus *Nothofagus*.

Beecham, Sir Thomas (1869–1961) English conductor, one of the greatest of his era. He founded (1906) the New Symphony Orchestra, the London Philharmonic (1932), and the Royal Philharmonic (1947). In 1933 Beecham became artistic director of Covent Garden Opera, introducing the operas of Richard Strauss to English audiences. He was widely respected as an interpreter of Delius and Sibelius.

Beecher, Henry Ward (1813–87) US Congregational minister, outstanding preacher and influential advocate of social reform, grandfather of Harriet Beecher STOWE. In 1847 Beecher became pastor of the Plymouth Congrega-tional Church, Brooklyn, New York. Famed for his opposi-tion to slavery, he supported women's voting rights and the scientific theory of evolution. He wrote several books of sermons, a life of Jesus Christ, and a novel *Norwood: A Tale of Village Life in New England* (1867).

bee-eater Tropical BIRD of the Eastern Hemisphere that catches flying bees and wasps. It has a long, curved beak, bright, colourful plumage, and a long tail. It nests in large colonies and builds a tunnel to its egg chamber. Length: 15–38cm (6–15in). Family Meropidae.

Beelzebub Name for Satan or the Devil. The word was originally *Beelzebul* ('Lord of demons') but was corrupted deliberately in Syrian texts and the (Latin) Vulgate to *Beelzebub* ('Lord of flies') as a gesture of contempt. Origi-nally an aspect of Baal, it was used in its present sense in the New Testament (Matthew 10, Mark 3 and Luke 11).

beer Alcoholic beverage produced by the soaking, boiling, and fermentation of a cereal extract (often malted barley) flavoured with a bitter substance (hops). Other ingredients are water, sugar, and yeast. The alcohol content of most beer ranges from *c*.2.5% to 12%. Among the major types of beer are: **ales**, which classically have fewer hops added; **stouts** and **porters**, which are darker and have a persistent head; **lagers** and **pilsners**, usually fizzy and matured over a longer period of time; **bitter**, which has additional hops; **mild**, which has few hops and is low in alcohol; and **brown ale**, similar to stout.

Beersheba (Be'er Sheva) Chief city of the Negev region, S Israel. It was the southernmost point of biblical PALES-TINE. It flourished under Byzantine rule, but declined until restored by the Ottoman Turks *c*.1900. Industries: chemi-cals, textiles, ceramics. Pop. (1997) 160,363.

beet Vegetable native to Europe and parts of Asia, and culti-vated in most cool regions. Its leaves are green or red and edi-ble, though it is generally grown for its thick red or golden root. Some varieties are eaten as a vegetable, others are a source of sugar, and some are used as fodder. Family Chenopodiaceae; species *Beta vulgaris*. See also SUGAR BEET

Beethoven, Ludwig van (1770–1827) German compos-er, a profound influence on the development of Western classical music. He provides a link between the formal CLASSICAL style of HAYDN and MOZART and the ROMANTI-CISM of WAGNER, BRAHMS and BRUCKNER. Born in Bonn, Beethoven visited Vienna in 1787, and was taught briefly by Mozart. He made Vienna his home from 1792, and took lessons from Haydn. Beethoven's early works, such as the piano sonatas *Pathétique* (1789) and *Moonlight* (1801), betray the influences of his teachers. The year 1801 marks the onset of Beethoven's deafness and a shift in style. His third SYMPHONY (Eroica, 1804) was a decisive break from the classical tradition, both in terms of its form and its dedi-cation to Napoleon I. This middle period also includes his fifth piano concerto (Emperor, 1809) and his only opera, *Fidelio* (1805). Beethoven's final period coincides with his complete loss of hearing (1817) and is marked by works of even greater length and complexity. These include the Ham-merklavier Sonata (1818) and his ninth symphony (*Ode to Joy*, 1817–23). Beethoven increased the dramatic scope of the symphony and expanded the size of the orchestra.

beetle Insect characterized by horny front wings that serve as protective covers for the membranous hind wings. These pro-tective sheaths are often brightly coloured. Beetles are usually stout-bodied and their mouthparts are adapted for biting and chewing. They are poor fliers, and (like all insects) are protect-ed from injury and drying up by an EXOSKELETON. Beetles are the most numerous of the insects. More than 250,000 species are known and new ones are still being discovered. They include SCARAB BEETLES, LADYBIRDS, and WEEVILS. Most feed on plants, some prey on small animals, including other insects, whereas others are scavengers. Beetles undergo complete METAMORPHOSIS. Their larvae (grubs) usually have three pairs of legs and distinct heads, usually dark in colour. Length: 0.5mm-6cm (0.02–6.3in). Order Coleoptera.

Begin, Menachem (1913–92) Israeli statesman, prime minister (1977–83), b. Belarus. A Zionist, Begin was sen-tenced to eight years' slave-labour but was released in 1941 to fight in the new Polish army. As commander of the para-military *Irgun Zeva'i Leumi*, he led resistance to British rule until Israeli independence in 1948. As leader of the Freedom Party (Herut), Begin clashed with David BEN-GURION and the animosity between the two men only eased in the SIX-DAY WAR (1967). In 1973 Begin became leader of the Likud Party. In 1977 Likud formed a coalition gov-ernment with Begin as prime minister. Although a fervent nationalist, he sought reconciliation with Egypt and signed the CAMP DAVID ACCORD with Anwar SADAT in 1979. In recognition of their efforts they shared the 1978 Nobel Peace Prize. Re-elected by a narrow margin in 1981, Begin maintained a hardline stance towards the West Bank and Gaza Strip. His popularity waned after Israel's 1982 invasion of Lebanon and he was succeeded by Yitzhak Shamir.

Behan, Brendan (1923–64) Irish writer, notorious for his riotous lifestyle. Behan became a member of the IRA at the age of 14 and served several years in reform school, as described in his autobiography *Borstal Boy* (1958). His first play, *The Quare Fellow*, was produced in 1954. Influenced by the work of BRECHT, his second play was *The Hostage* (1959).

behavioural ecology Study of the complex relationship between environment and animal behaviour. This involves drawing on natural history to study the adaptive features of an organism within its habitat. Human behaviour is similarly studied. *See also* ADAPTATION; ECOLOGY; ETHOLOGY

behaviourism School of psychology that seeks to explain all animal and human behaviour primarily in terms of observable and measurable responses to stimuli. Its method of research often involves laboratory experiments. PAVLOV's work on conditioned reflexes was a source for the early behaviourists such as J.B. WATSON. They rejected the evidence introspection gives of conscious feelings, motives and will. Later behaviourists, such as B.F. Skinner, explain learning and development by "operant conditioning". *See also* DEVELOPMENTAL PSYCHOLOGY

Behn, Aphra (1640–89) English playwright, poet, and novelist – the first English professional female writer. A proto-feminist, Behn attracted much contemporary scandal. She produced 15 risqué comic plays, making her one of the most prolific dramatists of the Reformation. The most well-known is *The Rover* (1677). She also wrote poetry under an assumed name, but is principally remembered for the first English philosophical novel, *Oroonoko* (1688), an anti-slavery love story.

Behring, Emil Adolph von (1854–1917) German bacteriologist and pioneer immunologist. In 1901 he received the first Nobel Prize in physiology or medicine for his work on serum therapy, developing immunization against DIPHTHERIA (1890) and TETANUS (1892) by injections of antitoxins. His discoveries led to the treatment of many childhood diseases.

Beijing (Peking) Capital of the People's Republic of CHINA, on a vast plain between the Pei and Hun rivers, NE China. A settlement since *c.*1000 BC Beijing served as China's capital from 1421 to 1911. After the establishment of the Chinese Republic (1911–12), Beijing remained the political centre of China. The seat of government was transferred to NANJING in 1928. Beijing ('northern capital') became known as Pei-p'ing ('northern peace'). Occupied by the Japanese in 1937, it was restored to China in 1945 and came under Communist control in 1949. Its name was restored as capital of the People's Republic. The city comprises two walled sections: the Inner (Tatar) City, which houses the Forbidden City (imperial palace complex), and the Outer (Chinese) city. Beijing is the political, cultural, educational, financial, and transport centre of China. Heavy industry expanded after the end of the Civil War, and products now include textiles, iron, and steel. Pop. (2005) 10,849,000. *See also* TIANANMEN SQUARE

Beirut (Bayrut) Capital and chief port of Lebanon, on the Mediterranean coast at the foot of the Lebanon Mountains. The city was taken by the Arabs in AD 635. In 1110 it was captured by Christian crusaders, and it remained part of the Latin Kingdom of Jerusalem until 1291. In 1516, under DRUSE control, Beirut became part of the Ottoman Empire. During the 19th century, it was the centre of MUHAMMAD ALI's revolt against the Ottoman Empire. In 1830 Beirut was captured by Egyptians, but in 1840 British and French forces restored Ottoman control. In 1920 it became capital of Lebanon under French mandate. With the creation of Israel, thousands of Arabs sought refuge in Beirut. During the 1950s and 1960s, Beirut was a popular tourist destination. In 1976, civil war broke out and Beirut rapidly fractured along religious lines. In 1982, Israel devastated West Beirut in the war against the PALESTINE LIBERATION ORGANIZATION (PLO). Three years later, Israel began a phased withdrawal. In 1987, Syrian troops entered Beirut as part of

an Arab peacekeeping force. In 1990, Syrian troops dismantled the 'Green Line' separating Muslim West from Christian East Beirut, and reopened the Beirut-Damascus highway. By 1991, all militias withdrew from the city and restoration work began. The infrastructure, economy, and culture of Beirut suffered terribly during the civil war and only small-scale industries remain. Pop. (2000) 2,070,000.

Béjart, Maurice Jean (1927–2007) French ballet dancer and choreographer. One of the most innovative modern choreographers. He experimented with avant-garde modern dance techniques and acrobatics, incorporating them into classical movements. He founded and became director of the Ballet of the 20th Century in Brussels in 1960.

Belarus Republic in NE Europe. *See* country feature, p. 144.

Belau (formerly Palau) Self-governing island group in the Caroline Islands of the W Pacific, consisting of about 200 islands, only eight of which are inhabited; the capital is Melekeok. A Spanish possession (1710–1898), Belau was then held by Germany until 1914, when Japan occupied it. At the end of World War 2 control passed to the USA, which administered Belau as part of the US Trust Territory of the Pacific Islands. Self-government was instituted in 1981 and full independence followed in 1994. Most of the population are Micronesian, engaged in subsistence agriculture. Commercial fishing and copra processing are important economic activities. Area: 460sq km (189sq mi). Pop. (2000) 12,000.

Belfast Capital of Northern Ireland, at the mouth of the River Legan on Belfast Lough. The city was founded in 1177, but did not develop until after the Industrial Revolution. Belfast is now the centre for the manufacture of Irish linen. Since the 19th century, religious and political differences between Protestants and Catholics have been a source of tension. In the late 1960s, these differences erupted into violence and civil unrest. Shipbuilding is a major industry and Belfast's harbour includes the Harland and Wolff yard, which has produced many of the world's largest liners. Other industries: aircraft, machinery, tobacco. Pop. (2001) 277,391.

Belgium Kingdom in NW Europe. *See* country feature, p.146

Belgrade (Beograd) Capital of SERBIA, at the confluence of the Sava and Danube rivers. Belgrade became capital of Serbia in the 12th century, but fell to the Ottoman Turks in 1521. Freed from Ottoman rule in 1867, it became capital of the newly created Yugoslavia in 1929. The city suffered much damage under German occupation in World War 2. In 1999 Belgrade was further damaged by Allied air strikes after Milosevic sent federal troops into Kosovo. In October 2000, more

◀ **Beethoven** A seminal figure in the development of Western classical music, Beethoven's work is often divided into three periods. His piano sonatas are most representative of the early period (1795–1801). His third symphony, *Eroica* (1804), was originally dedicated to Napoleon I. This middle period (1801–16) also includes his sixth (*Pastoral*) symphony. From 1817 Beethoven was completely deaf. This last period is marked by his ninth symphony (with a finale based on Schiller's "Ode to Joy") and a great mass *Missa Solemnis* (1823).

than 300,000 people marched through the streets of Belgrade, forcing Milosevic to step down as president. Industries: chemicals, metals, machine tools, textiles. Pop. (2005) 1,160,000.

Belize (formerly British Honduras) Republic in Central America, on the Caribbean Sea. *see* country feature, p. 146.

Bell, Alexander Graham (1847–1922) US scientist, inventor of the TELEPHONE, b. Scotland. He first worked with his father, inventor of a system for educating the deaf. The family moved to America in 1870, and Bell taught speech at Boston University (1873–77). His work on the transmission of sound by electricity led to the first demonstration of the telephone in 1876, and the founding of Bell Telephone Company in 1877.

belladonna *See* ATROPINE; NIGHTSHADE

Bellini, Giovanni (*c.*1430–1516) Italian painter, from a famous artistic family. Giovanni's father, **Jacopo** (*c.*1400–*c.*1470), was a pupil of GENTILE DA FABRIANO. His major surviving works are two sketchbooks – the source of many works by his son-in-law Andrea MANTEGNA and his two sons Giovanni and Gentile. **Gentile** (*c.*1429–1507) was famous for his narrative works (such as *The Miracle of the True Cross*) which became the prototype of the genre in Venice. **Giovanni** was the greatest painter of the family, and single-handedly transformed Venice into a great centre of the RENAISSANCE. The most important influences on his work were Mantegna and ANTONELLO DA MESSINA. In Bellini's early works, the treatment of nature was precise and realistic but it gradually became poetic and monumental. Despite an extraordinary series of allegorical and mythological paintings, he is chiefly remembered as a religious painter. His pictures emphasize light and colour as a means of expression. Many of the leading painters of Venice trained in his studio, including TITIAN, Palma Vecchio, Sebastiano del Piombo, and possibly GIORGIONE.

Bellini, Vincenzo (1801–35) Italian composer of operas. His most notable works were *Norma* and *La Sonnambula* (both in 1831), and *I Puritani* (1835). His characteristically flowing melodies require great vocal skill. These *bel canto* operas were widely popular during the 19th century.

BELARUS

The Republic of Belarus is a landlocked country in Eastern Europe, formerly part of the SOVIET UNION. The land is low-lying and mostly flat. In the S, much of the land is marshy. This area contains Europe's largest marsh and peat bog, the Pripet Marshes.

A hilly region extends from NE to SW and includes the highest point in Belarus, situated near the capital Minsk. This hill reaches a height of 342m [1,122ft] above sea level. Over 1,000 lakes, mostly small, dot the landscape. Forests cover large areas. Belarus and Poland jointly control a remnant of virgin forest, which contains a herd of rare wisent (European bison). This is the Belovezha Forest, which is known as the Bialowieza Forest in Poland.

CLIMATE

The climate of Belarus is affected by both the moderating influence of the Baltic Sea and continental conditions to the E. The winters are cold and the summers warm.

HISTORY

Slavic people settled in what is now Belarus about 1,500 years ago. In the 9th century, the area became part of the first E Slavic state, Kievan Rus, which became a major European power in the 10th and 11th centuries. MONGOL invaders captured the E part of Kievan Rus in 1240, while Germanic tribes threatened from the W. Belarus allied itself with Lithuania, which became a powerful state. In 1386, the Lithuanian Grand Duke married the queen of Poland and Lithuanian-Polish kings ruled both countries until 1569, when The Livonian War (1558–63) between Lithuania and Muscovy forced the union of Lithuania and Belarus with Poland. In the 18th century, Russia took most of E Poland, including all of modern Belarus, by the Partitions of Poland (1772, 1793, 1795). Yet the people of Belarus continued to maintain their individuality. In the NAPOLEONIC WARS, Belarus was razed by the retreating Russian army in 1812. Belarus was again devastated by conflict in WORLD WAR I.

Following the Russian Revolution of 1917, a Communist government replaced tsarist rule in Russia, and, in March 1918, Belarus unilaterally declared itself an independent, non-Communist republic. Later that year, Russian Communists invaded Belarus, renaming it Byelorussia, a name derived from the Russian Belaya Rus, or White Russia. They established a Communist government there in 1919, though in the Treaty of Riga (1921), W Byelorussia was handed to Poland. In 1922, the remaining part of the country became a founder republic of the Soviet Union. In 1939, Russia occupied what is now W Belarus, which had been part of Poland since 1921. Nazi troops occupied the area between 1941 and 1944, during which a quarter of the population died. Byelorussia became a founding member of the United Nations in 1945.

POLITICS

In 1990 the Byelorussian parliament declared that its laws took precedence over those of the Soviet Union. In 1991, many observers were surprised when the country's conservative and Communist-dominated parliament declared its independence and helped form the COMMONWEALTH OF INDEPENDENT STATES (CIS). In September 1991, the republic changed its name from the Russian form Byelorussia to Belarus, its Belarusian form.

Communists retained control in Belarus after independence. A new constitution introduced in 1994 led to presidential elections

AREA 207,600sq km [80,154sq mi]	
POPULATION 9,725,000	
CAPITAL (POPULATION) Minsk (1,709,000)	
GOVERNMENT Multiparty republic	
ETHNIC GROUPS Belarusian 81%, Russian 11%, Polish, Ukrainian, others	
LANGUAGES Belarusian, Russian (both official)	
RELIGIONS Eastern Orthodox 80%, others 20%	
CURRENCY Belarusian rouble = 100 kopecks	

that brought Alexander Lukashenko to power. Economic reform began, although the country remained pro-Russian. Lukashenko favoured a union with Russia and, in 1999, signed a union treaty committing the countries to setting up a confederal state. However, Russia insisted that a referendum would have to take place before any merger could occur.

In 2001, Lukashenko was re-elected as president amid accusations of electoral fraud. A referendum in 2004 showed overwhelming support for the removal of the two-term limit on his rule, while Western observers alleged further fraud, claiming that the vote was neither free nor fair. In 2005 Belarus was listed as Europe's last remaining outpost of tyranny by the US.

In 2006, Russian attempts to end gas subsidies escalated into a major dispute. Belarus briefly blocked Russian oil pipelines to the EU, and in 2007 Lukashenko rejected earlier plans for union with Russia.

ECONOMY

The World Bank classifies Belarus as an 'upper-middle-income' economy. Like other former republics of the Soviet Union, it faces many problems in turning from Communism to a free-market economy.

Under Communist rule many manufacturing industries were set up, making such things as chemicals, trucks and tractors, machine tools and textiles. Farming is important and major products include barley, eggs, flax, meat, potatoes and other vegetables, rye and sugar beet. Leading exports include machinery and transport equipment, chemicals and food products.

Belloc, (Joseph) Hilaire (Pierre-René) (1870–1953) British writer, b. France. Belloc became a British citizen in 1902, and was a Liberal MP (1906–10). A versatile writer, his work includes satirical novels (some illustrated by his long-term collaborator, G.K. CHESTERTON), biographies, historical works and travel writing. He is best-known for his light verse, especially the children's classic, *Cautionary Tales* (1907).

Bellow, Saul (1915–2005) US novelist, b. Canada. His novels, usually set in Chicago, are concerned with the conflict between private and public, and the sense of alienation in 20th-century urban life. His debut novel was *The Dangling Man* (1944). Bellow won National Book awards for *The Adventures of Augie March* (1953), *Herzog* (1964), and *Mr Sammler's Planet* (1970). He won a Pulitzer Prize for *Humboldt's Gift* (1975). Other works include the novella *Seize the Day* (1956), *The Dean's December* (1982) and *Something to Remember Me By* (1993). He was awarded the 1976 Nobel Prize in literature.

Bellows, George Wesley (1882–1925) US painter and printmaker. Bellows was taught by Robert HENRI and worked with the ASHCAN SCHOOL. He is best known for his paintings of boxing matches and street scenes such as the impressionistic *Stag at Sharkey's* (1907), which depicts an illegal boxing match. He helped to organize the ARMORY SHOW (1913).

Bell's palsy Paralysis of a facial nerve causing weakness of the muscles on one side of the face. The condition, which may be due to viral infection, usually disappears spontaneously, or may be treated with drugs or, rarely, surgery.

Belmopan Capital of Belize, on the River Belize. It replaced Belize City, 80km (50mi) upstream, as capital in 1970, the latter having been largely destroyed by a hurricane in 1961. The building of Belmopan began in 1966. Pop. (2005) 12,000.

Belo Horizonte City in E Brazil; capital of Minas Gerais state. Built in 1895–97, it was Brazil's first planned city. Today, it is a popular resort, and distribution and processing centre for a prosperous farming and mining region whose

BELGIUM

The Kingdom of Belgium is a densely populated country in W Europe. Behind the 63km [39mi] long coastline on the North Sea lie its coastal plains. Some low-lying areas, called polders, are protected from the sea by dykes (sea walls).

Central Belgium consists of low plateaux, and the only highland region is the ARDENNES in the SE. The Ardennes, reaching a height of 694m [2,277ft], consists largely of moorland, peat bogs and woodland. The country's chief rivers are the Schelde, which flows through Tournai, Gent (or Ghent) and Antwerp in the W, and the Sambre and the Meuse, which flow between the central plateau and the Ardennes.

CLIMATE
The moderating effects of the sea give much of Belgium a temperate climate, with mild winters and cool summers. Moist winds from the Atlantic Ocean bring significant amounts of rainfall throughout the year, especially in the Ardennes. During January and February, much snow falls in the Ardennes, where temperatures are more extreme. Brussels has mild winters and warm summers.

HISTORY
One of the Low Countries, Belgium has often been called the 'cockpit of Europe' due to its strategic position. In the Middle Ages, the area was split into small duchies such as BRABANT but, with the Netherlands and Luxembourg, it was united and made prosperous by the dukes

of BURGUNDY in the 14th and 15th centuries. From 1482 to 1794 Belgium was, at various times, ruled by Austria, Spain, France and the Netherlands. Occupied during the FRENCH REVOLUTIONARY WARS, it passed to France in 1797.

From 1815, following the NAPOLEONIC WARS, Belgium was subsumed into the Netherlands. Dutch discrimination led to rebellion, and in 1830 a National Congress proclaimed independence from the Dutch. The division between Belgium and the Netherlands rested on history rather than geography. Belgium was a mainly Roman Catholic country while the Netherlands was mainly Protestant. In 1831, Prince Leopold of Saxe-Coburg became Belgium's king LEOPOLD I. His successor, LEOPOLD II, encouraged industrialization and colonialism, notably in the Congo.

In August 1914, Germany invaded Belgium, prompting British entry into World War 1. Belgium stoutly resisted German occupation and it became a major battleground in the war. After the war, Belgium took over former German colonial possessions in Africa. In May 1940, Germany again invaded Belgium, which was occupied by the Nazis until September 1944.

Despite the damage inflicted during World War 2, the economy recovered quickly, first through collaboration with the Netherlands and Luxembourg – which formed a customs union called Benelux – and later as a founder member of what is now the European Union. In 1960, Belgium granted independence to its colony of the Belgian Congo (now the Democratic Republic of Congo) and in 1962 it lost control of Ruanda-Urundi (now Rwanda and Burundi).

POLITICS
Belgium has always been an uneasy marriage of two peoples: the majority Flemings, who speak a language closely related to Dutch, and the WALLOONS, who speak French. The dividing line between the two communities runs EW, just s of Brussels, although the capital is officially bilingual.

Since the inception of the country, the Flemings have caught up and overtaken the Walloons

AREA 30,528sq km [11,787sq mi]
POPULATION 10,392,000
CAPITAL (POPULATION) Brussels (964,000)
GOVERNMENT Federal constitutional monarchy
ETHNIC GROUPS Belgian 89% (Fleming 58%, Walloon 31%), others
LANGUAGES Dutch, French, German (all official)
RELIGIONS Roman Catholic 75%, others 25%
CURRENCY Euro = 100 cents

in numbers and cultural influence. In 1971, the constitution was revised and three economic regions were established: FLANDERS (Vlaanderen), Wallonia (Wallonie) and BRUSSELS. However, tensions remained. In 1993, Belgium adopted a federal system of government, with each of the three regions being granted its own regional assembly. Further changes in 2001 gave the regions greater powers.

In June 2007 elections the ruling coalition led by prime minister Guy Verhofstadt suffered major losses, but no clear winner emerged and no party was able to form a successful coalition. Political deadlock arose, and observers speculated that the country might divide. In March 2008 Yves Leterme of the Christian Democrats managed to form a broad coalition government and became prime minister.

ECONOMY
Belgium is a major trading nation, with a highly developed economy. Almost 75% of its trade is with other EU nations. With few natural resources it must import a large percentage of the raw materials required for industry. Its main products include chemicals, processed food and steel. The steelworks lie near to ports because they are powered by petroleum. In 2002, parliament voted to phase out the use of nuclear energy by 2025.

Agriculture employs less than 2% of the people, but Belgian farmers produce most of the country's food requirements. The chief crops are barley and wheat, but the most valuable activities are dairy farming and livestock rearing.

B

mineral deposits include iron ore, manganese and diamonds. Industries: steel, textiles, cement. Pop. (2005) 5,304,000.

Belsen Village in Lower Saxony, Germany, site of a CONCENTRATION CAMP established by the Nazis during World War 2. Originally it housed Jews for exchange for Germans interned overseas, but was later converted into a death camp. Between 30,000 and 50,000 people were murdered or died of starvation and disease before the camp was liberated in 1945.

Belshazzar In the Old Testament, the son of NEBUCHADNEZZAR and last king of BABYLON. The Book of DANIEL relates how Belshazzar organized a great feast during which a disembodied hand wrote upon the wall, "*Mene, mene tekel upharsin*". Daniel translated it as "Thou art weighed in the balance and found wanting." and said it signified Babylon's downfall. Modern archaeological investigations identified Belshazzar with Bel-shar-usur (d.539BC), the son of Nabonidus, King of Babylon (556–539BC).

beluga (white whale) Small, toothed Arctic WHALE that is milky white when mature. It preys on fish, squid, and crustaceans and is valued by Eskimos for its meat, hide and blubber. Length: *c*.4m (13ft). Species: *Delphinapterus leucas*. Beluga is also a type of sturgeon, whose roe is sold as CAVIAR.

Benares *See* VARANASI

Ben Bella, (Muhammad) Ahmed (1916–) Algerian statesman, prime minister (1962–63), president (1963–65). He was director (1952–56) of the *Front de Libération Nationale* (FLN). Imprisoned (1956–62) by the French, Ben Bella was released to become the first prime minister of an independent Algeria. He was deposed in a coup (1965) led by Houari Boumedienne. After 15 years in prison, he went into exile (1980–90) in France where he formed the Movement for Democracy in Algeria (MDA).

bends (decompression sickness) Syndrome, mostly seen in divers, featuring pain in the joints, dizziness, nausea, and paralysis. It is caused by the release of nitrogen into the tissues and blood. This occurs if there is a too rapid return to normal atmospheric pressure after a period of breathing high-pressure air (when the body absorbs more nitrogen). Treatment involves gradual decompression in a hyperbaric chamber.

Benedict (of Nursia), Saint (480–547) Roman Christian figure, founder of Western monasticism and of the BENEDICTINE order. Saint Benedict was of noble birth and educated in Rome. Shocked by the city's lawlessness, he retired to a cave above Subiaco, where he acquired a reputation for austerity and sanctity. A community grew up around him and he established 12 monasteries. His feast day is July 11.

Benedict XVI (1927–) Pope (2005–), b. Joseph Ratzinger in Bavaria, Germany. After a career in academic theology, he became Cardinal of Munich in 1977. From 1981 he was head of the Congregation for the Doctrine of the Faith (formerly the Inquisition). He is known for his conservative views.

Benedictines Monks and nuns of the monastic Order of Saint Benedict, who follow the Rule laid down by Saint BENEDICT (OF NURSIA) in the 6th century. The order played a leading role in bringing Christianity and civilization to Western Europe in the 7th century and in preserving the traditions of Christianity throughout the medieval period. During the REFORMATION most Benedictine monasteries and nunneries in Europe were suppressed. The order revived in France and Germany during the 17th century.

BELIZE

Belize is a small country in Central America, lying on the Caribbean Sea. It is a monarchy whose head of state is Britain's monarch. A governor-general represents the monarch, while an elected government, headed by a prime minister, actually rules the country day-to-day.

Behind the swampy coastal plain in the s, the land rises to the low Maya Mountains, which reach 1,120m [3,675ft] at Victoria Peak. N Belize is mostly low lying and swampy. The main river, the River Belize, flows across the centre of the country. Rainforest covers large areas. A barrier reef stretches 297km (185mi) along the coast, the longest of its kind in the Western Hemisphere.

CLIMATE

Belize has a humid tropical climate with high temperatures all year round. The average annual rainfall ranges from 1,300mm [52in] in the N to over 3,800mm [150in] in the S. Hurricanes sometimes occur. One in

AREA 8,867sq miles [22,966sq km]
POPULATION 294,000
CAPITAL (POPULATION) Belmopan (12,000)
GOVERNMENT Constitutional monarchy
ETHNIC GROUPS Mestizo 49%, Creole 25%, Mayan Indian 11%, Garifuna 6%, others 9%
LANGUAGES English (official), Spanish, Creole
RELIGIONS Roman Catholic 50%, Protestant 27%, others
CURRENCY Belizean dollar = 100 cents

2001 killed 22 people and left 12,000 homeless.

HISTORY

Between 300 BC and AD 1000 Belize was part of the MAYAN Empire, which was in decline long before Spanish explorers reached the coast in the 16th century. Spain claimed the area but did not settle. In 1638 the first European settlement was founded by shipwrecked soldiers. Over the next 150 years Britain gradually took control of Belize and established sugar plantations using slave labour.

In 1862 Belize became the colony of British Honduras. Renamed Belize in 1973 it gained full independence in 1981. Guatemala, which had claimed the area since the early 19th century, opposed Belize's independence and British troops remained to prevent a possible invasion.

POLITICS

In 1983, Guatemala reduced its claim to the southern half of Belize. Improved relations in the early 1990s led Guatemala to recognize Belize's independence and in 1992, Britain agreed to withdraw its troops from the country. Mayan land rights remain a contentious political issue.

High levels of unemployment are a major problem, as is a growing involvement in the South American drug trade, which has brought with it increasing levels of violent crime.

ECONOMY

The World Bank classifies Belize as a 'lower-middle-income' developing country. Tourism has become the mainstay of the economy and in recent years cruise ships have called here,

bringing extra income. Fishing has become only the second biggest earner. Agriculture is still important, and cane sugar is the chief commercial crop and export. Other crops include bananas, beans, citrus fruits, maize and rice. Forestry is of longstanding importance, and the timber trade is even featured on the nation's coat of arms.

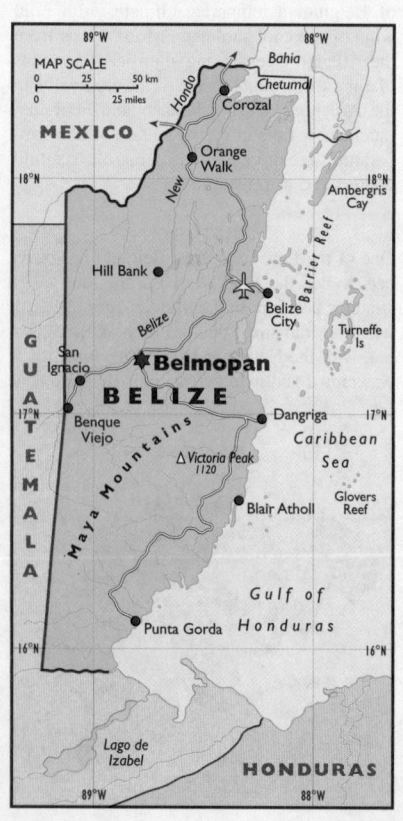

Benedictine monks and nuns returned to England in the late 19th century and the Benedictine Order spread to North and South America. *See also* MONASTICISM

Beneš, Eduard (1884–1948) Czech statesman, president (1935–38). A follower of Tomás MASARYK, Beneš promoted Czech independence while abroad during World War 1, and became Czechoslovakia's first foreign minister (1918–35). He resigned (1938) from the presidency in protest against the MUNICH AGREEMENT. Re-elected in 1946, he resigned again in 1948 after the communist takeover.

Bengal Former province of India. It is now a region of the Indian subcontinent that includes WEST BENGAL in India and East Bengal (now part of BANGLADESH). Much of Bengal lies in the deltas of the Ganges and Brahmaputra rivers. Bengal was the richest region in the 16th-century Mogul Empire of AKBAR I (THE GREAT). Conquered by the British in 1757, it became the centre of British India, with KOLKATA as the capital. It was made an autonomous region in 1937 and the present boundaries were fixed in 1947. Area: 200,575sq km (77,442sq mi).

Bengal, Bay of North-east gulf of the Indian Ocean, bounded by India and Sri Lanka (W), India and Bangladesh (N), Burma (E), and the Indian Ocean (S). Many rivers empty into the Bay, including the GANGES, BRAHMAPUTRA, Krishna, and Mahanadi. The chief ports are MADRAS and KOLKATA.

Bengali Major language of the Indian subcontinent. It is spoken by virtually all of the *c.*129 million citizens of Bangladesh, and by 45 million in the Indian province of West Bengal. It belongs to the Indic branch of INDO-EUROPEAN LANGUAGES.

Benghazi (Banghazi) City on the NE shore of the Gulf of Sidra, Libya. Founded by the Greeks in the 6th century BC Benghazi was captured by the Italians in 1911. Libya's second largest city, Benghazi is a commercial and industrial centre for Cyrenaica province. Industries: salt processing, shipping, oil refining. Pop. (2000) 829,000.

Ben-Gurion, David (1886–1973) Israeli statesman, prime minister (1948–53, 1955–63), b. Poland as David Grün. He settled in Palestine in 1906. In 1930 he became leader of the Mapai (Labour) Party, a socialist arm of the Zionist movement. After World War 2, he headed the campaign for an independent Jewish state and supported the use of violence to remove the British from Palestine. In 1948 he became Israel's first prime minister.

Benin Republic in W Africa. *See* country feature, page 149

Benin Kingdom that flourished in W Nigeria between the 14th and 17th centuries. Benin's bronze sculptures and wood and ivory carvings, are among the finest art produced in Africa. Ruled autocratically by a divine sovereign, Benin was prosperous and peaceful until the advent of firearms and the slave trade, when central authority disintegrated.

Benn, Tony (Anthony Neil Wedgwood) (1925–) British politician. Elected to Parliament in 1950, in 1963 Benn disclaimed an inherited peerage in order to remain a member of the House of Commons. He served as minister of technology (1966–70), secretary for industry (1974–75), and secretary for energy (1975–79). A committed pacifist, he was a leading spokesman on the left wing of the Labour Party.

Bennett, Alan (1934–) English playwright, actor, and director. Bennett's gentle, satiric observations of British eccentricities began in *Beyond the Fringe* (1960). His first play was *Forty Years On* (1968). Other plays include *Kafka's Dick* (1986). His series of monologues *Talking Heads* (1987) and an autobiography *Writing Home* (1994) were highly successful. He also wrote the screenplay for *The Madness of King George* (1995).

Bennett, (Enoch) Arnold (1867–1931) English writer who made a significant contribution to realism. He is best known for his novels of the "Five Towns", which portray provincial life in the industrial Midlands, England. They include *Anna of the Five Towns* (1902), *The Old Wives' Tale* (1908), and a trilogy – *Clayhanger* (1910), *Hilda Lessways* (1911), and *These Twain* (1916). He also wrote plays and short stories.

Ben Nevis Highest peak in the British Isles, Highlands region, W central Scotland. Ben Nevis is in the central Grampian Mountain range (overlooking Glen Nevis), near Fort William. It rises to 1343m (4406ft).

Bentham, Jeremy (1748–1832) English philosopher, jurist, and social reformer. Bentham developed the theory of UTILI-

TARIANISM based on the premise that "the greatest happiness of the greatest number" should be the object of individual and government action. This philosophy was defined in his *Introduction to the Principles of Morals and Legislation* (1789). His theories influenced much of England's early reform legislation.

Bentley, John Francis (1839–1902) English architect. His most famous design is the Byzantine-style, Roman Catholic Westminster Cathedral, London (1895–1903).

Benton, Thomas Hart (1889–1975) US realist painter. Benton painted rural and small-town life in the USA. His work includes the murals in the New School for Social Research, New York City (1930–31), and *The Arts of Life in America* (1932, now in the Museum of American Art, New Britain, Connecticut). Jackson POLLOCK was his most famous pupil.

Benz, Karl (1844–1929) German pioneer of the INTERNAL COMBUSTION ENGINE. After some success with an earlier TWO-STROKE ENGINE, he built a FOUR-STROKE ENGINE in 1885. Benz achieved great success when he installed the engine in a four-wheel vehicle in 1893. Benz was the first to make and sell light, self-propelled vehicles built to a standardized pattern.

benzene Colourless, volatile, sweet-smelling, flammable liquid HYDROCARBON (C_6H_6), a product of petroleum refining. A benzene molecule is a hexagonal ring of six unsaturated carbon atoms (benzene ring). It is a raw material for manufacturing many organic chemicals and plastics, drugs and dyes. Properties: r.d. 0.88; m.p. 5.5°C (41.9°F); b.p. 80.1°C (176.2°F). Benzene is carcinogenic and should be handled with caution.

benzodiazepine Any of a group of mood-altering drugs, such as librium and valium, that are used primarily to treat severe anxiety or insomnia. They intervene in the transmission of nerve signals in the CENTRAL NERVOUS SYSTEM and were originally developed as muscle relaxants. Today, they are the most widely prescribed tranquillizers.

benzoin Fragrant, resinous polymer, once obtained from the balsam resin found in the trees of the genus *Styrax* in tropical SE Asia, now made synthetically. It is used in perfumes and decongestant cough linctus.

Ben-zvi, Itzhak (1884–1963) Israeli statesman, president (1952–63). After fleeing his native Russia, he settled in PALESTINE in 1907. Exiled (1915–18), he worked with David BEN-GURION and other Zionist leaders to create the institutions basic to the formation of the state of Israel, including Histadrut, the leading labour organization, and the Mapai (Labour) Party.

Beowulf Oldest English epic poem, dating from around the 8th century, and the most important surviving example of Anglo-Saxon verse. It tells how a young prince, Beowulf, slays the monster Grendel and his vengeful mother. Some 50 years later, Beowulf (now King of the Geats) fights and slays a fire-breathing dragon but dies from his wounds. The text, which exists in a single 10th century manuscript, was transcribed by more than one hand, and the many explicitly Christian interpretations were probably added by monks.

berberis (barberry) Genus of *c.*450 species of shrubs native to temperate regions. The bark and wood are yellow, the stems are usually spiny, and the golden flowers give way to sour blue berries. The stamens are sensitive to touch. It is a host for the plant disease rust. Family Berberidaceae.

Berbers Caucasian Muslim people of N Africa and the Sahara Desert. Some are herdsmen and subsistence farmers; others, like the TUAREG, roam the desert with their animal herds. The farmers live in independent villages, governed

◀ **Ben-Gurion** Known as the 'Father of the Nation', Ben-Gurion was Israel's first prime minister, and played a key role in cementing the establishment of a Jewish state. He sanctioned the use of force to remove the British from Palestine and took a hardline stance against the new state's Arab neighbours.

INTERNET

Benin
▸ www.afrika.no/index/ Countries/Benin/index.html
▸ www.benintourism.com

Beowulf
▸ etext.lib.virginia.edu/toc/ modeng/public/AnoBeow. html

▲ **Bergman** A three-time Oscar winner, Ingrid Bergman began an affair with Roberto Rossellini after making the film *Stromboli* (1949) together. The ensuing scandal almost wrecked her career, although she and Rossellini later married.

by tribesmen. Their remarkably stable culture dates back to before 2400 BC. Berber languages are spoken by more than 10 million people. *See also* ALMOHAD; ALMORAVID

Berg, Alban (1885–1935) Austrian composer. A student of Arnold SCHOENBERG, he composed his later works in a complex, highly individualized style based on Schoenberg's TWELVE-TONE MUSIC technique. His *Wozzeck* (1925) is regarded as one of the masterpieces of 20th-century opera. He also composed a fine violin concerto (1935). Another opera, *Lulu*, unfinished at his death, was completed by Friedrich Cerha.

bergamot Herb of the genus *Monarda*, including horsemint and Oswego tea. Family Labiatae. Also refers to the pear-shaped fruit of *Citrus bergamia*, grown in Italy for its oil, which is used in perfumery. Family Rutaceae.

Bergen Atlantic port, capital of Hordaland county, SW Norway. Founded in the 11th century, Bergen was Norway's royal residence in the Middle Ages. It is now Norway's second largest city, with a university (1948), national theatre (1850), and 13th-century Viking hall. Industries: shipbuilding, textiles, fishing. Pop. (2000) 229,496.

Bergman, Ingmar (1918–2007) Swedish film director. With a versatile company of actors and a strong personal vision, Bergman created dark allegories, satires on sex, and complex studies of human relationships. Major films include *The Seventh Seal* (1956), *Wild Strawberries* (1957), *The Virgin Spring* (1960), *Persona* (1966), *Scenes from a Marriage* (1974), and *The Magic Flute* (1975). The intimate and poignant *Fanny and Alexander* (1983) is considered his finest achievement.

Bergman, Ingrid (1915–82) Swedish stage and film actress. Bergman's first major film was *Intermezzo* (1936). In 1939 she moved to Hollywood, starring in films such as *Casablanca* (1943). She won an Academy Award for best actress in *Gaslight* (1944). Other classics followed, such as *Spellbound* (1945) and *Notorious* (1946). She gained another best actress Oscar for *Anastasia* (1956). She won a third Oscar as best supporting Actress in *Murder on the Orient Express* (1974). She was married (1950–58) to director Roberto ROSSELLINI.

Bergson, Henri (1859–1941) French philosopher of evolution. He saw existence as a struggle between a person's life-force (*élan vital*) and the material world: people perceive the material world through the use of intellect, whereas the life-force is perceived through intuition. Bergson received the Nobel Prize in literature in 1927. His works include *Time and Free Will* (1889) and *Creative Evolution* (1907).

beriberi Disease caused by a deficiency of vitamin B$_1$ (thiamine), and other vitamins in the diet. Symptoms include weakness, oedema (waterlogging of the tissues) and degeneration of nerves. The disease is rare in the developed world.

Bering, Vitus Jonassen (1680–1741) Danish naval officer and explorer in Russian service who gave his name to the Bering Strait and Bering Sea. In 1728, he sailed from NE Siberia, to the Bering Strait to discover whether Asia and North America were joined. He turned back before he was certain, but set out again in 1741, this time reaching Alaska. Returning, he was shipwrecked and died on what is now Bering Island.

Bering Sea Northernmost reach of the Pacific Ocean, bounded by Siberia (NW), Alaska (NE), and separated from the Pacific by the ALEUTIAN ISLANDS; it is connected to the Arctic Ocean by the BERING STRAIT. It is icebound in the winter months. Vitus BERING's explorations in the early 18th century drew international attention to the seal-fur resource. Widespread disagreement over the protection of seals resulted in the BERING SEA CONTROVERSY (1886). Seal hunting regulations were imposed in 1893. Area: *c.*2.292 million sq km (885,000sq mi).

Bering Sea Controversy Dispute between various nations concerning control of the E Bering Sea and its lucrative seal-fur trade. After 1867 US hunters endangered the seal population of the region by overhunting. In 1881 US citizens demanded control of the entire region, seized British ships, and weakened Canadian commercial interests. In 1893, an international board of arbitration ruled in favour of the British. An agreement (1911) between Britain, Japan, Russia, and the USA limited hunting and made concessions to Canadian interests.

Bering Strait Strait at the N end of the Bering Sea separating W Alaska from E Siberia and connecting the BERING SEA

to the ARCTIC OCEAN. It was named after Vitus BERING, who sailed through it in 1728. Min. width: 85km (53mi).

Berio, Luciano (1925–2003) Italian composer. He was in the forefront of post-war avant-garde composers, and used electronic and chance effects in many of his works.

Berkeley, George (1685–1753) Irish philosopher and cleric. Drawing on the EMPIRICISM of John LOCKE, he argued that there is no existence independent of subjective perception (*esse est percipi*). For Berkeley, the apparently ordered physical world is the work of God. This view is often called subjective IDEALISM.

berkelium (symbol Bk) Radioactive metallic element, of the ACTINIDE SERIES. It does not occur in nature and was first made in 1949 by alpha-particle bombardment of americium-241 at the University of California at Berkeley (after which it is named) by a research team led by the US nuclear chemist Glenn Seaborg (1912–99). Nine isotopes are known. Properties: at.no. 97; r.d. (calculated) 14; m.p. 986°C (1807°F); most stable isotope Bk^{247} (half-life 1.410^3 yr).

Berkshire Former county in S central England, now split into six unitary authorities; the county town was READING. Berkshire lies almost entirely within the River Thames basin, which marks the N border. The Berkshire Downs run across the county. Area: 1255sq km (485sq mi). Pop. (1998) 788,422.

Berlin Capital and largest city of Germany, lying on the River Spree, NE Germany. Berlin was founded in the 13th century. It became the residence of the Hohenzollerns and the capital of Brandenburg, and later of Prussia. It rose to prominence as a manufacturing town and became the capital of the newly formed state of Germany in 1871. In the early 20th century, it was the second-largest city in Europe. Virtually destroyed at the end of World War 2, Berlin was divided into four sectors; British, French, US, and Soviet. On the formation of East Germany, the Soviet sector became East Berlin and the rest West Berlin. In 1961 East Germany erected the BERLIN WALL, which divided the city until 1989. On the reunification of Germany in 1990, East Berlin and West Berlin amalgamated. Sights include the Brandenburg Gate, the ruins of Kaiser Wilhelm Memorial Church, and the Victory Column in Tiergarten Park. Parts of the Berlin Wall remain as a monument. Berlin has two universities, important museums and art galleries, a famous opera house, and the Berlin Philharmonic Orchestra. Industries: chemicals, electronics. Pop. (2000) 3,387,000.

Berlin, Congress of (1878) Meeting of European powers to revise the Treaty of San Stefano (1878), which had increased Russian power in SE Europe to an extent unacceptable to other powers. The purpose of the Congress, under the presidency of BISMARCK, was to modify its terms. The main territorial adjustment was to reduce the Russian-sponsored Greater Bulgaria.

Berlin, Irving (1888–1989) US songwriter and composer. A prolific artist, he wrote nearly 1,000 songs. His most popular include "God Bless America" and "There's No Business Like Show Business".

Berlin, Sir Isaiah (1909–97) British philosopher and historian of ideas, b. Latvia. Berlin and A.J. AYER introduced logical positivism into British philosophy. He was a staunch defender of pluralism and liberalism.

Berlin Airlift (1948–49) Operation to supply BERLIN with food and other supplies after the Soviet Union closed all road and rail links between the city and West Germany. British and US aircraft flew more than 270,000 missions in 15 months.

Berlin Wall Heavily fortified and defended wall, more than 150km (100mi) long, that surrounded West BERLIN. About 45km (28mi) of it ran between East and West Berlin. It was built by East Germany in 1961 to prevent refugees fleeing to West Germany. A few thousand people succeeded in crossing the wall; 193 were killed in the attempt. It was dismantled in 1989 after the collapse of East Germany's communist regime

Berlioz, (Louis) Hector (1803–69) French composer, a leading figure in the French Romantic movement. He is noted for innovative orchestral writing, and the emphasis he laid on orchestral colour. His *Symphonie Fantastique* (1830) is an example of PROGRAMME MUSIC. Other works include *Harold in Italy* for viola and orchestra (1834), the operas *Benvenuto Cellini* (1838) and *The Trojans* (1855–58), and the *Requiem* (1837).

Berlusconi, Silvio (1936–) Italian prime minister (1994, 2001–6) and business tycoon. In the 1980s Berlusconi built a media empire, launching three television stations and acquiring Italy's largest publishing house. In 1994 he formed a political party, Forza Italia, and headed a coalition government. Berlusconi resigned amid charges of corruption and nationwide strikes. He regained power in 2001. In 2003, he appeared in court on corruption charges, but the trial was halted after Parliament granted him immunity from prosecution. In 2004, the Constitutional Court rejected the immunity law and the trial continued. In 2006 he lost a general election and was succeeded as prime minister by Romano PRODI. Berlusconi returned to power in 2008 elections after Prodi's government collapsed.

Bermuda (formerly Somers Island) British dependency, consisting of *c.*300 islands in the w Atlantic Ocean, 940km (580mi) E of North Carolina; the capital is Hamilton (Bermuda Island). Discovered in *c.*1503, the islands were claimed for Britain by Sir George Somers in the early 17th century. They became a crown colony in 1684, eventually achieving self-government in 1968. Tourism is important. Agricultural products include vegetables, bananas and citrus fruits. Area: 53sq km (21sq mi). Pop. (2000) 64,000.

Bern (Berne) Capital of Switzerland, on the River Aare in Bern region. Founded in 1191 as a military post, it became part of the Swiss Confederation in 1353. Bern was occupied by France during the French Revolutionary Wars (1798). It has a Gothic cathedral, a 15th-century town hall, and is the headquarters of the Swiss National Library. Industries: precision instruments, chemicals, textiles, chocolate, tourism. Pop. (2000) 122,484.

Bernard of Clairvaux, Saint (1090?-1153) French mystic and religious leader. He was abbot of the Cistercian monastery of Clairvaux from 1115 until his death. He was canonized in 1174. His feast day is August 20.

BENIN

The Republic of Benin, formerly called Dahomey, is one of Africa's smallest countries. It extends N to s for about 620km [390mi]. The coastline on the Bight of Benin, which is about 100km [62mi] long, is lined by lagoons. It lacks natural harbours and the harbour at COTONOU, the main port and commercial centre, is artificial.

Behind the coastal lagoons is a flat plain. Beyond this plain is a marshy depression, but the land rises to a low plateau in central Benin. The highest land is in the NW.

Savanna covers most of N Benin and is home to savanna animals such as buffaloes, elephants and lions. The N has two national

parks, the Penjari and the 'W', which Benin shares with Burkina Faso and Niger.

CLIMATE

Benin has a hot, wet climate. The average annual temperature on the coast is 25°C [77°F], while the average annual rainfall is 1,330mm [52in]. The forested inland plains are wetter than the coast, but the rainfall decreases to the N, which has rainy summer season and a very dry winter.

HISTORY

The ancient kingdom of Dahomey, a prominent w African kingdom that developed in the 15th century, had its capital at Abomey in what is now sw Benin. In the 17th century, the kings of Dahomey became involved in supplying slaves to European slave traders, and by 1700 more than 200,000 slaves were being annually transported from the 'Slave Coast'. The Portuguese shipped many Dahomeans to Brazil and, despite the British abolition of slavery, the trade persisted well into the 19th century. Traces of the culture and religion of the slaves still survive in parts of the Americas. For example, the voodoo cult in Haiti originated in Dahomey.

After slavery was ended in the 19th century, France began to gain influence in the area. Around 1851, France signed a treaty with the kingdom of Dahomey and, in the 1890s, the area, which also included some other small African states, became a French colony. From 1904, they ruled Dahomey as part of a huge region called French West Africa, which also included what are now Burkina Faso, Guinea, Ivory Coast, Mauritania, Mali, Niger and Senegal. The French developed the country's infrastructure and institutions. Dahomey became an overseas territory of France in 1946 and a self-governing nation in the French Community in 1958. Full independence was achieved in 1960.

POLITICS

Dahomey suffered from instability and unrest in the early years of independence. The first president, Hubert Maga, was removed in 1963 in a military coup led by General Christophe Soglo. A presidential council was set up in 1970 and Hubert Maga became one of three

AREA 112,622sq km [43,483sq mi]
POPULATION 8,078,000
CAPITAL (POPULATION) Porto-Novo (233,000)
GOVERNMENT Multiparty republic
ETHNIC GROUPS Fon, Adja, Bariba, Yoruba, Fulani
LANGUAGES French (official), Fon, Adja, Yoruba
RELIGIONS Traditional beliefs 50%, Christianity 30%, Islam 20%
CURRENCY CFA franc = 100 centimes

rotating presidents, but this regime was overthrown in 1973 by a coup led by Lt-Col Matthieu Kérékou. In 1975, Kérékou renamed the country Benin after the powerful historical state in sw Nigeria. Benin became a Marxist-Leninist People's Republic and, in 1977, it became a one-party state. This regime was maintained until 1989, when Kerekou declared that Benin would follow the lead of Eastern Europe in abandoning Communism. Marxism-Leninism was replaced by liberal economic policies.

In 1990, a new democratic constitution with a presidential system was introduced. Presidential elections were held in 1991 and Nicéphore Soglo, a former World Bank executive and prime minister, defeated Kérékou. In 1996 elections, Kérékou returned to power. He was re-elected in 2001, worked to restore Benin's fragile economy. In 2006 elections Kérékou was replaced by a political newcomer, Yayi Boni, with an anti-corruption stance. Many observers have praised Benin's transition from a Marxist-Leninist state into one of Africa's most stable democracies.

ECONOMY

Benin is a poor developing country. About half of the population depends on agriculture, but farming is largely at subsistence level. The main food crops include beans, cassava, millet, rice, sorghum and yams. The chief cash crops are cotton, palm oil and palm kernels. Forestry is also important.

Benin produces some oil, but manufacturing remains on a small scale. It depends heavily upon Nigeria for trade.

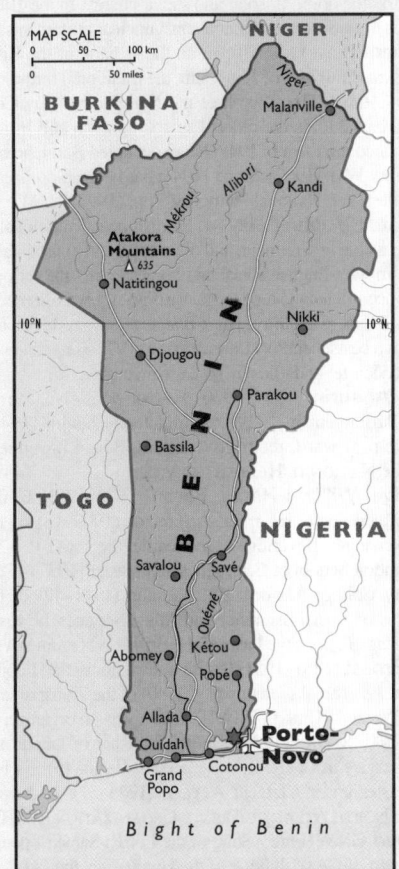

MAP SCALE
0   50   100 km
0   50 miles

NIGER
BURKINA FASO
Malanville
Niger
Kandi
Alibori
Mékrou
Atakora Mountains
△ 635
Natitingou
10°N   10°N
Nikki
Djougou
Parakou
Bassila
TOGO
NIGERIA
Savalou
Savé
Ouémé
Abomey
Kétou
Pobé
Allada
Ouidah
Grand Popo
Cotonou
Porto-Novo
Bight of Benin

B

Bernhardt, Sarah (1845–1923) French actress. The greatest tragedienne of her era, Bernhardt rose to prominence in the Comédie Française (1872–80). Her superb portrayals in *Phédre* (1874) and *Hernani* (1877) earned her the title 'Divine Sarah'. In 1899 she founded the Théatre Sarah Bernhardt in Paris, where she played the lead in *Hamlet* (1899) and *L'Aiglon* (1901).

Bernini, Gian Lorenzo (1598–1680) Italian architect and sculptor. The outstanding personality of the Italian BAROQUE, his work combines astonishing, flamboyant energy with great clarity of detail. His architecture was splendid in conception, lavish in use of marble and dramatic lighting, and often grand in scale. The favourite of several popes, his large-scale commissions in and around St Peter's include the *baldacchino* (canopy) above the high altar (1633), Barbarini Palace (1638), Cathedra Petri (1657–66), and (from 1656 onwards) the great elliptical piazza and enclosing colonnades in front of ST PETER'S.

Bernoulli, Daniel (1700–82) Swiss mathematician and physicist. His work on hydrodynamics demonstrated that pressure in a flowing FLUID decreases as the flow velocity increases. This fact, known as Bernoulli's principle, explains the LIFT of an aircraft. Bernoulli also formulated BERNOULLI'S LAW and made the first statement of the KINETIC THEORY of gases.

Bernoulli's law For a steadily flowing fluid, the sum of the pressure, kinetic energy, and potential energy per unit volume is constant at any point in the fluid. Using this relationship, formulated by Daniel BERNOULLI, it is possible to measure the velocity of a liquid by measuring its pressure at two points.

Bernstein, Leonard (1918–90) US conductor, composer and pianist. He was conductor with the New York Philharmonic (1957–58) and then musical director (1958–69), winning large audiences and world fame through his recordings. His compositions include three symphonies, the oratorio *Kaddish* (1963), the *Chichester Psalms* (1965) and *Mass* (1971), ballets, and the musicals *Candide* (1956) and *West Side Story* (1957).

Berryman, John (1914–72) US poet and critic. His major work, *The Dream Songs* (1969), combines *77 Dream Songs* (1964), winner of the 1965 Pulitzer prize, and *His Toy, His Dream, His Rest* (1968), winner of the 1969 National Book Award.

Bertolucci, Bernardo (1940–) Italian film director. His spectacular, poetic epics often dealt with the conflict between the personal and the political. Bertolucci began his career as assistant director to Pier PASOLINI. His full directorial debut was *The Grim Reaper* (1962). His most influential film was probably *The Conformist* (1969). *Last Tango in Paris* (1972) was his first commercial success. *The Last Emperor* (1987) gained Oscars for best director and best film.

beryl Mineral, beryllium silicate. Its crystals are usually hexagonal prisms of the hexagonal system. Gemstone varieties are aquamarine (pale blue-green) from Brazil; emerald (deep green) from Colombia; and morganite (pink) from Madagascar. Cut stones have little brilliance, but are valued for their intense colour. Hardness 8; r.d. 2.6–2.8.

beryllium (symbol Be) Silver-grey, metallic alkaline-earth element, first isolated in 1828 by Friedrich Wöhler and A.A.B. Bussy. It occurs in many minerals (mostly forms of BERYL) and is used in alloys that combine lightness with rigidity. Specific usages include in computer parts, gyroscopes, and nuclear reactors (to control the speed of neutrons). Properties: at.no. 4; r.a.m. 9.012; r.d. 1.85; m.p. 1285°C (2345°F); b.p. 2970°C (5378°F); most common isotope Be^9 (100%).

Berzelius, Jöns Jakob, Baron (1779–1848) Swedish chemist, one of the founders of modern chemistry. His accomplishments include the discovery of CERIUM, SELENIUM, and THORIUM; the isolation of the elements SILICON, ZIRCONIUM, and TITANIUM; the determination of relative atomic masses; and the devising of a modern system of chemical symbols. He prepared the first PERIODIC TABLE of relative atomic masses.

Bessel, Friedrich Wilhelm (1784–1846) German astronomer and mathematician. Bessel devised a system for analysing and reducing astronomical observations, made the first accepted measurements of the distance of a star (61 Cygni), and accurately predicted that SIRIUS and PROCYON are binary stars. He devised Bessel functions, a type of mathematical function, after observing perturbations of the planets.

Bessemer process First method for the mass production of STEEL. English engineer Sir Henry Bessemer (1813–98) patented the process in 1856. In a Bessemer converter, cast iron is converted into steel by blowing air through the molten iron to remove impurities. Precise amounts of carbon and metals are then added to give the desired properties to the steel.

Best, Charles Herbert (1899–1978) Canadian physiologist. In 1921 Best and F.G. BANTING discovered INSULIN. Best was head of the department of physiology at the University of Toronto (1929–65) and chief of the Banting-Best Department of Medical Research there after Banting's death.

beta-blocker Any of a class of DRUGS that block impulses to beta nerve receptors in various tissues throughout the body, including the heart, airways, and peripheral arteries. These drugs are mainly prescribed to regulate the heartbeat, reduce blood pressure, and relieve ANGINA.

Beta Israel Ethnic group of black Jews in Ethiopia, probably descended from early converts to JUDAISM. The Beta Israel are frequently known as Falashas, a term some consider derogatory. Their form of religion relies solely on observance of the OLD TESTAMENT. Israel acknowledged them as Jews in 1975 and many, suffering discrimination at home, migrated to Israel. By the 1980s, there were *c.*30,000 still in Ethiopia, but amid the war and famine of that decade thousands were airlifted to Israel.

beta particle Energetic electron emitted spontaneously by certain radioactive ISOTOPES. Beta decay results from the breakdown of a neutron to a proton, electron and anti-neutrino. *See also* RADIOACTIVITY

Betelgeuse (Alpha Orionis) Red supergiant star, the second-brightest in the constellation of Orion. It is a pulsating variable whose diameter fluctuates between 300 to 400 times that of the Sun. Characteristics: apparent mag. 0.85 (mean); absolute mag. 25.5 (mean); spectral type M2; distance 500 light years.

Bethe, Hans Albrecht (1906–2005) US physicist, b. Germany. Bethe left Germany when Hitler came to power and was professor of theoretical physics at Cornell University (1935–75). He worked on stellar energy and helped develop the atomic bomb. Bethe was awarded the 1967 Nobel Prize in physics for work on the origin of solar and stellar energy. In the 1980s and 1990s he was a campaigner against nuclear armaments.

Bethlehem (Bayt Lahm) Town on the w bank of the River Jordan, 8km (5mi) ssw of Jerusalem, the traditional birthplace of JESUS CHRIST. The Church of the Nativity, built by Constantine in AD 330, is the oldest Christian church still in use. Jordan gained the town in 1948. Israel occupied Bethlehem in the SIX-DAY WAR (1967). Since 1994 it has been administered by the Palestinian National Authority. Pop. (1997) 21,947.

Betjeman, Sir John (1906–84) English poet. Traditional in form, accessible in sentiment, and often apparently parochial in his concern with English social and domestic life, the seriousness and accomplishment of Betjeman's poetry has often been obscured by its popularity. His *Collected Poems* (1958; rev. 1962) was a bestseller. Poet Laureate from 1972, Betjeman was also a broadcaster and idiosyncratic architectural critic.

Bevan, Aneurin (1897–1960) British politician. Bevan entered Parliament in 1929. As minister of health (1945–51) in the post-war Labour government, Bevan introduced (1948) the NATIONAL HEALTH SERVICE.

Beveridge, William Henry, Baron (1879–1963) British academic and social reformer. A director (1909–16) of the labour exchanges, Beveridge later became director (1919–37) of the London School of Economics and master (1937–45) of University College, Oxford. As chairman (1941–42) of the Committee on Social Insurance and Allied Services, he wrote the *Beveridge Report*, the basis of the British WELFARE STATE.

Bevin, Ernest (1881–1951) British trade unionist and Labour politician. As general secretary (1922–40) of the Transport and General Workers' Union (TGWU), Bevin was an organizer of the GENERAL STRIKE (1926). He was minister of labour and national service in Churchill's war cabinet (1940–45). As foreign minister under Clement ATTLEE (1945–51), he helped create the NORTH ATLANTIC TREATY ORGANIZATION (NATO).

Bhagavad Gita (Hindi, 'Song of the Lord') Sanskrit poem, forming part of the sixth book of the Hindu epic, the MAHABHARATA. Probably written in the 1st or 2nd century AD it is

INTERNET

Bernini, Gian Lorenzo
▶ www.vatican.va/ phome_en.htm
▶ www.galleriaborghese.it

perhaps the greatest philosophical expression of HINDUISM. In the Bhagavad Gita, Lord KRISHNA (as an incarnation of VISHNU) instructs Prince Arjuna on the importance of absolute devotion (*bhakti*) to a personal god as a means of salvation.

Bharatiya Janata Party (BJP) Indian political party. In the "emergency" of 1975–77, most of the non-communist left-of-centre and right-wing parties formed the coalition Janata Party in opposition to Indira GANDHI's ruling CONGRESS PARTY. The alliance collapsed in 1979, and the BJP emerged as one of the principal remnants. Broadly right-wing, the BJP is in favour of the creation of a Hindu state, Hindustan. The BJP won the 1996, 1998, and 1999 parliamentary elections.

Bhopal State capital of MADHYA PRADESH, central India. Founded in 1728, it is noted for its terraced lakes, mosques and prehistoric paintings. In 1984 poisonous gas from the Union Carbide insecticide plant killed *c.*2500 people, the world's worst industrial disaster. Bhopal is an industrial and trade centre with food processing, electrical engineering, flour milling and cotton textile industries. Pop. (2005) 1,656,000.

Bhutan Kingdom in the E Himalayas. *see* country feature.

Bhutto, Benazir (1953–2007) Pakistani stateswoman, prime minister (1988–90, 1993–96), daughter of Zulfikar Ali BHUTTO. Benazir was long considered the leader of the Pakistan People's Party, but was subject to house arrest and forced into exile. Jubilation and violence marked her return in 1986. Two years later, Bhutto proclaimed a "people's revolution" and become the first woman prime minister of Pakistan. President Khan dismissed her on charges of corruption. Re-elected in 1993, further claims of corruption led to her second dismissal in 1996. She left Pakistan in 1998. In 2007 she returned to contest elections, but was assassinated in Rawalpindi while campaigning.

Bhutto, Zulfikar Ali (1928–79) Pakistani president (1971–73) and prime minister (1973–77), father of Benazir BHUTTO. In 1970 elections, Bhutto gained a majority in West Pakistan but the Awami League won in East Pakistan. Bhutto's refusal to grant autonomy to East Pakistan led to civil war in 1971, and defeat saw the formation of BANGLADESH. He was overthrown in a military coup led by General Zia, convicted of conspiracy to murder and executed.

Bible Sacred scriptures of Judaism and Christianity. Partly a history of the tribes of Israel, it is regarded as a source of divine revelation and of prescriptions and prohibitions for moral living. The Bible consists of two main sections. The OLD TESTAMENT, excluding the APOCRYPHA, is accepted as sacred by both Jews and Christians. The NEW TESTAMENT is accepted as sacred only by Christians.

bicycle Two-wheeled vehicle propelled by a rider. The earliest design (a hobbyhorse-type bicycle) dates from *c.*1790. In 1816 German engineer Karl Drais von Sauerbronn invented a steerable bicycle. Scottish blacksmith Kirkpatrick Macmillan is usually credited with the invention of the first pedal bicycle in 1839. In *c.*1861, French engineers Pierre and Ernest Michaux demonstrated their 'boneshaker' velocipede, with pedals attached to the front wheel. In 1871 James Starley produced his 'penny-farthing' bicycle. In 1873 J.H. Lawson invented the chain drive, which John Starley incorporated into his modern safety bicycle with tangential-spoked wheels in 1885. *See also* CYCLING

biennial Plant that completes its life cycle in two years, producing flowers and seed during the second year, such as an onion. This distinguishes it from an ANNUAL and a PERENNIAL.

Bierce, Ambrose Gwinett (1842–1914) US satirical writer and journalist. A one-time associate of Mark TWAIN, Bierce is best-known for *The Devil's Dictionary* (1906), a collection of epigrammatic definitions.

Big Bang In COSMOLOGY, theory advanced to explain the origin of the Universe, developed from the ideas of Georges LEMAÎTRE and advanced in the 1940s by George GAMOW. According to 'Big Bang' theory, a giant explosion 10 to 20 thousand million years ago began the expansion of the Universe, which still continues. Everything in the Universe once constituted an exceedingly hot and compressed gas with a temperature exceeding 10,000 million degrees. As it cooled, nuclear reactions took place that led to material emerging from the fireball consisting of about 75% hydrogen and 25% helium by mass, the composition of the Universe as we observe it today.

There were local fluctuations in the density or expansion rate. Slightly denser regions of gas, the expansion rates of which lagged behind the mean value, collapsed to form galaxies when the Universe was perhaps a tenth of its present age. *See also* OSCILLATING UNIVERSE THEORY; STEADY-STATE THEORY

Bihar State in NE India; the capital is Patna. Bihar was a centre of Indian civilization from the 6th century BC to the 7th century AD. It became a province in the Mogul Empire. A rich agricultural region, drained by the River Ganges, it produces more than 40% of India's total mineral output. In 2000 the state of Jharkand was carved out from part of Bihar. Industries: mica, coal, copper and iron ore. Area: 94,163sq km (36,356sq mi). Pop. (2001) 82,878,796.

Bikini Atoll Group of 36 small islands in the W central Pacific and part of the US-administered MARSHALL ISLANDS. The USA used the area to conduct atomic weapons tests (1946–56), resulting in heavy fallout. The islands were evacuated.

Biko, Steve (Stephen) (1946–77) South African political activist. In 1969 Biko founded the South African Students Organization. In 1972 he co-founded the Black People's Convention, a black consciousness movement. In 1973 the APARTHEID regime severely curtailed his freedoms of speech and association. Biko died in police custody at Port Elizabeth and became a symbol of the cruelty and injustice of apartheid.

Bilbao Seaport on the estuary of the River Nervión, near the Bay of Biscay; capital of the BASQUE COUNTRY province of Vizcaya, Spain. Founded in *c.*1300, it grew prosperous through the export of wool and later by trade with Spain's American colonies. Lying at the centre of an industrial region, it is now Spain's major port. Industries: iron and steel, fishing, shipbuilding, oil refining, chemicals. Pop. (2001) 349,972.

BICYCLE

New designs of mountain bikes reduced weight without sacrificing strength, and added suspension units to both front (1) and rear wheels (2) to allow greater speed over rough terrain. In the front forks, the suspension has twin pistons with elastomer cores (3) that allow travel and absorb vibration. Oil and air can also be used in the pistons. The rear suspension has a single, oil-filled piston (4) that damps the spring (5). Rear suspension units come in different forms (6). New frame materials include carbon fibre, titanium, and aluminium. A V-shaped frame (7) allows bike designers to incorporate the more exotic substances that are difficult to use in a traditional tubular frame. Some bikes have softer compounds of rubber for the back wheels to give greater grip on steep slopes.

bilberry (blueberry or whortleberry) Deciduous evergreen shrub native to N Europe and E North America, which produces a small, dark purple fruit. Family Ericaceae; genus Vaccinium.

bile Bitter yellow, brown or green alkaline fluid, secreted by the LIVER and stored in the GALL BLADDER. Important in digestion, it enters the duodenum via the bile duct. The bile salts it contains emulsify fats (allowing easier digestion and absorption) and neutralize stomach acids.

Bill of Rights (1689) British statute enshrining the constitutional principles won during the GLORIOUS REVOLUTION. It confirmed the abdication of JAMES II and bestowed the throne on WILLIAM III and MARY II. It excluded Roman Catholics from the succession and outlawed some of James' abuses of the royal prerogative, such as manipulation of the legal system and use of a standing army. In general, its provisions hastened the trend towards the supremacy of Parliament over the Crown.

Bill of Rights Name given to the first ten amendments to the CONSTITUTION OF THE UNITED STATES, ratified in 1791. Several states had agreed to ratify the Constitution (1787) only after George Washington promised to add such a list of liberties. The main rights confirmed were: freedom of worship, of speech, of the press, and of assembly; the right to bear arms;

freedom from unreasonable search and seizure; the right to a speedy trial by jury; and protection from self-incrimination.

binary star Two stars in orbit around a common centre of mass. **Visual** binaries can be seen as separate stars. In an **eclipsing** binary, one star periodically passes in front of the other, so that the total light output appears to fluctuate. Most eclipsing binaries are also spectroscopic binaries. A **spectroscopic** binary is a system too close for their separation to be measured visually and must be measured spectroscopically.

binary system In mathematics, number system having a BASE of 2 (the DECIMAL SYSTEM has a base of 10). It is particularly appropriate to computers since it is simple and corresponds to the open (0), and closed (1) states of switch, or logic gate, on which computers are based (*see* BIT).

binomial nomenclature (Linnaean system) System of categorizing organisms by a two-part Latin name. The first part of is the GENUS and the second part the SPECIES. For example, *Homo sapiens* categorizes humans. The system was developed by the LINNAEUS in the 18th century. *See also* TAXONOMY

binomial theorem Mathematical rule for expanding (as a series) an algebraic expression of the form $(x + y)^n$, where x and y are numerical quantities and N is a positive integer.

BHUTAN

The Kingdom of Bhutan is a small, landlocked country in the eastern Himalayas, between India and the Tibetan plateau of China. S Bhutan, along the border with India, is the lowest land region, ranging between about 50 and 900m [160 to 2,950ft] above sea level. N of the plains is a mountainous region between about 1,500 and 4,250m [4,920 to 13,940ft]. The northernmost region lies in the Great Himalayan range, reaching more than 7,300m [23,950ft]. Most people live in the fertile valleys of rivers, which flow generally from N to S.

CLIMATE
The altitude determines the climate. The S plains have a subtropical, rainy climate, with an average annual rainfall of around 5,000mm [197in]. Dense vegetation covers much of the region, with savanna in the far S. Central Bhutan has a moderate climate, though winters are cold.

HISTORY
Tibetan invaders settled in the area around 1,200 years ago. In the early 17th century, Bhutan unified under the leader of the Drukpa Kagyu ("Thunder Dragon") sect of TIBETAN BUDDHISM, who was both a spiritual and temporal ruler. Villages developed around the *dzong* (castle-monastery), and many Bhutanese

continue to live in monastic communities. The 19th century was plagued by civil wars in which rival governors battled for power. War with Britain (1865) resulted in the British annexation of S Bhutan In 1907, with British support, Bhutan became a hereditary monarchy; Ugyen Wangchuk, the powerful governor of Tongsa district, made himself Maharajah (now King) and set up the country's first effective central government. His successors have ruled the country ever since.

Britain took control of Bhutan's foreign affairs in 1910, but it did not interfere in internal affairs. This treaty was renewed with newly independent India in 1949. India also returned the parts of Bhutan that had been annexed by Britain and agreed to help Bhutan develop its economy and, later, its defence.

POLITICS
Bhutan's remote but strategic position cut it off from the outside world for centuries and it only began to open up to outsiders in the 1970s. Slow reforms began 1952, when Jigme Dorji Wangchuk succeeded to the throne and a national assembly was established to advise the king. Slavery was abolished in 1958 and, in 1959, Bhutan admitted several thousand refugees after China had annexed Tibet. The first cabinet was set up in 1968.

In 1972, King Jigme Dorji Wangchuk died and was succeeded by his son, Jigme Singye Wangchuk. The new king continued Bhutan's policy of slow modernization. The first foreign tourists were admitted in 1974, although tourism was restricted to people on prepackaged or guided tours. Independent travel was discouraged, as Bhutan sought to preserve its majority Buddhist culture. A television service was not introduced until 1999.

The king gave up some of the monarch's absolute powers in 1998, stepping down from his role as head of the government. Instead, he ruled in conjunction with the government, a National Assembly and a royal advisory council. In 2005 the government published a new draft constitution, which would make Bhutan a

AREA 47,000sq km [18,147sq mi]
POPULATION 2,328,000
CAPITAL (POPULATION) Thimphu (35,000)
GOVERNMENT Constitutional monarchy
ETHNIC GROUPS Bhutanese 50%, Nepalese 35%
LANGUAGES Dzongkha (official)
RELIGIONS Buddhism 75%, Hinduism 25%
CURRENCY Ngultrum = 100 cetrum

democracy with a parliament consisting of two elected houses.

Ethnic conflict has marred Bhutan's recent history. In 1986, a new law came into force declaring citizenship dependent on length of residence in Bhutan,which made many ethnic Nepalis illegal immigrants. Laws emphasizing Buddhist culture further antagonized the minority Nepalis, and violence in 1990 caused many to flee. In 2005 the king declared that the country would become a democracy in 2008. In 2006 he abdicated in favour of his son, Prince Namgyal. 2007 saw Bhutan's first ever elections, though both parties were pro-monarchy.

ECONOMY
Bhutan is a poor country. The rugged terrain makes the building of roads and other infrastructure difficult. Agriculture, mainly subsistence farming, cattle rearing and forestry, accounts for 93% of the workforce. Barley, rice and wheat are the chief food crops. Other products include citrus fruits, dairy products and maize. Industry is small scale, although some coal is mined in the south.

The country's economy is closely linked to that of India, with nearly 90% of Bhutan's total exports going to India. Bhutan has considerable hydroelectric power potential and electricity is exported to India. However, economic development is hampered by Bhutan's desire to maintain its traditional culture. The controls placed by the government on outside groups have inevitably restricted foreign investment.

For $n = 2$, its expansion is given by $(x + y)^2 = x^2 + 2xy + y^2$. The theorem was published in 1676 by Sir Isaac NEWTON.

biochemistry Science of the CHEMISTRY of life. It attempts to use the methods and concepts of organic and physical chemistry to investigate living matter and systems. Biochemists study the structure and properties of all the constituents of living matter (such as FATS, PROTEINS, ENZYMES, HORMONES, VITAMINS, DNA, CELLS, MEMBRANES, and ORGANS) together with the complex reactions and pathways of these in METABOLISM. Biochemistry is an essential part of medical and agricultural research.

biodegradable Property of a substance that enables it to be decomposed by microorganisms. The end result of decay is stable, simple compounds (such as water and carbon dioxide). This aids refuse disposal and reduces pollution.

bioengineering Application of engineering techniques to medical and biological problems such as devices to aid or replace defective or inadequate body organs, as in the production of artificial limbs, heart valves, hip joints, and hearing aids.

biography Literary form that describes the events of a person's life. The first known biographies were *Lives* by PLUTARCH in the 1st century AD. In English literature the first biographies appeared in the 17th century, notably *Lives* (1640–70) by Izaak Walton and *Lives of Eminent Men* (1813) by John Aubrey. The first 'modern' biography was the *Life of Samuel Johnson* (1791) by James BOSWELL. *See also* AUTOBIOGRAPHY

biological clock Internal system in organisms that relates behaviour to natural rhythms. Functions, such as growth, feeding, or reproduction, coincide with external events including day and night, tides, and seasons. These seem to be set by environmental conditions, but if organisms are isolated from these conditions they still function according to the usual rhythm.

biological warfare Use of disease microbes and their toxins in warfare. The extensive use of mustard gas during World War 1 prompted the prohibition of biological warfare by the GENEVA CONVENTION (1925). However, many nations have maintained costly research programmes for the production of harmful microorganisms. *See also* CHEMICAL WARFARE

biology Science of life and living organisms. Its branches include BOTANY (plants), ZOOLOGY (animals), ECOLOGY (habitats and species' interaction), PHYSIOLOGY (structure of living things), CYTOLOGY (cells), GENETICS (inheritance), TAXONOMY (classification), embryology (embryos), and MICROBIOLOGY (microorganisms). These sciences deal with the origin, history, structure, development, and function of living organisms, their relationships to each other and their environment, and the differences between living and non-living organisms.

bioluminescence Production of light, with very little heat, by some living organisms. Its biological function is varied: in some species, such as fireflies, it is a recognition signal in mating; in others, such as squids, it is a method of warding off predators; and in angler fish it is used to attract prey. The light-emitting substance (luciferin) in most species is an organic molecule that emits light when it is oxidized by molecular oxygen in the presence of an enzyme (luciferase).

biomass Total mass (excluding water content) of the plants and/or animals in a particular place. The term is often used to refer to the totality of living things on Earth; or those occupying a part of the Earth, such as the oceans. It may also refer to plant material that can be exploited, either as fuel or as raw material.

biome Extensive community of animals and plants whose make-up is determined by soil type and climate. There is generally distinctive, dominant vegetation, and characteristic climate and animal life in each biome. Ecologists divide the Earth (including the seas, lakes, and rivers) into ten biomes.

biophysics Study of biological phenomena in terms of the laws and techniques of physics. Techniques include X-ray diffraction and SPECTROSCOPY. Subjects studied include the structure and function of molecules, the conduction of electricity by nerves, the visual mechanism, the transport of molecules across cell membranes, muscle contraction (using electron microscopy) and energy transformations in living organisms.

biopsy Removal of a small piece of tissue from a patient for examination for evidence of disease. An example is the cervical biopsy ('smear test'), performed in order to screen for pre-cancerous changes that can lead to cervical cancer.

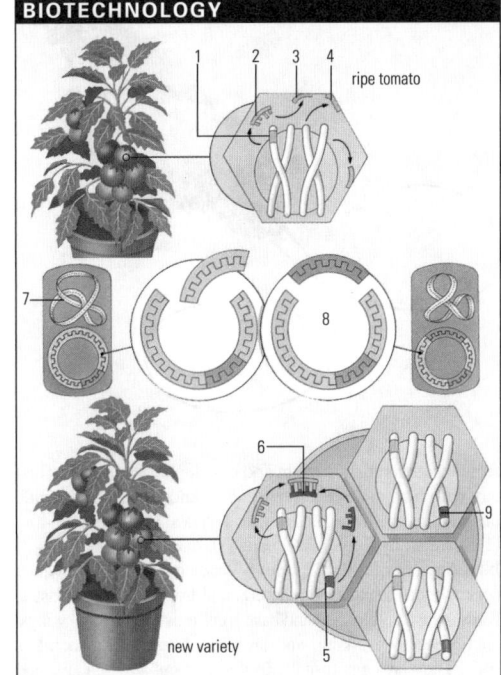

BIOTECHNOLOGY

In a ripe tomato, rotting is caused by an enzyme formed by the copying of a gene in the plant DNA (1) in a messenger molecule mRNA (2). The mRNA is changed into the enzyme (3), which damages the cell wall (4). In a genetically modified (GM) tomato, a mirror duplicate of the gene that starts the process is present (5). The result is that two mirror-image mRNA molecules are released (6) and they bind together, preventing the creation of the rotting enzyme.

The result is longer-lasting tomatoes. Introducing the necessary DNA through the rigid cell wall is accomplished by using a bacteria (7) that naturally copies its own DNA onto that of a plant. It is easy to introduce the mirror DNA (8) into the bacteria, and once the bacteria has infected the cell the DNA is transferred (9). All cells then replicated have the new DNA in their chromosomes and can be grown to create the new variety.

biosphere Portion of the Earth from its crust to the surrounding atmosphere that contains living organisms. It includes the oceans, a thin layer of the Earth's crust, and the lower reaches of the atmosphere.

biosynthesis Process in living cells by which complex chemical substances, such as PROTEIN, are made from simpler substances. A GENE 'orders' a molecule of RNA to be made, which carries the genetic instructions from the DNA. On the RIBOSOMES of the cell, the protein is built up from molecules of AMINO ACIDS, in the order determined by the genetic instructions carried by the RNA.

biotechnology Technologies making use of biological processes. Until the 1970s the term was mostly used in the food industry, where yeasts and bacterial cultures have long been used for brewing, baking, and cheesemaking. The late 20th and early 21st centuries saw a revolution in the field as GENETIC ENGINEERING techniques of cloning, splicing, and mixing genes allowed organisms to be adapted for medical, industrial, or manufacturing purposes. An early success in the area adapted microorganisms to produce the hormone INSULIN for treating diabetes. Later work allowed the production of many new drugs and chemicals and the alteration of plants to improve crop yields or produce medicines.

birch Any of *c.*40 species of trees and shrubs native to cooler areas of the Northern Hemisphere. The double-toothed leaves are oval or triangular with blunt bases and arranged alternately along branches. The smooth, resinous bark peels off in papery sheets. Male catkins droop, whereas smaller

▲ **birch** From the Betulaceae family, birches are found throughout the Northern Hemisphere. The paper birch (*Betula papyriferia*) is found in many regions of North America, and grows to a height of 39m (130ft). Native Americans used the tree to make birch-bark canoes.

B

▶ **bird of paradise** The magnificent bird of paradise (*Diphyllodes magnificus*) inhabits the tropical forests of New Guinea. Like other species of bird of paradise, the male performs elaborate courtship displays, involving ruffling the feathers on his breast and neck. Before he displays, he clears an area on the ground, using the branches of young saplings as perches. The name derives from 16th-century Spanish explorers, who believed the birds must be visitors from paradise. During the 19th century, the birds' skins were highly prized.

female catkins stand upright and develop into cone-like clusters with tiny, one-seeded nuts. Well-known species include the grey, silver, sweet, and yellow birches. Height: up to 40m (130ft). Family Betulaceae; genus *Betula*.

bird Any one of *c*.8600 species of feathered vertebrates, which occupy most habitats from deserts and tropics to polar wastes. Birds are warm-blooded and have forelimbs modified as wings, hind-limbs for walking, and jaws elongated into a toothless beak. They lay eggs (usually in nests), incubate the eggs, and care for young. As a group they feed on seeds, nectar, fruit and carrion, and hunt live prey ranging from insects to small mammals, although individual species may be very specialized in their diet. Size ranges from the bee HUMMINGBIRD, 6.4cm (2.5in) to the wandering ALBATROSS, whose wingspread reaches 3.5m (11.5ft). The 2.4m (8ft) tall OSTRICH is the largest of living birds, but several extinct flightless birds were even bigger. Of the 27 orders of birds, the perching birds (Passeriformes) include more species than all others combined. A bird's body is adapted primarily for flight, with all its parts modified accordingly. There are several species of large, flightless birds, including the OSTRICH, RHEA, EMU, CASSOWARY, KIWI, and PENGUIN. Birds are descended from Theocodonts (reptiles), and the first fossil bird, ARCHAEOPTERYX, dates from the late Jurassic period. Class Aves. *See* individual speciesbird flu *see* INFLUENZA.

bird of paradise Brightly coloured, ornately plumed, perching bird of New Guinea, Australia, and nearby regions. Most species have stocky bodies, rounded wings, and short legs. The males' plumes are raised during elaborate courtship rituals. Length: 12.5–100cm (5–40in). Family Paradisaeidae.

bird of prey Bird that usually has a sharp, hooked beak and talons with which it captures its prey. Two orders fit this description: the HAWKS, FALCONS, EAGLES, VULTURES, and SECRETARY BIRD (order Falconiformes); and the OWLS (order Strigiformes).

Birdseye, Clarence (1886–1956) US industrialist and inventor, who developed a technique for deep-freezing foods. He experimented on freezing food in 1917, and sold frozen fish in 1924. He was a founder of General Foods Corporation.

Birmingham Britain's second-largest city, in the West Midlands, England. A small town in the Middle Ages, during the Industrial Revolution it became one of Britain's chief manufacturing cities. James WATT designed and built his steam-engine here. Later it became known for the manufacture of cheap goods ('Brummagem ware'). The city possesses a symphony orchestra, and three universities. Industries: car manufacture, engineering, machine tools, metallurgy. Pop. (2000) 2,373,000.

Birmingham Largest city in Alabama, USA. Founded in 1871, Birmingham developed as a steel town. In 1963, Martin Luther King, Jr., led a large civil rights demonstration to protest racial segregation in the city. On September 15, 1963, four young black girls died when a bomb exploded at the 16th Street Baptist Church. Two members of the Ku Klux Klan were later convicted of the crime. Industries: iron and steel, metalworking, construction materials. Pop. (2000) 242,820.

Birmingham Six Six Irishmen convicted by an English court in 1974 of carrying out terrorist bombings in two public

houses in Birmingham, England. Their life sentences were quashed in 1991. The Court of Appeal ruled that methods used by the police in obtaining some written statements were inappropriate. The court also found that much of the circumstantial forensic evidence given by expert witnesses was unreliable. Five of the men were duly released; the sixth had died in prison. Their case became notorious as a modern miscarriage of British justice. *See also* GUILDFORD FOUR

birth, Caesarean (Caesarean section) Delivery of a baby by a surgical incision made through the abdomen and UTERUS of the mother. It is carried out for various medical reasons; nowadays the mother usually recovers quickly, without complications. The procedure is named from Latin *caedere* "to cut" and not, despite the myth, Julius CAESAR.

birth control Alternative term for CONTRACEPTION

Birtwistle, Harrison (1934–) English composer. Influenced by Igor STRAVINSKY and by medieval and Renaissance music, Birtwistle works include the instrumental motet *The World is Discovered* (1960), *Verses for Ensembles* (1970), and *The Triumph of Time* (1972). He also composed four operas including *Punch and Judy* (1967) and *The Second Mrs Kong* (1995).

Biscay, Bay of Inlet of the Atlantic Ocean, W of France and N of Spain. It is noted for its strong currents, sudden storms and sardine fishing grounds. The chief ports are BILBAO, San Sebastián and Santander in Spain, and LA ROCHELLE, Bayonne and Saint-Nazaire in France.

Bishkek (formerly Frunze) Capital of Kyrgyzstan, central Asia, on the River Chu. Founded in 1862 as Pishpek, it was the birthplace of a Soviet general, Mikhail Frunze, after whom it was renamed in 1926 when it became administrative centre of the Kirghiz Soviet Republic. Its name changed to Bishkek in 1991, when Kyrgyzstan declared independence. The city has a university (1951). Industries: textiles, food processing, agricultural machinery. Pop. (2005) 828,000.

bishop In Christian churches, the highest order in the ministry. Bishops are distinguished from priests chiefly by their powers to confer holy orders and to administer CONFIRMATION.

Bismarck State capital of North Dakota, USA, overlooking the Missouri River. It originated in the 1830s, becoming a distribution centre for grain and cattle and was later an important stop on the Northern Pacific Railroad. Industries: livestock raising, dairying, woodworking. Pop. (2000) 55,532.

Bismarck, Otto von (1815–98) German statesman, responsible for 19th-century German unification. He was born into a wealthy Prussian family and made an impression during the REVOLUTIONS OF 1848 as a diehard reactionary. In 1862 Wilhelm I named him chancellor of Prussia. Victory in the FRANCO-PRUSSIAN WAR (1870–71) brought the s German states into the Prussian-led North German Confederation, and in 1871 Bismarck became the first chancellor of the empire. In 1882 he formed the TRIPLE ALLIANCE with

▶ **bison** European settlers hunted the American bison (*Bison bison*) to near extinction in order to free the land for farming and deprive the Plains Native Americans of their herds. Strict conservation programmes subsequently ensured the survival of large numbers of this animal in protected areas.

Austro-Hungary and Italy. Bismarck encouraged industry and a programme of social welfare at home, and colonization overseas. He found it difficult to work with Wilhelm II, who forced the 'Iron Chancellor' to resign in 1890.

bismuth (symbol Bi) Metallic, silvery-white element of group V of the PERIODIC TABLE, first identified as a separate element in 1753. The chief ores are bismite (Bi_2O_3) and bismuthnite (Bi_2S_3). A poor heat conductor, it is put into low-melting alloys for automatic sprinkler systems. Bismuth is also used in insoluble compounds to treat gastric ulcers and skin injuries. It expands when it solidifies, a property exploited in several bismuth alloys for castings. Properties: at.no. 83; r.a.m. 208.98; r.d. 9.75; m.p. 271.3°C (520.3°F); b.p. 1560°C (2840°F); most common isotope Bi^{209} (100%).

bison Two species of wild oxen formerly ranging over the grasslands and open woodlands of most of North America and Europe. Once numbered in millions, the American bison (often incorrectly called a BUFFALO) is now almost extinct in the wild. The wisent (European bison) was reduced to two herds by the 18th century. Both species now survive in protected areas. The American species is not as massive or as shaggy as the European. Length: to 3.5m (138in); height: to 3m (118in); weight: to 1350kg (2976lb). Family Bovidae; species American *Bison bison*; wisent *Bison bonasus*.

Bissau Capital of Guinea-Bissau, near the mouth of the River Geba, w Africa. Established by the Portuguese as a slave-trading centre in 1687, Bissau became a free port in 1869. It replaced Bonama as capital in 1941. The port has recently been improved. Industries: oil processing. Pop. (2002 est.) 288,300.

bit Abbreviation for binary digit, a 1 or 0 used in the BINARY SYSTEM. In computing, a bit is the smallest element of storage. Groups of bits form a BYTE of binary code representing letters and other characters. Binary code is used in computing because it is easy to represent each 1 or 0 by the presence or absence of an electrical voltage. The code is also easy to store on disk as a magnetic or optical pattern.

bittern Rare, solitary, heron-like wading bird with a characteristic booming call found in marshes. A heavy-bodied bird, it is brownish with streaks and spots which help to disguise it. The female lays 3–6 eggs. Length: 25–90cm (10in-3ft). Family Ardeidae, species *Botaurus stellaris*.

bitumen (asphalt) Material used for roadmaking and for proofing timber against rot. It consists of a mixture of hydrocarbons and other organic chemical compounds. Some bitumen occurs naturally in pitch lakes, notably in Trinidad. The material is also made by distilling tar from coal or wood.

bivalve Animal that has a shell with two halves or parts hinged together. The term most usually applies to a class of MOLLUSCS – Pelecypoda or Lamellibranchiata – with left and right shells, such as clams, cockles, mussels, and oysters. It also refers to animals of the phylum BRACHIOPODA with dorsal and ventral shells. Length: 2mm-1.2m (0.17in-4ft).

Biwa-ko Lake in w central Honshu, Japan, and namesake of the Japanese musical instrument whose shape it resembles. It is the largest lake in Japan and yields freshwater fish. Length: 64km (40mi); width 3–19km (2–12mi); depth 96m (315ft).

Bizet, Georges (1838–75) French Romantic composer. His opera *Carmen* (1875), although a failure at its first performance, is one of the most popular operas of all time.

Bizet also composed other operas, notably *Les pêcheurs de perles* (1863) and orchestral works, including the Symphony in C (1855) and *L'arlésienne* suites (1872).

Black, Joseph (1728–99) Scottish chemist and physicist. Rediscovering 'fixed air' (carbon dioxide), Black found that this gas is produced by respiration, burning of charcoal and FERMENTATION, that it behaves as an ACID, and that it is probably found in the atmosphere. He also discovered hydrogen carbonates (bicarbonates). He investigated LATENT HEAT and specific heat but was unable to reconcile it with the PHLOGISTON theory.

black bear BEAR found in North America and Asia. The **American** black bear lives in forests from Canada to central Mexico. It eats a variety of plant and animal foods, including carrion. It is timid and avoids humans. Length: 1.5–1.8m (5–6ft); weight: 120–150kg (265–330lb). Species *Euarctos americanus*. The **Asiatic** black bear lives in bush or forest areas of E and S Asia. Smaller than the American black bear, it has a white crescent marking on its chest. It has been known to kill livestock and people. Species *Selenarctos thibetanos*.

blackberry (bramble) Fruit-bearing bush, native to northern temperate regions. The prickly stems may be erect or trailing, the leaves oval, and the blossoms white, pink or red. The edible berries are black or dark red. Family Rosaceae; genus *Rubus*.

blackbird Songbird of the THRUSH family, common in gardens and woodland throughout most of Europe, the Near East, Australia, and New Zealand. The male has jet-black plumage and a bright orange bill. The female is brown, with a brown bill. The blackbird feeds on earthworms and other invertebrates. Length: to 25cm (10in). Species *Turdus merula*.

black body In physics, an ideal body that absorbs all incident radiation and reflects none. Such a body would look 'perfectly' black. Wien's law, Stefan's law, and PLANCK's law of black body radiation grew out of this study, as did Planck's discoveries in QUANTUM MECHANICS.

blackbuck (Indian antelope) Medium-sized ANTELOPE of the open plains of India. Females and young are fawn coloured and males are dark. The underparts are white, and there are also patches of white on the muzzle. Only males carry long, spiral horns. Length: to 1.2m (47in); height: to 81cm (32in) at the shoulder. Family Bovidae; species *Antilope cervicapra*.

Black Codes (1865–66) Laws passed in former US Confederate states restricting the rights of newly freed blacks. They limited freedom of employment, freedom of movement, right to own land, and freedom to testify in court. The 14th Amendment to the US Constitution (1868) outlawed the Black Codes.

Black Death (1347–52) Pandemic of PLAGUE, both bubonic and pneumonic, which killed about one-third of the population of Europe (200 million) in two years. It was first carried to Mediterranean ports from the Crimea and spread throughout Europe, carried by fleas infesting rats. Plague recurred less severely in 1361 and other years, until the 18th century.

blackfly See APHID

Blackfoot Nomadic, warlike Native North American tribes. They consist of three Algonquian-speaking tribes: the Siksika or Blackfeet proper, the Kainah, and the Pikuni (Piegan). Living E of the Rockies, on the N Great Plains, they depended largely on the bison (buffalo), which was hunted on horseback. Something of their richly ceremonial

INTERNET

Bizet, Georges
▶ www.classical.net

▼ **Black Death** Originating in China (*c.*1333), the Black Death spread w across Asia and Europe via trade and pilgrimage routes, reaching the Crimea in 1347. Rats were the disease's original hosts, but when they died their infected fleas would transfer to humans. Contemporary descriptions suggest that the infection was bubonic plague, a disease characterized by swollen lymphatic glands (buboes), and an extremely high mortality rate. Recurring for short spells throughout much of the late 1300s, by 1400 it is estimated that the European population had declined by 50%.

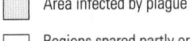

Area infected by plague

Regions spared partly or wholly from the plague

➡ Route of plague's spread

▬ Approximate extent of plague in Europe at six monthly intervals from December 31, 1347, to June 30, 1350

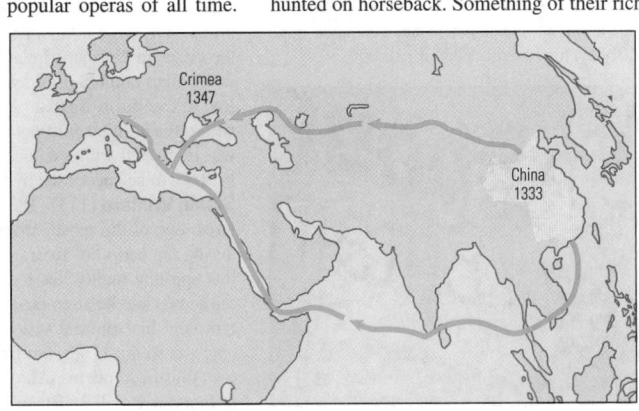

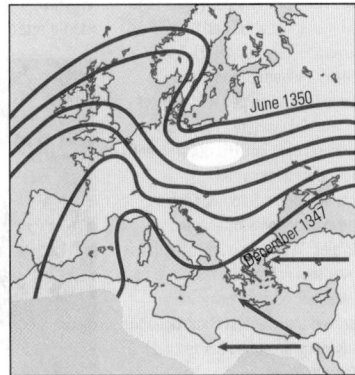

▲ **black widow** The European black widow spider (*Latrodectus tredecimguttatus*) has characteristic red marks on its rounded abdomen that warn other animals that it is poisonous. On rare occasions, the female will eat the male once he has fertilized her eggs.

INTERNET

Black Mountain Poets
▶ www.lib.virginia.edu/ speccol/exhibits/sixties/ list.html

Blair, Tony (Anthony Charles Lynton)
▶ www.number-10.gov.uk

Blake, William
▶ www.blakearchive.org.uk
▶ www.tate.org.uk/britain/ exhibitions/blakeinteractive

▶ **Blair** Britain's youngest Prime Minister since the Earl of Liverpool (elected 1812), Tony Blair's modernization of the Labour Party helped it to achieve a landslide victory in the 1997 general election. His government introduced important constitutional reforms, such as devolution for Scotland and Wales. War in Iraq and questions over that country's possession of weapons of mass destruction proved the greatest challenges to his leadship during his second term in office.

culture survives among the *c.*8000 Blackfeet living today on reservations in Alberta, Canada, and Montana, USA.

Black Forest (Schwarzwald) Mountainous region between the rivers Rhine and Neckar, Baden-Württemburg, sw Germany. It is heavily forested in the higher areas, particularly around the sources of the Danube and the Neckar. The highest peak is Feldberg, 1493m (4898ft). Industries: tourism, timber, mechanical toys, clocks. Area: *c.*6000sq km (2320sq mi).

Black Friday (September 24, 1869) Day of financial panic in the USA. Financiers Jay Gould and James Fisk attempted to corner the gold market and drove the price of gold up. The price fell after the US government sold part of its gold reserve, and many speculators were ruined.

black hole Postulated end-product of the total gravitational collapse of a massive star into itself following exhaustion of its nuclear fuel; the matter inside is crushed to unimaginably high density. It is an empty region of distorted space-time that acts as a centre of gravitational attraction; matter is drawn towards it, and once inside nothing can escape. Its boundary (the event horizon) is a demarcation line, rather than a material surface. Black holes can have an immense range of sizes. Since no light or other radiation can escape from black holes, they are extremely difficult to detect. Not all black holes result from stellar collapse. During the BIG BANG, some regions of space might have become so compressed that they formed so-called **primordial black holes** Such black holes would not be completely black, because radiation could still 'tunnel out' of the event horizon at a steady rate, leading to the evaporation of the hole. Primordial black holes could therefore be very hot.

Black Hole of Calcutta Prison in Calcutta (now KOLKATA), India, where 64 or more British soldiers were placed by the Nawab Siraj-ad-Dawlah of Bengal in June 1756. The cell was 5.5 × 4.5m (18 × 15ft) and most of the soldiers died of suffocation.

Blackmore, R.D. (Richard Doddridge) (1825–1900) English novelist and poet. Blackmore wrote several novels and many volumes of poetry, but is chiefly known for the historical romance *Lorna Doone* (1869).

Black Mountain Poets Designation for writers affiliated with Black Mountain College, North Carolina, in the 1950s. There the writers came under the influence of Charles Olson. Poets from this school include Robert Creeley, Robert Duncan, Denise Levertov, and Joel Oppenheimer.

Black Muslims African-American nationalist movement in the USA. It aims to establish a separatist black Muslim state. Founded in Detroit by Wallace Farad in 1930, the movement was led (1934–76) by Elijah MUHAMMAD. Helped by the rhetorical power of the preacher MALCOLM X, the organization grew rapidly between 1945 and 1960. Factions developed within the movement, and Malcolm was suspended in 1963. In 1976, the movement split into the American Muslim Mission and the Nation of Islam. The former (led by Elijah's son, Wallace Muhammad) preached a more integrationist message. The Nation of Islam, led by Louis FARRAKHAN, claimed to uphold the true doctrines of Elijah Muhammad, and preached a more racially exclusive message. During the 1980s and 1990s, the Nation of Islam gained greater popularity in the USA. Mass demonstrations, such as the 'Million Man March' (1995) in Washington, D.C., and controversial speeches generated huge media attention. Today, total membership is *c*10,000.

Black Panthers Revolutionary party of African-Americans in the 1960s and 1970s. It was founded by Huey Newton and Bobby Seale in 1966. The Black Panthers called for the establishment of an autonomous black state, armed resistance to white repression, and the provision of social welfare organizations in poor black areas. Armed clashes with police occurred and several leaders, including Newton, fled abroad to escape prosecution. Leadership conflicts and the decline of black militancy reduced the influence of the Panthers in the 1970s.

Blackpool Town on the Irish Sea, Lancashire, NW England. A popular resort, it has 11km (7mi) of sandy beaches, a 158m (520ft) tower (built 1895), many indoor and outdoor entertainments and a promenade which is illuminated every autumn. Industries: tourism. Pop. (2001) 142,284.

Black Sea (Kara Sea) Inland sea between Europe and Asia, connected to the Aegean Sea by the Bosporus, the Sea of Marmara and the Dardanelles. It receives many rivers (including the Danube) and is a major outlet for Russian shipping. Subject to violent storms in winter, it remains free of ice except in the remote NW. The Black Sea yields large quantities of fish (especially sturgeon). Area: 413,365sq km (159,662sq mi).

blackthorn Tree or shrub of the ROSE family, which bears white flowers early in the year and has small plum-like fruits (sloes) and long black thorns. The flowers appear before the leaves in spring. Family Rosaceae; species *Prunus spinosa*.

black widow Common name for a small SPIDER found in many warm regions of the world. It is black and has red hour-glass-shaped marks on the underside. Its bite is poisonous, though rarely fatal to humans. Length: 25mm (1in); the male is smaller. Family Theridiidae; genus *Latrodectus*.

bladder Large, elastic-walled organ in the lower abdomen in which URINE is stored. Urine passes from each KIDNEY by way of two narrow tubes (ureters) to the bladder, where it is stored until it can be voided. When pressure in the bladder becomes too great, nervous impulses signal the need for emptying. Urine leaves the bladder through a tube called the URETHRA.

bladderwort Mat-like, aquatic INSECTIVOROUS PLANT found in bogs and ponds. It has feathery thread-like leaves with small bladders in which insects and other small creatures are trapped and drowned. Upright stems bear purple or dark pink flowers. Family Lentibulariaceae; genus *Utricularia*.

Blaine, James Gillespie (1830–93) US statesman, secretary of state (1881, 1889–92). An influential Republican from Maine, he served as state legislator (1858–62), Congressman (1863–76), speaker of the house (1869–75), and US senator (1876–81). He ran for president in 1884, but lost the election to the Democrat candidate, Grover CLEVELAND, partly because of the defection of reform Republicans.

Blair, Tony (Anthony Charles Lynton) (1953–) British statesman, prime minister (1997–2007). He entered Parliament in 1983. Blair became leader of the LABOUR PARTY after the death (1994) of John Smith. His support for reform of the party's structure and constitution ('new Labour') helped defeat John MAJOR's Conservative government in the 1997 general election. He was re-elected in 2001. Blair undertook constitutional reforms such as devolution for Scotland and Wales, and reform of the HOUSE OF LORDS. Aided by a buoyant economy, he sought to improve health and education provision, while keeping a tight grip on public expenditure. In foreign affairs, he devoted much energy to solving the crises in Northern Ireland, Kosovo, and Afghanistan. In 2003, Blair and US president George W. Bush sent troops to Iraq to overthrow Saddam Hussein and his regime. He faced widespread criticism of his decision to go to war in Iraq. He was re-elected with a reduced majority in 2005 and resigned in 2007, to be succeeded by Gordon BROWN.

Blake, William (1757–1827) English poet, philosopher, and artist, one of the most extraordinary personalities to emerge during the period of ROMANTICISM. A visionary, he believed that spiritual reality lies hidden behind the visible world of the senses and he attempted to create a symbolic language to represent his spiritual visions. He worked as a commercial engraver in the 1780s, but from *c.*1787 he began printing his own illustrated poems in colour. The first example was *Songs of Innocence* (1789). Blake's two patrons, Thomas Butts and

John Linnell, enabled him to pursue his individual path as a poet-illustrator, producing notable engravings for *Jerusalem* (1804–20). Towards the end of his life, he joined a circle of younger artists who appreciated his remarkable powers, notably Samuel PALMER and Edward Calvert. It was not until the late 19th century that Blake's work achieved general recognition. He was extremely prolific and his prints, illustrations, and TEMPERA paintings can be found in several important public collections in England and the USA. Among his other productions were *Songs of Experience* (1794), prophetic books portraying his private mythologies such as *The Book of Urizen* (1794) and *The Four Zoas* (1797), and illustrations to *The Book of Job* and to the *Divine Comedy* by DANTE.

Blanc, Mont *See* MONT BLANC

Blankers-Koen, Fanny (Francina) (1918–2004) Dutch track and field athlete, b. Francina Elsje Koen. At the 1948 Olympic Games in London, England she became the first woman to win four gold medals on the track at a single Olympics (100m, 200m, 80m hurdles, 4100m). At the 1946 European Championships, she won gold medals in the 80m hurdles and 4100m relay. She won three more gold medals (100m, 200m, 80m hurdles) at the 1950 European Championship. She retired from competitive athletics in 1955, and managed the Dutch national team at the 1968 Olympics. In 1999, she was voted woman athlete of the century.

blank verse Unrhymed verse, especially iambic pentameter or unrhymed heroic couplets, widely used in English dramatic and epic poetry. Henry HOWARD introduced blank verse into England in the 16th century with his translation of Virgil's *Aeneid*. Christopher Marlowe and William SHAKESPEARE transformed it into the characteristic medium of Elizabethan and JACOBEAN drama. John MILTON employed it in *Paradise Lost* (1667) and William WORDSWORTH used it in his long autobiography *The Prelude* (1850). It continues to be popular as a form and technical device in contemporary poetry.

Blanqui, Louis Auguste (1805–81) French socialist leader. A legendary revolutionary who spent much of his life in prison. He participated in the revolutions of 1830 and 1848, and in the overthrow of NAPOLEON III in 1870. He became a symbol for European socialists and was president of the PARIS COMMUNE.

Blasco Ibáñez, Vicente (1867–1928) Spanish novelist, influenced by ZOLA and MAUPASSANT. His best works, such as *The Cabin* (1898) and *Reeds and Mud* (1902), deal with rural life in Valencia and express his fervent Republican beliefs. *Blood and Sand* (1908) and *The Four Horsemen of the Apocalypse* (1916) established his international reputation.

blasphemy Speech or action manifesting contempt for God or religion. Severe penalties were prescribed for it in the Old Testament and also by medieval CANON LAW. Jesus Christ was crucified for blasphemy against Judaism. The statutes of many secular countries still include laws against blasphemy. Britain, for example, retains its law, originally designed to ensure social conformity to Anglicanism.

blast furnace Cylindrical smelting furnace. It is used in the extraction of metals, mainly iron and copper, from their ores. The ore is mixed with coke and a flux (limestone in the case of iron ore). A blast of hot, compressed air is piped in at the bottom of the furnace to force up temperatures so that the oxide ore is reduced to impure metal. The molten metal sinks to the bottom and is tapped off. Waste 'slag' floats to the top of the metal and is piped off. *See also* OXIDATION-REDUCTION

blastula Stage in the development of the EMBRYO in animals. The blastula consists of a hollow cavity (blastocoel) surrounded by one or more spherical layers of cells. Commonly called the 'hollow ball of cells' stage, it occurs at or near the end of cleavage and precedes the gastrulation stage.

Blaue Reiter, Der Loosely organized group of German expressionist painters. Formed in 1911, it took its name from a picture by Wassily KANDINSKY, one of the group's members. Other members included Paul KLEE, August MACKE, Alexei von Jawlensky, and Franz Marc. Influenced by CUBISM, Blaue Reiter was the most important manifestation of German modern art before World War 1. They sought to express the struggle of inner impulses and a repressed spirituality, which they felt IMPRESSIONISM had overlooked. *See also* EXPRESSIONISM

Blenheim, Battle of (1704) Decisive battle in the War of the SPANISH SUCCESSION. The Duke of MARLBOROUGH and Prince EUGÈNE OF SAVOY defeated the French at Blenheim in Bavaria. Vienna was saved and Bavaria taken by the anti-French allies. Marlborough was rewarded with a royal manor near Oxford, where he built Blenheim Palace, birthplace of his descendant Winston Churchill.

Blériot, Louis (1872–1936) French aircraft designer and aviator. In 1909 Blériot became the first man to fly an aircraft across the English Channel. The flight from Calais to Dover took 37 minutes. As a designer, he was responsible for various innovations, including the first successful monoplane.

Bleuler, Paul Eugen (1857–1939) Swiss psychiatrist, pioneer in the diagnosis and treatment of PSYCHOSIS. Bleuler coined the term SCHIZOPHRENIA and attributed the symptoms to psychological rather than physiological origins.

Bligh, William (1754–1817) British naval officer. He was captain of the *Bounty* in 1789, when his mutinous crew cast him adrift. With a few loyal companions, he sailed nearly 6500km (4000mi) to Timor. While governor of New South Wales (1805–08), he was arrested by mutineers led by his deputy, and sent back to England. He was exonerated.

blight Yellowing, browning, and withering of plant tissues caused by various diseases; alternatively, the diseases themselves. Blights may be caused by microorganisms, such as bacteria and fungi, or by environmental factors such as drought. Common blights induced by microorganisms include fire, bean, late, and potato blight. They typically affect leaves more severely than other parts.

blindness Severe impairment (or absence of) vision. It may be due to heredity, accident, disease, or old age. Worldwide, the commonest cause of blindness is TRACHOMA. In developed countries, it is most often due to severe DIABETES, GLAUCOMA, CATARACT or degenerative changes associated with ageing.

blind spot Small area on the retina of the EYE where no visual image can be formed because of the absence of light-sensitive cells, the rods and cones. It is the area where the optic nerve leaves the eye.

Bliss, Sir Arthur (1891–1975) English composer. He was a pupil of Charles Villiers Stanford, Ralph Vaughan Williams, and Gustav Holst. Bliss' works include the *Colour Symphony* (1932), quintets for oboe (1927) and clarinet (1931), a piano concerto (1938), two operas and a number of choral works. From 1953 he was Master of the Queen's Music.

Blitz, the Name used by the British to describe the night bombings of British cities by the German *Luftwaffe* (air force) in 1940–41. It is an abbreviation of *Blitzkrieg* (lightning war), the name used by the German army to describe hard-hitting, surprise attacks on enemy forces.

Blixen, Karen *See* DINESEN, ISAK

Bloch, Felix (1905–83) US nuclear physicist, b. Switzerland. He shared the 1952 Nobel Prize in physics with the US physicist Edward Mills Purcell for their separate development of the technique of nuclear MAGNETIC RESONANCE (NMR), used to study the interactions between atomic nuclei. Bloch was the first director (1954–55) of the *Conseil Européen pour la Recherche Nucléaire (CERN)*, the European centre in Geneva for research into high-energy PARTICLE PHYSICS.

Bloemfontein City and judicial capital of South Africa, capital of FREE STATE. Dutch farmers settled here in the early 19th century. It contains the oldest Dutch Reformed church in

◄ **The Blitz** The aerial bombardment of London and other major cities in Britain, such as Coventry (shown here) by the German airforce in World War 2. It was most intense during the Battle of Britain (July–December 1940). The Blitz aimed not only to destroy key industrial centres, but also to undermine the spirit of British civilians and overseas forces. Some 23,000 civilians died during the Blitz.

BLOOD

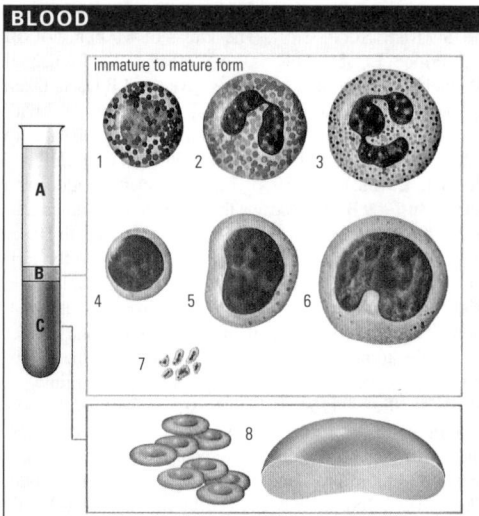

immature to mature form

Spun in a high-speed centrifuge, blood separates out into plasma (A), layers of white cells and platelets (B) and red cells (C). Fluid plasma, almost 90% water, contains salts and proteins. Three main types of white cells (shown in magnification) are polymorphonuclearcytes (1–3), responsible for the destruction of invading bacteria and removal of dead or damaged tissue, small and large lymphocytes (4 and 5), which assist in the body's immune system, and monocytes (6), which form a further line of the body's defence. Platelets (7) are vital clotting agents. Red cells (8) are the most numerous, and are concerned with the transport of oxygen around the body.

South Africa. The modern city is an important educational centre. Industries: furniture, glassware. Pop. (2002) 371,200.

blood Fluid circulating in the body that transports oxygen and nutrients to all the cells and removes wastes such as carbon dioxide. In a healthy human, it constitutes *c*.5% of the body's total weight; by volume, it comprises *c*.5.5 litres (9.7 pints). It is composed of a colourless, transparent fluid called plasma in which are suspended microscopic ERY-THROCYTES, LEUCOCYTES, and PLATELETS.

blood clotting Protective mechanism that prevents excessive blood loss after injury. A mesh of tight fibres (of insoluble FIBRIN) coagulates at the site of injury through a complex series of chemical reactions. This mesh traps blood cells to form a clot which dries to form a scab. This prevents further loss of blood, and also prevents bacteria getting into the wound. Normal clotting takes place within five minutes. The clotting mechanism is impaired in some diseases, such as HAEMOPHILIA.

blood group Any of the types into which blood is classified according to which ANTIGENS are present on the surface of its red cells. There are four major types: A, B, AB, and O. Each group in the ABO system may also contain the rhesus factor (Rh), in which case it is Rh-positive; otherwise it is Rh-negative. Such typing is essential before BLOOD TRANSFUSION, since using blood of the wrong group may produce a dangerous or even fatal reaction. *See also* LANDSTEINER, KARL

bloodhound Hunting DOG with long tapered head, loose hanging jowls and ears, and a characteristically wrinkled skin. The smooth coat may be black, tan, or red and tan. Weight: up to 50kg (110lb). Height: (at shoulder) up to 69cm (27in).

blood poisoning (septicaemia) Presence in the blood of bacteria or their toxins in sufficient quantity to cause illness. Symptoms include chills and fever, sweating and collapse. It is most often seen in people who are already in some way vulnerable, such as the young or old, the critically ill or injured, or those whose immune systems have been suppressed.

blood pressure Force exerted by circulating BLOOD on the walls of blood vessels due to the pumping action of the HEART. This is measured, using a gauge known as a SPHYG-MOMANOMETER. It is greatest when the heart contracts and lowest when it relaxes. High blood pressure is associated with an increased risk of heart attacks and strokes; abnormally low blood pressure is mostly seen in people in shock or following excessive loss of fluid or blood.

blood transfusion Transfer of blood or a component of blood from one body to another to make up for a deficiency. This is possible only if the BLOOD GROUPS of the donor and recipient are compatible. It is often done to treat life-threatening SHOCK following excessive blood loss. Donated blood is scrutinized for readily transmissible diseases such as HEPATITIS B and ACQUIRED IMMUNE DEFICIENCY SYNDROME (AIDS).

blood vessel Closed channels that carry blood throughout the body. An ARTERY carries oxygenated blood away from the heart; these give way to smaller arterioles and finally to tiny capillaries deep in the tissues, where oxygen and nutrients are exchanged for cellular wastes. The deoxygenated blood is returned to the heart by way of the VEINS.

Bloody Assizes (1685) Trials held in the w of England following MONMOUTH's Rebellion against James II. Judge Jeffreys conducted the trials. He sentenced about 200 people to be hanged, 800 to transportation, and hundreds more to flogging, imprisonment or fines.

bloom Dense population of microscopic algae or CYANOBACTERIA on the surface of lakes or seas, often colouring the water. They may appear suddenly through migration of the population to the water surface. This occurs when the cells (previously mixed down into the water column by wind action) float or swim to the surface under calm conditions. They may arise also through rapid multiplication in response to large increases in nutrients. This happens when sewage, or other mineral-rich water, enters a lake or sea. Some blooms produce toxins, which can be harmful to marine life.

Bloomer, Amelia Jenks (1818–94) US women's rights campaigner. She published *Lily*, the first US magazine for women, between 1849 and 1854. She subsequently continued as editor, and wrote articles on education, marriage laws and

BLOOD VESSELS

Arteries (A) and veins (B) conduct blood around the body. They have a common structure consisting of four layers: a protective fibrous coat (1); a middle layer of smooth muscle and elastic tissue (2), which is thickest in the largest arteries; a thin layer of connective tissue (3); and a smooth layer of cells – endothelium (4). Arteries have thicker walls and a smaller diameter. In veins, inner coat layers are often indistinguishable. A comparison of the two vessels is shown in half sections of arteries and veins found in the body. Arteries divide into smaller ones, and finally into arterioles (5), where the blood flow can be controlled by autonomic nerves supplying the layer of smooth muscle.

female suffrage. As part of her campaign, she popularized the full trousers for women that became known as "bloomers".

Bloomsbury Group Intellectuals who met in Bloomsbury, London, from *c*.1907. They included the art critics Roger Fry and Clive Bell; novelists E.M. FORSTER and Virginia WOOLF; her husband Leonard Woolf, a publisher; economist John Maynard KEYNES, and biographer Lytton STRACHEY. The group's attitudes were influenced by the empiricist philosopher G.E. Moore, and are encapsulated in his statement: "the rational ultimate end of human progress consists in the pleasures of human intercourse and the enjoyment of beautiful objects."

bluebell Spring-flowering blue flower, native to Europe. It grows from a bulb, especially in woodlands, and bears a drooping head of bell-shaped flowers. Height: 20–50cm (8–20in). Family Liliaceae; species *Hyacinthoides non-scripta*.

blueberry *See* BILBERRY

bluebird North American songbird with blue plumage, a member of the thrush subfamily. There are three species. Typically, a bluebird lays its eggs (usually four to six) in a grass-and-weed-lined nest in a hole in a tree or fence post. Length: 7in (17.8cm). Genus *Sialia*.

bluebottle Black or metallic blue-green FLY, slightly larger but similar in habits to the house fly. The larvae (maggots) usually feed on carrion and refuse containing meat. Like the greenbottle, it is often also called a blowfly. Family Calliphoridae. Genus *Calliphora*. Length: 6–11mm (0.23–0.43in).

bluefish Marine fish found in most tropical and temperate seas. A voracious predator, it travels in large schools. Fished widely for food and sport, it has an elongated blue/green body, and a large mouth with sharp teeth. Length: 1.2m (4ft). Family Pomatomidae; species *Pomatomus saltatrix*.

bluegrass Type of GRASS that grows in temperate and Arctic regions and is used extensively for food by grazing animals. Family Poaceae/Gramineae; genus *Poa*.

blue-green algae *See* CYANOBACTERIA

Blue Ridge Mountains East and SE range of the APPALACHIAN Mountains, extending from S Pennsylvania into Georgia, USA. A narrow ridge, 15km (10mi) wide in the N, widens to 110km (70mi) in North Carolina. Heavily forested, with few lakes, it includes Great Smoky Mountains National Park, North Carolina, and Shenandoah National Park, Virginia. The Appalachian Trail runs across the top of range. The highest peak is Mount Mitchell, North Carolina, at 6684ft (2039m).

blues Form of African-American music, originating in the late 19th-century folk traditions of the American South. It evolved from gospel and work songs. The standard verse pattern is the 12–bar blues: three sets of four bars, the second set being a repetition of the first. The first published blues piece was "The Memphis Blues" by W.C. HANDY (1912). 'Jelly Roll' MORTON incorporated a jazzier style in "Jelly Roll Blues". Great vocalists such as Bessie Smith ('Empress of the Blues'), Robert Johnson, Leadbelly (Huddie LEDBETTER) and 'Ma' Rainey, helped popularize the blues. The northerly migration of African-Americans in the 1930s saw the emergence of a brasher, urban blues tradition based around Chicago. After World War 2, instruments were amplified, and the electric guitar became the dominant voice, with artists such as Muddy Waters and John Lee Hooker. In the 1950s, new forms such as rhythm and blues, and rock and roll drew on the blues. During the 1960s, rock and pop bands, such as the Rolling Stones, were also directly influenced by the tradition.

blue shift In astronomy, an effect in which the lines in the SPECTRUM of a celestial object are displaced towards the blue end of the spectrum. It results from the DOPPLER EFFECT because the object and the observer are moving towards each other. The closing speed can be calculated from the extent of the shift. *See also* RED SHIFT

blue whale Baleen WHALE, related to the rorquals. The blue whale is the largest animal that has ever lived, reaching up to 30m (100ft) in length and weighing as much as 120 tonnes. In summer it lives in polar seas. Mating occurs at the end of winter and the whales migrate to warmer latitudes to give birth. A single calf is born every two or three years, after a 10–11 month gestation period. They live up to 50 years. Overhunting has led to threat of extinction. Species *Balaenoptera musculus*.

Blum, Léon (1872–1950) French statesman, prime minister (1936–37). He served in the chamber of deputies (1919–40) as a leader of the Socialist Party. Blum formed the Popular Front, which became a coalition government. His administration rapidly embarked on a programme of nationalization. Opposed by Conservatives, Blum was forced to resign and became deputy prime minister. He opposed the MUNICH AGREEMENT (1938). Interned by the VICHY GOVERNMENT (1940–45), he briefly led a provisional government (1946–47).

Blunt, Anthony (1907–83) English art historian, director (1947–74) of the Courtauld Institute of Art, London, and surveyor of the King's (later Queen's) pictures (1945–72). Blunt was a formidable scholar, earning praise for his work on Nicolas POUSSIN. In 1979, his reputation was destroyed when it was disclosed that he had been a Soviet spy during the Cold War .

boa Large constricting SNAKE that gives birth to live young. The boa constrictor (*Constrictor constrictor*) of the American tropics can grow to 3.7m (12ft) in length. The iridescent rainbow boa, the emerald tree boa, and the rosy boa are smaller species. Most boas are tree-dwellers, but the rubber boa of the W USA is a burrowing species. Family Boidae.

Boadicea (Boudicca) (d. AD 62) Queen of the ICENI in East Britain. She was the wife of King Prasutagus who, on his death, left his daughters and the Roman Emperor as co-heirs. The Romans seized his domain and Boadicea led a revolt against them. After initial successes, during which her army killed as many as 70,000 Roman soldiers, she was defeated and poisoned herself. *See also* ROMAN BRITAIN

boar Male domestic PIG (particularly one that has not been castrated) or, more specifically, the wild pig of Europe, Africa, and Asia. In almost all its habitats it is hunted, either for food or for sport. The European wild boar is species *Sus scrofa*.

boat Vehicle for passenger and freight transport by water. Today, it usually refers to a craft that can be removed from the water – a larger vessel is called a SHIP. The first boats, made in prehistoric times, included rafts, hollowed-out logs and vessels made from plaited reeds. Among the first maritime peoples were the Phoenicians. They built fleets of galleys, propelled by sails and oars, for their extensive trading in the Mediterranean and adjoining areas. The later Viking long-boats, also square-sailed, were slimmer and speedier. Lateen (triangular) sails were probably imported from the Persian Gulf and introduced to the West by the empire-building Arabs. Modern boats include launches, motorboats, and some SAILING vessels used mainly for pleasure.

boat people Refugees that flee their country by sea to avoid political persecution, or to find greater economic opportunities. The term is closely associated with South Vietnamese refugees, of whom, since 1975, *c*.150,000 sailed to Hong Kong and other Southeast Asian countries. Other boat people include Cubans and Haitians attempting to reach the USA, usually Florida.

bobcat (wild cat or red lynx) Vicious, short-tailed cat found throughout swamp, forest and grassland regions of the USA, S Canada, and Central America. Its reddish-brown coat has black spots with white underparts. The bobcat feeds on rodents and gives birth to 2–4 young following a gestation period of 50–60 days. Length: body 64–76cm (25–30in). Family Felidae; species *Lynx rufus*.

Boccaccio, Giovanni (1313–75) Italian poet, prose writer, and scholar, considered to be one of the founders of the Italian Renaissance. His early work, the *Filocolo* (*c*.1336), is considered by many to be the first European novel, but he is best known for his masterpiece the *Decameron* (1348–58), a series of prose stories which exercised a tremendous influence on the

▲ **bluebell** A spring-flowering bulb, the bluebell (*Endymion nonsciptus*) is a monocotyledon. The bulb is a storage organ for the plant and provides a means of vegetative reproduction.

INTERNET

Blue Ridge Mountains
▸ www.nps.gov/blri

blue whale
▸ www.wdcs.org

◄ **boa** The boa constrictor (*Constrictor constrictor*) is found in many areas of South America. It feeds on birds and small mammals, such as rats and agoutis, which it kills by restricting their ability to breathe. A large snake, it grows to *c*.3.6m (12ft) in length.

▲ **Bolsheviks** Following the October Revolution of 1917, the Bolsheviks, led by Lenin, gained power. A significant element of support was provided by soldiers and sailors returning home from World War 1, seen here at a rally in the Catherine Hall of the Tauride Palace, Petrograd (now St Petersburg).

development of RENAISSANCE literature. His poetry includes *Il Filostrato* (*c*.1338). Boccaccio was a friend of PETRARCH and biographer of DANTE. *See also* ITALIAN LITERATURE

Bode's law In astronomy, empirical numerical relationship for the mean distances of the planets from the Sun, named after the German astronomer Johann Bode (1747–1826). If 4 is added to the sequence 0, 3, 6, 12, 24, 48, 96, and 192, the result corresponds reasonably with the mean planetary distances – Earth's distance being equal to 10. This aided the discovery of Uranus (1781), but does not work for Neptune.

Bodhidharma (active 6th century AD) Indian Buddhist monk who travelled to China and founded ZEN Buddhism.

bodhisattva (bodhista) In THERAVADA Buddhism, an individual who is about to reach NIRVANA. In MAHAYANA Buddhism, the term is used to denote an individual on the verge of enlightenment who delays his salvation in order to help mankind.

Bodin, Jean (1530–96) French lawyer and political philosopher. In *Six Books of the Republic* (1576), Bodin treated anarchy as the supreme political evil and order as the supreme human need. He supported absolute monarchy and an unrestricted secular sovereignty residing in the state.

Boer (Afrikaans, farmer) Alternative name for AFRIKANER

Boer Wars *See* SOUTH AFRICAN WARS

Boethius (*c*.480–524) (Anicius Manlius Severinus) Roman statesman and philosopher under Emperor Theodoric. He was imprisoned on a charge of conspiracy. In prison at Pavia, where he was subsequently tortured and executed, he wrote *On the Consolation of Philosophy* (523). Next to the Bible, this was medieval Europe's most influential book.

bog Spongy wet soil consisting of decayed vegetable matter; often called a peat bog. It develops in a depression with little or no drainage, where the water is cold and acidic and almost devoid of oxygen and nitrogen. Bogs support plants such as cranberry and the carnivorous SUNDEW.

Bogart, Humphrey DeForest (1899–1957) Legendary US film actor, often cast as a cynical, wisecracking anti-hero. In 1941, an association with FILM NOIR and John HUSTON began with roles in *High Sierra* and *The Maltese Falcon*. He starred in *Casablanca* (1942). In 1945 he married Lauren Bacall; their sexual magnetism was evident in the *film noir* classic *The Big Sleep* (1946). In 1948 Bogart starred in another two Huston classics, *The Treasure of the Sierra Madre* and *Key Largo*. He won a best actor Oscar for *The African Queen* (1951).

Bogotá Capital of Colombia, in the centre of the country on a fertile plateau. Bogotá was founded in 1538 by the Spanish on the site of a CHIBCHA Indian settlement. In 1819 it became the capital of Greater Colombia, part of which later formed Colombia. Today, it is a centre for culture, education and finance. Industries: tobacco, sugar, flour, textiles, engineering, chemicals. Pop. (2005) 7,594,000.

Bohemia Historic region which (with MORAVIA) now comprises the CZECH REPUBLIC. Its borders with Germany are

formed (NW) by the Ore Mountains and (SW) by the Bohemian Forest. The plateau region is drained by the rivers ELBE and Vltava. The major cities are PRAGUE and PLZEN. Bohemia was established as an independent principality at the end of the 9th century. In the 920s, Saint WENCESLAS successfully resisted Germanic invasion, but by the end of the 10th century Bohemia formed part of the Holy Roman Empire. In 1198 Ottocar I formed an independent kingdom. At the height of its power during the reign (1253–78) of Ottocar II, Bohemia stretched from the Oder to the Adriatic. Bohemia's golden age was in the reign (1347–78) of Emperor CHARLES IV, who made Prague his capital. In the reigns of WENCESLAS and SIGISMUND, Bohemia was at the centre of nationalist and religious revolts against imperial domination, including the rebellion of Jan HUS. In 1526 Bohemia was inherited by the HABSBURG dynasty. In 1618 the Defenestration of Prague sparked the THIRTY YEARS' WAR. The process of Germanization was continued by MARIA THERESA and JOSEPH II. Leopold II was the last King of Bohemia. The formation of the AUSTRO-HUNGARIAN EMPIRE failed to satisfy Czech demands for autonomy; independence was finally achieved at the end of World War 1 under Tomás MASARYK. In the MUNICH AGREEMENT (1938), CZECHOSLOVAKIA was forced to cede the SUDETENLAND to Germany. In 1993, the dissolution of Czechoslovakia saw Bohemia and Moravia join to form the Czech Republic.

Bohr, Aage Niels (1922–1962) Danish physicist, son of Niels BOHR. With Benjamin Mottelson and James Rainwater, Bohr shared the 1975 Nobel Prize in physics for devising a "collective model" of the atomic nucleus that assumes the collective vibration of all nucleons and their individual motion.

Bohr, Niels Henrik David (1885–1962) Danish physicist, a major contributor to QUANTUM THEORY. Bohr worked with J.J. THOMSON and Ernest RUTHERFORD in Britain before teaching theoretical physics at the University of Copenhagen. He escaped from German-occupied Denmark during World War 2, and worked briefly on developing the atom bomb in the USA. Bohr used the quantum theory to explain the spectrum of hydrogen and in the 1920s helped develop the 'standard model' of QUANTUM THEORY, known as the Copenhagen Interpretation. He received the 1922 Nobel Prize in physics for his work on atomic structure, and gained the first Atoms for Peace Award in 1957.

bohrium (symbol Bh) Synthetic, radioactive, ELEMENT of the transactinide series. It is very unstable, and few atoms have ever been detected. Its discovery was made by German physicists Peter Armbruster and Gottfried Münzenberg and collegues by bombarding bismuth-209 nuclei with chromium-54 nuclei. It is named after Danish physicist Niels BOHR. Properties: at.no. 107.

boil (furuncle) Small, pus-filled swelling on the skin, often around a hair follicle or SEBACEOUS GLAND. Most boils are caused by infection from a bacterium (STAPHYLOCOCCUS).

boiling point Temperature at which a substance changes phase (state) from a liquid to a vapour or gas. The boiling point increases as the external pressure increases and falls as pressure decreases. It is usually measured at standard pressure of one atmosphere (760mm of mercury). The boiling point of pure water at standard pressure is 100°C (212°F).

Boise Capital and largest city of Idaho, USA, in the valley of the Boise River. Founded in 1863 as a supply post for gold miners, it is now a trade centre for the agricultural region of SW Idaho and E Oregon. Crops: sugar beets, potatoes, alfalfa, onions. Industries: steel, sheet metal, furniture, electrical equipment, timber products. Pop. (2000) 185,787.

Bokassa, Jean Bedel (1921–96) Emperor of the Central African Empire (1977–79). Bokassa came to power in 1966 in a military coup. After serving as president (1966–77) of the CENTRAL AFRICAN REPUBLIC, he crowned himself emperor. His regime was brutal. A 1979 coup (with French military aid) removed Bokassa, who went into exile in France, and replaced him with his cousin David Dacko.

boletus Genus of terrestrial fungi, whose spore-bearing parts are tubes instead of the usual gills. There are many species, all of which have a fleshy cap on a central stem and many of which are edible. Some poisonous kinds have red tube mouths. The edible cep is *Boletus edulis*.

Boleyn, Anne (1507–1536) Second wife of HENRY VIII of England, mother of ELIZABETH I. She married Henry in 1533, when his marriage to CATHERINE OF ARAGON had been annulled. Henry was desperate for an heir and following the birth of a stillborn boy, Anne was accused of adultery and executed for treason. It is thought that her Protestant sympathies, as well as Henry's need for a divorce, pushed the king towards the break with Rome that unleashed the English REFORMATION.

Bolingbroke *See* HENRY IV (of England)

Bolingbroke, Henry St John, Viscount (1678–1751) English politician. A prominent Tory minister under Queen ANNE, in 1714 Bolingbroke fled to France and joined the JACOBITES. In 1723 he was allowed to return to England, and continued to oppose the Whig regime, attacking political corruption under Robert WALPOLE. The best known of his many philosophical and political writings is *The Idea of a Patriot King* (1749), upholding the role of monarchy in government.

Bolívar, Simón (1783–1830) Latin American revolutionary leader, known as 'the Liberator'. His experience in Napoleonic Europe influenced his untiring attempts to free South America from Spanish rule. He achieved no real success until 1819, when his victory at Boyacá led to the liberation of New Granada (later Colombia) in 1821. The liberation of

Venezuela (1821), Ecuador (1822), Peru (1824), and Upper Peru (1825) followed, the latter renaming itself Bolivia in his honour. Despite the removal of Spanish hegemony from the continent, his hopes of uniting South America into one confederation were dashed by rivalry between the new states.

Bolivia Republic in South America. *See* country feature

Bologna City at the foot of Apennines, N central Italy; capital of Bologna and Emilia-Romagna province. Originally an Etruscan town, Felsina, it was colonized by Rome in the 2nd century BC. It has an 11th-century university, the incomplete Church of San Petronio (1390) and the Palazzo Comunale. Industries: mechanical and electrical engineering, agricultural machinery, publishing, chemicals. Pop. (2001) 380,000.

Bolsheviks (Rus. 'majority') Marxist revolutionaries, led by LENIN, who seized power in the RUSSIAN REVOLUTION of 1917. They narrowly defeated the MENSHEVIKS at the Second Congress of the Social Democratic Labour Party in London (1903). The split, on tactics as much as doctrine, centred on the means of achieving revolution. The Bolsheviks believed it could be obtained only by professional revolutionaries leading the PROLETARIAT. The Bolsheviks were able to overthrow the Provisional government of KERENSKY through their support in the SOVIETS of Moscow and Petrograd. *See also* MARXISM

Bolshoi Ballet One of the world's leading ballet companies. It adopted its present name in 1825, but was founded

BOLIVIA

The Republic of Bolivia is a landlocked country in South America. It can be divided into two regions. The W is dominated by two parallel ranges of the Andes Mountains. The W cordillera forms Bolivia's border with Chile. The E range runs through the heart of Bolivia. Between the two lies the Altiplano. The Altiplano is the most densely populated region of Bolivia and the site of its famous ruins, it includes the seat of government, LA PAZ, close to Lake TITICACA. SUCRE, the legal capital, lies in the Andean foothills.

The E is a relatively unexplored region of lush, tropical rainforest, inhabited mainly by Native South Americans. The windswept Altiplano is a grassland region. In the SE lies the semi-arid GRAN CHACO, which is a largely unpopulated vast lowland plain, drained by the River Madeira, a tributary of the AMAZON. The region is famous for its

quebracho trees which are a major source of tannin.

CLIMATE
Bolivia's climate varies greatly according to altitude, with the highest Andean peaks permanently covered in snow. In contrast, the E plains have a humid tropical climate. The main rainy season takes place between December and February.

HISTORY
Native Americans have lived in Bolivia for at least 10,000 years. The ruins of Tiahuanaco indicate that the Altiplano was the site of one of the great pre-Colombian civilizations. Before the Spanish invasion in 1532, the QUECHUA had subsumed the AYMARÁ into the Inca Empire. The main groups today are still the Aymara and Quechua people.

When Spanish soldiers arrived in the early 16th century, Bolivia was part of the Inca empire. Following the defeat of the Incas, Spain ruled from 1532 to 1825, exploiting the Andean silver mines with native forced labour. In 1824 Antonio José de SUCRE, one of revolutionary leader Simón BOLÍVAR's generals, defeated the Spaniards and completed the liberation of the country from Spanish rule.

For the next 100 years, corruption and instability plagued the new nation and Bolivia lost territory to its neighbours. War with Paraguay for control of the Gran Chaco region (1932–35) cost c.100,000 lives. Bolivia lost and most of this area passed to Paraguay in 1938. During World War 2 the need for tin revived Bolivia's economy.

POLITICS
Following the Chaco War, Bolivia entered a long period of instability. It had ten presidents, six military, between 1936 and 1952, when the Revolutionary Movement took power. In the 1950s the revolutionaries broke up large estates and granted land to Amerindian farmers. The

AREA 1,098,581sq km
[424,162sq mi]
POPULATION 9,119,000
CAPITAL (POPULATION)
La Paz (seat of government, 1,533,000); Sucre (legal capital/seat of judiciary, 177,000)
GOVERNMENT Multiparty republic
ETHNIC GROUPS Mestizo 30%, Quechua 30%, Aymara 25%, White 15%
LANGUAGES
Spanish, Aymara, Quechua (all official)
RELIGIONS Roman Catholic 95%
CURRENCY Boliviano = 100 centavos

revolutionaries were toppled by a military uprising in 1964. Elections were held in 1980, but the military again intervened until 1982.

Presidential elections were held from 1989. In 1997 General Suárez, who had ruled as a dictator in the 1970s, became president. In 2005 Evo Morales, a left-wing Aymaran Indian and peasant leader, replaced him. In 2006 Morales nationalized the oil and gas industries and began reforms he claimed would aid indigenous peoples and the poor, which led to a divide between the government and the wealthier E provinces.

ECONOMY
Bolivia is one of the poorest countries in South America. It has several natural resources, including tin, silver and natural gas, but the chief activity is agriculture, which employs 47% of the people. Potatoes, wheat and a grain called quinoa are important crops on the Altiplano, while bananas, cocoa, coffee and maize are grown at the lower, warmer levels.

Manufacturing is small-scale and the main exports are mineral ores and fossil fuels. Coca, which is used to make cocaine, is exported illegally. In 2002–3 the production of coca plummeted, causing social unrest. In 2004 the people voted in favour of a government plan to export natural gas via a port in Peru.

▼ **bone** A magnified cross-section of bone (A) shows that it is composed of rod-like units (1) which when further magnified (B) are seen to have a central channel (2) containing blood vessels (3). These are surrounded by concentric layers, or lamellae, of collagen fibres, each arranged in a different direction from those in adjacent layers. Calcium salt crystals and bone cells (4) are embedded between the fibres.

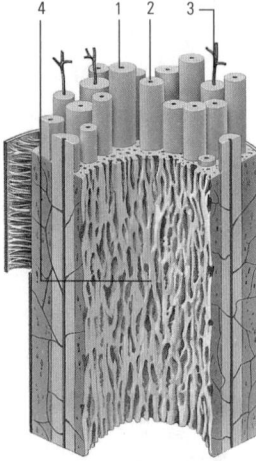

as the Petrovsky Theatre in 1776. Based at the Bolshoi Theatre, its choreographers have included Yuri Grigorovich, Marius PETIPA, and Alexander Gorsky, and its leading dancers Galina ULANOVA and Mikhail Lavrovsky.

Bolshoi Opera Leading Russian opera company, founded in 1780 in Moscow. It performs mostly Russian works.

Boltzmann, Ludwig (1844–1906) Austrian physicist, acclaimed for his contribution to statistical mechanics and to the kinetic theory of gases. His research extended the ideas of James MAXWELL. Boltzmann's general law asserts that a system will approach a state of thermodynamic equilibrium because that is the most probable state. He introduced the 'Boltzmann equation' (1877) relating the kinetic energy of a gas atom or molecule to temperature. Symbol K in the formula, the gas constant per molecule, is called the 'Boltzmann constant'. In 1884 he derived a law, often termed the 'Stefan-Boltzmann law', for BLACK BODY radiation discovered by his teacher, Josef Stefan (1835–93). Boltzmann suffered from depression, probably worsened by bitter struggles to gain acceptance for his ideas, and committed suicide.

Bombay *See* MUMBAI

Bonaparte, Joseph (1768–1844) King of Spain (1808–13), b. Corsica. He was the eldest brother of NAPOLEON I. He participated in the Italian campaign (1797) and later served as diplomat for the First Republic of France. Napoleon made him king of Naples (1806). After Napoleon's defeat at Waterloo, he resided in the USA (1815–32).

Bonaparte, Louis (1778–1846) King of Holland (1806–10), brother of NAPOLEON I and father of NAPOLEON III. He accompanied his brother in the Italian and Egyptian campaigns, became a general (1804) and governor of Paris (1805). Forced by Napoleon to assume the Dutch throne, he worked to restore its economy and welfare, but the French Continental System proved ruinous to Dutch trade. Napoleon felt he was too lenient and the conflict led Louis to abdicate.

Bonaparte, Napoleon *See* NAPOLEON I

Bonar Law, Andrew *See* LAW, (ANDREW) BONAR

bond Promissory note guaranteeing the repayment of a specific amount of money on a particular date at a particular fixed rate of interest. Bonds may be issued by corporations, states, cities, or the federal government. The quality of the bond, and the interest rate paid on it, is determined by the period of the outstanding loan and the risk involved. Thus the US federal government normally pays a lower rate of interest than cities because US bonds are relatively risk-free. Bonds pay out fixed amounts of interest on a regular basis and appeal to investors seeking a regular income.

Bond, Edward (1935–) English playwright. Bond's early works, such as *Saved* (1965), were controversial in their use of violent imagery. *Early Morning* (1968) was the last play to be banned in the UK by the Lord Chamberlain. Other major plays include *Lear* (1971) and *War Plays* (1985). He has also written several film scripts, including *Blow Up* (1966).

Bondfield, Margaret Grace (1873–1953) English Labour politician and trade unionist. In 1923 she became chairman of the TRADES UNION CONGRESS (TUC) and entered Parliament. As minister of labour (1923–31), Bondfield was the first British woman to hold cabinet office.

bone CONNECTIVE TISSUE that forms the skeleton of the body, protects its internal organs, serves as a lever during locomotion and when lifting objects, and stores calcium and phosphorus. Bone is composed of a strong, compact layer of COLLAGEN (tough protein) and calcium phosphate and a lighter, porous inner spongy layer containing MARROW, in which ERYTHROCYTES (red blood cells) and some LEUCOCYTES (white blood cells) are produced.

bone china Hard-paste PORCELAIN, consisting of kaolin, china stone, and bone ash. Josiah SPODE perfected the manufacture of bone china in the 19th century and was largely responsible for its popularity.

Bonhoeffer, Dietrich (1906–45) German theologian. A Lutheran pastor, he opposed the rise of fascism in Germany. Arrested by the Nazis in 1943, he was executed for treason after documents linked him with a failed conspiracy to assassinate Adolf Hitler in 1944. Among his works

are the posthumously published *Letters from Prison* (1953) and *Christology* (1966).

Boniface, Saint (*c.*675–754?) English missionary. In 716 he left England to convert the pagan Germans. For his success, Boniface received the Archbishopric of Mainz in 751. In 754 he was martyred by pagans in Friesland. He is buried in Fulda, Bavaria, and is venerated as the Apostle of Germany. His feast day is June 5.

Boniface VIII (1235–1303) Pope (1294–1303), b. Benedetto Gaetani. To bring order to Rome and prevent schism, he imprisoned his predecessor Celestine V. He offered the first plenary indulgence (1300) for all who made a pilgrimage to Rome.

bonito Speedy, streamlined tuna-like fish found in all warm and temperate waters, usually in schools. Bonitos are blue, black and silver. They are highly valued as food and game fish. The ocean bonito (*Katsuwonus pelamis*) is also called skipjack tuna or bluefin. Family Scombridae.

Bonn City and capital of former West Germany on the River Rhine, North Rhine-Westphalia, W Germany. Founded in the 1st century AD as a Roman military establishment, it later became the seat of the electors of Cologne (1238–1797) and was awarded to Prussia by the Congress of Vienna (1815). Bonn was capital of West Germany from 1949 until German reunification in 1990. Sights include a Romanesque cathedral and the Poppelsdorf Palace. Beethoven was born here. Industries: engineering, laboratory equipment. Pop. (1999) 304,100.

Bonnard, Pierre (1867–1947) French painter and graphic artist. Together with his friend, Jean-Edouard Vuillard, he adapted the traditions of IMPRESSIONISM to create a repertoire of sensuous domestic interiors. Known as *intimiste*, his paintings are drenched in gorgeous colours and generate an atmosphere of exuberant well-being. Examples include *The Terrasse Family*, *Luncheon* (1922), and *Martha in a Red Blouse* (1928).

Bonnie Prince Charlie *See* STUART, CHARLES EDWARD

bonsai Japanese art of dwarfing woody plants and shrubs by pruning and restraining root growth; they are primarily outdoor plants and occur naturally in cliff areas. This art, which has been practised for centuries in the Far East, is most successful with plants that have a substantial tapering trunk, naturally twisted branches and small leaves. Bonsai can be 5–60cm (2–24in) tall, depending on the plant used.

Bonus Army (1932) Group of unemployed veterans who marched on Washington, D.C., and demanded cash payment of bonus certificates. The 17,000 veterans camped out during June and July until President Herbert HOOVER sent regular troops, led by Douglas MACARTHUR, to disperse them. In 1936, the veterans were given cashable bonds.

boogie-woogie Type of JAZZ popular in the 1930s. It has a rapid, driving beat, uses BLUES themes and is generally played on the piano. The melody is played over a consistently repeated bass motif played by the left hand.

book Primarily a bound volume of printed pages, it may also be a division within a book (as in the BIBLE) or a statement of accounts. The earliest books were Egyptian writings on papyrus scrolls, of which the BOOK OF THE DEAD is the most famous. Roman books were mostly in the form of rolled scrolls, although the later Roman period also saw the emergence of the codex – the forerunner of the paged book. Early monasteries developed the form. In the Middle Ages a fine parchment made from calfskin, vellum, became the standard material for books. By the 15th century they were often written on paper. Modern printed books date to *c.*1454, when GUTENBERG conceived of using moveable type in conjunction with early forms of the PRINTING press. Movable type had been independently invented earlier in China and Korea but did not cause a similar revolution there. The first printed book was a German Latin Bible (1455).

Booker Prize British literary prize. The Booker is the most prestigious award for new English-language novels published by UK, Commonwealth or Irish writers. The annual award generates much media attention, controversy and increased sales for short-listed writers. Recipients of the prize, first presented in 1969, have included Kazuo ISHIGURO, Iris MURDOCH, V.S. NAIPAUL and Pat BARKER. In 1993 Salman RUSHDIE's *Midnight's Children* won the 'Booker of Bookers'.

book-keeping Regular and systematic recording in ledgers of the amounts of money involved in business transactions. These records provide the basis for accountancy.

Book of Changes (I Ching) Ancient Chinese book of wisdom. Although the oldest parts of the text are thought to pre-date CONFUCIUS, he is credited with the commentaries that form a part of the collection.

Book of Common Prayer *See* COMMON PRAYER, BOOK OF

book of hours Book containing the prescribed order of prayers, rites for the canonical hours and readings from the Bible. Such books, developed in the 1300s, were often lavishly decorated by miniaturists and served as status symbols. The most celebrated book of hours to survive is the *Très Riches Heures du Duc de Berry* (1413–15), illustrated in part by the LIMBOURG brothers.

Book of Kells Illuminated manuscript of the four GOSPELS in Latin. Probably begun in the late 8th century at the Irish monastery of Iona, which later migrated to Kells, County Meath, Ireland, its intricate illumination and superb penmanship have earned it the epithet of 'the most beautiful book in the world'. After its collation in 1621 by James Usher, it was presented to Trinity College, Dublin, where it has remained.

Book of the Dead Collection of Old Egyptian texts probably dating from the 16th century BC. The papyrus texts, which exist in many different versions and incorporate mortuary texts from as early as 2350 BC were placed in the tombs of the dead in order to help them combat the dangers of the afterlife.

Boole, George (1815–64) English mathematician. Largely self-taught, he was appointed (1849) professor of mathematics of Cork University. He is best-known for his invention of Boolean algebra, a set of symbols which can be manipulated to represent logical operations. It is mostly used in COMPUTERS.

boomslang Venomous snake of the African savannas. It is green or brown with a slender body and a small head. Commonly found in trees or bushes, it lies in wait for lizards and birds, often with the front of its body extended motionless in mid-air. Length: to 1.5m (4.9ft). Species *Dispholidus typus*.

Boone, Daniel (1734–1820) US frontier pioneer. In 1775 he blazed the famous Wilderness Road from Virginia to Kentucky, and founded the settlement of Boonesborough. The Shawnee captured Boone during the American Revolution, but he escaped and reached Boonesborough in time to prevent it falling to the British and their Native American allies.

Booth, John Wilkes (1838–65) US actor and assassin of Abraham LINCOLN. He was a Confederate sympathizer. On April 14, 1865, during a performance at Ford's Theater, Washington, D.C., he shot Lincoln, who died the next day. Booth escaped but was either shot, or killed himself, two weeks later.

Booth, William (1829–1912) English religious leader, founder and first general of the SALVATION ARMY. A Methodist revivalist, he preached regularly at the Methodist New Connection from 1852 to 1861. He started his own revivalist movement, which undertook evangelistic and social work among the poor. Named the Salvation Army in 1878, the movement gradually spread to many countries. On his death, Booth was succeeded by his son William Bramwell Booth.

bootlegging Illegal supply and sale of goods that are subject to government prohibition or taxation. Bootleg also refers to unlicensed copies of goods that are packaged to deceive the buyer into thinking they are the original. The name is said to derive from the practice of American frontiersmen who carried bottles of illicit liquor in the tops of their boots. In its original sense, bootlegging blossomed during the PROHIBITION era in the USA (1920–33), increasing government corruption and helping fuel the rise of organised crime.

borage Hairy, annual plant native to s Europe. It has rough, oblong leaves and drooping clusters of pale blue flowers, and is cultivated as a food and flavouring. Height: up to 60cm (2ft). Family Boraginaceae; species *Borago officinalis*.

borax The most common borate mineral (hydrated sodium borate, $Na_2B_4O_7.10H_2O$), used to make heat-resistant glass, pottery glaze, water softeners in washing powders, fertilizers, and pharmaceuticals. It is found in large deposits in dried-up alkaline lakes in arid regions as crusts or masses of crystals. It may be colourless or white, transparent or opaque.

Bordeaux City and port on the River Garonne; capital of Gironde department, sw France. There is an 11th-century Gothic cathedral, a university (1441), and many fine 18th-century buildings – a period when the slave trade brought considerable prosperity. Bordeaux is a good, deepwater inland port and serves an area famous for its fine wines and brandies. Industries: shipbuilding, oil refining, pharmaceuticals, flour, textiles, glass. Pop. (2000) 754,000.

Borders Region of SE Scotland; its s boundary forms the border between Scotland and England. The administrative centre is Newtown St Boswells, other towns include Hawick and Jedburgh. The rivers Tweed and Teviot flow E through Borders and meet near Kelso. The Cheviot Hills forms most of its s border, and the Southern Uplands its E border with STRATHCLYDE and DUMFRIES AND GALLOWAY. Livestock farming and forestry are the major economic activities. Due to its strategic location it was the scene of many battles between the English and the Scots. Area: 4714sq km (1820sq mi). Pop. (2001 est.) 106,950.

boreal forest Wooded zone of northern latitudes with a cold dry climate and a poor sandy soil. It consists primarily of conifers and stretches like a broad ribbon across the Northern Hemisphere. Its northern edge is bordered by frozen tundra.

Borg, Björn (1956–) Swedish tennis player. The dominant player in the late 1970s, Borg won five consecutive men's singles titles at Wimbledon (1976–80). He also helped Sweden win its first Davis Cup (1975). He retired in 1983.

Borges, Jorge Luis (1899–1986) Argentinian short-story writer, poet, and critic. Borges is best known for his short-story collections *Dreamtigers* (1960), *The Book of Imaginary Beings* (1967) and *Dr Brodie's Report* (1970). Dream-like and poetic, they established Borges as one of the most significant figures in 20th-century fiction. Often using intellectual puzzles, they dramatize the extreme difficulty of achieving knowledge,

Borghese Italian princely family, originally of Siena, later Rome. Camillo Borghese (1552–1621) became Pope as Paul V in 1605. Another Camillo (1775–1832) married Marie Pauline Bonaparte, the sister of NAPOLEON I, and was made Governor of Piedmont.

Borgia, Cesare (1475–1507) Italian general and political figure, brother of Lucrezia BORGIA. He was made a cardinal (1493) by his father, Pope Alexander VI, but forsook the Church to embark on a military campaign (1498–1503) to establish his dominion in central Italy. His ruthless campaigns lend credence to the theory that he was the model for Machiavelli's *The Prince*. His political fortunes collapsed with Alexander's death (1503). Imprisoned by Pope Julius II, he escaped to Spain, where he was killed in battle.

Borgia, Lucrezia (1480–1519) Daughter of Pope Alexander VI and sister of Cesare BORGIA. Her marriage to Giovanni Sforza (1493) was annulled by Alexander in 1497 when it failed to produce anticipated political advantages. Her marriage to Alfonso, nephew of Alfonso II of Naples, ended with Alfonso's murder (1500) by Cesare's henchman. After the collapse of Borgia aspirations in 1503, she forsook the political intrigue for which she was notorious and lived quietly, a patron of art, at Ferrara with her third husband, Alfonso d'Este.

Borglum, (John) Gutzon (1867–1941) US sculptor. From a six-ton marble block he fashioned a head of Abraham Lincoln, which now stands in the Capitol rotunda in Washington, D.C. His last and most exacting project was to carve the heads of George Washington, Thomas Jefferson, Abraham Lincoln and Theodore Roosevelt in a rock face at MOUNT RUSHMORE, South Dakota. The final details were completed by his son.

boric acid (boracic acid) Soft, white crystalline solid (H_3BO_3) that occurs naturally in certain volcanic hot springs. It is used as a metallurgical flux, preservative, mild antiseptic, insecticide for ants and cockroaches, and to manufacture heat-resistant glass and enamels.

Born, Max (1882–1970) German-British physicist. He was professor of physics at Göttingen University from 1921 but left Germany in 1933, teaching at the universities of Cambridge (1933–36) and Edinburgh (1936–53). He returned to Germany in 1954. For his work in QUANTUM MECHANICS, he shared the 1954 Nobel Prize in physics with Walther BOTHE.

INTERNET

Borges, Jorge Luis
▶ www.themodernword.com/borges

B

▲ **Borobudur** One of the world's greatest Buddhist shrines, Borobudur was built in about the middle of the 9th century to a unique plan involving colossal resources; 570,000cu m (2 million cu ft) of stone were moved from a river bed, dressed, positioned, and carved with countless spouts, urns and other embellishments. The walls are covered with reliefs relating to Buddhist doctrine and there are altogether 504 shrines with seated Buddhas.

▶ **Bosch** A detail of the "Hell" section of The Garden of Earthly Delights. The triptych by Hieronymus Bosch shows the surreal nature of his work. Among his patrons was the devout Catholic Philip II of Spain, and it is thought that Bosch's work was to serve as a warning against sin.

Borneo Island in the Malay Archipelago, 640km (400mi) E of Singapore, SE Asia. Mostly undeveloped, Borneo is the world's third-largest island. It consists of four political regions: SARAWAK (W) and SABAH (N) are states of Malaysia; BRUNEI (NW) is a former British protectorate; KALIMANTAN (E central and S) covers 70% of the island and forms part of Indonesia. Industries: timber, fishing, oil and coal extraction. Area: 743,330sq km (287,000sq mi).

Borobudur Ruins of a Buddhist monument in Central JAVA, built c.850, under the Sailendra dynasty. It comprises a stupa (relic mound), mandalas (ritual diagrams) and the temple mountain, all forms of Indian GUPTA DYNASTY religious art.

Borodin, Alexander Porfirevich (1833–87) Russian composer and chemist, one of the RUSSIAN FIVE group of composers. His most popular works include the tone poem *In the Steppes of Central Asia* (1880) and the 'Polovtsian Dances' from his opera *Prince Igor* (completed after his death by GLAZUNOV and RIMSKY-KORSAKOV).

boron (symbol B) Nonmetallic element of group III of the PERIODIC TABLE, first isolated in 1808 by English chemist Sir Humphry DAVY. It occurs in several minerals, notably kernite (its chief ore) and BORAX. It has two allotropes: **amorphous** boron is an impure brown powder; **metallic** boron is a black to silver-grey hard crystalline material. It is used in semiconductor devices and the stable isotope B^{10} is a good neutron absorber, used in nuclear reactors and particle counters. Properties: at.no. 5; r.a.m. 10.81; r.d. 2.34 (cryst.), 2.37 (amorph.); m.p. 2079°C (3774°F); sublimes 2550°C (4622°F); most common isotope B^{11} (80.22%).

Borromini, Francesco (1599–1667) Italian BAROQUE architect. Borromini was the most inventive figure of the three masters of Roman baroque (the others were BERNINI and Pietro da Cortona). His hallmark was a dynamic hexagonal design based on intersecting equilateral triangles and circles, such as the spectacular Sant'Ivo della Sapienza (begun 1642). His masterpieces include San Carlo alle Quattro Fontane (1638–41) and Sant'Agnese in Piazza Navona (1653–55).

borzoi (Russian wolfhound) Keen-sighted, speedy hunting DOG. It has a long, narrow head and powerful jaws. The body is deep and streamlined, with long legs and curved tail. The coat is long and silky, and is usually white with darker markings. Height: (at shoulder) up to 79cm (31in).

Bosch, Hieronymus (c.1450–1516) Flemish painter, b. Jerome van Aken in Hertogenbosch. His paintings of grotesque and fantastic visions based on religious themes led to accusations of heresy, but greatly influenced 20th-century SURREALISM. The majority of his pictures explore the distressing consequences of human sin: innocent figures are besieged by horrifying physical torments. About 40 examples of his work survive, but his most famous works are *The Temptation of St Anthony*, *The Garden of Earthly Delights* (often considered his masterpiece), and the *Adoration of the Magi*.

Bose, Satyendranath (1894–1974) Indian physicist and mathematician who contributed to the theory of QUANTUM MECHANICS and STATISTICAL MECHANICS. Bose made the initial advances to describe the statistical properties of certain ELEMENTARY PARTICLES (now called BOSONS). These particles all have the property that any number of them can occupy the same quantum state: that is they do not obey Enrico FERMI's EXCLUSION PRINCIPLE. Bose's work was developed by EINSTEIN and the statistics that such particles obey are called **Bose-Einstein statistics**.

Bosnia-Herzegovina Balkan republic in SE Europe. *See* country feature

boson ELEMENTARY PARTICLE that has an integer SPIN. Named after the Indian physicist Satyendranath BOSE, bosons are those particles not covered by the EXCLUSION PRINCIPLE which says no two electrons in an atom can have the same energy and spin. This means that the number of bosons occupying the same quantum state is not restricted. Bosons are force-transmitting particles, such as PHOTONS and gluons (the particles that hold QUARKS together). *See also* FERMION

Bosporus (Karadeniz Bogazi) Narrow strait joining the Sea of Marmara with the Black Sea, and separating European and Asiatic Turkey. It is an important strategic and commercial waterway, controlled by the Turks since 1452, and refortified after the Montreux Convention of 1936. Length: 30km (19mi).

Boston State capital and seaport of Massachusetts, USA, at the mouth of the Charles River, on Massachusetts Bay. Founded in 1630, it became a Puritan stronghold and the scene of several incidents leading to the outbreak of the American Revolution. A religious and cultural centre, Boston is the home of many important educational establishments. Harvard University and the Massachusetts Institute of Technology (MIT) are situated nearby. Industries: publishing, banking and insurance, shipbuilding, electronics, fishing, clothing. Pop. (2000) 4,032,000.

Boston Massacre (1770) Riot by American colonists, angered over the quartering of troops in private homes. Starting with some snowballing, it was put down by British soldiers and resulted in the death of five civilians, including Crispus Attucks. The riot was exploited for anti-British propaganda by Samuel ADAMS and the Boston radicals. The soldiers were tried for murder, defended by John Adams, and acquitted.

Boston Tea Party (1773) Protest by a group of Massachusetts colonists, disguised as Mohawks and led by Samuel ADAMS, against the Tea Act and, more generally, against "taxation without representation". The Tea Act (1773), passed by the British Parliament, withdrew duty on tea exported to the colonies. It enabled the EAST INDIA COMPANY to sell tea directly to the colonies without first going to Britain and resulted in colonial merchants being undersold. The protesters boarded three British ships and threw their cargo of tea into Boston harbour. The British retaliated by closing the harbour.

Boswell, James (1740–95) Scottish biographer and writer. As a young man, he travelled widely in Europe, meeting VOLTAIRE and Jean-Jacques ROUSSEAU. An inveterate hero-worshipper, Boswell found his vocation as the

friend and biographer of Samuel JOHNSON. His monumental *Life of Samuel Johnson* (1791) is regarded not only as his masterpiece but also one of the greatest biographies in English. Boswell's other works include *An Account of Corsica* (1768) and *The Journal of a Tour to the Hebrides* (1785), an account of his travels with Johnson. *See also* BIOGRAPHY

Bosworth Field English battleground, near Leicester, England, where RICHARD III was defeated by Henry Tudor (1485). Henry, who claimed to represent the Lancastrian royal house, which had competed with the Yorkists during the Wars of the ROSES, invaded England from France. Richard was killed, and Henry claimed the throne as HENRY VII.

botanical garden Large, garden preserve for display, research and teaching purposes. Wild and cultivated plants from all climates are maintained. The first botanical gardens were established during the Middle Ages. In the 16th century, gardens existed in Pisa, Bologna, Padua, and Leiden. Aromatic and medicinal herbs still exist in the Botanical Garden of Padua. The first US botanical garden was established by John Bartram in Philadelphia in 1728. Famous botanical gardens include the Royal Botanical Gardens in Kew, near London (1759), the Botanical Gardens of Berlin-Dahlem (1646), and the Botanical Gardens in Schönbrunn, Vienna (1753).

botany Study of PLANTS and ALGAE, including their classification, structure, physiology, reproduction, and evolution. The discipline used to be studied in two halves: lower (non-flowering) plants, which included the algae (now in the kingdom Protoctista), MOSS and FERNS; and higher (seed-bearing) plants, including most flowers, trees and shrubs.

Botany Bay Large, shallow inlet immediately s of Port Jackson, Sydney Harbour, New South Wales, Australia. It was visited in 1700 by Captain James COOK, who named it because of its flora. It is fed by the Georges and Woronora rivers, and is *c.*1.6km (1mi) wide at its mouth.

botfly Any of several families of stout, hairy, black-and-white to grey fly. Its larvae are parasites that feed on livestock, small animals and even humans. Eggs are laid on the host and the larvae cause damage to the skin or internal systems. The botfly that attacks deer is believed to be the world's swiftest insect, flying at 80km/h (50mph). Order Diptera; family Oestridae.

Botha, Louis (1862–1919) South African politician and military leader. During the SOUTH AFRICAN WAR (1899–1902), Botha was an outstanding commander and led the Transvaal delegation at the peace conference. A moderate, he advocated reconciliation with the British, and in 1910 became first prime minister of the Union of SOUTH AFRICA.

Botha, P.W. (Pieter Willem) (1916–2006) South African statesman. The longest-serving member of the APARTHEID regime, he entered parliament in 1948. As defence minister (1966–78), he increased South Africa's armed forces and was responsible for the military involvement in Angola. He became prime minister (1978) and undertook limited reform of apartheid, adopting a new, racial constitution which still excluded the black majority. In 1980 he established the Southwest Africa Territorial Force, as part of a destabilization policy of South Africa's neighbours. He became the state's first president (1980) and was re-elected in 1987. In 1989 he suffered a stroke and, amid increasing National party factionalism, resigned and was replaced by the more reform-minded F.W. DE KLERK.

Botham, Sir Ian Terence (1955–) English cricketer. He made his county debut for Somerset in 1974, and made his test debut in 1977. In 1979 he became the first player to score a century and take ten wickets in a test, and in 1981 he almost single-handedly helped England regain the Ashes.

Bothe, Walther Wilhelm Georg Franz (1891–1957) German physicist. During World War 2, Bothe worked on Germany's nuclear energy project and built its first cyclotron. He shared the 1954 Nobel Prize in physics with Max BORN for his development of the coincidence method, which can detect two particles emitted simultaneously from the same nucleus during radioactive decay.

Bo tree (Bodhi tree) In BUDDHISM, the pipal under which BUDDHA found enlightenment at Bodh Gaya, near Varanasi, N India. A pipal at Anuradhapura, N Sri Lanka, is said to have grown from a cutting taken from the original tree by Ashoka in the 3rd century BC. Family Moraceae; species *Ficus religiosa*.

Botswana Landlocked republic in s Africa; the capital is GABORONE. *see* country feature.

Botticelli, Sandro (1444–1510) (Alessandro di Mariano Filipepi) Florentine RENAISSANCE painter. Loved by the PRE-RAPHAELITE BROTHERHOOD and an important influence on ART NOUVEAU, he was part of a late 15th-century movement which admired the ornamental, linear qualities of Gothic painting. Botticelli is best known for his mythological allegories, *Primavera* (*c.*1478), *The Birth of Venus* and *Pallas and the Centaur*. He was one of the few to decorate the Sistine Chapel in Rome (1481) and, at the height of his career, was the most popular painter in Florence. He made a series of delicate pen drawings for a copy of Dante's *Divine Comedy*. From 1500, his style was superseded by the inspired naturalism of LEONARDO DA VINCI.

botulism Rare, but potentially lethal, form of food-poisoning caused by a toxin produced by the bacterium *Clostridium botulinum*. The toxin attacks the nervous system, causing paralysis and cessation of breathing. Botulinum toxin (Botox) is used medicinally as a treatment for some neuromuscular disorders and in plastic surgery.

Boucher, François (1703–70) French painter, decorator, and engraver. His style was the epitome of ROCOCO frivolity and was distinctly risqué in tone. He was immensely successful and widely imitated. He produced more than 11,000 historical, mythological, genre, and landscape paintings. Boucher became director of the GOBELINS tapestry works (1755), and was also First Painter to LOUIS XV.

Boucicault, Dion (Dionysius Lardner) (*c.*1822–90) Anglo-Irish playwright and actor-manager. He was responsible for the development of the touring company. A prolific dramatist, Boucicault wrote and adapted nearly 300 plays. The most successful were his comedies and romantic melodramas, such as *London Assurance* (1841) and *The Octoroon* (1859). He was one of the greatest figures of Victorian theatre.

Bougainville Volcanic island in the sw Pacific Ocean, E of New Guinea; a territory of PAPUA NEW GUINEA. It was

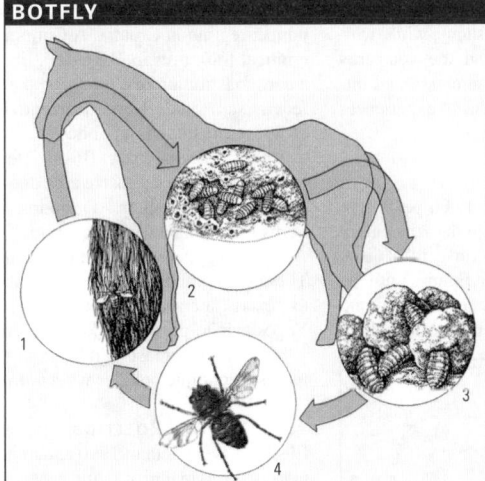

BOTFLY

The families of botflies (Cuterebridae, Oestridae, and Gaterophilidae) are parasitic on humans, sheep and horses. The life cycle of the common horse botfly (*Gasterophilus intestinalis*) begins (1) as eggs are glued by the adult to the hairs, usually on the front legs of the horse. The stimulus of the moisture and friction provided by the horse's tongue when cleaning itself near the eggs causes the larvae to emerge and attach themselves to the animal's tongue and lips. The larvae pass to the stomach (2) where they attach themselves to the walls. The fully developed larvae release their hold on the walls and pass out with excrement (3). The larvae pupate in the ground and emerge as adults (4).

discovered in 1768 by Louis de BOUGAINVILLE. The island was under German control from 1884, and then under Australian administration after 1914. It was occupied by Japan occupation in WW2. It was torn by guerrilla warfare in the 1980s and 90s. Kieta is the chief port. Industries: copper mining, copra, cocoa, timber. Area: 10,049sq km (3880sq mi). Pop. (2002 est.) 204,800.

Bougainville, Louis Antoine de (1729–1811) French maritime explorer. A veteran of the French and Indian Wars, a diplomat, mathematician and soldier, he commanded the frigate *La Boudeuse* on the first French voyage around the world (1766–69). It included a long interlude in TAHITI, which, among other Pacific islands, he claimed for France. Important botanical and astronomical studies were made during the voyage, of which Bougainville published an account in 1771–72.

bougainvillea Tropical, flowering woody vine native to s America, often grown as a garden plant in warm climates. Its flowers have showy purple or red bracts. It was named after the French explorer Louis de BOUGAINVILLE. Family Nyctaginaceae; genus *Bougainvillea*.

Boulanger, Nadia (1887–1979) French music teacher. One of the foremost teachers of composition in the 20th century. her pupils included Aaron Copland, Darius Milhaud and Jean Fran-

çaix. In the 1930s, she became the first woman to conduct the Boston Symphony Orchestra and the New York Philharmonic.

Boulez, Pierre (1925–) French conductor and composer. Influenced by Olivier MESSIAEN and Anton von WEBERN, he aimed to extend serialism into all aspects of a composition, including rhythm and dynamics. His works for voice and orchestra have received much attention, especially *Le Marteau sans maître* (1954) and *Pli selon pli* (1960). Renowned for conducting complex 20th-century works, Boulez became director of the French Institute for Acoustic and Musical Research (IRCAM) in 1975.

Boulle (Buhl), André Charles (1642–1732) French cabinet-maker, one of a number of skilled craftsmen maintained in the Louvre Palace by LOUIS XIV to design for the court. Boulle created a distinctive marquetry of tortoise-shell and gilded brass, to which he gave his name.

Boult, Sir Adrian (1889–1983) English conductor, widely known for his interpretation of early 20th-century English composers, such as Elgar, Holst and Vaughan Williams. He was musical director and principal conductor of the BBC Symphony Orchestra (1930–50).

Bounty, Mutiny on the (April 28, 1789) British mutiny that took place near Tonga in the South Pacific Ocean.

BOSNIA-HERZEGOVINA

Bosnia-Herzegovina is one of the five republics to emerge from the former Federal People's Republic of Yugoslavia. Much of the country is mountainous or hilly, with an arid limestone plateau in the sw. The River Sava, which forms most of the N border with Croatia, is a tributary of the River Danube. Because of the country's odd shape, the coastline is limited to a short stretch of 20km [13mi] on the Adriatic coast.

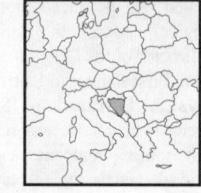

CLIMATE
The coast benefits from a Mediterranean climate. Summers are dry and sunny, while winters are moist and mild. Inland, the weather is more severe, with hot, dry summers and bitterly cold, snowy winters. The N experiences the most severe weather.

HISTORY
SLAVS settled in the region *c*.1,400 years ago. Bosnia was settled by Serbs in the 7th century and conquered by Ottoman Turks in 1463. It remained part of the Ottoman Empire until the 19th century. The persistence of serfdom into the 19th century led to a peasant revolt in

1875. In 1878, the AUSTRO-HUNGARIAN EMPIRE gained temporary control over Bosnia-Herzegovina at the Congress of Berlin, and it formally took over the area in 1908. The assassination of Archduke FRANZ FERDINAND of Austria-Hungary in Sarajevo in June 1914 was the catalyst for the start of World War 1. In 1918, Bosnia-Herzegovina was annexed by SERBIA as part of the Kingdom of the Serbs, Croats and Slovenes, renamed Yugoslavia in 1929. Germany occupied the region during World War 2, and Bosnia-Herzegovina came under a puppet regime in Croatia. A Communist government took over in Yugoslavia in 1945 and a new constitution in 1946 made the country a federal state, with Bosnia-Herzegovina as one of its six constituent republics.

Under Communism, Bosnia-Herzegovina was a potentially explosive area due to its mix of Bosnian Muslims, Orthodox Christian Serbs and Roman Catholic Croats, as well as Albanian, gypsy and Ukrainian minorities. These ethnic and religious differences started to exert themselves after the death of Yugoslavia's president Josip Broz Tito in 1980, among increasing indications that Communist economic policies were not working.

POLITICS
Elections were held in 1990 and non-Communists won a majority, with a Muslim, Alija IZETBEGOVIC, as president. In 1991, Croatia and Slovenia declared themselves independent republics and seceded from Yugoslavia. Bosnia-Herzegovina held a referendum on independence in 1992. Most Bosnian Serbs boycotted the vote, but Muslims and Croats voted in favour and Bosnia-Herzegovina proclaimed its independence. War then broke out.

At first, the Muslim-dominated government allied itself uneasily with the Croat minority, but it was at once under attack by local Serbs, supported by their co-nationals from beyond Bosnia-Herzegovina's borders. In their 'ethnic cleansing' campaign, heavily

AREA 51,197sq km [19,767sq mi]
POPULATION 4,552,000
CAPITAL (POPULATION) Sarajevo (529,000)
GOVERNMENT Federal republic
ETHNIC GROUPS Bosnian 48%, Serb 37%, Croat 14%
LANGUAGES Bosnian, Serbian, Croatian
RELIGIONS Islam 40%, Serbian Orthodox 31%, Roman Catholic 15%, others 14%
CURRENCY Convertible marka = 100 convertible pfenniga

equipped Serb militias drove poorly-armed Muslims from towns they had long inhabited. By early 1993, the Muslims controlled less than a third of the former federal republic. Even the capital, SARAJEVO, became disputed territory suffering constant shelling.

The Muslim-Croat alliance rapidly disintegrated and a million people became refugees. Tougher economic sanctions on Serbia in April 1993 had little effect on the war in Bosnia. A small UN force attempted to deliver relief supplies to civilians and maintain 'safe' Muslim areas to no avail.

In 1995, the warring parties agreed to a solution to the conflict, the Dayton Peace Accord. The country was split into two self-governing provinces, one Bosnian Serb and the other Muslim-Croat, under a central, unified, multi-ethnic government. A NATO-led force helped stabilize the country. European forces took over in 2004, and began to leave in 2007 as stability returned and the new government became stronger.

ECONOMY
The economy of Bosnia-Herzegovina was shattered by the war in the early 1990s. Manufactures include electrical equipment, machinery and transport equipment, and textiles. Farm products include fruits, maize, tobacco, vegetables and wheat, but the country has to import food.

Fletcher Christian led a rebellion against Captain William BLIGH. Christian and the mutineers founded a colony on Pitcairn Island.

Bourbons European dynastic family, descendants of the CAPETIANS. The ducal title was created in 1327, and continued until 1527. A cadet branch, the Bourbon-Vendôme line, won the kingdom of Navarre. The Bourbons ruled France from 1589 (when Henry of Navarre became HENRY IV) until the FRENCH REVOLUTION (1789). Two members of the family, LOUIS XVIII and CHARLES X, reigned after the restoration of the monarchy In 1700 the Bourbons became the ruling family of Spain, when PHILIP V (grandson of LOUIS XIV of France) assumed the throne. His descendants continued to rule Spain until the declaration of the Second Republic (1931). JUAN CARLOS I, a Bourbon, was restored to the Spanish throne in 1975.

bourgeoisie (middle class) Term originally applied to artisans and craftsmen who lived in medieval French towns. Up to the late 18th century it was a propertied but relatively unprivileged class, often of urban merchants and tradesmen, who helped speed the decline of the feudal system. The 19th-century advent of CAPITALISM led to the expansion of the bourgeoisie and its division into the high (industrialists and financiers) and petty (tradesmen, clerical workers) bourgeoisie.

Bourguiba, Habib (1903–2000) First president of Tunisia (1957–87). In 1934, Bourguiba founded the nationalist Neo-Destour Party. He began negotiations that culminated in Tunisian independence in 1956. In 1975 he was proclaimed president-for-life. Bourguiba maintained a pro-French, autocratic rule until, overthrown in a coup led by Ben Ali.

Bourke-White, Margaret (1906–71) US photo-journalist She produced dramatic photo-essays for *Time, Life,* and *Fortune* magazines on a variety of subjects, including the rural South of the 1930s, World War 2, concentration-camp victims, the Korean War, South Africa, and India.

Boutros-Ghali, Boutros (1922–) Egyptian politician, sixth secretary-general (1992–96) of the UNITED NATIONS (UN). As Egypt's foreign affairs minister (1977–91), he was involved in Middle East peace negotiations. He was briefly prime minister of Egypt (1991–92), before becoming the first African secretary-general of the UN. In his term he faced civil-war crises in the Balkans, Somalia, and Rwanda. Fiercely independent, Boutros-Ghali managed to alienate US opinion and was blamed for the failure of UN peacekeeping in Somalia and Bosnia.

bovine spongiform encephalopathy (BSE) In cattle, degeneration of the brain caused by PRIONS, transmitted by feeding infected meat. It is also known as 'mad cow disease'. *See also* CREUTZFELDT-JAKOB DISEASE (CJD)

bowerbird Forest bird of New Guinea and Australia. The male builds a simple but brightly ornamented bower to attract the female. After mating, the female lays one to

▲ **bowerbird** The tooth-billed bowerbird (*Scenopoeetes dentirostris*) is found in NE Australia. The male builds a nest as part of a courtship ritual.

INTERNET

Boutros-Ghali, Boutros
▶ www.un.org/Overview/SG/sg6bio.html

BOTSWANA

The Republic of Botswana is a landlocked country that lies in the heart of s Africa. The majority of the land is flat or gently rolling, with an average height of about 1,000m [3,280ft]. More hilly country lies in the E. The KALAHARI, a semi-desert area, covers much of Botswana.

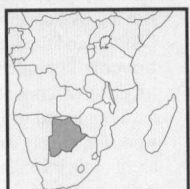

Most of the s has no permanent streams, but large depressions occur in the N. In one, the Okavango River – which flows from Angola – forms a large delta, an area of swampland. Another depression contains the Makgadikgadi Salt Pans. During floods, the Botletle River drains from the Okavango Swamps into the Makgadikgadi Salt Pans.

CLIMATE
Temperatures are high during the summer, which runs from October to April, but the winter months are much cooler. Night-time temperatures in winter sometimes drop below freezing. The average rainfall ranges from over 400mm [16in] in the E to less than 200mm [8in] in the sw.

Gaborone, the capital of Botswana, lies in the wetter E part of the country, where the majority of the population lives. The rainy season occurs during summer, between the months of November and March. Frosts sometimes occur in parts of the E when temperature drops below freezing.

HISTORY
The earliest inhabitants of the region were the SAN, who are also called Bushmen. They had a nomadic way of life, hunting wild animals and collecting plant foods.

The Bantu-speaking Tswana, cattle owners, settled in E Botswana more than 1,000 years ago and now form the majority of the population. Their arrival displaced the San s into the Kalahari desert region. Today the San form a tiny minority, most of whom live in permanent settlements and work on cattle ranches. San land rights remain a contentious issue.

POLITICS
Britain ruled the area as the Bechuanaland Protectorate between 1885 and 1966. When the country became independent, it adopted the name of Botswana. Since then, unlike many African countries, Botswana has been a stable multiparty democracy.

The economy has undergone a steady process of diversification under successive presidents. Botswana's first president, Sir Seretse Khama, who died in 1980, was succeeded by Sir Ketumile Masire, who served from 1980 until 1998 when he retired in favour of Festus Mogae. Despite a severe drought, the economy expanded and the government introduced major social programmes. Tourism also grew as huge national parks and reserves were established.

By the early 2000s Botswana had one of the world's highest rates of HIV infection –

AREA 581,730sq km [224,606sq mi]
POPULATION 1,816,000
CAPITAL (POPULATION) Gaborone (186,000)
GOVERNMENT Multiparty republic
ETHNIC GROUPS Tswana (or Setswana) 79%, Kalanga 11%, Basarwa 3%, others
LANGUAGES English (official), Setswana
RELIGIONS Traditional beliefs 85%, Christianity 15%
CURRENCY Pula = 100 thebe

around one in five of the population had the virus. The average life expectancy fell to 40 years. Botswana does, however, have one of Africa's most progressive programmes in place to deal with the disease.

ECONOMY
In 1966 Botswana was one of Africa's poorest countries, depending on meat and live cattle for its exports. The discovery of minerals, including coal, cobalt, copper and nickel, has helped to diversify the economy. The mining of diamonds at Orapa started in 1971 and was the chief factor in the transformation of the economy. By 1997 Botswana had become the world's leading producer, overtaking Australia and the Democratic Republic of Congo. Diamonds accounted for about 74% of Botswana's exports, followed by copper-nickel matte, textiles and meat products. Another major source of income comes from tourists, the majority of whom come from South Africa, which continues to have a great influence on Botswana.

The development of mining and tourism has reduced the relative importance of farming, although agriculture still employs about a fifth of the population. The most important type of farming is livestock raising, particularly cattle, which are mostly reared in the wetter E. Crops include beans, maize, millet, sorghum and vegetables.

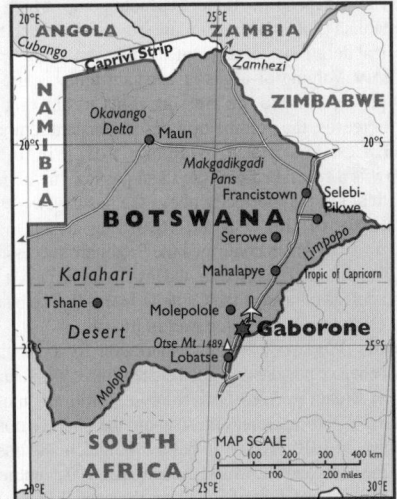

three eggs in a cup-shaped nest. Adults, mainly terrestrial, have short wings and legs, and variously coloured plumage. Length: 25–38cm (10–15in). Family Ptilonorhynchidae.

Bowie, David (1947–) British pop singer, b. David Jones. Fusing a bizarre theatricality and progressive pop, he graduated to international stardom with his album *Ziggy Stardust* (1972). His subsequent work has embraced many styles. Other albums include *Hunky Dory* (1972) and *Heroes* (1977). He made his film debut in *The Man Who Fell to Earth* (1976).

Bowie, Jim (James) (1796–1836) US frontiersman. He moved to Texas from Louisiana in 1828, and married the daughter of the Mexican vice-governor. By 1832 he had joined the US colonists who opposed the Mexican government. He was appointed a colonel in the Texas Army (1835), and was killed at the Alamo (1836).

bowling Indoor sport in which a ball is bowled at pins. An ancient game, it originated in Germany and was brought to the USA by Dutch immigrants in the 17th century. Known as ninepins, it soon became a popular gambling game and, when it was banned, a tenth pin was added to circumvent the law. Two players or teams bowl at pins set on a triangular base, scoring according to the number of pins knocked over.

bowls Game popular in Britain and Commonwealth countries, in which a series of bowls (woods) are delivered underarm to stop as close as possible to a small white target ball (jack). A point is scored for each bowl closer to the jack than the best opposition bowl.

box Evergreen tree or shrub found in tropical and temperate regions in Europe, North America and w Asia. The shrub is popular for TOPIARY, and box wood is used for musical instruments. The 100 species include English or common *Buxus sempervirens* and larger *Buxus balearica* that grows to 24m (80ft). Family *Buxaceae*.

boxer Smooth-haired working DOG bred originally in Germany. It has a broad head with a deep, short, square muzzle, and its deep-chested body is set on strong, medium-length legs. The tail is commonly docked, and its coat is generally red or brown, with black and white markings. Height: to 61cm (24in) at the shoulder.

Boxer Rebellion (1898–1900) Anti-western uprising in China. The OPIUM WARS resulted in greater European involvement in China. Defeat in the first of the SINO-JAPANESE WARS further weakened the Qing dynasty. In a bid to restore Manchu authority, the Empress Dowager CIXI supported the attempts of the Society of Righteous and Harmonious Fists (hence the 'Boxers') forcibly to remove Western influence from China. Nationwide attacks on foreigners and Chinese Christians left more than 200 dead. In June 1900, the Boxers began a two-month long siege of Beijing. An international expeditionary force relieved the foreign legations and suppressed the rising. China agreed to pay an indemnity.

boxing Sport of fist fighting between two people wearing padded gloves within a roped-off ring. Boxers are classified in eight divisions according to weight: minimumweight (under 48kg/105lb), fly, bantam, feather, light, welter, middle and heavyweight (more than 88kg/195lb). Professional bouts are scheduled for four to 15 rounds of three minutes' duration. A fight is controlled by a referee in the ring, and ends when there is a knock-down (a boxer is unable to get to his feet by a count of ten) or if one fighter is seriously injured. If both boxers finish the scheduled number of rounds, the winner is determined by a ringside referee or three judges. Boxing developed from bareknuckle fighting when the Marquess of Queensberry's rules introduced timed rounds and padded gloves in 1866. Despite worldwide popularity, boxing is under pressure to introduce further safety measures or be abolished, with brain damage, comas and deaths worryingly regular. The international sport is now controlled by three major rival organizations: the World Boxing Association (WBA), the World Boxing Council (WBC), and the International Boxing Federation (IBF).

boycott Refusal to deal with a person, organization or country, either in terms of trade or other activities, such as sport. The term originated in 1880, when Irish tenant farmers refused to work for, supply or speak with Captain Charles Boycott, an agent of their landlord. Boycotts can be powerful protest tools, if they have sufficient support. *See also* EMBARGO

Boycott, Geoffrey (1940–) English cricketer. He was captain of Yorkshire (1971–79). In 1971, Boycott became the first English batsman to average more than 100 runs in a first-class season. He played in 108 tests. His 8114 test runs for England is surpassed only by Graham Gooch and David Gower. In 1982 he was banned from test cricket after touring South Africa. Boycott is now a sports commentator for television.

Boyd, William (1952–) British novelist and short story writer, b. Ghana. His sometimes grimly comic works are often set in Africa, where he grew up. These include *A Good Man in Africa* (1981), *An Ice-cream War* (1982) ,and *Brazzaville Beach* (1990). His most ambitious novel, *The New Confessions* (1987), ranges across the whole history of the 20th century.

Boyle, Robert (1627–91) British chemist, b. Ireland, often regarded as the father of modern chemistry. Boyle conducted research into air, vacuum, metals, combustion, and sound. His *Sceptical Chymist* (1661) proposed an early atomic theory of MATTER. He made an efficient vacuum pump, which he used to establish (1662) BOYLE'S LAW. Boyle formulated the first chemical definitions of an element and a reaction.

Boyle's law Volume of a gas at constant temperature is inversely proportional to the pressure. This means that as pressure increases, the volume of a gas at constant temperature decreases. First stated by Robert BOYLE in 1662, Boyle's law is a special case of the ideal gas law (involving a hypothetical gas that perfectly obeys the gas laws).

Boyne, Battle of the (July 11, 1690) Engagement near Drogheda, Ireland, which confirmed the Protestant succession to the English throne. The forces of the Protestant WILLIAM III of England defeated those of the Catholic JAMES II. The battle led to the restoration of English power in Ireland.

Boy Scouts Worldwide social organization for boys that encourages outdoor pursuits and good citizenship. It was founded (1908) in Britain by Lord BADEN-POWELL with the motto "Be prepared". A companion organization, the GIRL GUIDES, was founded in 1910. Today, it has *c*.14 million members (including the Cubs and Brownies) in more than 100 countries.

Brabant Province of central Belgium; the capital is BRUSSELS. ANTWERP is one of the world's largest ports. Brabant is

BRACHIOPODA

The marine animal known as a brachiopod, or lampshell, lives in holes in mud flats. It comprises (A) a hinged shell and a stalk with which it grips the rocks. The cross-section (B) shows; lophophore (1) which bears ciliated tentacles for feeding; digestive gland (2); mouth (3) and stalks (4).

Lingula (C), which resembles fossil forms of 500 million years ago, feeds from the surface of its burrow using feathery cilia to filter water for food particles. When disturbed, its stalk contracts, drawing the animal into the burrow (D), out of sight and reach of its potential predator.

INTERNET

Boxer Rebellion
▶ www.history.navy.mil/ faqs/faq86-1.htm

B

a densely populated and fertile agricultural region. Industries: chemicals, metallurgy. Area: 3372sq km (1302sq mi). Pop. (2000) 1,014,704 (Flemish region); 349,884 (Walloon region).

brachiopoda (lampshells) Phylum of *c.*260 species of small, bottom-dwelling, marine invertebrates. They are similar in outward appearance to BIVALVE MOLLUSCS, having a shell composed of two valves; however, unlike bivalves, there is a line of symmetry running through the valves. They live attached to rocks by a pedicle (stalk), or buried in mud or sand. There are 75 genera including *Lingula*, the oldest known animal genus. Most modern brachiopods are less than 5cm (2in) across. More than 30,000 fossil species have been found and described.

bracken Persistent, weedy FERN found worldwide. It has an underground stem that can travel 1.8m (6ft) and sends up fronds that may reach 4.6m (15ft) in some climates. The typica variety is widespread in Britain. Family Dennstaedtiaceae; species *Pteridium aquilinum.*

bracket fungus (shelf fungus) Any of a large family (Polyporaceae) of common arboreal fungi that have spore-bearing tubes under the cap. Bracket fungi are usually hard and leathery or wood-like and have no stems. They often cover old logs and their parasitic activity may kill living trees. Some are edible when young.

bract Modified leaf found on a flower stalk or the flower base. Bracts are usually small and scale-like. In some species they are large and brightly coloured, such as DOGWOOD and POINSETTIA.

Bradbury, Ray Douglas (1920–) US novelist and short story writer. Best known for his imaginative science fiction, Bradbury's most celebrated work includes: *The Martian Chronicles* (1950), a collection of short stories; *Fahrenheit 451* (1953), an unhappy vision of a book-burning future world; and the fantasy *Something Wicked This Way Comes* (1962). He has also written plays, poetry, children's stories, screenplays, and volumes of essays, such as *Journey to Far Metaphor* (1994).

Braddock, Edward (1695–1755) British general in the FRENCH AND INDIAN WARS. As commander in chief of the British forces in North America, Braddock led the attack on the French stronghold of Fort Dequesne (1755). Progress was slow and, on the advice of George WASHINGTON, Braddock led an advance party. Ambushed by Native Americans, the party was routed and Braddock killed.

Bradford City in the Aire Valley, West Yorkshire, N England. Since the 14th century, it has been a centre for woollen and worsted manufacturing, but industry has recently greatly diversified. The city is home to one of England's largest Asian communities. It has a university (established 1966). Industries: textiles, textile engineering, electrical engineering, micro-electronics. Pop. (2001) 467,668.

Bradford, William (1590–1657) American colonial governor and signatory of the Mayflower Compact. He emigrated to America as one of the PILGRIMS on the *Mayflower* (1620), being one of the organizers of the voyage. He was elected governor of Plymouth Colony in 1621, and re-elected for 30 years thereafter. He helped draw up a body of laws for the colony in 1636, and wrote a *History of Plymouth Plantation, 1620–46.*

Bradley, Omar Nelson (1893–1981) US general. In World War 2, Bradley commanded the 2nd Corps in N Africa and the invasion of Sicily (1943), and led the 1st Army in the Normandy invasion (1944). After the war, he served as chief of staff of the US Army (1948–49) and first chairman of the joint chiefs of staff (1949–53).

Bradman, Sir Don (Donald George) (1908–2001) Australian cricketer and sports administrator, probably the greatest batsmen the game has ever seen. Bradman made his test debut for Australia in 1928, and acted as captain from 1936 until his retirement in 1948. His scored 6996 runs in 52 tests (an average of 99.94), including 29 centuries and a highest score of 334 (against England at Leeds in 1930). During his first-class career, Bradman made a total of 28,067 runs (averaging 95.14), including 117 centuries. He was knighted in 1949.

Brady, Mathew B. (1823–96) Pioneer US photographer After studying the daguerreotype process with Samuel F.B. Morse, he became the leading US portraitist of his day. President Lincoln was a frequent subject. Brady organized a staff of photographers to make a record of the Civil War. Much of this early war photography is in the Library of Congress.

Braganza Ruling dynasty of Portugal (1640–1910). The dynasty was founded by the Duke of Braganza, who ruled (1640–56) as JOHN IV. During the NAPOLEONIC WARS, the royal family fled to Brazil, then a Portuguese colony. A branch of the house ruled as emperors of Brazil from 1822–89.

Bragg, Sir (William) Lawrence (1890–1971) English physicist, b. Australia. He was director (1938–53) of the Cavendish Laboratory at Cambridge. With his father, Sir William Henry Bragg (1862–1942), he determined the mathematics involved in X-ray DIFFRACTION, showed how to compute X-ray wavelengths and studied CRYSTAL structure by X-ray diffraction. For these advances, they were jointly awarded the 1915 Nobel Prize in physics.

Brahe, Tycho (1546–1601) Danish astronomer. Under the patronage of King Frederick II of Denmark he became the most skilled observer of the pre-telescope era, expert in making accurate naked-eye measurements of the stars and planets. He built an observatory on the island of Hven (1576) and calculated the orbit of the comet seen in 1577. This, together with his study of the supernova, showed that ARISTOTLE was wrong in picturing an unchanging heaven. Brahe could not, however, accept the world system put forward by COPERNICUS. In his own planetary theory (the Tychonian system), the planets move around the Sun, and the Sun itself, like the Moon, moves round the stationary Earth. In 1597 he settled in Prague, where Johannes KEPLER became his assistant.

Brahma Creator god in HINDUISM, later identified as one of the three gods in the Trimurti. Brahma is usually thought equal to the gods VISHNU and SHIVA, but later myths tell of him being born from Vishnu's navel. There is only one major temple to Brahma, located at Pushkar, Rajasthan, NW India.

Brahman (Atman) In HINDUISM, the supreme soul of the universe. The omnipresent Brahman sustains the Earth. According to the UPANISHADS, the individual soul is identified with Brahman. Brahman is not God, but rather is *neti neti* (not this, not that) or indescribable.

Brahmanism Term denoting an early phase of HINDUISM. It was characterized by acceptance of the VEDAS as divine revelation. The Brahmanas, the major text of Brahmanism, are the ritualistic books comprising the greater portion of Vedic literature. They were complemented by the UPANISHADS. In the course of time deities of post-Vedic origin began to be worshipped and the influence of Brahmanist priests declined.

Brahmaputra River in S Asia. Rising in SW Tibet, it flows E into China, then S into India and WSW across India into Bangladesh (where it becomes the River YAMUNA). Before emptying into the Bay of BENGAL, it forms (with the GANGES and Meghna rivers) a vast delta. Length: *c.*2900km (1800mi).

Brahmin (Brahman) Priestly CASTE that was the highest-ranking of the four *varnas* (social classes) in India during the late Vedic period, the era of BRAHMANISM. The term also denotes a member of that caste. Brahmin were believed to be ritually purer than other castes, and they alone could perform certain spiritual and ritual duties. The recitation of the VEDAS was their preserve, and for hundreds of years they were the only caste to receive an education and so controlled Indian scholarship. With the later development of HINDUISM as a popular religion, their priestly influence declined, but their secular influence grew, and their social supremacy and privileged status have changed little over the centuries. Brahmins maintain ritual cleanliness through strict dietary laws and tightly regulated contact with other castes.

Brahms, Johannes (1833–97) German composer. Encouraged by his friends Robert and Clara SCHUMANN, he began to earn his living as a composer at the age of 30. He used classical forms, rather than the less-strict programmatic style that was becoming popular, and was a master of contrapuntal HARMONY. He composed in all major musical genres except opera. Among his major works are the *German Requiem* (1868), the *Variations on the St Antony Chorale* (1863), the Violin Concerto in D (1878), four symphonies (1876–1885), two piano concertos (1858 and 1881) and the orchestral *Hungarian Dances* (1873). He also wrote many songs.

Braille System of reading and writing for the blind. It was invented by French educationalist Louis Braille (1809–52), who lost his sight at the age of three. Braille was a scholar, and later a teacher, at the National Institute of Blind Youth, Paris. He developed a system of embossed dots to enable blind people to read by touch. This was first published in 1829, and a more complete form appeared in 1837. There are also Braille codes for music and mathematics.

brain Mass of nerve tissue which regulates all physical and mental activity; it is continuous with the spinal cord. Weighing about 1.5kg (3.3lb) in the adult (about 2% of body weight), the human brain has three parts: the hindbrain, where basic physiological processes such as breathing and the heartbeat are co-ordinated; the midbrain links the hindbrain and the forebrain, which is the seat of all higher functions and attributes (personality, intellect, memory, emotion), as well as being involved in sensation and initiating voluntary movement. The forebrain includes the highly fissured cerebrum that is the brain's most highly developed part. *See also* CENTRAL NERVOUS SYSTEM; CEREBRUM

brain damage Result of any harm done to brain tissue causing the death of nerve cells. It may arise from a number of causes, such as oxygen deprivation, brain or other disease or head injury. The nature and extent of damage varies. Sudden failure of the oxygen supply to the brain may result in widespread (global) damage, whereas a blow to the head may affect only one part of the brain (local damage). Common effects of brain damage include weakness of one or more limbs, impaired balance, memory loss and personality change; epilepsy may develop. While brain cells do not regenerate, there is some hope of improvement following mild to moderate brain damage, especially with skilled rehabilitation. The survivor of major brain injury is likely to remain severely disabled, possibly even permanently unconscious.

brain disorder Disturbances of physical or mental function due to abnormality or disease of the brain. Brain disorders should be distinguished from psychological (psychogenic) mental disturbances in which the functioning of the brain itself is not impaired. Brain disorders are associated with impairment of memory, orientation, comprehension and judgment, and also by shallowness of emotional expression. Secondary personality changes may occur, depending upon such factors as the strength and type of personality and the amount of psychological and social stress present. Brain disorders are divided into two types. **Acute** disorders are temporary, and are generally due to disruption of brain function rather than destruction of brain tissue. They may be caused by such things as infection, drug or alcohol intoxication, and brain trauma. **Chronic** brain disorders are irreversible, and include such things as congenital defects, hereditary diseases, senility, and brain damage. *See also* BRAIN DAMAGE; CONGENITAL DISORDER

brain stem Stalk-like portion of the brain in vertebrates that includes everything except the CEREBELLUM and the CEREBRAL HEMISPHERES. It provides a channel for all signals passing between the spinal cord and the higher parts of the brain. It also controls automatic functions such as breathing and heartbeat, digestion, and respiration.

Brain Trust (1933–35) Name given to the advisers of US President Franklin ROOSEVELT. It first described his closest advisers in the presidential campaign of 1932. Later, the term was applied more widely to members of his administration who advised on the policies of the NEW DEAL.

brake Device for slowing the speed of a vehicle or machine. Braking can be accomplished by a mechanical, hydraulic (liquid), or pneumatic (air) system that presses a non-rotating part into contact with a rotating part, so that friction stops the motion. In a car, the non-rotating part is called a shoe or pad, and the rotating part is a disc or drum attached to a wheel. Some vehicles use electromagnetic effects to oppose the motion and cause braking. A 'power' brake utilizes a vacuum system.

Bramante, Donato (1444–1514) Italian architect and painter. He is best known as the greatest exponent of High RENAISSANCE architecture. His first building, Santa Maria presso San Satiro in Milan (*c.*1481), uses perspective to give an illusion of deeply receding space in the choir. In 1506, he started rebuilding St Peter's, Rome. His influence was enormous and many Milanese painters took up his interest in perspective and *trompe l'oeil*.

bramble *See* BLACKBERRY

Branagh, Kenneth (1960–) Northern Irish actor and director. An immediate young acting success, he worked with the ROYAL SHAKESPEARE COMPANY (RSC) before leaving to form his own Renaissance Theatre Company. He moved into directing with the film *Henry V* (1989), receiving Academy Award nominations for best actor and best director. His success in popularizing Shakespeare was demonstrated further in *Much Ado About Nothing* (1993), *Othello* (1996) and *Hamlet* (1997).

Branch Davidians Late 20th-century religious CULT. A breakaway branch of the SEVENTH-DAY ADVENTISTS, the cult had its headquarters in Waco, Texas, and was led by the David Koresh, who claimed to be the reincarnated Jesus Christ. In 1993, following the shooting of federal officers, the cult was besieged by FBI agents. Fire suddenly broke out and more than 80 cult members, including Koresh, were killed.

Brancusi, Constantin (1876–1957) French sculptor. His primitive style is revealed in a series of wooden sculptures, including *Prodigal Son* (1914), *Sorceress* (1916), and *Chimera* (1918). In 1919, his *Bird in Space* was not permitted

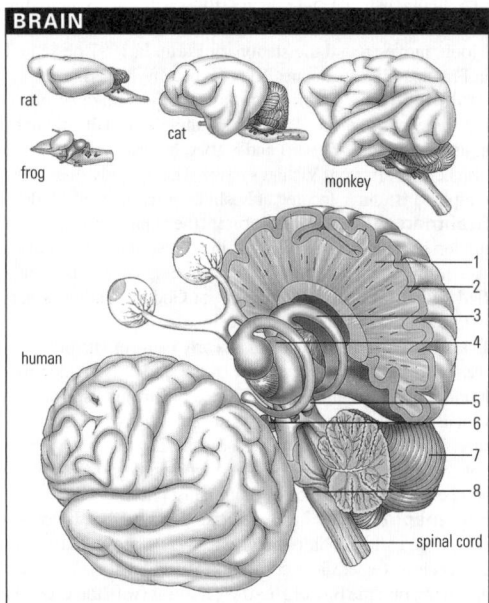

BRAIN

rat

cat

frog

monkey

human

1
2
3
4
5
6
7
8

spinal cord

The veterbrate brain has three major structural and functional regions – the forebrain, the midbrain and the hindbrain. In primitive animals, such as amphibians, the forebrain is concerned with smell, the midbrain with vision and the hindbrain with balance and hearing. In higher animals, such as rats, cats, monkeys and humans, parts of the brain have adapted to meet the needs of the organism. Most notably, part of the forebrain, the cerebrum (1), developed into a complex, deeply fissured structure. It comprises large regions concerned with association, reasoning and judgement. Its outer layer, the cortex (2), contains areas that coordinate movement and sensory information. The limbic system (3) controls emotional responses, such as fear. The thalamus (4) coordinates sensory and motor signals, and relays them to the cerebrum: the hypothalamus (5) along with the pituitary glands control the body's hormonal system. Visual, tactile and auditory inputs are coordinated by the tectum (6), part of the midbrain. In the hindbrain, the cerebellum (7) controls the muscle activity needed for refined limb movements and maintaining posture. The medulla (8) contains reflex centres that are involved in respiration, heartbeat regulation and gastric function.

into the USA as a work of art, but was taxed on its value as raw metal. This decision was reversed in a suit filed by Brancusi, and the sculpture is now housed in the Museum of Modern Art, New York City. Other works include *The Kiss* (1908), *Sculpture for the Blind* (1924) and *Flying Turtle* (1943).

Brandenburg State in NE Germany; the capital is POTS-DAM. The region formed the nucleus of the kingdom of Prussia. The March of Brandenburg was founded in 1134 by Albert I (the Bear). It came under the rule of the Hohen-zollerns in 1411, and in 1417 Frederick I became the first Elector of Brandenburg. Frederick II became the first King of Prussia in 1701. Pop. (1999) 2,601,207.

Brando, Marlon (1924–2004) US actor. A brooding presence with an inimitable mumbling vocal style, he trained at the ACTORS' STUDIO. In 1951, a reprise of his Broadway role for the film *A Streetcar Named Desire* earned him the first of four consecutive Oscar nominations. He finally won his first best actor Oscar as the isolated docker in *On the Waterfront* (1954). By the end of the 1950s, he was the first actor to command a million-dollar appearance fee. He was awarded a second Best Actor Oscar for his lead performance in *The Godfather* (1971), but refused the award in protest against the persecution of Native Americans. He received another Oscar nomination for *The Last Tango in Paris* (1972). Other credits include *Missouri Breaks* (1976), *Apocalypse Now* (1979), and an Oscar-nominated performance in *A Dry White Season* (1989).

Brandt, Bill (1904–83) British photographer, b. Germany. He assisted Man RAY in Paris (1929–30), before returning to London where he developed a reputation as a social commentator, as shown in his collection of photographs *The English at Home* (1936). During World War 2, he documented life through the Blitz in a series of atmospheric wartime landscapes. He is perhaps better known for his nudes, many of which can be found in his book *Perspective of Nudes* (1961).

Brandt, Willy (1913–92) German politician, chancellor of West Germany (1969–74), b. Karl Herbert Frahm. An active Social Democrat, he fled to Norway and then Sweden during the Nazi era. He returned to Germany after World War 2, and was elected mayor of West Berlin in 1957. In national politics, he became foreign minister in 1966. As chancellor, Brandt initiated a programme of cooperation with states in the communist bloc, for which he was awarded the Nobel Peace Prize in 1971. He resigned after a close aide was exposed as an East German spy. He chaired the Brandt Commission on international development issues, which published *North-South: A Programme for Survival* (1980) and *Common Crisis* (1983).

Brant, Joseph (1742–1807) Mohawk chief. He served in the FRENCH AND INDIAN WARS (1754–63) and in PONTIAC'S REBELLION (1763–66). He attended an Anglican school and became an interpreter for missionaries. In return for securing an alliance between the Iroquois and the British, Brant gained a commission in the British Army in 1775. He fought with great courage for the British during the American Revolution.

Braque, Georges (1882–1963) French painter who created CUBISM with PICASSO. Having tried FAUVISM without success, Braque's interest in analytical painting was sparked by the work he saw in Paul CÉZANNE's 1907 memorial show. *Head of a Woman* (1909), *Violin and Palette* (1909–10), and *The Portuguese* (1911) show his transition through the early phases of cubism. Braque was badly wounded in World War 1, and afterwards evolved a gentler style which earned him enormous prestige. He concentrated on still-life subjects but also produced book illustrations, stage sets, and decorative ceramics.

Brasília Capital of Brazil, w central Brazil. Although the city was originally planned in 1891, building did not start until 1956. The city was laid out in the shape of an aircraft, and Oscar Niemeyer designed the modernist public buildings. It was inaugurated as the capital in 1960, in order to develop Brazil's interior. Pop (2005) 3,341,000.

brass Alloy of mainly copper (55%-95%) and zinc (5%-45%). Brass is yellowish or reddish, malleable, and ductile, and can be hammered, machined, or cast. Its properties can

be altered by varying the amounts of copper and zinc, or by adding other metals, such as tin, lead, and nickel. Brass is widely used for pipe and electrical fittings, screws, musical instruments, and ornamental metalwork.

brass Family of musical wind instruments made of metal and played by means of a cupped or funnel-shaped mouthpiece. Simple brass instruments, such as the BUGLE, produce a limited range of notes, which are the harmonics corresponding to the length of the tube. In most other brass instruments, the length of the air column can be altered by valves or slides to produce the full range of notes. The chief brass instruments of a symphony orchestra are the TRUMPET, FRENCH HORN, TROMBONE, and TUBA. Other members of the family include the cornet.

Brassäi (1899–1984) French photographer and painter, b. Hungary as Guyla Halasz. Arriving in Paris in 1923, he worked as a journalist and painter, associating with Picasso and Dalí. In 1930 Brassäi turned to photography, concentrating on pictures of Parisian nightlife and portraits, the latter being remarkable for their static quality.

brassica Genus of plants with edible roots or leaves. It includes cabbages, cauliflowers, Brussels sprouts (all subspecies of *Brassica oleracea*), turnip (*B. rapa*), swede (*B. napobrassica*). Some, such as broccoli, have edible flowerheads. Family Brassicaceae/Cruciferae.

Bratislava Capital of Slovakia, on the River Danube, w Slovakia. It became part of Hungary after the 13th century, and was the Hungarian capital from 1526–1784. Incorporated into Czechoslovakia in 1918, it become the capital of Slovakia in 1992. Industries: oil refining, textiles, chemicals, electrical goods. Pop. (2001) 428,672.

Brattain, Walter Houser (1902–87) US physicist. As research physicist with the Bell Telephone Laboratories he focused on solid-state physics. In 1956, he shared the Nobel Prize in physics with John BARDEEN and William SHOCKLEY for their development of the TRANSISTOR and research into semiconductivity. In 1967 Brattain became professor at Whitman College in Walla Walla, Washington.

Braun, Eva (1912–45) Mistress of Adolf HITLER. She met Hitler in the early 1930s, and they lived together for the rest of their lives. On April 29, 1945, Braun and Hitler married in Berlin. The next day, the couple committed suicide.

Braun, Wernher von (1912–77) US rocket engineer, b. Germany. He perfected the V-2 rocket missiles in the early 1940s. In 1945 he went to the USA, becoming a US citizen in 1955. In 1958, von Braun was largely responsible for launching the first US satellite *Explorer 1*. He later worked on the development of the *Saturn* rocket (for the Apollo program), and was deputy associate administrator (1970–72) of NATIONAL AERONAUTICS AND SPACE ADMINISTRATION (NASA).

Brazil Republic in E South America. *See* country feature, page 172–73.

Brazil nut Seed of an evergreen tree, which has leathery leaves and grows to 41m (135ft) tall. Its flowers produce a thick-walled fruit 10–30.5cm (4–12in) in diameter which contain 25–40 large seeds. Family Lecythidaceae; species *Bertholletia excelsa*.

Brazzaville Capital and largest city of the Congo, w Africa, on the River Congo, below Stanley Pool. Founded in 1880, it was capital of French Equatorial Africa (1910–58) and a base for Free French forces in World War 2. It has a university (1972) and a cathedral. It is a major port, connected by rail

▲ **Brazil nut** Brazil nut trees (genus *Bertholletia*) are found along the banks of the Amazon and Orinoco rivers in Brazil. They grow in clumps and are a valuable source of natural oils.

The Federative Republic of Brazil is the world's fifth largest country. Structurally, it has two main regions. In the N is the vast AMAZON basin, once an inland sea and now drained by a river system that carries one-fifth of the world's running water. The largest area of river plain is in the upper part of the basin, along the frontiers with Bolivia and Peru. Downstream, the flood plain is relatively narrow.

The Brazilian Highlands make up the country's second main region and consist largely of hard crystalline rock dissected into rolling uplands. They include the heartland (MATO GROSSO) and the whole w flank of the country, from the bulge to the border with Uruguay. The undulating plateau of the northern highlands carries poor soils.

The typical vegetation is thorny scrub that, in the S, merges into wooded savanna. Conditions are better in the S, where rainfall is more reliable. More than 60% of the population lives in the four S and SE states, the most developed part of Brazil, although these account only for 17% of Brazil's total area.

CLIMATE

Manaus has high temperatures all through the year. The rainfall is heavy, though the period from June to September is drier than the rest of the year. The capital, BRASÍLIA, and the city RIO DE JANEIRO also have tropical climates, with much more marked dry seasons than Manaus. The far S has a temperate climate. The NE interior is the driest region, with an average annual rainfall of only 250mm [10in] in places. The rainfall is also unreliable and severe droughts are common in this region.

The Amazon basin contains the world's largest rainforests, which the Brazilians call the *selvas*. The forests contain an enormous variety of plant and animal species, but many species are threatened by loggers and those who wish to exploit the forests. The destruction of the forest is also ruining the lives of the last surviving groups of Amazonian Indians.

Forests grow on the NE coasts, but the dry interior has large areas of thorny scrub. The SE contains fertile farmland and large ranches.

HISTORY

The Portuguese explorer Pedro Alvarez CABRAL claimed Brazil for Portugal in 1500. While Spain was occupied in W South America, the first Portuguese colonists settled in the NE in the 1530s. They were followed by other settlers, missionaries, explorers and prospectors who gradually penetrated the country during the 17th and 18th centuries. They found many groups of Amerindians, some of whom lived semi-nomadic lives, hunting, fishing and gathering fruits, while others lived in farming villages, growing cassava and other crops.

Brazil was more than 90 times larger than Portugal and development was achieved by the use of Native American and c.4 million African slaves to work on the sugar plantations and in the mines. For many decades following the early settlements, Brazil was mainly a sugar-producing colony, with most plantations centred on the rich coastal plains of the NE. These areas later produced cotton, cocoa, rice and other crops. In the S, colonists penetrated the interior in search of slaves and minerals, especially gold and diamonds. The city of Ouro Preto in Minas Gerais was built and Rio de Janeiro grew as a port for

BRAZIL

the area. The growth of mining saw the capital move from Salvador to Rio de Janeiro in 1763.

Initially little more than a group of rival provinces, Brazil began to unite in 1807 after Napoleon's defeat of Portugal led the Portuguese king JOHN VI to flee to Brazil. His eldest son was chosen as the 'Perpetual Defender' of Brazil by a national congress. In 1822, he proclaimed the independence of the country and was chosen as the constitutional emperor with the title of PEDRO I. He became increasingly unpopular and was forced to abdicate in 1831. He was succeeded by his five-year-old son, PEDRO II, who officially took office in 1841. Pedro's liberal policies included the gradual abolition of slavery, which finally ceased in 1888.

During the 19th century, São Paulo state became the centre of a huge coffee-growing industry. The second half of the 19th century saw the development of the wild rubber industry in the Amazon basin, where the city of Manaus served as a centre and market. Although Manaus lies 1,600km [1,000mi] from the mouth of the Amazon, rubber from the hinterland could be shipped out directly to world markets in ocean-going steamers. The boom in the coffee and rubber industries spurred an increase in European immigration, and Brazil enjoyed a virtual monopoly of the rubber trade until Malaya began to compete in the early 20th century.

Brazil became a republic in 1889 after a bloodless revolution. Until 1930, the country experienced very strong economic expansion and prospered, but social unrest in 1930 resulted

in a major revolt. President Getulio VARGAS siezed power and established a strong corporate state based on fascist Italy, although Brazil entered World War 2 on the side of the Allies. In 1945 Vargas was forced to resign, but rampant inflation led to his return to power (1950–54).

As part of the development of the interior, the capital was transferred to Brasília in 1960. In 1964 the military seized power, maintaining control through repression and torture. Civilian government was finally restored in 1985, and a new constitution (1988) brought liberal reforms and the transfer of powers to Congress.

POLITICS
A new constitution, the eighth since Brazil's independence, came into force in October 1988. The constitution transferred powers from the president to the congress and paved the way for a return to democracy. In 1989 Fernando Collor de Mello was elected to cut inflation and combat corruption, but made little progress. In 1992 his vice-president Itamar Franco replaced him. He served until 1994 when the Social Democrat Fernando Henrique Cardoso, a former finance minister, was elected president.

In elections in 2002 Luiz Inácio Lula da Silva, leader of the left-wing Workers' Party, was elected president. Popularly known as 'Lula', he promised many social reforms. In office, he proved to be a pragmatist, following moderate economic policies. In 2005 his government was damaged by corruption charges, but in 2006 he was re-elected in a landslide victory.

AREA 8,514,215sq km [3,287,338sq mi]
POPULATION 190,011,000
CAPITAL (POPULATION) Brasilia (3,341,000)
GOVERNMENT Federal republic
ETHNIC GROUPS White 55%, Mulatto 38%, Black 6%, others 1%
LANGUAGES Portuguese (official)
RELIGIONS Roman Catholic 80%
CURRENCY Real = 100 centavos

ECONOMY
Brazil's total volume of production is one of the largest in the world, but few share in the country's fast economic growth. Widespread poverty, together with high inflation and unemployment, cause political problems. Industry is the most valuable activity, employing about 20% of the workforce. Brazil is among the world's top producers of bauxite, chrome, diamonds, gold, iron ore, manganese and tin. Its manufactures include aircraft, cars, chemicals, processed food, raw sugar, iron and steel, paper and textiles.

Agriculture employs 28% of workers. Coffee is a major export. Other leading products include bananas, citrus fruits, cocoa, maize, rice, soya beans and sugar cane. Brazil is the top producer of eggs, meat and milk in South America. Forestry is a major industry, although the exploitation of the rainforests, with 1.5% to 4% of Brazil's forest being destroyed every year, is a disaster for the entire world.

---

to the main Atlantic seaport of Pointe-Noire. Industries: foundries, chemicals, shipyards. Pop. (2005) 1,153,000.

bread Staple food made by mixing flour (containing a little yeast, salt, and sugar) with water to make a dough, allowing the yeast to ferment carbohydrates in the mixture (thus providing carbon dioxide gas which leavens the bread), and finally baking in an oven. Yeast fermentation not only lightens the texture of the bread but also adds to its taste. Bicarbonate of soda ($NaHCO_3$) may be used instead of yeast. Unleavened bread, favoured in many Asian countries, is flat in shape and heavy in texture by comparison.

Breakspear, Nicholas *See* ADRIAN IV

bream Freshwater fish of E and N Europe. Its stocky body is green-brown and silver, and anglers prize it for its tasty flesh. Length: 30–50cm (12–20in); weight: 4–6kg (9–13lb). Family Cyprinidae; species *Abramis brama*.

Bream, Julian Alexander (1933–) English guitarist and lutenist. He studied at the Royal College of Music (1945–48). An outstanding classical guitarist, he has had pieces composed for him by, among others, Benjamin BRITTEN and William WALTON. He has transcribed lute music for the guitar.

breast (mammary gland) Organ of a female mammal that secretes milk to nourish new-born young. In males, the glands are rudimentary and nonfunctional. A woman's breast, which develops during puberty, is made up of *c*.15–20 irregularly shaped lobes separated by connective and fat tissues. Lactiferous ducts lead from each lobe to the nipple, a small cone-shaped structure in the centre of the breast.

breathing Process by which air is taken into and expelled from the LUNGS for the purpose of GAS EXCHANGE. During inhalation, the intercostal muscles raise the ribs, increasing the volume of the THORAX and drawing air into the lungs. During exhalation, the ribs are lowered, and air is forced out through the nose, and sometimes also the mouth. Breathing provides oxygen for the chemical process of RESPIRATION, although both terms are informally used for breathing.

BREAST

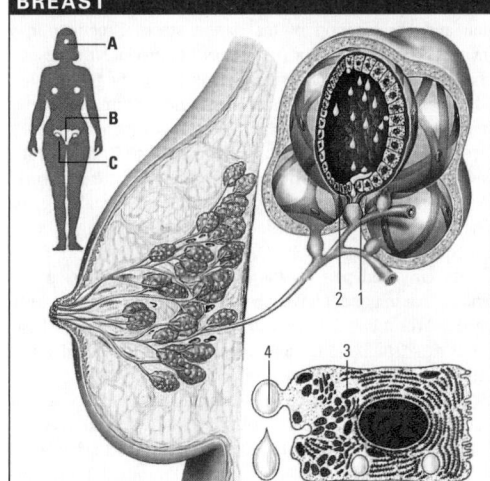

In humans, there is one pair of mammary glands, which are composed of a mass of epithelial ducts (1, shown magnified) surrounded by a fibrous tissue. In women, these ducts enlarge and spread, differentiating into milk-producing tissue. This process occurs under complex hormonal control from the anterior and posterior pituitary glands (A), the placenta during pregnancy (B), and from the ovaries (C). Full development of the glands involves extensive growth of mammary ducts from which specialized lobules proliferate (2). Each lobule, lined by milk-producing cells (3), opens into the ducts leading to the gland nipple. Three to four days after childbirth, the hormone prolactin enables milk containing fat droplets (4) and protein to become available to the child.

breccia Rock formed by the cementation of sharp-angled fragments in a finer matrix of the same or different material. It is formed either inside the Earth by movements of the crust, from scree slopes, or from volcanic material. *See also* CONGLOMERATE

Brecht, Bertolt (1898–1956) German playwright, poet, and drama theorist. One of the most influential dramatists of the 20th century, his controversial early plays, such as *Baal* (1918), won praise for their radicalism. In the 1920s, Brecht developed his distinctive, politicized theory of epic theatre. An attempt to move away from Western theatrical realism, it encouraged audiences to see theatre as staged illusion via a range of "alienation" techniques. Music played an important part in this foregrounding of artifice. Brecht's major works were written in collaboration with composers: Kurt WEILL, *The Threepenny Opera* (1928) and *The Rise and Fall of the City of Mahagonny* (1927); Hanns Eisler, *The Mother* (1931); and Paul Dessau, *The Caucasian Chalk Circle* (1948). With the rise of Hitler in 1933, Brecht's Marxist views forced him into exile. While in the USA, he wrote *Mother Courage and Her Children* (1941) and *The Good Woman of Setzuan* (1943). In 1949, Brecht returned to East Germany to direct the Berliner Ensemble.

Breckinridge, John Cabell (1821–75) US vice president (1857–61). He was a major in the MEXICAN WAR and a congressman (1851), before being elected vice president under James BUCHANAN. Defeated as a pro-slavery presidential candidate in 1860 by Abraham LINCOLN, he became a Confederate general and secretary of war in Jefferson DAVIS' cabinet (1865).

Breda City in Noord-Brabant province, s Netherlands. A historically important town, it is noted for the 1566 Compromise of Breda (a Dutch alliance against Spanish rule) and Charles II's Declaration of Breda (1660) before the Restoration. Industries: engineering, textiles. Pop. (2002) 163,283.

Breda, Treaty of (1667) Peace agreement that ended the Second DUTCH WARS with England. England gave up its claim to the Dutch East Indies but gained New York and New Jersey.

breeding Process of producing offspring, specifically the science of changing or promoting certain genetic characteristics in animals and plants. This is done through careful selection and combination of the parent stock. Breeding may involve cross-breeding or INBREEDING to produce the desired characteristics in the offspring. Scientific breeding has resulted in disease-resistant strains of crops, and in animals that give improved food yields. *See also* GENE; GENETIC ENGINEERING

Bremen City on the River Weser; capital of Bremen state, N Germany. Bremen suffered severe damage during World War 2, but many of its original buildings (including the Gothic city hall) survived. Industries: shipbuilding, electrical equipment, textiles. Pop. (1999) 542,300.

Brest City and port on the Atlantic coast of Brittany, W France. An important naval base, the town was severely damaged in World War 2, when used as a German submarine base. Industries: shipbuilding and repair, chemical manufacture, electronic equipment, wine, fruit, coal. Pop. (1999) 149,649.

Brest-Litovsk, Treaty of (March 1918) Peace treaty between Russia and the CENTRAL POWERS, signed in Brest-Litovsk in what is now Belarus, confirming Russian withdrawal from World War 1. The Ukraine and Georgia became independent and Russian territory was surrendered to Germany and Austria-Hungary. The treaty was declared void when the war ended in November.

Breton Celtic language spoken in Brittany, on the NW coast of France. It is a descendant of British, an old Celtic language, and is closely related to Welsh. Its *c.*500,000 users usually also speak French, which is rapidly replacing it.

Breton, André (1896–1966) French poet and theorist. A founder and poet of SURREALISM, he wrote *Manifeste du surrealisme* (1924) and *Le Surrealisme et la Peinture* (1928). His fictional works reflect surrealist theories. *See also* DADA

Bretton Woods Conference Officially the United Nations Monetary and Financial Conference, it met at Bretton Woods, New Hampshire, in July 1944. It was summoned on the initiative of US President Franklin ROOSEVELT to establish a system of international monetary cooperation and prevent financial crises such as that of 1929, which had precipitated the GREAT DEPRESSION. Representatives of 44 countries agreed to establish the INTERNATIONAL MONETARY FUND (IMF), to provide cash reserves for member states faced by deficits in their balance of payments, and the International Bank for Reconstruction and Development, or WORLD BANK, to provide credit to states requiring financial investment in major economic projects.

Breuer, Marcel (1902–81) US architect and designer, b. Hungary. One of the great innovators of modern furniture design, Breuer studied and taught at the BAUHAUS (1920–28), where he created his famous tubular steel chair. In 1937, he settled in the USA and subsequently worked with Walter GROPIUS as a partner in architectural projects. He designed the Whitney Museum of American Art, New York City (1966).

brewing Preparation of BEER and stout by using yeast as a catalyst in the alcoholic fermentation of liquors containing malt and hops. In beer brewing, a malt liquor (wort) is made from crushed, germinated barley grains. Hops are added to the boiling wort, both to impart a bitter flavour and also to help to clarify the beer and keep it free from spoilage by microbes. The clear, filtered wort is cooled and inoculated with brewer's yeast, which ferments part of the sugar from malt into alcohol.

Brezhnev, Leonid Ilyich (1906–82) Soviet statesman, effective ruler from the mid-1960s until his death. He rose through party ranks to become secretary to the central committee of the Soviet COMMUNIST PARTY (1952) and a member of the Presidium (later Politburo) (1957). In 1964 he helped plan the downfall of Nikita KHRUSHCHEV and became party general secretary, at first sharing power with Aleksei KOSYGIN. In 1977 he became president of the Soviet Union. After the Soviet invasion of CZECHOSLOVAKIA (1968), he promulgated the 'Brezhnev Doctrine' confirming Soviet domination of satellite states, as seen in the 1979 invasion of Afghanistan.

Brian Boru (940?-1014) King of Ireland (1002–14). From a power base in Munster, he gained control of the whole of s Ireland. Brian was killed in the aftermath of his victory over the Norsemen at the Battle of Clontarf.

Briand, Aristide (1862–1932) French statesman. A moderate, Briand was premier of 11 governments between 1909 and 1929. He advocated international cooperation and was one of the instigators of the LOCARNO PACT (1925), for which he shared the Nobel Peace Prize with Gustav STRESEMANN in 1926. He was also one of the authors of the KELLOGG-BRIAND PACT (1928), and favoured a form of European union.

brick Hardened block of clay used for building and paving. Usually rectangular, bricks are made in standard sizes by machines that either mould bricks or cut off extruded sections of stiff clay. They are baked at temperatures of up to 1300°C (2372°F). The first (sun-dried) bricks were used in the Tigris-Euphrates basin *c.*5000 years ago.

bridge Structure providing a continuous passage over a body of water, roadway or valley. Bridges are built for people, vehicles, pipelines, or power transmission lines. Bridges are prehistoric in origin, the first probably being merely logs over rivers or chasms. Modern bridges take a great variety of forms including beams, arches, cantilevers, suspension bridges and cable-stayed bridges. They can also be movable or floating pontoons. They can be made from a variety of materials, including brick or stone (for arches), steel or concrete.

Bridgeport City on Long Island Sound, sw Connecticut, USA. Settled in 1639 as a fishing community, it is now a port of entry and the chief industrial city in Connecticut. Industries: electrical appliances, transport equipment, helicopters, machine tools. Pop. (2000) 139,529.

Bridgetown Capital and port of Barbados, in the West Indies. Founded in 1628, it is the seat of the parliament and has a college of the University of the West Indies. Industries: rum distilling, sugar processing, tourism. Pop. (2000) 97,500.

Bright, John (1811–89) British parliamentary reformer. A Quaker and mill owner, he and his fellow radical, Richard COBDEN, were leaders of the ANTI-CORN LAW LEAGUE (founded 1839). First elected to Parliament in 1843, he subsequently represented Manchester, the home of FREE TRADE. He lost his seat in 1857 after opposing the Crimean War but was re-elected for

Birmingham. After the repeal of the CORN LAWS (1846), Bright worked tirelessly in the cause of parliamentary reform.

Brighton and Hove City on the English Channel, East Sussex, s England. Originally a fishing village, Brighton was popularized as a resort by the Prince Regent (George IV), who had the Royal Pavilion rebuilt here in oriental style by John NASH. It is the seat of the University of Sussex (1961) and the University of Brighton (1992). It gained city status in 2000. Industries: food processing, furniture, tourism. Pop. (2001) 247,817.

Brindley, James (1716–72) English canal-builder who constructed the Bridgewater Canal, the first major canal in England. It linked Worsley, Lancashire, to Manchester and was commissioned by Francis Egerton, 3rd Duke of Bridgewater (1736–1803). The design included an aqueduct over the River Irwell. Brindley was responsible for c.565km (350mi) of canals that hastened the INDUSTRIAL REVOLUTION.

Brisbane City and seaport on the River Brisbane; capital of QUEENSLAND, E Australia. First settled in 1824 as a penal colony, it became state capital in 1859. It is the location of Parliament House (1869) and the University of Queensland (1909) and is a major shipping and rail centre. Industries: oil refining, shipbuilding, car assembly. Pop. (2005) 1,769,000.

Bristol City and unitary authority at the confluence of the rivers Avon and Frome, sw England. An important seaport and trade centre since achieving city status in 1155, it was a major centre for the wool and cloth industry. From the 15th-18th century, it was England's second city and the base for many New World explorations. The 19th century witnessed a gradual decline in the city's economy due to competition from LIVERPOOL. Bristol suffered intensive bombing during World War 2. Clifton Suspension Bridge (designed by BRUNEL) was completed in 1864. Industries: aircraft engineering, chemicals, tobacco. City pop. (2001) 380,615.

Britain (Great Britain) Kingdom in NW Europe, officially the UNITED KINGDOM of Great Britain and NORTHERN IRELAND. It comprises ENGLAND, SCOTLAND, WALES, NORTHERN IRELAND, the CHANNEL ISLANDS, and the Isle of MAN.

Britain, ancient British history from PREHISTORY to ROMAN BRITAIN. Old STONE AGE remains have been found at Cheddar Gorge, Somerset, s England. During the NEOLITHIC age, hunter-gatherers gradually turned to sedentary farming. There are numerous examples of New Stone Age burial mounds. During the BRONZE AGE (c.2300BC), an advanced civilization, the Beaker culture, produced the stone circles at STONEHENGE and Avebury, s England. The IRON AGE was dominated by the CELTS.

Britain, Battle of (1940) Series of battles fought in the skies over Britain. Early in World War 2 the Germans hoped to destroy Britain's industrial and military infrastructure and civilian morale by a sustained series of bombing raids, as a prelude to invasion. Failure to eliminate the fighters of the Royal Air Force in August-September resulted in the abandonment of the plans for invasion, though bombing raids continued.

British Antarctic Territory British colony in ANTARCTICA, comprising the mainland and islands within a triangular area bounded by latitude 60°S and longitudes 20° and 80°W. It includes the South Shetland Islands, South Orkney Islands, and Graham Land. Formerly part of the FALKLAND ISLANDS, the territory became a British Crown colony in 1962, although Argentina and Chile claim parts of it. There are no permanent settlements, but teams of scientists occupy meteorological stations and other establishments of the British Antarctic Survey. Area: 1,725,000sq km (666,000sq mi).

British Broadcasting Corporation (BBC) UK state-financed radio and television network. Its directors are appointed by the government but, in terms of policy and content, the BBC is largely independent. It receives its finances from a television licence fee. The BBC was set up in 1927 to replace the British Broadcasting Company, which had been in operation since 1922. Its first director-general (1927–38) was Lord Reith, whose philosophy of the BBC as an instrument of education greatly shaped the corporation's policies. In recent times, John Birt was appointed director-general in 1992. His controversial reforms included rationalizing the BBC, exposing it to the influence of market forces and developing the use of independent production companies. In 2000, Greg Dyke was appointed director-general. His reforms included spending more BBC money on programme-making and less on the corporation itself. Dyke also encouraged the development of digital television. In 2004, Dyke resigned after the BBC was criticized by the Hutton report.

British Columbia Province of w Canada, on the Pacific coast, bounded N by Alaska, s by Washington state. The Rocky Mountains run N to s through the province. The capital is VICTORIA, other major cities include VANCOUVER. The region was first sighted by Sir Francis Drake in 1578. Captain Cook landed here in 1778, and George Vancouver took possession of the island that bears his name for Britain in 1794. In 1846 the border with the USA was finally settled. The completion (1885) of the Canadian Pacific Railway spurred the development of the province. The many rivers (principal of which is the Fraser) provide abundant hydroelectric power. Three-quarters of the land is forested, making timber an important industry. Mineral deposits include copper, silver, gold, lead, zinc, and asbestos. Dairying and fruit-growing are the chief farming activities, practised mainly in the s. Industries: fishing, paper, tourism, transport equipment, chemicals. Area: 948,600sq km (366,255sq mi). Pop. (2001) 3,907,738.

British Empire Overseas territories ruled by Britain from the 16th to the 20th century. Historians distinguish two empires. The first, based mainly on commercial ventures (such as sugar and tobacco plantations), missionary activities and slave trad-

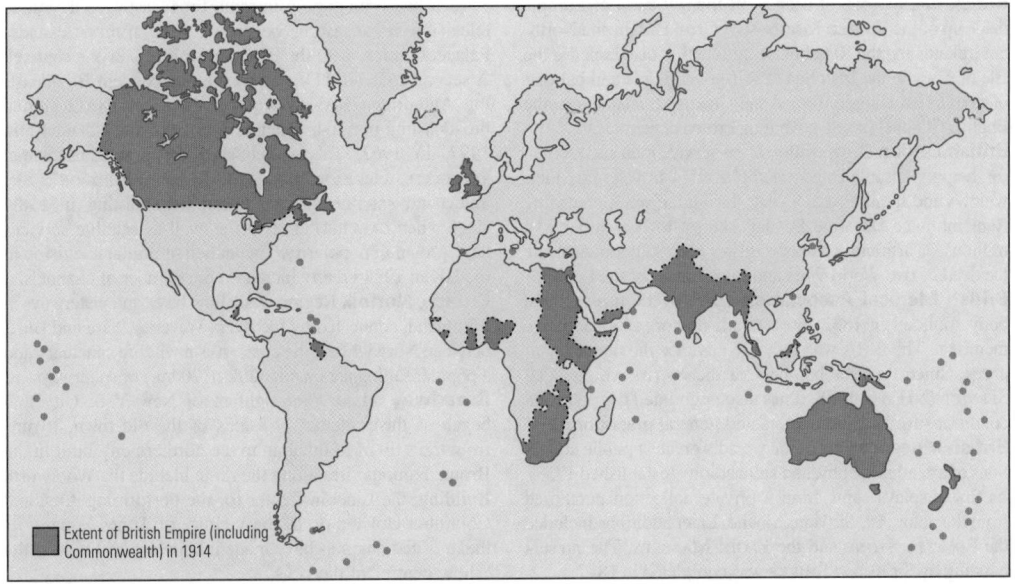

Extent of British Empire (including Commonwealth) in 1914

◄ **British Empire** Despite the loss of the USA (1783) and the strong anti-imperialist pressure of the free trade faction, the British Empire continued to expand throughout the 19th century. By 1914 (shown here), the Empire included all of India, Canada, Australia, most of the Cape to Nile 'corridor', which ran up E Africa, and many small islands of strategic importance.

B

▶ **bromeliad** Many bromeliads, such as *Aechmea fasciata*, are epiphytes (air plants), plants that use other plants for support but are not parasitic. Its broad leaves catch water as it drips through the canopy of the tropical forest. Bromeliads are members of the pineapple family (Bromeliaceae).

ing, resulted in the creation of British colonies in the Caribbean and North America in the 17th century. This 'First Empire' was curtailed by the loss of 13 US colonies, at the end of the AMERICAN REVOLUTION (1775–81). The 'Second Empire' was created in the 19th century, with Queen VICTORIA its empress. The EAST INDIA COMPANY acquired a larger trading empire as a result of the NAPOLEONIC WARS. COLONIALISM increased dramatically from the 1820s. British expansion was predominantly in the Far East, Australia (initially with the penal colonies), Africa and India. As a result of the INDIAN MUTINY (1857), the British government assumed direct responsibility for the administration of India. In the "scramble" for Africa, imperialists such as Cecil RHODES were thwarted in their desire to create a continent-wide empire by the SOUTH AFRICAN WARS. By 1914 the empire comprised *c*.25% of the Earth's land surface and population. Virtually all the constituent members gained independence in the period after World War 2. Most subsequently became members of the COMMONWEALTH.

British Empire, Order of the (OBE) Military and civil order or knighthood, bestowed as a reward for public service to the Commonwealth of Nations. Created in 1917, it has five different classes for men and women: Knights (or Dames) Grand Cross, Knights (or Dames) Commander, Commanders, Officers and Members.

British Honduras See BELIZE

British Indian Ocean Territory British colony in the Indian Ocean comprising the islands of the Chagos Archipelago, 1900km (1200mi) NE of MAURITIUS. In 1814 France ceded the territory to Britain, and it was administered by Mauritius. In 1965, Britain bought it from Mauritius in order to build a joint US-UK naval base on Diego Garcia island. In 1976, the islands of Aldabra, Farquhar, and Desroches reverted to SEYCHELLES administration. Industries: coconuts, fishing. Area: 80sq km (31sq mi). There is no permanent population.

British Isles Group of islands off the NW coast of Europe, made up of the UNITED KINGDOM of Great Britain and Northern Ireland, and the Republic of IRELAND. It also includes the Isle of MAN in the Irish Sea (a self-governing island but part of the United Kingdom); and the CHANNEL ISLANDS in the English Channel (a self-governing crown dependency).

British Legion Organization of ex-service men and women for helping disabled and unemployed war veterans, their widows and families. Each year, during the week preceding Remembrance Day (the Sunday nearest to November 11), millions of artificial red poppies are sold to commemorate the dead of two World Wars and raise funds for the Legion.

British Medical Association (BMA) UK professional body founded in 1832; 66% of all doctors in Britain are members. The BMA was set up to advance the medical sciences. Since the establishment of the NATIONAL HEALTH SERVICE (NHS) in 1948, it has also negotiated over pay and conditions for hospital doctors and general practitioners.

British Museum One of the world's greatest public collections of art, ethnography, and archaeology (established 1753). Its first displays came from a private collection purchased from the naturalist, Sir Hans Sloane. Later additions included the ROSETTA STONE and the ELGIN MARBLES. The present building by Sir Robert SMIRKE was completed in 1847.

British North America Act (1867) Act of the British Parliament that created the Dominion of CANADA. It resulted from a series of conferences and provided a constitution similar to that of Britain. Residual British powers were surrendered in the Canada Act of 1982, when the act was renamed the Constitution Act.

British Summer Time (BST) *See* SUMMER TIME

Brittany (Bretagne) Former duchy and province in NW France, forming the peninsula between the Bay of Biscay and the English Channel. Under Roman rule from 56 BC to the 5th century AD it was later inhabited by CELTS who provided its name, language (BRETON), and distinctive costume and culture. It was formally incorporated within France in 1532, and the years that followed saw the deliberate suppression of Breton culture, to the extent that the language was banned. In more recent times, the French government has improved the region's infrastructure. Pop. (1999) 2,907,178.

Britten, (Edward) Benjamin (1913–76) English composer. He is best known for his operas, which rank him among the foremost composers of the 20th century. He also wrote numerous songs, many especially for Peter PEARS. Britten's operas include *Peter Grimes* (1945), *Billy Budd* (1951), *The Turn of the Screw* (1954), and *Death in Venice* (1973). Other works include the popular *Young Person's Guide to the Orchestra* (1945) and *War Requiem* (1962). In 1948, he established the music festival held annually at his home town of Aldeburgh, on the E coast of England. He was made a peer in 1976.

brittle star (serpent star) Marine ECHINODERM with a small central disc body and up to 20 (though typically five) long, sinuous arms; these break off easily and are replaced by REGENERATION. Class Ophiuroidea; genera include the phosphorescent *Amphiopholis* and the small *Ophiactis*.

Brno (Brünn) Capital city of central Jihomoravsky (MORAVIA) region, SE Czech Republic. Founded in the 10th century, it has a 15th-century cathedral. The Bren Gun was designed here. Industries: armaments, engineering, textiles, chemicals. Pop. (2001) 379,185.

broadband High-speed computing data transmission system that uses a single circuit (such as a telephone connection) to carry several channels (such as data, voice and video) at once. The signals travel over a wide range of frequencies. Broadband provides greater INTERNET access speeds when using standard telephone systems. Wireless broadband has been developed using point-to-point microwave and satellite systems. See also COMPUTER NETWORK

broadcasting Transmission of sound or images to a widely dispersed audience through RADIO or TELEVISION receivers. The first US commercial radio company, KDKA, began broadcasting in Pittsburgh in 1920. In the UK, the British Broadcasting Company (later the BRITISH BROADCASTING CORPORATION) began transmissions in 1922. Until 1973 it had a monopoly in radio broadcasting. UK public television broadcasting began in 1936 from Alexandra Palace, London, with the BBC transmitting on one channel. A second channel, ITV, run by the Independent Broadcasting Authority (IBA), was set up in 1955. BBC2 started broadcasting in 1964, Channel 4 in 1982 and Channel 5 in 1997. In 1962, Telstar delivered the first transatlantic, SATELLITE television broadcast. Rupert MURDOCH's Sky Television satellite service began broadcasting in 1989, since when CABLE TELEVISION as well as satellite services have grown in popularity. The launch of digital television in the UK in 1998 greatly increased the number of channels.

Broads, Norfolk Region of shallow lakes and waterways in E England, connected by the rivers Waveney, Yare and Bure, between Norwich and the coast. It is a wildlife sanctuary and a popular sailing area, with 320km (200mi) of waterways.

Broadway Major thoroughfare of New York City that began as the principal N-S axis of the old town. It runs from the S tip of Manhattan to the northern city limit in the Bronx. Famous sites along the route include the Woolworth Building, the Lincoln Center for the Performing Arts, and Columbia University. In the vicinity of Times Square, its theatres and cinemas have made it known worldwide as the "show-centre" of the USA.

Brod, Max (1884–1968) Czech novelist, critic, and philosopher. Although chiefly remembered for bringing to public attention the work of Franz KAFKA, of whom he also wrote a biography, Brod was also a novelist in his own right. He was a Zionist and settled in Palestine as a refugee in 1939, where he later became director of the Habina Theatre.

Brodsky, Joseph (1940–96) US poet, b. Russia, winner of the 1987 Nobel Prize in literature and US poet laureate (1991–92). Before his exile from the Soviet Union in 1972, he was accused of being a "social parasite" and sent to a Soviet labour camp. His works include *Less than One: Selected Essays*, which won the 1986 US National Book Critics award, and *History of the Twentieth Century* (1986).

Broglie, Prince Louis Victor de (1892–1987) French physicist who theorized that all ELEMENTARY PARTICLES have an associated wave. He devised the formula that predicts this wavelength, and its existence was proven in 1927. Broglie developed this form of QUANTUM MECHANICS, called WAVE MECHANICS, and was awarded the 1929 Nobel Prize in physics. Erwin SCHRÖDINGER advanced Broglie's ideas with his equation that describes the wave function of a particle.

bromeliad Any of the 1700 species of the PINEAPPLE family (Bromeliaceae). Most are native to the tropics and subtropics and, besides the pineapple, include many of the larger EPIPHYTES of trees of the rainforests.

bromide Salt of hydrobromic acid or certain organic compounds containing bromine. The bromides of ammonium, sodium, potassium and certain other metals were once extensively used medically as sedatives. Silver bromide is light-sensitive and is used in photography.

bromine (symbol Br) Volatile liquid element of the halogen group (elements in group VII of the PERIODIC TABLE), first isolated in 1826 by the French chemist A.J. Balard. Bromine is the only liquid form of a nonmetallic element. It is extracted by treating seawater or natural brines with CHLORINE. A reddish-brown fuming liquid having an unpleasant odour, it is used in commercial compounds, such as those used to manufacture photographic film and additives for petrol. Chemically it resembles chlorine but is less reactive. Properties: at.no. 35; r.a.m 79.904; r.d. 3.12; m.p. −7.2°C (19.04°F); b.p. 58.8°C (137.8°F); the most common isotope is Br^{79} (50.54%).

bronchitis Inflammation of the bronchial tubes, most often caused by a viral infection such as the common cold or influenza but exacerbated by environmental pollutants. Symptoms include coughing and the production of large quantities of mucus. It can be acute (sudden and short-lived) or chronic (persistent), especially in those who smoke.

bronchus (pl. bronchi) One of two branches into which the TRACHEA or windpipe divides, with one branch leading to each of the LUNGS. The bronchus divides into smaller and smaller branches, called bronchioles, which extend throughout the lung, opening into the air sacs or ALVEOLI. *See also* BRONCHITIS

Brontë, Anne (1820–49) English novelist and poet. The youngest of the Brontë sisters, she became a governess, an experience reflected in *Agnes Grey* (1847). All of her work was published under the male pseudonym Acton Bell and her best-known novel is *The Tenant of Wildfell Hall* (1848).

Brontë, Charlotte (1816–55) English novelist and poet. Her personal life was unhappy and she persistently suffered from ill health. Born into genteel poverty, her mother, four sisters, and dissolute brother Branwell died early. She died in childbirth within a year of her marriage. Her four novels, *The Professor* (1846), *Jane Eyre* (1847), *Shirley* (1849), and *Villette* (1853) are works of remarkable passion and imagination. Her writings initially appeared under the male pseudonym Currer Bell.

Brontë, Emily (1818–48) English novelist and poet. Like her sisters she wrote under a male pseudonym, Ellis Bell. Her love for her native Yorkshire moors and insight into human passion are manifested in her poetry and her only novel, *Wuthering Heights* (1847).

brontosaurus Now known as apatosaurus, a DINOSAUR of the Jurassic and early Cretaceous periods. It had a long neck and tail, and a small head with the eyes and nostrils on top so that it could remain presumably almost completely immersed in water. Length: 21m (70ft); weight: to 30 tonnes.

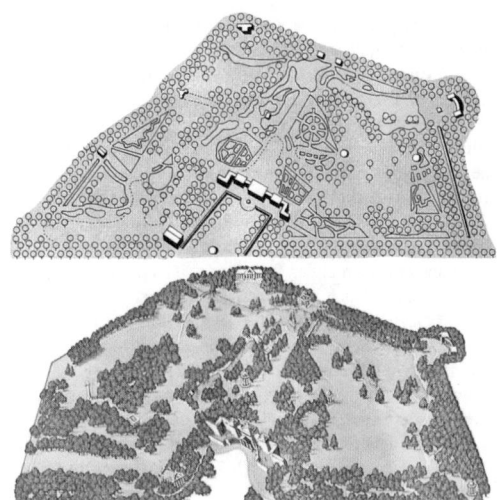

bronze Traditionally an ALLOY of COPPER and no more than 33% tin. It is hard and resistant to corrosion, but easy to work. It has long been used in sculpture and bell-casting. Other metals are often added for specific properties and uses, such as aluminium in aircraft parts and tubing, silicon in marine hardware and chemical equipment, and phosphorus in springs, gunmetal, and electrical parts.

Bronze Age Period in human cultural development between the NEOLITHIC period and the discovery of iron-working techniques (the IRON AGE). In Mesopotamia, BRONZE tools were used from *c*.3200 BC and the Bronze Age lasted until *c*.1100 BC. In Britain, bronze was used after 2000 BC and iron technology did not become widespread until *c*.500 BC.

Brook, Peter Stephen Paul (1925–) British director of theatre, opera, and film. He joined the ROYAL SHAKESPEARE COMPANY (RSC) as co-director in 1962. His most notable productions were *King Lear* (1962, filmed 1969), *Marat/Sade* (1964), and *Midsummer Night's Dream* (1970). In 1970 he established the experimental and collaborative International Centre for Theatre Research in Paris. Their productions include *The Conference of the Birds* (1973). Brook's film work includes *Lord of the Flies* (1963).

Brooke, Rupert Chawner (1887–1915) English poet. Brooke wrote some of the most anthologized poems in the English language, including "The Soldier" and "The Old Vicarage, Grantchester", but the romantic image created by his early death during World War 1 has tended to distort his status as a fairly typical poet of the Georgian school. His collections include *Poems* (1911) and *1914 and Other Poems* (1915).

Brooklyn Borough of New York City, coextensive with Kings County in sw Long Island; it is connected to Manhattan and Staten Island by bridges, underground railways and ferries. First settled in 1645, it became a borough in 1898. It is the home of Coney Island. Industries: shipbuilding, warehousing, brewing. Area: 184sq km (71sq mi). Pop. (2000) 2,465,326.

Brooks, Louise (1906–85) Legendary US film actress. Brooks achieved the majority of her success in Germany under the direction of G.W. Pabst in his *Diary of a Lost Girl* (1929), and as Lulu in *Pandora's Box* (1929). She was never able to recapture this early brilliance, and retired in 1938.

broom Any of various deciduous shrubs of the PEA family (Fabaceae/Leguminosae). They have yellow, purple or white flowers, usually in clusters. Many belong to the genus *Genista*, which gave its name to the Plantagenet kings of England (from the Latin *Planta genista*), who used the broom as their emblem.

Brown, 'Capability' (Lancelot) (1715–83) English landscape gardener who revolutionized garden and parkland layout in the 1700s. He designed or remodelled nearly 150 estates, including gardens at Blenheim and Kew. He worked to achieve casual effects, with scattered groups of trees and gently rolling hills. He earned his nickname from a habit of saying that a place had "capabilities of improvement".

Brown, Ford Madox (1821–93) English painter, closely associated with (although not a member of) the PRE-

◄ **Brown** The 18th-century gardens of Stowe, Buckinghamshire, s England, were worked on successively by Charles Bridgeman, William Kent and 'Capability' Brown. Bridgeman's layout moved some way from the formal geometric patterns of the French and Italian gardens, but was still characterized by a rigidity of outline. Kent's work (above) softened these outlines considerably, introducing the concept of naturalism, harmonizing house and temples with the landscape. It can be seen, however, that a certain formality persisted. The transformation of the gardens into their superbly landscaped state (below) is attributed to 'Capability' Brown. The stilted outlines have gone, the whole setting has a deceptively natural breadth and ease as well as a generous fullness.

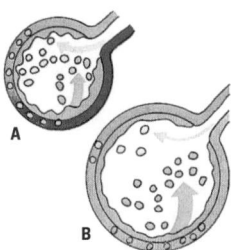

▲ **bronchitis** A common disease of industrialized areas with a cool damp climate, bronchitis involves inflammation of air passages and air sacs of the lungs. Mild attacks lasting only a few days are usually due to a cold, spreading to the chest. Chronic bronchitis is caused by heavily polluted air irritating the lining of the lungs. The lung air sacs become inflamed and lose their elasticity and air passages become constricted [normal air sac (A); diseased (B)]. Less oxygen (yellow dots) enters the blood stream and carbon dioxide (green dots) accumulate. Rapid shallow breathing arises to compensate.

Raphaelite Brotherhood. A meticulous draughtsman, he was in contact with the German Nazarenes before settling in England in 1845. The Pre-Raphaelite influence can be seen in *The Last of England* (1855) and *Work* (1852–63). Towards the end of his career, he produced a cycle of paintings on the history of Manchester (1878–93). He was the grandfather of the writer Ford Madox Ford.

Brown, Gordon (1951–) British statesman, prime minister (2007–), b. Scotland. Brown entered Parliament in 1983. Brown became shadow chancellor under John Smith and maintained the post under Tony Blair. His promise to freeze income tax did much to secure Labour's victory in the 1997 general election. His first act as chancellor was to give the Bank of England independence in interest rate policy. He became prime minister when Blair left office.

Brown, James (1933–2006) US singer and songwriter. An energetic performer, renowned for his dance routines, Brown is hailed as the "Godfather of Soul" and a pioneer of funk. His album *Live at the Apollo* (1962) is one of the best-selling pop albums of all time. Brown's hit singles include "Please, Please, Please" (1956), "Papa's Got a Brand New Bag" (1965) and "Say it Loud, I'm Black and I'm Proud" (1968).

Brown, John (1800–59) US anti-slavery crusader, hero of the song "John Brown's Body". Hoping to start a slave revolt, he led 21 men in the capture of the US arsenal at Harper's Ferry, Virginia, in 1859. They were driven out the next day by troops under General Robert E. Lee. Brown was captured, charged with treason and hanged. The trial aggravated North-South tensions on the eve of the American Civil War.

brown bear *See* bear

Browne, Robert (*c.*1550–1633) English clergyman, founder of the "Brownists", a separatist religious sect. In *Reformation without Tarrying for Any* (1582), he presented the first argument for Congregationalism. In 1584, he was imprisoned and late excommunicated. By 1591, Brown had been reconciled to the Church of England.

Brownian motion Random, zigzag movement of particles suspended in a fluid (liquid or gas). It is caused by the unequal bombardment of larger particles, from different sides, by the smaller molecules of the fluid. The movement is named after the Scottish botanist Robert Brown (1773–1858), who in 1827 observed the movement of plant spores floating in water.

Browning, Elizabeth Barrett (1806–61) English poet. In 1846 she secretly married Robert Browning and, from 1847, the couple lived in Italy. She began to write verse early in life. Her first volume, *The Battle of Marathon*, was published privately in 1820. *The Seraphim and Other Poems* (1838) and *Poems* (1844) established her widespread popularity, later confirmed by her collection of 1850, which included *Sonnets from the Portuguese*, and *Aurora Leigh* (1857). She was regarded as the pre-eminent English woman poet of her age.

Browning, Robert (1812–89) English poet. "My Last Duchess" and "Soliloquy of the Spanish Cloister", both published in *Bells and Pomegranates* (1846), display his characteristic use of dramatic monologue. In 1846, he and Elizabeth Barrett (Browning) secretly married and moved to Florence, Italy, in 1847. He published the volumes *Christmas Eve and Easter Day* (1850) and *Men and Women* (1855) before returning to London after Elizabeth's death in 1861. His popularity increased with *Dramatis Personae* (1864) and *The Ring and the Book* (1868–69), the latter often considered to be his masterpiece. One of the foremost poets of the 19th century, Browning is also at times one of the most obscure.

Bruch, Max (1838–1920) German Romantic composer. He composed operas and was a prominent conductor, but he is remembered primarily for three orchestral works – the Violin Concerto No. 1, *Scottish Fantasy* for violin and orchestra, and the *Kol Nidrei* for cello and orchestra.

Brücke, Die (1905–13) (The Bridge) First group of German expressionist painters. Founded in Dresden by E.L. Kirchner, the group chose their name because they wanted their work to form a bridge with the art of the future. They produced paintings and drawings, but their greatest strength lay in the art of woodcut. Members of the group included Emil Nolde, Karl Schmidt-Rottluff, Max Pechstein, and Erich Heckel. Inspired by Munch, Van Gogh, and Gauguin, jagged edges, harshly distorted figures, and a simplification of colour and form characterized their work. *See also* expressionism

Bruckner, Anton (1824–96) Austrian composer. An intensely pious man, he wrote a great deal of church music – cantatas, masses and a *Te Deum* (1881–84) – and nine symphonies. His symphonies are lengthy, monumental creations greatly influenced by Romanticism. His use of complex musical form infuses his work.

Bruegel (the Elder), Pieter (1525–69) Netherlandish landscape painter and draughtsman. The greatest 16th-century Dutch artist. He travelled extensively in France and Italy. His return journey through the Alps influenced him profoundly, and he produced a series of remarkably sensitive drawings of the region. In 1563, he moved to Brussels and for the rest of his life concentrated on painting. The characteristic rural scenes crowded with tiny peasant figures of his early years gave way during his last six years to paintings with larger figures which illustrated proverbs. His son, **Pieter Bruegel (the Younger)** (1564–1637), sometimes copied his father's work. Another son, **Jan** (1568–1625), specialized in highly detailed flower paintings and earned the nickname 'Velvet Bruegel' because of his skill in depicting delicate textures.

Bruges (Brugge) Capital of West Flanders province, NW Belgium. Built on a network of canals, it was a great trading centre in the 15th century. Its importance declined after 1500, but trade revived when the Zeebrugge ship canal was opened in 1907. It has many medieval buildings, including churches, a town hall and a market hall. Industries: engineering, brewing, lace, textiles, tourism. Pop. (2000) 133,859.

Brunei Sultanate in N Borneo, SE Asia; the capital is Bandar Seri Begawan. **Land and climate** Bounded in the NW by the South China Sea, Brunei consists of humid plains with forested mountains running along its S border with Malaysia. Brunei has a moist, tropical climate. **History and politics** During the 16th century, Brunei ruled over the whole of Borneo and parts of the Philippines, but gradually lost its influence in the region. It became a British protectorate in 1888. Brunei achieved independence in 1983. The Sultan has executive authority. **Economy** Oil and gas are the main source of income, accounting for 70% of GDP. Recently, attempts have been made to increase agricultural production. Area: 5765sq km (2226sq mi). Pop. (2006 est.) 379,000.

Brunel, Isambard Kingdom (1806–59) English marine and railway engineer. A man of remarkable foresight, imagination and daring, Brunel revolutionized British engineering. In 1829, he designed the Clifton Suspension Bridge (completed 1864). Brunel is also famous for designing the ships *Great Western* (1837), the first trans-Atlantic wooden steamship, *Great Britain* (1843), the first iron-hulled, screw-driven steamship, and *Great Eastern* (1858), a steamship powered by screws and paddles, which was the largest vessel of its time.

Brunelleschi, Filippo (1377–1446) Florentine architect, first of the great Renaissance architects and a pioneer of perspective. He influenced many later architects, including Michelangelo. In 1420, he began to design the dome of Florence Cathedral, the largest since the Hagia Sophia. Other works include the Ospedale degl'Innocenti (1419–26), the Basilica of San Lorenzo (begun 1421) and the Pazzi Chapel (*c.*1440), all in Florence.

Bruno, Frank (Franklin Roy) (1961–) English boxer. He turned professional in 1982, and in 1985 won the European heavyweight title and challenged Tim Witherspoon for the WBA crown. He retired after losing to Mike Tyson in 1989, but staged a comeback only to lose another world title challenge to Lennox Lewis in 1993. In 1995 he beat Oliver McCall on points to win the WBC title, but lost his defence against Tyson and retired again.

Brussels (Bruxelles) Capital of Belgium and of Brabant province, central Belgium. During the Middle Ages, it achieved prosperity through the wool trade and became capital of the Spanish Netherlands. In 1830 it became capital of newly independent Belgium. Sites include a 13th-century cathedral, the town hall, splendid art nouveau buildings, and academies of fine arts. The main commercial, financial, cultural and administrative centre of Belgium, it is also the headquarters of the EUROPEAN COMMUNITY (EC) and of the NORTH ATLANTIC TREATY ORGANIZATION (NATO). Industries: textiles, chemicals, electronic equipment, electrical goods, brewing. Pop. (2005) 964,000.

Brussels, Treaty of (1948) Agreement signed by Britain, France, and the Low Countries for cooperation in defence, politics, economics, and cultural affairs for 50 years. The defence agreement merged into the NORTH ATLANTIC TREATY ORGANIZATION (NATO) in 1950. In 1954 Italy and West Germany joined the original signatories, and the name was changed to the Western European Union. It was a forerunner of the EUROPEAN COMMUNITY (EC).

brutalism Architectural movement of the 1950s and early 1960s. It took its inspiration from LE CORBUSIER's pilgrimage chapel at Ronchamp and his High Court building at Chandigarh, India. Corbusier designed both buildings as a reaction to the sterility of the INTERNATIONAL STYLE. A number of young architects, such as James STIRLING, tried to extend Le Corbusier's experiments into aggressive and chunky designs of their own. It should not be confused with the 1950s movement of **new brutalism**, in which Alison and Peter Smithson adopted the uncompromising simplicity of MIES VAN DER ROHE.

Bruton, John Gerard (1947–) Irish prime minister (1995–97). Bruton was elected to the Dáil in 1969. A member of FINE GAEL, he rose steadily through the ministerial ranks, earning a reputation as a right-winger. He became leader of Fine Gael in 1990, and succeeded Albert REYNOLDS as prime minister. Bruton was succeeded by Bertie AHERN.

Brutus (85–42 BC) (Marcus Junius Brutus) Roman republican leader, one of the principal assassins of Julius CAESAR. He sided first with POMPEY against Caesar, but Caesar forgave him and made him governor of Cisalpine Gaul in 46 BC and city praetor in 44 BC. After taking part in Caesar's assassination, he raised an army in Greece but was defeated at Philippi by Mark ANTONY and OCTAVIAN. He committed suicide.

Bryant, William Cullen (1794–1878) US poet and editor. His debut volume, *Poems* (1821), contained some of his most famous verse, including "Thanatopsis" and "To a Waterfowl". In 1826 he joined the *New York Evening Post*, soon rising to editor (1829) and part-owner. Under his editorship, the *Post* emerged as a powerful liberal voice. Later volumes include *The Fountain* (1842) and *Thirty Poems* (1864).

bryophyte Group of small, green, rootless non-VASCULAR PLANTS (phylum Bryophyta), including MOSS and LIVERWORT. Bryophytes grow on damp surfaces exposed to light, including rocks and tree bark, almost everywhere from the Arctic to the Antarctic. There are c.24,000 species. *See also* ALTERNATION OF GENERATIONS

BSE *See* BOVINE SPONGIFORM ENCEPHALOPATHY

bubble chamber Device for detecting and identifying SUBATOMIC PARTICLES. It consists of a sealed chamber filled with a liquefied gas, usually liquid hydrogen, kept just below its boiling point by high pressure in the chamber. When the pressure is released, the boiling point is lowered and a charged particle passing through the superheated liquid leaves a trail of tiny gas bubbles that can be illuminated and photographed before the pressure is restored. If a magnetic field is applied to the chamber, the tracks are curved according to the charge, mass and velocity of the particles, which can thus be identified. The US physicist Donald GLASER received the 1960 Nobel Prize in physics for inventing the bubble chamber, and it was developed by Luis ALVAREZ.

Buber, Martin (1878–1965) Austrian Jewish philosopher. An ardent early advocate of ZIONISM, he edited *Der Jude* (1916–24), the leading journal of German-speaking Jewish intellectuals. He opposed the Nazis in Germany until forced to move to Palestine in 1938. His most important published work is *I and Thou* (1922), on the directness of the relationship between man and God within the traditions of HASIDISM. He also wrote on the ideals of the state of Israel.

bubonic plague *See* PLAGUE

Buchan, John, 1st Baron Tweedsmuir (1875–1940) Scottish writer and politician. Buchan is best known for his adventure novels, such as *The Thirty-Nine Steps* (1915). He

also wrote a four-volume history of World War 1 (1915–19) and biographies of Walter Scott (1932) and Oliver Cromwell (1934). He was governor-general of Canada (1935–40).

Buchanan, James (1791–1868) 15th US president (1857–1861). Buchanan entered Congress in 1821, and acted as senator (1834–45). President POLK appointed him secretary of state (1845–49). Under President Franklin PIERCE, Buchanan served as minister to Great Britain (1853–56). After securing the DEMOCRATIC PARTY nomination, he defeated John FRÉMONT of the newly formed REPUBLICAN PARTY and Millard FILLMORE in the presidential election. Buchanan's administration was unpopular, his attempt to compromise between pro- and anti-SLAVERY factions floundered. His efforts to purchase Cuba and acceptance of a pro-slavery constitution in Kansas, contributed to his electoral defeat by Abraham LINCOLN. The Southern states seceded and, shortly after Buchanan left office, the American CIVIL WAR began.

Bucharest (Bucuresti) Capital and largest city of Romania, on the River Dimbovita, s Romania. Founded in the 14th century on an important trade route, it became capital in 1862 and was occupied by Germany in both World Wars. It is an industrial, commercial and cultural centre. The seat of the patriarch of the Romanian Orthodox Church, it has notable churches, museums and galleries. There are two universities. Industries: oil refining, chemicals, textiles. Pop. (2005) 1,764,000.

Buchenwald Site of a Nazi concentration camp, near Weimar in Germany. Established in 1937, it became notorious for the medical experiments conducted on its inmates, of whom c.50,000 died. It was liberated by US forces in 1945.

Buck, Pearl S. (Sydenstricker) (1892–1973) US novelist. Buck was brought up in China, which she used as the setting for many of her novels, including *The Good Earth* (1931), which won a Pulitzer Prize in 1932. Her other works include *Sons* (1932), *The Mother* (1934), *A House Divided* (1935) and *Dragon Seed* (1942). She also wrote plays, screenplays, verse and children's fiction. Buck received the 1938 Nobel Prize in literature.

Buckingham, George Villiers, 1st Duke of (1592–1628) English statesman and court favourite of JAMES I and CHARLES I. Buckingham joined the court of James I in 1614, and rapidly acquired a series of titles. In 1623, he was largely responsible for the breakdown in negotiations of marriage between Prince Charles and the Spanish Infanta Maria. In 1624, he arranged Charles' marriage to Henrietta Maria. Buckingham's failure to provide adequate supplies for an English expedition to the Palatinate led to charges of political incompetence. The disastrous expedition to capture Cádiz (1625) led to his impeachment, but Charles dissolved Parliament. In 1627 he led another unsuccessful campaign to relieve the HUGUENOTS at La Rochelle. He was murdered by a discontented naval officer.

Buckingham, George Villiers, 2nd Duke of (1628–87) English courtier and political figure, son of the 1st Duke of BUCKINGHAM. He was educated with Charles I's sons and supported the Royalists in the CIVIL WAR (1642–48). A dashing, rakish courtier in RESTORATION England, he was a member of the group of ministers known as the CABAL, but later joined the opposition to Charles II. He wrote several comedies, notably *The Rehearsal* (1671).

Buckingham Palace London residence of British sovereigns since 1837. Formerly owned by the Dukes of Buckingham, it was purchased by George III in 1761, and remodelled into a 600–room palace by John NASH in 1825. Sir Aston Webb redesigned the east front in 1913.

Buckinghamshire County in SE central England; the county town is Aylesbury. In the Vale of Aylesbury to the N, cereal crops and beans are grown. Livestock and poultry are reared in the s. Industries: furniture, printing, building materials. Area: 1877sq km (725sq mi). Pop. (2001) 479,028.

bud In plants, a small swelling or projection consisting of a short stem with overlapping, immature leaves covered with scales. Leaf buds develop into leafy twigs, and flower buds develop into blossoms. A bud at the tip of a twig is a terminal bud and contains the growing point; lateral buds develop in leaf axils along a twig.

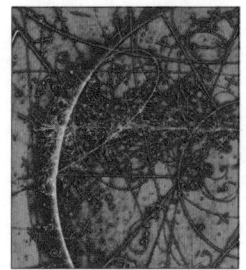

▲ **bubble chamber** Coloured image showing a collection of tracks left by subatomic particles in a bubble chamber. A charged particle leaves behind a trail of tiny bubbles as the liquid hydrogen boils in its wake. The tracks are curved due to an intense, applied magnetic field. The tightly wound spiral tracks are due to electrons and positrons.

B

► **Buddhism** Founded in NE India in the 6th century, Buddhism has more than 300 million followers in Japan, Sri Lanka, Nepal, Thailand, and other parts of the Far East. Its philosophy that human happiness cannot be found through material wealth is finding increasing support from some in the West.

INTERNET

Bulgaria
► www.government.bg
► www.bulgariatravel.org

Budapest Capital of Hungary, on the River Danube. It was created in 1873 by uniting the towns of Buda (capital of Hungary since the 14th century) and Pest on the opposite bank. It became one of the two capitals of the AUSTRO-HUNGARIAN EMPIRE. In 1918, it was declared capital of an independent Hungary. Budapest was the scene of a popular uprising against the Soviet Union in 1956. The old town contains a remarkable collection of buildings, including Buda Castle, the parliament building, the National Museum, and Roman remains. Industries: iron and steel, chemicals, textiles. Pop. (2005) 1,670,000.

Buddha (Enlightened One) Title adopted by Gautama Siddhartha (c.563–c.483BC), the founder of BUDDHISM. Born at Lumbini, Nepal, Siddhartha was son of the ruler of the Sakya tribe, and his early years were spent in luxury. At the age of 29, he realized that human life is little more than suffering. He gave up his wealth and comfort, deserted his wife and small son, and took to the road as a wandering ascetic. He travelled south, and sought truth in a six-year regime of austerity and self-mortification. After abandoning asceticism as futile, he sought his own middle way towards enlightenment. The moment of truth came in c.528 BC as he sat beneath a banyan tree in the village of Buddha Gaya, Bihar, India. After this incident, he taught others about his way to truth. The title 'buddha' applies to those who have achieved perfect enlightenment. Buddhists believe that there have been several buddhas before Siddhartha, and there will be many to come. The term also serves to describe a variety of Buddha images.

Buddhism Religion and philosophy founded (c.528BC) in India by Gautama Siddhartha, the BUDDHA. Buddhism is based on Four Noble Truths: existence is suffering; the cause of suffering is desire; the end of suffering comes with the achievement of NIRVANA, and Nirvana is attained through the Eightfold Path: right views, right resolve, right speech, right action, right livelihood, right effort, right mindfulness and right concentration. There are no gods in Buddhism. KARMA, one of Buddhism's most important concepts, says good actions are rewarded and evil ones are punished, either in this life or throughout a long series of lives resulting from **samsara**, the cycle of death and rebirth by REINCARNATION. The achievement of nirvana breaks the cycle. Buddhism is a worldwide religion. Its main divisions are THERAVADA or Hinayana in SE Asia, MAHAYANA in N Asia, Lamaism or TIBETAN BUDDHISM in Tibet, and ZEN in Japan. Today, there are c.300 million Buddhists worldwide.

budding Method of asexual reproduction that produces a new organism from an outgrowth of the parent. Hydras, for example, often bud in spring and summer. Yeasts also reproduce by budding. A small bulge appears on the parent and grows until it breaks away as a new individual.

Budge, (John) Don (Donald) (1915–2000) US tennis player. Regarded as one of the greatest players of all time, Budge was the first man to complete the Grand Slam of the four major singles titles (Wimbledon, USA, Australia, France) in one year (1938). In 1937–38, he also won both the mixed and men's doubles titles at Wimbledon and the US Open.

budgerigar (parakeet) Small, brightly coloured seed-eating PARROT native to Australia. A popular pet, it can be taught to mimic speech. The sexes look alike but the coloration of the cere (a waxy membrane at the base of the beak) may vary seasonally. Size: 19cm (7.5in) long. Species *Melopsittacus undulatus*.

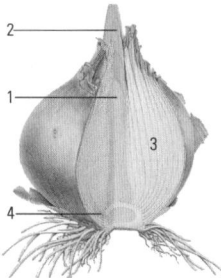

▲ **bulb** As well as serving as underground storage organs, bulbs can also provide flowering plants with a means of vegetative reproduction. In spring, the flower bud (1) and young foliage leaves (2) develop into a flowering plant, using the food and water stored in the bulb's fleshy scale leaves (3). When the flower dies, the leaves live on, and continue to make food which is transported downwards to the leaf bases. These swell and develop into new bulbs. Axillary buds (4) may develop into daughter bulbs, which break off to form new independent plants.

budget Plan for the financial expenditure of an individual, corporation or government, matching it against expected income. National budgets determine the level of direct and indirect TAXATION against projected expenditure and economic growth. The complexity of modern trade and finance has sometimes forced governments to make two or more budgets in a single year.

Buenos Aires Capital of Argentina, on the estuary of the Río de la Plata, 240km (150mi) from the Atlantic Ocean. Originally founded by Spain in 1536, it was refounded in 1580 after being destroyed by the indigenous population. It became a separate federal district and capital of Argentina in 1880. Buenos Aires later developed as a commercial centre for beef, grain and dairy products. It is the seat of the National University (1821). Industries: meat processing, flour milling, textiles, metal works, car assembly. Pop. (2005) 13,349,000.

Buffalo Industrial city and port on the E shore of Lake Erie, NW New York, USA. It was first settled in 1803 by the Holland Land Company. Its rapid industrial growth was encouraged by its position at the W terminus of the Erie Canal (opened 1825). President William MCKINLEY was assassinated at the Pan-American Exposition held here in 1901. It is home to the Albright-Knox Art Gallery and has two universities. Industries: flour milling, motor vehicles, chemicals, railway engineering. Pop. (2000) 977,000.

buffalo Any of several horned mammals and a misnomer for the North American BISON. The massive ox-like Indian, or water, buffalo (*Bubalus bubalis*) is often domesticated for milk and hides. Height: 1.5m (5ft). Family Bovidae.

buffer solution Solution to which a moderate quantity of a strong acid or a strong base can be added without making a significant change to its pH value (acidity or alkalinity). Buffer solutions usually consist of either a mixture of a weak acid and one of its salts, a mixture of an acid salt and its normal salt or a mixture of two acid salts.

bug Any member of the INSECT order Hemiptera, although in the USA any insect is commonly called a bug. True bugs are flattened insects that undergo gradual or incomplete metamorphosis, have two pairs of wings and use piercing and sucking mouthparts. Most feed on plant juices, such as the greenfly, although a number attack animals and are carriers of disease.

bugle BRASS wind instrument resembling a small TRUMPET without valves, capable of playing notes of only one harmonic series. Because its penetrating tones carry great distances, it was often used for military signalling.

Buhl, André Charles *See* BOULLE, ANDRÉ CHARLES

building society In the UK, financial institution primarily for providing mortgage loans to house-buyers. The money lent by a building society comes from savings invested by the public in deposits and shares. Since the Building Societies Act (1986), they have been allowed to offer a wider range of financial services, putting them in competition with banks.

Bujumbura (formerly Usumbura) Capital and chief port of Burundi, E central Africa, at the NE end of Lake TANGANYIKA. Founded in 1899 as part of German East Africa, it was the capital of the Belgian trust territory of Ruanda-Urundi after World War 1 and remained capital of Burundi when the country achieved independence in 1962. It is an administrative and commercial centre. Industries: textiles, cotton, coffee, cement. Pop. (2002 est.) 846,000.

Bukhara (Buchara) Ancient city in W Uzbekistan, capital of the Bukhara region. Founded c.1st century AD it was ruled by Arabs (7th-9th century), by Turks and Mongols (12th-15th century) and annexed to Russia in 1868; it was included in Uzbekistan (1924). It is an important Asian trade and cultural centre. Monuments include the 10th-century Mausoleum of Ismail Samani and the Ulugbek (1417–18). Industries: silk processing, rugs, handicrafts, textiles. Pop. (2002 est.) 268,000.

Bukharin, Nikolai Ivanovich (1888–1938) Russian communist political theorist. After the 1917 Revolution he became a leading member of the COMMUNIST INTERNATIONAL (Comintern) and editor of *Pravda*. In 1924, he became a member of the politburo. He opposed agricultural collectivization and was executed for treason by STALIN in 1938.

Bulawayo City in SW Zimbabwe, SE Africa; capital of Matabeleland North province. Founded by the British in

1893, it was the site of the Matabele revolt in 1896. It is the second- largest city in the country. Industries: textiles, motor vehicles, cement, electrical equipment. Pop. (2005) 824,000.

bulb In botany, a food storage organ consisting of a short stem and swollen scale leaves. Food is stored in the scales, which are either layered in a series of rings, as in the onion, or loosely attached to the stem, as in some lilies. Small buds between the scale leaves give rise to new shoots each year. New bulbs are produced in the axils of the outer scale leaves. *See also* ASEXUAL REPRODUCTION

Bulfinch, Charles (1763–1844) US architect. Bulfinch is noted for his public buildings, such as the State House in Boston; University Hall at Harvard, Cambridge, Massachusetts; and Massachusetts General Hospital, Boston. In 1818–30 he completed the building of the Capitol in Washington, D.C.

Bulganin, Nikolai (1895–1975) Soviet statesman and soldier, prime minister (1955–58) and defence minister (1947–49, 1953–55). He served in the army during World War 2. Bulganin became prime minister after the fall of MALENKOV. Nikita KHRUSHCHEV dismissed him.

Bulgaria Balkan republic in SE Europe. *See* country feature.

Bulgars Ancient Turkic people originating in the region N and E of the Black Sea. In *c.*AD 650 they split into two groups. The W group moved to Bulgaria, where they became assimilated into the Slavic population and adopted Christianity. The other group moved to the Volga region and set up a Bulgar state, eventually converting to Islam. The Volga Bulgars were conquered by the Kievan Rus in the 10th century.

Bulge, Battle of the Final German offensive of WORLD WAR 2. The Germans drove a wedge through the Allied lines in the Ardennes forest on the French-Belgian frontier in December 1944. Allied forces converged to extinguish the "bulge" in their lines in January 1945, and the advance into Germany was renewed.

bulimia nervosa Eating disorder that takes the form of compulsive eating, then purging by induced vomiting or the use of a LAXATIVE or DIURETIC. More common in girls and women, the disorder often reflects serious psychological problems or feelings of loss of control. Social pressure to be thin, particularly as a result of media images, is a contributing factor.

bulldog English bull-baiting breed of DOG with a distinctive large head, a short upturned muzzle and a projecting lower

▲ **bulldog** The history of the bulldog goes back many centuries. It was initially bred in England for bear-baiting and dog-fighting, but these pursuits were banned in 1835. The French bulldog (shown here) is considerably smaller than the pure bulldog.

BULGARIA

The Republic of Bulgaria is a country in the Balkan Peninsula, facing the Black Sea in the E. There are two main lowland regions. The Danubian lowlands in the N consist of a plateau that descends to the DANUBE, which forms much of the boundary with Romania. The other lowland region is the warmer valley of the River Maritsa, where cotton, fruits, grains, rice, tobacco and vines are grown.

Separating the two lowland areas are the BALKAN MOUNTAINS (Stara Planina), rising to heights of over 2,000m [6,500ft]. N of the capital SOFIA (Sofiya), the Balkan Mountains contain rich mineral veins of iron and non-ferrous metals.

In s-facing valleys overlooking the Maritsa Plain, plums, tobacco and vines are grown. A feature of this area is Kazanluk, from where attar of roses is exported worldwide to the cosmetics industry. South and west of the Maritsa Valley are the Rhodope (or Rhodopi) Mountains, which contain lead, zinc and copper ores.

CLIMATE

The average temperature in Sofia is 15°–21° C (60–70° F) in the summer and between –1° and 5° C (30°–40° F) in the winter. Other regions of the country experience more extreme ranges of temperature but winters are rarely severe. Rainfall is moderate all through the year.

HISTORY

In the late 7th century, BULGAR tribes crossed the Danube and subjugated the SLAVS. The first Bulgarian Empire (681–1018) quickly became a major Balkan power. In 870, Constantinople recognized the independence of the Bulgarian Christian Church. The Empire was at its height in the early 10th century, but in 1018 it was annexed to the BYZANTINE EMPIRE by Basil II. A second Bulgarian Empire (1186–1396) encompassed the whole of the Balkan peninsula, before it was subsumed into the OTTOMAN EMPIRE, which ruled the area until the 19th century. Ethnic Turks still form a sizeable minority in the country.

Ottoman attempts to undermine Bulgarian religion and language created national resentment. The brutal crushing of a native rebellion (1876) brought Russian assistance, and Bulgaria gained autonomy in 1879. In 1908 Prince FERDINAND declared Bulgaria an independent monarchy. Bulgaria was victorious in the first of the BALKAN WARS (1912–13), but fell out with its allies in the second. An ally of Germany in World War 1, defeat led to the abdication of Ferdinand (1918). His successor, Boris III, established a dictatorship in 1935, and allied with Germany in World War 2. In 1944, Soviet troops invaded. Todor Zhivkov led a coup against the monarchy and declared war on Germany.

In 1946, Bulgaria became a Communist republic. Industry was nationalized and agriculture collectivized. In 1949, Bulgaria joined the Council for Mutual Economic Assistance (COMECON) and was a founder member of the WARSAW PACT (1955).

POLITICS

In the period after World War 2, and especially under President Zhivkov from 1954, Bulgaria became dependent on the Soviet Union. In 1990 the Communist Party held on to power under increasing pressure by ousting Zhivkov, renouncing its leading role in the nation's affairs and changing its name to the Socialist Party. It won the first free elections since the war, albeit unconvincingly and against con-

AREA 110,912sq km [42,823sq mi]
POPULATION 7,322,000
CAPITAL (POPULATION) Sofia (1,045,000)
GOVERNMENT Multiparty republic
ETHNIC GROUPS Bulgarian 84%, Turkish 9%, Gypsy 5%, Macedonian, Armenian, others
LANGUAGES Bulgarian (official), Turkish
RELIGIONS Bulgarian Orthodox 83%, Islam 12%, Roman Catholic 2%, others
CURRENCY Lev = 100 stotinki

fused opposition. With improved organization, the Union of Democratic Forces defeated the old guard in the following year and began the transition to a free-market economy. Subsequent governments faced problems including inflation, food shortages, rising unemployment, strikes, a large foreign debt, a declining manufacturing industry and increased prices for raw materials. In 2001 former king Siméon Saxe-Coburg-Gotha, who had left Bulgaria in 1948 when the monarchy was abolished, became prime minister. He left office when his party lost the elections in 2005. Bulgaria joined the EU in early 2007, but six months on was criticized by EU officials for making little progress at reducing corruption.

ECONOMY

According to the World Bank, Bulgaria in the 1990s was a 'lower-middle-income' developing country. Bulgaria has some deposits of minerals, including brown coal, manganese and iron ore. Manufacturing is the leading economic activity, although outdated industrial technology has caused problems. The main products are chemicals, processed foods, metal products, machinery and textiles. Another leading export is energy, but the EU's demands to shut down ageing nuclear power plants threaten to cripple output.

Wheat and maize are the chief crops of Bulgaria. Fruit, oilseeds, tobacco and vegetables are also important. Livestock farming, particularly the rearing of dairy and beef cattle, sheep and pigs, is an important source of revenue.

B

jaw. The body is large, with muscular shoulders, a broad chest and short stout legs; the tail is short. The smooth coat may be white, tan or brindle. Height: (at shoulder) up to 38cm (15in).

bullfighting National sport of Spain and also popular in Latin America and s France. Classically, there are six bulls and three matadors, who are assigned two bulls each. Each matador has five assistants – two *picadors* (mounted on armoured horses) and three *peones* or *banderilleros*. A bullfight starts when the picadors stab the bull to weaken it. The peones then plant *banderillas* (barbed sticks) on the withers of the bull. The matador makes several passes with his red cape (*muleta*) before attempting to kill the bull by thrusting a sword between its shoulder blades. In Spain, bullfighting is regarded as an art, to many others worldwide it is a cruel spectacle.

bullfinch Northern European and Asian finch, with a stout, rounded beak. Males have a crimson and grey body and a black head; females have duller colours. It grows to 14cm (5.5in) long; species *Pyrrhula pyrrhula*.

bullfrog FROG found in streams and ponds in the USA; it is green or brown. The largest North American frog; it can jump long distances and gets its name from its loud bass voice. Family Ranidae, genus *Rana*. Length: up to 20cm (8in).

bullhead Freshwater catfish, originally found throughout E USA. Now farmed as food, it has been introduced in Europe and Hawaii. It has four pairs of fleshy mouth whiskers and a square tail. Length: to 24in (61cm); weight: to 8lb (3.6kg). Family Ictaluridae; species include yellow *Ictalurus natalis* and brown *Ictalurus nebulosus*.

Bull Run, First Battle of (July 21, 1861) American CIVIL WAR conflict, fought near Manassas, Virginia. Under-trained Union troops led by General Irvin McDowell, at first successful, were eventually routed by Confederate troops under General P.G.T. BEAUREGARD, reinforced by General Thomas J. JACKSON, who earned his nickname 'Stonewall' at the battle.

Bull Run, Second Battle of (August 28, 1862) American CIVIL WAR battle. On the old battleground of 1861, 48,000 Confederates under General Robert E. LEE defeated 75,000 Union soldiers under General John Pope, and once more, Lee threatened Washington, D.C. Union losses were 16,000 to the Confederates' 9000. Pope was dismissed as commander of the Union army, and General George McClellan, the former commander, reassumed control.

bull terrier Strongly built sporting DOG, originating from England and once used for bear-baiting; it has a large oval head with small, erect ears. The broad-chested body is set on strong legs and the tail is short. The "coloured" variety can be any colour, but the "white" is pure white, often with darker head markings. Height (at shoulder): up to 56cm (22in).

Bülow, Bernhard von, Prince (1849–1929) Chancellor of the German Empire (1900–09). Bülow was conservative in

INTERNET

Bull Run, First Battle of
▶ www.nps.gov/mana/home.htm

BURKINA FASO

The Democratic People's Republic of Burkina Faso is a landlocked country, a little larger than the United Kingdom, in w Africa. Burkina Faso consists of a plateau, between about 300 and 700m [650–2,300ft] above sea level. The plateau is cut by several rivers. Most of the rivers flow s into Ghana or E into the River Niger. During droughts some of the rivers stop flowing, becoming marshes.

The N part of the country is covered by savanna, consisting of grassland with stunted trees and shrubs. It is part of a region called the SAHEL, where the land merges into the Sahara Desert. Overgrazing of the land and deforestation are common problems in the Sahel, causing desertification in many areas of the country.

Woodlands border the rivers and parts of the SE region are swampy. The SE contains the 'W' National Park, which Burkina Faso shares with Benin and Niger, and the Arly Park. A third wildlife area is the Po Park, situated south of Ouagadougou.

CLIMATE
Burkina Faso has three main seasons. From October to February, it is relatively cool and

dry. From March to April, it is hot and dry, while it is hot and humid from May to September.

HISTORY
The people of Burkina Faso are divided into two main groups. The Voltaic group includes the Mossi – the largest single group – and the Bobo. The other main group is the Mande. Some FULANI herders and HAUSA traders also live in Burkina Faso; both groups are related to the people of N Nigeria. From c.1100, the Mossi invaded the region and established small, highly complex kingdoms. The Moro Naba, a Mossi absolute monarch, ruled the powerful Ouagadougou state from the 13th century. These semi-autonomous states fiercely resisted domination by the larger Mali and Songhai Empires.

During the 1890s 'scramble for Africa' France gained control of the area, capturing Ougadougou in 1897. In 1919, the region became the French protectorate of Upper Volta. In 1947, Upper Volta gained semi-autonomy within the French Union, and in 1958 became an autonomous republic within the French Community.

POLITICS
Upper Volta achieved independence in 1960 and adopted a strong presidential form of government. Persistent drought and austerity measures led to a military coup in 1966. Civilian rule partially returned in 1970 but the military, led by Sangoule Lamizana, regained power in 1974. Lamizana became president after elections in 1978, but was overthrown in 1980. Parliament and the constitution were suspended and a series of military regimes ensued. In 1983 Thomas Sankara gained power in a bloody coup.

In 1984, as a symbolic break from the country's colonial past, Sankara changed Upper Volta's name to Burkina Faso – 'land of the incorruptible'. In 1987, Sankara was

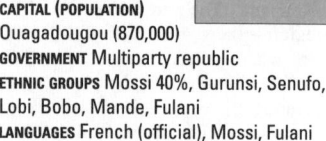

AREA 274,000sq km [105,791sq mi]
POPULATION 14,326,000
CAPITAL (POPULATION) Ouagadougou (870,000)
GOVERNMENT Multiparty republic
ETHNIC GROUPS Mossi 40%, Gurunsi, Senufo, Lobi, Bobo, Mande, Fulani
LANGUAGES French (official), Mossi, Fulani
RELIGIONS Islam 50%, traditional beliefs 40%, Christianity 10%
CURRENCY CFA franc = 100 centimes

assassinated and Captain Blaise Campaore seized power. Campaore became president in unopposed elections in 1991. Elections in 1992 were the first multiparty ballots since 1978, but Campaore remained in power then and in subsequent polls, most recently in 2005. Burkina Faso struggles with one of the world's highest rates of HIV infection.

ECONOMY
Burkina Faso is one of the world's 20 poorest countries and has become extremely dependent on foreign aid. Approximately 90% of the people earn their living by farming or by raising livestock. Grazing land covers around 37% of the land and farmland covers around 10%.

Most of Burkina Faso is dry with thin soils. The country's main food crops are beans, maize, millet, rice and sorghum. Cotton, groundnuts and shea nuts, whose seeds produce a fat used to make cooking oil and soap, are grown for sale abroad. Livestock is also important.

The country has few resources and manufacturing is on a small scale. There are deposits of manganese, zinc, lead and nickel in the north of the country, but exploitation awaits improvements to the transport system. Many young men work abroad in Ghana and Ivory Coast. The money they send to their families is important to the country's economy.

domestic policy, but his aggressiveness in foreign policy left Germany isolated and heightened the tensions in Europe that preceded the outbreak of World War 1. In 1908 Bülow lost the favour of Emperor WILLIAM II and was forced to resign.

bulrush Grass-like plant of the SEDGE family, found in marshes or beside water in Europe, Africa and North America. The common British bulrush (reed mace), *Typha latifolia*, reaches 1.8–2.1m (6–7ft) and bears both male and female flowers. Family Cyperaceae.

bumblebee (humble bee) Robust, hairy, black BEE with broad yellow or orange stripes. The genus *Bombus* lives in organized groups in ground or tree nests, where the queen lays her first eggs after the winter hibernation. These become worker bees. Later, the queen lays eggs to produce drones (males) and new queens which develop before the colony dies. The cycle is then repeated. The genus *Psithyrus*, or cuckoo bee, lays its eggs in the nests of *Bombus*, which rear them. Length: up to 2.5cm (1in). Order Hymenoptera; family Apidae.

Bunche, Ralph Johnson (1904–71) US diplomat. Bunche joined the staff of the United Nations in 1947, and helped negotiate a ceasefire in the Arab-Israeli conflict (1949), for which he received the Nobel Peace Prize (1950). He directed UN peacekeeping forces in Suez (1956), the Congo (1960) and Cyprus (1964) and was UN under secretary general (1967–71).

Bunin, Ivan Alekseievich (1870–1953) Russian writer. He was opposed to the 1917 Revolution and emigrated to France. Influenced by TURGENEV, his works lament the passing of the old Russian order. They include the novel *The Village* (1910) and the short story *The Gentleman from San Francisco* (1916). In 1933 he became the first Russian to be awarded the Nobel Prize in literature.

Bunker Hill, Battle of (June 17, 1775) Battle in the AMERICAN REVOLUTION fought on Boston's Charlestown peninsula. The first large-scale battle of the war, it was actually fought s of Bunker Hill on Breed's Hill. Although the Americans were driven from their position, they inflicted heavy losses on the British.

Bunsen, Robert Wilhelm (1811–99) German chemist, professor at Heidelberg (1852–99). He did important work with organo-arsenic compounds and discovered an arsenic poisoning antidote and evolved a method of gas analysis. With Gustav KIRCHHOFF, he used SPECTROSCOPY to discover two new elements (caesium and rubidium). He invented various kinds of laboratory equipment, including the bunsen burner.

Bunshaft, Gordon (1909–90) US architect, chief designer of the Skidmore, Owings and Merrill group. Influenced by MIES VAN DER ROHE, Bunshaft is best known for Lever House, New York (1952), a glass, curtain-walled skyscraper that created an international style.

bunting FINCH found almost worldwide. Males of the genus *Passerina* are brightly coloured, whereas the females are smaller and duller. Members of the genus *Emberiza* are larger and dull coloured, although the snow bunting is almost white. Family Fringillidae.

Buñuel, Luis (1900–83) Spanish film director. Buñuel and Salvador DALÍCôte collaborated on the surrealist masterpiece *Un Chien Andalou* (1928). *L'Age d'Or* (1930) was ferociously critical of the church and social hypocrisy. Other films include *Viridiana* (1961), *Belle de Jour* (1966), and *The Discreet Charms of the Bourgeoisie* (1974).

Bunyan, John (1628–88) English preacher and writer. During the English CIVIL WAR (1642–52), Bunyan fought as a Parliamentarian. In 1653, he began preaching at a Baptist Church in Bedford. In 1660, he was arrested for unlicensed preaching. Bunyan spent the next 12 years in prison, where he wrote the spiritual autobiography *Grace Abounding* (1666). In 1672 he was reimprisoned and started work on his masterpiece, the Christian ALLEGORY *The Pilgrim's Progress* (1684).

buoyancy Upward pressure exerted on an object by the fluid in which it is immersed. The object is subjected to pressure from all sides. The result of all these pressures is a force acting upwards that is equal to the weight of the fluid displaced. *See also* ARCHIMEDES' PRINCIPLE

burdock Oil-yielding weed found throughout Europe, North Africa and North America. It has large basal leaves

and thistle-like purple flower heads covered by stiff, hooked bracts. Common burdock, *Arctium pubens*, is biennial and grows to 0.9m (3ft). Family Asteraceae/Compositae.

Burger, Warren Earl (1907–95) Chief justice of the US Supreme Court (1969–86). He served as a judge of the US Court of Appeals in Washington, D.C. (1956–69), before his appointment as chief justice. He led a court that reversed or limited liberal decisions. In *Gregg* v. *Georgia* (1976), capital punishment for murder was declared constitutional.

Burgess, Anthony (1917–93) English novelist. Burgess' early works are set in Malaya, where he served (1954–60) as part of the colonial service. In his subsequent novels, Burgess demonstrated an interest in social trends, linguistic effects, and religious symbolism. His best-known work, *A Clockwork Orange* (1962), is a nightmare vision of a modern dystopia in which he deploys a macabre, invented language. Later novels include *Earthly Powers* (1980) and *The Kingdom of the Wicked* (1985).

Burgess shale Layer of siltstone in a quarry in Yoho National Park, E British Columbia, Canada. Discovered in 1909 by US scientist Charles Walcott, it contains a large number of animal fossils from the CAMBRIAN period. The silt has preserved traces of many of the soft bodies of sea creatures. The fossils include the oldest known chordate – a forerunner of all animals with backbones. They also include a number of kinds of animals that have completely vanished, and apparently do not belong to any of the 32 or so phyla of animals we know today.

Burghley, William Cecil, 1st Baron (1520–98) English statesman and chief minister of ELIZABETH I of England. He was secretary of state (1550–53) under EDWARD VI but failed to win MARY I's favour on her accession to the throne. On Mary's death, Elizabeth I made Burghley secretary of state (1558–72) and then lord high treasurer (1572–98). An able administrator, he helped steer a moderate course between Catholicism and Protestantism. In 1587, he was responsible for ordering the execution of MARY, QUEEN OF SCOTS.

Burgos Capital of Burgos province, N Spain. Founded in the 9th century, it was capital of the former kingdom of CASTILE. Burgos was General FRANCO's headquarters during the Spanish CIVIL WAR. Sites includes a fine Gothic cathedral (1221) and the burial place of El CID. It is an important trade and tourist centre. Pop. (2001) 166,187; 348,934 (province).

Burgundy (Bourgogne) Historical region and former duchy of E central France; it now includes the departments of Yonne, Côte-d'Or, Saône et Loire, Ain and Nièvre. Dijon is the historical capital. Burgundy's golden age began in 1364 when John II of France made his son, Philip the Bold, Duke of Burgundy. The succeeding dukes created a state that extended across the Rhine and included the Low Countries. The last Duke, Charles the Bold (r 1467–77), failed to have himself crowned king by the Holy Roman Emperor, and Burgundy was divided up after his death, France annexing the largest part. The region has many Romanesque churches. It is a rich agricultural region renowned for its wine. Pop. (1999) 1,610,407.

Burke, Edmund (1729–97) British statesman and writer, b. Ireland. He played a major part in the reduction of royal influence in the House of Commons and sought better treatment for Catholics and American colonists. He was involved in the impeachment of Warren HASTINGS in an attempt to reform India's government in 1788. Burke deplored the excesses of the FRENCH REVOLUTION in his most celebrated work, *Reflections on the Revolution in France* (1790).

Burke, Robert O'Hara (1820–61) Irish explorer. In 1860, he led the first expedition to cross Australia from s to N. At the Barcoo River, Burke left most of the party and continued with three companions. They reached N Australia in 1861. Only one of the group survived the return journey.

Burkina Faso Republic in west Africa. *See* country feature

burlesque (It. 'ridicule') Form of literary or dramatic entertainment that achieves its effect by caricature, ridicule and distortion, often of celebrated literary genres or works. A later form, in the USA, became synonymous with strip shows.

Burlington City on Lake Champlain, NW Vermont, USA. Settled in 1773, it was the scene of a British naval attack in

▲ **bullfinch** The stout-beaked bullfinch (*Pyrrhula pyrrhula*) is well adapted to its woodland habitats where it feeds on the buds and flowers found on trees.

▲ **bunting** The black-headed bunting (*Emberiza melanocephala*) is found in SE Europe and SW Asia. A type of finch this species grows to about 16cm (6in) long.

▲ **bull terrier** A sporting dog bred for dog-fighting and bear-baiting, the bull terrier was a cross between a bulldog and a type of terrier. No longer bred for their aggression, today's bull terriers are intelligent, loyal dogs, and make good family pets.

INTERNET

Burgess shale
▶ www.nmnh.si.edu/paleo/shale

Burkina Faso
▶ burkinaembassy-usa.org

the WAR OF 1812. The largest city in the state, it is the site of the University of Vermont and of Trinity College. Industries: missile parts, textiles, wood products. Pop. (2000) 38,889.

Burlington, Richard Boyle, 3rd Earl of (1694–1753) English architect. Burlington was an important exponent of PALLADIANISM in England. He promoted the style through his own buildings, such as his villa at Chiswick, London. He also published drawings by PALLADIO and Inigo JONES.

Burma Republic in SE Asia. *See* country feature

Burmese Official language of Burma, spoken by 75% of the population. It belongs to the Tibeto-Burman branch of the Sino-Tibetan family of languages.

burn Injury caused by exposure to flames, scalding liquids, caustic chemicals, acids, electric current, or ionizing radiation. Its severity depends on the extent of skin loss and the depth of tissue damage. A **superficial** burn, involving only

the EPIDERMIS, causes redness, swelling and pain; it heals within a few days. A **partial thickness** burn (epidermis and DERMIS) causes intense pain, with mottling and blistering of the skin; it takes a couple of weeks to heal. In a **full thickness** burn, involving both the skin and the underlying flesh, there is charring, and the damaged flesh looks dry and leathery; there is no pain because the nerve endings have been destroyed. Such a burn, serious in itself, is associated with life-threatening complications, including dehydration and infection. Treatment includes fluid replacement and antibiotics; skin grafting may be necessary.

Burne-Jones, Sir Edward Coley (1833–98) English painter and designer. Burne-Jones was influenced by Dante Gabriel ROSSETTI and William MORRIS, and was associated with the PRE-RAPHAELITE BROTHERHOOD's Romanticism and escapism. He often depicted scenes from Arthurian and

BURMA

The Union of Burma has been officially known as the Union of Myanmar since 1989 but is more usually referred to as Burma. Mountains border the country in the E and W, with the highest mountains in the N. Burma's highest mountain is Hkakabo Razi, which is 5,881m [19,294ft]

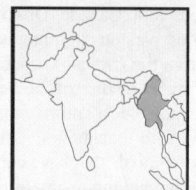

high. Between these ranges is central Burma, which contains the fertile valleys of the IRRAWADDY and Sittang rivers. The Irrawaddy delta on the Bay of Bengal is one of the

world's leading rice-growing areas. Burma also includes the long Tenasserim coast in the SE.

CLIMATE

Burma has a tropical monsoon climate. There are three seasons. The rainy season runs from late May to mid-October. A cool, dry season follows, between late October and the middle part of February. The hot season lasts from late February to mid-May, although temperatures remain high during the humid rainy season.

AREA 676,578sq km [261,227sq mi]
POPULATION 47,374,000
CAPITAL (POPULATION) Rangoon (4,082,000), Naypyidaw (seat of government)
GOVERNMENT Military regime
ETHNIC GROUPS Burman 68%, Shan 9%, Karen 7%, Rakhine 4%, Chinese, Indian, Mon
LANGUAGES Burmese (official), minority ethnic groups have their own languages
RELIGIONS Buddhism 89%, Christianity, Islam
CURRENCY Kyat = 100 pyas

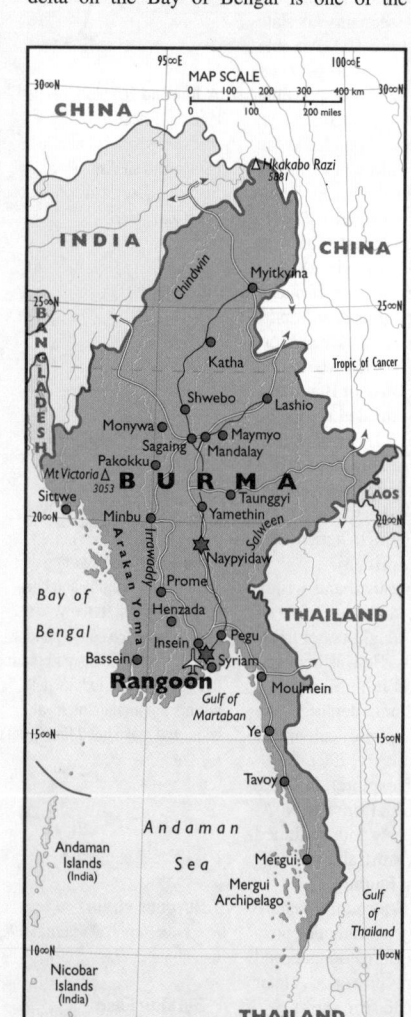

HISTORY

Conflict between the Burmans and Mons dominated Burma's early history. In 1044 the Burman King Anawratha unified the Irrawaddy delta region. In 1287 KUBLAI KHAN conquered the Burman capital, Pagan. Burma was divided: the Shan controlled N Burma, while the resurgent Mons held the S. In the 16th century, the Burmans subjugated the Shan. In 1758 Alaungapaya reunified Burma, defeating the Mons kingdom and establishing the Konbaung dynasty.

Wars with British India marked much of the 19th century. The first war (1824) resulted in the British gaining the coastal regions of Tenasserim and Arakan. The second war (1852) saw the British gain control of the Irrawaddy delta. British India annexed Burma in the third war (1885). In 1937 Burma gained limited self-government. Helped by the Burmese Independent Army, led by AUNG SAN, Japan conquered the country in 1942. The installation of a puppet regime led Aung San to form a resistance movement. In 1947 Aung San was murdered. Burma achieved independence in 1948.

POLITICS

The socialist AFPFL government, led by U NU, faced secessionist revolts by communists and Karen tribesmen. In 1958 U Nu invited General NE WIN to re-establish order. Civilian rule returned in 1960, but in 1962 Ne Win mounted a successful coup. His military dictatorship faced mass insurgency. In 1974 Ne Win became president. Mass demonstrations forced Ne Win to resign in 1988, but the military retained power under the guise of the State Law and Order Restoration Council (SLORC), led by General Saw Maung. In

1989 the country's name changed to Myanmar. The National League for Democracy (NLD) led by AUNG SAN SUU KYI won elections in 1990, but SLORC annulled the result and placed Aung San Suu Kyi under house arrest. In 1997 SLORC became the State Peace and Development Council (SPDC). In 1998, NLD calls for the reconvening of Parliament led to mass detention of political opponents by the SPDC.

Aung San Suu Kyi, effectively leader of the opposition, was released in 2002 but arrested again from 2003. Her continued imprisonment, along with that of thousands of other political prisoners, attracted widespread international criticism.

In 2006 the government abruptly moved the administrative capital to Naypyidaw, in the Pyinmana area 400km (250mi) north of Rangoon. The newly built city is closed to the Burmese public and to most international visitors, and is specifically designed for easy military access to allow demonstrations to be rapidly suppressed. Secrecy is high and little information is available. September 2007 saw mass protests, the largest since the 1980s, which were brutally suppressed.

ECONOMY

Agriculture is the main activity, employing 66% of the workforce. The chief crop is rice. Groundnuts, maize, plantains, pulses, seed cotton, sesame seeds and sugar cane are also produced. Forestry is important and teak is a major product. Fish and shellfish are another industry. The varied natural resources are mostly underdeveloped, but Burma is famous for its precious stones, especially rubies. It is almost self-sufficient in oil and natural gas.

other mediaeval legends, and was considered an outstanding designer of stained glass windows.

Burnett, Frances (1849–1924) US writer, b. England. Burnett is chiefly remembered as the author of the children's classics *Little Lord Fauntleroy* (1886), *The Little Princess* (1905), and *The Secret Garden* (1911). She also wrote novels and plays for older audiences.

Burney, Fanny (1752–1840) English novelist, dramatist, and diarist. The daughter of the musicologist Dr Charles Burney, she achieved fame with her debut novel, *Evelina* (1778), a semi-satirical, semi-sentimental look at polite society through the eyes of a young innocent. This was followed by similar works such as *Cecilia* (1782), *Camilla* (1796), and *The Wanderer* (1814). Her writing greatly influenced Jane AUSTEN.

Burnham, Daniel Hudson (1846–1912) US architect and city planner. With his partner John W. Root, Burnett pioneered the development of early steel-frame and modern commercial architecture. Designs include the Reliance Building (1890) and the Masonic Temple Building (1891), both in Chicago.

Burns, Robert (1759–96) Scottish poet. The success of *Poems, Chiefly in the Scottish Dialect* (1786), which includes "The Holy Fair" and "To a Mouse", enabled Burns to move to Edinburgh, where he was admired as "the heaven-taught ploughman". Although popular, he could not support himself from his poetry and so became an excise officer. Scotland's unofficial national poet, his works include "Tam o'Shanter" (1790) and the song "Auld Lang Syne". An annual Burns Night is held on his birthday, January 25.

Burnside, Ambrose Everett (1824–81) US Civil War general. He participated in the First Battle of BULL RUN (1861). Burnside led the Union's Army of the Potomac to defeat at Fredericksburg (1862). He was relieved of command of the 9th Corps following Petersburg (1864). After the war, he was governor of Rhode Island and a senator (1875–81).

Burr, Aaron (1756–1836) US statesman, vice president (1801–05). A veteran of the American Revolution, Burr was senator for New York (1791–97). His contribution to the formation of a Republican legislature in New York (1800), ensured the election of a Republican president. Burr was meant to become vice president, but confusion in the ELECTORAL COLLEGE resulted in a tie for president between Burr and Thomas JEFFERSON. Jefferson was elected with the support of Alexander HAMILTON. This mix-up led to the adoption of the 12th Amendment to the US Constitution. Burr proved an able vice president and was nominated for governor of New York. Hamilton led public attacks on Burr's suitability, which resulted in a duel (1804). Burr killed Hamilton and his political career was effectively ended. Embittered, he embarked on an apparent conspiracy to establish an independent republic in sw USA. Burr was tried for treason, but acquitted in 1807.

Burra, Edward John (1905–76) English painter. Fascinated with the urban life of Harlem, New York, and the Marseilles docks, some of Burra's most famous paintings are the Harlem scenes (1933–34). In the mid-1930s, he turned to fantastic imagery, akin to SURREALISM. His later paintings, such as *Soldiers* and *War in the Sun*, were provoked by the tragedies of the Spanish Civil War and World War 2.

Burroughs, Edgar Rice (1875–1950) US author of adventure novels. A prolific writer, he is best known as the creator of the apeman Tarzan, who featured in a series of books, beginning with *Tarzan of the Apes* (1912).

Burroughs, William S. (Seward) (1914–97) US novelist, regarded as one of the founders of the BEAT MOVEMENT. Burroughs's best-known work, *Naked Lunch* (1959), deals in part with his heroin addiction. Other works, experimental in style, include *The Ticket That Exploded* (1962), *The Wild Boys* (1971), and *The Western Lands* (1987).

bursitis Inflammation of the fluid-filled sac (bursa) surrounding a joint. It is characterized by pain, swelling and restricted movement. Treatment generally includes rest, heat and gentle exercise. 'Housemaid's knee', 'tennis elbow', and bunions are common forms of bursitis.

Burton, Richard (1925–84) Welsh stage and film actor, remembered for his deep, passionate, and fiery voice. By the 1950s, he had a reputation as a leading Shakespearian actor. Burton made his film debut in *The Last Days of Dolwyn* (1948). From 1952 he concentrated on cinema, appearing in *The Robe* (1953), *Look Back in Anger* (1959), and *Becket* (1964). He made a number of films with Elizabeth Taylor, notably *Who's Afraid of Virginia Woolf?* (1966). The couple had a tempestuous relationship and married each other twice.

Burton, Sir Richard Francis (1821–90) English explorer and scholar. In 1853 he travelled in disguise to Medina and Mecca, one of the first Europeans to visit the holy cities. On his second trip to E Africa, with John SPEKE in 1857, he discovered Lake Tanganyika. The author of many books, he was best known for his translation of the *Arabian Nights* (1885–88).

Burundi Republic in E central Africa. *See* country feature.

Busby, Sir Matt (1909–94) Scottish football player and manager. Busby played for Manchester City, Liverpool, and Scotland, before becoming manager (1945–69) of Manchester United. He survived the 1958 Munich air disaster (in which most of the famous 'Busby Babes' died) to build his third great side, and the first English club to win the European Cup (1968).

Bush, George Herbert Walker (1924–) 41st US president (1989–93). Bush served as a fighter pilot during World War 2. In 1966, he entered Congress as a representative of Texas. Under President Richard Nixon, he held several political offices, including ambassador (1971–73) to the United Nations. Under President Gerald Ford, Bush was head (1976–77) of the Central Intelligence Agency (CIA). In 1980, after failing to secure the presidential nomination, he became vice president (1981–88) to Ronald REAGAN. When Reagan retired, Bush gained the Republican nomination. In the 1988 presidential election, he easily defeated the challenge of Michael Dukakis. For many Americans, the collapse of Soviet communism was a vindication of the hawkish policies of the Reagan-Bush years. In 1989, the US military invaded Panama and seized General Manuel NORIEGA. Iraq's invasion (1990) of Kuwait provided the first test of Bush's "new world order" and threatened America's oil supplies. The Allied forces, led by General SCHWARZKOPF, won the GULF WAR (1991) but failed to remove Saddam HUSSEIN. At home Bush faced a stagnant economy, high unemployment, and a massive budget deficit, forcing him (1990) to break his election pledge and raise taxes. This factor, combined with a split in the conservative vote, led to victory for his Democratic successor Bill CLINTON.

Bush, George W. (Walker) (1946–) 43rd US president (2001–), son of the 41st president George Bush. He made a personal fortune from the sale of the Texas Rangers baseball team and was Republican governor of Texas from 1995 to 2000. In the controversial 2000 presidential elections, Bush defeated the Democrat candidate Al Gore by the narrowest of margins. The US Supreme Court ruled against a further recount of votes in the crucial state of Florida after accusations of faulty counting and electoral fraud. Faced with economic recession, Bush passed a tax-cutting budget. After the terrorist attacks on the United States on September 11, 2001, he sent US troops into Afghanistan to destroy the AL-QAEDA terrorist network, believed to be responsible, and to topple the Taliban regime accused of supporting al-Qaeda. He increased military expenditure to fight the 'war on terror'. In 2003 US and other (particularly British) troops invaded Iraq and overthrew Saddam HUSSEIN and his regime. In 2004 Bush was re-elected, defeating John Kerry.

bushbaby (galago) Primitive, squirrel-like PRIMATE of African forests and bushlands. It is usually grey or brown with a white stripe between its large eyes. It is a gregarious nocturnal tree-dweller which can be domesticated. Length: (excluding tail) to 38cm (15in). Family Lorisidae; genus *Galago*.

bushido (Jap. way of the samurai) Moral discipline important in Japan between 1603 and 1868. It arose from a fusion of Confucian ethics and Japanese feudalism. Requiring loyalty, courage, honour, politeness and benevolence, Bushido paralleled European chivalry. Although not a religion, Bushido involved family worship and SHINTO rites.

bushmaster Largest pit VIPER, found in central America and N South America. It has long fangs and large venom glands,

▲ **Bush** 43rd US President George Walker Bush began his business career in his family's oil business. His first attempt to gain high political office was an unsuccessful run for the US House of Representatives in 1978. Known for his informal manner, he has achieved both the highest and the lowest opinion poll ratings of any US president.

and is pinkish and brown with a diamond pattern. Length: up to 3.7m (12ft). Family Viperidae; subfamily Crotalidae.

bustard Large bird found in arid areas of the Eastern Hemisphere. Its plumage is grey, black, brown and white and its neck and legs are long; in appearance it is quite ostrich-like. A swift runner and a strong, though reluctant flier, it feeds on small animals and lays up to five eggs. Family Otidae. Height: 1.3m (4.3ft).

butane (C_4H_{10}) Colourless flammable gas, the fourth member of the ALKANE series of HYDROCARBONS. It has two ISOMERS: n-butane is obtained from natural gas; isobutane is a by-product of PETROLEUM refining. Butane can be liquefied under pressure at normal temperatures and is used in the manufacture of fuel gas and synthetic rubber. Properties: b.p. (n-butane) $-0.3°C$ (31.5°F) and (isobutane) $-10.3°C$ (13.46°F).

Buthelezi, Mangosuthu Gatsha (1928–) ZULU chief and politician. Buthelezi was installed as chief of the Buthelezi tribe in 1953 and became chief minister of KwaZulu, a 'bantustan' within APARTHEID South Africa in 1970. In 1975, he founded INKATHA. Accusations of complicity in apartheid led

INTERNET

Butler, Samuel
▶ www.victorianweb.org/
science/butler.html

to violence between Inkatha and the rival AFRICAN NATIONAL CONGRESS (ANC) in the early 1990s. Buthelezi acted as minister for home affairs (1994–2004) in the ANC government.

Butler, Samuel (1835–1902) British satirical writer. His famous novel *Erewhon* (1872) is a classic utopian criticism of contemporary social and economic injustice. He produced a sequel to his early masterpiece, *Erewhon Revisited* (1901), and the autobiographical *The Way of All Flesh* (1903), a biting attack on Victorian life and the values of his own upbringing.

butter Edible fat made from milk. A churning process changes the milk from a water-in-oil emulsion to an oil-in-water emulsion. The fat (oil) globules of the milk collide and coalesce, losing their protective shield of protein and turning into butter, thus separating out from the more watery whey. Commercial butter contains about 80% fat, 1–3% added salt, 1% milk solids and 16% water.

buttercup Herbaceous flowering plant found worldwide; the many species vary considerably according to habitat, but usually have yellow or white flowers and deeply-cut leaves. Family Ranunculaceae; genus *Ranunculus*.

BURUNDI

The Republic of Burundi is a small country in E-central Africa. A section of the Great RIFT VALLEY lies in the W. It contains part of Lake TANGANYIKA, whose shoreline is 772m [2,533ft] above sea level. E of the Rift Valley is a mountain zone, rising to 2,670m [8,760ft]. The land descends to the E in a series of steppe-like plateaux. Burundi forms part of the Nile-Congo watershed and contains the headwaters of the River Kagera, the most remote source of the Nile.

Grassland covers much of Burundi, because much of the original forest has been cleared by farming and overgrazing. New forests are now being planted to halt the loss of soil fertility caused by erosion.

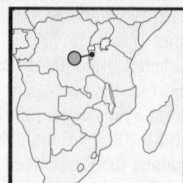

CLIMATE
Bujumbura has an average annual temperature of 23°C [73°F]. The months of June to August and December to January are dry, but the rest of the year is rainy. The mountains and the central plateaux are distinctly cooler and wetter than the Rift Valley floor, but rainfall decreases to the E.

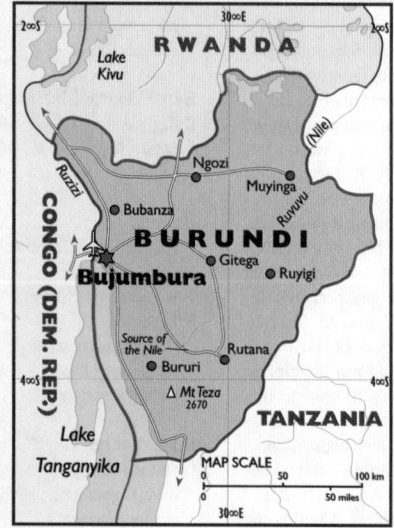

HISTORY
The first known inhabitants of the area were the Twa, a pygmy group of hunting and gathering people, who now make up just 1% of the population. Around 1,000 years ago, the Hutu, a Bantu-speaking, iron-using farming people from the W, began to settle, pushing the Twa into remote areas. A third group, the cattle-owning Tutsi from the NE, arrived around 600 years ago. They gradually took control of the area and, although in the minority, formed the ruling class. The Tutsi created a feudal state, making the Hutu serfs. The explorers Richard Burton and John Hanning Speke visited the area in 1858 in their quest to find the source of the Nile.

A powerful Tutsi kingdom under Mwami (king) Rugamba developed in the late 18th century, but broke up by the 1880s. Germany conquered what are now Burundi and Rwanda in the late 1890s. The area, called Ruanda-Urundi, became part of German East Africa. But after Germany's defeat in World War 1, Belgium took control.

In 1961, the people of Urundi voted to become a monarchy under Mwami Mwambutsa IV, who had ruled since 1915, while the people of Ruanda voted to become a republic.

POLITICS
The two territories finally became fully independent as Burundi and Rwanda on 1 July 1962. Since then, Burundi has suffered great conflict caused by ethnic rivalry between the Hutu majority and the Tutsi. Around 300,000 people have been killed, and a great many more displaced or made refugees. In 1965, Mwambutsa refused to appoint a Hutu prime minister, although the Hutu were in the majority. An attempted coup was brutally put down. In 1966, Mwambutsa was deposed by his son who became Mwami Ntare V, but Tutsi prime minister Michel Micombero deposed Ntare and declared Burundi to be a republic with himself as president.

Between 1966 and 1972, most Hutu and some Tutsi were removed from high office. This culminated in a rebellion, when between 100,000 and 200,000 mostly Hutu were

AREA 27,834sq km [10,747sq mi]
POPULATION 8,391,000
CAPITAL (POPULATION) Bujumbura (235,000)
GOVERNMENT Republic
ETHNIC GROUPS Hutu 85%, Tutsi 14%, Twa (Pygmy)
LANGUAGES French, Kirundi (both official)
RELIGIONS Roman Catholic 62%, traditional beliefs 23%, Islam 10%, Protestant 5%
CURRENCY Burundi franc = 100 centimes

killed. In 1976, Jean-Baptiste Bagaza, a Tutsi, deposed Micombero. In 1981, Burundi became a one-party state, but Bagaza was deposed in 1987 by a coup led by Pierre Buyoya. Another uprising in 1988 led to the slaughter of thousands of Hutus.

In 1992, a new constitution gave the country a multiparty system. In 1993 Melchior Ndadaye, a Hutu, beat Buyoya in presidential elections, but was assassinated by supporters of Bagaza. In 1994 the new president, Cyprien Ntaryamira, a Hutu, was killed in a plane crash together with the Rwandan president, causing more ethnic violence. In 1996, Buyoya staged another coup and suspended the constitution. In 1999 peace talks began which led, in 2001, to the setting up of a transitional power-sharing government. However, some Hutu rebel groups refused to sign the ceasefire. In 2003, Domitien Ndayizeye became president under the power-sharing agreement. In 2004, the disarming of rebels and soldiers began. In 2005 the people voted in favour of a new power-sharing constitution. In 2006 the last rebel group signed a ceasefire, but peace remains fragile.

ECONOMY
Burundi is one of the world's poorest countries. 94% of the people depend on farming, mainly at subsistence level. The main food crops are bananas, beans, cassava, maize and sweet potatoes. Cattle, goats and sheep are raised and fish is important.

The economy depends on coffee and tea, which account for 90% of foreign exchange earnings, and cotton.

butterfly Day-flying INSECT of the order Lepidoptera. The adult has two pairs of scale-covered wings that are often brightly coloured. The female lays eggs on a selected food source and the (CATERPILLAR) larvae emerge within days or hours. The larvae have chewing mouthparts and often do great damage to crops until they reach the "resting phase" of the life cycle, the pupa (chrysalis). Within the pupa, the adult (imago) is formed with wings, wing muscles, antennae, a slender body and sucking mouthparts. The adults mate soon after emerging from the chrysalis, and the four-stage life cycle begins again. *See also* METAMORPHOSIS

butterwort Large group of carnivorous bog plants that trap and digest insects in a sticky secretion on their leaves. They bear single white, purple or yellow flowers on a leafless stalk. The sides of the leaves roll over to enclose the insect while it is digested. Family Lentibulariaceae; species *Pinguicula*. *See also* INSECTIVOROUS PLANT

buttress Mass of masonry built against a wall to add support or reinforcement. Used since ancient times, buttresses became increasingly complex and decorative in medieval architecture. GOTHIC architecture often featured marvellously daring flying buttresses.

Buxtehude, Diderik (Dietrich) (1637–1707) Danish organist and composer known for his organ and church music. He was organist at Lübeck, Germany, and became well-known for his evening concerts, *Abendmusik*, for which he composed many works. He wrote many sacred choral works, especially cantatas, a large number of organ compositions and much chamber music. J.S. BACH was greatly influenced by him.

buzzard Slow-flying bird with broad, rounded wings, fan-shaped tail, sharp, hooked beak, and sharp talons. The name is used in reference to many BIRDS OF PREY, as in North America for hawks and vultures. Family Accipitridae; genus *Buteo*.

Byatt, A.S. (Antonia Susan) (1936–) English novelist and critic, sister of Margaret DRABBLE. Byatt was primarily an academic literary scholar until the publication of her third novel, *The Virgin in the Garden* (1978). *Possession*, a literary mystery story and romance spanning two centuries, won the 1990 Booker Prize. She has written studies of Wordsworth, Coleridge, and Iris Murdoch. She received a CBE in 1990.

Byblos Ancient city of the Phoenicians, in Lebanon, 27km (17mi) N of BEIRUT. Byblos was a centre of Phoenician trade with Egypt from the 2nd millennium BC and was particularly famous as a source of PAPYRUS. The Greek word for 'book' derived from its name. Byblos was abandoned after its capture by the Crusaders in 1103.

Byrd, Richard Evelyn (1888–1957) US polar explorer. A naval officer and aviator, Byrd led five major expeditions to the Antarctic (1928–57), surveying more than 2,200,000sq km (845,000sq mi) of the continent. Among other feats, he claimed to be the first man to fly over both the North Pole (1926) and the South Pole (1929).

Byrd, William (1543–1623) English composer. He was appointed by Elizabeth I to be joint organist of the Chapel Royal with Thomas TALLIS, whom he succeeded in 1585. With Tallis, he was granted England's first monopoly to print music. Byrd was a master of all the musical forms of his day, but was especially celebrated for his madrigals and church music.

Byron, George Gordon Noel Byron, 6th Baron (1788–1824) English poet. After a childhood scarred by the handicap of a clubfoot and maltreatment by his mother, he went to Trinity College, Cambridge (1805). Although Byron achieved notice with the satire *English Bards and Scotch Reviewers* (1809), it was the first two cantos of *Childe Harold's Pilgrimage* (1812) that brought him fame. His romantic image and reputation for dissolute living and numerous sexual affairs vied with his poetic reputation. By 1816 he was a social outcast and went into permanent exile. Abroad, Byron wrote Cantos III and IV of *Childe Harold* (1816, 1818) and *Don Juan* (1819–24), an epic satire often regarded as his masterpiece. In 1823 he travelled to Greece to fight for Greek independence against the Turks and died of fever at Missolonghi.

byte Binary number used to represent the letters, numbers and other characters in a computer system. Each byte consists of the same number of BITS (binary digits). Each bit has

BUTTERFLY

The life-cycle of the European swallowtail (*Papilio machoan*) is typical of most butterflies. The female adult (1) lays her eggs (2) on the underside of leaves in batches of 100 or more. The eggs hatch into the first stage larva or caterpillar (3). The caterpillar moults several times before it is fully grown (4). After the final moult the caterpillar's skin hardens (4, 5) to form the case of the pupa or chrysalis (6). Within the case the tissues of the caterpillar reorganize before the adult butterfly emerges (1).

two possible states, represented by the binary numbers 0 and 1. Byte is a contraction of "by eight", and originally meant an eight-bit byte, such as 01101010 (representing j). Some computers now use 16– or 32–bit bytes.

Byzantine art and architecture Art produced in the Byzantine empire E of the Balkans. Its greatest achievements fall within three periods. The **first Golden Age** coincided with the reign of JUSTINIAN I (527–65), and saw the construction of the HAGIA SOPHIA. The **second Golden Age** refers to the artistic revival that occurred during the time of the Macedonian emperors (867–1057), and which followed the terrible destruction of art caused by the Iconoclastic Controversy which forbade the worship of religious images. Finally, the last years of the empire, under the rule of the Palaeologs (1261–1453), are often referred to as the **Byzantine Renaissance**. Most Byzantine art was religious in subject matter and combined Christian imagery with an oriental expressive style. The MOSAIC and ICON were the most common forms. Byzantine church architecture is typically central rather than longitudinal, and the central dome (surrounded by groupings of smaller or semi-domes) is supported by means of pendentives. Construction is of brick arranged in decorative patterns and mortar. Interiors are faced with marble slabs, coloured glass mosaics, gold leaf, and fresco decoration.

Byzantine Empire Christian, Greek-speaking, Eastern ROMAN EMPIRE, which outlasted the Roman Empire in the West by nearly 1000 years. Constantinople (Byzantium or ISTANBUL) was established by the Roman Emperor CONSTANTINE I in AD 330. The area of the Byzantine Empire varied greatly, and its history from *c*.600 was marked by continual military crisis and heroic recovery. At its height, under JUSTINIAN I in the 6th century, it controlled, besides Asia Minor and the Balkans, much of the Near East and the Mediterranean coastal regions of Europe and North Africa. Of its many enemies, the most formidable were the Arabs, who overran the Near Eastern provinces in the 7th century; the Slavs and BULGARS, who captured most of the Balkans, and the Seljuk Turks. From 1204 to 1261, it was controlled by usurping Crusaders from W Europe and, although Constantinople was recovered, Byzantine territory shrank under pressure from the West and from the Ottoman Turks, who finally captured Constantinople in 1453, extinguishing the Byzantine Empire.

INTERNET

Byron, George Gordon Noel Byron, 6th Baron
▶ www.englishhistory.net/byron.html

Byzantine art and architecture
▶ www.guideistanbul.net/sultanahmet.htm
▶ www.culture.gr

C

C/c, third letter of the Roman alphabet; it comes from the same root as the letter G/g. It is derived from the Semitic word gimel, *meaning throwing stick. It is thought to have been adapted from the Egyptian hieroglyph for a boomerang.*

▲ **cabbage** Cabbage (1), broccoli (2), cauliflower (3), and brussels sprouts (4) all belong to the same Brassica species although they differ greatly in appearance. Like curly kale (5), they are all hardy and some varieties can stand quite cold winters.

Cabal Advisers to CHARLES II of England, 1667–74. The five members of this group, which is sometimes considered the first CABINET, were Clifford, Arlington, Buckingham, Ashley (later Earl of SHAFTESBURY) and Lauderdale; the first letters of their names spell 'cabal'. When it became known that two of them plotted with the king to tolerate Catholicism, the Cabal split up.

cabbage Low, stout vegetable of the genus *Brassica*. Members include Brussels sprouts, cauliflowers, broccoli, kohlrabi and turnips. They are biennials that produce 'heads' one year and flowers the next. The common cabbage (*B. oleracea capitata*) has an edible head and large, fleshy leaves. Family Brassicaceae/Cruciferae.

cabbage white butterfly BUTTERFLY, the green caterpillar of which is a common pest on cabbage plants. The female adult is almost completely white except for black spots on its wings; the male has no forewing spots. Species *Pieris brassicae.*

cabbala (kabbala) Form of Jewish MYSTICISM holding that every word, letter, number and accent of the Bible contains mysteries to be interpreted, often in codes for YAHWEH. The earliest extant cabbalist work is the 3rd-century *Sefir Yezirah* ("Book of Creation"). Cabbalism spread throughout Europe in the 13th century, and is still practised by some Hasidic Jews.

Cabeza de Vaca, Álvar Núñez (1490–1557) Spanish explorer. In 1528, he was shipwrecked off the Texas coast. He and three fellow survivors became the first Europeans to explore the American Southwest, eventually settling in Mexico in 1536. His *Comentarios* (1555) recount hardships endured in South America, where he served as governor (1542–45) of the province of Río de la Plata.

Cabinda Province of Angola, SW Africa, N of the River Congo, bounded W by the Atlantic Ocean and separated from the rest of Angola by D.R. Congo; the seaport and chief town is Cabinda. The Simulambuco Treaty (1885) politically unified Cabinda with Angola. Cabinda refuses to recognize the treaty and claims independence from Angola. There are important offshore oilfields. Industries: oil refining, palm, timber, cacao. Area: 7270sq km (2808sq mi). Pop. (2002 est.) 208,900.

cabinet Body of people collectively responsible to the legislature for government in a parliamentary system. Most cabinet ministers have individual responsibility for the management of a department of state. In the UK, cabinet ministers are chosen by the PRIME MINISTER, but officially appointed by the crown. A cabinet minister need not sit in either House of Parliament, but usually sits in the HOUSE OF COMMONS. In a presidential system, cabinets may be formed out of heads of major departments, but have only advisory status in relation to the PRESIDENT. Most present-day cabinets have about 20 members.

cable Wire for mechanical support, for conducting electricity or carrying signals. In civil and mechanical engineering, a cable is made of twisted strands of steel wire. They range in size from small bowden cables to massive supporting cables on the decks of suspension bridges. In electrical engineering, a cable is a CONDUCTOR of electricity and consists of one or more insulated wires, which may be either single or multi-stranded. They range greatly in size, from cables used for domestic wiring to the large, armoured underwater cables. These are used for telephone, radio, television and data signals. In a COAXIAL CABLE, one conductor is cylindrical and surrounds the other. OPTICAL FIBRES carry signals in the form of coded pulses of light.

cable television Generally refers to community antenna television (CATV). CATV does not broadcast, but picks up signals at a central ANTENNA and delivers them to individual subscribers via COAXIAL or OPTICAL-FIBRE cables. Originally designed for areas with poor reception and no local station, cable television, run by private franchise, increasingly relays satellite transmissions from the central antenna.

Cabot, John (*c.*1450–98) Italian navigator, b. Giovanni Caboto. Backed by HENRY VII of England, he sailed in search of a W route to India, and reached NEWFOUNDLAND (1497). His discovery served as the basis for English claims in North America. His account of the Newfoundland fisheries encouraged fishermen from European Atlantic ports to follow his route.

Cabral, Pedro Álvares (1467–1520) Portuguese navigator who discovered Brazil. In 1500, he led an expedition to the East Indies on the route pioneered by Vasco da GAMA. To avoid contrary winds and currents, he took a westward course in the Atlantic and touched on the coast of Brazil, which he claimed for Portugal.

Cabrini, Saint Frances Xavier (1850–1917) US foundress of orphanages, hospitals, schools and convents, b. Italy; the first US citizen to be canonized (1946). She became a nun in 1877, founded the Institute of Missionary Sisters of the Sacred Heart (1880), and moved to the USA (1889). Her feast day is December 22.

cacao *See* COCOA

cactus Any of 2000 or so species of SUCCULENTS, found particularly in hot desert regions of the Western Hemisphere. A cactus' long roots enable it to absorb moisture from desert terrains and the fleshy green stem is adapted for water storage with a waxy coating to restrict evaporation. Stems are usually spiny, cylindrical and branched. Cactus flowers are usually borne singly in a wide range of colours. Height: from less than 2.5cm (1in) to more than 15m (50ft). *See also* XEROPHYTE

Cadbury, George (1839–1922) English manufacturer and social reformer. In 1861, he and his brother Richard (1835–99) took control of their father's cocoa and chocolate factory. In 1879, Cadbury established a model housing estate for the factory workers at Bourneville.

caddis fly Any of several moth-like insects of the order Trichoptera. Adults have long, many-jointed antennae, hold their wings tent-like over the body, and usually grow to about 25mm (1in) long.

cadence In music, ending of a melodic phrase and/or its accompanying CHORD progression. In Western classical theory, the main kinds of chordal cadence are: **perfect** (dominant to tonic chords); **imperfect** (tonic or other chord to dominant); **plagal** (subdominant to tonic); and **interrupted** (dominant to chord other than tonic, often submediant).

Cádiz Port in SW Spain, on the Gulf of Cádiz; capital of Cádiz province (founded 1100BC). It became an important port for shipping routes to the Americas, and in 1587 a Spanish fleet was burned here by Sir Francis DRAKE. It has a 13th-century cathedral, art and archaeological museums. Industries: shipbuilding, sherry, olives, salt, fishing. Pop. (2000) 138,006.

cadmium (symbol Cd) Silvery-white metallic element in group II of the periodic table, first isolated in 1817 by the German chemist Friedrich Stromeyer. Cadmium is mainly obtained as a by-product in the extraction of ZINC and LEAD. Malleable and ductile, it is used in ELECTROPLATING, as an absorber of neutrons in nuclear reactors, and in nickel-cadium batteries. Properties: at.no. 48; r.a.m. 112.4; r.d. 8.65; m.p. 320.9°C (609.6°F); b.p. 765°C (1409°F); most common isotope Cd^{114} (28.86%).

caecilian Underground burrowing amphibian found in Central and South America, S Asia and Africa. Its worm-like body varies from *c.*18–135cm (7–53in) in length and its colour from black to pink. There are sensory tentacles between the eyes, which are tiny and often useless.

caecum Dilated pouch at the junction of the small and large intestines, terminating in the APPENDIX. It has no known function in humans. In rabbits and horses, the caecum contains microorganisms which help to break down the cellulose cell-walls of the plants they eat.

Caedmon Earliest known English poet, dating from around the 7th century. According to BEDE, he was an illiterate herdsman of Whitby Abbey, Yorkshire, who was commanded in a vision to turn the scriptures into poetry. His only surviving work is the fragmentary *Hymn on the Creation.*

Caernarvon (Caernarfon) Market town on the Menai Strait, Gwynedd, NW Wales. It has a 13th-century castle built by Edward I, whose son, Edward II, was crowned the first Prince of Wales (1301). The Princes of Wales are invested here. Pop. (1992 est.) 9600.

Caesar Name of a powerful family of ancient Rome. The most illustrious representative was Julius CAESAR. The name became the title for the Roman emperor in 27 BC on the accession of Octavian (later AUGUSTUS), adopted son of Julius Caesar. *Tsar* and *kaiser* are derived from it.

Caesar, (Gaius) Julius (100–44 BC) Roman general and statesman. A great military commander and brilliant politician, he defeated formidable rivals to become dictator of Rome. After the death of SULLA, Caesar became military tribune. As *pontifex maximus*, he directed reforms in 63 BC that resulted in the Julian CALENDAR. He formed the First Triumvirate in 60 BC with POMPEY and CRASSUS, instituted agrarian reforms and created a PATRICIAN-PLEBEIAN alliance. He conquered Gaul for Rome (58–49BC) and invaded Britain (54BC). Refusing Senate demands to disband his army, he provoked civil war with Pompey. Caesar defeated Pompey at Pharsalus in 48 BC and pursued him to Egypt, where he made CLEOPATRA queen. After further victories, he returned to Rome in 45 BC and was received with unprecedented honours, culminating in the title of dictator for life. He introduced popular reforms, but his growing power aroused resentment. He was assassinated in the Senate on March 15 by a conspiracy led by CASSIUS and BRUTUS. Caesar bequeathed his wealth and power to his grandnephew, Octavian (later AUGUSTUS) who, together with Mark ANTONY, avenged his murder.

Caesarean section *See* BIRTH, CAESAREAN

caesium (symbol Cs) Rare silvery-white metallic element in group I of the PERIODIC TABLE; the most alkaline and electropositive element. Discovered in 1860 by German chemist Robert BUNSEN and German physicist Gustav KIRCHHOFF, caesium is ductile and used commercially in PHOTOELECTRIC CELLS. The isotope Cs^{137} is used in cancer treatments. The decay rate of its most common isotope Cs^{133} is the standard for measuring time. Properties: at.no. 55; r.a.m. 132.9055; r.d. 1.87; m.p. 28.4°C (83.1°F); b.p. 678°C (1252.4°F). *See also* ALKALI METALS; ATOMIC CLOCK

caffeine ($C_8H_{10}N_4O_2$) White, bitter substance that occurs in coffee, tea and other substances, such as cocoa and ilex plants. It acts as a mild, harmless stimulant and DIURETIC, although an excessive dose can cause insomnia and delirium.

Cage, John (1912–92) US avant-garde composer. He experimented with new sound sources, believing that all sounds, including noise and silence, are valid compositional materials. He worked with percussion orchestras and invented the 'prepared piano', modified by fixing objects to the strings. He used chance in his compositions: *Imaginary Landscape* (1951) is written for 12 randomly tuned radios; *Reunion* (1968) consists of electronic sounds created by chess moves on an electric board; *4'33"* (1952) has no sound, except for the environment in which it is performed.

Cain First-born son of ADAM and EVE, brother of Abel. His story is recounted in Genesis 4. God accepted Abel's offering in preference to Cain's, who murdered Abel in anger. Marked by God to preserve him from being murdered, Cain was driven from the Garden of EDEN and lived in exile in the land of Nod.

Cairngorms Range of mountains in NE central Scotland, in the Grampian region. The highest peak, Ben Macdhui, 1309m (4296ft), is the second highest point in the British Isles.

Cairo (Al-Qahirah) Capital of Egypt and port on the River Nile. The largest city in Africa, Cairo was founded in AD 969 by the Fatimid dynasty and subsequently fortified by SALADIN. Medieval Cairo became capital of the MAMLUK empire, but declined under Turkish rule. During the 20th century it grew dramatically in population and area. Nearby are world-famous archaeological sites, the SPHINX and the PYRAMIDS of GIZA; museums include the Museum of Egyptian Antiquities and Museum of Islamic Art. Old Cairo is a world heritage site containing over 400 mosques and other fine examples of ISLAMIC ART AND ARCHITECTURE. Its five universities include the world's oldest, housed in the mosque of Al Azhar (972) and the centre of SHI'ITE Koranic study. Industries: tourism, textiles, leather, iron and steel, sugar refining. Pop. (2005) 11,146,000. *See also* EGYPTIAN ARCHITECTURE

Cajun French-speaking settlers in Louisiana. They were driven from NOVA SCOTIA (then Acadia) by the British in the 18th century. Cajun music is a popular style.

calabash gourd (bottle gourd) Tropical vine with oval leaves and white flowers. It grows to 9–12m (30–40ft). Its smooth, hard fruit is bottle-shaped and grows to 180cm (6ft) long. Family Cucurbitaceae; species *Lagenaria vulgaris*.

Calabria Region in s Italy, including the provinces of Catanzaro, Cosenza and Reggio di Calabria. The capital is Catanzaro. The local economy is almost exclusively agricultural. Area: 15,080sq km (5822sq mi). Pop. (2001) 2,043,288.

Calais City and seaport in Pas-de-Calais department, NW France. An important port and commercial centre since the Middle Ages, it was captured by the English king EDWARD III in 1347, but was retaken in 1558. It suffered much damage during WORLD WAR 2. Calais lies *c*.34km (21mi) across the English Channel from DOVER, and is the site of the CHANNEL TUNNEL connection to Folkestone. Industries: lace making, chemicals, paper. Pop. (1999) 77,300.

calcium (symbol Ca) Common silvery-white metallic element of the ALKALINE-EARTH METALS; first isolated in 1808 by English chemist Sir Humphry DAVY. It occurs in many rocks and minerals, notably LIMESTONE and GYPSUM, and in bones. Calcium helps regulate the heartbeat and is essential for strong bones and teeth. The metal, which is soft and malleable, has few commercial applications but its compounds are widely used. It is a reactive element, combining readily with oxygen, nitrogen and other non-metals. Properties: at.no. 20; r.a.m. 40.08; r.d. 1.55; m.p. 839°C (1542°F); b.p. 1484°C (2703°F); most common isotope Ca^{40} (96.95%). *See also* HARDNESS OF WATER

calcium carbide (calcium acetylide) Chemical (CaC_2) made commercially by heating coke and calcium oxide (CaO) in an ELECTRIC FURNACE. It reacts with water to yield ETHYNE. Calcium carbide is also used to manufacture ETHANOIC ACID and ETHANAL, as well as fertilizers.

calcium carbonate ($CaCO_3$) White compound, insoluble in water, that occurs naturally as MARBLE, CHALK, LIMESTONE and calcite. Crystals are in the hexagonal system and vary in form. Calcium carbonate is used in the manufacture of cement, iron, steel and lime, to neutralize soil acidity and as a constituent of antacids. Properties: r.d. 2.7 (calcite).

calcium oxide (quicklime) White solid (CaO) made by heating CALCIUM CARBONATE ($CaCO_3$) at high temperatures. It is used industrially to treat acidic soil and to make porcelain and glass, bleaching powder, caustic soda, mortar and cement. Calcium oxide reacts with water to form calcium hydroxide ($Ca(OH)_2$).

calcium sulphate Chemical compound ($CaSO_4$) that occurs naturally as the mineral anhydrite. The HARDNESS OF WATER results when calcium sulphate dissolves in water. The hydrated form is GYPSUM, which loses water when heated to form plaster of Paris.

calculus Area of mathematics dealing with continuously changing quantities, rates of change, infinite series and limits. Its major branches are DIFFERENTIAL CALCULUS, based on rates of change, and INTEGRAL CALCULUS, based on summations. Gottfried LEIBNIZ and Sir Isaac NEWTON developed calculus independently, each discovering the relationship between differentials and integrals. Calculus has developed into a large body of mathematical techniques with many practical applications.

▼ **Caesar** Successful campaigns were waged by Julius Caesar between 58 and 51 BC against the Helvetii, Belgae, Veneti and the Aquitani. He conquered the whole of Gaul and made it a new province, Transalpine Gaul. He twice landed in Britain, near Walmer or Deal in 54 BC. The second expedition was on quite a large scale and Caesar penetrated northward beyond St Albans.

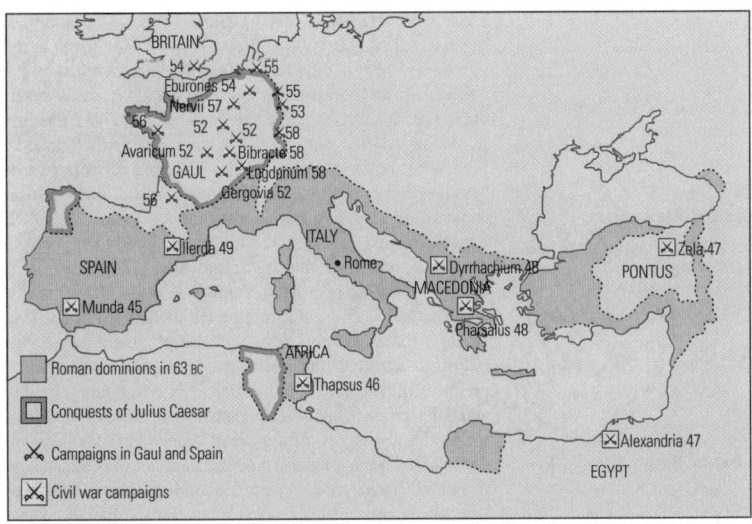

C

CALIFORNIA
Statehood :
September 9, 1850
Nickname :
The Golden State
State bird :
California valley quail
State flower :
Golden poppy
State tree :
California redwood
State motto :
Eureka!

Calcutta *See* KOLKATA.

Calder, Alexander (1898–1976) US sculptor. Calder created the mobile, a type of delicate, colourful, kinetic sculpture with parts that move either by motors or air currents. He also developed non-moving sculptures called 'stabiles'.

caldera Large, shallow crater formed when a VOLCANO collapses and the MAGMA migrates under the Earth's crust. The caldera of an extinct volcano, if fed by floodwater, rain or springs, can become a crater lake.

calendar Way of reckoning time for regulating religious, commercial and civil life, and for dating events in the past and future. Ancient Egyptians had a system based on the movement of the star SIRIUS and on the seasons. Calendars are based on natural and astronomical regularities: tides and seasons, movements of the Sun and Earth, and phases of the Moon. The basic units are day, month and year. The main difficulty in compiling a calendar is that the year is not a whole number of days, so it cannot be divided into months of constant length. For convenience, months and days are assigned a whole number of days, and extra days (**intercalations**) are added at intervals to compensate. In the modern **Gregorian**, or New Style, calendar, an extra day (February 29) is added to every year evenly divisible by four, known as "leap years". However, the ends of centuries, such as 1900, are not leap years unless divisible by 400. The Gregorian calendar was based on the **Julian**, or Old Style, solar calendar. This used leap years but did not omit those divisible by 100, causing it to very gradually fall out of synchronisation with the natural year. It was introduced by Julius Caesar in the 1st century BC and was developed from an earlier Moon-based calendar. The **Jewish calendar** is semilunar, made up of 12 common years and 7 leap years. The leap years have an additional month (Adar II). The **Muslim calendar** is wholly lunar, the year always consisting of 12 months without intercalations. The months have alternately 30 and 29 days, except for the twelfth month (Dulhajj) which has one intercalary day in 11 years out of a cycle of 30 calendar years.

Calgary City at the confluence of the Bow and Elbow rivers, s Alberta, Canada. It was founded in 1875 as a post of the Royal Canadian Mounted Police. It is an industrial and commercial centre, and has a university (1945). Industries: flour milling, timber, brick, cement, oil refining. Pop. (2005) 1,074,000.

Calhoun, John Caldwell (1782–1850) US statesman and vice president (1825–32). After serving in the House of Representatives (1811–17), he was secretary of war (1817–25). He was vice president under John Quincy ADAMS and Andrew JACKSON before resigning over a dispute about a state's right to nullify federal laws. Calhoun was elected to the Senate and, except for a brief period as secretary of state (1844–45), served until 1850. An advocate of SLAVERY and states' rights, he was an important spokesman for the South.

California State in w USA, on the Pacific coast; the largest state by population and the third largest in area. The capital is SACRAMENTO. Other major cities include LOS ANGELES, SAN FRANCISCO, SAN DIEGO and Oakland. In the w, coast ranges run N to S, paralleled by the Sierra Nevada Mountains in the E; between them lies the fertile Central Valley, drained by the Sacramento and San Joaquin rivers. In the SE is a broad desert area. The Spanish explored the coast in 1542, but the first European settlement was in 1769, when Spaniards founded a Franciscan mission at San Diego. The area became part of MEXICO and huge cattle ranches were established. Settlers came from the USA and, during the MEXICAN WAR, US forces occupied California (1846); it was ceded to the USA at the war's end. After gold was discovered (1848), the GOLD RUSH swelled the population from 15,000 to 250,000 in just four years. In 1850, California joined the Union. In the 20th century, the discovery of oil and development of service industries attracted further settlers. California is the leading producer of many crops in the United States. Poultry, fishing and dairy produce are also important. Forests cover *c.*40% of the land and support an important timber industry. Mineral deposits include oil, natural gas, and a variety of ores valuable in manufacturing (the largest economic sector). Industries: aircraft, aerospace equipment, electronics, missiles, wine.

Tourism is also a vital industry. Area: 403,971sq km (155,973sq mi). Pop. (2000) 33,871,648.

California redwood (*Sequoia sempervirens*) Conifer that grows to a height of more than 100m (330ft), and is one of the tallest trees. Its close relative (also from California) is the less common Big Tree or Wellingtonia (*Sequoiadendron giganteum*), the heaviest tree in the Western world. SEQUOIAS live to be more than 4000 years old. Family Taxodiaceae.

californium (symbol Cf) Radioactive metallic element of the ACTINIDE SERIES, first made in 1950 by US nuclear chemist Glenn Seaborg (1912–99) and colleagues at the University of California, Berkeley, by alpha-particle bombardment of the curium isotope Cm^{242}. Californium presents biological dangers because one microgram releases 170 million neutrons a minute. Properties: at.no. 98; most stable isotope Cf^{251} (half-life 800 yr). *See also* TRANSURANIC ELEMENTS

Caligula (AD 12–41) (Gaius Caesar) Roman emperor (37–41). Son of Germanicus Caesar, he became emperor after the death of TIBERIUS. He was highly autocratic, made his horse a consul to mock the Senate, and was said to be insane. He was murdered by an officer of the Praetorian Guard and succeeded by his uncle, CLAUDIUS I.

caliph Leader of the Muslim community. After the death of MUHAMMAD, ABU BAKR was chosen to be his caliph (successor). The role was originally elective but later became hereditary. The title remained with the Ottoman sultans (1517–1924), after which it was abolished. SUNNI Muslims recognize the first four caliphs: ABU BAKR, OMAR, OTHMAN and ALI. Shiites accept authority as passing directly from Muhammad to Ali.

Callaghan, (Leonard) James, Baron (1912–2005) British statesman, prime minister (1976–79). Callaghan entered Parliament in 1945, and succeeded Harold WILSON as LABOUR PARTY leader in 1976. He is the only prime minister in British history to have held all three major offices of state: chancellor of the exchequer (1964–67), home secretary (1967–70) and foreign secretary (1974–76). Callaghan is only the second post-war prime minister never to have won a general election. His tenure was marked by negotiations with David STEEL in the Lib-Lab Pact, and strife with the trade unions which culminated in the 'winter of discontent'. He was defeated by Margaret THATCHER in the 1979 general election and became a life peer in 1987.

Callas, Maria (1923–77) Greek soprano. Her successes at LA SCALA, Milan, and the ROYAL OPERA HOUSE, Covent Garden, established her reputation as a leading singing actress. She was particularly admired in the Italian repertoire, especially as PUCCINI's *Tosca*.

calligraphy Art of fine freehand writing. In Europe, there was a marked difference between **uncial** hands used for literary works, which are rounded, easily inscribed letters, and **cursive** hands, used for documents and letters, which are more regularized. Fragments on papyrus from the 3rd century BC show a variety of cursive hands. Several different types of Greek uncials were used in Roman times. During the 8th century, the **minuscule** superseded the uncial for ordinary, commercial purposes. Intentional complexity was developed to prevent forgeries. The 20th century saw a revival of calligraphy.

Callisto Second-largest and outermost of Jupiter's GALILEAN SATELLITES, with a diameter of 4800km (3000mi). It is the most heavily cratered object known. As well as the dark dense craters, there are large, multi-ringed impact features, the largest of which is Valhalla, with a diameter of 4000km (2500mi).

callus In botany, a protective mass of undifferentiated plant cells formed at the site of a wound in a woody plant. Callus tissue also forms at the base of cuttings as they start to take root. Important as the starting point for TISSUE CULTURE in plants.

calorie Unit of heat. A calorie is the amount of heat required to raise one gram of water one degree CELSIUS between 14.5 -15.5°C (58.1–59.9°F). The SI system of units uses the JOULE (1 calorie = 4.184 joules) instead of the calorie. A dietitian's 'calorie' is the kilocalorie, 1,000 times larger than a calorie.

Calvin, John (1509–64) French theologian of the REFORMATION. He prepared for a career in the Roman Catholic Church but turned to the study of classics. In *c.*1533 he became a Protestant and began work on his *Institutes of the Christian Religion*. In this work he presented the basics of what came to be known as CALVINISM. To avoid persecution, he went to live in Geneva, Switzerland (1536), where he advanced the Reformation.

Calvin, Melvin (1911–97) US chemist. He used radioactive carbon-14 as a trace to label carbon dioxide, and track the process by which plants turned it into glucose by means of PHOTOSYNTHESIS. The series of reactions that take place during photosynthesis is known as the Calvin cycle. Calvin received the Nobel Prize in chemistry in 1961.

Calvinism Set of doctrines and attitudes derived from the Protestant theologian John CALVIN. The Reformed and Presbyterian churches were established in his tradition. Rejecting papal authority and relying on the Bible as the source of religious truth, Calvinism stresses the sovereignty of God and PREDESTINATION. Calvinism usually subordinates state to church, and cultivates austere morality. The development of these doctrines, particularly predestination, and the rejection of consubstantiation in its eucharistic teaching, caused a split in PROTESTANTISM

between LUTHERANISM and PRESBYTERIANISM. Important Calvinist leaders include John KNOX and Jonathan Edwards.

cambium In botany, layer of cells parallel to the surface of stems and roots of plants. It divides to produce new cells that allow for growth in diameter of the stem and roots. There are two main types of cambium. **Vascular** cambium produces new PHLOEM on the outside and XYLEM on the inside, leaving narrow bands of thin-walled cells through which nutrients and gases diffuse to the centre of the plant. **Cork** cambium forms a cylinder just below the EPIDERMIS, and produces cork cells to replace the epidermis, which ruptures as the stem and root expand, forming the bark and corky outer layer of the older root. *See also* MERISTEM

Cambodia Kingdom in SE Asia, *see* country feature

Cambrian Earliest period of the PALAEOZOIC era, lasting from *c.* 590 million to 505 million years ago. Cambrian rocks are the earliest to preserve the hard parts of animals as fossils. They contain a large variety of fossils, including all the animal phyla, with the exception of the vertebrates. The

INTERNET

Cambodia
▶ www.embassy.org/ cambodia

CAMBODIA

The Kingdom of Cambodia is a country in SE Asia. Low mountains border the country, except in the SE. Most of Cambodia consists of plains drained by the River MEKONG, which enters Cambodia from Laos in the N and exits through Vietnam in the SE. The NW contains Tonlé Sap (or Great Lake). In the dry season, this lake drains into the River Mekong. In the wet season the level of the Mekong rises and water flows in the opposite direction, from the river into Tonlé Sap. The lake then becomes the largest freshwater lake in Asia.

CLIMATE
Cambodia has a tropical monsoon climate, with high temperatures all through the year. The dry season, when winds blow from the N or NE, runs from November to April. During the rainy season, from May to October, moist winds blow from the S or SE. The high humidity and heat often make conditions unpleasant. The rainfall is heaviest near the coast, and rather lower inland.

HISTORY
From 802 to 1431, the Hindu-Buddhist Khmer people ruled a great empire. Its zenith came in the reign of Suryavarman II (1113–50), who built the great funerary temple of Angkor Wat. Together with Angkor

Thom, the ANGKOR site contains the world's largest group of religious buildings. The wealth of the kingdom rested on fish from the lake and rice from the flooded lowlands, for which an extensive system of irrigation channels and strong reservoirs was developed.

Thai forces captured Angkor in 1431 and forests covered the site. Following its rediscovery in 1860, it has been gradually restored and is now a major tourist attraction. After the capture of Angkor, the capital moved to Phnom Penh. In the 17th and 18th centuries, Cambodia was a battleground for the empires of Siam and Annam.

France ruled the country from 1863 as part of the French Union of INDOCHINA. Japan occupied it during World War 2, after which it returned to French control until it achieved independence in 1954 as a kingdom ruled by King NORODOM SIHANOUK. In 1955 he abdicated to become prime minister. In a short period of stability during the late 1950s and 1960s, the country developed its small-scale agricultural resources and rubber plantations. It remained predominantly rural but achieved self-sufficiency in food, with some exports.

POLITICS
In 1969, during the VIETNAM WAR, US planes bombed North Vietnamese targets in Cambodia. In 1970, King Norodom Sihanouk was overthrown and Cambodia became a republic. Under assault from South Vietnamese troops, the Communist Vietnamese withdrew deep into Cambodia. US raids ended in 1973, but fighting continued as Cambodia's Communists in the KHMER ROUGE fought against the government. The Khmer Rouge, led by POL POT, were victorious in 1975. They began a reign of terror, murdering government officials and educated people. Up to 2 million are estimated to have been killed. After the overthrow of Pol Pot by Vietnamese forces in 1979, civil war raged between the Vietnamese-backed government led by Heng Samrin and the US-backed Democratic Kampuchea faction. This was a coalition of

AREA 181,035sq km
[69,898sq mi]
POPULATION 13,996,000
CAPITAL (POPULATION)
Phnom Penh (1,174,000)
GOVERNMENT Constitutional monarchy
ETHNIC GROUPS Khmer 90%, Vietnamese 5%, Chinese 1%, others
LANGUAGES Khmer (official), French, English
RELIGIONS Buddhism 95%, others 5%
CURRENCY Riel = 100 sen

Prince Sihanouk, the Khmer Liberation Front, and the Khmer Rouge who, from 1982, claimed to have abandoned their Communist ideology.

Devastated by war and denied almost any aid, Cambodia continued to decline. It was only the withdrawal of Vietnamese troops in 1989, sparking fear of a Khmer Rouge revival, that forced a settlement. In October 1991, a UN-brokered peace plan for elections in 1993 was accepted by all parties. A new constitution was adopted in September 1993, restoring democracy and the monarchy. Sihanouk again became king, with his son Prince Norodom Ranariddh as prime minister. However, the Khmer Rouge continued hostilities and were banned in 1994. In 1997, Hu Sen engineered a coup against prime minister Ranariddh, exiling him and taking his place. In 1998 Ranariddh returned, alleging electoral fraud when elections resulted in victory for Hu Sen. In 2001, the government set up a court to try leaders of the Khmer Rouge. In 2004, Sihanouk abdicated due to ill health and was succeeded by his son Prince Norodom Sihamoni.

ECONOMY
Cambodia is a poor country, whose economy has been wrecked by war. By 1986, it was only able to supply 80% of its needs. Recovery has been slow, though textile exports have begun to earn foreign revenue. Farming is the main activity and rice, rubber and maize are important crops. Tourism is increasing, and the impressive Angkor temples are a major attraction. In 2005, promising oil and gas deposits were discovered in Cambodian territorial waters.

commonest animal forms were TRILOBITES, BRACHIOPODA, sponges and snails. Plant life consisted mainly of seaweeds.

Cambridge City on the River Cam, county town of Cambridgeshire, E England. The University of CAMBRIDGE is one of the world's leading institutions. Industries: precision engineering, electronics, printing, publishing. Pop. (2001) 108,879.

Cambridge, University of Founded in 1209 (with claims for an earlier origin), it is one of the oldest academic institutions in England. It has a collegiate system, the oldest college being Peterhouse (1284). A centre of Renaissance learning and theological debate in the Reformation, it now has faculties for studying almost every discipline. In the 20th century it excelled in scientific research.

Cambridgeshire County in E central England; the county town is CAMBRIDGE. The area is mainly fenland with chalk hills to the S and is drained by the Ouse and Nene rivers. Ely and Peterborough both have cathedrals. Agriculture is the most important economic activity; crops include wheat, barley and oats. Area: 3400sq km (1312sq mi). Pop. (2001) 552,655.

camel Large, hump-backed, UNGULATE mammal of the family Camelidae. There are two species – the two-humped **Bactrian** of central Asia and the single-humped Arabian **dromedary**. Its broad, padded feet and ability to travel long periods without water make the camel a perfect desert animal. Genus *Camelus*.

camellia Genus of evergreen trees or shrubs of the family Theaceae, native to E Asia. It has oval, dark green leaves and waxy, rose-like flowers which may be pink, red, white or variegated. *Camellia japonica* is the most common species.

Camelot In English mythology, the seat chosen by King ARTHUR for his court. Its site is not known, although many believe it was Cadbury Castle, Somerset, SW England.

cameo Relief carving, usually on striated gemstones, semi-precious stones or shell. Decoration is generally cut on the light-coloured vein, the dark vein being left as a background. Cameos originated from the carved stone seals bearing the symbol of the scarab beetle used by Ancient Egyptians, Greeks and Etruscans.

camera Apparatus for taking photographs, traditionally consisting of a light-proof box containing photographic film. When a shutter is opened, usually briefly, light from the scene is focused by a lens system onto the film. The amount of light falling on the film is controlled by the shutter speed and by the diameter of the lens APERTURE, their settings usually determined by a built-in exposure meter. Most cameras can manually or automatically focus, varying the lens' distance from the film to produce a sharp image of a specific object distance. Both focus and exposure are nowadays usually fully automated except in professional camera equipment. The newer digital cameras have no film but use a built-in computer to record electronic images. An image sensor behind the lens converts the incoming light into electrical charges. The common sensor is a semiconductor, a charge-coupled device (CCD). It can contain millions of photosensitive dots called pixels to record

CAMEROON

The Republic of Cameroon in West Africa got its name from the Portuguese word camarões, or prawns. This name was used by Portuguese explorers who fished for prawns along the coast.

Behind the narrow coastal plains that lie on the Gulf of Guinea, the land rises to a series of plateaux. In the N, the land slopes down towards the Lake CHAD (Tchad) basin. The mountain region located in the SW of the country includes Mount Cameroon, a volcano that erupts from time to time. The vegetation varies greatly from N to S. The deserts in the N merge into dry and moist savanna in cen-

tral Cameroon, with dense tropical rainforests in the humid S.

CLIMATE
The rainfall is heavy, especially in the highlands. The rainiest months near the coast are from June to September. The rainfall decreases to the N and the far N has a hot, dry climate. Temperatures are high on the coast, whereas the inland plateaux are cooler.

HISTORY
Among the early inhabitants of Cameroon were groups of Bantu-speaking people. There are now more than 160 ethnic groups, each with its own language. Bantu-speakers predominate in coastal areas, such as DOUALA. Islam is the dominant force in the N, where major tribal groupings include the FULANI.

In 1472 Portuguese explorers seeking a sea route to Asia around Africa reached the Cameroon coast. From the 17th century, S Cameroon was a centre of the slave trade, but SLAVERY was ended in the early 19th century. The ivory trade became important, led by Britain. In 1884 the area became a German protectorate, but was captured by Allied troops during World War 1. After the war Cameroon was divided into two zones, ruled by Britain and France.

POLITICS
In 1960, French Cameroon became the independent Cameroon Republic. In 1961, after a vote in British Cameroon, part of the territory joined the Cameroon Republic to become the Federal Republic of Cameroon. The other part joined Nigeria. In 1972, Cameroon became a unitary state called the United Republic of Cameroon. It adopted the name Republic of Cameroon in 1984. Opposition parties were legalized in 1992, and Paul Biya was elected president in 1993 and 1997. In 1995, partly to placate the English-speaking part of the

AREA 475,442sq km [183,568sq mi]
POPULATION 18,060,000
CAPITAL (POPULATION)
Yaoundé (1,727,000)
GOVERNMENT Multiparty republic
ETHNIC GROUPS Cameroon Highlanders 31%, Bantu 27%, Kirdi 11%, Fulani 10%, others
LANGUAGES French and English (both official), many others
RELIGIONS Christianity 40%, traditional beliefs 40%, Islam 20%
CURRENCY CFA franc = 100 centimes

population, Cameroon became the 52nd member of the COMMONWEALTH OF NATIONS. In 2002 the International Court of Justice gave Cameroon sovereignty over the disputed oil-rich Bakassi peninsula, but Nigeria failed to reach the 2004 deadline for the handover.

Presidential elections in 2004 saw Paul Biya win a new seven-year term with more than 70% of the vote. The result was accepted by Commonwealth observers, although opposition parties alleged fraud. In 2006 Nigerian troops finally withdrew from the Bakassi peninsula, but parts remain under Nigerian administration.

ECONOMY
Like most countries in tropical Africa, Cameroon's economy is based on agriculture, which employs 73% of the people. The chief food crops include cassava, maize, millet, sweet potatoes and yams.

Cameroon's chief exports are oil and bauxite. Although Cameroon has few manufacturing and processing industries, its mineral exports and its self-sufficiency in food production make it one of the wealthier countries in tropical Africa. Another important industry is forestry, ranking second among the exports, after oil. Other exports are cocoa, coffee, aluminium and cotton.

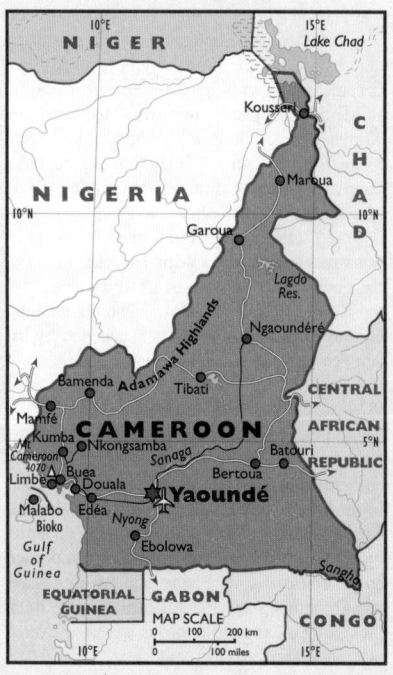

the picture. Most digital cameras also have a monitor at the back of the camera that displays the picture just taken. Since digital images use the BINARY SYSTEM to store information, they can be stored and manipulated by computers.

Cameroon Republic in w Africa. *See* country feature

Campaign for Nuclear Disarmament (CND) Movement in Britain, founded by Bertrand RUSSELL and Canon John Collins (1958). Advocating unilateral nuclear disarmament, during the 1960s it organized an annual march between the atomic research centre at Aldermaston and Trafalgar Square, London. Membership and activities declined in the 1970s, but CND revived in the early 1980s in response to the escalation of the East-West nuclear arms race and the siting of CRUISE MISSILES at Greenham Common, s England. The end of the COLD WAR and disarmament treaties between the USA and the former Soviet Union, have lessened CND's political prominence.

Campania Region of sw Italy on the Tyrrhenian Sea, including the provinces of Avellino, Benevento, Caserta, Napoli and Salerno. The capital is NAPLES. It is a mountainous area with fertile plains yielding agricultural products such as wheat, potatoes, fruit, tobacco, flowers and wine. Area: 13,595sq km (5249sq mi). Pop. (2001) 5,782,244.

Campanulaceae Bellflower family of herbaceous flowering plants. There are *c*.300 species, including HAREBELL, Canterbury bell, peach bellflower and Coventry bell.

Campbell, Donald Malcolm (1921–67) British world speed record holder. Son of Sir Malcolm CAMPBELL, he set seven new world records on water. In 1964, he broke the world water and speed records in Australia. On Lake Dumbleyung, Campbell achieved 444.7km/h (276.28mph), while on the salt flats of Lake Eyre he reached 648.72km/h (403mph). He died trying to set a new record. In 1984, his daughter Gina set a new women's water speed record.

Campbell, Sir Malcolm (1885–1948) British world speed record holder. In 1935, he became the first man to reach a land speed of 300mph (483km/h), accomplished in *Bluebird* at Utah's Bonneville Salt Flats, USA. He also set a water record of 227km/h (141mph).

Camp David Accord (September 1978) Significant step towards Arab-Israeli reconciliation. The agreement resulted from a meeting between Anwar SADAT of Egypt and Menachem BEGIN of Israel, mediated by US President Jimmy CARTER at the US presidential retreat in the mountains of Maryland. Condemned by other Arab leaders, the agreement formed the basis of a 1979 treaty between Egypt and Israel. Sadat and Begin shared the 1978 Nobel Peace Prize.

Campese, David Ian (1962–) Australian rugby football player. A flamboyant player, who played regularly in Italy as well as Australia, he holds the world record for the number of tries scored in international rugby (63). He retired from international rugby in 1996, after more than 100 test appearances.

camphor Organic chemical compound ($C_{10}H_{16}O$). It has a strong odour, which also occurs in the camphor tree, *Cinammonum camphora*, native to Taiwan. Camphor is used in medicine for liniments, in the manufacture of celluloid, lacquers and explosives, and as an ingredient of mothballs.

Campion, Jane (1955–) New Zealand film director and screenwriter. A sensitive and poetic film-maker, Campion's film *The Piano* (1993) shared the Palme d'Or and won her an Oscar for Best Screenplay. She also directed an adaptation of Henry James' novel *Portrait of a Lady* (1997).

Campion, Saint Edmund (1540–81) English Jesuit priest and martyr. He was ordained deacon in the Church of England (1569), but became a Roman Catholic (1571) and later a Jesuit missionary. In 1581, he published the pamphlet *Decem Rationes*, defending the Roman Catholic position against Protestantism. He was charged with treason and executed. His feast day is December 1.

Camus, Albert (1913–60) French novelist, playwright, and essayist. An active figure in the French Resistance, Camus achieved recognition with his debut novel *The Outsider* (1942), a work permeated with the sense of individual alienation that underlies much of his writing. His later work include the novels *The Plague* (1947) and *The Fall*

◀ **Canaletto** The *Punta della Dogana* (1730) by Giovanni Caneletto is one of his famous series of views of Venice. The incredible attention to detail is characteristic of his work.

C

(1956), and the essay *The Rebel* (1951). Camus has been associated with EXISTENTIALISM and the Theatre of the ABSURD. He received the 1957 Nobel Prize in literature.

Canaan Historical region occupying the land between the Mediterranean and the Dead Sea. The Canaanites were a Semitic people, identified with the Phoenicians from *c*.1200 BC. Canaan was the Promised Land of the Israelites, who settled here on their return from Egypt.

Canada Federation in N North America. *See* country feature, pages 194–195

Canadian literature Literary work can be divided into two distinct (yet interrelated) traditions, reflecting Canada's dual French and English linguistic and cultural history. A French-language tradition really began in opposition to English colonialism and cultural dominance. During the 1860s a Québec group emerged, characterized by nationalist romanticism. In the early 20th century Québec was again the focus for a parochial pastoralism. In Montréal a more innovative poetic SYMBOLISM developed. The first English-language works were accounts of the Canadian landscape by explorers, such as Alexander MACKENZIE. The first North American novel, *The History of Emily Montague* (1769), was an account of Québec by Frances Moore Brooke. The Confederation of 1867 produced the first national literary movement, the Confederation school of poets. At the turn of the 19th century, prose tended to pastoral romanticism, such as L.M. Montgomery's classic *Anne of Green Gables* (1908). Literature in the 1920s was more critical of Canadian society and post-1945 literature reflected and nurtured a burgeoning national consciousness. Major poets of the period include Earle Birney, Dorothy Livesay, and Jay Macpherson. Recent novelists include Margaret ATWOOD, Robertson DAVIES, and Mordecai RICHLER. Canada also has a healthy tradition of literary criticism, major figures include Northrop Frye and Marshall McLUHAN.

canal Artificial waterway for irrigation, drainage, navigation or in conjunction with hydroelectric dams. Canals were built 4000 years ago in ancient Mesopotamia. Today, the longest canal able to accommodate large ships connects the Baltic and White Seas in N Europe and is 227km (141mi) long. The heyday of canal building in England was in the late 18th-early 19th century.

Canaletto (1697–1768) (Giovanni Antonio Canal) Italian painter of the VENETIAN SCHOOL, famous for his perspectival views of Venice. His early work is more dramatic and free-flowing than his smoother, accurate mature style. He portrayed festivals and ceremonies in his Venetian views. In 1746 he travelled to England, where he painted views of London and country houses. He used a camera obscura to make his paintings more precise, sometimes making the finished work seem stiff and mannered. Canaletto managed to infuse his best work with energy, light and colour. He had an enormous influence in Italy, central Europe, and England.

canary Popular cage-bird that lives wild in the Azores, Canary and Madeira islands. These yellowish finches feed on fruit, seeds and insects, and lay spotted greenish-blue eggs. The pure yellow varieties have been domesticated since the 16th century, although they are difficult to breed in captivity. Family Fringillidae; species *Serinus canarius*.

Canary Islands The Canary Islands are seven large islands and many small volcanic islands situated off S Morocco. The climate is subtropical, dry at sea level, wetter

C

A vast confederation of ten provinces and three territories, Canada is the world's second largest country after Russia, with an even longer coastline – about 250,000km [155,000mi]. It is sparsely populated because it contains vast areas of virtually unoccupied mountains, cold forests, tundra and polar desert in the N and W. About 80% of the population of Canada lives within about 300km [186mi] of the S border.

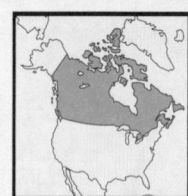

Forests of cedars, hemlocks and other trees grow on the W mountains, with firs and spruces at the higher levels. The mountain forests provide habitats for bears, deer and mountain lions, while the sure-footed Rocky Mountain goats and bighorn sheep roam above the tree line (the upper limit of tree growth).

The interior plains were once grassy prairies. While the drier areas are still used for grazing cattle, the wetter areas are used largely for growing wheat and other cereals. N of the prairies are boreal forests, which in turn merge into the treeless tundra and Arctic wastelands in the far N. The lowlands in SE Canada contain forests of deciduous trees, such as beech, hickory, oak and walnut.

CLIMATE
Canada has a cold climate. In winter, temperatures fall below freezing point throughout most of the country. But the SW coast has a relatively mild climate. Along the Arctic Circle the temperatures are, on average, below freezing for seven months of the year. By contrast, hot winds from the Gulf of Mexico warm S ONTARIO and the ST LAWRENCE River lowlands in summer. As a result, S Ontario has a frost-free season of nearly six months.

The coasts of BRITISH COLUMBIA are wet, with an average annual rainfall of more than 2,500mm [98in] in places. The prairies however are arid or semi-arid, with an average annual rainfall of 250 to 500mm [10–20in]. The rainfall in SE Canada ranges from around 800mm [31in] in southern Ontario to about 1,500mm [59in] on the coasts of NEWFOUNDLAND and NOVA SCOTIA. Heavy snow falls in E Canada in winter.

HISTORY
Canada's first people, ancestors of present-day Native Americans, arrived from Asia c.10–15,000 years ago. Later arrivals were the INUIT, also from Asia. The first Europeans to reach the Canadian coast were VIKINGS in c.AD 1000, but their settlements were short lived. John CABOT rediscovered the Canadian coast in 1497, and a race between France and Britain for the riches in this new land began. France gained an initial advantage when Jacques CARTIER discovered the St Lawrence River in 1534 and claimed Canada for France.

The French established the first European settlement in 1605 and founded QUÉBEC in 1608. The empire was extended by explorers such as LA SALLE. French settlement in the W was generally much slower than English development on the Atlantic coast. The FRENCH AND INDIAN WARS (1689–1763)

were a protracted battle for colonial domination of Canada. In 1713, the province of Nova Scotia was ceded by the Treaty of Utrecht. In 1759, Québec was captured by Britain, and France surrendered all of its Canadian lands in the Treaty of Paris (1763). In 1774 the French-Canadian population of Québec gained territory to the Ohio River and the CONTINENTAL CONGRESS responded by invading Canada. During the American Revolution, Canada remained loyal to the English crown, and American attempts to capture it failed. In 1784 the province of NEW BRUNSWICK was created out of Nova Scotia. The Constitutional Act of 1791 divided Canada along linguistic and religious lines: Upper Canada (now Ontario) was English and Protestant; Lower Canada (now Québec) was French and Catholic.

Explorers such as Alexander MACKENZIE, James Cook and George Vancouver enabled

Britain to form the crown colony of British Columbia in 1858. Border disputes with the USA (see AROOSTOOK WAR, WAR OF 1812) continued into the 19th century. Large-scale immigration from Ireland and Scotland

AREA
9,970,610sq km
[3,849,653sq mi]
POPULATION
33,390,000
CAPITAL (POPULATION)
Ottawa (1,120,000)
GOVERNMENT
Federal multiparty constitutional monarchy
ETHNIC GROUPS British origin 28%, French origin 23%, other European 15%, Amerindian/Inuit 2%, others
LANGUAGES English and French (both official)
RELIGIONS Roman Catholic 46%, Protestant 36%, Judaism, Islam, Hinduism
CURRENCY Canadian dollar = 100 cents

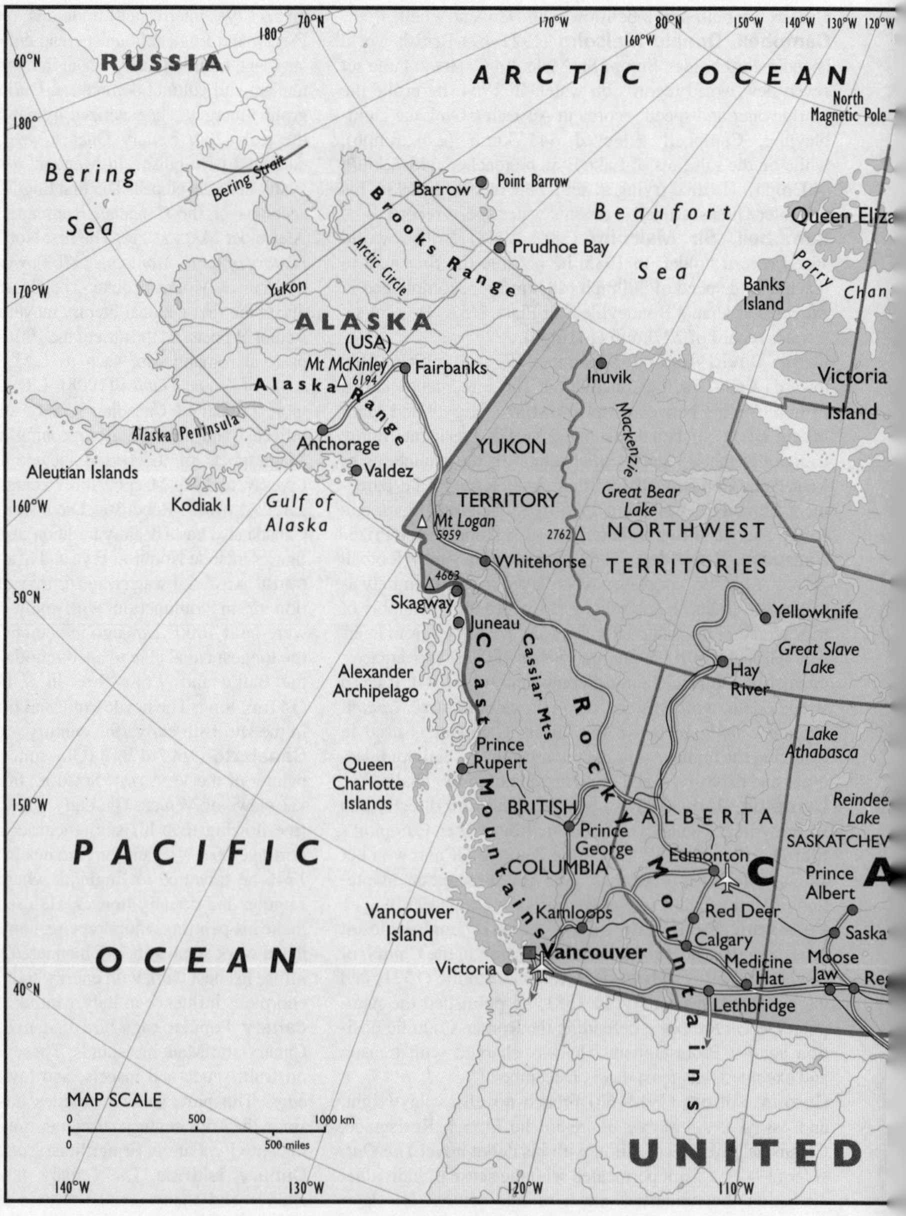

increased tension and conflict between the English-speaking majority and the French-speaking minority. In an attempt to reduce conflict, the British passed the British North America act (1867). This constitutional act established the federation or Dominion of Canada, consisting of Québec, Ontario, Nova Scotia and New Brunswick. In 1869 it acquired the lands of the HUDSON'S BAY COMPANY and other provinces were added: Manitoba (1870), British Columbia (1871), PRINCE EDWARD ISLAND (1873), Alberta and Saskatchewan (1905) and Newfoundland (1949). The Dominion's first prime minister, Sir John A. MACDONALD, established the Canadian Pacific Railway, which proved disastrous to his career but provided the means for 3 million Europeans to emigrate to Canada between 1894 and 1914.

Canadians fought as part of Allied forces in both World Wars, and in 1949 Canada was a founding member of NATO. Under the leadership of W.L. Mackenzie King, national unity was strengthened and industry

developed. In 1963, Lester PEARSON became prime minister and, as a sign of Canada's growing national confidence, adopted a new national flag. Pierre TRUDEAU's first administration (1968–79) faced violent separatist demands for Québec's independence, and martial law was imposed in 1970. In 1976, Montréal hosted the summer Olympic Games. In Trudeau's second administration (1980–84), Québec voted to remain part of the federation (1980). Under the Constitution Act of 1982, Queen Elizabeth II is head of state and a symbol of the close ties between Canada and Britain. The British monarch is represented by an appointed governor-general, but the country is ruled by a prime minister, and an elected, two-chamber parliament.

POLITICS

Canada combines the cabinet system with a federal form of government, with each province having its own government. The federal government can reject any law passed by

a provincial legislature, though this seldom happens in practice. The territories are self-governing, but the federal government plays a large part in their administration.

Canada and the United States of America have the largest bilateral trade flow in the world. Economic co-operation was further enhanced in 1993 when Canada, the United States and Mexico set up the North American Free Trade Agreement, NAFTA.

A constant problem facing those who want to maintain the unity of Canada is the persistence of French culture in Québec, which has fuelled a separatist movement seeking to turn the province into an independent French-speaking republic. More than two-thirds of the population of Québec are French speakers. In 1994, the people of Québec voted the separatist Parti Québécois into provincial office. The incoming prime minister announced that independence for Québec would be the subject of a referendum in 1995. In that referendum, 49.4% voted 'Yes' for separation while 50.5% voted 'No'.

Provincial elections in 1998 resulted in another victory for the Parti Québécois, but while the separatist party won 75 out of the 125 seats in the provincial assembly, it won only 43% of the popular vote compared with 44% for the anti-secessionist Liberal Party and 12% for the floating Action Démocratique de Québec. Canada's highest court ruled that, under Canadian law, Québec does not have the right to secede unilaterally. The court ruled that, should a clear majority of the people in the province vote by 'a clear majority' to a 'clear question' in favour of independence, the federal government and the other provinces would have to negotiate Québec's secession. In 2006 the national parliament symbolically recognized Québec as "a nation within a united Canada" in an attempt at reconciliation.

Other problems involve the rights of the aboriginal Native Americans and the Inuit, who together numbered about 470,000 in 1991. In 1999, a new Inuit territory was created. Called Nunavut, it is made up of 64% of the former Northwest Territories, and covers 2,201,400sq km [649,965sq mi]. The population in 1991 was about 25,000, 85% of whom were Inuit. Nunavut, whose capital is Iqaluit (formerly Frobisher Bay), will depend on aid. Mineral extraction and eco–tourism will be developed in the region to lessen dependence.

ECONOMY

Canada is a highly developed and prosperous country. Although farmland covers only 8% of the country, Canadian farms are highly productive, Canada is one of the world's leading producers of barley, wheat, meat and milk. Forestry and fishing are other important industries. It is rich in natural resources, especially oil and natural gas. Canada exports minerals, including copper, gold, iron ore, uranium and zinc. Manufacturing is important, mainly in the cities where 79% of the population lives. Canada processes farm and mineral products. It also produces cars, chemicals, electronic goods, machinery, paper and timber products. Tourism is an important source of income with winter and summer both popular tourist seasons.

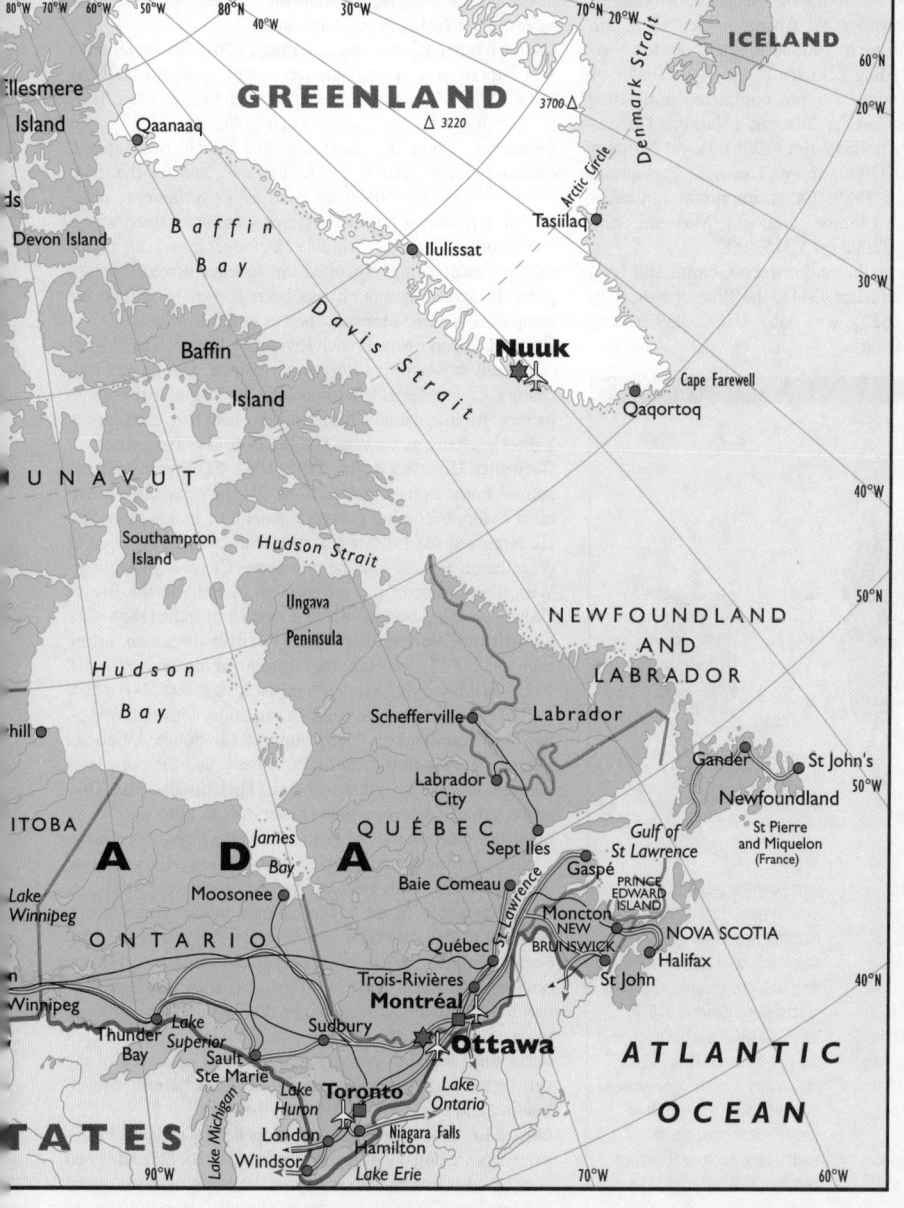

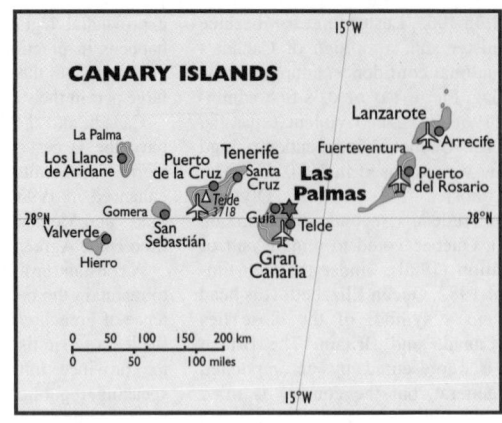

CANARY ISLANDS

in the mountains. Claimed by Portugal in 1341, they were ceded to Spain in 1479. Since 1927 they have constituted two Spanish provinces, LAS PALMAS and SANTA CRUZ DE TENERIFE, which were given autonomous government in the early 1980s. Tourism is the major industry, directly employing a third of the population, and farming and fishing are also important.

Canberra Capital of Australia on the River Molonglo, Australian Capital Territory, SE Australia. Settled in the early 1820s, it was chosen in 1908 as the new site for Australia's capital (succeeding MELBOURNE). The transfer of all governmental agencies was not completed until after World War 2. Canberra has the Australian National University (1946), Royal Australian Mint (1965), Royal Military College and Stromlo Observatory. The new Parliament House was opened in 1988. Other important buildings include the National Library, National Museum, and National Gallery. Pop. (2002 est.) 315,400.

Cancer Northern constellation between Gemini and Leo. It contains two open clusters: M44, the Praesepe or Beehive Nebula (NGC 2632), and M67 (NGC 2692). The brightest star is Beta Cancri.

CANCER

Cancer can spread in two ways. First, by direct growth into adjacent tissues, called "direct extension" (A), when cancer cells penetrate into bone, soft connective tissue and the walls of veins and lymphatic vessels. Alternatively, a cancer cell separates from its tumour and is transported to another part of the body. This spread of cancer is called "metastasis" (B). In metastasis after the tumour has grown to some size, cancer cells or small groups of cells enter a blood or lymph vessel through the vessel wall (1). They travel through the vessel until they are stopped by a barrier, such as a lymph node, where additional tumours may develop, before releasing more cells which may develop on other lymph nodes. Such cancers, usually carcinomas, may also invade the blood stream and establish more distant secondary growths. Another type of cancer, sarcomas, tend to spread via venous blood vessels frequently establishing tumours in the lungs, gastrointestinal tract or the genito-urinary tract (2). In abdominal cancers, metastases may also arise as a result of travel across body cavities, such as the peritoneal, oral or pleural cavities (3).

cancer Group of diseases featuring the uncontrolled proliferation of cells (tumour formation). Malignant (cancerous) cells spread (metastasize) from their original site to other parts of the body. There are many different cancers. Known causative agents (carcinogens) include smoking, certain industrial chemicals, asbestos dust and radioactivity. Viruses are implicated in the causation of some cancers. Some people have a genetic tendency towards particular types of cancer. Treatments include surgery, chemotherapy with cell-destroying drugs and radiotherapy (or sometimes a combination of all three). Early diagnosis holds out the best chance of successful treatment.

Cancer, Tropic of Line of latitude, c.23.5° N of the Equator, which marks the N boundary of the tropics. It indicates the farthest N position at which the Sun appears directly overhead at noon. The Sun is vertical over the Tropic of Cancer on about June 21, the summer SOLSTICE in the Northern Hemisphere.

candela (symbol cd) SI unit of luminous intensity. It is defined as 1/60 of the luminous intensity of a BLACK BODY (which looks black) at atmospheric pressure and the temperature of solidification of platinum, 1,772°C (3,222°F).

Canetti, Elias (1905–94) British writer, b. Bulgaria. His first-hand experience of violent anti-Semitism in the 1930s inspired his masterpiece, *Crowds and Power* (1960). His fear of the destructive power of mass psychology also informed his only novel, *Auto da Fé* (1935). In 1981 he received the Nobel Prize in literature.

Canis Major (Great Dog) Southern constellation situated s of Monoceros. It contains the bright open cluster M41 (NGC 2287). The brightest star is Alpha Canis Majoris or Sirius (Dog Star), the brightest star in the sky.

cannabis Common name for the Indian hemp plant, *Cannabis sativa* (family Cannabidaceae), and for the dried plant or extracted resin when used as a psychotropic drug. The drug produces NARCOTIC effect sometimes allied with a feeling of well-being. It is highly carcinogenic and can induce mild psychosis; long term effects include an increased risk of paranoid schizophrenia. It has been shown to relieve the symptoms of some illnesses, such as multiple sclerosis.

Cannes Resort on the French Riviera, SE France. The old part of the city has a 16th-17th century church. During the 19th century, Cannes became fashionable with visiting British aristocracy. An international film festival is held here each spring. Industries: tourism, flowers, textiles. Pop. (1999) 67,406.

Canning, Charles John, Earl (1812–62) British imperial administrator. Son of George CANNING, he served in government before becoming governor general of India (1856–58). He repressed the INDIAN MUTINY and followed a policy of conciliation earning him the nickname 'Clemency Canning'. With the transfer of the government of India to the British Crown, Canning became the first viceroy of India (1858–62).

Canning, George (1770–1827) British statesman, prime minister (1827) He was Tory foreign minister (1807–10, 1822–24), favouring vigorous measures against NAPOLEON I. He became prime minister in coalition with the Whigs, but died four months later. Support for South American independence and opposition to slavery and the corn laws marked him as relatively liberal. This divided the Tory party, some of whom refused to serve with him.

cannon One of several forms of large ARTILLERY piece working on the principle of the GUN. The earliest cannon, used from the 14th century, were smooth-bore, muzzle-loaded weapons made of bronze or iron. They used GUNPOWDER to fire spherical iron shot. By the end of the 15th century cannon had become a dominant weapon in Europe both on land and at sea. Their form, handling, carriages and methods of manufacture were gradually improved, producing a reliable and efficient weapon. Radical changes did not occur until the 19th century technological advances of the INDUSTRIAL REVOLUTION. By 1900 rifled barrels, breech loading and explosive shells were the norm.

canoe Light, shallow-draft boat propelled by paddles. Primitive types are dug out of logs or made of skin or bark stretched over wooden frames. Modern types are made of wood, metal or fibreglass. Canoeing became an Olympic sport in 1936.

canon In music, form of COUNTERPOINT using strict imitation. All the voices or parts have the same melody, but each voice starts at a different time, at the same or a different pitch.

canon Term used in Christian religion with several meanings. The basic meaning is a rule or standard. In this sense, a canon is something accepted or decreed as a rule or regulation, such as the official list of saints or the list of books accepted as genuine parts of the BIBLE. This is the meaning embraced by the term canon law. Initially a canon was also a priest in a cathedral or collegiate church, whose life was regulated by the precepts of CANON LAW. They were distinct from secular canons, who lived outside the cathedral and, although ordained, played a largely administrative role.

canonization Official action by which a member of a Christian Church is created a cult figure or SAINT and added to the CANON. In the Orthodox Church, a person's sainthood may be proclaimed by a bishop after examining the candidate's case. In the Anglican Church, a commission determines whether someone is to be admitted into the list of saints. In the Roman Catholic Church, officials analyse the evidence of a candidate's reputation for sanctity or virtue and seek out evidence for any MIRACLE performed. The results are submitted to the Congregation for the Causes of Saints and, after their findings are ratified by the pope, the candidate is beatified. Further proof of additional miracles is required before full canonization.

canon law In the Roman Catholic, Anglican, and Orthodox Churches, a body of ecclesiastical laws relating to faith, morals and discipline. It is based on custom and regulations laid down by church councils, popes or bishops.

Canopus (Alpha Carinae) Second-brightest star in the sky. It is 14,000 times as lumionous as the sun and lies 313 light years away.

Canova, Antonio (1757–1822) Italian sculptor. His work expresses the grave elegance and allusions to antique art which characterize NEO-CLASSICISM, but retains a high degree of individuality. Two important pieces of the 1780s, *Theseus and the Minotaur* and Pope Clement XIV's tomb, catapulted Canova into the limelight. He worked for many distinguished European patrons, notably the papal court.

cantata Musical work consisting of vocal solos and choruses, often alternating with passages of recitative, and accompanied by an orchestra. It was a popular form in the 17th and 18th centuries, when Alessandro Scarlatti and J.S. Bach wrote numerous cantatas, both secular and religious.

Canterbury City on the River Great Stour, Kent, SE England. It is the seat of the archbishop and primate of the Anglican Church. The present cathedral (built in the 11th-15th centuries) replaced the original Abbey of St Augustine. Thomas à BECKET was murdered in the cathedral in 1170; after his canonization, Canterbury became a major pilgrimage centre. It contains the University of Kent (1965). Tourism is a major industry. Pop. (2001) 135,287.

Canterbury, Archbishop of Primate of All England and spiritual leader of the worldwide ANGLICAN COMMUNION. The archbishopric was established in 597, when Pope GREGORY I sent a mission to England to convert the Anglo-Saxons. Saint AUGUSTINE of Canterbury, leader of the mission, became the first Archbishop. During the Reformation, Archbishop Thomas CRANMER accepted the decision of the English Crown to end papal jurisdiction in England (1534). The Archbishop of Canterbury traditionally crowns British monarchs and officiates at other religious ceremonies of national importance. He presides over the Lambeth Conference of worldwide Anglicanism, but exercises no jurisdiction outside his own ecclesiastical province.

cantilever bridge BRIDGE in which each half of the main span is rigidly supported at one end only. The other ends are joined in the middle of the bridge, where there is no supporting structure.

Canton *See* GUANGZHOU

canton Unit of government and administration that make up the Swiss Confederation (Switzerland). Each canton sends two members to the Council of State, which (with the National Council) forms the country's federal parliament.

Cantonese One of the major languages of China. Within the Chinese People's Republic it is spoken by *c.*50 million people, mainly in the extreme southern provinces of Guangdong and GUANGXI. It is also the language spoken by most Chinese in Southeast Asia and the USA.

Canute II (the Great) (*c.*994–1035) King of Denmark (1014–28), England (1017–35), and Norway (1028–29). He accompanied his father, Sweyn, on the Danish invasion of England (1013). After his father's death (1014), he was accepted as joint king of Denmark with his brother and later became sole king. He invaded England again (1015) and divided it (1016) with the English king Edmund Ironside. He was accepted as king after Edmund's death. His rule was a just and peaceful one. He restored the church and codified English law. His reign in Scandinavia was more turbulent. He conquered Norway (1028), made one son king of Denmark (1028) and another king of Norway (1029).

canyon Deep, narrow depression in the Earth's crust. Land canyons are the result of EROSION by rivers flowing through arid terrain. Marine canyons may be formed when a river bed and the surrounding terrain is submerged, or by turbulence produced by deep water currents. *See also* GRAND CANYON

Capa, Robert (1913–54) US photojournalist, b. Hungary. He is best remembered for his haunting photos of the brutality of war, in particular one of a Loyalist soldier in the Spanish Civil War falling at the moment of his death. Capa covered World War 2 for *Life* magazine and was a founder (1946) of the Magnum photographic agency. He was killed by a landmine in Vietnam.

capacitance (symbol *C*) Property of an electrical circuit or component that describes its ability to store charge in its CAPACITOR. Capacitance is measured in farads: one farad is a capacitance needing a charge of 1 coulomb to raise its potential by 1 volt. Most capacitances are small enough to be measured in microfarads (one millionth of a farad).

capacitor (condenser) Electrical circuit component that stores charge. It has at least two metal plates and is used principally in alternating current (AC) circuits. The various types include parallel-plate condensers and electrolytic capacitors, the latter having a thin layer of oxide on one electrode. *See also* ELECTRIC CURRENT

Cape Canaveral Low sandy promontory in E Florida, USA, extending E into the Atlantic Ocean. It is the site of the John F. Kennedy Space Center which, since 1950, has been NASA's main US launch site for space flights and long-range missiles.

Cape Cod Hook-shaped sandy peninsula in SE Massachusetts, USA. The Pilgrim Fathers landed here in 1620. Of glacial origin, it extends into the Atlantic Ocean, forming Cape Cod Bay. It was originally a centre for fishing, whaling and salt extraction; tourism is now the major industry.

Cape Horn Southernmost point of South America in S Chile. It was sighted by Francis Drake in 1578, and first rounded in 1616 by Cornelis van Schouten.

Cape of Good Hope Peninsula, 50km (30mi) S of Cape Town, South Africa. The first European to sail around it was Bartholomeu Diaz in 1488. The Cape sea route between India and Europe was established by Vasco da Gama in 1497–99.

Cape Province Formerly the largest province in South Africa. In 1994 it was divided into the separate provinces of EASTERN CAPE, WESTERN CAPE and NORTHERN CAPE. The first colony was established by the Dutch EAST INDIA COMPANY in 1652 and slaves were imported to work the land. The BOER settlers' expansion led to territorial wars with indigenous tribes, such as the XHOSA (1779). In 1806 Britain established control and renamed the region, Cape of Good Hope Colony. The new British settlers clashed with the Boers, precipitating the GREAT TREK (1835). Diamonds were discovered near KIMBERLEY in 1867. The British attempt to incorporate TRANSVAAL and Orange FREE STATE into a single state with NATAL and Cape Colony, resulted in the SOUTH AFRICAN WARS (1899–1902). In 1910 the colony became a province of the Union of South Africa. During the 1960s, the apartheid government created the separate tribal areas (bantustans) of Transkei and Ciskei. In 1994 these were integrated to form Eastern Cape Province.

▲ **Capone** Born in Naples, S Italy, Al Capone grew up in Brooklyn, New York. During the prohibition era, 'Scarface' Capone established himself as the head of a organized crime syndicate in Chicago.

Capetians French royal family forming the third dynasty providing France with 15 kings. It began with Hugh Capet, Duke of Francia (987), and ended with Charles IV (1328). Hugh Capet was elected king after the death of Louis V, the last of the CAROLINGIANS. Capetians dominated the feudal forces, extending the king's rule over the country. It was succeeded by Philip VI of the House of Valois.

Cape Town City and seaport at the foot of Table Mountain, South Africa. It is South Africa's legislative capital and the capital of WESTERN CAPE province. Founded in 1652 by the Dutch EAST INDIA COMPANY, it came under British rule in 1795. Places of interest include the Union Parliament, a 17th-century castle, the National Historic Museum, and the University of Cape Town (founded 1829). It is an important industrial and commercial centre. Industries: clothing, engineering equipment, motor vehicles, wine. Pop. (2000) 2,930,000.

Cape Verde Republic in the E Atlantic Ocean, the most westerly point of Africa. It is made up of 15 islands divided into two groups (Windward and Leeward). The capital is Praia on São Tiago. Cape Verde was colonized by the Portuguese in 1462, and served as a base for the slave trade. The islands gained independence in 1975. Industries: agriculture, fishing and salt. Area: 4033sq km (1557sq mi). Pop. (2002 est.) 412,000.

capillary Smallest of BLOOD VESSELS, connecting arteries and veins. They are about 0.1mm (0.004in) in diameter. Capillary walls consist of only a single layer of cells, so that water containing dissolved oxygen and other nutrients (as well as carbon dioxide and other wastes) can pass easily between the blood and surrounding tissues.

capital In architecture, the block of masonry at the top of a column, often elaborately carved. The design of the capital is characteristic of the ORDERS OF ARCHITECTURE.

capital In ECONOMICS, different forms of wealth. **Fixed** capital refers to such things as buildings, tools and equipment; **working** capital (variable or circulating capital) includes raw materials, stock and cash. In accounting, capital is the obligation a business enterprise has to its owners. Capital includes not only the owner's contribution but also the profits retained within the business for future use.

capitalism Economic system in which property and the means of production are privately owned. Capitalism is based on profit motive, free enterprise, efficiency through competition and a notion of freedom of choice. It was first articulated by Adam SMITH in his treatise *The Wealth of Nations* (1776). Its development dates from the INDUSTRIAL REVOLUTION and the rise of the BOURGEOISIE. In practice, capitalist governments participate in economic regulation although to a lesser extent than a government within COMMUNISM or SOCIALISM. *See also* FREE TRADE; KEYNES, JOHN MAYNARD; LAISSEZ-FAIRE; MARXISM; MERCANTILISM; MONETARISM

capital punishment Punishing a criminal offence by death. Usual methods of execution include hanging, electrocution, lethal injection, lethal gas or firing squad. The death penalty has been abolished in many Western countries. In the USA, capital punishment was effectively in abeyance during the 1970s after several rulings by the US Supreme Court, but today 38 states have the death penalty. Britain effectively abolished capital punishment in 1965. The use of capital punishment is the subject of much debate: supporters claim that such punishment can be deserved and has a deterrent effect, while opponents state that it is inhuman, does not deter and that miscarriages of justice cannot be rectified.

Capitol Building in WASHINGTON, D.C., in which the US CONGRESS convenes. The original architect was William Thornton, and the cornerstone was laid by George Washington in 1793. The British burned it down in 1814. Benjamin LATROBE and Charles BULFINCH worked on the restoration, which was completed in 1830. The dome reaches a height of 88m (288ft).

Capone, Al (Alphonse) (1899–1947) US gangster of the PROHIBITION era, b. Italy. He inherited a vast crime empire from the gang leader Johnny Torio. Capone was suspected of involvement in many brutal crimes, but ironically was only ever convicted and imprisoned for income tax evasion (1931).

Capote, Truman (1924–84) US writer. His works, typified by keen social observation and characters on the fringes of

society, include the novella *Breakfast at Tiffany's* (1958), the novel *The Grass Harp* (1951) and volumes of shorter pieces such as *Music for Chameleons* (1980). Capote claimed that *In Cold Blood* (1966) was the first non-fiction novel.

Capra, Frank (1897–1991) US film director, b. Sicily. During the 1930s Depression, Capra made a string of successful screwball comedies. His central theme was the unlikely triumph of idealism and the common man over materialism and bureaucracy. He won three Academy Awards for best director: *It Happened One Night* (1934), *Mr Deeds Goes to Town* (1936), and *You Can't Take It With You* (1938). During World War 2 he directed propaganda films. *It's a Wonderful Life* (1947), perhaps Capra's best film, was a commercial failure.

Capricorn, Tropic of Line of latitude, *c.*23.27° S of the Equator which marks the southern boundary of the tropics. It indicates the farthest southern position at which the Sun appears directly overhead at noon. The Sun is vertical over the Tropic of Capricorn on about December 22, which is the summer SOLSTICE in the Southern Hemisphere.

Capricornus (Sea Goat) Southern constellation situated on the ecliptic between Sagittarius and Aquarius; the tenth sign of the zodiac, identified with the Greek god PAN. Usually referred to as Capricorn only for astrological purposes, this constellation contains the faint globular cluster M30 (NGC 7099).

capsicum *See* PEPPER

capuchin Small diurnal monkey found in South and Central America. It is generally brown or black and is a tree-dweller. Omnivorous, but preferring fruit, it may grow to 55cm (22in) with a furry, prehensile tail of similar length. Family Cebidae.

Capuchins (officially Friars Minor of St Francis Capuchin, O.F.M.Cap.) Roman Catholic religious order, founded in 1525 as an offshoot of the FRANCISCANS. Capuchins are named after the pointed cowl (*capuche*), which forms part of their habit. They re-emphasized Franciscan ideals of poverty and austerity, and played an important role in the COUNTER-REFORMATION.

capybara Largest living RODENT, native to Central and South America; it is semi-aquatic with webbed feet, a large, nearly hairless, body, short legs and a tiny tail. Length: 1.2m (4ft). Species *Hydrochoerus hydrochoeris*.

car *See* AUTOMOBILE

Caracalla (188–217) (Marcus Aurelius Antoninus) Roman Emperor (211–17). He murdered his brother, Geta, along with many of his supporters (212). Excessive expenditure on war caused economic crisis. During his reign, Roman citizenship was extended to all free men in the Empire. Caracalla was assassinated by his successor, Macrinus.

Caracas Capital of Venezuela, on the River Guaire. Caracas was under Spanish rule until 1821. It was the birthplace of Simón BOLÍVAR. The city grew after 1930, encouraged by the exploitation of oil. It has the Central University of Venezuela (1725) and a cathedral (1614). Industries: motor vehicles, oil, brewing, chemicals, rubber. Pop. (2005) 3,276,000.

Caravaggio, Michelangelo Merisi da (1571–1610) Italian painter, the most influential and original painter of the 17th century. His work brought a new, formidable sense of reality at a time when a feeble MANNERISM prevailed. Caravaggio's early works were mainly experimental and include the erotic half-length figures of *The Young Bacchus* and *Boy with a Fruit Basket* (both *c.*1595). The majestic *Supper at Emmaus* (*c.*1598–1600) with its beautifully modelled images of Christ and his disciples shows Caravaggio gaining confidence. His mature phase (1599–1606) began with two large-scale religious paintings of Saint Matthew. The use of dramatic shadows (CHIAROSCURO) and a living model, show Caravaggio's revolutionary approach to religious themes. *The Crucifixion of St Peter* and *The Conversion of St Paul* (both 1600–01) are masterpieces of psychological realism.

caraway Biennial herb native to Eurasia and cultivated for its small, brown seed-like fruits that are used for flavouring foods. It has feathery leaves and white flowers. Family Apiaceae/Umbelliferae; species *Carum carvi*.

carbide Inorganic compound of carbon with metals or other more electropositive elements. Many transition metals form carbides, in which carbon atoms occupy spaces between adjacent atoms in the metal lattice. Some electropositive metals form ionic carbon compounds; the best known is CALCIUM CARBIDE. Carbides are commonly used as abrasives.

carbohydrate Organic compound of carbon, hydrogen and oxygen that is a constituent of many foodstuffs. The simplest carbohydrates are SUGARS. GLUCOSE and FRUCTOSE are monosaccharides, naturally occurring sugars; they have the same formula ($C_6H_{12}O_6$) but different structures. One molecule of each combines with the loss of water to make sucrose ($C_{12}H_{22}O_{11}$), a disaccharide. Starch and cellulose are polysaccharides, carbohydrates consisting of hundreds of glucose molecules linked together. *See also* SACCHARIDE

carbon (symbol C) Common, nonmetallic element of group IV of the periodic table. Carbon forms more compounds than all the other elements together. With hydrogen-hydocarbons and other nonmetals, it forms the basis of organic CHEMISTRY. Until recently, it was believed there were two crystalline allotropes: GRAPHITE and DIAMOND. In 1996 a third type, 'bucky balls' (named after US engineer Richard Buckminster Fuller), which are shaped like geodesic domes, was discovered. Various amorphous (noncrystalline) forms of carbon also exist, such as coal, coke, and charcoal. A recently made synthetic form of carbon is CARBON FIBRE. The isotope C^{14} is used for CARBON DATING of archaeological specimens. Properties: at.no. 6; r.a.m. 12.011; r.d. 1.9–2.3 (graphite), 3.15–3.53 (diamond); m.p. *c*.3550°C (6422°F); sublimes at 3367°C (6093°F); b.p. *c*.4200°C (7592°F); most common isotope C^{12} (98.89%).

carbonate Salt of carbonic acid, formed when carbon dioxide (CO_2) dissolves in water. Carbonic acid is an extremely weak acid and both it and many of its salts are unstable, decomposing readily to release CO_2. Nevertheless, large parts of the Earth's crust are made up of carbonates, such as CALCIUM CARBONATE and DOLOMITE.

carbon cycle Circulation of carbon in the biosphere. It is a complex chain of events. The most important elements are the taking up of carbon dioxide (CO_2) by green plants during PHOTOSYNTHESIS, and the return of CO_2 to the atmosphere by the respiration and eventual decomposition of animals which eat the plants. The burning of fossil fuels has also, over the years, released CO_2 back into the atmosphere. *See* diagram.

carbon dating (radiocarbon dating) Method of determining the age of organic materials by measuring the amount of radioactive decay of an ISOTOPE of carbon, carbon-14 (C^{14}). This radio-isotope decays to form nitrogen, with a half-life of 5730 years. When a living organism dies, it ceases to take carbon dioxide into its body, so that the amount of C^{14} it contains is fixed relative to its total weight. Over the centuries, this quantity steadily diminishes. Refined chemical and physical analysis is used to determine the exact amount remaining, and from this the age of a specimen is deduced.

carbon dioxide (CO_2) Colourless, odourless gas that occurs in the atmosphere (0.03%) and as a product of the combustion of fossil fuels and respiration in plants and animals. In its solid form (dry ice) it is used in refrigeration; as a gas it is used in carbonated beverages and fire extinguishers. Research indicates that its increase in the atmosphere leads to the GREENHOUSE EFFECT and GLOBAL WARMING. Properties: m.p. −56.6°C (−69.9°F); sublimes −78.5°C (−109.3°F).

carbon fibre Form of carbon made by heating textile fibres to high temperatures. The result is fibres (typically 0.001cm in diameter) which are, weight-for-weight, some of the strongest of all fibres. They are too short to be woven into a super-strong yarn. Instead they are incorporated into plastics, ceramics and glass, which give the materials great strength.

Carboniferous Fifth geological division of the PALAEOZOIC era, lasting from 360 to 286 million years ago. It is often called the 'Age of Coal' because of its extensive swampy forests of conifers and tree ferns that turned into most of today's coal deposits. Amphibians flourished, marine life abounded in warm, inland seas, and the first reptiles appeared.

carbon monoxide Colourless, odourless poisonous gas (CO) formed during the incomplete combustion of fossil fuels, occurring for example in coal gas and the exhaust fumes of cars. Carbon monoxide poisons by combining with the HAEMO-

GLOBIN in red blood cells and thus preventing them from carrying oxygen around the body. (This happens if the inhaled air contains only 0.1% of carbon monoxide by volume). It is used as a reducing agent in metallurgy. Properties: density 0.968 (air = 1); m.p. −205°C (−337°F); b.p. −191.5°C (−312.7°F).

carboxylic acid Member of a class of organic chemical compounds containing the group COOH. The commonest example is ETHANOIC ACID (acetic acid, CH_3COOH), which is present in vinegar. These acids are weakly acidic, forming salts with bases and esters with alcohols. Esters of high-molecular weight, carboxylic acids, such as stearic, lauric and oleic acids, are present in animal and vegetable fats; for this reason carboxylic acids are often called FATTY ACIDS.

carburettor Component of some petrol-powered INTERNAL COMBUSTION ENGINES, used to vaporize and mix fuel with air in the correct proportion for proper combustion. No carburettor is needed in engines that use fuel injection.

carcinogen External substance or agent that causes CANCER, including chemicals, such as the tar present in cigarette smoke, large doses of radiation and some viruses, such as polyoma.

carcinoma Form of CANCER arising from the epithelial cells present in skin and the membranes lining the internal organs. It is a malignant growth that can invade surrounding tissues, in turn giving rise to metastases (secondary cancers). *See also* MELANOMA; SARCOMA

cardamom Pungent spice made from seeds of a plant of the GINGER family (Zingiberaceae), often mixed with turmeric to make a type of curry. Species *Elettaria cardamomum*.

cardiac muscle *See* MUSCLE

Cardiff (Caerdydd) Capital of Wales and port on the River Severn estuary at the mouth of the rivers Taff, Rhymney and Ely, s Glamorgan. The construction of docks in 1839 led to the rapid growth of the city, and, until the early 20th century, it was a major coal exporting centre. It is the seat of the Welsh National Assembly and the University College of South Wales and Monmouthshire (1893). The Millennium Stadium hosted the 1999 Rugby World Cup. Industries: steel manufacturing, engineering, chemicals, food processing. Pop. (2001) 305,340.

▲ **capybara** Found in central and South America, the capybara (*Hydrochoerus hydrochaeris*) is the largest rodent in the world. It grows to more than 1m (3ft).

C

CARBON CYCLE

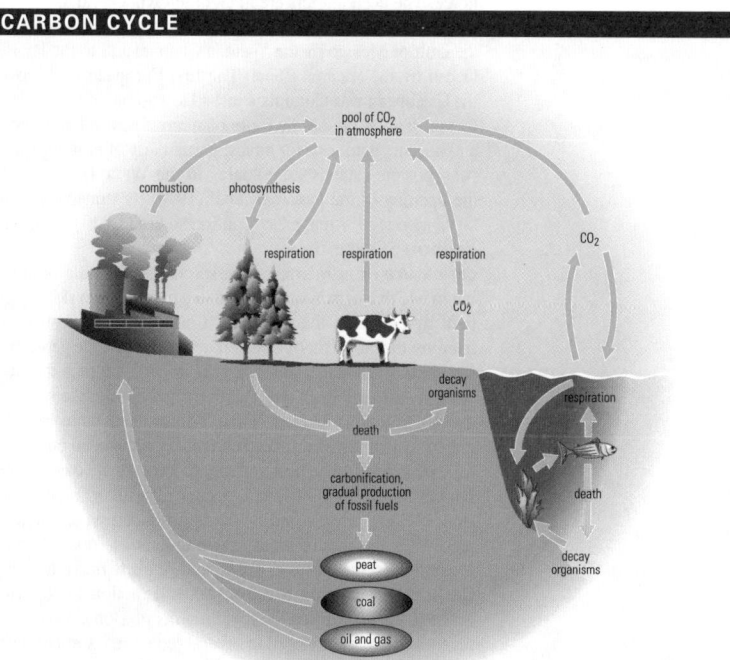

pool of CO_2 in atmosphere

combustion | photosynthesis

respiration | respiration | respiration

CO_2

CO_2

decay organisms

respiration

death

death

carbonification, gradual production of fossil fuels

decay organisms

peat

coal

oil and gas

Elemental carbon is in constant flux. Gaseous carbon dioxide (CO2) is first incorporated into simple sugars by photosynthesis in green plants. These may be broken down (respired) to provide energy, a process that releases CO2 back into the atmosphere. Alternatively, animals which eat the plants also metabolize the sugars and release CO2 in the process. Geological processes also affect the Earth's carbon balance, with carbon being removed from the cycle when it is accumulated within fossil fuels such as coal, oil and gas. Conversely, large amounts of carbon dioxide are released into the atmosphere when such fuels are burned.

C

▲ **carnation** Native to the Mediterranean region, carnations are a species of pink (*Dianthus caryophyllaceus*). A great number of hybrids have been developed to be grown in gardens in many tempertate regions.

cardinal Highest ranking priest in the hierarchy of the Roman Catholic Church after the pope. Some cardinals are heads of departments of the church administration, whereas others are PRIMATES of national churches or other senior bishops. They are nominated by the pope, whom they advise. On the death of a pope they meet in secret CONCLAVE to elect his successor.

cardiology Branch of medicine that deals with the diagnosis and treatment of the diseases and disorders of the HEART and vascular system.

Carew, Thomas (1595–1639) English poet. His poetry was largely influenced by his friend Ben JONSON and John DONNE, to whom he wrote an elegy. His work includes *A Rapture* and the MASQUE *Coelum Britannicum*.

Carey, George Leonard (1935–) Anglican Archbishop of Canterbury and primate of all England (1991–2002). After serving for four years as curate of St Mary's Church, Islington, he became bishop of Bath and Wells (1988). Carey was on the evangelical wing of the CHURCH OF ENGLAND. He favoured the ordination of women priests and supported environmental conservation. His books include *I Believe in Men* (1975) and *The Great God Robbery* (1989). In 2002 he was succeeded as Archbishop by Dr Rowan WILLIAMS. *See also* EVANGELICALISM

Carey, Peter (1943–) Australian novelist and short-story writer. Beside J.M. COETZEE, Carey is the only writer to receive two Booker Prizes – for *Oscar and Lucinda* (1988) and *The True History of the Kelly Gang* (2001). Other novels include *Bliss* (1981), *Illywacker* (1985), and *Jack Maggs* (1997).

Carib Major language group and Native American tribe. They entered the Caribbean region from NE South America. About 500 Caribs still live on the island of Dominica; 5000 migrated to the E coast of Central America, notably around Honduras, where their descendants still live.

Caribbean Community and Common Market (CARICOM) Caribbean economic union. CARICOM was formed in 1973 by the Treaty of Chaguaramas to co-ordinate economic and foreign policy in the WEST INDIES. Most members rely on the export of sugar and tropical fruits and are heavily dependent on imports, so competition for foreign markets is fierce. The headquarters are in Georgetown, Guyana.

Caribbean Sea Extension of the N Atlantic Ocean linked to the Gulf of Mexico by the Yucatán Channel and to the Pacific Ocean by the Panama Canal. The first European to discover the Caribbean was Columbus in 1492, who named it after the CARIB. It soon lay on the route of many Spanish expeditions and became notorious for piracy, particularly after other European powers established colonies in the WEST INDIES. With the opening of the Panama Canal (1914) its strategic importance increased. Area: *c.*2.64 million sq km (1,020,000sq mi).

caribou *See* REINDEER

caricature (It. *caricare*, load or surcharge) Painting or drawing in which a person is presented in a comic, often ridiculous, light by distorting their features. Caricature may be used to interpret the character of a person, event or age. The genre first appeared in the late 16th century. HOGARTH attempted to distinguish between depicting character and comic likeness, but the two traditions merged. In the 20th century, many popular graphic artists have combined caricature with social and political satire, and today most political CARTOONS are caricatures.

caries Decay and disintegration of teeth or BONE substance. Caries are caused by acids produced when bacteria present in the mouth break down sugars in food. Regular brushing, a reduced sugar intake and fluoride prevent decay.

Carlists Reactionary Spanish political faction in the 19th century. They favoured the royal claims of Don CARLOS and his successors, and figured in several rebellions, sometimes in alliance with BASQUES and CATALANS. The remnants of the Carlists eventually merged with the fascist FALANGE in 1937.

Carlos (1788–1855) Spanish prince and pretender to the throne. His elder brother, Ferdinand VII, changed Spanish law so that his daughter ISABELLA II succeeded him (1833). Carlos was proclaimed king by the CARLISTS, and civil war ensued. Isabella won (1840), and Carlos went into exile. In 1845 he resigned his claim in favour of his son Don Carlos II.

Carlson, Chester (1906–68) US physicist, inventor of XEROGRAPHY (1938). He patented it in 1940, but few were convinced of its commercial value. In 1947, he signed an agreement with the Haloid Company (now Rank Xerox).

Carlyle, Thomas (1795–1881) Scottish philosopher, critic and historian. His most successful work, *Sartor Resartus* (1836), combined philosophy and autobiography. His histories include *The French Revolution* (1837). Influenced by Goethe and the German Romantics, he was a powerful advocate of the significance of great leaders in history. He was also an energetic social critic and a proponent of moral values.

Carmelites (officially Order of Our Lady of Mount Carmel) Order founded by Saint Berthold in Palestine *c.*1154. An order of Carmelite sisters was founded in 1452. The Carmelites devote themselves to contemplation and missionary work.

carnation Slender-stemmed herbaceous plant native to Europe. It has narrow leaves, characteristic swollen stem joints, and produces several dense blooms with serrated (pinked) petals which range from white to yellow, pink and red. Family Caryophyllaceae; species *Dianthus caryophyllus*.

Carnegie, Andrew (1835–1919) US industrialist and philanthropist, b. Scotland. A telegraph operator with the Pennsylvania Railroad (1853–65), he foresaw the demand for iron and steel, and founded the Keystone Bridge Company. From 1873 he concentrated on steel manufacture, pioneering mass production techniques. By 1901 the Carnegie Steel Company was producing 25% of US steel. Carnegie endowed 2800 libraries and donated more than $350 million to charitable foundations.

carnivore Any member of the order of flesh-eating mammals. Mustelids – weasels, martens, minks and the wolverine – make up the largest family. CATS are the most specialized killers among the carnivores; dogs, bears and raccoons are much less exclusively meat eaters; and civets, mongooses and their relatives also have a mixed diet. Related to the civets, but in a separate family, are the hyenas, large dog-like scavengers. More distantly related to living land carnivores are the seals, sea lions and walruses; they evolved from ancient land carnivores who gave rise to early weasel- or civet-like forms. Other extinct carnivores include the sabretooth cats, which died out during the Pliocene epoch, 2 million years ago.

carnivorous plant *See* INSECTIVOROUS PLANT

Carnot, Lazare Nicolas Marguerite (1753–1823) French general. Carnot was the outstanding commander of the FRENCH REVOLUTIONARY WARS, his strategy being largely responsible for French victories. Ousted in 1797, he was recalled by Napoleon (1800), who made him minister of war.

Carnot, (Marie François) Sadi (1837–94) French statesman, political leader, president of the Third Republic (1887–94). After quashing the anti-republican movement, he successfully defended the regime during the Panama Canal scandal (1892). He was stabbed to death by an Italian anarchist.

Carnot, (Nicolas Léonard) Sadi (1796–1832) French engineer and physicist whose work laid the foundation for the science of THERMODYNAMICS. His major work, *Réflexions sur la puissance motrice du feu* (1824), provided the first theoretical background for the STEAM ENGINE and introduced the concept of the second law of thermodynamics (involving ENTROPY), which was formulated later by Rudolf CLAUSIUS. Carnot's work was extended in 1834 by the railway engineer Emile Clapeyron and recognized in 1848 by William KELVIN.

Carnot cycle In THERMODYNAMICS, a four-stage cycle (named after Sadi CARNOT) involving alternate **adiabatic** and **istothermal** processes. The former take place without gaining or losing heat, the latter without changing temperature. For example: 1) adiabatic compression of a gas increases its temperature. 2) the gas is then expanded isothermally. 3) Adiabatic expansion of the gas lowers the temperature. 4) The gas is compressed isothermally, lowering the temperature and completing the cycle. In practical terms, it demonstrates the impossibility of total efficiency in heat engines. Some heat energy always remains unused in a 'cold sink'. In an internal combustion engine, this can be thought of as the engine itself.

Caro, Sir Anthony (1924–) British sculptor. He is best known for distinctive 'structures' made from 'found' metal objects welded together in such a way that they keep their original identity, but also create a definite mood. They go beyond CONSTRUCTIVISM in their expressiveness. He often places his work on the floor so as to involve the spectator on an intimate level. He worked as an assistant to Henry MOORE.

carob Plant of the E Mediterranean. It belongs to the pea family (Fabaceae/Leguminosae) and bears leguminous fruits. These long juicy pods are a foodstuff. Its seeds are used as a substitute for coffee beans. Species *Ceratonia siliqua*.

carol Traditional song usually of religious joy and associated with Christmas. Earliest examples date from the 14th century.

Carol I (1839–1914) Prince of Romania (1866–81); first king (1881–1914). He aided Russia in the first Russo-Turkish War (1877–78). The Congress of Berlin (1878) recognized Romanian independence and Carol's sovereignty. By 1913 Romania had become the strongest power in the Balkans. He preserved the neutrality of Romania at the start of World War 1, but sympathized with Germany.

Carol II (1893–1953) King of Romania (1930–40), grandnephew of CAROL I. In 1925 he renounced the throne. He returned in 1930 and supplanted his son Michael as king, despite liberal opposition and economic crisis. Carol II supported FASCISM. He aimed to become dictator, but German pressure forced him to abdicate in favour of his son Michael in 1940, leaving power in the hands of the Romanian fascist leader, Ion ANTONESCU.

Caroline Islands Archipelago of *c*.600 volcanic islands, coral islets and reefs in the W Pacific Ocean, N of the Equator; part of the US Trust Territory of the Pacific Islands. Politically the islands exist as two entities. In 1979 all the islands except the BELAU group became the Federated States of MICRONESIA. Area: 1130sq km (450sq mi).

Carolingian renaissance Cultural revival in France and Italy under the encouragement of CHARLEMAGNE. Having enlarged and enriched the Frankish kingdom and organized an efficient government, the illiterate monarch gathered notable educators and artists from all over the world. He promoted Catholicism, art, and learning by founding abbeys and encouraging church building. As the first Roman Emperor in the West for more than 300 years, he imposed a new culture in Europe, combining Christian, Roman and Frankish elements.

Carolingians Second Frankish dynasty of early medieval Europe. Founded in the 7th century by Pepin of Landen, it rose to power under the weak kingship of the MEROVINGIANS. In 732 Charles Martel defeated the Muslims at Poitiers; in 751 his son PEPIN III (THE SHORT) deposed the last Merovingian and became king of the Franks. The dynasty reached its peak under Pepin's son CHARLEMAGNE (after whom the dynasty is called), who united the Frankish dominions and much of W and central Europe, and was crowned Holy Roman Emperor by the pope in 800. His empire was later subdivided and broken up by civil wars. Carolingian rule finally ended in 987.

Carothers, Wallace Hume (1896–1937) US chemist who discovered the synthetic polyamide fibre now called NYLON.

carp Freshwater fish native to temperate waters of Asia. Introduced to the USA and Europe, it is an important food fish. It is brown or golden and has four fleshy mouth whiskers called barbels. Unlike other species of carp, the mirror carp has only a few scales and the leather carp has none. Length: to 1m (3.2ft). Family Cyprinidae; species *Cyprinus carpio*.

Carpaccio, Vittore (1460–1525) Venetian painter. His narrative paintings relate incidents against a background of an idealized Venice. His cycle of scenes from the legend of St Ursula has an exceptional vitality. Carpaccio's range of subjects varied from religious paintings, such as *The Presentation of Christ in the Temple*, to the enchanting *Two Venetian Ladies*.

Carpathian Mountains Mountain range in central and E Europe, extending NE from the central Czech Republic to the Polish-Czech border and into Romania and the Ukraine. The N Carpathians (Beskids and Tatra) run E along the border and SE through W Ukraine; the S Carpathians (Transylvanian Alps) extend SW to the River Danube. The highest peak is Gerlachovka, 2655m (8711ft). Industries: timber, mining, tourism. Length: 1530km (950mi).

carpel Female reproductive part of a flowering plant. A carpel consists of a STIGMA, a STYLE and an OVARY. A group of carpels make up the **gynoecium**, the complete female reproductive structure within a flower.

Carranza, Venustiano (1859–1920) Mexican political leader. As first chief of the constitutionalist army during the MEXICAN REVOLUTION, Carranza defeated Victoriano HUERTA (1914). Interim president in 1915, he allowed the Pershing expedition to pursue 'Pancho' VILLA, resulting in the US occupation of Veracruz. Elected president in 1917, he was unable to impose a civilian successor. Carranza was murdered.

Carreras, José Maria (1946–) Spanish tenor. He made his debut in Barcelona (1970), going on to sing in opera houses worldwide. At the height of his career he developed leukaemia. After treatment, he successfully returned to the stage in 1988, becoming a household name as one of the Three Tenors, with Placido DOMINGO and Luciano PAVAROTTI.

Carroll, Lewis (1832–98) (Charles Lutwidge Dodgson) British mathematician, photographer and children's writer. An Oxford don, much of his output consisted of mathematical textbooks. He is more widely remembered for the whimsical novel *Alice's Adventures in Wonderland* (1865) and its sequel, *Through the Looking Glass* (1872). Along with his poem *The Hunting of the Snark* (1876), they have attracted much serious scholarly criticism.

carrot Herbaceous, generally BIENNIAL, root vegetable, cultivated widely as a food crop. The edible orange taproot is the plant's store of food for the following year. The plant is topped by delicate fern-like leaves and white or pink flower clusters. Family UMBELLIFERAE; Species *Daucus carota*.

Carson, Edward Henry, Baron (1854–1935) Northern Irish political leader. A famous barrister and powerful orator, he was the leader of resistance to Irish Home Rule. Organizing the paramilitary Ulster Volunteers (1912) and proclaiming "Ulster will fight, and Ulster will be right", he forced the British government to exclude the Protestant provinces from the Home Rule Agreement of 1914.

Carson, Kit (Christopher) (1809–68) US guide and soldier. He originally lived as a trapper and hunter but achieved fame for his work as a guide on FRÉMONT's expeditions (1842–46). In 1854 he became an Indian agent in New Mexico and in 1861 became a colonel in the US army, fighting against Confederate forces. In 1868, he became superintendent of Indian affairs for the Colorado Territory.

Carson City State capital of Nevada, USA, 50km (30mi) s of Reno. The city grew rapidly after silver was discovered in the Comstock Lode in 1859. It was named after Kit CARSON. Gambling is the main industry. Pop. (2000) 52,457.

Cartagena City and port in NW Colombia, on the Bay of Cartagena in the Caribbean Sea; capital of the department of Bolívar. It is the principal oil port of Colombia. There is a university (founded 1824). Industries: oil refining, sugar, tobacco, textiles, tourism. Pop. (2005) 1,002,000.

Cartagena Major seaport in SE Spain, on the Mediterranean Sea. Founded in *c*.255 BC by the Carthaginians, the settlement later fell to the Romans. Moors captured it in the 8th century, but it was retaken by Spaniards in the 13th century. In 1585, it was destroyed by Francis Drake. It is the site of the medieval Castillo de la Concepción and a modern naval base. Industries: shipbuilding, lead, zinc, iron. Pop. (2000) 179,930.

Carte, Richard D'Oyly (1844–1901) English impresario and producer of the operas of GILBERT and SULLIVAN. He founded the Savoy Theatre, London (1881).

cartel Formal agreement among the producers of a product to fix the price and divide the market among themselves. Cartels

◀ **carp** Bony fish belonging to the order Cypriniformes, carps have large bodies usually covered evenly with scales, but these may be missing in cultivated types such as the mirror carp.

C

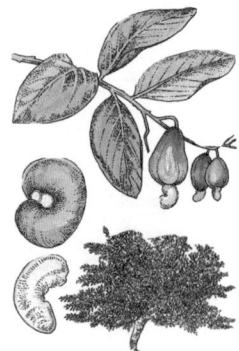

▲ **cashew** Grown in tropical regions, the cashew bears bean-shaped nuts that form beneath an apple-like fruit, and which have an inner and an outer shell which are removed before roasting.

▲ **cassava** Grown widely throughout the tropics, cassava (*Manihot utilissama*) is one of the world's most important tubers. A processed form of meal is produced from its roots, and used as a cereal substitute.

usually result in higher prices for consumers and extra profits for the producers. They are illegal in many countries.

Carter, Angela (1940–92) English novelist and short story writer. Renowned for her daring and innovative style, Carter is closely associated with MAGICAL REALISM. Her writing draws on legend and myth, and mixes past and present, a technique apparent in *Nights at the Circus* (1984), whose central character is half-woman, half-bird. Other writings include the novels *The Magic Toyshop* (1967) and *The Passion of New Eve* (1977), and short-story collections such as *The Bloody Chamber* (1979) and *Fireworks* (1987).

Carter, Elliott Cook, Jr (1908–) US composer, widely regarded as the leading modern American composer. His works are notable for their elaborate COUNTERPOINT, complex structures and use of tempo as an aspect of form. Compositions include a piano (1946) and a cello (1948) sonata, *Variations* (1953–55) and *Concerto* (1970) for orchestra, and four string quartets (1951, 1959, 1971 and 1986). In 1960 he received a Pulitzer Prize for his second string quartet.

Carter, Jimmy (James Earl), Jr (1924–) 39th US president (1977–81). Carter was a Democrat senator (1962–66) and governor (1971–74) for the state of Georgia. In 1976 he defeated President Gerald FORD. Carter had a number of foreign policy successes, such as the CAMP DAVID ACCORD (1979). These were overshadowed by a disastrous attempt to free US hostages in Iran (1980). Following the Soviet invasion of Afghanistan, Carter backed a US boycott of the 1980 Moscow Olympics. An oil price rise contributed to spiralling inflation, which was dampened only by an increase in interest rates. In 1980 elections, Carter was defeated by Ronald REAGAN. He subsequently promoted human rights and acted as an international peace broker. In 2002 he received the Nobel Peace Prize.

Cartesian co-ordinates System in which the position of a point is specified by its distances from intersecting lines (axes). In the simplest type – rectangular co-ordinates in two dimensions – two axes are used at right angles: x and y. The position of a point is then given by a pair of numbers (x, y). The abscissa, x, is the point's distance from the y axis, measured in the direction of the x axis, and the ordinate, y, is the distance from the x axis. The axes in such a system need not be at right angles but should not be parallel to each other. Three axes represent three dimensions. Cartesian co-ordinates are often used in generating computer graphics.

Carthage Ancient port on a peninsula in the Bay of Tunis, N Africa. It was founded in the 9th century BC by Phoenician colonists. It became a great commercial city and imperial power controlling an empire in North Africa, S Spain and the W Mediterranean islands. The rise of ROME in the 3rd century resulted in the PUNIC WARS and, in spite of the victories of Hannibal, ended with the destruction of Carthage in the Third Punic War (149–146BC). It was resettled as a Roman colony, and in the 5th century AD was the capital of the VANDALS.

Carthusian Monastic order founded by St Bruno in 1084. It is based at the Grande Chartreuse Monastery near Grenoble, France. It is a mainly contemplative order, in which monks and nuns solemnly vow to live in silence and solitude.

Cartier, Jacques (1491–1557) French explorer who discovered the St Lawrence River (1535). He sailed up the river to what is now Québec and continued on foot to Hochelaga (now Montréal). He laid the basis for French settlements in Canada.

Cartier-Bresson, Henri (1908–2004) French photographer. In the 1930s Cartier-Bresson was an assistant to Jean Renoir. He co-founded the agency Magnum Photos. His photos, all in black-and-white, are composed with a deep sense of drama, often capturing fleeting images. His images of post-war Europe are historically important works of photo-journalism. His books include *The Decisive Moment* (1952), *The World of Henri Cartier-Bresson* (1968) and *About Russia* (1974).

cartilage Flexible supporting tissue made up of the tough protein COLLAGEN. In the vertebrate EMBRYO, the greater part of the SKELETON consists of cartilage, which is gradually replaced by BONE during development. In humans, cartilage is also present in the larynx, nose and external ear.

cartoon Originally a preparatory drawing. Italian Renaissance painters made very thorough cartoons, such as RAPHAEL for the Sistine Chapel. Its more common, modern usage in reference to a humorous drawing or satirical picture is derived from a 19th-century competition for fresco designs for Parliament parodied in *Punch* magazine. *See also* CARICATURE

Cartwright, Edmund (1743–1823) English inventor of the power loom. It was patented in 1785, but not used commercially until the early 19th century. He also invented a wool-combing machine (patented 1789) and an alcohol engine (1797).

Caruso, Enrico (1873–1921) Italian tenor, one of the most widely acclaimed opera singers of all time. He made his debut in Naples (1894), but settled in the USA. He appeared in leading European opera houses and made many recordings.

Carver, George Washington (1864–1943) US agricultural chemist. He is best known for his scientific research on the peanut, from which he derived more than 300 products. Born into an African-American slave family, his chief motive was to benefit the impoverished farmers of the South.

Carver, Raymond (1938–88) US short story writer and poet. Carver's fiction depicts, with uncompromising realism, the lives of US citizens. His short stories are collected in *Will You Please Be Quiet, Please?* (1976), *What We Talk About When We Talk About Love* (1981) and *Cathedral* (1983). He also wrote five books of poetry.

Cary, (Arthur) Joyce (Lunel) (1888–1957) British novelist, b. Northern Ireland. His experiences in colonial service in Nigeria (1914–20) are reflected in novels such as *Mister Johnson* (1939). His best-known novel is *The Horse's Mouth* (1944).

Casablanca (Dar el-Beida) City in W MOROCCO, on Africa's Atlantic coast. Resettled in 1515 by the Portuguese after their destruction of the old town. An earthquake damaged the city (1755). Today, Casablanca is Morocco's largest city and a busy commercial centre, exporting phosphates and importing petroleum. Industries: tourism, textiles. Pop. (2005) 3,743,000.

Casals, Pablo (Pau) (1876–1973) Spanish (Catalan) cellist and conductor. He founded his own orchestra in Barcelona in 1919, and organized the annual Casals Festival in Puerto Rico from 1957. His virtuoso playing influenced many cellists.

Casanova de Seingalt, Giovanni Giacomo (1725–98) Italian libertine and adventurer. From 1750 he travelled through Europe leading a dissolute existence. His exploits are recounted in *Memoirs*, which were not published in original form until 1960. His name is synonymous with the amorous adventurer.

Cascade Range Mountain range in W North America, extending from NE California across Oregon and Washington into Canada. The Cascade Tunnel, at 13km (8mi) the longest rail tunnel in the USA, passes through them. Crater Lake National Park is in the Cascades. The highest peak is Mount RAINIER, at 4395m (14,410ft). The range also includes Mount ST HELENS, at 2549m (8363ft).

casein Principal protein in milk, containing about 15 amino acids. Its curds are used to make cheese. Obtained by the addition of either acid or the enzyme rennet, casein is used to make plastics, cosmetics, paper coatings, adhesives, paints, textile sizing, cheese, and animal feed.

Casement, Sir Roger David (1864–1916) Irish humanitarian and revolutionary. While a British consul (1895–1912) he exposed the exploitation of rubber-gatherers in the Belgian Congo and similar iniquities in South America. During World War 1 he sought aid for an Irish nationalist uprising, and was executed for treason after the British secret service had tried to destroy his reputation by publishing the Casement diaries.

cash crop Agricultural crop cultivated for its commercial value, as opposed to one grown for subsistence. The term is often encountered in development economics. Cash crops, such as coffee, sugar or cotton, were introduced into Africa, Asia and the Americas as part of the colonialist project and intensively farmed via plantation systems.

cashew Evergreen shrub or tree grown in the tropics, important for its nuts. The wood is used for boxes and boats, and produces a gum similar to gum arabic. Height: to 12m (39ft). Family Anacardiaceae; species *Anacardium occidentale*.

cashmere Woolly hair of a goat native to Kashmir, India. The warm but lightweight wool is woven for clothing.

CASTING

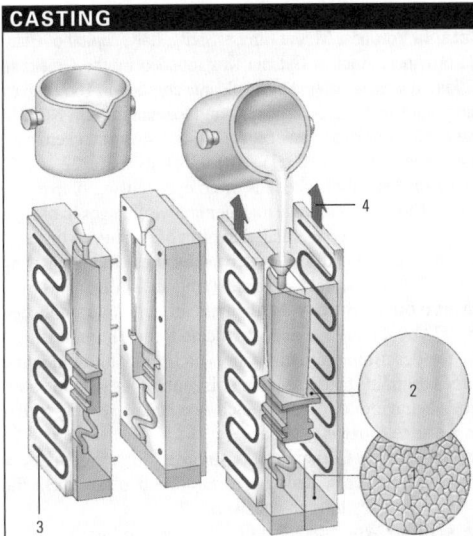

Metal alloys used to make turbine blades must withstand the huge temperatures and forces inside jet engines. The random crystalline structure formed when the alloy cools normally (as seen in the overflow, 1) can be a source of weakness. The strongest structure is achieved by making a blade from a single crystal (2). This can be done by using heating elements (3). After the molten alloy is poured, the elements move up the sides of the mold (4) ensuring the alloy cools from the bottom and forms a single crystal.

Caspian Sea Shallow salt lake, the world's largest inland body of water. The Caspian Sea is enclosed on three sides by Russia, Kazakhstan, Turkmenistan and Azerbaijan. The S shore forms the N border of Iran. It has been a valuable trade route for centuries. It is fed mainly by the River Volga; there is no outlet. The chief ports are BAKU and ASTRAKHAN. It has important fisheries. Area: *c.*371,000sq km (143,000sq mi).

Cassandra In Greek mythology, the daughter of PRIAM, skilled in the art of prophecy, but condemned by Apollo never to be taken seriously. Her warning that the Greeks would capture Troy went unheeded. She was raped by Ajax the lesser, and then carried off as a concubine by AGAMEMNON; they were murdered by his wife CLYTEMNESTRA and her lover Aegisthus.

Cassatt, Mary (1845–1926) French painter and printmaker, b. USA. She was influenced by DEGAS and IMPRESSIONISM. Her finest paintings include *The Bath* (1892). She also made many fine DRYPOINT and AQUATINT studies of domestic life.

cassava (manioc) Tapioca plant native to Brazil. It is a tall woody shrub with small clustered flowers. A valuable cereal substitute is made from the tuberous roots. Height: up to 2.7m (9ft). Family Euphorbiaceae; species *Manihot esculenta*.

Cassini, Giovanni Domenico (1625–1712) French astronomer, who ran the Paris Observatory. He was the first to accurately measure the dimensions of the SOLAR SYSTEM, and discovered four satellites and also the division in the rings of SATURN that now bear his name. He measured Jupiter's rotation period, and also improved the tables of satellites.

Cassiopeia Distinctive N constellation, representing in mythology the mother of ANDROMEDA.

Cassius (Longinus), Gaius (d.42BC) Roman general who led the plot to assassinate Julius CAESAR. He sided with POMPEY against Caesar but was pardoned after Caesar defeated Pompey at Pharsalus (48BC). After the assassination of Caesar in 44 BC he left for Sicily. Believing he had lost against Mark ANTONY and AUGUSTUS at Philippi, Cassius committed suicide.

cassowary Flightless bird of rainforests in Australia and Malaysia. It has coarse black plumage, a horny crest on its brightly coloured head, large feet and sharp claws. Height: to 1.6m (65in). Family Casuariidae; species *Casuarius casuarius*.

caste Formal system of social stratification based on factors such as race, gender or religious heritage, and sanctioned by tradition. An individual is born into and remains in a fixed social position. It is prevalent in Hindu society, in which the four main divisions (*varnas*) are BRAHMINS (priests and professionals), Kshatriyas (nobles), Vaishyas (farmers and merchants) and Sudras (servants). A fifth group, the 'Untouchables' (*harijan* or *dalit*), traditionally lie outside the caste system.

Castile Region and former kingdom in central Spain, traditionally comprising Old Castile (N) and New Castile (S). Old Castile was part of the kingdom of León until 1230. The Castilians captured New Castile from the Moors. Queen ISABELLA I established the union with ARAGÓN in 1479, and in the 16th century Castile became the most influential power in Spain and the core of the Spanish monarchy.

Castile-La Mancha Region in central Spain; includes the provinces of Albacete, Ciudad Real, Cuenca, Guadalajara and Toledo; the capital is TOLEDO. It was captured from the Moors in 1212. Chief products are olive oil and grapes. Area: 79,226sq km (30,590sq mi). Pop. (2001) 1,760,516.

Castile-León Region in N Spain; includes the provinces of Ávila, Burgos, León, Palencia, Salamanca, Segovia, Soria, Valladolid and Zamora; the capital is Valladolid. Formerly part of the kingdom of León, Castile and Aragón united in 1479. Extreme climate and poor soil allow limited grain growing and sheep raising. Area: 94,147sq km (36,350sq mi). Pop. (2001) 2,456,474.

casting Forming objects by pouring molten metal into moulds and allowing it to cool and solidify. Specialized processes, such as plastic moulding, composite moulding, CIRE PERDUE casting and die casting give greater dimensional accuracy, smoother surfaces and finer detail.

castle Fortified house or fortress, usually the medieval residences of European kings or nobles. Castles evolved from a need for fortresses that could accommodate several households and provide shelter in war. Heavily built of wood or masonry, castles were located on a raised site and sometimes surrounded by a ditch or moat.

Castlereagh, Robert Stewart, 2nd Viscount (1769–1822) British politician. Castlereagh was chief secretary of Ireland (1799–1801), helping to pass the Act of Union with Britain in 1800. As war secretary (1805–06, 1807–09), he vigorously opposed Napoleon but resigned after a duel with George CANNING. Castlereagh was a brilliant foreign secretary (1812–22), backing WELLINGTON in war and securing long-term peace in Europe at the Congress of Vienna (1814–15).

Castor and Pollux (Dioscuri) In Greek mythology, the twin sons of LEDA. They were invoked by sailors seeking favourable winds. Zeus, father of Pollux, transformed them into the Gemini constellation after Castor died and Pollux refused to be parted from him.

castration Removal of the sexual glands (testes or ovaries) from an animal or human. In human beings, removal of the testes has been used as a form of punishment, a way of sexually incapacitating slaves to produce EUNUCHS, a way of artificially creating soprano voices (CASTRATO) and as a method of stopping the spread of cancer. It can also make animals tamer.

castrato Male voice in the soprano or mezzo-soprano register, produced in adult males by CASTRATION during boyhood. Castratos were much used in operas in the 17th and 18th centuries and in music for the Roman Catholic Church. The most famous castrato was Farinelli. *See also* COUNTERTENOR

Castro (Ruz), Fidel (1926–) Cuban revolutionary leader and politician, premier (1959–2006). In 1953, he was sentenced to 15 years' imprisonment after an unsuccessful coup against the BATISTA regime. Two years later, he was granted an amnesty and exiled to Mexico. In January 1959, his guerrilla forces overthrew the regime. He quickly instituted radical reforms, collectivizing agriculture and dispossessing foreign companies. In 1961, after the failed BAY OF PIGS US invasion attempt, Castro allied Cuba more closely with the Soviet Union. In 1962, the CUBAN MISSILE CRISIS saw the USA and Soviet Union on the brink of nuclear war. Castro's attempt to spread revolution in Latin America was largely crushed by the capture (1967) of his ally 'Che' GUEVARA. In 1980 he lifted the ban on emigration and 125,000 people left for Florida. While Castro maintained political independence from the Soviet Union, the Cuban

▲ **cassowary** The several species of large ground-dwelling birds – ostrich, rhea, emu, and cassowary (*Casuarius casuarius*) – all resemble each other quite closely but are thought to have arisen independently and as such are examples of a phenomenon called convergent evolution.

▲ **Castro** Cuba's political leader from 1959 to 2006, Fidel Castro enjoyed huge support from the Cuban people. However, US trade embargoes and withdrawal of economic support from the former Soviet Union brought about public demand for economic and political reforms.

INTERNET

Cascade Range
▶ www.nps.gov/crla

Castro (Ruz), Fidel
▶ www.cubaheritage.com

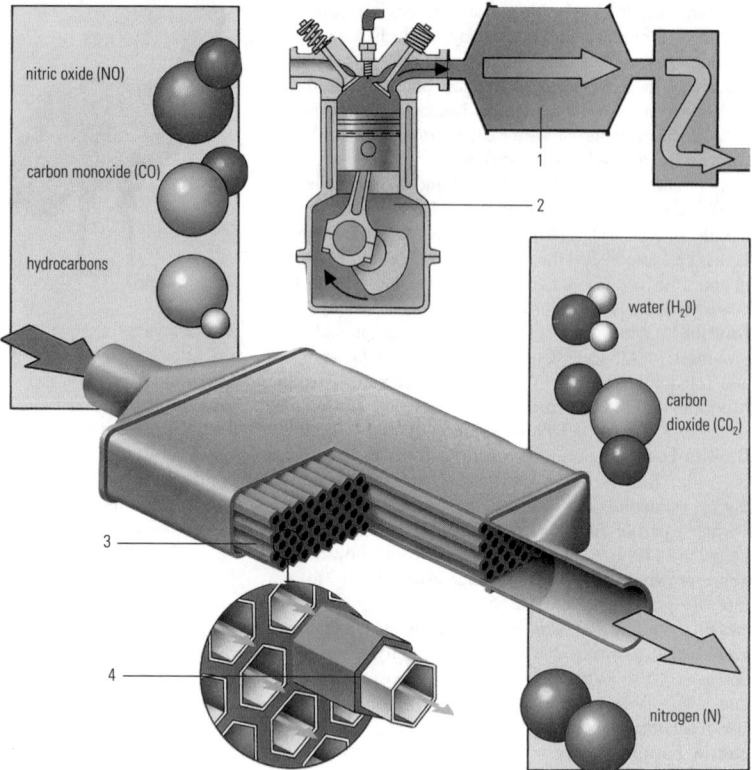

nitric oxide (NO)

carbon monoxide (CO)

hydrocarbons

water (H₂O)

carbon dioxide (CO₂)

1

2

3

4

nitrogen (N)

▲ **catalytic converter** A catalytic converter is placed in the exhaust system (1) to reduce the pollution produced by combustion engines (2). It comprises a ceramic honeycomb structure (3), which maximizes the surface area of the converter, covered in catalysts – normally platinum and rhodium (4). As exhaust gases, primarily carbon monoxide, nitric oxide and hydrocarbons from the cylinder, pass through the converter they react under the influence of the catalysts. The platinum and rhodium accelerate oxidation and reduction in the hot gases. The pollutants are oxidized into water, carbon dioxide and nitrogen.

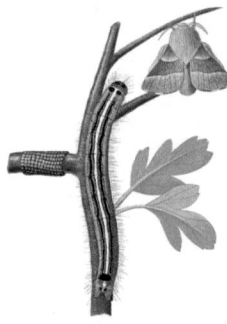

▲ **caterpillar** The lackey moth (*Malacosoma neustria*) is found throughout Europe. Its colourfully striped caterpillars live communally on hawthorn and similar bushes, which they may strip of their leaves. Eggs are laid in a collar around a twig.

economy was heavily dependent on Soviet economic aid. The collapse of European communism and the continuing US trade embargo dramatically worsened the Cuban economy, forcing Castro to introduce economic reforms. In 2006 failing health led him to retire from politics. He passed power to his brother Raul, and in 2008 declared that he would not return to the presidency.

cat Carnivorous, often solitary and nocturnal mammal of the family Felidae, ranging in size from the Indian tiger (3m, 10ft) to the domestic cat (40cm, 14in). It has specialized teeth and claws for hunting, a keen sense of smell, acute hearing, sensitive vision, and balances well with its long tail. Cats all have fully retractile claws, except for the cheetah which needs greater purchase on the ground to run at high speeds. One of the first animals to be domesticated, cats appear frequently in myth and religion. Order Carnivora. *See also* CARNIVORE

catabolism *See* METABOLISM

Catalan Romance language spoken mainly in NE Spain, but also in the Balearic Islands, Andorra, and S France. There are *c*.6 million speakers.

Catalonia (Sp. Cataluña) Region in NE Spain, extending from the French border to the Mediterranean Sea. The capital is BARCELONA. Catalonia includes the provinces of Barcelona, Gerona, Lérida and Tarragona. United with Aragón in 1137, it retained its own laws and language. During the Spanish Civil War it was a Loyalist stronghold, and recently it has been a focus of separatist movements. The Costa Brava is an important tourist area. Products: grain, fruit, olive oil, wool, wine. Area: 31,932sq km (12,329sq mi). Pop. (2001) 6,343,110.

catalyst Substance that speeds up the rate of a chemical reaction without itself being consumed. Many industrial processes rely on catalysts, such as the HABER PROCESS for manufacturing AMMONIA. Metals or their compounds catalyse by adsorbing gases to their surface, forming intermediates that then readily react to form the desired product while regenerating the original catalytic surface. The METABOLISM of all living organisms depends on biological catalysts called ENZYMES.

catalytic converter Anti-pollution device used in internal combustion engines. It consists of a bed of catalytic agents through which flow the gaseous exhaust of fuel combustion. Converters located in mufflers reduce harmful unburned hydrocarbons and carbon monoxide. These converters are adversely affected by tetraethyl lead found in some gasolines.

catalytic cracking *See* CRACKING

Catania Port near Mount Etna, E Sicily, Italy, capital of Catania province. Ancient Catania was founded by the Greeks in 729 BC. It was devastated by a volcanic eruption in 1669 and an earthquake in 1693. It has Greek and Roman ruins, a Norman cathedral (1091) and a university (1444). Industries: chemicals, cement, textiles. Pop. (2001) 1,101,936; (city) 336,222.

cataract Opacity in the lens of an eye, causing blurring of vision. Most cases are due to degenerative changes in old age but it can also be congenital, the result of damage to the lens, or some metabolic disorder such as diabetes. Treatment is by removal of the cataract and implanting an artificial lens.

catastrophe theory Mathematical technique published in 1972 by the French mathematician René Thom. It is useful for describing situations in which gradually changing forces or inputs cause a sudden discontinuous leap in a system's behaviour or output – such as when increasing forces on a bridge cause it to collapse.

catechism In Christianity, a summary of religious doctrine and church teachings. A catechism often takes the form of set questions and answers.

caterpillar Worm-like larva of a butterfly or moth; it has a segmented body, short antennae, simple eyes, three pairs of true legs and chewing mouthparts. Nearly all caterpillars feed voraciously on plants and are serious crop pests.

catfish Any member of a large family of slow-swimming scaleless fish found in tropical and subtropical waters; it has fleshy barbels on the upper jaw, sometimes with venomous spines. Most species live in freshwater and can be farmed. Length: up to 3.3m (10ft). Order Siluriformes.

cathedral (Gk. *kathedra*, 'throne' or 'seat') Main church of a bishop's province, the church containing his throne. In the ROMANESQUE period, cathedrals started to become very large and many Gothic cathedrals are gigantic structures. The prototype of the true Gothic cathedral is the Abbey Church of St.-Denis near Paris. Suger, the abbot, enlarged the existing Romanesque building in the 12th century, adding a chapel and pointed groin VAULT. Bigger windows and slender arches gave it a sense of lightness very different from the static solidity of the Romanesque. Among the most remarkable of the great cathedrals of western Europe that followed are NOTRE-DAME, Paris (begun 1163), and CHARTRES (begun 1194) in France, COLOGNE Cathedral in Germany, and MILAN Cathedral (begun 1386) in Italy. Some of the finest English examples, such as Canterbury and York, combine Romanesque and Gothic features. St Mark's, VENICE, is a magnificent Byzantine example. Central and Eastern European cathedrals often amalgamate Byzantine and western features, while many Spanish cathedrals combine Romanesque, French, German and Moorish features. In Latin America, cathedrals are often of Portuguese or Spanish RENAISSANCE and BAROQUE origin. The Episcopal Cathedral of St John the Divine in New York is the world's largest Gothic cathedral. *See also* BYZANTINE ART AND ARCHITECTURE; GOTHIC ART AND ARCHITECTURE

Cather, Willa (1876–1947) US novelist and short story writer. She grew up among immigrant Nebraskan farmers who became the subject of her work. Her fiction explores the pioneer spirit: love of the land, loyalty to family, and the struggle with nature. Her books, often featuring strong characters who lead life as a noble endeavour, include *O Pioneers* (1913), *A Lost Lady* (1923), and *Death Comes for the Archbishop* (1927).

Catherine II (the Great) (1729–96) Empress of Russia (1762–96). A German princess, she married Peter III in 1745 and succeeded him after he was murdered. She began as an 'enlightened despot', with ambitious plans for reform. Her economic improvements, patronage of the arts and vast extension of Russian territory (chiefly at the expense of the Ottoman Turks) raised national prestige, but did little for Russian peasants. After the revolt of 1773–74, led by the Cossack Pugachev, she became increasingly conservative.

Catherine de' Medici (1519–89) Queen of France, wife of Henry II and daughter of Lorenzo de' MEDICI. She exerted considerable political influence after her husband's and first son's deaths in 1559. In 1560 she became regent for her second

C

son, CHARLES IX, and remained principal adviser until his death (1574). Her initial tolerance of the HUGUENOTS turned to enmity at the beginning of the French Wars of RELIGION. Her concern for preserving the power of the monarchy led to a dependence on the Catholic House of GUISE, whose growing power she failed to control. Fearing the decline of her power at court, due to the rise of the Huguenot leader Gaspard de Coligny, she planned the SAINT BARTHOLOMEW'S DAY MASSACRE (1572). When her third son, HENRY III, acceded in 1574, her effectiveness in policy-making had been compromised.

Catherine of Aragon (1485–1536) Daughter of FERDINAND and ISABELLA, she was the first queen of HENRY VIII of England (1509). Her only surviving child was a daughter (MARY I). The need to produce a male heir, combined with Henry's desire for Anne BOLEYN, induced him to seek an annulment (1527) on the grounds of her previous marriage to his brother Arthur. Pope CLEMENT VII's procrastination led to the break with Rome and to the English REFORMATION. The annulment was granted by Thomas CRANMER in 1533.

cathode In chemistry, the negative ELECTRODE of an electrolytic CELL or electron tube. It attracts positive ions (CATIONS) during ELECTROLYSIS.

cathode ray Radiation emitted by the cathode of a thermionic electron valve containing a gas at low pressure. In 1897 J.J. THOMSON identified the rays as streams of charged, elementary particles having extremely low mass, later called ELECTRONS. Some electrons are emitted because the CATHODE is heated but most because of collisions between the cathode and positive ions formed in the valve.

cathode-ray oscilloscope *See* OSCILLOSCOPE

cathode-ray tube Evacuated electron tube used for television picture tubes, oscilloscopes and display screens in radar sets and computers. An electron gun shoots a beam of electrons, focused by a grid. The electrons strike a fluorescent screen and produce a spot of light. In a television tube, an electrostatic or magnetic field deflects the beam so that it scans a number of lines on the screen, controlled by the incoming picture signals.

Catholic Church Term used in Christianity with one of several connotations: (1) It is the Universal Church, as distinct from local Churches. (2) It means the Church holding 'orthodox' doctrines, defined by St Vincent of Lérins as doctrines held "everywhere, always, and by all" – in this sense the term is used to distinguish the church from heretical bodies. (3) It is the undivided Church as it existed before the schism of East and West in 1054. Following this, the Western Church called itself 'Catholic', the Eastern Church 'Orthodox'. (4) Since the REFORMATION, the term has usually been used to denote the ROMAN CATHOLIC CHURCH, although the ANGLICAN COMMUNION and the OLD CATHOLICS use it for themselves as well.

Catholic Emancipation, Act of (1829) Measure by which the statutes (dating back to the REFORMATION) barring Roman Catholics in Britain from holding civil office or sitting in Parliament were repealed. Emancipation was achieved through a series of acts. In 1778 restrictions against land purchase and inheritance were lifted. In 1791 further restrictions were removed, and by 1793 Catholics were allowed in the services, universities and judiciary. Daniel O'CONNELL wrung the final concession, allowing catholics to sit in Parliament, from the Duke of WELLINGTON's government.

cation Positive ION that is attracted to the CATHODE during the process of ELECTROLYSIS.

Cato (the Elder), Marcus Porcius (234–149 BC) Roman leader. As censor, from 184 BC he worked to restore the old ideals of Rome – courage, honesty and simple living. His constant urging in the Senate that CARTHAGE should be destroyed helped initiate the Third PUNIC WAR.

Cato (the Younger), Marcus Porcius (95–46 BC) Roman politician, great-grandson of CATO THE ELDER. A supporter of the republic, he opposed Julius CAESAR and forced the creation of the First Triumvirate. He favoured POMPEY in the civil war (49BC) and, when Caesar was victorious, committed suicide.

CAT scan (computed axial tomography) X-ray technique for displaying images of cross-sections through the human

body. X-ray sources and detectors slowly move around the patient's body on opposite sides, producing a changing 'view' of an organ. The data from the detectors is processed through a computer to display only the details relating to a specific 'slice' through the body.

Catskill Mountains Plateau of the Appalachian system on the W bank of the Hudson River, SE New York, USA. The highest peak is Slide Mountain, 1282m (4204ft). Site of the Rip Van Winkle legend, its numerous forests, streams and lakes attracted the painters of the Hudson River School. Today, the Catskills are a popular resort area.

cattle Large, ruminant mammals of the family Bovidae, including all the varieties of modern domestic cattle (*Bos taurus*), the brahman (*Bos indicus*) and hybrids of these two. The family also includes the YAK, the wild GAUR, the wild banteng and the kouprey. Different terms are used to indicate the sex and age of domestic cattle. The male is born as a bull calf and

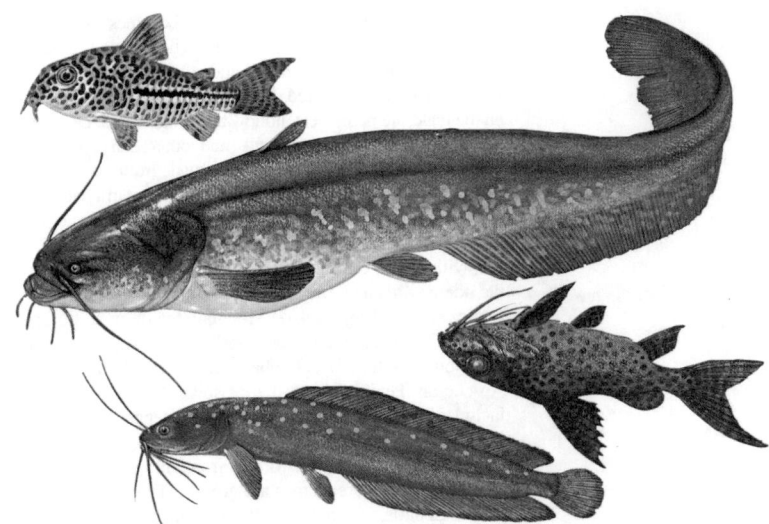

▲ **catfish** The name 'catfish' is applied to a very large family of freshwater fish, which includes the unusual upside down catfish. They tend to be sluggish and have barbels (whiskers).

INTERNET

Catholic Emancipation, Act of

▶ britishhistory.about.com/ cs/politicalreform

CATHODE-RAY TUBE

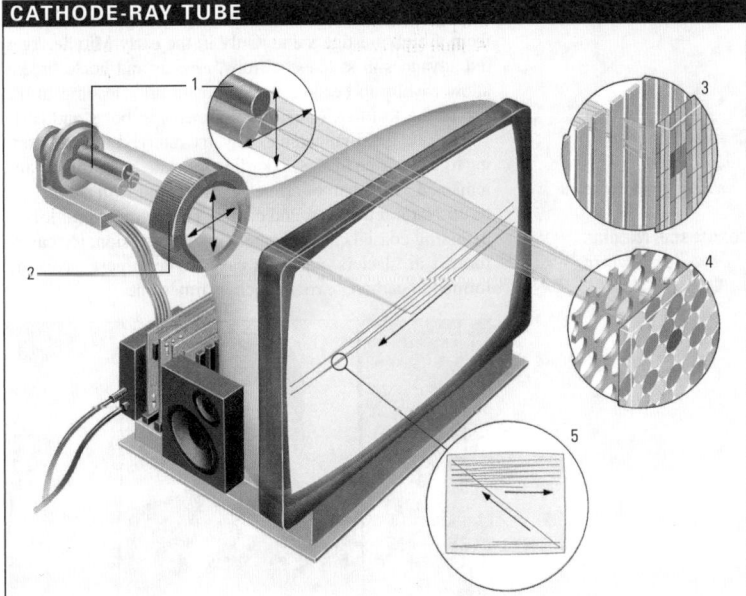

Television receivers are a type of cathode-ray tube. Three electron guns (1) receive colour signals from a colour decoder which splits the colour signal into red, green and blue. The guns fire three beams of electrons through vertical and horizontal deflection coils (2) onto the screen of a 'shadow mask tube' (3). This is made up of about a million dots (4), a third of which glow red when bombarded, a third blue and the remaining third, green. The dots compose the colour picture received by the television. The beam of electrons scans hundreds of lines on the screen (525 in the USA, 625 in Europe) making up the moving pictures. The beam scans from left to right, starting top left and finishing at the bottom right (5).

becomes a bull if left intact; if castrated, it becomes a steer, bullock or ox if used as a draught animal. The female is a heifer calf, growing to become a heifer and, after calving, a cow. In Hinduism, the cow is sacred. Horns, sometimes appearing only on the male, are permanent, hollow and unbranched. Domestic cattle are raised for meat, milk and other dairy products. Leather, glue, gelatin and fertilizer are made from the carcass.

Catullus, Gaius Valerius (84–54 BC) Roman lyric poet. He is best known for his short love lyrics, the most famous of which refer to Lesbia, depicting the Roman woman, Clodia, with whom Catullus was in love. His longer works are the poems *Attis* and *The Marriage of Peleus and Thetis*.

Caucasus (Bol'soj Kavkaz) Mountain region in SE Europe, Russia, Georgia, Armenia and Azerbaijan, extending SE from the mouth of the River Kuban on the Black Sea to the Apscheron Peninsula on the Caspian Sea. The system includes two major regions: N Caucasia (steppes) and TRANSCAUCASIA. It forms a natural barrier between Asia and Europe. There are deposits of oil, iron and manganese, and cotton, fruit and cereal crops are grown. The highest peak is Mount ELBRUS, 5637m (18,493ft). Length: 1210km (750mi).

cauliflower Form of CABBAGE with a short thick stem, large lobed leaves and edible white or purplish flower clusters that form tightly compressed heads. Family Brassicaceae; species *Brassica oleracea botrytis*.

caustic soda (sodium hydroxide, NaOH) Strong ALKALI prepared industrially by the ELECTROLYSIS of salt (sodium chloride, NaCl). It is a white solid that burns skin, with a slippery feel because it absorbs moisture from the air. It also absorbs atmospheric carbon dioxide, forming a crust of sodium carbonate (Na_2CO_3). Caustic soda is used in many industries, such as soapmaking and in bauxite-processing to make ALUMINIUM.

Cavalier (Fr. *chevalier*) Name adopted by the Royalists during the English CIVIL WAR in opposition to the ROUNDHEADS (Parliamentarians). It was originally a derogatory term applied by their opponents. The court party retained the name after the RESTORATION, until superseded by TORY PARTY.

Cavalry Mounted troops. The first cavalry were developed during the BRONZE AGE in central Asia, and the idea spread rapidly. Early cavalry were limited to supporting roles in an ARMY, but their expense and impressive appearance gave them a high prestige value. Only in the early Middle Ages did advances in saddles, stirrups, armour and horse breeds allow cavalry to become the dominant arm, leading to the rise of the KNIGHT. Later, developments in bows and early guns made them vulnerable. Cavalry returned to a supporting role, working in close coordination with other forces, and remained a vital part of armies until the mid 19th century.

cave Natural underground cavity. There are several kinds, including coastal caves, formed by wave erosion, ice caves, formed in glaciers, and lava caves. The largest caves are formed in carbonate rocks such as limestone.

► **Ceauşescu** The former president of Romania, Nicolae Ceauşescu, attempted massive social and political reforms while in power (1978–89), many of which were hugely unpopular. With the demise of Communism in Eastern Europe, he was deposed, and executed along with his wife Elena.

Cavendish, Henry (1731–1810) English chemist and physicist, b. France. He discovered HYDROGEN and the compositions of water and air, and estimated the Earth's mass and density. He also discovered NITRIC ACID (HNO_3), the gravitational constant, measured the specific gravity of carbon dioxide (CO_2) and hydrogen, and stated the inverse square law for the interaction of charged particles.

caviar Roe (eggs) of a STURGEON and three less common fish (also occasionally a salmon) which, salted and seasoned, is a gastronomic delicacy, especially in Russia. The roe is extracted from the fish before it can spawn.

Cavour, Camillo Benso, Conte di (1810–61) Piedmontese politician, instrumental in uniting Italy under Savoy rule. From 1852 he was prime minister under VICTOR EMMANUEL II. He engineered Italian liberation from Austria with French aid, expelled the French with the help of Giuseppe GARIBALDI, and finally neutralized Garibaldi's influence. This led to the formation of the kingdom of Italy (1861). *See also* RISORGIMENTO

cavy (wild guinea pig) Herbivorous South American rodent from which domestic GUINEA PIGS are descended. Small, with dark fur, cavies live in burrows and often form large colonies for protection. Family Caviidae; species *Cavia aperea*.

Caxton, William (1422–91) First English printer. Following a period in Cologne (1470–72), where he learned printing, he set up his own press in 1476 at Westminster. He published more than 100 items many of them his own translations from French, Latin and Dutch. Among his most influential publications were editions of CHAUCER, GOWER, and MALORY.

Cayley, Sir George (1773–1857) English inventor who founded the science of AERODYNAMICS. He built the first glider to carry a man successfully, developed the basic form of the early aeroplane and invented a caterpillar tractor.

Cayman Islands British dependency in the West Indies, comprising Grand Cayman, Little Cayman, and Cayman Brac, *c*.325km (200mi) NW of Jamaica, in the Caribbean Sea. The capital is Georgetown. The islands were discovered by Columbus in 1503, and ceded to Britain in the 17th century. The islanders voted against independence in 1962. Industries: tourism, international finance, turtle and shark fishing, timber, coconuts, oil trans-shipment. Area: 264sq km (102sq mi). Pop. (2002 est.) 42,000. *See* WEST INDIES map

CBI Abbreviation of CONFEDERATION OF BRITISH INDUSTRY

CD-ROM (compact disc read-only memory) Optical storage for computer data and programs. A form of COMPACT DISC, they are cheaper and more durable than most digital media.

Ceauşescu, Nicolae (1918–89) Romanian statesman, the country's effective ruler from 1965 to 1989. He became a member of the politburo in 1955, general secretary of the Romanian Communist Party in 1965 and head of state in 1967. He promoted Romanian nationalism, pursued an independent foreign policy, but instituted repressive domestic policies. He was deposed and executed in the December 1989 revolution.

Cecil, Robert, 1st Earl of Salisbury (1563–1612) English statesman, son of Lord BURGHLEY. He became secretary of state to ELIZABETH I on his father's retirement in 1596. Cecil was chiefly responsible for negotiating the accession of JAMES I (1603).

cedar Evergreen tree native to the Mediterranean and Asia, but found in warm temperate regions worldwide; it has clustered needle-like leaves, long cones and fragrant, durable wood. It is a popular ornamental tree. Height: 30–55m (100–180ft). Family Pinaceae; genus *Cedrus*.

Celebes Former name of SULAWESI, Indonesia

celery Biennial plant, native to the Mediterranean and widely cultivated for its long stalks used as a vegetable. Its fruits are used as food flavouring and in medicine. Family Apiaceae/Umbelliferae; species *Apium graveolens*.

celestial mechanics Branch of ASTRONOMY concerned with the relative motions of stars and planets that are associated in systems (such as the Solar System or a binary star system) by gravitational fields. Introduced by Isaac NEWTON in the 17th century, celestial mechanics, rather than general RELATIVITY, is usually sufficient to calculate the various factors determining the motion of planets, satellites, comets, stars, and galaxies around a centre of gravitational attraction.

celestial sphere Imaginary sphere of infinite radius used to define the positions of celestial bodies as seen from Earth, the centre of the sphere. The sphere rotates, once in 24 hours, about a line that is an extension of the Earth's axis. The position of a celestial body is the point at which a radial line through it meets the surface of the sphere. The position is defined in terms of co-ordinates, such as declination and right ascension or altitude and AZIMUTH, which refer to great circles on the sphere, such as the celestial EQUATOR or the ecliptic.

celibacy Commitment to abstention from sexual relations. The status of celibacy as a religious obligation is found in Christianity and Buddhism. From the 4th century, it gradually became compulsory for Roman Catholic priests, monks and nuns.

cell Basic biological unit of which all plant and animal tissues are composed. The cell is the smallest unit of life that can exist independently, with its own self-regulating chemical system. Most consist of a MEMBRANE surrounding jelly-like CYTOPLASM with a central NUCLEUS. The nucleus is the main structure in which DNA is stored in CHROMOSOMES. Animal cells vary widely in shape. A red blood cell, for instance, is a biconcave disc, while a nerve cell has a long fibre. The cells of plants and algae are enclosed in a cell wall, which gives them a more rigid shape. PROKARYOTAE cells, as in bacteria, also have a cell wall but do not have nuclei or chromosomes; instead, they have a loop of DNA floating in the cytoplasm. More advanced cells, with nuclei, often have other membrane-bounded structures inside the cell such as CHLOROPLASTS within a plant cell. Cells divide by duplicating the DNA and splitting the nucleus. This takes place by MEIOSIS in sexual reproduction, and by MITOSIS in asexual reproduction. *See also* EUKARYOTE; MITOCHONDRION

cell, electrolytic Device from which electricity is obtained due to a chemical reaction. A cell consists of two electrodes (a positive ANODE and a negative CATHODE) immersed in a solution (electrolyte). A chemical reaction takes place between the electrolyte and one of the electrodes. In a **primary** cell, current is produced from an irreversible chemical reaction, and the chemicals must be renewed at intervals. In a **secondary** cell (BATTERY), the chemical reaction is reversible, and the cell can be charged by passing a current through it.

cell division Process by which living cells reproduce and enable an organism to grow. In EUKARYOTE cells, a single cell splits in two, first by division of the NUCLEUS (occurring by MITOSIS or MEIOSIS), then by fission of the CYTOPLASM. For growth and asexual reproduction, where the daughter cells are required to be genetically identical to their parents, mitosis is used. Meiosis results in daughter cells having half the number of chromosomes (HAPLOID). This type of division results in the production of GAMETES (sex cells), which allow genetic information from two parents to be combined at FERTILIZATION, when the DIPLOID number of chromosomes is restored. *See also* ALTERNATION OF GENERATIONS

cello (violoncello) Musical instrument, member of the violin family. It has a soft, mellow tone, one octave below the viola; its strings are tuned to C-G-D-A. It is played with a bow and supported by the knees of a seated player. It was developed in the 16th-century by the AMATI family. Celebrated 20th century players include Pablo CASALS and Jacqueline DU PRÉ.

cellophane Flexible, transparent film made of CELLULOSE and used mostly as a wrapping material. It is made by dissolving wood pulp or other plant material in an ALKALI, to which carbon disulphide is added to form viscose. This is forced through a narrow slit into a dilute acid where it precipitates as a film of cellulose. It is then dried and waterproofed.

celluloid Hard plastic invented (1869) in the USA by John Hyatt. Hyatt made the PLASTIC by mixing cellulose nitrate with pigments and fillers in a solution of camphor and alcohol. When heated, it can be moulded into a variety of shapes and hardens on cooling. It was the first major plastic, and was used for early motion pictures. It is highly flammable.

cellulose POLYSACCHARIDE, CARBOHYDRATE $(C_6H_{10}O_5)_n$ that is the structural constituent of the cell walls of plants and algae. Consisting of parallel unbranched chains of GLUCOSE units cross-linked together into a stable structure, it forms the basic material of the paper and textile industries. The first synthetic cellulose was produced in 1996 by Japanese chemists.

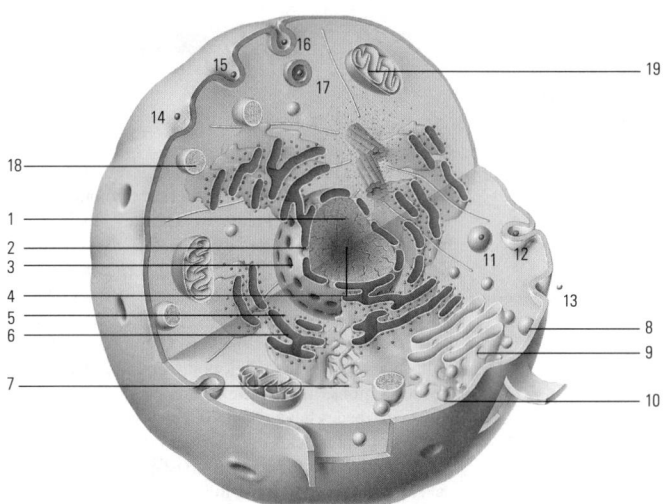

Celsius Temperature scale, devised in 1742 by the Swedish astronomer Anders Celsius. On this scale, the difference between the reference temperatures of the freezing and boiling points of water is divided into 100 degrees. The freezing point is 0°C and the boiling point is 100°C. The name Celsius officially replaced centigrade in 1948. Degrees Celsius are converted to degrees FAHRENHEIT by multiplying by 1.8 and then adding 32. *See also* THERMOMETER

Celt Someone who speaks one of the CELTIC LANGUAGES or is descended from a Celtic language area. After 2000 BC early Celts spread from E France and W Germany over much of W Europe, including Britain. They developed a village-based, heirarchical society headed by nobles and DRUIDS. Conquered by the Romans, the Celts were pushed into Ireland, Wales, Cornwall, and Brittany by Germanic peoples. Their culture remained vigorous, and Celtic churches were important in the early spread of Christianity in N Europe.

Celtic art Artworks produced by Celts during the prehistoric LA TÈNE period. This period is normally subdivided into four periods: Early Style (after *c.*480BC); Waldalgesheim Style (after *c.*350BC); Plastic Style (after *c.*290BC); and Hungarian Sword Style (after *c.*190BC). Characterized by swirling, abstract design, Celtic art found its fullest expression in metalwork and jewellery. The term is also applied to the La Tène-influenced early Christian art of W Europe, such as the BOOK OF KELLS.

Celtic languages Indo-European languages spoken in parts of Britain, Ireland and France, forming a division within the Italo-Celtic subfamily. There are two branches of Celtic languages: Brittonic, which includes WELSH, BRETON and Cornish; and Goidelic, including Irish and Scots GAELIC and MANX. The Brittonic or Celtic languages were dominant in the British Isles until the 5th century AD.

Celtic mythology Legends of local deities of the Celtic tribes. Each tribe had an omnipotent god, similar to Dagda, who possessed all-embracing power. The gods' world was seen as a reflection of the world of men, while female divinities were more closely identified with nature.

Cenozoic Most recent era of geological time, beginning about 65 million years ago and extending up to the present. It is subdivided into the TERTIARY and Quaternary periods. It is the period during which the modern world, with its present geographical features and plants and animals, developed.

censor Public official of ancient Rome (443–22BC). Two censors were elected for 18–month terms. Besides taking the census, they supervised public works, finance and morals, and filled senatorial vacancies.

censorship System whereby a government-appointed body or official claims the right to protect the public interest by influencing the release of any item of mass communication. Censorship usually falls into four broad categories – politics, religion, pornography or violence. Material may be censored before dissemination or seized by the authorities. Censorship damages freedom of speech. Communications technology and the Internet has made policing more problematic.

▲ cell Animal cells are made up of many different components called organelles. The most prominent is the nucleus (1), which contains all the information of the cell in the form of chromosomes. It is surrounded by the nuclear membrane (2) which contains many pores (3) which allow the nucleus to communicate with the rest of the cell. The centre of the nucleus, the nucleolus (4), generates ribosomes (5), which provide the cell with protein. They are found on the rough endoplasmic reticulum (6), a system of flattened sacs and tubes connected to the nuclear membrane. It brings the messenger RNA molecules, which control the creation of protein, to the ribosomes. The smooth endoplasmic reticulum (7) produces small spheres called vesicles (8) which provide the Golgi apparatus (9) with protein. The Golgi apparatus modifies, sorts and packs large molecules into other vesicles which bud off (10). They are sent to other organelles or secreted from the cell. The fusion of such vesicles with the cell membrane allows particles to be transported out of the cell (exocytosis) (11–13) or brought in (endocytosis) (14–17). Lysosomes (18) break down the molecules entering the cell into enzymes. The mitochondria (19) power the cell, using oxygen and food to generate energy in the form of ATP. ATP is then used in many metabolic processes essential for the cell to function.

C

▶ **centipede** Despite its name the centipede rarely has 100 legs. They are placed in the class *Chilopoda*. The house centipede (*Scutigera coleoptrata*) is found in damp indoor places, and measures up to 5cm (2in) long.

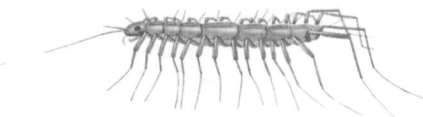

centaur In Greek mythology, a creature half-human, half-horse. One of a warlike and lustful race of mountain-dwellers who roamed Mount Pelion in Thessaly, their debauched behaviour was exacerbated by wine. *See also* CHIRON

Centaurus (Centaur) Brilliant southern constellation representing a centaur. Its brightest star is ALPHA CENTAURI.

centigrade *See* CELSIUS

centipede (lit. hundred-legged) Common name for many arthropods of the class Chilopoda. Found in warm and temperate regions, they have flattened, segmented bodies. Most centipedes have about 70 legs (one pair per segment). Many tropical species are 15–30cm (6–12in) long; temperate ones are about 2.5cm (1in). Fast-moving predators, they eat small insects and other invertebrates.

Central African Republic *see* country feature.

Central America Geographical term for the narrow strip of land that connects NORTH AMERICA to SOUTH AMERICA and divides the Caribbean Sea from the Pacific Ocean; it consists of GUATEMALA, EL SALVADOR, HONDURAS, NICARAGUA, COSTA RICA, BELIZE and PANAMA. Highly developed by the Mayas, the region (excluding Panama) was conquered and ruled by the Spanish from the 16th century until 1821. In 1823 the Central

American Federation was formed, but broke up in 1838, the individual states (except Belize) declaring themselves independent. The terrain is mostly mountainous; the climate tropical. It enjoys an economic, ethnic and geological unity. Spanish is the main language. Area: 715,876sq km (276,400sq mi).

Central and South American mythology Traditional beliefs of the native peoples of Mexico and Central and South America. The AZTECS had a rich and complex mythology, much of it based on the earlier cultures of the TOLTECS and MAYAS. The **Aztecs** believed that there had been four eras (suns) before the one in which they were living, and that each sun had ended in universal destruction. They expected that their own era, the fifth, would end with an earthquake. The Aztec pantheon was headed by HUITZILOPOCHTLI. Other important deities included QUETZALCÓATL, Tezcatlipoca (god of the night sky) and Tlaloc (rain-god). The underworld was ruled by Mictlantecuhtli, the god of death. Human sacrifice was a central feature of Aztec culture. They believed that the Sun would cease to rise unless constantly supplied with human blood. Religious festivals in which sacrificial victims were offered to the gods were held throughout the year. The **Mayas** of the Yucatán peninsula in Central America had a god of creation, Hunab Ku, remote from human affairs. His son, Itzamna, usually depicted as a toothless old man, was the inventor of drawing and writing, and also offered help to the sick. Another important god was Cukulan, the bird snake – the Mayan equivalent of Quetzacóatl. In Guatemala there were creator divinities and also the ancient god Huracán who gave the Mayas fire. In South America the vast INCA empire of Peru wor-

INTERNET

Central African Republic
▶ www.afrika.no/index/
Countries/Central_African
_Republic/index.html

CENTRAL AFRICAN REPUBLIC

The Central African Republic is a remote landlocked country in central Africa. It lies on a plateau, mostly 600–800m (1,970–2,620ft) above sea level, forming a watershed between the headwaters of two river systems. In the S, the rivers flow into the navigable River Ubangi (a tributary of the CONGO). The Ubangi and the Bomu form much of its S border. In the N, most rivers are headwaters of the River Chari, which flows N into Lake CHAD.

Wooded savanna covers much of the country, with open grasslands in the N and rainforests in the SW. The country has many forest and savanna animal species, such as buffalo, leopards, lions and elephants, and many bird species. About 6% of the land is protected in national parks and reserves, but tourism is on a small scale because of the republic's remoteness.

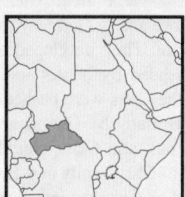

CLIMATE

The climate is warm throughout the year, with an average annual rainfall in Bangui totalling 1,574mm [62in]. The N is drier, with an average annual rainfall total of about 800mm [31in].

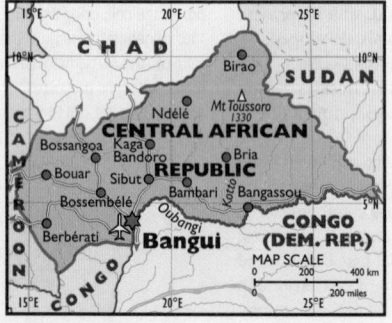

HISTORY

Little is known of the country's early history. Between the 16th and 19th centuries, the population was greatly reduced by slavery, and the country is still thinly populated. France first occupied the area in 1887, and in 1894 established the colony of Ubangi-Shari at Bangui. In 1906 the colony was united with Chad, and in 1910 was subsumed into French Equatorial Africa, which included Chad, Congo and Gabon. Forced-labour rebellions occurred in 1928, 1935 and 1946. During World War 2 Ubangi-Shari supported the Free French. Post-1945 the colony received representation in the French parliament. In 1958 the colony voted to become a self-governing republic within the French community, and became the Central African Republic.

POLITICS

In 1960 Central African Republic declared independence. The next six years, under President David Dacko, saw a deterioration in the economy and increasing government corruption and inefficiency. The country became a one-party state in 1962. In 1966 Colonel Jean Bédel BOKASSA assumed total power in a bloodless coup and dissolved the National Assembly.

In 1976 Bokassa declared the republic an Empire and himself Emperor Bokassa I. His rule became increasingly brutal, and in 1979 he was deposed in a French-backed coup. Dacko returned to power but, faced with continuing unrest, was replaced by André Kolingba in 1981. The army quickly banned all political parties.

The country adopted a new, multiparty constitution in 1991. Elections were held in 1993. An army rebellion in 1996 was finally put down in 1997 with the assistance of French troops. In 2001 President Ange-Félix Patassé, who had served as president since 1993,

AREA 622,984sq km [240,534sq mi]
POPULATION 4,369,000
CAPITAL (POPULATION)
Bangui (553,000)
GOVERNMENT Multiparty republic
ETHNIC GROUPS Baya 33%, Banda 27%, Mandjia 13%, Sara 10%, Mboum 7% Mbaka 4%, others
LANGUAGES French (official), Sangho
RELIGIONS Traditional beliefs 35%, Protestant 25%, Roman Catholic 25%, Islam 15%
CURRENCY CFA franc = 100 centimes

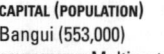

stopped a coup attempt with help from Libya. A 2003 coup brought General François Bozize to power and Patassé went into exile in Togo. In 2006 the country descended into civil war between Bozize's forces and a guerrilla movement associated with the Patassé government. The country has also struggled to cope with refugees from neighbouring Sudan.

ECONOMY

The World Bank classifies the Central African Republic as a 'low-income' developing country. Approximately 10% of the land is cultivated and over 80% of the workforce is engaged in subsistence agriculture. The main food crops are bananas, maize, manioc, millet and yams. Coffee, cotton, timber and tobacco are the main cash crops

Diamonds, the only major mineral resource, are the most valuable single export. Manufacturing is on a very small scale. Products include beer, cotton fabrics, footwear, leather, soap and sawn timber. The Central African Republic's development has been greatly impeded by its remote position, its poor transport system and an untrained workforce. The country is heavily dependent on aid, especially from France.

shipped Inti, the sun god and ancestor of the ruling dynasty. Another important deity was Viracocha, the creator god. ANCESTOR WORSHIP played a central role in Inca religious observances. The dead were venerated and the mummies of previous emperors accorded special honours. Tribal peoples have evolved elaborate magical practices in order to control spirits. In these groups the shaman still enjoys considerable authority.

central bank Institution that regulates and sets policy for a nation's banking system. The US central bank is the FEDERAL RESERVE SYSTEM, and in the UK it is the BANK OF ENGLAND.

Central Criminal Court In the UK, the CROWN COURT of central London. Housed in the Old Bailey, the Central Criminal Court is responsible for trying all serious offences in the City of London and Greater London area.

Central Intelligence Agency (CIA) US government agency established to co-ordinate the intelligence activities of government departments and agencies responsible for US national security. Founded in 1947, it played a major role during the COLD WAR, supporting anti-communist movements. At times the CIA has come under attack for overstepping its mandate and interfering in the internal affairs of foreign nations. Having no domestic jurisdiction, it was severely criticized for its involvement in the WATERGATE AFFAIR. It advises and is directed by the National Security Council (NSC) and should report any action it proposes to take to Congress and gain presidential authorization.

central nervous system (CNS) Term embracing the brain and spinal cord, as distinct from the PERIPHERAL NERVOUS SYSTEM. The CNS co-ordinates all nervous activity, sending messages to muscles and glands. *See also* NERVOUS SYSTEM

Central Powers Alliance of Germany and Austria-Hungary (with Bulgaria and Turkey) during World War 1. The name distinguished them from their opponents (Britain, France and Belgium) in the W, with Russia and others in the E.

central processing unit (CPU) Part of a digital COMPUTER circuit that controls all operations. In most modern computers, the CPU consists of one complex INTEGRATED CIRCUIT (IC), a chip called a MICROPROCESSOR. A CPU contains temporary storage circuits that hold data and instructions; an arithmetic and logic unit (ALU) that works out problems; and a control unit that organizes operations.

centre of gravity Point at which the weight of a body is considered to be concentrated, and around which its weight is evenly balanced. An object in free-flight spins around its centre of gravity (that is moving in a straight line). In a uniform gravitational field, the centre of gravity is the same as the CENTRE OF MASS.

centre of mass Point at which the whole mass of an object or group of objects is considered to be concentrated. A centre of mass would therefore exist for colliding elementary particles. Isaac NEWTON first proved his inverse-square law of gravitation by assuming the respective masses of the Earth and Moon were located at their centres.

centrifugal force *See* CENTRIPETAL FORCE

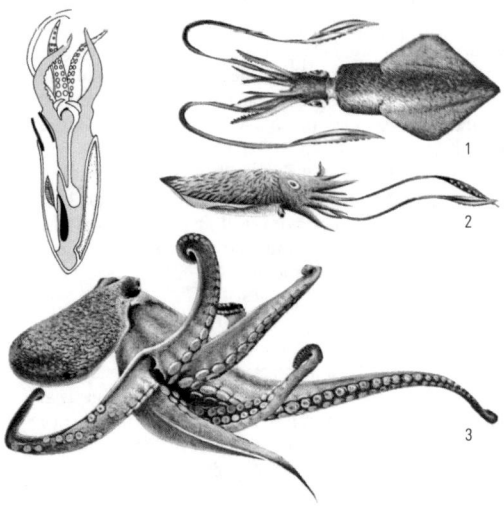

CENTRIFUGE

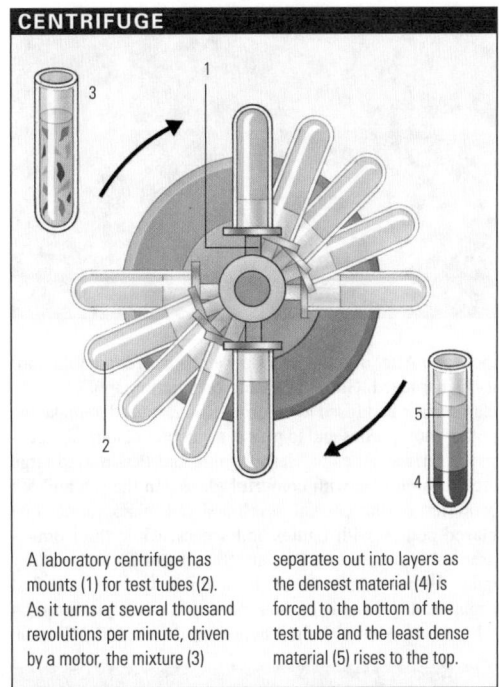

A laboratory centrifuge has mounts (1) for test tubes (2). As it turns at several thousand revolutions per minute, driven by a motor, the mixture (3) separates out into layers as the densest material (4) is forced to the bottom of the test tube and the least dense material (5) rises to the top.

centrifuge Rotating device used for separating substances. In laboratories, centrifuges separate particles from suspensions, and red blood cells from plasma. In the food industry, centrifuges separate cream from milk and sugar from syrup. In each case, the denser substance is forced to the outside of a rotating container. A spin dryer uses the same principle to remove water from clothes.

centripetal force In circular or curved motion, the force acting on an object that keeps it moving in a circular path. For example, if an object attached to a rope is swung in a circular motion above a person's head, the centripetal force acting on the object is the tension in the rope. Similarly, the centripetal force acting on the Earth as it orbits the Sun is gravity. In accordance with NEWTON's laws, the reaction to this, the (theoretical) centrifugal force, is equal in magnitude and opposite in direction.

cephalopod Any member of the advanced class of predatory marine molluscs Cephalopoda, including SQUID, NAUTILUS, OCTOPUS, and CUTTLEFISH. Each has eight or more arms surrounding the mouth, which has a parrot-like beak. The nervous system is well developed, permitting great speed and alertness; the large eyes have an image-forming ability equal to that of vertebrates. Most squirt an inky fluid to alarm attackers. Cephalopods move by squirting water from their mantle edge. Their heavily yolked eggs develop into larval young that resemble the adults. Members of this class vary dramatically in size from 4cm (1.5in) to the giant squid, which may reach 20m (65ft). There are more than 600 species.

cephalosporin Class of ANTIBIOTIC drugs derived from fungi of the genus *Cephalosporium*. Similar to PENICILLIN, they are effective against a wide spectrum of BACTERIA, including some which have become resistant to penicillin.

cepheid variable One of an important class of VARIABLE STARS that pulsate in a regular manner, accompanied by changes in luminosity. Cepheids can expand and contract up to 30% in each cycle. The average luminosity is 10,000 times that of the Sun. Cepheids became important in cosmology (1912) when US astronomer Henrietta Leavitt discovered a relationship between the period of light variation and the absolute magnitude of a cepheid. This period-luminosity law enables the distances of stars to be ascertained.

ceramics Objects made of moistened clay that are shaped and then baked. Earthenware, terracotta, brick, tile, faience, majolica, stoneware, and porcelain are all ceramics. Ceramic ware is ornamented by clay inlays, relief modelling on the surface, or by incised, stamped, or impressed designs. A creamy mixture of clay and water (slip) can be used to coat

◄ **cephalopod** The squid (1), cuttlefish (2), and octopus (3) are all swimming molluscs of the Cephalopoda class. They have advanced, powerful eyes, tentacles lined with sucker pads which are used to catch fish and small crustaceans. The horny jawed mouth is powerful enough to break up their prey before it is digested in the gut.

C

▶ **Cézanne** *Mountains in Provence* (c.1879). The mountains near L'Estaque, Provence, sw France, were one of Cézanne's favourite landscape subjects. His use of interlocking flat planes of colour, representing land, water and buildings, greatly influenced abstract artists.

the ware. After drying, ceramic ware is baked in a kiln until it has hardened. Glaze, a silicate preparation applied to the clay surface and fused to it during firing, is used to make the pottery non-porous and to give it a smooth, colourful, decorative surface. Ancient Mesopotamia and Persia used large architectural tiles with colourful glazes. In the 6th and 5th centuries BC the Greeks developed red, black, and white glazed pottery with figures and scenes, while the Romans used relief decoration. Persian, Syrian and Turkish pottery made further improvements. In Spain, lustreware – the first sophisticated ceramic of the modern era – was produced by 9th-century Moors. Italian majolica, Dutch delft, German

Meissen, and English Wedgewood were further refinements. Chinese porcelain dates from the T'ang dynasty, and Chinese stoneware goes back to *c.*3000 BC.

cereal Any grain of the grass family (Gramineae) grown as a food crop. Wheat, corn, rye, oats, and barley are grown in temperate regions. Rice, millet, sorghum, and maize require more tropical climates. Cereal cultivation was the basis of early civilizations, and with the development of high-yielding strains, remains the world's most important food source.

cerebellum Part of the brain located at the base of the CEREBRUM. It is involved in maintaining muscle tone, balance, and finely co-ordinated movement. It is divided into hemispheres, and each controls a side of the body.

cerebral cortex Deeply fissured outer layer of the CEREBRUM. The cortex (grey matter) is the most sophisticated part of the brain, responsible for the appreciation of sensation, initiating voluntary movement, emotions, and intellect.

cerebral haemorrhage Form of STROKE in which there is bleeding from a blood vessel in the BRAIN into the surrounding tissue. It is usually caused by ARTERIOSCLEROSIS and high blood pressure. Symptoms may vary from temporary numbness and weakness down one side of the body to deep coma. A major haemorrhage may be fatal. There is a high risk of repeated strokes.

cerebral hemispheres Lateral halves of the CEREBRUM, the largest parts of the BRAIN and the sites of higher thought. Due to

CHAD

Chad is Africa's fifth largest country. It is more than twice as big as France (its former colonial power). S Chad is crossed by rivers that flow into Lake CHAD, on the w border with Nigeria. The capital, NDJAMENA, lies on the banks of the River Chari. Beyond a large depression (NE of Lake Chad) are the Tibesti Mountains, which rise steeply from the sands of the SAHARA Desert. The mountains contain Chad's highest peak, Emi Koussi, at 3,415m [11,204ft]. The far S contains forests, while central Chad is a region of savanna, merging into the dry grasslands of

the SAHEL. Plants are rare in the N desert. Droughts are common in N central Chad. Long droughts, over-grazing, and felling for firewood have exposed the Sahel's soil and wind erosion is increasing desertification.

CLIMATE

Central Chad has a hot tropical climate. There is a marked dry season from November to April. The S is wetter, with an average annual rainfall of about 1,000mm [39in]. Conversely, the hot N desert has an average annual rainfall of less than 130mm [5in].

AREA 1,284,000sq km [495,752sq mi]
POPULATION 9,886,000
CAPITAL (POPULATION) Ndjamena (530,000)
GOVERNMENT Multiparty republic
ETHNIC GROUPS 200 distinct groups: mostly Muslim in the north and centre; mostly Christian or animist in the south
LANGUAGES French and Arabic (both official), many others
RELIGIONS Islam 51%, Christianity 35%, animist 7%
CURRENCY CFA franc = 100 centimes

HISTORY

Chad straddles two, often conflicting, worlds: the N, populated by nomadic or semi-nomadic Muslim peoples such as Arabs and Tuaregs, and the dominant S, where a sedentary population practises Christianity or traditional religions such as animism. Lake Chad was an important watering point for the trans-Saharan caravans. Around AD 700 North African nomads founded the Kanem Empire. In the 14th century, the kingdom of Bornu expanded to incorporate Kanem. In the late 19th century the region fell to Sudan.

The first major European explorations were by the French in 1890. The French defeated the Sudanese in 1900, and in 1908 Chad became the largest province of French Equatorial Africa. In 1920 it became a separate colony.

POLITICS

In 1958 Chad gained autonomous status within the French Community, and in 1960 achieved full independence. Divisions between N and S rapidly surfaced. In 1965, President François Tombalbaye declared a one-party state and the N Muslims, led by the Chad National Liberation Front (Frolinat), rebelled. By 1973 the revolt was crushed with French help. In 1980 Libya occupied north-

ern Chad. In 1982 two leaders of Frolinat, Hissène Habré and Goukouni Oueddi, formed rival regimes. Libya's bombing of Chad in 1983 led to the deployment of 3,000 French troops and the Libyans retreated, although they held the uranium-rich Aozou Strip until 1994. A ceasefire took effect in 1987. In 1990, Habré was removed in a coup led by Idriss Déby. In 1996, a new constitution was adopted and multi-party elections confirmed Déby as president. In 2002 a peace treaty, signed by the government and the Movement for Democracy and Justice, ended three years of civil war but stability proved elusive. From 2004, Chad's forces clashed with pro-Sudanese militia as the conflict in Sudan's Darfur province spilled over the border. Clashes worsened in 2006-7, and the arrival of large numbers of Sudanese refugees posed major problems.

ECONOMY

Chad is one of the world's poorest countries. Agriculture dominates the economy and occupies more than 80% of the workforce, mostly at a subsistence level. Groundnuts, millet, rice and sorghum are major crops. Exports include cotton and, since 2003, oil.

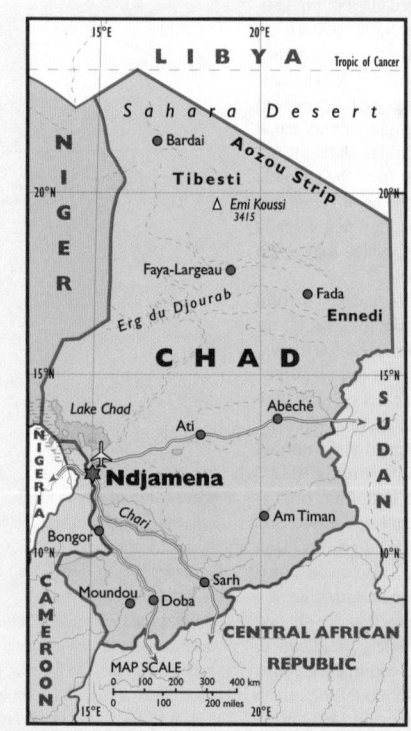

the crossing over of nerve fibres from one cerebral hemisphere to the other, the right side controls most of the movements and sensation on the left side of the body, and vice-versa. Damage to cerebral hemispheres can produce personality changes.

cerebral palsy Disorder mainly of movement and coordination caused by damage to the BRAIN during or soon after birth. It may feature muscular spasm and weakness, lack of coordination and impaired movement or paralysis and deformities of the limbs. Intelligence is not necessarily affected. The condition may result from a number of causes, such as faulty development, oxygen deprivation, birth injury, haemorrhage or infection.

cerebrospinal fluid Clear fluid that cushions the brain and spinal cord, giving some protection against shock. It is found between the two innermost meninges (membranes), in the four ventricles of the brain and in the central canal of the spinal cord. A small quantity of the fluid can be withdrawn by lumbar puncture to aid diagnosis of some brain and spinal cord diseases.

cerebrum Largest and most highly developed part of the BRAIN, consisting of the CEREBRAL HEMISPHERES separated by a central fissure. It is covered by the CEREBRAL CORTEX. It co-ordinates all higher functions and voluntary activity. The cerebrum is divided into hemispheres and four lobes, including paired frontal lobes that are involved in learning and personality.

Cerenkov, Pavel Alekseievich (1904–90) Russian physicist. Working at the Institute of Physics in the Soviet Academy of Science, he discovered that light (CERENKOV RADIATION) is emitted by charged particles travelling at very high speeds. He was awarded the 1958 Nobel Prize in physics with his co-workers, I.M. Frank and I.Y. Tamm.

Cerenkov radiation A form of light, emitted when energetic particles such as electrons travel through a transparent medium at high speeds. In materials such as water the velocity of light is much slower than in a vacuum, and particles' speed can exceed it. A cone of light is emitted in the path of the particle, an action called the Cerenkov effect. It is analogous to a SONIC BOOM , and is named after Pavel CERENKOV who discovered it in 1934. The principle of Cerenkov radiation is used in a Cerenkov counter, a detector of highly energetic particles.

Ceres Largest ASTEROID and the first to be discovered (January 1, 1801, by Guiseppe Piazzi). Ceres' diameter measures 913km (567mi). It orbits in the main asteroid belt, at an average distance from the Sun of 414 million km (257 million mi), the distance of the 'missing' planet predicted by BODE'S LAW.

cerium (symbol Ce) Soft, ductile, iron-grey metallic element, the most abundant of the LANTHANIDE SERIES (rare-earth metals), first isolated in 1803. The chief ore is monazite. It is used in alloys, catalysts, nuclear fuels, glass and as the core of carbon electrodes in arc lamps. Properties: at.no. 58; r.a.m. 140.12; r.d. 6.77; m.p. 798°C (1468°F); b.p. 3257°C (5895°F). The most common isotope is Ce^{140} (88.48%).

CERN (European Laboratory for Particle Physics) Nuclear research centre located on the Franco-Swiss border w of Geneva. Founded in 1954 as an intergovernmental organization, it was called *Conseil Européen pour la Recherche Nucléaire*. It is the main European centre for research into PARTICLE PHYSICS.

Cervantes, Miguel de (1547–1616) Spanish novelist, poet, and dramatist. Cervantes published two volumes of his masterpiece *Don Quixote de la Mancha* (1605, 1615). Don Quixote is a great archetype of Western fiction; the picaresque hero who misapplies the logic of high Romance to the mundane situations of modern life. It established Cervantes as a main figure in Spanish letters. Other works include two surviving plays and a collection of short stories, *Novelas Ejemplares* (1613).

cervical smear (pap test) Test for CANCER of the CERVIX, established by George Papanicolaou. In this diagnostic procedure, a small sample of tissue is removed from the cervix and examined under a microscope for the presence of abnormal, pre-cancerous cells. Treatment in the early stages of cervical cancer can prevent the disease from developing.

cervix Neck of the UTERUS, projecting downwards into the VAGINA. It dilates (expands) widely to allow the passage of the baby during childbirth.

Ceylon Former name of SRI LANKA

Cézanne, Paul (1839–1906) French painter. A friend of PISSARRO, Cézanne exhibited at the first Impressionist show in 1874. *House of the Hanged Man* (1873–74) is characteristic of his Impressionist period. He later shifted away from IMPRESSIONISM in favour of a deeper, more analytical approach, using colour to model and express form. Figure paintings, such as *The Card Players* (1890–92), *Madame Cézanne* (c.1885), and *The Bathers* (1895–1905), as well as landscapes, such as *Mont Sainte Victoire* (1904–06), were painted on this principle. Cézanne ranks as one of the great influences on modern art, especially CUBISM. *See also* POST-IMPRESSIONISM

Chaco War (1932–35) *See* GRAN CHACO

Chad Republic in N central Africa. *See* country feature.

Chad, Lake (Tchad) Lake in N central Africa, lying mainly in the Republic of Chad and partly in Nigeria, Cameroon and Niger. The chief tributary is the River Chari; the lake has no outlet. Depending on the season, the area of the surface varies from c.10,000 to 26,000sq km (3850–10,000sq mi). Max. depth: 7.6m (25ft).

Chadwick, Sir James (1891–1974) English physicist who discovered and named the NEUTRON. Chadwick worked on radioactivity with Ernest RUTHERFORD at the Cavendish Laboratory, Cambridge. In 1920, Rutherford had predicted a particle without electric charge in the nucleus of an ATOM, and, in 1932, Chadwick proved the neutron's existence and calculated its mass. For this, he received the 1935 Nobel Prize in physics. Chadwick also constructed Britain's first particle accelerator (1935). During World War 2, he moved to the USA to head British research on the MANHATTAN PROJECT.

chaffinch Small songbird common throughout Europe. It generally perches on low trees, bushes and fences, feeding on plants and insects. The blue and buff colours and pink breast belong to the male only, although the drab female shares his white markings. In winter, flocks consisting solely of males can be seen. Family Fringillidae; species *Fringilla coelebs*.

Chagall, Marc (1887–1985) Russian-French painter, b. Belarus. His paintings, with their dream-like imagery, considerably influenced SURREALISM. He worked using ceramics, mosaics and tapestry, and in theatre design. He designed stained-glass windows for Hadassah-Hebrew Medical Centre, Jerusalem (1962), murals for the Paris Opéra and the Metropolitan Opera House, New York (1966), and mosaics and tapestries for the Knesset in Jerusalem (1969).

Chain, Sir Ernst Boris (1906–79) British biochemist, b. Germany. He shared the 1945 Nobel Prize in physiology or medicine with Howard FLOREY and Alexander FLEMING for the isolation and development of penicillin as an antibiotic. He also studied spreading factor, an enzyme that aids the dispersal of fluids in tissue.

chain reaction Self-sustaining nuclear FISSION reaction in which one reaction (splitting an atomic nucleus) is the cause of a second, the second of a third and so on. The initial conditions are critical, as the quantity of fissionable material must exceed the CRITICAL MASS, which is the minimum mass needed of fissionable material. The explosion of an atom bomb is an uncontrolled chain reaction.

Chalcedon, Council of (451) Meeting of all the bishops of the Christian church in the city of Chalcedon, Asia Minor. It was convoked by the Emperor Marcian to settle controversial theological questions. It reaffirmed the doctrine of two natures (divine and human) in Christ and condemned NESTORIANISM.

chalcedony Microcrystalline form of QUARTZ. When cut and polished, it is used by gem engravers. It is waxy, lustrous and there are white, grey, blue and brown varieties. Often coloured by artificial methods, some varieties contain impurities giving a distinctive appearance, such as AGATE (coloured bands), ONYX (striped) and bloodstone (dark green with red flecks).

chalcopyrite (copper pyrites) Opaque, brass-coloured, copper iron sulphide ($CuFeS_2$); the most important copper ore. It is found in sulphide veins and in igneous and contact metamorphic rocks. The crystals are tetragonal but often occur in masses. Hardness 3.5–4; r.d. 4.2.

Chaliapin, Fyodor Ivanovich (1873–1938) Russian operatic bass. He made his debut at LA SCALA, Milan, in 1901 and at the METROPOLITAN OPERA COMPANY, New York, in 1907.

C

▲ **Chagall** Belarus-born artist Marc Chagall influenced many later 'surrealist' painters. His paintings draw heavily from folklore and have a fairy tale or dreamlike appeal.

C

▲ **Chamberlain** Having been instrumental in the formation of the National Government (1931), British Prime Minister Neville Chamberlain's firm belief in appeasement resulted in Britain's slow preparation for war. The resulting initial victories for the Axis powers in the early stages of World War 2 forced Chamberlain to resign.

His differences with the Soviet government caused him to leave Russia in 1921 and join the Metropolitan. He was particularly noted for the title role in Mussorgsky's *Boris Godunov*.

chalk Mineral, mainly calcium carbonate ($CaCO_3$), formed from the shells of minute marine organisms. It varies in properties and appearance; pure forms, such as calcite, contain up to 99% calcium carbonate. It is used in making putty, plaster and cement, and harder forms are occasionally used for building. Blackboard chalk is now made from calcium sulphate ($CaSO_4$) or chemically produced calcium carbonate.

Challenger expedition (1872–76) British expedition in oceanographic research. The *Challenger* ship comprised a staff of six naturalists headed by Charles Wyville Thompson. She sailed *c*.128,000km (69,000 nautical mi) making studies of the life, water and seabed in the three main oceans.

Chamberlain, Sir (Joseph) Austen (1863–1937) British statesman, son of Joseph CHAMBERLAIN. He entered Parliament in 1892, and served as chancellor of the exchequer (1903–05, 1919–21) in the governments of Arthur BALFOUR and David LLOYD GEORGE. In 1921, he succeeded Bonar LAW as Conservative Party leader. He acted as foreign minister (1924–29) in Stanley BALDWIN's administration. For his work on the LOCARNO PACT, he shared the 1925 Nobel Peace Prize.

Chamberlain, Joseph (1836–1914) British political leader, father of Neville CHAMBERLAIN. He entered Parliament as a Liberal in 1876. In 1880, he became president of the board of trade. In 1886 he resigned over GLADSTONE's Home Rule Bill, and was leader of the Liberal Unionists from 1889. In 1895, he returned to government as colonial secretary, where his aggressive, imperialist stance helped provoke the SOUTH AFRICAN WAR (1899). He resigned again in 1903 in order to argue freely for tariff reforms.

Chamberlain, (Arthur) Neville (1869–1940) British prime minister (1937–40). Son of Joseph CHAMBERLAIN, he was a successful businessman before entering Parliament in 1918. During the 1920s, he served as chancellor of the exchequer (1923–24, 1931–37) and minister of health (1924–29). He succeeded Stanley BALDWIN as Conservative prime minister. He confronted the threat to European peace posed by Adolf Hitler with a policy of APPEASEMENT and signed the MUNICH AGREEMENT (1938). After Hitler's invasion of Poland, Chamberlain declared war in September 1939. After the loss of Norway, he was replaced by Winston CHURCHILL in May 1940.

chamber music Music intended for performance in intimate surroundings, rather than a concert hall. It is usually written for two to eight instruments (or voices). The string quartet (two violins, viola and cello) is the most common arrangement. The term dates from the 17th century, and was applied to music played privately in the homes of wealthy patrons. The form has been revived in the late 20th century.

chameleon Arboreal LIZARD, found chiefly in Madagascar, Africa and Asia, notable for its ability to change colour. The compressed body has a curled, prehensile tail and bulging eyes that move independently. Length: 17–60cm (7–24in). Family Chamaeleontidae; genus *Chamaeleo*; there are 80 species.

chamois Nimble, goat-like RUMINANT that lives in mountain ranges of Europe and W Asia. It has coarse, reddish-brown fur with a black tail and horns. Its skin is made into chamois leather. Length: up to 1.3m (50in); weight: 25–50kg (55–110lb). Family Bovidae; species *Rupicapra rupicapra*.

chamomile (camomile) Low-growing, yellow- or white-flowered herb. Several species are cultivated as ground cover. Flowers of the European chamomile (*Chamaemelum nobile*) are used to make herbal tea. Family Asteraceae; genus *Chamaemelum*.

Chamorro, Violeta Barrios de (1939–) Nicaraguan stateswoman, president (1990–96). She entered politics in 1978 when her husband, Pedro Joáin Chamorro, was assassinated. In 1989, supported by the USA, she became leader of the right-wing coalition, the National Opposition Union (UNO). She became president after defeating the SANDINISTA government in February 1990. Her early presidency was marked by unemployment, strikes and skirmishes between CONTRA rebels and Sandinista militants. Many of Chamorro's

policies were blocked by reactionary elements in the UNO and by members of the Sandinista Liberation Front.

Champagne District in NE France, made up of the Aube, Marne, Haute-Marne, and Ardennes departments. The major city is REIMS. It was a centre for European trade and commerce in the 11th-13th centuries. During World War 2 there was heavy fighting along the River Marne. It is an arid region, renowned for its champagne, a sparkling white wine that can only be produced in the district. Area: 25,606sq km (9886sq mi). Pop. (1999) 1,342,202.

Champaigne, Philippe de (1602–74) French painter, b. Flanders. He was the greatest French portraitist of the 17th century and a remarkable religious painter. In 1628 he became artist to Queen Marie de' Medici and Cardinal Richelieu. After 1643 his beliefs in JANSENISM produced religious paintings characterized by a serene realism. His best-known works include portraits and frescos at Vincennes and in the Tuileries.

Champlain, Lake Lake that lies on the border of New York State and Vermont, USA, and extends into Québec, Canada. It serves as a link in the Hudson-St Lawrence waterway. Explored by Samuel de CHAMPLAIN (1609), it was the scene of many battles in the French and Indian Wars, the American Revolution, and the defeat of the British in the War of 1812. Today, the lake is a popular resort area. Area: 1100sq km (435sq mi).

Champlain, Samuel de (1567–1635) French explorer, founder of New France (Canada). Following the discoveries of Jacques CARTIER, he made 12 visits to New France. Besides seeking a NORTHWEST PASSAGE, he encouraged settlement and the fur trade, established friendly relations with ALGONQUIN peoples (at the cost of antagonizing the Iroquois), and vastly increased geographical knowledge during his extensive travels. In 1608, he founded Québec.

Champollion, Jean François (1790–1832) French scholar, one of the founders of Egyptology. In 1822, he revealed his decipherment of Egyptian HIEROGLYPHICS through study of the ROSETTA STONE.

chancellor of the exchequer British minister responsible for national finances. The office evolved from the 13th-century clerk of the court of exchequer, assistant to the chancellor. Until the mid-19th century, the office was departmentally inferior to the first lord of the treasury. Since Gladstone's tenure of the office in 1850s, it has become probably the second most high-profile cabinet office (after the prime minister).

Chancery In England, court developed in the 15th century for the lord chancellor to deal with petitions from aggrieved persons for redress when no remedy was available in the COMMON LAW courts. By the mid-17th century, Chancery had become a second system of law (equity) rather than a reforming agency. By the Supreme Court of Judicature Act (1925), the court of Chancery was merged into the HIGH COURT OF JUSTICE, of which it is now known as the Chancery Division.

Chandigarh City at the foot of the Siwalik Hills, NW India. The joint capital of Punjab and Haryana states, it is a planned city, designed by LE CORBUSIER and built in the 1950s. Pop. (2005) 896,000.

Chandler, Raymond Thornton (1888–1959) US crime writer. After a career in journalism and business, Chandler turned to writing detective fiction. Many of his novels featuring tough private eye Philip Marlowe, such as *The Big Sleep* (1939), *Farewell, My Lovely* (1940) and *The Long Goodbye* (1953), have been made into successful films. His crackling dialogue and seedy plots are distinctive and much copied.

Chandragupta Founder of the Maurya Empire in India (r. *c*.321–297BC) and grandfather of ASHOKA. He seized the throne of Magadha and defeated SELEUCUS, gaining dominion over most of N India and part of Afghanistan. His reign was characterized by religious tolerance. He established a vast bureaucracy and secret service based at Patna. He abdicated and, it is thought, became a Jain monk before dying.

Chandrasekhar, Subrahmanyan (1910–95) US astrophysicist, b. India. He formulated theories about the creation, life and death of stars, and calculated the maximum mass of a white dwarf star before it becomes a neutron star; the Chandrasekhar limit. It equals 1.4 times the mass of the Sun. He shared the 1983 Nobel Prize in physics with William Fowler.

INTERNET

Challenger expedition
▶ www.oceansonline.com

Chamberlain, (Arthur) Neville
▶ www.number-10.gov.uk

CHANNEL TUNNEL

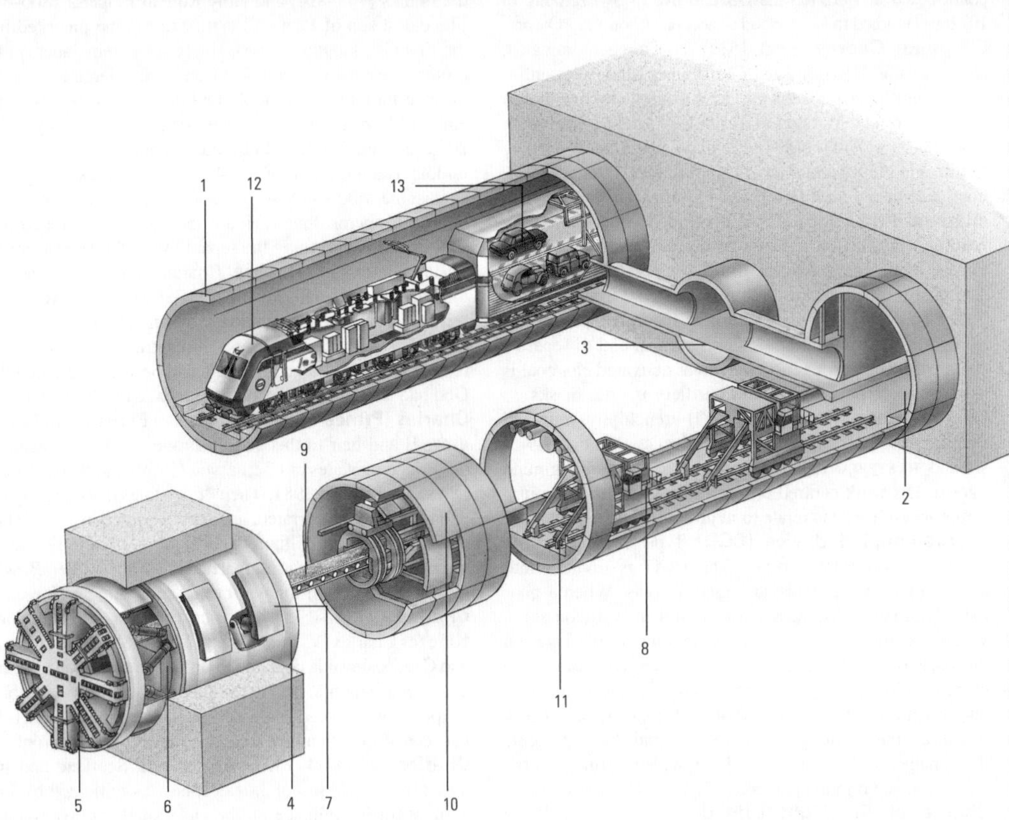

The Channel Tunnel is made up of three separate tunnels – two railway tunnels (1 and 2) and a central service tunnel (3) that allows maintenance and evacuation. They were excavated by giant tunnel boring machines (TBMs) (4). The rotating cutter heads (5) at the front of the TBMs had a diameter of up to 9m (30ft) and were moved forward by hydraulic rams (6) as they cut. When the rams were fully extended the gripper pads (7) that anchored the machines were withdrawn and the body of the TBM moved forward. Behind the TBMs was a train 260m (850ft) long (8). A conveyor belt (9) removed the cut rock to wagons at the rear of the train which were then pulled to the surface. As the TBM advanced, one part of the train lined the walls of the tunnel with concrete segments (10). The train also laid its own rails (11). In operation, electric locomotives (12) pull passengers, freight or specially built vehicle wagons (13) through the tunnel.

Chanel, 'Coco' (Gabrielle) (1883–1971) French fashion designer. She revolutionized women's fashion, borrowing many elements of her designs from men's clothing. She is associated with the Chanel suit, jersey dresses, bell-bottom trousers, trench coats, and Chanel No. 5 perfume.

Chaney, Lon, Sr. (1883–1930) US silent-film actor. The son of deaf-mutes, Chaney was a brilliant mime noted for his complex disguises in horror films. His major films include *The Hunchback of Notre Dame* (1923) and *The Phantom of the Opera* (1925). His son, Lon Chaney, Jr. (1906–73), also was a film actor.

Changchun (Ch'ang-ch'un) Capital of Jilin, NE China. As Hsinking it was the capital (1932–45) of the Japanese-occupied state of Manchukuo. It is an industrial city. Industries: chemicals, textiles, motor vehicles. Pop. (2005) 3,092,000.

Channel Islands Group of islands at the SW end of the English Channel, *c.*16km (10mi) off the W coast of France. The main islands are JERSEY, GUERNSEY, Alderney, and SARK; the chief towns are St. Helier (on Jersey) and St. Peter Port (on Guernsey). A dependency of the British crown since the Norman Conquest, they were under German occupation during World War 2. They are divided into the administrative bailiwicks of Guernsey and Jersey, each with its own legislative assembly. The islands have a warm, sunny climate and fertile soil. The major industries are tourism and agriculture. Area: 194sq km (75sq mi). Pop. (2000) 144,400.

Channel Tunnel (Chunnel) Railway tunnel under the English Channel, 49km (30.6mi) long. The first Channel tunnel was proposed in 1802 by a French engineer. A start was made in 1882, but abandoned for defence reasons. Another false start was made in the 1970s. In 1985, Eurotunnel, a joint French-English private company, was granted a 55–year concession to finance and operate the tunnel. The French and English sections were linked in 1990, and the tunnel became operational in 1994. Consisting of two railway tunnels and one service tunnel, it links Folkestone, S England, with Calais, N France.

chansons de geste (Fr. 'songs of deed') Epic poems, written in Old French between the 11th and 14th centuries,

generally dealing with the campaigns of CHARLEMAGNE. These anonymous narratives, of which some 80 survive, describe semi-fictional events in the lives of Guillaume d'Orange, Girart de Roussillon, Roland and others.

chant Unaccompanied liturgical singing, especially of PSALMS. Anglican chant developed from the earlier Gregorian tones, which were melody formulas defining pitch relationships only. Later, harmonies were added to the melodies and note values designated to English texts of the psalms. The chant is adjustable in length to fit different verses by repeating one note for any number of words, a process known as pointing.

chaos theory Theory that attempts to describe and explain the highly complex behaviour of apparently chaotic or unpredictable systems which show an underlying order. The behaviour of some physical systems is impossible to describe using the standard laws of physics – the mathematics needed to describe these systems being too difficult for even the largest supercomputers. Such systems are sometimes known as 'nonlinear' or 'chaotic' systems, and they include complex machines, electrical circuits, and natural phenomena such as the weather. Non-chaotic systems can become chaotic, such as when smoothly flowing water hits a rock and becomes turbulent. Chaos theory provides mathematical methods needed to describe chaotic systems, and even allows some general prediction of a system's behaviour. However, chaos theory also shows that even the tiniest variation in a system's starting conditions can lead to enormous differences in the later state of the system. Because it is impossible to know the precise starting conditions of a system, accurate prediction is also impossible.

Chaplin, Charlie (Sir Charles Spencer) (1889–1977) English actor and film-maker, often considered the greatest silent film comedian. In his short films, such as *The Immigrant* (1917) and *A Dog's Life* (1918), he developed his famous character; a jaunty, wistful figure of pathos in baggy trousers and bowler hat, with a cane and a moustache. His films include *The Kid* (1920), *The Gold Rush* (1924), *City Lights* (1931), *Modern Times* (1936), *The Great Dictator* (1940), *Monsieur Verdoux*

▲ **Chaplin** Although he made several talking pictures, Charlie Chaplin will always be remembered as one of the most notable figures of the silent movie era. His films, although comedies, were sophisticated enough to evoke sympathy and romance, unlike many of his contemporaries who relied solely on slapstick.

C

(1947), and *Limelight* (1952). He was attacked for his liberal politics, and in 1952 left the USA to live in Switzerland. In 1972, he returned to Hollywood to accept an honorary Oscar.

Chapman, George (1560–1634) English poet, dramatist, and translator. He completed Christopher Marlowe's unfinished poem *Hero and Leander* (1598), and worked with Ben JONSON and John Marston. His own works include the poem *The Shadow of Night* (1594), the plays *The Blind Beggar of Alexandria* (1598) and *Bussy D'Ambois* (1604), and translations of Homer's *Iliad* (1611) and *Odyssey* (1614–15).

charcoal Porous form of CARBON, made traditionally by heating wood in the absence of air, and used in western Europe until late medieval times for smelting iron ore. Artists still use sticks of traditional charcoal for sketching. Today, charcoal is chiefly used for its absorptive properties, to decolourize food liquids such as syrups, and to separate chemicals. The porous form known as activated charcoal is used to absorb poisons in water purifiers and gas masks.

Charcot, Jean Martin (1825–93) French physician and founder of neurology. He made classical studies of HYPNOSIS and HYSTERIA, and taught Pierre Janet and Sigmund FREUD. His work centred on discovering how behavioural symptoms of patients relate to neurological disorders.

charge-coupled device (CCD) Type of silicon CHIP designed to capture images. The CCD is divided into microscopic areas, pixels, arranged in rows. When a photon hits a pixel it displaces an electron from a silicon atom, which becomes charged. An opposite charge in a layer on the base of the CCD confines this charged atom, so a charge builds up in each pixel relative to the number of photons hitting it. The charge of each pixel is read off, a row at a time, forming an electrical signal that represents the image. CCDs are found in video cameras, fax machines, and digital cameras.

Charge of the Light Brigade (October 25, 1854) British cavalry charge in the CRIMEAN WAR, one of the most notorious mistakes in British military history. It stemmed from Lord Lucan's misreading of an ambiguous order by the British commander, Lord Raglan. As a result, Lord Cardigan led the unsupported Light Brigade straight at a battery of Russian guns. More than 600 men took part, nearly half of whom were casualties. The incident is commemorated in a famous poem by Lord TENNYSON.

charismatic movement Movement within the Christian Church. It emphasizes the presence of the Holy Spirit in the life of an individual and in the work of the church. It is particularly associated with PENTECOSTAL CHURCHES.

INTERNET

Charge of the Light Brigade
▶ www.pinetreeweb.com/13th-balaclava2.htm

Charlemagne
▶ www.chronique.com/Library/MedHistory/charlemagne.htm
▶ sunsite.berkeley.edu/OMACL/Roland

▼ **Charles V** The map illustrates how Charles V gained his vast European empire. In 1506, he succeeded his father, Philip, as Duke of Burgundy. In 1516, Charles inherited much of s Europe from his grandparents, Ferdinand and Isabella and, in 1519, he became Holy Roman Emperor.

From Mary of Burgundy 1506
From Ferdinand and Isabella of Castile (1516)
From Maximilian of Austria (1519)
boundary of Holy Roman Empire

NETHERLANDS
HOLY ROMAN EMPIRE
AUSTRIA
Franche Comté
Charolais
Tyrol
FRANCE
Navarre
Castile
Aragon
Catalonia
Naples
PORTUGAL
Valencia
Sardinia
Balearic islands
Sicily
Granada

Charlemagne (742–814) (lit. Charles the Great) King of the Franks (768–814) and Holy Roman Emperor (800–14). The eldest son of PEPIN III (THE SHORT), he inherited half the Frankish kingdom (768), annexed the remainder on his brother Carloman's death (771), and built a large empire. He invaded Italy twice and took the Lombard throne (773). He embarked on a long and brutal conquest of Saxony (772–804), annexed Bavaria (788) and defeated the Avars of the middle Danube (791–96, 804). He undertook campaigns against the Moors in Spain. In 800 Pope Leo III consecrated him as Emperor, thus reviving the concept of the Roman Empire, and confirming the separation of the West from the Eastern BYZANTINE EMPIRE. Charlemagne encouraged the intellectual awakening of the CAROLINGIAN RENAISSANCE, set up a strong central authority and maintained provincial control through court officials. His central aim was Christian reform, both of church and laity, and he was convinced that God had made him emperor to undertake this holy work.

Charles (Prince of Wales) (1948–) Eldest son of ELIZABETH II and heir to the British throne. He was invested as the Prince of Wales at Caernarvon (1969). He married Lady DIANA Spencer in 1981. Their 'fairy-tale' marriage rapidly and publicly disintegrated, and they divorced in 1996. Their eldest son, Prince William (b. 1982), is second in line to the throne. In 2005, Charles married Camilla Parker Bowles (1947–). He is well-known for his work with charities.

Charles I (1887–1922) Austrian Emperor (1916–18) and King (as Charles IV) of Hungary (1916–18). When Hungary and Czechoslovakia declared their independence and Austria became a republic in 1918, Charles, the last Habsburg Emperor, was forced into exile in Switzerland. In 1921, he unsuccessfully attempted to regain the Hungarian throne.

Charles I (1600–49) King of England, Scotland and Ireland (1625–49). Son of JAMES I, he was criticized by Parliament for his reliance on the Duke of BUCKINGHAM and for his Catholic marriage to Henrietta Maria. Although he accepted the PETITION OF RIGHT, Charles' insistence on the "divine right of kings" provoked further conflict with Parliament, and led him to rule without it for 11 years (1629–40). With the support of the Archbishop of Canterbury, William LAUD, Charles imposed harsh penalties on nonconformists. When attempts to impose Anglican liturgy on Scotland led to the Bishops' War, Charles was forced to recall Parliament to raise revenue. The LONG PARLIAMENT insisted on imposing conditions, and impeached Charles' chief adviser, the Earl of STRAFFORD, and in 1641 it presented the GRAND REMONSTRANCE. Relations worsened and Charles' attempt to arrest five leading opponents in the Commons precipitated the English CIVIL WAR. After the defeat of the Royalists, attempts by Oliver CROMWELL and other parliamentary and army leaders to reach a compromise with the king failed, and he was tried and executed.

Charles II (the Bald) (823–77) King of the West Franks (843–77) and Holy Roman Emperor (875–77). Younger son of Emperor Louis I, he was involved in the ambitious disputes of his elder brothers. The Treaty of Verdun (843) made him king of the West Franks, in effect the first king of France. Continuing family conflict, rebellion and Viking attacks resulted in territorial losses. Yet, after the death of Emperor Louis II, Charles was recognized as Holy Roman Emperor.

Charles II (1630–85) King of England, Scotland and Ireland (1660–85). After the execution of his father, CHARLES I, he fled to France, but in 1650 was invited to Scotland by the COVENANTERS and crowned king in 1651. Charles' attempted invasion of England was repulsed by CROMWELL, and he was forced back into exile. In 1660, Charles issued the Declaration of Breda, in which he promised religious toleration and an amnesty for his enemies. Parliament agreed to the Declaration and Charles was crowned king in May 1660, ushering in the RESTORATION. He attempted to preserve royal power, accepting secret subsidies from LOUIS XIV in exchange for promoting Roman Catholicism. Charles' support of Louis led to a war with the Netherlands (1672–74). He clashed with Parliament over both the war and his support of the Catholics. Conflict was further fuelled by anti-Catholic feeling, manifest in the 'Popish

Plot' rumour spread by Titus OATES and the Exclusion Crisis (1679–81), when attempts were made to exclude Charles' brother, the Catholic Duke of York (later JAMES II), from the succession. Unable to resolve his differences with Parliament, Charles dissolved it and ruled with financial support from Louis XIV. Known as the Merry Monarch, Charles had many mistresses (including Nell Gwyn), but left no legitimate heir.

Charles III (the Fat) (839–88) Holy Roman Emperor (881–87) and King of France (884–87) as Charles II. Through the death or incapacity of relatives, he inherited the kingdoms of the East and West Franks. He almost reunited the territories of Charlemagne in the 880s, but was deposed by his nephew, Arnulf.

Charles III (1716–88) King of Spain (1759–88) and of Naples and Sicily (1735–59), the son of Philip V and Elizabeth Farnese. He conquered Naples and Sicily in 1734, and inherited the Spanish crown from his half-brother Ferdinand VI. He handed Naples and Sicily to his son Ferdinand, who ruled as Ferdinand I of the Two Sicilies. Charles was a highly competent ruler. He encouraged commercial and agrarian reform, and brought the Spanish Catholic Church under state control, expelling the Jesuits in 1767. Allied with France in the SEVEN YEARS' WAR, he received LOUISIANA in 1763. He was succeeded by his son Charles IV.

Charles IV (1316–78) Holy Roman Emperor (1355–78) and King of Bohemia (1347–78). Supported by Pope Clement VI, he was a rival of the Wittelsbach Emperor Louis IV, and when Louis died, was elected King of the Germans (Emperor-elect). A skilful diplomat, he blocked or appeased his Wittelsbach and Habsburg rivals and improved relations with the papacy. In 1356, he introduced a stable system of imperial government. He ruled from PRAGUE, his birthplace, where he founded Charles University (1348) and built the Charles Bridge. Czech culture reached a peak under his patronage. He was succeeded by his son, WENCESLAS.

Charles IV (1748–1819) King of Spain (1788–1808), son and successor of CHARLES III. Unable to cope with the upheavals of Napoleon Bonaparte, Charles virtually turned over government to his wife María Luisa and her lover Manuel de Godoy. Godoy formed an alliance with France, but Spain was nevertheless occupied by French troops in the PENINSULAR WAR. Charles was forced to abdicate in favour of his son, Ferdinand VII, who in turn was forced from the throne by Napoleon.

Charles V (1500–58) Holy Roman Emperor (1519–56) and King of Spain, as Charles I (1516–56). He ruled the Spanish kingdoms, s Italy, the Netherlands, and the Austrian Habsburg lands by inheritance and, when elected Emperor in succession to his grandfather, MAXIMILIAN I, headed the largest European empire since CHARLEMAGNE. In addition, the Spanish CONQUISTADORS made him master of a New World empire. Charles' efforts to unify his possessions were unsuccessful, largely due to the hostility of FRANCIS I of France, the Ottoman Turks in central Europe, and the conflicts arising from the advance of LUTHERANISM in Germany. The struggle with France was centred in Italy: Spanish control was largely confirmed by 1535, but French hostility was never overcome. The Turks were held in check but not defeated, and Charles' attempt to capture Algiers failed (1541). In Germany, Charles, who saw himself as the defender of the Catholic Church, nevertheless recognized the need for reform, but other commitments prevented him following a consistent policy, and LUTHERANISM expanded. Charles increasingly delegated power in Germany to his brother Ferdinand I, his successor, and in 1554–56 surrendered his other titles to his son, Philip II of Spain.

Charles V (the Wise) (1337–80) King of France (1364–80). He regained most of the territory previously lost to the English during the HUNDRED YEARS' WAR, stabilized the coinage, and endeavoured to suppress anarchy and revolt in France. He strengthened royal authority further by introducing a regular taxation system, standing army, and powerful navy. He established a royal library, encouraged literature and art, and built the BASTILLE. He was succeeded by his son, CHARLES VI.

Charles VI (1685–1740) Holy Roman Emperor (1711–40) and King of Hungary as Charles III. His claim to the Spanish throne against the grandson of Louis XIV, Philip V, supported by the powers opposed to Louis, caused the War of the SPANISH SUCCESSION. After his election as emperor (1711), he gave up his Spanish claim as international support for it fell away. He spent much of his reign trying to secure the succession of his daughter, MARIA THERESA, to his Austrian possessions.

Charles VI (the Mad) (1368–1422) King of France (1380–1422). Until 1388 he was controlled by his uncle, Philip the Bold of Burgundy, whose policies drained the treasury and provoked uprisings. After ruling effectively for four years, Charles suffered recurrent bouts of insanity. Philip and Louis d'Orléans, the king's brother, fought for control of the kingdom. Louis was murdered in 1407, and Philip allied himself with Henry V of England. English victories at Agincourt (1415) and elsewhere forced Charles to sign the Treaty of Troyes (1420), acknowledging Henry as his successor.

Charles VII (1403–61) King of France (1422–61). The son of CHARLES VI, he was excluded from the throne by the Treaty of Troyes (1420). When his father died, Charles controlled French lands s of the River Loire, while the N remained in English hands. With the support of JOAN OF ARC, he checked the English at Orléans and was crowned king at Reims (1429). The Treaty of Arras (1435) ended the hostility of Burgundy, and by 1453 the English had been driven out of most of France. Charles strengthened his authority by re-establishing regular taxation and creating a standing army.

Charles VIII (1470–98) King of France (1483–98). He succeeded his father Louis XI, and until 1491 was controlled by his sister Anne de Beaujeu and her husband. Obsessed with gaining the kingdom of NAPLES, he invaded Italy in 1494, beginning the long Italian Wars, and in 1495 he entered Naples. A league of Italian states, the Papacy and Spain forced him to retreat. One positive result was the introduction of Italian Renaissance culture into France. He was succeeded by his cousin LOUIS XII.

Charles IX (1550–74) King of France (1560–74). Charles succeeded his brother FRANCIS II in 1560, and his mother CATHERINE DE' MEDICI became regent. Her authority waned when, in 1571, the young king fell under the influence of Gaspard de Coligny, leader of the HUGUENOTS. Coligny and thousands of followers were slain in the SAINT BARTHOLOMEW'S DAY MASSACRE (1572), ordered by Charles at the instigation of his mother. He was succeeded by his brother HENRY III.

Charles X (1757–1836) King of France (1824–30). Brother of LOUIS XVI and LOUIS XVIII, he fled France at the outbreak of the FRENCH REVOLUTION (1789). He remained in England until the BOURBON restoration (1814), and thereafter opposed the ensuing moderate policies of Louis XVIII. After the assassination of Charles' son in 1820, his reactionary forces triumphed. In 1825 he signed a law indemnifying émigrés for land confiscated during the Revolution. In 1830 he issued the July Ordinance, which restricted suffrage and press freedom, and dissolved the newly elected chamber of deputies. The people rebelled and Charles was forced to abdicate. He designated his grandson Henry as successor, but the Duc d'Orléans, LOUIS PHILIPPE, was selected.

Charles X (1622–60) King of Sweden (1654–60). He ascended the throne when his cousin Queen Christina abdicated in his favour. His efforts to complete Swedish domination of the Baltic resulted in a reign of continuous military activity. He invaded Poland unsuccessfully and twice invaded Denmark. He established the natural frontiers in Scandinavia, recovering the s provinces of Sweden from Denmark. He was succeeded by his son, Charles XI.

Charles XII (1682–1718) King of Sweden (1697–1718). His father, Charles XI, trained him in all aspects of administration, and he became king when 14 years old. Charles XII was one of the greatest military leaders in European history. He defeated Denmark, Poland, Saxony and Russia in a series of brilliant campaigns. Leading the troops, he destroyed the army of PETER I (THE GREAT) at Narva (1700). In 1708 he renewed his assault on Russia, but his army, depleted by the severe winter, was decisively defeated at Poltava (1709). He fled to the Ottomans and persuaded the Sultan to attack Russia (1711). The Sultan turned against him and, in disguise, he escaped back to Sweden and devoted his energy to the domestic economy. Weakened by war and opposed by many

▶ **cheetah** Also known as the hunting leopard, the cheetah (*Acinonyx jubatus*) is well adapted to catching its prey of antelope, hares and some species of birds, such as guinea fowl and young ostriches. It has long legs (height to shoulder, 1m/3ft), a supple but strong back (1.5m/5ft long) and well-developed eyesight; the cheetah hunts by sight not scent. It is distinguished by its pattern of solid black spots, a striped tail and a dark line running from the inner eye to the mouth. It is the fastest land animal.

enemies, he was killed, while fighting in Norway, and succeeded by his sister, Ulrica Eleanora.

Charles XIV (1763–1844) (Jean Baptiste Bernadotte) King of Sweden (1810–44), b. France. He fought in the French Revolution and was chosen by the Swedish legislature in 1810 to succeed Charles XIII. In the Treaty of Kiel, he forced Denmark to cede Norway to Sweden, and became king of Norway as Charles III John (1818–44). He joined the Allies against Napoleon at the Battle of Leipzig (1814). His subsequent reign brought peace and prosperity to Sweden.

Charles Edward Stuart *See* STUART, CHARLES EDWARD

Charles' law Volume of a gas at constant pressure is directly proportional to its absolute temperature. As temperature increases, the volume of a gas also increases at a constant pressure. The relationship was discovered by a French scientist Jacques Charles in 1787. The law is a special case of the ideal gas law. It is sometimes called Gay-Lussac's law, because Joseph GAY-LUSSAC established it more accurately in 1802.

Charleston City and port in SE South Carolina, USA. Founded in the 1670s by William Sayle, it soon became the major SE seaport. The South Carolina Ordinance of Secession was signed here (1860), and the firing on FORT SUMTER was the first engagement of the American Civil War. It has many fine colonial buildings and the Fort Sumter National Monument. It is the site of an important naval base. Industries: paper, textiles, chemicals, steel. Pop. (2000) 96,650.

Charleston Capital of West Virginia, USA, in the w of the state, on the River Kanawha. The city grew around Fort Lee in the 1780s. It is an important trade and transport centre for the industrialized Kanawha Valley. Industries: chemicals, glass, metallurgy, timber, oil, gas, coal. Pop. (2000) 53,421.

Charlton, Sir Bobby (Robert) (1937–) English footballer. Charlton played for Manchester United and was voted European Footballer of the Year (1966). He was a member of England's World Cup winning team. He won 106 international caps, scoring an English record of 49 goals. On retiring, Bobby pursued a career in football administration and became a director of Manchester United.

Charon In Greek mythology, boatman of the Lower World who ferried the souls of the dead across the STYX to HADES.

Charpentier, Gustave (1860–1956) French composer, taught by MASSENET. His best-known compositions are the operas *Louise* (1900) and *Julien* (1913), and the orchestral *Impressions d'Italie*.

Chartism (1838–48) British working-class movement for political reform. Combining the discontent of industrial workers with the demands of radical artisans, the movement adhered to the People's Charter (1838), which demanded electoral reform including universal male suffrage. As well as local riots and strikes, the Chartists organized mass petitions (1839, 1842, 1848). The movement faded away after a major demonstration in 1848.

Chartres Town on the River Eure, NW France; capital of Eure-et-Loire department. The stained glass and sculptures in the 12th-13th century gothic Cathedral of Notre Dame, make it one of Europe's finest cathedrals. It is a world heritage site. Industries: brewing, leather, agricultural equipment, radio and televison parts. Pop. (1999) 40,402.

Charybdis In Greek mythology, a female monster of the Straits of Messina, opposite SCYLLA. Daughter of Poseidon and Gaea, Zeus hurled her into the sea for stealing Heracles' cattle. A whirlpool formed where she lay under the water.

Chase, Salmon Portland (1808–73) Chief justice of the US Supreme Court (1864–73). Known as a defender of fugitive slaves, President LINCOLN appointed him chief justice. Chase reorganized the federal courts, and presided over the impeachment of President Andrew JOHNSON (1868). His decision in the Slaughterhouse Cases (1873) became a standard judgement on the restrictive clause of the 14th Amendment.

Chateaubriand, François René, Vicomte de (1768–1848) French writer and diplomat, whose works contributed to French ROMANTICISM. *The Genius of Christianity* (1802) was a reaction to ENLIGHTENMENT attacks on Catholicism and established his literary reputation. *Atala* (1801) and *René* (1805) are tragic love stories set in the American

wilderness. After 1803, he held important diplomatic posts for both NAPOLEON and the Bourbons and was minister of foreign affairs (1823–24). In 1830, he resigned from politics and wrote his *Memoirs from Beyond the Grave*.

Chattanooga City on the Tennessee River, SE Tennessee, USA. Founded as a trading post in the early 19th century, it was an important strategic centre in the American Civil War. Since 1935 it has been the headquarters of the Tennessee Valley Authority (TVA). Industries: iron and steel, food processing, synthetic fibres, tourism. Pop. (2000) 155,554.

Chatterton, Thomas (1752–70) English poet and forger of antiquities. He achieved posthumous fame for poems such as "Bristowe Tragedie" and "Mynstrelles Songe", supposedly composed by Thomas Rowley, an imaginary 15th-century monk. An erratic talent, his early suicide established him as a hero of the Romantic movement. William Wordsworth described him as "the marvellous boy".

Chaucer, Geoffrey (1346–1400) English medieval poet. His writings are remarkable for their range, narrative sense, power of characterization, and humour. They include *The Book of the Duchess* (1369), *The House of Fame* (c.1375), *The Parliament of Fowls,* and *Troilus and Criseyde* (both c.1385). His most famous and popular work is *The Canterbury Tales* (c.1387–1400), an extraordinarily varied collection of narrative poems, each told by one of a group of pilgrims while travelling to the shrine of Thomas à Becket. Ranging from the courtly "Knight's Tale" to the bawdy "Miller's Tale", they provide a panoramic view of 14th-century English society and are a landmark in medieval fiction. Influenced by both French and Italian literary traditions, Chaucer's writings exercised a powerful influence on the future direction of ENGLISH LITERATURE, not least in confirming SE English as its principal language.

Chávez, Cesar Estrada (1927–93) US labour leader. Born of Mexican-American parents, Chavez migrated to California as a field worker. In 1962 he founded the National Farm Workers Association (NFWA), which in 1966 merged with the Agricultural Workers Organizing Committee of the AFL-CIO, to become the United Farm Workers Organizing Committee. In 1968–70, he led a successful national boycott of California grapes, and later a lettuce boycott. Disputes over farm labourer representation continued into the 1980s.

Chechnya Republic of the Russian Federation, in the N Caucasus; the capital is GROZNY. The region's chief rivers are the Terek and Sunzha, whose fertile valleys support farming. Grozny oil field is a major source of Russian oil. Chechens, who are mostly Sunni Muslims, constitute 50%

INTERNET

Chartres
▶ www.chartres-csm.org/
us_fixe/index.html

Chaucer, Geoffrey
▶ www.luminarium.org/
medlit/chaucer.htm

of the population. The Chechens fiercely resisted tsarist RUSSIA's conquest of the Caucasus, even after absorption in 1859. In the 1920s, separate autonomous regions were created by the Soviet Union for the Chechen and Ingush peoples. In 1936, the two were united to form the Chechen-Ingush Autonomous Republic. The republic was dissolved in 1943–44 because of alleged collaboration with German occupying forces in World War 2. The region was reconstituted in 1957. In 1991 the Chechen-Ingush Republic split in two. General Dudayev was elected president of Chechnya, but a declaration of independence was not recognized by the Russian government. In December 1994, Russia invaded but met fierce resistance. In February 1995, Russian troops completed the capture of Grozny at the cost of *c.*25,000 civilian lives. A protracted guerrilla war ensued. In 1999, the Russians launched a second concerted attack, attempting to crush Chechen resistance. In 2003, the Kremlin approved a new constitution granting more autonomy to the region. Industries: oil refining and equipment, chemicals. Area: 19,301sq km (7452sq mi). Pop. (2000 est.) 573,900.

cheese Food made by processing curdled milk. The commonest source is cows' milk. Blue cheeses are pierced to channel air to a reactive fungus previously introduced. The simplest product is cottage cheese, formed when skimmed milk coagulates.

cheetah Spotted large CAT found in hot, arid areas of Africa, the Middle East and India. A long-legged animal with blunt, non-retractable claws, the cheetah has a tawny brown coat with round black spots. Capable of running at more than 95km/h (60mph), it hunts gazelles and antelopes by sight. Length: body: 140–150cm (55–60in); tail: 75–80cm (30–32in); weight: 60kg (132lb). Family Felidae; species *Acinonyx jubatus*.

Cheever, John (1912–82) US short story writer and novelist. Cheever's works satirize the morals of American suburban life, particularly 1940s Manhattan. His novel *The Wapshot Chronicle* (1957) won a National Book award. His short-story collection *The Stories of John Cheever* (1978) won a Pulitzer Prize.

Cheka First secret police of the Soviet Union. Formed shortly after the RUSSIAN REVOLUTION, its purpose was to seek out and punish all anti-BOLSHEVIK activity.

Chekhov, Anton Pavlovich (1860–1904) Russian dramatist, who worked closely with Konstantin STANISLAVSKY at the MOSCOW ART THEATRE. His major plays, *The Seagull* (1896), *Uncle Vanya* (1897), *The Three Sisters* (1901) and *The Cherry Orchard* (1904), display a deep understanding of human nature and a fine blend of comedy and tragedy. The main action usually takes place off-stage. Characters often reveal as much by what they leave unsaid as the subtleties of the dialogue itself.

chemical bond Mechanism that holds together atoms to form molecules. There are several types which arise either from the attraction of unlike charges, or from the formation of stable configurations through electron-sharing. The number of bonds an atom can form is governed by VALENCE. The main types are IONIC, COVALENT, metallic and hydrogen bonds.

chemical engineering Application of engineering principles to the making of chemical products on an industrial scale. Unit processes of chemical engineering include oxidation and reduction, nitration and sulphonation, electrolysis, polymerization, ion exchange and fermentation.

chemical equation Set of symbols used to represent a CHEMICAL REACTION. Equations show how atoms are rearranged as a result of a reaction, with reactants on the left-hand side and products on the right-hand side. For example, the formation of magnesium oxide when magnesium burns in oxygen is represented by $2Mg + O_2 \rightarrow 2MgO$. The number of atoms of an element on the left-hand side of an equation must equal the number on the right.

chemical equilibrium Balance in a REVERSIBLE REACTION, when two opposing reactions proceed at constant equal rates with no net change in the system. The initial rate of the reactions falls off as the concentrations of reactants decrease and the build-up of products causes the rate of the reverse reaction to increase. This is seen in the HABER

PROCESS where ammonia formed by nitrogen and hydrogen immediately breaks down again into those elements.

chemical reaction Change or process in which chemical substances convert into other substances. This involves the breaking and formation of chemical bonds. Reaction mechanisms include endothermic, exothermic, replacement, combination, decomposition and oxidation reactions.

chemical warfare Use of chemical weapons such as poison and nerve gases, defoliants and HERBICIDES. Poison gas and mustard gas was used in World War 1. Chemical weapons were not used in World War 2, but the Germans developed a nerve gas. A defoliant, Agent Orange, was employed by the US in the Vietnam War. Although the use of chemical and biological weapons is prohibited by the Geneva Convention (1925), their production, possession and exchange are not. In 1990, the USA and Soviet Union agreed to reduce their stockpiles of chemical weapons by 80%. *See also* BIOLOGICAL WARFARE

chemistry Branch of science concerned with the properties, structure and composition of substances and their reactions with one another. **Inorganic** chemistry studies the preparation, properties and reactions of all chemical elements and their compounds, except those of CARBON. **Organic** chemistry studies the reactions of carbon compounds, which are *c.*100 times more numerous than nonorganic ones. It also studies an immense variety of molecules, including those of industrial compounds such as plastics, rubbers, dyes, drugs and solvents. BIOCHEMISTRY deals with living processes and **Analytical** chemistry deals with the composition of substances. PHYSICAL CHEMISTRY deals with the physical properties of substances, such as their boiling and melting points. Its subdivisions include ELECTROCHEMISTRY, thermochemistry and chemical KINETICS.

chemoreceptor Tiny region on the outer membrane of some biological cells that is sensitive to chemical stimuli. The chemoreceptor transforms a stimulus from an external molecule into a sensation, such as smell or taste.

chemotherapy Treatment of a disease (usually cancer) by a combination of chemical substances, or DRUGS, that kill or impair disease-producing organisms in the body. Specific drug treatment was introduced in the early 1900s by Paul EHRLICH.

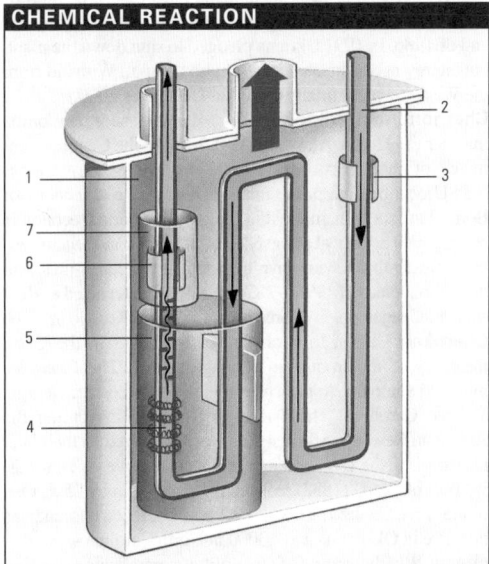

CHEMICAL REACTION

Calorimeters measure the amount of heat absorbed or let out during a chemical reaction. In a high-pressure flow calorimeter, the apparatus is contained in a vacuum (1) for insulation. A constant flow of liquid or gas enters the calorimeter (2). A platinum resistance thermometer (3) measures the temperature of the substance on entry. A heater (4) puts a known amount of energy into the liquid or gas inside a radiation shield (5), which further lessens any dispersion of energy. The change in temperature is measured by a second thermometer (6) again shielded (7).

C

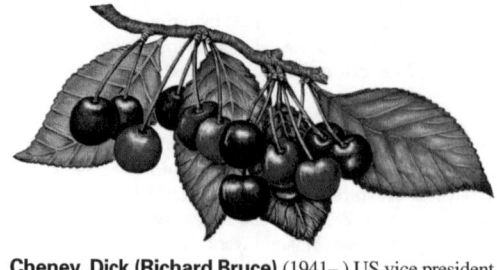

► **cherry** Grown for their fruit in many parts of the world, the cherry forms a type of fruit known as a drupe. It takes the form of a single seed surrounded by fleshy fruit. Cherries date from Roman times and the one shown is the black Early Rivers variety. The Japanese have a annual national festival to celebrate the arrival of cherry blossom.

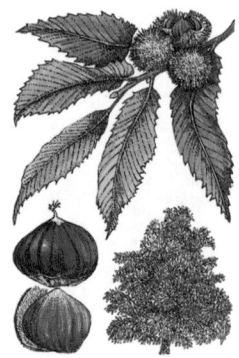

▲ **chestnut** Sweet chestnuts may be roasted, boiled or ground into flour or fed to livestock. The best quality chestnuts grow in Italy. Chestnut wood is extremely durable. The American chestnut *C. dentata* is almost extinct.

Cheney, Dick (Richard Bruce) (1941–) US vice president (2001–) under George W. BUSH. He was White House chief of staff (1974–77) under President Gerald FORD, and served as Republican Congressman for Wyoming (1978–89). Secretary of defense (1989–93) under President George BUSH, Cheney directed the invasion of Panama (1989) and the GULF WAR (1991) against Iraq. As vice president, Cheney steered legislation through Congress and contributed to the 'war on terror'.

Chennai (formerly Madras) City in SE India, on the Bay of Bengal; capital of Tamil Nadu state. India's second-largest port and fourth-largest city, Chennai was founded in 1639 as a British trading post. As Fort St. George, it became the seat of the EAST INDIA COMPANY and rapidly developed as a commercial centre. It was occupied by the French in 1746, but returned to Britain in 1748. The harbour was constructed in the second half of the 19th century. Industries: textiles, Tamil films, railroad stock, transport equipment. Pop. (2005) 6,915,000.

Chernenko, Konstantin Ustinovich (1911–85) Soviet statesman, president (1984–85). An ally of Leonid BREZHNEV, he joined the Politburo in 1978. Chernenko succeeded Yuri ANDROPOV as president and general secretary of the Communist Party of the Soviet Union (CPSU). He died after only 13 months in office and was succeeded by Mikhail GORBACHEV.

Chernobyl (Chornobyl) City on the River Pripyat River, N central Ukraine. It is 20km (12mi) from the Chernobyl power plant. On April 26, 1986, an explosion in one of the plant's reactors released eight tonnes of radioactive material into the atmosphere. Within the first few hours, 31 people died. Fallout spread across E and N Europe, contaminating agricultural produce. The long-term effects of contamination are inconclusive, but 25,000 local inhabitants have died prematurely. Two of the three remaining reactors were reworking by the end of 1986. In 1991 Ukraine pledged to shut down the plant, but energy needs dictated its continued output. With aid from the West, the plant finally closed in December 2000.

Chernomyrdin, Viktor (1938–) Russian statesman, prime minister (1992–98). A member (1986–90) of the Central Committee of the COMMUNIST PARTY OF THE SOVIET UNION (CPSU), he became prime minister despite the objections of Boris YELTSIN. Chernomyrdin broadly supported economic reform but was critical of the pace of privatization. Yeltsin's illness meant that Chernomyrdin acted as caretaker-president throughout much of 1996–97. Chernomyrdin later acted as Russia's chief negotiator in efforts to end the war in Kosovo in 1999.

Cherokee Largest tribe of Native Americans in the USA, members of the Iroquoian language family. The Cherokee migrated s into the Appalachian region of Tennessee, Georgia and the Carolinas. They sided with the British during the American Revolution. When gold was discovered on their land in Georgia in the 1830s, they were forced to move W. This tragic 'Trail of Tears' (1838) reduced the population by 25%. One of the 'Five Civilized Tribes', *c.*47,000 Cherokee descendants now live in Oklahoma and *c.*3000 in North Carolina.

cherry Widely grown fruit tree of temperate regions, probably native to W Asia and E Europe. Various types are grown for their fruit – round yellow, red or almost black with a round stone. The wood is used in furniture. Height: to 30m (100ft). Family Rosaceae; genus *Prunus*; there are about 50 species.

Chesapeake Bay Inlet of the Atlantic Ocean in Virginia (S) and Maryland (N), USA, at the mouth of the Susquehanna River. Linked to the Delaware River by the Chesapeake and Delaware Canal, the first permanent English settlement in North America was on Chesapeake Bay, at Jamestown, Virginia, (1607). In 1608 John Smith explored and charted the bay. Length: 311km (193mi). Width: 5–40km (3–25mi).

Cheshire County in NW England, bounded W by Wales and N by Greater Manchester and Merseyside. The county town is Chester. Cheshire is drained by the Mersey, Weaver and Dee rivers. It is an important industrial and dairy farming region, noted for its cheese. Industries: salt mining, chemicals, textiles, motor vehicles, oil refining. Area: 2331sq km (900sq mi). Pop. (2001) 673,777.

chess Board game of strategic attack and defence, played on a 64–square chequered board. Two players start with 16 pieces each, white or black, set out along the outer two ranks (rows) of the board. With a black square in the left corner, white's pieces are set out: rook (castle), knight, bishop, queen, king, bishop, knight, rook. Black's pieces align directly opposite. Pawns stand on the second rank. White takes first move, and players move pieces alternately on either rank (horizontal), file (vertical), or diagonal as appropriate, until the king is captured (checkmate). Chess originated in India, and the earliest extant references date the game back to the 6th century AD. Modern chess is a high-profile, international game which has been subjected to a great deal of analysis. Since 1950 all but one of the male world champion grandmasters have come from Russia or the former Soviet Union; the exception was Bobby Fisher of the USA in 1975.

Chester City and county district on the River Dee, NW England, Cheshire. A Roman garrison town, it has been of strategic importance throughout British history. It was a major port until the Dee became silted and Liverpool's port facilities were expanded. Notable buildings include the city wall, a Roman amphitheatre and a medieval cathedral. Industries: tourism, engineering. Area: 448sq km (173sq mi). Pop. (2001) 118,207.

Chesterton, G.K. (Gilbert Keith) (1874–1936) English essayist, novelist, biographer, and poet. Best known for his *Father Brown* stories, which began in 1911, he also wrote literary criticism and essays on social and political themes. His novels include *The Napoleon of Notting Hill* (1904) and *The Man who was Thursday* (1908). He became a Catholic (1922) and wrote *St Francis of Assisi* (1923) and *St Thomas Aquinas* (1933). His *Collected Poems* was published in 1933.

chestnut Deciduous tree native to temperate areas of the Northern Hemisphere. It has lance-shaped leaves and furrowed bark. Male flowers hang in long catkins, females are solitary or clustered at the base of catkins. The prickly husked fruits open to reveal two or three edible nuts. Family Fagaceae; genus *Castanea*; there are four species. *See also* HORSE CHESTNUT

Cheyenne Native North American tribe. During the 18th century, many abandoned sedentary farming for hunting buffalo. The tribe split in *c.*1830, with the Northern Cheyenne remaining near the Platte River, and the Southern Cheyenne settling near the Arkansas River. The Colorado Gold Rush (1858) brought rapid white migration and the Cheyenne were restricted to a reservation. War broke out following a US army massacre of Cheyenne (1864). General George CUSTER crushed Southern Cheyenne resistance, but the Northern Cheyenne helped in his defeat at LITTLE BIGHORN. They surrendered in 1877. Today, there are *c.*2000 Cheyenne.

Cheyenne State capital of Wyoming and county seat of Laramie County. Founded in 1867 as a centre for transporting goods and livestock by railway, it became famous for its lawlessness and connections with figures such as Buffalo Bill, Calamity Jane, and Wild Bill Hickok. Industries: packing plants, oil refineries. Pop. (2000) 53,001.

Chiang Kai-shek (1887–1975) (Jiang Jieshi) Chinese nationalist leader. After taking part in resistance against the QING dynasty, he joined the KUOMINTANG, succeeding SUN YAT-SEN (1925). From 1927 he purged the party of communists, and headed a Nationalist government in Nanking. The Japanese invasion (1937) forced a truce between nationalists and communists, and during World War 2, with US support, Chiang led the fight against Japan. Civil war resumed in 1945. Chiang was elected president of China (1948), but in 1949 the victorious communists led by MAO ZEDONG drove his government into exile in TAIWAN. Chiang established a dictatorship, and maintained that the Kuomintang were the legitimate Chinese government. The United Nations finally accepted the Chinese COMMUNIST

PARTY as the official government in 1972. Chiang Kai-shek remained President of Taiwan until his death.

chiaroscuro Term for the opposition of light and dark in painting and drawing. CARAVAGGIO and REMBRANDT were masters of the dramatic use of chiaroscuro.

Chiba City and port in Japan, on Tokyo Bay, central Honshu; capital of Chiba prefecture. Chiba has an 8th-century Buddhist temple. Industries: textiles, paper. Pop. (2000) 887,000.

Chibcha (Muisca) Late prehistoric culture in South America. Bogotá and Tunja were the main centres. The Chibcha culture flourished between 1000 and 1541, and rivalled the INCA in political sophistication. The inhabitants, c.750,000, developed remarkable city-states. Their pottery, weaving and goldsmithing were inferior to Inca work. The Chibcha were conquered by the Spanish (1536–41). In modern times, Chibcha refers to a Native American language family, whose speakers inhabit s Panama and n Colombia.

Chicago City on the sw shore of Lake Michigan, NE Illinois, USA. In the late 18th century it was a trading post and became Fort Dearborn military post (1803). With the construction of the Erie Canal and railways, and the opening up of the prairies, Chicago attracted settlers and industry. Large areas of the city were destroyed by fire in 1871, but its expansion continued. It became a noted cultural centre in the late 19th century with the establishment of the Chicago Symphony Orchestra (1891) and several literary magazines. It is the major industrial, commercial, cultural and shipping centre of the Midwest. It has many colleges and universities, the largest rail terminal in the world and one of the world's busiest airports, O'Hare. Chicago is renowned for its architecture. The

CHILE

The Republic of Chile stretches 4,260km [2,650mi] from N to s, while the greatest E to w distance is only 430km [270mi]. The ANDES mountains form Chile's E borders with Argentina and Bolivia. Ojos del Salado, at 6,863m [22,516ft], is the second–highest peak in the continent. EASTER ISLAND lies 3,500km

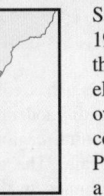

[2,200mi] off Chile's w coast. w Chile contains three main regions. In the N is the sparsely populated ATACAMA DESERT, stretching 1,600km [1,000mi] s from the Peruvian border. The Central Valley, which contains the capital, SANTIAGO, VALPARAÍSO and Concepción, is by far the most densely populated region. In the s, the land has been heavily glaciated. The coastal uplands have been worn into islands, while the inland valleys are arms of the sea.

In the far s, the Strait of MAGELLAN separates the Chilean mainland from TIERRA DEL FUEGO. Punta Arenas is the world's southernmost city.

CLIMATE

Chile is divided into three main climate zones. The Atacama Desert in the north has an arid climate, but temperatures are moderated by the cold Peru Current. Central Chile has a Mediterranean climate with hot, dry summers and mild, moist winters. The south has a cool and stormy climate, prone to alpine conditions.

HISTORY

ARAUCANIANS reached the s tip of South America at least 8,000 years ago. In 1520 Portuguese navigator Ferdinand MAGELLAN became the first European to sight Chile. In 1541, Pedro de Valdivia founded Santiago. Chile became a Spanish colony, ruled as part of the Viceroyalty of Peru. Under Spain, the economy in the N was based on mining. Huge ranches or haciendas were set up in central Chile, on which the Native Americans served as bonded labour.

In 1817 an army fighting for separation from Spain and led by José de SAN MARTÍN surprised the Spanish by crossing the Andes. In 1818, Bernardo O'HIGGINS proclaimed Chilean independence. His dictatorship was followed by democratic reforms. Chile gained mineral-rich areas from Peru and Bolivia in the War of the Pacific (1879–84). In the late 19th century, Chile's economy rapidly industrialized, fuelled by revenue from nitrate exports, but a succession of autocratic regimes hampered growth.

POLITICS

After World War 2 Chile faced economic problems, partly caused by falls in world copper prices. A Christian Democrat was elected president in 1964, but was replaced by

Salvador ALLENDE Gossens in 1970. Allende's administration, the world's first democratically elected Marxist government, was overthrown in a CIA-backed coup in 1973. General Augusto PINOCHET Ugarte took power as a dictator, banning all political activity in a repressive regime. A new constitution took effect from 1981, allowing for an eventual return to democracy. Elections took place in 1989. President Patricio Aylwin took office in 1990, but Pinochet secured continued office as commander-in-chief of the armed forces. Eduardo Frei was elected president in 1993 and was succeeded by a socialist, Ricardo Lagos, who narrowly defeated a conservative candidate in January 2000. In 1999, General Pinochet, who was visiting Britain for medical treatment, was faced with extradition to Spain to answer charges that he had presided over acts of torture when he was Chile's dictator. In 2000, he was allowed to return to Chile where, in 2001, he was found to be too ill to stand trial. New charges were brought against him in 2004, and he was under house arrest until his death in 2006. In 2006 elections Michelle Bachelet became Chile's first woman president.

ECONOMY

The World Bank classifies Chile as a 'lower-middle-income' developing country. Mining is important. Minerals dominate Chile's exports. The most valuable economic activity is manufacturing. Products include processed foods, metals, iron and steel, wood products and textiles.

Agriculture employs 18% of the workforce. The chief crop is wheat. Beans, fruits, maize and livestock products are also important. The fishing industry is one of the world's largest.

AREA 756,626sq km [292,133sq mi]
POPULATION 16,285,000
CAPITAL (POPULATION) Santiago (5,623,000)
GOVERNMENT Multiparty republic
ETHNIC GROUPS Mestizo 95%, Amerindian 3%
LANGUAGES Spanish (official)
RELIGIONS Roman Catholic 89%, Protestant 11%
CURRENCY Chilean peso = 100 centavos

The People's Republic of China is the world's third largest country. Most people live on the eastern coastal plains, in the highlands or the fertile valleys of the rivers HUANG HE and YANGTZE. The latter is Asia's longest river, at 6,380km [3,960mi].

Western China includes the bleak Tibetan plateau, which is bounded by the HIMALAYAS. EVEREST, the world's highest peak, lies on the Nepal-Tibet border. Other ranges include the TIAN SHAN and Kunlun Shan. China also has deserts, such as the GOBI.

Large areas in the W are covered by sparse grasses or desert. The most luxuriant forests are in the SE, such as the bamboo forest habitat of the rare giant panda.

CLIMATE

The capital, BEIJING, in NE China, has cold winters and warm summers, with moderate rainfall. SHANGHAI, in the E-central region, has milder winters and more rain. The SE region has a wet, subtropical climate. In the W, the climate is colder and more severe.

HISTORY

The first documented dynasty was the Shang (1523–1030 BC), when bronze casting was perfected. The ZHOU dynasty (1030–221 BC)

was the age of Chinese classical literature, in particular CONFU-CIUS and LAO TZU. China was unified by QIN SHIHUANGDI, whose tomb near XIAN contains the famous terracotta army. The QIN dynasty (221–206 BC) also built the majority of the GREAT WALL. The HAN dynasty (202 BC–AD 220) developed the Empire, a bureaucracy based on CONFUCIANISM, and also introduced BUDDHISM. China then split into three kingdoms (Wei, Shu, and Wu) and the influence of Buddhism and TAOISM grew. The T'ANG dynasty (618–907) was a golden era of artistic achievement, especially in poetry and fine art. GENGHIS KHAN conquered most of China in the 1210s and established the MON-GOL empire. KUBLAI KHAN founded the YÜAN dynasty (1271–1368), an era of dialogue with Europe. The MING dynasty (1368–1644) re-established Chinese rule and is famed for its fine porcelain. The Manchu QING dynasty (1644–1912) began by vastly extending the empire, but the 19th century was marked by foreign interventions, such as the OPIUM WAR (1839–42), when Britain occupied HONG KONG. Popular disaffection culminated in the BOXER REBELLION (1900). The last Emperor (Henry PU YI) was overthrown in a revolution led by SUN YAT-SEN and a republic established (1912).

AREA
9,596,961sq km
[3,705,387sq mi]
POPULATION
1,321,852,000
CAPITAL (POPULATION) Beijing (10,717,000)
GOVERNMENT Single-party Communist republic
ETHNIC GROUPS Han Chinese 92%, many others
LANGUAGES Mandarin Chinese (official)
RELIGIONS State officially atheist
CURRENCY Renminbi yuan = 10 jiao = 100 fen

China rapidly fragmented between a Beijing government supported by warlords, and Sun Yat-sen's nationalist KUOMINTANG government in GUANGZHOU. The Chinese COMMU-NIST initially allied with the Kuomintang. In 1926, the Kuomintang, led by CHIANG KAI-SHEK, emerged victorious and turned on their Communist allies. In 1930 a rival communist government was established, but was uprooted by Kuomintang troops and began the LONG MARCH (1934). Japan established the puppet state of MANCHUKUO (1932). Chiang was forced to ally with the Communists. Japan launched a full-scale invasion in 1937, and conquered much of N and E China. From 1941 Chinese forces, with Allied support, began to regain territory. At the end of World War 2, civil war resumed: nationalists supported by

CHINA

the USA and Communists by Russia. The Communists, with greater popular support, triumphed and the Kuomintang fled to TAIWAN.

POLITICS

MAO ZEDONG established the People's Republic of China in 1949 and seized Tibet in 1950. Mao began to collectivize agriculture and nationalize industry. In 1958 the GREAT LEAP FORWARD failed to boost industrial production. The CULTURAL REVOLUTION (1966–76) promoted indoctrination, purged intellectuals and destroyed cultural heritage. By 1971 China

had nuclear arms and a seat on the UN security council. Following Mao's death (1976), a power struggle developed between the GANG OF FOUR and moderates led by DENG XIAOPING. Xiaoping emerged victorious and began a process of modernization, forging closer links with the West. In 1989 a pro-democracy demonstration was crushed in TIANANMEN SQUARE. Jiang Zemin succeeded Deng as paramount leader in 1997, and in 2002 was succeeded by Hu Jintao. The government remains authoritarian, exercising heavy censorship and repressing all opposition.

ECONOMY

China's economy has grown extraordinarily rapidly in recent years, and has become one of the world's largest. The rise of private enterprise has led to massive investments in manufacturing, making China a major exporter of every class of goods. Economic inequality is increasing, although a middle class has arisen and is growing rapidly. The countryside has seen few of the economic benefits and remains very poor, leading to mass migration to cities and attendant social problems. Industrial growth has led to severe and widespread environmental damage.

---

world's first SKYSCRAPER was built here in 1885 and, until 1996, the Sears Tower was the world's tallest building, 443m (1454ft). Industries: steel, chemicals, machinery, metalworking. Pop. (2000) 8,308,000.

Chichester County town of West Sussex, s England. It is a market centre for the surrounding agricultural region and has a sheltered harbour. There are Roman remains, a Norman cathedral, and a modern theatre. An annual drama festival is held here. Pop. (2001) 106,445.

Chichester, Sir Francis Charles (1901–72) English yachtsman and aviator. He embarked on a solo flight between England and Australia in a Gypsy Moth biplane (1929). He began ocean sailing in the 1950s, and won his first solo transatlantic race in 1960. In 1966–67, he circumnavigated the globe single-handed in his boat *Gypsy Moth IV*.

Chickasaw Muskogean-speaking NATIVE AMERICANS, who originated in Mississippi-Tennessee (near present-day MEMPHIS). One of the 'Five Civilized Tribes', the US government established the Ohio River as their boundary in the Hopewell Treaty (1786). In the 1830s, the Chickasaw were resettled in Indian Territory (now Oklahoma). Today, they number *c*.9000.

chicken *See* POULTRY

chickenpox (varicella) Infectious disease of childhood caused by a virus of the HERPES group. After an incubation period of two to three weeks, a fever develops and red spots (which later develop into blisters) appear on the trunk, face and limbs. Recovery is usual within a week, although the possibility of contagion remains until the last scab has been shed.

chickpea (dwarf pea, garbanzo, chich or gram) Bushy annual plant cultivated from antiquity in s Europe and Asia for its pea-like seeds. It is now also grown widely in the Western Hemisphere. The seeds are boiled or roasted before eating. Family Fabaceae/Leguminosae; species *Cicer arietinum*.

chicory Perennial weedy plant whose leaves are cooked and eaten, or served raw in salads. The fleshy roots are dried and ground for mixing with (or a substitute for) COFFEE. Chicory has bright blue, daisy-like flowers. Height: 1.5m (5ft). Family Asteraceae/Compositae; species *Chichorium intybus*.

chigger (harvest mite or red bug) Tiny, red larva of some kinds of MITES found worldwide. Adults lay eggs on plants and hatched larvae find an animal host. Length: 0.1–16mm (0.004–0.6in). Order Acarina; family Trombiculidae.

Chihuahua Largest state in Mexico, on the N Mexican plateau; the capital is Chihuahua. Other cities include CIUDAD JUÁREZ. The climate and terrain vary from the cool mountains of the Sierra Madre (W) to the arid desert (E). Industries: mining, forestry, tourism, cotton. Area: 247,086sq km (95,400sq mi). Pop. (2000) 3,047,867; (city) 670,208.

child abuse Emotional and/or physical (often sexual) maltreatment of a child. Neglect is considered a form of abuse. Physical abuse may be apparent in bruising and lacerations, burns or scars. Sexual abuse is often concealed by the abused either out of fear or guilt. Physical effects of sexual abuse may be apparent to a medical practitioner. Mental effects may result in remoteness or crudely violent outbursts. It is argued that victims of abuse are more likely to be abusers later in life.

childbirth *See* LABOUR

child psychology *See* DEVELOPMENTAL PSYCHOLOGY

Children's Crusade Name given to two 13th-century CRUSADES by children. One group of French children were offered free transport from Marseilles to the Holy Land, but were sold as slaves in North Africa. Another group of German children bound for the Holy Land travelled to Italy, where the crusade floundered, many dying of starvation and disease.

Chile Republic in South America. *See* country feature, p.219

chilli (chili) Hot, red PEPPER. It is an annual with oval leaves and white or greenish-white flowers that produce red or green seedpods. When dried, the pods are ground to powder. Cayenne pepper comes from the same plant. Height: 2– 2.5m (6–8ft). Family Solanaceae; species *Capsicum annuum*.

chimaera (ratfish or ghost shark) One of about 28 species of cartilaginous, deep-sea FISH with a long, poisonous, dorsal spine and a slender tail. An oil, derived from its liver, is used as a lubricant. Length: 60cm-2m (23–80in). Families Chimaeridae, Collorhinchidae and Rhinochimaeridae. The term also refers to an animal formed from several different embryos.

Chimera In Greek mythology, a monster with a lion's head, goat's body, and dragon's tail. She was the sister of Cerberus, HYDRA, and the SPHINX, and was slain by Bellerophon.

chimpanzee Gregarious, intelligent great APE of tropical Africa. Chimpanzees are mostly black and powerfully built. A smaller chimpanzee of the Congo region is sometimes classified as a separate species. Chimpanzees often nest in trees, but are mostly on the ground searching for fruit and nuts. They are communicative and, in controlled situations, have learned a limited human vocabulary in sign language. Height: *c*.1.3m (4.5ft); weight: *c*.68kg (150lb). Family Pongidae. Species *Pan troglodytes*, Congo *Pan paniscus*. *See also* PRIMATES

Ch'in Alternative transliteration for the QIN dynasty

China Republic in E Asia. *See* country feature, pages 220–21

China Sea Western part of the Pacific Ocean, divided by Taiwan into the SOUTH CHINA SEA and the EAST CHINA SEA.

chinchilla Genus of small, furry RODENTS native to South America. Chinchillas were hunted almost to extinction. They are now bred in captivity for their long, close-textured and soft fur, the most expensive of all animal furs. Length: 23–38cm (9–15in); weight: 450–900g (1–2lb). Family Chinchillidae.

Chinese Group of languages spoken by *c*.95% of the population of China and by millions more in Taiwan, Hong Kong, SE Asia and elsewhere. There are six major languages, which are not mutually intelligible; the most common is MANDARIN, spoken by *c*.66% of the Chinese population. All Chinese languages are written in a single common non-alphabetic script, whose characters number in the thousands and in some cases date back several thousand years. This single writing-system leads to the traditional classification of all Chinese languages as dialects of one language. Chinese has twice as many users as any other language in the world. *See also* CANTONESE

Chinese architecture Style that as early as the Neolithic period, used columns to support roofs, faced houses s, and used bright colours. The characteristic Chinese roof with wide overhang and upturned eaves was probably developed in the ZHOU period (1030–221BC). A walled complex with a central axis for

INTERNET

Chile
▶ www.chile-usa.org

▲ **chickpea** A staple crop in certain regions of India, the chick pea (*Cicer arietinum*) is grown for its seed, which is then boiled.

C

INTERNET

China
▶ www.china-embassy.org/
eng
▶ www.cnto.org.au

temples and palaces was established in the HAN (202BC–AD 220), and the practice of building residential units around a central courtyard with elaborately planned garden became standard. The pagoda derives from Buddhist influences, notably the Indian stupa, and dates from the 6th century.

Chinese art Longest pedigree of any school in world art, its earliest artefacts (painted pottery) date back to the late Neolithic period. By the time of the SHANG dynasty (*c.*1523–1030BC), native craftsmen were proficient at casting bronze and making jade carvings, many of which have survived as grave goods. The most elaborate of these early tombs belonged to the first emperor of the QIN dynasty, QIN SHI-HUANGDI (d.210BC). It contains a fabulous Terracotta Army of *c.*7500 life-sized figures and horses. Painting and sculpture were established during the HAN dynasty, though little survives. The T'ANG dynasty (618–907) marked China's artistic zenith. Sculpture reached a peak of refinement, and there were early attempts at landscape painting. The SUNG dynasty saw the introduction of the first true porcelain. Important technical advances, most notably in the application of coloured ENAMELS, took place during the MING period (1368–1644). Chinese porcelain became highly valuable in European markets, a trend which accelerated under the QING dynasty. Communism created a rift in this long tradition, as artists adopted Soviet-inspired SOCIALIST REALISM.

Chinese literature Earliest literary texts date from the ZHOU dynasty (*c.*1030–221BC). This period produced the canonical writings of CONFUCIANISM: the Five Classics, including the first poetry anthology *Shih ching* (Classic of Odes); and the Four Books, containing doctrinal writings, such as *The Book of Mencius*. Traditionally attributed to CONFUCIUS, the *Shih ching* is probably earlier still. In this era, LAO TZU is credited with founding TAOISM. During the HAN dynasty (202BC–AD 220), elaborate *fu* prose poems which praised the dynasty flourished. The T'ANG dynasty (618–907) marked the golden age of Chinese literature. LI PO, TU FU and Wang Wei were the outstanding poets of the period. In the SUNG dynasty (960–1279), the novel (often historical) and drama (stressing conflicts such as filial versus national loyalty) came into being. From the late 17th to early 19th century, much emphasis was placed on formal technique. Ts'ao Chan produced the most memorable work of the period, the novel *Dream of the Red Chamber*. The lyric poem has been the dominant form in Chinese literature. It is normally philosophical, with a quietness of tone and an emphasis on simple, routine experiences. In the first half of the 20th century, Chinese literature became greatly modernized, with the new republic striving to formulate a new, politicized literary language to reflect its doctrine. During the CULTURAL REVOLUTION, strict censorship was imposed. Recent years have seen a slight liberalization.

Chinese mythology During the SHANG dynasty, divination by means of animal bones was used to consult the spirits of royal ancestors on matters such as harvests, rainfall, and the prospects of success in battle. These ancestors were divine and provided a means of communication with the spirit world. A supreme god, Shang Ti, ruled in heaven as Chinese sovereigns did on earth. During the ZHOU dynasty, Shang Ti was replaced by T'ien ('Heaven') as the supreme being. The Emperor, the 'Son of Heaven', was responsible for maintaining harmony on earth and assumed the role of

both priest and monarch. Chinese creation myths are essentially the reduction of chaos to order. Later, in conjunction with popular mythology, there existed a formal Chinese pantheon ruled by a father-god, the August Personage of Jade. His heavenly court was an almost exact replica of the imperial court at BEIJING. The Sun and the Moon were the objects of an official cult, and the Festival of the Moon was a major annual celebration. Another popular divinity was the Thunder God who punished those guilty of great crimes.

Chinese theatre In its purest form, the traditions of Chinese theatre date back to the SUNG dynasty (960–1279). Traditional theatre is highly stylized and the symbolism of the various dramatic parts, the actors' costumes, make-up and gestures are considered of far greater importance than the dialogue. Although much recent Chinese theatre has become Westernized, the old dramatic tradition remains enormously popular.

Ch'ing Alternative transliteration of the QING dynasty

Chinook Native American tribe living along the Pacific coast from the Columbia River to The Dalles, Oregon. Although numbering fewer than 1,000, the Chinook travelled widely and the Chinook language was used by others, native and European, during the settlement of the West. The name is also given to a warm, dry wind on the E side of the Rocky Mountains.

chip, silicon See SILICON CHIP

chipmunk Small, ground-dwelling SQUIRREL native to North America and Asia. It carries nuts, berries and seeds in cheek pouches, to store underground. Active tree-climbers in summer, they hibernate in winter. Most chipmunks are brown with black-bordered, light stripes. Length: 13–15cm (5–6in), excluding tail. Family Sciuridae; genera *Eutamias* and *Tamias*.

Chippendale, Thomas (1718–79) English furniture designer. One of the greatest craftsmen of his day, much of his fame rested upon the wide circulation of his *The Gentleman and Cabinet Maker's Directory* (1754–62), a trade catalogue illustrating the designs of his factory. Many of Chippendale's finest pieces were marquetry and inlaid items in neo-classical vein.

Chirac, Jacques (1932–) French statesman, president (1995–2007). Chirac was elected to the National Assembly in 1967 and held a number of ministerial posts. In 1974 he was appointed prime minister by President GISCARD D'ES-TAING. In 1976 he resigned and formed a new Gaullist party, the Rally for the Republic (RPR). In 1977 he became mayor of Paris. He was again prime minister (1986–88), this time under President MITTERRAND. In 1995 he succeeded Mitterrand as president. Confronted by tough economic decisions in the lead-up to European economic and monetary union, Chirac called a surprise prime ministerial election (1997). Victory for the socialists, led by Lionel JOSPIN, was a personal setback for Chirac. Chirac won a landslide victory in 2002 elections.

Chirico, Giorgio de (1888–1978) Italian painter, b. Greece. Chirico was founder of the quasi-surrealist 'metaphysical painting' movement. He painted still lifes and empty, dream-like landscapes in exaggerated perspective. In the 1930s he repudiated all modern art in favour of paintings in the style of the Old Masters. *See also* SURREALISM

Chiron In Greek mythology, wisest and most famous CENTAUR. He taught many of the lesser gods and heroes, including ACHILLES, and was accidently killed by Hercules with a poisoned arrow. He was placed among the stars by ZEUS.

chiropractic Non-orthodox medical practice based on the theory that misalignments of the spine are the cause of much or most disease. While such claims are backed by little or no scientific evidence, chiropractic can be successful in the treatment of some forms of back pain, and headaches. However, some of its techniques carry a risk of dangerous accidents.

Chisinau (Kishinev) Capital of Moldova, in the centre of the country, on the River Byk. Founded in the early 15th century, it came under Turkish then Russian rule. Romania held the city from 1918 to 1940 when it was annexed by the Soviet Union. In 1991 it became capital of independent Moldova. It has a 19th-century cathedral and a university (1945). Industries: plastics, rubber, textiles, tobacco. Pop. (2002 est.) 776,700.

chitin Hard, tough substance that occurs widely in nature, particularly in the shells (exoskeletons) of arthropods such as

▶ **Chirac** Elected president of France in 1995, Jacques Chirac's major task was to ensure the French economy met the stringent criteria for entry into the European single currency (the euro) in 1999. He persisted with an austere economic programme despite rising unemployment and a general strike in 1995. Chirac faced international criticism for authorizing French nuclear tests in the Pacific in 1995 and 1996. In 2002 presidential elections, he received 82% of the vote, after a split in the socialist vote led to a second round contest against Jean-Marie Le Pen, leader of the far-right National Front.

crabs, insects and spiders. The walls of hyphae (microscopic tubes of fungi) are composed of slightly different chitin. Chemically chitin is a polysaccharide, derived from glucose.

chiton (coat-of-mail shell) MOLLUSC that lives attached to, or creeping on, rocks along marine shores. Bilaterally symmetrical, its upper surface has eight overlapping shells. Underneath is a large fleshy foot and a degenerate head with mouth, gills and mantle. Length: to 33cm (13in). Class Amphineura; order Polyplacophora; family Chitonidae.

Chittagong Seaport on the River Karnaphuli, near the Bay of Bengal, SE Bangladesh. Under Mogul rule in the 17th century, it was ceded to the British EAST INDIA COMPANY in 1760. It is Bangladesh's chief port. Its facilities were badly damaged in liberation struggle with Pakistan (1971). Industries: jute, tea, oil, engineering, cotton, steel. Pop. (2005) 4,171,000.

chivalry (Fr. *chevalerie*, knighthood) Code of ethics and behaviour of the knightly class that developed from the FEUDAL SYSTEM. A combination of Christian ethics and military codes of conduct, the main chivalric virtues were piety, honour, valour, chastity, and loyalty. A KNIGHT swore loyalty to God, king and his love. Chivalry was always prone to corruption, and the traditions died out in the 15th century.

chive Perennial herb whose long hollow leaves have an onion-like flavour used for seasoning. The flowers grow in rose-purple clusters. Family Liliaceae; species *Allium schoenoprasum*.

chlamydia Small, virus-like BACTERIA that live as PARASITES in animals and cause disease. One strain, *C. trachomatis*, is responsible for TRACHOMA and is also a major cause of pelvic inflammatory disease (PID) in women. *C. psittaci* causes PSITTACOSIS. Chlamydial infection is the most common SEXUALLY TRANSMITTED DISEASE in many developed countries.

chloride Salt of HYDROCHLORIC ACID or some organic compounds containing CHLORINE, especially those with the negative ion Cl. The best-known example is common salt, sodium chloride (NaCl). Most chlorides are soluble in water, except mercurous and silver chlorides.

chlorine (symbol Cl) Common nonmetallic element that is one of the HALOGENS, discovered in 1774 by the Swedish chemist K.W. Scheele. It occurs in common salt (NaCl). It is a greenish-yellow poisonous gas extracted by the electrolysis of brine (salt water) and is widely used to disinfect drinking water and swimming pools, to bleach wood pulp and in the manufacture of plastics, chloroform and pesticide. Chemically it is a reactive element, and combines with most metals. Properties: at.no. 17; r.a.m. 35.453; m.p. 101°C (149.8°F); b.p. 34.6°C (30.28°F). The most common isotope is Cl^{35} (75.53%).

chlorofluorocarbon (CFC) Chemical compound in which hydrogen atoms of a HYDROCARBON, such as an alkane, are replaced by atoms of fluorine, chlorine, carbon and sometimes bromine. CFCs are inert, stable at high temperatures and are odourless, colourless, nontoxic, noncorrosive and nonflammable. Under the trade name of Freons, CFCs were widely used in aerosols, fire-extinguishers, refrigerators, and in the manufacture of foam plastics. The two most common are Freon 11 (trichlorofluoromethane, $CFCl_3$) and Freon 12 (dichlorodifluoromethane, CF_2Cl_2). CFCs slowly drift into the stratosphere and are broken down by the Sun's ultraviolet radiation into chlorine atoms that destroy the ozone layer. It often takes more than 100 years for CFCs to disappear from the atmosphere. Growing environmental concern led to an international agreement in 1990 to reduce and eventually phase out the use of CFCs, and to develop safe substitutes.

chloroform (trichloromethane) Colourless, volatile, sweet-smelling liquid ($CHCl_3$) prepared by the chlorination of methane. Formerly a major anaesthetic, it is used in the manufacture of fluorocarbons, in cough medicines, for insect bites and as a solvent. Properties: r.d. 1.48; m.p. -63.5°C (-82.3°F); b.p. 61.2°C (142.2°F).

chlorophyll Group of green pigments present in the CHLOROPLASTS of plants and ALGAE that absorb light for PHOTOSYNTHESIS. There are five types: chlorophyll *a* is present in all photosynthetic organisms except bacteria; chlorophyll *b*, in plants and GREEN ALGAE; and chlorophylls *c*, *d* and *e*, in some algae. It is similar in structure to HAEMOGLOBIN, with a magnesium atom replacing the iron atom.

chloroplast Microscopic green structure within a plant cell in which PHOTOSYNTHESIS takes place. The chloroplast is enclosed in an envelope formed from two membranes and contains internal membranes to increase the surface area for reactions. Molecules of the light-absorbing pigment CHLOROPHYLL are embedded in these internal membranes.

chocolate Like COCOA, chocolate was originally a drink (introduced to Europe in the 1500s) produced from the seeds of the tropical tree *Theobroma cacao*. The seeds are beans contained in an elliptical pod, and do not have the flavour or colour of chocolate until they have been fermented and roasted. The beans are then ground up to make chocolate powder. The first chocolate bar was produced in the late 1700s.

Choctaw One of the largest tribes of Muskogean-speaking NATIVE AMERICANS, located in SE Mississippi and part of Alabama. An agricultural people, they were generally at peace with European settlers, and remained neutral during the Revolution. As large slave-owners, they supported the South during the Civil War. Some 40,000 still reside in Oklahoma.

choir Group of singers who perform as a musical unit. The earliest choirs were ecclesiastical and sang the PLAINSONG in church services. From the 10th century onwards, polyphonic composition gradually replaced unharmonized plainsong in liturgical use. In the 16th and 17th centuries, pieces were written for two or more contrasting choirs. The birth of OPERA marked the development of the secular choir, or CHORUS. Most modern choirs, apart from some all-male cathedral choirs, are mixed.

Choiseul, Etienne François, Duc (1719–85) French statesman, chief minister of LOUIS XV (1758–1770). As ambassador to Vienna (1757–58), he negotiated the marriage of Marie Antoinette and the future Louis XVI. As minister of foreign affairs, he negotiated the Family Compact (1761), which allied the BOURBON rulers of France and Spain, and the Treaty of Paris (1763), in which France was forced to surrender French Canada and India to Britain.

Chola Dynasty of S India. Between 985 and 1024, they established an empire that included Sri Lanka, Bengal, and parts of Sumatra and Malaya. The dynasty declined and ended in 1279. The Cholas marked a great era of Hindu culture in S India.

cholera Infectious disease caused by the bacterium *Vibrio cholerae*, transmitted in contaminated water. Cholera, prevalent in many tropical regions, produces almost continuous, watery diarrhoea often accompanied by vomiting and muscle cramps, and leads to severe dehydration. Untreated it can be fatal, but proper treatment, including fluid replacement and antibiotics, result in a high recovery rate. There is a vaccine.

cholesterol White, fatty STEROID, occurring in large concentrations in the brain, spinal cord and liver. It is synthesized in the liver, intestines and skin, and is an intermediate in the synthesis of vitamin D and many hormones. GALLSTONES are composed mainly of cholesterol. Meat-rich diets may produce Low-density lipoprotein cholesterol (LDL-cholesterol), which can become high cholesterol in the blood vessels and lead to atherosclerosis (hardening of the arteries) and ARTERIOSCLEROSIS (degenerative disease of the arteries). High-density lipoprotein cholesterol (HDL-cholesterol) is a beneficial form that reduces LDL-cholesterol and fat by transporting them to the liver which breaks them down. Certain diets, such as those reducing saturated fat, can lower the dangers of cholesterol. Home kits are available to check cholesterol levels.

Chomsky, (Avram) Noam (1928–) US professor of LINGUISTICS. In *Syntactic Structures* (1957), he developed the concept of a transformational grammar, embodying his theories about the relationship between language and mind, and an underlying universal structure of language. Chomsky argued that the human capacity for language is partially innate, unlike supporters of BEHAVIOURISM. His ideas greatly influenced psychologists concerned with language acquisition. Chomsky is a consistent critic of US imperialism, and his political works include *American Power and the New Mandarins* (1969).

Chongjin City on the Sea of Japan, NE North Korea. From 1910 to 1945, it was controlled by the Japanese, who developed the Musan iron mines. Industries: iron, steel, shipbuilding, chemicals, textiles. Pop. (2002 est.) 674,000.

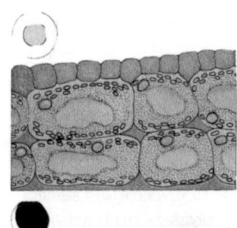
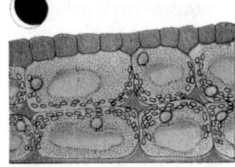

▲ **chloroplast** Found mostly in the cells of plant leaves, chloroplasts absorb sunlight and use it to manufacture special types of sugar. They are able to move about in order to receive the maximum amount of light possible. A section through a leaf reveals that during the day (top) chloroplasts have moved to the outer and inner walls in the direct line of light. During the night (bottom) they move to the inner and side walls only.

► **Chopin** As well as being a successful composer, Frédéric Chopin was a virtuoso pianist. He left his native Poland due to political repression, and moved to Paris in 1831. Much of his music reflects traditional Polish folk songs. Chopin had a stormy relationship with the woman novelist George Sand.

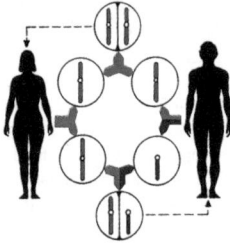

▲ **chromosome** The 46 chromosomes in somatic (non-reproductive) cells contain a single sex-determining pair, which consists of an X and Y chromosome in males, or an XX pair in females. Ova contain only the X chromosome, while spermatazoa contain X or Y chromosomes in equal proportions. At fertilization, therefore, there is a 50% chance of an XX or XY pair being formed.

▲ **chrysanthemum** Native to E Asia, the chrysanthemum, along with the cherry blossom, is the national flower of Japan. Today, there are some 200 species cultivated around the world.

INTERNET

Chopin, Frédéric François
► www.classical.net

Chrétien, (Joseph-Jacques) Jean
► pm.gc.ca

Christmas Island
► www.christmas.net.au

Chopin, Frédéric François (1810–49) Composer for the piano, b. Poland. He gave his first recital in Warsaw at the age of eight. Political repression forced him to move (1831) to Paris, where he endeared himself in the *salons*. His restrained and delicate style contrasted strongly with contemporary trends. In 1836, LISZT introduced Chopin to the novelist George SAND. In 1838 the couple moved to Majorca, and he composed 24 preludes. Chopin composed almost exclusively for the piano and established it as a solo instrument. His major works include two piano concertos and three piano sonatas.

choral music Music written for several voices. Choral compositions were originally religious, CANTATA and ORA-TORIO being the most usual forms. The foremost composer of cantatas was J.C. BACH, and of oratorios HANDEL. Choral music varies greatly in size and style, from the small-scale, secular madrigals of the 16th century to the large-scale works of the 19th and 20th centuries, such as Verdi's *Requiem* (1874), Elgar's *Dream of Gerontius* (1900), and the choral symphonies of Mahler.

chord In music, the simultaneous occurrence of three or more musical tones of different pitch. Chords are categorized as anomalous, characteristic, common, inverted or transient. *See also* HARMONY

chordate Any member of the Chordata, a large phylum of VERTEBRATES and some marine invertebrates, which, at some stage, have rod-like, cartilaginous supporting structures (**notochords**). Invertebrate chordates are divided into three subphyla: tunicates (seasquirts); Cephalochordata (amphioxus); and Hemichordata (acorn worms).

chorus In Greek tragedy, the *choros* danced and chanted commentary. Today, a chorus refers to a group of voices. Major works with chorus parts include CANTATAS, OPERAS and ORATORIOS. *See also* CHOIR

Chou Alternative name for the ZHOU dynasty

Chouteau, (Jean) Pierre (1758–1849) US fur trader and politician. With **René Auguste** Chouteau, he controlled the important trade with the Osage Native Americans. In 1804, he became US agent for all Native American tribes w of the Mississippi. Chouteau founded the first permanent white settlement in Oklahoma.

Chrétien, (Joseph-Jacques) Jean (1934–) 20th prime minister (1993–2003) of Canada. He entered Parliament in 1963, and was a member of Pierre TRUDEAU's cabinet. In 1990 he became leader of the Liberal Party. Chrétien won a landslide victory in the 1993 elections and was re-elected, with a much reduced majority, in 1997 and again in 2000. His main challenges were to reduce unemployment and to maintain the federation against the threat of secession from Québec. In 2003, Chrétien retired and was succeeded by Paul Martin.

Chrétien de Troyes (active1160–85) Romance writer of N France, noted for his tales of King Arthur and his knights. He influenced Geoffrey CHAUCER and Thomas

MALORY, and wrote at least five romances including the enormously influential *Lancelot*, *Yvain* and *Perceval*.

Christ (Gk. *christos*, 'anointed one') Epithet for the MES-SIAH in Old Testament prophecies. Later applied to JESUS CHRIST, in recognition that he was the expected Messiah.

Christchurch City on South Island, New Zealand; main town of Canterbury. It was founded as a Church of England settlement (1850). The University of Canterbury (1873) is here. Industries: fertilizers, rubber, woollen goods, electrical goods, furniture. Pop. (2001) 316,227.

christening *See* BAPTISM

Christian Follower of JESUS CHRIST. The major Christian Churches regard belief in the divinity of Christ and the Holy TRINITY as the minimum requirement for a Christian. This definition excludes religious bodies such as UNITARIANISM.

Christian IV (1577–1648) King of Denmark and Norway (1588–1648), the son of Frederick II. Despite a costly war with Sweden (1611–13) and his disastrous participation (1625–29) in the THIRTY YEARS' WAR, he was a popular monarch who kept the nobility in check. His reign brought culture and economic prosperity, and he founded the city of Oslo in Norway.

Christian X (1870–1947) King of Denmark (1912–47) and Iceland (1919–44), succeeding Frederick VIII. During his reign universal suffrage was established (1915) and social welfare policies were consolidated. He tried to remain neutral during World War 1 and defied the Germans during occupation (1940–45).

Christian Democrats Political group combining Christian conservative principles with progressive social responsibility. Christian Democrats have achieved power in many European countries, notably Germany and Italy. Its political principles include: individual responsibility allied with collective action; social equality within a welfare state; progress through evolutionary change; and a competitive society responsive to democratic debate and economic planning. Christian Democrats are also represented outside Europe.

Christianity Religion based on faith in JESUS CHRIST as the Son of God. The orthodox Christian faith, summarized in the APOSTLES' and NICENE CREEDS, affirms belief in the TRINITY and Christ's incarnation, atoning death on the cross, resurrection and ascension. The moral teachings of Jesus are contained in the NEW TESTAMENT. The history of Christianity has been turbulent and often sectarian. The first major schism took place in 1054, when the Eastern and Western churches separated. The next occurred in the 16th-century REFORMATION, with the split of PROTES-TANTISM and the ROMAN CATHOLIC CHURCH. In recent times, the ECUMENICAL MOVEMENT, which aims at the reunion of all Christians, has gained strength. Today, there are more than 1000 million Christians. *See also* BIBLE

Christian Science (Church of Christ Scientist) Religious sect founded in 1879 by Mary Baker EDDY, and based on her book *Science and Health With Key to the Scriptures*. Its followers believe that physical illness and moral problems can only be cured by spiritual and mental activity. They usually refuse medical treatment, a practice which has led to major ethical controversies.

Christie, Dame Agatha Mary Clarissa (1891–1976) English author. A prolific writer of detective stories, *The Mysterious Affair at Styles* (1920) introduced her most famous character, Hercule Poirot. *Murder at the Vicarage* (1930) featured the aged sleuth Miss Marple. Other novels include *The Murder of Roger Ackroyd* (1926), *Murder on the Orient Express* (1934), and *And Then There Were None* (1939). Her plays include *The Mousetrap* (1952). Many of her novels have been made into films.

Christie, Linford (1960–) British athlete, b. Jamaica. He captained the British men's team at the 1992 Olympic Games and won the 100m gold medal. He repeated this feat in the World Championships (1993). Christie also won gold medals in the European Championships (1986, 1990) and the Commonwealth Games (1990, 1994). He retired in 1997.

Christina (1626–89) Queen of Sweden (1632–54). An intellectual of great energy, Christina brought foreign scholars, such as DESCARTES, to her court. Ruling a Lutheran country, she abdicated to become a Roman Catholic, and settled in Rome. She tried unsuccessfully to obtain the crown of Poland (1667).

Christmas Feast in celebration of the birth of JESUS CHRIST, common in Christendom since the 4th century. Although the exact date of Christ's birth is unknown, the feast takes place on December 25 within all Christian churches. Christmas is also a secular holiday, marked by the exchange of presents.

Christmas Island *See* KIRITIMATI

Christmas Island Island in the E Indian Ocean, 320km (200mi) s of JAVA. Once under British domination, it was annexed to Australia in 1958. It has important lime phosphate deposits. Area: 135sq km (52sq mi). Pop. (2001 est.) 2771.

Christophe, Henri (1767–1820) Haitian revolutionary leader, president (1806–11) and king (1811–20). Born a free black on the island of Grenada, he participated in struggle against the French in Haiti and fought a civil war with the partisans of the mulatto Pétion. He ordered the construction of the citadel of La Ferrière, the building of which cost many lives.

chromatic Musical term used in melodic and harmonic analysis to refer to notes which do not occur in the scale of the KEY of a passage. Such notes are marked with accidentals; the chords in which they occur are termed chromatic. A chromatic scale is one containing all 12 notes of an octave rather than the seven notes of a diatonic scale.

chromatography Techniques of chemical analysis by which substances are separated from one another, identified and measured. All involve a **mobile** phase consisting of a liquid or gaseous mixture of the substances to be separated, and a **stationary** phase consisting of a material that differentially absorbs the substances in the mixture. The two major types are gas and paper chromatography. *See also* ELECTROPHORESIS

chromite Black mineral, ferrous chromic oxide ($FeO.Cr_2O_3$), separated from magma in the formation of igneous rock. It is weakly magnetic and opaque. Hardness 5.5; r.d. 4.6.

chromium (symbol Cr) Dull grey metal, one of the TRANSITION ELEMENTS, first isolated in 1797 by the French chemist Louis Vauquelin. Its chief ore is CHROMITE. It is extensively used as an electroplated coating. It is also an ingredient of many special steels, such as stainless steel. Polished chromium plate (chrome) is used to enhance the look of cars. Chromium compounds are used in tanning and dyeing. Properties: at.no. 24; r.a.m. 51.996; r.d. 7.19; m.p. 1890°C (3434°F); b.p. 2672°C (4842°F); most common isotope Cr^{52} (83.76%).

chromosome Structure carrying genetic information, found only in the cell nucleus of EUKARYOTES. Thread-like and composed of DNA, chromosomes carry a specific set of GENES. Each species usually has a characteristic number of chromosomes; these occur in pairs, members of which carry identical genes, so that most cells are DIPLOID (two sets of chromosomes in one cell). Gametes carry a HAPLOID (a single set) number of chromosomes. *See also* HEREDITY

chromosphere Layer of the Sun's atmosphere between the PHOTOSPHERE and the CORONA. It is *c.*10,000km (6000mi) thick and is briefly visible near the beginning and end of a total solar eclipse as a spiky red rim around the Moon's disk. At its base the temperature of the chromosphere is *c.*4000K, rising to 100,000K at the top.

Chronicles Two historical books of the OLD TESTAMENT. They trace the history of Israel and Judah from the Creation to the return of the Jews from exile in Babylon (538BC). *See* BABYLONIAN CAPTIVITY

chrysalis Intermediate or pupal stage in the life cycle of all insects that undergo complete METAMORPHOSIS. The chrysalis is usually covered with a hard case, but some pupae, such as the silk moth, spin a silk cocoon. Within the chrysalis, feeding and locomotion stop and the final stages of the development take place. *See also* LEPIDOPTERA

chrysanthemum Large genus of annual and perennial plants native to temperate Eurasia and now widely cultivated. Centuries of selective breeding have modified the original plain daisy-like flowers, and most species have large white, yellow, bronze, pink or red flower-heads. Family Asteraceae/COMPOSITAE.

Chrysostom, Saint John (*c.*347–407) Doctor of the Church, Patriarch of Constantinople. In 386 he was ordained in Antioch, and his sermons earned him the epithet *Chrysostom* (Gk. golden-mouthed). In 398 he was made Archbishop of Constantinople. His *Homilies* are an invaluable record of religious thought. His feast day is January 27.

chub Freshwater CARP found in flowing waters. It has a large head, wide mouth and is grey-brown. Length: 10–60cm (4–25in). Family Cyprinidae. Chub is also the name of a marine fish of warm seas – oval-shaped with a small mouth and bright colours. Family Kyphosidae.

Chungking (Chongqing, Ch'ung-ch'ing) City on the River YANGTZE, s China. From the 14th century it was part of a unified China. It became a treaty port in 1891, and was the wartime capital of China (1937–45). It is a transport and shipping centre. Industries: chemicals, steel, iron, silk, cotton textiles, plastics. Pop. (2002 est.) 2,311,500.

church Community of believers. Although adopted by non-Christian movements such as SCIENTOLOGY, it is usually used in reference to CHRISTIANITY. The characteristics of the Christian Church as the whole body of Christ's followers are described in the NICENE CREED. The church is also

◄ **Christie** In 1992, Linford Christie became the oldest man ever to win the blue-ribbon race of the Olympic Games, the 100m. He is the only European athlete to run under 10 seconds in the event. Christie defended his title in the finals of the 1996 Olympics, but made three false starts and was automatically disqualified. He retired in 1997, and became coach of an elite group of British athletes.

▼ **chromatography** Gas-liquid chromatographs can separate the components of tiny amounts of an unknown mixture. The chromatograph shown here is a flame ionisation detector. A sample of the mixture (1) is injected (2) into a stream of helium (3), or another inert gas. Heating ensures the vaporized gas mixes fully with the helium. After impurities are removed (4), the gas mixture passes into a tube (5) packed with coated granules of silica (6). A liquid with a very high boiling point (7) covers the 4mm (0.15in) granules. The components of the vaporized mixture have different solubilities (8) and so pass through the liquid around the silicon, and the whole tube, at different speeds. The tube is kept at a high temperature to prevent the vaporized gas condensing. As the now separated parts of the mixture exit the tube (9) they enter a detector (10). Hydrogen (11) and oxygen (12) are added, and the gas stream is burnt (13). During burning, each compound produces ions that pass a charge between an anode (14) and a cathode (15). This charge is measured and can be compared to known results to determine the composition of the initial mixture.

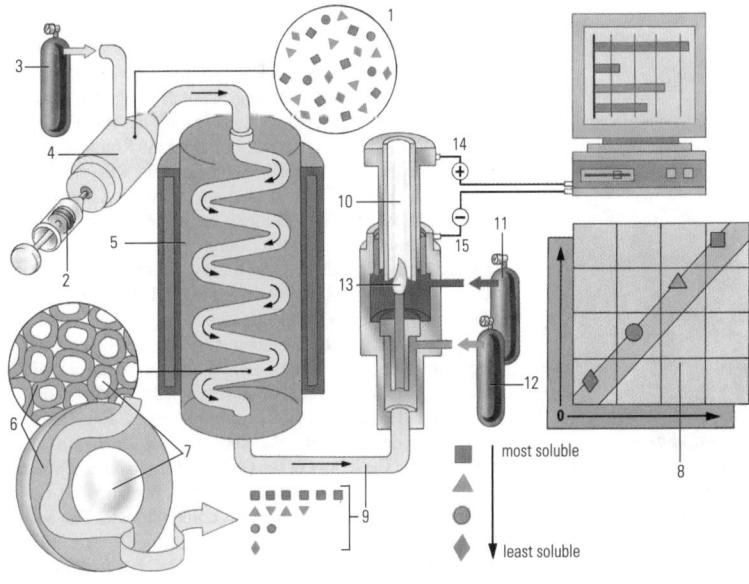

C

► **Churchill** British Prime Minister Winston Churchill was an inspiring leader during World War 2. His charismatic public speeches and broadcasts encouraged a 'bulldog' spirit of resistance to the German forces that had amassed in Europe. Even in the darkest days of the Blitz (1940–41), Churchill remained steadfast in his opposition to fascism and totalitarianism.

the name of the building used for worship by Christians. Churches vary from the stark plainness of some Protestant chapels to the grandeur of the world's major CATHEDRALS.

Churchill, Lord Randolph Henry Spencer (1849–95) British statesman, secretary of state for India (1885–86) and chancellor of the exchequer (1886). A gifted speaker and loyal member of the Tory Party, he nevertheless attempted widespread party reform, in particular encouraging mass participation in the Conservative Associations. His popularity ensured his appointment to government. His first budget as chancellor proposed deep cuts in military expenditure and was defeated. Churchill was forced to resign. He married Jennie Jerome, a US citizen, in 1874. Their son, Winston CHURCHILL, was to achieve the success denied his father.

Churchill, Sir Winston Leonard Spencer (1874–1965) British statesman, prime minister (1940–45, 1951–55). Son of Lord Randolph CHURCHILL, he was a reporter in the SOUTH AFRICAN WARS. Elected to Parliament in 1900 as a Conservative, he crossed the floor to join the Liberals in 1904. As first lord of the admiralty under Herbert ASQUITH, Churchill expanded Britain's navy in preparation for World War 1. In LLOYD GEORGE's cabinet, he served as secretary of state for war (1918–21) and, as colonial secretary (1921–22), he oversaw the creation of the Irish Free State. He returned to power as chancellor of the exchequer (1924–29) in Stanley BALDWIN's Conservative government. Out of office (1929–39), he spoke out against the rising threat of Nazi Germany. On the outbreak of WORLD WAR 2, he once more became first lord of the admiralty. In 1940 he replaced Neville CHAMBERLAIN as prime minister. He proved an inspiring war leader, resolute in his opposition to fascism. Cultivating close relations with President ROOSEVELT, Churchill was the principal architect of the grand alliance of Britain, the USA and Soviet Union (*see* YALTA; POTSDAM), which eventually defeated the Axis Powers. In 1945 Churchill was succeeded by Clement ATTLEE, but he was re-elected in 1950 and reversed some of Labour's nationalizations. He remained a MP until 1964. His extensive writings include a history of World War 2 and the *History of the English-Speaking Peoples* (1956–58). He received the Nobel Prize in literature in 1953.

Church of England Christian Church in England, established by law in the 16th century. During the reign of King HENRY VIII, a process of separation from the Roman Catholic Church began. The initial impetus for this was the pope's refusal to grant Henry a divorce from CATHERINE OF ARAGON. By the Act of Supremacy (1534), the English monarch became head of the Church. Henry wanted to retain the use of the Roman Catholic liturgy, but outside papal control. As the REFORMATION extended to England, the Church of England finally emerged independent of papal jurisdiction and adopted the Elizabethan Settlement. This agreement, while espousing PROTESTANTISM, aimed at preserving religious unity by shaping a national Church acceptable to all persons of moderate theological views. This middle course found expression in the doctrinal formulae known as the *Thirty-nine Articles* (1571). The liturgy of the Church of England is contained in the Book of COMMON PRAYER (1662), but since the 1960s alternative forms of worship have come into use. The sovereign bears the title Supreme Governor of the Church of England, and formally nominates the bishops, but this does not

confer any spiritual powers on the sovereign. The Church is episcopally governed, but priests and laity share in all major decisions by virtue of their representation in the General Synod. Territorially, the Church divides into two provinces, Canterbury and York. The Archbishop of CANTERBURY is the Primate of All England: the Archbishop of YORK the Primate of England. The overseas expansion of the Church of England, in line with the growth of the British Empire, resulted in the development of the worldwide ANGLICAN COMMUNION. The Church of England is the only part of the Anglican Communion still established by law as an official state Church. In 1992, the General Synod voted in favour of the ordination of women as priests. The first women priests were ordained in 1994. The issue of homosexual priests remains divisive.

Church of Ireland Anglican Church in Ireland. It claims to be heir to the ancient Church of the island of Ireland. At the time of the REFORMATION, it ended papal jurisdiction and introduced doctrinal and disciplinary reforms similar to the CHURCH OF ENGLAND. It is territorially divided into two provinces, Armagh and Dublin. The Archbishop of Armagh is Primate of All Ireland. The Church of Ireland was the legally established Church until 1869.

Church of Scotland National non-episcopal form of CHRISTIANITY in Scotland, adopting PRESBYTERIANISM by constitutional act in 1689. The Church arose as a separate entity during the REFORMATION. Under the leadership of John KNOX, it abolished papal authority and accepted many of the teachings of John CALVIN. The doctrinal position of the Church is based on the Scottish Confession (1560) and the Westminster Confession of 1643. The highest authority of the Church of Scotland resides in the General Assembly, presided over by an annually elected moderator. The Disruption of 1843 led to about one-third of its ministers and members leaving to form the FREE CHURCH OF SCOTLAND. The spiritual independence of the Church was recognized by an act of parliament in 1921, although this did not affect its status as the established Church in Scotland. The Church has *c.*850,000 members.

CIA Abbreviation of CENTRAL INTELLIGENCE AGENCY

cicada GRASSHOPPER-like insect found in most parts of the world. Males make a loud sound by the vibration of a pair of plates in their abdomen. Females lay eggs in tree branches. The dog-day cicada appears annually in summer. The larvae of the 17–year locust spends up to 17 years in the ground feeding on roots and lives only a week as a winged adult. Length: up to 5cm (2in).

Cicero, Marcus Tullius (106–43 BC) Roman politician, philospher, and orator. A leader of the Senate, he exposed Catiline's conspiracy (63BC). He criticized Mark ANTONY in the Senate, and when Octavian came to power Antony persuaded him to have Cicero executed. Cicero's fame rests largely on his political philosophy and oratory. Among his greatest speeches were *Orations Against Catiline* and the *Phillipics*. His rhetorical and philosophical works include *De Amicitia* and *De Officiis*.

CID Abbreviation of CRIMINAL INVESTIGATION DEPARTMENT

Cid, El (1043–99) (Rodrigo Díaz de Vivar) Spanish national hero. He was a knight in the service of the king of Castile who spent his whole life fighting against various opponents, principally the Moors. His greatest achievement was the conquest of Valencia (1094) which he ruled until his death, officially for Castile but effectively as an independent kingdom. His exploits have been romanticized in Spanish legend.

cigarette Roll of shredded TOBACCO wrapped in thin paper for inhalation by smoking. Because of tar, nicotine (the addictive substance) and other chemicals in the smoke, cigarettes are CARCINOGENS. However, cigarettes continue to represent a huge industry and source of taxation for governments despite increasing controls, including clear warnings on packets, bans, limits on advertising, and nonsmoking areas in public places.

cilia Small, hair-like filaments on cell walls whose wafting motion is used for propulsion or moving matter along a surface. Cilia are present in great quantities on some lining cells of the body, such as those along the respiratory tract. Cilia are also found on single-celled PROTOZOA known as CILIATES.

C

ciliate One of a large class of PROTOZOAN found in freshwater, characterized by hair-like CILIA used for locomotion and food collecting. Subclasses include the Holotrichs (*Paramecium*); Spirotrichs (*Stentor*); and Peritrichs (*Vorticella*).

Cimabue, Giovanni 13th-century Florentine painter, an important transitional link between the rigid Byzantine style of painting and the greater realism of the 14th-century School of Florence. His best-known work is *Madonna and Child Enthroned*. Cimabue is said to have taught GIOTTO.

Cimarosa, Domenico (1749–1801) Italian composer. He wrote more than 60 operas, his most famous being *Il matrimonio segreto*, which was first performed in Vienna in 1792. He also wrote seven cantatas and six oratorios.

cinchona Genus of evergreen trees native to the Andes and grown in South America, Indonesia and Congo. The dried bark of the trees is a source of QUININE and other medicinal products. Family Rubiaceae.

Cincinnati City on the Ohio River, sw Ohio, USA. Originally named Losantiville, it grew around Fort Washington (established 1789). The completion of the Miami and Erie Canal in 1832 made the city a shipping centre for farm produce. In order to compete with CHICAGO and ST LOUIS, Cincinnati built its own railway (1880). The city has a university (1819) and other colleges. Industries: machine tools, soap products, brewing, meat packing, aircraft engines. Pop. (2000) 1,503,000.

cine camera Apparatus that takes a number of consecutive still photographs or frames, on film. The illusion of motion is created when the developed film is projected on to a screen. Big-screen cine cameras use 70mm cine film, most professional cameras 35mm, and some smaller cameras 16mm. The amateur 8mm standard is largely obsolete, replaced by digital video cameras. Digital equipment is also becoming widespread in professional use.

cinema Motion pictures as an industry and artistic pursuit. For much of its history, cinema has been commercially dominated by HOLLYWOOD. Public showings of silent moving pictures, with live musical accompaniment, began in the 1890s, but speech was not heard in a full-length film until *The Jazz Singer* (1927). By then cinema was big business with mass appeal. In Germany and Russia, startling technical innovations showed the creative possibilities of the medium. The 1930s saw the widespread introduction of colour. The growth of television in the USA during the 1940s profoundly altered film economics; the decline of Hollywood led to the rise of the independent producer and director. In post-war Europe film-makers explored social and psychological themes with often disturbing candour. British cinema flourished in the 1950s and early 1960s, but has suffered since from a lack of finance and resources. The 1990s, with the development of computer-generated images, brought a new dimension to film. *See also* ANIMATION, CINEMA, CINE CAMERA; CINEMATOGRAPHY; CINÉMA VÉRITÉ; DOCUMENTARY

cinematography Technique of taking and projecting cine film, the basis of the CINEMA industry. Based on the experiments and inventions pioneered during the 1880s and 1890s by Thomas EDISON in the United States and the LUMIÈRE brothers in France, cinematography was applied professionally to the taking and showing of films soon after the turn of the century.

cinéma vérité Style of film-making, popular during the 1960s, but first practised by Dziga Vertov in the 1920s. It attempted to record truthful action, employing a documentary-like style, often using 16mm cameras. The style was also used in dramas, particularly by TRUFFAUT and GODARD.

cinnamon Light-brown SPICE made from the dried inner bark of the cinnamon tree. Its delicate aroma and sweet flavour make it a common ingredient in food, and it was once extremely expensive. The tree is a bushy evergreen native to India and BURMA and cultivated in the West Indies and South America. Family Lauraceae; species *Cinnamomum zeylanicum*.

cipher *See* CRYPTOGRAPHY

circadian rhythm Internal 'clock' mechanism found in most organisms. It normally corresponds with the 24–hour day, relating most obviously to waking and sleeping cycles, but is also involved in other cyclic variations, such as body temperature, hormone levels, metabolism and mental performance.

Circe In Greek mythology, seductive but baleful enchantress whose spells could change men into animals. Mistress of the island of Aeaea, she kept Odysseus with her for a year, changing his men into pigs.

circle Plane geometric figure that is the locus of points an equal distance from a fixed point (the centre). This distance is the radius (r). The area of a circle is πr^2 and its perimeter (circumference) is $2\pi r$.

circuit System of electric conductors, appliances or electronic components connected together so they form a continuously conducting path. In modern electronics, circuits are often printed in copper on plastic card (printed circuit). Circuit components are also manufactured on SILICON CHIPS. *See also* CAPACITOR; INTEGRATED CIRCUIT (IC); TRANSISTOR

circulation, atmospheric In climatology, the movement of air in the troposphere, the lowest region of Earth's ATMOSPHERE. The circulation towards the poles due to CONVECTION – hot air rising at the equator – gives rise to large-scale eddies, such as CYCLONES and ANTICYCLONES, low-pressure troughs and high-pressure ridges. The eddies are also caused by the Earth's rotation maintaining E winds towards the Equator and w winds towards the poles due to the CORIOLIS EFFECT. *See also* JET STREAM; OCEANIC CURRENT; TRADE WINDS; WIND

circulatory system Means by which oxygen and nutrients are carried to the body's tissues, and carbon dioxide and other waste products are removed. It consists of BLOOD VESSELS that carry the BLOOD, propelled by the pumping action of the HEART. In humans and other mammals, blood travels to the lungs, where it picks up OXYGEN and loses CARBON DIOXIDE. It then flows to the heart, from where it is pumped out into the AORTA, which branches into smaller arteries, arterioles and CAPILLARIES. Oxygen and other nutrients diffuse out of the blood, and carbon dioxide and other tissue wastes pass into the capillaries, which join to form veins leading back to the heart. Blood then returns to the lungs and the entire cycle is repeated. This is known as a double circulatory system, as the blood is pumped first to the lungs, and then to the rest of the body. In fish and many other animals, there is a single circulatory system, with blood passing through the GILLS and on to the rest of the body without an extra boost from the heart. Both these circulatory systems are closed; the blood remains confined within the blood vessels. Insects and many other invertebrates have an open circulatory system, where the blood flows freely within the body cavity, but passes through a series of open blood vessels and heart(s), whose pumping maintains a directional flow.

circumcision Operation of removing part or the whole of the foreskin of the penis or of removing the clitoris. Male circumcision is ritual in some groups, notably Jews and Muslims, and is said to have sanitary benefits. Female circumcision is intended to reduce sexual pleasure and has no medical benefit.

circumference Distance round the boundary of a plane geometric figure, nearly always applied to a circle, for which it has the value $2\pi r$, where r is the radius.

▲ **cinchona** The medicinal significance of the 40 or so species of the genus *Cinchona* lies in its bark which yields quinine and cinchona. Until relatively recently, quinine was the major drug used in the treatment and prevention of malaria, while cinchona eased coughs. However, with ever increasingly sophisticated ways of synthesizing natural products, cheaper man-made drugs are now available.

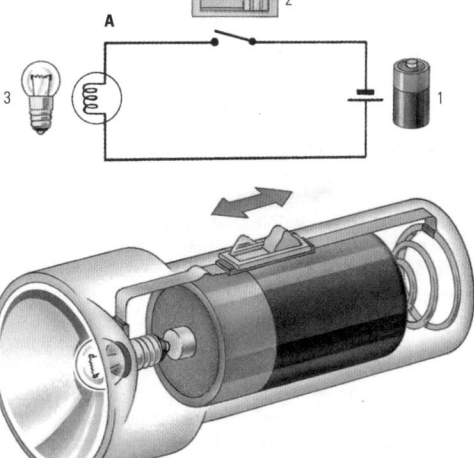

◄ **circuit** This simple electric circuit (A) represents a torch. The power source is a battery (1). The on/off switch (2) breaks the circuit when it is in the off position. When closed, in the on position, electrons flow to the resistor (3), the bulb, which emits light.

C

▶ **citrus** Most fruits belonging to the genus Citrus originated in China and SE Asia. The fruits are commercially important throughout the world, and some hybrids have been created to increase the number of varieties available. The orange (1) is probably the most economically important and popular citrus fruit. It is sweet and contains a great amount of vitamin C. The largest producer is Brazil. The grapefruit (2) is less sweet, and has been crossed with the tangerine to produce the sweet, juicy fruit known as the ugli (3). The lemon (4) is one of the few citrus fruits with a sour taste. The world's largest producer of grapefruits and lemons is the United States.

cire perdue (Fr. 'lost wax') Method of casting metal objects (usually bronzes) used since classical antiquity. First the object is covered in wax then covered in a heat-proof mould. When heated, the wax melts and the metal is poured into the space.

cirque (corrie, cwm) Bowl-shaped, steep-sided hollow in a mountainous region formed by glaciation. A hollow is scoured out of the rock by ice and freeze-thaw activity. When the ice melts, a lake may form at the base of the cirque. Such lakes are often fed by the retreating GLACIER.

cirrhosis Degenerative disease in which there is excessive growth of fibrous tissue in an organ, most often the LIVER, causing inflammation and scarring. Cirrhosis of the liver may be caused by viral hepatitis, prolonged obstruction of the common bile duct, chronic abuse of alcohol or other drugs, blood disorder, heart failure or malnutrition.

Cistercian Order of monks founded (1098) in Citeaux, France, by BENEDICTINE monks led by St Robert of Molesme. St BERNARD OF CLAIRVAUX was largely responsible for the growth of the order in the 12th century. In the 17th century the order split into two communities: Common Observance and Strict Observance, the latter popularly known as TRAPPISTS.

citric acid Colourless, crystalline solid ($C_6H_8O_7$) with a sour taste. It is found in a free form in citrus fruits such as lemons and oranges, and is used for flavouring, in effervescent salts, and as a mordant (colour-fixer) in dyeing. Properties: r.d. 1.54; m.p. 153°C (307.4°F).

citrus Important group of trees and shrubs of the genus *Citrus* in the rue family. They include GRAPEFRUIT, kumquat, LEMON, LIME, ORANGE, tangerine and ugli, and are native to subtropical regions. The stems are usually thorny, the leaves bright green, shiny and pointed. The flowers are usually white, waxy and fragrant. The fruit (hesperidium) is usually ovoid with a thick, aromatic rind. The inside of the fruit is pulpy and juicy and is divided into segments that contain the seeds. Most citrus fruits contain large amounts of vitamin C. Family Rutaceae.

Ciudad Juárez City on the Río Bravo del Norte (Río Grande), Chihuahua state, N Mexico. Lying on the US-Mexico border, it is connected by bridges to El Paso, Texas. It has processing industries for the surrounding cotton-growing region. Pop. (2005) 1,469,000.

civet Small, nocturnal, carnivorous mammal, related to the GENET and MONGOOSE, found in Africa, Asia and S Europe. It has a narrow body set on long legs, and its coat is grey-yellow with black markings. There are c.20 species. Overall length: 53–150cm (21–59in). Family Viverridae.

civil engineering Field of engineering dealing with large structures and systems. Civil engineers provide facilities for living, industry and transportation, such as roads, bridges, airports, dams, harbours and tunnels.

civil law Legal system derived from ROMAN LAW. It is different from COMMON LAW, the system generally adhered to in England and other English-speaking countries. Civil law is based on a system of codes, the most famous of which is the *Code Napoléon* (1804), and decisions are precisely worked out from general basic principles *a priori*. Thus the civil law judge follows the evidence and is bound by the conditions of the written law and not by previous judicial interpretation. Civil law influences common law in jurisprudence and in admiralty, testamentary and domestic relations; it is also the basis for the system of equity. It is prevalent in continental Europe.

civil liberties Rights possessed by citizens intended to protect them from abuse by the state. Examples include the right

to a fair trial, and freedoms of speech and assembly. The extent of civil liberties is widely debated and even the core rights are frequently threatened by government action. Few countries have truly effective mechanisms for defending civil rights; in many, the legal system is intended to ensure freedom from government control or restraint except as the public good may require. In the USA, civil liberties are theoretically guaranteed by a BILL OF RIGHTS. Similar constitutional legislation is being prepared in the UK. *See also* CIVIL RIGHTS

civil list Annual grant voted by Parliament to supply the expenses of the royal establishment in Britain. In 1993, the number of royal family members on the civil list was reduced to the Queen, the Duke of Edinburgh, and the Queen Mother.

civil rights Rights conferred legally upon the individual by the state. There is no universal conception of civil rights. The modern use of the phrase is most common in the USA, where it refers to relations between individuals as well as between individuals and the state. It is especially associated with the movement to achieve equal rights for African-Americans. Although that struggle dates back to the Civil War, the modern civil-rights movement may be said to have begun with the foundation of the NATIONAL ASSOCIATION FOR THE ADVANCEMENT OF COLORED PEOPLE (NAACP) in 1910. It gathered pace after the 1954 Supreme Court decision against segregation in schools (enforced by federal troops in Arkansas in 1957), and the foundation of organizations such as the CONGRESS OF RACIAL EQUALITY (CORE), the Southern Christian Leadership Conference led by Martin Luther KING, Jr, and the Student Non-violent Coordinating Committee (SNCC). Subsequently, a series of CIVIL RIGHTS ACTS protected individuals from discrimination.

Civil Rights Acts (1866, 1870, 1875, 1957, 1960, 1964, 1968, 1991) US legislation. The **Civil Rights Act (1866)** gave African-Americans citizenship and extended civil rights to all persons born in the USA except Native Americans. The **1870 Act** was passed to re-enact the previous measure, which was considered to be of dubious constitutionality. In 1883, the US Supreme Court declared unconstitutional the 1870 law. The **1875 Act** was passed to outlaw discrimination in public places because of race or previous servitude. The act was declared unconstitutional by the Supreme Court (1883–85), which stated that the 14th Amendment, the constitutional basis of the act, protected individual rights against infringement by the states, not by other individuals. The **1957 Act** established the CIVIL RIGHTS COMMISSION to investigate violations of the 15th Amendment. The **1960 Act** enabled court-appointed federal officials to protect black voting rights. An act of violence to obstruct a court order became a federal offence. The **1964 Act** established as law equal rights for all citizens in voting, education, public accommodations and in federally assisted programmes. The **1968 Act** guaranteed equal treatment in housing and real estate to all citizens. The **1991 Act** provided for damages in cases of intentional discrimination in the workplace.

Civil Rights Commission US federal commission that investigates complaints alleging that citizens are being deprived of their right to vote because of their race, colour, religion, sex or national origin, or, in the case of federal elections, by fraudulent practices. It appraises the laws and policies of the federal government and submits reports of its activities, findings and recommendations to the president and Congress.

civil service Administrative establishment for carrying on the work of government. In the UK, the modern service was developed between 1780 and 1870, as the weight of parliamentary business became too heavy for ministers to attend to both policy-making and departmental administration. The Treasury got its first permanent secretary in 1805, the Colonial Office a permanent official in 1825. The two main divisions of the civil service are the Home and Diplomatic services. Since 1968 the civil service has been controlled by the Prime Minister (as minister of the civil service), but day-to-day management is undertaken by the Lord Privy Seal. In 1981 the Secretary to the Cabinet was made Head of the Home Civil Service. In 1996 the Senior Civil Service was created. The UK civil service has grown away from its centre in

Whitehall, London, and now has many regional offices. In 1998, there were c.468,180 permanent civil servants in the UK. In the USA, the civil service evolved from the ineffective 'SPOILS SYSTEM' (1828) established during Andrew JACKSON's presidency, whereby posts were given as rewards for political support. This system remained in place until the Pendleton Act (1883) created the Civil Service Commission. The Commission created a merit system, and following the Hatch Acts (1939, 1940), federal employees can no longer play an active role in party politics.

Civil War, American (1861–65) War fought in the USA between the northern states (the Union) and the forces of the 11 southern states that seceded from the Union to form the CONFEDERATE STATES OF AMERICA (Confederacy). Its immediate cause was the determination of the southern states to withdraw from a Union that the northern states regarded as indivisible. The more general cause was the question of SLAVERY, a well-established institution in the South but one which the northern ABOLITIONISTS opposed. By the 1850s, slavery, abolition and states' rights had created insurmountable divisions between North and South. There was political polarization with the abolitionists forming the new REPUBLICAN PARTY and those campaigning for the rights of southern states remaining in the DEMOCRATIC PARTY. The 1860 election of a Republican, Abraham LINCOLN, virtually assured southern withdrawal from the Union. The Unionists had superior numbers, greater economic power and command of the seas. The Confederates had passionate conviction and superior generals, such as Robert E. LEE and 'Stonewall' JACKSON. The war began on April 12, 1861, when Confederate forces attacked FORT SUMTER, South Carolina. The Union's first objective was to take the Confederate capital at Richmond, Virginia, in the First Battle of BULL RUN (July 1861). This campaign was unsuccessful, and the Confederates continued to be victorious with Lee winning the Peninsular Campaign (April-June 1862) and Jackson carrying off a brilliant campaign in the Shenandoah Valley (March-June 1862). The Confederates were also victorious at the Seven Days' Battles (June-July 1862) and the Second Battle of BULL RUN (August 1862). However, Lee's army was checked by the strengthening Union troops (led by General George McClellan), in the Battle of ANTIETAM (September 1862). The Union was defeated at the Battle of FREDERICKSBURG (December 1862) under Ambrose BURNSIDE, and at Chancellorsville (May 1863) under Joseph Hooker. The Union victory in the Battle of GETTYSBURG (June-July 1863) was a turning point. The Union Navy had blocked southern ports, thereby denying the Confederacy essential trade with Europe. The strategy was to divide the South by taking control of the Mississippi, Tennessee and Cumberland rivers. The first big Union victory was at Fort Donelson on the Tennessee River (February 1862) under the command of Ulysses S. GRANT. Grant won a victory in the siege of VICKSBURG (November 1862–July 1863), which, with the fall of Memphis (June 1862), gave Union troops control of the Mississippi. In 1864 Grant became supreme commander. He confronted Lee's army in the Wilderness Campaign (May-June 1864) and began the long siege of Petersburg, Virginia – the defence of which was vital to the survival of RICHMOND. Meanwhile, the Unionist General SHERMAN cut a devastating swathe across Georgia, burning ATLANTA on the way. The Union victory at the battle of Five Forks blocked the retreat route for Confederate troops in Richmond. Petersburg fell two days later and Richmond was indefensible. The war ended with Lee's surrender to Grant at Appomattox Court House village, Virginia in April 1865. The South was economically ruined by the war, and RECONSTRUCTION policies poisoned relations between North and South for a century.

Civil War, English (1642–45, 1648, 1651) Conflicts between Crown and Parliament. Following years of dispute between the King and State, essentially over the power of the monarchy, war began when the King CHARLES I raised his standard at Nottingham. Royalist forces were at first successful at Edgehill (1642) but despite hard fighting there were no decisive engagements. Parliament's position was stronger, as it controlled the SE (including London) and the navy and managed to form an alliance with Scotland. Parliament's victory at Marston Moor (1644) was a turning point, and in 1645 FAIRFAX and CROMWELL won a decisive victory at Naseby with their NEW MODEL ARMY. The Royalists were driven back to Wales and Cornwall and Charles surrendered to the Scots in 1646. While negotiating with Parliament, he secretly secured an agreement with the Scots that led to the Second Civil War (1648). A few local Royalist risings came to nothing, and the Scots, invading England, were swiftly defeated. The execution of Charles I (1649) provoked further conflict in 1650, in which Scots and Irish Royalists supported the future CHARLES II. Cromwell suppressed the Irish and the Scots, the final battle being fought at Worcester (1651).

Civil War, Spanish (1936–39) Conflict developing from a military rising against the republican government in Spain. The revolt began in Spanish Morocco, led by General FRANCO. It was supported by conservatives and reactionaries, collectively known as the Nationalists and including the fascist FALANGE. The leftist POPULAR FRONT government was supported by republicans, socialists and various poorly co-ordinated leftist groups, collectively known as Loyalists or Republicans. The Nationalists swiftly gained control of most of rural w Spain, but not the main industrial regions. The war, fought with great savagery, became a serious international issue, representing the first major clash between the forces of the extreme right and the extreme left in Europe. Franco received extensive military support, especially aircraft, from the fascist dictators MUSSOLINI and HITLER. The Soviet Union provided more limited aid for the Republicans. Liberal and socialist sympathizers from countries such as Britain and France fought as volunteers for the Republicans, but their governments remained neutral. The Nationalists extended their control in 1937, while the Republicans were increasingly weakened by internal quarrels. In 1938, despite some Republican gains, the Nationalists reached the Mediterranean, splitting the Republican forces. The fall of Madrid, after a long siege, in March 1939 brought the war to an end, with Franco supreme. More than one million Spaniards died in the conflict.

Cixi (1835–1908) (Tz'u Hsi or Zi Xi) Empress Dowager of China. As mistress of the Emperor Xian Feng and mother of his only son, Cixi became co-regent in 1861 and remained in power until her death by arranging for the succession of her infant nephew in 1875, and displacing him in a palace coup in 1898. Ruthless and reactionary, she abandoned the modernization programme of the 'Hundred Days of Reform' and supported the BOXER REBELLION (1900).

clam Bivalve mollusc found mainly in marine waters. It is usually partly buried in sand or mud with the two parts of the shell slightly open for feeding. With a large foot for burrowing,

▼ **Civil War** Loyalties to South or North crossed state lines and divided families during the American Civil War. Three of Abraham Lincoln's brothers-in-law died fighting for the Confederates. The 'border states', the slave states of Kentucky, Maryland and Missouri, were most divided. Their allegiance to the 'Stars and Stripes' proved to be stronger than their purely regional interests. Often seen as the beginning of modern warfare, the Civil War claimed c.620,000 lives (360,000 Union troops, 260,000 Confederate), almost as many as the combined American dead in all other conflicts between 1775 and 1975. It cost billions of dollars and fuelled resentment and hostility towards the Northern states and central government.

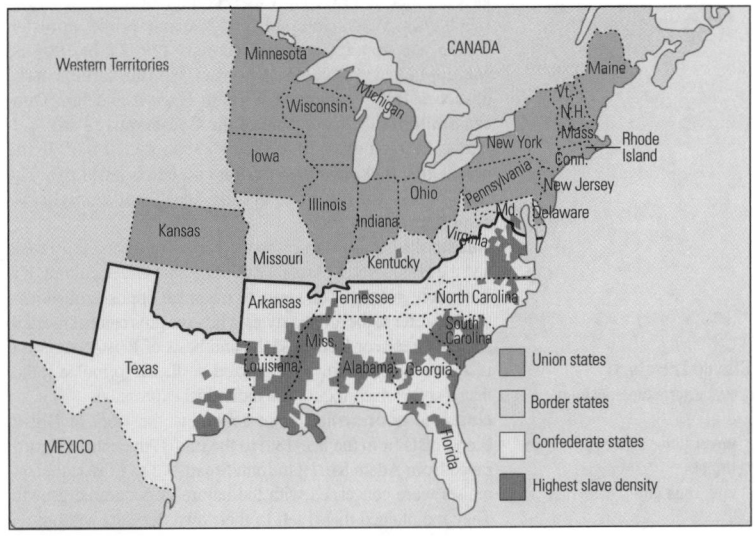

its soft, flat body lies between two muscles for opening and closing the shells. A fleshy part called the mantle, lies next to the shells. Clams feed on PLANKTON. Class Pelecypoda.

Clapham Sect (*c*.1790–*c*.1830) Group of British evangelical reformers. Many of them, including William WILBERFORCE, lived in Clapham, s London, and several were MPs. Originally known as the "Saints", they were especially influential in the abolition of SLAVERY and in prison reform.

Clare County between Galway Bay and the River Shannon estuary, Munster province, w Republic of Ireland. Ennis is the county town. The chief crops are oats and potatoes. Sheep, cattle, pigs and poultry are raised, and fishing is important. Area: 3188sq km (1231sq mi). Pop. (2002) 103,333.

Clare, John (1793–1864) English poet. The son of an agricultural laborer, his verse contained vivid descriptions of the countryside from the viewpoint of a class that seldom found a poetic voice. His works include *Poems Descriptive of Rural Life and Scenery* (1820), *The Village Minstrel* (1821), and *The Rural Muse* (1835). Briefly lionized as a 'peasant' poet, he was declared insane in 1837.

Clarendon, Constitutions of (1164) Sixteen articles issued by HENRY II of England to limit the temporal and judicial powers of the Church. The most controversial article required clergy who had been convicted in church courts to be punished by royal courts. They played a significant role in the dispute between Henry and Thomas à BECKET.

Clarendon, Edward Hyde, 1st Earl of (1609–74) English statesman and historian. A leading adviser to Charles I, he joined CHARLES II in exile, and negotiated the RESTORATION (1660). As chief minister to Charles II, he initiated (but disapproved of) four statutes collectively known as the Clarendon Code. The statutes restricted gatherings of PURITANS and Nonconformists, and the movement of their ministers. In addition, municipal and church officers were required to be professed Anglicans, and all ministers were forced to use the Anglican Book of COMMON PRAYER. Following disagreements with Charles II he was impeached and forced into exile in 1667, where he completed his *History of the Rebellion* and wrote an autobiography. *See also* NONCONFORMISM

clarinet Single-reed WOODWIND instrument. It is commonly pitched in B flat (also A) and has a range of more than three octaves. Other members of the family include the alto clarinet in E flat, the bass in B flat and the high sopranino in E flat.

Clarke, Sir Arthur C. (Charles) (1917–2007) English science fiction writer. He is noted for the scientific realism of his works, such as *Childhood's End* (1953), *A Fall of Moondust* (1961) and *Voices from the Sky* (1965). Stanley Kubrick's film *2001: A Space Odyssey* (1969) was based on his short story *The Sentinel* (1951). Clarke has since written two sequels – *2010: Odyssey Two* (1982) and *2061: Odyssey Three* (1987).

Clarke, Kenneth Harry (1940–) British statesman, chancellor of the exchequer (1993–97). Clarke became a Conservative MP in 1970, and joined Margaret THATCHER's cabinet in 1985. He was secretary of state for health (1988–90). When John MAJOR became prime minister, Clarke was appointed home secretary (1992). In 1993 he was appointed chancellor. An outspoken Europhile, Clarke unsuccessfully challenged William HAGUE and Iain Duncan Smith for the leadership of the Conservative Party.

class In biology, part of the CLASSIFICATION of living organisms, ranking above ORDER and below PHYLUM. The class names for plants all end in 'idae', but animal class names are more varied.

classical Literally, it refers to the period between the Archaic and the HELLENISTIC AGE phases of ancient Greek culture. It is used more generally, however, to mean the opposite of romantic or to refer to the artistic styles whose origins can be traced in ancient Greece or Rome. As the antithesis of ROMANTICISM, it is an art which follows recognized aesthetic formulae rather than a style which focuses on individual expression.

classical economics Term applied to the work of British economists from the late-18th to the mid-19th century, figures range from Adam SMITH to John Stuart MILL. Classical economists were concerned with the nature of economic growth. They maintained that if left to their own devices, without the interference of government, markets would find a natural equilibrium. *See also* CAPITALISM; MALTHUS, THOMAS

classical music Music composed between *c*.1750 and 1820, whose style is characterized by emotional restraint, the dominance of homophonic melodies (melodies with accompaniment), and clear structures and forms underlying the music. The classical period saw the development of forms such as concerto, sonata, symphony and string quartet, and the piano replace the harpsichord as the most popular keyboard instrument. The greatest classical composers of this period were HAYDN, MOZART, BEETHOVEN, and SCHUBERT.

classical revival Art and architecture in the style of the Ancient Greeks and Romans. The style reflects simplicity, harmony and balance. The Italian RENAISSANCE and the neo-classical style of the early 19th century are examples of classical revivals. *See also* CLASSICISM; NEO-CLASSICISM

classicism Art history term used to describe both an aesthetic attitude and an artistic tradition. The artistic tradition refers to the classical antiquity of Greece and Rome, its art, literature and criticism, and the subsequent periods that looked back to Greece and Rome for their prototypes, such as the CAROLINGIAN RENAISSANCE, RENAISSANCE, and NEO-CLASSICISM. Its aesthetic use suggests the classical characteristics of clarity, order, balance, unity, symmetry, and dignity.

classification Organization of organisms into categories based on appearance, structure, genetic sequence or evolution. The categories, from the most inclusive to the most exclusive are KINGDOM, PHYLUM, CLASS, ORDER, family, GENUS, SPECIES, and sometimes variety. For example, the domestic dog is classified as kingdom Animalia, phylum Chordata, class Mammalia, order Carnivora, family Canidae, genus *Canis,* species *Canis familiaris*.

Claude Lorrain (*c*.1604–82) (Claude Gellée) French landscape painter, the most influential ideal landscapist. After settling in Rome (1627), he developed a style that combined poetic idealism inspired by antique models and his own observations. His mature style evolved between 1640 and 1660, when he explored the natural play of light on different textures. TURNER was among those to absorb his ideas, and he inspired the style known as picturesque.

Claudius I (10 BC–AD 54) (Tiberius Claudius Nero Germanicus) Roman Emperor (AD 41–54), nephew of TIBERIUS. As successor to CALIGULA, he was the first emperor chosen by the army. He had military successes in Germany, conquered Britain in AD 43, and built both the harbour of Ostia and the Claudian aqueduct. Agrippina the Younger (his fourth wife) supposedly poisoned him and made her son, NERO, emperor.

Clausius, Rudolf Julius Emanuel (1822–88) German physicist, regarded as the founder of THERMODYNAMICS. Using the work of Sadi CARNOT, Clausius formulated the second law of thermodynamics that heat cannot pass from a colder to a hotter object. He also introduced the term ENTROPY.

clavichord Earliest stringed musical instrument with mechanical action controlled by a keyboard. Possibly originating in the 13th century, it was used extensively from the 16th to 18th centuries. The clavichord has a delicate, expressive tone; it was superseded by the HARPSICHORD and then by the PIANO.

clavicle (collarbone) Thin, slightly curved bone attached by ligaments to the top of the STERNUM (breast-bone). The clavicle and SHOULDER-blade make up the shoulder girdle, linking the arms to the axis of the body.

clay Group of hydrous silicates of aluminium and magnesium, including kaolinite and halloysite, usually mixed with some quartz, calcite or gypsum. It is formed by the weathering of surface granite or the chemical decomposition of feldspar. Soft when wet, it hardens on firing and is used to make ceramics. It is also used for bricks and cement, as well as the manufacture of electrical insulators, pipes and paper.

Clay, Cassius Marcellus Former name of Muhammad ALI

Clay, Henry (1777–1852) US statesman He served in both the House of Representatives (1811–14, 1815–21, 1823–25), several times as speaker, and in the Senate (1831–42, 1849–52). He was one of the 'war hawks' who favoured the WAR OF 1812. He ran for president (1824), and when the election went to the House of Representatives, he threw his support behind the eventual winner, John Quincy ADAMS. One of the founders of the WHIGS, he ran against Andrew JACKSON (a bitter political enemy) in 1832. He ran for president again (1844) but was defeated by James POLK. Clay's last years in the Senate were spent trying to work out a compromise between the slave-owning states of the South and the free Northern states. The COMPROMISE OF 1850 was one result of those efforts.

cleavage In embryology, progressive series of cell divisions that transform a fertilized egg into the earliest embryonic stage (BLASTULA). The egg is divided into blastomeres (smaller cells), each containing a DIPLOID number of chromosomes.

cleft palate Congenital deformity in which there is an opening in the roof of the mouth, causing direct communication between the nasal and mouth cavities. It is often associated with HARELIP and makes normal speech difficult. Usual treatment includes surgical correction, followed by special dental care and speech therapy if necessary.

clematis Genus of perennial, mostly climbing shrubs found worldwide. Many have attractive deep blue, violet, white, pink or red flowers or flower clusters. The leaves are usually compound. Family Ranunculaceae.

Clemenceau, Georges (1841–1929) French statesman. A moderate republican, he served in the Chamber of Deputies (1876–1893), attempted compromise during the revolt of the PARIS COMMUNE (1871) and strongly supported Dreyfus. He returned to the Senate in 1902 and was twice premier (1906–09, 1917–20). He led the French delegation at the VERSAILLES Peace Conference. *See also* DREYFUS AFFAIR

Clement VII (1478–1534) Pope (1523–34), b. Giulio de Medici. He sided with Francis I in the League of Cognac, thus opposing the Holy Roman Emperor CHARLES V. The imperial troops attacked Rome, and a compromise was won. His indecisiveness over the divorce of Catherine of Aragon and Henry VIII is thought to have hastened the REFORMATION.

Clement I, Saint (active late 1st century AD) (Clement of Rome) Pope (c.88–97). His epistle to the Church at Corinth (c.96) stated the need for unity within the Church. He was executed for refusing to pledge allegiance to the Roman emperor. His feast day is November 23.

Cleopatra (69–30 BC) Queen of Egypt (51–30BC). In 48 BC she overthrew her husband, brother and co-ruler Ptolemy XIII with the aid of Julius CAESAR, who became her lover. She went to Rome with Caesar, but after his assassination in 44 BC she returned to Alexandria. Mark ANTONY followed her to Egypt, and they married (37BC). The marriage infuriated Octavian

(later AUGUSTUS), the brother of Mark Antony's former wife. Rome declared war on Egypt in 31 BC and defeated Antony and Cleopatra's forces at the Battle of ACTIUM. Mark Antony committed suicide, and Cleopatra surrendered to Octavian but failed to win his affections and she too killed herself.

clergy Collective organization of ordained or consecrated priests and ministers, especially of the Christian Church. In the Roman Catholic, Orthodox, and Anglican Churches, the clergy comprise the orders of bishop, priest and deacon, and may also include members of religious orders. In these churches, bishops exercise authority over priests and deacons. In non-episcopal Protestant Churches, the clergy consist of pastors and ministers. Functions of the clergy include administration of the sacrament, preaching and the exercise of spiritual guidance. *See also* ORDINATION

Cleveland City and port at the mouth of the Cuyahoga River, on Lake Erie, NE Ohio, USA. Founded in 1796 by Moses Cleaveland, it grew rapidly with the opening of the Ohio and Erie Canal and the arrival of the railway in 1851. John D. Rockefeller founded Standard Oil Company here in 1870. Cleveland has a symphony orchestra, three universities, and an art institute. It is a major Great Lakes shipping port, and an important iron and steel centre. NASA maintains a research centre here. Industries: chemicals, oil refining, engineering, electronics. Pop. (2000) 1,787,000.

Cleveland, (Stephen) Grover (1837–1908) 22nd and 24th US president (1885–89, 1893–97). Cleveland rose to prominence as a reforming Democratic mayor of Buffalo (1881–82) and governor of New York (1883–84). With the help of Republican "mugwumps", he defeated James G. BLAINE to become the first Democratic president since the Civil War. His attempt to reduce the tariff contributed to Benjamin HARRISON's electoral victory in 1888. In his second term, Cleveland faced a monetary crisis (1893), and was forced to send troops to crush the Pullman Strike (1894) called by Eugene V. DEBS. His attempt to maintain the gold standard angered radical Democrats and tariff reform proposals were shelved.

click language Any of several s African languages belonging chiefly to the Khoisan group and characterized by the use of suction speech sounds called clicks. Several clicks can be distinguished, each being a distinct consonant. Clicks are also found in some Bantu languages.

cliff dwellers *See* PUEBLO

climate Weather conditions of a place or region prevailing over a long time. The major factors influencing climate are

▼ **climate** This map of the Eastern and Western Hemispheres shows the world's various major climatic regions. Latitude is a major factor in determining the amount of solar radiation, with the greatest in equatorial regions and the least in polar regions.

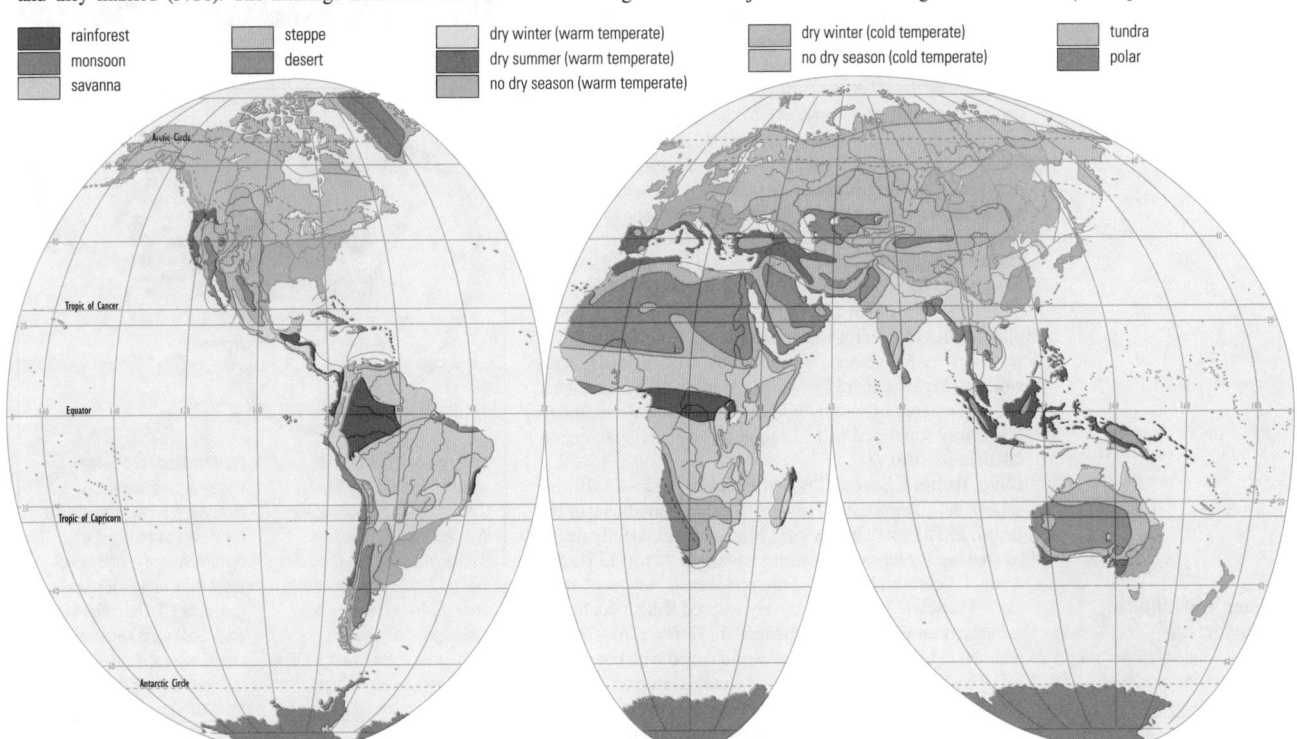

temperatures, air movements, incoming and outgoing radiation and moisture movements. Climates are defined on different scales, ranging from macroclimates, which cover the broad climatic zones of the globe, down to microclimates, which refer to the conditions in a small area, such as a wood or a field. World-wide climate change, and in particular GLOBAL WARMING, is an increasingly important issue.

climatology Scientific study of Earth's CLIMATES. Physical climatology investigates relationships between temperature, pressure, winds, precipitation, and other weather phenomena. Regional climatology considers latitude and other geographical factors in the climatic study of a particular place or region.

Clinton, Bill (William Jefferson) (1946–) 42nd US president (1993–2001). Clinton became the youngest-ever US governor when he was elected to represent Arkansas (1978–80, 1983–92). Economic recession and Clinton's centrist agenda led to an easy electoral victory (1992) over the incumbent president, George BUSH. As president, Clinton made health-care an immediate priority, appointing his wife, Hillary CLINTON, to head a commission on reform. Clinton was a leading advocate of the NORTH AMERICAN FREE TRADE AGREEMENT (NAFTA), which won congressional approval in 1993. His first term was dogged by the Whitewater investigation and the blocking of reforms and appointments by a Republican-dominated Congress. Despite allegations of financial and personal impropriety, a buoyant domestic economy and Bob DOLE's lacklustre campaign enabled Clinton to become the first Democratic president since Franklin D. ROOSEVELT to serve successive terms in office. The priorities for his second term were education and welfare reforms, and the expansion of NATO. His second term was dogged by sexual scandal. Following the investigations of special prosecutor Kenneth Starr, Clinton was forced to admit that he had an improper relationship with Monica Lewinsky, a White House intern. In 1998, facing charges of perjury over the affair, he became only the second US president (after Andrew JOHNSON) to be impeached. Clinton refused to resign and launched Operation Desert Fox (December 1998), a concerted bombing campaign against Iraq for failing to comply with UN resolutions. In 1999, the Senate cleared him of impeachment charges. George W. BUSH, son of his predecessor in office, succeeded him as president.

Clinton, Hillary Rodham (1947–) US Senator (2000–) from New York, attorney and first lady (1993–2001), wife of 42nd US President Bill CLINTON. In 1993, she drafted a plan to provide health insurance for all Americans, but it was not implemented. Clinton involved herself with women's rights around the world. Along with her husband, she was cleared of wrongdoing in the Whitewater scandal. She firmly supported Bill Clinton during his impeachment.

clitoris *See* VULVA

Clive, Robert, Baron Clive of Plassey (1725–74) British soldier and administrator. He went to India as an official of the British EAST INDIA COMPANY (1743), and successfully resisted growing French power with his capture of Arcot (1751). By taking Calcutta and defeating the pro-French Nawab of Bengal at Plassey (1757) he effectively assured British control of N India. He was governor of Bengal (1757–60, 1765–67). He returned to England in 1773, and was charged with but acquitted of embezzling state funds. He committed suicide.

cloaca Cavity into which intestinal, urinary, and genital tracts open in fish, reptiles, birds and some primitive mammals.

clock Instrument for measuring time. The earliest timekeeping instruments had no moving parts, being designed to measure the movements of the Sun, Moon and stars. Examples include neolithic stone columns, and ancient Egyptian sundials and water clocks. Candle clocks and sandglasses were later types of non-mechanical clocks. The central feature of all mechanical clocks is an **escapement** mechanism, which enables a clock to tick off time at discrete intervals. This movement is transmitted through a series of gears to the hands, which are pushed forward a small distance with every escapement movement. Motive power for mechanical clocks has been provided variously by falling weights, pendulums and coiled springs. Other modern clocks include those using an electrically oscillated quartz crystal as the basis of time-division. Even more accurate are ATOMIC CLOCKS, which rely upon the natural oscillations of atoms (usually those of the metal, caesium) and which measure time to an accuracy of thousandths of a second per year.

cloisonné Enamelling technique in which the design is constructed out of wires soldered to a plate, and the cells (*cloisons*) thus formed are filled with coloured ENAMEL paste and fired. The technique was developed in Mycenaean Greece, and was popular in Byzantine art of the 10th and 11th centuries. It flourished in China during the Ming and Qing dynasties and was also adopted in Japan.

clone Set of organisms obtained from a single original parent either by ASEXUAL REPRODUCTION or by ARTIFICIAL SELECTION. Clones are genetically identical and may arise naturally from PARTHENOGENESIS in animals. Cloning is often used in plant propagation (including TISSUE CULTURE) to produce new plants from parents with desirable qualities such as high yield. In 1997 scientists in Scotland produced a sheep embryo from a single cell of an adult sheep using nuclear-transfer technology (transfer of a cell NUCLEUS). Since then, cloning experiments have been carried out with many other species. *See also* GENETIC ENGINEERING

cloud Masses of water particles or ice crystals suspended in the lower atmosphere. Clouds are formed when water from the Earth's surface becomes vapour through EVAPORATION. As the water vapour rises, it cools and condenses around microscopic salt and dust particles, forming droplets. There are ten different classifications of clouds: **cirrus** are high (above 6000m/20,000ft), white and thread-like. **Cirrocumulus** are also high clouds, but are often thin sheets. **Cirrostratus** are white, almost transparent, sheets.

CLOCK

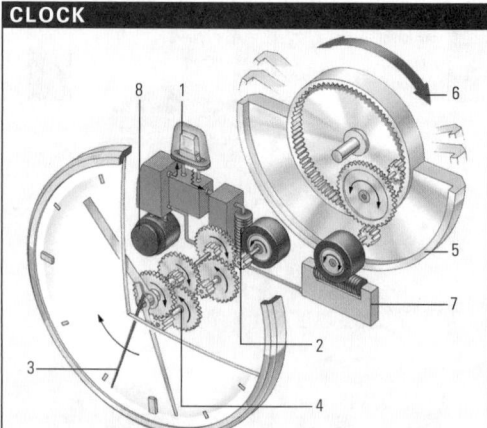

Many modern clocks and watches use a quartz crystal (1) to tell the time accurately. When electricity is passed through the quartz, it oscillates exactly 32,768 times each second. The oscillations are counted and on every 32,768th, a pulse of electricity is sent to a motor (2) that moves the hands (3) via gears (4). The need for a battery to power the motor can be removed if a swinging weight (5) is used to generate a current. As the watch moves the weight rotates (6) turning a generator (7). The current produced by the generator is stored in a capacitor (8) and is smoothed before reaching the quartz crystal.

Altocumulus are greyish-white globular clouds found between 2400m (8000ft) and 6000m (20,000ft). **Altostratus** are grey/blue and streaky, and often cover the whole sky. **Nimbostratus** are low, thick and dark, and shed rain or snow. **Stratocumulus** are masses of white, grey or dark cloud. **Stratus** are low-lying and grey. **Cumulus** are white and fluffy-looking. **Cumulonimbus** are towering, dark clouds that often produce thunderstorms. Their bases almost touch the ground and extend upward to 23,000m (75,000ft). By day, clouds reflect the rays of the Sun back into the atmosphere, keeping the ground cool. At night, clouds trap and re-radiate heat rising from the Earth, keeping surface temperatures warm. *See also* FOG; HYDROLOGICAL CYCLE

cloud chamber Instrument used to detect and identify charged particles, invented in the 1880s by C.T.R. WILSON to study atomic radiation. The principle is the same as the BUBBLE CHAMBER, except liquefied gas is replaced by air supersaturated with water or alcohol vapour. This is cooled quickly to create droplets whose tracks form around the ionizing particle. The tracks are deflected by a magnetic field and photographed for analysis. In a diffusion cloud chamber, a large temperature difference is maintained between the top and bottom.

clove Tall, aromatic, evergreen tree native to the Moluccan Islands. The small purple flowers appear in clusters; the dried flower buds are widely used in cookery. Height: to 12m (40ft). Family Myrtaceae; species *Syzygium aromaticum*.

clover Low-growing annual, biennial, and perennial plants, native to temperate Europe, but now found throughout warmer regions of the N Hemisphere. The leaves have three leaflets, rarely four, and the dense flower clusters are white, red, purple, pink or yellow. Some species are grown for cattle, others by beekeepers as a source of nectar. Most species are good nitrogen-fixers, due to bacteria in their ROOT NODULES, which help to enrich soil. Family Fabaceae/Leguminosae; genus *Trifolium*. *See also* NITROGEN CYCLE; NITROGEN FIXATION

Clovis I (465–511) Frankish king of the MEROVINGIAN dynasty. He overthrew the Romanized kingdom of Soissons and conquered the Alemmani near Cologne. He and his army later converted to Christianity in fulfilment of a promise made before the battle. In 507 he defeated the Visigoths under Alaric II near POITIERS. By the time Clovis died, he controlled most of GAUL and had firmly established Merovingian power.

club moss Any of about 200 species of small evergreen spore-bearing plants which, unlike the more primitive true MOSSES, have specialized tissues for transporting water, food and minerals. They are related to FERNS and HORSETAILS. The small leaves are arranged in tight whorls around the aerial stems. Millions of years ago their ancestors formed the large trees that dominated CARBONIFEROUS coal forests. Phylum LYCOPODOPHYTA, Family Lycopodiaceae.

cluster, stellar *See* GLOBULAR CLUSTER; OPEN CLUSTER

clutch Device placed between the rotating parts of an engine or motor and the drive-shaft to facilitate their connection or disconnection. In a car, temporary disengagement of the engine is essential during gear-changes. The clutch usually consists of a pair of friction plates, although there are fluid clutches as well.

Clwyd County in N Wales, bordered by the Irish Sea, Cheshire, Shropshire, Powys and Gwynedd. The county town is Mold. The Vale of Clwyd is a rich agricultural region. Industries: iron and steel, tourism, chemicals, quarrying. Area: 2426sq km (937sq mi). Pop. (1991) 408,090.

Clyde River in SW Scotland. It rises in the Southern Uplands, passing over the Falls of Clyde (which provide hydroelectric power) near Lanark and widening into the Firth of Clyde at Dumbarton. Clydebank, below GLASGOW, was Scotland's main shipbuilding region. Length: 170km (106mi).

Clytemnestra In Greek legend, the unfaithful wife of AGAMEMNON, King of Mycenae, and mother of his son ORESTES. On Agamemnon's return from TROY he was murdered by Clytemnestra and her lover Aegisthus.

CND Abbreviation of CAMPAIGN FOR NUCLEAR DISARMAMENT

cnidarian (coelenterate) Any one of the 9,000 species of marine invertebrates of the phylum Cnidaria. The phylum includes JELLYFISH, SEA ANEMONE and CORAL. Characterized by a digestive cavity that forms the main body, they may

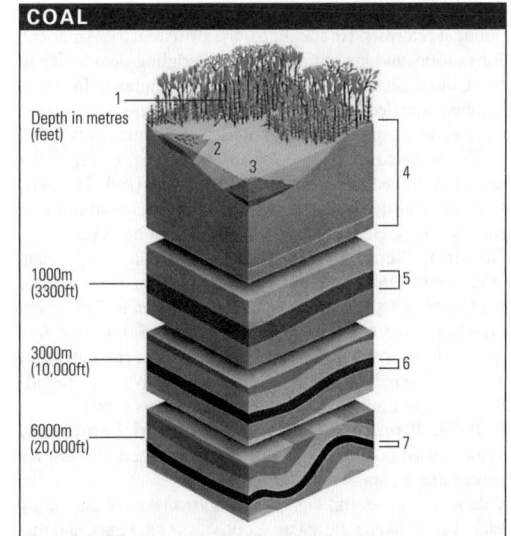

COAL

1 — Depth in metres (feet)

1000m (3300ft) — 5
3000m (10,000ft) — 6
6000m (20,000ft) — 7

The process of making coal begins with plant debris (1). Dead vegetation lies in a swampy environment and forms peat (4), the first stage of coal formation. Underwater bacteria remove some oxygen, nitrogen and hydrogen from the organic material. Debris carried elsewhere and deposited by water forms a product called cannel coal (2). Algal material collected underwater forms boghead coal (3). If the dead organic material is buried by sediment, the weight on top of the peat and the higher temperature will turn the peat into lignite (5). With more heat and pressure at increasing depths, lignite becomes bituminous coal (6) and then anthracite (7).

have been the first animal group to reach the tissue level of organization. Cnidarians are radially symmetrical, jelly-like and have a nerve net and one body opening. Reproduction is sexual and asexual; REGENERATION also occurs.

coal Blackish, solid fuel formed from the remains of fossil plants. In the carboniferous and tertiary periods, swamp vegetation subsided to form PEAT bogs. Sedimentary deposits buried the bogs, and the resultant increase in pressure and heat produced lignite (brown coal), then bituminous coal and finally ANTHRACITE if temperature increased sufficiently. This is termed the coal rank series; each rank of coal represents an increase in carbon content and a reduction in the proportion of natural gas and moisture. Lignite is a poorer fuel than anthracite.

coal tar By-product from the manufacture of coke. Coal tar comes from bituminous coal used in the distillation process. It is a volatile substance, important for its organic chemical constituents (coal-tar crudes), which are extracted by further distillation. These include xylene, toluene, naphthalene and phenanthrene, and are the basic ingredients for the synthesis of many products, such as explosives, drugs, dyes and perfumes.

coati (coatimundi) Three species of raccoon-like rodents of the SW USA and South America. Most have long, slender reddish-brown to black bodies with tapering snouts and long ringed tails. Length: 67cm (26in); weight: 11.3kg (25lb). Family Procyonidae; genus *Nasua*.

coaxial cable Communications CABLE consisting of a central conductor with surrounding insulator and tubular shield. They are used to transmit high-frequency signals. Most domestic television aerials use coaxial cables.

cobalt (symbol Co) Metallic element, a transition metal, discovered *c.*1735. It is found in cobaltite and smaltite, but mostly obtained as a by-product during the processing of other ores. Cobalt is a constituent of vitamin B^{12}. It is used in high-temperature steel, artists' colours (cobalt blue), jet engine manufacture, cutting tools and magnets. Cobalt-60 (half-life 5.26yr) is an artificial isotope used as a source of gamma rays in radiotherapy and tracer studies. Properties: at.no. 27; r.a.m. 58.9332; r.d. 8.9; m.p. 1495°C (2723°F); b.p. 2870°C (5198°F); most common isotope Co^{59} (100%).

▲ **coca** Native to regions of South America, the leaves of the coca tree (*Erythroxylon coca*) have been used for centuries as medicine and to relieve hunger. The leaves are harvested and used in the illegal manufacture of cocaine.

▲ **cockle** Bivalves, such as the cockle (*Cardium* sp.), have calcareous shells, the two halves of which are hinged, and can be closed by muscular action.

▲ **coconut palm** Their ability to survive in sandy, salty soil makes the coconut palm (*Cocus nucifera*) a common sight close to beaches. The nut is found within an outer skin and thick fibrous layer or husk. A hard shell covers the edible white 'meat'.

Cobbett, William (1763–1835) English journalist and political reformer. He fought for the British in the American Revolution, and his criticism of the fledgling democracy in the United States forced his return to England. In 1802, Cobbett founded the weekly newspaper *Political Register*. He was an outspoken critic of abuses of political power and was imprisoned (1810–12) for his attack on flogging in the army and forced into exile (1817–19) in the USA. His masterpiece, *Rural Rides* (1830), describes the conditions of rural workers. He was elected to Parliament in 1832.

Cobden, Richard (1804–65) British Radical politician. With John BRIGHT, he led the campaign for the repeal of the CORN LAWS and was the chief spokesman in Parliament (1841–57, 1859–65) for the 'Manchester School' of free trade. He opposed Britain's participation in the CRIMEAN WAR, supported the Union in the US Civil War and negotiated a major trading agreement with France (1860).

COBOL (Common Business-Oriented Language) Widely used COMPUTER LANGUAGE developed in 1959 for processing business data.

cobra Any of several highly poisonous snakes in the family Elapidae, including the MAMBA, CORAL SNAKE, kraits, and true cobras. It can expand its neck ribs to form a characteristic hood. Found primarily in Africa and Asia, they feed on snakes, rats, toads, and small birds. The king cobra (*Ophiophagus hannah*) reaches 5.5m (18ft) in length, and is the largest venomous snake in the world. The Indian cobra (*Naja naja*) has spectacle-like markings on its hood. Some African species have forward-facing fangs and can spit venom into a victim's eyes from more than 2m (7ft), causing temporary or permanent blindness.

coca Shrub native to Colombia and Peru which contains the drug COCAINE. Native Americans chew the leaves for pleasure and to relieve hunger or tiredness. The plant has yellow-white flowers growing in clusters, and red berries. Height: *c*.2.4m (8ft). Family Erythroxylaceae; species *Erythroxylon coca*.

cocaine White, crystalline ALKALOID extracted from the leaves of the COCA plant. Once used as a local anaesthetic and an early ingredient in Coca-Cola, it is now primarily an illegal narcotic, with stimulant and hallucinatory effects. It is psychologically habit-forming, and the body does not develop tolerance. Habitual use of cocaine results in physical and nervous deterioration, and subsequent withdrawal results in severe depression. The drug CRACK is a cocaine derivative.

coccus Small spherical or spheroid bacterium. Average diameter: 0.5–1.25 micrometres. Some, such as *Streptococcus* and *Staphylococcus*, are common causes of infection.

cochineal Crimson dye produced from the pulverized dried bodies of certain female scale insects, found in Central America. The dye is still used in cosmetics and foodstuffs, although now often replaced by aniline dyes.

Cochise (1815–1874) Chief of the Chiricahua APACHE. In 1861, the US Army falsely imprisoned him, killing five of his relatives. He escaped to lead an 11–year war against the US Army in Arizona. A war of extermination was waged against his people. Cochise concluded a treaty that created a tribal reservation where he lived peacefully until his death, after which the treaty was broken and his people forcibly moved.

cochlea Fluid-filled structure in the inner EAR. It has a shape like a coiled shell, and is lined with hair cells which move in response to incoming sound waves, stimulating nerve cells to transmit impulses to the BRAIN. Different groups of hair cells are stimulated by different pitches of sound.

cockatoo Large PARROT with a long, erectile crest. Cockatoos live mainly in Australia and sw Asia. Most are predominantly white, tinged with pink or yellow. They feed on fruit and seeds. Females lay 1–4 white eggs in a tree hole nest. Length: 38cm (15in). Family Psittacidae.

cockchafer (maybug, June beetle) Any of various large, SCARAB BEETLES whose white grubs feed on the roots of trees and crops. One of the most destructive pests facing farmers, they emerge as adults in the spring. Family Scarabaeidae.

Cockcroft, Sir John Douglas (1897–1967) English physicist who, with Ernest WALTON, first split the ATOM. He and Walton constructed a particle ACCELERATOR, and created the first man-made nuclear reaction by bombarding lithium atoms

▲ **cockroach** The *Blaberus giganticus* species of cockroach is found in central America. Its wingspan measures 8cm (3in).

with protons (1932). They shared the 1951 Nobel Prize in physics for using particle accelerators to study atomic nuclei.

cockle Bivalve mollusc found in marine waters. Its varicoloured, heart-shaped shell has 20–24 strong, radiating ribs. There are *c*.200 recognized species, many of which are edible. Average length: 4–8cm (1.5–3in). Class Bivalvia; family Cardiidae; species include *Cardium aculeatum*.

cockroach (roach) Member of a group of insects with long antennae and a flat, soft body found worldwide, but mostly in the tropics. Its head is hidden under a shield (pronotum) and it may be winged or wingless. Eggs are laid in considerable numbers in special egg cases. Some species are serious household pests. Length: 13–50mm (0.5–2in). Family Blattidae.

cocoa Drink obtained from the seeds of the tropical American evergreen tree *Theobroma cacao*. The seeds are crushed and some fatty substances are removed to produce cocoa powder. Cocoa is the basic ingredient of CHOCOLATE. The Ivory Coast is the world's largest producer. Family Sterculiaceae.

coconut palm Tall palm tree native to the shores of the Indo-Pacific region and the Pacific coast of South America; commercially the most important of all palms. Growing to 30m (100ft) tall, it has a leaning trunk and a crown of feather-shaped leaves. Copra, the dried kernel of the coconut fruit, is valuable as a source of oil used in foods and soap. The fibrous husk is used for matting as well as a peat substitute (coir) in composts. Family Arecacae/Palmae; species *Cocos nucifera*.

cocoon Case or wrapping produced by larval forms of animals (such as some MOTHS, BUTTERFLIES, and WASPS) for the resting or pupal stage in their life cycle. Some spiders spin a cocoon that protects their eggs. Most cocoons are made of SILK, and those of the domestic silkworm provide most of the world's commercial silk. *See also* CHRYSALIS; PUPA

Cocteau, Jean (1889–1963) French writer and film-maker, an experimental leader of the French avant-garde. He was associated with many leading artistic figures of the 1920s, such as APOLLINAIRE, PICASSO, DIAGHILEV, and STRAVINSKY. His many successful works of surrealist fantasy include the novel *Les enfants terribles* (1929; filmed 1950); the plays *Orphée* (1926; filmed 1950) and *La Machine Infernale* (1934); and the films *Le sang d'un poète* (1930) and *La belle et la bête* (1946).

cod Bottom-dwelling, marine fish found in cold to temperate waters of the Northern Hemisphere. It is grey, green, brown or red with darker speckled markings. Cod is one of the chief food fishes. Length: up to 1.8m (6ft). Family Gadidae.

codeine White, crystalline ALKALOID extracted from OPIUM by the methylation of MORPHINE, with the properties of weak

▲ **cod** The characteristic configuration of the fins – three dorsal fins, two anal fins – reveal this to be a species of cod, in this instance an Atlantic cod (*Gadus morhua*). Carnivorous fish, cod can grow up to 1.8m (6ft).

morphine. It is used in medicine as an analgesic to treat mild to moderate pain, as a cough suppressant and to treat diarrhoea.

Code Napoléon French CIVIL LAW, first introduced (1804) by NAPOLÉON I. Based on ROMAN LAW, the Code was intended to end the disunity of French law and was applied to all French territories. It banned social inequality, permitted freedom of person and contract and upheld the right to own private property. It was revised in 1904 and remains the basis of French civil law.

Coe, Sebastian Newbold (1956–) English athlete. In the 1980 and 1984 Olympic Games, he won gold medals in the 1500m and silver medals in the 800m. His 800m world record stood for 16 years. He retired in 1990, and became a Conservative MP (1992–97). He acted as an adviser to William HAGUE.

coefficient In mathematics, the number or symbol in an algebraic expression that multiplies an unknown quantity. In the expression $1 + 5x + 2x^2$, 5 and 2 are the coefficients of x and x^2 respectively. In physics or chemistry, it is a numerical measure of a property that remains constant under particular conditions – e.g. the coefficent of friction.

coelacanth Bony fish of the genus *Latimeria*. Thought to have become extinct 60 million years ago, it was found in deep waters off the African coast in 1938. It is grey-brown with lobed fins that have fleshy bases. The scales and bony plates are unlike those of modern fish. Length: 1.5m (5ft). Order Crossopterygii; species *Latimeria chalumnae*.

Coetzee, J.M. (John Michael) (1940–) South African novelist and critic. His novels deal with life under forms of imperialism, including the South African apartheid system in *In the Heart of the Country* (1977) and *Age of Iron* (1990). Beside Peter CAREY, Coetzee is the only writer to be awarded two Booker Prizes – for *Life and Times of Michael K* (1983) and *Disgrace* (1999). Other novels include *Waiting for the Barbarians* (1980), *Foe* (1986), and *The Master of Petersburg* (1994).

coffee Plant and the popular CAFFEINE beverage produced from its seeds (coffee beans). The plants of the genus *Coffea* are evergreen with white fragrant flowers. Originally native to Ethiopia, they are now cultivated in the tropics, especially Brazil, Colombia and the Ivory Coast. Family Rubiaceae.

cognitive psychology Broad subject area of psychology concerned with perceiving, thinking and knowing. It investigates such matters as the way in which people perceive by sight or hearing; how they organize, remember and use information; and the use they make of language.

cognitive therapy Form of PSYCHOTHERAPY that aims to treat psychological problems through changing patients' attitudes and beliefs. It is based on the theory that behaviour is learned, and beliefs and attitudes that lead to negative behaviour can be altered by relearning and CONDITIONING. It is used in the treatment of various behavioural problems, phobias, and sometimes for children with learning problems.

Cohen, William (1940–) US statesman, secretary of defence (1997–2001). A former Republican senator from Maine, President Bill CLINTON appointed Cohen partly as an attempt to ensure closer support for foreign policy initiatives from a Republican-dominated Senate. He supported the expansion of NATO and a new missile defence system.

coin Stamped metal discs of standard sizes used in commercial transactions. The earliest coins are of Lydian origin, from the 7th century BC. Early coinage also appeared in China and India. Ancient coins usually contained a specific quantity of precious metal, often gold or silver, and were stamped with the symbol of the issuing authority. With the introduction of banknotes in the late 17th century and the decline of the quantity of precious metal in each coin, the role of coins changed.

Coke, Sir Edward (1552–1634) English jurist. As chief justice of the King's Bench (1613), he championed the COMMON LAW and, after 1620, developed it in Parliament to oppose the king's assumption of 'divine right'. He helped to draft a declaration of civil liberties, PETITION OF RIGHT (1628), and wrote the influential *Institutes of the Laws of England* (1628).

Colbert, Jean Baptiste (1619–83) French statesman, the principal exponent of MERCANTILISM. He came to prominence as an adviser to Cardinal MAZARIN. From 1661, when LOUIS XIV began his personal rule, Colbert controlled most aspects of government: reforming taxation and manufacturing,

reducing tariffs, establishing commercial companies such as the French EAST INDIA COMPANY, and strengthening the navy. He also enacted legal reforms and encouraged arts and sciences.

Colchester Town on the River Colne, Essex, SE England. The first Roman colony in Britain was settled here in AD 43, and was attacked by Boadicea in AD 61. It has a Roman wall and a fine Norman castle. It is a market centre for the surrounding agricultural and horticultural area. Pop. (2001) 155,794.

colchicum Genus of *c*.30 species of flowering plants, including *C. autumnale*. Species grow throughout Eurasia, and have pink, white, or purple crocus-like flowers in bloom during the autumn. The CORM contains colchicine, an ALKALOID used to treat rheumatism and gout. Colchicine's ability to inhibit MITOSIS make it a valuable IMMUNOSUPPRESSIVE DRUG and aid to cancer research. Family Liliaceae.

cold, common Minor disease of the upper respiratory tract caused by viral infection. Symptoms include inflammation of the nose, headache, sore throat and a cough. A cold usually disappears within a few days. Fever-reducing and pain-relieving drugs, as well as decongestants, may relieve symptoms; rest is recommended for heavy colds. Antibiotics may be prescribed where a bacterial infection is also present.

cold-blooded *See* POIKILOTHERMIC

Cold War Political, ideological and economic confrontation between the United States and the SOVIET UNION and their allies from the end of World War 2 until the late 1980s. Despite incidents such as the BERLIN AIRLIFT (1948–49) and the CUBAN MISSILE CRISIS (1962), open warfare never occurred between the NORTH ATLANTIC TREATY ORGANIZATION (NATO) and the WARSAW PACT – although indirect confrontation occurred in the KOREAN WAR and the VIETNAM WAR. the Cold War ended with the collapse of COMMUNISM in the late 1980s and the dissolution of the Warsaw Pact in 1990.

Cole, Nat King (Nathaniel Adams) (1917–65) US singer and pianist. He was a jazz pianist in the King Cole Trio from 1939, but achieved popularity as a singer with his

▲ **coffee** The Arabian coffee plant (*Coffea arabica*) is the most common kind of coffee plant. It is a small, evergreen tree which can grow to a height of 7.5m (25ft), but is pruned to 3m (10ft) on plantations. Its leaves are *c*.7.5–15cm (3–6in) long. The white blossoms are followed by tiny green berries, each holding two tough-skinned, greenish beans. The berries ripen to a deep red after six or seven months and are then ready for picking. Instant coffee often uses another genus, *Coffea robusta*.

▼ **Cold War** The map shows the division of Europe in 1955, between the members of NATO and the Soviet-dominated Warsaw Pact.

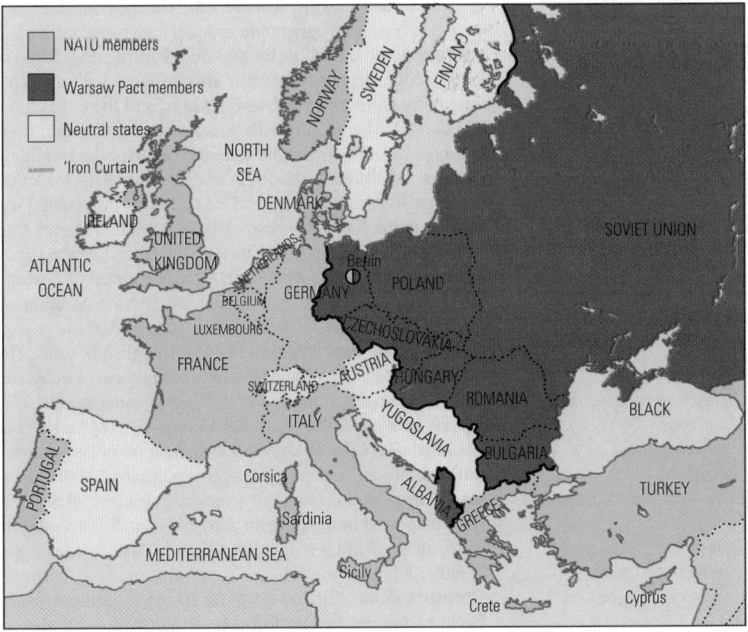

C

▲ **Cole** Popular US singer and jazz pianist, Nat King Cole had a string of successful songs during the 1950s and 1960s.

▲ **collie** Bred in Scotland during the 17th and 18th centuries, the collie is still used on farms for rounding up livestock, most commonly sheep. Collies are highly intelligent dogs and one of the most popular breeds.

velvety soft and rich voice. Cole's many hit songs include "Unforgettable", "Mona Lisa" and "Nature Boy".

Cole, Thomas (1801–48) US landscape painter, b. England. A founder of the HUDSON RIVER SCHOOL, his romantic landscapes depict the grandeur of the Hudson River valley.

Coleridge, Samuel Taylor (1772–1834) English poet, critic, and philosopher. In 1798 Coleridge and William WORDSWORTH published *Lyrical Ballads*, a fundamental work of English ROMANTICISM that opened with Coleridge's ballad "The Rime of the Ancient Mariner". *Christabel and Other Poems* (1816) included the ballad "Christabel" and the fragment "Kubla Khan". In 1800 Coleridge moved to the Lake District, where he fell in love with Wordsworth's sister-in-law Sara Hutchinson. Battling with opium-addiction, Coleridge produced little poetry in his later life, concentrating instead on his lectures. *Biographia Literaria* (1817) is both a meditation on German philosophy and a work of literary criticism.

Colette (1873–1954) French novelist. Her early works, including the first four *Claudine* novels (1900–03), appeared under her first husband's pseudonym, Willy. Other works include *Chéri* (1920), *The Last of Chéri* (1926), and *Gigi* (1944).

colic Severe pain in the abdomen, usually becoming intense, subsiding and then recurring. Intestinal colic may be associated with obstruction of the intestine or constipation.

colitis Inflammation of the lining of the colon, or large intestine, that produces bowel changes, usually diarrhoea and cramp-like pains. In severe chronic ulcerative colitis, the colon lining ulcerates and bleeds.

collage Composition made up of various materials (such as cardboard, string and fabric), pasted on to a canvas or other background. Cubist artists, such as PICASSO, BRAQUE, and GRIS developed it into a serious art form. Collage was also used by members of the DADA movement, such as SCHWITTERS.

collagen Protein substance that is the main constituent of bones, tendons, cartilage, connective tissue and skin. It is made up of inelastic fibres that form a mesh.

collective unconscious According to C.G. JUNG's psychological theory, the inherited aspect of the UNCONSCIOUS that is common to all members of the human race. The collective unconscious has evolved over many centuries and contains images (archetypes), which are found in dreams and numerous religious and mystical symbols.

collectivism Political and economic theory, opposed to individualism. It emphasizes the need to replace competition with cooperation. SOCIALISM and COMMUNISM are both expressions of the collectivist idea.

collectivization Agricultural policy enforced in the SOVIET UNION under STALIN in 1929, and adopted by China after the Communist takeover in 1949. With the object of modernizing agriculture and making it more efficient, peasant holdings were combined and agriculture brought under state control.

collie Smooth-coated or long-haired working dog. It has a lean, wedge-shaped head with small triangular ears. The long body is set on strong straight legs, and the tail is long and curved. The coat, usually black-and-white or tan, may be rough or smooth. Height: to 66cm (26in) at the shoulder.

Collins, Michael (1890–1922) Irish revolutionary, leader of the IRISH REPUBLICAN ARMY (IRA). He was imprisoned for his role in the EASTER RISING (1916). A leading member of SINN FÉIN, he helped establish (1918) the Dáil Eireann (Irish assembly). He and Arthur GRIFFITH negotiated the treaty (1921) that created the Irish Free State and the partition of Ireland. He was assassinated by extremist republicans.

Collins, (William) Wilkie (1824–89) English novelist. He made important contributions to the development of detective fiction, especially in his two enduringly popular novels, *The Woman in White* (1860) and *The Moonstone* (1868). He collaborated with Charles DICKENS in writing plays and stories.

colloid Substance composed of fine particles which can be readily dispersed throughout a second substance. A sol is a solid dispersed in a liquid, an aerosol is a solid or liquid in a gas, an emulsion is a liquid in a liquid, and a foam is a gas in either a solid or liquid.

Cologne (Köln) City on the River Rhine, Nordrhein Westfalen, W Germany. The Romans established a fortress at

Cologne in AD 50. It was made an archbishopric by Charlemagne in 785 and enjoyed great influence during the Middle Ages. It was heavily bombed during World War 2. Notable buildings include a cathedral and the Gürzenich (a Renaissance patrician's house). Its university was founded in 1388. Cologne is a commercial, industrial, and transport centre. Industries: oil refining, chemicals, engineering, textiles. Pop. (2000) 963,000.

Colombia Republic in NW South America. *See* country feature

Colombo Capital and chief seaport of Sri Lanka, on the SW coast. Settled in the 6th century BC it was taken by Portugal in the 16th century and later by the Dutch. It was captured by the British in 1796, and gained its independence in 1948. Colombo has one of the world's largest artificial harbours. Sites include a town hall and the Aqua de Lupo Church. Apart from shipping, the city has light industries. Pop. (2001) 642,020.

Colombo Plan International organization with headquarters in COLOMBO, Sri Lanka, which seeks to promote the economic and social development in S and SE Asia. Initiated by the Commonwealth of Nations (1951), it now includes 26 states including Canada, Japan, UK, and the USA. It fosters bilateral agreements providing various kinds of aid.

colon Part of the large INTESTINE in mammals that extends from the small intestine to the RECTUM. In humans, it is about 1.5m (60in) long. The colon absorbs water from digested food and allows bacterial action for the formation of faeces. *See also* DIGESTIVE SYSTEM

colonialism Control by one country over a dependent area or people. Although associated with modern political history, the practice is ancient. In European colonial history, economic, political and strategic factors were involved in the colonial enterprise, which created the world empires of countries such as Britain and France, subjugating mainly African and Asian states and often creating artificial boundaries. After World War 2, colonialist exploitation was widely recognized, and powers conceded independence to their colonies. *See also* IMPERIALISM

Colorado State in W USA; the state capital is DENVER. Other major cities include Colorado Springs and Pueblo. It is the highest state in the USA, with an average elevation of 2073m (6800ft). In the W half are the ranges of the ROCKY MOUNTAINS, and in the E the GREAT PLAINS. Major rivers are the Colorado, Rio Grande, Arkansas, and South Platte. The USA acquired the E of the state from France in the LOUISIANA PURCHASE (1803). The remainder was ceded by Mexico after the MEXICAN WAR (1848). The discovery of gold and silver encouraged immigration and Colorado was made a territory in 1861. It achieved statehood in 1876. Important agricultural activity includes sheep and cattle rearing on the Plains. Sugar beet, maize and hay are grown using irrigation. Industries: tourism, transport and electrical equipment, mining, chemicals. Area: 268,658sq km (103,729sq mi). Pop. (2000) 4,301,261.

Colorado River Major river in SW USA, which rises in the Rocky Mountains of N Colorado, and flows generally SW into the Gulf of California, passing through the GRAND CANYON. There are many national parks, irrigation and hydroelectric power schemes along the river. Length: 2,333km (1,450mi).

Colosseum Amphitheatre in Rome, built AD 72–81 by the Emperor Vespasian. One of the most awe-inspiring examples of ancient Roman architecture, it measures 189 × 156m (620 × 513ft) by 45.7m (150ft) high, and seated c.50,000 people. Citizens of Rome came here to watch gladiatorial contests and, according to tradition, the martyrdom of Christians.

Colossians, Epistle to the Book of the New Testament taking the form of a letter written by either St PAUL or a disciple to the Church at Colossae in SW Phrygia (central Turkey). The letter, written from prison in Rome (c.AD 61), is a warning to the Colossians not to adopt ideas from other faiths and philosophies that may undermine the supremacy of JESUS CHRIST.

Colossus of Rhodes One of the SEVEN WONDERS OF THE WORLD, a bronze statue of the Sun god overlooking the harbour at Rhodes. It stood more than 30.5m (100ft) high. It was built, at least in part, by Chares of Lindos between c.292 BC and c.280 BC and destroyed by an earthquake c.224 BC.

colostomy Operation to bring the COLON out through the abdomen wall in order to bypass the lower section of the bowel. An artificial opening is created so that faecal matter is passed into a bag, worn outside the body. The site of the colostomy varies according to the disease's location. *See also* DIGESTION

colour Sensation experienced when light of sufficient brightness and of a particular wavelength strikes the retina of the eye. The colour of an object is normally the colour it reflects. A red car absorbs all colours except red which is reflected. Normal daylight (white light) is made up of a spectrum of colours, each a different wavelength. These colours can be placed in seven bands – red, orange, yellow, green, blue, indigo and violet – of decreasing wavelength. A pure spectral colour is called a **hue**. If the colour is not pure but contains some white, it is 'desaturated' (**tint**). Saturation is the degree to which a colour departs from white and approaches a pure hue. A colour may also have luminosity (brightness) which determines its shade. Any colour is seen as a mixture of three primary colours: red, green, and blue in light; or red, yellow, and blue in paint. A colour created by combining two primary colours is called a **secondary colour**.

colour blindness General term for various disorders of colour vision. The most common involves red-green vision, a hereditary defect almost exclusively affecting males. Total colour blindness (achromatic vision), an inherited disorder in which the person sees only black, white and grey, is very rare.

Coltrane, John William (1926–67) US jazz saxophonist, one of the leading innovators of the 1950s and 1960s. He played with Dizzy GILLESPIE (1949–51) and Miles DAVIS (1955–57) before forming his own seminal quartet in 1960.

He established a reputation as an intense musician and technical virtuoso. He was a primary exponent of the 'modal' improvisation technique. *A Love Supreme* (1964) is his masterpiece.

Colum, Padraic (1881–1972) Irish writer. A key figure in the Irish literary renaissance, he was an associate of James JOYCE, of whom he wrote a memoir, and author of many poems. From 1914 he lived mainly in the USA, where he developed an interest in myth and folklore. His output includes many plays and a novel, *The Flying Swans* (1957).

Columba, Saint (521–97) Irish Christian missionary in Ireland and Scotland. He founded several monasteries throughout Ireland. In 563, he left Ireland and founded an important monastery on the island of Iona. As Abbot of Iona, he strove to convert the PICTS of N Scotland to Christianity. His feast day is June 9.

Columbia Capital of South Carolina, USA, on the Congaree River in the centre of the state. Founded as state capital in 1786, it was nearly destroyed in the American Civil War. It is home to the University of South Carolina (1801), Columbia College (1854), Allen University (1870) and the Woodrow Wilson Museum. Industries: textiles, printing, electronic equipment. Pop. (2000) 116,278.

Columbia, District of *See* WASHINGTON, D.C.

Columbia River River in SW Canada and NW USA. It flows from Columbia Lake in British Columbia, Canada, through Washington and Oregon, USA, and enters the Pacific Ocean N of Portland, Oregon. It has one of the

COLORADO
Statehood :
August 1, 1876
Nickname :
The Centennial State
State bird :
Lark bunting
State flower :
Rocky Mountain
columbine
State tree :
Blue spruce
State motto :
Nothing without
providence

COLOMBIA

Colombia is the only South American country to have coastlines on both Pacific Ocean and Caribbean Sea. CARTAGENA is the main Caribbean port. Colombia is dominated by three ranges of the Andean Mountains. On the edge of the W Cordillera lies the city of Cali. The Central Cordillera is a chain of volcanoes dividing the valleys of the rivers Magdalena and Cauca. It includes the city of Medellín. The E Cordillera contains the capital, BOGOTÁ, at 2,800m [9,200ft]. E of the Andes lie plains drained by headwaters of the AMAZON and ORINOCO rivers.

Vegetation varies from dense rainforest in the SE to tundra in the snow-capped Andes.

Coffee plantations line the W slopes of the E Cordillera. The ancient forests of the Caribbean lowlands have mostly been cleared. Savanna (*llanos*) covers the NE plains.

CLIMATE

Altitude greatly affects the climate. The Pacific lowlands have a tropical, rainy climate, but Bogotá has mild annual temperatures. The lowlands of the Caribbean and the Magdalena valley both have dry seasons.

AREA 1,138,914sq km [439,735sq mi]
POPULATION 44,380,000
CAPITAL (POPULATION)
Bogotá (7,594,000)
GOVERNMENT Multiparty republic
ETHNIC GROUPS Mestizo 58%, White 20%, Mulatto 14%, Black 4%
LANGUAGES Spanish (official)
RELIGIONS Roman Catholic 90%
CURRENCY Colombian peso = 100 centavos

HISTORY

The pre-Colombian CHIBCHA civilization lived undisturbed in the E Cordillera for thousands of years. In 1525 the Spanish established the first European settlement at Santa Marta. By 1538 conquistador Gonzalo Jiménez de Quesada had conquered the Chibcha and established the city of Bogotá. Colombia became part of the New Kingdom of Granada, whose territory also included Ecuador, Panama, and Venezuela.

In 1819 Simón BOLÍVAR defeated the Spanish at Boyacá, and established Greater Colombia. Bolívar became president. In 1830, Ecuador and Venezuela gained independence. In 1885, the Republic of Colombia was formed. Differences between republican and federalist factions proved irreconcilable and the first civil war from 1899–1902 killed nearly 100,000 people. In 1903, aided by the United States, Panama gained independence. The second civil war, *La Violencia* (1949–57), was even more bloody. In 1957 Liberal and Conservative parties formed a National Front Coalition, which held power until 1974.

POLITICS

Throughout the 1970s, Colombia's illegal trade in cocaine grew steadily, creating wealthy drug

barons. In the 1980s, armed cartels such as the Cali destabilized Colombia with frequent assassinations of political and media figures.

A new constitution in 1991 aimed to protect human rights. Social Conservative Party (PSC) leader Andrés Pastrana Arango won the 1998 presidential elections and, in an effort to end the 30-year guerrilla war, negotiated with the Revolutionary Armed Forces of Colombia (FARC) and the National Liberation Army (ELN). Pastrana granted FARC a safe haven in SE Colombia.

In 1999, the worst earthquake in Colombia's history killed more than 1,000 people and left thousands homeless. In 2002 Pastrana declared war on FARC, sending the army into FARC's 'safe haven'. Alvaro Uribe defeated Pastrana in 2002 presidential elections. Uribe promised even tougher action against terrorism.

ECONOMY

Colombia is a lower-middle income developing country. It is the world's second-largest coffee producer. Other crops include bananas, cocoa and maize. Colombia also exports coal, oil, emeralds, and gold. In 1997 a collapse in the world coffee and banana markets led to a budget deficit. In 1998 Colombia devalued the peso, triggering a 20-day general strike, the longest in Colombia's history.

C

▲ **Columbus** Although Columbus was not the first European to sail to the New World (the Vikings visited in c.1000), his voyages mark the start of intensive European exploration of the Americas. On his final voyage (1502), he sailed past Hispaniola and south along the coast of Honduras. Attempting to return to Hispaniola, he was shipwrecked on Jamaica and forced to return to Spain, abandoning his travels.

largest drainage basins on the continent, c.668,220sq km (258,000sq mi). Length: 1953km (1214mi).

columbine Any of c.100 species of perennial herbaceous plant native to cool climates of the Northern Hemisphere. They have five-petalled, spurred flowers and notched leaflets. Height: to 90cm (3ft). Family Ranunculaceae; genus *Aquilegia*.

columbium *See* NIOBIUM

Columbus Capital of Ohio, USA, on the Scioto River. Founded in 1812, it grew rapidly with the arrival of the railway in 1850. It is a major transport, industrial and trading centre for a rich agricultural region. Columbus has numerous universities and colleges. The Battelle Memorial Institute (1929) conducts technological and economic research. Industries: machinery, aircraft, printing and publishing. Pop. (2000) 1,133,000.

Columbus, Christopher (1451–1506) Italian explorer credited with the discovery of America. He believed he could establish a route to China and the East Indies by sailing across the Atlantic since, along with many learned contemporaries, he believed the circumference of the Earth to be much smaller than it actually is. After several disappointments, he secured Spanish patronage from Ferdinand and Isabella. He set out with three ships (*Niña*, *Pinta*, and *Santa Maria*) in 1492 and made landfall in the Bahamas, the first European to reach the Americas since the Vikings, whose achievement was then unknown. Believing he had reached the East, he called the inhabitants "Indians". On a second, larger expedition (1493), a permanent colony was established in Hispaniola. He made two more voyages (1498 and 1502), exploring the Caribbean region without reaching the North American mainland. He never surrendered his belief that he had reached Asia. His discoveries laid the basis for the Spanish empire in the Americas.

column In architecture, a vertical post, supporting part of a building. A column may be free-standing, with a capital, base and shaft, or it may be partly attached to a wall. Triumphal columns such as Trajan's Column in Rome, have narrative reliefs to depict battle victories. Annulated columns, clustered together by rings or bands, were popular in medieval England. *See also* ORDERS OF ARCHITECTURE

coma State of unconsciousness brought about by head injury, brain disease, drugs, or lack of blood supply to the BRAIN.

Comanche Shoshonean-speaking NATIVE AMERICAN nation. They separated from the parent SHOSHONE in the distant past and migrated from E Wyoming into Kansas. Conflict with US forces resulted in their near extinction by 1874. Today, c.4500 Comanche live on reservations in SW Oklahoma.

Combination Acts British Acts of Parliament of 1799 and 1800 making combinations (trade unions) of workers illegal. The government feared that such organizations were potentially subversive. Trade unions nevertheless multiplied after 1815, and in 1824 the acts were repealed. A later Combination Act (1825) restricted the right to strike and, as the TOLPUDDLE MARTYRS (1834) demonstrated, trade-union organizers could still be prosecuted.

combustion Burning, usually in oxygen. The combustion of fuels is used to produce heat and light. An example is a fire. Industrial techniques harness the energy produced using combustion chambers and furnaces.

COMECON Acronym for the COUNCIL FOR MUTUAL ECONOMIC ASSISTANCE

Comédie-Française French national theatre, founded in 1680. It is organized according to a charter granted by Louis XIV and revised by Napoléon I. There are two kinds of members: *pensionnaires*, chosen by audition, and *sociétaires* – to which the *pensionnaire* can be elevated only upon the death, retirement, or resignation of a *sociétaire*.

comedy One of the two main types of DRAMA. It differs from TRAGEDY in its lightness of style and theme and its tendency to resolve happily. It originated in early Greek fertility rites and, in modern usage, refers not only to a humorous play or film, but also to the growing tradition of stand-up routines. As theatre has developed over the centuries, the once clear division between the two dramatic forms has been blurred, as fusions and a variety of sub-divisions of the two have been developed. *See also* ARISTOPHANES; GREEK DRAMA

Comenius, John Amos (1592–1670) Czech religious leader and educational reformer, who influenced modern education. Comenius believed in equal education for all children. His best-known book was *Orbis Sensualum Pictus* (*The Visible World in Pictures*, 1658).

comet Small, icy Solar System body in orbit around the Sun. The solid nucleus of a comet is small, that of HALLEY'S COMET measures just 16×8km (10×5mi), and comprises rock and dust particles embedded in ice. As the comet approaches the Sun, evaporation begins, and jets of gas and dust form the luminous coma. Later, radiation pressure from the Sun and SOLAR WIND may send dust and gas streaming away as a tail, as much as 150 million km in length. There are three main types of comet: **short-period** comets often have their aphelia at approximately the distance of Jupiter's orbit. **Long-period** comets have aphelia near or beyond Neptune's orbit. The third type are either called **non-periodic**, or **hyperbolic**. Their periods may be as much as several million years. *See also* METEOR

comfrey Any plant of the genus *Symphytum* of the BORAGE family (Boraginaceae), native to Eurasia. Comfreys have small yellow or purple flowers and hairy leaves. Boiled concoctions of *S. officinale* were once used to treat wounds.

comic Magazine consisting of stories told by means of strip cartoons with 'balloons' containing the characters' speech. Comics evolved from the comic-strip in the 1930s, and cover many subjects – from war and science fiction to school and family life. A tradition of adult, politicized, subversive and often erotic comics, along with explicit graphic novels, has established itself during the latter part of the 20th century.

comic opera Musico-dramatic work with some spoken dialogue and a light or amusing plot. The term is used indiscriminately and includes musical comedy and OPERETTA. In operatic works, it approximates most closely to early 18th-century Italian OPERA BUFFA (notably the operas of PERGOLESI), but bears little relation to the French OPÉRA COMIQUE.

Comintern *See* COMMUNIST INTERNATIONAL

commedia dell'arte Style of Italian comedy, popular from the mid-16th to late-18th century, which spread throughout Europe. Professional players performed on street stages or at court functions. Plays were comic, often coarse, and crudely improvized on briefly outlined scenarios. Commedia produced several (now standard) masked characters: Harlequin (clown), Capitano (braggart soldier), Pantalone (deceived father or cuckolded husband), Colombina (maid) and Inamorato (lover).

commensalism Situation in nature in which two species live in close association but only one partner benefits. One of the species (the commensal) may gain from increased food supply, or by procuring shelter, support or means of locomotion, but the other (the host) neither gains nor loses from the relationship. For example, silverfish clean the nests of army ants by scavenging on refuse without harming the ants. Commensalism is a type of SYMBIOSIS. In the other type, MUTUALISM, both organisms gain from the relationship.

commodity market Market in which goods or services are bought and sold. Commodities are raw materials such as tea, rubber, tin or copper, which generally need processing to reach their final state. The actual commodities are seldom present, and what is traded is their ownership. The largest commodity exchange in the world is in Chicago, Illinois.

Common Agricultural Policy (CAP) System of support for agriculture within the EUROPEAN UNION (EU). The Treaty of ROME created CAP in 1957. CAP was designed to increase food production within the EU, and to ensure a reasonable income for farmers. The EU set target prices for commodities. If prices fell below target, to a level known as 'intervention prices', the EU bought up surplus product creating the so-called 'beef mountains' and 'wine lakes'. In 1988, to prevent over-production, the EU introduced a policy of paying farmers to set aside part of their land as fallow. Prices for imports from outside the EU are kept above target by means of levies. By 1994, the CAP accounted for 51% of the total EU budget, having soared to 75% in the 1970s. Between 2005 and 2012 it is being reformed in an attempt to subsidize improvements in environmental standards rather than simple quantity of production. Reform of the CAP is one of the most contentious issues in the Union.

common law Legal system developed in England and adopted in most English-speaking countries. Distinguished from CIVIL LAW, its chief characteristics are judicial precedents, trial by jury and the doctrine of the supremacy of law. Based originally on the King's Court, "common to the whole realm", rather than local or manorial courts, it dates back to the Constitutions of CLARENDON (1164). It is the customary and traditional element in the law accumulating from court decisions. Swift changes in society and public opinion have resulted in a proliferation of statutes which have come to supersede common law. *See also* ROMAN LAW

Common Market *See* EUROPEAN UNION (EU)

Common Prayer, Book of Official liturgy of the Church of England. Originally prepared as a reformed version of the old Roman Catholic liturgy for Henry VIII by Thomas CRANMER in 1549. Three years later it underwent revision under the Protestant government of Edward VI. The final version (1559), a combination of the two, was produced by Elizabeth I's Archbishop of Canterbury, Matthew Parker. The Prayer Book was further revised in 1662 after the RESTORATION of Charles II.

Commons, House of *See* HOUSE OF COMMONS

Commonwealth (1649–60) Official name of the republic established in England after the execution of CHARLES I in 1649. After a series of unsuccessful attempts to find a suitable constitution, the PROTECTORATE was set up in 1653, in which Oliver CROMWELL was given almost regal powers. The Commonwealth ended with the RESTORATION of CHARLES II.

Commonwealth Games Sporting event originating as the British Empire Games (1930). Competitors are members of the COMMONWEALTH OF NATIONS. Based on the OLYMPIC GAMES, they are held every four years.

Commonwealth of Independent States (CIS) Alliance of 12 of the former republics of the SOVIET UNION (Armenia, Azerbaijan, Belarus, Georgia, Kazakhstan, Kyrgyzstan, Moldova, Russia, Tajikistan, Turkmenistan, Ukraine, and Uzbekistan). The CIS formed in 1991. The Baltic states (Estonia, Latvia, and Lithuania) did not join. In 1993 all members, except Ukraine, signed a treaty of economic union, creating a free-trade zone. Russia is the dominant power, with overall responsibility for defence and peacekeeping. It is also the main provider of oil and natural gas.

Commonwealth of Nations Voluntary association of 53 states, consisting of English-speaking countries formerly part of the BRITISH EMPIRE. Headed by the British monarch, it exists largely as a forum for discussion of issues of common concern. A Commonwealth Secretariat is located in London.

communications Processes for sharing information and ideas. Facial expressions, hand signals, writing, and speech are examples. The 15th-century invention of the printing press revolutionized communications. The 20th century witnessed a communications revolution, primarily in terms of increased access. TELECOMMUNICATIONS inventions, such as the TELEPHONE, RADIO, TELEVISION, and COMPUTER NETWORK, facilitated rapid, global, mass communication. The INTERNET is the latest in a long line of technological innovations.

Communications Satellite (COMSAT) Private company that provides worldwide satellite communications systems. COMSAT, established by the US Congress, began with the launch of the Early Bird satellite in 1965. Many other nations now participate in COMSAT projects.

communism Political outlook based on the principle of communal ownership of property. The theory derives from the interpretation of the course of human history defined by Karl MARX and Friedrich ENGELS. As outlined in the *Communist Manifesto* (1848), *Capital* (vol. 1, 1867), and other writings, Marx asserted that social and political relations depend ultimately upon relations of economic production. All value (and so wealth) is produced by labour, yet, in a capitalist system, workers' salaries do not represent the full value of their labour. Thus, the working class (PROLETARIAT) and the class that is in control of CAPITAL and production (BOURGEOISIE) have conflicting interests. CAPITALISM, it is asserted, is merely one stage in the progress of human

institutions. As the forces of production (technology and capital stock) increase, the relations of production must change in order to accommodate them. Conflicting interests within capitalism would inevitably lead to the overthrow of the bourgeoisie by the proletariat and so the collapse of the system itself. This would be replaced, first by SOCIALISM and eventually by a communist society in which production and distribution would be democratically controlled, summarized in the slogan "From each according to their ability, to each according to their need". A socialist experiment was attempted by LENIN in Russia following the RUSSIAN REVOLUTION (1917). STALIN turned communism into an ideology to justify the use of dictatorial state power to drive rapid economic development. This process was used as a model for other communist countries, such as China and Cuba.

Communist International (Comintern, Third International) Communist organization founded by LENIN in 1919. He feared that the reformist Second International might re-emerge and wished to secure control of the world socialist movement. The Comintern was made up mainly of Russians, and failed to organize a successful revolution in Europe in the 1920s and 1930s. The Soviet Union abolished the Comintern in 1943 to placate its World War 2 allies.

Communist Party, Chinese Political organization founded in July 1921 by Li Dazhao and Chen Duxiu. The party was strengthened by its alliance (1924) with CHIANG KAI-SHEK's nationalist KUOMINTANG, but virtually shattered when the communists were expelled from the alliance in 1927. MAO ZEDONG was the guiding force in revitalizing the party in the early 1930s. Under his leadership, solidified during the LONG MARCH (1934–35), the party revised the Soviet proletariat-based model to fit the peasant-oriented economy of China and, after another four years of civil war from 1945, the People's Republic was proclaimed in TIANANMEN SQUARE (October 1949). The party had achieved complete political and military power. Its structure and hierarchy was nearly destroyed during the CULTURAL REVOLUTION, but re-established after Mao's death (1976) by DENG XIAOPING. Following pro-democracy demonstrations (May 1989), the party swung away from political reform and hardline conservatives consolidated power. Yet, its flexible approach to economic reform enabled it to survive the collapse of Soviet COMMUNISM. Jiang ZEMIN became president in 1993. The National People's Congress is the supreme legislative body, and nominally elects the highest officers of state. Today, there are more than 40 million members.

Communist Party of the Soviet Union (CPSU) Former ruling party of the SOVIET UNION. It wielded all effective political power in the country and, via the COMMUNIST INTERNATIONAL, had considerable influence over Communist parties in other countries. At its height the CPSU had *c.*15 million members, organized into *c.*400,000 local units (cells) throughout the Soviet Union. Party organization paralleled the hierarchy of local government administration, thus enabling party control of every level of government. There were party cells in almost all areas of Soviet life, such as the school system, armed forces, factories, collective farms and the media. After the break up of the Soviet Union in 1991, the party was dissolved by Boris YELTSIN. There remains a strong, traditional conservative power base of ex-party members who are politically active in Russia. The 1996 presidential elections revealed popular support for the communist leader, Gennady ZYUGANOV. *See also* COMMUNISM; LENIN; individual party leaders

community In ECOLOGY, naturally occurring group of plants or animals living within a particular HABITAT. A community in a particular ECOSYSTEM is interdependent in many ways, such as the FOOD CHAIN. During ecological SUCCESSION, the structure of a community is constantly shifting until a stable, climax community is established.

commutative law Rule of combination in mathematics; it requires that an operation on two terms is independent of the order of the terms. Addition and multiplication of numbers is commutative, since $a + b = b + a$ and $ab = ba$. Vector cross-multiplication does not obey the commutative law.

COMPACT DISC

A compact disc player reads digital information from a compact disc (1) using a focused laser (2). Music or other information is written on the underside of the disc in a spiral track of pits (3), representing a digital code of zeros and ones. The disc spins and the laser, mounted on a swing arm (4), moves as the disc plays. The laser passes through a semi-silvered mirror (5) and is focused on the disc (6). When the laser hits a flat area it is reflected back via the mirror to a sensor (7) and the information sent to a chip. When the laser hits a pit, it is scattered.

Comoros (Comores) Independent republic off the E coast of Africa between Mozambique and Madagascar in the Indian Ocean, made up of a group of volcanic islands. The three major islands are Grande Comore (site of the capital, Moroni), Anjouan, and Mohéli. The islands are mountainous, the climate tropical, and the soil fertile. Coconuts, copra, vanilla, cocoa, and sisal are the main crops and exports. France owned the islands between 1841 and 1909. They gained their independence in 1975. Area: 2235sq km (863sq mi). Pop. (2000 est.) 633,000.

compact disc (CD) Disc used for high-quality digital sound reproduction. It is a plastic disc with a shiny metal layer and a transparent protective plastic coating. The sound signal consists of millions of minute pits, pressed into one side of the metal. On replay, a narrow laser beam is reflected from the rotating disc's surface. A sensor detects changes in the beam, and forms an electrical signal of pulses. This is processed and decoded to form a sound signal that can be amplified for reproduction on loudspeakers. *See also* CD-ROM

company Group of people who agree to work together as a firm or business. The legal responsibility of running a company rests with its board of directors which, if the business has raised finance by selling shares in the company, has to account to its shareholders. In a **private** company, the directors sell shares to whomever they please (sometimes the only shareholders are the directors). The shares of a **public** company can be bought and sold by anyone through a STOCK EXCHANGE. In a **public limited company (plc)**, the legal liability of its shareholders is limited to the value of their shares. *See also* CORPORATION

compass Direction-finding instrument also used to show direction of a MAGNETIC FIELD. It is a horizontal magnetic needle on a vertical pivot whose north-seeking end can turn to point towards the Earth's magnetic N. Adjustments can be made to give true N. The compass has been used in Europe since the 12th century when the 'needle' was a piece of lodestone. A compass, however, can give an incorrect reading if magnetic metals are nearby. In navigation today, the magnetic compass is often replaced by the motor-driven GYROCOMPASS.

compiler Computer PROGRAM that translates the symbols of a programming language into instructions readable directly by a computer. Most programs are written in a COMPUTER LANGUAGE, such as C++, made up of words and symbols easily comprehended by humans. A compiler takes these programs and renders them into a form that is readable by the circuits of the computer itself.

complex number Number of the form $a + bi$, where $i = \sqrt{-1}$, and a and b are REAL NUMBERS. In order to obtain a solution to the equation $x^2 + 1 = 0$, we need to introduce a new number i such that $i^2 = -1$. The solutions to similar equations then give rise to a set of numbers of the general form $a + bi$. These are known as the complex numbers. Since b can be equal to zero, the set of complex numbers includes the real numbers.

Compositae Family of $c.20,000$ species of plants in which the 'flower' is actually a composite flower-head consisting of a cluster of many, usually tiny, individual flowers (florets). In a typical composite, such as the DAISY, the flower-head has a central yellow disc, consisting of a cluster of tiny bisexual florets lacking visible petals. The outer ring of female, ray florets has large white petals. In composites such as the DANDELION and ENDIVE, the flower-head consists entirely of ray florets. Others, such as THISTLES, consist entirely of disc florets. Composites make up by far the largest family of plants, and include food plants, such as ARTICHOKES, and many popular garden flowers. The Compositae are often known as the Asteraceae.

compound Substance formed by chemical combination of two or more elements that cannot be separated by physical means. Compounds are produced by the rearrangement of valency ELECTRONS (outer electrons of an atom) seeking more stable configurations. They usually have properties different from their constituent elements. Ionic compounds have IONIC BONDS – they are collections of oppositely charged ions. They have high melting and boiling points, due to the electrostatic forces of attraction holding their crystal lattice together. COVALENT BONDS occur where non-metal atoms share electrons. Such compounds can be classified as simple molecular structures, such as carbon dioxide, with low melting and boiling points; or giant molecular structures, such as graphite and diamond. Their properties depend on the arrangement of the atoms in the macromolecule. *See also* MOLECULE; VALENCE

comprehensive school System of secondary education based on the notion of inclusivity rather than selectivity. In principle, comprehensive schools admit any child regardless of ability or aptitude. In practice, a degree of selection or 'streaming' according to ability often occurs.

Compromise of 1850 Set of balanced resolutions by Senator Henry CLAY to prevent civil war. The US Congress agreed to admit California as a free state, organize New Mexico and Utah as territories without mention of slavery, provide for a tougher fugitive slave law, abolish the slave trade in Washington, D.C., and assume the Texas national debt.

Compton, Arthur Holly (1892–1962) US physicist. He discovered that wavelengths of X-rays increase when the rays collide with electrons (the 'Compton effect'). This helped prove that X-rays could act as particles. He shared the 1927 Nobel Prize in physics with C.T.R. WILSON. Head of the early phase of the MANHATTAN PROJECT to develop the atom bomb, Compton helped create the first sustained nuclear CHAIN REACTION.

computed axial tomography *see* CAT SCAN.

computer Device that processes data (information) by following a set of instructions called a PROGRAM. All digital computers work by manipulating data represented as numbers. The tallying principle of the ABACUS was mechanized in calculating machines, such as those devised by Charles BABBAGE, in which complex calculations were processed by means of geared wheels. From the 1930s on, mechanical calculations began to be replaced by electronic versions using electromagnetic switches called relays to register binary numbers. At any instant each switch could be either on or off, corresponding to the digits 1 or 0 in the BINARY SYSTEM. The first true computers, Colossus in 1945 and ENIAC in 1946, used electronic VALVES instead of relays. Programming them to do a particular task was a lengthy process of changing wired connections. John von NEUMANN helped to develop techniques for storing programs electronically to avoid this problem. In 1951, UNIVAC 1 became the first computer offered for general sale, and one of the first to use the TRANSISTOR to perform the same role as valves. Transisters were smaller, cheaper and cooler and, as a result, computers became smaller and more commonplace. In the 1960s, a third generation of computers appeared with the invention of INTEGRATED CIRCUITS, leading to a further reduction in size. By the 1980s, computers used powerful MICROPROCESSORS containing a complete central processing unit (CPU) which controls operations, and this allowed them to make the transition from room-sized mainframes to small desktop units. The latest microprocessors contain hundreds of millions of transistors and other components, all in a package little bigger than a postage stamp. Read-Only Memory (ROM) and Random Access Memory (RAM) chips act as permanent and temporary electronic memories for storing data. A typical modern desktop computer unit contains a central processor, memory chips, storage devices, and a graphics control chip to drive the monitor. Computer programs are usually stored on magnetic DISKS, such as the HARD DISK, and transferred to the machine's RAM when required. Other storage devices are optical, such as the CD-ROM and DVD-ROM drives, or based on solid-state flash memory. The main **input devices**, the keyboard and mouse, have changed little in design since the 1970s. The **keyboard** enables the user to enter letters, numbers and other symbols. The **mouse** is a small device moved by hand, which causes corresponding movements of a pointer on screen and enables the user to control the computer's GRAPHICAL USER INTERFACE (GUI). Many other **peripherals** are available to input data, especially for COMPUTER GRAPHICS and audio.

COMPUTER

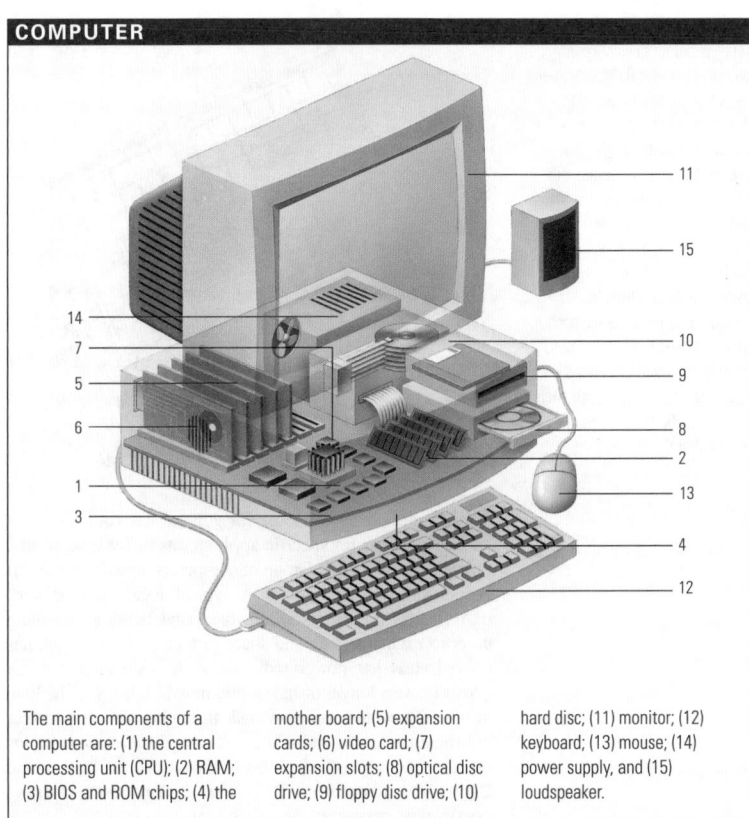

The main components of a computer are: (1) the central processing unit (CPU); (2) RAM; (3) BIOS and ROM chips; (4) the mother board; (5) expansion cards; (6) video card; (7) expansion slots; (8) optical disc drive; (9) floppy disc drive; (10) hard disc; (11) monitor; (12) keyboard; (13) mouse; (14) power supply, and (15) loudspeaker.

COMPUTER

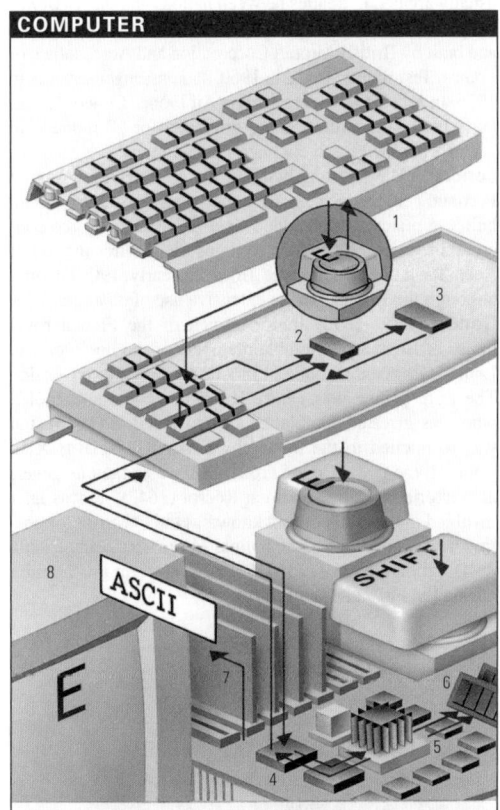

Pressing a key (1) or pair of keys changes the current flowing through the key's circuit. A microprocessor (2) scans the circuits and detects when they change. A scan code is transmitted by the microprocessor to the memory buffer in the keyboard (3). The scan code then travels through the cable connecting the keyboard to its controller chip (4), in the body of the computer. The controller chip informs the CPU (5) which finds the keyboard program in ROM (6) and cancels the scan code in the keyboard's memory buffer. The ROM converts the scan code into the PC's language, ASCII (7), and then instructs the monitor (8) to display the character, an uppercase E.

Physical parts of the computer system are known as HARD-WARE, while the programs that exist in its memory are termed SOFTWARE. The modern computer market is dominated by PCs, a generic term used to refer to machines based on the original IBM personal computer produced in the early 1980s. Most of these machines use the commercial operating system known as Windows, produced by the giant software corporation Microsoft, but some use free varieties of the powerful UNIX system. The Windows PC's main competitor is the Apple Macintosh, which also runs a UNIX-derived operating system.

computer-aided design (CAD) Use of COMPUTER GRAPHICS to assist the design of physical products such as fabrics, electronic circuits, buildings and vehicles. With CAD, designers can make alterations and analyse their effect. Structures and colours can be varied and the effect judged on the computer screen. *See also* VIRTUAL REALITY

computer graphics Modern computer programs are able to manipulate existing images or create entirely new ones. **Raster graphics** software is used to edit two-dimensional images such as paintings and photographs. **Vector graphics** programs have replaced traditional drawing tools to create graphic layouts, line drawings and diagrams. **3–d graphics** programs, the most complex type, create a simulation of a scene in the computer's memory and then realistically calculate its appearance from a chosen viewpoint. They are used for cinematic special effects, and to create modern VIDEO GAMES.

computer language System of words and rules used to PROGRAM a computer. Most COMPUTERS use internal **machine code** based on the BINARY SYSTEM, but this is time consuming for a human to program. Instead, a synthetic language with a very precise structure can be used to instruct a computer. Another program, such as a COMPILER, assembler, or interpreter, then translates this into machine code. Some languages, described as **low level**, use instructions closely corresponding to small amounts of machine code. This allows the programmer to create efficient high-speed programs, but requires a great deal of time and experience. **High level** languages can use instructions more easily understood by the user, allowing easier and faster programming at the expense of longer computing time. Hundreds of programming languages have been designed

▶ **computer graphics** Touch-screens detect physical contact with the screen (1). Most screens have two plastic layers with a thin transparent coating of a conducting material (2). The pressure of a finger brings the two sheets slightly closer together (3). The screen reads the position of the touch horizontally and vertically (4) to ascertain its position. In consumer touch-screens, such as automated teller machines, a small selection of options is presented to the user with each section of the screen relating to one of them.

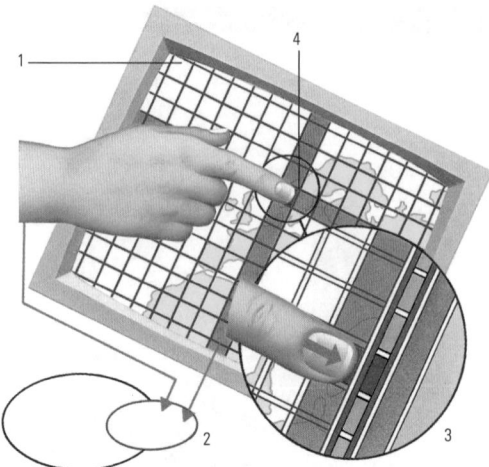

for different purposes, some for general use such as C++ and Java, others for specific applications or for education.

computer network Group of computers linked together for COMMUNICATIONS purposes. A typical local area network (LAN) links computers within the same building, enabling users to exchange data and share printers. LANs sometimes use **wireless** low-power radio links. A wide area network (WAN) covers longer distances and may link LANs. The long distance interconnections are made through FIBRE OPTIC cables or orbital SATELLITE radio links. Shorter distance connections often use high-speed telephone services such as Asymmetric Digital Subscriber Line (ADSL). *See also* INTERNET, MODEM

computer program *See* PROGRAM

computer virus A computer PROGRAM designed to destroy user data, steal information, or allow the computer to be remotely controlled for use in criminal activity. Many spread through the INTERNET by exploiting technical vulnerabilities in users' software and operating systems. Others trick users into installing them by imitating useful programs.

Comte, Auguste (1798–1857) French philosopher, the founder of POSITIVISM. He proposed the law of the three stages (theological, metaphysical, and positive) that represent the development of the human race. In the first two stages, the human mind finds religious or abstract causes to explain phenomena. While in the third, explanation of a phenomenon is found in a scientific law. He influenced John Stuart MILL and was the founder of SOCIOLOGY. His works include *System of Positive Polity* (1830–42) and *Politique Positive* (1851–54).

Conakry Capital city of Guinea, W Africa, on Tombo Island, in the Atlantic Ocean. Founded in 1884, it is a major port and the administrative and commercial centre of Guinea. It exports alumina and bananas. Pop. (2005) 1,465,000.

concentration camp Detention centre for military or political prisoners. The first were set up by the British for Afrikaner civilians during the SOUTH AFRICAN WARS (1899–1902). The most notorious were established by the German Nazi regime in the 1930s for political opponents, and people considered racially or socially undesirable. Some of these camps provided slave labour while others were the sites of mass execution. In Poland, more than 6 million people (mostly Jews) were murdered in the gas chambers. GULAGS were widely employed during Stalin's purges, and reeducation camps were used in the Chinese CULTURAL REVOLUTION and by the KHMER ROUGE. *See also* AUSCHWITZ; BELSEN; BUCHENWALD; DACHAU

conceptual art Art giving primacy to idea over craftsmanship. DUCHAMP first asserted the notion, but a movement only began to take shape in the 1960s. Conceptual art questions the nature of art and emphasizes the elimination of art as an object or commodity for reproduction. The 'viewer' is often implicated in the production of art as performance or 'happening'. Artists include Claes OLDENBURG and Joseph Beuys.

conceptualism Philosophical theory in which the universal is found in the particular, a position between NOMINALISM and REALISM. It asserts that the mind is the individual that univer-

salizes by experiencing particulars, finding common factors in them, and conceptualizing these common factors as universals.

concerto Musical work for instrumental soloists accompanied by orchestra. The earliest concertos are the 17th-century *Concerto grosso* (a small section of soloists on various instruments, the *concertino*, is contrasted with the full orchestra, the *ripieno*) written by CORELLI and Torelli. J.S. BACH's Brandenburg Concertos are fine examples of this form. VIVALDI composed most of his concertos for one soloist and orchestra and used the three-movement form (fast-slow-fast) which was to become standard in CLASSICAL MUSIC, such as the brilliant concertos of MOZART and BEETHOVEN. In the 19th century, concertos involved increasing virtuosity, particularly in the works of LISZT and RACHMANINOV. Concertos have also been written for two or three soloists (double and triple concertos).

conclave Originally a place of private or secret assembly, then the assembly itself. More particularly, the term denotes the assembly of CARDINALS that meets to secretly elect a new pope.

Concord Capital of New Hampshire, USA, on the Merrimack River. Founded as a trading post (1660), it was settled in 1727. It was the scene of New Hampshire's ratification of the Constitution as the ninth and deciding state on June 21, 1788, and designated state capital in 1808. Quarries N of the city produce the famous white granite used for the Library of Congress (Washington, D.C.) and the Museum of Modern Art (New York City). An industrial and financial centre, industries include electrical equipment and printing. Pop. (2000) 40,687.

concordat Agreement between Church and State, a term usually applied to treaties between nations and the VATICAN.

Concorde Supersonic passenger aircraft. Jointly developed and built by British Aircraft Corporation and Aerospatiale of France. Test flights started in 1969, and passenger services in 1976. In July 2000, the crash of an Air France Concorde near Paris led to the aircraft being grounded for 17 months. In 2003 Concorde ceased commercial operations.

concrete Hard, strong building material made by mixing Portland cement, sand, gravel, and water. It is an important building material. Embedded steel rods can reinforce concrete. Pre-stressed concrete contains piano wires instead of steel. Its modern use dates from the early 19th century, although the Romans made extensive use of concrete.

Condé (1530–1830) Junior branch of the French royal house of BOURBON. Notable members of the line included Louis I, Prince de Condé (1530–69), a HUGUENOT leader. The third prince was Henry II (1588–1646), a Catholic, who was arrested for blackmail and sedition (1616), but was reconciled to the monarchy under King LOUIS XIII. Louis II, the Great Condé (1621–86), was a famous general. Victorious against Spain at Rocroi (1643), he was later involved in the civil conflict known as the FRONDES, opposing the Regent Anne and Cardinal MAZARIN. Louis Joseph de Bourbon-Condé (1736–1818) led the émigré nobility during the FRENCH REVOLUTION.

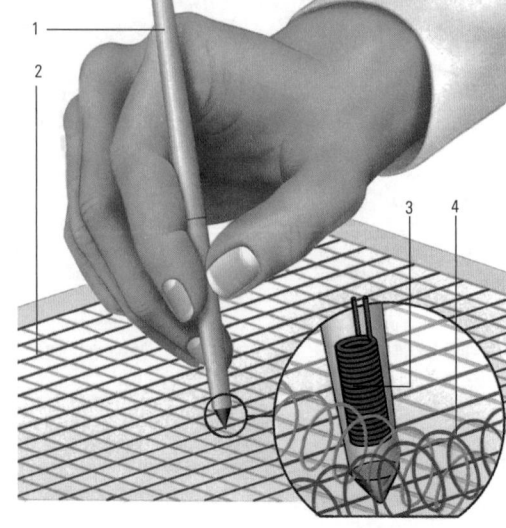

▶ **computer graphics** A graphics pad is a method for inputting information to a computer. It allows the operator to 'draw' on the computer with a pen or stylus (1) via the pad (2). Just below the surface of the pad are current-carrying filaments (shown blue and green). The pen has a magnet in the tip (3). As the pen moves across the pad, the magnet interferes with the magnetic fields (4) created by the filaments, sending the location of the pen to the computer. The location of the interference is read hundreds of times a second by a chip, providing a constant stream of co-ordinates.

condensation Formation of a liquid from a gas or vapour, caused by cooling or an increase in pressure. Commonly, it is the changing of water vapour in the air into water droplets, forming mist, cloud, rain, or drops on cold surfaces (see DEW POINT). The reverse process is EVAPORATION.

conditioning In experimental psychology, learning in which human or animal subjects learn to respond in a certain way to a stimulus. Most of the procedures and terminology of classical conditioning stem from the work of Ivan PAVLOV, while B.F. Skinner first described operant conditioning.

condor Common name for two species of the American VULTURE: the black Andean condor (*Vultur gryphus*) and the rare grey-brown California condor (*Gymnogyps californianus*). Length: up to 127cm (50in). Wing-span: up to 3.5m (10ft).

conductance (symbol G) Ability of a material to conduct ELECTRICITY. In a direct current (DC) circuit, it is the reciprocal of electrical RESISTANCE that opposes the flow. For example, a conductor of resistance R has a conductance of 1/R. In an alternating current (AC) circuit, it is the resistance divided by the square of impedance (the opposition of a circuit to the passage of a current; $G = R/Z^2$. SI units of conductance are siemens (S).

conduction Transfer of heat within a body. If one end of a metal rod is placed in a flame, the heat energy received causes increased vibratory motion of the molecules in that end. These molecules bump into others farther along the rod, and the increased motion is passed along until finally the end not in the flame becomes hot.

conductivity Measure of the ease with which a material allows electricity or heat to pass through it. For a solid substance, the electrical conductivity is the CONDUCTANCE. *See also* ELECTRIC CURRENT

conductor In music, a person who co-ordinates the performance of a band, orchestra or choir and directs and inspires the interpretation of the music. Before the 19th century, a harpsichordist or first violinist 'directed' orchestral playing. As the size of orchestras increased it became common practice for a musician to stand before the players and conduct with a baton.

conductor Substance or object that allows easy flow of electricity. Conductors have low electrical RESISTANCE that opposes the flow. Metals, the best conductors, have free electrons that become an ELECTRIC CURRENT when moved. The resistance of metal conductors increases with temperature because the vibrations of atoms increase and scatter the free electrons.

cone Solid, three-dimensional geometric figure that is a pyramid over a circular base. It is swept out by a line (generator) that joins a point moving in a closed curve in a plane, to a fixed point (vertex) outside the plane. In a right circular cone, the vertex lies above the centre of a circle (base), and the cone's generators join the vertex to points on the circle. Such a cone has a volume $\frac{1}{3}\pi r^2 h$ and a curved surface area πrs, where h is vertical height, s the slant height, and r the radius of the base.

▲ **condor** The Andean condor (*Vultur gryphus*) is a type of vulture. With a wing span of up to 3m (10ft), the Andean condor feeds mainly on carrion, but also preys on lambs and deer.

CONGO

The Republic of Congo lies on the River CONGO in w-central Africa. The equator runs through the centre of the country. Congo has a narrow coastal plain on which stands its main port, Pointe Noire, which itself lies in the sw of the country on the Gulf of Guinea. Behind the plain are forested highlands through which the River Niari has carved a fertile valley. To the E lies Malebo (formerly known as Stanley) Pool, a large lake where the River Congo widens.

Central Congo consists of luxuriant savanna. Tree species include the valuable okoumé and mahogany. The N contains large swamps in the tributary valleys of the Congo and Ubangi rivers.

CLIMATE
Most of the country has a humid, equatorial climate, with rain throughout the year. Brazzaville has a dry season between June and September. The narrow treeless coastal plain is drier and cooler than the rest of the country, because the cold Benguela current flows N along the coast.

HISTORY
The Loango and Bakongo kingdoms dominated the Congo when the first European arrived in 1482. Between the 15th and 18th centuries, part of Congo belonged to the huge Kongo kingdom, whose centre lay to the south. Portuguese explorers reached the coast of Congo in the 15th century and the area soon became a trading region, the main commodities being slaves and ivory. The slave trade continued until the 19th century.

European exploration of the interior did not occur until the late 19th century. In 1880 Pierre Savorgnan de Brazza explored the area and it became a French protectorate. It became known as Middle Congo, a country within French Equatorial Africa, which also included Chad, Gabon and Ubangi-Shari (now called Central African Republic). In 1910 Brazzaville became the capital of French Equatorial Africa. In 1960 the Republic of Congo gained independence.

POLITICS
In 1964 Congo adopted Marxism-Leninism as the state ideology. The military, led by Marien Ngouabi, seized power in 1968. Ngouabi created the Congolese Workers Party (PCT) but was assassinated in 1977. The PCT retained power under Colonel Denis Sassou-Nguesso. In 1990 it renounced Marxism and Sassou-Nguesso was deposed. The Pan-African Union for Social Democracy (UPADS), led by Pascal

AREA 342,000sq km [132,046sq mi]
POPULATION 3,801,000
CAPITAL (POPULATION) Brazzaville (1,153,000)
GOVERNMENT Military regime
ETHNIC GROUPS Kongo 48%, Sangha 20%, Teke 17%, M'bochi 12%
LANGUAGES French (official), many others
RELIGIONS Christianity 50%, animist 48%, Islam 2%
CURRENCY CFA franc = 100 centimes

Lissouba, won multi-party elections in 1992. However, in 1997, Sassou-Nguesso, assisted by his personal militia and also by troops from Angola, launched an uprising that overthrew the government. Lissouba fled the country, taking refuge in Burkina Faso, but forces loyal to him fought back and started a civil war. Ceasefires were agreed in 1999. Sassou-Nguesso took the presidency after rigged elections in 2002. A peace accord was signed in 2003, but militias have not yet fully disarmed.

ECONOMY
The World Bank classifies Congo as a 'lower-middle-income' developing country. Agriculture is the most important activity, employing about 60% of the workforce, but many only farm at a subsistence level. The chief food crops include bananas, cassava, maize, plantains, rice and yams, while cash crops include cocoa, coffee and sugar cane.

Congo is one of Africa's major producers of oil, and oil remains the major export, but production has begun to decline. Timber is also exported. Manufacturing is relatively unimportant, hampered by poor transport links. Inland, rivers form the main lines of communication, and BRAZZAVILLE is linked to the port of Pointe-Noire by the Congo-Ocean Railway.

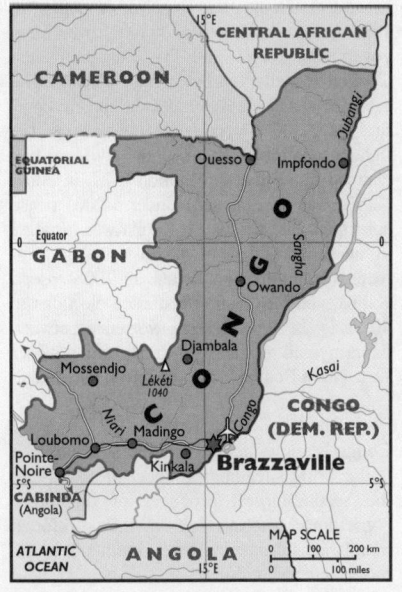

Confederate States of America (Confederacy) Southern states that seceded from the Union following the election of Abraham LINCOLN. South Carolina left in December 1860, and was followed by Alabama, Florida, Georgia, Louisiana, Mississippi and Texas. In March 1861, Jefferson DAVIS was elected president and a new constitution protected STATES' RIGHTS and retained SLAVERY. A capital was established at MONTGOMERY, Alabama. On April 12, the US CIVIL WAR began and Arkansas, North Carolina, Tennessee and Virginia joined the Confederacy. The capital was moved to RICHMOND, Virginia. The Confederacy received little external support, and internal division contributed to its defeat and dissolution in April 1865.

Confederation of British Industry (CBI) UK organization founded in 1965 to promote the prosperity and interests of British industry. Financed by *c*.250,000 companies, which are its members, the CBI advises the government on policy.

confession Acknowledgement of sins. In the Jewish and Christian traditions, it may be made by a congregation in the course of worship, or by individual penitents.

CONGO, DEMOCRATIC REPUBLIC OF (DRC)

The Democratic Republic of Congo is Africa's third-largest country. It is dominated by the River CONGO. N-central Congo consists of a high plateau. In the E, the plateau rises to 5,109m [16,762ft] in the RUWENZORI mountains. Lakes Albert and Edward form much of Congo's border with Uganda. Lake Kivu lies along its border with Rwanda. Lake TANGANYIKA forms the border with Tanzania. All the lakes lie in an arm of the Great RIFT VALLEY. Dense equatorial rainforests grow in the N, with savanna and swamps in the S.

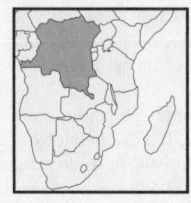

CLIMATE
Much of Congo has an equatorial climate with high temperatures and heavy rainfall throughout the year. The S has a more subtropical climate.

HISTORY
By *c.* AD 1000, Bantu-speakers had largely displaced the native pygmy population. From the 14th century, large Bantu kingdoms emerged. In 1482, a Portuguese navigator became the first European to reach the mouth of the River Congo. In the 19th century, traders in slaves and ivory formed powerful states. Henry Morton STANLEY's explorations (1874–77) established the route of the Congo. In 1878, King LEOPOLD II of Belgium employed Stanley to found colonies along the Congo. In 1885, Leopold established the Congo Free State. Leopold's empire grew, and concessionaires gained control of the lucrative rubber trade. The trade received international criticism after Sir Roger CASEMENT denounced its exploitation of the native population. In 1908, Belgium responded by establishing direct control as the colony of Belgian Congo. European companies exploited African labour to develop copper and diamond mines. In 1958, France offered the Congo a vote on independence. Nationalists in Belgian Congo demanded similar elections.

AREA
2,344,858sq km
[905,350sq mi]
POPULATION
65,752,000
CAPITAL (POPULATION)
Kinshasa (5,717,000)
GOVERNMENT Single-party republic
ETHNIC GROUPS Over 200; the largest are Mongo, Luba, Kongo, Mangbetu-Azande
LANGUAGES French (official), tribal languages
RELIGIONS Roman Catholic 50%, Protestant 20%, Islam 10%, others
CURRENCY Congolese franc = 100 centimes

POLITICS
In 1960, the Belgian Congo gained independence and Patrice LUMUMBA became prime minister. Joseph MOBUTU, commander in chief of the Congolese National Army, seized power later that year and Lumumba was murdered. In 1964, the country plunged into civil war and Belgian troops intervened. In 1965, Mobutu proclaimed himself president and began a campaign of 'Africanization'. The country and river were renamed Zaïre in 1971, and Mobutu adopted the name Mobutu Sese Seko. Zaïre became a one-party state. Mobutu finally accepting opposition parties in 1990, although elections were repeatedly deferred. In 1995, millions of Hutus fled from Rwanda into east Zaïre to escape Tutsi reprisals. In 1996, rebels led by Laurent Kabila overthrew Mobuto. Zaïre became the Democratic Republic of Congo. In 1998, Congo descended into civil war between government forces and the Tutsi-dominated Congolese Rally for Democracy (RCD). The 1999 Lusaka Peace Agreement brought a ceasefire and 5,500 UN peace-keeping troops, but fighting continued. By 2001 the civil war had claimed more than 2.5 million lives. In 2001, Kabila was assassinated. Under a 2003 peace agreement his son Joseph Kabila was installed as interim president of a transitional government, but fighting continued. In 2006 Joseph Kabila won DRC's first contested elections in 40 years. In 2007 fighting worsened between the army and militia loyal to opposition leader Jean-Pierre Bemba, who was driven into exile.

ECONOMY
Congo is a low-income developing country. It is the world's leading producer of cobalt and the second-largest producer of diamonds. Agriculture employs 71% of the workforce, mainly at subsistence level. Palm oil is the most vital cash crop.

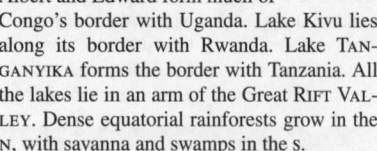

confirmation Sacrament of the Christian Church by which the relationship between God and an individual, established by BAPTISM, is confirmed or strengthened in faith. Candidates for confirmation take the baptismal vows previously made on their behalf by godparents, and confirm the intention to keep them.

Confucianism Philosophy that dominated China until the early 20th century and still has many followers, mainly in Asia. It is based on the *Analects*, sayings attributed to CONFUCIUS. Strictly an ethical system to ensure a smooth-running society, it gradually acquired quasi-religious characteristics. Confucianism views man as potentially the most perfect form of *li*, the ultimate embodiment of good. It stresses the responsibility of sovereign to subject, of family members to one other, and of friend to friend. Politically, it helped to preserve the existing order, upholding the status of the Mandarins. When the monarchy was overthrown (1911–12), Confucian institutions were ended, but after the Communist Revolution (1949), many Confucian elements were incorporated into Maoism.

Confucius (551–479 BC) (K'ung-fu-tzu) Founder of CONFUCIANISM. Born in Lu, he was an excellent scholar and became an influential teacher of the sons of wealthy families. He is said to have been prime minister of Lu, but he resigned when he realized the post carried no real authority. In his later years he sought a return to the political morality of the early ZHOU dynasty. *See also* CHINESE LITERATURE

congenital disorder Abnormal condition present from birth caused by faulty development, infection, or the mother's exposure to drugs or other toxic substances during pregnancy. SPINA BIFIDA is such a condition.

conglomerate In geology, a sedimentary rock made up of rounded pebbles embedded in a fine matrix of sand or silt, commonly formed along beaches or on river beds.

Congo *See* country feature.

Congo (formerly Zaïre River) River in central and W Africa; the second-longest in the continent. It rises in S D.R. Congo and flows in a massive curve to the Atlantic Ocean for 4670km (2900mi). Its rate of flow and size of drainage basin make it Africa's largest untapped source of hydroelectric power. The chief ocean port is Matadi, and the major river ports are KINSHASA and KISANGANI. The main headstream is the Lualaba, and the Kasai and Ubangi are among its many large tributaries.

Congo, Democratic Republic of *See* country feature.

congregationalism Christian church denomination in which local churches are autonomous; members have been called Brownists, Separatists, and Independents. It is based on the belief that Christ is the head of the Church and all members are God's priests. Congregationalism began in England in *c*.1580. In the UK, the Congregational Church in England and Wales merged with others to form the United Reformed Church (1972). In the USA, the Congregational Christian Churches united with others to form the United Church of Christ (1957).

Congress Legislative branch of the US federal government established by the US CONSTITUTION (1789). The first meeting of Congress took place in 1789 in New York City. Congress comprises the SENATE (the Upper House) and the HOUSE OF REPRESENTATIVES (the Lower House). The main powers of Congress include the right to assess and collect taxes, introduce legislation, regulate commerce, propose constitutional amendments, mint money, raise and maintain armed forces, establish lower courts and declare war. Legislation must be passed by both Houses and the President to become law. If the President uses his power of veto, Congress can still pass the bill with a two-thirds majority in each house. A resident commissioner from Puerto Rico, and delegates from Guam, the Virgin Islands, and the District of Columbia complete the composition of Congress. The Senate can approve treaties and presidential appointments, and tries the president if he is impeached. The House of Representatives initiates all tax bills and has the power to impeach the president. The Constitution requires that Congress meet at least once every year, and the president may call special sessions. The preparation and consideration of legislation is largely accomplished by the 17 standing committees in the Senate and the 21 in the House of Representatives.

Congress of Industrial Organizations (CIO) *See* AMERICAN FEDERATION OF LABOR AND CONGRESS OF INDUSTRIAL ORGANIZATIONS (AFL-CIO)

Congress of Racial Equality (CORE) US civil rights organization, founded in 1942 by James Farmer. It employed sit-ins, picketing, and boycotting tactics to combat discrimination in employment.

Congress Party (officially Indian National Congress) Oldest political party in India, whose fortunes have often been intertwined with the Nehru dynasty. Founded in 1885, Congress was not prominent until after World War 1, when 'Mahatma' GANDHI transformed it into a mass independence movement, agitating by means of civil disobedience. Jawaharlal NEHRU became president of the Congress in 1929. In the 1937 provincial elections it gained power in many states. During World War 2 (after the British refused to grant self-government) it remained neutral. At independence (1947), Nehru became prime minister. Nehru's daughter Indira GANDHI became prime minister in 1966, but in 1969 was challenged by a right wing faction (led by Moraji Desai) causing a split in the party. Indira's Congress (I) suffered a landslide defeat at the elections of 1977. They returned to power in 1979, and in 1984 (after Indira's assassination) her son Rajiv GANDHI became leader, securing the party's re-election in that year. Congress lost the 1989 elections, and Rajiv Gandhi was assassinated in 1991. The Congress Party lost the 1996, 1998, and 1999 elections to the BHARATIYA JANATA PARTY (BJP).

congress system Attempt during the early 19th century to conduct diplomacy through regular conferences between the European allies that had defeated Napoleonic France. It originated in the Treaty of PARIS (1815). The four powers (Austria, Britain, Prussia, and Russia) met in 1818, 1820, and 1821. Britain withdrew from the Congress of Verona (1822) after opposing proposals to intervene against revolutionary forces in South America and elsewhere. In 1825, differences between the three remaining powers at a meeting in St Petersburg, Russia, caused the abandonment of the system.

Congreve, William (1670–1729) English dramatist who wrote comedies such as *Love for Love* (1695) and *The Way of the World* (1700). His satire is at the peak of RESTORATION DRAMA. He also wrote a tragedy, *The Mourning Bride* (1697).

conic (conic section) Curve found by the intersection of a plane with a cone. Circles, ellipses, parabolas or hyperbolas are conic sections. Alternatively a conic is the locus of a point that moves so that the ratio of its distances from a fixed point (the focus) and a fixed line (the directrix) is constant. This ratio is called the eccentricity (e): $e = 1$ gives a parabola, $e > 1$ a hyperbola, $e < 1$ an ellipse, and $e = 0$ a circle.

conifer Large group of cone-bearing trees, generally evergreen, such as pines, firs and redwoods. Some are the Earth's largest plants, reaching heights up to 99m (325ft). They are a major natural resource of the Northern Hemisphere. *See* picture, page 246

Connecticut State in NE USA; its state capital and largest city is HARTFORD. One of the original 13 colonies, Connecticut was first settled by the English in the 1630s. Puritans flocked to the area, and in 1662 the colony received a charter from Charles II. Connecticut was one of the first states to ratify the US Constitution and was admitted to the union in 1788. The Connecticut River valley separates the W and E highlands. Manufacturing is the mainstay of the state economy. Industries: transport equipment, machinery, chemicals, metallurgy. Hartford is one of the world's leading insurance centres. Dairy produce, eggs and tobacco are the main farm products. Fishing is also important. Area: 12,549sq km (4845sq mi). Pop. (2000) 3,405,565.

connective tissue Supporting and packing tissue that helps to maintain the body's shape and hold it together. Its main component is the tough protein COLLAGEN. Bones, ligaments, cartilage and skin are all types of connective tissue.

C

CONNECTICUT
Statehood :
January 9, 1788
Nickname :
Constitution State
State bird :
Robin
State flower :
Mountain laurel
State tree :
White oak
State motto :
He who transplanted still sustains

INTERNET

Congo, Democratic Republic of
▶ www.un.int/drcongo

Connecticut
▶ www.ct.gov

Connery, Sean (1930–) Scottish film actor. Connery starred in *Dr No* (1962), the first adaptation of Ian FLEMING's James Bond spy stories. He went on to make a further six Bond films. Keen to escape typecasting, Connery established himself as a versatile character actor in films such as *The Name of the Rose* (1986). He won an Academy Award as best supporting actor for *The Untouchables* (1987).

Connolly, James (1870–1916) Irish nationalist leader. He went to the USA in 1903, and helped establish the Industrial Workers of the World (IWW). Returning to Ireland, he united Belfast's dock workers and then helped organize the Dublin transport workers' strike (1913). He was a leader in the EASTER RISING of 1916, and was executed by the British.

Connors, Jimmy (James Scott) (1952–) US tennis player. Connors won more Grand Prix singles titles (109) than any other player. In 1974, he won the US, Australian, and Wimbledon singles titles. He went on to win the US Open four more times (1976, 1978, 1982–83) and Wimbledon in 1982. He also won doubles titles with Ilie Nastase.

conquistador Leader of the Spanish conquest of the New World in the 16th century. Conquistadores ('conquerors') were often ex-soldiers unemployed since the completion of the Christian reconquest of Spain. The most famous were Hernán CORTÉS and Francisco PIZARRO.

Conrad IV (1228–54) German king (1237–54) and King of Sicily and Jerusalem (1250–54). Son of FREDERICK II, he was elected German king (Emperor-elect, 1237). When Pope Innocent IV deposed Frederick in 1245 and named an anti-king to replace Conrad in 1246, Germany was plunged into war. Conrad inherited Sicily and Jerusalem upon Frederick's death, but was never crowned Emperor. *See also* HOLY ROMAN EMPIRE

Conrad, Joseph (1857–1924) British novelist and short-story writer, b. Poland. His eventful years as a ship's officer in Asian, African, and Latin American waters informed the exotic settings of many of his novels. He was a central figure in the development of literary MODERNISM. His major works include *Lord Jim* (1900), *Heart of Darkness* (1902), *Nostromo* (1904), *The Secret Agent* (1907), and *Chance* (1914).

conscription (draft) Compulsory enlistment of people for service in the armed forces. In its modern form, conscription originates with the FRENCH REVOLUTION and its struggles against the other European powers. In Britain, conscription was used in both World Wars and continued as National Service until 1962. In the United States, conscription was used during the American CIVIL WAR and again from 1940–73.

conservation Preservation of nature and natural resources. Conservation includes protecting the landscape from change due to natural erosion; using soil conditioners and artificial fertilizers to maintain soil fertility; replacing topsoil and landscaping spoiled land and protecting threatened species of animals and plants by law or in wildlife parks and reservations.

conservation, laws of Physical laws stating that some property of a closed system is unaltered by change in the system; it is conserved. The most important are the laws of conservation of matter and energy. Mass and energy are interconvertible according to the equation $E = mc^2$; what is conserved is the total mass and its equivalent in energy.

conservatism Political philosophy seeking to preserve the continuity of a society's laws, social structure, and institutions. Its modern expression derives from the response, first evident in Germany, to the liberal doctrines of the Enlightenment and French Revolution. Originally conservatives supported MERCANTILISM in preference to LAISSEZ-FAIRE economics, but in the 20th century they adopted the principles of the free-market and MONETARISM. *See also* BURKE, EDMUND; CHRISTIAN DEMOCRATS; CONSERVATIVE PARTY; LIBERALISM; SOCIALISM

Conservative Party (officially Conservative and Unionist Party) The oldest political party in Britain, its origins lie in the transformation of TORY PARTY into the Conservative Party under Sir Robert PEEL in the 1830s. Until the late 19th century, it was mainly a party of landed interests, electorally dependent on the county constituencies. After the Reform Act (1867) and the establishment of a Central Office in 1870, the urban and commercial element in the party increased. In 1886 the split in the LIBERAL PARTY over Irish home rule brought Liberal Unionists into the party. It was in power for 31 of the years 1834–1905, and either alone or in coalition for most of the 1920s and 1930s . It held office in 1951–64 and 1970–74. In 1979, the party swung to the right under the leadership (1975–90) of Margaret THATCHER. With the support of traditional Labour Party voters, it was able (under Thatcher and John MAJOR) to win four consecutive elections but was then defeated in 1997, 2001 and 2005.

Constable, John (1776–1837) English painter, a leading western landscapist. He attended the Royal Academy (1795–1802) and studied the paintings of CLAUDE LORRAIN. He considered every effect of clouds and light on water, often using broken colour and a thick impasto texture. His first success came when *The Haywain* (1821) and *View on the Stour* (1817) were shown at the 1824 Paris Salon, although recognition in England only came after his death. He had a great impact on French romantic artists, notably DELACROIX.

Constance, Council of (1414–18) Ecumenical council that ended the GREAT SCHISM. It was convoked by the antipope John XXIII. Martin V was elected in 1417.

constant In mathematics, a quantity or factor that does not change. It may be universal, such as PI, or it may be particular, such as a symbol that has a fixed value in an algebraic equation.

Constant (de Rebecque), (Henri) Benjamin (1761–1830) French political writer, b. Switzerland. A member of Napoléon's tribunate (1799–1802), he went into exile in 1803. After the BOURBON restoration he was leader of the liberal opposition (1819–22, 1824–30). His chief work was

---

CONIFER

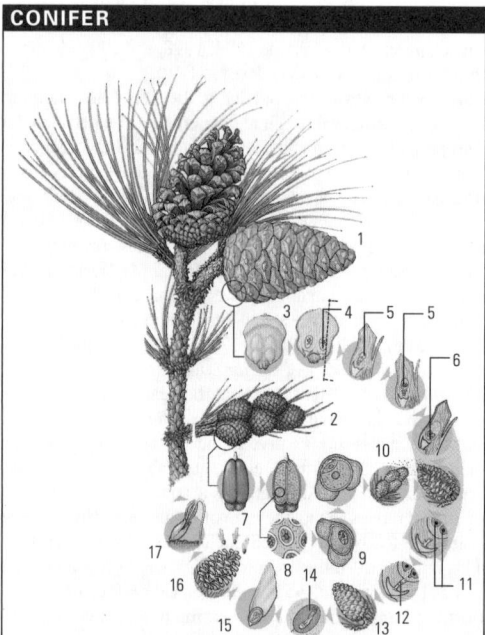

The reproductive cycle of the ponderosa pine is typical of many conifers. In summer, the mature tree bears both female cones (1) and male cones (2). A scale from the female cone (3) contains two ovules (4). Within each ovule, a spore cell (5) divides to develop into a female gametophyte (6). A scale from the male cone (7) contains many spores (8). Each of these develops into a male gametophyte within a winged pollen grain (9). This process lasts one year. Pollination occurs early the next summer, when female cones open so that airborne pollen grains enter an ovule. Inside the ovule, the female gametophyte develops two ova (11). Fertilization occurs during the spring of the following year, after the male gametophyte has matured and grown a pollen tube, and the cone closes (13). Within the female gametophyte, the fertilized ova (zygote) develops into an embryo (14); and around it, a tough, winged seed case is formed (15). In the autumn of the second year, the female cone opens (16), and seeds are dispersed by wind; ready to germinate (17).

the psychological novel *Adolphe* (1816), a fictionalized account of his relationship with Madame de STAËL.

Constanta City in E Romania, on the Black Sea. Founded in the 7th century BC as a Greek colony. It is Romania's chief port and a major trade centre. It has Roman and Byzantine ruins, several mosques, and a naval and air base. Industries: shipbuilding, oil refining, textiles. Pop. (2002 est.) 337,800.

Constantine I (the Great) (285–337) Roman Emperor (306–37) and founder of the Christian empire. A series of feuds for control of Italy ended when Constantine adopted Christianity and defeated Maxentius (312). Constantine and Licinius signed the Edict of Milan (313), which extended tolerance to Christians throughout the Empire. In 324 Constantine defeated Licinius and became sole ruler of the Empire. He presided over the first council of the Christian Church at NICAEA (325), which condemned ARIANISM. Constantine rebuilt (330) Byzantium as his capital and renamed it Constantinople (modern-day ISTANBUL). Constantine centralized imperial power, but divided the empire on his death. Historians debate whether his Christianity was born of conviction or political expediency.

Constantinople Former name of ISTANBUL

constellation Grouping of stars, forming an imaginary figure traced on the sky. The groupings have no physical basis as each star is a different distance from Earth. There are 88 constellations that have been assigned boundaries on the CELESTIAL SPHERE by the International Astronomical Union in 1930.

constitution Code of laws or collection of customary practices delineating the powers and organization of the various organs of government within a nation, and some of the rights and obligations of its citizens. In states with a written constitution, courts often have specific powers relating to the constitution. In the US, where there is a federal system of government, the SUPREME COURT resolves conflict between the individual states and the central government. In countries without a written constitution, such as Britain, constitutional law is less precise and problems are addressed within the political process.

Constitutional Convention (1787) Meeting of delegates, in Philadelphia, from 12 of the 13 US states (Rhode Island abstained), which resulted in the creation of the US Constitution. The Convention convened to revise the ARTICLES OF CONFEDERATION and to redress the lack of power wielded by the existing government structure. The major disagreement centred on how each state should determine its share of this centralized power. It agreed a bicameral system, whereby the House of Representatives was elected according to population, and the Senate was chosen by the states.

constitutional law Procedures and doctrines defining the operation of the constitution of a state. In states with a written constitution, courts often have specific powers relating to the constitution and likely points of conflict. In the USA, where there is a federal system of government, the SUPREME COURT often resolves conflict between the individual states and the central government. In countries without a written constitution, such as Britain, constitutional law is more imprecise and problems are addressed within the political process.

Constitution of the United States Fundamental laws and basis of government of the USA. Adopted by the CONSTITUTIONAL CONVENTION in Philadelphia in September 1787, it was ratified by the 13 states in 1788–90. It replaced the ARTICLES OF CONFEDERATION (1781), which had proved inadequate, giving too much power to each state at the expense of central government. It was designed to create a system of 'checks and balances', to prevent one branch of government gaining dominance over others. Opponents who feared the federal government would be too powerful and the rights of the individual unprotected succeeded in having ten amendments, collectively known as the BILL OF RIGHTS, added to the Constitution. The US Constitution was designed not as a code of laws, but as a statement of principles to which laws should adhere, thus allowing considerable flexibility in judicial interpretation.

constructivism Russian ABSTRACT ART movement founded in c.1913 by Vladimir TATLIN. Other leading members were the painter and photographer Alexander RODCHENKO and the brothers Naum GABO and Antoine PEVSNER, both sculptors. Influenced by CUBISM and FUTURISM, their works were less purely abstract than Tatlin's geometric constructions and attempted to relate to contemporary technology. From 1921 the Soviet regime condemned the movement, and Gabo and Pevsner left Russia. Through them, and other exiles, constructivism influenced modern European architecture and sculpture.

consul Highest civil and military office of the ancient Roman Republic. According to Roman tradition the office was established in 510 BC, although it did not become a continuous institution until somewhat later. Consuls were elected each year. All Roman citizens were eligible to vote, but over time the election process became biased in favour of the aristocracy. After 367 BC one consul was a PATRICIAN, the other a PLEBEIAN, each having the power to veto the other's decisions. The office continued in the Imperial period, although no longer effective head of state, and most emperors declared themselves Consul repeatedly. The title of Consul has been used by later governments, not always for comparable roles.

consumption *See* TUBERCULOSIS

contact lens Lens worn on the CORNEA to aid defective vision. Invented in 1887, lenses were initially made of glass. Modern contact lenses, developed (1948) by Kevin Tuohy, are made of plastic. Hard (corneal) lenses cover the pupil and part of the cornea. They are usually gas-permeable (allowing oxygen to reach the cornea). Soft (hydrophilic) lenses cover the whole cornea and are hydrated in saline solution.

continent Large land masses on the Earth's surface. The continents are EUROPE and ASIA (or Eurasia), AFRICA, NORTH AMERICA, SOUTH AMERICA, AUSTRALIA, and ANTARCTICA. They cover c.30% of the Earth above sea level and extend below sea level forming continental shelves. All continents have four components which make up the continental crust. **Shields** are areas of relatively flat land less than a few hundred metres above sea level, and consist of crystalline rocks. **Stable platforms** are areas that have a thin covering of sedimentary rock. **Sedimentary basins** are broad, deep depressions filled with sedimentary rocks formed in shallow seas. **Folded mountain** belts are younger sedimentary rocks in long, linear zones of intensely folded and faulted rocks that have been metamorphosed and intruded by igneous and volcanic activity. The continental crust is composed of rocks, less dense than the basaltic rocks in ocean basins, moving very slowly across the surface of the Earth by CONTINENTAL DRIFT. Its thickness is mainly between 30 and 40km (20–25mi), except under large mountain chains where its thickness can be 70km (45mi). *See also* PLATE TECTONICS

Continental Congress Federal legislature of the American colonies during the AMERICAN REVOLUTION and the period of Confederation. Its first meeting (Philadelphia, September 1774) resulted in unified opposition to British rule and agreed on a boycott of trade with Britain. The Congress reconvened in May 1775, and appointed George WASHINGTON commander of the army. In July 1776, the Second Congress adopted the DECLARATION OF INDEPENDENCE and drafted the ARTICLES OF CONFEDERATION. Adoption of the US CONSTITUTION (1787) made the Congress redundant, although it met until 1789.

continental drift Theory that the continents change position very slowly, moving over the Earth's surface at a rate of a only a few centimetres per year, but this adding up to

◀ **Connery** Sean Connery appeared in seven Bond films: *Dr No* (1962), *From Russia with Love* (1963), *Goldfinger* (1964), *Thunderball* (1965), *You Only Live Twice* (1967), *Diamonds Are Forever* (1971), and *Never Say Never Again* (1983). His performance in *The Untouchables* (1987) led to a succession of roles in Hollywood action films, such as *Indiana Jones and the Last Crusade* (1989).

thousands of kilometres over time. Early supporters of continental drift claimed that the jigsaw shapes of the present day continents could be pieced together to form an ancient land mass which, at sometime in the past, split and drifted apart. Evidence for this theory included matching the outlines of continents, rock types, geological structures and fossils. Continental drift became accepted with the development of PLATE TECTONICS in the 1960s. In recent years, continental movement has been measured by global positioning satellites. *See also* GONDWANALAND; PANGAEA

continental margin Region of the ocean floor that lies between the shoreline and the abyssal ocean floor. It includes the continental shelf, the continental slope, and the continental rise. The continental shelf slopes gently seawards, between the shoreline and the top of the continental slope. Between the continental shelf and the continental rise is the continental slope which leads into deep water. The continental rise, at the foot of the slope, is an area of thick deposits of sediments.

Continental System Trade blockade of Britain introduced (1806) by NAPOLEON I to cripple the British economy and force peace terms in the NAPOLEONIC WARS. Extended to Russia by the Treaty of Tilsit (1807) and to Spain and Portugal (1808), the Continental System also included neutral countries and prompted a retaliatory British blockade against France and its allies. The system was unpopular, and the economic war probably caused more deprivation on continental mainland than in Britain. The restrictions contributed to the WAR OF 1812.

Contra Right-wing Nicaraguan revolutionary group active between 1979 and 1990. Supporters of the former dictator General Anastasio SOMOZA, ousted in 1979, the Contra aimed to overthrow the elected, left-wing SANDINISTA government. The Contra received financial and military assistance from the US government from mid-1986. Elections were subsequently held in Nicaragua in 1990, at which the US-funded Union of National Opposition (UNO), effectively the political wing of the Contra, was victorious. The Contra were officially disbanded, but social conditions within Nicaragua remained unstable. *See also* IRAN-CONTRA AFFAIR

contraception (birth control) Use of devices or techniques to prevent pregnancy. The PILL is a hormone preparation that prevents the release of an egg (OVUM) and thickens the cervical mucus. The intra-uterine device (IUD) is a small spring made from plastic or metal inserted into the womb. It stops the fertilized egg embedding itself in the uterine lining. Barrier methods include the male and female condom and the diaphragm. The male condom is a latex sheath that covers the penis and collects the ejaculated semen; the female condom lines the inside of the vagina, preventing any sperm entering the womb. The use of condoms is widely advocated because they protect against some sexually transmitted diseases, including ACQUIRED IMMUNE DEFICIENCY SYNDROME (AIDS). Devices such as diaphragms or caps cover the cervix, thus preventing sperm entering the womb. Less effective is the "rhythm method", which involves the avoidance of sex on days when conception is most likely (when the woman is ovulating). It is not a reliable method as ovulation cannot always be predicted accurately. Emergency contraception, known as the "morning-after pill", can be taken up to 72 hours after unprotected sexual intercourse; it prevents the fertilized ovum embedding itself in the womb. It is not suitable to be used regularly. *See also* SEXUAL REPRODUCTION

contralto Lowest range (below SOPRANO and MEZZO-SOPRANO) of the female singing voice. A male voice in this range is called a COUNTERTENOR. *See also* ALTO

convection Transfer of heat by flow of currents within fluids (gases or liquids). Warm fluids have a natural tendency to rise (because they are less dense), whereas cooler fluids tend to fall. This movement subsides when all areas of the fluid are at the same temperature. Convection in the form of winds is the main method of heat transfer from one part of the Earth to another. Liquid convection is used in a car's cooling system and some domestic central-heating systems.

convection current In geology, heat generated from radioactivity deep within the Earth's MANTLE causing rock to flow towards the CRUST. At the top of the mantle the rising rock is deflected laterally below the crust before sinking. This mantle convection is thought to drive PLATE TECTONICS.

Cook, James (1728–79) British naval officer and explorer. He demonstrated his remarkable navigational talent charting the approaches to Québec during the Seven Years' War. In 1768–71, he led an expedition to Tahiti to observe the transit of Venus and investigate the strategic and economic potential of the South Pacific. This accomplished, he conducted a survey of the unknown coasts of New Zealand and charted the E coast of Australia, naming it New South Wales and claiming it for Britain. On a second expedition to the S Pacific (1772–75), Cook charted much of the Southern Hemisphere and circumnavigated Antarctica. On his last voyage (1776–79), he discovered the Sandwich (Hawaiian) Islands, where he was killed in a dispute with the inhabitants. Cook is generally regarded as the greatest European explorer of the Pacific in the 18th century.

Cook, Robin (1946–2005) British statesman, foreign secretary (1997–2001), leader of the House (2001–2003). He entered Parliament in 1974, and held various posts (1987–97) in Labour's shadow cabinet. As foreign secretary, Cook sought to promote a greater ethical dimension to British foreign policy. In 2003, he resigned in protest at the US and UK led war in Iraq. He died of heart failure whilst mountain climbing in Scotland.

Cook Islands Group of 15 islands in the S Pacific Ocean, NE of New Zealand, consisting of the Northern (Manihiki) Cook Islands and the Southern (Lower) Cook Islands; a self-governing territory in free association with New Zealand. Discovered (1773) by Captain James COOK, the islands became a British protectorate in 1888 and were annexed to New Zealand in 1901. They became self-governing in 1965. Products: copra, citrus fruits. Area: 293sq km (113sq mi). Pop. (2001) 18,027.

Coolidge, (John) Calvin (1872–1933) 30th US president (1923–29). Stern action in the Boston police strike of 1919 earned him the Republican nomination as vice president in 1920. He became president on the death of Warren HARDING in 1923 and was re-elected in 1924. His conservative administration was characterized by minimal government interference in business and commerce, summed up by his phrase "the business of America is business".

Cooper, James Fenimore (1789–1851) US novelist. One of the earliest American novelists and among the first to gain international recognition. His most successful works were the romantic 'Leatherstocking Tales' about the frontier, of which the best known are *The Pioneers* (1823), *The Last of the Mohicans* (1826) and *The Deerslayer* (1841). He also wrote a number of novels about life at sea, including *The Pilot* (1823).

cooperative movement Variety of worldwide organizations, founded to provide mutual assistance in economic enterprises for the benefit of their members. The first such movement was founded (1844) in England by the Rochdale Pioneers, who established a cooperative retail society to eliminate the middleman and share profits among its members. The

INTERNET

Cook Islands
▸ www.ck

Coolidge, (John) Calvin
▸ www.whitehouse.gov/ history/presidents

Cooper, James Fenimore
▸ external.oneonta.edu/ cooper
▸ www.classicbookshelf. com

▼ **continental drift** About 200 million years ago, the original Pangaea land mass began to split into two continental groups, which further separated over time to produce the present-day configuration.

—— trench
—— rift
—— new ocean floor
—— zones of slippage

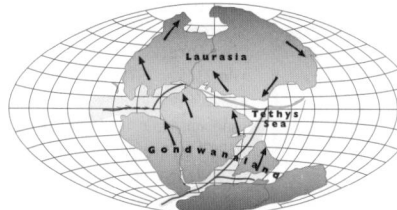

180 million years ago

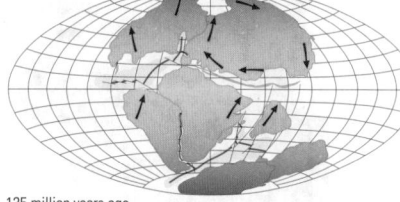

135 million years ago

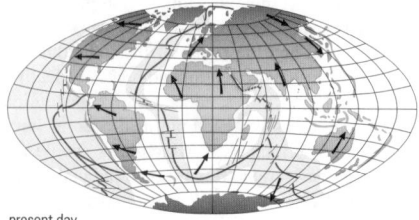

present day

cooperative movement has been extended to include cooperative agriculture, manufacturing, banking and finance. *See also* COOPERATIVE PARTY; COOPERATIVE WHOLESALE SOCIETY

Cooperative Party British political party, formed in 1917 as the political arm of the Cooperative Union. Associated with the LABOUR PARTY, since 1946 all of its parliamentary candidates have stood for election jointly as Labour co-operative candidates. Since 1959, it limited the number of its candidates to 30.

Cooperative Wholesale Society Organization formed in the north of England in 1863 to provide for consumer cooperation. It was a development of the early cooperative experiments of Robert Owen and the Rochdale Pioneers, which encouraged consumers to form their own retail societies and share the profits among themselves, eliminating the middleman.

coordinate geometry (algebraic geometry) Branch of mathematics combining the methods of pure GEOMETRY with those of ALGEBRA. Any geometrical point can be given an algebraical value by relating it to co-ordinates, marked off from a frame of reference. Thus, if a point is marked on a square grid so that it is x_1 squares along the x axis and y_1 squares along the y axis, it has the co-ordinates (x_1, y_1). Polar co-ordinates can also be used. It was first introduced in the 17th century by René Descartes. *See also* CARTESIAN CO-ORDINATES

coot Aquatic bird of freshwater marshes. Related to the RAILS, it is a strong swimmer and diver. All coots have white bills and foreheads. The female lays 8–12 buff-coloured, brown-spotted eggs on a floating reed nest. Family Rallidae; genus *Fulica*.

Copenhagen (København) Capital and chief port of Denmark on E Sjaelland and N Amager Island, in the Øresund. A trading and fishing centre by the early 12th century, it became Denmark's capital in 1443. It has a 17th-century stock exchange, the Amalienborg palace (home of the royal family) and the Christianborgs Palace. Other sights include the Tivoli Amusement Park and the Little Mermaid sculpture. The commercial and cultural centre of the nation, it has shipbuilding, chemical and brewing industries. Pop. (2005) 1,091,000.

Copernicus, Nicolas (1473–1543) (Mikolaj Kopernik) Polish astronomer. Through his study of planetary motions, Copernicus developed a heliocentric (Sun-centred) theory of the universe in opposition to the accepted geocentric (Earth-centred) theory conceived by PTOLEMY nearly 1500 years before. In the **Copernican system** (as it is now called) the planets' motions in the sky were explained by their orbit of the Sun. The motion of the sky was simply a result of the Earth turning on its axis. An account of his work, *De revolutionibus orbium coelestium*, was published in 1543. Most astronomers considered the new system as merely a means of calculating planetary positions, and continued to believe in ARISTOTLE's view of the world. *See also* GALILEO; KEPLER

Copland, Aaron (1900–90) US composer, especially known for combining folk and jazz elements with 20th-century symphonic techniques. His highly popular ballet music includes *Billy the Kid* (1938), *Rodeo* (1942) and *Appalachian Spring* (1944), which won a Pulitzer Prize. He wrote symphonies, chamber music and overtly patriotic pieces such as *A Lincoln Portrait* (1942). Less well known are Copland's experiments with serial techniques, as in *Piano Fantasy* (1957). He was also a conductor and an admired teacher.

Copley, John Singleton (1738–1815) US painter. An extraordinarily gifted draughtsman and colourist, he produced portraits and historical action scenes. His notable paintings include *Colonel Epes Sargent* (c.1760), *The Boy with a Squirrel* (1765), and the history paintings *Brook Watson and the Shark* (1778) and *The Death of Major Peirson* (1783).

copper (symbol Cu) Metallic element, one of the transition metals. Reddish copper occurs native (free or uncombined) and in several ores including cuprite (an oxide) and chalcopyrite (a sulphide). The metal is extracted by smelting and is purified by ELECTROLYSIS. It is malleable, a good thermal and electrical conductor, second only to silver, and is extensively used in boilers, pipes, electrical equipment and alloys, such as brass and bronze. Copper tarnishes in air, oxidizes at high temperatures and is attacked only by oxidizing acids. Properties: at.no. 29; r.a.m. 63.546; r.d. 8.96; m.p. 1.083°C (1981°F); b.p. 2567°C (4653°F); most common isotope Cu^{63} (69.09%).

copperhead Any of various species of snakes, so-called because of their head colour. The N American copperhead is a pit viper, rarely more than 1m (3ft) long. The Australian copperhead is a venomous snake of the cobra family, often reaching 1.5m (5ft) in length. The Indian copperhead is a rat snake.

Coppola, Francis Ford (1939–) US film director, producer, and screenwriter. In 1969 Coppola established Zoetrope, an independent production company. He won an Academy Award for best picture for *The Godfather* (1972). Its sequel, *Godfather II* (1974), won him Oscars for best picture and best director. Coppola followed this success with *Apocalypse Now* (1975). Other films include *Rumble Fish* (1983), *Peggy Sue Got Married* (1986), and *Dracula* (1992).

Coptic Church Largest Christian Church in Egypt. Its members form 5–10% of Egypt's population. Of ancient origin, the Copts trace the history of the church to Saint MARK. As a result of its Monophysite creed (denying the humanity of Christ), the Coptic Church was declared heretical by the Council of Chalcedon (451) and was isolated from other Christian Churches. The Arab conquest of Egypt brought mass conversion to Islam.

copyright Legal authority protecting works of art, literature, music and computer programs from reproduction or publication without the consent of the owner of the copyright. Since the Universal Copyright Convention (1952), works must carry the copyright symbol (©) followed by the owner's name and the first year of publication. Computer software and programs are protected in the US by the Copyright Act (1976) and Computer Software Act (1980), and in the UK by the Copyright (Computer Software) Amendment Act (1985). In the UK, the Copyright, Designs and Patents Act (1988) introduced the concept of 'intellectual property'.

coral Small, CNIDARIAN marine animal of class Anthozoa, often found in colonies. The limestone skeletons secreted by each animal polyp accumulate to form a CORAL REEF. Reef-building corals are found only in waters with temperatures in excess of 20°C (68°F).

coral reef Rock formation found in shallow tropical seas. Such reefs are formed from the calcium carbonate secreted by living CORAL organisms as protection against predators and wave action. The way in which the coral, and therefore the reef, grows is strongly influenced by the prevailing currents and the temperature of the surrounding sea water.

Coral Sea Arm of the sw Pacific Ocean between the Great Barrier Reef off the E coast of Australia, Vanuatu (E) and New Guinea (NW). It was the scene of a US naval victory over the Japanese in 1942.

coral snake Poisonous burrowing snake of the Americas and SE Asia. It is shy and docile, but has fatal venom. Most species are brightly coloured, ringed with red, yellow, and black. It feeds on lizards, frogs, and other snakes. Family Elapidae.

cor anglais (English horn) Reed instrument of the OBOE family. Longer than the oboe, its range is a fifth lower. Its bell is

◄ **Coolidge** His honesty and homespun philosophy made Calvin Coolidge a popular president. His term in office was distinguished by a laissez-faire approach to business. Many argue that his attitude towards commerce was partly responsible for the unsustainable bullishness of the US stock market in the 1920s.

▲ **Coppola** His Godfather trilogy on the history of the Corleone mafia family earned him a place in cinema history. In 1970, Francis Coppola won his first Academy Award for co-writing the screenplay *Patton*. *Apocalypse Now* (1975) was both a creative updating of the Joseph Conrad novel *Heart of Darkness*, and an expression of the horrors of the Vietnam War. His daughter, Sofia Coppola (1971–), who starred in *The Godfather, Part III* (1990), made an auspicious directorial feature film debut with *The Virgin Suicides* (2000).

C

▲ **cormorant** The common cormorant (*Phalacrocorax carbo*) is the largest of the cormorant species. It grows to a height of up to 1m (3ft). This particular species is found in or near coastal regions of N Europe, Iceland, W Greenland, Africa, Asia, Australia and New Zealand.

pear-shaped and its double reed is inserted in a curved mouthpiece. A modern counterpart for the curved oboe da caccia in the music of J.S. BACH, parts have been scored for it in 19th-century works, especially those of BERLIOZ and WAGNER.

Corbusier, Le *See* LE CORBUSIER

Córdoba (Cordova) City on the River Guadalquivir, Andalusia, S Spain; capital of Córdoba province. A flourishing centre of learning under Abd ar-Rahman III (first caliph of Córdoba), it was captured by Ferdinand III of Castile in 1236, who imposed Christian culture on the city. The Great Mosque (8th-10th century) is a world heritage site. Industries: tourism, coal and lead mining, engineering. Pop. (2001) 308,072.

core Central area of the Earth from a depth of 2885km (1790mi). It accounts for 16% of the Earth's volume and 31% of its mass. Information about the core is obtained from the measurement of seismic waves. These indicate that the outer part of the core is liquid, because shear (S) waves will not travel through it, whereas the inner core from 5150km (3200mi) to the centre of the Earth is interpreted as solid because seismic velocities are lower. It is believed that the change from liquid to solid core occurs because of immense pressure conditions. The core is thought to be composed of iron-nickel alloy (90% iron, 10% nickel). Temperature estimates for the core vary from 4000 to 7000°C (7200–12,600°F). Convection in the iron liquid outer core is thought to be responsible for producing the Earth's magnetic field.

Corelli, Arcangelo (1653–1713) Italian BAROQUE composer. He achieved early distinction as a violinist under the guidance of Giovanni Benvenuti. He helped to develop the CONCERTO grosso, composed many sonatas and did much to consolidate the principles behind modern violin playing.

Corfu (Kérkyra) Island in NW Greece, second largest of the Ionian island group; the major town is Corfu. In 433 BC the island was allied with Athens against Corinth. The Romans held Corfu from 229 BC and it was part of the Byzantine Empire until the 11th century. It was occupied by the Venetians (1386–1797), and then fell under British protection (1809–64), when it passed to Greece. Products: olives, fruit, livestock, wine. Tourism and fishing are important industries. Area: 593sq km (229sq mi). Pop. (2001) 111,975.

coriander Strong-smelling herb of the CARROT family native to the Mediterranean and Near East. The leaves, the ground seeds and oil from the seeds are used as aromatic flavourings in foods, medicines and liqueurs. Family Apiaceae/Umbelliferae; species *Coriandrum sativum*.

Corinth (Kórinthos) Capital of Corinth department, NE Peloponnesos, at the SW tip of the Isthmus of Corinth, Greece. One of the largest and most powerful cities in ancient Greece, it was a rival of Athens and friend of Sparta, with which it was allied in the PELOPONNESIAN WARS. Destroyed by the Romans in 146 BC it was rebuilt by Caesar in 44 BC. Ruled by the Venetians (1687–1715), then by the Turks, it became part of Greece in 1822. The city is 5km (3mi) NE of ancient Corinth, which was destroyed by an earthquake in 1858. The ruins include a temple of Apollo and amphitheatre. It is a transport centre and has chemical and winemaking industries. Pop. (2002 est.) 32,900.

Corinthian order One of the five ORDERS OF ARCHITECTURE

Coriolis effect (force) Apparent force on particles or objects due to the rotation of the Earth under them. The motion of particles or objects deflects towards the right in the Northern Hemisphere and towards the left in the Southern, but their speed is unaffected. The effect is named after French physicist Gustave Gaspard de Coriolis (1792–1843) who discovered it.

Cork County and county town in Munster province, S Republic of Ireland. Largest of the Irish counties, Cork has a rugged terrain with fertile valleys and a rocky coastline. The chief occupations are farming and fishing. The Danes occupied Cork in the 9th century, but Dermot McCarthy drove them out in 1172, and then he swore allegiance to the English throne. Oliver Cromwell occupied Cork in 1649. Many public buildings were destroyed in nationalist uprisings in 1920. The city has Catholic and Protestant cathedrals, the University College of Cork (1845), and a large harbour. Cork is renowned for its tweed and linen. Area: 7462sq km (2881sq mi). Pop. (2002) 448,181.

cork Outer, dead, waterproof layer of the BARK of woody plants. The bark of the cork oak, native to Mediterranean countries, is the chief source of commercial cork. Family Fagaceae; species *Quercus ruber*.

corm Fleshy, underground stem that produces a plant such as the CROCUS. In most plants, new corms form on top of old ones, which last for one season. *See also* ASEXUAL REPRODUCTION

cormorant Bird found in coastal and inland waters throughout the world. It has a hooked bill, a black body and webbed feet. It dives well and, in some areas of SE Asia, it is trained to catch and retrieve fish. There are 30 species. Length: to 1m (3.3ft). Family Phalacrocoracidae; genus *Phalacrocorax*.

corn Main CEREAL plant of a country or region. In Britain, corn normally refers to WHEAT, in North America to MAIZE, and in Scandinavia to BARLEY.

corncrake Bird of the RAIL family common in grain fields of N Europe. It has a brown body and a short bill, and its specific name describes its call. Family Rallidae; species *Crex crex*.

cornea Transparent membrane at the front of the EYE. It is curved and acts as a fixed LENS, so that light entering the eye is to some extent focused before it reaches the lens.

Corneille, Pierre (1606–84) First of the great French classical dramatists. His plays include the tragedy *Médée* (1635), the epic *Le Cid* (1637), and a comedy *Le Menteur* (1643). He was elected to the French Academy in 1647.

cornet BRASS musical instrument similar to a TRUMPET. It was one of the first brass instrumnets to have valves and, therefore, capable of playing a full range of notes. Hector BERLIOZ was one composer to take advantage of this ability. Its range is about the same as a trumpet's, but its tone is mellower.

cornflower ANNUAL of the composite family common in many parts of Europe. Family Asteraceae/Compositae; species *Centaurea cyanus*.

Corn Laws Series of Acts regulating the import and export of grain in Britain. The Act of 1815, intended to protect British farmers, prevented the import of wheat until the domestic price exceeded a certain figure. The result was to keep the price of bread high. Opposition led to repeal by the ANTI-CORN LAW LEAGUE (1846).

Cornwall County in SW England, on a peninsula bounded by the Atlantic Ocean, the English Channel and Devon; the county town is Truro. Major towns include Bodmin, St Austell and Penzance. A rocky coast with hills and moors inland, it is drained by the Camel, Fowey, Tamar, and Fal rivers. It is a popular tourist region. Area: (including Scilly Isles) 3512sq km (1356sq mi). Pop. (2001) 499,114.

Cornwallis, Charles, 1st Marquess (1738–1805) British general and statesman. In 1778 he became second in command of British forces in the AMERICAN REVOLUTION. His surrender at the Siege of YORKTOWN (1781) signalled the end of the war. As governor general of India (1786–93, 1805), he reformed the civil service and defeated Tipu Sahib of Mysore. Cornwallis resigned as viceroy of Ireland (1798–1801) after GEORGE III refused to accept the Act of CATHOLIC EMANCIPATION.

corona Outermost layer of the SUN's atmosphere, extending for many millions of kilometres into space. The corona emits strongly in the X-ray region, and has been studied by X-ray satellites. The corona has a temperature of 1–2 million K.

coronary heart disease ARTERIOSCLEROSIS of the coronary ARTERIES. It is the most common cause of death in the West. Atheriosclerosis can lead to the formation of a blood clot in one or other of the coronary arteries supplying the HEART (**coronary thrombosis**). The patient experiences sudden pain in the chest (ANGINA) and the result may be a HEART ATTACK (**myocardial infarction**), when the flow of blood to the heart is stopped. Smokers are more likely to die suddenly from atheriosclerosis. Evidence suggests that a high intake of POLYUNSATURATES can protect against coronary heart disease.

coronation Ceremony of crowning a monarch. The form of coronation used in Britain was first drafted by Saint Dunstan, who crowned King Edgar in 973, but has been substantially reinvented several times. Since 1066, British sovereigns have been crowned in Westminster Abbey in London. The Merovingian kings of the Franks were probably the first to introduce Christian coronation to Europe in *c.*5th century AD.

coroner Public official who inquires into deaths that have apparent unnatural causes by means of an inquest and/or post-mortem. The office dates to 12th-century England. Coroners in Britain also inquire into cases of 'treasure trove' (coins, gold, silver, or bullion with no known owner) which by law are the property of the crown. In both the USA and England, coroners are often assisted by a jury.

Corot, Jean-Baptiste Camille (1796–1875) French painter, a leading 19th-century landscapist. He had more sympathy for the French CLASSICAL tradition than for the attitudes of the BARBIZON SCHOOL, but was more natural than most classicists. After 1827, he gained success at the Paris Salon with more traditionally romantic paintings executed in a soft-edged style, unlike the precisely observed scenes of his earlier work. He was an important influence on Paul CÉZANNE and POST-IMPRESSIONISM in general.

corporation Business organization that is legally a separate entity, which gives it limited liability, as compared to a proprietorship or partnership. The owners or shareholders are not individually responsible for the legal dealings of the corporation, except in the extent of their holdings. The corporation form is most usual in large organizations, especially in the USA. In Britain, the term COMPANY is often used.

Correggio (c.1490–1534) (Antonio Allegri) Italian painter from Correggio who worked mainly in Parma. His oil paintings and frescos produced daring (although anatomically exact) foreshortening effects inspired by those of MICHELANGELO and RAPHAEL. One of the first painters to experiment with the dramatic effects of artificial light, Corregio is the major link between the early illusionism of Andrea MANTEGNA and the great Baroque ceiling painters.

correlation In STATISTICS, a number that summarizes the direction and degree of relationship between two or more dimensions or variables. Correlations range between 0 (no relationship) and 1.00 (a perfect relationship), and may be positive (as one variable increases, so does the other) or negative (as one variable increases, the other decreases).

corrie See CIRQUE

corrosion Gradual tarnishing of surface or major structural decomposition by chemical action on solids, especially metals and alloys. It commonly appears as a greenish deposit on copper and brass, RUST on iron, or a grey deposit on aluminium, zinc, and magnesium. Rust is the most important form of corrosion because of the extensive use of iron and its susceptibility to attack. Some metals, such as aluminium and magnesium, corrode readily forming an oxide, which then protects the undersurface from further corrosion.

Corsica (Corse) Mountainous island in the Mediterranean Sea, c.160km (100mi) SE of the French coast. It is a region of France comprising two departments. The capital is Ajaccio. It was a Roman colony, before passing into the hands of a series of Italian rulers. In 1768 France purchased all rights to the island. Napoleon was born here in 1769. Products: grapes, olives, mutton, cheese, wool, fish. Area: 8681sq km (3352sq mi). Pop. (1999) 260,196.

Cortés, Hernán (1485–1547) Spanish CONQUISTADOR and conqueror of Mexico. In 1518, Cortés sailed from Cuba to Central America with 550 men. They marched inland toward the AZTEC capital, Tenochtitlán (now Mexico City), gaining allies among the subject peoples of the Aztec king, Montezuma II. While he was absent, conflict broke out. In 1521 Cortés captured the city after a three-month siege, thereby gaining the Aztec empire for Spain.

cortex In animal and plant anatomy, outer layer of a gland or tissue. Examples are the cortex of the ADRENAL GLANDS the renal cortex of a kidney; the cerebral cortex or outer layer of the brain; the cortical layers of tissue in plant roots and stems lying between the bark or EPIDERMIS and the hard wood or conducting tissues.

cortisone HORMONE produced by the cortex of the ADRENAL GLANDS and essential for carbohydrate, protein and fat metabolism, kidney function and disease resistance. Synthetic cortisone is used to treat adrenal insufficiency, rheumatoid arthritis and other inflammatory diseases and rheumatic fever.

corundum Translucent to transparent mineral, aluminium oxide (Al_2O_3). It is found in igneous, pegmatitic and metamorphic rocks, occurring as pyramidal or prismatic crystals in the rhombohedral class and as granular masses. It is the hardest natural substance after DIAMOND. Gemstone varieties are sapphire and ruby. It is an industrial abrasive. Hardness 9; r.d. 4.

cosecant In TRIGONOMETRY, ratio of the length of the hypotenuse to the length of the side opposite an acute angle in a right-angled triangle. The cosecant of angle A is usually abbreviated cosec A and is equal to the reciprocal of its SINE.

Cosgrave, William Thomas (1880–1965) Irish statesman, first president (1922–32) of the Irish Free State. A member of SINN FÉIN, he took part in the EASTER RISING (1916). Cosgrave served in the provisional government of the Dáil Éireann in 1919. Eamon DE VALERA defeated him in 1932 elections, and Cosgrave became leader (1932–44) of the FINE GAEL opposition. His son **Liam Cosgrave** (1920–), served as taoiseach (1973–77) of the Republic of Ireland.

cosine In TRIGONOMETRY, ratio of the length of the side adjacent to an acute angle to the length of the HYPOTENUSE in a right-angled triangle.

cosmic radiation (cosmic rays) Streams of SUBATOMIC PARTICLES from space that constantly bombard the Earth at velocities approaching the speed of light. Primary cosmic rays are high-energy RADIATION that comes from the Sun and other sources in outer space. This includes ultraviolet rays, X-rays and radio waves. They consist mainly of atomic nuclei and PROTONS. When primary cosmic rays strike gas molecules in the upper atmosphere they yield showers of secondary cosmic rays, which consist of energetic protons, NEUTRONS, and pions. Further collisions yield muons, ALPHA PARTICLES, POSITRONS, ELECTRONS, GAMMA RADIATION, and PHOTONS.

cosmology Branch of scientific study that brings together astronomy, mathematics and physics in an effort to understand the make-up and evolution of the universe. Once considered the province of theologians and philosophers, it is now an all-embracing science, which has made great strides in the 20th century. The discovery by Edwin HUBBLE in the 1920s that galaxies are receding from each other promoted the BIG BANG theory. Associated with this is the OSCILLATING UNIVERSE THEORY. The other main theory is the STEADY-STATE THEORY.

Cosmos (Gk. 'order') Universe considered as an ordered whole. PLATO and ARISTOTLE conceived of the universe as ordered by an intelligent principle. The conviction of an ordered nature became the basis of modern natural science.

Cossacks Bands of Russian adventurers who undertook the conquest of Siberia in the 17th century. Of ethnically mixed origins, they were escaped serfs, renegades and vagabonds who formed independent, semi-military groups on the fringe of society. After the Russian Revolution (1917), the Cossacks opposed the BOLSHEVIKS and strongly resisted collectivization.

Costa Rica See country feature.

Costner, Kevin (1955–) US film actor and director. Costner's breakthrough film was *The Untouchables* (1987).

▲ **Costner** After the success of films such as *Dances with Wolves* (1990), Kevin Costner suffered a huge setback with the spectacular flop *Waterworld* (1995), one of the most expensive films ever made.

INTERNET

Corot, Jean-Baptiste Camille
▸ www.metmuseum.org
▸ www.nationalgallery.org.uk
▸ www.clevelandart.org

Correggio
▸ www.getty.edu
▸ www.nationalgallery.org.uk
▸ www.nga.gov

Corsica
▸ www.visit-corsica.com
▸ www.corsica.net

Costa Rica
▸ centralamerica.com/cr

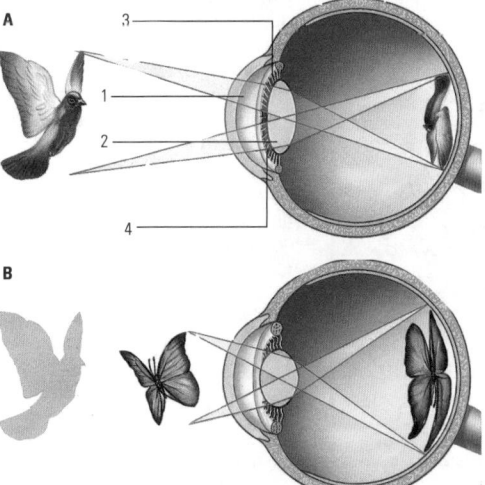

◀ **cornea** Focusing of light rays from distant objects (A) is mainly done by the cornea (1) with a little help from the lens (2). Ciliary muscles (3) encircling the lens relax and stretch ligaments (4), which pull the lens flat. Rays from a near object (B) are bent by a thick lens produced when the ligaments slacken as the ciliary muscles contract. This process, which is called accommodation, is essential for sharp focusing.

C

Other leading roles followed, such as *Bull Durham* (1988). Costner won Academy Awards for Best Director and Best Actor in his directorial debut *Dances With Wolves* (1990), an epic Civil War-era Western. Other acting credits include *JFK* (1991), *The Bodyguard* (1992), and *The Postman* (1998).

cotangent Ratio of the length of the side adjacent to an acute angle, to the length of the side opposite the angle in a right-angled triangle. The cotangent of angle *A* is usually abbreviated cot *A* and is equal to the reciprocal of its TANGENT.

cot death (sudden infant death syndrome) Sudden, unexpected death of an infant less than two years old. In the UK, it accounts for *c.*20% of infant mortality. It appears that babies who sleep on their fronts have an increased risk.

Cotman, John Sell (1782–1842) British landscape painter and etcher, co-founder (with John Crome) of the Norwich School. One of Britain's most important 19th-century watercolourists. He used broad, flat colour washes and built up his images in sharply defined planes and simple shapes. His paintings include *Greta Bridge* (*c.*1805) and *Chirk Aqueduct*.

cotoneaster Genus of *c.*50 species of deciduous shrubs of the ROSE family (Rosaceae), mostly native to China. They have small white flowers and small, red or black, round berry-like fruit, and are often cultivated as ornamental plants.

Cotopaxi Volcano in N central Ecuador, 65km (40mi) s of Quito, in the Andes Mountains. It is the highest continually active volcano in the world and its frequent eruptions often cause severe damage. Height: 5896m (19,344ft).

Cotswolds Range of limestone hills in w England, lying mainly in Gloucestershire and extending 80km (50mi) NE from Bath. The local stone is widely used as a building material and the region is also known for its breed of sheep.

cotton Annual shrub native to subtropical regions. Most cotton is grown for the fibres that envelop the seeds and are made into fabric. Family Malvaceae; genus *Gossypium*.

cotton gin Machine for separating cotton lint from seeds, a task previously done by hand. The gin, patented in 1794 by Eli Whitney, could clean more than 20kg (50lb) per day. It contributed to the prosperity of US cotton plantations and to the industrialization of the textile industry.

cottonmouth *See* WATER MOCCASIN

cotyledon First leaf or pair of leaves produced by the embryo of a flowering plant. Its function is to store and digest food for the embryo plant, and, if it emerges above ground, to photosynthesize for seedling growth. *See also* DICOTYLEDON; MONOCOTYLEDON

cougar *See* PUMA

Coulomb, Charles Augustin de (1736–1806) French physicist. He invented the torsion balance which led to experiments in electrostatics and the discovery of 'Coulomb's law': the force between two charged particles is proportional to the product of the charges, and inversely proportional to the square of the distance between them.

Council for Mutual Economic Assistance (COMECON) International organization (1949–91) aimed at the coordination

COSTA RICA

The Republic of Costa Rica in Central America is bordered by Nicaragua to the N and Panama to the s. It has coastlines on both the Pacific Ocean and on the Caribbean Sea.

Central Costa Rica consists of several mountain ranges and plateaux with many volcanoes. The Meseta Central – where the capital, San José itself, is situated – and the Valle del General in the SE have rich volcanic soils and are the most thickly populated parts of Costa Rica.

The highlands descend to the Caribbean lowlands and the Pacific Coast region, with its low mountain ranges. San José stands at about 1,170m [3,840ft] above sea level.

Evergreen forests cover around 50% of Costa Rica. Oaks grow in the highlands, palm trees along the Caribbean coast and mangrove swamps are common on the Pacific coast.

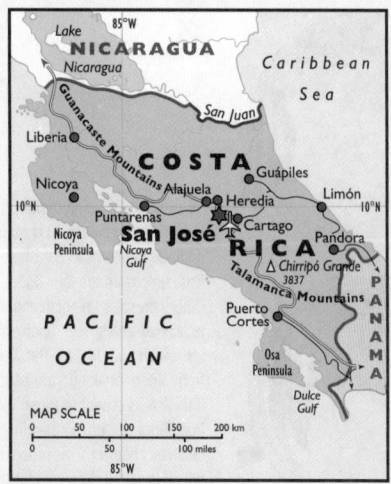

CLIMATE
The Meseta Central benefits from a pleasant climate and an average annual temperature of 20°C [68° F], compared with more than 27°C [81° F] on the coast. The coolest months are December and January. The NE trade winds bring heavy rain to the Caribbean coast. There is only half as much rainfall in the the highlands and on the Pacific coastlands as occurs on the Caribbean coast.

HISTORY
Christopher Columbus reached the Caribbean coast in 1502 and named the land Costa Rica, Spanish for 'rich coast'. Rumours of treasure attracted many Spaniards to settle in the country from 1561. Spain ruled the country until 1821, when Spain's Central American colonies broke away to join the Mexican empire in 1822. In 1823, the Central American states broke with Mexico and set up the Central American Federation, the members of which were Costa Rica, Guatemala, Honduras, Nicaragua, and El Salvador. Later, this large union broke up and Costa Rica became fully independent in 1838.

From the late 19th century, Costa Rica experienced a number of revolutions, with both periods of dictatorship and democracy. In 1917–19 General Tinoco formed a dictatorship. In 1948, following a revolt, the armed forces were abolished.

POLITICS
Jose Figueres Ferrer served as president from 1953 to 1958 and again from 1970 to 1974. In 1987 President Oscar Arias Sanchez was awarded the Nobel Peace Prize for his efforts to end the civil wars in Central America.

In 2002 Abel Pancho won the presidential elections. Costa Rica's image was tarnished in

AREA 51,100sq km [19,730sq mi]

POPULATION 4,134,000

CAPITAL (POPULATION) San José (1,145,000)

GOVERNMENT Multiparty republic

ETHNIC GROUPS White (including Mestizo) 94%, Black 3%, Amerindian 1%, Chinese 1%, others

LANGUAGES Spanish (official), English

RELIGIONS Roman Catholic 76%, Evangelical 14%

CURRENCY Costa Rican colón = 100 céntimos

2004 when two former presidents were imprisoned on charges of corruption, but the country remains an exemplar of political stability in the region and continues to maintain this without resorting to armed forces. In 2006 Oscar Arias was re-elected president.

ECONOMY
Costa Rica is classified by the World Bank as a 'lower-middle-income' developing country. It is one of the most prosperous countries in Central America. There are high educational standards, and a high average life expectancy of 78 years.

Agriculture employs 24% of the workforce. Major crops include coffee, pineapples, bananas and sugar. Other crops include beans, citrus fruits, cocoa, potatoes, rice and maize. Cattle ranching is important.

The country's resources include its forests, but it lacks minerals apart from some bauxite and manganese. Manufacturing is increasing with electronics to the fore. It also has hydropower.

Tourism is a fast-growing industry with eco–tourism gaining in importance. The United States is Costa Rica's chief trading partner.

of economic policy among communist states, especially in Eastern Europe. Led by the Soviet Union, its original members were Bulgaria, Czechoslovakia, East Germany, Hungary, Poland, and Romania; later joined by Cuba, Mongolia, and Vietnam. Cooperation took the form of bilateral trade agreements rather than the establishment of a single market or a uniform price system.

Council of Europe European organization founded in 1949 with the aim of strengthening pluralist democracy and human rights, and promoting European cultural identity. Originally a Western European organization, it admitted former communist countries in the 1990s. It adopted *c*.150 conventions, the most important of which is the EUROPEAN CONVENTION ON HUMAN RIGHTS. It is based in Strasbourg, France.

council tax Tax levied on British households to pay for local services. Introduced in 1993, it was the successor to community charge (POLL TAX). The level of tax paid is assessed with reference to a range of eight price bands based on house value.

counterfeiting Illegal manufacture of coins or printed 'money'. Although counterfeiting is a form of forgery, it is considered a more serious offence as it is perpetrated against the government rather than an individual or company.

counterpoint In music, technique in composition involving independent melodic lines that are sung or played simultaneously to produce HARMONY. The term derives from the medieval practice of adding an accompanying note to each note of a melody. Counterpoint writing reached its height in the 16th century in the work of William Byrd, Orlando di Lasso, and Giovanni Palestrina, organ compositions of J.S. Bach in the 18th century, and in the late works of Beethoven.

Counter-Reformation Revival of the Roman Catholic Church in Europe during the 16th and early 17th centuries. It began as a reaction to the Protestant REFORMATION and was intended to strengthen the Church against PROTESTANTISM and the prevailing HUMANISM of the RENAISSANCE. The reforms were essentially conservative, trying to remove many of the abuses that had crept into the late medieval church and win new prestige for the papacy. The major impetus for reform emerged from the pontificate of PAUL III and the founding of the Society of Jesus (JESUITS). The Council of Trent (1545–63) was the engine of the Counter-Reformation. It eradicated simony (such as the sale of indulgences), standardized Roman Catholic theology, and undertook institutional reforms. The second phase (1563–90) of the Counter-Reformation was administered by PIUS V, GREGORY XIII and Sixtus V. *See also* CAMPION, SAINT EDMUND; VINCENT DE PAUL, SAINT

countertenor Male voice of the same register as the female CONTRALTO. It is most common in Britain, where some of the more traditional church choirs still prefer male altos.

country and western Popular music originally associated with rural areas of s USA. The music typically features sentimental lyrics and instrumental music played with stringed instruments such as the guitar, banjo, or fiddle. Its origins were in the folk music of British immigrants (although in Texas, the blues were also an influence). NASHVILLE, Tennessee, is the music's spiritual home.

county One of the main administrative divisions of local government in the UK, the USA, and some Commonwealth countries. Counties are responsible for policing, local judicial administration, maintaining public roads, and other public facilities, such as a fire service and keeping record offices.

coup d'état Swift stroke of policy, either against the ruling power of a state or by the state against an element within it. Of the former, the most usual is a military takeover of civilian government, such as 'the Colonels' in Greece (1967). An example of the latter is Hitler's murder of the *Sturm Abteilung* (SA) leaders in Germany (1934).

Couperin, François (1668–1733) French composer. He was organist and harpsichordist at the court of Louis XIV. 'Le Grand', as he was known, is now principally remembered for his many harpsichord pieces.

Courbet, Gustave (1819–77) French painter, the leading exponent of REALISM. Largely self-taught, Courbet rejected traditional subject matter and instead painted peasant groups and scenes from life in Paris. His nudes, splendid in their richness of colour and textural contrast, shocked contemporary society.

His controversial political activity forced him into exile in Switzerland in 1873. Courbet's rejection of both Romantic and Classical ideals prepared the way for IMPRESSIONISM.

Court, Margaret (1942–) Australian tennis player. She won more Grand Slam titles (62) than any other player in the history of women's tennis. In 1970, Court became only the second woman (after Maureen Connolly) to complete the Grand Slam.

Courtauld, Samuel (1876–1947) English industrialist and art collector. The family firm of Courtaulds, founded in 1816, specialized in the production of silks. From 1904 it developed artificial fibres such as viscose, rayon and nylon and made Courtauld immensely wealthy. This allowed Courtauld to become a major art collector. In 1931, he bequeathed his London home (Home House) and collection of 19th-century French painting to the University of London to form the Courtauld Institute for the research and study of art.

court martial Court of the armed services for trial of service persons accused of breaking military law. Offences range from murder and robbery to those specific to the armed services, such as desertion. Court martials do not utilize the TRIAL BY JURY system. Members of the court martial are serving officers, in certain cases advised by a judge advocate.

courts of law Judicial assemblies established to try legal cases and to impose punishment for wrongdoing or to remedy a damage. The history of the court system lies in the English assumption of COMMON LAW as its legal basis (which Britain introduced to its former colonies, including the USA and Canada) as opposed to ROMAN LAW, which is the judicial basis of many other countries around the world. In the UK and the USA, courts are hierarchically organized, and try suits of two different types, CIVIL or CRIMINAL. In the UK, civil law cases are heard by county courts and the HIGH COURT OF JUSTICE, while those of criminal law are heard by CROWN COURTS or magistrates' court. In the USA, **federal** courts including the SUPREME COURT administer cases involving the nation, federal laws, interstate disputes and non-US nationals. **State** courts handle matters specific to one state.

Cousteau, Jacques Yves (1910–97) French oceanographer. Best known as the co-inventor (with Emile Gagnan) of the AQUALUNG, he also invented a process of underwater television and conducted a series of undersea living experiments (1962–65). Many of the expeditions made by his research ship *Calypso* were filmed for television.

covalent bond Chemical bond in which two atoms share a pair of electrons, one from each atom. Covalent bonds with one shared pair of electrons are called single bonds; double and triple bonds also exist. The molecules tend to have low melting and boiling points and to be soluble in nonpolar solvents. Covalent bonding is most common in organic compounds.

Covenanters Scottish Presbyterians pledged by the National Covenant (1638) to uphold their religion. They opposed CHARLES I's efforts to impose an Anglican episcopal system and supported Parliament in the English CIVIL WAR, in exchange for a promise to introduce PRESBYTERIANISM in England and Ireland. The Scots changed sides when this promise was broken, but were defeated by Oliver CROMWELL. Covenanter revolts against Charles II were suppressed, but Presbyterianism was restored in Scotland in 1688.

Coventry City and county district in West Midlands, central England. An important weaving centre in the Middle Ages, it later became known for its clothing manufacture. The city was badly damaged by bombing during World War 2, and the 14th-century cathedral was destroyed. A new cathedral (designed by Sir Basil Spence) was completed in 1962. It is the home of the University of Warwick (1965) and Coventry University (1992). Industries: motor vehicles, mechanical and electrical engineering, telecommunications. Pop. (2001) 300,844.

Coverdale, Miles (1488–1569) English cleric who issued the first printed English Bible (1535) and the 'Great Bible' (1539). Influenced by the REFORMATION, he helped William TYNDALE on his Bible translation.

cow Mature female CATTLE that produce more than one calf. It also applies to other mammals, such as elephants and seals.

Coward, Sir Noel Pierce (1899–1973) English playwright, composer, and performer. He first attracted notice as a

▲ **cotton** The cotton plant (*Gossypium* sp.) is a shrub-like annual native to the world's subtropical regions. After rapid flowering, small green seedpods (bolls) develop. The cotton seeds within the bolls sprout a mass of fine fibre hairs. When mature, the bolls rupture and soft cloud of cotton erupts. The crop is either harvested by hand or machine and then taken to be ginned (separating the seed from the fibres), cleaned, carded and spun into yarn.

C

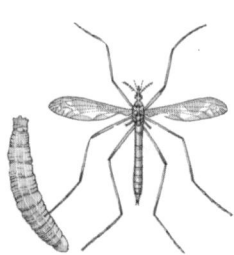

▶ **coypu** Native to swamps, lakes and streams of central and South America, the coypu (*Myocastor coypus*) is now found in the wetter regions of the USA and Europe, a number having escaped from fur farms.

▲ **crane fly** The hindwings of crane flies have evolved into small balancing organs known as halterers. In flight they vibrate with the wings, detecting and helping to correct any deviation from the stable flight path.

▲ **crab** Fiddler crabs (*Uca* sp.), like most crustaceans, recognize potential mates by sight. During courtship, the male waves his one enormous claw in a complex series of signals, while at the same time raising and lowering his body.

playwright with his drama *The Vortex* (1924), and later with his urbane comedies such as *Hay Fever* (1925), *Bitter Sweet* (1929), *Private Lives* (1930), and *Blithe Spirit* (1941). His plays frequently lampooned drab high-society etiquette. Other works include the films *In Which We Serve* (1942) and *Brief Encounter* (1945). He also composed hundreds of songs, such as "Mad Dogs and Englishmen" and "Mad About the Boy".

cowboy (cowhand) US ranch hand. Traditionally living and working in the West, cowboys increased after the Civil War. They have been romanticized in books and films as a symbol of the rugged independence, colour and vigour of the old 'Wild West'. *See also* GAUCHO

Cowper, William (1731–1800) English poet and hymn writer. Despite bouts of near insanity, Cowper's poetry is lucid and direct, often drawing engagingly on the countryside or the details of domestic life, as in the long blank-verse poem *The Task* (1785). Some of his contributions to *Olney Hymns* have become standards of the Anglican Church.

cowrie (cowry) Gastropod MOLLUSC identified by an ovoid, highly polished shell with a long toothed opening and varied markings. It is found on tropical coral shores. Length: 8.3–152mm (0.33–6in). Family Cypraeidae; more than 160 species, including the map cowry *Cypraea mappa*.

cowslip Herb of the PRIMROSE family (Primulaceae), with a hanging yellow flower head; species *Primula veris*. In the USA cowslip is a marsh marigold (*Caltha palustris*).

coyote Wild DOG originally native to w North America. Coyotes have moved into many E areas of the USA formerly inhabited by wolves. Usually greyish-brown, they have pointed muzzles, big ears, and bushy tails. Length: 90cm (35in); weight: *c.*12kg (26lb). Species *Canis latrans*.

coypu Large, aquatic RODENT, native to South America. It now also lives in North America and parts of Europe, both wild and on fur farms. Coypus have brown outer fur and soft grey underfur, commercially known as nutria. Overall length: 1.06m (3.5ft); weight: 8kg (18lb). Species *Myocastor coypus*.

crab Flattened, triangular, or oval ten-legged crustacean covered with a hard shell. Primarily marine, some crabs are found in freshwater and a few are terrestrial. Their short abdomen, often called a tail, is bent under. Most have a pair of large foreclaws, a pair of movable eyestalks and a segmented mouth. Crabs usually move sideways. Size: pea-sized to 3m (12ft). Order Decapoda.

Crabbe, George (1754–1832) English poet. His poetry, such as *The Village* (1783), is imbued with the atmosphere of his native Suffolk and is unflinchingly anti-sentimental.

Crab Nebula NEBULA located *c.*6500 light years away in the constellation of Taurus. It is the remnant of a supernova noted by Chinese astronomers in July 1054, when it shone as brightly as Venus, visible even in daylight. The nebula was discovered in 1731 by the English astronomer John Bevis, and independently by Charles Messier in 1758.

crack Street DRUG that is a COCAINE derivative. It is supplied in the form of hard, crystalline lumps, which are heated to produce smoke inhaled for its stimulant effects. It imposes considerable strain on the heart and blood vessels, and may result in heart failure or a stroke. Psychotic episodes may also occur.

cracking Stage in oil-refining during which the products of the first distillation are treated to break up large hydrocarbons into smaller molecules by the controlled use of heat, catalysts and often pressure. The cracking of petroleum yields heavy oils, petrol, and gases such as ethane, ethylene, and propene (propylene), which are used in the manufacture of plastics, textiles, detergents, and agricultural chemicals. Cracking is,

therefore, a means of yielding greater amounts of lighter hydrocarbons from heavier fractions such as lubricating oil.

Craig, James (1871–1940) Northern Irish soldier and politician, first prime minister of Northern Ireland (1921–40). An extreme Unionist, he helped Sir Edward CARSON to keep the province part of Britain.

crake *See* RAIL

Cranach (the Elder), Lucas (1472–1553) German painter and engraver, court artist to the Electors of Saxony. A friend and follower of Martin LUTHER, Cranach designed many propaganda woodcuts for the Protestant cause. He also produced some of the first full-length portraits and developed a style of painting female nudes in a unique, enamel-like finish.

cranberry Plant of the HEATH family, distributed widely in N temperate regions. It is a creeping or trailing shrub and bears red berries with an acid taste used to make sauce and juice. Family Ericaceae; Genus *Vaccinium*.

crane Any of several species of tall wading birds found in most parts of the world except s America. It has brownish, greyish, or white plumage with a bright ornamental head. After courtship dances, the female lays two eggs in a bulky nest. Height: to 150cm (60in). Family Gruidae.

Crane, (Harold) Hart (1899–1932) US poet. Acclaimed as one of the most brilliant and creative 20th-century US poets, he published his first volume, *White Buildings*, in 1926. His major work, *The Bridge* (1930), is a series of related poems in which New York City's Brooklyn Bridge serves as a mystical symbol of the creative power of civilization.

Crane, Stephen (1871–1900) US writer, poet, and war correspondent. His best-known work is *The Red Badge of Courage* (1895), a grimly realistic story of an American Civil War soldier. Other works include a novel, *Maggie: A Girl of the Streets* (1893), a collection of short stories, *The Open Boat and Other Tales of Adventure* (1898), and poems collected in *The Black Riders* (1895) and *War is Kind* (1900).

crane fly True fly of the order Diptera. It has a slender body, long fragile legs, and one pair of wings. The hindwings are reduced to special balancing organs called halteres. The larvae, leatherjackets, live in the soil where they feed on plant roots and stems, frequently becoming serious agricultural pests. Family Tipulidae; species *Tipula simplex*. Length: to 3cm (1.2in). The name is also given to the HARVESTMAN.

cranesbill Common name for certain species of wild GERANIUM. Some species are cultivated for ornamental ground cover.

cranium The SKULL, especially the dome-shaped part that protects the brain. It is composed of eight bones that are fused together.

Cranmer, Thomas (1489–1556) English prelate and religious reformer. HENRY VIII appointed him Archbishop of Canterbury in 1533. Cranmer secured the annulment of Henry's marriage to Catherine of Aragon, despite opposition from the Pope. A friend of Thomas CROMWELL, Cranmer promoted the introduction of Protestantism into England and compiled the first Book of COMMON PRAYER in 1549. Following the accession of the Roman Catholic MARY I in 1553, Cranmer's reforms were halted and he was burned at the stake.

Crassus, Marcus Licinius (*c.*115–53 BC) Roman political and military leader. He commanded an army for SULLA in 83 BC amassed a vast personal fortune, and raised and led the troops who defeated the slave rebellion of Spartacus in 71. With POMPEY and Julius CAESAR he formed the First Triumvirate in 60 BC and was governor of Syria in 54 BC.

crater Roughly circular depression found on the surface of many bodies in the SOLAR SYSTEM, notably SATELLITES, PLANETS, and ASTEROIDS. It is formed either by meteoric impact, when shock waves blast out a hole in the ground, or at the vent of a volcano, when lava is expelled explosively.

crater lake Accumulation of water, usually by precipitation of rain or snow but sometimes groundwater, in a volcanic crater (CALDERA). Should an eruption occur, the resulting mud flow (lahar) is often more destructive than a lava flow, owing to its greater speed. Crater Lake in Crater Lake Park, Oregon, USA, was formed by precipitation. The lake is maintained solely by rain and snow. It is the second deepest lake in North America.

Crawford, Joan (1904–77) US film actress, b. Lucille Fay le Sueur. Determined and versatile, Crawford remained a star for almost 50 years. She started in musicals, such as *Our Dancing Daughters* (1928), before graduating to dramatic roles in films such as *Grand Hotel* (1932) and *The Women* (1939). She won a best actress Academy Award for *Mildred Pierce* (1945). Other films include *Possessed* (1947), *Johnny Guitar* (1954), and *What Ever Happened to Baby Jane?* (1962).

Crawford, Thomas (1814–57) US sculptor who studied in Rome and brought a neo-classical style to his art. His most famous works are the equestrian statue of George Washington, and the enormous *Freedom* statue on top of the US Capitol.

crayfish Edible, freshwater, ten-legged crustacean that lives in rivers and streams of temperate regions. Smaller than lobsters, crayfish burrow into the banks of streams and feed on animal and vegetable matter. Some cave-dwelling species are blind. Length: normally 8–10cm (3–4in). Families Astacidae (Northern Hemisphere), Parastacidae (Southern Hemisphere), Austroastacidae (Australia).

Crazy Horse (1842–77) Chief of the Oglala SIOUX. He was a leader of Sioux resistance to the advance of white settlers in the Black Hills, and assisted SITTING BULL in the destruction of General CUSTER at the Battle of LITTLE BIGHORN in 1876. Persuaded to surrender, he was killed a few months later.

Crécy, Battle of (1346) First major battle of the HUNDRED YEARS' WAR. The English led by EDWARD III and his son, EDWARD THE BLACK PRINCE, defeated the French of PHILIP VI. The English longbow and superior tactics produced the victory.

Cree People belonging to the ALGONQUIN language family of Native Americans in Canada, who ranged from James Bay to the Saskatchewan River. Like the closely related Chippewa, the Cree served as guides and hunters for French and British fur traders. Many of the Plains Cree intermarried with the French. Today, there are *c*.130,000 Cree.

creed (Lat. *credo*, 'I believe') In Christian churches, personal yet formal statement of commitment to doctrinal belief. *See also* APOSTLES' CREED; ATHANASIAN CREED; NICENE CREED

Creek Confederation of NATIVE AMERICANS, part of the Muskogean-language group. One of the largest groups of SE USA, they ranged from Georgia to Alabama. They formed a settled, agricultural society, with land owned communally.

▲ **crane** The crowned crane (*Balearica pavonina*) is a tall, elegant bird of desert and grassland regions of Africa, s from the Nile Valley. It grows to a height of 95cm (3ft).

Within the confederacy, individual settlements had a degree of autonomy. After the Creek Wars (1813–14), they were removed to Oklahoma, where *c*.60,000 remain today.

cremation Ritual disposal of a corpse by burning. It was a common custom in parts of the ancient civilized world, and is still the only funeral practice among Hindus and Buddhists. Early Christians rejected cremation because of their belief in the physical resurrection of the body. It was not until the 19th century that it was revived in the Western world. Its legitimacy is now recognized by all Christian Churches.

Creole Person born in the West Indies, Latin America, or s USA, but of foreign or mixed descent. Generally, a Creole's ancestors were either African slaves or French, Spanish or English settlers. In the USA, it also refers to someone of mixed European and African ancestry. Creole language is a PIDGIN, adopted as the native language of a community (English, French, Portuguese) and influenced by the native languages of the community's ancestors.

crescent Symbol of the MOON in its first quarter. It has been associated with ISLAM since the capture of Constantinople by the Ottoman Turks in 1453. It appears on the Turkish standard and other Islamic nation flags.

cress Any of several small, pungent-leaved plants of the mustard family (Brassicaceae/Cruciferae), generally used in salads and as garnishes. The best known is WATERCRESS. Species *Nasturtium officinale*.

Cretaceous Last period of the MESOZOIC era, lasting from 144 to 65 million years ago. The first true placental and MARSUPIAL mammals appeared and modern flowering plants were common. DINOSAURS became extinct at the end of this period.

Crete (Kreti, Kríti) Largest island of Greece, in the E Mediterranean Sea, SSE of the Greek mainland; the capital is IRÁKLION. MINOAN CIVILIZATION flourished on Crete from 2000 BC and the palace of KNOSSOS was built *c*.1700 BC. Crete was conquered by Rome in *c*.68 BC and later came under Byzantine (395), Arab (826) and Venetian (1210) rule. In 1669, Crete fell to Turkey. Foreign intervention forced Turkey to evacuate Crete (1898), and it was eventually united with Greece (1908). It was occupied by German forces in World War 2. Crete has a mountainous terrain upon which sheep and goats are raised. The mild climate supports the cultivation of cereals, grapes, olives and oranges. Products: wool, hides, cheese, olive oil, wine. Tourism is important. Area: 8336sq km (3218sq mi). Pop. (2001) 601,159.

Creutzfeldt-Jakob disease (CJD) Rare, degenerative brain disease that causes physical deterioration and dementia, usually progressing to death within a year of onset. Caused by an abnormal protein called a PRION, it is related to SCRAPIE in sheep, and BOVINE SPONGIFORM ENCEPHALOPATHY (BSE) – 'mad cow disease'. Typically it affects older people, but in 1996 scientists found a new variant form of CJD (nvCJD) in younger victims. In 1997 research confirmed that the agent responsible for this variant was identical to that of BSE, confirming the link between CJD and the consumption of infected beef. There is no known cure.

Crick, Francis Harry Compton (1916–2004) English biophysicist. In the 1950s, with James WATSON and Maurice Wilkins, Crick established the double-helix molecular structure of deoxyribonucleic acid (DNA). The three were jointly awarded the Nobel Prize in physiology or medicine in 1962.

cricket Brown to black insect with long antennae and hind legs adapted for jumping, found worldwide. Males produce a chirping sound by rubbing their wings together. Length: 3–50mm (0.8–2in). Family Gryllidae.

cricket Bat-and-ball game popular in Britain and other Commonwealth nations since *c*.1700. Two teams of 11 players

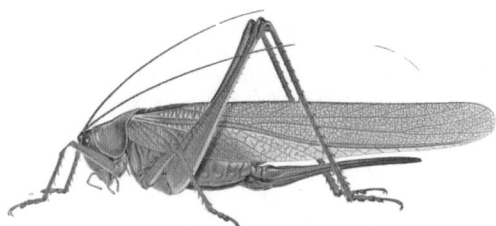

◄ **cricket** The great green bush cricket (*Tettigonia viridissima*) of s Europe, N Africa, and Asia is bright green in colour to blend in well with its surroundings. Large examples of this insect can reach 7cm (3in) long. The chirping of tree crickets increases with temperature.

C

compete on an oval or round pitch. The game revolves around two wickets, 20.1m (66ft, 22yd) apart. In an *innings*, all the players of one team bat once, while the other team fields and bowls. A batsman stands within a marked area (crease) on the pitch, 1.2m (4ft) from the wicket. Fielders are placed around the ground. In an "over", a bowler makes six consecutive over-arm deliveries at the wicket defended by a batsman. The next over follows from the opposite end of the pitch by a different bowler. Bowlers may be slow (relying mostly on spin) or fast (relying on speed to beat the batsman). A run is usually scored by a batsman striking the ball, and running between the wickets with his partner before the ball can be returned to either wicket. If the ball reaches the boundary of the pitch it scores four, or six runs if it does not bounce. A batsman can be given out in a number of ways: by being bowled (when the ball delivered by a bowler hits the wicket); by being caught (the ball struck by the bat or glove is caught on the full by a player); by being run out or 'stumped' (a player dislodges the bails with the ball when a batsman is outside the crease), by being 'leg before wicket' (the ball pitches in line with the stumps and hits a batsman's padded leg); or by hitting his own wicket. Leading nations compete against each other in a series of test matches,

the most famous of which is The ASHES. A test match is held over a maximum of five days and two innings per side, although shortened one-day games are increasingly popular.

Crimea (Krym) Peninsula in s Ukraine that extends into the Black Sea, w of the Azov Sea and joined to the mainland by the Perekop Isthmus. Simferopol is the capital. The Crimea was inhabited from the 10th to 8th centuries BC by the Cimmerians. During the 5th century, it was colonized by the Greeks and then by Romans, Ostrogoths, Huns, Mongols, Byzantines and Turks, before being annexed to Russia in 1783. In 1921 it became an autonomous republic of Russia, and in 1954 was transferred to the Ukraine as the Krymskaya oblast. In 1991 it was made an autonomous republic of an independent Ukraine. The region has many mineral resources, notably iron and gypsum, and intensive agriculture. Area: *c.*27,000sq km (10,425sq mi). Pop. (2001) 2,031,000.

Crimean War (1853–56) Fought by Britain, France, and the Ottoman Turks against Russia. In 1853, Russia occupied Turkish territory and France and Britain, determined to preserve the Ottoman Empire, invaded the Crimea (1854) to attack SEVASTOPOL. The war was marked on both sides by incompetent leadership and organization. The CHARGE OF

INTERNET

Crimean War
▶ www.crimeanwar.org

CROATIA

The Republic of Croatia was part of YUGOSLAVIA until becoming independent in 1991. The region bordering the Adriatic Sea is called DALMATIA. It includes the coastal ranges, which contain large areas of bare limestone, reaching 1,913m [6,276ft] at Mount Troglav. Other highlands lie in the NE. Most of the rest of the country consists of the fertile Pannonian Plains, which are drained by Croatia's two main rivers, the Drava and the Sava.

CLIMATE
The coastal area has a climate akin to that of the Mediterranean, with hot, dry summers and mild, moist winters. Inland, the climate becomes more continental. Winters are cold, while temperatures often soar to 38°C [100°F] in the summer months.

HISTORY
Slav peoples settled in the area *c.*1400 years ago. In 803 Croatia became part of the HOLY ROMAN EMPIRE. Croatia was an independent kingdom in the 10th and 11th centuries, but in 1102 the king of Hungary also became king of Croatia, creating a union that lasted 800 years.

In 1526, part of Croatia fell to the Ottoman Empire, while the remainder came under the Austrian HABSBURGS. In 1699, the Habsburgs drove out the Turks and all of Croatia came under their rule. In 1809, Croatia became part of the Illyrian provinces of NAPOLEON I of France, but the Habsburgs took over in 1815.

In 1867, the Habsburg Empire became the AUSTRO-HUNGARIAN EMPIRE. During WORLD WAR I, Austria-Hungary fought on the side of the defeated Axis powers, and, in 1918, the empire was broken up. Croatia declared its independence and joined with neighbouring states to form the Kingdom of the Serbs, Croats and Slovenes. Serbian domination provoked Croatian opposition. In 1929, the king changed the country's name to Yugoslavia and began to rule as a dictator. He was assassinated in 1934 by a Bulgarian employed by a Croatian terrorist group, provoking more hostility between Croats and Serbs.

In WORLD WAR 2, Yugoslavia was occupied by Germany, and Croatia was proclaimed independent, although in reality it was a pro-Nazi puppet state (*Ustashe*). After the war, communists took power, and Josip Broz TITO became the country's leader and held it together until his death (1980). During the 1980s, economic and ethnic problems (including a deterioration in relations between Croatia and Serbia) threatened the country's stability. In 1990 The Croatian Democratic Union (HDZ), led by Franjo TUDJMAN, won Croatia's first democratic elections. A 1991 referendum voted overwhelmingly in favour of Croatia becoming an independent republic. The Yugoslav National Army was deployed and Serb-dominated areas took up arms in favour of remaining in the federation.

POLITICS
After Serbia supplied arms to Serbs living in Croatia, war broke out between the two republics, causing great damage, large-scale movements of refugees and disruption of the economy. In 1992, the United Nations sent a

AREA 56,538sq km [21,829sq mi]
POPULATION 4,493,000
CAPITAL (POPULATION) Zagreb (1,067,000)
GOVERNMENT Multiparty republic
ETHNIC GROUPS Croat 90%, Serb 5%, others
LANGUAGES Croatian 96%
RELIGIONS Roman Catholic 88%, Orthodox 4%, Islam 1%, others
CURRENCY Kuna = 100 lipas

peace-keeping force to Croatia, effectively ending the war with Serbia. However, war broke out in Bosnia-Herzegovina and Bosnian Croats occupied parts of the country. In 1994, Croatia helped to end the Croat-Muslim conflict in Bosnia-Herzegovina. In 1995, after retaking some areas occupied by Serbs, it contributed to the drawing up of the Dayton Peace Accord which ended the civil war.

Croatia's arch-nationalist president, Franco Tudjman, died in December 1999. In January 2000 elections, his Croatian Democratic Union (CDU) party was defeated by a westward-leaning alliance of Social Democrats and Social Liberals. Stipe Mesic, the last head of state of the former Yugoslavia in 1991, became president. In 2000, the government announced that it would prosecute suspected war criminals and co-operate with the war crimes tribunal in The Hague which indicted former Yugoslav president Slobodan MILOŠEVIĆ. In 2005 Croatia began negotiations to join the EU. 2007 parliamentary elections left a CDU-led coalition in power.

ECONOMY
The wars of the early 1990s disrupted Croatia's economy. Tourism on the Dalmatian coast has gradually recovered and is once again thriving. The manufacturing industries include cement, chemicals, refined oil and oil products, ships, steel and wood products, provide the chief exports.

Agriculture is important, and major farm products include fruits, livestock, maize, soya beans, sugar beet and wheat.

THE LIGHT BRIGADE is the best-known example. Sevastopol was eventually captured (1855). At the Treaty of Paris (1856) Russia surrendered its claims on the Ottoman Empire.

Criminal Investigation Department (CID) Non-uniformed branch of the London Metropolitan Police (founded 1878) dealing with the prevention and investigation of crime, and with the preparation of information on criminal trends. There are *c*.1600 CID officers, whose headquarters are at New Scotland Yard.

criminal law Body of law that defines crimes, lays down rules of procedure for dealing with them, and establishes penalties for those convicted. Broadly, a crime is distinguished from a TORT by being deemed injurious to the state. In many countries the criminal law has been codified. Among the best-known modern codes are the *Constitutio Criminalis Carolina* (1532) promulgated by Charles II for the Holy Roman Empire, Joseph II's code for Austria (1786), and the CODE NAPOLÉON. Criminal law remains part of COMMON LAW, although since the 18th century it has been greatly added to by statute law.

Cripps, Sir (Richard) Stafford (1889–1952) British statesman. He belonged to the left wing of the LABOUR PARTY and was ambassador to Russia (1940–42), later serving in Winston CHURCHILL's war cabinet. As chancellor of the exchequer (1947–50) in the reforming government of ATTLEE, he played a significant role in reconstruction of the post-war economy.

critical angle Angle at which a significant transition occurs. In optics, it is the angle of incidence with a medium at which total internal REFLECTION occurs. In telecommunications, it is the angle at which the IONOSPHERE reflects radio waves.

critical mass Minimum mass of fissionable material required in a fission bomb or nuclear reactor to sustain a CHAIN REACTION. The fissionable material of a fission bomb divides into portions less than the critical mass; when brought together at the moment of detonation they exceed the critical mass. *See also* FISSION, NUCLEAR

Croatia Balkan republic in SE Europe. *See* country feature

Croce, Benedetto (1866–1952) Italian idealist philosopher and politician. He wrote the idealistic *Philosophy of the Spirit* (1902–17) and was a senator (1910–20) and minister of education (1920–21). When Mussolini came to power, Croce retired from politics in protest against fascism. He re-entered politics following the fall of Mussolini in 1943 and, as leader of the Liberal Party, played a prominent role in resurrecting Italy's democratic institutions.

Crockett, Davy (David) (1786–1836) US politician and frontiersman. He served in the Tennessee legislature (1821–26) and the US Congress (1827–31, 1833–35). A Whig, he opposed the policies of Andrew JACKSON and the Democrats. He died at the ALAMO.

crocodile Carnivorous lizard-like REPTILE found in warm parts of every continent except Europe. Most crocodiles have a longer snout than ALLIGATORS. All lay hard-shelled eggs in nests. Length: up to 7m (23ft). There are about 12 species including two dwarf species in Africa. The Asian saltwater crocodile (*Crocodylus porosus*) sometimes attacks humans. Family Crocodylidae.

crocus Hardy PERENNIAL flowering plant. It is low growing with a single, tubular flower and grass-like leaves rising from an underground corm. Family Iridaceae; genus *Crocus*.

Croesus King of Lydia in Asia Minor (r. *c*.560–546BC). Renowned for his wealth, he was overthrown by CYRUS THE GREAT of Persia but served in his court.

Cro-Magnon Tall, Upper Paleolithic race of HUMANS, possibly the earliest form of modern *Homo sapiens*. Cro-Magnon people settled in Europe *c*.35,000 years ago. They manufactured a variety of sophisticated flint tools, as well as bone, shell, and ivory jewellery and artifacts. Cro-Magnon artists produced cave paintings in France and N Spain. Cro-Magnon remains were first found in 1868 in a rock shelter in Les Eyzies-de-Tayac, Dordogne, France. *See also* HUMAN EVOLUTION

Crompton, Richmal (1890–1969) English writer. She created one of the most popular characters in children's fiction, William, the scruffy, prankish schoolboy. The stories were first collected as *Just William* (1922), and more than 30 William novels followed. She also wrote adult fiction.

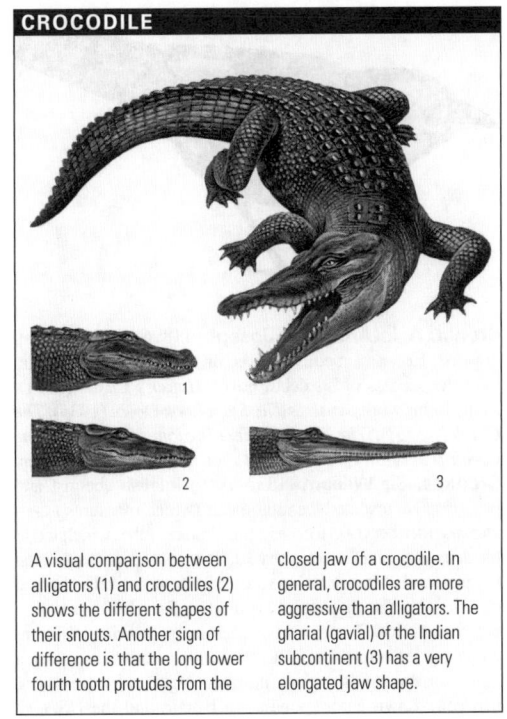

CROCODILE

A visual comparison between alligators (1) and crocodiles (2) shows the different shapes of their snouts. Another sign of difference is that the long lower fourth tooth protudes from the closed jaw of a crocodile. In general, crocodiles are more aggressive than alligators. The gharial (gavial) of the Indian subcontinent (3) has a very elongated jaw shape.

Crompton, Samuel (1753–1827) English inventor of a spinning machine. His 'spinning mule' of 1779 proved a boon to the textile industry reducing the amount of thread-breakage and made possible the production of very fine yarn.

Cromwell, Oliver (1599–1658) Lord Protector of England (1653–58). A committed Puritan, Cromwell entered Parliament in 1628 and was an active critic of CHARLES I in the LONG PARLIAMENT (1640). His tactical and organizational abilities became apparent in the first of the English CIVIL WAR, when his Ironsides helped defeat the Cavaliers at MARSTON MOOR (1644). In 1645 he was made second in command to Sir Thomas FAIRFAX, and helped form the NEW MODEL ARMY. After a decisive victory at NASEBY (1645), Cromwell emerged as the leading voice of the army faction. At first he favoured a compromise with Charles I, but eventually Charles' duplicity convinced him of the need to execute the king. In the Second Civil War, he defeated the Scottish Royalists at Preston (1648). Cromwell's political influence was strengthened in PRIDE'S PURGE (1648) of Parliament. The RUMP PARLIAMENT pressed for Charles' execution and established the COMMONWEALTH republic (1649). Cromwell ruthlessly suppressed opposition in Ireland, and defeated CHARLES II in the Third Civil War (1651). The failure of BAREBONE'S PARLIAMENT (1653) led to the "Instrument of Government" that established the PROTECTORATE. Cromwell became a virtual military dictator as "Lord Protector". The Humble Petition and Advice (1657) offered Cromwell the throne, but he refused. Cromwell's expansionist foreign policy was both anti-Stuart and pro-Protestant. The first of the DUTCH WARS (1652–54) and the war with Spain (1655–58) were both major drains on the country's resources. He was succeeded by his son Richard CROMWELL.

Cromwell, Richard (1626–1712) Lord Protector of England (1658–59). Son of Oliver CROMWELL, Richard lacked his father's leadership and lasted only eight months in power before going into exile in 1660. He returned to England in 1680.

Cromwell, Thomas, Earl of Essex (1485–1540) English statesman. Cromwell was secretary to Cardinal WOLSEY and succeeded him as HENRY VIII's chief minister in 1531. He was responsible for the acts of the REFORMATION parliament that established the CHURCH OF ENGLAND with the king as supreme head. Cromwell's ruthless management of the DISSOLUTION OF THE MONASTERIES (1536–40) was demonstrated by the Pilgrimage of Grace (1536). He made vital reforms of local government. Cromwell fell from power after the failure of Henry's marriage to ANNE OF CLEVES, and was executed.

▲ **crocus** Native to Europe and Asia, the crocus is grown in temperate climates, usually appearing in spring months.

► **crow** The American crow (*Corvus brachyrhynchas*) is found throughout North America. A large crow, its wingspan can reach up to 90cm (3ft). It feeds on some eggs and nesting chicks as well as insects and small rodents.

C

Cronin, A.J. (Archibald Joseph) (1896–1981) Scottish novelist. He was a medical inspector of mines and physician until the success of his debut novel, *Hatter's Castle* (1931). Many of his works, such as *The Stars Look Down* (1935), *The Citadel* (1937), *The Keys of the Kingdom* (1942) and *The Green Years* (1944), were filmed soon after they were written.

Crookes, Sir William (1832–1919) English chemist and physicist. He invented the radiometer (which measures ELECTROMAGNETIC RADIATION) and the Crookes tube, which led to the discovery of the electron by J.J. THOMSON. He was the first to suggest that CATHODE RAYS consist of negatively charged particles. He also discovered THALLIUM. *See also* X-RAY

crop rotation Practice of successively growing different crops on the same field. Rotated crops complement each other, some replenishing soil nutrients required by the others.

croquet Lawn game, popular in Britain and the USA, in which wooden balls are hit with wooden mallets through a series of six wire hoops towards a peg. The first player to complete all 12 hoops (each hoop in both directions) and reach the peg wins the game. On the way, a player can 'roquet' an opponent, by hitting the opponent's ball to a position of disadvantage on the lawn (usually the 'wrong' side of a hoop). Croquet developed in France in the 17th century.

Crosby, 'Bing' (Harry Lillis) (1904–77) US popular singer and actor. Following Crosby's film debut in *King of Jazz* (1930), he became one of the most successful 'crooners'. He worked with Bob HOPE on the acclaimed *Road* series and won a best actor Academy Award for *Going My Way* (1944). His recording of the Irving BERLIN song "White Christmas" (1942) is one of the best-selling records of all time.

crossbill Parrot-like, forest FINCH found mainly in the N of the Northern Hemisphere. It has a heavy, curved, scissor-like bill it uses to prise seeds from cones of evergreens. Length: 15cm (6in). Family Fringillidae; genus *Loxia*.

croup Respiratory disorder of children caused by inflammation of the LARYNX and airways. It is triggered by viral infection. Symptoms are a cough, difficult breathing, and fever.

Crow Large tribe of Siouan-speaking Native Americans who separated in the early 18th century from the Hidatsa. They migrated into the Rocky Mountains region from the upper Missouri River. Today, they occupy a large reservation area in Montana, where they were settled in 1868. They are noted for their fine costumes, artistic culture and complex social system.

crow Large, black bird found in many temperate woodlands and farm areas worldwide. Living in large flocks, crows prey on small animals and eat plants and carrion. They can be crop pests. They are intelligent birds and can sometimes be taught to repeat phrases. The female lays three to six greenish eggs. Family Corvidae. *See also* JAY; MAGPIE; RAVEN; ROOK

crown courts In England, courts established in 1971 to replace the assize courts and courts of quarter session. They are superior courts with a general jurisdiction, presided over by High Court judges. *See also* COURTS OF LAW

Cruelty, Theatre of French dramatic movement of the late 1920s. It developed under the influence of Antonin ARTAUD, who advocated a physical theatre expressing stark emotions rather than complex dialogue. Violence was used as a theatrical device to disturb audience perception. Artaud's theories emphasized the ritual and the surreal, and performance was considered more important than a specific text.

Cruikshank, George (1792–1878) English illustrator and cartoonist, known for his political and theatrical illustrations.

He first gained fame with his caricatures of the leading figures in George IV's divorce proceedings. He also illustrated more than 800 books, of which the best-known are Dickens' *Sketches by Boz* (1836) and *Oliver Twist* (1839).

Cruise, Tom (1962–) US film actor. He rose to fame in *Top Gun* (1986). After supporting roles in *The Color of Money* (1986) and *Rain Man* (1988), Cruise earned an Academy Award nomination for his performance in *Born on the Fourth of July* (1990).

cruise missile Self-propelled, GUIDED MISSILE that travels, generally at low altitudes, following the contours of the terrain. It is able to fly low enough to avoid conventional radar defences. The siting of American cruise missiles on European soil during the 1980s led to large-scale public demonstrations.

Crusades Military expeditions from Christian Europe to recapture the Holy Land (Palestine) from the Muslims in the 11th-14th centuries. Among the motives for the Crusades were rising religious fervour, protection of pilgrims to the Holy Land and aid for the BYZANTINE EMPIRE against the Seljuk Turks. Self-advancement of individual Crusaders and commercial motives were also significant. The **First Crusade** (1096–99), initiated by Pope URBAN II, captured Jerusalem and created several Christian states. Later Crusades had the objective of supporting or regaining these states. The **Third Crusade** (1189–91) was a response to the victories of SALADIN. Its leaders included the Holy Roman Emperor and the Kings of France and England. It had some successes, but failed to reconquer JERUSALEM. Although Crusader states survived for another century, later Crusades were less successful. In the 13th century, the Church sponsored crusades against other foes, such as the ALBIGENSES in France. *See also* CHILDREN'S CRUSADES

crust In geology, the thin, outermost solid layer of the Earth. The crust represents less than 1% of the Earth's volume and varies in thickness from *c*.5km (3mi) beneath the oceans to *c*.70km (45mi) beneath mountain chains. Oceanic crust is generally thinner averaging 7km (4.5mi) thick and is basaltic in composition, whereas continental crust is mainly between 30–40km (20–25mi) thick and of granitic composition. The crust is defined by its seismicity. The lower boundary of the crust is defined by a marked increase in seismic velocity, known as the Mohorovicic discontinuity. *See also* MOHO

crustacean Any member of the class Crustacea, comprising *c*.30,000 species of ARTHROPODS. The class includes the decapods (crabs, lobsters, shrimps and crayfish), isopods (pill millipedes and woodlice) and many varied forms, most of which have no common names. Most crustaceans are aquatic and breathe through gills or the body surface. They are typically covered by a hard exoskeleton. They range in size from the Japanese spider crab up to 3m (12ft) across to the ocean plankton, as little as 1mm (0.04in) in diameter.

cryogenics Branch of physics that studies materials and effects at temperatures approaching ABSOLUTE ZERO. Some materials exhibit highly unusual properties such as SUPERCONDUCTIVITY or SUPERFLUIDITY at such temperatures. The **Joule-Thomson effect** can be used to reduce temperatures to 0.3K. To cool gases even further requires magnetic process such as the **adiabatic process**. Cryogenics has been used to freeze human bodies in the uncertain hope that future technology may be able to revive the subjects.

cryptography Form of written message in which the original text (plaintext) is replaced by a series of other signs according to a prearranged system, in order to keep the message confidential. Unlike a **code**, in which each letter of the plaintext is replaced by another sign, a **cipher** cannot be 'cracked' without a key. Typically, a key is a complex pattern of letters or symbols forming the basis upon which the plaintext is enciphered. The receiver reverses this process to decipher the message. Ciphers were used by the ancient Greeks and were employed widely for military and diplomatic messages during the medieval and Renaissance periods. Mechanical devices for producing complex ciphers were developed between the two World Wars. The best-known cipher machine was the German Enigma device. Modern fast computers are today used by

INTERNET

Cruikshank, George
► www.famsf.org
► collage.nhil.com

Crusades
► crusades.boisestate.edu

cryptography
► www.bletchleypark.org.uk

Cuba
► www.cubagob.cu/ingles
► www.cubaheritage.com

intelligence services for constructing and breaking constantly changing complex ciphers. The same system is used for keeping credit card information secret.

crystal Solid with a regular geometrical form and with characteristic angles between its faces, having limited chemical composition. There are 32 classifications of crystals using the combinations of symmetry. The external form is called the **crystal habit**. The structure of a crystal, such as common salt, is based upon a regular 3–D arrangement of atoms, ions or molecules (a crystal or ionic lattice). Crystals are produced when a substance passes from a gaseous or liquid phase to a solid state, or comes out of solution by evaporation or precipitation. The rate of crystallization determines the size of crystal formed. Slow cooling produces large crystals, whereas fast cooling produces small crystals.

crystallography Study of the formation and structure of crystalline substances. Includes the study of crystal formation, chemical bonding in crystals and the physical properties of solids. Crystallography is particularly concerned with the internal structure of crystals. X-RAY CRYSTALLOGRAPHY uses X-rays to discover the molecular structure of crystals.

Crystal Palace First building of its size, 124 × 564m (408 × 1850ft), to be made of glass and iron. Sir Joseph PAXTON designed it for the Great Exhibition held in Hyde Park, London (1851). It was the first building prefabricated in sections and assembled on site. After the Exhibition, it was dismantled and re-erected on Sydenham Hill, SE London, where it stood until accidentally destroyed by fire in 1936.

Cuba Caribbean island republic at the entrance to the Gulf of Mexico. *See* country feature

CUBA

The Republic of Cuba is the largest island country in the Caribbean Sea. It consists of the large island of Cuba, the Isle of Youth (*Isla de la Juventud*) and about 1,600 islets. Mountains and hills cover about a quarter of Cuba. The highest mountain range, the Sierra Maestra in the SE, reaches 2,000m [6,562ft] above sea level at the Pico Real del Turquino. The rest of the land consists of gently rolling country or coastal plains, crossed by fertile valleys that have been carved by the short, mostly shallow and narrow rivers.

Farmland covers about half of Cuba and 66% of this is given over to sugar cane. Pine forests still grow, especially in the SE. Mangrove swamps line some coastal areas.

CLIMATE

Cuba lies in the tropics, but sea breezes moderate the temperature, warming the land in winter and cooling it in summer.

HISTORY

Christopher Columbus discovered Cuba in 1492, and Spanish settlers arrived in 1511. The indigenous population was quickly killed and replaced by African slave labour. Cuba formed a base for Spanish exploration of the American mainland, and became a prime target for pirates. Discontent at Spanish rule erupted into war in 1868. Slavery was abolished in 1886. In 1895, a second war of independence was led by José MARTÍ. In 1898, the sinking of the US battleship Maine precipitated the SPANISH-AMERICAN WAR. From 1898 Cuba was under US occupation. It became an independent republic in 1902, electing Tomás Estrada Palma as president, though American influence remained strong.

During WORLD WAR I, Cuba's economy flourished as the price of sugar rose dramatically. In 1933, an army sergeant named Fulgencio BATISTA seized power and ruled as dictator, maintaining good relations with the US. However, under a new constitution, he was elected president in 1940, serving until 1944. He again seized power in 1952 and became dictator once more. Fidel CASTRO (supported by Che GUEVARA) launched a revolution in 1956 and became premier in 1959. Castro nationalized many US-owned industries and many Cubans who were opposed to Castro left the country, settling in the United States. Castro nationalized many US-owned industries, and in 1961 the US broke off diplomatic ties and imposed a trade embargo. Cuban exiles, supported by the US government, launched the disastrous BAY OF PIGS invasion.

POLITICS

The United States opposed Castro's policies, so he turned to the Soviet Union for assistance. In 1962, the US learned that nuclear missile bases armed by the Soviet Union had been established in Cuba, initiating the CUBAN MISSILE CRISIS. The US ordered the Soviet Union to remove the missiles and bases. After a few days, during which many people feared that a world war might break out, the Soviet Union agreed to American demands.

Cuba's relations with the Soviet Union remained strong until 1991, when the Soviet Union was broken up. The loss of Soviet aid greatly damaged Cuba's economy and undermined Castro's social achievements, although the government remained popular. In 1998 hopes of a thaw in relations with the United States were

AREA 110,861sq km [42,803sq mi]
POPULATION 11,394,000
CAPITAL (POPULATION) Havana (2,192,000)
GOVERNMENT Socialist republic
ETHNIC GROUPS Mulatto 51%, White 37%, Black 11%
LANGUAGES Spanish (official)
RELIGIONS Christianity
CURRENCY Cuban peso = 100 centavos

raised when the US government announced that it was lifting the ban on flights to Cuba. The Pope, making his first visit to Cuba, criticized the 'unjust and ethically unacceptable' US blockade. In 2000, the United States lifted its food embargo on Cuba. The last Russian base in Cuba closed in 2002. In 2004 relations with the US again worsened and Cuba declared that US dollars would no longer be accepted on the island. Fidel Castro handed power to his brother Raul during a health crisis in 2006 and formally stepped down in 2008. The government remains repressive.

ECONOMY

The World Bank classifies Cuba as a 'lower-middle-income' country. Sugar cane remains Cuba's outstandingly important cash crop, accounting for more than 60% of the country's exports. It is grown on more than half of the island's cultivated land and Cuba is one of the world's top ten producers of the product. Before 1959, the sugar cane was grown on large estates, many of them owned by US companies. Following the Revolution, they were nationalized and the Soviet Union and Eastern European countries replaced the United States as the main market. The other main crop is tobacco, which is grown in the NW. Cattle raising, milk production and rice cultivation have also been encouraged to help diversify the economy, and the Castro regime has devoted considerable efforts to improving the quality of rural life, making standards of living more homogeneous throughout the island.

Minerals and concentrates rank second to sugar among Cuba's exports, followed by fish products, tobacco and tobacco products, including the famous cigars, and citrus fruits. In the 1990s, Cuba sought to increase its trade with Latin America and China. Tourism is a major source of income, but the industry was badly hit following the terrorist attacks on the United States in 2001.

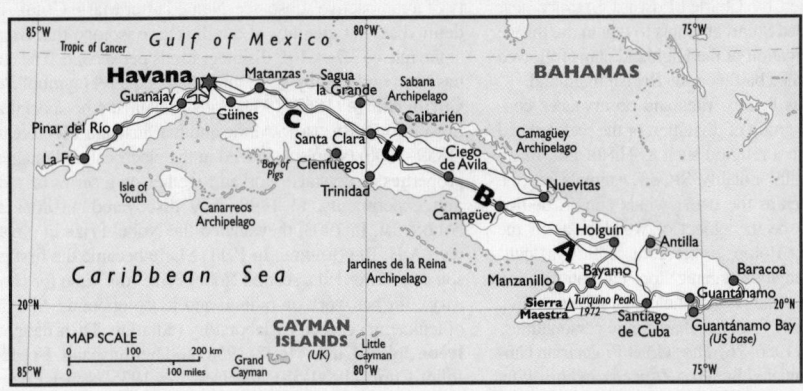

▲ **cuckoo** The common European cuckoo (*Cuculus canorus*) is famous for its parasitic behaviour. The female lays its egg in a smaller host's nest. The young cuckoo ejects its smaller nest mates and receives all the attention of its foster parents.

▲ **cucumber** Large, watery fruits are a common feature of the cucumber (*Cucumis sativus*) and its relatives. The plants are generally large and covered in coarse hairs and many have tendrils that help them climb.

INTERNET

Cuban Missile Crisis
▶ www.hpol.org/jfk/cuban

Culloden, Battle of
▶ www.highlanderweb.co.
uk/culloden/home.htm

Cuban Missile Crisis (October 1962) US and Soviet Union confrontation over the installation of Soviet nuclear rockets in Cuba, perhaps the closest the world has yet come to nuclear war. Photographs taken by US reconnaissance aircraft revealed the construction of ballistic missile bases in Cuba. President John F. KENNEDY warned Premier Nikita KHRUSHCHEV that any missile launched from Cuba would be met by a full-scale nuclear strike on the Soviet Union. On October 24, Cuba-bound Soviet ships bearing missiles turned back, and Khrushchev ordered the bases to be dismantled.

cube In mathematics, the result of multiplying a given number by itself twice. Thus, the cube of a is $a \times a \times a$, written a^3. A cube is also described as the third power of a number. The cube root is the number that must be multiplied by itself twice over to give a specified number. A cube is also a regular six-sided solid figure (all its edges are equal in length and all its faces are squares).

cubism Revolutionary, 20th-century art movement. It originated in c.1907 when PICASSO and BRAQUE began working together to develop ideas for changing the scope of painting. Abandoning traditional methods of creating pictures with one-point PERSPECTIVE, they built up three-dimensional images on the canvas using fragmented solids and volumes. In 1908, Braque held an exhibition of his new paintings that provoked the critic Louis Vauxcelles to describe them as bizarre arrangements of 'cubes'. The initial experimental, 'analytical', phase (1907–12), of which Picasso and Braque were the main exponents, was inspired mainly by African sculpture and the later works of CÉZANNE. They treated their subjects in muted grey and beige so as not to distract attention from the new concept. The 'synthetic' phase (1912–14) introduced much more colour and decoration and the techniques of COLLAGE and papiers collés were very popular. Cubism attracted many painters as well as sculptors. These included LÉGER, Robert DELAUNAY and Sonia DELAUNAY-TERK and Frantisek KUPKA. The most important cubist sculptors (apart from Picasso) were ARCHIPENKO, LIPCHITZ and Ossip Zadkine. Although it was not an abstract idiom, cubism revolutionized artistic expression, and lent itself easily to adaptation and development. It is probably the most important single influence on 20th-century progressive art.

cuckoo Widely distributed forest bird. Related species are the ani, ROAD RUNNER and coucal. Noted for parasitic behaviour. Their chief food is insects. True Old World cuckoos are generally brownish, although a few species are brightly coloured. Length: 15–75cm (6–30in). Family Cuculidae; genus *Cuculus*.

cuckoopint (wake robin or lords-and-ladies) Tuberous plant native to Europe. It has arrow-shaped leaves and sends up stout SPATHES, each of which unfurls to reveal a SPADIX that gives off a fetid carrion scent, attractive to insects, especially carrion-feeders. Later red poisonous berries form as the spathe dies off. Family Araceae; species *Arum maculatum*.

cucumber Trailing annual vine covered in coarse hairs; it has yellowish flowers and the immature fruit is eaten raw or pickled. Family Cucurbitaceae; species *Cucumis sativus*.

Culloden, Battle of (April 16, 1746) Decisive conflict of the JACOBITE rising of 1745. Government forces under the Duke of Cumberland, son of George II, defeated the Jacobites (largely Highlanders) led by Charles Edward STUART near Inverness. Culloden ended Stuart attempts to regain the throne by force. Ruthless subjugation of the Highland clans followed the conflict, the last pitched battle on the British mainland.

cult System of religious beliefs, rites and observances connected with a divinity or group of divinities, or the sect devoted to such a system. Within a religion such as HINDUISM, many gods have their own cults, notably SHIVA. Animals are the focus of some cults, such as the INUIT whale cult. A deified human being may also be the object of worship, as in the emperor cults of ancient Rome. In the 20th century, a 'cult' often denotes a quasi-religious organization that controls and exploits its followers by means of psychological manipulation. Leaders of cults are usually forceful, charismatic personalities.

Cultural Revolution (1966–76) The "Great Proletarian Cultural Revolution" was initiated by MAO ZEDONG and his wife, JIANG QING, to purge the Chinese COMMUNIST PARTY of his

opponents and instil 'correct' revolutionary attitudes after dissent over the failure of the GREAT LEAP FORWARD. Mao mobilized China's youth (*see* RED GUARDS) who held rallies, and violently attacked reactionary ideas. Senior party officials were purged (*see* LIU SHAOQI), intellectuals and others suspected of revisionism were victimized and humiliated and many murdered. By 1968, China was approaching civil war and the Cultural Revolution transformed into a struggle for the succession to Mao with the moderates led by DENG XIAOPING against the GANG OF FOUR. It ended with the defeat of the Gang of Four and the accession of Deng as paramount leader in 1976.

culture In ANTHROPOLOGY, all knowledge that is acquired by human beings through their membership of a society. A culture incorporates all the shared knowledge, expectations and beliefs of a group. Culture in general distinguishes human beings from animals, since only humans can pass on accumulated knowledge by means of symbolic systems such as language.

Cumbria County in NW England, bounded by the Solway Firth (N), and the Irish Sea (W); the county town is Carlisle. The region includes the LAKE DISTRICT and the Cumbrian Mountains. Area: 6808sq km (2629sq mi). Pop. (2001) 487,607.

Cummings, E.E. (Edward Estlin) (1894–1962) US poet. His first work was a novel, *The Enormous Room* (1922), which describes his imprisonment in a French detention centre. His reputation rests on his poetry, which is famously characterized by unconventional spelling, punctuation and typography.

cuneiform System of writing developed in Mesopotamia by c.3000 BC. It consists of wedge-shaped strokes, derived from writing on soft clay with a triangular stylus as a 'pen'. Cuneiform developed from pictograms. The pictograms came to serve as an 'ALPHABET', eventually consisting of more than 500 characters. Most stood for words, but there were also some that stood for syllables or speech-sounds.

Cunningham, Merce (1919–) US modern dancer and choreographer. In 1952, he formed the much-acclaimed Merce Cunningham Dance Company. His productions were highly experimental and include *Antic Meet* (1958) and *How to Pass, Kick, Fall, and Run* (1965).

Cupid In Roman mythology, god of love, equivalent to the Greek god EROS.

cuprite Reddish-brown, brittle, translucent oxide mineral, cuprous oxide (Cu_2O). Formed by the oxidation of other ores, such as copper sulphide, it is an important source of copper.

Curaçao Largest island of the NETHERLANDS ANTILLES in the West Indies, in the S Caribbean Sea; the capital is Willemstad. Most inhabitants are descended from African slaves imported during the 17th and 18th centuries; the indigenous Arawak are now extinct. Curaçao derives most of its income from tourism and oil-refining. Products: groundnuts, tropical fruits, Curaçao liqueur, phosphates. Area: 444sq km (171sq mi). Pop. (1998 est.) 205,693.

curare Poisonous resinous extract obtained from various tropical South American plants of the genera *Chondodendron* and *Strychnos*. Most of its active elements are ALKALOIDS. Causing muscle paralysis, it is used on the poisoned hunting arrows of Native South Americans and has been applied in surgery.

curie (symbol *Ci*) Unit formerly used to measure the activity of a radioactive substance. Named after Marie CURIE, it is defined as that quantity of a radioactive isotope that decays at the rate of 3.7×10^{10} disintegrations per second. The curie has been replaced by an SI unit, the becquerel (symbol *Bq*).

Curie, Marie (1867–1934) Polish scientist who specialized in work on RADIATION. Marie and her husband **Pierre** Curie (1859–1906) (who specialized in the electrical and magnetic properties of crystals) worked together on a series of radiation experiments. In 1898, they discovered RADIUM and POLONIUM. In 1903, they shared the Nobel Prize in physics with A.H. BECQUEREL. In 1911, Marie became the first person to be awarded a second Nobel Prize (this time for chemistry), for her work on radium and its compounds. She died of leukaemia caused by laboratory radiation. Their daughter, **Irène Joliot-Curie** (1897–1956) and her husband, **Frédéric** Joliot-Curie (1900–58), received the 1935 Nobel Prize in chemistry for producing artificial radioactive substances.

curium (symbol Cm) Synthetic radioactive metallic element of the ACTINIDE SERIES in the periodic table. It was first made in 1944 by the US nuclear chemist Glenn Seaborg and his colleagues by the alpha-particle bombardment of plutonium-239 in a cyclotron. Silvery in colour, curium is chemically reactive, intensely radioactive and is toxic if absorbed by the body. It provides power for orbiting satellites. Properties: at.no. 96; r.d. (calculated) 13.51; m.p. 1340°C (2444°F); 14 isotopes, most stable Cm^{247} (half-life 1.6×10^7 yr).

curlew Long-legged wading bird with a down-curved bill and mottled brown plumage. Often migrating long distances, it feeds on small animals, insects and seeds, and nests on the ground, laying two to four eggs. Length: to 48–62cm (19–25in). Species *Numenius arquata*.

curling Game resembling bowls on ice that is a major winter sport of Scotland, and popular in Canada, N USA, and Nordic countries. The game is played by two teams of four players on an ice surface, 42m (138ft) $\times$ 4.3m (14ft). Each player has two smooth circular stones – dished at the base and on top, and with a handle. At each end of the ice is a circular target with a central area known as the tee. One player sends his stone towards the tee, team-mates use brooms to sweep the surface in front of it to give it a smoother surface over which to glide. Each player delivers two stones. One point is scored for each stone lying nearer the tee than an opponent's stone.

currant Any of several mainly deciduous shrubs and their fruits, rich in vitamin C. Black, red, and white currants are included in the genus *Ribes*: they are popular plants, cultivated widely. The fruits are used in pies, preserves, and syrups. Family Grossulariaceae.

current *See* OCEANIC CURRENT

current, electric *See* ELECTRIC CURRENT

Cushing, Harvey (1869–1939) US surgeon. His pioneering techniques for surgery on the brain and spinal cord helped advance neurosurgery. He first described the syndrome produced by over-secretion of adrenal hormones that is now known as 'Cushing's syndrome'. It is characterized by weight-gain in the face and trunk, high blood pressure, excessive growth of facial and body hair, and diabetes-like effects.

Custer, George Armstrong (1839–76) US military leader. A flamboyant, headstrong character, Custer served with the Union and became the youngest brigadier general in the US Civil War. Following the war, he was posted to the frontier, but was court-martialled for disobeying orders in 1867 and suspended. In 1868, he returned to service and led attacks on the CHEYENNE. In 1876, at the Battle of the LITTLE BIGHORN, his force was attacked by the SIOUX and every man killed.

cuticle Exposed, outer layer of an animal. In humans, this refers to the EPIDERMIS, especially the dead skin at the edge of fingers. In botany, it refers to the waxy layer on the outer surface of epidermal cells of leaves and stems of vascular plants. It helps to prevent excessive water loss.

cuttlefish Cephalopod MOLLUSC related to the SQUID and OCTOPUS. Like squid, cuttlefish swim rapidly by the propulsion of a jet of water forced out through a siphon. They have ten sucker-covered arms on the head, two much longer than the rest. Their flattened bodies contain the familiar chalky cuttle-bone. Capable of rapid colour changes, they can also eject blue-black 'ink' as a means of protection. Family Sepiidae; species *Sepia officinalis*.

Cuvier, Georges, Baron (1769–1832) French geologist and zoologist, a founder of comparative anatomy and palaeontology. His scheme of classification stressed the form of organs and their correlation within the body. He applied this system of classification to fossils, and came to reject the theory of gradual evolution, favouring instead a theory of catastrophic changes.

Cuyp, Albert (1620–91) Dutch painter, son and pupil of **Benjamin Gerritsz** Cuyp (1612–52). His father was a genre painter much influenced by REMBRANDT. Albert is regarded as one of the greatest Dutch landscape painters. His calm, colourful river scenes and landscapes with cows use glowing light effects.

Cuzco City in s central Peru; capital of Cuzco department. An ancient capital of the Inca Empire from *c.*1200, it fell to the Spaniards in 1533. Cuzco was destroyed by earthquakes in 1650 and then rebuilt. It is a centre of archaeological research;

nearby sites include the fortress of Sacsahuáman and the Inca terraces at Pisac and MACHU PICCHU. Pop. (2002 est.) 282,600.

cyanide Salt or ester of hydrocyanic acid (prussic acid, HCN). The most important cyanides are sodium cyanide (NaCN) and potassium cyanide (KCN), both of which are lethal poisons. Cyanides have many industrial uses – in electroplating, for the heat treatment of metals, in the extraction of silver and gold, in photography, and in insecticides and pigments.

cyanobacteria (formerly blue-green algae) One of the major BACTERIA phyla, distinguished by the presence of the green pigment CHLOROPHYLL and the blue pigment phycocyanin. They perform PHOTOSYNTHESIS with the production of oxygen. Analysis of the genetic material of chloroplasts shows that they evolved from cyanobacteria, by ENDOSYMBIOSIS. Many cyanobacteria perform NITROGEN FIXATION. They occur in soil, mud, and deserts; they are most abundant in lakes, rivers, and oceans. Some produce toxic BLOOMS.

cybernetics Study of communication and control systems in animals, organizations and machines. It makes analogies between the BRAIN and nervous system, and COMPUTERS and other electronic systems, such as the analysis of the mechanisms of FEEDBACK and data processing. A household thermostat might be compared with the body's mechanisms for temperature control and respiration. Cybernetics combines aspects of mathematics, neurophysiology, computer technology, INFORMATION THEORY, and psychology.

cycad Phylum (Cycadophyta) of primitive palm-like shrubs and trees that grow in tropical and subtropical regions. Although they are GYMNOSPERMS, they have feathery palm- or fern-like leaves (poisonous in most species) at the top of stout (usually unbranched) stems. In addition to their main roots, they also have special roots containing CYANOBACTERIA that carry out NITROGEN FIXATION. These plants first flourished *c.*225 million years ago. Most of the 100 or so surviving species are less than 6m (20ft) tall.

cyclamen Genus of 20 species of low-growing perennial herbs, native to central Europe and the Mediterranean region. They have swollen, tuberous corms, drooping blooms and heart- or kidney-shaped leaves. Family Primulaceae.

cycling Sport for individuals and teams competing on BICYCLES. Now a regular event at the Olympic Games, cycle racing first became popular following the invention of the pneumatic tyre (1888). There is a diversity of formats and events, road racing being the best-known form. The most famous cycle race is the TOUR DE FRANCE (inaugurated 1903).

cyclone System of winds, or a storm, that rotates inwards around a centre of low atmospheric pressure (depression). The winds flow anti-clockwise in the Northern Hemisphere and clockwise in the Southern Hemisphere. Cyclones in middle latitudes are associated with cloudiness and high humidity, and the development of a FRONT. Strong tropical cyclones can give rise to HURRICANES. The term is also used for a DEPRESSION or, especially in the USA, for a TORNADO. *See also* ANTICYCLONE

Cyclopes In Greek mythology, three demons, each having one eye in the centre of its forehead, who forged the thunderbolts of ZEUS. They were depicted by Homer as giant herdsmen living on an island. ODYSSEUS escaped from the cannabalistic Cyclops Polyphemus by blinding him.

cyclotron *See* ACCELERATOR, PARTICLE

Cygnus One of the most distinctive constellations, often nicknamed the Northern Cross.

cylinder Solid figure or surface with straight parallel sides and a circular or oval cross section. It is formed by rotating a rectangle using one side as an axis. If the vertical height is h and the radius of the base r, then the volume is $\pi r^2 h$ and the curved surface area $2\pi rh$.

Cymbeline (Cunobelinus) (d. *c.*AD 42) Ancient British king. An ally of the Romans, he was king of the Catuvellauni tribe. After conquering the Trinovantes, he became the strongest ruler of s Britain.

Cynewulf English poet of the early 8th century, presumed to be the author of *Elene*, *The Fates of the Apostles*, *The Ascension*, and *Juliana*. Little is known about him, but the poems suggest that he was a priest in Mercia or Northumbria.

▲ **Custer** The youngest Union general in the American Civil War, George Custer received the Confederate flag of truce. A controversial figure in US history, he was accused later of abandoning a detachment of his troops, who were massacred at Washita (1868). Custer's decision to divide his regiment and attack a superior force of Sioux at the Battle of Little Bighorn resulted in the killing of Custer and his entire regiment. Custer became a national hero.

▲ **cyclamen** Often cultivated for its pink or white flowers, cyclamen (genus *Cyclamen*) is a member of the primrose family. It has petals that are twisted at the base and bent back.

▲ **cypress** The Lawson cypress (*Chamaecyparis lawsoniana*) is a false cypress. The name *Chamaecyparis* derives from the Greek *chamai* (dwarf) and *kuparissos* (cypress). It grows to a height of 60m (200ft), and lives for up to 600 years. It is native to Oregon and California.

Cynics School of philosophy founded (*c.*440BC) by Antisthenes, a pupil of SOCRATES. Cynics considered virtue to be in knowledge and action and rejected material pleasures. Its teachings were developed by DIOGENES. *See also* STOICS

cypress Tall, evergreen tree native to North America and Eurasia, and growing best in warmer climates. It has scale-like leaves, roundish cones and a distinctive symmetrical shape. The wood is durable and fragrant and is of value commercially. Height: 6–24m (20–80ft). Family Cupressaceae; genus *Cupressus*. There are *c.*20 species.

Cyprus Mediterranean republic. *see* country feature.

Cyrano de Bergerac, Savinien (1619–55) French writer. His novels and plays combine free thinking, humour and burlesque romance. His two posthumously published prose fantasies, *Journey to the Moon* (1656) and *The Comical Tale of the States and Empires of the Sun* (1662), contain many scientific predictions. He is also the eponymous hero of a popular but historically inaccurate play by Edmond ROSTAND.

Cyril, Saint Greek Christian missionary. With his brother, Methodius, he is one of the two so-called "Apostles to the Slavs" who were sent to convert the Khazars and Moravians to Christianity. Cyril is said to have invented the CYRILLIC alphabet. His feast day is February 14 (West); May 11 (East).

Cyrillic ALPHABET based on Greek letter forms that is now used for writing several Slavic languages, notably Russian.

Cyrus the Great (*c.*590–529 BC) King of Persia, founder of the ACHAEMENID Empire in Persia. He overthrew the Medes, then rulers of Persia, in 549 BC defeated King CROESUS of Lydia (*c.*546BC), captured BABYLON (539BC) and the Greek cities in Asia Minor. Although he failed to conquer Egypt, Cyrus' empire stretched from the Mediterranean to India. He delivered the Jews from their BABYLONIAN CAPTIVITY, sending them home to Palestine. His decree, held in the British Museum, is regarded as the first declaration of human rights.

cystic fibrosis Hereditary glandular disease in which the body produces abnormally thick mucus that obstructs the breathing passages, causing chronic lung disease. There is a deficiency of pancreatic enzymes and a general failure to gain weight. The disease is treated with antibiotics, pancreatic enzymes and a high-protein diet; sufferers must undergo vigorous physiotherapy to keep the chest as clear as possible.

cystitis Inflammation of the urinary bladder caused by bacterial infection. It is more common in women. Symptoms include frequent and painful urination, low back pain and slight fever.

cytokinin (kinetin or kinin) Any of a group of plant hormones that stimulate CELL DIVISION. Cytokinins work in conjunction with AUXINS to promote swelling and division in the plant cells producing lateral buds. They can also slow down the aging process in plants, encourage seeds to germinate and plants to flower, and are involved in plant responses to drought and water-logging. They are used commercially to produce seedless grapes, to stimulate germination of barley in brewing, and to prolong the life of green-leaf vegetables.

cytology Study of living CELLS and their structure, behaviour and function. Cytology began with English physicist Robert HOOKE's microscopic studies of cork in 1665, and the microscope is still the main tool. In the 19th century, a

CYPRUS

The Republic of Cyprus is an island nation which lies in the NE Mediterranean Sea. Geographers regard it as part of Asia, but it resembles S Europe in many ways. Cyprus has scenic mountain ranges, including the Kyrenia Range in the north and the Troodos Mountains in the S, which rise to 1,951m [6,401ft] at Mount Olympus.

The island also contains fertile lowlands used extensively for agriculture, including the broad Mesaoria Plain. Pine forests grow on the mountain slopes.

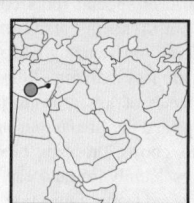

CLIMATE

Cyprus experiences hot, dry summers and mild, wet winters. Summers are hotter than those further W in the Mediterranean, as Cyprus lies close to the hot mainland of SW Asia.

HISTORY

The history of Cyprus dates back to 7000 BC. Greeks settled on Cyprus *c.*3,200 years ago. By 1050 BC Cyprus was fully established as a Greek island having embraced the language and culture of Greece. In 333 BC it became part of the empire of Alexander the Great and in

58 BC part of the Roman Empire. From AD 330, the island was under the Byzantine empire.

Cyprus was defeated in 1191 by Richard the Lionheart and the island was sold to the Knights Templar. Catholicism became the official religion. The island was under Venetian control from 1489 and fortifications were added to the towns of Nicosia and Famagusta. In the 1570s, it became part of the Turkish Ottoman Empire and Islam was introduced.

Turkish rule continued until 1878 when Cyprus was leased to Britain, although it was still part of the Ottoman Empire. When the Ottomans entered World War 1 in 1914 on the side of Germany, the island was annexed by Britain. It was proclaimed a Crown colony in 1925.

In the 1950s, Greek Cypriots, who made up *c.*80% of the population, led by Greek Orthodox Archbishop Makarios, began a campaign for *enosis* (union) with Greece. A secret guerrilla force called EOKA attacked the British, who responded by exiling Makarios.

POLITICS

Cyprus became an independent country in 1960 with Makarios as president. Britain retained two military bases. The constitution of Cyprus provided for power-sharing between the Greek and Turkish Cypriots, but this arrangement proved unworkable and fighting broke out. In 1964 the UN sent in a peace-keeping force.

In 1974, Cypriot forces led by Greek officers overthrew Makarios. This led Turkey to invade N Cyprus, a territory occupying about 40% of the island. Many Greek Cypriots fled from the N, which, in 1983, was proclaimed an independent state called the Turkish Republic of Northern Cyprus. However, the only country to recognize its status was Turkey. The UN regards

AREA 9,251sq km [3,572sq mi]
POPULATION 788,000
CAPITAL (POPULATION) Nicosia (198,000)
GOVERNMENT Multiparty republic
ETHNIC GROUPS Greek Cypriot 77%, Turkish Cypriot 18%, others
LANGUAGES Greek and Turkish (both official), English
RELIGIONS Greek Orthodox 78%, Islam 8%
CURRENCY Euro = 100 cents

Cyprus as a single nation under the Greek-Cypriot government in the S. It is estimated that more than 30,000 Turkish troops are deployed in N Cyprus. Despite UN-brokered peace negotiations, reunification efforts remain stalled.

In 2002, the European Union invited Cyprus to become a member. In April 2004, the people voted on a UN plan to reunify the island. The Turkish Cypriots voted in favour of the plan, but the Greek Cypriots voted against. As a result of this, only the S was admitted to membership of the EU on 1 May 2004. In 2008 the S adopted the Euro as the official currency.

ECONOMY

Cyprus got its name from the Greek word *kypros*, meaning copper, but little copper remains. The chief minerals are asbestos and chromium. The most valuable activity in Cyprus is tourism.

Industry employs 37% of the workforce and manufactures include cement, clothes, footwear, tiles and wine. In the early 1990s the UN reclassified Cyprus as a developed rather than developing country, though the economy of the Turkish-Cypriot N lags behind that of the more prosperous Greek-Cypriots.

theory was developed which suggested that cells are the basic units of organisms. Recently cytochemistry has focused on the study of the chemistry of cell components.

cytoplasm Jelly-like matter inside a CELL and surrounding the NUCLEUS. Cytoplasm has a complex constituency and contains various bodies known as organelles, with specific metabolic functions. The proteins needed for cell growth and repair are produced in the cytoplasm.

Czech Language spoken in the CZECH REPUBLIC (Bohemia and Moravia) by *c.*10 million people. A Slavic language, it is closely related to SLOVAK.

Czechoslovakia Former federal state in central Europe. Formed after World War 1 from parts of the old AUSTRO-HUNGARIAN EMPIRE, Czechoslovakia was formally recognized as a new republic by the Treaty of St Germain (1918). A democratic constitution was established in 1920, and the nation was led first by Tomás MASARYK and then by Eduard BENEŠ. Nationalist tensions caused unrest: the Slovaks had long wanted autonomy and the large German population in the N wanted to join with Germany. Hitler's rise to power and annexation of Austria led to the Munich Agreement (1938), which ceded Czech land to Germany. Poland and Hungary also acquired territory and Beneš resigned. In 1939 Hitler occupied the country, and Beneš

formed a government in exile in London. In 1945, Soviet and US troops liberated the country and restored Beneš as president. The communists gained a majority in the coalition after 1946 elections, and by 1948 they assumed complete control. Beneš resigned, and Czechoslovakia became a Soviet-style state with greatly reduced political and cultural freedom. Unrest during the 1950s led to some liberalization, but it was not until the PRAGUE SPRING of 1968, with the reforms of Alexander DUBČEK, that any major moves towards democratization occurred. Soviet troops crushed the movement. There were mass arrests and all reforms reversed. When Gorbachev introduced democratic reforms in the Soviet Union in the late 1980s, Czechs also demanded reforms. In 1989, anti-government demonstrations and the democratization of Eastern Europe finally led to the resignation of Communist Party leaders. Non-communists came to power, and the 'Velvet Revolution' ended with the election of Vaclav HAVEL. Free elections were held in 1990, but differences between the Czechs and Slovaks led to the partitioning of the country on January 1, 1993. The break was peaceful and the two new nations, the CZECH REPUBLIC and the SLOVAK REPUBLIC, retain many ties. *See also* BOHEMIA; MORAVIA

Czech Republic Republic in Europe. *See* country feature.

INTERNET

Cyprus
▶ www.cyprustourism.org
▶ kypros.org/PIO/cyprus/ index.htm
▶ www.cypnet.com/.ncyprus

Czech Republic
▶ www.czech.cz
▶ cz.avisit.com

CZECH REPUBLIC

The Czech Republic is the w three-fifths of the former country of Czechoslovakia. It contains two regions: BOHEMIA in the w and MORAVIA in the E. Mountains border much of the country in the w. The Bohemian basin in the N-centre is a fertile lowland region, with PRAGUE, the capital city, as its main centre. Highlands cover much of the centre of the country, with lowlands in the SE. Some rivers, such as the ELBE (Labe) and Oder (Odra) flow N into Germany and Poland. In the s, rivers flow into the DANUBE Basin.

CLIMATE

The climate of the Czech Republic is influenced by its landlocked position in E-central Europe. The country experiences a humid continental climate, with warm summers and cold winters. The average rainfall is moderate, with 500 to 750mm [20 to 30in] annually in lowland areas.

HISTORY

The ancestors of the Czech people began to settle in what is now the Czech Republic around 1,500 years ago. Bohemia, in the w, became important in the 10th century as a kingdom within the Holy Roman Empire. By the 14th century, Prague was one of Europe's major cultural centres. Religious wars in the first half of the 15th century led many Czech people to become Protestants. From 1526, the Roman

Catholic HABSBURGS from Austria began to rule the area, but in 1618 a Czech Protestant rebellion started the THIRTY YEARS' WAR. From 1620, most Czechs were forced to convert to Catholicism and adopt German as their language. German culture dominated the area until the late 18th century.

Although Austria continued to rule Bohemia and Moravia, Czech nationalism grew throughout the 19th century. During World War 1, Czech nationalists advocated the creation of an independent nation. At the end of the war, when Austria-Hungary collapsed, the new republic of CZECHOSLOVAKIA was founded. The 1920s and 1930s were generally a period of stability and economic progress, but problems arose concerning the country's minority groups. Many Slovaks wanted a greater degree of self-government, while Germans living in Sudetenland in w Czechoslovakia were unhappy under Czech rule.

In 1938, Sudetenland was turned over to Germany. In March 1939, Germany occupied the rest of the country. In 1945, following the Nazi defeat, a coalition government including Czech Communists was formed to rule the country. In 1948, Communist leaders seized control and made the country an ally of the Soviet Union in the Cold War. In 1968, the Communist government introduced reforms, which were known as the 'PRAGUE SPRING'. However, Russian and other East European troops invaded and suppressed the reform group.

POLITICS

When democratic reforms were introduced in the Soviet Union in the 1980s, the Czechs also demanded change. In 1989, the Federal Assembly elected Václav HAVEL, a noted playwright and dissident, as the country's president and, in 1990, free elections were held. The smooth transition from Communism to democracy was called the 'Velvet Revolution'. The road to a free-market economy was not easy, resulting in inflation, falling production, strikes and unemployment, although tourism has partly made up

AREA 30,450sq km [78,866sq mi]
POPULATION 10,229,000
CAPITAL (POPULATION) Prague (1,164,000)
GOVERNMENT Multiparty republic
ETHNIC GROUPS Czech 81%, Moravian 13%, Slovak 3%, Polish, German, Silesian, Gypsy, Hungarian, Ukrainian
LANGUAGES Czech (official)
RELIGIONS Atheist 40%, Roman Catholic 39%, Protestant 4%, Orthodox 3%, others
CURRENCY Czech koruna = 100 haler

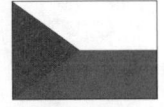

for some of the economic decline. Political problems also arose when Slovaks began to demand independence. Finally, on 1 January 1993, the more statist Slovakia broke away from the free-market Czech Republic. However, the split was generally amicable and border adjustments were negligible. The Czechs and Slovaks maintained a customs union and other economic ties. Meanwhile the Czech government continued to develop ties with Western Europe when it became a member of NATO in 1992. On 1 May 2004 the Czech Republic became a member of the EU.

ECONOMY

Under Communist rule the Czech Republic became one of the most industrialized parts of E Europe. The country has deposits of coal, uranium, iron ore, magnesite, tin and zinc. Manufactures include such products as chemicals, iron and steel and machinery, but the country also has light industries making such things as glassware and textiles for export. Manufacturing employs about 40% of the Czech Republic's entire workforce.

Farming is important. The main crops include barley, fruit, hops for beer-making, maize, potatoes, sugar beet, vegetables and wheat. Cattle and other livestock are raised. The country was admitted into the Organization for Economic Co-operation and Development (OECD) in 1995.

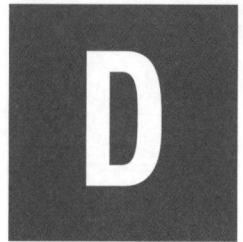

D/d, fourth letter of the Roman alphabet. It is derived from the Semitic daleth, meaning door, and the Greek delta. It took its current form c.AD 114. In Roman numerals, D stands for 500.

▲ **daffodil** Originally native to Europe and N Africa, the daffodil (*Narcissus* genus) is grown worldwide for its attractive, yellow, trumpet-shaped flower. In many regions, it heralds the beginning of spring.

▲ **dahlia** Numbering more than 7,000 varieties, the dahlia (*Dahlia* genus) is named after the Swiss botanist Anders Dahl. Most varieties have been developed from the original s American species *D. pinnata*.

dace Any of several small, freshwater fish of the carp family, Cyprinidae. The common European dace (*Leuciscus leuciscus*) is silvery and may grow 30cm (12in) long. The Moapa dace (*Moapa coriacea*) is an endangered species.

Dachau Town in Bavaria, SW Germany, site of the first Nazi CONCENTRATION CAMP established in March 1933. Up to 70,000 people were killed here before liberation in 1945. The site is preserved as a memorial.

Dacia Ancient region of Europe (now in Romania). It was colonized (101–106) by TRAJAN. Dacia was later overrun by Goths, Huns and Avars. The language was retained, and forms the basis of modern Romanian.

Dada (Dadaism) Movement in literature and the visual arts, started in Zürich (1915). Contributors included Jean ARP, Marcel DUCHAMP, Max ERNST and Man RAY. The group, repelled by war and bored with CUBISM, promulgated complete NIHILISM, espoused satire and ridiculed civilization. Dadaists participated in deliberately irreverent art events designed to shock a complacent public. They stressed the absurd, and the importance of the unconcious. In the early 1920s, conflicts of interest led to the demise of Dadaism. *See also* SURREALISM

Dadd, Richard (1817–61) English painter. Dadd showed early promise as an artist, but murdered his father in 1843 and spent the rest of his life in asylums. He continued to paint, specializing in highly imaginative fairy and fantasy pictures. His finest work is *The Fairy Feller's Master-Stroke* (1855–64), a minutely detailed piece of whimsical invention.

daddy-longlegs European name for the CRANE FLY

Daedalus In Greek mythology, a masterly architect and sculptor. He constructed the LABYRINTH for King MINOS of Crete. When denied permission to leave the island, he made wings of wax and feathers to escape with his son ICARUS.

daffodil Bulbous flowering plant, family Amaryllidaceae. Long leaves grow from the base and the single flowers are yellow or yellow and white, with a bell-like central cup and oval petals. Height: to 45cm (18in). Genus *Narcissus*.

Dagestan Republic in the Russian Federation, bounded on the E by the CASPIAN SEA, SE European Russia. The capital is Makhachkala. Islam was introduced in the 7th century, and the majority of the present population is Muslim. Annexed by Russia in the early 19th century, Dagestan's native population resisted Russian rule until autonomy was granted in 1921. In 1991 it claimed full republic status. The CAUCASUS mountains dominates the region. Lowlands to the N support wheat, maize and grapes. The rivers Samur and Sulak provide hydroelectric power. Difficulty of access leaves mineral resources untapped. Industries: engineering, oil, chemicals. Area: 50,300sq km (19,416sq mi). Pop. (2000) 2,148,800.

Daguerre, Louis Jacques Mandé (1789–1851) French painter and inventor. In 1829, Daguerre and Niepce invented the daguerreotype, an early photographic process in which a unique image is produced on a copper plate without an intervening negative. Their process was announced in 1839, shortly before William Fox TALBOT developed the calotype. *See also* PHOTOGRAPHY

Dahl, Roald (1913–90) British writer, chiefly of short stories. He is remembered for his witty, imaginative children's fiction. His books, such as *James and the Giant Peach* (1961) and *Charlie and the Chocolate Factory* (1964), are popular with all ages. He is also noted for his adult stories, which regularly feature a grotesque, moral twist, such as *Someone Like You* (1953) and *Kiss, Kiss* (1959). *Boy* (1984) and *Going Solo* (1986) are volumes of autobiography.

dahlia Genus of perennial plants with tuberous roots and large flowers. The common garden dahlia (*Dahlia pinnata*) has been developed into more than 2000 varieties. Height: to 1.5m (5ft). Family Asteraceae/Compositae.

Dáil Éireann Lower House of the two-chamber Parliament of the Republic of Ireland (the Upper House is the *Seanad Éireann*). It has 166 members elected for five-year terms by a system of proportional representation.

Daimler, Gottlieb (1834–1900) German engineer and automobile manufacturer. In 1883, with Wilhelm Maybach, Daimler developed an INTERNAL COMBUSTION ENGINE and powered a motorcycle and then his first car (1886). In 1890, he founded

the Daimler Motor Company, which made Mercedes cars, and became Daimler-BENZ (1926), then Daimler-Chrysler (1998).

daisy Any of several members of the family Asteraceae/Compositae, especially the common English garden daisy, *Bellis perennis*. It has basal leaves and long stalks bearing solitary flower heads, each of which has a large, yellow, central disc and small radiating white petal-like florets.

Dakar Capital and largest city of Senegal, W Africa. Founded in 1857 as a French fort, the city grew rapidly with the arrival of a railroad (1885). A major Atlantic port, it later became capital of French West Africa. There is a Roman Catholic cathedral and a presidential palace. Dakar has excellent educational and medical facilities, including the Pasteur Institute. Industries: textiles, oil refining, brewing. Pop. (2005) 2,313,000.

Dakota *See* NORTH DAKOTA and SOUTH DAKOTA

Daladier, Édouard (1884–1970) French statesman, prime minister (1933, 1934, 1938–40). In 1934, Daladier was forced to resign after failing to quell riots. As prime minister and minister of defence, he signed the MUNICH AGREEMENT (1938). Daladier again resigned after his failure to help Finland repel the Russian advance. In 1940 he was arrested by the new VICHY GOVERNMENT, and was deported to Germany in 1942. He was released at the end of World War 2, and became a member of the National Assembly (1946–58).

Dalai Lama (Grand Lama) Supreme head of the Yellow Hat Buddhist monastery at LHASA, TIBET. The title was bestowed upon the third Grand Lama by the Mongol ruler Altan Khan (d.1583). In 1642, the Mongols installed Ngawang Lopsang Gyatso (1617–82), fifth Dalai Lama, as political and spiritual ruler of Tibet. Dalai Lamas thereafter retained political leadership, but spiritual supremacy was later shared with the PANCHEN LAMA. In 1950–51, **Tenzin Gyatso** (1935–), 14th Dalai Lama, temporarily fled Tibet after it was annexed by the People's Republic of China. Following a brutally suppressed Tibetan uprising (1959), he went into exile in India. In TIBETAN BUDDHISM, the Dalai Lama is revered as the BODHISATTVA *Avalokitesvara*. When a Dalai Lama dies, his soul is believed to pass into the body of an infant, born 49 days later.

Dalí, Salvador (1904–89) Spanish artist. His style, a blend of meticulous realism and hallucinatory transformations of form and space, made him an influential exponent of SURREALISM. His dream-like paintings exploit the human fear of distortion, as in *The Persistence of Memory* (1931). Dalí collaborated with Luis BUÑUEL on the films *Un Chien andalou* (1928) and *L'Age d'or* (1930).

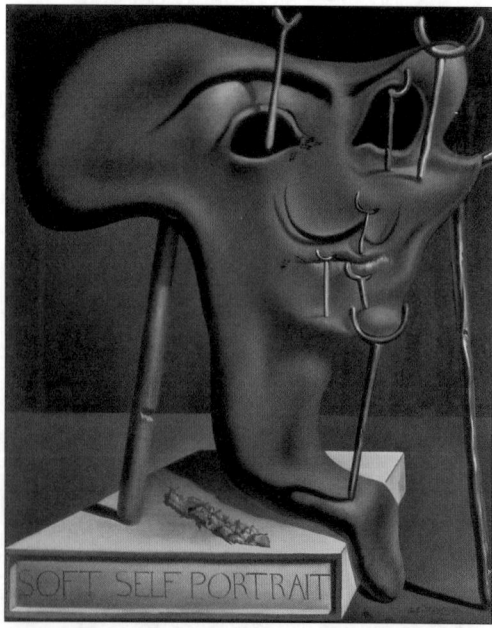

▲ **Dalí** *Soft Self Portrait* (1941) by Salvador Dalí. The Spanish painter Dalí was influenced by the work of Sigmund Freud, and his surrealist images convey powerful dream and hallucinatory elements.

Dallas City in NE Texas, USA. First settled in the 1840s, Dallas expanded with the 20th-century development of its oilfields. President John F. KENNEDY was assassinated here on November 22, 1963. A leading commercial and transport centre of SW USA, it has many educational and cultural institutions. Industries: oil refining, electronic equipment, clothing, aircraft. Pop. (2000) 4,146,000.

Dalmatia Region of CROATIA on the E coast of the Adriatic; the provincial capital is SPLIT. From the 10th century it was divided N/S between Croatia and Serbia. By 1420, after centuries of war, most of Dalmatia was controlled by Venice. The Treaty of Campo Formio (1797) ceded the region to Austria. After World War 1 it became part of Yugoslavia. The coastline, a popular tourist destination, stretches along the Adriatic from Rijeka to the border with Montenegro. Most of the inland area is mountainous. In 1991, following Croatia's secession from the Yugoslav federation, Dalmatia was the scene of heavy fighting between Croats and Serbs. Other major cities in the region include Zadar (the historic capital) and DUBROVNIK. Area: 4524sq km (1747sq mi). Pop. (2001) 467,899

dalmatian Dog, characterized by its white coat with black or dark-brown spots. It has a long, flat head with long muzzle and high-set ears. Its powerful body is set on strong legs and the tail is long and tapered. Height: to 58cm (23in) at the shoulder.

Dalton, John (1766–1844) English chemist, physicist, and meteorologist. He researched TRADE WINDS, the cause of rain, and the AURORA borealis. He described COLOUR BLINDNESS based on personal experience. His study of gases led to Dalton's law of partial pressures: the total pressure of a gas mixture is equal to the sum of the partial pressures of the individual gases, provided no chemical reaction occurs. His atomic theory states that each element is made up of indestructible, small particles. He also constructed a table of relative atomic masses.

dam Barrier built to confine water (or check its flow) for irrigation, flood control or electricity generation. The first dams were probably constructed by the Egyptians 4,500 years ago. **Gravity** dams are anchored by their own weight. **Single-arch** dams are convex to the water they retain, supported at each end by river banks. **Multiple-arch** and buttress dams are supported by buttresses rooted in the bedrock. The cheapest commercial source of electricity comes from hydroelectric projects made possible by dams, such as the ASWAN High Dam, Egypt.

Damascus Capital of Syria, on the River Barada, SW Syria. Thought to be the oldest continuously occupied city in the world, in ancient times it belonged to the Egyptians, Persians and Greeks, and under Roman rule was a prosperous commercial centre. It was held by the Ottoman Turks for 400 years, and after World War 1 came under French administration. It became capital of an independent Syria in 1941. Sites include the Great Mosque and the Citadel. It is Syria's administrative and financial centre. Industries: damask fabric, metalware, leather goods, refined sugar. Pop. (2005) 2,317,000.

Damocles In Greek history, a courtier of Dionysius I of Syracuse (Sicily). Dionysius suspended a sword by a thread above Damocles' head to make him realize that wealth and power were transient and fragile.

damselfly Delicate insect resembling the DRAGONFLY. Almost all have a slender, elongated, blue abdomen and one pair of membranous wings that are held vertically over the body when at rest. Length: to 5cm (2in). Order Odonata.

damson Small tree and its edible fruit. The name is often applied to varieties of PLUM (*Prunus domestica*), especially *P.d. insititia*. The fleshy DRUPE is generally borne in clusters, has a tart flavour, and is made into jam. Family Rosaceae. The damson-plum of tropical America is a separate species, *Chrysophyllum oliviforme*, Family Sapotaceae.

dance Ancient art of ordered, stylized body movements, normally performed to the accompaniment of music or voices. In its most primitive form, dance was probably part of courtship and religious ritual. In China, Japan, and India, graceful MIME is the distinctive feature, whereas the dances of Africa are characterized by rapid, athletic movements. In 18th-century Europe, Bach and Handel, among others, composed music for formal courtly dances, such as the

gavotte and minuet. Ballroom dances, such as the waltz, foxtrot, tango and quickstep, became popular in the 19th and early 20th centuries. In the 1950s, dances such as the jive and the twist were introduced. Many different styles have emerged from MODERN DANCE. *See also* BALLET

dandelion Widespread perennial weed, with leaves growing from the base and yellow composite flowers. It reproduces by means of parachute seeds. The leaves are used in salads; the flowers in winemaking. Family Asteraceae (COMPOSITAE); species *Taraxacum officinale*.

Danelaw Large region of NE England, occupied by Danes in the late 9th century. In 886, Alfred and Guthrum's Pact formally confirmed its independence. Alfred's son, Edward the Elder, and grandson, Athelstan, restored it to English control in the early 10th century.

Daniel Legendary Jewish hero and visionary of the 6th century BC who was at the court of the kings of Babylon, Nebuchadnezzar and Belshazzar. The Old Testament Book of Daniel, probably written *c.*165 BC relates events in Daniel's life during the BABYLONIAN CAPTIVITY. The book also gives an account of Belshazzar's Feast. The last six of its 12 chapters consist of visions and prophesies.

Dante Alighieri (1265–1321) Italian poet. In his early years Dante wrote many *canzoni* to Beatrice Portinari, who remained the inspiration for much of his life's work. In 1300, he became one of the rulers of Florence, but was exiled in 1302 after a feud between the White and Black GUELPHS. He never returned to Florence, but wrote under the patronage of various nobles until he died impoverished in Ravenna. His writings include *The New Life* (*c.*1293), *Banquet* (*c.*1304–07), *On Monarchy* (*c.*1313), and *De Vulgari Eloquentia* (1304–07). His masterpiece, *The Divine Comedy*, a three-book epic in *terza rima*, represents one of the pinnacles of Western literature and places Dante among the greatest writers of all time.

Danton, Georges Jacques (1759–94) French politician and a leader of the FRENCH REVOLUTION. He played the role of moderator in the turbulent 1790s, seeking conciliation between the GIRONDINS and Montagnards. Briefly head of the JACOBINS in 1793 and a member of the Committee of Public Safety, he was arrested during the REIGN OF TERROR and guillotined.

Danube (Donau) River in central and SE Europe. Europe's second-longest river (after the Volga), it rises in SW Germany, flows NE then SE across Austria to form the border between Slovakia and Hungary. It then flows S into Serbia, forming part of Romania's borders with Serbia and Bulgaria. It continues N across SE Romania to the Black Sea. It is an international waterway, run by the Danube Commission. Length: *c.*2,859km (1,770mi).

Danzig *See* GDANSK

Daphne Nymph in Greek mythology. APOLLO, struck by a gold-tipped arrow of EROS, fell in love with Daphne. She had been shot with one of Eros' leaden points, and so scorned all men. To protect her from Apollo, the gods transformed her into a laurel tree.

Dardanelles (Çanakkale Bogazi) Narrow strait between the Sea of Marmara and the Aegean Sea, separating Çanakkale (in Asian Turkey) from GALLIPOLI (in European Turkey). With the BOSPORUS Strait, the Dardanelles forms a waterway, whose strategic and commercial importance has been recognized since ancient times (then known as Hellespont). In the Byzantine and Ottoman empires and both World Wars, it was vital to the defence of Constantinople (ISTANBUL). Since the early 14th century it has been almost continuously controlled by Turkey. The strait was the scene of the GALLIPOLI CAMPAIGN in World War 1. The Treaty of Sévres (1920) demilitarized the straits, but by 1936 Turkey had remilitarized the zone. Length: 61km (38 mi). Width: 1.2–6km (0.75–4mi).

Dar es Salaam Former capital of Tanzania, on the Indian Ocean, E Tanzania. Founded in the 1860s by the sultan of Zanzibar, it was capital of German East Africa (1891–1916) and of Tanganyika (1916–74). It is Tanzania's commercial centre, largest city and port. Industries: textiles, chemicals, oil products. Pop. (2005) 2,683,000.

Darío, Rubén (1867–1916) (Félix Rubén García Sarmiento) Nicaraguan poet, father of the *modernismo* movement. His early works, such as *Blue* (1881) and

▲ **dalmatian** Perhaps best known from the Disney animated film *101 Dalmatians* (1961), dalmatians are thought to have been developed as carriage dogs in the Croatian region of Dalmatia.

▲ **dandelion** Found throughout the Northern Hemisphere, the leaves of the common dandelion (*Taraxacum officinale*) have teeth-shaped edges. It is from this shape that the dandelion derives its name (Fr. *dents de lion*, 'teeth of the lion'.)

D

Profane Hymns (1896), show the influence of the French Parnassians and symbolists. Darío's masterpiece, *Songs of Life and Hope* (1905), is more historical and political.

Darius I (the Great) (*c.*558–486 BC) King of Persia (521–486BC) of the ACHAEMENID dynasty. He extended the Persian Empire, and divided it into provinces (satrapies). He made great improvements to transport infrastructure, and was tolerant of religious diversity. The Greeks defeated Darius at MARATHON in 490 BC. *See also* PERSIAN WARS

Darius III (*c.*380–330 BC) King of Persia (336–330BC). He underestimated ALEXANDER THE GREAT, and brought about the demise of the ACHAEMENID Persian Empire. Defeated at Issus (333BC) and Gaugamela (331BC), he fled to Ecbatana and then to Bactria, where he was killed.

Darjeeling City at the foot of the Himalayas, West Bengal, NE India. A former British hill station, it is noted for its teas and its views of Kanchenjunga and Everest. Pop. (2001) 107,530.

Dark Ages Period of European history from the fall of the Roman Empire in the 5th century to the 9th or 10th century. The term appears to imply cultural and economic backwardness after the classical civilization of Greece and Rome, but indicates more an ignorance of the period due to the paucity of historical evidence.

Darmstadt City in Hesse state, W central Germany. The old town dates from the Middle Ages. The city was severely damaged during World War 2. It is a cultural centre, with a notable international music school. Industries: chemicals, aerospace engineering, steel. Pop. (1999) 137,600.

Darwin Port in N Australia, on the Beagle Gulf, an inlet of the Timor Sea; capital of Northern Territory. Founded in the late 1860s as Palmerston, it became Port Darwin in 1911. The Allied headquarters in N Australia during World War 2, it was bombed by the Japanese in 1942. In 1974 most of the city was destroyed by a cyclone. Darwin's harbour is the major shipping point for the sparsely populated and relatively undeveloped N region of Australia. Pop. (1999 est.) 88,100.

Darwin, Charles Robert (1809–82) English naturalist, originator of a theory of EVOLUTION based on NATURAL SELECTION. In 1831, he joined an expedition on HMS BEAGLE and observations made of the flora and fauna of South America (especially the GALÁPAGOS ISLANDS) formed the basis of his work on animal variation. The development of a similar theory by A.R. WALLACE led Darwin to present his ideas to the Linnean Society in 1858, and in 1859 he published *The Origin of Species*, one of the world's most influential science books.

dasyurus Genus of mainly nocturnal, carnivorous marsupials found in Australia, New Guinea, and Tasmania. They have large canine teeth, separate digits and long tails. The female's pouch is normally shallow. Family Dasyuridae.

data Information, such as lists of words, quantities or measurements. A computer PROGRAM works by processing data, which may be entered on the keyboard, or stored in code as a data file on a DATABASE, magnetic disk or tape.

database Collection of DATA produced and retrieved by computer. The data is usually stored on magnetic disk or tape. A database PROGRAM enables the computer to generate files of data and later search for and retrieve specific items or groups of items. For example, a library database system can list, on screen, all the books on a particular subject and can then display further details of any selected book.

data processing Systematic sequence of operations performed on DATA, especially by a COMPUTER, in order to calculate or revise information stored on magnetic disk or tape. This involves retrieving and classifying information. The main processing operations performed by a computer are: arithmetical addition, subtraction, multiplication and division, and logical operations that involve decision-making based on comparison of data. For example, data processing is used to predict population growth.

date palm Tree native to the Near East. It has feather-shaped leaves and large flower clusters that produce the popular edible fruit. Height: up to 30m (100ft). Family Arecacae/Palmae.

dating, radioactive (radiometric dating) Any of several methods using RADIOACTIVE DECAY to assess the ages of archaeological remains, fossils and rocks. The specimens must contain a very long-lived radioisotope of known HALF-LIFE (time taken for one half of its nuclei to decay), which, with a measurement of the ratio of radioisotope to a stable ISO-TOPE (usually the decay product), gives the age. In **potassium-argon** dating, the ratio of potassium-40 to its stable decay product argon-40 gives ages more than 10 million years. In **rubidium-strontium** dating, the ratio of rubidium-87 to its stable product strontium-87 gives ages to several thousand million years. In CARBON DATING, the proportion of carbon-14 (half-life 5,730 years) to stable carbon-12 absorbed into once-living matter gives ages to several thousand years.

Daumier, Honoré (1808–79) French painter, sculptor, and caricaturist. He produced more than 4,000 lithographs in a vigorous style, lampooning French middle-class society.

David (d. *c.*962BC) King of ancient Israel (*c.*1010–970BC), successor of SAUL. His career is related in the OLD TESTAMENT books of SAMUEL. As king, he united Judah and Israel. David captured Jerusalem, making it his capital. The later part of his reign was marked by the revolts of his sons ABSALOM and Adonijah. David was succeeded by SOLOMON, his son by Bathsheba. According to the Jewish Prophets, the MESSIAH must be a descendant of David.

David, Gerard (1460–1523) Flemish painter. Influenced by van EYCK and van der WEYDEN, David has a distinctive austere grace. He was commissioned by the town of BRUGES to paint several works: *The Judgement of Cambyses* and *The Flaying of Sisamnes* warned officials of the retribution for injustice. Other works include *Madonna Enthroned* and *Annunciation*.

David, Jacques Louis (1748–1825) French painter, a leader of NEO-CLASSICISM. Influenced by POUSSIN and Greek and Roman art, David's work was closely tied to his Jacobin views and support for Napoleon during the French Revolution. His most famous work is *Oath of the Horatii* (1784). Other works include *Death of Marat* (1793), and *Madame Recamier* (1799).

David, Saint (d. *c.*600) Patron saint of Wales. He founded a monastery at what is now St Davids. Little is known of his life, but legends abound. His feast day is March 1.

David I (*c.*1084–1153) King of Scotland (1124–53), son of Malcolm III. He strengthened the monarchy by granting land to the aristocracy and developing the burghs. In 1136, David invaded England in support of his niece Matilda's claim to the throne. He was defeated at the Battle of the Standard (1138). In 1141, David gained control of Northumberland.

Davies, Sir Peter Maxwell (1934–) British composer. Prolific and varied in his compositions, he has written seven operas, including *Taverner* (1970), *The Martyrdom of St Magnus* (1976), and *Resurrection* (1987). His symphonies include the *Antarctic Symphony* (2000, Symphony No. 8). Much of his work, reflects the landscape and culture of his adopted home, the remote Orkney Islands, N Scotland.

Davies, Robertson (1913–95) Canadian novelist, dramatist, and journalist. Davies is best known for *The Deptford Trilogy* (1970–75), a characteristic mixture of

▲ ▶ **date palm** Today, grown as an ornament as well as for its fruit, the date palm (*Phoenix dactylifera*) has been cultivated for more than 4000 years. The tallest examples reach a height of 30m (100ft). The fruit is often dried.

myth, satire and symbolism. Other works include *The Salterton Trilogy* (1951–58) and a number of plays.

Da Vinci, Leonardo *See* LEONARDO DA VINCI

Davis, Bette (1908–89) US film actress. She is remembered for her intense character portrayals and evocative screen presence. She won two best actress Academy Awards for *Dangerous* (1935) and *Jezebel* (1938). Other films include *All About Eve* (1950) and *What Ever Happened to Baby Jane?* (1962). She was the first woman to receive (1977) a Life Achievement Award from the American Film Institute.

Davis, Sir Colin Rex (1927–) English conductor. He was principal conductor of the BBC Symphony Orchestra (1967–71), musical director at the Royal Opera House (1971–86), principal conductor of the Bavarian Radio Symphony Orchestra (1983–92), and principal conductor of the London Symphony Orchestra (1995– 2006).

Davis, Jefferson (1808–89) American statesman, president (1862–65) of the CONFEDERATE STATES OF AMERICA during the US CIVIL WAR. Davis was elected to Congress in 1845, but resigned to fight in the Mexican War. He was a strong advocate of the extension of SLAVERY and acted as senator for Mississippi (1849–51). In 1853 Franklin PIERCE made him secretary of war. In 1857 he rejoined the Senate and acted as leader of the Southern bloc. He resigned when Mississippi seceded from the Union (1861) and was soon elected leader of the Confederacy. Davis assumed authoritarian political power and also participated in military decision-making. Following Lee's surrender, Davis was captured and imprisoned (1865–67). He wrote *The Rise and Fall of Confederate Government* (1881).

Davis, Miles Dewey (1926–91) US jazz trumpeter, one of the most influential modern jazz musicians. During the 1940s, he played BE-BOP with Charlie PARKER. Eager to experiment with diverse musical forms, he changed the course of jazz with the sophisticated and reflective *Birth of the Cool* (1949), and played with the saxophonist John COLTRANE on the seminal *Kind of Blue* (1959). During the late 1960s, he switched to electric instrumentation, and was a pioneer of jazz-rock. In the 1970s and 1980s he gained considerable commercial success.

Davis, Stuart (1894–1964) US painter, the leading American exponent of CUBISM. Although influenced by the ASH-CAN SCHOOL, the greatest impact on his mature style was the ARMORY SHOW (1913). After a visit to Paris (1928–29), he turned towards cubism's synthetic phase, introducing natural forms arranged in flat areas of pattern in bright, contrasting colours. His later abstract style used lettering that resembled advertising slogans, such as *Owh! in San Pao* (1951).

Davitt, Michael (1846–1906) Irish nationalist. Imprisoned in 1870 as a member of the FENIAN MOVEMENT, Davitt and PARNELL established the Irish Land League to organize Irish tenant farmers against exploitive landlords. The League gained concessions of fair rents, fixed tenure and freedom of sale in the Land Act (1881).

Davy, Sir Humphry (1778–1829) English chemist, a founder of ELECTROCHEMISTRY. He was invited to join the Royal Institution after discovering the anaesthetic nitrous oxide (laughing gas). In 1807, using the process of ELECTROLYSIS, Davy discovered potassium. In 1808 he isolated the elements sodium, barium, strontium, calcium, and magnesium. His investigation of how firedamp (methane and other gases) and air explode, led to his invention of the miner's safety lamp.

Dawes, Charles Gates (1865–1951) US statesman, vice president (1925–29). He served (1897–1902) as comptroller of the currency under William MCKINLEY. Dawes received the 1925 Nobel Peace Prize for his work that produced the DAWES PLAN (1924) for stabilizing the German economy.

Dawes Plan (1924) Measure devised by a committee chaired by Charles DAWES to collect and distribute German reparations after World War 1. It established a schedule of payments and arranged for a loan of 800 million marks by US banks to stabilize the German currency.

Day, Doris (1924–) US singer and film actress. Her recordings, such as "Sentimental Journey" (1945) and "Secret Love" (1954), sold millions during the 1940s and 1950s. Her

wholesome, energetic performances in films such as *Calamity Jane* (1953), *Pajama Game* (1957), and *Send Me No Flowers* (1964) won her an even greater audience.

Dayan, Moshe (1915–81) Israeli army officer and politician. Dayan served with the British and led a Palestinian Jewish company against the Vichy French in World War 2. He led the invasion of the Sinai Peninsula in 1956 and, as minister of defence, became a hero of the SIX-DAY WAR (1967). Active in Israeli policy-making, he served as foreign minister (1977–79).

Day-Lewis, Cecil (1904–72) British poet and critic. He was associated with the leftist AUDEN circle. His concern for social justice is evident in *Transitional Poem* (1929), *Magnetic Mountain* (1933), *Overtures to Death* (1938) and *Collected Poems* (1954). He was poet laureate from 1968. He also wrote detective fiction under the pseudonym Nicholas Blake.

Day-Lewis, Daniel Michael (1957–) Irish actor, b. London. Day-Lewis first gained public recognition for his performance in *My Beautiful Laundrette* (1986). In 1989 he won a Best Actor Academy Award for his extraordinary physical role in *My Left Foot*. Other films include *The Age of Innocence* (1993) and *In the Name of the Father* (1993).

Dayton City at the confluence of the Great Miami and Stillwater rivers, SW Ohio, USA. Settled in 1796, it is a commercial centre of an agricultural region. In 1995, the Dayton Peace Accord ended the war in Bosnia. Pop. (2000) 166,179.

D-day (June 6, 1944) Codename for the Allied invasion of Normandy during WORLD WAR 2. Commanded by General EISENHOWER, Allied forces landed on the French coast between Cherbourg and Le Havre. It was the largest amphibious operation in history, involving *c*.5,000 ships. Despite fierce resistance, bridgeheads were established by June 9. It was the first step in the liberation of Europe.

DDT (dichlorodiphenyltrichloroethane) Organic compound used as an insecticide. It acts as a contact poison, disorganizing the nervous system. Effective against most insect pests, it proved to have long-lasting toxic effects and many species developed resistance. It is now banned in many countries.

deacon (Gk. *diakonos*, 'helper') Ordained minister who serves as a priest's assistant in Christian churches. The institution of the diaconate can be traced to the New Testament, which describes the ordination of seven deacons (Acts 6) to carry out the administrative work of the early Church.

deadly nightshade Poisonous perennial plant native to Europe and W Asia. It has large leaves, purple flowers, and black berries. ALKALOIDS, such as ATROPINE, are obtained from its roots and leaves. Eating the fruit can be fatal. Family Solanaceae; species *Atropa belladonna*.

Dead Sea (Al-Bahr-al-Mayyit) Salt lake in the Jordan valley, on the Jordan-Israel border. It is fed by the River JORDAN. The surface, 403m (1,320ft) below sea level, is the lowest point on Earth. It is situated in a hot, dry region, and much water is lost through evaporation. One of the world's saltiest waters, large amounts of its salts are extracted. It supports no life.

Dead Sea Scrolls Ancient manuscripts discovered from 1947 in caves at Qumran near the DEAD SEA. Written in Hebrew or Aramaic, they date from between the 1st century BC and the 1st century AD. They include versions of much of the OLD TESTAMENT and other types of religious literature. Some are a thousand years older than any other biblical manuscript.

deafness Partial or total hearing loss. **Conductive** deafness, faulty transmission of sound to the sensory organs, is usually due to infection or inherited abnormalities of the middle ear. **Perceptive** deafness may be hereditary or due to injury or disease of the COCHLEA, auditory nerve or hearing centres in the brain. Treatment ranges from removal of impacted wax to delicate microsurgery. Hearing aids, sign language, and lip-reading are techniques which help deaf people to communicate.

Dean, James (1931–55) US film actor. He played the restless son in the film (1954) of John Steinbeck's *East of Eden*, and appeared as a misunderstood teenager in *Rebel Without a Cause* (1955). Dean died in a car crash, a year before the release of his final film *Giant*. He became a cult hero.

death Cessation of life. In medicine, death has traditionally been pronounced on cessation of the heartbeat. However, modern resuscitation and life-support techniques have enabled the

▲ **Davis** Trumpeter Miles Davis was among the first jazz musicians to experiment with other contemporary forms of music, such as funk and rap. Beginning in the 1940s be-bop era, his musical career spanned half a century.

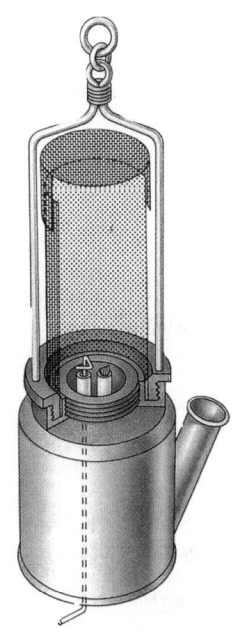

▲ **Davy** Perhaps best known for the invention of the miner's safety lamp (Davy lamp), English scientist Sir Humphry Davy was a significant chemist who inspired Michael Faraday.

▶ **Death Valley** The desert region of SE California, known as Death Valley, is among the hottest places on Earth. It acquired its name from gold and silver prospectors, many of whom lost their lives trying to cross it.

revival of patients whose hearts have stopped. In a tiny minority of cases, while breathing and heartbeat can be maintained artificially, the potential for life is extinct. In this context, death may be pronounced when it is clear that the brain no longer controls vital functions. The issue is highly controversial.

death cap (deadly amanita) Highly poisonous FUNGUS that grows in woodland. It has a yellowish-green cap and a white stem with a drooping ring and sheathed base. If eaten, the poison causes great pain, serious liver damage and, in most cases, death. Species *Amanita phalloides*.

death penalty *See* CAPITAL PUNISHMENT

Death Valley Desert basin in E California, USA. It has the lowest point in the Western Hemisphere, 86m (282ft) below sea level. Temperatures can reach 57°C (134°F), the highest in the USA. Gold and silver were mined in the 1850s, and borax in the late 19th century. It is surrounded by the Panamint mountains (W) and the Armagosa (E). Length: 225km (140mi).

deathwatch beetle Small beetle that tunnels through wood. It makes a faint ticking sound, once said to presage death. It is actually the mating signal of the female as it taps its head against the wood. Length: to 0.9cm (0.3in). Family Anobiidae; species *Xestobium rufovillosum*.

de Beauvoir, Simone *See* BEAUVOIR, SIMONE DE

Debs, Eugene Victor (1855–1926) US labour organizer. President of the American Railway Union (1893–97), he was imprisoned during the Pullman Strike (1894). He organized the Social Democratic Party (1898), and was five times a presidential candidate (1900–20), even while imprisoned for violation of the Espionage Act (1918). He was a founder of the Industrial Workers of the World (IWW).

Debussy, Claude Achille (1862–1918) French composer, exponent of IMPRESSIONISM. Debussy wrote highly individual music that was delicate and suggestive. He explored new techniques of harmony and orchestral colour. Some critics cite his *Prélude à l'après-midi d'un faune* (1894) as the beginning of 20th-century music. Other orchestral works are *Nocturnes* (1899), *La Mer* (1905), and *Images* (1912). His piano works, such as *Suite Bergamasque* (1890) and *Etudes* (1915), are among the most important in the repertoire. His one completed opera was *Pelléas and Mélisande* (1902).

Debye, Peter Joseph Wilhelm (1884–1966) US chemist, b. Netherlands. He was best known for his work on molecular structure and ionization. He pioneered X-ray CRYSTALLOGRAPHY and received the 1936 Nobel Prize in chemistry.

decathlon Sports event comprising ten different track and field activities: 100m, long jump, shot-put, high jump, 400m, 110m hurdles, discus, pole vault, javelin, and 1,500m.

Deccan Plateau in central India, S of the River Narmada. It has been a region of conflict since early times. In attempting to conquer it in the 17th century, Aurangzeb fatally weakened the MOGUL dynasty. In the late 18th century, the British defeated the French here. On its E and W edges, the Deccan rises to the GHATS. The plateau is covered with rich volcanic soils. Cotton, cereal, coffee, and tea are grown.

decibel (symbol dB) Logarithmic unit, one tenth of a bel, used for comparing two power levels and for expressing the loudness of a sound. The faintest audible sound (2×10^{-5} pascal) is given an arbitrary value of 0dB. The human pain threshold is *c.*120dB. Ordinary conversations occur at 50–60 dB.

deciduous Annual or seasonal loss of all leaves from a tree or shrub; it is the opposite of EVERGREEN.

decimal system Common system of writing numbers using a base ten and the Arabic numerals 0 to 9. It is a positional number system, each position to the left representing an extra power of ten. Thus 6741 is $(6 \times 10^3) + (7 \times 10^2) + (4 \times 10^1) + (1 \times 10^0)$: note that $10^0 = 1$. Decimal fractions are represented by negative powers of ten placed to the right of a decimal point.

Declaration of Independence (July 4, 1776) Statement of the principles with which the THIRTEEN COLONIES of North America justified the AMERICAN REVOLUTION and separation from Britain as the United States of America. Its blend of high idealism and practical statements ensured its place as one of the world's most important political documents. The Declaration was drafted by a committee that included Thomas JEFFERSON, and was based on the theory of NATURAL RIGHTS propounded by John LOCKE to justify the GLORIOUS REVOLUTION in England. It was approved by the Continental Congress on July 4. The Declaration states the necessity of government having the consent of the governed, of government's responsibility to its people, and contains the famous paragraph: "We hold these truths to be self-evident, that all men are created equal, that they are endowed by their Creator with certain unalienable Rights, that among these are Life, Liberty, and the Pursuit of Happiness."

Declaration of Rights *See* BILL OF RIGHTS

Declaration of the Rights of Man and Citizen Statement of principles of the French Revolution, adopted by the National Assembly, accepted by Louis XVI and included in the 1791 constitution. Influenced by the American DECLARATION OF INDEPENDENCE and the ideas of Jean Jacques ROUSSEAU, it established the sovereignty of the people and the principles of "liberty, equality, and fraternity".

decoder In telecommunications and electronics, a device that converts the information content of a signal into a more intelligible form. In a satellite TV receiver, for example, it transforms satellite signals into TELEVISION ones.

decomposition Natural degradation of organic matter into simpler substances, such as carbon dioxide and water. Organisms of decay are usually bacteria and fungi. Decomposition recycles nutrients by releasing them back into the ecosystem.

decompression sickness *See* BENDS

deconstruction Key approach in literary criticism. It was pioneered by Jacques DERRIDA (1930–2004), who resisted a precise definition of the term. Techniques include searching for pairs of ideas stated or implied as opposed, which are then broken apart to question the implied hierarchies between them. The process of deconstruction is text-centred, and its critics claim it excludes the role of history in literary work. The term is also used in architecture early 1980s work that explored ways of reconciling traditional oppositions in building design, such as structure-decoration and abstract-figurative.

Decorated style Style of English Gothic architecture which flourished from *c.*1250 to 1350. The most exuberant phase of English Gothic, it featured the double-curving ogee arch and intricate, curvilinear window tracery. Its French equivalent, the FLAMBOYANT STYLE, came much later. The windows of EXETER Cathedral are excellent examples of Decorated stone carving. *See also* GOTHIC ART AND ARCHITECTURE

deer Long-legged, hoofed, RUMINANT. There are 53 species in 17 genera distributed worldwide. In most species, the male (buck, hart or stag) bears antlers. Only in reindeer does the female (hind or doe) bear antlers. Deer often gather in herds. They are generally brown, with spotted young (fawns) and eat bark, shoots, twigs and grass. Humans exploit them for their meat (venison), hides and antlers (for hunting trophies). The deer family Cervidae has existed since the Oligocene epoch. The Chinese water deer is the smallest, measuring 55cm (22in) tall at the shoulder; the largest is the ELK, at 2m (6.5ft).

Defence, Ministry of (MoD) British department of state. First formed in 1940, in 1964 it was reorganized to combine the old War Office, Admiralty and Air Ministry. It is presided over by a secretary of state and two ministers of state.

Defender of the Faith (Lat. *Fidei Defensor*) Title claimed by the monarchs of England since 1521. The title was first given to HENRY VIII by Pope Leo X after the publication of a tract by Henry attacking the protestant Martin Luther.

INTERNET

Death Valley
www.nps.gov/deva

Declaration of Independence
memory.loc.gov/const/declar.html

Declaration of the Rights of Man and Citizen
www.constitution.org/fr/fr_drm.htm

Degas, (Hilaire Germain) Edgar
www.metmuseum.org
www.nationalgallery.org.uk

Defense, US Department of (DOD) US government department. It consists of the secretary of defence, Joint Chiefs of Staff (JCS), service departments and operational military commands. The secretary of defence, with the president, is responsible for all operational military activities, providing civilian control for the ARMY, NAVY and AIR FORCE. First formed in 1789, it reorganized in 1949.

deflation Falling prices, accompanied by falls in output and employment; the opposite of INFLATION. It normally occurs during a RECESSION or DEPRESSION, and can be measured by the price index. Excess production capacity leads to an excess of supply, in which manufacturers supply more goods than consumers wish to buy, and usually causes deflation.

Defoe, Daniel (1660–1731) English journalist and novelist. He championed William III in his first notable poem, *The Trueborn Englishman* (1701). A politically controversial journalist, he was twice imprisoned, once for *The Shortest Way with the Dissenters* (1702). His reputation now rests on his fiction. His enduringly popular novels include *Robinson Crusoe* (1719), *Moll Flanders* (1722), *Colonel Jack* (1722), and *Roxana* (1724). A man of remarkably varied interests, Defoe is among the most prolific writers in the English language.

De Forest, Lee (1873–1961) US inventor of the audion triode valve (1907), an important electronic invention. It could amplify signals, and had many applications. Valves became essential in radio, television, radar, and computer systems. The TRANSISTOR largely replaced valves. *See also* THERMIONICS

deforestation Clearing away of forests and their ECOSYSTEMS, usually on a large scale, by humans. It may be done to create open areas for farming or building, or for timber. There is an immediate danger that the vital topsoil will be eroded by wind (such as the DUST BOWL, USA) or, in hilly areas, by rain. Proposals to clear whole regions of the Amazonian RAINFORESTS, which play a key role in maintaining the oxygen balance of the Earth, could cause an environmental catastrophe.

Degas, (Hilaire Germain) Edgar (1834–1917) French painter and sculptor. Classically trained and an admirer of INGRES, Degas combined the discipline of classic art with the immediacy of the modern. After meeting Édouard MANET, he took part in exhibitions of IMPRESSIONISM and shared an interest in scenes of everyday life, especially ballet and horse-racing. A brilliant draughtsman, he found inspiration in Japanese prints and photography. He made sculptures of dancers and horses to master the expression of movement. His subtle use of colour and light became concentrated in his later pastels.

De Gasperi, Alcide (1881–1954) Italian statesman, prime minister (1945–53). De Gasperi was born in Trentino, then under Austrian rule. He struggled successfully for its reunification with Italy. A staunch anti-fascist, De Gasperi was imprisoned twice in the 1920s. During World War 2, he founded the Italian Christian Democratic Party. De Gasperi is regarded as the chief architect of Italy's post-war recovery. He led Italy into NATO, and championed closer relations with the USA.

De Gaulle, Charles André Joseph Marie (1890–1970) French general and statesman, first president (1959–69) of the Fifth Republic. De Gaulle's experience of World War 1 (captured 1916), convinced him of the need to modernize the French army. In 1940 he became undersecretary of war, but fled to London after the German invasion. He organized French Resistance (Free French) forces, and in June 1944 was proclaimed president of the provisional French government. Following liberation he resigned, disenchanted with the political settlement. In 1958, he emerged from retirement to deal with the war in Algeria. In 1959 a new constitution was signed, creating the French Community. In 1962, De Gaulle was forced to cede Algerian independence. France gained an independent nuclear capability, but alienated the UK and USA by its temporary withdrawal from NATO and by blocking British entry into the EEC. De Gaulle's devaluation of the franc brought relative domestic prosperity. He was re-elected (1965), but resigned following defeat in a 1969 referendum.

degree In mathematics, unit of angular measure equal to 1/360 of a complete revolution. One degree is written 1°, and can be divided into 60 parts called minutes (e.g. 20′) which may in turn be divided into 60 parts called seconds (e.g. 25″). Three hundred and sixty degrees are equal to 2π radians. In physics and engineering, a degree is one unit on any of various scales, such as the CELSIUS temperature scale.

dehydration Removal or loss of water from a substance or tissue. Water molecules can be removed by heat, catalysts or a dehydrating agent such as concentrated sulphuric acid. Dehydration is used in FOOD PRESERVATION, such as the freeze-drying process of such items as coffee and meat. In medicine, excessive water loss is often a symptom or result of disease or injury.

Deighton, Len (Leonard Cyril) (1929–) English novelist. His spy thrillers *The Ipcress File* (1962) and *Funeral in Berlin* (1964) were made into films. Bernard Samson is the central character of the *Game, Set and Match* trilogy: *Berlin Game* (1983), *Mexico Set* (1984), and *London Match* (1986).

deism System of natural religion, first developed in England in the late 17th century. It affirmed belief in one God, but held that He detached himself from the universe after its creation and made no revelation. Reason was man's only guide. The deists opposed revealed religion in general, and Christianity in particular. Deist writings include John Toland's *Christianity not Mysterious* (1696) and Matthew Tindal's *Christianity as Old as the Creation* (1730). VOLTAIRE, ROUSSEAU, and DIDEROT were the main deists of the ENLIGHTENMENT period.

de Klerk, F.W. (Frederik Willem) (1936–) South African statesman, president (1989–94). De Klerk entered parliament in 1972 and joined the cabinet in 1978. In 1989, de Klerk led a 'palace coup' against P.W. BOTHA, and became president and National Party leader. Following a narrow electoral victory, de Klerk began the process of dismantling APARTHEID. In 1990, the ban on the AFRICAN NATIONAL CONGRESS (ANC) was lifted and Nelson MANDELA was released. In 1991, the principal apartheid laws were repealed and victory in a 1992 whites-only referendum marked the end of white minority rule. In 1993, he shared the Nobel Peace Prize with Nelson Mandela. Following the 1994 elections, de Klerk became deputy president in Mandela's government of national unity. In 1996, he resigned and led the Nationalists out of the coalition. He retired as leader of the National Party in 1997.

de Kooning, Willem (1904–97) US painter, b. Netherlands. De Kooning was greatly influenced by PICASSO and Arshile GORKY. In 1948, he became one of the leaders of ABSTRACT EXPRESSIONISM. Unlike Pollock, he kept a figurative element in his work and shocked the public with violently distorted images, such as the *Women* series (1953). His emphasis on technique became known as ACTION PAINTING.

Delacroix, (Ferdinand Victor) Eugène (1798–1863) French painter, the greatest French artist of ROMANTICISM. Success came at his first Paris salon (1822), when he sold *The Barque of Dante* and, two years later, *The Massacre at Chios*. A

▼ **Degas** The French painter Degas was an unusual impressionist, because of the emphasis he placed on drawing and composition of indoor scenes. Perhaps his most popular theme was movement, in particular dance, such as *Dancers on a Bench* (1898).

DELAWARE
Statehood :
December 7, 1787
Nickname :
The First State
State bird :
Blue hen chicken
State flower :
Peach blossom
State tree :
American holly
State motto :
Liberty and independence

INTERNET

Delaware
▶ www.delaware.gov

Deng Xiaoping
▶ chineseculture.about.com/
cs/dengxiaoping

visit to Morocco (1832) inspired a rich collection of sketches. His work underwent a major change in the 1830s, when he began to exploit divisionism (placing complementary colours side by side to obtain greater vibrancy). He was one of France's best monumental history painters and influenced many late 19th-century progressive artists, especially Van Gogh.

de la Mare, Walter (1873–1956) English poet, short-story writer and anthologist. His technically accomplished collections of poems include *Songs of Childhood* (1902), *Peacock Pie* (1913), *Winged Chariot* (1951), and the anthology *Come Hither* (1923). His prose includes the novel *Memoirs of a Midget* (1921) and the collection of stories *On the Edge* (1930).

Delaunay, Robert (1885–1941) French painter, co-founder (with his wife Sonia DELAUNAY-TERK) of ORPHISM. Delaunay was a major influence on der BLAUE REITER. Many of his works are abstract cityscapes, principally of his native Paris. The *Eiffel Tower* series is his most famous.

Delaunay-Terk, Sonia (1885–1979) French painter, b. Russia. Co-founder (with her husband Robert DELAUNAY) of ORPHISM. Among her most notable works are the lyrical *Simultaneous Contrasts* (1912) and delightful abstract illustrations for the *Prose du Trans-Sibérien* by Blaise Cendrars.

Delaware Confederation of Algonquian-speaking NATIVE AMERICANS. The main members were the Unami, Munsee and Unalachtigo, who occupied territory from Long Island to Pennsylvania and Delaware. Under pressure from settlers and the IROQUOIS CONFEDERACY, they migrated to the Ohio region in the 18th century. They lost these lands by a treaty of 1795, and subsequently became widely scattered.

Delaware State in E USA, on the Atlantic coast, occupying a peninsula between Chesapeake and Delaware bays; the capital is DOVER, the largest city is WILMINGTON. Discovered by Henry Hudson in 1609, it was named after the British governor of Virginia, Baron De la Warr. Delaware was settled by Swedes in 1638. The Dutch, under Peter STUYVESANT, conquered the territory by 1655. Although the Dutch briefly recaptured Delaware in 1673, it was under effective English control from 1664 to 1776. One of the original THIRTEEN COLONIES, it was the first to ratify the Articles of Confederation (1789). Despite being a slave state, it maintained a fragile loyalty to the Union during the American Civil War. It is the second smallest US state by area (after Rhode Island), and most of its land is coastal plain. The Delaware River, an important shipping route, forms part of the E boundary. Industries: chemicals, rubber, plastics, metallurgy. Agriculture: cereal crops, soya, dairy produce. Area: 5,328sq km (2,057sq mi). Pop. (2000) 783,600.

Delft City in South Holland province, SW Netherlands. Founded in the 11th century, it was an important commercial centre until the 17th century. It has a 13th-century Gothic church and a 15th-century church. Industries: Delftware pottery, ceramics, china, tiles, pharmaceuticals. Pop. (2001) 96,556.

Delhi Former capital of India, on the River Yamuna, union territory of Delhi, N central India. Delhi has held a key position throughout India's history, and is built on the site of at least seven settlements, dating back more than 2,000 years. In the 17th century, it was capital of the MOGUL EMPIRE. In 1912, it became capital of British India (replacing Calcutta) and remained so until independence in 1947, when the capital became NEW DELHI. Sites include the Red Fort, Qutb Minar, the Rajghat (a shrine where Gandhi was cremated), the Jamii Masjid, and the Jai Singh Observatory. Industries: cotton textiles, handicrafts, tourism. Pop. (2005) 15,334,000.

Delian League Confederation of Greek city-states formed (478BC) under Athenian leadership after the losses of the PERSIAN WARS. The treasury was initially held on the island of Delos, but was moved to Athens by PERICLES and later appropriated to fund Athens' imperial ambitions. It was disbanded after the PELOPONNESIAN WARS.

Delibes, (Clément Philibert) Léo (1836–91) French composer. He was famous for his ballet music, especially *Coppélia* (1870), and also wrote several operas (*Lakmé*, 1883), as well as sacred and secular choral works.

DeLillo, Don (1936–) US novelist. A leading figure in POST-MODERNISM, his complex works examine the state of contemporary American society. Novels include *White Noise* (1986), *Libra* (1988), and *Underworld* (1997).

delirium State of confusion in which a person becomes agitated and incoherent and loses touch with reality; often associated with delusions or HALLUCINATIONS. It may be seen in various disorders, brain disease, fever, and drug or alcohol intoxication.

Delius, Frederick (1862–1934) English composer. He combined elements of ROMANTICISM with IMPRESSIONISM, most notably in orchestral pieces, such as *Brigg Fair* (1907) and *On Hearing the First Cuckoo in Spring* (1912). His interest in nature is evident in the operas *A Village Romeo and Juliet* (1901) and *Fennimore and Gerda* (1910).

Delphi Ancient city state in Greece, near Mount Parnassus. The presence of the oracle of Apollo made it a sacred city. The Pythian Games, celebrating Apollo's destruction of the monster Python, were held at Delphi every four years. The Temple of Apollo was sacked in Roman times, and the oracle closed (AD 390) with the spread of Christianity.

delphinium (larkspur) Any of *c*.250 species of herbaceous plants native to temperate areas, with spirally arranged leaves and loose clusters of flowers. Petals form a tubular spur, which contains nectar. Garden delphiniums are varieties of *Delphinium elatum*. Family Ranunculaceae.

delta Fan-shaped body of ALLUVIUM deposited at the mouth of a river. A delta is formed when a river deposits sediment as its speed decreases while it enters the sea. Most deltas are extremely fertile areas, but are subject to frequent flooding.

dementia Deterioration of personality and intellect that can result from disease of or damage to the brain. It is characterized by memory loss, impaired mental processes, personality change, confusion, lack of inhibition and deterioration in personal hygiene. Dementia can occur at any age, although it is more common in the elderly. *See also* ALZHEIMER'S DISEASE

Demeter In Greek mythology, the goddess of nature, sister of ZEUS and mother of PERSEPHONE.

De Mille, Agnes George (1906–93) US dancer and choreographer. Her choreography for the Broadway musical *Oklahoma* (1943) rendered dance integral to the plot and turned them into a serious art form. Other musicals include *Carousel* (1945), *Brigadoon* (1947), *Gentlemen Prefer Blondes* (1949), *Paint Your Wagon* (1951) and *Come Summer* (1969). She also created ballets that combined classical and modern elements, such as *Rodeo* (1942) and *Fall River Legend* (1948).

De Mille, Cecil B. (Blount) (1881–1959) US film producer and director, noted for his lavish dramatic presentations. His debut film, *The Squaw Man* (1913), established Hollywood as the world's film production capital. Much of his best-known work deals with biblical themes, such as *The Ten Commandments* (two versions, 1923 and 1956) and *King of Kings* (1927). Other major films include *Forbidden Fruit* (1921), *Union Pacific* (1939), and *The Greatest Show on Earth* (1952).

Demirel, Süleiman (1924–) Turkish statesman, prime minister (1965–71, 1975–77, 1979–80, 1991–93) and president (1993–2000). In 1964, he became leader of the centre-right Justice Party. Demirel was twice ousted by military coups (1971, 1980). He led the Truth Path Party (1987–93). Ahmet Necdet Sezer succeeded Demirel as president.

democracy (Gk. *demos kratia*, 'people authority') Rule of the people, as opposed to rule by one (autocracy) or a few (oligarchy). Ancient GREECE is regarded as the birthplace of democracy, in particular ATHENS (5th centuryBC). Small Greek city-states enabled direct political participation, but only among its citizens (a small political elite). As societies grew, more refined systems of representative democracy were needed. In a FEUDAL SYSTEM, the king selected tenants-in-chief to provide counsel. In late 13th-century England, a PARLIAMENT evolved, but remained answerable to the monarchy. Changes in land ownership and the growth of a mercantile class widened the representative base of parliament. The Parliamentarians' victory in the English CIVIL WAR was, in general terms, a victory for parliamentary sovereignty. A fundamental shift in emphasis was the transition from natural law to **natural rights**, as expounded by John LOCKE: in addition to responsibility (to crown or church), people possessed inalienable rights. ROUSSEAU developed

▲ **Dempsey** The first boxer to generate a $1 million gate, Dempsey will always be remembered for his 'Battle of the Long Count' fight with Gene Tunney (1927). After flooring Tunney, Dempsey failed to return to a neutral corner, and delayed the start of the referee's count. Tunney won the fight.

these notions into the SOCIAL CONTRACT, which influenced the FRENCH and AMERICAN REVOLUTIONS: government was limited by law from impinging on individual freedoms. During the 19th century, the franchise was extended. In the 20th century, democratic representation has been a matter of debate and sometimes bloody dispute. Common to modern liberal democracy is the principle of free multi-party elections with universal adult suffrage.

Democratic Party US political party, the descendant of the ANTI-FEDERALIST PARTY and the DEMOCRATIC REPUBLICAN PARTY. From the election of Thomas JEFFERSON (1801) until James BUCHANAN in 1857, the Democratic Party was the dominant force in US politics, gathering support from farmers and white-collar workers. The party was split by the Civil War (1861–65), with support mainly restricted to the South and West. It regained power in 1932 with Franklin D. ROOSEVELT's 'New Deal' policy. Democratic presidents were in office from 1961–69 (John F. KENNEDY, Lyndon JOHNSON), a period marked by progressive economic and social policy, such as the passing of CIVIL RIGHTS legislation. The 1970s and 1980s were more barren years, only Jimmy CARTER (1977–81) held the presidency. The REPUBLICAN PARTY dominated the political landscape until Bill CLINTON recaptured the centre ground.

Democratic Republican Party Early US political party, and the precursor to the modern DEMOCRATIC PARTY. It was formed in the late 1790s in opposition to the Federalist Party, and led by Thomas JEFFERSON and James MADISON. It opposed strong central government and Alexander HAMILTON's economic policies, and advocated a liberal agrarian democracy, while also appealing to poor townsfolk. It became the Democratic Party in the era of Andrew JACKSON.

democratic socialism Political movement that arose in late 19th- and early 20th-century Europe, out of the evolutionary wing of the Second COMMUNIST INTERNATIONAL. Broadly speaking, democratic SOCIALISM is committed to the principles of: equality and social justice, parliamentary government, redistribution of wealth (through progressive taxation) and social protection. Democratic socialist parties have held power in most Western European countries, as well as Australasia, Canada and some Latin American countries. After the collapse of Soviet communism in the late 1980s, many communist parties reconstituted themselves as 'democratic socialist' parties.

Democritus (c.460–c.370 BC) Greek philosopher and scientist. Only fragments of his work remain. He contributed to the theory of ATOMISM, propounded by his teacher Leucippus, by suggesting that all matter consisted of tiny, indivisible particles.

demography Term introduced (1855) by Achille Guillard for the scientific study of human populations and their changes, movements, size, distribution and structure. The primary sources of data are the census and vital statistics. Demographic methods are used for gauging and anticipating public needs.

Demosthenes (c.384–322 BC) Athenian orator and statesman. In 351 BC he delivered the first of his famous *Philippics*, urging the Greeks to unite and resist PHILIP II of Macedon.

Dempsey, Jack (1895–1983) US heavyweight boxer. Hugely popular with the public, Dempsey became the world heavyweight champion after knocking out Jess Willard (1919). He lost the title to Gene Tunney (1926) on points. Dempsey won 64 of his 79 professional fights.

Dench, Dame Judi (Judith) Olivia (1934–) English actress. Dench began her career with the Old Vic (1957–61) before joining the Royal Shakespeare Company. She received an Academy Award nomination for her performance as Victoria in *Mrs Brown* (1997), and won an Oscar for Best Supporting Actress for her role as Elizabeth I in *Shakespeare in Love* (1998). Other films include *84 Charing Cross Road* (1986), *A Handful of Dust* (1987), and *Iris* (2001).

dendrochronology Means of dating archaeological remains by examination of the ANNUAL RINGS in trees. It is used to calibrate other dating methods. Chronology based on the bristle-cone pine extends back more than 7000 years.

Deneb (Alpha Cygni) White supergiant and brightest star in the constellation Cygnus. It is a quarter of a million times more luminous than the Sun and located c.3230 light years away.

dengue Infectious virus disease transmitted by the *Aedes aegypti* mosquito. Occurring in the tropics and some temperate areas, it produces fever, headache and fatigue, followed by severe joint pains, aching muscles, swollen glands, and a rash.

Deng Xiaoping (1904–97) Chinese statesman. He took part in the LONG MARCH, served in the Red Army, and became a member of the Central Committee of the Chinese COMMUNIST PARTY in 1945. After the establishment of the People's Republic (1949) he held several important posts, becoming general secretary of the party in 1956. During the CULTURAL REVOLUTION, Deng was denounced for capitalist tendencies and dismissed. He returned to government in 1973, was purged by the GANG OF FOUR in 1976, but reinstated in 1977 after the death of MAO ZEDONG. Within three years Deng had ousted HUA GUOFENG to become the dominant leader of party and government. He introduced rapid economic modernization, encouraging foreign investment, but without social and political liberalization. Deng officially retired in 1987, but was still essentially in control at the time of the TIANANMEN SQUARE massacre (1989). In 1993, JIANG ZEMIN became president.

De Niro, Robert (1943–) US film actor. An intense, powerful player, he first gained critical acclaim in Martin SCORSESE's *Mean Streets* (1973). In 1974, he won an Oscar for best supporting actor in *The Godfather, Part II*. Another critical triumph in *Taxi Driver* (1976) was followed by a nominated role in *The Deer Hunter* (1978). He finally won an Oscar for best actor in *Raging Bull* (1981). He made his directorial debut with *A Bronx Tale* (1993). Other films include *Goodfellas* (1990), *Heat* (1995), and *Jackie Brown* (1997).

Denmark Kingdom in W Europe. *See* country feature

density Ratio of mass to volume for a given substance usually expressed in SI UNITS as kilograms per cubic metre (kg/m^3). It is an indication of the concentration of particles within a material. The density of a solid or liquid changes little over a wide range of temperatures and pressures. RELATIVE DENSITY (R.D.) is the ratio of the density of one substance to that of a reference substance (usually water) at the same temperature and pressure. The density of a gas depends on both pressure and temperature.

dentistry Profession concerned with the care and treatment of the mouth, particularly the teeth and their supporting tissues, the gums and oral bones. As well as general practice, dentistry specialities includes oral surgery, periodontics (structures around the teeth) and orthodontics (irregular teeth and jaws).

dentition Type, number, and arrangement of TEETH. An adult human has 32 teeth. In each jaw are four **incisors**, two **canines**, four **premolars**, four **molars** and, in most adults, up to four **wisdom** teeth. Children lack the premolars and four molars. The incisors are used for cutting; the canines for gripping and tearing; the molars and premolars for crushing and grinding food. A HERBIVORE has relatively unspecialized teeth that grow throughout life to compensate for wear, and are adapted for grinding. A CARNIVORE has a range of specialized teeth related to killing, gripping,

▲ **Deng Xiaoping** Chinese political leader for much of the 1980s and paramount leader during the 1990s, Deng saw the advantage of introducing economic reforms to China, and encouraged a more open and free market. However, he was still deeply opposed to political reforms, and cracked down heavily on the pro-democracy movement.

▲ **De Niro** Academy Award-winning actor Robert De Niro is famed for his 'method' approach to acting. Many of his most complex performances have been as Italian-American gangsters in Martin Scorsese films, such as *The Godfather, Part II* (1974).

and crushing bones. In carnivores, unspecialized milk teeth are replaced by specialized adult teeth.

Denver Capital and largest city of Colorado state, USA, at the foot of the ROCKY MOUNTAINS. At an altitude of 1,608m (5,280ft), it is called the 'Mile High City'. Founded in 1860, it became state capital in 1867. The discovery of gold and silver and the building of the Denver Pacific Railroad (1870) boosted its prosperity. Places of note are the Denver Art Museum, the Boettcher Botanical Gardens, and a university (1864). After World War 2, Denver's fast growth and high altitude led to pollution problems. During the 1970s, exploitation of oil deposits created further growth, but the worldwide slump in oil prices in the 1980s temporarily stagnated its economy. It has the world's largest airport, Denver International. Its proximity to the Rockies and the ski resort of Aspen make it a major tourist centre. Denver is a processing, shipping and distribution centre and the location of many high-technology industries, especially aerospace and electronics. Pop. (2000) 1,985,000.

deodar (Indian CEDAR) Conical, evergreen, coniferous tree from the snowy slopes of the w Himalayas, where it has religious significance. Hindus refer to it as the 'tree of God'. Its spreading branches droop or 'weep' at their ends. The leaves are bright green needles, *c*.5cm (*c*.2in) long, produced in whorls of about 20. The bark is very dark brown to black and the cones are held upright. The deodar also grows well in temperate climates. Its wood is used for timber and it yields a fragrant oil. Height: to 61m (200ft). Family Pinaceae; species *Cedrus deodara*.

deoxyribonucleic acid *See* DNA

DENMARK

The Kingdom of Denmark is the smallest country in Scandinavia. It consists of a peninsula called Jutland (*Jylland*), which is joined to Germany, and more than 400 islands, 89 of which are inhabited. The land is flat and mostly covered by rocks dropped there by huge ice sheets during the last Ice Age. The highest point in Denmark is on Jutland and is only 173m [568ft].

CLIMATE
Denmark has a cool but pleasant climate. During cold spells in the winter The Sound between Sjælland and Sweden may freeze over. Summers are warm. Rainfall occurs throughout the year.

HISTORY
In *c*.2000 BC, the Danes developed an advanced Bronze Age culture. Between the 9th and 11th centuries, VIKINGS conquered much of W Europe and Danes were among the invaders who conquered much of England. In the 11th century King CANUTE ruled over Denmark, Norway and England. Control of the entrances to the Baltic Sea contributed to the power of Denmark in the Middle Ages, when the kingdom dominated its neighbours and expanded its territories to include Norway, Iceland, Greenland and the Faroe Islands. Queen Margaret unified the crowns of Denmark, Sweden and Norway in 1397. Sweden broke away in 1523, Norway was lost to Sweden in 1814, and Iceland separated in 1944. GREENLAND and the FARÖE ISLANDS retain connections with Denmark. The granite island of Bornholm, off the southern tip of Sweden, also remains a Danish possession. Denmark adopted LUTHERANISM as the national religion in 1536 and Danish culture flourished in the 16th and early 17th centuries. CHRISTIAN IV led Denmark into costly wars with Sweden, and the Thirty Years War (1618–48) weakened the Danish aristocracy. Serfdom was abolished in 1788. In 1866, SCHLESWIG-HOLSTEIN was lost to Prussia.

In the late 19th century, Denmark developed its economy and its education system. Danes set up cooperatives and improved farming techniques. The Social Democratic Party dominated 20th-century Danish politics. Denmark remained neutral in World War 1. In 1918, Iceland gained independence. During the 1920s, Denmark adopted progressive social welfare policies. In 1940, Germany occupied Denmark. In 1943, CHRISTIAN X was arrested and martial law declared. Many Jews escaped to Sweden. In 1945, British forces liberated Denmark and the Danes set about rebuilding their industries and restoring their economy.

POLITICS
Denmark is a constitutional monarchy, ruled by a prime minister and parliament. Traditionally parliament had two equal houses, the conservative Landsting and more liberal Folketing, but in 1953 the Landsting was abolished. Most post-war governments have been coalitions.

The government granted home rule to the Faeroe Islands in 1948. In 1998, the government of the Faeroes announced plans for independence. In 1979, home rule was also granted to Greenland, which demonstrated its new-found independence by withdrawing from the European Community in 1985.

Denmark is one of the 'greenest' of the developed nations, with a pioneering Ministry of Pollution. In 1991, it became the first government anywhere to fine industries for emissions of carbon dioxide, the primary 'greenhouse' gas.

It joined the North Atlantic Treaty Organization (NATO) in 1949, and in 1973 it joined the European Community (now the European Union). However, it remains one of the European Union's least enthusiastic members and was one of the four countries that did not adopt the euro, the single EU currency, on 1 January 2002. In 1972, in order to join the EC, Denmark had become the first Scandinavian country to break away from the other major economic grouping in Europe, the European Free Trade Association (EFTA), but it continued to co-operate with its five Scandinavian partners through the consultative Nordic Council, which was set up in 1953.

The Danes enjoy some of the world's highest living standards, although the cost of welfare provisions is high. The election of a Liberal-Conservative coalition in 2001 led to cutbacks. Under Prime Minister Anders Fogh Rasmussen, who won a second term in 2005, the government also tightened immigration controls, causing criticism from the UN High Commissioner for Refugees. In 2007 Rasmussen's centre-right government narrowly won a snap election and announced a second referendum on adopting the Euro.

ECONOMY
Denmark has few mineral resources, although there is now some oil and natural gas from the North Sea. It is one of Europe's wealthiest industrial nations. Farming employs only 4% of workers, but it is highly industrialized and productive with dairy farming and pig and poultry breeding chief areas.

From a firm agricultural base, Denmark has developed a wide range of industries. Some, including brewing, meat canning, fish processing, pottery, textiles and furniture making, use Danish products, but others, such as shipbuilding, oil refining, engineering and metalworking, depend on imported raw materials. Copenhagen is the chief industrial centre and draws more than a million tourists each year. At the other end of the scale is Legoland, the famous miniature town of plastic bricks, built at Billand, NW of Vejle in E Jutland. It was here that Lego was created before it became the world's best-selling construction toy and a prominent Danish export.

AREA 43,094sq km [16,639sq mi]
POPULATION 5,468,000
CAPITAL (POPULATION)
Copenhagen (1,091,000)
GOVERNMENT
Parliamentary monarchy
ETHNIC GROUPS
Scandinavian, Inuit, Faeroese, German
LANGUAGES Danish (official), English, Faerose
RELIGIONS Evangelical Lutheran 95%
CURRENCY Danish krone = 100 øre

Depardieu, Gérard (1948–) French film actor. Burly and charismatic, he was France's principal actor in the 1980s. He has an extraordinary range, equally adroit at playing an historical figure such as *Danton* (1982), or a hunchback tax-collector, *Jean de Florette* (1986). *Green Card* (1990) was his first major English-speaking role. His performance as *Cyrano de Bergerac* (1990) was definitive. Other films include *Germinal* (1993).

depression In economics, a time of economic hardship, more severe than a RECESSION. It is commonly measured by a fall in output and a rise in unemployment. The most severe and widespread depression was the GREAT DEPRESSION of the 1930s.

depression In meteorology, a region of low atmospheric pressure with the lowest pressure at the centre. It usually brings unsettled or stormy weather. *See also* CYCLONE

depression Disorder characterized by feelings of guilt, failure, worthlessness or rejection. Frequently a response to a difficult life-situation, depression leads to low self-esteem, self-recrimination and obsessive thoughts. Insomnia, loss of appetite and lethargy are often present, and in severe cases there is a risk of suicide. *See also* MANIC DEPRESSION

De Quincey, Thomas (1785–1859) English essayist and critic. An associate of WORDSWORTH and COLERIDGE, whom he memorialized in *Recollections of the Lakes* and *The Lake Poets* (1834–39), De Quincey is best known for *Confessions of an English Opium Eater* (1822).

Derby City and county district on the River Derwent, Derbyshire, central England. Known for its Derby ware china, manufactured here since *c*.1750. Industries: railway and aerospace engineering, textiles, ceramics. Pop. (2001) 221,716.

Derby, Edward George Geoffrey Smith Stanley, 14th Earl of (1799–1869) British statesman, three times prime minister (1852, 1858–59, 1866–68). He entered Parliament as a Whig in 1827, and acted as chief secretary for Ireland (1830–33). He resigned soon after becoming colonial secretary (1833), and joined the CONSERVATIVE PARTY. He was colonial secretary under PEEL (1841–45), but resigned over the CORN LAWS. From 1846 to 1868, Derby led the Tory protectionists. In 1866, he became prime minister for the last time, introducing the REFORM ACT (1867). Benjamin DISRAELI succeeded him.

Derbyshire County in N central England; the county town is DERBY, other major towns are Chesterfield and Alfreton. Low-lying in the S, it rises to the PEAK DISTRICT in the N and is drained by the River Trent and its tributaries (the Dove, Derwent, and Wye). Agriculture is important, such as dairy farming, livestock rearing, wheat, oats, and market gardening. There are coal deposits in the E. Industries: steel, textiles, paper, pottery. Area: 2,631sq km (1,016sq mi). Pop. (2001) 734,581.

derivative A measurement of the rate at which the output of a continuous mathematical FUNCTION changes when its input, the dependent VARIABLE, changes. In general it is itself a function of the variable, and it is usually obtained by *differential calculus*. For a function with a single variable for which every result is a REAL NUMBER, the derivative at a single point can be represented on a graph of the function by the TANGENT to the graph at that point. Derivatives have many practical applications. For example, in MECHANICS, the VELOCITY of an object is the derivative of its position – the rate at which its position changes – and the ACCELERATION is the derivative of the velocity.

dermatitis Inflammation of the skin. In acute form, it produces itching and blisters. In chronic form, it causes thickening, scaling and darkening of the skin. *See also* ECZEMA

dermis Thick, inner layer of the SKIN, which lies beneath the EPIDERMIS. It consists mainly of loose CONNECTIVE TISSUE richly supplied with BLOOD and lymph vessels, nerve endings, sensory organs and sweat glands.

Derrida, Jacques (1930–2004) French philosopher, born Algeria. He was widely influential and is best known for developing the ideas of DECONSTRUCTION. He wrote and lectured prolifically, and held academic posts in France and the United States. Key works include *Writing and Difference* (1967) and *Dissemination* (1972).

Derry City and administrative district on the River Foyle near Lough Foyle, NW Northern Ireland. In AD 546 St

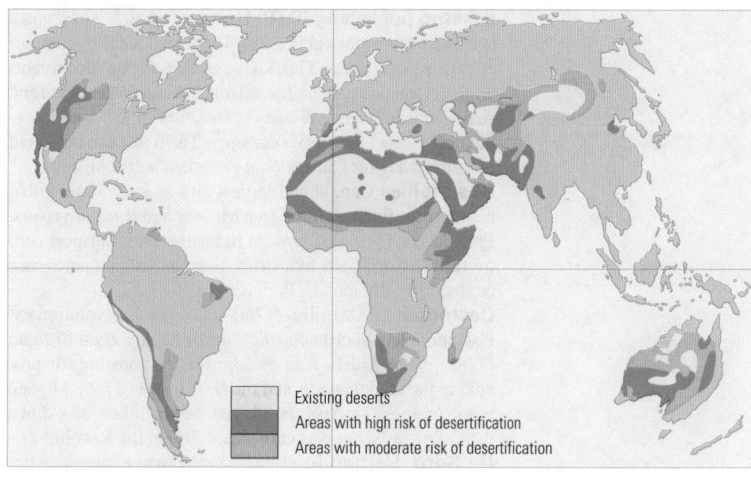

Existing deserts
Areas with high risk of desertification
Areas with moderate risk of desertification

Columba founded a monastery here, and a settlement grew up around it. In 1311, Derry was granted to the Earl of Ulster. In 1600 English forces seized the city, and in 1613 James I granted Derry to the citizens of London. It was renamed **Londonderry**, a new city was laid out, and Protestant colonization began. In 1688–89, James II unsuccessfully besieged the city. Sectarian violence plagued the city in the latter half of the 20th century. In 1984 its name reverted to Derry. Industries: clothing manufacture. Area: 347sq km (149sq mi). Pop. (2001) 105,066.

dervish Member of a Muslim fraternity. Communities arose within SUFISM, and by the 12th century had established themselves in the Middle East. The Bektashi order acted as companions to the Ottoman JANISSARIES, and were suppressed by ATATÜRK. The chief devotion of dervishes is *dhikr* ('remembering of God'). Its encouragement of emotional display and hypnotic trances has earned dervishes the epithet 'whirling'.

desalination Extraction of pure water (for drinking, industrial and chemical uses, or for irrigation) from water containing dissolved salts, usually sea water. The commonest and oldest method is DISTILLATION. Another method is to freeze the salt solution; salt is excluded from the ice which can then be melted. In reverse OSMOSIS, pure water passes through a semipermeable membrane against which salt water is pressurised. Other methods include electrodialysis.

Descartes, René (1596–1650) French philosopher and mathematician. Often regarded as the father of modern philosophy. In 1619, he described an all-embracing science of the universe. His works include *Discourse on Method* (1637), *Meditations on the First Philosophy* (1641) and *Principles of Philosophy* (1644). Descartes' methods of deduction and intuition inform modern metaphysics. By doubting all his ideas, he reached one indubitable proposition: "I am thinking", and from this that he existed: *cogito ergo sum* ("I think, therefore I am"). He also founded analytic geometry, introduced the CARTESIAN CO-ORDINATE system and helped establish the science of optics.

desert Arid region of the Earth characterized by rainfall of less than 25cm (10in) per year, and little or no vegetation. Regions with 25 to 50cm (10–20in) of rainfall are semi-deserts. Cold deserts, areas almost permanently ice or snow covered, extend over one-sixth of the Earth, and hot deserts over one-fifth. Most desert regions lie in the horse latitudes between 20° and 30° N and S of the Equator. These include the KALAHARI and SAHARA (the world's largest desert). Deserts, such as the ATACAMA and NAMIB, occur in W coastal regions where offshore currents make the land very dry. There are also deserts in the middle of the largest continents where no onshore winds can reach to bring rain, such as the GOBI and MOJAVE deserts. *See also* TUNDRA

desertification Process by which a desert gradually spreads into neighbouring areas of semi-desert. The change may result from a natural event, such as fire or climatic change, but occurs most frequently as a result of human activity. Once vegetation is removed (usually by over-grazing or for firewood), the soil is easily eroded and the land rendered infertile.

▲ **desertification** The true causes of desertification are still not entirely understood, but it is generally accepted that recent desertification is directly attributable to increased human intervention. On a large scale, the burning of fossil fuels is likely to shift climatic belts and increase areas of desert. More localized problems have occurred due to overgrazing of livestock and ill-conceived irrigation projects.

INTERNET

Denmark
▶ www.denmark.dk
▶ www.visitdenmark.com

Derby, Edward George Geoffrey Smith Stanley, 14th Earl of
▶ www.number-10.gov.uk

desertification
▶ www.unccd.int
▶ www.fao.org/ desertification

D

desktop publishing (DTP) Use of a COMPUTER to prepare text and pictures for publication. The technique uses computer PROGRAMS, such as QuarkXpress, that display documents on the computer screen. The operator controls the type font, size, line length, and column organization of text, and incorporates scanned images if necessary. The result can be output in forms ready for conventional PRINTING and publishing.

Des Moines Capital and largest city of Iowa state, USA, near the confluence of the Des Moines and Raccoon rivers. Founded in 1843, it is now an industrial and transport centre for the Corn Belt. Industries: mechanical and aerospace engineering, chemicals. Pop. (2000) 198,682.

Desmoulins, Camille (1760–94) French revolutionary. His pamphlets, such as *Révolutions de France et de Brabant* (1789), were widely read and he was responsible for provoking the mob that attacked the BASTILLE in 1789. Aligned with Georges DANTON, he played a part in bringing down the GIRONDINS, but was guillotined during the Revolution.

De Soto, Hernando (1500–42) Spanish explorer. After taking part in the conquest of the Incas under Francisco PIZARRO, he was appointed governor of Cuba (1537) with permission to conquer North America. His expedition landed in Florida (1539), and advanced as far N as the Carolinas and as W as the Mississippi. The search for treasure and the extreme brutality towards the native inhabitants led to a costly battle at Maubilia (1540). They returned to the Mississippi, where De Soto died.

Dessalines, Jean Jacques (1758–1806) Haitian ruler. He succeeded Toussaint L'Ouverture as leader of the revolution in 1802. Having driven out the French, he declared independence in 1804, changing the country's name from St Domingue to Haiti. As Emperor Jacques, he ruled despotically and was assassinated after a two-year reign.

detergent Synthetic chemical cleansing substance. The most common type is alkyl sulphonate. Detergents have molecules that possess a long hydrocarbon chain attached to an ionized group. This chain attaches to grease and other nonpolar substances, while the ionized group has an affinity for water (so the grease is washed away with the water).

determinism Philosophical thesis that every event is the necessary result of its causes. Nothing is accidental. It usually involves the denial of free will, though Thomas HOBBES and David HUME struggled to reconcile the two ideas. CALVIN's concept of PREDESTINATION is a form of determinism.

Detroit City on the Detroit River, SE Michigan, USA. Founded as a French trading post (1710), the British captured it in 1760, and used it as a base during the American Revolution. It was lost to Britain in the WAR OF 1812, but retaken by US forces in 1813. The largest city in Michigan, Detroit is a major GREAT LAKES centre and headquarters of General Motors, Chrysler and Ford. Industries: motor vehicles, steel, pharmaceuticals, machine tools, tyres, paint. Pop. (2000) 3,903,000.

deuterium ISOTOPE (D or H^2) of hydrogen whose nuclei contain a neutron in addition to a proton. Deuterium occurs in water as D$_2$O (heavy water), from which it is obtained by ELECTROLYSIS. Heavy water is used in some NUCLEAR REACTORS as a moderator that slows down free neutrons to increase nuclear fission. Properties: r.a.m. 2.0144.

Deuteronomy Biblical book, fifth and last of the PENTATEUCH or TORAH. It contains three discourses ascribed to Moses, which frame a code of civil and religious laws.

De Valera, Eamon (1882–1975) Irish statesman, taoiseach (1932–48, 1951–54, 1957–59). De Valera was active in the Irish independence struggle and, after the Easter Rising (1916), was elected president of SINN FÉIN while imprisoned in England. He opposed William COSGRAVE's Irish Free State ministry and founded FIANNA FÁIL in 1924. He defeated Cosgrave in 1932. In 1959, De Valera became president of the republic. He retired in 1973.

devaluation Lowering the value of one nation's currency with respect to that of another or to gold. The decision to devalue is made by a central government usually when the nation is having BALANCE OF PAYMENTS problems. Devaluation stimulates the economy by reducing the foreign currency price of exports and raising the domestic price of imports.

developmental psychology Study of changes in behaviour through all life stages from the fetus to old age. Psychologists study normal growth, change, and self-actualization, and also life-stage related problems. *See also* CHILD PSYCHOLOGY

devil Evil spirit considered in many religions to be the archenemy of the Supreme being. In Christianity, the Devil is the chief of the fallen angels cast out of heaven for their sins. The devil was named as SATAN, BEELZEBUB or the Prince of Darkness. The biblical account of Christ's temptation in the desert leads to the perception of the Devil as the tempter of souls. In Islam, Iblis is the name of the devil figure, the supreme tempter.

devolution Delegation of authority and political power from a central legislature to a regional government. Central government retains overall constitutional control. In the UK, central government has devolved power to Scotland, Wales and Northern Ireland with the establishment of separate Parliaments. The Scottish Parliament has tax-varying powers.

Devon County in SW England, bounded by the English Channel (S) and the Bristol Channel (N); the county town is EXETER. There are Bronze and Iron Age remains. During the Middle Ages, tin mining was a major industry. Devon is a hilly region that includes Dartmoor and Exmoor. The principal rivers are the Ex, Tamar, Dart and Teign. Cattle farming is important. Industries: tourism, fishing, dairy products, cider, textiles. Area: 6,711sq km (2,591sq mi). Pop. (2001) 704,499.

Devonian Fourth-oldest period of the PALAEOZOIC era, lasting from 408 to 360 million years ago. Numerous marine and freshwater remains include jawless fishes and forerunners of today's bony and cartilaginous fishes. The first known land vertebrate, the amphibian Ichthyostega, appeared at this time. Land animals included scorpions, mites, spiders, and the first insects. Land plants included club moss, scouring rushes, and ferns.

De Vries, Hugo (1848–1935) Dutch botanist. De Vries introduced the concept of MUTATION into the study of GENETICS. He wrote *The Mutation Theory* (1901–03), which influenced concepts of the role of mutation in evolution.

Dewar, Sir James (1842–1923) Scottish chemist and physicist who researched materials at extremely low temperatures. In 1872, he invented the Thermos flask. He also built a device that could produce liquid oxygen.

Dewey, John (1859–1952) US educator and philosopher. Influenced by PRAGMATISM and UTILITARIANISM. Dewey proposed a philosophy of **instrumentalism**. He regarded intelligence as an instrument to overcome problems. In *Democracy and Education* (1916), Dewey emphasized the importance of experimentation and practical application in education and was leading figure in the development of PROGRESSIVE EDUCATION.

Dewey decimal system Means of classifying books, created by US librarian Melvil Dewey in the 1870s. It is popular because of its subject currency and simplicity.

dew point Temperature at which a vapour begins to condense. Particularly, it refers to water vapour in the air condens into into cloud, mist, dew or fog. *See also* CONDENSATION

Dhaka (Dacca) Capital of Bangladesh, a port on the Ganges delta, E Bangladesh. Its influence grew as the 17th century Mogul capital of Bengal. In 1765 it came under British control. At independence (1947) it was made capital of the province of East Pakistan. Severely damaged during the war of independence from Pakistan, it became capital of Bangladesh (1971). Sites include the Dakeshwari Temple, Bara Katra Palace (1644) and mosques. It is in the centre of the world's largest jute-producing area. Industries: engineering, textiles, printing, glass, chemicals. Pop. (2005) 12,560,000.

dharma Religious concept relating to what is true or right, found in the principal religions of India. In HINDUISM, it is the moral law or code governing an individual's conduct. In BUDDHISM, dharma is the doctrine of universal truth proclaimed by the BUDDHA. In JAINISM, dharma is moral virtue and is also the principle that gives beings the power of movement.

diabetes Disease characterized by lack of INSULIN needed for sugar METABOLISM. This leads to HYPERGLYCAEMIA and an excess of SUGAR in the blood. Symptoms include abnormal thirst, over-production of urine and weight loss; degenerative changes occur in blood vessels. Untreated, the condition progresses to diabetic coma and death. There are two forms of the disease. **Type 1** usually begins in childhood and is an autoimmune disease. Those affected owe their survival to insulin injections. **Type 2** diabetes mostly begins in middle-age; there is some insulin output but not enough for the body's needs. The disease is managed with dietary restrictions, tablets to lower blood sugar levels and insulin injections. Susceptibility to *diabetes mellitus* is inherited and more common in males.

diagenesis Physical and chemical processes whereby sediments are transformed into solid rock, usually at low pressure and temperature. Pressure results in compaction, forcing grains together and eliminating air and water.

Diaghilev, Sergei Pavlovich (1872–1929) Russian ballet impressario. Diaghilev was active in the Russian avant-garde after 1898 and formed (1911) the BALLETS RUSSES, acting as its director until his death. He revolutionized BALLET, integrating music and scene design with innovative choreography.

dialectic Method of argument through conversation and dialogue; based on the philosophy of SOCRATES, in particular the *Dialogues*. HEGEL went on to argue that ordinary LOGIC, governed by the law of contradiction, is static and lifeless. In the *Science of Logic* (1812–16) he claimed to satisfy the need for a dynamic method, whose two moments of thesis and antithesis are cancelled and reconciled in a higher synthesis. Logic was to be dialectical, or a process of resolution by means of conflict of categories. *See also* DIALECTICAL MATERIALISM

dialectical materialism Scientific theory and philosophical basis of MARXISM. It asserts that everything is material, and that change results from the struggle of opposites according to definite laws. Its main application was in the analysis of human history. Karl MARX agreed with HEGEL that the course of history is logically dialectical, so that true social change can only occur when two opposing views are resolved through a new synthesis, rather than one establishing itself as true. Marx believed that Hegel was wrong to define DIALECTICS as purely spiritual or logical. For Marx, the proper dialectical subject was material experience. According to his theory of historical materialism, history derived from economic or social realities.

dialysis Process for separating particles from a solution by virtue of differing rates of diffusion through a semipermeable membrane. In an artificial KIDNEY, unwanted molecules of waste products are separated out to purify the blood. Electrodialysis employs a direct electric current to accelerate the process, especially useful for isolating proteins.

diamond Crystalline form of carbon (C). The hardest natural substance known, it is found in kimberlite pipes and alluvial deposits. Appearance varies according to its impurities. Bort, inferior in crystal and colour, carborondo, an opaque grey to black variety, and other non-gem varieties are used in industry. Industrial diamonds are used as abrasives, bearings in precision instruments such as watches, and in the cutting heads of drills for mining. Synthetic diamonds, made by subjecting GRAPHITE, with a catalyst, to high pressure and temperatures of *c.*3,000°C (5,400°F) are fit only for industry. Diamonds are weighed in carats (0.2gm) and points (1/100 carat). The largest producer is Australia. Hardness 10; r.d. 3.5.

Diana In Roman religion, the virgin huntress and patroness of domestic animals. She was identified with Artemis. A fertility deity, she was invoked to aid conception and childbirth.

Diana, Princess of Wales (1961–97) Former wife of the heir to the British throne. The daughter of Earl Spencer, Diana married CHARLES, Prince of Wales in 1981, and they had two sons, William and Harry. A popular, glamorous figure, she worked for many charities. Their marriage fell apart acrimoniously, and they divorced in 1996. She continued to campaign for humanitarian causes until her death in a car crash in Paris.

diaphragm Sheet of muscle that separates the abdomen from the THORAX. During exhalation, it relaxes and allows the chest to subside; on inhalation it contracts and flattens, causing the chest cavity to enlarge.

diarrhoea Frequent elimination of loose, watery stools, often accompanied by cramps and stomach pains. It arises from various causes, such as infection, intestinal irritants or food allergy. Mild attacks can be treated by replacement fluids.

Diaspora (Gk. 'dispersion') Jewish communities outside Palestine. Although there were communities of Jews outside Palestine from the time of the Babylonian Captivity (6th centuryBC), the Diaspora essentially dates from the destruction of Jerusalem by the Romans (AD 70). *See also* ZIONISM

diatom Any of a group of tiny microscopic single-celled ALGAE (phylum Bacillariophyta) characterized by a shell-like cell wall made of silica. Diatoms live in nearly all bodies of salt and freshwater, and even soil and tree bark.

Diaz, Bartholomeu (1450–1500) Portuguese navigator, the first European to round the CAPE OF GOOD HOPE. In 1487, under the commission of King John II of Portugal, Diaz sailed three ships around the Cape, opening the long-sought route to India. He took part in the expedition of Cabral that discovered Brazil, but was drowned when his ship foundered.

Díaz, Porfirio (1830–1915) Mexican statesman, president (1876–80, 1884–1911). After twice failing to unseat President JUÁREZ, he succeeded against Lerdo in 1876. Díaz provided stable leadership for 30 years. Growing opposition crystallized under Francisco MADERO in 1911, and Díaz resigned.

Dickens, Charles John Huffam (1812–70) English novelist. He began his writing career as a parliamentary reporter for the *Morning Chronicle*. His first success were satirical pieces collected as *Sketches by Boz* (1836). *The Pickwick Papers* (1836–37) launched his literary career. All of Dickens' novels first appeared in serial form. His early work includes *Oliver Twist* (1838), *Nicholas Nickleby* (1839), *The Old Curiosity Shop* (1841) and *Barnaby Rudge* (1841). In 1843, he finished *Martin Chuzzlewit* and wrote *A Christmas Carol*. His mature novels included *David Copperfield* (1850), *Bleak House* (1853), *Hard Times* (1854), *Little Dorrit* (1857), and *A Tale of Two Cities* (1859). Dickens' last novels, *Great Expectations* (1861), *Our Mutual Friend* (1865), and the incomplete *The Mystery of Edwin Drood*, are bleak depictions of the destructive powers of money and ambition. His output provided some of the most memorable characters in ENGLISH LITERATURE.

Dickinson, Emily Elizabeth (1830–86) US poet. From the age of 30 she lived in almost total seclusion in Amherst, Massachusetts. Dickinson wrote 1775 short lyrics, only seven of which were published in her lifetime. *Poems by Emily Dickinson* appeared in 1890, and her collected works were not published until 1955. They rank among the greatest works in AMERICAN LITERATURE. Her rich verse explores the world of emotion and the beauty of simple things.

dicotyledon Larger of the two subgroups of flowering plants or ANGIOSPERMS, characterized by two seed leaves (COTYLEDONS) in the seed embryo. Other general features

◀ **Diana, Princess of Wales**
Diana's 'fairy-tale' marriage to Charles (Prince of Wales) ended in a bitter divorce and left Diana without a clear public role. Her frankness about her personal difficulties struck an emotional chord. Diana's iconic beauty and glamour ensured the constant, often intrusive, presence of the media. Her self-appointed role as 'Queen of Hearts' saw her campaign for a worldwide ban on landmines. An unprecedented outpouring of public emotion followed her tragic death with Dodi Fayed in a car crash in Paris.

D

INTERNET

Dien Bien Phu
▶ www.dienbienphu.org

include broad leaves with branching veins; flower parts in whorls of fours or fives; and a taproot. There are *c*.250 families of dicotyledons, such as the ROSE, DAISY, and MAGNOLIA.

dictatorship Absolute rule without the consent of the governed. In many modern dictatorships, all power resides in the dictator, with representative DEMOCRACY abolished or existing as mere formality. Personal freedom is severely limited, censorship is generally enforced, education is tightly controlled, and legal restraints on governmental authority are abolished.

dictionary Book that lists in alphabetical order, words and their definitions. A dictionary may be general or subject oriented. In the former category, Samuel JOHNSON's *A Dictionary of the English Language* (1755) is the pioneering work in English; its two most comprehensive descendants are (in the UK) the *Oxford English Dictionary*, published from 1884, and (in the USA) *Webster's Dictionary*, published from 1828.

Diderot, Denis (1713–84) French philosopher and writer. He was chief editor of the *Encyclopédie* (1751–72), an influential publication of the ENLIGHTENMENT. A friend of ROUSSEAU, he was imprisoned briefly (1749) for irreligious writings. He broadened the scope of the *Encyclopédie* and with d'ALEMBERT recruited contributors, such as VOLTAIRE. As a philosopher, Diderot progressed from Christianity through DEISM to ATHEISM. His books *On the Interpretation of Nature* (1754) and *D'Alembert's Dream* (1769) reveal his scientific MATERIALISM. *Jacques the Fatalist* (1796) and *Rameau's Nephew* illustrate his DETERMINISM. He wrote plays, and art and literary criticism.

Dido In Greek and Roman legend, Phoenician princess and founder of CARTHAGE. Carthage prospered and Dido's hand was sought by the king of Libya. To escape him she stabbed herself. VIRGIL made Dido a lover of AENEAS, and attributes her suicide to his decision to abandon her.

Diem, Ngo Dinh (1901–63) Vietnamese statesman, prime minister of South Vietnam (1954–63). In 1955 he formed a republic, forcing Bao Dai into exile. At first, Diem received strong US support but corruption and setbacks in the VIETNAM WAR led to growing discontent. With covert US help, army officers staged a coup in which he was murdered.

Dien Bien Phu Fortified village in N Vietnam. In 1954, the the Vietnamese Viet Minh captured the French stronghold after a siege lasting 55 days. French casualties were *c*.15,000. The resultant ceasefire ended eight years of war.

diesel engine INTERNAL COMBUSTION ENGINE, invented by Rudolf Diesel (1897). Heat for igniting the light fuel oil is produced by compressing air.

diet Range of food and drink consumed by an animal. The human diet falls into five main groups of necessary nutrients: PROTEIN, CARBOHYDRATE, FAT, VITAMIN, and MINERAL. An adult's daily requirement is about one gram of protein for each kilogram of body weight. Beans, fish, eggs, milk, and meat are important protein sources. Carbohydrates (stored as GLYCOGEN) and fat are the chief sources of energy and are found in cereals, root vegetables and sugars. Carbohydrates make up the bulk of most diets. Fats are a concentrated source of energy and aid the absorption of fat-soluble vitamins (vitamins A, D, E, and K). Water and minerals, such as iron, calcium, potassium and sodium, are also essential.

Dietrich, Marlene (1904–92) German film star and cabaret singer. Her glamorous, sultry image evolved in films directed by Josef von Sternberg, such as *The Blue Angel* (1930) and *Blonde Venus* (1932). Other films include *Destry Rides Again* (1939) and *Rancho Notorious* (1956).

differential In mathematics, small change occurring in the value of a mathematical expression due to a small change in a VARIABLE. If $f(x)$ is a FUNCTION of x, the differential of the function, written df, is given by $f'(x)dx$, where $f'(x)$ is the DERIVATIVE of $f(x)$.

differential In mechanics, a set of circular gears that transmits power from an engine to the wheels. When a car is turning a corner, the differential allows the outside drive wheel to rotate faster than the inner one.

differential calculus (differentiation) Form of CALCULUS used to calculate the rate of change (DERIVATIVE) of one quantity with respect to another of which it is the FUNCTION.

diffraction Spreading of a wave, such as a light beam, on passing through a narrow opening or hitting an obstacle, such as sound being heard around corners. It is evidence for the wave nature of light. Diffraction provides information on the wavelength of light and the structure of CRYSTALS.

diffusion Movement of a substance in a mixture from regions of high concentration to regions of low concentration, due to the random motion of individual atoms or molecules. It is used to separate the isotopes of uranium to produce enriched fuel for fast nuclear reactors. Diffusion ceases when there is no longer a concentration gradient. Its rate increases with temperature, since average molecular speed also increases with temperature.

digestion Process of the DIGESTIVE SYSTEM, in which food is broken down mechanically and chemically into smaller molecules that can be readily absorbed by an organism. Digestion occurs mainly by means of chemical agents called ENZYMES.

digestive system (alimentary system) Group of organs of the body concerned with the DIGESTION of food. In humans, it begins with the mouth, and continues into the OESOPHAGUS, which carries food to the STOMACH. The stomach leads to the

DIGESTIVE SYSTEM

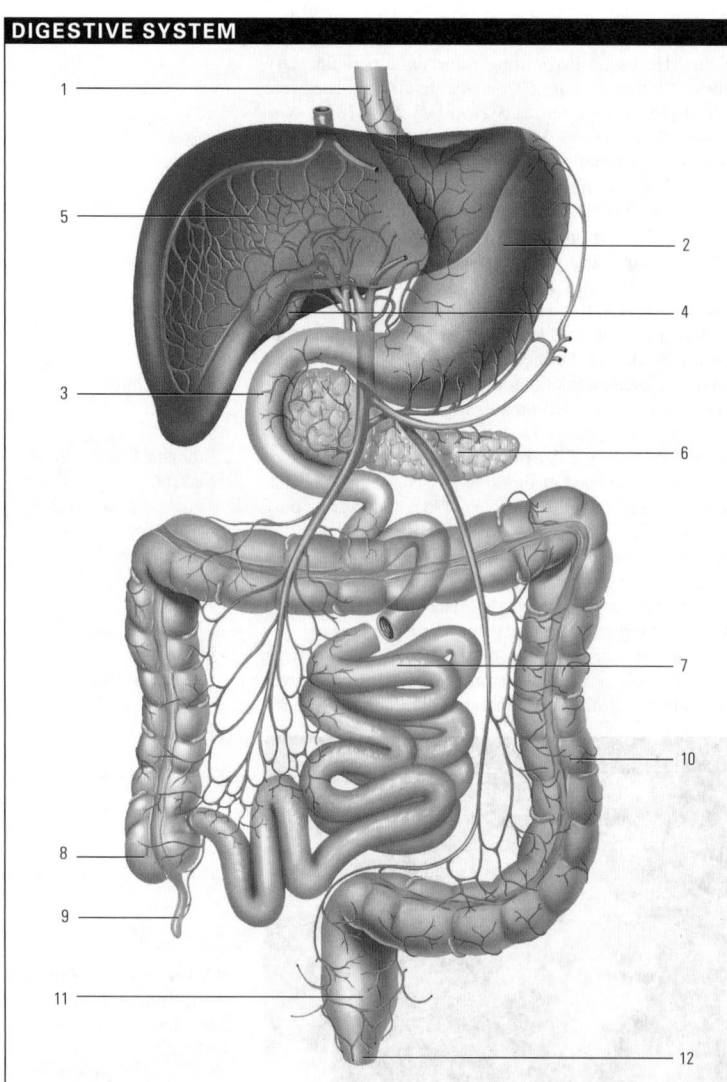

The digestion and absorption of food takes place within the digestive tract, a coiled tube some 10m (33ft) long which links mouth to anus. Food is passed down the oesophagus (1) to the stomach (2), where it is partially digested. Chyme is released into the duodenum (3), the first part of 7m (23ft) of small intestine. The duodenum receives bile secreted by the gall bladder (4) in the liver (5), and enzymes secreted by the pancreas (6). Most absorption occurs in the jejunum and ileum, the remaining parts of the small intestine (7). Any residue passes into the caecum (8), the pouch at the start of the large intestine. At one end of the caecum is the 10cm (4in) long vermiform appendix (9), which serves no useful purpose in man. Water is reabsorbed in the colon (10). Faeces form and collect in the rectum (11) before being expelled as waste through the anus (12).

small intestine, which then opens into the COLON. Food is pushed through the digestive tract by PERISTALSIS (muscle contractions). On its journey, food is transformed into small molecules that can be absorbed into the bloodstream and carried to the tissues. CARBOHYDRATE is broken down to sugars, PROTEIN to AMINO ACIDS, and FAT to FATTY ACIDS and GLYCEROL. Indigestible matter, passes into the rectum, and is eliminated from the body through the anus as faeces.

Diggers (1649–50) English millenarian social and religious sect in England, an extreme group of the LEVELLERS. They formed an egalitarian agrarian community at St George's Hill, Surrey. It was destroyed by local farmers. The main Digger theorist, Gerrard Winstanley, proposed communalization of property to establish social equality in *Law of Freedom* (1652).

digital Data or information expressed in terms of a few discrete quantities, often associated with a digital COMPUTER. Data is represented as a series of zeros and ones in a BINARY SYSTEM. Digital can also refer to displaying information in numbers, as opposed to continuously varying analogue.

digital audio tape (DAT) Technology for recording sound in DIGITAL form on magnetic TAPE. The original sound signal is encoded to form patterns of equal-strength pulses. These DIGITAL SIGNALS are recorded onto tape. On playback, the patterns are detected and decoded to produce an identical signal.

digital camera *See* CAMERA

digitalis Drug obtained from the leaves of the FOXGLOVE (*Digitalis purpurea*), used to treat HEART disease. It increases heart contractions and slows the heartbeat.

digital signal Group of electrical or other pulses in a COMPUTER or COMMUNICATIONS system. They may represent data, sounds or pictures. Pulses in a stream of digital signals are represented by zeros and ones in the BINARY SYSTEM. This is distinctly different from an ANALOGUE SIGNAL.

digital video disc (DVD) Optical disc that can store 15 times as much data as a COMPACT DISC (CD). Using the MPEG-2 compression format, a DVD is capable of storing a movie up to 133 minutes long. DVDs come in two formats: DVD-Video and DVD-ROM. DVD drives are downward compatible, so they can read conventional CD-ROMs and play music CDs. DVDs have a capacity of 4.7 gigabytes (GB), 8.5GB, or 17GB.

Dijon City in E France; capital of Côte-d'Or department. In the 11th century, the Dukes of Burgundy made it their capital. It was annexed to France (1477). Sites include Dijon University (1722), Cathedral of St Bénigne and the Church of Notre Dame. Exports: wine, mustard, cassis. Pop. (1999) 153,813.

dill Aromatic annual herb native to Europe. Its small oval seeds and feathery leaves are used in cooking. Family Apiaceae/Umbelliferae; species *Anethum graveolens*.

DiMaggio, Joe (Joseph Paul) (1914–99) US baseball player. DiMaggio played for the New York Yankees (1936–42, 1946–51), and holds the record for hitting safely in 56 consecutive games. He had a lifetime batting average of .325. DiMaggio married Marilyn MONROE (1954) and was elected to the Baseball Hall of Fame (1955).

dimensions In mathematics, numbers specifying the extent of an object in different directions. A figure with length only, is one-dimensional; a figure having area but not volume, two-dimensional; and a figure having volume, three-dimensional.

diminishing returns, law of (law of increasing costs) In economics, if more of a variable input, such as labour, is added to the production process, while all other factors are held constant, the addition to total output per unit input begins to decline.

Dinaric Alps (Dinara Planina) Mountain range running parallel to the E coast of the Adriatic Sea. Forming part of the E Alps, it extends from the Istrian peninsula (Croatia) to NW Albania, with peaks over 2,400m (7,900ft). Length: 640km (400mi).

D'Indy, Vincent (1851–1931) French composer and teacher. He co-founded the *Schola Cantorum* for the study of church music (1894), which became a general music school. His pupils included SATIE. He composed operas, orchestral, choral, chamber and piano music.

Dinesen, Isak (1885–1962) Danish writer. She described her life on a Kenyan coffee plantation in *Out of Africa* (1937). Her collections of short stories include *Seven Gothic Tales* (1934), *Winter's Tales* (1942) and *Shadows on the Grass* (1960).

dingo Yellowish-brown wild DOG found in Australia; it is probably a descendant of early domestic dogs introduced by Native Australians. It feeds mainly on rabbits and other small mammals. Family Canidae; species *Canis dingo*.

dinosaur Any of a large number of REPTILES that lived during the MESOZOIC era, between 225 and 65 million years ago. They appeared during the Triassic period, survived the JURASSIC, and became extinct at the end of the Cretaceous. There were two orders: **Saurischia** ('lizard hips'), included the bipedal carnivores and the giant herbivores; the **Ornithiscia** ('bird hips') were smaller herbivores. Their posture, with limbs vertically beneath the body, distinguish them from other reptiles. Many theories are advanced to account for their extinction. It is possible that, as the climate changed, they were incapable of swift adaptation. A more catastrophic theory is that they died because of the devastating atmospheric effects from the impact of a large METEORITE. *See also* BRONTOSAURUS; DIPLODOCUS; TYRANNOSAURUS.

Diocletian (245–313) Roman Emperor (284–305). Of low birth, the army appointed him. He reorganized the empire to resist the Barbarians, dividing it into four divisions and sharing power with Maximilian, Constantius I, and Galerius. He ordered the last great persecution of the Christians (303).

diode Electronic component with two electrodes, used as a RECTIFIER to convert alternating current (AC) to direct current (DC). Semiconductor diodes have largely replaced electron-tubes, and allow ELECTRIC CURRENT to flow freely in only one direction; only a small current flows in the reverse direction. A Zener diode blocks current until a critical voltage is reached.

Diogenes (active 4th centuryBC) Greek philosopher. Diogenes founded the CYNIC school of philosophy. He believed that by reducing personal needs, one can control one's soul.

Dionysius the Elder (*c*.430–367 BC) Tyrant of Syracuse (405–367BC). His ambitions were to spread Hellenism. Dionysius tried to form an empire in Lower Italy by seizing Rhegium (387), Caulonia and Croton (379). A patron of the arts and an erstwhile playwright, he once sold Plato as a slave.

Dionysus Greek god of wine and fertility, identified with the Roman god BACCHUS. The son of ZEUS and Semele.

Dior, Christian (1905–57) French fashion designer. In the spring of 1947, he launched the New Look, whose wide shoulders and long shapely skirts signalled an end to war austerity.

dioxin Any of various poisonous chemicals. The compound most commonly known as dioxin is 2,3,7,8–tetrachlorodibenzo-p-dioxin (TCDD), a by-product and impurity in the manufacture of various disinfectants and HERBICIDES. It is also produced in the burning of chlorinated chemicals and plastics. Dioxin causes skin disfigurement and is associated with birth defects, cancer and miscarriages. Accidental releases of dioxin from chemical plants have caused several major disasters.

dip, magnetic Angle between the direction of the Earth's magnetic field and the horizontal. A freely suspended magnetic needle in London dips, with its north pole pointing down, at an angle of 71.5° to the horizontal.

diphtheria Acute infectious disease characterized by the formation of a membrane in the throat which can cause

◄ **dinosaur** The first dinosaurs roamed the Earth *c.*225 million years ago. They were the dominant land animals until they died out suddenly, *c.*65 million years ago. The stegosaurus (left) was a plant-eating dinosaur that lived *c.*140 million years ago. It grew to 6m (20ft) long and 2.4m (8ft) high at the hip. The bony plates along the spine and the spikes on the tail are thought to have offered protection against carnivorous dinosaurs, but may also have acted like radiators, regulating the animal's temperature.

asphyxiation; there is also release of a toxin which can damage the nerves and heart. Caused by a bacterium, *Corynebacterium diphtheriae*, which often enters through the upper respiratory tract, it is treated with antitoxin and antibiotics

Diplodocus DINOSAUR that lived in N USA during the Jurassic period. The longest land animal ever found. It had a long slender neck and tail and was a swamp-dwelling herbivore. Length: 25m (82ft).

diploid CELL that has its CHROMOSOMES in pairs. Diploids are found in almost all animal cells, except GAMETES which are haploid (a single set of chromosomes). Cells of flowering plants and gymnosperms are also diploid. Algae and lower plants, such as ferns, have two generations (ALTERNATION OF GENERATIONS) in their life cycle, one diploid, the other haploid. In diploids, the chromosomes of each pair carry the same GENES.

dipole Separation of electric charge in a molecule. In a COVALENT BOND, the electron pair is not equally shared. In hydrogen chloride (HCl), electrons are attracted towards the more electro-negative chlorine atom, giving it a partial negative charge and leaving an equal positive charge on the hydrogen atom. Dipoles contribute to the chemical properties of molecules.

dipper Bird found near fast-flowing mountain streams, where it dives for small fish and aquatic invertebrates. It has a thin, straight bill, short wings, and greyish-brown plumage. Length: to 19cm (7.5in). Family Cinclidae; genus *Cinclus*.

Dirac, Paul Adrien Maurice (1902–84) English physicist. He made valuable contributions to the development of QUANTUM THEORY. In 1928 Dirac introduced a notation for quantum equations that combined SCHRÖDINGER's use of DIFFERENTIAL CALCULUS with HEISENBERG's use of matrices. In 1930 he applied EINSTEIN's theory of RELATIVITY to quantum mechanics in order to describe the SPIN of an ELECTRON. The resultant equation predicted the existence of ANTIMATTER. Dirac shared the 1933 Nobel Prize in physics with Schrödinger.

direct current (DC) *See* ELECTRIC CURRENT

disarmament Refers principally to attempts post-1918 (and especially post-1945) to reach international agreements to reduce armaments. The United Nations established the Atomic Energy Commission (1946), and the Commission for Conventional Armaments (1947). In 1952, these merged to form the Disarmament Commission. It produced no results and the Soviet Union withdrew in 1957. The USA and the Soviet Union signed the Nuclear Test Ban Treaty (1963) and the Nuclear Non-Proliferation Treaty (1968), which provided for an international inspectorate. A series of STRATEGIC ARMS LIMITATION TALKS (SALT) followed. In the early 1980s, intensification of the COLD WAR froze all disarmament efforts. In 1986 START (strategic arms reduction talks) superseded SALT, resulting in the Intermediate Nuclear Forces (INF) Treaty (1987), which reduced the superpowers' arsenal of short-range, intermediate missiles by *c*.2000 (4% of the total stockpile) and provided for on-site inspection. Following the break-up of the Soviet Union, the focus shifted to non-nuclear disarmament. The Conventional Forces in Europe Treaty (1990) set limits on equipment and troop levels. Attempts to sign a Test Ban Treaty have been thwarted by China, France, India, and Pakistan.

disciple One of the followers of Jesus Christ during his life on earth, especially one of his 12 close personal associates. These 12 men were his first APOSTLES.

Disciples of Christ US Protestant church, claiming to derive all its beliefs from the BIBLE. It strives to return to the purity of the Scriptures. Beginning in the 19th-century religious revival movements of frontier America, there is no single founder and no creed but Christ. There are *c*.1.2 million members.

discus Field athletics event, in which a wooden and metal disc is thrown by competitors. The thrower rotates in a circle (diameter 2.5m/8.2ft) before releasing the discus. An ancient Greek sport, it featured in the first modern Olympic Games (1896).

disease Any departure from health, with impaired functioning of the body. Disease may be **acute**, severe symptoms for a short time; **chronic**, lasting a long time; or **recurrent**, returning periodically. There are many types and causes of disease: infectious, caused by harmful BACTERIA or VIRUSES; hereditary and metabolic; growth and development; IMMUNE SYSTEM diseases; neoplastic (TUMOUR-producing); nutritional; deficiency; ENDOCRINE SYSTEM diseases; or diseases due to environmental agents, such as lead poisoning. Treatment depends on the cause and course of the disease. It may be **symptomatic** (relieving symptoms, but not necessarily combating a cause) or **specific** (attempting to cure an underlying cause). Disease prevention includes eradication of harmful organisms, VACCINES, public health measures and routine medical checks.

disk Form of computer data storage. Disks come in many different forms, some using magnetic methods to store data, such as the HARD DISK, while others use optical systems like the COMPACT DISC (CD) and CD-ROM.

disk operating system (DOS) Family of computer operating system SOFTWARE developed from 1979. The version created by Bill GATES' Microsoft Corporation for use with early International Business Machines (IBM) personal computers and was dominant in the 1980s and early 1990s. Like other operating systems it organized storage and provided a framework for programs to access the computer's hardware.

Disney, Walt (Walter Elias) (1901–66) US film animator, producer and executive. Disney has become synonymous with family entertainment and a menagerie of cartoon characters, such as Mickey Mouse, Donald Duck, and Pluto. *Steamboat Willie* (1928) was the first cartoon to use sound and featured Walt Disney's own voice as Mickey. Disney's first feature was *Snow White and the Seven Dwarfs* (1937). A series of classics followed: *Pinocchio* (1940), *Fantasia* (1940), *Dumbo* (1941), and *Bambi* (1942). In 1950, Disney diversified into live-action films with *Treasure Island* (1950), and began a nature series with *The Living Desert* (1953). In 1955, Disneyland amusement park opened in Anaheim, California. Disney collected 29 Academy Awards. The Walt Disney Company (founded 1923) is one of the world's most powerful media corporations.

Disraeli, Benjamin, 1st Earl of Beaconsfield (1804–81) British statesman and novelist, prime minister (1868, 1874–80). Disraeli was elected to Parliament in 1837. His brand of Toryism is expressed in the trilogy of novels *Coningsby* (1844), *Sybil* (1846), and *Tancred* (1847). Following the split in the Tory Party over the repeal of the CORN LAWS (1846), Disraeli became leader of the land-owning faction. His opposition to Robert PEEL was rewarded when he became chancellor of the exchequer (1852, 1858–59, 1866–68) under Lord DERBY. Disraeli succeeded Derby as prime minister, but was soon ousted by William GLADSTONE. His second term coincided with the greatest expansion of the second BRITISH EMPIRE. In 1876, Queen VICTORIA was proclaimed empress of India. Disraeli led Britain into the Zulu War (1879), the second Afghan War (1878–79), and sought to diminish the strength of Russia. In 1875 Britain purchased the Suez Canal from Egypt. In 1880 Disraeli was defeated for a second time by Gladstone.

Dissolution of the Monasteries (1536–40) Abolition of English MONASTICISM in the reign of HENRY VIII. The operation, managed by Thomas CROMWELL, was a result of the break with Rome, but also provided additional revenue, since the monasteries owned *c*.25% of the land in England, all of which passed to the Crown. The smaller religious houses were closed in 1536, larger ones in 1538–40. The Dissolution caused hardship and revolt, while providing estates for wealthy gentry.

distemper Contagious, often fatal, disease of young dogs, wild canines and weasels. Symptoms include fever, shivering, muscular spasms, and loss of appetite. Death is caused by inflammation of the brain. Puppies can be immunized.

distillation Extraction of a liquid by boiling a solution in which it is contained and cooling the vapour so that it condenses and can be collected. Distillation is used to separate liquids in solution, or liquid solvents from dissolved solids, to yield drinking water from sea water, or to produce alcoholic spirit. Fractional distillation, which uses a vertical column for condensation, is used in OIL refining to separate the various fractions of crude oil.

distilling Production of liquor by DISTILLATION, especially of ethyl ALCOHOL. In wine, yeast FERMENTATION produces a maximum alcohol content of *c*.15%. Distillation concentrates alcohol to a much higher degree to produce spirit. Most spirits are *c*.40% proof.

distributive law Rule of combination in mathematics, in which an operation applied to a combination of terms is equal to the combination of the operation applied to each individual term. Thus, in arithmetic $3 \times (2 + 1) = (3 \times 2) + (3 \times 1)$ and, in algebra $a(x + y) = ax + ay$.

District of Columbia US federal district, coextensive (since 1890) with the capital, WASHINGTON, D.C. It was created in 1790–91, from land taken from the states of Maryland and Virginia. The Virginia portion was returned in 1846. Area: 179sq km (69sq mi)

diuretic Drug used to increase the output of urine. It is used to treat raised blood pressure and oedema.

divination Foretelling the future by interpreting various signs. Omens are often thought to be found in cards, palms, or the entrails of sacrificed animals.

diving Water sport in which acrobatic manoeuvres are performed off a springboard or highboard, set at varying heights. Points are awarded for level of difficulty, technique and grace of flight, and cleanness of entry into the water. Techniques include tuck, pike, twist and somersault. *See also* SCUBA DIVING

Diwali Festival of lights in HINDUISM. Homes are lit with numerous tiny clay lamps in commemoration of the defeat of Ravana by RAMA, and the festival marks the resumption of social activities, such as pilgrimages and marriages. The story is symbolic of the return of light after the monsoon.

Dix, Otto (1891–1969) German painter and engraver. He was a pitiless satirist of inhumanity, notably in a series of 50 etchings called *The War* (1924) and his portrayal of prostitutes. The Nazis banned him from teaching (1933),

and he was jailed for an alleged plot to kill Hitler (1939). After World War 2, he concentrated on religious themes.

Dixieland Style of JAZZ music originating in NEW ORLEANS in the 1900s. It consists of a steady beat with interweaving melodic lines played by a small group (typically, clarinet, trumpet, trombone and rhythm section). King Oliver and Louis ARMSTRONG were two of its most famous exponents.

Djibouti *see* country feature.

Djibouti (Jibuti) Capital of DJIBOUTI, on the s shore of the Gulf of Tadjoura, NE Africa. Founded in 1888, it became capital in 1892, and a free port in 1949. Ethiopian emperor Menelik II built a railway from ADDIS ABABA, and Djibouti became the chief port for handling Ethiopian trade. While ERITREA was federated with Ethiopia (1952–93), it lost this status to the Red Sea port of Assab. Pop. (2002 est.) 524,700.

DNA (deoxyribonucleic acid) Molecule found in all cells, and in some viruses, which is responsible for forming the GENETIC CODE. It consists of two long chains of alternating deoxyribose SUGAR molecules and PHOSPHATE groups linked by nitrogenous bases. A base and its associated sugar are known as a nucleotide; the whole chain is a polynucleotide chain. The genetic code is formed in terms of the sequence of nucleotides: three nucleotides code for one specific amino acid and a series of them constitute a GENE. A single human CELL contains 4m (13ft) of DNA made up of all the information needed to make a human being. Each CHROMOSOME is believed to involve more than 100,000 different genes each representing one of the instructions needed to make and maintain the organism from which it originated. DNA directs development and maintains life of an organism by instructing cells to make PROTEINS – the versatile molecules on which all life depends. DNA is permanently locked into the nucleus. But the machinery for

▲ **Disney** Creator of the world's most famous cartoon characters, Walt Disney first introduced Mickey Mouse in a series of short cartoons in 1928. He went on to make full-length cartoons, the first of which, *Snow White and the Seven Dwarfs* (1937) became one of the most popular movies ever made. The Walt Disney Company, with theme parks in the USA, and Paris, France, and merchandizing, home-video, publishing and recording interests, is one of the most successful entertainment companies in the world.

DJIBOUTI

The Republic of Djibouti is a small country on the NE coast of Africa. The capital is also DJIBOUTI. Djibouti occupies a strategic position around the Gulf of Tadjoura, where the Red Sea meets the Gulf of Aden. Behind the coastal plain lie the Mabla Mountains, rising to Moussa Ali at 2,028m [6,654ft]. Djibouti contains the lowest point on the African continent, Lake Assal, at 155m [509ft] below sea level. Nearly 90% of the land is semi-desert, and shortage of pasture and water make farming difficult.

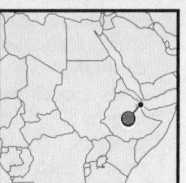

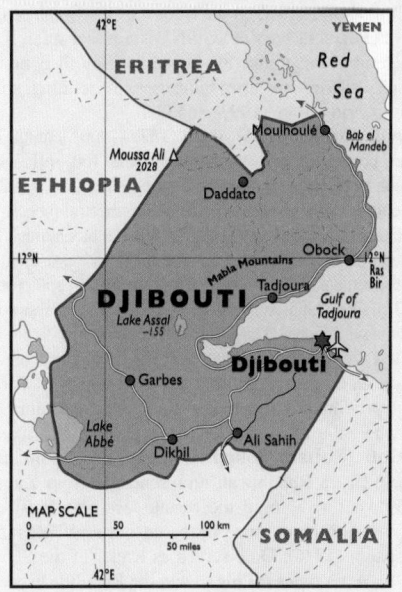

CLIMATE
Djibouti has one of the world's hottest and driest climates with summer temperatures regularly exceeding 42°C [100°F]. Average annual rainfall is only 130mm [5in]. In the wooded Mabla Mountains, the average annual rainfall reaches 500mm [20in].

HISTORY
Islam arrived in the 9th century. The subsequent conversion of the Afars led to conflict with Christian Ethiopians who lived in the interior. By the 19th century, Somalian Issas moved north and occupied much of the Afars' traditional grazing land. France gained influence in 1862, with its interest centred around Djibouti, the French commercial rival to the port of Aden. French Somaliland was established in 1888.

A referendum in 1967 saw 60% of the electorate vote to retain links with France, although most Issas favoured independence. The country was renamed the French Territory of the Afars and Issas.

POLITICS
In 1977 the Republic of Djibouti gained full independence, and Hassan Gouled Aptidon of the Popular Rally for Progress (RPP) was elected president. He declared a one-party state in 1981. Protests against the Issas-dominated regime forced the adoption of a multiparty constitution in 1992. The Front for the Restoration of Unity and Democracy (FRUD), supported primarily by Afars, boycotted 1993 elections, and Aptidon was re-elected for a

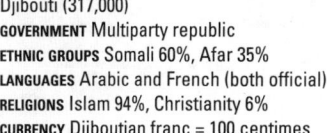

AREA 23,200sq km [8,958sq mi]
POPULATION 496,000
CAPITAL (POPULATION) Djibouti (317,000)
GOVERNMENT Multiparty republic
ETHNIC GROUPS Somali 60%, Afar 35%
LANGUAGES Arabic and French (both official)
RELIGIONS Islam 94%, Christianity 6%
CURRENCY Djiboutian franc = 100 centimes

fourth six-year term. FRUD rebels continued an armed campaign for political representation. In 1996, government and FRUD forces signed a peace agreement, recognizing FRUD as a political party.

In 1999, Ismael Omar Gelleh succeeded Aptidon as president in the country's first multi-party presidential elections. He pursues closer links with France, which still has a strong military presence in Djibouti, and with the US. The only US military base in sub-Saharan Africa is stationed here. In 2005 elections Gelleh was the only candidate.

ECONOMY
Djibouti is a poor nation, heavily reliant on food imports and revenue from the capital city. A free-trade zone, it has no major resources and manufacturing is on a very small scale. The only important activity is livestock raising, and 50% of the population are pastoral nomads.

Its location at the mouth of the Red Sea is of great economic importance as it serves as a vital trans-shipment point.

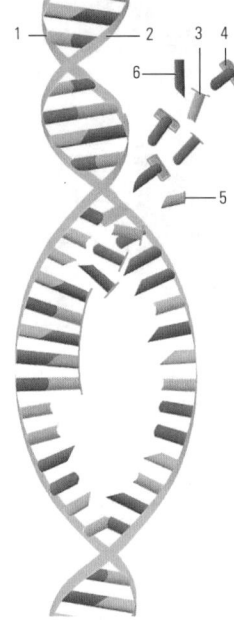

protein synthesis is situated in the cytoplasm – outside the cell membrane. DNA communicates with this machinery through a messenger molecule known as RNA. In EUKARY-OTE cells, DNA is stored in chromosomes inside the nucleus. Loops of DNA also occur inside chloroplasts and mitochondria. In 2003, the international Human Genome Project completed the sequence of the 3 billion DNA bases in the human GENOME that carries all the genetic information of an individual. *See also* RECOMBINANT DNA RESEARCH

Dnieper (Dnepr) River in E Europe. Rising in the Valdai Hills, W of Moscow, it flows s through Belarus and Ukraine to the Black Sea. It is the third longest river in Europe. The Dneproges dam (completed 1932) made the river entirely navigable. It is linked by canal to the River Bug, and has several hydroelectric power stations. Length: 2,286km (1,420mi).

doberman Strong guard dog, bred in late 19th-century Germany. It has a long, wedge-shaped head and short erect ears. Its deep-chested body is set on straight legs. The smooth coat may be black, red or fawn. Height: to 71cm (28in) at the shoulder.

Dobzhansky, Theodosius (1900–75) US geneticist and authority on human evolution, b. Russia. He was influential in the development of population GENETICS. His writings include *Genetics and the Origin of Species* (1937), *Mankind Evolving* (1962), and *Genetics of the Evolutionary Process* (1970).

dock Any of more than 200 species of flowering plants native to N USA and Europe. Curled dock (*Rumex crispus*) has brown flowers and oblong leaves with curly margins. Dock leaves are a country remedy for nettle stings. Family Polygonaceae.

Doctorow, E.L. (Edgar Lawrence) (1931–) US writer. Doctorow's novels have a strong political edge and incisive concern for history. *Ragtime* (1975), his best known novel, deals with late 19th-century racism in the USA. Other works include *Welcome to Hard Times* (1960), *The Book of Daniel* (1971), *Loon Lake* (1980), *Billy Bathgate* (1988), *The Waterworks* (1994), and *City of God* (2000).

documentary Factual film. The term was first applied to Robert Flaherty's *Nanook of the North* (1921), a first-hand account of life among the Inuit. Documentaries soon rivalled

newspapers and became a major means of television news, current affairs and science presentation. Other ground-breaking documentaries include D.A. Pennebaker's *Don't Look Back* (1967) and Marcel OPHÜLS' *A Sense of Loss* (1972).

dodder Leafless, parasitic, twining plant with a thread-like stem and clusters of small yellow flowers. It feeds using haustoria, modified roots that enter the host plant. Family Convolvulaceae; species *Cuscuta europaea*.

Dodecanese (Dhodhekánisos) Group of c.20 islands forming a department of Greece, in the SE Aegean Sea, between Turkey and Crete. The capital and largest island is RHODES. The islands were under Ottoman control (1500–1912), before passing to Greece (1947). The main occupation is agriculture, such as fruit growing, livestock raising, and diving for sponges. Area: 2,174sq km (839sq mi). Pop. (2001) 190,071.

dodo Extinct, flightless bird that lived on the Mascarene Islands in the Indian Ocean. The last dodo died by c.1690. The true dodo (*Raphus cucullatus*) of Mauritius and the similar Réunion solitaire (*Raphus solitarius*) were heavy-bodied birds with large heads and large hooked bills. Weight: to 23kg (50lb).

Dodoma Capital of Tanzania, central Tanzania. In 1974 Dodoma replaced DAR ES SALAAM as capital. It is in an agricultural region, crops include grain, seeds, and nuts. Pop. (2002 est.) 157,300.

dog Domesticated carnivorous mammal, closely related to the jackal, wolf and fox. Typically, it has a slender, muscular body; long head with slender snout; small paws, five toes on the forefeet, four on the hind; non-retractile claws; and well-developed teeth. Smell is the dog's keenest sense; its hearing is also acute. The gestation period is 49–70 days; one or more puppies are born. Dogs developed from the tree-dwelling *miacis*, which lived c.40 million years ago, through intermediate forms to *tomarctus*, which lived c.15 million years ago. The dog was domesticated c.10–14,000 years ago. There are c.400 breeds, classified in various ways, such as TERRIER, sporting, hound, working, and toy. Length: 34–135cm (13–53in); tail 11–54cm (4–21in); weight: 1kg-68kg (2–150lb). Family Canidae; species *Canis familiaris. See also* individual breeds

dogfish SHARK found in marine waters worldwide. Generally greyish with white spots, it lacks a lower tail lobe. Eggs are laid in cases (mermaids' purses). Dogfish are divided into two groups: spiny, with a stout, sharp spine in front of each dorsal fin; and spineless, without a spine in front of the second dorsal fin. A food fish, they are sold as rock salmon. Length: spiny, 0.6–1.2m (2–4ft); spineless, 7.3m (24ft). Suborder Squalidae.

dogwood Any of several small trees and shrubs in the genus *Cornus* of the dogwood family (Cornaceae). Wild flowering dogwoods are found in deciduous forests. They have small flowers, enclosed by four large, petal-like, white bracts.

Doha Capital of QATAR, on the E coast of the Qatar peninsula, in the Persian (Arabian) Gulf. Doha was a small fishing village until oil production began in 1949. It is now a modern city and trade centre. Industries: oil refining, shipping, engineering. Pop. (1997) 264,009.

Dohnányi, Ernst (Ernö) von (1877–1960) Hungarian composer, conductor, and pianist. Hungarian folk influences are evident, such as the piano suite *Ruralia Hungarica* (1926). He also composed operas, concertos and orchestral pieces.

Doisy, Edward Adelbert (1893–1986) US biochemist. He researched BLOOD buffers, VITAMINS and METABOLISM. He also isolated the female sex HORMONES, oestrone (1929) and oestradiol (1935). Doisy shared the 1943 Nobel Prize in physiology or medicine with Henrik Dam, for their analysis of vitamin K.

doldrums Region of the ocean near the EQUATOR, characterized by calms, and light and variable winds. It corresponds approximately to a belt of low pressure around the Equatorwhere the TRADE WINDS converge.

Dole, Bob (Robert Joseph) (1923–) US politician. Dole served as a Republican representative from Kansas (1960–69), before joining the Senate. He was President Gerald FORD's running mate in the unsuccessful Republican campaign (1976). Dole served as leader of the Senate (1984–96). After twice failing to win the Republican presidential nomination (1980, 1988), he finally secured the

▲ **DNA** molecules form a double helix, with two spiral backbones (1,2). These are made of sugar and phosphate units. Linking the backbones, like rungs on a ladder, are the bases; adenine (3), thymine (4), guanine (5) and cytosine (6). Each backbone contributes one base to each rung, which are strictly paired; adenine with thymine, and cytosine with guanine.

DNA FINGERPRINTING

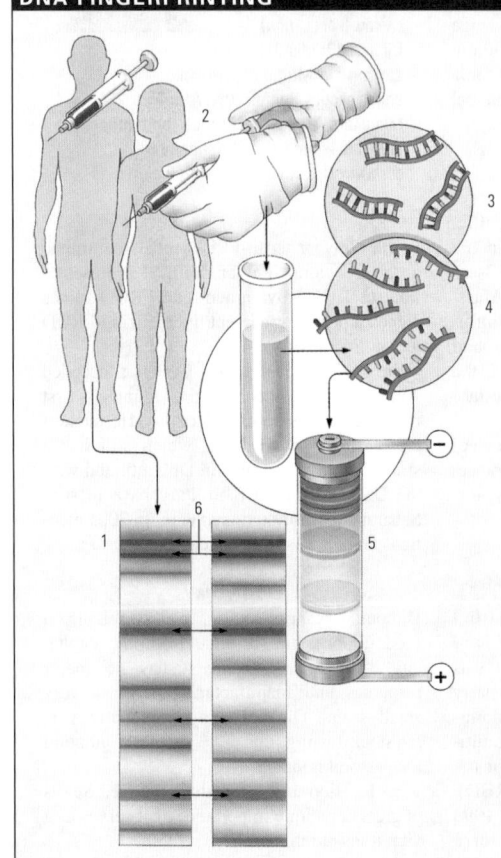

Using a technique known as DNA fingerprinting, a person can be accurately identified. The process allows a person's DNA to be represented in visual form (1). Each DNA pattern is unique (like a fingerprint) _ with the exception of identical twins. In a case of disputed paternity, DNA fingerprinting allows the relationship to be settled beyond doubt. DNA is present in all cells, so a sample can be taken from blood (2), skin or even sweat. DNA is separated out (3) and an enzyme that divides DNA is added. The enzyme attacks the minisatellite region between the genes (4). The genes are then sorted by size by an electric field (5). Gel electrophoresis exploits the fact that snippets of DNA carry a charge to force them through a gel. The size of the snippets controls how far they travel, giving a pattern unique to each individual. A child combines DNA from both parents, so will have a partially similar pattern. Paternity is confirmed by the matching marks (6).

vote in 1996. Dole ran a lacklustre campaign and lost the election to President Bill CLINTON.

dollar ($) Standard monetary unit of the US since 1792. It was derived from the Spanish *dolar*, the most widely used coin in the American colonies. Divided into a hundred cents, the value of the US dollar was based on the gold price until 1934. Many other countries have adopted the dollar as their currency.

Dollfuss, Engelbert (1892–1934) Austrian statesman, chancellor (1932–34). Determined to preserve Austrian independence, he dissolved the National Socialist (Nazi) Party, which had demanded union with Germany (1933), crushed a socialist rising, and assumed authoritarian powers. He was assassinated by Austrian Nazis in an unsuccessful coup.

dolmen Megalithic monument comprising a stone lintel supported by upright stones. Dolmens were originally used as burial chambers and covered by a BARROW. They are most common in Cornwall, sw England, and Brittany, NW France.

dolomite Carbonate mineral, calcium-magnesium carbonate, $CaMg(CO_3)_2$, found in altered limestones. It is usually colourless or white. A rhombohedral class prismatic crystal, it is often found as a gangue mineral in hydrothermal veins. It is also a sedimentary rock, probably formed by the alteration of limestone by seawater, where calcite has been replaced by calcium magnesium carbonate. Hardness 3.5–4; r.d. 2.8.

Dolomites (Dolomiti or Dolomiten) Alpine range in NE Italy. The Dolomites are composed of dolomitic limestone, eroded to form a striking landscape popular with mountaineers and tourists. There are several hydroelectric power stations. The highest peak is Marmolada, 3,342m (10,964ft) high.

dolphin Family of small-toothed aquatic WHALES; there are salt and freshwater species. The best-known are the dark blue-backed common dolphin, the blue-grey bottlenose and the KILLER WHALE. They map their environment by ECHOLOCATION and swim in hierarchically organized pods, feeding on fish and crustacea. Bottlenose dolphins (*Tursiops truncatus*) have a distinct beak and slender body, a tail fin for propulsion, pectoral fins for steering and a dorsal fin for stability. They breathe through a single blowhole, and can remain underwater for 8 minutes. They can achieve speeds of up to 35km/h (20mph) for short periods and leaps of 9m (30ft). Their language is complex, and each individual has an identifiying whistle. They have a gestation period of 12 months, and the mother nurtures her calf for two years. They are highly intelligent: off Mauritania they fish cooperatively with fishermen. They grow to 4m (13ft) with cold-water populations reaching larger sizes. Family Delphinidae.

domain In mathematics, a set of values that can be assigned to the independent VARIABLE in a function or relation; the set of values of the dependent variable is called the **range**. For example, let the function be $y = x^2$, with x restricted to 0, 1, 2, 3 and −3. Then y takes the values 0, 1, 4, 9 and 9 respectively. The domain is {0, 1, 2, 3, −3} and the range is { 0, 1, 4, 9 }.

domain In TAXONOMY, some experts recognize the domain as a higher category than KINGDOM. In this scheme, the two sub-kingdoms of PROKARYOTES (ARCHAEBACTERIA and EUBACTERIA) constitute two domains, called Archaea and Bacteria, while all other living organisms are in a third domain, EUKARYOTES. *See also* PHYLOGENETICS; PLANT CLASSIFICATION

dome In architecture, a hemispherical roof. One of the earliest monumental domes is the PANTHEON, Rome. It was an important element in ISLAMIC ART AND ARCHITECTURE, especially MOSQUES. Eclipsed in importance in Gothic architecture, it was a significant element in Renaissance and Baroque styles.

Domenichino (1581–1641) Leading painter of the Italian BAROQUE. In 1602, he worked with Annibale Carracci on the FARNESE Palace. Domenichino's landscape paintings, such as *The Hunt of Diana* and *Landscape with St John Baptizing*, influenced Nicolas POUSSIN and CLAUDE LORRAIN.

Dome of the Rock (*Qubbat al-Sakhrah*) MOSQUE and shrine built (685–692) by Abd al-Malik on a Jewish temple site in JERUSALEM. The Dome covers the summit of Mount Moriah, where the prophet MUHAMMAD is believed to have ascended to Heaven. According to the Old Testament, the Rock is also where ABRAHAM was to have sacrificed ISAAC. *See also* TEMPLE, JERUSALEM

Domesday Book (1085–86) Census of the English kingdom commissioned by WILLIAM I (THE CONQUERER). Its purpose was to ascertain potential crown revenue. The most complete survey in medieval Europe, it is an important primary historical source. It lists property and resources manor by manor.

Domingo, Plácido (1941–) Spanish tenor, one of the leading opera singers of his generation. He made his debut at Monterrey, Mexico (1961), and has since toured extensively. He is an outstanding interpreter of the Italian romantic repertoire. In the 1990s, he achieved popularity as one of the Three Tenors. *See also* CARRERAS, JOSÉ; PAVAROTTI, LUCIANO

Dominic, Saint (1170–1221) (Domingo de Guzmán) Spanish priest, founder of the DOMINICANS. In 1203, Pope Innocent III sent him to s France to preach to the ALBIGENSES. He founded a monastery at Prouille. He developed an order based on scholastic and democratic principles, and rules derived from Saint AUGUSTINE. His feast day is August 4.

Dominica Independent island nation in the E Caribbean Sea, West Indies; the capital and chief port is ROSEAU. The largest of the Windward Islands, it was named after *dies dominica* (Sunday), the day it Christopher Columbus discovered it in 1493. The original inhabitants were CARIB, but the present population are mainly the descendants of African slaves. Dominica is mountainous and heavily forested, and the climate is tropical. Britain and France disputed Dominica until Britain asserted full control in 1783. It became a British crown colony in 1805, and was a member of the Federation of the West Indies (1958–62). It achieved complete independence as a republic within the Commonwealth of Nations in 1978. Eugenia Charles was the first woman prime minister (1980–95) in the West Indies. Dominica is one of the poorest Caribbean countries (2000 GDP per capita US$4000). Agriculture dominates the economy. In 1979 and 1980, hurricane damage severely reduced production. Exports: copra, bananas, citrus fruit. Area: 751sq km (290sq mi). Pop. (2000) 70,000. *See* WEST INDIES map

Dominican Republic *see* country feature, p. 282.

Dominicans (officially *Ordo Praedicatorum*, Order of Preachers, O.P.) Roman Catholic religious order, founded (1215) by Saint DOMINIC. They are also known as Black Friars or Jacobins. Dominicans are one of the four great mendicant orders of Roman Catholicism. Devoted to preaching and study, the order operates worldwide and includes a contemplative order of nuns. Noted scholars include Saint Thomas AQUINAS.

domino theory Political doctrine that affected US foreign policy during the COLD WAR, especially in Southeast Asia. It held that if one country became communist, its neighbours would inevitably follow. The doctrine was widely used in support of US military involvement in VIETNAM.

Domitian (AD 51–96) Roman Emperor (81–96). A son of VESPASIAN, he succeeded his brother TITUS. His rule was at first orderly but became increasingly tyrannical and paranoid. After several failed attempts, he was assassinated. Domitian was partly responsible for building the COLOSSEUM.

▲ **dock** The curled dock (*Rumex crispus*) of Europe and Asia, is related to sorrel. It gets its name from the wavy margins of its leaves. Application of dock leaves is a country remedy for nettle stings.

INTERNET

dolphin
► www.wdcs.org

Domenichino
► www.nationalgallery.org.uk

Dominica
► www.avirtualdominica.com

Dominican Republic
► www.dominicanrepublic.com/Tourism

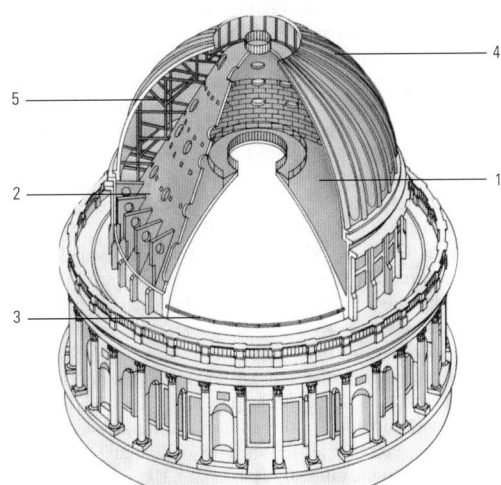

◄ **dome** Sir Christopher Wren designed the dome of St Paul's Cathedral, London. To make it as airy and as light as possible it has a triple construction: a brick inner dome (1), its 'eye' rises 65m (213ft) above the floor; an intermediate, brick cone (2), reinforced with iron chains (3); and an outer dome (4), resting on the intermediate cone, and built out with timber framing (5) and lead covering to obtain the desired silhouette.

DOMINICAN REPUBLIC

The Dominican Republic is the second largest of the Caribbean nations in both area and population. It shares the island of Hispaniola with Haiti, with the Dominican Republic occupying the E two-thirds.

Of the steep-sided mountains that dominate the island, the country includes the N Cordillera Septentrional, the huge Cordillera Central, which rises to Pico Duarte, at 3,175m [10,414ft] the highest peak in the Caribbean, and the southern Sierra de Baoruco. Between them and to the E lie fertile valleys and lowlands, including the Vega Real and the coastal plains where the main sugar plantations are found.

CLIMATE

Typical of the Caribbean region, the climate is humid and hot throughout the year close to sea level, while cooler conditions prevail in the mountains. Rainfall is heavy, especially in the NE.

HISTORY

Christopher COLUMBUS visited the island on 5 December 1492. The city of Santo Domingo,

now the capital and chief port, was founded by Columbus's brother Bartholomew four years later and is the oldest in the Americas. For a long time a Spanish colony, Hispaniola was initially the centrepiece of their empire, but was later to become a poor relation.

In 1795 the whole island came under French rule, but the E part was returned to Spain in 1809. In 1821, when it was called Santo Domingo, it won its independence. It was quickly annexed by Haiti, which held the territory from 1822 until 1844 when it won independence again as the Dominican Republic. Its subsequent history was one of anarchy and civil war, punctuated by dictatorships and US military interventions.

Growing American influence culminated in occupation between 1916 and 1924. This was followed by a period of corrupt dictatorship. From 1930 until his assassination in 1961, the country was ruled by Rafael Trujillo, one of Latin America's most notorious dictators, who imprisoned or killed many of his opponents. A power struggle developed between the military, the upper class, those who wanted the country to become a democracy and others who favoured making it a Communist regime.

POLITICS

In 1962 Juan Bosch became president, but was ousted in 1963. Bosch supporters tried to seize power in 1965, but were met with strong military opposition. This led to US military intervention in 1965. In 1966, a new constitution was adopted and Joaquín Balaguer was elected president (1966–78, 1986–96). Elec-

AREA 48,511sq km [18,730sq mi]
POPULATION 9,366,000
CAPITAL (POPULATION) Santo Domingo (2,563,000)
GOVERNMENT Multiparty republic
ETHNIC GROUPS Mulatto 73%, White 16%, Black 11%
LANGUAGES Spanish (official)
RELIGIONS Roman Catholic 95%
CURRENCY Dominican peso = 100 centavos

tions have been known to be violent and the United States has kept a watchful eye.

Leonel Fernandez was elected president for a second time in 2004. He had campaigned on a ticket that promised to tackle inflation, and once in office he introduced austerity measures including cuts to state spending.

ECONOMY

The World Bank describes the Dominican Republic as a 'lower-middle-income' developing country. In the 1990s, industrial growth that exploited the country's huge hydroelectric potential, mining and tourism has augmented the traditional agricultural economy, though the country is far from being politically stable. Agriculture is a major activity. Leading crops include avocados, bananas, beans, mangoes, oranges, plantains, rice, sugar cane and tobacco.

Gold and nickel are mined. Sugar refining is a major industry, with the bulk of production exported to the United States. Leading exports are ferronickel, sugar, coffee, cocoa and gold. Its main trading partner is the United States.

▲ **donkey** Smaller than a horse, the donkey has a large head and long ears in proportion to its body. Its coarse hair is tight and matted giving the coat a very rough appearance. Male donkeys are crossed with female horses to breed mules.

Don River of SW Russia. Rising SE of Tula, it flows S, then SW to the Sea of Azov. Rostov is the major port. Annual floods are controlled by the Tsimlyansk Reservoir. The Don is navigable for 1,370km (850mi), and is an important shipping route for grain, timber and coal. It is linked by canal to the River VOLGA. Length: 1,930km (1,200mi).

Donatello (c.1386–1466) Greatest European sculptor of the 15th century, joint creator of the RENAISSANCE style in Florence. His work is a turning point in European sculpture, moving from a formulaic GOTHIC style to a more vital means of expression. Inspired by HUMANISM, his initial innovations included standing figures of saints in the Church of Or San Michele. His reliefs and free-standing statues, have been likened to 'drawing in stone'. After a visit to Rome (1430–32), his work, such as the *Cantoria* for Florence Cathedral and the bronze *David*, adopted a more CLASSICAL feel. His late work, such as *Judith and Holofernes* and his wood carving of *Mary Magdalene* (1455), shows even greater emotional intensity. Donatello greatly influenced MICHELANGELO.

Donegal County in NW Republic of Ireland, bounded by Northern Ireland (E) and the Atlantic Ocean (N and W). The county town is Lifford. There is a rocky, indented coastline and much of the county is hilly. The chief rivers are the Finn, Foyle and Erne. Agriculture is the main activity, but only 33% of the land is fertile. Tourism and fishing are also important. Area: 4,830sq km (1,865sq mi). Pop. (2002) 137,383.

Donets Basin Industrial region in E Ukraine and S Russia; the capital is Donetsk. It is a major coal and steel producer, close to the mineral deposits in E Ukraine. Development of area began in c.1870. By 1989, it produced more

than 200 million tonnes of coal a year. In the 1990s, there was a slump in production due to exhausted seams and antiquated technology. Area: c.25,900sq km (10,000sq mi).

Donizetti, Gaetano (1797–1848) Italian composer. He wrote 75 comic and serious operas. Initially influenced by Gioacchino ROSSINI, he formed his own melodic style with rich harmonies and orchestration. Operas include *L'Elisir d'Amore* (1832), *Lucia di Lammermoor* (1835), *Roberto Devereux* (1837), *La Fille du Régiment* (1840), and *Don Pasquale* (1843).

donkey Domesticated ASS, used by humans since well before 3000 BC. Crossed with a horse it produces a MULE.

Donleavy, J.P. (James Patrick) (1926–) Irish writer, b. USA. His first novel, *The Ginger Man* (1955), was not published in uncensored form in Britain and the USA until 1963. Other novels include *A Singular Man* (1963), *The Beastly Beatitudes of Balthazar B.* (1968), *The Onion Eaters* (1971), and *That Darcy, That Dancer, That Gentleman* (1991).

Donne, John (1572–1631) English poet and cleric. Donne's METAPHYSICAL POETRY is among the greatest work in ENGLISH LITERATURE. His early poetry, mostly written in the 1590s, consists mainly of love poems, elegies and satires while later work, such as *An Anatomy of the World* (1611) and *Of the Progress of the Soul* (1612), became more philosophical. Donne's rejection of Catholicism and conversion to Anglicanism is evident in the prose-work *Pseudo-Martyr* (1610). He was ordained in 1615 and became Dean (1621) of St Paul's Cathedral, London.

Doolittle, Hilda (1886–1961) (H.D.) US poet associated with Ezra POUND and IMAGISM. Her published verse includes *Sea Garden* (1916) and *The Flowering of the Rod* (1946). Her *Collected Poems 1914–44* were published in 1983. She also wrote prose, such as *Hermione* (1927 but unpublished until 1981), a novel of lesbian love.

Doppler, Christian Johann (1803–53) Austrian physicist and mathematician. Doppler is famous for his prediction of the DOPPLER EFFECT in a paper on DOUBLE STARS (1842).

Doppler effect Change in frequency of a wave, when there is relative motion between the wave source and the observer. The amount of change depends on the velocities of the wave, source and observer. With a sound wave, the effect is demonstrated by the drop in pitch of a vehicle's siren as it passes an observer. With light, the velocity of the source or observer must be large for an appreciable effect to occur, such as the red shift of a rapidly receding galaxy. This effect was first described in 1842 by the Austrian physicist Christian Johann DOPPLER. *See also* NAVIGATION

Dordogne River in SW France. Rising in the AUVERGNE hills, it is formed by the convergence of the Dor and Dogne rivers. It flows SW then W to meet the River Garonne, and forms the Gironde estuary. It has famous vineyards along its 471km (293mi) course, and is a vital source of hydroelectric power.

Doré, Gustave (1832–83) French illustrator, painter and sculptor. He is best known for his engraved illustrations, many of them grotesque fantasies, for books such as *Inferno* (1861), *Don Quixote* (1862) and the Bible (1866). His drawings of London slums (1869–71) inspired VAN GOGH.

Dorians Greek-speaking people, who settled N Greece *c.*1200 BC as the MYCENAEAN CIVILIZATION completed its decline. Their arrival marks the beginning of a so-called 'dark age' of ancient Greece, lasting about 400 years, in which writing in LINEAR SCRIPT disappeared but technologies such as ironworking were developed.

Doric order One of the five ORDERS OF ARCHITECTURE

dormouse Squirrel-like RODENT of Eurasia and Africa that hibernates in temperate climates. Most dormice are active at night and sleep by day. They eat nuts, fruit, seeds, insects and other tiny animals. They were once bred for human food. Length: 10–20cm (4–8in), excluding tail. Family Gliridae.

Dorset County on the English Channel, SW England; the county town is Dorchester. Dorset's most famous monument is the Iron Age hill fort, Maiden Castle. After the defeat of the Romans, Dorset became part of the West Saxon kingdom. It is traversed W to E by the North and South Dorset Downs, and drained by the rivers Frome and Stour. Cereal crop cultivation and livestock-raising is important. Industries: tourism, marble quarrying. Area: 2,654sq km (1,025sq mi). Pop. (2001) 390,986.

Dortmund City and port on the Dortmund-Ems Canal, Nordrhein-Westfalen state, NW Germany. In the 13th century Dortmund flourished as a member of the HANSEATIC LEAGUE. It declined in the late 17th century but grew as an industrial centre from the mid-19th century. Industries: iron and steel, brewing, engineering. Pop. (1999) 590,300.

dory (John Dory) Marine fish found worldwide. It is deep-bodied with a large mouth. The species *Zeus faber* of the Mediterranean Sea and Atlantic Ocean is a valuable food fish. Length: to 1m (3.3ft). Family Zeidae.

Dos Passos, John Roderigo (1896–1970) US novelist. The first novel to attract critical acclaim was *Manhattan Transfer* (1925). His best known work is the trilogy *United States* (1930–36), in which he deploys innovatory techniques (such as stream of consciousness, news headlines and biographies) to portray early 20th-century American life. Later fiction includes the trilogy *District of Columbia* (1939–43).

Dos Santos, José Eduardo (1942–) Angolan statesman, president (1979–). Dos Santos' succession to the presidency was marked by escalating violence between the Cuban-backed People's Movement for the Liberation of Angola (MPLA) government, and the South African-backed National Union for the Total Independence of Angola (UNITA). UNITA leader Jonas SAVIMBI refused to recognize Dos Santos' narrow election victory in 1992 and fighting resumed. The Lusaka Protocol (1994) paved the way for a unified government which was inaugurated in

◄ **dormouse** Found in Europe and Asia, the dormouse (*Glis glis*) usually lives in trees. The hands and feet of the dormouse are equipped with rough pads which assist in climbing. The diet is chiefly vegetarian, but may include insects and small birds.

D

1997, headed by Dos Santos. In 2002, after the death of Savimbi, Dos Santos declared an end to the civil war.

Dostoevsky, Fyodor Mikhailovich (1821–81) Russian novelist, one of the greatest 19th-century writers. After completing *Poor Folk* and *The Double* (both 1846), he joined a revolutionary group, was arrested, and sentenced to death (1849). He was reprieved at the eleventh hour, and his sentence was commuted to four years' hard labour. He returned to St Petersburg in 1859, where he wrote *Notes from the Underground* (1864). After his classic work on sin and redemption *Crime and Punishment* (1866), he left Russia, partly to escape creditors. While abroad, he wrote *The Idiot* (1868–69) and *The Devils* (or *The Possessed*) (1872). His last major work was his masterpiece *The Brothers Karamazov* (1879–80).

Douala Chief port of Cameroon, on the Bight of Biafra, W Africa. As Kamerunstadt, it was capital of the German Kamerun Protectorate (1885–1901), became Douala (1907), and was capital of French Cameroon (1940–46). Industries: ship repairing, textiles and palm oil. Pop. (2005) 1,980,000.

double bass Largest stringed instrument. It has four strings tuned in fourths (E-A-D-G) and sounds one OCTAVE below the musical notation. It resembles a large violin, but has sloping shoulders (it was originally a member of the VIOL family). The double bass is held vertically. A bow is generally used for classical music, but the strings are usually plucked in jazz.

double bassoon (contrabassoon) *See* BASSOON

double star Two stars that appear close together in the sky. There are two types of double star: BINARY STARS and **optical doubles** (two stars that are quite distant from each other, but appear close together as a result of chance alignment).

Douglas, Gavin (1475–1522) Scottish medieval poet, important in the emergence of Scots as a distinct language. His rhymed couplet version of Virgil's *Aeneid* in Scots (1513) was the first translation of a classic into an English-based language. His other surviving work is *The Palace of Honour* (1553).

Douglas, Michael (1944–) US actor and producer, son of Kirk Douglas. His acting career soared after the adventure-comedy *Romancing the Stone* (1984). Douglas won a best actor Oscar for *Wall Street* (1987). Other films include *Fatal Attraction* (1986), *Basic Instinct* (1992), and *Traffic* (2000).

Douglas, Stephen Arnold (1813–61) US statesman. Douglas served in the House of Representatives (1843–47), before becoming Senator for Illinois (1847–61). He tried to unite the Democratic Party on the issue of SLAVERY, and was instrumental in the COMPROMISE OF 1850. He sponsored the Kansas-Nebraska Act (1854), that promoted popular sovereignty. In the Lincoln-Douglas debates (1858), Douglas defeated the challenge of Abraham LINCOLN. In 1860 he gained the Democratic presidential nomination, but lost the election to Lincoln. He supported Lincoln at the start of the American CIVIL WAR.

Douglas-Home, Sir Alec (Alexander Frederick) (1903–95) British statesman, prime minister (1963–64). He entered Parliament in 1931, and served as private secretary (1937–39) to Neville CHAMBERLAIN. He joined the House of Lords as Lord Home of the Hirsel (1951), and had a succession of posts, including foreign secretary (1960–63). He renounced his peerage to succeed Harold MACMILLAN as prime minister. He was also foreign secretary (1970–74) under Ted HEATH.

Douglass, Frederick (1817–95) African-American social reformer and abolitionist. An escaped slave, he was a lecturer for the Massachusetts Anti-Slavery Society and managed to buy his freedom. He published an abolitionist paper, *North Star* (1847), and recruited African American soldiers for the Union side in the American Civil War. He later held several government posts, such as minister to Haiti (1889–91).

Douro (Duero) River in Spain and Portugal. Rising in N central Spain, it flows W to form part of the Spain-Portugal

INTERNET

Dos Santos, José Eduardo
► www.angola.org.uk/ facts_bio_pres.htm

Douglas-Home, Sir Alec (Alexander Frederick)
► www.number-10.gov.uk

D

► **dragonfly** An incomplete metamorphosis, such as occurs in dragonflies (order Odonata), may be an adaptation to take advantage of different habitats. The adult form (A) of *Anax imperator* is a fast-flying predator on other insects, while the nymph (B) is aquatic, preying on a variety of life in freshwater ponds.

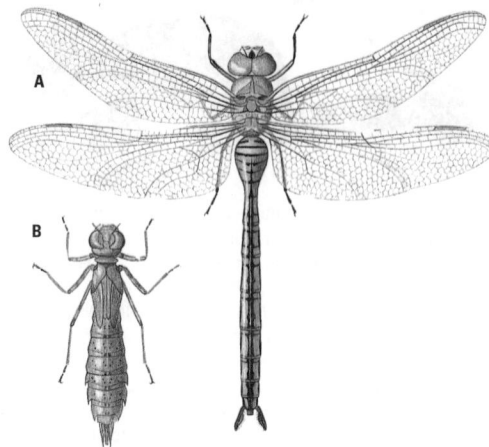

A

B

► **Drake** This portrait of Sir Francis Drake by Samuel Lane, reflects Drake's life as an explorer, adventurer and mariner. He was the first Englisman to circumnavigate the world (1577–80), and to cross the Strait of Magellan. Along the way, Drake plundered a fortune in Spanish treasure. In 1587, he 'singed the King of Spain's beard' by sinking 30 ships in Cadiz harbour, thus postponing the Spanish Armada.

border. It then turns W through N Portugal to empty into the Atlantic Ocean near OPORTO. Length: 895km (556mi).

dove Cooing, plump-bodied bird found almost worldwide. Doves are related to PIGEONS, and have small heads, short legs and dense, varied plumage. They feed mostly on vegetable matter. Length: 15–83cm (6–33in). Family Columbidae.

Dover Seaport on the Strait of Dover, Kent, SE England. One of the cinque ports, Dover is a resort and cross-Channel ferry port. The nearest point to France on mainland Britain, it was fortified by the Romans. In World War 1, it was an important naval base, and suffered intensive bombing during World War 2. Its medieval castle contains the remains of a Roman lighthouse and Saxon stronghold. Pop. (2001) 104,490.

Dover Capital of Delaware state, USA, on the St Jones River. Founded in 1683, it was first laid out in 1717 and has been state capital since 1777. Dover contains fine examples of Georgian architecture. It is a shipping and canning centre for the surrounding agricultural region. It is also the site of Dover Air Force Base. Industries: gelatin food products, synthetic polymers, adhesives, chemicals. Pop. (2000) 32,135.

Dowland, John (1563–1626) English composer of songs and lute music. His songs, written for voice and lute, are widely considered to be the finest of his generation, due to their great emotional range. He also composed much instrumental music, such as the famous set of variations, *Lachrimae*.

Down District on the Irish Sea coast, SE Northern Ireland; the administrative centre is Downpatrick. Anglo-Normans invaded (12th century), and 16th and 17th century English and Scottish settlers made their home here. A hilly region, the Mountains of Mourne lie in the S. Agriculture dominates, such as livestock and crop farming. Industries: agricultural machinery and textiles. Area: 650sq km (250sq mi). Pop. (2001) 63,828.

Downing Street Street in London, off Whitehall, named after the diplomat Sir George Downing (1623–84). It includes the official residence of the British prime minister at No. 10, chancellor of the exchequer at No. 11, chief whip at No. 12.

Downing Street Declaration (December 15, 1993) Issued by the then prime minister John MAJOR and the Irish taoiseach Albert REYNOLDS. Continuing the momentum of the ANGLO-IRISH AGREEMENT, it set a framework for peace talks in Northern IRELAND. It stated all democratically mandated political parties (including SINN FÉIN) could be involved in an all-Ireland forum if they were committed to ending paramilitary violence. The UK and Irish governments also agreed that the status of Northern Ireland could only change with majority consent, and Ireland's future would be determined by the peoples of Ireland.

Down's syndrome Human condition caused by a chromosomal abnormality. It gives rise to varying degrees of mental retardation, decreased life expectancy, and perhaps physical problems, such as heart and respiratory disorders. The syndrome was first described by a British physician, J.L.H. Down. It is caused by the presence of an extra copy of CHROMOSOME 21, and detected by counting chromosomes in the cells of the FETUS during pre-natal testing. There is evidence that the risk of having a Down's child

increases with maternal age. Originally called 'Mongolism' by Down, this term is now obsolete.

Doyle, Sir Arthur Conan (1859–1930) Scottish novelist and physician. The novel *A Study in Scarlet* (1887) introduced his characters Sherlock Holmes and Dr Watson. A succession of hugely popular Sherlock Holmes stories followed, including *The Adventures of Sherlock Holmes* (1892), *The Memoirs of Sherlock Holmes* (1894) and *The Hound of the Baskervilles* (1902). Other works include *The Lost World* (1912).

D'Oyly Carte, Richard *See* CARTE, RICHARD D'OYLY

Drabble, Margaret (1939–) English novelist, sister of A.S. BYATT. Her debut novel was *The Summer Birdcage* (1963). *The Millstone* (1965) was filmed as *A Touch of Love*. Later work includes the trilogy *The Radiant Way* (1987), *A Natural Curiosity* (1989), and *The Gates of Ivory* (1991).

Draco (Dragon) Long, winding N constellation, representing the dragon slain by Hercules. It extends between URSA MAJOR and URSA MINOR, with the dragon's head near the star VEGA.

drag (air resistance) Force opposing the motion of a body through a gas or liquid. Aircraft experience drag as the friction of air over external surfaces. To combat drag, aircraft and cars have streamlined designs.

dragon Mythical scaly lizard, snake or fire-breathing monster. Often depicted with wings, talons and a lashing tail. In some traditions it has many heads, or changes shape at will. Sometimes, such as the tale of St GEORGE and the dragon, it is used symbolically as the personification of evil. In China and Japan, the dragon is identified with a beneficent force of nature.

dragonfly Swift-flying insect of the order Odonata. It has a long, slender, often brightly coloured abdomen, and two pairs of large membranous wings. Like the DAMSELFLY, it mates while flying. The carnivorous nymphs, which hatch from eggs laid on water plants, are aquatic. Wingspan: to 17cm (7in).

Drake, Sir Francis (*c*.1540–96) English mariner. In 1577–80, he circumnavigated the world in the *Golden Hind*, looting Spanish ships and settlements in the Pacific, and claiming California for England. Elizabeth I knighted Drake on his return. In 1587, his famous raid on CADIZ postponed the Spanish ARMADA, which he helped to defeat in 1588. He died during a raid on the Spanish colonies.

drama Art form, probably derived from primitive religious rituals. In the West, drama developed into a sophisticated art form in 5th-century BC Greece with the plays of AESCHYLUS, SOPHOCLES, EURIPIDES and ARISTOPHANES. GREEK DRAMA followed the unity of action, defined by ARISTOTLE in his *Poetics*. Classical Roman drama relied heavily on Greek models, and these in turn strongly influenced ELIZABETHAN and JACOBEAN drama, such as the plays of Thomas Kyd, Francis BEAUMONT, John FLETCHER, Christopher MARLOWE, Ben JONSON, and William SHAKESPEARE. In Spain, Lope de VEGA established the *comedia*, written in verse with three acts. NEO-CLASSICISM flourished in the reign of LOUIS

XIV with the tragedies of CORNEILLE and RACINE. The comedies of MOLIÈRE reflected the influence of the COMMEDIA DELL'ARTE. Twentieth-century drama received its impetus from the NATURALISM of CHEKHOV, IBSEN and STRINDBERG. The verse dramas of T.S. ELIOT marked the beginnings of MODERNISM. These experiments were extended by epic theatre, theatre of CRUELTY and theatre of the ABSURD. SURREALISM influenced the work of PIRANDELLO and Samuel BECKETT. *See also* CHINESE THEATRE; COMEDY; INDIAN THEATRE; JAPANESE THEATRE; TRAGEDY

Dravidian Family of languages spoken in S India by *c.*10 million people. The four major Dravidian languages are Telugu, Tamil, Kannada (Kanarese) and Malayalam. Tamil is also spoken in Sri Lanka. Brahui is spoken in Pakistan. Dravidian languages are unrelated to Indic languages, such as HINDI, which are a branch of INDO-EUROPEAN LANGUAGES.

Dreiser, Theodore Herman Albert (1871–1945) US writer. His first novel, *Sister Carrie* (1900), was considered immoral by its publisher and Dreiser distributed it himself. The *Cowperwood* trilogy includes *The Financier* (1912), *The Titan* (1914), and *The Stoic* (1947). Dresier's greatest work, *An American Tragedy* (1925), is based on the Chester Gillette-Grace Brown murder case of 1906.

Dresden City on the River Elbe, capital of Saxony state, SE Germany. First settled by Germans in the early 13th century. It suffered almost total destruction from Allied bombing during World War 2. Dresden china, famous since the 18th century, is in fact manufactured in Meissen. Industries: optical and precision instruments, glass, chemicals. Pop. (1999) 477,700.

Dreyfus Affair French political crisis arising from the conviction of Captain Alfred Dreyfus (1859–1935) for treason in 1894. Dreyfus was a Jewish army officer, convicted on evidence later proved false. In 1898, publication of *J'accuse*, an open letter by Émile ZOLA in defence of Dreyfus, provoked a bitter national controversy in which the opposing forces of republicanism and royalism almost resulted in civil war. Dreyfus, initially imprisoned, later received a presidential pardon.

drug In medicine, any substance used to diagnose, prevent or treat disease or aid recovery from injury. Although many drugs are still obtained from natural sources, scientists are continually developing synthetic drugs which work on target cells or microorganisms. Such drugs include ANTIBIOTICS. Some drugs interfere in physiological processes, such as anti-coagulants which render the blood less prone to clotting. Drugs also may be given to make good some deficiency, such as hormone preparations which compensate for an underactive gland.

drug addiction Psychological or physical dependence on a DRUG. **Physical** addiction is often manifested by withdrawal symptoms. Long-term drug use often produces tolerance. Physical addiction has been medically proven for NARCOTICS (such as HEROIN), depressants (such as BARBITURATES or ALCOHOL) and some STIMULANTS (such as NICOTINE). Other drugs, such as hallucinogens or hashish, are not thought to be physically addictive, but can produce PSYCHOSIS or PARANOIA. Two of the most common addictions are alcohol and nicotine, since these are easily available. Unlike narcotics, alcohol is physically harmful, especially to the brain and liver, and cigarette smoking annually accounts for more than 100,000 premature deaths in the United Kingdom alone. Addiction to 'hard' drugs (such as HEROIN or COCAINE) is not common, but drug-related crime makes up a significant percentage of crime statistics in many countries.

druids Pre-Christian Celtic religious leaders in ancient Britain, Ireland, and Gaul. Little is known of them, but they appear to have been judges and teachers as well as priests. In Britain and Gaul, the Romans suppressed druidism, but it survived in Ireland until the 5th century.

drum PERCUSSION instrument, generally a hollow cylinder or vessel with a skin stretched across the openings. It is struck with hands or a variety of sticks. Drums were among the earliest musical instruments; examples have been found dating from 6000 BC. Drums first appeared in European CLASSICAL MUSIC in the 18th century. In the 20th century, the role of drums in popular music greatly expanded. Electronic drum machines shape much contemporary dance music. *See also* TIMPANI

◄ **Dublin** One of the world's most famous cultural centres, Dublin is the capital of the Republic of Ireland. It is closely associated with many literary figures, in particular George Bernard Shaw, W.B. Yeats, Oscar Wilde and James Joyce. Each year, hundreds of tourists visit the city to follow the route around Dublin taken by Leopold Bloom, the central character in Joyce's modernist masterpiece *Ulysses* (1922).

drupe (stone fruit) Any FRUIT with a thin skin, fleshy pulp and hard stone or pip enclosing a single seed. Examples are plums, cherries, peaches, olives, almonds and coconuts.

Druse (Druzes) Members of a Middle Eastern religious sect. A breakaway group of the ISMAILIS, the Druse originated in the reign of al-Hakim (996–1021), sixth Fatimid CALIPH of Egypt, who claimed to be divine. They are named after al-Darazi, the first to proclaim the cult publicly. Stressing pure MONOTHEISM, they emphasize the possibility of direct communication with divinity as a living presence. They were persecuted in Egypt, fought against both Turks and local Christians, and against French rule in Syria in the 1920s. There are about 500,000 Druses living in Syria, LEBANON, and Israel.

Dryden, John (1631–1700) English poet and playwright. He became known for his *Heroic Stanzas* on Oliver Cromwell's death (1658); diplomatically followed by *Astraea Redux* (1660), praising Charles II. He was poet laureate from 1668 to 1688, when James II was ousted in the Glorious Revolution. Other poems include *Annus Mirabilis* (1667), the satires *Absalom and Achitophel* (1681), the allegory *The Hind and the Panther* (1687), and the ode *Alexander's Feast* (1693). Dryden also wrote numerous fine plays, his best-known are *All for Love* (1678) and *Marriage á la mode* (1673).

drypoint Quick ENGRAVING technique, probably originating in the 15th century, using a sharply pointed tool to draw lines in a metal plate. The drypoint steel can produce different qualities of line according to the amount of pressure.

dualism Doctrine in philosophy and metaphysics that recognizes two basic and mutually independent principles, such as mind and matter, body and soul, or good and evil. Dualism contrasts with MONISM. Both PLATO and DESCARTES were dualists, but more modern philosophers, influenced by the discoveries of science, have tended towards monism.

Dubai One of the seven federated states of the UNITED ARAB EMIRATES (UAE), on the Persian (Arabian) Gulf, SE Arabia; the capital is Dubai. First settled in the late 18th century, it was a dependency of Abu Dhabi until 1833. At the end of the 19th century, it became a British Protectorate. Dubai was at war with Abu Dhabi from 1945–48. In 1971 it became a founder member of the UAE. Oil was discovered in the early 1960s, and is the largest sector of its prosperous, export-driven economy. Area: *c.*3890sq km (1500sq mi). Pop. (2006) *c.* 1.4m.

Dubček, Alexander (1921–92) Czechoslovak statesman, Communist Party secretary (1968–69). Dubček was elected party leader at the start of the PRAGUE SPRING. His liberal reforms led to a Soviet invasion in August 1968, and Dubček was forced to resign and expelled from the party. Following the collapse of Czech communism, he was publicly rehabilitated and served as speaker of the federal parliament (1989–92).

Dublin (Baile Átha Cliath) Capital of the Republic of Ireland, at the mouth of the River Liffey on Dublin Bay. In 1014,

INTERNET

Dubai
► www.dubaitourism.co.ae
► www.godubai.com

Dubček, Alexander
► www.age-of-the-sage.org/
alexander_dubcek.html

Brian Boru recaptured it from the Danish. In 1170, it was taken by the English and became the seat of colonial government. Dublin suffered much bloodshed in nationalist attempts to free Ireland from English rule. Strikes beginning in 1913 finally resulted in the EASTER RISING (1916). Dublin was the centre of the late 19th-century Irish literary renaissance. It is now the commercial and cultural centre of the Republic. Notable sites include Christ Church Cathedral (1053), St Patrick's Cathedral (1190), Trinity College (1591), and the ABBEY THEATRE (1904). Industries: brewing, textiles, clothing. Pop. (2005) 985,000. *See* photo, page 285.

dubnium (symbol Db) Synthetic, radioactive transactinide element. Six isotopes have been synthesized. It was first reported by a Soviet team at Dubna in 1967. They claimed the isotopes of mass numbers 260 and 261, as a result of bombarding AMERICIUM with neon ions. In 1970, a team at the University of California claimed the isotope 260 (half-life 1.6 seconds) obtained by bombarding CALIFORNIUM with nitrogen nuclei. It was previously named HAHNIUM. Properties: at.no. 105; r.a.m. 262.

Du Bois, W.E.B. (William Edward Burghardt) (1868–1963) US civil-rights leader, writer, and educator. In 1905, he co-founded the Niagara movement that evolved into the NATIONAL ASSOCIATION FOR THE ADVANCEMENT OF COLORED PEOPLE (NAACP). He also helped organize the First Pan-Africanist Congress (1919). His works include *The Souls of Black Folk* (1903). *See also* PAN-AFRICANISM.

Dubrovnik Adriatic seaport in Dalmatia, Croatia. As a free city, it was an important trading post between the Ottoman empire and Europe, and a traditional place of asylum for persecuted peoples. It was devastated by an earthquake (1979), and a 1991 Serbian siege. Sites include a 14th-century mint, Franciscan and Dominican monasteries. It is an important tourist centre. Products: grapes, cheese, olives. Pop. (2001) 45,830.

Dubuffet, Jean (1901–85) French painter and sculptor. His best-known works are assemblages of materials (such as glass, sand, rope) arranged into crude shapes, called *pâtes*. He collected the work of untrained artists, coining the phrase *art brut*.

Duccio di Buoninsegna (c.1265–1319) Italian painter, first great artist of the Sienese School. He infused the rigid Byzantine style of figure painting with humanity and lyricism. Notable for dramatic depiction of religious subjects, he is often compared unfavourably with GIOTTO. Surviving works include *Rucellai Madonna* (1285) and Maestà altarpiece (1308–11).

Duchamp, Marcel (1887–1968) French painter. A radical art theorist, his *Nude Descending a Staircase* outraged visitors to the ARMORY SHOW. He produced few paintings, concentrating on abolishing the concept of aesthetic beauty. He was a leading member of New York DADA, inventing the concept of the 'ready-made'. His *Fountain* consisted of nothing but a urinal. His main work, *The Bride Stripped Bare by her Bachelors, Even* (1915–23), is a 'definitively unfinished' painting of metal collage elements on glass.

duck Worldwide waterfowl, related to the SWAN and GOOSE. Most nest in cool areas and migrate to warm areas in winter. All have large bills, short legs and webbed feet. Their colour is varied, and dense plumage is underlaid by down and waterproof feathers. There are two groups: **dabbling** ducks, which feed from the surface, and **diving** ducks. All eat seeds, insects, crustacea and molluscs. Most engage in complex courtship, and lay a large clutch of eggs. There are seven tribes: EIDERS, shelducks, dabbling ducks, perching ducks, pochards, sea ducks and stiff-tailed ducks. There are c.200 species. Length: 30–60cm (1–2ft); weight: to 7.2kg (16lb). Family Anatidae.

duck-billed platypus *See* PLATYPUS

duckweed Family (Lemnaceae) of four genera including 25 species of tiny, floating, aquatic flowering plants. The disc-like leaflets have a single 15cm (6in) trailing root.

due process of law Formal legal procedure to ensure that no one is deprived of life, freedom or property before proper legal authority has been obtained. It is enshrined in England's MAGNA CARTA and the 5th and 14th Amendments of the US CONSTITUTION. A major element of the process is a TRIAL.

Dufay, Guillaume (1400–74) Burgundian composer. He composed many motets and settings of the liturgy. His motets were grand, complex compositions written for specific events. He wrote some outstanding masses and secular songs.

Dufy, Raoul (1877–1953) French painter. He was associated with IMPRESSIONISM and FAUVISM, and is famous for his decorative racing and boating scenes.

dugong (sea cow) Large plant-eating aquatic mammal found in shallow coastal waters of Africa, Asia, and Australia. Grey and hairless, the dugong has no hind legs, and its forelegs are weak flippers. Length: 2.5–4m (8–13ft); weight: 270kg (600lb). Family Dugongidae.

duiker (duikerbok) Small, sub-Saharan African ANTELOPE usually found in scrubland. The female is larger than the male and occasionally carries stunted horns; the horns of the male are short and spiky. Duikers are grey to reddish-yellow. Height: up to 66cm (26in) at the shoulder; weight: up to 17kg (37lb). Family Bovidae; species *Sylvicapra grimmia*.

Duisburg City at the confluence of the Rhine and Ruhr rivers, Nordrhein-Westfalen, NW Germany. Chartered in 1129, it remained a free imperial city until the late 13th century. During World War 2, it was the centre of the German armaments industry, and suffered extensive bomb damage. Industries: iron, steel, textiles, chemicals. Pop. (1999) 521,300.

Dukas, Paul (1865–1935) French composer. His best-known work, the orchestral scherzo *The Sorcerer's Apprentice* (1897), shows his skilful orchestration and individual style. He also wrote the opera *Ariane et Barbe-Bleue* (1907).

dulcimer Medieval stringed instrument, originally Persian, with a flat, triangular sounding board and ten or more strings struck with hand-held hammers.

Dulles, John Foster (1888–1959) US statesman, secretary of state (1953–59) under Dwight D. EISENHOWER. A powerful opponent of communism, he became a back-room influence on the Republican Party in the 1940s, and served briefly in the Senate. He was a member of the US delegation at the San Francisco Conference that founded the United Nations (1945).

Dumas, Alexandre (1802–70) (*père*) French novelist and dramatist. He achieved success with romantic historical plays, such as *La Tour de Nesle* (1832). He is better known today for his swashbuckling novels, such as *The Count of Monte Cristo*, *The Three Musketeers* (1844–45) and *The Black Tulip* (1850).

Dumas, Alexandre (1824–95) (*fils*) French dramatist and novelist, illegitimate son of Alexandre DUMAS (*père*). His work stands in stark contrast to his father's exuberant historical romances. His first great success was *La Dame aux Camélias* (1852), which forms the basis of Verdi's opera *La Traviata*. His didactic later plays, such as *Les idées de Madame Aubray* (1867), helped to provoke French social reform.

Du Maurier, Daphne (1907–89) English novelist. Her romantic novels include *The Loving Spirit* (1931), *Jamaica Inn* (1936), *Rebecca* (1938), *Frenchman's Creek* (1941), and *My Cousin Rachel* (1951). She also wrote plays, short stories (including *The Birds*), and a biography of Branwell Brontë.

Dumfries and Galloway Region in SW Scotland, bounded SE by England and S by the Solway Firth; the capital is Dumfries. Major towns include Castle Douglas, Lockerbie and Stranraer. An agricultural region, with forestry and livestock raising. Area: 6396sq km (2470sq mi). Pop. (2001) 147,780.

dump In computing, information copied from computer memory to an output or storage device. It may be the entire contents of a file copied to another disk, or a print-out of the screen (screen dump).

Dunbar, Paul Laurence (1872–1906) US writer. His poetry, written in African-American dialect, is a bittersweet mixture of sadness and humour. His *Lyrics of Lowly Life* (1896) concerns Southern black life before the Civil War. His novels include *The Love of Landry* (1900).

Duncan, Isadora (1877–1927) US dancer, pioneer of MODERN DANCE. She achieved fame in Europe for her emotional, expressive style. Duncan died tragically when her scarf caught in the wheel of her car and strangled her. She wrote an autobiography, *My Life* (1926–27).

▲ **duck** Ducks were domesticated more than 3000 years ago. The picture shows Muscovy (A), buff Orpington (B), Aylesbury (C), khaki Campbell (D), Peking (E), Rouen (F) and Indian runner white (G).

Dundee City on the N shore of the Firth of Tay, Tayside, E Scotland. A centre of the Reformation in Scotland, Dundee is an important port and has a university (founded 1881). Industries: textiles, confectionery, engineering. Pop. (2001) 145,460.

dune Ridge of wind-blown particles, most often sand. They occur in deserts in many shapes: **barchans** (crescent-shaped) are formed by a constant wind; **seifs** are narrow ridges.

Dunedin City in SE South Island, New Zealand. Founded in 1848 by Scottish Free Church settlers, Dunedin grew after the discovery of gold in the 1860s. It is home to the University of Otago (1871). Industries: agricultural machinery and engineering. Pop. (2001) 114,342.

dung beetle Small to medium-sized SCARAB BEETLE. Some species form balls of dung as food for their larvae, and may roll the balls some distance before burying them. Family Scarabaeidae; species *Geotrupes stercorarius*.

Dunkirk (Dunkerque) Port at the entrance to the Straits of Dover, Nord department, NW France. It came under French rule in 1662. In World War 2, more than 300,000 Allied troops were evacuated from its beaches, many in small, privately owned boats, between May 29 and June 3, 1940, when the German army broke through to the English Channel. Today, it is France's third-largest port and one of the principal iron and steel producers in W Europe. Industries: oil refining, shipbuilding. Pop. (1999) 70,850.

Duns Scotus, John (1265–1308) Scottish theologian and scholastic philosopher. His main works were commentaries on the writings of the Italian theologian Peter Lombard. He founded a school of SCHOLASTICISM called 'Scotism'.

Dunstable, John (*c.*1390–1453) Important 15th-century English composer. Little is known about him, but masses, motets, and a few secular works survive. He gained recognition for his experiments in COUNTERPOINT and influenced Guillaume DUFAY and Gilles de Binchois.

duodenum First section of the small INTESTINE, shaped like a horseshoe. The pyloric sphincter, a circular muscle, separates it from the STOMACH. Alkaline BILE and pancreatic juices are released into the duodenum to aid the DIGESTION of food.

Du Pont de Nemours, Eleuthère Irénée (1771–1834) US industrialist, b. France. Founder of a huge chemical company and family business empire. He came to the USA in 1799 with his father, Pierre Samuel Du Pont de Nemours (1739–1817). They started a business producing high-quality gunpowder, and prospered from the War of 1812. The company, E.I. Du Pont de Nemours and Co., continues to trade.

Du Pré, Jacqueline (1945–87) English cellist. Soon after her London debut (1961), Du Pré became widely acknowledged as a remarkable talent. Multiple sclerosis cut short her career in 1973, but she continued to teach.

Duras, Marguérite (1914–96) French novelist and playwright, b. Indochina. Novels include *The Sea Wall* (1950), *The Sailor from Gibraltar* (1952), *Destroy, She Said* (1969), *The Lover* (1984) and *Summer Rain* (1990). Her best-known screenplay is *Hiroshima Mon Amour* (1959).

Durban Seaport on the N shore of Durban Bay, South Africa. Founded in 1835, the national convention initiating the Union of South Africa was held here. The University of Natal (1949) and Natal University College (1960) are here. Industries: shipbuilding, oil refining, and chemicals. Pop. (2005) 2,391,000.

Dürer, Albrecht (1471–1528) German painter, engraver, and designer of woodcuts, the greatest artist of the N RENAISSANCE. During Dürer's visits to Italy, he was influenced by artists such as LEONARDO DA VINCI. His personal synthesis of N and S European traditions deeply affected European art. Dürer's album of woodcuts, *The Apocalypse* (1498), established him as a supremely talented graphic artist. His paintings include *The Feast of the Rose Garlands* (1506) and *Four Apostles* (1526), which reveal his preoccupation with LUTHERANISM.

Durga In the Hindu pantheon, one of the names of the wife of SHIVA. Depicted as a 10–armed goddess, she is both destructive and beneficent but is worshipped today as a warrior against evil. Her festival, the Durga-puja, which occurs in September or October, is an occasion for family reunions.

Durham City and administrative district on the River Wear, NE England; the county town of Co. Durham. Founded by

◄ **Dürer** German artist, Albrecht Dürer's *Self-portrait* (1500), depicts the artist resembling Christ. The greatest artist of the northern Renaissance, he is perhaps best known for his albums of woodcuts, such as *The Apocalypse* (1498). These have a remarkably dense and subtle texture, creating paint-like tones. The Emperor Maximilian was a patron, and commissioned his famous *Rhinoceros* woodcut.

monks in the 10th century, it became a defensive outpost against the Scots and the seat of prince-bishops. Its cathedral (1093) contains the tomb of the Venerable BEDE, and an 11th-century castle is now part of the university (founded 1832). Durham is is home to the Gulbenkian Museum of Oriental Art and Archaeology (1960). Industries: textiles, carpet-weaving, engineering. Pop. (2001) 493,470.

Durham, John George Lambton, 1st Earl of (1792–1840) British statesman. One of the drafters of the Great REFORM ACT of 1832, he led the radical wing of the Whig Party. As governor general of Canada (1838), he produced a report which became the basis of British colonial policy.

Durkheim, Emile (1858–1917) French sociologist. Influenced by the POSITIVISM of Auguste COMTE, Durkheim used the methods of natural science to study human society, and is considered (along with Max WEBER) a founder of sociology. In *The Division of Labour in Society* (1893) and the *Elementary Forms of Religious Life* (1912), Durkheim argued that religion and labour were basic organizing principles of society. *The Rules of the Sociological Method* (1895) set out his methodology. *Suicide* (1897) outlines his theory of alienation (*anomie*).

Durrell, Gerald Malcolm (1925–95) British naturalist and author, b. India. Brother of Lawrence DURRELL, his humorous and stylish novels include *My Family and Other Animals* (1956) and *A Zoo in My Luggage* (1960). Other works include *Beasts in the Belfry* (1973) and *The Aye-Aye and I* (1992).

Durrell, Lawrence George (1912–90) British novelist and poet, b. India. Brother of Gerald DURRELL, his life in Greece and Egypt provided inspiration for most of his writing. His major work is the inventive tetralogy, *The Alexandria Quartet: Justine* (1957), *Balthazar* (1958), *Mountolive* (1958), and *Clea* (1960). Other novels include *Avignon Quintet* (1992). His *Collected Poems 1931–74* appeared in 1980.

Dürrenmatt, Friedrich (1921–90) Swiss dramatist, novelist and essayist. Influential in the post-1945 revival of German theatre, Dürrenmatt's works are ironic and display a nihilistic, black humour. His first play was *It is Written* (1947). *Woyzeck* (1972) is his most frequently performed play

Dushanbe (Dusanbe) Capital of Tajikistan, at the foot of the Gissar Mountains, Central Asia. Founded in the 1920s, it was known as Stalinabad from 1929–61. An industrial, trade and transport centre, it is the site of Tadzhik University and Academy of Sciences. Industries: cotton milling, engineering, leather goods, food processing. Pop. (2002 est.) 580,800.

Düsseldorf Capital of North Rhine-Westphalia, at the confluence of the rivers RHINE and Düssel, NW Germany. Founded in the 13th century, it was the residence of the dukes of Berg in the 14th-16th centuries. It became part of Prussia in 1815 and was under French occupation 1921–25. It is a cultural centre, with an Academy of Art and an opera house. Industries: chemicals, textiles, iron, steel. Pop. (1999) 568,500.

D

▲ **Dvořák** Czech composer Antonín Dvořák drew heavily on folk music, both Czech (for the polka rhythms) and American. While he was director (1892–95) of the National Conservatory, New York, he wrote his famous Ninth Symphony ("From the New World"). Although he was intrigued by opera, it is generally accepted that his stage works are of less significance than his orchestral pieces.

dust bowl Area of *c.*40 million ha (100 million acres) of the GREAT PLAINS, USA, that suffered extensively from wind erosion. Due to drought, overplanting and mismanagement, much of the topsoil was blown away in the 1930s. Subsequent soil conservation programmes have helped restore productivity.

Dutch Official language of the Netherlands, spoken by almost all of the country's 16 million inhabitants, and also in Netherlands Antilles and Surinam. Dutch is a Germanic language, belonging to the Indo-European family.

Dutch art Before the 16th century, the Church commissioned most Dutch art. Artists, such as LUCAS VAN LEYDEN, produced elaborate altarpieces. After independence the chief patrons were the merchant class. The 17th century was a golden age in portraiture, landscape, and genre painting, producing artists of the calibre of REMBRANDT, Jan VERMEER, Frans HALS, and Jacob van RUISDAEL. The 19th-century Hague School rekindled the landscape tradition. VAN GOGH, though Dutch-born, had close links with French art. In the 20th century, the main contributions came from Piet MONDRIAN and the De STIJL group.

Dutch East India Company *See* EAST INDIA COMPANY

Dutch East Indies Until 1949, the part of Southeast Asia that is now INDONESIA. An overseas territory of the Netherlands, it comprised the Malay Archipelago, SUMATRA, JAVA, BORNEO (except North Borneo), SULAWESI, MOLUCCAS, and the Lesser Sunda Islands (except Portuguese TIMOR). The Dutch colonized the islands in the early 17th century.

Dutch Wars Three 17th-century naval conflicts between Holland and England arising from commercial rivalry. The first war (1652–54) ended inconclusively, but with England holding the advantage. The second war (1665–67) followed England's seizure of New Amsterdam (New York). The Dutch inflicted heavy losses, and destroyed Chatham naval base in Kent; England modified its trade laws. The third war (1672–74) arose from English support of a French invasion of the Netherlands. The Dutch naval victory forced England to make peace.

Duvalier, 'Baby Doc' (Jean-Claude) (1951–) President of Haiti (1971–86). He succeeded his father, 'Papa Doc' DUVALIER as president-for-life. Though he introduced reforms and

disbanded the *Tonton Macoutes*, he retained his father's brutal methods. Civil unrest forced his exile to France in 1986.

Duvalier, 'Papa Doc' (François) (1907–71) President of Haiti (1957–71). He declared himself president-for-life and relied on the feared *Tonton Macoutes*, a vigilante group, to consolidate his rule. Under his ruthless regime, the longest in Haiti's history, the country's economy severely declined. He was succeeded by his son 'Baby Doc' DUVALIER.

Dvořák, Antonín (1841–1904) Czech composer. He adapted Czech FOLK MUSIC to a classical style. Best known for his orchestral works, his Cello Concerto (1895) is one of the supreme achievements of the form. His stay in the USA (1892–95) inspired his most popular work, the Symphony in E minor ("From the New World").

dye Substance, natural or synthetic, used to impart colour to various substances. Natural dyes have mostly been replaced by synthetic dyes, many derived from coal tar. Dyes are classified according to their application: **direct** dyes, such as sulphur and vat dyes, can be applied directly to fabric because they bind to the fibres. **Indirect** dyes, such as ingrain and mordant dyes, require a secondary process to fix the dye.

Dyfed-Powys Region in SW Wales; the administrative centre is Carmarthen. The Cambrian Mountains extend to the coast. Agriculture is based on livestock rearing, and the cultivation of crops. Industries: fishing, timber, woollen textiles and tourism. Area: 5765sq km (2226sq mi). Pop. (1999) 480,663.

dyke In engineering, a barrier or embankment designed to confine or regulate the flow of water. Dykes are used in reclaiming land from the sea by sedimentation (as practised in the Netherlands), and also as controls against river flooding. In geology, a dyke (dike) is an intrusion of igneous rock whose surface is different from that of the adjoining material.

Dyke, Sir Anthony van *See* VAN DYCK, SIR ANTHONY

Dylan, Bob (1941–) US popular singer and composer, b. Robert Allen Zimmerman. During the 1960s, Dylan successfully combined social protest poetry and FOLK MUSIC on albums such as *The Times They Are A-Changin'* (1963). His switch to ROCK music initially alienated many fans. Classic albums include *Highway 61 Revisited* (1965) and *Blood on the Tracks* (1975). Dylan's tunes include "All Along the Watchtower".

dynamics Branch of MECHANICS that deals with objects in motion. Its two main branches are: kinematics, which examines motion without regard to cause; and KINETICS, which also studies the causes of motion. *See also* INERTIA; MOMENTUM

dynamite Solid, blasting EXPLOSIVE. It contains NITROGLYCERINE incorporated in an absorbent base, such as charcoal or wood-pulp. Dynamite is used in mining, quarrying and engineering. Its properties are varied by adding ammonium nitrate or sodium nitrate. Alfred NOBEL invented dynamite in 1866.

dynamo (GENERATOR) Device that converts mechanical energy into electrical energy by the principle of ELECTROMAGNETIC INDUCTION that uses magnetism to produce an electric current. In a simple dynamo, a CONDUCTOR, usually an open coil of wire (armature), is placed between the poles of a permanent magnet. This armature is rotated within the magnetic field, inducing an ELECTRIC CURRENT. *See also* ALTERNATOR

dysentery Infectious disease characterized by DIARRHOEA, bleeding, and abdominal cramps. It spreads in contaminated food and water, especially in the tropics. There are two types: **bacillary** dysentery, caused by BACTERIA of the genus *Shigella*; and **amoebic** dysentery, caused by a type of PROTOZOA. Both forms are treated with antibacterials and fluid replacement.

dyslexia Impairment in reading ability. Dyslexia is usually diagnosed when difficulty in learning to read is clearly not due to inadequate intelligence, brain damage, or emotional problems. Its specific causes are disputed, but is probably due to a neurological disorder. Symptoms may include difficulty with writing, especially in spelling correctly.

dysprosium (symbol Dy) Silvery-white metallic element of the LANTHANIDE SERIES, first identified by Lecoq de Boisbaudran (1886). Its chief ores are monazite and bastnaesite. Its capacity to absorb neutrons makes it important in nuclear technology. Its compounds are also used in lasers. Properties: at.no. 66; r.a.m. 162.5; r.d. 8.54; m.p. 1409°C (2568°F); b.p. 2335°C (4235°F); most common isotope Dy^{164} (28.18%).

DYSENTERY

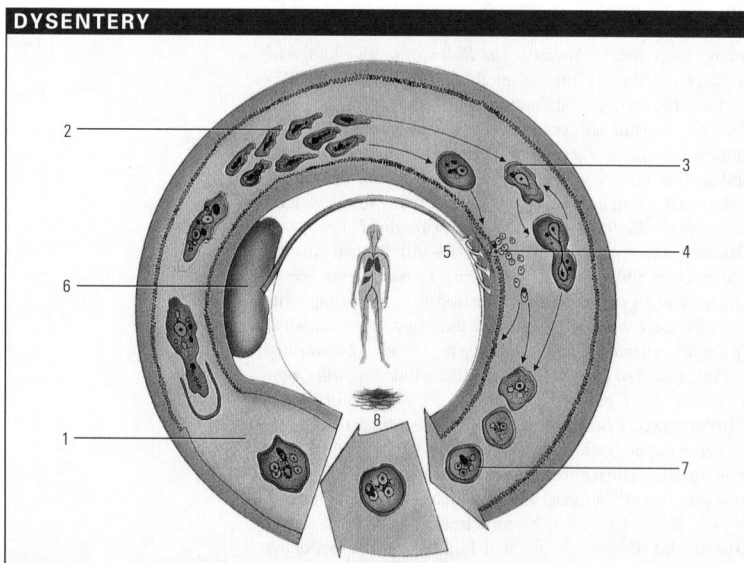

Amoebic dysentery is a widespread disease caused by a microscopic organism (Entamoeba histolytica), found in contaminated water and food. Entamoeba is a natural inhabitant of the gut, however, under certain conditions invasion of the gut wall occurs. Ingested Entamoeba cysts undergo division and

multiplication in the large intestine (1). After division, eight trophozoites (feeding protozoa) are produced (2), non-infective trophozoites remain in the intestine (3) feeding on bacteria and food particles. Infective trophozoites invade the gut wall (4), multiply and dissolve away tissues by producing protein-digesting enzymes. If organisms

enter the blood stream (5) they can be carried to the lungs (6), liver and brain where abscesses develop. Those released from gut abscesses reinvade tissues or form cysts (7) and are passed in the faeces. The disease is transmitted if flies carry cysts from faeces to food or, more commonly, by drinking contaminated water (8).

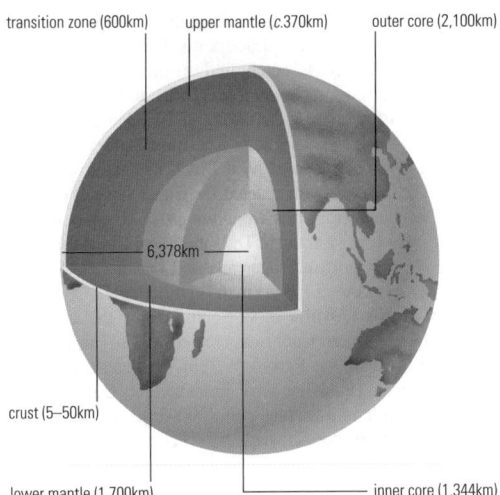

transition zone (600km) upper mantle (c.370km) outer core (2,100km)

6,378km

crust (5–50km)

lower mantle (1,700km) inner core (1,344km)

▲ **Earth** Formed c.4,600 million years ago, The Earth consists of concentric rings, from the uppermost crust to a solid inner core of nickel and iron. The intermediate layers, the mantle, are composed of hot and molten rock.

eagle Strong, carnivorous diurnal BIRD OF PREY. Sea and fishing eagles, such as the American bald eagle, are large birds found on sea coasts and inland bodies of water, where they feed on fish, small animals and carrion. Serpent eagles are reptile-eating birds. Large, harpy eagles inhabit tropical forests. Some Asian and African eagles are open-country predators. True (booted) eagles (Aquila) have long hooked bills, broad wings, powerful toes with long curved talons and feathered legs. They are usually brownish, black or grey with light or white markings. Length: 40–100cm (16–40in). Family Accipitridae. *See also* FALCON

Eakins, Thomas (1844–1916) US painter and photographer, regarded as one of the greatest artists of the 19th century. Eakins' painstaking search for anatomical accuracy aroused much controversy. His most celebrated paintings are *Gross Clinic* (1875), *The Chess Players* (1876), *The Swimming Hole* (1883), and *Agnew Clinic* (1889). He had a profound impact on the ASHCAN SCHOOL. *See also* LUMINISM

ear Organ of hearing and balance. In most mammals, it consists of the outer, middle and inner ear. The **outer** ear carries sound to the eardrum. The air-filled **middle** ear passes on and amplifies sound vibrations to the fluid-filled **inner** ear, where vibrations in the COCHLEA and semi-circular canals stimulate tiny hairs, which cause impulses to be sent via the auditory nerve to the brain.

Early, Jubal (1816–94) Confederate general in the US CIVIL WAR. A Virginian lawyer with military training, he opposed secession. He led a daring raid on Washington, D.C. (1864), but later suffered defeats and was relieved of his command after being crushed by superior forces at Waynesboro (March 1865).

Early English First phase of English GOTHIC architecture (13th century). It followed NORMAN ARCHITECTURE. In c.1250, French-inspired English stonemasons developed a native Gothic idiom: CANTERBURY Cathedral is an early example. Later works emphasized appearance: builders ornamented visible walls, such as Rievaulx Abbey, or made prominent use of VAULT ribbing, such as Lincoln Cathedral. *See also* DECORATED STYLE; PERPENDICULAR STYLE

Early English (Anglo-Saxon, or Old English) ENGLISH language from c.450 to 1100. It was the earliest form of English, descended from the Germanic languages of the ANGLO-SAXONS. It had a vocabulary of c.50,000 words and comprised four main dialects: Northumbrian, Mercian, Kentish, and West Saxon. The best Early English literature, such as BEOWULF, was written in Northumbrian. West Saxon became the chief dialect through ALFRED THE GREAT's unification of England.

Earp, Wyatt Berry Stapp (1848–1929) US law officer. In 1879, he became deputy sheriff of Tombstone, Arizona. The Earp brothers and Doc Holliday fought the Clanton gang in the famous gunfight at the O.K. Corral in 1881.

Earth Third major planet from the Sun, and the largest of the four inner, terrestrial planets. Water covers c.70% of the Earth's surface, at which the average temperature is 13°C (55°F). Continental land masses make up the other 30%. Earth has one natural satellite, the MOON. The dense CORE, rich in iron and nickel, is surrounded by a MANTLE of silicate rocks. The thin, outermost layer of lighter rock is the CRUST, which varies in depth from between 50km (30mi) – the thickest **continental** crust – to 5km (3mi) – the thinnest **oceanic** crust. The boundary between crust and mantle is called the MOHO (Mohorovičić) discontinuity. The solid, inner core rotates at a different rate from the molten outer layers, giving rise to the Earth's MAGNETIC FIELD. The crust and the uppermost mantle form the **lithosphere**, which consists of tightly fitting slabs called **plates**. The plates, which float on a semi-molten layer of mantle called the **asthenosphere**, move in interactions called PLATE TECTONICS. *See also* ATMOSPHERE

earthquake Tremor below or at the surface of the Earth which causes shaking in the crust. Shaking may last for only a few seconds, but widespread devastation can result. Earthquakes are caused by the Earth's crustal plates slipping against each other. Three different waves are created: primary/push (P), secondary/shake (S), and longitudinal/surface (L). P and s waves originate from the hypocentre (site of the rupture), up to 640km (400mi) deep. On the Earth's surface, they travel as L waves. The surface point directly above the hypocentre is the epicentre, where most damage is concentrated. A large earthquake is usually followed by smaller 'aftershocks'. An earthquake beneath the sea may cause a TSUNAMI. Earthquake prediction is a branch of SEISMOLOGY. Present methods indicate only a probability of earthquake activity, and cannot be used to predict actual events. The world's largest recorded earthquake (1960), in Chile, measured magnitude 9.5.

Earth Summit (1992) UNITED NATIONS Conference on Environment and Development, held in Rio de Janeiro, Brazil. The first serious global acknowledgement of the problems created by the impact of industrial society on the ENVIRONMENT. The Rio Declaration laid down principles of environmentally sound development and imposed limits on the emission of gases responsible for the GREENHOUSE EFFECT. A second summit (1997) in New York, USA, called for practical progress in reducing CARBON DIOXIDE emissions and strict enforcement of the Convention on Biodiversity. The EUROPEAN UNION pledged to cut CO_2 emissions to 15% below 1990 levels. The US agreed only to maintain its level of emissions. A third summit (2002) in Johannesburg, South Africa, raised the issue of

E/e, fifth letter of the Roman alphabet. Derived from an Egyptian hieroglyph of a man rejoicing, it entered the Semitic alphabet as the letter he. It was adopted by the Greeks as the letter epsilon before taking its present form.

EARTH: DATA

Diameter (equatorial): 12,756km
Mass: 5378 billion billion tonnes
Volume: 1083 billion km3
Density (water =1): 5.52
Orbital period: 365.3 days
Rotation period: 23h 56m 04s
Surface temperature: 290K

INTERNET

earthquake
▶ neic.usgs.gov

Earth Summit
▶ www.
johannesburgsummit.org

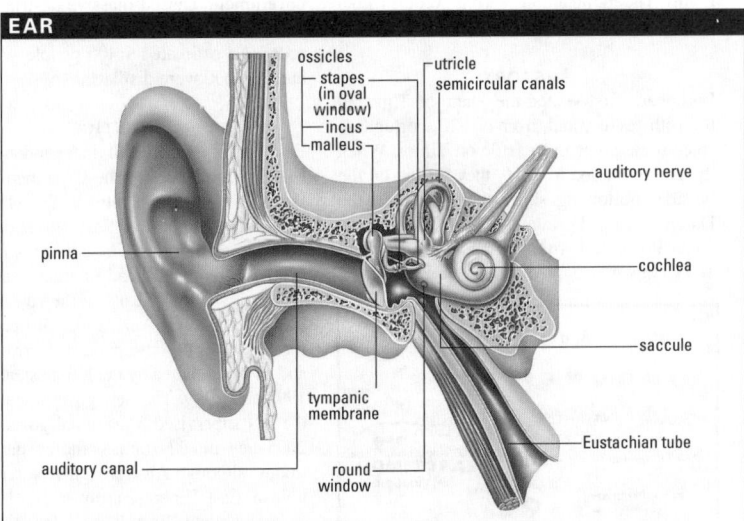

EAR

ossicles
stapes (in oval window)
incus
malleus
utricle
semicircular canals
auditory nerve
pinna
cochlea
saccule
tympanic membrane
Eustachian tube
auditory canal
round window

The ear divides into three parts – the outer, middle, and inner ear. The outer consists of the pinna and the auditory canal. The pinna funnels sound waves via the canal to the tympanic membrane. Tiny bones, called ossicles, amplify and transmit sound waves, which cause the oval window to vibrate, setting the fluids of the inner ear in motion. Hair cells in the cochlea and semicircular canals generate nerve impulses interpreted by the brain as sound. The semicircular canals also maintain balance and orientation.

sustainable development programmes in Africa as a way to beat poverty and protect the environment. *See also* ECOLOGY

earthworm Annelid with a cylindrical, segmented body and tiny bristles. Most worms are red, pink or brown, and live in moist soil. Their burrowing loosens and aerates the soil, helping to make it fertile. Length: 5cm-33m (2in-11ft). There are several hundred species. Class Oligochaeta; genus *Lumbricus*.

earwig Slender, flattened, brownish-black insect found in crevices and under tree bark. There are some 900 winged and wingless species worldwide. All have a pair of forceps at the hind end of the abdomen. Order Dermaptera; genus *Forficula*.

East Anglia Region of E England, made up of NORFOLK, SUFFOLK and parts of CAMBRIDGESHIRE and ESSEX. It was a powerful Anglo-Saxon kingdom of the late 6th century. Farming on its fertile land includes grain, vegetables and livestock. Industries: market gardening, tourism and fishing.

East China Sea Northern branch of the China Sea, bordered by Korea and Japan (N), China (W), Taiwan (S) and the Ryukyu Islands (E). Area: *c.*1,249,160sq km (482,300sq mi).

Easter Feast celebratiing the resurrection of JESUS CHRIST on the third day after his crucifixion. It is the oldest and greatest Christian feast, celebrated on the Sunday following the first full moon between March 21 and April 25.

Easter Island (Isla de Pascua) Volcanic island in the SE Pacific; the chief town is Hanga Roa. The most isolated island in Polynesia, it was discovered by a Dutch navigator on Easter Day, 1722. Chile has administered the island since 1888. It is famous for the hieroglyphs (*rongorongo*) and stone statues, standing up to 12m (40ft) high. The subtropical climate allows a variety of crops, such as sugarcane and bananas. Industries: farming, tourism. Area: 163sq km (63sq mi). Pop. (2000) 3,618.

Eastern Cape Province in SE South Africa; the capital is East London. Eastern Cape was created in 1994 from the E part of the former CAPE PROVINCE. It incorporates the former, apartheid-created homelands of Transkei and Ciskei. Area: 169,600sq km (65,466sq mi). Pop. (2000 est.) 6,978,387.

Eastern Orthodox Church *See* ORTHODOX CHURCH, EASTERN

EAST TIMOR

The Democratic Republic of East Timor is a small island nation in South-east Asia. It became part of Indonesia in 1975, but achieved independence in 2002, ending almost 500 years of foreign domination.

The Timor Sea separates East Timor from Australia, which lies about 500km [310mi] away. East Timor occupies the NE part of the island of Timor. It also includes some small islands and the enclave of Oscùsso-Ambeno on the NW coast of West Timor, the Indonesian part of the island. The land is largely mountainous, rising to about 2,960m [9,711ft].

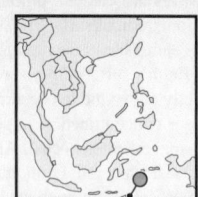

CLIMATE

East Timor has a monsoon climate, with high temperatures throughout the year. The average temperature is more than 24°C [75°F], although the mountainous zone is cooler. The monsoon extends from November to May. The average annual rainfall is less than 1,500mm [59in]. The mountainous zone is wetter, with a shorter dry period of four months.

HISTORY

Europeans first visited the island of Timor in the 16th century and, from *c.*1520, Portuguese spice traders began to settle on Timor. When the Dutch landed in 1620, they settled on the W side. Following skirmishing between the Dutch and the Portuguese, East Timor came under Portuguese rule by treaties in 1859 and 1893. Japan occupied Timor between 1942

and 1945 during World War 2, but the Portuguese returned after Japan was defeated. Following a coup in 1974, the Portuguese government declared its intention to abandon its colonies. The Portuguese withdrew from East Timor in August 1975 and FRETILIN (the Revolutionary Front for an Independent East Timor) declared the territory independent. In December 1975, Indonesia seized the territory, which became the 27th province of Indonesia named Timor Timur.

Indonesian rule proved oppressive and guerrilla resistance, led by the independence movement FRETILIN, grew. In 1999, Indonesia agreed to let the people of East Timor vote on independence or local autonomy in a UN-supervised referendum. The people voted by almost 99% for independence. East Timor declared itself independent. However, pro-Indonesian militias, who were widely believed to have the backing of the Indonesian government, caused massive destruction until an international peace-keeping force restored order. An estimated 1,400 people were killed and 250,000 were displaced.

POLITICS

East Timor gained full independence on 20 May 2002 and became the 191st member of the United Nations in September. The UN set up a Mission of Support in East Timor to help the Timorese authorities. The country's first president, a ceremonial head of state, was Xanana Gusmao who took 82.6% of the votes in a presidential election in April 2002. Gusmao was the former leader of the separatist guerrilla fighters and had been jailed by the Indonesians between 1992 and 1999. The new government replaced the UN-supervised transitional government. In 2005 the United Nations withdrew the last of its troops, although Australian troops remained to train an East Timorese army.

Independent East Timor faced problems bringing to trial those responsible for atrocities committed during the country's violent transition. An Indonesian court tried people for human rights abuses in East Timor in 1999 and a joint Indonesian and East Timorese Truth and Friendship Commission was established.

AREA 14,874sq km
[5,743sq mi]
POPULATION 1,085,000
CAPITAL (POPULATION)
Dili (52,000)
GOVERNMENT Multiparty republic
ETHNIC GROUPS Austronesian
(Malayo-Polynesian), Papuan
LANGUAGES Tetum, Portuguese (both official),
Indonesian, English
RELIGIONS Roman Catholic 90%, Muslim 4%,
Protestant 3%
CURRENCY US dollar = 100 cents

Organizations including the UN have criticized the Truth and Friendship Commission, describing it as an attempt to bury the past rather than providing justice.

Violence broke out in 2006 after 600 members of the army were sacked, causing a national crisis, but it was brought under control with Australian assistance. In 2007 support for the FRETILIN government declined and Gusmao became prime minister at the head of a newly formed party, but the country remained unstable. Both Gusmao and José Ramos-Horta, the country's president, survived assassination attempts in early 2008.

ECONOMY

Agriculture is the main activity. Arable farms cover about 5% of the land and coffee is widely grown. Crops include bananas, cassava, maize, rice, soya beans and sweet potatoes. Coffee, sandalwood and marble are exported.

Following independence, the new country, with its shattered economy and infrastructure, was heavily dependent on foreign aid. However, offshore oil and gas deposits hold out hope for future development. Production of natural gas began in 2004. The oil and gas deposits are located under the Timor Sea and, following independence, East Timor denounced the maritime boundary given to Australia by Indonesia because it gave Australia control over what was thought to be the richest oil field region. In 2005 Australia agreed on a division of the expected revenues on the oil and gas deposits, while East Timor agreed to postpone discussions on the disputed maritime boundary.

Easter Rising (April 24, 1916) Rebellion by Irish nationalists against British rule, led by Patrick PEARSE of the Irish Republican Brotherhood (IRB) and James CONNOLLY of SINN FÉIN. The British Navy intercepted an arms shipment from Germany and arrested Roger CASEMENT, but the insurrection went ahead as planned. On Easter Monday, c.1,500 volunteers seized buildings in Dublin and proclaimed Ireland a republic. By April 29, the British had crushed the rising: 16 of the were executed and 2,000 others imprisoned. In 1917, Eamon DE VALERA was granted an amnesty and nationalist sentiment produced an electoral victory for Sinn Féin.

East India Company Name of several organizations set up by European countries in the 17th century to trade E of Africa. Louis XIV founded the French company in 1664, and it set up colonies on several islands in the Indian Ocean. It was abolished in 1789. The Dutch company was founded (1602), with headquarters in Jakarta from 1619. It dissolved in 1799. The British company was set up in 1600 to compete for the East Indian spice trade. In the 18th century, Robert CLIVE defeated the French company and captured BENGAL (1757). Corruption and mismanagement led William PITT (the Younger) to make the company responsible to Parliament: it became an administrative arm of colonial government in India and lost its commercial monopolies in 1813. The INDIAN MUTINY (1857) led to its powers being transferred to the British Crown and the company dissolved in 1873.

Eastman, George (1854–1932) US photographic inventor and manufacturer, who popularized affordable amateur still and motion picture PHOTOGRAPHY. He introduced innovations in photographic technology during the late 1800s and founded the Eastman Kodak Company (1892).

East Sussex County of SE England. The county town is Lewes, other major towns include BRIGHTON, Hastings and Eastbourne. Its S border is the English Channel. The chalky South Downs run parallel to the coast. In the N, the Weald is drained by the Ouse and Rother. Most of the region was included in the kingdom of WESSEX. In 1066, William the Conqueror met the forces of Harold II in the Battle of HASTINGS. The local economy is dominated by agriculture, services and tourism. Area: 1,795sq km (693sq mi) Pop. (2001) 492,324.

East Timor Independent state established after the overthrow of Indonesian rule in 1999. For history, *see* TIMOR

Eastwood, Clint (1930–) US film actor and director. Following the television series *Rawhide*, Eastwood played the drifter in the 'spaghetti WESTERNS' *A Fistful of Dollars* (1964), *For a Few Dollars More* (1965) and *The Good, the Bad and the Ugly* (1967). *Dirty Harry* (1971) and its four sequels were uncompromising. As a director, he earned praise for *The Outlaw Josey Wales* (1976) and *Bird* (1988). Eastwood won Academy Awards for best director, best actor, and best picture for *Unforgiven* (1992).

ebola Virus that causes haemorrhagic fever. The ebola virus was first identified in humans during an outbreak in Congo in 1976. It is acquired through contact with contaminated body fluids. Death rates can be as high as 90%.

ebony Hard, fine-grained dark heartwood of various Asian and African trees of the genus *Diospyros* in the ebony family (Ebenaceae). Its major commercial tree is the macassar ebony (*D. ebenum*) of S India and Malaysia. It is valued for woodcarving, cabinetwork, and parts of musical instruments.

Ebro River, N Spain. Rising at Fontibre in the Catabrian Mountains, it flows ESE, then SE through Logrono and ZARAGOZA, and into the Mediterranean below Tortosa. It is the longest river whose entire course is in Spain. Length: 910km (565mi).

eccentricity (symbol *e*) One of the elements of an ORBIT. It indicates how much an elliptical orbit departs from a circle. It is found by dividing the distance between the two foci of the ellipse by the length of the major axis. A circle has an eccentricity of 0, a parabola an eccentricity of 1.

Ecclesiastes OLD TESTAMENT book of aphorisms, compiled under the pseudonym 'the Preacher, the son of David'. Evidence suggests that the book dates from after the BABYLONIAN CAPTIVITY. Its theme is the vanity and emptiness of human life and aspirations, relieved only by faith in God.

Ecclesiasticus Book of the APOCRYPHA, an example of Jewish WISDOM LITERATURE. The work of a Jewish scribe, Jesus ben Sirach, written in c.180 BC. Although originally in Hebrew, it found its way into the SEPTUAGINT and not the Jewish canon. A handbook of practical and moral advice, the central theme is the relationship between wisdom and God.

echidna (spiny anteater) MONOTREME related to the PLATYPUS, found in Australia and New Guinea. It is a primitive egg-laying mammal with a CLOACA, spines on the upper body, and an elongated snout. Length: 30–77cm (12–30in).

echinoderm Phylum of spiny-skinned marine invertebrate animals. Radially symmetrical with five axes, their skin consists of calcareous plates. Their hollow body cavity includes a complex, internal fluid-pumping system and tube feet. They reproduce sexually, and produce a bilaterally symmetrical larva resembling that of chordates; regeneration also occurs. Species include SEA URCHIN, SEA CUCUMBER, and STARFISH.

Echo In Greek mythology, a mountain nymph condemned to speak only in echoes because her chattering distracted the goddess HERA from the infidelity of ZEUS. Unable to declare her love for NARCISSUS, Echo pined away in solitude until her bones turned to stone and only her voice remained.

echo Reflected portion of a wave, such as SOUND or RADAR, from a surface so that it returns to the source and is heard after a short interval. High notes provide a better sound echo than low notes. Echoes are useful in NAVIGATION.

echolocation In animals, system of orientation used principally by WHALES and BATS. The animal emits a series of short, high-frequency sounds, and from the returning ECHO it gauges its environment. Bats also use the system for hunting.

eclipse In astronomy, partial or total obscuration of the light from one celestial body as it passes behind another body: the most familiar are lunar and solar eclipses. Within any year, a maximum of seven eclipses can occur, either four solar and three lunar or five solar and two lunar. A **solar** eclipse occurs when the MOON passes between EARTH and the SUN, blocking the Sun's light from the part of the Earth on which the Moon's shadow falls. It can only happen at new Moon. The maximum duration of a **total** solar eclipse is 7min 8sec. A **lunar** eclipse occurs when the Earth lies between the Sun and the Moon, blocking the Sun's light from the Moon. It can only happen at full Moon. The longest duration of a lunar eclipse is 1hr 42min. The Earth and Moon both cast a shadow into space away from the Sun. The shadow consists of a region of total darkness (**umbra**) and partial darkness (**penumbra**).

Eco, Umberto (1932–) Italian writer and academic. He lectured on aesthetics, architecture, visual communications, and SEMIOTICS, and his writing is based on these themes. His best-known work is the erudite philosophical thriller *The Name of the Rose* (1981). Other novels include *Foucault's Pendulum* (1989) and *The Island Before Time* (1994).

ecology Biological study of relationships of organisms to their ENVIRONMENT and to one another. The term was coined (1866) by Ernst Haeckel. Ecologists study **populations** (groups of individual organisms), **communities** (different organisms sharing the same environment), or ECOSYSTEMS. The maximum population that can be sustained by an environment's resources is called its **carrying capacity**. Within the BIOSPHERE, natural cycles (CARBON CYCLE, HYDROLOGICAL CYCLE, NITROGEN CYCLE and oxygen cycle) are assisted when

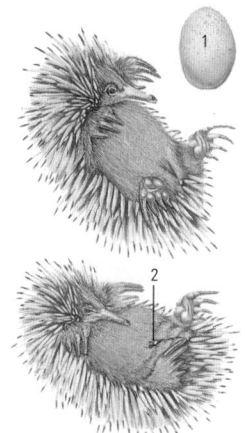

▲ **echidna** An example of a primitive mammal, the echidna (spiny anteater) is classified as a monotreme. Instead of giving birth to live young like other mammals, it lays a tiny egg. The egg (1) is soft-shelled and resembles a reptile's egg. Once the egg is laid, the echidna uses its hind limbs to roll it to a special incubation groove (2). The minute hatchling is about 1.25cm (0.5in) long.

INTERNET

Eastern Cape
▶ www.ecprov.gov.za

East Timor
▶ www.gov.east-timor.org

▼ **eclipse** When the Moon passes between the Sun and the Earth, it causes a partial eclipse of the Sun if the Earth passes through the Moon's outer shadow, or a total eclipse if the inner cone shadow crosses the Earth's surface. In a lunar eclipse, the Earth's shadow crosses the Moon and, again, provides either a partial or total eclipse. Eclipses of the Sun and the Moon do not occur every month because of the 5° difference between the plane of the Moon's orbit and the plane in which the Earth moves.

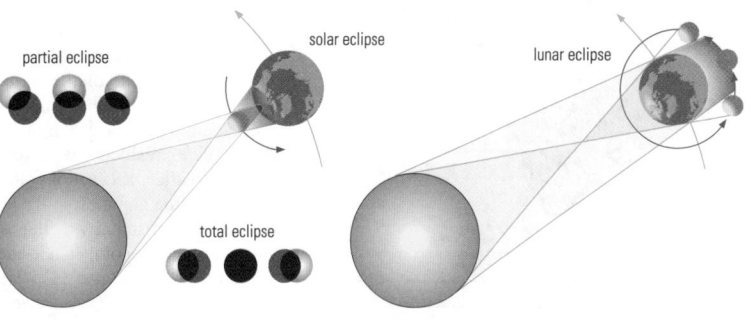

E

the biological diversity of species fills ecological niches. This diversity produces **climax communities**, and an extensive climax **community** is called a BIOME. **Applied ecology** is the practical management of natural resources and environments.
economics Social science studying the allocation of resources in the production of commodities, and the distribution of these commodities for CONSUMPTION in society. Adam SMITH's *The Wealth of Nations* (1776) is often cited as the first economic treatise. Smith's arguments in favour of FREE TRADE form the basis of CLASSICAL ECONOMICS. Refinements to classical economics included the theory of marginal utility, which argued that need determined value. John Maynard KEYNES' *General Theory of Employment, Interest and Money* (1936) was an attempt to deal with economic DEPRESSION and mass UNEMPLOYMENT. The pressures of INFLATION led to the development of MONETARISM and the re-emergence of high UNEMPLOYMENT. Economics developed into two areas: **microeconomics** studies the economics of firms and individuals, and the workings of individual market mechanisms; and **macroeconomics** studies whole economic systems. *See also* CONSERVATISM; DEFLA-

TION; FEUDAL SYSTEM; LAISSEZ-FAIRE; MERCANTILISM; SOCIALISM; SUPPLY AND DEMAND, LAW OF
ecosystem Interacting community of organisms and their physical ENVIRONMENT. It includes all organic life in an area with the soil, water and other inorganic components, and the ecological interactions that take place within and between the organic and inorganic. It is a complete ecosystem only if it can incorporate energy into organic compounds and pass it from organism to organism, and if it recycles elements for re-use. Examples include meadows, woodland and ponds.
ecstasy (MDMA) (3,4–methylnedioxymethylamphetamine) An AMPHETAMINE-based drug, which raises body temperature and blood pressure by inducing the release of adrenaline and targeting the neurotransmitter SEROTONIN. Users experience short-term feelings of euphoria, rushes of energy and increased tactility. Withdrawal can involve bouts of DEPRESSION and insomnia. Some deaths have resulted from use of ecstasy.
ectopic Occurrence of a pregnancy outside the UTERUS, such as in the FALLOPIAN TUBE. The EMBRYO cannot develop normally, and spontaneous ABORTION often occurs. If not, urgent surgery is needed to save the mother from serious haemorrhage.

ECUADOR

The Republic of Ecuador straddles the Equator on the w coast of South America. Three ranges of the high Andes Mountains form the backbone of the country. Between the towering, snow-capped peaks of the mountains, some of which are volcanoes, lie a series of high plateaux, or basins. Nearly half of Ecuador's population lives on these plateaux.

w of the Andes lie the flat coastal lowlands, which border the Pacific Ocean and average 100 km [60 mi] in width. The E alluvial lowlands, often called the Oriente, are drained by headwaters of the River AMAZON.

They introduced their language, Quechua, which is widely spoken today. In 1532, Spanish forces, under Francisco PIZARRO, defeated the Incas at Cajamarca and established the Spanish viceroyalty of QUITO. The country became independent in 1822, following a war of independence in which a Spanish force was defeated near Quito by an army led by General Antonio Jose de SUCRE. Ecuador joined Gran Colombia, a confederation which also included Colombia and Venezuela, but it became a separate nation in 1830.

In 1832, Ecuador annexed the volcanic GALAPAGOS ISLANDS, which lie 970 km [610 mi] w of Ecuador, of which they form a province. The archipelago, which contains six main islands and more than 50 smaller ones, later became world-famous through the writings of Charles Darwin, who visited the islands in 1835. His descriptions of the unique endemic flora and fauna gave him crucial evidence for his theory of natural selection.

AREA 283,561sq km (109,483sq mi)
POPULATION 13,756,000
CAPITAL (POPULATION) Quito (1,514,000)
GOVERNMENT Multiparty republic
ETHNIC GROUPS Mestizo (mixed White/Amerindian) 65%, Amerindian 25%, White 7%, Black 3%
LANGUAGES Spanish (official), Quechua
RELIGIONS Roman Catholic 95%
CURRENCY US dollar = 100 cents

CLIMATE

The climate in Ecuador is greatly influenced by the altitude. The coastal lowlands are hot, despite the cooling effect of the cold offshore Peru Current. The Andes have spring temperatures throughout the year, while the E lowlands are hot and humid. The rainfall is heaviest in the E lowlands and the N coastal lowlands.

HISTORY

The Inca people of Peru conquered much of what is now Ecuador in the late 15th century.

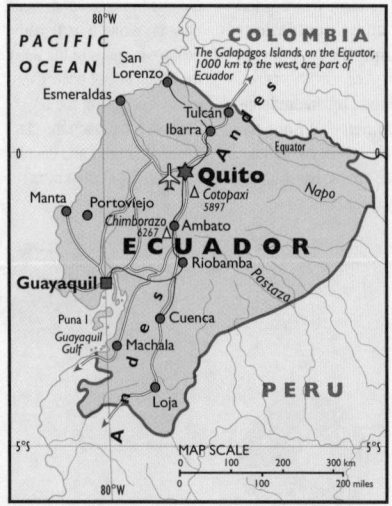

MAP SCALE
0   100   200   300 km
0   100   200 miles

POLITICS

The failure of successive governments to tackle the country's many social and economic problems caused great instability in Ecuador throughout the 20th century. A war with Peru in 1941 led to loss of territory and border disputes flared up again in 1995, although the two countries eventually signed a peace treaty in January 1998.

Military regimes ruled the country between 1963 and 1966 and again from 1976 to 1979. The second of these military juntas restored civilian government under a new constiution. Civilian governments have ruled Ecuador since multiparty elections in 1979, but politics remained volatile throughout the 1980s and 1990s. A state of emergency, albeit of short duration, was declared in 1986. In 1995, the vice-president was forced to leave the country after accusations that he had bribed opposition deputies.

In 1996 the president was deposed on the grounds of mental incompetence and, in 1998, accusations of fraud marred the victory of

President Jamil Mahaud of the centre-right Popular Democracy Party. The early years of the 21st century were marked by political instability as successive presidents faced opposition from the military and public demonstrations. In 2000, economic problems led Ecuador to adopt the US dollar as its sole unit of currency. In 2006 elections, Raffael Correa became president, promising anti-corruption measures. He embarked on a programme of socialist reforms funded by an increase in the government's share of oil revenues.

ECONOMY

The World Bank classifies Ecuador as a 'lower-middle-income' developing country. Agriculture employs 10% of the populous. Bananas, cocoa and coffee are all important export crops. Other products in the hot coastal lowlands include citrus fruits, rice and sugar cane, while beans, maize and wheat are important in the highlands. Cattle are raised for dairy products and meat, while fishing is important in the coastal waters. Forestry is a major activity. Ecuador produces balsa wood and such hardwoods as mahogany. Mining is important and oil and oil products now play a major part in the economy. Ecuador started to export oil in the early 1970s and is a member of the Organization of Petroleum Exporting Countries. Manufactures include cement, Panama hats, paper products, processed food and textiles. Major exports are food, live animals, and mineral fuels. Ecuador's main trading partners are the United States and Colombia.

Ecuador Republic in NW South America. *See* country feature

ecumenical council (general council) Ecclesiastical convention of worldwide Church representatives. Pronouncements are considered binding on all church members. All Christians recognize the first seven councils, the last of which was held in NICAEA in 787. The Roman Catholic Church recognizes 21 ecumenical councils convened by various popes. Since the REFORMATION, the councils have been restricted to Roman Catholics. The most recent was the Second Vatican Council (1962–65).

ecumenical movement Movement to restore the lost unity of Christendom. In its modern sense, it began with the Edinburgh Missionary Conference of 1910, and led to the foundation of the WORLD COUNCIL OF CHURCHES in 1948. *See also* BASEL, COUNCIL OF; CHALCEDON, COUNCIL OF; CONSTANCE, COUNCIL OF; LATERAN COUNCILS; TRENT, COUNCIL OF

eczema Inflammatory condition of the skin, a form of DERMATITIS characterized by dryness, itching, rashes and blister formation. It can be caused by contact with a substance, such as a detergent, to which the skin has been sensitized, or a general ALLERGY. Treatment is usually with a corticosteroid ointment.

Eddington, Sir Arthur Stanley (1882–1944) English astronomer and physicist. He pioneered the use of atomic theory to study the constitution of stars. Among his discoveries were the mass-luminosity relationship and the degeneration of matter by WHITE DWARFS. Eddington helped popularize the theory of RELATIVITY, and in 1919 obtained proof of the general theory that gravity bends light by measuring stars close to the Sun during a solar ECLIPSE.

Eddy, Mary Baker (1821–1910) US founder of CHRISTIAN SCIENCE (1879). She claimed to have rediscovered the secret of primitive Christian healing after an instantaneous recovery from serious injury. She expounded her system in *Science and Health With Key to the Scriptures* (1875).

edelweiss Small PERENNIAL native to the Alps and other Eurasian mountains. It has white, downy leaves and small,yellow flower heads enclosed in whitish-yellow bracts. Family Asteraceae (COMPOSITAE); species *Leontopodium alpinum.*

Eden, Sir (Robert) Anthony, 1st Earl of Avon (1897–1977) British statesman, prime minister (1955–57) and Britain's youngest foreign secretary (1935). He resigned (1938) in protest at the of APPEASEMENT policy of Neville CHAMBERLAIN. He served again as foreign secretary (1940–45, 1951–55), and succeeded Winston CHURCHILL as Conservative prime minister. Ill health and his mishandling of the SUEZ CANAL Crisis (1956) forced Eden to resign. He was succeeded by Harold MACMILLAN.

Eden, Garden of In GENESIS 2, garden created by God as the home of ADAM and EVE. They lived in the garden and enjoyed its fruits without toil, until they were banished for eating the forbidden fruit from the tree of knowledge. The Garden of Eden is mentioned in the KORAN and is equated with paradise.

edentate (Lat. 'with all the teeth removed') Any member of the small order Edentata of North and South American mammals found from Kansas to Patagonia. There are *c.*30 species, including ARMADILLO, SLOTH, and ANTEATER. Only the anteaters are truly toothless.

Edgar (943–75) King of England (959–75), younger son of EDMUND I. In 957 he succeeded his brother Edwy as king of Mercia and Northumberland. In 958 he recalled Saint Dunstan from exile and assisted in the revival of monasticism. His CORONATION (973) at Bath was the first of its kind. He was succeeded by his son, EDWARD THE MARTYR. *See also* DANELAW

Edgehill, Battle of (October 23, 1642) First encounter of Parliamentarians and Royalists in the English CIVIL WAR, near Banbury, Oxfordshire. The Royalists were outnumbered (11,000 men to the Parliamentarians' 13,000), but the result was to their advantage.

Edinburgh Capital of Scotland, in Lothian region. The city grew steadily when Malcolm III made Edinburgh Castle his residence (11th century), and became the capital of Scotland in the early 15th century. It flourished as a cultural centre in the 18th and 19th centuries around figures such as David HUME, Adam SMITH and Sir Walter SCOTT. The new, devolved

Scottish Parliament is in the city. Industries: brewing, tourism, chemicals, printing and publishing. Pop. (2001) 449,020.

Edinburgh, Duke of *See* PHILIP, PRINCE

Edison, Thomas Alva (1847–1931) US inventor. Edison made many important inventions, such as the telegraph, phonograph (1877), the first commercially successful electric light (1879) and improvements to the electricity distribution system. By the time of his death, he patented more than 1,000 inventions. During World War 1, he worked for the US government on anti-submarine weapons. Most of his companies merged into the General Electric Company (GEC) in 1892.

Edmonton Capital of ALBERTA province, on the North Saskatchewan River, SW Canada. Founded in 1795, it developed with the arrival of the railway in 1891 and became capital in 1905. Edmonton enjoyed a boom with the discovery of oil after World War 2. Industries: coal mining, natural gas, petrochemicals, oil refining. Pop. (2005) 1,005,000.

Edmund I (921–46) King of Wessex (939–46). Faced with a Viking invasion, he relinquished Northumbria and much of the E Midlands. Between 942 and 944, he regained most of the territory and reunited the kingdom.

Edmund II (*c.*980–1016) (Edmund Ironside) King of the English (1016), son of ETHELRED II (THE UNREADY). In 1015 he became ruler of the Danelaw. Edmund resisted the Danish King CANUTE II, who defeated him at the Battle of Ashingdon (1016). Forced to divide the kingdom, retaining only Wessex, Edmund died shortly after, leaving Canute as sole ruler.

Edo Japanese city, renamed TOKYO when it became the official capital and imperial residence in 1868. Edo was the seat of government under the TOKUGAWA shogunate (1603–1868), when the emperor lived at Kyoto. The Edo period was an era of unparalleled peace, economic advance and culture.

Education and Skills, UK Department for (DfES) British government department responsible for education in England. Headed by the secretary of state for education, its function is the broad allocation of capital resources for education, provision and training of teachers, and the setting of educational standards. The department works in cooperation with local education authorities (LEAs), which administer the day-to-day running of schools, and with the University Grants Committee which administers the universities.

Edward I (1239–1307) King of England (1272–1307), son and successor of HENRY III. His suppression of the BARONS' WAR, led by Simon de MONTFORT, made him de facto king. In 1270 he joined the Ninth Crusade, and was crowned on his return (1274). He conquered Wales and incorporated it into England (1272–84). In 1296 he captured the Scottish coronation stone from Scone, but William WALLACE and ROBERT I led Scottish resistance. Edward's reforms are central to British legal and constitutional history. The Statutes of WESTMINSTER codified common law. Edward's foreign ambitions led to the formation of the MODEL PARLIAMENT (1295). His son, EDWARD II, inherited high taxation and the enmity of Scotland.

Edward II (1284–1327) King of England (1307–27), son and successor of EDWARD I. His reliance on his friend Piers Gaveston alienated his barons who drafted the Ordinances of 1311, which restricted royal power and banished Gaveston, whom they killed in 1312. Edward was routed at BANNOCKBURN (1314). In 1321, Thomas, Earl of Lancaster, led a failed revolt against the king. In 1326, his estranged Queen, Isabella, formed an army with her lover, Roger Mortimer, which invaded England and forced Edward to abdicate in favour of his son, EDWARD III. Edward II was murdered in Berkeley Castle, Gloucestershire.

Edward III (1312–77) King of England (1327–77), son and successor of EDWARD II. For the first three years of his reign, Edward was king only in name: his mother, Isabella, and Roger Mortimer held power. In 1330, Edward mounted a successful coup. The outbreak (1337) of the HUNDRED YEARS' WAR dominated his reign. He led several campaigns to France, won a famous victory at CRÉCY (1346) and claimed the title King of France – although conquering only Calais. In his old age, EDWARD THE BLACK PRINCE and JOHN OF GAUNT, governed. His grandson, RICHARD II, succeeded him.

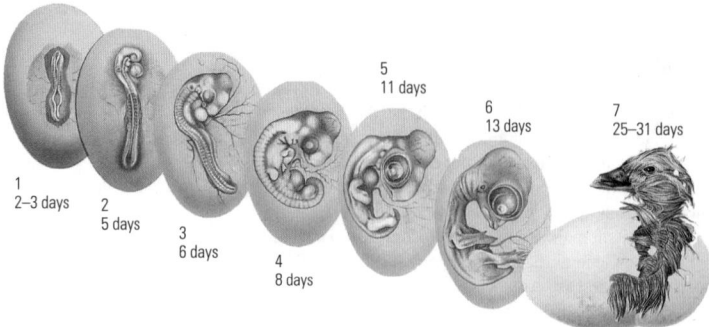

1 2–3 days
2 5 days
3 6 days
4 8 days
5 11 days
6 13 days
7 25–31 days

▲ **egg** A duck embryo grows from a patch of cells on the surface of the egg yolk. The yolk is its food store. First, a network of tiny blood vessels spreads over the yolk and a simple heart develops. The developing embryo (enlarged here for clarity) begins to elongate and develops a vertebral column (1). A head and bulging eye start to form, and the heart folds around into its final position (2). The gut forms, the brain begins to enlarge and the embryo starts to curl (3–4). The limbs appear as tiny buds; and the tail and mouth form (5). By 13 days (6), it is possible to identify the bird from its bill. Some species of bird hatch shortly after this stage, others, such as the mallard duck (7) continue to develop in the egg. Feathers grow, limbs become stronger and the bird hatches with its eyes open and able to see.

Rebus pectoral

signet ring

shell pendant

bezel ring

faience collar

▲ **Egyptian art**
Examples of the work of ancient Egyptian jewellers survive as evidence of their fine craftsmanship. Gold was the major material. Silver, the alloy electrum, and semi-precious stones, such as carnelians, turquoise, and lapis lazuli, were also used.

Edward IV (1442–83) King of England (1461–70, 1471–83). On the death (1460) of his father, Richard, Duke of York, in the Wars of the ROSES, Edward became the Yorkist candidate for the throne. He became king after the defeat of the Lancastrians at Towton. When the Earl of WARWICK changed sides, Edward was exiled, but returned to defeat Warwick at Barnet (1471). He encouraged trade, restored order, and enforced royal absolutism. He died leaving two young sons, but the throne was usurped by his brother, RICHARD III.

Edward V (1470–83) King of England for 77 days in 1483. He succeeded his father, EDWARD IV. His uncle, the Duke of Gloucester, imprisoned Edward and his younger brother, Richard, in the Tower of London, and assumed the throne as RICHARD III. Both boys disappeared, and HENRY VII accused Richard III of having killed them in order to legitimate his rule.

Edward VI (1537–53) King of England (1547–53), only legitimate son of HENRY VIII. Edward reigned under two regents, the Dukes of Somerset (1547–49) and Northumberland (1549–53). During his reign, the introduction of Protestant liturgy consolidated the REFORMATION. He died at 16 after willing the crown to Northumberland's daughter-in-law, Lady Jane GREY, in an attempt to exclude the Catholic MARY I.

Edward VII (1841–1910) King of Great Britain and Ireland (1901–10). As Prince of Wales, his dissolute lifestyle led to his exclusion from government by his mother Queen VICTORIA. As king, he contributed to the ENTENTE CORDIALE with France and reluctantly cooperated with Herbert ASQUITH's reform of the House of Lords. He was succeeded by his son, GEORGE V.

Edward VIII (1894–1972) King of Great Britain and Ireland (1936), then Duke of Windsor. Edward's proposed marriage to American divorcee, Wallis Simpson, was opposed by Stanley BALDWIN's government. Edward refused to back down, and abdicated. Controversy surrounds his links with Nazi Germany.

Edward the Black Prince (1330–76) Prince of Wales (1343–76), eldest son of EDWARD III. He distinguished himself at the Battle of CRÉCY (1346) and captured JOHN II (THE GOOD) of France at Poitiers (1356). As ruler (1362–71) of Aquitaine, Edward was responsible for the massacre at Limoges (1371). He ensured the accession of his son as RICHARD II.

Edward the Confessor, Saint (1002–66) King of England (1042–66), son of ETHELRED II (THE UNREADY). His favouritism to Normans led his father-in-law, Godwin, to rebel. His reign is noted for the rebuilding of WESTMINSTER ABBEY. Having taken a vow of chastity, Edward produced no heir. Although he is said to have promised the throne to WILLIAM I (THE CONQUEROR), Edward acknowledged HAROLD II as his heir. He was canonized in 1161. His feast day is October 13.

Edward the Elder (d.925) King of Wessex (899–925), son and successor of ALFRED THE GREAT. Edward completed the reconquest of the s DANELAW (918).

Edward the Martyr (d.978) King of England (975–78). He was murdered, perhaps by his stepmother, and succeeded by his step-brother ETHELRED II (THE UNREADY).

eel Marine and freshwater fish found worldwide in shallow temperate and tropical waters. Eels have snake-like bodies, dorsal and anal fins continuous with the tail, and an air bladder connected to the throat. Length: up to 3m (10ft). Types include freshwater, moray and conger. Order Anguilliformes.

eelworm Tiny, thread-like nematode found worldwide. Most species are parasitic, and can cause extensive damage to crops. They have been used to control other pests. *See* ROUNDWORM

EFTA Acronym for the EUROPEAN FREE TRADE ASSOCIATION

egg (OVUM) Reproductive cell of female organism. Its nucleus supplies half the chromosome complement of a future ZYGOTE cell, and almost all the CYTOPLASM, upon union with the male gamete (SPERM). Once fertilized, an animal egg is surrounded as it develops by ALBUMIN (egg white), shell, egg case, or MEMBRANE, depending on the species. The egg provides a reserve of food for the EMBRYO in the form of yolk.

ego Self or 'I' which the individual consciously experiences. According to Sigmund FREUD, it is the conscious level of personality that deals with the external world, and also mediates the internal demands made by the impulses of the ID and the prohibitions of the SUPEREGO.

egret White HERON of temperate and tropical marshy regions. It is known for its plumes. Egrets are long-legged, long-necked, slender-bodied, wading birds with dagger-like bills. Height: 50–100cm (20–40in). Family Ardeidae; genus *Egretta*.

Egypt Republic in NE Africa. *See* country feature

Egypt, ancient Civilization that flourished along the River Nile in NW Africa from *c.*3400 BC to 30 BC. The dynasties number from 1 to 30. MENES united the kingdoms of Upper and Lower Egypt in *c.*3100 BC. The highlight of the **Old Kingdom** was the building of the pyramids of GIZA during the 4th dynasty. The Great Pyramid was Khufu's; the other two pyramids were those of his son Khafre and grandson Menkaure. After the death of Pepy II in the 6th dynasty, central government disintegrated. This was the **First Intermediate Period**. Central authority returned in the 11th dynasty, and the capital moved to Thebes (now LUXOR). The **Middle Kingdom** (*c.*2040–1640BC) saw Egypt develop into a great power. Amenemhet I, founder of the 12th dynasty (*c.*1991BC) secured Egypt's borders, and created a new capital. Art, architecture, and literature flourished. At the end of this period, Egypt once again fell into disarray (**Second Intermediate Period**) and the HYKSOS seized control. The **New Kingdom** began in *c.*1550 BC when Ahmose I founded the 18th dynasty. The New Kingdom brought great wealth. Huge temples and tombs, such as TUTANKHAMEN's, were built. Wars with the Hittites under RAMSES II drained Egypt, and later weak rulers led to the decline of the New Kingdom. The 21st to 25th dynasties (**Third Intermediate Period**) culminated in Assyrian domination. The Persians ruled from 525 until 404 BC when the Egyptians revolted, and the last native dynasties appeared. In 332 BC Egypt fell to the armies of ALEXANDER THE GREAT, who moved the capital to ALEXANDRIA. After Alexander's death, his general became ruler of Egypt, as PTOLEMY I. The Ptolemies maintained a powerful empire for three centuries until Ptolemy XII asked POMPEY for aid in 58 BC Rome took control. CLEOPATRA tried to assert independence through links with Julius CAESAR and Mark ANTONY, but she was defeated at ACTIUM. Her son, Ptolemy XV (whose father was probably Julius Caesar), was the last Ptolemy; he was killed by OCTAVIAN (Augustus), and Egypt became a province of Rome.

Egyptian architecture Architecture developed since 3000 BC and characterized by post and lintel construction, massive walls covered with hieroglyphic and pictorial carving, flat roofs, and structures such as the mastaba, obelisk, pylon and the PYRAMIDS. Houses were built of clay or baked bricks. Tombs and temples reproduced features of domestic architecture, but on a massive scale using permanent materials. Perhaps the great architect of the period was Imhotep.

Egyptian art Works were chiefly relief sculpture and painting, characterized by front and side views of the human figure, flat colour tones, symmetry in sculpture, and static figures. Relief-decorated private tombs and temples portrayed the daily life of subjects. With the decline of Egyptian power, the country's art styles formed hybrids with those of its Greek and Roman rulers.

Egyptian mythology Polytheistic mythology that developed in small agricultural communities, each with its own local deities, united under the Pharaohs. A vast pantheon of gods and a multiplicity of myths emerged. Each religious centre had its own creation myth justifying itself as the centre of existence.

During the 3,000 year span of ancient Egypt's civilization Egyptian mythology gradually became more unified, but added ever–increasing levels of complexity.

Egyptology Study of ancient EGYPT, its people, and its antiquities. Mystery still surrounds ancient EGYPTIAN ART and EGYPTIAN ARCHITECTURE (such as the significance of the PYRAMIDS) and the religion of its ancient peoples. Important landmarks include the discovery of the ROSETTA STONE, the temple of AMUN and tomb of TUTANKHAMEN at LUXOR.

Ehrlich, Paul (1854–1915) German bacteriologist. He shared with Ilya Metchnikoff the 1908 Nobel Prize in physiology or medicine for his work on immunization, which included the development of basic standards and methods for studying toxins and antitoxins, especially DIPHTHERIA antitoxins. His subsequent search for a 'magic bullet' against disease, and his discovery of salvarsan (a chemical effective against syphilis microorganisms) introduced CHEMOTHERAPY.

Eichmann, (Karl) Adolf (1906–62) German Nazi, head of the notorious section IV-B-4 of the Reich Central Security Office in WORLD WAR 2. Eichmann supervised the Nazi policies of deportation, slave labour, and mass murder in the CONCENTRATION CAMPS that led to the death of c.6 million Jews. In 1945, he escaped to Argentina but was abducted by the Israel secret police in 1960, and tried and executed in Israel.

eider Large, sea DUCK found in N Europe and North America. Its down is used as a filling for pillows and quilts. In the breeding season, the male grows striking black and white plumage. Family Anatidae; genus *Somateria*.

Eiffel Tower Landmark built for the Paris *Exposition* (1889). Designed by Alexandre Gustave Eiffel, the iron tower rises 300m (984ft). Lifts and stairs lead to observation platforms.

Einstein, Albert (1879–1955) US physicist, b. Germany, who devised the famous theories of RELATIVITY. Einstein published many important theoretical papers. He produced

▲ **Einstein** Albert Einstein devised the special and general theories of relativity and revolutionized physics.

EGYPT

The Arab Republic of Egypt is Africa's second largest country by population after Nigeria. Most of Egypt is desert. Almost all the people live either in the NILE Valley and its fertile delta or along the SUEZ CANAL, the artificial waterway between the Mediterranean and Red seas. This canal shortens the sea journey between the United Kingdom and India by 9,700km [6,027mi]. Recent attempts have been made to irrigate parts of the Western Desert.

Apart from the Nile Valley, Egypt has three other main regions. The W and E deserts are part of the SAHARA. The SINAI Peninsula (Es Sina) – to the E of the Suez Canal – is sparsely populated, very mountainous and contains Egypt's highest peak, Gebel Katherina (2,637 m [8,650 ft]).

CLIMATE

Egypt has a desert climate and is one of the world's sunniest countries. The low rainfall occurs in winter, if at all, and winters are mild. In summer conditions are hot, and become unpleasant when hot and dusty winds blow from the deserts into the Nile Valley.

HISTORY

The Egyptian state was formed c.3100 BC. The Old Kingdom saw the building of the PYRAMIDS at GIZA (c.2500 BC). The ruins of the Middle Kingdom's capital at LUXOR bear

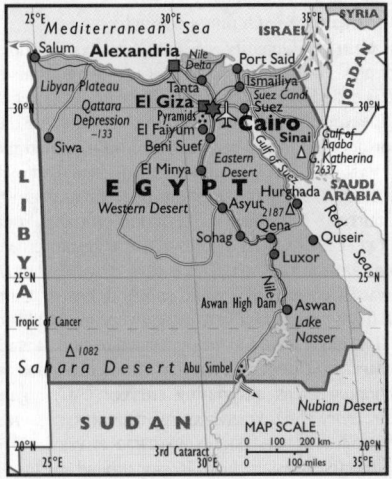

testament to Egypt's imperial power (see EGYPT, ANCIENT). In 332 BC, it was conquered by ALEXANDER THE GREAT and the capital moved to ALEXANDRIA. After CLEOPATRA, the ROMAN EMPIRE took control. In AD 642 Egypt was conquered by the UMAYYAD dynasty, who were later supplanted by the ABBASIDS. ARABIC became the official language and ISLAM the dominant religion. Under the FATIMIDS, Cairo became a centre of SHI'ITE culture. SALADIN's rule (1169–93) was notable for the defeat of the CRUSADES. His dynasty was overthrown (1250) by MAMLUK soldier slaves.

In 1517, Egypt was conquered by the OTTOMANS, who ruled for nearly three centuries. Egypt was occupied (1798–1801) by Napoleon I. France was expelled by MUHAMMAD ALI, who established the modern Egyptian state. The construction of the Suez Canal (1867) encouraged British imperial ambitions. Britain subdued Cairo and took control of the country (1882) and the British army remained even after Egypt became a partially independent monarchy under FUAD I (1922). Fuad was succeeded by FAROUK (1936–52). The creation of Israel (1948) saw the involvement of Egypt in the first of the ARAB-ISRAELI WARS.

POLITICS

In 1952, following a military revolution led by General Muhammad Naguib, the monarchy was abolished and Egypt became a republic. Naguib became president, but he was overthrown in 1954 by Colonel Gamal Abdel NASSER. President Nasser sought to develop Egypt's economy, and he announced a major project to build a new dam at Aswan to provide electricity and water for irrigation. When Britain and the United States failed to provide finance for building the dam, Nasser seized the Suez Canal Company in July 1956. In retaliation, Israel, backed by British and French troops, invaded the Sinai Peninsula and the Suez Canal region. However, under international pressure, they were forced to withdraw. Construction of the Aswan High Dam began in 1960 and it was fully operational by 1968.

In 1967 Egypt lost territory to Israel in the SIX-DAY WAR. Nasser tendered his resignation, but the people refused to accept it. After his death in 1970, Nasser was succeeded by his

AREA 1,001,449sq km [386,659sq mi]	
POPULATION 80,335,000	
CAPITAL (POPULATION) Cairo (11,146,000)	
GOVERNMENT Republic	
ETHNIC GROUPS Egyptians/Bedouins/Berbers 99%	
LANGUAGES Arabic (official), French, English	
RELIGIONS Islam (mainly Sunni Muslim) 94%, Christian (mainly Coptic Christian) and others 6%	
CURRENCY Egyptian pound = 100 piastres	

vice-president, Anwar el-SADAT. In 1973 Egypt launched a surprise attack in Sinai, but its troops were forced back to the Suez Canal. In 1977, Sadat began negotiations with Israel, and in 1979 Egypt and Israel signed a peace treaty. The Sinai Peninsula was returned to Egypt. Extremists opposed contacts with Israel, and in 1981 Sadat was assassinated. He was succeeded as president by Hosni MUBARAK.

In the 1990s attacks on foreign visitors severely damaged tourism, despite efforts to curb the activities of Islamic extremists. In 1997 terrorists killed 58 foreign tourists near Luxor. Unrest continued in the 21st century. In 2005 Mubarak was victorious in the first contested presidential elections, but members of the banned Muslim Brotherhood, standing as independents, made gains in parliament. In 2007 Mubarak altered the constitution to strengthen his control, increase police powers and further outlaw the Muslim Brotherhood.

ECONOMY

Egypt is Africa's second most industrialized country after South Africa, but remains a developing country. The people are poor; farming employs 34% of the workers. Most fellahin (peasants) grow food crops such as beans, maize, rice, sugar cane and wheat, but cotton is the chief cash crop

Egypt depends, as it always has, on the Nile. Its waters are seasonal, and control and storage have become essential in the last 100 years. The Aswan High Dam is the largest Nile dam, and the water behind it in Lake Nasser makes desert reclamation possible. The electricity produced is important for industrial development.

ELECTRICITY SOURCES

A combined-cycle power station burns gas to generate electricity. It is considerably more efficient than traditional fossil fuel power stations. The first turbine (1) sucks in air (2), compressing it before mixing it with the fuel (3) and burning the mixture (4). Exhaust gases spin a second turbine, connected to the first turbine and a generator (5). A second multiple turbine (6), connected to another generator (7), harnasses the energy of the gases. Gases superheat water (8), which loops through a special vessel (9). To maximize power generation, superheated steam (10) turns a high-pressure turbine (11), before passing (at a slightly lower temperature) into a lower-pressure turbine (12). Steam feeds directly into the turbine from the heating loops (13), and cools (14) before going back into the circuit.

INTERNET

Eisenhower, Dwight David ('Ike')
▶ www.eisenhower.utexas. edu
▶ www.whitehouse.gov/ history/presidents

El Alamein
▶ www.historylearningsite. co.uk/battle_of_el_ alamein.htm

▲ **elder** Native to Europe, the elder (family Caprifoliaceae, commonly honeysuckle) grows to a height of 12m (40ft). In early summer, the tree bears clusters of white flowers. The species shown here is *Sambucus nigra*.

the first satisfactory explanation of BROWNIAN MOTION, whch helped confirm the reality of atoms. He successfully modelled the photoelectric effect by treating light as quantized, which won him the 1921 Nobel Prize in physics and led to the discovery of the PHOTON. In 1905 Einstein devised the special theory of relativity, which completely revolutionized physics through its equivalence of MASS and ENERGY ($E = mc^2$). In 1916, Einstein produced the general theory of relativity, which linked gravity to the curvature of space.

einsteinium (symbol Es) Radioactive, synthetic metallic element of the ACTINIDE SERIES. The isotope, Es^{253}, was first identified in 1952 by US nuclear scientist Albert Ghiorso (1915–) and colleagues at the University of California at Berkeley; this was after it was found as a decay product of U^{238} produced by the first large hydrogen bomb explosion. Eleven isotopes have been identified. Properties: at.no. 99; most stable isotope Es^{254} (half-life 276 days). *See also* TRANSURANIC ELEMENTS

Eire *See* IRELAND, REPUBLIC OF

Eisenhower, Dwight David ('Ike') (1890–1969) 34th US president (1953–61). Eisenhower served as aide (1935–40) to General Douglas MACARTHUR. As supreme commander of the Allied Expeditionary Force from 1943, he was largely responsible for the integration of Allied forces in the liberation of Europe. In 1950, he became Supreme Allied Commander (Europe) and helped establish the NORTH ATLANTIC TREATY ORGANIZATION (NATO). In 1952, he gained the Republican Party nomination, and secured victory over Adlai Stevenson in the presidential election. Eisenhower enforced a prompt end to the KOREAN WAR and, with John Foster DULLES, established a staunchly anti-communist foreign policy. Eisenhower was re-elected in 1956. In 1957, he ordered Federal troops into Little Rock, Arkansas, to end segregation in schools. The escalation of the COLD WAR marked his second term. John F. KENNEDY succeeded Eisenhower.

Eisenstein, Sergei (1898–1948) Soviet film director and theorist. Although he completed just six films in 25 years, he is one of cinema's most influential artists. He developed a strong political and aesthetic style, enhanced by the use of creative editing (*see* MONTAGE). His films include *The Battleship Potemkin* (1925) and *October* (or *Ten Days That Shook the World*, 1928).

El Alamein Village in N Egypt. In October 1942, the British 8th Army, led by General MONTGOMERY, launched a successful attack on Axis forces here, and eventually

drove them back to Tunisia. The battle was a turning point in the North Africa campaign of WORLD WAR 2.

Elam Ancient country of MESOPOTAMIA; the capital was Susa. Elamite civilization became dominant *c.*2000 BC with the capture of BABYLON. It continued to flourish until the Muslim conquest in the 7th century. Susa was an important centre under the ACHAEMENID kings of Persia and contained a palace of DARIUS I; archaeological finds include the Stele of HAMMURABI.

eland Largest living ANTELOPE, native to central and s Africa. Elands have heavy, spiralled horns. Height: up to 1.8m (5.8ft) at the shoulder; weight: up to 900kg (1984lb). Family Bovidae.

elasticity Capability of a material to recover its size and shape after deformation by STRESS and strain. When an external force is applied, a material develops stress, which results in strain (a change in dimensions). If a material passes its elastic limit, it will not return to its original shape. If more stress causes a material to snap, this is its **breaking point**. *See also* HOOKE'S LAW

Elat (Eilat) Seaport town in s Israel, on the Gulf of AQABA. A popular holiday resort, it is also the site of an oil pipeline terminal. Its location close to the SINAI Peninsula and deep, manmade harbour make it a vital gateway for Israel's trade with Africa. Industries: fishing, tourism. Pop. (2002 est.) 43,100.

Elba Italian island in the Tyrrhenian Sea; largest of the Tuscan Archipelago; the chief port and town is Portoferraio. Napoleon I was exiled here (1814–15). Industries: iron ore, fisheries, wine, tourism. Area: 223sq km (86sq mi). Pop. (2000 est.) 35,000.

Elbe River in central Europe. It rises as the Labe on the s slopes of the Riesengebirge in the Czech Republic, flows N and NW through Germany and enters the North Sea at Cuxhaven. Length: 1167km (725mi).

Elbert, Mount Mountain in the Sawatch Range of the Rocky Mountain system, central Colorado, USA. It is the highest peak in the ROCKY MOUNTAINS, at 4402m (14,433ft).

Elbrus, Mount (Gora El'Brus) Two peaks in s European Russia, in the Caucasus range, on the border with Georgia. Extinct volcanoes, the w peak, rising to 5633m (18,481ft), is the highest in Europe. The E peak is 5595m (18,356ft) high.

El Cid *See* CID, EL

elder Shrub or small tree found in temperate and subtropical areas. It has divided leaves and small, white flowers. Its shiny black berries are used for making wine, jelly, and in medicine. There are 40 species. Family Caprifoliaceae, genus *Sambucus*.

El Dorado (Sp. 'The Golden One') Mythical city of fabulous wealth, supposedly located in the interior of South America, the focus of many Spanish expeditions in the 16th century.

electoral college Body, elected by the states, which casts the votes to elect the US president and vice president. The number of electors from each state equals the number of its representatives in both Houses of Congress. In each state, people vote for a list of electors, each list representing a particular party. Therefore, a party wins all or none of a state's electoral votes.

Electra In GREEK MYTHOLOGY, the daughter of AGAMEMNON and CLYTEMNESTRA. She helped her brother Orestes avenge their father's death by plotting to kill Clytemnestra and their stepfather Aegisthus.

Electra complex *See* OEDIPUS COMPLEX

electric charge Quantity of ELECTRICITY. A moving charge creates an ELECTRIC CURRENT. A charge that does not move is called a **static charge** and creates STATIC ELECTRICITY. Electric charges (measured in coulombs) are either positive or negative. They can be stored on insulated metal spheres (VAN DE GRAAFF GENERATOR), insulated plates (CAPACITOR) or in chemical solutions (electric BATTERY).

electric current Movement of ELECTRIC CHARGES, usually the flow of ELECTRONS along a CONDUCTOR or the movement of ions through an ELECTROLYTE. This is caused by freely moving particles usually charged by a mains supply or battery. Current (symbol I) flows from a positive to a negative terminal, although electrons flow along a wire in the opposite direction. It is measured in AMPERES. **Direct current** (DC) flows continuously in one direction, whereas **alternating current** (AC) regularly reverses direction. The frequency of AC current is measured in HERTZ (Hz). *See also* ELECTRICITY; PARTICLE PHYSICS

electric field (electrostatic field) Region around an ELECTRIC CHARGE in which any charged particle experiences a force.

The strength of the field (E) upon unit charge at a distance r from a charge Q is equal to $Q/4\pi r^2\epsilon_0$, where ϵ is the vacuum permittivity (degree to which molecules polarize). A changing MAGNETIC FIELD can also create an electric field.

electric furnace Enclosure heated to a very high temperature by an ELECTRIC CURRENT. Electric furnaces are used in industry for melting metals and other materials. Three main methods of heating are used: striking an ARC between electrodes in the furnace; producing currents in the material by ELECTROMAGNETIC INDUCTION; and passing a high current through the material, heat being produced because of its RESISTANCE.

electricity Form of energy associated with static or moving charges. Charge has two forms – positive and negative. Like charges repel, and unlike attract; as described by Charles COULOMB in Coulomb's law. ELECTRIC CHARGES are acted upon by forces when they move in a MAGNETIC FIELD, this movement generates an opposing magnetic field (FARADAY'S LAWS). Electricity and MAGNETISM are different aspects of ELECTROMAGNETISM. The flow of charges constitutes a current, which in a CONDUCTOR consists of negatively charged ELECTRONS. For an ELECTRIC CURRENT to exist in a conductor there must be an ELECTROMOTIVE FORCE (EMF) or POTENTIAL DIFFERENCE between the ends of the conductor. If the source of potential difference is a BATTERY, the current flows in one direction as a direct current (DC). If the source is the mains, the current reverses direction twice every cycle, as alternating current (AC). The AMPERE is the unit of current, the coulomb is the unit of charge, the OHM the unit of RESISTANCE and the VOLT is the unit of ELECTROMOTIVE FORCE. OHM'S LAW and the laws of KIRCHHOFF are the basic means of calculating circuit values.

electricity sources Devices that convert other forms of energy into ELECTRICITY. Most of the world's electricity is produced in power stations from the chemical energy of fossil fuels. The heat from burning coal, oil, or natural gas turns water into steam. The steam drives a TURBINE, linked to an electricity GENERATOR. In a nuclear power station, heat comes from the FISSION of nuclei in a NUCLEAR REACTOR. A BATTERY and fuel cell converts chemical energy directly into electricity. SOLAR CELLS convert SOLAR ENERGY into electricity. Wind generators and water turbines produce electricity

---

ELECTRIC MOTOR

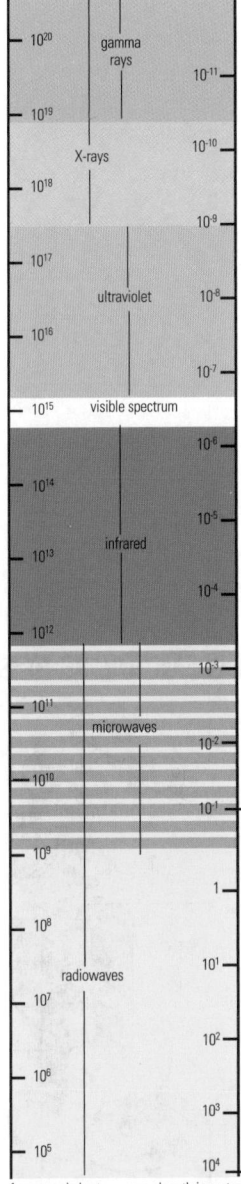

Electric motors work using the interaction of a magnet (1) and a wire with a current passing through it (2). With the current flowing, the magnetic field produced by the loop interacts with the field of the magnet. A downward force acts on the right side, an upward force on the left side. When the loop reaches the vertical, the split ring (through which the current reaches the loop) (3) reverses the current and so the magnetic field. Electric motors use multiple coils (4) to ensure constant torque. In an electric drill, the turning shaft (5) emerges from the magnetic coils, and is then geared (6) through to a chuck (7) to the drill bit (8).

carbon brush

---

from the energy of movement in wind and water. *See also* ENERGY SOURCES; HYDROELECTRICITY; RENEWABLE ENERGY

electric light Artificial light produced by a flow of electricity in a wire or gas. In an ordinary light-bulb, an electric current heats a filament, such as tungsten-alloy wire, producing light by INCANDESCENCE. In a fluorescent tube, the ELECTRIC CURRENT passes through a gas. The gas atoms give off invisible ultraviolet rays. These strike a coating on the inside of the tube, causing it to emit light by FLUORESCENCE.

electric motor Machine that converts electrical energy into mechanical energy. In a simple form of electric MOTOR, an ELECTRIC CURRENT powers a set of ELECTROMAGNETS on a rotor in the MAGNETIC FIELD of a permanent MAGNET. Magnetic forces between the permanent magnet and the electromagnet cause the rotor to turn. Electric motors are convenient and quiet, and have replaced many other forms of motive power. They may use alternating current (AC) or direct current (DC).

electrocardiogram (ECG) Recording of the electrical activity of the heart, traced on a moving strip of paper by an electrocardiograph. It is used to diagnose heart disease.

electrochemistry Branch of chemistry concerned with the relationship between ELECTRICITY and chemical changes. It includes the properties and reactions of IONS in solution, the CONDUCTIVITY of ELECTROLYTES and the study of the processes occurring in electrolytic CELLS and in ELECTROLYSIS.

electrocution Death caused by the passage of an ELECTRIC CURRENT through the body. The current may come from a low- or (more often) a high-voltage source, or from lightning. A major shock either causes chaotic disruption of the heartbeat (fibrillation) or stops the heart completely, in which case breathing also ceases. Severe burns may be visible where the current has entered the body and also at its point of exit. Electrocution is still used as a form of execution in some US states.

electrode CONDUCTOR, usually a wire or rod, through which an ELECTRIC CURRENT flows into or leaves a medium. In ELECTROLYSIS, two electrodes – a positive (ANODE) and a negative (CATHODE) – are immersed in an ELECTROLYTE.

electroencephalogram (EEG) Recording of electrical activity of the brain. Electrodes are attached to the scalp to pick up the tiny oscillating currents produced by brain activity. The visual trace is recorded on paper or an oscilloscope screen. The result is used mainly in the diagnosis and monitoring of EPILEPSY. The machine is called an **electroencephalograph**.

electrolysis Chemical reaction caused by passing a direct current (DC) through an ELECTROLYTE. This results in positive IONS migrating to the negative ELECTRODE (CATHODE) and negative ions migrating to the positive electrode (ANODE). Electrolysis is an important method of obtaining chemicals, particularly reactive elements such as sodium, magnesium, aluminium and chlorine. A commercial use is in ELECTROPLATING.

electrolyte Solution or molten salt that can conduct ELECTRICITY, as in ELECTROLYSIS. In electrolytes, current is carried by IONS, rather than by ELECTRONS. In a lead-acid car battery, the electrolyte is dilute sulphuric acid, which contains negative sulphate ions and positive hydrogen ions.

electromagnet Magnet constructed from a soft iron core around which is wound a coil of wire. A MAGNETIC FIELD is set up when an ELECTRIC CURRENT is passed through the wire. Electromagnets are used in such items as switches and electric bells, while power stations have rotating electromagnets.

electromagnetic force One of four FUNDAMENTAL FORCES. Within an atom, the electromagnetic force binds the negatively charged electrons to the positively charged nucleus. *See also* GRAND UNIFIED THEORY (GUT); UNIFIED FIELD THEORY

electromagnetic induction Use of MAGNETISM to produce an ELECTROMOTIVE FORCE (EMF). If a bar magnet is pushed through a wire coil, an ELECTRIC CURRENT is induced, in the coil, as long as the magnet is moving. By the same principle, an electric current is induced in the coil if it is rotated around the magnet, as in a DYNAMO, ELECTRIC MOTOR, or transformer. *See also* INDUCTANCE; INDUCTION

electromagnetic radiation ENERGY in the form of transverse waves. It travels through free space at close to the speed of light, *c.*300,000km (186,000mi)/sec. These are oscillating electric and magnetic fields travelling together. In

---

gamma rays

X-rays

ultraviolet

visible spectrum

infrared

microwaves

radiowaves

10^{20} — 10^{-11}
10^{19} — 10^{-10}
10^{18} — 10^{-9}
10^{17} — 10^{-8}
10^{16} — 10^{-7}
10^{15} — 10^{-6}
10^{14} — 10^{-5}
10^{13} — 10^{-4}
10^{12} — 10^{-3}
10^{11} — 10^{-2}
10^{10} — 10^{-1}
10^9 — 1
10^8 — 10^1
10^7 — 10^2
10^6 — 10^3
10^5 — 10^4

frequency in hertz   wavelength in metres

▲ **electromagnetic radiation** can be ordered either by frequency or wavelength, to make up the electromagnetic spectrum. The spectrum ranges from low-frequency (high-wavelength) radio waves, through microwaves, infrared waves, light (the visible spectrum – red, orange, yellow, green, blue, indigo, and violet), continuing with ultraviolet waves and X-rays, to very high-frequency (short-wavelength) gamma rays.

E

general, electromagnetic waves are set up by electrical and magnetic vibrations that occur in ATOMS. The WAVELENGTH of electromagnetic radiation varies inversely with the WAVE FREQUENCY. These waves make up the **electromagnetic spectrum**, which includes (in ascending order of frequency): RADIO waves (including MICROWAVES), INFRARED RADIATION, LIGHT, ULTRAVIOLET RADIATION, X-RAYS, and GAMMA RADIATION. They can undergo REFLECTION, REFRACTION (change of direction), INTERFERENCE, DIFFRACTION (spreading or bending), and polarization (restricting vibrations to one direction). In some cases, such as the PHOTOELECTRIC EFFECT, electromagnetic radiation behaviour can only be explained by assuming the radiation is composed of quanta of energy (photons). *See also* QUANTUM THEORY

electromagnetism Branch of physics dealing with the laws and phenomena that involve the interaction or interdependence of ELECTRICITY and MAGNETISM. The region in which the effect of an electromagnetic system can be detected is known as an **electromagnetic field**. When a magnetic field changes, an ELECTRIC FIELD can always be detected. When an electric field varies, a magnetic field can always be detected. Either type of energy field can be regarded as an electromagnetic field. A particle with an ELECTRIC CHARGE is in a magnetic field if it experiences a force only while moving; it is in an electric field if the force is experienced when stationary.

ELECTRON MICROSCOPE

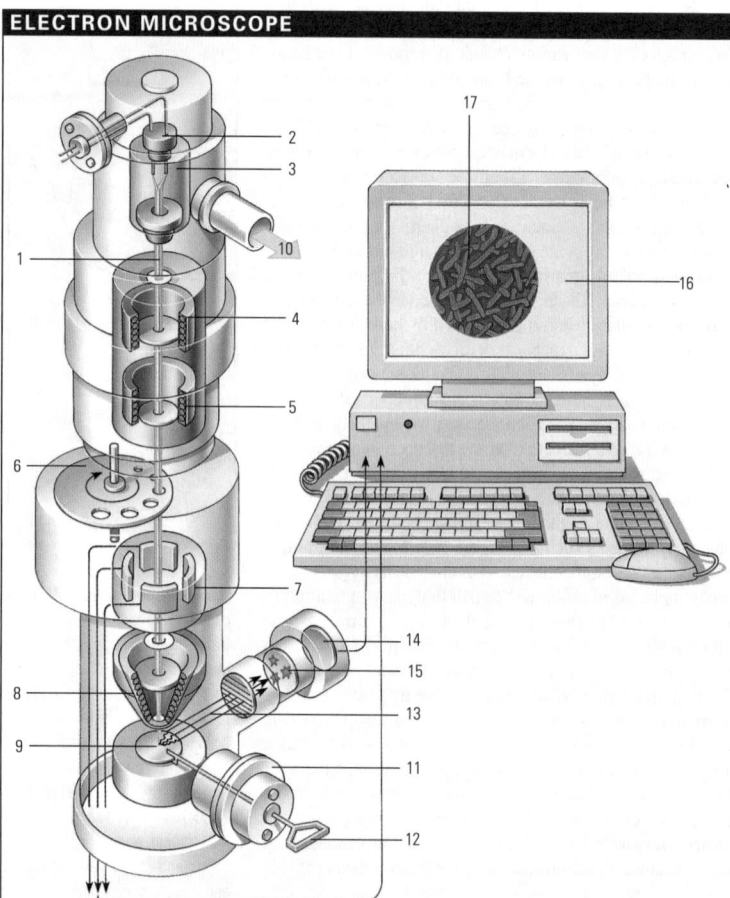

In an electron microscope, a beam of electrons (1) streams from the heated tungsten cathode (2) of an electron gun (3), and is focused by upper (4) and lower (5) electromagnetic lenses. It then passes through an aperture ring (6) and a scan coil (7) before being focused by a projector lens (8) onto the sample (9). The process takes place in a vacuum with air evacuated (10) by a pump. A computer controls the scan coil, which directs the beam across the sample. The sample is placed in an airlock (11) and manipulated into position (12). An image of the sample is created by detecting electrons dislodged (13) from the sample. These electrons correlate to the topography of the sample and are measured by a flash detector (14) when they hit a fluorescent target (15). The image is displayed on a computer monitor (16): here Lactobacillus bulgaricus magnified 1000 times (17).

electromotive force (emf) Potential difference between the terminals in a source of ELECTRIC CURRENT, measured in volts. It equals the energy liberated when this voltage drives the current round an electric circuit. *See also* ELECTRICITY

electron (symbol *e*) Stable ELEMENTARY PARTICLE with a negative charge (1.602×10^{-19}C), a rest mass of 9.1×10^{-31} kg. It is one of the LEPTONS. J.J. THOMSON first identified electrons in 1897. They are not made up of smaller particles and are one of the three primary constituents of ATOMS. They form ORBITALS that surround the positively charged NUCLEUS. In a free atom, the electrons' total negative charge balances the positive charge of the PROTONS in the nucleus. Removal or addition of an atomic electron produces a charged ION. **Free electrons** (not bound to an atom) produce electrical conduction. Electronic devices, such as CATHODE-RAY TUBES, OSCILLOSCOPES and ELECTRON MICROSCOPES, use beams of electrons. An electron is a LEPTON (light particle). Its anti-particle is the POSITRON (positive particle). *See also* BROGLIE, PRINCE LOUIS VICTOR DE; CHEMICAL BOND; MATTER; NEUTRONS; PARTICLE PHYSICS; PHOTOELECTRIC EFFECT; VALENCE

electronic mail (e-mail) Correspondence sent via a COMPUTER NETWORK. In a simple system, messages produced using word-processing programs are transmitted over a network (such as a local-area network or the INTERNET) and stored in a computer called a mail server. People connected to the network can contact the mail server to collect their mail and transfer it to their own computer.

electronic music Music in which electronic methods are used to generate or modulate sounds. The first pieces produced on tape recorders were composed in the 1920s. In Paris, Pierre Schaeffer and Pierre Henry manipulated recorded sounds, producing one of the first major works, *Symphonie pour un homme seul* (1950). The invention of the SYNTHESIZER inspired many composers, particularly Karlheinz STOCKHAUSEN. In the 1960s, it became possible to use computers for complex electronic sounds; Yannis XENAKIS and Pierre BOULEZ are two of many composers to have used computers.

electronic publishing Production of publications by electronic means, generally using a COMPUTER. Word-processing and graphics PROGRAMS are used to assemble 'pages' on a computer screen. The publication may be printed on paper, produced as a CD-ROM or put on the INTERNET. Electronic distribution of 'e-books' has gained some popularity on the internet.

electronics Study and use of CIRCUITS based on the conduction of ELECTRICITY through valves and SEMICONDUCTORS. The DIODE valve, invented by John FLEMING, and the triode valve, invented by Lee DE FOREST, provided the basic components for all the electronics of RADIO, TELEVISION and RADAR until the end of World War 2. In 1948, a team led by William SHOCKLEY produced the first semiconducting TRANSISTOR. Semiconductor devices do not require the high operating voltages of valves and can be miniaturized as an INTEGRATED CIRCUIT (IC). This has led to the production of COMPUTERS and automatic control devices. *See also* CATHODE-RAY TUBE; ELECTRON; MICROELECTRONICS; PRINTED CIRCUIT; THERMIONICS

electron microscope MICROSCOPE used for producing an image of a minute object. It 'illuminates' the object with a stream of electrons, and the 'lenses' consist of magnets that focus the electron beam. Smaller objects can be seen because electrons have shorter wavelengths than light, and thus provide greater resolution. The image is obtained by converting the pattern (made by electrons passing through the object) into a video display, which may be photographed. These microscopes can magnify from 2,000 to a million times.

electrophoresis Movement of electrically charged colloidal particles through a fluid from one ELECTRODE to another when a voltage is applied across the electrodes. It is used in the analysis and separation of colloidal suspensions, especially colloidal proteins. *See also* CHROMATOGRAPHY; COLLOID

electroplating Deposition of a coating of metal on another by making the object to be coated the CATHODE in ELECTROLYSIS. Positive ions in the ELECTROLYTE are discharged at the cathode and deposited as metal. Electroplating is used to produce a decorative or corrosion-resistant layer, as in silver-plated tableware and chromium-plated motor-car parts.

electroscope Instrument for detecting the presence of an ELECTRIC CHARGE or radiation. The commonest type is the gold-leaf electroscope, in which two gold leaves hang from a conducting rod held in an insulated container. A charge applied to the rod causes the leaves to separate, and the amount of separation indicates the amount of charge.

electrostatics *See* STATIC ELECTRICITY

element Substance that cannot be split into simpler substances by chemical means. All atoms of a given element have the same ATOMIC NUMBER (at.no.) and thus the same number of PROTONS and ELECTRONS. The atoms can have different ATOMIC MASS NUMBERS and a natural sample of an element is generally a mixture of ISOTOPES. The known elements range from hydrogen (at.no. 1) to unnilenium (at.no. 109); elements of the first 95 atomic numbers exist in nature, the higher numbers have been synthesized. *See also* PERIODIC TABLE

element 104 *See* DUBNIUM

element 105 *See* HAHNIUM

element 106 *See* RUTHERFORDIUM

elementary particle In physics, a SUBATOMIC PARTICLE that cannot be subdivided. Such particles are the basic constituents of matter. There are three groups of elementary particles: QUARKS, LEPTONS (light particles), and gauge BOSONS (messenger particles). All elementary particles have an associated antiparticle which make up ANTIMATTER.

elephant Largest land animal, the only surviving member of the mammal order Proboscidea, which included the MAMMOTH and the MASTODON. It is native to Africa (*Loxodonta africana*) and India (*Elephas maximus*). The tusks, the source of ivory, are elongated upper incisors. The Indian cow (female) elephant has no tusks. The trunk is an elongated nose and upper lip that it uses for drinking and picking up food. The African elephant is taller and heavier than the Indian. A bull (male) elephant may weigh as much as 7000kg (eight tonnes), and can charge at speeds up to 40km/h (25mph). It also has much larger ears, up to 100cm (40in) in diameter. Elephants are herbivores and browse in herds led by a bull. The cow (female) gives birth to its calf after 18 to 22 months gestation. Elephants live for 60 to 70 years. Indian elephants are used as beasts of burden but do not breed in captivity. The hunting of elephants for their tusks saw the population reduce from 1.3 million in 1979 to 600,000 in 1989. A ban on hunting led to a resurgence.

elephantiasis Condition in which there is gross swelling of the tissues due to blockage of lymph vessels. It is usually caused by parasitic worms, as in FILARIASIS.

Eleusinian Mysteries Religious rites performed in ancient Greece at Eleusis, Attica, to honour DEMETER and PERSEPHONE. The rites probably arose out of a rural fertility festival.

Elgar, Sir Edward (1857–1934) English composer. His individual style is first evident in his set of 14 orchestral variations, the *Enigma Variations* (1899). Elgar's oratorio, *The Dream of Gerontius* (1900), established him as a leading European composer. Other works include a violin concerto (1910), a cello concerto (1919) and two symphonies. His third symphony was completed (1998) by Anthony Payne. Elgar is perhaps best-known for the patriotic piece "Land of Hope and Glory", one of the five *Pomp and Circumstance* marches (1901–30).

Elgin Marbles Group of sculptures from the Acropolis of Athens, including sculptures of the PARTHENON. They were transported (1803–12) by the 7th Earl of Elgin (1766–1841), sold to the British Government in 1816, and are now on display in the British Museum, London. The Greek government continues to campaign for their return.

El Greco *See* GRECO, EL

Elijah (active 9th century BC) Old Testament prophet. He rebuked King Ahab for his attitude to the Phoenician cult of Baal, promoted by Ahab's wife, Jezebel (1 Kings 17, 2 Kings 2) at the expense of the cult of YAHWEH. Elijah, aided by his disciple ELISHA, contested that there was no God but Yahweh.

Eliot, George (1819–80) English novelist, b. Mary Ann Evans. Her unconventional relationship with G.H. LEWES began in 1853. Eliot's first work of fiction was the collection, *Scenes of Clerical Life* (1858). Three novels of provincial life followed: *Adam Bede* (1859), *The Mill on the Floss* (1860), and *Silas Marner* (1861). *Romola* (1862–63) was her only his-

◀ **elephant** Over many thousands of years, the numerous front teeth of the elephant reduced to two upper incisors, which form two long tusks. The nose also extended to form the trunk. The African elephant (*Loxodonta africana*) is found over much of the continent and, while it was once relatively rare due to destruction of its habitat and hunting for its ivory, numbers are now increasing.

torical romance. *Middlemarch* (1871–72) is regarded as Eliot's masterpiece. Her last novel was *Daniel Deronda* (1874–76).

Eliot, John (1604–90) American missionary, b. England. He travelled to Massachusetts (1631) as the first Christian missionary in New England. He became known as the 'Apostle of the Indians' for his evangelistic work.

Eliot, T.S. (Thomas Stearns) (1888–1965) British poet, playwright and critic, b. USA. His poem *The Waste Land* (1922), with its complex language and bleak view of contemporary life, is one of the keystones of literary MODERNISM. Later poems, notably *Ash Wednesday* (1930) and the *Four Quartets* (1935–43), held out hope through religious faith. An influential literary critic, Eliot also wrote verse plays, including *Murder in the Cathedral* (1935) and *The Cocktail Party* (1950). His children's poems, *Old Possum's Book of Practical Cats* (1939), formed the basis for the musical *Cats*. He received the 1948 Nobel Prize in literature.

Elisha Old Testament prophet of Israel, disciple and successor of ELIJAH (2 Kings 2–13). He appeared in the 9th century BC and accomplished the destruction of the Phoenician cult of Baal. Elisha is portrayed as a miracle-worker, healer and fulfiller of God's commissions to his master Elijah.

Elizabeth (1709–62) Empress of Russia (1741–62). The daughter of PETER I (THE GREAT), she came to the throne after overthrowing her nephew, Ivan VI. She reduced German influence in Russia, waged war against Sweden (1741–43), and annexed the s portion of Finland (1743). A great patron of the arts, she was succeeded by her nephew, Peter III.

Elizabeth I (1533–1603) Queen of England (1558–1603), daughter of HENRY VIII and Anne BOLEYN. During the reigns of EDWARD VI and MARY I, her half-brother and half-sister, she avoided political disputes. Once crowned, she reestablished Protestantism. The Elizabethan Settlement saw the CHURCH OF ENGLAND adopt the 39 Articles (1571). Various plots to murder Elizabeth and place the

◀ **Elizabeth I** Her reign was a 'Golden Age' of increasing prosperity and a flowering of the arts. Elizabeth I became known as 'Good Queen Bess' or the 'Virgin Queen'. Throughout her reign, friction with Spain grew, culminating in the Armada, and there were attempts to place the Catholic Mary, Queen of Scots, on the throne.

EMBRYO

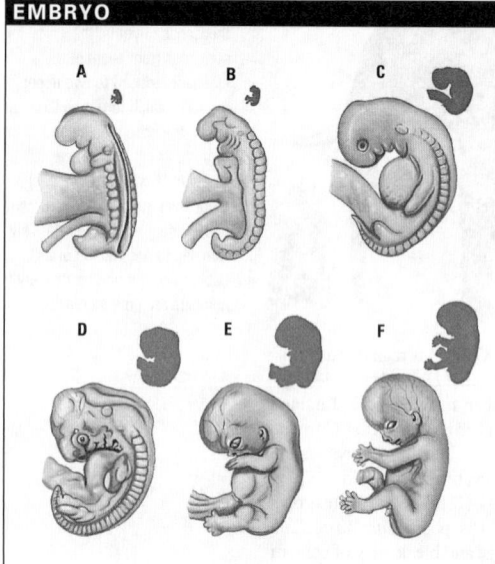

After three weeks a human embryo bears a primitive heart and head (A). By the fourth week, the heart is pumping blood around the body and into the placenta and 25 pairs of tissue blocks (somites) appear, which later give rise to bone and muscle tissue (B). After five weeks, limb buds and rudimentary eyes are visible (C). The limbs become well developed and the tail region recedes by the sixth week (D). The head grows rapidly; eyes, ears and teeth buds appear by the seventh week (E). The tail portion vanishes and almost all the organs and tissues have developed by the eighth week (F). It is now known as a fetus.

Catholic MARY, QUEEN OF SCOTS on the throne resulted in Mary's imprisonment and execution (1587), and increasing discrimation against Catholics. Elizabeth adhered to a small group of advisers, such as Lord BURGHLEY and Sir Francis WALSINGHAM. For most of her reign, England was at peace, and commerce and industry prospered. The expansion of the navy saw the development of the first BRITISH EMPIRE. The hostility of Spain resulted in war and the defeat of the Spanish ARMADA (1588). Despite pressure to marry, Elizabeth remained single. Her favourites included Robert Dudley, Earl of LEICESTER, and Robert Devereux, 2nd Earl of Essex, who later attempted to overthrow her. Elizabeth was the last of the TUDORS, and she was succeeded by JAMES I, a STUART.

Elizabeth II (1926–) Queen of Great Britain and Northern Ireland (1952–), daughter and successor of GEORGE VI. Elizabeth married PHILIP Mountbatten in 1947, and the couple had four children, CHARLES (Prince of Wales), Anne, Andrew, and Edward. Her coronation (June 2, 1953) was the first to be televised. Elizabeth travels extensively, especially in the COMMONWEALTH. Expanded media coverage demystified the monarchy and encouraged criticism of her personal wealth (2001 est. £1.1 billion), and the behaviour of the younger royals. In 1993, she voluntarily agreed to pay income tax. The marriage failures of her children, particular that of Charles to DIANA, PRINCESS OF WALES, intensified public criticism. In 2002 Elizabeth celebrated her Golden Jubilee.

Elizabeth (1900–2002) (Queen Mother) British Queen Consort of GEORGE VI, b. Lady Bowes-Lyon. Elizabeth married George in 1923. They had two children, Elizabeth (later ELIZABETH II) and Margaret (1930–2002). In 1936 she unexpectedly became Queen when George's elder brother, EDWARD VIII, abdicated. She was a popular figure, respected for her steadfastness during the Blitz, and large celebrations marked her 100th birthday.

Elizabethan drama Drama staged in England during the reign of ELIZABETH I (1558–1603). Drawing on classical and medieval thought, as well as folk drama, Elizabethan drama is characterized by a spiritual vitality and creativity. Masters of the period include SHAKESPEARE, MARLOWE, and JONSON.

elk Name of two different species of DEER: the European elk (*Alces alces*), known in North America as the moose; and the American elk, or WAPITI. The elk, found in N Eurasia, is the largest of all deer. Height at the shoulder: to 1.9m (6ft); weight: 820kg (1800lb). Family Cervidae.

Ellesmere Island Mountainous island in the Arctic Ocean, NW of Greenland, forming part of the Northwest Territories of Canada. It is the second largest and northernmost island of the Arctic Archipelago. Area: 196,236sq km (75,767sq mi).

Ellice Islands Former name of TUVALU

Ellington, 'Duke' (Edward Kennedy) (1899–1974) US jazz composer, pianist, and bandleader. His early pieces, performed (1927–32) at the Cotton Club, New York, include "Black and Tan Fantasy" (1927) and "Mood Indigo" (1930). The 'jungle' style gave way to the elegance of the Blanton-Webster years (1939–42), and standards such as "Take the A Train" and "I Got It Bad". *Black, Brown and Beige* (1943) was written for a concert at Carneige Hall, New York.

ellipse A geometrical figure with the shape like a circle seen from an angle. It is a CONIC section formed by cutting a right circular cone with a plane inclined at such an angle that the plane does not intersect the base of the cone. When the intersecting plane is parallel to the base, the conic section is a circle. In rectangular Cartesian co-ordinates its standard equation is $x^2/a^2 + y^2/b^2 = 1$. Most planetary orbits are ellipses.

Ellis Island Island in Upper New York Bay, near MANHATTAN, SE New York, USA. It acted as the main US immigration centre (1892–1943); at the height of immigration it was handling one million applicants annually. From 1943 to 1954, it was a detention centre for aliens and deportees. It is estimated that more than 20 million immigrants entered the United States via Ellis Island. Area: 11ha (27 acres).

elm Hardy, DECIDUOUS tree of N temperate zones. The simple leaves are arranged alternately along the stem, and the flowers are greenish and inconspicuous. Species include the American (*Ulmus americana*), English (*U. procera*) and Scotch elm (*U. glabra*). Height: more than 30m (100ft). Family Ulmaceae.

El Niño (Sp. (Christ) 'child') Warm surface current that flows in the equatorial Pacific Ocean towards the South American coast. It occurs around Christmas time. An easing or reversing of the TRADE WINDS over the S Pacific Ocean, causes warm surface waters that have 'piled-up' in the W Pacific to flow back and warm the coastal waters of South America by 2 to 3°C. It has a dramatic effect on climate patterns in Australia and Southeast Asia, and may affect rainfall as far away as Africa. In normal years, trade winds blow E to W along the Equator, dragging warm surface waters into a pool off N Australia and monsoon rains to Indonesia. In the W Pacific, the Humboldt Current pushes the surface waters away from the coast of Peru, bringing cold water to the surface. This upwelled, nutrient-rich water stimulates phytoplankton production and swells the population of anchovies, a mainstay of the Peruvian fishing industry. In an El Niño year, the upwelling ceases and the biological productivity of the area collapses. In addition, mean sea-level along the coast of Latin America may increase by as much as 50cm (20in), causing widespread flooding. Some scientists believe that the frequency (presently every 2–10 years) and effects of El Niño may be increasing.

El Salvador Republic in Central America. *See* country feature

Elysium In Greek mythology, the Elysian fields. The abode of blessed mortals after their removal from the Earth, it is the realm to which heroes departed to live a life of happiness.

Emancipation Proclamation Declaration issued by President Abraham LINCOLN giving freedom to slaves in the CONFEDERATE STATES OF AMERICA from January 1, 1863. Lincoln's primary aim was to preserve the Union. The Proclamation, which he announced in September 1862, had little immediate effect, but did establish the abolition of SLAVERY as a Union war aim. The 13th Amendment to the Constitution (December 1865) finally abolished slavery.

embargo Obstruction of the movement of cargo to prevent its delivery. In modern terms, it refers to complete suspension of trade with a country or withholding crucial goods.

Embargo Act (1807) Act passed under President JEFFERSON to force England and France to remove restrictions on US trade. It forbade international trade to and from US ports.

embolism Blocking of a blood vessel by an obstruction called an embolus, usually a blood clot, air bubble or particle of fat. The effects depend on where the embolus lodges; a cerebral embolism causes a STROKE. Treatment is with anticoagulants or surgery. *See also* ARTERIOSCLEROSIS

embryo Early developing stage of an animal or plant. In animals, the embryo stage starts at FERTILIZATION. In mammals, an embryo is sustained through blood supplied by the mother via the PLACENTA. In humans, the embryo is called a FETUS after the first eight weeks of pregnancy. In invertebrate animals the embryo is usually called a LARVA. In plants, the embryo is found in the seed, and the embryo stage ends on GERMINATION. An embryo results when the nuclei of GAMETES, an EGG (OVUM) and a SPERM or male sex cell fuse to form a single cell, called a ZYGOTE. The zygote then divides into a ball of cells called a BLASTULA. In 2004, thirty human embryos were cloned in South Korea. *See also* MEIOSIS; MITOSIS

emerald Variety of BERYL, highly valued as a gemstone. The colour varies from light to dark green due to the presence of small amounts of chromium.

Emerson, Ralph Waldo (1803–82) US essayist and poet. He was an exponent of TRANSCENDENTALISM, the principles of which are expressed in his book *Nature* (1836). His belief in the soul, the unity of God with man and nature, self-reliance and hope is articulated in his *Essays* (1841, 1844), *Poems* (1847), *The Conduct of Life* (1860), *Society and Solitude* (1870), and many other influential works.

Emilia-Romagna Region in N central Italy, bordering the Adriatic Sea; the capital is BOLOGNA. It was incorporated in the Kingdom of Italy in 1860. The N part of Emilia-Romagna forms a vast plain. In the S lies the central part of the APENNINES, from which flow its main rivers. Agriculture is important, products include cereals, rice, vegetables and dairying. Industries: tourism, motor vehicles, refined petroleum, chemicals. Area: 22,124sq km (8542sq mi). Pop. (1999) 3,959,770.

Empedocles (*c.*490–*c.*430 BC) Greek scientist and philosopher. He taught the doctrine of the four elements (earth, water, air, and fire) and, anticipating modern physics, he explained change as alterations in the proportions of these four elements.

emphysema Accumulation of air in tissues, most often occurring in the lungs (pulmonary emphysema). Pulmonary emphysema, characterized by marked breathlessness, is the result of damage to and enlargement of the ALVEOLUS. It is associated with chronic bronchitis and smoking.

Empire State Building Skyscraper in New York City. Completed in 1931, it was the highest building in the world until 1972. It is 381m (1250ft) tall, or 449m (1472ft) to the top of its television mast. .

Empire style Neo-classical style in interior decoration, associated with the reign of NAPOLEON I of France. It made affected use of Egyptian decorative motifs and corresponded to the REGENCY STYLE in England.

empiricism Philosophical doctrine that all knowledge is derived from experience. It was developed mainly by a school of British philosophers, LOCKE, BERKELEY, and HUME, in reaction to the RATIONALISM of DESCARTES, SPINOZA, and LEIBNIZ, who claimed the existence of *a priori* knowledge (innate ideas). *See also* LOGICAL POSITIVISM

emu Large, dark-plumed, flightless Australian bird. It is a strong runner with powerful legs. Large greenish eggs (8–10) are hatched by the male in a ground nest. Height: 1.5m (5ft); weight: to 54kg (120lb). Species *Dromaius novaehollandiae*.

emulator COMPUTER configured in such a way that it acts like another type of computer. Emulators are often used in the development of new microprocessors, allowing a designer to assess a new design without building an expensive prototype.

enamel Decorative or protective glazed coating produced on metal surfaces, or a type of paint. Ceramic enamels are made from powdered glass and calx, with metal oxides to add colour. Enamel paints consist of zinc oxide, lithopone, and high-grade varnish. The finish is hard, glossy, and highly durable.

EL SALVADOR

El Salvador is the smallest and most densely populated country in Central America. It has a narrow coastal plain along the Pacific Ocean. The majority of the interior is mountainous with many extinct volcanic peaks overlooking a heavily populated central plateau. Earthquakes are common; in 1854, an earthquake destroyed the capital, SAN SALVADOR. In October 1986, another earthquake killed 400 people and caused widespread damage.

Grassland and some virgin forests of original oak and pine are found in the highlands. The central plateau and valleys have areas of grass and deciduous woodland, while tropical savanna or forest cover the coastal regions.

CLIMATE
The coast has a hot tropical climate. Inland, the climate is moderated by altitude. The centre region has similar temperatures by day, but nights are cooler. Rain falls during most afternoons between May and October.

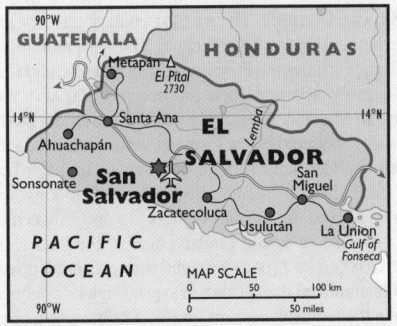

HISTORY
In 1524–26 Spanish explorer Pedro de Alvarado conquered Native American tribes such as the Pipil, and the region became part of the Spanish Viceroyalty of Guatemala. Independence was achieved in 1821, and in 1823 El Salvador joined the Central American Federation. The federation dissolved in 1839.

El Salvador declared independence in 1841, but was continually subject to foreign interference, especially from Guatemala and Nicaragua. It was at this time that El Salvador's coffee plantations developed.

POLITICS
Following a collapse in the world coffee market, Maximiliano Hernández Martínez seized power in a palace coup in 1931. In 1944 a general strike overthrew his brutal dictatorship. After a period of progressive government, a military junta headed by Julio Adalberto Rivera from 1962 to 1967 and Fidel Sánchez Hernández from 1967 to 1972 seized power. Honduras' discriminatory immigration laws exacerbated tension on the border between the two countries. The 'Soccer War' of 1969 broke out following an ill-tempered World Cup qualifying match. Within four days, El Salvador captured much of Honduras. Troops withdrew after a ceasefire.

In the 1970s, the repressive National Republican Alliance (ARENA) regime compounded El Salvador's problems of overpopulation, unequal distribution of wealth and social unrest. Civil war broke out in 1979 between US-backed government forces and the Farabundo Marti National Liberation Front (FMLN). The 12-year war claimed 75,000

AREA 21,041sq km [8,124sq mi]	
POPULATION 6,948,000	
CAPITAL (POPULATION) San Salvador (1,472,000)	
GOVERNMENT Republic	
ETHNIC GROUPS Mestizo 90%, White 9%, Amerindian 1%	
LANGUAGES Spanish (official)	
RELIGIONS Roman Catholic 83%	
CURRENCY US dollar = 100 cents	

lives and made millions homeless. A ceasefire held from 1992, and the FMLN became a recognized political party. In 1993 a UN Truth Commission led to the decommissioning of FMLN arms and the removal of senior army officers for human rights abuses. Armando Calderón Sol became president in 1994 elections; Francisco Flores succeeded him in 1999.

In 2001, massive earthquakes killed about 1,200 people and left one million homeless. Tony Saca won 2004 presidential elections to become the fourth successive ARENA president.

ECONOMY
El Salvador is a lower-middle-income developing country. Farmland and pasture account for approximately 60% of land use. El Salvador is the world's 10th largest producer of coffee. Its reliance on the crop caused economic structural imbalance. Sugar and cotton grow on the coastal lowlands. Fishing is important, but manufacturing is on a small scale. The civil war devastated the economy. Between 1993 and 1995, El Salvador received more than US$100 million of credit from the International Monetary Fund.

▲ **Engels** A founder of 19th-century communism, Friedrich Engels' success in the textile industry helped finance the work of Karl Marx, and they collaborated on the *Communist Manifesto* (1848). Engels' work on dialectical materialism informed much subsequent Marxist philosophy. *The Origin of the Family, Private Property and the State* (1884) is a seminal work.

INTERNET

endangered species
▸ www.redlist.org
▸ www.cites.org

Engels, Friedrich
▸ www.anu.edu.au/polsci/ marx/classics/manifesto. html

encephalitis Inflammation of the brain, usually associated with a viral infection; often there is an associated MENINGITIS. Symptoms include fever, headache, lassitude, and intolerance of light; in severe cases there may be sensory and behavioural disturbances, paralysis, convulsions, and coma.

enclosure In European history, the fencing-in by landlords of common land. Complaints against this practice date from the 13th century. Enclosure usually led to increased agricultural productivity at the cost of depriving people of free grazing and firewood. It was a cause of popular rebellions, especially in the 16th century. The AGRICULTURAL REVOLUTION of the 18th century produced another spurt of enclosure.

endangered species Animals or plants threatened with extinction as a result of such activities as habitat destruction and overhunting. In 1948, the International Union for the Conservation of Nature and Natural Resources (IUCN) was founded to protect endangered species. The IUCN publishes the *Red Data Book*, which currently lists more than 1,000 animals and 20,000 plants considered endangered. *See also* CONSERVATION; ECOLOGY; HABITAT; WETLAND

endive Leafy, ANNUAL or BIENNIAL plant widely cultivated for its sharp-flavoured leaves. There are two main types: curly CHICORY (escarole), with slender, wavy-edged leaves and a variety with broad, flat leaves. Family Asteraceae/Compositae.

endocrine system Body system made up of all the endocrine (ductless) glands that secrete HORMONES directly into the bloodstream to control body functions. The endocrine system (together with the NERVOUS SYSTEM) controls and regulates all body functions. The chief endocrine glands are the PITUITARY GLAND (in the brain), the THYROID GLAND (in the neck), the ADRENAL GLAND (in the abdomen), and the sex gland or GONAD (in the female abdomen and male testes).

endometriosis Gynaecological disorder in which tissue similar to the ENDOMETRIUM is found in other parts of the pelvic cavity. It is treated with analgesics, hormones or surgery.

endometrium Mucous membrane, well supplied with blood vessels, that lines the UTERUS. The endometrium sheds each month as part of the MENSTRUAL CYCLE.

endoplasmic reticulum (ER) Network of membranes and channels in the CYTOPLASM of EUKARYOTE cells. It helps transport material, such as proteins, inside CELLS. Minute granules called RIBOSOMES, consisting of protein and a form of ribonucleic acid (RNA), cover parts of the endoplasmic reticulum.

endorphin (endogenous MORPHINE) Naturally occurring PEPTIDE neurotransmitter found in the PITUITARY GLAND that has similar pain-relieving effects as morphine and other derivatives of OPIUM. Endorphins block the sensation of pain by binding to pain-receptor sites. Two endorphins (**enkephalins**) occur in the brain, spinal cord and gut. *See also* ANALGESIC; NEURON; NEUROTRANSMITTER

endoscope Instrument used to examine the interior of the body. Early types of endoscope, such as the opthalmoscope, were developed in the 19th century. FIBRE OPTICS has revolutionized the design of endoscopes. The modern endoscope is a flexible, fibreglass instrument that can be swallowed by a patient or introduced through a tiny incision in the body. Most endoscopy is for diagnostic purposes, but modern instruments are used in biopsy and MINIMAL ACCESS SURGERY.

endosperm Tissue that surrounds the developing embryo of a seed and provides food for growth. It is triploid (each cell has three sets of chromosomes), being derived from the fusion of one of the male gametes from the germinated pollen grain and two of the haploid nuclei in the embryo sac. *See also* ALTERNATION OF GENERATIONS

endosymbiosis Mutually beneficial relationship in which one organism lives inside another. For example, bacteria were engulfed by EUKARYOTE cells and formed symbiotic relationships with them, eventually becoming so interdependent that the cells behaved as a single organism; the bacteria became MITOCHONDRIA and CHLOROPLASTS. *See also* SYMBIOSIS

endothermic reaction Chemical reaction in which heat is absorbed from the surroundings, causing a fall in temperature – as in the manufacture of water-gas from coal and steam. *See also* EXOTHERMIC REACTION

energy In physics, capacity for doing WORK. It is measured in JOULES (J). POWER, the rate at which energy is produced or consumed, is measured in WATTS (W). POTENTIAL ENERGY is an object's ability to do work because of a change in the object's position or shape. KINETIC ENERGY is the energy an object has because it is moving. Many forms of energy include electrical, NUCLEAR, thermal, LIGHT and chemical. Energy can be transferred from one body to another through work processes, heating, ELECTROMAGNETIC RADIATION and ELECTRICITY. The law of CONSERVATION of energy states energy cannot be created or destroyed. Albert EINSTEIN established the idea that MASS is a form of energy, recognizing that energy (E) and mass (m) could be transformed into each other according to the relation $E = mc^2$, where c is the velocity of light.

energy sources Naturally occurring substances, processes and phenomena from which we obtain ENERGY. The vast majority of energy derives from the Sun. FOSSIL FUELS are the remains of life that depended for growth on SOLAR ENERGY. HYDROELECTRICITY also derives from solar energy, which maintains the Earth's HYDROLOGICAL CYCLE, while uneven heating of the atmosphere generates wind, whose energy harnessed by wind farms. The movements of the oceans, namely waves and tides, controlled by wind and the pull of the Sun and Moon, have been used successfully in some regions to create energy. Increasingly, solar energy is being used to heat some domestic water supplies directly, and for providing electricity from PHOTOELECTRIC CELLS. GEOTHERMAL ENERGY is energy obtained from underground hot rocks. *See also* NUCLEAR ENERGY; RENEWABLE ENERGY

Engels, Friedrich (1820–95) German political philosopher. Engels and MARX formulated the theory of DIALECTICAL MATERIALISM and co-wrote the *Communist Manifesto* (1848). Engels' materialist reworking of HEGEL is most evident in *Anti-Dühring* (1878) and *Socialism, Utopian and Scientific* (1882). From 1870 until Marx's death in 1883, Engels helped financially with Marx's research and continued to assist him with his writings, particularly *Das Kapital*. His works include *Condition of the Working Class in England in 1844* (1845).

engine A machine that produces useful energy of motion from some other form of energy. The term is usually restricted to combustion engines, which burn fuel. These machines include the STEAM ENGINE, DIESEL ENGINE, JET ENGINE, and ROCKET engine. Combustion engines are of two main kinds: an **external** combustion engine burns its fuel outside the chamber in which motion is produced. In a steam LOCOMOTIVE, for example, the fire box is separate from the cylinders. An INTERNAL COMBUSTION ENGINE burns its fuel and develops motion in the same place.

engineering Application of scientific principles for practical purposes, such as construction and developing power sources. There are many different fields in engineering including MECHANICAL, CIVIL, CHEMICAL, electrical, and nuclear. Academic training starts with a grounding in the fundamentals of science and general engineering. *See also* ELECTRONICS

England Largest nation within the United Kingdom, bounded by the North Sea (E), the English Channel (S), Wales and the Irish Sea (W), and Scotland (N); the capital is LONDON. **Land and economy** The landscape is complex. In general, the N and W are higher and geologically older than the S and E. The chief rivers are the SEVERN, THAMES, TRENT, Ouse, Humber and Mersey. Principal lakes include WINDERMERE and Derwentwater in the LAKE DISTRICT. The S of the country has low hills, while much of E England is flat fenland. The N is predominantly upland, and includes the PENNINES, Cheviot Hills, and Cumbrian Mountains. **History** There are traces of PALAEOLITHIC settlements in England. Occupied by the CELTS from *c*.400 BC England was conquered by the Romans, whose rule lasted until the 5th century. Germanic tribes began arriving in the 3rd century AD and gradually established independent kingdoms. Christianity arrived in the 6th century. In the 9th century, ALFRED THE GREAT united England against the Danes. The NORMAN CONQUEST (1066) brought strong central government and inaugurated the FEUDAL SYSTEM. England conquered IRELAND in the late 12th century, and WALES became a principality of England in 1284. The 13th century saw the foundations of parliamentary government and the development of statute law. The Wars of the ROSES curbed the power of the English nobility. Under the TUDORS, England was united politically with Wales and became a strong Protestant monarchy. The reign of ELIZABETH I was one of colonial expansion. In 1603, JAMES I merged the English and Scottish crowns. For the subsequent history of England, *see* UNITED KINGDOM. Area: 130,362sq km (50,333sq mi). Pop. (2001) 49,138,831.

English Language belonging to the Germanic branch of the INDO-EUROPEAN family. It may be said to have come into existence with the arrival of the ANGLO-SAXONS in England in the 5th century AD. During more than 1,500 years of development, it transformed from an inflected language with grammatical gender to a language with very few inflections and employing a sex-correlated gender system. The inclusion of numerous foreign, technical and slang words massively expanded the vocabulary of English. It is the mother tongue of *c.*300 million people, and a second language for hundreds of millions more worldwide.

English architecture Between the 6th and the 17th centuries, there were at least five distinct styles of architecture: SAXON, NORMAN, GOTHIC, RENAISSANCE and BAROQUE. Inigo JONES brought his revolutionary Renaissance ideas relatively late to the 17th-century STUART court, and Christopher WREN introduced Baroque forms to England at the end of his career. GEORGIAN ARCHITECTURE (1702–1830) subdivides into English Baroque, PALLADIANISM, and NEO-CLASSICISM. In the 19th century, the Victorian age marked an earnestness and solidity of architecture, while the Great Exhibition (1851) paved the way for MODERNISM. William Morris and the ARTS AND CRAFTS MOVEMENT encouraged purity of design in the late 19th century, a concept that was maintained in the early 20th-century work of LUTYENS and Voysey. In the late 20th century, MODERNISM and POST-MODERNISM, in particular the work of Richard ROGERS and Norman FOSTER, have been challenged by proponents of more classical styles.

English art England's earliest artistic traditions were shaped by invading forces. The ANGLO-SAXONS had an enduring influence. Their most notable achievement came with the BAYEUX TAPESTRY. The Church remained the dominant patron of the arts until the arrival of Hans HOLBEIN at the court of HENRY VIII. In the 17th century, RUBENS and VAN DYCK worked in the courts of James I and Charles I. A native tradition emerged in the 18th century, with William HOGARTH and Thomas GAINSBOROUGH. The ROYAL ACADEMY OF ARTS (RA) was founded in 1768, and Joshua REYNOLDS was the first president. In the 19th century, England's two most influential artists were J.M.W. TURNER and John CONSTABLE. The work of the PRE-RAPHAELITE BROTHERHOOD bridged ROMANTICISM and SYMBOLISM, while William MORRIS was a seminal influence on the ARTS AND CRAFTS MOVEMENT. Major 20th-century figures were Stanley SPENCER and Francis BACON. Modern English sculptors, including Jacob EPSTEIN, Henry MOORE, and Barbara HEPWORTH, exerted a broad influence.

English Channel Arm of the Atlantic Ocean between France and Britain, joining the North Sea at the Strait of Dover. A cross-channel train-ferry service was started in 1936, and the CHANNEL TUNNEL was completed in 1994. Width: 30–160km (20–100mi); length: 564km (350mi).

English literature The earliest surviving works are from the Old English period (475–1000). Mainly poems in the heroic mould, epics such as BEOWULF belong to an oral tradition but were written down in the 7th century. ALFRED THE GREAT translated a number of Latin works into the vernacular and initiated the *Anglo Saxon Chronicle*. Norman French replaced Old English as the language of the ruling classes after 1066, and the influence of French literature was reflected in the numerous romances centred around the stories of Charlemagne and the legends of King Arthur. The native tradition of alliterative poetry re-emerged in the 14th century in the works of LANGLAND, MALORY and Geoffrey CHAUCER, whose talent was unrivalled until the 16th century. Humanism and the Renaissance influenced English writing in the 16th century. William SHAKESPEARE and Christopher MAR-

LOWE were the leading figures in ELIZABETHAN DRAMA. Shakespeare's late works formed a bridge with the JACOBEAN era. Edmund SPENSER and Philip SIDNEY ensured the period was also a golden age for poetry. John DONNE and the METAPHYSICAL poets continued this tradition, but the poetry of MILTON was unsurpassed in the 17th century. English prose flourished with the production of the Authorized Version of the Bible in 1611. After the RESTORATION, drama revived in the comedies of CONGREVE, while the satiric prose of SWIFT, the poetry of POPE, the drama of GOLDSMITH and the criticism of Samuel JOHNSON typify the classical ideals of the Augustan age (*c.*1690–1740). The NOVEL emerged during the early 18th century, with works by DEFOE, RICHARDSON, FIELDING, STERNE and SMOLLETT, and was developed further in the 19th century by Jane AUSTEN, Walter SCOTT, THACKERAY, the BRONTË, ELIOT, and DICKENS. The Romantic movement, presaged by BLAKE's visionary poetry, gained full expression with WORDSWORTH and COLERIDGE and was developed by KEATS, BYRON, and SHELLEY. The major Victorian poets were TENNYSON and Robert and Elizabeth BROWNING. The wit of SHAW and WILDE and the bleak novels of HARDY gave way to the cynicism of war poets such as Siegfried SASSOON. The novels of James JOYCE, Virginia WOOLF, and D.H. LAWRENCE, and the poetic dramas of T.S. ELIOT, best realized the formal inventions of MODERNISM. W.B. YEATS looked back to the visions of Blake. The novel diversified with the writings of Aldous HUXLEY, Evelyn WAUGH, and Graham GREENE. In the 1930s, W.H. AUDEN produced explicitly political poems and Noel COWARD lampooned the British class system. The 1950s saw the emergence of the 'ANGRY YOUNG MEN', including John OSBORNE and Kingsley AMIS, and the absurdist plays of Samuel BECKETT. Postwar novelists include Anthony BURGESS, William GOLDING, Iris MURDOCH, Angela CARTER, and Salman RUSHDIE; dramatists include Harold PINTER, Tom STOPPARD, Joe

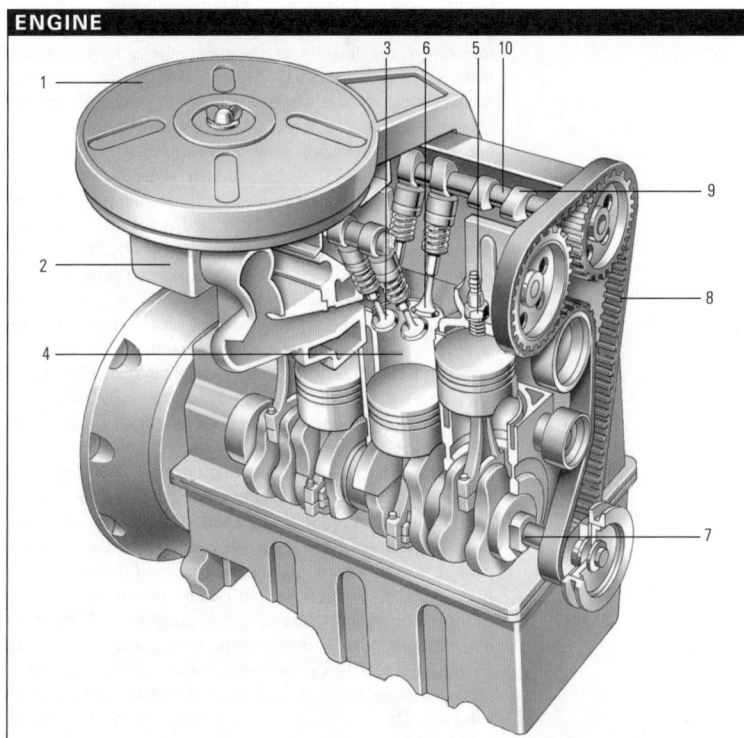

ENGINE

In an in-line, four cylinder petrol engine, a filter (1) sucks air into the carburettor (2), where it mixes with petrol. This mixture then enters the cylinders through the dual inlet valves (3) on each cylinder (4). The spark plug (5) ignites the mixture, forcing the piston rapidly down. The burnt gases expel through the outlet valves (6), and the crankshaft (7) converts the reciprocating motion of the pistons into rotation. The crankshaft also turns the timing belt (8), which controls the opening of the valves, through the cams (9) located on the camshaft (10), and also the firing of the spark plugs.

ORTON and David HARE; poets include Dylan THOMAS, Philip LARKIN, Ted HUGHES, and Seamus HEANEY.

English National Opera (ENO) English opera company with a policy of performing all operas in English. The ENO moved from Sadler's Wells to its present location at the London Coliseum in 1968. They have given the first British performance of numerous operas.

engraving INTAGLIO printing process; it describes various methods of making prints by cutting lines into metal or wood. Variations include ETCHING and AQUATINT. In modern engraving, different processes are frequently combined in a single plate. *See also* WOODCUT

Enlightenment (Age of Reason) Intellectual temper of Western Europe in the 18th century. It developed from the spirit of rational enquiry of the Scientific Revolution and from political theorists of the late 17th-century Age of Reason, such as John LOCKE. Its leaders thought that all things could be understood or explained by reason. Their emphasis on human reason and perfectibility often brought conflct with the Church.

Enoch Name of several Old Testament figures. One was the father of METHUSELAH, and writer of PSEUDEPIGRAPHA, such as the Books of Enoch. Another was the eldest son of CAIN.

Entebbe City on the NW shore of Lake Victoria, s central Uganda, E Africa. Founded in 1893, it was capital of the British protectorate of Uganda (1894–1962). Pop. (2002 est.) 57,400.

Entente Cordiale Anglo-French alliance, formalized in April 1904. Outstanding differences, especially over colonies, were solved and the basis laid for future cooperation. The Entente was the first step leading to the TRIPLE ENTENTE.

enthalpy (symbol H) In THERMODYNAMICS, amount of HEAT energy possessed by a substance. The enthalpy of a system equals the sum of its internal energy and the product of pressure and volume. In an ENDOTHERMIC REACTION, there is an increase in enthalpy. The reverse occurs in an EXOTHERMIC REACTION.

entomology (Gk. *entomon*, 'insect') Term for the scientific study of INSECTS, coined by ARISTOTLE. The ancient Greeks were the first serious entomologists (4th centuryBC).

entropy Quantity that specifies the disorder of a physical system; the greater the disorder, the greater the entropy. In THERMODYNAMICS, it expresses the degree to which thermal energy is available for WORK – the less available it is, the greater the entropy. According to the second law of thermodynamics, a system's change in entropy is either zero or positive in any process.

Enver Pasha (1881–1922) Turkish general and political leader. Involved in the Young Turk revolution (1908), he became virtual dictator after a coup (1913). He was instrumental in bringing Turkey into World War 1 as an ally of Germany. He was killed leading an anti-Soviet expedition in Bukhara.

environment Physical and biological surroundings of an organism. The environment covers non-living (**abiotic**) factors such as temperature, soil, atmosphere and radiation, and also living (**biotic**) organisms such as plants, microorganisms and animals. The study of the relationship of organisms to their environment is called ECOLOGY, and protecting the environment involves CONSERVATION.

enzyme (Gk. *zymosis*, 'fermentation') PROTEIN that functions as a CATALYST in biochemical reactions. They remain chemically unaltered in these reactions and so are effective in tiny quantities. The FERMENTATION properties of yeast cells, for example, have long been utilized in the brewing trade. Chemical reactions can occur several thousand or million times faster with enzymes than without. They operate within a narrow temperature range, usually 30°C to 40°C (86°F to 104°F) and have optimal pH ranges. Many enzymes have to be bound to non-protein molecules to function. These molecules include **trace elements** (such as metals) and **co-enzymes** (such as vitamins).

Eocene Second of the five epochs of the TERTIARY period, *c.*55–38 million years ago. The fossil record shows members of modern plant genera, including beeches, walnuts, and elms, and indicates the apparent dominance of mammals, including the ancestors of camels, horses, rodents, bats, and monkeys.

Eos In Greek mythology, the goddess of dawn, identified with the Roman goddess Aurora. Daughter of HYPERION, and sister of HELIOS and SELENE, she rode the sky in a chariot.

Ephesus (Efes) Ancient Ionian city of w Asia Minor (modern Turkey). A prosperous port under the Greeks and Romans, it was a centre of the cult of Artemis (Diana). The Temple of Artemis was the largest Greek temple ever built and was one of the SEVEN WONDERS OF THE WORLD. Ephesus was captured by CROESUS (*c.*550BC), CYRUS THE GREAT (*c.*546BC) and by ALEXANDER THE GREAT (334BC), falling eventually into Roman control (133BC). Today, it is one of the world's principal archaeological sites.

epic Long, narrative poem in grandiose style. The earliest known form of Greek literature, epics were originally used to transmit history orally. Using highly formalized language, epics tend to involve gods, men and legendary battles. HOMER is the author of two of the most famous epics, the *Iliad* and the *Odyssey*, which effectively established the scope and conventions of the form.

Epicureanism School of Greek philosophy founded by EPICURUS. He proposed that the sensations of pleasure and pain were the ultimate measures of good and evil, and that pleasure should be actively pursued. He also embraced a theory of physics derived from the ATOMISM of DEMOCRITUS, and a theology denying the existence of an afterlife.

Epicurus (*c.*341–*c.*270 BC) Greek philosopher, founder of EPICUREANISM. Born on the island of Samos, he began teaching philosophy at the age of 32. Epicurus settled in Athens in 306 BC and taught students in his garden. He wrote many books and letters, only fragments remain.

epidemic Outbreak of an infectious disease rapidly spreading to many people. The study of epidemics, which includes causes, patterns of contagion and methods of containment, is known as **epidemiology**. An epidemic sweeping across many countries, such as the BLACK DEATH, is termed a pandemic.

epidermis In animals, outer layer that contains no blood vessels. In many invertebrates, it is only one cell thick. In vertebrates, it may comprise several layers and forms part of the SKIN. In plants, the epidermis is the outermost layer of a leaf or of an unthickened stem or root; it is usually coated in a waxy layer, the CUTICLE, which reduces water loss.

epiglottis Small flap of CARTILAGE projecting upwards behind the root of the tongue. It closes off the LARYNX during swallowing to prevent food entering the airway.

epilepsy Disorder characterized by abnormal electrical discharges in the brain which provoke seizures. It is seen both in generalized forms, involving the whole of the CEREBRAL CORTEX, or in partial (focal) attacks arising in one small part of the brain. Attacks are often presaged by warning symptoms, the 'aura'. Seizure types vary from the momentary loss of awareness seen in *petit mal* attacks to the major convulsions of *grand mal* epilepsy. They may be triggered by a number of factors, including sleep deprivation, flashing lights or excessive noise.

Epiphany Christian feast celebrated on January 6. It originated in the Eastern Church as an observance of the baptism of Jesus. In the West, it became associated with the manifestation of Christ to the Gentiles and more particularly it has come to celebrate the coming of the Magi (Three Wise Men).

epiphyte (air plant) Plant that grows on another plant, but is not a PARASITE. Epiphytes usually have aerial roots and produce their own food by PHOTOSYNTHESIS. They are common in tropical forests. Examples are some FERNS, ORCHIDS, Spanish moss, and many BROMELIADS.

Episcopal Church US Anglican Church. CHURCH OF ENGLAND services were held in the first American colonies. With the AMERICAN REVOLUTION, the Church of England disestablished, and a national church organized in its place. Known as the Protestant Episcopal Church, its constitution and version of the Book of COMMON PRAYER were established in 1789. In 1873, a breakaway group of clergy and laity founded the Reformed Episcopal Church .

epistemology Branch of philosophy that critically examines the nature, limits and validity of knowledge, and the difference between knowledge and belief. DESCARTES showed that many previously 'philosophical' questions would be better studied scientifically, and that what remained of metaphysics should be absorbed into epistemology.

INTERNET

Entente Cordiale
▶ www.yale.edu/lawweb/
avalon/entencord.htm

Ephesus
▶ www.sailturkey.com/
panoramas/ephesus

Epistles Collection of 20 letters forming most of the middle section of the New Testament. More than half of them are attributed to Saint PAUL while the rest are by various writers: two by Peter, three by John, one by James and one by Jude. The author of the Epistle to the Hebrews is unknown. The Epistle to the Romans contains the single most complete formulation of Paul's teachings.

epithelium Layer of cells, closely packed to form a surface for a body tube or cavity. Epithelium covers the SKIN, and various internal organs and surfaces such as the intestines, nasal passages and mouth. Epithelial cells may also produce protective modifications such as hair and nails, or secrete substances such as ENZYMES and mucus.

epoxy resin Group of thermosetting polymers with outstandingly good mechanical and electrical properties, stability, heat and chemical resistance and adhesion. Epoxy resins are used as adhesives, in casting and as protective coatings.

Epstein, Sir Jacob (1880–1959) British sculptor, b. USA. He made his most audacious sculptural statements before 1920, starting with a series of 18 nude figures (1907–08), whose explicit representation caused a public outcry. He scandalized Paris with the angel carved for Oscar Wilde's tomb (1912). His most revolutionary sculpture was *The Rock Drill* (1913–14), a modernist form which suggests both ape and machine and which caused much controversy.

equation Mathematical statement of VARIABLES, equal to some subset of all possible variables. The equation $x^2 = 8 - 2x$ is true only for certain values (solutions) of x ($x = 2$ and $x = -4$). This type of equation is contrasted with an identity, such as $(x+2)^2 = x^2 + 4x + 4$, which is true for all values of x. Equations are said to be linear, QUADRATIC, cubic, quartic, etc., according to whether their degree (the highest power of the variable) is 1, 2, 3, 4, etc. *See also* SIMULTANEOUS EQUATIONS

equator Name given to two imaginary circles. The **terrestrial** equator lies midway between the North Pole and South Pole and is the zero line from which LATITUDE is measured. It divides the Earth into the Southern and Northern Hemispheres. The **celestial** equator lies directly above the Earth's equator, and is used as a reference to determine the position of a star using the astronomical co-ordinate system of right ascension and declination.

Equatorial Guinea (formerly Spanish Guinea) Republic in W central Africa,. *see* country feature.

equilibrium In physics, a stable state in which any variety of forces acting on a particle or object negate each other, resulting in no net force. While equilibrium is often thought of as a state of balance or rest, an object with constant velocity is also said to be in equilibrium. The term can also be ascribed to a body with a constant temperature; this is known as **thermic equilibrium**.

EQUATORIAL GUINEA

The Republic of Equatorial Guinea is located in W central Africa and is one of the smallest countries on the African continent. It consists of a mainland territory between Cameroon and Gabon, called Río Muni (Mbini), and five islands in the Bight of Biafra (Bonny), the largest of which is Bioko (Fernando Póo).

Bioko is a volcanic island with fertile soils and a steep rocky coast. MALABO's harbour is part of a submerged volcano. Bioko is mountainous, rising to a height of 3,008m [9,869ft] at the Pico de Santa Isabel. It has varied vegetation with trees such as teak, mahogany, oak, walnut and rosewood, and grasslands at higher levels.

Mainland Río Muni (90% of all land) consists mainly of hills and plateaux behind the coastal plains. Its main river, the Lolo, rises in Gabon. Dense forest covers most of Río Muni and provides a habitat for animals such as lions, gazelles and elephants .

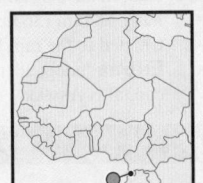

CLIMATE
Situated on the equator, Equatorial Guinea has a tropical climate. High temperatures and high humidity are the norm with an average annual temperature of 25°C [77°F]. Bioko has heavy rainfall and there is a dry

season from December to February. Río Muni has a similar climate to Bioko, though rainfall diminishes inland.

HISTORY
In 1472 Portuguese navigator Fernão do Pó sighted the largest island of Bioko. In 1778, Portugal ceded the islands and commercial mainland rights to Spain in exchange for some Brazilian territories. Yellow fever hit Spanish settlers on Bioko, and they withdrew in 1781. In 1827, Spain leased bases on Bioko to Britain, and the British settled some freed slaves. Descendants of these former slaves (Fernandinos) remain on the island. Spain returned in the mid-19th century and developed plantations on Bioko.

In 1956 Bioko and Mbini, the islands in the Gulf of Guinea, became Spanish Overseas Provinces. In 1959, the territory was divided into two provinces, Fernando Póo and Río Muni, and named Spanish Guinea. The two territories reunified in 1963 and attained partial self-government as the Autonomous Territories of Equatorial Guinea. In 1968 the territory gained full independence and became a republic.

POLITICS
In 1969, after social unrest caused by ethnic conflict and economic problems, President Francisco Macías Nguema annulled the constitution. A military dictatorship ensued, and up to 100,000 refugees fled to neighbouring countries. Nguema's dictatorship endured from until 1979, by which time more than 40,000 people had been killed.

In 1979, Lieutenant-Colonel Teodoro Obiang Nguema Mbasogo deposed Nguema in a military coup. A 1991 referendum voted to set up a multiparty democracy, consisting of the ruling Equatorial Guinea Democratic Party (PDGE) and ten opposition parties. The main parties and most of the electorate boycotted elections in 1993, and the PDGE formed a

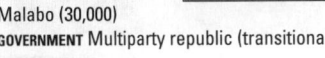

AREA 28,051sq km
[10,830sq mi]
POPULATION 551,000
CAPITAL (POPULATION)
Malabo (30,000)
GOVERNMENT Multiparty republic (transitional)
ETHNIC GROUPS
Bubi (on Bioko), Fang (in Rio Muni)
LANGUAGES Spanish and French (both official)
RELIGIONS Christianity
CURRENCY CFA franc = 100 centimes

government. In 1996 elections, again boycotted by most opposition parties, President Obiang claimed 99% of the vote. Human rights organizations accuse his regime of routine arrests and torture of opponents and the president is seen to control all the political parties.

In 2004, a coup attempt by foreign mercenaries was foiled and the leaders were arrested.

ECONOMY
Equatorial Guinea is a poor country. Agriculture employs around 60% of the people, though many farmers live at subsistence level, making little contribution to the economy. The main food crops are bananas, cassava and sweet potatoes. The chief cash crop is cocoa, grown on Bioko, although this has been hit by a worldwide dip in cocoa prices.

Oil has been produced off Bioko since 1966. By 2002 it accounted for more than 80% of exports. Despite the rapid expansion of the economy and massive increase in revenue, a UN human rights report stated that 65% of the people still live in extreme poverty.

The government has promised that agriculture will benefit from the large amounts of revenue gained from oil, but this has yet to materialize. Other natural resources that have yet to be developed include titanium, iron ore, manganese and uranium. The country has forfeited much aid from the World Bank and the IMF due to corruption and mismanagement.

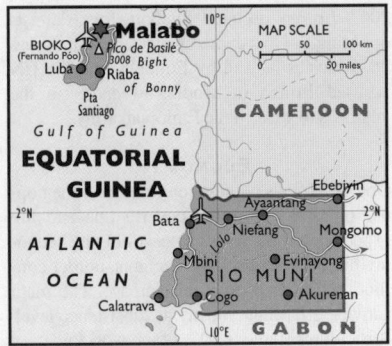

▲ **Erasmus** *Portrait of Desiderius Erasmus* by Hans Holbein (the Younger). Erasmus criticized clerical abuse and Church involvement in material matters. *The Education of a Christian Prince* (1515) is Erasmus' greatest work.

INTERNET

Eritrea
▶ www.afrika.no/index/
Countries/Eritrea/index.html

equinox Either of the two days each year when day and night are of equal duration. They occur on the two occasions, (one spring, one autumn) when the Sun crosses the celestial equator. In the Northern Hemisphere, the **Vernal** (spring) Equinox occurs around March 21 and the **Autumnal** Equinox around September 23.

equity In law, a field of jurisdiction that enables the judiciary to apply principles or morals in cases where strict adherence to the law would result in unjust sentencing. In some systems, equity is considered before the jury makes its decision.

Erasmus, Desiderius (1466–1536) (Gerhard Gerhards) Dutch scholar and teacher, the greatest of the RENAISSANCE humanists. His Latin translation of the Greek New Testament revealed flaws in the VULGATE text. He edited the writings of Saint JEROME and other patristic literature. Among his original works, *Enchiridion militis* ('*Manual of the Christian Knight*', 1503) emphasized simple piety as an ideal of CHRISTIANITY and called for reform of the Church. His works influenced Martin LUTHER and other Protestant reformers, although Erasmus sought change from within the Catholic Church and disagreed with the course of the REFORMATION. In *On Free Will* (1524), he clashed openly with Luther. *See also* HUMANISM

Erastianism Complete control of Church affairs by the State. It is named after Thomas Erastus (1524–85), a Swiss physician and theologian, who denied that the Church alone had disciplinary powers, especially of excommunication. Hence, Erastianism is a distortion of his position, which assumed cooperation between Church and State.

Eratosthenes (*c.*276–*c.*194 BC) Greek scholar who first measured the Earth's circumference by geometry. He administered the library of ALEXANDRIA and was renowned for his work in mathematics, geography, philosophy and literature.

erbium (symbol Er) Silvery, metallic element of the LANTHANIDE SERIES. There are six isotopes naturally occurring, and the chief ores are monazite and bastnaesite. Nine radioactive isotopes have been identified. Soft and malleable, erbium is used in some specialized alloys, and erbium oxide is used as a pink colourant for glass. Properties: at.no. 68; r.a.m. 167.26; m.p. 1522°C (2772°F); r.d. 9.045; b.p. 2863°C (5185°F); most common isotope Er^{166} (33.41%).

erica Genus of more than 500 species of mostly low, evergreen shrubs comprising true heaths and heathers. Most species are native to Africa, but many grow on moors in Britain and other parts of Europe. Blossoms are colourful and tube-shaped or bell-shaped. Family Ericaceae.

Eric the Red (active late 10th century) Norse chieftain, who settled on Greenland. Born in Norway, he was then banished from Iceland after a murder. He set off to the west, and discovered the land he named Greenland in *c.*981. Returning to Iceland, he organized a party of colonists who set out for Greenland in *c.*985.

Erie, Lake Great Lake in North America, bordered by Ontario (W), New York (E), Ohio and Pennsylvania (S), and Michigan (SW); part of the GREAT LAKES-ST LAWRENCE SEAWAY. It was the site of a British defeat by the USA in the WAR OF 1812. It has been polluted by the cities on its shores. Government regulations are now aiding its recovery. Area: 25,667sq km (9910sq mi). Max. depth: 64m (210ft).

Erie Canal Waterway in New York state, between Buffalo and Albany, USA. It was built in 1817–25, and was originally 584km (363mi) long. A commercial success, it contributed to the rapid growth of the MIDWEST.

Eritrea Independent state in NE Africa, on the Red Sea; the capital is ASMARA. *see* country feature.

ERITREA

Eritrea occupies a strategic position on the Red Sea in NE Africa. The coastal plain extends inland for between 16 and 64km [10–40mi]. Inland are mountains. In the SW, the mountains descend to the Danakil Desert, which contains Eritrea's lowest point at 75m [246ft] below sea level.

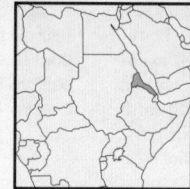

CLIMATE
The temperature ranges from 16°C [61°F] in the highlands to 27°C [81°F] on the coastal plain. Rainfall on the coastal plain is between 150 and 250mm [6–10in] with up to 610mm [24in] in the highlands. The rainy season is from June to September.

HISTORY
The first settlers were from Africa, followed by others from the Arabian peninsula. Between AD 50 and 600, Eritrea was part of the Ethiopian kingdom of Axum. The people were converted to Christianity in the 4th

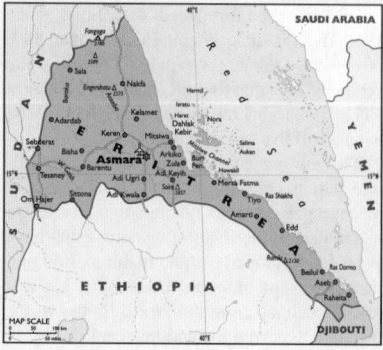

century, and Islam was introduced to the coastal areas in the 7th century. Christianity survived inland.

In the 16th century, the Ottoman Empire took over the coastal area. During the 19th century control of the region was disputed between Ethiopia, Egypt and Italy. Eritrea became an Italian colony in 1890, and in 1935 Italy also conquered Ethiopia. During World War 2, British drove the Italians out of NE Africa. From 1941–52, Eritrea was under British military administration. In 1952 the UN made Eritrea a self-governing part of Ethiopia. Ethiopian rule proved unpopular and, in 1958, Eritrean nationalists formed the Eritrean Liberation Front (ELF). War broke out in 1961 between the ELF and the Ethiopians. In 1962, Ethiopia declared Eritrea to be a province, sparking off a war of independence.

The Eritrean People's Liberation Front (EPLF) was formed in 1970, replacing the ELF as the main anti-Ethiopian organization. In 1974, Ethiopian Emperor Haile Selassie was overthrown and a military government took power. EPLF victories gradually weakened Ethiopia's government. and the regime collapsed in 1991. The EPLF then formed a provisional government.

POLITICS
Eritrea declared independence in 1993, with Isaias Afewerki as president. The government has been criticized for the repression of opposition and for closing the private press in 2001.

Eritrea's relations with Ethiopia deteriorated in 1998 over a border dispute around the town of Badme on the SW border. Ethiopia bombed

AREA 45,405sq miles [117,600sq km]
POPULATION 4,907,000
CAPITAL (POPULATION) Asmara (358,000)
GOVERNMENT Transitional government
ETHNIC GROUPS Tigrinya 50%, Tigre and Kunama 40%, Afar 4%, Saho 3% and others
LANGUAGES Afar, Arabic, Tigre and Kunama, Tigrinya
RELIGIONS Islam, Coptic Christian, Roman Catholic
CURRENCY Nakfa = 100 cents

Asmara airport, Eritrea attacked Mekele in N Ethiopia, and war broke out. In 2000 the UN intervened to support a peace plan. In 2001 the two countries agreed to a UN-proposed mediator to demarcate the border, which in 2003 ruled that Badme lies in Eritrea, but both sides refused to accept the new borders. Tension continued and, in late 2005, Eritrea ordered UN peace-keeping troops to leave the country. In 2007 Eritrea declared support for Islamists opposing the transitional government in Somalia, which is backed by Ethiopia, and the UN accused Eritrea of sending weapons to the Islamists to weaken the Ethiopian army.

ECONOMY
One of Africa's poorest countries, half the population lives below the poverty line and life expectancy is 52 years. Since 1993, the economy has been set back by droughts, border conflict, and high population increase. The main activity is farming, mostly at subsistence level. Agriculture employs 80% of the workforce.

ermine Known as a STOAT in Eurasia, or short-tailed WEASEL in North America.

Ernst, Max (1891–1976) German painter and sculptor, founder of Cologne DADA (1919), later influential in SURREALISM. Ernst was a prolific innnovator and developed ways of adapting COLLAGE, photomontage and other pictorial techniques. His most important works include *L'Eléphant Célèbes* (1921). Ernst left the surrealist movement in 1938 and lived in New York (1941–48), where he collaborated on the periodical *VVV* with André BRETON and Marcel DUCHAMP.

Eros Elongated asteroid with an irregular orbit. In 1931 and 1975, it approached to within 24 million km (15 million mi) of Earth. Longer diameter, 27km (17mi); mean distance from the Sun, 232 million km (144 million mi); mean sidereal period 1.76yr.

Eros In GREEK MYTHOLOGY, god of love, equivalent to the Roman god Cupid. Depicted as a winged boy carrying a bow and arrows, and often blindfold, he was the youngest and most mischievous of the gods. He married PSYCHE.

erosion Alteration of landforms by the wearing away of rock and soil, and the removal of any debris. Erosion is carried out by the actions of wind, water, glaciers and living organisms. In **chemical** erosion, minerals in the rock react to other substances, such as acids found in rainwater, and are broken down. In **physical** erosion, powerful forces such as rivers and glaciers wear rock down and transport it. Erosion can have disastrous economic results, such as the removal of topsoil, the gradual destruction of buildings and the alteration of water systems. Inland, erosion occurs most drastically by the action of rivers, and in coastal regions, by waves.

erratic In geology, a rock that has been transported some distance from its source by glacial action, and is therefore of a different type to the surrounding rocks. The tracing of erratics can give important information about the movement of ice.

erythrocyte Red blood cell, usually disc-shaped and without a nucleus. It contains HAEMOGLOBIN, which combines with oxygen and gives blood its red colour. Normal human blood contains an average of 5 million such cells per cu mm of blood.

Esaki, Leo (1925–) Japanese physicist, who developed the tunnel DIODE, a SEMICONDUCTOR that allows electrons to cross normally impassable electronic barriers. US physicist Ivar Giaever extended Esaki's research to the field of SUPERCONDUCTIVITY. For this work, they shared the 1973 Nobel Prize in physics with Brian JOSEPHSON. The Esaki diode is used in computer data storage.

Esau Old Testament figure who sold for refreshment his future inheritance to his scheming brother JACOB. The story probably derives from an attempt to give an ancient background to the enmity between the Israelites and the Edomites.

escape velocity Minimum velocity required to free a body from the gravitational field of a celestial body or stellar system. Escape velocities are: for the Earth, 11.2km/sec (7mi/s); and for the Moon, 2.4km/sec (1.5mi/s). They can be calculated from the formula: $v = (2G\,M/R)^{1/2}$ where G is the gravitational constant, M the mass of the planet or system, and R the distance of the rocket from the centre of mass of the system.

Escher, Maurits Cornelis (1898–1972) Dutch graphic artist. He is best known for his prints based on mathematical premises. These contain bizarre metamorphoses, illusions and paradoxical structures as in *Ascending and Descending* (1960).

Escorial Monastery and palace near Madrid, central Spain. Built between 1563 and 1584 for PHILIP II, it comprises a massive group of buildings arranged in a square plan, dominated by church towers. Escorial houses a notable art collection.

Esfahan *See* ISFAHAN

Eshkol, Levi (1895–1969) Israeli statesman, prime minister (1963–69), b. Ukraine. Eshkol established one of the first *kibbutzim* (cooperative farms), became minister of finance (1952–53), created the Israel Labour Party, and succeeded David BEN-GURION as prime minister.

Eskimo (Algonquian, eaters of raw flesh) Aboriginal inhabitants (c.60,000) of Arctic and sub-Arctic regions of North America (the INUIT), Greenland and Siberia. Sharing the common language family of Eskimo-ALEUT, Eskimos have adapted to harsh climates and are proficient hunters of sea

mammals. In some areas, a nomadic existence has been replaced by village settlements and work in the oil and mining industries. The eating of raw meat preserves scarce resources and provides essential nutrients. In winter, igloos (snow huts) provide temporary shelter. In summer, tents are made from animal skins. Eskimos are skilled artisans, producing kayaks and finely crafted tools from skin, ivory, bone, copper or stone. Their spiritual life is dominated by invisible forces of nature (*innua*). SHAMANISM plays an important role in everyday life.

Esperanto Language devised in 1887 by Ludwik Zamenhof (1859–1917), as a language of international communication. Its spelling and grammar are regular and consistent, and its vocabulary mostly derived from W European languages.

essay (Fr. *essai*, 'attempt') Usually short, non-fictional prose composition, written expressing a personal point of view. The essay form originated with the 16th-century French writer Montaigne. British essayists include Francis BACON, Henry FIELDING, Samuel JOHNSON, Oliver GOLDSMITH and Charles LAMB. Noted US essayists include Ralph Waldo EMERSON, Henry David THOREAU, Oliver Wendell HOLMES, James THURBER, George SANTAYANA, and Dorothy PARKER.

Essen City on the River Ruhr, Nordrhein-Westfalen, NW Germany. Essen developed around a 9th-century Benedictine convent. Prussia annexed it in 1802. Lying at the centre of a major coalfield, it underwent a huge industrial expansion

EROSION

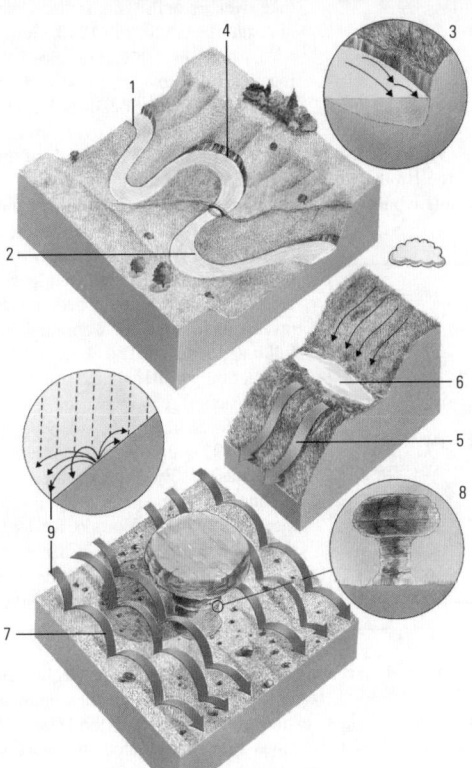 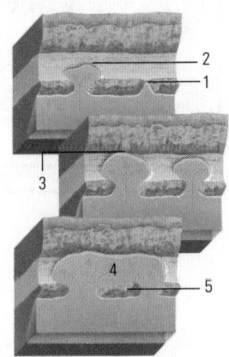

▼ **coastal erosion** The powerful action of the waves produces recognizable features. Horseshoe bays (below), for example, form when rock layers of different hardness lie parallel to the coast. The erosive power of the sea exploits areas of weakness in a hard rock deposit (1). Waves will then cut away any softer rock behind (2), eroding back until they reach another strata of harder rock (3). When bays join (4), islands of hard rock can be left across the mouth (5).

Erosion is the breakdown and transportation of rock due to the action of an outside agent. There are three main forms: river, glacial, and wind. Rivers (1) erode their channels through the flow of water and the abrasion of banks and riverbed by the material they carry. Erosion is most forceful at the outside of bends (2), where the banks are undercut (3), often creating cliffs or bluffs (4) down which material

moves. Flood surges dramatically increase the power of the river and correspondingly magnify the erosive force. On a smaller scale, rainwater moves material down a hillside (5). Rivulets carry particles of soil and the impact of raindrops throws soil down slope. Vegetation reduces such erosion by binding the soil together. Where vegetation is removed, as on tracks (6),

erosion increases. In arid conditions, wind erosion can carve distinctive features. Sand and stones blown by the wind (7) have the same effect as shot-blasting. Mushroom-shaped formations, pedestals, (8) are often the result. This is due to the maximum height at which the erosive sand is carried by the wind as it bounces across the surface (9). Above this height, the rock remains untouched.

ESTONIA

The Republic of Estonia is the smallest of the three states on the E coast of the Baltic Sea, formerly part of the Soviet Union, which became independent in the early 1990s. Estonia consists of a generally flat plain which was covered by ice sheets during the Ice Age. The land is strewn with moraine rocks deposited by the ice.

The country is dotted with more than 1,500 small lakes. Water, including the large Lake Peipus (Ozero Chudskoye) and the River Narva, makes up much of Estonia's E border with Russia. Estonia has more than 800 islands, which together comprise about a tenth of the country. The largest island is Saaremaa (Sarema). Farmland and pasture account for more than 33% of land use.

CLIMATE
Despite its N position, Estonia has a fairly mild climate due to its proximity to the sea. Sea winds tend to warm the land during winter and cool it in summer. Rainfall averages from 480 to 580mm (19–23in).

HISTORY
The ancestors of the Estonians, who are related to the Finns, settled in the area several thousand years ago. Divided into several separate states, they were vulnerable to Viking attacks. In 1217 the German order of the Brothers of the Sword conquered S Estonia (Livonia) and

introduced Christianity. Germany took control of the S part of Estonia and Denmark took control of the N. The Danes sold the N to the Germans in 1324 and by 1346 the TEUTONIC KNIGHTS controlled the country. Estonia became part of the Holy Roman Empire, and by the 16th century German nobles owned much of the land.

In 1561, Sweden took over N Estonia and Poland ruled the S. Sweden controlled the entire country from 1625 until 1721 but, following the victory of Peter the Great over Sweden in the Great Northern War (1700–21), the area became part of the Russian Empire. On 24 February 1918, Estonia declared its independence. A democratic form of government was established in 1919. However, a fascist coup in 1934 ended democratic rule.

POLITICS
In 1939, Germany and the Soviet Union agreed to take over large areas of E Europe, and it was agreed that the Soviet Union would take over Estonia. The Soviet Union forcibly annexed the country in 1940. Germany invaded Estonia in 1941, but the Soviet Union regained control in 1944 and created the Estonian Soviet Socialist Republic. Many Estonians opposed Soviet rule and were deported to Siberia. Hundreds of thousands of Russians were settled in Estonia.

Resistance to Soviet rule was fuelled in the 1980s when the Soviet leader Mikhail Gorbachev began to introduce reforms and many Estonians called for independence. In 1990, the Estonian parliament declared Soviet rule invalid and called for a gradual transition to full independence. The Soviet Union regarded this action as illegal, but finally the Soviet State Council recognized the Estonian parliament's proclamation of independence in September 1991, shortly before the Soviet Union itself was dissolved in December 1991.

Since independence, Estonia has sought to increase links with Europe. It was admitted to the Council of Europe in 1993; has been a member of the World Trade Organization since 1999 and a member of NATO and the

AREA 45,100sq km [17,413sq mi]
POPULATION 1,316,000
CAPITAL (POPULATION) Tallinn (418,000)
GOVERNMENT Multiparty republic
ETHNIC GROUPS Estonian 65%, Russian 28%, Ukrainian 2%, Belarusian 2%, Finnish 1%
LANGUAGES Estonian (official), Russian
RELIGIONS Lutheran, Russian and Estonian Orthodox, Methodist, Baptist, Roman Catholic
CURRENCY Estonian kroon = 100 senti

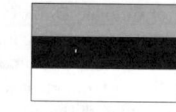

European Union since 2004. Other problems facing Estonia include crime, rural under-development and the status of its non-Estonian citizens, including Russians, who make up about 30% of the population. In the country's first free elections in 1992, only Estonians were permitted to vote and all Russians were excluded. Tension on this issue continued through the 1990s as dual citizenship was outlawed, while restrictions were placed on Russians applying for Estonian citizenship.

ECONOMY
Despite having had the highest standard of living of the 15 former Soviet republics, Estonia found the transition to a free–market economy difficult. After initial problems the economy entered rapid growth, particularly in IT and finance. This has brought high inflation, which has postponed Estonia's intended adoption of the Euro.

The timber industry is still important, alongside metal-working, shipbuilding, clothing, textiles, chemicals and food processing. Food processing is based on efficient dairy farming and pig breeding, and oats, barley and potatoes suit the cool climate. Like the other Baltic states, Estonia is poor in natural resources, although oil shale is an important mineral deposit; enough gas is extracted to supply St Petersburg, Russia's second largest city. The leading exports are mineral fuels and chemical products, followed by food, textiles, cloth, wood and paper products. Finland and Russia are the main trading partners.

during the 19th century and is home to the Krupp steelworks. It has a cathedral (begun 11th century). Industries: mining, iron and steel, glass, textiles, chemicals. Pop. (1999) 600,700.

Essenes Jewish religious sect that existed in Palestine from the 2nd century BC to the end of the 2nd century AD. Members of the sect, adult men, lived in communal groups isolated from society. A secrecy developed about the sect, and they shunned public life and temple worship. The DEAD SEA SCROLLS are said to contain their sacred books.

essential oil Oil found in flowers, fruits or plants. It is the source of their characteristic odour and is widely used in aromatherapy, potpourri, and perfumed toiletries. Many are obtained from plants that originate in dry, Mediterranean climates. These oils are usually produced by special GLANDS.

Essex County in SE England; the county town is Chelmsford. Colonized by the Romans at COLCHESTER, the Anglo-Saxons invaded it in the 5th century, and later came under Danish control. Low lying on the E coast, the land rises to the NW, providing pasture for dairy and sheep farming. Wheat, barley, and sugar beet are grown. Industries: machinery, electrical goods. Area: 3674sq km (1419sq mi). Pop. (2001) 1,310,922.

ester Any of a class of organic compounds formed by reaction between an ALCOHOL and an ACID. Water is eliminated in the process. The **esterification** reaction is the opposite of HYDROLYSIS.

Esther Old Testament book narrating how the legendary Queen Esther averted the killing of her people, the Jews, by the Persians in Babylon. She persuaded king Xerxes I of Persia to ignore his grand vizier Haman, who advocated their extermination. The Jewish feast of Purim celebrates Haman's overthrow.

Estonia Republic on the E coast of the Baltic Sea, *see* country feature.

estuary Coastal region where a river mouth opens into the ocean and freshwater from the land mixes with saltwater from the sea. Estuaries usually provide good harbours and breeding grounds for many kinds of marine life.

etching Method of incised printing used for black-and-white designs. A metal plate, usually copper, is coated with an acid-proof ground. A design is etched with a needle through the ground. The plate is placed in an acid that eats away the exposed line so it will hold ink. When the plate is finished, it is rolled with ink and placed in a press to be printed.

ethanal (acetaldehyde) Colourless volatile flammable liquid (CH_3CHO) manufactured by catalytic oxidation of ethene or ethanol, or catalytic hydration of acetylene. It is used in the breathalyser test and to silver mirrors. Properties: r.d. 0.788; m.p. $-123.5°C$ ($-190.3°F$); b.p. $20.8°C$ ($69.4°F$).

ethane Colourless odourless gas (CH_3CH_3), the second member of the ALKANE series of HYDROCARBONS. It is a minor constituent of natural gas. *See also* SATURATED COMPOUND

ethanoate (acetate) Salt or ester of ethanoic acid. A compound containing the ion CH_3COO or the group CH_3COO-. It is used in synthetic fibres, lacquers and acetate film.

ethanoic acid (acetic acid) Colourless, corrosive liquid (CH_3COOH) made by the oxidation of ethanol, either by catalysis or by the action of bacteria. It is the active ingredient in VINEGAR, and has many uses in the organic chemicals industry. Properties: r.d. 1.049; m.p. $16.6°C$ ($61.9°F$); b.p. $117.9°C$ ($244.4°F$).

ethanol (ethyl alcohol) Colourless, volatile ALCOHOL (C_2H_5OH), produced by the fermentation of sugars, molasses and grains, or by the catalytic hydration of ethylene. Also known as grain alcohol, its uses include alcoholic beverages, cleaning solutions, antifreeze, rocket fuels, cosmetics and pharmaceuticals. Properties: r.d. 0.789; b.p. $78.5°C$ ($173.3°F$).

Ethelbert (d.616) King of Kent (560–616). He was the strongest ruler in England s of the River Humber, and was the first Christian king in Anglo-Saxon England. He allowed AUGUSTINE and his monks to settle and preach in Canterbury.

Ethelred II (the Unready) (968–1016) (Old English, evil *rede*, 'counsel') King of England (978–1013; 1014–16). Fol-

lowing continuous Danish attacks, he paid off the raiders with money raised by the Danegeld (994). The Danes returned nevertheless in 997, and again in 1002 when they were massacred by Ethelred's forces. The Danish King Sweyn retaliated and conquered England (1013). Ethelred was made king again on Sweyn's death, but was succeeded by Sweyn's son CANUTE II.

ethene (ethylene) Colourless gas (C_2H_4) derived from the cracking of propane and other compounds. Vast quantities are used in polyethylene production. Ethene is also used for many other chemical syntheses.

ether In physics, hypothetical medium that was supposed to fill all space and offer no resistance to motion. It was postulated as a medium to support the propagation of electromagnetic radiations, but was disproved.

ether (diethyl ether) Colourless volatile inflammable liquid ($C_2H_5OC_2H_5$) prepared by the action of sulphuric acid on ethanol followed by distillation. It is used as an industrial solvent, fuel additive and decreasingly as an anaesthetic. Diethyl ether is a typical member of the ethers with the general formula ROR', where R,R' are hydrocarbon radicals. Properties: m.p. $-116.2°C$ ($-117.2°F$); b.p. $34.5°C$ ($94.1°F$).

ethics (moral philosophy) Study of voluntary human actions, according to moral precepts. For ARISTOTLE, happiness was achieved through cultivation of virtue. PLATO's ethical system was based on metaphysical IDEALISM. HEDONISM taught that the pursuit of pleasure was the highest good. STOICS advocated virtue through harmony with nature. RATIONALISM postulated conscience as the basis of moral behaviour. EMPIRICISM argued that conscience was acquired by experience. KANT put moral

INTERNET

Etna
▶ boris.vulcanoetna.com

ETHIOPIA

Ethiopia is dominated by the Ethiopian Plateau, a block of volcanic mountains. Its average height is 1,800 to 2,450m [6,000 to 8,000ft], rising in the N to 4620m [15,157ft], at Ras Dashen. The Great RIFT VALLEY bisects the plateau. The E Highlands include the Somali Plateau and the desert of the Ogaden Plateau. The W Highlands include the capital, ADDIS ABABA, the Blue NILE (Abbay) and its source, Lake Tana (Ethiopia's largest lake). The Danakil Desert forms Ethiopia's border with Eritrea. Grass, farmland, and trees cover most of the highlands. Semi-desert and tropical savanna cover parts of the lowlands. Dense rainforest grows in the SW.

CLIMATE

Ethiopia's climate is greatly affected by altitude. Addis Ababa, at 2,450m [8,000ft], has an average annual temperature of 20°C [68°F]. Rainfall

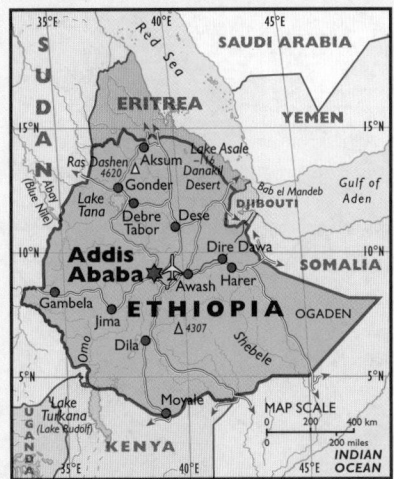

is generally over 1,000mm [39in], with a rainy season from April to September. The NE and SW lowlands are extremely hot and arid with less than 500mm [20in] rainfall, and frequent droughts.

HISTORY

According to legend, Menelik I, son of King Solomon and the Queen of Sheba, founded Ethiopia in about 1000 BC. In AD 321, the northern kingdom of Axum introduced Coptic Christianity. Judaism flourished in the 6th century. The expansion of Islam led to the isolation of Axum, and the kingdom fragmented in the 16th century.

In 1855, Kasa reestablished unity and proclaimed himself Negus (Emperor) Theodore, founding the modern state. European intervention marked the late 19th century, and Menelik II became emperor with Italian support. He expanded the empire, made Addis Ababa his capital (1889) and defeated an Italian invasion (1895). In 1930, Menelik II's grandnephew, Ras Tafari Makonnen, was crowned Emperor HAILE SELASSIE I. In 1935, Italian troops invaded. In 1936, Italy combined Ethiopia with Somalia and Eritrea to form Italian East Africa. During World War 2, British and South African forces recaptured Ethiopia, and Haile Selassie was restored as emperor in 1941.

POLITICS

Eritrea federated with Ethiopia in 1952, but the 1960s saw violent demands for Eritrean secession. In 1962 Ethiopia annexed Eritrea. Following famine in N Ethiopia, Selassie was killed in 1974. The Provisional Military Administrative Council (PMAC) abolished the monarchy. Military rule was repressive, and civil war broke out. The new PMAC leader, Mengistu Mariam, recaptured territory in Eritrea and the Ogaden

AREA 1,104,300sq km [426,370sq mi]
POPULATION 76,512,000
CAPITAL (POPULATION) Addis Ababa (2,899,000)
GOVERNMENT Federation of nine provinces
ETHNIC GROUPS Oromo 40%, Amhara and Tigre 32%, Sidamo 9%, Shankella 6%, Somali 6% , others
LANGUAGES Amharic (official), many others
RELIGIONS Islam 47%, Ethiopian Orthodox 40%, traditional beliefs 12%
CURRENCY Birr = 100 cents

with Soviet military assistance. In 1984–5 widespread famine received global news coverage and 10,000 of the Ethiopian Jewish BETA ISRAEL were airlifted to Israel.

In 1991, the Ethiopian People's Revolutionary Democratic Front and Eritrean People's Liberation Front deposed Mengistu. In 1995 the Federal Democratic Republic of Ethiopia was created, with Meles Zenawi as prime minister. Border disputes with Eritrea led to war from 1998–2000. Elections in 2005 led to protests and a crackdown on the opposition and press. Ethiopia intervened against Somalia's Islamist government in 2006, and in 2007 sent troops to support the transitional government.

ECONOMY

Having been afflicted by drought and civil war in the 1970s and 1980s, Ethiopia is now one of the world's poorest countries. Agriculture is the main activity. In 2004, a UN report stated that Ethiopia remained on the brink of disaster, with spiralling population growth, slow economic growth and environmental degradation. Coffee is the leading cash crop and export, followed by hides, skins and pulses.

▼ **Europe** Earth's second smallest continent is, strictly speaking, a peninsula of the vast Eurasian land mass. Traditionally, it is separated from Asia by the Urals (E), the Caucasus and the Caspian Sea (SE), and the Black Sea (S). Europe is home to more than 500 million people. The ancient civilizations of Greece and Rome were the cradle of democracy. European languages, culture and religion were disseminated by migration, imperialism and colonialism. Throughout human history, Europe has witnessed many destructive wars. In the 19th century, vast European empires crumbled with the rise of nationalism. The antagonism of these new nation-states led to both World Wars. Europe lay at the heart of the Cold War between capitalism and communism. The collapse of Soviet communism saw the emergence of new nations. The European Union (EU) was formed to promote pan-European co-operation and development.

duty above happiness. He argued that an act is only truly moral if it is motivated solely by duty. The ethics of UTILITARIANISM are based on the principle of the greatest good for the greatest number. *See also* AYER, A.J.; DEWEY, JOHN

Ethiopia Landlocked republic in E Africa. *See* country feature, page 309.

ethnography Study of the culture of an ethnic group or society. Ethnographers gather anthropological data by direct observation of a group's economic and social life. *See also* ANTHROPOLOGY; ETHNOLOGY

ethnology Comparative study of cultures. Historical ethnology was developed in the late 19th century in an attempt to trace cultural diffusion.

ethology Study of animal behaviour, such as courtship, mating and self-defence, especially in the natural environment, first outlined in the 1920s by Konrad LORENZ.

ethylene *See* ETHENE

ethyne (acetylene) Colourless, flammable gas (C_2H_2), manufactured by CRACKING of petroleum fractions. The simplest ALKYNE, it is explosive if mixed with air. When burned with oxygen, it produces very high temperatures up to 3,480°C (6,300°F) and is used in oxyacetylene torches. It is polymerized to manufacture plastics, synthetic fibres, resins and neoprene. It is used to produce ethanal and ethanoic acid. Properties: r.d. 0.625; m.p. −80.8°C (−113.4°F); b.p. −84°C (−119.2°F).

Etna Volcano in E Sicily, Italy. The first known eruption was in 475 BC with others in 1169, 1669 and 1971. It is the highest active volcano in Europe. Height: *c.*3340m (10,958ft).

Etruscan Inhabitant of ancient Etruria (Tuscany and Umbria), Italy. They organized their sophisticated society into city-states. Etruscan civilization reached its peak in the

6th century BC – their wealth and power based primarily on skill at ironworking and control of the iron trade. The Etruscan 'cult of the dead' led them to produce elaborate tombs. From the 5th to the 3rd century BC they were gradually overrun by neighbouring peoples, particularly the Romans.

etymology Branch of PHILOLOGY dealing with the origin and history of words. The word telephone, for example, is a combination of two elements derived from Greek, *tele* ('distant') and *phone* ('sound' or 'voice').

eubacteria Subkingdom of the kingdom PROKARYOTAE, sometimes considered a separate DOMAIN. Eubacteria include all multicellular BACTERIA, including those that photosynthesize, deriving their carbon from the air. They do not have the unique types of cell walls, RIBOSOMES and RNA of the other subkingdom, ARCHAEBACTERIA. *See also* PHOTOSYNTHESIS

Euboea (Évvoia) Island in the W Aegean Sea, SE central Greece; the administrative centre is Khalkís. Under Athenian domination (506–411BC), it was taken by Philip II of Macedon in 338 BC then held successively by the Romans, Byzantines, the Venetians and the Turks, before being incorporated into independent Greece in 1830. Industries: livestock, grapes, timber, grain, marble quarrying, lignite and magnesite mining. Area: 3654sq km (1411sq mi). Pop. (2001) 215,136.

eucalyptus (gum tree) Genus of evergreen shrubs and trees, native to Australia. They are valuable sources of hardwood and oils. Leaves are blue/white, and they bear woody fruits and flowers without petals. Height: to 122m (400ft). There are *c.*600 species. Family Myrtaceae.

Eucharist Central act of Christian worship, in which the priest and congregation partake in Holy Communion – one of the principal SACRAMENTS. The Eucharist is a

commemorative re-enactment of the LAST SUPPER. Among Roman Catholics, the rite is also called Mass; among Protestants, it is the Lord's Supper. *See also* TRANSUBSTANTIATION

Euclid (*c*.330–*c*.260 BC) Greek mathematician who taught at Alexandria, Egypt. He is remembered for his classic textbook on GEOMETRY *Elements* (Lat. pub. 1482). His axioms – that parallel lines never meet and the angles of a triangle always add up to 180° – remained the basis for geometry until the development of **non-Euclidean geometry** in the 18th century.

Eugène of Savoy (1663–1736) French-born prince and Austrian general. Rejected by LOUIS XIV, he displayed extraordinary courage and leadership for Austria against the Ottoman Turks at Vienna (1683) and Zenta (1697). In the War of the SPANISH SUCCESSION (1702–13), he cooperated with the Duke of MARLBOROUGH in victories over the French at BLENHEIM (1704), Oudenarde (1708), and Malplaquet (1709).

eugenics Study of human improvement by selective breeding, founded in the 19th century by English scientist Sir Francis Galton. It proposed the genetic 'improvement' of the human species through encouraging parents who are above average in certain traits to have more children, while ensuring those who are below average have fewer. It was discredited in the early 20th century, owing to its ethical implications and its racist and class-based assumptions.

euglenophyte Any member of the phylum Euglenophyta comprising single-celled ALGAE, including the genus *Euglena*. Members of this group have both animal and plant characteristics. They swim by means of flagella. Many species contain CHLOROPLASTS and employ PHOTOSYNTHESIS, but some are colourless and feed on BACTERIA and DIATOMS.

eukaryote Organism whose CELLS have a membrane-bound NUCLEUS, with DNA contained in CHROMOSOMES. Making up one of the three DOMAINS, eukaryotes include all ANIMALS, PLANTS, FUNGUS, and PROTOCTISTA. They have a complex CYTOPLASM with an ENDOPLASMIC RETICULUM, and most of them possess MITOCHONDRIA. Most plants and algae also possess CHLOROPLASTS. Other structures specific to eukaryotic cells include microtubules, GOLGI BODIES, and membrane-bound flagella. *See also* KINGDOM; PROKARYOTE

Euler, Leonhard (1707–83) Swiss mathematician. He is best known for his geometric theorem, which states that for any polyhedron (many-sided figure), $V - E + F = 2$, where V is the number of vertices, E the number of edges, and F the number of faces. Euler conducted much research into the number E, the base of natural LOGARITHMS.

eunuch Castrated man, originally a keeper of a HAREM. Employed as servants in royal and wealthy households, especially in the Byzantine and Ottoman Empires, they were often African slaves. *See also* CASTRATO

Euphrates (Firat) River of sw Asia. Formed by the confluence of the Murat and Karasu, it flows from E Turkey across Syria into central Iraq, where it joins the TIGRIS NW of BASRA to form the SHATT AL-ARAB, and eventually flows into the PERSIAN GULF. BABYLONIA and ASSYRIA developed along its lower reaches. Length: 2,800km (1,740mi).

eurhythmics System of musical and dance training which influenced ballet and acting. Developed in Switzerland and Germany by Emile Jaques-Dalcroze in the early 20th century, and also applied by Rudolf STEINER, it evolved from a series of interpretive gymnastic exercises in response to music.

Euripides (*c*.480–*c*.450 BC) Greek playwright. One of the great writers of Greek tragedy. His plays, with their cynical depiction of human motivation, caused controversy. The significance of the CHORUS was reduced in favour of a more complex examination of individual behaviour, especially women. His works include *Medea*, *Electra*, *Hecuba*, and the anti-war satire *Trojan Women*. Only 18 plays are extant.

euro Currency unit of the EUROPEAN UNION (EU). The MAASTRICHT TREATY (1992) established a timetable for economic and monetary union (EMU). The European Currency Unit (ECU) acted as a theoretical unit until the birth of the Euro on January 1, 1999. In this first stage, 11 member states (Austria, Belgium, Finland, France, Germany, Ireland, Italy, Luxembourg, Netherlands, Portugal, and Spain) fixed their exchange rates against each other and against the ECU. The

European Central Bank took control of a single monetary policy. Greece joined the first stage in 2001. The euro entered public circulation on January 1, 2002, and circulated alongside national currencies for six months, after which these were abolished. The ten new EU members have yet to join the euro. *See also* EUROPEAN MONETARY SYSTEM (EMS)

Europa Smallest of Jupiter's GALILEAN SATELLITES, with a diameter of 3138km (1950mi). Mainly rock, Europa's smooth water-ice crust is criss-crossed by a network of light and dark linear markings. A form of ice tectonics might be operating on the planet, since there are very few craters.

Europe Earth's second smallest continent, comprising the western fifth of the Eurasian landmass. It is separated from Asia by the URALS (E), CASPIAN SEA and the CAUCASUS (SE), BLACK SEA and DARDANELLES (S), and from Africa by the MEDITERRANEAN SEA. **Land** Europe is dominated by the Alpine mountain chain, the main links of which are the PYRENEES, ALPS, CARPATHIAN MOUNTAINS, BALKAN MOUNTAINS, and the Caucasus. Between the Scandinavian peninsula and the Alps is the great European plain, which extends from the Atlantic coast in France to the Urals. Much of the plain is fertile farmland. Major islands include the British Isles, Sicily, Sardinia, Corsica and Iceland. **Structure and Geology** Much of N Europe consists of large sedimentary plains overlying an ancient Precambrian shield, outcrops of which remain in N Scandinavia, Scotland and the Urals. There are also worn-down Palaeozoic highlands. Many upland areas N of the Alps were formed during the Carboniferous period, including Ireland, the moorlands of Devon and Cornwall and the PENNINES, England. Southern Europe is geologically younger. Alpine folding began in the Oligocene period. Europe's longest river is the VOLGA; other major rivers are (from W to E) the TAGUS, LOIRE, RHÔNE, RHINE, ELBE, and DANUBE. The Caspian Sea is the world's largest lake. **Climate and Vegetation** Europe's climate varies from subtropical to polar. The Mediterranean climate of the S is dry and warm. Much of the land is scrub (*maquis*), with some hardwood forests. Further N, the climate is mild and quite humid, moderated by prevailing westerly winds and the GULF STREAM. The natural vegetation is mixed forest, but this has been greatly depleted. Mixed forest merges into boreal forests of conifers. In SE European Russia, wooded and grass steppe merge into semidesert to the N of the Caspian Sea. In the far N, lies the tundra. **History** The Mediterranean region was the cradle of the ancient Greek and Roman civilizations. The collapse of the Western Roman Empire and the Barbarian invasions brought chaos to much of Europe. During the Middle Ages, Christianity was the unifying force throughout the continent. The post-medieval period witnessed the SCHISM in the Catholic Church and the emergence of the nation-state. European powers began to found vast empires in other parts of the globe (*see* COLONIALISM; IMPERIALISM), and the FRENCH REVOLUTION ushered in an era of momentous political changes. During the 20th century, a period overshadowed by two World Wars and the rise of COMMUNISM, Europe began to lose some of its pre-eminence in world affairs. After World War 2, the countries of Europe divided into two ideological blocs: Eastern Europe, dominated by the Soviet Union; and Western Europe, closely aligned with the USA (*see* COLD WAR) The NORTH ATLANTIC TREATY ORGANIZATION (NATO) was established to act as a deterrent to the spread of COMMUNISM; the WARSAW PACT was its E European counterpart. Several economic organizations, in particular the EUROPEAN COMMUNITY (EC), worked towards closer intra-national cooperation. The collapse of Soviet communism in 1991 added to the momentum for a kind of supranational union in the form of a EUROPEAN UNION (EU). **Economy** Almost half of European land is unproductive because of climate, relief, soil or urbanization. A quarter of land is forested; the lumber industry is particularly important in Scandinavia and the mountains of E Europe. Fishing is a major industry in countries with Atlantic or North Sea coastlines. Two-thirds of cultivated land is arable. Cereals are the principal crop: wheat is the most important, with oats in the N, and maize in the S. Sheep graze on many upland areas, but dairy farming is by far the most important form of animal husbandry. Many fruits, early vegetables and grapes (mainly used for wine) grow in Mediterranean areas. Europe produces more than one-third of the world's coal. Germany, Poland, Czech Republic and Russia are the leading producers. Other minerals include bauxite, mercury, lead, zinc, oil and potash. Europe is highly industrialized. The largest industrial areas are in N and NE France, the RUHR, and around the North Sea ports of ANTWERP, AMSTERDAM, ROTTERDAM, and HAMBURG. *Area c.*10.36 millionsq km (4 millionsq mi) *Highest mountain* Mount Elbrus (Russia) 5633m (18,481ft) *Longest river* Volga 3750km (2330mi) *Population* (2000 est.) 728,887,000 *Largest cities* MOSCOW (8,296,000); LONDON (7,172,036); ST PETERSBURG (4,661,000); BERLIN (3,388,434) *See also* individual countries

European Atomic Energy Commission (Euratom)
Organization that formed following the second of the Treaties of ROME (1958). Euratom was founded to co-ordinate non-military nuclear research and production, and provide capital for investment, specialists and equipment. It is administered by the European Commission.

European Commission
Institution responsible for initiating and implementing EUROPEAN UNION (EU) policy. The Commission drafts policies, which it submits to the EUROPEAN COUNCIL OF MINISTERS and the EUROPEAN PARLIAMENT. It was established (1967) with the creation of the EUROPEAN COMMUNITY (EC). It is responsible to the European Parliament, which can remove it on a censure motion carried by a two-thirds majority. Since 2005, when 10 new countries joined the EU, there have been 25 commissioners, one from each member state. Each commissioner has responsibility for a different policy area and pledges loyalty to the EU rather than individual states. A secretariat of *c.*15,000 civil servants is based in Brussels. The commissioners elect their President for a four-year term.

European Community (EC)
Historical organization of Western European countries dedicated to closer economic and political cooperation in Europe. In 1952, the European Coal and Steel Community (ECSC) was established to integrate the coal and steel industries primarily of France and West Germany. The success of the ECSC led to the Treaties of ROME (1957) that established the **European Economic Community** (EEC), and the EUROPEAN ATOMIC ENERGY COMMISSION (EURATOM). The aim was to create a common economic approach to agriculture, employment, trade and social development, and to give Western Europe more influence in world affairs. Original members included France, West Germany, Italy, Belgium, Netherlands and Luxembourg. In 1962, the COMMON AGRICULTURAL POLICY (CAP) came into effect. In 1967, the EEC, ECSC, and EURATOM merged to form the European Community (EC). The United Kingdom, Ireland, and Denmark joined in 1973; Greece in 1981; Spain and Portugal in 1986; and Austria, Finland and Sweden in 1995. In 1993, the EUROPEAN UNION (EU) superseded the EC.

European Convention on Human Rights (1950)
Agreement to protect the rights of the individual, signed by the members of the COUNCIL OF EUROPE. It listed 12 basic rights, including the right to life, to a fair trial, to peaceful assembly and association, and to freedom of expression, and freedom from slavery and torture. An additional protocol provides for the abolition of the death penalty. *See also* HUMAN RIGHTS

European Council of Ministers
Policy-making body of the EUROPEAN UNION (EU). The Council, which meets in Brussels, consists of ministers from each of the member states. Council decisions are made by qualified majority vote, simple majority or unanimity. Unanimity votes are taken on sensitive issues, such as taxation and constitutional matters. Qualified majority voting is weighted according to the relative population sizes of each of the member states. The **European Council**, comprising the heads of government of the member states, meets twice a year to provide overall policy direction.

European Court of Human Rights
Created in 1959, the court is presided over by a judge from each of the member states that are signatories of the EUROPEAN CONVENTION ON HUMAN RIGHTS. It decides whether or not an individual's rights have been disregarded by a member state in cases when the two parties have already failed to reach a settlement through the European Commission of Human Rights.

European Court of Justice
(officially Court of Justice of the European Communities) Court responsible for interpreting and implementing European Union laws. The court also rules on alleged breaches of EU laws by member states.

European Economic Area (EEA)
Economic union agreed (1992) between the 12 members of the EUROPEAN COMMUNITY (EC) and six of the seven members (Switzerland rejected the notion) of the EUROPEAN FREE TRADE ASSOCIATION (EFTA). The EEA extended the EU's Single Market principles to EFTA. In 1995, Austria, Finland, and Sweden joined the EUROPEAN UNION (EU), leaving only Norway, Iceland, and Liechtenstein as non-EU members.

European Free Trade Association (EFTA)
Organization promoting free trade among its European members. Established in 1960, it comprised Austria, Denmark, Ireland, Norway, Portugal, Sweden, Switzerland, and the UK. By 1995, all but Norway and Switzerland had joined the EUROPEAN UNION (EU), while Iceland and Liechtenstein joined EFTA in 1970 and 1991, respectively. *See also* EUROPEAN ECONOMIC AREA (EEA)

European Monetary System (EMS)
System set up in 1979 to bring about monetary stability among the nine members of the EUROPEAN COMMUNITY (EC). The EMS's main components were the European Currency Unit (ECU), a monetary unit weighted according to the size of each member state's economy and trade value; the Exchange Rate Mechanism (ERM), where each state agreed to keep its currency within set margins of a central rate of exchange against the ECU; and credit mechanisms. The MAASTRICHT TREATY (1992) set a timetable for achieving economic and monetary union (EMU) and the establishment of a single currency (the EURO). In 1998, 11 states chose to participate in the first stage of EMU. On January 1, 1999, the euro was born and a European Central Bank gained control of a single monetary policy.

European Parliament
Institution of the EUROPEAN UNION (EU). The Parliament forms part of the permanent structure of the European Union, along with the Council of Ministers, the Commission, the Court of Justice, and the Court of Auditors. It meets in Strasbourg, Brussels and Luxembourg. It has 732 members, representing the 25 member states, elected for five-year terms. It has limited legislative powers.

European Space Agency (ESA)
Organization founded by several European nations in 1962 as the European Space Research Agency (ESRO) to promote international cooperation in space research. Australia was admitted in 1965.

European Union (EU)
Organization of 27 European countries established (1993) following the ratification of the MAASTRICHT TREATY (1992) by Austria, Belgium, Denmark, Finland, France, Germany, Greece, Ireland, Italy, Luxembourg, Netherlands, Portugal, Spain, Sweden and the United Kingdom. The EU assumed control of the framework and institutions of the EUROPEAN COMMUNITY (EC), such as the EUROPEAN COMMISSION and EUROPEAN PARLIAMENT, but extended the role and scope beyond that of the EC. The member states agreed to greater cooperation, particularly in areas such as foreign and security policies (*see* WESTERN EUROPEAN UNION), and internal and judicial policies. The single European currency, the EURO, was adopted by 12 countries in January 2002. In 2004, ten new countries joined the EU: Cyprus (not northern Cyprus), Czech Republic, Estonia, Hungary, Latvia, Lithuania, Malta, Poland, Slovak Republic and Slovenia. Bulgaria and Romania joined at the beginning of 2007. In addition to the Commission and Parliament, the EU's institutional structure comprises the EUROPEAN COUNCIL OF MINISTERS, the European Central Bank, and the EUROPEAN COURT OF JUSTICE. *See also* EUROPEAN MONETARY SYSTEM (EMS)

europium
(symbol Eu) Silvery-white metallic element of the LANTHANIDE SERIES. Its chief ores are monazite and bastnaesite. The metal is used in the manufacture of colour television screens, lasers, and in control rods in nuclear reactors. Properties: at.no. 63; r.a.m. 151.96; r.d. 5.25; m.p. 822°C (1512°F); b.p. 1597°C (2907°F); most common isotope Eu[153] (52.18%).

Eurydice In Greek mythology, nymph married to ORPHEUS.

Eustachian tube Channel connecting the middle EAR to the back of the throat. It opens when swallowing to allow the pressure in the middle ear to remain the same as that outside the body.

Euston Road School School of painting and drawing founded in London in 1937. Its return to a more straightforward naturalism was inspired by SICKERT and CÉZANNE, and was a response to the prevalent abstract or surrealist styles.

euthanasia (Gk. 'good death') Inducing the painless death of a person, often by a drug. It is illegal in most countries. **Voluntary** euthanasia, the taking of life with the consent of the patient, is legal in the Netherlands. **Passive** euthanasia is the withholding of life-supporting treatment.

eutrophication Process by which a stream or lake becomes rich in inorganic nutrients by agricultural run-off or other artificial means. Compounds of nitrogen, phosphorus, iron, sulphur and potassium are vital for plant growth in water; in excess they overstimulate the growth of surface ALGAE or CYANOBACTERIA producing BLOOM that can consume all available dissolved oxygen with devastating effects on marine life.

evangelicalism (Gk. *euangelos*, 'good news' or 'gospel') Term applied to several, generally Protestant, tendencies within the Christian Church. Evangelicalism denotes the school which stresses personal conversion and witness of salvation by faith in the atoning death of Jesus Christ.

evangelist Person who preaches the gospel, announcing the good news of redemption through Jesus Christ and the hope of everlasting life. The word also applies by extension to the Saints MATTHEW, MARK, LUKE, and JOHN.

evaporation Process by which a liquid or solid becomes a vapour. The reverse process is CONDENSATION. Solids and liquids cool when they evaporate because they give up energy (LATENT HEAT) to the escaping molecules. Evaporation of sweat on the skin is a cooling device of the human body.

Eve In the Bible (GENESIS 2), the first woman, created by God from Adam's rib. Eve disobeyed God by eating the fruit of the tree of the knowledge and sharing it with Adam. For this act, the couple were banished from the garden of EDEN. She was the mother of CAIN, ABEL, and Seth.

evening primrose Any of various plants of the genus *Oenothera*, many of which are native to w North America. They have yellow, pink or white flowers that open in the evening. Height: 1.8m (5.3ft). Family Onagraceae.

event horizon Boundary of a BLACK HOLE, from which nothing can escape. Observers outside the event horizon can therefore obtain no information about the black hole's interior. The radius of the event horizon is called the **Schwarzschild radius**. At the event horizon, the ESCAPE VELOCITY equals the velocity of light with the consequence that all ELECTROMAGNETIC RADIATION is trapped.

Everest, Mount (Nepalese *Sagarmatha*; Tibetan *Chomo-Langma*, Mother Goddess of the World) World's highest mountain, in the central Himalayas on the borders of Tibet and Nepal. It is named after George Everest, first surveyor general of India. It was first climbed on May 29, 1953, by Sir Edmund HILLARY and Tenzing Norgay. Height: 8850m (29,035ft).

Everglades Large marshland in s Florida, USA, extending from Lake Okeechobee to Florida Bay; it includes the Everglades National Park. The region comprises mangrove forests, saw grass and hummocks (island masses of vegetation), and supports tropical animal life, including alligators, snakes, turtles, egrets and bald eagles. Area: *c*.10,000sq km (4000sq mi).

evergreen Plant that retains its green foliage for a year or more, unlike DECIDUOUS plants. Evergreens are divided into two groups: narrow-leaved, or CONIFERS, and broad-leaved. Conifers include fir, spruce, pine and juniper. Among the broad-leaved evergreens are holly and rhododendron. Not all conifers are evergreens; exceptions include the larch (*Larix*).

evolution In biology, theory that a SPECIES undergoes gradual changes to survive and reproduce in a competitive, and often changing, environment, and that a new species is the result of change from the ancestral forms. In the early 1800s French biologist Jean LAMARCK began to develop evolutionary theory. In the mid-1800s English naturalists Charles DARWIN and A.R. WALLACE developed the same theory on evolution and in 1859 Darwin published the ground-breaking *On the Origin of Species*. Darwin observed that organisms produce far more offspring than they need to maintain the population, yet most populations remain relatively constant in numbers because of predation, disease and starvation. Consequently, individuals compete for survival. Darwin argued that each organism was a unique combination of genetic VARIATIONS. Each individual has different GENES and is distinct from the others. Some individuals will be better suited to survive in the existing conditions: these 'fitter' individuals are more likely to breed and pass their advantageous genes on to their offspring through the process of HEREDITY. Over many generations, individuals with favourable characteristics will build up at the expense of those lacking them. This process is called NATURAL SELECTION. In time, more variations will lead to the evolution of a new species. Evidence for the theory of natural selection is that dated FOSSIL remains show that life did not arise at once, but as a gradual change from one type of organism into another. Other evidence for evolution involves the structures of different animals or plants that show such similarity it is highly probable they evolved from a common ancestor. The bones in the wing of a bird, the arm of a primate and the paddle of a whale, for example, show remarkable similarity. Equally, many proteins in organisms are fundamentally the same and we share common genes. Present-day evolutionary theory is largely derived from the work of Darwin and Austrian naturalist Gregor MENDEL and maintains that in any population or gene pool, there is variation, including random MUTATION, in genetic forms and characteristics. *See also* ADAPTATION; ADAPTIVE RADIATION; GENETICS; GOULD, STEPHEN JAY; HUMAN EVOLUTION; NEO-DARWINISM; WILSON, EDWARD O. (Osborne)

exchange rate In economics, the rate at which one nation's currency can be converted to that of another.

exclusion principle Basic law of QUANTUM MECHANICS, proposed by Wolfgang PAULI in 1925, stating no two ELECTRONS in an atom can possess the same energy and SPIN. More precisely, the set of four QUANTUM NUMBERS characterizing certain ELEMENTARY PARTICLES called FERMIONS must be unique.

excommunication Formal expulsion from the communion of the faithful, from sacraments and rites of a religious body.

excretion Elimination of materials from the body that have been involved in METABOLISM. In mammals, these wastes excrete mainly as URINE, and to some extent by sweating. Carbon dioxide excretes through the lungs during breathing. Defaecation is not excretion, as faeces consist mostly of material that has never been part of the body.

Exeter City on the River Exe; county town of Devon, sw England. Many ancient buildings remain, notably the Norman cathedral (*c*.1275), the 12th-century Guildhall and the remains of Roman walls. Industries: tourism, textiles, leather goods, metal products, pharmaceuticals. Pop. (2001) 111,078.

existentialism Philosophical systems concerned with the nature of existence or being. Søren KIERKEGAARD is regarded as the founder of the movement. He rejected METAPHYSICS, arguing an individual is forced to make their own ethical decisions. Martin HEIDEGGER developed these ideas in relation to the PHENOMENOLOGY of Edmund HUSSERL. Karl JASPERS argued that the greatest insights into existence were experienced in extreme situations. For

◀ **Everest** The world's highest peak, at 8850m (29,035ft). Since Everest was first climbed in 1953, more than 1500 people have reached the summit. Climbing technology has greatly improved, and the Himalayan summit is now sometimes reached without the use of oxygen tanks. Climbing Everest is still highly dangerous. The mountain is imbued with local religious significance.

EYE

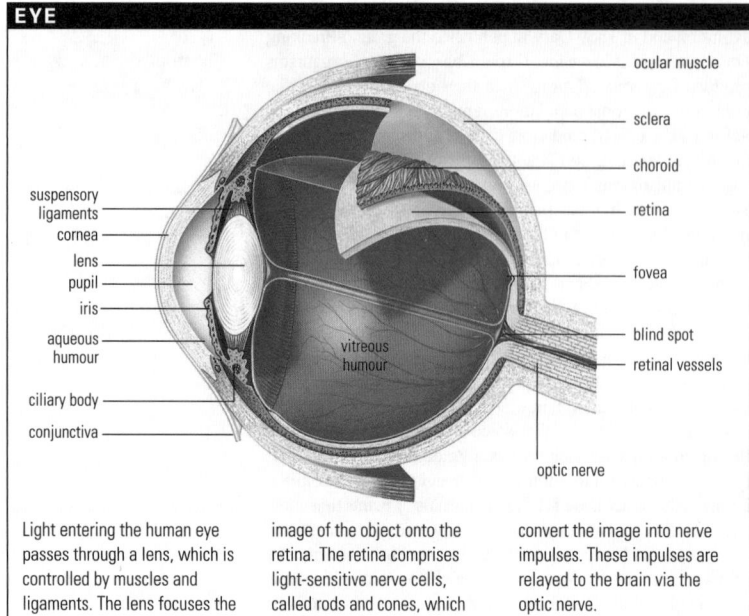

ocular muscle
sclera
choroid
retina
fovea
blind spot
retinal vessels

suspensory ligaments
cornea
lens
pupil
iris
aqueous humour
ciliary body
conjunctiva

vitreous humour

optic nerve

Light entering the human eye passes through a lens, which is controlled by muscles and ligaments. The lens focuses the image of the object onto the retina. The retina comprises light-sensitive nerve cells, called rods and cones, which convert the image into nerve impulses. These impulses are relayed to the brain via the optic nerve.

Jean-Paul SARTRE, the central tenet of existentialism was that existence precedes essence.

exobiology Search for life on other planets. Exobiology attempts to detect environmental conditions and possible biochemical and evolutionary pathways to life beyond Earth. Examples include the probes sent in 2003 by NASA and the European Space Agency to detect evidence of water on Mars.

Exodus Old Testament book of the Bible, the second book of the PENTATEUCH or TORAH. The first part details the flight of the Israelites from Egypt; the second part contains a catalogue of religious instructions that formed the basis of Mosaic law.

exoskeleton Protective skeleton or hard supporting structure forming the outside of the soft bodies of certain animals, notably ARTHROPODS and MOLLUSCS. In arthropods, it consists of a thick horny covering attached to the outside of the body and may be jointed and flexible. The exoskeleton is shed periodically and the animal generates a new one.

exothermic reaction CHEMICAL REACTION in which heat is evolved. A common example is COMBUSTION. *See also* ENDOTHERMIC REACTION

expanding Universe Theory of the origin and direction in time of the UNIVERSE. Physicists have attempted to explain RED SHIFT as resulting from a single, huge explosion which causes everything to be moving away from our section of the Universe. The red shift occurs when, due to the DOPPLER EFFECT, the perceived wavelengths of light from some stars are lengthened because of their outwards movement. There is also the opposite effect, a BLUE SHIFT, but this does not occur as often. Today, the balance of opinion is in favour of the theory of the Universe expanding following the BIG BANG. *See also* HUBBLE'S LAW

expansion Change in the size of an object with change in temperature. Most substances expand on heating, although there are exceptions (ice expands on cooling). The expansivity (coefficient of expansion) of a substance is its increase in length, area or volume per unit temperature rise. For a gas, the coefficient of expansion is the ratio of the rates of change of volume to temperature (at constant pressure), or of volume to pressure (at constant temperature).

explosive Substances that react rapidly and violently, emitting heat, light, sound, and shock waves. Chemical explosives are mostly highly nitrated compounds or mixtures that are unstable and decompose violently with the evolution of much gas. Nuclear explosives are radioactive metals, the atoms of which can undergo nuclear FISSION or FUSION to release radiant energy and devastating shock waves.

exponent Superscript number placed to the right of a symbol indicating its power, e.g. in a^4 (= $a \times a \times a \times a$), 4

is the exponent. Certain laws of exponents apply in mathematical operations. For example, $3^2 \times 3^3 = 3^{(2+3)} = 3^5$; $3^4/3^3 = 3^{(4-3)} = 3^1$; $(3^2)^3 = 3^{(2 \times 3)} = 3^6$; $3^{-5} = 1/3^5$.

exponential In general, a function of x of the form ax, where a is a constant. The exponential function ex' where E is the base of natural logarithms, 2.7182818..., can be represented by a power series $1 + x + x2/2! + x3/3! + ...$

expressionism Style of art in which NATURALISM is replaced by exaggerated images to express intense, subjective emotion. The term is often used in relation to a radical German art movement between the 1880s and $c.$1905. The inspiration for this new focus came from many different sources, including the work of VAN GOGH, GAUGUIN, MUNCH and those within SYMBOLISM, as well as from folk art. German expressionism reached its apogee in the work of the BLAUE REITER group. The term also applies to performance arts, such as the works of STRINDBERG and WEDEKIND.

extinction Dying out of a species or population. Extinction is part of the process of EVOLUTION in which certain species of plants and animals die out, often to be replaced by others.

extrasensory perception (ESP) Perception that takes place outside the known sensory systems. No scientific evidence for any form of ESP has yet been found.

extroversion Personality type characterized by outgoing behaviour; the opposite of INTROVERSION. The term was popularized by Carl JUNG, according to whose theory of PERSONALITY, extroverts are sociable, impulsive, and more interested in the outside world than in their own emotions.

extrusion In geology, the breaking-out of IGNEOUS ROCK from below the Earth's surface. Any volcanic product reaching the surface becomes extrusive material whether it is ejected through a VOLCANO's cone or through pipe-like channels or fissures in its crust. In industry, the forcing of metals or plastics at optimum temperature through a die to make rods, tubes and various hollow or solid sections.

Eyck, Jan van ($c.$1390–1441) Flemish painter. His best-known work is the altarpiece for the Church of St Bavon, Ghent, which includes the *Adoration of the Lamb* (1432) and the *Arnolfini Wedding* (1434). He is said to have perfected the manufacture and technique of oil paint. His brother, **Hubert van Eyck** ($c.$1370–1426) is thought to have worked in Ghent and assisted Jan on the St Bavon altarpiece. No other works are definitely his, and some art historians think he never existed.

eye Organ of vision. It converts light energy to nerve impulses that are transmitted to the visual centre of the brain. Most of the mass of a human eye lies in a bony protective socket, called the orbital cavity. The eyeball is spherical and composed of three layers: the **sclera** (white of the eye), which contains the transparent CORNEA; the **choroid**, which connects with the IRIS, PUPIL and LENS, and contains blood vessels to provide nutrients and oxygen; and the RETINA, which contains rods and cones for converting the image into nerve impulses. The aqueous humour (a watery liquid between the cornea and iris) and the vitreous humour (a jelly-like substance behind the lens) help to maintain the shape of the eye. *See also* SIGHT

Eyre, Lake Salt lake in NE South Australia. It is the lowest point on the continent, $c.$15m (50ft) below sea level, and its largest salt lake. Area: 9,324sq km (3,600sq mi). Max. depth: 1.2m (4ft).

Eysenck, Hans Jurgen (1916–97) British psychologist and pioneer of behaviour therapy, b. Germany. Much of his work focused on a scientific definition of personality, based on experimental and psychometric methods. Eysenck founded (1955) the psychological department of the Institute of Psychiatry, Maudsley Hospital, London. Many of his works, such as *Uses and Abuses of Psychology* and *Know Your Own IQ*, were bestsellers.

Ezekiel Old Testament prophet who was among the Jews deported during the BABYLONIAN CAPTIVITY. He is traditionally considered the author of the Old Testament Book of Ezekiel. He was the third and last of the 'greater' Old Testament prophets, the successor of ISAIAH and JEREMIAH.

Ezra In the Old Testament, a continuation of Chronicles I and II. It records the priest Ezra's journey from Babylon to Jerusalem to spread the law of Moses.

Fabergé, Peter Carl (1846–1920) Russian jeweller. He took over his father's business in 1870, making decorative objects in gold and precious stones. Famed for his designs of flowers and animals, he made many jewelled Easter eggs for European royalty, the first for Tsar Alexander III in 1884. Fabergé left Russia after the Revolution of 1917.

Fabian Society British society of Socialists, founded in 1883. Careful to remain separate from Marxists, Fabians believed that SOCIALISM could be attained through gradual political change. With George Bernard SHAW and Sidney and Beatrice WEBB as leaders, the society gained widespread recognition and helped found the Labour Representation Committee in 1900, which became the LABOUR PARTY in 1906. The Fabian Society is affiliated to the Labour Party and publishes a journal and pamphlets.

fable Literary genre which takes the form of a short allegorical tale, intended to convey a moral. The oldest extant fables are the Greek tales of AESOP and the Indian stories of the *Panchatantra*. Other notable collections of fables were made by Jean de LA FONTAINE and John GAY. *See also* ALLEGORY

facies In geology, all the features of a rock or that show the history of its formation. Geologists often distinguish age by facies. The term is also applied to gradations of IGNEOUS ROCK.

factor In mathematics, any number that divides exactly into a given number. For example, the factors of 72 are 1, 2, 3, 4, 6, 8, 9, 12, 18, 24, and 36.

factory farming Intensive rearing of livestock, such as pigs, poultry, and calves, in densely populated enclosures. Feeding is usually automatically dispensed, and the emphasis is on 'mass-production' of the food products rather than the well-being of the animals involved. ANIMAL RIGHTS campaigns encouraged less intensive rearing, such as free-range chickens.

Fahrenheit, Gabriel Daniel (1686–1736) German physicist and instrument-maker. He invented the alcohol THERMOMETER (1709), the first mercury thermometer (1714) and devised the FAHRENHEIT TEMPERATURE SCALE. He also showed the boiling points of liquids vary with changes in pressure and that water can remain liquid below its freezing point.

Fahrenheit temperature scale System for measuring temperature based on the freezing point of water (32°F) and the boiling point of water (212°F). The interval between them is divided into 180 equal parts. Although replaced in Britain by CELSIUS, Fahrenheit is still used in the USA for nonscientific measurements. Fahrenheit is converted to Celsius by subtracting 32 and then dividing by 1.8. *See also* THERMOMETER

fainting (syncope) Temporary loss of consciousness accompanied by general weakness of the muscles. A faint may be preceded by giddiness, nausea and sweating. Its causes include insufficient flow of blood to the brain and shock.

Fairbanks, Douglas (1883–1939) US film actor, b. Julius Ullman. In 1919, he founded United Artists (UA) with Charlie CHAPLIN, D.W. GRIFFITH, and his wife Mary PICKFORD. Fairbanks' swashbuckling acrobatics made him a screen idol in adventures such as *The Mark of Zorro* (1920) and *Robin Hood* (1922). His son, **Douglas Fairbanks, Jr** (1909–2000), appeared in films such as *The Dawn Patrol* (1930), *Catherine the Great* (1934), and *The Prisoner of Zenda* (1937).

Fairfax of Cameron, Thomas, 3rd Baron (1612–71) Parliamentary commander in the English CIVIL WAR. He succeeded Essex as commander-in-chief (1645), but in 1650 he refused to march against the Scots, and was replaced by Oliver CROMWELL. He later headed the commission to the Hague to arrange the RESTORATION of Charles II (1660).

Falange Spanish political party founded in 1933 by José Antonio Primo de Rivera. Modelled on other European fascist parties, it was merged with other groups under the FRANCO regime and became the sole legal political party. It was heavily defeated in free elections in 1977. *See also* FASCISM

Falashas *see* BETA ISRAEL.

falcon Widely distributed, hawk-like bird of prey, sometimes trained by man to hunt game. Falcons have keen eyesight, short hooked bills, long pointed wings, streamlined bodies, strong legs with hooked claws, and grey or brownish plumage with lighter markings. The females are much larger than the males. Falcons feed on insects, smaller birds, and small ground animals. They can kill on the wing, using their talons. They lay two to five brown-spotted white eggs, often in abandoned nests. Length: 15–64cm (6–25in). Family Falconidae.

Faldo, Nick (Nicholas Alexander) (1957–) English golfer. He won the British Open (1987, 1990, 1992) and the US Masters (1989, 1990, 1996); the only player apart from Jack Nicklaus to win in successive years. Faldo was a member of winning European Ryder Cup teams (1995, 1997).

Falkland Islands (Islas Malvinas) British crown colony in the s Atlantic Ocean, c.520km (320mi) off the E coast of Argentina; the capital is STANLEY (on East Falkland). It includes two large islands (East and West Falkland) and 200 smaller ones. First explored by Europeans in the late 16th century, the Falklands were at various times under Spanish, French and British control. Argentinian denials of British sovereignty led to the FALKLANDS WAR (1982). The main activity is sheep farming; wool and hides are exported. Area: c.12,173sq km (4,700sq mi). Pop. (2002 est.) 3,000.

Falklands War (April-June 1982) Military conflict between Great Britain and Argentina on the issue of sovereignty over the FALKLAND ISLANDS. On April 2, after the breakdown of negotiations, Argentine forces invaded and occupied the Falklands, South Georgia, and South Sandwich Islands, which had been administered and occupied by Great Britain since the 19th century. Despite attempts by the UN to negotiate a settlement, the Argentine government refused to withdraw. The British established a blockade of the islands and staged an amphibious landing at Port San Carlos. They surrounded the Argentine troops at the capital, Port Stanley, and forced them to surrender (June 14). The war cost 254 British and 750 Argentine lives. Although Britain resumed administration of the islands, the basic issue of sovereignty remains unresolved. Britain's victory helped secure a second term for Margaret THATCHER.

Falla, Manuel de (1876–1946) Spanish composer. He developed a Spanish style by using folksongs combined with rich modern harmonies. Among his works are the opera *La Vida Breve* (1905), *Nights in the Gardens of Spain* (1916) for piano and orchestra, and the music for the ballets *Love the Magician* (1915) and *The Three-Cornered Hat* (1919).

Fallopian tube (oviduct) In mammals, either of two narrow ducts leading from the upper part of the UTERUS into the pelvic cavity and ending near each OVARY. After ovulation, the OVUM enters and travels through the Fallopian tube where FERTILIZATION can occur. The fertilized ovum, or EMBRYO, continues into the uterus where it becomes implanted.

family planning Alternative term for CONTRACEPTION

famine Extreme prolonged shortage of food, produced by both natural and man-made causes. If it persists, famine results in widespread starvation and death. Famine is often associated with drought, or alterations in weather patterns, which leads to crop failure and the destruction of livestock. However, warfare and complex political situations resulting in the mismanagement of food resources are equally likely causes.

Fangio, Juan Manuel (1911–95) Argentine racing driver. One of the best drivers of all time, he was Formula One world champion five times (1951, 1954–57), and on his retirement (1958) had won a total of 24 Grands Prix.

FAO *See* FOOD AND AGRICULTURE ORGANIZATION

F/f, sixth letter of the Roman alphabet. It is derived from the Semite letter waw, *meaning hook. It entered the Greek alphabet as* digamma. *The Greeks used it to represent the sound w in English. It gained its present form c.AD 114.*

◀ **Faldo** Famed for his powers of concentration and attention to detail, Faldo was the first home player to win the British Open three times (1987, 1990, 1992) for more than 50 years. His success in the USA saw him play less golf on the European circuit.

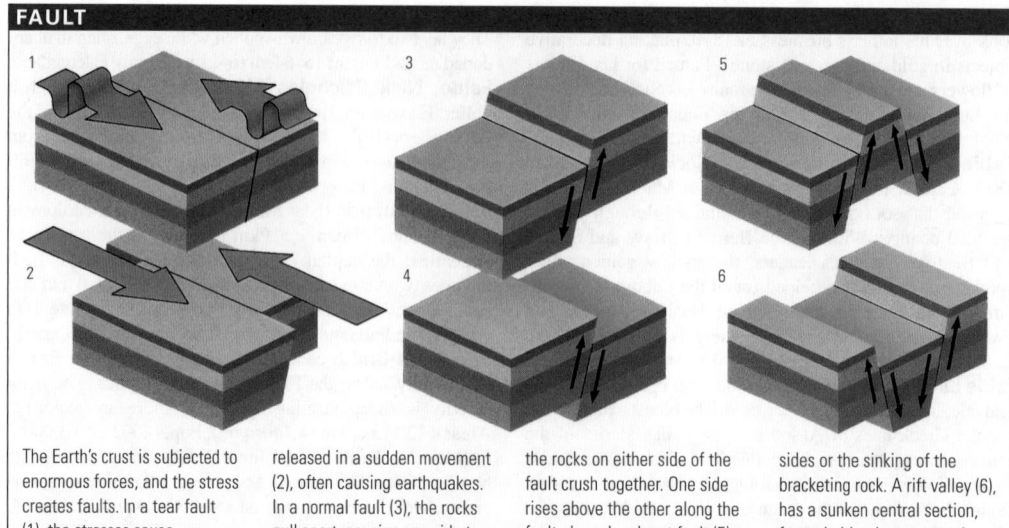

FAULT

The Earth's crust is subjected to enormous forces, and the stress creates faults. In a tear fault (1), the stresses cause horizontal movement. The forces build up until they are released in a sudden movement (2), often causing earthquakes. In a normal fault (3), the rocks pull apart, causing one side to slip down along the plane of the fault. In a reverse fault (4), the rocks on either side of the fault crush together. One side rises above the other along the fault plane. In a horst fault (5), the central section protrudes due to compression from both sides or the sinking of the bracketing rock. A rift valley (6), has a sunken central section, formed either by compression or the outward movement of the two valley sides.

Faraday, Michael (1791–1867) English physicist and chemist. Faraday worked as Sir Humphry DAVY's assistant at the Royal Institution in London, where, in 1825 he became director of the laboratories. Faraday liquefied chlorine, discovered benzene (1825), and enunciated the laws of electrolysis (FARADAY'S LAWS). He also discovered ELECTROMAGNETIC INDUCTION, made the first DYNAMO, built a primitive electric motor, and studied nonconducting materials (dielectrics). The unit of capacitance (the farad) is named after him.

Faraday's laws Two laws of ELECTROLYSIS and three of ELECTROMAGNETIC INDUCTION, formulated by Michael FARADAY. The electrolysis laws state that (1) the amount of chemical change during electrolysis is proportional to the charge of electricity passed, and (2) the amount of chemical change produced in a substance by a certain amount of electricity is proportional to the electrochemical equivalent of that substance. Faraday's laws of induction state that (1) an electromagnetic force is induced in a CONDUCTOR if the MAGNETIC FIELD surrounding it changes, (2) the electromagnetic force is proportional to the rate of change of the field, and (3) the direction of the induced electromagnetic force depends on the field's orientation.

farce Comic drama typified by stereotypical characterizations, improbable plot lines and emphasis on physical humour. One of the earliest examples is Shakespeare's *Comedy of Errors* (c.1593). French dramatist Georges FEYDEAU developed the 'bedroom farce'. Oscar Wilde's *The Importance of Being Earnest* (1895) opened up new dramatic possibilities.

Fargo, William George (1818–81) US businessman. In 1844, Fargo and Henry Wells organized a carrier service between Buffalo and the West. Wells, Fargo and Company then set up an express service between New York and San Francisco to cater for the gold rush. The company merged with two others to form the American Express Company in 1850.

farming *See* AGRICULTURE

Farnese Italian family who ruled the Duchy of Parma and Piacenza (1545–1731). **Alessandro** Farnese (1468–1549) became pope as PAUL III in 1534. His grandson, **Alessandro** Farnese (1545–92), was a general in the service of PHILIP II of Spain. In 1578, he was appointed governor general of the Spanish Netherlands. He captured Antwerp (1585), and secured possession of the s Netherlands.

Faroe Islands (Faeroe Islands) Group of 22 mountainous, volcanic islands (17 inhabited) in the N Atlantic between Iceland and the Shetland Islands. The largest are Streymoy and Esturoy. Settled in the 7th century, they were part of Norway from the 11th century to 1380, when they were ceded to Denmark. In 1852 parliament was restored, and since 1948 they have enjoyed a degree of autonomy. Capital and chief port: Tórshavn (Streymoy), pop. (2000) 16,700; Language: Faroese; Industries: fishery, sheep-rearing. Area: 1,339sq km (540sq mi). Total pop. (2000) 46,000.

Farouk (1920–65) King of Egypt (1936–52), son of King FUAD I. He alienated many Egyptians by his personal extravagance and corruption. His ambitious foreign policy ended with defeat in the first ARAB-ISRAELI WAR (1948), and he was overthrown in a military coup led by Gamal Abdel NASSER.

Farquhar, George (1678–1707) Irish dramatist associated with RESTORATION DRAMA. His comedies were distinguished by their combination of humour and depth of character. Among his plays are *The Constant Couple* (1699), *The Recruiting Officer* (1706), and *The Beaux' Stratagem* (1707).

Farrakhan, Louis (1933–) US leader of the Nation of Islam, a black separatist organization. A controversial figure, he was recruited into the BLACK MUSLIMS in the 1950s by MALCOLM X. Farrakhan was a charismatic advocate of its racial exclusivity. In 1976 he formed the Nation of Islam, which claimed greater adherence to the teachings of Elijah MUHAMMAD. His powerful oratory stresses the importance of self-discipline, family values and community regeneration. His speeches often contain inflammatory anti-white, anti-Semitic and anti-homosexual remarks. In 1995, he organized a large political demonstration, assembling 400,000 men in a 'Million Man March' on Washington, D.C.

Farrell, J.T. (James Thomas) (1904–79) US writer. He is best known for his trilogy about Studs Lonigan (1932–35). Set in a poor Irish community in Chicago, it is typical of his harshly realistic treatment of modern inner city life. Later fiction includes a five-volume series of novels which revolves around Danny O'Neill, a character from the earlier trilogy, and ten novels of a projected 25–volume series called *A Universe of Time*.

Farrell, Terry (1938–) British post-modern architect known for his witty imagery and anthropomorphism. His projects include the redevelopment of Charing Cross Station, London (1991), and the Edinburgh International Conference Centre, Scotland (1995). His hallmarks include strategies for breaking down the verticality of buildings. *See also* POST-MODERNISM

fascism Political movement founded in Italy by Benito MUSSOLINI (1919), characterized by NATIONALISM, TOTALITARIANISM and anti-communism. The term also applied to the regimes of Adolf HITLER in Germany (1933), and Francisco FRANCO in Spain (1936). A reaction to the RUSSIAN REVOLUTION (1917) and the spread of communist influence, the movement based its appeal on the fear of financial instability among the middle classes and on a wider social discontent. Basic to fascist ideas were glorification of the state and total subordination to its authority; suppression of all political opposition; preservation of a rigid class structure; stern enforcement of law and order; the supremacy of the leader as the embodiment of high ideals; and an aggressive militarism aimed at achieving national greatness. It also typically encouraged racist and xenophobic attitudes and policies. Discredited by defeat in World War 2, fascism was insignificant in Western European politics for many years. In recent years, however, far-right nationalist groups re-emerged in many countries. *See also* NATIONAL SOCIALISM

Fassbinder, Rainer Werner (1946–82) German film director. A leading figure in modern German cinema, Fassbinder directed his first feature in 1969, and became known for his radical, low-budget, hypnotic style. Fiercely political, his films include *The Bitter Tears of Petra von Kant* (1972), *The Marriage of Eva Braun* (1979) and *Veronika Voss* (1982).

fat Semi-solid organic substance made and used by plants and animals to store energy. Fats dissolve in organic solvents such as ether, carbon tetrachloride, chloroform and benzene. Most common fats are triglycerides: ESTERS in which one molecule of GLYCEROL is bound to three molecules of FATTY ACIDS, each having 12 to 18 carbon atoms. Animal fats are esters of **saturated** fatty acids. Vegetable OILS are esters of **unsaturated** fatty acids, that is, they have a higher proportion of molecules with double carbon-carbon bonds in the chain. In animals, fat resides in the subcutaneous layer beneath the skin and deep within the body as a specialized ADIPOSE TISSUE. It serves as an insulator and protects internal organs. Research indicates that the consumption of high levels of SATURATED FAT can increase the risk of heart disease. Foods high in fat include butter, margarine, and most oils. Almost all fats found in plant sources are unsaturated. *See also* LIPID

Fates In Greek mythology, the three goddesses of human destiny. Called the *Moirae* by the Greeks, they correspond to the Roman *Parcae* and the Germanic Norns. Clotho spun the thread of life; Lachesis, the element of chance, measured it; and Atropos, the inevitable, cut it.

Fatima (606–32) Daughter of the prophet MUHAMMAD, and wife of ALI. She is revered by the SHI'ITE sect of ISLAM, who believe that ABU BAKR usurped Ali. *See also* FATIMID

Fatimid SHI'ITE dynasty who claimed the caliphate on the basis of their descent from FATIMA. The dynasty was founded by Said ibn Husayn. The Fatimids quickly overthrew the SUNNI rulers in most of NW Africa. By ibn Husayn's death (934), the Fatimid Empire expanded into s Europe, and in 969 they captured Egypt and established the Mosque and University of Al-Azhar, one of the most influential educational establishments in contemporary Islam. By the end of the 11th century, Egypt was all that remained of the Fatimid Empire.

fatty acid Organic compound consisting of a CARBOXYLIC ACID group (-COOH) bound to a hydrocarbon chain. Examples of **saturated** fatty acids (those with only single bonds in their hydrocarbon chain) are acetic acid and palmitic acid; **unsaturated** fatty acids (one double bond) include oleic acid; **polyunsaturated** fatty acids (two or more double bonds) include linoleic acid. **Essential** fatty acids (EFAs) are polyunsaturated fats that are essential to the human DIET because they cannot be manufactured by the body.

Faulkner, William Cuthbert (1897–1962) US novelist. Faulkner's debut novel was *Soldier's Pay* (1925). *Sartoris* (1929) was the first in a series of novels set in the fictional Mississippi county of Yoknapatawpha. *The Sound and the Fury* (1929) and *As I Lay Dying* (1930) utilize a STREAM OF CONSCIOUSNESS style to explore the relationship of past to present. *Light in August* (1932) and *Absalom, Absalom!* (1936) examine the effects of racism in the Deep South. Faulkner received the 1949 Nobel Prize in literature. He won Pulitzer Prizes for *A Fable* (1951), and his final novel *The Reivers* (1962).

fault In geology, a fracture in the Earth's crust along which movement occurs. The result of PLATE TECTONICS, faults are classified according to the type of movement. Vertical movements in the crust cause normal and reverse faults, while horizontal movements result in tear faults. Faults can occur in groups creating horsts, block mountains, grabens, or rift valleys.

Fauré, Gabriel Urbain (1845–1924) French Romantic composer renowned for his intimate, restrained compositions.

They include many songs, such as *Clair de lune* (1889); chamber music, such as his *Elégie* (1883); and the *Requiem* (1887). He was director of the Paris Conservatoire (1805–22).

fauvism Expressionist style based on extremely vivid non-naturalistic colours. MATISSE was the leading figure and, with SIGNAC and Derain, exhibited at the Salon d'Automne (1905). A critic described their work as something produced by wild animals (Fr. *fauves*). Other members included Albert Marquet, George Rouault, VLAMINCK, and BRAQUE. Although fauvism was short-lived, its influence on EXPRESSIONISM was profound.

Fawcett, Dame Millicent Garrett (1847–1929) British feminist. As president of the National Union of Women's Suffrage Societies (1897–1919), Fawcett was a leading figure in the SUFFRAGETTE MOVEMENT. She also founded Newnham College, Cambridge, one of the first women's colleges of higher education in Britain.

Fawkes, Guy (1570–1606) English conspirator in the GUNPOWDER PLOT of 1605. Roman Catholic traitors enlisted him in a plot against JAMES I and Parliament. The plot was betrayed, and Fawkes, surrounded by barrels of gunpowder, was arrested in a building adjacent to the House of Lords. He was later executed. Traditionally, an effigy called a 'guy', is burned on November 5, the date of the intended explosion.

fax (facsimile transmission) Equipment by which text and images can be transmitted and received through a TELEPHONE system. The image, on paper, is scanned to translate it into electrical pulses. A MODEM converts the pulses into an analogue form that can be transmitted through the telephone system. At the receiving end, the fax machine's modem converts the signals back into digital pulses, and prints these as dots to build up a copy of the original document. Faxes may also be sent using personal computers. *See also* SCANNING

FBI Abbreviation of the FEDERAL BUREAU OF INVESTIGATION.

▲ **Faulkner** Much of William Faulkner's work describes the effects of social disintegration on family life in s USA. He also wrote the screenplays for the films *To Have and Have Not* (1945) and *The Big Sleep* (1946).

INTERNET

Fawkes, Guy
▶ www.bonefire.org/guy

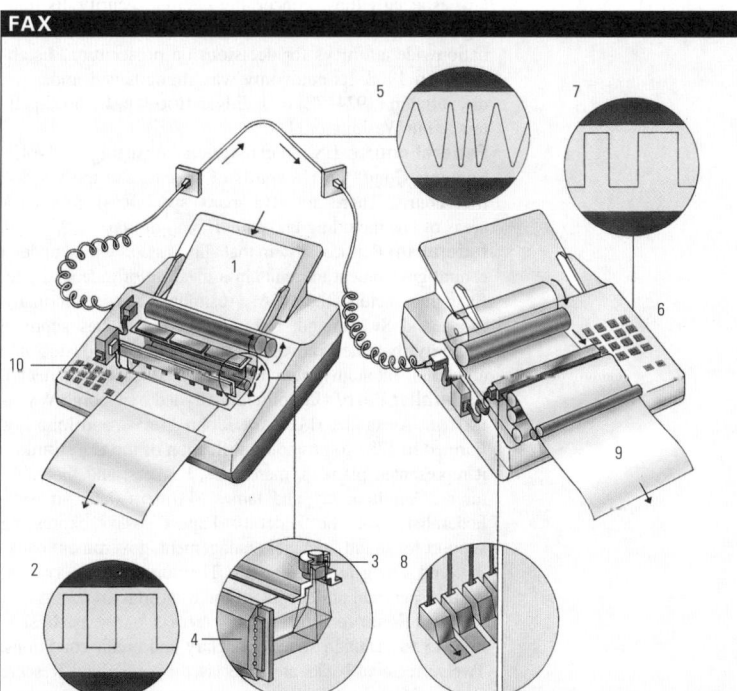

FAX

A fax machine converts text or images fed into the machine (1) into a digital code (2). The code is created by shining light on tiny strips of the document in turn (3). Sensors (4) detect the amount of light that bounces back. Where ink is present, little light is reflected – creating an electrical pulse of low voltage. A high voltage results when light reflects from blank paper. A modem converts the digital code in the fax into an analogue signal (5), and transmits it to the receiving fax machine (6) via the telephone network. A modem in the second machine converts the analogue code back into a digital code (7). A printer (8) interprets the digital code and produces the hard facsimile copy (9). Each machine has its own number, dialled via a keyboard (10) on the sending machine.

FEATHER

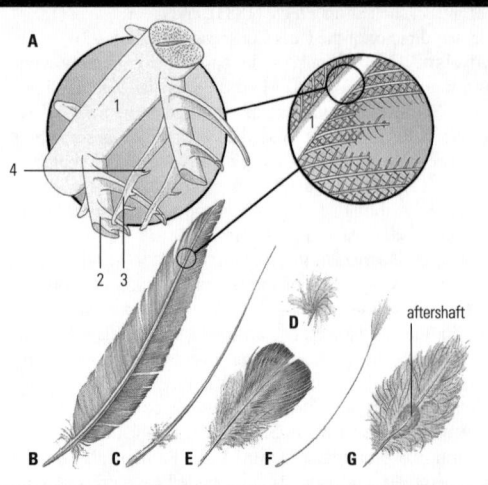

The structure of a bird's feather (A) shows how barbs (2) extend from the central midrib (1). Barbules (3) project from both sides of the barb, one side of which has tiny hooks (hamuli, 4), which catch on the next barbule. The interlocking construction adds strength and helps the feather to retain its shape. Types of feather include: flight (B); bristle (C); down (D); contour feathers (E), which insulate; filoplumes (F), hair-like feathers that are either sensory or decorative; and body contour feathers (G), which have a smaller feather (aftershaft) growing from the base.

feather One of the skin appendages that makes up the plumage of BIRDS. They are composed of the fibrous protein KERATIN, and provide insulation and enable flight. They are usually replaced at least once a year.

February Revolution (1848) French insurrection that overthrew the government of LOUIS PHILIPPE. The revolution began in Paris following the economic crisis of 1847–48 and agitation for parliamentary reform. Led by bourgeois radicals and working-class revolutionaries, it created the short-lived Second Republic in France, and set off popular uprisings and unrest throughout Europe. *See also* REVOLUTIONS OF 1848

Federal Bureau of Investigation (FBI) US federal government agency that investigates violations of federal law, especially those concerning internal security. Its findings are reported to the ATTORNEY GENERAL and various nationwide attorneys for decisions on prosecution. Established in 1908, its autonomy was strengthened under the directorship (1924–72) of J. Edgar HOOVER. Its headquarters are in Washington, D.C.

Federal courts US judicial system consisting of the US Supreme Court, the US courts of appeals and the US district courts. There are also many specialized courts for areas of law including tax, patents, and military law.

federalism Political system that allows states united under a central government to maintain a measure of independence. Examples include the USA, Australia, Canada, Germany, India, and Switzerland. Central government has supreme authority, but the component states retain a considerable amount of autonomy in such matters as education and health.

Federalist Party US political party led by George WASHINGTON, Alexander HAMILTON, John ADAMS, and John Jay. Formed in 1787 to promote ratification of the Constitution, it represented planters, merchants, bankers, and manufacturers. Hamilton, Jay, and James MADISON (later an Anti-Federalist) wrote the 'Federalist Papers' essays, expressing support for sound financial management, government banking, and strong federal powers. They opposed the STATES' RIGHTS, agrarian philosophy of the REPUBLICAN PARTY.

Federal Reserve System US CENTRAL BANK, established in 1913 to maintain sound monetary and credit conditions. Twelve regional banks are supervised by a Federal Reserve Board of Governors. All national banks are members, as are many state and commercial banks. The Federal Reserve System regulates money flow and credit by varying its discount rate on loans to member banks and by varying the percentage of total deposits member banks must keep in reserve.

feedback In technology, process by which an electronic or mechanical control system monitors and regulates itself. A governor device that restricts the speed of a vehicle regulates the fuel supply, decreasing it as speed increases. Feedback works by returning part of the 'output' of the system to its 'input'.

Feininger, Lyonel (1871–1956) US painter. He left the USA for Europe in 1887 and became involved with CUBISM in 1912.

He evolved a distinctive style of figurative scenes in straight-edged patterns of interconnecting planes, coloured to resemble prisms. He exhibited with the BLAUE REITER (1913) and taught at the BAUHAUS (1919–33). In 1937 he returned to the USA and produced some of his best work, such as *Dawn* (1938).

Feldman, Morton (1926–87) US composer. In the 1950s, he worked with John CAGE and was influenced by contemporary New York painters. Works include *Rothko Chapel* (1971) and *The Viola in my Life* (1970–71).

feldspar Group of common rock-forming minerals that all contain aluminium, silicon and oxygen, but with varying proportions of potassium, sodium and calcium. They are essential constituents of IGNEOUS ROCKS. Hardness 6–6.5; r.d. 2.5–2.8.

Fellini, Federico (1920–93) Italian film director. Fellini's full directorial debut was *The White Sheik* (1952). His next film, *I Vitelloni* (1953), established the elements of satire, autobiography, and humanism common to many of his films. *La Strada* (1954) won an Academy Award for best foreign film. Fellini won a second Oscar for *Le notti di Cabiria* (1957). He won two more Oscars for *8½* (1963) and *Amarcord* (1974). His last film was *Voices of the Moon* (1990).

feminism Movement that promotes equal rights for women. One of the first feminist texts was Mary WOLLSTONECRAFT's *Vindication of the Rights of Women* (1792). In the USA, Elizabeth Cady Stanton organized (1848) the Seneca Falls Convention on WOMEN'S RIGHTS. The SUFFRAGETTE MOVEMENT formed in late 19th-century Britain. Its leaders included Emily PANKHURST and Millicent FAWCETT. The women's movement gained impetus during the two World Wars as women took on employment previously reserved for men. The **women's liberation** movement grew out of texts such as *The Second Sex* (1949) by Simone de BEAUVOIR, *The Golden Notebook* (1962) by Doris LESSING, *The Feminine Mystique* (1963) by Betty FRIEDAN, and *The Female Eunuch* (1970) by Germaine GREER. Practical demands focused on attaining social and economic equality. In the USA, the Equal Employment Opportunity Commission was created (1964). In the UK, the Equal Pay Act (1970), the Sex Discrimination Acts (1975, 1976) and the creation (1975) of the Equal Opportunities Commission gave legal force to many feminist demands.

femur Thigh bone, extending from the hip to the knee. It is the longest and strongest bone of the human skeleton. In four-legged animals, it is the upper bone in the hind legs.

fencing Sport of swordsmanship, using blunt weapons: the foil, épée and sabre. Fencers wear protective jackets, breeches, gloves and wire-mesh masks. In competitions, electronic sensors register hits. It has been an Olympic sport since 1896.

Fenian movement Secret Irish-American revolutionary society. The Great Potato Famine (1845–49) spurred the Young Ireland Uprising (1848), the failure of which prompted many revolutionaries to emigrate. In the USA, John O'Mahoney founded (1848) the Fenian Brotherhood. In Ireland, James Stephens formed (1858) the **Irish Republican Brotherhood (IRB)**. The growing strength of the transatlantic movement led the British government to arrest the leaders of the IRB. In 1867, James Kelly led the abortive Fenian Rising. The Fenians split into factions: the HOME RULE and Land League movements led by Charles Stewart PARNELL and Michael DAVITT; and SINN FÉIN led by Arthur GRIFFITH. Patrick PEARSE led the IRB in the abortive EASTER RISING (1916). In 1919, Michael COLLINS formed the IRISH REPUBLICAN ARMY (IRA).

fennel Tall, perennial herb of the PARSLEY family, native to s Europe. The seeds and extracted oil are used to add a liquorice flavour to medicines, liqueurs and foods. It grows to 1m (3.2ft). Family Apiaceae/Umbelliferae; species *Foeniculum vulgare*.

Fens Lowland region of E England, including parts of Lincolnshire, Cambridgeshire, Suffolk, and Norfolk. This marshy area is intensively cultivated for fruit and vegetables.

Fenton, Roger (1819–69) English photographer whose carefully composed portraits and landscape studies earned him enduring acclaim. In 1855, he became one of the first war photographers, with a series of plates of the Crimean War.

Ferdinand (1861–1948) Prince (1887–1908) and Tsar (1908–18) of Bulgaria. In 1908, he declared Bulgaria independent of the Ottoman Empire and himself tsar. He allied Bulgaria with

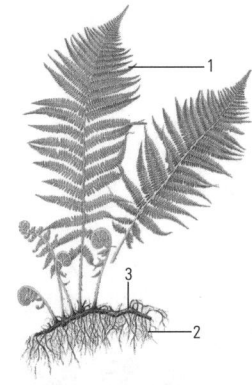

Serbia, Greece and Montenegro in the first BALKAN WAR (1912–13), but largely lost Bulgaria's territorial gains to its former allies in the second war (1913). This led Ferdinand to join the CENTRAL POWERS in World War 1. After the defeat, Ferdinand abdicated in favour of his son, Boris III.

Ferdinand I (1503–64) Holy Roman Emperor (1558–64), King of Bohemia and of Hungary (1526–64). His rule in Hungary was contested by John I, then by John II, both of whom were aided by the Ottoman Sultan. In Bohemia, Ferdinand secured the absolute rule of his HABSBURG dynasty. In Germany, he helped to defeat the Protestant Schmalkaldic League (1546–47). Although a devout Catholic, Ferdinand negotiated the Peace of AUGSBURG (1555).

Ferdinand II (1578–1637) Holy Roman Emperor (1619–37) and HABSBURG King of Bohemia (1617–37) and Hungary (1621–37). He championed the COUNTER-REFORMATION. In 1619, the mainly Protestant diet of Bohemia chose FREDERICK V as their ruler, precipitating the THIRTY YEARS' WAR. The entry of GUSTAVUS II of Sweden into the war turned the tide against Ferdinand. His son succeeded him as FERDINAND III.

Ferdinand III (1608–57) Holy Roman Emperor (1637–57), son of FERDINAND II. In 1634, he succeeded Albrecht WALLENSTEIN as commander of the imperial armies in the THIRTY YEARS' WAR. After Ferdinand's accession, the HABSBURG empire suffered a devastating series of defeats. He was forced to conclude the Peace of WESTPHALIA (1648), marking the end of Habsburg dominance in Germany.

Ferdinand V (1452–1516) (Ferdinand the Catholic) King of Castile and León (1474–1504), of Aragon (as Ferdinand II) (1479–1516), of Sicily (1468–1516), and of Naples (as Ferdinand III) (1504–16). He became joint king of Castile and León after marrying ISABELLA I in 1469, and inherited Aragon from his father, John II, in 1479. After he and Isabella conquered Granada in 1492, they ruled over a united Spain. In 1492 they sponsored the voyage of Christopher COLUMBUS to the New World, expelled the Jews from Spain, and initiated the Spanish INQUISITION. After Isabella's death (1504), Ferdinand acted as regent in Castile for their insane daughter, Joanna, and later for her son, Charles I (who ruled as Emperor CHARLES V).

Ferlinghetti, Lawrence (1919–) US writer. A BEAT MOVEMENT poet, he opened (1953) the City Lights bookstore in San Francisco and began publishing beat authors, such as Allen GINSBERG. His works include *A Coney Island of the Mind* (1958) and *Starting from San Francisco* (1961).

Fermanagh District in sw Northern Ireland; the county town is Enniskillen. During the 17th century, English people settled here as part of the Plantation of Ulster. The district is hilly in the NE and sw. Area: 1,876sq km (724sq mi). Pop. (2001) 57,527.

Fermat, Pierre de (1601–65) French mathematician. With PASCAL, Fermat formulated the theory of probability and, by showing that light travels along the shortest path (**Fermat's principle**), founded the science of geometric optics. In mathematics, he is known for his development of modern NUMBER THEORY and for the contribution some of his ideas made to the development of DIFFERENTIAL CALCULUS.

Fermat's last theorem Theory that, for all integers n 2, there are no non-zero integers x, y and z that satisfy the equation $xn + yn = zn$. Fermat wrote that he had found a proof, but he died without revealing it. Subsequent attempts at a valid proof enriched the area of algebraic number theory. In 1995, English Mathematician Andrew Wiles completed a proof.

fermentation Energy-yielding metabolic process by which sugar and starch molecules are broken down to carbon dioxide and ethanol in the absence of air (ANAEROBIC respiration). Catalysed by ENZYMES, it is used for bread-making, wine- and beer-brewing and cheese maturation. The intoxicating effect of fermented fruits has been known of since 4000 BC.

Fermi, Enrico (1901–54) US physicist, b. Italy. He spent his early career in Italy developing, independently of Paul DIRAC, a form of quantum statistics now known as **Fermi-Dirac statistics**. In 1940 Fermi produced the first synthetic transuranic element, NEPTUNIUM. In 1942, he built the world's first nuclear reactor and produced the first controlled, self-sustaining nuclear CHAIN REACTION. At Los Alamos, Fermi worked on the MANHATTAN PROJECT to develop the atomic bomb.

Fermi received the 1938 Nobel Prize in physics for his work on the bombardment of uranium by neutrons. The element FERMIUM was named after him.

fermion SUBATOMIC PARTICLE that has a half-integer SPIN. Fermions are particles that obey the EXCLUSION PRINCIPLE that no two electrons can have the same energy and spin. Nuclear structures tend to be made up of fermions, of which there are two classes, LEPTONS and QUARKS. *See also* BOSON

fermium (symbol Fm) Radioactive metallic TRANSURANIC ELEMENT of the ACTINIDE SERIES. US nuclear scientist Albert Ghiorso (1915–) and colleagues identified it in 1952 as a decay product of U^{255} from the first large hydrogen bomb explosion. Ten isotopes have subsequently been identified. Properties: at.no. 100; most stable isotope Fm^{257} (half-life 80 days).

fern Non-flowering plant. Ferns grow mainly in warm, moist areas; there are *c.*10,000 species. The best-known genus *Pteridium* (BRACKEN) grows on moorland and in open woodland. Ferns are characterized by two generations: the conspicuous SPOROPHYTE, which possesses leafy fronds, stems, RHIZOMES and roots, and reproduces by minute SPORES usually clustered on the leaves; and the inconspicuous GAMETOPHYTE, which resembles moss and produces sperm and ova. Phylum Filicinophyta. *See also* ALTERNATION OF GENERATIONS

Ferrari, Enzo (1898–1988) Italian racing and sports car designer and manufacturer. He began racing with Alfa Romeo in 1920. In 1939, he founded his own company and the first Ferrari racing car was produced in 1947. Ferrari have won more Formula One championships than any other team.

ferret Semi-domesticated albino form of POLECAT. WEASEL-like animals, ferrets have long necks, slender bodies, and long tails. They are agile killers. Body length: 36cm (14in); weight: 700g (1.5lb). Family Mustelidae; species *Mustela putorius*.

fertility drugs Drugs taken to increase a woman's chances of conception and pregnancy. One cause of female sterility is insufficient secretion of pituitary HORMONES; this can be treated with human chorionic gonadotropin or clomiphene citrate, although use of the latter can result in multiple births. In cases where FERTILIZATION occurs, but where the uterine lining is unable to support the fetus, the hormone PROGESTERONE may be used. Infertility cannot always be corrected with drugs.

fertilization Key process in SEXUAL REPRODUCTION during which the nuclei of female and male GAMETES (sex cells) fuse to form a ZYGOTE. The zygote contains the genetic material (CHROMOSOMES) from both parents (*see* HEREDITY). In animals, the female sex cell is called the

▲ **fern** A typical fern, such as the lady fern (*Athyrium filix-femina*) shown here, has upright leaves called fronds (1) which uncurl as they grow, and roots (2) which grow from the underground stem (3). The first ferns grew in the Devonian period, *c.*400 million years ago.

F

FERTILIZATION

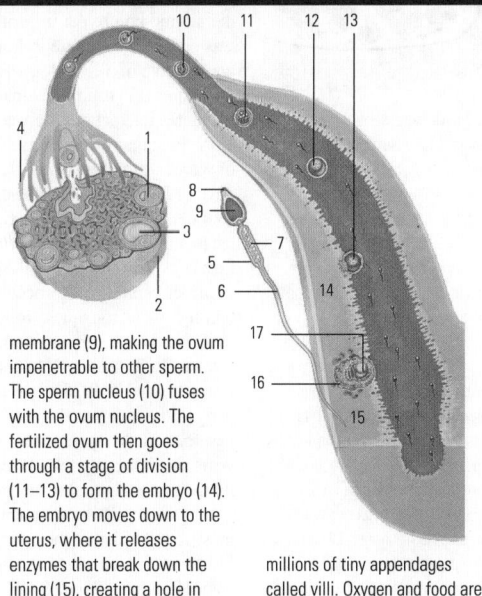

Mammalian fertilization begins with ovulation, in which an ovum or egg (1) develops in an ovary (2) into a follicle (3). The follicle consists of the ovum, a sac of liquid and follicle cells. The pressure in the follicle increases until it bursts, releasing the ovum into the Fallopian tube (4). During ovulation, oestrogen is produced by the collapsed follicle, which causes the lining of the uterus to thicken and extend its network of blood vessels, from which the ovum will be nourished. Fertilization occurs when sperm (5) ejaculates from the penis during copulation. The sperm use their tail-like flagella (6), powered by mitochondria (7), to swim up the uterus. The first to reach the ovum penetrates the ovum membrane with enzymes secreted by the acrosomal vesicle (8). This triggers the formation of a

membrane (9), making the ovum impenetrable to other sperm. The sperm nucleus (10) fuses with the ovum nucleus. The fertilized ovum then goes through a stage of division (11–13) to form the embryo (14). The embryo moves down to the uterus, where it releases enzymes that break down the lining (15), creating a hole in which the embryo sits (16). The embryo (17) develops an organ, the placenta, that comprises of

millions of tiny appendages called villi. Oxygen and food are absorbed from the mother's blood, via capillaries in the villi, into the embryo's blood.

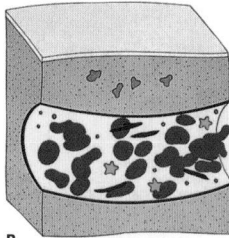

- ⬦ tissue factor
- ☆ plasma factor
- ✦ fibrinogen
- · platelet
- ⬭ erythrocyte
- ✦ fibrin

A

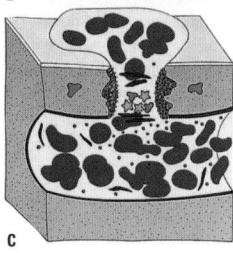

B

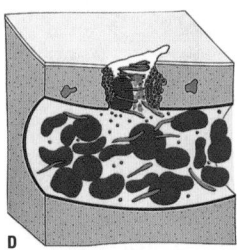

C

D

▲ **fibrin** An essential component of blood clotting, fibrin prevents excessive blood loss from a wound. Normally, circulating blood contains erythrocytes (red blood cells), platelets, plasma, clotting factors, and fibrinogen. Tissue-clotting factors lie trapped within cells surrounding each blood vessel (A). When damage occurs, blood escapes from the broken vessel. Platelets congregate at the site and help to plug the wound. Tissue-clotting factors are released (B). The reaction of the platelets with plasma and tissue-clotting factors converts the soluble fibrinogen into insoluble threads of fibrin. The fibrin forms a mesh across the break (C). Platelets and blood cells become trapped in the mesh. The jelly-like mass shrinks and serum oozes out, leaving a clot (D).

OVUM and the male cell SPERM. After fertilization, the zygote divides to form an EMBRYO. Fertilization of the female OVUM by the male SPERM can be external (as in most fish, amphibians and aquatic invertebrates) or internal (as in reptiles, birds, mammals and insects). In PLANTS, the male gamete is found in POLLEN, and for most higher plants, POLLINATION occurs before fertilization.

fertilizer Organic or inorganic substance added to soil to improve plant growth by increasing fertility. Manure and compost were the first fertilizers. Other organic fertilizers include bone meal, ashes, guano and fish. Modern chemical fertilizers, containing the nutrients nitrogen, phosphorus or potassium, are now widely used.

Fessenden, Reginald Aubrey (1866–1932) US engineer, physicist and inventor, a pioneer in radio and echo-sounding. He is thought to have broadcast the first radio programme (using speech signals, not Morse code) in 1906. Among his more than 500 patents were AMPLITUDE MODULATION (AM), the high-frequency alternator, the electrolytic detector, the heterodyne system of radio reception, and the fathometer.

fetus (foetus) Stage of EMBRYO development in a mammal at which the main adult features become recognizable, although most are still far from their later forms. In humans, it is reached in approximately the ninth week after conception, at which time the fetus is about 30 mm (1.2 inches) long.

feudal system Social system that prevailed in most of Europe from the 9th century to the late MIDDLE AGES, based on the tenure of land. The system originated from the need to provide for a permanent group of knights to assist the king in his wars. All land was theoretically owned by the monarch and leased out to tenants-in-chief in return for their attendance at court and military assistance; and they, in turn, let out fiefs to knights in return for military service and other obligations. The Church too was sometimes required to render military service for its land. Feudalism collapsed in 16th-century England, but persisted into the 18th century in other parts of Europe.

fever Elevation of the body temperature above normal, that is 37°C (98.6°F). It is mostly caused by bacterial or viral infection and can accompany virtually any infectious disease.

Feydeau, Georges (1862–1921) French playwright. He wrote many extremely popular plays, with absurd plots and sparkling dialogue, in which he pioneered 19th-century French FARCE. Among these plays were *Hotel Paradiso* (1894), *The Lady from Maxim's* (1899), and *A Flea in Her Ear* (1907).

Feynman, Richard Phillips (1918–88) US theoretical physicist. He worked on the MANHATTAN PROJECT to develop the atomic bomb. An inspiring teacher and orator, Feynman was professor of theoretical physics (1950–88) at the California Institute of Technology. In 1949, he introduced a graphic technique (**Feynman diagrams**) for illustrating the electromagnetic interactions between ELEMENTARY PARTICLES. In 1957, Feynman and Murray GELL-MANN proposed the theory of WEAK NUCLEAR FORCE. He shared the 1965 Nobel Prize in physics for his part in the development of QUANTUM ELECTRODYNAMICS (QED). In 1986, he was a member of the committee that investigated the *Challenger* space-shuttle disaster.

Fez (Fès) City in N central Morocco. Founded in *c*.790, it is a former capital of Morocco and a sacred city of Islam containing many mosques. Industries: leather goods, pottery, traditional crafts, metal-working. Pop. (1994) 771,740.

Fianna Fáil (Gaelic, Soldiers of Destiny) Irish political party. It was formed in 1926 by those opposed to Irish partition. The party came to power in 1932 under Eamon DE VALERA, and has formed the government alone or in coalition for most years since then. It seeks the reunification of Ireland by peaceful means, believes that the government should take an active role in economic development, and has traditionally been the most conservative of the main parties. *See also* FINE GAEL

Fibonacci, Leonardo (*c*.1170–*c*.1240) Italian mathematician. He wrote *Liber abaci* (*c*.1200), the first Western work to propose the adoption of the Arabic numerical system. He produced the mathematical sequence named after him, in which each term is formed by the addition of the two terms preceding it. The sequence begins 0, 1, 1, 2, 3, 5, 8, 13, 21....

and so on. Many natural forms, such as spiral shells and leaf systems, are delimited by the Fibonacci series.

fibre Any of various materials consisting of thread-like strands. Natural fibres can be made into yarn, textiles and other products, including carpets and rope. The fibres consist of long narrow cells. **Animal** fibres are based on protein molecules and include WOOL, SILK, mohair, angora, and horsehair. **Vegetable** fibres are based mainly on CELLULOSE and include COTTON, LINEN, FLAX, JUTE, SISAL, and KAPOK. The mineral ASBESTOS is a natural, inorganic fibre. **Regenerated** fibres are manufactured from natural products, modified chemically. For example, RAYON is made from cellulose fibre from cotton or wood. **Synthetic** fibres are made from a molten or dissolved plastic resin by forcing it through fine nozzles (spinnerets). These fibres can be used as single-strand yarn, or spun to form multi-strand yarn and woven into textiles. Synthetic fibres include NYLON and other polyamides, POLYESTERS, and ACRYLICS.

fibreglass Spun glass used as a continuous filament in textiles and electrical insulation, and in a fibrous form to reinforce plastics or for sound or heat insulation. Molten glass is drawn through spinnerets or spun through holes in a revolving dish. Combined with layers of resin, fibreglass is a popular medium for car bodies, boats, aircraft parts, and containers.

fibre optics Branch of OPTICS concerned with the transmission of data and images by reflecting light through fine glass OPTICAL FIBRES. Data can travel at very high speeds.

fibrin Insoluble, fibrous protein that is essential to BLOOD CLOTTING. Developed in the blood from a soluble protein, fibrinogen, fibrin is laid down at the site of a wound in the form of a mesh, which then dries and hardens so the bleeding stops.

fibula Long, thin outer bone of the lower leg of two- and four-legged VERTEBRATES, including humans. It articulates with the other lower leg bone, the TIBIA, just below the knee.

Fidei Defensor *See* DEFENDER OF THE FAITH

Fielding, Henry (1707–54) English novelist and playwright. During the 1730s, he wrote a number of satirical plays, such as *Pasquin* (1736). His first work of fiction, *An Apology for the Life of Mrs Shamela Andrews* (1741), was a parody of Samuel RICHARDSON's *Pamela* (1740). *Joseph Andrews* (1742) was his first NOVEL. His masterpiece is the picaresque novel *Tom Jones* (1749). Fielding was responsible for the foundation of Britain's first organized police force, the Bow Street Runners.

Fields, W.C. (William Claud) (1880–1946) US music-hall, film and radio comedian. He was famous for his portrayal of hard-drinking, misanthropic braggarts in such films as *My Little Chickadee* (1940) and *Never Give a Sucker an Even Break* (1941).

Fife Region in E central Scotland between the firths of Tay and Forth; the capital is Glenrothes. The central part is mostly low-lying farmland. Coalfields are situated in the W and E. Along the North Sea coast there are many fishing villages. ST ANDREWS is the seat of Scotland's oldest university (1410), and the home of the Royal and Ancient Golf Club. Area: 1,305sq km (504sq mi). Pop. (2001) 349,770.

fig Tree, shrub, or climber of the MULBERRY family, growing in warm regions, especially from the E Mediterranean to India and Malaysia. The common fig (*Ficus carica*) has tiny flowers without petals that grow inside fleshy flask-like receptacles; these become the thick outer covering holding the seeds, the true, edible fruit of the fig tree. Height: to 11.8m (39ft). Family Moraceae, genus *Ficus*.

Fiji Independent nation in the S Pacific Ocean, consisting of more than 800 mostly volcanic islands and islets; the capital is Suva. Settlement dates back to the second millennium BC. Discovered by Abel TASMAN in 1643, the islands became a British crown colony in 1874. Indians were imported to work on sugar plantations, and by the 1950s outnumbered native Fijians. In 1987 the election of an Indian-majority government prompted a military coup, led by Colonel Sitiveni Rabuka. He proclaimed a republic, and in 1992 became prime minister. In 1997 Fiji approved a new multiracial constitution and was readmitted to the Commonwealth. Mahendra Chaudhry, an ethnic Indian, defeated Rabuka in 1999 elections. In May 2000, George Speight led a coup, the Great Council of Chiefs dismissed Chaudhry, and the army declared martial law. The Commonwealth suspended Fiji. In July 2000, Speight was arrested after freeing the hostages. Ratu Iloilo became president. Laisenia Qarase became prime minister in 2001 elections, and the Commonwealth readmitted Fiji. In 2002 Speight was found guilty of treason and imprisoned. The crisis devastated Fiji's economy, which relies heavily on tourism and aid (2006 PPP GDP per capita, US$6100). In 2006 Commodore Bainimarama led a military coup, and US aid and Fiji's Commonwealth membership were again suspended. Agriculture: copra, sugar, and rice. Gold and silver are mined. Area: 18,274sq km (7,056sq mi). Pop. (2005) 906,000.

filariasis Group of tropical diseases caused by infection with a nematode worm, *filaria*. The parasites, which are transmitted by insects, infiltrate the lymph glands, causing swelling and impaired drainage. Drug treatment reduces the symptoms. *See also* ELEPHANTIASIS

filibuster Method of frustrating the action of a legislative assembly by making long speeches. It has particular reference to debates in the US Senate, which did not have any method for voting to end debate until 1917. Since then a two-thirds majority is required to close a debate, thereby allowing a minority to prevent a vote on legislation that they oppose.

Fillmore, Millard (1800–74) Thirteenth US president (1850–53). Fillmore served (1833–43) in the House of Representatives, and in 1834 joined the newly formed WHIGS. In 1848, he was elected vice president to Zachary TAYLOR, and succeeded as president when Taylor died. In a bid to mediate between pro- and anti-slavery factions, Fillmore agreed to the COMPROMISE OF 1850. His attempt to enforce the Fugitive Slave Law embittered abolitionists and split the party. Fillmore failed to win renomination in 1852, and was succeeded by Franklin PIERCE. In the 1856 elections Fillmore stood for the Know-Nothing movement, but was defeated by Abraham LINCOLN.

film noir Genre of cynical, bleak films, originating in Hollywood during the 1940s and 1950s. Often bathed in gloomy shadows, the ominous mood of the films mirrored the corruption and paralysis of the underworld characters they presented. Influenced by the effects of World War 2, it

INTERNET

Fiji
▶ www.fiji.gov.fj
▶ www.bulafiji.com

Fillmore, Millard
▶ www.whitehouse.gov/ history/presidents

FINLAND

The Republic of Finland (*Suomi*) has four geographical regions. In the s and w, on the Gulfs of Bothnia and Finland, is the low, narrow coastal strip where most Finns live. The capital and largest city, HELSINKI, is here. The ÅLAND ISLANDS lie in the entrance to the Gulf of Bothnia. Most of the interior is a beautiful wooded plateau, with more than 60,000 lakes. The Saimaa area is Europe's largest inland water system. A third of Finland lies within the Arctic Circle; this 'land of the midnight sun' is called *Lappi* (LAPLAND).

Forests (birch, pine, and spruce) cover 60% of Finland. The vegetation becomes more and more sparse to the N, until it merges into Arctic tundra.

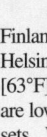

CLIMATE
Finland has short, warm summers; Helsinki's July average is 17°C [63°F]. In Lapland, the temperatures are lower, and in June the sun never sets. Winters are long and cold; Helsinki's January average is –6°C [21°F]. The North Atlantic Drift keeps the Arctic coasts free of ice.

HISTORY
In the 8th century, Finnish-speaking settlers forced the LAPPS to the north. Between 1150 and 1809, Finland was under Swedish rule. The close links between the countries continue today. Swedish remains an official language in Finland and one of the legacies of this period is a Swedish-speaking minority of 6% of the total population. Finnish bears little relation to the Swedish or any other Scandinavian language. It is closest to Magyar, the language of Hungary.

Lutheranism arrived in the 16th century. Wars between Sweden and Russia devastated Finland, and following the NORTHERN WAR (1700–21), Russia gained much Finnish land. In the NAPOLEONIC WARS Russia conquered Finland and, in 1809, it became a grand duchy of the Russian Empire. Nationalist feelings developed during the 19th century, but in 1899 Tsar NICHOLAS II began a programme of Russification, seeking to force Russian culture on the Finns, who resisted fiercely. In 1903, the Russian governor suspended the constitution and became dictator, although following much resistance, self-government was restored in 1906.

Following the Russian Revolution (1917), Finland declared independence. Civil war (January–May 1918) broke out between the Russian-backed Red Guard and the German-backed White Guard led by Carl MANNERHEIM. The White Guard triumphed, and a republic was established in 1919.

At the outbreak of World War 2, Finland declared its neutrality. A Soviet invasion (November 1939) resulted in the Russo-Finnish War and, in March 1940, Finland ceded part of KARELIA and Lake LADOGA to Russia. In 1941, Finland allied itself to Germany and Finnish troops regained s Karelia.

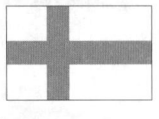

AREA 338,145sq km [130,558sq mi]
POPULATION 5,238,000
CAPITAL (POPULATION) Helsinki (937,000)
GOVERNMENT Multiparty republic
ETHNIC GROUPS Finnish 93%, Swedish 6%
LANGUAGES Finnish and Swedish (both official)
RELIGIONS Evangelical Lutheran 89%
CURRENCY Euro = 100 cents

At the end of the war, Russia regained s Karelia and other parts of Finland.

After World War 2, Finland pursued a policy of neutrality acceptable to the Soviet Union. In 1955, Finland joined the UN and the Nordic Council. Finland also strengthened its links with other north European countries and became an associate member of the European Free Trade Association (EFTA) in 1961. Urho Kaleva Kekkonen led (1956–81) Finland through reconstruction and Finland became a full member of EFTA in 1986, in a decade when its economy was growing rapidly.

POLITICS
After the fall of the Soviet Union, Finland no longer needed to remain neutral. In 1992 the country applied to join the European Union, officially becoming a member in 1995. On 1 January 2002 the euro became Finland's official sole currency. Finland has also discussed the possibility of joining NATO, but polls since 2001 suggest that the majority of Finns favour non-alliance. Tarja Halonen became Finland's first female president in 2000 elections and was re-elected in 2006.

ECONOMY
Although the fall of the Soviet Union caused a major recession, Finland recovered rapidly and has a prosperous economy. Engineering, high technology electronics, and paper and wood products are the major sectors and the largest exports. Within these, shipbuilding and mobile telephones are particularly important. Forests are Finland's most valuable natural resource, and most other raw materials are imported. Farming employs less than 5% of the workforce.

INTERNET

Finland
▶ virtual.finland.fi
▶ www.visitfinland.com

F

▲ **fir** The Douglas fir (*Pseudotsuga menziesii*) shown here is not a true fir, rather it is a false hemlock. Named after the Scottish botanist David Douglas, the largest of the species grow to some 90m (300ft) and can live for more than 400 years. In damp conditions, a Douglas fir will grow 1m (3ft) a year for the first 30 years of its life.

depicted an uneasy world, lacking ideals or moral absolutes. John HUSTON's *The Maltese Falcon* (1941) was the blueprint for other genre classics, such as *The Big Sleep* (1946) and *Touch of Evil* (1958).

filter Porous device for separating solid particles from a liquid or gas through filtration. A coffee filter is a simple example, and many complex forms of filter have been devised for various uses. Most cars have a number of filters, for air, petrol, and oil. These operate either by trapping solid particles in porous materials such as paper or meshes, or by circulating the material to be filtered through a maze, the pockets of which trap particles, as in the air filter.

finch Any of a family (Fringillidae) of small or medium-sized birds, including the SPARROW, cardinal, CANARY, BUNTING, and GROSBEAK. They are found in most parts of the world, except for Australia, New Zealand, and the Pacific islands. Most have a cone-shaped bill and feed on seeds, although some eat fruit or insects. Some British 'finches', such as the bullfinch and goldfinch, belong to another family, Ploceidae.

Fine Gael Irish political party. It was founded in 1933, as a successor to the party under William COSGRAVE that had held power since the inception of the Irish Free State. Overshadowed by FIANNA FÁIL, Fine Gael has held office only four times, always in coalition with the Labour Party (1948–51, 1954–57, 1973–77, 1994–97).

fingerprint Pattern of ridges in the dermis or deeper skin on the end of the fingers and thumbs. Fingerprints are specific to an individual and remain unchanged in pattern throughout life. In 1901, the British police force introduced fingerprinting as a means of identifying criminals. *See also* FORENSIC SCIENCE

Finland Republic in N Europe. *See* country feature, page 321

Finnish One of the two official languages of Finland and a member of the FINNO-UGRIC group of languages. It is spoken by over 4.5 million people in Finland, and by nearly a million people in Sweden, Russia and the USA. SWEDISH is the other official language of Finland, spoken by *c.*300,000 inhabitants.

Finn Mac Cumhail (Finn MacCool or Fingal) (active 2nd or 3rd century AD) Semi-mythical Irish leader of a group of soldiers known as the Fianna. Their exploits were recorded in many poems, including those in the 12th-century *Book of Leinster* and others said to have been written by his son, Ossian.

Finno-Ugric Group of related languages spoken by more than 22 million people in Finland and N Norway, in Estonia and Karelia, in various areas at the N end of the River Volga and each side of the Ural Mountains, and in Hungary. The languages are unrelated to the INDO-EUROPEAN family. The Finnic branch includes FINNISH, Estonian, Lappish, Mordvinian, Mari, Komi, Votyak, Cheremiss and Zyrian; the Ugric branch comprises HUNGARIAN, Ostyak and Mansi (Vogul). Together with the Samoyed languages, Finno-Ugric makes up the Uralic family.

fir Any of a number of evergreen trees of the PINE family, native to alpine regions of the Northern Hemisphere. The pyramid-shaped trees are prized for their beauty and fragrance. They have flat needles and cylindrical cones that shed their scales when mature. The North American balsam fir is the source of Canadian BALSAM. Height: 15–90m (50–300ft). Family Pinaceae; genus *Abies*.

Firdausi (935–1020) Persian poet. He wrote the *Shah Nama*, an epic poem of more than 50,000 couplets about the history of Persia. The work, which created the traditions of Persian poetry, was presented to Mahmud of Ghazni in 1010.

firearm Term used usually to describe a small arm – a weapon carried and fired by one person. The first effective firearms were made *c.*1425, when a primitive trigger to bring a burning cord known as a match into contact with the gunpowder charge was invented. Such firearms, called matchlocks, were heavy and cumbersome, and needed a constantly lit match and careful loading with loose gunpowder. The lighter flintlock (which used the spark produced by flint striking steel to ignite the powder) superseded the matchlock in the mid-17th century and remained essentially the same for a further 150 years. During the 19th century there were great changes. In 1805, the explosive properties of mercury fulminate were discovered; it was used in the percussion cap (invented 1815) to provide a surer, more efficient means of detonation. This permitted the development by 1865 of the centre-fire cartridge, which has been the basic type of ammunition used in firearms ever since. Faster breech loading became practical. Rifling – the cutting of spiral grooves along the inside of a barrel in order to make the bullet spin in flight, stabilising it – became widespread with the development of new machine tools. During the 1830s Samuel Colt perfected the revolver, a PISTOL which could fire several shots without the need to reload. Magazine RIFLES were in use by 1880 and became more effective with the introduction of a bolt action after 1889. Development of a weapon that could fire a continuous stream of bullets began with the manually operated GATLING GUN, but the first modern MACHINE GUN was the Maxim gun, invented in the 1880s. In the twentieth century guns became lighter, faster firing and cheaper to manufacture.

fireball (bollide) Exceptionally bright METEOR. Fireballs have been loosely defined as meteors brighter than the planets; with the modern estimate of the maximum brightness of Venus, this would mean that all meteors brighter than magnitude −4.7 should be classified as fireballs.

firefly Light-emitting beetle found in moist places of temperate and tropical regions. Organs underneath the abdomen usually give off rhythmic flashes of light that are typical of the species. The luminous larvae and wingless females of some species are called GLOW-WORMS. Length: to 25mm (1in). There are 1,000 species. Family Lampyridae.

Fire of London (September 2–6, 1666) Accidental fire that destroyed most of the City of London, England. It started in a baker's shop in Pudding Lane, a site now marked by the Monument, and a strong wind spread it quickly through the closely packed wooden houses. The fire provided an opportunity for rebuilding London on a more spacious plan, but, for the most part, only the famous churches of Christopher WREN (including ST PAUL's Cathedral) were built.

First World War *See* WORLD WAR I

Fischer, Hans (1881–1945) German biochemist who received the 1930 Nobel Prize in chemistry for his structural studies of CHLOROPHYLL and of the red blood pigment haemin. His research indicated the close relationship between the two substances. He was able to synthesize haemin, and he almost completely synthesized one of the chlorophylls.

Fischer-Dieskau, Dietrich (1925–) German baritone. One of the foremost operatic singers of the 20th century, and an outstanding interpreter of Lieder. He was an extremely versatile singer, appearing in recitals, as soloist with orchestras, in operatic roles and on numerous recordings.

fish Cold-blooded, aquatic vertebrate animal characterized by fins, gills for breathing, a streamlined body almost always covered by scales or bony plates on to which a layer

FISH

swim bladder
epineural spine
vertebral column
gill cover
muscle blocks
tail fin
dorsal fin
gill raker
gill arch
lateral line
gill filaments
kidney
liver
intestine
stomach
overlapping scales
heart
pelvic fin
ovary (cutaway to show eggs)

There are more than 22,000 species of bony fish. Although they vary in shape and the way they swim, they share many common features. All have a tail with equal upper and lower lobe sizes, which provides neither up nor down thrust. Such fish achieve natural buoyancy by adjusting their density using the swim bladder. The fish can expand or contract the swim bladder by secreting gas into or absorbing gas out of it, so adjusting the volume and external pressure, and counteracting the tendency to sink or float to the surface.

of mucus is secreted, and a two-chambered heart. Fish are the most ancient form of vertebrate life, with a history of about 450 million years. They reproduce sexually, and fertilization may be external or internal. The eggs develop in water or inside the female, according to species. Fish have lateral line organs, which are fluid-filled pits and channels that run under the skin of the body. Sensitive fibres link these channels to the central nervous system and detect changes of pressure in the water and changes of strength and direction in currents. About 75% of all fish live in the sea; the remainder are freshwater species that live in lakes, rivers and streams. A few fish, such as the SALMON and EEL, divide their lives between salt and freshwater habitats. The classification of fish varies. They are usually divided into three classes: Agnatha, which are **jawless** fish, including the hagfish and LAMPREY; Chondrichthyes (**cartilaginous** fish), which includes SHARK, SKATE, RAY and CHIMERA; and the much more numerous Osteichthyes (**bony** fish), including subclasses of soft-rayed fish (LUNGFISH and lobefin) and the very successful teleost fish, such as salmon and COD. There are more than 22,000 species of bony fish, and they represent *c*.40% of all living vertebrates. They divide into 34 orders and 48 families.

Fisher, Saint John (1469–1535) English Roman Catholic prelate. Fisher opposed Henry VIII's proposed divorce from Catherine of Aragon in 1529. He was tried and executed for denying that Henry was supreme head of the Church under the Act of Supremacy. He was canonized in 1935. His feast day is July 9.

fishing and **fisheries** Harvesting fish for commercial uses. Commercial fishing boats and fleets employ several methods for catching fish, including pole and line, purse seine, gill netting, trawling and stunning. About 70% of the commercial fish catch is taken in the Northern Hemisphere, with the greatest catches taken between the Philippines and Japan. Other fishing areas include the North Atlantic, North Pacific and North Sea. The most significant Southern Hemisphere areas are the Pacific coast of Peru and the South African coast. Herrings, sardines and anchovies make up the largest percentage of the total catch. Other species caught in commercial quantities include cod, haddock, hake, redfish, sea bream, mackerel, tuna, and salmon. The major fishing nations (by catch) are China, Japan, Peru, Chile, Russia, and the United States. By the late 1970s, fish stocks were severely depleted. While attempts have been made to allow fish stocks to return to previous levels, such as the 1983 United Nations' 'Law of the Sea' resolution that allowed countries to enforce an exclusive 320km (200mi) limit around their coastlines, fish stocks remain low. *See also* ANGLING

fission In biology, form of ASEXUAL REPRODUCTION in unicellular organisms. The parent cell divides into two or more identical daughter cells. Binary fission produces two daughter cells (as in bacteria). Multiple fission produces 4, 8, or, in the case of some protozoa, more than 1,000 daughter cells, each developing into a new organism.

fission, nuclear In physics, form of nuclear reaction in which a heavy atomic NUCLEUS splits into two, with the release of two or three NEUTRONS and large amounts of heat and nuclear RADIATION. Fission may occur spontaneously or be made to occur by bombarding certain nuclei with low-energy (slow) neutrons or PROTONS. The only naturally occurring fissionable material is URANIUM-235. Natural uranium is not capable of sustaining a CHAIN REACTION because its major isotope, U^{238}, tends to absorb neutrons before they can split another atom. Currently, there are two main methods of creating a sustained chain reaction in uranium fuel. In the first, the neutrons released by fission of U^{235} are slowed down by a **moderator** composed of light atoms, such as DEUTERIUM, which does not absorb neutrons. Most NUCLEAR REACTORS use this method. Alternatively, the uranium may be **enriched** (increasing the amount of fissionable material). Fast-breeder reactors employ this process. Nuclear fission and nuclear FUSION are used in NUCLEAR WEAPONS.

Fitzgerald, Ella (1917–96) US jazz singer. Chick Webb discovered the "First Lady of Song" at Harlem's Apollo Theater

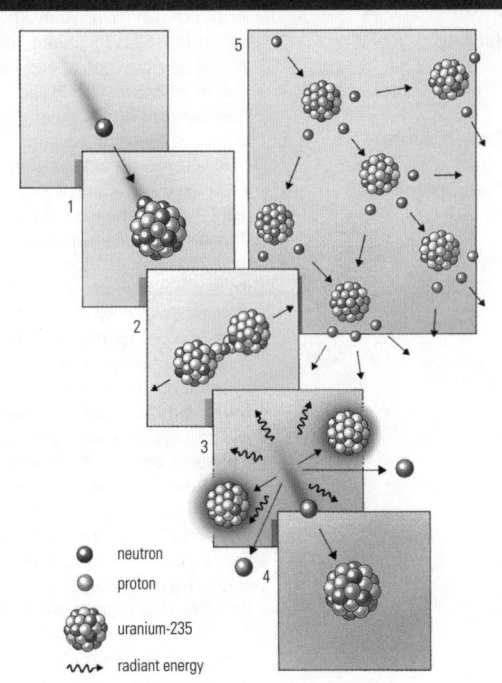

FISSION

Most nuclear power stations use uranium-235 as fuel. When a uranium-235 nucleus strikes a slow-moving neutron (1), it absorbs the neutron to form uranium-236. This is unstable and splits violently (2) forming two smaller nuclei, generating radiant energy (some in the form of heat), and releasing several neutrons (3). These neutrons can then start the process again (4), splitting further nuclei, which in turn release yet more neutrons (5). Such a process is known as a chain reaction and can spread at lightning speed. In a nuclear reactor, many of the neutrons are absorbed to prevent the chain reaction from running out of control and causing an excessive release of energy. Atomic bombs are designed to encourage the chain reaction to spread extremely rapidly.

- ● neutron
- ○ proton
- uranium-235
- ∿∿ radiant energy

in 1934. Fitzgerald's first hit was "A-Tisket A-Tasket" (1938). Her *Songbook* series of renditions of popular 'standards' by George Gershwin, Jerome Kern and Cole Porter have become definitive. She worked with most of the jazz greats of her era, including Duke Ellington, Count Basie, and Louis Armstrong.

Fitzgerald, F. Scott (Francis Scott Key) (1896–1940) US writer. He began his debut novel, *This Side of Paradise* (1920), while in the US Army. Along with *The Beautiful and Damned* (1922), this established him as a chronicler of what he christened the 'Jazz Age'. He spent much of the 1920s in Europe, mingling with wealthy and sophisticated expatriates. Fitzgerald published his masterpiece, *The Great Gatsby*, in 1925. His last novels were *Tender is the Night* (1934) and the unfinished *The Last Tycoon* (1941).

Fitzgerald, George Francis (1851–1901) Irish physicist who researched ELECTROLYSIS and ELECTROMAGNETISM and who is noted for his theory of ELECTROMAGNETIC RADIATION. As an explanation of the MICHELSON-Morley experiment to determine the Earth's movement through the ETHER, Fitzgerald suggested the theory that objects change length (the LORENTZ-**Fitzgerald contraction**) due to this type of movement. This theory was incorporated into Albert EINSTEIN's special theory of RELATIVITY.

Fitzgerald, Penelope Mary (1916–2000) British novelist and biographer. Her first novel, *The Golden Child*, did not appear until 1977. *Offshore* (1979), a portrait of a houseboat community, won the Booker Prize. Her later works, including *At Freddie's* (1982), *Innocence* (1986) and *The Gate of Angels* (1990), show a similarly deft handling of character and detail.

fjord (fiord) Narrow, steep-sided inlet on a sea coast. They were formed by GLACIERS moving towards the sea, and were flooded when the ice melted and sea levels rose.

flagellant Religious zealot who uses flagellation, or flogging, for disciplinary or devotional purposes. Now almost obsolete, the practice of flagellation has been part of many religions, including those of ancient Greece and Rome, some Native American cultures, and Christianity. In most cases, flagellants have used beatings as a form of penance or purification.

flagellate Any member of the class Mastigophora. Flagellates are PROTOZOA that possesses, at some stage of their development, one or several whip-like structures (flagellum) for locomotion and sensation. There are two major groups; the **phytoflagellates** resemble plants (in that they obtain their energy through PHOTOSYNTHESIS), the **zooflagellates** resemble animals (in that they obtain energy through feeding).

▲ **Fitzgerald** US jazz singer Ella Fitzgerald's smooth, effortless, 'scat' vocalizing is best heard on her interpretations of standards by Cole Porter, Jerome Kern and George Gershwin.

Flaherty, Robert Joseph (1884–1951) Pioneer US director of DOCUMENTARY films. In Canada, he made *Nanook of the North* (1922) about Inuit life, followed by *Moana* (1926), an idyllic treatment of Samoa. Other major films include *Industrial Britain* (1932) and *Louisiana Story* (1948).

flamboyant style Final phase of French GOTHIC architecture (14th-16th century). The name comes from the flame-like forms of the elaborate tracery used in cathedrals, as on the west façade of Rouen Cathedral (1370). The English DECORATED STYLE is a close equivalent.

flamenco Traditional song, dance, and instrumental music, thought to have developed from an amalgam of Romany, Jewish, and Arab cultures in Andalusia, s Spain. Flamenco consists of improvisation within strict rules. There are three types of song, of which the most demanding is *cante hondo*. The dances epitomize pride, poise, and sensuality. They are accompanied by handclaps, finger-snapping, and rhythmic rolls on the guitar.

flamingo Long-necked, long-legged wading bird of tropical and subtropical lagoons and lakes. They have webbed feet and a plumage that varies in colour from pale to deep pink. Their bills have fine hair-like filters which strain food from the muddy water. Height: to 1.5m (5ft). Family Phoenicopteridae.

Flanders Historic region now divided between Belgium and France. Between the 13th and 15th centuries, Flanders prospered on trade, and the old nobility lost authority to the towns. By 1400, it was part of Burgundy, passing to the Habsburgs in 1482, before becoming part of the Spanish Netherlands. It was frequently fought over by France, Spain and later Austria. It was the scene of devastating trench warfare in World War 1.

flare, solar *See* SOLAR FLARE

flash memory Form of solid–state computer data storage. Invented in the 1980s, it became widespread in the 2000s when large capacities became cheaply available. Its robustness and low power use has made it popular in portable devices.

flat (symbol *b*) In musical notation, an accidental sign placed before a note or immediately after the clef to indicate that the note it refers to should be sounded a semitone lower.

flatfish Any of more than 500 species of bottom-dwelling, mainly marine fish found worldwide. Most have oval flattened bodies. Both eyes are on the upper side; the lower side is generally white. Examples include the HALIBUT, PLAICE, TURBOT, and SOLE. Order Pleuronectiformes.

flatworm Simple, carnivorous, ribbon-like creature which, having no circulatory system and sometimes no mouth or gut, feeds by absorption through its body wall. The FLUKE and TAPEWORM are both animal parasites. Order Platyhelminthes.

Flaubert, Gustave (1821–80) French novelist of the 19th-century realist school. An extremely craftsmanlike and elegant writer, he remains one of the most highly respected of European novelists. *Madame Bovary* (1857), his masterpiece, represents the transition from ROMANTICISM to REALISM in the development of the NOVEL. Other fiction includes *The Temptation of*

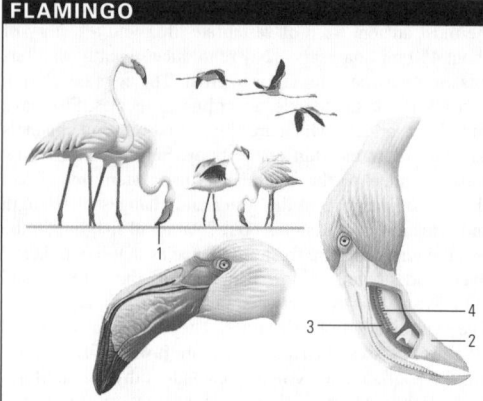

FLAMINGO

1

3 — 4
2

Flamingos feed by lowering their heads into the water so that their bills are upside down (1). The bill's crooked shape allows the front half of the bill to lie horizontally in the water (2). Tiny, hook-like lamellae (3) strain food as the

water is pumped through them by a backward and forward motion of the tongue. Protuberances on the tongue (4) scrape the particles of food off the lamellae for ingestion as the tongue moves back and forth.

St Anthony (1847), *Salammbô* (1862), *A Sentimental Education* (1869), and the short stories *Three Tales* (1877).

flax Slender, erect, flowering plant cultivated for its fibres and seeds. After harvesting, the stems are retted (soaked in water) to soften the fibres and wash away other tissues. The fibres are spun into yarn to make linen. The seeds yield linseed oil. Family Linaceae; species *Linum usitatissium*.

flea Any of 1,000 species of wingless, leaping insects found worldwide. They are external parasites on warm-blooded animals. In moving from one host to another, they can carry disease. Length: to 1cm (0.4in). Order Siphonaptera.

Fleming, Sir Alexander (1881–1955) Scottish bacteriologist, discoverer of PENICILLIN. In 1922, Fleming discovered lysozyme, a natural antibacterial substance found in saliva and tears. During research on staphylococci in 1928, Fleming noticed that a mould, identified as *Penicillium notatum*, liberated a substance that inhibited the growth of some bacteria. He named it penicillin; it was the first ANTIBIOTIC. Howard FLOREY and Ernst CHAIN refined the drug's production and it was first produced commercially in 1941. In 1945, Fleming, Florey and Chain shared the Nobel Prize in physiology or medicine.

Fleming, Ian Lancaster (1908–64) English novelist. After a career as a journalist and banker, he wrote 13 escapist spy thrillers about James Bond, secret agent '007'. The novels won great popularity for their escapist fantasy, sex, and violence. The subsequent films based on, or inspired by, his novels became a cinematic institution.

Fleming, Sir John Ambrose (1849–1945) English electrical engineer, inventor of the thermionic valve. Fleming's valve was a RECTIFIER, or DIODE, consisting of two electrodes in an evacuated glass envelope. The diode permitted current to flow in one direction only. It could detect RADIO signals but could not amplify them. *See also* FLEMING'S RULES

Fleming's rules In physics, ways of remembering the relationships between the directions of the current, field and mechanical rotation in electric motors and generators. In the **left-hand** rule (for motors), the forefinger represents magnetic field, the second finger current, and the thumb, force; when the digits are extended at right-angles to each other, the appropriate directions are indicated. The **right-hand** rule applies the same principles to generators. John FLEMING devised the rules.

Flemish One of two official languages of Belgium (the other being French). It is spoken, mainly in the N of the country, by *c.*50% of the population. It is virtually the same as DUTCH.

Flemish art (Netherlandish art) Loose art history term used to describe artists working in what roughly corresponds to modern-day Netherlands, Belgium and Luxembourg. In the 14th and early 15th centuries, Flemish artists were masters

▲ **flax** Cultivated in moist, temperate climates, only one of several species of flax (*Linum* sp.) is grown for its fibre and rich oil seeds. After harvesting, flax stems are retted (soaked in water) to soften the fibres which are then spun into yarn.

▶ **Florence** Located among the Tuscan foothills of N Italy, Florence is one of Italy's oldest intellectual and cultural centres. In the centre of the photograph is the Duomo of Santa Maria del Fiore, designed by Brunelleschi, and to its left a campanile (bell-tower) designed by Giotto.

of the International GOTHIC style, brilliantly characterized by the illuminated manuscripts of the LIMBOURG brothers. Naturalism became a hallmark of Flemish art, such as the portraits and altarpieces of van EYCK and van der WEYDEN and the LANDSCAPE PAINTINGS of BRUEGEL. The greatest figures of the next era were Anthony VAN DYCK, who spent much of his career in England, and Peter Paul RUBENS, the chief exponent of BAROQUE art in N Europe. After 1650, Flemish art went into a long decline. In the 19th century, the leading Belgian artist was James Ensor, a precursor of EXPRESSIONISM. In the 20th century, MAGRITTE and Paul Delvaux both made significant contributions to the SURREALISM movement. *See also* DUTCH ART

Fletcher, John (1579–1625) English dramatist and poet. From *c.*1607 to 1616, he collaborated with Francis BEAUMONT on romantic tragicomedies, such as *Philaster*, *The Maid's Tragedy*, and *A King and No King*. He may have collaborated with Shakespeare on *Henry VIII* and *The Two Noble Kinsmen*. His own work includes *The Faithful Shepherdess* (1608).

flight *See* AERODYNAMICS; AEROFOIL; AERONAUTICS; AIRCRAFT

flight recorder (black box) Device for automatically recording data during the operation of an aircraft. Investigators analyse the data after a crash or malfunction. A small aircraft may have a simple cockpit voice recorder (CVR), which records all cockpit sounds and all radio contact with air traffic control. Larger aircraft carry a separate flight data recorder (FDR). Control settings, instrument readings and other data are recorded.

flint Granular variety of QUARTZ (SiO_2) of a fine crystalline structure. It is usually brown or dark grey, although the variety known as chert is a paler grey. It occurs in rounded nodules and is found in chalk or other sedimentary rocks containing calcium carbonate. Of great importance to early humans during the STONE AGE, flint flakes when struck a glancing blow, leaving sharp edges appropriate for tools and weapons; two flints struck together produce a spark which can be used to make fire.

Flood, The Primeval deluge, sent by God to devastate the Earth as a punishment for wickedness. As related in the Old Testament (Genesis 6–9), God sent rain upon the Earth for 40 days and nights, destroying everything he had created. Only NOAH, his family, and a pair of every living creature, contained in the floating Ark he had built, were spared to start creation afresh. Similar myths occur in many cultures. The Flood also appears in the Koran and it bears some resemblance to a section of the Mesopotamian Epic of GILGAMESH.

Flora In Roman mythology, personification and goddess of springtime. She was honoured as a fertility goddess.

Florence (Firenze) Capital of Tuscany and Firenze province, on the River Arno, Italy. Initially an Etruscan town, it was a Roman colony from the 1st century BC to 5th century AD. In the 12th century, it became an independent commune and major trading centre. The site of many factional power struggles, especially the 13th-century war between the GUELPH and GHIBELLINES, it nevertheless became the cultural and intellectual centre of Italy. Florence's period of dominance coincided with the rule of the Medici family. It became a city-state and a leading centre of the RENAISSANCE. Artists who contributed to the flourishing city included MICHELANGELO, LEONARDO DA VINCI, RAPHAEL, and DONATELLO. In 1569 Florence became the capital of the Grand Duchy of Tuscany. Opera developed here in the late 16th century. From 1865 to 1871, it was the capital of the kingdom of Italy. Its many notable churches include: the Duomo gothic cathedral (1296); San Lorenzo, Florence's first cathedral rebuilt in 1425 by BRUNELLESCHI, including a New Sacristy built by Michelangelo; and the monastery San Marco which holds masterpieces by FRA ANGELICO. Major art collections include the UFFIZI and the Bargello Palace. Industries: tourism, craft, fashion. Pop. (2000) 374,501.

Florence, school of Painters and sculptors who flourished in Florence during the RENAISSANCE. Major figures include GIOTTO, Fra ANGELICO, LEONARDO DA VINCI, MICHELANGELO, BOTTICELLI, and RAPHAEL. The finest achievements of the school were in the early 15th and early 16th centuries.

Florey, Sir Howard Walter (Baron Florey of Adelaide) (1898–1968) British pathologist, b. Australia. He shared, with Alexander FLEMING and Ernst CHAIN, the 1945 Nobel Prize in physiology or medicine for his part in the development of PENICILLIN. Florey isolated the antibacterial agent from the mould, making large-scale preparation of penicillin possible.

Florida State in the extreme SE USA, occupying a peninsula between the Atlantic Ocean and the Gulf of Mexico; the capital is TALLAHASSEE. Florida forms a long peninsula with thousands of lakes, many rivers and vast areas of swampland. At the S tip there is a chain of small islands, the Florida Keys, stretching W. The biggest attractions are the EVERGLADES, Florida Keys, and Disney World in ORLANDO. Discovered in 1513, the first permanent settlement in Florida was at St Augustine. Originally Spanish, the land passed to the English (1763), then returned to the Spanish (1783). America purchased Florida in 1819 and, although the state seceded from the Union in 1861, it was little affected by the Civil War. It developed rapidly after 1880. Florida's historic ties with Cuba are particularly evident in MIAMI, Florida's second-largest city (after JACKSONVILLE). Industries focus on the John F. Kennedy Space Center at CAPE CANAVERAL. Chief agricultural products are citrus fruits, sugar cane and vegetables. Area: 151,670sq km (58,560sq mi). Pop. (2000) 15,982,378.

flour Fine or coarse powder prepared by sifting and grinding GRAIN. Most flour is made from WHEAT and is used to bake BREAD. The main protein in wheat is GLUTEN. Self-raising flour contains a leavening agent, SODIUM BICARBONATE. Flour dough is often bleached and enriched with vitamins and minerals.

flower Reproductive structure of a FLOWERING PLANT. It has four sets of organs set in whorls on a short apex (receptacle). The leaf-like sepals protect the bud and form the calyx. The brightly coloured petals form the corolla. The stamens are stalks (filaments) tipped by anthers (pollen sacs). The carpels form the pistil, with an ovary, style and stigma. Flowers are bisexual if they contain stamens and carpels, and unisexual if only one of these is present. Reproduction occurs when POLLEN transfers from the anthers to the stigma. A pollen tube grows down into the ovary where FERTILIZATION occurs and a seed is produced. The ovary bearing the seed ripens into a FRUIT and the other parts of the flower wilt and fall.

flowering plant Any of *c.*250,000 species of plants that produce FLOWERS, FRUITS, and SEEDS. *See* ANGIOSPERM

flu Abbreviation of INFLUENZA

fluid Any substance that has no fixed state and is able to flow. Of the three common states of matter, GAS and LIQUID are considered fluid, while a SOLID is not.

fluid mechanics Study of the behaviour of liquids and gases. **Fluid statics** is the study of fluids at rest and includes the study of pressure, density and the principles of PASCAL and ARCHIMEDES. **Fluid dynamics** is the study of moving fluids and includes the study of streamline flow, BERNOULLI'S LAW (used to measure a fluid's velocity) and the propagation of waves. Engineers use fluid mechanics in the design of bridges, dams and ships. AERODYNAMICS, the study of the motion of gases, and **hydrodynamics**, the study of the motion of liquids, are branches of fluid mechanics.

fluke FLATWORM, an external or internal parasite of animals. Flukes have suckers for attachment to the host. Human infection can result from eating uncooked food containing encysted larvae, or from penetration of the skin by larvae in infected waters. The worms enter various body organs, such as the liver, lungs and intestines, causing oedema (swelling) and decreased function. Phylum Platyhelminthes, class Trematoda.

fluorescence Emission of radiation, usually light, from a substance when its atoms have acquired excess energy from a bombarding source of radiation, usually ultraviolet light or electrons. When the source of energy is removed, the fluorescence ceases. Mercury vapour is a fluorescent substance used in motorway lights; television tubes use fluorescent screens.

fluoride Any salt of hydrogen fluoride (HF); more particularly, fluoride compounds added to drinking water or toothpaste in order to build up resistance to tooth decay. Fluoride protection appears to result from the formation of a fluorophosphate complex in the outer tooth layers, making them resistant to penetration by acids made by mouth

FLORIDA
Statehood:
March 3, 1845
Nickname:
Sunshine State
State bird:
Mockingbird
State flower:
Orange blossom
State tree:
Sabal palm
State motto:
In God we trust

F

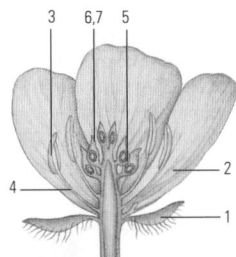

▲ **flower** A typical flower has four main parts: sepals, petals, stamens, and carpels. The sepals (1) form a protective covering (the calyx) over the developing flowerbud and lie outside the showy petals (2), which collectively are called the corolla. Each male stamen is made up of an anther (3), which contains the pollen grains, borne on a filament (4). The female carpels, which together form the pistil, are found at the centre of the flower, each containing ovaries (5) that bear ovules, and a style (6) that supports the stigma (7) – the structure on which pollen is deposited.

▲ **flute** Flutes, although called woodwind instruments, are metallic and covered in silver or gold plate. The illustration shows three members of the flute family; piccolo (1), flute (2), and bass flute (3).

▲ **flycatcher** Like all flycatchers, the paradise flycatcher (*Terpsiphone viridis*) shown here catches its prey of small insects on the wing. It sits on its perch waiting to dart out after insects, rather than trying to catch them in continual flight.

bacteria. Some public concern exists about water authorities using fluoridation, but research has shown that the ratio used, 1 part of fluoride to per million tap water, is harmless.

fluorine (symbol F) Gaseous toxic element of the halogen group (elements in group VII of the periodic table), isolated in 1886 by Henri Moissan. Chief sources are fluorspar and cryolite. The pale yellow element, obtained by ELECTROLYSIS, is the most electronegative element and the most reactive nonmetallic element. It is in FLUORIDE in drinking water and is used in making FLUOROCARBONS and in extracting URANIUM. Properties: at.no. 9; r.a.m. 19; m.p. $-219.6°C$ ($-363.3°F$); b.p. $-188.1°C$ ($-306.6°F$); single isotope F^{19}.

fluorite (fluorspar) Mineral, calcium fluoride (CaF_2). It has cubic system crystals with granular and fibrous masses. Brittle and glassy, it can be yellow, purple or green. It is used as a flux in steel production and in ceramics and chemical industries. Hardness 4; r.d. 3.1.

fluorocarbon Organic compound that is produced by replacing some hydrogen atoms of a hydrocarbon with FLUORINE. Their inertness, low toxicity, and ability to withstand high temperatures, make them ideal for use in plastics, such as PTFE (POLYTETRAFLUOROETHYLENE) or Teflon. Many of these chemicals also contain CHLORINE and are called CHLOROFLUOROCARBONS (CFCs).

flute WOODWIND musical instrument. Air is blown across a mouth-hole near one end of a horizontally held tube. It has a range of three octaves, with a mellow tone in the lower register and a brighter tone in the higher.

fly Any of a large order (Diptera) of two-winged insects. They range in size from midges, 1.6mm (0.06in) long, to robber flies more than 76mm (3in) in length. There are between 60,000 and 100,000 species worldwide. All flies undergo METAMORPHOSIS. A female lays between one and 250 eggs at a time. The larva (MAGGOT) typically lives on rotting flesh or plants. Adult flies have compound eyes and sucking mouthparts. Many are pests and spread disease, for example the HORSEFLY, MOSQUITO, and TSETSE FLY. The common housefly is *Musca domestica*.

flycatcher Any of several small birds of the order Passeriformes, found worldwide, that catch insects in midflight.

flying bomb Popular name for the V-1 missile used by Germany in World War 2. *see* V-WEAPONS.

flying fish Tropical marine fish. It is dark blue and silver, and uses its enlarged pectoral and pelvic fins to glide above the water surface for several metres. Length: to 45.7cm (18in). Family Exocoetidae; species *Cypselurus opisthopus*.

flying fox Fruit-eating bat with a fox-like head that lives in SE Asia. The largest of all bats, it does substantial damage to fruit crops. Length: to 40cm (16in); wingspan: to 1.5m (5ft). Genus *Pteropus*.

flying squirrel Small, gliding rodent that lives in forests of Eurasia and the USA. It glides by means of furry flaps of skin that stretch out flat and taut on both sides of the body when the limbs are extended. Genus *Pteromys*. The African flying squirrel is of a separate genus (*Anomalurus*).

Flynn, Errol (1909–59) US film actor, b. Tasmania. He made his name with *Captain Blood* (1935), and won worldwide fame playing swashbuckling heroes, as in *The Adventures of Robin Hood* (1938). He had a scandalous off-screen reputation, and published an autobiography, *My Wicked, Wicked Ways* (1959).

FM Abbreviation of FREQUENCY MODULATION

Fo, Dario (1926–) Italian playwright and director. Inspired by the traditions of the COMMEDIA DELL' ARTE and the 'alienation' techniques of Bertolt BRECHT, Fo's drama includes elements of farce and the carnivalesque. His best-known works are *Accidental Death of an Anarchist* (1970) and *Can't Pay? Won't Pay!* (1975). He received the Nobel Prize for literature in 1997.

focal length Distance from the midpoint of a curved mirror or the centre of a thin lens to the focal point of the system. For converging systems, it is given a positive value; for diverging systems, a negative value.

Foch, Ferdinand (1851–1929) French general. In WORLD WAR I, he helped repel the German advance at the MARNE (1914), but the disastrous offensives at YPRES (1915) and the SOMME (1916) led to his dismissal. In 1917, Foch returned as chief of the French general staff. In April 1918, he became

commander-in-chief of all Allied forces in France and led the counter-offensive that ended in German surrender.

fog (mist) Water vapour in the atmosphere that has condensed around particles of dust at or near the ground, as opposed to water vapour condensed as clouds. Fog forms when moist air is cooled below its DEW POINT.

Fokine, Michel (1880–1942) Russian choreographer. He revolutionized BALLET through his efforts at unity of music, drama, dance, and décor. From 1909, Fokine was chief choreographer for DIAGHILEV and his BALLETS RUSSES in Paris. In 1932, he became a naturalized American. His best-known works include *Les Sylphides* (1909), *Firebird* (1910), and *Petrushka* (1916).

fold In geology, a bend in a layer of rock. An upfold is an ANTICLINE; a downfold a SYNCLINE. The line around which the rock is folded is termed the fold axis. The fold system may be symmetrical, asymmetrical, overturned or recumbent (with the axis of the fold horizontal). A single folding is a monocline.

folic acid Yellow, crystalline derivative of glutamic acid, it forms part of the vitamin B complex. Found in liver and green vegetables, it is crucial for growth and is used in the treatment of ANAEMIA. Ensuring an adequate intake of folic acid during preganancy helps to avoid spina bifida.

folk art Term used to describe the art of folk cultures, especially those of rural and ethnic minority communities. It is usually practised by people who have not had formal training and who use local craft processes. The decoration of everyday objects features strongly in folk art, often with motifs handed down from generation to generation.

folklore Traditions, customs and beliefs of people. The most prevalent form of folklore is the **folk tale**. In contrast to LITERATURE, which is transmitted through written texts, the folk tale has an oral basis and is transmitted mainly through memory and tradition. Often the tales take the form of myths, fables and fairy tales. The best-known study of folklore is Sir James Frazer's anthropological study *The Golden Bough* (1890).

folk music Music deriving from, and expressive of, a particular national, ethnic, or regional culture. The musical structure is often the repetition of a tune to accompany verse (with or without chorus), sometimes with a freedom of rhythm that follows the natural metre of the words.

follicle-stimulating hormone (FSH) HORMONE produced by the anterior PITUITARY GLAND found in the brain of mammals. In females, it regulates ovulation by stimulating the Graafian follicles found in the OVARY to produce eggs (ova). In males, FSH promotes spermatogenesis. FSH is an ingredient in most fertility drugs.

Fonda, Henry (1905–82) US actor. Cast as a model of American decency and homespun wisdom, Fonda appeared in a series of John FORD films, such as *Young Mr Lincoln* (1939), *The Grapes of Wrath* (1940), and *Twelve Angry Men* (1957). He won his first and only Academy Award for his performance opposite his daughter, Jane FONDA, in *On Golden Pond* (1981). Other films include *The Lady Eve* (1941), *My Darling Clementine* (1946), and *Mister Roberts* (1955).

Fonda, Jane (1937–) US film actress, daughter of Henry FONDA. Following a lauded performance in *They Shoot Horses, Don't They?* (1969), Fonda won a Best Actress Academy Award for *Klute* (1971). A second award followed for *Coming Home* (1978). She starred opposite her father in *On Golden Pond* (1981). Her personal fitness programme, *Jane Fonda's Workout Book* (1981), was a worldwide bestseller.

Fontainebleau Town in the Forest of Fontainebleau, Seine-et-Marne department, N France. It is famed for its 16th-century royal palace, commissioned by Francis I. Built on the site of a previous royal residence, it is a world heritage site and a masterpiece of French Renaissance architecture. Napoleon's imperial headquarters, it was also the location for the signing of his first abdication (1814). It is now a museum and the presidential summer residence. The town was headquarters of the military branch of NATO from 1945 to 1965. Pop. (1999) 44,421.

Fontainebleau School Style of painting associated with a group of artists working at the French court in the 16th century. In a bid to match the magnificence of the Italian courts, Francis I gathered international artists to decorate his palace at Fontainebleau. Led by the Florentine artists Fiorentino

Rosso and Francesco Primaticcio, the group evolved a unique style of MANNERISM, blending sensuality and elegance.

Fonteyn, Dame Margot (1919–91) English ballerina. She was a member of the Royal Ballet (1934–59), and a guest artist with every major US and European ballet company. Fonteyn made her debut (1935) in Sir Frederick ASHTON's production of *The Fairy's Kiss*. She was acclaimed as one of the most exquisite classical dancers of the 20th century. Fonteyn continued to dazzle audiences late in her career, especially in partnership with Rudolf NUREYEV.

food Material ingested to maintain life and growth. Important substances in food include PROTEINS, FATS, CARBOHYDRATES, MINERALS and VITAMINS. *See also* FOOD CHAIN

food additive Substance introduced into food to enhance flavour, to act as a preservative, to effect a better external coloration or more appetizing appearance, or to restore or increase nutritional value. Other additives include thickeners, stabilizers and anti-caking agents. The use of food additives is strictly regulated by law and requires prominent labelling. The 330–plus food additives approved for use in the EU carry an **E number**.

Food and Agriculture Organization (FAO) Specialized agency of the UNITED NATIONS (UN), established in 1946. It aims to eliminate hunger and improve world nutrition. Its headquarters are in Rome, Italy.

Food and Drug Administration (FDA) US federal agency within the Department of Health and Human Services, established in 1979. Its purpose is to protect against impure and unsafe foods, drugs and cosmetics, and other potential hazards. The FDA divides into several bureaux.

food chain Transfer of energy through a series of organisms, each organism consuming the previous member of the chain. Its main sequence is from green plants (producers) to HERBIVORES (primary consumers) and then to CARNIVORES (secondary consumers). Decomposers, such as bacteria and fungi, act at each stage, breaking down waste and dead matter into forms that can be absorbed by plants, thus perpetuating the chain. *See also* DECOMPOSITION; PHOTOSYNTHESIS

food poisoning Acute illness caused by consumption of food that is itself poisonous or which has become poisoned or contaminated with bacteria. Frequently implicated are SALMONELLA bacteria, found in cattle, pigs, poultry, and eggs, and listeria, sometimes found in certain types of cheese. Symptoms include abdominal pain, DIARRHOEA, nausea, and vomiting. Treatment includes rest, fluids to prevent dehydration and, possibly, medication. *See also* BOTULISM; GASTROENTERITIS

food preservation Treatment of foodstuffs to prolong the time for which they can be kept before spoiling. Salting, pickling, and FERMENTATION preserve food chemically. Chemical preservatives, such as sodium benzoate, can also be added to foods. In canning, meats and vegetables are sterilized by heat after being sealed into airtight cans. Cold storage at 5°C (41°F) prolongs the life of foods temporarily, while deep-freezing at −5°C (23°F) or below greatly extends the acceptable storage period. In the technique of freeze-drying, frozen foods are placed in a vacuum chamber and the water in them is removed as vapour; the foods can be fully reconstituted at a later date. Since the early 1990s IRRADIATION, the preservation of food by subjecting it to low levels of radiation in order to kill micro-organisms, has been increasingly used.

food technology Application of scientific techniques to the generation, mass production, packaging and preservation of all types of food. Generating new and better forms of food often involves GENETIC ENGINEERING. The genetic material in edible plants is improved in order to achieve greater yield and resistance to disease. Improving genetic strains is also important in the mass production of all forms of meat farming. The scientific provision of an idealized environment can increase the size and quality of vegetables and animals. Animals can be further scientifically bioengineered through the careful introduction of hormones intended to cause effects beneficial to the eventual consumer. *See also* BIOTECHNOLOGY; FOOD PRESERVATION; GENETICALLY MODIFIED FOOD (GM)

foot In poetry, unit of verse metre. Each foot is composed of a group of two or more syllables, some of which are stressed. Most commonly used are anapest, dactyl, iamb, and trochee.

foot-and-mouth disease (FMD) (hoof-and-mouth disease) Highly infectious viral disease affecting most cloven-hoofed mammals, including cattle, sheep, pigs (not carriers), and goats. The disease does not affect humans. It is characterized by fever, followed by the eruption of blisters mainly in the mouth and around the hoofs. Lameness is the most noticeable sign. The average incubation period is 3–8 days. Foot-and-mouth is often fatal for young animals and reduces the yield from milk-producing animals. The virus is present in the discharge from blisters, and also occurs in the saliva, milk and dung of infected animals. Wind may also spread the virus over large distances. The mortality rate ranges from 5 to 50%. The traditional method of controlling the disease has been to quarantine areas of outbreak, and quickly slaughter and dispose of all infected or susceptible animals. An alternative or complementary method is vaccination, but this is costly and not effective against all seven strains of foot-and-mouth. An outbreak in the UK in 2001 led to the slaughter of more than 3 million animals. In the USA, the last major outbreak was in 1929.

football, American Contact sport played mainly in the USA. It is second in popularity only to baseball. It is played by two teams of 11 people on a field 100 × 53yd (91.5 × 49m). The field is marked off by latitudinal stripes every 5yd (4.6m), and is flanked on each end by an end zone, 10yd (9.1m) long. At each end of the end zone are H-shaped goal posts. An inflated leather, spheroid ball is used, with the object of moving the ball – by the ground or air – across the opponent's goal line. A game consists of two halves, each having two 15–minute quarters. Each half starts with a kick-off, and after the receiving team has run back the ball, it must advance 10yd (9m) in four attempts (downs) or turn the ball over to the opponents. The defending team must stop the ball carrier by pushing him out of bounds or by bringing him to the ground (tackling). The ball is usually turned over by punting (kicking) on the last down or attempting a field goal. If a player fumbles and loses possession of the ball during the series of downs, the opposition takes over the ball. Scoring can occur in four ways: a **touchdown** (crossing the opponent's goal line) scores six points; a **conversion** (kicking the ball through the uprights of the goal post after a touchdown) scores one; a **field goal** (kicking the ball through the uprights in normal play) scores three; and a **safety** (downing the ball carrier behind his own goal line) scores two points. Except for certain instances in professional football, games can end in a tie. Substitutions are freely allowed. Football has its roots in England and has similarities to rugby and soccer. Professional football began in the 19th century. The winners of the two US professional leagues, the American Football Conference (AFL) and the National Football Conference (NFL), play off each January for the Super Bowl.

football, association (soccer) Arguably the most popular worldwide sport. It involves two teams of 11 players who attempt to force a round ball into their opponents' goal. It is played on a rectangular pitch of maximum size 120 × 90m (390 × 300ft), minimum 90 × 45m (300 × 150ft). The goals, two uprights surmounted by a crossbar, are 7.32m × 2.44m (8ft × 24ft) wide. Only the goalkeeper may handle the

▲ **flying fox** The grey-headed flying fox (*Pteropus poliocephalus*) of Australia grows to 40cm (16in), and has a wingspan of more than 1m (3.3ft). They feed in groups on various wild and cultivated fruits.

◄ **Fonda** Her political activities included a campaign for the return of US troops from Vietnam. Among her many films, Jane Fonda starred in the cult classic *Barbarella* (1968), directed by her first husband Roger Vadim. In 1991, Fonda married for the third time. Her husband was Ted Turner, founder of Cable News Network (CNN). The couple separated in 2000.

F

ball, and then only in the penalty area of the goal he is defending. The other players may play the ball in any direction with any other part of the body, essentially it is kicked or headed. A game is played over two 45–minute periods and controlled by a referee. Modern football rules were formulated in 19th-century England, and the Football Association (FA) was founded in 1863. The FA Cup, established in 1872, is the world's oldest knockout football competition. The introduction of professionalism in 1885 led to the foundation (1888) of the Football League Championship. In 1904, *Fédération internationale de football association* (FIFA) was formed to control the sport at world level. Football has been played at the Olympic Games since 1908. The first of the four-yearly World Cup competitions was held in 1930. In Europe, the winners of each national league annually compete in the European Champions League (established 1955). Recent years have seen an increase in commercial sponsorship and television coverage. In 1992, the English FA changed the 'four-divisions' structure of the Football League, primarily to raise the commercial profile of leading clubs. This structure consists of the Premier League, the Championhip and the First and Second Divisions of the Football League.

football, Australian rules Type of football popular in Australia and Papua New Guinea. It is played over four 25–minute quarters between two teams of 18 players using an oval-shaped ball on an oval pitch 135–185m (440–600ft) long and 110–155m (345–504ft) wide. The ball may be kicked or punched, and although players can run with the ball, they must bounce it on the ground every 10m (33ft). The object of the game is to score points by kicking the ball between goalposts 6.4m (21ft) apart (six points). There are two other posts farther apart, one 6.4m (21ft) each side of the goalposts; a ball passing between one of these and a goal post scores a behind (1 point).

football, Canadian Game similar to American FOOTBALL. The main differences are that teams have 12 players, are allowed only three downs, and play on a larger field, 100 × 59m (330 × 195 ft). The Grey Cup is the principal trophy.

football, Gaelic Sport popular in Ireland and dating from the 16th century. Each side has 15 players who may kick, punch, or pass the ball, but not throw it. Players may not pick the ball up from the ground; it may be carried for four paces, and then has to be bounced, kicked or punched away. The pitch is 128m (420ft) and 146m (480ft) long and between 77m (252ft) and 91m (300ft) wide with goalposts at each end. One point is scored for putting the ball over the bar, and three for driving it under the bar. The game lasts 60 minutes (except in the All-Ireland semi-finals and final when it lasts 80 minutes) with two halves, and is controlled by a referee and four goal umpires.

foraminiferan Amoeboid protozoan animal that lives among plankton in the sea. They have multi-chambered chalky shells (tests), which may be spiral, straight or clustered, and vary in size from microscopic to 5cm (2in) across. Many remain as fossils and are useful in geological dating. When they die, their shells sink to the ocean-floor to form large deposits, the source of chalk and limestone. Order Foraminiferida.

force Push, pull, or turn. A force acting on an object may: (1) balance an equal but opposite force or a combination of forces so that it does not move, (2) change the state of motion of the object (in magnitude or direction), or (3) change the shape or state of the object. There are four FUNDAMENTAL FORCES: gravitation, electromagnetic force, weak nuclear force and strong nuclear force.

Ford, Ford Madox (1873–1939) English novelist, poet and critic, b. Ford Madox Hueffer. He provided influential support to such writers as Ezra POUND, while editing the *Transatlantic Review* in Paris, and Joseph CONRAD and D.H. LAWRENCE during his editorship of the *English Review*. He was also a prolific writer; his most remembered works are the novels *The Good Soldier* (1915) and the tetralogy *Parade's End* (1924–28).

Ford, Gerald Rudolph (1913–2006) 38th US President (1974–77). Elected to the House of Representatives in 1948, Ford gained a reputation as an honest and hard-working Republican. He was nominated by President NIXON to replace the disgraced Spiro AGNEW as vice president (1973).

When Nixon resigned, Ford became president – the only person to hold the office without winning an election. One of his first acts was to pardon Nixon. His attempts to counter economic recession with cuts in social welfare and taxes were hindered by a Democrat-dominated Congress. Renominated in 1976, he narrowly lost the election to Jimmy CARTER.

Ford, Henry (1863–1947) US industrialist. He developed a gas-engined car in 1892, and founded Ford Motors in 1903. In 1908 Ford designed the Model T. His introduction of an assembly line (1913) revolutionized industrial MASS PRODUCTION. In 1914, Ford raised the minimum wage to $5 a day and reduced the workday to eight hours. He refused, however, to allow union organization in his factories until 1941. In 1945, with the company losing *c.*$9 million per month, he handed control of the company to his grandson, **Henry Ford II** (1917–87).

Ford, John (1586–1639) English playwright who, with Cyril Tourneur, pioneered post-JACOBEAN drama. His major plays include *The Broken Heart* (*c.*1630), *Love's Sacrifice* (*c.*1630), *'Tis Pity She's a Whore* (*c.*1633) and *Perkin Warbeck* (1634). Incest and thwarted passion are common themes, and plays emphasize the difference between public and private morality.

Ford, John (1895–1973) US film director. Ford won four Academy Awards for best director: *The Informer* (1935), *The Grapes of Wrath* (1940), *How Green Was My Valley* (1941) and *The Quiet Man* (1952). A prolific film-maker, he made a significant contribution to the development of the WESTERN. His genre classics include *Stagecoach* (1939), *My Darling Clementine* (1946), *The Horse Soldiers* (1959), and *The Searchers* (1956).

Foreign Legion Professional military group, created in 1831 to serve in French colonies. In 1962, after fighting in two World Wars and later French colonial struggles, the Legion moved its headquarters from Algeria to S France.

forensic science (medical jurisprudence) Application of medical, scientific, or technological knowledge to the investigation of crimes. Forensic medicine involves examination of living victims and suspects, as well as the pathology of the dead. The cause of death, if there is doubt, is established at an autopsy. Forensic science developed in the early 1900s in England as a collaboration between police work and medicine. Modern developments include DNA fingerprinting.

Forester, C.S. (Cecil Scott) (1899–1966) British writer, b. Egypt. Forester is perhaps best remembered for a 12–novel saga about Horatio Hornblower, a naval officer during the Napoleonic Wars; the series began with *The Happy Return* (1937). His other works include *The Gun* (1933) and *The African Queen* (1935).

forget-me-not Any of *c.*50 species of hardy perennial and annual herbs of the genus *Myosotis*, found in temperate parts of Europe, Asia, Australasia and North America. The typical five-petalled flowers are sky blue but may change colour with age. Family Boraganacea (BORAGE).

forging Shaping of metal by hammering, or by applying pressure against a shaped die. Blacksmiths forge horseshoes and other iron items by hammering the red-hot metal on an anvil. In mass-manufacturing processes, pressure from an hydraulic forging press or blows from a forging hammer shape metal parts by forcing them against hard-metal die.

formaldehyde Alternative name for METHANAL

Forman, Milos (1932–) Czech film director. Forman made several films in Czechoslovakia, including *Fireman's Ball* (1967), before moving to the USA in 1968. *One Flew Over the Cuckoo's Nest* (1975) is one of only three films (*It Happened One Night* and *Silence of the Lambs*) to gain Academy Awards for best film, best director, best actor, and best actress. He also won a further Oscar as best director for *Amadeus* (1984).

Former Yugoslav Republic of Macedonia, The *See* MACEDONIA, THE FORMER YUGOSLAV REPUBLIC OF

formic acid Alternative name for METHANOIC ACID

Formosa *See* TAIWAN

Forster, E.M. (Edward Morgan) (1879–1970) English novelist. He wrote six novels before giving up fiction at the age of 45: *Where Angels Fear to Tread* (1905), *The Longest Journey* (1907), *A Room with a View* (1908), *Howards End* (1910), *A Passage to India* (1924) – widely seen as his masterpiece –

and the posthumously published homosexual love story, *Maurice* (1971). He made a significant contribution to the development of REALISM, and *Aspects of the Novel* (1927) is a collection of literary criticism. *Abinger Harvest* (1936) and *Two Cheers for Democracy* (1951) comprise various essays.

forsythia Genus of hardy deciduous shrubs of the OLIVE family Oleaceae, named after the British botanist William Forsyth. They are commonly cultivated in temperate regions. The masses of small yellow flowers look like golden bells and appear in early spring before the leaves. Height: to 3m (10ft).

Fort-de-France Capital of the French overseas department of Martinique, on Fort-de-France Bay. First settled in the 17th century, it remained undeveloped until the beginning of the 20th century, when a volcanic eruption destroyed St. Pierre, Martinique's commercial centre. It is now a popular tourist resort. Exports: sugar cane, rum, cacao. Pop. (1999) 94,152.

Fort Lauderdale City on the Atlantic coast of SE Florida, USA; seat of Broward county. It was established as a military post in 1838 by Major William Lauderdale during the wars with the SEMINOLE. There are more than 435km (270mi) of waterways. Port Everglades is one of the world's largest passenger ports. Today, Fort Lauderdale is a popular holiday resort. Industries: tourism, computing. Pop. (2000) 152,397.

Fort Sumter Fort in South Carolina, scene of the first hostilities of the American CIVIL WAR. In 1861 it was held by Federal forces. The Confederate authorities, having failed to negotiate a peaceful evacuation, felt compelled to take it by force. The Confederate General BEAUREGARD opened fire on April 12, and the fort surrendered the following day.

Fort Wayne City in NE Indiana, USA, at the confluence of the St Joseph and St Mary rivers. It was captured by the British during the French and Indian War (1755–63) and held by Native Americans (1763) during Pontiac's Rebellion. Development was spurred in the 1850s by the Wabash and Erie canals and the railroad. Industries: heavy vehicles, copper wire, stainless steel, mining machinery, pumps. Pop. (2000) 205,727.

Fort Worth City in N central Texas, USA, *c.*50km (30mi) W of Dallas. It was settled in 1843. The US army set up a post here in 1847. In the 1870s, Fort Worth was a supply centre on the cattle route from Texas to Kansas. It is famous for its oil and cattle. Industries: aerospace, electronics. Pop. (2000) 534,694.

fossil Remnant of an organism more than 10,000 years old. Fossils document evolution and enable geologic dating. The original structures, such as bones, shells, or wood, are often altered through mineralization or preserved as casts, Imprints, such as tracks and footprints are also found. Leaves are often preserved as a carbonized film outlining their form. Occasionally organisms (such as mammoths) are totally preserved in frozen soil, peat bogs and asphalt lakes, or trapped in hardened

FOSSIL

Animal fossils are not only made from their bones or shells, often their tracks can also be fossilized. Typically, a footprint (1) is left behind in soft mud, which partially hardens to form a cast. If the mud becomes flooded (2), sediment is laid over the mud especially quickly (3), helping to preserve the shape of the footprint. Over the course of time, the mud and sediment become compressed and turn to rock (4). The original mud-based rock forms a mould of the footprint (5) and the sediment-based rock forms a cast (6).

resin (such as insects in amber). Fossil excrement (coprolite) frequently contains undigested and recognizable hard parts.

fossil fuels Term to describe COAL, OIL, and NATURAL GAS – FUELS that were formed millions of years ago from the fossilized remains of plants or animals. Fossil fuels supply much of the energy used by industry and almost all used in road transport. They cause enormous POLLUTION (contributing particular to the GREENHOUSE EFFECT). Fossil fuels are non-RENEWABLE ENERGY, and supplies are limited.

Foster, Jodie (1962–) US film actress and director. Foster was a precocious talent. In 1976, aged 13, she received an Academy nomination for her role in *Taxi Driver*. She has won two best actress Oscars, for *The Accused* (1988) and *The Silence of the Lambs* (1991). She made her directorial debut with the personal *Little Man Tate* (1991). Other films include *Sommersby* (1993), *Nell* (1994), and *Panic Room* (2002).

Foster, Sir Norman (1935–) English architect. He formed Team 4, with his wife Wendy and Sue and Richard ROGERS. Foster is noted for his use of advanced engineering technology, and his huge glass and steel exoskeletons aim to exemplify modernist ideals of efficiency. Foster's works include the HSBC building, Hong Kong, (1986), Stansted Airport terminal, Essex (1991), and the German Reichstag, Berlin (1999).

Foster, Stephen Collins (1826–64) US songwriter. Influenced by the Negro spiritual, his popular songs include "Camptown Races" (1850), "My Old Kentucky Home" (1853), and "Jeanie with the Light Brown Hair" (1854).

Foster, William Zebulon (1881–1961) US labour leader and politican. He was affiliated with the Socialist Party, the Industrial Workers of the World (IWW) and the American Federation of Labor (AFL). He led a steel strike (1919), and was the Communist Party presidential candidate (1924, 1928 and 1932). He became national party chairman (1945–61).

Foucault, Jean Bernard Léon (1819–68) French physician and physicist who invented the GYROSCOPE. He used a PENDULUM ("Foucault's pendulum") to prove that the Earth spins on its axis and devised a method to measure the absolute speed of light (1850). With Armand Fizeau, he took the first

INTERNET

Fort Sumter
▶ www.civilwarhome.com/
ftsumter.htm

◀ **Foster** When only 13 years old, Foster starred in *Taxi Driver* and *Bugsy Malone* (1975). A deranged fan, John Hinckley, Jr, tried to assassinate Ronald Reagan in a bid to impress her.

F

▲ **fowl** Commercial hybrid poultry are bred for eggs and meat from pure breeding birds. The most productive egg-laying strains derive from leghorns (1) and Rhode Island reds (2), while the Dorking (3) and Cornwall (4) are popular British meat breeds.

▲ **foxglove** Native to Old World countries, particularly those of Europe, N Africa and Asia, foxgloves are hardy plants that bear purple and white, or less commonly, golden flowers.

clear photograph of the Sun. He also noted the occurrence of eddy currents, which became known as Foucault currents.

Foucault, Michel (1926–84) French philosopher and social historian. Foucault was professor of the history of systems of thought at the *Collège de France* (1970–84). He examined the social and historical contexts of ideas and institutions, such as school, prison, police force and asylum. For Foucault (like NIETZSCHE), social scientific knowledge and power are inextricably linked. His main theme was how Western systems of knowledge (such as psychiatry) have changed humans into subjects. His works include *Madness and Civilization* (1961), *Discipline and Punish* (1975), and *The Order of Things* (1966).

Fouquet, Jean (1420–80) French court painter. His work is monumental and sculptural, with figures modelled in broad planes. Notable works include a portrait of Charles VII (*c.*1447), Books of Hours (1450–60), and the *Pietá* at Nouans.

Four Freedoms Expression of war aims in World War 2 enunciated by US President Franklin D. ROOSEVELT in his State of the Union address (January 1941). They were: freedom of speech and worship, and freedom from want and fear. These aims were echoed in the ATLANTIC CHARTER (1941).

Fourier, Jean Baptiste Joseph (1768–1830) French mathematician and physicist, scientific adviser (1798–1801) to Napoleon in Egypt. Fourier's application of mathematics to the study of heat led him to discover a technique (**Fourier analysis**) of expressing complex periodic functions in terms of sums of SINE and COSINE waves. He also developed the **Fourier series** of sine and cosine functions, which can be used to represent many periodic phenomena.

four-stroke engine Engine in which the operation of each piston is in four stages, each stage corresponding to one movement of a piston along a cylinder. The stages are: induction, in which the fuel-air mixture enters the cylinder; compression; expansion, in which the exploding mixture forces the piston along the cylinder; and exhaust. This system is called the four-stroke cycle, or the Otto cycle, after its inventor, Nickolaus Otto (1832–91), and is used by many INTERNAL COMBUSTION ENGINES, including DIESEL ENGINES.

Fourteen Points Programme presented (January 1918) by US President Woodrow WILSON for a just peace settlement of World War 1. In general, the programme required greater liberalism in international affairs and supported the principle of national self-determination. It made useful propaganda for the Allies, and was the basis on which Germany sued for peace in 1918. Some points found expression in the Treaty of VERSAILLES, others were modified or rejected at the peace conference. The 14th Point laid the basis for the LEAGUE OF NATIONS.

Fourth of July US national holiday. It celebrates the signing of the DECLARATION OF INDEPENDENCE, July 4, 1776, and has been a national holiday since then.

fowl Term applied to domestic birds, such as chicken or turkey, and game such as pheasant and duck. *See also* POULTRY

Fowler, H.W. (Henry Watson) (1858–1933) English lexicographer and grammarian. With his brother F.G. Fowler (1870–1918), he compiled the first *Concise Oxford Dictionary* (1911). Fowler is best known for his *Dictionary of Modern English Usage* (1926), which continues to be published.

Fowler, William Alfred (1911–95) US physicist and astrophysicist best known for his explanation of how chemical elements are built up (from heavier to lighter) within stars as they evolve. He developed these ideas (published 1957) while working with three British astronomers: Fred HOYLE, and Geoffrey and Margaret Burbidge. In 1983, he shared the Nobel Prize in physics with Subrahmanyan CHANDRASEKHAR.

Fowles, John Robert (1926–2005) English novelist. His debut novel, *The Collector* (1963), about an obsessive who kidnaps a young woman, was made into a feature film. *The Magus* (1966) and *The French Lieutenant's Woman* (1969) were also filmed. Later novels include *A Maggot* (1985) and works on natural history, such as *A Short History of Lyme Regis* (1982).

fox Any of several carnivores of the DOG family. The red fox (*Vulpes vulpes*) is typical. Height: 38cm (15in); weight: *c.*9kg (20lb). Distinguished by its sharp features, large ears and long, bushy tail, foxes feed on insects, fruit, small birds

and mammals, and carrion. They are solitary animals, living in dens only for the mating season. Family Canidae.

Fox, Charles James (1749–1806) British statesman, the main parliamentary proponent of liberal reform in the late 18th century. Fox entered Parliament in 1768, and served as Lord of the Admiralty (1770–72) and Lord of the Treasury (1773–74). GEORGE III dismissed Fox for his opposition to government policy on North America. He became foreign secretary (1782) in Rockingham's government and formed a short-lived coalition government (1783) with Lord NORTH. Thereafter, he led Whig opposition to William PITT's government, urging the abolition of slavery and the extension of the franchise.

Fox, George (1624–91) English religious leader, founder of the QUAKERS. He embarked upon his evangelical calling in 1646 in response to an 'inner light'. Imprisoned eight times between 1649 and 1673, his missionary work included visits to Quaker colonies in Caribbean and America (1671–72). His *Journal* (1694) is a record of the early Quaker movement.

Foxe, John (1516–87) English Anglican clergyman and historian, whose writings promoted Protestantism and influenced policy towards Roman Catholics. He returned from exile in France during Elizabeth I's reign and wrote *Actes and Monuments of these latter and perillous Dayes*, better known as *Foxe's Book of Martyrs* (1563).

foxglove Hardy Eurasian biennial and perennial plants of the genus *Digitalis*. They have long, spiky clusters of drooping tubular flowers. The common biennial foxglove (*D. purpurea*), source of the heart stimulant DIGITALIS, is grown for its showy purple or white flowers. Family Scrophulariaceae.

foxhound Medium-sized dog (sporting group) used in foxhunting. The coat is short and smooth, the ears droop and the tail is carried erect. They are black, tan and white, and are noted for their speed and stamina. The American foxhound, recognized as a separate breed, is slighter than the English variety. Height: 53.3–63.5cm (21–25in) at the shoulder.

fractal Geometrical figure in which an identical motif is repeated on a reducing scale; the figure is 'self-similar'. Coined by Benoit MANDELBROT, fractal geometry is closely associated with CHAOS THEORY. Fractal objects in nature include shells, cauliflowers, mountains and clouds. Fractals are also produced mathematically in computer graphics.

fraction Quotient written in the form of one number divided by another. A fraction is a/b, where a is the **numerator** and b the **denominator**. If a and b are whole numbers, the quotient is a **simple** fraction. If a is smaller than b, it is a **proper** fraction; if b is smaller than a, it is an **improper** fraction. In an **algebraic** fraction the denominator, or the numerator and denominator, are algebraic expressions, e.g. $x/(x^2+2)$. In *composite* fractions, both the numerator and denominator are themselves fractions.

Fragonard, Jean-Honoré (1732–1806) French painter. He was a student of Jean Chardin and François BOUCHER. Fragonard is best known for the lighthearted spontaneity of his amorous scenes, rustic landscapes and decorative panels.

Frame, Janet (1924–2004) New Zealand short-story writer and novelist. Her works draw on first-hand experience of the treatment of mental health patients. Her autobiographical work, *An Angel at My Table* (1984), was filmed by Jane CAMPION.

France Republic in W Europe. *See country feature, page 332*

France, Anatole (1844–1924) (Jacques Anatole François Thibault) French writer. He achieved recognition with the novels *The Crime of Sylvester Bonnard* (1881) and *Thaïs* (1890). He supported Emile ZOLA during the DREYFUS AFFAIR, and his writing grew more political, such as the four-volume novel series *Contemporary History* (1897–1901) and *Penguin Island* (1908). He received the 1921 Nobel Prize in literature.

Francesca, Piero della *See* PIERO DELLA FRANCESCA

Franche-Comté Historic region of E France; its capital was Dôle until 1674 and Besançon thereafter. Founded in the 12th century as the 'free county' of the Burgundians, it was disputed throughout the Middle Ages between the Holy Roman Empire, France, Burgundy, Spain, and Switzerland. After Louis XIV's conquest of 1674, it was finally recognized as part of France in 1678. Area: 16,202sq km (6256sq mi). Pop. (1999) 1,117,059.

Francis I (1708–65) Holy Roman Emperor (1745–65), Duke of Lorraine (1729–35) and Tuscany (1737–65). In 1736, he married the Habsburg heiress MARIA THERESA. Her accession (1740) precipitated the War of the AUSTRIAN SUCCESSION against FREDERICK II. Francis succeeded Charles VIII as Emperor, but Maria Theresa effectively wielded power.

Francis I (1494–1547) King of France (1515–47). A leader of the Renaissance, he is best remembered for his patronage of the arts and his palace at FONTAINEBLEAU. Persecution of the WALDENSES, centralization of monarchical power and foolish financial policies earned the dissatisfaction of his people. A costly struggle with the Emperor CHARLES V over the imperial crown led to a defeat at Pavia in 1525. Francis was imprisoned and forced to give up Burgundy as a condition of the Treaty of Madrid (1526). Two more wars (1527–29, 1536–38) ended ingloriously. In 1542, Francis concluded a treaty with SULEIMAN I and attacked Italy for a fourth time. He lost further territory. His son succeeded him as HENRY II.

Francis II (1768–1835) Last Holy Roman Emperor (1792–1806), first emperor of Austria, as Francis I (1804–35), and King of Bohemia and of Hungary (1792–1835). The armies of NAPOLEON I repeatedly defeated Francis in the FRENCH REVOLUTIONARY WARS, and his territory steadily diminished, culminating in the abolition of the HOLY ROMAN EMPIRE. In 1810 Prince METTERNICH secured the marriage of Francis' daughter, Marie Louise, to Napoleon. Austria was preserved by this alliance, and in 1813 Francis joined the coalition that defeated Napoleon. He then formed the HOLY ALLIANCE.

Francis II (1544–60) King of France (1559–60), eldest son of HENRY II and CATHERINE DE' MEDICI. Married to MARY, QUEEN OF SCOTS at the age of 14, he was a sickly youth and the GUISE family controlled his kingdom.

Franciscans Friars belonging to an itinerant religious order founded by Saint FRANCIS OF ASSISI. The first order, known as the Friars Minor now comprises three subdivisions: the Observants; the CAPUCHIN; and the Conventual, who are allowed to own property corporately. The second order, Poor Clares, an order of nuns founded by Saint Francis and Saint Clare, came into being in 1212.

Francis of Assisi, Saint (1182–1226) Italian founder of the FRANCISCANS, b. Giovanni di Bernardone. The son of a wealthy merchant in Assisi, Francis renounced his worldly life for one of poverty and prayer in 1205. In 1209, he received permission from Pope INNOCENT III to begin a monastic order. The Franciscans were vowed to humility, poverty and devotion to the task of helping people. In 1212, with St CLARE, he established an order for women, popularly called the Poor Clares. In 1224, while Francis prayed on Monte della Verna, near Florence, the stigmata wounds of the Crucifixion appeared on his body. He was canonized in 1228. His feast day is October 4.

Francis Xavier, Saint (1506–52) Early JESUIT missionary, often called the Apostle to the Indies. He was an associate of St IGNATIUS OF LOYOLA, with whom he took the vow founding the Society of Jesus (JESUITS). From 1541 he travelled through India, Japan, and the East Indies, making many converts. He died while on a journey to China. His feast day is December 3.

francium (symbol Fr) Radioactive metallic element, discovered (1939) by French physicist Marguerite Perey (1909–75). It occurs naturally in uranium ores and is a decay product of actinium. Properties: at.no. 87; most stable isotope Fr^{223} (half life 22 minutes).

Franck, César Auguste (1822–90) French composer, b. Belgium. He is best remembered for the *Symphonic Variations* for piano and orchestra (1885), the popular *Symphony in D Minor* (1888) and significant chamber works.

Franck, James (1882–1964) US physicist, b. Germany. With Gustav Hertz, he experimented in electron bombardment of gases, providing support for the theory of atomic structure proposed by Niels BOHR and information for the quantum theory of Max PLANCK. Franck and Hertz shared the 1925 Nobel Prize in physics. He worked on the MANHATTAN PROJECT to develop the atomic bomb, and presented the 'Franck report' about the future of nuclear weaponry.

Franco, Francisco (1892–1975) Spanish general and dictator of Spain (1939–75). He joined the 1936 military uprising that led to the Spanish CIVIL WAR and assumed leadership of the fascist FALANGE. In 1939, with the aid of Nazi Germany and fascist Italy, he won the war and become Spain's dictator. He kept Spain neutral in World War 2, after which he presided over accelerating economic development, while maintaining rigid control over its politics. In 1947, he declared Spain a monarchy with himself as regent. In 1969, he designated JUAN CARLOS as heir to his throne.

Franco-Prussian War (1870–71) Conflict engineered by the Prussian Chancellor Otto von BISMARCK. The nominal cause was a dispute over the Spanish succession. Bismarck's aim was to use the prospect of French invasion to frighten the s German states into joining the North German Confederation dominated by Prussia. When the French declared war (July 14, 1870), the Prussian General von Moltke launched an offensive into Alsace. The French were defeated at Sedan, NAPOLEON III abdicated, and Paris was besieged. An armistice was agreed in January 1871, and Alsace and Lorraine were ceded to the new German empire, led by WILLIAM I. Paris refused to surrender its weapons, and the PARIS COMMUNE was formed.

Frank, Anne (1929–45) German Jew who became a symbol of suffering under the Nazis. Born in Frankfurt-am-Main, she fled with her family to the Netherlands in 1933. The Franks were living in Amsterdam at the time of the German invasion in 1940, and went into hiding from 1942 until they were betrayed in August 1944. Anne died in Bergen-Belsen concentration camp. The diary she kept during her years in hiding was published in 1947, and attracted worldwide readership.

Frankenthaler, Helen (1928–) US painter, sculptor, and graphic artist who provides the link between ABSTRACT EXPRESSIONISM and colour-field painting. Her early work shows the influence of Jackson POLLOCK. She evolved a modified drip technique, staining her unprimed canvases with thinned-down paint. Her seminal work is *Mountains and Sea* (1952). She was married (1958–71) to Robert MOTHERWELL.

Frankfort State capital of Kentucky, USA, on the Kentucky River, N central Kentucky. First settled in 1779, it was made the state capital in 1792. Notable buildings include Kentucky State College (1886), 'Liberty Hall' (1796) – reportedly designed by Thomas Jefferson, and the Old Capitol (1827–30). Industries: tobacco, whisky distilling, textiles, electronic parts, furniture. Pop. (2000) 27,741.

Frankfurt City and port, on the River Main, Hesse state, W Germany. One of the royal residences of Charlemagne, Holy Roman Emperors were elected here, and the first German National Assembly met at Frankfurt in 1848. Notable buildings include a Gothic cathedral, an art museum and a university. Frankfurt is Germany's banking centre and a venue for international fairs. Industries: chemicals, electrical equipment, telecommunications, publishing. Pop. (1999) 644,700.

Frankfurter, Felix (1882–1965) US jurist and educator. An assistant US attorney (1906–11) and law officer in the War Department (1911–14), he helped found (1920) the American Civil Liberties Union (ACLU). He was an adviser to President Franklin D. Roosevelt, who appointed him associate justice of the Supreme Court (1939–62).

frankincense (olibanum) Gum resin extracted from the bark of trees of the genus *Boswellia*, found in Africa and parts

▲ **foxhound** Foxhounds are medium-sized dogs that have been bred for their speed and stamina.

INTERNET

Fourteen Points
▶ usinfo.state.gov/usa/
infousa/facts/democrac/
51.htm

France
▶ www.premier-ministre.
gouv.fr/en

◄ **Franco** The Spanish dictator Francisco Franco ruled Spain for 36 years. Although he allied himself with Nazi Germany and fascist Italy, he kept Spain neutral during World War 2. Towards the end of his dictatorship, his regime adopted a more liberal stance.

The Republic of France is the largest country in Western Europe. The scenery is extremely varied. The Vosges Mountains overlook the Rhine Valley in the NE, the JURA MOUNTAINS and the ALPS form the borders with Switzerland and Italy in the SE, while the PYRENEES straddle France's border with Spain. The only large highland area entirely within France is the MASSIF CENTRAL between the RHÔNE-Saône Valley and the basin of Aquitaine. This dramatic area, covering one-sixth of the country, has peaks rising to more than 1,800m [5,900ft]. Volcanic activity dating back 10 to 30 million years ago appears in the form of steep-sided volcanic plugs.

Brittany (Bretagne) and Normandy (Normande) form a scenic hill region. Fertile lowlands cover most of N France, including the densely populated Paris Basin. Another major lowland area, the Aquitanian Basin, is in the SW, while the Rhône-Saône Valley and the Mediterranean lowlands are in the SE.

CLIMATE

The climate varies both from W to E and from N to S. The W comes under the moderating influence of the Atlantic Ocean, giving generally mild weather. To the E, summers are warmer and winters colder. The climate also becomes warmer as one travels from N to S. The Mediterranean Sea coast experiences hot, dry summers and mild, moist winters. The Alps, Jura and Pyrenees mountains have snowy winters. Winter sports centres are found in all three areas. Large glaciers occupy high valleys in the Alps.

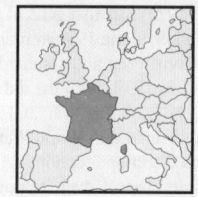

HISTORY

Julius Caesar completed the Roman conquest of France, then known as Gaul, in 51 BC. The Roman Empire began to decline in the 3rd century AD. In 486 the Franks, led by CLOVIS I, established a Christian kingdom and the MEROVINGIAN dynasty. Following his death, the kingdom fragmented. In 687, the CAROLINGIANS reunited Gaul and PEPIN III (THE SHORT) overthrew the Merovingians (757). His son, CHARLEMAGNE, succeeded in 768 and was crowned Emperor of the West (800). Through conquest, his empire extended from central Italy to Denmark, and from eastern Germany to the Atlantic Ocean. Following his death the empire was divided up, and in 843 his grandson CHARLES II (THE BALD) became ruler of the area of present-day France. Hugh Capet is often seen as the first king of France (987), and the CAPETIANS gradually subdued the nobility. The NORMAN CONQUEST (1066) marked the start of a long history of Anglo-French rivalry. PHILIP II regained land lost through dowry to the English. In 1328, the first Valois king, PHILIP VI, acceded to the throne.

The HUNDRED YEARS' WAR (1337–1453) was a series of battles for the French succession. By 1422, England controlled most of France. JOAN OF ARC helped to crush the siege of Orléans (1428) and by 1453 England had been expelled from France. In the course of the war the French kings lost much power to the nobility, but LOUIS XI (r. 1461–83) laid the foundations for absolute monarchy by restoring royal authority and crushing the ANGEVINS.

FRANCIS I's reign marked the beginning of the Renaissance in France and the struggle with the Habsburgs. The rise of the HUGUENOTS led to the Wars of RELIGION (1562–98). The Guise faction lost, and HENRY IV became the first Bourbon king (1589). Cardinals RICHELIEU and MAZARIN led France to victory in the THIRTY YEARS' WAR (1618–48). Louis XIV's court at VERSAILLES was the richest in Europe. Yet the *ancien régime* of LOUIS XV and LOUIS XVI was bankrupted by war and incapable of reform.

The FRENCH REVOLUTION (1789–99) saw the execution of the king and ROBESPIERRE's brutal REIGN OF TERROR and set up a government known as the Directory. In 1799 NAPOLEON I overthrew it and proclaimed himself Emperor (1799). The success of the NAPOLEONIC WARS was wiped out at WATERLOO (1815). Napoleon was forced into exile and the Bourbons restored to the throne. The FEBRUARY REVOLUTION (1848) established a Second Republic. Napoleon I's nephew seized power as NAPOLEON III (1852). His defeat in the FRANCO-PRUSSIAN WAR (1870–71) led to the formation of the Third Republic (1875–1940). The PARIS COMMUNE (1871) was violently suppressed.

France was the battleground for most of WORLD WAR I. CLEMENCEAU and BRIAND led France to peace, but Léon BLUM and Édouard DALADIER failed to halt the rise of Germany. In June 1940, German troops conquered France, and established the VICHY GOVERNMENT. Charles DE GAULLE became head of a government-in-exile. Paris was liberated in August 1944, and a Fourth Republic founded in 1946. Political instability and colonial war, especially in Algeria, slowed the post-war recovery. The problems in Algeria caused considerable unrest in France in the 1950s and, in 1958, de Gaulle was recalled to power as prime minister. His government prepared a new constitution and he became president. He resigned in 1969, replaced first by Georges POMPIDOU, then by Valéry GISCARD D'ESTAING. François MITTERRAND's presidency brought nationalization, civic rebuilding, decentralization, and advocacy of the EUROPEAN UNION (EU). After Mitterrand's death in 1995, his rival Jacques CHIRAC was elected president

POLITICS

A socialist government under Lionel Jospin was elected in 1997. He increased the minimum wage, shortened the working week, and adopted the euro. However, in 2002 centre-right parties won a resounding victory and Jean-Pierre Raffarin replaced Jospin as Prime Minister.

France has a long record of independence in foreign affairs, and in 2003 it angered the US and some of its allies in the EU by opposing the invasion of Iraq, arguing that the UN weapons inspectors should be given more time to search for weapons of mass destruction.

France is a major force in the politics of the European Union, and Raffarin's government strongly supported the proposal for an EU constitution. France's referendum on the adoption of the proposed constitution was held in May 2005, and the resounding 'no' vote led to the resignation of Raffarin and his replacement by Dominique de Villepin.

FRANCE

Disputes over Britain and France's respective benefits and subsidies from the EU fuelled further decline in the relationship between Jacques Chirac and Tony BLAIR.

Unemployment is a major problem, particularly among the young and among the large population of immigrants from northern Africa. Civil unrest in poor suburban districts is a recurring problem. Certain 2006 laws which attempted to force weaker employment contracts on the young were withdrawn after widespread rioting.

In 2007 elections Nicolas Sarkozy, of the centre-right UMP party, became president. He promised pro-market reforms and tax cuts to boost economic growth.

ECONOMY

France is one of the world's most developed countries. Its post-war economic growth was built on a high level of state control and national ownership of major industries, a policy known as *dirigiste*. Since the 1980s the country has mostly made the transition to a free-market system, but adjustments have been difficult. Unemployment is persistently high, and economic growth remains slow. The government still holds major stakes in sectors such as energy, defence, transport and communications.

In addition to large services and design sectors, France has managed to retain a large manufacturing base. Major manufactures include aircraft, cars, chemicals, electronic products, machinery, metal products, processed food, steel, and textiles. Some natural resources are exploited, including bauxite, coal, iron ore, natural gas, and potash.

Agriculture employs only about 2% of the population, but France is the largest producer of farm products in w Europe, producing most of its own food and extensive exports. Wheat,

AREA 551,500sq km
[212,934sq mi]
POPULATION 60,876,000
CAPITAL (POPULATION)
Paris (9,630,000)
GOVERNMENT
Multiparty republic
ETHNIC GROUPS
Celtic, Latin, Arab, Teutonic, Slavic
LANGUAGES French (official)
RELIGIONS Roman Catholic 85%, Islam 8%, others
CURRENCY Euro = 100 cents

livestock and dairy farming, and grapes for wine production are all of major importance. Fishing and forestry are significant industries. Tourism is also a major source of income, and France is a popular year-round destination both for its cities and its countryside.

---

of the Middle East. Used in religious ceremonies, and one of the gifts of the MAGI, it is burned as incense. The fine spicy oil extracted from the resin is used as a fixative in perfumes.

Franklin, Aretha (1942–) US gospel and soul singer. Known as the 'Queen of Soul', Aretha has had more million-selling singles than any other female artist. Her classic songs include "I Never Loved a Man (The Way I Love You)" (1967), "Respect" (1967), and "I Say a Little Prayer" (1967).

Franklin, Benjamin (1706–90) US statesman, scientist, and inventor. A successful printer in Philadelphia, where he published *Poor Richard's Almanac* (1732–57), he gave the business up to devote his life to scientific research. His experiments in electricity, which he identified in lightning, were influential. Franklin was deputy paymaster general (1753–74) of the colonies. At the ALBANY CONGRESS (1754), he proposed a union of the colonies. Franklin argued for moderate opposition to the STAMP ACT (1768). A leading delegate to the CONTINENTAL CONGRESS, he became an architect of the new republic. When war broke out, Franklin went to Paris and negotiated a treaty of alliance (1778). His peace proposals formed the basis of the final Treaty of Paris (1783) with Great Britain. Franklin was president of Pennsylvania's executive council (1785–88) and, as a member of the CONSTITUTIONAL CONVENTION (1787), helped form the US constitution.

Franklin, Sir John (1786–1847) English Arctic explorer. Franklin served as a naval officer in the Battle of Trafalgar (1805). His first overland exploration of N Canada (1819–22) crossed from Great Slave Lake to the Arctic coast. Franklin's second expedition (1825–27) descended the Mackenzie River. He served as governor of Tasmania (1836–43). In 1845, he embarked on a fated search for the NORTHWEST PASSAGE. The first of 40 search parties was launched in 1848. These expeditions greatly advanced knowledge of the Arctic and eventually established (1859) that Franklin died with his entire 129–man crew after they became caught in the ice in Victoria Strait.

Franks Germanic people who settled in the region of the River Rhine in the 3rd century. In the late 5th century, under CLOVIS I, they overthrew the remnants of Roman rule in Gaul and established the MEROVINGIAN Empire. This was divided into the kingdoms of Austrasia, Neustria and Burgundy, but was reunited by the CAROLINGIANS, notably by CHARLEMAGNE. The partition of his empire into the East and West Frankish kingdoms is the origin of Germany and France.

Franz Ferdinand (1863–1914) Archduke of Austria. Nephew of FRANZ JOSEPH, he became heir apparent in 1889. On June 28, 1914, on an official visit to Sarajevo, Bosnia-Herzegovina, Franz and his wife were assassinated by Serb nationalist Gavrilo Princip. The incident led directly to the outbreak of WORLD WAR I.

Franz Josef Land (Zemlya Frantsa Iosifa) Archipelago in the Arctic Ocean, forming part of Russia's Archangel'sk oblast. A group of c.187 islands, it includes Alexandra Land, George Land and Graham Bell Island. It was discovered in 1873 by an Austrian expedition, and was incorporated into the Soviet Union in 1926. Area: c.20,700sq km (8,000sq mi).

Franz Joseph (1830–1916) (Francis Joseph) Emperor of Austria (1848–1916) and King of Hungary (1867–1916). He succeeded his uncle Ferdinand, who abdicated during the REVOLUTIONS OF 1848, and quickly brought the revolutions under control, defeating the Hungarians under Louis KOSSUTH in 1849. With the formation (1867) of the AUSTRO-HUNGARIAN EMPIRE, Franz Joseph was forced to grant Hungary co-equal status. He died in the midst of World War 1, two years before the final collapse of the HABSBURG Empire.

Frasch process *See* SULPHUR

Fraser, (John) Malcolm (1930–) Australian statesman, prime minister (1975–83). In 1955, Fraser entered Parliament, becoming the youngest-ever Liberal MP. He served in the cabinet (1966–71) before becoming Liberal Party leader (1975) and forming a coalition government. Bob HAWKE defeated Fraser in 1983 elections, and he resigned from Parliament.

Fraunhofer, Joseph von (1787–1826) German physicist and optician, founder of astronomical spectroscopy. By studying the DIFFRACTION of light through narrow slits, he developed the earliest form of diffraction grating. He observed and began to map the dark lines in the Sun's spectrum (1814), now called **Fraunhofer lines**. Fraunhofer solved many of the scientific and technical problems of astronomical telescope-making.

Frazier, Joe (1944–) US heavyweight boxer. In 1968, Frazier won a version of the world's heavyweight title when he beat Buster Mathis and was undisputed champion after he defeated Jimmy Ellis (1970). He lost the title to George Foreman (1973). His bouts with Muhammad ALI, whom he defeated in 1971, were his most notable. After losing again to Foreman and twice to Ali, he retired in 1976.

Frederick I (Barbarossa) (1123–90) Holy Roman Emperor (1155–90), King of Germany (1152–90); successor to Conrad III. He was crowned emperor by ADRIAN IV. In 1156 Frederick restored Bavaria to HENRY THE LION. In 1158, he captured Milan and declared himself king of the Lombards. Frederick set up an antipope to ALEXANDER III, who excommunicated him and formed the LOMBARD LEAGUE. In 1176, Frederick was defeated at Legnano by the League and was forced to recognize Alexander as pope and make peace (1183). In 1180, he defeated Henry the Lion and partitioned Bavaria. Frederick died on the Third Crusade. His son succeeded as HENRY VI.

Frederick II (1194–1250) Holy Roman Emperor (1215–50), king of Germany (1212–20), Sicily (1198–1250) and Jerusalem (1229–50); son of Emperor HENRY VI. Frederick

INTERNET

Franklin, Benjamin
▶ www.whitehouse.gov/
history/presidents

Fraser, (John) Malcolm
▶ www.nma.gov.au/
primeministers/10.htm

F

devoted himself to Italy and Sicily. He promised to make his son, Henry, King of Sicily but gave him Germany (1220) instead. Frederick's claims on Lombardy and postponement of a crusade angered Pope Honorius III, who excommunicated him and revived the LOMBARD LEAGUE. Frederick finally embarked on a crusade in 1228, and was crowned King of Jerusalem. In Sicily, he set up a centralized royal administration. In Germany, he devolved authority to the princes; Henry rebelled against his father, and in 1235 Frederick imprisoned him and gave the throne to CONRAD IV. In 1245, Innocent IV deposed Frederick and civil war ensued in Germany and Italy.

Frederick II (the Great) (1712–86) King of Prussia (1740–86). Succeeding his father, FREDERICK WILLIAM I, he made PRUSSIA a major European power. In the War of the AUSTRIAN SUCCESSION (1740–48), Frederick gained the province of Silesia from Austria. During the SEVEN YEARS' WAR (1756–63), his brilliant generalship preserved the kingdom from a superior hostile alliance. In 1760, Austro-Russian forces reached Berlin, but Russia's subsequent withdrawal from the war enabled Frederick to emerge triumphant. He directed Prussia's remarkable recovery from the devastation of war. Gaining further territory in the first partition of Poland (1772), he renewed the contest against Austria in the War of the Bavarian Succession (1778–79). Artistic and intellectual, he built the palace of Sans Souci, and was a gifted musician.

Frederick III (1415–93) Holy Roman Emperor (1440–93). He attempted to win the thrones of Bohemia and Hungary after the death (1458) of his ward, Ladislas V. Instead he lost Austria, Carinthia, Carniola, and Styria to Matthias Corvinus of Hungary, recovering them only on Matthias' death (1490). By marrying his son Maximilian to Mary, heiress of Burgundy, in 1477, he acquired an enormous inheritance for the HABSBURGS.

Frederick III (1831–88) Emperor of Germany (1888). Son of William I, he married (1858) Victoria, eldest daughter of the British Queen VICTORIA. Liberal and popular, he died 90 days after his accession and was succeeded by his son, William II.

Frederick V (1596–1623) (Winter King) Elector Palatine (1610–20), King of Bohemia (1619–20). A Calvinist prince of the Wittelsbach family, he married the daughter of James I of England (1613). In 1619, he was chosen as King in preference to the Holy Roman Emperor FERDINAND II, provoking the outbreak of the THIRTY YEARS' WAR. Defeat at the Battle of the White Mountain (1620) resulted in the loss of Frederick's titles.

Fredericksburg City on the Rappahannock River, N Virginia, USA. Planned in 1727, the many historic landmarks make it a major tourist attraction. It is particularly associated with the American Revolution and Civil War. From 1760, the Rising Sun Tavern was a meeting place for American patriots. Many sites are connected to George WASHINGTON, including the site of the signing of a 1775 resolution of American Independence. The US Civil War battle of Fredericksburg (1862) was a victory for the 72,500–strong Confederate army of Northern Virginia, led by General Robert E. LEE, over the 114,000–strong Union Army of the Potomac, led by Major General Ambrose BURNSIDE. Nearly 13,000 Union troops were killed or wounded. In comparison, the Confederate troops of Stonewall JACKSON and James Longstreet lost about 5,300 men. Industries: tourism, clothing, shoes, cement, cinder blocks. Pop. (2000) 19,279.

Frederick William (1620–88) (Great Elector) Elector of Brandenburg (1640–88). He inherited a collection of small, disparate and impoverished territories ravaged by the THIRTY YEARS' WAR. By the end of his reign, Frederick's organizational powers had created a unified state with a sound, centralized tax system and a formidable standing army. The powers of the provincial estates (assemblies) were reduced, and he encouraged commerce and industry. Frederick acquired Eastern Pomerania at the Peace of WESTPHALIA and, by his interventions in the war between Poland and Sweden (1655–60), gained sovereignty over Prussia, formerly a Polish fief.

Frederick William I (1688–1740) King of Prussia (1713–40). Succeeding his father, Frederick I, he strengthened the army and economy and centralized the government, laying the basis for the rise of Prussia as a great power. He treated his

son, the future FREDERICK II (THE GREAT), with brutality, but bequeathed him a full treasury and the finest army in Europe.

Frederick William II (1744–97) King of Prussia (1786–97), nephew and successor of FREDERICK II (THE GREAT). He joined (1792) the alliance against France, but made peace in 1795 in order to consolidate his acquisitions in the E as a result of the Second (1793) and Third (1795) Partitions of Poland. He kept an extravagant court and left the country virtually bankrupt.

Frederick William III (1770–1840) King of Prussia (1797–1840), son and successor of FREDERICK WILLIAM II. He declared war on France (1806), suffered a disastrous defeat at Jena and was forced to sign the Treaty of Tilsit (1807). In Prussia, some progressive reforms were made, but a constitution, although promised, was never produced, and the king became increasingly reactionary. The reorganized Prussian army re-entered the NAPOLEONIC WARS in 1813 and played a major part in NAPOLEON I's eventual defeat.

Frederick William IV (1795–1861) King of Prussia (1840–61), son and successor of FREDERICK WILLIAM III. He granted a constitution in response to the REVOLUTIONS OF 1848, but later amended it to eliminate popular influence. He refused the crown of Germany (1849) because it was offered by the Frankfurt Parliament, a democratic assembly. From 1858, the future Emperor WILLIAM I ruled as regent.

Free Church Any of a number of Protestant churches that are independent of the established church of a country. In England, CONGREGATIONALISM, METHODISM, PRESBYTERIANISM and the BAPTIST movements formed a National Council of Evangelical Free Churches.

Free Church of Scotland Grouping of Scottish Presbyterians formed as a result of the secession of nearly one-third of the membership of the established CHURCH OF SCOTLAND in the Disruption of 1843. In 1900, all but a small minority of this Free Church joined the United Presbyterian Church to become the United Free Church of Scotland. In 1929, after the acceptance of the Church of Scotland's spiritual independence, the United Free Church of Scotland reunited with it. The tiny Presbyterian minority who had opposed the initial union retained their independence and kept the name United Free Church.

Freedmen's Bureau US government agency established in 1865, at the end of the CIVIL WAR, to aid newly freed African-Americans. Administered by the War Department, the agency provided relief work and educational services, as well as legal protection for African-Americans in the South. It was a powerful instrument of RECONSTRUCTION. The Bureau also acted as a political machine, recruiting voters for the Republican Party.

Freedom of Information Act (1967) US law giving greater public access to government records. It permits government agencies to exercise full discretion about disclosure of information only in such areas as national defence, confidential financial information and law enforcement. Other countries, including the United Kingdom (2000), have adopted similar laws.

Freedom Rides Civil rights trips to the South in 1961 sponsored by the CONGRESS OF RACIAL EQUALITY (CORE). They led to the desegregation of interstate terminals and subsequently to the Interstate Commerce Commission's ruling providing "non-racial" seating in buses.

Free French Group formed by Charles DE GAULLE on the creation of the VICHY GOVERNMENT in 1940. Its purpose was to continue French opposition to Germany. Operating outside France, the group was soon aligned with internal resistance groups. The Free French aided the Allies throughout the war forming a provisional government after the D-DAY invasion.

freemasonry Customs and teachings of the secret fraternal order of Free and Accepted Masons, an all-male secret society with national organizations all over the world. Freemasonry is most popular in the UK and some countries in the Commonwealth of Nations. It evolved from the medieval guilds of stonemasons and cathedral builders. The first Grand Lodge (meeting place) was founded in England in 1717. Historically associated with liberalism, freemasonry teaches morality, charity and law-abiding behaviour. Its ceremonies, which use many symbolic gestures and allegories, demand a belief in God as the architect of the universe. In recent times, they have incurred criticism because of their strict secrecy, male exclusivity and alleged use of influence within organizations, such as the police or local government, to benefit members. It is estimated that there are *c*.6 million masons worldwide.

free port Area in which goods may be landed and reshipped without customs intervention. Free ports aid quicker movement of ships and goods. When the goods are moved to the consumer, they then become subject to customs duties. Free ports include Copenhagen, Singapore, Stockholm, and New York City.

freesia Genus of perennial herbs of the IRIS family, native to South Africa. Species of freesia are widely cultivated for their fragrant yellow, white, or pink tubular flowers. They are grown in cool greenhouses for winter blooming.

Free State (formerly Orange Free State) Province in E central South Africa; the capital is BLOEMFONTEIN. The region consists principally of fertile high plains, with the Drakensberg Range as part of its E border with Lesotho. The River ORANGE forms its S border with Northern Cape. Boers began to settle in large numbers after the GREAT TREK (1836). In 1848, the British annexed the region as the Orange River Sovereignty and, in 1854, it achieved independence as Orange Free State. After its involvement in the SOUTH AFRICAN WARS (1899–1902), it was again annexed by Britain. Regaining independence in 1907, the Orange Free State joined the Union of South Africa in 1910. The economy is dominated by agriculture and gold. Pop. (2000 est.) 2,817,076.

freethinkers People whose opinions and ideas, especially on matters of religion, are not influenced by CANON law or dogma. The original freethinkers were part of a post-Reformation movement that sought to assert reason over religious authority. DEISM emerged as the chief expression of freethought during the 17th and 18th centuries. *See also* ATHEISM; HUMANISM

Freetown Capital and chief port of Sierra Leone, W Africa. First explored by the Portuguese in the 15th century and visited by Sir John Hawkins in 1562. Freetown was founded by the British in 1787 as a settlement for freed slaves from England, Nova Scotia and Jamaica. It was the capital of British West Africa (1808–74). West Africa's oldest university, Fourah Bay, was founded here in 1827. Freetown was made capital of independent Sierra Leone in 1961. Industries: platinum, gold, diamonds, oil refining, palm oil. Pop. (2005) 1,007,000.

free trade Commerce conducted between nations without restrictions on imports and exports. In modern history, its origins lie in the 19th-century attack (especially in Britain) on the traditional mercantile control of trade. The repeal of the CORN LAWS (1846) and the Anglo-French free trade treaty (1860) were the hallmarks of the mid-Victorian faith in free trade. Twentieth-century free trade agreements include the EUROPEAN FREE TRADE ASSOCIATION (EFTA) in 1959, and the 1994 NORTH AMERICAN FREE TRADE AGREEMENT (NAFTA). Protectionists oppose free trade, advocating import duties and restrictive quotas to safeguard domestic industry.

free verse Verse with no regular metre and no apparent form, relying primarily on cadence. The unsystematized rhythm is close to that of prose. Early users were Walt WHITMAN and Arthur RIMBAUD. It became common in the 20th century.

freezing *See* FOOD PRESERVATION

freezing point Temperature at which a substance changes state from LIQUID to SOLID. The freezing point for most substances increases with pressure. Melting point is the change from solid to liquid and is the same as freezing point. The freezing point for water at sea level is 0C (32F or 273.15K).

Frege, Gottlob (1848–1925) German philosopher, professor of mathematics at the University of Jena (1879–1918). With George BOOLE, Frege was one of the founders of modern symbolic LOGIC. In his *Foundations of Arithmetic* (1884), Frege attempted to derive all mathematics from logical axioms.

Frei (Montalva), Eduardo (1911–82) Chilean statesman, president (1964–70). In 1964, he defeated Salvador ALLENDE to become the first Christian Democrat leader of Chile. Frei's ambitious package of reforms, including the nationalization of Chile's copper industry and the redistribution of land and wealth, floundered amid economic recession. In 1970, Frei was defeated by Allende. His son, Eduardo **Frei Ruiz-Tagle**, also served as president (1993–2000).

Frémont, John Charles (1813–90) US explorer and general. Following his exploration and mapping of the Oregon Trail (1842), Frémont crossed the Sierra Nevada in the winter of 1843–44. A second expedition (1845) led to the Bear Flag Revolt by American settlers, and Frémont became civil governor. He resigned his commission in 1848, and made a fortune in the gold rush. He served briefly (1850–51) as one of California's first two senators and was the first REPUBLICAN PARTY presidential candidate losing to James BUCHANAN. He was removed from office during the Civil War, and became governor of Arizona (1878–83).

French Major language, spoken in France and parts of Belgium, Switzerland, Canada, Haiti, Africa and other areas. There are *c*.80–100 million French speakers worldwide. Descended from Latin, it is one of the Romance languages and part of the Indo-European family. It is one of the six official languages of the United Nations.

French and Indian Wars (1689–1763) Collective name for four colonial wars in North America, fought between Great Britain and France with Native American nations fighting on both sides. The aim of the wars in North America was for control of the E part of the continent, with ports and forts that controlled trade to the Old World. **King William's War** (1689–97) ended inconclusively. **Queen Anne's War** (1702–13) corresponds to the War of the SPANISH SUCCESSION in Europe. Britain gained Newfoundland, Acadia and Hudson Bay. **King George's War** (1744–48) grew out of the War of the AUSTRIAN SUCCESSION. It ended inconclusively. The **French and Indian War** (1754–63) was the most significant conflict, forming part of the SEVEN YEARS' WAR. British efforts (1754–55) to capture French forts in W America were unsuccessful. After 1756, British resources improved, and forts at Louisburg and Duquesne (1758) were captured. Ticonderoga fell in 1759. In the battle for Québec on the Plains of Abraham (1759), both the French and English generals, Louis Joseph de Montcalm and James WOLFE, were killed, but Britain emerged victorious. In 1760, the British captured Montréal. The Treaty of Paris (1763) established British control of Canada.

French architecture From the 8th to early 19th centuries, French architects depended on royal patronage, although the 10th-century Benedictine abbey at Cluny had an influence on church architecture. During the 11th and 12th centuries, CATHEDRALS in the ROMANESQUE style were constructed. In the 13th century, Gothic cathedrals, such as CHARTRES and NOTRE-DAME, were built. From 1494 the influence of Italian RENAISSANCE ARCHITECTURE grew, inspiring kings such as Francis I and Henry IV to commission magnificent palaces, including FONTAINEBLEAU and the LOUVRE. Royal influence climaxed in the 17th century with Louis XIV's palace at VERSAILLES In the mid-18th century, official architecture turned to NEO-CLASSICISM, introducing designs based on the Doric order. In the 19th century, patronage shifted from the court to the bourgeoisie. Baron George-Eugène Haussman designed the wide boulevards of Paris, and between 1850 and 1870, mansard roofs and pavilions marked a Renaissance revival. The skeletal frame of the EIFFEL TOWER (1889) heralded MODERNISM. ART NOUVEAU faded quickly. In the 1920s and 1930s, BAUHAUS had a large influence, and the Domino frame buildings of LE CORBUSIER spearheaded the INTERNATIONAL STYLE. French architects took an active role in the Congrès Internationaux d'Architecture Moderne (CIAM), which created a forum for serious discussions from 1928.

French art Studies of French art usually begin with the 12th century, when the kingdom was starting to take a recognizable shape. There were several important centres of manuscript illumination in Cistercian abbeys, but for many centuries FRENCH ARCHITECTURE was more prominent than the visual arts. During the RENAISSANCE, the art of the court was heavily influenced by Italian trends, as is evident from the output of Jean FOUQUET and the FONTAINEBLEAU SCHOOL. It was not until the 17th century that artists of international stature emerged. Dominant figures were CLAUDE LORRAIN and Nicolas POUSSIN, both masterful exponents of classical

F

▲ **freesia** Now cultivated commercially worldwide, freesias are native to South Africa. They grow to a height of 75cm (30in).

FRENCH GUIANA

French Guiana is a French overseas department and the smallest country in mainland South America. The coastal plain is swampy in places, but dry areas are cultivated, particularly near the capital Cayenne. The River Maroni forms the border with Suriname, and the River Oyapock its E border with Brazil. Inland lies a plateau, with the low Tumuchumac Mountains in the south. Most of the rivers run N towards the Atlantic Ocean.

Rainforest covers approximately 90% of the land and contains valuable hardwood species. Mangrove swamps line parts of the coast; other areas are covered by tropical savanna.

CLIMATE

French Guiana has a hot equatorial climate with high temperatures throughout the year. Rainfall is heavy, especially between December and June, but it is dry between August and October. NE trade winds blow across the country constantly.

HISTORY

The original inhabitants of the area were Native Americans, but today only a few remain in the interior. Europeans first explored the coast in 1500, and they were followed by adventurers seeking EL DORADO. The French were the first settlers (1604), and French merchants founded Cayenne in 1637. It became a French colony in the late 17th century, with a plantation economy dependent on African slaves. It remained French except for a brief period in the early 19th century. Slavery was abolished in 1848, and Asian labourers were introduced to work the land. From the time of the French Revolution, France used the colony as a penal settlement, and between 1852 and 1945 the country was notorious for the harsh treatment of prisoners. Alfred DREYFUS was imprisoned on Île du Diable.

POLITICS

In 1946, French Guiana became an overseas department of France, and in 1974 it also

AREA 90,000sq km
[34,749sq mi]
POPULATION 200,000
CAPITAL (POPULATION)
Cayenne (51,000)
GOVERNMENT
Overseas department of France
ETHNIC GROUPS Black or Mulatto 66%, East Indian/Chinese and Amerindian 12%, White 12%, others 10%
LANGUAGES French (official)
RELIGIONS Roman Catholic
CURRENCY Euro = 100 cents

became an administrative region. An independence movement developed in the 1980s, but most of the people want to retain links with France and continue to obtain financial aid to develop their territory.

ECONOMY

Although it has rich forest and mineral resources, such as bauxite (aluminium ore), French Guiana is a developing country with high unemployment. It depends greatly on France for money to run its services and the government is the country's biggest employer. Since 1975, Kourou has been the European Space Agency's rocket-launching site and has earned money for France by sending communications satellites into space.

The main industries are fishing, forestry, gold mining and agriculture. Crops include bananas, cassava, rice and sugar cane. French Guiana exports shrimps, timber, and rosewood essence.

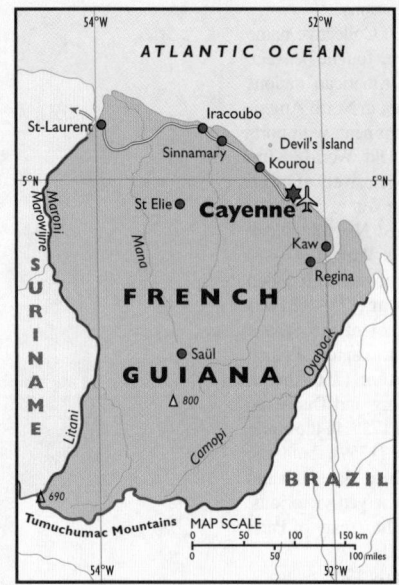

landscape painting. The latter was particularly important, and his rigorous draughtsmanship was used as a benchmark for academic standards until well into the 19th century. The twilight years of the *ancien régime* were celebrated in the lighthearted ROCOCO fantasies of François BOUCHER and Jean-Honoré FRAGONARD. As the revolution drew near, however, these gave way to the stern moralizing of neo-classical painters such as Jacques Louis DAVID. He remained influential into the Romantic period, when the leading French artist was Eugène DELACROIX. In the second half of the 19th century, there were a succession of movements which increased artistic freedom. These began with the REALISM of Gustave COURBET, and culminated in IMPRESSIONISM, POST-IMPRESSIONISM, and SYMBOLISM. This creativity continued into the 20th century,

▶ **French Revolution** Shortly before the Revolution, Paris' city limits were extended by the building of the "tax-farmers' wall" (1785), authorized by the finance minister Charles de Calonne to facilitate the collection of tolls from those entering the city. The wall, 3m (7ft) high, ran concentrically with the old city boundaries and took in several of the surrounding districts (*faubourgs*). Access was gained through 54 gates (*barrières*), which were largely destroyed by the crowds during the Revolution. The city's population in 1789 was approximately 600,000.

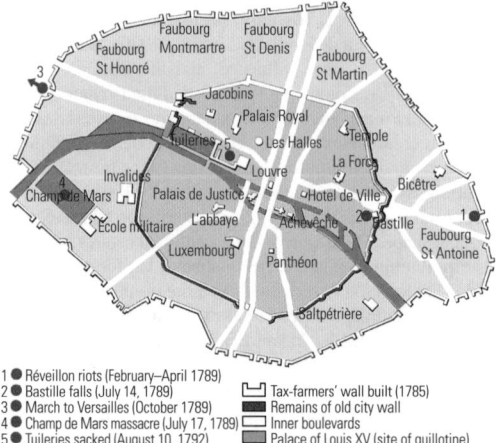

1 ● Réveillon riots (February–April 1789)
2 ● Bastille falls (July 14, 1789)
3 ● March to Versailles (October 1789)
4 ● Champ de Mars massacre (July 17, 1789)
5 ● Tuileries sacked (August 10, 1792)

⌐⌐ Tax-farmers' wall built (1785)
■ Remains of old city wall
☐ Inner boulevards
■ Palace of Louis XV (site of guillotine)

when the School of Paris fostered many new developments. France remained the leading force in avant-garde art until after World War 2, when its mantle passed to the USA.
French Guiana French overseas department in South America. *see* country feature.
French horn Brass musical instrument. It has a flared bell, long coiled conical tube, three or four valves, and a funnel-shaped mouthpiece. Its romantic, mellow tones were favoured by Richard WAGNER, Johannes BRAHMS and Richard STRAUSS.
French literature Although the earliest surviving works of French literature, written in the *langue d'oil*, date from the 10th century, major works date from the 12th century when the CHANSONS DE GESTE (Fr. 'songs of deeds') celebrated the military exploits of the nobility. Allegorical romances by Chrétien de TROYES and others gave way to more intimate poetry in the 15th century by writers such as François VILLON. The poems of the 16th century poet Pierre de RONSARD (leader of La PLÉIADE) rivalled that of Renaissance Italy, and in prose, the comic genius of RABELAIS contrasted with the pithy originality of the essayist Montaigne. The great dramatists CORNEILLE, RACINE, and MOLIÈRE, and the writings of philosophers DESCARTES and PASCAL ensured that the 17th century was a golden age of French literature. They were succeeded in the 18th century by the writers of the ENLIGHTENMENT, the rationalists ROUSSEAU, DIDEROT, and VOLTAIRE; and BEAUMARCHAIS, who wrote social farces. The romantic movement of the early 19th century produced novels and poems by the prolific Victor HUGO, Lamartine, and DUMAS (*père* and *fils*). Writers such as STENDHAL, BALZAC, FLAUBERT, MAUPASSANT, and ZOLA reacted against ROMANTICISM, producing works of NATURALISM and REALISM. Poets BAUDELAIRE and RIMBAUD paved the way for SYMBOLISM and modern

poetry, typified by the works of VERLAINE, and of VALÉRY and APOLLINAIRE in the 20th century. PROUST and GIDE dominated French fiction until 1940, backed up by MAURIAC and Duhamel, with SARTRE, BEAUVOIR, CAMUS, MALRAUX, and SAINT-EXUPÉRY producing the finest post-war work. The most original dramatists of the second-half of the 20th century were GENET, IONESCO, and BECKETT, with their abstract, poetic and unconventional works.

French Polynesia French overseas territory in the s central Pacific Ocean, consisting of more than 130 islands, divided into five scattered archipelagos: SOCIETY ISLANDS, MARQUESAS ISLANDS, Tuamotu Archipelago, Gambier Islands, and the Tubuai Islands; the capital is Papeete on TAHITI (Society Islands). The larger islands are volcanic with fertile soil and dense vegetation. The more numerous coral islands are low lying. The climate is tropical. Missionaries arrived in Tahiti at the end of the 18th century, and in the 1840s France began establishing protectorates. In 1880–82, France annexed the islands and they became part of its colony of Oceania. In 1958, they received the status of an overseas territory. In recent years, there have been demands for autonomy in Tahiti – the largest and most populous island. In the 1960s, the French government began nuclear testing on Mururoa atoll, leading to worldwide protests. In 1995, the French government put forward proposals to grant Polynesia the status of an autonomous overseas territory. Copra and vanilla are the leading agricultural products, and cultured pearls are exported. Tourism has grown considerably in recent years. Area: 4,000sq km (1,544sq mi). Pop. (2002) 262,000

French Revolution (1789–99) Series of events that removed the French monarchy, transformed government and society, and established the First Republic. Suggested causes include economic pressures, an antiquated social structure, weakness of the (theoretically absolute) royal government and the influence of the ENLIGHTENMENT. Beginning in June 1789, when the STATES-GENERAL met at VERSAILLES during a political crisis caused by attempts to tax the nobility, representatives of the bourgeoisie demanded reform and proclaimed themselves a National Assembly. Popular resistance, epitomized by the storming of the BASTILLE, forced the government to accede to demands which included the abolition of the aristocracy, reform of the clergy, and a DECLARATION OF THE RIGHTS OF MAN AND CITIZEN. The Legislative Assembly was installed (October 1791) and, faced with growing internal and external pressure, declared war on Austria (April 1792). It was soon in conflict with most other European states, the governments of which viewed events in France with fear. The war hastened political change: LOUIS XVI was deposed (August 1792) and the National Convention met to proclaim a republic (September 1792). After a period of rivalry between JACOBINS and GIRONDINS (November 1792–June 1793), strong central government, marked by fanaticism and violence, was imposed during the REIGN OF TERROR, and Louis was executed. Social anarchy and runaway inflation characterized the Thermidorean Reaction (July 1794–October 1795), which followed the fall of ROBESPIERRE. Another new constitution imposed a five-man executive called the 'Directory' (1795). It lasted until 1799, when the Consulate (1799–1804), dominated by NAPOLEON, put an end to the decade of revolution.

French Revolutionary Wars (1792–1802) Series of campaigns in which the popular armies of revolutionary France fought combinations of their European enemies. Fear and hatred of the FRENCH REVOLUTION fuelled the hostility of Austria in particular. The French declared war on Austria and Prussia in 1792, and their success at Valmy and Jemappes provoked other states, including Britain, the Netherlands and Spain, to form the First Coalition (1793). It was no more successful against France's conscript army and soon fell apart with Austria making peace at Campo-Formio. Britain remained at war, and NELSON won significant naval victories, but a Second Coalition was again unsuccessful on land in 1799–1800, NAPOLEON winning a notable victory at Marengo. Britain made peace at Amiens in 1802, but it marked only an interval before the NAPOLEONIC WARS.

frequency Rate of occurrence. In statistics, the number of times something occurs in a population in a given time, such as the births in a country per year. In physics, the number of oscillations occurring in a given time (measured in HERTZ), such as sound, light and radio waves, or a swinging PENDULUM, or vibrating springs. Frequency is the RECIPROCAL of period.

frequency modulation (FM) Form of RADIO transmission. It is the variation of the FREQUENCY of a transmitted radio carrier wave by the signal being broadcast. The technique makes radio reception fairly free from static interference and, although restricted in range to receivers in line-of-sight of the transmitter, has become the most favoured transmission method. *See also* AMPLITUDE MODULATION (AM)

fresco Method of painting on freshly spread plaster while it is still damp. In true fresco (*buon fresco*), paint combines chemically with moist plaster so that, when dry, the painted surface does not peel. Dry fresco (*fresco secco*) involves the application of paint in a water and glue medium to a dry plaster wall. It does not last as well as true fresco. The palace at Knossos, Crete (*c.*1700BC), was decorated with frescos. GIOTTO and MICHELANGELO are considered to be masters of the form.

Fresnel, Augustin Jean (1788–1827) French physicist and engineer. His pioneering work in OPTICS was instrumental in establishing the wave theory of light. He researched the conditions governing interference phenomena in POLARIZED LIGHT, studied double refraction and devised a way of producing circularly polarized light. The **Fresnel lens**, consisting of a series of stepped concentric lenses, focuses light more efficiently than a standard convex lens.

Freud, Lucian (1922–) British painter, b. Germany, grandson of Sigmund FREUD. He is regarded as one of the strongest contemporary British figure painters. His most characteristic subjects are portraits, such as *Francis Bacon* (1952), and nudes, often painted in strikingly realistic close-up.

Freud, Sigmund (1856–1939) Austrian physician and founder of PSYCHOANALYSIS. With Josef Breuer he developed new methods of treating mental disorders by free association and the interpretation of dreams. These methods derived from his theories of the ID, EGO and SUPEREGO, and emphasized the unconscious and subconscious as agents of human behaviour. He developed theories of neuroses involving childhood relationships to one's parents and stressed the importance of sexuality in behaviour. He believed that each personality had a tripartite structure: the id, the unconscious emotions, desires and fears which may surface in dreams or madness; the ego, the conscious rationalizing section of the mind; and the superego, which may be compared to the conscience. As he saw it, a very young baby is largely id, full of unchecked desires; the ego develops from the id, enabling the child to negotiate realistically with the world; and the superego evolves as the child internalizes the moral values of society. The ego comes to mediate the selfish needs of the id and the idealistic demands of the superego. The adoption of a satisfactory superego is dependent on the resolution of the OEDIPUS COMPLEX. His works include *The Interpretation of Dreams* (1900), *The Psychopathology of Everyday Life* (1904), and *The Ego and the Id* (1923).

friar Member of certain religious orders. The four main orders – the DOMINICANS, FRANCISCANS, CARMELITES, and AUGUSTINIANS – were founded in the 13th century. Friars differ from cloistered monks in that they are involved in widespread outside activity and are more centrally organized.

friction Resistance encountered when surfaces in contact slide or roll against each other, or when a fluid flows along a surface. Friction is directly proportional to the force pressing the surfaces together and the surface roughness. When the movement begins, it is opposed by a static friction up to a maximum 'limiting friction' and then slipping occurs. **Rolling friction** is friction between a wheel and the surface on which it is moving.

Friedan, Betty (1921–2006) US feminist writer. Through her best-selling book, *The Feminine Mystique* (1963), she prompted women to examine their roles in society. She was a founder and first president (1966–70) of the National

▲ **Freud** The Austrian doctor Sigmund Freud is considered the founder of psychoanalysis. His methods of dream interpretation and employment of free association were considered highly revolutionary.

F

INTERNET

French Polynesia
▶ www.pacificislandtravel.
  com/fr_polynesia/
  introduction.html

French Revolution
▶ chnm.gmu.edu/revolution

FROG

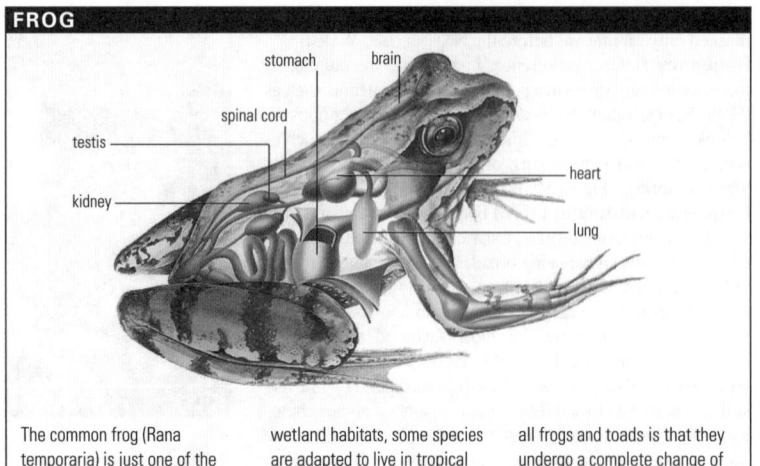

The common frog (Rana temporaria) is just one of the 2500 or so species of frog or toad. Although most live in wetland habitats, some species are adapted to live in tropical forests, grassland and even deserts. A common feature of all frogs and toads is that they undergo a complete change of form (metamorphosis) during their life cycle.

some terrestrial living in trees or underground. Most have teeth in the upper jaw and all have long sticky tongues attached at the front of the mouth to capture live food, usually insects. Length: 2.5–30cm (1–12in). Subclass Salientia (or Anura), divided into 17 families; the most typical genus is *Rana*. See also TOAD

Froissart, Jean (1335–1401) French poet and chronicler. He travelled widely in Europe, visiting several famous courts. He is best known for his *Chronicles*, a lively if not always reliable account of events in Europe (1325–1400).

Fromm, Erich (1900–80) US psychoanalyst and writer, b. Germany. Fromm applied PSYCHOANALYSIS to the study of peoples and cultures, stressing the importance of interpersonal relationships in an impersonal, industrialized society. His books include *Escape from Freedom* (1941) and *The Art of Loving* (1956).

Fronde (1648–53) Series of rebellions against oppressive government in France. The Fronde of the Parlement (1648–49) began when ANNE OF AUSTRIA tried to reduce the salaries of court officials. It gained some concessions from the regent, LOUIS XIV. The Fronde of the Princes (1650–53) was a rebellion of the aristocratic followers of the Great CONDÉ, and forced the unpopular Cardinal MAZARIN into temporary exile. Condé briefly held Paris, but the rebellion soon collapsed, and promised reforms were withdrawn. The Fronde succeeded in moderating the financial excesses of royal government, but under Louis XIV royal absolutism triumphed.

front In meteorology, the boundary between two air masses of different temperatures or different densities. **Cold** fronts occur when a relatively cold and dense air mass moves under warmer air. With a **warm** front, warmer air is pushing over colder air and replacing it. An **occluded** front consists of two fronts: a cold front overtakes a warm or stationary front. In a **stationary** front, air masses remain in the same areas and the weather is mostly unchanged.

frontier In US history, the westernmost region of white settlement. In the 17th century, the frontier began at the foothills of the APPALACHIAN mountains and gradually moved westwards until the late 19th century, when no new land remained for pioneer homesteaders. In the USA, Frederick Jackson Turner promoted the frontier notions of rugged individualism and free enterprise as central to US society in *The Significance of the Frontier in American History* (1893). The existence of a frontier region, where a dominant group was able to expand (usually at the expense of native inhabitants), has been an important factor in the history of other countries, such as South Africa.

frost In meteorology, atmospheric temperatures below 0°C (32°F) at the Earth's surface. The visible result of a frost is usually a deposit of minute ice crystals formed on exposed surfaces from dew and water vapour. In freezing weather, the 'degree of frost' indicates the number of degrees below freezing point. When white **hoar-frost** is formed, water vapour passes directly from its gaseous state to a solid, without becoming a liquid.

Frost, Robert Lee (1874–1963) US poet. His work was shaped by the landscape of his native New England and by the fusion of colloquial idioms and traditional rhythms. His first two volumes of lyric poems, *A Boy's Will* (1913) and *North of Boston* (1914), established his reputation. His best-known poems include: "Stopping by Woods on a Snowy Evening", "The Road Not Taken", and "Mending Wall". He received the Pulitzer Prize for poetry (1924, 1931, 1937, 1943).

frostbite Freezing of living body-tissue in sub-zero temperatures. Frostbite is an effect of the body's defensive response to intense cold, which is to shut down blood vessels at the extremities in order to preserve warmth at the core of the body. Consequently, it mostly occurs in the face, ears, hands, and feet. In superficial frostbite, the affected part turns white and cold; it can be treated by gentle thawing. In deep frostbite, ice crystals form in the tissues. The flesh hardens and sensation is lost. It requires urgent medical treatment. No attempt should be made at rewarming if there is a risk of refreezing, as this results in the death of body tissue (gangrene).

fructose (fruit sugar, $C_6H_{12}O_6$) Simple white monosaccharide, found in honey, sweet fruits, and flower nectar. Sweeter than SUCROSE, it is made commercially by the HYDROLYSIS of beet

A

B

C

D

▲ **front** Fronts form in temperate latitudes where a cold air mass meets a warm air mass (A). The air masses spiral round a bulge causing cold and warm fronts to develop (B). The warm air rises above the cold front and the cold air slides underneath the warm (C). Eventually, the cold air areas merge, and the warm air is lifted up or occluded (D).

Organization for Women (NOW). *The Second Stage* (1981) called for new directions in the women's movement.

Friedman, Milton (1912–2006) US economist. An influential member of the Chicago School of Economics, he supported MONETARISM as the best means of controlling the economy. His works include: *A Monetary History of the United States 1867–1960* (1963), written with Anna Schwartz and a key book in monetary economics; *A Theory of the Consumption Function* (1957); *Essays in Positive Economics* (1953); and *Capitalism and Freedom* (1962). He received the 1976 Nobel Prize in economic science.

Friedrich, Caspar David (1774–1840) German painter. One of the greatest German Romantic painters, he created eerie, symbolic landscapes, such as *Shipwreck on the Ice* (1822) and *Man and Woman Gazing at the Moon* (1824).

friendly societies Associations established in Britain to provide insurance against sickness, old age and funeral expenses. Started in the 17th century, they became a conventional alternative to parish relief and charitable assistance. They spread quickly, and in the Victorian age were the most important form of insurance for the working-class. In the USA, benefit societies filled a similar role.

Friends, The Religious Society of See QUAKERS

Frisch, Karl von (1886–1982) Austrian zoologist. He shared the 1973 Nobel Prize in physiology or medicine with K. LORENZ and N. TINBERGEN for his pioneering work in ETHOLOGY. He deciphered the 'language' of bees by studying their dance patterns in which one bee tells others in the hive the direction and distance of a food source. In his earlier work, he showed that fish and bees see colours, fish can hear and that bees can distinguish various flower scents.

Frisch, Max (1911–91) Swiss novelist and dramatist. His early plays, greatly influenced by BRECHT, are experimental in form and often satirical. They include: *The Chinese Wall* (1946), and *Andorra* (1961). His later plays, including *Biography* (1968) and *Triptych* (1979), and the novels *Stiller* (1954) and *A Wilderness of Mirrors* (1964), deal with man's quest for identity.

fritillary Common name for several genera of butterflies including large fritillaries (silverspots) of the genus *Speyeria* and small fritillaries of the genus *Boloria*. The larvae (caterpillars) are largely nocturnal. Family Nymphalidae.

Froebel, Friedrich Wilhelm August (1782–1852) German educator and influential educational theorist. His main interest was in pre-school age children and, in 1841, he opened the first kindergarten. He stressed the importance of pleasant surroundings, self-directed activity, physical training, and play in the development of the child.

frog Tailless AMPHIBIAN, found worldwide. Frogs have long hind limbs, webbed feet, and external eardrums behind the eyes. Most begin life as TADPOLES after hatching from gelatinous eggs, usually laid in water. Some frogs remain aquatic,

or cane sugar, and is used in foods as a sweetener. Its derivatives play a crucial role in providing energy for organisms.

fruit Seed-containing mature OVARY of a flowering plant. Fruits serve to disperse plants and are an important food source (they provide vitamins, acids, salts, calcium, iron, and phosphates). They can be classified as simple, aggregate or multiple. Simple fruits, dry or fleshy, are produced by one ripened ovary of a single pistil (unit comprising a stigma, style, and ovary) and include legumes (peas and beans) and nuts. **Aggregate** fruits develop from several simple pistils; examples are raspberry and blackberry. **Multiple** fruits develop from a flower cluster; each flower produces a fruit which merges into a single mass at maturity; examples are pineapples and figs. Although considered fruits in culinary terms, apples and pears are regarded botanically as 'false' fruits, as the edible parts are created by the RECEPTACLE and not the carpel walls.

Frunze Former name for BISHKEK

Fry, Christopher (1907–2005) English dramatist, real name Christopher Harris. His witty blank-verse plays are often set in ancient or medieval times. They include *A Phoenix Too Frequent* (1946), *The Lady's Not for Burning* (1948), and *Venus Observed* (1950).

Fry, Elizabeth (1780–1845) English social worker and prison reformer. A committed Quaker, she agitated for more humane treatment of women prisoners and convicts transported to Australia. She was also involved in attempts to improve working conditions for nurses and facilities for women's education.

Fuad I (1868–1936) Sultan (1917–22), first King (1922–36) of modern Egypt, son of ISMAIL PASHA. During Fuad's reign, Egypt remained under strong British influence and conflict with the nationalist Wafd Party led him to suspend (1928–35) the constitution. His grandson reigned briefly (1952–53) as Fuad II, before FAROUK assumed the throne.

Fuchs, Klaus (1912–88) German physicist. Klaus worked on the atom bomb in the USA (1943) and moved to Britain (1946) to head the theoretical physics division of the Atomic Research Centre at Harwell. He was imprisoned (1950) for passing secrets to the Soviet Union. After release (1959), he went to Germany to work at a nuclear research centre.

fuchsia Genus of shrubby plants found wild in tropical and subtropical America and parts of New Zealand. They are widely cultivated. Named after the German herbalist Leonard Fuchs (1501–66), they have oval leaves and pink, red or purple trumpet-shaped, waxy flowers. The 100 or so species include the crimson-purple *Fuchsia procumbens* and *F. speciosa*. Family Onagraceae.

fuel Substance that is burned or otherwise modified to produce energy, usually in the form of heat. Apart from fossil hydrocarbons (coal, oil and gas) and firewood and charcoal, the term also applies to radioactive materials used in nuclear power stations. *See also* FOSSIL FUELS

Fuentes, Carlos (1928–) Mexican novelist and short story writer. His first two novels, *Where the Air is Clean* (1958), and *The Death of Artemio Cruz* (1962), share a critical view of Mexican society and helped to establish his international reputation. Other fiction includes *The Hydra Head* (1978) and *Distant Relations* (1980), the novels *The Campaign* (1991) and *Diana, The Goddess Who Hunts Alone* (1995), and the essay-collection *Geography of the Novel* (1993).

Fugard, Athol (1932–) South African playwright, director and actor. Fugard achieved international acclaim for his plays *The Blood Knot* (1961), *Sizwe Bandi is Dead* (1972), and *My Children! My Africa* (1990). His work often explores the effects of apartheid on South Africa's black population and the country's rapidly changing modern politics. He published an autobiography, *Cousins: A Memoir*, in 1997.

fugue In music, a composition of several parts or voices where the same melodic line or theme is stated and developed in each voice so that interest in its overall development becomes cumulative. Generally the theme begins in one part and others are added in sequence. Popular in the BAROQUE period, fugue writing reached its peak in the music of J.S. BACH and has been revived by composers of the 20th century.

Fujiyama (Mount Fuji) Highest mountain in Japan, in the Fuji-Hakone National Park. An extinct volcano, it is seen as the most sacred mountain in Japan. It is a summer and winter sports area. Height: 3776m (12,389ft).

Fukuoka City on the SE shore of Hakata Bay, N Kyushu, S Japan. In medieval times, Hakata was one of Japan's major ports. There is a rich agricultural region to the N. Industries: textiles, machinery, chemicals, fishing. Pop. (2000) 1,341,000.

Fulani (Fulah or Fulbe) West African people, numbering *c.*6 million. Their language belongs to the NIGER-CONGO group. Originally a pastoral people, they helped the spread of Islam throughout W Africa from the 16th century, establishing an empire lasting until British colonialism in the 19th century.

Fuller, Richard Buckminster (1895–1983) US architect and engineer. Believing that only technology can solve modern world problems, he invented several revolutionary designs. The most widely used is the GEODESIC DOME. His books include *Operating Manual for Spaceship Earth* (1969) and *Earth Inc.* (1973).

Fuller, Roy Broadbent (1912–91) English poet and novelist. The progress of Fuller's verse from Audenesque works to a more individual voice can be traced in *Collected Poems 1936–61* (1962) and *New and Collected Poems* (1985). Novels include *Image of a Society* (1956), *My Child, My Sister* (1965) and *Stares* (1990). He also wrote an autobiography, *Spanner and Pen* (1991).

fuller's earth Clay-like substance containing over 50% SILICA. Once used for fulling (removing oil and grease from wool), it is now used to bleach petroleum and refine vegetable oils.

Fulton, Robert (1765–1815) US inventor and engineer. Designing torpedoes and other naval weapons, his main interest was in navigation and, as early as 1796, he was urging the USA to build canals. In 1807, he pioneered the use of steamboats for carrying passengers and freight, when his craft, *Clermont*, travelled between New York City and Albany.

Funchal Capital and chief port of Madeira. Founded in 1421, it was ruled by Spain from 1580 to 1640 and was briefly under British administration in the early 19th century. It is now an industrial and resort centre for the Madeira archipelago. Industries: sugar-milling, distilling, wine. Pop. (2001) 102,500.

function In mathematics, rule that assigns a unique value to each element of a given SET. The given set is the **domain** of the function, and the set of values is the **range**. Two or more elements of the DOMAIN may be assigned the same value, but a function must assign only one value to each element of the domain. A function f maps each element x of the domain to a corresponding element (or value) y in the range. Here x and y are variables, with y dependent on x through the functional relationship f. The dependent variable y is said to be a function of the independent variable x. For example, the square-root is a function, its domain and range being the non-negative real numbers. *See also* TRIGONOMETRIC FUNCTION

functionalism In art and architecture, an early 20th-century style based on UTILITARIANISM. Functionalism rejected ornamentation and stressed the basic structure of the work and of the materials used. Major proponents of functionalism included GROPIUS, BAUHAUS, and LE CORBUSIER.

functionalism Sociological and anthropological theory outlined by Emile DURKHEIM. The theory attempts to understand the function of each part of society (customs, institutions, objects, roles, religion) in relation to each other and to the whole society. It attempts to explain how each separate cultural phenomenon corresponds to the "needs" of the whole society.

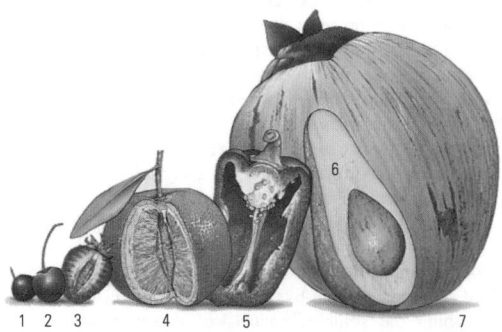

◀ **fruit** A fruit is the ripened ovary of a flowering plant, enclosed by the fruit wall, which is known as the pericarp. Most fruits, such as blackcurrants (1), cherries (2), strawberries (3), oranges (4), and peppers (5), contain more than one seed. The avocado (6), however, contains only one seed, about the size of a golf ball. The largest fruit, the double coconut (7), is also single-seeded.

F

FUSION

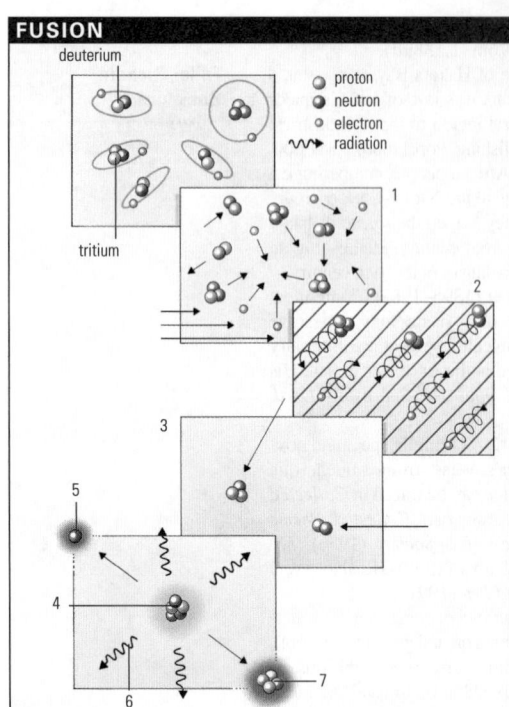

deuterium

tritium

- proton
- neutron
- electron
- ⌇⌇⌇ radiation

1
2
3
5
4
6
7

In experiments to generate power by nuclear fusion, the aim is usually to produce energy by fusing tritium and deuterium. These are isotopes of hydrogen and the process can occur only at a temperature above 100 million°C and under enormous pressure. Deuterium has one proton, one neutron, and one electron, whereas tritium has one proton, two neutrons, and an electron. In a fusion reactor, the mixture of the two isotopes is heated by intense radio emissions, ion bombardment, and electrical pulses (1). The plasma that results is suspended in a magnetic field (2). The tritium and deuterium nuclei fuse (3), creating a helium nucleus (4), a loose neutron (5), radiation (6), and energy when the products hit the edge of the plasma (7).

fundamental forces Four basic forces that exist in physics. The most familiar, and the weakest, is GRAVITATION. The gravitational force between the Earth and an object accounts for the object's WEIGHT. Much stronger is the ELECTROMAGNETIC FORCE, which 'binds' particles together. The two other forces operate only on the subatomic level: the WEAK NUCLEAR FORCE, associated with the decay of particles, is intermediate in strength between the gravitational and electromagnetic force; the STRONG NUCLEAR FORCE, associated with the 'glue' that holds nuclei together, is the strongest natural force.

fundamentalism Movement within some Protestant denominations, particularly in the USA, which originated in the late 19th and early 20th centuries as a reaction against biblical criticism and contemporary theories of evolution. The name is derived from *The Fundamentals*, a series of 12 tracts published in 1909–15 by eminent US evangelical leaders. The term "fundamentalism" is also often used to refer to any extreme orthodox tendency within a religion.

Fundamental Orders Code of laws adopted by representatives of the settlements in Connecticut in 1639 to govern the Connecticut Colony. It was similar to a system in Massachusetts, but did not demand church membership from voters. Sometimes called the first written constitution, it remained in force until superseded by the Connecticut Charter (1662).

fungicide Chemical that kills fungi in plants and humans. In medicine this includes some antibiotics. In plants, for example, creosote is used on wood to prevent dry rot.

fungus Any of a wide variety of organisms of the KINGDOM Fungi, which are unable to photosynthesize and which reproduce by means of spores and never produce cells with flagella. They include MUSHROOMS, MOULDS, and YEASTS. There are c.100,000 species. Fungi have relatively simple structures, with no roots, stems, or leaves. Their cell walls contain the polysaccharide CHITIN. The main body of a typical multicellular fungus consists of an inconspicuous network (mycelium) of fine filaments (hyphae), which contain many nuclei and may or may not be divided into segments by cross-walls. The hypha nuclei are HAPLOID. The mycelia may develop spore-producing, often conspicuous, fruiting bodies, mushrooms and TOADSTOOLS. Fungal PARASITES depend on living animals or plants: SAPROPHYTES utilize the materials of dead plants and animals, and symbionts obtain food in a mutually beneficial relationship with plants. Fungi feed by secreting digestive ENZYMES onto their food, then absorbing the soluble products of digestion. All three groups are of great importance to man. Many cause diseases in crops, livestock and humans (athlete's foot). Moulds and yeasts are used in the production of BEER and CHEESE; some fungi, such as *Penicillium*, are sources of ANTIBIOTICS.

funk Style or energy of popular music. It was originally employed in the 1950s to summarize a form of modern JAZZ which, although influenced by BE-BOP harmonies, emphasized modern melodies. Funk developed into an independent form with artists such as James BROWN and George Clinton.

fur Soft, dense hair covering the skin of certain mammals. Such mammals include mink, fox, ermine, musquash, wolf, bear, squirrel and rabbit. Some are hunted and killed for their pelts which, when manufactured into clothing, may command high prices. Some fur-bearing animals are now protected by law because overhunting has threatened extinction.

Furies (Erthyes and Eumenides) In Greek mythology, three hideous goddesses of vengeance whose main task was to torment those guilty of social crimes.

furnace Enclosed space raised to a high temperature by the combustion of fuels or by electric heating. Most furnaces are used in the extraction of metals or the making of alloys. An **arc** furnace relies on the heat generated by an electric arc (spark), often between two large carbon electrodes, which are slowly consumed. A **resistance** furnace is heated by passing an electric current through a heating element, or directly through metallic material. An **induction** furnace uses ELECTROMAGNETIC INDUCTION to cause a current to flow in a metallic charge. The resulting heat is sufficient to melt the metal.

Furtwängler, Wilhelm (1886–1954) German conductor. He became conductor of the Berlin Philharmonic Orchestra in 1922 (life appointment in 1952), and of the Vienna Philharmonic Orchestra in 1930. He appeared frequently at the Bayreuth and Salzburg Festivals, and was a specialist in the works of Beethoven and Wagner. His ambiguous relationship with the Nazi regime aroused controversy.

furze *See* GORSE

fuse In electrical engineering, a safety device to protect against overloading. Fuses are commonly strips of easily melted metal placed in series in an electrical circuit such that when overloaded, the fuse melts, breaking the circuit and preventing systemic damage.

fusel oil Poisonous, clear, colourless liquid with a disagreeable smell. It consists of a mixture of amyl alcohols, obtained as a by-product of the fermentation of plant materials containing sugar and starch. It is used as a solvent for waxes, resins, fats and oils, and in the manufacture of explosives.

fusion, nuclear Form of nuclear reaction in which nuclei of light atoms (such as hydrogen) combine to form one or more heavier nuclei with the release of large amounts of energy. The process takes place in the Sun and other stars, and has been reproduced on Earth in the HYDROGEN BOMB. Efforts have since been concentrated on producing controlled fusion reaction in a thermonuclear reactor. Two main methods have been employed. In the first, a PLASMA of tritium and deuterium is raised to a temperature above 100 million°C in a tokamak reactor. The second method is laser fusion, in which a laser implodes a pellet of tritium and deuterium. At present, both methods fail to produce more energy from fusion than is put into the system. *See also* FISSION, NUCLEAR; NUCLEAR ENERGY

futurism Art movement that originated in Italy (1909) with the publication of the first futurist manifesto. It aimed to glorify machines and to depict speed and motion by means of an adapted version of CUBISM. It was violently opposed to the study of art of the past and embraced the values of modernity. Leading futurists include the poet MARINETTI. Its ideas were absorbed by the DADA movement and by SURREALISM.

Fuzhou (Foo-chow or Fu-chou) City and port on the River Min Chiang, capital of Fukien province, SE China. Fuzhou was founded in the T'ang dynasty (618–907). It was one of the first treaty ports to be opened to foreign trade (1842) and flourished as China's largest tea-exporting centre. It declined in the early 20th century. In 1949, after the communist takeover, Fuzhou was blockaded by the nationalists. Industries: engineering, chemicals, textiles. Pop. (2005) 1,398,000.

G Symbol for the universal constant of GRAVITATION. g is also the symbol for acceleration of free fall due to Earth's gravity. One g is $c.9.8 \text{m/s}^2$ (32ft/s^2).

G8 Abbreviation of GROUP OF EIGHT

Gable, Clark (1901–60) US film actor. He was a popular leading man, and was declared 'king' of 1930s Hollywood. Gable won an Academy Award for best actor in *It Happened One Night* (1934) but is probably best known for his performance as Rhett Butler in *Gone With the Wind* (1939). His best post-war acting was in the posthumously released *The Misfits* (1961).

Gabo, Naum (1890–1977) US sculptor and architect, b. Russia as Naum Pevsner. A founder of CONSTRUCTIVISM, he published the *Realist Manifesto* (1920) with his brother Antoine PEVSNER.

Gabon The Gabonese Republic lies on the Equator in w central Africa. *see* country feature.

Gabor, Dennis (1900–79) British physicist, b. Hungary. He received the 1971 Nobel Prize in physics for his invention (1947) of HOLOGRAPHY. He developed the basic technique of creating a three-dimensional image, but it was not until the invention (1960) of the LASER by Charles H. TOWNES that holography became commercially feasible.

Gaborone Capital of Botswana, s Africa. First settled in the 1890s, it served as the administrative headquarters of the former Bechuanaland Protectorate. In 1966 it became the capital of an independent Botswana. Pop. (2001) 186,007.

Gabriel In the OLD TESTAMENT Book of Daniel, an angel who serves as God's messenger. In Christian tradition, he is one of the Archangels.

Gabrieli Two Italian composers, uncle and nephew. **Andrea** Gabrieli (*c.*1533–86) was organist at St Mark's, Venice. He wrote vocal and organ music, developing the antiphonal use of several choirs. His nephew **Giovanni** (*c.*1553–1612) succeeded him as organist at St Mark's. He developed the new CONCERTO style and was a major influence on the early BAROQUE.

Gaddafi, Muammar al *See* QADDAFI, MUAMMAR AL-

Gaddi, Taddeo (*c.*1300–*c.*1366) Leading member in a family of Florentine artists. Taddeo's father, **Gaddo di Zanobi** (*c.*1259–*c.*1330), was a noted painter and mosaicist. **Taddeo** served as an apprentice to GIOTTO. His best-known work is the fresco series *Life of the Virgin* (completed in 1338). Taddeo's son, **Agnolo** (d.1396), also painted frescos; the most famous is the *Legend of the True Cross* (*c.*1380).

gadolinium (symbol Gd) Silvery white metallic element of the LANTHANIDE SERIES. Chief ores are gadolinite, monazite and bastnaesite. Its uses include neutron absorption and the manufacture of certain alloys. Properties: at.no. 64; r.a.m. 157.25; r.d. 7.898; m.p. 1,311°C (2,392°F); b.p. 3,233°C (5,851°F); most common isotope Gd[158] (24.87%).

Gaelic Language spoken in parts of Ireland and Scotland. The two branches diverged in the 15th century and are mutually unintelligible. The Irish variety is one of the official languages of the Republic of Ireland. In Scotland, Gaelic has no official status. The number of speakers of both is diminishing.

Gagarin, Yuri Alekseyevich (1934–68) Russian cosmonaut, the first man to orbit Earth (April 12, 1961) and regarded as the first man in space. Gagarin became an international celebrity. He died in an aeroplane crash during training.

gag rules Series of rules adopted by US Congress in the 1830s to prevent discussion of slavery. John Quincy ADAMS led the fight against the rules, and they were repealed in 1844.

Gaia (Gaea) In Greek mythology, mother goddess of the Earth. Wife (and in some legends, mother) of URANUS, she bore the TITANS and the CYCLOPES.

Gainsborough, Thomas (1727–88) English portrait and landscape painter. Influenced by the Dutch landscape painters, he developed a style remarkable for its characterization and use of colour. His portraits, such as *Viscount Kilmorey* (1768) and *Blue Boy* (*c.*1770), rivalled those of Sir Joshua REYNOLDS. Among his best landscapes is *The Watering Place* (1777).

Gaitskell, Hugh Todd Naylor (1906–63) British statesman, Labour Party leader (1955–63). Gaitskell entered Parlia-

G/g, seventh letter of the Roman alphabet. Like c, it probably derived from the Egyptian hieroglyph for a boomerang. The Greeks made it the third letter of their alphabet, **gamma***. G is the symbol for gravity and g that for gram.*

▲ **Gable** Actor Clark Gable was one of the biggest stars of 1930s Hollywood.

GABON

The Gabonese Republic lies on the Equator in w-central Africa. It is a little larger than the United Kingdom in area, with a coastline 800km [500mi] long. Behind the narrow, partly lagoon-lined coastal plain, the land rises to hills, plateaux and mountains divided by deep valleys carved by the River Ogooué and its tributaries.

Dense rainforest covers about 75% of Gabon, with tropical savanna in the E and S. The forests teem with wildlife, and Gabon has several national parks and wildlife reserves.

CLIMATE

Most of Gabon has an equatorial climate. There are high temperatures and humidity throughout the year. The rainfall is heavy and the skies are often cloudy.

HISTORY

Explorers from Portugal reached the Gabon coast in the 1470s, and the area later became a source of slaves. In 1839, France established the first European settlement. In 1849 freed slaves founded LIBREVILLE. Gabon became a French colony in the 1880s and achieved full independence in 1960.

Léon Mba was Gabon's first president from 1960 to 1967. In 1964, an attempted coup was put down when French troops intervened and crushed the revolt. Following the death of Léon Mba in 1967, Bernard-Albert Bongo became president. He later renamed himself El Hadj Omar Bongo, and made Gabon a one-party state in 1968.

POLITICS

Elections took place in 1990. The Gabonese Democratic Party (PDG) won a majority in the National Assembly. President Bongo, of the PDG, won the presidential elections in 1993, although accusations of fraud and corruption led to riots. The international community condemned Bongo for his harsh suppression of popular demonstrations. He claimed victory again in 1998 elections. In 2003, constitutional changes enabled Bongo to stand as president as

AREA 267,668sq km [103,347sq mi]
POPULATION 1,455,000
CAPITAL (POPULATION) Libreville (362,000)
GOVERNMENT Multiparty republic
ETHNIC GROUPS Bantu tribes: Fang, Bandjabi, Bapounou, Eshira, Myene, Nzebi, Obamba and Okande
LANGUAGES French (official), Fang, Myene, Nzebi, Bapounou/Eschira, Bandjabi
RELIGIONS Christianity 75%, animist, Islam
CURRENCY CFA franc = 100 centimes

many times as he wished. In November 2005 he was again elected president. Despite the opposition's protestations of unfairness, the elections were deemed acceptable by international observers. Opposition parties remain weak.

ECONOMY

Gabon's abundant natural resources include its forests, oil and gas deposits near Port Gentil, together with manganese and uranium. These mineral deposits make Gabon one of Africa's wealthier countries.

However, agriculture still employs about 75% of the workforce, most farmers producing little more than they need to support their families. Crops include bananas, cassava, maize, and sugar cane. Cocoa and coffee are grown for export. Other exports include oil, manganese, timber and wood products and uranium.

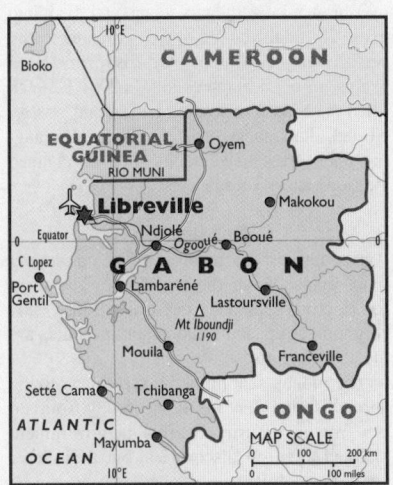

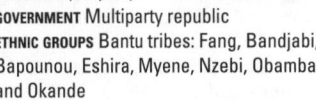

ment in 1945, joining the cabinet in 1947. In 1950, he became minister of state for economic affairs and then chancellor of the exchequer (1950–51). In the 1950 leadership elections, he led Labour's right to victory over Aneurin BEVAN's challenge. In 1960, Gaitskell refused to accept the conference's decision to adopt a policy of unilateral disarmament and defeated a leadership challenge from his eventual successor Harold WILSON.

Galápagos Islands (Sp. *Archipiélago de Colón*) Pacific archipelago on the Equator; a province of Ecuador; *c*.1050km (650mi) w of mainland South America. The capital is Baquerizo Moreno, on San Cristóbal. Other main islands include Santa Cruz, San Salvador and Isabela. There are numerous smaller islands. The islands are volcanic with sparse vegetation, except for dense forests on the high lava craters, which rise to 1,707m (5,633ft) at Volcán Wolf (Isabela). Mangrove swamps and lagoons teem with wildlife. Many animal species are unique to the islands, such as the giant land tortoises. Other native creatures include marine and land iguanas and flightless cormorants. The Galápagos National Park is a world heritage site, established in 1935 to protect the wildlife. In 1832 Ecuador annexed the archipelago and established a settlement. In 1835, Charles DARWIN spent six weeks studying the fauna which provided much support for his theory of natural selection. Area: 7,845sq km (3,029sq mi) Pop. (2000 est.) 16,917.

galaxy Huge assembly of STARS, dust and gas. There are three main types, as classified by Edwin HUBBLE in 1925. **Elliptical** galaxies (E) are round or elliptical systems, showing a gradual decrease in brightness from the centre outwards. **Spiral** galaxies (S) are flattened, disc-shaped systems in which young stars, dust and gas are concentrated in spiral arms coiling out from a central bulge, the nucleus. **Barred spiral** galaxies (SB) have a bright, central bar from which the spi-

ral arms emerge. In addition to these three main classes are **lenticular** galaxies, systems with a disc and nucleus but with no apparent spiral arms. **Irregular** galaxies, such as the MAG-ELLANIC CLOUDS, are systems with no symmetry. Galaxies can exist singly or in clusters. About one galaxy in a million is a RADIO GALAXY, emitting strong ELECTROMAGNETIC RADIA-TION. A SEYFERT GALAXY has a bright, compact nucleus and is a strong emitter of INFRARED RADIATION. Current theories suggest all galaxies were formed from immense clouds of gas soon after the BIG BANG. Our galaxy is spiral or barred spiral and *c*.100,000 light years in diameter. The SOLAR SYSTEM lies at the edge of one of the spiral arms, *c*.30,000 light years from the centre. The stars of the spiral arms form the MILKY WAY.

galaxy cluster Group of associated galaxies, consisting of several separate systems moving together through space. Our galaxy belongs to the Local Group of galaxies, which includes the ANDROMEDA GALAXY and MAGELLANIC CLOUDS. A concentration of galactic clusters is called a galactic supercluster.

galena (lead sulphide, PbS) Grey metallic mineral, major ore of LEAD. It is found in hydrothermal veins and as a replacement in limestone and dolomite rocks. Hardness 2.5–2.7; r.d. 7.5.

Galicia Region of SE Poland (Western Galicia) and w Ukraine (Eastern Galicia), on the slopes of the Carpathian Mountains (N) and bordering the Czech Republic (S). The major cities are KRAKÓW (Poland) and LVOV (Ukraine). After passing to Austria in 1772, Galicia became the centre of HASIDISM. After World War 1, Poland seized Western Galicia and was awarded Eastern Galicia at the 1919 Paris Peace Conference. The 1939 partition of Poland between Nazi Germany and the Soviet Union gave most of Eastern Galicia to the Ukraine, a position ratified by the 1945 Polish-Soviet Treaty. The region is predominantly agricultural. Area: 78,500sq km (30,309sq mi).

GAMBIA

The Republic of the Gambia is the smallest country in mainland Africa. It consists of a narrow strip of land bordering the River Gambia. The Gambia is almost entirely enclosed by Senegal, except along the short Atlantic coastline. The land is flat near the sea.

Mangrove swamps line the river banks. Much tropical savanna has been cleared for farming. The Gambia is rich in wildlife and has six national parks and reserves as well as several forest parks.

CLIMATE
The Gambia has hot and humid summers, but winter temperatures (November to May) drop to around 16°C [61°F]. In the summer, moist winds heading sw bring rain, which is heaviest on the coast.

HISTORY
Portuguese mariners reached Gambia's coast in 1455, when the area was part of the Mali empire. In the 16th century, Portuguese and English slave traders operated in the area.

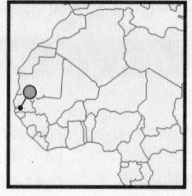

English traders bought rights to trade on the River Gambia in 1588, and in 1664 the English established a settlement on an island in the river estuary. In 1765 the British founded a colony called Senegambia, which included parts of present-day Gambia and Senegal. In 1783, Britain handed this colony over to France.

During the 1860s and 1870s, Britain and France discussed the exchange of the Gambia for some other French territory. No agreement was reached and Britain made the Gambia a British colony in 1888. It remained under British rule until 1965, when it achieved full independence with Dawda Jawara as prime minister. In 1970 the Gambia became a republic.

POLITICS
Relations between the French-speaking Senegalese and the English-speaking Gambians form a major political issue. In 1981 an attempted coup in the Gambia was put down with Senegalese help. In 1982 The Gambia and Senegal set up a defence alliance, called the Confederation of

AREA 11,295sq km [4,361sq mi]
POPULATION 1,688,000
CAPITAL (POPULATION) Banjul (42,000)
GOVERNMENT Military regime
ETHNIC GROUPS Mandinka 42%, Fula 18%, Wolof 16%, Jola 10%, Serahuli 9%, others
LANGUAGES English (official), Mandinka, Wolof, Fula
RELIGIONS Islam 90%, Christianity 9%, traditional beliefs 1%
CURRENCY Dalasi = 100 butut

Senegambia, though this alliance was dissolved in 1989. In 1992 Jawara was re-elected as president for a fifth term. In July 1994 he was overthrown in a military coup and fled into exile. The coup was led by Yahya Jammeh who was elected president in 1996. His regime faced charges of political repression. In 2001 Jammeh lifted the ban on opposition parties and was re-elected, although he is still criticized for impinging upon press freedom. In 2006 he claimed election victory yet again.

ECONOMY
Agriculture is the main activity, employing more than 80% of the workforce. The main food crops include cassava, millet and sorghum, but peanuts and peanut products are the chief exports.

The money sent home by Gambians living abroad is important for the economy. Tourism is a growing industry. In 2004 the government claimed large oil discoveries, but these have yet to be exploited.

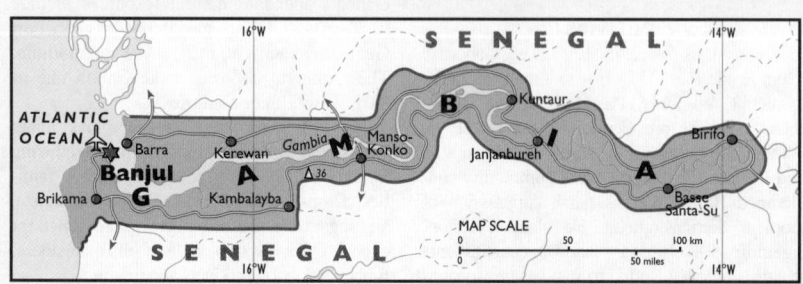

Galicia Autonomous region in NW Spain, comprising the provinces of La Coruña, Lugo, Orense and Pontevedra; the capital is Santiago de Compostela. It was a centre of resistance to the Moorish invasions in the 8th century, and passed to Castile in the 13th century. Galicia has a mountainous interior. Its economy is based on livestock, fishing, and mining. Area: 29,434sq km (11,361sq mi). Pop. (2001) 2,695,880.

Galilean satellites Four chief SATELLITES of JUPITER: GANYMEDE, CALLISTO, Io and EUROPA, named after GALILEO.

Galilee, Sea of (Lake Tiberius or Yam Kinneret) Freshwater lake in N Israel, fed by the River JORDAN. Israel's major reservoir, it is an important fishing ground and the source of water for irrigation of the NEGEV Desert. The surface is *c.*215m (705ft) below sea level. Area: 166sq km (64sq mi).

Galileo (1564–1642) (Galileo Galilei) Italian physicist and astronomer. According to legend, Galileo observed that a hanging lamp in Pisa Cathedral took the same time to complete one oscillation however long the swing, and he suggested the pendulum could be used for timekeeping. He later studied falling bodies, and disproved ARISTOTLE's view that they fall at different rates according to weight. He also discovered the parabolic flight path of projectiles. In 1609, Galileo used one of the first astronomical telescopes to discover sunspots, lunar craters, Jupiter's major satellites, and the phases of Venus. In *Sidereus Nuncius* (1610), he supported COPERNICUS' heliocentric theory that the Earth moves around the Sun. Galileo was forbidden by the Roman Catholic Church to teach that this system represented physical reality but, in *Dialogue on the Two Great World Systems* (1632), he defied the pope by making his criticism of PTOLEMY's system even more explicit. As a result, Galileo was brought before the Inquisition and forced to recant.

gall Abnormal swelling of plant tissue stimulated by an invasion of any of a wide variety of parasitic or symbiotic organisms, including bacteria, fungi, insects and nematodes. Most gall organisms stunt but do not kill the affected plants.

Galla Hamitic people who make up 40% of the population of Ethiopia, living mainly in the south. Characteristically tall and dark-skinned, they are predominantly nomadic pastoralists. Their religions include Christianity, Islam and animism.

gall bladder Muscular pear-shaped sac, found in most vertebrates, which stores BILE. In humans, it is beneath the right lobe of the LIVER. It stores bile created in the liver and releases it into the DUODENUM through the bile duct. A painful inflammation of the gall bladder can be caused by a GALLSTONE, a hard crystalline mass, blocking the duct.

Gallic Wars (58–51BC) Campaigns in which the Romans, led by CAESAR, conquered GAUL. By 57 BC Caesar had subdued SW and N Gaul. In 56 BC he conquered the Veneti, leaders of an anti-Roman confederation He defeated a united Gallic revolt in 52 BC.

Gallipoli (Gelibolu) Peninsula and port in W Turkey, on the European side of the DARDANELLES. Colonized by the Ancient Greeks, it has been of strategic importance in the defence of Istanbul (Constantinople). It was the first European city to be conquered by the Ottoman Turks (1354). In 1915–16, it was the scene of the GALLIPOLI CAMPAIGN. Pop. (1997) 21,900.

Gallipoli Campaign (1915–16) Allied operation against the Turks during WORLD WAR I. Some 45,000 British and French and 30,000 ANZAC troops were involved. After eight months of inconclusive fighting and more than 145,000 casualties on both sides, the Allies withdrew.

gallium (symbol Ga) Grey metallic element of group III of the periodic table. It was discovered in 1875. Chief sources are bauxite and some zinc ores. The metal is used in lasers, semiconductors and high-temperature thermometers. Properties: at.no. 31; r.a.m. 69.72; r.d. 5.9; m.p. 29.78°C (85.60°F); b.p. 2,403°C (4,357°F); most common isotope Ga[69] (60.4%).

gallstone (cholelithiasis) Hard mass, usually composed of cholesterol and calcium salts, which forms in the GALL BLADDER. Gallstones may cause severe pain or become lodged in the common bile duct, causing obstructive JAUNDICE or cholecystitis. Treatment is by removal of the stones or of the gall bladder.

Galsworthy, John (1867–1933) English novelist and playwright. Galsworthy is best known for a quartet of novels, *The Forsyte Saga* (1906–21), that traces three generations of a fictional English upper-middle-class family. Other chronicles include *A Modern Comedy* (1924–28) and *End of the Chapter* (1931–33). He received the 1932 Nobel Prize in literature

Galvani, Luigi (1737–98) Italian physician and physicist. His experiments with frogs' legs indicated a connection between muscular contraction and electricity. He believed a new type of electricity was created in the muscle and nerve.

galvanizing Coating of iron or steel articles with zinc in order to protect from CORROSION. The coating can be applied directly in a bath of molten zinc, electroplated from cold zinc sulphate solutions, or dusted on and baked.

Galway County in the province of Connaught, W Republic of Ireland; the county town is Galway. Bounded by the Atlantic (W), it has an indented coastline with many islands. It is mountainous in the W, low-lying in the E, and drained by the River Shannon. It is an agricultural region. Industries: tourism, agriculture, cotton-spinning, sugar-refining, handicrafts. Area: 5,939sq km (2,293sq mi). Pop. (2002) 208,826.

Gama, Vasco da (1469–1524) Portuguese navigator. He was charged with continuing Bartholomeu DIAZ's search for a sea route to India. Da Gama's successful expedition (1497–99) rounded the Cape of Good Hope, and sailed across the Indian Ocean to Calicut. In 1502–03, he led a heavily armed expedition of 20 ships to Calicut, and brutally avenged the killing of Portuguese settlers left there by CABRAL.

Gambia, The Republic in Africa. *See* country feature

gamelan Traditional Indonesian orchestra using xylophones, marimbas, gongs and drums. Used to accompany ceremonies, the rhythmically complex music has inspired Western composers, such as Claude DEBUSSY and Philip GLASS.

gamete Reproductive sex cell that joins with another sex cell to form a new organism. Female gametes (ova) are usually motionless; male gametes (SPERM) often have a tail (flagellum) enabling them to swim to the OVUM. All gametes are HAPLOID having a single set of CHROMOSOMES in each cell.

game theory In mathematics, analysis of problems involving conflict. Initially it was based on the assumption that participants in conflict adopt strategies that maximize personal gain and minimize loss. Later, more complex motivations, such as morality, were included. Applications of game theory include business management, sociology, economics and military strategy. The theory was introduced by French mathematician Émile Borel and developed by John von NEUMANN in 1928.

gametophyte Generation of plants and algae that bears the female and male GAMETES. In flowering plants, these are the germinated pollen grains (male) and the embryo sac (female) inside the ovule. *See also* ALTERNATION OF GENERATIONS; FERN

gamma radiation Form of very short wavelength ELECTROMAGNETIC RADIATION emitted from the nuclei of some radioactive atoms. High-energy gamma rays have even greater powers of penetration than X-RAYS. They are used in medicine to treat cancer and in the food industry to kill microorganisms. *See also* RADIOACTIVITY

Gamow, George (1904–68) US nuclear physicist, b. Russia. He developed the BIG BANG theory and explained (with Ralph Alpher and Hans BETHE) the abundance of chemical elements in the universe. In molecular biology, Gamow deduced the triplet code (codon) of bases in DNA. With Edward TELLER, he established the Gamow-Teller theory of beta decay.

Gandhi, Indira (1917–84) Indian stateswoman, primeminister (1966–77, 1980–84), daughter of Jawaharlal NEHRU. She was president of the CONGRESS PARTY (1959–60) before succeeding Lal Shastri as prime minister. In 1975, amid growing social unrest, Gandhi was found guilty of breaking electoral rules in 1971. She refused to resign, invoked emergency powers, and imprisoned many opponents. In 1977 elections, the Congress Party was defeated and the party split. In 1980, leading a faction of the Congress Party, Gandhi returned to power. In 1984, after authorizing the use of force against Sikh dissidents in the Golden Temple at AMRITSAR, she was killed by a Sikh bodyguard. Her eldest son, Rajiv GANDHI, succeeded her.

Gandhi, 'Mahatma' (Mohandas Karamchand) (1869–1948) Indian political and spiritual leader. A lawyer, he practised in South Africa (1893–1914), where he led equal-rights

▲ **Gandhi** advocated a policy of non-violent resistance to British rule in India. He endured long hunger-strikes to highlight the injustices of British colonialism, the caste system, and communal violence. 'Mahatma' (Sanskrit, 'Great Soul') Gandhi lived an ascetic life, rejecting materialism and industrialization in favour of cottage industries.

G

INTERNET

Gabon (page 341)
▶ afrika.no/links/Countries

Gagarin, Yuri Alekseyevich (page 341)
▶ www.abamedia.com/rao/gallery/gagarin

Gainsborough, Thomas (page 341)
▶ www.npg.org.uk
▶ www.nationalgallery.org.uk

Galápagos Islands (page 341)
▶ www.galapagos.org
▶ www.darwinfoundation.org
▶ www.galapagos-islands.net

Galileo
▶ galileo.rice.edu

Gallipoli Campaign
▶ www.firstworldwar.com/battles

Gambia, The
▶ www.gambia.gm

Gandhi, 'Mahatma' (Mohandas Karamchand)
▶ www.mkgandhi.org

▲ **Ganges** The River Ganges holds great religious significance for the world's Hindu population. Certain points along the river, known as *tirath*, are holy places where bathing festivals (*mela*) occur annually. The best-known *tirath* are at Varanasi, Allahabad, and Hardwar.

▲ **gannet** The Atlantic gannet (*Sula bassana*) is found in some coastal regions of N Europe and E North America. It grows to a length of 100cm (40in). Gannets spot their prey of surface-swimming fish from the air, before dropping in a near-vertical dive to catch the fish. They snatch and swallow the prey before re-emerging.

campaigns, before returning to his native India in 1914. Following the massacre at AMRITSAR (1919), Gandhi organized several non-cooperation campaigns and was imprisoned (1922–24) for conspiracy. Resistance methods included strikes, refusal to pay taxes and non-respect of colonial law. After his release, Gandhi served as president (1925–34) of the Indian National CONGRESS. In 1930, he made his famous 400km (250mi) protest march against a salt tax. In 1934, Jawaharlal NEHRU succeeded Gandhi as leader of the Congress. In 1942, Gandhi launched the Quit India movement. He was then interned until 1944. He played a major role in the post-war talks with Nehru, Lord MOUNTBATTEN and Muhammad Ali JINNAH that led to India's independence (1947). He opposed partition and the creation of a separate Muslim state (Pakistan). When violence flared between Hindus and Muslims, Gandhi resorted to fasts for peace. A figure of huge international and moral stature, he was assassinated by a Hindu fanatic in New Delhi.

Gandhi, Rajiv (1944–91) Indian statesman, prime minister (1984–89). The elder son of Indira GANDHI, Rajiv Gandhi was an airline pilot before reluctantly entering politics. He became prime minister after his mother's assassination. He worked to placate India's Sikh extremists, but a bribery scandal tarnished his reputation. Defeated in the 1989 election, Gandhi was assassinated while campaigning for re-election in 1991.

Ganesh Elephant-headed Hindu god, son of SHIVA and PARVATI. He is the patron of learning and is said to have written down the MAHABHARATA. *See also* HINDUISM

Ganges (Ganga) River of N India. It rises in the Himalayas, then flows SE, and empties into the Bay of Bengal through the BRAHMAPUTRA-Ganges delta. The plains of the Ganges are extremely fertile and support the densely populated cities of DELHI, AGRA, VARANASI, and LUCKNOW. In HINDUISM, it is the earthly form of the Goddess Ganga and pilgrims purify themselves in its waters. Length: 2,512km (1,560mi).

ganglion Cluster of nerve-cell bodies and SYNAPSES (nerve connections), usually enclosed in a fibrous sheath. In VERTEBRATES, most ganglia occur outside the CENTRAL NERVOUS SYSTEM. The term is used in medicine for a harmless abnormal swelling on a tendon sheath, normally at the wrist.

Gang of Four Faction that tried to seize power in China after the death of both Chairman MAO ZEDONG and Prime Minister ZHOU ENLAI. in 1976. The Gang of Four, Zhang Chunjao, Wang Hungwen, Yao Wenyuan, and their leader JIANG QING (Mao's widow), tried to launch a military coup, but were arrested by HUA GUOFENG and were sentenced to life imprisonment.

gannet Diving seabird related to the tropical booby. Gannets are heavy-bodied with tapering bills, long pointed wings, short legs and webbed feet. They nest in huge colonies on rocky islands. Length: 63–100cm (25–40in). Family Sulidae.

Gansu (Kansu) Province in NW central China, bordered E by Inner Mongolia; the capital is Lanzhou. The region

became Chinese territory in the 3rd century BC. Wheat, cotton, rice, maize, and tobacco grow under irrigation. Mineral deposits include iron ore, oil, and coal. Area: 366,625sq km (141,550sq mi). Pop. (2000) 25,620,000.

Ganymede Largest of Jupiter's GALILEAN SATELLITES, with a diameter of 5,262km (3,270mi). Its cratered terrain is covered with grooves suggesting recent geological activity.

gar Primitive, freshwater bony fish found in shallow waters of North America. Bony, diamond-shaped plates cover its long, cylindrical body. Its snout is studded with teeth. Length: to 3m (10ft); weight: to 135kg (300lb). Family Lepisosteidae.

Garbo, Greta (1905–90) Swedish film actress. Garbo's aura of mystery and enigmatic beauty made her an adored screen idol. Her first lead role was in *Torrent* (1926). Her first 'talkie' was *Anna Christie* (1930). She played the leads in the classics *Anna Karenina* (1935) and *Camille* (1937), and the comedy *Ninotchka* (1939). She retired in 1941.

García Lorca, Federico *See* LORCA, FEDERICO GARCÍA

García Márquez, Gabriel (1928–) Colombian novelist. His popular novel *One Hundred Years of Solitude* (1967) achieves a unique combination of realism, lyricism and mythical fantasy, making it a central text of MAGICAL REALISM. Later works include *The Autumn of the Patriarch* (1975), *Love in the Time of Cholera* (1985), and *The General in his Labyrinth* (1989). He received the 1982 Nobel Prize in literature.

Garda, Lake Largest lake in Italy, forming the border between Lombardy and Venetia. It has many popular tourist resorts along its shoreline. Area: 370sq km (143sq mi).

gardenia Genus of more than 60 species of evergreen shrubs and small trees, native to tropical and sub-tropical Asia and Africa. They have white or yellow, fragrant, waxy flowers. Height: to 5.5m (18ft). Family Rubiaceae.

Gardner, Erle Stanley (1889–1970) US writer. He wrote 80 novels featuring the detective lawyer Perry Mason, the first of which was *The Case of the Velvet Claws* (1933).

Garfield, James Abram (1831–81) 20th US president (1881). He served in the Civil War until 1863, when he was elected to the House of Representatives. In 1876, he became the Republican Leader of the House. The 1880 Republican convention was deadlocked and, on the 36th ballot, he became the compromise presidential candidate. His four-month administration was characterized by party squabbles over federal jobs and political patronage. He was assassinated on July 2, 1881, and was succeeded by his Vice President, Chester A. ARTHUR.

Garibaldi, Giuseppe (1807–82) Italian patriot and guerrilla leader who helped to bring about Italian unification. Influenced by MAZZINI, he participated in a republican rising in 1834, subsequently fleeing to South America. Garibaldi returned to fight against the Austrians in the REVOLUTIONS OF 1848, and in the unsuccessful defence of Rome against the French. In 1860, he led his 1,000–strong band of 'Red Shirts' against the Kingdom of the Two Sicilies, a dramatic episode in the RISORGIMENTO. He handed his conquests to King VICTOR EMMANUEL II to be incorporated into the new kingdom of Italy.

Garland, Judy (1922–69) US singer and film actress, b. Frances Gumm. Her performance as Dorothy in *The Wizard of Oz* (1939) made her a worldwide star. Her other films include *Meet Me in St Louis* (1944), *Easter Parade* (1948), and *A Star is Born* (1954). Her daughter is actress **Liza Minnelli** (1946–).

garlic Bulbous herb native to S Europe and central Asia. It has onion-like foliage and a bulb made up of sections called cloves, which are used for flavouring. It is also claimed to have medicinal properties. Family Liliaceae; species *Allium sativum*.

garnet Two series of orthosilicate minerals found in metamorphic rocks and pegmatites. Some varieties are important as gemstones. Hardness 6.5–7.5; r.d. 4.

Garrick, David (1717–79) English actor, theatre manager and dramatist. A pupil of Samuel JOHNSON, he is credited with replacing the formal declamatory style of acting with natural speech. Garrick made his acting debut (1741) in *Richard III*. He was manager (1747–76) of Drury Lane Theatre, London.

Garrison, William Lloyd (1805–79) US ABOLITIONIST. In 1831, he started the influential, anti-slavery journal *Liberator* in Boston. After the Civil War, he concentrated on other reforms, including temperance and women's suffrage.

Garter, Order of the Most ancient of chivalric orders in Britain, created by Edward III in 1348. The monarch is the Grand Master and there are usually 25 Knights of the Order.

garter snake Non-venomous SNAKE native to North and Central America. They are usually olive-brown with yellow, orange, red or blue stripes, often spotted with black. Length: to 60cm (24in). Family Colubridae; genus *Thamnophis*.

Garvey, Marcus (1887–1940) US black nationalist leader, b. Jamaica. In 1914, he founded the Universal Negro Improvement Association (UNIA). Garvey believed that black people could not achieve equality within white-dominated, Western countries. He created a 'back-to-Africa' movement, establishing the Black Star Line shipping company as a means of transport. By the 1920s, Garvey was the most influential US black leader. In 1922, the Black Star Line and the UNIA collapsed. Garvey was convicted of fraud and jailed (1925). He was pardoned by President Calvin Coolidge and deported to Jamaica (1927). RASTAFARIANISM is influenced by his philosophy.

gas State of MATTER in which molecules are free to move in any direction; a gas spreads by DIFFUSION. Any quantity of gas will occupy its entire container. Because of their low densities, most gases are poor conductors of heat and electricity (although at high voltages a gas may be ionized and become electrically conductive). When cooled, gases become LIQUIDS. Some, such as carbon dioxide, can be liquefied by pressure alone. All gases follow certain laws, such as AVOGADRO'S law, BOYLE'S LAW, CHARLES' LAW, GRAHAM'S law, and the IDEAL GAS LAWS. All involve volume and pressure, with Graham's law particularly concerned with diffusion. *See also* PLASMA; SOLID

Gascony Former province in sw France, bounded to the s by the PYRENEES and to the w by the Bay of BISCAY. Part of Roman Gaul, it was later overrun by the Visigoths and the Franks. In the 6th century, it was conquered by the Vascones. It passed to Aquitaine in the 11th century. In 1154, Gascony fell to the English. It was a major battleground in the Hundred Years' War, and was finally restored to France in 1453.

gas exchange In biology, the uptake and output of gases, especially oxygen and carbon dioxide, by living organisms. In animals and other organisms that obtain their energy by AEROBIC respiration, gas exchange involves the uptake of oxygen and the output of carbon dioxide. In plants, algae and bacteria that carry out PHOTOSYNTHESIS, the opposite may occur, with a carbon dioxide uptake and oxygen output. At the cellular level, gas exchange takes place by DIFFUSION across cell MEMBRANES in solution. *See also* BREATHING; CIRCULATORY SYSTEM; RESPIRATION; RESPIRATORY SYSTEM; VENTILATION

Gaskell, Elizabeth Cleghorn (1810–65) English writer. She explored the problems of the industrial poor in her novels *Mary Barton* (1848) and *North and South* (1855). Other works include *Cranford* (1853), *Wives and Daughters* (1866), and an acclaimed biography of her friend Charlotte BRONTË (1857).

Gasperi, Alcide de (1881–1954) Italian statesman, prime minister (1945–53). Gasperi was elected to the Austro-Hungarian parliament in 1911, and in 1921 entered the Italian parliament as a founder of the Italian People's Party. A strong opponent of fascism, he was imprisoned during MUSSOLINI's regime. During World War 2, he was active in the resistance and helped to create the Christian Democratic Party. As prime minister, he contributed greatly to Italy's postwar recovery.

gastric juice Fluid comprising a mixture of substances, including PEPSIN and hydrochloric acid, secreted by GLANDS of the stomach. Its principal function is to break down proteins into polypeptides during DIGESTION.

gastroenteritis Inflammation of the stomach and intestines causing abdominal pain, diarrhoea, and vomiting. It may be caused by infection, food poisoning, or allergy. Severe cases can cause dehydration. Treatment includes fluid replacement.

gastropod Member of the Gastropoda class of MOLLUSCS, which includes the SNAIL, SLUG, WHELK, LIMPET, ABALONE and SEA SLUG. Many possess a single spiral shell produced by chemical precipitation from the mantle. Many types of gastropod live immersed in seawater, breathing through gills. Some freshwater snails, however, breathe through lungs and surface periodically for air. Sea slugs are entirely without shells.

Gates, Bill (William Henry) (1955–) US businessman. In 1975 he co-founded Microsoft Corporation, which in the 1980s became the leading computer software producer. Gates is noted for his innovative thinking and aggressive business tactics. In 2000, he fought to prevent the break-up of Microsoft after the corporation was found guilty of breaking US anti-monopoly laws for the software it produced for the Internet.

Gates, Horatio (1727–1806) American general, b. England. He served in the British Army under General BRADDOCK in the FRENCH AND INDIAN WARS before emigrating to Virginia in 1772, and joining the colonists' cause in the AMERICAN REVOLUTION. In 1776, Gates became commander of the army in the north and defeated the British at SARATOGA (1777). He lost his command after the defeat at Camden, South Carolina (1780).

Gatling gun Early MACHINE GUN invented by Richard Gatling in 1862. It had several barrels mounted in a cylinder that was rotated manually by a crank so each barrel fired in turn.

GATT Acronym for the GENERAL AGREEMENT ON TARIFFS AND TRADE

gaucho Colourful COWBOY of the Argentine, Paraguayan, and Uruguayan pampas. Originally nomadic, the mixed-blood gauchos became farmhands and superb horse soldiers. They were an important political force in the 18th and 19th centuries.

Gaudí (y Cornet), Antonio (1852–1926) Spanish architect. An idiosyncratic exponent of ART NOUVEAU, Gaudí employed sculptural forms and ceramic ornamentation on buildings such as the Palau Güell (1885–89), Caso Battló (1905–07) and the unfinished Church of the Sagrada Familia, all in Barcelona.

Gaudier-Brzeska, Henri (1891–1915) French sculptor, who lived in England from 1911. A friend of Ezra POUND, he was part of the VORTICISM movement. His works include *Red Stone Dancer* (1913) and *Bird swallowing Fish* (1914).

Gauguin, (Eugène Henri) Paul (1848–1903) French painter, one of the greatest artists of POST-IMPRESSIONISM. In his early career, Gauguin exhibited (1881–86) with the impressionists in Paris. *The Vision After the Sermon* (1888) is a key work in Gauguin's break with the naturalism of IMPRESSIONISM. His belief that form and pattern should represent mental images influenced SYMBOLISM. Gauguin developed his own 'synthetist' style of EXPRESSIONISM characterized by bold contours and large areas of unmodulated colour. Inspired by 'primitive' art, he left France for Tahiti in 1891. The late works, often of South Sea islanders, convey a sense of mystery and myth. They include *Where do we come from? What are we? Where are we going?* (1897) and *Faa Iheihe* (1898).

Gaul Ancient Roman name for the land N of the Pyrenees, s and w of the Rhine and w of the Alps. In 900 BC tribes of CELTS began to migrate across the Rhine and spread s. In 222 BC the Romans conquered the region s of the Alps, calling it **Cisalpine** Gaul. By 121 BC Rome captured the area N of the Alps, known as **Transalpine** Gaul. In the GALLIC WARS (58–51BC), Caesar completed the conquest of Gaul.

gaur (seladang) Species of wild cattle found in forested hilly country in India and Malaysia. Gaurs are dark brown in colour with a white 'sock' on each leg. Length: up to 3.8m (12.4ft). Family Bovidae; species *Bos gaurus*.

Gauss, Karl Friedrich (1777–1855) German mathematician. Gauss made many discoveries that were not credited to him, such as non-Euclidean geometry and quaternions. In 1801, he calculated the orbit of the asteroid Ceres. From 1821, he worked on the first worldwide survey of the Earth's magnetic field. In 1833, Gauss invented the electric telegraph. The unit of magnetic flux density is named after him.

Gauteng Province in N central South Africa; the capital is JOHANNESBURG. Formed in 1994 from the TRANSVAAL as PWV (PRETORIA-WITWATERSRAND-Vereeniging), the province was renamed Gauteng in 1995. It is South Africa's smallest but most populous province. Area: 18,810sq km (7,260sq mi). Pop. (2002 est.) 8,106,190.

Gautier, Théophile (1811–72) French poet, novelist, and critic. His poems, such as *Albertus* (1833), *España* (1845), and *Enamels and Cameos* (1852), exhibit the formalist aesthetic theory of art that influenced SYMBOLISM.

gavial Reptile native to N India. It has a long, narrow snout, an olive or brownish back, and a lighter belly. It feeds almost

▲ **Gaudí** The *Sagrada Familia* (Holy Family) cathedral in Barcelona is a fine example of the Spanish architect Antonio Gaudí's extraordinary style. The cathedral, although started in 1883, remains unfinished. Gaudí's plans reveal a vast central spire, surrounded by 12 smaller spires (four are visible here). The building represents Christ surrounded by his 12 disciples. Funding for the cathedral is still uncertain, and there is no definite completion date.

▲ **gazelle** The Thomson's gazelle (*Gazella thomsoni*) inhabits the savanna of E Africa. Its relatively small size and unremarkable colouring make it less attractive to poachers and hunters than other African herbivores, and for this reason large populations still exist. The males' long, elegant horns are more often used for stylized, display fighting, but serious disputes do occur, often resulting in significant injury.

▶ **gecko** The banded gecko (*Coleonyx variegatus*) is one of a great many species of gecko inhabiting desert regions. It is nocturnal, hiding under rocks during the day and foraging for insects at night.

exclusively on fish. Length: to 5m (16.4ft). Family Gavialidae; species *Gavialis gangeticus*. *See also* CROCODILE

Gay, John (1685–1732) English poet and dramatist. His verse includes *The Shepherd's Week* (1714). His best-known work is the ballad-opera *The Beggar's Opera* (1728).

Gaya City on the Phalgu River, Bihar state, NE India. It is a pilgrimage centre sacred to both Hindus and Buddhists. Buddha received enlightenment nearby, and the God Vishnu is said to have sacrificed the demon of Gaya. Pop. (2001) 383,197.

Gaye, Marvin (1939–84) US singer-songwriter. His hit singles included "I Heard It Through The Grapevine" (1968) and "Too Busy Thinking 'Bout My Baby" (1968). Gaye released a string of classic soul albums, including *What's Going On* (1971), *Let's Get It On* (1973) and *Midnight Love* (1982). Gaye was shot dead by his father during an argument.

Gay-Lussac, Joseph Louis (1778–1850) French chemist and physicist. He discovered (1808) the law that gases combine in a simple ratio by volume (Gay-Lussac's law). Gay-Lussac also discovered the law of gas expansion, often attributed to J.A.C. CHARLES.

Gaza Strip Strip of territory in SW ISRAEL, bordering on the SE Mediterranean Sea. It became an Egyptian possession after the first ARAB-ISRAELI WAR (1948–49), and later served as a centre for Palestinian refugees. The Gaza Strip was occupied by Israel from 1967, and it was the scene of the INTIFADA against Israel in 1988. In 1994 the Palestinian Authority took over the administration of Gaza. In 2000, the Intifada renewed. In 2005, Israel withdrew troops and settlers from the area. Area: 363sq km (140sq mi). Pop. (1997) 1,001,569.

gazelle Any of several species of graceful, small-to-medium antelopes native to Africa and Asia, often inhabiting plains. Most are light brown with a white rump and horns. Some can run at up to 80km/h (50mph). Family Bovidae; genus *Gazella*.

Gdansk (Danzig) City and seaport on the Gulf of Gdansk, N Poland; capital of Gdansk county. Settled by Slavs in the 10th century, it was a member of the HANSEATIC LEAGUE. It was taken by Poland in the 15th century but passed to Prussia in 1793. The Treaty of VERSAILLES (1919) established it as a free city, and annexation by Germany in 1939 precipitated World War 2. The SOLIDARITY movement led by Lech WALESA was founded by strikers in Gdansk's shipyards in 1980. Industries: metallurgy, chemicals, machinery, timber. Pop. (1999) 457,900.

GDP Abbreviation of GROSS DOMESTIC PRODUCT

gear Wheel, usually toothed, attached to a rotating shaft. The teeth of one gear engage those of another in order to transmit and modify speed of rotation and TORQUE.

gecko Any of *c*.650 species of LIZARDS, native to warm regions of the world. They owe their remarkable climbing ability to minute hooks on their feet. They make chirping calls. Length: 3–15cm (1–6in). Family Gekkonidae.

Gehrig, (Henry) Lou (Louis) (1903–41) US baseball player. Gehrig played for the New York Yankees (1925–39), notching up a record 2,130 consecutive appearances. He had a lifetime batting average of .340 and hit 493 home runs. His career was cut short by amyotrophic lateral sclerosis, a degenerative muscular disease that became known as 'Gehrig's disease'. He was elected to the Baseball Hall of Fame in 1939.

Geiger, Hans (Johannes Wilhelm) (1882–1945) German physicist who, with Ernest RUTHERFORD, devised the GEIGER COUNTER (1908). In 1909, Geiger and Ernest Marsden studied the deflection of alpha particles by thin metal foil, providing the basis of Rutherford's discovery of the atomic nucleus.

Geiger counter (Geiger-Müller counter) Instrument used to detect and measure the strength of radiation by counting the number of ionized particles produced. It is named after the German physicist Hans GEIGER who developed the modern particle counter with Walter Müller at Kiel University.

gel Homogeneous mass consisting of minute particles dispersed in a liquid to form a fine network throughout the mass. A gel's appearance can be elastic or jellylike, as in GELATIN, or quite rigid and solid, as in silica gel.

gelatin Colourless or yellowish protein obtained from COLLAGEN in animal cartilage and bones. It is used in photographic film emulsions, capsules for medicines, as a culture medium for bacteria, and in foodstuffs such as jellies.

Geldof, Bob (Robert Frederick Xenon) (1954–) Irish rock musician. He was the lead singer (1975–86) with the Boomtown Rats. In 1984, Geldof organized the pop charity "Band Aid", which raised £8 million for famine-relief in Africa. The 1985 "Live Aid" concerts raised more than £48 million. Geldof received an honorary knighthood in 1986.

Gell-Mann, Murray (1929–) US physicist. In 1954, he introduced the concept of 'strangeness' to account for the relative longevity of HADRONS. In 1962, Gell-Mann predicted the existence of a new particle (**omega-minus**). In 1964, he coined the term 'QUARK' to describe the basic constituent of the BARYON and MESON. Gell-Mann received the 1969 Nobel Prize in physics for his work on ELEMENTARY PARTICLES.

gem Any of about 100 minerals valued for their beauty, rarity and durability. Transparent stones, such as DIAMOND, RUBY, EMERALD and SAPPHIRE, are the most highly valued.

Gemini (the Twins) Northern constellation situated on the ecliptic between Taurus and Cancer; the third sign of the zodiac. The brightest star is Beta Geminorum (Pollux).

gemma In botany and zoology, a bud that will give rise to a new individual. The term also refers to a multicellular reproductive structure found in algae, liver worts and mosses.

gender In linguistics, any of several categories into which nouns and pronouns can be divided for grammatical purposes. In some languages, adjectives or verbs may take different forms to agree with the different genders. A three-gender system, with categories labelled masculine, feminine and neuter, exists in such languages as German, Latin and Russian, while a two-gender system, with masculine and feminine, operates in such languages as French and Welsh.

gene Unit by which hereditary characteristics pass from one generation to another in plants and animals. A gene is a length of DNA that codes for a particular protein or peptide. Genes are found along the CHROMOSOMES. In most cell nuclei, genes occur in pairs, one located on each of a chromosome pair. Where different forms of a gene (ALLELES) exist in a population, some forms may be recessive to others and will not be expressed unless present on both members of a chromosome pair. The arrangement of information in a gene is called its GENETIC CODE. The manipulation of genetic material through GENETIC ENGINEERING is a controversial subject.

General Agreement on Tariffs and Trade (GATT) United Nations agency of international trade, subsumed into the new WORLD TRADE ORGANIZATION in 1995. Founded in 1948, GATT was designed to prevent 'tariff wars' (the retaliatory escalation of tariffs) and to work towards the reduction of tariff levels. Most non-communist states were party to GATT.

General Strike (May 4–12, 1926) Nationwide strike in Britain involving *c*.3 million members of the Trades Union Congress (TUC). It was called in support of the National Union of Mineworkers (NUM), the members of which had been locked out of the mines after refusing to accept a reduction in pay and an increase in working hours. Stanley BALDWIN's government employed special constables and volunteers to run essential services and issued an anti-strike propaganda journal, *The British Gazette*. The TUC called off the strike and the Trade Union Act (1927) restricted trade union rights.

generator Device for producing electrical energy. The most common is a machine that converts the mechanical energy of a TURBINE or INTERNAL COMBUSTION ENGINE into ELECTRICITY by employing ELECTROMAGNETIC INDUCTION. There are two types of generators: alternating current (an alternator, such as found in power stations) and direct current (a dynamo). Each has an armature (or ring) that rotates within a magnetic field creating an induced ELECTRIC CURRENT.

gene replacement therapy (GRT) Medical treatment involving the replacement or alteration of faulty GENES by means of GENETIC ENGINEERING. Although first used on humans in 1990, it remains a largely experimental procedure. A healthy gene is packaged into some kind of vector (usually a suitably doctored virus) so that it can be targeted at the affected cells. Initially, gene therapy was restricted to the treatment of hereditary disorders such as CYSTIC FIBROSIS and SICKLE-CELL DISEASE. Research is being conducted into its suitability as a method for the treatment of certain cancers.

Genesis First book of the OLD TESTAMENT and of the PENTATEUCH or TORAH. It probably achieved its final form in the 5th century BC but parts may be much older. It relates the creation of the universe, from ADAM and EVE to ABRAHAM, and from Abraham to JOSEPH, and the descent into Egypt.

genet Cat-like carnivore of the CIVET family, native to W Europe and S and E Africa. Solitary and nocturnal, genets have slender bodies, short legs, grey to brown spotted fur and banded tails. Length: body – to 58cm (22in), tail – to 53cm (21in); weight: to 2kg (4.4lb). Family Viverridae; genus *Genetta*.

Genet, Jean (1910–86) French dramatist and novelist. His experiences as a homosexual are recounted in *Our Lady of the Flowers* (1944), *Miracle of the Rose* (1946), and *The Robber's Journal* (1949). A leading exponent of the Theatre of the ABSURD, Genet used violent eroticism and bizarre illusion in plays such as *The Maids* (1947) and *The Balcony* (1957).

genetically modified food (GM) Food made from crops that have been bred using GENETIC ENGINEERING. The genetic makeup of crops is altered for such characteristics as resistance to insects and disease, resistance to herbicides, or increased protein content. Opponents of GM food question whether such crops may carry risks to health and may spread to the wild. The first approved GM food, a tomato developed for a longer shelf life, was sold in the USA in 1993.

genetic code Arrangement of information stored in GENES. It is the ultimate basis of HEREDITY and forms a blueprint for the entire organism. The genetic code is based on the genes that are present, which, in molecular terms, depends on the arrangement of nucleotides in the long molecules of DNA in the cell CHROMOSOMES. Each group of three nucleotides specifies, or codes, for an amino acid, or for an action such as start or stop. By specifying which PROTEINS to make and in what quantities, the genetic code directly controls production of structural materials. It also codes for ENZYMES, which regulate all the chemical reactions in the cell, thus indirectly coding for the production of other cell materials as well. *See also* GENOME

genetic engineering Construction of a DNA molecule containing a desired GENE. The gene is then introduced into a bacterial, fungal, plant or mammalian cell, so that this cell produces the desired protein. It has been used to produce substances such as human growth hormone, insulin and enzymes for biological washing powder. There are concerns about the ethics of genetic engineering both in human medicine and FOOD TECHNOLOGY. Many believe that GENETICALLY MODIFIED FOOD is dangerous, despite government assurances concerning its safety. *See also* BIOTECHNOLOGY; CLONE

genetic fingerprinting Forensic technique pioneered by Alec Jeffreys, using genetic material, specifically the DNA within sample body cells, to identify individuals. It is used in paternity suits to detect the true father of a child, and sometimes in rape cases. The technique was first used in a court of law in the late 1980s. *See illustration*, page 280

genetics Study of HEREDITY. Geneticists study how the characteristics of an organism depend on its GENES; how these characteristics pass down to the next generation, and how changes may occur through MUTATION. A person's behaviour, learning ability, and physiology may be explained partly by genetics, although the environment has a considerable influence too. Austrian naturalist Gregor MENDEL established the basic laws of inheritance. The discovery (1953) of DNA by English biophysicist Francis CRICK, US geneticist James WATSON and British physicist Maurice Wilkins revealed the molecular structure of heredity. *See also* GENETIC CODE; GENETIC ENGINEERING

Geneva City at the S end of Lake Geneva, SW Switzerland. A Roman town, it was taken by the Franks in the 6th century and passed to the HOLY ROMAN EMPIRE in the 12th century. During the REFORMATION, it became the centre of PROTESTANTISM under John CALVIN. It joined the Swiss Confederation in 1814 and was the scene of the GENEVA CONVENTION in 1864. It was the seat of the LEAGUE OF NATIONS (1919–46), and is the headquarters of the Red Cross and the World Health Organization. Industries: banking, watch-making and jewellery, precision instruments, tourism, enamelware. Pop. (2000) 175,000.

Geneva, Lake (Fr. Lac Léman, Ger. Genfersee) Lake in SW Switzerland and E France. Crescent-shaped, it lies between the ALPS and the JURA MOUNTAINS. Its S shore forms part of the French-Swiss border. It is drained to the W by the River Rhône. Length: 72km (45mi). Width: up to 14km (9mi). Area: 580sq km (224sq mi).

Geneva Conventions Series of agreements, beginning in 1864, on the treatment of wounded soldiers and prisoners during war, and on the neutrality of the medical services.

Genghis Khan (*c.*1162–1227) Conqueror and founder of the MONGOL Empire, b. Temüjin. In 1206, he united Mongolia and was proclaimed Genghis Khan ('Universal Ruler'). Organizing his cavalry into a highly mobile and disciplined squadron (*ordus*, hence 'hordes'), Genghis Khan demonstrated his military genius by capturing Beijing (1215) and subjugating most of N China. He went on to create one of the largest empires ever known, by annexing Afghanistan, Iran, Uzbekistan, and invading Russia as far as Moscow. On his death, the empire divided among his sons.

Genoa (Genova) Seaport on the Gulf of Genoa, NW Italy; capital of Liguria region. It has a university (1471) and an Academy of Fine Arts (1751). Industries: oil refining, motor vehicles, textiles, chemicals, paper. Pop. (2000) 803,000.

genocide Systematic and deliberate destruction of a racial, religious or ethnic group in times of war or peace. The HOLOCAUST during World War 2 is an example of genocide.

genome Entire complement of genetic material carried within the CHROMOSOMES of a single cell. In effect, a genome carries all the genetic information about an organism in the DNA of the chromosomes. The term has also been applied to the whole range of GENES in a particular species. In 2003, a 13–year international Human Genome Project was completed that sequenced the 3 billion DNA bases in the human GENOME that carries all genetic information about an individual. In the

G

GENE REPLACEMENT THERAPY (GRT)

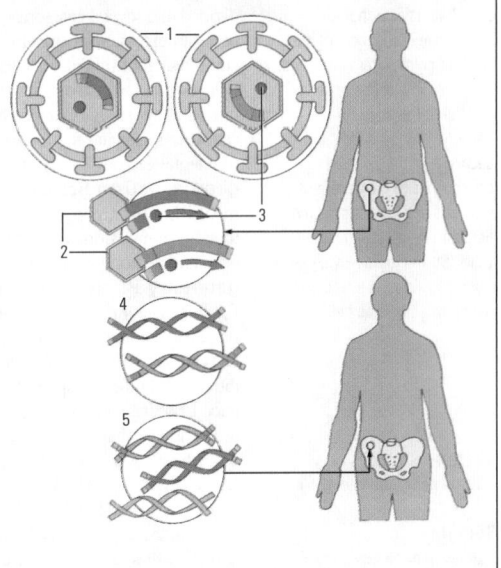

GRT is used to treat severe combined immunodeficiency disease (SCID), where the gene responsible for production of the enzyme adenosine deaminase (ADA) is missing. As ADA is essential for white blood cell production, this renders the body open to infection. Two retroviruses (1) are introduced into the bone marrow. These have the ability to produce RNA from their DNA (2) using a reverse transcriptase enzyme (3). This DNA is then incorporated into the chromosomes (4). When these chromosomes multiply, new viral RNA, viral proteins, and ADA are produced (5). The first two produce more new viruses, while the body uses ADA to produce white blood cells. The process repeats and spreads throughout the bone marrow.

▶ **geological time** The 4,600 million years since the formation of the Earth are divided into four great eras, which are further split into periods and, in the case of the most recent era, epochs. The present era is the Cenozoic ('new life'), extending backwards through 'middle life' and 'ancient life' to the Precambrian. Although traces of ancient life have since been found, it was largely the proliferation of fossils from the beginning of the Palaeozoic era onwards (*c.*570 million years ago), which first allowed precise sub-divisions to be made.

G

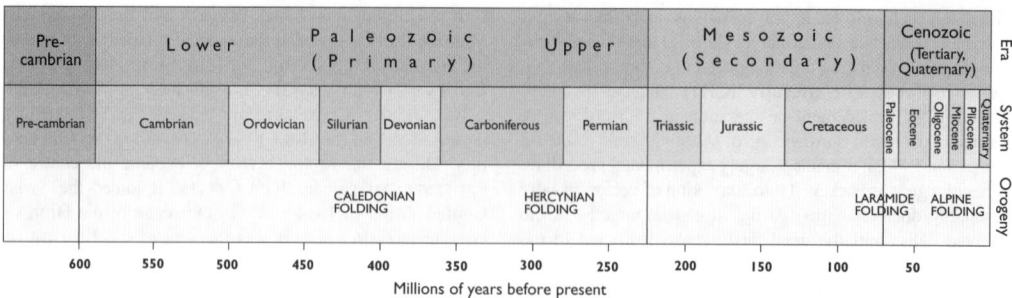

Pre-cambrian	Lower		Paleozoic (Primary)			Upper		Mesozoic (Secondary)			Cenozoic (Tertiary, Quaternary)				Era
Pre-cambrian	Cambrian	Ordovician	Silurian	Devonian	Carboniferous		Permian	Triassic	Jurassic	Cretaceous	Paleocene	Eocene	Oligocene	Miocene / Pliocene / Quaternary	System
			CALEDONIAN FOLDING			HERCYNIAN FOLDING					LARAMIDE FOLDING		ALPINE FOLDING		Orogeny

600	550	500	450	400	350	300	250	200	150	100	50

Millions of years before present

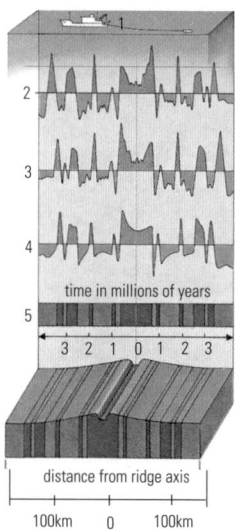

time in millions of years

3 2 1 0 1 2 3

distance from ridge axis

100km   0   100km

▲ **geomagnetism** A magnetic survey from a research ship (1) sailing back and forth over a mid-oceanic ridge gives readings (2, 3, 4) that indicate that the magnetism of the rocks of the seafloor points alternately north and south in a series of bands parallel to the ridge. The pattern of bands is identical at each side of the axis and corresponds to the pattern of reversals in the Earth's magnetic field for the last few million years (5). The rocks moving away from the axis carry a record of the Earth's magnetic field.

future, this should help with the detection and treatment of inherited genetic disorders and diseases. *See also* GENETICS

genotype Genetic makeup of an individual. The particular set of GENES present in each cell of an organism is distinct from the PHENOTYPE, the observable characteristics of the organism.

genre painting Art term used to define paintings that portray scenes of everyday life. It was first used in the late 18th century to define the small paintings of household interiors popularized by 17th-century DUTCH ART.

Gentile da Fabriano (*c.*1370–1427) Italian painter. A leader of the International Gothic style, he greatly influenced Florentine art with frescos and the *Adoration of the Magi* (1423) for the Church of Santa Trinita, Florence.

genus Part of the TAXONOMY of living organisms, ranking below family and above species.

geochemistry Study of the chemical composition of Earth. It is concerned with the abundance, distribution and migration of the elements in Earth's atmosphere, mantle, crust and core.

geodesic dome Architectural structure made up of polygonal (often triangular) facets. It combines optimal structural strength with an efficient use of materials. Geodesic domes were originated (1947) by R. Buckminster FULLER.

Geoffrey of Monmouth (1100–54) Welsh priest and chronicler. He is best known for his *History of the Kings of Britain* (*c.*1136), which combined historical accounts with folk tales. The book was the chief source for the legend of King ARTHUR, and was Shakespeare's source for *King Lear* and *Cymbeline*.

geography Science studying the physical nature of the Earth and people's relationship to it. It includes land masses and features, seas, resources, climate and population.

geological time Time scale of the history of Earth. Until recently, only methods of relative dating were possible, by studying the correlation of rock formations and fossils. The largest divisions of geologic time are called eras, each of which is broken down into periods, which, in turn, are sub-divided into series or epochs.

geology Study of the materials of the Earth, their origin, arrangement, classification, change and history. Geology is divided into several categories, the major ones being MINERALOGY (arrangement of minerals), PETROLOGY (rocks and their combination of minerals), STRATIGRAPHY (succession of rocks in layers), PALAEONTOLOGY (study of fossilized remains), geomorphology (study of landforms), structural geology (classification of rocks and the forces that produced them), and environmental geology (study of use of the environment).

geomagnetism Branch of GEOPHYSICS that studies Earth's magnetic field. Geomagnetism is thought to be caused by the metallic composition of Earth's core. The gradual movements of magnetic north result from currents within the MANTLE.

geometry Branch of mathematics concerned with shapes. Euclidean geometry deals with simple plane and solid figures. **Analytic** geometry (co-ordinate geometry), introduced by DESCARTES (1637), applies algebra to geometry and allows the study of more complex curves. **Projective** geometry, introduced by Jean-Victor Poncelet (1822), concerns itself with projection of shapes and with properties that are independent of such changes. More abstraction occurred in the early 19th century with formulations of non-Euclidean geometry by Janos Bolyai and N.I. Lobachevsky, and differential geometry, based on the application of calculus. *See also* TOPOLOGY

geophysics Study of the characteristic physical properties of the Earth as a whole system. It uses parts of CHEM-ISTRY, GEOLOGY, ASTRONOMY, SEISMOLOGY, METEOROLOGY, and many other disciplines. From the study of seismic waves, geophysicists deduced the Earth's interior structure.

George, Saint (active 3rd-4th century AD) Christian martyr who became patron saint of England in the late Middle Ages. Many stories grew up about him, including the 12th-century tale of his killing a dragon to save a maiden. His feast day is April 23.

George I (1660–1727) King of Great Britain and Ireland (1714–27), and Elector of Hanover (1698–1727). A Protestant, he succeeded Queen ANNE as the first monarch of the House of HANOVER. He favoured the WHIGS over the Tories, suspecting the latter of JACOBITE sympathies. As King of England, he preferred his native Hanover and spoke little English. As a result, power passed increasingly to Parliament and ministers such as Sir Robert WALPOLE.

George I (1845–1913) King of the Hellenes (1863–1913). Made king by Great Britain, France and Russia, with the approval of the Greek National Assembly, he backed the constitution of 1864 giving power to an elected Parliament. He gained territory through the Balkan Wars. He was assassinated in 1913 and was succeeded by his son Constantine I.

George II (1683–1760) King of Great Britain and Ireland and Elector of Hanover (1727–1760), son of GEORGE I. Like his father, he was more German than English. Sir Robert WALPOLE dominated politics early in the reign. George survived a JACOBITE revolt (1745) and was the last British king to lead his army in battle, at Dettingen (1746). George witnessed great victories overseas in the SEVEN YEARS' WAR.

George III (1738–1820) King of Great Britain and Ireland (1760–1820), and King of Hanover (1760–1820), grandson of GEORGE II. He was the first thoroughly English monarch of his line. George shared the blame with Lord NORTH for the loss of the American colonies in the AMERICAN REVOLUTION (1775–83), but was quick to appreciate the talents of William PITT (THE YOUNGER). His reign witnessed the beginnings of the INDUSTRIAL REVOLUTION. In 1765, he suffered his first attack of apparent insanity, now known to be symptoms of PORPHYRIA. The attacks grew worse and, in 1811, his son, the future GEORGE IV, became Prince Regent.

George IV (1762–1830) King of Great Britain and Ireland (1820–30). He served as Regent for his father, GEORGE III, from 1811. Self-indulgent and extravagant, government bored him but he was a strong patron of the arts. His marriage to Caroline of Brunswick (1795) was a source of scandal and he contracted a legally invalid marriage with Mrs Fitzherbert in 1785.

George V (1865–1936) King of Great Britain and Northern Ireland and Emperor of India (1910–36), second son of EDWARD VII. He married Princess Mary of Teck in 1893. In 1917, George changed the name of the royal house from the German SAXE-COBURG-GOTHA to Windsor. Honourable and devoted to duty, he maintained the popularity of the monarchy.

George VI (1895–1952) King of Great Britain and Northern Ireland (1936–52) and Emperor of India (1936–47), son of GEORGE V. He became king when his brother, EDWARD VIII, abdicated. In 1923, he married Lady ELIZABETH Bowes-Lyon. In an inspirational display of solidarity, he refused to move his family away from London during the BLITZ. In 1949, he became head of the newly formed COMMONWEALTH.

Georgetown Capital and largest city of Guyana, at the mouth of the River Demerara. Founded in 1781 by the British, it was the capital of the united colonies of Essequibo and Demerara and was known as Stabroek during the brief Dutch occupation from 1784. It was renamed Georgetown in 1812. Industries: shipbuilding, brewing. Pop. (2002 est.) 225,800.

Georgetown *See* PENANG

Georgia Republic in central Europe. *See* country feature

Georgia State in SE USA, on the Atlantic Ocean, N of Florida; the capital is ATLANTA. Other major cities are Columbus, Macon, and Savannah. In the S and E of the state is a broad coastal plain. The central area consists of the Piedmont plateau beyond which, in the N, are the Blue Ridge Mountains and the Appalachian plateau. The area is drained by the Savannah, Ogeechee and Altamaha rivers. First settled in 1732, it was one of the original six states of the Confederacy in the CIVIL WAR. Ravaged by the armies of General Sherman in 1864, Georgia rejoined the Union in 1870. Cotton, once the chief crop, declined in favour of tobacco, peanuts, livestock, and poultry. Textiles are historically a major industry, but chemicals, paper and timber, and the manufacture of ships, aircraft, and truck bodies are increasingly significant. Area: 152,488sq km (58,876sq mi). Pop. (2000) 8,186,453.

Georgian architecture Building styles in Britain and its colonies (1714–1830). The name derives from the Hanoverian kings who reigned during this period (George I-IV). The various Georgian styles include ROCOCO, Greek revival, NEO-CLASSICISM, GOTHIC REVIVAL, and REGENCY STYLE.

geostationary orbit Location of an artificial SATELLITE so that it remains above the same point on a planet's surface because it completes one ORBIT in the same time it takes that planet to rotate once on its axis. Communications and remote-sensing satellites are often placed in geostationary orbits.

geothermal energy Heat contained in the Earth's crust. It is produced by RADIOACTIVITY within the Earth's core and by the movement of tectonic plates. It is released naturally by GEYSERS and VOLCANOES and hot springs, and can be used as a power source for generating electricity. *See also* PLATE TECTONICS

geranium (Pelargonium) Genus of 400 perennial plants. They bear pink, purple or white flowers. Family Geraniaceae.

gerbil (desert rat) Nocturnal rodent native to arid areas of Asia and Africa. It has long hind legs and tail, with fawn, grey, brown or red fur. It is a subterranean herbivore. Gerbils are popular as pets. Family Cricetidae.

Géricault, (Jean Louis André) Théodore (1791–1824) French painter. A forerunner of the Romantic movement, he began by painting battles. His most famous work, *Raft of the Medusa* (1817), depicts the survivors of a shipwreck.

GEORGIA
Statehood :
January 2, 1788
Nickname :
Empire state of the South
State bird :
Brown thrasher
State flower :
Cherokee rose
State tree :
Live oak
State motto :
Wisdom, justice and moderation

G

GEORGIA

Georgia is located on the borders of Europe and Asia, facing the Black Sea. The land is rugged with the CAUCASUS Mountains forming its northern border. The highest mountain in this range, Mount Elbrus (5,642m [18,506ft]), lies over the border in Russia.

Lower ranges run through S Georgia, through which pass the borders with Turkey and Armenia. The Black Sea coastal plains are in the W. In the E a low plateau extends into Azerbaijan. The main river in the E is the River Kura, on which the capital TBILISI stands.

CLIMATE
The Black Sea plains have hot summers and mild winters, when the temperature seldom drops below freezing. Rainfall is heavy, but inland Tbilisi has moderate rainfall, with the heaviest rains in the spring and early summer.

HISTORY
The land of the legendary Golden Fleece, Georgia has a strong national culture and a long literary tradition. From the 6th century BC, the two Black Sea kingdoms of Iberia and Colchis developed in E and W Georgia respectively. In 66 BC the Roman Empire conquered both kingdoms. Christianity was introduced in AD 330 and most Georgians are now members of the Georgian Orthodox Church. The area was ruled successively by Romans, SASSANID Persians, Byzantines, Arabs, and Seljuk Turks before Georgia finally freed itself from foreign rule in the 11th century. The 12th century was Georgia's greatest period of cultural, econom-

ic, and military expansion. Mongol armies invaded in the 13th century and, from the 16th to the 18th centuries, Iran and the Turkish OTTOMAN EMPIRE struggled for control of the area.

In the late 18th century, Georgia sought the protection of Russia and, by the early 19th century, it was part of the Russian Empire. After the Russian Revolution of 1917, Georgia declared itself independent and was recognized by the League of Nations. However, Russian troops invaded in 1921, making Georgia part of the Soviet regime. From 1922, Georgia, Armenia and Azerbaijan were linked, forming the Republic of TRANSCAUCASIA. In 1936 the territories became separate republics within the SOVIET UNION. Renowned for their longevity, the people of Georgia are famous for producing Josef Stalin, who was born in Gori, 65km [40mi] NW of the capital Tbilisi. Stalin ruled the Soviet Union from 1929 until his death in 1953.

POLITICS
In April 1991 Georgia was the first Soviet republic to declare independence. It deferred joining the COMMONWEALTH OF INDEPENDENT STATES (CIS) until 1993.

In 1991 Zviad Gamsakhurdia, a non-Communist who had been democratically elected president of Georgia in 1990, was besieged in Tbilisi's KGB headquarters by rebel forces. They represented widespread opposition to his government's policies, ranging from the economy to the imprisonment of his opponents. In January 1992, following the break-up of the Soviet Union, Gamsakhurdia fled the country and a military council took power.

Georgia contains three regions of minority peoples. In South Ossetia, in N central Georgia, civil war broke out in the early 1990s, when nationalists demanded the right to set up their own governments. ABKHAZIA in the NW proclaimed its sovereignty in 1994, with fierce fighting continuing until the late 1990s. Adjaria (Adzharia), in the SW, gained its autonomy which was recognized in Georgia's constitution in 2000.

AREA 9,700sq km
[26,911sq mi]
POPULATION 4,646,000
CAPITAL (POPULATION)
Tbilisi (1,406,000)
GOVERNMENT Multiparty republic
ETHNIC GROUPS Georgian 70%, Armenian 8%, Russian 6%, Azeri 6%, Ossetiam 3%, Greek 2%, Abkhaz 2%, others
LANGUAGES Georgian (official), Russian
RELIGIONS Georgian Orthodox 65%, Islam 11%, Russian Orthodox 10%, Armenian Apostolic 8%
CURRENCY Lari = 100 tetri

In March 1992, Eduard SHEVARDNADZE, former Soviet Foreign Minister, was named head of state. He was elected, unopposed, later that year. In 2001, Georgia and Abkhazia signed a peace accord and agreed to the safe return of refugees. In 2002, Russian and Georgian troops attacked Chechen rebels in Pankisi Gorge in NE Georgia. In 2004 Mikhail Saakashvili was elected president, but his authority was challenged by separatists in the three minority regions. In 2006 Saakashvili criticized Russian support for the separatists as relations with Russia worsened. In 2007 discontent with Saakashvili's rule and accusations of corruption led to large demonstrations. He declared a state of emergency, and postponed elections until 2008, claiming victory despite opposition allegations of fraud.

ECONOMY
Georgia is a developing country. Agriculture is important. Major products include barley, citrus fruits, grapes for wine-making, maize, tea, tobacco and vegetables. Food processing, and silk- and perfume-making are other important activities. Sheep and cattle are reared.

Barite (barium ore), coal, copper and manganese are mined, and tourism is a major industry on the Black Sea coast. Georgia's mountains have huge potential for generating hydroelectric power, but most of Georgia's electricity is generated in Russia or Ukraine.

The Federal Republic of Germany lies in the heart of Europe. It is the fifth-largest country in Europe. Germany divides into three geographical regions: the N German plain, central highlands, and the s Central Alps.

The rivers ELBE, Weser, and Oder drain the fertile N plain, which includes the industrial centres of HAMBURG, BREMEN, HANOVER, and KIEL. In the E lies the capital, BERLIN, and the former East German cities of LEIPZIG, DRESDEN and MAGDEBURG. NW Germany (especially the RHINE, RUHR and Saar valleys) is the country's industrial heartland. It includes the cities of COLOGNE, ESSEN, DORTMUND, DÜSSELDORF and DUISBURG.

The central highlands include the HARZ MOUNTAINS and the cities of MUNICH, FRANKFURT, STUTTGART, NUREMBERG and AUGSBURG. S Germany rises to the Bavarian ALPS on the border with Switzerland and Germany's highest peak, Zugspitze (2,963m [9,721ft]).

The BLACK FOREST, overlooking the Rhine valley, is a major tourist attraction. The region is drained by the River DANUBE.

CLIMATE

Germany has a temperate climate. The NW is warmed by the North Sea. The Baltic lowlands in the NE are cooler. In the s, the climate becomes more continental.

HISTORY

Around 3,000 years ago, various tribes from N Europe began to settle in what is now Germany, occupying the valleys of the Rhine and the Danube. The Romans called this region Germania after the Germani, the name of one of the tribes. In the 5th century BC, the Germanic tribes attacked the Roman Empire and plundered Rome. The w part of the Roman Empire split up into several kingdoms, the largest of which was the Kingdom of the Franks.

In 486 the MEROVINGIAN king CLOVIS I conquered s and w Germany, THURINGIA and Gaul (now France), introducing Christianity. His son CHARLEMAGNE came to power in 768, established his capital at Aachen, expanded his territory to the Elbe and was crowned Emperor in 800. His empire rapidly fragmented, and the FEUDAL SYSTEM created powerful local duchies. In 918 HENRY I (THE FOWLER) began a century of SAXON rule, and his son OTTO I (THE GREAT) established the Holy Roman Empire (first reich, 962).

In 1152, FREDERICK I founded the HOHENSTAUFEN dynasty. FREDERICK II's conflict with the papacy created civil war. In 1273, Rudolf I founded the HABSBURG dynasty. City-states formed alliances, such as the HANSEATIC LEAGUE. CHARLES V's reign (1519–58) brought religious and civil unrest, such as the PEASANTS' WAR. In 1517, a German monk, Martin LUTHER, began to criticize many of the practices and teachings of the Roman Catholic Church. A Protestant movement called the REFORMATION soon attracted much support, and by the early 17th century Germany was deeply divided by political and religious rivalries. Catholic and Protestant conflict culminated in the devastating THIRTY YEARS' WAR (1618–48) which ravaged much of the country, with Germany losing territory to France and Sweden and being split into hundreds of states and free cities. It took almost 200 years for Germany to recover

In the 17th century, the Hohenzollern family began to assume importance in E Germany, gradually extending their power and building a professional civil service and army. The reign (1740–86) of FREDERICK II (THE GREAT) saw the emergence of PRUSSIA. Prussia stayed out of the NAPOLEONIC WARS until 1806, but, following defeats by Napoleon, lost its territories west of the Elbe. Prussia did help defeat Napoleon's armies at the battles of Leipzig (1813) and Waterloo (1815) and following the Napoleonic wars gained the Rhineland, Westphalia and much of Saxony at the Congress of VIENNA.

The 19th century brought growing nationalism, fuelled by German ROMANTICISM. The REVOLUTIONS OF 1848 led the Prussian HOHENZOLLERN king, Wilhelm (WILLIAM I), to appoint Otto von BISMARCK as chancellor. Bismarck set about strengthening Prussian power through three short wars. One conflict led to the acquisition of Schleswig-Holstein from Denmark, another to the annexation of territory from Austria in the AUSTRO-PRUSSIAN WAR. The third was the FRANCO-PRUSSIAN WAR (1870–1), through which Prussia acquired Alsace and part of Lorraine. In 1871, Wilhelm I was crowned the first Kaiser of the new German Empire (or second reich) and Bismarck became head of government. Bismarck sought to consolidate German power and avoid conflict with Austria-Hungary and Russia, but was forced to resign in 1890 when Wilhelm II (WILLIAM II) wanted to establish his own authority and extend Germany's influence in the world. Wilhelm's ambitions led Britain and France to establish the Entente Cordiale in 1904, with Britain and Russia signing a similar agreement in 1907. This left Europe divided, with Germany, Austria-Hungary and Italy forming the Triple Alliance.

Prince von BÜLOW's imperial ambitions were a cause of WORLD WAR I (1914–18). The

G

GERMANY

Treaty of VERSAILLES (1919) placed a heavy price on German defeat. Wilhelm II was forced to abdicate, overseas colonies were lost to the victors and the WEIMAR REPUBLIC (1919–33) was created. Germany's humiliation under the terms of the Versailles Treaty caused much resentment, made worse by the economic collapse of 1922–23. Mass unemployment, crippling inflation, war reparations and worldwide economic depression created the conditions for FASCISM. Support grew for the Nazi Party and its leader Adolf HITLER, who became chancellor in 1933 and declared a THIRD REICH.

NATIONAL SOCIALISM pervaded all areas of society, the GESTAPO crushed dissent and opposition parties and elections were banned. Hitler, as *Führer*, became the father of the nation through GOEBBELS' propagandizing. CONCENTRATION CAMPS were set up and armaments stockpiled. Hitler remilitarized the RHINELAND (1936), aided Franco in the SPANISH CIVIL WAR (1936–39), and annexed Austria (1938). The MUNICH AGREEMENT (1938) marked the failure of appeasement; Germany invaded Czechoslovakia (March 1939) and Poland (September 1939), precipitating WORLD WAR 2. Initial success was halted by failure in the Battle of BRITAIN, and Hitler's disastrous Soviet offensive (June 1941). The blanket bombing of German cities devastated German industry and morale. Faced with defeat, Hitler committed suicide (April 1945). Germany surrendered (May 8, 1945), and leading Nazis faced the NUREMBERG TRIALS.

The country was left in ruins. Germany was obliged to transfer the area E of the Oder and Neisse rivers to Poland and the Soviet Union. German-speaking inhabitants were expelled and the remainder of Germany was occupied by the four victorious Allied powers, each controlling a military zone. COLD WAR tension increased. Following the BERLIN AIRLIFT (1948–49), American, British and French zones joined to make the Federal Republic of Germany (West Germany); the Soviet zone formed the German Democratic Republic (East Germany). Berlin was divided by the BERLIN WALL. E Berlin became capital of East Germany; BONN de facto capital of West Germany.

POLITICS

The post-war partition of Germany, together with its geographical position, made it a central focus of the Cold War. West Germany had become a showpiece of the West through its phenomenal recovery and sustained growth, the so-called 'economic miracle'. It played a major part, together with France, in the revival of Western Europe through the development of the European Community (now the EUROPEAN UNION). Although East Germany had achieved the highest standard of living in the Soviet bloc, it fell short of Western Europe. East Germany dissolved itself in 1990, at the start of the fall of Communism, and was reunited with the rest of Germany in October of that year.

Following reunification, the new country adopted the name the Federal Republic of Germany. Massive investment was needed to rebuild the East's industrial base and transport system, leading to an increased tax burden on the West. In addition, the new nation found itself funnelling aid into Eastern Europe. Germany led the EU in recognizing the independence of Slovenia, Croatia and the former Soviet republics. The transition to a free market economy in the East caused rapid de-industrialization, leading to large scale unemployment and its attendant social problems. The creation of a unified state was far more complicated, expensive and lengthy an undertaking than had been envisaged when the Berlin Wall came down.

In 1998 the centre-right government of Helmut KOHL, who had presided over reunification, was defeated by the left-of-centre Social Democratic Party (SPD), led by Gerhard SCHRÖDER. Schröder led an SPD-GREEN PARTY coalition which aimed to tackle Germany's high unemployment and a sluggish economy. Following the attacks on the United States on 11 September 2001, Schröder announced Germany's support for the campaign against terrorism, although Germany opposed the invasion of Iraq in 2003. In 2005, Schröder was narrowly defeated in elections. A broad left-right coalition was set up, and the conservative Angela MERKEL became Germany's first female Chancellor.

AREA 357,022sq km [137, 846sq mi]
POPULATION 82,400,000
CAPITAL (POPULATION)
Berlin (3,387,000)
GOVERNMENT Federal multiparty republic
EETHNIC GROUPS
German 92%, Turkish 3%, Serbo-Croatian, Italian, Greek, Polish, Spanish
LANGUAGES German (official)
RELIGIONS Protestant (mainly Lutheran) 34%, Roman Catholic 34%, Islam 4%, others
CURRENCY Euro = 100 cents

ECONOMY

Despite the problems associated with reunification, Germany has one of the world's largest economies and is one of the largest exporters of manufactured goods. The foundation of the 'economic miracle' that led to Germany's astonishing post-war recovery was manufacturing. Germany's industrial strength was based on its coal reserves, though oil-burning and nuclear generating plants have become increasingly important since the 1970s. Lower Saxony has oilfields, while southern Germany has some hydroelectricity. In the early 2000s the government resolved to phase out nuclear power by 2020, but this plan was questioned in 2007 after oil supplies from Russia were disrupted.

The leading industrial region is the Ruhr, which produces iron and steel, chemicals, and textiles. Germany is a major producer of cars, while other manufactures include electronic equipment, fertilizers, processed food, plastics, scientific instruments, ships, tools, and wood and pulp products. Mineral resources include potash, rock salt, and smaller quantities of copper, lead, tin, uranium and zinc.

Agriculture employs 2.4% of the workforce, but is extremely productive, and the country produces a majority of its own food. Barley, fruits, grapes, oats, potatoes, rye, sugar beet, vegetables and wheat are the major crops. Beef and dairy cattle are raised, together with pigs, poultry and sheep.

---

germ Popular term for any infectious agent. Germs can be bacteria, fungi or viruses. In biology, it denotes a rudimentary stage in plant growth.

German Indo-European language spoken by *c.*120 million people in Germany, Austria, and Switzerland, and by German communities in many other countries. **High** German (*Hochdeutsch*), of S Germany and Austria, is now the standard dialect. **Low** German (*Plattdeutsch*) was spoken widely in the N, but is now declining.

German architecture Architecture of Germany including, in its early days, that of Austria. The earliest surviving buildings date from CHARLEMAGNE. They are in the ROMANESQUE style, at its best in Worms Cathedral (built *c.*1180). Romanesque was superseded by GOTHIC, seen in ecclesiastical architecture and provincial buildings, such as the *Rathaus* (Ger. 'town hall') typical of NE German towns. There is little RENAISSANCE architecture in Germany, an exception being the rebuilt façade of the *Rathaus* in Bremen. The BAROQUE period extended into the ROCOCO, examples including the elaborate Church of the *Vierzehnheiligen* ('Fourteen Saints', 1772) by Balthasar Neuman, and master-

pieces by Fischer von Erlach and Matthaeus Pöppelmann. In the late 1700s, NEO-CLASSICISM inspired buildings in Berlin and Munich by Friedrich Schinkel, Leo von Klenze and others. New materials such as cast iron were exploited, as in Vienna's *Dianabad* by Karl Etzel (1843). Walter GROPIUS and the BAUHAUS dominated the beginning of the 20th century. In the 1930s, MIES VAN DER ROHE exemplified the INTERNATIONAL STYLE, which was replaced by the re-adoption of neo-classicism under HITLER, with 'official' Nazi architect Albert SPEER. After World War 2, most new buildings adopted principles of EXPRESSIONISM or MODERNISM.

German art National tradition dating back to the illuminated manuscripts of the 9th and 10th centuries. By the end of the Middle Ages, a flourishing tradition in wood-carving had grown up in the S with the work of Veit Stoss and Tilman Riemenschneider. In the 16th century, Germany was at the forefront of the N Renaissance, led by Albrecht DÜRER and Hans HOLBEIN the Younger. This was a golden age for German painting and, although Caspar FRIEDRICH made an important contribution to ROMANTICISM, it was only in the 20th century that EXPRESSIONISM and BAUHAUS achieved comparable status.

INTERNET

Géricault, (Jean Louis André) Théodore
▸ www.louvre.fr (page 349)

Germany
▸ eng.bundesregierung.de
▸ www.germany-tourism.de

Gettysburg, Battle of
(page 352)
▸ www.gettysburg.com

Gettysburg Address (page 352)
▸ www.loc.gov/exhibits/gadd

G

▲ **Getty** As well as being one of the world's richest men, Jean Paul Getty was considered an important patron of the arts.

A

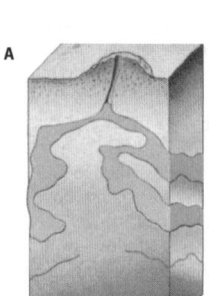

B

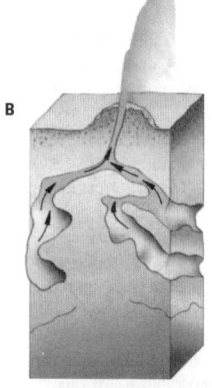

C

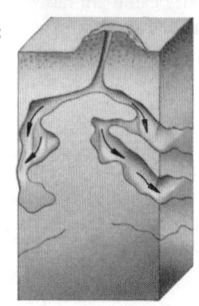

▲ **geyser** A plume of hot water and steam, a geyser is the result of the boiling of water at depth by volcanic heat in a series of interconnecting chambers (A). The expansion of steam produced drives the water and steam above it out at the surface (B), and this is followed by a period of refilling and heating making it a periodic phenomenon (C).

Germanic languages Group of languages, a sub-division of the INDO-EUROPEAN family. One branch (West Germanic) includes English, German, Yiddish, Dutch, Flemish, Frisian, and Afrikaans; another (North Germanic) includes Swedish, Danish, Norwegian, Icelandic, and Faroese.

germanium (symbol Ge) Grey-white metalloid element of group IV of the PERIODIC TABLE, discovered in 1886 by German chemist Clements Winkler. A by-product of zinc ores or the combustion of certain coals, it is important in semiconductor devices. In compounds, it is used in transistors, alloys, and as catalysts. Properties: at.no. 32; r.a.m. 72.59; r.d. 5.35; m.p. 937°C (1,719 °F); b.p. 2,830°C (5,126°F); most common isotope Ge^{74} (36.54%).

German literature German literature has a long tradition, dating back to the Middle High German period and the 13th-century courtly poems of WOLFRAM VON ESCHENBACH and Gottfried von Strassburg, as well as the *Minnesang* of WALTHER VON DER VOGELWEIDE and the heroic epic, the *Nibelungenlied*. During the next centuries, the classical conventions of FRENCH LITERATURE dominated German writing. In the late 18th century, a truly national literary movement, STURM UND DRANG, emerged. Two of Germany's greatest writers, the Weimar classicists GOETHE and SCHILLER were early proponents of the movement. CLASSICISM found its major literary exponent in the poet Friedrich Hölderlin. ROMANTICISM flourished in the late 18th and early 19th centuries, when writers such as SCHLEGEL, NOVALIS, E.T.A. HOFFMANN, Kleist, and the GRIMM BROTHERS encouraged a romanticization of German history and folklore. Heine's work marks the beginnings of German REALISM. At the start of the 20th century, RILKE's lyrical poetry was in part a reaction against the prevailing realist tone. Among anti-naturalist novelists were major figures like Thomas MANN, Erich REMARQUE, and Hermann HESSE. German EXPRESSIONISM was a combination of formal experimentation and political content. Major figures in the movement included Franz KAFKA and Bertolt BRECHT. During the Third Reich, many writers were branded as 'undesirable'. Post-war German writers, such as Günter GRASS and Heinrich Böll, examined aspects of German complicity during the Nazi period.

German measles (rubella) Viral disease usually contracted in childhood. Symptoms include a sore throat, slight fever and pinkish rash. Women developing rubella during the first three months of pregnancy risk damage to the fetus. Immunization is recommended for those who have not had the disease.

German shepherd (Alsatian) Working dog first bred in Germany in *c.*1900. It has woolly underhair and is black, grey, or black and tan. Height: *c.*64cm (25in) at the shoulder; weight: 27–38kg (60–85lb).

Germany Republic in Europe. *See* country feature, p.350–51

germination Growth of the EMBRYO in the SEED of a new plant. To germinate, a seed or spore needs favourable conditions of temperature, light, moisture and oxygen.

Geronimo (1829–1908) Chief of the Chiricahua Apaches. He led his tribe against white settlers in Arizona for more than ten years. In 1886, he surrendered his tribe to General Miles, and they were taken to Fort Sill, Oklahoma. He became a farmer and national celebrity.

gerrymander Practice of redrawing electoral boundaries to favour a particular party. It is named after Elbridge Gerry, Governor of Massachusetts (1810–12), whose party employed the practice. One of his redefined districts was said to resemble a salamander, hence gerrymander.

Gershwin, George (1898–1937) US popular composer, b. Jacob Gershovitz. His brother **Ira** Gershwin (1896–1983) mostly wrote the lyrics. George composed musicals, such as *Lady Be Good* (1924), a jazz opera *Porgy and Bess* (1935), and some orchestral works, such as *Rhapsody in Blue* (1924).

gestalt psychology School of psychology characterized by the expression 'the whole (*gestalt*) is greater than the sum of its parts'. It opposed the dominant theories of BEHAVIOURISM. It was founded (*c.*1912) in Germany by Max Wertheimer, Wilhelm WUNDT, Wolfgang KÖHLER, and Kurt KOFFKA.

Gestapo (Geheime Staatspolizei) State secret-police of Nazi Germany. Founded in 1933 by GOERING, it became a

powerful, national organization under HIMMLER from 1934, as an arm of the SS. With up to 50,000 members by 1945, the Gestapo and SS ran the CONCENTRATION CAMPS.

gestation (PREGNANCY) Period during which a developing EMBRYO is carried in the UTERUS. Gestation periods are specific to each mammalian species; it is about 266 days, or nine months, for humans, 330 days for horses, 284 days for cows, and 63 days for domestic cats.

Getty, Jean Paul (1892–1976) US businessman and art collector. In 1930, he became president of his father's oil business. After 1959 he lived in England. He was one of the world's richest men, with a fortune estimated at more than $1,000 million. He founded the J. Paul Getty Museum in Malibu, California.

Gettysburg, Battle of (1–3 July, 1863) Decisive campaign of the American CIVIL WAR, fought over three days near Gettysburg, Pennsylvania. The Union army of George Gordon Meade checked the invasion of Pennsylvania by the Confederate forces of Robert E. LEE. The battle was a turning point. The heavy casualties (*c.*20,000 each side) prompted Abraham Lincoln's GETTYSBURG ADDRESS.

Gettysburg Address (November 19, 1863) Speech by US President Abraham LINCOLN at the dedication of the national cemetery on the battlefield of GETTYSBURG. It ended by describing democracy as 'government of the people, by the people, and for the people'.

Getz, Stan (1927–91) US jazz saxophonist. Influenced by Lester YOUNG, he played with Woody Herman in the 1940s, then formed his own groups and developed his soft, breathy sound. Albums include *At Storyville* (1951) and *Focus* (1965).

geyser Hot spring that erupts intermittently, throwing up jets of superheated water and steam to a height of *c.*60m (200ft), followed by a shaft of steam with a thunderous roar. Geysers occur in Iceland, New Zealand and the USA.

Ghana Republic in W Africa. *See* country feature

Ghats Two mountain systems in India running parallel to the coast on both sides of the Deccan Plateau. The **Western** Ghats extend from the Tapti River to Cape Comorin. The **Eastern** Ghats extend from the Mahanadi River to the Nilgiri Hills. Height: (W) 900–1,500m (2,950–4,920ft); (E) 600m (1,970ft). Length: (W) 1,600km (1,000mi); (E) 1,400km (875mi).

Ghazali, al- (1058–1111) Muslim scholar and mystic. He wrote on law, philosophy, theology and mysticism. His greatest work, *The Revival of the Religious Sciences*, made SUFISM an acceptable part of orthodox ISLAM.

Ghent (Gent, Gand) City in NW central Belgium. Ghent came under Austrian control from 1714 and was captured by the French in 1792, becoming part of independent Belgium in 1830. Textile factories revived its prosperity in the 19th century, and it was occupied by Germany in both World Wars. Notable buildings include the 12th-century Cathedral of St Bavon and the 16th-century town hall. Industries: plastics, chemicals, steel, electrical engineering, motor vehicles. Pop. (2000) 224,180.

Ghent, Treaty of (1814) Agreement ending the WAR OF 1812 between Britain and the USA. It appointed a commission to settle the dispute about the USA-Canada boundary.

Ghibelline Political faction in 13th-century Italy that supported the HOHENSTAUFEN dynasty of the HOLY ROMAN EMPIRE and opposed the pro-papal GUELPHS. During the struggles between FREDERICK II and the Popes in the mid-13th century, Ghibellines came to designate those on the Imperial side. Defeated by the Guelphs in 1268, the family went into decline.

Ghiberti, Lorenzo (1378–1455) Italian sculptor, goldsmith, architect, painter, and writer; a major transitional figure between the late GOTHIC and RENAISSANCE worlds. He made two pairs of bronze doors for the Baptistery in Florence. One pair, the 'Doors of Paradise', is considered his masterpiece.

Ghirlandaio, Domenico (1449–94) Florentine painter, best known for his frescos. He worked on the Sistine Chapel with BOTTICELLI and others, his major contribution being *Christ Calling the First Apostles* (1482).

Ghose, Aurobindo (1872–1950) (Sri Aurobindo) Indian mystic philosopher and nationalist leader. In 1908, he was imprisoned for agitating against British rule in Bengal. After his release, Ghose devoted himself to Hindu philosophy. His works include *The Synthesis of Yoga* (1948).

Giacometti, Alberto (1901–66) Swiss sculptor and painter, influenced by SURREALISM. During the 1940s and 1950s, he produced his most characteristic works: emaciated, dream-like figures built of plaster on a wire base.

Giant's Causeway Promontory on the N coast of Northern Ireland in County Antrim. It extends 5km (3mi) along the coast and consists of thousands of basalt columns of varying height.

gibberellin Any of a group of plant HORMONES that stimulate cell division, stem elongation and response to light and temperature. They have been used to increase crop yields.

gibbon Ape, native to forests in SE Asia. It has a shaggy brown, black or silvery coat and is very agile. It has long, powerful arms for swinging from branch to branch. Height: 41–66cm (16–26in). Family Pongidae, genus *Hyloblates*.

Gibbon, Edward (1737–94) English historian. He conceived of his great work, *The Decline and Fall of the Roman Empire* (1776–88), while among the ruins of ancient Rome.

Gibbons, Grinling (1648–1721) British wood carver, b. Holland. His decorative carvings of fruit, flowers, and cherubs' heads adorn the choir stalls of St Paul's Cathedral, London. His patrons included Charles II and George I.

Gibbons, Orlando (1583–1625) English composer. He wrote viol fantasies and madrigals, such as *The Silver Swanne*. A master of POLYPHONY, he composed mostly church music.

Gibbs, James (1682–1754) Scottish architect who was inspired by Sir Christopher WREN. Gibbs was an individualist, fitting neither into the BAROQUE style, which preceded

him, nor the later Palladian. His best-known work is the church of St Martin in the Fields, London (1722–26).

Gibbs, Josiah Willard (1839–1903) US theoretical physicist and chemist. His application of thermodynamics to physical processes led to statistical mechanics. He devised the phase rule and developed vector analysis.

Gibraltar British crown colony, a rocky peninsula on the s coast of Spain. The MUSLIM conquest of Spain began in 711, and Gibraltar remained Moorish property until 1462. In 1704, an Anglo-Dutch fleet captured the Rock, and Spain ceded it to Britain in the Treaty of UTRECHT (1713). A Spanish siege (1769–83) caused great destruction. In 1830 Gibraltar became a British Crown Colony. In a 1967 referendum, the islanders rejected Spanish sovereignty, and in 1969 Gibraltar gained self-government. In 2002, Gibraltarians resisted a proposal for joint sovereignty. Industries: tourism, petroleum re-exportation. Area: 6.5sq km (2.5sq mi). Pop. (2002 est.) 29,300.

Gibson, Mel (1956–) Australian film actor and director, b. USA. International recognition followed his roles in *Mad Max* (1979) and *Gallipoli* (1981) and *Hamlet* (1990). In 1995, he won Oscars for best director and best picture for *Braveheart*.

Gide, André Paul Guillaume (1869–1951) French novelist, playwright and critic. His novels and *Journals* (1885–1950) show the struggle between his puritan and pagan elements. Mature works, such as *Les Faux-monnayeurs* (1926), dramatize a search for spiritual truth. He received the 1947 Nobel Prize in literature.

G

GHANA

The Republic of Ghana faces the Gulf of Guinea in W Africa. This hot country, N of the Equator, was formerly called the Gold Coast. Behind the thickly populated southern coastal plains, which are lined with lagoons, lies a plateau region in the sw.

N Ghana is drained by the Black and White VOLTA rivers, which flow into Lake Volta, behind the Akosombo Dam and one of the world's largest artificially created lakes. Rainforests grow in the sw. To the N, the forests merge into savanna. More open grasslands dominate in the far N.

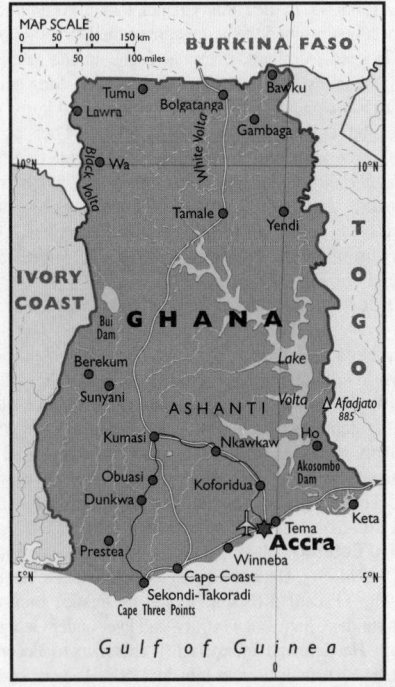

CLIMATE
Ghana has a tropical climate. A cool offshore current reduces temperatures on the coast, and the N is hotter. The heaviest rains occur in the sw. There are marked dry seasons in N and E Ghana.

HISTORY
Ghana was a great African empire which flourished to the NORTH-WEST of present-day Ghana between the AD 300s and 1000s. Various African kingdoms existed here before the arrival of Portuguese explorers in 1471, who named it the Gold Coast after its precious mineral resource. In 1642 the Dutch took control, and the Gold Coast became a centre of the 17th-century slave trade. Following the abolition of slavery (1860s), the European powers withdrew with the advance of the Ashanti. In 1874, Britain colonized the region excluding Ashanti, which fell in 1901. The British began to develop cacao plantations.

After World War 2, nationalist demands intensified and Kwame NKRUMAH became prime minister in 1951 elections. In 1957, Gold Coast became the first African colony to gain full independence. British Togoland was incorporated into the new state. The country was renamed Ghana after the medieval kingdom.

POLITICS
After independence, attempts were made to develop the economy by creating large state-owned manufacturing industries. Debt and corruption, together with falls in the price of the chief export, cocoa, caused economic problems. This led to instability and frequent coups. In 1981 power was invested in a Provisional National Defence Council, led by Flight Lieutenant Jerry Rawlings.

The government steadied the economy and introduced several new policies, including the relaxation of government controls. In 1992, a new constitution was introduced which

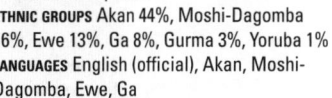

AREA 238,533sq km [92,098sq mi]
POPULATION 22,931,000
CAPITAL (POPULATION) Accra (1,970,000)
GOVERNMENT Republic
ETHNIC GROUPS Akan 44%, Moshi-Dagomba 16%, Ewe 13%, Ga 8%, Gurma 3%, Yoruba 1%
LANGUAGES English (official), Akan, Moshi-Dagomba, Ewe, Ga
RELIGIONS Christianity 63%, traditional beliefs 21%, Islam 16%
CURRENCY Cedi = 100 pesewas

allowed for multiparty elections. Rawlings was re-elected later that year, and served until his retirement in 2000. The economy expanded in the 1990s as the government followed World Bank policies. When Rawlings retired the opposition leader, John Agyekum Kufuor, leader of the New Patriotic Party, was elected president, defeating Rawlings' vice-president. Kufuor was re-elected in 2004.

ECONOMY
The World Bank classifies Ghana as a 'low-income' developing country. Most people are poor, and farming employs 59% of the population. Food crops include cassava, peanuts, maize, millet, plantains, rice and yams. Cocoa is the most valuable export crop; timber and gold are also exported. Other valuable crops include tobacco, coffee, coconuts and palm kernels.

Many small factories produce goods such as beverages, cement and clothing for local consumption. The aluminium smelter at Tema, a port near the capital ACCRA, is the country's largest factory. There are plans to construct around 600km [378mi] of pipeline which will form part of the West African Gas Pipeline Project. The aim is to lessen the dependence of electricity production on hydroelectric stations.

G

INTERNET

Giotto (di Bondone)
▶ www.san-francesco.org
▶ www.kfki.hu/~arthp/html/
   g/giotto/assisi

▼ **glacier** In spite of a return to warmer conditions, ice still covers some regions of the world, namely those nearer the Poles. The movement of ice greatly alters the landscape of these areas. Erosion and deposition are the main processes in glaciated regions. Erosion takes place mainly in highland areas, leaving features such as pyramidal peaks, cirques, *roches moutonnées*, truncated spurs and hanging valleys. Most deposition occurs on lowlands, where, after the retreat of the ice, moraines, drumlins, eskers, erratic boulders, and alluvial fans remain.

Key:
1 pyramidal peak
2 firn (granular snow)
3 cirque
4 tarn (corrie lake)
5 arête
6 marginal crevasse
7 lateral moraine
8 medial moraine
9 terminal moraine
10 sérac
11 subglacial moraine
12 glacial table
13 *roche moutonnée*
14 drumlin
15 esker
16 glacial lake
17 finger lake
18 U-shaped valley
19 erratics
20 truncated spur
21 hanging valley
22 outwash fan

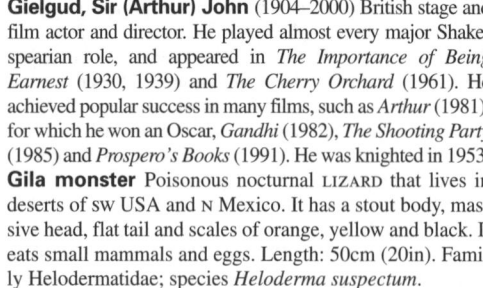

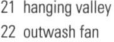

Gielgud, Sir (Arthur) John (1904–2000) British stage and film actor and director. He played almost every major Shakespearian role, and appeared in *The Importance of Being Earnest* (1930, 1939) and *The Cherry Orchard* (1961). He achieved popular success in many films, such as *Arthur* (1981), for which he won an Oscar, *Gandhi* (1982), *The Shooting Party* (1985) and *Prospero's Books* (1991). He was knighted in 1953.

Gila monster Poisonous nocturnal LIZARD that lives in deserts of sw USA and N Mexico. It has a stout body, massive head, flat tail and scales of orange, yellow and black. It eats small mammals and eggs. Length: 50cm (20in). Family Helodermatidae; species *Heloderma suspectum*.

Gilbert, Cass (1859–1934) US architect, inspired by NEO-CLASSICISM. He designed the US Supreme Court Building, Washington, D.C., and the Woolworth Building, New York City, which influenced the development of skyscrapers.

Gilbert, William (1544–1603) English physicist and physician to Queen Elizabeth I. In *De Magnete*, he was the first to recognize terrestrial MAGNETISM, and coined the terms magnetic pole, electric attraction, and electric force.

Gilbert, Sir W.S. (William Schwenck) (1836–1911) English librettist and playwright. He collaborated with Sir Arthur SULLIVAN on an immensely successful series of 14 comic operettas, nearly all first performed by the D'Oyly CARTE company. Their works include *The Mikado* (1855), *HMS Pinafore* (1878) and *The Pirates of Penzance* (1879).

Gilbert and Ellice Islands Two groups of coral islands in the w Pacific Ocean, 4000km (2500mi) NE of Australia. In 1915, the islands became a British colony. Separated from the Ellice Islands in 1975, the Gilbert Islands are now part of KIRIBATI. The Ellice Islands are now called TUVALU.

Gilgamesh Hero of the great Assyro-Babylonian myth, the Epic of Gilgamesh. He went in search of the secret of immortality. Having overcome monsters and gods, he found the flower of life, only to have it snatched from him by a serpent.

gill Organ through which most fish, some larval amphibians and many aquatic invertebrates obtain oxygen from water. When a fish breathes, it opens its mouth, draws in water and shuts its mouth again. Water is forced through the gill slits, over the gills, and out into the surrounding water. Oxygen is absorbed into small blood vessels, and at the same time, waste carbon dioxide carried by the blood diffuses into the water.

Gill, (Arthur) Eric (Rowton) (1882–1940) English engraver and sculptor. He designed many typefaces, including Gill sans serif (1927). Gill's sculptures include the *Stations of the Cross* (1914–18) in Westminster Cathedral, London.

Gillespie, 'Dizzy' (John Birks) (1917–93) US jazz trumpeter and bandleader. With Charlie PARKER and Bud POWELL, 'Dizzy' was a pioneer of BE-BOP. His dazzling tone and harmonic invention is evident on *Shaw 'Nuff* (1946).

Gillray, James (1757–1815) English caricaturist. His political and social satire was wider in scope than that of HOGARTH. Gillray lampooned George III as 'Farmer George'. William Pitt and Napoleon I appear in 'The Plum Pudding in Danger'.

ginger Herbaceous perennial plant native to tropical E Asia and grown commercially elsewhere. It has fat, tuberous roots and yellow-green flowers. The kitchen spice is made from the tubers of *Zingiber officinale*. Family Zingiberaceae.

ginkgo (maidenhair tree) Oldest living species of GYMNOSPERM, native to temperate regions of China. It dates from the late Permian period. It has fan-shaped leaves, small, foul-smelling fruits and edible, nut-like seeds. Height: to 30m (100ft). Phylum Ginkgophyta; species *Ginkgo biloba*.

Ginsberg, Allen (1926–97) US poet. Zen Buddhism, meditation, and the use of drugs all influenced Ginsberg's work. His first collection of verse, *Howl and Other Poems* (1956), a condemnation of American society, established him as the leading poet of the BEAT MOVEMENT. Other works include *Kaddish and Other Poems* (1961), a lament for his mother.

ginseng Either of two perennial plants found in the USA (*Panax quinquefolius*) and E Asia (*P. ginseng*). It has yellow-green flowers and compound leaves. Height: to 51cm (20in). Family Araliaceae.

Giolitti, Giovanni (1842–1928) Italian statesman, five times prime minister between 1892 and 1921. Giolitti introduced measures of social welfare and broadened the franchise. Although Giolitti instigated the Italo-Turkish War of 1911, he opposed Italy's entry into World War 1. He initially backed MUSSOLINI, withdrawing support in 1924.

Giorgione (c.1478–1510) Italian painter, b. Giorgio da Castlefranco. A pupil of BELLINI, he became one of the major painters of the Venetian High RENAISSANCE. He had an enigmatic romantic style, as in *Tempest* (c.1505). His *Sleeping Venus* was probably completed (c.1510) by TITIAN.

Giotto (di Bondone) (c.1266–1337) Florentine painter. A pupil of CIMABUE, he is a central figure of the early RENAISSANCE. Giotto rejected the stylized form of Italo-Byzantine art in favour of a more realistic style, best represented by the frescos (c.1305–08) in the Arena Chapel, Padua. As architect of Florence, he designed the campanile of the Duomo.

giraffe Hoofed, ruminant mammal found in the African savannas; the tallest living mammal. It has a very long neck, a short tufted mane, and two to four skin-covered horns on the head. The legs are long, slender and bony. Their coats are pale brown with red-brown blotches. Height: to 5.5m (18ft). Family Giraffidae; species *Giraffa camelopardalis*.

Giraudoux, Jean (1882–1944) French novelist and dramatist. He is best known for his stylized plays based on Greek myths, including *Amphitryon '38* (1929), *Intermezzo* (1933), and *Tiger at the Gates* (1935).

Girl Guides Organization for girls founded (1910) in England by Agnes Baden-Powell, sister of Lord BADEN-POWELL, founder of the BOY SCOUTS. There are c.7 million guides worldwide, including c.870,000 in Britain.

Girondins Political group in the FRENCH REVOLUTION named after deputies from Gironde, sw France. From 1792 the relatively moderate and middle-class Girondins tried to prevent the execution of LOUIS XVI, and reduce the power of Paris. The JACOBINS expelled the Girondins from the National Congress in 1793, and executed their leaders.

Giscard d'Estaing, Valéry (1926–) French statesman, president (1974–81). He was elected to the National Assembly in 1956. Giscard d'Estaing served as finance minister (1962–66) under Charles DE GAULLE and later under Georges POMPIDOU. He defeated François MITTERRAND to become president, but narrowly lost to him in 1981. He was leader (1988–1996) of the Union for French Democracy (UDF).

Giulio Romano (1492–1546) Italian painter and architect, b. Giulio Pippi. One of the founders of MANNERISM, he was the chief assistant to RAPHAEL in his youth. His later work was considered pornographic, and he had to flee from Rome to Mantua where, in 1526, he began his famous *Palazzo Te*.

Giza (Al-Jizah) City in N Egypt, a suburb of Cairo. It is the site of the Great SPHINX, the PYRAMID of Khufu (Cheops), the University of Cairo (relocated in 1924), and Egypt's film industry. It is a resort and agricultural centre. Industries: cotton textiles, footwear, cigarette-manufacturing. Pop. (1996) 2,221,868.

glacier Large mass of ice, mainly recrystallized snow, which moves slowly by creep downslope or outward in all directions due to the stress of its own weight. The flow terminates where the rate of melting is equal to the advance of the glacier. There are three main types: the **mountain** or **valley** glacier, originating above the snow line in mountain regions; the **piedmont**, which develops when valley glaciers spread out over lowland; and the **ice-sheet** and ICE-CAP.

gladiator In ancient Rome, volunteer, prisoner of war, slave or condemned convict trained to fight humans or wild animals in public arenas. Gladiatorial contests were officially abolished by Constantine I in AD 325, but persisted into the 5th century.

gladiolus Genus of *c*.250 species of perennial flowering plants native to Europe and Africa but cultivated widely. A gladiolus passes the dry season as a CORM, which sprouts in spring to produce a spike of funnel-shaped flowers and tall, lance-shaped leaves. Height: to 0.91m (3ft). Family Iridaceae.

Gladstone, William Ewart (1809–98) British statesman, prime minister (1868–74, 1880–85, 1886, 1892–94). He was elected to Parliament as a Tory in 1832. Gladstone served as chancellor of the exchequer (1852–55, 1857–66). In 1867, he succeeded PALMERSTON as leader of the LIBERAL PARTY. In 1874, he was defeated by Benjamin DISRAELI and resigned as Liberal leader. His criticism of Disraeli's imperialist tendencies won him the 1879 elections. Gladstone passed two Irish Land Acts and several REFORM ACTS (1884, 1885), extending the franchise. The government's failure to help General GORDON in Khartoum forced him to resign. Gladstone's last ministries were dominated by his advocacy of HOME RULE for Ireland.

Glamorganshire (Morganwg) Former county in S Wales, divided into West, Mid, and South Glamorgan. The Romans invaded in the 1st century AD and constructed roads to link their fortified settlements. Christianity spread in the 6th century. In Norman times Glamorgan became a border territory owing allegiance to the English crown. In the 15th century it suffered during the rebellion of GLYN DŴR. It was created as a county in 1536, and underwent rapid industrialization owing to its coal industry. Area: 2,119sq km (818sq mi).

gland Cell or tissue that manufactures and secretes special substances. There are two basic types. **Exocrine** glands make such substances as hydrochloric acid, mucus, sweat, sebaceous fluids and ENZYMES, and secrete these usually through ducts to an external or internal body surface. **Endocrine** glands contain cells that secrete HORMONES directly into the bloodstream. *See also* ENDOCRINE SYSTEM

glandular fever (infectious mononucleosis) Acute disease, usually of young people, caused by the Epstein-Barr virus. Glandular fever produces an increased number of white cells (monocytes) in the blood. Symptoms include fever, painful enlargement of the LYMPH nodes, and pronounced lassitude.

Glaser, Donald Arthur (1926–) US physicist who invented (1953) the BUBBLE CHAMBER, and used it to devise a new method for studying ELEMENTARY PARTICLES. He received the 1960 Nobel Prize in physics for this work.

Glasgow Largest city and port in Scotland on the River Clyde, Strathclyde Region. Founded in the 6th century, it developed commercially with the American tobacco trade in the 18th century and the cotton trade in the 19th century. Nearby coalfields and the Clyde estuary promoted the growth of heavy industry, chiefly iron, steel and shipbuilding. Glasgow is a cultural centre, with three universities, the Glasgow School of Art, and the Kelvingrove Art Gallery. Industries: shipbuilding, heavy engineering, flour milling, brewing, textiles, tobacco, chemicals, textiles, printing. Pop. (2005) 832,000.

glasnost (Rus. 'openness') Term adopted (1986) by Mikhail GORBACHEV to refer to the adoption of a more liberal social policy. One result was widespread criticism of the Soviet system and the COMMUNIST PARTY, leading to the break-up of the SOVIET UNION. *See also* PERESTROIKA

glass Brittle, transparent material. It behaves like a solid, but is actually a liquid that is cooled to prevent particles forming a regular pattern. It is made by melting together SILICA (sand), sodium carbonate (SODA), and CALCIUM CARBONATE (limestone). It can only be worked while hot. There are many types of glass. **Soda-lime** glass is used for bottles and drinking vessels. **Flint** glass refracts light well, and is used in lenses and prisms. **Toughened** glass (laminated with plastic) is used in car windscreens. Glass is also used in fibre optic cables.

Glass, Philip (1937–) US composer. Glass studied with Nadia BOULANGER in Paris, where he met Ravi SHANKAR and became interested in non-Western music. Glass was a pioneer of MINIMALISM, his style characterized by hypnotic repetition of short motifs within a simple harmonic idiom. He has written operas, notably *Einstein on the Beach* (1976) and *Akhnaten* (1984), and instrumental works including the first symphony (1992) and the second symphony (1994).

glass snake (glass lizard) Legless LIZARD found in North America, Eurasia, and Africa. The cylindrical body has a groove along each side and is mostly brown or green. Length: 60–120cm (24–48in). Family Anguidae; genus *Ophisaurus*.

glaucoma Incurable condition in which pressure within the EYE is increased due to an excess of aqueous humour, the fluid within the chamber. It occurs when normal drainage of fluid is interrupted, posing a threat to vision. Most frequently found in the over 40s, glaucoma is managed with drugs and surgery.

Glazunov, Alexander Constantinovich (1865–1936) Russian composer in the Romantic tradition of TCHAIKOVSKY. His works include eight symphonies, two violin concertos and the ballets *Raymonda* (1897) and *The Seasons* (1898).

Glendower, Owen *See* GLYN DŴR, OWAIN

Glenn, John Herschel, Jr (1921–) US astronaut. On February 20, 1962, aboard the spacecraft *Friendship 7*, he became the first American to orbit Earth. Glenn became a US Senator (Democrat) from Ohio (1974–99). In 1998, Glenn flew his second space mission on the space shuttle *Discovery*.

gliding Leisure activity involving flight in a glider. The unpowered glider is launched off the ground by a sling mechanism or towed by a small aircraft and then released. Once airborne, gliders descend relative to the surrounding air. If this air is a rising updraft, a glider may gain altitude for a while, thus prolonging its flight. *See also* HANG GLIDING

global warming Trend towards higher average temperatures on Earth's surface. During the last few million years,

INTERNET

Gladstone, William Ewart
▶ www.number-10.gov.uk

Glenn, John Herschel, Jr
▶ www.nasa.gov/centers/ glenn/about/johnglen.html

global warming
▶ yosemite.epa.gov/oar/ globalwarming.nsf

G

▲ **giraffe** The world's tallest mammal, the giraffe (*Giraffa camelopardalis*) reaches a height of 5.5m (18ft). The giraffe's long neck makes up about half its height, and enables it to browse from the higher branches of trees of the African savanna.

◀ **global warming** Short-wave solar radiation passes easily through Earth's atmosphere and warms the planet, although some is reflected by cloud cover (1). Earth re-radiates the heat at longer wavelengths, but this radiation passes relatively easily through the atmosphere (2). Increased industrialization pollutes the atmosphere with 'greenhouse gases' – particularly carbon dioxide from burning fossil fuels and methane (3), The greenhouse gases absorb the longer-wavelength radiation and re-radiate it back down to Earth (4). This is known as the 'greenhouse effect' because the gases act like the glass of a greenhouse. On a global scale, scientists believe the greenhouse effect will raise the temperature of the Earth, resulting in the melting of the polar ice-caps and subsequent sea-level rise and flooding of low-lying areas (5).

temperature rise in 1 °C increments

1550 1600 1650 1700 1750 1800 1850 1900 1950 2000 2050

there have been several periods when surface temperatures have been significantly higher or lower than at present. During cold periods (ICE AGES), GLACIERS covered much of the land. The Earth is currently in the middle of a warm period (interglacial), which began c.10,000 years ago. Since the 1960s, many scientists have called attention to signs that the Earth is becoming unnaturally warmer as the result of an increased GREENHOUSE EFFECT caused by human activity. The international 1997 Kyoto Protocol set targets for industrial nations to cut industrial emissions that cause global warming.

Globe Theatre Elizabethan public theatre associated with William SHAKESPEARE. Built in 1599 on Bankside, London, it had polygonal walls with a roof over the stage and galleries. Destroyed by fire in 1613 and rebuilt in 1614, it was closed by the Puritans in 1642 and demolished in 1644. The theatre was rebuilt and reopened in 1995, staging period performances.

globular cluster Near-spherical cluster of very old stars in the halo of our GALAXY and others. Globular clusters contain anything from 100,000 to several million stars, concentrated so tightly near the centre that they cannot be separately distinguished by ground-based telescopes.

glockenspiel Percussion instrument with a bell-like sound. Its tuned metal bars are struck with a hammer, either freehand or from a miniature keyboard.

glomerulonephritis Group of KIDNEY disorders featuring damage to the glomeruli (clusters of blood vessels in the kidney NEPHRONS). Chronic forms may progress to kidney failure.

Glorious Revolution (1688–89) Abdication of JAMES II of England and his replacement with WILLIAM III (OF ORANGE) and MARY II. After James antagonized powerful subjects by his favour towards Roman Catholics, political leaders invited William to take the throne. William landed in November and James fled to France. It was called "Glorious" because it occurred virtually without violence. In 1689, William and Mary ratified the BILL OF RIGHTS. In 1690, William defeated James at the Battle of the BOYNE.

Gloucester County town of GLOUCESTERSHIRE on the River SEVERN, W England. It was the Roman city of Glevum and acted as capital of Mercia in Saxon times. There is an 11th-century cathedral where Edward II is buried. A market town, its industries include agricultural machinery, aircraft components, railway equipment, and fishing. Pop. (2001) 109,888.

Gloucestershire County in SW England; the county town is GLOUCESTER. Other important towns include Cheltenham and Stroud. There was a strong Roman presence in the county and in later periods it became important for coal-mining and the wool industry. The COTSWOLDS, to the E, sustain dairy and arable farming. The fertile Severn River valley is home to dairying. Industries: engineering, scientific instruments, plastics. Area: 2,642sq km (1,020sq mi). Pop. (2001) 564,559.

glow-worm Any of a number of wingless female BEETLES or beetle larvae of the genus *Lampyris* that possess light-emitting organs, especially the European beetle *Lampyris noctiluca*. A winged male is known as a FIREFLY. Family Lampyridae.

Gluck, Christoph Willibald von (1714–87) German operatic composer. His early operas were composed in the Italian tradition. In *Orfeo ed Euridice* (1762), Gluck attempted to reform opera by unifying musical and dramatic components. He turned to the French tradition in *Iphigénie en Tauride* (1779). His reforms influenced Mozart.

glucose (dextrose) Colourless crystalline SUGAR ($C_6H_{12}O_6$) occurring in fruit and honey. It requires no digestion before absorption. INSULIN lowers the blood-glucose level by causing the liver to convert glucose into GLYCOGEN. A monosaccharide sugar, it is prepared commercially by the hydrolysis of STARCH using hydrochloric acid.

glue Adhesive traditionally made by boiling animal skin, bones, horns, and hooves. Vegetable glues are made from starch (flour and water), rubber, soybeans, and other sources. Synthetic adhesives include EPOXY RESINS, a group of POLYMERS with good properties of heat and chemical resistance.

gluten Main protein substance in WHEAT flour. Not present in barley, oats, or maize, gluten contributes the elasticity

to dough. It is used in gluten bread for diabetics, and as an additive to chocolate and coffee.

glycerol (glycerine) Thick, syrupy, sweet liquid (1,2,3–trihydroxypropane, $CH_2OHCH(OH)CH_2OH$) obtained as a by-product of SOAP, and synthesized industrially from PROPENE. It is used in the manufacture of various products, including paints, cosmetics, and EXPLOSIVES.

glycogen CARBOHYDRATE stored in the body, principally by the LIVER and muscles. Glycogen is a polymer of GLUCOSE. When the body needs energy, it breaks down glycogen into glucose. *See also* RESPIRATION

Glyndebourne Estate in East Sussex, England, site of an annual opera festival. John Christie built an opera theatre here in 1931. A larger theatre opened in 1994.

Glyn Dŵr, Owain (c.1359–1416) (Owen Glendower) Welsh leader. A member of the house of Powys, he led a rebellion (1401) against HENRY IV. Proclaimed Prince of Wales, Glyn Dŵr allied himself with Henry's English enemies, Sir Henry PERCY and the Mortimer family. He captured Harlech and Aberystwyth castles, but lost both by 1409 and retreated to the hills to maintain guerrilla warfare against the English.

GMT Abbreviation of GREENWICH MEAN TIME.

gnat Common name for several small flies, mainly of the family Culicidae, the female of which bites human beings.

gneiss METAMORPHIC ROCK with a distinctive layering or banding. The darker minerals are likely to be hornblende, augite, mica, or dark feldspar. Before metamorphism, gneiss was an IGNEOUS ROCK, possibly a granite.

Gnosticism Religious movement, embracing numerous sects, based on *gnosis* (Gk. 'knowledge'). This was occult knowledge that released the spiritual part of human beings from the evil bondage of the material world. Gnosticism became widespread by the 2nd century AD.

gnu (wildebeest) Large, ox-like African ANTELOPE. The white-tailed gnu (*Connochaetes gnou*) is almost extinct. The brindled gnu (*Connochaetes taurinus*) lives in E and S Africa, where large herds migrate annually. It has a massive, buffalo-like head and a slender body. Both sexes are horned. Length: up to 2.4m (7.8ft); height: 1.3m (4ft); weight: up to 275kg (600lb). Family Bovidae.

Goa State in SW India, on the Arabian Sea; the capital is Panaji. It was ruled by Hindu dynasties until it came under Muslim domination in the 15th century. Captured by the Portuguese in 1510, it became the hub of Portugal's Asian empire. It was annexed by India in 1962 and made a Union territory. In 1987, Goa became a separate state. Products: rice, cashews, spices, pharmaceutical products, footwear, pesticides. Area: 3,702sq km (1,429sq mi). Pop. (2001) 1,344,000.

goat Horned RUMINANT raised for milk, meat, leather and hair. They are brown or grey in colour. The male is a ram or billy, the female a doe or nanny, and the young a kid. Wild species are nomadic, living in rugged mountain areas. The five species include the IBEX (*Capra ibex*), markhor (*Capra falconeri*), and the pasang (*Capra aegagrus*). Length: to 1.4m (4.5ft); height: to 0.85m (2.8ft). Family Bovidae; genus *Capra*.

goatsucker Common name for various large-mouthed, nocturnal birds of the order Caprimulgiformes. They include the frogmouth, nighthawk, NIGHTJAR, whip-poor-will, and potoo. Length: 15–30cm (6–12in). Family Caprimulgidae.

Gobbi, Tito (1915–84) Italian baritone. In 1938, he made his debut in Verdi's *La Traviata* in Rome. Gobbi sang in most of the great opera houses and was acclaimed for his acting ability.

Gobelins, Manufacture nationale des State-controlled TAPESTRY factory in Paris, founded c.1440 by Jean Gobelin. The factory converted from a dyeworks to making tapestry in 1601. In 1662 Louis XIV bought the premises to create a royal tapestry and furniture works. It was directed (1663–90) by Charles LE BRUN.

Gobi (Sha-moh) Desert area in central Asia, extending over much of S Mongolia and N China. One of the world's largest deserts, it is on a plateau, 900–1,500m (3,000–5,000ft) high. The fringes are grassy and inhabited by nomadic Mongolian tribes who rear sheep and goats. The Gobi has cold winters, hot summers, and fierce winds and sandstorms. Area: c.1.3 million sq km (500,000sq mi).

▲ **goat** Bred mainly in countries where the pasture is too poor for sheep, goats are an important source of milk and meat in many desert and mountain regions worldwide. Angora goats (A) originated in Turkey, near Ankara. They have now spread to other parts of the world, and are bred for their fleece, known as mohair. The quality of mohair is important and animals are carefully bred to produce long, fine-haired fleece. The Granada (B) is a black, hornless Spanish breed, kept for its milk. Although still popular in Spain, it has not spread further afield. The Toggenburg (C) is a hardy, hornless breed. It originated in Switzerland, but is now used in many countries for cross-breeding.

Gobind Singh (1666–1708) Tenth and last Sikh guru, who laid the foundations of Sikh militarism. In 1699 he created the *Khalsa*, a military fraternity of devout Sikhs, which became the basis of the Sikh army he led against the MOGUL EMPIRE. The wearing of the turban and the common attachment of Singh ('lion') to Sikh names date from his reign.

god One of the supernatural, divine and usually immortal beings worshipped by followers of polytheistic religions. Also, the single supreme being, creator, and mover of the universe, as worshipped by the followers of monotheistic religions such as JUDAISM or ISLAM. ALLAH is God of Islam and YAHWEH is God of Judaism. CHRISTIANITY, a monotheistic religion, conceives of one God with three elements – Father, Son, and Holy Spirit. In HINDUISM, BRAHMA is considered the soul of the world, but there are lesser gods. *See also* AGNOSTICISM; ATHEISM; DEISM; MONOTHEISM; POLYTHEISM

Godard, Jean-Luc (1930–) French film director. His contributions to *Cahiers du Cinéma* established him as a leader of the *nouvelle vague*. Godard's debut feature *A Bout de Souffle* (1960) revolutionized film-making with its jump cuts and shaky hand-held shots. After making *Alphaville* (1965), *La Chinoise* (1967), and *Weekend* (1965), Godard collaborated on propaganda films such as *Tout va bien* (1972). Other films include *Bande à Part* (1964).

Goddard, Robert Hutchings (1882–1945) US physicist and pioneer in ROCKET development. Goddard developed and launched (1926) the first liquid-fuelled rocket, and produced the first smokeless powder rocket and the first automatic steering for rockets.

Gödel, Kurt (1906–78) US logician, b. Moravia. He is best known for his 'undecidability' or 'incompleteness' theorem, first published in 1931. **Godel's theorem** states any AXIOM-based mathematical system contains statements that can neither be proved or disproved within the system. In 1940, he emigrated to the USA, joining Albert EINSTEIN at the Institute of Advanced Study at Princeton. *See also* NUMBER THEORY

Godiva, Lady (d. *c*.1080) English benefactress, wife of Leofric, Earl of Mercia. According to tradition, Lady Godiva rode naked through the streets of Coventry in 1040 to persuade her husband to reduce the burden of taxation.

Godthåb Danish name for NUUK, capital of Greenland

Godunov, Boris (1551–1605) Tsar of Russia (1598–1605). The chief minister (and brother-in-law) of IVAN IV (THE TERRIBLE), he became Regent to Ivan's imbecile son Fyodor after Ivan's death, and was popularly supposed to have murdered Fyodor's brother and heir, Dmitri, in 1591. On Fyodor's death in 1598, Boris was elected Tsar. He gained recognition for the Russian Orthodox Church as an independent patriarchate.

Goebbels, (Paul) Joseph (1897–1945) German Nazi leader. He joined the Nazi Party in 1924, and in 1926 founded the newspaper *Der Angriff*. When the Nazis came to power in 1933, he became minister of propaganda. He took total control of the media, which he exploited to support Nazi aims. He committed suicide with his entire family in April 1945.

Goering, Hermann Wilhelm (1893–1946) German Nazi leader. As commander of the LUFTWAFFE (Ger. 'air force') from 1933 and overall director of economic affairs from 1936, he was second in command to HITLER. His reputation declined during World War 2 with the failure of the Luftwaffe to subdue the British or the Russians. Captured in 1945, he was sentenced to death at the NUREMBERG TRIALS but committed suicide.

Goes, Hugo van der (*c*.1440–82) Flemish painter, one of the greatest 15th-century artists. In 1474, he was elected Dean of the painter's guild in Ghent and in 1475 entered a monastery. His triptych the *Portinari Altarpiece* (the only work definitely ascribed to him) is a masterpiece of emotional intensity.

Goethe, Johann Wolfgang von (1749–1832) German poet, dramatist, novelist, and statesman. While studying law at Strasbourg, HERDER inspired him to appreciate Shakespeare. Goethe's first play, *Götz von Berlichingen* (1773), was in the tradition of STURM UND DRANG. His epistolary novel *The Sorrows of Young Werther* (1774) won him international fame. His visits to Italy (1786–88, 1790) fired his enthusiasm for

classicism, evidenced in the historical drama *Egmont* (1788). Goethe's novel *Wilhelm Meister's Apprenticeship* (1796) became the model for the German *bildungsroman*. Goethe's most enduring work, the dramatic poem *Faust*, was published in two parts (1808, 1832). *See also* GERMAN LITERATURE

Gogol, Nikolai (1809–52) Russian novelist and dramatist whose work marks the transition from ROMANTICISM to early realism. Gogol made his reputation with stories, such as *The Nose* (1835), and the drama *The Government Inspector* (1836). He turned to religion and lived mostly in Rome from 1836–48. Here he wrote the first part of his major work, *Dead Souls* (1842), and the story *The Overcoat* (1842).

Goh Chok Tong (1941–) Prime minister of Singapore (1990–2004). An economist, Goh became a member of Parliament for the People's Action Party in 1976. He rose steadily through the ministerial ranks and suceeded Lee Kuan Yew.

Golan Heights (Ramat Ha Golan) Range of hills in SW Syria on the border with Israel. Israel occupied the area in the SIX-DAY WAR (1967), and later annexed it. Of great strategic importance to Israel, it remains a source of conflict between the two countries. Area: 1,150sq km (444sq mi). Pop. (2000 est.) 14,000.

gold (symbol Au) Naturally occurring metallic element. It is also obtained as a by-product in the refining of copper. It is used in jewellery, connectors for electronic equipment, and as a form of money. Gold in the form of a COLLOID is sometimes used in colouring glass. The isotope A^{198} (half-life 2.7 days) is used in RADIOTHERAPY. The metal is unreactive but dissolves in aqua regia, a mixture of nitric and hydrochloric acids. Properties: at.no. 79; r.a.m. 196.9665; r.d. 19.30; m.p. 1,063°C (1,945°F); b.p. 2,800°C (5,072°F); most common isotope Au^{197} (100%).

goldcrest Smallest British bird. Its head is capped with bright orange and a black stripe. Its body is green and its wings are black with a white stripe. Length: *c*.8.4cm (3.3in). Family Muscicapidae; species *Regulus regulus*.

Golden Horde Mongol state established in S Russia in the early 13th century, derived from the conquests of GENGHIS KHAN and extended by his successors, who took over the whole of the Russian state, centred on Kiev. It was conquered by TAMERLANE in the late 14th century and then split up.

goldfinch Any of various small, seed-eating birds of the genus *Carduelis*. The red-faced European goldfinch (*C. carduelis*) has a brownish body with yellow and black wings. Male American goldfinches (such as *C. tristis*) have yellow body plumage in the summer. Family Fringillidae.

goldfish Freshwater CARP originally found in China. The most popular aquarium fish, it was domesticated in China *c*.1,000 years ago. The wild form is plain and brownish, but selective breeding has produced a variety of colours. Family Cyprinidae; species *Carassius auratus*.

Golding, Sir William Gerald (1911–93) English novelist. He achieved fame with his allegorical debut novel, *Lord of the Flies* (1954). Other novels include *The Spire* (1964) and the trilogy *The Ends of the Earth* (1991), which incorporates the Booker Prize winning *Rites of Passage* (1980). He received the 1983 Nobel Prize in literature.

gold rush Rapid influx of population in response to reports of the discovery of gold. The largest gold rush brought *c*.100,000 prospectors to California (1849–50). Some of the miners, known as Forty-Niners, went on to Australia (1851–53). There were also gold rushes to Witwatersrand, South Africa (1886), Klondike in the Yukon, Canada (1896), and Alaska (1898).

Goldsmith, Oliver (1730–74) Anglo-Irish poet, novelist, essayist, and dramatist. After a colourful but penurious early life, he became known as a lively comic writer. His work includes the essay collection *The Citizen of the World* (1762), the poem *The Deserted Village* (1770), the novel *The Vicar of Wakefield* (1766), and the play *She Stoops to Conquer* (1773).

gold standard Monetary system in which the gold value of currency is set at a fixed rate and currency is convertible into gold on demand. It was adopted by Britain in 1821, by France, Germany and the USA in the 1870s, and by most of the rest of the world by the 1890s. Internationally it produced nearly fixed EXCHANGE RATES and was intended to foster monetary stability.

INTERNET

Goddard, Robert Hutchings
▸ www-istp.gsfc.nasa.gov/
stargaze/Sgoddard.htm

Goethe, Johann Wolfgang von
▸ www.everypoet.com

G

▲ **goose** Unlike most species of birds, geese mate for life. Found in freshwater habitats all over the world, geese have been domesticated for their eggs and down. The species shown here are the Roman (A), the Egyptian (B), the Chinese (C), the greylag (D), and the embden (E).

▲ **gooseberry** The green, hairy fruit of the gooseberry (*Ribes grossularia*) is excellent for bottling, jam, and baking in pies.

The GREAT DEPRESSION forced many countries to depreciate their exchange rates in an attempt to foster trade and, by the mid-1930s, all countries had abandoned the gold standard.

Goldwyn, Samuel (1882–1974) US film producer, b. Poland. He was noted for his commercially successful films, including *Wuthering Heights* (1939), *The Best Years of Our Lives* (1946), *Guys and Dolls* (1955), and *Porgy and Bess* (1959). He formed Goldwyn Pictures in 1917 and later merged with Louis B. Mayer to form Metro-Goldwyn-Mayer (1924).

golf Game in which a small, hard ball is struck by a club. The object of the game is to hit the ball into a sequence of holes (usually 18), in the least number of shots. The length of each hole varies from *c.*100–550yd (*c.*90–500m) and consists of a **tee**, from where the player hits the first shot; a **fairway** of mown grass bordered by trees and longer grass, known as the **rough**; and a **green**, a putting area of smooth, short grass and the site of the hole. A player may have to circumvent course hazards, such as lakes or bunkers. Each hole is given a par, the number of shots it should take to complete the hole. Competition is usually over 18, 36 or 72 holes; the winner decided by the lowest total of strokes (stroke play) or the most holes won (match play). In 1754, the Royal and Ancient Golf Club, ST ANDREWS, Scotland, was formed and the basic rules of the game codified. Major tournaments are the US Open, British Open, US Professional Golfer's Association (PGA), and the US Masters.

Golgi body Collection of microscopic vesicles or packets observed near the nucleus of many living CELLS. It is a part of a cell's ENDOPLASMIC RETICULUM, specialized for the purpose of packaging and dispatching proteins made by the cell.

Goliath In the OLD TESTAMENT, the PHILISTINE giant slain by the shepherd boy DAVID (1 Samuel 17). David killed Goliath with a stone from his catapult.

gonad Primary reproductive organ of male and female animals, in which develop the GAMETES or sex cells. Thus, the gonad in the male is a TESTIS and in the female an OVARY. HERMAPHRODITE animals possess both types.

Goncourt, Edmond de (1822–96) French novelist and social historian. He collaborated with his brother **Jules** (1830–70) on *The Journal of the Goncourts* (1836–40), a personal account of Parisian society, and the novels *Germinie Lacerteux* (1864) and *Madame Gervaisais* (1869). In his will, he provided for the Prix Goncourt, France's top literary award.

Gondwanaland Southern supercontinent. It began to break away from the single land mass PANGAEA *c.*200 million years ago. It became South America, Africa, India, Australia and Antarctica. The northern supercontinent, Laurasia, eventually became North America and Eurasia without India.

gonorrhoea SEXUALLY TRANSMITTED DISEASE caused by the bacterium *Neisseria gonorrhoeae*, giving rise to inflammation of the genital tract. Symptoms include pain on urination and the passing of pus. Some infected women experience no symptoms. The condition is treated with antibiotics. If not treated, it may spread, causing sterility and ultimately threatening other organs in the body.

Good Friday Friday before EASTER Day. It is observed by Christians as marking the day of the crucifixion of Jesus. For many Christians, it is a day of fasting and abstinence.

Good Friday Agreement (April 10, 1998) Northern IRELAND peace accord signed by British Prime Minister Tony BLAIR, Irish Taoiseach Bertie AHERN, and representatives from eight political parties in Northern Ireland. The Agreement provided for a new, 108–seat Northern Ireland Assembly with legislative powers devolved from the British Parliament. It created a Ministerial Council to co-ordinate policies between the Republic of IRELAND and Northern Ireland, and a 'Council of the Isles' to replace the intergovernmental conference established by the ANGLO-IRISH AGREEMENT (1985). The Assembly met for the first time in July, but the peace process stalled when First Minister David TRIMBLE refused to appoint two SINN FÉIN members to the executive committee until the IRISH REPUBLICAN ARMY (IRA) began decommissioning weapons. US Senator George Mitchell conducted a review of the Agreement and secured concessions that, in December 1999, produced home rule in Northern Ireland for the first time since 1974. *See also* ADAMS, GERRY; HUME, JOHN; PAISLEY, IAN

goose Widely distributed waterfowl, related to the DUCK and SWAN. Geese have blunt bills, long necks, shortish legs, webbed feet and, in the wild, a combination of grey, brown, black and white dense plumage underlaid by down. They live near fresh or brackish water and spend time on land, grazing on meadow grasses. Wild geese breed in colonies, mate for life, and build grass-and-twig, down-lined nests for 3–12 eggs. They migrate in summer, flying in skeins in V-formation. There are 14 species. Weight: 1.4–5.9kg (3–13lb). Family Anatidae.

gooseberry Hardy, deciduous, spiny shrub and its edible fruit. It is generally green and hairy, and fairly acidic. Family Grossulariaceae; species *Ribes grossularia*.

gopher Small, stout, burrowing rodent of North and Central America. It has fur-lined external cheek pouches and long incisor teeth outside the lips. It lives underground, digging tunnels to find roots and tubers and for shelter and food storage. Length: 13–46cm (5–18in). Family Geomyidae.

Gorbachev, Mikhail Sergeievich (1931–) Soviet statesman, president of the SOVIET UNION (1988–91) and general secretary of the Soviet Communist Party (1985–91). After succeeding CHERNENKO as leader, Gorbachev embarked on a programme of reform based on PERESTROIKA (restructuring) and GLASNOST (openness). He played a major role in the nuclear DISARMAMENT process, withdrew Soviet troops from Afghanistan, and acquiesced to the demise of communist regimes in Eastern Europe (1989–90), effectively ending the COLD WAR. In Russia, the benefits of radical socio-economic change were slow to take effect, and Gorbachev's popularity fell as prices rose. In August 1991, Communist hardliners mounted an unsuccessful coup. In December 1991, the Communist Party was abolished. Gorbachev was forced to dissolve the Soviet Union and hand power to his rival Boris YELTSIN. Gorbachev received the Nobel Peace Prize in 1990.

Gordimer, Nadine (1923–) South African writer. Her works, critical of apartheid, are concerned with contemporary politics and social morality. Among her collections of short stories are *Face to Face* (1949) and *Jump* (1991). Gordimer won the Booker Prize for *The Conservationist* (1974). Other novels include *The Lying Days* (1953) and *My Son's Story* (1990). She received the 1991 Nobel Prize in literature.

Gordon, Charles George (1833–85) British soldier and administrator. He fought in the CRIMEAN WAR and OPIUM WAR, and was employed by the Chinese government in the TAIPING REBELLION. Governor-general of the Sudan (1877–80), he returned to Khartoum in 1884 to evacuate Egyptian forces threatened by the MAHDI and was killed.

Gordon Riots (1780) Violent demonstrations against Roman Catholics in London, England. Protestant extremists led by Lord George Gordon (1751–93) marched on Parliament to protest against the Catholic Relief Act (1778), which lifted some restrictions on Catholics. The march degenerated into a week-long riot in which *c.*450 people were killed or injured.

Gore, Al (Albert Arnold) (1948–) US statesman, vice president (1993–2001). He was a Democratic congressman (1977–85) and senator (1985–93) for Tennessee. As vice president to Bill CLINTON, Gore championed environmental issues. In 1999 he gained the DEMOCRATIC PARTY nomination for president, but was defeated by Republican challenger George W. BUSH in a highly controversial and closely fought election. Gore shared the 2007 Nobel Peace Prize for his work spreading knowledge about climate change.

Górecki, Henryk (1933–) Polish composer. His early works were influenced by WEBERN and SERIAL MUSIC, but his later output, such as his third symphony (1976), is inspired more by medieval Polish chants, Renaissance polyphony, and the richness of the Wagnerian orchestra.

Gorgons In Greek mythology, three monsters named Stheno, Euryale, and MEDUSA. They had gold wings, snakes for hair, and turned anyone who looked directly at them to stone. PERSEUS killed Medusa by using his shield as a mirror.

gorilla Powerfully built great APE native to the forests of equatorial Africa. The largest PRIMATE, it is brown or black, with long arms and short legs. It walks on all fours and is herbivorous. Height: to 175cm (70in); weight: 140–180kg (308–396lb). Family Pongidae; species *Gorilla gorilla*.

Gorky, Arshile (1905–48) US painter, b. Armenia. He bridged SURREALISM and ABSTRACT EXPRESSIONISM. In 1920, he emigrated to the USA, joining a group of European surrealists in New York in the 1940s. Gorky became fascinated by the work of Joan MIRÓ, who inspired paintings, such as the versions of *Garden in Sochi* (1940) and *Mojave* (1941–42).

Gorky, Maxim (1868–1936) Russian writer, b. Aleksei Madsimovich Peshkov. He championed the worker in *Sketches and Stories* (1898), the play *The Lower Depths* (1902), and the novel *Mother* (1907). Gorky was imprisoned for his role in the Russian Revolution of 1905, and lived much of his life in exile. He is best known for an autobiographical trilogy (1913–23).

gorse (furze) Any of several dense thorny shrubs found mainly in Europe; genus *Ulex*; family Fabaceae/Leguminosae. The common European species, *U. europaeus*, bears yellow flowers and thrives in open hilly regions.

gospel Central content of the Christian faith, the good news (*god spell* in Old English) that human sins are forgiven and that all sinners are redeemed. The first four books of the NEW TESTAMENT, ascribed to the Evangelists Matthew, Mark, Luke, and John, are known as the four Gospels.

gospel music African-American vocal church music. It arose in the depression of the 1930s from the fusion of Protestant hymn harmony with African rhythms and melody. Gospel music emphasizes the 'good news' aspect of revivalist Christianity. Powerfully expressive, it often uses a call-and-response form, with a choir answering a soloist/preacher.

Gothenburg (Göteborg) City in sw Sweden, situated where the River Göta meets the Kattegat. It is the country's chief seaport and second-largest city. Founded by Gustavus II (1619), it flourished as a commercial centre. Industries: shipbuilding, vehicles, chemicals, textiles. Pop. (2005) 829,000.

Gothic art and architecture Gothic architecture developed in medieval Europe from the 12th to 16th centuries. It is characterized by the pointed ARCH and ribbed VAULT, and is principally ecclesiastical. Its greatest and most characteristic expression is the CATHEDRAL. The introduction of flying BUTTRESSES was a technical advance that made larger windows possible. An early prototype is the Abbey Church of St Denis (1140–44). Ever higher and lighter structures followed, with increasingly intricate vaulting and tracery. Gothic sculpture was elegant and more realistic than the Romanesque, emphasizing line and silhouette. In painting, the Gothic style manifested itself most successfully in manuscript ILLUMINATION. See also GOTHIC REVIVAL

Gothic novel Genre of English fiction popular in the late 18th and early 19th centuries. Gothic novels often rely on eerie medieval externals, such as old castles, monasteries and hidden trapdoors, for their symbolism. Horace WALPOLE wrote an important prototype, *The Castle of Otranto* (1764). Later examples include *The Mysteries of Udolpho* (1794) by Ann Radcliffe and *Frankenstein* (1818) by Mary SHELLEY.

Gothic revival Architecture based on the GOTHIC ART AND ARCHITECTURE of the Middle Ages. Beginning in the late 18th century, it peaked in 19th-century Britain and the USA, also appearing in many European countries. British exponents, notably the critic John RUSKIN and the writer and architect A.W.N. PUGIN, insisted on the need for authentic, structural recreation of medieval styles. Notable examples are the Houses of Parliament in London by Pugin and Sir Charles BARRY, and Trinity Church in New York City by Richard Upjohn.

Goths Ancient Germanic people, groups of whom settled near the Black Sea in the 2nd-3rd centuries AD. In 376 the HUNS drove the **Visigoths** westwards into Roman territory and the Visigoths, led by ALARIC, sacked Rome in 410. They settled in sw France, but the Franks expelled them in the early 6th century, and they migrated in Spain. Some groups united to create the **Ostrogoths**, who conquered Italy under THEODORIC THE GREAT (489). They held Italy until conquered by the Byzantines under Belisarius and Narses (536–53).

Gottlieb, Adolph (1903–74) US painter, an exponent of ABSTRACT EXPRESSIONISM. His early work shows the influence of EXPRESSIONISM and SURREALISM. Best known for a series of *Pictographs* (1941–51), he portrayed Freudian or mythological concepts compartmentalized in different areas of the canvas.

gouache Watercolour paint made opaque by the addition of white. It lightens in colour when dry and cracks if used thickly. Popular among manuscript illuminators in the Middle Ages, gouache has been used by 20th-century artists.

Gould, Glenn (1932–82) Canadian pianist and composer. Gould is chiefly celebrated for his interpretations of J.S. Bach and Beethoven. His first string quartet premiered in 1956.

Gould, Stephen Jay (1941–2002) US palaeontologist. He proposed that EVOLUTION could occur in sudden spurts rather than gradually. Gould's theory of PUNCTUATED EQUILIBRIUM suggested that sudden accelerations in the evolutionary process could produce rapid changes in species over the comparatively short time of a few hundred thousand years. His many popular science books include *Bully for Brontosaurus* (1992).

Gounod, Charles François (1818–93) French composer and organist. He composed church and choral music and is best known for his operas, which include *Faust* (1859), *Mireille* (1863), and *Roméo et Juliette* (1864).

gourd Annual vine and its ornamental, hard-shelled fruit. These range from almost spherical, as in *Cucurbita pepo*, to irregular or bottle-shaped, as in *Lagenaria siceraria*. The rind may be smooth or warty. Family Cucurbitaceae.

gout Form of ARTHRITIS, featuring an excess of uric acid crystals in the tissues. More common in men, it causes attacks of pain and inflammation in the joints, most often those of the feet or hands. It is treated with anti-inflammatories.

Gower, John (1330–1408) English poet. Ranked in his time with Lydgate and CHAUCER, his work includes *Vox Clamantis* (1379–82), an attack on social injustice, and his most famous work, *Confessio Amantis* (1386–93), a collection of allegorical tales on the subject of Christian and courtly love.

Goya y Lucientes, Francisco José de (1746–1828) Spanish painter and engraver. A severe illness (1791) provoked a vein of fantastic works, one of the most vicious and sinister of which is *Los caprichos*, a series of 82 engravings published in 1799. Goya enjoyed the royal patronage of Charles IV despite mercilessly realistic paintings such as *The*

G

▲ **Gorbachev** The former president (1988–91) of the Soviet Union, Mikhail Gorbachev was responsible for the two radical socio-economic reforms of *glasnost* ('openness') and *perestroika* ('restructuring'). Although Gorbachev initially enjoyed huge popular support, his economic reforms resulted in massive price rises, and he was eventually forced to resign.

◀ **Gothic art and architecture** Cologne Cathedral, Germany, was begun in 1248, but the present building dates from between 1842 and 1880. The largest Gothic church in N Europe, the illustration shows the w façade. The cathedral's grandeur lies predominantly in its highly decorated, spiny twin towers, which rise to 152m (502ft).

G

▶ **Graf** German tennis star
Steffi Graf is among the greatest
women tennis players of all
time. She dominated women's
tennis from 1987 to 1997,
ranking as number one in the
world every year (apart from
1991 and 1992, when Monica
Seles surpassed her). Graf won a
career total of 107 titles,
including 22 Grand Slams. In
2001, she married fellow tennis
player Andre Agassi.

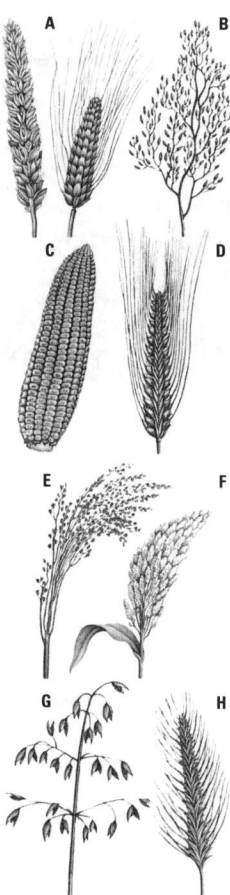

▲ **grain** The fruits of various
cereal plants, the various grains
together are the most important
food. Wheat (A), corn or maize
(C), and barley (D) are grown in
the world's temperate regions.
Rice (B) needs a tropical climate
to grow successfully. Millet (E) is
one of the oldest cultivated grains
in the world and, along with
sorghum (F), is grown extensively
in Africa. Oats (G) and rye (H) are
grown extensively in Europe, and
rye especially is well suited to
poorer soils than those required
for most cereal grains.

family of Charles IV (1800). His bloody scenes *The Second of
May, 1808* and *The Third of May, 1808* portray the Spanish
resistance to the French invasion. Still obsessed with the dark
side of the human psyche, his last works are the so-called
Black paintings, 14 murals in sombre colours in which Goya
unleashed yet more horrors from his tortured imagination.

Gozzoli, Benozzo (1421–97) Italian painter. He is
famous for his numerous frescos, such as *The Journey of
the Magi* (1459–61) in the Medici Palace, Florence.

Gracchus, Gaius Sempronius (*c.*153–*c.*121 BC) Roman
statesman. As tribune (123–112BC) he organized the social
reforms of his brother **Tiberius** (d.133BC). He sought to
check the power of the Senate by uniting the plebeians and
the equites, and by reforming agrarian laws to benefit the
poor. These reforms were short-lived; he was defeated in the
election of 121 BC and killed during the riots that ensued.

Grace, W.G. (William Gilbert) (1848–1915) English
cricketer. He played for England, Gloucestershire, and London County. He scored 54,896 runs (including 126 centuries),
took 2,876 wickets, and held 877 catches in first-class matches. He led England in 13 of his 22 test matches (1880–99).

Graces In Greek mythology, three goddesses who represented intellectual pleasures: beauty, grace, and charm.
Associated especially with poetry, Aglaia, Euphrosyne and
Thalia were often linked with the MUSES. They were also
described as daughters or granddaughters of ZEUS.

grackle Several species of stout-billed, New World blackbirds within the genera *Quiscalus* and *Cassidix* of the family
Icteridae. Sometimes called crow blackbirds, they have blackish, iridescent plumage. The common grackle, *Q. quiscula*, of
the USA, may reach 30cm (12in) in length. Species of Asian
mina birds of the genus *Gracula* are also called grackles.

Graf, Steffi (Stephanie) (1969–) German tennis player.
Graf succeeded Martina Navratilova as the world's No. 1
woman tennis player in 1987. In 1988, she won all four
Grand Slam tournaments. Graf's powerful serve and fore-
hand play dominated the women's game, despite her injury
problems. She won the Australian Open (1988–90, 1994),
the French Open (1987–88, 1993, 1995–96), Wimbledon
(1988–89, 1991–93, 1995–96), and the US Open (1988–
89, 1993, 1995–96). Graf retired in 1999.

grafting In horticulture, method of plant propagation. A twig
of one variety (the **scion**) is established on the roots of a related
variety (the **stock**). Most fruit trees are propagated by a similar
process called budding, in which the scion is a single bud.

Graham, Billy (William Franklin) (1918–) US evangelist.
A charismatic preacher, he led Christian revivalist crusades all
over the world, including communist countries. He was consulted by several US presidents, especially Richard NIXON.

Graham, Martha (1894–1991) US choreographer and
dancer, a leading figure in MODERN DANCE. In the early
1920s, she began to break with traditional BALLET, employing highly individual forms based on natural movement.

Graham, Thomas (1805–69) Scottish chemist, best remembered for **Graham's law**, which states that the diffusion rate of
a gas is inversely proportional to the square root of its density.
This law is used in separating isotopes by the diffusion method
and has industrial applications. He also discovered DIALYSIS.

Grahame, Kenneth (1859–1932) Scottish writer of children's books. He created Mole, Rat, Badger and Mr Toad
in the classic *Wind in the Willows* (1908), which formed the
basis for the A.A. MILNE play *Toad of Toad Hall* (1929).

grain Fruits of various CEREAL plants, or the plants themselves. The main kinds of grain are WHEAT, MAIZE, and
RICE. It is an important food, rich in carbohydrates and also
containing proteins and vitamins.

Grainger, (George) Percy (Aldridge) (1882–1961)
Australian composer and pianist. He was a pupil of Ferruc-
cio Busoni and a protégé of Edvard Grieg, who encouraged
him to edit and arrange folk music. His arrangements of
Country Gardens and *Shepherd's Hey* were both published
in 1908. He also wrote highly experimental music.

grammar Branch of LINGUISTICS that studies the structure of
words (**morphology**) and how words combine into phrases,
clauses and sentences (SYNTAX). It can also include SEMAN-
TICS. **Prescriptive** grammar is a value-based subject that
establishes conventions of 'correct' usage. **Descriptive** grammar describes actual usage patterns. In 1957 Noam CHOMSKY
developed the concept of **generative** grammar, which aims to
provide a formal description of the finite set of linguistic rules
that generate the infinite number of grammatical sentences in
a language. **Transformational** grammar is a form of generative grammar which seeks to explain the structural relationship between words in a sentence and sentences themselves.

Grampian Region in NE Scotland, bordered by the North
Sea, the Grampian Highlands and the CAIRNGORMS; the capital is ABERDEEN. The W of the region is mountainous, rising to
1,311m (4,301ft) at Ben Macdhui. The E is drained by the
Spey, Dee, and Don rivers. Along the banks of the Spey lie
many whisky distilleries. Industries: beef farming, fishing, and
tourism. Area: 8,707sq km (3361sq mi). Pop. (1996) 531,000.

Grampians Mountain range in N central Scotland. It is
the highest mountain system in Britain, running SW-NE
between Glen More and the Scottish Lowlands. Rivers rising in the Grampians include the Spey and Findhorn (flowing N), the Don and Dee (flowing E), and the Tay and Forth
(flowing S). Highest peak: BEN NEVIS, 1,343m (4,406ft).

Granada City in Andalusia, S Spain; capital of Granada
province. Founded in the 8th century as a Moorish fortress,
it became the capital of the independent Muslim kingdom
of Granada in 1238. The last Moorish stronghold in Spain, it
surrendered to the Christian armies of Ferdinand and Isabella in 1492. The central splendour of Granada is the ALHAM-
BRA. Industries: tourism and textiles. Pop. (2001) 240,661.

Gran Chaco Lowland plain of central South America,
stretching across the borders of Argentina, Bolivia, and
Paraguay. Arid and largely unpopulated, the region is famous
for its quebracho trees, a major source of TANNIN. The discovery of oil in the Chaco Borea, and Bolivia's subsequent need
for a route to the sea, led to the Chaco War (1932–35) between
Bolivia and Paraguay. The war killed more than 100,000 soldiers before an agreement gave 75% of Gran Chaco to
Paraguay, and allowed Bolivia use of the Paraguay River.

Grand Canal Ancient inland waterway in NE China, between
Beijing and Hangzhou. The first part, between the Yangtze and
Huai Ho rivers, was built in the 6th century BC. It was extended
to Hangzhou in the 6th century AD and to Beijing by KUBLAI
KHAN in the 13th century. Total length: *c.*1,600km (1,000mi).

Grand Canyon Deep gorge in NW Arizona, USA, carved
by the Colorado River. It is 450km (280mi) long, and varies
from 6km (4mi) to 18km (11mi) in width. With its magnificent multicoloured rock formations revealing hundreds of
millions of years of geological history, the Grand Canyon
is one of the great wonders of the natural world.

Grand Remonstrance (November 1641) Statement of grievances by the LONG PARLIAMENT presented to King CHARLES I in November 1641. It listed numerous objections to the royal government and demanded parliamentary approval of ministers. It was passed in the House of Commons by only 11 votes, and Charles rejected it. It hardened the division between the crown and Parliament, which culminated in the CIVIL WAR.

grand unified theory (GUT) Theory that would demonstrate that three of the four FUNDAMENTAL FORCES are actually different aspects of the same fundamental force. The WEAK NUCLEAR FORCE and ELECTROMAGNETIC FORCE have been incorporated as the electroweak force, as demonstrated by particle accelerator experiments. In order to prove the GUT, the electroweak force must be unified with the STRONG NUCLEAR FORCE. If the gravitational force could be incorporated, then a UNIFIED FIELD THEORY would be produced.

granite Coarse-grained, light-grey, durable IGNEOUS ROCK, composed chiefly of feldspar and quartz, with some mica or hornblende. It is thought to have solidified from magma (molten rock). It is a valuable construction material.

Grant, Cary (1904–86) US film star, b. Britain as Archibald Leach. A handsome and charming actor, he specialized in playing romantic leads. Grant's films include sophisticated comedies such as *Bringing Up Baby* (1938) and *His Girl Friday* (1940), and stylish thrillers such as *North by Northwest* (1959).

Grant, Duncan James Corrow (1885–1978) Scottish painter and designer, one of the first British artists to be influenced by POST-IMPRESSIONISM. He was a member of the BLOOMSBURY GROUP. A pioneer of British abstract art, his paintings include *Abstract kinetic collage painting* (1914).

Grant, Ulysses S. (Simpson) (1822–85) US Civil War general and 18th US president (1869–77). He served in the MEXICAN WAR (1846–48) and the CIVIL WAR. He masterminded the Vicksburg Campaign (1862–63). In 1864, Abraham LINCOLN gave him overall command of the Union forces. He co-ordinated the final campaigns and accepted the surrender of Robert E. LEE (1865). He served under President Andrew Johnson as secretary of war (1867–68). As president, Grant achieved foreign policy successes, but failed to prevent the growth of domestic corruption. He was easily re-elected in 1872, but members of his administration were implicated in a corruption scandal and he retired at the end of his second term.

grape Vines that grow in temperate and subtropical climates, producing fruit that is eaten raw, dried or used for making WINE. The classical European vine (*Vitis vinifera*) has its origins in Asia. The climate, soil, topography, and methods of cultivation all determine the quality of the crop. Family Vitaceae.

grapefruit Evergreen CITRUS fruit tree and its yellow, edible fruit, which is a valuable source of vitamin C. The tree may reach 6m (20ft), and is grown mainly in subtropical climates in the USA, Israel, South Africa and Argentina. Family Rutaceae.

graph Diagram representing a relationship between numbers or quantities. Many graphs use the CARTESIAN CO-ORDINATE system. Other forms include bar charts, where a series of figures is represented by lines of various lengths, and pie charts, in which quantities are represented by sectors of a circle.

graphical user interface (GUI) Computer PROGRAM enabling a user to operate a COMPUTER using simple symbols. Early personal computers used operating systems that were text based. Commands were often obscure combinations of letters and numbers, which made using the systems difficult. A GUI replaces these commands with a screen containing symbols called icons. The user manipulates these using a 'mouse'.

graphite (plumbago) Dark-grey, soft, crystalline form of CARBON. It occurs naturally in deposits of varying purity and is made synthetically by heating petroleum coke. It is used in pencils, lubricants, electrodes, brushes of electrical machines, rocket nozzles, and as a moderator that slows down neutrons in nuclear reactors. Graphite is a good conductor of heat and electricity. Hardness 1–2; r.d. 2.1–2.3.

grass Herbaceous plants with fibrous roots that have long, narrow leaves enclosing hollow, jointed stems. The stems may be upright or bent, lie on the ground, or grow underground.

The flowers are small, without PETALS and SEPALS. The leaves grow from the base, and so removal of the tips does not inhibit growth, making grass suitable for lawns and pastures. CEREAL grasses, such as rice, millet, maize and wheat, are cultivated for their seeds. Others are grown as food for animals and for erosion control and ornament. There are *c.*9,000 species. Family Poaceae/Gramineae. *See also* MONOCOTYLEDON

Grass, Günter Wilhelm (1927–) German novelist, poet and dramatist. He combined evocative description with historical documentation in a mannerist style. He used powerful techniques to grotesque comic effect in *The Tin Drum* (1959) and *Cat and Mouse* (1961), and satirized the Nazi era in *Dog Years* (1963). Later works include *The Flounder* (1977) and *The Rat* (1986). He received the Nobel Prize in literature in 1999.

grasshopper Plant-eating insect. Its enlarged hind legs make it a powerful jumper. The forewings are leathery and the hind wings are membranous and fan-shaped; when the insect is at rest, the wings are folded over its back. Length: 8–11cm (0.3–4.3in). Order Orthoptera; families Acrididae and Tettingoniidae. *See also* CRICKET; LOCUST *See* illustration, page 362

Grattan, Henry (1746–1820) Irish statesman. He entered the Irish Parliament in 1775. A compelling orator, he became leader of the Patriotic Party. In 1782, Grattan helped to obtain legislative independence. He strongly opposed the Act of UNION (1801), which merged the Irish and British Parliaments. As a member of the Westminster Parliament (1805–20), Grattan fought for CATHOLIC EMANCIPATION.

Graves, Robert von Ranke (1895–1985) English poet, novelist, and critic. His early poetry, such as *Fairies and Fusiliers* (1917), relates his experiences in World War 1. After writing an autobiographical farce, *Goodbye To All That* (1929), Graves emigrated to Majorca. He is best known for the historical novels *I, Claudius* (1934) and *Claudius the God* (1939).

gravitation Force of attraction that is exercised by every particle of MATTER as a result of its MASS. Gravitation is the weakest of the four FUNDAMENTAL FORCES, but it is apparent because of the great mass of the Earth. The Moon has only 1/6 of the Earth's gravitational force. Gravitation was first described (1687) by Sir Isaac NEWTON, whose **law of gravitation** stated that gravitational force is directly proportional to the masses of the interacting bodies and inversely proportional to the square of the distance between them. Thus, the gravitational force will decrease by 1/4 if the distance between two objects is doubled. Albert EINSTEIN developed a more complete treatment of gravitation, showing in his general theory of RELATIVITY that gravitation is a manifestation of SPACE-TIME.

gray (symbol Gy) SI unit of absorbed radiation dose. One gray is equivalent to supplying 1 joule of energy per kilogram of irradiated material. It superseded the rad (1 gray = 100 rad).

Gray, Elisha (1835–1901) US inventor. He patented the self-adjusting telegraph relay, the telegraphic repeater and the type-printing telegraph. He claimed priority as the inventor of the telephone, but Alexander Graham BELL's patent rights were upheld by the US Supreme Court.

Gray, Thomas (1716–71) English poet. His masterpiece was "Elegy Written in a Country Churchyard" (1751). Other poems include "Ode on the Death of a Favourite Cat" (1748), and "The Descent of Odin" (1768).

Graz City at the foot of the Schlossberg Mountain, on the River Mur, SE Austria; capital of Styria. Its historic buildings include a 15th-century Gothic cathedral, the *Uhrturm* clock tower (1561), and the Renaissance *Landhaus* (provincial parliament). Johannes KEPLER taught at the university (founded 1586) and Emperor Frederick II is buried here. Industries: iron and steel, paper, leather, glass, chemicals. Pop. (2001) 226,424.

Great Awakening Series of 18th-century religious revivals in the American colonies. It was inspired in the 1730s by the preaching of Jonathan Edwards and George WHITEFIELD. Baptist revivals occurred in 1760, and METHODISM evolved in the pre-Revolutionary period. The movement led to Christian missionary work among the Native American tribes.

Great Barrier Reef World's largest CORAL REEF, in the Coral Sea off the NE coast of Queensland, Australia. It was first explored by James COOK in 1770. It forms a natural breakwater and is up to 800m (2,600ft) wide. The reef is

▲ **Grant** US general and president, Ulysses S. Grant served under Zachary Taylor and Winfield Scott in the Mexican War (1846–48). Grant gained the first major victory for the Union (Fort Donelson, February 1862) in the Civil War, but was widely blamed for the defeat at Shiloh (April 1862). He was hailed as a hero after forcing Robert E. Lee's surrender at Appomattox. His presidency was tainted by the Crédit Mobilier corruption scandal.

▲ **grass** Meadow grass (*Poa pratensis*) is an important hay and green pasture grass in North America and Europe, and as such it is an economically valuable member of the large and widespread grass family (Gramineae). The flower of the grass is a minute spikelet, usually arranged in open branching clusters known as panicles. The flowers are cross-fertilized by the wind and the single ovule then develops into a seed or grain. Grassland will evolve readily wherever forest or scrub cover is sparse, and where there is sufficient moisture and nutrients in the soil. Vast areas of the world are natural grasslands, such as the steppes of Asia and the prairies of North America.

G

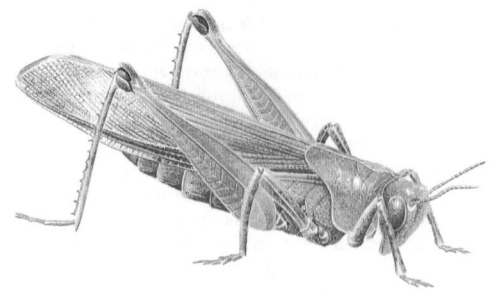

separated from the mainland by a shallow lagoon, 11–24km (7–15mi) wide. It is a world heritage site. Length: 2,000km (1,250mi). Area: *c.*207,000sq km (80,000sq mi).

Great Basin Desert area in w USA comprising most of Nevada and parts of Utah, Idaho, California, Wyoming and Oregon. This sparsely populated area includes DEATH VALLEY and the MOJAVE DESERT. The few streams drain into saline lakes, the largest being GREAT SALT LAKE. Mineral deposits include gold, magnesite, mercury, and beryllium ore. Area: *c.*492,000sq km (190,000sq mi).

Great Bear Lake Lake in Northwest Territories, NW Canada; the largest lake in Canada and fourth largest in North America. It was first explored in 1825 by John FRANKLIN. It is drained in the w by the Great Bear River. Although the lake is one of North America's deepest, it is icebound for eight months of the year. Area: *c.*31,800sq km (12,300sq mi).

Great Britain Island of Britain, comprising ENGLAND, SCOTLAND, and WALES. Wales united with England in 1536. The Act of UNION (1707) united Scotland with England, and the Act of Union (1801) established the UNITED KINGDOM of Great Britain and Ireland.

great circle Circle on a spherical surface, the centre of which is coincident with the centre of the sphere. On the celestial sphere, the EQUATOR is a great circle, as are all MERIDIANS. The shortest distance between any two points on a sphere, great circles are used for mapping aircraft routes.

Great Dane (German mastiff) Large hunting dog, originally bred in Germany more than 400 years ago. One of the largest dog breeds, it has a narrow head and blunt muzzle. Its deep-chested body is set on long, strong legs. The smooth coat may be various colours. Height: up to 92cm (36in) at the shoulder.

Great Depression Severe economic DEPRESSION that afflicted the USA throughout the 1930s. At the close of the 1920s, economic factors such as over-production, unrealistic credit levels, stock market speculation, lack of external markets, high corruption, US financial isolationism, and unequal distribution of wealth all contributed to the prolonged economic crisis. The dramatic collapse of the stock market in October 1929 saw US$30,000 million wiped off stock values in the first week. Bank failures became commonplace. At the depth of the Depression (1932–33), unemployment stood at 16 million, almost 33% of the total workforce. The gross national product fell by almost 50%. The Hawley-Smoot Tariff Act increased US tariffs and effectively spread the depression worldwide. Franklin D. ROOSEVELT, sensing the national emergency, instituted the NEW DEAL, which helped to mitigate the worst effects of the crisis. The economy only significantly recovered with increased defence spending in the 1940s.

Great Dividing Range (Eastern Highlands) Series of mountain ranges along the E coast of Australia. They extend S from the Atherton Tableland in Queensland to the Grampian Mountains in Victoria. The highest peak is Mount Kosciuszko, 2,230m (7,316ft). Length: 3,703km (2,300 mi).

Greater Antilles Largest of three major island groups in the WEST INDIES, between the Atlantic Ocean and the Caribbean Sea. The group includes CUBA, HISPANIOLA, JAMAICA, PUERTO RICO, and the CAYMAN ISLANDS.

Great Exhibition (1851) See CRYSTAL PALACE

Great Lakes Five lakes in central North America, between Canada and the USA; the world's largest expanse of freshwater. They are (from w to E): Lakes SUPERIOR, MICHIGAN, HURON, ERIE, and ONTARIO. They interconnect by straits, rivers, and canals, providing a continuous waterway. They are

drained by the ST LAWRENCE River, the deepening of which opened up the lakes to world shipping. Industrial and commercial growth led to pollution. Major cities include CHICAGO, TORONTO, DETROIT, BUFFALO, CLEVELAND, and MILWAUKEE. Total surface area: *c.*245,300sq km (94,700sq mi).

Great Leap Forward Five-year economic plan begun by MAO ZEDONG in China in 1958. It aimed to double industrial production and boost agricultural output in record time. The plan mobilized tens of millions of workers to smelt steel in primitive pig-iron furnaces, but most of the steel was poor quality and useless. Collective farms merged into communes, but a succession of poor harvests dashed progress. After four years, the government admitted the failure of the plan.

Great Plains Extensive region of grassland in central North America. The Great Plains extend from the Canadian provinces of Alberta, Saskatchewan, and Manitoba, through w central USA to Texas. The plateau slopes down and E from the Rocky Mountains. It is a sparsely populated region with a semi-arid climate, prone to high winds. The chinook wind warms the bitter winter. Most of the land is prairie. Cattle-ranching and sheep-rearing are the main economic activities; wheat is the principal crop. Native Americans roamed the Great Plains before Europeans destroyed the BISON. The railroads brought settlers in the late 19th century. In the 1930s, drought and soil mismanagement resulted in the DUST BOWL.

Great Red Spot *See* JUPITER

Great Salt Lake Large, shallow saltwater lake in NW Utah, USA. Fed by the Bear, Weber, and Jordan rivers, its depth and area vary with climatic changes. The heavy brine supports only shrimp and algae. It is the remnant of the prehistoric Lake Bonneville, which covered much of the GREAT BASIN of North America. Bonneville Salt Flats, famous for land speed records, lies in the Great Salt Desert. Area: varies from *c.*2,500sq km (960sq mi) to *c.*6,200sq km (2,400sq mi).

Great Schism (1378–1417) Split within the Roman Catholic Church following the election of two rival popes to succeed Gregory XI. In 1309, Pope Clement V moved the papacy from Rome to AVIGNON, France. The attempt to return the papacy to Rome saw the Italian cardinals elect an Italian pope, URBAN VI, and the French cardinals elect a rival 'ANTIPOPE', Clement VII. The SCHISM ended with the Council of CONSTANCE, which established MARTIN V as sole pope.

Great Slave Lake Second-largest lake in Canada, w Northwest Territories; the deepest lake in North America. It is named after the Slave tribe of Native Americans. The first European discovery was in 1771. Gold is mined on its N shore. It is drained by the Mackenzie River. Area: *c.*28,400sq km (10,980sq mi). Max. depth: 615m (2,015ft).

Great Smoky Mountains Part of the APPALACHIANS, on the North Carolina-Tennessee border, USA. One of the oldest ranges on Earth, it includes the largest virgin forest of red spruce. The region is renowned for its flora and fauna. Early 20th-century exploitation of the region was restricted by the establishment of a national park. The highest point is Clingmans Dome, 2,026m (6,643ft). Area: 2,090sq km (806sq mi).

Great Trek (1835–40) Migration of *c.*12,000 BOERS from Cape Colony into the South African interior. Their motives were to escape British control and to acquire cheap land. The majority settled in what became Orange FREE STATE, TRANSVAAL, and NATAL.

Great Wall of China Defensive frontier and world heritage site, *c.*2,400km (1,500mi) long, extending from the Huang Hai (Yellow Sea) to the Central Asian Desert, N China. It is an amalgamation of fortifications constructed by various dynasties.The Warring States built the first sections of the wall. In 214 BC QIN SHIHUANGDI ordered that they should be joined to form a unified boundary. The present wall was mostly built 600 years ago by the MING dynasty. It averages 7.6m (25ft) high, and is up to 9m (30ft) thick.

Great Zimbabwe Ruined city and world heritage site, SE Zimbabwe. It was the capital of a Bantu-speaking kingdom (12th-15th century). At the height of its power, the city's population probably numbered more than 15,000.

grebe Brown, grey and black freshwater diving bird found worldwide. It flies laboriously and has legs set so far back that it cannot walk. There are five common species of grebes in Britain and W Europe. Length: to 48cm (19in). Family Podicepididae; genus *Podiceps*.

Greco, El (1541–1614) Cretan painter, b. Domenikos Theotokopoulos. He studied under TITIAN in Venice. By 1577, he had settled in Toledo, Spain. His earliest work here, *The Assumption of the Virgin*, combines Spanish influences with Italian. His characteristically elongated and distorted figures disregard normal rules of perspective. His later paintings, such as *Burial of Count Orgasz* (1586), *Agony in the Garden* (1610) and *Assumption* (1613), express his profound religious conviction. *See also* MANNERISM

Greece Republic in SE Europe. *See* country feature

Greece, Ancient Period beginning with the defeat of the second Persian invasion in 479 BC and ending with the establishment of Macedonian power in 338 BC. Warring city-states flourished as centres of trade. ATHENS, the most wealthy and powerful, developed a democratic system under the guidance of PERICLES. Its main rival was the military state of SPARTA. Classical Greece was the birthplace of many ideas in art, literature, philosophy and science – among them those of PLATO and ARISTOTLE. It is traditionally regarded as the birthplace of Western civilization. *See also* HELLENISTIC AGE

Greek INDO-EUROPEAN LANGUAGE spoken in Greece since *c.*2000 BC. In ancient Greece there were several dialects: Attic, spoken in Athens, is the most common in literary records. Greek was widely spoken in the Middle East during the HELLENISTIC AGE. It was the official language of the Byzantine Empire, and it began to evolve into its modern form in *c.*1000 AD. After the fall of Byzantium, it developed two forms: 'demotiki', the spoken language also used in most literary forms, and 'katharevousa', used in official documents.

Greek art and architecture Greek architecture came into its own in the 6th century BC when stone replaced wood as the building material for civic and temple buildings. Distinct ORDERS OF ARCHITECTURE began to emerge. The earliest remaining Doric temple is the Temple of Hera at Olympia (late 7th century BC), and the most outstanding example is the PARTHENON. Among Ionic temples, the Erechtheum is considered the most perfect. The Corinthian mausoleum at HALICARNASSUS (350 BC) was one of the SEVEN WONDERS OF THE WORLD. Greek art may be divided into four periods: Geometric (late 11th–late 8th century BC), Archaic (late 8th century–480 BC), Classical (480–323 BC), and Hellenistic (323–27 BC). Only a few small bronze horses survive from the **Geometric** period. During the **Archaic** period, stone sculpture appeared, vase painting proliferated, and the human figure became a common subject. Civic wealth and pride was a feature of the **Classical** period, and sculpture reached its peak of serene perfection. The **Hellenistic** period is noted for increasingly dramatic works.

G

GREECE

The Hellenic Republic, the official name of Greece, is a rugged country lying at the southern end of the Balkan Peninsula. OLYMPUS (Ólimbos), at 2,917m [9,570ft], is the highest peak. Nearly a fifth of the land area is made up of around 2,000 islands, mainly in the Aegean Sea, east of the main peninsula, but also in the Ionian Sea to the west. Only 154 are inhabited. The island of CRETE is structurally related to the main Alpine fold mountain system to which the mainland Pindos Range belongs.

CLIMATE
Low-lying areas in Greece have mild, moist winters and hot, dry summers. The E coast has more than 2,700 hours of sunshine a year and only about half of the rainfall of the W. The mountains have a more severe climate, with snow on the higher slopes in winter.

HISTORY
Crete was the centre of the MINOAN CIVILIZATION, a BRONZE AGE culture which made use of LINEAR SCRIPT, between about 3000 and 1400 BC. Following the end of the related MYCAENEAN period on the mainland (1580–1200 BC), the DORIANS settled, inaugurating an IRON AGE but non-literate era which lasted until the adoption of a script derived from Phoenician characters in about 800 BC. In about 750 BC, the Greeks began to colonize the Mediterranean, creating wealth through trade. Powerful city-states emerged, such as SPARTA and Athens, in which Solon established the first DEMOCRACY (5th century AD). The revolt of the IONIANS started the PERSIAN WARS (499–479 BC). See GREECE, ANCIENT. The city-state of Athens reached its peak in the 461–431 BC, but Corinth and Thebes gained control after Athens' defeat in the Peloponnesian War (431–404 BC). In 338 BC, MACEDON, led by PHILIP II, became the dominant power. His son, ALEXANDER THE GREAT, conquered a vast empire and began the HELLENISTIC AGE. In 146 BC, Greece fell to the Romans. Greece formed part of the BYZANTINE EMPIRE from AD 330 until its fall in 1453. In 1456, the OTTOMAN EMPIRE conquered Greece.

The European powers supported the Greek War of Independence (1821–27), and an independent monarchy emerged in 1832. As King of the Hellenes (1863–1913), GEORGE I recovered much Greek territory. In 1913, Greece took control of Crete. Greece finally entered World War 1 on the Allied side in 1917. In 1923, 1.5 million Greeks from Asia Minor resettled in Greece. In 1936, Joannis METAXAS became premier. His dictatorial regime remained neutral at the start of World War 2. By May 1941, Germany occupied Greece. Resistance movements recaptured most territory by 1944, and the Germans withdrew.

From 1946–49, a civil war raged between communist and royalist forces. In 1951, Greece joined NATO. In 1955, KARAMANLIS became prime minister. The economy slowly improved, but tension surfaced with Turkey about the status of Cyprus. In 1964 a republican, Andreas PAPANDREOU, became prime minister. In 1967, a military dictatorship seized power. The 'Colonels' imposed harsh controls on dissent. In 1973, they abolished the monarchy, and Greece became a presidential republic. In 1974 civil unrest led to the restoration of civilian government, headed by Karamanlis.

AREA 131,957sq km [50,949sq mi]
POPULATION 10,706,000
CAPITAL (POPULATION) Athens (3,238,000)
GOVERNMENT Multiparty republic
ETHNIC GROUPS Greek 98%
LANGUAGES Greek (official)
RELIGIONS Greek Orthodox 98%
CURRENCY Euro = 100 cents

POLITICS
Greece joined the EC in 1981. Despite efforts to develop the economy, Greece remained one of the poorer countries in the European Union. The euro became the sole currency in 2002.

Relations with Turkey have long been difficult. In 1999, the two countries helped each other when both were hit by major earthquakes. In 2000 Greece and Turkey signed agreements aimed at improving relations between them, but boundary disputes in the Aegean continued.

ECONOMY
Manufacturing is important. Products include processed food, cement, chemicals, metal products, textiles and tobacco. Lignite, bauxite and chromite are mined.

Farmland and grazing land cover about 75% of the land. Major crops include barley, grapes for wine-making, dried fruits, olives, potatoes, sugar beet and wheat. Poultry, sheep, goats, pigs and cattle are raised. The vital tourist industry is based on the warm climate, beautiful scenery, and historical sites dating back to the days of classical Greece.

G

INTERNET

greenhouse effect
▶ www.epa.gov/
globalwarming/kids/
greenhouse.html

Greenland
▶ www.greenland-guide.gl

Greek drama First form of DRAMA in Western civilization. It took three forms – TRAGEDY, COMEDY and satyr plays. Tragedy and comedy were the two main forms. **Tragedy** developed from religious festivals, at which a CHORUS sang responses to a leader. AESCHYLUS introduced a second actor, and SOPHOCLES added a third. The other major tragedian was EURIPIDES. Greek tragedy usually dealt with mythical subjects, but sometimes (as in Aeschylus' *The Persians*) used recent history for its setting. A tradition of Greek **comedy** arose in the 5th century BC. It was often highly topical and lampooned politics and the conventions of tragedy; its best-known exponent was ARISTOPHANES. Comedy flourished in the HELLENISTIC AGE (323–27BC), especially in the work of MENANDER. **Satyr** plays were bawdy works written to accompany tragedies.

Greek literature One of the longest surviving traditions in world literature. The earliest Greek literature took the form of EPIC songs, as epitomized by the *Iliad* and the *Odyssey* of HOMER, and the didactic poetry of Hesiod, such as *Theogony*. It also saw the development of lyric poetry, exemplified by the choric lyrics and odes of PINDAR. Throughout the Classical period (*c*.480–*c*.323BC) there was a tradition of fine literature in poetry and prose writing. During the Hellenistic Age (323–27BC), epic, epigrammatic and didactic poetry flourished in the works of Apollonius of Rhodes, Aratus and Callimachus. Herodus revitalized the art of MIME. During the Roman period (*c*.27BC–*c*.AD 330) important figures included PLUTARCH, MARCUS AURELIUS, and PTOLEMY. Writing in Greek died out after the Turkish invasions of the 15th century, and only revived after their overthrow in 1828. Prominent among the new generation were Dionysios Solomos and Andreas Kalvos. Modern Greek writers of international stature include Nikos KAZANTZAKIS.

Greek mythology Collection of stories mainly concerning the adventures of gods and heroes. In the myths, the gods are not wholly admirable figures: they have similar weaknesses to humans and are capable of great vindictiveness, revenge, and favouritism. Greek myths were often explanatory, offering answers to questions of human nature and the universe, clarifying abstract ideas, or explaining religious matters in a more rational manner. From the time of HOMER (9th century-BC), Greek polytheism formed a coherent system with a pantheon of 12 deities who dwelt on Mount OLYMPUS: ZEUS, HERA, POSEIDON, ATHENA, APOLLO, ARTEMIS, APHRODITE, HEPHAESTUS, ARES, DEMETER, HESTIA, and HERMES. Major religious centres included Delphi and Olympia.

Greeley, Horace (1811–72) US journalist and political leader. In 1841 Greeley founded and edited the *New York Tribune*. He advocated progressive social reforms and opposed slavery. His advocacy of Western settlement was encapsulated in his advice, "Go West, young man, go West". Ulysses S. GRANT defeated Greeley's bid for the presidency in 1872.

green algae Large group of marine and freshwater ALGAE (phylum Chlorophyta). They are distinct from other algae by virtue of possessing cup-shaped CHLOROPLASTS that contain chlorophyll b, and by producing cells with flagella at some stage in their lives. Green algae range in size from microscopic single-cell types to large, complex SEAWEEDS. *See also* LICHEN

Greenaway, Peter (1942–) Welsh film director and screenwriter. An innovative and painterly director, his breakthrough film was *The Draughtsman's Contract* (1983). Other films include *The Cook, the Thief, His Wife and Her Lover* (1989), *Prospero's Books* (1991) and *The Pillow Book* (1996).

greenback Paper money issued by the US government during the Civil War. Authorized by Congress as legal tender, they could not be redeemed in gold or coins. A total of US$450 million was issued. In 1878, they became convertible to gold.

green belt Area of open land maintained as a barrier between adjoining built-up areas. The concept of green belts was first put forward (1898) by Ebenezer Howard in his plans for Britain's garden cities. Howard used them to distinguish residential from industrial sections. Green belts provide protection from factories and intensive commercial areas.

Greene, (Henry) Graham (1904–91) English novelist and dramatist. Greene converted to Catholicism in 1926; religion,

guilt and the search for redemption are consistent themes in his novels. His psychological thrillers are among the most popular and critically acclaimed works of 20th-century fiction. His first novel was *The Man Within* (1929). Important works include *Brighton Rock* (1938), *The Power and the Glory* (1940), *The Heart of the Matter* (1948), *The Quiet American* (1955), the 'entertainment' *Our Man in Havana* (1958), *The Honorary Consul* (1973), and *Travels with My Aunt* (1978).

Greene, Nathanael (1743–86) American general. He was George WASHINGTON's second-in-command in the AMERICAN REVOLUTION. In 1776, he skilfully led the left wing of the American forces at Trenton, Princeton, and Brandywine. Greene assumed command of the Southern army in 1780. His reorganization and strategy ensured the success of the Carolina Campaign (1780–82), resulting in numerous British defeats.

greenhouse effect Raised temperature at a planet's surface as a result of heat energy being trapped by gases in the ATMOSPHERE. As the Sun's rays pass through the atmosphere, some heat is absorbed but most of the short-wave SOLAR ENERGY passes through. This energy is re-emitted from the ground as long-wave radiation, which cannot pass easily through the certain gases in the atmosphere, most notably carbon dioxide, but also methane, CHLOROFLUOROCARBONS (CFCs) – this is unconnected to their effect on the OZONE LAYER) and other gases. On Earth in the last 100 years, the level of greenhouse gases has increased as a result of industrialisation. Of particular concern is carbon dioxide (CO_2) from the burning of FOSSIL FUELS. Scientists of the Intergovernmental Panel on Climate Change (IPCC) estimate that present patterns of carbon dioxide and methane emissions could lead to GLOBAL WARMING on the scale of an average surface temperature rise of between 1.4 to 5.8°C by 2100. *See also* EARTH SUMMIT

Greenland World's largest island, in the NW Atlantic Ocean, lying mostly within the Arctic Circle. It is a self-governing province of Denmark; the capital is NUUK (Godthåb). PERMAFROST covers more than 85% of Greenland, with an average depth of 1,500m (5,000ft). Settlement is confined to the SW coast, which is warmed by Atlantic currents. Most of Greenland's inhabitants are INUIT. Its European discovery is credited to ERIC THE RED, who settled in 982, founding a colony that lasted more than 500 years. Greenland became a Danish possession in 1380, and was incorporated into the kingdom in 1953. Following a referendum, Greenland achieved home rule in 1979 and self-government in 1981. In 1985, it withdrew from the European Union. Greenland's economy depends heavily on subsidies from Denmark. Fish forms the basis of the economy. Lead and zinc are mined in the NW, and the S has untapped reserves of uranium. Tourism is increasing. Area: 2,175,600sq km (838,999sq mi). Pop. (2000) 56,000.

green movement Campaign to preserve the environment, and to minimize pollution or destruction of the Earth's natural habitat. The green movement formed its own active pressure groups, GREENPEACE and Friends of the Earth, in the 1970s. It gained political representation shortly afterwards in the form of various European Green Parties. In affluent Western societies, effects of the movement included campaigns for environmentally safe products and a concern with the recycling of waste products such as glass, paper and plastics.

Green Party Any of a number of European political parties embodying the principles of the GREEN MOVEMENT. Major Green parties were founded in the early 1970s. In the UK, traditional political parties adopted many Green policies in the 1990s and the Green vote declined. The Greens in Germany were the junior partners in a coalition govenment (1998–2005).

Greenpeace International pressure group. It was founded in 1971, initially to oppose US nuclear testing in Alaska. Greenpeace promotes environmental awareness and campaigns against environmental abuse. It gains wide media coverage for its active, non-violent demonstrations against whaling, toxic-waste dumping and nuclear testing.

green revolution Intensive plan of the 1960s to increase crop yields in developing countries by introducing higher-yielding strains of plant and new fertilizers. The scheme began in Mexico in the 1940s, and was successfully introduced in parts of India, SE Asia, the Middle East and Latin America.

▲ **Greek art** A collection of classical Greek jewellery dating from the 4th century BC. The items include a bracelet (A) showing lions' heads in chased gold with filigree collars; a central element of a diadem (B) decorated with gold filigree work; a golden earring (C) shaped in a spiral tube, ending in a lion's head; a second earring (D) in the form of a gold filigree rosette with delicately chased female head suspended from the disc; and two gold rings, one carved in intaglio with a female figure (E), the other carved with a woman's profile (F).

Greenwich Borough in SE London, England. The former Royal Observatory (founded 1675) is in Greenwich Park. The prime meridian forms the basis of GREENWICH MEAN TIME (GMT). Greenwich has a rich maritime history. The Royal Naval College, partly designed (1696) by Sir Christopher WREN, stands on the site of a Tudor royal palace, birthplace of Henry VIII. The Millennium Dome was built here to celebrate the dawning of the third millennium. Pop. (2001) 214,540.

Greenwich Mean Time (GMT) Local time at GREENWICH, London, situated on the prime MERIDIAN (0° LONGITUDE) that passes through the Old Royal Observatory. It has been used as the basis for calculating standard time in various parts of the world since 1884.

Greer, Germaine (1939–) Australian feminist writer. Her controversial book *The Female Eunuch* (1970) portrayed marriage as a legalized form of female slavery and questioned a number of gender-oriented stereotypes. Other works include *Sex and Destiny: the Politics of Human Fertility* (1984), *The Change: Women, Ageing and the Menopause* (1991), and *The Whole Woman* (1999). *See also* FEMINISM

Gregory I (the Great), Saint (540–604) Pope (590–604), one of the Fathers of the Church. Gregory devoted himself to alleviating poverty and hunger among the Romans. His reforms included changes in the Mass. He also initiated the conversion of the LOMBARDS, sent Saint AUGUSTINE OF CANTERBURY to convert the ANGLO-SAXONS, and encouraged monasticism. His feast day is March 12.

Gregory XIII (1502–85) Pope (1572–85), b. Ugo Buoncompagni. He supported education, training for the clergy, and missionary activity, especially the JESUITS. He promoted Church reform and sought to carry out the decrees of the Council of TRENT. He is best known for reforming the Julian CALENDAR.

Gregory VII, Saint (1020–85) Pope (1073–85), b. Hildebrand. He condemned lay investiture, simony and clerical marriage. Emperor HENRY IV opposed the reforms and deposed Gregory (1076). Gregory responded by excommunicating Henry. Gregory failed to establish the independence of the papacy, but his example inspired the Concordat of WORMS (1122). His feast day is May 25.

Grenada Independent island nation in the SE Caribbean Sea, the most southerly of the WINDWARD ISLANDS, *c.*160km (100mi) N of Venezuela. It consists of Grenada and the smaller islands of the Southern Grenadines dependency; the capital is St George's. The country is volcanic in origin, with a ridge of mountains running N-S. It has a tropical climate with occasional hurricanes. First sighted in 1498 by Christopher COLUMBUS, the islands were then inhabited by the Carib. In the mid-17th century, France settled Grenada. It became a permanent British possession in 1783, and a Crown Colony in 1877. It was a member of the West Indian Federation (1958–62). In 1974, it became an independent Commonwealth state. In 1979, the New Jewel movement seized power and in 1983, following a military coup, US forces invaded the island. They were withdrawn in 1985 after the re-establishment of a democratic government. The New National Party, led by Dr Keith Mitchell, won elections in 1995 and 1999. The economy is largely agricultural, based on cocoa, bananas, sugar, spices, and citrus fruits. It depends greatly on tourism. Area: 344sq km (133sq mi). Pop. (2000) 89,000.

Grenadines Group of *c.*600 small islands in the S Windward Islands, Caribbean Sea, WEST INDIES. The S Grenadines are included in GRENADA. The N Grenadines form part of ST VINCENT AND THE GRENADINES.

Grenville, Sir Richard (1541–91) English naval commander and hero. He commanded the fleet that carried Sir Walter Raleigh's colonists to Roanoke, Virginia, in 1585. His adventurous career ended when he was fatally wounded and his ship, *Revenge*, captured in a 15-hour battle off the Azores (1591).

Gretzky, Wayne (1961–) ('the Great One') Canadian ice hockey player. He led the Edmonton Oilers to four consecutive Stanley Cups before being traded to the Los Angeles Kings in 1988. In 1981–82, Gretzky scored the most goals (92) in a single season. He heads the NHL all-time scoring record with 2,857 career points (894 goals and 1,963 assists).

Grey, Charles, 2nd Earl (1764–1845) British Prime Minister (1830–34). During his administration, the First REFORM Act was passed (1832) and slavery was abolished throughout the British Empire (1833). Grey supported limited parliamentary reform, though as a Whig aristocrat he was no radical.

Grey, Lady Jane (1537–54) (Nine-Day Queen) Queen of England (1553). Great-granddaughter of Henry VII, she was married to the son of the Duke of NORTHUMBERLAND, regent for the ailing EDWARD VI. On Edward VI's death, she was proclaimed queen, but the rightful heir, MARY I, was almost universally preferred. Lady Jane and her husband were executed.

greyhound Coursing dog traditionally used to hunt hares and also used for racing. It has a long tapered head and muzzle. Its muscular back and well-arched loins are set on long, lean legs. The smooth coat may be almost any colour. Height: 66cm (26in) at the shoulder; weight 29kg (65lb).

Grieg, Edvard Hagerup (1843–1907) Norwegian composer. He used Norwegian folk themes in his compositions, many of which are for piano or voice. Among his best-known works are the song *I Love Thee* (1864), the two *Peer Gynt* suites for orchestra (1876), and the Piano Concerto (1868).

Griffith, Arthur (1872–1922) Irish statesman, president of the Irish Free State (1922). From 1899 he edited the republican newspaper, *United Irishman*. In 1905, Griffith founded SINN FÉIN. He took no part in the EASTER RISING (1916), but the British imprisoned him (1916–18). In 1919, he became vice president of the unofficial Irish parliament, the *Dáil Éireann*. Griffith and Michael COLLINS were the chief negotiators of the Anglo-Irish Treaty (1921), which created the Irish Free State and *de facto* acceptance of partition. Eamon DE VALERA rejected the settlement and Griffith became president.

Griffith, D.W. (David Wark) (1875–1948) US film director. His expressive use of the camera, lighting and dramatic editing established film as an independent art form. In 1915, Griffith released the Civil War epic *The Birth of a Nation*, often cited as the most important document in cinematic history, but also condemned as racist. *Intolerance* (1916) was his response, examining the persistence of prejudice. In 1919, he co-founded United Artists, and in 1935 he won an honorary Oscar.

griffon vulture Carrion-eating bird of prey of Eurasia and N Africa, with gold or sandy-brown plumage. It is gregarious and nests in large flocks. Length: 1m (3.3ft). Family Accipitridae; species *Gyps fulvus*.

Grimm brothers German philologists and folklorists. **Jakob Ludwig Karl** (1785–1863) formulated **Grimm's law** relating to the regular shifting of consonants in INDO-EUROPEAN LANGUAGES. He and his brother **Wilhelm Karl** (1786–1859) are popularly known for their collection of folk tales, *Grimm's Fairy Tales* (1812–15). It was a major text of ROMANTICISM.

Grimond, Jo (Joseph), Baron (1913–93) British politician, Liberal Party leader (1956–67). Grimond became a member of Parliament in 1950. He modernized the Liberal Party and proposed a political realignment, which captured new supporters. He opposed nuclear weapons and favoured Britain's entry into the EUROPEAN COMMUNITY (EC). After the forced resignation of Jeremy Thorpe (1976), Grimond became caretaker leader of the Party until David STEEL took over.

Gris, Juan (1887–1927) Spanish painter. In 1906 Gris settled in Paris and, with PICASSO and BRAQUE, became a leading exponent of synthetic CUBISM, as seen in *Homage to Picasso* (1912). Later works include collages, architectonic paintings, stage sets and costumes for DIAGHILEV.

grizzly bear Large BEAR, generally considered to be a variety of brown bear (*Ursus arctos*) although sometimes classified as a separate species (*U. horribilis*). Once widespread in W North America, the grizzly is now rare except in W Canada, Alaska, and some US national parks. Length: to 2.5m (7ft); weight: 410kg (900lb).

Gromyko, Andrei (1909–89) Soviet statesman, foreign minister (1957–85), president (1985–88). As Soviet ambassador to the USA (1943–46), Gromyko took part in the Yalta and Potsdam peace conferences (1945). He acted as the permanent Soviet delegate to the United Nations (1946–48). As foreign minister, Gromyko represented the Soviet Union throughout most of the COLD WAR and helped to arrange the

G

▲ **Gretzky** Canadian ice hockey star Wayne Gretzky was the first player ever to exceed 200 points (goals and assists) in a single season (1981–82). He was voted Most Valuable Player in the National Hockey League nine times (including every year from 1980 to 1987). He retired in 1999, and within months was inducted into the NHL Hall of Fame. He scored a total of 1072 goals in his professional career. He played for the Edmonton Oilers (1979–88), the Los Angeles Kings (1988–96), the St Louis Blues (1995–96), and the New York Rangers (1996–99).

▲ **guava** The fruit of the tropical American tree (*Psidium guajava*) is high in vitamin C. It is most commonly made into guava jelly, but it can also be stewed and canned.

G

summits between BREZHNEV and NIXON. He was given the largely honorary role of president by Mikhail GORBACHEV.

Groningen City at the confluence of the Hoornse Diep and the Winschoter Diep, NE Netherlands; capital of Groningen province. A member of the HANSEATIC LEAGUE from 1284, it controlled most of Friesland. Groningen remained loyal to the Habsburgs, but was forced to surrender to the Dutch in 1594. It has 15th- and 17th-century churches and a university (1614). The surrounding fertile agricultural land makes it one of the country's biggest markets. Industries: shipbuilding, electrical equipment. Pop. (2002) 175,484.

Gropius, Walter (1883–1969) German-US architect, founder of the BAUHAUS (1919–28). Gropius transformed the Weimar School of Art into the Bauhaus, which relocated to his newly designed buildings at Dessau in 1926. He fled Germany in 1934, and headed the Harvard School of Architecture (1937–52). Gropius pioneered functional design and the INTERNATIONAL STYLE in particular. The results of his cooperative, group-work design methods can be seen in the Harvard Graduate Center (1949) and the US Embassy, Athens (1960).

grosbeak Any of several birds of the FINCH family (fringillidae). They have short, thick, seed-cracking beaks. Found in woodlands of the Americas, Europe and Asia, species include the rose-breasted grosbeak (*Pheucticus ludovicianus*) of North and South America, and the pine grosbeak (*Pinicolor enucleator*) of Canada and N Europe. Length: 18–25cm (7–10in).

gross domestic product (GDP) Total amount of goods and services produced by a country annually. It does not include income from investments or overseas possessions. GDP gives an indication of the strength of national industry. *See also* GROSS NATIONAL PRODUCT (GNP)

gross national product (GNP) Total market value of all goods and services produced by a country annually, plus net income from abroad. GNP is a universal indicator of economic performance, and provides an assessment of different economic sectors. GNP is the sum of four types of spending: private consumption (goods and services bought by the community), government expenditure, balance of trade, and business investment. *See also* GROSS DOMESTIC PRODUCT (GDP)

Gros Ventre (Fr. 'Big Belly') French settlers' name for two tribes of Native North Americans: the Hidatsa and the Atsina.

Grosz, George (1893–1959) German illustrator and painter. A founder of the DADA movement in Berlin, Grosz mercilessly satirized capitalist decadence, German militarism and the rise of fascism in drawings and caricatures, such as *Ecce Homo* (1923). In 1932 he fled to the USA.

groundnut *See* PEANUT

ground squirrel (gopher) Small, terrestrial SQUIRREL native to Eurasia and North America. Ground squirrels eat plants, seeds, insects, small animals and sometimes eggs. Most have greyish-red to brown fur and some are striped or spotted. Length: to 40.5cm (16in); weight: 85–1,000g (0.1–2.2lb). Family Sciuridae; genus *Citellus* (and others).

groundwater Water that lies beneath the surface of the Earth. It comes chiefly from rain, although some is of volcanic or sedimentary origin. It moves through porous rocks and soil and can be collected in wells. Ground water can dissolve minerals and leave deposits, creating structures such as CAVES, STALAGMITES, and STALACTITES. *See also* WATER TABLE

grouper Tropical marine fish found from the coast of Florida to South America, and in the Indian and Pacific Oceans. It has a large mouth, sharp teeth, a mottled body and the ability to change colour. Length: to 3.7m (12ft); weight: to 450kg (1,000lb). Family Serranidae; species: giant, *Epinephelus itajara*; Australian, *Epinephelus lanceolatus*. *See also* BASS

Group of Eight (G8) (formerly Group of Seven, G7) Eight nations that meet for an annual economic summit meeting. In 1975, the heads of government of what were the world's seven wealthiest nations – the USA, Japan, Germany, Britain, France, Canada, and Italy – met in the first of these meetings. The changing world economy led other countries to seek membership. In 1997, Russia was formally admitted to the group.

grouse Plump gamebird of N areas of the Northern Hemisphere. Grouse are fowl-like, but have feathered ankles and toes and brightly coloured air sacs on the neck. Family Tetraonidae.

Grozny City in the Caucasus Mountains, SW Russia, the capital of CHECHNYA. Founded in 1818, it has been an oil-producing centre since 1893 and has a pipeline to the Black Sea and the Donets Basin. Grozny was severely damaged in fighting between Russian forces and Chechen rebels from 1994 to 2000. Industries: oil, petrochemicals. Pop. (1994) 364,000.

Grünewald, Matthias (1470–1528) German painter, b. Mathis Gothardt. A contemporary of DÜRER, he was court painter at Mainz (1508–14) and Brandenburg (1515–25). Grünewald's masterpiece is the altarpiece at Isenheim, Alsace (*c.*1515). His use of dazzling colour and distorted figures was a major influence on EXPRESSIONISM.

Guadalajara City in SW Mexico; capital of Jalisco state and second-largest city in Mexico. Founded in 1531, it has some fine Spanish colonial architecture, such as the cathedral and governor's palace. Noted for its mountain scenery and mild climate, it is a popular health resort. Industries: engineering, textiles, pottery, glassware. Pop. (2005) 3,905,000.

Guadalcanal Largest of the Solomon Islands, *c.*970km (600mi) E of New Guinea, W central Pacific Ocean; the capital is Honiara. Guadalcanal was the scene of heavy fighting between Japanese and US troops in World War 2. The chief products are coconuts, fish, fruit, and timber. Area: 5,302sq km (2,047sq mi). Pop. (2002 est.) 120,100.

Guadalupe-Hidalgo, Treaty of (1848) Peace settlement ending the MEXICAN WAR. Mexico ceded the present US states of Texas, New Mexico, Arizona, California, Nevada, Utah, and parts of Colorado and Wyoming. The USA paid US$15 million in compensation.

Guadalupe Mountains National Park Park in W Texas, USA. It became a national park in 1966. The mountains contain portions of an extensive Permian limestone fossil reef. Area: 328sq km (127sq mi).

Guadeloupe French overseas department (since 1946), consisting of the islands of Basse-Terre (W), Grande-Terre (E), and several smaller islands in the Leeward Islands, E WEST INDIES. Discovered in 1493 by Columbus, France settled Guadeloupe in 1635. Briefly held by Britain and Sweden, it reverted to French rule in 1816. The chief crops are sugar cane and bananas. Industries: distilling, tourism. Area: 1,705sq km (658sq mi). Pop. (1999) 440,000.

Guam Southernmost and largest of the MARIANA ISLANDS in the W Pacific Ocean; the capital is Agaña. An unincorporated US territory, Ferdinand Magellan discovered Guam in 1521. Spain ceded the island to the USA in 1898. Guam was the first US territory to be occupied by the Japanese during World War 2. Industries: oil refining, palm oil, fish products. Area: 549sq km (212sq mi). Pop (2000) 164,000.

Guangxi (Kwangsi) Autonomous region in S China; the capital is Nanning. It was established in 1958 for the Zhuang, China's largest minority nationality. Its mountainous terrain limits cultivation. Minerals include manganese, zinc, tin, tungsten, and antimony. Industries: oil refining, fertilizers. Area: 220,495sq km (85,133sq mi). Pop. (2000) 44,890,000.

Guangzhou (Canton) Largest city in S China, on the Pearl River; capital of Guangdong province. It has been an important trading port since 300 BC. The birthplace of SUN YAT-SEN, it was the focal point of the nationalist revolution (1911). It is S China's leading industrial and commercial city. Industries: textiles, rubber products, shipbuilding. Pop. (2005) 3,881,000.

guano Dried excrement, mainly of sea birds and bats, that accumulates along coastlines and in caves. It contains phosphorous, nitrogen, and potassium and is a natural fertilizer. It is found mainly on islands off South America and Africa.

Guaraní Native South American tribe and language. The tribe's population has decreased greatly, although most Paraguayans descend from Guaraní, and their language survives as Paraguay's second national language.

Guardi, Francesco (1712–93) Venetian painter. He produced vivid and fluidly painted views of Venice, appreciated after the impressionists 'discovered' them in the 19th century. His work is much freer than that of CANALETTO.

Guatemala Republic in Central America. *See* country feature

Guatemala City (Ciudad Guatemala) Capital of Guatemala, on a plateau in the Sierra Madre; largest city in Central America. Founded in 1776, the city was the capital of the Central American Federation from 1823–39. It was badly damaged by earthquakes in 1917–18 and 1976. Industries: mining, furniture, textiles, handicrafts. Pop. (2005) 3,242,000.

guava Any of 100 species of fruit-bearing trees or shrubs native to tropical America and the West Indies. The large white flowers produce a berry-like fruit, usually yellow with white, pink or yellow flesh. Family Myrtaceae.

Guayaquil City on the River Guayas, near the Gulf of Guayaquil, W Ecuador; chief port and largest city of Ecuador. It was founded by the Spanish in the 1530s. Industries: textiles, pharmaceuticals, leather goods, cement, iron products, oil refining, fruit. Pop. (2005) 2,387,000.

gudgeon Freshwater CARP found in rivers from Britain to China. It has a small mouth with barbels, an elongated body and variable colour. Length: 20cm (8in). Species *Gobio gobio*.

guelder rose Plant of the HONEYSUCKLE family (Caprifoliaceae). It has globular clusters of white or pink flowers. Species *Viburnum opulus*.

Guelph Political faction in medieval Italy, opposed to the GHIBELLINE. The two factions were linked to rival families contending for the HOLY ROMAN EMPIRE in the 12th century. In 1198, OTTO IV (a Guelph) became Holy Roman Emperor. In the battle for control of Italy, the Guelphs took the side of the papacy, while the Ghibellines backed the emperor FREDERICK II. In 1268, the Guelphs defeated the Ghibellines at Tagliacozzo, but the feud smouldered on. *See also* HOHENSTAUFEN

guenon Any one of 10 to 20 species of long-tailed, slender, medium-sized African MONKEYS found s of the Sahara Desert. Guenons are omnivorous tree-dwellers, living in small troops dominated by an old male. Genus *Cercopithecus*.

Guernica Town in Vizcaya province, N Spain. It is a centre of BASQUE nationalism. The bombing of Guernica's civilian population by German aircraft during the Spanish CIVIL WAR inspired Picasso's masterpiece *Guernica* (1937).

Guernsey Second-largest island in the CHANNEL ISLANDS; the capital is St Peter Port. It constitutes a bailiwick with several smaller islands, including Alderney and SARK. Its mild, sunny climate is ideal for dairy farming and horticulture. Tourism is also important. Area: 78sq km (30sq mi). Pop. (1996) 58,681.

guerrilla warfare Small-scale, ground combat operations usually designed to harass, rather than destroy, the enemy. Such tactics are often employed by insurgents or irregular soldiers. The tactics are especially suited to difficult terrain, and rely on lightning attacks and aid from civilian sympathizers. In the 20th century, many nationalist and communist movements, such as TITO's Yugoslavian partisans in World War 2, used guerrilla tactics.

Guevara, 'Che' (Ernesto) (1928–67) Argentine revolutionary leader. He became associated with Fidel CASTRO in Mexico, and returned with him to Cuba in 1956 to conduct guerrilla activities against the BATISTA regime. He disappeared from public view in 1965. Two years later, he was captured and killed while trying to establish a communist guerrilla base in Bolivia. His remains were returned to Cuba in 1997.

▲ **Guevara** The revolutionary leader 'Che' Guevara was closely associated with Castro's seizure of power in Cuba, where Guevara held several government posts. In 1965–66, he helped anti-Mobutu forces in Congo. A committed Marxist, he was eventually killed by Bolivian government forces while attempting to foment a peasants' revolution in that country. His actions and violent death made him a heroic figure for many revolutionaries.

G

GUATEMALA

The Central American republic of Guatemala contains a densely populated fertile mountain region. The capital, GUATEMALA CITY, is situated here. The highlands run E–W and contain many volcanoes. Guatemala is subject to frequent earthquakes and volcanic eruptions. Tajumulco, an inactive volcano, is the highest peak in Central America, at 4,211m [13,816ft].

S of the highlands lie the Pacific coastal lowlands. N of the highlands is the thinly populated Caribbean plain and the vast Petén tropical forest. Guatemala's largest lake, Izabal, drains into the Caribbean Sea.

Hardwoods, such as mahogany, rubber, palm, and chicozapote (from which chicle, used in chewing gum, is obtained), grow in the tropical

forests in the N, with mangrove swamps on the coast. Oak and willow grow in the highlands, with fir and pine at higher levels. Much of the Pacific plains is farmland.

CLIMATE

Guatemala lies in the tropics. The lowlands are hot and wet, with the central mountain region being cooler and drier. Guatemala City – at about 1,500m [5,000ft] above sea level – has a pleasant, warm climate, with a marked dry season between November and April.

HISTORY

Between AD 300 and 900, the QUICHÉ branch of the MAYA ruled much of Guatemala, but inexplicably abandoned their cities on the N plains. The Quiché ruins at Tikal are the tallest temple pyramids in the Americas. In 1523–24, the Spanish conquistador Pedro de Alvarado defeated the native tribes. In 1821, Guatemala became independent. From 1823–39, it formed part of the Central American Federation. Various dictatorial regimes interfered in the politics of other Central American states, arousing resentment and leading to the creation of the Central American Court of Justice. Guatemala nationalized German-owned coffee plantations in 1941 and the remainder after World War 2.

POLITICS

In 1960, the mainly Quiché Guatemalan Revolutionary National Unity Movement (URNG) began a guerrilla war that claimed more than 200,000 lives. Most atrocities were carried out by the security forces, rather than guerrillas. During the 1960s and 1970s, terrorism and political assassinations beset Guatemala.

AREA 108,889sq km [42,042sq mi]
POPULATION 12,728,000
CAPITAL (POPULATION) Guatemala City (3,242,000)
GOVERNMENT Republic
ETHNIC GROUPS Ladino (mixed Hispanic and Amerindian) 55%, Amerindian 43%, others 2%
LANGUAGES Spanish (official), Amerindian languages
RELIGIONS Christianity, indigenous Mayan beliefs
CURRENCY US dollar; Quetzal = 100 centavos

In 1985, Guatemala elected its first civilian president for 15 years. In 1996 a peace agreement with the URNG ended 35 years of civil war, and US$35 million was paid in damages to victims of the civil war in 2004, but efforts to bring the killers to justice were very slow.

In 2007 elections, which were marred by violence, centre-left candidate Alvaro Colom became president.

ECONOMY

The World Bank classifies Guatemala as a 'lower-middle-income' developing country. Agriculture employs nearly half of the workforce and coffee, sugar, bananas and beef are the leading exports. Cardamom and cotton are also exported. Maize is the chief food crop, but is insufficient to feed the population, leaving the country dependent on food imports. Tourism and manufacturing are growing in importance. Manufactures include processed farm products, textiles, wood products, and handicrafts. Money sent home by Guatemalans working in the US is the primary source of foreign income.

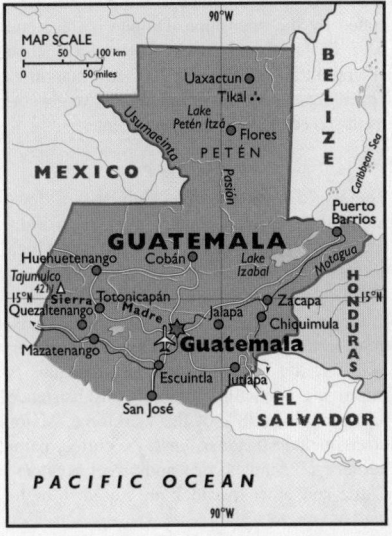

Guggenheim US family of industrialists and philanthropists. **Meyer** Guggenheim (1828–1905), b. Switzerland, emigrated to Philadelphia (1847) and prospered in lace importing, and bought silver and lead mines in Colorado. He retired leaving control of his enterprises to seven living sons. **Daniel** Guggenheim (1856–1930) took the lead in expanding the businesses. A philanthropist, he established the Daniel and Florence Guggenheim Foundation. **Solomon R.** Guggenheim (1861–1949) endowed a foundation for non-objective art: the Guggenheim Museum opened in New York City in 1959. **Simon** Guggenheim (1867–1941) was a US senator. In memory of his son, he established the John Simon Guggenheim Memorial Foundation. **Harry Frank** Guggenheim (1890–1971) was US ambassador to Cuba (1929–33). **Peggy** Guggenheim (1898–1979) was a patron and collector of modern art.

guided missile MISSILE controlled throughout its flight by exterior or interior control systems. There are four types: surface-to-surface, surface-to-air, air-to-air, air-to-surface. The first guided missiles were the V-WEAPONS launched (1944) by Germany during World War 2. Postwar developments included the huge intercontinental ballistic missiles (ICBMs), with nuclear warheads and ranges of 10,000km (6000mi). Submarine systems included Polaris and Trident. The multiple independently targeted re-entry vehicles (MIRVs) – ICBMs with many sub-missiles – were developed in the late 1960s. The CRUISE MISSILE has small wings, making it capable of flying at low altitudes.

guild Association of craftsmen or merchants in medieval Europe. Merchant guilds probably developed from earlier religious associations and sometimes became more or less synonymous with municipal government. Guilds controlled economic conditions in the interest of their members, but were eclipsed by the development of capitalism.

Guildford Four Three men and a woman of Irish extraction convicted in an English court of terrorist bombings in Guildford and Woolwich, s England, in 1975. The life sentences were quashed on appeal in 1989. *See also* BIRMINGHAM SIX

guillemot Small, usually black-and-white seabird of the AUK family (Alcidae). It lives on cold Northern Hemisphere coastlines and dives for food. Nesting in colonies, it lays two eggs. Length: *c*.43cm (17in). Genera *Cepphus* and *Uria*.

guillotine Mechanized device for execution by beheading adopted during the FRENCH REVOLUTION. It was first used in 1792, and *c*.1400 died under it during the REIGN OF TERROR. It remained in use in France until the abolition of CAPITAL PUNISHMENT in 1981. The term also describes a British parliamentary procedure (first used in 1887) by which a set time is allotted to various stages of a bill in order to speed its passage into law.

Guinea Republic in West Africa. *See* country feature
Guinea-Bissau Small republic in West Africa; the capital and chief port is BISSAU. *See* country feature.

GUINEA

The Republic of Guinea, which faces the Atlantic Ocean in w Africa, can be divided into four regions: an alluvial coastal plain, which includes the capital, CONAKRY; the highland region of the Fouta Djallon, the source of one of Africa's longest rivers, the NIGER; the NE savanna; and the SE Guinea Highlands, which rise to 1,752m [5,748ft] at Mount Nimba.

Mangrove swamps grow along parts of the coast. Inland, the Fouta Djallon is largely open grassland. NE Guinea is tropical savanna, with acacia and shea scattered across the grassland. Rainforests of ebony, mahogany, and teak grow in the Guinea Highlands.

CLIMATE
Guinea has a tropical climate. Conakry, on the coast, has heavy rains during the relatively cool season between May and November. Hot, dry harmattan winds blow sw from the SAHARA in the dry season. The Fouta Djalon is cooler than the coast. The driest region is in the NE. This region and the SE highlands have greater temperature variations than on the coast.

HISTORY
The NE Guinea plains formed part of the medieval Empire of Ghana. The Malinke formed the Mali Empire, which dominated the region in the 12th century. The SONGHAI Empire supplanted the Malinke in the 15th century. Portuguese explorers arrived in the mid-15th century, and the slave trade began soon afterwards. From the 17th century, other European nations' slave traders became active in Guinea. In the early 18th century, the FULANI embarked on a *jihad* (holy war) and gained control of the Fouta Djallon. Following a series of wars, France won control in the mid-19th century, later establishing the colony of French Guinea (1891). France exploited the nation's bauxite deposits, and mining unions developed.

In 1958, Guinea voted to become an independent republic and France severed all aid. Its first president, Sékou Touré (1958–84), adopted a Marxist programme of reform and embraced Pan-Africanism. Opposition parties were banned, and dissent brutally suppressed. In 1970, Portuguese Guinea (now Guinea-Bissau) invaded Guinea. Conakry later acted as the headquarters for independence movements in Guinea-Bissau. A military coup followed Touré's death in 1984, and Colonel Lansana Conté established the Military Committee for National Recovery (CMRN). Conté improved relations with the West and introduced free enterprise policies.

POLITICS
Civil unrest forced the introduction of a multiparty system in 1992. Elections in 1993 confirmed Conté as president, amid claims of voting fraud. In February 1996, Conté foiled an attempted military coup. He was re-elected in 1998.

AREA 245,857sq km
[94,925sq mi]
POPULATION
9,948,000
CAPITAL (POPULATION)
Conakry (1,465,000)
GOVERNMENT Multiparty republic
ETHNIC GROUPS Peuhl 40%, Malinke 30%,
Soussou 20%, others 10%
LANGUAGES French (official)
RELIGIONS Islam 85%, Christianity 8%,
traditional beliefs 7%
CURRENCY Guinean franc = 100 cauris

By 2000, Guinea was home to about 500,000 refugees from the wars in neighbouring Sierra Leone and Liberia. In 2000, rebel incursions from these countries killed more than 1,000 people, caused massive population displacement, and threatened to destablilize Guinea. Conté was re-elected in 2003, although the poll was boycotted by the opposition. Despite his age and poor health Conté survived an assassination attempt in 2005. 2006 and 2007 saw mass riots protesting against his corrupt, repressive government and economic mismanagement.

ECONOMY
The World Bank classifies Guinea as a 'low-income' developing country. It is the world's second-largest producer of bauxite, which accounts for 90% of its exports. Guinea has 25% of the world's known reserves of bauxite.

Other natural resources include diamonds, gold, iron ore and uranium. Due to the mining industry, the rail and road infrastructure is improving. Agriculture, mainly at subsistence level, employs 78% of the workforce. Major crops include bananas, cassava, coffee, palm kernels, pineapples, rice and sweet potatoes. Cattle and other livestock are raised in highland areas.

guinea fowl Pheasant-like game bird of Africa and Madagascar. The common domestic guinea hen (*Numida meleagris*) is blue, grey or black with white spots and an ornamental crest. Length: to 50cm (20in). Family Phasianidae.

guinea pig CAVY found in South America. The domestic *Cavia porcellus* is a popular pet. It has a large head, short legs and no tail. *Cavia aperea* is a wild species. Family Caviidae.

Guinevere In Arthurian legend, King ARTHUR's queen who was loved by LANCELOT OF THE LAKE. In Thomas MALORY's *Morte d'Arthur* she betrayed the king, and was sentenced to die. She was rescued by Lancelot and later restored to Arthur.

Guinness, Sir Alec (1914–2000) British actor. He is best-known for his film performances in the Ealing Studios comedies, such as *Kind Hearts and Coronets* (1949), *The Lavender Hill Mob* (1951) and *The Ladykillers* (1955). He won an Academy Award for best actor in *Bridge on the River Kwai* (1957). Other films include *Lawrence of Arabia* (1962), *Doctor Zhivago* (1965), *Star Wars* (1977), *A Passage to India* (1984), and *Little Dorrit* (1988). He was knighted in 1959.

Guise, House of Ducal house of Lorraine, the most powerful family in 16th-century France. **Claude**, Duke of Lorraine (1496–1550), founded the house in 1528. His eldest son, **Francis** (1519–63), supervised the massacre of HUGUENOTS at Vassy in 1562, precipitating the French Wars of RELIGION. His second son, **Charles** (1524–74), Cardinal of Guise, played an important role at the Council of TRENT. His daughter **Mary of Guise**, married JAMES V, and was the mother of MARY, QUEEN OF SCOTS. Francis' son, **Henri** (1550–88), helped to organize the SAINT BARTHOLOMEW'S DAY MASSACRE (1572) and led the Holy League, which vehemently opposed Protestantism. Guise power declined when HENRY IV acceded to the throne.

guitar Plucked stringed musical instrument. The early guitar had four double strings and was similar to the LUTE. The modern guitar has six strings. The virtuoso playing of Andrés SEGOVIA inspired compositions by Manuel de FALLA and VILLA-LOBOS. In 1946, Les Paul invented the electric guitar,

now a standard instrument in blues, pop and rock music. Acoustic and semi-acoustic guitars are used in folk and jazz.

Guizhou (Kweichow) Province in S China; the capital is Guiyang. Guizhou became a Chinese province in the Ming dynasty. There were frequent rebellions against Chinese rule in the 19th and 20th centuries. During World War 2, it served as a military base for Allied forces. It was taken by Chinese communists in 1950. Industries: coal mining, iron ore, mercury. Area: 174,060sq km (67,204sq mi). Pop. (2000) 35,250,000.

Gujarat State in W India, on the Arabian Sea; the capital is Gandhinagar. Absorbed into the MAURYA EMPIRE in the 3rd century BC it was a centre of JAINISM under the Maitraka dynasty (5th-8th centuries AD). In the early 15th century, it was an autonomous Muslim sultanate. Under British rule, it became a province (1857). After independence, it was established as a separate state. It is highly industrialized, with substantial reserves of oil and gas. Industries: cotton textiles, salt mining, electrical engineering, petrochemicals. Area: 195,984sq km (75,669sq mi). Pop. (2001) 50,596,992.

Gujarati (Gujerati) Modern language of N India, the official language of GUJARAT. Belonging to the Indic branch of INDO-EUROPEAN LANGUAGES, it began to evolve in *c.*AD 1000. More than 30 million inhabitants of Gujarat and other Asian communities worldwide speak Gujarati.

gulag Network of detention centres and forced-labour prisons within the former Soviet Union. The term is an acronym in Russian for Chief Administration of Corrective Labour Camps. Established in 1918, gulags were secret CONCENTRATION CAMPS used to silence political and religious dissenters.

Gulf States Countries around the Persian (Arabian) Gulf, including IRAN, IRAQ, KUWAIT, SAUDI ARABIA, QATAR, the UNITED ARAB EMIRATES, and the BAHRAIN islands. Since the 1960s, the extensive exploitation of oil reserves blostered the political and economic importance of the states.

Gulf Stream Relatively fast-moving current of the N Atlantic Ocean. It flows from the straits of Florida, USA, along the E coast of North America, then E across the

GUINEA-BISSAU

The Republic of Guinea-Bissau is a small country in W Africa. The land is mostly low-lying, with a broad, swampy, coastal plain and many flat offshore islands, including the Bijagós Archipelago. Mangrove forests line the coasts, and dense rainforest covers much of the coastal plain.

CLIMATE

The country has a tropical climate, with its dry season from December to May and its rainy season from June to November.

HISTORY

It was first visited by Portuguese navigators in 1446. From the 17th to the early 19th century,

Portugal used the coast as a slave-trading base. In 1836, Portugal appointed a governor to administer Guinea-Bissau and the CAPE VERDE islands. In 1879, the two territories separated, and Guinea-Bissau became the colony of Portuguese Guinea. Development was slow, partly because the territory did not attract settlers on the same scale as Portugal's much healthier African colonies of Angola and Mozambique.

In 1956, Amilcar Cabral founded the African Party for the Independence of Guinea and Cape Verde (PAIGC). Portugal's determination to keep its overseas territories led the PAIGC to begin a guerrilla war in 1963, and by 1968 it held two-thirds of the country. In 1972, a rebel National Assembly, elected by the people in the PAIGC-controlled areas, voted to make the country independent as Guinea-Bissau. Formal independence came in 1974.

POLITICS

The independent nation faced many problems arising from its under-developed economy and a lack of trained personnel. Guinea-Bissau's leaders favoured union with Cape Verde. This objective was abandoned in 1980 when an army coup, led by Major João Vieira, overthrew the government. The Revolutionary Council which took over opposed unification with Cape Verde; it concentrated on national policies and socialist reforms.

AREA 36,125sq km [13,948sq mi]
POPULATION 1,473,000
CAPITAL (POPULATION) Bissau (200,000)
GOVERNMENT Interim government
ETHNIC GROUPS Balanta 30%, Fula 20%, Manjaca 14%, Mandinga 13%, Papel 7%
LANGUAGES Portuguese (official), Crioulo
RELIGIONS Traditional beliefs 50%, Islam 45%, Christianity 5%
CURRENCY CFA franc = 100 centimes

In 1991, the government voted to introduce a multiparty system. They won 1994 elections, and Vieira was elected president. In 1998 an army rebellion sparked a civil war. Army rebels took power in 1999, but elections were held in 1999–2000. Kumba Ialá became president in 2000 but was overthrown in a coup in 2003. Civilian government was restored in 2004. Elections in 2005 made Vieira president once again.

ECONOMY

Guinea-Bissau is a poor country. Agriculture employs more than 70% of the workforce, mostly at subsistence level. Fishing is also important. The transhipment of illegal drugs occurs on a large scale, dwarfing the country's legal export earnings which are derived mainly from cashew nuts.

Atlantic (as the North Atlantic Drift) to the NW European coast. The current warms coastal climates along its course.

Gulf War (January 16, 1991–February 28, 1991) Military action by a US-led coalition of 32 states to expel Iraqi forces from KUWAIT. Iraqi forces invaded Kuwait (August 2, 1990) and claimed it as an Iraqi province. On August 7, 1990, Operation Desert Shield began a mass deployment of coalition forces to protect Saudi oil reserves. Economic sanctions failed to secure a withdrawal, and the UN Security Council set a deadline of January 15, 1991, for the peaceful removal of Iraqi forces. Iraqi President Saddam HUSSEIN ignored the ultimatum, and General Norman SCHWARZKOPF launched Operation Desert Storm. Within a week, extensive coalition air attacks secured control of the skies and weakened Iraq's military command. Iraqi ground forces were defenceless against the coalition's technologically advanced weaponry. Iraq launched Scud missile attacks on Saudi Arabia and Israel, in the hope of weakening Arab support for the coalition. On February 24, the war began on the ground. Iraqi troops burned Kuwaiti oil wells as they fled. Kuwait was liberated two days later, and a ceasefire declared on February 28. Saddam Hussein remained in power in Iraq. The Gulf War claimed the lives of 234 Allied troops and between 85,000 and 150,000 Iraqi soldiers. Some 33,000 Kuwaitis were killed or captured.

gull (seagull) Any of various ground-nesting birds found along coastlines. They eat carrion, refuse, fish, shellfish, eggs, and young birds. The herring gull (*Larus argentatus*) is grey and white with black markings, hooked bill, pointed wings and webbed feet. It grows to 56–66cm (22–26in). The black-headed gull (*Larus ridibundus*) is smaller, with black feathers on its head in summer. Family Laridae.

gum Secretions of plants. Gums are chemically complex, consisting mainly of various saccharides bound to organic acids. Common examples are gum arabic (used as an adhesive on envelopes and postage stamps), agar and tragacanth. Chewing gum is traditionally derived from the sapodilla tree, but most is now synthetic. *See also* EUCALYPTUS; RESINS

gun Tubular weapon firing a projectile by force of explosion. The term is now restricted to pieces with a high muzzle velocity and, usually, a flat trajectory. PISTOLS, RIFLES , MACHINE GUNS and CANNON are usually described as guns,

GUYANA

The Co-operative Republic of Guyana borders the Atlantic Ocean. It is the only English-speaking country in mainland South America. The coastal plain, where the majority lives, is between 3 and 48km [2–30mi] wide, much of it below sea level. Dykes prevent flooding. Inland is hilly and forested, and this terrain makes up Guyana's largest region. The land rises to 2,810m [9,219ft] in the Pakaraima Mountains, part of the Guiana Highlands on Guyana's western border. Other highlands are in the S and SW. Guyana has impressive waterfalls, such as the King George VI Falls (488m [1,601ft], the Great Falls (256m [840ft]), and Kaieteur Falls (226m [741ft]).

The coastal plain is largely farmed, but wet savanna covers some areas. Inland, rainforests, rich in plant and animal species, cover about 85% of the country. Savanna occurs in the SW.

CLIMATE
Guyana has a hot, humid equatorial climate. Rainfall ranges from 2,280mm [90in] on the coast to 3,560mm [140in] in the rainforest region. Rainfall decreases to the W and S.

HISTORY
The first inhabitants of Guyana were Arawak, Carib and Warrau Amerindians. The Dutch founded a trading post in what is now Guyana in 1581 and, in 1620, the Dutch West India Company began to set up armed bases. In 1658 they began to establish sugar plantations, importing African slaves as workers. In the 18th century the plantations were expanded. However, between 1780 and 1813, the territory changed hands between the Dutch, French and British. Britain occupied Guyana in 1814 during the Napoleonic Wars, and, in 1831, Britain founded the colony of British Guiana. After slavery was abolished in 1834, many former slaves set up their own farms. East Indian and Chinese labourers were introduced to replace them. Gold was discovered in 1879. In 1889, Venezuela claimed part of the territory, but its claims were over-ruled by an international arbitration tribunal. In 1952 Guyana adopted a new constitution. In 1953 the left-wing Guyanese Progressive People's Party (PPP), led by East Indian Cheddi Jagan, won the elections. Britain then sent in troops and set up an interim administration. The constitution was restored in 1957, when the PPP split into a mostly Indian party, led by Jagan, and another group, led by a black lawyer, Forbes Burnham. Burnham's party, the more moderate People's National Congress (PNC), consisted mainly of the descendants of Africans. In 1961 British Guiana became self-governing, with Jagan as prime minister. Riots, strikes and racial conflict broke out in the early 1960s. Elections in 1964 were won by the PNC and its ally the United Force, and Burnham became prime minister.

AREA 214,969sq km [83,000sq mi]	
POPULATION 769,000	
CAPITAL (POPULATION) Georgetown (213,000)	
GOVERNMENT Multiparty republic	
ETHNIC GROUPS East Indian 50%, Black 36%, Amerindian 7%, others	
LANGUAGES English (official), Creole, Hindi, Urdu	
RELIGIONS Christianity 50%, Hinduism 35%, Islam 10%, others	
CURRENCY Guyanese dollar = 100 cents	

POLITICS
British Guiana became independent as Guyana on 26 May 1966, with Burnham as prime minister. In 1970 Guyana became a republic, but remained a member of the Commonwealth. In 1980 Burnham became president and served in that post until his death in 1985. He was succeeded by the prime minister Desmond Hoyte, but, in 1992, the PPP won the elections and Cheddi Jagan was elected president. On his death in 1997 he was succeeded by his wife Janet, who herself retired on health grounds in 1999. Her successor Bharrat Jagdeo, a former finance minister, was re-elected in 2001 and again in 2006 when the PPP won both presidential and parliamentary elections.

In 2007 a long-standing dispute with Suriname over sea boundaries, which run through a potentially important offshore oilfield, was resolved with a sharing arrangement by a UN tribunal. Disputes remain with Venezuela over the border in the Essequibo region, which is rich in timber and minerals.

ECONOMY
Guyana is a poor developing country. Its resources include gold, bauxite (aluminium ore) and other minerals, its forests and fertile soils. Agriculture and mining are the chief activities. The leading crops are sugar cane and rice, but citrus fruits, cocoa, coffee and plantains are also important. Farmers also produce beef, pork, poultry and dairy products. Other activities include fishing and forestry.

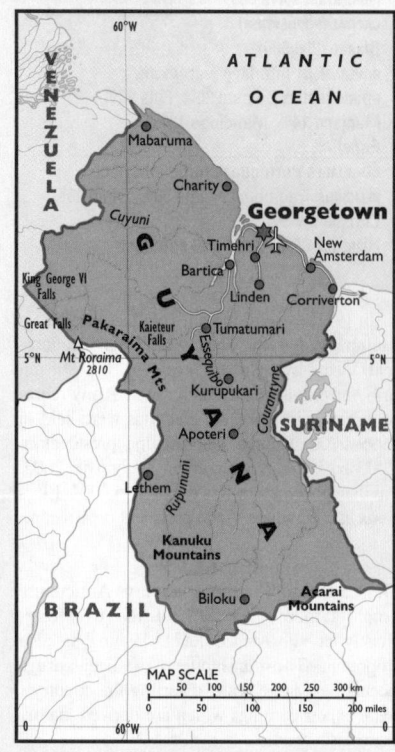

VENEZUELA
60°W
ATLANTIC OCEAN
Mabaruma
Charity
Cuyuni
Georgetown
King George VI Falls
Timehri
New Amsterdam
Bartica
Linden
Corriverton
Great Falls
Pakaraima Mts
Kaieteur Falls
Tumatumari
Mt Roraima 2810
5°N
Essequibo
Courantyne
Kurupukari
SURINAME
Apoteri
G U Y A N A
Lethem
Rupununi
Kanuku Mountains
Biloku
Acarai Mountains
BRAZIL
MAP SCALE
0 50 100 150 200 250 300 km
0 50 100 150 200 miles
60°W

whereas ARTILLERY devices such as mortars, which fire slow shot at high angles, are not.

Gunnell, Sally Janet Jane (1966–) British athlete. In the 1992 Olympic Games, Gunnell captained the British women's team, and won a gold medal in the 400m hurdles. She repeated this success in the 1993 World Championships, breaking the world record. A foot injury prevented her defence of the world title in 1995, and forced her retirement from the 1996 Olympics.

gunpowder EXPLOSIVE mixture of potassium nitrate (saltpetre), charcoal and sulphur. When ignited, it expands violently due to the almost instantaneous conversion of solid ingredients into gases. It was used exclusively in firearms until *c.*1900, when it was replaced by smokeless powders such as DYNAMITE.

Gunpowder Plot (November 1605) Failed Roman Catholic conspiracy to blow up JAMES I of England and his Parliament. The leader of the plot was Robert Catesby, and its chief perpetrator Guy FAWKES. The plotters were arrested on November 5, a date now celebrated in Britain as Bonfire Night.

Gupta dynasty (*c.*AD 320–*c.*550) Ruling house whose kingdom covered most of N India. Founded by Chandragupta I, the Gupta dynasty embraced Buddhism and is seen as a golden age. It reached its greatest extent at the end of the 4th century, but declined at the end of the 5th century under concerted attack from the HUNS.

gurdwara (Sanskrit, 'Guru's doorway') Sikh temple housing a copy of the *Adi Granth*, the holy scripture of SIKHISM. There are several historically important *gurdwaras*, such as the Golden Temple of AMRITSAR, Punjab.

Gurkha Member of a Hindu caste of Nepal. The Gurkhas conquered Nepal from the early to mid-18th century. They speak a SANSKRIT language. The name also denotes soldiers in Nepalese regiments of the British and Indian armies.

gurnard Tropical, marine, bottom-dwelling fish. It has a large spiny head and enlarged pectoral fins. Length: to 50cm (20in). Family Triglidae.

guru Personal teacher and spiritual master. In traditional Hindu education, boys lived in the home of a *guru*, who guided their studies of the VEDAS and saw to their physical health and ethical training. The first ten leaders of SIKHISM assumed the title of *guru*. Guruship terminated in 1708.

Gustavus I (Vasa) (1496–1560) King of Sweden (1523–60) and founder of the Vasa dynasty. He led a victorious rebellion against the invading Danes in 1520. In 1523, he was elected King and the Kalmar Union destroyed. During his reign, Sweden gained independence, the Protestant Church was established, and the Bible translated into Swedish.

Gustavus II (Adolphus) (1594–1632) King of Sweden (1611–32). He succeeded his father, Charles IX, during a constitutional crisis. Gustav's reign was distinguished by constitutional, legal, and educational reforms. He ended war with Denmark (1613) and Russia (1617). Hoping to increase Sweden's control of the Baltic and to support Protestantism, he entered the THIRTY YEARS' WAR (1618–48) and died in battle.

Gutenberg, Johann (1400–68) German goldsmith and printer, credited with the invention of PRINTING from movable metallic type. He experimented with printing in Mainz, Germany, in the 1430s. He made the first printed Bible, known as the *Gutenberg Bible* or *Mazarin Bible* (*c.*1455).

Guthrie, 'Woody' (Woodrow Wilson) (1912–67) US folk singer, guitarist and songwriter. His social-protest poetry captured the spirit of the Great Depression and championed workers' rights. His most famous tunes include "This Land Is Your Land" and "So Long, It's Been Good to Know You".

Guyana South American republic. *See* country feature.

Gwent Former county in SE Wales. It was formed in 1974 from most of Monmouthshire, part of Breconshire, and Newport. In 1996 Gwent was abolished and Monmouthshire was reconstituted with new boundaries and four new county boroughs, including Blaenau Gwent.

Gwyn, Nell (1650–87) English actress. She made her first appearance in John Dryden's *The Indian Emperor* (1665), after being discovered selling oranges. She attracted the attention of CHARLES II, and became his mistress.

Gwynedd County in NW Wales, on the Irish Sea coast; the administrative centre is CAERNARVON. It is the site of a medieval principality. Gwynedd is rugged and mountainous, and includes most of the Snowdonia National Park. To the N of the mountains lie the Lleyn Peninsula and the island of Anglesey. Industries: slate quarrying, hydroelectric power, tourism. Area: 3,866sq km (1,493sq mi). Pop. (2001) 116,838.

gymnastics Multidisciplined sport requiring suppleness, strength and poise in a variety of regulated athletic exercises. Men and women compete separately in individual and team events. Men perform in six events: vault, parallel bars, horizontal bars, pommel horse, rings, and floor exercises. Women perform in four events: vault, balance beam, asymmetrical bars, and floor exercises. Exercises are rated in terms of difficulty, and points awarded for technical skills and artistry. World championships began in 1950, and women's gymnastics became an Olympic sport in 1952.

gymnosperm Seed plant with naked seeds borne on scales, usually cones. Most EVERGREENS are gymnosperms. However, LARCH and some other CONIFERS are DECIDUOUS. All living seed-bearing plants are divided into two main groups: gymnosperms and ANGIOSPERMS. In the Five KINGDOMS classification system, gymnosperms comprise three distinct phyla: Coniferophyta (such as PINE, SPRUCE, and CEDAR); Ginkgophyta (a single species, the GINKGO); and Gnetophyta (strange plants such as *Welwitschia*, *Ephedra* and *Gnetum*).

gynaecology Area of medicine concerned with the female reproductive organs. Its study and practice is often paired with obstetrics.

gypsum (hydrated calcium sulphate, $CaSO_4.2H_2O$) Most common sulphate mineral. Huge beds of gypsum occur in sedimentary rocks, where it is associated with HALITE. It crystallizes in the monoclinic system. Varieties are ALABASTER, selenite (transparent and foliated) and satinspar (silky and fibrous). It is a source of plaster of Paris. Hardness 2; r.d. 2.3.

gypsy *See* ROMANY

gypsy moth Small, tussock MOTH with black zigzag markings; the larger female is lighter in colour. The caterpillar feeds on forest and fruit trees, and can be a serious pest. Length: 5cm (2in). Family Lepidoptera; species *Lymantria dispar*.

gyrocompass Navigational aid incorporating a continuously driven GYROSCOPE. The spinning axis of the gyroscope is horizontal and its direction indicates true N, irrespective of the course or attitude of the craft. *See also* COMPASS

gyroscope Symmetrical spinning disc that can adapt to any orientation, being mounted in gimbals (a pair of rings with one swinging freely in the other). When a gyroscope spins, a change in the orientation of the gimbals does not change the orientation of the spinning wheel. This means that changes in direction of an aircraft or ship can be determined without external references. A gyrostabilizer is used to stabilize the roll of a ship or aircraft. *See also* AUTOPILOT

G

GYROCOMPASS

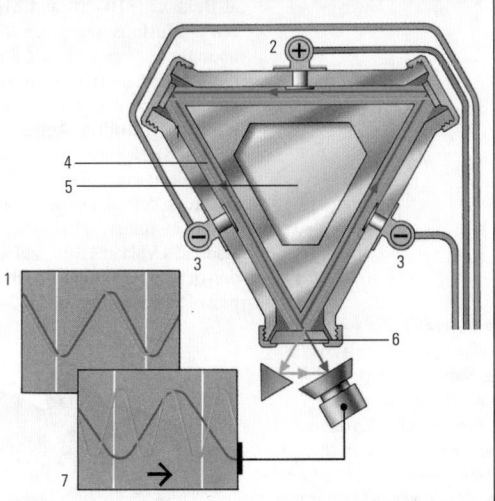

A laser gyrocompass measures rotation by comparing the wavelength of lasers (1). A current is passed from a cathode (2) to two anodes (3) creating two lasers in a gas-filled triangular chamber (4) drilled in a solid glass block (5). Part of the lasers are bled out at one end of the gyrocompass (6), and the wavelength measured. If the gyrocompass rotates to the left, the path of the laser travelling to the left is reduced fractionally, thereby reducing its wavelength. The opposite occurs to the other laser. A sensor (7) compares the two lasers to measure the rotation.

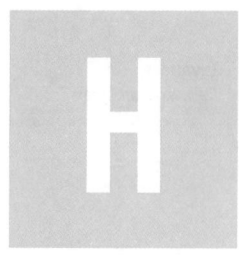

H

H/h, eighth letter of the Roman alphabet. It is derived from an Egyptian hieroglyph for rope. The Semites modified it to form the letter cheth. It was taken into the Greek alphabet (c.600 BC) as the letter eta.

Haakon IV (1204–63) King of Norway (1247–63). He conquered Iceland and Greenland. A patron of the arts, he reigned at the beginning of Norway's 'golden age' (1217–1319). He died in the Orkneys after a campaign against the Scots.

Haarlem City on the River Spaarne, W Netherlands; capital of North Holland province. By the 12th century, Haarlem was a fortified town. A centre of Dutch painting in the 16th and 17th centuries, it is famous for its tulip bulbs. Industries: electronic equipment, publishing and printing. Pop. (2002) 147,795.

habeas corpus (Lat. 'you have the body') Writ in English law for the protection of the liberty of the individual.

Haber process Industrial process for converting atmospheric nitrogen into AMMONIA. A mixture of nitrogen and hydrogen is passed over a heated CATALYST at a pressure of $c.1,000$ atmospheres. The chemical reaction $N_2 + 3H_2 \rightarrow 2NH_3$ occurs. 'Fixing' atmospheric nitrogen, makes it possible to convert ammonia to NITRIC ACID, and produce the NITRATES used in fertilizers and explosives. It was invented (1908–09) by German chemists Fritz Haber and Carl Bosch. *See also* NITROGEN FIXATION

habitat Place in which an organism normally lives. A habitat is defined by characteristic physical conditions and the presence of other organisms. *See also* ECOSYSTEM

Habsburg (Hapsburg) Royal dynasty, a leading house in Europe from the 13th to 19th century. It became a major force when RUDOLF I was chosen king of the Germans (1273) by the electors of the HOLY ROMAN EMPIRE. He established the core dominions in AUSTRIA. The Habsburgs ruled the Empire from 1438 to 1806. Under CHARLES V, their dominions included Spain, the Low Countries and parts of Italy. From 1556, the house divided into Austrian and Spanish branches. The Spanish branch ended in 1700, and the male line of the Austrian in 1740. MARIA THERESA reestablished the house as Habsburg-Lorraine. By 1867, the Habsburg Empire was reduced to the AUSTRO-HUNGARIAN EMPIRE. It ended in 1918, when CHARLES I was deposed.

haddock Marine fish found in cold and temperate waters, primarily in the Northern Hemisphere. Dark grey and silver, it has a dark blotch near the pectoral fins. Length: to $c.1m$ (36in); weight: to 11kg (25lb). Family Gadidae; species *Melanogrammus aeglefinus*.

Hades In Greek mythology, the world of the dead, ruled by PLUTO and PERSEPHONE; also another name for Pluto. CHARON ferried the dead across the river STYX to Hades. In Hades, the virtuous went to ELYSIUM, while the wicked were condemned to Tartarus – the bottomless pit.

Hadith Sayings and acts attributed to the Prophet MUHAMMAD, second only to the KORAN as a source of authority in ISLAM. Hadith formalizes the *sunna* (right behaviour) of Muslims. It consists of the text and the chain of transmitters (*isnad*) that authenticate the traditions as arising from the Prophet. Of the six collections accepted as canonical by Sunnis, the most important texts are those of al-Bukhari (810–70) and Muslim ibn al-Hajjaj (817–75). Shi'a Muslims recognize five Hadith collections based upon the authority of the Caliph *Ali*. The Hadith constitutes the primary source of information on the early doctrinal development of Islam. *See also* SHARIA

Hadrian, Publius Aelius (AD 76–138) Roman Emperor (117–138). Nephew of Emperor TRAJAN, he adopted a policy of retrenchment, discouraging conquests, relinquishing territory hard to defend, and ordering the construction of HADRIAN'S WALL in Britain. He erected many fine buildings, notably Hadrian's Villa at Tivoli, and rebuilt the PANTHEON. The erection of a shrine to Jupiter on the site of the Temple in Jerusalem provoked a Jewish revolt (132–35), which was suppressed.

Hadrian's Wall Defensive fortification in N England, Erected (AD 122–36) on the orders of Emperor HADRIAN. It extended 118.3km (73.5mi), and was about 2.3m (7.5ft) thick and 1.8–4.6m (6–15ft) high. Forts were built along its length.

hadron Group of SUBATOMIC PARTICLES that are influenced by STRONG NUCLEAR FORCE. Made up of QUARKS, the group can be divided into BARYONS, such as the NEUTRON and PROTON, and MESONS. More than 150 hadrons have been discovered, and, with the exception of the proton and antiproton, they are all unstable. Unlike LEPTONS, they have a measurable size.

haemoglobin Red-coloured PROTEIN present in the ERYTHROCYTES (red-blood cells) of vertebrates. It carries oxygen to all cells in the body by combining with it to form oxyhaemoglobin. Oxygen attaches to the haem part of the PROTEIN, which contains iron; the globin part is a globular PROTEIN.

haemophilia Hereditary BLOOD clotting disorder causing prolonged external or internal bleeding, often without apparent cause. **Haemophilia A** is caused by inability to synthesize blood factor VIII, a substance essential to clotting. This can be managed with injections of factor VIII. The rarer **haemophilia B** is caused by a deficiency of blood factor IX. The gene for both types is passed on almost exclusively from mother to son.

haemorrhage Loss of BLOOD from a damaged vessel. It may be external, flowing from a wound, or internal, as from internal injury or a bleeding ulcer.

haemostasis Process by which bleeding stops. BLOOD vessels constrict, platelets aggregate, and plasma coagulates to form filaments of FIBRIN.

Hafiz (c.1325–c.1390) (Shams ed-Din Muhammad) Persian poet, one of the finest lyricists in the Persian language. His verse, in rhyming couplets, deals with sensual pleasures, most famously in the *Divan*. He was a devout Sufi and DERVISH, and much of his poetry is religious in content. *See also* SUFISM

hafnium (symbol Hf) Silvery metallic element, one of the TRANSITION ELEMENTS. Dutch physicist Dirk Coster and Hungarian chemist Georg von Hevesy discovered it in 1923. Its chief source is as a by-product of producing ZIRCONIUM. It is used as a neutron absorber in reactor control-rods. Properties: at.no. 72; r.a.m. 178.49; r.d. 13.31; m.p. 2,227°C (4,041°F); b.p. 4,602°C (8,316°F); most common isotope Hf^{180} (35.24%).

Haganah (Heb. 'defence') Jewish militia formed in 1920 to protect Jewish interests in Palestine. Allied with the extreme Irgun group in 1945, it tried to change British policy on Jewish immigration, receiving financial and military aid from US Zionists. In 1948 it became ISRAEL's army. *See also* ZIONISM

Haggadah Story of the Exodus and redemption of the people of Israel by God, read during PASSOVER services. Developed over centuries, it includes excerpts from the Bible, rabbinical writings, psalms, stories, and prayers.

Haggai (active 6th century BC) Old Testament prophet. He is probably not the author of the Book of Haggai, the tenth of the 12 books of the Minor Prophets. The book records four prophesies made by Haggai in 521 BC in which he urged the Jews to make haste in rebuilding the TEMPLE.

Haggard, Sir (Henry) Rider (1856–1925) English novelist. He wrote popular romantic adventure novels, such as *King Solomon's Mines* (1885), and *Allan Quatermain* (1887).

Hagia Sophia (Aya Sofia) Byzantine church in Istanbul. It was built (532–37) for the Emperor JUSTINIAN I. A supreme masterpiece of Byzantine architecture, it was the first building to use pendentives to support a central dome. A series of domes extends the lofty interior space. The interior contains columns of marble and porphyry. The church was converted into a mosque in 1453. The Hagia Sophia now acts as a museum.

Hague, The ('s-Gravenhage, Den Haag) City in the W Netherlands; capital of South Holland. It is the seat of the Dutch government. Founded in the 15th century, it has been an intellectual and political centre since the 17th century and has been the seat of the International Court of Justice since 1945. Much of its economy depends on diplomatic activities. Industries: textiles, pottery, furniture, chemicals. Pop. (2002) 458,286.

Hague, William Jefferson (1961–) British politician, leader of the CONSERVATIVE PARTY (1997–2001). He entered Parliament in 1989. In 1995, he joined John MAJOR's cabinet. After a landslide defeat in the 1997 general election, Hague

▶ **haddock** One of the mainstay species of the world's commercial fish catch, the haddock (*Melanogrammus aegelfinus*) is found in cold and temperate waters of the Northern Hemisphere. It has been at risk of overfishing and stocks are now monitored carefully.

became the youngest Tory leader since William PITT (THE YOUNGER). He resigned after losing the 2001 general election.

Hahn, Otto (1879–1968) German physical chemist who studied RADIOACTIVITY with Ernest RUTHERFORD and William RAMSAY. In 1906, he began to work with Lise MEITNER. In 1917, they discovered PROTACTINIUM. Hahn and Meitner investigated Enrico FERMI's work on the NEUTRON bombardment of URANIUM. He received the 1944 Nobel Prize in chemistry.

hahnium (symbol Ha) The former name of both DUBNIUM and HASSIUM. It was named after German chemist Otto HAHN.

Haifa (Hefa) City on Mount Carmel, Israel. It is the centre of BAHA'I. It is Israel's major port and third-largest city. Industries: textiles, shipbuilding, oil-refining. Pop. (2005) 948,000.

Haig, Douglas, 1st Earl (1861–1928) British field marshal. In World War 1, he served as commander-in-chief (1915–18) of British forces in France. His policies led to appalling losses on British troops. Under the supreme command of Marshal FOCH, he led the final assault on the Hindenburg line. In 1921 he helped establish the Royal BRITISH LEGION.

haiku In JAPANESE LITERATURE, a poetic form consisting of 17 syllables in five-seven-five pattern. Haikus originally evoked a moment in nature. Matsuo Basho (1644–94) is considered to be the finest exponent of the form.

hail PRECIPITATION from cumulonimbus CLOUDS in the form of balls of ice. Hailstorms are associated with atmospheric turbulence combined with warm, moist air nearer the ground. A hailstone normally has a diameter of less than 1.3cm (.5in).

Haile Selassie I (1892–1975) (Ras Tafari Makonnen) Emperor of Ethiopia (1930–74). When Italy invaded Ethiopia in 1935, he was forced into exile (1936), despite appeals to the League of Nations. He drove out the Italians with British aid in 1941. He became a leader among independent African nations, helping to found the ORGANIZATION OF AFRICAN UNITY (OAU) in 1963. In 1974 he was deposed by a military coup. He died while under arrest. *See also* RASTAFARIANISM

Hainan Island off s China, separated from the mainland by the Hainan Strait; the capital is Haikou. It has been under Chinese authority from the 2nd century BC. In 1988, it was designated a special economic zone. Its products include rubber, coffee, rice, timber, tin, copper, iron, steel and bauxite. Area: 33,991sq km (13,124sq mi). Pop. (2000) 7,870,000.

Haiphong Port on the Red River delta, N Vietnam. Founded in 1874, Haiphong became the chief naval base of French Indochina. It was occupied by the Japanese during World War 2 and bombed by the French in 1946. During the Vietnam War it was heavily bombed by the USA, and its harbour was mined. Industries: cement, glass, chemicals. Pop. (2005) 1,817,000.

hair Threadlike structure covering the SKIN of mammals. It has insulating, protective and sensory functions. Hair grows in a follicle, extending down through the EPIDERMIS to the DERMIS. New cells are added to the base; older cells become impregnated with KERATIN and die. Hair colour depends on the presence of MELANIN. An erector muscle attached to the base of the hair

▲ **Hagia Sophia** One of the finest examples of Byzantine architecture in the world, the Hagia Sophia (Gk. 'holy wisdom'), has been an Eastern Orthodox church, a Catholic cathedral, and a mosque. Now a museum and World Heritage site, the building is undergoing intensive restoration, which has revealed previously hidden Christian mosaics and decorations.

HAITI

The Republic of Haiti occupies the w third of Hispaniola, the Caribbean's second largest island. It is best known for political instability and for voodoo, which is practised by around 80% of the people. The land is mainly rugged, with mountain chains forming peninsulas in the N and s. The highest peak. 2,680m [8,793ft] is in Massif de la Selle in the SE. Between the peninsulas is the Golfe de la Gonâve, which contains the large Isle de la La Gonâve. Haiti's long coastline, which extends about 1,770km [1,100mi], is deeply indented.

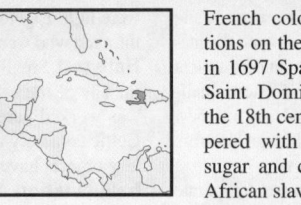

CLIMATE
Haiti has a hot, humid tropical climate. Annual rainfall in the N highlands is about 2,000mm [79in], more than twice that of the s coast. The country is subject to tropical storms, which frequently cause widespread damage.

HISTORY
In 1496, Spain established a settlement at Santo Domingo, now capital of the neighbouring Dominican Republic. This was the first European settlement in the Western Hemisphere. Within decades most of the native Arawaks were killed by the Spanish or died of imported disease. In the 17th century,

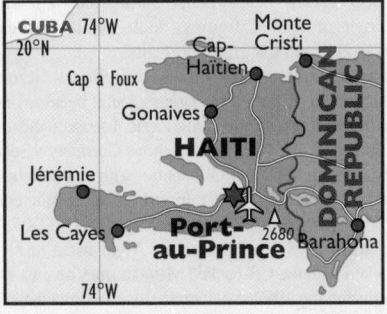

French colonists set up plantations on the w of the island, and in 1697 Spain ceded Haiti (then Saint Dominque) to France. In the 18th century, the region prospered with the development of sugar and coffee plantations by African slaves, who soon formed the majority of the population.

In 1801, former slave TOUSSAINT L'OUVERTURE led a revolt and proclaimed himself governor-general. A French force failed to conquer the interior of Haiti and the country became independent in 1804. Another former slave, Jean-Jacques DESSALINES, declared himself emperor. In the 19th century, assassinations, revolutions and dictatorships plagued Haiti. In 1915, following conflict between black and mulatto Haitians, the United States invaded the country to protect its interests and virtually governed. American troops finally withdrew in 1934, although the United States maintained firm control over the economy until 1947.

In 1956, François DUVALIER ('Papa Doc') seized power in a military coup. He was elected president in 1957. Duvalier established a corrupt and brutal dictatorship. He died in 1971 and his son Jean Claude Duvalier ('Baby Doc') became president. Like his father, Baby Doc used a murderous militia, the Tontons Macoutes, to conduct a reign of terror and maintain rule. In 1986, popular unrest forced Baby Doc to flee into exile and a military regime took over.

POLITICS
The country's first multiparty elections were held in December 1990. The winner was radical Roman Catholic priest, Father Jean-Bertrand Aristide, who promised sweeping reforms. Aristide was re-elected in 1994, but stood down in 1995 and was succeeded by René Préval. Violence and poverty prevailed

AREA 27,750sq km [10,714sq mi]
POPULATION 8,706,000
CAPITAL (POPULATION) Port-au-Prince (2,090,000)
GOVERNMENT Multiparty republic
ETHNIC GROUPS Black 95%, Mulatto/White 5%
LANGUAGES French and Creole (both official)
RELIGIONS Roman Catholic 80%, Voodoo
CURRENCY Gourde = 100 centimes

and, in 1999, Préval dissolved parliament and declared that he would rule by decree. In the elections of 2000 Aristide again became president amid accusations of electoral irregularitie. He survived an attempted coup in 2001.

In 2004, rebels seized several towns and cities in an anti-government uprising. Aristide fled the country, accusing the United States of forcing him into exile. The UN sent a peacekeeping force to stabilize the country. An interim president, Boniface Alexandre, was sworn in and an interim government took control under prime minister Gerald Latortue, a former foreign secretary and UN official. Floods in May 2004 caused major loss of life in Haiti, and later that year, Hurricane Jeanne killed nearly 3,000 people in the NW. The interim government failed to solve the country's problems and was accused of a poor human rights record. By 2006 UN forces had managed to suppress gangs and political violence enough to hold elections. René Préval became president.

ECONOMY
Haiti is the poorest country in the Western Hemisphere; 80% of the people live below the poverty line. Agriculture is the occupation of two-thirds of the people, but coffee is the only significant cash crop. Money-laundering, corruption and drug-trafficking are rife.

▲ **Handel** Although born in Germany, George Frideric Handel spent most of his working life in England under the patronage of George I, King of England and Elector of Hanover. Among Handel's best-known works are the oratorios, including the *Messiah* (1742), and orchestral pieces such as the *Water Music* (1717), which was written for George I. He was the first director of the Royal Academy of Music, London.

responds to nerve signals sent to the follicle, trapping a layer of air close to the skin, which acts as INSULATION. *See also* FUR

Haiti Caribbean nation. *See* country feature, page 373.

Haitink, Sir Bernard (1929–) Dutch conductor, principal conductor of the Amsterdam Concertgebouw Orchestra (1961–88) and the London Philharmonic (1967–79). In 1987, he became musical director of the ROYAL OPERA HOUSE, London, where he was noted for superb WAGNER performances.

Hajj (Arabic, 'migration') Pilgrimage to MECCA, made in the 12th month of the Muslim year. All Muslims are required to undertake the Hajj. It is the last of the Five Pillars of ISLAM.

hake Marine fish found in cold and temperate waters. Its streamlined body is silver and brown. Length: to 1m (40in); weight: to 14kg (30lb). Family Gadidae or Merluccidae; species Atlantic *Merluccius bilinearis*; Pacific *M. productus*.

Halcyon Greek mythological figure, daughter of Aeolus and wife of Ceyx, King of Thessaly. When Ceyx drowned in a shipwreck, Halcyon ran to the seashore to find his body and drowned herself. The gods changed them into kingfishers.

Hale, George Ellery (1868–1938) US astronomer who organized a number of observatories, including the YERKES OBSERVATORY (1897), the Mount Wilson Observatory (1917) and PALOMAR Observatory, which entered service in 1949. Each observatory featured the largest telescope of its day. Hale was an able solar observer; he invented the spectroheliograph.

half-life Time taken for half of the nuclei in a given amount of radioactive ISOTOPE to decay (change into another element or isotope). The half-life is measured because the decay is never considered to be total. Half-lives remain constant under any temperature or pressure, but there is a great variety among different isotopes. Oxygen-20 has a half-life of 14 seconds and uranium-234 of 250,000 years. A radioactive isotope disintegrates by giving off alpha or beta particles, and measurement of this rate of emission is used to record decay. The term 'half-life' also refers to particles that spontaneously decay into new particles, such as a free neutron transforming into an electron. *See also* DATING, RADIOACTIVE; RADIOACTIVITY

halibut Flatfish found worldwide in deep, cold to temperate seas. Important commercially, it is brownish on the eye side and white below. Family Pleuronectidae; species, Atlantic *Hippoglossus hippoglossus*, giant Pacific *H. stenolepis*.

Halicarnassus Ancient Greek city in sw Asia Minor. Under Persian rule from the 6th century BC its advantageous trading position made it rich. In the 4th century BC it was a semi-independent state under the Persian governor, Mausolus, whose tomb was one of the SEVEN WONDERS OF THE WORLD.

halide Salt of one of the HALOGENS (elements in group VII of the periodic table), or a compound containing a halogen and one other element; examples are sodium fluoride and potassium chloride. The alkyl halides (haloalkanes) are organic compounds, such as methyl chloride (chloromethane, CH_3Cl).

Halifax City and seaport in E Canada, on the Atlantic Ocean; capital of Nova Scotia. Founded in 1749, it developed as naval base. In 1917, it was the scene of a huge explosion on a munitions ship, which killed 2,000 people. Industries: fishing, shipbuilding, oil refining. Pop. (2001) 359,183.

halite (NaCl) Sodium chloride, in common (rock) salt. It is found in some sedimentary rocks, and in salt domes and dried lakes. It is colourless, white or grey with a glassy lustre. It has a system of interlocking cubic crystals, granules and masses. It is important as a source of CHLORINE. Hardness 2.5; r.d. 2.2.

Hall, Granville Stanley (1846–1924) US psychologist. He founded the first US psychology journal (1887) and the American Psychological Association (1892). His books include *The Contents of Children's Minds* (1883) and *Adolescence* (1904).

Hall, Sir Peter Reginald Frederick (1930–) English theatrical director. He was director of the ROYAL SHAKESPEARE COMPANY (1961–73). He directed opera at Glyndebourne and the Royal Opera House. His films include *Akenfield* (1974). He was director of the National Theatre of Great Britain (1973–88) and formed the Peter Hall Company in 1987.

Hallé, Sir Charles (1819–95) British conductor and pianist, b. Germany. In 1857 he formed a symphony orchestra in Manchester, England, which later became the Hallé Orchestra. In 1893 he helped found the Royal Manchester College of Music.

Haller, Albrecht von (1708–77) Swiss biologist, physician and poet. As a botanist he was celebrated for his descriptions of alpine flora and as a poet for *The Alps* (1729). In 1736, he researched the properties of muscle tissue, and his treatise (1757–66) laid the foundations of neurology and physiology.

Halley, Edmond (1656–1742) English mathematician and Astronomer Royal (1720–42). His most famous discovery (1696) was that COMETS have periodic ORBITS. In 1705, he accurately predicted the return (1758) of the comet now known as HALLEY'S COMET. Halley charted variations in Earth's magnetic field and established the magnetic origin of the AURORA borealis and showed that atmospheric pressure decreases with altitude. He financed Isaac NEWTON to write *Principia* (1687).

Halley's comet Bright periodic COMET. It takes 76 years to complete an orbit that takes it from within Venus' orbit to outside Neptune's. It was observed by Edmond HALLEY in 1682; later he deduced that it was the same comet that had been seen in 1531 and 1607, and predicted its return in 1758. There are records of every return since 240 BC. In 1986, the Giotto probe showed the nucleus to be an irregular object, measuring 15×8km (9×5mi), and consisting of dust and ice.

hallmark Official stamp used by British government ASSAY offices to mark the standard of gold and silver articles. The mark has four elements: the standard mark, showing the purity of the metal; the office mark, bearing the assay office's cipher; the date mark; and the maker's mark.

Hallowe'en (hallowed or holy evening) In medieval times, a holy festival observed on October 31, the eve of All Saints' Day. It merged with the ancient Celtic festival of Samhain, which marked the beginning of the year. On Samhain, fires were lit to frighten away evil spirits and to guide the souls of the dead who were supposed to revisit their homes on this day.

Hallstatt Small town in w central Austria, believed to be the site of the earliest IRON AGE culture in w Europe. Iron was worked here from *c.*700 BC. The site contains a large Celtic cemetery and a deep salt mine. Fine bronze and pottery objects have also been discovered.

hallucination Apparent perception of something that is not present. Although they may occur in any of the five senses, auditory hallucinations and visual hallucinations are the commonest. While they are usually symptomatic of psychotic disorders, hallucinations may result from fatigue or emotional upsets and can also be a side effect of certain drugs.

hallucinogen Drug that causes HALLUCINATIONS. Hallucinogenic drugs, such as mescaline, were used in primitive religious ceremonies. Today, drugs such as LSD are illicitly taken.

halogen Elements (FLUORINE, CHLORINE, BROMINE, IODINE and ASTATINE) belonging to group VII of the periodic table. They react with most other elements and with organic compounds. Fluorine is the most reactive and radioactive astatine is the least reactive. Halogens are electronegative; they react strongly because they require only one electron to achieve the 'stable 8' inert gas configuration. They produce crystalline salts (HALIDES) containing negative ions of the type F and Cl.

halon Any of several organic gases used in fire extinguishers, but banned in 1994 because they destroy the OZONE LAYER. Chemically halons can be considered as simple HYDROCARBONS that have had some or all of their hydrogen atoms replaced by a HALOGEN. Similar to CHLOROFLUOROCARBONS (CFCs), they are even more destructive to the ozone layer.

halophyte Any plant that is able to live in salty conditions.

Hals, Frans (*c.*1580–1666) Dutch painter, best known for his paintings of robust figures, such as the *Laughing Cavalier* (1624), and his group portraits.

Hamburg City, state, and port on the River Elbe, N Germany. Founded in the 9th century by Charlemagne, it became one of the original members of the HANSEATIC LEAGUE. Severely bombed during World War 2, it is now Germany's second largest city. It is a notable cultural centre, with an opera house, art gallery and university (1919). Industries: electronic equipment, brewing, publishing, chemicals. Pop. (2000) 1,705,000.

Hamid Karzai (1957–) President of Afghanistan (2004–). Karzai worked with the US-backed MUJAHEDDIN against Russian forces during the 1980s Soviet invasion of Afghanistan, but went into exile when the TALIBAN took power in 1996. When the US deposed the Taliban in 2001 he became interim president. In 2004 he won elections and became full president. His pro-US administration struggled to unify the country.

Hamilcar Barca (d.228BC) Carthaginian commander. Initially successful in the first of the PUNIC WARS, he was defeated in 241 BC. He suppressed a revolt of Carthaginian mercenaries in 238 BC and the following year conquered much of Spain. He was the father of HANNIBAL and Hasdrubal Barca.

Hamilton Capital and chief seaport of Bermuda, on Great Bermuda, at the head of Great Sound. Founded in 1790, it became the capital in 1815 and was made a free port in 1956. Tourism is the major industry. Pop. (2002 est.) 1400.

Hamilton City in SE Ontario, Canada, 65km (40mi) sw of Toronto. Founded in 1813, it is an important communication and manufacturing centre. Industries: iron, steel, vehicles, electrical equipment, textiles. Pop. (2001) 618,820.

Hamilton, Alexander (1755–1804) US statesman. During the American Revolution, he served as George WASHINGTON's aide-de-camp and secretary. He was the leading writer of *The Federalist Papers* (1788), advocating the new US CONSTITUTION. As first secretary of the treasury (1789–95), he founded the national currency and the BANK OF THE UNITED STATES (1791). In 1800, he alienated many within the FEDERALIST PARTY by backing Thomas JEFFERSON's bid for the presidency. In 1804, he thwarted Aaron BURR's campaign for governor of New York. Burr challenged him to a duel and killed him.

Hamilton, James Hamilton, 1st Duke of (1606–49) Scottish leader. He fought in the Thirty Years' War. As Charles I's commissioner in Scotland (1638–39), he failed to reach a compromise with the COVENANTERS and led an army against them (1639). He fought for Charles in the English CIVIL WAR, but was imprisoned for his plotting (1644–45). In 1648, he led Scottish forces in support of the king. He was defeated by CROMWELL at Preston and executed.

Hamilton, Richard (1922–) English artist, a leader of the POP ART movement. He produced collages using images taken from commercial art. His best-known work is *Just what is it that makes today's homes so different, so appealing?* (1956).

Hamito-Semitic *See* AFRO-ASIATIC LANGUAGES

Hammarskjöld, Dag (1905–61) Swedish diplomat and second secretary-general of the United Nations (1953–61), an office to which he brought great moral force. In 1956 he played a leading part in resolving the Suez Crisis. He sent a UN peacekeeping force to the Congo and later died there in an air crash. He was posthumously awarded the 1961 Nobel Peace Prize.

hammer In athletics, men's field event in which a spherical weight attached to a steel wire is thrown. The 'hammer' weighs 7.26kg (16lb) and the wire is 1.2m (3.8ft) long. The thrower stands within a circle 2.13m (7ft) in diameter.

hammerhead SHARK found in tropical marine waters and warm temperate zones. Its head is extended sideways into two lobes, with one eye and one nostril located at the tip of each. It is grey above and white below. Length: to 6.1m (20ft); weight: to 906kg (2,000lb). Family Sphyrnidae.

Hammerstein II, Oscar (1895–1960) US lyricist and librettist. He collaborated with Jerome KERN on *Show Boat* (1927) and with Richard RODGERS on *Oklahoma!* (1943), *Carousel* (1945), *South Pacific* (1949), *The King and I* (1951), and *The Sound of Music* (1959).

Hammett, Dashiell (1894–1961) US writer, the originator of hard-boiled detective fiction. Hammett drew on his own experience as a Pinkerton detective to create the investigators Sam Spade and Nick Charles. His books include *Red Harvest* (1929), *The Maltese Falcon* (1930), and *The Thin Man* (1934).

Hammurabi King of BABYLONIA (r. *c*.1792–*c*.1750BC). By conquering neighbours, such as SUMERIA, he extended his rule in Mesopotamia and reorganized the Empire under the Code of HAMMURABI.

Hammurabi, Code of Ancient laws compiled under HAMMURABI. A copy is in the Louvre, Paris. It has 282 provisions with harsh penalties for offenders and includes the maxim "An eye for an eye, a tooth for a tooth". It provides information on social and economic conditions in ancient Babylonia.

Hampden, John (1594–1643) English parliamentarian, a leader of the opposition to CHARLES I. Hampden was one of five members whom the king tried to arrest in the House of Commons in 1642, an act that spurred the English CIVIL WAR.

Hampshire County in s England, on the English Channel; the county town is WINCHESTER. There are traces of Iron Age hill forts and Roman settlements. Mainly agricultural, Hampshire contains the port of SOUTHAMPTON and PORTSMOUTH naval base. Its resorts and the NEW FOREST are tourist attractions. Industries: agriculture, oil refining, chemicals, electronics. Area: 3,782sq km (1,460sq mi). Pop. (2001) 1,240,032.

Hampton Seaport in SE Virginia, USA, on the James River. First settled in 1610, it is reputedly the oldest continuous English settlement in the USA. Industries: defence, tourism, seafood packing, fertilizers. Pop. (2000) 146,437.

Hampton Court Palace Palace situated beside the River Thames, 23km (14mi) from Westminster, London. It was begun in 1515 by Cardinal WOLSEY, who gave it to HENRY VIII in 1526, hoping to regain his favour. Christopher WREN rebuilt and extended parts of the palace between 1696 and 1704.

hamster Small, mainly nocturnal, burrowing RODENT native to Eurasia and Africa. It has internal cheek pouches for carrying food. The golden hamster (*Mesocricetus auratus*) is a domestic pet and all are descended from one female captured in Syria in 1930. Length: up to 18cm (7in). Family Cricetidae; species *Cricetus mesocricetus*.

Hamsun, Knut (1859–1952) Norwegian novelist, playwright, and poet. A proponent of individualism, his work reflected his suspicion of modern Western culture. In 1920, Hamsun received the Nobel Prize in literature for *The Growth of the Soil* (1917). Other important novels include *Hunger* (1890), *Victoria* (1898), and *Vagabonds* (1927).

Han Imperial Chinese dynasty (202BC–AD 220). Liu Pang, a peasant, overthrew the QIN dynasty and established the Han's dynastic capital at Chang'an. CONFUCIANISM became the state philosophy, and China achieved unprecedented power, prosperity, technological invention and cultural growth – especially under Han Wu Ti in the 2nd century BC. A usurper, WANG MANG, interrupted the dynasty between AD 8 and 25; this period divides the dynasty into the Former Han and Later Han.

handball Name of two games. One is played with a hard, small ball by two or four gloved players on courts of one, three, or four walls. A variant of this game that uses wooden rackets is called **paddleball**. The other game, sometimes called **team handball**, is played on a court where, between two goals and two goalkeepers, players catch, pass and throw a ball with the object of hurling the ball into the opposing goal.

Handel, George Frideric (1685–1759) English composer, b. Germany. In 1712, he moved from Italy to England. He wrote (*c*.1717) the *Water Music* for GEORGE I's procession on the River Thames. In 1720, he became the first director of the Royal Academy of Music, London. From 1729 to 1734, he wrote a series of operas for the King's Theatre, London, including *Orlando* (1733). From 1739, Handel concentrated on creating a new form, the ORATORIO, producing such works as *Saul* (1739), *Messiah* (1742) and *Judas Maccabaeus* (1747). In 1749, he composed *Music for the Royal Fireworks*.

Handy, W.C. (William Christopher) (1873–1958) US composer and musician, known as the 'father of the BLUES'. Handy published the first blues piece, "Memphis Blues" (1912), and composed many hits including "St. Louis Blues" (1914).

hang gliding GLIDING using a lightweight craft, usually with a triangular wing that is stabilized by the weight of the pilot's body. The wing is usually made of fabric. The pilot hangs from a harness and using a control bar to steer.

Hanging Gardens of Babylon One of the SEVEN WONDERS OF THE WORLD. The gardens are thought to have been spectacular, rising in a series of terraces (rather than hanging) and ingeniously irrigated by water pumped up from the Euphrates. They were probably built (*c*.600BC) by NEBUCHADNEZZAR. Nothing now remains of them.

hanging valley Valley that ends high up the face of a larger valley, possibly with a stream running through it and ending in a waterfall. Most hanging valleys result from glacial deepening of the main valley. *See also* GLACIER

Hanks, Tom (1956–) US film actor and director. Initially typecast in comedy roles, his early films included *Splash*

▲ **Hanks** Tom Hanks is one of only two actors (the other is Spencer Tracy) to win Oscars for best actor in consecutive years, with *Philadelphia* (1993) and *Forrest Gump* (1994). Other films include *Sleepless in Seattle* (1993), *Apollo 13* (1995), *The Green Mile* (1999), and *Cast Away* (2000). He is the voice of Woody, the cowboy doll, in *Toy Story* (1995).

INTERNET

Hannibal
▶ www.barca.fsnet.co.uk

Harding, Warren Gamaliel
▶ www.whitehouse.gov/history/presidents

(1984) and *Big* (1988). Hanks' performance as a gay AIDS victim in *Philadelphia* (1993) won him an Academy Award for best actor. He won a second Oscar for *Forrest Gump* (1994). In 1996 he made his directorial debut with *That Thing You Do!* He was acclaimed for his role in Steven SPIELBERG's *Saving Private Ryan* (1998). Other films include *Road to Perdition* (2002).

Hannibal (*c.*247–*c.*183 BC) Carthaginian general in the second of the PUNIC WARS, son of HAMILCAR BARCA. One of the greatest generals of ancient times, in 218 BC he invaded N Italy after crossing the Alps with 40,000 troops and a force of elephants. Hannibal won a series of victories, but was unable to capture Rome. Recalled to CARTHAGE to confront the invasion of SCIPIO AFRICANUS, he was defeated at Zama (202 BC). After the war, as chief magistrate of Carthage, he alienated the nobility by reducing their power. They sought Roman intervention, and Hannibal fled to the Seleucid kingdom of ANTIOCHUS III. Defeated fighting for Antiochus against the Romans, Hannibal committed suicide.

Hanoi Capital of Vietnam and its second largest city, on the River Red. In the 7th century the Chinese ruled Vietnam from Hanoi; it later became capital of the Vietnamese empire. Taken by the French in 1883, the city became the capital of French Indochina (1887–1945). In 1946–54, it was the scene of fierce fighting between the French and the Viet Minh. The US Air Force heavily bombed Hanoi during the VIETNAM WAR. Industries: engineering, vehicles, textiles, rice milling, food processing. Pop. (2005) 4,147,000.

Hanover (Hannover) City on the River Leine, N Germany; capital of Lower Saxony. Chartered in 1241, it joined the HANSEATIC LEAGUE in 1386. In 1636 it became the residence of the Dukes of Brunswick-Lüneberg (predecessors of the House of Hanover); GEORGE I was Elector of Hanover. Allied bombing badly damaged Hanover during World War 2, but the city reconstructed many old buildings. Industries: machinery, steel, textiles, rubber, chemicals. Pop. (1999) 512,200.

Hanover (Hannover) Former kingdom and province of Germany. In 1692, Ernest Augustus, Duke of Brunswick-Lüneberg, was created Elector of Hanover; his lands were known thereafter as Hanover. His son succeeded to the British throne as GEORGE I in 1714. Divided during the Napoleonic era, Hanover was reconstituted as a kingdom in 1815. Allied with Austria in the AUSTRO-PRUSSIAN WAR (1866), it was annexed by Prussia after Austria's defeat. After World War 2 it became part of the state of Lower Saxony.

Hanover, House of German royal family and rulers of Britain from 1714 to 1901. The Electors of Hanover succeeded to the English throne in 1714, under the terms of the Act of Settlement (1701) and the Act of Union (1707).

GEORGE I, the first Elector also to be King of England, was succeeded in both England and Hanover by GEORGE II, GEORGE III, GEORGE IV, and WILLIAM IV. Salic law forbade Queen Victoria's accession in Hanover; her uncle, the Duke of Cumberland, inherited the Hanoverian title and the crowns of Britain and Germany separated.

Hansard Colloquial name for the daily record of the proceedings of the British Houses of Parliament. Named after Luke Hansard (1752–1828), printer to the Commons, who compiled unofficial reports, these verbatim records have continued to be referred to as 'Hansard', even though the family sold their publishing interest in 1889. The responsibility now rests with The Stationery Office.

Hanseatic League Commercial union formed in 1241 by *c.*160 N German cities (Hanse towns), including Bremen, Cologne, Hamburg, and Lübeck. The League protected its merchants by controlling the trade routes from the Baltic region to the Atlantic. It began to decline in the late 15th century, with the opening up of the New World and aggressive trading by the British and Dutch.

Hanukkah (Chanukah or Feast of Lights) Eight-day festival celebrated in JUDAISM. It commemorates the re-dedication of the Jerusalem TEMPLE in 165 BC and the miracle of a one-day supply of oil lasting for eight days.

Hanuman In Hindu mythology, the monkey general who helped RAMA to find and rescue his wife, Sita. His attributes include great strength, agility, and wisdom. He remains a favourite deity in rural India.

haploid Term describing a CELL that has only one member of each CHROMOSOME pair. All human cells except GAMETES are DIPLOID, having 46 chromosomes. Gametes are haploid, having 23 chromosomes. The body cells of many lower organisms, including many algae and single-celled organisms, are haploid. *See also* ALTERNATION OF GENERATIONS; MEIOSIS

Hapsburg *See* HABSBURG

Harare (formerly Salisbury) Capital of Zimbabwe, in the NE part of the country. Settled by Europeans in 1890 as Fort Salisbury, it became capital of Southern Rhodesia in 1902. The city served as capital of the Federation of Rhodesia and Nyasaland (1953–63) and of Rhodesia (1965–79). It has a university (1957) and two cathedrals. Industries: gold mining, textiles, steel, tobacco, chemicals, furniture. Pop. (2005) 1,527,000.

Harbin (Haerbin) City on the River Sungari, NE China; capital of Heilungkiang province. It was a place of refuge for White Russians after the Revolution of 1917. Ruled by Japan from 1932 to 1945, it was then briefly occupied by Soviet forces before falling to the Chinese communists in 1946. Industries: oil, coal, turbines and generators, mining equipment, sugar refining, food processing, paper. Pop. (2005) 2,898,000.

hard disk Rigid magnetic disk for storing computer PROGRAMS and DATA. A built-in hard disk drive in a typical personal COMPUTER consists of a number of hard platters, coated with a magnetic material set on a common spindle. They are housed inside a sealed container, with a motor to spin the stack of platters, a head to write (record) and read (replay) each side of each platter, and associated electronic circuits. Hard disk capacity is continually being increased: most computers are now sold with a disk of at least 80Gb (8,000 million bytes) capacity.

Hardie, (James) Keir (1856–1915) Scottish socialist politician. In 1888, he founded the Scottish Parliamentary Labour Party. In 1892, Hardie entered Parliament as the first socialist MP. In 1893, he founded the Independent Labour Party. In 1906, he became a co-founder and first leader (1906–08) of the LABOUR PARTY. A committed pacifist, he withdrew from Labour politics in World War 1.

Harding, Warren Gamaliel (1865–1923) Twenty-ninth US president (1921–23). A senator (1915–21), he was a compromise Republican presidential candidate. His campaign for a return to 'normalcy' easily won the election. He handed government to his cabinet, and his administration, known as the 'Ohio Gang', was one of the most corrupt in US history. The Teapot Dome Scandal forced a Congessional investigation. Harding died before the worst excesses became public knowledge, and his vice president, Calvin COOLIDGE, succeeded him.

HARD DISK

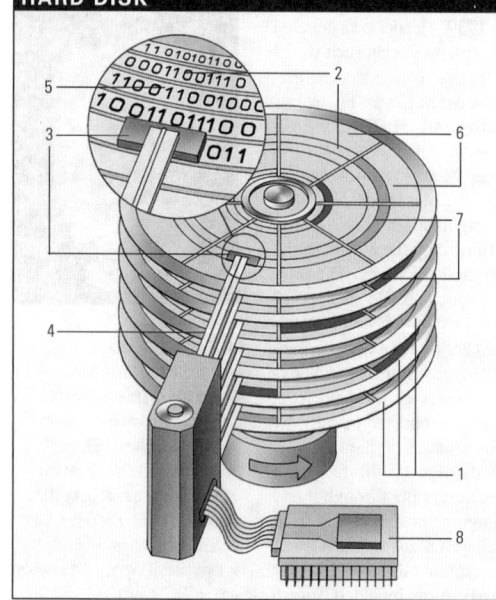

A computer hard disk consists of multiple rotating platters (1), each of which has circular magnetic tracks (2) that are read and written on by a magnetic head (3) held by an arm (4). The disks spin at 100 times per second. Tiny electromagnetic heads align magnetic particles on the surface of the platters to represent a digital code of zeros and ones (5). The magnetic tracks on the platters divide into sectors (6) and, when information is written to the hard disk, files split into different sectors on the platters (7). A file-allocation table tells the chip (8) controlling the hard disk where information is held on each platter.

hardness Resistance of a material to abrasion, cutting, or indentation. The **Mohs' scale** is a means of expressing the comparative hardness of materials, particularly minerals, by testing them against ten standard materials. These range from (1) talc to (10) diamond (the hardest). A mineral hard enough to scratch material 3, but soft enough to be scratched by material 5, would be rated as having hardness 4 on the Mohs' scale.

hardness of water Reluctance of water to produce a lather with soap, due to various dissolved salts, mainly those of calcium and magnesium. These salts give rise to an insoluble precipitate, which causes 'fur' or 'scale' in boilers, pipes and kettles. Lather is inhibited until all the dissolved salts are precipitated as scum, which floats on the surface. Hardness may be temporary (removed by boiling), caused by calcium bicarbonate; or permanent (not affected by boiling), caused by calcium sulphate.

Hardouin-Mansart, Jules (1646–1708) French architect to LOUIS XIV. His bold Baroque style made him an ideal person to carry out the king's vast building works. His major achievements include the Hall of Mirrors (1678–84), the Orangerie (1681–86), and the Grand Trianon (1687–88), all at Versailles, and the dome of the Hôtel des Invalides, Paris (1680–91).

hardware In computing, equipment as opposed to the programs, or SOFTWARE, with which a COMPUTER functions. The computer, keyboard, printer and electronic circuit boards are examples of hardware.

Hardy, Thomas (1840–1928) English novelist and poet. His birthplace, Dorset, SW England, formed the background for most of his writing. His first major success was *Far from the Madding Crowd* (1874). The often tragic tales that followed remain among the most widely read 19th-century novels and include *The Return of the Native* (1878), *The Mayor of Casterbridge* (1886), *Tess of the d'Urbervilles* (1891), and *Jude the Obscure* (1895). Critics attacked the latter for its immoral tone, and thereafter Hardy devoted himself to poetry, including *Wessex Poems* (1898) and *The Dynasts* (1903–08).

hare Large member of the RABBIT family (Leporidae). Unlike rabbits, true hares (genus *Lepus*) have ears that are longer than their heads, and their young are born with open eyes and a full coat of fur. Length: to 76cm (30in); weight: to 4.5kg (10lb). Hares include the JACK RABBIT and snowshoe rabbit.

Hare, David (1947–) English playwright and director. He collaborated with Howard Brenton on *Pravda* (1985), a study of media corruption. Hare wrote a 'State of the Nation' trilogy on the British establishment: *Racing Demon* (1990) on the Church of England; *Murmuring Judges* (1991) on the legal system; and *The Absence of War* (1993) on politics. His screenplays include *Plenty* and *Wetherby* (both 1985). Other works include *Via Dolorosa* (1998) and *The Blue Room* (1999).

harebell Flowering plant of the bellflower family (CAMPANULACEAE) widespread as a wild flower of pastures and also cultivated in gardens. It has drooping, bell-shaped, mid-blue flowers. Species *Campanula rotundifolia*.

Hare Krishna (International Society for KRISHNA Consciousness) Hindu sect, founded (1965) in New York by Swami Prabhupada (A.C. Bhaktivedanta). The movement is based on the philosophy that Krishna is the supreme God and stresses the importance of asceticism. Public perception of the movement has been enhanced by the proselytizing of its shaven-headed, saffron-robed devotees, who practise self-denial, vegetarianism, meditation and chanting of MANTRAS. *See also* HINDUISM

harelip Congenital cleft in the upper lip caused by the failure of the two parts of the palate to unite. It is a congenital condition, often associated with CLEFT PALATE.

harem Women's quarters in a Muslim household. It contained a man's wives, concubines, and female servants. The most famous harems were those of the Turkish sultans in ISTANBUL, which often had several hundred women guarded by EUNUCHS.

Hargreaves, James (1722–1778) English inventor and industrialist. In 1764 he invented the spinning jenny, a machine that greatly speeded the production of cotton by simultaneously spinning eight threads. In 1768 local spinners destroyed the machine, fearing that it threatened their jobs. Hargreaves moved to Nottingham and, with Thomas James, built a spinning mill and became one of the first great factory owners.

HARDNESS OF WATER

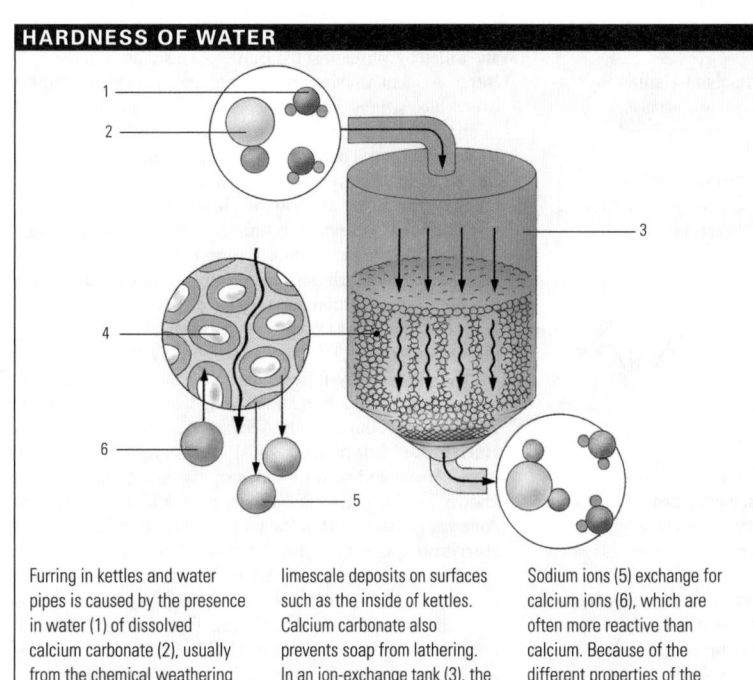

Furring in kettles and water pipes is caused by the presence in water (1) of dissolved calcium carbonate (2), usually from the chemical weathering of limestone. Calcium carbonate precipitates in hot or boiling water, forming solid limescale deposits on surfaces such as the inside of kettles. Calcium carbonate also prevents soap from lathering. In an ion-exchange tank (3), the tank contains grains of sodium-coated material with which the water comes into contact (4). Sodium ions (5) exchange for calcium ions (6), which are often more reactive than calcium. Because of the different properties of the sodium ions, the resultant sodium salts remain in solution even when boiled.

Harlem Residential area of New York City, USA, a political and cultural focus for African-Americans. The Center for Research in Black Culture is located here, next to the Countee Cullen Library, which has been a meeting place for black writers since the 1920s.

Harlem Renaissance Period of creativity, particularly in literature, among African-Americans in the 1920s. Centred in HARLEM, New York City, the Renaissance produced many fine writers, such as Countee Cullen, Langston HUGHES, and Claude McKay.

harlequin English name derived from the character Arlecchino of the COMMEDIA DELL'ARTE, who was a quick-witted, unscrupulous serving man. A harlequin nowadays appears in pantomine and comedy as a mute jester, dressed in diamond-patterned, multi-coloured tights.

harmonica (mouth organ) Musical instrument consisting of a metal cassette containing metal reeds. The reeds are vibrated as the player blows or inhales through slots along one edge of the cassette.

harmonics (overtones) In acoustics, additional notes whose frequencies are multiples of a basic (fundamental) note. When a violin string is plucked, the sounds correspond to vibrations of the string. The loudest note corresponds to the fundamental mode of vibration. Other weaker notes, corresponding to subsidiary vibrations, sound at the same time. Together these notes make up a harmonic series.

harmony In music, structure of chords and the relationships between them. The diatonic scale (from one C to the next on a piano, for example) is the basis of chord construction, and a **harmonic progression** from one chord to the next is defined by the KEY. The **tonic, dominant**, and **subdominant** chords are the primary chords of a key (C, G, and F chords in the key of C). *See also* SCALE

Harold I (d.1040) (Harold Harefoot) Danish king and ruler of England (1035–40). An illegitimate son of CANUTE II, he claimed the throne, ruling as regent (1035–37). Elected king at Oxford, he disposed of his rival, Alfred the Aethling, and displaced the heir, his half-brother, Hardecanute.

Harold II (1022–66) Last Anglo-Saxon King of England (1066). He was elected King following the death of EDWARD THE CONFESSOR, despite having pledged to support William of Normandy's (WILLIAM I) claim to the throne. He immediately had to contend with the invasion of Harold III of Nor-

▲ **hare** The wide range of the various species of hare, from cold polar climates to warmer, temperate regions, brought about physical adaptations. To conserve as much heat as possible, the Arctic hare (*Lepus timidus*) (top) has shorter ears and a more spherical body than its relative the Mediterranean brown hare (*L. capensis*). The Arctic hare also has thicker fur which turns white in winter for camouflage.

▲ **harvestman** The North African harvestman (*Phalangium africanum*) has many relatives throughout the world, including North America where it is known as the daddy-long-legs. This minute scavenger measures up to 12mm (0.5in).

▲ **Havel** President of the Czech Republic, Vaclav Havel was imprisoned under the former communist regime, and his plays, which centre around the lives of political dissidents, were banned.

▲ **hawthorn** An ideal tree for hedge-planting because of its hardiness and its display of thorns, the hawthorn (family Rosaceae) can grow to 11.5m (35ft) if left untrimmed. Its heavily scented blossom is conspicuous in late spring and early summer in the hedgerows of Europe.

way, whom he defeated. Three days later, he was defeated and killed by William at the Battle of Hastings.

harp Ancient musical instrument consisting of a frame over which strings are stretched. Variations have been found in civilizations as diverse as Egyptian, Greek and Celtic. A modern orchestral harp has a large triangular frame that carries 47 strings. Seven pedals ensure the whole chromatic range is covered by altering the pitch of the strings.

harpsichord Keyboard instrument. Its metal strings are mechanically plucked by quill plectrums. Its volume can barely be regulated, although stops may be used to bring extra strings into use. Historic instruments may have had two or, rarely, three keyboards. The harpsichord was the principal keyboard instrument from 1500 to 1750, but was replaced by the PIANO.

harrier Bird of prey. It frequents grasslands where it preys on small animals. It has a small bill, long wings and tail. Length: 38–50cm (15–20in). Family Accipitridae; genus *Circus*.

Harris, Joel Chandler (1848–1908) US writer. A journalist in the American South for much of his career, Harris is best known for the *Uncle Remus* stories, retellings of African-American folk-tales. Brer Rabbit is his most famous character.

Harrisburg Capital of Pennsylvania, USA, in the SE of the state, on the Susquehanna River. Established as a trading post in *c*.1718, by 1785 a town was established, and it was later the scene of the Harrisburg Convention (1788). It became the state capital in 1812. Industries: textiles, machinery, electronic equipment. Pop. (2000) 48,950.

Harrison, Benjamin (1833–1901) Twenty-third US president (1889–93). He was a grandson of William Henry HARRISON. After one term in the US Senate, he was selected (1888) as the Republican presidential nominee against President Grover CLEVELAND. He won with a majority of the electoral votes, although Cleveland had the most popular votes. As president, Harrison signed the Sherman Antitrust Act and the McKinley Tariff Act. Cleveland defeated him in 1892 elections.

Harrison, William Henry (1773–1841) Ninth US president (1841). Harrison is chiefly remembered for his military career, especially his victory against Native Americans at Tippecanoe (1811). He was elected president in 1840, with John Tyler as vice president, under the slogan "Tippecanoe and Tyler too." Harrison died only a month after taking office.

Hart, Moss (1904–61) US dramatist. He collaborated with George S. KAUFMAN on many comedies, including *You Can't Take It With You* (1936). His most successful musical was *Lady in the Dark* (1941), written with Kurt WEILL and Ira Gershwin. In 1956, he directed *My Fair Lady*.

hartebeest Large ANTELOPE native to sub-Saharan African grasslands. They have sharply rising horns united at the base. Length: up to 200cm (80in); height: to 150cm (60in); weight: up to 180kg (400lb). Family Bovidae.

Hartford State capital of Connecticut, USA, on the Connecticut River. More than 25 insurance companies have their headquarters here. Manufactures include precision instruments and electrical equipment. Pop. (2000) 852,000.

Hartford Convention (1814–15) Secret meeting of leaders from five New England states opposed to the WAR OF 1812 because it disrupted trade. Convention resolutions sought to strengthen states' rights over conscription and taxation; some delegates favoured withdrawal from the Union.

Hartley, L.P. (Lesley Poles) (1895–1972) English novelist, short-story writer, and critic. Hartley first won acclaim with his trilogy of novels *The Shrimp and the Anemone* (1944), *The Sixth Heaven* (1946), and *Eustace and Hilda* (1947). *The Go-Between* (1953) presents a picture of the sexual desires beneath the surface of aristocratic Edwardian society.

Hartmann, Nicolai (1882–1950) German realist philosopher. Although influenced by PLATO and Immanuel KANT, he proposed, in *Outlines of a Metaphysics of Knowledge* (1921), that existence is an essential prerequisite for knowledge, a reversal of Kant's idea. He finally rejected Kantian ideas in his book *New Ways of Ontology* (1942). *See also* REALISM

Harun al-Rashid (764–809) Most famous of the ABBASID caliphs of Baghdad (786–809). His reign gained romantic lustre from the stories of the *Thousand and One Arabian Nights*. He engaged in successful war with the BYZANTINE

EMPIRE, but civil war ensued from his effort to reconcile competing interests by dividing the empire between his sons.

Harvard University Oldest US college, founded in 1636 by John Harvard at Cambridge, Massachusetts. It was originally intended for the instruction of Puritan ministers. Today, there are two colleges, Harvard College for men and Radcliffe College for women.

harvestman ARACHNID with legs that may be several times its body length. It feeds on insects and plant juices. Body length: 2.5–13mm (0.1–0.5in). Family Phalangidae.

Harvey, William (1578–1657) English physician and anatomist who discovered the circulation of the blood. His findings, published in *De Motu Cordis et Sanguinis* (1628), were ridiculed at first. He also studied embryology.

Haryana State in N central India; the capital is Chandigarh. It was formed in 1966 from part of the state of Punjab. Irrigation and fertilization increased the agricultural land. Industries: machine tools, farming implements, cement, paper, bicycles. Area: 44,222sq km (17,074sq mi). Pop. (2001) 21,082,989.

Harz Mountains Mountain range in central Germany, extending 96km (60mi) between the Weser and Elbe rivers. The highest peak is the Brocken, at 1,142m (3,747ft).

Hasdrubal Barca Name of two Carthaginian generals. The **Elder** (d.221BC) expanded Carthaginian power, and founded Cartagena, Spain. The **Younger** (d.207BC) was the son of HAMILCAR BARCA and the brother of HANNIBAL.

Hašek, Jaroslav (1883–1923) Czech novelist and short story writer. He wrote the best-selling satirical novel *The Good Soldier Schweik* (1920–23).

Hashemite Arab princely family descended from the Prophet MUHAMMAD, including the fourth caliph ALI and King HUSSEIN of Jordan.

hashish Resin obtained from the flowering tops of the hemp plant *Cannabis sativa* and used as a psychotropic drug. When smoked or eaten it generally induces heady sensations and often a feeling of detachment. It is not considered addictive. Possession of the drug is illegal in the UK and the USA. *See also* CANNABIS; MARIJUANA

Hasidism Popular pietist movement within JUDAISM founded by Israel ben Eliezer (*c*.1699–*c*.1761), known as the Baal Shem Tov (Master of the Good Name). The movement, centred in E Europe until World War 2, strongly supports Orthodox Judaism. Its main centres are now in Israel and the USA.

Hassan II (1929–99) King of Morocco (1961–99), son and successor of Muhammad V. He dissolved the National Assembly in 1965, and introduced a new constitution, approved by referendum (1971), which left his authority supreme. He eliminated foreign ownership of business in 1973, and in 1975 made claims to much of Western Sahara.

hassium (symbol Hs) Synthetic, radioactive transactinide element. It is a very unstable element that is produced by high-energy atomic collisions. It was discovered in 1984 by German physicists Peter Armbruster and Gottfried Münzenberg. Named after the Latin *Hassia* for 'Germany', it was formerly named hahnium. Properties: at.no. 108; r.a.m. 277.

Hastings, Battle of (October 14, 1066) Engagement fought near Hastings, SE England, by King HAROLD II of England against the invasion of WILLIAM, Duke of Normandy. The Norman victory and death of Harold marked the end of the Anglo-Saxon monarchy and produced a social revolution.

Hastings, Warren (1732–1818) First British governor general of India (1774–85). He successfully defended British territory against several Indian opponents. He made many enemies and returned to England in 1785 to face a variety of charges. Although eventually acquitted, his career was ruined.

hatchetfish Marine fish found in deep temperate and tropical seas. There are light-emitting organs along the underside of its deep, muscular abdomen. Length: to 10cm (4in). Family Sternoptychidae (or Characidae).

Hathor Ancient Egyptian goddess of love, happiness, music, and dance. She is depicted as a cow or with a cow's horns.

Hatshepsut (d.1482BC) Queen of Egypt (*c*.1494–1482BC). Daughter of THUTMOSE I, she married Thutmose II and, after his death (*c*.1504BC), ruled first as regent for her nephew, then in her own right – the only woman to rule as pharaoh.

Haughey, Charles (1925–2006) Irish statesman, prime minister (1979–81, 1982, 1987–92). A member of FIANNA FÁIL, Haughey entered Parliament in 1957. Dismissed from the cabinet in 1970 for alleged conspiracy in IRISH REPUBLICAN ARMY (IRA) gun-running, he was later acquitted. He retired in 1992.

Hauptmann, Gerhart (1862–1946) German dramatist, poet, and novelist. His play *Vor Sonnenaufgang* (1889) marked the birth of German naturalist drama. He received the 1912 Nobel Prize in literature. He is chiefly remembered for his early, naturalistic works.

Hausa Predominantly Muslim people, inhabiting NW Nigeria and S Niger. Hausa society is feudal and based on patrilineal descent. Its language is the official language of N Nigeria and a major trading language of W Africa. Hausa crafts include weaving, leatherwork and silversmithing.

Havana (La Habana) Capital of CUBA, on the NW coast; largest city and port in the West Indies. It was founded by the Spanish explorer Diego Velázquez in 1515, and moved to its present site in 1519. Havana became Cuba's capital at the end of the 16th century. Industries: oil refining, textiles, sugar and cigars. Pop. (2005) 2192,000.

Havel, Vaclav (1936–) Czech statesman and dramatist. He wrote a series of plays, such as *The Garden Party* (1963), that were critical of Czechoslovakia's communist regime. Havel was the leading spokesman for the dissident group Charter 77 and was imprisoned (1979–83). In 1989, he founded Civic Forum. Following the 'Velvet Revolution' (December 1989), Havel was elected president of Czechoslovakia. He resigned (1992) in protest at the partition of Czechoslovakia, but returned by popular demand as president of the Czech Republic. He was re-elected in 1998 and resigned in 2003.

Hawaii US state in the N Pacific Ocean, *c.*3,350km (2,100mi) WSW of San Francisco; the capital is HONOLULU. It consists of eight large and 124 small volcanic islands. The highest point is MAUNA KEA, at 4,205m (13,678ft). There is an important US naval base at PEARL HARBOR. Settled by Polynesians in the 9th century AD King KAMEHAMEHA united the islands in the late 18th century. In 1893, the monarchy was overthrown. The USA annexed by Hawaii in 1898 and, in 1900, Hawaii became a US territory. It the last state to be admitted (1959) to the Union. Agriculture and tourism are the mainstays of the economy. Exports: bananas, pineapples, nuts, coffee. Area: 16,705sq km (6,450sq mi). Pop. (2000) 1,211,537.

hawfinch Largest European FINCH, nesting in temperate regions. Its large bill cracks nuts and fruit stones. It has mostly chestnut plumage, with black and white patches. Length: 18cm (7in). Species *Coccothraustes coccothraustes*.

hawk BIRD OF PREY of the family Accipitridae, which includes the true hawks, BUZZARDS, EAGLES, HARRIERS, KITES, OSPREYS and VULTURES. They range in size from the tiny sparrow hawk to the harpy eagle. Hawks have short, hooked bills for tearing meat and strong claws for killing prey. Common coloration is red, brown or grey plumage with streaks on the wings. Length: 28–46 cm (11–26in). Order Falconiformes. *See also* FALCON

Hawke, Bob (Robert) (1929–) Australian statesman, prime minister (1983–91). He entered Parliament in 1980, and in 1983 became leader of the Australian Labor Party. Hawke held office for an unprecedented four terms. He was succeeded by Paul KEATING.

Hawking, Stephen William (1942–) English theoretical physicist. He used the general theory of RELATIVITY and QUANTUM MECHANICS to produce theories on BIG BANG and the formation of BLACK HOLES. He found the powerful gravitational field around super dense black holes can radiate matter. Hawking wrote the science bestseller *A Brief History of Time* (1988).

Hawkins, Coleman (1904–69) US jazz saxophonist. His definitive recording of "Body and Soul" was one of the first recordings of an extended jazz solo. From 1934 to 1939, he lived in Europe, where he recorded with 'Django' REINHARDT.

Hawkins, Sir John (1532–95) English naval commander. With the support of Queen Elizabeth I, he led two lucrative expeditions to Africa and the West Indies (1562–63, 1564–65), but on his third expedition (1567–69) the Spanish destroyed most of his ships. He played an important role in the defeat of the Spanish ARMADA in 1588.

Hawksmoor, Nicholas (1661–1736) English BAROQUE architect. He assisted Christopher WREN on the construction of St Paul's, London, and worked with John VANBRUGH at Castle Howard and Blenheim Palace. He is celebrated for his six London church designs, including St Mary's, Woolnoth (1716–27), and St George's, Bloomsbury (1716–31).

hawthorn Any of more than 200 species of thorny DECIDUOUS shrubs and trees of the genus *Crataegus*, growing in N temperate parts of the world. Their flowers are white or pink, and small berries are borne in clusters. Family Rosaceae.

Hawthorne, Nathaniel (1804–64) US novelist and short-story writer. Hawthorne's debut novel was *Fanshawe* (1829). His short-story collections include *Twice-Told Tales* (1837) and *Mosses from an Old Manse* (1846). His masterpiece is the psychological novel *The Scarlet Letter* (1850). Other works include *The House of the Seven Gables* (1851), *The Blithedale Romance* (1852), and the children's books *A Wonder Book* (1852) and *Tanglewood Tales* (1853).

Hay, John Milton (1838–1905) US secretary of state (1898–1905) under Presidents William McKINLEY and Theodore ROOSEVELT. His 'open-door policy' demanded equal trading status for foreign powers in China. He negotiated the HAY-PAUNCEFOTE TREATY ensuring US control of the Panama Canal.

Haydn, Franz Joseph (1732–1809) Austrian composer. Haydn brought the SONATA form to masterful fruition in more than 100 symphonies, notably the 'Military', the 'Clock' and the 'London' (all 1793–95). His most famous choral works are the oratorios *The Creation* (1798) and *The Seasons* (1801). He also wrote many string quartets, chamber works, concertos and masses.

Hayek, Friedrich August von (1899–1992) British economist, b. Vienna. He was professor at London (1931–50), Chicago (1950–62), and Freiburg (1962–69). He wrote many books on law, economics, and philosophy, and received the 1974 Nobel Prize in economics.

Hayes, Rutherford Birchard (1822–93) Nineteenth US President (1877–81). As governor of Ohio, he won the Republican nomination for president in 1876. Some of the electoral votes were disputed, but an electoral commission awarded all of them to Hayes, giving him victory over Samuel J. Tilden. As president, Hayes removed all federal troops from the South and tried to promote civil-service reform. He retired after one term.

hay fever Seasonal ALLERGY induced by grass or tree POLLENS. Symptoms include ASTHMA, itching of the nose and eyes, and sneezing. Symptoms are controlled with an ANTIHISTAMINE.

Hay-Pauncefote Treaty (1901) Agreement promising equal rates through the PANAMA CANAL to all nations and all vessels. It also granted the USA the full right to build and manage the canal. John HAY and Lord Pauncefote, British ambassador to the USA, negotiated the treaty.

Hayworth, Rita (1918–87) US film actress. *Blood and Sand* (1941) established her sultry, temptress image. She was the dancing partner of both Gene KELLY in *Cover Girl* (1944), and Fred ASTAIRE in *You Were Never Lovelier* (1941). Orson WELLES (one of her four husbands) directed her in *The Lady From Shanghai* (1948).

hazel Any of *c.*15 bushes or small trees of the genus *Corylus*, native to temperate regions of Europe, Asia and America.

▲ **Hawking** The author of the best-selling *A Brief History of Time* (1988), Professor Stephen Hawking's work has concentrated on the nature of black holes. Since the 1960s he has suffered from a motor neuron disease.

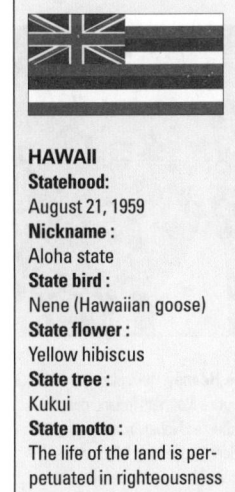

HAWAII
Statehood:
August 21, 1959
Nickname :
Aloha state
State bird :
Nene (Hawaiian goose)
State flower :
Yellow hibiscus
State tree :
Kukui
State motto :
The life of the land is perpetuated in righteousness

INTERNET

Havel, Vaclav
▶ www.hrad.cz

Hawaii
▶ www.state.hi.us

Hawke, Bob (Robert)
▶ www.nma.gov.au/primeministers/12.htm

Hayes, Rutherford Birchard
▶ www.whitehouse.gov/history/presidents

◀ **Hayworth** A cousin of Ginger Rogers, the US actress and dancer Rita Hayworth came from a show-business family. Known as the 'Love Goddess', she was best known for her roles as the sultry temptress, and as the fun-loving female lead in musicals such as *Cover Girl* (1944).

H

▲ **Heaney** The violence in his native Northern Ireland deeply affected Nobel Prize-winning poet Seamus Heaney. Much of his poetry examines the violence and its impact on communities. He left Northern Ireland because of 'the Troubles', and taught in Dublin, becoming professor of rhetoric and oratory (1985–95) at Harvard, USA, and professor of poetry (1989–1994) at Oxford, UK. Volumes include *Electric Light* (2001).

There are separate male and female flowers. The fruit is a hazelnut, also called cobnut or filbert. Family Betulaceae.

Hazlitt, William (1778–1830) English critic and essayist. A friend to many leading talents of the Romantic movement, his volumes of critical essays include *Lectures on the English Poets* (1818), *Table Talk* (1821–22), and *The Spirit of the Age* (1825).

Health, UK Department of Government department responsible for the administration of the NATIONAL HEALTH SERVICE and local authority social services. It also provides information on public and environmental health and is responsible for public ambulance services. The head of the department is the secretary of state for health.

Health and Safety Commission British government body created by the Health and Safety at Work Act (1974) to instigate and monitor measures to protect people in work and the public at large from industrial or commerical hazards. The Health and Safety Executive has an inspectorate to enforce health and safety law in working premises.

Heaney, Seamus (1939–) Irish poet, b. Northern Ireland. His early volumes, such as *Death of a Naturalist* (1966), establish a link between soil and language. Later works, such as *North* (1975), *Field Work* (1979), and *Station Island* (1984), examine the political and historical connotations of words. He won the Whitbread Prize for *The Spirit Level* (1996). His essay collections include *The Government of the Tongue* (1988). Heaney received the 1995 Nobel Prize in literature. In 1999, he won a second Whitbread Prize for a translation of the Anglo-Saxon epic *Beowulf*.

hearing Process by which sound WAVES are experienced. SOUND waves enter the auditory canal of the EAR and vibrate the eardrum. The vibrations are transmitted by three small bones to the COCHLEA, where receptors generate nerve impulses that pass via the auditory nerve to the brain to be interpreted.

Hearst, William Randolph (1863–1951) US media tycoon. He built a nationwide publishing empire that included newspapers, magazines, news services, radio stations, and film studios. With his rival, Joseph Pulitzer, Hearst practised sensational journalism and promoted the Spanish-American War. His career inspired Orson Welles' film *Citizen Kane* (1941).

heart Muscular ORGAN that pumps BLOOD through the body. In humans, the heart MUSCLE is located behind the STERNUM. Divided longitudinally by a muscular wall, the right side contains only deoxygenated blood, the left side only oxygenated blood. The pulmonary ARTERY carries deoxygenated blood from the heart to the lungs. Each side divides into two chambers, an atrium and a ventricle. The average heart beat rate for an adult at rest is 70–80 beats per minute.

heart attack (myocardial infarction) Death of part of the HEART muscle due to the blockage of a coronary ARTERY by a blood clot (thrombosis). It is accompanied by chest pain, sweat-

ing and vomiting. Modern drugs treat abnormal heart rhythms and dissolve clots in the coronary arteries. **Heart failure** occurs when the heart is unable to pump blood at the rate necessary to supply body tissues and may be due to high BLOOD PRESSURE or CORONARY HEART DISEASE. Symptoms include shortness of breath, oedema, and fatigue. Treatment is with a DIURETIC and heart drugs. *See also* ANGINA; ARTERIOSCLEROSIS

heart-lung machine Apparatus used during some surgery to take over the function of the heart and lungs. It consists of a pump to circulate blood around the body and special equipment to add oxygen to the blood and remove carbon dioxide.

heat (symbol Q) Form of ENERGY that transfers as a consequence of a difference in TEMPERATURE. The amount of heat gained or lost by a body equals the product of its heat capacity and the temperature through which it rises or falls. Heat transfers in three forms: CONVECTION (within fluids), CONDUCTION (within objects), and RADIATION. The total KINETIC and POTENTIAL ENERGY of a body is its internal energy (U). If this body changes temperature, there is a corresponding change (ΔU) in its internal energy. According to the first law of THERMODYNAMICS, $\Delta U = Q - w$, where Q is the heat and w is the WORK. The SI unit of heat and energy is the JOULE (J).

heat capacity (thermal capacity) Ratio of the heat supplied to an object to the rise in its temperature. It is measured in joules/kelvin. *See also* SPECIFIC HEAT CAPACITY

heath Any of various woody evergreen shrubs of the genus *Erica*, found in Europe, Africa, and North America. They generally have bell-shaped blue or purple flowers. Family Ericaceae. The term also applies to land that supports heath.

Heath, Sir Edward Richard George (1916–2005) British statesman, prime minister (1970–74). He entered Parliament in 1950. In 1965, he became leader of the CONSERVATIVE PARTY, succeeding Harold WILSON as prime minister. Heath secured Britain's membership of the EUROPEAN COMMUNITY (EC) (1973), but poor industrial relations led to a bitter miners' strike and the introduction of a 'three-day week' (1974). Defeated in two elections in 1974, the following year Margaret THATCHER replaced Heath as Conservative Party leader. Heath remained an outspoken advocate of European integration even after his retirement from the Commons in 2001.

heather (ling) Evergreen shrub native to Europe and Asia. It has small bell-shaped flowers of pink, lavender, or white. Family Ericaceae; species *Calluna vulgaris*. *See also* ERICA

heatstroke Condition in which the body temperature rises above 41°C (106°F). It is brought on by exposure to extreme heat. In mild cases there may be lassitude and fainting; in severe cases, collapse, coma and death may ensue.

heaven Abode of divine beings or a world of bliss beyond death. In the later Jewish tradition (after the 3rd or 2nd centuryBC), it was the dwelling place of God and the angels, and of those human beings who had died after leading a virtuous life. Christian theology adopted this conception but modified it to be the destination after death of the true followers of Jesus Christ. *See also* HADES; HELL; LIMBO; NIRVANA; PURGATORY

heavy metal Metal of high density or high relative atomic weight, such as platinum or lead. It may also refer to metallic pollutants in soil that restrict plant growth.

heavy water *See* DEUTERIUM

Hebrew Language of the SEMITIC branch of the AFRO-ASIATIC family. Orginally spoken in Palestine, it is the language of the OLD TESTAMENT. It declined during the BABYLONIAN CAPTIVITY, supplanted by ARAMAIC. Hebrew persisted as a literary and liturgical language among Jews. The 19th-century Zionist movement revived Hebrew as a spoken language. It became the official language of ISRAEL in 1948. *See also* YIDDISH

Hebrews, Epistle to the Part of the NEW TESTAMENT. It contains a letter of encouragement to a group of Jewish converts to Christianity and a review of Israel's history and Jesus' place in it. Its author is unknown.

Hebrides (Western Isles) Group of more than 500 islands off the W coast of Scotland. They divide into the Inner Hebrides (Skye, Rhum, Eigg, Islay, Mull) and the Outer Hebrides (Lewis, Harris, North Uist, and South Uist). First inhabited in the 4th millennium BC Picts settled on the islands from the 3rd century AD and the Scots arrived later. In the 8th

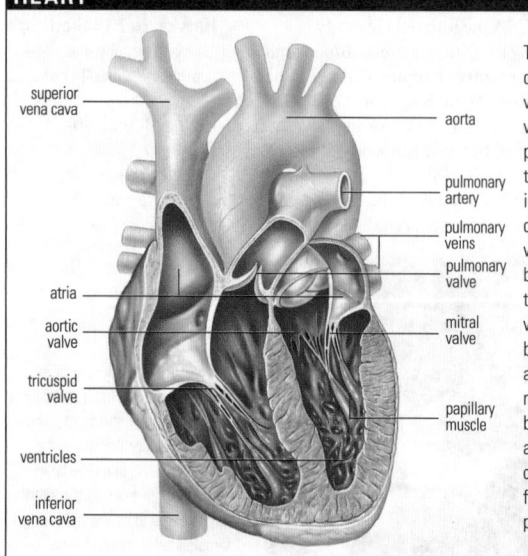

HEART

The human heart contains four chambers – two atria and two ventricles – and four sets of valves. Blood from the body passes into the right atrium, via the vena cavae. Flow of blood into the right ventricle is controlled by the tricuspid valve. Pulmonary arteries carry blood from the right ventricle to the lungs, while pulmonary veins carry oxygenated blood back from the lungs to the left atrium. In a similar way, the mitral valve controls the flow of blood between the left atrium and the left ventricle. The aorta conducts the oxygenated blood from the left ventricle to all parts of the body.

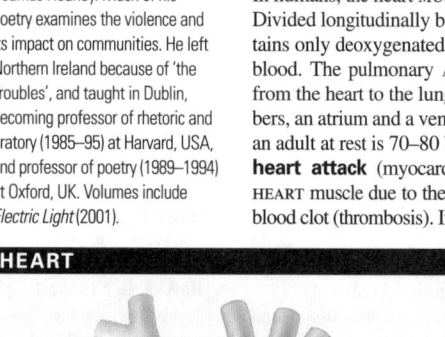

superior vena cava
aorta
pulmonary artery
pulmonary veins
pulmonary valve
atria
mitral valve
aortic valve
tricuspid valve
papillary muscle
ventricles
inferior vena cava

century, the Vikings invaded and the Hebrides became a Norwegian dependency. In the 13th century, Norway ceded the islands to Scotland. Less than 100 of the islands are inhabited. Industries: fishing, farming, woollen clothing.

Hebron (El Khalil) City in the Israeli-occupied WEST BANK. An ancient city, it came under Arab control in the 7th century AD and was occupied by the Crusaders (12th-13th centuries) before reverting to Arab rule. It later became part of the Ottoman Empire. In 1948, Jordan annexed Hebron but Israel occupied it during the SIX-DAY WAR (1967). It witnessed much Israeli-Arab tension, especially during the INTIFADA. The ISRAELI-PALESTINIAN ACCORD granted Palestinian self-rule to 85% of Hebron. It is sacred to both Jews and Muslims. The Tomb of the Patriarchs (the Cave of Machpelah) is the traditional burial place of Abraham, Sarah, Isaac, Rebecca, Jacob, and Leah. Industries: tanning, glass making. Pop. (1997) 119,200.

Hecate Goddess in Greek mythology. Associated with ARTEMIS, she bestowed wealth and blessings, and presided over witchcraft, graveyards, and crossroads.

Hector In Greek legend, the greatest of the Trojan heroes, eldest son of PRIAM. Hector was slain by ACHILLES.

hedgehog Small, nocturnal Eurasian mammal of the family Erinaceidae. It has short, sharp spines above, lighter-coloured fur below, and a pointed snout. It feeds on insects and other small animals, and defends itself by rolling into a ball with the spines outermost. Species *Erinaceus europaeus*.

hedonism Pursuit of pleasure, or any of several philosophical or ethical doctrines associated with it. Aristippus (c.435-c.356BC) taught that pleasure was the highest good. EPICURUS advocated discrimination in the seeking of pleasure. John LOCKE believed that the idea of 'good' can be defined in terms of pleasure. BENTHAM and J.S. MILL adapted a psychological view of hedonism in formulating UTILITARIANISM.

Hegel, Georg Wilhelm Friedrich (1770-1831) German philosopher, whose method of dialectical reasoning had a strong influence on his successors, notably Karl MARX. In 1818, he succeeded Johann Fichte as professor of philosophy at Berlin University. He developed a metaphysical system that traced the self-realization of spirit by dialectical movements towards perfection. These progressions took the form of battles between a thesis and an antithesis, eventually resolved in a synthesis at a higher level of truth. Hegel wrote two major books, *Phenomenology of Mind* (1807) and *Science of Logic* (1812-16). *See also* DIALECTICAL MATERIALISM

hegemony Leadership or dominance of one state over others. The term originated in ancient Greece where the cities of Athens, Sparta and Thebes held hegemony over Greece in the 5th and 4th centuries BC. Italian Marxian theorist Antonio Gramsci (1891-1937) also employed the term hegemony to refer to the phenomenon of one social class monopolizing the creation and transmission of values.

Hegira (Arab. 'Exodus') Flight of MUHAMMAD from MECCA to MEDINA in AD 622 to escape persecution. OMAR set this date as the start of the Islamic CALENDAR.

Heidegger, Martin (1889-1976) German philosopher. A founder of EXISTENTIALISM and a major influence on modern philosophy, his most important work was *Being and Time* (1927). Influenced by PHENOMENOLOGY and Christian ONTOLOGY, his central concern was how human self-awareness depends on the concepts of time and death. For him, Western science and philosophy led to NIHILISM. His later work focused more on the role of language.

Heidelberg City on the River Neckar, Baden-Württemberg, SW Germany. Founded in the 12th century, it has the oldest university in Germany (1386) and a medieval castle. Industries: printing machinery, precision instruments, publishing, textiles, leather goods. Pop. (1999) 139,400.

Heimlich manoeuvre First-aid technique, developed by Dr Henry J. Heimlich for relieving blockage in the windpipe. The rescuer uses his or her arms to encircle the choking person's chest from behind, positioning one fist in the space just beneath the breastbone and covering it with the other hand. The rescuer then thumps the fist into the person's midriff.

◄ **hedgehog** The spines of the European hedgehog (*Erinaceus europus*) are actually hairs, modified into hollow tubes with reinforcing ridges on the inside walls, making for a strong but light structure. The spines are raised when the animal is threatened.

Heisenberg, Werner Karl (1901-76) German physicist, one of the pioneers of QUANTUM MECHANICS. He studied under Max BORN and Niels BOHR, and in 1926 developed a form of QUANTUM THEORY based on matrix ALGEBRA, known as matrix mechanics. Paul DIRAC showed that Heisenberg's theory was equivalent to Erwin SCHRÖDINGER's notion of WAVE MECHANICS. In 1927, Heisenberg published his famous UNCERTAINTY PRINCIPLE. He received the 1932 Nobel Prize in physics.

Hejaz Region in NW Saudi Arabia, on the Red Sea coast. The centre of ISLAM, it contains the Muslim holy cities of MECCA and MEDINA. It has been part of Saudi Arabia since 1932. Area: 388,500sq km (150,000sq mi).

Hejira (Arab. *Hegira*, 'breaking off of relations') Flight of MUHAMMAD from MECCA to MEDINA in AD 622 in order to escape persecution. The Islamic calendar begins in 622.

Helen In Greek legend, the beautiful daughter of LEDA and ZEUS. She married Menelaus, King of Sparta, but was carried off by PARIS, Prince of TROY, thus provoking the TROJAN WAR.

Helena Capital of Montana, USA, in the W central part. It was settled by prospectors in 1864. By 1868 the population was 7500 and US$16 million worth of gold had been mined. In 1875 it was made capital of Montana Territory, becoming state capital in 1889. Industries: mineral smelting, bakery equipment, ceramics, paints. Pop. (2000) 25,780.

helicopter AIRCRAFT that gains lift from **rotors** (rotating AEROFOILS), and is capable of vertical takeoff and landing, hovering, and forwards, backwards and lateral flight. At takeoff, all blades have a steep pitch in order to achieve maximum LIFT. The circular movement of the blades generates an opposite, reactive force on the helicopter that is overcome by another set of opposite-turning rotors, or by another small rotor in

HELICOPTER

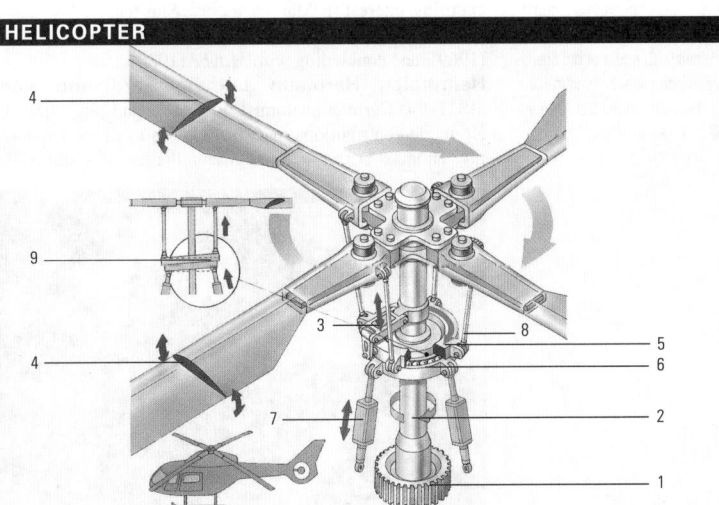

A helicopter rotor head transfers the power of the engines to the rotor blades via gears (1) and the rotor shaft (2). The swash plate controls the tilt of the rotor (3) and also the pitch of the blades (4). The upper (5) and lower (6) swash plates are controlled by hydraulic cylinders, (7) attached to the lower plate. The upper plate connects to the rotor blades by control rods (8). The pitch of the blades controls the amount of lift generated, while the attitude of the whole rotor controls how the helicopter moves horizontally. If the rear of the swash plate is raised (9), the rotor dips towards the nose of the helicopter causing it to travel forward.

▲ **Hemingway** US novelist Ernest Hemingway was constantly seeking adventure, and was a correspondent in the Spanish Civil War and World War 2. Between the wars, Hemingway spent time big-game hunting or deep-sea fishing. During his later life he suffered increasingly from severe bouts of depression, and it is thought that this illness, combined with a fear of old age, drove him to shoot himself in 1961. He won the Pulitzer Prize in 1953, and received the Nobel Prize in literature in 1954.

the tail generating THRUST in the opposite direction. Igor Sikorsky (1889–1972) built the first successful helicopter in 1939.

Helios In Greek mythology, god of the Sun, identified with the Roman god APOLLO. Helios appears driving a four-horse chariot through the sky.

helium (symbol He) Nonmetallic element, a NOBLE GAS, discovered in 1868 by Jules Janssen. First obtained in 1895 from the mineral clevite, the chief source today is from natural gas. It is also found in some radioactive minerals and in the Earth's atmosphere (0.0005% by volume). It has the lowest melting and boiling points of any element. It is colourless, odourless and nonflammable, and is used in light-air balloons, to make artificial 'air' (with oxygen) for deep-sea divers and in welding, semiconductors and lasers. Liquid helium is used in cryogenics (physics dealing with low temperatures). Properties: at.no. 2; r.a.m. 4.0026; r.d. 0.178; m.p. −272.2°C (−458°F); b.p. −268.9°C (−452.02°F); single isotope He⁴.

helix Curve generated when a point moves over the surface of a cylinder so that it traces a path inclined at a constant angle to the cylinder's axis, as in a coil spring.

hell Abode of evil spirits, and the place or state of eternal punishment after death for the wicked. In modern Christian theology, hell is conceived as eternal separation from God. Hell is parallelled in other religions and mythologies, for example, the Hebrew *sheol* or the Greek HADES. *See also* HEAVEN; LIMBO; PURGATORY

hellebore Any of *c*.20 species of poisonous herbaceous plants of the genus *Helleborus*, native to Eurasia. Best known is the Christmas rose, *H. niger*, which bears white flowers from mid-winter to early spring. Family Ranunculaceae.

Hellenistic Age (323–30BC) Period of classical Mediterranean history from ALEXANDER THE GREAT to the reign of AUGUSTUS. Alexander's conquests helped to spread Greek civilization over a wide area east of the Mediterranean. The age was distinguished by remarkable scientific and technological advances, especially in ALEXANDRIA, and by more elaborate and naturalistic styles in the visual arts.

Heller, Joseph (1923–99) US writer. His first novel, *Catch-22* (1961), was a brilliant satire on military administration. Other works include the play *We Bombed in New Haven* (1968) and the novels *Something Happened* (1974), *God Knows* (1984) and *Closing Time* (1994), a sequel to *Catch-22*.

Hellespont *See* DARDANELLES

Hellman, Lillian (1905–84) US dramatist and writer. Her debut play, *The Children's Hour* (1934), set the tone for her enduring interest in Marxist theory. She received acclaim for her memoirs, beginning with *An Unfinished Woman* (1969), and concluding with *Maybe* (1980).

Helmholtz, Hermann Ludwig Ferdinand von (1821–94) German anatomist, physicist, and physiologist. He made contributions in ACOUSTICS and OPTICS, expanding Thomas YOUNG's three-colour theory of vision. His

experiments on the speed of nerve impulses led him to formulate a principle of conservation of energy.

Helsinki (Helsingfors) Capital of Finland, in the s of the country, on the Gulf of Finland. Founded in 1550 by GUSTAVUS I (VASA), it became the capital in 1812. It has two universities (1849, 1908), a cathedral (1852), museums and art galleries. The commercial and administrative centre of the country, it is Finland's largest port. Industries: shipbuilding, engineering, food processing, ceramics, textiles. Pop. (2005) 937,000.

Helvétius, Claude Adrien (1715–71) French philosopher and educator. His best-known work, *On the Mind* (1758), attacked the religious basis of morality, arousing opposition. He claimed that everybody is intellectually equal but some have less desire to learn than others. This led him to claim, in *Of Man* (1772), that human problems can be solved by education.

hematite One of the most important iron ores, containing mainly ferric oxide, Fe₂O₃. Containing 70% iron by weight, it occurs in several forms and from steel-grey to black in colour.

Hemingway, Ernest Miller (1899–1961) US writer. After serving as an ambulance driver in World War 1, Hemingway became a journalist, first in Paris and later as a war correspondent in the Spanish Civil War and World War 2. The novel *The Sun Also Rises* (1926), published in the UK as *Fiesta* (1927), chronicled the Lost Generation and established his reputation. Later works include a non-fiction work about bullfighting, *Death in the Afternoon* (1932), *A Farewell to Arms* (1929), *For Whom the Bell Tolls* (1940), and the novella *The Old Man and the Sea* (1952). Hemingway was also an acclaimed short-story writer. He received the 1954 Nobel Prize in literature.

hemlock Poisonous herbaceous plant found in Eurasia. It has a long taproot and flat clusters of white flowers. The leaf stalks have purple spots. Family Apiaceae/Umbelliferae; species *Conium maculatum*. Hemlock also refers to species of conifers of the genus *Tsuga*, family Pinaceae.

hemp Herb native to Asia and cultivated throughout Eurasia, North America and parts of South America. It has hollow stems with fibrous inner bark, also called hemp, which is used to make ropes and cloth. The flowers, leaves and resinous juice are used to produce MARIJUANA and HASHISH. Height: to 5m (16ft). Family Cannabinaceae; species *Cannabis sativa*.

Hendrix, Jimi (James Marshall) (1942–70) US rock guitarist, songwriter and singer. Hendrix's improvised guitar solos have influenced generations of rock and jazz musicians. His debut album was *Are You Experienced?* (1967). His band, The Jimi Hendrix Experience, played live at Woodstock (1970). Other albums include *Band of Gypsies* (1970).

Hendry, Stephen Gordon (1969–) Scottish snooker player. In 1987, he became the youngest player to win a major title. In 1988, he became British Open champion. The youngest-ever world champion in 1990, Hendry won the world title a further six times in the 1990s (1992–96, 1999).

Henley Royal Regatta Oldest rowing regatta in the world, begun (1839) in Henley-on-Thames, Oxfordshire, England. Held every July, it is also a social event. Trophies include the Grand Challenge Cup and Diamond Challenge Sculls.

henna (Egyptian privet) Small shrub, native to the Middle East and N Africa. Since ancient times, people have extracted a red-brown dye from the leaves to colour hair and skin. Family Lythraceae; species *Lawsonia inerma*.

Hennepin, Louis (1640–1701) French explorer and missionary. He sailed to Canada in 1675, and became chaplain to René LA SALLE. He accompanied him on the 1679. His exaggerated account, *Description de la Louisiane* (1683), was very popular.

Henri, Robert (1865–1929) US painter, a member of the ASHCAN SCHOOL. One of the most influential artists of his time, he is best known for his realistic urban scenes.

Henrietta Maria (1609–69) Queen consort of CHARLES I of England. Daughter of Henry IV of France, her Catholicism and her support for Charles' absolutist tendencies incurred Parliament's hostility. After 1644 she lived in France, except for a brief return to England after the RESTORATION in 1660.

Henry I (the Fowler) (*c*.876–936) German king (918–36). Duke of Saxony, he was elected to succeed Conrad I as king. He asserted his authority over the German Princes

▶ **Hendrix** Considered by many to be the most influential rock guitarist of all time, Jimi Hendrix enjoyed greater initial success in the UK than his native USA. Although left handed, he played a right-handed guitar turned upside down. Hendrix died, age 28, following a drug overdose.

and reconquered Lotharingia (Lorraine, 925). He was succeeded by his son OTTO I, the first Holy Roman Emperor.

Henry I (1068–1135) King of England (1100–35), youngest son of WILLIAM I (THE CONQUEROR). Henry rescinded unpopular taxes and married a Scottish princess of Anglo-Saxon descent. He thus won the support that helped him to defeat his brother ROBERT II, Duke of Normandy, and regain Normandy for the English crown (1106). Henry settled the dispute over the investiture involving Archbishop ANSELM.

Henry II (1133–89) King of England (1154–89), son of Geoffrey of Anjou and Matilda (daughter of HENRY I). Henry inherited the ANGEVIN lands and obtained Aquitaine by marrying Eleanor in 1152. He re-established stable royal government in England, instituting reforms in finance, local government and justice. His efforts to extend royal justice to priests led to his quarrel with Thomas à BECKET. The rebellions of his sons, RICHARD I and JOHN, troubled his later reign.

Henry II (1519–59) King of France (1547–59). Son and successor of FRANCIS I, he married CATHERINE DE' MEDICI but was dominated by his mistress, Diane de Poitiers, and the rival families of GUISE and Montmorency. After bankrupting the royal government, the war with Spain ended with the Peace of Cateau-Cambrésis (1559).

Henry III (1017–56) German King (1039–56) and Holy Roman Emperor (1046–56). He succeeded his father, Conrad II. Imperial power reached its zenith in his reign as he subdued rebellious vassals in Saxony and Lorraine, and compelled the rulers of Poland, Bohemia and Hungary, as well as the s Italian princes, to pay him homage.

Henry III (1207–72) King of England (1216–72). The influence of foreigners on Henry's administration antagonized the nobles. He was forced to accept the Provisions of Westminster (1259), giving more power to his councillors, but renounced them in 1261, provoking the BARONS' WAR. Henry's son, later EDWARD I, defeated Simon de MONTFORT, the leader of the barons, in 1264, and thereafter ruled on his father's behalf.

Henry III (1551–89) King of France (1574–89). As Duke of Anjou, he fought against the HUGUENOTS in the Wars of RELIGION. By making peace with the Huguenots (1576), he antagonized extremist Roman Catholics, who formed the Catholic League led by the House of GUISE. After the League provoked a revolt in 1588, Henry had the Guise leaders killed and made an alliance with the Huguenot, Henry of Navarre (later HENRY IV). The king was assassinated by a member of the League.

Henry III (the Lion) (1129–95) Duke of Saxony (1142–80) and of Bavaria (1156–80). A GUELPH, he regained lands lost by his father, Henry the Proud, to Emperor Conrad III. As Duke of Saxony, he promoted German expansion beyond the River Elbe. In 1180, after refusing to support the Italian campaign of Emperor FREDERICK I, he was deprived of most of his lands.

Henry IV (1050–1106) German King (1056–1106) and Holy Roman Emperor (1084–1106). Embroiled in the dispute with the papacy over the lay investiture of clerics, he deposed Pope GREGORY VII and was in turn excommunicated by the Pope (1076). Rebellion in Germany weakened Henry's position. In 1077, he was forced to do penance at Canossa. In 1084, Henry captured Rome, deposed Gregory and set up an antipope, Clement III. In 1105 Henry's son, HENRY V, deposed him.

Henry IV (1367–1413) King of England (1399–1413). Son of JOHN OF GAUNT, Henry was one of the five 'lords apellant' who ruled England in 1388–89. He betrayed his fellow lords, but was exiled by RICHARD II in 1398. Henry mounted a successful invasion and usurped the throne. He faced revolts, notably by Owain GLYN DŴR and the PERCYS of Northumberland. His son succeeded him as HENRY V.

Henry IV (1553–1610) King of France (1589–1610), first of the BOURBON dynasty. From a Protestant upbringing, Henry was recognized as leader of the HUGUENOTS. The SAINT BARTHOLOMEW'S DAY MASSACRE (1572) marred Henry's marriage to Margaret of Valois. Henry survived, but was forced to convert to Catholicism. In 1584 he became legal heir to HENRY III. On Henry's death, the GUISE family refused to recognize his claim, but were subdued. In 1593, Henry willingly converted to Roman Catholicism – allegedly remarking that "Paris is well worth a Mass". He ended the Wars of RELIGION

◄ **Henry VIII** Portrait of Henry VIII by Hans Holbein (the Younger). The historic schism between the papacy and the Church in England dates from Henry's reign. Replacing the Pope as the head of the Church in England, Henry obtained a divorce from his first wife, Catherine of Aragon, who was unable to provide him with a male heir.

H

by the Edict of NANTES (1598), but remained sympathetic to Protestantism, secretly supporting the revolt of the Protestant Netherlands against Spain. A popular king, with a keen sense of social justice, he was assassinated by François Ravaillac.

Henry V (1081–1125) German King (1105–25) and Holy Roman Emperor (1111–25). After deposing his father, HENRY IV, he resumed the quarrel with the papacy over investiture, while antagonizing German princes by the ruthless assertion of his power. Henry was defeated in Germany and compelled to compromise with the papacy. The Concordat of WORMS (1122) ended the investiture conflict.

Henry V (1387–1422) King of England (1413–22). Son of HENRY IV, he helped defeat Owain GLYN DŴR and the PERCYS. As King, Henry reopened the HUNDRED YEARS' WAR and won a decisive victory at AGINCOURT in 1415. Further conquests in 1417–19 resulted in the Treaty of Troyes (1420), in which CHARLES VI of France recognized him as his heir. He died on his third invasion of France. His military success and popular appeal made him a national hero.

Henry VI (1165–97) German King (1190–97) and Holy Roman Emperor (1191–97), son of FREDERICK I (BARBAROSSA). Henry married Constance, heiress of the Kingdom of Sicily, in 1186 and devoted much of his reign to securing that inheritance. After 1194, the Empire was at the height of its power. Although he failed to make the Empire hereditary, his infant son FREDERICK II was accepted as his successor.

Henry VI (1421–71) King of England (1422–61, 1470–71). He succeeded his father, HENRY V, as a baby and came of age in 1437. In 1445 Henry married MARGARET OF ANJOU, who thereafter dominated government. His reign was characterized by military disasters in France, and by the dynastic conflict in England known as the Wars of the ROSES. Deposed by the Yorkists led by EDWARD IV (1461), he returned to power in 1470, but was soon deposed and murdered.

Henry VII (1457–1509) King of England (1485–1509), founder of the TUDOR dynasty. Having come to the throne by defeating RICHARD III in the final battle of the Wars of the ROSES at BOSWORTH FIELD (1485), Henry united the houses of LANCASTER and YORK by marrying the Yorkist heiress, Elizabeth. His financial acumen restored England's fortunes after the devastation of civil war. He defeated pretenders to his throne, securing the succession of his son HENRY VIII.

Henry VIII (1491–1547) King of England (1509–47). Second son of HENRY VII, he became heir on the death of his

H

▲ **herbivore** Mammalian herbivores may conveniently share a habitat without competing for resources. On the African plains, giraffes (1) browse in branches up to 6m (20ft) above the ground. Elephants (2) also browse in tree canopies, using their trunks to pluck off vegetation. Eland (3) attack the middle branches with their horns, twisting twigs to break them off, while gerenuk (4) stand on their hind legs to reach higher branches. The black rhino (5) uses its hook-like upper lip to feed on bark, twigs, and leaves (white rhinos have lengthened skulls and broad lips for grazing the short grasses that they favour). The wart hog (6) and dik-dik (7) eat buds and flowers, and will also dig up roots and tubers. Such sharing of resources also occurs among grazers. Migrating zebra (8) crop the taller, coarse grasses; wildebeest (9) feed on the leafy centre layer, allowing small gazelles (10) to reach the tender new shoots.

elder brother, Arthur, in 1502. His aggressive foreign policy, administered by Cardinal WOLSEY, depleted the royal treasury. Henry, supported by Thomas CROMWELL, presided over the first stages of the English REFORMATION. He managed to obtain a divorce from his first wife, CATHERINE OF ARAGON, and married Anne BOLEYN (1533), mother of the future ELIZABETH I. In 1535, he executed Anne for adultery. Thomas MORE, Henry's former chancellor, was also executed for refusing to accept Henry as head of the Church. Henry then married Jane Seymour, who died shortly after the birth of the future EDWARD VI. His next marriage, to ANNE OF CLEVES, ended in divorce in 1540, and with the execution of Cromwell. Shortly after, he married Catherine HOWARD (executed 1542) and finally Catherine Parr in 1543 who survived him. Henry's reign will also be remembered for the DISSOLUTION OF THE MONASTERIES (1536–40), which brought temporary relief from financial problems, but at the cost of great social unrest.

Henry, Joseph (1797–1878) US physicist, whose work on ELECTROMAGNETISM was essential for the development of the telegraph. His work on INDUCTION led to the production of the TRANSFORMER. The unit of inductance is named after him.

Henry, O. (1862–1910) US short-story writer, b. William Sydney Porter. Supposedly taking his pseudonym from a contraction of Ohio Penitentiary, where he served a sentence for embezzlement, he produced popular short stories.

Henry, Patrick (1736–99) American patriot and statesman. As a member of the CONTINENTAL CONGRESS, he called the colonists to arms in March 1775 with the demand, "Give me liberty or give me death". Henry served as governor of Virginia (1776–79, 1784–86). A strong believer in STATES' RIGHTS, he opposed ratification of the US CONSTITUTION in 1787.

Henry the Navigator (1394–1460) Portuguese prince. A son of JOHN I, he sponsored Portuguese voyages of discovery to the Atlantic coast of Africa, which later led to the discovery of the route to India via the Cape of Good Hope.

Henze, Hans Werner (1926–) German composer. Influenced by TWELVE-TONE MUSIC, he is best-known for his operas, such as *Elegy for Young Lovers* (1961).

hepatitis Inflammation of the liver, usually due to a generalized infection. Early symptoms include lethargy, nausea, fever and muscle and joint pains. Five hepatitis viruses are known: A, B, C, D and E. The most common single cause is the hepatitis A virus (HAV). More serious is infection with the hepatitis B virus (HBV), which can lead to chronic inflammation or complete failure of the liver and, in some cases, to liver cancer.

Hepburn, Audrey (1929–93) US actress, b. Belgium. Her ingénue performance in *Roman Holiday* (1953) won her an

Academy Award for best actress. A succession of similiar roles in films such as *Sabrina* (1954) and *Funny Face* (1957) earned her further popular success. Other credits include *Breakfast at Tiffany's* (1961) and *My Fair Lady* (1964). She later became involved in charitable and humanitarian work.

Hepburn, Katharine (1909–2003) US stage and film actress. She made her film debut in 1932 and won her first best actress Academy Award for *Morning Glory* (1933). She made nine films with Spencer TRACY, beginning with *Woman of the Year* (1952) and ending with an Oscar-winning performance in *Guess Who's Coming to Dinner* (1967). In 1968 she won a third best actress Oscar for *The Lion in Winter*. Her performance in *On Golden Pond* (1981) gained her a fourth award. Other films include *Bringing Up Baby* (1938), *The Philadelphia Story* (1940), *The African Queen* (1951), *Suddenly Last Summer* (1959), and *Long Day's Journey Into Night* (1962).

Hephaestus Ancient Greek god of fire and crafts. Son of ZEUS and HERA, he is equivalent to the Roman VULCAN. Blacksmith and armourer to the Olympian gods, with a forge under Etna, he is depicted as crippled and uncouth.

Hepplewhite, George (d.1786) English furniture designer and cabinet-maker. His chairs often have tapered legs with shield backs, and his furniture combines pale woods with mahogany, often in the form of inlay.

heptathlon Athletics discipline for women consisting of seven events contested over two days. *See also* DECATHLON

Hepworth, Dame Barbara (1903–76) English sculptor. She shared Henry MOORE's interest in the techniques of carving. Her early pieces were mainly in wood and stone, using their natural qualities to produce fluid forms such as *Figure in sycamore* (1931). She married (1932–51) the abstract painter Ben NICHOLSON. In the 1950s, Hepworth began to work in bronze. Later works include the memorial to Dag Hammerskojd, *Single form* (1963).

Hera In Greek mythology, queen of the Olympian gods, sister and wife of ZEUS. She appears as a jealous scold who persecuted her rivals but helped heroes such as JASON and ACHILLES.

Heracles (Roman, Hercules) Greatest of the Greek mythological heroes. Condemned to serve King Eurystheus, he performed 12 labours: he killed the Nemean lion and the Hydra; caught the Erymanthian boar and the Cerynean hind; drove away the Stymphalian birds; cleaned the Augean stables; caught the Cretan bull and Diomedes' horses; stole the girdle of Hippolyte; killed Geryon; captured Cerberus and stole the golden apples of Hesperides. After death, he was allowed to ascend as a god to Olympus.

Heraclitus (*c.*536–*c.*470 BC) Greek philosopher, b. Ephesus, Asia Minor. He believed that the outward, unchanging face of the universe masked a dynamic equilibrium in which all things were constantly changing, but with opposites remaining in balance. The elemental substance connecting everything was fire. Two sayings sum up his world view: "All things change" and "You cannot step into the same river twice".

Heraclius (575–641) Byzantine Emperor (610–41). An outstanding military leader, Heraclius came to power at a time of economic, political and military crisis. He re-established government and army, defeated the Persians and took the Byzantine Empire to unrivalled power. By the time of his death, however, the Arabs had conquered much of the Empire.

herb Seed-bearing plant, usually with a soft stem that withers away after one growing season. Most herbs are ANGIOSPERMS. The term is also applied to any plant used as a flavouring, seasoning or medicine, such as thyme, sage, and mint.

Herbert, George (1593–1633) English poet and cleric. His verse, some of the finest METAPHYSICAL POETRY, was published after his death as *The Temple*. It is remarkable for its devotional tone and formal complexity.

herbicide PESTICIDE used to kill weeds and other unwanted plants. Selective herbicides kill the weeds growing with crops, leaving the crops unharmed; non-selective herbicides, such as paraquat, kill all the vegetation. There are concerns over their toxicity to humans and their persistence in the environment.

herbivore Animal that feeds solely on plants. The term is most often applied to MAMMALS, especially RUMINANTS. Herbivores are characterized by broad molars and blunt-edged teeth, which they use to pull, cut, and grind their food. Their digestive systems are adapted to digest cellulose. *See also* RODENT

Herculaneum Ancient city on the Bay of Naples, Italy, the site of modern Resina. Devastated by an earthquake in AD 62, it was buried by the eruption of VESUVIUS in 79. Archaeological excavations unearthed the Villa of the Papyri, which contained a library, furniture, and the bodies of victims.

Herder, Johann Gottfried von (1744–1803) German philosopher and poet. He believed human society to be an organic, secular totality that develops as the result of a historical process. Herder was a founder of German ROMANTICISM and a critic of KANT. *Outlines of a Philosophy on the History of Man* (1784–91) is regarded as his masterpiece.

heredity Transmission of characteristics from one generation of plants or animals to another. Characteristics, such as red hair, may be specific to individuals within a group; others, such as the possession of external ears, may be typical of a group as a whole. The combination of characteristics that makes up an organism and makes it different from others is set out in the organism's GENETIC CODE, passed on from its parents. Austrian naturalist Gregor MENDEL conducted the first studies of heredity.

Herefordshire Unitary authority in w central England, bounded w and sw by Wales; the administrative headquarters is Hereford. It is drained by the Severn, Wye and Teme rivers. The Malvern Hills divide the county into two lowland plains. The Vale of Evesham in the s provides rich soil for market gardening. Agriculture and dairy farming are important activities. Industries: agricultural machinery, fruit canning and processing. Area: 2,288sq km (884sq mi). Pop. (2001) 174,844.

heresy Denial of, or deviation from, orthodox religious belief. The concept exists in most organized religions with a rigid, dogmatic system.

hermaphrodite Organism that has both male and female sexual organs. Most hermaphrodite animals are invertebrates, such as the EARTHWORM and SNAIL. They reproduce by the mating of two individuals, each of which receives SPERM from the other. Some hermaphrodites are self-fertilizing.

Hermes In Greek mythology, god identified with the Roman Mercury. Represented with winged hat and sandals and carrying a golden wand, Hermes was the messenger of the gods and patron of travellers and commerce.

hermit crab Small, crab-like CRUSTACEAN found in tidal pools and shallow water worldwide. It uses sea-snail shells to protect its soft abdomen, changing shells as it grows. Some are terrestrial and do not use shells as adults. Family Paguridae.

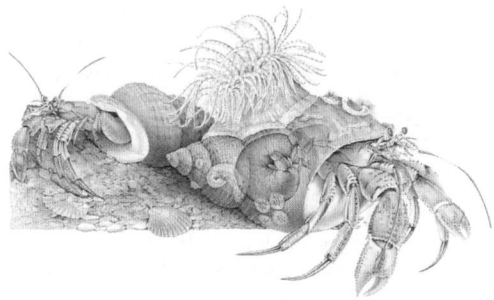

hernia Protrusion of an organ, or part of an organ, through its enclosing wall or connective tissue. Common hernias are a protrusion of an intestinal loop through the umbilicus (umbilical hernia), or protrusion of part of the stomach or oesophagus into the chest cavity (hiatus hernia).

Herod Agrippa I (AD 10–44) King of Judaea (41–44), grandson of HEROD THE GREAT. He attracted the favour of CALIGULA, who confirmed him as ruler of most of Palestine. He imprisoned St PETER and executed St James.

Herod Agrippa II (27–93) King of Chalcis (50–93) and of Judaea (53–70). Son of HEROD AGRIPPA I and last of the Herodian dynasty, he tried to prevent the Jewish revolt (66) and afterwards sided with Rome.

Herodotus (*c.*485–*c.*425 BC) Greek historian. Regarded as the first historian, Herodotus' *Histories* are the first great prose work in European literature. His main theme was the struggle of Greece against the Persian Empire in the PERSIAN WARS, but he also provides an insight into the Mediterranean world.

Herod the Great (73 BC–4 BC) King of Judaea (37–04BC). Supported by Mark ANTONY and AUGUSTUS, he endeavoured to reconcile Jews and Romans and was responsible for many public works, including the rebuilding of the temple in Jerusalem. He later became cruel and tyrannical, executing three of his sons and his wife. According to the New Testament, Herod was King of Judaea when JESUS was born.

heroin Drug derived from MORPHINE. It produces similar effects to morphine, but acts more quickly and is effective in smaller doses. It is prescribed to relieve pain in terminal illness and severe injuries. Widely used illegally, it is more addictive than morphine. *See also* DRUG ADDICTION

heron Any of several species of wading bird that live near rivers. Herons have white, grey, or brown plumage, long neck and legs, and a sharp bill. They feed mainly on fish, and nest in large groups. Height: to 1.8m (6ft). Family Ardeidae.

herpes Infectious disease caused by one of the herpes viruses. **Herpes simplex 1** infects the skin and causes cold sores. **Herpes zoster** attacks nerve ganglia, causing SHINGLES. The same virus is responsible for CHICKENPOX.

Herrick, Robert (1591–1674) English poet, disciple of Ben JONSON. Ordained in 1623, Herrick was ejected from his post (1647) for royalist sympathies. He regained the position after the RESTORATION. His poems, most notably the collection *Hesperides* (1648), have great lyrical freshness.

herring Marine fish found worldwide. One of the most important food fish, various species are canned as PILCHARD or SARDINE, or sold fresh, pickled, or smoked (as kippers and bloaters). Herrings have a laterally compressed body and a deeply forked tail fin. Length: 8–46cm (3–18in). Family Clupeidae; the 190 species include *Clupea harengus*.

Herschel, Sir John Frederick William (1792–1871) English astronomer, son of Sir William HERSCHEL. He extended his father's work on DOUBLE STARS and NEBULAE. In 1834, at the Cape of Good Hope, Herschel undertook a systematic survey of the southern sky, discovering more than 1,200 doubles and 1,700 nebulae and clusters. He combined these and his father's observations into a *General Catalog of Nebulae and Clusters* (1864).

Herschel, Sir William (1738–1822) English astronomer, b. Germany. He discovered URANUS (1781) and later two SATELLITES of Uranus (1787) and two of Saturn (1789). Herschel observed many DOUBLE STARS and more than 2,000 NEBULAE and clusters, and published catalogues of

◀ **hermit crab** Unlike most other species of crab, the hermit crab (*Eupagurus* sp.) has a soft body. To protect itself, the hermit crab uses the empty shells of whelks or sea snails as a home. It has a modified abdomen with a twisted shape to fit a spiral shell, and its last two legs and hind appendages (uropods) are specialized for gripping the shell. When the hermit crab has grown too large for its shell, it waits until it has found a suitable larger shell before risking the changeover.

H

◀ **heron** The purple heron (*Ardea purpurea*) is found in reed-grown waters in open country of southern Europe and Asia, and Africa. It grows to a length of 80cm (2.5ft) and, like many other species of heron, feeds on fish.

H

them. Herschel realized that the Milky Way is the plane of a disc-shaped universe, whose form he calculated by counting the numbers of stars visible in different directions. In 1800, he discovered and investigated infrared radiation.

Hertfordshire County in London's 'commuter belt', SE England; the county town is Hertford. Other major towns include St Albans (built on the site of a Roman settlement), Watford, Hatfield, and Letchworth (Britain's first garden city). The terrain is flat, apart from an extension of the Chiltern Hills in the NW. The main rivers are the Lea, Stort, and Colne. Agriculture is important. Industries: engineering, electrical equipment, printing. Area: 1,636sq km (631sq mi). Pop. (2001) 1,033,977.

hertz (symbol Hz) SI unit of FREQUENCY named after German physicist Heinrich HERTZ. A periodic phenomenon with a period of one second (such as one oscillation per second) is equivalent to 1Hz.

Hertz, Heinrich Rudolf (1857–94) German physicist. In his early career, he worked as an assistant to Hermann HELMHOLTZ. In 1888, Hertz discovered, broadcasted and received the RADIO waves predicted by James Clerk MAXWELL. He also demonstrated that heat and light are kinds of ELECTROMAGNETIC RADIATION. The unit of FREQUENCY, the HERTZ (Hz), is named for him.

Hertzog, James Barry Munnik (1866–1942) South African statesman, prime minister (1924–39). He led the Orange Free State forces in the second of the SOUTH AFRICAN WARS (1899–1902). A member (1910–12) of the first Union government under Louis BOTHA, Hertzog founded the opposition National Party in 1914. He led two coalition governments. In 1939, he resigned from the coalition with Jan SMUTS in protest against South Africa's support for Britain in World War 2.

Hertzsprung-Russell diagram (H-R diagram) Plot of the absolute MAGNITUDE of stars against their spectral type; this is equivalent to plotting their LUMINOSITY against their surface temperature or colour index. Brightness increases from bottom to top, and temperature increases from right to left. Henry Norris Russell devised the diagram in 1913, independently of Ejnar Hertzsprung, who had the same idea some years before. The H-R diagram reveals a pattern in which most stars lie on a diagonal band, the **main sequence**.

Herzegovina See BOSNIA-HERZEGOVINA

Herzl, Theodor (1860–1904) Founder of modern ZIONISM, b. Hungary. As a journalist reporting on the Dreyfus Affair, Herzl became convinced of the need for a Jewish national state. In 1897, he published *Der Judenstaat* and organized the first Zionist World Congress. Herzl acted as its president (1897–1904). In 1949, his body moved from Vienna to Jerusalem, where he was reburied with Israeli state honours.

Heseltine, Michael Ray Dibdin (1933–) British statesman, deputy prime minister (1995–97). He entered Parliament in 1966. In Margaret THATCHER's cabinet, he was secretary of state for the environment (1979–83) and defence secretary (1983–86), resigning over the Westland Affair. Heseltine rejoined the cabinet as secretary of state for the environment (1990–92) under John MAJOR's leadership. As secretary of state for trade and industry (1992–95), he announced a drastic programme of pit closures. Despite a heart attack, Heseltine continued as deputy prime minister. Following electoral defeat (1997), he took a less active rôle in Conservative Party politics.

Hess, Rudolf (1894–1987) German Nazi leader. He joined the Nazi Party in 1921, and took part in the abortive MUNICH PUTSCH. Hess was nominal deputy leader under Adolf HITLER from 1933. In 1941, he flew to Scotland in a mysterious one-man effort to make peace with the British. In 1945, he was sentenced to life imprisonment at the NUREMBERG TRIALS and died in Spandau Prison, Berlin, for many years its sole inmate.

Hess, Victor Francis (1883–1964) US physicist, b. Austria. As a result of his investigations into the ionization of air, he suggested that radiation similar to X-rays, later named COSMIC RADIATION, comes from space. He shared the 1936 Nobel Prize in physics with Carl ANDERSON.

Hesse, Hermann (1877–1962) German novelist. Hesse studied Indian mysticism and Jungian psychology, subjects that find expression in novels such as *Demian* (1919), *Siddhartha* (1922), and *Steppenwolf* (1927). Other novels include *Narcissus and Goldmund* (1930) and *The Glass Bead Game* (1943). He received the 1946 Nobel Prize in literature.

Hessen Region of central Germany. It was divided by a strip of Prussian territory until 1945. Industries: chemicals, manufacturing, electrical engineering, cereal cropping. Area: 21,114sq km (8,150sq mi). Pop. (1999) 6,051,350.

Hestia In Greek mythology, goddess of the burning hearth. The daughter of Cronus and Rhea, she scorned the attentions of Apollo and Poseidon, and ZEUS installed her in Olympus. In Rome, she was worshipped as Vesta. *See also* VESTAL VIRGINS

heterosexuality Attraction of a male or female to members of the opposite SEX. The word is used to distinguish such attraction from HOMOSEXUALITY.

heterozygote Organism possessing two contrasting forms (ALLELES) of a GENE in a CHROMOSOME pair. In cases where one form is dominant and the other recessive, only the dominant form is expressed in the PHENOTYPE (physical characteristics). A HOMOZYGOTE has identical forms of a gene.

Hewish, Antony (1924–) English astronomer He shared the 1974 Nobel Prize in physics for his work on PULSARS.

hexagon Six-sided plane figure. Its interior angles add up to 720°. In a regular hexagon, whose sides and interior angles are all equal, each interior angle is 120°.

Heyerdahl, Thor (1914–2002) Norwegian ethnologist who, with five companions, drifted on the balsa raft *Kon Tiki* c.8,000km (5,000mi) across the Pacific Ocean from Peru to Polynesia (1947) in an attempt to prove the Polynesians came from South America and not from Southeast Asia. He also sailed (1970) from Africa to the West Indies in a papyrus boat *Ra II*, and travelled (1977) from Iraq to Djibouti in a reed boat, *Tigris*.

Hiawatha (active 16th century) Native American leader of the Onondaga. In c.1575, he founded the five-nation IROQUOIS CONFEDERACY to halt intertribal wars. His semi-mythic reputation is partly the result of association with the fictional hero of the LONGFELLOW poem, *The Song of Hiawatha* (1855).

hibernation Dormant (sleep-like) condition adopted by some animals, such as bears, bats and squirrels, to survive harsh winters. Adaptive mechanisms to avoid starvation and extreme temperatures include reduced body temperature, slower heartbeat, breathing rate, and metabolism.

hibiscus Genus of plants, shrubs and small trees native to tropical and temperate regions and cultivated worlwide. Their large white, pink, yellow, blue or red bell-shaped flowers have darker or variegated centres. Family Malvaceae.

Hickok, 'Wild Bill' (James Butler) (1837–76) US frontiersman. A renowned marksman, he was a scout first with the Union Army during the American CIVIL WAR, and then with George CUSTER. He served as US marshal in Kansas (1869–71), and later toured with the Wild West show of 'Buffalo Bill'. He was shot dead while playing poker.

hickory Deciduous tree of the WALNUT family native to E North America. Hickories are grown for ornament, timber, and for their nuts. Height: 25m (80ft). Family Juglandaceae; genus *Carya*. *See also* PECAN

Hidalgo y Costilla, Miguel (1753–1811) Mexican priest and revolutionary. Of Creole birth, he was a priest in Dolores, Guanajuato, where he plotted a revolt against Spain. With an untrained army of 80,000, he captured Guanajuato and Valladolid, but failed to generate support among the ruling class. Defeated by government forces at Calderón Bridge, Hidalgo fled but was later captured and executed.

hieroglyphics Writing system of pictorial characters used in ancient EGYPT and, by analogy, those of ancient Crete, Asia Minor, Central America and Mexico. The Egyptian system of hieroglyphics began to develop before 3000 BC. Most of the symbols represent a consonant sound, or group of sounds, and are composed into groups to form words. Some symbols represent categories or concepts to clarify the meaning of the adjacent word. Only a small proportion of hieroglyphs are literal picture writing. Hieroglyphs were later developed into cursive scripts called hieratic and demotic for business and literary purposes. As ancient

Egyptian was supplanted by Greek, hieroglyphics died out. The discovery of the ROSETTA STONE in 1799 allowed them to be deciphered, and most Egyptian texts can now be read.

Higginson, Thomas Wentworth Storrow (1823–1911) US social reformer. A Unitarian minister, he worked for abolition of slavery and for women's rights. He was colonel of the first black regiment during the Civil War, an experience recorded in *Army Life in a Black Regiment* (1870). Higginson was a close friend of many writers, notably Emily DICKINSON, and the biographer of other poets.

High Court of Justice In English law, court established primarily to hear civil cases. It also hears appeals from the magistrates' courts. It consists of three divisions: the Queen's Bench, the CHANCERY, and the Family Division.

high-definition television (HDTV) Form of television on which the picture is made up of 1,250 or 1,125 scanning lines instead of 625 or 525. The increased number of scanning lines makes the TV image sharper. It relies on digital transmission down OPTICAL FIBRES, rather than the transmission of electronic signals by radio waves. The use of cables increases the total number of available channels.

high jump Track-and-field event in which a competitor attempts to jump over a bar supported between two uprights. An Olympic sport since 1896, a competitor may have a maximum of three attempts to clear each height to which the bar is raised. The record for men's high jump was set at 2.45m (8ft ½in) in 1993, and women's at 2.09m (6ft 10¼in) in 1987.

Highland Scottish mountain and moorland region, lying N of a line running roughly SW to NE from Dumbarton to Stonehaven; the administrative centre is Inverness. The area is split into the Northwest Highlands and the Grampian Highlands (separated by Glen More). Hydroelectric power and forestry schemes have been introduced in an effort to halt the decline in population through emigration. Industries: tourism, forestry, fishing. Area: 25,396sq km (9,804sq mi) Pop: (2001) 208,920.

Highland Games Series of athletics competitions featuring traditional Scottish events. The term specifically refers to the autumn Royal Braemar Games or Braemar Gathering, held annually since 1819. The programme includes highland dancing, bagpipe playing, and the tossing of the caber.

high-level language COMPUTER LANGUAGE that is reasonably close to spoken English. The higher the level, the further the language is removed from the BINARY SYSTEM of many other computer languages.

Hilbert, David (1862–1943) German mathematician, b. Russia. He was professor of mathematics (1895–1943) at the University of Göttingen. Hilbert's *Foundations of Geometry* (1899) had the most profound influence on the study of GEOMETRY since EUCLID, establishing a rigorous axiomatic basis for the subject. Kurt GÖDEL later discredited his attempt to ground all mathematics on axioms. Hilbert's *On Numbers* (1897) systematized all the known results of algebraic NUMBER THEORY. His work on integral equations led to the concept of **Hilbert space**, crucial to the development of QUANTUM MECHANICS. In 1900, Hilbert proposed 23 problems for the mathematicians of the 20th century to tackle. Most of these were solved, and led to profound new understandings in mathematics.

Hill, Geoffrey (1932–) English poet. Hill usually writes on historical and religious themes. His volumes of poetry include *For the Unfallen* (1959), *King Log* (1968), *Mercian Hymns* (1971), *Tenebrae* (1978), and *The Mystery of the Charity of Charles Péguy* (1983).

Hill, Graham (1929–75) English motor racing driver. Hill's long Formula 1 career included 14 wins in 176 starts. In 1962, racing for BRM, he won his first Grand Prix and the world driver's championship. In 1968 he won his second title, racing for Lotus. In 1972, he became the first Formula 1 world champion to win the Le Mans 24–hour race. His son, **Damon** (1960–), was also a successful Formula 1 driver, becoming world champion in 1996. He retired in 1999.

Hill, Sir Rowland (1795–1879) English administrator and postal reformer. Hill invented the nationwide 'penny post', adopting the first adhesive, pre-paid postage stamp.

Hillary, Sir Edmund Percival (1919–2008) New Zealand explorer and mountaineer. On May 29, 1953, Hillary and his Sherpa guide, Tenzing Norgay, were the first men to reach the summit of Mount EVEREST. He led (1955–58) the New Zealand arm of the Commonwealth Trans-Antarctic Expedition.

Hilliard, Nicholas (1547–1619) English miniaturist and goldsmith. Hilliard portrayed many of the leading figures of the time in an exquisitely graceful style.

Himachal Pradesh State in the W Himalayas, NW India; the capital is Simla. It suffered numerous invasions before coming under British rule in the 19th century. The state is mountainous and heavily forested, with highly cultivated valleys. Timber provides the main source of income. Area: 55,673sq km (21,495sq mi). Pop. (2001) 6,077,248.

Himalayas System of mountains in S Asia, extending *c.*2,400km (1,500mi) N-S in an arc between Tibet and India-Pakistan. The mountains are divided into three ranges: the Greater Himalayas (N), which include Mount EVEREST and K2; the Lesser Himalayas; and the Outer Himalayas (S).

Himmler, Heinrich (1900–45) German Nazi leader. In 1929, he became head of the SS. After the Nazis came to power in 1933, Himmler assumed control of the German GESTAPO and of the CONCENTRATION CAMPS. Captured by the British in 1945, he committed suicide before the NUREMBERG TRIALS.

Hindemith, Paul (1895–1963) German composer. Among his works are symphonies, concertos, ballets, chamber music and operas. In the 1930s, with Kurt WEILL, he developed *Gebrauchsmusik* (Ger. utility music) written for amateur performance. Hindemith's best-known work is the symphony he derived from his opera *Mathis der Maler* (1934).

Hindenburg, Paul Ludwig Hans von Beneckendorf und von (1847–1934) German statesman and general, president (1925–34). Commanding the army on the E front in World War 1, he defeated the Russians in the Battle of Tannenberg. In 1916, Hindenburg became supreme commander and, with his chief-of-staff, Erich LUDENDORFF, directed the German retreat on the Western Front (to the **Hindenburg line**). As second president of the WEIMAR REPUBLIC, he reluctantly appointed Adolf HITLER as chancellor in 1933.

Hindi Most widespread language in India, spoken in the north-central area by 154 million people. Hindi and English are the official languages of India. It derives from SANSKRIT and belongs to the Indo-European family.

Hinduism Traditional religion of India, characterized by a philosophy and a way of life rather than by a dogmatic structure. It was not founded by an individual and has been

INTERNET

Hillary, Sir Edmund Percival
▶ www.nzedge.com/heroes/hillary.html

Hilliard, Nicholas
▶ www.metmuseum.org
▶ www.npg.org.uk

H

◀ **Hinduism** Hindus practice a complex set of rites, ceremonies and festivals based around a pantheon of gods. The religion first appeared in N India *c.*4000 years ago. The three chief gods (the Trimurti) are Brahma, Vishnu and Siva, creator, preserver and destroyer respectively. Central to Hinduism is the belief in reincarnation, which is seen as the cycle of rebirth and suffering. To escape this cycle is the chief aim for all Hindus.

H

▲ **hippopotamus** The common hippopotamus, *Hippopotamus amphibius*, has the largest mouth of any mammal. Its canine teeth can reach 60cm (2ft) in length. The female produces a single calf. Hippos usually travel in herds of 10 to 15 animals.

▶ **Hitchcock** Known as the 'master of suspense', Alfred Hitchcock is widely regarded as one of the greatest directors of all time. His films were often visually spectacular and contained brooding, threatening undertones. Criticized for remaining faithful to the melodramatic genre, Hitchcock never received an Academy Award for best director.

developing gradually since *c.*3000 BC, absorbing external influences. There are several schools within Hinduism, but all Hindus recognize the VEDAS as sacred texts. DHARMA is the eternal moral law underpinning existence. KARMA is the law of cause of effect that energizes REINCARNATION. Liberation from the cycle of suffering and rebirth (*moksha*) and a return to BRAHMAN is the chief aim in life. One of the features of Hindu society is the CASTE system, but modern Hindu scholars maintain that it is not part of the religion. The main Hindu gods are BRAHMA, VISHNU, and SHIVA (the Trimurti). Popular deities include KRISHNA, GANESH, PARVATI, LAKSHMI, and INDRA. BRAHMANISM, the early phase of Hinduism, culminated in the classic texts of the MAHABHARATA (incorporating the BHAGAVAD GITA) and the RAMAYANA (relating the adventures of RAMA). Today, there are *c.*800 million Hindus worldwide. *See also* ADVAITA; AHIMSA; HARE KRISHNA; MANTRA; UPANISHADS; VEDANTA

Hindu Kush Mountain range in central Asia, a continuation of the Himalayas extending WSW for 800–960km (500–600mi) from N Pakistan and NE Afghanistan. The highest peak is Tirich Mir, at 7,700m (25,260ft).

Hindustani Member of the Indo-Iranian branch of INDO-EUROPEAN LANGUAGES, closely related to HINDI and URDU. More than 300 million people are thought to speak or understand Hindustani in India and Pakistan.

hip Joint on each side of the lower trunk, into which the head of the femur fits; the hip bones form part of the PELVIS.

hip-hop RAP music and its associated culture, originating in New York in the early 1980s. The music is characterized by a strong drumbeat, percussive 'scratching' of vinyl records, and rap vocals.

Hipparchus (active 2nd century BC) Greek astronomer. Hipparchus estimated the distance of the Moon from the Earth and drew the first accurate star map. He developed an organization of the universe that, although it had the Earth at the centre, provided for accurate prediction of the positions of the planets.

Hippocrates (*c.*460–377 BC) Greek physician, often called 'the father of medicine'. Hippocrates emphasized clinical observation and provided guidelines for surgery. He is credited with the **Hippocratic oath**, a code of professional conduct still followed by doctors.

Hippolytus In Greek mythology, son of Theseus and Hippolyta. When he spurned the advances of his stepmother, Phaedra, she turned his father against him. He was put to death, but came back to life when his innocence was proved.

hippopotamus Bulky, herbivorous mammal, native to Africa. *Hippopotamus amphibius* has a massive grey or brown body with a large head, short legs and short tail, and spends much time in water. Males weigh up to 4.5 tonnes. **Pygmy** hippopotamuses, *Choeropsis liberiensis*, are much smaller and spend more time on land. Family Hippopotamidae.

hire-purchase (HP) Method of acquiring goods by making a deposit, then paying the rest, with interest, in regular instalments. The vendor usually has an agreement with a financer who pays the full price of the goods. The buyer becomes full owner of the goods only after repaying the financer.

Hirohito (1901–89) Emperor of Japan (1926–89). He was the first Crown Prince to travel abroad (1921). Although Hirohito generally exercised little political power during his reign, he persuaded the Japanese government to surrender to the

Allies in 1945. Under the new constitution of 1946, he lost all power and renounced the traditional claim of the Japanese emperors to be divine. He was succeeded by his son AKIHITO.

Hiroshige, Ando (1797–1858) Japanese master of UKIYO-E (coloured WOODCUT). With HOKUSAI and UTAMARO, he was one of the leading Japanese printmakers of his day. He is best known for his landscapes, which influenced IMPRESSIONISM.

Hiroshima City on the delta of the River Ota, SW Honshu island, Japan; the river divides the city into six islands, connected by 81 bridges. Founded in 1594, it was a military headquarters in the SINO-JAPANESE and RUSSO-JAPANESE Wars. In August 1945, it was the target of the first atomic bomb dropped on a populated area. The bomb obliterated the city centre, killing more than 70,000 people. The city's Peace Memorial Park commemorates the event. Industries: brewing, shipbuilding, motor vehicles, chemicals. Pop. (2000) 1,126,000.

Hirst, Damien (1965–) English sculptor. He made his name by exhibiting sculptures of animals preserved in formaldehyde. One of these pieces, *Mother and Child Divided* (1993), which consists of the severed halves of a cow and calf displayed in four tanks, helped him to win the Turner Prize in 1995.

Hispaniola Island in the West Indies, in the N central Caribbean Sea, between Cuba (W) and Puerto Rico (E). The second-largest island in the West Indies, Christopher COLUMBUS discovered Hispaniola in 1492. HAITI occupies the W third and the DOMINICAN REPUBLIC the remaining portion. It is a mountainous, agricultural region with a subtropical climate. Industries: coffee, cacao, tobacco, rice, sugar cane, mining. Area: 76,480sq km (29,521sq mi). *See* West Indies map

histamine Substance derived from the amino acid histidine, occurring naturally in many plants and in animal tissues, and released on tissue injury. It is implicated in allergic reactions that can be treated with ANTIHISTAMINE drugs.

histology Biological, especially microscopic, study of TISSUES and structures in living organisms.

history Written record of the human past, often used to mean the events themselves rather than the record of them. The Western historical tradition began with the Greek historians HERODOTUS and THUCYDIDES. China (and countries influenced by it) had a different, even older historical tradition in which the past was seen as the source of wisdom and historians strove to distinguish comprehensible patterns in it.

Hitchcock, Sir Alfred (1899–1980) English film director. His full debut was *The Pleasure Garden* (1925). His appearances as an extra, the thrilling chases, sinister mood and sudden shocks, greatly influenced the French *nouvelle vague*. *The Man Who Knew Too Much* (1934) was an international success. After *The 39 Steps* (1935) and *The Lady Vanishes* (1938), Hitchcock left for Hollywood. *Rebecca* (1940) won an Academy Award for best picture. Though less consistent in the 1940s, his credits included *Suspicion* (1941) and *Spellbound* (1945). An extraordinary sequence began with *Strangers on a Train* (1951), followed by the classic thrillers *Rear Window* (1954), *Vertigo* (1958), *North by Northwest* (1959), and *Psycho* (1960).

Hitler, Adolf (1889–1945) German fascist dictator (1933–45), b. Austria. He served in the German army during World War 1, receiving a decoration for bravery. In 1921, Hitler became leader of the small National Socialist Workers' Party (Nazi Party). While imprisoned for his role in the failed MUNICH PUTSCH, he set out NATIONAL SOCIALISM's extreme racist and nationalist views in *Mein Kampf* (1925). Economic distress and dissatisfaction with the WEIMAR REPUBLIC led to electoral gains for the Nazis and, by forming an alliance with orthodox Nationalists, Hitler became chancellor in January 1933. He made himself dictator of a one-party state in which the SS and GESTAPO ruthlessly suppressed all opposition. The racial hatred he incited led to a policy of extermination of Jews and others in the HOLOCAUST. Hitler pursued an aggressive foreign policy aimed at territorial expansion in E Europe. The invasion of Poland finally goaded Britain and France into declaring war on Germany in September 1939. Hitler himself played a large part in determining strategy during WORLD WAR 2. In April 1945, with Germany in ruins, he committed suicide.

Hittites People of Asia Minor who controlled a powerful empire in the 15th-13th centuries BC. They founded a kingdom in Anatolia (Turkey) in the 18th century BC; their capital was Hattusas (Bogazköy). They expanded E and S in the 15th century BC and conquered N Syria before being checked by the Egyptians under RAMSES II. Under attack from ASSYRIA, the Hittite Empire disintegrated in c.1200 BC.

HIV See HUMAN IMMUNODEFICIENCY VIRUS (HIV)

hives (urticaria or nettle rash) Transient, itchy reddish or pale raised skin patches. Hives may be caused by an ALLERGY, by irritants such as sunlight, or by stress.

Hizbollah (Hezbollah) Iranian-backed, Islamic fundamentalist group. Formed in the early 1980s, to encourage the integration of SHI'ITE religious militants into Middle Eastern politics, Hizbollah engaged in terrorist actions against Israel, including missile attacks from within Lebanon.

Hobart Port and state capital of TASMANIA, SE Australia. Founded as a penal colony in the early 1800s, it became capital in 1812. It has one of the world's best natural harbours. Industries: fruit processing, textiles, zinc. Pop. (1999 est.) 194,200.

Hobbema, Meindert (1638–1709) Dutch painter. Hobbema's serene landscapes, especially the masterpiece *Avenue of Middelharnis* (1689), were highly influential on 18th- and early 19th-century English landscape artists.

Hobbes, Thomas (1588–1679) English philosopher. In *De Corpore* (1655), *De Homine* (1658) and *De Cive* (1642), he maintained that matter and its motion comprise the only valid subjects for philosophy. His greatest work, *Leviathan* (1651), argued that man is inherently selfish but obeys a SOCIAL CONTRACT in order to maintain civilized society.

Hobbs, Sir Jack (John Berry) (1882–1963) English cricketer. His first-class record of 61,237 runs (including 197 centuries) remains unbeaten. He played cricket for Surrey (1904–30) and England (1908–30). Hobbs scored 5,410 runs (3,636 against Australia) in 61 tests. He was knighted in 1953.

Ho Chi Minh (1890–1969) (Nguyen That Thanh) Vietnamese statesman, president of North Vietnam (1954–69). He founded the Vietnamese Communist Party in 1930. Forced into exile, he returned to Vietnam in 1941 to lead the VIET MINH against the Japanese. In 1945, Ho Chi Minh declared Vietnamese independence. After the French defeat at DIEN BIEN PHU (1954), Vietnam split and he became president of North Vietnam. Ho Chi Minh organized and supported the VIET CONG against South Vietnam and committed North Vietnamese forces against the USA in the VIETNAM WAR.

Ho Chi Minh City (Saigon) City at the mouth of the River Saigon in the Mekong delta, S Vietnam; the largest city in Vietnam. An ancient Khmer settlement, Saigon was seized by the French in 1859 and made capital of Cochin China, then French INDOCHINA (1887–1902). In 1954 it became capital of independent South Vietnam. During the VIETNAM WAR, it served as military headquarters for US and South Vietnamese forces. Taken by the North Vietnamese in 1975, it was later renamed Ho Chi Minh City. It is the commercial, industrial and transport centre of Vietnam. Industries: shipbuilding, textiles, pharmaceuticals. Pop. (2005) 5,030,000.

hockey (field hockey) Game played by two teams of 11 players, in which a hooked stick is used to strike a small, solid ball into the opponents' goal. The field of play classically measures 91.47 × 54.9m (300 × 180ft), usually grassed. There are two 35–minute halves. To score, a player must be within the semi-circle marked out in front of the goal. Body contact is forbidden and a ball cannot be hit above shoulder height. The modern game dates from the formation of the English Hockey Association in 1875, and has been an Olympic sport since 1908. Recent developments in the UK include the introduction of a national club league system. *See also* ICE HOCKEY

Hockney, David (1937–) English painter, the most acclaimed British artist of his generation. He first attracted attention with witty POP ART paintings, such as *Flight into Italy-Swiss Landscape* (1962). The swimming-pool was a common theme, such as *A Bigger Splash* (1967). His portraits in spacious interiors, such as *Mr and Mrs Clark and Percy* (1970), are almost period pieces. His graphic work is often regarded as being more innovative than his painting.

Hodgkin's disease Rare type of cancer causing painless enlargement of the lymph glands, lymphatic tissue, and spleen, with subsequent spread to other areas. Named after English pathologist Thomas Hodgkin (1798–1866), its treatment consists of RADIOTHERAPY, surgery, drug therapy, or a combination. It is curable if caught early. *See also* LYMPHATIC SYSTEM

Hoffa, Jimmy (James Riddle) (1913–?75) US trade union leader, president of the International Brotherhood of Teamsters (1957–71). In 1967, he was imprisoned for jury tampering, mail fraud, and mishandling of union funds. In 1971, President Richard NIXON commuted his sentence. In 1975, Hoffa disappeared and is presumed dead.

Hoffman, Dustin (1937–) US film actor. Hoffman's debut performance in *The Graduate* (1967), earned him an Academy nomination for best actor. A dedicated character actor, he won further nominations for his roles as a derelict in *Midnight Cowboy* (1969) and as comedian Lenny Bruce in *Lenny* (1974). He finally won a best actor Oscar for *Kramer vs Kramer* (1979). After a startling performance in *Tootsie* (1982), he won a second best actor award for *Rain Man* (1988).

Hoffmann, E.T.A. (Ernst Theodor Amadeus) (1776–1822) German Romantic writer, musician, and music critic. He wrote many fantastic gothic stories, several of which later formed the basis for the opera *The Tales of Hoffmann* (1881) by OFFENBACH. Tchaikovsky based his *Nutcracker Suite* (1892) on another of his stories. His two novels are *The Devil's Elixir* (1815–16) and *The Educated Cat* (1820–22).

Hofstadter, Robert (1915–90) US physicist. He proposed that PROTONS and NEUTRONS have a positively charged core surrounded by a cloud of ELEMENTARY PARTICLES (pions). Hofstadter shared the 1961 Nobel Prize in physics.

Hogarth, William (1697–1764) English painter and engraver. Hogarth established his reputation with *A Harlot's Progress* (1731–32), the first in a series of 'modern moral subjects'. He painted narrative pictures that satirically exposed the follies and vices of his age. Hogarth is best known for *A Rake's Progress* (1733–35) and the masterpiece *Marriage à la Mode* (1743–45). He reached a wider audience by producing engravings of his paintings. He also excelled at portraiture, such as *Captain Coram* (1740).

Hohenstaufen Dynasty that exercised great power in Germany and the HOLY ROMAN EMPIRE from 1138 to 1254. It is named after the castle of Staufen, built by Frederick, Count of Swabia, whose son became Conrad III of Germany and Holy Roman emperor in 1138. From Conrad III to CONRAD IV, the family occupied the Imperial throne, except for the years 1209–15 (when the GUELPH Otto IV was Emperor). The greatest of the dynasty was FREDERICK II.

Hohenzollern German dynasty that ruled BRANDENBURG, Prussia and Germany. The family acquired Brandenburg in 1415, and gained Prussia in 1618. FREDERICK WILLIAM expanded their territories, and his son, Frederick I, adopted the title 'King in Prussia'. FREDERICK WILLIAM I built up the Prussian army, and FREDERICK II used it to great effect against the Habsburgs. Germany finally united in 1871, under the Hohenzollern Emperor WILLIAM I.

Hokkaido (formerly Yezo) Most northerly and second largest of the main islands of Japan, bounded W by the Sea of Japan and E by the Pacific Ocean; the capital is Sapporo. Until the late 19th century, it was the homeland of the Ainu aboriginals. It is mountainous and forested, with some active volcanoes. Linked to HONSHU by the Seikan Tunnel, Hokkaido is Japan's chief farming region and coal-producer, and a winter sports resort. Area: 83,451sq km (32,212sq mi). Pop. (2000) 5,683,000.

Hokusai, Katsushika (1760–1849) Japanese master of UKIYO-E (coloured WOODCUT), especially famous for his landscapes. Hokusai had an enormous influence on late 19th-century European painters. His most famous print is *The Wave*.

Holbein (the Younger), Hans (1497–1543) German painter. His early work included religious paintings, such as *Dead Christ* (1521) and woodcuts such as *Dance of Death* (c.1523–25). Holbein's portraits of his friend ERASMUS earned him the patronage (1526–28) of Sir Thomas MORE. In 1532, he settled permanently in London and became (1536) court painter to HENRY VIII. Holbein's masterpieces include *The*

▲ **Holbein** *Portrait of Thomas Cromwell wearing the Order of St George* (c.1534) by Hans Holbein (the Younger). Best known for his woodcuts and portraits, Holbein painted many influential people in both German and English society, including Desiderius Erasmus and Thomas More. He was court painter to Henry VIII.

H

INTERNET

Hockney, David
▶ www.tate.org.uk

Hokusai, Katsushika
▶ www.book-navi.com/ hokusai/hokusai-e.html
▶ www.thebritishmuseum. ac.uk

Holbein (the Younger), Hans
▶ www.metmuseum.org
▶ www.nationalgallery.org.uk
▶ www.nga.gov

▶ **Hollywood** One of the most famous signs in the world, Hollywood, Los Angeles, is home to legendary film studios including MGM, Paramount, 20th-Century Fox, and Colombia Pictures. Once the world centre of cinema, an increasing number of films are being made outside Hollywood as film production facilities become more dispersed.

Ambassadors (1533) and superb portraits of *Christina of Denmark, Duchess of Milan* (1538), and *Anne of Cleves* (1540).

Holguín City in SE Cuba, its port on the Atlantic Ocean. Founded *c.*1720, it was the focus for rebellions against Spanish rule (1868–78, 1895–98). Located on a fertile plateau, it exports tobacco and cattle products. Industries: sugar cane, coffee, timber, furniture. Pop. (1995 est.) 243,240.

Holiday, Billie (1915–59) US blues and jazz singer, nicknamed Lady Day. She became famous in the 1930s with the bands of Count Basie and Artie Shaw. Her melancholic renditions of "My Man, Mean to Me" (1937) and "God Bless the Child" (1941) are legendary in the history of jazz.

Holland Popular name for the NETHERLANDS, but properly referring only to a historic region, now divided into two provinces. A fief of the Holy Roman Empire in the 12th century, Holland united with the county of Hainaut in 1299. It passed to Burgundy in 1433 and to the Habsburgs in 1482. In the 16th century, Holland led the Netherlands in their long struggle for independence from Spain.

Hollerith, Herman (1860–1929) US COMPUTER pioneer. In 1890, he invented a mechanical tabulating machine that used punched cards to record and process data. These gave rise to the Hollerith code (later employed by early computers) that uses 12 bits per alphanumeric character. Hollerith's firm, the Tabulating Machine Company, later expanded to become International Business Machines (IBM).

Holly, Buddy (1936–59) US singer and songwriter, b. Charles Hardin Holley. Holly and his group, the Crickets, achieved success in 1957 with "That'll be the Day", "Oh Boy", and "Peggy Sue". He was a pioneer of double-tracking and the standard rock grouping of drums, bass, rhythm and lead guitar. He died in a plane crash.

Hollywood Suburb of LOS ANGELES, California, USA. After 1911 it became the primary centre for film-making in the USA, and by the 1930s its studios dominated world cinema. From the 1950s onwards, television became increasingly important.

Holmes, Oliver Wendell (1809–94) US writer and physician. Holmes' best literary work takes the form of humorous table talk, such as *The Autocrat of the Breakfast Table* (1857–58), *The Professor at the Breakfast Table* (1860), and *The Poet at the Breakfast Table* (1872). He was also a respected professor of medicine at Harvard University.

HONDURAS

The Republic of Honduras is the second largest country in Central America. It has two coastlines. The N coast extends for about 600km (375mi) by the Caribbean; its deep offshore waters prompted the Spanish to name the country Honduras ('depths'). To the S it has a narrow 80km (50mi) long Pacific outlet to the Gulf of Fonseca. Along the N coast are vast banana plantations. To the E lies the MOSQUITO COAST. The Cordilleras highlands form 80% of Honduras, and include the capital, TEGUCIGALPA.

Pine forests cover 75% of Honduras. The N coastal plains contain rainforest and tropical savanna. The Mosquito Coast contains mangrove swamps and dense forests. Mahogany and rosewood forest grow on lower mountain slopes.

CLIMATE
The climate is tropical, though the uplands, where the capital Tegucigalpa is situated, are cooler than the coastal plains. The heaviest rainfall occurs from November to May. The coast is often battered by hurricanes. In October 1998, Honduras and Nicaragua were hit by Hurricane Mitch, which caused floods and mudslides.

HISTORY
From AD 400 to 900, the MAYA civilization flourished. Christopher Columbus sighted the coast in 1502, and by 1524 the first Spanish settlements had been founded by Pedro de Alvarado. The Spanish gradually subdued the native population and established gold and silver mines. They discovered the magnificent ruins at Copán in W Honduras in 1576, but these became covered in dense forest and were only rediscovered in 1839. In 1821 Honduras gained independence, forming part of the Mexican Empire. From 1823 to 1838, Honduras was a member of the Central American Federation. Throughout the rest of the 19th century, Honduras was subject to continuous political interference, especially from Guatemala. Britain controlled the Mosquito Coast.

In the 1890s US companies developed banana plantations which soon became the country's chief source of income. The companies exerted great political influence, and Honduras became known as a 'banana republic', a name later extended to other Latin American nations. After World War 2, demands grew for greater national autonomy and workers' rights. A military coup overthrew the Liberal government in 1963. Honduras' expulsion of Salvadorean immigrants after an ill-tempered World Cup qualifier led to the brief 'Soccer War' (1969) with El Salvador.

POLITICS
Civilian government returned in 1982. In the 1980s Honduras, dependent on US aid, allowed US-backed Nicaraguan Contra rebels to operate in Honduras against Nicaragua's left-wing Sandinista government. A state of emergency was declared during popular demonstrations against the Contras in 1988. After Nicaragua reached a ceasefire the Contra bases were closed.

AREA 112,088sq km [43,277sq mi]
POPULATION 7,484,000
CAPITAL (POPULATION) Tegucigalpa (1,061,000)
GOVERNMENT Republic
ETHNIC GROUPS Mestizo 90%, Amerindian 7%, Black (including Black Carib) 2%, White 1%
LANGUAGES Spanish (official), Amerindian dialects
RELIGIONS Roman Catholic 97%
CURRENCY Honduran lempira = 100 centavos

In 1992 Honduras signed a treaty with El Salvador, settling the disputed border. Carlos Flores became president in 1997 elections. In 1998, Hurricane Mitch killed more than 5,500 people and left 14 million homeless. Human rights organizations estimated that 'death squads', often backed by the police, killed more than 1,000 street children in 2000. Ricardo Maduro became president in 2001 elections but was unable to stem rising violent crime. In 2005 Manuel Zelaya was elected president.

ECONOMY
Honduras is the least industrialized country in Central America, and the poorest developing nation in the Americas. Unemployment is very high, leading to crime and drug trafficking. The country's few mineral resources consist of silver, lead and zinc. Agriculture is dominant, providing 78% of exports and employing 38% of the workforce. Bananas and coffee are the leading exports, and maize the principal food crop. Cattle are raised in the mountain valleys and on the S Pacific plains. Fishing and forestry are also important. Lack of an adequate transport infrastructure hampers development.

holmium (symbol Ho) Metallic element of the LAN-THANIDE SERIES (rare-earth metals), first identified spectroscopically in 1878 by Swiss chemists and in 1897 by Swedish chemist Per Cleve (1840–1905) who named it after the Latin name for Stockholm (*Holmia*). Its chief ore is monazite. The element has few commercial uses. Properties: at.no. 67; r.a.m. 164.9304; r.d. 8.795 (25°C); m.p. 1,474°C (2685°F); b.p. 2,695°C (4,883°F); most common isotope Ho^{165} (100%).

Holocaust, the (1933–45) Extermination of European Jews and others by the Nazi regime in Germany. The Nazi persecution reached its peak in the 'Final Solution', a programme of mass extermination adopted in 1942, and carried out with murderous efficiency by Adolf EICHMANN. Jews, as well as others considered racially inferior by the Nazis, were killed in CONCENTRATION CAMPS such as AUSCHWITZ, BELSEN, DACHAU, Majdanek, and Treblinka. Total Jewish deaths are estimated at more than 6 million, about three-quarters of the population of European Jews. The Holocaust raised moral problems about the course of European civilization.

Holocene (Recent epoch) Division of geological time extending from *c*.10,000 years ago to the present. It includes the emergence of humans as settled members of communities; the first known villages date from *c*.8,000 years ago.

holography Process of making a 3–D **hologram**. One or more photographs form on a single film or plate by INTERFERENCE between two parts of a split LASER beam. The photograph appears as a flat pattern until light hits the plate in the correct position; it then becomes a 3–D image. British physicist Dennis GABOR proposed the theory of holography in 1947, but it only became practicable with the invention of the laser.

Holst, Gustav (Gustavus Theodore von) (1874–1934) English composer. His early works were often influenced by Hinduism, as in the opera *Sita* (1906), and English folksong, as in *Somerset Rhapsody* (1907). Among his works are several operas, including *The Perfect Fool* (1922), songs, chamber music, and the popular orchestral suite *The Planets* (1914–16).

Holy Alliance (1815) Agreement signed at the Congress of VIENNA by the crowned heads of Russia, Prussia, and Austria. Its purpose was to re-establish the principle of hereditary rule and to suppress democratic and nationalist movements, which sprung up in the wake of the FRENCH REVOLUTION. The agreement was later signedby every European dynasty except the King of England and the Ottoman Sultan.

Holy Communion *See* EUCHARIST

Holy Grail In medieval times, the cup supposedly used by Jesus at the LAST SUPPER and by JOSEPH OF ARIMATHEA at the crucifixion to catch the blood from Jesus' wounds. The quest for the Grail, especially by the knights of Arthurian legend, became a search for mystical union with God.

Holy Roman Empire European Empire centred on Germany (10th-19th centuries), which echoed the Empire of ancient ROME. It was founded (962) when the German king OTTO I (THE GREAT) was crowned in Rome, although some historians date it from the coronation of CHARLEMAGNE in 800. The Emperor, elected by the German Princes, claimed to be the temporal sovereign of Christendom, ruling in cooperation with the spiritual sovereign, the Pope. However-er, the Empire never encompassed all of western Christendom, and relations with the papacy were often difficult. From 1438, the title was virtually hereditary in the HABS-BURG dynasty. After 1648, the Empire became little more than a loose confederation. NAPOLEON I finally abolished the Holy Roman Empire in 1806.

Holy Sepulchre Tomb in the old city of Jerusalem traditionally held to be the site of the burial and resurrection of Jesus Christ. It was believed to have been discovered by Saint Helena, mother of Emperor Constantine I, who built the first 'Church of the Holy Sepulchre' there in *c*.336. Several churches have been built, destroyed, and rebuilt on the site over the centuries. Most of the church dates from the 18th century.

Holy Spirit (Holy Ghost) Third Person of the TRINITY in Christian theology. The Holy Spirit represents the spiritual agent through whom God's grace is given. The NEW TES-TAMENT contains many references to the Holy Spirit, firstly as the agent by whom Mary conceived JESUS CHRIST and later as the divine power imparted to the church.

Holy Week Seven-day period preceding EASTER. It begins with Palm Sunday, commemorating Christ's entry into Jerusalem; Maundy Thursday marks his institution of the EUCHARIST; Good Friday marks his betrayal and crucifixion.

Home, Sir Alec Douglas- *See* DOUGLAS-HOME, SIR ALEC (ALEXANDER FREDERICK)

Home Counties Counties surrounding London, England, consisting of HERTFORDSHIRE, SURREY, ESSEX, KENT, BERKSHIRE, and BUCKINGHAMSHIRE.

Home Office British department of state, dating from 1782. The Home Office's present duties cover all matters of national administration not entrusted to another minister. The head of the department, the Home Secretary, is a cabinet position; there are separate secretaries of state for Scotland and Wales. There is also a separate Northern Ireland Office.

homeopathy Unorthodox medical treatment that involves administering infinitesimal doses of a remedy which, in large doses, causes effects or symptoms similar to those that are being treated. Invented in the 18th century, there is little or no scientific evidence for its effectiveness.

homeostasis In biology, processes that maintain constant conditions within a cell or organism in response to either internal or external changes. An example is the regulation of body temperature by the skin and liver.

homeothermic (endothermic or warm-blooded) Describes an animal whose body temperature does not fluctuate with the changing temperature of its surroundings. Mammals and birds are warm-blooded. They maintain their body temperature through metabolism. *See also* POIKILOTHERMIC

Homer (active 8th century BC) Greek poet. Homer is considered to be the author of the the *Iliad* and the *Odyssey*, the great early epics of GREEK LITERATURE. Nothing factual is known about Homer; he is supposed have been blind and lived in Ionia. Literary scholarship revealed that the Homeric poems are a synthesis of oral, bardic stories. The *Iliad* relates the siege of Troy in the TROJAN WAR. The *Odyssey* tells of the post-war wanderings of ODYSSEUS on his way back to Penelope in Ithaca.

Homer, Winslow (1836–1910) US painter and illustrator. He won international acclaim for his coverage of the American Civil War in *Harper's Weekly* and recognition as a painter with *Prisoners from the Front* (1866). He is best known for his oil and watercolour paintings, such as *Northeaster* (1895).

Home Rule, Irish Movement to gain Irish legislative independence from the British Parliament in the 19th century. In the 1830s and 1840s, Daniel O'CONNELL's Repeal Association unsuccessfully challenged the Act of UNION (1800) between Britain and IRELAND. In the 1870s, Isaac Butt began the Home Rule League. His successor, Charles PARNELL, won GLAD-STONE's support, but the first Home Rule Bill of 1886 split the LIBERAL PARTY and sent Liberal Unionists into the arms of the CONSERVATIVE PARTY. This coalition defeated a second bill in 1893. In 1912, Parliament passed a third bill, presented by Herbert ASQUITH, but the outbreak of World War 1 postponed implementation. A guerrilla war led by the IRISH REPUBLICAN ARMY (IRA) and the landslide victory for SINN FÉIN in Irish elections followed the EASTER RISING (1916). In 1919, the *Dáil Éireann* claimed independence. In 1920, LLOYD GEORGE's government passed a fourth Home Rule Bill establishing separate parliaments in Dublin and Belfast. In 1921 Arthur GRIF-FITH and Michael COLLINS signed the Anglo-Irish Treaty that created the Irish Free State and gave *de facto* recognition to Northern IRELAND. Eamon DE VALERA opposed the agreement and the Irish Free State plunged into civil war.

Homo Genus to which humans belong. Modern humans are classified *Homo sapiens sapiens*. *See also* CRO-MAGNON; HOMO ERECTUS; HOMO HABILIS; HOMO SAPIENS; HUMAN EVOLUTION; NEANDERTHAL

Homo erectus ('upright man') Species of early human, presumably evolved from HOMO HABILIS, dating from *c*.1.5 million to 0.2 million years ago. **Java Man** was the first early human fossil to be found, late in the 19th century. Both it and **Peking Man**, another early discovery, represent more advanced forms of *Homo erectus* than older fossils found more

INTERNET

Honduras
▶ www.hondurasemb.org

Hong Kong
▶ www.info.gov.hk
www.discoverhongkong.com

H

recently in Africa. Our own species, HOMO SAPIENS, probably evolved from **Heidelberg Man**. *See also* HUMAN EVOLUTION

Homo habilis (Lat. 'handy man') Species of early human, discovered in 1964 by English palaeoanthropologist Louis LEAKEY in the OLDUVAI GORGE, East Africa. Its fossil remains are between *c.*1.8 and *c.*1.2 million years old, contemporary with those of *Australopithecus*. The physical development is much more like that of modern human and it is thought they evolved into HOMO ERECTUS. *See also* HUMAN EVOLUTION

homology In biology, similarity in essential structure of organisms based on a common genetic heritage. It often refers to organs that now have a different superficial appearance and function in different organisms. For example, a human arm and a seal's flipper are homologues, having evolved from a common origin. *See also* EVOLUTION

homophony In music, the sounding in unison of voices or instruments. It also refers to a musical texture with a predominant melody part and an accompaniment, as opposed to monophony (music in a single part) or POLYPHONY.

Homo sapiens ('wise man') Our own species, which is thought to have evolved *c.*500,000 years ago from HOMO ERECTUS. The earliest fossils of *H. sapiens* have been discovered in Africa. Modern man, *H. sapiens sapiens*, developed sophisticated tools (*c.*40,000 years ago) that enabled it to colonize all Earth's continents, except Antarctica, by *c.*10,000 years ago.

homosexuality Emotional or sexual attraction to members of one's own sex. Male and female homosexuals are popularly known as gays and lesbians respectively. Historically, homosexuality was seen as a pathological condition; however, doctors now agree that homosexuality is a normal aspect of sexuality. In the UK, gay liberation groups, such as Stonewall, struggled for an end to discrimination. The pressure group Outrage created controversy in its policy to 'out' public figures. After much political argument, homosexual marriages are gaining legal recognition in much of the West.

homozygote Organism possessing identical forms of a gene on a CHROMOSOME pair. It is a purebred organism and always produces the same kind of GAMETE. *See also* HETEROZYGOTE

Honduras Republic in Central America. *See* country feature, page 390

Honecker, Erich (1912–94) East German communist leader (1971–89). Imprisoned by the Nazis (1935–45), Honecker rose rapidly in the East German Communist Party after World War 2, and succeeded Walter ULBRICHT as party leader, pursuing policies approved by Moscow. With the reforms under Mikhail GORBACHEV and the collapse of European communism, the ailing Honecker resigned.

Honegger, Arthur (1892–1955) French composer. One of a group of Parisian composers known as *Les Six*, he caused a sensation with *Pacific 231* (1923), an orchestral description of a steam locomotive. His other compositions include five symphonies, two operas, and the psalm *King David* (1921).

honey Sweet, viscous, nutritious liquid manufactured by honeybees from nectar. It consists of the sugars laevulose and dextrose, traces of minerals, and *c.*17% water.

honeyeater (honey sucker) Any of a group of Australian songbirds. They have long tongues for feeding on nectar and fruit, and pollinate flowers they feed on. Family Meliphagidae.

honeysuckle Woody twining or shrubby plant that grows in temperate regions worldwide. It has oval leaves and tubular flowers. A common species in Eurasia, *Lonicera periclymenum*, climbs to 6m (20ft). Family Caprifoliaceae.

Hong Kong (Xianggang Special Administrative Region) Former British Crown Colony off the coast of SE China; the capital is Victoria on Hong Kong Island. Hong Kong comprises: Hong Kong Island, ceded to Britain by China in 1842; the mainland peninsula of KOWLOON, acquired in 1860; the New Territories on the mainland, leased for 99 years in 1898; and some 230 islets in the South China Sea. The climate is sub-tropical, with hot, dry summers. In 1984, the UK and China signed a Joint Declaration in which it was agreed that China would resume sovereignty over Hong Kong in 1997. It also provided that Hong Kong would become a special administrative region, with its existing social and economic structure unchanged for 50 years. It would remain a free port.

The last British governor Chris Patten (1992–97) introduced a legislative council. The handover to China completed on July 1, 1997, and Chief Executive Tung Chee-hwa was sworn in and a provisional legislative council appointed. Hong Kong is a vital international financial centre with a strong manufacturing base (2000 GDP per capita, US$25,400). In 1997 the financial crisis in SE Asia caused the Hang Seng index to lose half of its value. In 1998 the administration spent more than US$15.2 billion defending the Hong Kong dollar. Industries: textiles, electronic goods, cameras, toys, plastic goods, printing. Pop. (2005) 7,182,000; urban core *c.* 1.5 million.

Honolulu Capital and chief port of Hawaii, on SE Oahu Island. It became the capital of the Kingdom of Hawaii in 1845, and remained the capital after the annexation of the islands by the USA in 1898. Landmarks include the Iolani Palace, Waikiki Beach, and the Diamond Head Crater. There are two universities and several colleges. Tourism is of major importance. Industries: sugar refining, pineapple canning. Pop. (2000) 371,657. *See also* PEARL HARBOR

Honshu Largest of Japan's four main islands, lying between the Sea of Japan (W) and the Pacific Ocean (E). It includes FUJIYAMA and BIWA-KO. It is highly industrial and has six of Japan's largest cities, including TOKYO. The majority of the population inhabit the coastal lowlands. Industries: shipbuilding, oil refining, chemicals, textiles, rice, tea, fruit. Area: 230,782sq km (89,105sq mi). Pop. (1999 est.) 102,049,000.

Honthorst, Gerard (1590–1656) Dutch painter. Influenced by CARAVAGGIO, Honthorst was skilled in depicting dramatic candle-lit interiors, notably *Samson and Delilah* (*c.*1620). He made his name, however, after abandoning the Caravaggesque style, becoming a successful portrait painter.

Hooch, Pieter de (1629–84) Dutch genre painter. He is best known for his paintings of serene, domestic interiors and courtyards. His best works, such as *The Courtyard of a House in Delft* and *The Pantry*, date from the 1650s.

Hooke, Robert (1635–1703) English philosopher, physicist, and inventor. Interested in astronomy, Hooke claimed to have stated the laws of planetary motion before Isaac NEWTON. He studied elasticity of solids, which led to HOOKE'S LAW. Among his inventions were a practical telegraph system and the Gregorian (reflecting) MICROSCOPE.

Hooke's law Law applying to an elastic material when it is stretched. The law states that the stress (internal tension) is proportional to the strain (a change in dimensions). Robert HOOKE discovered the relationship in 1676. *See also* ELASTICITY

hookworm Two species (*Necator americanus* and *Ancyclostoma duodenale*) of ROUNDWORM. A human PARASITE, hookworm larvae usually enter the host through the skin of the feet and legs and attach to the wall of the small intestine. Symptoms can include anaemia and constipation. Phylum Nematoda.

hoopoe Striped, fawn-coloured bird that lives in open areas throughout warmer parts of Eurasia. It has a fan-like crest, a long, curved bill, and feeds on small invertebrates. Length: 30cm (12in). Family Upupidae; species *Upupa epops*.

Hoover, Herbert Clark (1874–1964) 31st US President (1929–33). Acclaimed for his work with victims of war, he was secretary of commerce under presidents HARDING and COOLIDGE. After winning the Republican nomination for president in 1928, Hoover easily defeated Alfred E. Smith. During his first year in office, the economy was shattered by the Wall Street Crash and the ensuing GREAT DEPRESSION. With his belief in individual enterprise and distrust of government interference, Hoover failed to provide sufficient government resources to deal with the Depression. In 1932, he was defeated by Franklin D. ROOSEVELT's promise of a NEW DEAL.

Hoover, J. (John) Edgar (1895–1972) US administrator, director (1924–72) of the US FEDERAL BUREAU OF INVESTIGATION (FBI). Hoover reorganized the Bureau, compiling a vast file of fingerprints and building a crime laboratory. During the 1930s, he fought organized crime. After World War 2, he concentrated on what he saw as the threat of communist subversion, harassing public figures such as Martin Luther King, Jr.

Hoover Dam One of the world's largest dams, on the Colorado River between Arizona and Nevada, USA. Opened in

1935, its waters irrigate land in s California, Arizona, and Mexico. Height: 221m (726ft). Length: 379m (1,244ft).

hop Twining vine native to Eurasia and the Americas. It has rough stems, heart-shaped leaves and small male and female flowers on separate plants. The female flowers of *Humulus lupulus* are used to flavour BEER. Family Cannabiaceae.

Hope, Bob (1903–2003) US comedian, b. England. After appearing on radio and in vaudeville, Hope made his film debut in *The Big Broadcast of 1938* (1939). *Road to Singapore* (1940) was the first of seven 'Road' pictures he made with Bing CROSBY and Dorothy Lamour. Other films include *The Paleface* (1947). Hope's work for charity and humanitarian causes earned him a Presidential Medal of Freedom (1969).

Hopi Shoshonean-speaking tribe of Native Americans. They are famous for having retained the purest form of pre-Columbian life to have survived in the USA today. Today, c.6,000 Hopi live in Arizona.

Hopkins, Sir Anthony (1937–) Welsh film and stage actor. His film career experienced several false starts before a dramatic resurgence in the 1990s. His hypnotic performance in *The Silence of the Lambs* (1991) won him an Academy Award for best actor. He also starred in *Shadowlands* (1993) and *Nixon* (1995). *August* (1995) was his directorial debut.

Hopkins, Gerard Manley (1844–89) English poet and Jesuit priest. Hopkins contributed the principle of 'sprung rhythm' to English poetry. His writing concerns itself with problems of faith. The sinking of a German ship carrying five nuns inspired "The Wreck of the *Deutschland*" (1875). All of his poems were published posthumously.

Hopper, Edward (1882–1967) US realist painter. A pupil of Robert HENRI, he was greatly influenced by the ASHCAN SCHOOL. His paintings of scenes in New England and New York City, such as *Early Sunday Morning* (1930), convey a unique sense of melancholic romanticism.

Horace (c.65–08 BC) Roman poet, b. Quintus Horatius Flaccus. His first *Satires* appeared in c.35 BC and were followed by *Epodes* (c.30BC), *Odes* (c.23BC), *Epistles* (c.20BC), and *Ars Poetica* (c.19BC). His simple Latin lyrics provided a vivid picture of the Augustan age.

horizon, celestial GREAT CIRCLE on the CELESTIAL SPHERE. It lies midway between the observer's ZENITH and NADIR.

hormone Chemical substance secreted by living cells. Hormones affect the metabolic activities of cells in other parts of the body. In MAMMALS, glands of the ENDOCRINE SYSTEM secrete hormones directly into the bloodstream. Hormones exercise chemical control of physiological functions, regulating growth, development, sexual functioning, METABOLISM, and (in part) emotional balance. They maintain a delicate equilibrium that is vital to health. The HYPOTHALAMUS, adjacent to the PITUITARY GLAND at the base of the BRAIN, is responsible for overall coordination of the secretion of hormones. Most hormones are PROTEINS or STEROIDS. Hormones include THYROXINE, ADRENALINE, INSULIN, OESTROGEN, PROGESTERONE, and TESTOSTERONE. In PLANTS, hormones control many aspects of metabolism, including cell elongation and division, direction of growth, initiation of flowering, development of fruits, leaf fall, and responses to environmental factors. The most important plant hormones include AUXIN, GIBBERELLIN, and CYTOKININ. *See also* HOMEOSTASIS

hormone replacement therapy (HRT) Use of the female HORMONES progestogen and OESTROGEN in women who are either menopausal or who have had both ovaries removed. HRT relieves symptoms of the MENOPAUSE; it also gives some protection against heart disease and OSTEOPOROSIS. The oestrogen causes a thickening of the lining of the uterus, which may increase risk of cancer of the ENDOMETRIUM. The progestogen causes a regular shedding of the lining, similar to menstruation, which may lessen this risk.

horn BRASS musical instrument traditionally used in hunting and ceremonies. They appeared in the opera orchestras of 17th-century Europe and in the 19th century with Wagner and Strauss. The modern instrument (French horn) consists of a coiled tube of conical bore that widens to a flared bell; most have three valves. It has a mellow tone.

◄ **hornbill** The great hornbill (*Buceros bicornis*) is just one of the 45 species of hornbill, all of which are found in tropical Asia and Africa. The enormously developed bill seen in the great hornbill is used for display and nesting purposes rather than for feeding.

hornbill Brownish or black-and-white bird, native to tropical Africa and SE Asia. It has a large, brightly coloured bill. The female lays one to six eggs in a hole high up in a tree trunk and then sometimes erects a barricade, imprisoning herself and her eggs there for 4 to 11 weeks. The male feeds her through a slit in the wall. There are several species. Length: 38–152cm (15–60in). Family Bucerotidae.

hornblende Black or green mineral found in IGNEOUS and METAMORPHIC ROCKS. It is the commonest form of AMPHIBOLE, and contains iron and silicates of calcium, aluminium and magnesium. Hardness 5.5; r.d. 3.2.

Horne, Marilyn (1934–) US mezzo-soprano. She studied with Lotte LEHMANN and made her debut in *The Bartered Bride*, Los Angeles (1954). Horne's career included a cycle of Rossini and Bellini operas with Joan SUTHERLAND.

hornet Large, orange and brown wasp native to Europe. They build egg-shaped paper nests with one queen and many nectar-gathering workers. They have a powerful sting, but are less aggressive than the common wasp. Family Vespidae.

horoscope Map of the stars and planets at the time of a person's birth. It shows the position of the celestial bodies in relation to the 12 signs of the ZODIAC and is the basis of ASTROLOGY. Today the term is more commonly used to describe the written predictions of an astrologer.

Horowitz, Vladimir (1904–89) US concert pianist, b. Russia. He first performed in public in 1921, and was world-famous by the age of 20 for his virtuoso technique and great sensitivity. From 1950, he was an infrequent concert performer, but continued to make recordings.

horse Hoofed mammal that evolved in North America but became extinct there during the late Pleistocene epoch. Early horse forms crossed the land bridge across the Bering Strait, dispersed throughout Asia, Europe and Africa, and produced the modern horse family. The only surviving true wild horse is Przewalski's horse. The horse was first domesticated about 5,000 years ago in central Asia and played a crucial role in agricultural and military development. Horses returned to the New World with the Spanish conquistadores in the 1500s. Horses are characterized by one large functional toe, molars with crowns joined by ridges for grazing, an elongated skull and a simple stomach. All are fast runners and all can interbreed. Family Equideae; species *Equus caballus*.

horse chestnut Any of 25 species of deciduous trees that grow in temperate regions, especially the common horse chestnut, *Aesculus hippocastanum*. It has large leaves, long flower spikes, and round prickly fruits containing one or two inedible nuts. Family Hippocastanaceae. Height: to 30m (100ft).

horsefly Any of several species of flies in the family Tabanidae, especially *Tabanus lineola*. The female inflicts a painful bite and sucks blood. Length: to 3cm (1.2in).

horsepower (hp) Unit indicating the rate at which work is done, adopted by James WATT in the 18th century. He defined it as the weight, 250kg (550lb), a horse could raise 0.3m (1ft) in one second. The electrical equivalent of 1 hp is 746 watts.

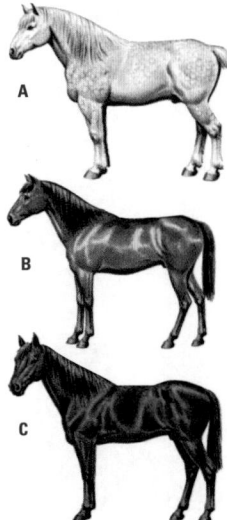

▲ **horse** Domesticated for more than 5000 years, the horse played a significant role in the development of both agriculture and war. The breeds shown here are the Percheron (A) a medium-weight draught horse, first bred in France. The Holstein (B) is a saddle and harness horse bred in Germany. The Hanover (C) also originated in Germany.

H

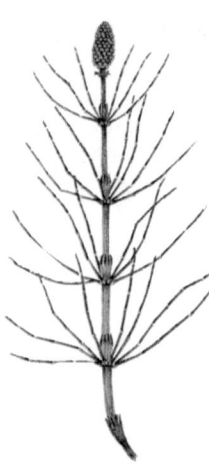

▲ **horsetail** Considered in the same group as ferns, horsetails have cylindrical 'leaves', borne in whorls, and jointed stems. The spores appear in cone-like structures at the tips of the fertile stems. They are 'living fossil' relatives of giant Carboniferous trees.

▲ **Horus** One of the principal deities of ancient Egypt, Horus is depicted as a hawk or falcon, or a man's body with a falcon's head. Horus was identified with Ra, and was the son of Isis and Osiris, who avenged his father's death and rightfully took the throne. For this reason, the Egyptian pharaohs were all considered Horus incarnate.

horse racing Sport in which horses, guided by jockeys, race over a course of predetermined length. Most popular is thoroughbred racing, although harness racing (in which horses draw a light two-wheeled carriage) is also popular. In the UK, thoroughbred racing includes **flat racing** organized by the Jockey Club, and hurdle racing and **steeplechasing** organized according to National Hunt rules. Horse racing began in Assyria in *c*.1500 BC. The world's oldest flat race is the English Derby, held annually at Epsom, Surrey, since 1780. It is one of the five English Classics: 1,000 Guineas, 2,000 Guineas, Oaks, and St Leger. The Grand National steeplechase dates from 1839.

horseradish Perennial plant native to Eastern Europe. It is cultivated for its pungent, fleshy root, which is a useful seasoning. It has lance-shaped, toothed leaves, white flower clusters, and egg-shaped seed-pods. Height: 1.2m (4ft). Family Brassicaceae/Cruciferae; species *Armoracia rusticana*.

horsetail Any of *c*.30 species of flowerless, rush-like plants allied to ferns, which grow in all continents except Australasia. The hollow jointed stems have a whorl of tiny leaves at each joint. Spores are produced in a cone-like structure at the top of a stem. Horsetails date from the Carboniferous period. Phylum Sphenophyta, genus *Equisetum*.

Horthy, Miklós Nagybánai (1868–1957) Hungarian political leader, regent (1920–44). He commanded the Austro-Hungarian fleet in World War 1. Horthy took part in the counter-revolution that overthrew Béla KUN, becoming regent and effective head of state. His highly conservative regime suppressed political opposition and resisted the return of CHARLES I. Allied with the Axis Powers in 1941, he tried to arrange a separate peace with the Allies in 1944 but was arrested by the Germans. After the war he settled in Portugal.

horticulture Growing of vegetables, fruits, seeds, herbs, shrubs, and flowers on a commercial scale. Techniques employed include propagation by leaf, stem, and root cuttings, and by stem and bud grafting. Fruit trees, shrubs, and vines are usually propagated by grafting the fruiting stock on to a hardier rootstock. SEED is a major horticultural crop. Close scientific control of POLLINATION is essential for producing crops of specific quality.

Horus In Egyptian mythology, falcon-headed god, son of ISIS and OSIRIS. He came to be closely identified with all the pharaohs, who used his name as the first of their titles and were thought to rule as him on Earth.

Hosea (Osee) (8th centuryBC) OLD TESTAMENT prophet. The Book of Hosea uses the adultery of his wife as an allegory of the unfaithfulness of Israel to God.

Hospitaller *See* KNIGHTS HOSPITALLERS

Hottentot (Khoikhoi) KHOISAN-speaking people of S Africa, now almost extinct. Traditionally nomadic, many were displaced or exterminated by Dutch settlers. Descendants have mostly been absorbed into the South African population.

Houdini, (Harry) (1874–1926) US escapologist, b. Erich Weiss in Hungary. He escaped from packing cases, handcuffs, and straitjackets, often while underwater in a tank. He also specialized in exposing fraudulent mediums. Author of *The Unmasking of Robert-Houdin* (1908), his extensive library on magic resides in the Library of Congress, Washington, D.C.

Houphouët-Boigny, Félix (1905–93) Ivory Coast statesman, first president (1960–93). He served in the French colonial government, becoming president on independence. His control remained almost absolute. Maintaining close relations with France, the Ivory Coast became one of the more affluent countries in West Africa. In the 1980s, a recession, exacerbated by expenditure on grandiose projects, caused mounting unrest and he was forced to legalize opposition parties in 1990.

house music Form of dance music popular in the USA and Britain from the late-1980s. Using drum machines and sampled sound effects, often put into repetitive loops, house music increased the creative role of the disc jockey (dj). It also inspired a number of other forms of dance music.

House of Commons Lower House of the British PARLIAMENT. The Upper House is the unelected HOUSE OF LORDS. The House of Commons dates from the 13th century. It is

the major forum for discussion and voting on intended legislation and questioning of ministers. Constituents elect its 659 members in a secret ballot, usually in general elections that must be held at least every five years. The PRIME MINISTER is the leader of the majority party in the Commons, and most members of the CABINET are drawn from the Commons, although some may be from the Lords. The speaker controls debates and proceedings of the House. Select committees scrutinize legislation.

House of Lords Upper House of the British PARLIAMENT. In its legislative capacity, the Lords is completely subordinate to the HOUSE OF COMMONS. The Parliament Acts of 1911 and 1949 checked virtually all its power, except to delay passage of a bill for one year. Members of the House of Lords include the Lords Spiritual (26 archbishops and bishops), Lords Temporal (*c*.1,000 hereditary and life peers) and the Lords of Appeal (Law Lords). The Law Lords form Britain's highest court of appeal. In 1999, the number of hereditary peers was reduced to 92 as a first step in the major reform of the House.

House of Representatives Lower House of the US legislature, which together with the SENATE forms the CONGRESS. It has 435 members. Each state has at least one representative; the larger the population of a state, the more representatives are allowed. Representatives must be more than 25 years old, US residents for no less than seven years, and resident in the state they represent. They are directly elected and serve two-year terms. The House considers bills, and has exclusive authority to originate revenue bills, initiate impeachment proceedings, and elect the president if the electoral college is deadlocked.

Houses of Parliament (Palace of Westminster) First large-scale public building of the GOTHIC REVIVAL in Britain. After a fire destroyed the old Palace of Westminster, Charles BARRY won a competition for its replacement. Together with Augustus PUGIN, a passionate Gothic specialist, he created a building that combined a functional plan and modern technology with Gothic detail. The Palace was finished in 1868.

Housman, A.E. (Alfred Edward) (1859–1936) English poet and scholar. Housman is best known for *A Shropshire Lad* (1896), a series of 63 lyrics on nature and love. Its idealized view of the English countryside proved extremely popular. His *Collected Poems* appeared in 1939.

Houston City and port in SE Texas, USA, connected to the Gulf of Mexico by the Houston Ship Canal. Founded in 1836, it was capital of the Republic of Texas (1837–39, 1842–45). Its greatest growth came after the building of the canal (1912–14), as the coastal oil fields provided a rich source of income and Houston developed as a deep-water port. The largest city in the state, it is a major cultural centre with five universities, a symphony orchestra, and many art galleries and museums. It is also a leading industrial, commercial, and financial centre, with vast oil refineries and a massive petrochemical complex. Industries: space research (the Johnson Space Center is nearby), shipbuilding, meat-packing, electronics, chemicals, brewing, sugar and rice processing, synthetic rubber, printing and publishing. Pop. (2000) 3,823,000.

hovercraft (AIR-CUSHION VEHICLE) Fast, usually amphibious craft. A horizontal fan produces a cushion of air supporting the craft just above the ground or water. Vertical fans propel the craft. Most hovercraft are powered by gas turbine or diesel engines. Hovercraft travel at speeds up to *c*.160km/h (100mph). Christopher Cockerell built the first hovercraft in 1959. They are used as marine ferries and as military vehicles.

Hovhaness, Alan (1911–2000) US composer. Influenced by Far Eastern music, Hovhaness gained recognition as an original and exotic composer. His works, some of which reflect his Armenian ancestry, include *Mysterious Mountain* (1955), *Magnificat* (1957), and *And God Created Great Whales* (1970). He wrote 67 symphonies.

Howard, Catherine (1520–42) Fifth Queen of HENRY VIII. She was brought to Henry's attention by opponents of Thomas CROMWELL. Henry married her in July 1540, but supposed evidence of her premarital indiscretions led to her execution.

Howard, Henry *See* SURREY, HENRY HOWARD, EARL OF

Howard, John Winston (1939–) Australian statesman, prime minister (1996–). Howard was elected to the House of

Representatives in 1974. In 1982 he became deputy leader of the Liberal Party, and was made leader in 1985. He held many shadow cabinet positions, and in 1995 was appointed Leader of the Opposition. Howard led the Liberal-National coalition to victory against Paul KEATING's ruling Labor Party government. He was re-elected in 1998 and 2001.

Howard, Trevor (1916–88) English actor. Howard made his film debut in *The Way Ahead* (1944). His first major role was in David LEAN's *Brief Encounter* (1945). Other films include *Sons and Lovers* (1960), *Ryan's Daughter* (1970), *Kidnapped* (1971), *The Missionary* (1982), and *Gandhi* (1982).

Howe, Sir Geoffrey (1926–) British statesman, chancellor of the exchequer (1979–83), foreign secretary (1983–89), deputy prime minister and leader of the House of Commons (1989–90). A leading figure in the Conservative cabinet of Margaret THATCHER, Howe made a damning resignation speech after Thatcher had voiced her hostility to the EURO.

Howe, Sir William (1729–1814) British general during the AMERICAN REVOLUTION. He fought at Bunker Hill and became commander in chief of British forces in North America in 1775. He captured New York (1776) and occupied Philadelphia (September 1777). After defeat at Saratoga (1777), he resigned and returned to England (1778).

Hoxha, Enver (1908–85) Albanian statesman, prime minister (1946–54), first secretary of the Communist Party (1954–85). In 1941 he founded the Albanian Communist Party, and led the resistance to Italian occupation during World War 2. In 1946, the Republic of Albania was established and Hoxha became prime minister. His dictatorial control of party, army and state led to accusations of Stalinism. In 1961, Hoxha withdrew from the WARSAW PACT. The later break with Peking led to Albania's isolation and economic impoverishment.

Hoyle, Sir Fred (Frederick) (1915–2001) English astrophysicist and cosmologist. He developed the STEADY-STATE THEORY, which, although superseded by the BIG BANG theory, sparked important research into nucleosynthesis in stars. Hoyle often attracted controversy with unorthodox ideas.

Hua Guofeng (*c.*1920–) (Hua Kuofeng) Chinese statesman, premier (1976–80), chairman (1976–81) of the Chinese COMMUNIST PARTY. After the death (1976) of MAO ZEDONG and ZHOU ENLAI, Hua was responsible for the arrest of the GANG OF FOUR. His pragmatic approach to domestic and foreign policy led to his isolation within the party. The rising power of DENG XIAOPING led to Hua being replaced by ZHAO ZIYANG as premier and HU YAOBANG as party chairman.

Huang Hai (Yellow Sea) Shallow branch of the Pacific Ocean, N of the East China Sea between the Chinese mainland and the Korean peninsula. It connects to the Chihli and Liaodong gulfs by the Strait of Chihli. The HUANG HE, Liao, and Yalu rivers drain into it; the yellow loess (fine-grained silt) from these rivers give the sea its popular name. Such deposits, along with shifting sandbanks and notorious fogs, make navigation perilous. Area: *c.*466,200sq km (180,000sq mi).

Huang He (Huang Ho or Yellow) River in N central China; China's second longest (after the YANGTZE). It rises in the Kunlun mountains, QINGHAI province, and flows E to LANZHOU. It then takes a 'great northern bend' around the Ordos Desert. Near Baotau, it turns S through Shanxi province. It then flows E through Henan province and NE through Shandong to enter the Bo Hai Gulf, an arm of the HUANG HAI. The river gets its popular name from the huge amounts of yellow silt it collects in its middle course. The silting of the riverbed makes it prone to serious flooding, but the threat has been greatly reduced by dykes and dams. Length: *c.*5,500km (3,400mi).

Hubble, Edwin Powell (1889–1953) US astronomer. In 1925, he published his classification of GALAXIES and his discovery that spiral NEBULAE were resolvable as independent star systems. Using the telescope at Mount Wilson Observatory, he measured the distance to the ANDROMEDA GALAXY. He attributed the RED SHIFT of the spectral lines of galaxies to their recession, and hence to the EXPANDING UNIVERSE. In 1929 he proposed a linear relation between the distance of a galaxy from Earth and their velocity of recession (HUBBLE'S LAW).

Hubble's law Proposed by Edwin HUBBLE (1929), it claimed a linear relation between the distance of galaxies from us and

their velocity of recession, deduced from the RED SHIFT in their spectra. The **Hubble constant** (symbol H_0) is the rate at which the velocity of recession of galaxies increases with distance from us. The inverse of the Hubble constant is the **Hubble time**, which gives a maximum age for the Universe on the assumption that there has been no slowing of the expansion.

Hubble Space Telescope (HST) Optical telescope that was placed in Earth orbit by the SPACE SHUTTLE in 1990. Images transmitted back to Earth revealed that the telescope's main mirror was incorrectly shaped. A repair team corrected the fault in 1993, and it was again repaired in 1997. Hubble now produces acurate images of bodies that cannot be observed clearly by terrestrial telescopes due to atmospheric distortion.

Hudson River in E New York state. It rises in the ADIRONDACK MOUNTAINS, and flows S to New York Bay, NEW YORK CITY. First explored by Henry HUDSON in 1609, it became one of the world's most important waterways. The New York State Barge Canal connects the Hudson with Lake Champlain, the Great Lakes and the St Lawrence River. Length: *c.*493km (306mi).

Hudson, Henry (d.1611) English maritime explorer. He made several efforts to find a NORTHEAST PASSAGE. Employed by the Dutch EAST INDIA COMPANY (1609), ice blocked Hudson's progress and he crossed the Atlantic to search for a NORTHWEST PASSAGE. He was the first European to sail up the HUDSON River, reaching as far as ALBANY. In 1610, he embarked on another voyage to discover the Northwest Passage and reached HUDSON BAY. Forced by ice to winter in the Bay, his mutinous crew set him adrift to die in an open boat.

Hudson Bay World's largest inland sea, in E Northwest Territories, Canada, also bounded by Québec (E), Ontario (S), and Manitoba (SW). It connects to the Atlantic by the Hudson Strait (NE), and to the Arctic Ocean by the Foxe Channel (N). Explored in 1610 by Henry HUDSON, the bay contains Southampton, Mansel, and Coats islands. The Churchill and Nelson rivers drain into the bay, which is ice-free from July to October. Area: *c.*1,243,000sq km (480,000sq mi).

Hudson River School (*c.*1825–75) Group of US landscape painters influenced by European ROMANTICISM. They were so named because of their idealized scenes of the HUDSON River valley. The group included Thomas COLE, Frederick E. Church, Henry Inman, and Asher B. Durand.

Hudson's Bay Company English company chartered in 1670 to promote trade in the HUDSON BAY region of North America and to seek a NORTHWEST PASSAGE. The Company had a fur trading monopoly and was virtually a sovereign power in the region. Throughout the 18th century, it fought with France for control of the bay. In 1763, France ceded control of CANADA to England and the North West Company was formed. Intense rivalry forced the Hudson's Bay Company into a more active role in W exploration, and in 1771 Samuel Hearne proved the lack of a short Northwest Passage out of the Bay. The companies merged in 1821,

INTERNET

Hubble Space Telescope (HST)
▶ www.stsci.edu

H

◀ **Hubble Space Telescope**
One of the most ambitious and expensive pieces of astronomical equipment ever made, the Hubble Space Telescope initially was unable to relay working images back to Earth due to an optical aberration of its main mirror. A shuttle mission in 1993, repaired this fault. A further mission in 1997 corrected problems with the telescope's power supply. Images now received on Earth provided astronomers with the clearest-ever images of distant objects.

H

▲ **Hughes** The son of a wealthy industrialist, Howard Hughes' passion was for film-making. Between 1926 and 1932, Hughes made six films, including *Hell's Angels* (1930) and *Scarface* (1932). He left Hollywood to pursue his other passion for flying and designing aircraft, building the largest-ever wooden aircraft. Hughes returned to the movie industry, directing his most notorious film *The Outlaw* in 1943. He spent the last ten years of his life as a total recluse.

▼ **human evolution** Although the fossil record is not complete, we know that humans evolved from ape-like creatures. Our earliest ancestor, *Australopithecus afarensis* (A), lived in NE Africa some 5 million years ago. Over the next 3–4 million years *A. africanus* (B) evolved. *Homo Habilis* (C), who used primitive stone tools, appeared *c.*500,000 years later. *H. erectus* (D) is believed to have spread from Africa to regions all over the world from *c.*750,000 years ago. Records indicate that from *H. erectus* evolved two species, Neanderthal man (E), who died out 40,000 years ago, and who could have been made extinct by the other species, the earliest modern man *H. sapiens sapiens* (F).

with the new company controlling a territory from the Atlantic to the Pacific. After the Confederation of Canada (1867), challenges to its monopoly power increased, and in 1869 it was forced to cede all its territory to Canada for £300,000. As the fur trade declined in the early 20th century, the company diversified, and in 1930 was divided up.

Huerta, Victoriano (1854–1916) Mexican general and president (1913–14). Instructed by President Francisco MADERO to suppress the revolt led by Félix Díaz, Huerta instead joined forces with the rebels. Madero was arrested and killed, and Huerta became president. Defeated by the Constitutionalists led by CARRANZA, Huerta fled to the USA.

Hughes, Howard Robard (1905–76) US industrialist, aviator and film producer. He inherited an industrial corporation (1923) and became a billionaire as head of the Hughes Aircraft Company. In 1935, he set the world speed record of 567km/h (352mph) in an aircraft of his own design. Hughes occasionally produced films, including *Hell's Angels* (1930), starring Jean Harlow, and *The Outlaw* (1941), starring Jane Russell. He was famed for his reclusive lifestyle.

Hughes, Langston (1902–67) US poet and leading figure of the HARLEM RENAISSANCE. His debut volume was *The Weary Blues* (1926). Hughes' distinctive musical style combined African-American dialect with the rhythms of jazz and blues. Other works include *Shakespeare in Harlem* (1942) and *One-Way Ticket* (1949).

Hughes, Ted (Edward James) (1930–98) English poet. He succeeded Sir John BETJEMAN as poet laureate in 1984. One of the most distinctive voices in contemporary English verse, Hughes focused on the raw, primal forces of nature. Collections include *Hawk in the Rain* (1957), *Lupercal* (1960), *Wodwo* (1967), *Crow* (1970), *Moortown* (1979), and *Wolfwatching* (1989). His creative translation of the Greek poet *Tales from Ovid* (1997) won the Whitbread Prize. Hughes married (1956–62) fellow poet Sylvia PLATH. His last volume, *Birthday Letters* (1998), was a personal reflection on their relationship and posthumously won him a second Whitbread Prize. His books for children include *The Iron Man* (1968).

Hughes, Thomas (1822–96) English novelist. A Christian socialist, Hughes is best known for the novel *Tom Brown's Schooldays* (1857), a semi-fictional account of his education under Thomas Arnold at Rugby School.

Hugo, Victor Marie (1802–85) French poet, dramatist, and novelist. A major force in 19th-century French literature, Hugo received a pension from Louis XVIII for his first collection of *Odes* (1822), and presented his manifesto of ROMANTICISM in the preface to his play *Cromwell* (1827). Later works include the plays *Hernani* (1830) and *Ruy Blas* (1838), and the novels *The Hunchback of Notre Dame* (1831) and *Les Misérables* (1862). Some of his most important works were written whilst in exile, such as the satirical poems *The Punishments* (1853). On the fall of the Second Republic, he returned to Paris where he became a senator.

Huguenots French Protestants who arose in Roman Catholic France during the REFORMATION and suffered persecution. In 1559, a national synod of Huguenot congregations adopted an ecclesiastical structure highly influenced by John CALVIN. During the Wars of RELIGION (1562–98), Huguenots continued to face persecution and thousands died. HENRY IV, a Huguenot, came to the throne in 1589 and, despite adopting the Roman Catholic faith in 1593, promulgated the Edict of NANTES (1598) that recognized Catholicism as the official religion but gave Huguenots certain rights. In 1685 LOUIS XIV revoked the edict, and thousands of Huguenots fled France. In 1789, their civil rights were restored and the CODE NAPOLÉON (1804) later guaranteed religious equality.

Huitzilopochtli Chief deity of the AZTEC, revered as a Sun god, god of war and protector of the fifth era. He is usually shown in armour decorated with humming-bird feathers. His cult required a daily nourishment of human blood. *See also* CENTRAL AND SOUTH AMERICAN MYTHOLOGY

Hull (officially Kingston upon Hull) City and unitary authority on the N bank of the Humber estuary, NE England. Britain's third largest port, it was founded in the late 13th century and grew around its fishing industry. Hull gained city status in 1897. The decline of the fishing industry has been partly offset by the construction of the Humber Bridge (1981), one of the world's longest single-span suspension bridges. The city is home to the University of Hull (1954) and the University of Humberside (1992). Pop. (2001) 243,595.

human Primate MAMMAL of the genus *Homo*, the only living species of which is *Homo sapiens*. When compared with near relatives, the CHIMPANZEE, GORILLA and ORANG-UTAN, humans have several distinct features. They walk upright, their body is only patchily hairy, their big toes are not opposable to the other toes, their backbone is more S-shaped than straight, and their forehead is higher than that of any ape. Humans are also distinct from great apes by the size, number, and shape of their chromosomes. Another distinction is the human capacity for language. Socially, humans are similar to lesser primates, preferring a family or other small group. Humans have always made great changes to their immediate environment and to ecosystems.

human body Physical structure of a HUMAN. It consists of water, PROTEIN and other organic compounds, and some minerals. The SKELETON consists of more than 200 bones, sheathed in voluntary MUSCLE to enable movement. A SKULL surrounds the large BRAIN. The body is fuelled by nutrients absorbed from the DIGESTIVE SYSTEM and oxygen from the LUNGS, which the CIRCULATORY SYSTEM pumps around the body by Metabolic wastes are eliminated mainly by EXCRETION. SEXUAL REPRODUCTION enables continuation of the species. The NERVOUS SYSTEM, working closely with the ENDOCRINE SYSTEM, exerts overall control. A protective layer of SKIN covers the body's surface.

human evolution Process by which humans developed from pre-human ancestors. The FOSSIL record of human

Modern man
Homo sapiens sapiens

ancestors is patchy and unclear. Some scientists believe that our ancestry traces back to one or more species of *Australopithecines* that flourished in S and E Africa *c.*4–1 million years ago. Other scientists believe that we descend from some as yet undiscovered ancestor. The earliest human fossils are those of HOMO HABILIS (handy people) which date from 2 million years ago. The next evolutionary stage was HOMO ERECTUS (upright people), who first appeared *c.*1.5 million years ago. The earliest fossils of our own species, HOMO SAPIENS (wise people), date from *c.*250,000 years ago. An apparent side-branch, the NEANDERTHALS, *Homo sapiens neanderthalensis*, existed in Europe and W Asia *c.*130,000–40,000 years ago. Modern humans, *Homo sapiens sapiens*, first appeared *c.*100,000 years ago. All human species apart from *Homo sapiens sapiens* are now extinct. *See also* EVOLUTION

human immunodeficiency virus (HIV) Organism that causes ACQUIRED IMMUNE DEFICIENCY SYNDROME (AIDS). A RETROVIRUS identified in 1983, HIV attacks the IMMUNE SYSTEM, leaving the person unable to fight off infection. There are two distinct viruses: HIV-1, which has now spread worldwide; and HIV-2, which is concentrated almost entirely in West Africa. Both cause AIDS. There are three main means of transmission: from person to person by sexual contact; from mother to baby during birth; and by contact with contaminated blood or blood products (for instance, during transfusions or when drug-users share needles). People can carry the virus for many years before developing symptoms.

humanism Philosophy based on a belief in the supreme importance of human beings and human values. The greatest flowering of humanism came during the RENAISSANCE, spreading from Italy to other parts of Europe. Early adherents included PETRARCH and ERASMUS. Modern humanism developed as an alternative to traditional Christian beliefs. This movement, associated with social reform, was championed by Bertrand RUSSELL. *See also* ATHEISM; EXISTENTIALISM

human rights Entitlements that an individual may arguably possess by virtue of being human and in accordance with what is natural. The concept of the inalienable rights of the human being has traditionally been linked to the idea of natural law, on which commentaries were written by several Greek and Roman writers. John LOCKE helped to shape ideas of fundamental human rights and liberal DEMOCRACY in *Two Treatises on Government* (1690). The concept of human rights has been most notably formulated in a number of historic declarations, such as the US DECLARATION OF INDEPENDENCE (1776), the US CONSTITUTION (1789) and particularly its first amendments in the BILL OF RIGHTS (1791), and the French DECLARATION OF THE RIGHTS OF MAN AND CITIZEN (1789). These documents owed much to the English PETITION OF RIGHT (1628) and BILL OF RIGHTS (1689), which extended the concept of individual freedom proclaimed earlier in the MAGNA CARTA (1215). The Charter of the United Nations (1945) and the Universal Declaration of Human Rights (1948) proclaims the responsibility of the international community for the protection of human rights. *See also* CIVIL RIGHTS

Humber Estuary in Humberside, NE England, formed by the confluence of the rivers TRENT and OUSE near Goole. HULL lies on its N shore. It is crossed by the Humber Bridge (opened 1981), the second longest single-span suspension bridge in the world. Main span: 1410m (4626ft). Length: 64km (40mi).

Humboldt, Friedrich Heinrich Alexander, Baron von (1769–1859) German naturalist and explorer. He explored (1799–1804) South America, studying volcanoes, tropical storms and the increase in magnetic intensity from the Equator towards the poles. His five-volume *Kosmos* (1845–62) describes the physical universe.

Hume, David (1711–76) Scottish philosopher, historian, and man of letters. Hume's publications include *A Treatise of Human Nature* (1739–40), *History of England* (1754–63), and various philosophical 'enquiries'. Widely known for his humanitarianism and philosophical SCEPTICISM, Hume's phi-

losophy was a form of EMPIRICISM that affirmed the contingency of all phenomenal events. He argued that it was impossible to go beyond the subjective experiences of impressions and ideas. *See also* BERKELEY, GEORGE; LOCKE, JOHN

Hume, John (1937–) Northern Irish politician, leader (1983–2001) of the nationalist SOCIAL DEMOCRATIC LABOUR PARTY (SDLP). He was a founding member and president (1964–68) of the Credit Union League. He entered Parliament in 1983. His commitment to peace in Northern Ireland helped secure an IRA ceasefire. Hume shared the 1998 Nobel Peace Prize with David TRIMBLE, leader of the ULSTER UNIONIST PARTY.

humerus Bone in the human upper arm, extending from the scapula (shoulder blade) to the elbow. A depression on the posterior, roughened lower end of the humerus provides the point of articulation for the ULNA bone of the forearm.

humidity (relative humidity) Measure of the amount of water vapour in air. It is the ratio of the actual amount of vapour to the amount of vapour at which water condenses, and is usually expressed as a percentage. Relative humidity is 100% at DEW POINT. Humidity is measured by a HYGROMETER.

hummingbird Popular name for small, brilliantly coloured birds of the family *Trochilidae*, found in S and N America. Hummingbirds feed in flight on insects and nectar, usually by hovering in front of flowers. Their speed can reach 100km/h (60mph) and their wings, which beat 50–75 times a second, make a humming sound. Length: 6–22cm (2.2–8.6in).

Humperdinck, Engelbert (1854–1921) German music teacher and composer. His works include incidental music, songs, and seven operas, of which the first, *Hansel and Gretel* (1893), is his most popular work. He worked with WAGNER in the preparation of *Parsifal* (1880–81).

Humphrey, Hubert Horatio (1911–78) US statesman, vice president (1965–69). As Lyndon JOHNSON's deputy, Humphrey's support of the VIETNAM WAR incurred much hostility. He won the Democratic nomination in 1968, but lost the ensuing election to Richard NIXON, and returned to the Senate.

humus Dark brown, organic substance resulting from partial decay of plant and animal matter. It improves soil by retaining moisture, aerating and increasing mineral nutrient content and bacterial activity. Types include peat moss, leaf mould, and soil from woods.

Hunan Province in SE central China, S of Tungting Lake; the capital is Changsha. The region is largely forested, but agriculture is important; products include rice, tea, rape seed, and tobacco. Hunan has valuable mineral resources. Area: 210,570sq km (81,301sq mi). Pop. (2000) 64,400,000.

Hundred Days (March 20–June 28, 1815) Period between the escape of NAPOLEON I from Elba and the second restoration of Louis XVIII, following the Allied victory at WATERLOO.

Hundred Years' War (1337–1453) Sporadic conflict between France and England. In 1328, PHILIP VI of France was crowned. In 1337, he captured Aquitaine, prompting King EDWARD III of England to invade France. English victories at CRÉCY (1346) and POITIERS (1356) led to the Peace of Brétigny (1360), which ceded large territories to Edward. The accession of HENRY VI to the English throne

◀ **hummingbird** The sword-billed hummingbird (*Ensifera ensifera*) is one of the 300 or so species of hummingbird found in the Americas. Hummingbirds live largely on nectar, which their long bills are perfectly suited to extracting from deep within flowers.

H

INTERNET

Hudson River School
▶ www.pbs.org/wnet/ihas/ icon/hudson.html
▶ www.albanyinstitute.org/ collections/hudson_river. htm

human evolution
▶ www.talkorigins.org/faqs/ homs

human rights
▶ www.un.org/aboutun/ charter/index.html
▶ www.un.org/Overview/ rights.html

▲ **Huston** US actor and director John Huston was one of the most colourful of Hollywood characters. His directorial debut was *The Maltese Falcon* (1941). His father, Walter Huston, won an Academy Award for best supporting actor in his film *The Treasure of the Sierra Madre* (1946). The early 1950s were a golden period, with movies such as *The Asphalt Jungle* (1950), *African Queen* (1951), and *Moulin Rouge* (1952). His daughter, Anjelica Huston, won an Oscar as best supporting actress in his film *Prizzi's Honor* (1985). Huston also appeared in front of the camera, gaining an Academy nomination for best supprting actor in *Chinatown* (1974).

revived French fortunes. In 1429, the siege of ORLÉANS was broken by JOAN OF ARC. In 1453, the French captured Bordeaux, leaving only Calais in English hands (until 1558). *See also* AGINCOURT

Hungarian (Magyar) Official language of Hungary, spoken by the country's 10.2 million inhabitants and by *c.*3 million more in parts of Romania, Slovakia, and other countries bordering Hungary. Part of the Ugric branch of the FINNO-UGRIC languages.

Hungary Republic in central Europe. *See* country feature

Huns Nomadic people of Mongol or Turkic origin who expanded from central Asia into E Europe. Under ATTILA, they overran large parts of the Roman empire in 434–53, exacting tribute, but after his death they disintegrated.

Hunt, (William) Holman (1827–1910) English painter, who was one of the founders of the PRE-RAPHAELITE BROTHERHOOD in 1848. Hunt's works, such as *The Light of the World* (1854) and *The Scapegoat* (1856), combine meticulous precision with heavy, didactic symbolism.

Hunt, (James Henry) Leigh (1784–1859) English critic, journalist, and poet. Hunt was instrumental in introducing the work of SHELLEY and KEATS to the public. He founded the literary periodical *The Examiner,* and also contributed to *The Indicator* and *The Liberal.*

hunting and gathering Practice of small societies in which members subsist by hunting and by collecting plants rather than by agriculture. The groups are always small bands and have sophisticated kinship and ritualistic systems. Today, hunting-gathering societies are most numerous in lowland South America and parts of Africa. *See also* NOMAD

Huntington's disease (Huntington's chorea) Acute degenerative disorder. It is genetically transmitted and usually occurs in early-middle life. It is caused by the presence of abnormally large amounts of glutamate and aspartate. Physical symptoms include loss of coordination. Mental deterioration can take various forms.

hurling (hurley) One of the national sports of Ireland. It is played by two teams of 15 on a field 137 × 82m (450 × 270ft), at each end of which are goalposts. The object is to score points by propelling the ball between the goal uprights, either above (1 point) or below (3 points) the crossbar. Every player carries a hurley (hooked stick), on which the ball may be balanced as the player runs, or with which it may be batted upfield towards a team-mate; the ball also may be kicked.

Huron Confederation of Iroquoian-speaking tribes of Native Americans who once occupied the St Lawrence Valley E of Lake Huron. In wars with the IROQUOIS CONFEDERACY for control of the fur trade (1648–50), their numbers fell from 15,000 to *c.*500. After much wandering, they settled in Ohio, the Great Lakes area, and Kansas. Today, *c.*1,250 Huron live on reservations in Ohio and Oklahoma, USA, and Ontario, Canada.

Huron, Lake Second largest of the GREAT LAKES of North America, forming part of the boundary between the USA and Canada. It drains Lake SUPERIOR, and feeds Lake ERIE as part of the GREAT LAKES-ST LAWRENCE SEAWAY system and is navigable by ocean-going vessels. Area: 59,596sq km (23,010sq mi). Max. depth: 230m (750ft).

Hurrians Ancient people of Mesopotamia. They established a kingdom to the N of SUMERIA by 2000 BC. By 1500 BC this had become organized into the kingdom of Mitanni, which established an empire in Syria and warred with Egypt. The power of the Hurrians was eventually destroyed by ASSYRIA in *c.*1200, but they had considerable influence over HITTITE culture. They spoke a language unrelated to any other Mesopotamian language and used a CUNEIFORM script.

hurricane Wind of force 12 or greater on the BEAUFORT WIND SCALE; intense tropical cyclone with winds ranging from 120 to 320km/h (75 to 200mph), known also as a typhoon in the Pacific. Originating over oceans around the Equator, hurricanes have a calm central hole, or eye, surrounded by inward spiralling winds and cumulonimbus clouds.

Hus, Jan (1369–1415) Bohemian religious reformer. He studied and later taught at Prague, where he was ordained

priest. Influenced by the writings of John WYCLIFFE, Hus was excommunicated by Pope Gregory XII in 1411. In *De Ecclesia* (1412), Hus outlined his case for reform of the Church. He was tried by the Council of CONSTANCE (1415) and burned at the stake as a heretic. His followers, known as HUSSITES, launched a civil war against the Holy Roman Empire.

Hussein I (1935–99) HASHEMITE king of Jordan (1953–99). He sought to maintain good relations with the West while supporting the Palestinians' cause in the ARAB-ISRAELI WARS. In 1967, Hussein led Jordan into the SIX-DAY WAR, losing the WEST BANK and East JERUSALEM to Israel. In 1970, he ordered his army to suppress the activities of the PALESTINE LIBERATION ORGANIZATION (PLO) in Jordan. In 1974, he relinquished Jordan's claim to the West Bank to the PLO. In the 1990s, Hussein supported efforts to secure peace in the Middle East, signing a treaty with Israel in 1994, and attending the funeral of Yitzhak RABIN in 1995. His son Abdullah (1962–) succeeded him as King.

Husserl, Edmund (1859–1938) German philosopher, founder of modern PHENOMENOLOGY. He studied man's consciousness as it related to objects and the structure of experience. His works include *Ideas: General Introduction to Pure Phenomenology* (1913) and *Cartesian Meditations* (1931).

Hussites Bohemian and Moravian followers of the 15th-century religious reformer Jan HUS. The execution of Hus in 1415 provoked the Hussite Wars against Emperor SIGISMUND. The Council of Basel (1431) brought peace, but the Taborites, the radical wing of the Hussites, rejected the terms. Sigismund defeated the Taborites at the Battle of Lipany in 1434.

Huston, John (1906–87) US film director, writer, and actor. His debut feature was *The Maltese Falcon* (1941). In 1946, he won a best director Academy Award for *The Treasure of the Sierra Madre*. Other classics followed, such as *Key Largo* (1948), *The Asphalt Jungle* (1950), and *The African Queen* (1951). After a series of critical failures, Huston returned to form with *The Man Who Would Be King* (1975) and *Prizzi's Honor* (1985). His last film was *The Dead* (1987).

Hutter, Jakob (*d.* 1536) Austrian ANABAPTIST and founder of the HUTTERITES. When Anabaptists in the Tyrol were persecuted, Hutter led many followers into Moravia. Charged with heresy, he was burned at the stake.

Hutterites German-speaking Anabaptists practising communal living. The sect originated in Moravia in the 16th century under the leadership of Jacob HUTTER, moved to the Russian Ukraine, and in 1874 to the w USA. Some also live in w Canada. All things are held by them in common ownership and they stress family life, simple ways and pacifism.

Hutton, James (1726–97) Scottish geologist. He sought to formulate theories of the origin of the Earth and of atmospheric changes. Concluding that the Earth's history could be explained only by observing forces currently at work within it, he laid the foundations of modern geological science.

Hutton, Sir Len (Leonard) (1916–90) English cricketer. An opening batsman for Yorkshire, in 1938 he scored 364 against Australia, a world record for 20 years. In 1953 he was the first professional captain of the England team.

Huxley, Aldous Leonard (1894–1963) English novelist, grandson of Thomas HUXLEY. Huxley began his career as a journalist and published several volumes of poetry before his debut novel, *Crome Yellow* (1921). *Point Counter Point* (1928) satirized the hedonism of the 1920s. Huxley's best-known work, *Brave New World* (1932), presents a nightmarish vision of a future society. *Island* (1962) invokes a utopian community. *Eyeless in Gaza* (1936) and *The Doors of Perception* (1954) explore his interest in mysticism and states of consciousness. Among his finest works are the *Collected Short Stories* (1957).

Huxley, Sir Julian Sorell (1887–1975) English biologist, grandson of Thomas HUXLEY, his researches were chiefly on the behaviour of birds and other animals in relation to evolution. Huxley's books include *The Individual in the Animal Kingdom* (1911) and *Evolutionary Ethics* (1943).

Huxley, Thomas Henry (1825–95) English biologist. Huxley was an early champion of Charles DARWIN's theory of evolution. His works include *Zoological Evidences as to Man's*

Place in Nature (1863), *Manual of Comparative Anatomy of Vertebrate Animals* (1871), and *Evolution and Ethics* (1893).

Huysmans, Joris Karl (1848–1907) French novelist of Dutch parentage. He was much admired by Oscar WILDE and other figures of the 1890s for his aestheticism, as revealed in his best known novel *À rebours* (1884; translated as *Against Nature*, 1922), in which the hero experiments with decadence to alleviate his boredom. Huysmans' other work includes the novel *Là bas* (Down There) (1891), a central character of which reappears in his last trilogy (1895–1903) as a loose representation of Huysmans himself.

Hu Yaobang (1915–89) Chinese statesman, general secretary of the Chinese COMMUNIST PARTY (1980–87). He joined the Communists in 1933, and took part in the LONG MARCH. Hu became associated with DENG XIAOPING in the war against Japan (1937–45), during which he served as a political commissar. In 1952 he became head of the Young Communist League, but lost his post (1966) during the CULTURAL REVOLUTION. Hu was rehabilitated after MAO ZEDONG's death (1976). Accused of sympathizing with student demonstrations for democracy, Hu was dismissed. The TIANANMEN SQUARE protests followed his death.

Huygens, Christiaan (1629–95) Dutch physicist and astronomer. In 1655 he discovered Saturn's largest satellite, Titan, and explained that the planet's appearance was due to a broad ring surrounding it. He introduced the convergent eyepiece for telescopes and constructed the first pendulum clock.

hyacinth Bulbous plant native to the Mediterranean region and Africa. It has long, thin leaves and spikes of bell-shaped flowers, which may be white, yellow, red, blue, or purple. Family Liliaceae; genus *Hyacinthus*.

hybrid Offspring of two parents of different GENE composition. It often refers to the offspring of different species of the cross between two separate species. Most inter-species hybrids, such as a MULE (offspring of a female horse and a male ass) are unable to produce fertile offspring.

hybridization Cross-breeding of plants or animals between species to produce offspring that differ in

HUNGARY

The Republic of Hungary is a landlocked country in central Europe. The land is mostly low-lying and drained by the DANUBE (Duna) and its tributary, the Tisza. Most of the land E of the Danube belongs to a region called the Great Plain (*Nagyalföld*), which covers about half of Hungary.

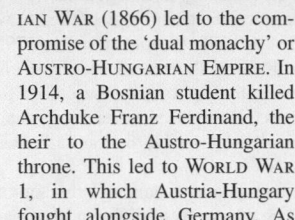

To the W of the Danube is a hilly region, with some low mountains, called Transdanubia. This region contains the country's largest lake, BALATON. In the NW is a small, fertile and mostly flat region called the Little Plain (*Kisalföld*). Much of Hungary's original vegetation has been cleared. Large forests remain in the scenic NE highlands.

CLIMATE
Hungary lies far from the moderating influence of the sea. As a result, summers are warmer and sunnier than in W Europe, and the winters colder.

HISTORY
MAGYARS first arrived in the 9th century. In the 11th century Hungary's first king, Saint STEPHEN, made Roman Catholicism the official religion. In 1222 a parliament was established. In the 14th century, the ANGEVINS extended the Empire. In the Battle of Mohács (1526), the Turks defeated the Hungarians and the country became part of the Ottoman Empire. In 1699, LEOPOLD I expelled the Turks and established HABSBURG control.

Lajos KOSSUTH declared independence in 1848, but FRANZ JOSEPH reasserted control in 1849. Austrian defeat in the AUSTRO-PRUSS-IAN WAR (1866) led to the compromise of the 'dual monachy' or AUSTRO-HUNGARIAN EMPIRE. In 1914, a Bosnian student killed Archduke Franz Ferdinand, the heir to the Austro-Hungarian throne. This led to WORLD WAR 1, in which Austria-Hungary fought alongside Germany. As defeat loomed nationalist demands intensified and, in 1918, Hungary declared independence. The treaty of Versaiiles saw the loss of all non-Magyar territory (60–70% of Hungarian land) to Czechoslovakia, Yugoslavia and Romania. In 1919 communists, led by Béla KUN, briefly held power. In 1920, Miklós HORTHY became regent.

In 1941 Hungary allied with Nazi Germany to regain much of its lost territory. Virulent anti-Semitism saw the extermination of many Hungarian Jews. Hungary's withdrawal from the war led to German occupation in March 1944. The Soviet expulsion of German troops (October 1944–May 1945) devastated much of Hungary. In 1946 Hungary became a republic, headed by Imre NAGY. Despite failing to win a majority in the 1947 elections, the Communist Party took control in 1948 and forced Nagy's resignation.

POLITICS
Hungary became a Communist state in 1949, with a constitution based on that of the Soviet Union. The first leader of the Communist government was Mathias Rákosi, who was replaced in 1953 by Imre Nagy. Nagy sought to relax Communist policies and was forced from office in 1955. He was replaced by Rákosi in 1956 and this led to a major uprising in which many Hungarians were killed or imprisoned. Nagy and his co-workers were executed for treason in 1958. Janos KÁDÁR came to power in the wake of the suppression, but his was a relatively progressive leadership, including elements of political reform and economic liberalism. Despite this, the economic situation worsened in the late 1970s.

Kádár resigned in 1989 and the central Committee of the Socialist Workers' Party (the Communist Party) agreed to sweeping reforms, including the introduction of a pluralist system and a democratic parliament, which had formerly been little more than a rubber-stamp assembly. The trial of Imre Nagy and his co-workers was declared unlawful and their bodies were reburied with honour in June 1989.

In 1990, Hungarians voted into office a centre-right coalition headed by the Democratic Forum. In 1994 the Hungarian Socialist Party, made up of former Communists, won a majority and governed in coalition. In 1998 elections Victor Orbán and the right-wing Fidesz-Hungarian Civic Party took power. In 2002, the Socialists and the Free Democrat coalition, led by Peter Medgyessy, won a majority in parliament. Hungary became a member of NATO and the EU in 2004. In 2006 Socialist PM Ferenc Gyurcsany's frank admissions of government failings and lies led to massive protests, but he refused to resign.

ECONOMY
Under communism the economy was transformed from agrarian to industrial. The new factories were owned by the government, as was most of the land. From the late 1980s, the government worked to increase private ownership. This change of policy caused many problems, including inflation and high rates of unemployment.

Manufacturing is the most valuable activity. The major products include aluminium made from local bauxite, chemicals, electrical and electronic goods, processed food, iron, steel and vehicles. Agriculture remains important, major crops include grapes, maize, potatoes, sugar beet and wheat.

AREA 93,032sq km [35,920sq mi]
POPULATION 9,956,000
CAPITAL (POPULATION) Budapest (1,670,000)
GOVERNMENT Multiparty republic
ETHNIC GROUPS Magyar 90%, Gypsy, German, Serb, Romanian, Slovak
LANGUAGES Hungarian (official)
RELIGIONS Roman Catholic 68%, Calvinist 20%, Lutheran 5%, others
CURRENCY Forint = 100 fillér

genetically determined traits. Changes in climate or in the environment of an organism may give rise to natural hybridization, but most hybrids are produced by human intervention to create organisms that may be hardier or more economical than the original.

Hyderabad City in the River Musi valley, s India; capital of Andhra Pradesh state. Founded in 1589, Hyderabad has a number of notable buildings dating from that time. Industries: tobacco, textiles, handicrafts, vehicle parts. Pop. (2005) 6,145,000.

Hyderabad City on the River INDUS, Sind province, SE Pakistan. Founded in 1768, Hyderabad was the capital of Sind until captured by the British in 1843. Industries: chemicals, pottery, shoes, furniture, handicrafts. Pop. (2005) 1,392,000.

Hydra Largest constellation in the sky. It represents the water snake killed by HERACLES in classical mythology.

hydra Popular name for a group of small, freshwater organisms including the JELLYFISH, CORAL and SEA ANEMONE.

hydrangea Genus of 80 deciduous woody shrubs, small trees ,and vines, native to the w Hemisphere and Asia. They are grown for their showy clusters of flowers, which may be white, pink, or blue. Family Hydrangeaceae.

hydraulics Physical science and technology of the behaviour of FLUIDS in both static and dynamic states. In 1795, English inventor Joseph Bramah created the hydraulic press. In the 19th century, hydraulic power was used for cranes and swing-bridges. Oil replaced water as the main working fluid. Most modern cars have hydraulic brakes. *See also* FLUID MECHANICS

hydrocarbon Organic compound containing only CARBON and HYDROGEN. There are thousands of different hydrocarbons, including open-chain compounds, such as the alkanes (paraffins), alkenes (olefins) and acetylenes. Petroleum, natural gas and coal tar are sources of hydrocarbons.

hydrocephalus Increased volume of cerebrospinal fluid (CSF) in the brain. A condition that exerts dangerous pressure on brain tissue, it can be due to obstruction or a failure of natural reabsorption. In babies, it is congenital; in adults, it may arise from injury or disease. It is treated by insertion of a shunting system to drain the CSF into the abdominal cavity.

hydrochloric acid Solution of hydrogen chloride (HCl) gas in water. It is obtained by the action of sulphuric acid on common salt, as a byproduct of the chlorination of hydrocarbons, or by combination of HYDROGEN and CHLORINE. Hydrochloric acid is used in industry and is produced by humans cells in the stomach lining to allow the enzyme PEPSIN to digest proteins.

hydroelectricity ELECTRICITY generated from the motion of water. In all installations, this ENERGY of movement, or kinetic energy, is first converted into mechanical energy in the spinning blades of a water TURBINE, and then into electricity by the spinning rotor of a GENERATOR. Many power stations are driven by water held back by large DAMS to regulate flow, such as the HOOVER DAM in the USA. Hydroelectric power (HEP) provides cheap energy for mountainous areas with high rainfall.

hydrofoil Boat or ship whose hull is lifted clear of the water, when moving at speed, by submerged wings. They usually have gas-turbine or diesel engines that power propellers or water jets. Speeds range from 30 to 60 knots.

hydrogen (symbol H) Gaseous, nonmetallic element, first identified as a separate element in 1766 by English chemist and physicist Henry CAVENDISH. Colourless and odourless, hydrogen is the lightest and most abundant element in the universe (76% by mass), mostly found combined with oxygen in water. It is used to manufacture AMMONIA by the HABER PROCESS and in rocket fuels. Liquid hydrogen is used in CRYOGENICS, including freezing human bodies with the hope of reviving them in the future. Properties: at.no. 1; r.a.m. 1.00797; r.d. 0.0899; m.p. $-259.1°C$ ($-434.4°F$); b.p. $-252.9°C$ ($-423.2°F$); most common isotope H^1 (99.985%).

hydrogen bomb (H-bomb) NUCLEAR WEAPON developed by the USA in the late 1940s, and first exploded in 1952 in the Pacific. The explosion results from NUCLEAR FUSION when hydrogen nuclei are joined to form helium nuclei, releasing great destructive energy and radioactive fallout. An atomic bomb is used as the trigger.

hydrogen peroxide Liquid compound of hydrogen and oxygen (H_2O_2). It is prepared by electrolytic oxidation of sulphuric acid, and by methods involving reduction of oxygen. Hydrogen peroxide is used as a bleach, a disinfectant, and an oxidizer for rocket fuel and submarine propellant. Properties: r.d. 1.44; m.p. $-0.9°C$ (30.4°F); b.p. 150°C (302°F).

hydrogen sulphide Colourless, poisonous gas (H_2S) with the smell of bad eggs. It is found in crude oil, and can be produced by decaying matter. Industrially it is prepared by the action of sulphuric acid on metal sulphides. Properties: m.p. $-85.5°C$ ($-121.9°F$), b.p. $-60.7°C$ ($-77.3°F$).

hydrological cycle (water cycle) Circulation of through land, air, and sea. Water evaporates from the sea; most falls back into the oceans, but CLOUD carries some over land. There it falls as precipitation, and by surface run off or infiltration and seepage, it gradually finds its way back to the sea. Less than 1% of the world's water is involved in this cycle.

hydrology Study of the Earth's waters, their sources, circulation, distribution, uses, and chemical and physical composition. The HYDROLOGICAL CYCLE is the Earth's natural water circulation system. Hydrologists concern themselves with the provision of freshwater, building dams and irrigation systems, and controlling floods and water pollution.

hydrolysis Chemical reaction in which molecules are split into smaller molecules by reaction with water; often assisted by a CATALYST. For example, in digestion, ENZYMES catalyse the hydrolysis of CARBOHYDRATES, PROTEINS, and FATS into smaller, soluble molecules that the body can assimilate.

hydrophyte (aquatic plant) Plant that grows only in water or in damp places. Examples include WATER LILIES, WATER HYACINTH, DUCKWEED, and various PONDWEEDS.

hydroponics (soil-less culture or tank farming) Plants grow with their roots in a solution or a moist inert medium (such as gravel) containing the necessary nutrients, instead of soil.

hydrotherapy Use of water within the body or on its surface to treat disease. It is often used in conjunction with PHYSIOTHERAPY.

hydroxide Inorganic chemical compound containing the group -OH, which acts as a BASE. Household ammonia is an example. The strong inorganic bases such as potassium hydroxide (KOH) dissociate (break down) in water almost completely to provide many hydroxyl ions.

hydrozoa Class of animals without backbones, all living in water, belonging to the phylum Coelenterata. They vary

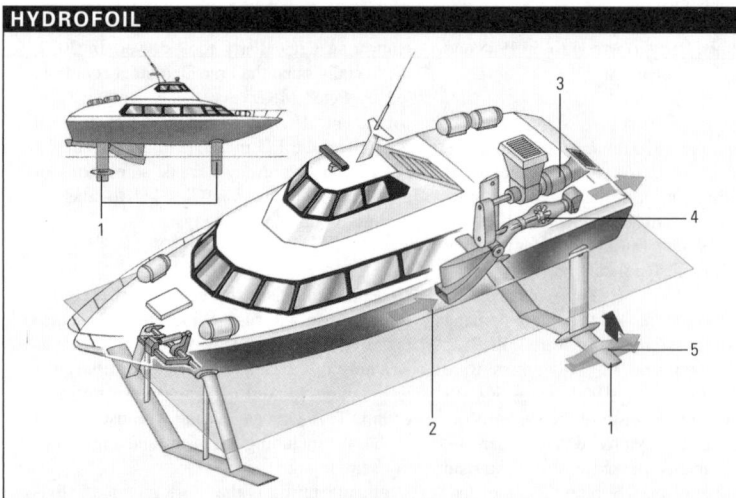

HYDROFOIL

Hydrofoils use the lift of underwater wings (1) to push the body of the boat out of the water. This lessens the drag allowing the boat to travel faster. The Boeing Jetfoil (shown) scoops up water (2) and uses gas turbines (3) to drive high-pressure pumps (4) that throw the water from the rear, creating thrust. The jetfoil can reach speeds of up to 75km/h (45 mph). The hydrofoil works in water the same way an aerofoil does in air. A low-pressure zone is created above the top surface of the hydrofoil, sucking and pushing the wing upwards (5).

in shape and size from the large PORTUGUESE MAN-OF-WAR to the simple HYDRA.

hyena Predatory and scavenging carnivore native to Africa and s Asia. The spotted or laughing hyena (*Crocuta crocuta*) of the sub-Sahara is the largest. Other species include the brown hyena (*Hyaena brunnea*) of s Africa. Weight: 27–80kg (60–176lb). Family Hyaenidae.

hygrometer Instrument used to measure the HUMIDITY of the atmosphere or a gas. One type, the psychrometer, compares the wet and dry bulb temperatures of the air; other types measure absorption or condensation of moisture from the air, or chemical or electrical changes caused by that moisture.

Hyksos Invaders, probably from Palestine, of EGYPT in the 17th century BC. They are attributed with the first use of horses and chariots. They ruled Egypt from *c*.1674 to 1567 BC as the 15th and 16th dynasties. A native revolt overthrew the Hyskos.

Hymen In Greek mythology, god of marriage. Son of APOLLO, he is represented as a youth attending APHRODITE.

hymn Song of praise or gratitude to a god or hero. The oldest forms are found in ancient Egyptian and Greek writings and in the Old Testament psalms of rejoicing. In strict Christian church usage, hymns are religious songs sung by the choir and congregation in a church, distinct from a psalm or a canticle. Hymns, both old and new, are now regular features of church services.

Hypatia (*d*. 415) Early female philosopher. A Greek living in Alexandria, she was one of the first women to practice and teach mathematics, philosophy and astronomy. A pagan, she followed NEOPLATONISM but encouraged rational, rather than mystical, thought. She was killed by a Christian mob.

hyperbola Curve (a CONIC section) formed by cutting a right circular cone with a plane so the plane has a smaller angle with its axis than the side of the cone. The plane curve traced out by a point that moves so that its distance from a fixed point bears a constant ratio, greater than one, to its distance from a fixed straight line. The fixed point is the focus, the ratio is the eccentricity, and the fixed line is the directrix. Its standard equation in Cartesian co-ordinates x and y is $x^2/a^2y^2/b^2 = 1$.

hyperbole Rhetorical device in which an obvious exaggeration is used to create an effect without being meant literally, such as "the music is loud enough to wake the dead".

hyperglycaemia Condition in which blood-sugar level is abnormally high. It can occur in a number of diseases, most notably DIABETES. *See also* HYPOGLYCAEMIA

Hyperion In Greek mythology, sometimes said to be the original Sun god. He was one of the TITANS, the son of URANUS and Gaea, and the father of HELIOS (the Sun), SELENE (the Moon) and Eos (the dawn). He is the subject of an incomplete epic poem (1818–19) of the same name by John KEATS.

hypertension Persistent high BLOOD PRESSURE. It can damage blood vessels and may increase the risk of strokes or heart disease. *See also* HYPOTENSION

hyperthermia Abnormally high body temperature, usually defined as being 41°C (105.8°F) or more. It is usually due to over-heating (as in HEATSTROKE) or FEVER.

hyperthyroidism Excessive production of thyroid HORMONE, with enlargement of the THYROID GLAND. Symptoms include protrusion of the eyeballs, rapid heart rate, high blood pressure, accelerated metabolism, and weight loss. *See also* HYPOTHYROIDISM

hyperventilation Rapid breathing that is not brought about by physical exertion. It reduces the carbon dioxide level in the blood, producing dizziness, tingling and tightness in the chest; it may cause loss of consciousness.

hypnosis State of relaxation and suggestibility brought about by interaction between a hypnotist and a subject. The exact nature of hypnosis is unclear. Hypnosis is put to many uses, from stage entertainment to treatment for pain and addiction, and it is sometimes used in PSYCHOANALYSIS.

hypochondria (hypochondriasis) Neurotic condition characterized by an exaggerated concern with ill health. Hypochondriacs imagine they have serious diseases and often consult several doctors in the hope of a 'cure'.

hypodermic syringe Surgical instrument for injecting fluids beneath the skin into a muscle or blood vessel. It

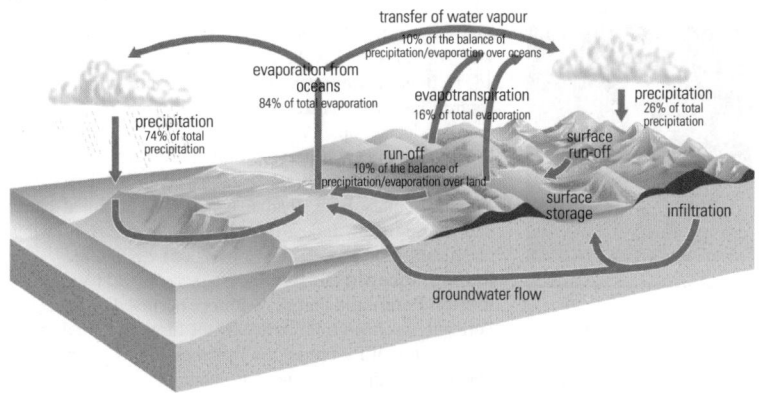

comprises a graduated tube containing a piston plunger, connected to a hollow needle. *See also* INJECTION

hypoglycaemia Abnormally low level of sugar in the blood. It may result from fasting, excess INSULIN in the blood, or various metabolic and glandular diseases, notably DIABETES. Symptoms include dizziness, headache, sweating, and mental confusion. *See also* HYPERGLYCAEMIA

hypotension Condition in which BLOOD PRESSURE is abnormally low. It is commonly seen after heavy blood loss or excessive fluid loss due to prolonged vomiting or diarrhoea. It also occurs in many serious illnesses. Temporary hypotension may cause sweating, dizziness, and fainting. *See also* HYPERTENSION

hypotenuse Side opposite the right angle in a right-angled triangle. It is the longest side of the triangle and is important for PYTHAGORAS theorem

hypothalamus Region at the base of the brain containing centres that regulate body temperature, fluid balance, hunger, thirst, and sexual activity. It is also involved in emotions, sleep, and the integration of HORMONE and nervous activity.

hypothermia Fall in body temperature to below 35°C. Most at risk are newborns and the elderly. Insidious in onset, it can progress to coma and death. Hypothermia is sometimes induced during surgery to lower the body's oxygen demand. It occurs naturally in animals during HIBERNATION.

hypothesis Assumption or proposal made in order to account for or correlate known facts. Consequences inferred from a hypothesis are put to further inquiry, thus enabling the assumption to be tested in a particular situation. A set of hypotheses, logically connected and leading to the prediction of a wide range of naturally occurring events or states, is called a theory.

hypothyroidism Deficient functioning of the THYROID GLAND. Congenital hypothyroidism can lead to cretinism in children. In adults, the condition is called **myxoedema**. More common in women, it causes physical and mental slowness, weight gain, sensitivity to cold, and susceptibility to infection. It can be due to a defect of the gland or a lack of iodine in the diet. It is treated with the hormone thyroxine.

hyrax Small, rodent-like, herbivorous, mammal of Africa and sw Asia, with a squat, furry body and short ears, legs and tail. Rock hyraxes (genus *Procavia*) living in deserts and hills are larger than the solitary, nocturnal, tree-dwelling hyraxes (genus *Dendrohyrax*). Length: to 50cm (20in). Family Procaviidae.

hysterectomy Removal of the UTERUS, possibly with surrounding structures. It is performed to treat fibroids or cancer or to put an end to excessive menstrual bleeding.

hysteresis Phenomenon occurring in the magnetic and elastic behaviour of substances in which the strain is greater when the stress is decreasing than when it is increasing because of a lag in the effect. When the stress disappears, a residual strain remains.

hysteria In traditional psychology, a group of disorders characterized by emotional instability, dissociation, hallucinations, and physical symptoms with no physiological cause. Hysteria is no longer used as a diagnostic term. Researchers in this field included Jean Martin CHARCOT, Pierre Janet, and Sigmund FREUD.

I/i, ninth letter of the Roman alphabet, is derived from the Semitic letter yod, meaning hand. It passed to the Greek alphabet, where it was known as iota. In the Roman alphabet it was pronounced ee.

▲ **ibis** The scarlet ibis (*Eudocimus ruber*) is found in marsh regions of tropical South America. It grows to a height of some 60cm (24in). It has distinctive scarlet plumage with black wing tips.

▲ **Ibsen** Norwegian playwright Henrik Ibsen is often considered the father of modern drama. He was among the first dramatists to tackle contemporary social issues in a naturalistic manner.

Iasi City in NE Romania, 16km (10mi) from the frontier with Moldova. It was the capital of Moldavia from 1562–1861. It is an important commercial and administrative centre. Industries: textiles, machinery, pharmaceuticals, food products. Pop. (1997) 348,399.

Ibadan City in SW Nigeria, *c.*145km (90mi) NNE of Lagos; capital of Oyo state. It was established in the 1830s as a Yoruba military base. Ibadan handles the regional cacao and cotton trades. Industries: plastics, cigarettes, brewing, chemicals, food processing. Pop. (2005) 2,375,000.

Ibañez, Vicente Blasco *See* BLASCO IBÁÑEZ, VICENTE

Iberian Peninsula Part of SW Europe occupied by Spain and Portugal, separated from Africa by the Strait of Gibraltar and from the rest of Europe by the Pyrenees. It was colonized by Phoenicians, then Carthaginians until the 2nd century BC when Rome dominated. The 4th-century Visigothic incursions were followed by Moorish invasions from North Africa. By the 15th century, the Christian reconquest of the Peninsula was virtually complete. Area: 596,384sq km (230,264sq mi).

ibex Any of several species of wild GOAT. The long, backward-curving horns grow up to 1.5m (5ft) long on the male, and both sexes have long, yellow-brown hair. Ibexes are renowned for their agility. Height: 85cm (3ft) at shoulder. Family Bovidae.

ibis Tropical lagoon and marsh wading bird with long, down-curved bill, long neck and lanky legs. Closely related to the SPOONBILL, it may be black, whitish or brightly coloured. It feeds on small animals, and nests in colonies. Length: 60–90cm (2–3ft). Subfamily: Threskiornithidae.

Ibiza Island of Spain, 130km (80mi) off the E coast, in the W Mediterranean; part of the Balearic group. The mild climate and beautiful scenery have made Ibiza a major tourist resort. Other activities: fishing, salt mining, cultivating figs and olives. Area: 572sq km (221sq mi). Pop. (2001) 94,334.

Ibn Batuta (1304?-68?) Arab traveller and writer. Born in Tangier, Morocco, he began his adventures in *c.*1325 with a pilgrimage to Mecca by way of Egypt and Syria. Travel was to occupy the next 30 years of his life, when he visited parts of Africa, Asia and Europe. In *c.*1350, he returned to Morocco to write an account of his travels.

Ibrahim Pasha (1789–1848) Egyptian general and governor, son of MUHAMMAD ALI. He campaigned (1816–18) against the Wahhabis of Arabia and fought the Greek insurgents until the Ottoman defeat at NAVARINO (1827). When his father defied Ottoman supremacy, Ibrahim conquered Syria (1832–33) and became its governor until forced to withdraw in 1841.

Ibsen, Henrik Johan (1828–1906) Norwegian playwright and poet. His first play was *Catilina* (1850), but he became internationally known for the drama, *Peer Gynt* (1867). The NATURALISM of Ibsen's presentation of social issues in tragedies such as *A Doll's House* (1879), *Ghosts* (1881) and *Hedda Gabler* (1890) established his reputation. His later works, such as *The Master Builder* (1892), are more symbolic.

Icarus In Greek mythology, the son of DAEDALUS, architect of the LABYRINTH for MINOS of Crete. Imprisoned by Minos, Daedalus made wings of feathers and wax in order for the pair to escape. He was successful, but Icarus flew too near the Sun, which melted his wings, and he fell into the sea and drowned.

ice Water frozen to 0°C (32°F) or below, when it forms complex six-sided crystals. It is less dense than water. When water vapour condenses below freezing point, ice crystals form. Clusters of crystals form snowflakes. *See also* GLACIER

Ice Ages Periods in the Earth's history when ice-sheets and GLACIERS advance to cover areas previously not affected by ice. There is evidence of at least six Ice Ages having occurred throughout the Earth's history, the earliest dating back to 2.3 billion years ago. The best known is the most recent Ice Age, which began *c.*2 million years ago and lasted until the retreat of the ice to its present extent *c.*10,000 years ago. The last Ice Age produced many of the landforms seen in northern continents and affected sea level on a global scale.

iceberg Large drifting piece of ice, broken from a GLACIER or polar ICE-CAP. In the N Hemisphere, the main source of icebergs is the SW coast of Greenland. In the S Hemisphere, glacial flow from Antarctica releases huge tabular icebergs.

ice-cap Small ice-sheet, often in the shape of a flattened dome, which spreads over the mountains and valleys of polar islands. The floating ice fields surrounding the North Pole are sometimes incorrectly called an ice-cap.

ice hockey Sport played on an ice rink, in which two teams of six players wearing ice skates and protective clothing use sticks to propel a vulcanized rubber disc (puck) into the opponents' goal. The rink is usually 61m × 26m (200ft × 85ft) and is evenly divided into three zones – attacking, neutral and defending – each 18.3m (60ft) long. The goals are within the playing area, 3 to 4m (10–15ft) from each back line. Games consist of three 20–minute periods of timed play. Substitutions are allowed at any time, and the game is controlled by a referee and two linesmen. A penalized player may be banished to the 'sin bin' for two or more minutes: his team meanwhile remains a player short on the ice unless their opponents score. The National Hockey League (NHL) of North America was instituted in 1917. The major trophy is the Stanley Cup. The sport has been included in the Winter Olympics since 1920.

Iceland Small Scandinavian republic in the North Atlantic Ocean. *See* country feature.

Icelandic Official language of Iceland, spoken by virtually all of the island's 282,849 inhabitants. It belongs to the Germanic family of INDO-EUROPEAN LANGUAGES. It is descended from Old Norse, which was taken to Iceland by Norwegian Vikings in the 9th and 10th centuries AD.

Icelandic literature Early Icelandic literature emerged in the 13th century from the oral tradition of Eadic and Skaldic poetry, both of which were influenced by ancient Icelandic mythology. Other early writings (14th-16th centuries) include the sagas of Norse monarchs, translations of foreign romances and religious works. From the 14th to 19th centuries, the *rímur*, a narrative verse poem, was the dominant form. The 19th century was probably the most important period in the development of Icelandic literature, with the rise of Icelandic realism late in the period. Important 20th-century writers include Gunnar Gunnarsson (1889–1975) and Halldór LAXNESS.

Iceni Ancient British tribe that occupied the area now known as Norfolk and Suffolk. The territory had been ruled by Prasutagus, a client-king, but on his death (AD 60) the Romans attempted to annex it. This led to a widespread revolt led by Prasutagus' queen, BOADICEA. The Iceni sacked Colchester, London and St Albans before they were crushed by the Roman governor, Suetonius Paulinus.

ice skating Winter leisure activity and all-year-round indoor sport in which participants use steel skates to glide on ice. In competition, **solo** and **pairs** skating comprise compulsory figure skating, a short programme of compulsory elements and free skating to music. **Ice dancing** is structured similarly but based on set styles of dancing. **Speed** skating has two disciplines: international-track and short-track.

I Ching *See* BOOK OF CHANGES

ichneumon fly Parasitic insect that attacks other insects and spiders. Found worldwide, they are characterized by an ovipositor that is often longer than the body. They are usually 1cm (0.4in) long. Family Ichneumonidae.

icon Religious painting or sculpture, often of Christ, the Virgin and Child or individual saints. The term is particularly used of Byzantine pictures and later Russian imitations. Icons were were produced as early as the 5th century and have been used as an aid to prayer from the 6th century. In the Eastern Christian Church the veneration of icons was banned (726–843).

iconography Study and interpretation of themes and symbols in the figurative arts. In the 18th century the term referred to the classification of ancient monuments by motifs and subjects, but by the 19th it was more specifically concerned with symbolism in Christian art. Modern iconographers also study secular art and that of religions other than Christianity.

id In psychoanalytic theory, the deepest level of the personality. It includes primitive drives (hunger, anger, sex) demanding instant gratification. Even after the EGO and the SUPEREGO develop and limit these instinctual impulses, the id is a source of motivation and often of unconscious conflicts.

Idaho State in NW USA, on the border with Canada; the capital and largest city is BOISE. The discovery of gold in 1860

ICELAND

The Republic of Iceland, though deemed part of Europe, is closer to Greenland than Scotland. In the N Atlantic Ocean, sits on the Mid-Atlantic Ridge, the geological boundary between Europe and N America. The island is slowly getting wider as the ocean is stretched apart by plate tectonics.

Iceland has around 200 volcanoes and eruptions are frequent. An eruption under the Vatnajökull ice cap in 1996 created a subglacial lake which subsequently burst, causing severe flooding. Geysers and hot springs are other volcanic features. During the thousand years that Iceland has been settled, between 150 and 200 volcanic eruptions have occurred. Ice caps and glaciers cover about one-eighth of the land. The only habitable regions are the coastal lowlands.

Vegetation is sparse or non-existent on 75% of the land. Treeless grassland or bogs cover some areas. Deep fjords fringe the coast.

CLIMATE

Although Iceland lies far to the N, its climate is moderated by the warmth of the Gulf Stream. The port of Reykjavik is ice-free all year.

HISTORY

Iceland was colonized by Vikings from Norway in AD 874, and the population grew as more settlers arrived from Norway and from the Viking colonies in the British Isles. In 930 the settlers

founded what is thought to be the world's first parliament, known as the Althing. One early settler was Erik the Red, a Viking who sailed to Greenland in about 982 and founded colony there in about 985. Iceland was an independent country until 1262 when, following a series of civil wars, the Althing recognized the rule of the king of Norway. When Norway united with Denmark in 1380, Iceland came under the rule of Danish kingdoms.

During the colonial period, Iceland lost much of its population due to migration, disease and natural disaster. The Black Death, which swept the island in 1402, killed two-thirds of the population. In the late 18th century, volcanic eruptions destroyed crops, farmland and livestock, causing a famine. Then, during the Napoleonic Wars in the early 19th century, food supplies from Europe failed to reach the island and many starved.

When Norway was separated from Denmark in 1814, Iceland remained under Danish rule. The late 19th century saw mounting demands for self-government. In 1918, Iceland was acknowledged as a self-governing sovereign state, but remained united with Denmark through a common monarch. During World War 2, when Germany occupied Denmark, British and American troops landed in Iceland to protect it from invasion by the Germans. Finally, following a referendum in which 97% of the people voted to cut all ties with Denmark, Iceland became a fully independent republic on 17 June 1944. In 1946, it joined the North Atlantic Treaty Organization (NATO). The USA maintained military bases on Iceland. In 1970, Iceland joined the European Free Trade Association.

POLITICS

Fishing, on which Iceland's economy is based, is a major political issue. From 1975 Iceland extended its territorial waters to 200 nautical miles, causing skirmishes between Icelandic and British vessels. The issue was resolved in 1977 when Britain withdrew. Problems developed in the late 1980s when overfishing caused depletion of cod stocks, leading Iceland to

AREA 103,000sq km [39,768sq mi]
POPULATION 302,000
CAPITAL (POPULATION) Reykjavik (110,000)
GOVERNMENT Multiparty republic
ETHNIC GROUPS Icelandic 97%, Danish 1%
LANGUAGES Icelandic (official)
RELIGIONS Evangelical Lutheran 87%, other Protestant 4%, Roman Catholic 2%, others
CURRENCY Icelandic króna = 100 aurar

reduce catch quotas. The reduction of the fish catch led to a slowdown in the economy and, eventually, to a recession. The economy recovered in the mid-1990s when the conservation measures appeared to have been successful. Iceland left the International Whaling Commission in 1992, because of its alleged anti-whaling policy. It rejoined in 2002, but in 2003 undertook its first whale hunt for 15 years, claiming that it was a scientific catch to study whales' impact on fish stocks.

Iceland has no armed forces of its own. However, it joined NATO in 1949 and, under a NATO agreement, the United States maintained a large base on the island. This became unpopular after the Cold War ended, and in 2006 the US agreed to withdraw.

ECONOMY

Iceland has few resources other than the fishing grounds that surround it. Fishing and fish processing are major industries which dominate Iceland's overseas trade. Overfishing is an economic problem.

Barely 1% of the land is used to grow crops, mainly root vegetables and fodder for livestock. However, 23% of the country is used for grazing sheep and cattle. Iceland is self-sufficient in meat and dairy products. Vegetables and fruits are grown in greenhouses heated by water from hot springs.

Manufacturing is important. Products include aluminium, cement, clothing, electrical equipment, fertilizers and processed foods. Geothermal power is an important energy source.

---

brought many immigrants, although the Native-American population was not subdued until 1877. The state was admitted to the Union in 1890 and soon began to develop its resources. The terrain is dominated by the Rocky Mountains and is drained chiefly by the Snake River, whose waters are used to generate hydroelectricity and for irrigation. Principal crops are potatoes, hay, wheat and sugar beet, and cattle are reared. Silver, lead, antimony and zinc are mined. Industries: timber. Area: 216,412sq km (83,557sq mi). Pop. (2000) 1,293,953.

ideal gas law Law relating pressure, temperature and volume of a hypothetical ideal (perfect) gas: $pV = NkT$, where N is the number of molecules of the gas, and k is a constant of proportionality. This law implies that at constant temperature (T), the product of pressure and volume (pV) is constant (BOYLE'S LAW); and at constant pressure, the volume is proportional to the temperature (CHARLES' LAW).

idealism Philosophical doctrine that assigns metaphysical priority to the mental over the material. It denies the claim within REALISM that material things exist independently of the MIND. Idealism in the West dates from the teachings of PLATO. The term is also applied to artistic pursuits to denote a rendering of something 'as it ought to be' rather than as it actually is.

ideology Collection of beliefs or ideas reflecting the interests and aspirations of a country or its political system. In the 20th century, the term has been applied to various political theories, including FASCISM, MARXISM, and COMMUNISM.

Ides Day in the Roman Republican calendar. They fell on the eighth day after the nones of each month, that is on the 15th of March, May, July and October and on the 13th of the other months. Julius CAESAR was assassinated on the Ides of March.

Igbo (Ibo) Kwa-speaking people of E NIGERIA. Originally, their patrilineal society consisted of politically and socially autonomous village units, but in the 20th century political unity developed in reaction to British colonial rule. In 1967, the Igbo attempted to secede from Nigeria as the Republic of Biafra.

Ignatius of Antioch, Saint (active 1st century AD) Bishop of Antioch, and influential theologian of the early Christian Church. On his way to Rome, where he died for his faith, he wrote his seven *Epistles*, which are valuable sources for an assessment of the doctrine of the early Church.

Ignatius of Loyola, Saint (1491–1556) Spanish soldier, churchman and founder of the JESUITS. In 1534, with FRANCIS XAVIER and other young men, he made vows of poverty, chastity and obedience. He was ordained to the priesthood in

IDAHO
Statehood :
July 3, 1890
Nickname :
Gem state
State bird :
Mountain bluebird
State flower :
Mock orange
State tree :
Western white pine
State motto :
It is perpetual

I

▲ **iguana** The common iguana (*Iguana iguana*) is one of the world's largest lizards, growing up to 2m (6.5ft) in length. It lives near rivers in tropical America. The young feed mainly on insects, adults on leaves and fruit.

ILLINOIS

ILLINOIS
Statehood:
December 3, 1818
Nickname:
Prairie state
State bird:
Cardinal
State flower:
Native violet
State tree:
Oak
State motto:
State sovereignty,
national union

1537 and moved to Rome where, in 1540, Paul III approved his request to found a religious order: the Society of Jesus, or Jesuits. He stayed in Rome supervising the order, which became the leading force in the COUNTER-REFORMATION.

igneous rock One of three major classes of rock produced by the cooling and solidifying of molten MAGMA. All igneous rocks are crystalline and most resist erosion. **Extrusive**, or volcanic, igneous rocks, such as BASALT, form by the rapid cooling of molten material at the surface. **Intrusive**, or hyperbyssal, rocks, such as dolerite, form in SILLS or dykes at intermediate depth. **Plutonic** rocks, such as GRANITE, form in BATHOLITHS at greater depth. The major chemical constituent is SILICA. **Acid** rocks contain high amounts of QUARTZ, FELDSPAR or MICA, and are light coloured. **Basic** rocks are darker and contain 45–55% silica, including minerals such as HORNBLENDE. *See also* METAMORPHIC ROCK; SEDIMENTARY ROCK

iguana Any of numerous species of terrestrial, arboreal (tree-dwelling), burrowing or aquatic LIZARDS that live in tropical America and the Galápagos Islands. The common iguana (*Iguana iguana*) is greenish-brown, with a serrated dewlap and a crest along its back. Length: to 2m (6.5ft). Family Iguanidae.

Ijsselmeer Large lake in the NW Netherlands. It was formed in 1932 by the completion of a dyke that divided the Zuider Zee into the saline Wadden Zee and the freshwater Ijsselmeer. Length of dyke: 32km (20mi). Area: 1200sq km (460sq mi).

ileum Major part of the small INTESTINE, *c*.4m (13ft) long. Its inner wall is lined with finger-like villi, which increase the area for the absorption of nutrients.

Iliescu, Ion (1930–) Romanian statesman and president (1990–96, 2001–2004). In 1971 he became propaganda secretary in Nicolae CEAUSESCU's regime, but was later banished to Timisoara for his opposition to Ceausescu's growing cult of the personality. Following the 'Christmas Revolution' (1989) and the execution of Ceausescu, Iliescu was elected president. He was succeeded by Emil Constantinescu, but re-elected in 2000.

Illinois State in N central USA, on the E bank of the Mississippi; the capital is SPRINGFIELD. Illinois was explored first by the French in 1673. Ceded to Britain in 1763, it was occupied by American troops during the American Revolution and became a state of the Union in 1818. The land is generally flat and is drained by rivers flowing SW to the Mississippi. Its fertile soil supports crops such as hay, oats and barley; livestock farming is also important. Mineral deposits are found in the S. CHICAGO is a transport centre and port on Lake MICHIGAN. Area: 146,075sq km (56,400sq mi). Pop. (2000) 12,419,293.

illiteracy Inability to read and write. It is estimated that about one billion adults in the world (about one in five of the world's population) are unable to read.

illumination Coloured decorations serving to beautify manuscripts of religious books, the earliest dating from about the 5th century. The style ranges from decoration of initial letters and borders to miniatures and full-page illustrations. Glowing colours and the use of gold leaf are common features. Early medieval illuminations were produced by monks. Illumination was at its height during the 14th and 15th centuries when the International Gothic style was in use by such Flemish and French artists as the LIMBOURG brothers and Jean FOUQUET.

Illyria Historic region on the N and E shores of the Adriatic Sea, now mainly in Albania. The tribes of Illyria were conquered by the Romans after 168 BC and the region was later divided into the provinces of Dalmatia and Pannonia.

image In optics, representation of an object produced when rays of light from the object are either reflected by a MIRROR or refracted by a LENS. A **real** image can be projected onto a screen and recorded in a photograph; a **virtual** image, such as that produced by a plane mirror, cannot.

imaginary number In mathematics, the SQUARE ROOT ($\sqrt{\,}$) of a negative quantity. The simplest, $\sqrt{-1}$, is usually represented by *i*. The NUMBERS are so called because when first discovered they were widely regarded as meaningless. But they are necessary for the solution of many QUADRATIC EQUATIONS, the roots of which can be expressed only as COMPLEX NUMBERS, which are composed of a real part and an imaginary part.

imagism Movement in poetry that flourished in the USA and England from 1912 to 1917. The imagists believed that poetry should use the language and flexible rhythms of common speech. Amy LOWELL, their principal exponent, produced three anthologies called *Some Imagist Poets* (1915–17). Among its most distinguished contributors was Ezra POUND.

imago Adult, reproductive stage of an insect that has undergone full METAMORPHOSIS. Imagos are the winged insects, such as butterflies and dragonflies, that emerge from PUPAS or develop from NYMPHS.

Imam Leader of a Muslim community invested with various forms of spiritual or temporal authority. It may describe a man who leads public prayers at a mosque. The word *Imam* is also a title of honour for Islamic theologians and religious leaders, such as the AGA KHAN. It is the title borne by any of a succession of spiritual guides and intercessors for the SHI'ITE Muslims.

IMF Abbreviation of INTERNATIONAL MONETARY FUND

Immaculate Conception Roman Catholic belief that the Blessed Virgin MARY was free of all ORIGINAL SIN from the moment of her conception. It was defined as a dogma by Pope PIUS IX in 1854.

immune system System by which the body defends itself against disease. It involves many kinds of LEUCOCYTES (white blood cells) in the blood, lymph and bone marrow. Some of the cells (B-cells) make ANTIBODIES against invading microbes and other foreign bodies (ANTIGENS), or neutralize TOXINS produced by PATHOGENS, while other antibodies encourage two types of leucocytes, PHAGOCYTES and MACROPHAGES, to attack and digest invaders. T-CELLS also provide a variety of functions in the immune system. *See also* INTERFERON

immunity In medicine, protection or resistance to DISEASE. Genetic factors and general health influence **Innate** immunity. **Acquired** immunity is the body's second line of defence. An infecting agent stimulates the IMMUNE SYSTEM to respond to the presence of ANTIGENS. In **cell-mediated** immunity sensitized cells react directly with the antigen. This form of immunity is suppressed by HUMAN IMMUNODEFICIENCY VIRUS (HIV). Immunity may be induced artificially by IMMUNIZATION.

immunization Conferring IMMUNITY against disease by artificial means. Passive immunity may be conferred by the injection of an antiserum containing antibodies. Active immunization involves vaccination with dead or attenuated (weakened) organisms to stimulate production of specific antibodies and so provide lasting immunity.

immunoglobulin PROTEIN found in the BLOOD that plays a role in the IMMUNE SYSTEM. Immunoglobulins act as ANTIBODIES for specific ANTIGENS. They can be obtained from donor plasma and injected into people at risk of particular diseases.

immunosuppressive drug Any drug that suppresses the body's immune responses to infection or 'foreign' tissue. Such drugs are used to prevent rejection of transplanted organs and to treat autoimmune disease and some cancers.

impala (or pala) Long-legged, medium-sized African antelope. Long, lyrate horns are found only on the males. Both sexes have sleek, glossy brown fur with black markings on the rump. Length: to 1.5m (5ft); height: to 1m (3.3ft) at the shoulder. Family Bovidae; species *Aepyceros melampus*.

impatiens (busy Lizzies) Genus of 450 species of succulent annual plants, mostly native to the tropics of Asia and Africa. They have white, red or yellow flowers and seedpods that, when ripe, pop and scatter their seeds. Some species are known as touch-me-not. Family Balsaminaceae.

impeachment Prosecution of a public official by the legislature of a state.

impedance (symbol Z) Property of a component in an electric CIRCUIT that opposes the passage of current. In a **direct current (DC)** circuit, the impedance corresponds to the RESISTANCE (R). In an **alternating current (AC)** circuit with CAPACITANCE or INDUCTANCE, the additional property of reactance (X) has to be allowed for, as expressed in the equation $Z^2 = R^2 + X^2$. All of these quantities are measured in *ohms*.

imperialism Domination of one people or state by another. Imperialism can be economic, cultural, political or religious. From the 16th century, trading empires were set up by major European powers such as the British, Spanish, French, Portuguese and Dutch. They penetrated Africa, Asia and N

America, their colonies serving as a source of raw materials and a market for manufactured goods. Imperialism often imposed alien cultures on native societies. *See also* COLONIALISM

imperial system System of WEIGHTS AND MEASURES based on the foot, pound and the second. It has largely been replaced by the METRIC SYSTEM of SI UNITS, but continues in the US, and to a lesser degree in the UK, for non-scientific measurements.

impetigo Contagious skin condition caused by streptococcal or staphylococcal infection. It causes multiple, spreading lesions with yellowish-brown crusts.

impotence In men, the inability to perform SEXUAL INTERCOURSE through lack of an erection. It may be temporary or permanent, brought about by illness, injury, the effects of certain drugs, fatigue or psychological factors.

Impressionism French anti-academic art movement of the late 19th century, gaining its name from a painting by MONET entitled *Impression, Sunrise* (1874). Impressionists aimed to create 'a spontaneous work rather than a calculated one'. In the 1860s, Monet, RENOIR, Sisley and Frédéric Bazille explored the possibilities of painting outdoors, analysing and interpreting the effects of light on nature. The first impressionist exhibition took place in 1874. Although not accepted at first, Impressionism became influential from the late 1880s. DEGAS and PISSARRO were prominent and CÉZANNE exhibited with them twice. MANET was influenced by and influenced Impressionism. Other Impressionists include Berthe Morisot and Mary CASSATT. RODIN has been called Impressionist because of his interest in the effects of light on sculpture. In music, the term Impressionism refers to a period lasting from roughly 1890 to 1930, and is usually applied to the work of Claude DEBUSSY. It tends to be subtle and atmospheric rather than overtly emotional. Many composers were influenced by Debussy, including Maurice RAVEL and Frederick DELIUS. *See also* ROMANTICISM

imprinting Form of LEARNING that occurs in a critical period in very young animals. A complex relationship develops between a newborn and the first animate object it encounters; this is usually a parent. The future emotional development of the infant depends upon this relationship. Imprinting in birds has been studied by Konrad LORENZ.

inbreeding Mating of two closely blood-related organisms. Over successive generations it causes much less variation in GENOTYPE (genetic makeup) and PHENOTYPE (physical characteristics) than is normal in a wild population. It usually has harmful results, although if carefully controlled it can be used to enhance specific traits in domesticated plants and animals.

Inca South American people who migrated from the Peruvian highlands into the CUZCO area in *c.*AD 1250. They consolidated their empire steadily until the reigns of Pachacuti (r.1438–71) and his son, Topa (r.1471–93), when Inca dominance extended over most of the continent W of the Andes. Although highly organized on bureaucratic lines, the Empire collapsed when the Spanish invasion (1532), led by PIZARRO, coincided with a civil war between ATAHUALPA and Huáscar. *See also* CENTRAL AND SOUTH AMERICAN MYTHOLOGY; MACHU PICCHU

incandescence Emission of light by a substance at a high temperature. An incandescent object is never at a temperature below about 400°C (750°F). An object such as a fluorescent lamp can emit bright light without being incandescent.

incarnation Act of appearing in or assuming bodily form, especially the assumption of human form by a divine being.

incest Sexual relations within a family or kinship group, the taboo on which varies between societies. In many countries, incest is a crime that carries a prison sentence.

Inchon City and port on the Yellow Sea, NW South Korea. It was first opened for foreign trade in the 1880s. It was the scene of a Russo-Japanese naval battle in 1904, and US forces landed there at the beginning of the Korean War in 1950. It is one of South Korea's major commercial centres. Industries: iron and steel, textiles and chemicals. Pop. (2000) 2,884,000.

income tax Federal or state annual assessment of tax on income, profits and financial gains of any type. It is a **direct** tax on money earned or acquired, as distinct from a tax levied on goods or services such as VALUE-ADDED TAX (VAT). Income tax is usually a **progressive** form of TAXATION, in the

sense that tax rates increase with levels of taxable income. The wealthy pay more tax in proportion to their income than the lower paid. Governments can use tax rates as a means of regulating consumption: if tax rates rise, consumers have less disposable income and less money to buy goods. In Britain, income tax is administered by the Board of Inland Revenue. It was first imposed by William PITT (THE YOUNGER) in 1798.

incubation Process of maintaining stable, warm conditions to ensure that eggs develop and hatch. Incubation is carried out by birds, and by some reptiles. It is accomplished by sitting on the eggs, by making use of volcanic or solar heat or the warmth of decaying vegetation or by covering the eggs with an insulating layer of soil or sand.

incubation period In medicine, time-lag between becoming infected with a disease and the appearance of the first symptoms. In many infectious diseases, the incubation period is quite short – anything from a few hours to a few days – although it may also be very variable. HUMAN IMMUNODEFICIENCY VIRUS (HIV) can remain in infected cells for up to 10 years before causing ACQUIRED IMMUNE DEFICIENCY SYNDROME (AIDS).

Independence Day *See* FOURTH OF JULY

Index Abbreviation for *Index librorum prohibitorum* (*Index of Prohibited Books*), a list of books banned by the Roman Catholic Church as being dangerous to the faith or morals of its members. It was first issued in 1559, and revised at intervals until it was finally discontinued in 1966.

India Republic in S Asia. *See* country feature, pages 406–07

Indiana State in N central USA, s of Lake Michigan; the capital is INDIANAPOLIS. Indiana was explored by the French in the early 18th century and ceded to the British in 1763. It passed to the USA after the American Revolution. The Native American population was not subdued until 1811. Access to Lake Michigan and to the Ohio River in the s ensures efficient distribution of the state's agricultural and manufacturing products. The area is a rich farming region. Indiana is a leading producer of machinery. Industries: grain, soya beans, livestock, coal, limestone, steel, electrical machinery, motor vehicles. Area: 93,993sq km (36,291sq mi). Pop. (2000) 6,080,485.

Indianapolis Capital of Indiana, USA, at the centre of the state, on the White River. Built on a specially selected site, it became the state capital in 1825. It is home to the Motor Speedway, where the Indianapolis 500 motor race takes place. The city is the major cereal and livestock market in a fertile agricultural area. Industries: electronic equipment, vehicle parts, pharmaceuticals, meat packing. Pop. (2000) 1,219,000.

Indian art and architecture Earliest examples of Indian art date from the ancient civilization of the Indus Valley (*c.*2300–1750BC). Excavations at Harappa (Punjab) and Mohenjo-daro (Sind) show fortified cities with a variety of buildings and sophisticated sanitation. Art in the MAURYA EMPIRE (321–185BC) was intensely Buddhist in motivation. It can be seen in the *chaitya* (shrines) and *vihara* (monastic halls hollowed out of solid rock) at Ajanta. The GUPTA DYNASTY (AD 320–550) was the golden age of Buddhist art. The Buddhist temple, with a porch and cella (main sanctuary), originated at this time. From the 6th century AD a typical Hindu temple plan developed. In S India in the 7th and 8th centuries AD a Dravidian style of Hindu temple emerged. ISLAMIC ART AND ARCHITECTURE was introduced after the Muslim conquest (1192). Between the 16th and 18th centuries, during the MOGUL EMPIRE, an Indo-Islamic style evolved, influenced by Persian prototypes. The TAJ MAHAL stands as the most perfect example of Mogul architecture. Persian influence was initially strong in drawing but, by the late 16th century, Indian taste was emerging in bright colouring and in detailed backgrounds. Under British rule, most Indian art declined to mere craftsmanship until the early 20th century. Major modern painters include Rabindranath TAGORE, Jamini Roy and Francis Souza.

Indian literature SANSKRIT LITERATURE divides into three periods: the **Vedic** period (*c.*1500–*c.*200BC) includes the VEDAS and the UPANISHADS; the **Epic** period (*c.*400BC–*c.*AD 400) includes the MAHABHARATA, the BHAGAVAD GITA, and the RAMAYANA; and the **Classical** period (from *c.*AD 200) includes the lyrics of Kalidasa. During the 19th century,

I

INDIANA
Statehood :
December 11, 1816
Nickname :
Hoosier state
State bird :
Cardinal
State flower :
Peony
State tree :
Tulip tree
State motto :
Crossroads of America

The Republic of India – the world's seventh largest country – extends from high in the HIMALAYAS, through the Tropic of Cancer, to the warm waters of the Indian Ocean at Cape Comorin. India is the world's second most populous nation after China, and the largest democracy. The N contains the mountains and foothills of the Himalayan range. Rivers such as the BRAHMAPUTRA, INDUS and GANGES (Ganga) rise in the Himalayas and flow across the fertile N plains. S India consists of a large plateau called the Deccan which is bordered by two mountain ranges, the W and E GHATS.

The Karakoram Range in the far N has permanently snow-covered peaks. The E Ganges delta has mangrove swamps. Between the gulfs of Kutch and Cambay are the deciduous forest habitats of the last of India's wild lions. The Ghats are clad in heavy rainforest.

CLIMATE

India has three seasons. The weather during the cool season – from October to February – is mild in the N plains. S India remains hot, though temperatures are a little lower than for the rest of the year. Temperatures on the N plains sometimes soar to 49°C [120°F] during the hot season from March to the end of June. The monsoon season starts in the middle of June and continues into September. At this time, moist SE winds from the Indian Ocean bring heavy rains to India. Darjeeling in the NE has an average annual rainfall of 3,040mm [120in], but parts of the Great Indian Desert in the NW have only 50mm [2in] of rain a year. The monsoon rains are essential for India's farmers. If they arrive late, crops may be ruined. If the rainfall is considerably higher than average, floods may cause great destruction.

HISTORY

One of the world's oldest civilizations flourished in the Lower Indus Valley, c.2500–1700 BC. In c.1500 BC, Aryans conquered India and established an early form of HINDUISM. In 327–25 BC, ALEXANDER THE GREAT conquered part of NW India. CHANDRAGUPTA founded the MAURYA empire. His grandson, ASHOKA, unified India and established BUDDHISM in the 3rd century BC. The CHOLA established a S trading kingdom in the 2nd century AD. In the 4th and 5th centuries AD, N India flourished under the GUPTA DYNASTY. The 7th century is the classical period of India's history. Islam was introduced from about AD 1000. In 1192, the DELHI Sultanate became India's first Muslim kingdom. In 1526, BABUR founded the MOGUL EMPIRE. In the 17th century, India became a centre of ISLAMIC ART AND ARCHITECTURE under SHAH JAHAN (who built the TAJ MAHAL) and AURANGZEB.

In the 17th century, the Maratha successfully resisted European imperial ambitions in the guise of the EAST INDIA COMPANY. European powers, particularly England and France, contested to increase their influence. In 1757, Robert CLIVE defeated the French-backed Nawab of Bengal and took Calcutta, allowing the East India Company to take control on behalf of Britain. India became one of the most important territories of the BRITISH EMPIRE. Civil unrest culminated in the INDIAN MUTINY (1857–58). Reforms failed to dampen nationalism, and the CONGRESS PARTY formed (1885). In 1906 the MUSLIM

INDIA

LEAGUE was founded to protect Muslim minority rights. Following World War 1, GANDHI led a popular campaign of non-violent disobedience and passive resistance to British rule. The AMRITSAR Massacre (1919) intensified Indian nationalism. In August 1947, British India was partitioned into two independent countries, India and the Muslim state of Pakistan. The ensuing migrations and disputes killed more than 500,000. Jawaharlal NEHRU of the Congress Party was India's first prime minister.

POLITICS

Gandhi was assassinated in 1948 by a Hindu extremist who hated him for his tolerant attitude towards Muslims. The country adopted a new constitution that year, making the country a democratic republic within the Commonwealth, and elections were held in 1951 and 1952. India's first prime minister was Jawaharlal Nehru. The government sought to develop the economy and raise living standards, while, on the international stage, Nehru won great respect for his policy of non-alignment and neutrality. The disputed status of Kashmir posed a difficult security problem.

In 1966 Nehru's daughter, Indira GANDHI, took office. Her Congress Party lost support because of food shortages, unemployment and other problems. In 1971, India helped the people of East Pakistan achieve independence from West Pakistan to become Bangladesh. India tested its first atomic bomb in 1974, but pledged to use nuclear power for peaceful purposes only. In 1977, Mrs Gandhi lost her seat in parliament and her Congress Party was defeated by the Janata Party, a coalition led by Morarji R. Desai. Disputes in the Janata Party led to Desai's resignation in 1979 and, in 1980, Congress-I (the I

standing for Indira) won the elections. Mrs Gandhi again became prime minister, but her government faced many problems. Many Sikhs wanted more control in Punjab, and Sikh radicals began to commit acts of violence to draw attention to their cause. In 1984, armed Sikhs occupied the sacred Golden Temple in AMRITSAR. In response, Indian troops attacked the temple, causing much damage and many deaths. In October, 1984, two of Mrs Gandhi's Sikh guards assassinated her. Her son Rajiv was chosen to succeed her as prime minister but, in 1989, Congress lost its majority in parliament and Rajiv resigned. During elections in 1991 he was assassinated by TAMIL extremists.

India is a vast country with an enormous diversity of cultures. It has more than a dozen major languages and many minor ones. The national language Hindi and the Dravidian languages of the south (Kannada, Tamil, Telugu and Malayam) are Indo-European. Sino-Tibetan languages are spoken in the N and E.

Hinduism is all-pervasive and Buddhism is slowly reviving in the country of its origin. Jainism is strong in the merchant towns around Mount Abu in the Aravallis hills north of Ahmadabad. Islam has contributed many mosques and monuments, the Taj Mahal being the best known, and India retains a large Muslim minority. The Punjab's militant Sikhs now seek separation. However, India's most intractable problem remains the divided region of Kashmir, the subject of a long conflict between India and Pakistan. In 2004 and 2005 both countries sought ways of easing the tension, including the opening up of cross-border transport services. In 2006, bombings in Mumbai were blamed on Pakistan, causing setbacks, but the peace process was resumed.

AREA 3,287,263sq km [1,269,212sq mi]
POPULATION 1,129,866,000
CAPITAL (POPULATION) New Delhi (295,000)
GOVERNMENT Multiparty federal republic
ETHNIC GROUPS Indo-Aryan (Caucasoid) 72%, Dravidian (Aboriginal) 25%, others (mainly Mongoloid) 3%
LANGUAGES Hindi, English, Telugu, Bengali, Marathi, Tamil, Urdu, Gujurati, Malayalam, Kannada, Oriya, Punjabi, Assamese, Kasmiri, Sindhi and Sanskrit (all official)
RELIGIONS Hinduism 82%, Islam 12%, Christianity 2%, Sikhism 2%, Buddhism and others
CURRENCY Indian rupee = 100 paisa

ECONOMY

India is a 'low-income' developing country. While it ranked 11th in total gross national product in 2004, its per capita GNP of US$440 placed it among the world's poorer countries. In the 1990s, the government introduced private enterprise policies to stimulate growth. Farming employs a high proportion of the people. The main crops are rice, wheat, millet, sorghum, peas and beans. India has more cattle than any other country; milk is produced, but Hindus do not eat beef. Manufacturing has expanded greatly since 1947 to include high-tech goods, iron and steel, machinery, textiles, jewellery and transport equipment. In the 2000s a booming IT and services sector has brought massive economic growth, but severe inequality remains a major problem.

---

various regional vernacular literatures emerged. **Bengali literature** was particularly influential in the development of a nationalist literature, including writers such as Rabindranath TAGORE.

Indian Mutiny (1857–58) Large-scale uprising against British rule. It is known in India as the first war of independence. It began (May 10, 1857) at Meerut as a mutiny among 35,000 Indian troops (sepoys) in the Bengal army. The immediate cause was the introduction of rifle cartridges allegedly greased with the fat of cows and pigs. A more general cause was resentment at Westernization. The mutineers captured Delhi and, with the support of local maharajahs and civilians in Uttar Pradesh and Madhya Pradesh, the British garrison at Lucknow was besieged. On 14 September 1857, British forces recaptured Delhi and the revolt petered out. The revolt resulted in the British government taking over control of India from the EAST INDIA COMPANY in 1858.

Indian National Congress See CONGRESS PARTY

Indian Ocean Third-largest ocean in the world, bounded by Asia (N), Antarctica (S), Africa (W) and Southeast Asia and Australia (E). Known in ancient times as the Erythraean Sea, the Indian Ocean was the first to be extensively navigated. Branches include the Arabian Sea, the Bay of BENGAL and the Andaman Sea. Its largest islands are MADAGASCAR and SRI LANKA. The average water depth is 4,000m (13,000ft) although there is a Mid-Oceanic Ridge, extending from Asia to Antarctica; several of its peaks emerge as islands. The deepest part is the Java Trench, reaching 7,725m (25,344ft). The climate of the nearby land masses is strongly influenced by the ocean's winds and currents. There are three wind belts: the monsoons, which pick up moisture from the ocean, bringing heavy rainfall to W India and Southeast Asia; the SE

TRADE WINDS; and the prevailing westerlies, bringing tropical storms. The currents are governed by the winds, the seasonal shift of the MONSOON dictating the flow of water N of the Equator. Area: c.73,600,000sq km (28,400,000sq mi).

Indians, American See NATIVE AMERICANS

Indian Territory Area set aside for Native Americans by the US government. The 1830 Indian Removal Act gave the President authority to designate specific Western lands for settlement by Indians removed from their native lands. In 1834, the Indian Intercourse Act set aside Kansas, Nebraska, and Oklahoma N and E of the Red River as Indian Territory. In 1854, Kansas and Nebraska were redesignated territories open to white settlement. West Oklahoma was opened to white settlement in 1889. In 1907, the last of the Indian Territory was dissolved when Oklahoma became a state.

Indian theatre Classical and modern dramatic traditions of the Indian subcontinent, including Sanskrit, Kutiyattam and Kathakali. Sanskrit (Hindu) classical drama, the two great epics of which are the MAHABHARATA and the RAMAYANA, can be traced back as far as the 3rd century BC and survived into the 11th century AD before dying out. Sanskrit was followed by a more eclectic tradition that emphasized music, poetry and dance in its performance. This developed in tandem with the endemic Indian folk drama. As a result of Western influence, modern drama appeared during the latter half of the 20th century. There is also a strong tradition of puppetry.

India-Pakistan Wars Three conflicts between India and Pakistan after independence in 1947. The **first** (1947–49) arose from a dispute over JAMMU AND KASHMIR. Fighting continued until January 1949, when the UN arranged a truce, leaving KASHMIR partitioned. This was the chief cause of the **second**

war (1965), over another territorial dispute. Each side invaded the other's territory and stalemate led to a ceasefire. The **third** war arose out of the civil war between East and West Pakistan in 1971. India intervened in support of East Pakistan (Bangladesh), and (West) Pakistan suffered a decisive defeat.

indicator In chemistry, substance used to indicate acidity or alkalinity. It does this usually by a change of colour. Indicators, such as the dye LITMUS, can detect a change of pH, which measures a solution's acidity (litmus turns red) or alkalinity (turns blue). **Universal indicator** (liquid or paper) undergoes a spectral range of colour changes indicating from pH 1 to 13.

indium (symbol In) Silvery-white, metallic element of group III of the PERIODIC TABLE. Its chief source is as a by-product of zinc ores. Malleable and ductile, indium is used in semiconductors and as a mirror surface. Its compounds are also used in dental alloys, transistors, and solar batteries. Properties: at.no. 49; r.a.m. 114.82; r.d. 7.31; m.p. 156.6°C (313.9°F); b.p. 2,080°C (3776°F); most common isotope In^{115} (95.77%).

Indochina Peninsula of SE Asia, including LAOS, THAILAND, BURMA, CAMBODIA, VIETNAM and West MALAYSIA. The name refers more specifically to the former federation of states of Vietnam, Laos and Cambodia, within the French Union (1945–54). European penetration of the area began in the 16th century. By the 19th century, France controlled Cochin China, Cambodia, ANNAM and Tonkin, which together formed the Union of Indochina in 1887; Laos joined in 1893. After World War 1, France announced plans for a federation within the French Union. Cambodia and Laos accepted this, but fighting broke out between the French and Annamese nationalists, who wanted independence for Annam, Tonkin and Cochin China as Vietnam. The war ended with the French defeat at DIEN BIEN PHU. French control of Indochina officially ended at the Geneva Conference of 1954.

Indo-European languages Family of languages spoken in Europe and SW and S Asia, and used in all areas of European settlement, such as Australia and New Zealand, South Africa, Canada, the USA and Latin America. It consists of the following subgroups: GERMANIC, CELTIC and Indo-Iranian (including Persian, Avestan and the Indic languages – SANSKRIT, Pali and modern HINDI). Other languages and groups in the family

INDONESIA

I

The Republic of Indonesia in SE Asia consists of about 13,600 islands, fewer than 6,000 of which are inhabited. The island of Java covers only 7% of the country's area but contains more than half of Indonesia's population. Three-quarters of the country is made up of five main areas: the Greater Sunda islands of SUMATRA, JAVA, SULAWESI (Celebes), KALIMANTAN (southern Borneo) and IRIAN JAYA or Papua (W New Guinea). The islands are mountainous and many have extensive coastal lowlands. Indonesia contains more than 200 volcanoes, but the highest peak is Puncak Jaya, which reaches 5,029m [16,503ft] above sea level, is in W Papua.

CLIMATE

Indonesia has a hot and humid monsoon climate. Only Java and the Sunda Islands have a relatively dry season. From December to March, moist prevailing winds blow from mainland Asia. Between mid-June and October, dry prevailing winds blow from Australia.

HISTORY

By the 8th century the area was ruled by early kingdoms including the Sailendra, which introduced BUDDHISM and built BOROBUDUR. The empire of Srivijaya, centred on Palembang, lasted until the end of the 13th century. It was replaced by the Hindu Madjapahit empire based in E-central Java. By the end of the 16th century Islam had become the main religion, and Indonesia is now the world's most populous Muslim nation. In 1511, the Portuguese seized MALACCA. By 1610 the Dutch EAST INDIA COMPANY acquired all of Portugal's holdings, except East Timor, and controlled the region until the end of the 18th century when its failure led to direct Dutch rule. In 1883, KRAKATOA erupted, claiming c.50,000 lives. In 1927, SUKARNO formed the Indonesian Nationalist Party (PNI). During World War 2, the Japanese expelled the Dutch (1942) and occupied Indonesia. In August 1945, Sukarno proclaimed independence; the Dutch resisted. In November 1949, Indonesia became an independent republic.

POLITICS

Indonesia's first president, the anti-Western Achmed Sukarno, plunged his country into chaos. In 1962, Indonesia invaded Dutch New Guinea (now West Papua), and between 1963 and 1966 sought to destabilize the Federation of Malaysia through incursions into northern Borneo. In 1965–7 Sukarno suppressed an allegedly Communist uprising at the cost of 80,000 lives. In 1967 General SUHARTO took over in a coup. His military regime, with US help, achieved significant economic growth though corruption was rife. In 1975, Indonesian troops invaded East Timor, opposed by the local people. Suharto was forced to stand down in 1998 and his deputy, Bacharuddin Jusuf Habibie, succeeded

AREA 735,354sq mi [1,904,569sq km]
POPULATION 234,694,000
CAPITAL (POPULATION) Jakarta (13,194,000)
GOVERNMENT Multiparty republic
ETHNIC GROUPS Javanese 45%, Sundanese 14|%, Madurese 7%, coastal Malays 7%, approximately 300 others
LANGUAGES Bahasa Indonesian (official), many others
RELIGIONS Islam 88%, Roman Catholic 3%, Hinduism 2%, Buddhism 1%
CURRENCY Indonesian rupiah = 100 sen

him. In June 1999, Habibie's ruling Golkar Party was defeated in elections and, in October, the parliament elected Abdurrahman Wahid as president. However, Wahid, charged with corruption and incompetence, was dismissed in 2001 and succeeded by the vice-president, Megawati Sukarnoputri, Sukarno's daughter.

East Timor seceded in 2002, while secessionists in Aceh province, northern Sumatra, and West Papua also demanded independence. Muslim-Christian clashes broke out in the Moluccas in 1999, while indigenous Dyaks in Kalimantan clashed with immigrants from Madura.

In 2004 elections former general Susilo Bambang Yudhoyono became president. In December 2004, more than 120,000 people were killed in Indonesia by a TSUNAMI. Worst hit was Aceh, though the tragedy was followed by peace talks in 2005. The separatist conflict ended and Aceh gained substantial autonomy. In 2006 Aceh held its first independent elections.

ECONOMY

Indonesia is a 'lower-middle-income' developing country. Agriculture employs more than 40% of the workforce and rice is the main food crop. Bananas, cassava, coconuts, peanuts, maize, spices and sweet potatoes are also grown. Major cash crops include coffee, palm oil, rubber, sugar cane, tea and tobacco. Fishing and forestry are also important.

There are important mineral reserves, including oil and natural gas. Bauxite, coal, iron ore, nickel and tin are also mined.

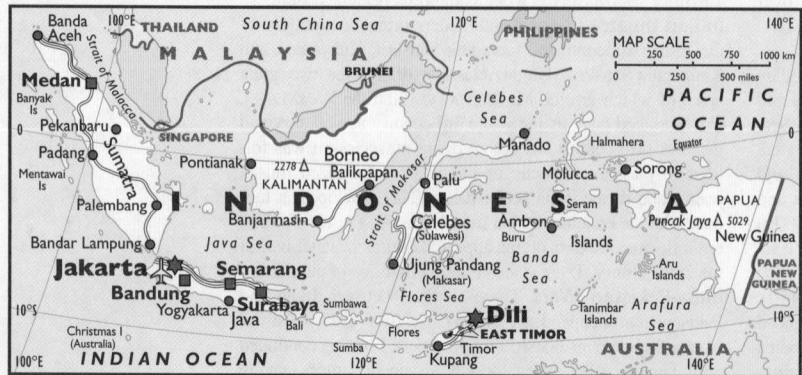

are Armenian, Albanian, GREEK, the Italic languages (including LATIN and its descendants, the ROMANCE LANGUAGES), the Baltic group (including Latvian and Lithuanian) and the Slavic group (including Old Church Slavonic, RUSSIAN, POLISH, CZECH, Serbian, Croatian and others). About half the world's population speaks an Indo-European language.

Indonesia Republic in the Malay archipelago, SE Asia. *See* country feature

Indra In Vedic mythology, the ruler of heaven, great god of storms, thunder and lightning, worshipped as rain-maker and bringer of fertility. In the creation myth, he slew Vritra, dragon of drought, to produce the Sun and water on the Earth.

inductance (symbol H) Property of an electric circuit or component that produces an ELECTROMOTIVE FORCE (EMF) after a change in the current. The SI unit is the henry (symbol H). **Self-inductance** (symbol L) occurs when the current flows through the circuit or component, and **mutual inductance** (symbol M) when current flows through two circuits or components that are linked magnetically. *See also* ELECTROMAGNETIC INDUCTION

induction In physics, process by which magnification or electrification is produced in an object. In ELECTROMAGNETIC INDUCTION, an electric current is produced in a CONDUCTOR when placed within a varying MAGNETIC FIELD. The magnitude of the current is proportional to the rate of change of MAGNETIC FLUX. In a TRANSFORMER, the alternating current in the primary coil creates a changing magnetic field that induces a current in the secondary coil. *See also* FARADAY'S LAWS; INDUCTANCE

indulgence In Roman Catholic theology, remission of temporal punishment for sin. An indulgence, once granted, obviates the need for the sinner to do PENANCE, although it does not necessarily remove guilt, and may be only a partial rather than a full (plenary) indulgence. Previously available from bishops, today they are granted only by the pope. The sale of indulgences was among the principal causes of the REFORMATION.

Indus River of S Asia. It rises in the Kailas mountain range in Tibet, and flows WNW through the Jammu and Kashmir region of India, then SW through Pakistan and into the Arabian Sea. The river is used chiefly for irrigation and hydroelectric power. In its lower valley, there are traces of an urban civilization that lived in the 3rd millennium BC. Length: *c*.3,060km (1,900mi).

Industrial Revolution Social and economic transformation of agricultural societies into industrial societies. It began in Britain in the 18th century. By 1870, France, Germany and the USA were rapidly developing industrial bases. The RUSSIAN REVOLUTION (1917) led to the rapid industrialization of the Soviet Union. In the UK, a rapid increase in population, which was both a cause and result of the AGRICULTURAL REVOLUTION, preceded the Industrial Revolution. The inventions of Richard ARKWRIGHT, Edmund CARTWRIGHT, Samuel CROMPTON, and James HARGREAVES revolutionized the production of textiles. The new machines necessitated the building of factories. The STEAM ENGINE, invented (1769) by James WATT, was the main driving force of the Industrial Revolution and led to the placing of factories near coalfields, which in turn led to the growth of large cities, especially in Scotland, the North, the Midlands, and South Wales. MASS PRODUCTION required an expansion of the network of CANALS and roads. The construction of RAILWAYS began in *c*.1830. At first, the economic doctrine of LAISSEZ-FAIRE allowed the growth of industrialization without restrictions on working conditions, but the Factory Acts (1802 onwards) brought regulations in employment of children and length of the working day. The Industrial Revolution produced major social changes, in particular the creation of a working class.

industry Businesses that produce goods or services. The term is also used to define a group of firms producing a similar kind of product, such as the computer industry. Industries are often classified into three groups: **manufacturing**, **agriculture** and **service**.

inequality Mathematical statement that one expression is less, or greater, than another. The symbol > stands for 'is greater than', and < stands for 'is less than'. The symbols ≤ and ≥ stand for 'greater than or equal to' and 'less than or equal to' respectively.

inert gas *See* NOBLE GAS

inertia Property possessed by all matter that is a measure of the way an object resists changes to its state of motion. Isaac NEWTON formulated the first law of motion, sometimes called the law of inertia, stating that a body will remain at rest or in uniform motion unless acted upon by external forces.

infection Invasion of the body by disease-causing organisms that become established, multiply and give rise to symptoms.

infertility Inability to reproduce. In a woman it may be due to lack of ovulation, obstruction of the FALLOPIAN TUBE, or disease of the ENDOMETRIUM; in a man it is due to inadequate SPERM production. In plants, the term refers to inability to reproduce sexually. Infertility occurs in a HYBRID between different species, which are unable to produce viable GAMETES.

infinity (symbol ∞) Abstract quantity that represents the magnitude of an object without limit or end. In algebra, $1/x$ approaches infinity as x approaches zero. In set theory, the set of all integers is an example of an infinite set.

inflammation Reaction of body tissue to infection or injury, with pain, heat, swelling and redness. Damaged cells release HISTAMINE, causing blood vessels to dilate. LEUCOCYTES engulf bacteria and MACROPHAGES remove dead tissue, sometimes with the formation of pus.

inflation Continual upward movement of prices. Although normally associated with periods of prosperity, inflation may also occur during RECESSIONS. It usually occurs when there is relatively full employment. Under 'cost-push' inflation, prices rise because the producers' costs increase. Under 'demand-pull' inflation, prices increase because of excessive consumer demand for goods.

inflection Variation in the form of a word that distinguishes its grammatical relationship to other words in a sentence without altering its part of speech. Commonly, affixes are added to to distinguish tense, person, number, gender, voice or case.

inflorescence FLOWER or flower cluster. Inflorescences are classified as belonging to two main types according to branching characteristics. A **racemose** inflorescence has a main axis and lateral flowering branches with flowers opening from the bottom up or from the outer edge in. A **cymose** inflorescence has a composite axis with the main stem ending in a flower and lateral branches bearing additional, later-flowering branches.

influenza (flu) Viral infection mainly affecting the airways, with chesty symptoms, headache, joint pains, fever and general malaise. It is treated by bed-rest and pain-killers. Vaccines are available to confer immunity to some strains. Dangerous strains of influenza crossing to humans from domestic birds ("bird flu") have caused concern.

information technology (IT) COMPUTER and TELECOMMUNICATIONS technologies used in processing information of any kind. Word processing, the use of a DATABASE and the sending of ELECTRONIC MAIL (E-MAIL) over a COMPUTER NETWORK are all examples of information technology. IT has revolutionized retailing and banking. In manufacturing, IT has enabled the development of computer-aided manufacture (CAM). *See also* ARTIFICIAL INTELLIGENCE

information theory Mathematical study of the laws governing communication channels, such as computer circuits and telecommunications systems. It is primarily concerned with the measurement of information and the methods of coding, transmitting, storing and processing this information.

infrared radiation (IR) ELECTROMAGNETIC RADIATION intermediate in energy between visible light and microwaves. Its wavelengths lie in the range between 750nm and 1mm. Some frequencies are commonly emitted by warm objects, and equipment to detect these has many military and commercial uses. Other frequencies are used in communications. Study of infrared radiation has led to many advances in astronomy.

Ingres, Jean Auguste Dominique (1780–1867) French neo-classical painter. One of the great figures of early 19th-century French art, he was an outstanding portraitist, especially of women in high society such as *Madame d'Haussonville* (1845). He also produced sensual nudes, such as *Bather of Valpinçon* (1808) and, much later, *The Turkish Bath* (1863).

Ingushetia Autonomous Russian republic; the capital is Nazran. It lies on the N side of the Caucasus Mountains. The population is (85%) Ingush with a Chechen minority.

INTERNET

Ingres, Jean Auguste Dominique
▶ www.louvre.fr
▶ www.metmuseum.org
▶ www.nationalgallery.org.uk

The economy is based on oil and cattle. For much of the 20th century, Ingushetia's history was tied to CHECHNYA. In 1991, the Chechen-Ingush Republic declared independence. The Ingush desire to distance itself from the Chechen-dominated decision led to the deployment of Russian troops and formal separation from Chechnya (1992). In 1993, Ingushetia became part of the Russian Federation. Pop. (2000 est.) 488,200.

injection In medicine, use of a syringe and needle to introduce drugs or other fluids into the body to diagnose, treat or prevent disease. Most injections are either **intravenous** (into a vein), **intramuscular** (into a muscle), or **intradermal** (into the skin).

ink Coloured liquid used for writing, drawing or printing. It may be coloured by a suspended pigment or a soluble dye. Some inks dry by evaporation of a volatile solvent.

Inkatha South African political organization, founded (1975) by Chief BUTHELEZI to represent South Africa's ZULU population. Its initial aim was to work towards a democratic, non-racial political system, but it was accused of complicity with the APARTHEID regime. In the early 1990s, Inkatha was involved in violent conflict with the AFRICAN NATIONAL CONGRESS (ANC). In terms of representation, it ranks third among political parties. Its strongest base is in KWAZULU-NATAL.

Innocent III (1161–1216) Pope (1198–1216), b. Lotario di Segni. He stressed moderation; increased papal control over civil matters; and established the courts of INQUISITION. During his papacy, TRANSUBSTANTIATION became part of Communion dogma. He allowed the Franciscan and Dominican orders to form and backed the crusade against the ALBIGENSES.

Innsbruck City in w Austria, on the River Inn, 135km (84mi) sw of Salzburg; capital of TIROL. Founded in the 12th century, the city grew rapidly because of its strategic position on a historic transalpine route. Innsbruck is a commercial and industrial centre, and an important winter sports resort. Industries: manufacturing, metalworking, textiles, Pop. (2001) 113,826.

Inns of Court Four legal societies in London: Lincoln's Inn, Inner Temple, Middle Temple, and Gray's Inn. They date from the 13th century, and have the exclusive right to admit persons to practise as barristers in English courts.

İnönü, İsmet (1884–1973) Turkish statesman, president (1938–50) and prime minister (1923–24, 1925–37, 1961–65). He was a leading figure in the Turkish nationalist movement and a formative influence on the development of the Turkish republic. He served as prime minister for most of ATATÜRK's presidency (1923–37) and succeeded him as president. İnönü's Republican People's Party lost the Republic's first free elections (1950). Following a military coup in 1960, Turkey's constitution was reformed and İnönü returned as prime minister.

inorganic chemistry *See* CHEMISTRY

inquest Inquiry into the death of a person who has been killed, or died unexpectedly or under suspicious circumstances.

Inquisition Court set up by the Roman Catholic Church in the Middle Ages to seek out and punish heresy. The accused were often tortured. Punishments ranged from penances to banishment or death. Kings and nobles supported the organized persecution of Jews, Protestants, and others considered enemies of church and state. The Inquisition was active in Europe from the 12th to the 15th centuries. The later **Spanish Inquisition** was instituted in 1483 at the request of the rulers of Spain and was not abolished until 1834. In 1542, a Roman Inquisition was set up to check the growth of Protestantism.

insect Any of more than a million species of small, invertebrate animals of the class Insecta, including the BEETLE, BUG, BUTTERFLY, ANT and BEE. There are more species of insects than all other species combined. Adult insects have three pairs of jointed legs, usually two pairs of wings, and a segmented body with a horny outer covering or EXOSKELETON. The head has three pairs of mouthparts, a pair of compound eyes, three pairs of simple eyes, and a pair of antennae. Most insects can detect a wide range of sounds through ultra-sensitive hairs. Some can 'sing' or make sounds by rubbing together parts of their bodies. Most insects are plant-eaters, many being serious pests. Some prey on small animals, especially other insects, and a few are scavengers. There are two main kinds of mouthparts – chewing and sucking. Reproduction is usually sexual. Most insects go through four distinct life stages, in METAMORPHOSIS. The stages are OVUM (egg), LARVA (caterpillar or grub), PUPA (chrysalis), and adult (IMAGO). Young grasshoppers and some other insects, called NYMPHS, resemble wingless miniatures of their parents. The nymphs develop during a series of moults (incomplete metamorphosis). SILVERFISH and a few other primitive, wingless insects do not undergo metamorphosis. Phylum Arthropoda *See also* ARTHROPOD

insectivore Any member of the order of carnivorous MAMMALS Insectivora, many of which eat insects. Almost worldwide in distribution, some species live underground, some on the ground and some in streams and ponds. Most insectivores have narrow snouts, long skulls and five-clawed feet. The order consists of three families: Erinaceidae (moon rats, gymures, HEDGEHOGS); Talpidae (MOLES, shrew moles, desmans); and Soricidae (SHREWS). Six other families, including tree shrews and solenodons, are also often part of the order.

insectivorous plant (carnivorous plant) Any of several plants that have poorly developed root systems and are often found in nitrogen-deficient sandy or boggy soils. They obtain nutrients by trapping, 'digesting' and absorbing insects. Some, such as Venus fly-trap (*Dionaea muscipula*), are active insect trappers. The sundews (*Drosera*) snare insects with a sticky substance. Bladderworts (*Utricularia*) suck insects into their underwater bladders. Other plants have vase-shaped leaves, such as the pitcher plant (*Sarracenia flava*).

instinct Behaviours that are innately determined, as opposed to behaviours that are learned. In the 19th century, instincts were often cited to explain behaviour, but the term fell into disrepute with the advent of BEHAVIOURISM. The term has been revived in the work of such ethologists as Konrad LORENZ.

insulation Technique for reducing or preventing the transfer of heat, electricity, sound or other vibrations. Wool, fibre-glass and foam plastic are good **heat** insulating materials because they contain air. This trapped air reduces the transfer of heat by CONDUCTION. Water is also a good heat insulator. A diver's wet suit keeps the wearer warm by trapping a layer of water around the body. **Electrical** insulation materials include rubber, PVC, polythene, glass and porcelain. **Sound** insulating materials absorb sound and change it to heat by FRICTION.

insulin HORMONE secreted by the islets of Langherhans in the PANCREAS and concerned with the control of blood-glucose levels. Insulin lowers the blood-GLUCOSE level by helping the uptake of glucose into cells, and by causing the liver to convert glucose to glycogen. In the absence of insulin, glucose accumulates in the blood and urine, resulting in DIABETES. Insulin was isolated in 1921 by Canadian physician Frederick BANTING and Canadian physiologist Charles BEST. Its structure was discovered in the 1940s by English biochemist Frederick SANGER.

insurance Procedure whereby one party (the insured) transfers the financial consequences of risk of loss to another (the insurer) for a consideration (the **premium**).

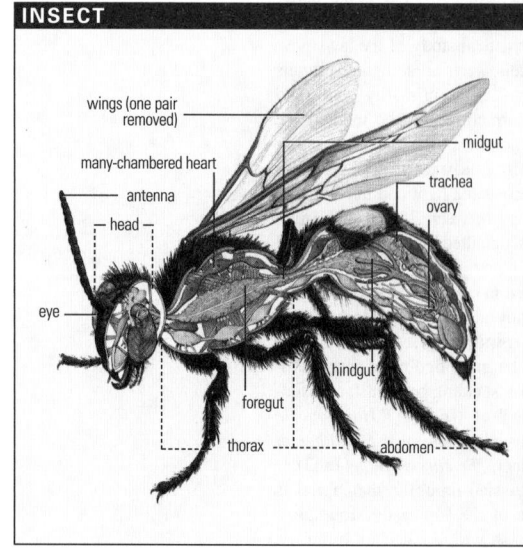

INSECT

The internal anatomy of all insects, such as the honey-bee, is contained and protected within the confines of the tough, flexible exoskeleton. The typical insect body contains organs of digestion, respiration, circulation, excretion, and reproduction. There are muscles through which movement is effected, and a nervous system that coordinates and controls an insect's actions on the basis of information received by the sense organs – most important of which are the large compound eyes, the feelers, and antennae. All insect bodies comprise three parts: the head, thorax, and abdomen.

wings (one pair removed)
midgut
many-chambered heart
trachea
antenna
ovary
head
eye
hindgut
foregut
thorax
abdomen

Each insured contributes to a common fund, and the losses of the few are reimbursed from the fund. Modern practices date back to the 16th and 17th centuries.

intaglio Incised carving on gemstones, hardstones or glass, in which the design is sunk below the surface. In printing, the term is used to describe processes in which ink is applied to incisions and hollows in a printing plate, as in ETCHING.

integer Any negative or positive whole number or zero, e.g. ... −3, −2, −1, 0, 1, 2, 3 ... There are a limitless (infinite) number of integers. The positive integers are the natural NUMBERS. The existence of negative integers and zero allow any integer to be subtracted from any other integer to give an integer result.

integral calculus In mathematics, branch of CALCULUS that deals with integration: the finding of a function, one or more derivatives of which are given. There are many applications of integral calculus. It is used to find the areas and volumes of curved shapes. In engineering calculations, differential equations are solved by integral calculus. Its principles are also incorporated in many measuring and control instruments.

integrated circuit (IC) Complete miniature electronic CIR-CUIT, incorporating semiconductor devices such as the TRANSISTOR and RESISTOR. It is used in such devices as microcomputers and pocket calculators. **Monolithic** integrated circuits have all the components manufactured into or on top of a single crystal of silicon (SILICON CHIP). **Hybrid** integrated circuits have separate components attached to a ceramic base. Components are joined by conducting film. *See also* PRINTED CIRCUIT

Integrated Services Digital Network (ISDN) High-speed telephone system that carries digital information over standard telephone lines. ISDN lines connect directly to a computer and do not need a MODEM. See also BROADBAND.

integration *See* INTEGRAL CALCULUS

intelligence General ability to learn and to deal with problems, new situations, and abstract concepts. It can be manifest in different ways, including skills in adaptability, memory and reasoning. Debate has raged over the roles of hereditary and environmental factors in developing intelligence. Intelligence tests measure abstract reasoning and problem-solving abilities.

intelligence quotient *See* IQ

intelligence service Government organization maintained in most countries to obtain information concerning activities that might endanger the state. In Britain, MI-5 (Military Intelligence-5) is responsible for domestic counterespionage; MI-6 is responsible for overseas intelligence. *See also* CENTRAL INTELLIGENCE AGENCY (CIA); FEDERAL BUREAU OF INVESTIGATION (FBI)

interdict Instrument of punishment in the Roman Catholic Church whereby sacraments and clerical offices are withdrawn from a place. Bishops have this power over individual parishes, but the pope has much wider powers.

interest Price paid to a lender by a borrower for the 'use' of money over a specified period of time, usually calculated as a percentage of the principal (sum lent). **Simple** interest is paid regularly and calculated as a percentage of the original principal. In **compound** interest, the interest calculated for one period (such as a year) is added to the original principal, and the interest for the next period is calculated as a percentage of this total. The **interest rate** is the percentage payable.

interface Way that a COMPUTER PROGRAM or system interacts with its user. The simplest form of computer interface is the keyboard, through which the user controls the computer by typing in commands. The most common type for personal computers is the GRAPHICAL USER INTERFACE (GUI).

interference In optics, the interaction of two or more WAVE motions, such as those of light, creating a disturbance pattern. **Constructive** interference is the reinforcement of the wave motion because the component motions are in PHASE. Interference is used in 3–D holography. **Destructive** interference is when two waves are out of phase and cancel each other.

interferometer Instrument in which a WAVE, such as a light wave, is split into waves that travel unequal distances to be recombined as INTERFERENCE patterns. Uses include quality control of lenses and prisms, and measuring WAVELENGTHS.

interferon PROTEIN produced by cells when infected with a VIRUS. Interferons can help uninfected cells to resist infection

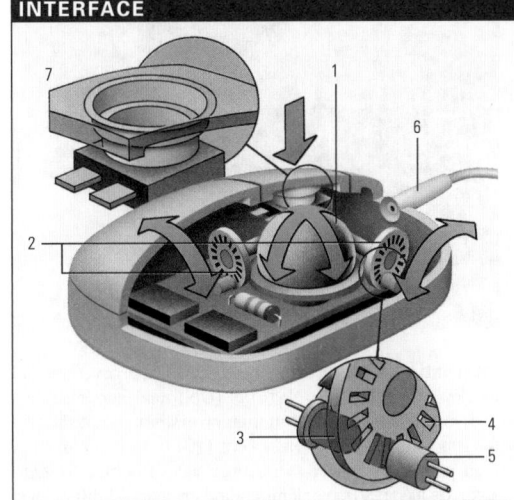

INTERFACE

Computer operators use a variety of means to interact with a computer. A hand-held mouse, for example, moves a cursor on a monitor screen. The central ball (1) rotates as the mouse moves. As the ball moves, spoked wheels (2) turn according to sideways and up-and-down movement. An LED (3) shines through the spokes (4). The rate of rotation of both wheels is detected by sensors (5), which send information to the computer via a cable (6), and move the cursor appropriately. Buttons at the front of the mouse (7) can be used to click on areas of the monitor screen or call up menus.

by the virus, and may also impede virus replication and protein synthesis. In some circumstances they can inhibit cell growth; human interferon is now produced by GENETIC ENGINEERING to treat some cancers, HEPATITIS and MULTIPLE SCLEROSIS.

interlude Short theatrical piece, prominent in the late 15th and early 16th centuries, which provided entertainment during royal and noble banquets. Performed by a small travelling company, it combined moral messages with clowning, and is sometimes seen as the starting point for English DRAMA.

intermezzo Light theatrical entertainment performed to music between the acts of a drama or OPERA. The earliest intermezzi date from the late 15th century. The 18th-century intermezzi of operas were the basis for the development of OPERA BUFFA. Today, the term most commonly refers to an instrumental interlude during the course of an opera.

internal combustion engine ENGINE in which fuel is burned inside, so that the gases formed can produce motion, widely used in AUTOMOBILES. It may be a TWO-STROKE ENGINE or a FOUR-STROKE ENGINE. In the most common type of engine, a mixture of PETROLEUM vapour and air is ignited by a spark. The gases produced in the explosion usually drive a piston along a cylinder. A crankshaft changes the reciprocating (to-and-fro) movement of the pistons into rotary motion. In the WANKEL ROTARY ENGINE, the gases produced in the explosions drive a triangular rotor. Nikolaus OTTO built the first practical internal combustion engine in 1867. Rudolf Diesel designed the first DIESEL ENGINE in 1897. Because combustion is incomplete and reliant on FOSSIL FUELS, internal combustion engines are a major cause of air pollution.

International Atomic Energy Agency (IAEA) Intergovernmental agency of the UNITED NATIONS (UN). It was founded in 1956 to promote peaceful uses of nuclear energy and to establish international control of nuclear weapons. The organization's headquarters are in Vienna, Austria.

International Court of Justice Supreme judicial body of the UNITED NATIONS (UN) for hearing disputes between countries involving treaties and INTERNATIONAL LAW. It replaced the League of Nations' Permanent Court of Justice in 1947. Its 15 judges are chosen by the UN, each coming from a different state and serving for nine years. The court sits at The Hague.

International Labour Organization (ILO) Specialized intergovernmental agency of the UNITED NATIONS (UN). Its aim is to facilitate improved industrial relations and conditions of work. It was formed as an agency of the LEAGUE OF NATIONS by the Treaty of VERSAILLES (1919) and has a membership comprising government, employer and worker representatives. Its headquarters are in Geneva, Switzerland.

international law Body of rules deemed legally binding that have resulted from treaties, agreements and customs between states. Its sources are also decisions by agencies, conferences or commissions of international organizations such as the UNITED NATIONS, as well as decisions of international tribunals such as those of the INTERNATIONAL COURT OF JUSTICE.

▶ **Intifada** The purpose of the first Intifada was to make the Israeli-occupied territories of Palestine, particularly the West Bank and Gaza Strip, ungovernable through concerted civil unrest. Street clashes between stone-throwing Palestinian youths and Israeli soldiers were frequent and attracted global attention. In November 2000, after the failure of peace talks, a second Intifada began. Both sides used far more force.

International Monetary Fund (IMF) Intergovernmental agency of the UNITED NATIONS (UN), and administrative body of the **international monetary system**, established by the BRETTON WOODS CONFERENCE (1944). Its main function is to provide assistance to member states troubled by BALANCE OF PAYMENTS problems and other financial difficulties. The IMF does not lend money; rather, it exchanges the member state's currency with its own **Special Drawing Rates (SDR)** in the hope that this will alleviate balance of payment difficulties. These exchanges are usually conditional upon the recipient country agreeing to pursue prescribed policy reforms. The organization is based in Washington, D.C.

International style (International modern style) Name for the architectural style that developed in Europe in the 1920s and 1930s. It characteristically features austere white walls, asymmetrical cubic shapes and large expanses of glass. LE CORBUSIER and Walter GROPIUS were early exponents.

Internet (Net) Worldwide communications system consisting of hundreds of small COMPUTER NETWORKS, interconnected by TELEPHONE systems. It is a network of networks in which messages and data are sent using short local links from place to place. The Internet or **Information Superhighway** started in 1969 with funds from the US Department of Defense. *See also* MODEM; WORLD WIDE WEB (WWW)

interplanetary matter Material in the space between the planets. It is made up of atomic particles (mainly PROTONS and ELECTRONS) ejected from the Sun via the SOLAR WIND, and dust particles mainly from COMETS.

Interpol (International Criminal Police Organization) Intergovernmental organization. Established in 1923, its main function is to provide member states with information about international criminals and to assist in their arrest. Its headquarters are in Lyon, France.

intersection Point, or LOCUS of points, common to two or more geometrical figures. Two non-parallel lines in the same plane meet in a point; two non-parallel planes meet in a line.

intestine Lower part of the ALIMENTARY CANAL, of the DIGESTIVE SYSTEM beyond the STOMACH. In the human, it is about 7m (24ft) long. Food is moved through the intestine by the wave-like action of PERISTALSIS. It undergoes the final stages of digestion and is absorbed into the bloodstream in the small intestine, which extends some 3m (10ft) from the stomach to the large intestine. In the large intestine (CAECUM, COLON and RECTUM) water is absorbed from undigested material, which is then passed out of the body through the anus.

Intifada (Arabic, 'uprising') The **first** Intifada, a campaign of civil disobedience by Palestinians in the Israeli-occupied territories of the WEST BANK of the River Jordan and the GAZA STRIP, began in 1987 as a sustained attempt to disrupt the Israeli occupation. It lost momentum after the ISRAELI-PALESTINIAN ACCORD, having claimed more than 1,400 Palestinian and 230 Jewish lives. In November 2000, after the collapse of peace negotiations, the **second** Intifada began. Palestinian groups attacked Israel with rockets and suicide bombs; Israeli counter-attacks failed to suppress these strikes, but caused extensive civilian casualties and attracted international criticism.

Intolerable Acts (1774) British legislation designed to punish the American colonists after the BOSTON TEA PARTY. Also known as the Coercive Acts, they closed the Boston port and moved the customs house to Salem. British officials accused

of capital offences would be tried in England (Administration of Justice Act); another law (the Massachusetts Government Act) annulled the Massachusetts Charter, giving the governor power to control town meetings and making the council and judiciary appointed bodies. The colonists' opposition resulted in the calling of the First CONTINENTAL CONGRESS.

intoxication Condition arising when the body is poisoned by any toxic substance, whether liquid, solid or gas. Symptoms vary according to the ingested substance.

intravenous drip Apparatus for delivering drugs, blood and blood products, nutrients or other fluids directly into the bloodstream. A hollow needle is inserted into a vein and then attached to tubing leading from a bag containing the fluid.

introversion Preoccupation with one's own responses and impressions, coupled with a preference for reflection over action and a dislike of social activity. The term was coined by C.G. JUNG as a polar opposite to EXTROVERSION.

intrusion In geology, process in which rock material is forced or flows into spaces among other rocks to form intrusive rocks. An igneous intrusion, sometimes called a pluton, consists of magma that never reached the Earth's surface but filled cracks and faults, then cooled and hardened.

Inuit Collective name for the ESKIMO people of Nunavut, Greenland, and the Northwest Territories, Arctic Québec, and N Labrador areas of Canada. Many Inuit still live by the traditional skills of fishing, trapping and hunting.

Inverness City at the head of the Moray Firth on the River Ness; capital of Highland region, N Scotland. A tourist centre with a boatbuilding history, Inverness lies at the NE end of the Caledonian Canal. Its castle was destroyed at the Battle of CULLODEN, but rebuilt in Victorian times. Pop. (2001) 43,100.

invertebrate An animal without a backbone. There are more than one million species of invertebrates, divided into 30 major groups. One of these is Arthropoda (joint-legged animals), the largest of all animal phyla in terms of numbers of species. Most are INSECTS, but it also includes crustaceans and ARACHNIDS. MOLLUSCS make up the second largest group of invertebrates. *See also* ARTHROPOD; CRUSTACEA; PHYLUM

in vitro fertilization (IVF) Use of artificial techniques to join an OVUM with SPERM outside (*in vitro*) a woman's body to help infertile couples to have children of their own. The basic technique of IVF involves removing ova from a woman's ovaries, fertilizing them in the laboratory, and then inserting them into her UTERUS. In **zygote intrafallopian transfer (ZIFT)**, a fertilized egg (ZYGOTE) is returned to the FALLOPIAN TUBE, from which it makes its own way to the uterus. The zygote then divides to form an EMBRYO. In **gamete intrafallopian transfer (GIFT)**, the ova are removed, mixed with sperm, then both ova and sperm are inserted into a Fallopian tube to be fertilized in the natural setting. The first 'test-tube baby' was born in England in 1978. *See also* FERTILIZATION; INFERTILITY

involuntary muscle One of three types of MUSCLE in the body, so called because, unlike SKELETAL MUSCLE, it is not under the conscious control of the brain but stimulated by the AUTONOMIC NERVOUS SYSTEM and by HORMONES. **Smooth muscle** is the muscle of the ALIMENTARY CANAL, blood vessels, and bladder. **Cardiac muscle** powers the HEART.

Io Large, innermost satellite of JUPITER. It was discovered by GALILEO in 1609–10, and is larger than the Moon. It is more than 3,600km (2,200mi) in diameter, and is 422,000km (262,000mi) above the surface of the planet.

iodine (symbol I) Nonmetallic element, the least reactive of the HALOGEN group. The black volatile solid gives a violet vapour and has an unpleasant odour that resembles CHLORINE. Iodine was discovered in 1811. Found in seawater, seaweeds and other plants, it is also extracted from Chile saltpetre and oil-well brine. Iodine is essential for the functioning of the THYROID GLAND. In medicine, it is used as an antiseptic. Properties: at.no. 53; r.a.m. 126.9; r.d. 4.93; m.p. 113.5°C (236.3°F); b.p. 184.4°C (363.9°F); most stable isotope I[127] (100%).

ion Atom or group of atoms with an electric (positive or negative) charge resulting from the loss or gain of one or more ELECTRONS. Positive ions are called **cations** and move towards the CATHODE in ELECTROLYSIS; negative ions are called **anions** and move towards the ANODE. **Ion exchange** is when a compound's ions are replaced by ions from another compound with the same charge, and this process is used to remove the HARDNESS OF WATER. The region of ions in the atmosphere is the IONOSPHERE. *See also* IONIC BOND; IONIC COMPOUND

Iona Island off the coast of w Scotland in the Inner HEBRIDES. Tourism is the main source of income. Area: 13sq km (5sq mi).

Ionesco, Eugène (1912–94) French dramatist. A major force behind the Theatre of the ABSURD, he had his first success with *The Bald Prima Donna* (1950), a satire on the futility of verbal communication.

Ionia Historic region on the w coast of Asia Minor (Turkey), including the neighbouring Aegean islands. The area was settled by people from Mycenae in Greece in the 11th and 10th centuries BC. Miletus and EPHESUS became the most important of the prosperous Ionian cities. Ionia was conquered by the Persians in the 6th century BC then fell

IRAN

The barren central plateau of the Islamic Republic of Iran covers about half the country. It includes the Great Salt Desert (*Dasht-e-Kavir*) and the Great Sand Desert (*Dasht-e-Lut*). The Elburz Mountains (Alborz), border the it to the N and contain Iran's highest peak, Damavand (5,604m [18,386ft]). N of the Elburz Mountains are the fertile, densely populated lowlands around the Caspian Sea, with a mild climate and abundant rainfall. Bordering the plateau to the w are the Zagros Mountains which separate the central plateau from the Khuzistan Plain, a region of sugar plantations and oil fields, which extends to the Iraqi border.

CLIMATE

Much of Iran has a severe, dry climate, with hot summers and cold winters. Rain falls on only about 30 days a year in Tehran and the annual temperature range is of more than 25°C [45°F]. The lowlands are generally milder.

HISTORY

In 550 BC CYRUS THE GREAT conquered the Median Empire, establishing the ACHAEMENID dynasty, rulers of the first Persian Empire. The Empire survived the Persian Wars (492–497 BC) against the Greek city-states, but fell to Alexander the Great in 331 BC. Persian rule was restored by the SASSANIDS in AD 224. Arabs conquered Iran in AD 641 and introduced ISLAM. For the next two centuries Iran was a centre of learning and of ISLAMIC ART AND ARCHITECTURE. SELJUK Turks conquered Iran in the 11th century, but the land was overrun by the MONGOLS in 1220.

The SAFAVID dynasty (1501–1722) was founded by Shah ISMAIL, who established the SHI'ITE theocratic principles of modern Iran. The despotic NADIR SHAH (1736–47) expelled Afghan invaders. The Qajar dynasty (1794–1925) witnessed the decline of the Iranian empire as Britain and Russia competed for influence in the area. The discovery of oil in sw Iran led to the Russian and British division of Iran (1907). In 1919 Iran effectively became a British protectorate. In 1921, Reza PAHLAVI seized power, annulled the British treaty and established the Pahlavi dynasty, naming the country Iran in 1935. In 1941 British and Soviet forces occupied the country and Reza Pahlavi abdicated in favour of his son Muhammad Reza PAHLAVI.

In 1951, the oil industry was nationalized. The Shah fled Iran, but soon returned with US backing and restored Western oil rights. Discontent surfaced over economic inequality and increasing westernization, as clerics led by Ayatollah KHOMEINI voiced their disapproval of secularism. In 1971 Britain withdrew its troops from the Arabian Gulf. Iran increased its defence spending to become the largest military power in the region. Khomeini, exiled in 1978, called for the abdication of the Shah. In 1979 the government was overthrown, the Shah fled, and Khomeini established an Islamic republic.

POLITICS

The IRAN-IRAQ WAR, fought over disputed borders from 1980–8, caused massive casualties and damaged the economy and vital oil industry. Khomeini died in 1989 but anti-Western attitudes continued to dominate. In 1997 and 2001 the liberal Mohammad KHATAMI was elected president, but the clerical establishment and institutions such as the judiciary and the Expediency Council blocked most of his reformist plans. From 2003 onwards the country began to develop a nuclear programme with Russian assistance, claiming it was for civilian power purposes, although the United States accused Iran of developing nuclear weapons. In 2005 elections Khatami was replaced as president by the highly conservative Mahmoud Ahmadinejad. In 2006 Iran began enriching uranium, causing disputes with the EU and US. In 2007, UN inspectors and US intelligence agencies both concluded that Iran was not developing an atomic bomb.

ECONOMY

Iran's prosperity is based on its oil, which accounts for 95% of the country's exports. Oil revenues have been used to develop a manufacturing sector, but agriculture still accounts for 25% of the gross domestic product even though farms cover only a tenth of the land. The main crops are wheat and barley. Livestock farming and fishing are also important.

AREA 1,648,195sq km [636,368sq mi]
POPULATION 65,398,000
CAPITAL (POPULATION) Tehran (7,352,000)
GOVERNMENT Islamic Republic
ETHNIC GROUPS Persian 51%, Azeri 24%, Gilaki and Mazandarani 8%, Kurd 7%, Arab 3%, Lur 2%, Baluchi 2%, Turkmen 2%
LANGUAGES Persian, Turkic 26%, Kurdish
RELIGIONS Islam (Shi'ite Muslim 89%)
CURRENCY Iranian rial = 100 dinars

under Athenian domination until the Persians regained control in the 4th century BC. After the conquests of ALEXANDER THE GREAT, Ionia was ruled by Hellenistic kings and from the 2nd century BC was part of the Roman Empire.

Ionians In ancient Greece, inhabitants of Attica, Boeotia, and IONIA. They spoke a dialect distinct from that of the DORIANS and Aeolians. The hostility between Ionians and Dorians, neither regarding the other as fully Greek, appears in the contest between Athens and Sparta in the PELOPONNESIAN WARS. The term is also applied to the inhabitants of Ionia alone.

ionic bond (electrovalent bond) Chemical bond in which IONS of opposite charge are held together by electrostatic attraction.

ionic compound Substance formed by ionic bonding, a chemical bond of positively and negatively charged IONS. Salts, bases and some acids are ionic compounds. As crystalline solids, they have high melting points and boiling points. As solids, they are nonconductors of electricity, and are usually soluble in water but insoluble in organic solvents. In the liquid and molten states, ionic compounds are good conductors.

Ionic order One of the classical ORDERS OF ARCHITECTURE

ionosphere Wide region of IONS in the ATMOSPHERE. It extends from about 60km (40mi) above the Earth to the limits of the atmosphere in the VAN ALLEN RADIATION BELTS (1,000km/620mi). Radio waves are deflected in the ionosphere, so making long-distance radio communication possible.

Iowa State in N central USA, lying between the Missouri and Mississippi; the capital is DES MOINES. First discovered in 1673, the land was claimed for France in 1682. The region was sold to the USA in the LOUISIANA PURCHASE of 1803. Iowa was admitted to the Union in 1846. Industrial development was encouraged after World War 2. Originally prairie that was ploughed to create farmland, the region is known for its fertile soil. Maize and other cereals are produced and Iowa stands second only to Texas in the raising of prime cattle. Industries: food processing, farm machinery. Area: 145,790sq km (56,290sq mi). Pop. (2000) 2,926,324.

Iphigenia In Greek legend, daughter of AGAMEMNON and CLYTEMNESTRA and sister of ELECTRA and ORESTES. She was sacrificed by her father to the goddess Artemis in exchange for her giving him favourable winds for his journey to Troy.

IRAQ

The Republic of Iraq is a SW Asian country at the head of the PERSIAN GULF. Deserts cover W and SW Iraq. Part of the Zagros Mountains forms the NE, where farming can be practised without irrigation. W Iraq contains a large slice of the Hamad (or Syrian) Desert, but essentially comprises lower valleys of the rivers EUPHRATES (Nahr al Furat) and TIGRIS (Nahr Dijlah). The region is arid, but has fertile alluvial soils. The Euphrates and Tigris join south of Al Qurnah to form the SHATT AL ARAB. The Shatt al Arab's delta is an area of irrigated farmland and marshes. This waterway is shared with Iran.

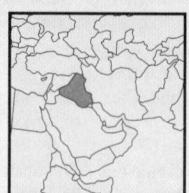

to ASSYRIA. In the 1st millennium BC the Assyrian kings SARGON II, SENNACHERIB and ASHURBANIPAL added to the splendour of NINEVEH. NEBUCHADNEZZAR conquered Jerusalem in 597 BC, beginning the BABYLONIAN CAPTIVITY. In 539 BC Babylon fell to CYRUS THE GREAT, who founded the ACHAEMENID dynasty. Mesopotamia became part of the Persian Empire. ISLAM was introduced via the Arab conquest in AD 637. In the 8th century, Baghdad became capital of the ABBASID caliphate (750–1258). Mongols captured Baghdad in 1258 and Mesopotamia went into decline. From 1534, Mesopotamia was part of the Ottoman Empire. Britain invaded Mesopotamia in 1916, and in 1920 it became a British mandated territory. Britain renamed the country Iraq, and set up an Arab monarchy. Iraq became independent in 1932.

As a member of the Arab League, Iraq participated in the 1948 ARAB-ISRAELI WAR. By the 1950s oil dominated Iraq's economy and in 1952 the government agreed to take 50% of the profits of the foreign oil companies to fund welfare services and national development programmes. In 1958, a proposal to form an Arab Union with Jordan precipitated a military coup. A republic was established and the king executed. In 1962, the Kurds of N Iraq demanded autonomy, beginning a protracted war of secession. In 1968 the BA'ATH PARTY emerged as the dominant power. Iraq participated in the 1973 Arab-Israeli War.

AREA 438,317sq km [169,234sq mi]
POPULATION 27,500,000
CAPITAL (POPULATION) Baghdad (5,910,000)
GOVERNMENT Republic
ETHNIC GROUPS Arab 77%, Kurdish 19%, Assyrian and others
LANGUAGES Arabic (official), Kurdish (official in Kurdish areas), Assyrian, Armenian
RELIGIONS Islam 97%, Christianity and others
CURRENCY New Iraqi dinar

In 2002 Iraq finally allowed the return of UN weapons inspectors. In 2003 a US-led coalition invaded and rapidly toppled Saddam's regime. Saddam Hussein was soon captured, but no biological or chemical weapons were found.

Attacks on the Coalition-backed Iraqi government by opposing insurgent forces escalated in 2004 and continue to the present. Attacks on civilians occur daily. Multiparty elections took place in 2005 but were boycotted by Sunni Arabs, 20% of the population. Reconstruction of damaged infrastructure was halted by widespread corruption. In 2006 a US Congress report urged withdrawal of American forces; President BUSH instead increased troop levels. Also in December, an Iraqi court executed Saddam by hanging for "crimes against humanity" committed against opposition groups during his rule. In 2007 the US accused Iran of backing insurgent groups. In 2008 Turkey attacked Kurds in northern Iraq, accusing them of supporting rebels in Turkey, but withdrew after pressure from the US.

CLIMATE
The climate of Iraq varies from temperate in the north to subtropical in the south and east. Baghdad, in central Iraq, has cool winters, with occasional frosts, and hot summers. Rainfall is generally low.

HISTORY
The ancient region of MESOPOTAMIA roughly corresponds with modern Iraq. SUMERIA was the first great civilization, c.3000 BC. In c. 2340 BC, Sargon I conquered Sumeria. In the 18th century BC, HAMMURABI established the first empire of Babylonia. In the 8th century BC, Babylonia fell

POLITICS
In 1979, SADDAM HUSSEIN became Iraq's president. Iraq invaded Iran in 1980, starting the eight-year IRAN-IRAQ WAR. Iraq used chemical weapons both against Iran and against Iraqi Kurds. In 1990 Iraqi troops occupied Kuwait, but an international force drove them out in the 1991 GULF WAR. From 1991 Iraqi troops attacked Shi'ite Marsh Arabs and Kurds.

In 1998, Iraq's failure to allow full access to UNSCOM, the UN body charged with disposing of Iraq's chemical and biological weapons, led to Western bombardment of military sites. Periodic bombardment and UN economic sanctions continued, but Iraq was allowed limited oil exports in exchange for food and medicines.

ECONOMY
Civil war and war damage in 1991 and 2003, UN sanctions, and economic mismanagement have all contributed to economic chaos. Oil remains Iraq's main resource, but the industry is severely disrupted. Although production is recovering, much oil is stolen or smuggled out to fund factions, militias and insurgencies. Farmland covers around a fifth of the land. Products include barley, cotton, dates, fruit, livestock, wheat and wool. Iraq still has to import food. Industries include oil refining, petrochemicals and consumer goods.

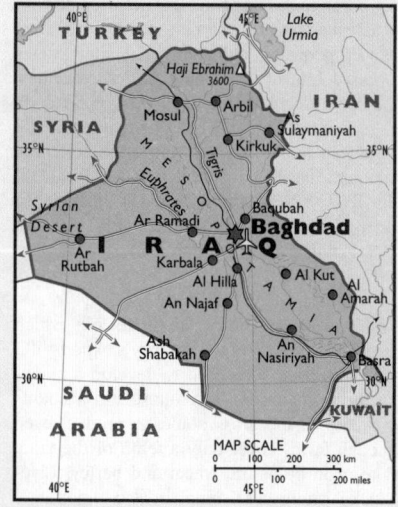

Ipswich City and port in E England; the county town of SUFFOLK. The wool trade brought it prosperity in the Middle Ages. Its fortunes revived in the 19th century with the introduction of light industry. Industries: milling, brewing, printing, agricultural machinery. Pop. (2001) 117,074.

IQ (Intelligence Quotient) Classification of the supposed intelligence of a person. It is computed by dividing the person's assessed 'mental age' by their real age, then multiplying by 100. The 'mental age' is determined by comparison to the average performance of people of various ages on a standard intelligence test. *See also* APTITUDE TEST

IRA Abbreviation of IRISH REPUBLICAN ARMY

Iráklion (Heraklion or Candia) Seaport and largest city on Crete, s Greece; capital of Iráklion prefecture. Founded in the 9th century by the Saracens, it was conquered by the Byzantines (961), the Venetians (1204) and the Ottoman Turks (1669). The ruins of KNOSSOS are nearby. Tourism is important. Exports: wine, olive oil, almonds and raisins. Pop. (2001) 263,868.

Iran Islamic republic in sw Asia. *See* country feature, page 413

Iran-Contra affair (Irangate) US political scandal (1985–86) in which weapons were illegally sold to Iran, in order to secure the release of US hostages in the Middle East and the profits diverted to support the Nicaraguan CONTRA, who were fighting the left wing SANDINISTA government. Colonel Oliver NORTH who negotiated the deal and several other officials were later convicted of various charges, including obstructing Congress. In 1992, they were pardoned by George BUSH.

Iranian languages Group of languages forming a subdivision of the Indo-Iranian family of INDO-EUROPEAN LANGUAGES. The major Iranian languages are Persian, Pashto, Kurdish, Mazanderani and Gilaki (of Iran), Baluchi (of Iran and Pakistan) and Tajik and Ossetic, spoken in the republic of Tajikistan and in South Ossetia (a part of Georgia) and North Ossetia (an autonomous region of the Russian Federation).

Iran-Iraq War (1980–88) Conflict between Iran and Iraq when Iraq, partly in response to Iranian encouragement of revolt among the SHI'ITES of s Iraq, invaded Iran, which was disorganized after the Islamic revolution of 1979. Iraq's objective was the SHATT AL ARAB waterway, but stiff Iranian resistance checked the Iraqi advance and forced their withdrawal (1982). The conflict bogged down in stalemate, with sporadic Iranian offensives. US-led intervention in 1987 was seen as tacit support for Iraq. A UN ceasefire resolution (1987) was accepted by Iraq and, after several Iraqi successes, by Iran also. Estimated total casualties were more than 1 million.

Iraq Republic in sw Asia. *See* country feature

Ireland Second largest island of the BRITISH ISLES. Ireland is w of Great Britain. The Irish Sea and St George's Channel run between the two islands. Politically, Ireland is divided in two: the Republic of IRELAND and Northern IRELAND. **Land and climate** The central area of Ireland is a lowland with a mild, wet climate. This area is covered with peat bogs (a source of fuel) and fertile limestone (the location of dairy farming). Most coastal regions are barren highlands. The interior of Ireland has many lakes and wide rivers (loughs). It boasts the longest river in the British Isles, the SHANNON. **History** From c.3rd century BC to the late 8th century, Ireland was divided into five kingdoms inhabited by Celtic and pre-Celtic tribes. In the 8th century AD the Danes invaded, establishing trading towns, including DUBLIN, and creating new kingdoms. In 1014, BRIAN BORU defeated the Danes, and for the next 150 years Ireland was free from invasion but subject to clan warfare. In 1171, HENRY II of England invaded Ireland and established English control. In the late 13th century, an Irish Parliament was formed. In 1315, English dominance was threatened by a Scottish invasion. In the late 15th century, HENRY VII restored English hegemony and began the plantation of Ireland by English settlers. Edward Poynings forced the Irish Parliament to pass Poynings Law (1495), stating that future Irish legislation must be sanctioned by the English Privy Council. Under JAMES I, the plantation of ULSTER intensified. An Irish rebellion (1641–49) was eventually thwarted by Oliver CROMWELL. During the GLORIOUS REVOLUTION, Irish Catholics supported JAMES II, while Ulster Protestants backed WILLIAM III. After James' defeat, the English-controlled Irish Parliament passed a series

of punitive laws against Catholics. In 1782, Henry GRATTAN forced trade concessions and the repeal of Poynings Law. William PITT's government passed the Act of UNION (1801), which abolished the Irish Assembly and created the United Kingdom of Great Britain and Ireland. In 1829, largely due to the efforts of Daniel O'CONNELL, the Act of CATHOLIC EMANCIPATION was passed, which secured Irish representation in the British Parliament. A blight ruined the potato crop and caused the Irish Famine (1845–49). Nationalist demands intensified. Gladstone failed to secure Irish HOME RULE amid mounting pressure from fearful Ulster Protestants. In 1905 Arthur GRIFFITH founded SINN FÉIN. In 1914 Home Rule was agreed, but implementation was suspended during World War 1. In the EASTER RISING (April 1916), Irish nationalists announced the creation of the Republic of Ireland. The British Army's brutal crushing of the rebellion was a propaganda victory for Sinn Féin and led to a landslide victory in Irish elections (1918). Between 1918 and 1921 the IRISH REPUBLICAN ARMY (IRA), founded by Michael COLLINS, fought a guerrilla war against British forces. In 1920, a new Home Rule Bill established separate parliaments for Ulster and Catholic Ireland. The Anglo-Irish Treaty (1921) led to the creation of an Irish Free State in January 1922 and *de facto* acceptance of partition. (For history post-1922, *see* IRELAND, NORTHERN; IRELAND, REPUBLIC OF)

Ireland, John Nicholson (1879–1962) British composer, influenced by Brahms, Dvorák and Ravel. His works, firmly grounded in ROMANTICISM and often inspired by places and landscape, include *The Forgotten Rite* (1913), *Mai-Dun* (1921), *These Things Shall Be* (1937), the overture *Satyricon* (1946) and many songs and piano pieces.

Ireland, Northern Part of the UNITED KINGDOM, 26 districts occupying the NE of IRELAND, traditionally divided into the six counties of ANTRIM, ARMAGH, DERRY, DOWN, FERMANAGH and TYRONE; the capital is BELFAST. Other major towns include DERRY, Coleraine, Ballymena, Lisburn, Enniskillen, Armagh and Newry. (For land and climate, and pre-1922 history, *see* IRELAND.) **History** In 1920, the six counties of Ulster became the self-governing province of Northern Ireland with a separate, Protestant-dominated parliament. The British government affirmed the inclusion of Northern Ireland within the UK under the principle of self-determination. The Irish Free State (now Republic of Ireland) constitution upheld the unity of the island of Ireland. In 1955, the IRISH REPUBLICAN ARMY (IRA) began a campaign of violence for the creation of an independent, unified Ireland. In 1962, the Republic of Ireland condemned the use of terrorism. Northern Catholics felt aggrieved at discrimination in employment, housing and political representation. In 1967, the Civil Rights Association was established to campaign for equal rights. In 1968, civil-rights marches resulted in violent clashes, especially in Derry. Catholic fear of the increasing Protestant domination of local security forces was compounded when the Royal Ulster Constabulary (RUC) was supplemented by the sectarian Ulster Defence Regiment (UDR). The British Army was brought in to protect the Catholic populations in Belfast and Derry. The IRA and Protestant LOYALIST paramilitary organizations, such as the Ulster Defence Association (UDA), increased their campaigns of sectarian violence. In 1972, the Northern Ireland parliament (Stormont) was suspended and replaced by direct rule from Westminster. On January 30, 1972 ('Bloody Sunday'), British troops shot and killed 13 civil-rights' demonstrators. In 1974 the Council of Ireland, formed by the British and Irish governments to promote cooperation between Ulster and the Irish Republic, quickly collapsed under pressure from a Unionist-led general strike. The IRA campaign widened to include terrorist attacks on Great Britain and British military bases in w Europe. In 1981, hunger strikes by IRA prisoners were more successful in gaining worldwide sympathy. In 1985, the ANGLO-IRISH AGREEMENT gave the Republic of Ireland a consultative role in the government of Northern Ireland. In 1986, a Northern Ireland Assembly was re-established, but quickly failed under the Unionists' boycott. In 1993, following secret talks between the British government and SINN FÉIN, the DOWNING STREET DECLARATION offered all-party negotiations following a cessation of violence. In 1994, Provisional

IOWA
Statehood :
December 28, 1846
Nickname :
Hawkeye state
State bird :
Eastern goldfinch
State flower :
Wild rose
State tree :
Oak
State motto :
Our liberties we prize and our rights we will maintain

I

IRA and Loyalist paramilitaries announced a ceasefire, raising hopes of an end to a sectarian conflict that had claimed more than 2,700 lives. In 1996, disputes over the decommissioning of arms stalled the process and the IRA resumed its terrorist campaign on the British mainland. In July 1997, another cease-fire was agreed and, in October, Sinn Féin and Unionists took part in joint peace talks for the first time since partition. On April 10, 1998, the GOOD FRIDAY AGREEMENT was signed. It provided for a devolved, elected Northern Ireland Assembly. The Republic of Ireland agreed to abandon its constitutional claim to Northern Ireland and processes were established for the decommissioning of weapons and releases of paramilitary prisoners. In May 1998, the Agreement was overwhelmingly approved in referenda in Northern Ireland and the Republic of Ireland. In June 1998, elections were held for the new Northern Ireland Assembly. David TRIMBLE of the Ulster Unionists became First Minister. The decommissioning of some IRA weapons in 2001 and 2002 seemed to open the way for a lasting peace but negotiations stagnated and the Assembly was suspended in 2002. It resumed in 2007. **Economy** More than 80% of Northern Ireland is farmed. Chief crops are potatoes and barley. Heavy industry is concentrated around the port of Belfast. Industries include shipbuilding, vehicle manufacture and textiles (especially linen). The majority population is Protestant; Catholics form a significant minority of 38%. Northern Ireland's economic prosperity is not equally shared: the Catholic community has a much higher rate of unemployment. The economy has been devastated by civil war. Area: 14,121sq km (5,452sq mi). Pop. (2001) 1,685,267.

Ireland, Republic of Country occupying most of the island of Ireland, NW Europe. *See* country feature

Irian Jaya (West Irian, or Irian Barat) Province of E Indonesia, comprising the W half of New Guinea and adjacent islands; the capital is Djajapura. First explored by Europeans in the 16th century, it was claimed by the Netherlands in 1828 and became known as Dutch New Guinea. It achieved independence in 1962, and was incorporated into Indonesia in 1963. In the centre of the province, a mountain range, rising to more than 5,000m (16,500ft), runs *c.*640km (400mi) E to W. Much of the region N of the range is covered by tropical rainforest. The economy is mainly agricultural, the chief products being copra, peanuts, rice and timber. Copper and crude oil are exported. Area: 422,170sq km (162,900sq mi). Pop. (1999) 1,691,800.

iridium (symbol Ir) Silver-white, metallic element discovered in 1804 by the English chemist Smithson Tennant. A platinum-type metal, iridium is hard and brittle and the most corrosion-resistant metal. It is used in making surgical tools, scientific instruments, pen tips and electrical contacts. Properties: at.no. 77; r.a.m. 192.22; r.d. 22.42; m.p. 2,410°C (4,370°F); b.p. 4,130°C (7,466°F); most common isotope Ir^{193} (62.6%).

iris Coloured part of the EYE. It controls the amount of light that enters the PUPIL in the centre of the eye by increasing or decreasing the size of the pupil. These changes are brought about by muscles in the iris contracting or relaxing.

iris Genus of about 300 species of flowering plants, widely distributed mostly in temperate areas. They are MONO-COTYLEDONS and have BULBS or RHIZOMES. Height: up to 90cm (3ft). Family Iridaceae. *See also* CROCUS; GLADIOLUS

IRELAND, REPUBLIC OF

The Republic of Ireland consists of a large lowland region surrounded by a broken rim of low mountains. The lowlands include peat bogs. The uplands include the Mountains of Kerry with Carrauntoohill, Ireland's highest peak (1,041m [3,415ft]). The River Shannon is the longest in the Ireland, flowing through three large lakes, loughs Allen, Ree and Derg. Forests cover approximately 5% of Ireland. Much of the land is under pasture and a very small percentage is set aside for crops.

CLIMATE

Ireland has a mild, damp climate influenced by the Gulf Stream current which warms the west coast, with Dublin in the east somewhat cooler. Rain occurs thoughout the year.

HISTORY

In 1920, the British parliament passed the Government of Ireland Act, partitioning Ireland. The six Ulster counties accepted the Act, but fighting broke out in southern Ireland. (See IRELAND for detail of pre-1922 history) In 1921, a treaty was agreed allowing southern Ireland to become a self-governing dominion, called the Irish Free State, within the British Commonwealth. Arthur GRIFFITH of SINN FÉIN became Taoiseach. Civil war (1922–23) ensued between supporters of the settlement, and those who refused to countenance the partition of Ireland and the creation of NORTHERN IRELAND. The anti-settlement party, led by Eamon DE VALERA, were defeated by Irish Free State forces led by Michael COLLINS. Collins was assassinated and William COSGRAVE became prime minister (1922–32). In 1926, De Valera formed a separate party, FIANNA FÁIL, and became Taoiseach (1932–48, 1951–54, 1957–59). In 1933, FINE GAEL was founded.

In 1937 a new constitution declared the sovereign nation of Éire to be the whole island of Ireland, and abolished the oath of loyalty to the English crown. During World War 2, Éire remained neutral. It opposed Allied operations in Northern Ireland and the IRISH REPUBLICAN ARMY (IRA) pursued a pro-German line

POLITICS

Ireland became a republic in 1949 and has subsequently played an independent role in Europe, joining the EEC in 1973 and adopting the euro as

AREA 70,273sq km [27,132sq mi]
POPULATION 4,109,000
CAPITAL (POPULATION) Dublin (985,000)
GOVERNMENT Multiparty republic
ETHNIC GROUPS Irish 94%
LANGUAGES Irish (Gaelic) and English (both official)
RELIGIONS Roman Catholic 92%, Protestant 3%
CURRENCY Euro = 100 cents

its currency in 2002. In 1998 the government of Ireland began to work with British governments in attempts to solve the problems of Northern Ireland. It supported the creation of a Northern Ireland Assembly and the amendment of the 1937 constitution, withdrawing the republic's claim to Northern Ireland. The Northern Ireland Assembly finally began to function in 2007, and the government of the Republic of Ireland has worked to strengthen links with the north.

Bertie AHERN was elected Taoiseach in 1997, and re-elected in 2002 and 2007 as the head of the country's longest-serving coalition government. He resigned as Taoiseach in May 2008.

ECONOMY

The 1990s and 2000s saw a substantial economic boom, and the Republic of Ireland is a prosperous developed country. Manufacturing is now the leading activity, with high-tech industries producing chemicals and pharmaceuticals, electronic equipment, machinery, paper and textiles. Aided by EU grants, farming is now relatively prosperous and includes cattle and dairy, sheep, pigs, potatoes and barley. Racehorses form a significant part of the rural economy. Tourism is also important.

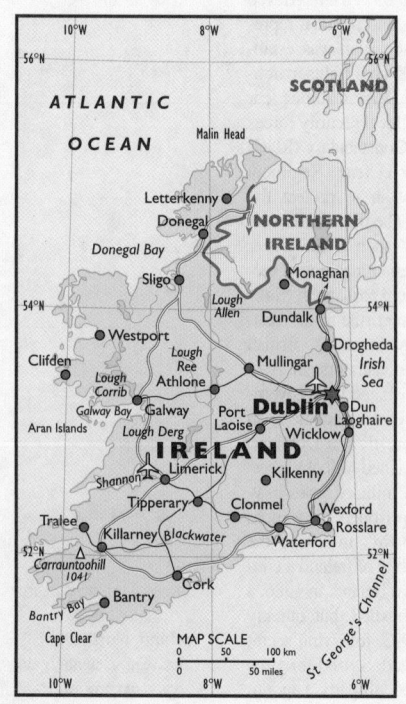

Iris In Greek mythology, goddess of the rainbow and the messenger of the gods. Depicted as swift-footed, golden-winged and robed in bright colours, she appears in numerous classical writings, including Euripides' *Herakles*.

Irish *See* GAELIC

Irish literature Body of work produced by inhabitants of Ireland. The earliest written works, mainly heroic sagas, date from the 7th to the 12th centuries and were composed in GAELIC. A number of lyric poets were also active during this period, writing on historical or religious subjects. Between the 13th and 17th centuries, Gaelic was gradually eroded by Norman and English encroachment, preserved only in poetic works commissioned by wealthy patrons. Leading figures in ENGLISH LITERATURE, such as Jonathan SWIFT, Laurence STERNE and Oscar WILDE, were of Irish descent. Inspired by the movement for Irish HOME RULE, the late 19th and early 20th centuries saw an Irish literary renaissance. Although largely writing in English, the movement drew on the traditions of Gaelic culture. The revival was led by W.B. YEATS. The ABBEY THEATRE hosted the resurgence in Irish drama, staging plays by J.M. SYNGE, George Bernard SHAW and Sean O'CASEY. James JOYCE and Samuel BECKETT reflected on Irish culture from self-exile. Leading contemporary Irish writers include Brian Friel and Seamus HEANEY.

Irish Republican Army (IRA) Guerrilla organization dedicated to the reunification of Ireland. Formed in 1919, the IRA waged guerrilla warfare against British rule. Some members ('irregulars') rejected the Anglo-Irish settlement of 1921, fighting a civil war until 1923. In 1970, the organization split into an 'Official' wing (which emphasized political activities), and a 'Provisional' wing (committed to armed struggle). Thereafter, the Provisional IRA became committed to terrorist acts in Northern Ireland and mainland Britain. It declared a ceasefire in 1994, but in 1996 resumed its campaign. Another ceasefire was declared in 1997. The decommissioning of IRA weapons was a major issue in the peace process.

Irish Sea Part of the Atlantic Ocean, lying between Ireland and Britain. It is connected to the Atlantic by the North Channel (N) and by St George's Channel (S). Scotland, Wales and England are on its E shore and Ireland on the w shore. Area: 103,600sq km (40,000sq mi).

Irkutsk City on the River Angara, E Siberia, Russia; capital of Irkutsk oblast. It began as a camp and trading centre in the mid-17th century. It grew as a result of trade with China and the completion of the Trans-Siberian Railway. Irkutsk is an important industrial and educational centre. Gold from the Lena goldfields is transshipped here, and there is also trade in furs. Industries: ship-repairing, timber, machine tools, heavy machinery, oil refining, hydroelectricity. Pop. (1994) 632,000.

iron (symbol Fe) Common metallic element of the first transition series, known from ancient times. Its chief ores are HEMATITE (Fe_2O_3), MAGNETITE (Fe_3O_4), and iron PYRITES (FeS_2). **Pig** iron is made in a BLAST FURNACE by SMELTING iron oxide with carbon monoxide from coke, using limestone to form a slag. **Cast** iron is made by remelting and cooling pig iron. Wrought iron is made by heating pig iron with ferric oxide. Iron corrodes to form RUST. Iron is alloyed with carbon and other elements in the various forms of STEEL used in cutlery, car parts, bridges, ships and buildings. Properties: at.no. 26; r.a.m. 55.847; r.d. 7.86; m.p. 1,535°C (2,795°F); b.p. 2,750°C (4,982°F); most common isotope Fe^{56} (91.66%).

Iron Age Period succeeding the BRONZE AGE, dating from about 1100 BC in the Near East, later in W Europe. During this period people learned to smelt IRON, although the HITTITES had probably developed the first significant iron industry in Armenia soon after 2000 BC.

Iron Curtain Term describing the barrier between communist East Europe and the capitalist West during the COLD WAR. The term passed into common use after its appearance in a speech by Winston CHURCHILL at Fulton, Missouri, in March 1946.

Iroquois Confederacy League of Native North Americans occupying the Mohawk Valley and the Lakes area of New York state. They called themselves Oñgwanósioñi (Hodinonhsioni), 'people of the long house', after the distinctive shape of their bark dwellings. The original tribes were the MOHAWK, SENECA, Onondaga, Cayuga and Oneida. The Tuscarora joined later. The Iroquois had a highly developed political system and were renowned warriors. Their total number has halved since 1600. Today, they number *c*.10,000, mostly living in New York, Wisconsin, Oklahoma, and Canada.

irradiation Exposure to nuclear or ELECTROMAGNETIC RADIATION. Materials are often irradiated with high-energy NEUTRONS in NUCLEAR REACTORS, to make them temporarily radioactive. More portable sources of such radiation are radioisotopes such as cobalt-60 and caesium-137, which are used in the irradiation treatment for cancer. Treatment also involves the use of particle ACCELERATORS, including PROTON and neutron beam machines. **Ionizing** radiation is used in FOOD PRESERVATION to destroy bacteria and microorganisms in some foodstuffs, while in other foods, such as soft fruits, it increases shelf-life. The process of irradiation in FOOD TECHNOLOGY is still being closely monitored.

irrational number In mathematics, any number that cannot be expressed as the ratio of two integers. An example is $\sqrt{2}$: like other irrational numbers, its expression as a decimal is infinite and non-repeating. Irrational numbers, together with the RATIONAL NUMBERS, make up the set of REAL NUMBERS.

Irrawaddy (Irawadi) River in central Burma (Myanmar), formed by the union of the Mali and Nmai rivers. A vast delta extends 290km (180mi) from Henzada to the Andaman Sea. One of Asia's major rivers, it lies at the centre of an important rice-producing region. Length: *c*.2,100km (1,300mi).

irrigation Artificial watering of land for growing crops. Irrigation enables crops to grow in regions with inadequate precipitation. The first irrigation systems date from before 3000 BC in Egypt, Asia and the Middle East. Today, most water for irrigation is surface water (from streams, rivers and lakes) or ground water (obtained from wells). In some regions, freshwater for irrigation is obtained by DESALINATION. Canals, ditches, pumps and pipes are used to convey water to fields.

Irving, Sir Henry (1838–1905) English actor-manager, real name John Henry Brodribb. He made his first stage appearance in 1856. In 1878, he became manager of the Lyceum Theatre, London. His last acting performance was in 1905.

Irving, Washington (1783–1859) US essayist and short-story writer. He wrote the burlesque *History of New York* (1809) under the pseudonym Dietrich Knickerbocker. He is most famous for the stories *Rip Van Winkle* and *The Legend of Sleepy Hollow*, which were written during his 17 years in Europe. He returned to the USA in 1832, where his continuing literary output included *Astoria* (1836).

Isaac Character of the Old Testament, and one of the PATRIARCHS. He was the son of ABRAHAM and Sarah. As a test of faith, Abraham was prepared to sacrifice Isaac, but at the last minute, he was told to sacrifice a lamb instead. In Islamic tradition ISHMAEL, not Isaac, was to be the sacrifice. Isaac married Rebecca and became the father of JACOB and ESAU.

Isabella I (1451–1504) Queen of Castile (1474–1504), whose marriage to Ferdinand II of Aragon (FERDINAND V of Castile and León) led to the unification of Spain and its emergence as a dominant European power. Daughter of John II, she won a dispute over the succession by 1468 and married Ferdinand (1469). With his support, she reformed royal administration in Castile and encouraged humanist scholarship in Spain, although she was also responsible for the Spanish INQUISITION (1487) and the expulsion of Jews (1492). Her popularity was enhanced by the conquest of Granada (1492). She supported the voyages of COLUMBUS, which led to the establishment of the Spanish Empire in the New World.

Isabella II (1830–1904) Queen of Spain (1833–68). The daughter of Ferdinand VII, she was challenged by her uncle, Don Carlos, which resulted in the first CARLIST civil war. A liberal revolt led by army officers forced her into exile (1868), and in 1870 she abdicated in favour of her son, Alfonso XII.

Isabella of France (1292–1358) Queen consort of EDWARD II of England (1308–27), daughter of PHILIP IV of France. In 1325 she returned to France. In 1326 Isabella and her lover, Roger de Mortimer, launched a successful invasion of England, forced Edward to abdicate and assassinated him. In 1327, Edward and Isabella's son acceded to

INTERNET

Irving, Washington
▶ www.online-literature.com /irving/

I

▲ **iris** Grown mainly in temperate regions for displays, the many plants of the genus *iris* usually feature narrow, pointed leaves. The flowers are either purple, white or yellow.

► **Islamic architecture** Much of Islamic architecture, such as this mosque in Tehran, Iran, is decorated with complex and colourful geometric shapes, often inscribing the name of the prophet Muhammad. Domes and minarets are common architectural forms.

the throne as EDWARD III, who in 1330 executed Mortimer and banished his mother to a nunnery.

Isaiah (Isaias) (active *c*.8th centuryBC) Old Testament prophet who was active in Jerusalem from the 740s until the end of the century, and gave his name to the Old Testament Book of Isaiah – although only part of it is attributed to him. The rest is thought to be the work of one or even two authors from a later period. The book contrasts Judah's perilous present-day state with glimpses into the future, when God shall send a king to rule over his people.

ISDN *See* INTEGRATED SERVICES DIGITAL NETWORK

Isfahan (Esfahan) City in central Iran, on the Zaindeh River. The ancient city of Aspadana, it was occupied successively by Arabs, Seljuk Turks and Mongols. In the late 16th century, the SAFAVID dynasty made it their capital and transformed it into one of the most beautiful cities of the age. After its capture by the Afghans in 1722, the city declined. It has steel and textile industries as well as the traditional crafts of carpets and rugs, metalwork and silverware. Pop. (2005) 1,547,000.

Isherwood, Christopher William Bradshaw (1904–86) English writer. His novels, characteristically dealing with the sensibility of the homosexual artist, include *All the Conspirators* (1928) and *Mr Norris Changes Trains* (1935), set in pre-war Germany. The musical *Cabaret* (1966) was based on a short story from *Goodbye to Berlin* (1939). He collaborated on three plays with W.H. AUDEN, including *The Ascent of F6* (1936). He emigrated to the USA in 1939, and became interested in Hinduism.

Ishiguro, Kazuo (1954–) Novelist, *b.* Japan, works UK writing in English. His early novels, *A Pale View of Hills* (1982) and *An Artist of the Floating World* (1986), are set in Japan. *The Remains of the Day* (1989) won the Booker Prize.

Ishmael Any of several biblical figures, most notably ABRAHAM's son by Hagar and half brother to ISAAC. He fathered 12 sons and one daughter, who married ESAU, Isaac's son.

Ishtar Principal goddess of Assyro-Babylonian mythology. She is the daughter of Anu, the sky god, and Sin, the moon god. Through the centuries, she came to exhibit diverse attributes, those of a compassionate mother goddess and of a lustful goddess of sex and war. Ishtar is identified with the Sumerian Inanna, Phoenician Astarte and the biblical Ashtoreth.

Isidore of Seville (560–636) Archbishop of Seville from *c*.600 and a distinguished administrator, teacher, and writer. His works include *Etymologies*, which was an encyclopedia, and books on history, natural science, linguistic studies, and theology. Pope Clement VIII canonized him in 1598.

isinglass Clear, almost pure gelatin that is prepared from the air bladders of sturgeon and other sources. It is used primarily to clarify wines and beers. The name also refers to an abundant silicate material, also called muscovite, used as an insulator.

Isis In Egyptian mythology, wife and sister of OSIRIS, and mother of Horus. After Osiris' murder, Isis put together the separate parts of Osiris's body and magically revived him.

Islam (Arabic, submission to God) Monotheistic religion originating in Arabia in the early 7th century. At the heart of Islam stands the KORAN, the divine revelation of God to MUHAMMAD. Members of the faith (MUSLIMS) date the beginning of Islam from AD 622, the year of the HEJIRA. Muslims submit to the will of Allah by five basic precepts (pillars). First, the *shahadah*, 'there is no God but Allah, and Muhammad is his prophet'. Second, *salah*, five daily ritual prayers. At a MOSQUE, a Muslim performs ritual ablutions before praying to God in a attitude of submission, kneeling on a prayer mat facing the KAABA at MECCA with head bowed, then rising with hands cupped behind the ears to hear God's message. Third, *zakat* or alms-giving. Fourth, *sawm*, fasting during RAMADAN. Fifth, HAJJ, the pilgrimage to MECCA. The rapid growth in Islam during the 8th century can be attributed to the unification of the temporal and spiritual. The community leader (CALIPH) is both religious and social leader. The Koran was soon supplemented by the informal, scriptural elaborations of the Sunna (Muhammad's sayings and deeds), collated as the Hadith. A Muslim must also abide by the SHARIA or religious law. While Islam stresses the importance of the unity of the *summa* (nation) of Islam, several distinctive branches have developed, such as SUNNI, SHI'ITE, and SUFISM. Today, there are *c*.1 billion Muslims worldwide.

Islamabad Capital of Pakistan, in the N of the country. Construction of a new capital to replace KARACHI began in 1960, and in 1967 Islamabad became the official capital. It lies at the heart of an agricultural region, but administrative and governmental activities predominate. Pop. (2005) 791,000.

Islamic art and architecture Islamic art began to develop as a unique synthesis of the diverse cultures of conquered countries from the 7th century. Early Islamic art and craft is best illustrated in the architecture of the MOSQUE. Two of the most impressive surviving examples of early Islamic architecture are the DOME OF THE ROCK (685–92) in Jerusalem and the UMAYYAD Mosque in Damascus (*c*.705). Common architectural forms, such as the DOME, MINARET, *sahn* (courtyard), and the often highly-decorated *mihrab* (prayer niche) and *mimbar* (prayer pulpit) developed in the 9th century. Mosques also acquired rich surface decorations of mosaic, carved stone and paint. In Spain, Moorish architecture developed independently after the Umayyads were forced to flee there by the ABBASID dynasty. It is characterized by its use of the horseshoe arch, faience and stone lattice screens, as seen in the ALHAMBRA. Islamic CAIRO is a world heritage site of Muslim architecture, often derived from Iranian innovation. The Ibn Tulun Mosque (879) is a fine example of early brick and stucco form. The Al-Azhar Mosque displays 10th-century developments. The masterwork of Persian mosques, with their distinctive onion-shaped domes and slender pencil minarets, is the ISFAHAN Imperial Mosque (1585–1612). The Iranians influenced the Islamic architecture of India and Turkey. Because of a religious stricture on the representation of nature, Islamic art developed stylized figures, geometrical designs and floral-like decorations (arabesques). The KORAN was the focus for much of the development of calligraphy and illumination. Many cursive scripts were developed in the 10th century, and the most commonly used, Nastaliq, was perfected in the 15th century. Muslim secular art included highly ornamented metalwork (often inlaid with red copper), which developed in the 13th century around Mosul, N MESOPOTAMIA. Pottery and ceramics were advanced, featuring glazes and decoration. The Islamic *minai* (enamel) technique reached its zenith in the 16th century in Isfahan, where entire walls were decorated in faience. Perhaps the best-known art of the Islamic world is that of rug-making.

Isle of Man *See* MAN, ISLE OF

Ismail (1486–1524) Shah of Persia (Iran) (1501–24), founder of the SAFAVID dynasty. A national and religious hero in Iran, he re-established Persian independence and established SHI'ITE Islam as the state religion. He warred successfully against the UZBEKS in 1510, but was defeated by Ottoman Sultan Selim I at the Battle of Chaldiran (1514).

Ismailis Smaller of the two SHI'ITE branches of ISLAM. Comprised of 'Twelvers', who trace the succession to the 12th IMAM, and 'Severners', who believe the succession halted with the 7th Imam, ISMAIL. Their leader is the AGA KHAN.

Ismail Pasha (1830–95) Viceroy and Khedive of Egypt (1863–79). He received the title of Khedive from the Ottoman Sultan in 1867. Profits from cotton enabled him to build in Alexandria and Cairo, but later financial difficulties forced him to sell Egypt's share in the Suez Canal Company to Britain and led to his resignation in favour of his son, Tewfik Pasha.

isobar Line on a weather map connecting points of equal pressure, either at the Earth's surface or at a constant height above it. The patterns of isobars depict the variation in atmospheric pressure, showing areas of high and low pressure on the map.

isolationism Avoidance by a state of foreign commitments and alliances, particularly applied to US policy in the early 20th century.

isomers Chemical compounds having the same molecular formula but different properties due to the different arrangement of atoms within the molecules. Structural isomers have atoms connected in different ways. Geometric isomers, also called cis-trans isomers, differ in their symmetry about a double bond. Optical isomers are mirror images of each other.

isotope One of two or more atoms with the same ATOMIC NUMBER but a different number of neutrons. Both ATOMIC MASS NUMBER and mass of the nucleus are different for different isotopes. The atomic mass of an element is an average of the isotope masses. The isotopes of an element have similar chemical properties, but physical properties vary slightly. Most elements have two or more naturally occurring isotopes, some of which are radioactive (radioisotopes). Hydrogen, for example, has two isotopes, deuterium and the

ISRAEL

The State of Israel is a small country in the E Mediterranean. Inland lie the Judaeo-Galilean highlands, from N Israel to the N tip of the NEGEV Desert in the S. To the E lie part of the Great Rift Valley, River JORDAN, Sea of GALILEE and DEAD SEA. At 403m [1,322ft] below sea level, this last is the world's lowest point on land.

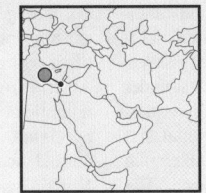

CLIMATE

Israel has hot, dry, summers. Winters are mild and moist on the coast. Annual rainfall decreases W to E and N to S with only 70mm [2.5in] in the Dead Sea region.

HISTORY

Israel comprises most of the Biblical Holy Lands (for history pre-1947, see PALESTINE). In the late 19th century, Zionists began to agitate for a Jewish homeland. Most modern Israelis are descendants of immigrants who began to settle from the 1880s. Britain ruled Palestine from 1917. Large numbers of Jews escaping Nazi persecution arrived in the 1930s, provoking an Arab uprising. In 1947, the United Nations (UN) agreed to partition Palestine into an Arab and a Jewish state, but Arabs rejected the plan and fighting broke out. On May 14, 1948, the State of Israel was proclaimed. Hundreds of thousands of Palestinians fled. In the first ARAB-ISRAELI WAR, Egypt, Iraq, Jordan, Lebanon and Syria invaded, but the HAGANAH successfully defended the state. An Israeli government was formed with Chaim WEIZMANN as president, and David BEN-GURION as prime minister. In 1949, Israel joined the United Nations and the capital moved from Tel-

Aviv to Jerusalem. In 1950, the Law of Return provided free citizenship for all immigrant Jews. Following Egypt's nationalization of the SUEZ CANAL, Israel captured Gaza and the SINAI PENINSULA. In 1957, Israel withdrew. In 1963 Ben-Gurion resigned, and Levi ESHKOL became prime minister (1963–69). In 1967, NASSER blockaded Elat. Israel's defence minister Moshe DAYAN launched a pre-emptive attack against Egypt and Syria. Within six days, Israel occupied the Gaza Strip, the Sinai Peninsula, the Golan Heights, the West Bank and East Jerusalem. Eshkol died in 1969, and Golda MEIR became prime minister (1969–74). On October 6, 1973 (YOM KIPPUR), Egypt and Syria attacked Israeli positions in Sinai and the Golan Heights. Israeli troops launched a counter-offensive and retained the territories gained in 1967. Yitzhak RABIN's government (1974–77) is chiefly remembered for the daring rescue of Israeli hostages at ENTEBBE.

POLITICS

Israel signed a treaty with Egypt in 1978 and returned the Sinai Peninsula in 1979, but conflict with the PLO continued. In 1993, the PLO and Israel agreed on Palestinian self-rule for the Gaza Strip and for Jericho on the West Bank. In 1995 this was extended to over 30% of the West Bank. Israel's prime minister Yitzhak Rabin, who had been seeking a 'land for peace' settlement, was assassinated in 1995 and replaced by right-wing hardliner Binyamin NETANYAHU.

In 1999 the left-wing Ehud Barak won elections, promising to resume the peace process. Problems included Jewish settlements in the occupied areas and attacks on Israel by the Lebanese militant Islamic group, Hezbollah. In 2001 former general Ariel Sharon was elected prime minister, adopting a hardline policy against the Palestinians.

Israel unilaterally withdrew from Gaza in 2005, forcibly evicting Israeli settlers. In early 2006 a stroke left Ariel Sharon in a permanent coma, and he was succeeded by his deputy, Ehud Olmert. Israel responded to Hezbollah kidnappings of Israeli soldiers with a massive invasion of Lebanon, but withdrew after a few months. In 2007-8 Israel responded to rocket attacks from Gaza, which was dominated by the anti-Israel faction Hamas, with airstrikes and a blockade.

AREA 20,600sq km [7,954sq mi]
POPULATION 6,427,000
CAPITAL (POPULATION) Jerusalem (724,000)
GOVERNMENT Multiparty republic
ETHNIC GROUPS Jewish 80%, Arab and others 20%
LANGUAGES Hebrew and Arabic (both official)
RELIGIONS Judaism 80%, Islam (mostly Sunni) 14%, Christianity 2%, Druze and others 2%
CURRENCY New Israeli shekel = 100 agorat

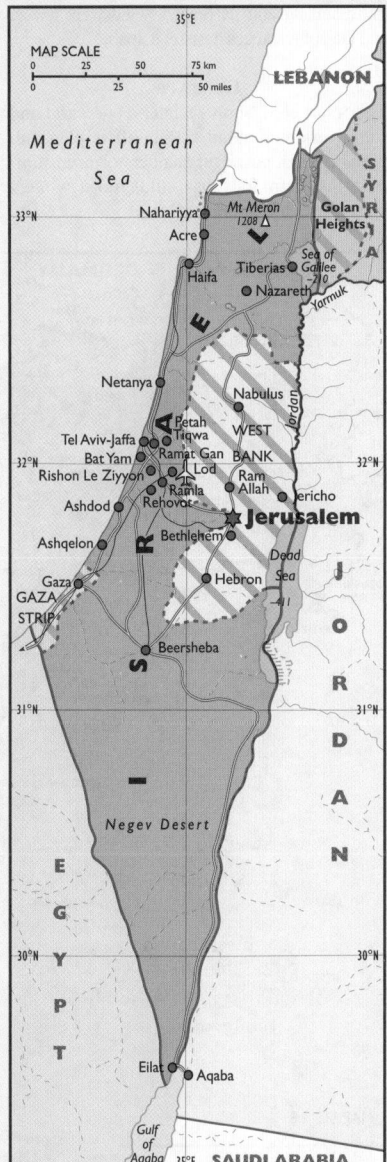

ECONOMY

Israel has a high standard of living, while Palestinian areas remain poor. Manufacturing is important. Israel produces potash, cotton, fruits, grain, poultry and vegetables.

The Republic of Italy is bordered to the N by the ALPS which overlook the N plains, Italy's most fertile and densely populated region, drained by the Po River. The APENNINES (Appennini), which form the backbone of s Italy, reach their highest peaks (3,000m [9,800ft]), in the Gran Sasso Range overlooking the the central Adriatic Sea, near Pescara. Limestones are the most common rocks. Between the mountains are long, narrow basins, some with lakes.

s Italy contains a string of volcanoes, stretching from Vesuvius, near Naples (Nápoli), through the Lipari Islands, to Mount Etna on SICILY. Traces of volcanic activity are found throughout Italy. Ancient lava flows cover large areas and produce fertile soils. Italy is still subject to earthquakes and volcanic eruptions. Sicily is the largest island in the Mediterranean. Sardinia is more isolated from the mainland and its rugged, windswept terrain and lack of resources have set it apart.

CLIMATE

The N has cold, snowy winters, but warm and sunny summer months. Rainfall is plentiful, with brief but powerful thunderstorms in summer. Southern Italy has mild, moist winters and warm, dry summers.

HISTORY

By tradition ROMULUS AND REMUS founded ancient ROME in 753 BC. The ETRUSCANS were overthrown by the Romans, who established a republic (509 BC). Rome gained a Mediterranean empire from the PUNIC WARS. POMPEY was defeated by Julius CAESAR, whose assassination led to the formation (27 BC) of the ROMAN EMPIRE under AUGUSTUS. The empire reached its peak in the AD 100s, then began to decline. DIOCLETIAN divided the Empire into Eastern (BYZANTINE EMPIRE) and Western sections. The western empire collapsed in the 400s. The PAPACY ensured the continuation of Rome's influence. PEPIN III (THE SHORT) expelled the LOMBARDS, and enabled the creation of the PAPAL STATES. His son CHARLEMAGNE was crowned emperor of the West (800).

In 962, OTTO I conquered Italy and established the HOLY ROMAN EMPIRE. Central and N Italy were controlled by powerful city-states, while the s established a FEUDAL SYSTEM under the HOHENSTAUFEN and Angevin dynasties. The 13th-century battle between imperial and papal power divided the cities and nobles into the GUELPH and GHIBELLINE factions. The 15th-century RENAISSANCE profoundly affected

AREA 301,318sq km [116,339sq mi]
POPULATION 58,148,000
CAPITAL (POPULATION) Rome (2,469,000)
GOVERNMENT Multiparty republic
ETHNIC GROUPS Italian 94%, German, French, Albanian, Slovene, Greek
LANGUAGES Italian (official),German, French, Slovene
RELIGIONS Roman Catholic
CURRENCY Euro = 100 cents

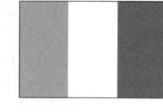

western civilization. ITALIAN ART AND ARCHITECTURE was an informing force across Europe.

In the 16th century, Spain gained Sicily, Naples and Milan. The FRENCH REVOLUTIONARY WARS failed to bring reunification. Nationalist groups, such as the RISORGIMENTO, emerged. Little progress was made until an alliance between France and Piedmont (then part of the Kingdom of Sardinia) drove Austria from Lombardy in 1859. MAZZINI's republicans were defeated by monarchists led by GARIBALDI and the Kingdom of Italy was unified under VICTOR EMMANUEL II (1861). Venetia was acquired from Austria in 1866 and Rome was finally annexed in 1871. Since then, Italy has been a unified state, though the pope and his successors disputed the takeover of the Papal States. This dispute was resolved in 1929, when VATICAN CITY was established as a fully independent state.

Since unification, the population has doubled, though the rate of increase is notoriously slow today. The rapid growth of population, in a poor country attempting to develop its resources, forced millions of Italians to emigrate during the first quarter of the 20th century. Large numbers settled in the United States, South America and Australia. More recently, large numbers of Italians have moved into northern Europe for similar reasons.

VICTOR EMMANUEL III's reign (1900–46) saw Italy enter World War 1 on the Allied side (1915). After the war, Italy was given nearly 23,000sq km [9,000sq mi] of territory that had belonged to Austria-Hungary. Italian discontent at the post-war settlement culminated in D'ANNUNZIO's seizure of TRIESTE, and the emergence of FASCISM. Benito MUSSOLINI became prime minister in 1922 and assumed dictatorial powers. His aggressive foreign policies included entering into an alliance with Hitler, sending forces to support General Franco in Spain (1936) and the seizure of Ethiopia (1936) and Albania (1939). During World War 2, Italy fought on the Axis side, but after losing its North African empire, Mussolini was dismissed and Italy surrendered (1943). Germany invaded and Italy declared war. Rome fell to the Allies in 1944. Mussolini was captured and shot by partisans in 1945, during an attempted escape to escape to Switzerland. Allied troops left in 1947.

The Christian Democrat Party emerged as the dominant post-war political force, with Alcide DE GASPERI as prime minister (1945–53). In 1948 Italy became a republic and was a founder member of NATO (1949) and the European Economic Community (1958). After the establishment of the EEC, Italy's economy began to expand. Much of the economic development

I

took place in the industrialized north. Central Italy is less developed and represents a transition zone between the developed north and the poor agrarian south known as the Mezzogiorno. Italy has been riven by political instability (50 governments since 1947), endemic corruption (often linked to the MAFIA), social unrest and the wealth gap between n and s.

POLITICS

In 1992, the old political establishment was driven from office with several prominent leaders accused of links to organized crime and some imprisoned. In 1996, the left-wing Olive Tree alliance led by Romano PRODI took office, but Prodi was forced to resign in 1998 following his rejection of demands made by his Communist allies. He was replaced by Massimo D'Alemo, the first former Communist to become prime minister. His attempts to create a two-party system in Italy failed in 1999.

By the late 1990s, it had the world's sixth largest economy and, on 1 January 2002, the euro became its currency. In 2001, Italy moved towards the political right when a coalition of centre-right parties won a substantial majority in parliament. Media tycoon Silvio BERLUSCONI became prime minister.

Accusations of corruption continued throughout his premiership and he was narrowly defeated by Prodi in 2006, but he returned to power in 2008 elections.

ECONOMY

Fifty years ago, Italy was a mainly agricultural society. Today it is a major industrial power. It imports most of the raw materials used in industry. Manufactures include cars, chemicals, processed food, machinery, textiles. Major crops include grapes for wine-making, and olives, citrus fruits, sugar beet and vegetables. Cattle, pigs, poultry and sheep are raised.

---

radioactive tritium. Radioisotopes are used in medicine, research and industry. Radioactive DATING also uses isotopes.

Israel Name given in the Old Testament to JACOB and to the nation that the Hebrews founded in Canaan. Jacob was renamed Israel after he had wrestled with the mysterious 'man' who was either an angel or God Himself (Genesis 32: 28). As a geographical name, Israel at first applied to the territory of Canaan captured or occupied by the Hebrews after the Exodus from Egypt. This territory united as a kingdom under DAVID in the early 10th century BC with its capital at JERUSALEM. Following the death of David's son, SOLOMON, the ten northern tribes seceded and the name Israel thereafter applied to the kingdom they founded in N Palestine; the remaining two tribes held the southern kingdom of JUDAH.

Israel Republic in SW Asia. *See* country feature, page 419

Israeli-Palestinian Accord Agreement that aimed to end hostilities between Palestinians and Israelis, especially in the WEST BANK and GAZA STRIP. Secret talks began in the mid-1980s. On September 13, 1993, a 'Declaration of Principles' was signed by Yitzhak RABIN and Yasir ARAFAT. The PLO recognized ISRAEL's right to exist and renounced terrorism. In return, Israel recognized the PLO as the representative of the Palestinians and agreed to a staged withdrawal of troops from parts of the occupied territories. On May 18, 1994, the Israeli army completed its redeployment in the Gaza Strip and withdrew from JERICHO. The Palestinian National Authority (headed by Arafat) assumed limited autonomy. In September 1995, Rabin agreed to withdraw Israeli troops from six more towns and 85% of HEBRON. In October 1995, Israel released 1,100 Palestinian prisoners. The assassination of Rabin and election of Benjamin NETANYAHU slowed the process, and Jewish settlement on the West Bank accelerated. In 1997, despite the withdrawal of most Israeli troops from Hebron and attempts by the US government to encourage dialogue, Israel's determination to build more Jewish settlements in E Jerusalem stalled the process. The Wye Accord (1998) appeared to break the deadlock, but met opposition within Israel. *See also* INTIFADA

Istanbul City and seaport in NW Turkey, astride the BOSPORUS, partly in Europe and partly in Asia, at the entrance to the Sea of Marmara. The city was founded by Greek colonists in the 7th century BC. It was known as **Byzantium** until AD 330 when CONSTANTINE I chose it as the capital of the Eastern Roman Empire and renamed it **Constantinople**. Captured by the OTTOMAN Turks in 1453, it was largely destroyed by an earthquake in 1509 and rebuilt by Sultan Beyazid II. When the Turkish Republic was established after World War 1, the capital was moved to ANKARA and Constantinople was renamed Istanbul. It is the financial and commercial centre of Turkey. Industries: shipbuilding, cement, textiles, glass, pottery, leather goods. Tourism is vital. Pop. (2000) 8,953,000.

Italian Language of Italy and of the Swiss canton of Ticino. It is one of the ROMANCE LANGUAGES and belongs to the Italic group of INDO-EUROPEAN LANGUAGES. There are many Italian dialects, and the official language is based on those of central Italy, particularly Tuscan. During the 20th century, broadcasting and the cinema standardized the language, but most Italians continue to use a regional dialect for everyday communication.

Italian art and architecture Painting, sculpture, and other art produced in Italy following the Roman period. By the 6th century, trade with the Byzantine Empire had brought a Byzantine influence to Italian art, which lasted through the 11th century. The chief centres of the Italo-Byzantine style were Venice, Tuscany, Rome and the deep south. Mosaics and stylized, geometric forms became standard. Icon panels were the main type of paintings during the 11th through the 13th centuries, with major schools in SIENA, Lucca and PISA. By the Renaissance, the emphasis was on balance and harmony, with such masters as LEONARDO DA VINCI, GHIBERTI, DONATELLO, BOTTICELLI and MICHELANGELO. MANNERISM developed in Florence late in the Renaissance but faded by the end of the 16th century, giving way to the 17th-century BAROQUE style, typified by artists such as the painter CARAVAGGIO and the architect BERNINI. In the 18th and 19th centuries, NEO-CLASSICISM was inspired by Classical Roman art, the subject of PIRANESI's engravings. The 20th century saw the birth of FUTURISM, as well as the more tranquil works of MODIGLIANI and de CHIRICO. Since the 1960s, Italian designers have been highly influential internationally.

Italian literature Italian vernacular literature emerged in the 13th century with the work of the Sicilian poets at the court of Frederick II; they extensively employed the SONNET. Religious poetry also flourished. Major figures of the 14th century were DANTE, PETRARCH and BOCCACCIO, who influenced the works of CHAUCER. The RENAISSANCE produced outstanding poetry and philosophy, especially in the work of Torquato TASSO, Lodovico Ariosto (1474–1533), and MACHIAVELLI. During the 18th century, a new literary language emerged to reflect modern experience. Carlo Porta (1775–1821) employed regional dialects, while Guiseppe Parini (1729–99) wrote in a more conventional style. The lyrical works of Giacomo Leopardi (1798–1837) and the novels of Alessandro MANZONI helped to take Italian literature into its Romantic period. The 19th-century political movement for Italian unification and independence inspired a literary flowering. The major figure to emerge was Gabriele D'Annunzio. Important 20th-century writers include Alberto MORAVIA, Cesare PAVESE and Eugenio MONTALE, and more recently Umberto ECO and Italo Calvino (1923–85).

italics Style of handwriting developed by the Florentine humanist Niccolò Niccoli in the 15th century. By the 16th century it had replaced Gothic script in most European countries. The 20th century has seen its revival. It is now used in printed works to indicate emphasis or foreign words.

Italy Republic in S Europe. *See* country feature.

Ito, Hirobumi (1841–1909) Japanese statesman. The leading figure in the modernization of Japan after the MEIJI RESTORATION (1868), he served in several government posts and took part in the Iwakura Mission (1871–73) to study Western governments. After the RUSSO-JAPANESE WAR (1904–05), he headed the Japanese administration in what was then the protectorate of Korea. He was assassinated by a Korean nationalist.

Ivan III (the Great) (1440–1505) Grand Duke of Moscow (1462–1505). He laid the foundations of the future Russian Empire. By 1480 Moscow's northern rivals, including Novgorod, were absorbed by conquest or persuasion, domestic rebellion was crushed, and the Tatar threat was ended. He began to use the title *Tsar* ('Caesar') and employed Italian artists in the buildings of the KREMLIN.

Ivan IV (the Terrible) (1530–84) Grand Duke of Moscow (1533–84) and tsar of Russia. Ivan was crowned in 1547 and married Anastasia, a ROMANOV. At first an able and progressive ruler, reforming law and government, after his wife's death in 1560, he became increasingly unbalanced, killing his own son in a rage. By annexing the Tatar states of Kazan and Astrakhan, he gained control of the Volga River. He established trade with W European states and began Russian expansion into Siberia. He established a personal dominion, the *oprichnina*, inside Russia. He also created a military force, the *oprichniki*, which he set against the boyars.

Ives, Charles (1874–1954) US composer who used American folk music as a basis, as in *Variations on America* for organ (1891). His works vary greatly in style, some are atonal, some quote from hymns or band music and some are conventional. He wrote four symphonies, chamber music and many songs. He received the 1947 Pulitzer Prize for music.

IVF Abbreviation of IN VITRO FERTILIZATION

ivory Hard, yellowish-white dentine of some mammals. The most valuable variety is obtained from elephant tusks. The term also refers to the teeth of hippopotamuses, walruses, sperm whales and several other mammals.

Ivory Coast (Côte d'Ivoire) Republic in W Africa. *See* country feature.

ivy Woody, EVERGREEN vine, native to Europe and Asia. Its long, climbing stems cling to upright surfaces, such as trees or walls, by aerial roots. Family Araliaceae.

Iwo Jima (formerly Sulphur Island) Largest of the Japanese Volcano Islands in the W Pacific Ocean. During World War 2, it was captured (1945) by US forces at great human cost. Iwo Jima was returned to Japan in 1968. Industries: sugar refining and sulphur mining. Area: 21sq km (8sq mi).

Izetbegović, Alija (1925–2003) Bosnian politician, president of Bosnia-Herzegovina (1992–2000). A Muslim, the Yugoslav government imprisoned him for supposed pan-Islamic activities (1945–48) and for his Islamic Declaration of 1970 (1983–88). Elected leader of the Party of Democratic Action (PDA) in 1990, Izetbegović advocated a multi-faith republic. He led Bosnia's coalition government from 1990 until independence in 1992, when he became president. He retained his position during the civil war, and signed the Treaty of Paris (1995) that ended it. Re-elected in 1996, he retired in 2000.

Izmir (formerly Smyrna) City and seaport on the Gulf of Izmir, W Turkey. It was settled by Greeks around 1000 BC. Izmir was part of the Ottoman Empire from 1424–1919, when it was assigned to Greece. It passed to Turkey under the Treaty of Lausanne (1923). Industries include tourism, tobacco, silk, carpets, cotton and woollen textiles. Pop. (2000) 2,250,000.

IVORY COAST

The Republic of the Ivory Coast, in West Africa, is officially known as Côte d'Ivoire. The SE coast is bordered by sand bars that enclose lagoons, on one of which the former capital and chief port of ABIDJAN is situated, but the SW coast is lined by rocky cliffs. Behind the coast is a coastal plain, but the land rises inland to high plains. The highest land is an extension of the Guinea Highlands in the NW, along the borders with Liberia and Guinea. Most of the country's rivers run N–S.

CLIMATE
Ivory Coast has a hot and humid tropical climate, with high temperatures throughout the year. There are two rainy seasons in the S: May–July, and October–November. Inland, the rainfall decreases. N Ivory Coast has a dry season and only one rainy season. As a result, the forests in central Ivory Coast thin out to the N, giving way to savanna.

HISTORY
The region came under successive African rulers until the late 15th century, when Europeans began to establish contacts along the coast to trade in ivory and slaves. Tribal kingdoms such as the Kong and Baule flourished inland and restricted European activity to the coastal region. French missionaries reached the area in 1637 and, by the end of the 17th century, the French had set up trading posts on the coast. In 1842, France brought the Grand-Bassam area under its protection and Ivory Coast became a French colony in 1893. From 1895, it was ruled as part of French West Africa that also included modern-day Benin, Burkina Faso, Guinea, Mali, Mauritania, Niger and Senegal. In 1946, Ivory Coast became a territory in the French Union. The port of Abidjan was built in the early 1950s, and the country achieved autonomy in 1958.

POLITICS
Ivory Coast became fully independent in 1960. Its first president, Félix Houphouët-Boigny, served until his death in 1993. He was a paternalistic, pro-Western leader who made his country a one-party state. In 1983 the National Assembly agreed to move the capital from Abidjan to YAMOUSSOUKRO, Houphouët-Boigny's birthplace.

Following the death of Houphouët-Boigny in 1993, the Speaker of the National Assembly, Henri Konan Bédié, proclaimed himself president. He was elected in 1995. In 1999, Bédié was overthrown during an army mutiny and a new administration was set up by General Robert Guei. Presidential elections, held after a new constitution was adopted in 2000, resulted in defeat for Guei by a veteran politician, Laurent Gbago. In 2002 economic problems and ethnic tensions led to civil war. In 2004 fighting died down, leaving the country divided into gov-

AREA 322,463sq km [124,503sq mi]
POPULATION 18,013,000
CAPITAL (POPULATION) Yamoussoukro (107,000)
GOVERNMENT Multiparty republic
ETHNIC GROUPS Akan 42%, Voltaiques 18%, Northern Mandes 16%, Krous 11%, Southern Mandes 10%
LANGUAGES French (official), many native dialects
RELIGIONS Islam 40%, Christianity 30%, traditional beliefs 30%
CURRENCY CFA franc = 100 centimes

ernment-held S and the rebel-held, mainly Muslim, N. UN peacekeeping attempts including French and west African troops struggled to prevent ethnic conflict. Elections were postponed in 2005–8. In 2007 new negotiations attempted to revive the peace process, and rebel leader Guillaume Soro was appointed prime minister so that both sides were represented in government.

ECONOMY
Ivory Coast is one of Africa's more prosperous countries, particularly in Abidjan and Yamoussoukro, but there are great social and regional inequalities. The country faces economic problems including unemployment, variations in the price of its export commodities, and high foreign debt. Its free-market economy has proved attractive to foreign investors, especially French firms, while France has given much aid. It has an agrarian economy, which employs about three-fifths of the workforce. The chief farm products are cocoa, coffee, and cotton and make up nearly half the value of the total exports. Food crops include cassava, maize, plantains, rice, vegetables and yams. Manufactures include processed farm products, timber and textiles.

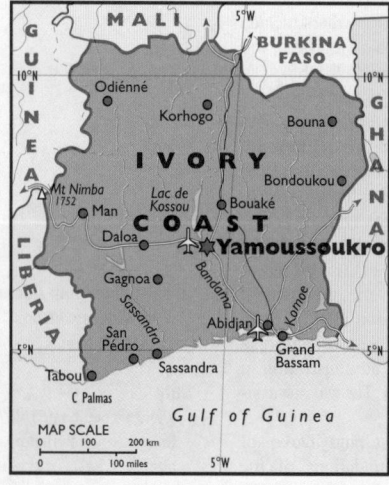

jabiru STORK of the New World, found in tropical swamps from Mexico to Argentina. Length: 1.5m (5ft); wingspan: 2m (7ft). Family Ciconiidae, species *Jabiru mycteria*.

jaçana (lily trotter) Long-toed water bird of tropical lakes with a slender body, narrow bill and tapered claws. It is black or reddish-brown. It feeds on aquatic plants and small animals. Length: to 50.8cm (20in). Family Jacanidae.

jackal Wild dog, found throughout Asia and Africa, that resembles a COYOTE. It eats small animals, fruit, and seeds. Length: to 74cm (29.1in). Family Canidae; genus *Canis*.

jackdaw Gregarious black-and-grey bird that frequents open country near buildings or cliffs. Smaller than its relative, the CROW, it has a grey head and white-rimmed eyes. It lives in colonies. Family Corvidae; species *Corvus monedula*.

jack rabbit Any of several large, slender, long-eared HARES of W North America. Jack rabbits rely on their great speed, powerful leaps and agility to escape from predators. Most are grey with white underparts. Family Leporidae; genus *Lepus*.

Jackson State capital and largest city of Mississippi, USA, on the Pearl River, SW Mississippi. Established as a trading post in the 1790s, it was chosen as state capital in 1821. Industries: natural gas, glass, textiles. Pop. (2000) 184,256.

Jackson, Andrew (1767–1845) Seventh US president (1829–37). Jackson became a national hero in the WAR OF 1812 when he defeated the British at New Orleans (1815). Jackson's popular appeal narrowly failed to defeat John Quincy ADAMS in the 1824 presidential election. His supporters built the basis of the new DEMOCRATIC PARTY and Jackson was elected with John C. CALHOUN as his vice president in 1828. Jackson faced staunch opposition from the establishment and set up a SPOILS SYSTEM of political appointments. Calhoun resigned over the nullification issue, and Jackson faced further conflict over STATES' RIGHTS, the expansion of the FRONTIER and the tariff. His second term (1832–37) was marked by his trenchant opposition to the BANK OF THE UNITED STATES.

Jackson, Jesse Louis (1941–) US politician and CIVIL-RIGHTS activist. He worked with Martin Luther KING, Jr., in the Southern Christian Leadership Conference (SCLC). Jackson served as national director (1967–71) of Operation Breadbasket, an economic arm of the SCLC. In 1971, he formed Operation PUSH (People United to Save Humanity) to combat racism in Chicago. Jackson mounted unsuccessful campaigns for the Democratic presidential nomination in 1984 and 1988. In 1986 he became president of the National Rainbow Coalition, which merged with PUSH to form the Rainbow/PUSH coalition in 1996.

Jackson, Michael (1958–) US pop singer and songwriter. At age five, he was the youngest member of his brothers' singing group, The Jackson Five. His albums, *Got to Be There* (1971) and *Off the Wall* (1979), launched a major solo career that peaked in the 1980s with elaborate worldwide concert tours and top-selling albums, such as *Thriller* (1982), *Bad* (1987), and *Dangerous* (1991).

Jackson, 'Stonewall' (Thomas Jonathan) (1824–63) Confederate general in the American CIVIL WAR. His stand against overwhelming odds at the first battle of BULL RUN (1861) gained him the nickname 'Stonewall'. He fought, again greatly outnumbered, in the Shenandoah Valley (1862) and played an important part in the Confederate victories after the second battle of BULL RUN. Jackson was accidentally shot and killed by his own men at Chancellorsville.

Jacksonville Seaport on St John's River, NE Florida, USA. The largest city in the state, it served as a CONFEDERATE base during the Civil War, and developed as a port in the 19th century. Fire devastated the city in 1901. Industries: cigars, fruit canning, wood products. Pop. (2000) 882,000.

Jacob Old Testament figure, grandson of ABRAHAM and, by tradition, ancestor of the nation of ISRAEL. He was the second-born son of ISAAC and Rebecca and younger twin brother of ESAU. Stories about him and his family form the last part of Genesis (25:19–50:13). The descendants of his 12 sons became the 12 tribes of Israel.

Jacobean (Lat. *Jacobus*, 'James') Artistic styles during the reign (1603–25) of JAMES I. The major literary form was drama, such as the works of WEBSTER and the late plays of

SHAKESPEARE. METAPHYSICAL POETRY, such as the work of John DONNE, was also a feature of the age. In architecture, the major achievement was the work of Inigo JONES.

Jacobins Political club of the FRENCH REVOLUTION. In 1789 Breton members of the STATES-GENERAL met in a Dominican (Fr. 'Jacobin') monastery to form the Jacobin Club. By 1791, it had branches throughout France. By 1792, ROBESPIERRE had seized control of the Jacobins and the club adopted more radical policies. In 1793, they engineered the expulsion of the GIRONDINS and the club became an instrument of the REIGN OF TERROR. It collapsed after Robespierre's downfall in 1794.

Jacobites Supporters of JAMES II of England and his STUART descendants, who attempted to regain the English throne after the GLORIOUS REVOLUTION of 1688. Jacobitism was strong in the Scottish Highlands and parts of Ireland. In 1715 (the "**Fifteen Rebellion**") a rising at Braemar proclaimed James Edward STUART as king. The movement collapsed with the defeat of the rebels at Preston. In 1745, a second rising (the "**Forty-Five Rebellion**"), led by Bonnie Prince Charlie (Charles Edward STUART), captured Scotland and advanced as far as Derby, before retreating. In 1746, the English decisively defeated the Highlanders at the battle of CULLODEN and embarked upon a policy of suppression of the Highland clans that ended the Jacobite threat.

jade Semi-precious silicate mineral of two major types: jadeite, which is often translucent; and nephrite, which has a waxy quality. Both types are extremely hard. Jade is found mainly in Burma and comes in many colours, most commonly green and white. Hardness 5–6; r.d. 3–3.4.

jaeger (skua) Gull-like, predatory seabird that breeds in the Arctic and winters in the subtropics. It has a dark, stocky body with pointed wings and long tail feathers. It feeds on small land animals and seabirds. Length: 33–51cm (13–20in). Genus: *Stercorarius*.

Jaffa (Yafo) City and port in W Israel, a suburb of TEL AVIV. Mentioned in the Bible, ALEXANDER THE GREAT captured it in 332 BC. The Jews regained Jaffa during the Hasmonean revolt, but Roman Emperor Vespasian destroyed the city in AD 68. It changed hands many times in the Middle Ages. The Israelis settled Jaffa in 1948, and united it with Tel Aviv in 1950. It became a focus of Palestinian resistance to Jewish settlement. Pop. (1995, Tel Aviv-Jaffa) 348,570.

Jagiello (Jagiello) Medieval Polish dynasty. It began with the marriage of Grand Duke Jagiello of Lithuania to Queen Jadwiga of Poland (1386), uniting Poland and Lithuania. Members of the dynasty reigned also in Hungary and Bohemia in the 15th-16th centuries.

jaguar Spotted big CAT found in wooded or grassy areas from SW USA to Argentina. It has a chunky body and a yellowish coat with black rosettes. It eats large mammals, turtles and fish. Length: body to 1.8m (5.9ft); tail to 91cm (35.8in); weight to 136kg (299.8lb). Family Felidae; species *Panthera onca*.

jaguarundi Small, ground-dwelling CAT found in Central and South America. It is black, brown, grey, or fox red. Length: to 67cm (26.4in), excluding the tail; weight: to 9kg (19.8lb). Family Felidae; species *Felis yagouaroundi*.

Jahangir (1569–1627) MOGUL Emperor of India (1605–27). He succeeded his father, AKBAR I, and continued the expansion of the Empire. He granted trading privileges to the Portuguese and the British, and was a patron of poetry and painting.

Jainism Ancient religion of India, originating in the 6th century BC as a reaction against BRAHMANISM. It was founded by Mahavira (599–527BC). Jains do not accept Hindu scriptures, rituals or priesthood, but they do accept the Hindu doctrine of

J/j, tenth letter of the Roman alphabet. It evolved from the letter i and was the last letter to be incorporated into the modern alphabet; its early history is the same as that of the letter i. The j developed from the tail form of the letter i.

▲ **Jackson** Raised in modest circumstances, Jesse Jackson became the first African-American to mount a sustained campaign for the presidency (1984 and 1988). Although he did not gain the Democratic nomination, Jackson inspired many African-Americans to vote for the first time. A charismatic Baptist preacher and civil-rights advocate, he later formed the National Rainbow Coalition, a political body made up of minority groups, environmentalists and peace activists.

INTERNET

Jackson, Andrew
▶ www.whitehouse.gov/ history/presidents

Jackson, Jesse Louis
▶ www.rainbowpush.org

◀ **jaguar** Largest cat in the Americas, the jaguar (*Panthera onca*) is now extinct in most of N America. It is a solitary and agile hunter, and an excellent swimmer and tree climber.

TRANSMIGRATION OF SOULS. Jainism lays special stress on *ahimsa* – non-injury to all creatures. There are *c*.4 million Jains.

Jaipur State capital of Rajasthan. Founded in 1727, it was enclosed by a wall (still extant), and there is a system of wide, regular streets. A transport and commercial centre, it is famous for its carpets, jewellery, enamels, and cloth. Pop. (2005) 2,796,000.

Jakarta Capital of Indonesia, on the NW coast of Java. It was founded (*c*.1619 as Batavia) by the Dutch as a fort and trading post, and it became the headquarters of the Dutch EAST INDIA COMPANY. It became the capital after Indonesia gained its independence in 1949. Industries: ironworking, printing, timber. Exports: rubber, tea, quinine. Pop. (2005) 13,194,000.

Jamaica Caribbean nation. *See* country feature.

James I (1566–1625) King of England (1603–25) and, as James VI, king of Scotland (1567–1625). Son of MARY, QUEEN OF SCOTS, he acceded to the Scottish throne as an infant on his mother's abdication. In 1589, he married Anne of Denmark. He inherited the English throne on the death (1603) of ELIZABETH I, and thereafter confined his attention to England. James supported the Anglican Church, thus antagonizing the PURITANS, and sponsored the publication (1611) of the Authorized, or King James, Version of the BIBLE. The GUNPOWDER PLOT (1605) was foiled and James suppressed the Catholics. In 1607, the first English colony in America (Jamestown) was founded. James's insistence on the divine right of kings brought conflict with Parliament. In 1611 he dissolved Parliament, and (excluding the 1614 Addled Parliament) ruled without one until 1621. The death (1612) of Robert CECIL saw James increasingly dependent on corrupt favourites such as Robert Carr and George Villiers, Duke of BUCKINGHAM. He was succeeded by his son, CHARLES I. *See also* JACOBEAN

James I (1394–1437) King of Scotland (1406–37). His father, Robert III, sent him to France for safety but he was intercepted by the English (1406). He was not ransomed until 1424. James then restored royal authority by ruthless methods. He carried out reforms of the financial and judicial systems and encouraged trade. His campaign against the nobility made him many enemies, and he was assassinated at Perth.

James II (1633–1701) King of England (1685–88), second son of CHARLES I, brother of CHARLES II. Following the English CIVIL WAR, James fought for the French and Spanish, before returning as lord high admiral after the RESTORATION (1660). He converted to Roman Catholicism (1669) and was forced to resign all his offices. As king, James was confronted by MONMOUTH's Rebellion (1685). His pro-Catholic policies inflamed popular opinion and the birth of a son, James STUART, precipitated the GLORIOUS REVOLUTION. His daughter, MARY II, and her husband, WILLIAM III OF ORANGE, acceded to the throne, and James fled to France. With French aid, James invaded Ireland but was defeated by William at the battle of the BOYNE (1690). *See also* JACOBITES

JAMAICA

Jamaica is the third largest Caribbean island. It is a parliamentary democracy, with the monarch of the UK as its head of state. The coastal plain is narrow and discontinuous. Inland are hills, plateaux and mountains. The country's central range culminates in the Blue Mountain Peak (2,256m [7,402ft]). The Cockpit Country in the NW of the island is an inaccessible limestone area, known for its many deep depressions (cockpits). Jamaica is a lush, green island.

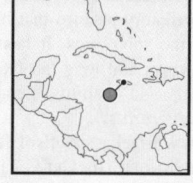

CLIMATE
The climate is hot and humid. Temperatures range from 25°C [77°F] in January to 27°C [81°F] in July. Moist SE trade winds bring rain to the more temperate highlands. Annual rainfall on the N slopes may reach 5,000mm [200in]. But the sheltered S coast is much drier, about 750mm [30in] per year. The island is prone to periodic hurricanes.

HISTORY
In 1494 Christopher Columbus discovered Jamaica, and in 1509 the island was occupied by the Spanish. Soon, the local Arawak Amerindian population had died out. The Spaniards imported African slaves to work the sugar plantations. The British took the island in 1655 and, with sugar as its staple product, it became a prized possession. Its sugar plantations brought prosperity, but the economy declined after the abolition of slavery in 1834. The African slaves were the forefathers of much of the present population, but the plantations on which they worked disappeared when the sugar market collapsed in the 19th century.

In 1865, after 200 years of having their own elected body to help the British rule the island, Jamaica came under direct British rule as a crown colony, following the Moranty Bay rebellion. This peasant uprising, led by Baptist deacon Paul Bogle, was staged by freed slaves who were suffering acute hardship, but it was put down by British troops. In the 1930s, Jamaican leaders called for more power and riots took place in 1938, with people protesting against unemployment and Britain's racial policies. In that year, the People's National Party (PNP) was founded. In 1944, Britain granted Jamaica a new constitution, providing for an elected House of Representatives. In 1958, the island became a member of the British-sponsored Federation of the West Indies, but it withdrew in 1961.

POLITICS
Jamaica became an independent nation and a member of the British Commonwealth in 1962. It joined the Organization of American States in 1969. In the 1970s, economic problems developed. Michael Manley, leader of the PNP, became prime minister in 1972 and he pursued socialist policies, advocating a policy of non-alignment. The PNP won a second term in office in 1976. It nationalized businesses and sought closer ties with Cuba. In 1980, the Jamaica Labour Party (JLP), led by Edward Seaga defeated the PNP in elections. Seaga privatized much state-owned business and distanced Jamaica from Cuba. His moderate policies led to increased investment and better relations with Western countries. In 1989, the PNP defeated the JLP and Manley was returned to power as prime minister. However, Manley broadly followed Seaga's moderate policies. Manley retired on health grounds in 1992 and

AREA 10,990sq km [4,244sq mi]
POPULATION 2,780,000
CAPITAL (POPULATION) Kingston (104,000)
GOVERNMENT Constitutional monarchy
ETHNIC GROUPS Black 91%, Mixed 7%, East Indian
LANGUAGES English (official), patois English
RELIGIONS Protestant 61%, Roman Catholic 4%
CURRENCY Jamaican dollar = 100 cents

was succeeded by Percival J Patterson. The PNP was re-elected in 1993, 1998 and 2002. In 2006 Patterson retired. The PNP chose Portia Simpson-Miller, Jamaica's first female prime minister, to replace him. She was defeated in 2007 elections and Bruce Golding of the opposition Labour party became prime minister.

Jamaica faces many problems, including drug trafficking. It has become a major transshipment point for cocaine being transported from South America to North America and Europe. Cannabis is produced in Jamaica. Corruption and money-laundering are major concerns. Price and tax increases led to riots in 1999, while in 2001, gun battles occurred with 27 people killed when the police searched for drugs in a poor district of Kingston. The murder rate remains very high.

ECONOMY
Jamaica is a developing country. Agriculture employs about 20% of the workforce. The chief crop is sugar cane, other products include allspice, bananas, citrus fruits, cocoa, coconuts, coffee, milk, poultry, vegetables and yams. The country's chief resource is bauxite (aluminium ore) and Jamaica is one of the world's top producers. Cement, chemicals, cigars, clothing and textiles, fertilizers, machinery, molasses and petroleum products are also produced. Service industries account for 60% of the gross domestic product. Tourism brings in vital revenue.

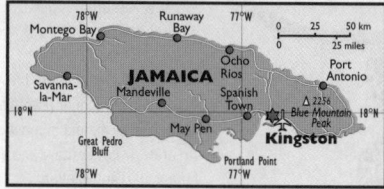

J

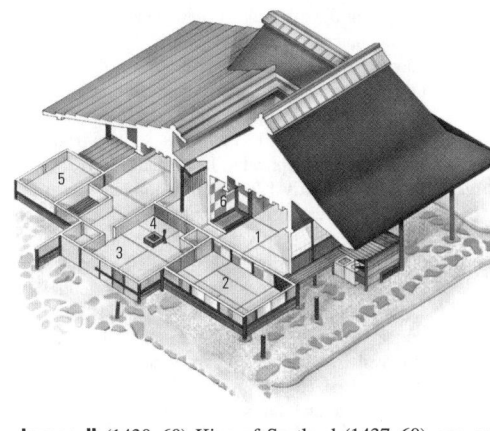

◄ **Japanese architecture**
The Shonkintei garden pavilion (1641) at the palace of Katsura in Kyoto is typical of Japanese period-architecture. It comprises two large rooms (1) and (2) divided by *shoji* (translucent screens), a tea room (3), lobby (4), and pantry section (5). The *tokonoma* (6) is an alcove for the display of flowers and objects of art.

James II (1430–60) King of Scotland (1437–60), son and successor of JAMES I. His minority was dominated by aristocratic factions, particularly the Douglases. In 1452, he killed the Earl of Douglas and seized control. During the Wars of the ROSES, James supported the Lancastrians against the Yorkists, and was killed by an exploding cannon at Roxburgh.

James III (1451–88) King of Scotland (1460–88), son of JAMES II. James was challenged by his brother, Albany, whom EDWARD IV of England recognized as king in 1482. Peace was arranged, but a new rebellion resulted in James's defeat and his subsequent murder.

James IV (1473–1513) King of Scotland (1488–1513). He succeeded his father, JAMES III, capturing and killing those nobles responsible for his death. James defended royal authority against the nobility and the Church and endeavoured to promote peace with England, marrying HENRY VIII's sister, Margaret Tudor. Henry's attack on Scotland's old ally, France, drew him into war (1513), and he was killed at Flodden.

James V (1512–42) King of Scotland (1513–42). He made a French alliance through marriage as a safeguard against his uncle, HENRY VIII. Lack of support from the nobility contributed to his defeat by the English at Solway Moss (1542). He was succeeded by his daughter, MARY, QUEEN OF SCOTS.

James Edward Francis Stuart *See* STUART, JAMES FRANCIS EDWARD

James, Henry (1843–1916) US novelist, brother of William JAMES. James settled (1876) in England and became a British subject in 1915. His early masterpiece *The Portrait of a Lady* (1881) contrasts the values of American and European society. The novels of his middle period, such as *The Bostonians* (1886), deal with political themes. His final novels, *The Wings of the Dove* (1902), *The Ambassadors* (1903) and *The Golden Bowl* (1904) show his mastery of the psychological novel. Other works include *The Turn of the Screw* (1898).

James, Jesse Woodson (1847–82) US outlaw. With his brother, Frank, he fought for the Confederacy during the Civil War. In 1867, they formed an outlaw band and terrorized the frontier. He was shot dead by Robert Ford, a member of his own gang, for a large reward.

James, William (1842–1910) US philosopher and psychologist, elder brother of Henry JAMES. He held that the feeling of emotion is based on the sensation of a state of the body; the bodily state comes first and the emotion follows. As a philosopher, he influenced PRAGMATISM. His most famous works are *The Principles of Psychology* (1890) and *Varieties of Religious Experience* (1902).

Jamestown First successful English settlement in America. It was established in 1607 on the James River, Virginia. On the verge of collapse from disease and starvation, it was saved by the leadership of Captain John SMITH (1608), and the timely arrival of new supplies and colonists (1610). From 1614 tobacco planting assured the colony's survival.

Jammu and Kashmir State in NW India, bounded N by Pakistan-controlled KASHMIR, W by Pakistan and E by China. The capitals are Srinagar (summer) and Jammu (winter). The state is largely mountainous, and the Himalayas tower above the heavily populated valleys of the Indus and Jhelum rivers. Industries: rice cultivation, animal husbandry, silk factories, rice and flour mills, tourism. Area: 100,569sq km (38,845sq mi). Pop. (2001) 10,069,917.

Janáček, Leoš (1854–1928) Czech composer. His compositions include orchestral works, such as *Taras Bulba* (1918) and the *Sinfonietta* (1926), two string quartets (1923, 1928), and the cantata *The Eternal Gospel* (1914). He also wrote several operas, including *Jenufa* (1904), *The Cunning Little Vixen* (1924), and *The Makropoulos Case* (1926).

Janissaries Elite corps of the Ottoman army, founded in the 14th century. The Janissaries were a highly effective fighting force until the 17th century, when discipline and military prestige declined. They were abolished by MAHMUD II in 1826.

Jansen, Cornelis (1585–1638) Dutch theologian. He studied problems raised for Catholics by Lutheran and Calvinist doctrine. He argued for a return to the views of Saint AUGUSTINE on grace and salvation. *See also* JANSENISM

Jansenism Theological school that grew up in the Roman Catholic Church in the 17th and 18th centuries. It was named after Cornelis JANSEN, but the movement was strongest in France. The Jansenists believed that man is incapable of carrying out the commandments of God without divine 'grace', which is bestowed only on a favoured few. French Jansenists incurred the hostility of the JESUITS and of the monarchy, and they were condemned by Pope Clement XI in 1713.

Jansky, Karl (1905–50) US engineer, who discovered (1931) unidentifiable radio signals from space. He concluded that they were stellar in origin and that the source lay in the direction of SAGITTARIUS. Jansky's discovery is considered to be the beginning of radio ASTRONOMY. The unit measuring radio emission is named after him.

Japan Archipelago state in E Asia. *See* country feature, p.426

Japanese Official language of Japan and the native tongue of more than 120 million people in Japan, and the Ryukyu and Bonin islands. Some scholars classify Japanese as a member of the Ural-Altaic family, which also includes Finnish, Hungarian and Turkish. Japanese uses a pitch accent. There are at least four different forms of spoken Japanese, and a modern literary style. Japanese writing uses a combination of some 1,850 Chinese characters with tables of syllabic symbols called *kana*.

Japanese art and architecture Earliest surviving examples of **Japanese art** are Jomon pottery figurines (*c.*1000BC). In the 6th century AD Chinese influence was strong. LACQUER work, sculpture and ink-painting developed during the **Nara period** (AD 674–794). The **Yamato-e** tradition was based on national, rather than Chinese, aesthetic standards. It flowered during the Kamakura military rule (1185–1333). The profound influence of ZEN Buddhism on Japanese art is particularly apparent in the Muromachi period (1333–1573). Many of the best-known examples of Japanese art were produced in the Edo (TOKUGAWA) period (*c.*1600–1868). The UKIYO-E prints of UTAMARO, HOKUSAI, HIROSHIGE and others date from this period. Modern Japanese artists have made important contributions to 20th-century art and design. **Japanese architecture** derives from 6th-century Chinese Buddhist structures. Temples have curved wooden columns, overhanging roofs and thin exterior wood and plaster walls. A gateway, drum tower, and pagoda are also built, usually on a picturesque wooded hillside. Domestic structures are traditionally built with interior wooden posts supporting the roof. The outer walls are movable panels of wood or rice paper that slide in grooves. The interior is subdivided by screens and decorated with simplicity and delicacy.

Japanese literature Earliest extant works are the *Kojiki* (712) and the *Nihongi* (720), which are histories written in Chinese characters used phonetically. The earliest recorded Japanese poetry is in the *Manyoshu* (760), which contains poems dating to the 4th century. The **Heian Period** (794–1185) is noted for the *Kokinshu* (905), an anthology of poetry commissioned by the emperor, which provided a pattern for *tanka* (short poems). Classical prose developed during this period and accounts of court life flourished. The most significant work was Murasaki Shikibu's *Genji Monogatari* (*c.*1010), Japan's first true novel. During the **Middle Ages** (1185–1603) NOH DRAMA was refined, and 'war tales', such as *Heike Monogatari*, were developed. In the **Tokugawa Period** (1603–1868)

▲ **Japanese art** The decorative arts in Japan were well developed by the end of the 8th century. Colour printing was particularly advanced, along with woodcuts, and ceramic glazes. *Kakemono* are hanging scrolls executed on thin silk or paper with Chinese ink, then mounted on silk brocade and rolled on a rod.

J

Japan is an island nation in NE Asia containing four large islands – HONSHU, HOKKAIDO, KYUSHU and SHIKOKU – which make up more than 98% of its land. Thousands of small islands, including the RYUKYU island chain, form the rest of the country.

The four main islands are mainly mountainous, while many of the small islands are the tips of volcanoes rising from the sea bed. Japan has more than 150 volcanoes, about 60 of which are active. Volcanic eruptions, earthquakes and tsunamis often occur.

Throughout Japan, complex folding and faulting has produced an intricate mosaic of landforms. Mountains and forested hills alternate with small basins and coastal lowlands, covered by alluvium deposited there by the short rivers that rise in the uplands. Most of the population lives on the coastal plains, one being the stretch from the Kanto Plain – where TOKYO is situated – along the narrow plains that border the S coasts of Honshu, to N Kyushu.

The pattern of landforms is further complicated by the presence of volcanic cones and calderas. The highest mountain in Japan, Fujisan (FUJIYAMA) (3,776m [12,388ft]), is a long dormant volcano which last erupted in 1707. It is considered sacred, and is visited by thousands of pilgrims every year.

CLIMATE

The climate of Japan varies greatly. Hokkaido in the N has cold, snowy winters. At Sapporo, temperatures below –20°C [4°F] have been recorded between December and March. Summers are warm, with temperatures often exceeding 30°C [86°F]. Rain falls throughout the year. Tokyo has the higher rainfall and temperatures while the islands of Shikoku and Kyushu in the S have warm temperate climates with hot summers and cold winters.

HISTORY

Most modern Japanese are descendants of early immigrants who arrived in successive waves from the Korean Peninsula and other parts of the Asian mainland. One of the earliest groups was the AINU, c.15,000 of whom still live on Hokkaido. The native religion was the polytheistic SHINTO, based on nature worship. According to legend, Japan's first emperor, Jimmu, ascended the throne in 660 BC.

By the 5th century AD Japan was divided among numerous clans. The largest and most powerful was the Yamato, who established the Japanese state in the 5th century and made Kyoto the capital. The chiefs of the Yamato clan are regarded as ancestors of the imperial family.

During the 5th century, new ideas and technology reached Japan from China. The Japanese adopted the Chinese system of writing. CONFUCIANISM was part of the profound cultural influence that China bestowed on JAPANESE ART AND ARCHITECTURE and JAPANESE LITERATURE. BUDDHISM, too, spread to Japan in the 550s.

From the early 12th century, political power passed increasingly to military aristocrats. Government was conducted in the name of the emperor by warrior leaders called shoguns. Civil warfare between rival groups of feudal lords was endemic over long periods, but, under the rule of the TOKUGAWA shoguns, between 1603 and 1867, Japan enjoyed a great period of peace and prosperity. Military families (the feudal lords and their retainers, or samurai) formed a powerful elite.

European contact began with the arrival of Portuguese sailors in 1543. In 1549 Spanish missionaries came to convert the Japanese to Christianity. In the 1630s Japan ordered all Christian missionaries to leave the country and forced Japanese converts to give up their faith. The only Europeans allowed to stay were Dutch traders. Japan only opened its ports to Western trade again in 1854 after American intervention led by Commodore Matthew PERRY. Western powers plotted the overthrow of the shogunate, and the re-establishment of imperial power with the MEIJI RESTORATION.

Emperor Meiji's reign (1868–1912) was marked by the adoption of Western ideas and technology. An educational system was set up, railways built and modern systems of banking and taxation introduced. Economic growth was driven by the formation of the ZAIBATSU. The samurai class was abolished and a modern army and navy established.

In 1889, Japan introduced its first constitution under which the emperor became head of state and supreme commander of the army and navy. The emperor appointed government ministers, responsible to him. The constitution allowed for a parliament, called the Diet, with two houses.

From the 1890s, Japan began to build up an overseas empire. In 1894–5, Japan fought China over the control of Korea in the first of the SINO-JAPANESE WARS. Under the Treaty of Shimonoseki (1895), Japan took Taiwan. Korea was made an independent territory, leaving it open to Japanese influence. Rivalry with Russia led to the RUSSO-JAPANESE WAR (1904–5) and decisive Japanese victory. Under the Treaty of Portsmouth, Japan gained the Liaodong peninsula, which Russia had leased from China, while Russia recognized the supremacy of Japan's interests in Korea. Thus Japan was established as a world power.

In World War 1 Japan supported the Allies. After the war, in 1920, Japan became a founding member of the League of Nations. During the 1920s, Japan built its economy, interrupted only by an earthquake (1923) that claimed 123,000 lives and devastated Tokyo and Yokohama. Militarists began to dominate Japanese politics. The army seized MANCHURIA in 1931 and made it a puppet state called MANCHUKUO, then extended Japanese influence into other parts of N China. In 1933, after the League of Nations condemned its actions in Manchuria, Japan was forced to rescind its membership

During the 1930s, and especially after the outbreak of the second Sino-Japanese war in

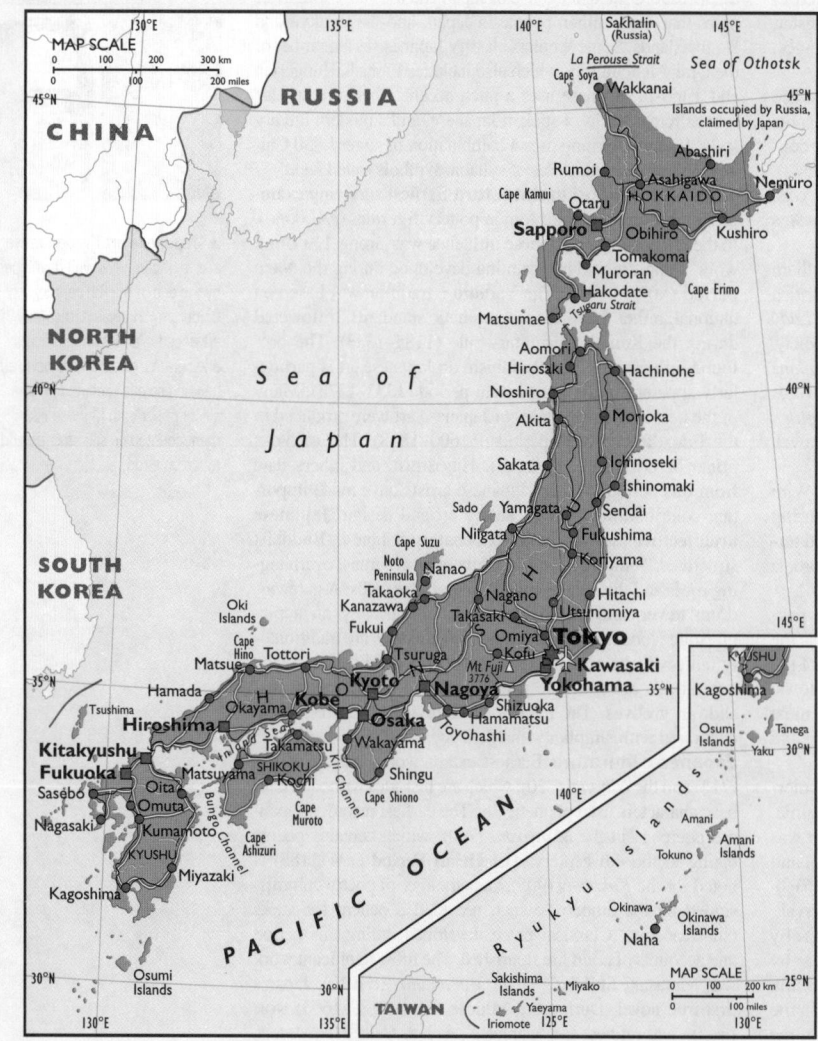

JAPAN

1937, militarist control of Japan's government grew steadily. By the end of 1938, when Japan controlled most of E China, Japan began to consider bringing all of E Asia under its control. In September 1939, Japan occupied the N part of French Indo-China and, later that month, signed an agreement with Italy and Germany, assuring their co-operation in building a 'new world order' and acknowledging Japan's leadership in Asia.

In 1941 Japan launched a surprise attack on the American naval base of PEARL HARBOR in Hawaii, an action that drew the United States into WORLD WAR 2. Japan conquered a huge swathe of Pacific territory, but gradually the Allies regained ground. On 6 August 1945, American bombers dropped the first atomic bomb on HIROSHIMA. The Soviet Union declared war on Japan and invaded Manchuria and Korea. On 9 August, the Americans dropped an atomic bomb on NAGASAKI. World War 2 ended on 2 September 1945 when Japan surrendered.

POLITICS

The US occupation of Japan under Douglas MACARTHUR (1945–52) demilitarized the country. Under a new constitution, which formally required the country to become pacifist, Emperor HIROHITO declaimed his divinity and became a constitutional monarch. Japan

signed a Treaty of Peace in 1952 and the allied occupation ended. The state of war between Japan and the Soviet Union did not formally end until a 1956 agreement, after which Japan became a member of the UN.

The conservative Liberal-Democratic Party was formed in 1955, made up of rival Japanese parties. The LDP controlled Japan's government until the 1990s, when a series of coalition governments were formed. A true opposition party emerged in the late 1990s, when the Democratic Party of Japan united with several small parties. The country underwent a serious economic crisis in 1997. In 2001, the LDP chose Junichiro Koizumi as prime minister. Koizumi promised drastic reforms to revive the economy, and sought to loosen Japan's commitment to pacifism. He won a landslide victory in 2005 elections after his plans to privatize Japan's postal system were defeated in the upper house. He was succeeded by Shinzo Abe in 2006, but Abe's period in office was dogged by political scandal and he was replaced by Yasuo Fukuda in 2007.

ECONOMY

Japan has one of the world's highest GDPs, second only to the USA. The most important sectors of the economy are financial services and manufacturing industry. Although Japan has to

AREA 377,829sq km [145,880sq mi]
POPULATION 127,433,000
CAPITAL (POPULATION) Tokyo (12,064,000)
GOVERNMENT Constitutional monarchy
ETHNIC GROUPS Japanese 99%, Chinese, Korean, Brazilian and others
LANGUAGES Japanese (official)
RELIGIONS Shintoism and Buddhism 84% (most Japanese consider themselves to be both Shinto and Buddhist), others
CURRENCY Yen = 100 sen

import raw materials, the development of high technology has given Japanese products a global market. Manufactures dominate its exports, which include machinery, electronic equipment, vehicles and chemicals. Economic growth, usually strong, was slowed by recession in the mid 1990s but recovered in the 2000s.

Japan has one of the world's largest fishing fleets. Only 15% of the land can be farmed due to its rugged nature, yet the country produces about 70% of the food it requires. Rice is the chief crop, taking up about half of the farmland. Other major products include fruits, sugar beet, tea and vegetables.

---

literature, once the preserve of the aristocracy, became the field of the commoners. HAIKU became popular; Matsuo Basho (1644–94) was the greatest poet of this form. In the **Modern Period**, foreign contacts and Western literature had a major influence. Poetry flourished, and writers such as Yosano Akiko (1878–1942), Ishikawa Takuboku (1885–1912) and Hagiwara Sakutaro (1886–1942) found new means of expression. Writers of modern fiction, such as MISHIMA Yukio, Abe Kobo and Kawabata Yasunari have an international reputation.

Japanese theatre Various dramatic forms, including NOH DRAMA, PUPPET THEATRE, and KABUKI THEATRE. Japanese theatre descended from ritual dances, and involves music, song and dance in addition to dialogue. More modern styles of drama, known as *shinpa* and *shingeki* (new theatre), which were influenced by Western theatre, developed out of the desire to portray modern events and ideas in a more realistic style.

Jarrow March (1936) British protest march of unemployed workers from Jarrow, County Durham, to London. Unemployment was especially high in Jarrow, a small shipbuilding town dependent on one company, which closed down in 1933. About 200 people took part in the march.

Jarry, Alfred (1873–1907) French playwright, poet, and satirist. He is chiefly remembered for his avant-garde farce *Ubu Roi* (1896). His work foreshadowed SURREALISM.

jasmine Any evergreen or deciduous shrub or vine of the genus *Jasminum*, common in the Mediterranean. It produces fragrant yellow, pink, or white flowers, and an oil that is used in perfumes. Height: to 6.5m (20ft). Family Oleaceae.

Jason In Greek mythology, hero and leader of the ARGONAUTS. Sent on a quest for the Golden Fleece, Jason sailed aboard the *Argo*. After surviving many perils, he found the fleece in Colchis and stole it, with the help of the sorceress MEDEA, whom he married.

Jaspers, Karl (1883–1969) German philosopher and psychopathologist. Jaspers was professor of psychology (1921–48) at the University of Heidelberg. His major work, *Philosophy* (1932), presents an individual interpretation of EXISTENTIALISM. Jaspers argued that the deepest insights into human nature are revealed in 'limit situations', such as death.

Jatakas (birth stories) Buddhist writings that drew moral conclusions from stories of the BUDDHA in a previous exis-

tence. The main character usually appears as an animal whose present circumstances are the result of past acts.

jaundice Yellowing of the skin and the whites of the eyes, caused by excess of BILE pigment in the blood. Mild jaundice is common in newborn babies. In adults, jaundice may occur when the flow of bile from the liver to the intestine is blocked by an obstruction such as a GALLSTONE, or in diseases such as CIRRHOSIS, HEPATITIS, or ANAEMIA.

Java Indonesian island, between the Java Sea and the Indian Ocean, SE of SUMATRA; its largest city is JAKARTA. In the early centuries AD the island was ruled by Hindu kingdoms. Islam began to spread in the 16th century. By the 18th century the island was mainly under Dutch control. It was occupied by the Japanese during World War 2. Java is a mountainous country, with a volcanic belt in the S and an alluvial plain to the N. It is thickly forested and has many rivers. It produces rice, tea, coffee, sugar cane, textiles, tobacco, and rubber. Silver, gold, and phosphate are mined in the N. Area: 126,501sq km (48,842sq mi). Pop. (2000) 117,319,419.

javelin Lightweight, tapered spear thrown in a field event: the longest throw wins, provided the javelin lands point-first. The modern javelin is made of a metal alloy, is up to 2.7m (8.9ft) long, and weighs a minimum of 800g (28.2oz) for men and 600g (21oz) for women.

jay Any of several species of harsh-voiced birds related to the MAGPIE and JACKDAW. It has blue wing markings. Length: 34.2cm (13.5in). Family Corvidae.

jazz Style of music that evolved in the USA in the late 19th century out of African and European folk music, and spiritual and popular songs. It is traditionally characterized by improvization, steady rhythm, and prominence of melody, often with elements derived from the BLUES. Early jazz developed in New Orleans, becoming known as DIXIELAND music. In the 1920s, it spread to Chicago and New York City. In the 1930s, SWING enjoyed great popularity, as did the BE-BOP style of the 1940s. Modern jazz incorporates many musical forms.

Jedda *See* JIDDAH

Jefferson, Thomas (1743–1826) Third US president (1801–09), vice president (1797–81). Jefferson was a leading member of the CONTINENTAL CONGRESS and the primary author of the DECLARATION OF INDEPENDENCE (1776).

The AMERICAN REVOLUTION halted his governorship of Virginia (1779–81). Jefferson returned to Congress (1783–84) before succeeding Benjamin FRANKLIN as minister to France (1785–89). George WASHINGTON persuaded Jefferson to serve as his first secretary of state (1789–93). Disagreements with Alexander HAMILTON saw the formation of the DEMOCRATIC REPUBLICAN PARTY led by Jefferson. Narrowly defeated by John ADAMS in the 1796 presidential election, Jefferson became vice president. He led opposition to the ALIEN AND SEDITION ACTS (1798). The landmarks of Jefferson's first presidency (1801–05) were the LOUISIANA PURCHASE (1803) and the LEWIS AND CLARK EXPEDITION (1804–06). His second administration (1805–09) overcame the Aaron BURR conspiracy. He managed to avoid war with Britain, instead passing an EMBARGO ACT (1807). He retired from office and James MADISON succeeded him. Jefferson was a slave owner, but in principle opposed slavery. He founded the University of Virginia (1825).

Jefferson City State capital of Missouri, on the Missouri River. It was chosen as state capital in 1821. The Capitol building (1911–18) contains some fine murals. Industries: shoes, clothes, electrical appliances. Pop. (2000) 39,636.

Jeffreys, George, 1st Baron (1648–89) English judge. He became lord chief justice in 1683, and lord chancellor in 1685. He presided over the BLOODY ASSIZES for JAMES II. After the GLORIOUS REVOLUTION (1688), he was caught trying to flee the country and was imprisoned in the Tower of London, where he died. *See also* MONMOUTH, JAMES SCOTT, DUKE OF

Jehovah's Witnesses Religious sect founded in the 1870s by Charles Taze Russell (1852–1916) of Pittsburgh. The sect believes in the imminent end of the world for all except its own members. They hold to the theory of a theocratic kingdom, membership of which cannot be reconciled with allegiance to any country. They deny most of the fundamental Christian doctrines. The sect is active worldwide.

jellyfish Marine CNIDARIAN found in coastal waters and characterized by tentacles with stinging cells. The adult form is the medusa. It has a bell-shaped body with a thick layer of jelly-like substance between two body cell layers, many tentacles and four mouth lobes surrounding the gut opening. Diameter: 7.5–30.5cm (3in-12in). Class Scyphozoa.

Jenner, Edward (1749–1823) English physician who pioneered VACCINATION. In 1796, aware that cowpox, a minor disease, seemed to protect people from smallpox, Jenner inoculated a healthy boy with cowpox from the sores of an infected dairymaid. The boy was later found to be immune to smallpox.

jerboa Nocturnal, herbivorous, burrowing RODENT of Eurasian and African deserts, with long hind legs developed for jumping. It has a satiny, sand-coloured body and a long tail. Length: to 15cm (6in), excluding the tail. Family Dipodidae.

Jeremiah (active *c*.626–*c*.586 BC) Old Testament prophet who gave his name to the Old Testament Book of Jeremiah. He preached that the sinful behaviour of his countrymen would be punished by God. When Babylon invaded Judah (587BC), Jeremiah saw this as divine retribution.

Jericho Ancient city of Palestine, on the WEST BANK of the River Jordan, N of the Dead Sea. It is one of the earliest known sites of continuous settlement, dating from *c*.9000 BC. According to the Old Testament, Joshua captured Jericho from the Canaanites (*c*.300BC). The city was destroyed and HEROD THE GREAT built a new city to the south. In 1993, following the Israel-PLO peace agreement, Jericho was selected as the centre for Palestinian self-rule. It lies in an agricultural area, producing citrus fruit and dates. Pop. (1997) 32,713.

Jerome, Jerome K. (Klapka) (1859–1927) English humorist, actor, and dramatist. His most successful works include the play *The Passing of the Third Floor Back* (1907) and the novel *Three Men in a Boat* (1889).

Jerome, Saint (347–420) Scholar and translator of the Bible into Latin, b. Eusebius Hieronymous. After a literary education at Rome, he spent two years of intense study as a hermit in the Syrian desert before being ordained a priest at Antioch. Later he returned to Rome. Pope Damasus I commissioned Jerome to prepare a standard text of the gospels for use by Latin-speaking Christians. His work was the basis for what later became the authorized Latin text of the Bible. In 384, Jerome left Rome and set up a monastic community in Bethlehem.

Jersey Largest of the CHANNEL ISLANDS, lying *c*.16km (10 mi) off the NW coast of Normandy in France; the capital is St Helier. It is administered as a bailiwick. Fruit and dairy farming (Jersey cattle) form the basis of the economy. Area: 117sq km (45sq mi). Pop. (1996) 85,200.

Jerusalem Capital of Israel, a sacred site for Christians, Jews and Muslims. Originally a Jebusite stronghold (2000–1500BC), King DAVID captured the city in *c*.1000 BC. Destroyed (*c*.587BC) by NEBUCHADNEZZAR, HEROD THE GREAT rebuilt the city in *c*.35 BC but TITUS destroyed it in AD 70. The Romans established the colony of Aelia Capitolina and banned Jews from the city until the 5th century. In 614 the Persians ended Christian control. In 1071 the SELJUKS conquered Jerusalem, and their maltreatment of Christians precipitated the CRUSADES. It was held by the OTTOMAN Turks from 1244 to 1917, before becoming the capital of the British-mandated territory of Palestine. In 1948, it was divided between Jordan (the east) and Israel (the west). In 1967, the Israeli army captured the Old City of East Jerusalem. In 1980, the united city became the capital of Israel, although this status is not recognized by the UN. Notable monuments within the old city include the DOME OF THE ROCK, the El Aqsa Mosque, and the WESTERN WALL. Jerusalem is an administrative and cultural centre. Industries: tourism, diamond-cutting. Pop. (2006) 724,000.

Jesuits (officially Society of Jesus) Members of a Roman Catholic religious order for men, founded by Saint IGNATIUS OF LOYOLA in 1534. They played a significant role in the COUNTER-REFORMATION. The Jesuits were active missionaries. They antagonized many European rulers because they gave allegiance only to their general in Rome and to the pope. In 1773 Pope Clement XIV abolished the order, under pressure from the Kings of France, Spain, and Portugal, but it continued to exist in Russia. The order was re-established in 1814, and remains an influential international religious organization.

Jesus Christ (active 1st century AD) Hebrew preacher who founded the religion of CHRISTIANITY, hailed and worshipped by his followers as the Son of God. Knowledge of Jesus' life is based mostly on the biblical gospels of St MATTHEW, St MARK, St LUKE, and St JOHN. MARY gave birth (*c*.4BC) to Jesus near the end of the reign of HEROD THE GREAT in Bethlehem, Judaea. Jesus grew up in Nazareth, and may have followed his father, JOSEPH, in becoming a carpenter. In *c*.AD 26, JOHN THE BAPTIST baptized Jesus in the River Jordan. Thereafter, Jesus began his own ministry, preaching to large numbers as he wandered throughout the country. He also taught a special group of 12 of his closest disciples, who were later sent out as his APOSTLES to bring his teachings to the Jews. Jesus' basic teaching, summarized in the SERMON ON THE MOUNT, was to "love God and love one's neighbour". He also taught that salvation depended on doing God's will rather than adhering to the letter and the contemporary interpretation of the Jewish Law. Such a precept angered the hierarchy of the Jewish religion. In *c*.AD 29,

▼ **Jerusalem** Dating from the 7th century, the Dome of the Rock was the first domed mosque. By tradition, it encloses the rock where Muhammad ascended to Heaven. The mosque stands within the Haram esh-Sharif. The wall of the Haram includes the Western (Wailing) Wall. The only extant piece of the Temple of Solomon, the site is sacred for Jews.

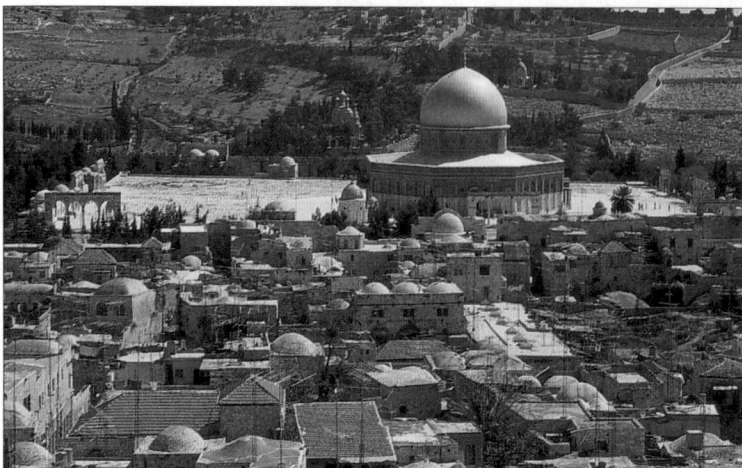

Jesus and his disciples went to Jerusalem. His reputation as preacher and miracle-worker went before him, and he was acclaimed by the people as the MESSIAH. A few days later, Jesus gathered his disciples to partake in the LAST SUPPER. At this meal, he instituted the EUCHARIST. Before dawn the next day, Jesus was arrested by agents of the Hebrew authorities accompanied by JUDAS ISCARIOT, a disaffected disciple, and summarily tried for sedition by the SANHEDRIN, who handed him over to the Roman procurator, PONTIUS PILATE. Roman soldiers crucified Jesus at Golgotha. After his death, his body was buried in a sealed rock tomb. Two days later, according to the gospel, he rose from the dead. Forty days after his resurrection, he is said to have ascended into heaven.

jet engine Form of gas turbine engine that derives forward motion by reaction to the rapid discharge of a jet of gas in the opposite direction. In a jet engine, fuel burns in oxygen from the air to produce a fast-moving stream of exhaust gases. These are ejected from the back of the jet engine and produce forward THRUST in accordance with NEWTON'S LAWS of motion. Frank WHITTLE patented the jet engine in 1930. In 1939 the He-178 became the first jet aeroplane to fly. Early commercial aircraft used **turboprop** engines, in which a propeller is driven by the turbine shaft. The **turbojet** engine provides greater efficiency at speeds in excess of 800km/h (500mph). The turbine drives one or more compressors but the remaining energy in the gas provides jet propulsion. The turbofan engine incorporates a large fan that compresses air outside the engine to provide greater acceleration. *See also* ROCKET

Jet Propulsion Laboratory (JPL) Space centre in Pasadena, California, for the development and control of unmanned spacecraft. The California Institute of Technology runs JPL for the NATIONAL AERONAUTICS AND SPACE ADMINISTRATION (NASA). JPL scientists sent the Surveyor probes to the Moon in the 1960s. Other notable achievements include the MARINER PROGRAM, VIKING SPACE MISSION, and VOYAGER PROGRAM.

jet stream Narrow, swift winds between slower currents at altitudes of 10–16km (6–10mi) in the upper troposphere or lower stratosphere, principally the zone of prevailing westerlies.

Jews Traditionally, the descendants of JUDAH, fourth son of JACOB, who settled in ancient Palestine towards the end of the 2nd millennium BC; historically, followers of the religion of JUDAISM. In *c.*1020 BC SAUL founded the HEBREW state of ISRAEL. DAVID united the kingdoms of Judaea and Israel. His son, Solomon, built the TEMPLE in JERUSALEM. In 587 BC NEBUCHADNEZZAR destroyed the Temple, and deported the Jews from Jerusalem, thus beginning the period of the BABYLONIAN CAPTIVITY. In 538 BC CYRUS THE GREAT delivered the Jews from Babylon. In the 2nd century BC the Maccabee dynasty gained political independence from the Greeks. In AD 70, the Temple was destroyed for a second time by the Romans and the DIASPORA began. In Christian Europe, Jews were victims of anti-Semitism. In 1290, Jews were driven out of England. In 1492, they were expelled from Spain. During World War 2 (1939–45), six million Jews were killed in the HOLOCAUST. In 1948, having struggled against British rule in modern Palestine, the modern state of ISRAEL was proclaimed, despite opposition from Arab and other Islamic states. Today, there are *c.*17.5 million Jews worldwide, including *c.*7 million in the USA and *c.*5 million in Israel. *See also* YIDDISH; ZIONISM

Jiang Qing (1914–92) Chinese actress and politician, the third wife of MAO ZEDONG. She became a high-ranking party official and the leader of the CULTURAL REVOLUTION. One of the radical GANG OF FOUR that sought power after Mao's death in 1976, she was arrested in 1977, convicted of treason and imprisoned.

Jiangsu (Kiangsu) Province in E China; the capital is NANJING. Under the rule of the Ming dynasty (1368–1644), it became a separate province in the 18th century. Taken by Japan in 1937, the province was freed by Chinese nationalists in 1945 but fell to the Chinese communists in 1949. One of China's smallest and most densely populated provinces, it is an extremely fertile region that includes the delta of the River YANGTZE. It is also highly industrialized. SHANGHAI (the largest city) is the chief manufacturing centre of China. Products: rice, cotton, wheat, barley, soya beans, peanuts, tea.

Industries: silk, oil refining, textiles, food processing, cement. Area: 102,240sq km (39,474sq mi). Pop. (2000) 74,380,000.

Jiang Zemin (1926–) Chinese statesman, general secretary of the Chinese Communist Party (1989–2002). A cautious proponent of reform, he was elected to the central committee in 1982, and served as mayor of Shanghai (1985–88). Jiang replaced ZHAO ZIYANG as general secretary. In 1997, he succeeded DENG XIAOPING as China's paramount leader. In 2003, Jiang Zemin was succeeded by Hu Jintao.

Jiddah (Jedda) Administrative capital and largest port of Saudi Arabia, on the Red Sea, 75km (45mi) W of Mecca. Under Turkish rule until 1916, it was taken in 1925 by ibn SAUD. It acts as a port of entry for the HAJJ. Oil wealth has also expanded the city and port. Industries: steel rolling, oil refining, cement and pottery manufacture. Pop. (2005) 3,807,000.

jihad (jehad) Religious obligation imposed upon Muslims through the Koran to spread ISLAM and protect its followers by waging war on non-believers. There are four ways in which Muslims may fulfil their jihad duty: by the heart, by the tongue, by the hand, and by the sword.

Jinnah, Muhammad Ali (1876–1948) Founder of Pakistan. A British-trained lawyer, he joined the Indian National Congress in 1906, but left it in 1920 when they rejected his demand for a separate Muslim electorate. Jinnah led the MUSLIM LEAGUE in campaigning for political equality for Indian Muslims, while continuing to seek agreement with Hindus. By 1940, he had adopted the aim of a separate Muslim state. This was realized when India was partitioned in 1947.

Joan of Arc, Saint (1412–31) (Jeanne d'Arc, Joan of Lorraine or the Maid of Orléans) National heroine of France. A peasant girl, she claimed to hear heavenly voices urging her to save France during the HUNDRED YEARS' WAR. In early 1429, she led French troops in breaking the English siege of Orléans. She drove the English from the Loire towns and persuaded the indecisive dauphin to have himself crowned at Reims as CHARLES VII. In 1430 she was captured and handed over to the English. Condemned as a heretic, she was burned at the stake.

Job Old Testament book describing the crises in the life of Job, a well-to-do man from a town E of Palestine. The main theme is that suffering comes to good and bad people alike.

Jodhpur (Marwar) Walled city on the edge of the THAR DESERT, Rajasthan, NW India. Founded in 1459, it was the capital of the former princely state of Jodhpur. It is now an important road and rail junction. Industries: textiles, lacquerware, bicycles. Pop. (2005) 954,000.

Jodrell Bank Site of the Nuffield Radio Astronomy Laboratories of the University of Manchester. It has one of the world's largest steerable radio telescopes. Diameter: 76m (250ft).

Joffre, Joseph Jacques Césaire (1852–1931) French general. Joffre was commander in chief of the French army at

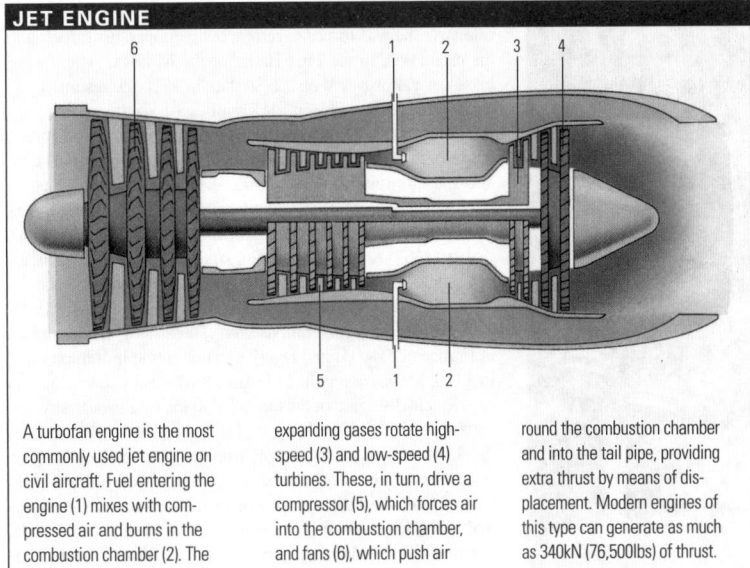

JET ENGINE

A turbofan engine is the most commonly used jet engine on civil aircraft. Fuel entering the engine (1) mixes with compressed air and burns in the combustion chamber (2). The expanding gases rotate high-speed (3) and low-speed (4) turbines. These, in turn, drive a compressor (5), which forces air into the combustion chamber, and fans (6), which push air round the combustion chamber and into the tail pipe, providing extra thrust by means of displacement. Modern engines of this type can generate as much as 340kN (76,500lbs) of thrust.

J

▲ **Jordan** Nicknamed 'Air Jordan', Michael Jordan began his professional basketball career in 1984, as guard for the Chicago Bulls. He went on to become one of the most successful players of all time, averaging a record 32.3 points per game. His sponsorship deals, including a famous series of adverts with director Spike Lee, made him one of the wealthiest sportsmen in the world.

the outbreak of World War 1 (1914). Determined to take the offensive, he was forced to retreat but recouped his forces, and his reputation, in the First Battle of the MARNE. After heavy losses at VERDUN and on the SOMME in 1916, he resigned.

Johannesburg City in NE Republic of South Africa; capital of GAUTENG province. It was founded in 1886. Today, it is South Africa's leading industrial and commercial city, and the administrative headquarters for gold-mining companies. Industries: pharmaceuticals, metal, machinery, textiles, engineering, diamond-cutting. Pop. (2000) 2,950,000.

John (1167–1216) King of England (1199–1216), youngest son of HENRY II. John ruled during RICHARD I's absence on the Third Crusade. Disgraced for intriguing against Richard, John nevertheless succeeded him as king. The loss of vast territories in France (1204–05) and heavy taxation made him unpopular. In 1215, he was compelled to sign the MAGNA CARTA, and his subsequent disregard of the terms led to the first BARONS' WAR.

John I (1357–1433) King of Portugal (1385–1433). After the death of his half-brother, Ferdinand I, he resisted the proposed regency of Ferdinand's daughter, and was elected king. His reign marked the start of Portugal's maritime expansion.

John II (the Good) (1319–64) King of France (1350–64), son of Philip VI. In the HUNDRED YEARS' WAR, he was captured (1356) at Poitiers and held in captivity in England. He was released on the promise of a large ransom, but failure to meet the terms forced his return to England, where he died.

John II (1609–72) King of Poland (1648–68). His reign was beset by wars against Sweden, Russia, and the Ottoman Turks. Territory was lost, Poland devastated, the royal government bankrupted, and John was forced to abdicate.

John III (1502–57) King of Portugal (1521–57). John's reign marked the climax of Portuguese expansion, including the colonization of Brazil, but the Empire began to decline by its end. He introduced (1536) the INQUISITION into Portugal and generally favoured clerical, particularly Jesuit, interests.

John III Sobieski (1624–96) King of Poland (1674–96). His ambition led him to conspire with the French against Polish interests, but his successful generalship against the Ottoman Turks gained him the throne. John's greatest triumph was ending the siege of Vienna (1683) and liberating Hungary by defeating the Ottoman Turks.

John IV (1605–56) King of Portugal (1640–56). As Duke of Braganza, he was a leader of the Portuguese revolt against Spanish rule (1640) and afterwards became king. Portuguese independence was confirmed by victory at Montijo (1644).

John VI (1767–1826) King of Portugal (1816–26). Owing to the insanity of his mother, Queen Maria, he was effectively sovereign from 1792 and officially regent from 1799. In 1807, he fled to Brazil to escape the invading French and did not return to claim the throne until 1822, when he accepted the constitutional government proclaimed in 1820.

John XXIII (1370–1419) ANTIPOPE (1410–15), b. Baldassare Cossa. He convoked the Council of CONSTANCE (1414) to end the GREAT SCHISM. The Council called for his resignation along with the other papal contenders, Gregory XII (Rome) and Benedict XIII (Avignon). He fled but was brought back and forced to resign. He was imprisoned until 1418, when he acknowledged MARTIN V as Pope.

John, Augustus Edwin (1878–1961) Welsh painter. Although he was influenced by the Old Masters and by POST-IMPRESSIONISM, John's high-toned colour and solidity of drawing were unique. His works include *Galway* (1916) and the portraits *Dorelia* and *Bernard Shaw* (c.1914).

John, Sir Elton (1947–) English rock singer and pianist, b. Reginald Kenneth Dwight. John collaborated with lyricist Bernie Taupin (1950–) on albums such as *Goodbye Yellow Brick Road* (1973), and singles "Rocket Man" and "Daniel" (both 1972), and "Candle in the Wind" (1973).

John, Gospel according to Saint Fourth and last gospel of the New Testament, recounting the life and death of JESUS CHRIST and believed to be the work of the Apostle JOHN. It is more concerned with the spiritual meaning of events than with historical facts or even historical sequence.

John, Gwen (Gwendolen Mary) (1876–1939) Welsh painter. The antithesis of her brother, Augustus JOHN, she cre-

ated restrained, grey-toned portraits of single figures. Her subtlety of characterization and tonal relationships is demonstrated in *Self Portrait* (c.1900) and *Portrait of a Nun* (c.1920–30).

John, Saint (active 1st century AD) APOSTLE of JESUS CHRIST, one of the original 12 disciples. Known also as St John the Apostle and St John the Evangelist, he is widely believed to be the author of the fourth GOSPEL and the three New Testament epistles of John. He is also identified with Saint John the Divine, the author of the Book of REVELATION. John was the brother of another apostle, Saint James the Greater. Together with his brother and Saint PETER, John belonged to the inner group of disciples. His feast day is December 27.

John the Baptist, Saint (active 1st century AD) Prophet who heralded the appearance of JESUS CHRIST and the coming of the kingdom of God. The son of ZECHARIAH and Elizabeth, he was born in Judaea six months before Jesus. John baptized Jesus in the River Jordan, recognizing him as the MESSIAH. Herod Antipas beheaded John, after SALOME asked for his head as a reward for her dance.

John of Austria (1545–78) (Don John) Spanish prince and military leader, illegitimate son of Emperor CHARLES V and half-brother of PHILIP II of Spain. In 1571, as head of the naval forces of the Holy League formed by Pope PIUS V, Spain and Venice, he defeated the Turks in the naval Battle of LEPANTO. He took Tunis from the Turks in 1573.

John of Gaunt (1340–99) English noble, Duke of Lancaster (1362–99), fourth son of EDWARD III and father of HENRY IV. In 1359 he acquired the Lancastrian estates through marriage to Blanche. John fought under his brother, EDWARD THE BLACK PRINCE, in the HUNDRED YEARS' WAR. His second marriage to Constance, daughter of Peter of Castile, gained him a claim to the throne of Castile. John was effective ruler of England during the senility of his father and the minority of RICHARD II. He supported the religious reforms of John WYCLIFFE.

John of the Cross, Saint (1542–91) Spanish poet and monk in the Carmelite order. He tried to reform the order to make it more austere, and became co-founder of the contemplative order of the Discalced Carmelites. He is best known for his spiritual poems, which are among the finest verses in Spanish literature. His feast day is December 14 or November 24.

John Paul I (1912–78) Pope (1978), b. Albino Luciani. He was the 263rd pope of the Roman Catholic Church. A modest but gregarious man, his reign lasted only 34 days.

John Paul II (1920–2005) Pope (1978–2005) b. Poland as Karol Wojtyla. Ordained in 1946, he became auxiliary bishop of Kraków (1958), archbishop (1964), and then cardinal (1967). The first non-Italian pope to be elected for more than 450 years. John Paul II travelled widely. Theologically conservative, he upheld papal infallibility and condemned CONTRACEPTION and the ordination of women priests.

Johns, Jasper (1930–) US painter, sculptor, and printmaker. Johns and Robert RAUSCHENBERG led the movement away from ABSTRACT EXPRESSIONISM towards POP ART and MINIMAL ART. Johns' canvases feature banal, everyday images, such as *Three Flags* (1958) and *Target With Four Faces* (1955).

Johnson, Amy (1903–41) English pilot, the first woman to fly solo from Britain to Australia (1930). In 1932 Johnson broke the record held by her husband, James Mollinson, for a solo flight to the Cape of Good Hope, South Africa. During World War 2, she was a pilot in the Air Transport Auxillary.

Johnson, Andrew (1808–75) Seventeenth US president (1865–69), vice president (1864–65). Jonhson was a Democrat governor (1853–57) and senator (1857–62) for Tennessee. He was the only Southerner to remain in the Senate after the outbreak of civil war. Johnson was elected with the incumbent Republican president Abraham LINCOLN on a National Union ticket, and became president when Lincoln was assassinated. His policy of RECONSTRUCTION saw the restoration of civil government to the South. His opposition to civil-rights for blacks, conciliation of Confederate leaders, and attempt to remove Edwin M. Stanton led to his impeachment for "crimes and misdemeanours". He was acquitted by one vote.

Johnson, Lyndon Baines (1908–73) 36th US president (1963–69), vice president (1960–63). Johnson represented

Texas as a Democrat in the House of Representatives (1937–48) and the Senate (1948–60). He served as vice president to John F. KENNEDY, and became president after Kennedy's assassination (1963). He secured the passage of the CIVIL RIGHTS ACT (1964) and was overwhelmingly re-elected in 1964. He carried out an ambitious domestic reform programme, but the VIETNAM WAR dominated his presidency. The war, coupled with severe race riots in 1965–68, dissuaded him from seeking re-election in 1968. His vice president, Hubert HUMPHREY, lost the ensuing election to Richard M. NIXON.

Johnson, 'Magic' (Earvin) (1959–) US professional basketball player. He won five National Basketball Association (NBA) championships (1980, 1982, 1985, 1987–88) with the Los Angeles Lakers and was named Most Valuable Player three times (1987, 1989, 1990). In 1991, Johnson announced he was HIV+ and retired, but he returned to win an Olympic gold medal (1992) in the US 'Dream Team'.

Johnson, Michael (1967–) US track athlete. Johnson became 200m world champion (1991), but was forced to retire from the 1992 Olympics. He was 200m and 400m world champion (1995). At the 1996 Olympics, he became the first man in Olympic history to win 200m and 400m gold medals. he successfully defended his 400m title at the 2000 Olympics.

Johnson, Philip Cortelyou (1906–2005) US architect. He studied under Marcel BREUER at Harvard University and became a proponent of the INTERNATIONAL STYLE. Johnson collaborated with MIES VAN DER ROHE on the Seagram Building, New York City, USA (1958). Other designs include the Lincoln Center, New York City (1964).

Johnson, Dr Samuel (1709–84) English lexicographer, poet, and critic. Most notable among his prolific array of works is the *Dictionary of the English Language* (1755), which established his reputation. *The Idler* (1758–61), and an edition (1765) of the plays of SHAKESPEARE. A discerning critic and trenchant conversationalist, he was co-founder with Joshua REYNOLDS of 'The Club' (1764), later known as 'The Literary Club'. James BOSWELL's life of Johnson contains invaluable biographical detail.

joint In anatomy, place where one BONE meets another. In movable joints, such as those of the knee, elbow and spine, the bones are separated and cushioned from one another by pads of CARTILAGE. In fixed joints, cartilage may be present in infancy

INTERNET

Jordan
▶ www.nis.gov.jo
▶ www.see-jordan.com

JORDAN

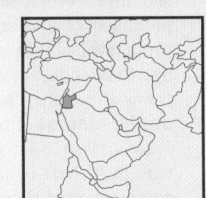

The Hashemite Kingdom of Jordan is an Arab country in SW Asia. The Great Rift Valley in the W contains the River JORDAN and the DEAD SEA. E of the RIFT VALLEY is the Transjordan Plateau, where most Jordanians live. To the E and S lie vast areas of desert. Jordan has a short coastline on an arm of the Red Sea, the Gulf of AQABA. The highest peak is Jabal Ram (1,754m [5,755ft]).

CLIMATE
About 90% of Jordan has a desert climate, with an average annual rainfall of less than 200mm [8in]. Summers are hot; winters can be cold, with snow on higher areas. The NW is the wettest region, with an average annual rainfall of 800mm [31in] in higher areas.

HISTORY
Jordan was first settled by Semitic peoples about 4,000 years ago, and later conquered by Egyptian, Assyrian, Chaldean, Persian and – in the 4th century BC – SELEUCID forces. In the 1st century BC the Nabatean Empire developed, with a capital at PETRA. The Romans captured the region in the 1st century AD. In AD 636, Arab armies conquered and introduced Islam and Islamic culture, which remain dominant.

After the First CRUSADE, the region became part of the Latin Kingdom of Jerusalem (1099). The crusaders were driven out by SALADIN in 1187. The Egyptian Mamelukes overthrew Saladin's successors in 1250 and ruled until 1517, when the area was conquered by the OTTOMANS. Jordan stagnated under their rule, but a railway in 1908 stimulated the economy. Arab and British forces defeated the Turks during World War 1, and after the war the area E of the River Jordan was awarded to Britain by the League of Nations as part of the territory of PALESTINE.

Britain created a territory called Transjordan, E of the River Jordan, in 1921. It became self-governing in 1923, but Britain retained control of its defences, finances and foreign affairs. In 1928, it became a constitutional monarchy ruled by the HASHEMITE dynasty. In 1946 ABDULLAH became King of the independent Hashemite Kingdom of Jordan.

Since the creation of Israel in 1948 Jordan has suffered instability from Arab-Israeli conflict. After the first ARAB-ISRAELI WAR (1948–9) Jordan acquired the remaining Arab parts of Palestine, the WEST BANK, which were incorporated into the state in 1950. This incensed the Palestinians and King Abdullah was assassinated in 1951. His son HUSSEIN I acceded in 1953. In 1958, Jordan formed the short-lived Arab Federation with Iraq. The West Bank, including east JERUSALEM, was lost to Israel in the SIX-DAY WAR of 1967, forcing many Palestinians to seek refuge in Jordan. Jordan became embroiled in a civil war with Palestinian independence movements (1970). By 1971 Jordan had ejected all guerrillas operating from its soil and restored peace.

POLITICS
In 1974 King Hussein suddenly renounced all responsibility for the West Bank, instead recognizing the PALESTINIAN LIBERATION ORGANIZATION as the legitimate representative of the Palestinian people. Palestinians were still a majority in the remaining part of Jordan. Refugees from the

AREA 89,342sq km [34,495sq mi]
POPULATION 6,053,000
CAPITAL (POPULATION) Amman (1,292,000)
GOVERNMENT Constitutional monarchy
ETHNIC GROUPS Arab 98% (Palestinians 50%)
Languages Arabic (official)
RELIGIONS Islam (mostly Sunni) 94%, Christianity (mostly Greek Orthodox) 6%
CURRENCY Jordanian dinar = 1,000 fils

Palestinian Territories, numbering around 900,000, placed a huge burden on an economy already weakened by the loss of trade links with Israel. Jordan was further undermined by the 1991 GULF WAR when, despite its official neutrality, the pro-Iraq, anti-Western stance of the Palestinians in Jordan damaged prospects of trade and aid deals with Europe and the United States. A ban on political parties was removed in 1991, and martial law lifted after 21 years. Multiparty elections were held in 1993. In 1994 Jordan and Israel signed a peace treaty, ending a 40-year war and restoring some land in the S to Jordan.

King Hussein, who had commanded great respect for his role in Middle Eastern affairs, died in 1999. He was succeeded by his eldest son, who became King Abdullah II. Following the path of his father, Abdullah sought to further the Israeli-Palestinian peace process. He also worked to consolidate his country's relations with other nations in the region. Despite local opposition to the invasion of Iraq in 2003, he supported the US-led war on terrorism and worked to improve relations with Israel. Suicide bombers linked to terrorist group al-QAEDA have been a problem.

ECONOMY
Jordan's economy depends substantially on aid. The World Bank classifies Jordan as a 'lower-middle-income' developing country. Less than 6% of the land is farmed. Jordan has no oil of its own, but does have a refining industry. Manufactures include ceramics, pharmaceuticals, processed food, fertilizers, shoes and textiles. Service industries, including tourism, employ more than 70% of the workforce.

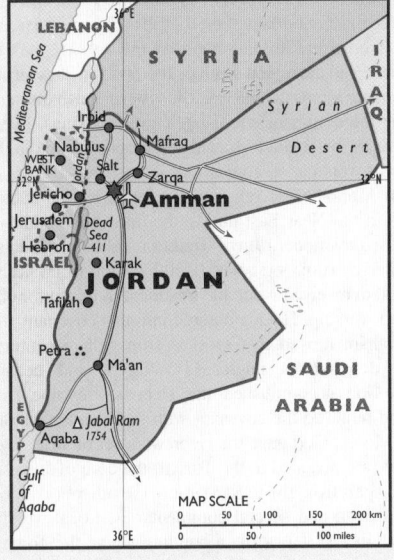

▲ **Joyce** Born in Dublin and educated first by Jesuits then at University College, Dublin, James Joyce was a voracious reader and an accomplished linguist. He was afflicted by glaucoma from a relatively early age, and was deeply troubled by his daughter's mental illness. His seminal novel, *Ulysses* (1922), was highly controversial at the time of its publication, but is now regarded as a ground-breaking work of modernism.

J

but disappear later as the bones fuse together, as in the SKULL. In the movable joints of bony VERTEBRATES, the bones are held together by LIGAMENTS. SYNOVIAL FLUID lubricates the joint.

Jolson, Al (1886–1950) US music hall singer, remembered for his sentimental renditions of "Swanee" and "Mammy". He starred in the first 'talkie', *The Jazz Singer* (1927).

Jonah Fifth of the 12 minor prophets and central character in the Old Testament Book of Jonah. This book relates how Jonah disobeyed God's command to preach to the Gentiles in Nineveh. He attempted to flee from the Assyrian capital in a ship, but was thrown overboard in a storm and swallowed by a whale. Three days later, Jonah was regurgitated alive on shore. He repented and carried out God's commandment.

Jones, Inigo (1573–1652) English architect, stage designer, and painter. Jones introduced a pure CLASSICAL style based on the work of Andrea PALLADIO. His knowledge of Italian architecture gained him enormous prestige in JACOBEAN and Carolingian England. Buildings include Queen's House, Greenwich (1616–35), and Banqueting House, Whitehall (1619–21).

Jongkind, Johan Barthold (1819–91) Dutch painter and etcher, whose work had close affinities with IMPRESSIONISM. Many of his oil paintings were based on landscape watercolours and drawings executed outside his studios.

Jonson, Ben (1572–1637) English dramatist, lyric poet, and actor. A friend of SHAKESPEARE, he was popular and influential in ELIZABETHAN and Stuart drama. His comedies of humours include *Volpone* (1606), *The Alchemist* (1610), and *Bartholomew Fair* (1614). He also wrote the neoclassical tragedies *Sejanus* and *Catiline*, and several court masques.

Joplin, Scott (1868–1917) US composer. He wrote ragtime piano music, such as *Maple Leaf Rag* (1900) and *The Entertainer* (1902), and the opera *Treemonisha* (1911).

Jordaens, Jacob (1593–1678) Flemish painter. He is known for his allegorical and mythological works and for his naturalistic depictions of peasant life.

Jordan Kingdom in sw Asia. *See* country feature, page 431

Jordan River in the Middle East, rising in the Anti-Lebanon mountains at the confluence of the Hasbani, Dan, and Baniyas rivers. It flows s through Israel and the Sea of Galilee, and empties into the Dead Sea. Since 1967, the s part of the river forms a section of the Israel-Jordan border. Length: 320km (200mi).

Jordan, Michael Jeffrey (1963–) US basketball player. Jordan led the Chicago Bulls to six National Basketball Association titles (1991–93, 1996–98) and was named Most Valuable Player five times (1988, 1991, 1992, 1996, 1997). Jordan played in the US teams that won gold medals at the 1984 and 1992 Olympics. In 1993 he switched to baseball, but returned to the Bulls in 1995.

Joseph In the Old Testament book of Genesis, 11th of the 12 sons of JACOB. Given a richly woven, multi-coloured coat by his father, Joseph was sold into slavery by his jealous elder brothers. He was taken to Egypt, where he gained the Pharaoh's favour by predicting the seven-year famine, thus allowing stores to be laid by from the previous seven good years. He was later reconciled with his brothers.

Joseph, Saint In the New Testament, husband of MARY and the legal father of JESUS CHRIST. He was a carpenter from Nazareth, N Palestine. His feast day is March 19 or May 1.

Joseph I (1678–1711) Holy Roman Emperor (1705–11). His reign was dominated by revolt in Hungary, where he was king from 1687, and by the War of the SPANISH SUCCESSION. He was succeeded by his brother, CHARLES VI.

Joseph II (1741–90) Holy Roman Emperor (1765–90). Co-ruler with his mother, MARIA THERESA, until 1780, he introduced sweeping liberal and humanitarian reforms while retaining autocratic powers. Some of his reforms were reversed by his successor, Leopold II.

Joséphine (1763–1814) Consort of NAPOLEON I and empress of the French (1804–09). Her first marriage, to Vicomte Alexandre de Beauharnais, ended (1794) with his death in the REIGN OF TERROR. She married Napoleon in 1796. Her inability to bear him a son caused Napoleon to seek and obtain annulment of their marriage in 1809.

Joseph of Arimathea, Saint Prosperous Jew who was a secret follower of JESUS CHRIST. He claimed Christ's body

from Pontius Pilate after the crucifixion and attended to its burial. His feast day is March 17 in the West, July 31 in the East.

Josephson, Brian David (1940–95) Welsh physicist. In 1962 he predicted that an electric current would flow between two superconductors separated by a thin layer of insulator (the **Josephson effect**). He shared the 1973 Nobel Prize in physics with Leo ESAKI and Ivar Giaever for its discovery. It helped in the understanding of SUPERCONDUCTIVITY.

Joshua Heroic figure among the Israelites, who became their commander after the death of MOSES and led them into CANAAN following their exodus from Egypt. His subsequent exploits and campaigns are recorded in the Book of Joshua.

Jospin, Lionel (1937–) French statesman, prime minister (1997–2002). Jospin joined the French Socialist Party (PS) in 1971. In 1981 he became first secretary of the PS. In 1995 he succeeded François MITTERRAND as leader of the PS, but lost the ensuing presidential election to Jacques CHIRAC. In the 1997 prime ministerial elections, Jospin won a surprise victory against the incumbent RPR prime minister, Alain Juppé. Jospin retired after losing a second presidential election in 2002.

Josquin Desprez (1445–1521) (Josquin Des Prés) Flemish composer. He wrote three books of masses, more than 100 motets and many secular songs. The expressiveness and inventiveness of his music marks him as the most prominent composer in Renaissance Europe.

joule (symbol J) SI unit of energy. One joule is the work done by a force of one NEWTON acting over a distance of one metre. It was named after James P. JOULE and replaced the erg.

Joule, James Prescott (1818–89) British physicist. Joule's law (1841) relates the current flowing through a wire to its heat loss. It laid the foundation for the law of conservation of energy. The JOULE is named after him.

Joyce, James (1882–1941) Irish novelist. In 1904 Joyce renounced Catholicism and left Ireland to live and work in Europe. Joyce's experiments with narrative form place him at the centre of literary MODERNISM. His debut was the short-story collection *Dubliners* (1914). *A Portrait of the Artist as a Young Man* (1916) was a fictionalized autobiography of Stephen Daedalus. His masterpiece, the novel *Ulysses* (1922), presents a day (June 16, 1904) in the life of Leopold Bloom. *Finnegan's Wake* (1939) is an allusive mix of Irish history and myth.

Juan Carlos (1938–) King of Spain (1975–), grandson of ALFONSO XIII. In 1975, Juan Carlos succeeded General FRANCO and set about the democratization of Spanish society. Juan survived an attempted military coup (1981). He is married (1962–) to Princess Sophia of Greece.

Juárez, Benito Pablo (1806–72) President of Mexico (1858–62, 1867–72). Juárez was exiled (1853–55) by SANTA ANNA. As president, he defeated the conservatives in the 'War of Reform' and headed resistance to the French invasion (1862) until the fall of MAXIMILIAN (1867).

Judah Fourth son of JACOB and his first wife Leah, and forefather of the most important of the 12 tribes of ancient ISRAEL. After the Exodus and Joshua's conquest of CANAAN, the tribe of Judah received the region south of JERUSALEM. This territory later became known as Judaea. The tribe of Judah eventually became the dominant one. Israel's greatest kings, DAVID and SOLOMON, belonged to Judah, and prophets foretold that the MESSIAH would arise from among its members.

Judaism Monotheistic religion developed by the ancient HEBREWS in the Near East during the third millennium BC and practised by modern JEWS. Tradition holds that Judaism was founded by ABRAHAM, who (*c.*20th centuryBC) was chosen by God to receive favourable treatment in return for obedience and worship. Having entered into this covenant with God, Abraham moved to CANAAN, from where centuries later his descendants migrated to Egypt and became enslaved. God accomplished the Hebrews' escape from Egypt, and renewed the covenant with their leader, MOSES. Through Moses, God gave the Hebrews a set of strict laws. These laws are revealed in the TORAH, the core of Judaistic scripture. Apart from the PENTATEUCH, the other holy books are the TALMUD and several commentaries. Local worship takes place in a SYNAGOGUE, a building where the Torah is read in public and preserved in a replica of the ARK OF THE

COVENANT. A RABBI undertakes the spiritual leadership and pastoral care of a community. Modern Judaism is split into four large groups: Orthodox, Reform, Conservative and Liberal Judaism. **Orthodox** Judaism, followed by most of the world's 18 million Jews, asserts the supreme authority of the Torah and adheres most closely to traditions, such as the segregation of men and women in the synagogue. **Reform** Judaism denies the Jews' claim to be God's chosen people, and is more liberal in its interpretation of certain laws and the Torah. **Conservative** Judaism is a compromise between Orthodox and Reform Judaism, adhering to many Orthodox traditions, but seeking to apply modern scholarship in interpreting the Torah. **Liberal** Judaism, also known as Reconstructionism, is a more extreme form of Reform Judaism, seeking to adapt Judaism to the needs of society.

Judas Iscariot (d.c.AD 30) Disciple who betrayed JESUS CHRIST to the Jewish hierarchy. In the New Testament, he was named as one of the 12 apostles originally chosen by Jesus, and served as the group's treasurer. In return for 30 pieces of silver, Judas agreed to assist the chief priests in arresting Jesus.

Judges Seventh book of the Old Testament. It covers a 200-year period in the history of ancient ISRAEL, from the death of JOSHUA to the establishment of the first Israelite kingdom (c.11th century BC). The judges are leaders inspired by God to fight battles on behalf of the fledgling nation. The Book of Judges contains some of the oldest material in the Bible.

judo Form of JUJITSU, and one of the most popular of the Japanese martial arts. It places great emphasis on physical fitness and mental discipline. A system of belt colours displays a practioner's standard. Manoeuvres include holds, trips, and falls. Scoring is according to the finality of a throw or hold.

jujitsu Method of unarmed self-defence used in hand-to-hand combat. It involves such techniques as striking, holding, throwing, choking and joint locking. There are c.50 systematized variants (including JUDO, KARATE, and AIKIDO) that have been refined over a period of 2,000 years in Japan, China, and Tibet. In the early 19th century, when the SAMURAI were forbidden to carry weapons, jujitsu became a form of self-defence.

jujube Either of two species of small thorny trees and their fruit of the genus *Zizyphus*. *Z. jujuba*, native to China, has elliptical leaves and reddish brown, plum-sized fruits, which have a crisp, white, sweet flesh. *Z. mauritanica* of India has smaller fruit. Family Rhamnaceae.

July Revolution (1830) Insurrection in France. The immediate cause was the July Ordinances, which dissolved the chamber of deputies, reduced the electorate and imposed rigid press censorship. CHARLES X was forced to abdicate and LOUIS PHILIPPE was proclaimed king with a more liberal constitution.

Juneau State capital of Alaska, USA; a seaport on the Gastineau Channel, bordering British Columbia. It grew rapidly after the discovery of gold in 1880, was made capital of Alaska territory in 1900, and state capital in 1959. Industries: mining, timber, salmon canning, tourism. Pop. (2000) 30,711.

Jung, Carl Gustav (1875–1961) Swiss psychiatrist. He worked closely (1907–13) with Sigmund FREUD, but disagreed that sexuality was the prime cause of NEUROSIS. Jung founded analytical psychology, based on psychic 'individuation'. He argued the UNCONSCIOUS had two dimensions: the personal and archetypes of a collective unconscious. He believed INTROVERSION and EXTROVERSION to be basic personality types.

juniper Any evergreen shrub or tree of the genus *Juniperus*, native to temperate regions of the Northern Hemisphere. Junipers have needle-like or scale-like leaves. The aromatic timber is used for making pencils, and the berry-like cones of common juniper for flavouring gin. Family Cupressaceae.

Junkers Landed aristocracy of Prussia. Descendants of knights who conquered large areas of E Germany in the Middle Ages, they came to dominate the government and army in Prussia and, after 1871, the German Empire. Intensely conservative, their hostility to the WEIMAR REPUBLIC contributed to the success of the Nazis.

Juno Asteroid discovered by Karl Harding in 1804. It is the tenth-largest asteroid, with a diameter of 244km (152mi).

Juno In Roman mythology, the principal female deity and consort of Jupiter, depicted as a statuesque, matronly figure.

Jupiter Fifth major planet from the Sun and the largest of the giant planets. It is one of the brightest objects in the sky. Through a telescope, Jupiter's yellowish elliptical disk is seen to be crossed by brownish-red bands, known as belts and zones. The most distinctive feature is the **Great Red Spot (GRS)**, first observed (1664) by Robert HOOKE. Jupiter's rapid rotation and turbulent atmosphere prouduces spots, streaks, and bands. Eddies give rise to the spots, which are cyclones or (like the GRS) anticyclones. Hydrogen accounts for nearly 90% of Jupiter's atmosphere and helium for most of the rest. The pressure at the cloud tops is c.0.5 bar. At 1,000km (600mi) below the cloud tops there is an ocean of liquid molecular hydrogen. At a depth of 20,000–25,000km (12,500–15,000mi), under a pressure of 3 million bars, the hydrogen becomes so compressed that it behaves as a metal. At the centre of Jupiter, there is probably a massive iron-silicate core surrounded by an ice mantle. The core temperature is estimated to be 30,000K. The deep, metallic hydrogen 'mantle' gives Jupiter a powerful magnetic field. It traps a large quantity of plasma (charged particles); high-energy plasma funnels into the radiation belts. Jupiter's magnetosphere is huge, several times the size of the Sun, and is the source of the planet's powerful radio emissions. Jupiter has 63 known SATELLITES, the four major ones being the GALILEAN SATELLITES. Knowledge of the planet owes much to visits by space probes: Pioneers 10 and 11, Voyagers 1 and 2, Ulysses and Galileo.

Jupiter King of the Roman gods, identified with the Greek god ZEUS. He could take on various forms: the light-bringer (Lucetius), god of lightning and thunderbolts (Fulgur), and god of rain (Jupiter Elicius).

Jura Mountains Mountain range in E France and NW Switzerland. Forming part of the Alpine system, it extends from the River Rhine at Basel to the River Rhône, SW of Geneva. It has several hydroelectric schemes.

Jurassic Central period of the MESOZOIC era, lasting from 213 to 144 million years ago. In this period there were saurischian and ornithischian DINOSAURS, such as *Allosaurus* and *Stegosaurus*, plesiosaurs, pterosaurs and ARCHAEOPTERYX. Primitive mammals had begun to evolve.

Justinian I (482–565) Byzantine Emperor (527–565), sometimes called 'the Great'. His troops, commanded by Belisarius, regained much of the old Roman Empire, including Italy, North Africa, and parts of Spain. Longer-lasting achievements were the Justinian Code (a revision of the whole body of Roman law) and his buildings in Constantinople. Heavy taxation to pay for wars, including defence against Sassanid Persia, drained the strength of the Empire.

Justin Martyr, Saint (100–165) Greek philosopher. He was one of the first Christian apologists in the early Church. Raised as a Jew, he converted to Christianity, probably while studying Platonic and Stoic philosophy at Ephesus. He strongly defended Christian doctrine and was put to death in Rome for his faith. His feast day is June 1.

jute Natural plant fibre obtained from *Corchorus capsularis* and *C. olitorius*, both native to India. The plants grow up to 4.6m (15ft) tall. The fibre is obtained from the bark by soaking (retting) and beating. Jute is used to make sacking, twine, and rope. Family Tileaceae.

Jutes Germanic people who invaded Britain in the 5th century along with Angles, Saxons and others. They settled mainly in Kent and the Isle of Wight.

Jutland, Battle of (1916) Naval battle in the North Sea between the British and Germans in World War 1. The only full-scale engagement of the war involving both main fleets, it ended indecisively. Although British losses were greater, the German fleet remained in harbour for the rest of the war.

Juvarra, Filippo (1678–1736) Italian architect, one of the finest exponents of the BAROQUE style. His greatest achievements are the Superga (1717–31), just outside Turin, and the Church of the Carmine (1732).

Juvenal, Decimus Junius (AD 55–140) Roman poet. Juvenal's satirical poems denounced the immorality of his time. He contrasted decadence in imperial Rome with the virtues of the republic.

JUPITER: DATA

Diameter (equatorial):
142,800km (88,700mi)
Mass (Earth = 1): 317.9
Volume (Earth = 1): 1319
Density (water = 1): 1.33
Orbital period: 11.86 years
Rotation period: 9hr 50m 30s
Temperature at cloud tops:
125K

▲ **jute** This tall, annual plant yields a fine bast fibre that is cheap, easy to bleach and dye, and can be readily woven into coarse fabrics such as hessian, scrim and burlap for sacking and furnishing uses.

433

K/k, eleventh letter of the Roman alphabet. It is derived from the Semitic letter kaph, *possibly from an earlier Egyptian hieroglyph for hand. In Greek it became* kappa *and in that form passed to the Roman alphabet.*

K2 (Godwin Austen) Mountain in NE Pakistan, on the border with China. It is the world's second-highest peak, and the highest in the Karakoram range. It was first climbed in 1954 by Ardito Desio. Height: 8,611m (28,251ft).

Kaaba (Ka'abah or Ka'ba) Central shrine of ISLAM, located in the Great Mosque in MECCA. Tradition believes it to have been built by ABRAHAM on a former site established by Adam. In prayer, Muslims face the meridian that passes through the Kaaba. Each pilgrim who undertakes the HAJJ circles the shrine seven times, touching the Black Stone for forgiveness.

Kabardino-Balkaria Republic of the Russian Federation in the N Caucasus Mountains; the capital is Nalchik. Annexed to Russia in 1827, constituted as a republic of the Soviet Union in 1936, it became a federal republic of Russia in 1991. The population consists of Muslim Kabardinos (48%), Russians (32%), and Turkic-speaking Balkars (10%). Industries: ore-mining, timber. Pop. (2000 est.) 791,600.

kabbala Variant spelling of CABBALA

kabuki theatre Stylized mixture of dance and music, mime and vocal performance; a major form of moralizing entertainment in Japan since the mid-17th century. In contrast to NOH DRAMA, which originated with the nobility, Kabuki was the theatre of the common people. *See also* JAPANESE THEATRE

Kabul Capital of Afghanistan, on the River Kabul, in the E part of the country. It is strategically located in a high mountain valley in the HINDU KUSH. It was taken by Genghis Khan in the 13th century. Later it became part of the Mogul Empire (1526–1738). The capital of Afghanistan since 1776, it was occupied by the British during the Afghan Wars in the 19th century. Following the Soviet invasion in 1979, Kabul was the scene of bitter fighting. Unrest continued into the mid-1990s as rival Muslim groups fought for control. Industries: textiles, leather goods, furniture, glass. Pop. (2005) 3,288,000.

Kádár, János (1912–89) Hungarian statesman, premier (1956–58, 1961–65) and first secretary of the Hungarian Socialist Workers' Party (1956–88). He fought in the resistance during World War 2, and later served as minister of the interior (1948–50). Kádár replaced Imre NAGY as premier after crushing the Hungarian uprising (1956). In 1968 he gave military support to the Soviet invasion of Czechoslovakia. Kádár's policy of 'consumer socialism' revitalized the domestic economy.

Kaddish Ancient Jewish prayer used particularly at services of mourning for the dead. It is a formal statement of praise and faith in the coming of God's Kingdom.

Kafka, Franz (1883–1924) German novelist, b. Czechoslovakia. He published only essays and short stories, such as *Metamorphosis* (1916), during his life. Kafka asked his friend Max BROD to destroy his works after his death, but Brod and published the trilogy of unfinished novels for which Kafka is best known today: *The Trial* (1925), *The Castle* (1926) and *Amerika* (1927). They are disturbing studies of alienation of the individual in a bureaucratic and totalitarian society.

Kahn, Louis Isadore (1901–74) US modernist architect. He followed the lead given by LE CORBUSIER, GROPIUS, and MIES VAN DER ROHE, using bare concrete to create his severely beautiful designs. Kahn's greatest statement is undoubtedly the Jonas Salk Institute of Biological Studies in La Jolla, California (1959–65). *See also* MODERNISM

Kaifeng City in Henan province, E central China. First settled in the 4th century BC it served as capital of China during the Five Dynasty period (907–60) and the Northern Sung dynasty (960–1126). It is the site of a Jewish settlement that flourished from 1163 until the 15th century. Industries: electrical goods, agricultural machinery, chemicals, silk. Pop. (2005) 810,000.

kaiser German title equivalent to Emperor. It derives from the Roman title 'Caesar' and was first connected with Germany when Otto I became Holy Roman Emperor in 962. The last Kaiser was Wilhelm II (r. 1888–1918), whose father had adopted the title after the Franco-Prussian War (1870–71).

Kalahari Desert region in S Africa, covering parts of BOTSWANA, NAMIBIA and SOUTH AFRICA, between the ORANGE and ZAMBEZI rivers. Thorn scrub and forest grow in some areas, and grazing is possible in the wet season. The SAN, and Africans and Europeans engaged in rearing cattle, live here. Area: *c.*260,000sq km (100,000sq mi).

kale Hardy, crop plant related to the CABBAGE. It is short-stemmed and has large, bluish-green, curly-edged leaves. It may reach a height of 61cm (24in). Family Brassicaceae; (sub)species *Brassica oleracea acephala.*

Kali Hindu goddess of destruction, consort of SHIVA. Also known as Chandi, DURGA, PARVATI, Sakti, Uma, and Mata, Kali represents the all-devouring aspect of Devi, the mother-goddess of India, who in other forms is calm and peaceful.

Kalimantan Region of Indonesia, forming the S part of the island of BORNEO. In the 16th century, Muslim states were created. In the 17th century, the Dutch gradually established colonial rule over what became part of the Netherlands East Indies. Kalimantan came under Indonesian control in 1950. Products: rice, copra, pepper, oil, coal, industrial diamonds, timber. Area: 539,460sq km (208,232sq mi). Pop. (2000) 11,014,372.

Kalinin, Mikhail Ivanovich (1875–1946) Soviet statesman, head of state of the Soviet Union (1919–46). He was a founder (1912) of the newspaper *Pravda* and fought in the RUSSIAN REVOLUTION (1917). A supporter of Stalin, Kalinin served in the Politburo (1925–46).

Kaliningrad (Königsberg) City and seaport in Russia, on the Baltic coast; capital of Kaliningrad oblast. Founded in 1255 as Königsberg, the city was a member of the Hanseatic League. It became the residence of the Dukes of Prussia in 1525. In 1946, it was incorporated into the Soviet Union. Following the break-up of the Soviet Union, Kaliningrad oblast is now separated from Russia proper. It shares a border with Poland and Lithuania. Industries: shipbuilding, fishing, motor vehicle parts. Pop. (1994 est.) 416,547.

Kalmykia Republic of the Russian Federation on the Caspian Sea, SE European Russia; the capital is Elista. The region was made an autonomous republic in 1936. In World War 2 its inhabitants were deported to Soviet Central Asia for alleged collaboration with the Germans. They returned in 1957. After the break-up of the Soviet Union, it became a republic within the Russian Federation, acquiring its present name in 1992. Industries: fishing, animal farming. Area: *c.*75,900sq km (29,300sq mi). Pop. (2000) 315,700.

Kamchatka Peninsula Peninsula in E Siberia, Russia, separating the Sea of Okhotsk (W) from the Bering Sea and the Pacific Ocean (E). The region has several active volcanoes. Mineral resources include oil, coal, gold and peat. Area: 270,034sq km (104,260sq mi).

Kamehameha Name of five kings of Hawaii. **Kamehameha I** (r. *c.*1758–1819) united all the Hawaiian islands. He instituted harsh laws, but abolished human sacrifice. His son, **Kamehameha II**, or Liholiho (r. 1819–25), admitted the first US missionaries. **Kamehameha III**, or Kauikeaouli (r. 1825–54), introduced a liberal constitution and land reform. **Kamehameha IV**, or Alexander Liholiho (r. 1854–63), made social and economic reforms and resisted US influence. His brother, **Kamehameha V** (r. 1863–72), abandoned the constitution and strengthened royal authority. The dynasty ended with his death.

Kamerlingh-Onnes, Heike (1853–1926) Dutch physicist. In 1908, using a liquid HYDROGEN cooling system, he liquefied HELIUM and achieved a temperature within one degree of ABSOLUTE ZERO. In 1911, Onnes discovered the property of SUPERCONDUCTIVITY in some metals. He received the 1913 Nobel Prize in physics.

kamikaze (Jap. 'divine wind') Name given to crews or their explosive-laden aircraft used by the Japanese during World War 2. Their suicidal method of attack was to dive into ships of the enemy fleet. Serious losses were inflicted on the US Navy.

Kampala Capital and largest city in UGANDA, on the N shore of Lake VICTORIA. Founded in the late 19th century on the remains of a royal palace of the Kings of Buganda, it replaced Entebbe as capital when Uganda attained independence in 1962. It is the trading centre for the agricultural goods and livestock produced in Uganda. Industries: textiles, food processing, tea blending, coffee, brewing. Pop. (2005) 1,345,000.

Kampuchea *See* CAMBODIA

Kanchenjunga (Kinchinjunga or Kanchanjanga) Third-highest mountain in the world, in the E Himalayas. It was first climbed in 1955 by a British expedition led by Charles Evans. The highest of its five peaks reaches 8,586m (28,169ft).

Kandahar (Qandahar) City and provincial capital in s Afghanistan, c.480km (300mi) sw of Kabul. Because of its location on important trade routes, it was occupied by many foreign conquerors before becoming the capital of the independent Afghani kingdom (1747–73). It was the scene of fighting after the Soviet invasion of Afghanistan in 1979 and became the headquarters of the TALIBAN in the 1990s. It is a commercial centre for the surrounding region. Pop. (2002 est.) 339,200.

Kandinsky, Wassily (1866–1944) Russian painter and theorist. His experiments with abstraction were revolutionary. His early abstract paintings, including the many numbered *Compositions*, express great lyricism. From 1911 he was an active member of the BLAUE REITER. His writings, especially *Concerning the Spiritual in Art* (1914), show the influence of Oriental art philosophy. After World War 1, his work became more controlled. *White Line* (1920) and *In the Black Circle* (1921) show the beginnings of a refinement of geometrical form that developed during his years at the BAUHAUS (1922–33).

Kandy City in Sri Lanka. Former capital of the ancient kings of Ceylon, it was occupied by the Portuguese and the Dutch before being captured by the British in 1815. The city is a market centre for a region producing tea, rice, rubber and cacao. The chief industry is tourism. Pop. (2001) 156,923.

kangaroo MARSUPIAL native to Australia, New Guinea and adjacent islands. The three main types are the grey kangaroo, the red kangaroo and the wallaroo, or euro. The thick, coarse fur is red, brown, grey or black. The front legs are small, the hind legs long and used in leaping. Height: to 1.8m (6ft) at the shoulder; weight: to 70kg (154lb). Family Macropodidae, genus *Macropus*.

kangaroo rat Tiny, desert-dwelling RODENT of w North America. It has long hind legs and a long tail, and hops. It stores seeds in its cheek pouches. Length: to 41cm (16in), including the tail. Family Heteromyidae; genus *Dipodomys*.

Kano City in N central Nigeria; capital of Kano state. The city dates from before the 12th century and became a Muslim possession in the 16th century. It was conquered by the FULANI in the early 19th century. Today Kano is a trading centre for a region producing cotton and nuts. Industries: textiles, leather goods, brewing, chemicals. Pop. (2005) 2,884,000.

Kanpur (Cawnpore) City on the River Ganges, Uttar Pradesh, N India. Kanpur was ceded to the British in 1801, and became a frontier post. During the INDIAN MUTINY, the entire British garrison in Kanpur was massacred. The city is now a major industrial and commercial centre. Industries: chemicals, leather goods, textiles. Pop. (2005) 3,040,000.

Kansas State in central USA; the capital is TOPEKA. Other major cities are Wichita and KANSAS CITY. First visited by Spanish explorers in the 16th century, the area passed from France to the new United States under the LOUISIANA PURCHASE of 1803. It was Native American territory until 1854, when the Territory of Kansas was created and the area opened up for settlement. Part of the Great Plains, the land rises from the prairies of the E to the semi-arid high plains of the w. The area is drained by the Kansas and Arkansas rivers. Kansas is the leading US producer of wheat. Corn, hay, and sorghum are also grown and cattle raising is important. Manufacturing is economically significant. Industries: transport equipment, chemicals, petroleum products, machinery. Area: 213,094sq km (82,276sq mi). Pop. (2000) 2,688,418.

Kansas City City in w Missouri, USA, on the Missouri River, adjacent to KANSAS CITY, Kansas. Established in 1821 as a trading post, it developed in the 1860s with the introduction of the railroad and the growth in cattle trade. Industries: aerospace equipment, vehicles, chemicals, petroleum products, livestock, grain. Pop. (2000) 1,362,000.

Kansas City City in NE Kansas, USA, at the confluence of the Kansas and Missouri rivers, adjacent to KANSAS CITY, Missouri. Part of a Native American reservation, it was acquired by Wyandotte Native Americans in 1843 and sold to the US government in 1855. The modern city was established in 1886. Industries: livestock, motor vehicles, metal products, chemicals. Pop. (2000) 146,866.

Kant, Immanuel (1724–1804) German metaphysical philosopher. He was a teacher and professor of logic and

◄ **Kandinsky** *Improvisation 28 (Second Version)* (1912). Throughout his life, the influential Russian painter Wassily Kandinsky explored what he saw as the deeply spiritual relationship between visual art and music. He is widely accepted as the founder of abstract art.

METAPHYSICS at the University of Königsberg. The order and modesty of Kant's life was undisturbed by the notoriety caused by his publications. Kant's philosophy of IDEALISM, outlined in *Critique of Pure Reason* (1781), sought to discover the nature and boundaries of human knowledge. Kant's system of ethics, described in the *Critique of Practical Reason* (1790), places moral duty above happiness and asserts the existence of an absolute moral law (the "categorical imperative"). His views on aesthetics are embodied in his *Critique of Judgment* (1790). Kant also produced several essays in support of religious liberalism and the ENLIGHTENMENT.

kaolin (china clay) Fine clay composed chiefly of KAOLINITE, a hydrous silicate of aluminium. It is used in the manufacture of coated paper, ceramics and fine porcelain.

kaolinite Sheet silicate mineral of the kaolinite group, hydrous aluminium silicate $[Al_2Si_2O_5(OH)_4]$. It is a product of the weathering of feldspar and has triclinic system tabular crystals. It is white with a dull lustre. Hardness 2–2.5; r.d. 2.6.

kapok Tropical tree with compound leaves and white or pink flowers. Its seed pods burst to release silky fibres, which are commonly used for stuffing and insulation. Height: to 50m (165ft). Family Bombacaceae; species *Ceiba pentandra*.

Karachai-Cherkassia Republic of the Russian Federation in the N Caucasus Mountains; the capital is Cherkessk. It was a autonomous region within the Soviet Union (1926–43) until Stalin deported much of the Muslim population. In 1957 it was established as an autonomous region. In 1992 it became a republic of the Russian Federation. Area: 14,100sq km (5,442sq mi). Pop. (2000 est.) 434,700.

Karachi City and seaport on the Arabian Sea, SE Pakistan; capital of Sind province. Settled in the early 18th century, in 1843 it passed to the British, who developed it as a major port. It was the first capital of Pakistan in 1947 and remains the country's largest city. Karachi is a trading centre for agricultural produce. Industries: steel, engineering, oil refining, motor vehicles, textiles, publishing. Pop. (2005) 11,819,000.

Karadžić, Radovan (1945–) Bosnian Serb politician. In 1990, he founded the Serbian Democratic Party. In 1992, Bosnia-Herzegovina voted for independence from the Serb-dominated Yugoslavia. Karadžić declared a separate Bosnian Serb state, Republika Srpska, with himself as president. With the support of Slobodan MILOŠEVIĆ, he instituted 'ethnic cleansing' of non-Serbs and a war against the Bosnian state. In 1995, Milosevic withdrew his support and Karadžić was forced to sign the Dayton Peace Accord with Bosnian President IZETBEGOVIĆ. In 1996, he was indicted by the United Nations (UN) for war crimes; he was apprehended in 2008.

Karajan, Herbert von (1908–89) German conductor. He conducted the Berlin State Opera (1938–45) and was director of the Vienna State Opera (1945–64). As musical director of the Berlin Philharmonic Orchestra (1955–89) and artistic director of the Salzburg Festival (1956–60), he dominated the European classical music scene.

Karakalpak Autonomous republic in w Uzbekistan; the capital is Nukus. Under Russian control at the end of the 19th century, it became an autonomous region of Kazakhstan in 1925, and an autonomous republic in 1933. In 1936 it became part of the Uzbek Soviet Republic and retained its autonomous status within independent Uzbekistan. Crops include alfalfa, rice, cotton and maize. Live-

K

KANSAS
Statehood :
January 29, 1861
Nickname :
Sunflower state
State bird :
Western meadowlark
State flower :
Sunflower
State tree :
Cottonwood
State motto :
To the stars through difficulties

INTERNET

Kansas
► www.state.ks.us

stock raising and the breeding of muskrats and silkworms are important, and there is some light industry. Area: 165,600sq km (63,940sq mi). Pop. (2002 est.) 1,633,900.

Karakoram Range Mountain range in central Asia, extending SE from E Afghanistan to Jammu and Kashmir in India. It includes some of the world's highest mountains, among them K2. Length: *c.*480km (300mi).

Karamanlis, Konstantinos (1907–98) Greek statesman, prime minister (1955–63, 1974–80), president (1980–85, 1990–95). He was elected to Parliament in 1935. On becoming prime minister, he formed his own party, the National Radical Union (ERE). He resigned in 1963 after an election defeat. During 11 years of self-imposed exile, he was an opponent of the Greek military junta, and when it fell in 1974 he returned as prime minister at the head of the new Democratic Party (ND).

karate Martial art popularized in Japan in the 1920s. It involves a method of physical and mental training, includes a variety of blows using the hand, legs, elbows and head. In competition, scoring depends on the finality of the blow.

Karelia Republic of the Russian Federation in NW European Russia; the capital is Petrozavodsk. In the Middle Ages, the region was an independent Finnish state. Split in the 12th century between Sweden and NOVGOROD, it was unified under Sweden in the 1600s. The E was returned to Russia in 1721, while the w was part of Finland until 1940. After the Soviet-Finnish War (1939–40), the E sector absorbed 36,000sq km (14,000sq mi) of Finnish land and became a constituent republic (Karelo-Finnish SSR). In World War 2, the Finns occupied most of Karelia but returned it to the Soviet Union in 1944. Declaring itself the Republic of Karelia, it became a constituent republic of the Russian Federation in 1992. Farming is in to the s, where vegetables and cereals are grown and livestock raised. Fishing and timber are the chief industries. The region has valuable mineral deposits. Area: 172,400sq km (66,564sq mi). Pop. (2000 est.) 766,400.

Karloff, Boris (1887–1969) English actor, b. William Henry Pratt. He is noted for his performances in horror films, including the portrayal of the monster in *Frankenstein* (1931).

karma (Sanskrit, action) Central moral doctrine in HINDUISM, BUDDHISM, and JAINISM. It is a natural, impersonal law of moral cause and effect, unconnected with divine punishment for sins. In Hinduism and Jainism, karma is the

KAZAKHSTAN

The Republic of Kazakhstan is a large country in w-central Asia. In the w, the CASPIAN SEA lowlands include the Karagiye Depression, which reaches 132 m [433 ft] below sea level. The lowlands extend E through the Aral Sea area. The N contains high plains, but the highest land is along the E and s borders. These areas include parts of the ALTAI and TIAN SHAN mountain ranges.

Eastern Kazakhstan contains several freshwater lakes, the largest of which is Lake BALKHASH (Balqash Köl). Many rivers have been diverted for use in irrigation, causing major ecological problems. The ARAL SEA, deprived of water, shrank from 66,900sq km [25,830sq mi] in 1960 to 33,642sq km [12,989sq mi] in 1993. Areas which once provided fish have dried up and are now barren desert.

Kazakhstan has very little woodland. Grassy steppe covers much of the N, while the s is desert or semi-desert. Large, dry areas between the Aral Sea and Lake Balkhash have become irrigated farmland.

CLIMATE

The extreme climate reflects position in the heart of Asia, far from the influence of the oceans. Winters are cold and snow covers the land for about 100 days, on average, at ALMATY (Alma Ata). Rainfall is generally low.

HISTORY

Little is known of the early history of Kazakhstan, except that it was the home of nomadic peoples. In 1218, the Mongol

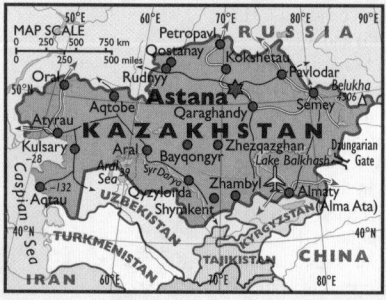

Emperor GENGHIS KHAN conquered the region. Following his death, the Empire was divided into khanates and feudal trading towns emerged beside the oases. In the late 15th century the towns formed a Kazakh state that fought for its independence from the neighbouring khanates and built up a large nomadic empire. In 1731, Kazakhstan appealed to Russia for protection and voluntarily acceded to the Russian Empire. By the mid-1740s Russia ruled most of the region. In the early 19th century Russia abolished the khanates and encouraged Russian settlement throughout Kazakhstan.

The conscription of Kazakhs during World War 1 aroused much resentment, and after the Russian Revolution (1917) demands for independence grew. In 1920, Kazakhstan became an autonomous Soviet republic, and in 1936 a full constituent republic of the Soviet Union. During the 1920s and 1930s the process of Russification increased. More than 1.5 million Kazakhs died of starvation under the agricultural policies of Joseph Stalin. Soviet minorities were transported to Kazakhstan in the 1930s. During World War 2, many people and industries from areas of western Russia threatened by German invasion were evacuated there. In the 1950s the 'Virgin Lands' project sought to turn vast areas of grassland into cultivated land to feed the Soviet Union. The Soviets placed many of their nuclear missile sites in Kazakhstan, sited the Baikonur cosmodrome there, and also built their first fast-breeder nuclear reactor at Mangyshlak. In 1986 nationalist riots were prompted by the imposition of a Russian to lead the republic.

POLITICS

Reforms in the Soviet Union in the 1980s led to its break-up in 1991. Kazakhstan kept contacts with Russia and most of the former Soviet republics by joining the COMMONWEALTH OF INDEPENDENT STATES (CIS) and in 1995 Kazakhstan announced that its army would unite with that of Russia. In 1997 the government moved the capital from Almaty to Aqmola, a town in the Russian-dominated north later

AREA 2,724,900sq km [1,052,084sq mi]
POPULATION 15,295,000
CAPITAL (POPULATION) Astana (322,000)
GOVERNMENT Multiparty republic
ETHNIC GROUPS Kazakh 53%, Russian 30%, Ukrainian 4%, German 2%, Uzbek 2%
LANGUAGES Kazakh (official). Russian, the former official language, is widely spoken
RELIGIONS Islam 47%, Russian Orthodox 44%
CURRENCY Tenge = 100 tiyn

renamed Astana. The move was intended to bring some Kazakh identity to the area.

Kazakhstan has emerged as a powerful entity, wealthier and more diversified than other Asian republics. It is the only former Soviet republic whose ethnic population is almost outnumbered by Russians, and its Muslim revival is relatively muted. Its first elected president, former Communist leader Nursultan Nazarbayev, introduced many reforms including a multiparty system. He has, however, been criticized for his authoritarian rule. International observers considered the elections of 2004 and 2005 to be seriously flawed. In 2007, constitutional reforms strengthened parliament and limited the number of terms future presidents could serve, but permitted Nazarbayev to stand indefinitely.

ECONOMY

The World Bank classifies Kazakhstan as a 'lower-middle-income' developing country. Livestock farming, especially sheep and cattle, is an important activity, and major crops include barley, cotton, rice and wheat.

The country is rich in mineral resources, including coal and oil reserves, together with bauxite, copper, lead, tungsten and zinc. Manufactures include chemicals, food products, machinery and textiles. The oil industry has grown rapidly, with exports both to Europe via a Russian-controlled Caspian Sea pipeline and to China by a direct link. Rising oil exports and prices made Kazakhstan one of the world's fastest growing economies in the mid 2000s.

sum of a person's actions which are passed on from one life to the next and determine the nature of rebirth.

Karpov, Anatoly (1951–) Russian chess player. In 1975 he became world champion by default after Bobby Fischer failed to play. Karpov successfully defending his title against Victor Korchnoi (1978, 1981). In 1985 he was defeated by Gary KASPAROV. Karpov suffered further defeats against Kasparov (1986, 1987, 1990) before Kasparov formed his own chess federation and forfeited the FIDE title (1993–99) to him.

Kashmir Region in N India and NE Pakistan; former Indian princely state. When the Indian subcontinent was partitioned in 1947, the maharaja of Kashmir acceded to India, precipitating war between India and Pakistan. A ceasefire left it divided between the Indian-controlled state of JAMMU AND KASHMIR and the Pakistan-controlled areas in the N and W of the region. The N area of Kashmir is ruled directly by the Pakistan government; the W area, Azad Kashmir, is partly autonomous. The Aksai Chin area of Kashmir, on the border with Tibet, is occupied by China. Indian Jammu and Kashmir has remained in a state of unrest. Kashmir includes parts of the Himalayas and the KARAKORAM RANGE. The Vale of Kashmir, in the River Jhelum valley, is the most populated area; wheat and rice are grown. Total area: 222,236sq km (85,806sq mi).

Kasparov, Gary (1963–) Russian chess player, b. Gary Weinstein. In 1985 he defeated Anatoly KARPOV to become the youngest-ever chess world champion. Kasparov successfully defended his title against Karpov in 1986, 1987, and 1990. In 1996, he defeated the IBM 'Deep Blue' chess computer, but lost a rematch in 1997. In 2000, Kasparov lost his world title to his former pupil, Vladimir Kramnik.

Katmandu (Kathmandu) Capital of Nepal, situated c.1,370m (4,500ft) above sea level in a valley of the HIMALAYAS. Founded in AD 723, it was independent from the 15th century to 1768, when Gurkhas captured it. Katmandu is Nepal's administrative, commercial, and religious centre. Pop. (2000) 1,176,000.

Katowice City in S Poland. Founded in the 16th century and chartered in 1865, it was occupied by Germany during World War 2. A leading industrial centre, it produces coal, iron and steel, heavy machinery and chemicals. Pop. (1999) 345,934.

Katz, Sir Bernard (1911–2003) British biophysicist, b. Germany. He shared the 1970 Nobel Prize in physiology or medicine for work on the chemistry of nerve transmission. He discovered how the NEUROTRANSMITTER acetylcholine is released by neural impulses, causing muscles to contract.

Kaufman, George Simon (1889–1961) US playwright. He collaborated with other writers, such as Edna Ferber on *Stage Door* (1936) and Moss HART on *You Can't Take It With You* (1936) and *The Man Who Came To Dinner* (1939). He also contributed to *Guys and Dolls* (1950).

Kaunas City and port in S Lithuania. Founded in the 11th century, it became part of Russia in 1795. From 1918–40, it was capital of independent Lithuania. Industries: iron and steel, electrical machinery, chemicals, textiles. Pop. (2001) 381,300.

Kaunda, Kenneth David (1924–) Zambian statesman, president (1964–91). In 1959, he was imprisoned for membership of the banned Zambia African National Congress. In 1960, he became leader of the United National Independence Party (UNIP). He led Northern Rhodesia to independence as Zambia, becoming its first president. In 1972, he imposed single-party rule. Kaunda was a staunch opponent of APARTHEID and played a leading role in establishing an independent Namibia (1990). In 1991, economic problems and unrest forced multiparty elections and he was defeated by Frederick Chiluba. In 1997, after a failed coup, Kaunda was imprisoned. In 1998, he was released and resigned as leader of UNIP.

Kawasaki City in SE Honshu Island, on Tokyo Bay, Japan. The city suffered extensive damage from bombing during World War 2. Industries: iron and steel mills, machinery, motor vehicles, petrochemicals, shipbuilding. Pop. (2000) 1,250,000.

Kazakh Turkic-speaking Muslim people who inhabit the Republic of Kazakhstan and the adjacent Sinkiang province

of China. Traditionally nomadic, in the 20th century they settled in the collective farm system of the former Soviet Union.

Kazakhstan Republic in central Asia. *See* country feature

Kazan Port on the River Volga, E European Russia; capital of the TATARSTAN. Founded in the 13th century, Kazan became the capital of the Tatar khanate (1438). Conquered by Ivan IV, it served as the E outpost of Russian colonization. Industries: electrical equipment. Pop. (2005) 1,108,000.

Kazan, Elia (1909–2003) US film director and novelist, b. Turkey. Kazan was one of the founders of the ACTORS' STUDIO. His work in the cinema includes *A Tree Grows in Brooklyn* (1945), *Gentleman's Agreement* (1947), and *On the Waterfront* (1954). He wrote two best-selling novels, *America, America* (1962) and *The Arrangement* (1967).

Kazantzakis, Nikos (1885–1957) Greek politician and writer. He wrote in a wide variety of genres, including lyric and epic poetry, literary criticism, and translations from DANTE and GOETHE. Kazantzakis is best known outside Greece for his novel *Zorba the Greek* (1946).

Keating, Paul John (1944–) Australian statesman, prime minister (1991–96). He entered Parliament in 1969, served in the government of Bob HAWKE from 1983, and succeeded Hawke as PM. He was defeated in 1996 by John HOWARD.

Keaton, Buster (1895–1966) US comic silent-film actor and director. *Our Hospitality* (1923), *Seven Chances* (1925) and *The General* (1926) are pre-eminent among the ten full-length features he released before 1928.

Keats, John (1795–1821) English poet, one of the major figures of ROMANTICISM. His first volume, *Poems* (1817), included 'On First Looking into Chapman's Homer'. Keats was savagely criticized for the four-volume romance *Endymion* (1818). *Lamia, Isabella, The Eve of St Agnes and Other Poems* (1820) included the ballad 'La Belle Dame sans Merci' and the magnificent lyrics 'Ode on a Grecian Urn', 'Ode to a Nightingale', and 'Ode to Autumn'. Keats died of tuberculosis in Rome, leaving unfinished the epic *Hyperion*. Percy SHELLEY mourned his passing in his elegy *Adonais* (1821).

Keillor, Garrison Edward (1942–) US writer and humorist best known for his bittersweet stories about the engaging fictional community of Lake Wobegon.

Keller, Helen Adams (1880–1968) US social worker, writer, and lecturer. With the help of her teacher Anne Sullivan, she overcame the loss of sight, hearing, and speech caused by an early illness. She mastered several languages and lectured throughout the world. Her books include *The Story of My Life* (1902), *The World I Live In* (1908), and *The Open Door* (1957).

Kellogg-Briand Pact (1928) International peace agreement negotiated by US secretary of state, Frank B. Kellogg, and French foreign minister, Aristide BRIAND. It renounced war as a means of settling international disputes and was subsequently signed by most of the world's governments.

Kelly, Gene (1912–96) US dancer, choreographer, film actor, and director. His greatest films, co-directed with Stanley Donen, were *On the Town* (1949), *An American in Paris* (1951), and the hugely popular *Singin' in the Rain* (1951).

Kelly, Grace Patricia (1929–82) US film actress. She appeared in *High Noon* (1952) and won an Academy Award for *The Country Girl* (1954). She retired from the screen after marrying Prince Rainier of Monaco in 1956.

kelp Any of several brown SEAWEEDS commonly found on Atlantic and Pacific coasts, a type of brown ALGAE. A source of iodine and potassium compounds, kelps are now used in a number of industrial processes. Giant kelp (*Macrocystis*) exceeds 46m (150ft) in length. Phylum Phaeophyta.

Kelvin, William Thomson, 1st Baron (1824–1907) British physicist and mathematician, b. Belfast, after whom the absolute scale of TEMPERATURE is named; this starts at absolute zero and degree intervals the same size as the degree Celsius. The freezing point of water is 273K (0°C/ 32°F) and the boiling point 373K (100°C/212°F).He resolved conflicting interpretations of the first and second laws of THERMODYNAMICS.

Kemal Atatürk *See* ATATÜRK, KEMAL

Kempis, Thomas à (1380–1471) German Augustinian monk and spiritual writer. Ordained in 1413, he remained in the Monastery of the Brethren of the Common Life, near

▲ **Keaton** A music-hall background provided the US comic actor and director Buster Keaton with many of the ideas for his sophisticated and completely visual slapstick style. Many of his films, including *The Navigator* (1924) and *The General* (1926), are becoming increasingly recognized for their comic inventiveness.

K

INTERNET

Kaunda, Kenneth David
▶ www.kaundachildrenof africa.org

Keating, Paul John
▶ www.nma.gov.au/ primeministers/16.htm

K

► **Kennedy** John F. Kennedy was badly wounded in World War2 and was discharged from the US Navy, receiving a medal for bravery. In 1957, he was awarded the Pulitzer Prize for *Profiles in Courage* (1956). Kennedy's youth and charisma helped him to defeat Richard Nixon in the 1960 elections, after the first-ever televised debates between presidential candidates. Kennedy, aged 43, was the youngest person and the first Roman Catholic ever to hold the highest national office. Kennedy was assassinated in Dallas, Texas. Lee Harvey Oswald was accused of being the assassin, but two days later was himself shot dead by Jack Ruby. The Warren Commission (1963–64) concluded that there was no plot to murder Kennedy and that Oswald had acted alone. In 1979, a special committee of the House of Representatives determined that there was probably more than one gunman and that a conspiracy was likely.

KENTUCKY
Statehood :
June 1, 1792
Nickname :
Bluegrass state
State bird :
Kentucky cardinal
State flower :
Goldenrod
State tree :
Kentucky coffee tree
State motto :
United we stand, divided we fall

INTERNET

Kennedy, John Fitzgerald
► www.whitehouse.gov/ history/presidents
► www.jfklibrary.org

Kentucky
► www.kentucky.com

Kenya
► www.kenyaweb.com/ government
► www.kenyaembassy.com

Zwolle, for most of his life. He wrote or edited numerous treatises on the life of the soul. The most famous work often attributed to him is *Imitation of Christ*. Other works include *Soliloquium Animae* and *De Tribus Tabernaculis*.

Kendall, Edward Calvin (1886–1972) US chemist. Kendall worked on the biological effects of the HORMONES of the ADRENAL GLANDS, in particular CORTISONE, which he isolated. He shared the 1950 Nobel Prize in physiology or medicine.

Keneally, Thomas Michael (1935–) Australian novelist. He drew on his training as a Catholic priest in early novels, including *The Place at Whitton* (1964). In *Bring Larks and Heroes* (1967), he turned to historical fiction. *Schindler's Ark* (1982), won the Booker Prize, and formed the basis of Steven Spielberg's film *Schindler's List* (1993).

Kennedy, John Fitzgerald (1917–63) 35th US president (1961–63). He was badly wounded while serving (1941–43) in the US Navy during World War 2. Kennedy served three terms as a Democrat representative from Massachusetts (1946–53). In 1953 he successfully ran for the Senate, and soon after married Jacqueline Lee Bouvier (later ONASSIS). In 1960 Kennedy gained the presidential nomination, and narrowly defeated his Republican challenger Richard NIXON. Kennedy adopted an ambitious and liberal program, and embraced the cause of CIVIL RIGHTS, but Congress frequently blocked his planned legislation. In foreign policy, he founded the "Alliance for Progress" in order to increase US influence in Latin America and created the Peace Corps. Adopting an anti-communist line, he was behind the BAY OF PIGS invasion of Cuba (1961), and stood firm against Nikita KHRUSHCHEV in the ensuing CUBAN MISSILE CRISIS (1962). He also increased military aid to South Vietnam in the VIETNAM WAR (1954–75). Perhaps Kennedy's greatest foreign policy success was the Nuclear Test Ban Treaty between the US, UK and Soviet Union. He was assassinated on November 22, 1963. Kennedy was succeeded by his vice president, Lyndon B. JOHNSON. *See also* COLD WAR

Kennedy, Robert Francis (1925–68) US lawyer and statesman. He served on the Senate Select Committee on Improper Activities (1957–59), where he clashed with the Teamsters' Union president Jimmy HOFFA. In 1960, he managed the successful presidential campaign of his brother John F. KENNEDY. He became US attorney general (1961–64), vigorously enforcing CIVIL RIGHTS laws and promoting the Civil Rights Act of 1964. After his brother's assassination, he left the cabinet and was elected senator for New York in 1964. While a candidate for the Democratic presidential nomination, he was assassinated in Los Angeles on June 6, 1968.

Kennedy Space Center *See* CAPE CANAVERAL

Kent County in SE England, S of the Thames and NW of the Strait of Dover; the county town is Maidstone. Roman settlement began in AD 43. It later became an Anglo-Saxon kingdom, and remained so until the 9th century. Apart from the North Downs, the area is mainly low-lying. It is drained by the Medway and Stour. Cereals, hops, fruit, and vegetables are grown, and sheep and cattle are reared. DOVER, Folkestone and Ramsgate are ports. Industries: paper making, shipbuilding, chemicals, brewing. Area: 3,732sq km (1,441sq mi). Pop. (2001) 1,329,653.

Kentucky State in SE central USA; the capital is FRANKFORT. Other cities include Lexington and Louisville. Ceded to Britain by France in 1763, the territory was admitted to

the Union in 1792. Its loyalties were divided at the outbreak of the CIVIL WAR. Most of the area is rolling plain. In the SE the Cumberland Mountains dominate a rugged plateau. The state is drained chiefly by the Ohio and Tennessee rivers. Tobacco is the chief crop, followed by hay, maize and soya beans. Cattle are reared and Kentucky is noted for breeding racehorses. Industries: electrical equipment, machinery, chemicals, metals. Kentucky is one of the country's major coal producers. Area: 104,623sq km (40,395sq mi). Pop. (2000) 4,041,769.

Kenya Republic on the E coast of Africa. *See* country feature

Kenya, Mount Extinct volcanic mountain in central Kenya. The second-highest mountain in Africa, it was first climbed in 1899. It consists of three peaks, the highest of which is Batian, rising to 5199m (17,057ft).

Kenyatta, Jomo (1893–1978) Kenyan statesman, first president of Kenya (1964–78). A KIKUYU, he led the struggle for Kenyan independence from 1946. In 1953, after a dubious trial, the British imprisoned Kenyatta for MAU MAU terrorism. As leader of the Kenya African National Union, he became president on Kenya's independence in 1964. Though he suppressed domestic opposition, he presided over a prosperous economy and generally followed pro-Western policies.

Kepler, Johannes (1571–1630) German mathematician and astronomer. He supported the heliocentric theory put forward by COPERNICUS. Kepler succeeded Tycho BRAHE as imperial mathematician to Emperor Rudolf II. From Brahe's observations, he concluded that Mars moves in an elliptical orbit, and he went on to establish his three laws of planetary motion: **law one** states that the orbit of a planet is an ellipse with the Sun at one of the foci; **law two** (law of areas) states that the line joining the planet to the Sun (radius vector) sweeps out equal areas in equal times; **law 3** states that the square of the period of revolution (P) is directly proportional to the cube of the mean distance of the planet from the Sun.

Kerala State on the Arabian Sea, SW India; the capital is Trivandrum. One of India's smallest states, Kerala is the most densely populated. Fishing is important. Chief products include rubber, tea, coffee, coconuts, cashew nuts, ivory, textiles, teak, chemicals and minerals. Area: 38,864sq km (15,005sq mi). Pop. (2001) 31,838,619.

keratin Fibrous PROTEIN present in large amounts in SKIN cells, where it serves as a protective layer. Hair and fingernails are made up of cells filled with keratin, which is also the basis of claws, horns, and feathers.

Kerensky, Alexander Feodorovich (1881–1970) Russian moderate politician. He became prime minister of the provisional government in July 1917, shortly after the overthrow of the Tsar. Deposed by the BOLSHEVIKS, he fled to France. *See also* RUSSIAN REVOLUTION

Kern, Jerome David (1885–1945) US songwriter of film and show music. His best-known musical, *Showboat* (staged 1927; filmed 1936, 1959), contains the song "Ol' Man River". Kern influenced Richard RODGERS and George GERSHWIN.

kerosene (paraffin) Distilled petroleum product heavier than petrol but lighter than diesel fuel. Kerosene is used in camping stoves, tractor fuels and fuels for jet and turboprop aircraft.

Kerouac, Jack (1922–69) US poet and novelist. Kerouac published his first novel, *The Town and the City*, in 1950, but it was *On the Road* (1957) that established him as the leading novelist of the BEAT MOVEMENT. Later works include *The Dharma Bums* (1958), *Desolation Angels* (1965) and the posthumously published *Visions of Cody* (1972).

Kerry County in Munster province, SW Republic of Ireland; the county town is Tralee. It is mountainous with an indented coastline and many lakes. Oats and potatoes are grown, and sheep and cattle raised. Industries: tourism, fishing, woollen goods. Area: 4,701sq km (1,815sq mi). Pop. (2002) 132,424.

Kertész, André (1894–1985) Hungarian-US photographer. He was one of the first to use a compact Leica camera. While in France, Kertész worked as a photo-journalist as well as taking portraits of artist-friends such as Mondrian and Colette. In 1936 he moved to the USA, where he worked for magazines such as *Vogue* and *Harper's Bazaar*. Kertész was a major influence on Robert CAPA and Henri CARTIER-BRESSON.

Kesselring, Albert (1885–1960) German general. During World War 2, he commanded the Luftwaffe, later becoming commander-in-chief in Italy (1943) and then supreme commander on the Western front (1945). Implicated in a 1943 massacre of Italian hostages, in 1947 he was sentenced to death, later commuted to imprisonment, by a British court.

kestrel Small FALCON that lives mainly in Europe, and hovers before attacking. It feeds mainly on rodents, insects and small birds. Length: 30cm (12in). Species *Falco tinnunculus.*

kettledrum *See* TIMPANI

Kew Gardens (Royal Botanic Gardens) Collection of plants and trees in sw London, UK. Founded in 1760 by George III's mother, they were given to the nation by Queen Victoria in 1840. Much plant research is carried out here.

key In music, term used to indicate TONALITY in a composition, based on one of the major or minor scales. The key of a piece of music is indicated by the key signature at the left hand end of the stave. The key of a passage may, however, change by the addition of accidentals before prescribed notes; a change of key is known as a modulation.

keyboard instrument Large group of musical instruments played by pressing keys on a keyboard. Notes are sounded by hitting or plucking a string (as in the PIANO or HARPSICHORD), passing air through a pipe or reed (as in the ORGAN or ACCORDION), or electronically (as in the SYNTHESIZER).

Keynes, John Maynard (1883–1946) English economist. In *The General Theory of Employment, Interest and Money* (1936), which was strongly influenced by the GREAT DEPRESSION, Keynes laid the foundation of modern MACROECONOMICS.

He advocated the active intervention of government in the economy to stimulate employment and prosperity. He was influential as an economic adviser in World War 2, and took a leading role in the BRETTON WOODS CONFERENCE of 1944.

KGB (*Komitet Gosudarstvennoye Bezhopaznosti*, Rus. Committee for State Security) Soviet secret police. In the 1980s, it employed an estimated 500,000 people and controlled all police, security, and intelligence operations in the Soviet Union. It also gathered military and political information about other countries. Opposing liberalization under GORBACHEV, its chief was a leader of the attempted coup against him in 1991. After the collapse of communism and the break-up of the Soviet Union, it underwent extensive reform.

Khafre, Great Sphinx of Monumental statue of the SPHINX at GIZA, Egypt. Its name derives from the pharaoh whose pyramid complex it may be part of and whose portrait is said to be represented by the sphinx's face.

Kharkov (Kharkiv) City in NE Ukraine. It was founded in the 17th century to serve as a stronghold for the Ukrainian Cossacks defending Russia's s border. During the 19th century it developed industrially, stimulated by nearby coalfields. From 1919 to 1934, it was capital of the Ukrainian Soviet Socialist Republic. Industries: mining machinery, ball-bearings, chemicals, electrical goods. Pop. (2000) 1,521,000.

Khartoum Capital of Sudan, at the junction of the Blue NILE and White Nile rivers. Khartoum was founded in the 1820s by MUHAMMAD ALI and was besieged by the Mahdists in 1885, when General GORDON was killed. In 1898, it became the seat

KENYA

The Republic of Kenya is located in E Africa, across the Equator. Behind the narrow coastal plain on the Indian Ocean, the land rises to high plains and highlands broken by volcanoes including Mount KENYA (5,199m) [17,057ft]. An arm of the Great RIFT VALLEY crosses the country, with several lakes including Baringo, Magadi, Naivasha, Nakuru and Turkana (formerly Lake Rudolf).

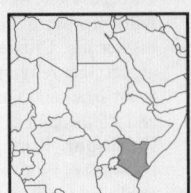

CLIMATE

The coast is hot and humid, but inland the climate is moderated by the height of the land. The thickly populated sw highlands have summer temperatures 10°C [18°F] lower than the coast. Nights can be cool, but temperatures

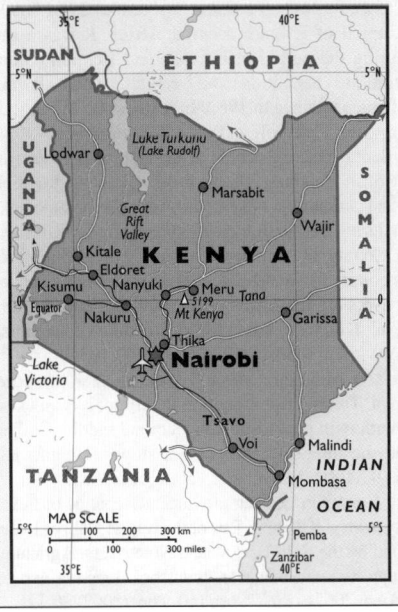

stay above zero. The main rainy season is from April to May. Only 15% of the country has a reliable rainfall of 800mm [31in].

HISTORY

Some of the earliest hominid fossils have been found in s Kenya. Kenya's coast has been a trading centre for more than 2,000 years, and in the 8th century the Arabs founded settlements to further trade with E Asia. Portuguese explorer Vasco da Gama reached the coast in 1498. In the 16th century Portuguese traders took over the area, but in 1729 Arab dynasties regained control.

Britain took over the Kenyan coast in 1895. Colonization began in 1903, and land was acquired from the KIKUYU for plantations and farms. The territory divided into the inland Kenya Colony and the coastal Protectorate of Kenya. European settlement intensified. The employment of Africans as plantation and farm labourers led to social unrest. Opposition to British rule mounted in the 1940s, and the MAU MAU uprising waged an armed struggle for land rights and independence from 1952 to 1956. Britain declared a state of emergency and imprisoned its leader, Jomo KENYATTA. Mau Mau was eventually defeated, but Kenya finally achieved independence in 1963, becoming a republic in 1964. Jomo Kenyatta was the first president.

POLITICS

Many Kenyan leaders felt that the division of the population into 40 ethnic groups might lead to instability. They argued that Kenya should have a strong central government and, as a result, Kenya has been a one-party state for much of the time since independence. Multiparty democracy was restored in the early 1990s. In the 1960s attempts by Kenya, Tanzania and

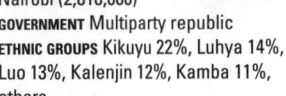

AREA 580,367sq km [224,080sq mi]
POPULATION 36,914,000
CAPITAL (POPULATION) Nairobi (2,818,000)
GOVERNMENT Multiparty republic
ETHNIC GROUPS Kikuyu 22%, Luhya 14%, Luo 13%, Kalenjin 12%, Kamba 11%, others
LANGUAGES Kiswahili and English (both official)
RELIGIONS Protestant 45%, Roman Catholic 33%, traditional beliefs 10%, Islam 10%
CURRENCY Kenyan shilling = 100 cents

Uganda to collaborate collapsed due to the deep differences between the political and economic policies of the countries. Hopes were revived in 1999, when a new East African Community was created. It aims to establish a customs union, a common market, and monetary union.

Jomo Kenyatta died in 1978 and was succeeded by the vice-president Daniel arap MOI, who stood down in 2002 after having been accused of corruption and criticized for his autocratic rule. The veteran Mwai Kibaki was elected president in 2002, promising to stamp out corruption, but little progress was made. International aid and loans were suspended. In 2006 Kibaki's government became caught up in a large-scale corruption scandal.

ECONOMY

Kenya is a 'low-income' developing country. Agriculture employs about 80% of the people, but many Kenyans are subsistence farmers. The chief food crop is maize. Bananas, beans, cassava and sweet potatoes are also grown. The main cash crops are coffee and tea. Manufactures include chemicals, leather, footwear, processed food, petroleum products and textiles.

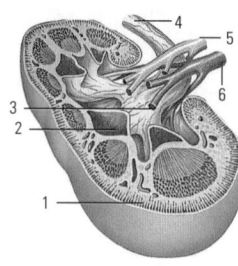

▲ **kidney** The human kidney is enclosed in a fibrous capsule, and consists of an outer cortex region (1), a medulla region (2) with pyramidal-shaped areas, and an inner pelvis region (3), which leads into the ureter (4). The renal artery (5) conducts blood into the kidney to be filtered; it is then carried away by the renal vein (6).

K

Khatami, Muhammad
▶ www.president.ir/eng

of government of the Anglo-Egyptian Sudan, and from 1956 the capital of independent Sudan. Industries: cement, gum arabic, chemicals, glass, cotton textiles. Pop. (2000) 2,742,000.

Khatami, Muhammad (1943–) Iranian statesman, president (1997– 2005). A leading opponent of Shah Muhammad Reza PAHLAVI, he was elected to Iran's national assembly after the Islamic Revolution (1979). In 1982 Khatami was appointed minister of culture by Ayatollah KHOMEINI. Conservative clerics criticized his liberal stance on press freedom and forced him to resign in 1992. Outgoing President Hashemi RAFSANJANI supported Khatami in the 1997 presidential elections, and Khatami's campaign for economic reform and greater social freedom gained him 70% of the vote. His moderate government faced opposition from the conservative establishment, whose blocking of reforms led to widespread unrest in 1999. Khatami was re-elected by a large majority in 2001 but lost to the conservative Mahmoud Ahmadinejad in 2004.

Khayyám, Omar *See* OMAR KHAYYÁM

Khazars Turkic people who first appeared in the lower Volga region in *c.*2nd century AD. Between the 8th and 10th centuries, their empire prospered and extended from N of the Black Sea to the River Volga and from W of the Caspian Sea to the River Dnieper. They conquered the Volga Bulgars, and fought the Arabs, Russians, and Pechenegs. In the 8th century, the ruling class adopted JUDAISM. Their empire was destroyed in 965.

Khmer Language of *c.*85% of the inhabitants of Cambodia. It belongs to a group of the **Mon-Khmer languages**. A Khmer empire existed from the 9th to the 15th centuries AD. Cambodia was renamed the Khmer Republic in 1970. When the Republic fell to the KHMER ROUGE in 1975, the country was renamed Kampuchea; the name Cambodia was restored in 1989.

Khmer Rouge Cambodian communist guerrilla organization. It gained control of Cambodia in 1975. Led by POL POT and Khieu Samphan, it embarked on a forced wholesale communist transformation of Cambodian society, during which an estimated 2 to 3 million people died. The regime lost power to the Vietnamese after a period of intense conflict in 1977–78. The Kampuchean National United Front for National Salvation founded a People's Republic in 1979. In 1982 the Khmer Rouge joined a coalition with Prince NORODOM SIHANOUK (the former Cambodian leader) and the Khmer Peoples National Liberation Front. From 1988 attempts were made to settle the political situation peacefully. In 1991 each faction signed a ceasefire agreement. After an election in 1993, in which the Khmer Rouge refused to take part, Prince Sihanouk's parliamentary monarchy was re-established. The Khmer Rouge continued hostilities and have been officially banned since 1994.

Khoisan Group of South African languages. The Khoikhoi and SAN are the two largest groups of native speakers of these languages. The Khoisan languages also include Sandawe and Hadza. *See also* CLICK LANGUAGE

Khomeini, Ruhollah (1900–89) Iranian ayatollah (religious leader). An Islamic scholar with great influence over his SHI'ITE students, he published (1941) an outspoken attack on Reza PAHLAVI and remained an active opponent of his son, Muhammad Reza PAHLAVI. Exiled in 1964, he returned to Iran in triumph after the fall of the Shah in 1979. His rule was characterized by strict religious orthodoxy, elimination of political opposition and economic turmoil. In 1989, Khomeini issued a *fatwa* ordiering the death of the Anglo-Indian writer Salman RUSHDIE. He was succeeded by Hashemi RAFSANJANI. *See also* IRAN-IRAQ WAR

Khrushchev, Nikita Sergeievich (1894–1971) Soviet politician, first secretary of the Communist Party (1953–64) and prime minister (1958–64). Noted for economic success and ruthless suppression of opposition in Ukraine, he was elected to the Politburo in 1939. After Stalin died, he made a speech denouncing him (1956). Favoring détente, he yielded to President John KENNEDY in the CUBAN MISSILE CRISIS (1962). Economic setbacks and trouble with China led to his replacement by Leonid BREZHNEV and Aleksei KOSYGIN in 1964.

Khyber Pass Mountain pass in the Safid Kuh range, on the frontier between Afghanistan and Pakistan, linking the

Kabul valley in Afghanistan (W) with Peshawar in Pakistan (E). Height: 1073m (3520ft). Length: 50km (30mi).

kibbutz Collective settlement in Israel that is owned by its members. The idea developed from the pioneering settlements established by Jewish settlers in a part of ancient Palestine that became Israel in 1948.

Kiddush Blessing recited before a meal on the eve of the Jewish Sabbath or of a festival. The head of the household says the prayer over a cup of wine, which is then passed around.

kidney In vertebrates, one of a pair of organs responsible for regulating blood composition and EXCRETION. The kidneys are at the back of the abdomen, either side of the backbone. Each is *c.*10cm (4in) long and 6.5cm (2.5in) wide. The human kidney consists of an outer cortex and an inner medulla with about one million tubules (NEPHRONS). Nephrons contain numerous capillaries, which filter the blood entering from the renal ARTERY. Some substances, including water, are reabsorbed into the blood. URINE remains, which is passed to the URETER and on to the BLADDER. One healthy kidney is needed to maintain life. A serious kidney disease may require a kidney transplant or DIALYSIS using a machine. *See also* CAPILLARY; HOMEOSTASIS

kidney machine (artificial kidney) Equipment designed to remove toxic wastes from the blood in kidney failure. Plastic tubing is used to pipe blood from the body into the machine, where waste products are filtered out by DIALYSIS.

Kiel City and seaport in N Germany, at the head of the Kiel Canal linking the North Sea and the Baltic Sea; capital of SCHLESWIG-HOLSTEIN state. Industries: shipbuilding, textiles, precision instruments, printed matter. Pop. (1999) 235,500.

Kierkegaard, Søren (1813–55) Danish philosopher and theologian, regarded as the founder of modern EXISTENTIALISM. He believed that the individual must exercise free will, making deliberate decisions about the direction of his/her life. Critical of HEGEL's speculative philosophy, he argued that religious faith was, at its best, blind obedience to an irrational God. His books include *Either/Or* (1843) and *Philosophical Fragments* (1844).

Kiesinger, Kurt Georg (1904–88) Chancellor of West GERMANY (1966–69), he maintained the conservative policy of his predecessors Konrad ADENAUER and Ludwig Erhard.

Kieslowski, Krzysztof (1941–96) Polish film director. He gained wide praise for the epic *Dekalog* (1988). Kieslowski's final work, *The Three Colours* trilogy – *Blue* (1993), *White* (1993) and *Red* (1994) – is a masterwork of European cinema.

Kiev (Kiyev) Capital of Ukraine and a seaport on the Dnieper River. Founded in the 6th or 7th century AD Kiev was the capital of Kievan Russia. It later came under Lithuanian, then Polish rule before being absorbed into Russia. It became the capital of the Ukrainian Soviet Socialist Republic in 1934, and of an independent Ukraine in 1991. Industries: shipbuilding, machine tools, footwear, furniture. Pop. (2000) 2,621,000.

Kigali Capital of Rwanda, central Africa. It was a trade centre during the period of German and Belgian colonial administration, becoming the capital when Rwanda achieved independence in 1962. Industries: tin mining, cotton, tanning, textiles, coffee. Pop. (2002) 608,141.

Kikuyu Bantu-speaking people of the highlands of Kenya, E Africa. British conquest strained the Kikuyu's traditional political and agricultural system; the result was an outbreak of terrorism during the 1950s by a group known as MAU MAU.

Kildare County in Leinster province, E Republic of Ireland; the county town is Naas. It is a low-lying region, and its chief rivers are the Liffey, Boyne and Barrow. Primarily agricultural, Kildare is noted for its breeding of racehorses. Area: 1,694sq km (654sq mi). Pop. (2002) 163,995.

Kilimanjaro Mountain in NE Tanzania, near the border with Kenya. The highest mountain in Africa, it is an extinct volcano with twin peaks joined by a broad saddle. Coffee is grown on the intensely cultivated S slopes. Height: Kibo 5,895m (19,340ft); Mawenzi 5,150m (16,896ft).

Kilkenny County in Leinster province, E Republic of Ireland; the county town is Kilkenny. Part of the central plain of Ireland, it is drained by the Suir, Barrow and Nore rivers. Agriculture: cereal crops, vegetables, cattle. Industries: brewing and coal mining. Area: 2062sq km (796sq mi). Pop. (2002) 80,421.

killer whale Toothed marine mammal of the DOLPHIN family that lives in all the world's oceans, especially colder regions. A fierce predator, it is black above and white below, with a white patch above each eye and a long, erect, dorsal fin. Length: 9m (30ft). Species: *Orcinus orca*.

kilogram (symbol kg) SI unit of mass, defined as the mass of the international prototype cylinder of platinum-iridium kept at the International Bureau of Weights and Measures near Paris. One kilogram is equal to 1,000g (2.2lb).

Kimberley City in South Africa; capital of Northern Cape province. It was founded in 1871 after the discovery of diamonds nearby. Today, it is one of the world's largest diamond centres. Other industries include the processing of gypsum, iron and manganese. Pop. (2002 est.) 189,500.

Kim II Sung (1912–94) Korean statesman, first premier of North Korea (1948–72) and president (1972–94). He joined the Korean Communist Party in 1931, and led a Korean unit in the Soviet Army during World War 2. In 1950, Kim led a North Korean invasion of South Korea, precipitating the KOREAN WAR (1950–53). Chairman of the Korean Workers' Party from 1948, Kim Il Sung suppressed all opposition and pursued communist policies. His son, KIM JONG IL, succeeded him.

Kim Jong II (1941–) North Korean politician, head of state (1994–). In 1980, he was officially named as the successor to his father, KIM IL SUNG, assuming a more important role in government and being included in the personality cult that surrounded his father. He succeeded on his father's death.

Ki-Moon, Ban (1944–) South Korean diplomat, Secretary-General of the United Nations (2007–). Ki-Moon joined South Korea's foreign ministry in 1970. In the 1980s he was posted to Korea's mission to the UN. After Korea joined the UN in 1991 he worked in UN as well as diplomatic roles. In 2007 Ki-Moon became the first Asian UN head in over 30 years.

Kim Young Sam (1927–) South Korean statesman, president (1992–98). In 1979 he was banned from politics for his opposition to President PARK CHUNG HEE: the ban was lifted in 1985. As leader of the Democratic Liberal Party (DLP), Kim Young Sam became the first civilian president of South KOREA. His efforts to reduce government corruption and abuses of power led to the arrests of former presidents Chun Doo Hwan and Roh Tae Woo. Kim's own government, however, became embroiled in a financial scandal and the economic crisis that swept through Southeast Asia in 1997 brought South Korea to the brink of financial collapse. Kim Dae Jung narrowly defeated Kim Young Sam in the 1997 elections.

kinetic energy (symbol K) Energy that an object possesses because it is in motion. It is the energy given to an object to set it in motion; it depends on the mass (*m*) of the object and its velocity (*v*), according to the equation $K = 1/2\ mv^2$. On impact, it is converted into other forms of energy such as heat, sound and light. *See also* POTENTIAL ENERGY

kinetics In physics, one of the branches of dynamics. In chemistry, a branch of physical chemistry that deals with the rates of chemical reactions.

kinetic theory In physics, a theory dealing with matter in terms of the forces between particles and the energies they possess. There are five principles to the kinetic theory: matter is composed of tiny particles; these are in constant motion; they do not lose energy in collision with each other or the walls of their container; there are no attractive forces between the particles or their container; and at any time the particles in a sample may not all have the same energy.

King, B.B. (Riley B.) (1925–) US rhythm-and-blues guitarist and singer-songwriter. Among his most notable albums is *There Must be a Better World Somewhere* (1981).

King, Martin Luther, Jr. (1929–68) US Baptist minister and CIVIL RIGHTS leader. He led the boycott of segregated public transport in Montgomery, Alabama, in 1956. King was founder (1960) and president of the Southern Christian Leadership Council (SCLC). He opposed the Vietnam War and demanded measures to relieve poverty, organizing a march on Washington D.C. (1963) where he made his famous "I have a dream..." speech. In 1964, King became the youngest person to receive the Nobel Peace Prize. He was assassinated in Memphis, Tennessee, on April 4 1968.

King, Stephen (1947–) US novelist and short-story writer. King is a master of the modern horror novel. Many of his books, such as *The Shining* (1977) and *Misery* (1987), have been made into successful films.

King, William Lyon Mackenzie (1874–1950) Canadian politician, prime minister (1921–30, 1935–48). His career was marked by the drive for national unity, culminating in the Statute of WESTMINSTER (1931). He made concessions to the Progressives, and he was conciliatory towards French-Canadian demands. In foreign policy, King's basic sympathies were isolationist and anti-British, but he cooperated closely with Britain and the USA during World War 2.

kingdom Topmost level (taxon) of the most widely adopted TAXONOMY for living organisms, the Five Kingdoms system. The Five Kingdoms are Animalia (ANIMAL), Plantae (PLANT), Fungi (FUNGUS), PROKARYOTAE, and PROTOCTISTA. Two subkingdoms are often recognized within Prokaryotae, ARCHAEBACTERIA and EUBACTERIA, but the bacteria are so diverse that many taxonomists think they comprise more than one kingdom. Some believe that they merit the status of a new, even higher category, DOMAIN. *See also* EUKARYOTE; PLANT CLASSIFICATION

kingfish Name applied to several varieties of fish valued for food or sport. They include *Scomberomorus cavalla*, a type of large mackerel, and *Menticirrhus saxitalis*, a member of the drum family, also known as whiting.

kingfisher Compact, brightly coloured bird with a straight, sharp bill. It dives for fish along rivers, streams and lakes. It nests in a horizontal hole in an earth bank. Length: 12.7–43.2cm (5–17in). Family Alcedinidae. *See* picture, page 442

King Philip's War (1675–76) War between English settlers and Native Americans in New England. The Wampanoags, under their chief Philip (Metacomet), rebelled against increasing white aggression. Colonial forces eventually gained the upper hand and wreaked still greater destruction on native settlements. King Philip was killed in 1676.

Kings I and II Two books in the OLD TESTAMENT, called Third and Fourth Kingdoms in the Greek SEPTUAGINT. These books recount the history of the kingdom of ISRAEL from the end of the reign of DAVID (*c*.970BC) to the fall of Judah and the destruction of Jerusalem by the Babylonians in 586 BC.

Kingsley, Charles (1819–75) English writer. He was one of the first clerics to support Charles DARWIN, whose ideas he partly incorporated into *The Water Babies* (1863). His popular historical novels include *Hereward the Wake* (1866).

Kingston Capital and largest city of Jamaica, founded in 1693. It is Jamaica's commercial centre, based on the export of raw cane sugar, bananas and rum. In 1872 it became the island's capital. Kingston is the cultural heart of Jamaica, the home of calypso and reggae music. Pop. (2002 est.) 538,900.

Kingstown Capital and chief port of St Vincent and the Grenadines, on the SW coast. Exports: cotton, sugar cane, molasses, cacao, fruit. Pop. (2002 est.) 17,400.

Kinsey, Alfred Charles (1894–1956) US zoologist, noted for his studies on human sexual behaviour. He was a director of the Institute for Sex Research, Indiana University, and is best known for *Sexual Behavior in the Human Male* (1948) and *Sexual Behavior in the Human Female* (1953).

Kinshasa (formerly Léopoldville) Capital of Democratic Republic of Congo, a port on the River Congo. Founded in 1881, it replaced Boma as the capital of the Belgian Congo in 1923. Its name was changed in 1966. Industries: tanning, chemicals, brewing, textiles. Pop. (2005) 5,717,100.

▲ **killer whale** The large triangular dorsal fin and the black and white body are the two obvious features of the killer whale (*Orcinus orca*). It is found mostly in polar seas and is generally considered to be the most ferocious of whales. Almost any creature in the sea is considered prey for the 9m (30ft) long killers.

K

▲ **King** US civil-rights leader Martin Luther King, Jr., was an inspiring orator of impressive moral impact. Often criticized by more militant activists, his policy of non-violent direct action was based on Gandhi's tactics in India. The Voting Rights Act (1965) was passed soon after state troopers in Selma, Alabama, broke up a SCLC march with tear-gas and nightsticks.

INTERNET

killer whale
▸ www.wdcs.org

King, Martin Luther, Jr.
▸ thekingcenter.com
▸ www.stanford.edu/group/King

K

▲ **kingfisher** The kingfisher (*Alcedo atthis*) is widespread throughout Europe, Asia, N Africa, and eastward to the Solomon Islands. The birds live on the banks of freshwater streams and lakes, feeding on small minnows and sometimes reptiles and crustaceans.

Kipling, (Joseph) Rudyard (1865–1936) British writer, b. India. His *Barrack Room Ballads and Other Verses* (1892), which include "If" and "Gunga Din", is a classic of British colonial literature. His novels include *The Light That Failed* (1890) and *Kim* (1901). His children's stories include *The Jungle Book* (1894) and the *Just So Stories* (1902). Kipling was the first English writer to receive the Nobel Prize in literature (1907).

Kirchhoff, Gustav Robert (1824–87) German physicist. With Robert BUNSEN, he developed the spectroscope, with which they discovered CAESIUM and RUBIDIUM in 1860. He is famous for two laws that apply to multiple-loop electric circuits. Kirchhoff's laws state that (1) at any junction the sum of the currents flowing is zero, and (2) the sum of the ELECTROMOTIVE FORCES (EMF) around any closed path equals the sum of the products of the currents and impedances (resistances).

Kirchner, Ernst Ludwig (1880–1938) German painter and printmaker, a leader of the expressionist artists known as Die BRÜCKE. Kirchner characteristically portrayed urban scenes. His art was condemned by the Nazis as degenerate and he committed suicide. *See also* EXPRESSIONISM

Kiribati (formerly Gilbert Islands) Independent nation in the W Pacific Ocean, comprising *c.*33 islands, including the Gilbert, Phoenix and Line Islands, and straddling the Equator over a vast area; the capital is Bairiki (on Tarawa). British navigators first visited in the late 18th century. They became a British protectorate in 1892. Kiribati achieved independence within the Commonwealth of Nations in 1979. Phosphate mining dominated the economy until 1980, when production ended. Agriculture is now the major economic activity. Land area: 726sq km (280sq mi). Pop. (2002 est.) 99,000.

Kiritimati (Christmas Island) Largest atoll in the world, one of the Pacific Line Islands, forming part of KIRIBATI. It was the site of nuclear tests by Britain (1956–62) and the USA (1962). Area: 575sq km (222sq mi). Pop. (2002 est.) 5,300.

Kirov Former name (1934–92) of VYATKA.

Kirov, Sergei Mironovich (1888–1934) Soviet politician. An effective speaker, he was elected to the Communist Party Politburo in 1930. His murder, probably on Stalin's orders, served as a pretext for the Stalin purges (1934–38).

Kirov Ballet Ballet company founded in 1735 at St Petersburg. Under the direction of PETIPA (1862–1903), the Kirov Ballet was the world's leading company, with principal dancers such as PAVLOVA and NIJINSKY. Later stars include Michel FOKINE, Rudolf NUREYEV, and Mikhail BARYSHNIKOV. **Kirov Opera** has also made a major contribution to Russian culture.

Kisangani (formerly Stanleyville) City and port on the River Congo, N central DR Congo. English explorer Henry M. STANLEY founded it in 1883. During the 1950s, it was the headquarters of the Congolese National Movement led by Patrice LUMUMBA. During the 1960s, it was the focus for a series of unsuccessful rebellions. In 1996 it was at the centre of the Hutu refugee crisis. Pop. (2002 est.) 510,300.

Kissinger, Henry Alfred (1923–) US statesman and political scientist, secretary of state (1973–77), b. Germany. In 1969 he became Richard NIXON's chief adviser on foreign policy, helping to establish the STRATEGIC ARMS LIMITATION TALKS (SALT) with the Soviet Union. As secretary of state, Kissinger shared the Nobel Peace Prize (1973) with Le Duc Tho for negotiating a ceasefire in the VIETNAM WAR. His diplomacy brought a ceasefire between Egypt and Israel in the 1973 Yom Kippur (October) War. After the fall of Nixon, Kissinger continued as secretary of state for President FORD.

Kitaj, R.B. (Ronald Brooks) (1932–2007) Painter, b. USA, worked in Britain. An individualist, he had loose links with the POP ART movement. Kitaj painted in flat, soft-edged areas of bright colour, often on very large canvasses.

Kitchener, Horatio Herbert, 1st Earl (1850–1916) British field marshal and statesman. Kitchener took part in the unsuccessful relief of General GORDON at Khartoum, but reconquered Sudan in 1898, becoming its governor general. He served as chief of staff in the second SOUTH AFRICAN WAR and established the first CONCENTRATION CAMPS. He was appointed secretary of state for war at the outbreak of World War 1. His image appeared on the recruitment posters.

kite Diverse group of HAWKS of the sub-family Milvinae, found in open country worldwide. Kites have hooked bills, long wings, and a long, forked tail. They are usually scavangers. The red kite, *Milvus milvus*, is common throughout rural Europe. Length: 60cm (24in). Family Accipitridae.

kiwi Any of three species of flightless, fast-running, forest and scrubland birds of New Zealand; especially the common brown kiwi, *Apteryx australis*. It has a long, flexible bill with which it probes for food in the ground. Family Apterygidae.

Klaus, Václav (1941–) Czech statesman, prime minister (1993–97), president (2003–). Following the 'Velvet Revolution' (1989) he became finance minister in Václav HAVEL's administration. In 1991 Klaus founded the Civic Democratic Party (ODS). He became prime minister of the Czech Republic following the break-up of Czechoslovakia, but was forced to resign by a financial scandal. He was replaced by Milos Zeman. In 2003 he suceeded Vaclav HAVEL as president.

Klee, Paul (1879–1940) Swiss painter and graphic artist. Klee evolved his own pictorial language based on correspondences between line, colour, and plane. Some of his images are entirely ABSTRACT ART, but some are recognizable figures. He taught at the BAUHAUS (1920–31) and at Düsseldorf Academy (1931–33), but returned to Switzerland in 1933 after the Nazis condemned his work as degenerate. Characteristic works include *Graduated Shades of Red-Green* (1921) and *Revolutions of the Viaducts* (1937).

Klein, Melanie (1882–1960) Austrian psychoanalyst who developed therapy for young children. In *The Psychoanalysis of Children* (1932), she presented her methods and ideas of child analysis; she believed play was a symbolic way of controlling anxiety and analysed it to gain insight into the psychological processes of early life.

Klemperer, Otto (1885–1973) German conductor, noted for his interpretations of Beethoven, Brahms, and Mahler. In 1933, with the rise of Nazism, he went to the USA and became conductor of the Los Angeles Philharmonic. He returned to Europe as director of the Budapest Opera (1947–50).

Klimt, Gustav (1862–1918) Austrian painter and designer, a founder of the Vienna SEZESSION and the foremost ART NOUVEAU painter in Vienna. Klimt's works include stylized nudes, bejewelled clothing and backgrounds reminiscent of Byzantine mosaics. His style considerably influenced the painters Egon SCHIELE and Oskar KOKOSCHKA. His works include *The Kiss* (1908).

Klondike Gold Rush (1896–1904) Mass migration of gold prospectors to the Klondike region, YUKON TERRITORY, NW Canada. The rich gold deposits discovered in the River Klondike in 1896 brought more than 30,000 prospectors to the territory. Within a decade, more than US$100 million worth of gold had been extracted. Workers exhausted the easily accessible lodes by *c.*1910, but mining continues.

Klopstock, Friedrich Gottlieb (1724–1803) German poet. He anticipated the STURM UND DRANG movement and influenced other poets, notably GOETHE, RILKE, and Hölderlin. While a student he began writing the epic poem *The Messiah*.

Kneller, Sir Godfrey (1646–1723) Painter, b. Germany, who settled in London (1674). His best-known works include 48 portraits, known as the *Kit Cat Series*. He founded the first English Academy of Painting (1711).

knight In medieval Europe, a mounted warrior of intermediate rank. The knight began as a squire and was knighted with

▶ **Kirov Ballet** *The Nutcracker* by Tchaikovsky was just one of the many ballets that ensured the enduring reputation of the Kirov Ballet. In recent years, however, many accused the company of falling standards. Some believe that the increased commercial profile of the company has been to the detriment of their art.

a sword touch on the shoulder after a period of trial. Knights were often landholders, owing military service to their over-lord. Honorary orders of knighthood, such as the Knights of the Garter (1349), were founded towards the end of the Mid-dle Ages, a tradition that continued into the modern era.

Knights Hospitallers (Order of the Hospital of St John of Jerusalem) Military Christian order recognized in 1113 by Pope Paschal II. In the early 11th century, a hospital was established in Jerusalem for Christian pilgrims. They adopted a military role in the 12th century to defend JERUSALEM. After the fall of Jerusalem (1187), they moved to Acre, then Cyprus, then Rhodes (1310), from where they were expelled by the Ottoman Turks (1522). The Pope then gave them Malta, where they remained until driven out by Napoleon in 1798.

Knights Templar Military religious order established in 1118, with headquarters in Jerusalem. With the KNIGHTS HOS-PITALLERS, the Templars protected routes to Jerusalem for Christians during the CRUSADES. The possessions of the Tem-plars in France attracted the envious attention of King PHILIP IV, who urged Pope Clement V to abolish the order in 1312.

Knossos Ancient palace complex in N Crete, 6.4km (4mi) SE of Iráklion. In 1900 Sir Arthur Evans began excavations that revealed that the site had been inhabited before 3000 BC. His main discovery was a palace from the MINOAN CIVILIZATION (built c.2000 BC and rebuilt c.1700 BC). Close to the palace were the houses of Cretan nobles. The complex also contains many frescos. Knossos dominated Crete c.1500 BC but the palace was occupied c.1400 BC by invaders from MYCENAE.

knot Unit of measurement equal to one nautical mile per hour – 1 knot equals 1.852km/h (1.15mph). The speeds of ships, aircraft, winds and currents are generally expressed in knots.

Knox, John (1514–72) Leader of the Protestant REFORMA-TION in Scotland. Ordained a Catholic priest, he later convert-ed to Protestantism and took up the cause of the Reformation. Captured by French soldiers in Scotland, he was imprisoned in France (1547), then lived in exile in England and Switzer-land. In 1559 Knox returned to Scotland, where he continued to promote the Protestant cause. In 1560 the Scottish Parlia-ment, under Knox's leadership, made PRESBYTERIANISM the state religion. In 1563, he was tried for treason but acquitted.

koala Small marsupial that lives in eucalyptus trees of Australia, eating the leaves. A single, immature young is born, nurtured in its mother's pouch until fully formed, then carried on her back for a further six months. Length: 85cm (33in). Species *Phascolarctos cinereus*.

Kobe City and seaport on SW Honshu island, Japan, on Osaka Bay. Kobe is Japan's leading port and a major industri-al centre. In January 1995, more than 5000 people were killed and 27,000 injured in an earthquake. Industries: shipbuilding, iron and steel, electronics, chemicals. Pop. (2000) 1,493,000.

Kodály, Zoltán (1882–1967) Hungarian composer. With BARTÓK he collected and systematized Hungarian folk music, which was the principal influence on his work. Among his best-known compositions are the *Psalmus Hun-garicus* (1923), and the comic opera *Háry János* (1927).

Koestler, Arthur (1905–83) British novelist and philosopher, b. Hungary. After living in many European capitals during the 1920s and 1930s, he went to Spain as a journalist to cover the Spanish CIVIL WAR. *Darkness at Noon* (1940), his best-known novel, is a biting indictment of Stalinist totalitarianism.

Koffka, Kurt (1886–1941) US psychologist, b. Germany. With Wolfgang KÖHLER and Max Wertheimer, Koffka was a founder of GESTALT PSYCHOLOGY. He wrote *The Growth of the Mind* (1921) and *Principles of Gestalt Psychology* (1935).

Kohl, Helmut (1930–) German statesman, chancellor (1982–98). Between 1976 and 1982, he led the Christian Democratic Union (CDU) opposition to Helmut SCHMIDT. Kohl succeeded Schmidt as chancellor. His conservative approach advocated strong support for NATO, and a return to the traditional values of the West German state. Kohl strongly supported closer integration in the European Union (EU) and the establishment of the EURO. In 1990, he presided over the reunification of East and West Germany and was elected as the first chancellor of unified Germany. Re-elected in 1994 and 1996, he lost the 1998 elections to Gerhard SCHRÖDER.

◄ **Klimt** *Hygieia* (1900–07) clearly shows the influence of the pre-Raphaelites on the Austrian painter Gustav Klimt. Much of his art, often erotic, features a bejewelled effect reminiscent of mosaics, a format in which he worked later in his life.

Köhler, Wolfgang (1887–1967) US psychologist, b. Estonia. With Kurt KOFFKA and Max Wertheimer, he was a key figure in GESTALT PSYCHOLOGY. His work on animal learning and prob-lem solving is summarized in *The Mentality of Apes* (1917).

Kokoschka, Oskar (1886–1980) Austrian painter. He was influenced by the elegance of Gustav KLIMT but soon devel-oped his own type of EXPRESSIONISM. His work is characterized by forceful, energetic draughtsmanship and restless brushwork.

Kolkata (Calcutta) City on the River Hooghly, E India; capital of West Bengal state. Founded c.1690 by the EAST INDIA COMPANY, it was the capital of India under British rule (1772–1912). The major port and industrial centre of E India, Kolkata has several important temples. Industries: jute milling, electrical equipment, chemicals, paper, cotton textiles. Pop. (2005) 14,299,544.

Kollwitz, Käthe (1867–1945) German graphic artist and sculptor. Kollwitz's works depict suffering, especially of women and children. Her economical style conveyed tragedy in the tradition of German EXPRESSIONISM. Her pieces include the series of etchings, *The Weavers' Revolt* (1897–98) and *Peasants' War* (1902–28). She also produced lithographs and woodcuts such as *War* (1922–23) and *Death* (1934–35).

Kommunizma Pik (Communism Peak) *See* PIK ISMAIL SAMANI

komodo dragon Monitor lizard that lives on four islands E of Java, Indonesia; it is the largest lizard in the world. Length: 3m (10ft). Family Varanidae; species *Varanus komodoensis*.

Königsberg *See* KALININGRAD

Konya City in S central Turkey. Known in ancient times as Iconium, it was first settled in the 8th century BC. The cap-ital of the SELJUK sultanate of Rum from 1099, it was annexed by the Ottoman sultan in 1472. It is the religious centre of the whirling DERVISHES. Industries include cotton and leather goods, and carpets. Pop. (2000) 761,000.

kookaburra Large KINGFISHER of Australia, known for its call, which resembles fiendish laughter. They feed on ani-mals. Species *Dacelo gigas*.

Koons, Jeff (1955–) US sculptor. He burst onto the art scene in the 1980s with a series of sexually explicit pieces. Other exhibits, such as his vacuum cleaners in perspex cases, were intended as a comment on modern consumer society and have their roots in the POP ART movement of the 1960s.

Koran (Qur'an) Sacred book of ISLAM which Muslims believe contains the actual word of God (Allah) as revealed by the angel Gabriel to the Prophet MUHAMMAD. Muhammad received these revelations over two decades beginning (c.AD 610) on the

Night of Power (commemorated at RAMADAN) and ending in 632, the year of his death. The 114 *suras* (chapters) of the Koran are the source of Islamic belief and a guide for the whole life of the community. The central teachings of the Koran are that there is no God but Allah and all must submit to Him, that Muhammad is the last of His many messengers, and that there will come a day of judgment. In addition to these teachings, the Koran contains rules that a Muslim must follow in everyday life.

Korda, Sir Alexander (1893–1956) British film director, b. Hungary, who was noted for his lavish productions. His films include *The Scarlet Pimpernel* (1935), *Lady Hamilton* (1941), and *Anna Karenina* (1948).

Korea Peninsula in E Asia, separating the Yellow Sea from the Sea of Japan. The rivers Yalu and Tumen form most of its N border with China. **Land and climate** The E seaboard is mountainous, rising in the NE to 2,744m (9,003ft) at Mount Paektu. The mountains descend in the W to coastal lowlands. The traditional capital, SEOUL, lies close to the 38th-parallel border between North KOREA and South KOREA. The Korean archipelago lies off the S coast and includes the province of Cheju-do. North Korea experiences long and severe winters but warm summers. South Korea has a more tropical climate with occasional typhoons in the rainy months (July-August). **History** Korea's calendar starts in 2333 BC. China was a dominant

influence. The first native Korean state was established in the 1st century AD and Korea unified under the Silla dynasty in the 7th century. Mongols invaded Korea in 1231, and the country eventually capitulated. The Yi dynasty ruled Korea from 1392 to 1910. Early in the Yi period, Seoul became the new capital and CONFUCIANISM became the official religion. In the 17th century, Korea was a semi-independent state, dominated by the MANCHU dynasty. A long period of isolationism followed. In the late 19th century, Korea became more active in foreign affairs, due to the growing power of Japan. After the RUSSO-JAPANESE WAR (1904–05), Korea was effectively a Japanese protectorate, and was formally annexed in 1910. Japan's enforced industrialization of Korea caused widespread resentment. Following Japan's defeat in World War 2, Korea divided into two zones of occupation: Soviet forces N of the 38th Parallel, and US forces S of the line. Attempts at reunification failed, and in 1948 two separate regimes were established: the Republic of Korea in the S and the Democratic People's Republic in the N. In June 1950, North Korea invaded South Korea. The ensuing KOREAN WAR (1950–53) devastated the peninsula.

Korea, North Republic in E Asia. *See* country feature
Korea, South Republic in E Asia. *See* country feature
Korean National language of North and South Korea. Some scholars classify it as one of the ALTAIC LANGUAGES.

KOREA, NORTH

The Democratic People's Republic of Korea occupies the N part of the Korean Peninsula extending S from NE China. Mountains form the country's heart. The highest peak, Paektu-san (2,744m [9,003ft]) is on the N border. E of the mountains lie the E coastal plains, which are densely populated, as are the coastal plains to the W which contain the capital, PYONGYANG. Another small highland region in the SE borders South Korea.

The coastal plains are mostly farmed, but some patches of chestnut, elm, and oak woodland survive on the hilltops. The mountains contain forests of such trees as cedar, fir, pine and spruce.

CLIMATE

North Korea has a fairly severe climate, with bitterly cold winters. Winds blowing from across central Asia bring snow. Rivers freeze over and sea-ice may block harbours on the coast. In summer, moist winds from the oceans bring rain.

HISTORY

(For pre-1953 history *see* KOREA and KOREAN WAR). North Korea was created in 1945, when the peninsula – a Japanese colony since 1910 – was divided in two. Soviet forces occupied the N, with US forces in the S. Soviet occupation led to a Communist government being established in 1948 under the leadership of KIM IL SUNG.

The Korean War began in June 1950 when North Korean troops invaded the S. North Korea, aided by China and the Soviet Union, fought with South Korea, which was supported by troops from the United States and other UN members. The war ended in July 1953. An armistice was signed but no permanent peace treaty was agreed. The war caused great destruction and loss of life, with 1.6 million Communist troops killed, wounded or reported missing.

POLITICS

Kim Il Sung ruled as dictator, in a style inspired by that of Stalin in the Soviet Union, until his death in 1994. After the war, North Korea adopted a hostile policy towards South Korea in pursuit of its aim of reunification.

The end of the Cold War in the late 1980s eased relations between N and S and they both joined the UN in 1991. The two countries made several agreements, including one in which they agreed not to use force against each other. However, the collapse of Communism in the Soviet Union meant that North Korea remained isolated. In 1993, North Korea triggered a new international crisis by announcing that it was withdrawing from the Nuclear Non-Proliferation Treaty, leading to suspicions that it was developing its own nuclear weapons.

Upon his death in 1994, Kim Il Sung was succeeded by his son, KIM JONG IL, who continued his repressive regime. In the early 2000s, uncertainty surrounding North Korea's nuclear capabilities cast unease across the entire region. Talks between North and South Korea continued in an attempt to normalize relations between

AREA 120,538sq km [46,540sq mi]
POPULATION 23,302,000
CAPITAL (POPULATION) Pyongyang (3,124,000)
GOVERNMENT Single-party people's republic
ETHNIC GROUPS Korean 99%
LANGUAGES Korean (official)
RELIGIONS Buddhist and Confucian with some Christianity, but religious expression now under government control.
CURRENCY North Korean won = 100 chon

them. In 2003 North Korea's relations with the United States deteriorated when the US accused the country of having a secret nuclear weapons programme. North Korea withdrew from international talks in early 2005 stating that it had already produced nuclear weapons.

Despite reports of widespread starvation and malnutrition, North Korea formally requested an end to food aid in September 2005. It was thought that the government might be worried that taking more food aid might be perceived as a sign of weakness. In 2006 North Korea tested a nuclear weapon, to widespread international condemnation; the UN imposed economic sanctions. In 2007 the country agreed to give up its nuclear programme in exchange for fuel oil and food aid, although deadlines for the shutdown were missed.

ECONOMY

North Korea's considerable resources include coal, copper, iron ore, lead, tin, tungsten and zinc. Under Communism, North Korea has concentrated on developing heavy, state-owned industries. Manufactures include chemicals, iron and steel, machinery, processed food and textiles. Agriculture employs about a third of the population and rice is the leading crop. Economic decline and mismanagement, aggravated by three successive crop failures caused by floods in 1995 and 1996 and a drought in 1997, led to famine on a large scale.

It is spoken by more than 50 million people. The Korean alphabet developed in the 15th century.

Korean War (1950–53) Conflict between North Korea (supported by China) and South Korea (backed by a US-dominated UN force). Northern forces invaded South Korea in June 1950. The United Nations Security Council voted to aid South Korea. UN forces landed under the overall command of General Douglas MACARTHUR. UN forces drove out the invaders, but when they advanced into North Korea, China intervened and drove them back, recapturing Seoul. After more heavy fighting, UN forces slowly advanced until virtual stalemate ensued near the 38th Parallel, the border between North and South Korea. Negotiations continued for two years before a truce was agreed in July 1953. The war claimed a total of *c.*4 million lives.

Kornberg, Arthur (1918–2007) US biochemist. In 1959, he shared (with Severo Ochoa) the Nobel Prize in physiology or medicine for work on the synthesis of RNA and DNA, an important contribution to the study of GENETICS.

Kosciuszko, Mount Mountain in SE Australia, in the Great Dividing Range, in SE New South Wales. The highest mountain in Australia at 2,228m (7,310ft), it lies inside a national park.

Kosciuszko, Thaddeus (1746–1817) Polish soldier and statesman. After the Second Partition of Poland in 1793, he led a revolutionary movement to regain Polish independence. The invading armies of Russia and Prussia proved too strong, and Kosciuszko was imprisoned (1794–96) and then exiled.

kosher Ritually correct or acceptable for Jews. A word of Hebrew origin, it is applied by Orthodox Jews to food that conforms to Jewish dietary laws and customs.

Kosovo Province in S SERBIA currently claiming independence; the capital is Priština. Ottoman victory in the Battle of Kosovo (1389) broke the power of Serbia. In 1913, it was reclaimed by Serbia and was incorporated into Yugoslavia in 1929. After World War 2, it became an autonomous province of Serbia. In 1974, it was granted some autonomy, but in 1990 the 80% Albanian population demanded more. Serbia imposed direct rule. The suppression of demonstrations escalated into a full-scale war in 1999. NATO bombardment of Yugoslavia led Serbia to withdraw and reinstate Kosovo's autonomous status. Kosovo officially became part of Serbia, but remained autonomous under UN administration. In 2008 it unilaterally declared its independence from Serbia. The EU and US recognized it as a country, but Serbia and Russia refused. Area: 10,887sq km (4,205sq mi). Pop. (2007 est.) 2,127,000.

Kossuth, Lajos (1802–94) Hungarian nationalist. Emerging as leader of the Revolution of 1848, Kossuth declared Hungarian independence (1849), but Russian intervention led to his defeat. He fled to rouse support in Europe and the USA. The compromise of 1867, which created the Dual Monarchy of the AUSTRO-HUNGARIAN EMPIRE, put an end to his hopes.

Kosygin, Aleksei Nikolaievich (1904–80) Soviet statesman, premier (1964–80). He was elected to the Communist

KOREA, SOUTH

The Republic of Korea, as South Korea is officially known, occupies the S part of the Korean Peninsula. Mountains cover much of the country. The S and W coasts are major farming regions. There are many islands along the W and S coasts. The largest of these is Cheju-do, with South Korea's highest peak, Halla-san (1,950m [6,398ft]).

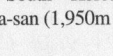

CLIMATE
South Korea is chilled in winter by cold, dry winds blowing from central Asia. Snow often covers the mountains in the E. The summers are hot and wet, especially in July and August.

HISTORY
The Chinese conquered the north in 108 BC and ruled until they were thrown out in AD 313. Mongol armies attacked Korea in the 13th century. In 1388 general Yi Songgye founded a dynasty of rulers that lasted until 1910.

From the 17th century Korea prevented foreigners from entering the country. This earned it the name 'Hermit Kingdom' until 1876, when Japan forced it to open some of its ports. Soon the United States, Russia and some European countries were trading with Korea. The Japanese gained dominance and, in 1910, forced Korea to become a Japanese colony.

After Japan's defeat in World War 2 North Korea was occupied by Soviet troops, while South Korea was occupied by United States forces. Attempts at reunification failed and, in 1948, a National Assembly was elected in South Korea. This Assembly created the Republic of Korea, while North Korea became a Communist state. North Korean troops invaded the South in June 1950, sparking off the Korean War (1950–53).

POLITICS
The story of South Korea after the civil war differs greatly from that of the North. Land reform based on smallholdings worked to produce some of the world's highest rice yields and self-sufficiency in food grains. Industrial expansion started in the early 1960s, leading to what became known as the "economic miracle". Initiated by a military government and based on limited natural resources, the country used its cheap, plentiful, well-educated labour force to transform the economy. The manufacturing base of textiles remained important, but South Korea also became a world leader in footwear, shipbuilding, consumer electronics, toys and vehicles.

AREA 99,268sq km [38,327sq mi]
POPULATION 49,045,000
CAPITAL (POPULATION) Seoul (9,888,000)
GOVERNMENT Multiparty republic
ETHNIC GROUPS Korean 99%
LANGUAGES Korean (official)
RELIGIONS No affiliation 46%, Christianity 26%, Buddhism 26%, Confucianism 1%
CURRENCY South Korean won = 100 chon

In 1988 a new constitution came into force, enabling presidential elections to be held every five years. Evidence of the new spirit of democracy came in 1997 presidential elections, when pro-democracy campaigner Kim Dae-jung narrowly defeated the governing party's candidate. In foreign affairs, a major breakthrough had occurred in 1991 when both North and South Korea were admitted as full members of the United Nations. The two countries signed several agreements, including one in which they agreed not to use force against each other, but tensions between them continued. In 2000 South Korea's President Dae-jung met with North Korea's KIM JONG IL in talks aimed at establishing better relations between the countries, but the prospect of reunification seemed as distant as ever. In 2003 Roh Moo-hyun became president.

ECONOMY
The World Bank classifies South Korea as an 'upper-middle-income' developing country. It is one of the world's fastest growing industrial economies. Resources include coal and tungsten. The main manufactures are computers, cars, televisions, processed food and textiles, while heavy industries include chemicals, fertilizers, iron, steel, and ships. Farming and fishing remain important activities, and rice is the chief food crop.

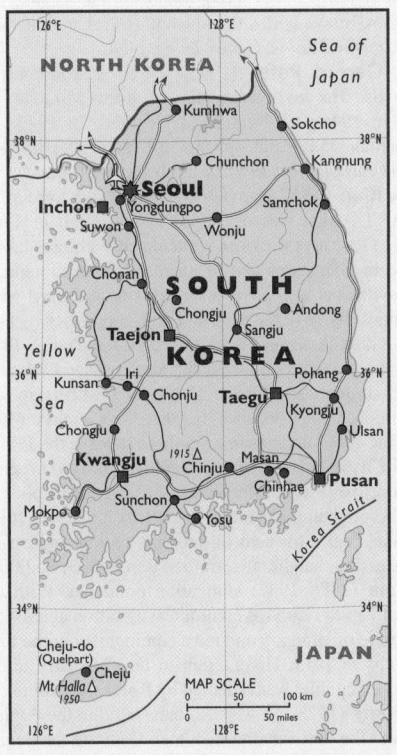

Party Central Committee in 1939 and the Politburo in 1948. Kosygin served as an economics adviser to Joseph STALIN. Removed on the accession of Nikita KHRUSHCHEV, Kosygin returned to share power with Leonid BREZHNEV.

Koussevitzky, Sergei Aleksandrovich (1874–1951) US musician, b. Russia. A virtuoso double-bass player, he was also conductor of the Boston Symphony Orchestra (1924–49).

Kowloon Peninsula on the SE coast of China, part of HONG KONG. One of the most densely populated areas of the world, it was ceded to Britain by China in 1860. Industries: shipbuilding. Area: 9sq km (3.5sq mi). Pop. (2001) 2,023,979.

Krakatoa Small, volcanic island in W Indonesia, in the Sunda Strait between Java and Sumatra. In 1883, one of the world's largest recorded volcanic eruptions destroyed most of the island. The resulting tidal waves caused 50,000 deaths and great destruction. Height: 813m (2667ft).

Kraków (Cracow) City in S Poland. Founded in the 8th century, it became a home of Polish kings in the 12th century and then capital of Poland. In 1795 it was ceded to Austria, from which it was independent 1815–46. It became part of Poland in 1919. Today, it is a manufacturing centre. Industries: chemicals, metals, machinery, printing. Pop. (2001 est.) 740,737.

Krasnodar City and port on the E bank of the River Kuban, SW European Russia; capital of Krasnodar Kray. Founded in 1794 by CATHERINE II as a frontier outpost, it was known as Yekaterinodar until 1920. Industries: oil refining, machine tools, textiles, metalworking. Pop. (2000 est.) 639,000.

Krasnoyarsk City and port on the W bank of the upper Yenisei River, W Siberian Russia; capital of Krasnoyarsk Kray. Founded in 1628 by the COSSACKS, it was attacked in the late 17th century by Tatars and other tribes. It underwent rapid development after the discovery of gold in the area. Industries: shipbuilding, heavy machinery, electrical goods, cement, timber, flour milling. Pop. (2000) 840,000.

Krebs cycle (citric acid or tricarboxylic acid cycle) Biochemical pathway by which most EUKARYOTE organisms, including animals and plants, obtain much of their energy by oxidizing foodstuffs. Occurring in the mitochondria of CELLS, the Krebs cycle comprises a number of complex chemical reactions, many of which release energy, in association with a process called the electron transport system, as **adenosine triphosphate** (ATP) becomes **adenosine diphosphate** (ADP). ATP provides chemical energy for metabolic reactions. The Krebs cycle is an essential part of the process of cell RESPIRATION and METABOLISM. It is named after British biochemist Sir Hans Krebs (1900–81). *See also* MITOCHONDRION

Kremlin (Rus. citadel) Historic centre of Moscow. It is a roughly triangular fortress covering *c.*37ha (90 acres). The Kremlin walls were built of timber in the 12th century, and its first stone walls were erected in 1367. Within the walls, several cathedrals face on to a central square; the Great Kremlin Palace was the Tsar's Moscow residence until the Revolution of 1917. In March 1918, the Supreme Soviet established the Kremlin complex as the location of all government offices. Today, the Kremlin is the home of the Russian presidential offices.

Krenek, Ernst (1900–91) US composer, b. Austria, who emigrated to the USA in 1938. Living in Vienna after 1930, he adopted the TWELVE-TONE MUSIC technique of Schoenberg. His jazz opera *Jonny spielt auf* (1925–26) created a sensation.

krill Collective term for the large variety of marine crustaceans found in all oceans. They are strained and used as food by the various species of baleen WHALE.

Krishna Most celebrated hero of Hindu mythology. He was the eighth AVATAR (incarnation) of VISHNU and primarily a god of joyfulness and fertility. Many devotional cults grew up around him, as well as legends and poems. *See also* HINDUISM

Kroeber, Alfred Louis (1876–1960) US anthropologist, one of the most influential cultural anthropologists of the early 20th century. Kroeber helped to advance the study of Native North American ethnology, linguistics, and folklore.

Kropotkin, Peter Alexeievich (1842–1921) Russian anarchist leader. He was jailed for seditious propaganda in 1874, but escaped into exile in 1876. Living mostly in Britain, he became one of the most important theorists of anarchist socialism, criticizing the centralizing tendencies of MARXISM. He

argued, in *Mutual Aid* (1902), that cooperation rather than competition is the natural order of things. *See also* ANARCHISM

Kruger, Paul (Stephanus Johannes Paulus) (1825–1904) South African statesman. After the British annexed Transvaal in 1877, Kruger worked for independence. In 1883 he was elected the first president of the South African Republic, and won again in 1888, 1893 and 1898. He fought in the first of the SOUTH AFRICAN WARS, and during the second he sought European support for the BOER cause. Following the British victory, Kruger died in exile.

Kruger National Park Game reserve in Northern Province, South Africa, on the Mozambique border. Founded in 1898 by Paul Kruger as the Sabi Game Reserve, it became a national park in 1926. Area: *c.*20,700sq km (8000sq mi).

krypton (symbol Kr) Gaseous nonmetallic element that is a NOBLE GAS. Discovered in 1898, krypton makes up about 0.0001% of the Earth's atmosphere by volume and is obtained by the fractional distillation of liquid air. It is used in fluorescent lamps, lasers and in electronic heart valves. Properties: at.no. 36; r.a.m. 83.80; r.d. 3.73; m.p. $-156.6°C$; ($-249.9°F$); b.p. $-152.3°C$ ($-242.1°F$); most common isotope Kr^{84} (56.9%).

Kuala Lumpur (Malay, 'estuary mud') Capital of Malaysia, S Malay Peninsula. Founded in 1857, it became the capital of the Federated Malay States in 1895, capital of the Federation of Malaya in 1957, and capital of Malaysia in 1963. A commercial city, its striking modern architecture includes one of the world's tallest buildings, the twin Petronas Towers, at 452m (1,483ft). Industries: tin, rubber. Pop. (2005) 1,392,000.

Kubelík Name of two Czech musicians. **Jan** (1880–1940) was a violinist and composer, highly regarded for his technical mastery. **Rafael** (1914–1996), his son, was an eminent conductor as well as a composer. He was musical director of the METROPOLITAN OPERA COMPANY in New York (1973–74).

Kublai Khan (1215–94) Mongol Emperor (1260–94). Grandson of GENGHIS KHAN, he completed the conquest of China in 1279, establishing the YÜAN dynasty, which ruled until 1368. He conquered the Southern SONG dynasty, and extended operations into SE Asia, although his attempt to invade Japan was thwarted by heavy storms.

Kubrick, Stanley (1928–99) US film director. His films include *Dr Strangelove* (1963), *2001: A Space Odyssey* (1968), *A Clockwork Orange* (1971) and *The Shining* (1980). His final film, *Eyes Wide Shut* (1999) was released after his death.

kudu Large African ANTELOPE found S of the Sahara. The body is grey-brown with vertical white stripes and the male bears long, spiral horns. Genus *Tragelaphus*.

Kuiper, Gerard Peter (1905–73) US astronomer, b. Netherlands. He discovered the satellites Miranda (of Uranus) in 1948 and Nereid (of Neptune) in 1949. He found methane in the atmospheres of Uranus, Neptune and Titan, and carbon dioxide in the atmosphere of Mars.

Ku Klux Klan (KKK) Name of two white, racist groups in the USA. The first was organized in the South in 1866. Opposed to RECONSTRUCTION, it attempted to enforce labour discipline in plantations and to maintain white supremacy. Klansmen dressed in white robes and hoods terrorized black communities. By 1872 the Klan had been suppressed by Federal authorities. A second Ku Klux Klan, founded in 1915, renewed racist attacks on blacks but also targeted Catholics, Jews and communists. By the 1920s, its membership was *c.*four million. It later declined, but there was a minor resurgence in the 1960s and in some Southern states in the 1990s.

Kumasi City in central Ghana; capital of ASHANTI region. The second-largest city in Ghana, it was the capital of Ashanti before being annexed by the British in 1901. It is a commercial centre for a cocoa-growing region. Industries: food processing, handicrafts, timber. Pop. (2005) 862,000.

Kun, Béla (1886–1937) Hungarian politician. With the support of LENIN, Kun led communist agitation against the new republic of Hungary and led a communist regime for a few months in 1919. His attempt to turn Hungary into a Soviet-style republic was defeated by Romanian troops.

Küng, Hans (1928–) Swiss Roman Catholic theologian. He became the first important Roman Catholic theologian to question the doctrine of papal infallibility and the dogma of the Virgin Mary. He was censured by the Vatican (1979) and forbidden to teach Catholic theology.

kung fu Ancient Chinese martial art based on the idea that the best form of defence against violence utilizes actions that combine attack and defence.

Kuniyoshi, Yasuo (1893–1953) Japanese painter. His work, which has been described as Oriental in spirit but Western in technique, includes *Child* (1923) and *Landscape* (1924).

Kuomintang Nationalist Party in China, the major political force during and after the creation of a republic in 1911. It was first led by SUN YAT-SEN. It cooperated with the Communist Party until 1927, when Sun's successor, CHIANG KAI-SHEK, turned against the communists, initiating a civil war. Cooperation was renewed in order to repel the Japanese (1937–45), after which the civil war was resumed. With the communists victorious, Chiang set up a rump state on the island of Taiwan, where the Kuomintang survives.

Kupka, František (1871–1957) Czech painter, etcher and illustrator, active mainly in Paris. He was among the first painters to develop purely abstract painting. His works include *Fugue in Red and Blue* (1912). *See also* ABSTRACT ART

Kurdistan Extensive mountainous and plateau region in SW Asia, inhabited by the KURDS and including parts of E Turkey, NE Iran, N Iraq, NE Syria, S Armenia and E Azerbaijan. Plans for the creation of a separate Kurdish state were put forward after World War 1 but were subsequently abandoned. Area: *c.*192,000sq km (74,000sq mi).

Kurds Predominantly rural Islamic population numbering some 18 million, who live in a disputed frontier area of SW Asia that they call KURDISTAN. Traditionally nomadic herdsmen, they are mainly SUNNI Muslims who speak an Iranian dialect. For 3,000 years, they maintained a unique cultural tradition, although internal division and constant external invasion prevented them from uniting into one nation. In recent times, their main conflicts were with Iran and Iraq. After the Iran-Iraq War (1988), Iraq destroyed many Kurdish villages and their inhabitants. The Iraqi response to a Kurdish revolt after the Gulf War caused 1.5 million Kurds to flee to Iran and Turkey. In 1996, Iraqi troops flooded the region and crushed the Kurdish city of Irbil. The USA responded by launching cruise missiles at Iraqi military installations. Currently about 8 million Kurds live in E Turkey, 6 million in Iran, 4 million in N Iraq, 500,000 in Syria, and 100,000 in Azerbaijan and Armenia.

Kuril Islands (Kurilskiye Ostrova) Chain of 56 islands in SAKHALIN region, Russia; extending 1200km (750mi) from the S Kamchatka Peninsula to NE Hokkaido, Japan, and separating the Sea of Okhotsk from the Pacific Ocean. The N islands were settled by Russians, the S islands by Japanese. In 1875, Russia gave the islands to Japan in exchange for full control of SAKHALIN island. After World War 2, the islands

▲ **krill** The shrimp-like krill, one of the most important types of plankton, are about 5cm (2in) long when fully grown. They belong to a group of crustaceans (found in all of the world's oceans) characterized by luminescent organs along their sides, on their undersides and heads. *Euphausia superba* (shown) is the most important species of the Antarctic seas, because it supports much of the warm-blooded life in the southern oceans.

INTERNET

Kuwait
▶ www.kuwait-info.org

KUWAIT

The State of Kuwait is a small, oil-rich Arab country at the head of the Persian Gulf. It consists of a mainland area and several offshore islands. The capital, Kuwait City, stands on a natural harbour called Kuwait Bay. Most of the land is a flat or gently undulating plain. The highest point is about 250m [820ft]. There are no rivers or lakes and water supply is a problem. Water is imported, but drinking water is also produced by desalination plants. Desert scrub covers some areas, but much of Kuwait has no vegetation.

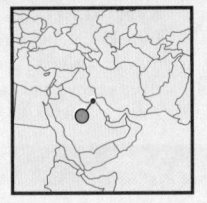

British interest in the area began near the end of the 18th century when Kuwait's leader, Sheikh Mubarak, feared Turkish domination. In 1899 Britain became responsible for Kuwait's defence and, in 1914, the territory became a British protectorate. Britain provided naval protection, while taking control of Kuwait's external affairs. Drilling for oil began in 1936 and large reserves were discovered by the US-British Kuwait Oil Company. Production was delayed by World War 2 (1939–45), but oil was produced commercially in 1946. Kuwait soon became a prosperous oil exporter. The country financed great improvements to the infrastructure, and Kuwaitis soon enjoyed a high standard of living.

AREA 17,818sq km [6,880sq mi]
POPULATION 2,506,000
CAPITAL (POPULATION) Kuwait City (879,000)
GOVERNMENT Constitutional monarchy
ETHNIC GROUPS Kuwaiti 45%, other Arab 35%, South Asian 9%, Iranian 4%, other 7%
LANGUAGES Arabic (official), English
RELIGIONS Islam 85%, Christianity, Hinduism
CURRENCY Kuwaiti dinar = 1000 fils

CLIMATE

Kuwait has a hot desert climate. Annual rainfall is around 125mm [5in] and most rain occurs November–March. Winters are mild and pleasant. Summers are hot, with average temperatures reaching 33°C–35°C [91–95°F] between June and September. Humidity is at its highest in August–September are the most uncomfortable months. Periodically, hot sandstorms or duststorms blow from central Arabia.

HISTORY

In the 17th century, the NW part of the Arabian peninsula became part of the Turkish Ottoman empire. But the area was thinly populated until about 1710, when people from Arabia settled there and built the port that later became Kuwait City. They elected the head of the Al Sabah family as their ruler, and this family still rules Kuwait today.

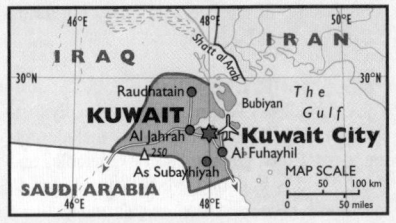

POLITICS

Kuwait became an independent state in 1961, and the Sheikh, the head of state, became an Emir. Kuwait joined the Arab League and Iraq renewed its claim that Kuwait was legally part of its territory. British military intervention forced Iraq to back down. In 1963, elections were held to the National Assembly under a new constitution. However, the Emir suspended the National Assembly in 1976. The National Assembly was restored in 1981 but dissolved again in 1986.

In the Iran-Iraq War, which began in 1980, Kuwait supported Iraq with huge loans. After the war, Iraq accused Kuwait of drilling across the border to take Iraqi oil. In August 1990, Iraq invaded Kuwait. The Emir and his cabinet fled to Saudi Arabia. Iraq refused to withdraw, and in 1991 a United States-led and UN-supported international force began an aerial bombing campaign. They took Kuwait City in late February and expelled the Iraqis, but not before they had set fire to more than 500 oil wells, causing massive pollution and destroying almost all the country's industrial installations. The fires took nine months to extinguish, and repairs cost over 5 billion dollars. After the war, Kuwait expelled many of its huge contingent of Palestinian

immigrant workers in retaliation for PLO leader Yasir ARAFAT's support for Iraq. In 1994, Iraq, under UN pressure, officially recognized Kuwait's independence and land boundaries. Marine boundaries remain ill-defined.

In 1992, elections were held for a new National Assembly. In 1999 the Emir, Jabir al-Ahmad al-Jabir al-SABAH, suspended the Assembly, but liberals and Islamists predominated in its replacement. In 2003 elections, the Islamists gained further seats. In 1999 the Assembly had narrowly rejected a proposal to give women full political rights, but parliament approved it in May 2005. Kuwait's first female cabinet minister was appointed in June. Recent problems include violence by Islamist militants, some allegedly linked to al-Qaeda, who have been accused of conspiring to attack Western targets. After Emir al-Sabah's death in 2006 he was succeeded by his half-brother Sabah.

ECONOMY

The economy is based on oil, which accounts for more than 90% of the exports. Kuwait has about 10% of the world's known reserves. Agriculture is practically non-existent, though the country has a small fishing fleet. Kuwait has to import most of its food. The shortage of water has inhibited the development of industries. However, industrial products include petrochemicals, cement, food products and construction materials. Another industry is shipbuilding and repair.

were ceded to the Soviet Union. Chief economic activities are sulphur mining and whaling. Area: 15,600sq km (6,023sq mi).

Kurosawa, Akira (1910–98) Japanese film director. In *Rashomon* (1950), he introduced the world of the samurai warriors to Western audiences. The popularity of this genre was confirmed by *The Seven Samurai* (1954). *Dersu Uzala* (1975) won an Academy Award for best foreign language film. Other classics include *Kagemusha* (1980) and *Ran* (1985).

Kursk City in w Russia, at the confluence of the Tuskoc and Seim. Founded in 1095, it was destroyed by the TATARS in 1240 and rebuilt as a frontier post in 1586. Industries: iron, steel, chemicals, synthetic fibres, shoes, electrical equipment. Pop. (1999 est.) 367,200.

Kush Kingdom and former state in NUBIA. Lasting from *c.*1000 BC to *c.* AD 350, it conquered Egypt in the 7th-8th centuries BC. It was later defeated by the Assyrians, and moved its capital to Meroë in the Sudan. After Roman and Arab attacks in the N, Meroë was captured by the Axumites around AD 350. The Kushites are thought to have fled w.

Kutusov, Mikhail Illarionovich (1745–1813) Russian general. Kutusov was supreme commander in the NAPOLEONIC WARS. After the French abandoned Moscow in 1812, he forced them to retreat in winter, harrying them by guerrilla attack.

Kuwait (Al Kuwayt) Independent state in the NE Arabian Peninsula. *see* country feature page 447.

KwaZulu-Natal Province in E South Africa, bordered by the Indian Ocean and the Drakensberg Mountains; the capital is Pietermaritzburg. It was created in 1994 from the Zulu homeland, KwaZulu, and the former province of Natal. Industries: sugar refining; textiles, tanning and oil refining. Area: 92,180sq km (33,578sq mi). Pop. (2000 est.) 9,070,458.

Kyoto City on w central Honshu island, Japan; capital of Kyoto prefecture. Founded in the 6th century, it was the capital of Japan for more than 1000 years. Industries: porcelain, lacquerware, textiles, precision tools. Pop. (2000) 1,468,000.

Kyoto Protocol International environmental treaty requiring member states to reduce their emissions of six gases that contribute towards the GREENHOUSE EFFECT, including Carbon dioxide. It was negotiated in 1997 and came into force in 2005. It has been widely criticized as too weak. The USA – the world's largest greenhouse gas emitter – refuses to ratify it, and its requirements are inadequate to meet its goals. However, the protocol contains provisions for increasing its requirements until successful and remains the only international legally binding basis for tackling climate change.

Kyrgyz Turko-Mongolian people who inhabit the Republic of Kyrgyzstan in central Asia. Of Muslim faith, they are Turkic-speaking nomadic pastoralists who began to settle in the TIAN SHAN region of Kyrgyzstan in the 7th century. They were colonized by the Russians during the 19th century. After fighting the BOLSHEVIKS in the Russian Civil War (1917–21), many Kyrgyz perished in the ensuing famine.

Kyrgyzstan Republic in NE Central Asia. *see* country feature

Kyushu Island in s Japan; the third-largest and southernmost of the four main Japanese islands. The terrain is mountainous, and the coastline has many natural harbours. It is the most densely populated Japanese island. The chief port is NAGASAKI. Products: rice, tea, tobacco, fruit, soya beans. Industries: mining, fishing, timber, textiles, porcelain, metals, machinery. Area: 42,149sq km (16,274sq mi). Pop. (2000) 14,764,000.

Kyzyl Kum (Kizil Kum) Desert of central Asia, situated in Uzbekistan and s Kazakhstan, between the Amudarya and Syrdarya rivers. Cotton and rice are grown in the irrigated river valleys and karakul sheep are raised by tribespeople. Area: *c.*230,000sq km (89,000sq mi).

KYRGYZSTAN

The Kyrgyz Republic is a landlocked country between China, Tajikistan, Uzbekistan and Kazakhstan. The country is mountainous, with spectacular scenery. The highest mountain, Pik Pobedy (Peak of Victory) in the Tian Shan Range, is 7,439m [24,406ft] above sea level in the E. Less than a sixth of the country is below 900m [2,950ft]. The largest of the country's many lakes is Lake Issyk Kul (Ysyk-Köl) in the NE.

CLIMATE

The lowlands have warm summers and cold winters. The altitude influences the climate in the mountains, where January temperatures drop to –28°C [18°F]. Kyrgyzstan has low rainfall.

HISTORY

The area was populated in ancient times by nomadic herders. MONGOL armies conquered the region in the early 13th century. They set up areas called khanates, ruled by chieftains, or khans. Islam was introduced in the 17th century.

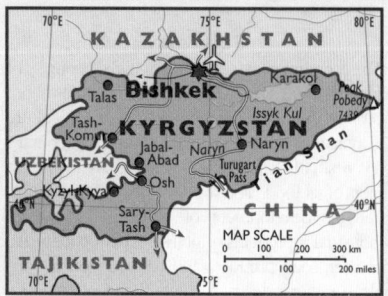

China gained control of the area in the mid-18th century, but in 1876 Kyrgyzstan became a province of Russia and Russian settlement in the area began. In 1916 Russia crushed a rebellion among the Kyrgyz, and many subsequently fled to China.

In 1922 the area became a self-governing region of the Soviet Union and, in 1936, it became one of the Soviet Socialist Republics. Under Communist rule, nomads were forced to work on government-run farms, while local customs and religious worship were harshly suppressed. However, education and health services were greatly improved.

POLITICS

In 1991, Kyrgyzstan became an independent country following the break-up of the Soviet Union. The Communist Party was dissolved, but the country retained ties with Russia through the Commonwealth of Independent States. Askar Akayev, president since 1990, introduced constitutional changes and other measures that limited press freedom and gave him greater powers. In 2000 Akayev was elected to a third five-year term as president. Alleged government interference in the parliamentary elections of March 2005 sparked massive popular protest, with the people demanding a rerun of the vote and the resignation of Akayev. Official buildings in the capital were seized and, with virtually no resistance from the security forces, Akayev fled to Russia. Kurmanbek Bakiyev was appointed acting president and prime minister and he subsequently won a

AREA 199,900sq km [77,181sq mi]
POPULATION 5,284,000
CAPITAL (POPULATION) Bishkek (828,000)
GOVERNMENT Multiparty republic
ETHNIC GROUPS Kyrgyz 65%, Russian 13%, Uzbek 13%, Ukrainian 1%, others
LANGUAGES Kyrgyz and Russian (both official)
RELIGIONS Islam 75%, Russian Orthodox 20%
CURRENCY Kyrgyzstani som = 100 tyiyn

landslide victory in a presidential election in July 2005. The election was deemed to have shown clear progress in democratic standards, according to independent foreign observers. In 2006 Bakiyev signed a new constitution limiting his powers as president, but he extended his powers in 2007, legitimizing them with a rigged referendum. In unfair 2007 elections Bakiyev's party took every parliamentary seat.

Kyrgyzstan suffers ethnic tensions with disenchanted Uzbeks, an influx of Chinese Muslim immigrants, and a large Russian minority who held positions of power in Soviet days. In the early 21st century, guerrillas staged border raids on Kyrgyzstan as they sought to set up an Islamic state in the Fergana valley bordering Uzbekistan and Tajikistan.

ECONOMY

The chief activity is agriculture, especially livestock rearing. The main products include cotton, eggs, fruits, grain, tobacco, vegetables and wool. Food is imported. Manufactures include machinery, processed food, metals and textiles.

Labor Party Social democratic party in Australia. Founded in 1891, it is the oldest surviving political party in Australia. It first held federal office in 1904. In 1916, the party split over involvement in World War 1. Prime Minister W.M. Hughes led the majority, pro-conscription wing into the breakaway National Party. In 1929, the Labor Party returned to office under J.H. Scullin, but it fractured again over policies to combat the GREAT DEPRESSION. Between 1939 and 1949, the Labor government introduced important social welfare reforms. In 1955, the party split again over attitudes to communism. In 1972, the party returned to power under Gough WHITLAM. Bob HAWKE held office for a record four terms. Paul KEATING succeeded Hawke as prime minister.

labour In childbirth, stage in the delivery of the FETUS at the end of pregnancy. In the first stage, contractions of the UTERUS begin and the CERVIX dilates in readiness; the sac containing the amniotic fluid ruptures. In the second stage, the contractions strengthen and the baby is propelled through the birth canal. The third stage is the expulsion of the PLACENTA and fetal membranes, together known as the afterbirth.

Labour Party Social democratic political party, traditionally closely linked with the trade-union movement. There are Labour Parties in many countries, including Australia, Britain, Canada, Israel, and New Zealand. The first British socialist parties, founded in the 1880s, united in the Independent Labour Party (ILP) in 1893, whose president was Keir HARDIE, the first socialist member of Parliament. The ILP created the Labour Representation Committee in 1900, which was renamed the Labour Party in 1906. In 1922, Labour became the second-largest party in Parliament. It formed a brief minority government in 1924 under Ramsay MACDONALD and again in 1929–31, but following a coalition with the Liberals in 1931, the party split and was defeated at the polls. Labour joined the wartime coalition of World War 2 and its leader, Clement ATTLEE, was deputy prime minister from 1942. After a landslide Labour victory in 1945, the Attlee government introduced a series of social reforms. Labour won the general election of 1964 under Harold WILSON and continued in power until 1970. From 1974 to 1979, it was in power, mostly as a minority administration. Following Wilson's resignation, James CALLAGHAN became prime minister. During the 1980s, led by Michael Foot and Neil Kinnock (1983–92), Labour remained in opposition. After the death of John Smith in 1994, Tony BLAIR stepped up the party's process of 'modernization' under the slogan 'new Labour'. In 1997, after 18 years in opposition, Labour regained power.

Labrador Mainland part of NEWFOUNDLAND province, E Canada, bordered W and S by Québec, and E by the Atlantic Ocean. John CABOT visited the coast in 1498. It passed to Britain under the Treaty of Paris (1736). In 1949, Labrador became part of Canada. It is mountainous with an indented coastline. The inland granite plateau is forested, with many lakes and rivers. Industries: timber, fishing, iron ore mining, hydroelectric power. Area: 292,220sq km (112,830sq mi).

laburnum Any of several Eurasian shrubs and small trees of the genus *Laburnum*, especially the common Laburnum, *L.anagyroides*, which has drooping clusters of bright yellow flowers. It bears pods, each of which contains round, black, poisonous seeds. Family Fabaceae/Leguminosae.

labyrinth In architecture, an intricate structure of chambers and passages, generally constructed with the object of confusing anyone within it. In Greek mythology, MINOS had a labyrinth built by DAEDALUS to confine the MINOTAUR.

lac Name of an insect and the sticky substance it secretes and deposits onto twigs; the deposit is harvested in Asia for use in shellac and red lac dye. Species *Laccifer lacca*.

lacemaking Manufacture of lace, an ornamental fabric made from fine threads of linen, cotton, silk or artificial fibres. **Needlepoint** lace was made with needle and thread, using embroidery on a linen backing. **Bobbin** lace was made using bobbins of thread. Most lace is now made by machine.

lacewing Any of numerous species of neuropteran insects, especially members of the families Chrysopidae and Hemerobiidae, which are found worldwide. Common

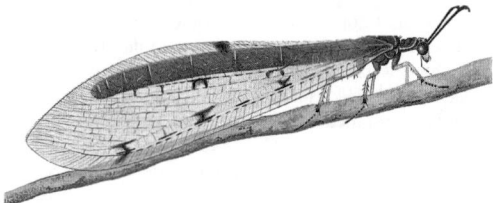

▲ **lacewing** The European lacewing (*Eurolean europaeus*), also known as the ant lion, grows to 2cm (0.8in). A member of the Neuroptera order, lacewings are found worldwide. The larva of the lacewing is a fierce predator of certain small insects, particularly aphids.

green lacewings have a slender greenish body, long antennae and two pairs of delicate, lacy, veined wings.

lachrymal gland Organ in the EYE that produces tears. It is located in the orbital cavity, and is controlled by the AUTONOMIC NERVOUS SYSTEM. It produces slightly germicidal tears, which flow through ducts to the surface of the eye to lubricate it.

Laclos, Pierre (Ambroise François) Choderlos de (1741–1803) French general and novelist. His one important work, *Les Liaisons Dangereuses* (1782), caused a sensation and was only belatedly recognized as a great work.

lacquer VARNISH used for coatings; it forms a film by loss of solvent through evaporation. Lacquer is usually composed of a CELLULOSE derivative in combination with a RESIN.

lacrosse Ball game that originated among the Iroquois Native Americans of Canada and the USA. It is played by teams of 10 male or 12 female players. The stick has a meshwork head like a flexible scoop, with which the ball may be conveyed, passed, kicked or hit, but only goalkeepers may handle the ball. Lacrosse became Canada's national game in 1867.

lactation Secretion of MILK to feed the young. In pregnant women, HORMONES induce the breasts to enlarge, and prolactin (a hormone of the PITUITARY GLAND) stimulates breast cells to begin secreting milk. The milk appears in the breast immediately after the birth of the baby. The hormone oxytocin controls the propulsion of milk from the breast.

lactic acid Colourless, organic acid (2–hydroxypropanoic acid, $CH_3CHOHCOOH$) formed from LACTOSE by the action of bacteria. It is also produced in muscles, where it causes muscle fatigue, when ANAEROBIC respiration occurs due to insufficient oxygen. Lactic acid is used in foods and beverages, in tanning, dyeing, and adhesive manufacture. Properties: r.d. 1.206; m.p. 18°C (64.4°F); b.p. 122°C (252°F).

lactose (milk sugar) Disaccharide in milk, made up of a molecule of GLUCOSE linked to a molecule of galactose. It is important in cheesemaking, when lactic bacteria turn it into LACTIC ACID, resulting in the production of cheese curd.

Ladoga (Rus. *Ladozhskoye Ozero*, Finnish *Laatokka*) Europe's largest lake, in NW Russia (near the Finnish border). It is drained by the River Neva. Formerly divided between Finland and the Soviet Union, it has been entirely within the Russian border since the Soviet invasion of Finland in 1940. Area: 17,678sq km (6,826sq mi).

ladybird (ladybug) Any of a large number of small, brightly coloured beetles; the most common are red with conspicuous black spots and a black and white head. Ladybirds and their larvae are regarded as useful by farmers because their diet consists primarily of aphids. Family Coccinellidae.

Lady Day Alternative name for ANNUNCIATION

lady's smock (cuckooflower) North American and Eurasian perennial flowering plant, common in moist meadows. It has a stout stem, fine leaves and clusters of pink or purplish flowers. Family Brassicaceae/Cruciferae; species *Cardamine pratensis*.

Lafayette, Marie Joseph Gilbert de Motier, Marquis de (1757–1834) French general and statesman. He fought for the colonists in the AMERICAN REVOLUTION, distinguishing himself in the Yorktown campaign (1781). Returning to France, Lafayette presented the DECLARATION OF THE RIGHTS OF MAN to the STATES-GENERAL (1789). After the storming of the Bastille, he commanded (1789–91) the National Guard in the first phase of the FRENCH REVOLUTION. In 1791 Lafayette lost popular support by

L/l, 12th letter of the alphabet, can be traced to the Semitic letter **lamedh***, which passed into Greek as* **lambda***. It became slightly modified in the Roman alphabet and in this form has passed into English.*

L

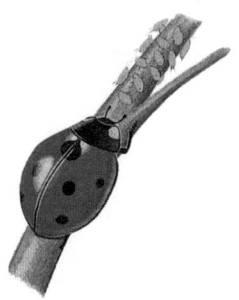

▲ **ladybird** The seven-spot ladybird or ladybug (*Coccinealla septempunctata*) is found throughout Europe. It is the largest of the European ladybirds, growing to 8mm (0.4in). Both the adults and larvae feed on aphids, making them popular with gardeners. During the winter, large numbers hibernate together.

INTERNET

Labrador
► www.gov.nf.ca

Lafayette, Marie Joseph Gilbert de Motier, Marquis de
► friendsoflafayette.org

▲ **Lamarck** French naturalist Jean-Baptiste Lamarck's theories of evolution were highly influential in the 19th century, but were proved false by the work of Charles Darwin. Lamarck believed that adaptations were caused by behaviour and were then passed on to offspring; for example the giraffe developed a long neck over generations because its ancestors were always reaching to feed on higher branches.

L

ordering his troops to fire on a riotous crowd. In 1792, hounded by the JACOBINS, he deserted to the Austrians. In 1799 he was rehabilitated by Napoleon and returned to France. He played a major role in the JULY REVOLUTION (1830) that installed LOUIS PHILIPPE as king of France.

La Fontaine, Jean de (1621–95) French poet noted for his fables, which are considered among the masterpieces of French literature. La Fontaine's *Fables choisies, mises en vers* (1668–94) consists of 12 books featuring some 240 fables. In 1683, he was elected to the Académie Française.

Lagerkvist, Pär Fabian (1891–1974) Swedish writer. One of the major 20th-century Scandinavian writers, his key works include *Anguish* (1916) and *The Hangman* (1933). International recognition came with *The Dwarf* (1944) and *Barabbas* (1950). His central theme is the brutality of man and the search for transcendental meaning. In 1951, he received the Nobel Prize in literature.

Lagerlöf, Selma (1858–1940) Swedish novelist. Her lyrical work *Story of Gösta Berling* (1891) became immensely popular. A visit to Palestine inspired her greatest novel, *Jerusalem* (1901). In 1909 she became the first Swedish writer to receive the Nobel Prize in literature.

lagoon Shallow stretch of seawater protected from waves and tides by a strip of land or coral.

Lagos Largest city and chief port of Nigeria, in the s of the country, on the Gulf of Guinea. From the 17th to the 19th centuries, Lagos grew as a YORUBA settlement. It came under British control in 1861, after years of Portuguese exploitation through the slave trade. It became the capital of independent Nigeria in 1960, but was replaced by ABUJA in 1982. UN estimates suggests that by 2015, Lagos will be the world's third-largest metropolis. Industries: brewing, ship repairing, textiles, crafts. Pop. (2005) 11,135,000.

Lagrange, Joseph Louis (1736–1813) French mathematician and astronomer, b. Italy. His early researches at the University of Turin included work on the calculus of variations and the harmonics of sound. In 1766, Lagrange succeeded Leonhard EULER as head of the Berlin Academy of Sciences. His major work is *Analytical Mechanics* (1788), developing a new approach to mechanics based entirely on ALGEBRA and CALCULUS. *See also* CELESTIAL MECHANICS; LAGRANGIAN POINTS

Lagrangian points Five points in space, defined in relation to two massive bodies orbiting one another, at which a third much lighter body can remain in a position of equilibrium.

Lahore City on the River Ravi, NE Pakistan; capital of Punjab province and Pakistan's second-largest city. An important city during the Ghazni and Ghuri sultanates of the 12th and 13th centuries, it was a royal residence under the Mogul Empire. It was part of the Sikh kingdom from 1767, and passed to the British in 1849. From 1955 to 1970, it was capital of West Pakistan. It is an important commercial and industrial centre. Industries: iron, steel, textiles, chemicals, rubber, leather, carpets, gold and silver jewellery. Pop. (2005) 6,373,000.

Laing, R.D. (Ronald David) (1927–1989) Scottish psychiatrist. He was an exponent of existential psychology and produced radical work on the nature of SCHIZOPHRENIA. He believed that the mentally ill are not necessarily maladapted: a psychotic disorder may be a reasonable reaction to the stresses of the world and of difficult family relationships.

laissez-faire The doctrine that an economic system functions best when self-interest and the profit motive are allowed free reign without government interference. French physiocrats developed the concept in the 18th century, in reaction to the dominant MERCANTILISM. Adam SMITH adopted the doctrine, arguing that FREE TRADE and competition were the basis of a healthy economy. John Stuart MILL and Jeremy BENTHAM developed Smith's ideas into the philosophy of UTILITARIANISM. In the 1840s, Richard COBDEN and John BRIGHT formed the 'Manchester school' that secured the repeal of the CORN LAWS. In the 20th century, the development of CAPITALISM led to state intervention to protect competition. In the 1930s, John Maynard KEYNES promoted the intervention of government to counter unemployment and recession.

lake Inland body of water, generally large and too deep to have rooted vegetation completely covering the surface.

Lake District Region of Cumbria, NW England, containing the principal English lakes. Its spectacular mountain and lakeland scenery and its literary associations make it a major tourist attraction. Among its 15 lakes are Derwent Water, Grasmere, Buttermere, and WINDERMERE. The highest point is SCAFELL PIKE at 978m (3,210ft). The Lake District National Park was established in 1951. Area: 2,243sq km (866sq mi).

Lake poets Three English poets (William WORDSWORTH, Samuel Taylor COLERIDGE, and Robert SOUTHEY) who lived in the LAKE DISTRICT around 1800.

Lakshmi (Padma or Sita) In Hindu mythology, the lotus goddess, wife of VISHNU, who existed at the beginning of creation, rising from the ocean borne by a lotus. Lakshmi is the goddess of beauty and youth, and is often depicted with (or as) a lotus.

Lalique, René (1860–1945) French jewellery designer. His work significantly contributed to the ART NOUVEAU movement. In 1920, he began to produce the popular Lalique glass.

Lamaism *See* TIBETAN BUDDHISM

Lamarck, Jean Baptiste Pierre Antoine de Monet, Chevalier de (1744–1829) French biologist. His theories of EVOLUTION, according to which acquired characteristics are inherited by offspring, influenced evolutionary thought throughout the 19th century, until they were disproved by DARWIN. One of his major works is *Philosophie zoologique* (1809).

Lamb, Charles (1775–1834) English writer. He is best known for his essays, most famously collected as *The Essays of Elia* (1820–23; 1833). He is also remembered for his children's books, which include *Tales from Shakespeare* (1807), on which he collaborated with his sister, **Mary** (1764–1847).

Lamb, Willis Eugene, Jr (1913–2008) US physicist who applied new techniques to measure the lines of the hydrogen SPECTRUM. He found that the actual positions (wavelengths) varied from the positions predicted by DIRAC's theory. For this research, he shared the 1955 Nobel Prize in physics.

Lambert, John (1619–84) English parliamentary general in the English CIVIL WAR. He commanded the cavalry in several victorious battles, including MARSTON MOOR (1644) and Preston (1648). Lambert headed the group that overthrew Richard CROMWELL and ruled the country as head of the 'Committee of Safety' until the RESTORATION. He was convicted of treason and sentenced to life imprisonment.

Lamentations Old Testament book bewailing the destruction of JERUSALEM and the TEMPLE in 587 or 586 BC; it is commonly attributed to the author of the Book of JEREMIAH. All five chapters of Lamentations are written in Hebrew verse.

Lammas Christian festival of thanksgiving for the harvest, celebrated on August 1 in medieval England. It was originally one of the quarter days.

Lamming, George (1927–) Caribbean novelist and poet. His native Barbados forms the background to his first novel, *In The Castle of My Skin* (1953). *The Emigrants* (1954) describes the problems facing West Indians in England, where he settled in the 1950s. Later novels include *Water with Berries* (1971) and *Natives of My Person* (1972).

lamp Form of artificial lighting. Early lamps burned fuels, such as animal fat, wax, or oil. Coal gas was used from the early 1800s. The ELECTRIC LIGHT became popular in the early 1900s. *See also* INCANDESCENCE, FLUORESCENCE

lamprey Eel-like, jawless vertebrate found in marine and fresh waters on both sides of the Atlantic. It feeds by attaching its mouth to fish and sucking their blood. Length: to 91cm (3ft). Family Petromyzondiae.

Lancashire County in NW England; the county town is Preston and the administrative centre, Lancaster. Occupied by the Romans, it later formed part of an Anglo-Saxon kingdom. Textile manufacturing became important in the 16th century and by the 19th, cotton was vital to Lancashire's economy. In the 20th century, cotton and its other traditional industry, coal, sharply declined. It is drained by the rivers Lune and Ribble. Lowland regions are predominantly agricultural. Major attractions include the seaside resort of BLACKPOOL and the PENNINES. Area: 3,064sq km (1,183sq mi). Pop. (2001) 1,134,976.

Lancaster, Burt (1913–94) US film actor and producer. A former circus acrobat, he made his film debut in *The Killers* (1946). He won a best actor Oscar for *Elmer Gantry* (1960).

Other films include *From Here to Eternity* (1953), *Bird Man of Alcatraz* (1962), *The Leopard* (1963) and *Atlantic City* (1981).

Lancaster, Duchy of English estate first given by HENRY III to his son Edmund in 1265. The revenues from the Duchy passed permanently to the monarchy in 1399 with the accession of the Lancastrian king HENRY IV.

Lancaster, House of English royal dynasty. The first Earl was Edmund 'Crouchback' (1245–96), son of HENRY III. In 1361, the Lancastrian title and lands passed to JOHN OF GAUNT via his wife. In 1399, their son was crowned Henry IV. During the Wars of the ROSES, the rival houses of Lancaster and York, both PLANTAGENETS, contended for the throne.

Lancelot of the Lake In Arthurian legend, the father of Galahad and one of the most famous knights; he is portrayed as the lover of GUINEVERE, wife of King ARTHUR.

Lanchow *See* LANZHOU

Landau, Lev Davidovich (1908–68) Soviet physicist. In 1927, he proposed a concept for energy called the density matrix, later used extensively in QUANTUM MECHANICS. He originated the theory that underlies the superfluid behaviour of liquid helium. In 1962, he received the Nobel Prize in physics for his research into condensed matter, especially helium.

Land League Irish association (1879) that campaigned for land reform and tenants' rights in Ireland. It was organized by Michael DAVITT and Charles PARNELL. Its aims were mainly realized in the Irish Land Act (1881). *See also* FENIAN MOVEMENT; HOME RULE, IRISH

Landor, Walter Savage (1775–1864) English writer. His works include *Gebir: a Poem in Seven Books* (1798) and *Heroic Idylls* (1863). Landor is chiefly remembered for his prose dialogues, *Imaginary Conversations of Literary Men and Statesmen* (1824–29).

Landowska, Wanda (1877–1959) Polish harpsichordist and pianist who lived in Paris from 1919, and in the USA from 1941. An authority on early music, she founded the École de Musique Ancienne (1925) in Paris. In her teaching and performances, she did much to promote interest in the HARPSICHORD.

landscape gardening Arranging gardens for effect. There are two main traditions: the Sino-English, with the apparent informality of nature; and the Franco-Italian, with geometric patterns in which nature is trimmed to art. The second tradition arose in Italy in the Renaissance and is exemplified in André LE NOTRE's *parterres* of VERSAILLES. In England, the naturalist style developed in the 18th century, with the work of William Kent, 'Capability' BROWN, and Humphrey Repton.

landscape painting Portrayal of natural scenery. While landscape painting was central to Eastern art, especially China, it came into full flower in the west only in the 16th century; Jacob van RUISDAEL is still regarded as the greatest Dutch landscape painter, while Italian Annibale Carracci invented the 'ideal landscape'. CLAUDE LORRAIN and Nicolas POUSSIN arranged natural elements into artificial compositions. In the 19th century, mystical and romantic landscapes were created by painters such as FRIEDRICH in Germany and TURNER in Britain. COROT and CONSTABLE introduced a more naturalistic approach, which led in turn to the enormous popularity that landscape achieved through IMPRESSIONISM. The 20th-century abstract and surrealist painters have reinvented the genre.

Landseer, Sir Edwin Henry (1802–73) English painter and sculptor. He achieved immense popularity with his sentimental paintings of animals, such as the stag in *Monarch of the Glen* (1851) and the dogs in *Dignity and Impudence* (1839). His best-known sculptures are the lions in Trafalgar Square, London.

Landsteiner, Karl (1868–1943) US pathologist, b. Austria. Landsteiner discovered the four different BLOOD GROUPS (A, B, AB, and O) and demonstrated that certain blood groups are incompatible with others. He received the 1930 Nobel Prize in physiology or medicine. In 1940, with A.S. Wiener, he identified the rhesus (Rh) factor in blood.

Lanfranc (*c.*1010–89) Italian theologian. A BENEDICTINE monk, his priory at Bec, Normandy, was a centre for European scholars in the 1040s. As a counsellor of WILLIAM I (THE CONQUEROR), he became Archbishop of Canterbury (1070–89).

Lanfranco, Giovanni (1582–1647) Italian painter, one of the pioneers of the high BAROQUE style in Rome. Born in

Parma and trained under Agostino Carracci in Bologna, in 1602 he moved to Rome to assist Annibale Carracci on the decorations in the Farnese Palace. After 1612, he executed a series of important frescos in Rome, including *The Assumption of the Virgin* (1625–27) at Sant'Andrea della Valle.

Lang, Fritz (1890–1976) Austrian director of silent and early sound films. His debut feature was *Halbblut* (1919). His first major success was the two-part crime thriller *Dr Mabuse* (1922). *Metropolis* (1926), is a science-fiction classic. Perhaps his greatest film was his first sound feature, *M* (1931), an expressionist, psychological thriller. Fleeing Nazism, Lang moved to the USA. His first film in Hollywood was *Fury* (1936). Later films include *The Big Heat* (1953).

Lange, Dorothea (1895–1965) US photographer. Her portraits of urban poor and migrant labourers in California during the GREAT DEPRESSION and her images of rural America are classics of documentary photography.

Langevin, Paul (1872–1946) French physicist. In 1905, Langevin was the first to interpret **paramagnetism** (weak MAGNETISM) and **diamagnetism** (opposition to a magnetic force) in terms of the behaviour of electrons in atoms. During World War 1, he built the first submarine detector based on ULTRASONICS. *See also* SONAR

Langland, William (1331–99) English poet. Langland's poem *Piers Plowman*, a late flowering of the alliterative tradition in English verse, is one of the most important works of medieval literature. It is remarkable for its sustained, complex, but profoundly Christian allegorical style.

Langley, Samuel Pierpont (1834–1906) US astronomer. He showed that mechanical flight was possible by building a large, steam-powered model aircraft (1896) that achieved the most successful flights up to that time. In 1880, he developed the bolometer, which could measure infrared emissions.

Langmuir, Irving (1881–1957) US physical chemist who invented a gas-filled tungsten lamp. He increased the life of the lamp by introducing nitrogen into the bulb instead of a high vacuum. He also devised the atomic hydrogen welding process and techniques to produce rain by cloud seeding. He received the 1932 Nobel Prize in chemistry.

Langton, Stephen (*c.*1150–1228) English cardinal and scholar, one of the most politically controversial and anti-royalist Archbishops of Canterbury. King JOHN opposed Langton's appointment to the see of Canterbury by Pope INNOCENT III in 1207, and prevented him from entering England until 1213. Langton supported the barons over the MAGNA CARTA (1215).

language System of human communication. Although there are more than 4,000 different languages, they have many characteristics in common. Almost every human language uses a fundamentally similar grammatical structure, or SYNTAX, even though they may not be linked in vocabulary or origin. **Families** of languages have been constructed (AFRO-ASIATIC, AUSTRONESIAN, DRAVIDIAN, INDO-EUROPEAN, NIGER-CONGO, SINO-TIBETAN) but their composition and origins are the subject of continuing debate. Historical studies

L

◀ **Lang** The work of Austrian film director Fritz Lang has been widely acclaimed for its dramatic composition and exacting detail. *Metropolis* (1926) is a powerful, futuristic vision of an urban dystopia. Lang used his expressionist style in a variety of genres, including crime melodramas and westerns. His last film was *The 1000 Eyes of Dr Mabuse* (1960).

L

of language are undertaken by the disciplines of ETYMOLOGY and PHILOLOGY. LINGUISTICS usually involves contemporary language. *See also* GRAMMAR; INFLECTION; SIGN LANGUAGE

Languedoc-Roussillon Region of S France, extending from the RHÔNE valley to the foothills of the PYRENEES; the capital is MONTPELLIER. Languedoc was part of the Carolingian Empire, before passing to the French monarchy in 1271. It is one of the world's major wine-producing regions. Area: 27,736sq km (10,706sq mi). Pop. (1999) 2,295,648.

langur Any of *c.*15 species of medium to large MONKEYS of SE Asia and the East Indies. Gregarious tree dwellers, they are active by day and are found from sea level to snowy Himalayan slopes up to an elevation of 4,000m (13,000ft). Length: 43–78cm (17–31in). Family Cercopithecidae; genus *Presbytis*.

lanolin Purified, fat-like substance derived from sheep's wool and used with water as a base for ointments and cosmetics.

Lansing State capital of MICHIGAN, USA, on the Grand River, S Michigan. First settled in the 1840s, it became the state capital in 1847. Industries: motor vehicles, trucks, tractors, metal goods, machinery. Pop. (2000) 119,128.

lantern fish Any of numerous species of marine fish in Atlantic and Mediterranean waters, especially *Diaphus rafinesquiei*. It has light organs along its sides, and lives in deep water during the day but near the surface at night. Length: 7.5cm (3in). Family Myctophidae.

lanthanide series (lanthanide elements, rare-earth metals) Series of 15 rare metallic elements with atomic numbers from 57 to 71. They are, in order of increasing atomic numbers: LANTHANUM (not always included), cerium, praseodymium, neodymium, promethium, samarium, europium, gadolinium, terbium, dysprosium, holmium, erbium, thulium, ytterbium, and lutetium. Their properties are similar. The shiny metals occur in monazite and other rare minerals and are placed in group III of the periodic table. Each element is analogous to the corresponding radioactive element in the ACTINIDE SERIES.

lanthanum (symbol La) Silvery-white metallic element of the LANTHANIDE SERIES, first identified in 1839. Its chief ores are monazite and bastnasite. Soft, malleable, and ductile, lanthanum is used as a catalyst in cracking crude oil, in alloys and to manufacture optical glasses. Properties: at.no. 57; r.a.m. 138.9055; r.d. 6.17; m.p. 920°C (1,688°F); b.p. 3,454°C (6,249°F); most common isotope La^{139} (99.91%).

Lanzhou City on the Huang He river, W China; capital of Gansu province. A walled city dating from the 6th century BC. The main industry is oil refining. The Chinese nuclear industry is based here. Pop. (2005) 1,788,000.

LAOS

The Lao People's Democratic Republic is a landlocked country in SE Asia. Mountains and plateaux cover much of the country. The highest point is Mount Bia in central Laos, which reaches 2,817m [9,242ft]. Most people live on the plains bordering the MEKONG and its tributaries. This river, one of Asia's longest, forms much of the country's NW and SW borders. The Annam Cordillera (Chaîne Annamatique) runs along the E border with Vietnam.

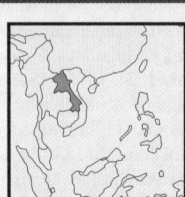

CLIMATE

Laos has a tropical monsoon climate. Winters are dry and sunny, with NE winds. Temperatures rise until April, when the wind direction reverses and moist SW winds reach Laos. This heralds the start of the wet monsoon season.

HISTORY

From the 9th century AD, Lao and Tai peoples set up a number of small states ruled by

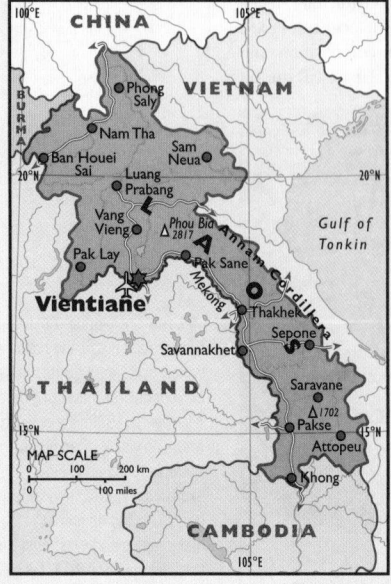

princes. In 1353 the area that is now Laos was united by Fa Ngoun in a kingdom called *Lan Xang* ('land of a million elephants'). Theravada BUDDHISM was the official religion. Apart from a period of Burmese rule (1574–1637), the Lan Xang ruled Laos until the early 18th century. The region was divided into three kingdoms, Champasak, Vientiane and Louangphrabang, which were vassals of Siam (Thailand).

In the 19th century Chao Anou, the king of Vientiane, united his kingdom with Vietnam in an attempt to break Siamese domination. He was defeated, and Vientiane became a Siamese province. In the late 19th century, France gradually gained control of all Siamese territory east of the River Mekong and made it a protectorate, ruling it as part of French INDOCHINA – a region that also included Cambodia and Vietnam. After France's surrender to Germany in 1945, Japanese forces moved into Indo-China. They allowed the French to continue as puppet rulers until 1945, when they interned all French authorities and military units. A Free Laos movement set up a government, but it collapsed when the French returned in 1946.

POLITICS

Under a new constitution, Laos became a monarchy in 1947 and, in 1949, the country became a self-governing state within the French Union. After full independence in 1954, Laos suffered from instability caused by a power struggle between royalist government forces and a pro-Communist group called the Pathet Lao. The Pathet Lao took power in 1975 after two decades of chaotic civil war in which the royalist forces were supported by American bombing and Thai mercenaries, while the Pathet Lao was assisted by North Vietnam. The king, Savang Vatthana, abdicated in 1975 and the People's Democratic Republic of Laos was proclaimed. Over 300,000 Laotians, including technicians and other experts as well as farmers and members of ethnic minorities, fled the

AREA 236,800sq km [91,428sq mi]
POPULATION 6,522,000
CAPITAL (POPULATION) Vientiane (700,000)
GOVERNMENT Single-party republic
ETHNIC GROUPS Lao Loum 68%, Lao Theung 22%, Lao Soung 9%
LANGUAGES Lao (official), French, English
RELIGIONS Buddhism 60%, traditional beliefs and others 40%
CURRENCY Kip = 100 at

country. Many opponents of the government who remained were sent to re-education camps. Communist policies brought isolation and stagnation under the domination of the Vietnamese government in Hanoi, which had used Laos as a supply line in their war against the US.

In 1986 the Laotian Politburo began to allow foreign tourism and open trade links with neighbours, notably China and Japan, but the economy remained weak. Laos became a member of the ASSOCIATION OF SOUTH-EAST ASIAN NATIONS (ASEAN) in 1997. In the 1990s and 2000s opposition to the government has led to sporadic bombings in Vientiane, attributed to rebels in the minority Hmong tribe. Dissent is dealt with harshly by the authorities. Choummaly Sayasone, the current president, was appointed by the Communist party in 2006.

ECONOMY

Laos is one of the world's poorest countries. Agriculture employs about 76% of the people, compared with 7% in industry and 17% in services. Rice is the main crop, and timber and coffee are both exported. The most valuable export is electricity, which is produced at hydroelectric power stations on the River Mekong and exported to Thailand. Laos also produces opium and in the early 1990s was thought to be the world's third biggest source of this illegal drug. Most enterprises are now outside state control. The government is working to develop alternative crops to opium.

Laos Landlocked republic in SE Asia. *See* country feature.

Lao Tzu (Laozi) (active 6th centuryBC) Chinese philosopher, credited as the founder of TAOISM. According to tradition, Lao Tzu was a contemporary of CONFUCIUS, and developed Taoism as a mystical reaction to CONFUCIANISM. He is said to have written *Tao Te Ching*, the sacred book of Taoism. In parables and verse, it advocates harmony with the *Tao* (path).

La Paz Administrative capital and largest city of Bolivia, in its W. Founded by the Spanish in 1548, it was one of the centres of revolt in the War of Independence (1809–24). At 3,600m (12,000ft), it is the world's highest capital city. Industries: chemicals, tanning, flour-milling, electrical equipment, textiles, brewing and distilling. Pop. (2005) 1,533,000.

Laplace, Pierre Simon, Marquis de (1749–1827) French astronomer and mathematician. Laplace made significant advances in PROBABILITY theory. His application of NEWTON's theory of GRAVITATION to the Solar System was summarized in his book *Celestial Mechanics* (1798–1827). Laplace proposed that the Solar System condensed out of a vast, rotating gaseous NEBULA (the **nebular hypothesis**).

Lapland Region in N Europe, lying almost entirely within the Arctic Circle and including N Norway, the northernmost parts of Sweden and Finland, and the W part of the Kola Peninsula of Russia. The land is mountainous in Norway and Sweden, but tundra predominates in the NE. The S regions are forested. Industries: hydroelectricity, fishing, tourism, mining for iron ore, copper and nickel. Area: *c.*388,500sq km (150,000sq mi).

La Plata City in E Argentina, 55km (35mi) ESE of Buenos Aires. Founded in 1882, it was called Eva Perón 1946–1955. It is Argentina's largest oil refining centre. Ensenada is a major exporter of oil, cereals and frozen meat. Pop. (1999) 556,308.

La Plata, Rio de *See* PLATA, RÍO DE LA

Lapps People inhabiting LAPLAND. The mountain Lapps are nomadic herders of reindeer, while those of the forest and coast are semi-nomadic and live by hunting, trapping, and fishing. Their racial origins are uncertain.

lapwing (peewit) Any of several species of birds, especially the Eurasian lapwing, *Vanellus vanellus*, a wading bird with a conspicuous crest. Length: 30cm (12in). Family Charadriidae.

Lara, Brian Charles (1969–) West Indian cricketer, b. Trinidad. A left-handed batsman, he made his debut for West Indies in 1990. In 1994, he scored 375 against England in Antigua, beating Gary SOBERS record (set in 1957) of the most runs in a single test innings (365). Also in 1994, playing English county cricket for Warwickshire, Lara scored a first-class record of 501 not out against Durham.

larch Any CONIFER tree of the genus *Larix*, native to cool and temperate regions of the Northern Hemisphere. Larches bear cones and needle-like leaves that, unusually for a conifer, are shed annually. Family Pinaceae.

lark Any of several small birds, known for their melodious songs. Most common in Europe are the woodlark (*Lullula arborea*), skylark (*Alauda arvensis*) and shore lark (*Eremophila alpestris*). All are mottled brown. Depending on where they live, they feed on insects, larvae, crustaceans or berries. Length: to 18cm (7in). Family Alaudidae.

Larkin, Philip Arthur (1922–85) English poet. His first verse collection was *The North Ship* (1945), but he found his characteristic voice in *The Less Deceived* (1955). Other works include *The Whitsun Weddings* (1964). He edited the *Oxford Book of Twentieth Century Verse* (1973). His *Collected Poems* were published in 1988, and his letters in 1992.

larkspur *See* DELPHINIUM

La Rochefoucauld, François, Duc de (1613–80) French writer, renowned for his literary maxims and epigrams. In 1635 he was involved in an intrigue against Cardinal RICHELIEU and took part in the FRONDES revolt (1648–53). His best-known work is *Réflexions ou Sentences et Maximes Morales* (1665).

La Rochelle Seaport on the Bay of Biscay, W France; capital of Charente-Maritime department. An English possession during the 12th and 13th centuries, it changed hands several times during the HUNDRED YEARS' WAR. In the 16th century, it was a HUGUENOT stronghold, but capitulated to Cardinal Richelieu in 1628. Industries: shipbuilding, oil refining, timber, fish-canning, cement, fertilizers, plastics. Pop. (1999) 76,711.

Larousse, Pierre (1817–75) French lexicographer. He founded the publishing firm Larousse, which produced *The Great Universal Dictionary of the 19th Century* (1866–76), the first of a famous series of dictionaries and encyclopedias.

larva Developmental stage in the life-cycle of many invertebrates and some other animals. A common life-cycle, typified by the BUTTERFLY, is EGG, larva, PUPA (with a protective outer casing), IMAGO (winged adult). The larva fends for itself and is mobile, but is different in form from the mature adult. It metamorphoses (or pupates) to become an adult. Names for the larval stage in different organisms include MAGGOT for a fly, CATERPILLAR for a butterfly and TADPOLE for a toad.

larynx (voice-box) Triangular cavity located between the trachea and the root of the tongue. Inside it are the vocal

◄ **Lara** West Indian cricketer Brian Lara is a prodigious left-handed batsman. He holds the record for the most runs scored in a single test innings, hitting 375 against England at Antigua before being bowled by Andrew Caddick. Born in Port of Spain, Trinidad, at his best Lara averaged more than 50 runs per innings in test matches.

▲ **lark** Found in many regions of Africa, Europe, and Asia, and some parts of North America and Australasia, larks (family *Alaudidae*) are notable for their songs. The crested lark (*Galerida cristata*, shown) has a sandy coloration suited for camouflage in the dry, dusty grassland habitats in which it lives.

L

INTERNET

Lapland
► www.laplandfinland.com

LARYNX

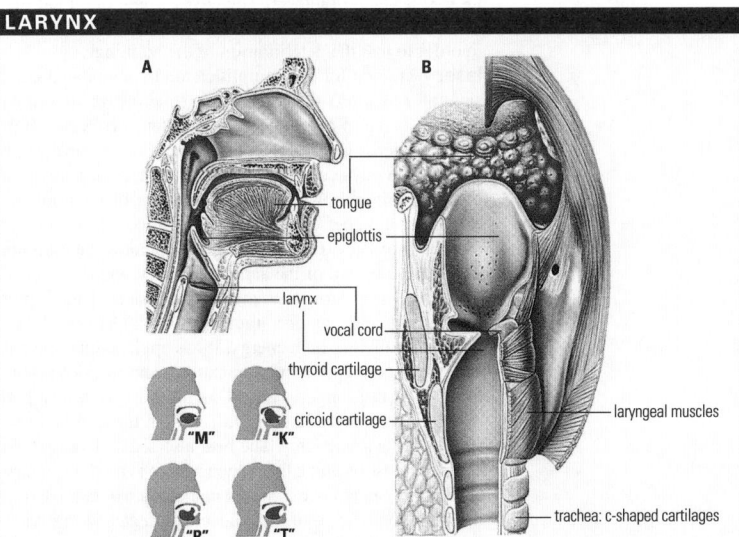

The larynx, epiglottis, tongue, mouth, and lips are the principal organs of speech. A side view (A) and back view (B) of these organs are shown. Air pushed out from the lungs through the larynx causes the vocal cords to vibrate, producing a continuous singing tone, the 'voice'. This tone can be altered in 'pitch' by varying the arrangement of the cartilages of the larynx (thyroid and cricoid) by action of the associated muscles. As air passes through the mouth, the voice is modulated and broken up by changing the position and shape of the other organs to produce speech. Altering the shape of the mouth produces different vowel sounds. Consonants (four shown) are formed when the stream of air is suddenly emitted or cut off.

Labels in figure: tongue, epiglottis, larynx, vocal cord, thyroid cartilage, cricoid cartilage, "M", "K", "R", "T", laryngeal muscles, trachea: c-shaped cartilages

► **laser surgery** Used for a number of surgical operations today, lasers were initially only used in surgery for operations involving the eye, notably to correct detached retinas. The ultra-fine beam of light is a much more delicate instrument than a scalpel, and the energy of the laser cauterizes an incision as soon as it is made.

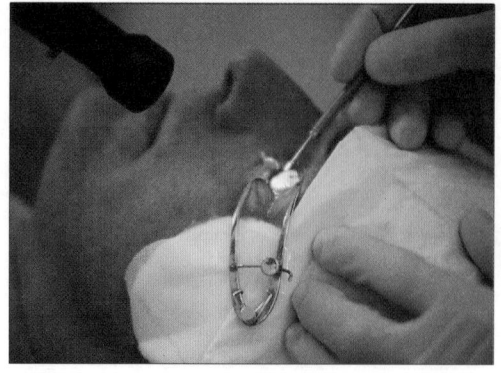

cords, which are thin bands of elastic tissue. The vocal cords vibrate when outgoing air passes over them, setting up resonant waves that are changed into sound by the action of throat muscles and the shape of the mouth. Inflammation of the larynx and vocal cords is called **laryngitis**. Symptoms include sore throat, coughing and breathing difficulties. It is usually due to a respiratory tract infection.

La Salle, René Robert Cavelier, Sieur de (1643–87) French explorer of North America. In 1668, he sailed for Canada to make his fortune in the fur trade. He explored the GREAT LAKES area and was governor of Fort Frontenac on Lake Ontario (1675). On his greatest journey, he followed the Mississippi to its mouth (1682), naming the land Louisiana and claiming it for France.

La Scala (*Teatro alla Scala*) One of the world's great opera houses, Milan, Italy. Designed by Giuseppe Piermarini, it opened in 1776, and has been the scene of many famous premieres, among them Bellini's *Norma*, Verdi's *Otello* and Puccini's *Madame Butterfly*.

Las Casas, Bartolomé de (1474–1566) Spanish missionary and historian of early Spanish America, known as the Apostle of the Indies. He went to Hispaniola in 1502, and spent his life alleviating the conditions of the Native Americans; his *History of the Indies* recounts their persecution by Spanish colonists.

Lascaux Complex of caves in the Dordogne in France, discovered in 1940. They contain examples of 13 different styles of PALAEOLITHIC wall paintings, depicting horses, ibex, stags and a reindeer. The caves, some of which may have been used for ritual ceremonies, were closed in 1963 in order to halt the deterioration of the paintings.

laser (acronym for **l**ight **a**mplification by **s**timulated **e**mission of **r**adiation) Optical MASER (microwave amplification), a source of a narrow beam of intense **coherent light** or ultraviolet or infrared radiation. The laser was invented in 1960 by US physicist Theodore H. Maiman. The source can be a solid, liquid or gas. A large number of its atoms are excited to a higher energy state. One PHOTON of radiation emitted from an excited atom then stimulates the emission of another photon, of the same frequency and direction of travel, which in turn stimulates the emission of more photons. The photon number multiplies rapidly to produce a laser beam of very high energy. It has applications in medicine, engineering, telecommunications, and HOLOGRAPHY.

laser surgery Surgery carried out using a LASER. The high energy in an narrow laser beam can burn through body tissues to make a fine 'cut'. The heat also seals blood vessels, so there is less bleeding than when a knife is used. Less powerful lasers can remove coloured marks, such as tattoos, from the skin. Some forms of skin cancer are treated in this way.

Laski, Harold Joseph (1893–1950) British political scientist and teacher. A prominent member of the FABIAN SOCIETY, he served on the national executive of the Labour Party (1937–49) and as party chairman (1945–46).

Las Palmas (Las Palmas de Gran Canaria) Spanish city in NE Grand Canary Island; capital of Las Palmas province. Founded in 1478, the city expanded considerably after the building of the port in 1883. It is now a tourist resort. Its port, Puerto de la Luz, is the chief port in the CANARY ISLANDS, exporting bananas, sugar, tomatoes and almonds. Pop. (2001) 354,863.

Lasso, Orlando di (1532–94) Flemish composer of madrigals, masses, and motets. He was famous throughout Europe, and is ranked with PALESTRINA as one of the greatest composers of the late 16th century. He was a prolific composer and wrote more than 2,000 pieces in all genres.

Last Supper (Lord's Supper) Final meal shared by JESUS CHRIST and his disciples in Jerusalem during or just before PASSOVER, in the course of which Jesus instituted the Christian EUCHARIST. According to the gospels of St Matthew, St Mark, and St Luke, Jesus warned the disciples of his imminent betrayal and blessed and shared bread and wine among them, telling them that these were his body and blood of the Covenant.

Las Vegas Largest city in S Nevada, USA. It is a world-famous gambling and entertainment centre, with more than 37 million visitors per year. The Mormons established a colony on the site in 1855–57. The modern city began with the arrival of the railway in 1905. Nevada legalized gambling in 1931, and the city grew rapidly. Its first big gambling casino opened in 1946, and by the 1970s gambling was earning the city more than US$1 million a day. Las Vegas is also the commercial centre for a mining and ranching area. Pop. (2005) 1,314,000.

La Tène Archaeological site in Switzerland, discovered in the 19th century. It gives its name to the second phase of CELTIC culture (*c.*500–*c.*50BC). The origin of the culture, which replaced the HALLSTATT, was contact with Greek and Etruscan influences. It was a highly war-like culture, hierarchically organized with kings, a priestly class (the DRUIDS), warriors, farmers and slaves. La Tène weaponry was Late IRON AGE. The La Tène Celts conquered central Europe in the 4th and 3rd centuries. By 50 BC they had submitted to German invaders from the N and Romans from the S.

latent heat (symbol L) Heat absorbed or given out by a substance as it changes its phase at constant temperature. When ice melts, its temperature remains the same until it has been completely transformed into water; the heat necessary to do this is called the latent heat of fusion.

Lateran Councils Five ECUMENICAL COUNCILS of the Western Church, held in the Lateran Palace, Rome. The **first** (1123) confirmed the Concordat of WORMS of 1122. The **second** (1139) condemned simony and the marriage of the clergy. The **third** (1179) decreed that the Pope was to be elected by a two-thirds majority of the College of Cardinals. The **fourth** (1215) defined the doctrine of the EUCHARIST, officially using the term 'TRANSUBSTANTIATION'. The **fifth** (1512–17) introduced minor reforms in the wake of the REFORMATION.

Lateran Treaty (1929) Agreement between ITALY and the VATICAN. The Italian government recognized the Vatican as an independent sovereign state with the Pope as its temporal head, and the Vatican surrendered the Papal States and Rome. Roman Catholicism was affirmed as Italy's state religion.

laterite Reddish soil found in the tropics. It results when hot, wet conditions wash away the nutrient content of the soil, leaving behind hydrated oxides of iron and aluminium. Some laterites contain sufficient iron to be of commercial value.

latex Milky fluid produced by certain plants, the most important being that produced by the RUBBER TREE. Rubber latex is a combination of gum resins and fats in a watery medium. It is used in paints, special papers and adhesives, and to make sponge rubbers. Synthetic rubber latexes are also produced.

Latimer, Hugh (1485–1555) English clergyman and Protestant martyr. He defended King HENRY VIII's divorce from Catherine of Aragon. In 1535 he was made Bishop of Worcester, but resigned his see in 1539 as a protest against the temporary reaction in favour of Catholicism. With the accession of EDWARD VI (1547), he resumed preaching. When the Roman Catholic MARY I came to the throne in 1553, he was charged with heresy and, refusing to recant, was burned at the stake.

Latin Language of ancient ROME, the ROMAN EMPIRE, and of educated medieval European society. It belongs to the family of INDO-EUROPEAN LANGUAGES. Its earliest written records are inscriptions and legal formulas of the late 6th century BC. As Rome extended its rule throughout Italy, Latin gained supremacy. The richest phase of LATIN LITERATURE was the Augustan age (43BC–AD 14). Spoken Latin was used throughout the Roman Empire. It eventually broke up into numerous

INTERNET

Lascaux
► www.culture.fr/culture/
arcnat/lascaux/en

dialects, which formed the basis of the ROMANCE LANGUAGES. Latin remained the language of the Church, science, medicine, law, education, and most written transactions in Europe throughout the Middle Ages. It was still used in some scholarly and diplomatic circles in the 19th century, and the Roman Catholic mass was in Latin until the 1960s.

Latin America Parts of the Western Hemisphere (but not French-speaking Canada) where the official or chief language is a ROMANCE LANGUAGE. Commonly it refers to the 18 Spanish-speaking republics and Brazil (Portuguese) and Haiti (French). Occasionally it includes those islands of the West Indies where Romance languages are the mother tongue.

Latin literature Literature of the ROMAN EMPIRE. The earliest works date from the 3rd century BC and were imitations of GREEK DRAMA and GREEK LITERATURE by Livius Andronicus and Naevius. In the 2nd century BC the influence of Greek drama was adapted to Roman themes by PLAUTUS. The 'Golden Age' of Latin literature (c.70BC–c.AD 14) was heralded in the prose works of CICERO and the poetry of CATULLUS and LUCRETIUS. The Augustan Age (43BC–AD 14) produced the *Metamorphoses* of OVID, the *Aeneid* of VIRGIL, the lyrics of HORACE, and the prose histories of LIVY. The writings of PLINY THE ELDER marked the reign of TRAJAN. The so-called 'Silver Age' (AD 98–138) saw the tragedies of SENECA, the satires of JUVENAL, and the sceptical histories of TACITUS. Generally, Latin literature declined until its revival in the 5th century as the *lingua franca* of Christian discourse by Saint AUGUSTINE. The trend was continued by BOETHIUS and BEDE. Latin writers of the Middle Ages included Pierre ABELARD, Thomas AQUINAS, and Thomas à KEMPIS. ERASMUS and Sir Thomas MORE revived Latin during the age of HUMANISM.

latitude Distance N or S of the EQUATOR, measured at an angle from the Earth's centre. All lines of latitude are parallel to the Equator, which is the zero line of latitude.

La Tour, Georges de (1593–1652) French painter of religious and genre scenes. An inspired follower of CARAVAGGIO, he is famous for nocturnal scenes lit by a single candle. Many art historians consider him to be one of the most important representatives of 17th-century French CLASSICISM. Examples of his work include *Christ and St Joseph in the Carpenter's Shop* (c.1645) and the *Lamentation over St Sebastian* (1645).

Latrobe, Benjamin Henry (1766–1820) US architect, b. England. He emigrated to the USA in 1796. He designed the neo-classical cathedral in Baltimore (1806–18), and worked on rebuilding the Capitol in Washington, D.C. (1815–17).

Latter Day Saints, Church of *See* MORMONS

Latvia Baltic republic in NE Europe. *see* country feature.

INTERNET

Latvia
▶ www.latvia-usa.org

LATVIA

The Republic of Latvia is one of the three states on the SE corner of the Baltic Sea known as the Baltic States. It has flat plains separated by low hills composed of moraine dumped there by ice sheets during the last Ice Age. The country's highest point is 311m [1,020ft] above sea level. Small lakes and peat bogs are common. The country's main river, the Daugava, is also known as the Western Dvina.

CLIMATE

Air masses from the Atlantic influence the climate of Latvia, bringing warm and rainy conditions in summer. Winters are cold. The average temperature range is 16° to18°C [61–64°F] in July, and –7° to –3°C [19-27°F] in January.

HISTORY

The ancestors of most modern Latvians settled in the area c.2,000 years ago. In the 9th–11th centuries the region was attacked by Vikings from the W and Russians from the E. In the 13th century German invaders took over, naming the country Livland.

In 1561 Latvia was partitioned and most of the land came under Polish or Lithuanian rule. A German duchy was also established there. In 1621 the Swedish king Gustavus II Adolphus took over Riga. In 1629 the greater part of the country north of the Daugava River was ceded to Sweden, with the SE remaining under Lithuanian rule. In 1710, PETER I (the Great) took control of Riga and, by the end of the 18th century, all of Latvia was under Russian control, although the German landowners and merchants continued to exercise considerable power. The 19th century saw the rise of Latvian nationalism and calls for independence became increasingly frequent.

After the Russian Revolution of March 1917 the Latvian National Political Conference demanded independence, but Germany occupied Riga in September. However, after the October Revolution, the Latvian National Political Conference proclaimed the country's independence in November 1918. Russia and Germany finally recognized Latvia's independence in 1920. In 1922, Latvia adopted a democratic constitution and the elected government introduced land reforms. However, a coup in May 1934 ended this period of democratic rule. In 1939, Germany and the Soviet Union agreed to divide up much of eastern Europe. Soviet troops invaded Latvia in June 1940 and Latvia was made a part of the Soviet Union. German forces invaded the area in 1941 and held it until 1944, when Soviet troops reoccupied the country. Many Latvians opposed to Russian rule were killed or deported.

POLITICS

Under Soviet rule many Russians settled in Latvia, leading Latvians to fear that the Russians would become dominant. From the mid-1980s, when Mikhail Gorbachev was introducing reforms in the Soviet Union, Latvian nationalists campaigned against Soviet rule. In the late 1980s the Latvian government ended absolute Communist rule, voted to restore the banned national flag and anthem and proclaimed Latvian the official language.

In 1990 Latvia established a multiparty political system. In elections in March, candidates in favour of separation from the Soviet Union won two-thirds of parliamentary seats. The parliament declared Latvia independent on 4 May 1990, although the Soviet Union declared this act illegal. However, the Soviet government recognized Latvia's independence in September 1991, shortly before the Soviet Union itself was dissolved. Latvia held its first free elections to its parliament, the Sacima, in 1993. Voting was limited only to those who were citizens on 17 June 1940 and their descendants. This meant that about 34% of Latvian residents were unable to vote. In 1994 Latvia restricted the naturalization of non-Latvians, denying them the vote and land ownership. In 1998 the government agreed that all children born since independence should have automatic citizenship, regardless of their parents' status. Latvia became a member of NATO and the EU in 2004.

AREA 64,600sq km [24,942sq mi]
POPULATION 2,260,000
CAPITAL (POPULATION) Riga (719,000)
GOVERNMENT Multiparty republic
ETHNIC GROUPS Latvian 58%, Russian 30%, Belarusian, Ukrainian, Polish, Lithuanian
LANGUAGES Latvian (official), Lithuanian, Russian
RELIGIONS Lutheran, Roman Catholic, Russian Orthodox
CURRENCY Latvian lat = 100 santimi

ECONOMY

The World Bank classifies Latvia as a 'lower-middle-income' country. The country's only natural resources are land and forests, so many raw materials have to be imported.

Its industries include electronic goods, farm machinery, fertilizers, processed food, plastics, radios, washing machines and vehicles. Latvia produces only about a tenth of its electricity needs. The rest has to be imported from Belarus, Russia and Ukraine. Farm products include barley, dairy, beef, oats, and rye.

L

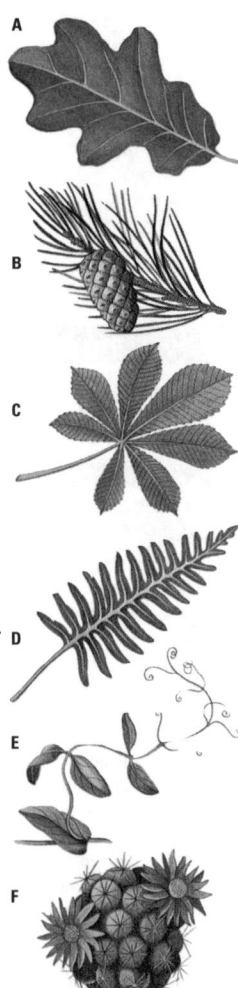

▲ **leaf** Leaves exhibit a wide variety of shapes. The pendunculate oak (*Quercus rober*) (A) and the Scots pine (*Pinus sylvestris*) (B) have simple leaves, with a single leaf blade, while the horse chestnut (*Aesculus hippocastrum*) (C) and ferns, such as Polypodium (D) have compound leaves. The leaflets of compound leaves either radiate from one point (palmate), as is the case with the horse chestnut, or are arranged in opposite pairs down the main stalk (pinnate) as is the case with ferns. The primary function of leaves is photosynthesis but, in addition, leaflets may be modified into climbing tendrils (E), or protective spines, as in the cactus *Mammillaria zeilmannia* (F).

Laud, William (1573–1645) English cleric, Archbishop of Canterbury (1633–45). As religious adviser to King Charles I, whom he supported during his period of non-parliamentary rule (1629–40), Laud imposed press censorship, enforced a policy regulating wages and prices, and sought to remove PURITANS from important positions in the Church. His attempt to impose the English Prayer Book upon the Scots was one of the immediate causes of the English Civil Wars. Laud was impeached (1640) by the LONG PARLIAMENT.

Lauda, Niki (Nikolas) (1949–) Austrian motor racing driver Racing for Ferrari, Lauda the world drivers' championship in 1975, 1977, and 1984. In 1976, he suffered near-fatal injuries in an accident at the German Grand Prix.

Laue, Max Theodor Felix von (1879–1960) German physicist. Using IONS in a crystal as a grating, Laue produced X-RAY interference patterns, thus showing that X-rays are waves, and providing a method of investigating crystal structure. For this discovery, he received the 1914 Nobel Prize in physics. *See also* X-RAY CRYSTALLOGRAPHY

Lauraceae Large family of flowering plants, mostly evergreen shrubs and trees, including LAUREL, CINNAMON, and SASSAFRAS; examples are found in warm and temperate regions worldwide. The flowers are generally green and are followed by berries.

laurel Evergreen shrubs and trees native to s Europe and cultivated in the USA. Included is the noble or BAY laurel (*Laurus nobilis*) with leathery, oval leaves, tiny yellowish flowers and purple berries. Height: 18–21m (60–70ft). Family LAURACEAE.

Laurel and Hardy US comedy team who starred in more than 200 films. **Stan Laurel** (1890–1965), b. Britain, played the thin, bumbling oaf. His US partner, **Oliver Hardy** (1892–1957), played the fat, pompous womanizer. Their best films include *Leave 'em Laughing* (1928), *The Music Box* (1932) and *Way Out West* (1937).

Lausanne City on the N shore of Lake Geneva, sw Switzerland; capital of Vaud canton. Originally a Celtic settlement, it became an episcopal see in the 6th century. Ruled by Prince-Bishops until 1536, when Bern conquered the city and it accepted the REFORMATION. Industries: leather, brewing, chemicals, printing, confectionery. Pop. (2000) 114,900.

Lautrec, Henri Toulouse *See* TOULOUSE-LAUTREC, HENRI MARIE RAYMOND DE

lava Molten rock or MAGMA that reaches the Earth's surface and flows out through a volcanic vent in streams or sheets. There are three main types of lava: vesicular, such as pumice; glassy, such as obsidian; and even-grained. Chemically, lavas range from acidic to ultrabasic. Basic lavas have a low viscosity and flow easily, covering large areas. Acidic lavas are highly viscous and rarely spread far.

Laval, Pierre (1883–1945) French statesman, prime minister (1931–32, 1935–36). His government fell as a result of the unpopularity of the Hoare-Laval Pact, which approved the Italian conquest of Ethiopia. In 1940, Laval joined the VICHY GOVERNMENT, becoming its head under Marshal PÉTAIN. His capitulation to German demands was seen as treason by the FREE FRENCH and he was executed after World War 2.

Laver, Rod (Rodney George) (1938–) Australian tennis player. Laver's major singles titles included the US (1962, 1969), French (1962, 1969) and Australian (1960, 1962, 1969) opens, and Wimbledon (1961, 1962, 1968, 1969). He was the first man to win the 'Grand Slam' twice (1962, 1969).

Lavoisier, Antoine Laurent (1743–94) French chemist who founded modern chemistry. He demolished the PHLOGISTON theory (which said that phlogiston was lost during combustion) by demonstrating the function of oxygen in combustion. He named oxygen and hydrogen, and showed how they combined to form water. In collaboration with Claude Berthollet, he published *Methods of Chemical Nomenclature* (1787), which laid down the modern method of naming substances.

law System of rules governing human society, enforced by punishments specified by society itself. The major systems of law are COMMON LAW, ROMAN LAW, and EQUITY.

Law, (Andrew) Bonar (1858–1923) British statesman, prime minister (1922–23), b. Canada. He entered Parliament in 1900, and in 1911 became the first leader of the Conservative

Party to come from a manufacturing background. He was chancellor (1916–19) before becoming prime minister.

Law and the Prophets Two major divisions of the OLD TESTAMENT. The **Law**, or Law of Moses, consists of the first five books of the Old Testament, known as the TORAH in Hebrew and the PENTATEUCH in Greek. The **Prophets** consists of several books grouped into different arrangements according to Jewish or Christian tradition. The groupings include: (a) Joshua, Judges, I and II Samuel, and I and II Kings; (b) Isaiah, Jeremiah, and Ezekiel; and (c) Hosea, Joel, Amos, Obadiah, Jonah, Micah, Nahum, Habakkuk, Zephaniah, Haggai, Zechariah and Malachi.

Lawrence, D.H. (David Herbert) (1885–1930) English novelist, short-story writer and poet. In 1909, Ford Madox FORD published Lawrence's first poems in the *English Review*. His debut novel was *The White Peacock* (1911). In 1912, Lawrence published his second novel, *The Trespasser*, and eloped to Germany with Frieda Weekley (*née* von Richthofen). His first major novel was the semi-autobiographical *Sons and Lovers* (1913). *The Rainbow* (1915), perhaps his greatest novel, was banned as obscene. *Women in Love* (1921) appeared in censored form. After completing *Aaron's Rod* (1922), Lawrence and Frieda went into self-imposed exile. *Kangaroo* (1923) was inspired by his travels in Australia, and *The Plumed Serpent* (1926) was set in Mexico. His last novel, *Lady Chatterley's Lover* was privately published (1928) in Florence, but until 1960 remained available only in expurgated form in England.

Lawrence, Ernest Orlando (1901–58) US physicist. In 1930, as professor at the University of California at Berkeley, he built the first cyclotron, a subatomic particle ACCELERATOR. He developed larger cyclotrons and received the 1939 Nobel Prize in physics. Lawrencium was named after him.

Lawrence, T.E. (Thomas Edward) (1888–1935) (Lawrence of Arabia) British soldier. He joined the army in World War 1, and in 1916 became a leader of the Arab revolt against the Turks. He proved a successful guerrilla commander, leading Arab forces into Damascus, Syria, in October 1918. He published his remarkable account of the Arab revolt, *The Seven Pillars of Wisdom*, privately in 1926.

Lawrence, Sir Thomas (1769–1830) English painter. Considered one of the most brilliant British portrait painters of his age, Lawrence's portrait of *Queen Charlotte* (1789) won immediate acclaim. He became Painter in Ordinary to the King, and was sent to Europe to paint the allied leaders involved in the defeat of Napoleon.

lawrencium (symbol Lr) Radioactive metallic element, one of the ACTINIDE SERIES. It was first made in 1961 at the University of California at Berkeley by bombarding CALIFORNIUM with boron nuclei. It is named after the US physicist Ernest Lawrence who established the laboratory where it was produced. Properties: at.no. 103; r.a.m. 262; most stable isotope Lr^{256} (half-life 27 seconds).

Law Society Either of two inclusive organizations of solicitors in Britain – the Law Society in England and Wales, and the Law Society of Scotland – as incorporated in 1831 by Act of Parliament. Each Law Society regulates and enforces the standards by which solicitors operate. It administers legal aid to those entitled to it and retains a fund from which compensation may be made in the case of a solicitor's fraud or negligence.

laxative Any agent used to counteract constipation. There are various kinds available, including bulk-forming drugs, stimulant laxatives, fecal softeners, and saline purgatives.

Laxness, Halldór Kiljan (1902–98) Icelandic novelist. He received the 1955 Nobel Prize in literature for his novels about the fishing villages and farms of Iceland. His fiction includes *Independent People* (1934–35), *The Atom Station* (1948), and *Paradise Reclaimed* (1960). The trilogy *Iceland's Bell* (1943–46) was influenced by traditional Icelandic sagas.

Lazarus Either of two men mentioned in the New Testament. In John 11, Lazarus is the brother of Mary and Martha of Bethany. Four days after his death, Jesus miraculously restored him to life. In Luke 16, Lazarus is the poor man in Christ's parable about a beggar and a rich man.

L

L-dopa (levodopa) Naturally occurring amino acid used to relieve some symptoms of PARKINSON'S DISEASE. It sometimes suppresses the trembling, unsteadiness, and slowness of movement that characterize the condition.

Leach, Bernard (1887–1979) English potter. He studied (1909–20) in Japan, before establishing a pottery studio at St Ives, Cornwall. Leach rediscovered traditional techniques of English pottery. His simple, beautifully proportioned designs are a mixture of English and Japanese influences.

lead (symbol Pb) Metallic element of group IV of the periodic table, known from ancient times. Its chief ore is GALENA (lead sulphide), from which lead is obtained by roasting. Exposure to lead from paints, pipes, petrol and other sources can lead to lead poisoning. Soft and malleable, it is used as a shield for X-rays and nuclear radiation, and in plumbing, batteries, cable sheaths, and alloys such as pewter and solder. Chemically, lead is unreactive and a poor conductor of electricity. Properties: at.no. 82; r.a.m. 207.19; r.d. 11.35; m.p. 327.5°C (621.5°F); b.p. 1,740°C (3,164°F); most common isotope Pb^{208} (52.3%).

Leadbelly Popular name of blues singer Huddie LEDBETTER

leaf Part of a plant, an organ that contains the green pigment CHLOROPHYLL and is involved in PHOTOSYNTHESIS and TRANSPIRATION. It usually consists of a blade and a stalk (petiole), which attaches it to a stem or twig. Most leaves are simple (undivided), but some are compound (divided into leaflets).

leaf hopper Any of numerous species of small, slender insects of the family Cicadellidae. Leaf hoppers feed by sucking the sap of plants and may, in large numbers, do a great deal of damage. Many species are brightly coloured.

leaf insect Any of several species of flat, green insects that bear a resemblance to leaves and are found throughout tropical Asia. The female has forewings with markings resembling leaf veins. Order Phasmida; family Phylliidae. *See also* STICK INSECT

League of Nations International organization (1920–46), forerunner of the UNITED NATIONS (UN). Created as part of the Treaty of VERSAILLES (1919) ending World War 1, the USA's refusal to participate impaired the League's effectiveness. The threats to world peace from Germany, Italy, and Japan caused the League to collapse in 1939, and it dissolved in 1946.

Leakey, Louis Seymour Bazett (1903–72) English palaeoanthropologist and archaeologist, who discovered fossils in East Africa that proved man to be older than previously thought. In 1931, Leakey began to research OLDUVAI GORGE, N Tanzania. Working with his wife **Mary** (1913–96), he found animal fossils and tools. Mary Leakey continued working in East Africa, often with her son Richard LEAKEY.

Leakey, Richard Erskine Frere (1944–) Kenyan palaeoanthropologist and archaeologist, son of Mary and

Louis LEAKEY. At Lake Turkana, Kenya, Leakey discovered (1972) a c.1.9 million year-old skull of *Homo habilis*. Other discoveries include a *Homo erectus* skeleton c.1.6 million years old. Leakey became director (1988–94) of the Kenyan Wildlife Service. In 1995, he co-founded the Safina Party. *See also* HUMAN EVOLUTION

Lean, Sir David (1908–91) English film director. His early films, such as *In Which We Serve* (1942) and *Brief Encounter* (1945), were collaborations with Noel COWARD. Lean followed these with the Dickens' adaptations, *Great Expectations* (1946) and *Oliver Twist'* (1948). He is best known for meticulously crafted spectaculars such as *The Bridge on the River Kwai* (1957) and *Lawrence of Arabia* (1962), for which he won an Academy Award. Other films include *Doctor Zhivago* (1965) and *Ryan's Daughter* (1970). In 1984 he made his final film, *A Passage to India*, and was knighted.

Lear, Edward (1812–88) English poet, painter, and draughtsman. Lear is famous for his tragi-comic nonsense verse for children. He invented such characters as the 'Pobble Which Had No Nose' and 'The Owl and the Pussycat'. Books include *The Book of Nonsense* (1846) and *Laughable Lyrics* (1877).

learning Acquisition of skills and concepts by a variety of processes. The oldest theories hold learning to be an associative process by which ideas, images and events become linked in the mind. Behaviourists believe that learning is related to conditioning. GESTALT PSYCHOLOGY deals with such learning potentials as problem solving; COGNITIVE PSYCHOLOGY concentrates on mental processes such as concept formation. Modern researchers tend to investigate particular problems, rather than formulating universal theories.

learning disability Disorder that prevents students from learning as well as would be expected from their ability, as measured on an intelligence test. It covers a range of problems, including difficulties with reading, writing, mathematics, or communication. In the UK, it is sometimes used with 'learning difficulties' to mean MENTAL HANDICAP. *See also* IQ

leather Animal hide, treated to make it hard-wearing and resistant to decay. Most leather comes from cattle hide, but many other kinds of skin are used too. The skin is first cured, via a drying process or the application of salt. It is then washed and prepared for tanning, a process that usually consists of treating the skin with a solution of chromium salts or plant extract (TANNIN). Other processes include dyeing, oiling and the application of various finishes, such as VARNISH.

Leavis, F.R. (Frank Raymond) (1895–1978) English literary critic. His works of criticism include *The Great Tradition* (1948), *The Common Pursuit* (1952), and *D.H. Lawrence, Novelist* (1955). His views on society and education are expounded in *Mass Civilization and Minority Culture* (1933) and *Education and the University* (1943).

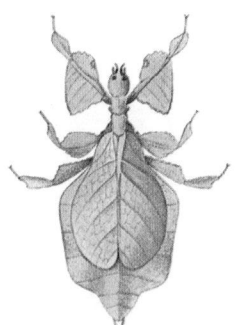

▲ **leaf insect** Masters of disguise, leaf insects such as *Phyllium crurufolium* (shown here), have legs and wings adapted to resemble leaves. In their tropical Asian habitats, predators find them difficult to spot. Some species have taken this adaptation a stage further, by laying eggs that resemble the seeds of various plants.

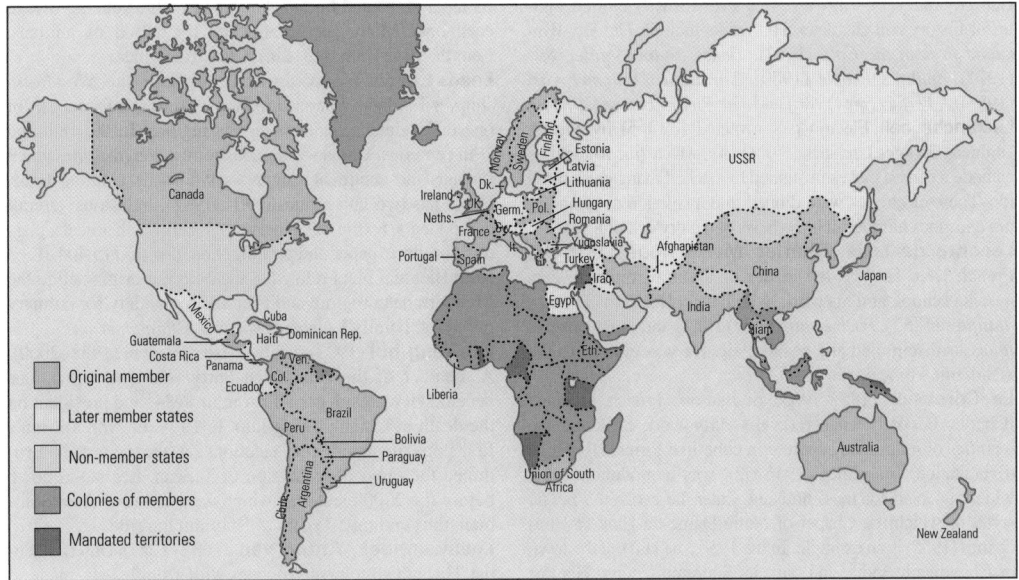

◀ **League of Nations** Set up following World War 1 to arbitrate in international disputes, the original members of the League of Nations were the 32 states that signed the Covenant and ratified it (although the USA did not ratify), and those states that joined by invitation. Other states were admitted at later dates by a two-thirds vote of the Assembly. The lack of US support weakened the league to such a degree that it became largely ineffectual as a forum for world peace.

Original member
Later member states
Non-member states
Colonies of members
Mandated territories

► **Le Corbusier** The pilgrimage Chapel of Notre-Dame-du-Haut, Ronchamp, E France, was built by Le Corbusier in 1955. The flowing, highly sculptural, concrete structure deliberately resembles a nun's headdress in both form and coloration. A combination of the southern wall of the chapel, which contains numerous stained glass windows, and structures of the northern wall, which break through the roof, suffuse the interior with light.

L

Lebanon Republic in SW Asia. *See* country feature

Lebed, Aleksander Ivanovich (1950–2002) Russian general and politician. As commander of the Tula Airborne Troops Division, he stood guard at the Supreme Soviet building during the attempted coup of August 1991. Running against YELTSIN in the 1996 presidential elections, Lebed's support was such that Yeltsin offered him a government position to win his votes. He was appointed national security adviser but dismissed later in 1996. Lebed died in a helicopter crash.

Leblanc, Nicolas (1742–1806) French chemist. In 1790, he devised a process for producing soda ash (sodium carbonate, Na_2CO_3) from salt (sodium chloride, NaCl) by treating it with sulphuric acid.

Le Brun, Charles (1619–90) French artist. He painted religious, mythological and historical subjects. He created the Galerie d'Apollon at the Louvre (1661) for Louis XIV and designed much VERSAILLES' interior, including the Hall of Mirrors (1679–84). He became director of the Académie Française and the GOBELINS tapestry factory in 1663.

Le Carré, John (1931–) English writer of espionage thrillers, b. David John Moore Cornwell. His first novel, *Call for the Dead* (1961), introduced his best-known character, George Smiley. Le Carré's stories are intricately plotted studies of history and character. His works include *The Spy Who Came in from the Cold* (1963), *Tinker, Tailor, Soldier, Spy* (1974), *Smiley's People* (1980), *The Little Drummer Girl* (1983), *A Perfect Spy* (1986) and *The Russia House* (1989).

Leclanché cell Electric cell invented (*c.*1865) by French engineer Georges Leclanché. Its ANODE was a zinc rod and its cathode a carbon plate surrounded by packed manganese dioxide. These electrodes were dipped into a solution of ammonium and zinc chlorides. It is the basis of the dry cell or BATTERY.

Leconte de Lisle, Charles Marie René (1818–94) French poet. He was the leader of the anti-romantic Parnassian school, and his work, which he collected as *Poèmes antiques* (1852), *Poèmes barbares* (1862) and *Poèmes tragiques*, is disciplined and pessimistic. He was elected to the Académie Française in 1866.

Le Corbusier (1887–1963) Swiss-born French architect (Charles Édouard Jeanneret). His early work exploited the qualities of reinforced concrete in cube-like forms. His Unité d'Habitation, Marseilles (1946–52), was a modular design widely adopted for mass housing. Later, he evolved a poetic style, of which the Chapel of Notre-Dame-du-Haut at Ronchamp (1955) is an example. In the 1950s, he laid out the town of Chandigarh, India, and built its Supreme Courts. His last major work was the Visual Arts Center at Harvard University, Cambridge, Massachusetts (1963). His book *Towards a New Architecture* (1923) is a key text of the INTERNATIONAL STYLE.

Leda In GREEK MYTHOLOGY, Queen of Sparta, the wife of Tyndareus and mother of CLYTEMNESTRA. She was also the mother of CASTOR AND POLLUX, and HELEN by ZEUS. The myth reveals that Zeus came to her in the form of a swan.

Ledbetter, Huddie (1888–1949) US composer and blues singer, better known as Leadbelly. Folklorist John A. Lomax discovered him in prison and used his songs in the book *Negro Folk Songs as Sung by Lead Belly* (1936). He is known as the composer of many classic blues songs including 'Goodnight Irene', 'The Midnight Special', and 'Rock Island Line'.

Lee, Ann (1736–84) English mystic, member of the United Society of Believers in Christ's Second Appearing, popularly called the SHAKERS. The Shaker sect was persecuted in Britain and, in 1774, Lee and eight others fled to the American colonies. In 1776, she founded a colony near Albany, New York State, and attracted many converts.

Lee, Laurie (1914–97) English writer. Lee's collections of poetry include *The Sun My Monument* (1944) and *My Many-Coated Man* (1955). He is best known for his autobiography *Cider with Rosie* (US: *The Edge of Day*, 1959), and his accounts of travels in Spain during the Spanish Civil War – *As I Walked Out One Midsummer Morning* (1969) and *A Moment of War* (1991). He also wrote short stories.

Lee, Robert E. (Edward) (1807–70) Commander of the Confederate forces in the American CIVIL WAR and military adviser to Jefferson DAVIS. In 1862, Davis appointed Lee as commander of the Army of Virginia. Lee defended Richmond and won the Second Battle of BULL RUN. Checked at Antietam (1862), he defeated the Union forces at Fredericksburg (1862) and Chancellorsville (1863). His invasion of the North ended in defeat at Gettysburg in July 1863. He was trapped by Ulysses S. GRANT and surrendered in April 1865.

Lee, Spike (Shelton Jackson) (1957–) US film director, screenwriter and actor. His first feature, the stylish comedy *She's Gotta Have It* (1986), was a box-office success. *Do the Right Thing* (1989) was a bleak meditation on urban racism in the USA. After the jazz film *Mo' Better Blues* (1990), Lee made the controversial *Jungle Fever* (1991), another piece on racial integration. Other films include *Malcolm X* (1992), *Clockers* (1996), *Summer of Sam* (1999), and *Bamboozled* (2000).

Lee, Tsung-Dao (1926–) US physicist, b. China. He and his colleague, Chen Ning YANG, showed that among the weak interactions of SUBATOMIC PARTICLES, the law of conservation of parity (that nature, in effect, makes no distinction between right- and left-handedness) does not always hold. Lee and Yang received the 1957 Nobel Prize in physics.

leech Any of numerous species of freshwater, marine and terrestrial annelids found in tropical and temperate regions. Its tapered, ringed body is equipped with a sucking disc at each end. Many species live on the blood of animals. Length: 13–51mm (0.5–2in). Class Hirudinea.

Leeds City and county district on the River Aire, West Yorkshire, N England. Founded in Roman times, it forms part of one of England's major industrial regions. In the 18th and 19th centuries, Leeds was famous for its cloth factories and it remains the centre of England's wholesale clothing trade. Leeds has two universities (1904, 1992). Industries: aircraft components, textile machinery, engineering, chemicals, plastics, furniture, paper and printing. Pop. (2001) 715,404.

leek Biennial plant related to the onion; it originated in the Mediterranean region, and is cultivated widely for culinary purposes. Family Liliaceae, species *Allium porrum*.

Lee Teng-hui (1923–) Taiwanese president (1988–2000). A member of the Nationalist Party (KUOMINTANG), Lee became vice president of Taiwan in 1984, and president on the death of Chiang Ching-kuo. In 1996, he won Taiwan's first popular presidential elections. A technocrat, Lee promoted the rapid liberalization of Taiwan. Lee stood down before the 2000 elections, which were won by Chen Shui-bian, thus ending 50 years of Kuomintang rule.

Leeuwenhoek, Anton van (1632–1723) Dutch scientist. He built simple microscopes with a single lens, made so accurately that they had better magnifying powers than the compound microscopes of his day. He investigated many microorganisms and their life histories, and described various microscopic structures, such as spermatozoa.

Leeward Islands Group of islands in the West Indies, the N section of the Lesser ANTILLES; it includes the US and British VIRGIN ISLANDS, GUADELOUPE, ANGUILLA, ANTIGUA AND BARBUDA, MONTSERRAT, ST KITTS-NEVIS, and St Martin. The islands are volcanic with a warm climate and tropical vegetation. Agriculture and tourism dominate the economy. Crops include fruits, sugar, cotton, and coffee. *See* WEST INDIES map

legal aid System by which those below a certain income can receive free or subsidized legal representation or advice.

Léger, Fernand (1881–1955) French painter. Influential in the School of Paris, he evolved a form of CUBISM called 'tubism' because of its emphasis on cylindrical forms. Examples include the series *Contrast of Forms* (1913). He directed the first non-narrative film *Ballet mécanique* (1924).

legion Basic organizational unit of the Roman army from the early Republic to the fall of the Empire in the West in the 5th century AD. During the great period of Rome's expansion, a legion was about 6,000 men strong, consisting mainly of heavy infantrymen (legionaries), with some light troops and cavalry in support. The legion was subdivided into cohorts (420 men each), maniples (120 men each) and centuries (100 men each).

legionnaire's disease Lung disease caused by infection with the bacterium *Legionella pneumophila*. It takes its name from the serious outbreak that occurred during a convention of the American Legion held in Philadelphia, USA, in 1976. The bacterium thrives in water and may be found in defective heating, ventilation and air-conditioning systems. It is inhaled in fine water droplets present in the air.

Legion of Honour (Légion d'Honneur) French award, created by Napoleon in 1802 to reward civil and military service. The highest class of award is the great cross (*grand-croix*). The most common level at which it is awarded is that of Knight of the Legion (*Chevalier de la Légion*).

legislation *See* LAW

legislature Representative assembly whose primary function is the enactment of laws. Legislatures can be either unicameral or bicameral (composed of one or two chambers). In most democracies, including Britain, the 'Lower' or more directly elected chamber is more powerful than the 'Upper' chamber filled by government appointees or hereditary members. In the USA, the SENATE is constitutionally more powerful than the HOUSE OF REPRESENTATIVES, and both Houses are elected. *See also* HOUSE OF COMMONS; HOUSE OF LORDS; PARLIAMENT

legume Member of the PEA family of flowering plants, including many trees, shrubs, vines and herbs whose roots bear nodules that contain nitrogen-fixing bacteria. The fruit is typically a pod (legume) containing a row of seeds. Important food species include the pea, runner BEAN, SOYA BEAN, LENTIL, broad bean, kidney bean, and haricot bean. *See also* NITROGEN CYCLE; NITROGEN FIXATION; ROOT NODULE

LEBANON

The Republic of Lebanon is a country on the E shores of the Mediterranean Sea. Behind the coastal plain are the rugged Lebanon Mountains (Jabal Lubnán), which rise to 3,088m [10,131ft]. Another range, the Anti-Lebanon Mountains (Al Jabal ash Sharqi), form the E border with Syria. Between the two ranges is the Bekaa (Beqaa) Valley, a fertile farming region.

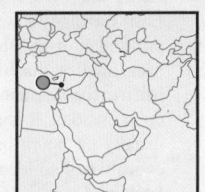

CLIMATE
The Lebanese coast has hot, dry summers and mild, wet winters. Inland, onshore winds bring heavy rain or snow to the W slopes of the mountains in winter.

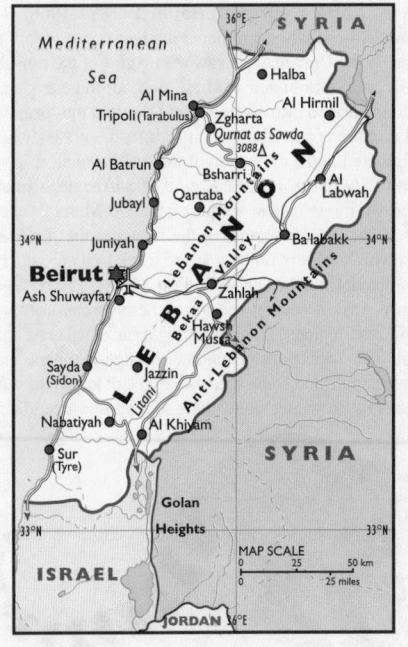

HISTORY
In *c.*3000 BC, the Canaanites founded the city of TYRE and established what became known as PHOENICIA. Invaders from *c.*800 BC included Egyptians, Hittites, Assyrians, Babylonians and Persians. Alexander the Great seized the area in 332 BC and the Romans in 64 BC. Christianity was introduced in AD 325, and in 395 the area became part of the Byzantine Empire. Muslim Arabs occupied the area in the 7th century; they converted many people to Islam, but Christian MARONITES still predominated.

European Crusaders arrived in Lebanon in about 1100, and the area became a battlefield between Christian and Muslim armies. The Muslim Mamelukes of Egypt drove the last of the Crusaders out of the area around 1300. In 1516, Lebanon was taken over by the Turkish Ottoman Empire. Turkish rule continued until World War 1, when British and French forces defeated the Ottoman Turks. France took over Lebanon's political affairs from 1923 until 1944 with Lebanon becoming independent in 1946.

POLITICS
Lebanon made rapid economic progress until the late 1950s, when periodic conflict between SUNNI and SHI'ITE Muslims, DRUZE and Christians slowed development. In March 1975, fierce civil war broke out between Christians, Muslims and Druzes. Lebanon sank into a state of chaos. Assassinations, bombings and kidnappings became routine as numerous factions fought for control. The situation was complicated by interventions by Palestinian refugees, the Syrian army, Western and then UN forces as the country became a patchwork of occupied zones and 'no-go areas'.

Although not directly involved, Lebanon was destabilized by the ARAB-ISRAELI WAR of 1967 and by the exile of the PLO leadership to Beirut

AREA 10,400sq km [4,015sq mi]
POPULATION 3,926,000
CAPITAL (POPULATION) Beirut (2,070,000)
GOVERNMENT Multiparty republic
ETHNIC GROUPS Arab 95%, Armenian 4%, others
LANGUAGES Arabic (official), French, English
RELIGIONS Islam 70%, Christianity 30%
CURRENCY Lebanese pound = 100 piastres

in 1970. By 1990 the Syrian army had crushed Christian rebels against the Lebanese government, but peace proved elusive. In 1996, Israeli forces launched a sustained attack on the pro-Iranian HIZBOLLAH group's positions in southern Lebanon, with heavy civilian casualties. Fighting continued in southern Lebanon in 1997 and again flared up in early 2000. In 2005 former prime minister Rafik Hariri, a critic of Syria's presence in Lebanon, was assassinated. Following demonstrations, Syria withdrew its forces in April and ended its occupation. Further assassinations of anti-Syrian politicians followed in 2006–7.

In 2006 Hizbollah launched rocket attacks on Israel from positions in Lebanon. Israeli counter-attacks caused extensive civilian casualties and damage to Lebanon's infrastructure.

In 2007 parliament failed to agree a successor to Emile Lahoud, the retiring President. A constitutional crisis resulted as Lahoud, the army, and the Prime Minister disputed authority. The resulting deadlock lasted into 2008.

ECONOMY
Civil war almost destroyed valuable trade and financial services which, together with tourism, had been Lebanon's chief source of income. Manufacturing was also hit. Manufactures include chemicals, electrical goods, processed food and textiles. Fruits, vegetables and sugar beet are farmed.

L

▶ **Leigh** Although she epitomized (in looks and manner) an English lady, the English actress Vivien Leigh is, in fact, most remembered for her two Academy Award winning roles as American, heroines, Scarlet O'Hara in *Gone with the Wind*, and Blanche du Bois in *A Streetcar Named Desire*. Suffering from tuberculosis for much of her career, Leigh was often exhausted while working on set. Born in Darjeeling, India, she attended the same convent school in England as Maureen O'Sullivan, who played Jane in the *Tarzan* films.

▶ **lemur** The ring-tailed lemur (*Lemur catta*), like the 16 or so other species of lemur, is found only in Madagascar and small neighbouring islands. The various species range in size, the smallest being no larger than a rat, while the largest reaches a similar size to a domestic cat. All species are arboreal and omnivorous, feeding on fruit, insects, and small mammals.

Lehár, Franz (1870–1948) Austrian composer, b. Hungary. Lehar wrote the first of his more than 30 operettas, *Kukuschka*, in 1896. Perhaps his most popular is *The Merry Widow* (1905).

Le Havre City and seaport in N France, at the mouth of the River Seine, on the English Channel. Founded in the 16th century on the site of a fishing village, it is France's second-largest port. It was briefly the base of the Belgian government in World War 2. The city was rebuilt after being almost completely destroyed during the war. It is the principal export point for Paris and a transatlantic and cross-Channel passenger port. Industries: chemicals, fertilizers, timber, food processing, oil-refining, shipbuilding. Pop. (1999) 193,259.

Lehmann, Lotte (1888–1976) US soprano, b. Germany. She was the most illustrious singer of her time. She sang with the Vienna State Opera (1914–38) and the Metropolitan Opera Company, New York, from 1934 until her retirement in 1961.

Leibniz, Gottfried Wilhelm (1646–1716) German philosopher and mathematician. Leibniz made many practical inventions, including a calculating machine (1671). His discovery of differential and integral CALCULUS was made independently of Sir Isaac NEWTON. Leibniz created a rationalist form of metaphysics, according to which the universe comprises a hierarchy of constituents (monads) with God at the top asserting a divine plan. This belief led him to argue that evil is divinely motivated. His major works include *New Essays Concerning Human Understanding* (1765) and *Monadology* (1898).

Leicester City in central England; county town of Leicestershire. It was founded in the 1st century AD as a Roman town (Ratae Coritanorum). Leicester was conquered by the Danes in the 9th century. The city is famous for the manufacture of hosiery and footwear. Pop. (2001) 279,923.

Leicester, Robert Dudley, Earl of (1532–88) English courtier. He was a favourite of Queen ELIZABETH I, who ennobled him and gave him Kenilworth Castle, Warwickshire, England. Leicester unsuccessfully led (1585–87) an English force in the Revolt of the Netherlands against Spain.

Leicestershire County in E central England; the county town is LEICESTER. The area is drained chiefly by the Soar and Wreak rivers. The uplands of the E are devoted to farming; the w has more industry. Wheat, barley, sheep and dairy cattle are important, and the region is famous for its hosiery, Stilton cheese and Melton Mowbray meat pies. Area: 2,553sq km (986sq mi). Pop. (2001) 609,579.

Leiden (Leyden) City on the River Oude Rijn, w Netherlands, 15km (9mi) NE of The Hague. Leiden received its city charter in the 13th century, and soon developed a flourishing textile industry. The Pilgrim Fathers lived in the city before setting out

for America in 1620. Industries: textiles, printing and publishing, food processing, metalworking. Pop. (2001) 117,479.

Leif Ericsson (c.970–1020) Norse adventurer and explorer. Son of ERIC THE RED, he sailed from Greenland in 1003 to investigate land in the west. He visited Helluland (probably Baffin Island), Markland (Labrador) and Vinland.

Leigh, Mike (1943–) English film director, playwright, and screenwriter. His debut feature, *Bleak Moments* (1971), established his reputation. After a long break, Leigh made the acclaimed *High Hopes* (1988), and the similarly satirical *Life is Sweet* (1990). *Naked* (1993) and *Secrets and Lies* (1995) gained him an international recognition. He won the Venice Film Festival's Leone d'Oro for *Vera Drake* (2004).

Leigh, Vivien (1913–67) British film and stage actress, b. India. She received an Academy Award for her performance as Scarlett O'Hara in *Gone With The Wind* (1939). She also received an Oscar for her moving portrayal of Blanche du Bois in *A Streetcar Named Desire* (1951). She was married to fellow actor Laurence OLIVIER from 1937 to 1960.

Leinster Province in E Republic of Ireland, comprising the counties of Carlow, Dublin, Kildare, Kilkenny, Laoighis, Longford, Louth, Meath, Offaly, Westmeath, Wexford and Wicklow. It is the most populous of Ireland's four provinces, and includes the most fertile farmland. The major city is DUBLIN. Area: 19,635sq km (7,581sq mi). Pop. (2002) 2,105,449.

Leipzig City in E central Germany, at the confluence of the Pleisse, White Elster and Parthe rivers. It was founded as a Slavic settlement in the 10th century. In 1813, it was the scene of the Battle of the Nations. It was home to J.S. Bach for 27 years, and is the birthplace of Richard Wagner. It was East Germany's second-biggest city (after Berlin). The printing industry (founded in 1480) is still important. Industries: textiles, machinery, chemicals. Pop. (1999) 490,000.

leitmotiv German word for a guiding theme in musical compositions. It is a theme that recurs throughout a work, usually an opera or a piece of programme music, and is evocative of an idea or a character on each occasion.

Leitrim County in Connacht province, N Republic of Ireland, narrowly bounded on the NW by Donegal Bay; the capital is Carrick-on-Shannon. Hilly in the N, undulating in the s, it is drained by the River Shannon and its tributaries. Although farming is the main occupation, the soil is not highly productive. Area: 1,525sq km (589sq mi). Pop. (2002) 25,815.

Lely, Sir Peter van der Faes (1618–80) Dutch portrait painter, active in England. Principal painter to CHARLES II, Lely established the tradition of the society portrait. His best-known paintings include two series, *The Windsor Beauties* (1660s) and the famous *Admirals* (1666–67).

Lemaître, Abbé Georges Édouard (1894–1966) Belgian astrophysicist who formulated the BIG BANG theory for the origin of the Universe. He saw the origins of the universe as analogous to a radioactive ATOM, with all the energy and matter concentrated into a kernel that he called the 'primeval atom'. Lemaître argued that an EXPANDING UNIVERSE would have originated in the explosion of the 'primeval atom'.

Le Mans City in NW France; capital of Sarthe department. It is world-famous as the venue of the Le Mans 24–hour race for sports cars. A feature of the race was the 'Le Mans start', in which drivers ran across the track to their cars, but this was discontinued after 1969. Pop. (1999) 150,605.

lemming Any of several species of herbivorous RODENTS, native to Arctic regions. They have brown fur, small ears, and a short tail. They occasionally migrate in large numbers when numbers are high, and some species have been known to suffer great losses by drowning while doing so. Family Cricetidae.

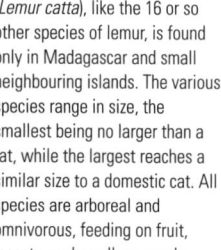

lemon Evergreen tree and its familiar, sour, yellow citrus fruit. Grown primarily in the USA and in subtropical regions, it is rarely eaten raw, but is used in cooking and in drinks. Height of tree: to 6m (20ft). Family Rutaceae; species *Citrus limon*.

lemur Any of several small primitive, mainly arboreal (tree-dwelling) and nocturnal, herbivorous PRIMATES that live in Madagascar. It resembles a squirrel, but has grasping monkey-like hands with which it climbs easily. Lemurs have changed little in 50 million years, closely resembling the ancestors of man and other primates. Family Lemuridae.

Lena River in E central Russia. Rising in the Baikal Mountains, it flows N through the central Siberian uplands and empties through a wide delta into the Laptev Sea (part of the Arctic Ocean). Yakutsk is the only major town on its course. Although navigable for 3,437km (2,135mi) of its 4,400km (2,730mi) route, it is frozen from early autumn to late spring.

Lenard, Philipp Eduard Anton (1862–1947) German physicist, b. Hungary. Lenard received the 1905 Nobel Prize in physics for his studies of cathode rays. His work was important in the development of ELECTRONICS and NUCLEAR PHYSICS. He researched ULTRAVIOLET RADIATION and PHOSPHORESCENCE.

lend-lease US programme of assistance during World War 2. The Lend-Lease Act was passed in March 1941, before the USA became a combatant. It empowered President Franklin D. ROOSEVELT to transfer military equipment to other countries in the US national interest. The first beneficiaries were Britain and China. The programme was later extended to other allies, notably the Soviet Union.

Lenin, Vladimir Ilyich (1870–1924) Russian revolutionary. He evolved a revolutionary doctrine, based on MARXISM, in which he emphasized the need for a vanguard party to lead the revolution. In 1900, Lenin went abroad and founded what became the BOLSHEVIKS (1903). After the first part of the RUSSIAN REVOLUTION of 1917, he returned to Russia. He denounced the liberal republican government of KERENSKY and demanded armed revolt. After the Bolshevik revolution (November 1917), he became leader of the first Soviet government. He withdrew Russia from World War 1, and reorganized government and economy. He founded the third COMMUNIST INTERNATIONAL in 1919. In 1921, the New Economic Policy (NEP) marked a return to a mixed economy. In 1922, he headed the newly formed SOVIET UNION. In 1923 a new constitution established the supremacy of the COMMUNIST PARTY OF THE SOVIET UNION (CPSU). Lenin's authority was

LENS

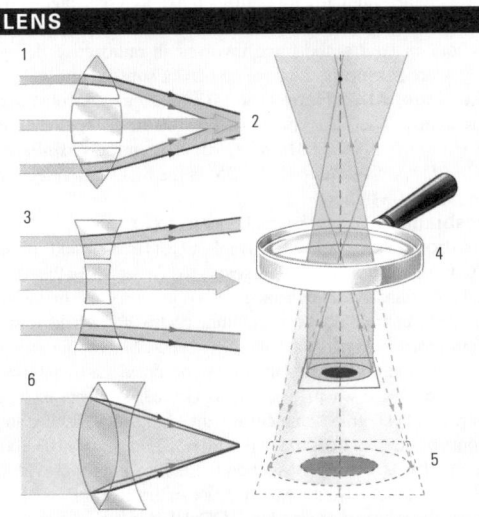

A convex lens (1) focuses light on a single point (2) by diffracting the beams of light towards each other. A concave lens (3) diffracts parallel rays of light, making them diverge. A magnifying glass (4) is a convex lens. The glass makes the rays of light diverge, making it appear that they come from a larger image (5) than is the actual case. Cameras use a combination of convex and concave lenses (6) to focus light on the film without separation of the colours of the spectrum.

unchallenged until he was crippled by a stroke in 1922. After his death, a struggle ensued between Trotsky and STALIN.

Leningrad Former name for ST PETERSBURG

Lennon, John (1940–80) English singer and songwriter, a member of The BEATLES. Lennon co-wrote the vast majority of The Beatles' songs with Paul McCARTNEY, and appeared in the band's films and in *How I Won the War* (1967). He published *In His Own Write* (1964) and *A Spaniard in the Works* (1965). A major figure in the peace movement, he married Yoko Ono (1933–) in 1969. His solo albums include *Imagine* (1971) and *Double Fantasy* (1980). On December 8, 1980, Lennon was shot dead by Mark Chapman in New York City.

Le Nôtre, André (1613–1700) French landscape gardener. His grandiose, architectural style established the French garden as the leading style in contemporary Europe. Le Nôtre became royal gardener in 1637 and, from the 1650s, created formal gardens for some of France's grandest châteaux and palaces, such as VERSAILLES, Chantilly, and Les Tuileries in Paris.

lens Piece of transparent glass, plastic, quartz, or organic matter, bounded by two surfaces (usually both spherical) that changes the direction of a light beam by REFRACTION (bending the wave). A convex lens bends light rays towards the lens axis. A concave lens bends rays away from the axis. The optical IMAGE may be right side-up or inverted, real or virtual, and magnified or reduced in size.

Lent Period in the Christian year that precedes EASTER. In the Western Churches it begins on Ash Wednesday and lasts 40 days (excluding Sundays); in the Eastern Church it lasts 80 days (excluding Saturdays and Sundays). Lent is a time of fasting, abstinence and penitence in preparation for the remembrance of the crucifixion and resurrection of Christ.

lentil Annual plant of the PEA family that grows in the Mediterranean region, SW Asia and N Africa. It has feather-like leaves and is cultivated for its nutritious seeds. Height: to 51cm (20in). Family Fabaceae/Leguminosae; species *Lens culinaris*.

Lenya, Lotte (*c*.1898–1981) Austrian singer and actress. Lenya became famous in two notable BRECHT plays with musical scores by her husband Kurt WEILL, namely *The Threepenny Opera* (1928) and *The Rise and Fall of the City of Mahagonny* (1930). She emigrated to the USA in 1935.

Leo I, Saint (390–461) (Leo the Great) Pope (440–61). He established important points of doctrine, including the dual nature of Christ, which he propounded at the Council of CHALCEDON (449). By personal meetings, he saved Rome from Attila (452) and the Vandal leader Gaiseric (455).

Leo III, Saint (*c*.750–816) Pope (795–816). With the help of CHARLEMAGNE, Leo imposed his rule on Rome, and

▲ **leopard** Leopards or panthers (*Panthera pardus*) live in sub-Saharan Africa and southern Asia. They are smaller and slimmer than their close relative, the jaguar. Powerful, agile hunters, leopards can jump up to 6.7m (22ft) long and 3m (10ft) high. They feed on any animal they can overpower. If they cannot consume their prey at one sitting, they drag the carcass into a tree out of reach of scavengers. The solid-coloured leopard or 'black panther' (left) is often more aggressive because spotted mothers tend to dislike solid-colour cubs, often driving them away prematurely.

L

crowned Charlemagne as Emperor on Christmas Day, 800. This historically important act strengthened papal authority in Rome, and led to recognition of the Pope and Emperor as religious and secular leaders of Western Christendom.

Leo X (1475–1521) Pope (1513–21), b. Giovanni de' Medici, son of Lorenzo de' MEDICI. He continued the artistic schemes of his predecessor, Julius II, and presided over the Fifth LATERAN COUNCIL. Leo's excommunication of LUTHER in 1521 marks the beginning of the REFORMATION.

León City in w Nicaragua, its second-largest city. It was founded near Lake Managua in 1524. In 1610, a severe earthquake forced the city's reconstruction on its present site. It served as the nation's capital until 1858. In 1821, when Nicaragua gained independence from Spain, a bitter rivalry between León and Granada led to civil war. León was the scene of bitter fighting between SANDINISTA guerrillas and government forces in the late 1970s. Industries: food processing, leather goods, cigars, cotton. Pop. (1995) 123,865.

León City in NW Spain; capital of León province. A military camp in Roman times, it was occupied by the Moors in the 8th century. Recaptured in 882 by Alfonso III of Asturias, it was capital of the medieval kingdom of Asturias and León until 1230. Industries: leather, cotton, textiles, iron, glass, pottery, tourism. Pop. (2001) 130,916.

Leonardo da Vinci (1452–1519) Florentine painter, sculptor, architect, engineer and scientist. By the 1470s, he developed his characteristic style of painting figures who seem rapt in sweet melancholy. In *c*.1482 Leonardo moved to Milan where he worked mainly for Ludovico SFORZA. While in Milan, he worked on an altarpiece, *The Virgin of the Rocks* (1483–85). Leonardo painted the *Last Supper* (*c*.1498) on the walls of Santa Maria delle Grazie, Milan, using a new mural technique that proved unstable. When the French invaded Milan in 1499, he left for Florence. From 1500–06, he created his finest easel paintings, including the enigmatic *Mona Lisa* (*c*.1504–05). His 19 notebooks contain detailed scientific drawings, including plans for a helicopter-like flying machine, a tank, and a submarine.

Leoncavallo, Ruggiero (1858–1919) Italian composer, mainly of operas. He travelled all over Europe working as an accompanist and composer of music-hall songs. Of his operas, *I Pagliacci* (1892) alone has withstood the test of time.

Leone, Sergio (1921–89) Italian film director, creator of the 'spaghetti western'. The "Man With No Name" trilogy of *A Fistful of Dollars* (1964), *For a Few Dollars More* (1965), and *The Good The Bad and The Ugly* (1966) revived Clint EASTWOOD's career. The epics *Once Upon a Time in the West* (1968) and *Once Upon a Time in America* (1984) were commercially unsuccessful but later reappraised as his masterworks.

leopard (panther) Solitary, big CAT found throughout Africa and S Asia, sometimes called a panther. The coat may be yellow and white with dark spots, or almost completely black. A good climber and swimmer, it feeds on birds, monkeys, antelopes, and cattle. Length: to 2.5m (8ft) including the tail; weight: to 90kg (200lb). Family Felidae; species *Panthera pardus*.

Leopold I (1640–1705) Holy Roman Emperor (1658–1705). Throughout his long reign, he was compelled to

defend the extensive HABSBURG dominions against foreign aggression. Leopold joined the European defensive alliances against LOUIS XIV of France in 1686, 1689 and 1701, but died before the end of the War of the SPANISH SUCCESSION.

Leopold I (1790–1865) First King of independent Belgium (1831–65). Son of the Duke of Saxe-Coburg-Saalfield, he became a British subject after marrying the daughter of the future King George IV (1816). He refused the throne of Greece in 1830, but accepted that of Belgium after it declared its independence from the Netherlands. He was an important influence on the young Queen VICTORIA, his niece, and was largely responsible for her marriage to Prince Albert.

Leopold II (1835–1909) King of Belgium (1865–1909). He initiated colonial expansion and sponsored the expedition (1879–84) of Henry STANLEY to the Congo. In 1885, he established the Congo Free State, under his own personal rule. Following Roger CASEMENT's reports of appalling exploitation, he was forced to cede the Congo to the Belgian state in 1908.

Leopold III (1901–83) King of Belgium (1934–51). When the Germans invaded Belgium (1940) during World War 2, he declined to accompany the government into exile and surrendered. He remained in Belgium during the war, until removed to Germany in 1944. On his return, he encountered such fierce opposition that he abdicated in favour of his son, Baudouin.

Lepanto, Battle of (October 7, 1571) Naval engagement in the Gulf of Patras, off Lepanto, Greece, between Christian and Ottoman fleets. The last great battle between war galleys, it was the first major victory of the Christians over the Turks.

lepidoptera Order of insects which includes MOTHS and butterflies found in every continent except Antarctica. Wingspan: 4–300mm (0.16–12in). *See also* BUTTERFLY

leprosy (Hansen's disease) Chronic, progressive condition affecting the skin and nerves, caused by infection with the microorganism *Mycobacterium leprae*. There are two main forms. **Lepromatous** leprosy is a contagious form in which raised nodules appear on the skin and there is thickening of the skin and peripheral nerves. In **tuberculoid** leprosy, there is loss of sensation in parts of the skin, sometimes with loss of pigmentation and hair. Now confined almost entirely to the tropics, leprosy can be treated with a combination of drugs, but the nerve damage is irreversible.

lepton One of a class of ELEMENTARY PARTICLES. There are 12 types, including the ELECTRON and electron-NEUTRINO, muon and muon-neutrino, tau and tau-neutrino, together with their antiparticles (anti-leptons). Leptons interact by electromagnetic interaction and are governed by the WEAK NUCLEAR FORCE, the force involved in radioactive decay. They are FERMIONS and have no QUARK substructure.

Le Sage, Alain René (1668–1747) French novelist and dramatist. The best known of his 100 or so comedies is *Crispin, Rival of his Master* (1707). His novel *Histoire de Gil Blas de Santillane* (1715–35) is the first masterpiece of PICARESQUE fiction.

lesbianism Term for female HOMOSEXUALITY

Lesbos (Lesvos or Mylini) Third-largest Greek island, 10km (6mi) off the NW coast of Turkey, in the Aegean Sea; the capital is Mitilíni. Aeolians settled Lesbos in *c*.1000 BC. In the 7th and 6th centuries BC it was a cultural centre. It was held at various times by Persia, the Greek city-states, Macedonia, Rome and Byzantium. The Ottoman Turks occupied the island from 1462 to 1913, when it passed to Greece. Products include olives, wheat, grapes and citrus fruits. Industries: fishing and tourism. Area: *c*.1,630sq km (630sq mi). Pop. (2001) 103,800.

Lesotho (formerly Basutoland) Enclave kingdom within the Republic of South Africa. *See* country feature.

less-developed countries (LDCs) Those nations (primarily in Africa, Asia, and Latin America) that have little or no industrial base. Characteristically, they have high rates of population growth, high infant mortality, short life expectancy, low levels of literacy, and poor distribution of wealth. Since the late 1980s, some countries, especially in Asia and Latin America, have experienced rapid economic development, resulting in greater differences between the less developed countries.

Lesseps, Ferdinand Marie, Vicomte de (1805–94) French diplomat and engineer. He conceived the idea of a

LESOTHO

The Kingdom of Lesotho is a landlocked country, surrounded by South Africa on all sides. The scenic Drakensberg Range covers most of the country and forms Lesotho's NE border with KwaZulu-Natal. It includes Lesotho's highest peak, Thabana Ntlenyana, at 3,482m [11,424ft].

Most people live in the w lowlands, site of Maseru, or in the s valley of the River Orange, which rises in NE Lesotho and flows through South Africa to the Atlantic Ocean. Grassland covers much of Lesotho. The King holds all land in Lesotho in trust for the SOTHO nation.

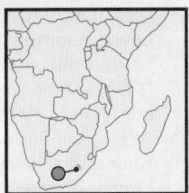

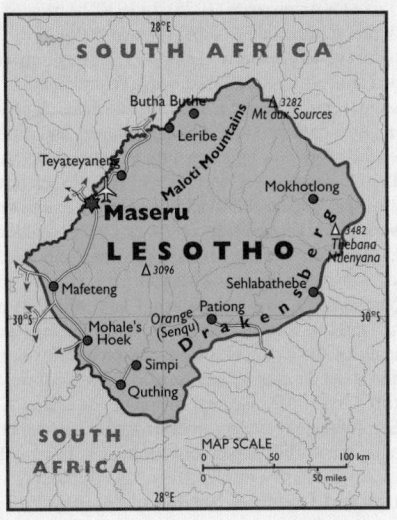

CLIMATE
The climate is greatly affected by altitude, with 66% of the country lying above 1,500m [4,921ft]. Maseru has warm summers, but the temperatures fall below freezing in the winter and the mountains are colder. Rainfall varies, averaging around 700mm [28in].

HISTORY
The Basotho nation was founded in the 1820s by King Moshoeshoe I, who united various groups fleeing from tribal wars in southern Africa. Moshoeshoe I was forced to yield to the British, and Britain made the area a protectorate in 1868. In 1871 it became part of the British Cape Colony in South Africa, but was reconstituted in 1884 as the British protectorate of Basutoland. Whites were not allowed to own land.

POLITICS
In 1966 Sotho opposition to incorporation into the Union of South Africa saw the creation of the independent Kingdom of Lesotho, with Moshoeshoe II, great-grandson of Moshoeshoe I, as its king. In 1970 Leabua Jonathan suspended the constitution and banned opposition parties. Civil conflict between the government and Basuto Congress Party (BCP) forces characterized the next 16 years. In 1986, a military coup led to the reinstatement of Moshoeshoe II. In 1990, he was deposed and replaced by his son, Letsie III, as monarch. The BCP won the 1992 multiparty elections, and the military council dissolved. In 1994 Letsie III attempted to overthrow the government. Moshoeshoe II returned to the throne in

AREA 0,355sq km [11,720sq mi]
POPULATION 2,125,000
CAPITAL (POPULATION) Maseru (180,000)
GOVERNMENT Constitutional monarchy
ETHNIC GROUPS Sotho 99%
LANGUAGES Sotho and English (both official)
RELIGIONS Christianity 80%, traditional beliefs 20%
CURRENCY Loti = 100 lisente

1995 but died in a car crash in 1996. Letsie III again became king. In 1997, a majority of BCP politicians formed a new governing party, the Lesotho Congress for Democracy (LCD).

In 1998, following an election in which the ruling party won 79 out of the 80 seats, the army led a revolt. South African forces intervened to maintain order, and in 2002 elections took place under a new democratic constitution. In 2004 the government declared a state of emergency following three years of drought. In 2006 a new flag was adopted.

ECONOMY
Lesotho is a 'low-income' developing country. It lacks natural resources apart from diamonds. Agriculture employs two-thirds of the workforce, but most farmers live at subsistence level. Livestock farming is important. Major crops include maize and sorghum. Tourism is developing. Another source of income consists of remittances sent home by Basotho working abroad, mostly in South Africa's mining industry.

L

---

canal through the isthmus of Suez, linking the Red Sea with the Mediterranean. He formed the SUEZ CANAL Company, securing finance from the French government. Digging began in 1859, and the canal opened in November 1869. His scheme to construct the PANAMA CANAL without using a system of locks began in 1879, but was abandoned seven years later with the failure of de Lesseps' company.

Lesser Antilles *See* ANTILLES

Lessing, Doris May (1919–) British novelist, b. Iran, who was brought up in Rhodesia. Her first novel, *The Grass Is Singing* (1950), is a story of racial hatred. Her *Children of Violence* quintet (1952–69) explores the social position of women; *The Golden Notebook* (1962) is a key feminist text. Lessing also wrote the science-fiction quintet *Canopus in Argos* (1979–83), which includes *The Making of the Representative for Planet 8* (1982). Other works include *The Good Terrorist* (1985).

Lessing, Gotthold Ephraim (1729–81) German philosopher, writer, and critic. He revealed his commitment to the German enlightenment in the verse play *Nathan the Wise* (1779). His other plays include *Miss Sara Sampson* (1755) and *Emilia Galotti* (1772), and the critical work *Laocoon* (1776).

Lethe In Greek mythology, the river of forgetfulness in HADES. All who drank from it lost their memories of past lives.

lettuce Edible annual plant that is widely cultivated for use in salads. Most varieties of *Lactuca sativa* are cool-weather crops. The large leaves form a compact head or loose rosette.

leucite Grey or white feldspar mineral, a potassium aluminium silicate, $KAl(SiO_3)_2$. Unstable at high pressures, it can be found in potassium-rich lava flows and volcanic plugs. Hardness 5.5–6; r.d. 2.5.

leucocyte (white BLOOD cell) Colourless structure containing a NUCLEUS and CYTOPLASM. There are two types of leucocytes – LYMPHOCYTES and PHAGOCYTES. Normal blood contains 5,000–10,000 leucocytes per cu mm. Excessive numbers of leucocytes are seen in such diseases as LEUKAEMIA. *See also* ANTIBODY; IMMUNE SYSTEM

leukaemia Any of a group of cancers in which the bone marrow and other blood-forming tissues produce abnormal numbers of immature or defective LEUCOCYTES. This overproduction suppresses output of normal blood cells and PLATELETS, leaving the person vulnerable to infection, anaemia and bleeding. **Acute lymphoblastic leukaemia** (ALL) is predominantly a disease of childhood; **acute myelogenous leukaemia** (AML) is mainly seen in older adults. Both forms are potentially curable.

Le Vau, Louis (1612–70) French architect. Inspired by contemporary Italian Baroque buildings, Le Vau evolved a classic 17th-century French style, seen most spectacularly in his designs for the Palace of VERSAILLES (1669–85).

levée Natural embankment formed alongside a river by the deposition of silt when the river is in flood. Levées can help to prevent flooding, and are sometimes built up and strengthened

◀ **Lessing** British novelist Doris Lessing drew heavily on her childhood experiences in Rhodesia (now Zimbabwe) to create her best-known work, *The Grass is Singing* (1950). The novel's exploration of racial and sexual themes made her unpopular with the white Rhodesian government. In 2007, she was awarded the Nobel Prize for Literature.

artificially. On some large rivers, such as the Mississippi, they may reach heights of more than 15m (50ft).

Levellers (1645–49) Members of a radical movement in England in the COMMONWEALTH period (*c.*1645–57). They wanted sweeping parliamentary reform, religious toleration, and a fairer, more egalitarian society. Their leaders, including John LILBURNE, presented a constitution to Oliver CROMWELL in 1647. When their demands were not met, several mutinies broke out in the army, resulting in their suppression. *See also* DIGGERS

lever Simple machine used to multiply the force applied to an object, usually to raise a heavy load. A lever consists of a rod and a point (fulcrum) about which the rod pivots. In a crowbar, for example, the applied force (effort) and the object to be moved (load) are on opposite sides of the fulcrum, with the point of application of the effort farther from the fulcrum.

Leverrier, Urbain Jean Joseph (1811–77) French astronomer. In 1845 he wrongly predicted that a planet (which he named Vulcan) lay within the orbit of Mercury. More successful was his prediction, independently of John Couch ADAMS, that an unknown planet (Neptune) was responsible for discrepancies between the calculated and observed orbital motion of Uranus.

Levi, Primo (1919–87) Italian writer. A Jew, Levi joined a guerrilla movement in World War 2. Captured and sent to Auschwitz, he survived but was haunted by the HOLOCAUST. Levi's books, such as *If This is a Man* (1947), *The Truce* (1963) and *The Periodic Table* (1984), are attempts to deal with his experiences. He committed suicide.

Leviathan In the Old Testament, an immense serpent living in the depths of the ocean. It embodied everything evil.

Levine, James (1943–) US pianist and conductor. Levine was principal conductor (1973) and then musical director (1975) of the New York METROPOLITAN OPERA, becoming its first artistic director in 1986. A leading interpreter of Wagner, he made his debut at Bayreuth in 1982.

Lévi-Strauss, Claude (1908–) French anthropologist. In *The Elementary Structures of Kinship* (1949) and *Structural Anthropology* (1958), Lévi-Strauss outlined the science of STRUCTURALISM. In 1959, he became professor of anthropology at the College of France. In 1973, he was elected to the Académie Française.

Levites Clan of religious officials in ancient Israel. It is possible that they once constituted one of the 12 tribes of Israel mentioned in the Old Testament, descended in this case from Levi, the third son of JACOB by his first wife Leah. After the building of the Temple of Jerusalem, Levites performed the lesser religious services. By the time of Jesus Christ, the Levites ran the entire Temple organization except the actual priesthood.

Leviticus Third book of the PENTATEUCH or TORAH. It is primarily a manual for the instruction of priests.

Lewes, George Henry (1817–78) English journalist and critic. He wrote dramatic criticism as well as philosophical works, including *A Biographical History of Philosophy* (1845) and the hugely successful *The Life and Works of Goethe* (1855). Separated from his wife, he lived with George ELIOT, whose work he encouraged and influenced.

Lewis, (Frederick) Carl (Carlton) (1961–) US track and field athlete. In a glittering career, Lewis won nine Olympic gold medals: 100m, 200m, 4 × 100m relay, and long jump (1984, Los Angeles), equalling Jesse OWENS' feat; 100m and long jump (Seoul, 1988); long jump and 4 × 100m relay (Barcelona, 1992); and long jump (Atlanta, 1996). Lewis set 100m world records at the Seoul Olympics (9.97sec) and the 1991 World Championships (9.86sec).

Lewis, C.S. (Clive Staples) (1898–1963) British critic and writer, b Northern Ireland. His scholarly works include *The Allegory of Love* (1936) and *The Discarded Image* (1964). He is best known, however, for the books on religious and moral themes written after his conversion to Christianity, particularly *The Screwtape Letters* (1942) and his autobiography *Surprised by Joy* (1955). He wrote a number of highly acclaimed children's books, including the seven 'Narnia' stories, beginning with *The Lion, the Witch and the Wardrobe* (1950).

Lewis, John Llewellyn (1880–1969) US labour leader. Lewis served as president (1920–60) of the United Mine Workers of America (UMW). After splitting with the American Federation of Labor (AFL) over the unionization of mass-production industries, he formed the Congress of Industrial Organizations (CIO) and was its president (1935–40).

Lewis, Lennox (1966–) British boxer. Raised in Canada, Lewis returned to Britain and later won the British title (1991) and the World Boxing Council (WBC) heavyweight title (1992, 1997) and the World Boxing Association (WBA) and International Boxing Federation (IBF) (1999). After several defences of his title, he retired in 2004.

Lewis, Meriwether (1774–1809) US explorer. An army officer, he was secretary to Thomas Jefferson, who chose him to lead the LEWIS AND CLARK EXPEDITION (1804). In 1808, he was appointed governor of Louisiana Territory.

Lewis, (Harry) Sinclair (1885–1951) US writer. Lewis' debut novel *Main Street* (1920) introduced his central theme, the hypocrisy and parochialism of small town, Midwestern society. *Babbitt* (1922), regarded as his greatest work, is the story of a businessman forced to conform. Lewis refused the Pulitzer Prize for *Arrowsmith* (1925). In 1930, he became the first US writer to receive the Nobel Prize in literature.

Lewis, (Percy) Wyndham (1884–1957) British novelist, painter, and critic, b. Canada. Lewis was a central figure in the VORTICISM movement; he and Ezra POUND founded its periodical *Blast*. Often criticized for his savage imagery and extremist politics, his work was influenced by FUTURISM and NIETZSCHE. Lewis' debut novel was *Tarr* (1918). Other novels include *The Apes of God* (1930) and *The Human Age* trilogy.

Lewis and Clark Expedition (1804–06) US expedition to seek a route by water from the Mississippi to the Pacific Ocean. Instigated by President Thomas JEFFERSON, it was led by army officers Meriwether LEWIS and William Clark, with the assistance of a Shoshone woman, Sacajawea. It reached the Pacific at the mouth of the Columbia River and produced valuable information about the country and peoples of the Northwest.

Lexington City in the bluegrass region of NE central Kentucky, USA. A famous breeding ground for thoroughbred horses, it also has the world's largest tobacco market. Other industries: electrical machinery, distilling. Pop. (2000) 260,512.

Lexington and Concord, battles of (April 1775) First engagements of the AMERICAN REVOLUTION. MINUTEMEN at Lexington Green intercepted British troops marching from Boston to Concord, Massachusetts. The British killed several minutemen and advanced to Concord, where they destroyed some military supplies. On their return to Boston, the British fought several skirmishes and suffered nearly 300 casualties.

Lhasa Capital of Tibet (Xizang Zizhiqu) Autonomous region, sw China, on a tributary of the Brahmaputra, at 3,600m (11,800ft) in the N Himalayas. An ancient religious centre, the Chinese occupied the city in 1951. After the Tibetan revolt against the occupation (1959–60), the Chinese closed many of Lhasa's temples and monasteries. The 17th-century Potala Palace was the home of the DALAI LAMA. Today, the city is an important trading centre, also manufacturing chemicals and processing gold and copper. Pop. (1999 est.) 121,568.

liana Any ground-rooting woody vine that twines and creeps extensively over other plants for support; it is common in tropical forests. Some species may reach a diameter of 60cm (24in) and a length of 100m (330ft).

Liaoning Coastal province in NE China, bordering North Korea; the capital is Shenyang. Japan conquered the Liaotung peninsula during the RUSSO-JAPANESE WAR (1904–05) and developed the province's industries and railroads. It later formed part of the Japanese puppet state of MANCHUKUO (1932–45). After World War 2, it fell under the joint control of Russia and China. A Chinese province since 1955. it is the chief site of China's heavy industry. The province has rich coal and iron ore reserves, and supplies 20% of China's electrical power. It includes the cities of Anshan, Fushun, and Dalian (China's major port). The principal river is the Liao. Area: 151,000sq km (58,300sq mi). Pop. (2000) 42,380,000.

Libby, Willard Frank (1908–80) US chemist. From 1941 to 1945, he worked on the separation of isotopes for the atomic bomb. In 1960, Libby received the 1960 Nobel Prize in chemistry for his development of CARBON DATING.

libel Permanent, false statement to a third person containing an untrue imputation against the reputation of another. Publications of any defamatory matter in permanent form (such as an article, picture, or broadcast statement) are treated as libel. Although usually a civil offence, libel may be considered criminal.

Liberal Democrats (LD) (officially Social and Liberal Democrats) British political party formed in March 1988 by the merger of the LIBERAL PARTY and the SOCIAL DEMOCRATIC PARTY (SDP). Its first leader (1988–99) was Paddy ASHDOWN. In the 1998 elections, it returned 20 MPs. The smallest of the three main political parties, it vigorously campaigned for PROPORTIONAL REPRESENTATION which would increase its influence. In the 2001 and 2005 general elections, the Liberal Democrats returned 52 and 62 MPs respectively.

liberalism Political and intellectual belief that advocates the right of the individual to make decisions, usually political or religious, according to the dictates of conscience. Its modern origins lie in the 18th-century ENLIGHTENMENT. In politics, it opposes arbitrary power and discrimination against minorities. In British history, its greatest influence was exercised in the 19th century. In the USA, liberalism has, since the 1930s, referred to a belief in government action to manage the economy and (from the 1960s on) to improve the position of women and racial minorities. *See also* LIBERAL PARTY

Liberal Party British political party. It grew out of the early 19th-century WHIGS. The first official use of the name was the National Liberal Federation founded (1877) by Joseph CHAMBERLAIN, although the administration

(1855–58) of Lord PALMERSTON is often regarded as Liberal. Its main interests were FREE TRADE, religious and individual liberty, financial retrenchment and constitutional reform. Its greatest leader was William GLADSTONE, who led four governments (1868–74, 1880–85, 1885–86, 1892–94). The government of (1905–08) Henry Campbell-Bannerman legalized TRADE UNIONS, reformed the House of Lords, and introduced progressive SOCIAL SECURITY measures. In 1908, Herbert ASQUITH became prime minister. In 1916, LLOYD GEORGE formed a coalition government with the CONSERVATIVE PARTY. After the formation (1980) of the SOCIAL DEMOCRATIC PARTY (SDP), the Liberal Party entered into an alliance, merging with it in 1987. In 1988, the Liberal members and most of the SDP formed the LIBERAL DEMOCRATS. A small Liberal Party still exists.

Liberal Party Australian political party. It was formed (1913) in opposition to the LABOR PARTY. In 1944, Robert MENZIES created a new Liberal Party from the remains of the United Australia Party. In 1949, Menzies became prime minister of a Liberal-Country coalition government. In 1966 Harold Holt succeeded Menzies as prime minister and leader of the Liberal Party. The Liberals returned to office under John Gorton (1968–71) and William McMahon (1971–72). In 1975, Malcolm FRASER defeated Gough WHITLAM to become prime minister (1975–83). In 1996, after five successive Labor governments, the Liberal Party regained power under John HOWARD.

Liberia Republic on the Atlantic coast of W Africa. *See* country feature

---

LIBERIA

The Republic of Liberia is located on the Atlantic coast of W Africa. Behind the coastline, 500km [311mi] long, lies a narrow coastal plain. Beyond, the land rises to a plateau region, with the highest land along the border with Guinea. The most important rivers are the Cavally, which forms the border with Ivory Coast, and the St Paul.

Mangrove swamps and lagoons line the coast, while inland forests cover nearly 40% of the land. Liberia also has areas of tropical savanna. Only 5% of the land is cultivated.

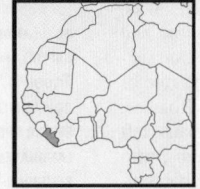

CLIMATE

Liberia has a tropical climate. There are high temperatures and humidity throughout the year. Rainfall is abundant all year round, but there is a particularly wet period from June to

November. Rainfall generally increases from E to W.

HISTORY

In the late 18th century, some white Americans in the United States wanted to help freed black slaves to return to Africa. They set up the AMERICAN COLONIZATION SOCIETY in 1820 and bought land in what is now Liberia.

In 1822 the Society landed former slaves at a settlement on the coast which they named Monrovia. In 1847 Liberia became a fully independent republic with a constitution much like that of the United States. For many years, the Americo-Liberians controlled the government. US influence remained strong and the American Firestone Company, which ran Liberia's rubber plantations covering more than 400,000ha [1 million acres], was especially influential. Foreign countries were also involved in exploiting Liberia's mineral resources, including its huge iron-ore deposits.

POLITICS

Under the leadership (1944–71) of William Tubman, Liberia's economy grew and it adopted social reforms. In 1980, a military force killed the Americo-Liberian president William R. Tolbert, Tubman's successor. An army sergeant, Samuel K. Doe, became president. In 1985, Doe's brutal and corrupt regime won a fraudulent election.

Civil war broke out in 1989, and the Economic Community of West African States (ECOWAS) sent a five-nation peace-keeping force. Doe was assassinated and an interim government, led by Amos Sawyer, took office. Civil war raged on, claiming 150,000 lives and leaving hundreds of thousands of people homeless by 1994. In 1995 a ceasefire was reached and the former warring factions formed a coun-

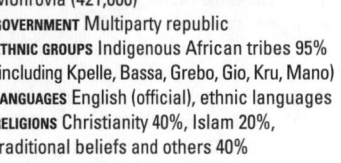

AREA 111,369sq km [43,000sq mi]
POPULATION 3,196,000
CAPITAL (POPULATION) Monrovia (421,000)
GOVERNMENT Multiparty republic
ETHNIC GROUPS Indigenous African tribes 95% (including Kpelle, Bassa, Grebo, Gio, Kru, Mano)
LANGUAGES English (official), ethnic languages
RELIGIONS Christianity 40%, Islam 20%, traditional beliefs and others 40%
CURRENCY Liberian dollar = 100 cents

cil of state. Former warlord Charles Taylor secured a resounding victory in 1997 elections.

In 2001 the UN imposed an arms embargo on Liberia for trading weapons for diamonds with rebels in Sierra Leone. In 2002 Taylor imposed a state of emergency as fighting intensified with rebels. In 2003 the fighting largely ended; Taylor went into exile. The UN helped to restore order and, in 2005, Ellen Johnson-Sirleaf was elected president. In 2006 Taylor was arrested in Nigeria and returned to face trial for war crimes.

ECONOMY

Liberia's civil war devastated the economy. Agriculture employs 75% of the workforce, but many families live at subsistence level. Food crops include cassava, fruits, rice and sugar cane. Rubber is grown on plantations and cash crops include cocoa and coffee.

Liberia's natural resources include its forests and iron ore, while gold and diamonds are also mined. Liberia has an oil refinery, but manufacturing is small-scale. Exports include rubber, timber, diamonds, gold and coffee. Revenue is also obtained from its 'flag of convenience', which is used by about one-sixth of the world's commercial shipping, exploiting low taxes.

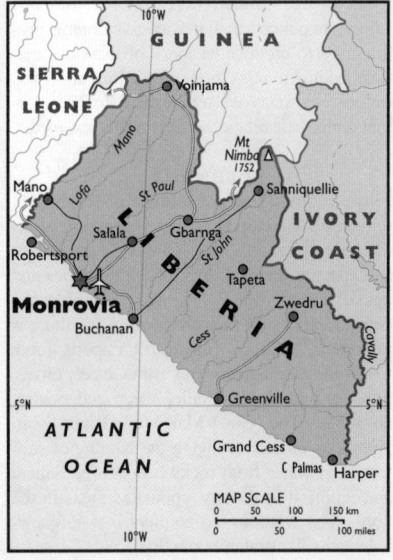

MAP SCALE
0   50   100   150 km
0   50   100 miles

Liberty, Statue of *See* STATUE OF LIBERTY

Liberty Bell US monument housed in Independence Hall, Philadelphia. According to legend, it was rung in July 1776 to celebrate the American DECLARATION OF INDEPENDENCE.

libido Term used by Sigmund FREUD to describe instinctive sexual energy. He later enlarged its meaning to include all mental energy (or life energy) that accompanies strong desires.

libretto Text of an opera or operetta. From 1597, libretti were printed to commemorate performances; by the mid-18th century, public audiences used them to follow the opera's story.

Libreville Capital and largest city of Gabon, w central Africa, at the mouth of the River Gabon, on the Gulf of Guinea. Founded by the French in 1843, and named Libreville (Fr. Freetown) in 1849, it was initially a refuge for escaped slaves. The city expanded with the development of the country's minerals and is now also an administrative centre. Other industries: timber (hardwoods), palm oil and rubber. Pop. (2002 est.) 541,000.

Libya Republic of N Africa. *See* country feature.

lice *See* LOUSE

lichen Plant consisting of a FUNGUS in which microscopic (usually single-celled) ALGAE are embedded. The fungus and its algae form a symbiotic association in which the fungus contributes support, water and minerals, while the algae contribute food produced by PHOTOSYNTHESIS. *See also* SYMBIOSIS

Lichtenstein, Roy (1923–97) US painter, sculptor, and graphic artist. Lichtenstein experimented with ABSTRACT EXPRESSIONISM, but is now regarded as a leading exponent of POP ART. Among his best-known paintings are *Whaam!* (1963) and *Good Morning, Darling* (1964).

Lie, Trygve Halvdan (1896–1968) Norwegian statesman, first secretary-general of the United Nations (1946–52). Lie blamed both sides for the COLD WAR, but antagonized the Soviet Union by his support for UN intervention in the Korean War (1950). He was replaced by Dag HAMMARSKJÖLD.

Liebig, Baron Justus von (1803–73) German chemist. He was the first to realize that animals use oxygen to get energy from food. Liebig also showed that plants derive their minerals from the soil, and introduced synthetic fertilizers.

Liebknecht, Karl (1871–1919) German communist revolutionary, son of Wilhelm LIEBKNECHT. He opposed Germany's participation in World War 1, and was imprisoned (1916–18). With Rosa LUXEMBURG, Liebknecht was a leader of the communist group known as the SPARTACISTS. After the failure of the Spartacist rising (1919), they were murdered while in police custody.

Liebknecht, Wilhelm (1826–1900) German revolutionary, father of Karl LIEBKNECHT. After taking part in the REVOLUTIONS OF 1848, he was exiled to England where he associated with MARX. In 1869, Liebknecht and August Bebel founded the Social Democratic Party (SPD). Otto von BISMARCK imprisoned (1872–74) them for opposing the FRANCO-PRUSSIAN WAR (1870–71). In 1874, he entered the Reichstag.

LIBYA

Libya, officially named the Great Socialist People's Libyan Arab Jamahiriya, is located in N Africa. The majority live on the Mediterranean coastal plains in the NE and NW. The SAHARA, the world's largest desert, occupies 95% of Libya, reaching the Mediterranean coast along the Gulf of Sidra (Khalíj Surt). The Sahara is virtually uninhabited except around scattered oases.

The land rises towards the s, reaching 2,286m [7,500ft] at Bette Peak (Bikku Bitti) on the border with Chad. Shrubs and grasses grow on N coasts, with some trees in wetter areas. Few plants grow in the desert, except at oases where date palms provide protection from the hot sun.

CLIMATE

The coastal plains experience hot summers. Winters are mild with some rain. Inland, the average yearly rainfall drops to around 100mm [4in] or less. Daytime temperatures are high but nights are cool.

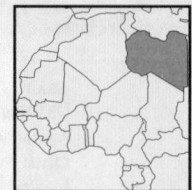

HISTORY

The earliest known inhabitants of Libya were the BERBERS. Between the 7th century BC and the 5th century AD the region successively came under the rule of Greeks, Carthaginians, Romans, and Vandals. The Romans left superb ruins, but the Arabs, who invaded the area in AD 642, imposed their culture and Islamic religion. From 1551 Libya was part of the Ottoman Empire, and power resided with local rulers or JANISSARIES. During the 17th century, Barbary pirates used bases on the Libyan coast to attack shipping.

In the 19th century, US, British, and French forces attempted to curb the pirates. Italy invaded Libya in 1911, and by 1914 conquered the whole territory. Italy made attempts at colonization in the 1930s, and in 1939 Libya was incorporated into Italy. Libya was a battleground for many of the North Africa campaigns in World War 2 and, after the Allied victory, it was placed under UN mandate. In 1951, it became an independent monarchy. Libya joined the Arab League in 1953 and became a member of the UN in 1955.

POLITICS

In 1969 a military group headed by Colonel Muammar al-QADDAFI deposed the king and set up a military government. Under Qaddafi, the government took control of the economy and used money from oil exports to finance welfare services and development projects. However, although Libya appears to be democratic, political parties are not permitted.

Qaddafi has attracted international criticism for his support for radical movements, such as the PLO (Palestine Liberation Organization) and various terrorist groups. In 1986 his policies led the United States to bomb installations in the capital and in Benghazi. In 1994 the International Court of Justice ruled against Libya's claim to an area in northern Chad.

AREA 1,759,540sq km [679,358sq mi]
POPULATION 6,037,000
CAPITAL (POPULATION) Tripoli (1,733,000)
GOVERNMENT Single-party socialist state
ETHNIC GROUPS Libyan Arab and Berber 97%
LANGUAGES Arabic (official), Berber
RELIGIONS Islam (Sunni Muslim) 97%
CURRENCY Libyan dinar = 1000 dirhams

In 1999 Qaddafi sought to restore good relations with the outside world by surrendering for trial two Libyans suspected of planting a bomb on a PanAm plane, which exploded over the Scottish town of Lockerbie in 1988. In addition Libya agreed to pay compensation to victims of the bombing. Qaddafi also accepted Libya's responsibility for the shooting of a British policewoman in London in 1984 and diplomatic relations with Britain were restored. In 2004 Libya announced that it was abandoning programmes to produce weapons of mass destruction, leading to relaxation of sanctions and visits to Libya by many Western leaders. In 2006 normal diplomatic relations with the US resumed.

ECONOMY

Libya is Africa's richest country, per capita, but remains a developing country because of its dependence on oil. Oil accounts for nearly all of its export revenues. Libya has oil refineries and petrochemical plants. It also manufactures cement, processed food and steel. Agriculture is important, although Libya still imports food. Crops include barley, citrus fruits, dates, olives, potatoes and wheat. Cattle, sheep and poultry are raised. The 'Great Man-Made River' is an ambitious project involving the tapping of subterranean water from rocks beneath the Sahara and piping it to the dry, populated areas in the north. The water in the aquifers is non-renewable and will eventually run dry.

Liechtenstein Independent principality in w central Europe, between Austria (E) and Switzerland (W); the capital is Vaduz. It was formed in 1719 through the merging of Vaduz and Schellenberg, but remained part of the Holy Roman Empire until 1806. A member of the German Confederation from 1815, it gained independence in 1866. In 1921, Liechtenstein entered into a currency union with Switzerland and, in 1923, a customs union. Until 1990 Switzerland also handled its foreign policy. In 1990, the principality joined the UN. Liechtenstein has a constitutional and hereditary monarchy; the ruling family is the Austrian House of Liechtenstein. Women received the vote in 1984. Liechtenstein is the fourth-smallest country in the world, but among the richest (1998 GDP per capita, US$23,000). After 1945, it developed a manufacturing base. Most revenue derives from multinationals attracted by the low taxation rates. In 2000 it reformed its banking laws after criticism that it encouraged money-laundering. Tourism is important. Area: 160sq km (62sq mi). Pop. (2000) 33,000.

lied (Ger. 'song') It has a more specific connotation in current usage as the art song of German Romantic composers – especially SCHUBERT, WOLF, BRAHMS, and SCHUMANN.

lie detector (polygraph) Device that may be capable of detecting lies when used by a trained examiner. It monitors such factors as heart rate, breathing rate and perspiration.

Liège (Flemish, Luik) City and river port in E Belgium, at the confluence of the rivers Meuse and Ourthe; capital of Liège province. Settled in Roman times, it became part of Belgium in 1830. During the 19th century, it was one of the first steel-making and coal-mining centres. The Germans occupied Liège in both World Wars, and fighting severely damaged the city in the Battle of the Bulge (1944–45). After 1945, Liège's steel industry drastically declined. It is a commercial centre. Industries: chemicals, electronics. Pop. (2000) 185,639.

life Feature of organisms that sets them apart from inorganic matter. Life can be regarded as the ability to obtain energy from the Sun or from food, and to use this energy for growth and reproduction. The various stages through which an organism passes make up its **life cycle**.

lift In AERODYNAMICS, force that acts upwards on the undersurface of an AEROFOIL, or wing. As it travels forwards, the leading edge of an aerofoil splits the airstream. Because the upper part of the airstream is forced to travel farther, its pressure falls. The lift force is a result of the upward pressure underneath the aerofoil being greater than the downward pressure on the top. *See also* BERNOUILLI'S LAW

ligament Bands of tough fibrous CONNECTIVE TISSUE that join bone to bone at the joints. Ligaments, which contain the protein COLLAGEN, form part of the supporting tissues of the body.

Ligeti, György (1923–2006) Hungarian composer whose avant-garde works involve shifting patterns of tone colours. After 1956, Ligeti's work on electronic sound influenced his compositions, especially *Atmosphères* (1961) and *Lux Aeterna* (1966). Since 1966, most of his work has been instrumental.

light ELECTROMAGNETIC RADIATION to which the human eye is sensitive. Visible light is in the wavelength range from c.400nm (violet) to 770nm (red). The speed (symbol c) at which electromagnetic radiation (including light) travels in a vacuum is 299,792,458ms⁻¹. The amount of light in an area is measured in LUMENS. Light exhibits typical phenomena of WAVE motion, such as REFLECTION, REFRACTION, DIFFRACTION, light polarization, and INTERFERENCE. Sir Isaac NEWTON investigated the properties of light in the 17th century, and he was the first to split white light into its component colours (SPECTRUM) with a PRISM. Newton believed in a corpuscular (particle) theory of light, but the wave theory was well established by the 1820s, thanks to the work of English physicist Thomas YOUNG and French physicist Augustin Jean FRESNEL. At the beginning of the 20th century, experiments on the PHOTOELECTRIC EFFECT and the work of German physicist Max PLANCK revived the idea that light can behave like a stream of particles. Albert EINSTEIN stated that this stream must be PHOTONS of electromagnetic energy. QUANTUM THEORY, according to which light consists of elementary particles called PHOTONS, resolved this dilemma. When light interacts with matter, as in the photoelectric effect, energy exchanges in the form of

photons and so light seems to be particles. Otherwise, it behaves as a wave. *See also* HOLOGRAPHY; LASER

lightning Electrical discharge between clouds or between clouds and the surface. The POTENTIAL DIFFERENCE causing the discharge can be as much as 1,000 million volts. *See also* THUNDERSTORM

light-year Unit of astronomical distance equal to the distance travelled in free space or a VACUUM by light in one tropical year. One light-year is equal to 9.4607×10^{12} km (5.88×10^{12} mi).

lignin Complex, non-carbohydrate substance that occurs in woody tissues (especially XYLEM of plants), often in combination with CELLULOSE. It is lignin that gives wood its strength. To obtain pure cellulose for the paper and rayon industries, the lignin has to be removed from wood.

lilac Any of 20 species of evergreen ornamental shrubs and small trees of the genus *Syringa*, which bear panicles (pointed clusters) of tiny white to purple flowers. Height: to 6m (20ft).

Lilburne, John (1614–57) English republican, leader of the LEVELLERS. Imprisoned (1638–40) under CHARLES I, he fought for Parliament during the CIVIL WAR (1642–45). Captured, he escaped execution in an exchange of prisoners. He left the army in 1645, refusing to sign the SOLEMN LEAGUE AND COVENANT. Demanding greater equality and religious freedom, he led protests against the government of Oliver CROMWELL. He spent his last years among Quakers.

Lilienthal, Otto (1849–96) German engineer and pioneer of glider design. A glider, designed by Sir George CAYLEY, had carried a passenger in 1853, but this aircraft had no controls. In 1891, Lilienthal became the first person to control a glider in flight. He made c.2,500 flights before his death in a crash.

Lille (Flemish, Lisle) City in NW France, near the Belgian border; capital of Nord department. It flourished in the 16th century under the Dukes of Burgundy. In the late 17th century, Lille became capital of French Flanders; the building of a stock exchange established its commercial reputation. It is a major industrial, commercial and cultural city. Industries: textiles, engineering, chemicals, brewing. Pop. (2000) 991,000.

Lilongwe Capital of Malawi, SE Africa, in the centre of the country, c.80km (50mi) W of Lake Malawi. It replaced Zomba as the capital in 1975, and rapidly became Malawi's second-largest city. Pop. (1998) 440,471.

lily Any of numerous species of perennial, BULB-producing plants of the genus *Lilium*, from temperate and subtropical regions. They have erect stems and various leaf arrangements. The showy flowers may be almost any colour.

lily of the valley Perennial woodland plant native to Europe, Asia and E USA. It has broad, elongated leaves and bears stalks of tiny, white, bell-shaped fragrant flowers. Family Liliaceae; species *Convallaria majalis*.

Lima Capital and largest city of Peru, on the River Rímac at the foot of the Cerro San Cristóbal. Francisco PIZARRO founded Lima in 1535. It was the capital of Spain's New World colonies until the 19th century. Chilean forces occupied it during the War of the Pacific (1881–83). It is the commercial and cultural centre of Peru. With the oil-refining port of Callao, the Lima metropolitan area forms the third-largest city of South America, and handles more than 75% of all Peru's manufacturing. Lima has the oldest university (1551) in the w hemisphere. Pop. (2005) 8,180,000.

limbic system Collection of structures in the middle of the brain. Looped around the HYPOTHALAMUS, the limbic system is thought to be involved in emotional responses, such as fear and aggression; basic drives like hunger and sex; mood changes; and the laying down of memories.

limbo In Roman Catholic theology, the abode of souls excluded from HEAVEN but not condemned to any other punishment. This view, which never became doctrine, stipulated that unbaptized infants go to limbo after death.

Limbourg, Pol de (active 1380–1416) Franco-Flemish manuscript illustrator. Pol and his brothers, Jan and Hermann, became court painters to Jean, duc de Berry in 1411. Their masterpiece is a Book of Hours known as *Les Très Riches Heures du Duc de Berry* (1413–15). *See also* ILLUMINATION

lime Any of the deciduous linden trees that grow throughout Earth's N temperate zone. The lime tree has serrated,

▲ **lily** Grown mainly in temperate and tropical regions, the showy displays of colour make lilies a popular garden plant in many regions of the world. Most lilies thrive in well-drained, moist soil, and a sunny location.

▲ **lime** The American lime or linden (*Tilia americana*), also known as American basswood, has some of the largest leaves of any deciduous tree, with examples reaching 30cm (12in) long. In the past, the wood was commonly used in carving, as it has both pliability and strength.

INTERNET

Limpopo
▶ www.limpopo.gov.za

Lincoln, Abraham
▶ www.whitehouse.gov/
history/presidents

Lindisfarne Gospels
▶ www.durham.anglican.
org/reference/lindisfarne

▲ **limpet** The conical shell of limpets (*Patella* sp shown) differs from most other gastropods, which have coiled shells. Found in rocky, coastal regions of the Pacific and Atlantic, limpets remain attached to the rock by a muscular 'foot', occasionally leaving their position to feed on seaweed.

L

▲ **Lincoln** US President Abraham Lincoln was born into a frontier family and received little formal education as a boy. After reading law, he was elected to the US House of Representatives in 1847. The highly publicized Lincoln-Douglas debates over the pro-slavery Kansas-Nebraska Act won Lincoln national fame. He went on to win the presidential election of 1860, and his dogged determination to retain the Union and refuse Southern secession brought about the start of the Civil War.

▶ **ling** A member of the cod family, the various species of ling (*Molva molva* shown) are commercially important fish. They are long-bodied fish, growing to 2m (7ft) and weighing up to 20kg (45lb).

heart-shaped leaves with small, fragrant, yellowish flowers borne in clusters. The common British linden, *Tilia vulgaris*, is one of three British species. The American lime, *T. americana*, is also called basswood. Family Tiliaceae.

lime Small tropical tree (*Citrus aurantifolia*) of the rue family (Rutaceae). The trees grow to 2.4–4.6m (8–15ft) tall and yield small green acid fruits. The juice was a valuable commodity in the 18th and 19th centuries for consumption on long sea voyages; the vitamin C helped to ward off scurvy.

Limerick City on the Shannon estuary, sw Republic of Ireland; capital of Limerick county, Munster province. Norse invaders sacked the city in the 9th century. At the beginning of the 11th century, Brian Boru made Limerick the capital of Munster. In the 17th century, the armies of Oliver Cromwell and William III besieged the city. Industries: lacemaking, salmon fishing. Pop. (2002) 54,058.

limestone SEDIMENTARY ROCK composed primarily of carbonates, such as calcite $CaCO_3$. Generally formed from deposits of the skeletons of marine invertebrates, it is used to make cement and lime and as a building material.

Limoges City on the River Vienne; capital of Haute-Vienne department, w central France. A Roman settlement, it was later a tribal capital of the Gauls. In 1370, Edward the Black Prince sacked the city. Its enamel industry culminated in the 16th-century craftsmanship of Léonard Limousin, but was devastated by the THIRTY YEARS' WAR. In the late 18th century, porcelain manufacturing flourished. Uranium has been mined here since 1945. Pop. (1999) 137,502.

limpet Primitive, gastropod MOLLUSC commonly found fixed to rocks along marine shores. It has a cap-like, rather than coiled, shell and a large muscular foot. Length: to 13cm (5in). Families: Patellacea, Acmaeidae and Fissurellidae.

Limpopo Province in N South Africa, formerly Northern Province (renamed 2002); the capital is Pietersburg. Northern Province was formed from the N part of the former province of TRANSVAAL in 1994. Area: 123,280sq km (46,970sq mi). Pop. (2002 est.) 5,857,622.

Limpopo (Crocodile) River in s Africa. It rises in NE South Africa, in the former Transvaal province. It then flows in a great curve N, forming part of the border between South Africa and Botswana, then E as the border of South Africa and Zimbabwe, before crossing Mozambique to enter the Indian Ocean NE of Maputo. Length: c.1,770km (1,100mi).

Lin Biao (1907–71) Chinese communist general and political leader. He defeated CHIANG KAI-SHEK in Manchuria (1948), thus helping to secure the victory of the communists in 1949. Lin was a leader of the CULTURAL REVOLUTION (1966–69), and compiled the book of quotations from MAO ZEDONG known as the *Little Red Book*. He was designated Mao's heir in 1969 but, after disagreements with Mao, was said to have died in an accident while fleeing to the Soviet Union.

Lincoln State capital and second-largest city of NEBRASKA, USA. Founded in 1856 as Lancaster, its name was changed in honour of Abraham Lincoln. The city was made state capital when Nebraska joined the Union in 1867. Lincoln is a centre for livestock and grain, and more recently for insurance. Industries: rubber products, pharmaceuticals Pop. (2000) 225,581.

Lincoln City in E England; the county town of LINCOLNSHIRE. The Romans founded the city as *Lindum Colonia*. As one of the five boroughs of the DANELAW, Lincoln thrived on its wool trade until the 14th century. The castle was begun (1068) in the reign of William I, and houses one of the original copies of the Magna Carta. Lincoln Cathedral (c.1073) has a tower 83m (271ft) high. Industries: farm machinery. Pop. (2001) 85,616.

Lincoln, Abraham (1809–65) Sixteenth US president (1861–65). Elected to the Illinois legislature for the WHIG PARTY in 1834, he studied law. He served (1847–49) in the House of Representatives and unsuccessfully ran for the Senate for the new REPUBLICAN PARTY against Stephen A. DOUGLAS in 1858. He was Republican candidate for president in 1860. Lincoln's victory made the secession of the Southern, slave-owning states inevitable, and his determination to defend FORT SUMTER began the CIVIL WAR. A strong commander-in-chief, he played a leading role in military planning. In September 1862, he issued the EMANCIPATION

PROCLAMATION, and in November 1863 delivered the GETTYSBURG ADDRESS. Re-elected in 1864, Lincoln saw the war to a successful conclusion. On April 14, 1865, five days after the surrender of Robert E. LEE, Lincoln was shot by John Wilkes BOOTH, a Southern sympathizer. He died the next day.

Lincolnshire County in E England, bordering the North Sea; the county town is LINCOLN. The area was settled by the Romans, and an Anglo-Saxon kingdom was later established in Lindsey. In the Middle Ages it was a prosperous farming region. Apart from the Wolds, the region is flat, drained by the Trent, Welland, and Witham rivers. Agriculture, mainly cereals, sugar beet and sheep, is the mainstay of the economy. Area: 5,886sq km (2,273sq mi). Pop. (2001) 646,646.

Lind, Jenny (1820–87) Swedish operatic soprano, b. Johanna Lind Goldschmidt. The 'Swedish nightingale' made her debut in 1838. Lind achieved worldwide success in coloratura roles. In c.1852, she settled in London and founded several musical scholarships.

Lindbergh, Charles Augustus (1902–74) US aviator. He became an international hero when, in *The Spirit of St Louis*, he made the first non-stop transatlantic solo flight, from New York to Paris (1927) in 33 hours 30 minutes. In 1932, his baby son was kidnapped and murdered.

Lindisfarne Gospels Manuscript illuminated in the Hiberno-Saxon style in the late 7th or 8th century. It may have been executed for Eadfrith, Bishop of Lindisfarne (698–721). It is now held in the British Museum, London.

linear script Early form of writing, found on clay tablets in Crete and Greece. **Linear A** was in extensive use during the middle period of the MINOAN CIVILIZATION (c.2100–c.1550BC). **Linear B** was an adaptation of Linear A, used by the MYCENAEAN CIVILIZATION of mainland Greece to write their early form of Greek. Linear B was used from c.1450 BC to the end of the Mycenaean period (c.1120BC). In 1952, Michael Ventris deciphered Linear B; Linear A still defies analysis.

linen Yarn and fabric made of fibres from the FLAX plant. The fibres are released from the substance that binds them by retting (soaking) the long stems in water. After sorting, the fibres are spun to form yarn, which is then woven.

ling *See* HEATHER

ling Food fish related to the COD found in the Atlantic Ocean. It is brown and silver and has long dorsal and ventral fins. Length: to 2m (7ft); weight: 3.6kg (8lb). Family Gadidae; species *Molva molva*.

lingua franca Language that serves as communication between people who otherwise lack a common tongue. A lingua franca may be a simplified form of the dominant language, such as PIDGIN English, or it may be a hybrid, such as SWAHILI, which consists of words of both Arabic and Bantu origins.

linguistics Systematic study of LANGUAGE, its nature, structure, constituent elements, and changes. As a discipline, linguistics embraces PHONETICS, phonology (the study of sound systems within languages), GRAMMAR (including SYNTAX), SEMANTICS and pragmatics (the study of language use). *See also* CHOMSKY, NOAM; SAUSSURE, FERDINAND DE; STRUCTURALISM

Linnaean system *See* BINOMIAL NOMENCLATURE

Linnaeus, Carolus (1707–78) (Carl von Linné) Swedish botanist and taxonomist. Linnaeus' *Systema Naturae* (1735) laid the foundation of TAXONOMY by including all known organisms in a single classification system. He was one of the first scientists to define clearly the differences between species, and he devised the system of BINOMIAL NOMENCLATURE, which gave standardized Latin names to every organism.

linnet Small songbird of the family Carduelidae. *Carduelis cannabina* of Europe inhabits hedgerows and thickets, moving to open country in colder seasons. Both sexes are brown and grey, but the male has a red breast and crown in the summer. Length: to 13cm (5in).

linseed *See* FLAX

linseed oil Oil pressed from seeds of cultivated FLAX (*Linum usitatissimum*). Because of its drying qualities, linseed is an important ingredient of oil paints and printing inks, and is used to make VARNISH and linoleum.

Linz City and major port on the Danube River; capital of Upper Austria, NW Austria. Founded in Roman times as Lentia, it became a provincial capital of the Holy Roman Empire in the late 15th century. Austria's third-largest city, Linz is a commercial and industrial centre. Manufactures include iron and steel, chemicals, and fertilizers. Pop. (2001) 186,298.

lion Large CAT that lives on African savannas s of the Sahara, and in SW Asia. It is golden yellow with light spots under the eyes. The male is instantly recognizable by its deep neck mane, which darkens with age. The female does most of the hunting and preys on antelopes, zebras, and bush pigs. Length: to 2.5m (8.5ft) overall. Family Felidae; species *Panthera leo*.

Lipchitz, Jacques (1891–1973) French sculptor, b. Lithuania. He created one of the first cubist sculptures, *Man with Guitar* (1914), exploring the concept of faceted planes and multiple viewpoints. After moving to the USA in 1941, his work became more spiritual and more solid in structure. Among his most representative works are *Sailor with a Guitar* (1914), *Harpist* (1928) and *Prayer* (1943). *See also* CUBISM

Li Peng (1928–) Chinese statesman, premier (1988–98). ZHOU ENLAI adopted him after his father was executed (1930) by the KUOMINTANG. Li was elected to the politburo in 1985. His support for DENG XIAOPING's policy of economic liberalization, while maintaining the Party's tight grip on politics and society, led him to succeed ZHAO ZIYANG as premier. In 1989, Li declared martial law during the student protests in TIANANMEN SQUARE, Beijing. Zhu Rongji succeeded him as premier. *See also* JIANG ZEMIN

lipid One of a large group of fatty organic compounds in living organisms. They include animal fats, vegetable oils, and natural waxes. Lipids form an important food store and energy source in plant and animal cells.

Li Po (701–62) Chinese poet of the T'ANG dynasty, regarded as one of the two greatest poets in CHINESE LITERATURE. Unlike his contemporary and rival, TU FU (a Confucian), Li Po was a Taoist and the influence of TAOISM can be seen in the sensual and spiritual aspects of his work.

Lippi, Filippino (1457–1504) Florentine painter, son of Fra Filippo LIPPI. He studied with BOTTICELLI. Lippi completed the frescos of MASACCIO in *Santa Maria del Carmine* (1484). His work is shown to full effect in his fresco cycles in the Caraffa Chapel, Santa Maria sopra Minerva, Rome (1488–93) and the Strozzi Chapel, Santa Maria Novella, Florence. He also painted altarpieces, notably *The Vision of St Bernard* (*c.*1480).

Lippi, Fra Filippo (1406–69) Florentine painter. His early work shows the influence of MASACCIO, but from *c.*1440 he developed his own style. His most characteristic subject was the Virgin and Child, which he sometimes painted in a circular format. His finest fresco cycle is in Prato cathedral and depicts the lives of St Stephen and St John. Lippi was a major influence on the 19th-century PRE-RAPHAELITE BROTHERHOOD.

liquid PHASE of MATTER intermediate between a GAS and a SOLID. A liquid substance has a relatively fixed volume but flows to take the shape of its container. A liquid changes into a vapour by heating or into a solid by cooling.

liquid crystal Substance that can exist half-way between the liquid and solid states with its molecules partly ordered.

By applying a carefully controlled electric current, liquid crystals turn dark. They are used in liquid crystal displays (LCDs) to show numbers and letters, as in pocket calculators and miniature television screens.

liquorice (licorice) Perennial plant of the PEA family, native to the Mediterranean region and cultivated in temperate and subtropical areas. It bears spikes of blue flowers. The dried roots are used to flavour confectionery, tobacco, beverages, and medicines. Height: to 90cm (3ft). Family Fabaceae/Leguminosae; species *Glycyrrhiza glabra*.

Lisbon (Lisboa) Capital, largest city, and chief port of Portugal, at the mouth of the River TAGUS, on the Atlantic Ocean. An ancient Phoenician settlement, the Romans conquered the city in 205 BC. After Teutonic invasions in the 5th century AD it fell to the Moors in 716. In 1147, the Portuguese reclaimed Lisbon, and in 1260 it became the capital. It declined under Spanish occupation (1580–1640). In 1755, an earthquake devastated the city and Marquês de POMBAL oversaw its reconstruction. An international port and tourist centre, sights include the 16th-century Tower of Belém and the 15th-century Jerónimos Monastery. Industries: steel, shipbuilding, chemicals. Pop. (2005) 1,977,000.

Lissitzky, El (Eliezor Markovich) (1890–1941) Innovative Russian painter. MALEVICH inspired him to create a series of paintings that simulate 3–D architectural constructs. In 1921, Lissitzky arranged an important exhibition of contemporary Russian ABSTRACT ART in Berlin. The BAUHAUS promoted his ideas. *See also* CONSTRUCTIVISM

Lister, Joseph, 1st Baron (1827–1912) English surgeon who introduced the principle of antisepsis, which complemented PASTEUR's theory that bacteria cause infection. Using carbolic acid (phenol) as the ANTISEPTIC agent, and employing it in conjunction with heat sterilization of instruments, he brought about a dramatic decrease in post-operative fatalities.

Liszt, Franz (1811–86) Hungarian composer and pianist, father-in-law of Richard WAGNER. He was the greatest pianist of his generation. Liszt's challenging compositions for piano include *Transcendental Studies* (1851). He invented the SYMPHONIC POEM. Although his output was predominantly piano

◀ **lion** Prides of lions (*Panthera leo*) are commonly seen lazing in the shade of a tree. Lionesses, which lack manes, do most of the killing, often working as a team to stalk prey. Lions themselves have no natural predators except humans.

LIQUID CRYSTAL

Liquid-crystal displays use the property of liquid crystals to twist the polarization of light to produce numbers or symbols. Incoming light (1) is first regimented in one plane by a polarizer (2) before it passes through the first of two plates of glass (3) on which are fixed electrodes (4). Seven electrodes are needed to represent Arabic numerals. The liquid crystal is between the two plates of glass and twists light (5) passing through uncharged electrodes (6). This light can pass through the second polarizer (7) and can be seen. The light passing through the charged electrodes (8) is not twisted (9), is blocked by the polarizer, and cannot be seen forming the components of the number (10).

INTERNET

Lithuania
▸ www.lrvk.lt/main_en.php
▸ www.litnet.lt/litinfo/litinfo.html

Little Bighorn, Battle of
▸ www.custerbattle.com

pieces, Liszt also wrote orchestral works, such as the *Faust Symphony* (1857), Hungarian rhapsodies, and choral music. He was patron to Frédéric CHOPIN and Edvard GRIEG.

literary criticism Discipline concerned with literary theory and the evaluation of literary works. It effectively began with PLATO's comments on the role of poets in his *Republic*; ARISTOTLE's response to this, the *Poetics*, represents the first systematic attempt to establish principles of literary procedure. Notable later contributions to the debate include Sir Philip SIDNEY's *The Defence of Poesie* (1595); DRYDEN's *Of Dramatick Poesie* (1668); WORDSWORTH's preface to *Lyrical Ballads* (1798); SHELLEY's *A Defence of Poetry* (1820); and the critical works of Matthew ARNOLD, in particular, *Culture and Anarchy* (1869). The 20th century witnessed an explosion of literary criticism, such as the writings of T.S ELIOT, I.A. Richards, William Empson and F.R. LEAVIS; also important are the writings of STRUCTURALISM and post-structuralism, notably Roland BARTHES, Michel FOUCAULT, and Jacques DERRIDA. The late 20th century saw the beginning of new critical approaches such as DECONSTRUCTION and FEMINISM.

literature Collections of writings, usually grouped according to language, period, and country of origin. Within such groupings, literature may be subdivided into forms, such as POETRY and PROSE, and within these again into categories, such as verse DRAMA, NOVELS, EPIC poems, TRAGEDIES, COMEDIES, SATIRES, and so on. *See also* LITERARY CRITICISM

lithium (symbol Li) Common, silvery metallic element, one of the ALKALI METALS, first isolated in 1817. Ores include lepidolite and spodumene. Chemically, it is similar to sodium. Lithium, the lightest of all metals, is used in alloys, glasses and glazes; its salts are used in medicine. Properties at.no. 3; r.a.m. 6.941; r.d. 0.534; m.p. 180.5°C (356.9°F); b.p. 1347°C (2456.6°F); most stable isotope Li^7 (92.58%).

lithography In art, method of printing from a flat, inked surface. In traditional lithography, invented in the 1790s, the design is made on a prepared plate or stone with a greasy pencil, crayon, or liquid. Water applied to the surface is absorbed where there is no design. Oil-based printing ink, rolled over the surface, sticks to the design, but not to the moist areas. Pressing paper onto the surface produces a print.

lithosphere Solid, upper layer of the EARTH which includes the CRUST and the uppermost MANTLE. Its thickness varies, but is *c*.60km (40mi); it extends down to a depth of *c*.200km (125mi). It is made up of a number of tectonic plates that move independently, giving rise to PLATE TECTONICS.

Lithuania Baltic republic in NE Europe. *See* country feature

litmus Dye that is purple in neutral aqueous solutions; it is used to indicate acidity (turning red) or alkalinity (turning

LITHUANIA

The Republic of Lithuania is the southernmost of the three Baltic states. The land is essentially flat, with the highest point a hill north-east of Vilnius (288m [945ft]). From the SE, the land slopes down to the fertile central lowland. In the W is an area of forested sandy ridges, dotted with lakes. s of Klaipeda, sand dunes separate a large lagoon from the Baltic Sea.

Most of the land is covered by moraine deposited by ice sheets during the Ice Age. Hollows in the moraine contain about 3,000 lakes. The longest river is the Neman, which rises in Belarus and flows through Lithuania to the Baltic Sea.

CLIMATE
Winters are cold, with temperatures averaging −3°C [27°F] in January. Summers are warm, with average temperatures in July of 17°C [63°F]. The average rainfall in the W is 630mm [25in]. Inland areas are drier.

HISTORY
The Lithuanian people were united into a single nation in the 12th century. The first great ruler was Mindaugas, who became king in 1251. By the 14th century, Lithuania's territory extended nearly to Moscow in the east and the

Black Sea in the south. In 1386 Lithuania entered into a dynastic union with Poland, and the two states finally unified in 1569. This state collapsed in the 18th century and, by 1795, Lithuania was under Russian control. Despite rebellions, Lithuania failed to regain its independence.

In 1905 a conference of elected representatives called for self-government, Russia refused. German troops occupied Lithuania during World War 1 and, in February 1918, Lithuania declared its independence from Germany and Russia. Russia briefly regained control, but retreated in 1919. Lithuania established a democratic form of government, and in 1920 Russia and Lithuania signed a peace treaty. Poland occupied Vilnius from 1920 until 1939, incorporating it into Poland in 1923. In 1926 a military coup overthrew Lithuania's democratic regime and established Antanas Smetona as dictator.

In 1939 Germany and the USSR secretly agreed to divide up much of eastern Europe. In 1940 the Soviet Union annexed Lithuania, including Vilnius, as a Soviet republic. German forces invaded in 1941 and held it until 1944, when Soviet troops reoccupied the country. Many Lithuanian guerrillas fought against Soviet rule between 1944 and 1952. Thousands of Lithuanians were killed and many more sent to labour camps.

POLITICS
From 1988, Lithuania led the way among the Baltic states in the drive to shed Communism and regain nationhood. In 1989, the parliament in Lithuania declared Soviet laws invalid unless approved by the Lithuanian parliament and made Lithuanian the official language. Religious freedom and the freedom of the press were restored, ending the Communist monopoly of power and creating a multiparty system.

Following parliamentary elections in 1990, in which pro-independence candidates won more than 90% of the seats, Lithuania declared itself independent. This declaration was reject-

AREA 65,200sq km [25,174sq mi]
POPULATION 3,575,000
CAPITAL (POPULATION) Vilnius (550,000)
GOVERNMENT Multiparty republic
ETHNIC GROUPS Lithuanian 80%, Russian 9%, Polish 7%, Belarusian 2%
LANGUAGES Lithuanian (official), Russian, Polish
RELIGIONS Mainly Roman Catholic
CURRENCY 1 litas = 100 centai

ed by Soviet leaders. Most of the capital was occupied by Soviet troops and a crippling economic blockade put in place. After negotiations to end the sanctions failed, Soviet troops moved into Lithuania and 14 people were killed when the troops fired on demonstrators. Finally, in September 1991, the Soviet government recognized Lithuania's independence.

Parliamentary elections in 1992 were won by the Lithuanian Democratic Labour Party, former Communists. Russian troops withdrew from the country in 1993. In 1996 elections, a coalition government was set up by the conservative Homeland Union and the Christian Democratic Party. In 1998 an independent, Valdas Adamkus, a Lithuanian-American who had fled in 1944, was elected president. Lithuania had better relations with Russia than the other two Baltic states, partly because ethnic Russians make up a lower proportion of the population than in Estonia and Latvia. Lithuania became a member of NATO and of the EU in 2004.

ECONOMY
The World Bank classifies Lithuania as a 'lower-middle-income' developing country. In the 2000s economic growth has been very rapid, leading to problems with inflation which have delayed the adoption of the Euro. Manufacturing is the most valuable activity. Products include chemicals, electronic goods, processed food and machine tools. Dairy and meat farming are important, as also is fishing.

blue). It is most familiar in the form of litmus-impregnated paper. The dye is extracted from lichens. *See also* pH

litre (symbol l or L) Metric unit equal to a cubic decimetre, one thousandth of a cubic metre. Another definition, used from 1901 to 1968, was that one litre equalled the volume of one kilogramme of pure water at 4°C (39°F). A litre is equivalent to 0.22 imperial gallons or 0.264 US gallons.

Little Bighorn, Battle of (June 25, 1876) Victory of SIOUX and CHEYENNE Native Americans against the US cavalry led by Colonel George CUSTER. Sometimes known as 'Custer's Last Stand', it was the last major victory of Native Americans against the US Army. The cavalry regiment of 225 men was annihilated by the Sioux, led by SITTING BULL and CRAZY HORSE, near the Little Bighorn River, Montana.

Little Richard (1935–) US singer-songwriter and pianist, b. Richard Penniman. He achieved fame in the late 1950s, with songs such as 'Tutti Frutti' (1956) and 'Good Golly Miss Molly' (1958). After a near-fatal plane crash, he was ordained in the Church of the Seventh-Day Adventists.

Little Rock Capital and largest city of Arkansas, USA, on the Arkansas River. Founded in 1814, it became the state capital in 1821. In 1957 federal troops enforced a US Supreme Court ruling against racial segregation in schools. Industries: electronics, textiles. Pop. (2000) 183,133.

liturgy Established order of the rituals of public ceremonies and worship, as laid down by the authorities of an organized religion. In Christianity, the term also refers to the Divine Office or to the rites proper to specific days, such as GOOD FRIDAY, or to particular sacraments, such as BAPTISM. In the Eastern Orthodox Church, the Divine Liturgy refers specifically to the celebration of the EUCHARIST.

Liu Shaoqi (1898–1974) Chinese statesman, chairman (1959–68) of the People's Republic of China. A leader of the trades union movement, Liu Shaoqi was the chief theorist of the early Chinese COMMUNIST PARTY. In 1949, he became chief vice-chairman of the party. Second-in-command to MAO ZEDONG from 1959, he was purged during the CULTURAL REVOLUTION and died in prison.

Lively, Penelope (1933–) British novelist, b. Egypt. Lively wrote numerous children's books, including the award-winning *The Ghost of Thomas Kempe* (1973) and *A Stitch in Time* (1976). Her first work for adults was *The Road to Lichfield* (1977). *Moon Tiger* (1987) won the Booker Prize. Other novels include *According to Mark* (1984).

liver Large organ located in the upper right abdomen of VERTEBRATES. Weighing up to 4.5lbs (2kg) in an adult human, it divides into four lobes. It is important in the control of the body's internal environment (HOMEOSTASIS). It receives nutrients from the intestine, and is a site of the metabolism of proteins, carbohydrates and fats. It synthesizes BILE and some vitamins, regulates the blood-glucose level, produces blood-clotting factors, breaks down worn-out ERYTHROCYTES and removes toxins from the blood. The metabolic reactions that occur in the liver are the body's main source of heat, which is distributed around the body by the blood. *See also* INSULIN

Liverpool City and seaport on the N side of the Mersey estuary, Merseyside, NW England. Liverpool was founded in the 10th century, and became a free borough in 1207. The first wet dock was completed in 1715, and the city expanded rapidly to become Britain's largest port. In the early 20th century, it was the major embarkation port for emigration to the New World. Liverpool suffered severe bomb damage during World War 2. The construction (1972) of a container terminal and the completion of a rail tunnel link with Birkenhead improved the city's trade and transport links. Inner-city regeneration schemes have included the Albert Dock. Liverpool Free Port (Britain's largest) opened in 1984. The sixth-largest city in England, Liverpool has more than 800ha (2,000 acres) of dockland. Pop. (2000) 852,000.

Liverpool, Robert Banks Jenkinson, 2nd Earl of (1770–1828) British statesman, prime minister (1812–27). He entered Parliament in 1790. Liverpool served as home secretary (1804–06, 1807–09) and secretary for war and the colonies (1809–12) before becoming Tory prime minister. His government oversaw the end of the NAPOLEONIC WARS

and the WAR OF 1812 with the USA. Liverpool resisted political reform and the CATHOLIC EMANCIPATION. He suspended HABEAS CORPUS after the PETERLOO MASSACRE (1819).

liverwort Any of *c*.9,000 species of tiny, non-flowering green plants, which, like the related MOSSES, lack specialized tissues for transporting water, food and minerals within the plant body. Liverworts belong to the plant phylum Bryophyta.

Livingstone, David (1813–73) Scottish explorer of Africa. He went to South Africa as a missionary in 1841, and became famous through his account of his journey across the continent from Angola to Mozambique (1853–56). He led a major expedition (1858–64) to the Zambezi and Lake Nyasa, and set off again in 1866 to find the source of the Nile. He disappeared until Henry STANLEY found him at Lake Tanganyika in 1871.

Livy (59 BC–AD 17) (Titus Livius) Roman historian. One of the greatest Roman historians, he began his *History of Rome* c.28 BC. Of the original 142 books, 35 have survived in full.

lizard REPTILE found on every continent; there are 20 families, *c*.3,000 species. Most have a scaly, cylindrical body with four legs, a long tail and moveable eyelids. Some species such as GLASS SNAKES, SLOW-WORM and some SKINKS, have reduced or absent limbs. Most lizards are terrestrial, and many live in deserts. There are also semi-aquatic and arboreal forms. Many lizards have an autotomic defence mechanism – they shed their tail when attacked. Most lay eggs rather than bear live young. They feed mainly on insects and vegetation. They range in size from the *c*.5cm (2in) GECKO to the 3m (10ft) KOMODO DRAGON. Order Squamata; sub-order Sauria. *See also* CHAMELEON; GECKO; IGUANA; MONITOR

Ljubljana (Laibach) Capital and largest city of Slovenia, at the confluence of the rivers Sava and Ljubljanica. In 34 BC Roman Emperor Augustus founded Ljubljana as Emona. From 1244 it was the capital of Carniola, an Austrian province of the Habsburg Empire. During the 19th century, it was the centre of the Slovene nationalist movement. The city remained under Austrian rule until 1918, when it became part of the Kingdom of Serbs, Croats, and Slovenes (later Yugoslavia). When Slovenia achieved independence in 1991, Ljubljana became capital. Industries: textiles, paper and printing. Pop. (2002) 257,338.

llama Domesticated, South American, even-toed, ruminant mammal. The llama has been used as a beast of burden by

▲ **lizard** The smooth-scaled agamid (*Leiolepis belliana*) is a lizard of SE Asia. Its body is flattened from top to bottom, an adaptation suited to its habit of burrowing up to 1m (39in) into the soil.

◄ **llama** Domesticated for more than a thousand years, llama (*Lama peruana*, shown) are used primarily as pack animals in S and W South America, from sea-level to elevations of 5000m (16,500ft). They thrive in a semi-desert habitat feeding on mountain grass. They grow to 1.2m (4ft) long, and to a height at the shoulder of 1.2m (4ft).

INTERNET

Lloyd George, David
► www.number-10.gov.uk

Native Americans for more than 1,000 years. It has a long, woolly coat and slender limbs and neck. The smaller alpaca is bred for its superb wool. Family Camelidae; genus *Lama*.

Lloyd, Harold (1893–1971) US film actor. Lloyd was hired by Hal ROACH in 1914 to star in comedy shorts. Lloyd modelled himself on Charlie CHAPLIN, but added cliff-hanging, death-defying stunts, such as hanging from the a skyscraper clockface in *Safety Last* (1923). His success waned in the sound era and he made his final film, *Mad Wednesday*, in 1947.

Lloyd George, David (1863–1945) British statesman, prime minister (1916–22). A Welsh Liberal, he entered Parliament in 1890. As chancellor of the exchequer (1908–15), Lloyd George increased taxation to pay for social measures such as old-age pensions. His 'People's Budget' (1909) provoked a constitutional crisis that led to a reduction of the powers of the House of Lords. He was an effective minister of munitions (1915) during World War 1. In 1916, he led a cabinet rebellion to dislodge the prime minister, Herbert ASQUITH. Lloyd George led a coalition government with the Conservatives for the rest of the war. He won by a landslide in 1918 elections and was a leading figure at the peace conference in VERSAILLES. In 1921, he negotiated with SINN FÉIN to create the Irish Free State and the Conservatives withdrew their support. Andrew BONAR LAW succeeded him as prime minister.

Lloyd's Insurance market in London, dealing especially in marine insurance. Lloyd's began in the 17th century as a coffee house where businessmen, who were willing to insure shipping, gathered. Lloyd's as an institution does not insure anything; it is merely the market where the individual underwriters ('names') can meet. Between 1988 and 1993, some syndicates sustained substantial losses, leading to a change in the regulations of names which allowed some to have limited liability.

Lloyd Webber, Andrew (1948–) English composer. He composed *Joseph and the Amazing Technicolour Dreamcoat* (1967) while still a student. The lyricist, Tim Rice, was also his collaborator on the rock opera *Jesus Christ Superstar* (1971) and on the musical *Evita* (1978). *Cats* (1981), using verse by T.S. Eliot, was a long-running hit, as were *The Phantom of the Opera* (1986) and *Sunset Boulevard* (1993). His brother, **Julian** (1951–), is a highly respected cellist.

Llywelyn ap Gruffydd (*c.*1225–82) (Llywelyn the Last) Prince of Wales. Allied with the rebellious English barons, he gained control of as much territory as his grandfather, LLYWELYN AP IORWERTH. He was recognized as Prince of Wales by the Treaty of Montgomery (1267). At the accession of EDWARD I, he renewed his rebellion in 1282 and died in battle.

Llywelyn ap Iorwerth (1173–1240) (Llywelyn the Great) Prince of Gwynedd, Wales. He overcame dynastic rivals and captured Mold from the English in 1199. He established his suzerainty in Gwynedd, subsequently gaining control of Powys also. He allied himself with the English barons against John and was recognized as suzerain by all the Welsh princes.

loach Small, freshwater fish that lives in mountain streams of central and s Asia and Europe; there are more than 200 species. British loaches are the stone loach (*Nemachilus barbatula*) and the spined loach (*Cobitis taenia*).

lobelia Genus of 365 species of flowering plants found worldwide, mainly trailing or bedding plants. The flowers may be blue, red or white and are irregularly shaped. The leaves are simple. Family Lobeliaceae.

lobster Large, long-tailed, marine decapod CRUSTACEAN. True lobsters (Homaridae) possess enlarged bulbous chelae (claws) and a segmented body. Some species are edible. Lobsters live in rocky crevices at the bottom of the ocean, feeding at night on seaweed and animals. Weight: up to 23kg (50lbs).

Locarno Pact (1925) Group of international agreements that attempted to solve problems of European security outstanding since the Treaty of VERSAILLES of 1919. The pact established Germany's w borders and enabled Germany to enter the LEAGUE OF NATIONS. Adolf HITLER's violations of the Treaty of Versailles disturbed the general peace established at Locarno.

loch (Scot. lake) *See* individual gazetteer articles

Lochner, Stefan (1410–51) German painter. His most important surviving work is *The Adoration of the Magi*, which is now in Cologne Cathedral. Dürer gazed "with wonder and astonishment" at the delicate naturalism of his style.

lock Structure built into a stretch of inland waterway to raise or lower water levels to correspond with the surrounding countryside. Each lock consists of two sets of lock gates. A vessel enters the lock, the gates are closed, and sluices are opened to admit or release enough water to bring the vessel to the same level as the water beyond the second pair of gates.

Locke, John (1632–1704) English philosopher and exponent of EMPIRICISM. In 1679 his friendship with the Earl of Shaftesbury, accused of conspiracy against Charles II, made him a target of suspicion and he went into exile in the Netherlands (1683–89). He returned to England only after the GLORIOUS REVOLUTION. He rejected the concept of 'innate ideas', arguing that all ideas are placed in the mind by experience. In 1690, he published *Two Treatises on Civil Government*, in which he advocated the SOCIAL CONTRACT, the right to freedom of conscience and the right to property.

lockjaw *See* TETANUS

locomotive Engine that draws a train, usually on a RAILWAY. In 1804, English engineer Richard TREVITHICK built the first STEAM ENGINE locomotive for transporting heavy loads at an ironworks. The first steam locomotive providing a railway service for passengers was George Stephenson's *Locomotion*, built in 1825. Electric-powered locomotives arrived in the late 19th century. Diesel, diesel-electric and gas-turbine locomotives were introduced in the 20th century.

locus In geometry, the path traced by a specified point when it moves to satisfy certain conditions. For example, a circle is the locus of a point in a plane moving in such a way that its distance from a fixed point (the centre) is constant.

locust Insect (type of large GRASSHOPPER) that migrates in huge swarms. Initially, the nymphs move in vast numbers on foot. As they feed, they develop into flying adults. Swarms may contain up to 40,000 million insects, and cover an area of *c.*1,000sq km (386sq mi). Length: 12.5–100mm (0.5–4in). Order Orthoptera; species *Schistocerca gregaria*.

Łódz Second-largest city in Poland, *c.*120km (75mi) sw of Warsaw. A small market town until the 19th century, Łódz grew under Russian occupation after 1820 to become the centre of the Polish textile industry. Taken by the Russians in 1815, the town returned to Poland in 1918. Industries: textiles, machinery. Pop. (2000) 815,000.

loess Fine-grained sedimentary clay. It is earthy, porous and crumbly, and usually yellowish or brown. Loess consists of mainly quartz and calcite from glaciated areas, blown by the wind and often built up into thick layers. The largest expanse is in the Huang He valley, N China.

Logan, Mount (officially Pierre Elliott Trudeau Mountain) Peak in the St Elias Mountains, Yukon, Canada. At 6,050m (19,849ft), it is the highest in Canada and the second-highest in North America. It was first climbed in 1925.

loganberry Biennial, hybrid, red-berried bramble. It is a cross between a blackberry and raspberry. Family Rosaceae; species *Rubus ursinus loganobaccus*.

logarithm Aid to calculation devised by John NAPIER in 1614, and developed by the English mathematician Henry

► **lobster** The Norway lobster (*Nephrops norvegicus*), a small burrowing form up to 20cm (8in) long found off NE Atlantic coasts, is a typical crustacean. With the crabs, crayfish, prawns, and shrimps, it is classified in a subgroup of the order Decapoda ('ten legs') called the Reptantia ('walking'; although they are able to swim short distances). The legs are borne in pairs (1–5), the first of which is enlarged to form nipping claws (chelae, 6). Of the two pairs of antennae (7, 8), the second may be far longer than the body. With the eyes (9), the antennae are the principal sense organs. The body segments are visible only on the abdomen (10) for the thorax is covered by a hard shell (the carapace, 11). The tail (12) is a characteristic fan shape.

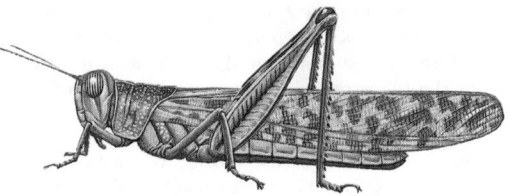

Briggs. A number's logarithm is the power to which a base must be raised to equal the number, i.e. if b^x = N, then $\log_b$ N = x, where N is the number, b the base and x the logarithm. Common logarithms have base 10, and so-called natural logarithms have base E (2.71828...). Logarithms to the base 2 are used in computer science and information theory.

logic Branch of philosophy that deals with the processes of valid reasoning and argument. Logic defines the way in which one thing may be said to follow from, or be consequent upon, another. This is known as **deductive** logic. **Inductive** logic is when a general conclusion is drawn from a particular fact or facts. Although logical systems were devised in China and India, the history of logic in the West began in the 4th century BC with the Greek philosopher ARISTOTLE. In the Middle Ages, Arab scholars rediscovered logic and in Europe Pierre ABÉLARD used logic in the synthesis of ideas that was the goal of SCHOLASTICISM. Various post-Renaissance scholars, including LEIBNIZ, developed the foundations of modern logic. In the 19th century, George BOOLE outlined **symbolic** (mathematical) logic, and Gottlob FREGE developed the system. Modern formal logic or symbolic logic utilizes symbols to represent precisely defined classes of proposition connected to each other by such operators as 'and', 'or', 'if... then'.

logical positivism Early 20th-century school of philosophy whose adherents consider that only empirically verifiable scientific propositions are meaningful. Its roots were in the LOGIC of Gottlob FREGE and Bertrand RUSSELL, the POSITIVISM of Ernst Mach and, above all, the claim of Ludwig WITTGENSTEIN that philosophy was the clarification of thought.

Loire Longest river in France. The Loire rises in the Cévennes range, on the SE edge of the MASSIF CENTRAL, and flows N and NW to Orléans. It then turns SW into a wide, fertile basin. The cities of Tours and Angers lie on its banks. It then flows through the Pays de la Loire to NANTES, emptying into the Bay of Biscay at St-Nazaire. It connects by canals to the RHÔNE and SEINE rivers. Length: 1,020km (635mi).

Lollards Followers of the 14th-century English religious reformer John WYCLIFFE. They helped to pave the way for the REFORMATION, and challenged many doctrines and practices of the medieval Church, including TRANSUBSTANTIATION, pilgrimages and clerical celibacy. They rejected the authority of the PAPACY and denounced the wealth of the Church. The first Lollards appeared at Oxford University, where Wycliffe was a teacher (c.1377). They went out among the people as 'poor preachers', teaching that the Bible was the sole authority in religion. From 1401 many Lollards were burned as heretics, and after mounting an unsuccessful uprising in London in 1414, many went into hiding.

Lombard League Defensive alliance of the cities of Lombardy in N Italy (1167). Its purpose was to resist the re-establishment of imperial authority by Emperor FREDERICK I. Led by Pope ALEXANDER III, the league defeated the Emperor at Legnano (1176). By the Peace of Constance (1183), the Italian cities retained independence while paying lip service to Frederick's authority. The League was active again in 1226, this time against Emperor FREDERICK II.

Lombards Germanic peoples who inhabited the area E of the lower River Elbe until driven W by the Romans in AD 9. In 568, they invaded N Italy under Alboin and conquered much of the country, adopting Catholicism and Latin customs. The Lombard kingdom reached its peak under Liutprand (d.744). It went into decline after defeat by the Franks under CHARLEMAGNE (775).

Lombardy (Lombardia) Region in N Italy, bordering Switzerland in the N; the capital is MILAN. Lombardy is Italy's most populous and industrial region. It consists of the provinces of Bergamo, Brescia, Como, Cremona, Mantova, Milano, Pavia, Sondrio, and Varese. North Lombardy is an Alpine region with many lakes. South Lombardy is dominated by the fertile plain of the River PO. The plains have been a major European battleground, from the Roman occupation of the 3rd century BC to the Italian takeover in 1859. Area: 23,834sq km (9,202sq mi). Pop. (1999) 9,028,913.

Lomé Capital and largest city of the Republic of Togo, W Africa, on the Gulf of Guinea. Made capital of German

Togoland in 1897, it later became an important commercial centre. It was the site of two conferences (1975, 1979) that produced a trade agreement (known as the Lomé Convention) between Europe and 46 African, Caribbean, and Pacific states. Its main exports are coffee, cocoa, palm nuts, copra and phosphates. Pop. (2002 est.) 658,100.

Lomond, Loch Long, narrow lake in Strathclyde and W central Scotland. It drains via the River Leven into the Firth of Clyde. The largest Scottish loch, it is 37km (21mi) long and up to 190m (625ft) deep. Ben Lomond (height 973m/3,192ft) towers over its N shore. Area: 70sq km (27.5sq mi).

London Capital of the United Kingdom, and the second-largest city in Europe, located on the River THAMES, 65km (40mi) from its mouth in the North Sea, SE England. Since 1965, it has been officially called Greater London, comprising the square mile of the City of London and 13 inner and 19 outer boroughs, covering a total of 1,580sq km (610sq mi). Little is known of London before the Romans set up camp in the 1st century AD. Called Londinium, it was their most important town in Britain. By the 3rd century, the population numbered c.40,000 and the town covered an area of 120ha (300 acres). After the Romans left Britain, London declined until the 9th century, when ALFRED THE GREAT made it the seat of government. The settlement of Westminster, W of the city walls, grew in the 10th century. Edward the Confessor built WESTMINSTER ABBEY and made Westminster his capital in 1042. The prosperity of England under the Tudors established London's wealth and importance. In the reign of Elizabeth I, the population increased from under 100,000 to almost 250,000. During the 17th century, the area between Westminster and the City was built up. The Plague of 1665 killed 75,000 Londoners, and in 1666 the FIRE OF LONDON destroyed many buildings. Sir Christopher WREN played an important role in the reconstruction of the city, designing many churches, including ST PAUL's. During the 19th century, the population reached 4 million. Much of E London was rebuilt after bomb damage during World War 2, and the largely derelict docklands regenerated in the late 1980s. Despite the problems of inner-city decay, experienced by most large western cities since the 1960s, London remains one of the world's most important administrative, financial, commercial and industrial cities. Industries: government administration, tourism, entertainment, engineering, printing and publishing, clothing, brewing. Pop. (2000) 8,089,000.

London, Jack (1876–1916) US novelist and short story writer. He is best known for his Alaskan novels, such as *Call of the Wild* (1903) and *White Fang* (1906). *The Iron Heel* (1907) is a dystopian novel inspired by his socialist beliefs.

London, University of Academic institution founded in 1836, originally comprising King's College and University College. The university now consists of 14 colleges, six medical schools and 11 postgraduate medical institutions, as well as various other academic institutes.

Londonderry *See* DERRY

Longfellow, Henry Wadsworth (1807–82) US poet. Longfellow's escapist poetry was extremely successful in his lifetime. He is best known for his long narrative poems, such as *Evangeline* (1847), *The Song of Hiawatha* (1855), *The Courtship of Miles Standish* (1858), and *Tales of a Wayside Inn* (1863), which includes 'Paul Revere's Ride'. Influenced by European Romanticism, Longfellow combined archaic rhythms to enliven American mythology. *Ballads and Other Poems* (1842) contains two of his most popular shorter poems, 'The Wreck of the Hesperus' and 'The Village Blacksmith'.

Longhi, Pietro (1702–85) Italian painter. He devoted himself chiefly to small-scale genre pictures, especially

▲ **Lorenz** Austrian scientist Konrad Lorenz studied the behaviour of animals for much of his life. Unlike animal psychologists, who studied animal behaviour in laboratories, Lorenz studied animals in their natural environments and arrived at radically different conclusions as to why animals behave in certain ways.

scenes of the domestic manners of the Venetian middle classes, such as *The Exhibition of a Rhinoceros at Venice*.

longhorn Almost extinct breed of beef cattle, originally from Mexico, descended from European cattle introduced by Spanish conquistadors. Once the mainstay of western US herds, they are now used only as rodeo and show animals.

Long Island Island in SE New York, USA, bounded on the S by the Atlantic Ocean and separated from MANHATTAN by the East River and from Connecticut by Long Island Sound. Originally inhabited by the Delaware Native Americans, it was settled by the Dutch West India Company and the Massachusetts Bay Colony in the 17th century. About 190km (120mi) long, it is used for commuter towns, light industry, market gardening, fishing, and holiday resorts. Area: 4463sq km (1,723sq mi). Pop. (2000) 7,448,618. *See also* BROOKLYN; QUEENS

longitude Angular measurement around the Earth, usually in degrees E or W of an imaginary N-S line through the prime MERIDIAN. All N-S lines are called either meridians or lines of longitude.

long jump Field event in which competitors run up to a take-off board and try to leap the farthest. Judges measure the length of the jump from the forward edge of the board to the rear imprint the jumper leaves in the cushioning sandpit.

Long March (1934–35) Enforced march of the Chinese Red Army during the war against the nationalist (KUOMINTANG) forces. Led by Zhu De and MAO ZEDONG, 90,000 communist troops, accompanied by *c*.15,000 civilians, broke through a Nationalist encirclement of their headquarters and marched some 10,000km (6,000mi) from JIANGSU province, SE China, to Shanxi province in the NW. Under frequent attack, the communists suffered 45,000 casualties. The march prevented the extermination of the COMMUNIST PARTY by the Nationalists.

Long Parliament English Parliament initially summoned by CHARLES I in November 1640 to raise revenue to combat Scotland in the 'Bishop's Wars'. It followed the SHORT PARLIAMENT, which lasted only weeks. Antagonism between Charles and Parliament resulted in the outbreak of the English CIVIL WAR. It sat, at intervals, for 20 years. Oliver CROMWELL expelled hostile members in PRIDE'S PURGE (1648), and thereafter it was known as the RUMP PARLIAMENT.

long-sightedness (hyperopia) Defect of vision that causes distant objects to be seen more clearly than nearby ones. In a long-sighted person, the focusing distance of the eyeball is too short and, as a result, light rays entering the eye strike the retina before they can be properly focused. Long-sightedness is corrected by convex lenses. *See also* MYOPIA

loom Frame or set of frames on which threads are woven into cloth. The loom enables a set of threads, called the weft, to be passed over and under a set of lengthwise threads, called the warp. The simplest kind of loom is a single frame on which WEAVING is done by hand. Such looms have been used for more than 7,000 years. In 1785, Edmund CARTWRIGHT invented a loom powered by a steam engine to speed cloth production. Today, most advanced commercial looms are computer-controlled and have mechanisms that thread the weft through the warp at speeds of *c*.100km/h (60mph).

loon (diver) Diving bird of the Northern Hemisphere, known for its harsh call. It has black, white, and grey plumage. An excellent swimmer, it often stays submerged while fishing. Length: 88cm (35in). Family Gaviidae.

Loos, Adolf (1870–1933) Czech architect who pioneered modern building design. He hated ART NOUVEAU, the prevailing style of the time, publishing his views in *Ornament and crime* (1908). His most important projects were houses built between 1904 and 1910; Steiner House, Vienna (1910) was one of the first to use concrete. *See also* MODERNISM

Loran (**Lo**ng **ra**nge **n**avigation) RADIO system of NAVIGATION for ships and aircraft. Pairs of transmitters emit signal pulses that are picked up by a receiver. By measuring the difference in time between the signals reaching the receiver, the vessel's position can be plotted.

Lorca, Federico García (1898–1936) Spanish poet and dramatist. His poetry, from *Gypsy Ballads* (1928) to *The Poet in New York* (1940), was internationally acclaimed. In theatre, his early balletic farces gave way to tragedies of frustrated

womanhood, such as the trilogy *Blood Wedding* (1933), *Yerma* (1935), and *The House of Bernarda Alba* (1936). He was killed by Nationalist soldiers at the start of the Spanish CIVIL WAR.

Lord Chancellor Head of the British legal system, an office of CABINET rank. The Lord Chancellor's duties include acting as head of the judiciary and as Speaker of the House of Lords.

Lord's CRICKET ground in London, UK. Founded by Thomas Lord in 1787, it has been at its present location in St John's Wood since 1814. It is the home of the Marylebone Cricket Club (MCC) and Middlesex County Cricket Club. Since 1884, every test series in England includes a match at Lord's.

Lord's Prayer Prayer JESUS CHRIST taught his disciples. It is found in Matthew 6:9–13, and slightly differently in Luke 11:2–4. It is also called *Pater Noster* (Lat. 'Our Father').

Lorelei Large rock in the River Rhine near Sankt Goarshausen, W Germany. According to legend, a beautiful maiden called Lorelei drowned herself in despair over her faithless lover, only to rise as a siren to lure fishermen to their doom on the rock.

Loren, Sophia (1934–) Italian film actress. Her sensuous performance in *The Black Orchid* (1959) set Hollywood alight. She won a best actress Academy Award for *Two Women* (1961). Other films include *Marriage Italian Style* (1964).

Lorentz, Hendrik Antoon (1853–1928) Dutch physicist and professor at Leiden. His early work concentrated on the theory of ELECTROMAGNETIC RADIATION devised by James Clerk MAXWELL. This led him to the **Lorentz transformation** and the prediction of the **Lorentz-Fitzgerald contraction**, both of which helped EINSTEIN to develop his special theory of RELATIVITY. Lorentz also worked on the ZEEMAN EFFECT, for which he and Pieter ZEEMAN gained the 1902 Nobel Prize in physics.

Lorenz, Konrad Zacharias (1903–89) Austrian zoologist, a founder of ETHOLOGY. He observed that INSTINCT played a major role in animal behaviour, as for example in IMPRINTING. He shared the 1973 Nobel Prize in physiology or medicine, with Nikolaas TINBERGEN and Karl von FRISCH.

loris Any of several species of primitive, tailless, tree-dwelling, nocturnal PRIMATES of S Asia and the East Indies. They have soft, thick fur and large eyes, and feed mainly on insects. Length: 18–38cm (7–15in). Family Lorisidae; genera *Loris* and *Nycticebus*.

Lorrain, Claude *See* CLAUDE LORRAIN

Lorraine (Ger. Lothringen) Region of NE France. The capital is Mietz. Lorraine consists of four departments: Meurthe-et-Moselle, Meuse, Moselle, and Vosges. In the 10th century, it divided into two duchies, Upper and Lower Lorraine. In 1766, it became a French province. In 1871, following the Franco-Prussian War, the E part of Lorraine joined to form the German territory of Alsace-Lorraine, which lay at the heart of Franco-German conflict in World Wars 1 and 2. Industries: brewing, winemaking. It also has rich deposits of iron-ore. Area: 23,547sq km (9,089sq mi). Pop. (1999) 2,310,376.

Los Alamos Town in New Mexico, USA, site of a large scientific laboratory. During World War 2, the laboratory was one of the centres for the MANHATTAN PROJECT, which produced the atomic bomb. After the war, the laboratory developed the HYDROGEN BOMB. Pop. (2000) 11,909.

Los Angeles (Sp. 'City of Angels') City on the Pacific coast, SW California, USA; the second-largest US city (after New York City) and the nation's leading manufacturing base.Mexican settlers founded the city in 1781. At the conclusion of the MEXICAN WAR (1848), the USA acquired Los Angeles. The city grew with the completion of the Southern Pacific (1876) and Santa Fe (1885) railways. The discovery of oil (1894) and the development of the HOLLYWOOD film and television industry encouraged further growth. During World War 2, Los Angeles' industry boomed with the need for aircraft and munitions, and many African Americans migrated to the city to work in the factories. In 1965, five days of riots in the Watts district left 34 dead and US$200 million damages. In 1992, the acquittal of four policemen on a charge of beating an African American suspect sparked off further race riots, which left 58 dead and US$1 billion damages. A 1994 earthquake killed 57 people and caused US$15–30 billion of damage. Air pollution is also a major

L

problem. Greater Los Angeles sprawls over 1,200sq km (465sq mi) joined by a freeway network. More than 600,000 Mexican-Americans live here, more than in any other US city, the majority in the overcrowded barrio of East Los Angeles. More than 500,000 African Americans also live in the city, concentrated especially in the south-central district of Watts. Central Los Angeles consists mainly of Hollywood. Beverley Hills is known for its opulent homes. Greater Los Angeles includes Anaheim (home of Disneyland) and Santa Monica. Industries: tourism, aerospace, film and television, oil refining, electronic equipment. Pop. (2000) 11,789,000.

Los Angeles, Victoria de (1923–2005) Spanish soprano. She gave her first public concert in Barcelona (1945) and made her debut at the Paris Opéra and La Scala, Milan, in 1949. In 1950 she made her American debut at Carnegie Hall and joined New York's Metropolitan Opera Company.

Lot Biblical character who was living in Sodom when God decided to destroy it (Genesis 11:31–14:16, 19). Lot survived, but his wife disobeyed instructions and looked back at the destruction of the city; she turned into a pillar of salt.

Lothair I (795–855) Frankish Emperor (840–55). Eldest son of LOUIS I, he was co-emperor with his father from 817. On Louis's death (840), war broke out between Lothair and his two brothers. Lothair was defeated at Fontenoy (841), and the Treaty of Verdun (843) split the Frankish Empire into three. Lothair retained the title of Emperor and ruled the Middle Kingdom, consisting of the Low Countries, N France, Switzerland, and N Italy

Lothair II (1070–1137) (Sometimes called Lothair III, 'the Saxon') King of the Germans and Holy Roman Emperor (1125–37). He secured the throne in a war (1125–35) against the HOHENSTAUFEN. He encouraged German E expansion, and supported Pope Innocent II against his opponents, invading Italy in 1136–37. Conrad III succeeded him.

Lothair II (826–869) King of LOTHARINGIA (855–869), son of LOTHAIR I. He inherited Lotharingia (Lorraine) from his father, and the kingdom of Provence from his brother (863).

Lotharingia Part of CHARLEMAGNE's empire inherited by his descendant LOTHAIR II, after whom it is named. Roughly, Lotharingia included modern LORRAINE (whose name is itself a corruption of Lotharingia), Alsace, NW Germany, Luxembourg, Belgium, and the Netherlands.

Lothian Region in E central Scotland, bounded N by the Firth of Forth, E by the North Sea, and S by the Lammermuir, Moorfoot and Pentland Hills; the capital is EDINBURGH. Industries: coal-mining, engineering, whisky distilling. Area: 1,755sq km (677sq mi). Pop. (2001 est.) 779,180.

lottery Form of gambling whereby participants pay to enter and winners are picked by a method based on chance. This method often involves participants choosing numbers. They win if their numbers correspond to numbers picked randomly by the lottery organizer during a subsequent draw.

lotus Common name for any WATER LILIES of the genus *Nelumbo* and several tropical species of the genus *Nymphaea*. The circular leaves and flowers of some species may be 60cm (2ft) across. *Nymphaea* is sacred to the Chinese, Indians and ancient Egyptians. Family Nymphaeaceae. The genus *Lotus* is made up of the trefoils that belong to the unrelated Fabaceae/Leguminosae family.

loudspeaker Device for converting changing electric currents into sound. The most common type has a moving coil attached to a stiff paper cone suspended in a strong MAGNETIC FIELD. By ELECTROMAGNETIC INDUCTION, the changing currents in the coil cause the cone to vibrate, thus creating sound waves. Many modern loudspeakers give faithful sound reproduction between 80 and 20,000 hertz. *See also* MICROPHONE; SOUND RECORDING

Louis I (the Pious) (778–840) Emperor of the Franks (814–840), only surviving son of CHARLEMAGNE. He struggled to maintain his father's empire. Louis' attempts to provide an inheritance for his four sons provoked civil war.

Louis VI (1081–1137) King of France (1108–37). He was the effective ruler for several years before he succeeded his father, Philip I. Louis re-established control of the royal domain, increased the authority of the royal courts, and

enjoyed the strong support of the Church. In 1137, he secured the marriage of his heir, LOUIS VII, to Eleanor of Aquitaine.

Louis VII (c.1120–80) King of France (1137–80). His marriage to Eleanor of Aquitaine extended the French crown's lands to the Pyrenees. As King, he consolidated royal power. Returning from the Second CRUSADE, Louis divorced Eleanor for alleged infidelity. She married HENRY II of England, whose French territories then became greater than those of Louis. Louis retaliated by supporting the rebellions of Henry's sons.

Louis VIII (1187–1226) King of France (1223–26). He invaded England (1216) at the invitation of barons opposing King JOHN but was defeated at Lincoln (1217) and returned to France. Louis successfully concluded the crusade against the heretical ALBIGENSES in S France.

Louis IX (1214–70) King of France (1226–70), later known as Saint Louis. His mother, Blanche of Castile, was regent from 1226 to 1236 and during his absence from France (1248–54). In 1242, Louis defeated the English at Taillebourg. He was captured on the Sixth CRUSADE.

Louis XI (1423–83) King of France (1461–83). Rebelling against his father, CHARLES VII, he was driven out of his province of the Dauphiné in 1456, and sought refuge at the court of Burgundy. As King, he suppressed rebellious nobles, largely by exploiting divisions between them. His greatest rival was Charles the Bold of Burgundy, but after Charles' death (1477), Louis gained Burgundy, and also, after another convenient death, Anjou. He strengthened the French monarchy.

Louis XII (1462–1515) King of France (1498–1515). On becoming king, Louis had his first marriage annulled in order to wed Anne of Britanny, resulting in the incorporation of Britanny into France. He succeeded his cousin, CHARLES VIII, and was involved throughout his reign in the dynastic wars arising from Charles's invasion of Italy in 1494. Louis continued this policy, invading Italy in 1499. In spite of some military successes, the Holy League defeated him and forced him to surrender all his Italian acquisitions (1513).

Louis XIII (1601–43) King of France (1610–43). Son of Henry IV and MARIE DE MÉDICIS, he forcibly ended his mother's regency in 1617 and exiled her. He relied on Cardinal RICHELIEU, who exercised total authority from 1624. Louis approved the policy of crushing the HUGUENOTS at home while making alliances with Protestant powers abroad, in opposition to the Habsburgs, during the THIRTY YEARS' WAR.

Louis XIV (1638–1715) King of France (1643–1715). Cardinal MAZARIN dominated the early part of his reign. From 1661, Louis was the epitome of absolute monarchy and was known as the 'Sun King' for the luxury of his court. As ministers, he chose men of low rank or the junior nobility, such as COLBERT. Louis' wars of aggrandisement in the Low Countries and elsewhere drained the treasury. His revocation of the Edict of NANTES drove Huguenots abroad, weakening the economy. In the War of the SPANISH SUCCESSION (1701–14), a European coalition decisively defeated the French armies.

Louis XV (1710–74) King of France (1715–74). Great-grandson and successor of LOUIS XIV, he failed to arrest the slow decline. Disastrous wars, especially the War of the AUSTRIAN SUCCESSION and the SEVEN YEARS' WAR, resulted in financial crisis and the loss of most of the French Empire. Louis encountered opposition from the *parlements* (supreme courts) and conflict with the followers of JANSENISM and court factions. The monarchy became deeply unpopular.

Louis XVI (1754–93) King of France (1774–92). Grandson and successor of LOUIS XV, he married the Austrian archduchess MARIE ANTOINETTE in 1770. Louis' lack of leadership qualities allowed the *parlements* (supreme courts) and aristocracy to defeat the efforts of government ministers, such as Jacques NECKER, to carry out vital economic reforms. The massive public debt forced Louis to convoke the STATES-GENERAL in order to raise taxation. His indecisiveness on the composition of the States-General led the third (popular) estate to proclaim itself a National Assembly, signalling the start of the FRENCH REVOLUTION. The dismissal of Necker and rumours that Louis intended to forcibly suppress the Assembly led to the storming of the BASTILLE (July 14, 1789). Louis was

▲ **loris** The slow loris (*Nycticebus coucang*) is found in the forests of SE Asia. Their tailless bodies grow to 30cm (12in). A nocturnal primate, the slow loris clings so closely to the branches of its arboreal habitat that it is able to climb upside down.

L

LOUISIANA
Statehood :
April 30, 1812
Nickname :
Pelican State
State bird :
Brown pelican
State flower :
Magnolia
State tree :
Bald cypress
State motto :
Union, Justice and
Confidence

forced to reinstate Necker, but continued to allow the Queen and court to conspire against the revolution. In October 1789, the royal family were confined to the Tuileries Palace. In June 1791, their attempt to flee France failed and Louis was forced to recognize the new constitution. Louis sought support from foreign powers. Early French defeats in the war against Austria and Prussia led to the declaration of a republic. Louis was tried for treason by the Convention and found guilty. He was guillotined on January 21, 1793.

Louis XVII (1785–95) Son of LOUIS XVI, proclaimed King of France by royalists in 1793. Placed in the care of a shoemaker by the Republican government after the execution of his father, he probably died of neglect.

Louis XVIII (1755–1824) King of France (1814–24), brother of LOUIS XVI. He fled from the FRENCH REVOLUTION to England. Louis was restored to the throne in 1814 but was forced to flee again during the HUNDRED DAYS until NAPOLEON I's final defeat at Waterloo (1815). He agreed to a constitution providing for parliamentary government and a relatively free society.

Louis, Joe (1914–81) US boxer, b. Joseph Louis Barrow. He was nicknamed the 'Brown Bomber'. In 1937, Louis won the world heavyweight title from James J. Braddock. He retired undefeated in 1949. Louis fought 25 successful defences and scored 21 knockouts, including the historic 1938 defeat of Max Schmeling. He returned to the ring, lost on points to Ezzard Charles (1950), and was knocked out by Rocky MARCIANO (1951). Louis held the title longer than any other heavyweight.

Louisiana State on the Gulf of Mexico, s central USA; the capital is BATON ROUGE. In 1699 the French colony of Louisiana was founded. It was later ceded to Spain but regained by France in 1800. In the LOUISIANA PURCHASE (1803) Napoleon sold the state to the USA. In 1861, it joined the Confederacy, being readmitted to the Union in 1868. The discovery of oil and natural gas in the early 20th century provided a great boost to the economy. Racial discrimination left the large African-American community (32% of the population) politically powerless until the 1960s. Louisiana consists of two main regions: the MISSISSIPPI alluvial plain and the Gulf coastal plain. The Mississippi Delta in the SE covers *c.*33,700sq km (13,000sq mi), about 25% of the state's total area. The tidal shoreline is 12,426km (7,721mi) long. Nearly 15% of the state is marshland. North of the marshes, prairies stretch to the Texas border. Almost half the state is forested. Louisiana has a subtropical climate. Low-lying land and heavy rainfall make it prone to flooding. It is a leading producer of soya beans, sweet potatoes, rice and sugar cane. Fishing is a major industry, particularly shrimps and crayfish. Louisiana is second only to Texas in US mineral production. Petroleum and coal account for more than 95% of mining income. Area: 125,674sq km (48,523sq mi). Pop. (2000) 4,468,976.

Louisiana Purchase (1803) Transaction between the USA and France, in which the USA bought, for 60 million francs (US$15 million), 2,144,500sq km (828,000sq mi) of land between the Mississippi River and the Rocky Mountains. With national security and the control of the Mississippi in mind, President Thomas JEFFERSON sent James MONROE to France to join US minister Robert Livingston. The two men negotiated the purchase from Napoleon, who had lost interest in a colonial empire in the New World. The Louisiana Purchase doubled the area of the USA, and 13 states were admitted from the territory.

Louis Philippe (1773–1850) King of France (1830–48). He returned to France from exile in 1814 and acquired a reputation as a liberal. He gained the throne after the JULY REVOLUTION. Although known as the 'Citizen King', Louis Philippe retained much personal power. He abdicated when revolution broke out again and the Second Republic was declared in February 1848. He died in exile in England.

Louisville City in NW Kentucky, USA, a port on the Ohio River; largest city in Kentucky. Established as a military base in 1778 by George Rogers Clark, it was named after LOUIS XVI of France. Host to the famous Kentucky Derby, the city has many stud stables. Industries: bourbon whiskey, tobacco, domestic appliances, synthetic rubber. Pop. (2000) 864,000.

Lourdes Town in sw France, in Hautes-Pyrénées department; a centre of religious pilgrimage. In 1858, a 14–year-old peasant girl called Bernadette Soubirous claimed to have had visions of the Virgin Mary in the nearby grotto of Massabielle, where there is an underground spring. In 1862, the Roman Catholic Church declared the visions to be authentic. The waters of the spring, believed to have healing powers, are the focus of pilgrimages by up to 5 million visitors a year. Pop. (1999) 40,000.

louse Common name for various small, wingless insects, parasitic on birds and mammals. The two main groups, are classified in different sub-orders of Phthiraptera. The chewing lice (Mallophaga) feed mainly on the feathers of birds. The biting or sucking lice (Anoplura) feed on the blood of mammals. Both are small, pale and flattened, with leathery or hairy skins.

Louth County in the NE Republic of Ireland, in Leinster province, bordering Northern Ireland (N) and the Irish Sea (E); the capital is Dundalk. It is a low-lying region, except in the hilly NW and the mountainous N, drained by the rivers Fane, Dee and Castletown. Industries: textiles, footwear, processed food. Area: 821sq km (317sq mi). Pop. (2002) 101,802.

Louvre France's national museum and art gallery in Paris. It holds a collection of more than 100,000 works, including paintings, drawings, prints, and sculpture from all over the world, from the prehistoric period to the late 19th century. Originally a royal palace, the Louvre became a fully fledged museum in the 18th century and opened as the first national public gallery during the Revolution in 1793.

Lovelace, Richard (1618–58) English CAVALIER poet. A flamboyant and ardent royalist, he was imprisoned in 1642 and 1648, during which time he wrote *To Althea, from Prison* and *To Lucasta, Going to the Wars*. Another collection, *Lucasta: Posthume Poems*, appeared in 1659.

Lovell, Sir (Alfred Charles) Bernard (1913–) English astronomer. From 1951 to 1981, Lovell was director of the JODRELL BANK experimental station for radio astronomy near Manchester, England, where he oversaw the construction of the world's first large steerable radio telescope.

Low Countries Region of NW Europe now occupied by the Netherlands, Belgium, and Luxembourg. Ruled by the Dukes of BURGUNDY from 1384 and the HABSBURGS from 1477, it was the most advanced and prosperous region of N Europe during the Middle Ages and Renaissance. The Dutch gained independence as the United Provinces in 1609. The southern Netherlands (Belgium), after a period united with the Dutch (1815–30), became an independent kingdom in 1830. The Dutch House of ORANGE ruled Luxembourg until 1890, when it passed to another branch.

Lowell, Amy (1874–1925) US poet and critic, sister of Percival LOWELL. Her first volume was the sensuous *A Dome of Many-Coloured Glass* (1912). Following the exit of Ezra POUND, Lowell became the leader of the IMAGISM movement. *Sword Blades and Poppy Seed* (1914) was an experiment with 'polyphonic prose', or free-verse.

Lowell, Percival (1855–1916) US astronomer, brother of Amy LOWELL. In 1894, he built an observatory at Flagstaff, Arizona. He studied the orbits of Uranus and Neptune and calculated that their orbital irregularities were caused by an undiscovered planet. His predictions led to the discovery of PLUTO in 1930. He also observed Mars, producing intricate maps of the 'canals', which he ascribed to intelligent beings.

Lowell, Robert (1917–77) US poet. Lowell was perhaps the most important voice in American poetry to emerge after World War 2. His early work, such as the Pulitzer Prize-winning *Lord Weary's Castle* (1946) is rich in Catholic symbolism. He is best known for his later, more intimate 'confessional' style, best represented by the autobiographical *Life Studies* (1959). Lowell and other 'confessional' poets, such as Sylvia PLATH, reappraised the gap between the private and the public. He won a second Pulitzer Prize for *The Dolphin* (1973).

Lower Saxony (Niedersachsen) Region of N Germany, formed in 1946 by the merging of the provinces of Hanover, Brunswick, Oldenberg, and Schaumberg-Lippe; the capital is HANOVER. Agriculture focuses on cereal crops. Industries: machine construction, electrical engineering. Area: 47,606sq km (18,376sq mi). Pop. (1999) 7,898,760.

Lowry, L.S. (Lawrence Stephen) (1887–1976) English painter known for his cityscapes of Salford, NW England.

INTERNET

Louisiana
▶ www.state.la.us

Louvre
▶ www.louvre.fr

Lowry, L.S. (Lawrence Stephen)
▶ www.thelowry.com

Loyalist In Northern Ireland, a person who wishes the province to remain part of the United Kingdom. In US history, Loyalists were those North American colonists who refused to renounce their allegiance to the British monarchy after the DECLARATION OF INDEPENDENCE (July 1776).

LSD (lysergic acid diethylamide) Hallucinogenic drug causing changes in mental state. Sensory confusion and behavioural changes result from the drug blocking the action of serotonin in the brain. First synthesized in the 1940s, LSD was made illegal in the UK and USA in the mid-1960s.

Luanda Capital, chief port, and largest city of Angola, on the Atlantic coast of sw Africa. First settled by the Portuguese in 1575, its economy thrived on the shipment of more than 3 million slaves to Brazil until the abolition of slavery in the 19th century. Today, it exports crops from the province of Luanda. Industries: oil refining, metalworking, building materials, textiles, paper, oil products. Pop. (2005) 2,839,000.

Lübeck Baltic port at the mouth of the Trave, Schleswig-Holstein, NE Germany. A Slavonic city in the 11th century, fire destroyed Lübeck in 1138. In 1143, it refounded as part of Holstein. In the 13th century, it held a pre-eminent position in the Hanseatic League. In the 16th century, it declined as trade with Scandinavia decreased. In 1937 it became part of Schleswig-Holstein. During World War 2, Allied bombing badly damaged the city. The port is the principal employer. Industries: shipbuilding, aeronautical equipment, steel, ceramics, fish canning, timber products. Pop. (1999) 213,800.

Lublin City in SE Poland. Founded in the late 9th century, Lublin developed as a trade centre along the SE route to the Ukraine. The city twice produced national governments: Poland's first Council of Workers' Delegates (a temporary authority) formed in 1918; and in 1944, following the retreat of the German army, the provisional government convened in Lublin. Today, it is the focus for a fertile farming region and a transport and industrial centre, producing heavy machinery, textiles and electrical goods. Pop. (2001 est.) 354,026.

Lucas, George (1944–) US film director and producer. Lucas began his career as an assistant to Francis Ford COPPOLA. *American Graffiti* (1973) was his breakthrough film. *Star Wars* (1977) was revolutionary in its use of special effects and became one of the biggest grossing films of all time. Lucas was executive producer of the *Star Wars* sequels *The Empire Strikes Back* (1980) and *Return of the Jedi* (1983) and the prequels *The Phantom Menace* (1999), *Attack of the Clones* (2002) and *Revenge of the Sith* (2005). He worked with Steven SPIELBERG on the 'Indiana Jones' trilogy.

Lucas van Leyden (1494–1533) Dutch painter and engraver. His engravings (which are regarded as second only to those of Dürer) include *Ecco Homo* and *Dance of the Magdalene* (1519). Among his paintings are *Moses Striking Water from the Rock* (1527) and *Last Judgement* (1526).

Lucerne (Luzern) City on Lake Lucerne, central Switzerland. It joined the Swiss Confederation in 1332. In 1803, Lucerne became the capital of the French-inspired Helvetic Republic but rejoined the Confederation in 1848. It is an important summer resort and plays host to a music festival. It is the centre of the cereal-growing canton of Lucerne. Industries: engineering, metal goods, chemicals, textiles. Pop. (2000) 57,000.

Lucifer Name given in Roman times to the planet Venus at dawn. In classical mythology, Lucifer's Greek counterpart was Phosphorus, and both were personified as male torch-bearers. In Christian mythology, Lucifer was an epithet of SATAN.

Lucknow City in N India, on the River Gomati; capital and largest city of Uttar Pradesh. The first Mogul Emperor of India conquered the city in 1528. It was the capital of the kingdom of Oudh (1775–1856), then of Oudh province (1856–77) and of the United Provinces (1887). Lucknow was the centre of the Muslim League's campaign (1942–47) for an independent Pakistan. Industries: papermaking, distilling, chemicals, printing, handicrafts. Pop. (2005) 2,589,000.

Lucretius (*c*.95–55 BC) (Titus Lucretius Carus) Latin poet and philosopher. His long poem *De rerum natura* (*On the Nature of Things*) is based on the philosophy of EPICURUS.

Luddites Unemployed workers, chiefly hand-loom weavers, in early 19th-century England who vandalized the machines that had put them out of work. The riots started in the Nottingham area in 1811, and spread to Lancashire and Yorkshire before dying out after 1815.

Ludendorff, Erich (1865–1937) German general. He played a major part in revising the Schlieffen Plan before World War 1. In 1914, Ludendorff masterminded the victory over the Russians at Tannenberg. In 1916, Ludendorff and Hindenburg gained supreme control of Germany's war effort. In the 1920s he was a member of the Nazi Party.

Luftwaffe German air force. In English-speaking countries, the term refers specifically to the air force of Nazi Germany. Built up rapidly in the 1930s, it was designed primarily as part of German *Blitzkrieg* tactics and was highly effective in support of ground forces in the early stages of WORLD WAR 2 and during the invasion of the Soviet Union (1941). It was less successful as an independent strategic bombing force in the Battle of BRITAIN (1940).

Lugosi, Bela (1884–1956) US film actor, b. Hungary. In 1927 he achieved fame on Broadway in the play *Dracula*. Lugosi reprised his role in the classic horror film *Dracula* (1931). He appeared with Boris KARLOFF in films such as *The Black Cat* (1934) and *The Raven* (1935).

lugworm Marine WORM that lives in the sand of the seabed. With the aid of bristles along its middle portion, it burrows a U-shaped tunnel in sand or mud, from which it rarely emerges. Length: up to 30cm (12in). Genus *Arenicola*.

Lukacs, György (1885–1971) Hungarian literary critic and philosopher. He joined the Communist Party in 1918, and was exiled after the abortive 1919 revolution. He returned to Budapest in 1945. Lukacs' writings include *History and Class Consciousness* (1923) and *The Historical Novel* (1955).

Luke, Gospel according to Saint Third book of the New Testament and one of the three SYNOPTIC GOSPELS. It is traditionally attributed to St LUKE. One of its sources is the Gospel according to St MARK, but it also seems to have relied on another source (now lost), which scholars refer to as 'Q'.

Luke, Saint Author, according to Christian tradition, of the gospel that bears his name and of the ACTS OF THE APOSTLES in the New Testament. He is said to have been a physician, to have been able to speak and write Greek, and may have been a non-Jew born in Antioch, Syria (modern-day Antakya, Turkey). He was a co-worker of the apostle Saint PAUL. Luke is the patron saint of painters. His feast day is October 18.

Lully, Jean Baptiste (1632–87) French composer, b. Italy. Lully was an early influence on the development of French opera. In 1652 he joined the court musicians to Louis XIV. After a series of comedy-ballets (1658–64), Lully wrote *Cadmus and Hermione* (1673), which has been called the first French lyrical tragedy. Other operas include *Alceste* (1674), *Proserpine* (1680), and *Acis et Galatée* (1686).

lumbago Pain in the lower (lumbar) region of the back. It is usually due to strain or poor posture. When associated with sciatica, it may be due to a slipped disc. *See also* RHEUMATISM

lumen (symbol lm) SI unit measuring the amount of light in an area for one second. The light emits in a unit solid angle (one steradian) from a source of unit intensity (one CANDELA).

Lumière, Louis Jean and Auguste Two brothers, Louis Jean (1864–1948) and Auguste (1862–1954), pioneers of CINEMATOGRAPHY. Together they invented an early combination of motion-picture camera and projector called the *Cinématographe*. Their film *Lunch Break at the Lumière Factory* (1895) is generally considered to be the first motion picture. They made numerous short films, each only 30 seconds or a minute in length. By 1895, the brothers had made improvements in colour photography; these eventually led to the AUTOCHROME process. *See also* CINEMA

luminescence *See* PHOSPHORESCENCE

luminism Art style followed by a group of 19th-century US painters. The luminists were principally concerned with the depiction of light and atmospheric effects. They used careful gradations of tone to achieve these, so that no brushwork was apparent. The leading figures were George Caleb Bingham, Asher Durand, and members of the HUDSON RIVER SCHOOL.

luminosity Absolute brightness of a star, given by the amount of energy radiated from its entire surface per second.

INTERNET

Lucas van Leyden
▶ www.famsf.org

L

▲ **Lumière** On March 22, 1895, Louis Lumière (pictured) and his brother, Auguste, produced their first film. On December 28, 1895, they projected several short films to a paying audience for the first time. This date is now considered by many to be the birth of modern cinema. Lumière initially shot his films himself, but later employed photographers, who were sent all over the world to record important events.

L

INTERNET

Luther, Martin
▶ www.luther.de/en/

Luxembourg
▶ www.luxembourg.co.uk

Luxor
▶ www.aegypten-fotos.de/
luxor_e.htm

It is expressed in watts (joules per second), or in terms of the Sun's luminosity. Bolometric luminosity is a measure of the star's total energy output, at all wavelengths. Absolute magnitude is an indication of luminosity at visual wavelengths.

lumpfish (lumpsucker) Marine fish of the North Atlantic coasts. A bottom-dwelling fish, it has a roughly spherical body and a modified sucking disk formed by pelvic fins, with which it attaches itself to rocks. Length: up to 61cm (2ft); weight: 6kg (13lb). Family Cyclopteridae

Lumumba, Patrice Emergy (1925–61) Congolese statesman, prime minister (1960–61) of Congo. He was leader of the Congolese nationalist movement against the Belgians and became first premier of the independent Republic of the Congo. The country plunged into civil war when the province of Katanga tried to secede. Lumumba appealed to the United Nations (UN) for assistance and a peace-keeping force was sent. MOBUTU dismissed and imprisoned him. Lumumba escaped, but was recaptured and killed.

lungfish Elongated fish from which the first amphibians developed, found in shallow freshwater and swamps in Africa, South America, and Australia. It has primitive lungs, and, during a dry season, the various species can breath air or survive total dehydration by burrowing into the mud and enveloping themselves in a mucous cocoon. Order Dipnoi.

lungs Organs of the RESPIRATORY SYSTEM of vertebrates, in which the exchange of gases between air and blood takes place. The lungs lie in the pleural cavity within the ribcage. Two sheets of tissue (the pleura) line this cavity: one coats the lungs, and the other lines the walls of the thorax. Between the pleura is a fluid that cushions the lungs and prevents friction. Light and spongy, lung tissue consists of

tiny air sacs, called ALVEOLI, which are served by networks of fine capillaries. *See also* GAS EXCHANGE; VENTILATION

lupin Any ANNUAL and PERENNIAL plants of the genus *Lupinus*, in the PEA family. They have star-shaped compound leaves and tall showy spikes of flowers. Height: to 2.4m (8ft). Family Fabaceae/Leguminosae.

lupus Autoimmune disease affecting the skin and connective tissue. The most common form, **lupus vulgaris**, is a tuberculous infection of the skin. **Lupus erythematosus (LE)** is an inflammation of tissues caused by the body's immune system. Discoid LE causes red patches covered with scales, often on the cheeks and nose. Nine times more common in women than in men, the disease is treated mainly with corticosteroids.

Lusaka Capital and largest city of Zambia, in the s central part of the country, at an altitude of 1,280m (4,200ft). Founded by Europeans in 1905 to service the local lead-mining, it replaced Livingstone as the capital of Northern Rhodesia (later Zambia) in 1935. A vital road and rail junction, Lusaka is the centre of a fertile agricultural region, and is a major financial and commercial city. Industries: textiles, shoe manufacture, cement, food processing, car assembly, brewing. Pop. (2005) 1,450,000.

lute Plucked stringed instrument most popular in 16th- and 17th-century Europe. It has an almond-shaped body and fretted neck and originally had 11 gut strings. Often played to accompany songs and stylized dances, recently it has been revived as a concert instrument.

lutetium (symbol Lu) Metallic element of the LANTHANIDE SERIES, isolated in 1907 from the element ytterbium. Chief ore is monazite (phosphate). It is used in the CRACKING of petroleum. It was named after the Latin name for Paris (*Lutetia*) by French chemist Georges Urbain who discovered it. Properties: at.no. 71; r.a.m. 174.97; r.d. 9.835; m.p. 1656°C (3013°F); b.p. 3315°C (5999°F); most common isotope Lu^{175} (97.41%).

Luther, Martin (1483–1546) German Christian reformer who was a founder of PROTESTANTISM and leader of the REFORMATION. He was deeply concerned about the problem of salvation, deciding that it could not be attained by good works but was a free gift of God's grace. In 1517 Luther affixed his *Ninety-five Theses*, which included statements challenging the sale of INDULGENCES, to the door of the Schlosskirche in Wittenberg. This action led to a quarrel between Luther and Church leaders, including the Pope. Luther decided that the Bible was the true source of authority and renounced obedience to Rome. He was excommunicated, but gained followers among churchmen as well as the laity. After the publication of the AUGSBURG CONFESSION (1530), he gradually retired from the leadership of the Protestant movement. *See also* LUTHERANISM

Lutheranism Doctrines and Church structure that grew out of the teaching of Martin LUTHER. The principal Lutheran doctrine is that of justification by faith alone (*sola fide*). He objected to the Catholic doctrine of TRANSUBSTANTIATION. Instead, Luther believed in the real presence of Christ 'in, with, and under' the bread and wine (consubstantiation). The essentials of Lutheran doctrine were set down by Philip MELANCHTHON in the AUGSBURG CONFESSION (1530), which has been the basic document of the Lutherans ever since. In 1947, the Lutheran World Federation was formed as a coordinating body for Lutheranism on a global scale.

Luthuli, Albert John Mvumbi (1898–1967) South African civil-rights leader. Elected chief of a Zulu community, he became president of the AFRICAN NATIONAL CONGRESS (ANC) in 1952, during a period of increasing militancy that led to the banning of the ANC in 1960. In 1960, Luthuli became the first African to receive the Nobel Peace Prize. Thereafter, the APARTHEID government restricted his movements and banned his publications in 1962.

Lutoslawski, Witold (1913–94) Polish composer. He gained international recognition with his *Concerto for Orchestra* (1954). Lutoslawski later experimented with serialism, notably in *Funeral Music* (1958), and aleatory techniques, as in *Venetian Games* (1961).

Lutyens, Sir Edwin Landseer (1869–1944) English architect. He built a reputation on original designs for houses. Lutyens developed a talent for more majestic commissions in

LUNGS

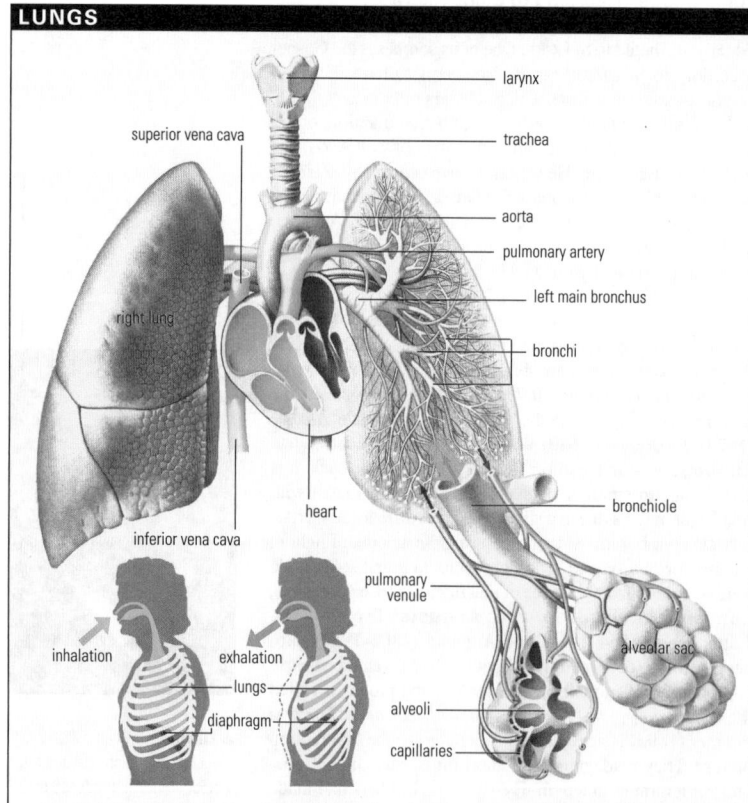

larynx

superior vena cava

trachea

aorta

pulmonary artery

left main bronchus

right lung

bronchi

heart

bronchiole

inferior vena cava

pulmonary venule

alveolar sac

inhalation   exhalation

lungs

diaphragm

alveoli

capillaries

The mechanism of breathing introduces air into the lungs for the exchange of oxygen and carbon dioxide. Air funnels into the trachea, a flexible windpipe ringed with cartilage. The trachea forks into the left and right bronchi, which enter their respective lungs. Each bronchus branches into several small segments, or bronchi, terminating ultimately in more than 250,000 respiratory bronchioles, each about 0.5mm (0.02in) in diameter. Beyond lie the alveolar ducts leading into hollow alveoli. Here in the alveoli, networked with capillaries only one cell in width, diffusion occurs across a fine membrane. Stale blood is re-oxygenated and makes its way back to the heart to be pumped to each living cell in the body. Carbon dioxide is eliminated from the lungs in expired air. The inset diagram shows the position of the diaphragm during breathing.

his World War 1 memorials, notably the Cenotaph (1922) in Whitehall, London. His most ambitious project was his plan for the imperial capital of New Delhi (1913–30).

Lutyens, (Agnes) Elisabeth (1906–83) English composer, daughter of Sir Edwin LUTYENS. She worked mainly within the TWELVE-TONE MUSIC system. Her works include various symphonies as well as *Quincunx for Orchestra* (1959–60) and the operas *The Numbered* and *Isis and Osiris* (both 1973).

lux (symbol lx) SI unit of illumination, equal to one LUMEN per square metre.

Luxembourg Independent Grand Duchy in w Europe. *See* country feature

Luxembourg Capital of the Grand Duchy of Luxembourg, at the confluence of the Alzette and Pétrusse rivers. Luxembourg was a Roman stronghold. The walled town developed around a 10th-century fortress. The Treaty of London (1867) dismantled the fortress and demilitarized the city. It is the seat of the European Court of Justice, the Secretariat of the Parliament of the European Union, the European Monetary Fund, the European Investment Bank, and the European Coal and Steel Union. Industries: iron and steel, chemicals, textiles, tourism. Pop. (2001) 81,800.

Luxemburg, Rosa (1871–1919) German socialist leader, b. Poland. She was an active revolutionary and anti-nationalist in Russian Poland before acquiring German citizenship by marriage. She founded the radical left-wing Spartacist League in 1916 with Karl LIEBKNECHT. Both she and Liebknecht are thought to have been murdered while under arrest in 1919.

Luxor (El Uqsur) City in E central Egypt, on the E bank of the Nile; known to the ancient Egyptians as Weset and to the ancient Greeks as **Thebes**. After the PYRAMIDS, Luxor's temples and tombs constitute Egypt's greatest pharaonic monuments. There are remains of many temples and tombs, dating back nearly 4,000 years. Luxor Temple lies on the banks of the Nile where, until the 19th century, it remained half buried. It was linked to the **Karnak** temple, 2.5km (1mi) N of Luxor, by an avenue of sphinxes. The temple complex covers 40ha (100 acres) and was built over 1,300 years. The greatest of the three temples is the Temple of AMUN. The Valley of the Kings, on the Nile's W bank, contains the tombs of many pharaohs. In 1997 Muslim fundamentalists killed 58 tourists outside HATSHEPSUT's Temple. Pop. (1996) 360,503.

Luzon Largest island of the Philippines, occupying the N part of the group; the main cities are QUEZON CITY and the nation's capital, MANILA. Luzon accounts for about one-third of the land mass of the Philippines and more than 50% of its population. The coastal areas are generally mountainous, the highest peak being Mount Pulog at 2,928m (9,606ft). The fertile central plain is a major rice-producing region. The indigenous Igorots also farm rice on the steep mountain terraces. The Bicol peninsula in the SE has many coconut plantations. Luzon has important mineral deposits, such as gold, chromite and copper. Manila Bay is one of the world's finest natural harbours and has been the landing point for countless invasions. Luzon has been at the epicentre of Philippine nationalism, leading revolts against first Spanish rule in 1896, and US rule in 1899. In 1941,

▲ **lute** The lute requires a high degree of skill on the part of the player. The instrument was once played throughout the Middle East and w Europe.

LUXEMBOURG

The Grand Duchy of Luxembourg is one of the smallest and oldest countries in Europe. The N belongs to an upland region that includes the Ardennes in Belgium and Luxembourg, and the Eiffel Highlands in Germany. This scenic region contains the country's highest point, a hill that reaches 565m [1,854ft] above sea level.

The s two-thirds of Luxembourg, geographically part of French Lorraine, is a hilly or rolling plateau called the Bon Pays or Gut Land ('Good Land'). This region contains rich farmland, especially in the fertile Alzette, Moselle and Sûre (or Sauer) valleys in the s and E.

Forests cover about a fifth of Luxembourg, mainly in the N, where deer and wild boar are found. Farms cover about 25% of the land and pasture another 20%.

CLIMATE

Luxembourg has a temperate climate. In the S of the country, summers and autumns are warm. This is when grapes ripen in the sheltered SE valleys. Winters are sometimes severe, particularly in the Ardennes, where snow can cover the land for weeks.

HISTORY

Luxembourg became an independent state in AD 963. By the 11th century, the County of Luxembourg formed one of the largest fiefs of the Holy Roman Empire. It became a duchy in 1354. In the 1440s Luxembourg came under the House of Burgundy then, in 1482, passed to the Habsburg dynasty. In the 16th century it became part of the Spanish Netherlands. From 1684, it came successively under France (1684–97), Spain (1697–1714) and then Austria until 1795, when it reverted to French rule.

In 1815, following the defeat of France in the the Napoleonic Wars, Luxembourg became a Grand Duchy ruled by the king of the Netherlands. Much of it passed to Belgium in the 1830s. It was not until 1867 that Luxembourg's independence was formally ratified, after a turbulent period which even included a brief time of civil unrest against plans to annex Luxembourg to Belgium, Germany or France. The crisis of 1867 almost resulted in war between France and Prussia over the status of Luxembourg. The issue was resolved by the second Treaty of London which guaranteed the perpetual independence and neutrality of the state.

Germany occupied Luxembourg in both World Wars. In 1944–5, northern Luxembourg was the scene of the Battle of the Bulge. Following World War 2, the economy recovered rapidly.

AREA 2,586sq km [998sq mi]	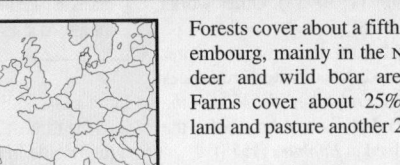
POPULATION 480,000	
CAPITAL (POPULATION)	
Luxembourg (80,000)	
GOVERNMENT Constitutional monarchy	
(Grand Duchy)	
ETHNIC GROUPS Luxembourger 71%,	
Portuguese, Italian, French, Belgian, Slav	
LANGUAGES Luxembourgish (official),	
French, German	
RELIGIONS Roman Catholic 87%, others 13%	
CURRENCY Euro = 100 cents	

POLITICS

In 1948 Luxembourg joined Belgium and the Netherlands in a union by the name of Benelux, and in the 1950s it was one of the six founders of what is now the European Union. The country's capital, a major financial centre, contains the headquarters of several international agencies including the European Coal and Steel Community and the European Court of Justice.

ECONOMY

Luxembourg has iron-ore reserves and is a major steel producer. It also has many high-technology industries, producing electronic goods and computers. Steel and other manufactures, including chemicals, glass and rubber products, are exported. Other activities include tourism and financial services. Half the land area is farmed, but agriculture employs only 3% of workers. Crops include barley, fruits, oats, potatoes and wheat. Cattle, sheep, pigs and poultry are reared.

▲ **lynx** The s European lynx (*Felis lynx*) is found only in inaccessible mountain sierras in s Spain and Portugal. It is the same species as the common lynx, which is found in North America and Asia as well as Europe, but has more clearly defined markings. The red lynx, or bobcat (*Felix rufus*), ranges throughout North America as far s as Mexico. It adapted to living in a variety of habitats, and is among the most common wild cats in the USA.

the Japanese invaded the island. US forces staged a last desperate stand on Bataan peninsula in 1942. In 1945, the US expelled the Japanese. Several US bases remain on the island. Area: 104,688sq km (40,420sq mi). Pop. (2000) 31,017,217.

Lvov (Lemberg) City in w Ukraine, on a tributary of the River Bug, close to the Polish border. Founded in 1256 by a Ukrainian prince, it was captured by Poland in 1340. Lvov became part of Austria in 1772, and in 1918 was briefly the capital of the independent Ukrainian Republic, before reverting to Poland. It was annexed by the Soviet Union (1945–91). Industries: heavy machinery, chemicals, oil refining. Pop. (2000) 794,000.

Lyceum School in classical Athens where ARISTOTLE taught. In later times, many educational institutions adopted the name.

Lycopodophyta Phylum of *c.*1,000 species of VASCULAR PLANTS related to ferns, which includes the club mosses, spike mosses and quillworts. They have branching underground stems (RHIZOMES) and upright shoots supported by roots. Some are EPIPHYTES.

Lycurgus (active *c.*625BC) Semi-mythical lawgiver of ancient Sparta. He has been cited as the author of the political and social system in Sparta. Many scholars now doubt that one individual was responsible for the Spartan social system.

Lydia Ancient kingdom of w Asia Minor. Under the Mermnad dynasty (*c.*700–547BC), it was a powerful and prosperous state, the first to issue a coinage, with its capital at Sardis. Its last King was CROESUS, famous for his wealth, who was defeated by the Persians under CYRUS THE GREAT in 547 BC.

Lyell, Sir Charles (1797–1875) Scottish geologist. He was influential in shaping 19th-century ideas about science and wrote *Principles of Geology* (1830–33). Other works include *Elements of Geology* (1838).

Lyly, John (1553–1606) English poet, dramatist, and writer of prose romances. His prose comedies and pastoral romances include *Sappho and Phao* (1584), *Endymion: the Man in the Moon* (1591), and *Midas* (1592). Lyly is best known for the elaborate prose style that he evolved in *Euphues* (1578).

lyme disease Condition caused by a spirochete (spiral-shaped bacterium) transmitted by the bite of a TICK that lives on deer. It begins with a red rash, often accompanied by fever, headache, and pain in the muscles and joints. Untreated, the disease can lead to chronic arthritis, and may affect the nervous system, heart, liver or kidneys. It is treated with ANTIBIOTICS.

lymph Clear, slightly yellowish fluid derived from the BLOOD and similar in composition to plasma. Circulating in the LYMPHATIC SYSTEM, it conveys LEUCOCYTES (white blood cells) and some nutrients to the tissues.

lymphatic system System of connecting vessels and organs in vertebrates that transport LYMPH through the body. Lymph flows into lymph capillaries and from here into lymph vessels (lymphatics). These extend throughout the body, leading to LYMPH GLANDS, storing some of the LEUCOCYTES (white blood cells). Lymph nodes empty into

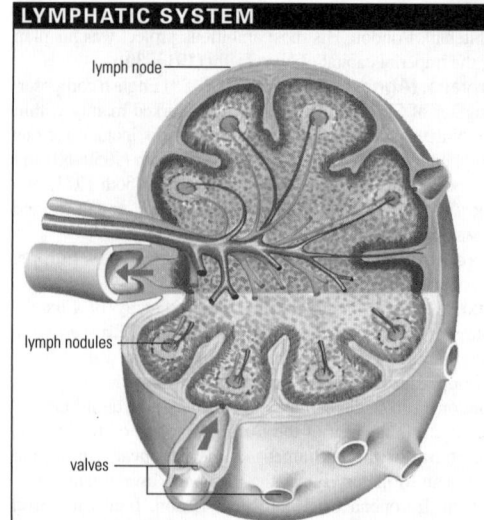

LYMPHATIC SYSTEM

lymph node

lymph nodules

valves

The lymphatic system is a network of lymphatic vessels that collects tissue fluid (the lymph) and conducts it back to the bloodstream. In the process it transports nutrients from blood to cells, and cell wastes back into capillaries. Lymph drains through the system, but the lymphatic nodes have valves to stop backflow. Lymphatic nodes are scattered along the lymph vessels but occur particularly in the neck, armpits, and groin. In the tissue around the nodes macrophage cells destroy micro-organisms, while lymph nodules produce antibody synthesizing white blood cells, the lymphocytes.

large vessels, linking up into lymph ducts that empty back into the CIRCULATORY SYSTEM. The lymphatic system plays a major role in the body's defence against disease.

lymph gland (lymph node) Mass of tissue along the major vessels of the LYMPHATIC SYSTEM. They filters and collect harmful material, notably bacteria and other disease organisms, and often become swollen when the body is infected.

lymphocyte Type of LEUCOCYTE (white blood cell) found in vertebrates. Produced in BONE marrow, they are mostly found in the LYMPH and blood and around infected sites. In human beings, lymphocytes form *c.*25% of white blood cells and play an important role in combating disease. **B-lymphocytes** produce ANTIBODIES and **T-lymphocytes** maintain IMMUNITY.

lynx Any of several small CATS found in forests of central and N Europe, along the French-Spanish border, and in the USA. It may be yellow-grey or reddish-brown. It has long legs, large feet, tufted ears, and characteristic beard-like hair on its cheeks. Length: to 116cm (46in). Family Felidae.

Lyon (Eng. Lyons) City and river port in SE France, at the confluence of the Rhône and Saône rivers; capital of Rhône department. The Romans founded Lyon in 43 BC and it became the capital of Gaul. Its historic association with silk began in the 15th century. It was also one of the first printing centres. In 1793, French Revolutionary troops devastated the city. During World War 2, Lyon was a stronghold of the French resistance. It is a major industrial area, and Europe's biggest producer of silk and rayon fabrics. Pop. (2000) 1,353,000.

lyre Ancient stringed musical instrument. Used originally by the Sumerians, it was introduced into Egypt and Assyria in the second millennium BC. In classical Greek times it had seven strings supported by a wooden frame and attached to a sound box; the strings were plucked with a plectrum. In Europe they were played with a bow. Today, the lyre also exists in various forms in E Africa and in Ethiopia.

lyrebird Either of two Australian songbirds; the superb lyrebird (*Menura superba*) and Albert's lyrebird (*M. alberti*). Males display lyre-shaped tails during courtship.

Lysander (d.395BC) Spartan general. Lysander led Sparta to victory over Athens during the PELOPONNESIAN WAR (429–404BC), defeating the Athenian fleet in 406 and 405 BC and obtaining Persian support for Sparta.

▶ **lyrebird** The superb lyrebird (*Menura superba*) of Australia is a secretive bird. It is rarely seen, as it hides in densely vegetated gullies in inaccessible parts of temperate forests. The male bird uses his impressive tail feathers in a spectacular courtship display. The female is remarkably fastidious – she carries all the droppings from the nest and puts them in a nearby stream.

L

Maastricht City on the River Maas (Meuse), SE Netherlands; capital of Limburg province. The city's strategic location, close to the Belgian and German borders, meant frequent occupation by foreign armies. In 1992, the MAASTRICHT TREATY was signed here. The city is the commercial, industrial, and transport centre for a wide region. Industries: dairy products, paper, leather goods, glass. Pop. (2001) 122,235.

Maastricht Treaty (February 7, 1992) Agreement on EUROPEAN UNION (EU) signed by the leaders of 12 European nations at MAASTRICHT, SE Netherlands. The treaty included a timetable for the introduction of a single currency (the EURO); a Common Foreign and Security Policy (CFSP), with the WESTERN EUROPEAN UNION (WEU) as a possible defence arm of the EU; a common European citizenship for nationals of all member states, and the extension of European cooperation in justice and home affairs. The treaty introduced the principle of subsidiarity, whereby decisions are taken at the most appropriate level: local, regional or national. It extended qualified majority voting in the EUROPEAN COUNCIL OF MINISTERS and increased the powers of the EUROPEAN PARLIAMENT over the budget and the EUROPEAN COMMISSION. Eleven states adopted a separate protocol on social policy (the social chapter), with the UK opting out. The UK signed up to the social chapter in the Amsterdam Treaty (1997).

Maazel, Lorin (1930–) US conductor, b. France. In 1960, he became the first American and the youngest-ever conductor at the Bayreuth Festival. He was director of Deutsche Oper (1965–71) and Vienna State Opera (1982–84). A lively performer, Maazel was music director of the Cleveland Orchestra (1971–82), and the Pittsburgh Symphony Orchestra (1988–1996). He became music director of the Bavarian Radio Symphony Orchestra in 1993.

Mabuse (1478–1536) (Jan Gossaert) Netherlandish painter. He began his career in the tradition of Gerard DAVID and Hugo van der GOES, but changed his style dramatically after a visit to Italy as an assistant to Philip of Burgundy in 1508–09. Italianate features appeared within his Netherlandish style, as seen in *Neptune and Amphitrite* (1516).

McAdam, John Loudon (1756–1836) Scottish engineer who invented the macadam road surface. McAdam proposed that roads should be raised above the surrounding ground, with a base of large stones covered with smaller stones and bound together with fine gravel. He was made surveyor general of roads in Britain in 1827.

Macadamia Genus of Australian trees of the family Proteaceae. Most species have stiff, oblong, lance-like leaves. The edible seeds are round, hard-shelled nuts, covered by thick husks that split when ripe. Height: to 18m (60ft).

Macao (Macau) Former Portuguese overseas province in SE China, 64km (40mi) W of Hong Kong, on the River Pearl estuary; it consists of the 6sq km (2sq mi) Macao Peninsula and the nearby islands of Taipa and Colôane. The city of Santa Nome de Deus de Macao (co-extensive with the peninsula) connects via a narrow isthmus to the Chinese province of GUANGZHOU. Vasco da GAMA discovered Macao in 1497, and the Portuguese colonized the island in 1557. In 1849, Portugal declared it a free port. In 1887, the Chinese government recognized Portugal's right of 'perpetual occupation'. Competition from Hong Kong and the silting of Macao's harbour led to the port's decline at the end of the 19th century. In 1974, Macao became a Chinese province under Portuguese administration. It returned to China in 1999. Gambling and tourism dominate the economy. Other industries: textiles, electronics, plastics. Pop. (2000) 656,000.

macaque Diverse group of omnivorous, medium-sized to large Old World MONKEYS found from NW Africa to Japan and Korea. Most are yellowish brown and are forest dwellers and good swimmers. Weight: to 13kg (29lb). Genus *Macaca. See also* BARBARY APE; RHESUS

MacArthur, Douglas (1880–1964) US general. A divisional commander in World War 1, he became army chief of staff in 1930, and military adviser to the Philippines in 1935, retiring from the US Army in 1937. Recalled in 1941, MacArthur conducted the defence of the Philippines until ordered out to Australia. As Supreme Allied Commander in the SW Pacific from 1942, he directed the campaigns that led to Japanese defeat. He became commander of UN forces on the outbreak of the KOREAN WAR in 1950. Autocratic and controversial, he was relieved of his command by President TRUMAN in 1951.

Macaulay, Thomas Babington (1800–59) English historian and statesman. He upheld liberal causes in Parliament (1830–38) and served on the British governor's council in India (1834–38), where he introduced a Western education system. He re-entered Parliament but spent his later years mainly in writing his *History of England* (1849–61).

macaw Any of several species of tropical American harsh-voiced PARROTS. All have sword-shaped tails and large powerful bills. Most species are brightly coloured, such as the scarlet macaw (*Ara macao*), which has a red tail and yellow wings with bright blue on its back and wings. Order Psittacidae.

Macbeth (d.1057) King of Scotland (1040–57). In 1040, he killed Duncan I, his cousin, in battle and seized the throne. English intervention on behalf of Duncan's son (Malcolm III Canmore) resulted in his defeat by Siward, Earl of Northumbria, at Dunsinane Hill, near Scone (1054). Macbeth fled north, and was eventually killed by Malcolm at Lumphanan. SHAKESPEARE based his tragedy on a 16th-century history of the king.

Maccabees, Books of Four historical books, the first two (I and II) of which are included in the Roman Catholic Deutero-canonical books of the Bible and the Protestant APOCRYPHA. **Maccabees I and II** are modelled on the OLD TESTAMENT books of CHRONICLES and are a valuable historical source. They record the Jewish dynasty of the Maccabees. In 165 BC **Judas Maccabee** led a revolt against the SELEUCID occupation of JERUSALEM. His reconsecration of the TEMPLE (165BC) is celebrated by the Jewish feast of HANUKKAH. Judas and his two brothers, Jonathan and Simon, were murdered (161 BC?, 143 BC, 135 BC respectively) in Judaea's resistance to Syrian domination. Maccabees III and IV are PSEUDEPIGRAPHA.

McCarthy, Joseph Raymond (1908–57) US Republican senator, leader of the crusade against alleged communists in the US government. Taking advantage of anti-communist sentiment in the COLD WAR, he widened his attack to other sectors of public life including the film industry. During the period of 'McCarthyism' many of those accused of communism were blacklisted. McCarthy polarized US society; many regarded his hearings as show trials or witch-hunts, while others considered him a hero. In 1954, his House Un-American Activities Committee (HUAC) turned its attention to the army. The hearings were televised, and McCarthy's accusations were shown to be baseless.

McCarthy, Mary (1912–89) US writer and drama critic. McCarthy wrote several novels, including *The Groves of Academe* (1952) and *The Group* (1963). Among her other works are *Venice Observed* (1956), and the autobiography *Memories of a Catholic Girlhood* (1957).

McCartney, Sir Paul (1942–) British singer and songwriter. McCartney was the bass player in The BEATLES and co-wrote most of their hit songs with John LENNON. The release of his solo album, *McCartney* (1970), marked the break-up of The Beatles. In 1971 he formed a new band, Wings, with his wife Linda (1942–98). "Mull of Kintyre" (1977) was the bestselling (2.5 million) UK single. In 1995, McCartney participated in a brief reformation of The Beatles. During the 1990s, he turned to classically inspired work, such as *Liverpool Oratorio* (1991) and *Standing Stone* (1997). He was knighted in 1997. *Driving Rain* (2001) marked a return to pop music.

McCullers, Carson (1917–67) US writer. Her remarkable debut novel, *The Heart is a Lonely Hunter* (1940), showed her to be a sensitive exponent of the 'southern gothic' style, epitomized by Tennessee WILLIAMS and William FAULKNER. Other poetic stories include *Reflections in a Golden Eye* (1941) and *The Ballad of the Sad Cafe* (1951).

McCullin, Don (Donald) (1935–) English photographer, best known for war photo-journalism for *The Observer* and *The Sunday Times*. McCullin produced haunting images of the horrors of conflict in Vietnam (1968) and Cambodia (1970).

MacDiarmid, Hugh (1892–1978) Scottish poet and critic, b. Christopher Murray Grieve. A nationalist and communist,

M/m, the 13th letter of the alphabet, is derived from the Semitic letter mem *(meaning water). The corresponding Greek letter was* mu, *which went via the Etruscan alphabet to Latin as m.*

M

MacDiarmid was the dominant poetic voice in Scotland from the early 1920s. His revival of Scots as a medium for poetry contributed to the 20th-century Scottish renaissance, of which *A Drunk Man Looks at the Thistle* (1926) is the masterpiece.

Macdonald, Flora (1722–90) Scottish JACOBITE heroine. After the battle of CULLODEN (1746), Macdonald smuggled the Young Pretender, Charles Edward STUART, to Skye, disguised as her maid. From there, he sailed safely to Europe.

MacDonald, (James) Ramsay (1866–1937) British statesman, prime minister (1924, 1929–31, 1931–35), b. Scotland. MacDonald became an MP in 1906, and leader of the LABOUR PARTY in 1911. His opposition to Britain's participation in World War 1 lost him the party leadership (1914), and his seat (1918). MacDonald was re-elected to Parliament and as Labour leader in 1922. In 1924, he became prime minister and foreign secretary in Britain's first Labour government. His administration was short-lived, as the LIBERAL PARTY withdrew its support and Stanley BALDWIN succeeded him as prime minister. Labour's second spell in office was also cut short, this time by the Great Depression. MacDonald, however, remained in office at the head of a Conservative-dominated 'National' government. MacDonald lost his seat in the 1935 elections, and Baldwin returned to power.

Macedon Ancient country in SE Europe, roughly corresponding to present-day MACEDONIA, Greek Macedonia, and Bulgarian Macedonia. The Macedonian King Alexander I (d.420BC) initiated a process of Hellenization. In 348 BC PHILIP II founded Thessaloníki. In 338 BC he became King of Greece. His son, ALEXANDER THE GREAT, built a world empire, but this rapidly fragmented after his death (323BC). The Romans eventually defeated Macedon in the Macedonian Wars, and the empire shrank to Macedonia proper. In 146 BC Thessaloníki became capital of the first Roman province. In AD 395, Macedonia became part of the Eastern Roman (Byzantine) Empire. Slavs settled in the 6th century. From the 9th to the 14th century, Bulgaria and the Byzantine Empire contested control of the area. A brief period of Serbian hegemony preceded Ottoman rule from the 14th to 19th century. In the late 19th century, Greece, Serbia and Bulgaria claimed Macedonia. In the first BALKAN WAR (1912–13), Bulgaria gained much of historic Macedonia, but was decisively defeated in the Second Balkan War, and the present-day boundaries were established.

Macedonia, The Former Yugoslav Republic of Balkan republic, SE Europe. *See* country feature

McEnroe, John Patrick, Jr (1959–) US tennis player, b. Germany. McEnroe was an exquisite stroke-maker, whose fiery temperament often brought him into conflict with referees. He won the US Open singles four times (1979–81, 1984), and Wimbledon three times (1981, 1983–84). McEnroe and Peter Fleming also captured ten Grand Slam doubles titles.

Machaut, Guillaume de (1300–77) French poet, musician and diplomat. His best-known poetry, in *Le livre de Voirdit*, influenced CHAUCER and anticipated the *ballade* and *rondeau*, is in A leading figure of the *ars nova*, he was among the first to compose polyphonic settings of poetry and the Mass.

Machiavelli, Niccolò (1469–1527) Florentine statesman and political theorist. From 1498 to 1512, he served as an

MACEDONIA

The Republic of Macedonia is in SE Europe. This landlocked country is largely mountainous or hilly, the highest point being Mount Korab (2,764m [9,068ft]) on the border with Albania. Most of the country is drained by the River Vardar and its many tributaries. In the SW, Macedonia shares two large lakes – Ohrid and Prespa – with Albania and Greece. Forests of beech, oak and pine cover large areas, especially in the W.

M

independence on 18 September 1991, avoiding the civil war that shattered other parts of the former Yugoslavia.

However, Macedonia ran into problems concerning recognition. Greece, considering Macedonia to be a Greek name, vetoed any acknowledgement of an independent Macedonia on its borders. It also objected to a symbol on Macedonia's flag associated with Philip of Macedon, and a reference in the country's constitution to the desire to reunite the three parts of the old Macedonia, which includes Greek territory. Macedonia adopted a new clause in its constitution rejecting all claims on Greek territory and, in 1993, joined the United Nations under the name of The Former Yugoslav Republic of Macedonia (FYROM). In late 1993 all EU countries, except Greece, established diplomatic relations with the FYROM. Greece barred Macedonian trade in 1994, but lifted the ban in 1995. Macedonia's stability was threatened in 1999 when Albanian-speaking refugees flooded into the country from Kosovo. In 2001, Albanian-

AREA 25,713sq km [9,928sq mi]
POPULATION 2,056,000
CAPITAL (POPULATION) Skopje (430,000)
GOVERNMENT Multiparty republic
ETHNIC GROUPS Macedonian 64%, Albanian 25%, Turkish 4%, Romanian 3%, Serb 2%
LANGUAGES Macedonian and Albanian (official)
RELIGIONS Macedonian Orthodox 70%, Islam 29%
CURRENCY Macedonian denar = 100 paras

speaking Macedonians in N Macedonia launched an armed struggle, which ended when the government introduced changes giving Albanian-speakers increased rights, including the recognition of Albanian as an official language. In 2004, the USA recognized the name Republic of Macedonia instead of FYROM. In 2005 relations with Greece improved and the EU agreed to consider Macedonia for membership.

CLIMATE

Summers are hot, although highland areas are cooler. Winters are cold and snowfall is often heavy. The climate is fairly continental with rainfall throughout the year. Average temperatures in Skopje range from 1°C [34°F] in January to 24°C [75°F] in July. The average annual rainfall in the city is 550mm [21in].

HISTORY

For history pre-1913, see MACEDON.

POLITICS

The BALKAN WARS (1912–13) ended with the flight of thousands of Macedonians into Bulgaria and the division of Macedonia into Greek Macedonia in the S, Bulgarian Macedonia in the SE and, largest, Serbian Macedonia in the N and centre. At the end of World War 1 Serbian Macedonia became part of the Kingdom of the Serbs, Croats and Slovenes, which was renamed Yugoslavia in 1929. Yugoslavia was conquered by Germany during World War 2, but when the war ended in 1945 partisan leader Josip Broz Tito set up a Communist government. Tito maintained Yugoslavian unity, but after his death in 1980 ethnic and religious differences began to reassert themselves. Yugoslavia broke apart into five sovereign republics; Macedonia declared its

ECONOMY

According to the World Bank, Macedonia ranks as a 'lower-middle-income' developing country. Macedonia mines coal, chromium, copper, iron ore, lead, manganese, uranium and zinc. Manufactures include cement, chemicals, cigarettes, cotton fabric, footwear, iron and steel, refrigerators, sulphuric acid, tobacco products and wool yarn.

Agriculture employs 9% of the workforce, as compared with 23% in manufacturing and mining. About a quarter of the land is farmed and major crops include cotton, fruits, maize, potatoes, tobacco, vegetables and wheat. Cattle, pigs, poultry and sheep are also raised. Forestry is another important activity in some areas.

official in the republican government of Florence, but lost his post when the Medici family regained power. His most famous work, *The Prince* (1513), offered advice on how the ruler of a small state might best preserve his power, including judicious use of force. The term Machiavellian, to describe immoral and deceitful political behaviour, arose from misunderstandings of his ideas.

machine Device that modifies or transmits a force in order to do useful work. In a basic (simple) machine, a force (**effort**) overcomes a larger force (**load**). The ratio of the load (output force) to the effort (input force) is the machine's **force ratio**, formerly called mechanical advantage. The ratio of the distance moved by the load to the distance moved by the effort is the distance ratio (formerly velocity ratio). The ratio of the work done by the machine to that put in it is the efficiency, usually expressed as a percentage. The three primary machines are the inclined plane (which includes the screw and the wedge), the LEVER, and the wheel (which includes the PULLEY and the WHEEL AND AXLE).

machine code In computing, instructions that the CENTRAL PROCESSING UNIT (CPU) of a COMPUTER can execute, without the need for translation. Machine-code statements are written in a binary-coded (low-level) COMPUTER LANGUAGE. Programmers usually write computer PROGRAMS in a high-level language (such as FORTRAN or C), which a COMPILER program then translates into code for execution. *See also* BINARY SYSTEM

machine gun Weapon that loads and fires automatically and is capable of sustained rapid fire. The firing mechanism is operated by recoil (backward thrust) or by gas from fired ammunition. The gun may be water- or air-cooled. Hiram MAXIM invented the first widely used machine gun, the maxim gun, in 1883. *See also* GATLING GUN

machine tools Power-driven machines for cutting and shaping metal and other materials. Shaping may be accomplished in several ways, including shearing, pressing, rolling, and cutting away excess material using lathes, shapers, planers, drills, milling machines, grinders, and saws. Other techniques include the use of machines that use electrical or chemical processes to shape the material. Advanced machine-tool processes include cutting by means of LASER beams, high-pressure water jets, streams of PLASMA (ionized gas), and ULTRASONICS. Today, computers control many cutting and shaping processes carried out by machine tools and ROBOTS.

Mach number Ratio of the speed of an object (or a fluid) to the speed of SOUND. Thus Mach 1 is the speed of sound, Mach 2 is twice the speed, and Mach 0.5 is half the speed. Mach numbers are named after the Austrian physicist Ernst Mach (1838–1916). *See also* SUPERSONIC SPEED

Machu Picchu Ancient fortified town, 80km (50mi) NW of Cuzco, Peru. The best-preserved of the INCA settlements, it lies on an Andean mountain saddle, 2,057m (6,750ft) above sea-level. A complex of terraces extends over 13sq km (5sq mi), linked by more than 3000 steps. US explorer Hiram Bingham discovered Machu Picchu in 1911, and dubbed it the 'lost city of the Incas'.

Macke, August (1887–1914) German painter. He was a prominent member of the BLAUE REITER group, and specialized in sensitive watercolours. During visits to Paris (1907–12), he was influenced by Robert DELAUNAY and by experimental groups, notably FAUVISM and ORPHISM. His own work remained basically in the style of EXPRESSIONISM.

Mackenzie River in NW Canada. The longest river in Canada, it flows *c.*1,800km (1,120mi) NW from the Great Slave Lake to the Arctic Ocean. Between the Great Slave and Athabasca lakes, the Mackenzie is called the Slave River. The Mackenzie River basin in Northwest Territories is heavily forested. During the 20th century, minerals have replaced fur as the principal economic resource of the basin.

Mackenzie, Sir Alexander (1764?–1820) Canadian fur trader and explorer, b. Scotland. Mackenzie moved to Montréal in 1778, and became a partner (1787) in the fur-trading North West Company. In 1789, searching for a route to the Pacific, he followed the river now named after him to the Arctic Ocean. On his second expedition (1793), Mackenzie became the first man to cross the American continent N of

Mexico. He travelled up the River Peace, discovered the River Fraser, and reached the Pacific coast at Bella Coola.

mackerel Fast-swimming, agile, marine food fish related to the TUNA, found in N Atlantic, N Pacific and Indian oceans. They have streamlined bodies and powerful tails. The body colour is silvery blue with dark side bars. It feeds on smaller fish and plankton. Length: 61cm (2ft). Family Scombridae.

Mackerras, Sir (Alan) Charles (1925–) Australian conductor, b. USA. He was musical director of English National Opera (1970–87) and Welsh National Opera (1987–92). Mackerras' most distinctive contribution has been as an interpreter of Czech music, notably Leoš JANÁČCEK.

McKinley, Mount Peak in S central Alaska state, USA, in the Alaska Range, and the highest peak in North America. Permanent snowfields cover more than half the mountain. Wildlife is abundant on the lower slopes, in particular the caribou and white Alaskan mountain sheep. It is included in Mount McKinley National Park (since 1980 known by the Aleutian name of Denali). Height: 6,194m (20,321ft).

McKinley, William (1843–1901) 25th US president (1897–1901). McKinley sat in the House of Representatives as a Republican (1876–90), and was elected governor of Ohio in 1891. He defeated William Jennings Bryan in the presidential election of 1896. A strong and effective president, he was largely preoccupied by foreign affairs. McKinley gained the support of Congress for the SPANISH-AMERICAN WAR (1898), and sanctioned US participation in suppression of the BOXER REBELLION in China (1900). McKinley declared that ISOLATIONISM was "no longer possible or desirable". Re-elected in 1900, he was shot dead by an anarchist on September 6, 1901. Theodore ROOSEVELT succeeded him as president.

Mackintosh, Charles Rennie (1868–1928) Scottish architect, artist, and designer. He was one of the most successful and gifted exponents of ART NOUVEAU. His buildings, such as the Glasgow School of Art (1898–1909), were notable for their simplicity of line and skilful use of materials. Mackintosh's ideas, some of which came from traditional Scottish buildings, had an enormous influence on early 20th-century European architecture, especially in Germany and Austria.

MacLeish, Archibald (1892–1982) US poet and playwright. One of the US expatriates in Paris during the 1920s, he was strongly influenced by Ezra POUND and T.S. ELIOT. The epic poem *Conquistador* (1932) and *Collected Poems* (1952) both won Pulitzer Prizes, as did the verse play *J.B.* (1958).

McLuhan, (Herbert) Marshall (1911–80) Canadian academic and expert on communications. His view that the forms in which people receive information (such as television, radio and computers) are more important than the messages themselves was presented in *The Mechanical Bride: Folklore of Industrial Man* (1951), *Understanding Media* (1964), and *The Medium is the Message* (1967).

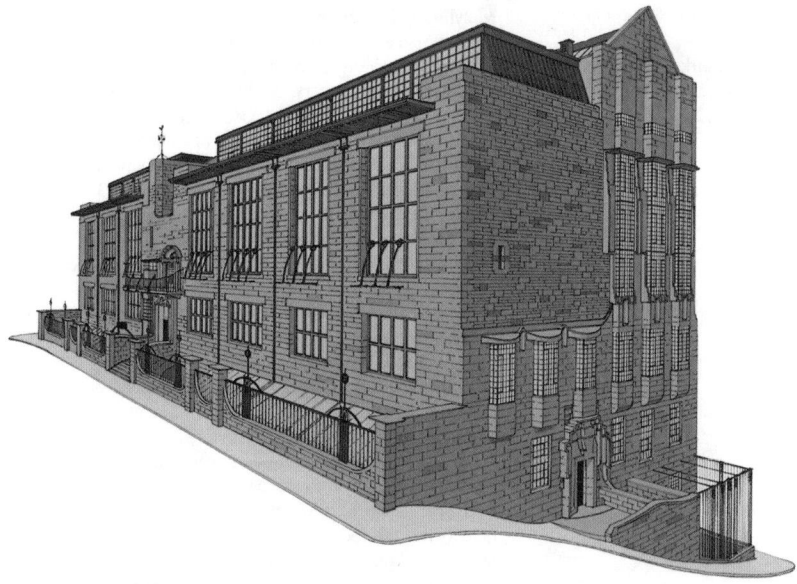

▲ **Mackintosh** Glasgow School of Art (1909). Scottish architect Charles Rennie Mackintosh based his work upon the tradition of Scottish baronial architecture, arriving at a simplified style stripped of all formal ornamentation. The clarity of line of the Glasgow School of Art shows art nouveau influences.

M

McMillan, Edwin Mattison (1907–91) US physicist. In 1951, he shared the Nobel Prize in chemistry with Glenn Seaborg for their discovery of the element neptunium and other TRANSURANIC ELEMENTS. McMillan worked on the atomic bomb at Los Alamos, New Mexico, then on the cyclotron with Ernest LAWRENCE at the University of California at Berkeley. McMillan developed the synchrocyclotron that led to modern nuclear accelerators, for which he shared the 1973 Atoms for Peace Prize with the Russian physicist V.I. Veksler.

Macmillan, Sir (Maurice) Harold (1894–1986) British statesman, prime minister (1957–63). Macmillan became a Conservative MP in 1924. He held a succession of cabinet posts, including minister of defence (1954–55) and chancellor of the exchequer (1955–57), before succeeding Anthony EDEN as prime minister. Macmillan improved Anglo-American relations, and sought a *rapprochement* between Moscow and Washington. His attempt to lead Britain into the European Economic Community (EEC) faltered in the face of DE GAULLE's opposition. Macmillan's campaign on the theme of domestic prosperity ('you've never had it so good') won him a landslide victory in the 1959 elections. His government was quickly beset by recession and the PROFUMO scandal. Macmillan resigned on grounds of ill health, and was succeeded by Alec DOUGLAS-HOME. He became Earl of Stockton in 1984.

MacNeice, Louis (1907–63) Northern Irish poet. MacNeice was a leading member of a left-wing group of writers of the 1930s, later dubbed the 'Auden circle'. MacNeice and W.H. AUDEN collaborated on *Letters from Iceland* (1937). Other volumes include *Autumn Journal* (1939) and *Solstices* (1961). Other works include the verse play *The Dark Tower* (1947).

macroeconomics Study of the economic system as a whole, rather than the study of individual markets as in MICROECONOMICS. It involves the determination of items such as GROSS NATIONAL PRODUCT (GNP) and the analysis of unemployment, INFLATION, growth, and the balance of payments. *See also* ECONOMICS; KEYNES, JOHN MAYNARD

macromolecule Molecule up to 1,000 times greater in diameter than the molecules of most substances. Many proteins, nucleic acids, plastics, resins, rubbers and natural and synthetic fibres are made up of such giant units.

macrophage Large white blood cell (LEUCOCYTE) found mainly in the liver, spleen and lymph nodes. It engulfs foreign particles and microorganisms by phagocytosis, in which PHAGOCYTES ingest them. Working with other LYMPHOCYTES, it forms part of the body's defence system.

Madagascar Island republic in the Indian Ocean. *See* country feature

mad cow disease Popular name for BOVINE SPONGIFORM ENCEPHALOPATHY (BSE)

Madeira Islands Archipelago and autonomous Portuguese region, off the NW African coast, *c.*420km (260mi) N of the Canary Islands, in the Atlantic Ocean; the capital and chief port

---

MADAGASCAR

The Republic of Madagascar lies 390km [240mi] off the SE coast of Africa and is the world's fourth largest island. In the W a wide coastal plain gives way to a central highland region, mostly between 600 and 1,220m [2,000–4,000ft]. This is Madagascar's most densely populated region and home of the capital, ANTANANARIVO. The land rises in the N to the volcanic peak of Tsaratanana, at 2,876m [9,436ft]. The land slopes off in the E to a narrow coastal strip.

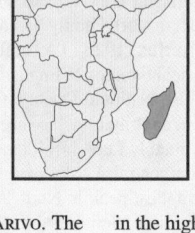

Grass and scrub grow in the s. Forest and tropical savanna once covered much of Madagascar, but farming has destroyed natural habitats and seriously threatens the unique and diverse wildlife.

CLIMATE

Altitude moderates temperatures in the highlands. Winters – April to September – are dry, but heavy rains occur in summer. Coastlands to the E are warm and humid. The W is drier, and the s and sw are hot and dry.

AREA 587,041sq km [226,657sq mi]
POPULATION 19,449,000
CAPITAL (POPULATION) Antananarivo (1,808,000)
GOVERNMENT Republic
ETHNIC GROUPS Merina, Betsimisaraka, Betsileo, Tsmihety, Sakalava and others
LANGUAGES Malagasy and French (both official)
RELIGIONS Traditional beliefs 52%, Christianity 41%, Islam 7%
CURRENCY Malagasy franc = 100 centimes

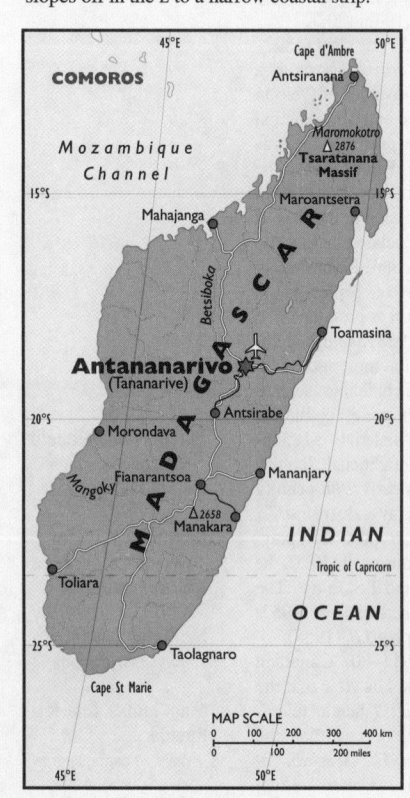

HISTORY

People from South-east Asia began to settle on Madagascar around 2,000 years ago. Subsequent influxes from Africa and Arabia added to the island's diverse heritage, culture and language. The Malagasy language is of SE Asian origin, though it included words from Arabic, Bantu languages and European languages.

The first Europeans to reach Madagascar were Portuguese missionaries in the early 17th century, who sought in vain to convert the native population. The 17th century saw the creation of small kingdoms, and later the French established trading posts along the east coast. The island became a haven for pirates from the late 18th to early 19th century. In the early 19th century, the Merina began to subdue smaller tribes, and by the 1880s they controlled nearly all the island. In 1817, the Merina ruler and the British governor of Mauritius agreed to the abolition of the slave trade. The island received British military and financial assistance, and British influence remained strong for several decades. France made contacts with the island in the 1860s. Finally, French troops defeated a Merina army in 1895 and Madagascar became a French colony. In 1942, the British overthrew Vichy colonial rule and the Free French reasserted control. In 1946–8 France brutally crushed a rebellion against colonial rule, killing perhaps as many as 80,000 islanders.

POLITICS

In 1960 the island achieved full independence as the Malagasy Republic. In 1972, the military took power. In 1975 Malagasy was renamed Madagascar and Didier Ratsiraka became president. He proclaimed martial law, banned opposition parties and nationalized many industries.

In 1992 Ratsiraka bowed to pressure and approved a democratic constitution. In 1993 multiparty elections Albert Zafy became president. He was impeached in 1996, and Ratsiraka regained the presidency in 1997. The country came to the brink of civil war in 2002 when Ratsiraka and his opponent, Marc Ravalomanana, both claimed victory in presidential elections. Ravalomanana was eventually recognized as president and Ratsiraka was exiled. In December 2006 elections Ravalomanana won a second term.

ECONOMY

Madagascar is one of the world's poorest countries. The land has been eroded due to the cutting down of forests and overgrazing of the grasslands. Farming, fishing and forestry employ about 80% of the people. The country's food crops include bananas, cassava, rice and sweet potatoes. Coffee is the leading export. Other exports include cloves, sisal, sugar and vanilla. There are few manufacturing industries.

is FUNCHAL (on Madeira). Madeira, the largest, and Porto Santo are the only inhabited islands. The region's warm and stable climate makes it a popular tourist destination. Industries: production of Madeira (a fortified wine), sugar cane, fruit, embroidery. Area: 794sq km (307sq mi). Pop. (2001) 253,482.

Maderna, Bruno (1920–73) Italian composer, conductor, and leader of the Italian avant-garde. In 1955 he founded, with BERIO, the electronic music studio of Italian Radio. Maderna often combined electronic media with live performance.

Madero, Francisco Indalecio (1873–1913) Mexican statesman, president (1911–13). Madero was imprisoned (1910) for his opposition to the dictatorship of Porfirio DÍAZ and was forced to flee to Texas, where he called for a MEXICAN REVOLUTION. With the aid of 'Pancho' VILLA and Emiliano ZAPATA, Madero overthrew Díaz. He was murdered during a military coup led by his former general Victoriano HUERTA.

Madhya Pradesh State in central India; the capital is BHOPAL. Other major cities include Gwalior and Indore. In the 16th and 17th centuries, the indigenous Gonds ruled the region. In the 18th century, the MARATHAS assumed control. The British occupied it in 1820, and from 1903 to 1950 it was known as Central Provinces and Berar. In 1956, Madhya Bharat, Vindhya Pradesh, and Bhopal incorporated to form the new state of Madhya Pradesh. Lying between the Deccan and Gangetic plains, it has the largest area of any state in India. In 2000 the state of Chhatisgarh was created out of part of Madhya Pradesh. Agriculture dominates the economy. Major crops include wheat, rice, and cotton. Madhya Pradesh is rich in mineral resources, such as bauxite, iron ore, and manganese. Bhopal has many chemical and electrical industries. Area: 308,245sq km (119,013sq mi). Pop. (2001) 60,385,118.

Madison State capital and second-largest city of Wisconsin, USA; on an isthmus between lakes Mendota and Monona. Founded as the territorial capital in 1836, it incorporated as a city in 1856. It is an educational and manufacturing centre in a dairy-farming region. Industries: agricultural machinery, meat and dairy products, medical equipment. Pop. (2000) 208,054.

Madison, James (1751–1836) Fourth US president (1809–17). Madison was a close adviser to George WASHINGTON until, dismayed by the growing power of the executive, he broke with the FEDERALIST PARTY. He became associated with Thomas JEFFERSON and the DEMOCRATIC REPUBLICAN PARTY. Jefferson made Madison secretary of state in 1801, and he succeeded him as president, winning the election easily in spite of his association with the EMBARGO ACT (1807). As president, he was unable to avoid the WAR OF 1812 with Britain, which provoked threats of secession in New England. The successful conclusion of the war restored prosperity.

Madonna Representation in painting or sculpture of the Virgin MARY, usually with the infant Jesus. The early Christians painted the Madonna in their catacombs, and she was a feature of many outstanding Byzantine ICONS. Renaissance representations were less stylized.

Madonna (1958–) (Madonna Louise Veronica Ciccone) US singer and actress. Madonna's first hit was 'Like A Virgin' (1984). After a promising debut in *Desperately Seeking Susan* (1985), her film career was less consistent. Other films include *Evita* (1996). The documentary *In Bed With Madonna* (1991) preceded the album *Erotica* (1992), and the book *Sex* (1992). She received critical acclaim for her albums *Ray of Light* (1998) and *Music* (2000).

Madras Former name of the Indian city of CHENNAI

Madrid Capital and largest city of Spain, lying on a high plain in the centre of Spain on the River Manzanares. It is Europe's highest capital city, at an altitude of 655m (2149ft). Founded as a Moorish fortress in the 10th century, Alfonso VI of Castile captured Madrid in 1083. In 1561, Philip II moved the capital to Madrid. The French occupied the city during the PENINSULAR WAR (1808–14). Madrid expanded considerably in the 19th century. During the Spanish CIVIL WAR, it remained loyal to the Republican cause and was under siege for almost three years. Its capitulation in March 1939 brought the war to an end. Modern Madrid is a thriving centre of commerce and industry. Industries: tourism, banking, publishing. Pop. (2000) 3,017,000.

madrigal Form of unaccompanied vocal music originating in Italy in the 14th century. Early madrigals feature two or three parts and a highly ornamented upper part. During the 16th and early 17th centuries, the number of voices increased and the style became more contrapuntal. Italian masters (Andrea GABRIELI; PALESTRINA) and Flemish composers such as Orlando di LASSO dominated the middle period of madrigal composition (*c*.1540–80). MONTEVERDI and English composers such as William BYRD, Orlando GIBBONS, and Thomas WEELKES commanded the late period (*c*.1580–1620).

Madurai City on the River Vaigai, Tamil Nadu, s India. Madurai was the capital of the Pandya dynasty (5th century-BC–11th century AD) and the Nayaka kingdom (*c*.1550–1736) before passing to the British in 1801. Industries: crafts, brassware, coffee, tea, tourism. Pop. (2005) 1,254,000.

Maeterlinck, Maurice (1862–1949) Belgian playwright. His plays include *The Princess Maleine* (1889) and *The Blue Bird* (1908), first produced in Moscow by STANISLAVSKY. Maeterlinck received the 1911 Nobel Prize in literature.

Mafia (It. 'boldness') Organized groups of Sicilian bandits. Originating in feudal times, the Mafia spread to the USA in the early 20th century and became involved in organized crime during the PROHIBITION era.

Magdalene, Mary *See* MARY MAGDALENE, SAINT

Magdeburg City-port on the River Elbe; capital of Saxony-Anhalt, central Germany. In the 13th century, Magdeburg received a charter and prospered as a leading member of the HANSEATIC LEAGUE. During the 16th century, it was one of the centres of the Protestant REFORMATION. In 1631, during the THIRTY YEARS' WAR, Magdeburg was sacked and destroyed by fire. The city also suffered heavy bomb damage in World War 2. A major inland port, the Mittelland Canal links it to the Rhine and the Ruhr. Industries: iron and steel, scientific instruments, chemicals. Pop. (1999) 238,000.

Magellan, Ferdinand (1480–1521) Portuguese explorer, leader of the first expedition to circumnavigate the globe. He sailed to the East Indies and may have visited the Spice Islands (Moluccas) in 1511. Subsequently he took service with Spain, promising to find a route to the Moluccas via the New World and the Pacific. In 1519, Magellan set out with five ships and nearly 300 men. He found the waterway near the s tip of South America that is now named Magellan's Strait. After severe hardships, the expedition reached the Philippines, where Magellan was killed in a local conflict. Only one ship, the *Victoria*, completed the round-the-world voyage.

Magellanic Clouds Two satellite galaxies of the MILKY WAY, visible in skies around the South Pole as misty stellar concentrations. The Small Cloud (**Nubecula Minor**), located in the constellation of Tucana, is irregular; the Large Cloud (**Nubecula Major**), mostly in the constellation of Dorado, is vaguely spiral. Their distance is *c*.150,000 light-years away. *See also* GALAXY

◄ **Madonna** US singer and actress Madonna trained briefly with the Alvin Ailey dance company before turning to pop music. Music videos and spectacular concerts accompanied hits like 'Material Girl' (1985). Her acting career was less consistent, although her performance as Eva Perón in *Evita* (1996) was widely acclaimed. Following the birth of her daughter Lourdes (1996–), she returned with the album *Ray of Light* (1998). In 2000, she married Guy Ritchie (1968–), an English director whose films include *Lock, Stock and Two Smoking Barrels* (1998) and *Snatch* (2000). Ritchie is the father of Madonna's second child, Rocco (2000–).

M

INTERNET

Madagascar
▶ www.embassy.org/madagascar

Madeira Islands
▶ www.madeiraonline.com
▶ www.madeira-web.com

Madison, James
▶ www.whitehouse.gov/history/presidents

▲ **magnolia** The flowers of the magnolia tree or shrub (*Magnolia stellata* shown) reveal it to be a relatively primitive plant. Like the earliest known flowering plants, its sepals resemble its petals. Native to E Asia and North America, they are popular in temperate gardens for their early white/pink flowers.

M

MAINE
Statehood:
March 15, 1820
Nickname:
Pine Tree State
State bird:
Chickadee
State flower:
White pine cone and flower
State tree:
White pine
State motto:
I direct

maggot Legless LARVA of a FLY. Maggot primarily refers to those larvae that infest food and waste material; others are generally called grubs. *See also* METAMORPHOSIS

Maghreb Arabic term for NW Africa, generally applied to MOROCCO, ALGERIA, TUNISIA and sometimes LIBYA.

Magi (sing. Magus) Members of a hereditary priestly class of ancient Persia, responsible for certain religious ceremonies. By the time of Christ, the term Magi applied to astrologers, soothsayers and practitioners of the occult. In the Western Church, the feast of **Epiphany** marks the coming of the Magi to Jesus. In the East, Christmas heralds the arrival of the Magi.

magic In history and anthropology, beliefs and practices intended to grant control over supernatural forces in order to indirectly affect people or events. In many cultures it is effectively a part of RELIGION, but in European history magic was traditionally regarded as opposed to religious beliefs. *See also* WITCHCRAFT

magical realism Twentieth-century literary form, particularly associated with post-1945 Latin American novelists. It is characterized by realistic and fantastical elements coherently interwoven into a highly subjective worldview. The fantastical is treated as matter-of-fact while everyday elements are described as if miraculous or extraordinary, creating a heightened sense of reality. Originally only highly formal works were described as magical realism, but recently the use of the term has broadened. Gabriel GARCÍA MÁRQUEZ's *One Hundred Years of Solitude* (1967) is a classic example of the form.

Maginot Line French fortifications on the border with Germany. Designed to prevent a German invasion, it was built between the World Wars and named after André Maginot, French minister of war (1929–32). It contained its own underground railway, hospitals and barracks, and was considered impregnable. When the Germans invaded France in 1940, they advanced through Belgium and outflanked the Maginot Line.

magma Molten material that is the source of all IGNEOUS ROCKS. Magma refers to this material while it is still under the Earth's crust. In addition to its complex silicate composition, magma contains gases and water vapour.

Magna Carta (June 1215) 'Great Charter' issued by King JOHN of England. Rebellious barons forced the King to sign the charter at Runnymede, an island in the River Thames. The 63 clauses of the Magna Carta primarily concerned the defining, and therefore limiting, of the feudal rights of the King and protecting the privileges of the Church. While it failed to prevent the first **Barons' War** (1215), it endured as a key text of the English constitution.

magnesia Magnesium oxide (MgO), a white, neutral, stable powder formed when magnesium is burned in oxygen. It is used industrially in firebrick and medicinally in stomach powders. Magnesium carbonate, found as magnesite and also used as an antacid, is often called magnesia.

magnesium (symbol Mg) Silvery-white metallic element, one of the ALKALINE-EARTH METALS. Magnesium's chief sources are magnesite and DOLOMITE. Scottish chemist and physicist Joseph BLACK first identified it as an element in 1755. Magnesium burns in air with an intense white flame, and is used in flashbulbs, fireworks, flares, and incendiaries. Magnesium alloys are light, and are used in aircraft fuselages, jet engines, missiles, and rockets. Chemically, the element is similar to CALCIUM. Hydrated magnesium sulphate is called Epsom salts. Properties: at.no. 12; r.a.m. 24.312; r.d. 1.738; m.p. 648.8°C (1,200°F); b.p. 1,090°C (1,994°F); most common isotope Mg^{24} (78.7%).

magnet Object that produces a MAGNETIC FIELD, an area around the magnet in which other magnetizable objects experience a force. Lodestones, which are naturally magnetic, were used as early magnets, and strong magnetic materials were later recognized as containing either iron, cobalt, nickel or their mixtures. A typical **permanent** magnet is a straight or horseshoe-shaped magnetized iron bar. The Earth is a giant magnet, its magnetic lines of force being detectable at all latitudes. An ELECTROMAGNET is much stronger than a permanent one and is used for raising heavy steel weights and scrap. A **superconducting** mag-

net, the strongest of all, has special alloys cooled to very low temperatures. *See also* ELECTRICITY; MAGNETISM

magnetic field Region surrounding a MAGNET, or a CONDUCTOR through which a current is flowing, in which magnetic effects, such as the deflection of a compass needle, can be detected. A magnetic field can be represented by a set of lines of force (flux lines) spreading out from the poles of a magnet or running around a current-carrying conductor. The direction of a magnetic field is the direction a tiny magnet takes when placed in the field. **Magnetic poles** are the field regions in which MAGNETISM appears to be concentrated. If a bar magnet is suspended to swing freely in the horizontal plane, one pole will point north; this is called the north-seeking or **north pole**. The other pole, the south-seeking or **south pole**, will point south. Unlike poles attract each other; like poles repel each other. The Earth's magnetic poles are the ends of the huge 'magnet' that is Earth.

magnetic flux (symbol Φ) Measure in webers (Wb) of the strength and extent of a MAGNETIC FIELD. The flux through an area A at right angles to a uniform magnetic field is $\Phi = \mu HA$, where μ is the magnetic permeability of the medium and H is the magnetic field intensity. Magnetic flux density, which is measured in TESLAS (T), is the flux per unit area (symbol B), which equals μH. Change of magnetic flux through a circuit induces an ELECTROMOTIVE FORCE.

magnetic recording Formation of a record of electrical signals on a wire or tape by means of magnetization. In an audio tape recorder, plastic tape coated with iron oxide is fed past an electromagnet that is energized by the amplified currents produced by a MICROPHONE. By ELECTROMAGNETIC INDUCTION, variations in magnetization (from the oscillating current produced by the sound) are induced in the particles of iron oxide on the tape. When played, the tape is fed past a similar electromagnet that converts the patterns into sound, which is in turn fed via an AMPLIFIER to a LOUDSPEAKER. *See also* SOUND RECORDING

magnetic resonance Absorption or emission of ELECTROMAGNETIC RADIATION by atoms placed in a MAGNETIC FIELD. Spectrometers for **nuclear magnetic resonance** (NMR) use radio frequencies for chemical analysis and research in nuclear physics, and medically to analyse body tissues.

magnetic resonance imaging (MRI) Diagnostic scanning system, based on the use of powerful MAGNETS, which produces images of soft tissues in the body. Magnetic resonance imaging (MRI) is invaluable for producing images of the brain and spinal cord in particular. The scanner's magnet causes the nuclei within the atoms of the patient's body to line themselves up in one direction. A brief radio pulse is then beamed at the nuclei, causing them to spin. As they realign themselves to the magnet, they give off weak radio signals that can be recorded and converted electronically into images.

magnetism Properties of MATTER and of electric currents associated with a field of force (MAGNETIC FIELD) and with a north-south polarity (magnetic poles). All substances possess these properties because orbiting ELECTRONS in their ATOMS produce a magnetic field; similarly, an external magnetic field affects the electron orbits. All substances possess weak magnetic (**diamagnetic**) properties and tend to align themselves with the field, but in some cases this diamagnetism is masked by the stronger forms of magnetism: paramagnetism and ferromagnetism. **Paramagnetism** is caused by electron SPIN, and occurs in substances having unpaired electrons in their atoms or molecules. The most important form of magnetism, **ferromagnetism**, is shown by substances such as iron and nickel, which can be magnetized by even a weak field due to the formation of tiny regions, called **domains**, that behave like miniature magnets and align themselves with an external field. In 1864, Scottish physicist James Clerk MAXWELL produced a unified mathematical theory of ELECTRICITY and magnetism (ELECTROMAGNETISM). The scientific branch concerned with the magnetic properties of the Earth is called **geomagnetism**.

magnetite Iron oxide mineral (Fe_3O_4). It is a valuable iron ore, found in igneous and metamorphic rocks. It is black, metallic and brittle. Permanently magnetized deposits are called lodestone. Hardness 6; r.d. 5.2.

magnification Measure of the enlarging power of a MICROSCOPE or TELESCOPE. It is the size of an object's image produced by the instrument compared with the size of the object viewed with the unaided eye.

magnitude Numerical value expressing the brightness of a celestial object on a logarithmic scale. **Apparent** magnitude is the magnitude as seen from Earth, determined by eye, photographically or photometrically. It ranges from positive through zero to negative values, the brightness increasing as the magnitude decreases. **Absolute** magnitude indicates intrinsic LUMINOSITY, and is defined as the apparent magnitude of an object at a distance of 10 PARSECS from the object.

magnolia Any of about 40 species of trees and shrubs of the genus *Magnolia*, native to North and Central America and E Asia. They are valued for their white, yellow, purple or pink flowers. Height: to 30m (100ft). Family Magnoliaceae.

magpie Bird of the CROW family, closely related to the JAY, found mostly in the Northern Hemisphere. The common magpie (*Pica pica*) has a chattering cry, a long greenish-black tail and short wings. It has a clearly defined white underside with black above. Length: 46cm (18in). Family Corvidae.

Magritte, René (1898–1967) Belgian painter. Influenced by DADA, Magritte's *The Menaced Assassin* (1926) is a landmark in the development of SURREALISM. He concentrated on the analysis of pictorial language, placing familiar objects in incongruous surroundings, and disturbing the link between word and image. Other works that explore paradox and ambiguity include *The Key of Dreams* (1930).

Magyars People who founded HUNGARY in the late 9th century. From their homeland in NE Europe, they moved S and occupied the Carpathian basin in 895, from where they raided the German lands to the west until checked by Otto I in 955. They adopted Christianity, and established a powerful state that included much of the N Balkans, but lost territory to the Ottoman Turks after the battle of Mohács (1526). The remainder of the kingdom subsequently fell to the HABSBURG Empire.

Mahabharata (Sanskrit, 'Great Epic of the Bharata Dynasty') Poem of almost 100,000 couplets, written between *c*.400 BC and *c*.AD 200. One of India's two major Sanskrit epics (the other is the RAMAYANA), the verse incorporates the BHAGAVAD GITA ('Song of the Lord'). It is important both as literature and as Hindu religious instruction.

Maharashtra State in W India, bordering on the Arabian Sea; the capital is MUMBAI. It is India's third-largest state in both area and population. Formed in 1960, Maharashtra consists of five sub-regions: Konkan, Deccan, Khandesh, Marathwada, and Vidarbha. Between the 14th and 17th century, the area was under Muslim rule. In the 17th century, it came under the control of the local Maratha tribe. Britain incorporated Maharashtra into its Indian empire in the early 19th century. Most of the land lies on the dry, W Deccan plateau where farming is poor. Rice grows along the coast. The area has rich mineral deposits, including manganese and coal. Industries, such as textiles and chemicals, concentrate in the major cities, especially Mumbai. Area: 307,762sq km (118,827sq mi). Pop. (2001) 96,752,247.

Mahatma (Sanskrit, 'Great Soul') Person of special holiness. The term is used by Hindus, but has no specific place in organized Hindu religion. The most famous 'Mahatma' of modern times was Mohandas K. GANDHI.

Mahayana (Sanskrit, 'Greater vehicle') One of the two main schools of BUDDHISM, the other being the THERAVADA or Hinayana. Mahayana Buddhism was dominant in India from the 1st to the 12th century and is now prevalent in Tibet, China, Korea, and Japan. Unlike the Hinayana (smaller vehicle) school, it conceives of BUDDHA as divine, the embodiment of the absolute and eternal truth.

Mahdi (Arabic, 'Rightly Guided One') Messianic Islamic leader. The title usually refers to Muhammad Ahmad (1844–85) of the Sudan, who declared himself the Mahdi in 1881, and led the attack on KHARTOUM (1885) in which British General Charles George GORDON died. The Mahdi set up a great Islamic empire with its capital at Omdurman. His reign lasted only about six months. The British eventually defeated his followers at Omdurman in 1898.

Mahfouz, Naguib (1911–2006) Egyptian novelist and short-story writer. He is celebrated especially for the 'Cairo Trilogy' (1956–57) of novels (*Palace Walk*, *Palace of Desire*, *Sugar Street*), which examines the fate of a middle-class family in Cairo between 1917 and the birth of the republic in 1952. His religious allegory *Children of Gebelawi* (1959) was banned in much of the Arab world. In 1988, Mahfouz became the first writer in Arabic to receive the Nobel Prize in literature.

Mahler, Gustav (1860–1911) Austrian composer and conductor. Mahler conducted the Vienna State Opera (1897–1907) and Metropolitan Opera (1908–10). He completed nine symphonies (the unfinished tenth was left as a full-length sketch). Other works include the song cycles *Das Lied von der Erde* (The Song of the Earth, 1908) and *Kindertotenlieder* (Songs on the Death of Children, 1902).

Mahmud II (1785–1839) Sultan of the OTTOMAN EMPIRE (1808–39). Mahmud's reign saw conflict with Greece, Russia and Egypt. He was initially successful against Greece in the Greek War of Independence, but Russian and British intervention forced him to capitulate (1829) and led to the Russo-Turkish War (1828–29). Mahmud then lost the support of the Viceroy of Egypt, Muhammad ALI, which led to the invasion of Turkey, precipitating Egyptian independence.

mahogany Any of numerous species of tropical American deciduous trees and their wood, valued for furniture making. Mahogany has composite leaves, large clusters of flowers, and winged seeds. Height: to 18m (60ft). Family Meliaceae.

Mailer, Norman (1923–2007) US novelist. Mailer's debut novel, *The Naked and the Dead* (1948), was one of the major works on World War 2. His combative political journalism, such as *Why are we in Vietnam?* (1967) and *The Prisoner of Sex* (1971), aroused great controversy. *Armies of the Night* (1968) and *The Executioner's Song* (1979) both won Pulitzer Prizes. Mailer has experimented with a variety of genres, from thrillers such as *Tough Guys Don't Dance* (1984), to historical novels such as *Ancient Evenings* (1983). *The Gospel According to the Son* (1997) was a political reworking of the life of Jesus.

Maillol, Aristide (1861–1944) French sculptor. Initially a painter and tapestry designer, after 1900 Maillol concentrated on sculpture and in particular the female nude. He rejected the fluid forms and Romanticism of RODIN in favour of classical ideals. Works include *Mediterranean* (1901) and *Night* (1902).

Maine State in NEW ENGLAND, extreme NE USA; the capital is AUGUSTA. The largest city is PORTLAND. The land is generally rolling country with mountains in the W and more than 2000 lakes. The chief rivers are the St John, Penobscot, Kennebec, and St Croix. Inhabited by Abnaki Native Americans, John CABOT explored Maine in 1498. The first British settlement, Fort St George, appeared in 1607 but was quickly abandoned. Firm colonization began in the 1620s, but French and Native American resistance hindered further British settlement. In 1652, Maine fell under the administration of the MASSACHUSETTS BAY COMPANY, and then of MASSACHUSETTS proper in 1691. In 1820, it became the 23rd state of the Union. Economic development was rapid, based on its trading ports and timber resources for shipbuilding. Three-quarters of Maine is forested. The major economic sector is the manufacture of paper and wood products. Economic development is hampered by poor soil, a short growing season, geographic remoteness and a lack of coal and steel. Broiler chickens and blueberries are the major agricultural products. Lobsters are the mainstay of the modern fishing industry. Tourism is increasingly important. Area: 86,026sq km (33,215sq mi). Pop. (2000) 1,174,923.

Mainz City at the confluence of the Rhine and Main rivers; capital of Rhineland-Palatinate, W Germany. Mainz was founded as a Roman camp in 1 BC. In AD 1118 it became a free city. In the 15th century, Mainz flourished as a major European centre of learning. In 1792 it fell to the French. Restored to Germany in 1815, Mainz was rapidly fortified. Today, it is a vital transport and commercial centre. Pop. (1999) 185,600.

maize (corn or sweet corn) CEREAL plant of the grass family. Originally from Central America, it is the key cereal in subtropical zones. Edible seeds grow in rows upon a cob, protected by a leafy sheath. Height: to 5m (16ft). Species *Zea mays*.

▲ **magpie** Found in temperate regions of Europe, Asia, North Africa and NW North America, magpies are members of the crow family. The common magpie (*Pica pica*) of Europe and North America, which grows to 46cm (18in), has gained an unfavourable reputation primarily due to its aggressive behaviour towards other birds.

▲ **Mailer** Norman Mailer's debut novel, *The Naked and the Dead* (1948), is both an uncompromising account of the brutality of war and a critique of American society. His characteristically rough and direct style often courted controversy, most infamously in his attack on feminism in *The Prisoner of Sex* (1971). His works of journalism include *Marilyn: A Biography* (1973), on Marilyn Monroe. His novels include *Harlot's Ghost* (1991) on the shady workings of the CIA.

INTERNET

Mahler, Gustav
▸ www.classical.net/music/
comp.lst/mahler.html

Maine
▸ www.state.me.us

Major, John

Major, John (1943–) British statesman, prime minister (1990–97). Major entered Parliament in 1979. In 1989, Margaret THATCHER made him foreign secretary, then chancellor of the exchequer. Following Mrs Thatcher's resignation, Major emerged as her compromise successor. He moderated the excesses of Thatcherism; such as scrapping the POLL TAX. Major lent full military support to the US in the GULF WAR (1991) and led the CONSERVATIVE PARTY to victory in the 1992 general election. Political scandals contributed to Tony BLAIR's landslide victory at the 1997 general election. Major resigned as party leader and was succeeded by William HAGUE.

Majorca (Mallorca) Largest of the BALEARIC ISLANDS, in the w Mediterranean, c.233km (145mi) off the Spanish coast; the capital is PALMA. The island is administered by Spain as part of the Baleares autonomous region. In 1229, James I of Aragon captured the island from the Moors and founded the kingdom of Majorca. During the Spanish Civil War, it served as a base for Italian forces supporting General Franco. Excluding the mountainous NW, the island has a mild climate, with fertile, rolling hills. Agricultural products include olives, figs and citrus fruits. The major industry is tourism. Area: 3,639sq km (1,405sq mi). Pop. (2001) 702,122.

Makarios III (1913–77) Greek-Cypriot leader. Appointed Greek Orthodox Archbishop of Cyprus in 1950, he led the movement for *enosis* (union with Greece), and the British deported him in 1956. Makarios was elected president when Cyprus gained independence in 1959, but was briefly overthrown (1974) by Greek Cypriots still demanding *enosis*. The coup provoked unrest among Turkish Cypriots and led to a Turkish invasion and the partition of Cyprus into Greek and Turkish sections, which Makarios was powerless to prevent.

Malabo Seaport capital of Equatorial Guinea, on Bioko island, in the Gulf of Guinea, w central Africa. Founded in 1827 as a British base to suppress the slave trade, it was known as Santa Isabel until 1973. Malabo stands on the edge of a volcanic crater that acts as a natural harbour. Industries: fish processing, hardwoods, cocoa, coffee. Pop. (2002) 112,800.

Malacca (Melaka) Malaysian state on the Strait of Malacca, SW Malay Peninsula; the capital is Malacca. The city was founded in 1403 and prospered as the leading trade centre for E Asia. The Muslim sultanate of Malacca became the region's most powerful empire, and the centre for the spread of Islam throughout Malaya. In 1511, Malacca was conquered by the Portuguese. In 1641, the Dutch seized the region and fortified the city. In 1824, it was ceded to Britain. In 1957, it became a state of independent Malaya and, in 1963, of Malaysia. Area: 1,658sq km (640sq mi). Pop. (2000) 602,867.

Malachi Last of the books of the 12 minor prophets and last book of all of the Old Testament in the Authorized Version. Probably written c.460 BC it addresses the Jews who had returned to Judaea after the Babylonian Captivity but were disillusioned with the continuing harshness of their existence.

Málaga City and seaport at the mouth of the River Guadalmedina; capital of Málaga province, Andalusia, s Spain. Founded in the 12th century BC by the Phoenicians, the Moors captured Malaga in AD 711, and it prospered as a major trading port. Spain regained Málaga in 1487. During the Spanish Civil War, Franco took the city from the Loyalists. After World War 2, tourism swelled Málaga's population and spilled over into the resorts of Torremolinos, Marbella, and Fuengirola. Industries: wine, beer, textiles. Pop. (2001) 531,565.

Malagasy *See* MADAGASCAR

Malamud, Bernard (1914–86) US novelist and short-story writer. The son of Russian Jewish immigrants, his common theme is the nature of a Jewish identity. His novels include *The Assistant* (1957) and *A New Life* (1961). Malamud won a Pulitzer Prize for his novel *The Fixer* (1966).

malaria Parasitic disease resulting from infection with one of four species of *Plasmodium* PROTOZOA. Transmitted by the *Anopheles* mosquito, it is characterized by sudden fever and enlargement of the spleen. Attacks of fever, chills, and sweating recur as new generations of parasites develop in the blood. The original antimalarial drug, QUININE, gave way to synthetics such as chloroquine. Malaria is one of the most widespread diseases, claiming two million lives a year.

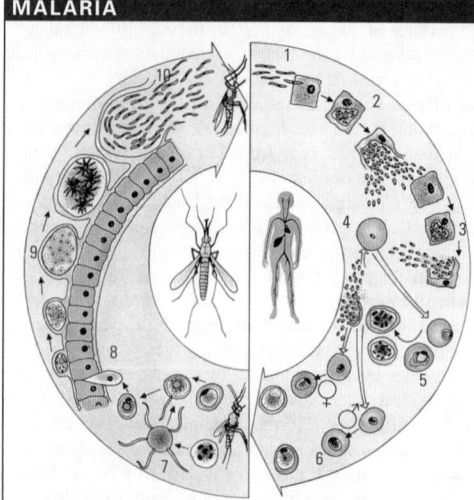

MALARIA

The life-cycle of the malaria parasite *Plasmodium* requires two hosts, the *Anopheles* mosquito and a human host, with adverse effects of infection only apparent in the human host. An infected mosquito injects thousands of *Plasmodium* organisms into the bloodstream when it bites a human (1). These penetrate liver cells, multiply and cause cell rupture (2). Released organisms may re-infect liver cells (3), but usually progress to infect red blood cells (4, 5). Male and female parasites shortly appear in the red blood cells (6). At this stage, another mosquito bites the human and takes infected blood from him/her (7). Fertilization occurs within the mosquito, the 'embryo' penetrating the stomach wall (8). Within the resulting cyst (9), thousands of organisms develop. The cyst ruptures, and the released organisms travel to the salivary glands, from where they are injected into a second human host (10).

Malawi Landlocked republic in SE Africa. *See* country feature

Malawi, Lake (formerly Lake Nyasa) Lake in the Great RIFT VALLEY of E central Africa, bordered by Tanzania (N), Mozambique (E) and Malawi (S and W). First sighted by the explorer Caspar Boccaro in 1616, the lake was visited by David LIVINGSTONE in 1859. The third-largest lake in Africa, it is fed chiefly by the River Ruhuhu and drained by the Shire.

Malayalam Language spoken on the W coast of extreme S India, principally in the state of Kerala. It belongs to the Dravidian family of languages and there are c.20 million speakers. It is one of the 15 constitutional languages of India.

Malayo-Polynesian languages Alternative name for the AUSTRONESIAN LANGUAGES

Malay Peninsula Promontory of SE Asia, stretching for c.1,100km (700mi) between the Strait of MALACCA and the South China Sea. The N part of the Peninsula is now s Thailand and the s part is Malaya (W MALAYSIA): SINGAPORE lies off its s tip. A mountain range forms the backbone of the Peninsula, rising to 2,190m (7,186ft) at Mount Gunong Tahang. Most of the vegetation is dense tropical rainforest. Malay Peninsula is one of the world's largest producers of tin and rubber. Today, it is populated equally by Malays and Chinese. The Buddhist Sailendra dynasty from SUMATRA controlled the region almost continuously from the 8th to the 13th century. In the 15th century, the Malaccan Empire held sway. For the next three centuries, the region came under the control of various European imperial powers. In 1909, Britain assumed control of a majority of the states and reached a border agreement with Siam (Thailand). Area: c.180,000sq km (70,000sq mi).

Malaysia Federation of SE Asian states. *See* country feature, page 490

Malcolm III (Canmore) (c.1031–93) King of Scotland (1058–93), son of Duncan I. He gained the throne after killing MACBETH. Malcolm launched five invasions of Norman England. In 1072, WILLIAM I of England compelled him to swear allegiance. He died in battle at Alnwick, N England.

▲ **Major** In 1990, John Major succeeded Margaret Thatcher as prime minister and leader of the Conservative Party. His consensual approach to government contrasted strongly with Mrs Thatcher's more autocratic style. In 1992, Major helped the Conservative Party secure a fourth consecutive election victory. Recession soon forced him to increase taxation. Internal wrangling over European policy dominated Major's second term. His 'back-to-basics' campaign floundered amidst accusations of sleaze and, despite an improving economy, the Conservative Party suffered a landslide defeat in the 1997 general election.

Malcolm X (1925–65) African-American nationalist leader, b. Malcolm Little. While in prison, Malcolm joined the BLACK MUSLIMS and, after his release (1953), became their leading spokesman. Following an ideological split with its leader, Elijah MUHAMMAD, he made a pilgrimage to MECCA, became an orthodox Muslim, and formed a rival group. His assassination may have been authorized by the Black Muslims.

Maldives Republic in the Indian Ocean, *c.*640km (400mi) sw of Sri Lanka, consisting of *c.*1,200 low-lying coral islands grouped into 26 atolls; the largest island and capital is MALE. The islands (200 inhabited) are prone to flooding. The climate is tropical, and the monsoon season lasts from April to October. The chief religion is Sunni Muslim. From the 14th century, the ad-Din dynasty ruled the Maldives. In 1518, the Portuguese claimed the islands. From 1665 to 1886, the Maldives were a dependency of Ceylon (Sri Lanka). In 1887, they

became a British protectorate. In 1965, they achieved independence as a sultanate. In 1968, the Sultan was deposed and a republic declared. Maumoon Abdul Gayoom has served as president since 1978. In 1982, Maldives joined the Commonwealth. In 1988, Indian troops helped suppress an attempted coup. Coconuts and copra are the primary crops. Fishing is the major industry, and the leading export-earner is the bonito (Maldives tuna). Since 1972 the growth in tourism boosted foreign reserves, but the Maldives remain one of the world's poorest countries (2000 GDP per capita, US$2000). Area: 298sq km (115sq mi). Pop. (2007) 369,000.

Male Largest of the Maldive islands, in the Indian Ocean. The island atoll forms the only urban area in the group. The extension of the airport boosted tourism. Pop. (2000) 74,069.

Malenkov, Georgi Maksimilianovich (1902–88) Soviet statesman, prime minister (1953–55). Malenkov succeeded

INTERNET

Major, John
▶ www.number-10.gov.uk

Malawi
▶ www.malawi.gov.mw

M

MALAWI

The Republic of Malawi in s Africa is a, landlocked country, no more than 160km [100mi] wide. Its dominant physical feature is Lake MALAWI, which is drained in the s by the River Shire, a tributary of the Zambezi. The land is mostly mountainous: the highest point is Mulanje, in the SE, which reaches 3,000m [9,843ft].

CLIMATE

The low-lying areas of Malawi are hot and humid all year round; the uplands have a pleasant climate. LILONGWE, at about 1,100m [3,609ft] above sea level, has a warm and sunny climate. Frosts sometimes occur in July and August, the middle of the long dry season. The wet season extends from November to May.

Wooded savanna and tropical grasslands cover much of the country, with swampy vegetation in many river valleys.

HISTORY

The Bantu-speaking ancestors of the people of Malawi first reached the area around 2,000 years ago, displacing the native SAN and introducing an iron age culture. They developed kingdoms in the region, eventually leading to the rise of the Maravi state (15th–18th centuries). In the first half of the 19th century two other Bantu-speaking groups – the Ngoni (or Angoni) and the Yao – invaded the area. The Yao took slaves and sold them to Arabs who traded along the coast. In 1859 the British missionary-explorer David Livingstone reached the area and was horrified by the cruelty of the slave trade. The Free Church of Scotland established a mission in 1875, while Scottish businessmen worked to found businesses to replace the slave trade.

The British made treaties with local chiefs on the western banks of what was then called Lake Nyasa and, in 1891, the area was made the British Protectorate of Nyasaland. They abolished slavery and established coffee plantations. In 1915 a rebellion against British rule was suppressed. The Federation of Rhodesia and Nyasaland was established by Britain in 1953. This included Northern Rhodesia (Zambia) and Southern Rhodesia (Zimbabwe). The people of Nyasaland opposed the creation of the federation, fearing domination by the white minority community in Southern Rhodesia. In 1958, Dr Hastings Banda took over leadership of the opposition to the federation and also to the continuance of British rule. Faced with mounting protests, Britain dissolved the federation in 1963. During 1964 Nyasaland became fully independent as Malawi and Banda became the country's first prime minister. In 1966, after the adoption of a new constitution, he made the country a single-party republic and took the post of president.

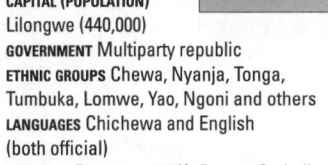

AREA 118,484sq km [45,747sq mi]
POPULATION 13,603,000
CAPITAL (POPULATION) Lilongwe (440,000)
GOVERNMENT Multiparty republic
ETHNIC GROUPS Chewa, Nyanja, Tonga, Tumbuka, Lomwe, Yao, Ngoni and others
LANGUAGES Chichewa and English (both official)
RELIGIONS Protestant 55%, Roman Catholic 20%, Islam 20%
CURRENCY Malawian kwacha = 100 tambala

POLITICS

Banda declared himself president for life in 1971. His autocratic regime differed from most of black Africa in being conservative and pragmatic, hostile to its socialist neighbours, but friendly with South Africa. His austerity programme and agricultural policies seemed to have wrought an economic miracle, but in the 1980s the country went into a swift decline. This, combined with the arrival of huge numbers of refugees from war-torn Mozambique, led to a return to poverty despite massive aid packages. Another immediate and ongoing problem was the high incidence of AIDS, which put pressure on the country's limited welfare services. Political dissent led to the restoration of a multiparty system in 1993. Banda and his party were defeated in the elections of 1994, and Bakili Muluzi became president. Banda was arrested and charged with murder, but he died in 1997.

ECONOMY

The overthrow of Banda led to a restoration of political freedoms. The abolition of school fees and school uniforms nearly doubled school enrolment. Malawi remains one of the world's poorest countries. Reforms in the 1990s included encouraging small farmers to diversify production, but free enterprise and privatization angered some farmers who have suffered from the ending of subsidies.

Although fertile farmland is limited, agriculture dominates the economy employing more than 80% of the workforce. Tobacco is the leading export, followed by tea, sugar and cotton. The main food crops include cassava, groundnuts, maize, rice and sorghum. Many farmers raise cattle, goats and other livestock.

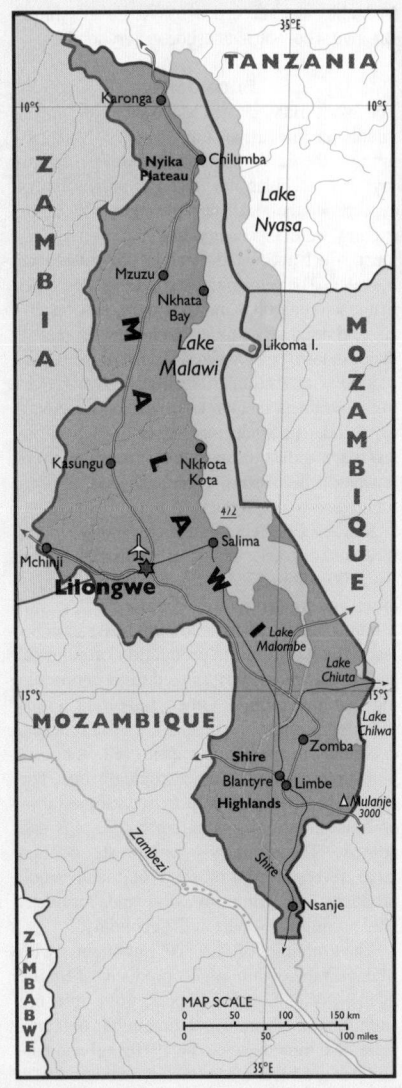

Malaysia consists of two parts, the Malay peninsula and N BORNEO. Peninsular Malaysia is made up of 11 states and 2 of the 3 components of the federal territory, KUALA LUMPUR and Putrajaya. N Borneo comprises two states and the remaining component of the federal territory, Labuan.

The peninsular is dominated by mountains that run n–s. The most important is the Main Range, which runs from the Thai border to se of Kuala Lumpur. At its highest, Gunong Kerbau, it is 2,182m [7,159ft]. s of the Main Range lie the flat, poorly drained lowlands of Johor. Short rivers have built up lowlands around the coast. n Borneo has a mangrove-fringed coastal plain backed by hill country, with e–w fold mountains in the interior. The most striking mountain, and Malaysia's highest point, is the 4,101 m [13,455 ft] granite peak of Mount Kinabalu in Sabah.

CLIMATE

Malaysia has a hot equatorial climate. Temperatures are high all year, though the mountains are much cooler than lowland areas. Rainfall affects the whole country and is heavy throughout the year.

HISTORY

For early history *see* MALAY PENINSULA, SABAH, and SARAWAK. The first Europeans to reach the area were the Portuguese, and MALACCA became a Portuguese possession in 1511. The Dutch took Malacca in 1641 and many people from Dutch-controlled Sulawesi and Sumatra settled in the peninsula, adding to the region's complex ethnic mix. The British EAST INDIA COMPANY led the British occupation of SINGAPORE in 1819, and Malacca fell under British rule by an Anglo-Dutch treaty of 1824.

In 1867 Penang (now Pinang), Malacca and Singapore together became a British colony called the Straits Settlement. British rule was gradually extended, with Sabah and Sarawak becoming a British protectorate in 1888. Under British rule the economy developed, and thousands of Chinese and Indians were brought in to work on rubber plantations and tin mines.

Japan occupied the area during World War 2, but British rule was restored in 1945 following Japan's defeat. In the late 1940s and 1950s, inspired by the Chinese revolution, communists fought the British authorities. Guerrilla warfare ended with the independence of the Federation of Malaya in 1957. In 1963 Malaya joined with Singapore, Sabah, and Sarawak to form the nation of Malaysia, with Tunku Abdul Rahman of the Alliance Party as prime minis-

ter. Brunei was invited to join, but no agreement was achieved on entry terms. Arguments between Singapore and the Malaysian government occurred from the outset, causing Singapore to withdraw in 1965 to become an independent sovereign state.

The nation has great ethnic and religious diversity, much of it a legacy of colonialism. There are also a number of aboriginal peoples, notably in Sabah and Sarawak. This patchwork has caused tensions, especially between the Muslim Malays and the politically dominant, mainly Buddhist, Chinese. Riots broke out in 1969 but did not escalate into armed conflict. Indonesia, which objected to Sabah and Sarawak joining Malaysia, adopted confrontational policies which drove Malaysia to increase its defence expenditure. Keen to remain independent of the Western bloc, by 1967 Malaysia was playing a major part in regional affairs through its membership of ASEAN (the Association of South-east Asian Nations).

POLITICS

From the 1970s Malaysia achieved rapid economic progress. This increased under the leadership of Dr Mahathir Mohamad, who became prime minister in 1981. Mahathir encouraged the development of industry in order to diversify the economy and reduce the country's reliance on agriculture and mining. The first Malaysian car, the Proton Saga, went into production in 1985 and by the early 1990s, manufacturing accounted for about 20% of the gross domestic product. By 1996 manufacturing's share of the GDP had risen to nearly 35%. However, as with many of the economic 'tigers' in Asia's eastern rim, Malaysia was hit by a recession from 1997–8. In response to the crisis, the government ordered the repatriation of many temporary foreign workers and initiated a series of austerity measures aimed at restoring confidence and avoiding the chronic debt problems affecting some other Asian countries. In 1998 the economy shrank by about 5%.

During the economic crisis, differences developed between Mahathir Mohamad and his deputy prime minister and finance minister, Anwar Ibrahim. Anwar wanted Malaysia to work closely with the International Monetary Fund (IMF) to promote domestic reforms and strict monetary and fiscal policies. By the summer of 1998 he had gone further, attacking corruption and nepotism in government. Mahathir, suspicious of international 'plots' to undermine Malaysia's economy, put much of the blame for the crisis on foreign

speculators. He sacked Anwar from the government and also from the ruling United Malays National Organization (UMNO). Anwar was jailed for corruption and alleged sexual misconduct, but these charges were later overturned.

In late 1999 Mahathir called a snap election to consolidate his power and strengthen his mandate to deal with the economy. With the economy appearing to be rebounding from recession, Mahathir's coalition retained its two-thirds majority in parliament. However, many Malays voted for the conservative Muslim Parti Islam and Mahathir had to rely more on the Chinese and Indian parties in his coalition. In 2003 Mahathir was succeeded by Abdullah Ahmad Badawi, who won a landslide victory in 2004.

ECONOMY

The World Bank classes Malaysia as an 'upper-middle-income' developing country. Manufacturing is the most important sector of the economy and accounts for a high proportion of exports. By the mid 1990s the country's leading exports were machinery and transport equipment, which accounted for about 55% of exports by value. The remaining exports included other manufactured goods, mineral fuels, raw materials and food. Electronic equipment is now a major industry, and Malaysia is one of the largest producers of consumer electronics. Other electronic products include communications equipment and semiconductors. Apart from electronics, major industries include chemicals, petroleum products, plastics, processed food, textiles, rubber and wood products.

Malaysia is becoming increasingly urbanized, mostly as a result of industrialization. By 2000, about 57% of the population lived in cities and towns. However, agriculture is still a major sector of the economy. The country leads the world in the production of palm oil and, in the mid-1990s, ranked third in producing natural rubber. Other important crops include apples, bananas, cocoa beans, coconuts, pepper, sugar cane, tea, tobacco, pineapples and many other tropical fruits. The country's chief food crop is rice. Some farmers raise livestock, including cattle, pigs and poultry. The country's rainforests contain large reserves of timber. Wood and wood products, including plywood and furniture, play an important part in the economy.

The mining of tin is important, with Malaysia the eighth largest producer of tin ore in the world. Bauxite, copper, gold, iron ore and ilmenite – from which titanium is obtained – are also mined. Since the 1970s, oil and natural gas production has steadily increased.

AREA 329,758sq km [127,320sq mi]
POPULATION 24,821,000
CAPITAL (POPULATION)
Kuala Lumpur (1,392,000), Putrajaya (administrative centre)
GOVERNMENT Constitutional monarchy
ETHNIC GROUPS Malay and other indigenous groups 58%, Chinese 24%, Indian 8%, others
LANGUAGES Malay (official), Chinese, English
RELIGIONS Islam, Buddhism, Daoism, Hinduism, Christianity, Sikhism
CURRENCY Ringgit = 100 cents

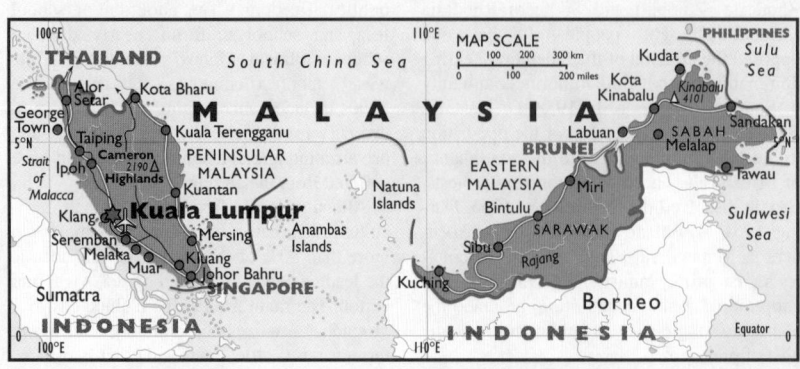

M

STALIN as prime minister and leader of the Communist Party. Nikita KHRUSHCHEV succeeded Malenkov as party leader and, in 1955, he also lost the premiership. Implicated in a coup against Khrushchev in 1957, he was sent to manage a power station in Siberia. He was expelled by the party in 1961.

Malevich, Kasimir (1878–1935) Russian painter, an important pioneer of geometric ABSTRACT ART. Malevich absorbed ideas from CUBISM (LÉGER in particular), and FUTURISM. His experiments with the fragmentation and multiplication of images include *The Knife Grinder* (1912). Malevich founded the SUPREMATISM movement (1913), and later concentrated on the development of CONSTRUCTIVISM.

Mali Landlocked republic in w Africa. *See* country feature

Malinowski, Bronislaw (1884–1942) British anthropologist, b. Poland. Considered a pioneer of social ANTHROPOLOGY, his work with 'primitive' societies led to the belief that every aspect of a society is a function vital to its existence.

mallard Large, common, freshwater duck. The male is black, white, brown and grey with a green head, whereas the female is mottled brown with blue wing markings. It feeds from the surface. Length: 63cm (28in). Species *Anas platyrhyncho*.

Mallarmé, Stephane (1842–98) French poet, leading exponent of SYMBOLISM and precursor of MODERNISM.

Mallarmé's allusive poetic style defies definitive statement in favour of sound associations. His best-known poems are *Hérodiade* (1869) and *L'Après-Midi d'un faune* (1876). Mallarmé's work was a defining influence on Paul VALÉRY.

Malle, Louis (1932–95) French film director. Malle's first feature, *Ascenseur pour l'Echafaud* (1957), was a landmark in the French *nouvelle vague*. Other films from this period include *Les Amants* (1958) and *Le Feu Follet* (1963). Malle first English language film was *Pretty Baby* (1978). Other US films include *Atlantic City* (1980) and *My Dinner with Andre* (1981). His best-known film is *Au Revoir Les Enfants* (1987). Malle's final film was *Uncle Vanya on 42nd Street* (1995).

malleability Property of metals (or other substances) that can be permanently shaped by hammering or rolling without breaking. In some cases it is increased by raising temperature.

mallow Annual and perennial plants occurring in tropical and temperate regions. The mallow family includes more than 900 species, of which cotton, okra and hibiscus are among the best known. Family Malvaceae; especially genus *Malva*.

Malmö Fortified port and city on the Øresund opposite Copenhagen, sw Sweden. Founded in the 12th century, Malmö is Sweden's third-largest city. It is a major industrial centre. Industries: shipbuilding, textiles. Pop. (2000) 259,711.

M

MALI

The Republic of Mali is the largest country in w Africa. It is mainly flat, with the highest land in the Adrar des Iforhas on the border with Algeria. Saharan Mali contains many wadis (dry river valleys). The old trading city of TIMBUKTU lies on the edge of the desert. The only permanent rivers are in the s, the main rivers being the Sénégal, which flows w to the Atlantic Ocean n of Kayes, and the Niger, which makes a large turn called the Niger Bend in s central Mali.

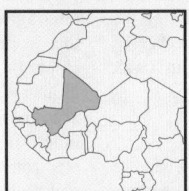

More than 70% of Mali is desert or semi-desert with sparse vegetation. Central and se Mali is a dry grassland region known as the Sahel. In prolonged droughts, the n Sahel dries up and becomes part of the SAHARA desert. Fertile farmland and tropical savanna covers s Mali, the most densely populated region.

CLIMATE

N Mali is part of the Sahara, with a hot, practically rainless climate. The s has enough rain for farming. In the sw of the country, unpleasant weather is experienced when dry and dusty harmattan winds blow from the Sahara Desert.

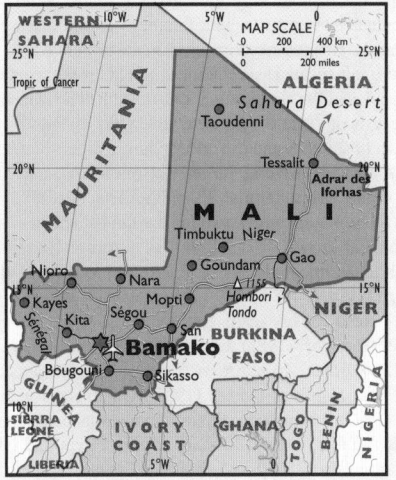

HISTORY

Mali lay at the heart of many of Africa's historic empires. From the 4th to the 11th centuries the region formed part of the ancient Empire of Ghana. It then became the heart of the medieval Empire of Mali, which at its height was West Africa's most powerful and prosperous state; its riches in gold were legendary. The 14th-century reign of Emperor Mansa Musa saw the introduction of Islam and the development of Timbuktu as a great centre of learning and trans-Saharan trade. The Songhai Empire dominated the region in the 15th century. but following its defeat by Morocco in 1591 the area became divided into small kingdoms.

In the 19th century, France gradually gained control. In 1893 the region became known as French Sudan, and was incorporated into the Federation of West Africa in 1898. Nationalist movements grew more vocal in their opposition to colonialism. In 1958, French Sudan voted to join the French Community as an autonomous republic. In 1959, it joined with Senegal to form the Federation of Mali.

Shortly after gaining independence Senegal seceded, and in 1960 Mali became a one-party republic. Its first president, Modibo Keita, committed Mali to nationalization and pan-Africanism. In 1962 Mali adopted its own currency. In 1963 it joined the ORGANIZATION OF AFRICAN STATES (OAS). Economic crisis forced Keita to revert to the franc zone, and permit France greater economic influence. Opposition led to Keita's overthrow in a military coup in 1968.

POLITICS

The military formed a National Liberation Committee and appointed Moussa Traoré as prime minister and later president. During the 1970s the Sahel suffered a series of droughts that contributed to a devastating famine in which thousands of people died.

In 1991 a military coup overthrew Traoré. A new constitution in 1992 saw the establishment of a multiparty democracy. Alpha Oumar Konaré

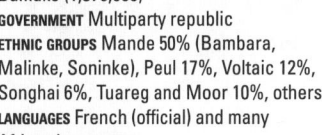

AREA 1,240,192sq km [478,838sq mi]
POPULATION 11,995,000
CAPITAL (POPULATION) Bamako (1,379,000)
GOVERNMENT Multiparty republic
ETHNIC GROUPS Mande 50% (Bambara, Malinke, Soninke), Peul 17%, Voltaic 12%, Songhai 6%, Tuareg and Moor 10%, others
LANGUAGES French (official) and many African languages
RELIGIONS Islam 90%, Traditional beliefs 9%, Christianity 1%
CURRENCY CFA franc = 100 centimes

won the ensuing presidential election. A political settlement provided a special administration for TUAREGS in n Mali. Konaré was re-elected in 1997. In 1999 he commuted Traoré's death sentence for corruption to life imprisonment. General Amadou Toumani Toure succeeded Konaré as president in 2002 elections and was re-elected in 2007. In 2007 unrest arose in the n among Tuaregs, who demanded greater autonomy.

ECONOMY

Mali is very poor, but recent stability has seen steady economic growth. 70% of the land is desert or semi-desert. Only about 2% of the land is used for growing crops, while 25% is used for grazing animals, but agriculture employs *c*.80% of the workforce. Many subsist by nomadic livestock rearing. Farming is hampered by water shortages, and the severe droughts in the 1970s and 1980s led to a great loss of animals and much human suffering. The farmers in the south grow millet, rice, sorghum and other food crops to feed their families.

The chief cash crops are cotton (the main export), peanuts and sugar cane. Many of these crops are grown on land irrigated with river water. Only a few small areas in the s are worked without irrigation, while the barren deserts in the n are populated only by a few poor nomads.

Fishing is an important economic activity. Mali has vital mineral deposits of gold and salt.

MALTA

The Republic of Malta is an archipelago republic in the Mediterranean Sea, 100km [60mi] s of Sicily. Malta consists of two main islands, Malta (246sq km [95sq mi]) and Gozo (67sq km [26sq mi]). The small island of Comino lies between them, and there are also two tiny islets.

The islands are low-lying. Malta island is composed mostly of limestone. Gozo is largely covered by clay, so its landscape is less arid. Malta has no forests, and 38% of the land is arable.

CLIMATE

Malta is typically Mediterranean. Summers are hot and dry, winters mild and wet. The

sirocco, a hot wind from North Africa, can raise temperatures considerably in the spring.

HISTORY

Malta has evidence of Stone Age settlement dating back 4,000 years. In *c.* 850 BC the Phoenicians colonized Malta. The Carthaginians, Greeks, and Romans followed. In AD 395 Malta became part of the Byzantine Empire. In 870 the Arab invasion brought Islam, but Roger I, Norman King of Sicily, restored Christian rule in 1091. In 1530 the Holy Roman Emperor gave Malta to the Knights Hospitallers. In 1565 the Knights, who had fought in the Crusades, held Malta against a Turkish siege. In 1798 the French captured Malta but, with help from Britain, they were driven out in 1800. In 1814 Malta became a British colony and a strategic military base.

During World War 1, Malta was an important naval base. In World War 2, Italian and German aircraft bombed the islands. In recognition of the bravery of the Maltese resistance, the British King George VI awarded the George Cross to Malta in 1942. Malta became a base for NATO in 1953.

POLITICS

Malta became independent in 1964, and a republic in 1974. Britain's military agreement with Malta expired in 1979, and Malta then ceased to be a military base. In the 1980s the

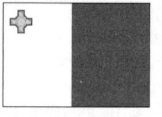

AREA	316sq km [122sq mi]
POPULATION	402,000
CAPITAL (POPULATION)	Valetta (9,000)
GOVERNMENT	Multiparty republic
ETHNIC GROUPS	Maltese 96%, British 2%
LANGUAGES	Maltese and English (both official)
RELIGIONS	Roman Catholic 98%
CURRENCY	Euro = 100 cents

people declared Malta neutral. Malta applied to join the European Union in the 1990s, but the bid was scrapped when the Labour Party won the elections in 1996. Following Labour's election defeat in 1998 the application was renewed, and Malta finally became a member in 2004. In 2008 the Euro became the official currency.

ECONOMY

The World Bank classifies Malta as an 'upper-middle income' developing country, although it lacks natural resources. Most of the workforce is employed in commercial shipbuilding, manufacturing and the tourist industry. Machinery and transport equipment account for more than 50% of exports. Manufacturing industries include chemicals, electronic equipment and textiles. The rocky soil makes farming difficult, and Malta produces only 20% of its food. It has a small fishing industry.

INTERNET

Malta
▶ www.gov.mt
▶ www.discover-malta.com

▲ **mammoth** The mammoth was a hairy, elephant-like mammal that inhabited the steppes and tundra of North America, Europe and Asia during the Ice Ages of the Pleistocene period. Complete specimens have been found preserved in ice formations in Russia. The mammoth was a herbivore and, while its body was of a similar size to modern elephants, it possessed a larger head and tusks, and a thick coat of hair to protect it from the cold.

MAMMALIAN FEET

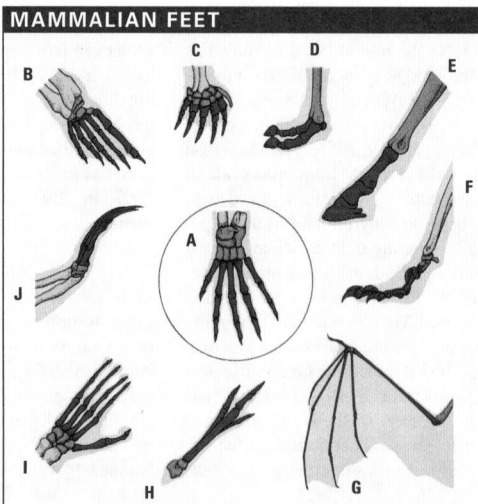

The feet of mammals evolved in many different ways from the basic mammalian foot (A) possessed by the earliest shrew-like mammal. Seals (B) developed evenly graduated toes for a webbed paddle. Moles (C) have truncated toes for leverage when digging. Camels have two padded toes (D) for walking on sand. Horses have hoofs (E) instead of claws. Horses and cheetahs (F) have elongated feet for speed. Bats (G) have enormously elongated digits to support wings. Kangaroos' toes (H) are designed for hopping. Lemurs (I) and sloths (J) have forelimbs for grasping trees.

Malory, Sir Thomas (active 1460–70) English author. He wrote *Le Morte d'Arthur*, which recounts the legends associated with King ARTHUR. The book was apparently written in prison and completed in 1469, but Malory's identity is obscure.

Malraux, André (1901–76) French novelist and politician. He witnessed (1925–27) the Communist uprising in China, and fought for the Republicans in the Spanish Civil War and the French resistance in World War 2. Malraux was a loyal supporter of Charles DE GAULLE and served (1959–69) as minister of cultural affairs. He is celebrated chiefly for his novels *La Condition humaine* (1933) and *L'Espoir* (1937).

malt Germinated grain, usually BARLEY, used in beverages, beer and foods. The grain is softened in water and allowed to germinate. This activates ENZYMES, which convert the starch to malt sugar (maltose). The grain is then kiln-dried.

Malta Republic in the Mediterranean Sea, *c.* 100km (60mi) s of Sicily; the capital is VALLETTA. *see* country feature.

Malthus, Thomas Robert (1766–1834) English economist and clergyman. In his famous *Essay on Population* (1798), Malthus argued that population increases geometrically but food supply can increase only arithmetically, so that population must eventually overtake it, with famine, war and disease as consequences. He prescribed controls on the birth rate.

maltose (malt sugar) Disaccharide ($C_{12}H_{22}O_{11}$) that contains two molecules of the simple sugar GLUCOSE. It is produced by the hydrolysis of STARCH by the enzyme AMYLASE and by the breakdown of starches and GLYCOGEN during digestion.

mamba Any of several large, poisonous African tree snakes of the cobra family, Elapidae. The deadly black mamba (*Dendroaspis polylepsis*) is the largest species. It is grey, greenish-brown or black and is notoriously aggressive; its bite is almost always fatal. Length: to 4.3m (14ft).

Mamet, David (1947–) US playwright and film director. Mamet is noted for his sharp, perceptive dialogue. His play *Glengarry Glen Ross* (1983) won a Pulitzer Prize. Screenplays include *The Postman Always Rings Twice* (1981). His directorial debut was *House of Games* (1987). Other plays include *Oleanna* (1992), a controversial play about sexual harassment.

Mamluk (Arabic, 'slave') Military elite in Egypt and other Arab countries. In 1250, the Mamluks of Egypt overthrew the Ayyubid dynasty. They halted the MONGOLS, defeated the

Crusaders and crushed the ASSASSINS. In 1517 Egypt was conquered by the Ottoman Turks, but the Mamluks continued to control Egypt until suppressed by MUHAMMAD ALI in 1811.

mammal Any member of the class Mammalia of VERTEBRATE animals characterized by mammary glands in the female and full, partial or vestigial hair covering. Mammals are warm-blooded. They have a four-chambered heart with circulation to the lungs separate from the rest of the body. Mammals usually bear fewer young than other animals, and give them longer and better parental care. Most mammals before birth grow inside the mother's body and are nourished from her by means of a placenta. When born, they continue to feed on milk from the mother's mammary glands. There is a wide range of features, shapes, and sizes among mammals. Mammals include 17 orders of placentals, one MARSUPIAL order – all live-bearing – and an order of egg-laying MONOTREMES. They probably evolved *c.*180 million years ago from a group of warm-blooded reptiles. Today, mammals range in size from shrews weighing a few grams to the blue whale, which can weigh as much as 150 tonnes.

mammary gland *See* BREAST

mammoth Extinct PLEISTOCENE ancestor of the ELEPHANT. Many were covered with long red or brown hair. The prominent tusks were long and curved, sometimes crossing in adult males. In summer months, the permafrost of Siberia has been known to yield whole specimens that have been frozen for as long as 30,000 years. Genus *Mammuthus*.

Man, Isle of Island off the NW coast of England, in the Irish Sea; the capital is Douglas. In the Middle Ages, it was a Norwegian dependency, subsequently coming under Scottish then English rule. It has been a British crown possession since 1828, but has its own government (the Tynwald). The basis of the economy is tourism although agriculture is important, the chief products being oats, fruit and vegetables. Area: 572sq km (221sq mi). Pop. (2001) 76,315.

Managua Capital of Nicaragua, on the s shore of Lake Managua, w central Nicaragua. It became the capital in 1855. Managua suffered damage from earthquakes in 1931 and 1962. It is the economic, industrial and commercial hub of Nicaragua. Industries: textiles, tobacco, cement. Pop. (2005) 1,159,000.

Manama (Al-Manamah) Capital of Bahrain, on the N coast of Bahrain Island, in the Persian Gulf. It was made a free port in 1958, and a deepwater harbour was built in 1962. It is the country's principal port and commercial centre. Industries: oil refining, banking, boatbuilding. Pop. (2002) 148,000.

manatee Any of three species of large, plant-eating, subungulate, aquatic mammals found primarily in shallow coastal waters of the Atlantic Ocean. It has a tapered body ending in a large rounded flipper; there are no hind limbs. Length: to 4.5m (14.7ft); weight: 680kg (1500lb). Family Trichechidae; genus *Trichechus*. *See also* DUGONG

Manchester City on the River Irwell, forming a metropolitan district in the Greater Manchester urban area, NW England. In AD 79, the Romans occupied the Celtic town, naming it Mancunium. The textile industry dates back to the 14th century. In 1830, the world's first passenger railway was constructed between LIVERPOOL and Manchester. In 1894 the Manchester Ship Canal opened, providing the city with its own access to the sea. In 1838, Manchester was incorporated as a borough. Modern Manchester has a diverse manufacturing base, including chemicals, pharmaceuticals, printing and publishing. It is the major financial centre of N England. Pop. (2000) 2,353,000.

Manchu Nomadic peoples of MANCHURIA. They established the QING dynasty.

Manchukuo Japanese puppet state in MANCHURIA (1932–45). It was under the nominal rule of the pretender to the Qing throne, Henry PU YI. Most foreign governments did not recognize the state of Manchukuo and, after the defeat of Japan in 1945, China regained Manchuria.

Manchuria Region of NE China, now in the provinces of Heilongjiang, Jilin, and Liaoning. Manchuria is rich in mineral deposits, and has become one of China's leading sites for heavy industry. It is a major agricultural area, whose chief product is soya beans. Dalian is the principal port. The Manchus conquered China in the 17th century. At the end of

the 19th century, the Chinese constructed the railways and the Russians developed the naval facilities at Port Arthur. In the RUSSO-JAPANESE WAR (1904–05), Japan seized control of s Manchuria and Port Arthur. In 1931, Japan occupied the whole of Manchuria and set up the puppet state of MANCHUKUO. The region's industry supplied the Japanese in World War 2. In 1945, Soviet forces occupied Manchuria, destroying many factories. In 1948, Chinese communists defeated the Manchurian nationalists and reconstruction began. From 1960 to 1990, the region was key in Sino-Soviet hostilities. Area: *c.*1,500,000sq km (600,000sq mi).

Manchurian Incident (1931) Japanese seizure of MANCHURIA. The Japanese captured Mukden in September 1931, and rapidly overran the province, setting up the puppet state of MANCHUKUO. The ensuing SINO-JAPANESE WAR later merged into World War 2. After the defeat of Japan (1945), Manchuria was returned to China.

Mandalay City in central Burma (Myanmar), on the River Irrawaddy; capital of Mandalay division. Founded in 1857, Mandalay was the last capital (1860–85) of the Burmese kingdom before Britain annexed it. Japan occupied Mandalay during World War 2, and the city suffered severe damage. Pop. (2005) 927,000.

Mandarin Major dialect of CHINESE, the spoken language of about 70% of China's population. It was the language of the imperial cour and is the basis of modern standard Chinese.

mandarin (mandarine) Type of orange popular because of its sweet flavour. The tangerine is a flattish, loose-skinned species of mandarin. Family Rutaceae; species *Citrus reticulata*.

Mandela, Nelson Rolihlahla (1918–) South African statesman, president (1994–99). He joined the AFRICAN NATIONAL CONGRESS (ANC) in 1944, and for the next 20 years led the campaign of civil disobedience against South Africa's APARTHEID government. Following the SHARPEVILLE Massacre (1960), Mandela formed *Umkhonte We Sizwe* (Spear of the Nation), a paramilitary wing of the ANC. In 1961, the ANC was banned. In 1962, Mandela was acquitted on charges of treason, but in 1964 he was sentenced to life imprisonment for political offences. He spent the next 27 years in prison on Robben Island, becoming a symbol of resistance to apartheid. International sanctions forced F.W. DE KLERK to begin the dismantling of apartheid. In February 1990, Mandela was released and resumed his leadership of the newly legalized ANC. In 1993, he and de Klerk shared the Nobel Peace Prize. In 1994, Mandela gained two-thirds of the popular vote in South Africa's first multiracial democratic elections. An advocate of the need for reconciliation, he made de Klerk deputy president (1994–96) in his government of national unity. In 1996, he divorced his wife, **Winnie** (1934–), who was convicted of kidnapping and of being an accessory to assault. Thabo MBEKI succeeded Mandela as president.

Mandelbrot, Benoit B. (1942–) US mathematician, b. Poland. He made major contributions to CHAOS THEORY, and is best known for coining the term FRACTAL. His book *The Fractal Geometry of Nature* (1982) contains many examples of natural fractals, such as ferns, trees and rivers. The Mandelbrot set, a well-known fractal object, is named after him.

◄ **manatee** The Florida manatee (*Trichechus manatus*), like all manatees, is a relative of the elephant. Manatees live in fresh or brackish estuarine waters. They form family groups consisting of parents and offspring. Peaceful, herbivorous animals, they feed on plants growing on the seafloor or river bed. It is supposed that manatees are the source of the mermaid legends.

INTERNET

Man, Isle of
▸ www.gov.im
▸ www.isle-of-man.com

Mandela, Nelson Rolihlahla
▸ www.anc.org.za/people/mandela.html
▸ www.nobel.se/peace/laureates/1993

M

▲ **Mandela** Former president Nelson Mandela struggled for a democratic South Africa for much of his life and spent 27 years in prison, charged with attempting to overthrow the government. He was largely responsible for the peaceful revolution that transformed South Africa into a multiracial 'rainbow nation'. Mandela's compassion and benevolence made him a figure of great moral stature. In 1998, he married Graca Machel, widow of Samora Machel, former president of Mozambique.

► **mandrill** A species of baboon, the mandrill (*Mandrillus sphinx*) lives in equatorial West Africa. The extraordinary colours of the mandrill's face intensify if the animal becomes annoyed or excited. Zoologists believe that this visual display replaced the baring of teeth to express anger that is common to most other baboons.

M

Manet, Édouard
► www.musee-orsay.fr
► www.metmuseum.org
► www.nga.gov

Manhattan Project
► www.atomicmuseum.com/tour/manhattanproject.cfm
► www.me.utexas.edu/~uer/manhattan

Manitoba
► www.gov.mb.ca

mandolin Stringed musical instrument related to the LUTE and associated with 18th-century Italy. It has four or six paired wire strings, which are played with a plectrum. It is most often used today as an accompaniment to folk songs and dances.

mandrake Plant of the potato family, native to the Mediterranean region and used since ancient times as a medicine. It contains the ALKALOIDS hyoscyamine, scopolamin, and mandragorine. The large greenish-yellow or purple flowers produce a many-seeded berry. Height: 40cm (16in); family Solanaceae; species *Mandragora officinarum*.

mandrill Large BABOON that lives in dense rainforests of central W Africa. Mandrills roam in small troops and forage for their food on the forest floor. The male has a red-tipped, pale blue nose, yellow-bearded cheeks and a reddish rump. Height: 75cm (30in) at the shoulder; weight: to 54kg (119lb). Species *Mandrillus sphinx*.

Manet, Édouard (1832–83) French painter. Although Manet is often linked with IMPRESSIONISM, he did not consider himself part of the movement. The famed *Le Déjeuner sur l'Herbe* (1863) was attacked by contemporary critics for its rejection of the refined Academic painting style then popular, and for placing a female nude in a contemporary setting. *Olympia* (1863), a portrait of a well-known courtesan, was similarly received. Manet finally achieved recognition with later works, such as *Le Bar aux Folies-Bergères* (1881).

manganese (symbol Mn) Grey-white, metallic element that resembles iron and was first isolated in 1774 by Swedish chemist Johan Gottlieb Gahn (1745–1818). Its chief ores are pyrolusite, manganite and hausmannite. The metal is used in alloy steels, ferromagnetic alloys, fertilizers, paints and as a petrol additive. Properties: at.no. 25; r.a.m. 54.938; r.d. 7.20; m.p. 1,244°C (2,271°F); b.p. 1,962°C (3,564°F); most common isotope Mn^{55} (100%). *See also* TRANSITION ELEMENTS

mango Evergreen tree native to SE Asia, and grown widely in the tropics for its fruit. It has lanceolate leaves, pinkish-white clustered flowers, and yellow-red fruit. Height: to 18m (60ft). Family Anacardiaceae; species *Mangifera indica*.

mangrove Common name for any one of 120 species of tropical trees or shrubs found in marine swampy areas. Its stilt-like aerial roots, which arise from the branches and hang down into the water, produce a thick undergrowth, useful in the reclaiming of land along tropical coasts. Some species also have roots that rise up out of the water. Height: to 20m (70ft). Major family: Rhizophoraceae.

Manhattan Borough of NEW YORK CITY, in SE New York state, USA; lying mainly on Manhattan Island and bounded w by the HUDSON River. In 1625, the Manhattan Indians sold the island to the Dutch West India Company and the town of New Amsterdam was built. The British captured the Dutch colony in 1664, and renamed it New York. In 1898, Manhattan became one of five boroughs established by the Greater New York Charter. Industries: electrical goods, chemicals, fabricated metals, finance, tourism, entertainment, broadcasting, publishing. Pop. (2000) 1,537,195.

Manhattan Project Code name given to the development of the US atomic bomb during WORLD WAR 2. Work on the bomb was carried out in great secrecy by a team including US physicists Enrico FERMI and J. Robert OPPENHEIMER. The first test took place on July 16, 1945, near Alamogordo, New Mexico, and the next month the US Air Force dropped bombs on Japan.

mania Mental illness marked by feelings of intense elation and excitement. Speech is rapid and physical activity frenetic. In extreme cases, violent behaviour accompanies mania.

manic depression (bipolar disorder) Mental illness marked by recurrent bouts of DEPRESSION, possibly alternating with periods of MANIA. Depressive and manic symptoms may alternate in a cyclical pattern, be mixed or be separated by periods of remission and disturbances of thought and judgement.

Manichaeism Religious teaching of the Persian prophet Mani (*c.*216–*c.*276) based on a primeval conflict between light and dark. The Manichaean sect, influenced by ZOROASTRIANISM and CHRISTIANITY, spread to Egypt and Rome, where it was considered a Christian heresy, and eastward to Chinese Turkestan, where it survived until the 13th century.

Manila Capital of the Philippines, on Manila Bay, sw Luzon island. Manila is the industrial, commercial, and administrative heart of the Philippines. The River Pasig bisects the city. On the s bank stands the old walled city (Intramuros), built by the Spanish in the 16th century on the site of a Muslim settlement. It became a trading centre for the Pacific area. On the N bank lies Ermita, the administrative and tourist centre. Japan occupied the city in 1942. In 1945 a battle between Japanese and Allied forces destroyed the old city. Pop. (2005) 10,677,000.

Manipur State in NE India, on the Burmese border; the capital is Imphal. The state of ASSAM governed Manipur until 1949, when it became a Union Territory. It was established as a state in 1972. Crops include rice, pulses, mustard, and sugar cane. Industries: cotton and silk weaving, carpentry. Area: 22,356sq km (8,632sq mi). Pop. (2001) 2,389,000.

Manitoba Province in s central Canada, the easternmost of the prairie provinces, bordered by Hudson Bay (NE) and the USA (S); the capital and largest city is WINNIPEG. In 1670, Charles II granted the land to the HUDSON'S BAY COMPANY, who, in 1869, sold it to the Confederation of Canada. Manitoba became a province in 1870. The s has prairie country and lakes, the NE the rugged upland of the Canadian Shield and the far N tundra. Manitoba is famous for its wheat fields. Dairy farming and the rearing of poultry are also important. Manufacturing includes food products, clothing, electrical products, machinery, metals, and transport equipment. Mineral deposits include nickel, copper, and zinc. There are large oilfields in the sw of the province and extensive timber reserves. Area: 649,947sq km (250,946sq mi). Pop. (2001) 1,119,583.

Mann, Thomas (1875–1955) German novelist and essayist. Perhaps the outstanding figure of 20th-century German literature, Mann linked individual psychological problems to the great decline in European culture. His first novel, *Buddenbrooks* (1901), is an epic family saga. Shorter works include the novella *Death in Venice* (1912), and the autobiographical essay *Reflections of a Non-political man* (1918). *The Magic Mountain* (1924) is widely acclaimed as his masterpiece. In 1933, Mann left Germany, first for Switzerland, then the United States. Other works include the tetralogy *Joseph and His Brothers* (1933–43), and *Confessions of Felix Krull, Confidence Man* (1955). Mann received the 1929 Nobel Prize in literature.

manna (flowering ash) Tree of the OLIVE family that grows in s Europe and Asia Minor. The pinnate leaves have rust-coloured hairs underneath. The flowers are white and showy with large petals. A sugary substance, mannite, is collected from cuts made in the bark and used medicinally. Height: to 18m (60ft); family Oleaceae: species *Fraxinus ornus*.

Mannerheim, Carl Gustav Emil von (1867–1951) Finnish statesman and general, president (1944–46). He served in the Russian army and was a general in World War 1. After the Russian Revolution (1917), he returned to Finland and led the anti-Bolshevik forces in the civil war. In 1918–19, he obtained international recognition of Finnish independence. He lost the

1919 presidential elections but, later, as head of the Defence Council, planned the fortified Mannerheim Line across Karelia.

mannerism Term generally applied to the art and architecture of Italy between the High RENAISSANCE and the BAROQUE. The style is typified by PARMIGIANO, PONTORMO and Giovanni LANFRANCO. Some theorists include El GRECO, the FONTAINEBLEAU SCHOOL or the Romanist painters of the Netherlands. The term implies a courtly, self-conscious style.

Mannheim City and river port on the E bank of the River Rhine, at the mouth of the River Neckar, Baden-Wüttemberg, central Germany. Originally a fishing village, Mannheim was fortified in 1606, and destroyed by the French in 1689. It was rebuilt in 1697, became the seat of the Rhine Palatinate (1719–77), and passed to Baden in 1803. Industries: chemicals, oil refining, engineering, paper, textiles. Pop. (1999) 308,400.

Manson, Charles (1934–) US cult leader. In 1967, he established a commune based on free love and complete subservience to him. In 1969 members of the cult committed a series of brutal murders, including that of Roman POLANSKI's wife Sharon Tate (1943–69). Manson and his accomplices were sentenced to death, later commuted to life imprisonment.

Mantegna, Andrea (1431–1506) Italian painter and engraver. In 1460, he became court painter to the Gonzaga family in Mantua, and decorated the Camera degli Sposi in the Duke's palace. This room contains the first example of illusionistic architecture to have been created since antiquity. Mantegna's other great work for the Gonzagas was his series of oil paintings, *The Triumph of Caesar* (c.1480–95).

mantis (praying mantis) Any of several species of mantids, insects found throughout the world. They have powerful front legs used to catch and hold their insect prey. Colours range from brown and green to bright pinks. Length: 25–150mm (1–6in). Family Mantidae.

mantissa Part of a LOGARITHM after the decimal point.

mantle Layer of the Earth between the CRUST and the CORE, which extends to a depth of 2,890km (1,795mi). The mantle forms the greatest bulk of the Earth: 82% of its volume and 68% of its mass. The uppermost part is rigid, solid and brittle and, together with the Earth's crust, forms the **lithosphere**. Between a depth of about 60–200km (40–125mi), the mantle has a soft zone that is called the **asthenosphere**. Here, temperature and pressure are in balance so that much of the material is near melting point or partly melted and flows. The remainder of the mantle is more solid but still capable of creeping flow. In the lower mantle, several changes in velocity can be detected. The chemical constitution of the mantle is uncertain, but it is thought to be made up of iron-magnesium silicates.

mantra Sacred word, verse, or formula recited during prayers or meditation in HINDUISM and BUDDHISM. Mantras include such chantings as the symbolic sound *Aum* (or *Om*).

Manx Language formerly spoken in the Isle of Man. Closely related to Scottish GAELIC, it was spoken by most of the native inhabitants until c.1700, when English was introduced. By 1900, there were only a few thousand speakers left.

Manzoni, Alessandro (1785–1873) Italian novelist and poet. His poetry expressed his religious faith, but his masterpiece is an historical novel, *The Betrothed* (1827), regarded as one of the most outstanding works of Italian literature.

Maori Polynesian population, the original inhabitants of New Zealand. Traditionally, Maori lived by agriculture, hunting and fishing. They retain much of their language, culture and customs. In Maori society, tattooing, carving and weaving were developed arts, and their war chants (*haka*) are still kept alive. Since the 1970s, Maori political activity increased, and some of their land has been restored. *See also* MAORI WARS

Maori Wars (1845–48, 1860–72) Two wars between British settlers and indigenous MAORI tribes in New Zealand. They arose when the settlers broke the terms of the Treaty of WAITANGI (1840) that guaranteed the Maori possession of their lands. As a result of the wars, a Native Land Court was established (1865), a Maori school system formed (1867), and four elected Maori admitted to the national legislature.

Mao Zedong (1893–1976) Chinese statesman, founder and chairman (1949–76) of the People's Republic of China. Mao was a founder member of the Chinese COMMUNIST PARTY in 1921. After the nationalist KUOMINTANG, led by CHIANG KAI-SHEK, dissolved the alliance with the communists in 1927, Mao helped established rural soviets. In 1931, he was elected chairman of the Soviet Republic of China, based in JIANGSU. The advance of nationalist forces forced Mao to lead the Red Army on the LONG MARCH (1934–35) NW to Shanxi. In 1937, the civil war was suspended as communists and nationalists combined to fight the second SINO-JAPANESE WAR. The communists' brand of guerrilla warfare gained hold of much of rural China. Civil war resumed in 1945, and by 1949 the nationalists had been driven out of mainland China. Mao became chairman of the People's Republic and was re-elected in 1954. ZHOU ENLAI acted as prime minister. In 1958, Mao attempted to distinguish Chinese COMMUNISM from its Soviet counterpart by launching the GREAT LEAP FORWARD. The programme ended in mass starvation, and the withdrawal of Soviet aid. Mao's leadership was challenged. The CULTURAL REVOLUTION was an attempt by Mao and his wife, JIANG QING, to reassert Maoist ideology. It encouraged the cult of the personality, dismissed political rivals, and Mao became supreme commander of the nation and army (1970). Mao and Zhou Enlai's death created a vacuum. A struggle developed between the GANG OF FOUR, HUA GUOFENG, and DENG XIAOPING. *Quotations from Chairman Mao Zedong* (popularly known as 'The Little Red Book', 1967) is a worldwide bestseller.

map Graphic representation of part or all of the Earth's surface. Maps are usually printed on a flat surface using various kinds of projections based on land surveys, aerial photographs and other sources.

maple Genus of deciduous trees native to temperate and cool regions of Europe, Asia, and North America. They have yellowish or greenish flowers and winged seeds. They are grown for ornament, shade or timber, depending on the species; the sugar maple is also tapped for maple syrup. A common British example is the sycamore tree. Height: 4.6–36m (15–120ft). Family Aceraceae; genus *Acer*.

Maputo (Lourenço Marques) Capital and chief port of Mozambique, on Maputo Bay, S Mozambique. It was visited by the Portuguese in 1502, and was made the capital of Portuguese East Africa in 1907, being known as Lourenço Marques until 1976. It is linked by rail to South Africa, Swaziland, and Zimbabwe, and is a popular resort area. Industries: footwear, textiles, rubber. Pop. (2005) 1,316,000.

Maracaibo City and port in NW Venezuela, between Lake Maracaibo and the Gulf of Venezuela. Founded in 1529, it was sacked in 1669. It expanded after the discovery of oil in 1917, and is now Venezuela's second-largest city. Industries: oil processing, coffee, cacao, sugar. Pop. (2005) 2,182,000.

Marat, Jean Paul (1743–93) French revolutionary. A physician, he founded *L'Ami du Peuple* ('*Friend of the People*'), a vitriolic journal that supported the JACOBINS. The Jacobins exploited his murder by Charlotte Corday, a member of the GIRONDINS, for propaganda purposes, and it thus contributed to the ensuing REIGN OF TERROR.

Maratha (Mahratta) Hindu warrior people of W central India, who rose to power in the 17th century. They extended their rule throughout W India by defeating the MOGUL EMPIRE and successfully resisting British supremacy in India during the 18th century. They were finally defeated in 1818.

marathon Long-distance race. The standard marathon is 42.2km (26.2mi) long, which was the distance run by the ancient Greek soldier who brought news to Athens of victory over the Persians at the Battle of MARATHON (490BC).

Marathon, Battle of (490BC) Victory of the Greeks, mainly Athenians, during the PERSIAN WARS. The defeat of a much larger Persian army on the Marathon plain, NE of Athens, secured Attica from the invasion of CYRUS THE GREAT.

marble Metamorphic rock composed largely of recrystallized limestones and dolomites. The colour is normally white, but when tinted by serpentine, iron oxide, or carbon can vary to shades of yellow, green, red, brown, or black. It has long been a favourite building and sculpting material.

Marche Region in E central Italy between the Apennines and the Adriatic Sea; the capital is Ancona. Except for a narrow

M

▲ **mango** The fruit of the mango tree has a delicate fragrance. Its juicy flesh surrounds a single, flat seed. The tree itself is grown as a garden plant throughout the tropical region.

coastal plain, Marche is mountainous. Farming is the principal economic activity; major crops include cereals, olives, and grapes. Area: 9,692sq km (3,743sq mi). Pop. (2001) 1,469,195.

Marciano, Rocky (1923–69) US boxer, b. Rocco Francis Marchegiano. In 1951, he became only the second boxer to knock out Joe Louis. In 1952, Marciano won the world heavyweight title by knocking out Joe Walcott. Marciano retired undefeated in 1956.

Marconi, Guglielmo (1874–1937) Italian physicist who developed RADIO. By 1897, he was able to demonstrate radio telegraphy over a distance of 19km (12mi). In 1899, he established radio communication between France and England. By 1901, radio transmissions were being received across the Atlantic Ocean. He received the 1909 Nobel Prize in physics.

Marco Polo *See* POLO, MARCO

Marcos, Ferdinand Edralin (1917–89) Philippine statesman, president (1965–86). Marcos was elected to the Philippine Congress in 1949. As president, he received support from the USA for his campaigns (1969) against communist guerrillas on Panay and Moro secessionists on MINDANAO. Continued civil unrest led to the imposition of martial law in 1972. A new constitution (1973) gave Marcos authoritarian powers. His regime acquired a reputation for corruption and repression, symbolized by the extravagance of his wife, **Imelda** (1930–). In 1983, his main rival, Benigno Aquino, was assassinated and political opposition coalesced behind Benigno's widow, Cory AQUINO. Marcos appeared to win the 1986 general election, but allegations of vote-rigging forced him into exile. In 1988, US authorities indicted both him and Imelda for fraud. Ferdinand was too ill to stand trial and died in Hawaii. Imelda was subsequently acquitted, but indicted for embezzlement upon her return to Manila in 1991. In 1992, Imelda unsuccessfully ran for president. In 1993, she was sentenced to 18 years' imprisonment, but appealed the judgement.

Marcus Aurelius Antonius (121–180) Roman Emperor (161–180) and philosopher of the STOIC school, b. Marcus Annius Verus. From 161 to 169, he ruled as co-emperor with his adoptive younger brother, Lucius Aurelius Verus (d.169). The much-admired *Meditations*, his one surviving work, is a collection of philosophical thoughts and ideas that occurred to him during his campaigns, on the last of which he died.

Marcuse, Herbert (1898–1979) US radical political philosopher, b. Germany. Marcuse is noted for his critical reinterpretations of MARXISM, and for his Freudian analysis of 20th-century industrial society. In the 1920s, he was a founder member of the Frankfurt Institute for Social Research. Fleeing Nazi Germany in 1933, he settled in the USA and worked for the US government (1941–50). Marcuse's advocacy of civil resistance found favour with left-wing students of the 1960s. His works include *Eros and Civilization* (1955) and *One-Dimensional Man* (1964). *See also* ALIENATION

Mardi gras Community festival or carnival held on Shrove Tuesday, the day before the beginning of Lent, in many Roman Catholic countries, particularly France. In the USA, most notably New Orleans, it includes parades, concerts and dances.

Mare, Walter de la *See* DE LA MARE, WALTER

Margaret of Anjou (1430–82) Queen consort of HENRY VI of England from 1445. She led the Lancastrian cause during the Wars of the ROSES, raising troops in France. After her only son, Edward, was killed at Tewkesbury (1471), Margaret was taken prisoner. Ransomed by LOUIS XII of France in 1476, she left England never to return.

margarine Butter-like substance made from vegetable fats blended with aqueous milk products, salt, flavouring, food colouring, emulsifier, and vitamins A and D. It is used for cooking and as a spread.

marguerite Perennial plant of the daisy family native to the CANARY ISLANDS. It has white-rayed, yellow-centred flower heads *c.*5cm (2in) across. Height: to 91cm (3ft). Family Asteraceae/COMPOSITAE; species *Argyranthemum frutescens*.

Mariana Islands Volcanic island chain in the W Pacific Ocean, stretching over 800km (500mi) of the Marianas Trench, *c.*2,400km (1,500mi) E of the Philippines. The group comprises GUAM and the islands of the Northern Marianas: Saipan, Tinian, Rota, Pagan, and 11 smaller islands. Discovered by Ferdinand

MAGELLAN in 1521, and named Islands of Thieves, the islands were renamed the Marianas in 1668. The Northern Marianas came under German control in 1898, subsequently passing to Japan. Taken by US forces in 1944, they became part of the US Trust Territory of the Pacific Islands in 1947. In 1978, the Commonwealth of the Northern Mariana Islands formed in association with the USA, and in 1986 the islanders acquired US citizenship. Trusteeship status ended in 1990. Exports include sugar cane, coconuts and coffee. Tourism is important. Area (excluding Guam): 464sq km (179sq mi). Pop. (2002) 78,400.

Maria Theresa (1717–80) Archduchess of Austria, ruler (1740–80) of the Austrian HABSBURG Empire. She succeeded her father, Emperor CHARLES VI, but neighbouring powers challenged her in the War of the AUSTRIAN SUCCESSION (1741–48). She lost Silesia to Prussia but secured the imperial title for her husband, FRANCIS I. She switched allegiances, but failed to regain Silesia in the SEVEN YEARS' WAR (1756–63).

Marie Antoinette (1755–93) Queen of France. Daughter of Emperor FRANCIS I and MARIA THERESA of Austria, she married the future LOUIS XVI in 1770. Her life of pleasure and extravagance contributed to the outbreak of the FRENCH REVOLUTION in 1789. She initiated the royal family's attempt to escape in 1791, was held prisoner, and then finally guillotined.

Marie de Médicis (1573–1642) Queen of France. A member of the Medici family, daughter of the Grand Duke of Tuscany, she married HENRY IV of France in 1600. He was assassinated the day after she was crowned queen in 1610, possibly with her connivance. As regent for her son, LOUIS XIII, she relied on Italian advisers and reversed Henry's anti-Habsburg policy. She was constantly at odds with Louis after 1614, and antagonized Cardinal RICHELIEU. Failing to have Richelieu dismissed in 1630, she was forced into exile in Brussels (1631).

Marie Louise (1791–1847) French Empress. Daughter of Emperor FRANCIS II, she married NAPOLEON I in 1810. A son, the future Napoleon II, was born in 1811, and she acted briefly as regent during Napoleon's absences on campaign. Alienated from him by 1814, she became Duchess of Parma.

marigold Any of several mostly golden-flowered plants, mainly of the genera *Chrysanthemum Tagetes* and *Calendula*, all of the daisy family (Asteraceae/COMPOSITAE). Those most commonly cultivated are the French marigold (*Tagetes patula*) and the African marigold (*T. erecta*).

marijuana NARCOTIC drug prepared from the dried leaves of the Indian hemp plant (*Cannabis sativa*); it is different from HASHISH, which is prepared from resin obtained from the flowering tops of the plant. Possession of the drug is illegal in many countries. *See also* ADDICTION

Marine Corps, US Branch of the armed forces that is a service within the Department of the Navy. It consists of *c.*196,000 personnel and conducts land operations connected with naval manoeuvres.

Mariner program Series of US space probes. **Mariner 2** flew past Venus in 1962. **Mariner 4** flew past Mars in July 1965, photographing craters on its surface. **Mariner 5** passed Venus in October 1967, making measurements of the planet's atmosphere. **Mariners 6 and 7** obtained further photographs of Mars in 1969. **Mariner 9** went into orbit around Mars in November 1971. It made a year-long photographic reconnaissance of the planet's surface and obtained close views of the moons, Phobos and Deimos. **Mariner 10**, the last of the series, passed Venus in February 1974 and then encountered Mercury three times: in March 1974, September 1974, and March 1975.

marines *See* MARINE CORPS, US; ROYAL MARINES

Marinetti, Filippo Tommaso (1876–1944) Italian poet, novelist, dramatist, and founder of FUTURISM. In such works as *Futurismo E Fascismo* (1924), he embraced fascism and advocated the glorification of machinery, speed and war. One of his earliest collections of poetry was entitled simply *Destruction*; another was called *War: the Only Hygiene of the World* (1915).

maritime law Branch of the law concerned with the sea and those who use it. It is quite distinct in its function and practice from domestic law.

Marius, Gaius (*c.*157–86 BC) Roman political and military leader. His policy of recruiting poor men helped the bond

M

between troops and their commanders. He also revised army training and equipment. His rivalry with SULLA forced him out of Rome, but he raised an army and recaptured the city in 87 BC.

marjoram Perennial herb of the mint family (Lamiaceae/Labiatae) *c*.60cm (24in) tall with purplish flowers. It is native to the Mediterranean region and W Asia, and cultivated as an annual in northern climates. Species *Origanum vulgare*.

Mark, Gospel according to Saint Second GOSPEL in the New Testament, but the earliest in composition. It was written in *c*.AD 55–65, and is believed to be one of two reference works (the other being 'Q') used by Saint MATTHEW and Saint LUKE in compiling their gospels. It is traditionally attributed to Saint MARK, and is one of the three SYNOPTIC GOSPELS – those presenting a common view of Jesus Christ's life.

Mark, Saint (active 1st century AD) Apostle and possibly one of the four evangelists of the New Testament. He is identified with John Mark (Acts 12:12. 15:37), the cousin of the apostle Saint BARNABAS. He accompanied both Barnabas and Saint PAUL on several missionary journeys until a disagreement with Paul caused him to detach himself. Christian tradition says that he went on to become secretary to Saint PETER and to write the first gospel. His feast day is April 25.

Mark Antony *See* ANTONY, MARK

market economy Economy in which the operation of free-markets (where the forces of supply and demand operate without interference) control resources. The opposite of a market economy is a command economy, where market forces are under governmental control; in a mixed economy, there is partial governmental control.

Markova, Dame Alicia (1910–2004) English ballerina, b. Lilian Alicia Marks. She joined the Vic-Wells Ballet in 1931, and was its first prima ballerina. Classical ballets in which she excelled include *Giselle*, *Les Sylphides*, and *Swan Lake*. In 1963 she became a Dame of the British Empire.

Marlborough, John Churchill, 1st Duke of (1650–1722) English general. Churchill helped JAMES II defeat MONMOUTH (1685), but switched allegiance in support of the Protestant GLORIOUS REVOLUTION (1688). Partly due to his wife's friendship with Queen ANNE, he was appointed Captain-General of Allied armies in the War of the SPANISH SUCCESSION. His strategic skill gained great victories at BLENHEIM (1704), Ramillies (1706), Oudenaarde (1708), and Malplaquet (1709). Churchill was rewarded with a dukedom and Blenheim Palace. When his wife lost the Queen's favour and the Tories regained power, Marlborough was dismissed (1711) and went into exile.

Marley, Bob (Robert Nesta) (1945–81) Jamaican singer-songwriter. Marley and his band, The Wailers, transformed REGGAE into an internationally popular music form with hit singles such as "Get Up, Stand Up" (1973) and "No Woman No Cry" (1974). He combined faith in RASTAFARIANISM with political statement. Marley's albums include *Natty Dread* (1975), *Exodus* (1977), and *Uprising* (1980).

marlin Any of several species of large marine fish found in warm waters of the Atlantic and Pacific Oceans, especially the blue marlin (*Makaira mitsukurii*); it is often fished for sport. The marlin is blue with a coppery tint and violet side markings. The fins and long snout are sharply pointed. Length: to 8m (26ft); weight: 635kg (1,400lb). Family Istiophoridae.

Marlowe, Christopher (1564–93) English playwright and poet. Marlowe helped make BLANK VERSE the vehicle of ELIZABETHAN drama. Much of his success derives from his ability to humanize his heroes, such as *Tamburlaine the Great* (1590), *The Tragical History of Doctor Faustus* (1604), and *The Jew of Malta* (1633). His masterpiece is the tragedy *Edward II* (1592). His greatest poems are *Hero and Leander* (1598) and *The Passionate Shepherd* (1599). Marlowe served as a spy in Francis WALSINGHAM's intelligence service.

marmoset Small, diurnal, arboreal MONKEY of tropical America. Among the smallest of the monkeys, marmosets are the size of small squirrels. They have soft, dense fur and sickle-shaped nails. Family Callitrichidae; typical genus *Callithrix*.

marmot Stocky, terrestrial rodent of the SQUIRREL family, native to North America, Europe and Asia. Most marmots have brown to grey fur, short, powerful legs, and furry tails.

Length, excluding tail: 30–60cm (12–24in); weight: 3–8kg (6.6–16.5lb). Family Sciuridae.

Marne, Battles of the Two engagements on the River Marne, N France, during WORLD WAR I. The first, in September 1914, was a counterattack directed by General JOFFRE, which checked the German drive on Paris. The second, in July 1918, was another Allied counter-stroke, which stopped the last German advance and preceded the final Allied offensive.

Maronites Christian community of Arabs in Lebanon and Syria, who emigrated to Egypt, Cyprus, S Europe, and North and South America. The Maronite Church claims origins from St Maron (d.407), a Syrian hermit. The Third Council of Constantinople (680) condemned the Maronites as Monotheletic heretics. They returned to communion with the Pope in 1182.

Marquesas Islands Volcanic archipelago in the Pacific Ocean, S of the Equator. The islands, part of FRENCH POLYNESIA, include Fatu Hiva, Hiva Oa, and Nuku Hiva; the capital is Taiohae (on Nuku Hiva). They were first discovered by a Spanish navigator in 1595. The French took possession in 1842. During the 19th century, European diseases killed many of the native Polynesians. The islands are mountainous, with fertile valleys and several good harbours. Exports: tobacco, vanilla and copra. Area: 1,049sq km (405sq mi). Pop. (2002) 9,400.

Márquez, Gabriel García *See* GARCÍA MÁRQUEZ, GABRIEL

Marrakech (Marrakesh) City in W central Morocco, at the NW foot of the Atlas Mountains. Founded in 1062 by the ALMORAVIDS, it was capital until 1147 and served as the sultan's residence. Industries: tourism, leather. Pop. (2005) 951,000.

marriage In the modern Western sense, the legal status of a man and a woman joined by ceremony as husband and wife. This is known as MONOGAMY, but some societies practise polyandry (having more than one husband) and POLYGAMY.

marrow Soft tissue containing blood vessels, found in the hollow cavities of BONE. The marrow found in many adult bones is yellowish and functions as a store of fat. The marrow in the flattish bones is reddish and contains cells that give rise to ERYTHROCYTES (red blood cells) as well as to most of the LEUCOCYTES (white blood cells). *See* picture, page 498.

Mars Fourth planet from the Sun. Mars appears red because of the high iron content of its surface crust, and is known as the Red Planet. The atmosphere consists of 95% carbon dioxide, 2.5% nitrogen, and 1.5% argon, with smaller quantities of oxygen, carbon monoxide and water vapour. Its axial tilt is similar to the Earth's, so it passes through a similar cycle of SEASONS. The surface temperature on Mars varies between extremes of 130K and 290K. Its surface reveals a long and complex history of geological activity. The N hemisphere has largely smooth, lowland volcanic plains and the S has heavily cratered uplands. The biggest volcanic structure on Mars is Olympus Mons, which is hundreds of kilometres across and 27km (17mi) high. Other geographical features, such as giant canyons, are channels in which rivers once flowed. The variable polar ice caps appear to be composed of solid carbon dioxide with underlying caps of water ice. Mars has two tiny SATELLITES in very close orbits, Phobos and Deimos. In 1996, scientists investigating a meteorite thought to have originated on Mars found what may be fossilized microorganisms that some believe indicate the presence of primitive life on the planet. In 2003, two separate missions to Mars were launched. The British-built probe Beagle 2 failed to make contact with Earth. In 2004, the NASA funded Opportunity rover found evidence that water, suitable for supporting life, once lay on the surface of Mars.

Mars Ancient Roman god of war, often depicted as an armed warrior; one of the three protector-deities of the city of Rome itself (with JUPITER and Quirinus). He was originally associated with agriculture but later took on his dominant military aspects; the wolf and woodpecker were sacred to him.

Marseilles (Marseille) City and seaport on the Gulf of Lyon, and connected to the River Rhône by an underground canal; capital of Bouches-du-Rhône department, SE France. The oldest city in France, Phocaean Greeks founded the settlement in 600 BC. During the CRUSADES, Marseilles was a commercial centre and shipping port for the Holy Land. The 19th-century French conquest of Algeria and the opening of

M

MARS: DATA

Diameter (equatorial): 6,787km (4,217mi)
Mass (Earth = 1): 0.11
Volume (Earth = 1): 0.15
Density (water = 1): 3.94
Orbital period: 687.0 days
Rotation period: 24h 37m 23s
Average temperature: 220K
Surface gravity (Earth=1): 0.38

▲ **marjoram** Wild marjoram (*Origanum vulgare*) is a pungent-flavoured herb much used in Mediterranean cooking to season meat, poultry, soups, and omelettes. It is known in its dried form as oregano.

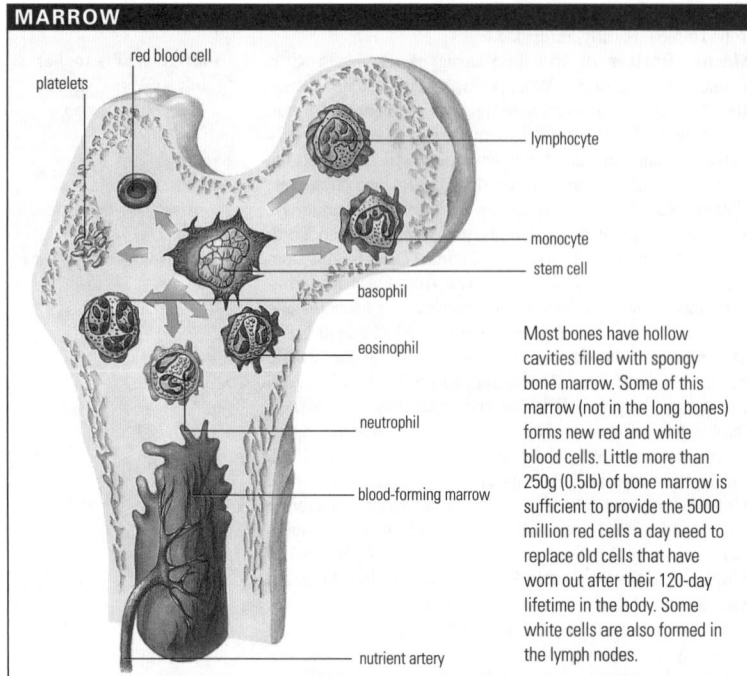

MARROW

platelets

red blood cell

lymphocyte

monocyte

stem cell

basophil

eosinophil

neutrophil

blood-forming marrow

nutrient artery

Most bones have hollow cavities filled with spongy bone marrow. Some of this marrow (not in the long bones) forms new red and white blood cells. Little more than 250g (0.5lb) of bone marrow is sufficient to provide the 5000 million red cells a day need to replace old cells that have worn out after their 120-day lifetime in the body. Some white cells are also formed in the lymph nodes.

the Suez Canal (1869) brought great prosperity to the city. Industries: flour milling, soap, vegetable oil, cement, sugar refining, chemicals, engineering. Pop. (2000) 1,290,000.

marsh Flat, wetland area, devoid of peat, saturated by moisture during one or more seasons. Typical vegetation includes grasses, sedges, reeds and rushes. Marshes are valuable WETLANDS and maintain water tables in adjacent ecosystems. Unlike BOGS, they have alkaline not acidic soil. *See also* SWAMP

Marshall, George Catlett (1880–1959) US general and statesman. Marshall served as a staff officer during World War 1 and, after various commissions including service in China (1924–27), became chief of staff during World War 2. After the war, he was secretary of state (1947–49) and defense secretary (1950–51). He inspired the MARSHALL PLAN.

Marshall Islands Republic in the W Pacific Ocean, E of the Caroline Islands, consisting of a group of atolls and coral reefs; the capital is Dalap-Uliga-Darrit (on Majuro Atoll). Spain first explored the islands in the early 16th century. Annexed to Germany in 1885, Japan occupied the group in 1914. US forces seized the islands in World War 2. In 1947, the islands became part of the US-administered Trust Territory of the Pacific Islands. Trusteeship ended in 1990, and in 1991 the islands became a full member state of the UN. They consist of two great chains, the Ralik (W) and the Ratak (E), which run almost parallel NW to SE, covering an ocean area of 11,650sq km (4,500sq mi). Products: copra, coconuts, tropical fruits, fish. Area: *c.*181sq km (70sq mi). Pop. (2000) 56,000.

Marshall Plan US programme of economic aid to European countries after World War 2. Promoted by US Secretary of State General MARSHALL, its purpose was to repair war damage and promote trade within Europe, while securing political stability. The Soviet Union and E European countries declined to participate. Between 1948 and 1951, 16 countries received a total of US$12,000 million under the plan.

Marston Moor, Battle of (July 2, 1664) Decisive engagement in the English CIVIL WAR, 11km (7mi) W of York. Parliamentarians, led by Thomas FAIRFAX and allied with Scots, defeated the Royalist forces under Prince RUPERT.

marsupial MAMMAL of which the female usually has a pouch (marsupium), within which the young are suckled and protected. At birth, the young are not fully formed. Most marsupials are Australasian, and include such varied types as the KANGAROO, KOALA, WOMBAT, TASMANIAN DEVIL, BANDICOOT, and marsupial MOLE. The only marsupials to live outside Australasia are the OPOSSUMS and similar species found in the Americas. *See also* MONOTREME

marten Any of several species of carnivorous mammals of the WEASEL family that live in forested areas of Europe, Asia and North and South America. They have a long body and short legs and are hunted for their fur. The skins of the SABLE, *Martes zibellina*, are the most valuable. Family Mustelidae.

Martí, José (1853–95) Cuban poet and essayist. His verse reflected his belief in the inseparability of poetry and politics. Martí was forced into exile and lived in New York before returning to Cuba, where he died fighting the Spanish. Many Latin Americans writers have been strongly influenced by his works. *Ismaelillo* (1882), *Versos libres* (published posthumously), and *Versos sencillos* (1891) contain his best poems.

martial law Maintenance of civic order by military personnel. Martial law may be declared on a local short-term basis by a government in an emergency, as when sending in the army to deal with pockets of civil unrest. It may also be declared on a nationwide, long-term basis following a military coup.

martin Fast-flying bird closely related to the SWALLOW and native to Europe and North America. It has long, pointed wings and short legs. Species include the house martin (*Delichon urbica*), purple martin (*Progne subis*) and sand martin (*Riparia riparia*). Family Hirundinidae.

Martin, Saint (315–97) Bishop of Tours. Born a heathen, he became a Christian in his youth. As a Roman soldier, Martin is reputed to have torn his cloak to share it with a beggar. From 360, he lived as a monk and was acclaimed Bishop in 371 (against his will). His feast day is known as Martinmas.

Martin V (1368–1431) Pope (1417–31), b. Oddone Colonna. After 39 years of schism, Martin tried to restore papal prestige and church unity through political means. He reorganized the Curia and sought unsuccessfully to reopen diplomatic links with the Eastern Orthodox Church in Constantinople.

Martin du Gard, Roger (1881–1958) French novelist. His major works, such as *Jean Barois* (1913) and the eight-novel series *Les Thibault* (1922–40), are treatments of moral and intellectual preoccupations. He received the 1937 Nobel Prize in literature.

Martineau, Harriet (1802–76) English writer. Deaf from birth, her works include the nine-volume *Illustrations of Political Economy* (1832–34). In 1834 she visited the USA and her anti-slavery views are contained in *Society in America* (1837).

Martini, Simone (1284–1344) Italian painter. His imposing fresco, the *Maestà* (1315), combines elements of BYZANTINE ART and GOTHIC ART and presages the RENAISSANCE. The *Annunciation* (1333) is his most accomplished work.

Martinique Caribbean island in the Windward group of the Lesser Antilles, forming an overseas department of France; the capital is Fort-de-France. Discovered in 1502 by Christopher COLUMBUS, Martinique was inhabited by Carib Indians until they were displaced by French settlers after 1635. Attacked in the 17th century by the Dutch and the British, the island became a permanent French possession after the Napoleonic Wars. Of volcanic origin, it is the largest of the Lesser Antilles. In 1902, a volcanic eruption completely destroyed the original capital, St Pierre. Industries: tourism, sugar, rum, fruits, cocoa, tobacco, vanilla, vegetables. Area: 1,102sq km (425sq mi). Pop. (1999) 426,000. *See* WEST INDIES map

Martins, Peter (1946–) Danish dancer, choreographer, and ballet director. His partnership with Suzanne Farrell was one of the greatest in the history of ballet. Martins was principal dancer (1969–83) with the New York City Ballet, before becoming its joint ballet master (with Jerome ROBBINS), then director (1990–). His choreographed works include *Les Gentilhommes* (1987) and *A Musical Offering* (1991).

Martinu, Bohuslav (1890–1959) Czech composer. Much of his music is based on Bohemian folk rhythms and Czech dances. Martinu's works include the opera *Julietta* (1938) and Symphony No. 6 (1955).

martyr Person who dies willingly rather than renounce his or her religious faith. The term, which is taken from the Greek word for 'witness', particularly applies to early Christians who suffered death for their beliefs. The first Christian martyr was Saint STEPHEN. In Judaism, the six million Jews murdered by the Nazis are regarded as martyrs. *See also* SAINT

M

Marvell, Andrew (1621–78) English metaphysical poet and satirist. In his lifetime, he was known for his withering satires on corruption and mismanagement in the court of Charles II. Today, Marvell is chiefly remembered for his lyric poetry, first collected in 1681 in a volume that included 'The Garden', "Bermudas" and his best-known poem, 'To His Coy Mistress'.

Marx, Karl Heinrich (1818–83) German social philosopher, political theorist, and founder (with Friedrich ENGELS) of international COMMUNISM. He produced his own philosophical approach of DIALECTICAL MATERIALISM. He proclaimed that religion was 'the opium of the people' and in *The German Ideology* (1845–46), written with Engels, described the 'inevitable laws' of history. In Brussels, he joined the Communist League and wrote with Engels the epoch-making *Communist Manifesto* (1848). Marx took part in the revolutionary movements in France and Germany, then went to London (1849), where he lived until his death. His work at the British Museum produced a stream of writings, including *Das Kapital* (3 vols, 1867, 1885, 1894; the last two edited by Engels), which became the 'Bible of the working class'. The International Workingmen's Association (the First International) formed in 1864, and Marx became its leading spirit. His expulsion of BAKUNIN from the Association in 1872 led to its collapse. Marx was one of the most important political theorists of modern times. *See also* MARXISM

Marx Brothers US team of vaudeville and film comedians. The Marx Brothers consisted of Chico (Leonard, 1891–1961), Harpo (Arthur, 1893–1964), Groucho (Julius, 1895–1977) and Zeppo (Herbert, 1901–79), the latter withdrew from the group in 1935. Marx Brothers' riotous, wisecracking comedies include *Animal Crackers* (1930), *Duck Soup* (1933), and *A Night at the Opera* (1935).

Marxism School of SOCIALISM that arose in 19th-century Europe as a response to the growth of industrial CAPITALISM. It is named after Karl MARX. According to Marxism, a communist society was historically inevitable. Capitalism, because of its emphasis on profits, would eventually so reduce the condition of workers that they would rebel, overthrow the capitalists, and establish a classless society in which the means of production were collectively owned. *The Communist Manifesto* (1848) and *Das Kapital* (1867, 1885, 1894) both contain ideas central to Marxism, which forms the basis of COMMUNISM and strongly influenced the related ideology, socialism. *See also* DIALECTICAL MATERIALISM; LENIN, VLADIMIR ILYICH; MAO ZEDONG

Mary (Blessed Virgin Mary) (active 1st century AD) Mother of JESUS CHRIST. She figures prominently in the first two chapters of the Gospels according to Saint MATTHEW and Saint LUKE, which record Christ's birth. Mary has always been held in high regard in Christendom. In the early Church, the principal Marian feast was the Commemoration of St Mary, from which developed the feast of the ASSUMPTION (August 15). Other Marian feasts are: the Nativity (September 8), the ANNUNCIATION or LADY DAY (March 25), the Purification or Candlemas (February 2), the Visitation (July 2), and (for Roman Catholics) the IMMACULATE CONCEPTION (December 8).

Mary, Queen of Scots (1542–87) Daughter of JAMES V, she succeeded him as queen when one week old. Mary was sent to France aged six, and married the future Francis II of France in 1558. On his death in 1560 she returned to Scotland, where, as a Catholic, she came into conflict with Protestant reformers. Her marriage to Henry Stuart (Lord Darnley) was also resented and soon broke down. After Darnley's murder (1567), she married Lord Bothwell, possibly her husband's murderer, which alienated her remaining supporters. Following a rebellion of Scottish nobles, she was imprisoned and forced to abdicate in favour of her infant son, James VI (later JAMES I of England). Although she escaped and raised an army, it was defeated at Langside (1568) and Mary fled to England. She was kept in captivity, but became involved in Spanish plots against ELIZABETH I and was eventually executed.

Mary I (Mary Tudor) (1516–58) Queen of England (1553–58). Daughter of HENRY VIII and CATHERINE OF ARAGON. During the reign of her half-brother, EDWARD VI, Mary remained a devout Catholic. On Edward's death, the Duke of NORTHUMBERLAND arranged the brief usurpation of Lady Jane GREY but Mary acceded with popular support. Her marriage (1554) to the future King PHILIP II of Spain secured a Spanish alliance. The union provoked a rebellion, led by Sir Thomas WYATT, and hostility intensified after England lost Calais to France (1558). Mary's determination to re-establish papal authority saw the restoration of heresy laws. The resultant execution of *c*.300 Protestants, including Thomas CRANMER, Hugh LATIMER and Nicholas RIDLEY, earned her the epithet 'Bloody Mary'. Mary's sister succeeded her as ELIZABETH I.

Mary II (1662–94) Queen of England, Scotland, and Ireland, eldest daughter of JAMES II. Despite her father's conversion to Catholicism, Mary was brought up a Protestant. In 1677, she married her cousin, William of Orange, and moved to Holland. The GLORIOUS REVOLUTION (1688–89) resulted in the exile of James II, and she and her husband were invited to assume the English throne as Mary II and WILLIAM III (OF ORANGE).

Maryland State in E USA, on the Atlantic Ocean; the capital is ANNAPOLIS. The largest city is BALTIMORE. The first settlements were founded in 1634. Maryland (one of the 13 original states) was active in the drive towards American independence. In 1791 it ceded an area of land on the Potomac River to create the District of Columbia, the site of the capital. During the American CIVIL WAR, Maryland was one of the border states that did not secede from the Union, but its citizens served in both armies. The W half of the state is part of the Piedmont plateau region. Chesapeake Bay and its coastal marshlands dominate. Maize, hay, tobacco and soya beans are the chief crops. Industries: iron and steel, shipbuilding, primary metals, transport equipment, chemicals, electrical machinery, fishing. Area: 25,316sq km (9,775sq mi). Pop. (2000) 5,296,486.

Mary Magdalene, Saint (active 1st century AD) Early follower of Jesus Christ, from the village of Magdala on the W shore of the Sea of Galilee. According to the gospels, Christ freed her of seven demons. Mary accompanied him on his preaching tours in Galilee, witnessed his crucifixion and burial, and was the first to see him after his resurrection. She is often identified as a repentant prostitute. Her feast day is July 22.

Masaccio (1401–28?) Florentine painter of the early RENAISSANCE, b. Tommaso Giovanni di Mone. His three most important surviving works are: a polyptych (1426) for the Carmelite Church, Pisa (now in London, Berlin, and Naples); a fresco cycle that he created with Masolino, portraying the life of Saint Peter, in the Brancacci Chapel, Santa Maria del Carmine, Florence (*c*.1425–28); and the *Trinity* fresco in Santa Maria Novella, Florence (*c*.1428).

Masada Fortified hill near the Dead Sea, SE Israel. It was the scene of the final defence of the Jewish ZEALOTS against the Romans during the Jewish revolt that began in AD 66. In 73, the defenders, *c*.1,000 in number, committed mass suicide rather than surrender.

Masai African people of Kenya and Tanzania, consisting of several subgroups who speak a Nilotic language. They are characteristically tall and slender. Their patrilineal, egalitarian society is based on nomadic pastoralism, cattle being equated with wealth. The traditional Masai *kraal* is a group of mud houses surrounded by a thorn fence. Today, there are *c*.250,000 Masai.

Masaryk, Tomás (1850–1937) Czech statesman and philosopher, first president of CZECHOSLOVAKIA (1918–35). In 1900, he founded the Czech Peoples Party to represent Czech interests in the AUSTRO-HUNGARIAN EMPIRE. Masaryk fled at the outbreak of World War 1, and (with Eduard BENEŠ) formed the Czechoslovak National Council. In 1918, he returned as president. Revered as the 'father of the nation', Masaryk enacted land reforms and pursued a liberal path on minority rights. Benes succeeded him.

Masefield, John (1878–1967) English poet and novelist. Masefield's early seafaring experiences inform much of his work. His debut volume *Salt-Water Ballads* (1902) includes 'Sea Fever'. He was Poet Laureate from 1930. Masefield is best-known for his long narrative poems, such as *The Everlasting Mercy* (1911) and *Reynard the Fox* (1919).

maser (acronym for **m**icrowave **a**mplification by **s**timulated **e**mission of **r**adiation) Device using atoms artificially kept in states of higher energy than normal to provide amplification

▲ **Marx Brothers** From top, Chico, Harpo, Groucho and Zeppo, the Marx Brothers, were born in New York City. After many unsuccessful years, they finally made it to Broadway with *I'll Say She Is* (1924). Zeppo left the team early but the remaining brothers each developed a distinctive style: Chico was the piano player with the broad Italian accent; Harpo was the harp player who never spoke a word; and Groucho was the moustached wisecracker.

M

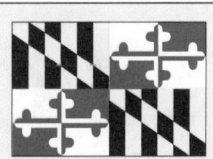

MARYLAND
Statehood :
April 28, 1788
Nickname :
Old Line State, Free State
State bird :
Baltimore oriole
State flower :
Black-eyed Susan
State tree :
White oak
State motto :
Manly deeds, womanly words

of high-frequency radio signals. Masers are used to amplify signals from spacecraft and as oscillators in ATOMIC CLOCKS. US physicist Charles Townes discovered the principle, for which he shared the 1964 Nobel Prize in physics with the Soviet physicists Nikolai BASOV and Aleksandr PROKHOROV. The first maser used electrostatic (charged) plates to separate high-energy ammonia atoms from low-energy ones. Radiation of a certain frequency stimulated the high-energy ammonium atoms to emit similar radiation and strengthen the signal. The principle is also applied to the LASER.

Maseru Capital of Lesotho, on the River Caledon, near the w border with South Africa. Originally a small trading town, it was capital of British Basutoland protectorate (1869–71, 1884–1966). It remained the capital when the Kingdom of Lesotho achieved independence in 1966. It is a commercial, transport and administrative centre. Pop. (2002) 169,200.

Mashhad (Arabic, 'shrine of martyrdom') City in NE Iran, close to the border with Turkmenistan; capital of Khorasan province. It is an Islamic holy city and a place of pilgrimage for SHI'ITE Muslims. In 809, the Abbasid Caliph HARUN AL-RASHID was buried here, and in 818 the Imam Ali Riza died while visiting Harun's grave. An ornate shrine was built over both their tombs. In the 18th century, Mashhad became the capital of Persia. Today, Mashhad is Iran's second-largest city and a major trade centre. It is famous for its carpet and textile manufacture. Pop. (2005) 2,147,000.

Mason-Dixon Line Border of Pennsylvania with Maryland and West Virginia, USA. It is named after the men who surveyed it in the 1760s. It was regarded as the dividing line between slave and free states at the time of the MISSOURI COMPROMISE (1820–21), and became the popular name for the boundary between North and South in the USA.

masque Dramatic presentation that originated in Italy but became popular in the English court and the great houses of the nobility during the late 16th and early 17th centuries. The masque consisted of verse, comedy and, as an essential feature, a dance for a group of masked revellers. The earliest masque text is *Proteus and the Adamantine Rock*, performed at Gray's Inn in 1594 in honour of Queen Elizabeth I.

mass Celebration of the EUCHARIST in the Roman Catholic Church and among some High Church Anglicans. The Catholic rite comprises the Liturgy of the Word and the Liturgy of the Eucharist, which includes the Offertory, the sacrifice of Christ's body and blood under the guise of bread and wine. In the late 20th century, the mass underwent a number of changes following the Second Vatican Council (1962–65).

mass A setting of the Roman Catholic religious service in Latin. Composers from all eras have written masses. One of the most famous is J.S. Bach's 'Mass in B minor'. In the 19th century, mass settings increased in scale until they began to be performed in concert halls rather than in church.

mass Measure of the quantity of matter in an object. The standard unit of mass is the kilogram (one kg = 1,000 grams). Scientists recognize two types of mass. The **gravitational** mass of a body is determined by its mutual attraction to another reference body, such as the Earth, as expressed in Newton's law of GRAVITATION. Spring balances and platform balances proved a measure of gravitational mass. The **inertial** mass of a body is determined by its resistance to a change in state of motion, as expressed in the second law of motion. INERTIA balances provide a measure of inertial mass. According to EINSTEIN's principle of equivalence, upon which his general theory of RELATIVITY is based, the inertial mass and the gravitational mass of a given body are equivalent. *See also* WEIGHT

Massachusetts State in NEW ENGLAND, on the Atlantic Ocean, NE USA; the capital and largest city is BOSTON. Other major cities are Worcester, Springfield, Cambridge, and New Bedford. The Pilgrim Fathers formed the first settlement, PLYMOUTH COLONY, on Massachusetts Bay in 1620. In 1630 English Puritans founded Boston, and it became the centre of the Massachusetts Bay Colony. The area played a leading role in events leading up to the American Revolution, and was the scene of the first battle. Massachusetts prospered after achieving statehood in 1788. In the E of the state is a low-lying coastal plain. The Connecticut River valley and the Berkshire

valley divided the uplands of the interior. The principal rivers are the Housatonic, Merrimack, and Connecticut. A highly industrialized region, Massachusetts is one of the most densely populated states. Agricultural produce includes cranberries, tobacco, hay, vegetables, and dairy products. Industries: electronic equipment, plastics, footwear, paper, machinery, metal and rubber goods, printing and publishing, fishing. Area: 20,300sq km (7838sq mi). Pop. (2000) 6,349,097.

Massachusetts Bay Company English company chartered in 1629. Its purpose was trade and colonization of the land between the Charles and Merrimack rivers in N America. A group of Puritans, led by John Winthrop, gained control of the company and founded the Massachusetts Bay Colony in 1630. They took the company's charter with them to Massachussetts and enjoyed considerable autonomy. Within ten years, *c*.20,000 people, mainly English Puritans, had settled.

Massenet, Jules Émile-Frédéric (1842–1912) French Romantic composer who dominated 19th-century French lyric opera. He composed many operas, including *Le Cid* (1885), *Werther* (1892). and *Thérèse* (1909). His two masterpieces are considered to be *Manon* (1884) and *Thaïs* (1894).

Massif Central Extensive mountainous plateau in SE central France. The volcanic AUVERGNE Mountains form the core of the region, which also includes the Cévennes (SE) and the Causses (SW). Sheep and goats graze on the slopes of the Massif Central. The region has hydroelectric plants and coal and kaolin mines. The highest peak is Puy de Sancy, at 1886m (6186ft). Area: *c*.85,000sq km (32,800sq mi)

Massine, Léonide (1896–1979) US choreographer and ballet dancer, b. Russia. His choreography includes *Le Soleil de Nuit* (1915), *La Boutique Fantasque* (1919), and *Three Cornered Hat* (1919). He also performed in the films *The Red Shoes* (1948) and *Tales of Hoffmann* (1951).

Massinger, Philip (1583–1640) English dramatist. He wrote more than 40 plays, often in collaboration, many of which are now lost. He is best known for his realistic yet highly symbolic satires of domestic life, such as *A New Way to Pay Old Debts* (1621–22) and *The City Madam* (*c*.1632).

mass number (nucleon number) The total number of PROTONS and NEUTRONS found in the NUCLEUS of an ATOM.

mass production Manufacture of goods in large quantities by standardizing parts, techniques and machinery. American inventor Eli WHITNEY introduced mass production in 1798 to produce weapons. The assembly line, a conveyor belt carrying the work through a series of assembly areas, was introduced in 1913 by Henry FORD. Many mass-production processes depend on computer control of machines, including ROBOTS.

mass spectrograph (mass spectrometer) Instrument for separating IONS according to their masses (or more precisely, according to their charge-to-mass ratio), used in chemical analysis. In the simplest types, an electric field accelerates ions, which a magnetic field then deflects; the lighter the ions the greater the deflection. By varying the field, ions of different masses can be focused in sequence onto a photographic plate or detector and a record of charge-to-mass ratios obtained.

mastectomy Surgical removal of all or part of the female breast. It is performed to treat CANCER. Simple mastectomy involves the breast alone; if the cancer has spread, radical mastectomy may be undertaken, removing also the lymphatic tissue from the armpit.

Masters, Edgar Lee (1868–1950) US poet and novelist. Although he published a number of volumes, he never repeated the success of his *Spoon River Anthology* (1915), a series of free-verse monologues spoken by the dead of a Midwest town.

Masters, William Howell (1915–2001) US physician who, with his psychologist wife (1971–93) Virginia (née Johnson) (1925–), became noted for studies of the physiology and anatomy of human sexual activity. Their works include *Human Sexual Response* (1966) and *Human Sexual Inadequacy* (1970).

mastiff (old English mastiff) Large fighting dog first bred in England more than 2,000 years ago. It has a broad, rounded head with a dark-coloured, square muzzle and small V-shaped ears. The deep-chested body is set on strong legs with large feet. The short, coarse coat may be brown, grey or brindle. Height: to 84cm (33in) at shoulder; weight: to 95kg (210lb).

MASSACHUSETTS
Statehood:
February 6, 1788
Nickname:
Bay State
State bird:
Chickadee
State flower:
Mayflower
State tree:
American elm
State motto:
By the sword we seek peace, but peace only under liberty

M

mastodon Any of several species of extinct elephantine mammals, all of which existed mainly in the PLEISTOCENE epoch. Mastodons had a long coat of red hair; the grinding teeth were notably smaller and less complex than those of modern ELEPHANTS, and the males had small tusks on the lower as well as the upper jaw. Genus *Mastodon*.

Mastroianni, Marcello (1923–96) Italian film actor. One of the greatest European character actors since the 1950s, he was often associated with the films of Federico FELLINI. Following international success in *La Dolce Vita* (1960), he appeared as Fellini's alter ego in *8½* (1963) and *Intervista* (1987). He finally made his Hollywood debut in *Used People* (1992).

masturbation Self-stimulation by manipulation of the genital organs for pleasure, usually to ORGASM. Once regarded as taboo, sinful or physically harmful, moderate masturbation is no longer considered abnormal.

Mata Hari (1876–1917) Dutch courtesan. Her real name was Margaretha Geertruida Zelle. In 1917, she was arrested in Paris as a German agent and subsequently executed. Although her conduct was suspicious, few people now believe she was the mysterious secret agent that the French authorities alleged.

materialism System of philosophical thought that explains the nature of the world as dependent on MATTER. The doctrine was formulated in the 4th century BC by DEMOCRITUS. PLATO developed the contrasting philosophy of IDEALISM. The early followers of BUDDHISM were also materialists. DIALECTICAL MATERIALISM as formulated by Karl MARX is a modern development of the older theory. *See also* EPICURUS; MONISM

mathematical induction Method of proving that a mathematical statement is true for any positive integer n by proving: (1) that it is true for a base value, for example 1; and (2) that if it is true for a value k then it is also true for $k + 1$. If (1) and (2) hold, then it follows in a finite number of steps that the statement is true for any positive integer n.

mathematics Study concerned originally with the properties of numbers and space; now more generally concerned with deductions made from assumptions about abstract entities. Mathematics is often divided into **pure** mathematics, which is purely abstract reasoning based on axioms, and **applied** mathematics, which involves the use of mathematical reasoning in other fields, such as engineering, physics, chemistry, and economics. The main divisions of pure mathematics are GEOMETRY, ALGEBRA, and analysis. The latter deals with the concept of limits and includes differential and integral CALCULUS. *See also* ARITHMETIC; TRIGONOMETRY

Mather, Cotton (1663–1728) Puritan minister in colonial Massachusetts. His father, **Increase** Mather (1639–1723) doubted the reliability of testimony at the SALEM witch trials, and his *Cases of Conscience* (1693) helped to stop the executions. In 1723, Cotton succeeded his father at the Boston ministry. He supported the SALEM witch trials, although not the subsequent executions, yet was sympathetic to scientific and philosophical ideas. He was one of the founders of Yale University and a member of the Royal Society, London.

Matisse, Henri Emile Benoît (1869–1954) French painter, sculptor, graphic artist and designer. Having experimented with NEO-IMPRESSIONISM in paintings such as *Luxe, calme et volupte* (1905), he developed the style of painting that became known as FAUVISM. After a brief flirtation with CUBISM, Matisse turned back to the luminous and sensual calmness that typified his art. In later life he produced one of his greatest works, the design of the Chapel of the Rosary at Vence (1949–51). He also started making coloured paper cut-outs, such as *L'Escargot* (1953). Matisse's most famous sculptures include a series of four bronzes *The Back* (1909–29).

Mato Grosso State in W central Brazil, bordered S by MATO GROSSO DO SUL, and W and SW by Bolivia; the capital is Cuiabà. First settled in the early 18th century by miners seeking gold and diamonds, it became a state in 1889. Much of the area lies on the central plateau of Brazil, but there is rainforest in the N and marshland in the SW. The W has good grazing land and cattle rearing is the chief occupation. Rice, maize, and sugar-cane are grown. There are extensive mineral deposits but most of them remain unexploited. Area: 881,000sq km (340,156sq mi). Pop. (2000) 2,498,150.

Mato Grosso do Sul State in SW Brazil, bordered N by MATO GROSSO, W by Bolivia, and W and S by Paraguay; the capital is Campo Grande. Early pioneers exploited the area's gold and diamonds but there was little permanent settlement until the late 20th century. In 1979, it was created a separate state from the S part of Mato Grosso. Most of Mato Grosso do Sul lies on an extension of the central plateau of Brazil. There is marshland to the NW and the state has extensive grazing land. There are vast mineral resources, including iron ore and manganese. Agriculture and livestock are important, and the main crops are groundnuts, rice, beans, maize, and cotton. Area: 350,548sq km (135,347sq mi). Pop. (2000) 2,075,275.

matriarchy Any society or group that is ruled by women. Matriarchal societies exist among some primitive peoples in South America. *See also* PATRIARCHY

matrix Rectangular array of numbers in rows and columns. The number of rows need not equal the number of columns. Matrices can be combined (added and multiplied) according to certain rules. They are useful in the study of transformations of co-ordinate systems and in the solving of sets of simultaneous equations.

matter Any material that takes up space. Ordinary matter is made up of ATOMS, which are combinations of ELECTRONS, PROTONS and NEUTRONS. Atoms, in turn, make up ELEMENTS – an ordered series of substances that have atoms with one proton in their nuclei (hydrogen) to a hundred or more. All matter exerts an attractive force on other matter, called GRAVITATION. Charged particles exert an attractive or repulsive ELECTROMAGNETIC FORCE that accounts for nearly all everyday phenomena. The strong interaction force is responsible for binding the protons and neutrons in an atomic NUCLEUS, and the weak interaction is responsible for beta decay. *See also* ANTIMATTER; FUNDAMENTAL FORCES; MATTER, STATES OF; MOLECULE

matter, states of Classification of MATTER according to its structural characteristics. Four states (or **phases**) of matter are generally recognized: solid, liquid, gas, and plasma. Any one ELEMENT or compound may exist sequentially or simultaneously in two or more of these states. SOLIDS may be crystalline or amorphous. LIQUIDS have molecules that can flow past one another but that remain almost as close as in a solid. In a GAS, molecules are so far from one another that they travel in relatively straight lines until they collide. In a PLASMA, atoms are torn apart into electrons and nuclei by the high temperatures.

Matterhorn (Monte Cervino) Mountain peak in Switzerland, in the Pennine Alps, on the Swiss-Italian border. It has a distinctive pyramidal peak formed from several cirques and was first climbed by English mountaineer Edward Whymper in 1865. Height: 4,478m (14,691ft).

Matthew, Gospel according to Saint Gospel placed first in the New Testament but probably written after those of Saint MARK and Saint LUKE. Written *c.*AD 70–75, it is ascribed to Saint MATTHEW, the tax gatherer who became one of the 12 disciples. It contains more of the teachings, parables and sayings of Jesus than the other gospels and is the only SYNOPTIC GOSPEL written in a Jewish, rather than a Hellenistic, style.

Matthew, Saint (active 1st century AD) Apostle and probably one of the four evangelists of the New Testament. In the lists of the disciples in the Synoptic Gospels, Matthew is sometimes called Levi. Before his calling, he was a tax collector for King Herod Antipas. Feast day: September 21 in the west, November 16 in the east.

Matthews, Sir Stanley (1915–2000) English footballer who played for Stoke City and Blackpool. Matthews made 786 appearances, including 54 caps for England, in a professional career that spanned from 1932 to 1965. He was the first European Footballer of the Year (1956).

Maugham, (William) Somerset (1874–1965) British novelist, short-story writer, and dramatist, b. France. He achieved fame initially as a dramatist with plays such as *Lady Frederick* (1912) and *The Circle* (1921). Maugham's first successful novel was the semi-autobiographical *Of Human Bondage* (1915). Other novels include *The Moon and Sixpence* (1919) and *Cakes and Ale* (1930). His experiences in British intelligence in World War 1 informs the short-story collection *Ashenden* (1928).

▲ **Matisse** One of the most influential artists of the 20th century, Matisse originally studied law, before quitting his studies to enter the studio of Gustave Moreau in Paris in 1892. His work culminates in the decorations for the Chapel of the Rosary at Vence, France. He designed the windows, ceramic tiles, and vestments as a gift to the nuns of the adjacent convent, who had looked after him during an illness.

M

INTERNET

Matisse, Henri Emile Benoît
▶ www.hermitagemuseum.org
▶ www.artsmia.org

Mau Mau Anti-colonial terrorist group of the KIKUYU of Kenya. In 1952, after repeated attacks on Europeans, Britain declared a state of emergency and drafted in troops. Within four years, the conflict claimed *c*.100 European and 2,000 anti-Mau Mau Kikuyu lives. More than 11,000 Mau Mau died before the state of emergency ended in 1960.

Mauna Kea (White Mountain) Dormant shield volcano in central Hawaii, USA. At 4,205m (13,796ft), Mauna Kea is the highest island mountain in the world. On the snow-capped peak of the volcano stands **Mauna Kea Observatory**.

Mauna Loa Volcano in central Hawaii, USA. The second highest active volcano in the world, Mauna Loa has many craters: Kilauea is the largest and Mokuaweoweo is at the summit. The greatest eruption was in 1881, with others in 1942, 1949, 1975 and 1984. Height: 4,169m (13,678ft).

Maundy Thursday In the Christian liturgical calendar, the day before GOOD FRIDAY, commemorating the institution of the EUCHARIST and the washing of the disciples' feet by Jesus, as described in the Gospel according to Saint JOHN.

Maupassant, Guy de (1850–93) French short-story writer and novelist. He produced one of his greatest short stories, 'Boule de suif' ('Ball of Fat'), for the collection *Les Soirées de Médan* (1880). He wrote more than 300 short stories; a number are collected in *La Maison Tellier* (1881), *Contes de la Bécasse* (1883), and *L'Inutile Beauté* (1890). *Pierre et Jean* (1887) is regarded as the best of his six novels.

Mauriac, François (1885–1970) French novelist and playwright. His novels, *A Kiss for the Leper* (1922), *Genitrix* (1923) and *The Desert of Love* (1925), portray the futility of pursuing fulfilment through material comfort and secular love. He also wrote poetry and volumes of memoirs and autobiography. He received the 1952 Nobel Prize in literature.

Mauritania Republic in NW Africa. *see* country feature.

Mauritius Republic in the Indian Ocean, *see* country feature.

Maurya Empire (321–185BC) Ancient Indian dynasty and state founded by CHANDRAGUPTA (r. *c*.321–*c*.291BC). His son, Bindusara (r. *c*.291–*c*.268BC), conquered the Deccan, and all of N India united under ASHOKA (r. *c*.264–*c*.238BC), Chandragupta's grandson. After Ashoka's death, the Empire broke up, and the last Emperor was assassinated in *c*.185 BC.

Maxim, Sir Hiram Stevens (1840–1916) US inventor of the Maxim MACHINE GUN (1883). His other inventions include a smokeless powder and a delayed-action fuse. He settled in England (1881) and was knighted in 1901.

Maximilian I (1459–1519) Holy Roman Emperor (1493–1519), son and successor of FREDERICK III. Maximilian was one of the most successful members of the HABSBURG dynasty. He gained Burgundy and the Netherlands by marriage, and defended them against France. He was less successful in asserting control over the German princes, and involvement in the Italian Wars led to his defeat by the Swiss in 1499. Maximilian strengthened the Habsburg heartland in Austria and through marriage diplomacy ensured that his grandson and successor, CHARLES V, inherited a vast European empire.

Maximilian, Ferdinand Joseph (1832–67) Emperor of Mexico (1864–67). An Austrian archduke, brother of the Emperor Francis Joseph, he was offered the throne of Mexico after the French invasion (1862). When the French

---

MAURITANIA

The Islamic Republic of Mauritania in NW Africa is nearly twice the size of France, although France's population is more than 28 times that of Mauritania. More than two-thirds of the land is barren, most of it being part of the SAHARA desert. Apart from a small nomadic population, most Mauritanians live in the S, either on the plains bordering the Senegal River in the SW or on the tropical savanna in the SE. The highest point is Kediet Ijill (915m [3,000ft]). It is an area rich in haematite, a high-quality iron ore.

CLIMATE

The amount of rain and the length of the rainy season increases from N to S. The desert has dry NE and E winds throughout the year. SW winds bring summer rain to the S.

HISTORY

Berbers migrated to the region in the first millennium AD. The Hodh basin lay at the heart of the ancient empire of Ghana (700–1200), and towns grew up along the trans-Saharan caravan routes. Mauritania was the cradle of the Almoravid dynasty, which spread Islam among the Saharan tribes. In the 14th and 15th century the region formed part of the ancient Mali Empire. Portuguese mariners explored the coast in the 1440s, but European colonialism did not begin until the 17th century. Trade in gum arabic, obtained from acacia trees, became important. Britain, France, and the Netherlands were all interested in exploiting this trade, and France finally took control and set up a protectorate in 1903. In 1920 the region became a separate colony within French West Africa. In 1958 Mauritania became a self-governing territory in the French Union. It achieved full independence in 1960.

POLITICS

In 1961 Mauritania's president, Mokhtar Ould Daddah, made the country a one-party state. In 1976 Spain withdrew from Spanish Sahara (now WESTERN SAHARA), which borders Mauritania to the N. Morocco occupied most of the territory, Mauritania the rest. Saharan guerrillas began an armed struggle for independence. In 1979 Mauritania withdrew from Moroccan-occupied Western Sahara.

From 1978 Mauritania was ruled by a series of military regimes. In 1991 the country adopted a new constitution when the people voted to create a multiparty democracy. In 1992 army colonel Maaouiya Ould Sidi Ahmed Taya, who had served as leader of a military administration since December 1984, was elected president. However, subsequent legislative elections in 1992 were boycotted by opposi-

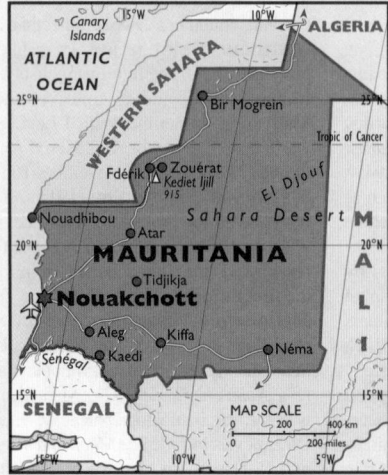

AREA 1,025,520sq km [395,953sq mi]
POPULATION 3,270,000
CAPITAL (POPULATION) Nouakchott (735,000)
GOVERNMENT Multiparty Islamic republic
ETHNIC GROUPS Mixed Moor/Black 40%, Moor 30%, Black 30%
LANGUAGES Arabic and Wolof (both official), French
RELIGIONS Islam
CURRENCY Ouguiya = 5 khoums

tion parties. Taya was re-elected in 1997 and 2003 but overthrown in a military coup led by Colonel Ely Ould Mohamed Vall in August 2005. Vall's administration had popular support and promised a swift return to democracy; parliamentary elections took place in 2006 and presidential elections in early 2007. Sidi Ould Cheikh Abdallahi became president and began a campaign to outlaw and end slavery.

ECONOMY

The World Bank classifies Mauritania as a 'low-income' developing country. Agriculture employs over half the workforce, with the majority living at subsistence level. Many are still cattle herders who drive their herds from the Senegal River through the SAHEL steppelands, coinciding with the seasonal rains. However, droughts in the 1980s greatly reduced the domestic animal populations, forcing many nomadic farmers to seek help in urban areas. Plagues of locusts in 2004 also caused severe damage. Farmers in the SE grow such crops as beans, dates, millet, rice and sorghum. Rich fishing grounds lie off the coast. The country's chief natural resource is iron ore; the vast reserves around Fderik provide a major source of revenue.

withdrew in 1867, the liberal forces of Benito JUÁREZ overthrew Maximilian and executed him.

Maxwell, James Clerk (1831–79) Scottish mathematician and physicist who did theoretical work on ELECTROMAGNETIC RADIATION. He used the theory of the electromagnetic field for **Maxwell's equations**, which linked light with electromagnetic waves, established the nature of Saturn's rings and worked on thermodynamics and statistical mechanics. The unit of magnetic flux, the maxwell (Mx), was named after him, but has since been replaced by the SI unit, the weber.

Maya Culture of classic American civilization. Occupying s Mexico and N Central America, it was at its height from the 3rd to 9th centuries. The Maya built great temple-cities, with buildings on step PYRAMIDS. They were skilful potters and weavers and productive farmers. They worshipped gods and ancestors, and blood sacrifice was an important element of religion. Maya civilization declined in the 10th century, and much was destroyed after the Spanish conquest in the 16th century. The modern Maya, numbering c.4 million, live in the same area and speak a variety of languages related to that of their ancestors.

Mayan Family of languages spoken on the Yucatán Peninsula of Mexico, as well as in Guatemala and part of Belize by the MAYA. There are several dozen of these languages, the most important being Yucatec (in Mexico), and Quiché, Cakchiquel, Mam, and Kekchi (in Guatemala). They derive from ancient Mayan.

May beetle Alternative name for the COCKCHAFER

Mayer, Louis B. (Burt) (1885–1957) US film executive. Mayer founded a film production company in 1917, and became vice president of Metro-Goldwyn-Mayer (MGM) in 1924. During the 1930s and 1940s, he was the most powerful magnate in Hollywood.

Mayflower Ship that carried the PILGRIMS from Plymouth, England to Massachusetts in September, 1620. It carried 102 English Puritans (some from the Netherlands) who established the PLYMOUTH COLONY.

mayfly Soft-bodied insect found worldwide. The adult does not eat and lives only a few days, but the aquatic larvae (NYMPH) may live several years. Adults have triangular front wings, characteristic thread-like tails, and vestigial mouth-

---

MAURITIUS

The Republic of Mauritius consists of the large island of Mauritius, which is situated 800km [500mi] E of Madagascar. This island makes up just over 90% of the country, which also includes the island of Rodrigues, about 560km [348mi] E of Mauritius, and several small islands. The main island is fringed by coral reefs, lagoons and sandy beaches. The land in the interior rises to a high lava plateau (828m [2,717ft]) enclosed by rocky peaks.

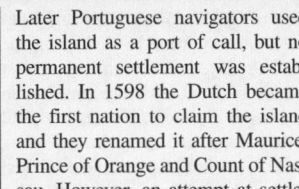

CLIMATE

Mauritius has a tropical climate, with heavy rains in the winter. SE winds bring rain to the interior plateau of the main island, which is also occasionally hit by destructive tropical cyclones in summer. Average annual rainfall on the interior plateau may reach 5,100mm [200in]. The SW is much drier, with about 890mm [35in]. Temperatures range from 22°C [72°F] in the winter (June to October) to 26°C [79°F] in the summer (November to April).

HISTORY

In 1498 the fleet of Vasco da Gama sighted the island, and in 1510 the Portuguese navigator Pedro Mascarenhas landed and named it Cimé.

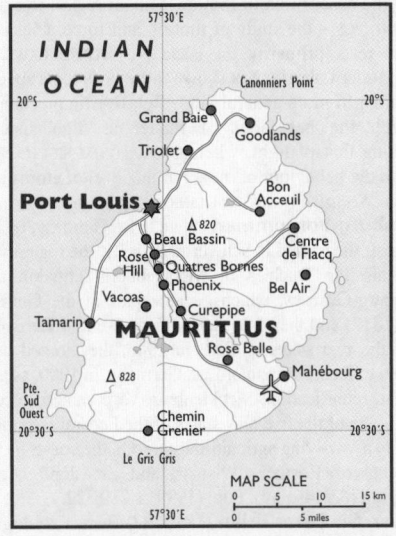

Later Portuguese navigators used the island as a port of call, but no permanent settlement was established. In 1598 the Dutch became the first nation to claim the island and they renamed it after Maurice, Prince of Orange and Count of Nassau. However, an attempt at settlement failed in the 1650s. A second attempt was abandoned in 1710, by which time the dodo – unique to Mauritius – had become extinct. Following the Dutch withdrawal, the island became a haven for pirates.

The French EAST INDIA COMPANY claimed Mauritius for France in 1715 and named it the Isle de France. The French developed the economy and imported African slaves. In 1767 control of the island passed to the French government, although the settlers revolted in 1796 when French government tried to abolish slavery.

British forces landed on Mauritius in 1810, starting a period of British rule. In 1834 Britain abolished slavery on the island and renamed it Mauritius. Most former slaves refused to work on the sugar plantations, so from 1837 Britain introduced indentured labourers from India. About 450,000 workers were brought in before indentured labour was ended in 1910.

In 1926 the first Indo-Mauritians were elected to the government council. In 1936, a Creole politician, Dr Maurice Cure, founded the Mauritian Labour Party (MLP). In 1942 representatives from all Mauritian communities were invited to serve on consultative committees and, in 1948, many Indians and Creoles were given the vote in elections to a new, enlarged legislature. Internal self-government was introduced in 1957. Elections were held under universal adult suffrage following the introduction of a new constitution in 1958. The MLP, led by Dr Seewoosagur Ramgoolam, won a majority. However, ethnic riots between Indians and Creoles occurred in 1964.

POLITICS

Mauritius became independent in 1968. In 1969 Paul Berenger founded the socialist Mauritian Militant Movement (MMM). In 1971 the MMM supported strikers and organized opposition to the government. In

AREA 2,040sq km [788sq mi]
POPULATION 1,251,000
CAPITAL (POPULATION) Port Louis (148,000)
GOVERNMENT Multiparty republic
ETHNIC GROUPS Indo-Mauritian 68%, Creole 27%, Sino-Mauritian 3%, Franco-Mauritian 2%
LANGUAGES English (official), Creole, French, Hindi, Urdu, Hakka, Bojpoori
RELIGIONS Hindu 50%, Roman Catholic 27%, Muslim (largely Sunni) 16%, Protestant 5%
CURRENCY Mauritian rupee = 100 cents

response, the government declared a state of emergency which lasted until 1976. The MMM won the 1992 elections and Anerood Jugnauth became prime minister.

Mauritius became a republic in 1992 and Caseem Uteem of the MMM was elected president. In 1995 an alliance led by Navin Ramgoolam and Paul Berenger won the elections and Ramgoolam became prime minister. But Jugnauth was returned to power in 2000. He served as prime minister until 2003, when he handed over to Paul Berenger, who had been his deputy. Berenger was the first non-Hindu to become prime minister. Navin Ramgoolam again became prime minister after elections in July 2005.

Despite tensions between the Indian and Creole communities, Mauritius is a stable democracy with free elections and a good human rights record. As a result, it has attracted foreign investment.

ECONOMY

Mauritius has become one of Africa's success stories. It is now a middle-income country with a diversified economy. Arable land covers more than half of the country and sugar cane plantations cover about 90% of the cultivated land. Sugar remains a major export, and tea and tobacco are also grown. Agriculture and fishing employ 14% of the workforce, compared with 36% in construction and industry. Textiles and clothing are the leading exports. Mauritius has growing industrial and financial sectors and is now a major tourist centre.

M

INTERNET

Mbeki, Thabo
▶ www.anc.org.za/people/
mbeki.html

parts; they often emerge from streams and rivers in swarms. Length: 10–25mm (0.4–1in). Order Ephemeroptera.

Mayo County in Connaught province, NW Republic of Ireland, bounded to the N and W by the Atlantic Ocean; the county town is Castlebar. A largely mountainous region, it has numerous lakes and is drained by the rivers Errif and Moy. Oats and potatoes are the chief crops. Cattle, sheep, pigs, and poultry are reared. Industries: woollen milling, toy manufacturing. Area: 5,397sq km (2,084sq mi). Pop. (2002) 117,428.

Mayotte (Mahore) French-administered archipelago in the Indian Ocean, E of the COMOROS. The two major islands are Grande Terre and Petite Terre (Pamanzi). Grande Terre includes the new capital, Mamoudzou. Pamanzi is the site of the old capital, Dzaoudzi. Mayotte was a French colony from 1843 to 1914, when it was attached to the Comoro group and collectively achieved administrative autonomy as a French Overseas Territory. In 1974, when the rest of the Comoros became independent, Mayotte voted to remain a French dependency. In 1976, it became an overseas collectivity of France. The economy is primarily agricultural; the chief products are bananas and mangoes. Area: 373sq km (144sq mi). Pop. (2002) 173,300.

Mazarin, Jules (1602–61) French cardinal and statesman, b. Italy. He was the protégé of Cardinal RICHELIEU and chief minister under ANNE OF AUSTRIA from 1643. During the civil wars of the FRONDES, he played off one faction against another and, although twice forced out of France, emerged in full control. As a former papal diplomat, he was a skilful negotiator of the treaties that ended the THIRTY YEARS' WAR.

Mazzini, Giuseppe (1805–72) Italian patriot and theorist of the RISORGIMENTO. A member of the *Carbonari* (Italian republican underground) from 1830, he founded the 'Young Italy' movement in 1831, dedicated to the unification of Italy. He fought in the REVOLUTIONS OF 1848, and ruled in Rome in 1849, but was then exiled. Unlike GARIBALDI or CAVOUR, Mazzini remained committed to popular republicanism.

Mbabane Capital of Swaziland, in the NW of the country, in the high veld region of S Africa. It is both an administrative and commercial centre, serving the surrounding agricultural region. Tin and iron ore are mined nearby. Pop. (2002 est.) 67,200.

Mbeki, Thabo (1942–) South African statesman, president (1999–). He went into exile in Europe when the AFRICAN NATIONAL CONGRESS (ANC) was banned in 1962. In 1975, Mbeki became the youngest member of the National Executive of the ANC. He returned to South Africa after President F.W. DE KLERK lifted the ban on the ANC (1990), succeeded Oliver TAMBO as chair (1993) and became deputy president to Nelson MANDELA (1994). In 1997, he succeeded Mandela as president of the ANC, and he won the 1999 elections in South Africa. As president, Mbeki faced criticism for slowness in tackling unemployment, poverty and violent crime, and his stance over the AIDS crisis. He was re-elected in 2004.

Mboya, Thomas Joseph (1930–69) Kenyan political leader. Mboya rejected Kenya's 1954 constitution and campaigned for independence. When Jomo KENYATTA established the African National Union (KANU), Mboya became general secretary. He served as minister for economic development and planning (1964–69) in Kenya's first post-colonial government. His assassination provoked rioting against the KIKUYU.

Mead, George Herbert (1863–1931) US philosopher and social psychologist. A founder of PRAGMATISM, influenced by John DEWEY, Mead studied the mind, the self, and society. His studies of the behaviour of individuals and small groups led to the sociological theories of symbolic interactionism.

Mead, Margaret (1901–78) US cultural anthropologist, curator of ethnology (1926–69) at the American Museum of Natural History. Mead conducted her fieldwork in the SW Pacific, particularly Samoa – the subject of her first and most famous work, *Coming of Age in Samoa* (1928). She was primarily interested in sexuality and adolescence, and helped develop the national-character approach to anthropology.

mean (arithmetic mean) Mathematical average. It is found by adding a group of numbers and dividing by the number of items in the group. Thus, for numbers a, b, c, and d, the mean is $(a + b + c + d)/4$.

meander Naturally occurring looplike bend of a RIVER or stream channel. Meanders form on a flood plain where there is little resistance in the alluvium. They lengthen the river, thus reducing its gradient and velocity. Meanders migrate slowly downstream, depositing sediment on one bank while eroding the opposite. Sometimes meanders make complete loops that, when cut off, form OXBOW LAKES.

measles (rubeola) Infectious viral disease. The symptoms (fever, catarrh, skin rash, spots inside the mouth and sensitivity to light) appear *c.*14 days after exposure. Complications such as pneumonia may occur, and middle-ear infection is also a hazard. Vaccination produces life-long IMMUNITY.

Meath County in Leinster province, E Republic of Ireland; the county town is Trim. A fertile, low-lying region, it is drained by the rivers Boyne and Blackwater. Cereal crops and potatoes are grown, and cattle are reared. Industries: textiles, paper-milling. Area: 2,338sq km (903sq mi). Pop. (2002) 133,936.

Mecca (Makkah) City in W Saudi Arabia and the holiest city of ISLAM. The birthplace of the prophet MUHAMMAD, only Muslims are allowed in the city. Mecca was originally home to an Arab population of merchants. When Muhammad began his ministry here, the Meccans rejected him. The flight or HEJIRA of Muhammad from Mecca to MEDINA in 622 marked the beginning of the Muslim era. In 630, Muhammad's followers captured Mecca and made it the centre of the first Islamic empire. Egypt controlled the city in the 13th century. The OTTOMAN Turks held it from 1517 to 1916, when Hussein Ibn Ali secured Arabian independence. In 1924, Mecca fell to the forces of Ibn SAUD, who later founded the Saudi Arabian kingdom. Much of Mecca's commerce depends on Muslim pilgrims undertaking the HAJJ. After World War 2, the city's wealth increased through oil revenues. Pop. (2005) 1,529,000.

mechanical advantage (force ratio) Factor by which any machine multiplies an applied force. It may be calculated from the ratio of the forces involved or from the ratio of the distances through which they move, as with simple machines such as the LEVER and PULLEY.

mechanical engineering Field of ENGINEERING concerned with the design, construction and operation of machinery. Mechanical engineers work in many branches of industry, including transportation, power generation and tool manufacture. Achievements in mechanical engineering include the development of wind and water TURBINES, STEAM ENGINES, and INTERNAL COMBUSTION ENGINES.

mechanics Branch of physics concerned with the behaviour of MATTER under the influence of FORCES. It may be divided into **solid** mechanics and **fluid** mechanics. Another classification is as STATICS – the study of matter at rest – and DYNAMICS – the study of matter in motion. In **statics**, the forces on an object are balanced and the object is said to be in equilibrium; static equilibrium may be stable, unstable or neutral. **Dynamics** may be further divided into kinematics – the description of motion without regard to cause – and KINETICS – the study of motion and force. Classical dynamics rests primarily on Isaac NEWTON'S LAWS of motion. Modern physics has shown these laws to be special cases similar to more general laws. **Relativistic** mechanics deals with the behaviour of matter at high speeds, approaching that of light, whereas QUANTUM MECHANICS deals with the behaviour of matter at the level of atoms and molecules. *See also* QUANTUM THEORY; RELATIVITY

Mecklenburg-Vorpommern State in NE Germany, on the Baltic coast; the capital is Schwerin. In 1621, the region was divided into the Duchies of Mecklenburg-Schwerin and Mecklenburg-Güstrow, which became part of the German Empire (1817) and then free states of the Weimar Republic. In 1934, the two states unified. In 1946, they joined with Pomerania to form a region of East Germany. In 1990, as part of German reunification, Mecklenburg-Vorpommern reconstituted as one of the five new states of the Federal Republic. It is mainly a low-lying agricultural state. On the coasts lie the Baltic ports of Rostock, Wismar, and Sreaslund. Area: 23,170sq km (8,944sq mi). Pop. (1999) 1,789,322.

Medawar, Sir Peter Brian (1915–87) British zoologist, b. Brazil. He shared the 1960 Nobel Prize in physiology or medicine with Sir Frank Macfarlane Burnet for their discovery of acquired immune tolerance. Medawar confirmed that if foreign tissue is introduced in the embryonic stages of development it may be reintroduced later without inducing a negative response from the IMMUNE SYSTEM.

Medea Daughter of Aeëtes, King of Colchis, whom she defied to help JASON retrieve the Golden Fleece.

Medellín City in NW central Colombia; capital of Antioquia department and the second-largest city in Colombia. Founded in the early 17th century by Spainish refugees, it became the cemtre of Colombia's illegal cocaine trade. The surrounding region has gold and silver mines. Industries: food processing, coffee, chemicals, steel. Pop. (2005) 3,236,000.

media General term for the modern channels of public information. Traditionally, they are radio, television, newspapers, and films, but the INTERNET is increasingly accepted as a form of media. These media disseminate information and entertainment on a wide scale and their powers of manipulating public opinion are the subject of much discussion and research.

median In statistics, the middle item in a group found by ranking the items from smallest to largest. In the series, 2, 3, 7, 9, 10, for example, the median is 7. With an even number of items, the MEAN of the two middle items is taken as the median. Thus in the series 2, 3, 7, 9, the median is 5.

Medici, Catherine de' *See* CATHERINE DE' MEDICI

Medici, Cosimo I de' (the Great) (1519–74) Duke of Florence (1537–74), Grand Duke of Tuscany (1569–74). Under Cosimo's authoritarian rule, Florence flourished and its territory swelled with the acquisition of Siena. He was given the title of Grand Duke by the Pope.

Medici, Cosimo de' (the Elder) (1389–1464) Ruler of Florence (1434–64). With the Medici banking fortune he led the oligarchy that was expelled from Florence in 1433 but returned to rule permanently the next year. He increased the Medici fortune, strengthened Florence by alliance with Milan and Naples, and was a great patron of the artists of the early Renaissance.

Medici, Lorenzo de' (the Magnificent) (1449–92) Ruler of Florence, grandson of Cosimo de' MEDICI (the Elder). In 1469 he succeeded his father, Piero. His power worried Pope Sixtus IV, who instigated a coup led by the Pazzi family. Lorenzo survived an assassination attempt and clamped down on his enemies. A notable poet, he encouraged writers.Girolamo SAVONAROLA attacked his autocratic rule.

medicine Practice of the prevention, diagnosis and treatment of disease or injury; the term also applies to any agent used in the treatment of disease. Medicine has been practised since ancient times, but the dawn of modern Western medicine coincided with accurate anatomical and physiological observations first made in the 17th century. By the 19th century, practical diagnostic procedures had been developed for many diseases; BACTERIA had been discovered and research undertaken for the production of immunizing serums in attempts to eradicate disease. The developments of the 20th century include the discovery of PENICILLIN and INSULIN, CHEMOTHERAPY, surgical procedures including organ transplants and diagnostic devices such as radioactive tracers and scanners.

Medina City in Saudi Arabia, N of MECCA. Originally called Yathrib, it was renamed Medinat an-Nabi ('Prophet's city') after MUHAMMAD fled Mecca and settled here in 622. Medina became his capital. In 661, the UMAYYAD caliphs moved their capital to DAMASCUS, and Medina's importance declined. It came under Turkish rule (1517–1916), before briefly forming part of the independent Arab kingdom of the Hejaz. In 1932, it became part of Saudi Arabia. Pop. (2005) 1,044,000.

Mediterranean Sea Largest inland sea in the world, lying between Europe and Africa, and extending from the Strait of Gibraltar in the W to the coast of SW Asia in the E. The Mediterranean was once a trade route for Phoenicians and Greeks, later controlled by Rome and Byzantium. In the Middle Ages Venice and Genoa were the dominant maritime powers until the rise of the Ottoman Turks. The opening of the Suez Canal in 1869 made the Mediterranean one of the world's busiest shipping routes and the development

of the Middle Eastern oilfields further increased its importance. The Mediterranean is connected to the Black Sea via the Dardanelles, the Sea of Marmara and the Bosporus, and to the Red Sea by the Suez Canal. It includes the Tyrrhenian, Adriatic, Ionian, and Aegean seas. It receives the waters of several major rivers, including the Nile, Rhône, Ebro, Tiber, and Po. There are *c.*400 species of fish in the Mediterranean, and tuna, sardines and anchovies are among those caught commercially. In recent years, pollution has become a major issue. Area: 2,509,972km (969,100sq mi).

Medusa In Greek mythology, one of the three gorgons, until Athena sent PERSEUS to decapitate her. From the wound sprang PEGASUS and Chrysaor, children of POSEIDON.

meerkat (suricate) Any of a number of small carnivorous mammals closely related to the MONGOOSE, native to the bush country of southern Africa. Length: 47cm (19in). Typical species *Suricata suricatta*.

megabyte (symbol Mb) Computing term to describe *c.*1 million BYTES. A **gigabyte** (Gb) is *c.*1,000 million bytes.

megalith (lit. huge stone) Prehistoric stone monument. Historians usually apply the term to the gigantic slabs that form stone circles, half circles and rows in N Europe. These constructions date from the NEOLITHIC and early BRONZE AGE. One of the best-known and complex examples is STONEHENGE (*c.*2100–2000BC). Megaliths existed long before the first stone buildings of Mycenean Crete. *See also* DOLMEN; MENHIR

Mehta, Zubin (1936–) Indian conductor. A flamboyant figure, Mehta has been music director of the Los Angeles Philharmonic Orchestra, the New York Philharmonic, the Israel Philharmonic, and the Bavarian State Opera.

Meiji, Mutsohito (1852–1912) Emperor of Japan (1867–1912). His reign saw the transformation of Japan into a modern industrial state. Mutsohito introduced sweeping reforms, including the abolition of the feudal system, a western-style constitution, the establishment of state education, and the encouragement of industrial growth.

Meiji Restoration Constitutional revolution in Japan (1868). Opposition to the shogunate built up after US Commodore PERRY ended Japan's policy of isolation in 1854. Pressure for modernization resulted in a new imperial government, at first dominated by former samurai, with the young Emperor MEIJI as its symbolic leader.

meiosis The process of cell division that reduces the CHROMOSOME number from DIPLOID (pairs) to HAPLOID (single set). The first division halves the chromosome number in the cells; the second then forms four haploid 'daughter' cells. In most higher organisms, the resulting haploid cells are the GAMETES, ova and SPERM. In this way, meiosis enables the genes from both parents to combine in a single cell without increasing the overall number of chromosomes. *See also* MITOSIS; OVARY

Meir, Golda (1898–1978) Israeli stateswoman, prime minister (1969–74), b. Ukraine as Golda Mabovitch. Her family emigrated to the USA in 1906, and Meir became active in ZIONISM. In 1921 she emigrated to Palestine. In 1936 she became head of the Jewish labour movement. After Israeli

◄ **Medici** Detail from *The Journey of the Magi* (1459–61) in Palazzo Medici-Riccardo by Benozzo Gozzoli, portraying Lorenzo de' Medici as one of the three Magi. Lorenzo the Magnificent, as he was also known, was a great patron of the Renaissance. A fine humanist poet and an astute politician, he was a generous supporter of many notable artists, among them Ghirlandaio, Botticelli, Leonardo da Vinci, and Michelangelo. His main collecting interest, however, was in antique coins and gems.

M

505

M

independence, Meir became minister of labour (1949–56) and foreign minister (1956–66). She succeeded Levi ESHKOL as prime minister. She resigned following criticism of lack of readiness for the 1973 ARAB-ISRAELI WAR.

Meistersinger German poet-musicians of the 15th-16th centuries. They formed guilds, which held competitions. Generally, the songs were religious and followed strict conventions. Some guilds continued into the 18th century. Richard Wagner immortalized a meistersinger, the cobbler Hans Sachs (1494–1576), in *Die Meistersinger von Nürnberg* (1868).

Meitner, Lise (1878–1968) Austrian physicist. She studied under Ludwig BOLTZMANN. In 1917, Meitner and Otto HAHN discovered the radioactive element PROTACTINIUM. In 1938 she was forced to flee Nazi Germany, shortly before Hahn discovered nuclear FISSION.

Mekong River in SE Asia. It rises in Tibet as the Lancang Jiang and flows s through Yünnan province, China. It forms the Burma-Laos border and part of the Laos-Thailand border and then flows s through Cambodia and Vietnam, creating a vast river delta that is one of the most important rice-producing regions in Asia. Length: *c.*4,180km (2,600mi).

Melanchthon, Philipp (1497–1560) German theologian and educator, considered with Martin LUTHER as a founder of PROTESTANTISM. Melanchthon wrote the *Confessions of Augsburg* (1530), a statement of Protestant beliefs.

Melanesia Collective term for a number of island groups in the w Pacific Ocean, generally s of the Equator, w of the International Date Line, N and E of Australia. It includes the Bismarck Archipelago, SOLOMON ISLANDS, New Hebrides, and the TONGA group. Melanesia is one of the subdivisions of OCEANIA. The others are POLYNESIA and MICRONESIA.

melanin Dark pigment found in the skin, hair, and parts of the eye. It helps protect skin from ultraviolet radiation. The amount of melanin determines skin colour.

melanoma Type of skin CANCER. Highly malignant tumour formed by melanocytes, cells that make MELANIN. They can occur in MUCOUS MEMBRANES and the eyes. Untreated, they may spread to the liver and lymph nodes. Excessive exposure to sunlight is a causative factor. Treatment is usually surgical.

Melba, Dame Nellie (1861–1931) Australian soprano, real name Helen Porter Mitchell. Initially a high coloratura soprano, she was famous in the roles of Lucia (Donizetti's *Lucia di Lammermoor*) and Gilda (Verdi's *Rigoletto*) and later for such lyric roles as Mimì (Puccini's *La Bohème*) and Marguerite (Gounod's *Faust*).

Melbourne City and port on the River Yarra at the N end of Port Phillip Bay; capital of Victoria state, SE Australia. Founded in 1835 by settlers from Tasmania, it was named after the British Prime Minister Lord Melbourne. It became the state capital in 1851, and later served (1901–27) as the seat of the Australian federal government. A centre of finance, commerce, communications, and transport, it is Australia's largest cargo-handling port. Manufacturing is also important. Industries: aircraft, motor vehicles, heavy engineering, shipbuilding, textiles, chemicals, agricultural machinery. Pop. (2005) 3,663,000.

Melbourne, William Lamb, 2nd Viscount (1779–1848) British statesman, prime minister (1834, 1835–41). He entered Parliament as a Whig in 1805 and joined the House of Lords in 1828. As home secretary (1830–34) in Earl GREY's administration, Melbourne was responsible for the suppression of the TOLPUDDLE MARTYRS. As prime minister, he oversaw reform of the POOR LAWS (1834), but resisted changes to the CORN LAWS. Melbourne gave Lord PALMERSTON control of foreign affairs and tutored Queen VICTORIA in statecraft. Sir Robert PEEL succeeded him.

melodrama Theatrical form originating in late 18th-century France, and achieving its greatest popularity during the following century. It relied on simple, violent plots in which virtue was finally rewarded.

melody In music, a sequence of notes that makes a recognizable musical pattern. The term is most commonly used of the dominant part or voice (the 'tune') in Romantic and light music, in which harmonic accompaniment is nearly always subordinate. Music featuring several melodies simultaneous-

ly and harmoniously is termed 'contrapuntal' or POLYPHONY, and is characteristic of the late BAROQUE period.

melon Annual vine and its large, fleshy edible fruit. Melons grow in warm temperate and subtropical climates. Family Cucurbitaceae.

melting point Temperature at which a substance changes from solid to liquid – the as the freezing point of the liquid.

Melville, Herman (1819–91) US novelist. Melville became a sailor in 1839, and joined a whaling ship in 1841. His debut novel, *Typee* (1846), recounts his experiences among remote island natives. In 1851 he wrote *Moby Dick*, an allegorical story of the search for a great whale. His short story *Billy Budd* (1924) was the inspiration for BRITTEN's eponymous opera. Melville's work was relatively neglected during his lifetime, but *Moby Dick* is now regarded as a classic of US literature.

membrane In biology, boundary layer or layers inside or around a living CELL or TISSUE. Cell membranes include the plasma membrane surrounding the cell, the network of membranes inside the cell (ENDOPLASMIC RETICULUM), and the double membrane surrounding the NUCLEUS. The multicellular membranes of the body comprise MUCOUS MEMBRANES of the respiratory, digestive and urinogenital passages, synovial membranes of the joints, and the membranes that coat the inner walls of the abdomen, thorax and the surfaces of organs. *See also* EPITHELIUM; SYNOVIAL FLUID

memory Capacity to retain information and experience and to recall or reconstruct them in the future. Modern psychologists often divide memory into two types, short-term and long-term. An item in short-term memory lasts for about 10–15 seconds after an experience, but is lost if not used again. An item enters long-term memory if the item is of sufficient importance or if the information is required frequently.

Memphis Ancient city of Egypt, s of Cairo, part of which is now occupied by the village of Mit Ra-hina. Founded in *c.*3100 BC by Menes, Memphis was formerly the royal residence and capital of Egypt. Material from its ruins was used by the Arabs for building Cairo.

Memphis City and river port on the Mississippi River, sw Tennessee, USA; largest city in Tennessee. Memphis was a French (1682), Spanish (1794) and US (1797) fort before the first permanent settlement in 1819. Today, it is a major transport centre and livestock market. Industries: timber, farm machinery, cotton, pharmaceuticals. Pop. (2000) 972,000.

Menander (*c.*342–292 BC) Greek playwright. Menander wrote more than 100 comedies, of which only one, *The Curmudgeon*, survives in full. As the outstanding exponent of the New Comedy of Hellenistic times, he is regarded as the founder of the domestic comedy of manners.

Mencius (*c.*372–289 BC) (Mengzi) Chinese philosopher of the Confucian school. He held that human beings are basically good but require cultivation to bring out the goodness. His teachings were recorded in the *Book of Mencius*, one of the Four Books in the canonical writings of CONFUCIANISM.

Mendel, Gregor Johann (1822–84) Austrian naturalist. He discovered the laws of HEREDITY, and in so doing laid the foundation for the science of GENETICS. He published his study of the inheritance of characteristics such as flower colour, height of plants and texture of the seeds of garden peas in *Experiments with Plant Hybrids* (1866). It was rediscovered in 1900.

mendelevium (symbol Md) Radioactive, metallic element that is the ninth of the TRANSURANIC ELEMENTS in the ACTINIDE SERIES. US physicist Albert Ghiorso (1915–) and colleagues at the University of California first synthesized it in 1955 by the alpha-particle bombardment of einsteinium-253. It is named after the Russian chemist Dmitri MENDELEYEV who devised the periodic table. Properties: at.no. 101; r.a.m. 258; most stable isotope Md^{258} (half-life, two months).

Mendeleyev, Dmitri Ivanovich (1834–1907) Russian chemist who devised the PERIODIC TABLE. Mendeleyev demonstrated that chemically similar elements appear at regular intervals if the elements are arranged in order by atomic weights. He classified the 60 known elements and left gaps in the table, predicting the existence and properties of several unknown elements later discovered.

Mendelsohn, Eric (1887–1953) German architect, who designed the Einstein Observatory at Potsdam (1920), perhaps the most famous example of EXPRESSIONISM in architecture. He later adopted FUNCTIONALISM, designing offices and other commercial buildings. During the 1930s, he practised in England, and in 1941 he settled in the USA, where his work includes the Maimonides Hospital, San Francisco (1946).

Mendelssohn (-Bartholdy), (Jakob Ludwig) Felix (1809–47) German composer and conductor. A child prodigy, at 16 he composed an octet, and at 17 he wrote his overture to *A Midsummer Night's Dream*. His performance (1829) of the *St Matthew Passion* revived 19th-century interest in J.S. BACH. His orchestral works include a famous violin concerto (1845) and five symphonies. He also wrote much piano and chamber music. His two oratorios, *St Paul* (1836) and *Elijah* (1846), are considered to be among the greatest of the 19th century. Mendelssohn's visit to Scotland inspired his popular orchestral overture *The Hebrides* (or 'Fingal's Cave', 1845).

Mendès-France, Pierre (1907–82) French statesman, prime minister (1955–56). He was imprisoned by the VICHY GOVERNMENT but escaped to London in 1941. He enlisted in the Free French air force, and later joined General DE GAULLE's government-in-exile. In 1946, he re-entered Parliament. After the defeat of the French army at DIEN BIEN PHU (1954), Mendès-France became prime minister and withdrew French troops from INDOCHINA. He also prepared the way for Tunisian independence. His austere economic plans led to his downfall.

Menem, Carlos Saúl (1935–) Argentinian statesman, president (1989–99). He was imprisoned (1976–81) by the military junta. Menem invoked the name of Juan PERÓN in his presidential campaign, but took office during an economic crisis and was forced to abandon Perónist tradition. He introduced austerity measures, encouraging business and the free market. Menem favoured moderation and compromise, freeing political prisoners and restoring good relations with Britain without sacrificing Argentina's claim to the FALKLAND ISLANDS. Ferdinand de la Rúa succeeded him as president.

Menes Egyptian king (*c*.3100BC), regarded as the first king of the First Dynasty. He unified upper and lower Egypt, establishing the Old Kingdom with its capital at Memphis.

menhir Archaeological term given to single standing stones found in W Europe. Probably of NEOLITHIC origin, they are usually tall and square in section, tapering towards the top. They are thought to mark places of religious or ritual significance. *See also* DOLMEN; MEGALITH

meningitis Inflammation of the **meninges** (membranes) covering the brain and spinal cord, resulting from infection. Bacterial meningitis is more serious than the viral form. Symptoms include headache, fever, nausea and stiffness of the neck. The disease can vary from mild to lethal.

Mennonites Christian sect founded by the Dutch reformer Menno Simons (1496–1561) and influenced by ANABAPTIST doctrines. They believe in the BAPTISM of adult believers instead of infants, and reject the doctrine of the EUCHARIST.

menopause Stage in a woman's life marking the end of her reproductive years, when the MENSTRUAL CYCLE becomes irregular and finally ceases, generally around the age of 50. It may be accompanied by side-effects such as hot flushes, excessive bleeding and emotional upset. HORMONE replacement therapy (HRT) is designed to relieve menopausal symptoms.

menorah Sacred, seven-branched candelabra that became a worldwide symbol of JUDAISM. Some interpret it in terms of the seven planets, the tree of life, or the six-day creation of the universe with the centre shaft representing the Sabbath.

Menotti, Gian Carlo (1911–2007) US composer, b. Italy. His operas, in modern OPERA BUFFA style, have been most successful and include *The Telephone* (1947). Menotti has also composed operas specifically for television such as *Amahl and the Night Visitors* (1951) and *Labyrinth* (1963).

Menshevik Moderate faction of the Russian Social Democratic Labour Party. The Mensheviks ('the minority') split from the more radical BOLSHEVIKS ('the majority') in 1903. They believed in 'scientific socialism' and favoured a gradual transformation of society, whereas the Bolsheviks wanted total revolution organized by a small, central group of disciplined revolutionaries. The Mensheviks were suppressed in 1922.

menstrual cycle In humans, and some higher primates, of reproductive age, the stage during which the body prepares for pregnancy. In human women, the average cycle is 28 days. At the beginning of the cycle, HORMONES from the PITUITARY GLAND stimulate the growth of an OVUM contained in a follicle in one of the two ovaries. At approximately mid-cycle, the follicle bursts, the ovum releases (**ovulation**) and travels down the FALLOPIAN TUBE to the UTERUS. The follicle (now called the **corpus luteum**) secretes the hormones, PROGESTERONE and OESTROGEN, during this phase, and the ENDOMETRIUM thickens, ready to receive the fertilized ovum. If fertilization (conception) does not occur, the corpus luteum degenerates, hormone secretion ceases, the endometrium breaks down and menstruation occurs. In the event of conception, the corpus luteum remains and maintains the endometrium with hormones until the PLACENTA is formed. In humans, the onset of the menstrual cycle occurs at PUBERTY; it ceases with the MENOPAUSE (around 50 years of age). *See also* OVARY

mental disorder Any failure of mental health that is severe enough for psychiatric treatment to be appropriate. Some mental disorders can be attributed to injury or organic disease of the BRAIN. Mental disorder may also be the result of a hereditary predisposition. Other disorders are psychogenic – without any clear evidence of any physiological cause. SCHIZOPHRENIA, severe DEPRESSION, and manic-depressive psychoses are the most widespread of mental disorders. Neurotic disorders, which can be severe but do not often warrant prolonged stays in hospital, include persistent anxiety, PHOBIAS, obsessions, and HYSTERIA.

▲ **Mendelssohn** A highly respected conductor, Felix Mendelssohn's concert tours took him all over Europe. His performance (1829) of the *St Matthew Passion* revived 19th-century interest in Bach. Mendelssohn's visit to Scotland inspired his popular orchestral overture, *The Hebrides* (1832; also known as 'Fingal's Cave'), and the Scottish Symphony (1845). Typical of German Romanticism, his compositions often have extra-musical associations, inspired by literature, historical events, or beautiful scenery.

M

MENSTRUAL CYCLE

oestrogen
progesterone
FSH
LH
chorionic gonadotrophin

Days →

The changes occurring during the menstrual cycle are controlled by the balance of the follicle stimulating hormone (FSH) and luteinizing hormone (LH) secreted by the pituitary. The diagram shows the changing levels of these, and of oestrogen and progesterone induction from the ovarian follicle, together with changes in the structure of the uterine wall (A) and development of the follicle (B), in a circular form through a normal 28-day cycle. The sharp increase in LH at about mid-cycle causes ovulation (C) and, if fertilization does not occur, the corpus luteum (D) formed degenerates around day 26 as pituitary hormone levels fall. The consequent withdrawal of oestrogen and progesterone causes the uterine wall to shed itself in the menstrual flow. The wall proliferates again under the influence of oestrogen from a new follicle. If fertilization and egg implantation do occur the placenta produces chorionic gonadotrophin, possibly as early as day 21, that allows the corpus luteum to continue to produce oestrogen and progesterone until the placenta takes over.

INTERNET

Mendelsohn, Eric
▶ www.open2.net/modernity/3_2_frame.htm

Mendelssohn (-Bartholdy), (Jakob Ludwig) Felix
▶ www.classical.net/music/comp.lst/mendelssohn.html

M

▶ **Messerschmitt** Founder of a successful aircraft manufacturing company, Messerschmitt designed the aircraft used by the Luftwaffe in World War 2, and joined Hitler's War Council in 1937.

mental handicap Intellectual functioning that is below the average, irrespective of cause. It is usually related to congenital conditions but can arise later in life through brain damage. It is classified on a severity scale ranging from borderline to profound, generally by means of an IQ test.

menthol ($C_{10}H_{19}OH$) White, waxy crystalline compound having a strong odour of peppermint. Its main source is oil of peppermint from the plant *Mentha arvensis*. It is an ingredient of decongestant ointments and nasal sprays, and as a flavouring in toothpaste and cigarettes.

Menuhin, Yehudi, Baron (1916–99) British violinist, b. USA. A child prodigy, he gave his first concert aged seven. In 1932, Menuhin recorded Elgar's violin concerto, the composer conducting. In 1942, Bela Bartók wrote his solo violin sonata for him. Menuhin was director (1959–68) of the Bath Festival, and in 1963 founded the Yehudi Menuhin School for young, gifted musicians. Menuhin was knighted in 1965. He was often accompanied on the piano by his sister **Hephzibah** Menuhin (1920–1981). Another sister, **Yaltah** (1921–2001) and Yehudi's son, **Jeremy** (1951–), were also pianists.

Menzies, Sir Robert Gordon (1894–1978) Australian statesman, longest-serving prime minister (1939–41, 1949–66). He encouraged British and US commitment to the security of Southeast Asia, and supported the ANZUS PACT and the SOUTHEAST ASIA TREATY ORGANIZATION (SEATO).

mercantilism Sixteenth- to 18th-century trade policy advocating state intervention in economic affairs, primarily to maximize exports. Foreign trade was publicly controlled to produce the maximum possible surplus in the nation's trade balance, thus increasing the country's store of silver and gold, which constitute the 'nation's wealth'.

Mercator, Gerardus (1512–94) Flemish cartographer. His huge world map of 1569 employed the system of projection now named after him, in which lines of longitude, as well as latitude, appear as straight, parallel lines.

merchant bank One of a number of UK specialist banks that offer financial services, primarily to corporate customers. They rose to prominence in the 18th and 19th centuries, involved in overseas trade. Today, they provide a range of services including: operating as issuing houses; sponsoring capital issues; offering corporate advisory work, such as advising on mergers and acquisitions; asset management; and foreign exchange.

merchant navy Section of a nation's fleet concerned with international commercial shipping. Today, 'flag-of-convenience' fleets carry most international cargo. These lines register ships in low-tax countries, such as Liberia or Panama.

Mercury Smallest of the four inner planets, and the planet closest to the Sun. It has no known satellite. Very little was known about Mercury's surface until the Mariner 10 probe made three close approaches to the planet in 1974 and 1975, and returned pictures of nearly half the surface. These showed a heavily cratered, lunar-like world marked by valleys and ridges. Radar mapping of Mercury's polar regions in 1991 and 1992 revealed what may be water-ice on the floors of craters permanently in shadow. There is a very tenuous atmosphere, mainly of helium and sodium, and a weak magnetic field.

mercury (quicksilver, symbol Hg) Liquid, metallic element. The chief ore is cinnabar (a sulphide), from which it is extracted by roasting. It is the only metal that is liquid at normal temperatures. The silvery element is poisonous, causing kidney and brain damage, as well as birth defects. Mercury is used in barometers, thermometers, laboratory apparatus, mercury-vapour lamps, and mercury cells. Mercury compounds are used in pharmaceuticals and in dentists' amalgams (alloys) to fill cavities in teeth. Properties: at.no. 80; r.a.m. 200.59: r.d. 13.6; m.p. 238.87°C; (237.97°F); b.p. 356.58°C (673.84°F); most common isotope Hg^{202} (29.8%).

Meredith, George (1828–1909) English novelist and poet. His verse includes the semi-autobiographical sonnets *Modern Love* (1862). He established his reputation as a novelist with *The Ordeal of Richard Feverel* (1859). Other novels include *Sandra Belloni* (1864). *The Egoist* (1879) and *Diana of the Crossways* (1885) are regarded as his finest.

merganser Any of several species of freshwater or marine ducks that dive for food, especially the red-breasted merganser (*Mergus serrator*), which has a hooked bill. The goosander (*M. merganser*) differs mainly in coloration. Family Anatidae.

meridian Circle that runs through the North and South Poles, at right angles to the Equator. *See also* LONGITUDE

Mérimée, Prosper (1803–70) French dramatist and short-story writer. He is best remembered for his historical novellas and short stories. These include the collection of short stories *Mosaïque* (1833), and the novellas *Colomba* (1841) and *Carmen* (1845), the latter of which is the basis for Bizet's opera.

meristem In plants, a layer of cells that divides repeatedly to generate new tissues. It is present at the growing tips of shoots and roots, and at certain sites in leaves. In MONOCOTYLEDONS, the leaf meristem is at the base, explaining why grasses continue to grow when the leaf tips are removed by grazing or mowing. *See also* CAMBIUM

Merkel, Angela (1954–) German politician, Chancellor of Germany (2005–). Angela Merkel acquired a doctorate in Physics before becoming leader of Germany's conservative Christian Democrat party in 2000. She took over from Gerhard SCHRÖDER in 2005 and became Germany's first female chancellor. She was victorious in elections later that year.

Merlin Legendary magician. His origins may be traced to early Celtic folklore, although his name is usually associated with the Arthurian legends as the mentor of King ARTHUR.

Merovingians Frankish dynasty (476–750). It was named after Merovech, a leader of the Salian Franks, whose grandson, CLOVIS I (r. *c.*481–511), ruled over most of France and established the common interests of the Frankish rulers. PEPIN III overthrew the last Merovingian king and founded the CAROLINGIAN dynasty.

Merseyside Metropolitan county in NW England, formed in 1974. It lies on both banks of the estuary of the River Mersey, and divides into five administrative districts. The major town is LIVERPOOL. In the 19th century, shipbuilding and ship repair grew in importance, and Liverpool became one of Britain's leading ports. Industries: motor vehicles, chemicals, electrical goods. Area: 655sq km (253sq mi). Pop. (2001) 1,362,034.

mesa Large, broad, flat-topped hill or mountain of moderate height and with steep, cliff-like sides. A mesa is capped with layers of resistant horizontal rocks which may then erode to form narrower **buttes**.

Mesmer, Franz (Friedrich Anton) (1734–1815) Austrian physician. Mesmer's interest in 'animal magnetism' led to his development of mesmerism (HYPNOSIS) as a therapeutic treatment. Ridiculed by fellow scientists, Mesmer died in obscurity.

Mesolithic (Middle Stone Age) In NW Europe, period in human development following the PALAEOLITHIC and preceding the NEOLITHIC. It followed an Ice Age (*c.*8000BC). As the environment changed, scrub gave way to forest, and small game proliferated. A nomadic life became unnecessary, and human settlement was a feature of this period, as were flint tools.

meson SUBATOMIC PARTICLE, member of a subgroup of HADRONS, all of which have either zero or integral SPIN. They include the pions, kaons, and eta mesons.

mesophyll Soft tissue located between the two layers of epidermis in a plant leaf. In most plants, mesophyll cells contain chlorophyll-producing structures called CHLOROPLASTS, which are essential to PHOTOSYNTHESIS.

Mesopotamia Ancient region between the rivers TIGRIS and EUPHRATES in SW Asia, roughly corresponding to modern Iraq. It was the site of one of the earliest human civilizations,

---

MERCURY: DATA

Diameter (equatorial):
4,878km (3,031mi)
Mass (Earth=1): 0.055
Volume (Earth=1): 0.056
Density (water=1): 5.44
Orbital period: 89.97 days
Rotation period: 68.646 days
Surface temperature: 100–800K
Surface gravity (Earth=1): 0.38

resulting from the development of irrigation in the 6th millennium BC and the extreme fertility of the irrigated land. The Sumerians established the first cities in *c.*2500 BC. The first empire-builders on a large scale were the people of Akkadia under SARGON, who conquered (*c.*2300BC) the Sumerian cities. BABYLONIA gained supremacy in the 18th century BC followed by others, most notably the Assyrians. Later ruled by the Persians, Greeks, and Romans, Mesopotamia gradually lost its distinctive cultural traditions. *See also* SUMERIA

Mesozoic Third era of GEOLOGICAL TIME, extending from *c.*248 to *c.*65 million years ago. It divides into three periods: the TRIASSIC, JURASSIC, and CRETACEOUS. For most of the era, the continents are believed to have been joined into one huge landmass called PANGAEA. The period was also characterized by the variety and size of its reptiles.

Messerschmitt, Willy (Wilhelm) (1898–1978) German aircraft designer, famous for the Messerschmitt Bf-109 fighter used by the LUFTWAFFE during World War 2. Messerschmitt also designed the Me-262, the first jet-propelled aircraft to be used in combat (1944).

Messiaen, Olivier (1908–92) French composer and organist. His organ works, including *L'Ascension* (1933) and *La Nativité du Seigneur* (1935), are important contributions to the repertoire of that instrument. Among other compositions is the monumental ten-movement *Turangalîla-symphonie* (1949) and an opera on the life of Francis of Assisi (1983).

Messiah (Heb. 'anointed') Saviour or redeemer. Specifically, the Messiah was the descendant of King DAVID expected by the Jews of ancient times to become their king, free them from foreign bondage, and rule over them in a golden age of glory, peace, and righteousness. It refers to the 'idealized' king as having been anointed by God or his representative in the way that David and his successors were. The title 'Christ', derived from the Greek version of the term Messiah, was probably applied to JESUS by his followers.

Messina Seaport city on the Strait of Messina; capital of Messina province, NE Sicily, Italy. The Greeks founded Messina in *c.*730 BC. The city was conquered by mercenaries, whose backing from Rome led directly to the first of the PUNIC WARS. From 241 BC Messina was a free city of Rome. The Muslim Saracen army conquered the city in the 9th century, followed by the Normans in 1061. In 1190 the Crusaders seized Messina, and Spain ruled the city from 1282 to 1714. In 1860 Giuseppe Garibaldi liberated Messina. In 1908 an earthquake killed more than 80,000 people, and destroyed most of the city. Exports: wine, citrus fruit, olive oil, chemicals. Industries: chemicals, pharmaceuticals, processed foods. Pop. (2001) 257,000.

metabolism Chemical and physical processes and changes continuously occurring in an organism. They include the breakdown of organic matter (**catabolism**), resulting in energy release and the synthesis of organic components (**anabolism**) to store energy and build and repair TISSUES. *See also* BASAL METABOLIC RATE (BMR); RESPIRATION

metal Element that is a good conductor of heat and electricity. Its atoms bond together within crystals in a unique way. Mix-tures of such elements (ALLOYS) are also metals. About three-quarters of known elements are metals. Most are hard, shiny materials that form oxides. MALLEABILITY and ductility are further metallic characteristics. Some metals have very high melting points and various high-temperature applications: TUNGSTEN, with the highest melting point of all at 3,410°C (6,170°F), is employed for incandescent-lamp filaments. ALUMINIUM and IRON are the two most abundant and useful metals. TITANIUM, although rarely seen as a metal, is more commonly distributed than the more familiar COPPER, ZINC, and LEAD. Other metals of economic importance, because they undergo nuclear FISSION, are URANIUM and PLUTONIUM.

metalloid ELEMENT having some properties typical of metals, and some associated with non-metals. They are sometimes called semi-metals or semi-metallic elements. Examples are silicon, germanium and arsenic. Some are SEMICONDUCTORS.

metallurgy Science and technology concerned with metals. Metallurgy includes the study of: methods of extraction of metals from their ores; physical and chemical properties of metals; ALLOY production, and the hardening, strengthening, corrosion-proofing and ELECTROPLATING of metals. *See also* ANODIZING; GALVANIZING

metamorphic rock Broad class of rocks that have been changed by heat or pressure from their original nature – SEDIMENTARY, IGNEOUS, or older metamorphic. The changes characteristically involve new crystalline structure, the creation of new minerals, or a radical change of texture. For example, the metamorphic rock slate is made from sedimentary shale.

metamorphosis Change of form during the development of various organisms, such as the changing of a caterpillar into a moth, or a tadpole into a frog. Sometimes the change is gradual, as with a grasshopper, and is known as incomplete metamorphosis. Complete metamorphosis usually involves the more distinct stages of LARVA (such as a caterpillar), PUPA (with a protective outer casing), and IMAGO (winged adult).

metaphor Figure of speech that draws a comparison. It differs from ordinary comparisons in its inventiveness, and from a **simile** in the complexity of the idea expressed. 'Fleece as white as snow', is a simile, whereas 'His political life was a constant swimming against the tide', is a metaphor.

metaphysical poetry English literary form of the 17th century, characterized by the combination of unlike ideas or images to create new representations of experience, and a reliance on wit and subtle argument. Although this method was by no means new, in the hands of such writers as George HERBERT, Andrew MARVELL and John DONNE it infused new life into English poetry.

metaphysics Branch of philosophy that deals with the first principles of reality and with the nature of the universe. Metaphysics divides into ONTOLOGY, the study of the essence of being, and COSMOLOGY, the study of the structure of the universe. Leading metaphysical thinkers include PLATO, ARISTOTLE, DESCARTES, LEIBNIZ, KANT, and A.N. WHITEHEAD.

Metaxas, Joannis (1871–1941) Greek general and statesman, prime minister (1936–41). Metaxas fought in the

INTERNET

Messiaen, Olivier
▶ www.oliviermessiaen.co.uk

M

▼ **metamorphosis** When common frogs mate, fertilization and egg laying occur in water (1). Within an hour, the jelly around the egg swells to produce frogspawn (2). The eggs develop (3) and produce embryos (4) that hatch as long-tailed tadpoles with external feathery gills six days after fertilization (5). Mouths and eyes develop later and the tails become powerful means of propulsion. Hind legs are well formed by week eight (6); meanwhile, the tadpole has changed from a herbivore to a carnivore. Via an intermediary gill and lung stage, the tadpole changes from gill- to lung-breathing, its internal lungs growing as its external gills are absorbed; the process is complete when the gills fully disappear at month three, by which time the forelegs are well developed (7). Metamorphosis is complete when the young frog (8) loses its tail.

BALKAN WARS (1912–13), but was dismissed for pro-German leanings during World War 1. As prime minister, Metaxas dissolved parliament and ruled as a virtual dictator. Despite fascist trappings, he led resistance to Mussolini's imperialism.

meteor (shooting star) Brief streak of light in the night sky caused by a meteoroid entering the Earth's upper atmosphere at high speed from space. A typical meteor lasts from a few tenths of a second to a few seconds, depending on the meteoroid's impact speed, which can vary from *c*.11–70km/s (7–45mi/s). At certain times of the year there are meteor showers, when meteors are more numerous than usual.

meteorite Part of a large meteoroid (a small particle or body following an Earth-crossing orbit) that survives passage through the Earth's atmosphere and reaches the ground. Most of a meteoroid burns up in the atmosphere to produce meteors, but *c*.10% reaches the surface as meteorites and micrometeorites. Meteorites generally have a pitted surface and a fused charred crust. There are three main types: iron meteorites (**siderites**), stony meteorites (**aerolites**), and mixed iron and stone meteorites. Some are tiny particles, but others weigh up to 200 tonnes.

meteorology Study of weather conditions, a branch of CLIMATOLOGY. Meteorologists study and analyse data from a network of weather ships, aircraft and satellites in order to compile maps showing the state of the high- and low-pressure regions in the Earth's atmosphere. They also anticipate changes in the distribution of the regions and forecast the future weather.

meter Instrument that measures a particular quantity. For example, a gas meter measures the amount of gas that flows in a certain time, and a voltmeter measures the voltage between two points in an electrical circuit.

methanal (formaldehyde, HCHO) Colourless, inflammable, poisonous gas with a penetrating odour. It is the simplest aldehyde and is produced by the oxidation of METHANOL by air. German chemist August von Hofmann (1818–92) discovered it in 1867. Most methanal is in the form of formalin. Methanal is used in the manufacture of dyes and plastics. Chief properties: r.d. 0.82; m.p. −92°C (−133.6°F); b.p. −19°C (−2.2°F).

methane (CH_4) Colourless, odourless HYDROCARBON, the simplest ALKANE (paraffin). It is the chief constituent of NATURAL GAS, from which it is obtained. It is produced by decomposing organic matter, such as in marshes, which led to its original name of 'marsh gas'. In the air, it contributes to the GREENHOUSE EFFECT and an increase in global temperature. Methane is used in the form of natural gas as a fuel. Properties: m.p. −182.5°C (−296.5°F); b.p. −164°C (−263.2°F).

methanoic acid (formic acid, HCOOH) Colourless, corrosive, pungent, liquid CARBOXYLIC ACID. It is used to produce insecticides and for dyeing, tanning, and electroplating. It occurs naturally in a variety of sources, such as stinging ants, nettles, pine needles, and sweat. The simplest of the carboxylic acids, it can be produced by the action of concentrated sulphuric acid on sodium methanoate. Properties: r.d. 1.22; m.p. 8.3°C (46.9°F); b.p. 100.8°C (213.4°F).

methanol (methyl alcohol, CH_3OH) Colourless, poisonous, flammable liquid, the simplest of the ALCOHOLS. It is obtained synthetically either from carbon monoxide and hydrogen by the OXIDATION of natural gas, or by the destructive distillation of wood. It is used as a solvent, petrol additive, and in rocket fuel and petrol. Properties: m.p. −93.9°C (−137°F); b.p. 64.9°C (148.8°F).

Methodism Worldwide religious movement that began in England in the 18th century. It was originally an evangelical movement within the CHURCH OF ENGLAND, started in 1729 by John and Charles WESLEY. John Wesley stayed within the Anglican Church until his death in 1791. In 1795, the Wesleyan Methodists became a separate body and divided into other sects, such as the Methodist New Connection (1797) and the Primitive Methodists (1811). The United Methodist Church reunited the New Connection with the smaller Bible Christians and the United Methodist Free Churches in 1907; in 1932 these united with the Wesleyans and Primitives. In the USA, the Methodist Episcopal Church was founded in 1784. Today, there are more than 50 million Methodists worldwide.

Methuselah In the Old Testament (Genesis 5:25–27), the longest-lived of all human beings; son of ENOCH and eighth in descent from ADAM and EVE. He is said to have died at the age of 969 and was the father of many children, including Lamech, the father of NOAH.

methylated spirit Industrial form of ETHANOL (ethyl alcohol). It contains 5% METHANOL (methyl alcohol), which is extremely poisonous, and enough pyridine to give it a foul taste. It is dyed purple and used as a solvent and fuel.

metre (symbol m) SI unit of distance. Conceived as being a ten-millionth of the surface distance between the North Pole and the Equator, it was formerly defined by two marks on a platinum bar kept in Paris. It is now defined as the length of the path travelled by light in a vacuum during 1/299,792,458 of a second. One metre equals 39.3701 inches.

metre In poetry, a regular rhythmic pattern. It imposes a regular recurrence of stresses, typically dividing a line into equal units called metrical feet. The most commonly used metrical feet are anapaest, dactyl, iamb, and trochee. The metre of a poem is described according to the kind and number of metrical feet per line: for example, iambic pentameters have five iambs per line.

metric system Decimal system of WEIGHTS AND MEASURES based on the METRE (m) and the KILOGRAM (kg). Larger and smaller metric units relate by powers of 10. Devised in 1791, the metric system is used internationally by scientists (particularly as SI UNITS) and has been adopted for general use by most Western countries, although the IMPERIAL SYSTEM is still commonly used in the USA and for certain measurements in Britain.

Metropolitan Museum of Art US art museum, New York City. Founded in 1870, the museum has a diverse permanent art collection, including numerous Egyptian, Greek, and Roman works. Much of the medieval collection is in a separate complex, The Cloisters. In addition to European sculpture, there are more than 4,600 European paintings ranging from the 15th century to the present, as well as many US paintings and sculptures. The Oriental art collection numbers 30,000 pieces.

Metropolitan Opera Company Company in New York City, USA, famous for the high standard of its productions. Operas premiered at 'the Met' include *Gianni Schicchi* (1918) and *The Girl of the Golden West* (1910), both by Puccini. The Metropolitan Opera House opened in 1883, and moved to the Lincoln Center for the Performing Arts in 1966.

Metternich, Klemens Wenzel Lothar, Prince von (1773–1859) Austrian statesman. As foreign minister (1809–48) and chancellor (1821–48), Metternich was a leading European statesman of the post-Napoleonic era. Following Austria's defeat in the NAPOLEONIC WARS (1809), he adopted a conciliatory policy towards France. After NAPOLEON I's retreat from Moscow (1812), Metternich formed the QUADRUPLE ALLIANCE (1813) that led to Napoleon's defeat. He was dominant at the Congress of VIENNA (1814–15) and at subsequent conferences held under the CONGRESS SYSTEM. In 1815, he secured peace and became increasingly autocratic, pressing the great powers to intervene in any revolutionary outbreak. He was driven from power in the REVOLUTIONS OF 1848.

Metz City on the River Moselle; capital of Moselle department, NE France. One of Roman Gaul's chief cities, it was burned by Vandals (406) and by Huns (451). After the 8th century, the Bishops of Metz ruled a vast empire. As a free imperial city in 12th century, Metz enjoyed considerable prosperity. Seized by France in 1552, it became part of Germany in 1871, after the Franco-Prussian War. The Treaty of Versailles (1919) restored it to France. Industries: metals, machinery, tobacco, wine, tanning, clothing. Pop. (1999) 123,704.

Mexican Revolution (1910–40) Extended political revolution that improved the welfare of the Mexican underprivileged. The dictatorial, elitist presidency of Porfirio DÍAZ prompted the Mexican Revolution. Díaz, who had agreed not to stand for re-election following the threat of armed revolt by Francisco MADERO, reneged on his agreement and was re-elected in 1910. In 1911, he was forced to resign by Madero, who was subsequently elected. Madero intended to make land-ownership more egalitarian, to strengthen labour organizations, and to lessen the influence of the Catholic Church. In 1913, he was assassinated by his former general Victoriano HUERTA. The repressive regime of Huerta caused massive unrest in the peasant community, who found leaders in Venustiano CARRANZA,

M

INTERNET

meteorite
▶ www.nmnh.si.edu/
minsci/meteor.htm

Metropolitan Museum of Art
▶ www.metmuseum.org

Metropolitan Opera Company
▶ www.metopera.org

Mexican War
▶ www.multied.com/
mexican

Francisco 'Pancho' VILLA, and Emiliano ZAPATA. Huerta resigned and Carranza became president (1914). Although some agrarian, educational and political reforms continued, it was Lázaro Cárdenas (1934–40) who finally began the process of land distribution, support of the labour movement, and improvements in health and education.

Mexican War (1846–48) War between Mexico and the USA. It broke out following US annexation of TEXAS (1845). The Mexicans were swiftly overwhelmed, and a series of US expeditions effected the conquest of the southwest. The war ended when General Winfield Scott, having landed at Vera Cruz in March 1847, defeated the army of SANTA ANNA and entered Mexico City on September 8. In the Treaty of GUADALUPE-HIDALGO (1848), Mexico ceded sovereignty over California and New Mexico, as well as Texas north of the Rio Grande.

Mexico Republic in N America. *See* country feature, page 512

Mexico City (Sp. *Ciudad de México*) Capital of Mexico, situated in a volcanic basin at an altitude of 2380m (7800ft), in the centre of the country. Mexico City is the nation's political, economic, and cultural centre. It suffers from overcrowding and high levels of pollution, and is vulnerable to earthquakes. Hernán Cortés destroyed the former AZTEC capital, known as Tenochtitlán, in 1521. A new city was constructed, which acted as the capital of Spain's New World colonies for the next 300 years. In 1847, during the MEXICAN WAR, US troops occupied the city. In 1863, French troops conquered the city and established MAXIMILIAN as Emperor. Benito JUÁREZ's forces recaptured it in 1867. Between 1914 and 1915, the revolutionary forces of Emiliano ZAPATA and Francisco VILLA captured and lost the city three times. The city is a major tourist centre. Pop. (2005) 19,013,000.

Meyerbeer, Giacomo (1791–1864) German composer, b. Jakob Liebmann Beer. His early operas, in the Italian tradition, were influenced by Gioacchino Rossini. Meyerbeer greatest acclaim, however, came in Paris where his works laid the foundations of French grand opera. With libretti by Eugene Scribe, these operas included *Robert le Diable* (1831), *Les Huguenots* (1836) and *Le Prophète* (1849).

mezzo-soprano (middle soprano) Range of the human voice falling between SOPRANO and CONTRALTO. It grew popular with opera composers in the 19th century, when the CASTRATO voice (which had a similar range) became less usual.

Miami City and port on Biscayne Bay in SE Florida, USA. Originally a small agricultural community, it developed quickly after 1895 when the railroad was extended and the harbour dredged. Modern Miami is a popular tourist resort, with luxury hotels and many sporting facilities. Industries: clothing, concrete, metal products, fishing, printing and publishing. Pop. (2000) 4,919,000.

mica Group of common rock-forming minerals characterized by a platy or flaky appearance. All contain aluminium, potassium and water; other metals, such as iron and magnesium, may be present. Micas have perfect basal cleavage. Common micas are muscovite and the biotite group. Muscovite is commonly found in coarse-grained acidic rocks, schists and gneisses, and in sedimentary rocks. The biotite micas are found in a wide range of IGNEOUS and METAMORPHIC ROCKS, but more rarely in SEDIMENTARY ROCKS.

Michael (1921–) King of Romania (1927–30, 1940–47). He succeeded his grandfather as a child, surrendered the throne to his father in 1930, and regained it when his father abdicated (1940). He backed the overthrow of the fascist Ion ANTONESCU in 1944, whereupon Romania joined the Allies in World War 2. Michael was forced to abdicate when the communists gained power (1947). His citizenship was restored in 1997.

Michael, Saint One of the archangels mentioned in the Bible, others being GABRIEL and RAPHAEL. In the Old Testament, Michael is the guardian of Israel and the highest of the archangels. In the New Testament book of Revelation, he is said to have thrown down the Dragon (Satan). His feast day is September 29 (MICHAELMAS). He is also given prominence in Islam.

Michaelmas Christian feast day of St Michael and All Angels, celebrated on September 29. Since the Middle Ages, Michaelmas has been one of the four quarter days of the financial year.

Michelangelo Buonarroti (1475–1564) Florentine sculptor, painter, architect, and poet. He was one of the outstanding figures of the High RENAISSANCE and a creator of MANNERISM. He spent five years in Rome where he made his name with a statue of *Bacchus* and the *Pietà* (now in St Peter's). In 1501 he returned to Florence, where he carved the gigantic *David*, a symbol of the new-found confidence of the Florentine Republic. In 1505, Pope Julius II called him to Rome to carry out two substantial commissions. The first, a magnificent tomb for Julius I, ended in disaster due to lack of funds from the Pope's heirs. The other, a vast painting for the Sistine Chapel ceiling, was Michelangelo's most sublime achievement. He added *The Last Judgment* later, starting in 1536. Among Michelangelo's other great (unfinished) works are the Medici Chapel and the Biblioteca Laurenziana, both for the church of San Lorenzo in Florence. For the last 30 years of his life, Michelangelo concentrated on architecture. He created the magnificent cathedral of ST PETER'S, Rome, but died before completing it.

Michelson, Albert Abraham (1852–1931) US physicist, b. Germany. In 1887, he conducted an experiment with Edward Morley to determine the velocity of the Earth through the ETHER, using an INTERFEROMETER of his own design. The negative result prompted the development of the theory of RELATIVITY. In 1907, Michelson became the first US scientist to receive a Nobel Prize.

Michener, James (1907–97) US writer. He won a Pulitzer Prize (1948) for his first collection of short stories, *Tales of the South Pacific* (1947). With *Hawaii* (1959), Michener established a pattern of panoramic novels, which he continued in later works such as *Chesapeake* (1978) and *Texas* (1985).

Michigan State in N central USA, bordered by four of the GREAT LAKES; the capital is LANSING. The largest city is DETROIT. First settled by the French in the 17th century, the region was ceded to Britain after the SEVEN YEARS' WAR. The British finally left the area in 1796, and Michigan became a US territory in 1805, achieving full statehood in 1837. The opening of the Erie Canal in 1825 aided its growth, but the real industrial boom came with the development of the motor vehicle industry in the early 20th century. Michigan is made up of two peninsulas separated by the Straits of Mackinac, which connect lakes Michigan and Huron. The Upper Peninsula has swampland on the NE lake shore and mountains in the W. Copper and iron ore are mined and timber is a valuable resource. The Lower Peninsula is also forested and mineral deposits include oil, gypsum, sandstone, and limestone. In the S cereal crops are cultivated and livestock rearing is important. Industries: motor vehicles, primary and fabricated metals, chemicals,

M

▼ **Michelangelo** Detail of the Sistine Chapel ceiling, Vatican Palace, Rome, showing 'Creation of Adam' (1510) by Michelangelo. Although he preferred sculpture to painting, Michelangelo worked almost single-handedly on the ceiling between 1508 and 1512. He learned the fresco technique from Ghirlandaio in Florence, although his most important lessons came from copying figures by Giotto and Masaccio.

food products. Area: 150,544sq km (58,110sq mi). Pop. (2000) 9,938,444.

Michigan, Lake Third-largest of the five GREAT LAKES of North America, and the only one entirely within the USA. Discovered by the French in 1634, it connects to Lake Huron by the Straits of Mackinac. The ST LAWRENCE SEAWAY opened up the lake to international trade. CHICAGO is on the sw shore. Area: 57,757sq km (22,300sq mi).

microbiology Study of microorganisms, their structure, function and significance. Mainly concerned with single-cell forms such as VIRUSES, BACTERIA, PROTOZOA and fungi, it has immense applications in medicine and the food industry. Microbiology began in the 17th century with the invention of the microscope, which first enabled scholars to view microorgan-

isms. Pioneers include Robert HOOKE, Anton van LEEUWENHOEK and Louis PASTEUR. *See also* BIOTECHNOLOGY; FUNGUS

microcomputer Small computer that has its CENTRAL PROCESSING UNIT (CPU) on an INTEGRATED CIRCUIT (chip) called a MICROPROCESSOR.

microeconomics Study of individual components of the economic system. It analyses individual consumers and producers, the market conditions and the law of SUPPLY AND DEMAND. It is one of the two major subdivisions of ECONOMICS; the other is MACROECONOMICS.

microelectronics In ELECTRONICS, systems designed and produced without wiring or other bulky components. They allow a high packing density, greatly reducing the size of component assemblies. Following World War 2, the appli-

---

MEXICO

The United Mexican States is the world's largest Spanish-speaking country. It is largely mountainous. The SIERRA MADRE Occidental begins in the NW state of CHIHUAHUA, and runs parallel to Mexico's W coast and the Sierra Madre Oriental. MONTERREY lies in the foothills of the latter.

Between the two ranges lies the Mexican Plateau. The southern part of the plateau contains a series of extinct volcanoes, rising to the 5,700m [18,701ft] Orizaba. The southern highlands of the Sierra Madre del Sur include the archaeological sites in OAXACA. Mexico contains two large peninsulas: the BAJA CALIFORNIA in the nw; and the YUCATÁN peninsula in the se.

CLIMATE

Mexico's climate is hugely varied according to altitude. Most rain occurs between June and September. More than 70% of Mexico experiences desert or semi-desert conditions.

HISTORY

One of the earliest NATIVE AMERICAN civilizations was that of the OLMEC (800–400 BC). The MAYA flourished between AD 300 and

900. The TOLTEC Empire ruled between 900 and c.1200, after which the AZTEC became dominant. They ruled the central plateau from their capital at Tenochtitlán (modern-day Mexico City). Many splendid PYRAMIDS and temples remain from these civilizations.

Fernández de Córdoba was the first European to explore Mexico in 1517. In 1519–21 Spanish *conquistadors*, led by Hernán CORTÉS, captured the capital and the Aztec emperor MONTEZUMA. In 1535, the territory became the Viceroyalty of New Spain. Christianity was introduced. Spanish colonial rule was harsh and divisive. HIDALGO Y COSTILLO's revolt (1810) failed to win the support of creoles. In 1821 Mexico gained independence from Spain and General Augustín de ITURBIDE became Emperor. In 1823 republicans seized power. In 1832 SANTA ANNA became president. War with Texas escalated into the MEXICAN WAR (1846–48) with the United States. Under the terms of the Treaty of GUADALUPE-HIDALGO (1848), Mexico lost 50% of its territory. A revolution led to the overthrow of Santa Anna in 1855, and civil war broke out. Liberal forces, led by Benito JUÁREZ, triumphed in the War of Reform (1858–61) but conserva-

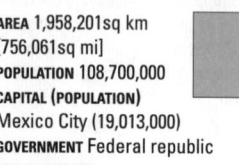

AREA 1,958,201sq km [756,061sq mi]
POPULATION 108,700,000
CAPITAL (POPULATION)
Mexico City (19,013,000)
GOVERNMENT Federal republic
ETHNIC GROUPS
Mestizo 60%, Amerindian 30%, White 9%
LANGUAGES Spanish (official)
RELIGIONS Roman Catholic 90%, Protestant 6%
CURRENCY Mexican peso = 100 centavos

tives, with support from France, installed MAXIMILIAN of Austria as Emperor in 1864. In 1867, republican rule was restored and Juárez became president. In 1876 an armed revolt gave Porfirio DÍAZ the presidency. Díaz's dictatorship lasted until 1910. Following an armed insurrection, Francisco MADERO became president in 1911. A weak leader, Madero was toppled by General HUERTA in 1913. Huerta's dictatorship prolonged the MEXICAN REVOLUTION (1910–40) and led to US intervention. The US-backed forces of CARRANZA battled with the peasant armies of VILLA and ZAPATA. After World War 2 Mexico's economy developed as relations with the US improved greatly, although economic migration became a problem.

POLITICS

The Institutional Revolutionary Party (PRI) ruled Mexico continuously from 1929 to 2000. In 1994 the Zapatista National Liberation Army (ZNLA) staged an armed revolt in the southern state of Chiapas, calling for land reforms and recognition of Native American rights. Vicente Fox became the first non-PRI leader of Mexico in 2000. In 2001, after a nationwide march by the Zapatistas, the Mexican parliament passed a new rights' bill for indigenous peoples. The 2006 elections, marred by fraud allegations, made the conservative Felipe Calderón president by a 0.5% margin. His socialist opponent Lopez Obrador contested the results, leading to months of disorder.

ECONOMY

The World Bank classifies Mexico as an 'upper-middle-income' developing country. Agriculture is important. Oil and oil products are the chief exports, while manufacturing is the most valuable activity. Many factories near the northern border, known as maquiladoras, assemble goods such as car parts and electrical products for US companies.

cation of such newly developed devices as the TRANSISTOR saw the beginnings of the microelectronics industry. This accelerated with the development of the PRINTED CIRCUIT. Even further reduction in size, or microminiaturization, was achieved with INTEGRATED CIRCUITS. Molecular electronics is a new development that promises a further size-reduction. Experimental NANOTECHNOLOGY, for example, has manipulated electrons and atoms for workable devices.

Micronesia Archipelago in the W Pacific Ocean, N of Polynesia. Micronesia includes BELAU, KIRIBATI, MARIANA ISLANDS, the Federated States of MICRONESIA, Nauru, and Tuvalu.

Micronesia, Federated States of Republic in the W Pacific Ocean, consisting of all the CAROLINE ISLANDS except BELAU. The 607 islands of the republic divide into four states: Chuuk, Pohnpei, Yap and Kosrae. The capital, Palikir, is on the island of Pohnpei. The archipelago is widely dispersed. Spain annexed the islands in 1874, and sold them to Germany in 1899. In 1914, Japan occupied the archipelago and was given a mandate to govern by the League of Nations in 1920. In 1944, US naval forces captured the islands, and in 1947 they came under US administration as part of the UN Trust Territory of the Pacific Islands. In 1979, the Federated States of Micronesia came into being, with Belau remaining a US trust territory. In 1986, a compact of free association with the USA was signed. In 1990 UN trust status was annulled, and in 1991 Micronesia became a full member of the UN. The economy depends heavily on US aid. Land use is limited to subsistence agriculture. Area: 702sq km (271sq mi). Pop. (2000) 108,000.

microphone Device for converting sound into varying electric currents of the same frequency. Live music performers often use a **moving coil** microphone, in which a coil attached to a diaphragm vibrates in a stationary magnetic field. The recording industry prefers the **condenser** microphone, which employs a CAPACITOR to store charge. **Crystal** microphones employ the PIEZOELECTRIC EFFECT that creates voltage between opposite faces of a crystal. *See also* SOUND RECORDING

microprocessor Complex INTEGRATED CIRCUIT (chip) used to control the operation of a computer or other equipment.

microscope Optical device for producing an enlarged image of a minute object. Anton van LEEUWENHOEK made the first simple microscope in 1668. The modern compound microscope has two converging lens systems, the objective and the eyepiece, both of short focal length. The **objective** produces a magnified image, which is further magnified by the **eyepiece** to give the image seen by the observer. Because of the nature of the visible spectrum of light, an optical microscope can magnify objects only up to 2,000 times. For extremely small objects, an ELECTRON MICROSCOPE is used. An **atomic force microscope** can magnify by up to a million times using a probe with a tip the size of a single atom.

microsurgery Delicate surgery performed under a binocular MICROSCOPE using specialized instruments, such as microneedles as small as 2mm (0.08in) long, ENDOSCOPES and LASERS. It is used in a number of specialized areas, including the repair of nerves and blood vessels; eye, ear and brain surgery; and the reattachment of severed parts.

microwave Form of ELECTROMAGNETIC RADIATION having a wavelength between 1mm (0.04in) and 1m (3.3ft) and a frequency range of about 255 to 300,000MHz. Microwaves are used in RADAR, RADIO and TELEVISION broadcasting, high-speed microwave heating and cellular telephones. See picture, page 514

Midas Name of several historical Phrygian rulers and one legendary foolish king in classical mythology. As a reward for rendering a service to a god, King Midas asked that everything he touched should become gold. Midas found he was unable to eat or drink because his food, too, was transformed.

Mid-Atlantic Ridge Underwater topographic feature along the margin between the diverging American crustal plate on one side and the European and African plates on the other. It runs for 14,000km (8,700mi) along the middle of the Atlantic Ocean. Iceland is located on the ridge itself, and was formed by the outpourings of volcanic lava.

Middle Ages Period in European history covering roughly 1,000 years between the disintegration of the Roman Empire in the DARK AGES of the 5th century and the period of the RENAISSANCE in the 15th century. The Middle Ages are sometimes divided into Early (up to the 10th century), High (10th-14th centuries) and Late Middle Ages. The Middle Ages were, above all, the age of the Christian Church, whose doctrine was widely accepted in Europe, and of the social-political structure known as the FEUDAL SYSTEM. In the arts, the Middle Ages encompassed the GOTHIC period (from the 11th century), and in science and learning, the predominance of ISLAM. *See also* CRUSADES; SCHOLASTICISM

Middle East Geographical term loosely applied to the predominantly Islamic countries of the E Mediterranean, NE Africa, and SW Asia. It usually includes: Bahrain, Cyprus, Egypt, Iran, Iraq, Israel, Jordan, Kuwait, Lebanon, Libya, Oman, Qatar, Saudi Arabia, Sudan, Syria, United Arab Emirates, and Yemen.

Middle English Form of the English language in use from *c*.1100 until *c*.1450. This period saw the borrowing of many words from NORMAN FRENCH. Grammatical GENDER was superseded by natural gender, and the use of an Anglo-Norman writing system caused radical changes in spellings. In literature, the Arthurian romances were influenced by the French TROUBADOUR tales of chivalry. The 'alliterative revival' in native poetry was led by LANGLAND, MALORY, GOWER and Geoffrey CHAUCER. Other forms include the MYSTERY PLAYS. *See also* ENGLISH LITERATURE

Middlesbrough Port and unitary authority on the River Tees estuary, NE England; former county town of Cleveland. Middlesbrough developed around its iron industry during the 19th century. Industries: steel, shipbuilding. Pop. (2001) 134,847.

MICHIGAN
Statehood :
January 26, 1837
Nickname :
Wolverine State
State bird :
Robin
State flower :
Apple blossom
State tree :
White pine
State motto :
If you seek a pleasant peninsula, look around you

M

MICROSCOPE

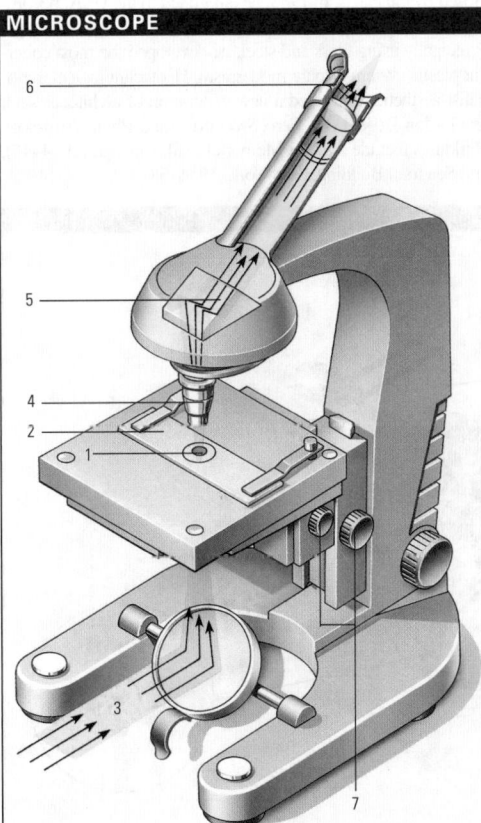

An optical microscope magnifies a sample (1) held on a slide (2). Light from below (3) illuminates the sample, magnified by a lens (4) that can be changed. Complicated lenses (5) directs the image onto an eyepiece (6). The position of the sample can be altered physically by turning knobs (7) that bring the image into position and focus.

Middlesex Former county of SE England, adjoining LONDON. The area was settled by the Saxons in the 5th century. Throughout history it was overshadowed by London. In 1888, it became an administrative county, losing much of its area to London. In 1965, most of the county was absorbed into Greater London, the remainder going to SURREY and HERTFORDSHIRE.

Middleton, Thomas (*c.*1570–1627) English dramatist. He collaborated with Thomas Dekker on the comedy *The Honest Whore* (1604). His comedies include *A Chaste Maid in Cheapside* (1611) and the satire *A Game at Chess* (1624). Middleton is chiefly remembered for his tragicomedies *The Changeling* (1622, written with William Rowley) and *Women Beware Women* (*c.*1625). Many critics believe he wrote *The Revenger's Tragedy* (1607), traditionally credited to Cyril Tourneur.

Midway Islands Coral atoll in the central Pacific Ocean, *c.*2,000km (1,250mi) WNW of Honolulu, consisting of two small islands, Easter and Sand. The islands were annexed to the USA in 1867, and were made an air base in 1935. They were the scene of the Battle of Midway (1942) during World War 2. The islands are administered by the US Department of the Interior. Area: 5sq km (2sq mi). Pop. (2001) 150.

Midwest (Middle West) Imprecise term referring to the interior plains of the USA around the W GREAT LAKES and the upper Mississippi River valley. It usually refers to the states of INDIANA, ILLINOIS, IOWA, KANSAS, MISSOURI, MINNESOTA, MICHIGAN, NEBRASKA, OHIO and WISCONSIN. Traditionally, the Midwest has been the manufacturing heartland of the USA. The Midwest is also one of the world's richest agricultural regions; the major crop is wheat.

Mies van der Rohe, Ludwig (1886–1969) US architect and designer, b. Germany. A leading exponent of MODERNISM and the INTERNATIONAL STYLE, Mies was the last director (1930–33) of the BAUHAUS, moving the school to Berlin before it was closed by the Nazis. In 1938, he emigrated to the USA, becoming director of the Illinois Institute of Technology, Chicago. Principally using glass and steel, he developed the most coherent plastic system of pure modernism. His technological, rationalist aesthetic influenced a new generation of architects, such as Gordon BUNSHAFT, Eero SAARINEN and Philip JOHNSON. Buildings include Alumni Memorial Hall, Chicago (1944–46), and Seagram Building, New York (1954–58).

▲ **migration** Remarkable annual migrations are made by birds of N temperate regions flying S in autumn to new breeding grounds, and returning N in spring to breed. The Arctic tern nests in polar regions, and flies S along one of the various routes shown to the islands of Antarctica – the round trip often totalling 32,000km (20,000mi).

M

migraine Recurrent attacks of throbbing headache, mostly on one side only, often accompanied by nausea, vomiting and visual disturbances. It results from changes in diameter of the arteries serving the brain. More common in women, it is seen usually in young adults and often runs in families. Attacks, which may last anything from two to 72 hours, are often associated with trigger factors, such as certain foods (especially chocolate), missed meals, consumption of alcohol, fatigue, exposure to glare or use of the contraceptive pill. It can be treated, or in some cases prevented, with various drugs.

migration Periodic movement of animals or humans, usually in groups, from one area to another, in order to find food, breeding areas, or better conditions. Animal migration involves the eventual return of the migrant to its place of departure. Fish migrate between fresh and salt water or from one part of an ocean to another. Birds usually migrate along established routes. Mammals migrate usually in search of food. For thousands of years, the deserts of central Asia widened inexorably resulting in the human migration of pre-historic tribes to China, the Middle East and Europe. Another migration occurred in the 14th century when the Maori left their overpopulated homes in the islands of central Polynesia to settle in New Zealand.

Milan (Milano) City in NW Italy; capital of Lombardy region. It was conquered by Rome in 222 BC. It was a free commune by the 12th century, and was a powerful Italian state under the Sforza family from 1447 to 1535, when the Spanish seized control. Ruled by Napoleon from 1796 to 1814, he claimed the city as capital of his Italian kingdom. It then fell to the Austrian HABSBURGS before becoming part of Italy in 1860. Milan is Italy's leading commercial, financial, and industrial centre. Sights include Leonardo da Vinci's *Last Supper* (1495–98) in the Convent of Santa Maria della Grazie, a white-marble cathedral (1386–1813), and LA SCALA opera house. Industries: motor vehicles, machinery, electrical goods, textiles, clothing, publishing. Pop. (2000) 1,813,000.

mildew External filaments and fruiting structures of numerous mould-like fungi. Mildews are PARASITES of plants and cause substantial damage to growing crops. *See also* FUNGUS

Milhaud, Darius (1892–1974) French composer. In the incidental music to Claudel's translation of Aeschylus' *Orestes*, (1913–22), Milhaud experimented with polytonality. He also included jazz elements in his compositions, notably *La Création du Monde* (1923). His most ambitious work was the opera *Christophe Colombe* (1930).

milk Liquid secreted from mammary glands by the females of nearly all mammals to feed their young. The milk of domesticated cattle, sheep, goats, horses, camels and reindeer has been used as food by humans since prehistoric times, both directly and to make BUTTER, CHEESE and yogurt. Milk is a suspension of fat and protein in water, sweetened with lactose sugar.

Milky Way Faint band of light visible on clear dark nights encircling the sky along the line of the galactic equator. It is the combined light of an enormous number of stars, in places obscured by clouds of interstellar gas and dust. It is in fact the disc of our GALAXY, viewed from our vantage point within it.

Mill, James (1773–1836) Scottish philosopher, father of John Stuart MILL. Mill became a friend of Jeremy BENTHAM, and together they evolved the doctrine of UTILITARIANISM. He wrote an *Analysis of the Phenomena of the Human Mind* (1829) and, among other works, a multi-volume history of the East India Company, for which he worked.

Mill, John Stuart (1806–73) Scottish philosopher who advocated UTILITARIANISM. His book *On Liberty* (1859) made him famous as a defender of human rights. *System of Logic* (1843) attempted to provide an account of inductive reason.

Millais, Sir John Everett (1829–96) English painter and illustrator, founder of the PRE-RAPHAELITE BROTHERHOOD. His Pre-Raphaelite works, such as *Christ in the House of his Parents* (1850), show the Brotherhood's liking for righteous subjects. His later, more sentimental style, included *Bubbles* (1886), which Pears Soap Company used as an advertisement.

millenarianism Belief, widespread in Christianity until the 4th century, that Christ's second coming will bring a

---

MICROWAVE

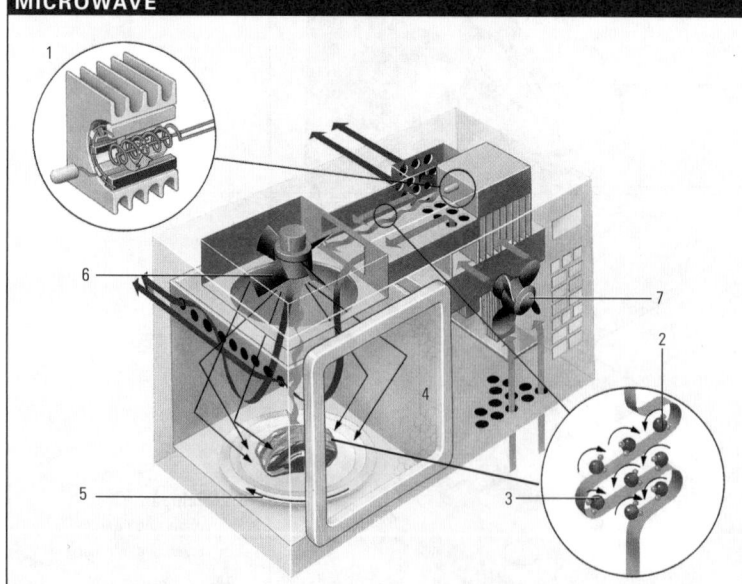

A microwave oven exploits the presence of water in food to cook things from the inside. An oven generates microwaves in a magnetron (1) and when the microwaves penetrate the food, they cause water molecules (2), which have a positive side and a negative side, to vibrate (3) generating heat. The oven is heavily insulated against radio energy (4) to prevent leakage of microwaves. A rotating plate (5) and paddles (6), which ensure a uniform distribution of microwaves, make sure the food cooks evenly. To dissipate the hot air generated by cooking and by the magnetron, a fan (7) pushes cold air around the oven.

thousand years of peace on Earth. It has its origins in the Judaic notion of the MESSIAH and a literal translation of the Book of REVELATIONS (20). Saint AUGUSTINE's allegorical interpretation of the kingdom of God supplanted millenarianism. Sects such as the ANABAPTISTS and the MORAVIAN CHURCH revived the belief during the REFORMATION. Since the 19th century, MORMONS and ADVENTISTS professed millenarian beliefs. Some sects, such as JEHOVAH'S WITNESSES, forecast the imminence of the second coming.

Miller, Arthur (1915–2005) US dramatist. Miller's Pulitzer Prize-winning play *Death of a Salesman* (1949) is a masterpiece of 20th-century theatre: an egocentric salesman, Willy Loman, has unrealistic aspirations, which he struggles to articulate. *The Crucible* (1953) is both a dramatic reconstruction of the SALEM witch trials and a parable of the McCARTHY era. Miller won a second Pulitzer Prize for *A View From the Bridge* (1955). Married (1955–61) to Marilyn MONROE, Miller wrote the screenplay for her film *The Misfits* (1961). *After the Fall* (1964) is a fictionalized account of their relationship. Other plays include *All My Sons* (1947), *Playing for Time* (1981), and *The Ryan Interview* (1995).

Miller, (Alton) Glenn (1904–44) US jazz trombonist and bandleader. During World War 2, his band played to servicemen all over the world. He composed such classics as 'Moonlight Serenade' and 'In the Mood' (both 1939). Miller's plane disappeared while flying from England to France.

Miller, Henry (1891–1980) US writer. Miller's sexually explicit novels, such as *Tropic of Cancer* (1934) and *Tropic of Capricorn* (1939), were considered obscene, and many were banned in the USA and Britain until the 1960s. Other works include *The Rosy Crucifixion* trilogy: *Sexus*, *Plexus*, and *Nexus* (1949–60).

Miller, Jonathan Wolfe (1934–) English stage director. Miller wrote parts for, and appeared in, *Beyond the Fringe* (1961). His first production for the British National Theatre was *The Merchant of Venice* (1970). Miller also directed definitive opera productions, notably Verdi's *Rigoletto* for English National Opera (1984). He was artistic director of the OLD VIC (1988–90). Miller also writes on neuropsychology.

millet CEREAL grass that produces small, edible seeds. The stalks have flower spikes and the hulled seeds are white. In Russia, W Africa, and Asia, it is a staple food. In W Europe, it is used mainly for pasture or hay. Pearl millet (*Pennisetum glaucum*) grows in poor soils, and is used as food in India and Africa. Height: 1m (39in). Family Poaceae/Gramineae.

Millet, Jean François (1814–75) French painter. He is best known for solemn, gritty scenes of rural life and labour such as *The Angelus* (1857–59). Millet's strengths as an artist show clearly in his drawings, which stress the dignity of his figures without any trivializing detail.

Millikan, Robert Andrews (1868–1953) US physicist. His **oil drop experiment** enabled him to determine the ELECTRIC CHARGE of an ELECTRON. Millikan went on to study the PHOTOELECTRIC EFFECT, verifying the equation of Albert EINSTEIN and gaining a precise value for Max PLANCK's constant. In 1923 he received the Nobel Prize in physics.

millipede Any of numerous species of elongated, invertebrate, arthropod animals with large numbers of legs. Found throughout the world, it has a segmented body, one pair of antennae, two pairs of legs per segment and can be orange, brown or black. All species avoid light and feed on plant tissues. Length: 2–280mm (0.2–11in). Class Diplopoda.

Milne, A.A. (Alan Alexander) (1882–1956) English essayist, dramatist and writer of children's books. He wrote the verses in *When We Were Very Young* (1924) and *Now We Are Six* (1927), and the stories in *Winnie-the-Pooh* (1926) and *The House at Pooh Corner* (1928).

Milošević, Slobodan (1941–2006) Serbian statesman, president of SERBIA (1989–97), president of Yugoslavia (1997–2000). In 1986, he became head of the Serbian Communist Party. As president, he confronted the breakup of the federation of Yugoslavia. After his re-election in 1992, he gave support to the Serb populations in CROATIA and BOSNIA-HERZEGOVINA, who fought for a Greater Serbia. Milošević gradually distanced himself from the brutal activ-

ities of the Bosnian Serbs MLADIĆ and KARADŽIĆ. In 1995, he signed the **Dayton Peace Accord** with Bosnian President IZETBEGOVIĆ and Croatian President TUDJMAN to end the civil war in the former Yugoslavia. In 1996, Milošević refused to recognize opposition victories in municipal elections. In 1997 he was forced to concede some of these victories after mass demonstrations in Belgrade. In 1998, Milošević ordered Yugoslav forces to crush the majority Albanian population in the province of KOSOVO, provoking NATO air attacks on Serbian military and industrial targets. In 1999, Milošević agreed to a peace plan and a United Nations' (UN) peacekeeping force was sent to Kosovo. Defeated by Vojislav Kostunica in 2000 elections, Milošević reluctantly stood down. In 2001, he was arrested on charges of corruption and abuse of power and sent to The Hague, the Netherlands, to face the International War Crimes Tribunal. He died in 2006 before the trial could be completed. For history of Yugoslavia, *see* SERBIA.

Milosz, Czeslaw (1911–2004) Polish poet and novelist, b. Lithuania. His novels, *The Valley of the Issa* (1955) and *The Usurpers* (1955), demonstrate an acute critical self-awareness. His celebrated volume of essays, *The Captive Mind* (1953), analyses the effects of communism on writers. His poetry is collected in *Selected Poems* (1973). He received the 1980 Nobel Prize in literature.

Milstein, César (1927–2002) British molecular biologist and immunologist, b. Argentina. He shared the 1984 Nobel Prize in physiology or medicine for helping to develop antibodies that can be commercially produced for drugs and diagnostic tests. In 1975, Milstein and the German immunochemist Georges Köhler developed a technique for cloning monoclonal antibodies (MABs) that combat diseases by targeting their sites.

Milton, John (1608–74) English poet. Milton first major pieces are the masque *Comus* (1634), and the pastoral elergy *Lycidas* (1637). He was committed to reform of the Church of England, and his pamphlet *Of Reformation in England* (1641) attacked episcopacy. A champion of the revolutionary forces in the English CIVIL WAR (1642–51), his *Areopagitica* (1644) is a classic argument for freedom of the press. Milton's defence of regicides in *The Tenure of Kings and Magistrates* (1649) earned him a position in CROMWELL's Commonwealth government. Blind from 1652, Milton was forced into hiding after the RESTORATION (1660). *Paradise Lost*, perhaps the greatest epic poem in English, was first published in 10 books (1667). In 1674, he produced a revised edition in 12 books. Written in blank-verse, it relates the theological stories of Satan's rebellion against God, and Adam and Eve in the Garden of Eden. Its sequel, *Paradise Regained* (1671), was published in four books and describes Christ's temptation.

Milton Keynes Town in Buckinghamshire, S central England. A new town, it was designed on a grid pattern by Richard Llewelyn-Davies in 1967. Milton Keynes is the headquarters of the Open University. The economy is based on retail and light industries. Pop. (2001) 207,063.

Milwaukee City and port of entry on the W shore of Lake Michigan, SE Wisconsin, USA. It was founded in 1836, and during the second half of the 19th century received many German settlers. Industries: brewing, diesel and petrol engines, construction, electrical equipment. Pop. (2000) 1,309,000.

mime In drama, the communication of mood, story and idea through the use of gestures, movements and facial expressions, without speech. It derives from Greek and Roman traditions.

mimicry Form of animal deception, either for protection or to lure prey. The mimic, generally a harmless edible species, protects itself by imitating the warning shape or coloration of a 'model', a poisonous or dangerous species. When coloration increases an animal's chances of survival, as seen in the chameleon, it is commonly referred to as **protective coloration**. Examples of mimicry to capture prey include the anglerfish that waves a fleshy wormlike extension from his snout, and spiders that resemble ants, their prey.

mimosa Genus of plants, shrubs and small trees native to tropical N and S America. they have showy featherlike

M

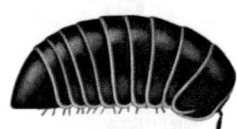

▲ **millipede** The pill millipede (*Glomeris marginata*) has the peculiar ability to roll up when disturbed, tucking its head in. The shell-like cuticle covering the segments of a millipede's body provides excellent protection against prying predators.

▲ **mimosa** Native to tropical and subtropical regions of Brazil, the leaves of the mimosa (*Mimosa pudica*) are sensitive. The plant shrinks when touched.

M

MINNESOTA
Statehood :
May 11, 1858
Nickname :
Gopher State
State bird :
Common loon
State flower :
Pink and white lady-slipper
State tree :
Norway pine
State motto :
Star of the North

leaves and heads or spikes of either white, pink or yellow flowers. Family Mimosaceae.

mina (myna or mynah) Any of several species of tropical birds of SE Asia, S Africa, Australasia, and the Pacific Islands; it is related to the STARLING. A natural mimic, especially the species *Gracula religiosa*, it imitates other birds. It feeds mainly on fruit. Length: to 33cm (13in). Family Sturnidae.

minaret Tower of a MOSQUE from which the MUEZZIN calls a Muslim to prayer. A mosque may have several minarets, and they vary enormously in shape and height. The earliest minarets (*c.*673) were built in Egypt as low square towers; later Persian developments included covered balconies and tiling.

mind Hypothetical faculty postulated to account for the ability of conscious beings to think, feel, will, or behave. The mind is considered to control, or consist of, so-called mental processes. Dualist philosophers, such as René DESCARTES, have distinguished between mind and matter as two totally independent entities. IDEALISM suggests that the world is a product of the mind and dependent on experience. MATERIALISM begins with a concept of a material world independent of experience; the mind is not separate from the physical but derives from it.

Mindanao Second-largest island of the PHILIPPINES, in the S of the archipelago; Davao is the major port and city. The island is forested and mountainous, rising to the active volcano of Mount Apo, at 2,954m (9,690ft), the highest peak in the Philippines. The jagged coastline features deep bays and islets. There are numerous inland waterways and lakes. The economy is primarily agricultural. Tin mining takes place around Mindanas. Area: 94,631sq km (36,537sq mi). Pop. (2000) 16,038,497.

mine Excavation from which minerals (mainly coal and metal ores) are extracted. Underground mines are of two main types: shaft mines and drift mines. **Shafts** are sunk vertically in the Earth's crust until they reach the depth of the seams to be exploited, which are then reached by tunnels or galleries. **Drift** mines are generally shallower, the seams being reached by a drift, or gradually sloping shaft, which leads on to a gallery system. In **open-cast** mining, the seams are near or on the surface and are exposed by giant dragline machines that dig away the topsoil; this is also called strip mining.

mineral Natural, homogeneous and, with a few exceptions, solid and crystalline material that form the Earth and make up its ROCKS. Most are formed through inorganic processes, and more than 3,000 minerals have been identified. They are classified on the basis of chemical make-up, crystal structure, and physical properties such as hardness, specific gravity, cleavage, colour, and lustre. Some minerals are economically important as ORES from which metals are extracted. *See* individual articles

mineral In nutrition, naturally occuring substances that are an important dietary element. The 'major' minerals are calcium and phosphorus as they are required in large amounts, particularly to aid growth of teeth and bones. 'Trace' minerals are needed in tiny amounts, and include iron, sodium, chlorine, sulphur, zinc, copper, manganese and magnesium. All minerals are consumed in a well-balanced diet. *See also* VITAMIN

mineralogy Investigation of naturally occurring inorganic substances found on Earth and elsewhere in the Solar System. *See* GEOCHEMISTRY; MINERAL; PETROLOGY

Minerva Roman goddess of the arts, professions and handicrafts, whose cult is believed to have originated in Etruria. She was identified with the Greek goddess ATHENA, and so became goddess of wisdom and later of war.

Ming Imperial Chinese dynasty (1368–1644). It was founded by a Buddhist monk and peasant leader, Chu Yüan-chang (r.1328–98), who expelled the Mongol YÜAN dynasty and unified China by 1382. Under the despotic rule of the early Ming Emperors, China experienced a period of great artistic and intellectual distinction and economic expansion. Decline began in the late 16th century, and in 1644 a rebel leader took Beijing. A Ming general summoned aid from the QING, who overthrew the dynasty and established their own.

Mingus, Charles (1922–79) US jazz bass player, composer, and bandleader. His large-scale compositions and use of overdubbing inspired a generation of modern jazz musicians. *The Black Saint and the Sinner Lady* (1963) is his masterpiece.

miniature painting Term that originally meant the art of manuscript ILLUMINATION, but was later applied to very small paintings, usually portraits. In Europe, the earliest miniatures were produced in the late 15th century, and executed in the same materials as illuminated manuscripts. During the 18th century, miniaturists usually painted in watercolour on ivory and sometimes worked in oils on metal.

minimal access surgery Operations that do not involve cutting open the body in the traditional way. Minimal access (**keyhole**) procedures are performed either by means of an ENDOSCOPE, or by passing miniature instruments through a catheter into a blood vessel. The surgical LASER is also used.

minimal art Movement in 20th-century painting and sculpture that used only the most fundamental geometric forms. It originated in the 1950s, as a reaction against the chaotic emotions provoked by ABSTRACT EXPRESSIONISM.

minimalism Trend in musical composition, beginning in the 1960s, in which short melodic or rhythmic fragments are repeated in gradually shifting patterns, usually in a simple harmonic context. The repetitive patterns of Indian and other non-Western music influenced many minimalist composers, such as Steve REICH and Philip GLASS.

mink Small, semi-aquatic mammal of the WEASEL family, with soft, durable, water-repellent hair of high commercial value. They have slender bodies, short legs, and bushy tails. Wild mink have dark brown fur with long black outer hair. Ranch mink have been bred to produce fur of various colours. They eat fish, rodents, and birds. Escaped ranch mink can be a serious threat to indigenous wildlife. Length to: 73cm (29in) including the tail; weight: 1.6kg (3.5lb). Family Mustelidae.

Minneapolis City and port on the Mississippi River, next to ST PAUL, SE Minnesota, USA; the largest city in Minnesota. First settled in the 1840s, it is now a processing and distribution centre for grain and cattle. Industries: farm machinery, food processing, electronic equipment, computers, printing and publishing. Pop. Minneapolis-St Paul (2000) 2,389,000.

minnesingers Medieval German poets or singers of courtly love (or *minne*), similar in style to the Provençal TROUBADOURS whom they originally copied. An individual German style developed in the 14th century, several of the poems are considered among the best of Middle High German lyric verse.

Minnesota State in N central USA, on the Canadian border; the capital is ST PAUL. Other major cities include MINNEAPOLIS and Duluth. French fur traders arrived in the 17th century. The area E of the Mississippi passed to Britain after the SEVEN YEARS' WAR, then to the USA after the AMERICAN REVOLUTION. The USA acquired lands W of the Mississippi from France in the LOUISIANA PURCHASE (1803). Minnesota organized as a territory in 1849, and acquired statehood in 1858. The terrain varies from the prairies of the S to the forests of the N. There are mountains in the E. The state is drained chiefly by the Minnesota, St Croix, and Mississippi rivers. Wheat and maize are the major crops, and many farms raise dairy cattle. There are rich deposits of iron ore in the Mesabi Range in the E. Since the 1950s, manufacturing replaced agriculture as the main economic activity. Industries: electronic equipment, machinery, paper products, chemicals, printing and publishing. Area: 206,207sq km (79,617sq mi). Pop. (2000) 4,919,479.

minnow Subfamily of freshwater fish found in temperate and tropical regions. It includes shiners, dace, chub, tench, and bream. The term includes small fish of the genera *Phoxinus* and *Leuciscus*. Length: 4–46cm (1.5–18in). Family Cyprinidae.

Minoan civilization Ancient AEGEAN CIVILIZATION that flourished *c.*3000–*c.*1100 BC on the island of Crete, named after the legendary King Minos. The Minoan period divides into three main eras: **Early** (*c.*3000–*c.*2100BC), **Middle** (*c.*2100–*c.*1550BC), and **Late** (*c.*1550–*c.*1100BC). In terms of artistic achievement and power, Minoan civilization peaked in the Late period. The prosperity of Bronze Age Crete is evident from the works of art and palaces excavated at KNOSSOS, Phaistos, and other sites. Its empire was based on trade and seafaring.

Minos In Greek mythology, the son of Europa and ZEUS, king of Crete. He was consigned at his death to HADES to judge

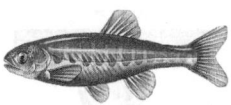

▲ **minnow** Found in freshwater habitats all over the world, the minnow (*Phoxinus* sp.) will swim in shoals to reduce the chance of individuals being preyed upon.

human souls. He angered POSEIDON who, in revenge, caused his wife, Pasiphaë, to give birth to the monstrous MINOTAUR.

Minotaur In Greek mythology, beast with the head of a bull and the body of a man, the issue of Pasiphaë, wife of MINOS, and a bull. He was confined by Minos in the LABYRINTH built by DAEDALUS. THESEUS killed the Minotaur.

Minsk Capital of Belarus, on the River Svisloc. Founded *c*.1060, it was under Lithuanian and Polish rule before becoming part of Russia in 1793. During World War 2, the occupying Germans exterminated the city's large Jewish population. In 1991, Minsk became the capital of the newly independent Belarus. Industries: textiles, machinery, motor vehicles, electronic goods. Pop. (2005) 1,709,000.

minstrel Itinerant musician and professional entertainer; more specifically, a secular musician, usually an instrumentalist. Minstrels were popular from the 12th to 17th centuries.

mint In botany, any species of aromatic herbs, with a characteristic flavour, of the genus *Mentha*. It is commonly used as a flavouring in cooking, confectionery, and medicines. Most species have oval leaves and spikes of purple or pink flowers. Family Lamiaceae/Labiatae. *See also* PEPPERMINT

minuet French dance fashionable at the court of Louis XIV from 1650. Graceful and precise, it is danced by couples and played in triple time. It was a familiar movement in the SUITES of composers such as HANDEL and MOZART.

minutemen Local militia units in the AMERICAN REVOLUTION. The first such units formed in Massachusetts in 1774, and minutemen took part in the opening battles of LEXINGTON AND CONCORD in 1775.

Miocene Geological epoch beginning *c*.5 million years ago and ending *c*.5 million years ago. It falls in the middle of the TERTIARY period, and is marked by a global increase in grasslands at the expense of forests and the development of most of the modern mammal groups.

Mir Soviet SPACE STATION orbiting the Earth. The main part of Mir launched in 1986. It weighed *c*.21 tonnes, and had six docking ports for the attachment of scientific modules or cargo vessels. Over the years, various modules attached to Mir, which was permanently manned by a succession of three-person crews. In 2001, Russia decommissioned the ageing space station and allowed it to burn up in Earth's atmosphere.

Mirabeau, Honoré (1749–91) French revolutionary. One of the most capable early leaders of the FRENCH REVOLUTION, Mirabeau was instrumental in establishing the National Assembly and became its leader. His goal was a parliamentary monarchy, but the obstinacy of the King on the one hand and the Assembly on the other frustrated his plans.

miracle Event that is contrary to the laws of nature and is assumed to be the result of supernatural or divine intervention. Most religions include a belief in miracles. The mythologies of ancient India, the Middle East, Greece and Rome abound with amazing wonders brought about by the gods, but in both Christianity and Judaism a human agent is generally involved.

mirage Type of optical illusion sometimes seen near the Earth's surface when light is refracted (bent) as it passes between cool dense air to warmer, less dense air. Mirages are most commonly seen shimmering on hot, dry roads; the shimmer is a refracted image of the sky.

Miró, Joan (1893–1983) Spanish painter and graphic artist. Early works reveal experimentation with FAUVISM, CUBISM, and DADA. His *Catalan Landscape* (1923) heralds his more mature work and a close affinity with ABSTRACT ART and PRIMITIVISM. In 1924 Miró became a member of the SURREALISM movement, producing works such as *Dog barking at the moon* (1926). His work is often playful, but the Spanish Civil War provoked him into creating darker, more savage images.

mirror Highly polished surface that produces an image of objects in front of it because of the laws of REFLECTION. Most mirrors are made of glass 'silvered' on one side with SILVER, MERCURY, or ALUMINIUM. They can be flat (plane) or curved (spherical or parabolic). **Plane** mirrors produce a virtual image that is the same size but turned sideways (left to right). **Spherical** mirrors may be concave (caving inwards) or convex (bulging outwards). The image can be right-way-up or inverted, real or virtual, depending on the position of the object in relation

to the focal point of the mirror; it may also be either magnified or reduced in size. A spherical mirror suffers spherical ABERRATION (a blurred image), which is absent in a concave parabolic mirror, as used in reflecting telescopes. *See also* IMAGE

miscarriage Popular term for a spontaneous ABORTION, the loss of a FETUS from the UTERUS

Mishima, Yukio (1925–70) Japanese writer. An early novel, *Confessions of a Mask* (1949), is a semi-autobiographical study of homosexuality. His final work, the four-volume *The Sea of Fertility* (1965), is an epic of modern Japan. He committed ritual suicide at Tokyo's military headquarters, which he occupied with his small, private army.

Mishna (Heb. 'instruction') Collection of Jewish legal traditions and moral precepts that form the basis of the TALMUD. The Mishna was compiled (*c*.AD 200) under Rabbi Judah ha-Nasi. It divides into six parts: laws pertaining to agriculture; the sabbath, fasts and festivals, family laws, civil and criminal laws, sacrifices, and laws on ceremonial regulations.

missile Unmanned and self-propelled flying weapon. Ballistic missiles travel in the outer atmosphere, and can be powered only by rockets. CRUISE MISSILES travel in the lower atmosphere, and can be powered by jet engines. GUIDED MISSILES carry self-contained guidance systems or are guided by radio.

missionary societies Organizations for the promotion of Christianity among non-Christians. The first such society was established in New England in 1649. In the 18th century, both the Baptists and Methodists established societies, and the 19th century saw the emergence of interdenominational and geographically specialized societies. The International Missionary Council formed in 1921. Today, governments or agencies, such as Christian Aid, carry out much of the missionary societies' traditional educational and medical work.

Mississippi State in s central USA, on the Gulf of Mexico; the capital and largest city is JACKSON. Other major cities are Meridian, Biloxi, Vicksburg, and Laurel. The French claimed the region in 1682, but it passed to Britain after the SEVEN YEARS' WAR. The Territory of Mississippi organized in 1798. The state seceded from the Union in 1861. It was a battleground during the American CIVIL WAR. Racial segregation remained in force until the 1960s, when the state was a focus of the civil-rights movement. The land slopes w from the hills of the NE to the Delta, a fertile plain between the Mississippi and Yazoo rivers. Pine forests cover most of the s of the state as far as the coastal plain. Primarily an agricultural state, Mississippi is the leading producer of cotton in the USA; hay and soya beans are also grown. Dairy farming is of great importance. There are valuable reserves of oil and natural gas. Other industries: clothing, wood products, chemicals. Area: 123,515sq km (47,689sq mi). Pop. (2000) 2,844,658.

Mississippi Principal river of the USA, second-longest national river (after the MISSOURI), *c*.3,780km (2,350mi) long. It rises in NW Minnesota and flows SE (forming many state boundaries along its course), emptying into the Gulf of Mexico via its huge marshland delta in SE Louisiana. Its chief tributaries include the Missouri, OHIO, ARKANSAS, and TENNESSEE rivers. A major transport route, it connects to the GREAT LAKES and the ST LAWRENCE SEAWAY (N), and the Intracoastal Waterway (E). Major ports on the river include MINNEAPOLIS, ST LOUIS, MEMPHIS, and NEW ORLEANS. In 1541, Hernando DE SOTO became the first European to discover the river. In 1682, La Salle sailed down the Mississippi to the Gulf of Mexico and gained control of the region. In 1803, the USA acquired it as part of the LOUISIANA PURCHASE. Since the 1950s, improvements to the river's channels enabled bulkier freight to be transported.

Mississippi Period In the USA, name given to the earlier part of the CARBONIFEROUS period

Missouri State in central USA, w of the Mississippi River; the capital is JEFFERSON CITY. The largest cities are ST LOUIS, KANSAS CITY, and Springfield. The French settled the area in the mid-18th century. The USA acquired the region in the LOUISIANA PURCHASE of 1803. Missouri Territory organized in 1812, and became a major corridor for westward migration. Missouri joined the Union in 1821 without restrictions on slavery, but when the CIVIL WAR began sympathies bitterly

▲ **mint** Long used as a food flavouring, many species of mint (*Mentha* sp.) are known, and they show subtle differences in the aroma they discharge. Crosses between water mint (*Mentha aquatica*) and spearmint (*M. spicata*) are the basis of cultivated peppermint (*M. x piperita*), commercially grown on a wide scale in the USA, and used to flavour gums, toothpaste, and a variety of drugs.

M

MISSISSIPPI
Statehood :
December 10, 1817
Nickname :
Magnolia State
State bird :
Mockingbird
State flower :
Magnolia
State tree :
Magnolia
State motto :
By valour and arms

divided and there was much violence. The state remained in the Union. Geographically it divides into two parts: to the N of the Missouri River is prairie country, where farmers grow maize and raise livestock. South of the river are the foothills and plateaus of the Ozarks. In the SW, is a small wheat-growing area and in the SE are the cotton fields of the Mississippi delta. The chief mineral resources are coal, lead, zinc and iron ore. Its economy is largely manufacturing. Industries: transport equipment, food processing, chemicals, printing and publishing, fabricated metals, electrical machinery. Area: 178,446sq km (68,898sq mi). Pop. (2000) 5,595,211.

Missouri ('Big Muddy') Longest river of the USA; the major tributary of the MISSISSIPPI. It rises at the confluence of the Jefferson, Madison and Gallatin rivers in the Rocky Mountains, Montana. It then flows E through Great Falls cataracts and Fort Peck reservoir. In North Dakota it turns SE across the Great Plains, passing through OMAHA and KANSAS CITY. It joins the Mississippi River, 27km (17mi) N of ST LOUIS. Sioux City, Iowa, is the head of navigation. The Missouri has seven major dams. Its major tributaries are the Yellowstone and Platte rivers. Native Americans used the river as a trade route for centuries before its discovery (1683) by the explorers Marquette and Jolliet. Mapped by the LEWIS AND CLARK EXPEDITION (1804–06), traders, gold seekers, and pioneers used the river as a route to the NW. Length: *c.*4,120km (2,560mi).

Missouri Compromise (1820–21) Effort to end the dispute between slave and free states in the USA. Largely the work of Henry CLAY, it permitted MISSOURI to join the union as a slave state at the same time as MAINE joined as a free state, preserving an equal balance between slave and free.

mistletoe Any of numerous species of evergreen plants that are semi-parasitic on tree branches. It has small, spatula-shaped, yellowish-green leaves and generally forms a large dense ball of foliage. The mistletoe taps into the branch of its host to sap its food supply, avoiding the necessity of growing roots itself. It also carries out photosynthesis, so is not entirely parasitic. Families: Loranthaceae and Viscaceae.

mistral Wind prevalent in the NW Mediterranean during the winter. It sweeps from the MASSIF CENTRAL, down the Rhône valley, reaching the Rhône delta as a strong, dry wind.

mite Minute ARACHNID found worldwide, many are PARASITES. The adult has four pairs of legs with claws at the tip, and a fused head and abdomen. Length: 0.5–3mm (0.02–0.1in). Class Arachnida; order Acarina. *See also* CHIGGER; TICK

Mitford Name of six British sisters, daughters of Lord and Lady Redesdale. The most famous, **Nancy** Freeman Mitford (1904–73), was a novelist and biographer. Her first successful novel was *The Pursuit of Love* (1945), followed by *Love in a Cold Climate* (1949). Her sister, **Jessica** Mitford (1917–96), also wrote, protesting about snobbery, as in *The American Way of Death* (1963) and *Kind and Usual Punishment* (1973). **Unity** Valkyrie (1914–48) and **Diana** (1910–96), turned to fascism, the former becoming a follower of Adolf HITLER in Germany, and the latter marrying Sir Oswald MOSLEY.

Mithras Solar deity of a popular mystery cult in the late Roman Empire. Initiation into the cult's seven levels of mysteries was limited to men, and many worshippers were in the military. Mithras was worshiped in cave-like temples, which featured a depiction of him slaying a sacred bull, but little is known about the cult's rites. Recent research, contrary to earlier views, has shown that Mithras bore little relation to the Persian MITRA.

Mithridates VI (*c.*132–63 BC) King of Pontus (120–63BC). He attempted to extend his rule S, but was repeatedly defeated by the Romans. Overwhelmed by the forces of SULLA in the war of 88–85 BC he lost his kingdom in a second campaign in 83–82. He reconquered it in 74, but POMPEY defeated him in 66 and he fled to the Bosporus. He was planning an invasion of Italy when his troops mutinied, and he committed suicide.

mitochondrion Structure (organelle) inside a CELL containing ENZYMES necessary for energy production. Mitochondria are present in the cytoplasm of most types of cell (but not in bacteria). *See also* RESPIRATION

mitosis CELL DIVISION resulting in two genetically identical 'daughter' cells with the same number of CHROMOSOMES as the

MOBILE TELEPHONE

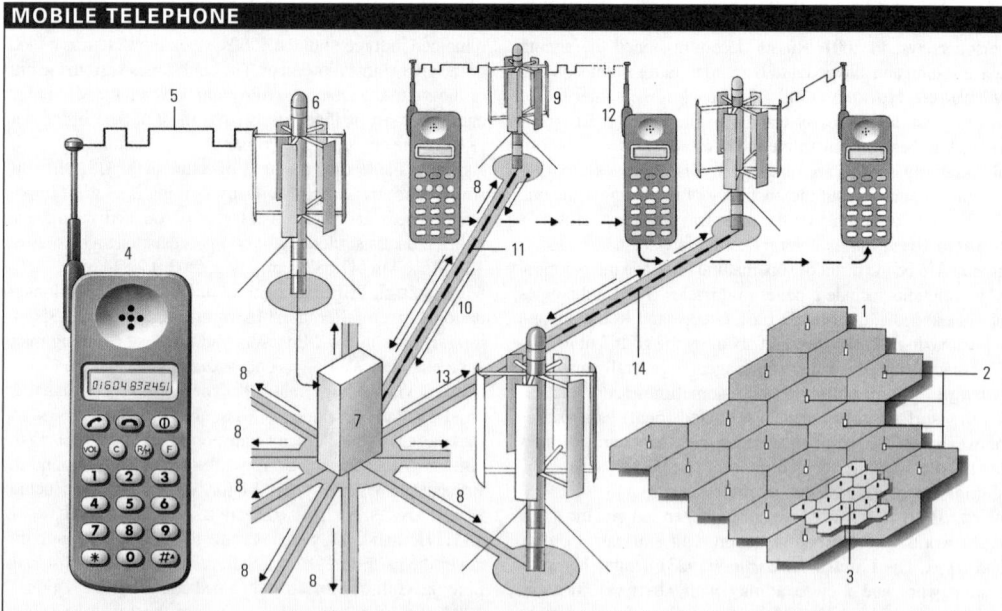

Mobile phone networks use a system of cells (1). By having a transmitter (2) in each cell, the same frequencies can be used in each cell allowing an enormous capacity for calls. Where there are many users, such as in the heart of a city (3), the cells are much smaller – further multiplying the number of frequencies available. A digital mobile phone (4) sends digital information (5) to a transmitter tower (6). Digital phones are better than analogue versions because they reduce background noise and interference, and are more difficult to bug. The transmitter passes the message to the systems' central exchange (7). If the call is for another mobile phone, the exchange sends a message (8) to the other transmitters, which in turn send out a message to locate the receiving phone. The transmitter locating the required phone (9) sends a confirmation message to the exchange (10), which then connects the conversation (11 – dotted line). When a phone moves out of range of a transmitter (12), a complicated procedure ensures the conversation can continue seamlessly. When the phone's signal to the transmitter becomes weaker, the exchange sends a message (13) to the transmitters in the surrounding cells to see which is receiving the strongest signal. It then transfers the conversation to that transmitter (14 – dotted line).

parent cell. Mitosis is the normal process of TISSUE growth, and is also involved in ASEXUAL REPRODUCTION. *See also* MEIOSIS

Mitra In Vedic mythology, Mitra was the spirit of the day, of the rain and of the sun, linked closely with VARUNA. The Persian Mitra was a popular deity of the ACHAEMENID empire, revered as the god of light and power. *See also* MITHRAS

Mitterrand, François Maurice Marie (1916–96) French statesman, president (1981–96). He was active in the French Resistance, and served in the government of the Fourth Republic. He united the parties of the left in 1964 and narrowly lost the 1974 presidential election. In 1981 elections, Mitterrand defeated the incumbent GISCARD D'ESTAING. Re-elected in 1988, Mitterrand introduced reforms, abolished capital punishment, and favoured state intervention in the economy. He was forced further right after 1986, when he had to cooperate with Gaullist prime minister Jacques CHIRAC, and some industries were returned to private ownership. Mitterrand supported the EUROPEAN UNION (EU). Jacques Chirac succeeded him.

mixture In chemistry, two or more substances that retain their specific identities when mixed (such as air containing oxygen, nitrogen, and other gases). The identities remain separate no matter in what proportion or how closely the components are mixed. *See also* COMPOUND; SOLUTION

Mladić, Ratko (1943–) Bosnian Serb general. As the aggressive commander of the Serbian army in the 1992 war in Bosnia, he earned the sobriquet "Butcher of the Balkans". In 1996 the UN indicted him as a war criminal.

mobile telephone (cellular phone) Portable radio that connects users to the public TELEPHONE system. They operate within a network of radio cells. The first generation operated with analogue signals, the second with digital signals, and the third generation includes high-speed data transfer and links to the INTERNET.

Möbius strip Shape or figure that can be modelled by giving a strip of paper a half-twist, then joining the ends together. It is of great interest in TOPOLOGY, being a single-edged one-sided surface (starting at any point a line can be drawn in one direction that to the starting-point). It was discovered by German mathematician August Ferdinand Möbius (1790–1868).

Mobutu Sese Seko (1930–97) Congolese statesman, president (1970–97), b. Joseph-Désiré Mobutu. He was defence minister under Patrice LUMUMBA. In 1960, he deposed Lumumba. Mobutu seized power in a military coup against Joseph Kasavubu in 1965. With the support of France, the CIA and his security forces, he maintained a dictatorship for more than 30 years. In May 1997, he was deposed in a Tutsi-dominated revolt, led by Laurent Kabila. He died in exile.

mockingbird Any of a group of New World birds, known for imitating other birds. The common mockingbird (*Mimus polyglottos*) of the USA is *c.*27cm (11in) long, ashy above with brownish wings and tail marked with white. Family Mimidae.

mock orange (Philadelphus or sweet syringa) Ornamental deciduous shrub native to the Western Hemisphere and Asia. It has solitary, white or yellowish, fragrant flowers. Family Hydrangeaceae; genus *Philadelphus*.

mode Classified scheme developed during the 4th to 16th centuries AD to systematize music. In the 4th century, from the SCALE worked out scientifically by PYTHAGORAS, St Ambrose is thought to have devised four 'authentic' modes: the **Dorian**, **Phrygian**, **Lydian**, and **Mixolydian**. All the modes comprised eight notes within the compass of an octave. Pope Gregory (6th century) added four 'plagal' modes, which were essentially new forms of the Ambrosian modes (Hypodorian, Hypophrygian etc.). Glareanus (16th century) added the Aeolian and Ionian modes, the basis of the minor and major scales respectively.

mode In statistics, a measure of central tendency. It is computed by determining the item that occurs most frequently in a data set. *See also* MEAN; MEDIAN

Model Parliament (November 1295) English Parliament summoned by EDWARD I. For the first time, knights of the shire and burgesses (representatives of the House of COMMONS) dealt with the affairs of the nation along with the king and barons. This enlargement of the Commons' function was held

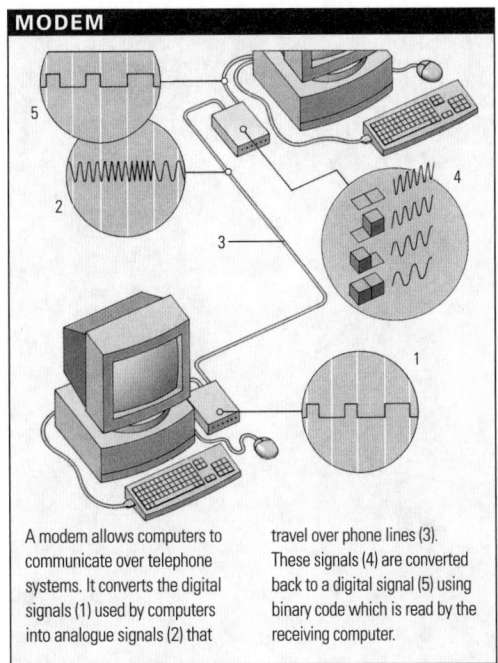

MODEM

A modem allows computers to communicate over telephone systems. It converts the digital signals (1) used by computers into analogue signals (2) that travel over phone lines (3). These signals (4) are converted back to a digital signal (5) using binary code which is read by the receiving computer.

to be the model for the future. They had previously merely agreed to what the king and the magnates had already decided.

modem (**mo**dulator-**dem**odulator) Electronic device for sending and receiving COMPUTER signals through a telephone system. The electrical pulses produced by a computer are fed into a modem, which uses the pulses to modulate a continuous tone (carrier) by a process called FREQUENCY MODULATION (FM). At the other end, another modem extracts the pulses (demodulation) for a receiving computer. The term is also used for the more complex equipment used for BROADBAND access, which works on similar principles at higher frequencies. *See also* COMPUTER NETWORK; INTERNET

modern dance Dance style that began to develop during the late 19th century as a protest against classical BALLET. It is often said to have been pioneered by Isadora DUNCAN. In Europe and the USA, such innovators as Rudolph von Laban, Ruth St. Denis and Ted Shawn attempted to make dance a viable contemporary art form.

modernism Twentieth-century movement in art, architecture, design and literature that, in general, concentrates on space and form, rather than content or ornamentation. In **architecture** and design, early influences were BAUHAUS (1919–33) and individuals such as Walter GROPIUS and MIES VAN DER ROHE. Modernism developed the use of new building materials, such as glass, steel, and concrete. While difficult to define and date precisely, the echoes of **literary** modernism can still be heard in late-20th-century fiction. The most recognizably distinct form is the STREAM OF CONSCIOUSNESS narrative, as evidenced in the work of Virginia WOOLF and James JOYCE's seminal novel, *Ulysses* (1922). The outstanding example of modernist poetry is the fragmentary "The Wasteland" (1922) by T.S. ELIOT. Literary modernism exhibits an increasing concern with psychological states and the subconscious. **Artists** such as PICASSO and Marcel DUCHAMP adopted new techniques of representation and worked in previously unexploited media. The movements of DADA and SURREALISM were vital to this new experimentation. In **music**, composers such as STRAVINSKY and SCHOENBERG challenged previously held notions of tonality. *See also* ABSTRACT ART; ABSTRACT EXPRESSIONISM; BLAUE REITER, DER; BRÜCKE, DIE; CONSTRUCTIVISM; CUBISM; DECONSTRUCTION; FAUVISM; FUTURISM; INTERNATIONAL STYLE; POST-MODERNISM; SUPREMATISM; VORTICISM

Modigliani, Amedeo (1884–1920) Italian painter, sculptor, and draughtsman. Many of his sculptures portray elongated heads, inspired by MANNERISM and AFRICAN ART. During World War 1 Modigliani returned to painting,

▶ **Modigliani** *Girl with Pigtails* (1901) Italian painter and sculptor Modigliani spent most of his life in Paris, but his studies of Renaissance masters in Italy had a strong influence on his work. Influenced by Brancusi, Modigliani's achievements may have been limited, but his legendary bohemian lifestyle, passion for work, and his tragic early death from tuberculosis ensured him a lasting reputation.

focusing on erotic female nudes and portraits, such as *Girl with Pigtails* (1901).

modulation In physics, the process of varying the characteristics of one wave system in accordance with those of another. It is basic to RADIO broadcasting. In AMPLITUDE MODULATION (AM), the amplitude of a high-frequency radio carrier wave varies in accordance with the frequency of a current generated by a sound wave. This means the wave will vary with a broadcast sound, such as a voice or music. FREQUENCY MODULATION (FM), in which the frequency of the carrier wave is modulated, is used for static-free, short-range broadcasting.

Mogadishu Capital and chief port of Somalia, on the Indian Ocean. Mogadishu was founded by Arabs in the 10th century. In the 16th century, the Portuguese captured the city and it became a cornerstone of their trade with Africa. In 1871, control passed to the Sultan of Zanzibar, who first leased (1892) and then sold (1905) the port to the Italians. Mogadishu became the capital of Italian Somaliland. During World War 2, the city was occupied by the British from 1941. In 1960, Mogadishu became the capital of independent Somalia. During the 1980s and early 1990s, civil war devastated the city, its population swelled by refugees escaping famine and drought in the outlying regions. In 1992, UN troops flew into Mogadishu to control aid distribution but withdrew in 1995 after little success. Pop. (2005) 1,257,000.

Mogul Empire (1526–1857) Muslim Empire in India founded by BABUR, who conquered Delhi and Agra in 1526. The Mogul Empire reached its height under AKBAR I (THE GREAT) (r.1556–1605), Babur's grandson, when it extended from Afghanistan to the Bay of Bengal and as far s as the Deccan. Akbar encouraged religious tolerance, which declined under his successors JAHANGIR (r.1605–27), SHAH JAHAN (r.1628–58), and AURANGZEB (r.1659–1707). Mogul art and architecture reached a peak under Shah Jahan, builder of the TAJ MAHAL. By the death of Aurangzeb, the Mogul dynasty was in decline. The British deposed the last Mogul Emperor in 1858, after the rising known as the INDIAN MUTINY.

Mohammed Alternative spelling of MUHAMMAD

M MOLDOVA

The Republic of Moldova is a small country lying between Ukraine and Romania. It was one of the 15 republics that made up the Soviet Union. Much of the land is hilly and the highest areas are near the centre of the country. The main river is the Dniester, which flows through E Moldova.

Forests of hornbeam and oak grow in n and central Moldova. In the drier s most of the country is now used for farming, with rich pasture along the rivers.

CLIMATE
Moldova has a moderately continental climate, with warm summers and fairly cold winters when temperatures dip below freezing point. Most of the rain falls in the warmer months.

HISTORY
(For history pre-1991, see MOLDAVIA)

POLITICS
Following independence in 1991, the majority Moldovan population wished to rejoin Romania. This alienated the Ukrainian and Russian populations east of the Dniester, who declared their independence from Moldova as the Transdniester Republic. War raged between the two, with Transdniester supported by the Russian 14th Army. In August 1992 a ceasefire was declared. The former Communists of the Agrarian Democratic Party won multiparty elections in 1994. A referendum rejected reunification with Romania. Parliament voted to join the COMMONWEALTH OF INDEPENDENT STATES (CIS).

In 1994 a new constitution established a presidential parliamentary republic. In 1995 Transdniester voted in favour of independence in a referendum. In 1996 Russian troops began their withdrawal and Petru Lucinschi was elected president. On 1 January 1997 a former Communist, Petru Lucinschi, became president. In 1998 and 2001 the Party of the Moldovan Communists (PCRM) won the highest share of the votes. The constitution was changed in 2000, turning Moldova from a semi-presidential to a parliamentary republic. In 2001 the Communist leader Vladimir Voronin was elected president. The Communist party was re-elected in 2005, though it now advocates close ties with the West. Disputes with Russia over Transdniester continue.

ECONOMY
According to the World Bank Moldova is a lower-middle income developing country and, in terms of GNP per capita, Europe's poorest country. It is fertile and agriculture remains central to the economy. Major products include fruits, maize, tobacco and grapes for winemaking. Farmers also raise livestock, including dairy cattle and pigs.

There are few natural resources in Moldova, and the government must import materials and fuels for its industries. Light industries, such as food processing and the manufacturing of household appliances, are expanding.

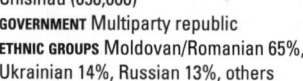

AREA 33,851sq km [13,070sq mi]
POPULATION 4,320,000
CAPITAL (POPULATION) Chisinau (658,000)
GOVERNMENT Multiparty republic
ETHNIC GROUPS Moldovan/Romanian 65%, Ukrainian 14%, Russian 13%, others
LANGUAGES Moldovan/Romanian, Russian (official)
RELIGIONS Eastern Orthodox 98%
CURRENCY Moldovan leu = 100 bani

Mohawk Iroquoian-speaking Native North American tribe of the IROQUOIS CONFEDERACY, formerly inhabiting central New York state. Today, there are c.2000 Mohawks. Most are farmers on two reservations in Ontario, Canada.

Mohican (Mahican) Algonquian-speaking tribe of Native North Americans, formerly inhabiting the upper Hudson valley in New York, and the area E of the Housatonic River in Connecticut, USA. They once numbered about 3000. Today, the surviving 525 Mohicans occupy the Stockbridge-Munsee Reservation in Wisconsin.

Moho (Mohorovicic discontinuity) Boundary between the Earth's CRUST and MANTLE. Identified by a sharp increase in the velocity of seismic waves passing through the Earth, it receive its name from the Croatian geophysicist Andrija Mohorovicic, who first recognized it in 1909. The velocity increase occurs because of the shift to more dense rocks in the mantle. The depth of the Moho varies from c.5km (3mi) to 60km (37mi) below the Earth's surface.

Moholy-Nagy, László (1895–1946) Hungarian designer, painter and sculptor. He was one of the most influential founders of CONSTRUCTIVISM. Moholy-Nagy taught at the BAUHAUS (1923–28), before working in Berlin as a stage designer and film-maker. He then moved to Paris, Amsterdam, and London. In 1937, he emigrated to the USA and became director of the short-lived New Bauhaus.

Moi, Daniel (Torotich) Arap (1924–) Kenyan statesman, president (1978–2003). He was the British-appointed representative to the Kenya Legislative Council from 1958 until independence in 1964. Moi succeeded Jomo KENYATTA as president in 1978 elections. He continued Kenyatta's liberal economic policies, but came under mounting international criticism for his repressive rule. He was re-elected in 1992 and 1997. Moi retired as president in 2003. He was succeeded by Mwai Kibaki.

Mojave Desert Arid region with low, barren mountains in S California, USA, surrounded by mountain ranges on the N and W, and the Colorado Desert on the SE. It was formed by volcanic eruptions and deposits from the Colorado River. Area: c.38,850sq km (15,000sq mi).

Moldavia Historic Balkan region, between the CARPATHIAN MOUNTAINS in Romania and the DNIEPER River in MOLDOVA. Major cities in the Romanian portion include Galati and Suceava. Moldavia is primarily an agricultural region. Under Roman rule it formed the major part of the province of DACIA, and today's population is Romanian-speaking. In the 14th century, it became an independent principality ruled by the Vlachs; its lands included Bessarabia and Bukovina. In 1504, the Turks conquered Moldavia, and it remained part of the Ottoman Empire until the 19th century. In 1775, the Austrians gained Bukovina, and in 1815 Russia conquered Bessarabia. After the Russo-Turkish War (1828–29), Russia became the dominant power. In 1856 the twin principalities of Moldavia and WALLACHIA gained considerable autonomy. Three years later, they united under one crown to form ROMANIA, but Russia re-occupied S Bessarabia in 1878. In 1920 Bessarabia and Bukovina incorporated into the Romanian state. In 1924 the Soviet republic of Moldavia was formed, which in 1947 enlarged to include Bessarabia and N Bukovina. In 1989 the Moldovans asserted their independence by making Romanian the official language; in 1991, following the dissolution of the Soviet Union, Moldavia became the independent republic of MOLDOVA.

Moldova Republic in E Europe. *see* country feature.

mole (symbol mol) SI unit of amount of substance. This is the amount of substance that contains as many elementary units, such as atoms and molecules, as there are atoms in 0.012kg of carbon-12. A mass of one mole of a compound is its relative molecular mass (molecular weight) in grams.

mole Any of several species of small, burrowing, mainly insectivorous mammals that live in various habitats worldwide. The European mole, *Talpa europaea*, has short brown or black fur, a short tail, and wide clawed forefeet for digging tunnels. Its eyes are sensitive only to bright light. Length: to 18cm (7in). Family Talpidae.

molecular biology Biological study of the make-up and function of molecules found in living organisms. Major areas of study include the chemical and physical properties of proteins and of nucleic acids such as DNA. *See also* BIOCHEMISTRY

molecular weight *See* RELATIVE MOLECULAR MASS

molecule Smallest particle of a substance (such as a compound) that exhibits the properties of that substance. Molecules consist of two or more atoms held together by CHEMICAL BONDS. For example, water molecules consist of two atoms of hydrogen bonded to one atom of oxygen (H_2O). A MACROMOLECULE can be up to 1,000 times greater in diameter. A molecule (unlike an ION) has no electrical charge. Molecules were first hypothesized in 1811 by Italian physicist Amedeo AVOGADRO and first detected by Scottish botanist Robert Brown.

Molière (1622–73) French playwright, b. Jean-Baptiste Poquelin. An acute observer of contemporary modern manners, Molière is regarded as the founder of modern French comedy. His best-known comedies include *Tartuffe* (1661), *The Misanthrope* (1667), and *The Miser* (1669). His work found favour with Louis XIV, but was unpopular with Church leaders. His last play was *The Imaginary Invalid*, during a performance of which he collapsed and died.

mollusc Any of more than 80,000 species of invertebrate animals in the phylum Mollusca. They include the SNAILS, CLAMS and SQUIDS. Originally marine, members of the group are now found in the oceans, in freshwater and on land. There are six classes: the GASTROPODS, CHITONS, univalves (SLUGS and snails), BIVALVES, tusk shells, and CEPHALOPOD. The mollusc bodydivides into three: the head, the foot, and the visceral mass. Associated with the body is a fold of skin (the mantle) that secretes the limy shell typical of most molluscs. The head is well developed only in snails and in the cephalopods. The visceral mass contains the internal organs. The sexes are usually separate but there are many hermaphroditic species.

Molotov, Vyacheslav Mikhailovich (1890–1986) Soviet statesman, premier (1930–41) and foreign minister (1939–49, 1953–56). A loyal ally of STALIN, he became a full member of the Politburo in 1926. As foreign minister, one of Molotov's first acts was to sign the Nazi-Soviet Pact (1939) with von

M

MOLECULE

| A | O_2 | H_2O | C_6H_6 |

Molecules are groups of bonded atoms. They can be groups of the same atoms as in oxygen (O_2), or combinations of different elements such as water (H_2O) and benzene (C_6H_6). Molecules can be illustrated in four ways. Line one (A), the chemical formula, lists the type and number of atoms in a molecule but does not show their structure. Line two (B) is the closest representation of the actual shape of the molecule but does not detail the bonds between the atoms. Line three (C) is less realistic but does show the bonding. Line four (D) combines the chemical formula, using the abbreviations of the periodic table, and symbolic representation of the bonding structure.

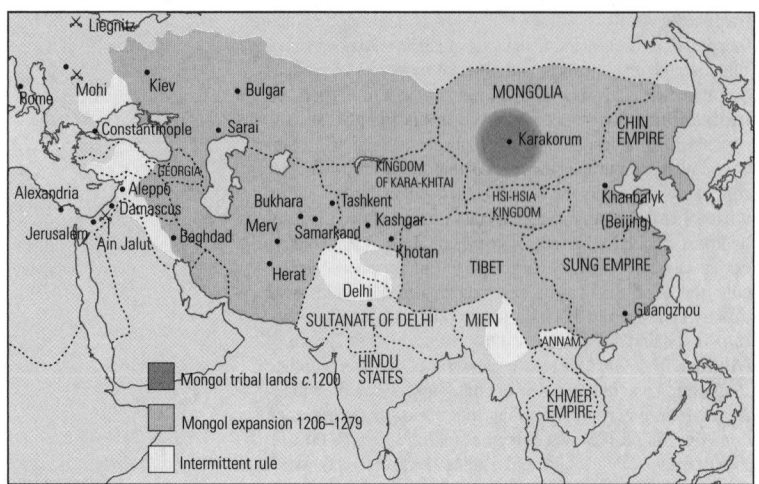

▲ **Mongol** In 1206, under the leadership of Genghis Khan, the Mongols extended the territory under their rule. By 1279, the Mongol Empire stretched from the Black Sea to the Pacific Ocean.

RIBBENTROP. His enthusiastic use of the veto in the UN Security Council contributed to the COLD WAR. He lost favour under Nikita KHRUSHCHEV, and was demoted and expelled from the Communist Party in 1962. Molotov was readmitted in 1984.

Moluccas (Maluku) Island group and province in E INDONESIA, between Sulawesi (W) and New Guinea (E); the capital is Ambon. The fabled Spice Islands were originally explored by Ferdinand Magellan in the early 16th century, and later settled by the Portuguese. The Dutch took the islands in the 17th century and monopolized the spice trade. The group includes the larger islands of Halmahera, Ceram, and Buru, and the island groups of Sula, Batjan, Obi, Kai, Aru, Tanimbar, Banda, Babar, and Leti. Products: spices, copra, timber, sago. Area: 74,505sq km (28,759sq mi). Pop. (2000) 1,977,570.

molybdenite (molybdenum sulphide, MoS_2) Sulphide mineral, found in pegmatites, IGNEOUS and METAMORPHIC rocks. It is a major ore of MOLYBDENUM. It has hexagonal system tabular prisms, flakes, and fine granules. It is lead-grey in colour with a metallic lustre. Hardness 1–1.5; r.d. 4.7.

molybdenum (symbol Mo) Silvery-white metallic element; one of the TRANSITION ELEMENTS. It was first isolated in 1781 by the Swedish chemist Karl SCHEELE. Its chief ore is molybdenite. Hard but malleable and ductile, it is used in alloy steels, X-ray tubes and missile parts; molybdenum compounds are used as catalysts and lubricants. It is one of the essential TRACE ELEMENTS for plant growth. Properties: at.no. 42; r.a.m. 95.94; r.d. 10.22; m.p. 2,610°C (4,730°F); b.p. 5,560°C (10,040°F); most stable isotope Mo^{98} (23.78%).

Mombasa City and seaport on the Indian Ocean, SW Kenya, partly on Mombasa Island and partly on the mainland (to which it connects by causeway). From the 11th to 16th centuries, Mombasa was a centre of the Arab slave and ivory

MONGOLIA

Mongolia, between China and Russia, is the world's largest landlocked country. It is mainly high plateaus, the highest of which are in the W between the Altai Mountains (Aerhtai Shan) and the Hangayn Mountains (Hangayn Nuruu). The Altai contain the country's highest peaks (4,362m [14,311ft]). The land descends towards the E and S, where part of the Gobi Desert is situated.

CLIMATE
Due to its remote position Mongolia has an extreme continental climate, with long, bitterly cold winters and short, warm summers. Annual rainfall ranges from no more than 500 mm [20 in] in the highlands to 125 mm [5 in] in the lowlands.

HISTORY
In the 13th century the great Mongol conqueror GENGHIS KHAN united the Mongol people, created a ruthless army, and founded the largest land empire in history. Under his grandson KUBLAI KHAN the Mongol empire stretched from Korea and China across Asia into what is now Iraq. In the NW, Mongol rule extended beyond the Black Sea into E Europe. Learning flourished under Kublai Khan, but after his death in 1294 the empire broke up into several parts. It was not until the late 16th century that Mongol princes reunited Mongolia. During their rule, the Mongols introduced a form of Buddhism known as Lamaism. In the early 17th century the Manchu leaders of Manchuria took over INNER MONGOLIA. They conquered China in 1644 and Outer Mongolia some 40 years later. Mongolia then became a remote Chinese province scarcely in contact with the outside world.

Outer Mongolia broke away from China following the collapse of the Qing Dynasty in 1911. The Mongols appointed a priest, the Living Buddha, as their king. Legally, Outer Mongolia remained Chinese territory, but China and Russia agreed to grant it control over its own affairs in 1913. Russian influence increased and, in 1921, Mongolian and Russian Communists took control of Outer Mongolia. They proclaimed the Mongolian People's Republic in 1924 and the Mongolian People's Revolutionary Party (MPRP) became the sole political party. The revolution in ownership prompted the Lama Rebellion of 1932, which saw the migration of thousands of peoples and millions of livestock into Inner Mongolia.

POLITICS
Mongolia became an ally of the Soviet Union, its support being particularly significant from the 1950s when the Soviet Union was in dispute with Mongolia's neighbour China. The Soviet Union helped develop Mongolia's mineral reserves, and by the late 1980s minerals had overtaken agriculture as the country's main source of revenue.

In 1990 the people, influenced by reforms taking place in the Soviet Union, held demonstrations demanding more freedom. Elections in June 1990 resulted in victory for the Communist Mongolian People's Revolutionary Party (MPRP). The new government began to move away from Communist policies, launching into privatization and developing a free-market economy. The 'People's Democracy' was abolished in 1992 and democratic institutions were introduced.

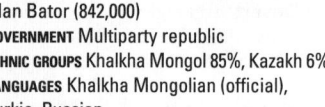

AREA 1,566,500sq km [604,826sq mi]
POPULATION 2,952,000
CAPITAL (POPULATION) Ulan Bator (842,000)
GOVERNMENT Multiparty republic
ETHNIC GROUPS Khalkha Mongol 85%, Kazakh 6%
LANGUAGES Khalkha Mongolian (official), Turkic, Russian
RELIGIONS Tibetan Buddhist Lamaism 96%
CURRENCY Tugrik = 100 möngös

The MPRP was defeated in elections in 1996 by the opposition Mongolian Democratic Union coalition. The Democratic Union ran into economic problems, and in the presidential elections of 1997 the MPRP candidate, Natasagiyn Babagandi, was victorious. Parliamentary elections in July 2000 resulted in a landslide victory for the MPRP, who gained 72 out of the 76 available seats in the Great Hural (parliament). The MPRP chairman, Nambaryn Enhbayar, became prime minister. Following disputed elections in 2004 a coalition government was set up. In 2006 the coalition broke down and the MPRP once again took power.

ECONOMY
The World Bank classifies Mongolia as a 'lower-middle-income' developing country. Many Mongolians were once nomads, moving around with their livestock. Under Communist rule, most were moved into permanent homes on government-owned farms. Livestock and animal products remain important.

The Communists developed mining and manufacturing and by 1996, mineral products accounted for nearly 60% of the country's exports. Minerals produced in Mongolia include coal, copper, fluorspar, gold, molybdenum, tin and tungsten. The leading manufactures are textiles and metal products.

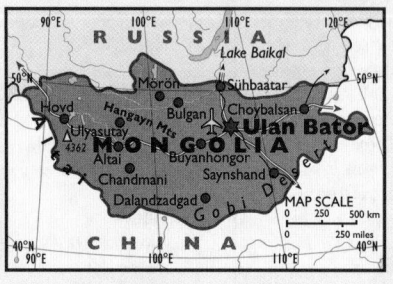

trades. From 1529 to 1648, the Portuguese held the port. Taken by Zanzibar in the mid-19th century, the city passed to Britain in 1887, when it became capital of the British East Africa Protectorate. Kenya's chief port, Mombasa exports coffee, fruit and grain. Industries: tourism, food processing, glass, oil refining, aluminium products. Pop. (2002) 707,400.

moment of force *See* TORQUE

moment of inertia (symbol I) For a rotating object, the sum of the products formed by multiplying the point masses of the rotating object by the squares of their distances from the axis of rotation.

momentum Product of the mass and linear velocity of an object. One of the fundamental laws of physics is the principle that the total momentum of any system of objects is conserved at all times, even during and after collisions.

Monaco Principality in s Europe, on the Mediterranean coast, forming an enclave in French territory near the border with Italy; the capital is Monaco-Ville. Ruled by the Grimaldi family from the end of the 13th century, it came under French protection in 1860. The chief source of income is tourism, attracted by the casinos of MONTE CARLO. There is some light industry, including printing, textiles and postage stamps. Area: 1sq km (0.4sq mi). Pop. (2000) 32,000.

Monaghan County in Ulster province, NE Republic of Ireland, on the boundary with Northern Ireland; the county town is Monaghan. The s and e are hilly, but the rest of the county is a fertile plain. The Blackwater and the Finn are the chief rivers. It is primarily an agricultural county and the main crops are potatoes, oats, and flax. Beef and dairy cattle are raised. Industries: linen-milling, footwear, furniture. Area: 1290sq km (498sq mi). Pop. (2002) 52,772.

monarchy Form of government in which one individual, whose power is usually hereditary, represents the state. There are few present-day monarchs holding absolute power. Most of those states that retain their royal families are governed by constitutional monarchies, with the sovereign performing only ceremonial functions and benefiting from few royal prerogatives.

monasticism Ascetic way of life followed by men or women who have taken religious vows and belong to a recognized religious order. Christian monasticism is said to have its origins in the late 3rd-century asceticism of the desert hermits of Egypt, Saint ANTHONY and Saint Pachomius. A communal approach replaced this solitary life, and community members followed a strict rule. The earliest such rule in Europe was that laid down by Saint BENEDICT (OF NURSIA) in the 6th century. Monasticism still embraces community life of such enclosed Christian orders, as the CISTERCIANS and the reformed CARMELITES. There are, however, many more orders that combine asceticism with social welfare work and spiritual guidance to society at large. Spiritual leadership provided through monasticism is also found in HINDUISM, BUDDHISM, JAINISM and TAOISM.

Monck, George, 1st Duke of Albemarle (1608–70) English soldier and diplomat. In the English CIVIL WAR, Monck fought for CHARLES I (1643–44). After his capture and imprisonment (1644–46), Monck changed sides and helped Oliver CROMWELL quell an Irish rebellion. Cromwell rewarded him with command of the forces in Scotland (1651). Monck was a general in the DUTCH WARS. After the collapse of the PROTECTORATE, he supported the return of the RUMP PARLIAMENT. Monck led the campaign for the RESTORATION of CHARLES II. His troops became the Coldstream Guards – the first permanent regiment of the British Army.

Mondrian, Piet (1872–1944) Dutch painter, co-founder (with Theo van Doesburg) of De STIJL and a pioneer of ABSTRACT ART. Influenced by CUBISM, Mondrian developed a distinctive, geometric style, which he dubbed neo-plasticism. He founded the art magazine *De Stijl* in 1917. Mondrian's art, such as *Composition in Yellow and Blue* (1925), informed the BAUHAUS movement and the INTERNATIONAL STYLE in architecture. In 1940 he moved to the USA where his pieces, such as *Broadway Boogie-Woogie* (1942–43), became more colourful, reflecting his interest in jazz and dance rhythms.

Monera *See* PROKARYOTE

Monet, Claude (1840–1926) French painter. A founder of IMPRESSIONISM, Monet's piece *Impression, Sunrise*

(1872) gave the movement its name. During the 1860s, he studied in Paris with RENOIR, Sisley, and Bazille. The group painted directly from nature, recording the transient effects of light. Monet often painted the same scene several times, such as the *Gare St-Lazare* (1876–78) and *Rouen Cathedral* (1892–94). In 1870 he stayed with PISSARRO in London, and made studies of the River Thames. In 1883, he settled in Giverny. Despite his failing eyesight, Monet's last series, *Water Lillies* (1906–26) is his most vibrant.

monetarism Economic and monetary theory that argues changes in monetary stability are the principal causes of changes in the economy. It asserts the importance of controlling the money supply as the means of achieving a non-inflationary, stable economy capable of supporting high employment and economic growth. This theory is associated particularly with the theories advanced by Milton FRIEDMAN in the 1950s and 1960s. Monetarism exerted great influence on government policy in the UK and the USA during the 1980s.

Mongolia Republic in central Asia. *See* country feature

mongolism *See* DOWN'S SYNDROME

Mongols Nomadic people of e central Asia who overran a vast region in the 13th and 14th centuries. In the early 13th century, GENGHIS KHAN united the different tribes in the areaand established an empire that stretched from the Black Sea to the Pacific Ocean and from Siberia to Tibet. Genghis Khan's possessions divided among his sons and developed into four khanates, one of which was the empire of the Great Khan (KUBLAI KHAN) that included China. In the 14th century, TAMERLANE, allegedly a descendant of Genghis, conquered the Persian and Turkish khanates and broke up the GOLDEN HORDE. By the end of the century, the true Mongol khanates had practically disappeared.

mongoose Small, agile, carnivorous mammal of the CIVET family, native to Africa, s Europe and Asia. It has a slender, thickly furred body and a long, bushy tail. Mongooses eat rodents, insects, eggs, birds, and snakes. Some may be domesticated, but most are highly destructive. Length: 46–115cm (18–45in). Family Viverridae.

monism In METAPHYSICS, doctrine that reality consists of a single unifying substance, or that the mental and physical are indivisible. SPINOZA saw this substance as God, while HEGEL believed it was the Spirit. German philosopher Christian Wolf (1679–1734) coined the term monism. It contrasts with DUALISM. *See also* PLURALISM

monitor Any of several species of powerful lizards that live in Africa, s Asia, Indonesia and Australia, including the KOMODO DRAGON (*Varanus komodoensis*). Most species are dull-coloured with yellow markings; many are semi-aquatic. Length: to 3m (10ft). Family Varanidae.

monk Member of a monastic community living under vows of religious observance such as poverty, chastity and obedience. *See* MONASTICISM

Monk, Thelonious Sphere (1917–82) US jazz pianist. Along with 'Dizzy' GILLESPIE and Charlie PARKER, Monk was a key figure in the development of BE-BOP. In the early 1950s, he formed his own band, featuring John COLTRANE. His distinctive, idiosyncratic chord structures and dissonances brought humour to the idiom. His greatest compositions, such as 'Round Midnight', 'Straight No Chaser', 'Epistrophy', and 'Crepuscule with Nellie' are jazz standards.

▲ **mongoose** The banded mongoose (*Mungos mungo*) is a formidable snake killer that lives in Africa and India. It relies on speed and agility to evade the poisonous fangs of its arch prey, the cobra. The snake becomes exhausted by its repeated failure to strike, and the mongoose crushes the snake's skull with its teeth. The mongoose is immune to ingested snake venom. It also feeds on small game.

▲ **monkey** The howler monkey (*Allouata caraya*) gets its name from its loud and persistent roars. It lives in the forests of tropical South America, feeding mainly on fruit and nuts, but also eating small animals. Its body grows to 1m (3ft) in length, with its tail reaching a similar length.

M

INTERNET

Monaco
▶ www.monaco.mc

Mondrian, Piet
▶ www. guggenheimcollection.org
▶ www.artsmia.org

Monet, Claude
▶ www.musee-orsay.fr
▶ www.nga.gov
▶ www.nationalgallery.org.uk

Mongolia
▶ www.embassyofmongolia. co.uk

► **Monroe** US actress Marilyn Monroe attained legendary status. A talented comedy actress, she will always be remembered as a vivacious sex symbol. Her career and private life were a constant source of public interest, particularly her marriages to such high profile men as Joe DiMaggio and Arthur Miller, and her alleged relationships with President John F. Kennedy and his brother, Bobby Kennedy. She died of a drug overdose.

MONTANA
Statehood:
November 8, 1889
Nickname:
Treasure State
State bird:
Western meadowlark
State flower:
Bitterroot
State tree:
Ponderosa pine
State motto:
Gold and silver

M

monkey Any of a wide variety of mostly tree-dwelling, diurnal, omnivorous PRIMATES that live in the tropics and sub-tropics. Most monkeys have flat, human-like faces, relatively large brains and grasping hands. They fall into two broad groups – Old World monkeys (family Cercopithecidae) and New World monkeys (Cebidae). The 60 **Old World** species include MACAQUES, BABOONS, BARBARY APES, and LANGUR monkeys. They all have non-prehensile (unable to grasp) tails. They range in distribution from Japan and N China through S Asia and Africa. The 70 species of **New World** monkeys include CAPUCHIN monkeys, SPIDER MONKEYS, and MARMOSETS. They are all tree dwellers, and most have grasping (prehensile) tails. They live in tropical forests of Central and South America. *See* picture, page 523.

monkey puzzle (Chilean pine) Evergreen tree native to the Andes mountains of South America. It has tangled branches, with spirally arranged, sharp, flat leaves. The female seeds are edible. Height to 45m (150ft). Family Araucariaceae; species *Araucaria araucana*.

Monmouth, James Scott, Duke of (1649–85) English noble, illegitimate son of CHARLES II. As captain general,Monmouth defeated the Scots at Bothwell Bridge (1679). Allied with the Earl of SHAFTESBURY, he became leader of the Protestant opposition to the succession of the Duke of York (later JAMES II). The discovery of a plot (1683) forced Monmouth into exile in Holland. Upon James' accession (1685), he launched a rebellion. Despite initial success, Monmouth lacked the support of the nobility and was defeated by the Duke of MARLBOROUGH at the Battle of Sedgemoor. He was executed.

monocotyledon Subclass of flowering plants (ANGIOSPERMS) characterized by one seed leaf (COTYLEDON) in the seed embryo; the leaves are usually parallel-veined. Examples include lilies, onions, orchids, palms, and grasses. The larger subclass of plants is DICOTYLEDON.

monogamy Relationship or MARRIAGE that is an exclusive union between two people. It is commonly supported by legal institutions. *See also* POLYGAMY

monomer Chemical compound composed of single molecules, as opposed to a POLYMER, which consists of repeated monomer units. For example, propene (propylene) is the monomer from which polypropene (polypropylene) is made.

mononucleosis, infectious *See* GLANDULAR FEVER

monopoly Sole supplier or producer of a product or service. A monopolistic industry has complete power over the market for its product and is able to determine levels of output and prices. In many countries, there are regulations to limit or prevent monopolies and mergers.

monotheism Belief in the existence of a single God, as followed in JUDAISM, CHRISTIANITY, and ISLAM.

monotreme One of an order of primitive mammals that lay eggs. The only monotremes are the PLATYPUS and two species of ECHIDNA, all native to Australasia. The eggs are temporarily transferred to a pouch beneath the female's abdomen where they eventually hatch and are nourished by

rudimentary mammary glands. *See also* MARSUPIAL

Monroe, James (1758–1831) Fifth US President (1817–25). Monroe fought in the American Revolution. He was governor of Virginia (1799–1802) before helping to negotiate the LOUISIANA PURCHASE (1803). He was secretary of state (1811–16) under James MADISON before becoming president. Disputes over SLAVERY marred his first term and resulted in the MISSOURI COMPROMISE. His foreign policy successes included the RUSH-BAGOT CONVENTION (1817), and the acquisition of Florida. He is chiefly remembered for the MONROE DOCTRINE.

Monroe, Marilyn (1926–62) US film actress, b. Norma Jean Baker. Her films include *Gentlemen Prefer Blondes* (1953), *The Seven Year Itch* (1955), *Bus Stop* (1956), *Some Like It Hot* (1959) and *The Misfits* (1961). She attended Lee STRASBERG's ACTORS' STUDIO and married playwright Arthur MILLER in 1956. She has lived on as an icon of beauty and has consistently inspired both analysis of and tributes to her life.

Monroe Doctrine Foreign policy statement made by US President James MONROE to Congress in 1823. It asserted US authority over the American continent, and declared that European interference in the Western Hemisphere would be regarded as "dangerous to peace and safety"; also, that the USA would not become involved in the internal conflicts of Europe.

Monrovia Capital and chief port of Liberia, West Africa, on the estuary of the River St Paul. In 1822 freed US slaves settled Monrovia, on a site chosen by the American Colonization Society. Monrovia exports latex and iron ore. Industries: bricks and cement. Pop. (2002) 543,000.

monsoon Seasonal reversal of winds, and their associated abrupt weather changes, that blow inshore in summer and offshore over nearby oceans in winter. The monsoon occurs annually in S Africa and E Asia, focusing on the Indian sub-continent where it occurs as a distinct rainy season – essential to agriculture, but sometimes causing severe flooding.

montage (Fr. *monter*, 'to mount') Cinematic film-editing and artistic technique. Images are cut and spliced in a particular way in order to obtain a desired structural or aesthetic effect.

Montale, Eugenio (1896–1981) Italian poet, journalist, critic, and translator. In 1922 Montale helped to found the literary magazine *Primo Tempo*, and from 1948 he was the literary editor of *Corriere della Sera*. His poetry is characteristically pessimistic in tone, especially in *Cuttlefish Bones* (1925). Montale received the 1975 Nobel Prize in literature.

Montana State in NW USA, on the Canadian border; the capital is HELENA. Other major cities include Billings and Great Falls. Until the USA acquired the area in the LOUISIANA PURCHASE (1803), it was relatively unexplored. In 1852 the discovery of gold brought a rush of immigrants. The Territory of Montana organized in 1864. The opening of the Northern Pacific Railroad in 1883 provided a stimulus to development. The ROCKY MOUNTAINS dominate the SW section of Montana. The E is part of the GREAT PLAINS, drained by the Missouri and Yellowstone rivers. Sheep and cattle graze on the plains. The principal crops (grown with irrigation) are wheat, hay, barley, and sugar beet. The Rockies have large mineral deposits including copper, silver, gold, zinc, lead, and manganese. Oil, natural gas and coal are found in the SE. Industries: timber, food processing, petroleum products; tourism is also important. Area: 381,086sq km (147,137sq mi). Pop. (2000) 902,105.

Mont Blanc Highest peak in the Alps and the second-highest peak in Europe, lying on the border between France and Italy. It was first climbed in 1786. The tunnel under it is 11km (7mi) long. Height: 4,807m (15,771ft).

Monte Carlo Town on the Mediterranean coast. N MONACO. It was founded (1858) by Prince Charles III of Monaco. Today, it is a popular resort noted for its scenery and mild climate. The Casino is a great tourist attraction. Pop. (2002) 15,300.

Montenegro (Črna Gora) Republic in Europe, formerly part of Yugoslavia. *See* country feature

Monteverdi, Claudio (1567–1643) Italian composer, the first great OPERA composer. Many of Monteverdi's operas are lost; the surviving ones include *L'Orfeo* (1607) and *L'Incoronazione di Poppea* (1642). He wrote much religious music and was the last and greatest master of the MADRIGAL.

Montevideo Capital of Uruguay, in the s part of the country, on the River Plate. Originally a Portuguese fort (1717), the Spanish captured Montevideo in 1726, and it became the capital of Uruguay in 1828. One of South America's major ports, it is the base of a large fishing fleet and handles most of the country's exports. Products include textiles, dairy goods, wine, and packaged meat. Pop. (2005) 1,353,000.

Montezuma Name of two AZTEC Emperors. **Montezuma I** (r.1440–69) increased the Empire by conquest. **Montezuma II** (r.1502–20) allowed the Spaniards under CORTÉS to enter his capital, Tenochtitlán, in 1519, and then was captured.

Montfort, Simon de, Earl of Leicester (1208–65) French-born leader of a revolt against HENRY III of England. Montfort distinguished himself on crusade. Resentful at being forced to cede power in Gascony to the future EDWARD I, Montfort led the rebel barons in the Barons' War (1263). He won the Battle of Lewes (1264), and formed a Parliament. Edward defeated and killed him at Evesham.

Montgolfier, Joseph Michel (1740–1810) and **Jacques Étienne** (1745–99) French inventors of the hot-air balloon. In 1782, the brothers experimented with paper and linen balloons filled with hot gases collected over a fire. In November 1783, the brothers launched the first balloon to carry humans.

Montgomery State capital of Alabama, USA, in SE central Alabama. Made state capital in 1847, in 1861 it became the first capital of the Confederate States. In the 1950s, it was the scene of the beginnings of the CIVIL RIGHTS movement. Industries: textiles, fertilizers, machinery. Pop. (2000) 201,568.

Montgomery, Bernard Law, 1st Viscount Montgomery of Alamein (1887–1976) British general. As commander of the British 8th Army in World War 2, he defeated ROMMEL and the AFRIKA KORPS at EL ALAMEIN (1942). He led the invasion of Sicily and Italy. 'Monty' helped to plan the Normandy landings (1944), and, under the overall command of General EISENHOWER, led the Allies in the initial stages. He was Deputy Supreme Allied Commander, Europe (1951–58).

month Time taken for the Moon to travel completely around the Earth. The **sidereal** month is the time of one revolution with respect to the stars, and is equal to 27.32 days. As the Earth is in motion around the Sun, the **synodic** month – from full moon to full moon – is longer (29.53 days) than the sidereal month.

Montpelier State capital of Vermont, USA, at the confluence of Winooski and North Branch rivers, N central Vermont. First settled in the 1780s, it became state capital in 1805. Industries: tourism, machinery, granite quarrying, timber products, maple sugar and syrup, plastics. Pop. (2000) 8035.

Montpellier City in s France, 10km (6mi) N of the Mediterranean coast; capital of Hérault department. Founded in the 8th century, it was a possession of the counts of Toulouse until the 13th century. In the 1960s, the population grew rapidly with an influx of refugees from Algeria. Industries: textiles, metal goods, wine, printing, chemicals. Pop. (1999) 229,055.

Montréal City on Montréal Island and the N bank of the St Lawrence River, Québec province, NE Canada; Canada's second-largest city and the country's chief port. The French settled the site in 1642. It remained in French hands until 1760, when the British seized control. Montréal's growth accelerated with the opening of the Lachine Canal in 1825, connecting it to the Great Lakes. Industries: aircraft, electrical equipment, rolling-stock, textiles, oil refining, metallurgy, chemicals. Pop. (2005) 3,511,000.

Mont-Saint-Michel Rocky isle in the Bay of Saint-Michel, 1.6km (1mi) off the coast of Normandy, NW France. It is the site of a Benedictine abbey built in 708. Ramparts, towers and bastions circle the base of the island and rise to support the Romanesque and Gothic abbey church. An island at high tide, a causeway first linked it to the mainland in 1875.

Montserrat British overseas territory in the West Indies; a volcanic island in the Leeward Islands, Lesser Antilles; the capital

M

MONTENEGRO

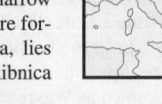

Montenegro separated from the union of Serbia and Montenegro after a 2006 referendum. The country is largely mountainous with a narrow coastal plain. Large areas are forest. The capital, Podgorica, lies at the confluence of the Ribnica and Morača rivers.

CLIMATE

The climate on the coastal plain is Mediterranean, with hot summers and mild, wet winters. Inland areas have warm summers, cold winters and high rainfall. The higher mountains are snow-covered during the winter months.

HISTORY

The region was part of the Serbian Empire until the Turkish invasion of 1355. Ottoman Turks decisively defeated Serbia in 1389, while Montenegro resisted the Sultan's rule. By 1500, most of the territory surrendered to the Ottomans.

In 1799, Turkey recognized Montenegro's independence. In 1851, a monarchy was established, and in 1878 the sovereignty of the state was formally recognized. In 1910, Nicholas I assumed the title of King and sought to expel the Turks. In 1914, he declared war on Austria, and Austro-German armies quickly overran Montenegro. Nicholas was deposed in 1918, and Montenegro united with Serbia.

In 1946, Montenegro became a republic of YUGOSLAVIA. When four Yugoslav republics voted to secede, in 1992 Montenegrins voted to remain part of a Yugoslav federation with Serbia. In 1999, many ethnic Albanians fled to Montenegro to escape Serb oppression in Kosovo.

POLITICS

In May 2006 a referendum was held on independence from Serbia. It was designed, moderated and closely monitored by the EU to ensure a fair process. A little more than the required 55% of Montenegrins voted for independence, following a campaign led by Prime Minister Milo Djukanović. The result was accepted by Serbia, and Montenegro formally became independent in June. The new country was immediately recognized by the rest of the world, and joined the United Nations. The

AREA 13,812sq km [5,331sq mi]
POPULATION 685,000
CAPITAL (POPULATION)
Podgorica (152,000)
GOVERNMENT Multiparty republic
ETHNIC GROUPS Montenegrin, Serbian, Bosniak, Albanian
LANGUAGES Serbian, Albanian
RELIGIONS Orthodox Christian, Muslim (18%)
CURRENCY Euro = 100 cents

government has declared an intention to join the European Union and NATO.

Parliamentary elections were held in September 2006, and parliament chose a new government in December. Djukanović's finance minister, Željko Šturanović, became president.

ECONOMY

The conflicts that followed the dismantling of former Yugoslavia did severe damage to the economy. Montenegro remains industrially underdeveloped, and unemployment and corruption remain serious problems. Bauxite mining and aluminium production form the largest industrial sector. The aluminium and financial sectors were privatized not long before independence. The fastest growth area is tourism, which is attracting substantial foreign investment.

Agriculture is concentrated in the Zeta Valley, and much of the rest of the country is suitable only for sheep farming. Agricultural products include tobacco, grain, and livestock.

INTERNET

Moore, Henry
▶ www.henry-moore-fdn.
co.uk

Moreau, Gustave
▶ www.artmuseums.harvard.
edu

Morocco
▶ www.mincom.gov.ma/
english/e_page.html

and chief port is Plymouth. An active volcano in the Soufrière Hills dominates the island. Christopher COLUMBUS. made the first European discovery in 1493. The British colonized in 1632. It formed part of the Leeward Island colony from 1871 until 1956, when it became a separate, dependent territory of the UK. In 1997, increased volcanic activity prompted the British government to offer aid to the remaining islanders for rehousing in the N or relocation to neighbouring islands. Industries: tourism, light industry and construction, offshore finance, cotton. Area: 102sq km (40sq mi). Pop. (2005) 4,5000. *See* WEST INDIES map

Moon Natural satellite of a planet; in particular the natural satellite of the planet Earth. Apart from the Sun it is the brightest object in the sky as seen from the Earth, being at a mean distance of only 384,000km (239,000mi). Its diameter is 3,476km (2,160mi). As the Moon orbits the Earth, it goes through a sequence of PHASES. Its surface features may be broadly divided into the darker maria, which are low-lying volcanic plains, and the brighter highland regions (sometimes called terrae), which are found predominantly in the s part of the Moon's near side and over the entire far side. The origin of the Moon is uncertain. A current theory is that a Mars-sized body collided with the Earth, and debris from the impact formed the Moon. On July 20, 1969, Neil Armstrong was the first person to walk on the Moon. The chemical composition of the Moon is mainly of silica, iron oxide, aluminium oxide, calcium oxide, titanium dioxide, and magnesium oxide. Lunar rocks are IGNEOUS ROCKS. The Moon has only the most tenuous of atmospheres; Apollo instruments detected traces of gases, such as helium, neon and

MOROCCO

The Kingdom of Morocco lies in NW Africa. Its name comes from the Arabic Maghreb-el-Aksa meaning 'the farthest west'. Behind the w coastal plain the land rises to a broad plateau and the ATLAS Mountains. The High (Haut) Atlas contains the highest peak, Djebel Toubkal, at 4,165 m [13,665 ft]. Other ranges include the Anti Atlas, the Middle (Moyen) Atlas and the Rif Atlas (or Er Rif). E of the mountains lies the arid SAHARA.

CLIMATE

The Atlantic coast is cooled by the Canaries Current. Inland, summers are very hot and dry while winters are mild. From October to April south-westerly Atlantic winds bring rain; there is frequent snowfall in the High Atlas.

HISTORY

BERBERS settled in the area *c.* 3,000 years ago. Jewish colonies were established under Roman rule. In *c.* AD 685 Arab armies invaded Morocco, introducing Islam and Arabic. In 711 Moroccan Muslims, the Moors, invaded Spain. In 788 Berbers and Arabs united in an independent Moroccan state. Fez became a

major religious and cultural centre. In the mid-11th century the ALMORAVIDS conquered Morocco, and established a vast Muslim empire. The ALMOHAD dynasty succeeded the Almoravids. In the 15th century the Moors were driven from Spain, and Spain and Portugal made advances into Morocco. The present ruling dynasty, the Alawite, came to power in 1660 and soon reclaimed most of the European-held territory.

In the mid-19th century, Morocco's strategic and economic potential began to attract European imperial interest. In 1912 Morocco was divided into French Morocco and the smaller protectorate of Spanish Morocco. Nationalist resistance was strong. Abd al-Krim led a revolt (1921–26) against European rule. In 1942 Allied forces invaded Morocco and removed the pro-Vichy colonial government. In 1947 the Sultan, Sidi Muhammad, called for the reunification of French and Spanish Morocco, but France refused and exiled the Sultan in 1953. Continuing civil unrest forced the French to accede to the return of the Sultan in 1955.

In 1956 Morocco gained independence, although Spain retained control of two small

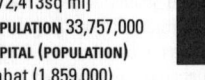

AREA 446,550sq km
[172,413sq mi]
POPULATION 33,757,000
CAPITAL (POPULATION)
Rabat (1,859,000)
GOVERNMENT Constitutional monarchy
ETHNIC GROUPS Arab-Berber 99%
LANGUAGES
Arabic (official), Berber dialects, French
RELIGIONS Islam 99%
CURRENCY Moroccan dirham = 100 centimes

enclaves at Ceuta and Melilla. In 1957, Morocco became an independent monarchy when Sidi Muhammad changed his title to King Muhammad V. In 1961 Muhammad's son succeeded as King HASSAN II. During the 1960s Morocco faced external territorial disputes, especially with Algeria, and internal political dissent. In 1965 Hassan II declared a state of emergency and assumed huge powers. While the 1972 constitution reduced royal influence, Morocco remains only nominally a constitutional monarchy, and effectively the King wields all political power.

In 1976 Spain finally relinquished its claim to Spanish Sahara, and the region became known as WESTERN SAHARA. Western Sahara divided between Morocco and Mauritania. In 1979 Mauritania withdrew from Western Sahara, and Morocco assumed control of the phosphate-rich region. It met fierce resistance from independence movements.

POLITICS

King Hassan II ruled the country in an authoritarian way until his death in 1999. His successor, King Mohamed VI, faced a number of problems, including finding a solution to the future of Western Sahara. Relations with Spain became strained in 2002 over the disputed island of Leila (Perejil in Spanish) in the Strait of Gibraltar. Diplomatic relations were restored in 2003. Another problem faced by Morocco is activity by Islamic extremists. Its opposition to extremism led the United States to designate Morocco as a major non-NATO ally in 2004.

ECONOMY

Morocco is classified as a 'lower-middle-income' developing country. It is the world's third largest producer of phosphate rock. Farming employs 38% of Moroccans. Fishing and tourism are important.

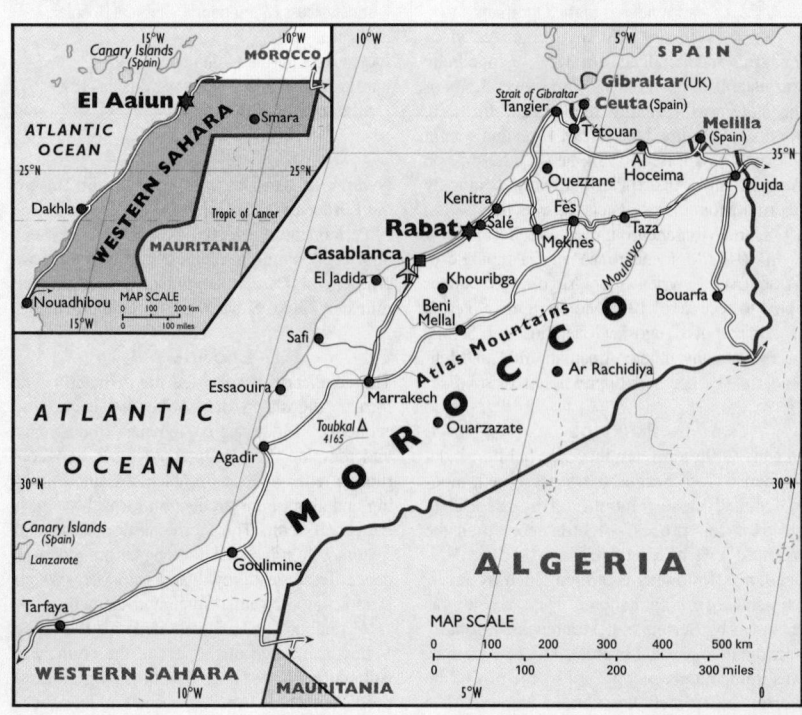

argon. The surface temperature variation is extreme, from 100 to 400K. In 1998, a probe discovered ice near the Moon's poles.

Moore, Henry (1898–1986) English sculptor and graphic artist. Moore is one of the greatest sculptors of the 20th century. The characteristic features of his art are hollowed-out or pierced spaces, such as *Reclining Figure* (1938). Moore based most of his work on natural forms and one of his favourite themes was the mother and child. Many of his sculptures are in parks rather than galleries.

Moore, Marianne (1887–1972) US poet. Her poetry is considered among the most distinguished US verse of the 20th century, with its wit, irony, and wide-ranging subject matter and its highly accomplished technical discipline. She received a Pulitzer Prize for *Collected Poems* (1951).

moorhen (waterhen) Common Old World aquatic bird of the RAIL family, so named because of its liking for rivers and ponds. It has black plumage and a yellow bill, and its long toes lack the webs or lobes typical of other water birds. Length: to 32.5cm (13in). Species *Gallinula chloropus*.

Moors Predominantly BERBER people of NW Africa. In Europe, the name applies particularly to the North African Muslims who invaded Spain in 711, and established a distinctive civilization that lasted nearly 800 years. It was at its height under the Cordoba CALIPHS in the 10th and 11th centuries. The Christian rulers of N Spain gradually reconquered the country until, after the ALMOHAD Empire broke up in the 13th century, Granada alone survived. Granada itself fell in 1492. *See also* ALHAMBRA

moose *See* ELK

moraine In geology, a mound, ridge, or other accumulation of unsorted glacial drift, predominantly TILL. **End** moraines form when a GLACIER is either advancing or retreating, and rock material accumulates at the glacier's edge. **Ground** moraines are sheets of debris left after a steady retreat of the glacier.

morality play *See* MYSTERY PLAY

Moravia Region of the CZECH REPUBLIC, bordered N by the Sudetes Mountains, E by the Carpathian Mountains, and W by Bohemia. Major cities include BRNO and Ostrava. In the 9th century, Moravia established a large empire and adopted Christianity. In the 10th century, the empire fell and the MAGYARS conquered Moravia. It was soon subsumed into the HOLY ROMAN EMPIRE. From the 11th to 16th centuries, it was part of the Kingdom of BOHEMIA. In 1526, it became Austrian HABSBURG territory, and a process of Germanification began. A failed revolution in 1849 led to Moravia becoming Austrian royal land. In 1918 the Habsburgs toppled, and Moravia became part of the new republic of Czechoslovakia. In 1938 Germany annexed S Moravia, and in 1939 Moravia became a German protectorate. Following World War 2, Moravia returned to Czechoslovakia control, and the German population was expelled. In 1960, Moravia divided into S Moravia and N Moravia. A fertile agricultural region, Moravia also has abundant mineral resources, especially coal and iron. These helped the region's rapid industrialization in the 20th century.

Moravia, Alberto (1907–90) Italian novelist. His early novels, including *The Time of Indifference* (1929) and *The Fancy Dress Party* (1940), were critical of fascism, and he was forced into hiding until 1944. Later works include *The Woman of Rome* (1947), *The Conformist* (1951), and *Two Women* (1957).

Moravian Church Protestant Church that originated in the 15th century in Bohemia and Moravia, among followers of Jan HUS. In the 18th century, Moravians began extensive missionary work. Several groups migrated to North America to settle in Bethlehem, Pennsylvania, and Winston-Salem, North Carolina. Today, there are Moravian communities in Europe, North and South America, Africa, and N India.

More, Sir Thomas (1478–1535) English statesman, humanist scholar, and writer of *Utopia* (1516). HENRY VIII knighted Morein 1521. Despite his opposition to Henry's divorce from CATHERINE OF ARAGON, More succeeded Cardinal WOLSEY as Lord Chancellor in 1529. He resigned in 1532, following policy disagreements with Henry. More's principled refusal to sign the Act of Supremacy (1534), which made Henry head of the English Church, led to his imprisonment and execution for treason. *Utopia* portrays an ideal state founded on reason.

Moreau, Gustave (1826–98) French painter and a leading practitioner of SYMBOLISM. His pictures are sensuous and notable for their use of jewel-like colours. Although Moreau spent much of his life in seclusion, he was professor at the École des Beaux-Arts, Paris.

Morgan, Sir Henry (1635–88) Welsh adventurer in the Caribbean. He led a band of buccaneers against Spanish colonies and ships, capturing and looting Panama (1671). In 1672, he was sent back to England on a charge of piracy, but was greeted as a hero and returned to the West Indies with a knighthood as lieutenant governor of Jamaica.

Morgan, Thomas Hunt (1866–1945) US biologist who received the 1933 Nobel Prize in physiology or medicine for the establishment of the CHROMOSOME theory of HEREDITY. His discovery of the function of chromosomes through experiments with the fruit-fly (*Drosophila*) is related in his book *The Theory of the Gene* (1926).

Mörike, Eduard Friedrich (1804–75) German poet. He published several volumes of subtle lyric poetry, including *Gedichte* (1938), a collection he added to in 1848, 1856, and 1867. It ranks among the finest examples of late German ROMANTICISM. His small but influential output also includes the novel *Maler Nolten* (1832).

Mormons ADVENTIST sect, the full name of which is the Church of Jesus Christ of Latter-day Saints. It was established (1830) in Manchester, New York, USA, by Joseph SMITH. Believing that they were to found Zion, or a New Jerusalem, Smith and his followers moved west. They tried to settle in Ohio, Missouri, and Illinois, but were driven out. Joseph Smith was murdered in Illinois in 1844. Brigham Young then rose to leadership, and in 1846–47 took the Mormons to UTAH.

Morocco Kingdom in NW Africa. *See* country feature

Moroni Capital of the COMOROS Islands, on SW Grande Comore. Founded by Arab settlers, it replaced Mayotte as capital in 1958. Chief exports are coffee, vanilla, cacao, and timber and metal products. Pop. (2002 est.) 42,200.

Morpheus In Greek and Roman mythology, the god of sleep and dreams.

morphine White, crystalline ALKALOID derived from OPIUM. It depresses the CENTRAL NERVOUS SYSTEM and is used as an ANALGESIC for severe pain. An addictive drug, its use is associated with a number of side-effects, including nausea. Morphine was first isolated in 1806. *See also* HEROIN

morphology Biological study of the form and structure of living things. It often focuses on the relation between similar features in different organisms.

Morricone, Ennio (1928–) Italian film composer who scored more than 400 films. He is best known for his work with director Sergio LEONE. He wrote the scores for Leone's 'spaghetti westerns': *A Fistful of Dollars* (1964), *The Good, the Bad and the Ugly* (1966), and *Once Upon a Time in the West* (1968). Other works include the classic scores for *The Untouchables* (1987) and *The Mission* (1986).

Morris, William (1834–96) English artist, craftsman, writer, social reformer, and printer. Associated with the PRE-RAPHAELITE BROTHERHOOD (PRB), he founded (1861) the ARTS AND CRAFTS MOVEMENT, a collection of

▲ **Moore** English sculptor Henry Moore was influenced more by ancient Mexican and Sumerian carving than the classical ideals of the Renaissance. He rejected academic techniques in favour of a method called 'truth to materials', which allowed the shape and texture of stone or wood to be an integral part of the work.

M

◀ **Morris** The Red House, Bexleyheath, near London, was designed in 1859–60 by the architect Philip Webb for (and in collaboration with) William Morris. The illustration shows the N and E of the house. It became one of the basic buildings of modern architecture. Morris and Webb created a simple brick building with echoes of traditional architecture in its high-pitched roof, Gothic arches, and Queen Anne windows. Among the house's more revolutionary features is the raising of the kitchen to the ground floor from its customary position in the basement, and the provision of windows to allow servants to overlook the gardens.

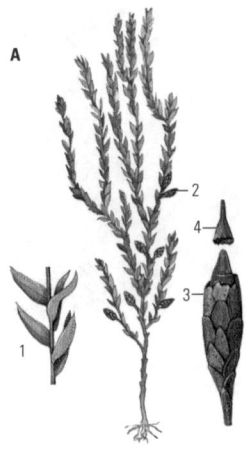

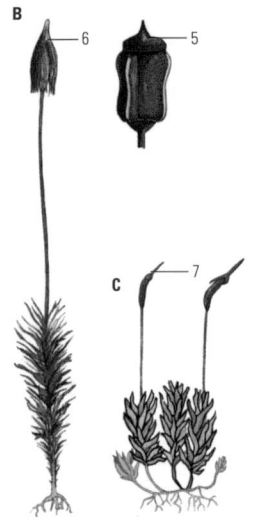

▲ **moss** Mosses vary in growth and colour according to species. *Fontinalis anti pyretica* (A) is an aquatic moss, whose boat-shaped leaves have a sharp keel (1); the capsules are oblong or cylindrical (2, 3) and there is a pointed cap (4). *Polytrichum commune* (B) is extremely common, and has a capsule (5) that looks like a four-sided box. It bears a long, golden brown cap (6) which is released before the spores are dispersed. *Atrichum undulatum* (C) is common on heaths and in woods, and has a capsule (7) with a long, pointed cap. *Schistostega pennata* (D) has flattened, translucent leaves.

decorators and designers influenced by medieval craftsmanship. Morris is perhaps best remembered for his wallpaper designs, which anticipated ART NOUVEAU in their use of the S-curve. In the 1880s he became interested in socialism, writing *The Dream of John Ball* (1886–87) and *News from Nowhere* (1890). In 1890, Morris founded Kelmscott Press.

Morrison, Toni (1931–) US writer, b. Chloe Anthony Wofford. Morrison's debut novel, *The Bluest Eye* (1970), established her as a major voice in AMERICAN LITERATURE. Her chronicles of African-American experience in the rural South include *Song of Solomon* (1977) and *Tar Baby* (1981). *Beloved* (1987), a powerful indictment of slavery, won a Pulitzer Prize. Other works include *Jazz* (1992). She was awarded the 1993 Nobel Prize in literature. She held a chair in humanities at Princeton University (1989–2006).

Morse, Samuel Finley Breese (1791–1872) US inventor of the **Morse code**. A successful artist, in *c.*1832 he became interested in developing a practical electric telegraph. His receiver was based on an electromagnet. Using a simple system of dots and dashes, he set up the first US telegraph from Washington to Baltimore in 1844.

Morton, 'Jelly Roll' (1885–1941) US jazz pianist, bandleader and composer, b. Ferdinand Joseph La Menthe. Morton played in the brothels of Storyville in New Orleans, before making some of the first jazz recordings (1923). Morton and his band, the Red Hot Peppers, combined blues, ragtime, and 'stomp' music on classics such as 'Wolverine Blues' (1923).

mosaic Technique of surface decoration using small pieces of coloured material set tightly together in an adhesive to form patterns or pictures. The technique was employed for floor and wall decorations in ancient Mesopotamia and Greece. Roman mosaics commonly featured a central design or a portrait, surrounded by a decorative geometric border. The art developed rapidly in early Christian times especially during the 4th-6th centuries and continues to be used for floors, church interiors, and wall decorations.

Moscow (Moskva) Capital of Russia and largest city in Europe, on the River Moskva. The site has been inhabited since Neolithic times, but Russian records do not mention it until 1147. It had become a principality by the end of the 13th century, and in 1367 the first stone walls of the KREMLIN were constructed. By the end of the 14th century, Moscow emerged as the focus of Russian opposition to the Mongols. Polish troops occupied the city in 1610, but were driven out two years later. Moscow was the capital of the Grand Duchy of Russia from 1547 to 1712, when the capital moved to ST PETERSBURG. In 1812 Napoleon and his army occupied Moscow, but were forced to flee when the city burned to the ground. In 1918, following the RUSSIAN REVOLUTION, it became the capital of the SOVIET UNION. The failure of the German army to seize the city in 1941 was the Nazis' first major setback in World War 2. The Kremlin is the centre of the city, and the administrative heart of the country. Adjoining it are Red Square, the Lenin Mausoleum, and the 16th-century cathedral of Basil the Beatified. Industries: metalworking, oil-refining, motor vehicles, film-making, precision instruments, chemicals, publishing, wood and paper products, tourism. Pop. (2005) 10,672,000.

Moscow, Grand Duchy of Historic Russian state, centred on the trading city of Moscow. In the late 15th century it emerged from Mongol and Tatar rule as the centre of a unified Russian state, defeating the principality of NOVGOROD and absorbing part of Lithuania.

Moscow Art Theatre Russian theatre, famous for its contribution to naturalistic theatre. It was founded in 1898 by STANISLAVSKY and Nemirovich-Danchenko. The original company consisted of amateur actors from the Society of Art and Literature, who were committed to adopting a more rigorous and professional approach to staging and acting. It was at the Moscow Art Theatre that Stanislavsky developed his influential method principle.

Moselle (Ger. Mosel) River in France and Germany, Rising in the Vosges Mountains, NE France, it flows NW past Remiremont, Epinal, and Toul, turning N to flow past METZ and Thionville and NE to form the Luxembourg-German border. It flows through Germany, emptying into the

River Rhine at Koblenz. The Moselle connects by canals to the rivers Rhine, Meuse, and Seine. Grapes grown along its steep banks between Trier and Koblenz are used to make Moselle wine. Length: 545km (340mi).

Moses (active *c.*13th centuryBC) Biblical hero who, as a prophet and leader of the ancient Hebrews, was the central figure in their liberation from bondage in Egypt and a formative influence in the founding of their nation-state, Israel. His story is recounted in the Old Testament books of Exodus and Numbers. An abandoned Hebrew child, Moses was brought up in the Pharaoh's court. As a man, Moses sought to lead the Hebrews out of Egypt, and eventually was permitted to lead the exodus. God revealed himself to Moses on Mount Sinai, but made the Israelites wander in the desert for a further 40 years before they entered the promised land of CANAAN.

Moses, Grandma (Anna Mary Robertson) (1860–1961) US primitive painter. Grandma Moses only began painting when she was in her late 70s. Her scenes of country life, based on recollections from her youth, became world-famous through prints and greeting cards. Well-known examples are *Out for the Christmas Tree* and *Thanksgiving Turkey*.

Moslem *See* MUSLIM

Mosley, Sir Oswald Ernald (1896–1980) British fascist leader. Mosley became a Conservative MP in 1918, but defected to Labour in 1924. He resigned as junior minister in 1929, and formed the leftist New Party in 1931. In 1932 he founded the British Union of Fascists. Modelled on German and Italian fascist parties, its rhetoric was virulently anti-Semitic. Mosley's blackshirts engaged in confrontational marches, especially in the East End of London. His support for Hitler led to his internment (1940–43). Following the defeat of fascism in World War 2, Mosley's pernicious influence declined.

mosque Islamic place of worship. Mosques are usually decorated with abstract and geometric designs, because ISLAM prohibits the imitation of God's creation. The building's parts include a DOME; a *mihrab* (prayer niche), which shows the direction of MECCA; a MINARET, from which the MUEZZIN calls the faithful to prayer; and a *sahn* (courtyard) often with a central fountain for ritual ablution. The complex often includes a *madressa* (school). *See also* ISLAMIC ART AND ARCHITECTURE

mosquito Long-legged, slender-winged insect found throughout the world. The female sucks blood from warm-blooded animals. Some species carry the parasites of diseases, including MALARIA, YELLOW FEVER, DENGUE, viral ENCEPHALITIS, and FILARIASIS. The larvae are aquatic. Adult length: 3–9mm (0.12–0.36in) Family Culicidae.

Mosquito Coast (Mosquitia) Coastal region bordering on the Caribbean Sea, *c.*65km (40mi) wide, now divided between Nicaragua and Honduras. A British protectorate from 1740, it returned to its original inhabitants in 1860. In 1894, it became part of Nicaragua. International arbitration awarded the N part to Honduras in 1960. The region, which consists mainly of tropical forest, swamp and lagoons, is only thinly populated.

moss Any of *c.*14,000 species of small, simple non-flowering green plants that typically grow in colonies, often forming

▲ **Moscow** The Lenin Mausoleum is on the w side of Red Square, Moscow. After the collapse of the Soviet Union in 1991, Moscow witnessed a growth in foreign business and tourism. There are plans to bury Lenin, rather than continue to preserve his body.

M

dense carpets. They reproduce by means of SPORES produced in a capsule on a long stalk. The spores germinate into branching filaments, from which buds arise that grow into moss plants. Mosses grow on soil, rocks and tree trunks in a wide variety of habitats, especially in shady, damp places. *See also* ALTERNATION OF GENERATIONS; BRYOPHYTE

Mössbauer, Rudolf Ludwig (1929–) German physicist. His doctoral thesis (1958) concerned the emission of GAMMA RADIATION by radioactive nuclei within crystals (the **Mössbauer effect**), which has been used to test Albert EINSTEIN's theory of general RELATIVITY. He shared the 1961 Nobel Prize in physics with the US physicist Robert HOFSTADTER.

motet Musical form prominent in all choral church music from *c.*1200 to 1600. In the 13th and 14th centuries, it consisted of three unaccompanied voice parts. The Renaissance motet of the 15th century, usually in four or five parts, was contrapuntal in style. PALESTRINA composed some of the purest examples of the form. After 1600, there were new developments in the form, including occasional instrumental parts and texts in vernacular languages.

moth Insect of the order LEPIDOPTERA, found in almost all parts of the world. It is distinguished from a BUTTERFLY mainly by its non-clubbed antennae, although there are a few exceptions. Most moths are nocturnal. Like a butterfly, a moth undergoes METAMORPHOSIS. It has a long coiled proboscis for sipping liquid food, particularly the nectar of flowers.

mother-of-pearl (nacre) Shiny substance lining many MOLLUSC shells. It consists of a form of calcium carbonate, deposited in layers interspersed with organic material. Diffraction of light causes the lustre and iridescence of mother-of-pearl. It is used in making buttons and jewellery, and for decorative inlay.

Motherwell, Robert (1915–91) US painter and writer. Motherwell was a pioneer of ABSTRACT EXPRESSIONISM. Perhaps his best-known work is the series *Elegies to the Spanish Republic*. He was the editor of the influential *The Documents of Modern Art* series (1944–57).

motor Mechanism that converts energy (such as heat or electricity) into useful WORK. The term is sometimes applied to the INTERNAL COMBUSTION ENGINE, but is more often applied to the ELECTRIC MOTOR. ROCKET engines are motors that can leave the Earth's atmosphere because they carry both fuel and oxidizer. Ion motors are in development, intended for spacecraft propulsion: a stream of ions, possibly from a nuclear reactor, is accelerated in a strong electrostatic field to produce a reaction that drives the spacecraft.

motorcycle Powered vehicle, usually with two wheels. Gottlieb DAIMLER is credited with building the first practical motorcycle in 1885. Motorcycles are classified in terms of engine capacity, usually 50cc to 1,200cc. Transmission of power to the rear wheel is by chain, shaft or belt. The clutch, accelerator, and front brake controls are on the handlebars. Foot pedals control the gear change and rear brake.

motor neuron NERVE carrying messages to the muscles from the BRAIN via the SPINAL CORD. The cell bodies of some motor NERVES form part of the spinal cord. Motor nerves are involved in both reflex action and voluntary muscular control. Motor neuron disease (MND) is a degeneration of nerve cells that causes muscle loss and eventual death.

motor racing Competitive racing of automobiles. The first organized race took place in 1894, from Paris to Rouen. The first Formula One Grand Prix took place in 1906. The world driver's championship started in 1950, and the constructors' trophy in 1956. The season (March-November) involves 16 Grands Prix. Formula One cars are purpose-built to strict specifications. With average speeds in excess of 240kph (150mph), Formula One circuits have rigorous safety procedures. Formula One is a worldwide sport which attracts major commercial sponsorship. The LE MANS 24–hour endurance race has been held annually since 1923. Other forms of motor racing include rallying and Indy car racing in the USA. Famous road races include the Monte Carlo Rally, the Paris-Dakar Rally and the Lombard-RAC Rally (first held 1927). The Indianapolis 500 was first held in 1911.

Motown Highly successful record company, whose artists made a major contribution to popular music of the 1960s.

Founded in Detroit ('Motor town'), Michigan, USA, in 1959 by Berry Gordy Jr, the company's original roster included Marvin GAYE, Stevie WONDER, Diana Ross, and Smokey Robinson. Berry sold Motown to the MCA company in 1988.

mould Mass composed of the spore-bearing mycelia (vegetative filaments) and fruiting bodies produced by numerous fungi. Moulds live off almost any dead organic material. Although many species are pathogenic (disease-causing), PENICILLIN and a few other ANTIBIOTICS are obtained from moulds. Blue CHEESES such as Roquefort and Stilton are made using mould species. *See also* FUNGICIDE; FUNGUS; SLIME MOULD

moulting Process involving the shedding of the outermost layers of an organism and their replacement. Mammals moult by shedding outer skin layers and hair, often at seasonal intervals. Birds moult their feathers, and amphibians and reptiles their skin. In all cases, HORMONES control the process. The moulting of insects and other arthropods, a process also called **ecdysis**, involves the resorption into the body of materials from the hard outer cuticle of the EXOSKELETON, making the cuticle more fragile. The arthropod then swells its body, and bursts free from the old cuticle and slowly reforms a new one around its swollen body, increasing in size. *See also* METAMORPHOSIS

mountain Part of the Earth's surface that rises to more than 2000ft (510m) above sea level. They are identified geologically by their most characteristic features, and are classified as FOLD, volcanic, or fault-block mountains. Mountains may occur as single isolated masses, as ranges or in systems or chains.

mountain lion *See* PUMA

Mountbatten, Louis, 1st Earl Mountbatten of Burma (1900–79) British admiral, great-grandson of Queen Victoria, uncle of Prince Philip. During World War 2, Mountbatten directed (1942–43) commando raids upon Norway and France. In 1943, he was appointed Allied commander-in-chief in SE Asia, and led operations against the Japanese in Burma. He accepted the Japanese surrender. Mountbatten was last viceroy (1947–48) of British India, overseeing the transition to independence. He died in an IRA bomb attack on his boat.

Mount Rushmore Mountain in the Black Hills, SW South Dakota, USA. From 1927 Gutzon BORGLUM carved out the colossal busts of US Presidents Washington, Jefferson, Lincoln, and Theodore Roosevelt from the granite face of Mount Rushmore. After Gutzon's death in 1941, his son completed the work. Area: 5sq km (2sq mi).

mouse Any of numerous species of small, common RODENTS found in a variety of habitats worldwide; especially the omnivorous, brown-grey house mouse (*Mus musculus*) of the family Muridae. This prolific nest-builder, often associated with human habitation, is considered a destructive pest and is believed to carry disease-producing organisms. It may grow as long as 20cm (8in) overall, and has been bred for use in laboratories and as a pet. Many species within the family Cricetidae are also called mice, as are pocket mice (Heteromyidae), jumping mice (Zapodidae) and marsupial mice (Dasyuridae).

mouse In computing, input device that can be operated with one hand. It is designed to fit in the palm of the hand, with one or more buttons that can be pressed by the fingers of the same hand. When the operator moves the mouse around on a flat surface, it controls the movement of a cursor or pointer on the COMPUTER screen. *See* INTERFACE *illustration*

mouth In animals, the anterior (front) end of the ALIMENTARY CANAL, where it opens to the outside. In humans and other higher animals, it is the cavity within the jaws, containing the teeth and tongue.

Mozambique Republic in SE Africa. *See* country feature, page 530

Mozart, Wolfgang Amadeus (1756–91) Austrian composer. A child prodigy on the piano, Mozart was taken by his father, Leopold, on performing tours in Europe (1762–65), during which he composed his first symphonies. In the 1770s, he worked at the Prince Archbishop's court in Salzburg. Masses, symphonies, and his first major piano concerto date from this time. Opera was his primary concern, and in 1780 he composed *Idomeneo*, which is impres-

▲ **moth** The male Madagascan moon moth (*Argema mittrei*) has a wingspan of 10cm (4in). It has feather antennae that are able to detect from many miles away the scent given off by a female when she is ready to mate.

M

▲ **mouse** The house mouse (*Mus musculus*) is found throughout the world. Due to its close association with people, the house mouse can be a transmitter of diseases. On average, it has a body length of up to 10cm (4in) and a similar length tail.

sive for its rich orchestral writing and depth of expression. In the 1780s, he moved to Vienna, where he became court composer to the Austrian Emperor in 1787. In this decade, he composed and performed his greatest piano concertos, the last eight of his 41 symphonies and the brilliant comic operas *Le Nozze di Figaro* (1786), *Don Giovanni* (1787) and *Così fan tutti* (1790). In the last year of his life, Mozart wrote the operas *Die Zauberflöte* and *La Clemenza di Tito*, the clarinet concerto, and the *Requiem* (completed by a pupil). In all, he composed more than 600 works, perfecting the CLASSICAL style and foreshadowing ROMANTICISM.

Mubarak, Hosni (1928–) Egyptian statesman, president (1981–). He was vice president (1975–81) under Anwar SADAT, and became president on his assassination. Mubarak continued Sadat's moderate policies, improving relations with Israel and the West. He gained Egypt's readmission to the Arab League in 1989, but struggled to stem the rise of Islamic fundamentalism in Egypt.

mucous membrane Sheet of TISSUE (or EPITHELIUM) lining all body channels that communicate with the air, such as the mouth and respiratory tract, the digestive and urogenital tracts, and the various glands that secrete mucus, which lubricates and protects tissues.

muezzin Person who calls MUSLIMS to prayer. In small MOSQUES, the call is given by the IMAM. In larger mosques, a muezzin is specially appointed for that purpose.

Mugabe, Robert Gabriel (1924–) Zimbabwean statesman, prime minister (1980–), president (1987–). In 1963, Mugabe went into exile and co-founded the Zimbabwe African National Union (ZANU). Imprisoned by Ian SMITH's white minority Rhodesian regime, he spent the next decade (1964–74) in detention. After his release, Mugabe, along with Joshua NKOMO, continued to agitate for majority rule. In 1976, ZAPU and ZANU merged to form the Patriotic Front, which became the first black majority government. Mugabe won Zimbabwe's first multi-party elections (1990). In 2000, Mugabe lost a referendum to amend the constitution to allow the government to confiscate white farmers' land. Mugabe attracted international criticism for his support of the subsequent illegal occupation of white-owned farms. Re-elected in 2002, the COMMONWEALTH suspended Zimbabwe after evidence of vote-rigging. In 2003, Mugabe withdrew Zimbabwe from the Commonwealth.

Mughal Alternative spelling of MOGUL

Muhammad (*c*.570–632) Arab prophet and religious leader who founded ISLAM. He was born in MECCA. At the age of 25

MOZAMBIQUE

The Republic of Mozambique borders the Indian Ocean in SE Africa. The coastal plains are narrow in the N but broaden to the S making up nearly half of the country. Inland lie plateaux and hills, which make up another two-fifths of the country, with highlands along the borders with Zimbabwe, Zambia, Malawi, and Tanzania.

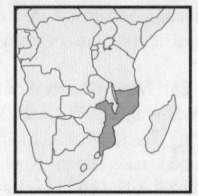

CLIMATE

Most of Mozambique has a tropical maritime climate, with two main seasons. The hot, wet season runs from November to March, with a dry, milder season between April and October. Rainfall varies, being greatest on the NW highlands and lowest on the SE lowlands. Temperatures in the lowlands vary from between 20°C and 30°C [79–86°F] in January, and can go as low as 11°C to 15°C [52–59°F] in July. The interior highlands are much cooler and generally less humid.

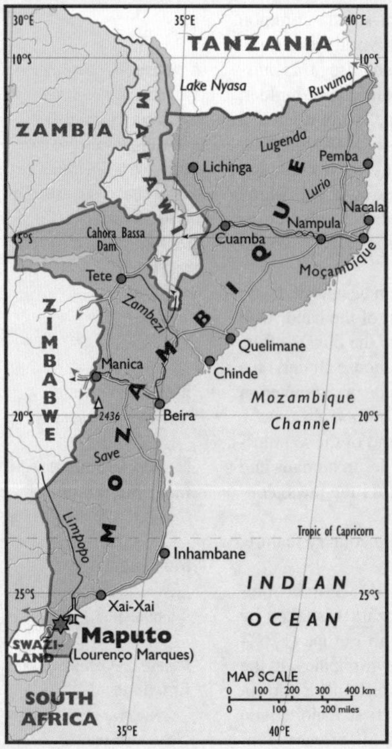

HISTORY

Bantu speakers arrived in the first century AD. Arab traders in gold and ivory settled in coastal regions from the 10th century AD. Vasco da Gama was the first European to discover Mozambique in 1498, and in 1505 Portugal established its first settlement. The area became a source of slaves, and was a major centre of the slave trade in the 18th and 19th centuries. When the European powers divided Africa in 1885 Mozambique was recognized as a Portuguese colony. Unfair land rights, forced labour, and social inequity led to rising nationalist opposition to European rule. In 1961 the Front for the Liberation of Mozambique (FRELIMO) was founded to drive out the Portuguese. FRELIMO launched a guerrilla war in 1964, and it continued for ten years. Mozambique achieved independence in 1975 and the Marxist-Leninist FRELIMO took over the government. Samora Machel became president.

POLITICS

After independence, Mozambique became a one-party state. Its government aided African nationalists in Rhodesia (now Zimbabwe) and South Africa. However, the white governments of these countries helped an opposition group, the Mozambique National Resistance Movement (RENAMO), to lead an armed struggle against Mozambique's government. This civil war, combined with severe droughts, caused much human suffering in the 1980s.

In 1989, FRELIMO declared that it had dropped its Communist policies and ended one-party rule. The war officially ended in 1992 and multiparty elections in 1994 were won by FRELIMO, whose leader, Joaquim Chissano, became president. RENAMO accepted the election

AREA 801,590sq km [309,494sq mi]
POPULATION 20,906,000
CAPITAL (POPULATION) Maputo (1,316,000)
GOVERNMENT Multiparty republic
ETHNIC GROUPS Indigenous tribal groups (Shangaan, Chokwe, Manyika, Sena, Makua, others) 99%
LANGUAGES Portuguese (official), many others
RELIGIONS Traditional beliefs 50%, Christianity 30%, Islam 20%
CURRENCY Metical = 100 centavos

results and stated that civil war would not resume. This led to a period of relative stability. In 1995 Mozambique joined the Commonwealth. In 2004 elections, which RENAMO accused of irregularities, FRELIMO's Armando Guebuza succeeded the presidency.

ECONOMY

In the early 1990s, Mozambique was one of the world's poorest countries. Civil war killed a million people and had driven 5 million from their homes. Combined with devastating droughts and floods, this caused the economy to collapse.

By the end of the twentieth century, economists were praising Mozambique for its economic recovery. Although 80% of the people are poor, support from the World Bank and other international institutions, combined with privatization and rescheduling of the country's foreign debts, led to an expansion of the economy and the bringing down of inflation to less than 10% by 1999. Massive floods at the start of 2000 made thousands homeless and devastated the economy, but in 2001 the currency stabilized and recovery began.

Agriculture is important. Crops include cassava, cotton, cashew nuts, fruits, maize, rice, sugar cane and tea. Fishing is important; shrimps, cashew nuts, sugar and copra are exported. Manufacturing is at a small scale. The large hydroelectric plant at the Cahora Bassa Dam on the ZAMBEZI exports electricity to South Africa.

Map labels: TANZANIA, Lake Nyasa, Ruvuma, ZAMBIA, Lugenda, Pemba, Lichinga, MALAWI, Lurio, Nacala, Cahora Bassa Dam, Cuamba, Nampula, Tete, Moçambique, Zambezi, ZIMBABWE, Quelimane, Manica, Chinde, Beira, Mozambique Channel, Save, MANICA, Limpopo, Tropic of Capricorn, Inhambane, INDIAN OCEAN, Xai-Xai, Maputo (Lourenço Marques), SWAZILAND, SOUTH AFRICA

MAP SCALE
0 100 200 300 400 km
0 100 200 miles

he began working as a trading agent for Khadijah, a wealthy widow of 40, whom he married. For 25 years, she was his closest companion and gave birth to several children. Only one brought him descendants – his daughter FATIMA, who married his cousin, ALI. In *c.*610, Muhammad claimed to have had a vision while meditating alone in a cave on Mount Hira. A voice three times commanded him to 'recite', and he felt his body compressed until he could hardly breathe. Then he heard the words of the first of many revelations that came to him in several similar visions over the next two decades. Muhammad's followers believe that they were passed to Muhammad from Allah or God through the angel Gabriel. At the core of this religion was the doctrine that there is no God but Allah and His followers must submit to Him – the word *islam* means 'submission'. Muhammad gained followers but also many enemies in Mecca. In 622 he fled to Yathrib (MEDINA). Muslims, later took this HEJIRA as initiating the first year in their calendar. Muhammad won more followers and organized rules for the proper worship of Allah and for Islam. Muhammad made war against his enemies and conquered Mecca in 630. Most of the Arab tribes allied with him. In Medina he married Aishah, the daughter of ABU BAKR, one of his strongest supporters. Muhammad is considered an ideal man by Muslims, but he never claimed supernatural powers and is not held to be divine. His tomb is in the Holy Mosque of the Prophet, Medina.

Muhammad, Elijah (1897–1975) Leader (1934–75) of the BLACK MUSLIMS, b. Elijah Poole. He became leader following the disappearance of the Black Muslims founder, Wallace D. Fard. During World War 2, he was imprisoned for encouraging draft-dodging. The rhetorical skills of MALCOLM X gained the movement national attention, and tensions grew until Malcolm was suspended. Under Muhammad's leadership, the Muslim doctrines were codified and membership increased.

Muhammad II (1429–81) Ottoman Sultan (1451–81), considered to be the true founder of the OTTOMAN EMPIRE. Muhammad captured Constantinople (1453) and made it the capital of the Ottoman Empire.

Muhammad Ali (1769–1849) Albanian soldier who founded an Egyptian dynasty. In 1798, he took part in an OTTOMAN expeditionary force to Egypt to drive out the French. He was unsuccessful, but (after the French left) quickly rose to power. In 1805, he was proclaimed viceroy to the Ottoman sultan. In 1811 he defeated the Mamelukes, who had ruled Egypt since the 13th century. Muhammad put down a rebellion in Greece in 1821, but his fleet was later destroyed by the European powers at the Battle of NAVARINO (1827). He challenged the sultan and began a conquest of Syria in 1831, but was compelled to withdraw by European powers.

Muhammad Ali *See* ALI, MUHAMMAD

Muhammad Reza Pahlavi *See* PAHLAVI, MUHAMMAD REZA

Mujaheddin Muslim militants dedicated to waging a holy war. The term is most often applied to the guerrilla fighters of Iran in the 1970s-80s, and of Afghanistan in the 1980s-90s.

mulberry Any member of the genus *Morus*, trees and shrubs that grow in tropical and temperate regions. They have simple leaves, and the male flowers are catkins, while the female flowers are borne in spikes. Several species are cultivated for their fleshy, edible fruits.

mule HYBRID, sterile offspring of a female horse and a male ass; it is different from the smaller **hinny**, which is the result of a cross between a male horse and a female ass. Brown or grey, it has a uniform coat and a body similar to a horse, but has the long ears, heavy head and thin limbs of an ass. The mule is commonly used as a pack animal. Height: 1.8m (5.8ft).

mule deer Game animal that inhabits W USA from Alaska to Mexico. It is red-brown with a black-tipped white tail; the male bears antlers. It is generally solitary, but often gathers in herds in winter. Height: to 1.1m (3.5ft) at the shoulder. Family Cervidae; species *Odocoileus hemionus*.

Muller, Hermann Joseph (1890–1967) US geneticist. Muller found that he could artifically increase the rate of MUTATIONS in the fruit fly (Drosophila) by the use of X-rays. He thus highlighted the human risk in exposure to radioactive material. He received the 1946 Nobel Prize in physiology or medicine.

mullet (grey mullet) Marine food fish found in shoals in shallow tropical and temperate waters throughout the world. Its torpedo-shaped body is green or blue and silver. Size: to about 90cm (3ft); weight: 6.8kg (15lb). Family Mugilidae.

Mulroney, Brian (1939–) Canadian statesman, prime minister (1984–93). In 1983, Mulroney became an MP and leader of the PROGRESSIVE CONSERVATIVE PARTY. In his first term, he signed the Meech Lake Accord (1985), which constitutionally made QUÉBEC a 'distinct society'. In 1987 he negotiated a free trade treaty with the US, which led to the 1992 NORTH AMERICAN FREE TRADE AGREEMENT (NAFTA). The status of Québec continued to vex his administration and, following defeat in a national referendum, Mulroney resigned. Kim Campbell succeeded him as prime minister and party leader.

multi-media COMPUTER system that includes text, audio (sound), and VIDEO (graphics) components. Often the user can interact with the system to interrogate it or even to control or contribute to what is happening on screen. A multi-media product is usually produced on a CD-ROM, which has the necessary high storage capacity for the audio and graphics elements. A multi-media computer must have a CD-ROM drive, a high-resolution colour monitor, and a sound card.

multiple sclerosis (MS) Incurable disorder of unknown cause in which there is degeneration of the myelin sheath that surrounds nerves in the brain and SPINAL CORD. Striking mostly young adults, symptoms may include unsteadiness, loss of coordination, and speech and visual disturbances. MS sufferers typically have relapses and remissions over many years.

Mumbai (Bombay) City centred on a peninsula on the W coast of India, capital of Maharashtra state. In 1534 it was ceded to the Portuguese. In 1661 the British gained control of Mumbai as part of Catherine of Braganza's dowry to Charles II. It was the headquarters of the British EAST INDIA COMPANY until 1858. After 1941 a population boom occurred as a result of immigration, rural migration, and an increasing birthrate. Mumbai has the largest population of PARSIS in India. The city has some fine Victorian public architecture. Mumbai is a cultural, educational, trade, and financial centre, and the site of the world's largest film industry. It is India's second-largest port, after KOLKATA. Educational establishments include the University of Mumbai (1857) and the Indian Institute of Technology (1958). Industries: chemicals, textiles, oil refining, motor vehicles. Exports: cotton, manganese. Pop. (2005) 18,336,000.

mumps Viral disease, most common in children, characterized by fever, pain and swelling of one or both parotid salivary glands (located just in front of the ears). The symptoms are more serious in adults, and in men inflammation of the testes (orchitis) may occur, with the risk of sterility. Vaccination produces life-long IMMUNITY.

Munch, Edvard (1863–1944) Norwegian painter and printmaker. Munch was one of the most influential of modern

▲ **mule** Traditionally common in regions where there is low mechanization, mules have been used as pack animals for many thousands of years. They need very little food and can endure harsh conditions. They are bigger than donkeys, and hardier and stronger than horses.

M

◄ **Munch** *Girls on the Bridge* (1901). Norwegian painter Edvard Munch is famous for his portrayals of mental anguish, which expressed his own deep sense of disillusionment with contemporary life. In 1908, Munch suffered a severe mental breakdown; his gradual recovery is reflected in the more optimistic tone of his later work.

M

artists, inspiring EXPRESSIONISM. Munch's tortured, isolated figures and violent colouring caused a scandal when he exhibited his work in Berlin in 1892, but his paintings inspired progressive artists to form the SEZESSION. Munch compiled a series of studies of love and death entitled a *Frieze of Life*, which included *The Scream* (1893). Other important works are *Ashes* (1894) and *Virginia Creeper* (1898).

Munich (München) City in s Germany, on the River Isar; capital of BAVARIA. Founded in 1158, Munich became the residence of the Dukes of Bavaria in 1255. Occupied by the Swedes in 1632 and the French in 1800, it developed rapidly in the 19th century, when its population grew to more than 100,000. From the early 1920s, Munich was the centre of the Nazi Party. It sustained heavy bomb damage in World War 2. Industries: chemicals, brewing, pharmaceuticals, motor vehicles, precision instruments, tourism. Pop. (2000) 1,195,000.

Munich Agreement (September 1938) Pact agreed by Britain, France, Italy, and Germany to settle German claims on Czechoslovakia. Hoping to preserve European peace, Britain and France compelled Czechoslovakia (not represented at Munich) to surrender the predominantly German-speaking SUDETENLAND to Nazi Germany on certain conditions. HITLER ignored the conditions and, six months later, his troops took over the rest of the country, an action that finally ended the Anglo-French policy of APPEASEMENT.

Munich Putsch (Beer-hall Putsch) Attempted coup in 1923 by Adolf HITLER and the Nazi Party to overthrow the republican government of Bavaria, which began in a beer-hall. The coup proved abortive, and Hitler was arrested and sentenced to five years in the Landsberg Fortress. He served nine months.

Munster Largest of the Republic of Ireland's four provinces, on the Atlantic coast. It includes the counties of CLARE, CORK, KERRY, LIMERICK, N and S TIPPERARY, and WATERFORD. Area: 24,126sq km (9,315sq mi). Pop. (2002) 1,101,266.

muntjac Small primitive Asian DEER. It is brown with cream markings and has tusk-like canine teeth and short, two-pronged antlers. There are two well known species, the Indian muntjac or barking deer (*Muntiacus muntjak*) and the Chinese muntjac (*M. reevesi*). Height: to 60cm (24in) at the shoulder; weight: to 18kg (40lb). Family Cervidae.

muon (symbol μ⁻) Negatively charged ELEMENTARY PARTICLE, originally thought to be a MESON but now classified as a LEPTON. It has SPIN $\frac{1}{2}$, a mass *c*.207 times that of the ELECTRON, and decays weakly into an electron, a NEUTRINO, and an antineutrino. *See also* ANTIMATTER

mural Painting or other design medium applied directly to a wall; a FRESCO is a type of mural. The Egyptians, Greeks and Romans produced murals in TEMPERA as well as fresco. In the Renaissance, mural painting allied with architecture in efforts to create illusions of space. The 20th century accorded more significance to the exterior mural, as exemplified by the works of the Mexicans José Clemente OROZCO and Diego RIVERA. Porcelain and liquid silicate enamels are among the media used in modern murals.

Murasaki, Shikibu (978–1014) Japanese diarist and novelist. Murasaki is best known for her novel, *The Tale of Genji*. Dating from *c*.1000, it is one of the first works of fiction written in Japanese. *See also* JAPANESE LITERATURE

Murcia Autonomous region in SE Spain; the capital is Murcia. It was settled in *c*.225 BC by the Carthaginians, who founded the port of Cartagena and the city of Murcia. The Moors captured the region in the 8th century. In the 11th century, Murcia became an independent kingdom, but in the 13th century it fell to Castile. Murcia is an arid, rugged province with desert vegetation. Historically, the region has been associated with the production of silk, concentrated around the city of Murcia. Area: 11,317sq km (4,368sq mi). Pop. (2000) 1,149,328.

murder Unlawful killing of a person, performed with malice or forethought. Committed accidentally, under sufficient provocation or in self-defence, a killing may not constitute murder.

Murdoch, (Jean) Iris (1919–99) British novelist and moral philosopher, b. Ireland. Murdoch created her own genre, the philosophical love story. Her early novels, culminating in *The Bell* (1958), are short and concise. Her later novels, such as *The Black Prince* (1973), the Booker Prize-winning *The Sea, the Sea* (1978), *The Good Apprentice* (1985), and *The Book and the Brotherhood* (1987), are longer and more elaborate. Recurrent themes include the difference between sacred and profane love and the nature of chance.

Murdoch, (Keith) Rupert (1931–) US media tycoon, b. Australia. In 1952, Murdoch assumed control of his late father's newspaper, *The Adelaide News*. He transferred his successful recipe of sensationalist journalism to the British newspapers *News of the World* (1969) and *The Sun* (1970). In 1973, he moved into the US newspaper market, acquiring the *Boston Herald* and *The Star*. In Britain, he bought *The Times* and the *Sunday Times*. In 1985, Murdoch became a US citizen. He began to diversify into other media industries, acquiring 50% of 20th Century Fox. In 1989, Murdoch launched the first satellite broadcasting network in the UK, Sky Television. He also monopolized the development of digital cable television.

Murillo, Bartolomé Estebán (1617–82) Spanish painter. Murillo made his name with a series of 11 pictures showing the lives of the Franciscan saints (1645–46). His mature style is characterized by soft, idealized figures.

Murray Longest river in Australia. It flows 2,590km (1,610mi) from the Australian Alps in SE New South Wales through Lake Alexandrina, and empties into the Indian Ocean at Encounter Bay, SE of Adelaide. It forms a large part of the border between New South Wales and Victoria.

MUSCLE

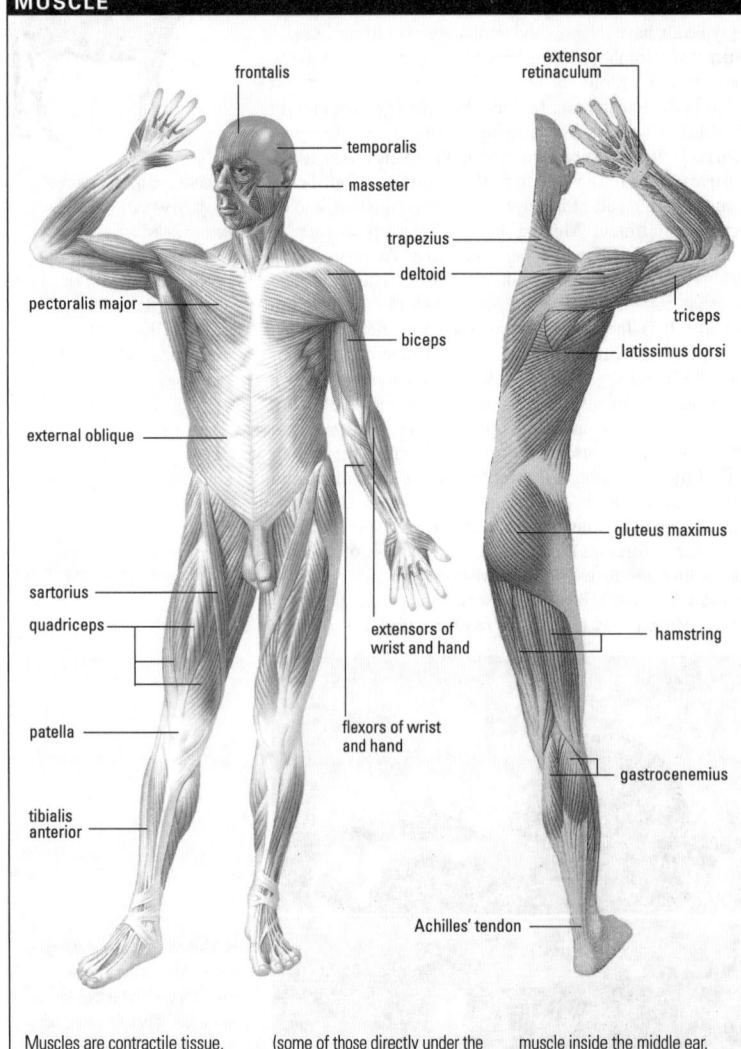

frontalis
temporalis
masseter
trapezius
deltoid
pectoralis major
biceps
triceps
latissimus dorsi
external oblique
extensor retinaculum
gluteus maximus
sartorius
quadriceps
extensors of wrist and hand
hamstring
patella
flexors of wrist and hand
gastrocenemius
tibialis anterior
Achilles' tendon

Muscles are contractile tissue, which can initiate or maintain movement in the body. Muscles comprise 35–40% of the total body weight and there are more than 650 human skeletal muscles (some of those directly under the skin are shown) controlled by the nervous system. Skeletal muscles may be massive, like the gluteus maximus in the buttock, or minute, like the stapedius muscle inside the middle ear. Most skeletal muscles join one bone to another, and have their 'origin' on one immobile bone, and their 'insertion' on the more mobile bone.

Its main tributary is the Darling. The Murray valley contains almost all the irrigated land in Australia.

Muscat (Masqat, Maskat) Capital of Oman, on the Gulf of Oman, in the SE Arabian Peninsula. The Portuguese held Muscat from 1508 to 1650, when it passed to Persia. After 1741 it became capital of Oman. In the 20th century, Muscat's rulers developed treaty relations with Britain. Industries: fish, dates, natural gas, chemicals. Pop. (2001 est.) 540,000.

muscle Tissue that has the ability to contract, enabling movement. There are three basic types: VOLUNTARY MUSCLE (or skeletal muscle), INVOLUNTARY MUSCLE (or smooth muscle), and cardiac muscle. **Voluntary** muscle is the largest tissue component of the human body, comprising *c*.40% by weight. It attaches by TENDONS to the BONES of the SKELETON, and is characterized by cross-markings known as striations; it typically contains many nuclei per cell. Most voluntary muscles require conscious effort for contraction. A muscle whose contraction causes a limb or a part of the body to straighten (extend) is called an extensor. A muscle whose contraction causes a limb or part of the body to bend is called a flexor. **Involuntary** muscle lines the digestive tract, blood vessels and many other organs. It is not striated and typically has only one nucleus per cell; it is not under conscious control. **Cardiac** muscle is found only in the HEART. It differs from the other types of muscle in that it beats rhythmically and does not need stimulation by a nerve impulse to contract. Cardiac muscle has some striations (but not as many as in voluntary muscle) and has only one nucleus per cell.

muscular dystrophy Any of a group of hereditary disorders in which the characteristic feature is progressive weakening and ATROPHY of the muscles. The commonest type, **Duchenne muscular dystrophy**, affects boys, usually before the age of four. Muscle fibres degenerate, to be replaced by fatty tissue.

muses In classical mythology, nine daughters of the Titan Mnemosyne (memory) and ZEUS. Calliope was the muse of epic poetry, Clio of history, Erato of love poetry, Euterpe of lyric poetry, Polyhymnia of song, Melpomene of tragedy, Terpsichore of dance, Thalia of comedy, and Urania of astronomy.

mushroom Any of numerous relatively large fleshy fungi, many of which are gathered for food. A typical mushroom consists of two parts: the mycelium – an extensive, underground cobweb-like network of fine filaments (hyphae), which is the main body of the FUNGUS – and a short-lived fruiting body (the visible mushroom).

music Sound arranged for instruments or voices, for many purposes, exhibiting a great variety of forms and styles. It can be split into categories, including ROCK, JAZZ, BLUES, FOLK MUSIC, SOUL MUSIC, RAP, HOUSE MUSIC, and COUNTRY AND WESTERN. Within classical music, there are distinct historical periods – medieval music (1100–1400), RENAISSANCE MUSIC (1400–1600), BAROQUE (1600–1750), CLASSICAL MUSIC (1750–*c*.1800) and Romantic (*c*.1800–1900) (*see* ROMANTICISM). In the 20th century, various techniques developed, notably SERIAL MUSIC, TWELVE-TONE MUSIC and IMPRESSIONISM. Composers also experimented with ELECTRONIC MUSIC.

musical Genre of popular dramatic light entertainment exemplified by firm plot, strong songs and vivacious dance numbers. It developed at the end of the 19th century from elements of light opera, revue and burlesque. The most popular musicals originated in the USA with the work of George GERSHWIN, Jerome KERN, Richard RODGERS, Oscar HAMMERSTEIN, and Stephen SONDHEIM. Audiences in the 1970s responded to the works of Andrew LLOYD WEBBER and Tim Rice, such as *Jesus Christ Superstar* (1971) and *Evita* (1978). Lloyd Webber was extremely successful in the 1980s with *Cats* (1981) and *The Phantom of the Opera* (1986). Successful film musicals, such as *West Side Story* (1961), *My Fair Lady* (1964) and *The Sound of Music* (1965), are generally based on stage originals. Original film musicals include *Forty-Second Street* (1933), *Meet Me in St Louis* (1944), and *Singin' in the Rain* (1952).

musical form Structural scheme that gives shape and artistic unity to a composition. The standard forms are binary, ternary, rondo, and sonata. Each consists of a number of musical sections or subsections. **Binary** form consists of two sections,

which may be contrasted in idea, key, or tempo, but which complement each other within the musical entity. **Ternary** form consists of a restatement of the first section after a middle section of contrasted material; an example is the MINUET and trio. In **rondo** form, the number of sections varies, but there is at least one restatement of the first section. **Sonata** form, as its name suggests, evolved with the **sonata** and is used most often for the first movement of a sonata or SYMPHONY. The exposition states two subjects, which are developed musically in the middle section, before being reworked in the recapitulation.

musical notation Method of writing down music – its language. Staff notation defines the absolute and relative pitches of notes; crotchets, quavers, etc., indicate their time values.

music hall Stage for popular variety shows, originally tavern annexes, devoted to comic song, acrobatics, magic shows, juggling, and dancing. The popularity of the music hall was at its height in late Victorian and Edwardian England, but declined with the advent of radio and motion pictures in the 1930s. In the USA, it was often known as VAUDEVILLE.

musicology Academic study of music. The term embraces various disciplines, including the study of music history, the analysis of compositions, acoustics, and ethnomusicology. The study of music history began in the 18th century. Musicological research in the 20th century is responsible for the increased interest and performance of early music.

Musil, Robert (1880–1942) Austrian novelist. His masterpiece is the epic novel *The Man Without Qualities* (1930–43), on the closing years of the Habsburg Empire.

musk ox Large, wild, shaggy RUMINANT, related to oxen and GOATS, native to N Canada and Greenland. Its brown fur reaches almost to the ground, and its down-pointing, recurved horns form a helmet over the forehead. When threatened, the herd forms a defensive circle round the calves. Length: to 2.3m (7.5ft); weight: to 410kg (903lb). Family Bovidae; species *Ovibos moschatus*. *See also* OX

musket Early GUN, the first portable firearm equipped with a shoulder stock and a lock (ignition mechanism). Developed in the 16th century, early muskets were less effective than a bow or crossbow, but rapidly became the dominant battlefield weapon due to the ease with which troops could be trained in their use. In the 19th century, they were superceded by the RIFLE.

muskrat Large, aquatic RODENT (a type of VOLE) native to North America. It is a good swimmer, with partly webbed hind feet and a long, scaly tail. Its commercially valuable fur (musquash) is glossy brown and durable. Length, including tail: to 53.5cm (21in); weight: to 1.8kg (4lb). Family Cricetidae; species *Ondatra obscura* and *O. zibethica*.

Muslim (Arabic, 'one who submits') Follower or believer in ISLAM. A Muslim is one who worships ALLAH alone and holds MUHAMMAD to be his final prophet. Today, there are *c*.1 billion Muslims worldwide.

Muslim League Political organization (founded 1906) to protect the rights of Muslims in British India. The League cooperated with the predominantly Hindu National Congress until the 1930s when, fearing Hindu domination, it turned to independent action under the leadership of Muhammad Ali JINNAH. Although pro-British, in 1940 it called for a separate Muslim state, which was achieved when the country was partitioned at independence (1947). At first, the League dominated politics in Pakistan but subsequently split into rival factions.

mussel Any of several species of bivalve MOLLUSCS with thin, oval shells. **Marine** species of the family Mytilidae are found throughout the world in colonies on sea walls and rocky shores,

◄ **muskrat** The scent of the muskrat (*Ondatra zebithicus*), from which it gets its name, comes from special glands located near its anus. The animal was originally a native of North America, but it has been introduced into other parts of the world for its fur.

▲ **mussel** The common mussel (*Mytilis edulis*) is edible and cultivated on ropes hanging from stakes or similar structures driven into seabeds, or on ropes suspended from floating rafts. Both methods involve the collection by settlement of mussel 'seed' or 'spat'. The seed may then be transferred to farming areas free from predators or pollution.

where they attach themselves by means of strands called **byssus** threads. The edible mussel, *Mytilus edulis*, is sometimes cultivated on ropes hanging from rafts. **Freshwater** mussels of the family Unionidae, found in N continents only, produce PEARLS.

Musset, Alfred de (1810–57) French poet and playwright. He is best remembered for his poems which, after 1834, appeared in the periodical *Revue des Deux Mondes*. His four lyrics *Les Nuits* (1835–37) are the most famous of his poems.

Mussolini, Benito (1883–1945) Italian fascist dictator, prime minister (1922–43). Mussolini turned to revolutionary nationalism in World War 1, and in 1919 founded the Italian fascist movement. The fascists' march on Rome in 1922 secured his appointment as prime minister. Mussolini imposed one-party government with himself as *Il Duce* (lit. 'the leader'), or dictator. His movement was a model for Adolf HITLER's Nazi Party, with whom Mussolini formed an alliance in 1936. Imperial ambitions led to the conquest of Ethiopia (1935–36) and the invasion of Albania (1939). Mussolini delayed entering World War 2 until a German victory seemed probable in 1940. A succession of defeats led to his fall from power. Mussolini was briefly restored by the Germans as head of a puppet government in N Italy, but in April 1945, fleeing Allied forces, he was captured and killed by Italian partisans.

Mussorgsky, Modest Petrovich (1839–81) Russian composer, one of the 'Russian Five' who promoted nationalism in Russian music. Mussorgsky's finest work is the opera *Boris Godunov* (1868–69). Other important pieces include the piano work *Pictures from an Exhibition* (1874, later orchestrated by several composers) and *A Night on the Bare Mountain* (1867). After his death, much of Mussorgsky's work was edited and revised, notably by Nikolai RIMSKY-KORSAKOV.

Mustafa Kemal *See* ATATÜRK, KEMAL

mustang Feral HORSE of the Great Plains of the USA, descended from horses that were imported from Spain. The mustang has short ears, a low-set tail and round leg bones. During the 17th century, there were 2–4 million mustangs. Today, only *c*.20,000 survive in SW USA.

mustard Any of various species of annual and perennial plants, native to the temperate zone. These plants have pungent-flavoured leaves, cross-shaped, four-petalled flowers and carry pods. The seeds of some species are ground to produce the condiment, mustard. Height: 1.8–4m (6–13ft). Family Brassicaceae/Cruciferae.

mutation Sudden permanent change in an inherited characteristic of an organism. This change occurs in the DNA of the GENES. Natural mutations during reproduction are rare, occur randomly, and usually produce an organism unable to survive in its environment. Occasionally, the change results in an organism being better adapted to its environment and, through NATURAL SELECTION, the altered gene may pass on to the next generation. Natural mutation is therefore one of the key means by which organisms evolve. The mutation rate can be increased by exposing genetic material to ionizing radiation, such as X-rays or UV light, or mutagenic chemicals, such as tobacco smoke. *See also* EVOLUTION

Muti, Riccardo (1941–) Italian conductor. He made his debut in 1968 with the Italian Radio Symphony Orchestra. In 1973 he became chief conductor of the Philharmonia Orchestra. He was principal conductor of the Philadelphia Orchestra (1981–92) and musical director of La Scala (1986–2005).

Mutter, Anne-Sophie (1963–) German violinist. She made her concerto debut with the Berlin Philharmonic in 1977, having come to the notice of Herbert von KARAJAN, with whom she later recorded all the major violin concertos.

mutualism Relationship with mutual benefits for the two or more organisms involved. An alternative term for SYMBIOSIS, it usually refers to two organisms of different species.

Muybridge, Eadweard (1830–1904) US photographer, b. Britain. After emigrating to the USA in 1852, he became a pioneer of motion photography. From 1878, Muybridge recorded the movements of animals and people by using a series of still cameras. In 1881 he invented the Zoopraxiscope, a forerunner of motion pictures, which projected animated pictures on a screen.

Myanmar Official name of BURMA since 1989.

Mycenae Ancient city in Greece, 11km (7mi) N of modern Argos, which gave its name to the MYCENAEAN CIVILIZATION. Dating from the third millennium BC Mycenae was at its cultural peak between *c*.1580 BC and 1120 BC. It was destroyed in the 5th century BC. Later restored, by the 2nd century AD it was once more in ruins. Heinrich SCHLIEMANN discovered the ruins of Mycenae in 1874–76.

Mycenaean art Greek art of the late Helladic period (*c*.1500–1100BC) of the BRONZE AGE, centred around the fortress-city of MYCENAE . Its greatest achievements came in architecture, which included both grand fortifications and beehive tombs, and in pottery, precious metalwork, and fresco.

Mycenaean civilization Ancient BRONZE AGE civilization (*c*.1580–1120BC) centred around MYCENAE, S Greece. The Mycenaeans entered Greece from the N, bringing with them advanced techniques particularly in architecture and metallurgy. By 1400 BC having invaded Crete and incorporated much of MINOAN CIVILIZATION, the Mycenaeans became the dominant power in the Aegean, trading as far as Syria, Palestine and Egypt, and importing luxurious goods for their wealthy and cultured citadel palaces. The reasons for the collapse of the Mycenaean civilization are uncertain, but it was most likely due to invasion by the DORIANS.

mycology Science and study of FUNGUS

mynah *See* MINA

myopia (short-sightedness) Common disorder of vision in which near objects are seen sharply, but distant objects are hazy. It is caused either by the eyeball being too long or the eye's lens being too powerful, so that light rays entering the eye focus in front of the RETINA. It is easily corrected with concave lenses in spectacles or contact lenses.

myrrh Aromatic, resinous, oily gum obtained from thorny, flowering trees such as *Commiphora myrrha* (family Burseraceae). Known and prized since ancient times, it has commonly been used as an ingredient in incense, perfumes, and medicines.

myrtle Any of numerous species of evergreen shrubs and trees that grow in tropical and subtropical regions, especially the aromatic shrub, *Myrtus communis*, of the Mediterranean region. Its leaves are simple and glossy; the purple-black berries, which follow the white flowers, were once dried and used like pepper. Family Myrtaceae.

mystery play (miracle play) Medieval English drama based on a religious theme. Mystery plays were originally used by the clergy to teach their illiterate congregation the principal stories of the Bible. By the 14th century, they had become a popular entertainment. Each year, the plays were performed by the various craft guilds in a town. In England, mystery plays from four towns have survived: Chester, York, Wakefield, and Coventry.

mysticism Belief in a perception of reality that is elevated above normal human understanding. It may involve some form of spiritual search for unity of self with God or the universe. It is found in most major religions, and exponents of mysticism (mystics) may experience trances, dreams, or visions. In India, mysticism has long been important in HINDUISM, and is based on YOGA. Mysticism in Judaism is apparent in HASIDISM and the CABBALA. Mystics in the Far East have mostly been followers of TAOISM or BUDDHISM.

mythology Literally, telling of stories, but usually collectively defined as the myths of a particular culture. A myth occurs in a timeless past, contains supernatural elements, and seeks to dramatize or explain such issues as the creation of the world (creation myth) and human beings, the institutions of political power, the cycle of seasons, birth, death and fate. Most mythologies have an established pantheon, or hierarchy, of gods who are more or less anthropomorphic. *See also* AFRICAN MYTHOLOGY; CELTIC MYTHOLOGY; CENTRAL AND SOUTH AMERICAN MYTHOLOGY; CHINESE MYTHOLOGY; EGYPTIAN MYTHOLOGY; GREEK MYTHOLOGY; NORTH AMERICAN MYTHOLOGY; OCEANIC MYTHOLOGY; PERSIAN MYTHOLOGY, ANCIENT; TEUTONIC MYTHOLOGY

myxoedema Disease caused by deficient function of the THYROID GLAND, resulting in fatigue, constipation, dry skin, a tendency towards weight-gain and, in the later stages, mental slowness. It mostly affects middle-aged women. Treatment involves administration of the thyroid hormone, thyroxine.

M

Nabokov, Vladimir (1899–1977) US novelist, b. Russia. His family emigrated in 1919, and he settled in Germany. His debut novel was *Mary* (1926). The rise of fascism forced Nabokov to flee, first to France then to the USA (1940). His first novel in English was *The Real Life of Sebastian Knight* (1938). *Bend Sinister* (1947) is a political novel on authoritarianism. His best-selling work, *Lolita* (1955), is a controversial, lyrical novel about an old man's desire for a 12–year old girl. Other works include *Pnin* (1957), *Pale Fire* (1962), and *Ada* (1969).

Nader, Ralph (1934–) US consumer affairs activist and lobbyist. His book *Unsafe at any Speed* (1965) revealed blatant compromise of passenger safety for the sake of costs in the US automobile industry. He subsequently examined issues concerned with mining, nuclear power, meat processing, and airlines. As the Green Party candidate in the 2000 US presidential elections, Nader gained 4% of the vote.

Nadi, Aldo (1899–1965) Italian fencer, regarded by many as the greatest of the 20th century. In 1920, he won Olympic gold in all three modern weapons (foil, epee and sabre). He acquired notoriety for his 1924 duel with Adolfo Contronei.

nadir Point on the CELESTIAL SPHERE vertically below the observer. It is diametrically opposite the ZENITH.

Nagaland State in NE India; the capital is Kohima. Briefly ruled by Burma in the early 19th century, it gradually came under British control, then became a separate state in 1963. The Nagas live in an underdeveloped tribal society with a strong separatist movement. Crops: rice, potatoes, sugar cane. Area: 16,579sq km (6,399sq mi). Pop. (2001) 1,988,636.

Nagasaki Seaport and prefecture in w Kyushu island, sw Japan. In the 16th century, Nagasaki was the first Japanese port to receive Western ships and became a centre of Christian influence. During Japan's isolation (1639–1859) it was the only port open to foreign trade. On August 9, 1945, a US atomic bomb destroyed the inner city, killing more than 70,000 people. Industries: shipbuilding, heavy engineering, fishing, mining. Pop. (2000) 438,635; 1,532,235 (prefecture).

Nagorno-Karabakh Autonomous region of Azerbaijan, between the Caucasus and Karabakh mountains. The capital is Stepanakert. During the 19th century the region was absorbed into the Russian empire. In 1921 it was annexed to the Azerbaijan republic. In 1991 the region declared its independence and Azerbaijan responded by imposing direct rule. The ensuing civil war claimed thousands of lives. In 1993 Armenian troops occupied the enclave and a peace agreement was reached in 1994. The main activities are farming and silk production. Area: 4,400sq km (1,700sq mi). Pop. (2002 est.) 143,100

Nagoya City and Pacific port on Honshu island, central Japan. Nagoya grew up around the 17th-century castle. Industries: iron and steel, textiles, motor vehicles, aircraft. Pop. (2000) 2,172,000.

Nagpur City in Maharashtra state, w central India. Founded in the 18th century as the capital of the Kingdom of Nagpur, it became the capital of Berar state (from 1903) and of Madhya Pradesh state (1947–56). Industries: metal goods, transport equipment, cigarettes, textiles, pottery, glass, leather, pharmaceuticals, brassware. Pop. (2005) 2,359,000.

Nagy, Imre (1896–1958) Hungarian statesman, premier (1953–55, 1956). He enacted liberal reforms of the Hungarian economy and society. Under pressure from the Soviet Union, Nagy was dismissed from the Hungarian Communist Party. The Hungarian Revolution (1956) led to Nagy's reinstatement as premier. Soviet tanks crushed the uprising and handed power to János KÁDÁR. Nagy was executed for treason.

Nahuatl Native American language of the UTO-AZTECAN linguistic family of s USA and Central America. Formerly the language of the Aztecs, today it is spoken by about one million people, mostly in Mexico.

naiad In Greek mythology, female figure or NYMPH, identified with streams, rivers, and lakes.

Naipaul, V.S. (Vidiadhar Surajprasad) (1932–) West Indian novelist and short-story writer. He was educated in his native Trinidad and at Oxford, but later settled in London. His novels include *A House for Mr Biswas* (1961), the Booker Prize-winning *In a Free State* (1971), and *A Bend in the River* (1979). His travelogues include *Among the Believ-

ers: An Islamic Journey* (1981) and *A Turn in the South* (1989). Naipaul received the 2001 Nobel Prize in literature.

Nairobi Capital and largest city of Kenya, in the s central part of the country. Founded in 1899, Nairobi replaced MOMBASA as the capital of the British East Africa Protectorate in 1905. Nairobi has a national park (1946), a university (1970) and several institutions of higher education. It is an administrative and commercial centre. Industries: cigarettes, textiles, chemicals, food processing, furniture, glass. Pop. (2005) 2,818,000.

Nakhichevan Autonomous republic of Azerbaijan, bounded N and E by Armenia, s and w by Iran, and w by Turkey; the capital is Nakhichevan. Under Persian domination from the 13th to the 19th century, it became part of Russia in 1828. In 1924, it was made an autonomous republic within the Soviet Union. In 1991, it became part of the independent republic of Azerbaijan, but was subsequently disputed between Armenia and Azerbaijan. Nakhichevan is mountainous and subject to earthquakes. Crops: grains, cotton, tobacco, fruit, grapes. Industries: mining, silk textile production, food processing. Area: 5,500sq km (2,120sq mi). Pop. (2002 est.) 366,500.

Namib Desert Coastal desert region of Namibia, between the Atlantic Ocean and the interior plateau. It has less than 1cm (0.4in) of rain a year and is almost completely barren. Diamonds are mined. Length: *c.*1,900km (1,200mi).

Namibia Republic in sw Africa. *See* country feature, p. 536.

Nanak (1469–1539) Indian spiritual teacher, founder and first guru of SIKHISM. Nanak preached a monotheistic religion that combined elements of both HINDUISM and ISLAM. In 1519, he founded the town of Kartarpur in Punjab, where he acquired many followers.

Nan-ch'ang (Nan-ch'ang-hsien) City in SE China; capital of Jiangxi province. It was founded as a walled city in the 3rd century BC. Army Day (August 1) commemorates the failed communist coup here in 1927. Industries: rice, tea, cotton textiles, machinery. Pop. (2005) 1,742,000.

Nanjing (Nanking) City on the River Yangtze, E China; capital of Jiangsu province. Founded in the 8th century BC it served as the capital of China at various times. The Treaty of Nanking (1842) ended the OPIUM WAR and opened five Chinese ports to foreign trade. It was the seat of SUN YAT-SEN's provisional presidency in 1912. In 1937, during the SINO-JAPANESE WAR, the city was captured by the Japanese, who massacred more than 100,000 of the population. Industries: iron and steel, oil refining, chemicals. Pop. (2005) 2,806,000.

nanometre (symbol nm) Unit of distance, equal to 10^{-9} metre. It is used in the measurement of intermolecular distances and wavelengths. It has superseded the ANGSTROM as the accepted unit for such measurements.

nanotechnology Range of technologies whose dimensions are on the NANOMETRE scale. The term is used both for the materials science of nano-scale particles, and for the more advanced idea of entire machines a few nanometres across. The former technologies are now beginning to enter practical use, while the latter are still largely theoretical. If nano-machines prove possible, they would be able to perform sophisticated chemical manipulations directly at a molecular level.

Nansen, Fridtjof (1861–1930) Norwegian explorer and statesman. After a pioneering crossing of Greenland in 1888, Nansen built a ship designed to withstand ice so that currents would carry her to the North Pole. She failed, but crossed the Arctic Ocean undamaged (1893–96). Nansen attempted to reach the Pole with skis and kayaks. He failed but set a record for farthest north. After 1918 Nansen was involved in humanitarian work. He received the Nobel Peace Prize in 1922.

Nantes City in w France, at the mouth of the River Loire; capital of Loire-Atlantique department. France's sixth-largest city, it has been a trading centre since Roman times. In the 10th century, it was captured from Norse invaders by the Duke of Brittany. Nantes remained a residence of the Dukes until 1524. The city developed around its port and the trade in sugar and ebony. By the 18th century, it was France's largest port. During World War 2, it was a centre of the resistance movement. Industries: shipbuilding, sugar refining. Pop. (1999) 277,728.

Nantes, Edict of (1598) French royal decree establishing toleration for HUGUENOTS (Protestants). It granted freedom

N/n, the 14th letter of the alphabet, is derived from the Semitic letter **nun,** *which was the pictorial representation of a fish. It was adopted by the Greeks as the letter* **nu** *and subsequently by the Romans.*

▲ **Napoleon I** As Emperor of the French, he spent his entire reign at war. He took control of most of Europe, but his invasion of Russia (1812) was a disaster. He was finally defeated at Waterloo (1815).

of worship and legal equality for Huguenots within limits, and ended the Wars of RELIGION. The Edict was revoked by LOUIS XIV in 1685, causing many Huguenots to emigrate.

napalm (naphthalene palmitate) Gelatinous petroleum used to make bombs and as fuel for flame-throwers. It was widely used by US forces in Vietnam. When napalm hits its target, it spreads out, clinging to and burning everything it touches.

naphtha Any of several volatile liquid-hydrocarbon mixtures. Naphtha first appears in the writings of Pliny the Elder in the 1st century. Alchemists used the word for various liquids of low boiling point. Several types of products are now called naphtha, including coal-tar naphtha and petroleum naphtha.

naphthalene ($C_{10}H_8$) Important hydrocarbon composed of two BENZENE rings sharing two adjacent carbon atoms. A white, waxy solid, naphthalene is soluble in ether and hot alcohol and is highly volatile. It is used in mothballs, dyes and synthetic resins, and in the high-temperature cracking process of petroleum. Properties: m.p. 80°C (176°F); b.p. 218°C (424°F).

Napier, John (1550–1617) Scottish mathematician. He developed 'Napier's bones', an early calculating apparatus, and LOGARITHMS (1614), a powerful mathematical technique.

Naples (Napoli) City on the Bay of Naples, s Italy; capital of CAMPANIA. Founded in c.600 BC as a Greek colony, it was conquered by Rome in the 4th century BC. Successively ruled by the Byzantines, Normans, Spanish and Austrians, it became the capital of the Kingdom of the Two Sicilies in 1734, joining the Kingdom of Italy in 1860. Industries: textiles, leather, steel, shipbuilding, aircraft, telecommunications, tourism. Pop. (2000) 993,000.

Napoleon I (1769–1821) (Napoleon Bonaparte) Emperor of the French (1804–15), b. Corsica. One of the greatest military leaders of modern times, he became a brigadier (1793) after driving the British out of Toulon. In 1796 he married JOSÉPHINE de Beauharnais and gained command in Italy, where he defeated the Austrians and Sardinians (see FRENCH REVOLUTIONARY WARS). In 1798 he launched an invasion of Egypt, but was defeated by NELSON at the Battle of Abukir Bay. In 1799 he returned to Paris, where his coup of 18 Brumaire (November 9) set up the Consulate. As First Consul, he enacted domestic reforms such as the CODE NAPOLÉON, while defeating the Austrians at Marengo (1800) and making peace with the British at Amiens (1802). Efforts to extend French

NAMIBIA

The Republic of Namibia lies on the Atlantic coast to the s of Angola and to the N of South Africa. The coastal region contains the arid NAMIB DESERT, mostly between 900 and 2,000m [2,950–6,560ft] above sea level, which is virtually uninhabited. Inland is a central plateau, bordered by a rugged spine of mountains stretching N–S.

E Namibia contains part of the KALAHARI, a semi-desert area which extends into Botswana. The ORANGE River forms Namibia's s border, while the Cunene and Cubango rivers form parts of the N borders.

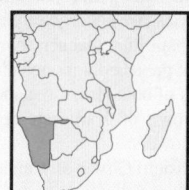

The Portuguese arrived in the early 15th century.

European colonization began in the 19th century. From 1868 Germans began to operate along the coast, and in 1884 Germany claimed the region as a protectorate and subsumed it into German South West Africa. In the 1890s the Germans forcibly removed the Damara and Herero from the Windhoek area. About 65,000 Herero were killed when they revolted against their eviction. The discovery of diamonds in 1908 increased European settlement. During World War 1 Namibia was occupied by South African troops from 1915. In 1920 the League of Nations gave South Africa a mandate to govern the country. After World War 2 South Africa refused to relinquish control, instead treating Namibia as a South African province. In 1966 the SOUTH WEST AFRICA PEOPLE'S ORGANIZATION (SWAPO) began a guerrilla war against South African rule. In 1968 the United Nations called on South Africa to withdraw and in 1971 the International Court of Justice declared that South Africa's rule over Namibia was illegal. South Africa refused to comply. International pressure forced South Africa to promise Namibia independence, but South Africa then qualified the terms. Civil war raged from 1977. A UN security council peace settlement was finally implemented in 1989. SWAPO won multi-party elections in November 1989. In March 1990 Namibia became an independent republic.

AREA 824,292sq km [318,259sq mi]
POPULATION 2,055,000
CAPITAL (POPULATION) Windhoek (147,000)
GOVERNMENT Multiparty republic
ETHNIC GROUPS Ovambo 50%, Kavango 9%, Herero 7%, Damara 7%, White 6%, Nama 5%
LANGUAGES English (official), Afrikaans, German, indigenous dialects
RELIGIONS Christianity 90% (Lutheran 51%)
CURRENCY Namibian dollar = 100 cents

became the scene of a rebellion in 1999 when a small band of rebels tried, unsuccessfully, to seize the regional capital, Kutima Mulilo, as part of an attempt to make the Caprivi Strip independent. The strip is populated mainly by Lozi people, who resent SWAPO rule. Lozi separatists also live in Botswana and Zambia.

ECONOMY

Namibia has important mineral reserves including diamonds, zinc, uranium, copper, lead and tin. Mining is the most valuable economic activity; by the mid-1990s minerals accounted for as much as 90% of exports, with diamonds making up over half the total revenue from minerals.

Farming employs around two out of every five Namibians, although many farmers live at subsistence level, contributing little to the economy. Because most of the land in Namibia has too little rainfall for arable farming, the principal agricultural activities are cattle and sheep raising. However, livestock raising has been hit in the last 20 years by extended droughts that have depleted the number of farm animals. The chief crops are maize, millet and vegetables.

Fishing in the Atlantic Ocean is also important, although overfishing has reduced the yields of Namibia's fishing fleet. The country has few manufacturing industries apart from jewellery-making, some metal smelting, the processing of farm products, such as karakul pelts – sheepskins used to make fur coats – and textiles. Tourism is developing, especially in the Etosha National Park in N Namibia, which is rich in wildlife.

CLIMATE

Namibia has a warm and largely arid climate. Daily temperatures range from about 24°C [75°F] in January to 20°C [68°F] in July. Annual rainfall ranges from about 500mm [20in] in northern areas to between 25 and 150mm [1–6in] in the s. Most of the rain falls in summer.

HISTORY

The earliest inhabitants of the region were the nomadic SAN. From the 14th century AD they were gradually displaced by Bantu-speakers such as the Ovambo, Kavango and Herero who migrated into Namibia from the north.

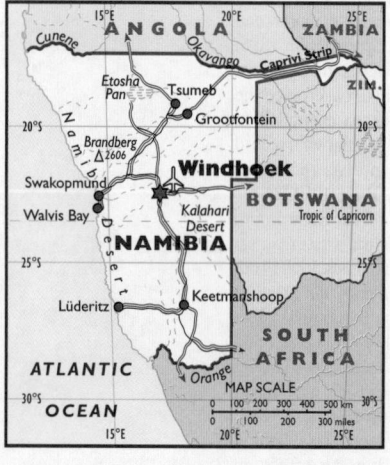

POLITICS

After achieving independence, the government pursued a policy of 'national reconciliation'. An enclave on Namibia's coast, called Walvis Bay (Walvisbaai), remained part of South Africa until 1994 when South Africa transferred it to Namibia. In 2004 Sam NUJOMA of the South West African People's Organization (SWAPO), who had been president since independence, retired. His successor was Hifikepunye Pohama.

Namibia's Caprivi Strip is a geographical oddity. The strip was given to Germany by European powers in the late 19th century so that Germany would have access to the River Zambezi. It

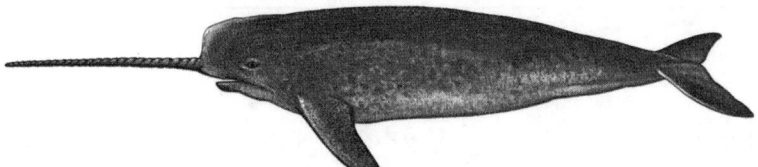

power led to the NAPOLEONIC WARS (1803–15). After the Battle of TRAFALGAR (1805) Britain controlled the seas, but Napoleon's Grande Armée continued to score notable land victories at AUSTERLITZ (1805) and Jena (1806). The CONTINENTAL SYSTEM attempted to defeat Britain by a commercial blockade that led indirectly to the PENINSULAR WAR. In 1810, after obtaining a divorce from Joséphine, Napoleon married MARIE LOUISE who bore him a son, the future NAPOLEON II. In 1812, Napoleon invaded Russia with a million-man army. Forced by hunger to retreat, more than 400,000 soldiers perished in the Russian winter. In 1813, Napoleon was routed by a European coalition at Leipzig. In March 1814, Paris was captured and he was exiled to ELBA. In March 1815, he escaped and returned to France, overthrowing the BOURBON King LOUIS XVIII. The HUNDRED DAYS of his return to power ended with defeat at the Battle of WATERLOO (June 1815). Napoleon was exiled to St Helena, where he died.

Napoleon II (1811–32) Son of NAPOLEON I and MARIE LOUISE. In 1814, he was taken by his mother to Austria, and in 1818 his grandfather, Francis I of Austria, conferred on him the title of Duke of Reichstadt.

Napoleon III (1808–73) (Louis Napoleon) Emperor of France (1852–70), nephew of NAPOLEON I. He twice tried coups in France (1836, 1840). Returning from exile after the FEBRUARY REVOLUTION (1848), he became president of the Second Republic. In 1851 he assumed autocratic powers and established the Second Empire (1852), taking the title Napoleon III. His attempt to establish a Mexican Empire under the Archduke MAXIMILIAN ended in disaster, and in 1870 he was provoked by BISMARCK into the FRANCO-PRUSSIAN WAR. His defeat at Sedan led to a republican rising.

Napoleonic Wars (1803–15) Campaigns by a series of European coalitions against French expansion under NAPOLEON I. In 1803, Britain declared war and formed the **Third Coalition** with Austria, Russia, and Sweden in 1804. Napoleon defeated the Austrians at Ulm, and the Russians and Austrians at AUSTERLITZ (both 1805), but the British under Admiral NELSON won a decisive naval victory at TRAFALGAR (1805). Prussia joined the **Fourth Coalition** (1806) but was decisively defeated at Jena. Resistance to the French occupation of Portugal (1807) began the PENINSULAR WAR. In 1808, French troops were sent to quell a Spanish rebellion, but were faced by the British army led by the Duke of WELLINGTON. The **Fifth Coalition** collapsed with the defeat of Austria at Wagram (1809). In 1812, Napoleon invaded Russia. Bitter winter forced his retreat from Moscow, and much of his army died of starvation, hypothermia or were killed by the pursuing Russian forces under Mikhail Kutuzov. The **Sixth Coalition** defeated Napoleon at Leipzig (October 1813). In March 1814, Allied forces entered Paris. While the coalition was negotiating at the Congress of VIENNA, Napoleon escaped from exile in Elba and overthrew LOUIS XVIII. War renewed during the HUNDRED DAYS of Napoleon's return to power and ended in his final defeat at the Battle of WATERLOO (June 1815).

Nara City on S Honshu island; capital of Nara prefecture, Japan. A centre of Japanese Buddhism, Nara was founded in 706. It was Japan's first imperial capital (710–784). Todaiji (East Great Temple) houses a 22m (72ft) tall bronze statue of Buddha. The 7th-century Horyuji temple is reputedly Japan's oldest building. Industries: textiles. Pop. (2000) 366,196.

Narcissus In Greek mythology, a beautiful youth who rejected the love of the nymph ECHO and was punished by being made to fall in love with his own reflection in a pond. He pined away and was turned into a flower.

narcissus Genus of Old World, bulb-forming, garden flowers, including daffodils and jonquils. The long, pointed leaves surround yellow, orange or white trumpet-like flowers. Family Amaryllidaceae.

narcotic Any drug that induces sleep and/or relieves pain. The term is used especially in relation to opium and its derivatives. These drugs have largely been replaced as sedatives because of their addictive properties, but they are still used for severe pain, notably in terminal illness. Other narcotics include alcohols and BARBITURATES.

narwhal Small, toothed Arctic WHALE. The male has a twisted horn, half as long as its body, which develops from a tooth and protrudes horizontally through one side of the upper lip. Length: up to 5m (16ft). Species *Monodon monoceros*.

NASA *See* NATIONAL AERONAUTICS AND SPACE ADMINISTRATION

Naseby, Battle of (June 14, 1645) Final battle of the first English CIVIL WAR. The Parliamentarian New Model Army, led by Oliver CROMWELL and Thomas FAIRFAX defeated the Royalist troops commanded by Prince RUPERT.

Nash, John (1752–1835) English architect and town planner, an important figure in the REGENCY STYLE. He designed Regent's Park and Regent Street, London, and rebuilt the Royal Pavilion, Brighton (1815–23).

Nash, Ogden (1902–71) US poet. Among his many volumes of humorous and satirical poetry are *Free Wheeling* (1931), *I'm a Stranger Here Myself* (1938), and *Everyone But Me and Thee* (1962). He also wrote the lyrics for the musical *One Touch of Venus* (1943).

Nash, Paul (1889–1946) English painter and graphic artist. Devoted to the English countryside, he was also closely in touch with European modernism. SURREALISM helped to stimulate the poetic, dream-like style of his landscapes, as in *The Menin Road* (1918) and *Landscape from a Dream* (1938).

Nash, Sir Walter (1882–1968) New Zealand statesman, prime minister (1957–60), b. England. Nash emigrated to New Zealand in 1909, and became a member of Parliament in 1929. As finance minister (1935–49), he helped to introduce the Labour Party's wide-ranging social security scheme.

Nashville Capital of Tennessee, USA, a port on the Cumberland River. Settled in 1779, it became state capital in 1843. During the Civil War, it was the scene of a decisive Union victory. The city merged with Davidson County in 1963. It is a country music centre and the home of the Country Music Hall of Fame (Grand Old Opry). The city has many neo-classical buildings. Industries: music, publishing. Pop. (2000) 569,891.

Nassau Capital of the BAHAMAS, West Indies, a port on the NE coast of New Providence Island. Founded in the 1660s by the British and named Charles Towne, it was renamed in 1695. It is a commercial centre and popular winter tourist resort. Pop. (2002 est.) 179,300.

Nasser, Gamal Abdel (1918–70) Egyptian soldier and statesman, prime minister (1954–56) and first president of the Republic of Egypt (1956–70). In 1942 Nasser founded the Society of Free Officers, which secretly campaigned against British imperialism and domestic corruption. He led the 1952 army coup against King FAROUK. He quickly ousted the nominal prime minister General Muhammad Neguib and assumed presidential powers. Nasser's nationalization of the SUEZ CANAL (1956) prompted an abortive Anglo-French and Israeli invasion. Nasser emerged as champion of the Arab world. He formed the short-lived United Arab Republic (1958–61) with Syria. He briefly resigned after Israel won the SIX-DAY WAR (1967). The crowning achievement of his brand of Arab socialism was the completion of the ASWAN DAM (1970).

Natal Former name (1910–94) of KWAZULU-NATAL

Nation, Carry Amelia Moore (1846–1911) US social reformer and temperance leader. Her alcoholic first husband turned her against liquor. Wielding a hatchet, which became her symbol, Nation began her anti-saloon campaign in the 1890s in Kansas, where saloons were illegal, and carried her crusade into several other states.

National Aeronautics and Space Administration (NASA) US government agency that organizes civilian aeronautical and space research programmes. It has departments throughout the USA. The Lyndon B. Johnson Space Center in Houston, Texas, is responsible for manned space flights. Space

▲ **narwhal** Generally found only in male narwhals, the distinctive tusk (*Monodon monoceros*) develops from a tooth in the upper jaw: its function remains unknown. Narwhals feed on fish and squid.

INTERNET

Namibia
▶ www.namibweb.com

Napoleon I
▶ www.napoleonguide.com

Nash, Ogden
▶ www.westegg.com/nash

Nash, Sir Walter
▶ www.labour.org.nz/labour_team/our_history/former_prime_ministers/index.html

N

▲ **Nasser** First president of the Republic of Egypt, Gamal Abdel Nasser was a British-trained soldier. In 1952 he led the army coup that ousted King Farouk. Becoming president in 1956, he provoked an international crisis by nationalizing the Suez Canal. Having fought in the 1948 Arab-Israeli War, he brought on the 1967 Arab-Israeli War by blocking the Israeli port of Elat.

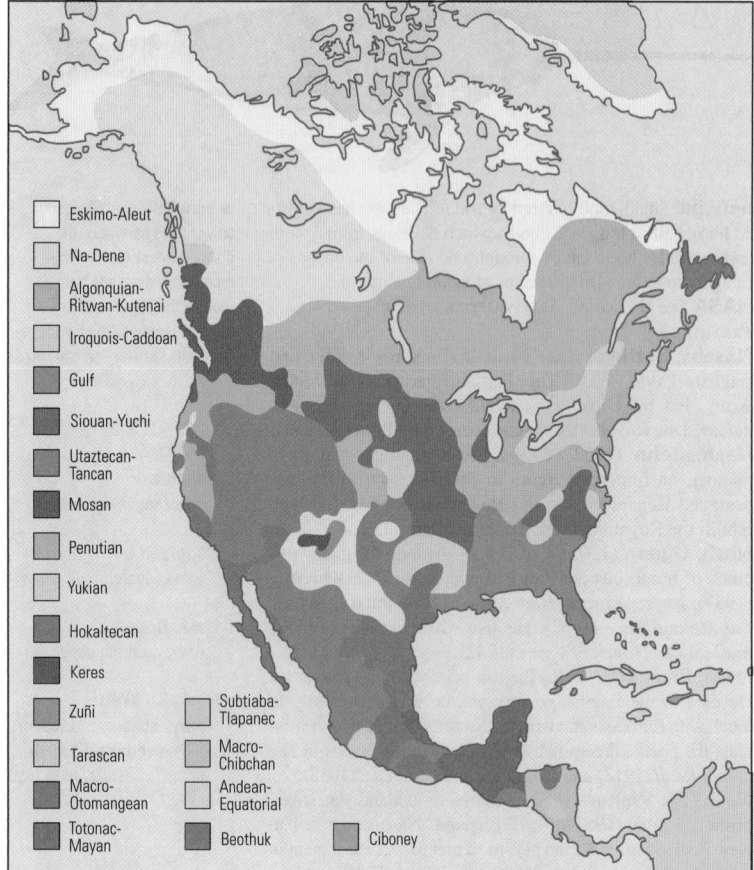

Eskimo-Aleut
Na-Dene
Algonquian-Ritwan-Kutenai
Iroquois-Caddoan
Gulf
Siouan-Yuchi
Utaztecan-Tancan
Mosan
Penutian
Yukian
Hokaltecan
Keres
Zuñi
Tarascan
Macro-Otomangean
Totonac-Mayan
Subtiaba-Tlapanec
Macro-Chibchan
Andean-Equatorial
Beothuk
Ciboney

▲ **Native Americans** A map of the main language groups of North America including the Caribbean area and Mexico.

rockets, both manned and unmanned, are launched from the John F. Kennedy Space Center at CAPE CANAVERAL, Florida.

National Association for the Advancement of Colored People (NAACP) US CIVIL-RIGHTS organization. Founded in 1909, its objectives are 'to achieve through peaceful and lawful means, equal citizenship rights for all American citizens by eliminating segregation and discrimination in housing, employment, voting, schools, the courts, transportation, and recreation'. Early leaders included W.E.B. DU BOIS.

National Front (NF) Extreme right-wing British political party founded in the 1960s. It has a racist doctrine advocating the repatriation of ethnic minorities irrespective of their place of birth and strongly opposing immigration.

National Health Service (NHS) In Britain, system of state provision of health care established in 1948. The NHS undertook to provide free, comprehensive coverage for most health services, including hospitals, general medical practice and public health facilities. It is administered by the Department of HEALTH.

National Insurance (NI) In Britain, state insurance scheme, founded by LLOYD GEORGE in 1911. More comprehensive proposals by Lord BEVERIDGE formed the basis of the National Insurance Act (1946). NI provides sickness, maternity, unemployment and child benefits as well as old-age pensions. It also contributes to the cost of the NATIONAL HEALTH SERVICE (NHS). The scheme is funded by compulsory contributions from employers and employees and is administered by the Department of SOCIAL SECURITY.

nationalism Ideology according to which all people owe a supreme loyalty to their nation and which holds that each nation should be embodied in a separate state. Nationalist sentiment, drawing upon and extolling a common culture, language and history, can be a powerful unifying force. With the possible exception of independence movements against COLONIALISM and IMPERIALISM, nationalism is essentially conservative.

nationalization Policy of acquiring for public ownership business enterprises that were formerly owned privately. Nationalization was an economic principle of early

SOCIALISM. Proponents of nationalization maintain that bringing essential industries under government control enhances social and economic equality.

national parks Protected areas where restraint on the killing of wildlife is enforced, and forests, waters and other natural environments are preserved from commercial use. The USA was the first country to set aside reserves for CONSERVATION and recreation. YELLOWSTONE NATIONAL PARK was the first national park (1872). In Africa, the main purpose of national parks is game preservation.

national service See CONSCRIPTION

National Socialism (Nazism) Doctrine of the National Socialist German Workers' (Nazi) Party, 1921–45. It was biologically racist (believing that the 'Aryan' race was superior to others; see EUGENICS), anti-Semitic, nationalistic, anti-communist, anti-democratic and anti-intellectual. It placed power before justice and the state before the individual. These beliefs were stated by the party's leader, Adolf HITLER, in his book *Mein Kampf* (1925). See also FASCISM; NATIONALISM

national theatre Permanent theatre company usually subsidized by the state and housed in one venue, where national classics of drama are performed in repertory. The oldest national theatre is the COMÉDIE-FRANÇAISE in Paris, founded in 1680. The National Theatre of Great Britain, first advocated by GARRICK, only became a reality in the 1960s. Its first production, *Hamlet*, took place on October 22, 1963, at the OLD VIC Theatre. Sir Peter HALL succeeded Laurence OLIVIER as artistic director (1973–88). In October 1976, new buildings designed by Sir Denys Lasdun were opened on London's South Bank.

Native Americans Indigenous peoples of the American continent. **North America** Native North Americans are believed to be descended from Asian peoples who crossed via the Bering Strait or the Aleutian Islands around 20,000 BC or earlier. They may be divided into eight distinct cultural and geographic groups: the Arctic area; the Northeastern-Mackenzie area; the Northwest Coast area; the South-western area; the Plains area; the California-Intermountain area; the Southwestern area; and the Mesoamerican area. *See* separate articles for individual tribes. **South America** Native South Americans derived from North American groups who migrated s. Three main culture groups inhabiting distinct geographic areas are recognized: (1) Native Americans of the Andean area developed the highest cultures of the continent. After AD 1300, the QUECHUA culture dominated almost the entire region. (2) Native Americans of the Amazon Basin are mainly isolated, primitive, agricultural communities of many localized tribes. (3) Native Americans of the pampas successfully resisted Inca and Spaniard alike. In the southernmost portion of the continent live the Tierra del Fuegans, who are now few in number.

Native Australians Indigenous peoples of Australia. Originally from SE Asia, Native Australians are thought to have colonized Australia 40,000–45,000 years ago. Before the arrival of Europeans (c.1788) they probably numbered more than 400,000, but many thousands died from European diseases when they were placed in reserves. All the 500 tribal groups led a nomadic life, hunting and gathering. They believe that the land is a religious phenomenon, inhabited by spirits of their ancestors, and these beliefs are celebrated in legends, song, mime, carving and painting. They were granted the right to full Australian citizenship in 1967, and were first included in the census in 1971, when their estimated numbers were 140,000. The Aboriginal Land Rights Act (1976) and the Aboriginal and Torres Islander Heritage Protect Act (1984) resulted in an increased population approaching 300,000 by the mid-1990s.

Native North American art Traditional art produced by the indigenous peoples of North America. The INUIT of the Arctic area have been producing ivory carvings since prehistoric times and are also noted for their ceremonial masks (made from driftwood or whalebone). The NW region is best known for its TOTEM POLES, while in California, basket-weaving and pottery were specialities. Similar crafts were practised by the PUEBLO people of the SW, who also created remarkable prehistoric wall paintings. The decoration of animal hides was popu-

N

lar in the Great Plains, while in the Eastern Woodlands, there was a preference for copper ornaments and stone carvings.

Native North American languages Any of more than 100 languages spoken in N and Central America by descendants of the various indigenous peoples. The languages fall into many different families. In the USA and Canada, languages include Algonquian (as spoken by the ALGONQUIN), ATHABASCAN and SIOUX. In the USA and Mexico, UTO-AZTECAN is the most common. In Mexico itself, Oto-Manguean is common, and in Mexico and Guatemala MAYAN. NAHUATL is the most widely spoken of this group.

Native South American languages Any of more than 1,000 languages spoken in South America by between 10 and 12 million people. Among the more important linguistic families are CHIBCHA, ARAWAK and Tupian. Widely spoken languages are QUECHUA (the language of the Incas) and Aymará, found in Peru and Bolivia. GUARANÍ is spoken in Paraguay.

nativity Birth of a New Testament figure as marked by a Christian feast. In general, the term refers to the birth of JESUS CHRIST in BETHLEHEM as described in the GOSPELS.

NATO Acronym for NORTH ATLANTIC TREATY ORGANIZATION

natrolite ($Na_2Al_2Si_3O_{10}.2H_2O$) Hydrated silicate mineral, hydrous sodium aluminium silicate. It has orthorhombic system, needle-like crystals, with radiating nodules or compact fibrous masses. It is colourless or white, glassy and brittle. Hardness 5–5.5; r.d. 2.2. *See also* ZEOLITE

natural In musical notation, an accidental sign placed before a note; it cancels a SHARP or FLAT.

natural gas Naturally occurring FOSSIL FUEL, consisting of HYDROCARBONS trapped in sedimentary rocks. Natural gas is the gaseous component of PETROLEUM and is extracted from OIL wells. The fossil history of gas and petroleum is the same, since they were both formed by the decomposition of ancient marine PLANKTON. Before natural gas can be used as a fuel, the heavier hydrocarbons of BUTANE and PROPANE are extracted; in liquid form, these hydrocarbons are forced into containers as bottled gas. The remaining 'dry gas' is piped to consumers for use as fuel. Dry gas is composed of METHANE and ETHANE.

naturalism Late 19th-century literary movement that began in France and was led by Émile ZOLA. An extension of REALISM, it emphasized the importance of documentation. Writers sought to represent unselective reality with all its emotional and social ramifications. A major exponent of naturalistic drama was August STRINDBERG. The movement declined by the beginning of the 20th century, but influenced the development of the modern US NOVEL and SOCIALIST REALISM.

natural rights Concept that human beings possess certain fundamental and inalienable rights, as described by John LOCKE. Among these rights were life, property ownership, and political equality. *See* HUMAN RIGHTS

natural selection In EVOLUTION, theory that advantageous change in an organism tends to be passed on to successive generations. Changes arise out of natural genetic VARIATION, especially MUTATION. Those that give an individual organism a greater capacity for survival and reproduction in a particular environment help it to produce more offspring bearing the same beneficial characteristic or trait. Thus white rabbits will survive better than brown ones in the snow. This theory was proposed by English naturalist Charles DARWIN in his book *The Origin of Species* (1859). It is still regarded as the key mechanism of evolution. When humans breed plants and animals to perpetuate desired traits, this is called ARTIFICIAL SELECTION.

Nauru Island republic in the W Pacific Ocean, a coral atoll located halfway between Australia and Hawaii, and the world's smallest independent state. Nauru was explored by a British navigator, John Fearn, in 1798. In 1888, the atoll was annexed to Germany. Australian forces occupied Nauru during World War 1. During World War 2, the Japanese held Nauru. In 1968, the island became an independent republic within the Commonwealth. Nauru had deposits of phosphate rock which made it wealthy, but with their exhaustion in the early 1990s the island has gone into severe economic decline (2000 GDP per capita, US$5000). Area: 21sq km (8sq mi). Pop. (2002 est.) 13,000.

nautilus (chambered nautilus) CEPHALOPOD mollusc found in W Pacific and E Indian Oceans at depths down to 200m (660ft). Its large, coiled shell divides into numerous, gas-filled chambers, which give it buoyancy. The foremost chamber contains the body. Its head has 60–90 retractable, thin tentacles without suckers, and it moves by squirting water from a funnel. Shell size *c*.25cm (10in). Family Nautilidae; genus *Nautilus*.

Navajo (Navaho) ATHABASCAN-speaking tribe, the largest group of NATIVE AMERICANS in the USA. Their reservation in Arizona and New Mexico is the biggest in the country. Today, the population numbers *c*.150,000.

Navarino, Battle of (1827) Naval conflict off the port of Navarino (Pylos), Greece. The combined British, French, and Russian fleets destroyed the Turkish-Egyptian fleet of IBRAHIM PASHA. The battle helped to ensure Greek independence (1829).

Navarre Autonomous region and ancient kingdom in N Spain, stretching from the River Ebro to the W Pyrenees border; the capital is PAMPLONA. For 400 years, the Kingdom of Navarre fended off successive invasions by the Visigoths, Arabs, and Franks. In 1512 Ferdinand II of Aragon annexed S Navarre. The N part was incorporated as French crown land in 1589. The Spanish region has historically maintained semi-autonomous status. It is a mountainous, agricultural region producing cattle, grapes, timber, cereals, vegetables, and sugar beet. Area: 10,421sq km (4,023sq mi). Pop. (2000) 543,800.

nave (Lat. *navis*, ship) Central, main area of a church or cathedral. It extends from the main entrance to the transepts and includes the main aisle. It is the congregation's seating area.

navigation Determining one's position and course, often while in a road vehicle, ship, or aircraft. Five main techniques are used: dead reckoning, piloting, celestial navigation, inertial guidance, and radio navigation. The last includes the use of radio beacons, LORAN, RADAR navigation, and SATELLITE navigation systems. Instruments and charts enable the navigator to determine position, expressed in terms of LATITUDE and LONGITUDE, direction in degrees of arc from true north, speed, and distance travelled. *See also* COMPASS; GYROCOMPASS; SEXTANT

Navigation Acts English 17th-century statutes placing restrictions on foreign trade and shipping. The first Navigation Act (1651) declared that English trade should be carried only in English ships; it was the main cause of the first Anglo-Dutch War. Later acts placed restrictions on the trade of the colonies.

navy *See* NAVY, US; ROYAL NAVY

Navy, US Naval service of the US armed forces. It consists of more than 500,000 personnel under the President, who is Commander in Chief of the armed forces. The navy

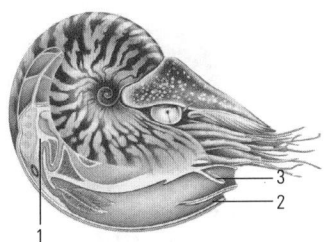

▲ **nautilus** The shell divides into about 30 compartments, but the body of the nautilus only occupies the first, largest chamber (1). All other chambers are self-contained buoyancy tanks filled with gas. The nautilus nevertheless is a poor shape for swimming. Water passes into the mantle (2) around its whole edge. It is expelled from the funnel (3) by the funnel muscles themselves, and by the animal expanding its body in the shell. Unlike its relatives squids, octopuses and cuttlefish, the nautilus cannot contract its mantle, which is attached to its shell.

NAVIGATION

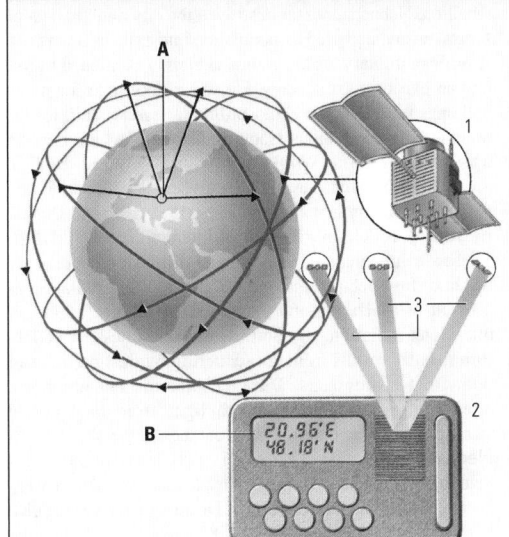

Twenty-four global positioning satellites, launched by the USA, ring the globe (1). At any time, four are above the horizon wherever you are on Earth (A). With a handheld receiver (2) that compares the time signals (3) from the satellite, your position can be fixed to a remarkable degree of accuracy. The receivers are now small enough to fit in the hand, and display either longitude and latitude (B) or a grid reference. Each satellite carries an atomic clock and transmits time signals to Earth. The receiver knows exactly where each satellite should be at any given time and, by simultaneously analysing the time signals from three satellites take to reach the receiver, it can compute its own position to within 10m (33ft). Aircraft and military users use a fourth satellite signal for even greater accuracy.

NEBRASKA
Statehood :
March 1, 1867
Nickname :
The Cornhusker State
State bird :
Western meadowlark
State flower :
Goldenrod
State tree :
Cottonwood
State motto :
Equality before the law

▲ **Nelson** British admiral
Horatio Nelson broke the rigid
naval tactics of his day. At the
Battle of St Vincent (1797), he
boldly, and without orders,
hauled out of line to confront the
Spanish head-on. At the battles
of Abukir (1798) and Copenhagen
(1801), Nelson annihilated the
enemy. His radical, 'pell-mell'
strategy at the Battle of Trafalgar
(1805) destroyed Napoleon's
plans for the invasion of Britain.

is under the general supervision of the Secretary of the Navy and his adviser, the Chief of Naval Operations (CNO), who is the navy's highest ranking officer. The Navy was established by Congress in 1798, although naval activities had begun during the Revolutionary War.

Nazareth (Nazerat) Town between Haifa and the Sea of Galilee, N Israel. According to the Gospels it was where JESUS spent most of his childhood. Today, Nazareth is a place of Christian pilgrimage. Industries: tourism. Pop. (1997) 55,494.

Nazism *See* NATIONAL SOCIALISM

Ndjamena Capital of Chad, N central Africa, a port on the River Chari. Founded by the French in 1900, it was known as Fort Lamy until 1973. Ndjamena grew rapidly after independence in 1960. It is an important market for the surrounding region, which produces livestock, dates, and cereals. The main industry is meat processing. Pop. (2002 est.) 601,500.

Neagh, Lough Lake in Northern Ireland, the largest freshwater lake in the British Isles. It has many feeder channels, the largest of which is the River Bann. The lake is noted for its fishing (especially trout and eels). Area: 396sq km (153sq mi).

Neanderthal Middle PALAEOLITHIC variety of human, known from fossils in Europe and Asia. Neanderthals were discovered when a skeleton was unearthed in the Neander Valley in W Germany in 1856. The bones were thick and powerfully built and the skull had a pronounced brow ridge. Neanderthals are now considered to be a separate species of human, possibly a local adaptation during the Ice Ages, and are not thought to be ancestral to modern humans. Neanderthals predated modern humans in Europe, but were superseded by them c.35,000 years ago. *See also* HUMAN EVOLUTION

Nebraska State in W central USA, in the Great Plains; the capital is LINCOLN. OMAHA is the largest city. The region was acquired under the LOUISIANA PURCHASE of 1803 and was unexplored until the LEWIS AND CLARK EXPEDITION (1804). The territory of Nebraska was created in 1854. Nebraska was admitted to the union in 1867. The land rises gently from the E to the foothills of the Rocky Mountains in the W, and is drained chiefly by the Platte River, a tributary of the MISSOURI. The E half of the state is farmland, where farmers grow grain and raise cattle and pigs. The economy is largely agricultural. Industries: food processing, oil, and sand, gravel and stone quarrying. Area: 199,113sq km (76,878sq mi). Pop. (2000) 1,711,263.

Nebuchadnezzar II (c.630–562 BC) Second and greatest king of the Chaldaean (New Babylonian) Empire (r.605–562BC) who changed the political map of the ancient Middle East. He subjugated Syria and Palestine but was himself defeated by Egyptian forces in 601 BC. He occupied JUDAH, capturing JERUSALEM in 597 BC and installing the puppet king Zedekiah on the throne of Judah. Following Zedekiah's rebellion, Nebuchadnezzar destroyed the city and TEMPLE of Jerusalem and deported its population into exile in BABYLON. A brilliant military leader, Nebuchadnezzar continued to follow an expansionist strategy. He was responsible for many buildings in Babylon, and (according to legend) built for his Median wife the famous Hanging Gardens, which became one of the SEVEN WONDERS OF THE WORLD. Biblical accounts of Nebuchadnezzar's involvement with Judah and the Jews appear principally in II Kings, Jeremiah and Daniel.

nebula (Lat. 'cloud') Region of interstellar gas and dust. There are three main types of nebula. **Emission** nebulae are bright diffuse nebulae that emit light and other radiation as a result of ionization and excitation of the gas atoms by ultraviolet radiation. In contrast, the brightness of **reflection** nebulae results from the scattering by dust particles of light from nearby stars. **Dark** nebulae are not luminous: interstellar gas and dust absorb light from background stars, producing apparently dark patches in the sky.

Necker, Jacques (1732–1804) French financier and statesman, b. Switzerland. A Protestant banker, he was finance minister (1776–81) under LOUIS XVI. Dismissed, he was recalled to deal with a financial crisis in 1788 and advised calling the STATES-GENERAL. The demands of the Third Estate caused his second dismissal, but the consequent riots and storming of the BASTILLE, forced LOUIS XVI to reappoint him. Unable to prevent the FRENCH REVOLUTION, he resigned in 1790.

nectar Sweet liquid secreted by flowering plants. It consists mainly of a solution of GLUCOSE, FRUCTOSE and SUCROSE in water. The glands (**nectaries**) that produce it usually lie at the base of the FLOWER petals but may be found also in parts of the stem or at the leaf bases. Nectar attracts insects, which help with cross-POLLINATION.

nectarine Variety of PEACH tree and its sweet, smooth-skinned, fleshy fruit. The tree and stone are identical to those of the peach. Family Rosaceae; species *Prunus persica nectarina*.

Nefertiti (active 14th centuryBC) Queen of Egypt as a wife of Akhenaten, frequently depicted as his co-regent. Her best surviving representation is a bust now in the Berlin Museum, Germany, which depicts her as exceptionally beautiful.

Negev (Hebrew, dry) Desert region in S Israel that extends from Beersheba to the border with Egypt at Elat, and accounts for more than 50% of Israeli land. An irrigation network has increased cultivation in the Negev. The region has good mineral resources, including copper, phosphates, natural gas, gypsum, and magnesium ore. Area: c.13,300sq km (5130sq mi).

Nehru, Jawaharlal (1889–1964) Indian statesman, prime minister of India (1947–64), father of Indira GANDHI. Educated in England, he succeeded his father Motilal Nehru (1861–1931) as president of the CONGRESS PARTY in 1929. Nehru and 'Mahatma' Gandhi led nationalist opposition to British rule in India. Nehru was imprisoned nine times for non-cooperation with the British between 1921 and 1945. He played a leading role in the negotiations with MOUNTBATTEN and JINNAH that led to the independence of India and Pakistan. As the first prime minister of an independent India, Nehru followed a foreign policy of non-alignment in the Cold War and became a respected leader of the Third World.

Nelson, Horatio, Viscount (1758–1805) British admiral. Joining the navy aged 12, he was a captain at 20. Nelson lost an eye in action in 1794, and lost his right arm in 1797. Having played a notable part in the victory at Cape St Vincent (1797), he again used unorthodox tactics in the Battle of Abukir Bay in 1798. He was killed at the moment of his greatest victory, when he destroyed the French and Spanish fleets at TRAFALGAR (1805). He is remembered for his courage and tactical ability, and for his love affair with Emma Hamilton.

nematode *See* ROUNDWORM

Nemesis In Greek mythology, personification of the gods' disapproval, jealousy, and retribution.

neo-classicism Movement in late 18th- and early 19th-century European art and architecture. Neo-classicism grew out of the Age of ENLIGHTENMENT, whose exponents admired the order and clarity of ancient Greek and Roman art. The archaeological discoveries at HERCULANEUM and POMPEII, Italy, in the 1740s helped to stimulate interest in these ancient civilizations. Many of the movement's pioneers congregated in Rome, notably Johann Winckelmann, CANOVA, John Flaxman, Gavin Hamilton, and Bertel Thorvaldsen. The most powerful neo-classical painter was Jacques Louis DAVID, whose work expressed a severity and grandeur. Concurrent **Greek Revival** architecture imitated the simplicity of ancient Greek buildings.

neo-Darwinism Development of Darwinism that incorporates the modern ideas of genetic HEREDITY with DARWIN's ideas of EVOLUTION through NATURAL SELECTION.

neodymium (symbol Nd) Silver-yellow metallic element of the LANTHANIDE SERIES (rare-earth metals). Discovered and named in 1885 by the Austrian chemist Carl von Welsbach (1858–1929), it is used to manufacture lasers, and its salts are used to colour glass. Properties: at.no. 60; r.a.m. 144.24; r.d. 7.004; m.p. 1,010°C (1,850°F); b.p. 3,068°C (5,554°F); most common isotope Nd^{142} (27.11%).

neo-fascism Revival of the principles of FASCISM. Neo-fascism has surfaced in a number of European countries since the 1980s, often feeding on social discontent. In the USA, neo-fascist elements exist in certain white supremacist groups.

neo-impressionism Late 19th-century painting style, originating in France and involving the use of POINTILLISM. The style is seen at its purest in the works of SEURAT.

Neolithic (New Stone Age) Period in human cultural development following the PALAEOLITHIC. The Neolithic began c.8000 BC in W Asia and c.4000 BC in Europe. During this period people first lived in settled villages, domesticated animals, cultivated cereal crops, and ground stone and flint.

neon (symbol Ne) Gaseous nonmetallic element, a NOBLE GAS. Colourless and odourless, it is present in the atmosphere (0.0018% by volume) and is obtained by the fractional distillation of liquid air. Discovered in 1898 by Scottish chemist William Ramsey and English chemist Morris Travers (1872–1961), its main use is in discharge tubes for advertising signs (emitting a red glow) and in gas lasers, geiger counters, and particle detectors. It forms no compounds. Properties: at.no. 10; r.a.m. 20.179; m.p. −248.67°C (−415.6°F); b.p. −246.05°C (−410.89°F); most common isotope Ne^{20} (90.92%).

Neoplatonism School of philosophy that dominated intellectual thought between c.AD 250 and 550. It combined the ideas of PYTHAGORAS, the STOICS, PLATO and ARISTOTLE, with strains from JUDAISM, oriental religions and Christianity. Fundamental to Neoplatonism was the concept of the 'One', something that transcends knowledge or existence but from which intelligence and the Soul derive. Neoplatonism's influence persisted through the Middle Ages and enjoyed a revival in the Renaissance, where it influenced early scientific ideas.

neo-realism Italian film movement (1945–50) that dealt with the harshness of life and death. Roberto ROSSELLINI directed the first such film, called *Open City* (1945), using non-professionals and real locations. Perhaps the finest example of neo-realism was Vittorio De Sica's *Bicycle Thieves* (1948). Neo-realist writers included Alberto MORAVIA and Cesare PAVESE.

Nepal Independent kingdom in central Asia; the capital is KATMANDU. *See* country feature, page 542.

nephritis (Bright's disease) Inflammation of the KIDNEY. It is a general term used to describe a condition rather than any specific disease. It can progress to kidney failure.

nephron Functional unit of the mammalian KIDNEY. There are c.1 million nephrons in a human kidney. Each consists of a cluster of tiny blood capillaries, cupped in a structure with an attached, narrow tubule. Blood enters the kidney under pressure, and water and wastes are forced into the tubule. Some water and essential molecules are reabsorbed into the bloodstream; the remaining filtrate, URINE, is passed to the BLADDER.

Neptune Eighth planet from the Sun. The mass, orbit, and position of an unseen planet had been calculated by LEVERRIER and, independently, by British astronomer John Couch Adams (1819–92). Neptune was first observed in 1846, and is invisible to the naked eye. Through a telescope it appears as a small, greenish-blue disc with very few details. The upper atmosphere is c.85% molecular hydrogen and 15% helium. Its predominant blue colour is due to a trace of methane, which strongly absorbs red light. Several different atmospheric features were visible at the time of the fly-by of the Voyager 2 probe in 1989. There were faint bands parallel to the equator, and spots, the most prominent of which was the oval Great Dark Spot (GDS), c.12,500km (8,000mi) long and 7,500km (4,500mi) wide, which is a giant anticyclone. White, cirrus-type clouds of methane crystals cast shadows on the main cloud deck c.50km (30mi) below. Neptune has the highest wind speeds recorded on any planet – more than 2,000km/h (1,250mph) in some places.

Neptune Roman god, originally associated with freshwater but later identified with the Greek god POSEIDON and hence the sea. He was often depicted carrying a trident and riding a dolphin. His festival was in July.

neptunium (symbol Np) Radioactive metallic element, the first of the TRANSURANIC ELEMENTS of the ACTINIDE SERIES. Discovered in 1940 by US physicists Edwin McMILLAN and Philip Abelson (1913–2004), this silvery element is found in small amounts in uranium ores, and is obtained as a by-product in nuclear reactors. Properties: at.no. 93; r.a.m. 237.0482; r.d. 20.25; m.p. 640°C (1,184°F); b.p. 3,902°C (7,056°F); most stable isotope Np^{237} (half-life 2.2 million years).

Nero (AD 37–68) Roman Emperor (54–68). One of the most notorious of rulers, he was responsible for the murders of his half-brother, his mother, and his first wife. Rome burned (64), according to rumour, at Nero's instigation. He blamed the Christians and began their persecution. Faced with widespread rebellion, Nero committed suicide.

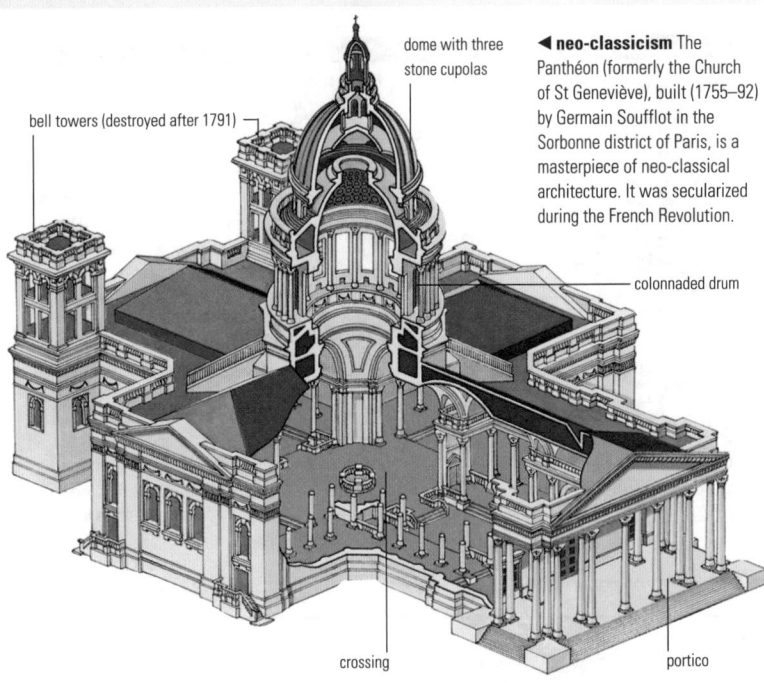

bell towers (destroyed after 1791)

dome with three stone cupolas

◀ **neo-classicism** The Panthéon (formerly the Church of St Geneviève), built (1755–92) by Germain Soufflot in the Sorbonne district of Paris, is a masterpiece of neo-classical architecture. It was secularized during the French Revolution.

colonnaded drum

crossing

portico

Neruda, Pablo (1904–73) Chilean poet, b. Neftalí Ricardo Reyes. Neruda's poetry presents the tragedy of the human condition through surreal imagery. His best-known work is the epic *Canto General* (1950). He received the 1971 Nobel Prize in literature.

nerve Collection of NEURONS providing a communications link between the vertebrate NERVOUS SYSTEM and other parts of the body. **Afferent** or sensory nerves transmit nervous impulses to the CENTRAL NERVOUS SYSTEM; **efferent** or MOTOR NEURONS carry impulses from the central nervous system to the muscles.

Nervi, Pier Luigi (1891–1979) Italian architect noted for his use of concrete. Nervi co-designed the UNESCO building, Paris (1954–58), and the Pirelli skyscraper, Milan (1958).

nervous breakdown Popular term for a mental and emotional crisis in which the person either is unable or feels unable to function normally. It is an imprecise term and refers to any of a range of conditions. *See also* MENTAL DISORDER

nervous system Communications system consisting of interconnecting nerve cells or NEURONS that co-ordinate all life, growth, and physical and mental activity. The mammalian nervous system consists of the CENTRAL NERVOUS SYSTEM (CNS) and the PERIPHERAL NERVOUS SYSTEM.

Ness, Loch Freshwater lake in N Scotland, running SW to NE along the geological fault of Glen More. It is 38km (24mi) long and 230m (754ft) deep and forms part of the Caledonian Canal. Accounts of a Loch Ness monster date back to the 15th century, but the veracity of the legend has never been established.

nest Structure built by a living organism to house itself, its eggs, or its young. Nest-builders include some invertebrates, particularly social insects, and members of all the larger groups of vertebrates. The nests of ants, bees, wasps, and termites may be highly elaborate and involve tunnels, passages and chambers. The nests of fish may be simple gravel scoops or enclosed structures, sometimes made of bubbles. Birds' nests vary enormously from simple, cup-shaped arrangements of twigs and other organic materials, to woven or knotted grass or leaves; some birds scrape a hollow in the ground to make a nest, others make nest-holes in cliffs, earth banks or trees. The most highly evolved animal to make a form of a nest is probably the gorilla, which builds a new sleeping platform of branches every night.

Nestorianism Christian heresy according to which JESUS CHRIST, the incarnate God, possesses two separate natures, one divine and the other human, as opposed to the orthodox belief that Christ is one person who is at once both God and man. The heresy was associated with Nestorius, Bishop of Constantinople, who died in c.451. It was condemned by the Councils of EPHESUS (431) and CHALCEDON (451). Nestorius was deposed

N

NEPTUNE: DATA

Diameter (equatorial): 49,528km (30,707mi)
Mass (Earth=1): 17.2
Volume (Earth=1): 57
Density (water=1): 2.06
Orbital period: 164.8 years
Rotation period: 16h 7m 0s
Temperature at cloud-tops: 55K
Surface gravity (Earth=1): 0.98

NERVOUS SYSTEM

spinal cord
sensory root
spinal nerve
vertebra
motor root
sympathetic ganglia of central nervous system

cerebrum
cranial nerves
cervical nerves (8 pairs)
thoracic nerves (12 pairs)
lumbar nerves (5 pairs)
sacral nerves (5 pairs)

The nervous system is divided into two parts: central and peripheral. The central nervous system (CNS) includes the brain and spinal cord (A). It receives information, makes decisions and transmits instructions. The peripheral nervous system (B) consists chiefly of nerve fibres leading to and from the CNS. It cannot make 'decisions', and acts only as a message transmitter.

INTERNET

Netherlands
▶ www.holland.com/uk
▶ www.overheid.nl/guest

and banished. His supporters gradually organized themselves into a separate church, which had its centre in Persia (Iran).
Netanyahu, Binyamin (1949–) Israeli statesman, prime minister (1996–99). He served as permanent representative (1984–88) to the United Nations (UN) before becoming deputy minister of foreign affairs. In 1993, he became leader of the right-wing Likud Party. He defeated Shimon PERES in the elections that followed the assassination of Yitzhak RABIN.

Netanyahu's uncompromising stance over Israeli settlement on the WEST BANK and Likud's opposition to the ISRAELI-PALESTINIAN ACCORD stalled the peace process in the Middle East. Netanyahu and Yasir ARAFAT signed the Wye Accord (1998), but the subsequent withdrawal of the religious right from the coalition prompted fresh elections (1999), in which Labour Party leader Ehud BARAK defeated Netanyahu. Ariel SHARON succeeded Netanyahu as leader of Likud.

netball Seven-a-side ball game. Invented in 1891, it is a variant of BASKETBALL. Only two players of each team are allowed in the shooting circle at goal, which is the same size and height as in basketball but without a backboard. The game is played chiefly in the English-speaking countries and the Commonwealth.

Netherlands Kingdom in NW Europe. *See* country feature

Netherlands Antilles Group of five main islands (and part of a sixth) in the West Indies, forming an autonomous region of the Netherlands; the capital is Willemstadt (on CURAÇAO). The islands were settled by the Spanish in 1527 and captured by the Dutch in 1634. They were granted internal self-government in 1954. The group includes Aruba, Bonaire, Curaçao, Saba, Saint Eustatius, and the s half of Saint Maarten. Industries: oil refining, petrochemicals, phosphates, tourism. Area: 800sq km (309sq mi). Pop. (2002) 216,000.

nettle Any of numerous species of flowering plants of the genus *Urtica*, especially the stinging nettle (*U. dioica*), which is typical of the genus in that it has stinging hairs along the leaves and stem. It has heart-shaped serrated leaves, small green flowers and is sometimes used for medicinal or culinary purposes. The stinging agent is formic acid. Family Urticaceae.

Neumann, John von *See* VON NEUMANN, JOHN

neuralgia Intense pain from a damaged nerve, possibly tracking along its course. Forms include trigeminal neuralgia,

NEPAL

The Kingdom of Nepal, in central Asia, lies between India to the s and China to the N. More than three-quarters of the country is in the Himalayan mountain heartland, culminating in the world's highest peak Mount EVEREST (Chomolongma) at 8,850m [29,035ft].

Nepal comprises three regions. A s lowland area (*terai*) of grassland and forests is the main location of Nepal's agriculture and timber industry. The central Siwalik mountains and valleys are divided between the basins of the Ghaghara, Gandak and Kosi rivers. Between the Gandak and Kosi lies Katmandu valley, Nepal's most populous area. The last region is the main section of the Himalayas. Vegetation varies widely according to altitude.

CLIMATE
The huge differences in altitude give Nepal a wide variety of climatic regions.

HISTORY
From the 10th to the 18th century the Malla dynasty ruled the region, though in 1482 the kingdom of was divided into three – Bhadgaon, Kathmandu and Patan. In 1768 the three kingdoms were reunited under Gurkha rule to form what is now known as Nepal.

Between 1815 and 1816 the Anglo-Nepalese War took place as a result of rivalry between Nepal and the British East India Company over the annexation of minor states bordering Nepal. In exchange for autonomy the Nepalese signed the Treaty of Sugauli, ceding parts of the Terrai and Sikkim to the British East India Company. From 1846 to 1951 hereditary prime ministers

from the Rana family ruled Nepal. In 1923 Britain recognized Nepal as a sovereign state. Gurkha soldiers fought in the British Army in both World Wars.

In 1951 the Rana government was overthrown and the monarchy re-established. A national constitution was adopted in 1959, and free elections were held. In 1960 King Mahendra dissolved parliament and introduced a political system based on village councils (panchayat). In 1972 Birendra succeeded his father as king.

POLITICS
In 1990, after protests, a new constitution limited the power of the monarchy. In 1991 the Nepali Congress Party won multiparty elections, but stability proved elusive as a Maoist revolt arose.

In 2001 King Birendra, his queen, and six other members of his family were shot dead by his heir Crown Prince Dipendra, who then took his own life. Gyanendra, Birendra's brother, became king. Increasing Maoist activity led him

AREA 56,827sq miles [147,181sq km]
POPULATION 28,902,000
CAPITAL (POPULATION) Katmandu (1,176,000)
GOVERNMENT Multiparty republic
ETHNIC GROUPS Rahman, Chetri, Newar, Gurung, Magar, Tamang, Sherpa and others
LANGUAGES Nepali (official), local languages
RELIGIONS Hinduism 86%, Buddhism 8%, Islam 4%
CURRENCY Nepalese rupee = 100 paisa

to take direct control of the government in 2005, but in 2006 he was forced to reinstate Parliament, which immediately voted to remove his power of veto. Parliament then reached a peace accord with the Maoists. About 12,000 had been killed in the revolt. Maoists finally joined parliament in 2007 after it promised to abolish the monarchy. They gained a strong majority in 2008 elections. In May 2008, the national assembly voted to make Nepal a republic.

ECONOMY
Agriculture employs over 80% of the workforce, much of it at subsistence level, and accounts for 40% of GDP. Export crops include herbs, jute, rice, spices and wheat. Tourism, which is centred around the high Himalayas, has grown in importance since the country first opened to foreigners in 1951. Nepal is highly dependent on foreign aid; the government plans to use part of it to improve the infrastructure and invest in hydroelectric power generation.

which features attacks of stabbing pain in the mouth area, and post-herpetic neuralgia following an attack of SHINGLES.

neurology Branch of medicine dealing with the diagnosis and treatment of diseases of the NERVOUS SYSTEM.

neuron (nerve cell) Basic structural unit of the NERVOUS SYSTEM, which enables rapid transmission of impulses between different parts of the body. It is composed of a cell body, containing a nucleus, and a number of trailing processes. The largest of these is the axon, which carries outgoing impulses; the rest are dendrites, which receive incoming impulses.

neurosis Emotional disorder such as anxiety, depression, or various phobias. It is a form of mental illness in which the main disorder is of mood, but the person does not lose contact with reality as happens in PSYCHOSIS.

neurotransmitter Any one of several dozen chemicals involved in communication between NEURONS or between a NERVE and muscle cells. When an electrical impulse arrives at a nerve ending, a neurotransmitter is released to carry the signal across the SYNAPSE (specialized junction) between the nerve cell and its neighbour. Some drugs work by disrupting neurotransmission. *See also* NERVOUS SYSTEM

neutrality Policy of non-involvement in hostilities between states. It is recognized by international law, mainly in the Declaration of Paris of 1856, and the Hague Conventions V and XIII of 1907. A state proclaiming its neutrality must be wholly impartial and refrain from helping or hindering any side.

neutralization In chemistry, the mixing, or TITRATION, of equivalent amounts of an acid and a base in an aqueous medium until the mixture is neither acidic nor basic (pH of 7).

neutrino (symbol v) Uncharged ELEMENTARY PARTICLE with little or no mass, SPIN $\frac{1}{2}$ and travelling at the speed of light. US physicist Wolfgang PAULI predicted its existence. Classified as a LEPTON, it reacts little with matter and is hard to detect. There are three species. The **electron** neutrino is closely associated with the electron, and is produced when protons and electrons react to form NEUTRONS, as in the Sun. The **muon** neutrino is associated with the muon, and occurs in high-energy reactions. The **tau** neutrino is associated with the tau particle.

▲ **nettle** The stinging nettle (*Urtica dioica*) has bristle-like stinging hairs. When the plant is touched they penetrate the skin, the tips break, and formic acid is released.

NETHERLANDS

The Kingdom of the Netherlands lies at the W end of the North European Plain, which extends to the Ural Mountains in Russia. The country is largely flat, about 40% being below sea level at high tide. To prevent flooding, dykes have been built to hold back the waves. There are large areas, called polders, of land reclaimed from the sea.

CLIMATE

Because of its position on the North Sea, the Netherlands has a temperate climate. Winters are mild, with rain coming from the Atlantic depressions which pass over the country. North Sea storms often batter the coasts. Storm waves have periodically breached the dykes, causing flooding and sometimes loss of life.

HISTORY

From the 4th to 8th century, the Franks ruled the region. In the 10th century, it became part of the Holy Roman Empire. Trade flourished through the HANSEATIC LEAGUE in the 14th and 15th centuries. In 1477, the region passed to the Habsburgs. Philip II's attempt to impose the Inquisition met with fierce resistance. The N Protestant provinces, led by WILLIAM I (THE SILENT), declared independence in 1581. The foundation of the Dutch EAST INDIA COMPANY in 1602 marked the beginnings of empire. After the THIRTY YEARS' WAR, the Peace of WESTPHALIA (1648) recognized the independence of the N and S provinces as the United Provinces. In 1652, Jan DE WITT formed a republic. In the remainder of the 17th century the Dutch built up a great overseas empire, especially in South-east Asia. Trading rivalry with England led to the DUTCH WARS, and the Treaty of BREDA (1667) confirmed Dutch imperial possessions. In 1672, France invaded and de Witt was murdered. The House of ORANGE regained control under WILLIAM III (OF ORANGE).

France conquered the Netherlands in 1795 during the French Revolutionary Wars, holding it until 1813. After the fall of Napoleon in 1815 the former United Provinces, Belgium, and Luxembourg united to form the Kingdom of the Netherlands under WILLIAM I. Belgium broke away in 1830. In 1890 Luxembourg seceded, and WILHELMINA began her long reign. The Netherlands was neutral in World War 1. Germany invaded in May 1940 and Queen Wilhelmina was exiled. Much of the Dutch fleet escaped and served with the Allies. About 75% of the country's Jews were deported to Poland and there murdered. By the end of the war about 270,000 Netherlanders had been killed or had died of starvation or forced labour.

POLITICS

In 1948 the Netherlands formed an economic union called Benelux with Belgium and Luxembourg, and in 1949 it became a member of NATO. Economic recovery was rapid and in 1957 the country became a founder member of the EEC.

After much fighting the Dutch recognized the independence of Indonesia, their largest overseas possession, in 1949. In 1954 Suriname and the NETHERLANDS ANTILLES were granted self-government. In 1962, the Dutch handed over Netherlands New Guinea to the United Nations, which handed it over, as Irian Jaya, to Indonesia in 1963. Suriname became fully independent in 1975.

AREA 41,526sq km [16,033sq mi]
POPULATION 16,571,000
CAPITAL (POPULATION) Amsterdam (1,157,000); The Hague (seat of government, 440,000)
GOVERNMENT Constitutional monarchy
ETHNIC GROUPS Dutch 83%, Indonesian, Turkish, Moroccan and others
LANGUAGES Dutch (official), Frisian
RELIGIONS Roman Catholic 31%, Protestant 21%, Islam 4%, others
CURRENCY Euro = 100 cents

In 1953 waves broke the coastal defences in the SW delta region, flooding vast areas, destroying or damaging more than 30,000 houses, and killing 1,800. Within three weeks, a commission of enquiry recommended the Delta Plan, a huge project to protect the region. Completed in 1986, it constructed massive dams and floodgates that are closed during severe storms.

The Maastricht Treaty, which transformed the EEC into the European Union, was signed in the Dutch city of Maastricht in 1991. In 2002 the Netherlands became one of the first countries to adopt the Euro currency.

ECONOMY

The Netherlands has the world's 14th largest economy and is a highly industrialized country. Manufacturing and commerce are the most valuable activities. Mineral resources include china clay, natural gas, oil and salt. It imports many of the materials needed by its industries. The products are wide-ranging, including aircraft, chemical products, electronic equipment, machinery, textiles and vehicles. In the area south of Rotterdam, the Dutch have constructed a vast port and industrial area, Europoort. Together with Rotterdam's own facilities, the complex is the largest and busiest in the world.

Agriculture employs only 5% of the workforce, but, through the use of scientific techniques, yields are high. The Dutch cut and sell more than 3 billion flowers a year. Dairy farming is the leading farming activity. In the areas above sea level, farming includes both cattle and crops. Major food crops include barley, potatoes, sugar beet and wheat.

NEVADA
Statehood :
October 31, 1864
Nickname :
The Silver State
State bird :
Mountain bluebird
State flower :
Sagebrush
State tree :
Pine nut
State motto :
All for our country

NEW HAMPSHIRE
Statehood :
June 21, 1788
Nickname :
The Granite State
State bird :
Purple finch
State flower :
Purple lilac
State tree :
White birch
State motto :
Live free or die

INTERNET

Nevada
► www.nv.gov

New Brunswick
► www.gnb.ca

New Caledonia
► www.sponline.com/nc

New Forest
► www.newforestcommittee.
org.uk

neutron (symbol n) Uncharged ELEMENTARY PARTICLE that occurs in the atomic nuclei of all chemical elements except the lightest isotope of HYDROGEN. It is classified as a BARYON with SPIN $\frac{1}{2}$. Outside the NUCLEUS, it is unstable, decaying with a half-life of 11.6 minutes into a PROTON, ELECTRON, and antineutrino. Its neutrality allows it to penetrate and be absorbed in nuclei and thus to induce nuclear TRANSMUTATION and FISSION. The neutron was discovered and named in 1932 by English physicist James Chadwick.

neutron bomb NUCLEAR WEAPON is a small hydrogen bomb producing a small blast but a very intense burst of high-speed NEUTRONS. The lack of heat and blast means that buildings are not heavily damaged. The neutrons, however, produce intense RADIATION SICKNESS in people located within a certain range of the explosion.

neutron star Extremely small, dense STAR that consists mostly of NEUTRONS. Neutron stars are formed when a massive star explodes as a SUPERNOVA, blasting off its outer layers and compressing the core so that its component PROTONS and ELECTRONS merge into neutrons. They are observed as PULSARS. They have masses comparable to that of the Sun, but diameters of only c.20km (12mi) and average densities of $c.10^{15}g/cm^3$.

Nevada State in w USA; the capital is CARSON CITY. The USA acquired the region in 1848 at the end of the MEXICAN WAR. When gold and silver were found in 1859, settlers flocked to Nevada. Much of the state lies in the Great Basin, but the SIERRA NEVADA rise steeply from its w edge. Hay and lucerne (alfalfa) are the chief crops; sheep and cattle grazing is important. Most of Nevada's economic wealth comes from its mineral deposits, which include copper, lead, silver, gold, zinc and tungsten. Industries: chemicals, timber, machinery, glass. It is a tourist area and, in cities such as LAS VEGAS and Reno, gambling provides an important source of state revenue. Area: 286,297sq km (110,539sq mi). Pop. (2000) 1,998,257.

Newark City in NE New Jersey, USA, on the Passaic River and Newark Bay, connected to nearby New York City by tunnel. Founded in 1666 by the Puritans, Newark began its industrial growth after the American Revolution. It is an important commercial and financial centre. Industries: electrical equipment, paints, chemicals. Pop. (2000) 273,546.

New Brunswick Maritime province on the US-Canadian border, E CANADA; the capital is Fredericton. The largest towns are St John and Moncton. First explored by Jacques CARTIER in 1534, France ceded the region to Britain in 1713. Many Loyalists entered the region from the American colonies during the AMERICAN REVOLUTION. Established in 1784, the province joined NOVA SCOTIA, QUÉBEC, and ONTARIO to form the Dominion of Canada in 1867. The land rises gradually from E to w, and is drained by the St John and Miramichi rivers. More than 75% of the province is forested. The chief crops are hay, clover, oats, potatoes, and fruit. Industries: timber, leather goods, pharmaceuticals, machinery. There are mineral deposits. Area: 73,437sq km (28,354sq mi). Pop. (2001) 729,500.

New Caledonia (Nouvelle Calédonie) French overseas territory in the sw Pacific Ocean, c.1200km (750mi) E of Australia, consisting of New Caledonia, Loyalty Islands, Isle des Pins, Isle Bélep, and Chesterfield and Huon Islands; the capital is NOUMÉA (on New Caledonia). Discovered in 1774 by Captain COOK, the islands were annexed by France in 1853. The group became a French overseas territory in 1946. In the 1980s, there was a growing separatist movement. Direct French rule was imposed in 1988. Products: copra, coffee, cotton, nickel, iron, manganese, cobalt, chromium. Area: 18,575sq km (7,172sq mi). Pop. (1996) 211,000

Newcastle upon Tyne City and major port on the River Tyne, NE England; administrative centre of Tyne and Wear. The site of a fort in Roman times, Newcastle acquired a Norman castle in the 11th century. It was a major woolexporting port in the 13th century, and later became a coalshipping centre. Its shipbuilding industry is in decline, but heavy engineering is still important. Industries: pharmaceuticals, engineering, aircraft. Pop. (2001) 259,573.

New Deal (1933–39) Programme for social and economic reconstruction in the USA following the GREAT DEPRES-

SION, launched by President Franklin D. ROOSEVELT. It was based on massive and unprecedented federal intervention in the economy. Early measures, including extensive public works, mainly dealt with relief. The New Deal encountered bitter resistance from conservatives and did not avert further recession in 1937–38. Industrial expansion, full employment, and agricultural prosperity were achieved less by the New Deal than by the advent of World War 2.

New Delhi Capital of India, in the N of the country, on the River Yamuna in DELHI Union Territory. Planned by the British architects Edwin LUTYENS and Herbert Baker, it was constructed in 1912–29 to replace Calcutta (now KOLKATA) as the capital of British India. Whereas Old DELHI is primarily a commercial centre, New Delhi has an administrative function. Industries: textile production, chemicals, machine tools, plastics, electrical appliances, traditional crafts. Pop. (2001) 294,783.

New England Region in NE USA, comprising the states of MAINE, NEW HAMPSHIRE, VERMONT, CONNECTICUT, MASSACHUSETTS, and RHODE ISLAND. In 1643, some of the British colonies set up the New England Confederation for the purposes of defence and to establish a common policy towards the Native Americans. New England was the centre of events leading up to the AMERICAN REVOLUTION. The region became highly industrialized after the WAR OF 1812. It was home to writers such as EMERSON, HAWTHORNE, and THOREAU and the literary movement TRANSCENDENTALISM.

New Forest Region of forest and heathland in s Hampshire, s England. It was established (1079) as a royal hunting ground by William I. The forest includes many species of trees. Pigs, cattle, and ponies are reared. Area: c.383sq km (148sq mi).

Newfoundland and Labrador Province in E Canada, on the Atlantic Ocean, consisting of the mainland region of LABRADOR and the island of Newfoundland plus adjacent islands; the capital is St John's (in Newfoundland). Norsemen are believed to have landed on the coast of Labrador c.AD 1000. John CABOT reached the island in 1497. The region became a British colony in 1824. It remained apart from the rest of Canada until 1949, when it became the country's tenth province. The island of Newfoundland is a plateau with many lakes and marshes. Labrador has tundra in the N, and the cold climate and lack of transport facilities have hindered economic development. There are, however, valuable mineral resources. Timber is an important industry, and the Grand Banks is one of the world's best cod-fishing areas. Area: 404,420sq km (156,185sq mi). Pop. (2001) 512,930.

New France Area of North America claimed by France in the 16th-18th centuries. It included the St Lawrence valley, the Great Lakes region and the Mississippi valley. Parts were lost during the Anglo-French wars of the 18th century, and the whole of New France passed to Britain in 1763.

New Frontier (1961–63) Term describing the legislative programme of US President John F. KENNEDY. The programme included massive expenditure on social reforms and welfare, as well as ambitious new projects such as the Peace Corps and SPACE EXPLORATION.

New Guinea World's second-largest island, part of the E Malay archipelago, in the w Pacific Ocean. Discovered in the early 16th century, New Guinea was colonized by the Dutch, the Germans and the British during the next two centuries. In 1904, the British-administered part transferred to Australia, and Australian forces seized German New Guinea during World War 1. The E half eventually achieved independence as PAPUA NEW GUINEA in 1975. The w half, IRIAN JAYA, became a province of Indonesia in 1969. The island has a tropical climate and is mountainous. Products: copra, cocoa, coffee, rubber, coconuts, tobacco. Area: 885,780sq km (342,000sq mi).

New Hampshire State in NE USA, on the Canadian border; the capital is CONCORD. The first settlement was made in 1623. Much of the land is mountainous and forested. The principal rivers are the Connecticut and the Merrimack, and there are more than 1,000 lakes. Farming is restricted by poor, stony soil, and is mostly concentrated in the Connecticut valley. Dairy and market garden produce, hay, apples, and potatoes are the chief products. New Hampshire is highly industrialized. There is hydroelectricity. Industries:

electrical machinery, paper and wood products, printing and publishing, leather goods, textiles. Area: 24,097sq km (9,304sq mi). Pop. (2000) 1,235,786.

New Haven City and port in s Connecticut, USA, on Long Island Sound. Founded by Puritans in 1638, it shared the role of capital of Connecticut with HARTFORD from 1701 to 1875. The presence of YALE UNIVERSITY (founded 1701) has made the city a cultural centre. Industries: firearms and ammunition, rubber products, locks, tools. Pop. (2000) 123,626.

Ne Win, U (1911–2002) Burmese general and statesman, prime minister (1958–60), head of state (1962–74), and president (1974–81). In 1943 he was appointed Chief of Staff of the Burmese army by AUNG SAN. In 1962 NE Win seized power in a military coup. He established a dictatorship and formed a one-party state, governed by the Burma Socialist Programme Party (BSPP). In 1988, NE Win retired as leader of the BSPP.

New Jersey State in E USA, on the Atlantic coast, s of New York; the capital is TRENTON. Other major cities include NEWARK, ATLANTIC CITY, and Paterson. Settlement began in the 1620s, when the Dutch founded New Netherland (later New York). The British took the colony in 1664, separated the land between the Hudson and Delaware rivers and named it New Jersey. The N part of the state is in the Appalachian highland region; SE of this are the Piedmont plains. More than half the state is coastal plain. Various crops are grown, and cattle and poultry are important. Industries: chemicals, pharmaceuticals, rubber goods, textiles, electronics, missile components, copper smelting, oil refining. Area: 20,295sq km (7,836sq mi). Pop. (2000) 8,414,350.

Newman, Barnett (1905–70) US painter, associated with ABSTRACT EXPRESSIONISM. He developed a distinctive kind of mystical abstraction, expressed in its earliest form in *Onement* (1948). This painting consists of a single tone of dark red with a narrow stripe of lighter red running vertically across the middle. With Mark ROTHKO, Newman pioneered monochromatic colour field painting and the use of huge canvases.

Newman, John Henry (1801–90) English theologian and cardinal. As leader of the OXFORD MOVEMENT (1833–45), Newman had a powerful effect on the Church of England, only equalled by the shock of his conversion to Roman Catholicism (1845). A great literary stylist, he is remembered especially for his autobiography, *Apologia pro vita sua* (1864).

Newman, Paul (1925–) US film actor, director, and producer. Newman made his big breakthrough in 1958 with *The Left-Handed Gun*, *The Long Hot Summer*, and *Cat on a Hot Tin Roof*. He was nominated for Academy Awards for *The Hustler* (1961), *Hud* (1963), and *Cool Hand Luke* (1967). In 1968 Newman made his directorial debut, *Rachel, Rachel*. He won a best actor Oscar for *The Color of Money* (1986). Other films include *Butch Cassidy and the Sundance Kid* (1969), *The Sting* (1973) and *The Hudsucker Proxy* (1994).

New Mexico State in sw USA, on the Mexican border; the capital is SANTA FE. The largest city is ALBUQUERQUE. The Spanish established the first permanent settlement at Santa Fe in 1610. The USA acquired the region in 1848, at the end of the MEXICAN WAR. In 1912, it entered the Union as the 47th state. The first atomic bomb exploded at Alamogordo in 1945. The Sangre de Cristo Mountains in the N flank the RIO GRANDE, which runs N to s through the state. The terrain includes desert, forested mountains, and stark mesa. In the s and sw are semi-arid plains. The s Pecos and Rio Grande rivers irrigate cotton crops; hay, wheat, dairy produce and chilli peppers are also important. A large proportion of the state's wealth comes from mineral deposits, including uranium, manganese, copper, silver, turquoise, oil, coal, and natural gas. Area: 314,334sq km (121,335sq mi). Pop. (2000) 1,819,406.

New Model Army Reformed parliamentary army in the English CIVIL WAR. Formed in 1645 by Oliver CROMWELL and Thomas FAIRFAX, it was better organized, trained, and disciplined than any Royalist force. After victory at NASEBY (1645), the army emerged as a political force and was responsible for PRIDE'S PURGE (1648) of the LONG PARLIAMENT. The radical LEVELLERS within the army were suppressed by Cromwell.

New Orleans City and river port in SE Louisiana, USA, between Lake Pontchartrain and the Mississippi River.

Founded by the French in 1718, it was ceded to Spain in 1763 and acquired by the USA under the LOUISIANA PURCHASE of 1803. Its industries expanded rapidly in the 20th century after the discovery of oil and natural gas. New Orleans made an important contribution to the development of JAZZ, and is also the home of the annual MARDI GRAS festival. In 2005 Hurricane Katrina devastated the city, flooding 80% of it. It caused around 2,000 deaths, mass evacuation and more than $40 billion of damage. Pop. (2000) 1,009,000; now estimated to be 300,000 lower.

New Orleans, Battle of (January 5, 1815) Last engagement in the WAR OF 1812. It took place two weeks after the Treaty of Ghent was signed because news of the treaty had not reached New Orleans. The Americans under General Andrew JACKSON won the battle with only 71 killed, while the British lost 2,500 lives.

Newport City and port in Narragansett Bay, SE Rhode Island, USA. Founded in 1639, it served as joint state capital with Providence until 1900. It is home to music festivals and for many years hosted the AMERICA'S CUP yachting races. Tourism is the chief industry. Other industries: shipbuilding and electronic instruments. Pop. (2000) 26,475.

New South Wales State in SE Australia, on the Tasman Sea; the capital is SYDNEY. Captain James COOK first visited the area in 1770, landing at Botany Bay. He claimed the E coast of Australia for Britain, naming it New South Wales. The colony developed in the 19th century with the growth of the wool industry. New South Wales achieved responsible government in 1855, becoming a state of the Commonwealth of Australia in 1901. The Great Dividing Range separates the narrow coastal lowlands from the w plains. The MURRAY River and its tributaries are used extensively for irrigation. Wheat, wool, dairy produce and beef are the principal agricultural products. The state has valuable mineral deposits. New South Wales is the most populous and industrialized state in Australia. Area: 801,430sq km (309,180sq mi). Pop. (2002) 6,599,500.

newspaper Periodical publication, usually daily or weekly, conveying news and comment on current events. Handwritten news-sheets were posted in public places in ancient Rome under such titles as *Acta Diurna* (Daily Events). In Europe, the invention and spread of printing in the 15th century facilitated the growth of newspapers. The earliest examples were printed in German cities, soon followed by Venice, the Low Countries and other states in the 16th century. The first daily newspaper in England was the *Daily Courant* (1702).

newt Any of numerous species of tailed AMPHIBIANS of Europe, Asia, and North America. The common European newt, *Triturus vulgaris*, is terrestrial, except during the breeding season, when it is aquatic and the male develops ornamental fins. Its body is long and slender and the tail is laterally flattened. Length: to 17cm (7in). Family Salamandridae.

New Testament Second part of the BIBLE, consisting of 27 books all originally written in Greek after AD 45 and concerning the life and teachings of JESUS CHRIST. It begins with the three SYNOPTIC GOSPELS (MATTHEW, MARK, and LUKE), which present a common narrative of Christ's life and ministry, and a fourth gospel (JOHN), which is more of a theological meditation. The ACTS OF THE APOSTLES follows, which records the early development and spread of Christianity. Next come 21 letters (the EPISTLES) addressed to specific early Church communities. The New Testament ends with the REVELATION of St John the Divine (otherwise known as the Apocalypse), which is an interpretation of history designed to demonstrate the sovereignty of God.

newton (symbol N) SI unit of FORCE. One newton is the force that gives a mass of one kilogram an acceleration of one metre per second. It is named after English scientist Isaac NEWTON.

NEW JERSEY
Statehood:
December 18, 1787
Nickname:
The Garden State
State bird:
Eastern goldfinch
State flower:
Purple violet
State tree:
Red oak
State motto:
Liberty and prosperity

NEW MEXICO
Statehood:
January 16, 1912
Nickname:
The Land of Enchantment
State bird:
Roadrunner
State flower:
Yucca flower
State tree:
Pine nut
State motto:
It grows as it goes

N

INTERNET

Newfoundland and Labrador
► www.gov.nf.ca

New Hampshire
► www.state.nh.us

New Jersey
► www.state.nj.us

New Mexico
► www.newmexico.org

New South Wales
► www.nsw.gov.au
► www.tourism.nsw.gov.au

◄ **newt** An amphibian from mountainous regions of central Europe, the alpine newt (*Triturus alpestris*) feeds on worms and insects. Normally dull brown or black, the male develops bright colours in the breeding season.

NEW YORK
Statehood :
July 26, 1788
Nickname :
The Empire State
State bird :
Bluebird
State flower :
Rose
State tree :
Sugar maple
State motto :
Ever upward

Newton, Sir Isaac (1642–1727) English scientist. He studied at Cambridge University and became professor of mathematics there (1669–1701). His main works were *Philosophiae Naturalis Principia Mathematica* (1687) and *Opticks* (1704). In the former, he outlined his laws of motion and proposed the principle of universal GRAVITATION; in the latter, he showed that white LIGHT is made up of colours of the SPECTRUM and proposed his particle theory of light. He created the first system of CALCULUS in the 1660s, but did not publish it until Gottfried LEIBNIZ published his own system in 1684. In c.1671, Newton built the first reflecting telescope. He was president of the Royal Society (1703–27). In 1705, he became the first person to be knighted for scientific work. His theory of CELESTIAL MECHANICS remained unchallenged until EINSTEIN's theory of RELATIVITY and QUANTUM MECHANICS. *See* NEWTON'S LAWS

Newton's laws Three physical laws of motion, formulated by the English scientist Isaac NEWTON. The **first** law states that an object remains at rest or moves in a straight line at constant speed unless acted upon by a FORCE. For example, the Moon does not move in a straight line because of the gravity of the Earth and Sun. This property is known as INERTIA. The **second** law, which enables FORCE to be calculated, states that force is proportional to the rate of change of MOMENTUM. If the mass of a body remains constant, the force F is equal to the product of mass m and acceleration a: $F = ma$. The **third** law states that every force has associated with it an equal and opposite force. For example, a computer remains at rest on a desk because the downward force of gravity is offset by the equal upward force of the desk. *See also* MECHANICS

new town Satellite town in the UK designed to re-house residents from a nearby large city and to create local employment. The construction of some 37 new towns began in 1946 and continued until 1975.

New York State in NE USA, bounded by the Canadian border, the Great Lakes, the Atlantic Ocean and three New England states; the capital is ALBANY. NEW YORK CITY is by far the largest city in the state. Much of the state is mountainous, the ADIRONDACK MOUNTAINS (NE) and Catskills (SE) being the principal ranges. The W consists of a rolling plateau sloping down to Lake Ontario and the St Lawrence valley. The HUDSON and its tributary, the Mohawk, are the chief rivers. Henry HUDSON discovered New York Bay in 1609, and sailed up the river that now bears his name. The New Netherland colony was established in the Hudson valley. In 1664, the British seized the colony and renamed it New York. It was one of the 13 original states of the Union. The opening of the ERIE CANAL in 1825 was an enormous

NEW ZEALAND

New Zealand lies c.1,600km [994mi] SE of Australia. It consists of two main islands and several small ones. New Zealand is mountainous and partly volcanic. The S Alps contain the country's highest peak, Aoraki (Mount COOK), at 3,753m [12,313ft]. Minor earthquakes are common and there are several areas of volcanic and geothermal activity, especially on NORTH ISLAND.

About 75% of New Zealand lies above the 200m [650ft] contour. In the SE, broad, fertile valleys have been cut by rivers between the low ranges. The only extensive lowland area of New Zealand is the Canterbury Plains. As a result of its isolation, almost 90% of the indigenous plants are unique to the country.

Much of the original vegetation has been destroyed and only small areas of the *kauri* forests have survived. Mixed evergreen forest grows on the western side of SOUTH ISLAND. Beech forests grow in the highlands and large plantations are grown for timber.

CLIMATE

AUCKLAND in the N has a warm, humid climate throughout the year. WELLINGTON has cooler summers, while in Dunedin, to the SE, temperatures sometimes dip below freezing in winter. The rainfall is heaviest on the western highlands.

HISTORY

Early MAORI settlers arrived in New Zealand more than 1,000 years ago. The Dutch navigator Abel Janszoon TASMAN reached the area in 1642, but after several of his men were killed by Maoris he made no further attempt to land. His discovery was not followed up until 1769, when the British Captain James COOK rediscovered the islands.

British settlers arrived in the early 19th century. A series of intertribal wars (1815–40) killed tens of thousands of Maoris. In 1840, under the Treaty of WAITANGI, Britain took possession of the islands. Increasing colonisation led to the MAORI WARS in the 1860s, but from the 1870s the Maoris and colonial society gradually integrated. In 1893 New Zealand became the first country in the world to give women the vote. In 1907 it became a self-governing dominion in the British Empire.

New Zealanders fought alongside the Allies in both World Wars. In 1952 New Zealand signed the ANZUS treaty, a mutual defence pact with Australia and the United States. Troops from New Zealand served in the Korean War of 1950–3, and a few units later served in the war in Vietnam.

POLITICS

After Britain joined the EEC (now the EU) in 1973, New Zealand's exports to Britain

AREA 270,534sq km [104,453sq miles]
POPULATION 4,116,000
CAPITAL (POPULATION) Wellington (167,000)
GOVERNMENT Constitutional monarchy
ETHNIC GROUPS New Zealand European 74%, New Zealand Maori 10%, Polynesian 4%
LANGUAGES English and Maori (both official)
RELIGIONS Anglican 24%, Presbyterian 18%, Roman Catholic 15%, others
CURRENCY New Zealand dollar = 100 cents

shrank dramatically, forcing the country to reassess its economic strategy. This has involved seeking new markets in Asia and cutting subsidies to farmers, followed in the 1990s by privatization and cutting back on the country's extensive welfare programmes.

The rights of Maoris and the preservation of their culture remain a major political issue. In 1998, New Zealand completed a NZ$170 million settlement with the Ngai Tahu group on South Island in compensation for forced land purchases in the 19th century.

Ties with Britain have been gradually reduced. In 2005, prime minister Helen Clark stated that the country would abolish the monarchy and become a republic. New Zealand has also gradually granted independence to its former colonies in the South Pacific, until by 2007 only Tokelau remained, having rejected independence in a referendum.

ECONOMY

Manufacturing now employs twice as many people as agriculture. Meat and dairy products are the most valuable agricultural products. The country has more than 45 million sheep, 4.3 million dairy cattle, and 4.6 million beef cattle. Major crops include barley, fruits, potatoes and other vegetables and wheat. Fishing is also important. The chief manufactures are processed food products, including butter, cheese, frozen meat and woollen products.

stimulus to New York's growth. Throughout US history its economic strength and large population have given it great influence in national affairs. Agricultural produce is varied. New York is the leading manufacturing and commercial state in the USA. Industries: clothing, machinery, chemicals, electrical equipment, paper, optical instruments. Area: 127,190sq km (49,108sq mi). Pop. (2000) 17,800,000.

New York City City and port in SE New York State, at the mouth of the HUDSON River; largest city population in the USA. Manhattan Island was settled in 1624 and was bought (1626) from Native Americans by the Dutch West India Company. New Amsterdam was founded at the S end. In 1664, the British took the colony and renamed it New York. The founding of the Bank of New York by Alexander HAMILTON, and the opening of the ERIE CANAL in 1825 made New York the main commercial and financial centre in the USA. After the American CIVIL WAR and in the early 20th century, the city received a great influx of immigrants. It is made up of five boroughs: MANHATTAN, the Bronx, BROOKLYN, QUEENS, and Staten Island. Sights include the STATUE OF LIBERTY, the EMPIRE STATE BUILDING, Rockefeller Center, the METROPOLITAN MUSEUM OF ART, the Museum of Modern Art, the Guggenheim Museum, Lincoln Center, and Carnegie Hall. It is one of the world's major ports and a vital financial centre. On September 11, 2001, terrorists piloted two hijacked airplanes into the twin towers of the World Trade Center, killing *c*.2,750 people and destroying the towers. Industries: clothing, chemicals, metal products, scientific instruments, shipbuilding, broadcasting, entertainment, tourism, publishing. Pop. (2000) 8,008,278.

New Zealand State in the S Pacific. *See* country feature

Ney, Michel (1769–1815) French general, one of the most brilliant of NAPOLEON I's commanders. Ney fought in the FRENCH REVOLUTIONARY WARS and the NAPOLEONIC WARS, notably at Friedland (1807) and in the retreat from Moscow (1812). He urged Napoleon to abdicate in 1814 and accepted the BOURBON restoration, but rejoined Napoleon during the HUNDRED DAYS and fought gallantly in the WATERLOO campaign. He was subsequently executed as a traitor.

Ngo Dinh Diem *See* DIEM, NGO DINH

Niagara Falls Waterfalls on the Niagara River on the border of the USA (W New York) and Canada (SE Ontario); divided into the Horseshoe, or Canadian, Falls, and the American Falls. The Canadian Falls are 48m (158ft) high and 792m (2,600ft), wide; the American Falls are 51m (167ft) high and 305m (1,000ft) wide.

Niamey Capital of Niger, West Africa, in the SW part of the country, on the River Niger. It became capital of the French colony of Niger in 1926. It grew rapidly after World War 2 and is now the country's largest city and its commercial and administrative centre. Manufactures include textiles, ceramics, plastics, and chemicals. Pop. (2002 est.) 723,200.

Nicaea, Councils of Two important ecumenical councils of the Christian Church held in Nicaea (modern Iznik, Turkey). The **first** was convoked in AD 325 to resolve the problems caused by the emergence of ARIANISM. It promulgated a creed, affirming belief in the divinity of Christ. The **second**, held in 787, was summoned by the patriarch Tarasius to deal with the problem of the worship of icons.

Nicaragua Republic in Central America. *See* country feature, page 548

Nice City on the Mediterranean coast, SE France; capital of Alpes-Maritimes department. Founded by Phocaean Greeks in the 4th century BC it was conquered by Rome in the 1st century AD. In the 10th century it passed to the counts of Provence. In 1388 it became a possession of the House of Savoy. Itbecame permanently part of France in 1860. It is a major centre of the French RIVIERA. Industries: tourism, olive oil, perfumes, textiles, electronics. Pop. (2000) 889,000.

Nicene Creed Statement of Christian faith named after the First Council of NICAEA (AD 325). Its exact origin is uncertain. The Nicene Creed defends the orthodox Christian doctrine of the TRINITY against the ARIAN heresy. It is subscribed to by all Christian Churches and is used in the celebrations of the EUCHARIST. *See also* APOSTLES' CREED; ATHANASIAN CREED

Nicholas, Saint (active 4th century) Patron saint of children and sailors. According to tradition, he was Bishop of Myra in Asia Minor. Nicholas is the subject of many legends. In one, he secretly gave gold to three poor girls as their dowry. From this came the custom of giving presents on his feast day, December 6, a habit later transferred to CHRISTMAS in most countries. His name in one Dutch dialect, *Sinter Claes*, became Santa Claus.

Nicholas I (1796–1855) Tsar of Russia (1825–55). As tsar, he was immediately confronted by the Decembrist revolt, during which a secret society of officers and aristocrats assembled some 3000 troops in St Petersburg, demanding a representative democracy. Having crushed the rebels, Nicholas ruthlessly suppressed rebellion in Poland and assisted Austria against the Hungarian REVOLUTIONS OF 1848. His pressure on Turkey led to the CRIMEAN WAR (1853–56).

Nicholas II (1868–1918) Last Tsar of Russia (1894–1917). Torn between the autocracy of his father, ALEXANDER III, and the reformist policies of ministers, such as Count Sergei Witte, he lacked the capacity for firm leadership. Defeat in the RUSSO-JAPANESE WAR was followed by the RUSSIAN REVOLUTION OF 1905. Nicholas agreed to constitutional government but, as danger receded, removed most of the powers of the Duma (Parliament). In WORLD WAR I he took military command (1915), but a succession of defeats provoked the RUSSIAN REVOLUTION (1917). Nicholas was forced to abdicate, and in July 1918 he and his family were executed by the BOLSHEVIKS.

Nichols, Mike (1931–) US stage and film director, b. Germany as Michael Peschkowsky. In 1939, his family fled to the US from Nazi Germany. Nichols began his career in theatre in Chicago. He achieved immediate success with his film debut *Who's Afraid of Virginia Woolf* (1966). Nicols won an Academy Award for best director for *The Graduate* (1967). He

INTERNET

New York
▶ www.state.ny.us

New Zealand
▶ www.govt.nz
▶ www.purenz.com

▲ **Nicholson** One of the most versatile of film actors, Jack Nicholson's films include *The Shining* (1980), *Reds* (1981), *The Postman Always Rings Twice* (1981), *Batman* (1989), and *As Good As It Gets* (1998). His roles are often that of an outsider.

◀ **Niagara Falls** Two spectacular waterfalls on the Niagara River are known as the Niagara Falls. They lie on the border between the USA and Canada, with Goat Island separating the Canadian Falls from the American (shown here). They provide hydroelectric power as well as attracting great numbers of tourists.

▲ **Nietzsche** The influential German philosopher Friedrich Nietzsche's work was distorted by the Nazis and used to defend their idea of an Aryan super-race.

earned further Academy nominations for *Silkwood* (1983) and *Working Girl* (1988). Other films include *Catch-22* (1971).

Nicholson, Ben (1894–1982) English painter, one of the champions of British ABSTRACT ART. Influenced by CUBISM and Piet MONDRIAN, Nicholson developed a geometric abstract style that he expressed in austere carved and painted reliefs, such as *White Relief* (1935). He later produced a series of freely abstracted still-lifes and landscapes, before returning to reliefs in the 1960s. Both he and his second wife, Barbara HEPWORTH, were leading members of the St Ives School.

Nicholson, Jack (1937–) US film actor. Charismatic and versatile, Nicholson won an Oscar-nomination for his supporting role in *Easy Rider* (1969). Other nominations followed for *Five Easy Pieces* (1970) and *Chinatown* (1974). He won best actor Oscars for *One Flew Over The Cuckoo's Nest* (1975) and *As Good As It Gets* (1998), and a best supporting actor award for *Terms of Endearment* (1983). His directorial credits include *The Two Jakes* (1990). *See* picture, page 547.

nickel (symbol Ni) Silvery-white metallic element, one of the TRANSITION ELEMENTS. Its chief ores are pentlandite and niccolite. Hard, malleable and ductile, nickel is used in stainless steels, other special alloys, coinage, cutlery, storage batteries and as a hydrogenation catalyst. Properties: at.no. 28; r.a.m. 58.71; r.d. 8.90 (25°C); m.p. 1,453°C (2,647°F); b.p. 2,732°C (4,950°F); most common isotope Ni^{58} (67.84%).

Nicosia (Levkosía) Capital of Cyprus, in the centre of the island. Known to the ancients as Ledra, the city was later held by Byzantines, French crusaders and Venetians. The Ottoman Turks occupied the city from 1571 to 1878, when it passed to Britain. It is now divided into Greek and Turkish sectors. Industries: cigarettes, textiles, footwear. Pop. (1999 est.) 195,300.

nicotine Poisonous ALKALOID obtained from the leaves of TOBACCO, used in agriculture as a pesticide and in veterinary medicine to kill external parasites. Nicotine is the principal addictive agent in smoking tobacco. *See also* CIGARETTE

Nielsen, Carl August (1865–1931) Danish composer. He developed the principle of progressive TONALITY. Nielsen wrote six symphonies, of which the fourth, 'The Inextinguishable' (1914–16), is perhaps the best known. He also composed concertos for violin, flute and clarinet, two operas, a woodwind quintet and four string quartets.

Nietzsche, Friedrich Wilhelm (1844–1900) German philosopher who rejected Christianity and the prevailing morality of his time and emphasized people's freedom to create their own values. He studied classical philology and taught Greek. In 1879 he abandoned PHILOLOGY for philosophy and worked out his view of the freedom of the individual over the next decade. In *Thus Spake Zarathustra* (1883–91), Nietzsche presented his notion of the *Übermensch* ('Superman'), the idealized man, strong, positive, and able to impose his wishes upon the weak and worthless. Other works include *Beyond Good and Evil* (1886) and *On the Genealogy of Morals* (1887). In 1889 Nietzsche was declared insane.

Niger Republic in N central Africa. *See* country feature

NICARAGUA

The Republic of Nicaragua is the largest country in Central America. The Central Highlands rise in the NW Cordillera Isabella to more than 2,400m [8,000ft] and are the source for many of the rivers that drain the eastern plain. The Caribbean coast forms part of the MOSQUITO COAST. Lakes Managua and Nicaragua lie on the edge of a narrow volcanic region which contains Nicaragua's major urban areas, including the capital MANAGUA and the second-largest city LEÓN. This region is highly unstable, with many active volcanoes, and is prone to earthquakes.

Rainforests cover large areas in the E, with trees such as cedar, mahogany and walnut. Tropical savanna is common in the drier W.

CLIMATE

Nicaragua has a tropical climate, with a rainy season from June to October. Cooler weather is found in the Central Highlands. The wettest part is the Mosquito Coast, with 4,200mm [165in] of rain.

HISTORY

The explorer Christopher Columbus reached Nicaragua in 1502 and claimed the land for Spain. *c.*100,000 Native Americans were killed by Spanish colonialism and imported disease. By 1518 Nicaragua had become part of the Spanish Captaincy-General of Guatemala, but in the 17th century Britain secured control of the Caribbean coast.

In 1821 Nicaragua gained independence, then formed part of the Central American Federation from 1825 to 1838. In the mid-19th century, civil war and US and British interference ravaged Nicaragua. The USA sought the construction of a trans-isthmian canal through Nicaragua. In 1855 William WALKER invaded and briefly established himself as president. José Santos Zemalya's dictatorship from 1893 to 1909 gained control of the Mosquito Coast and formed close links with the British. Following his downfall, civil war raged once more. In 1912 US marines landed to protect the pro-US regime, and in 1916 the USA gained exclusive rights to the canal. Opposition to US occupation resulted in guerrilla war, led by Augusto César Sandino. In 1933 the US marines withdrew, but set up a pro-US National Guard to help defeat the rebels.

In 1934 Anastasio SOMOZA, director of the National Guard, assassinated Sandino. Somoza became president in 1937, and his dictatorial regime led to political isolation. Somoza was succeeded by his sons Luis in 1956 and Anastasio in 1967. Anastasio's diversion of international relief aid following the devastating 1972 Managua earthquake cemented opposition.

POLITICS

In 1979 the SANDINISTA National Liberation Front (FSLN) overthrew the Somoza regime. Led by Daniel ORTEGA, they instigated wide-ranging socialist reforms. The USA, con-

AREA 130,000sq km [50,193sq mi]	
POPULATION 5,675,000	
CAPITAL (POPULATION) Managua (1,159,000)	
GOVERNMENT Multiparty republic	
ETHNIC GROUPS Mestizo 69%, White 17%, Black 9%, Amerindian 5%	
LANGUAGES Spanish (official)	
RELIGIONS Roman Catholic 85%, Protestant	
CURRENCY Córdoba oro (gold córdoba) = 100 centavos	

cerned about the Sandinista's ties with communist regimes, sought to destabilize the government by supporting the CONTRA rebels leading to a decade of devastating civil war.

In 1990 elections, Violeta CHAMORRO's National Opposition Union coalition defeated the Sandinistas. Coalition partners and Sandinista-controlled trade unions blocked many of her reforms. In 1996 elections, Liberal leader Arnoldo Aleman defeated Chamorro. In 1998, Hurricane Mitch killed *c.*4,000 and caused extensive damage. Enrique Bolanos became president in 2001 elections, and in 2003 Aleman was sentenced to 20 years in prison for corruption. The 2006 elections returned Daniel Ortega to the presidency. A deal in 2007 ended a long-standing dispute with Honduras over maritime borders.

ECONOMY

Nicaragua faces problems in rebuilding its economy and introducing free-market reforms. Agriculture is the main activity, employing 50% of the workforce and accounting for 70% of exports. Major cash crops include coffee, cotton, sugar and bananas. Rice is the main food crop.

There is some copper, gold, and silver, but mining is underdeveloped. Most of the country's small manufacturing base is near Managua.

Niger Major river of w Africa. It rises in the Fouta Djallon plateau in the sw Republic of Guinea and flows NE through Guinea into the Mali Republic, where it forms an extensive inland delta. It then flows in a great curve across the border into Nigeria and s into another vast delta before emptying into the Gulf of Guinea. Length: 4,180km (2,600mi).

Niger-Congo languages Group of *c.*1,000 languages spoken by more than 300 million people in sub-Saharan Africa. The main ones are BANTU (spoken in s Africa), FULANI (Guinea, Senegal, and other w African countries), SWAHILI (E coast), YORUBA (mainly Nigeria) and Malinke (Mali).

Nigeria Republic in w Africa. *See* country feature, page 550

nightingale Migratory Old World songbird of the THRUSH family (Turdidae). The common nightingale of England and Western Europe (*Luscinia megarhynchos*) is ruddy-brown with light grey underparts. Length: *c.*16.5cm (6.5in).

Nightingale, Florence (1820–1910) British nurse, b. Italy. She founded modern NURSING and is best known for her activities in the CRIMEAN WAR. In 1860, she founded the Nightingale School and Home for nurse training at St Thomas's Hospital, London.

nightjar Insect-eating, nocturnal bird found worldwide. It has a whirring cry. Length: 27cm (10.5in). Family Caprimulgidae.

nightshade Name given to various species of poisonous flowering plants, but especially to the DEADLY NIGHT-SHADE (*Atropa belladonna*) and its close relatives.

nihilism Philosophical belief that there are no basic moral values and that existence is without ultimate purpose or meaning. Nihilism is often linked to a rejection of authority and religion. The term is particularly associated with Friedrich NIETZSCHE and certain forms of EXISTEN-TIALISM. In 19th century Russia the term was used to criticize revolutionaries who were not in fact nihilist.

Nijinsky, Vaslav (1890–1950) Russian dancer, often regarded as the greatest male ballet dancer of the 20th century. Dancing with the BALLETS RUSSES, his most noted roles were in *Petrushka*, *Les Sylphides* and *Scheherazade*. From 1912, Nijinsky choreographed such ballets as *L'Après-midi d'un faune*, *Jeux*, *Le Sacre du printemps* for DIAGHILEV and STRAVINSKY's *The Rites of Spring* (1913).

Nile Longest river in the world, flowing *c.*6,700km (4,160mi) from the Kagera headstream, E Burundi, to its Mediterranean delta in NE Egypt. The **Kagera** flows generally N before emptying into Lake VICTORIA. The **Victoria** Nile flows from Lake Victoria to Lake ALBERT in Uganda. From Lake Albert to the Sudanese border, it is called the **Albert** Nile. It continues to

---

NIGER

The Republic of Niger is a landlocked nation in N central Africa. The N plateaus lie in the SAHARA, while N central Niger contains the rugged Aïr Mountains. These, near Agadez, reach a height of 2,022m [6,632ft] above sea level. The rainfall in the mountains – averaging *c.*175mm [7in] per year – is sufficient in places to permit the growth of thorny shrub. Severe droughts since the 1970s have crippled the traditional lifestyle of the nomads in N and central Niger as the Sahara has slowly advanced s. The s region has also been hit by droughts.

The s consists of broad plains. The Lake CHAD Basin lies in SE Niger on the borders with Chad and Nigeria. The only permanent rivers are the NIGER and its tributaries in the sw. The narrow Niger Valley is the country's most fertile and densely populated region and includes the capital, Niamey. Niger, a title which comes from a Tuareg word meaning 'flowing water', seems scarcely appropriate for a country which consists mainly of hot, arid, sandy and stony basins.

Buffaloes, elephants, giraffes. and lions are found in the 'W' National Park, which Niger shares with Benin and Burkina Faso. Most of s

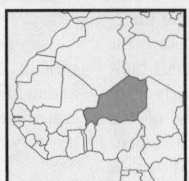

Niger lies in the SAHEL region of dry grassland. The Aïr Mountains support grass and scrub. The N deserts are generally barren.

CLIMATE

Niger is one of the world's hottest countries. The warmest months are March to May, when the HAR-MATTAN wind blows from the Sahara. Niamey has a tropical climate, with a rainy season from June to September. Rainfall decreases from s to N, and N Niger is practically rainless. The far s consists of tropical savanna.

HISTORY

Neolithic remains have been found in the northern desert. Nomadic TUAREG settled in the Aïr Mountains in the 11th century AD, and by the 13th century established a state centred around Agadez and the trans-Saharan trade. In the 14th century, the HAUSA settled in southern Niger. In the early 16th century the SONGHAI Empire controlled much of Niger, but the Moroccans supplanted the Songhai at the turn of the century.

Later on, the Hausa and then the FULANI set up kingdoms in the region. In the early 19th century the Fulani gained control of much of southern Niger. The first French expedition arrived in 1891, but Tuareg resistance prevented full occupation until 1914.

POLITICS

In 1922 Niger became a colony within French West Africa. In 1958 Niger voted to remain an autonomous republic within the French Community. It gained full independence in 1960, and Hamani Diori became Niger's first president. He maintained close ties with France.

Drought in the Sahel, beginning in 1968, killed many livestock and destroyed crops. In 1974 a group of army officers, led by Lieutenant Colonel Seyni Kountché, overthrew Hamani Diori and suspended the constitution. Kountché died in 1987 and was succeeded by his cousin General Ali Saibou. In 1991 the Tuareg in N Niger began an armed campaign for greater autonomy. A national conference removed Sai-

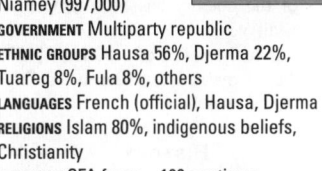

AREA 1,267,000sq km [489,189sq mi]
POPULATION 12,895,000
CAPITAL (POPULATION) Niamey (997,000)
GOVERNMENT Multiparty republic
ETHNIC GROUPS Hausa 56%, Djerma 22%, Tuareg 8%, Fula 8%, others
LANGUAGES French (official), Hausa, Djerma
RELIGIONS Islam 80%, indigenous beliefs, Christianity
CURRENCY CFA franc = 100 centimes

bou and established a transitional government. In 1993 multiparty elections, Mahamane Ousmane of the Alliance of Forces for Change (AFC) coalition became president. The collapse of the coalition led to fresh elections in 1995, which were won by the National Movement for a Development Society (MNSD), but a military coup, led by Colonel Ibrahim Bare Mainassara, seized power. In 1995 the government and the Tuaregs signed a peace accord. Elections in 1996 confirmed Mainassara as president. In 1999 bodyguards assassinated Mainassara and he was replaced briefly by Major Daouda Malam Wanke. Parliamentary rule was restored, and Tandjou Mamadou was elected president. He was re-elected in 2004. Renewed unrest occurred in 2007 from the Tuareg in the N.

ECONOMY

Droughts have caused great hardship and food shortages in Niger, and have destroyed much of the traditional nomadic lifestyle. Niger's chief resource is uranium, and it is the world's second-largest producer. Uranium, most of which goes to France, accounts for more than 80% of exports. Some tin and tungsten are also mined, but other mineral resources are largely unexploited.

Niger is one of the world's poorest countries, despite its resources. Farming employs 85% of the workforce, although only 3% of the land is arable and 7% is used for grazing. Food crops include beans, cassava, millet, rice, and sorghum. Cotton and groundnuts are leading cash crops.

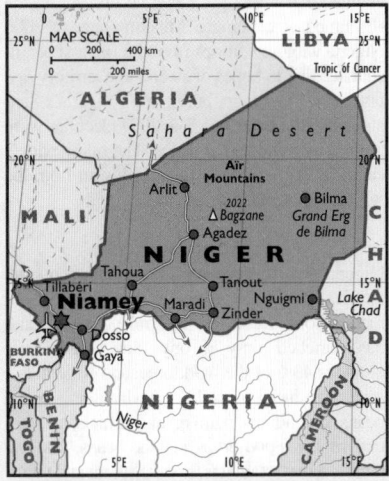

N

flow N through the S Sudanese swamps as the **Bahr el Jebel**. From Malakâl to KHARTOUM the river is called the **White** Nile. At Khartoum it converges with the **Blue** Nile. As the Nile, the river continues to flow N to the Egyptian border. It then flows into the man-made Lake Nasser, created by the damming of the river at ASWAN. From Aswan, the river flows through LUXOR to CAIRO. N of Cairo is the Nile Delta. The Nile empties into the Mediterranean at Damietta and Rosetta. As well as supporting the agriculture of Egypt and Sudan, the Nile is used for transport, hydroelectricity and tourism.

Nimitz, Chester William (1885–1966) US admiral. He served in submarines during World War 1, and commanded the Pacific fleet during World War 2, directing operations against the Japanese at Midway and subsequent battles.

Nin, Anaïs (1903–77) US novelist and diarist, b. France. She was part of the 'Lost Generation' of US expatriate writers in Paris during the 1920s. A student of Carl JUNG, her novels are psychological studies. They include *The House of Incest* (1936) and *Winter of Artifice* (1939). Her diaries (*Journals*, 1966–80) aroused admiration and controversy.

NIGERIA

The Federal Republic of Nigeria is the most populous nation in Africa. The country's main rivers are the NIGER and Benue, which meet in central Nigeria. N of the two river valleys are high plains and plateaux. The Lake CHAD Basin is in the NE, with the Sokoto plains in the NW. S Nigeria contains hilly uplands and broad coastal plains, including the swampy Niger Delta. Highlands form the border with Cameroon. Mangrove swamps line the coast, behind which are rainforests. The N contains large areas of savanna with forests along the rivers. Open grassland and semi-desert occur in drier areas.

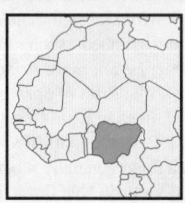

CLIMATE

The S of the country has high temperatures and rain all year. Parts of the coast have an average annual rainfall of 3,800mm [150in]. The N has a marked dry season and higher temperatures than the S.

HISTORY

Excavations around the Nigerian village of Nok have uncovered some of the oldest and most beautiful examples of African sculpture. The Nok civilization flourished between 500 BC and AD 200. In the 11th century the Kanem-

Bornu kingdom extended S from Lake Chad into Nigeria, and the HAUSA established several city-states. In SW Nigeria, the state of BENIN and the YORUBA kingdom of Oyo flourished in the 15th century. They produced superb brass, bronze and ivory sculptures. The SONGHAI Empire dominated N Nigeria in the early 16th century.

The Portuguese were the first Europeans to reach the Nigerian coast, and they established trading links with Benin in the late 15th century. Nigeria became a centre of the slave trade, with major European powers competing for control. The IGBO established city-states built on the wealth of the trade. In the early 19th century, the FULANI captured many of the Hausa city-states. Sokoto retained its independence. The SW began a protracted civil war. In 1807, Britain renounced the slave trade, but other countries continued the practice. In 1861 Britain seized LAGOS, ostensibly to stop the trade. By 1885 the British controlled all of S Nigeria and gradually extended N, conquering all of Nigeria by 1906. They divided the country into the Colony (Lagos) and Protectorate of Southern Nigeria and the Protectorate of Northern Nigeria. The two merged in 1914, and Britain ruled indirectly through colonial

AREA 923,768sq km [356,667sq mi]
POPULATION 135,031,000
CAPITAL (POPULATION) Abuja (339,000)
GOVERNMENT Federal multiparty republic
ETHNIC GROUPS Hausa and Fulani 29%, Yoruba 21%, Ibo (or Igbo) 18%, Ijaw 10%, Kanuri 4%
LANGUAGES English (official), Hausa, Yoruba, Ibo
RELIGIONS Islam 50%, Christianity 40%, traditional beliefs
CURRENCY Naira = 100 kobo

officials and local rulers. Cities, infrastructure and industries developed. In 1954 Nigeria federated into three regions (N, E, and W) plus the territory of Lagos.

POLITICS

Nigeria became independent in 1960 and a federal republic in 1963. The federal constitution, dividing the country into four regions in an attempt to prevent Nigeria's hundreds of ethnic, religious and linguistic groups from threatening national unity. In 1967, in an attempt to meet the demands of more ethnic groups, the regions were replaced by 12 states. The division of the E region provoked an uprising and in 1967 its governor, Colonel Odumegwu Ojukwu, proclaimed it an independent republic called Biafra. Civil war continued until Biafra's surrender in 1970.

In 1998–9 civilian rule was finally restored. Former military leader Olusegun Obasanjo was elected president. In the late 1990s and early 2000s riots broke out between Yorubas and Hausas in the SW, while the introduction of Islamic Sharia law in northern states has caused friction with Christians. In 2004 the government claimed that it had put down an uprising in the NE aimed at creating a Muslim state. In 2006 Nigeria withdrew troops from the Bakassi peninsula, leading to hopes of an end to a territory dispute with Cameroon, but in 2007 Nigeria's Senate halted the handover. The 2007 elections were marred by fraud and violence. The ruling party's candidate Umaru Yar'Adua, a Muslim from the N, became president.

ECONOMY

Nigeria is a 'low-income' developing economy despite many natural resources, including oil, metals, forests and fertile farmland. Oil wealth has enriched only a tiny elite. Agriculture employs 43% of the workforce, and Nigeria is a major producer of cash crops including cocoa beans, groundnuts, palm oil and kernels, and natural rubber. Food crops include beans, cassava, maize, millet, plantains, rice, sorghum and yams.

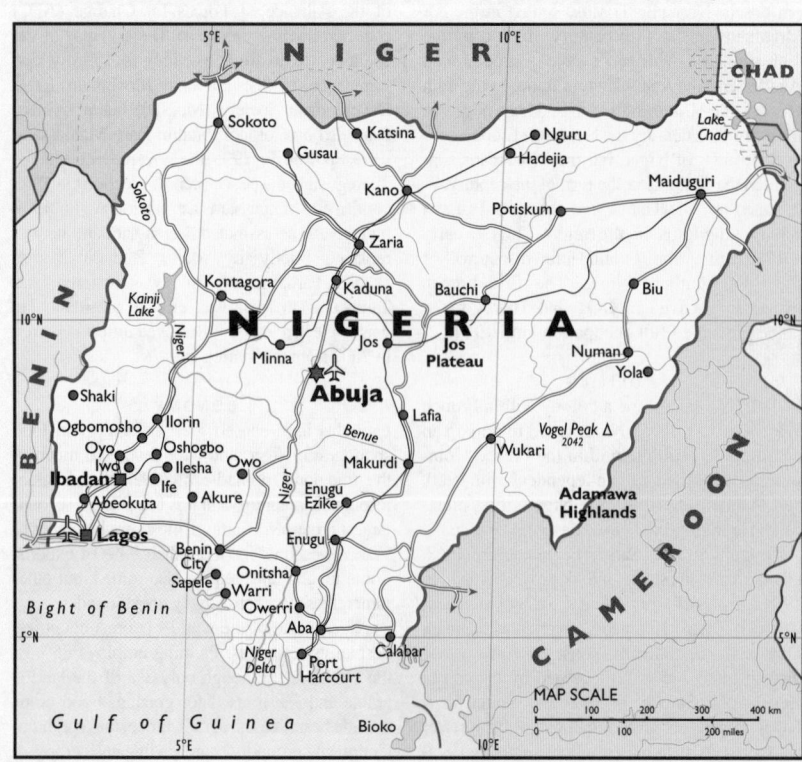

Nineveh Capital of ancient ASSYRIA, on the River Tigris (opposite modern Mosul, Iraq). First occupied in the 6th millennium BC Nineveh became the Assyrian capital under SENNACHERIB (r. 704–681BC). The city walls were more than 12km (7.5mi) long, and contained gardens irrigated by canals. Nineveh was sacked by the Medes in 612 BC but continued to be occupied until the Middle Ages.

niobium (symbol Nb) Shiny grey-white metallic element of the second transition series. Its chief ore is pyrochlore. Soft and ductile, niobium is used in special stainless steels and in alloys for rockets and jet engines. It was discovered in 1801 by the English chemist Charles Hatchett (1765–1847) who named it columbium; the name was changed to niobium in 1844. Properties: at.no. 41; r.a.m. 92.9064; r.d. 8.57; m.p. 2,468°C (4,474°F); b.p. 4,742°C (8,568°F); most common isotope Nb^{93} (100%).

Nirenberg, Marshall Warren (1927–) US biochemist who found the key to the GENETIC CODE by deciphering different combinations of three nucleotide bases (called 'codons') within long nucleotide chains in DNA and RNA. He shared the 1968 Nobel Prize in physiology or medicine.

nirvana Conception of salvation and liberation from rebirth in the religions of ancient India – HINDUISM, BUDDHISM, and JAINISM. To Hindus, *nirvana* is extinction in the supreme being, brought about by internal happiness, internal satisfaction and internal illumination. To Buddhists, it is the attainment of a transcendent state of enlightenment through the extinction of all desires. To Jainists, *nirvana* is a state of eternal blissful repose.

nitrate Salt of NITRIC ACID. Nitrate salts contain the nitrate ion (NO_3) and some are important, naturally occurring compounds such as saltpetre (potassium nitrate, KNO_3) and Chile saltpetre (sodium nitrate, $NaNO_3$). Nitrates are used as food preservers, fertilizers, explosives, and as a source of nitric acid. They can be an environmental hazard.

nitric acid (HNO_3) Colourless liquid that is one of the strongest mineral acids. Nitric acid attacks most metals, resulting in the formation of NITRATES, and is a strong oxidizing agent. It is used in the manufacture of agricultural chemicals, explosives, plastics, dyes and rocket propellants.

nitrogen (symbol N) Common, gaseous nonmetallic element of group V of the periodic table. Colourless and odourless, it is the major component of the atmosphere (78% by volume), from which it is extracted by fractional distillation of liquid air. It is necessary for life, being present in all plants and animals.English chemist Daniel Rutherford (1749–1819) isolated it in 1772. The main industrial use is in the HABER PROCESS. Nitrogen compounds are used in fertilizers, explosives, dyes, foods and drugs. The element is chemically inert. Properties: at.no. 7; r.a.m. 14.0067; r.d. 1.2506; m.p. −209.86°C (−345.75°F); b.p. −195.8°C (−320.4°F); most common isotope N^{14} (99.76%).

nitrogen cycle Circulation of NITROGEN through plants and animals in the BIOSPHERE. Plants obtain nitrogen compounds for producing essential proteins through ASSIMILATION. Nitrogen-fixing bacteria in the soil or plant root nodules take free nitrogen from the soil and air to form the nitrogen compounds (NITRATES) used by plants in assimilation (*see* NITROGEN FIXATION). HERBIVORES obtain their nitrogen from the plants, and CARNIVORES obtain nitrogen by eating herbivores (*see* FOOD CHAIN). SAPROPHYTES decompose the tissue of all the organisms concerned and the nitrogen is released back into the cycle.

nitrogen dioxide (NO_2) Oxide of NITROGEN. It is a pungent, brown gas that readily forms dinitrogen tetroxide (N_2O_4). It is made by the action of concentrated NITRIC ACID on copper, and dissolves in water to give a mixture of nitrous and nitric acids. It is also formed by the reaction of oxygen with nitrogen monoxide. Its presence in the atmosphere contributes to the formation of ACID RAIN and the depletion of the OZONE LAYER.

nitrogen fixation Incorporation of atmospheric NITROGEN into chemicals for use by organisms. Nitrogen-fixing microorganisms (mainly BACTERIA and CYANOBACTERIA) absorb nitrogen gas from the air, from air spaces in the soil or from water, and build it up into compounds of AMMONIA. Other bacteria can then change these compounds into NITRATES, which can be taken up by plants. *See also* NITROGEN CYCLE

nitroglycerine Oily liquid used in the manufacture of explosives. It is used in medicine (as glyceryl trinitrate) to relieve the symptoms of ANGINA.

nitrous oxide (dinitrogen oxide) Colourless gas (N_2O) that is used as an anaesthetic or analgesic during surgical or dental operations. It is known as 'laughing gas' since it produces exhilaration. It is also used in making pressurized foods. It is also used in making pressurized foods. It was first prepared in 1772 by English chemist Joseph PRIESTLEY.

Niue Island territory in the S Pacific Ocean, 2160km (1340mi) NE of New Zealand; the capital is Alofi. The largest coral island in the world, Niue was first visited by Europeans in 1774. In 1901, it was annexed to New Zealand. In 1974 it achieved self-government in free association with New Zealand. Its economy is mainly agricultural. The major export is coconut. Area: 260sq km (100sq mi). Pop. (2000) 2000.

Niven, David (1910–83) English film actor. He was regularly cast as the reticent but urbane Englishman. He gave fine performances in *Wuthering Heights* (1939) and *The First of the Few* (1942). Other films include *Around the World in Eighty Days* (1956). He also wrote two autobiographies, *The Moon's a Balloon* (1971) and *Bring On The Empty Horses* (1975).

Nixon, Richard Milhous (1913–94) 37th US President (1969–74). He was elected as a Republican to the House of Representatives in 1946, and the Senate in 1950. Nixon came to prominence as a member of the House Un-American Activities Committee (HUAC). He was vice president under Dwight D. EISENHOWER (1953–61), but lost the presidential elections of 1960 to John F. KENNEDY. In 1968, Nixon received the Republican nomination for a second time and narrowly defeated his Democrat challenger, Hubert Humphrey. As president, he adopted a policy of détente with the Soviet Union and opened US relations with communist China. Re-elected in 1972, he withdrew US troops from the VIETNAM WAR (1973). The WATERGATE affair revealed that he was implicated in the obstruction of justice, and he resigned to avoid impeachment.

Nkomo, Joshua (1917–99) Zimbabwean statesman, vice-president (1990–99). In 1961, he became leader of ZAPU. In 1976, Nkomo and Robert MUGABE formed the Patriotic Front in opposition to Ian Smith's white-minority government in Rhodesia. In 1982, he was dismissed from Mugabe's government, but returned in 1988.

Nkrumah, Kwame (1909–72) Ghanaian statesman, prime minister (1957–60), first president of Ghana (1960–66). He was the leading post-colonial proponent of PAN-AFRICANISM. In 1950 the British imprisoned Nkrumah, but released him when his party won the general election. He led the Gold Coast to independence in 1957, and became prime minister. In 1960, Gold Coast became the Republic of Ghana and Nkrumah was made president. Nkrumah gradually assumed absolute power and Ghana became a one-party state (1964). While on a visit to China, he was deposed in a military coup (1966).

Noah Old Testament patriarch, the only person righteous enough to be chosen by God to survive the destruction of the FLOOD. In Genesis 6–9, Noah built an ARK, in accordance with God's instructions, to carry and shelter himself, all his family, and selected animals and birds. Noah and his sons and their wives were the ancestors of the human race after the Flood.

Nobel, Alfred Bernhard (1833–96) Swedish chemist, engineer and industrialist. He invented DYNAMITE in 1866 and patented a more powerful explosive, gelignite, in 1876. With the fortune he made from the manufacture of explosives, he founded the NOBEL PRIZES.

nobelium (symbol No) Radioactive metallic element, one of the ACTINIDE SERIES of elements. Seven isotopes are known. It was discovered in 1958 by US nuclear scientist Albert Ghiorso (1915–) and colleagues at the Lawrence Radiation laboratory in Berkeley, California. Properties: at.no. 102, most stable isotope No^{255} (half-life 3 minutes). *See also* TRANSURANIC ELEMENTS

Nobel Prizes Awards given each year for outstanding contributions in the fields of physics, chemistry, physiology or medicine, literature, economics, and world peace. Established in 1901 by the will of Swedish scientist Alfred NOBEL,

INTERNET

Nobel Prizes
▶ www.nobel.se

Nolde, Emil
▶ www.famsf.org

Norfolk Island
▶ www.nf

N

the prizes are awarded annually on December 10. Committees based in Sweden and Norway select the winners.

Nobili, Leopoldo (1784–1835) Italian physicist who was a pioneer in electrochemistry. He generated electricity using platinum ELECTRODES in an alkaline nitrate ELECTROLYTE and devised the astatic galvanometer to measure the current.

noble gas (inert gas) HELIUM, NEON, ARGON, KRYPTON, XENON, and RADON – the elements (in order of increasing atomic number) forming group 0 of the PERIODIC TABLE. They are colourless, odourless, and unreactive. They have low reactivity because their outer electron shells are complete (two electrons for helium and eight each for the rest).

nocturne In music, a quiet piece endeavouring to reflect the atmosphere and mood of night-time. First used by John Field for some of his piano pieces, the title was later used by CHOPIN. DEBUSSY composed three orchestral nocturnes.

noh drama Form of JAPANESE THEATRE that developed between the 12th or 13th and the 15th centuries. It was influenced by ZEN, and the actors were originally Buddhist priests. The plots were taken chiefly from Japanese mythology and poetry. With little character or plot development, the Noh play seeks to convey a moment of experience or insight. It is highly stylized and uses masks, music, dance and song. Noh was central to the development of KABUKI THEATRE.

Nok Ancient African civilization that flourished 500 BC to 200 AD named after the village of Nok in central Nigeria where remains were found. Nok artists produced small clay figurines that are among the first African sculptures.

Nolde, Emil (1867–1956) German painter and graphic artist who exemplified EXPRESSIONISM. He trained as a wood-carver before turning to painting relatively late. He painted his subjects (often flowers or landscapes) with deep, glowing colours and simplified outlines, bringing the works to the borders of ABSTRACT ART. Although Nolde was a member of Die BRÜCKE (1905–07), he was essentially a solitary figure.

nomad Member of a wandering group of people who live mainly by hunting or herding. Nomadism is an intermediate state between hunter-gatherer and farming societies. Today, nomadic groups survive only in the more remote parts of Africa, Asia, and the Arctic. *See also* BEDOUIN; ESKIMO

nominalism Philosophical theory, opposed to REALISM, that denies the reality of universal concepts. Whereas realists claim that there are universal concepts, such as roundness or dog, that are referred to by the use of these terms, nominalists argue that such generalized concepts cannot be known, and that the terms refer only to specific qualities common to particular circles or dogs that have been encountered up to now. Nominalism was much discussed by philosophers of the Middle Ages.

nonalignment *See* NEUTRALITY

nonconformism Dissent from or lack of conformity with the religious doctrines or discipline of an established Church, especially the CHURCH OF ENGLAND. The term Nonconformist applies to all the sects of British Protestantism that do not subscribe to the principles of the established Anglican Church or the established CHURCH OF SCOTLAND. It arose in England in reaction to the Act of UNIFORMITY (1662). Movements such as CONGREGATIONALISM and PRESBYTERIANISM,

BAPTISTS and QUAKERS proliferated. Nonconformist Churches were eventually granted freedom of worship in 1689, and civil and political rights in 1828. METHODISM and UNITARIANISM swelled their ranks during the 18th century.

non-figurative (non-objective) Art that makes no attempt to represent objects from the physical world. The term comprises all ABSTRACT ART that does not rely on the appearance of the visual world for the source of its ideas.

nonjurors Clergy in England and Scotland who refused to take the oath of allegiance to WILLIAM III and MARY II in 1689. Anglo-Catholic in sympathy, they included bishops and about 400 priests in England and most of the Scottish episcopal clergy.

Nono, Luigi (1924–90) Italian composer. An early follower of Anton WEBERN, he gained international recognition with the *Canonic Variations* (1950), an orchestral work based on a note series of Arnold SCHOENBERG. He composed several political works, including the anti-fascist opera *Intolerance* (1960).

noradrenaline HORMONE secreted by nerves in the AUTONOMIC NERVOUS SYSTEM and by the ADRENAL GLANDS. It slows the heart rate and constricts small arteries, thus raising the blood pressure. It is used therapeutically to combat the fall in blood pressure that accompanies shock.

Norfolk County of E England; the county town is NORWICH. The region was home to the ICENI tribe in the 3rd century BC. After the departure of the Romans it became part of the ANGLO-SAXON kingdom of East Anglia. In the Middle Ages, Norfolk was a centre of the wool industry. The land is generally low-lying and is used mainly for agriculture. The region is drained by the rivers Waveney, Yare, Bure and Ouse, and by the BROADS. Today, Norfolk produces cereals and root vegetables; poultry farming and fishing are also important. Area: 5,372sq km (2,073sq mi). Pop. (2001) 796,733.

Norfolk City-port on Elizabeth River, SE Virginia, USA. Founded in 1682, with Newport News and Portsmouth it forms the port of Hampton Roads. It is the largest US naval complex. Exports: coal, grain, tobacco. Industries: shipbuilding, motor vehicles, chemicals. Pop. (2000) 234,403.

Norfolk Broads *See* BROADS, NORFOLK

Norfolk Island Territory of Australia in the SW Pacific Ocean, *c.*1,450km (900mi) E of Australia. Visited in 1774 by Captain James Cook, it was a British penal colony (1788–1814, 1825–55). Many people living on Pitcairn Island, descendants of the *Bounty* mutineers, resettled here in 1856. The chief economic activities are agriculture and tourism. Area: 34sq km (13sq mi). Pop. (2000) 2,000.

Noriega, Manuel (Antonio Morena) (1934–) Panamanian dictator and general. In 1963, he became head of Panama's National Defense Forces. Recruited as a CIA operative by the USA, Noriega became an important backstage powerbroker. For most of the 1980s, he was Panama's paramount leader, ruling behind puppet presidents. In 1988, he was indicted by a US court on drug-connected charges and accused of murder. In December 1989, US troops invaded Panama and installed a civilian government. Noriega surrendered to US forces, and was taken to the USA for trial on corruption, drug trafficking and money laundering. In April 1992, he received a 40–year prison sentence.

Norman architecture ROMANESQUE architectural style of the Normans in England, N France, and S Italy. Characteristic buildings include the cathedrals at St Étienne and Caen in France, and Durham in England. The style features massive proportions, square towers, round arches, and little decoration.

Norman Conquest (1066) Invasion of England by WILLIAM I (THE CONQUEROR), Duke of Normandy. William claimed that EDWARD THE CONFESSOR (d.1066) recognized him as heir to the throne of England, and he disputed the right of HAROLD II to be Edward's successor. William's army defeated and killed Harold at the Battle of HASTINGS (1066), then advanced on London, where William was accepted as king. The Normans gradually replaced the existing ruling class, lay and ecclesiastical, and Norman institutions appeared.

Normandy Region and former province of NW France, coextensive with the departments of Manche, Calvados, Orne, Eure and Seine-Maritime. Part of the Roman province

▶ **Nolde** *Flowers in a Garden.* Flowers were a favourite subject of the Expressionist painter, Emil Nolde. He was fascinated by the expressive potential of colour. The Nazis declared Nolde's art degenerate and forbade him to paint. His later works were small watercolours that he painted in secret.

of Gaul, it was absorbed into the Frankish kingdom of Neustria in the 6th century. It was the seat of William, Duke of Normandy (later WILLIAM I), who invaded England in 1066. France recovered Normandy from the English in 1204. It was the site of the NORMANDY CAMPAIGN. It is characterized by forests, flat farmlands and rolling hills. The economy is based on livestock rearing, dairy products, fruit, cider and fishing.

Normandy Campaign Allied invasion of German-occupied France, launched on June 6, 1944 (D-Day). Commanded by Dwight EISENHOWER, the invasion was the largest amphibious operation in history. The successful landings were the start of the final campaign of World War 2 in W Europe.

Norman French Dialect of Old French spoken by the Normans at the time of the conquest of England (1066). In Normandy, it was the general language, but it was also used by the Normans in England, where it coexisted with contemporary MIDDLE ENGLISH for about three centuries.

Normans Descendants of Vikings who settled in NW France in the 9th-10th centuries. They created a powerful state, with a strongly centralized feudal society and warlike aristocracy. In the 11th century, under Robert Guiscard and ROBERT II, they defeated the Muslims to create an independent kingdom in Sicily. In 1066 Duke William of Normandy conquered England and became WILLIAM I.

Norodom Sihanouk (1922–) Cambodian statesman, king (1941–55, 1993–2004), prime minister (1955–60) and head of state (1960–70, 1975–76, 1991–93). In 1965, he broke off diplomatic relations with the USA because of US military involvement in Indochina. In 1970, a right-wing military coup deposed Sihanouk. He returned from exile when the KHMER ROUGE assumed power in 1975, first supporting then opposing their regime. In 1979, after the Vietnamese invasion, Sihanouk formed a government-in-exile. In 1991, he returned to Cambodia. In 1993, UN peacekeepers withdrew and Sihanouk was reinstated as a constitutional monarch. In 2004 he abdicated, citing ill health, and was succeeded by his son Norodom Sihamoni.

Norse literature Literature of the Scandinavian Norsemen, written between the 9th and the 12th century. It consists mainly of mythological poetry and SAGAS. The works

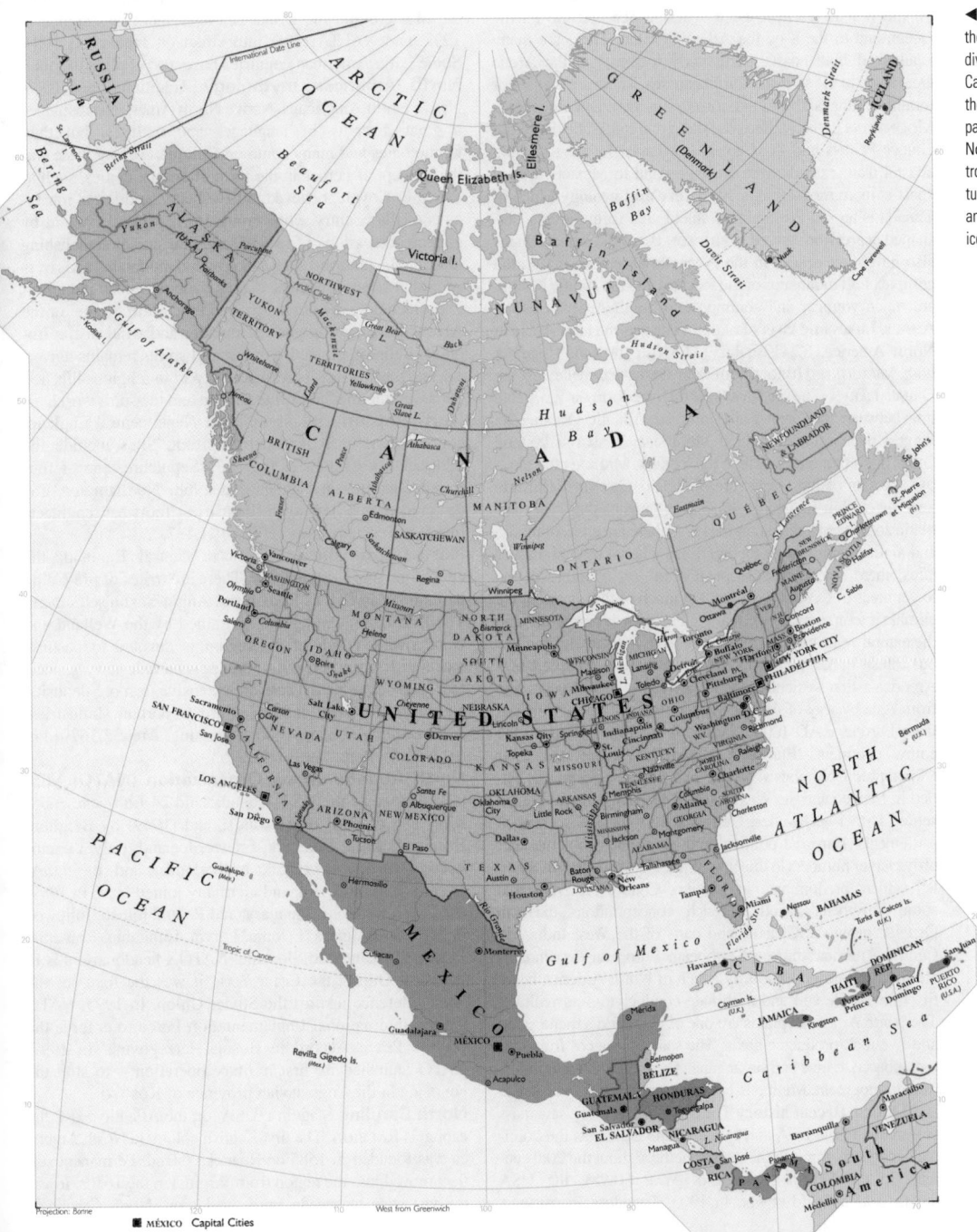

◀ **North America** The N part of the American continent is divided fairly evenly between Canada and the USA. Greenland, the largest island in the world, is part of Denmark. The climate of North America ranges from the tropical Caribbean islands to the tundra landscape of N Canada and Alaska, and the permanent ice-sheet covering Greenland.

INTERNET

North, Frederick, Lord
► www.number-10.gov.uk

North American Free Trade Agreement (NAFTA)
► www.nafta-sec-alena.org

North Atlantic Treaty Organization (NATO)
► www.nato.int

were set down in stone and wood, and survived orally to be recorded in the 12th-14th centuries.

North, Frederick, Lord (1732–92) British statesman, prime minister (1770–82). He entered Parliament in 1754. North was lord of the treasury (1759–65) and chancellor (1767–70) before becoming prime minister under King GEORGE III. His repressive measures against the North American colonies, particularly the INTOLERABLE ACTS, are seen as a precipitating factor for the AMERICAN REVOLUTION. In 1782, he formed a coalition with Charles James Fox, but was forced to resign in 1783.

North, Oliver Laurence (1943–) US marine lieutenant colonel. Recruited as an aide to the National Security Council, North managed several covert operations. The Congressional committee that investigated the notorious IRAN-CONTRA AFFAIR in 1987 revealed him as the central figure in the diversion of funds to the Contra, and he was subsequently convicted of three criminal charges. He was pardoned in 1992.

North America Continent, including the mainland and off-shore islands N of and including Panama. **Land** North America extends N of the Arctic Circle and S almost to the Equator. To the W it is bordered by the Bering Sea and the Pacific Ocean and to the E by the Atlantic Ocean. There are many islands off both coasts, particularly to the N in the Arctic Ocean and to the SE in the Caribbean Sea. There are two major mountain ranges: the APPALACHIANS in the E and the ROCKY MOUNTAINS in the W. Between these two ranges lie the fertile GREAT PLAINS and the Central Lowlands. In the E, a long coastal plain extends from New England to Mexico. The W coast is more mountainous. **Structure and geology** Much of Canada is an old Precambrian shield area forming a saucer-shaped depression centred in HUDSON BAY. The Appalachians also have their origins in the Precambrian era. In the W, the complex fold mountains of the Rockies and the Pacific Margin are much younger and continue into South America as the ANDES. **Lakes and rivers** Lake SUPERIOR is the largest lake in North America, 82,413sq km (31,820sq mi), and, together with MICHIGAN, HURON, ERIE and ONTARIO, makes up the GREAT LAKES. The ST LAWRENCE River forms a navigable link between the Great Lakes and the Atlantic Ocean. The longest river is the combined MISSISSIPPI-MISSOURI system. Other important rivers include the YUKON, MACKENZIE, COLORADO, COLUMBIA, Delaware, and RIO GRANDE. **Climate and vegetation** Its geographical range means that every climatic zone is represented. In the far N, there are areas of tundra and arctic conditions. In the interior, sheltered by high mountains, there are deserts. Tropical rainforest is found in the lower areas of Central America. On much of the continent the climate is temperate. The Great Plains region is temperate, and the natural vegetation is grass, bordered by mixed and coniferous forests in the mountains to the E, W, and N. **People** North America's first settlers probably arrived c.45,000 years ago from Asia by way of Alaska. By the time the Vikings arrived from Europe, c.AD 1000, NATIVE AMERICANS occupied the entire continent. European settlement accelerated after Christopher Columbus's voyage in 1492. The Spaniards settled in Mexico and the WEST INDIES. The English and French settled farther N; Swedes, Germans, and Dutch also formed settlements. Europe's political and economic problems later drove larger numbers to the New World. Descendants of Spanish settlers predominate in Mexico, Central America, and some Caribbean islands. French concentrations exist in QUÉBEC province, Canada, and parts of the West Indies. In Central America and the Caribbean, European descendants are in the minority. **Economy** Much of North America benefits from fertile soil and a climate conducive to agriculture. The North American plains are one of the world's major grain and livestock-producing areas. The S area produces fruit, cotton, tobacco, coffee and sugar cane. There is also major industrial development. Mining is important, particularly in Canada and Mexico. **Recent history** The early 20th century saw mass emigration to the USA and Canada. The USA was the dominant economic force on the continent throughout the 20th century. In the SPANISH-AMERICAN WAR (1898), the USA emerged as a world power. In 1903, Theodore ROOSEVELT

enforced construction of the PANAMA CANAL, which returned to Panama in 1999. The USA emerged from World War 2 as a world superpower. The ideological battle between CAPITALISM and COMMUNISM led to the COLD WAR, and US involvement in the KOREAN WAR and VIETNAM WAR. In 1994, Canada, the USA, and Mexico signed the NORTH AMERICAN FREE TRADE AGREEMENT (NAFTA). As the USA and Canada developed more service-based economies, some manufacturing transferred to Mexico. Economic inequality and instability remain major issues in Mexico. Since World War 2, many Caribbean islands gained independence. A US trade embargo since Fidel CASTRO's revolution (1959) crippled Cuba's economy. US interests also dominated Central America, characterized by repressive regimes and economic inequality. *Highest mountain* Mount McKINLEY (Denali) 6,194m (20,321ft) *Longest river* Mississippi-Missouri 6,050km (3,760mi) *Population* 464,000,000 *Largest cities* MEXICO CITY (8,605,239); NEW YORK CITY (8,008,278); LOS ANGELES (3,694,820) *See map page 553 and see also individual country articles*

North American Free Trade Agreement (NAFTA) Treaty designed to eliminate trade barriers between Canada, Mexico, and the USA. The agreement was signed in 1992, and NAFTA came into effect on January 1, 1994. Some Latin American countries have also applied to join.

North American mythology Traditional beliefs of Native North Americans. Native North Americans displayed a great diversity of languages and cultures, but their mythologies had many common features. Among these was the concept of heroes in the form of animal deities, such as Raven or Coyote, believed to have been the original inhabitants of the country. They brought order into the world by gaining possession of fire, wind and rain, and by establishing laws and institutions. They also created mountains and rivers and other natural features. Native Americans had numerous gods, including the Great Spirit and the Earth Mother of the Algonquins, and the gods of thunder and wind of the Iroquois. Belief in protective or harmful spirits remains universal, and the SHAMAN plays a central part in religious life, acting as an intermediary between man and the spirit world.

Northampton City on the River Nene, central England; county town of NORTHAMPTONSHIRE. Sites include the 12th-century Church of the Holy Sepulchre, one of four round churches in England. In 1968, Northampton was designated as a new town. Industries: footwear, engineering, leather goods. Pop. (2001) 194,477.

Northamptonshire County in central England; the county town is Northampton. There are traces of pre-Celtic habitations as well as Roman and Anglo-Saxon settlement. The land is undulating and is drained by the Welland and Nene rivers. Much of the region is devoted to pasture, wheat growing and forestry. Products include cereals, potatoes, and sugar beet. There are extensive iron ore deposits, and iron and steel industries are important. Industries: footwear, engineering, food processing. Area: 2,367sq km (914sq mi). Pop. (2001) 629,676.

North Atlantic Treaty Organization (NATO) Military alliance of the USA, Canada, and 24 European countries. The original treaty was signed (1949) by Belgium, Britain, Canada, Denmark, France, Iceland, Italy, Luxembourg, Norway, Portugal, Netherlands, and the USA. Greece, Turkey, Spain, and Germany joined later. In 1999, the Czech Republic, Hungary, and Poland joined, followed in 2004 by Bulgaria, Estonia, Latvia, Lithuania, Romania, Slovak Republic and Slovenia. NATO's headquarters is in Brussels. During the COLD WAR, it was the focus of the West's defence against the Soviet Union. In 1995, NATO led the International Implementation Force to enforce the Dayton Peace Accord in Bosnia-Herzegovina. In 1999, NATO launched its first military operation – to stop the genocide in the Yugoslavian province of KOSOVO.

North Carolina State in E USA, on the Atlantic coast; the capital is RALEIGH. The first English colony in North America was founded in 1585 on Roanoke Island. Permanent settlers moved into the region from Virginia in the 1650s. It was the last state to secede from the Union. North Carolina's

NORTH CAROLINA
Statehood :
November 21, 1789
Nickname :
The Tar Heel State
State bird :
Cardinal
State flower :
Flowering dogwood
State tree :
Pine
State motto :
To be, rather than to seem

N

coastal plain is swampy and low-lying. Its w edge rises to rolling hills; further w are the Blue Ridge and Great Smoky Mountains. It is the leading producer of tobacco in the USA. Important agricultural products are corn, soya beans, peanuts, pigs, chickens and dairy produce. Industries: textiles, timber, fishing, tourism, electrical machinery, chemicals. Mineral resources include phosphate, feldspar, mica and kaolin. Area: 136,523sq km (52,712sq mi). Pop. (2000) 8,049,313.

Northcliffe, Alfred Charles William Harmsworth, Viscount (1865–1922) British newspaper publisher, b. Ireland. In 1896 he launched the *Daily Mail*, whose concise, populist style of news presentation proved very successful. In 1905 he founded the *Daily Mirror*, the first picture paper, and in 1908 gained control of *The Times*.

North Dakota State in N central USA, on the Canadian border; the capital is BISMARCK. French explorers first visited the region in 1738. The USA acquired the w half of the area from France in the LOUISIANA PURCHASE (1803), and the rest from Britain in 1818 when the boundary with Canada was fixed. Dakota was divided into North and South Dakota in 1889. The region is low-lying and drained by the Missouri and Red rivers. Wheat, barley, rye, oats, sunflowers and flaxseed are the chief crops. Cattle rearing is the most important economic activity. Area: 183,022sq km (70,665sq mi). Pop. (2000) 642,200.

Northeast Passage Route from the Atlantic to the Pacific via the Arctic Ocean. Unsuccessful attempts were made to find the passage by Dutch and English mariners from the 16th century. The complete voyage was first made by Baron Nordenskjöld in 1878–80.

Northern Cape Province in sw South Africa; the capital is Kimberley. Northern Cape was created in 1994 from the N part of the former CAPE PROVINCE. Area: 361,800sq km (139,650sq mi). Pop. (2000 est.) 879,675.

Northern Ireland *See* IRELAND, NORTHERN

Northern Lights Popular name for the AURORA borealis

Northern Territory Territory in N central Australia bounded by the Timor and Arafura seas (N), and the states of Western Australia (W), South Australia (S) and Queensland (E); the capital is DARWIN. In 1863 it was annexed to South Australia but in 1911 was under the control of the federal government. In 1978, it achieved self-government. The territory lies mostly within the tropics. The coastal areas are flat with offshore islands, and the region rises inland to a high plateau, the Barkly Tableland. In the mainly arid s are the Macdonnell Ranges and AYERS ROCK. Today there is little farming but some government-aided stock-breeding. Manganese ore, bauxite and iron are mined. Area: 1,347,525sq km (520,280sq mi). Pop. (2000 est.) 196,300.

Northern War (1700–21) Conflict in N Europe between Sweden and its neighbours. It began with an attack on Sweden by Denmark, Saxony, Poland, and Russia. CHARLES XII of Sweden defeated all his opponents (1700–06), but war renewed in 1707 when Charles invaded Russia. The Swedes were decisively defeated at Poltava (1709). Charles took refuge with the Ottoman Turks, encouraging their attack on Russia in 1710–11. At the ensuing peace treaties (1719–21), Sweden lost virtually all its N empire.

North Island Smaller but more densely populated of the two main islands of New Zealand; separated from SOUTH ISLAND by Cook Strait. The chief cities are WELLINGTON, AUCKLAND, and Hamilton. The island contains several mountain ranges, Lake Taupu (New Zealand's largest lake), fertile coastal plains, and numerous hot springs. Most of New Zealand's dairy produce comes from North Island. Industries: wood pulp and paper, mining, fishing. Area: 114,729sq km (44,297sq mi). Pop. (2001) 2,829,798.

North Korea *See* KOREA, NORTH

North Pole Most northerly point on EARTH; the N end of the Earth's axis of rotation, 725km (450mi) N of Greenland. Geographic north lies at 90° latitude, 0° longitude.

North Sea Arm of the Atlantic Ocean, lying between the E coast of Britain and the European mainland and connected to the English Channel by the Straits of Dover. Generally shallow, it is *c.*960km (600mi) long, with a maximum width of 640km (400mi). It is a major fishing ground, ship-ping route, and (since 1970) an important source of oil and natural gas. Area: *c.*580,000sq km (220,000sq mi).

Northumberland County in NE England, on the border with Scotland; the county town is Morpeth. In the 2nd century AD HADRIAN'S WALL was built to defend Roman Britain from the northern tribes. In the 7th century, the region became part of the Saxon Kingdom of NORTHUMBRIA. The region is drained by the Tyne, Tweed, Blythe and Coquet rivers. The county is largely rural, the chief farming activities being cattle and sheep rearing. Barley and oats are grown and forestry is important. Coal is mined. Area: 5,033sq km (1,943sq mi). Pop. (2001) 307,186.

Northumberland, John Dudley, Duke of (1502–53) Effectively ruler of England (1549–53). He was one of the councillors named by HENRY VIII to govern during the minority of EDWARD VI. In 1553, he attempted to usurp the succession through his daughter-in-law, Lady Jane GREY, but was thwarted by popular support for the rightful queen, MARY I. He was subsequently executed for treason.

Northumbria, Kingdom of Largest kingdom in Anglo-Saxon England. Formed in the early 7th century, it included NE England and SE Scotland up to the Firth of Forth. In the age of the historian BEDE and the LINDISFARNE GOSPELS, Northumbria experienced a blossoming of scholarship and monastic culture. Its power declined in the 8th century.

North-West Frontier Province (NWFP) Province in NW Pakistan bounded by Afghanistan, located near the KHYBER PASS; the capital is PESHAWAR. Important during the time of ALEXANDER THE GREAT, in 1849 it became part of British India and was annexed to Pakistan in 1947. It is largely agricultural. Area: 106,200sq km (41,000sq mi). Pop. (1998) 17,555,000.

Northwest Ordinances (1787) Decree of the US CONTINENTAL CONGRESS, establishing the Northwest Territory. Based on plans proposed by a committee chaired by JEFFERSON, it created a government for the Territory, between the Ohio and Mississippi rivers, and laid down the policy for federal land sales.

Northwest Passage Western route from the Atlantic to the Pacific via N Canada. Many European explorers in the 16th and 17th centuries tried to find a passage through North America to the Pacific. The effort was renewed in the 19th century. The expedition of Sir John FRANKLIN, which set out in 1845, was lost with all hands, but during the search for survivors, the route was established. First to make the passage in one ship was Roald AMUNDSEN in 1903–06.

North-West Province Province in NW South Africa; the capital is Mmabatho. North-West Province was created from the SW part of the former province of TRANSVAAL and the NE part of former Cape Province. Area: 116,190sq km (44,489sq mi). Pop. (2000 est.) 3,604,472.

Northwest Territories Region in N Canada, covering more than 33% of the country and consisting of mainland Canada N of latitude 60°N, and hundreds of islands in the Arctic Archipelago. The capital is Yellowknife. Much of the N and E of the province is tundra, inhabited by INUIT and other native peoples. The HUDSON'S BAY COMPANY acquired the area under a charter from CHARLES II in 1670. In 1869, the Canadian government bought the land from the company. Most of the present boundary was set in 1912, but in 1999, part of the Northwest Territories became the Inuit land of NUNAVUT. Most economic development has occurred in Mackenzie district, which has large tracts of softwoods and rich mineral deposits. Area: 1,172,000sq km (453,000sq mi). Pop. (2003) 41,000.

North Yorkshire County in N England; the administrative centre is YORK. Other major towns include Scarborough, Whitby, and Harrogate. In the 9th century, Scandinavian invasions destroyed a thriving culture. In the Middle Ages, the region became noted for its monastic foundations. In the w of the county are the PENNINES. In the E are the North Yorkshire Moors. North Yorkshire is agricultural, with dairy farming, cereals, and hill sheep farming. There is some manufacturing industry. Area: 8,309sq km (3,208sq mi). Pop. (2001) 569,660.

Norway Kingdom in NW Europe. *See* country feature

Norwegian Official language of Norway, spoken by nearly all of its 4 million inhabitants. It belongs to the N branch of the Germanic family of INDO-EUROPEAN LANGUAGES.

NORTH DAKOTA
Statehood:
November 2, 1889
Nickname:
The Flickertail State
State bird:
Western meadowlark
State flower:
Wild prairie rose
State tree:
American elm
State motto:
Liberty and union, now and forever, one and inseparable

N

Norwich City and county town of NORFOLK, E England. There are many fine medieval churches and a Norman cathedral (begun 1096). Industries: textiles, machinery, chemicals, electrical goods, foodstuffs, footwear. Pop. (2001) 121,533.

nose In human beings, other primates and some vertebrates, the prominent structure between the eyes. It contains receptors sensitive to various chemicals (sense of SMELL), and serves as the opening to the respiratory tract, warming and moistening the air and trapping dust particles on the MUCOUS MEMBRANES.

Nostradamus (1503–66) French seer and astrologer, b. Michel de Nostredame. Originally a doctor, he began making astrological predictions in 1547. These were published in rhyming quatrains in *Centuries* (from 1555); they relate to 16th century political events and not, as is commonly supposed, to subsequent centuries.

notary (notary public) Public official who authenticates documents such as deeds and contracts by witnessing them.

notochord In CHORDATES, such as acorn worms, and the early embryonic stages of vertebrates, the flexible, primitive backbone; in mature vertebrates it is replaced by the SPINE.

Notre-Dame Early GOTHIC cathedral in Paris (1163–1250). One of the most daring constructions of its time, it has a wide nave and double ambulatory, and the W façade was imitated in many French churches.

Nottingham City and county town of NOTTINGHAMSHIRE, on the River Trent, N central England. Originally a 6th-century Anglo-Saxon settlement, it is the traditional birthplace of ROBIN HOOD. The city grew rapidly in the 19th century, becoming famous for its fine lace, cotton and hosiery. Industries: textiles, engineering, bicycles, electronic equipment, pharmaceuticals. Pop. (2001) 266,995.

Nottinghamshire County in central England; the county town is NOTTINGHAM. The land slopes down from the E ridges of the PENNINES in the W to the lowlands of the E. The principal river is the TRENT. Wheat, barley and sugar beet are the chief crops; beef and dairy cattle are important. There are rich deposits of coal, and it has long been noted for its textile industries. Area: 2,164sq km (836sq mi). Pop. (2001) 748,503.

Nouakchott Capital of MAURITANIA, NW Africa, in the SW part of the country, *c.*8km (5mi) from the Atlantic Ocean. Originally a small fishing village, it was chosen as capital when Mauritania became independent in 1960. Nouakchott now has an international airport and is the site of modern stor-

NORWAY

The Kingdom of Norway forms the W part of the mountainous Scandinavian Peninsula. The landscape is dominated by rolling plateaux, the vidda, which are generally between 300 and 900m [1,000–3,000ft] high. Some peaks rise from 1,500 to 2,500m [5,000–8,000ft] in the area between OSLO, BERGEN and TRONDHEIM. The highest areas retain permanent icefields, as in the Jotunheimen Mountains above Sognefjord.

Norway's jagged coastline is the longest in Europe. The vidda are cut by long, narrow, steep-sided FJORDS on the W coast. The largest of the fjords is Sognefjord, which is 203km [127mi] long and less than 5km [3mi] wide.

CLIMATE
The warm North Atlantic Drift flows off the coast and moderates the country's climate, with milder winters and cooler summers. Most of Norway's ports remain ice-free all year. Inland, away from the moderating effects of the sea, the climate becomes more severe. Winters are bitterly cold with snow cover for at least three months of the year.

HISTORY
Norway's seafaring tradition dates back to the VIKINGS, who raided W Europe between the 9th and 11th centuries and founded colonies around the coasts of Britain, Iceland and even North America. In about 900 AD Norway was united under Harold I, the country's first king. OLAF II introduced Christianity in the early 11th century, but was deposed by CANUTE II of Denmark. HAAKON IV re-established unity in the 13th century. In 1319 Sweden joined with Norway.

In 1397 Norway, Sweden, and Denmark were united in the Kalmar Union. For the next four centuries, Norway was subject to Danish rule. Sweden broke away in 1523 and in 1526 Denmark, which had become increasingly powerful, made Norway a Danish province. Lutheranism became the state religion in the mid-16th century. In 1814 Denmark ceded

Norway to Sweden, but retained Norway's colonies of Greenland, Iceland and the Faeroe Islands. Norway declared independence, but Swedish troops forced Norway to accept union under the Swedish crown.

Norway finally became an independent monarchy in 1905. The Norwegians chose as their king a Danish prince, who took the title Haakon VII. The

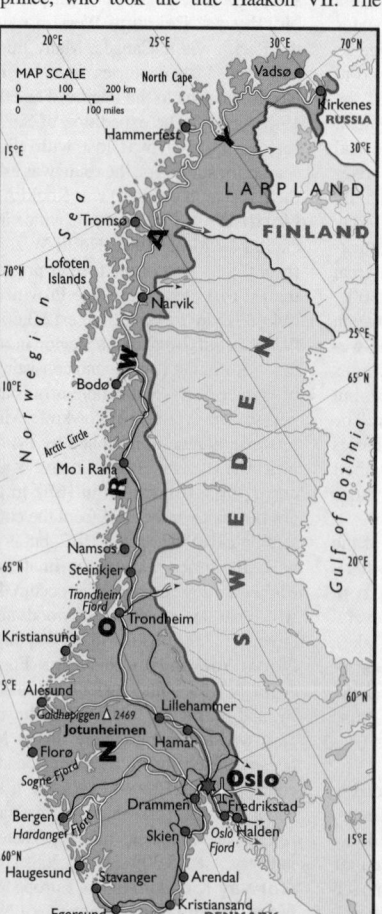

AREA 323,877sq km [125,049sq mi]
POPULATION 4,628,000
CAPITAL (POPULATION)
Oslo (808,000)
GOVERNMENT Constitutional monarchy
ETHNIC GROUPS Norwegian 97%
LANGUAGES Norwegian (official)
RELIGIONS Evangelical Lutheran 86%
CURRENCY Norwegian krone = 100 øre

country remained neutral in World War 1 and, in the 1920s and 1930s, Norway industrialized and adopted progressive social welfare provisions. In April 1940 German troops invaded. More than 50% of Norway's merchant fleet was destroyed in the resistance. The country was finally liberated in May 1945.

POLITICS
After World War 2, Norwegians worked to rebuild their economy and their merchant fleet. The economy was boosted in the 1970s, when Norway began producing petroleum and natural gas from wells in the North Sea. Rapid economic growth has ensured that Norwegians are among the most prosperous in Europe.

In 1949 it became a member of NATO, though neither NATO bases nor nuclear weapons were permitted on its soil for fear of provoking its neighbour, the Soviet Union. In 1960, Norway and six other countries formed the European Free Trade Association while continuing to work with its Scandinavian neighbours through the Nordic Council. In 1994 Norwegians again voted against membership of the EU. The 1990s–2000s saw Norwegian diplomats seeking to broker peace deals in Sri Lanka and Palestine.

ECONOMY
Norway's chief resources and exports are oil and natural gas. Dairy farming and meat production are the chief farming activities, although Norway has to import food. Industries include petroleum products, chemicals, aluminium, wood products, machinery and clothing.

age facilities for petroleum. Light industries have been developed and handicrafts are important. Pop. (2000) 611,883.

Nouméa City and seaport in SW New Caledonia island, S Pacific Ocean; the capital of NEW CALEDONIA. Originally called Port-de-France, it was made capital of New Caledonia in 1854. Local mining products include nickel, chrome and manganese. Pop. (2002 est.) 84,900.

noun Member of a linguistic class or category consisting of words that serve to name a person, place, thing, or concept. In traditional grammar, nouns form one of the so-called parts of speech. Modern linguistics experts, however, tend to define them in terms of their grammatical function.

nouveau roman (Fr. 'new novel') Experimental fictional form. Pioneered by Alain ROBBE-GRILLET, Samuel BECKETT, and Nathalie Sarraute during the 1950s, it drew on the writings of Franz KAFKA and James JOYCE, and the techniques of film-making. It is characterized by meticulously detailed description, the avoidance of value judgments, and a consciousness of the artificiality of time sequences.

nova (pl. novae) Faint star that undergoes unpredictable increases in brightness by several magnitudes, apparently due to explosions in its outer regions, and then slowly fades back to normal. *See also* VARIABLE STAR

Novalis (1772–1801) German Romantic poet and novelist, b. Friedrich Leopold, Baron von Hardenberg. He began his major work, the mythical romance *Heinrich von Ofterdingen*, in 1799, but had not completed it by the time of his death. His work influenced the development of German ROMANTICISM.

Nova Scotia Maritime province in SE Canada, consisting of a mainland peninsula, Cape Breton Island and a few smaller islands; the capital is HALIFAX. The first settlement was made by the French in 1605. The mainland was awarded to Britain in 1713, and Cape Breton Island was seized from the French in 1758. Nova Scotia joined NEW BRUNSWICK, QUÉBEC and ONTARIO to form the Dominion of CANADA in 1867. The land is generally low-lying and there are extensive forests. The principal crops are hay, apples, grain and vegetables. There are coal deposits on Cape Breton Island. Fishing is important. Industries: shipbuilding, pulp and paper, steelmaking, food processing. Area: 55,490sq km (21,425sq mi). Pop. (2001) 908,007.

novel Narrative fiction, usually in prose form, that is longer and more detailed than a short story. The word derives from the Latin word *novus* (new) and the Italian NOVELLA (a short tale with an element of surprise). The roots of the modern novel are generally traced to CERVANTES' *Don Quixote* (1605–15). Its development as a major literary form can be seen in 18th-century Britain in Daniel DEFOE's *Robinson Crusoe* (1719) and Samuel RICHARDSON's *Pamela* (1740). The 20th century has seen considerable formal experimentation, notably the STREAM OF CONSCIOUSNESS technique and the NOUVEAU ROMAN.

novella Short, highly structured prose narrative. The form was developed by Giovanni BOCCACCIO in the *Decameron* (1348–53), and has proved popular since the 18th century. In modern usage, the term broadly denotes a work of prose fiction that is longer than a short story but shorter than a NOVEL.

Novello, Ivor (1893–1951) Welsh composer, actor and dramatist, b. David Ivor Davies. He is best known as the writer of comedies and light musicals, including *The Dancing Years* (1939) and *Perchance to Dream* (1945). Novello composed the World War 1 anthem 'Keep the Home Fires Burning' (1914).

Novgorod City in NW Russia, on the River Volchov. It was supposedly founded by the Varangian Prince RURIK in the 9th century. Its inhabitants were forcibly converted to Christianity in 989. It subsequently became capital of a vast territory. After a long fight for supremacy, the city was forced to submit to Moscow in 1478. In 1570, IVAN IV (THE TERRIBLE) massacred the inhabitants. It declined in importance after the founding of ST PETERSBURG. During World War 2 it suffered great destruction. Industries: distilling, foodstuffs, electrical engineering, furniture, chinaware. Pop. (1994 est.) 239,700.

Novosibirsk City on the River Ob, S Siberia, Russia. Founded in 1896 after the construction of the Trans-Siberian Railway, it grew quickly. During World War 2 it received complete

◄ **Notre-Dame** The Early Gothic cathedral of Notre-Dame is situated on the Ile de la Cité in Paris, France, seen here from the Seine River. A fine example of Gothic architecture, it is noted for its flying buttresses, which were a technical advance providing support, and for the rose window in the west façade.

industrial plants moved from war-stricken areas of the W Soviet Union. It is now a centre for scientific research. Industries: agricultural and mining machinery, metallurgy, machine tools, chemicals, textiles, furniture. Pop. (2005) 1,425,000.

Nu, U (1907–95) Burmese statesman, prime minister (1948–56, 1957–58, 1960–62). Active in the struggle for independence, Nu became BURMA's first prime minister. Ousted by the military in 1958, he returned to power in 1960. In 1962 he was again deposed by a military coup led by U NE WIN. After years of exile, he returned to Burma in 1980, but was later placed under house arrest.

Nuba Group of several unrelated peoples inhabiting a region of S Sudan. Most Nuba peoples are farmers and many tribes cultivate terraces on rugged granite hillsides. Their religious rituals revolve around agricultural fertility rites.

Nubia Ancient state on the upper Nile, NE Africa. At its height, Nubia extended from Egypt to the Sudan. At first ruled by Egypt, it later controlled Egypt in the 8th and 7th centuries BC. It converted to Christianity in the 6th century AD and became part of Ethiopia in the 14th century.

nuclear disarmament *See* DISARMAMENT; STRATEGIC ARMS LIMITATION TALKS (SALT)

nuclear energy ENERGY released during a nuclear reaction as a result of the conversion of mass into energy according to EINSTEIN's equation $E = mc^2$. The conversion involves the binding energy of the *nucleus* of an ATOM. Nuclear energy is released in two ways: by FISSION (splitting a heavy atomic nucleus in two) and by FUSION (combining light atomic nuclei). **Fission**, discovered in 1938, is the process responsibile for the atomic bomb and for NUCLEAR REACTORS in nuclear power stations that produce electricity. In 1942, German-born US physicist Enrico FERMI achieved the first sustained nuclear CHAIN REACTION. **Fusion** provides the energy for the stars and the HYDROGEN BOMB. It also offers the prospect of cheap energy, once a method has been perfected for controlling fusion reactions. *See also* CRITICAL MASS; MANHATTAN PROJECT; NUCLEAR WEAPON

nuclear fission *See* FISSION, NUCLEAR

nuclear fuel Various chemical and physical forms of URANIUM and PLUTONIUM used in NUCLEAR REACTORS. Fluid fuels are required in homogeneous reactors; heterogeneous reactors use various forms of fuels – pure metals or alloys, as well as oxides or carbides. The fuel must have a high thermal conductivity, be resistant to radiation damage and be easy to fabricate.

nuclear fusion *See* FUSION, NUCLEAR

nuclear magnetic resonance (NMR) *See* MAGNETIC RESONANCE

nuclear physics Branch of physics concerned with the structure and properties of the atomic NUCLEUS. The principal means of investigating the nucleus is SCATTERING experiments carried out in particle ACCELERATORS, in which a nucleus is bombarded with a beam of high-energy ELEMENTARY PARTICLES, and the resultant particles analysed. Study of the nucleus has led to an understanding of the processes occurring inside stars and has enabled the building of NUCLEAR REACTORS.

nuclear reactor Device in which nuclear FISSION (and sometimes nuclear FUSION) reactions are used for power generation or for the production of radioactive materials. In the reactor, the fuel is a radioactive heavy metal: URANIUM-235, uranium-233 or PLUTONIUM-239. In these metals, ATOMS break down spontaneously, undergoing a process called RADIOACTIVE DECAY. Some NEUTRONS released in this process strike the nuclei of fuel atoms, causing them to undergo fission and emit more neutrons. These, in turn, strike more nuclei, and in this way a CHAIN REACTION is set up. Usually a material, called a **moderator**, is used to slow down the neutrons to a speed at which the chain reaction is self-sustaining. This process occurs within the reactor **core**. The chain reaction is regulated by inserting **control rods**, which contain neutron-absorbing material such as cadmium or boron, into the core. The heat generated by the nuclear reaction is absorbed by a circulating **coolant**, and transferred to a boiler to raise steam. The steam drives a TURBINE that turns a GENERATOR, that in turn produces electricity. There are a variety of nuclear reactors, named after the type of coolant they use. For example, a **boiling-water** reactor (BWR) and a **pressurized-water** reactor (PWR), presently the most common type of reactor, both use water as the coolant and the moderator. In **advanced gas-cooled** reactors (AGR), the coolant is a gas – most commonly carbon dioxide. **Fast** reactors do not use a moderator, and fission is caused by fast neutrons. This type of reactor generates greater temperatures, and the coolant used is a liquid metal (usually liquid sodium). Sometimes called 'fast-breeder' reactors, fast reactors produce ('breed') more fissionable material than they consume. Excess neutrons from the fission of a fuel such as Ur^{235}, instead of being absorbed in control rods, are used to bombard atoms of relatively inactive Ur^{238} which transmutes to the active ISOTOPE Pu^{239}. When the original fuel is spent, the plutonium can be used as a NUCLEAR FUEL in other reactors or NUCLEAR WEAPONS. *See also* ELECTRICITY SOURCES; TRANSMUTATION

nuclear waste Residues containing radioactive substances. After URANIUM, PLUTONIUM and other useful fission products have been removed, some long-lived radioactive elements remain, such as CAESIUM-137 and STRONTIUM-90. The storage of nuclear waste is a major environmental issue.

NUCLEAR REACTOR

A pressurized water reactor (PWR) is so named because the primary coolant (1) that passes through the reactor core (2) is pressurized to prevent it from boiling. The uranium-235 fuel is loaded into the reactor in pellets (3) contained by the fuel rods (4). To prevent an uncontrolled chain reaction, control rods of graphite (5) separate the fuel rods. All the rods are loaded into the reactor from above (6). The primary coolant is heated by the fission reaction in the fuel rods and circulates into a steam generator (7), where it superheats the secondary coolant (8). The secondary coolant leaves the protective containment vessel (9), and drives turbines (10) that produce electricity through a generator (11). A third coolant loop (12) cools the secondary coolant, transferring the heat to a sea, river or lake. Reducing the temperature of the secondary coolant increases the efficiency of the transfer from the primary to the secondary coolant.

primary coolant
superheated primary coolant
secondary coolant
third coolant

nuclear weapon Device whose enormous explosive force derives from the reactions of nuclear FISSION (splitting a heavy atomic nucleus in two) or FUSION (combining light atomic nuclei) reactions. In August 1945, the United States dropped the first **atomic bombs** on the Japanese cities of HIROSHIMA and NAGASAKI. The bombs consisted of two stable, sub-critical masses of URANIUM or PLUTONIUM which, when brought forcefully together, caused the CRITICAL MASS to be exceeded, thus initiating an uncontrolled nuclear CHAIN REACTION. In such detonations, huge amounts of energy and harmful radiation are released: the explosive force can be equivalent to 20,000 tonnes of TNT. The HYDROGEN BOMB consists of an atomic bomb that on explosion provides a temperature high enough to cause nuclear fusion in a surrounding solid layer, usually lithium deuteride. The explosive power can be that of several million tonnes (megatons) of TNT. Devastation from such bombs covers a wide area: a 15–megaton bomb will cause all flammable material within 20km (12mi) to burst into flame. A third type of weapon, the **neutron bomb**, is a small hydrogen bomb, also called an enhanced radiation weapon, that produces a small blast but a very intense burst of high-speed NEUTRONS. The lack of heat and blast means that buildings are not heavily damaged. The neutrons, however, produce intense radiation sickness in people located within a certain range, killing those affected within a week.

nucleic acid Chemical molecules present in all living cells and in viruses. They are of two types, DNA (deoxyribonucleic acid) and RNA (ribonucleic acid), both of which play fundamental roles in heredity. *See also* CHROMOSOME; GENE

nucleon Any of the particles found within the NUCLEUS of an atom: a NEUTRON or a PROTON.

nucleon number *See* ATOMIC MASS NUMBER

nucleus In biology, membrane-bound structure that, in most CELLS, contains the CHROMOSOMES. As well as holding the genetic material, the nucleus is essential for the maintenance of cell processes. It manufactures the RNA used to build RIBOSOMES. Other RNA molecules carry the GENETIC CODE from the DNA through pores in the nuclear membrane into the jelly-like CYTOPLASM, where it is used as a template for PROTEIN synthesis by the ribosomes. Cell division involves the splitting of the nucleus and CYTOPLASM. Cells without nuclei include BACTERIA and mammalian ERYTHROCYTES (red blood cells).

nucleus In physics, central core of an ATOM. Made up of NUCLEONS (PROTONS and NEUTRONS), the nucleus accounts for almost all of an atom's mass. Because protons are positively charged and neutrons have no charge, a nucleus has an overall positive charge; this is cancelled out, however, by the negatively charged ELECTRONS that orbit the nucleus.

Nuffield, William Richard Morris, 1st Viscount (1877–1963) English automobile manufacturer and philanthropist. Nuffield developed low-price, mass-produced cars and revolutionized the British car industry. In 1952 he became chairman of the British Motor Corporation (BMC).

Nujoma, Sam (1929–) Namibian statesman, president 1990–2005. A founder and leader of the SOUTH WEST AFRICA PEOPLE'S ORGANIZATION (SWAPO) from 1959, Nujoma was exiled by the South African government to Tanzania in 1960. Forced to resort to armed conflict from 1966, Nujoma controlled an army of highly effective SWAPO guerrillas. After negotiating Namibian independence through the auspices of the United Nations, he returned in 1989 to contest successfully its first free elections. He was re-elected in 1994 and 1999.

Nukualofa Capital of Tonga, in the SW Pacific Ocean, on the N coast of Tongatabu Island. The chief industry is copra processing. Pop. (2002 est.) 24,300.

number Symbol representing a quantity used in counting or calculation. All ancient cultures devised their own number systems for the purposes of counting and measuring. From the basic process of counting we get the natural numbers. This concept can be extended to define an INTEGER, a RATIONAL NUMBER, a REAL NUMBER and a COMPLEX NUMBER. *See also* BINARY SYSTEM; IRRATIONAL NUMBER; PRIME NUMBER

Numbers Fourth book of the Bible and of the PENTATEUCH. Its describes the Israelites' 40 years of wandering in the desert of the Sinai Peninsula, in search of the Promised

Land of CANAAN. Religious material is interwoven with their story, including laws concerning purification rituals.

number theory Branch of mathematics concerned with the properties of natural NUMBERS (whole numbers) or special classes of natural numbers such as PRIME NUMBERS and perfect numbers (which equal the sum of their FACTORS). For example, as early as the 4th century BC Greek mathematician EUCLID proved that the number of primes was infinite. One of the unresolved problems in number theory is to find formulae for the generation of the primes. FERMAT (in the 17th century) and EULER (in the 18th century) both explored number theory.

numeral Symbol used alone or in a group to denote a number. Arabic numerals are the 10 digits from 0 to 9. ROMAN NUMERALS consist of seven letters or marks.

nun Woman belonging to a religious order who has taken monastic vows (*see* MONASTICISM). Nuns may belong to either a closed order, or one that encourages its members to work for the welfare of society at large. BUDDHISM, CHRISTIANITY, and TAOISM all have orders of nuns. Nuns serve a preparatory period called a novitiate, after which they take their final vows.

Nunavut Territory in N Canada; the capital is Iqaluit. Once part of NORTHWEST TERRITORIES, it was granted self-government in 1999 as a homeland for the INUIT. Its first premier was Paul Okalit. The economy relies on fishing, hunting and mining lead, zinc and coal, and on central government subsidies. Area: *c.*2 million sq km (775,000sq mi). Pop. (2001) 26,745.

Nunn, Trevor (1940–) English stage director. He was artistic director of the ROYAL SHAKESPEARE COMPANY (RSC) (1968–96). Nunn directed the West End musicals *Cats* (1981) and *Starlight Express* (1984) and was artistic director of the NATIONAL THEATRE of Great Britain (1996–2002).

Nur-ad-Din (1118–74) (Nureddin) Ruler of Syria. He united Muslim forces in Syria to resist the Christians of the CRUSADES. He recaptured Edessa from the Christians in 1146 and in 1154 took Damascus from the Seljuk Turks.

Nuremberg (Nürnburg) City in Bavaria, s Germany. It began as a settlement around an 11th-century castle, later becoming a free imperial city. It was a centre of learning and artistic achievement in Germany during the 15th and 16th centuries. During the 1930s it was the location of the annual congress of the Nazi Party, and after World War 2 was the scene of the NUREMBERG TRIALS (1945–46). Today, Nuremberg is an important commercial and industrial centre. Industries: textiles, pharmaceuticals, electrical equipment, machinery, publishing and printing, motor vehicles, brewing. Pop. (1999) 486,400.

Nuremberg Trials (1945–46) Trials of Germans accused of WAR CRIMES during World War 2, held before a military tribunal. The tribunal was established by the USA, Britain, France, and the Soviet Union. Ten Nazi leaders were executed (including von RIBBENTROP). GOERING committed suicide before he could be executed. Rudolf HESS was one of six men sentenced to life imprisonment. *See also* HOLOCAUST

Nureyev, Rudolf (1938–93) Russian ballet dancer and choreographer. In 1961, he defected from the Soviet Union while on tour in Paris. He was noted for his spectacular technical virtuosity and dramatic character portrayal. Major ballets in which he had leading roles included *Sleeping Beauty*, *Giselle* and *Swan Lake*, and he regularly partnered Margot FONTEYN.

Nurhachi (1559–1626) Organizer and creator of the QING state, which later ruled China. He welded related tribes into a powerful unit, creating the Manchu military banner organization for control and mobilization. Among other innovations, he introduced a writing system for administrative purposes.

nursing Profession that has as its general function the care of people who, through ill-health, disability, immaturity or advanced age, are unable to care for themselves. The Christian Church emphasized caring for the sick and many religious orders performed such 'acts of mercy'. In the 19th century, Florence NIGHTINGALE revealed the need for reform; by the end of the 19th century, England and the USA had adopted some of her principles. Modern nursing provides a broad range of services, with standards set by relevant professional bodies.

nut Dry, one-seeded fruit with a hard, woody or stony wall. It develops from a flower that has petals attached above the OVARY. Examples include ACORNS and hazelnuts.

nutation Oscillating movement (period 18.6 years) superimposed on the steady precessional movement of the Earth's axis so that the precessional path of each celestial pole on the CELESTIAL SPHERE follows an irregular rather than a true circle. It results from the varying gravitational attraction of the Sun and Moon on the Earth. *See also* PRECESSION

nutcracker Crow-like bird of evergreen forests of the Northern Hemisphere. A projection inside the bill turns it into a highly efficient seed cracker or nutcracker. Family Corvidae. Length: 30cm (12in).

nuthatch Bird found in the Northern Hemisphere and occasionally in Africa and Australia. It is bluish-grey above and white, grey or chestnut underneath. It eats nuts, opening them with its sharp bill. It also feeds on insects, spiders, and seeds. Length: 9–19cm (3.5–7.5in). Family Sittidae.

nutmeg Evergreen tree native to tropical Asia, Africa and America. Its seeds yield the spice nutmeg. Height: up to 18m (60ft). Family Myristicaceae.

nutrition Processes by which plants and animals take in and make use of food substances. The science of nutrition involves identifying the kinds and amounts of nutrients necessary for growth and health. Nutrients are generally divided into PROTEINS, CARBOHYDRATES, FATS, minerals, and VITAMINS. Plants use materials from the **abiotic** (non-living) environment, a process known as **autotrophic nutrition**, while animals use food from the **biotic** (living) environment, a process called **heterotrophic nutrition**.

Nuuk (Danish, Godthåb) Capital and largest town of GREENLAND, at the mouth of a group of fjords on the sw coast. Founded in 1721, it is the oldest Danish settlement in Greenland. Industries: fishing and fish processing, scientific research. Pop. (2000) 13,400.

Nyerere, Julius Kambarage (1922–99) Tanzanian statesman and its first president (1964–85). In 1954, he founded the Tanganyika African National Union. In 1961, Nyerere led Tanganyika to independence. In 1964, he negotiated the union between Tanganyika and ZANZIBAR that created Tanzania. He established a one-party state. In 1979, Nyerere sent troops into Uganda to destabilize Idi AMIN. Under his autocratic but generally benign socialist government, Tanzania made progress in social welfare and education. Economic setbacks led to calls for greater democracy and he was forced to retire.

nylon Any of numerous synthetic materials consisting of polyamides (with protein-like structures). Introduced in the USA in 1938, nylon was the first totally synthetic fibre. It can be formed into fibres, filaments, bristles or sheets. It is characterized by elasticity and strength, and is used chiefly in yarn, cordage and moulded products.

Nyman, Michael (1944–) English composer. Influenced by John CAGE, he explored experimental music. His works include operas, notably *The Man who Mistook his Wife for a Hat* (1986), but he is best known for his film scores. These include *The Draughtsman's Contract* (1982) and *The Piano* (1993).

nymph In Greek mythology, a female nature spirit who was said to be a guardian of natural objects. Nymphs were identified with specific locations, often with trees and water.

nymph Young insect of primitive orders that do not undergo complete METAMORPHOSIS. The term designates all immature stages after the egg. The nymph resembles the adult and does so more closely with each moulting. Examples are the aquatic nymphs of dragonflies, mayflies, and damsel flies.

◄ **nuclear weapon** The detonation of a large nuclear weapon above ground creates a huge mushroom cloud of radioactive dust and debris above the explosion that can reach several kilometres in height. The hazardous airborne dust is then free to be carried in any direction by the prevailing winds. The devastation covers a wide area: a 15 megaton hydrogen bomb will cause all flammable material within 20km (12mi) to burst into flame.

O/o, the 15th letter of the alphabet, is derived from the Phoenician alphabet. It entered the Greek alphabet as omicron, "short o", and passed unchanged into the various languages in which it is used today.

oak Common name of *c.*600 species of the genus *Quercus,* which are found in temperate areas of the Northern Hemisphere and at high elevations in the tropics. Most species are hardwood trees that grow 18–30m (60–100ft) tall. Leaves are simple, often lobed, and sometimes serrated. The flowers are greenish and inconspicuous; male flowers hang in catkins. The fruit is an acorn, surrounded by a cup.

Oakley, Annie (1860–1926) US entertainer. From a poor family in rural Ohio, Oakley became an expert sharpshooter. In the 1880s her talents led her to a career in trick–shooting. She was the star of Buffalo Bill's 'Wild West Show' for 17 years.

oarfish Any of several deep water, marine, ribbon fish. Its long, thin body has a dorsal fin extending along its entire length. Two long oar-like pelvic fins protrude from beneath the head. Length: to 6m (20ft). Genus *Regalecus.*

OAS Abbreviation of ORGANIZATION OF AMERICAN STATES

OAS (Organisation de l'Armée Secrète) French terrorist group opposed to Algerian independence. Disaffected army officers and French settlers in Algeria founded the OAS after President Charles DE GAULLE opened negotiations with Algerian nationalists. Acts of terrorism in France and Algeria failed to prevent Algeria gaining independence in 1962.

oasis Fertile location that has water in an arid landscape. Usually, groundwater is brought to the surface in a well, but an oasis may occur where a river flowing from a wetter region crosses the desert on its way to the sea, such as the NILE.

oat Cereal plant native to W Europe, and cultivated worldwide. The flower comprises numerous florets that produce one-seeded fruits. Mainly fed to livestock, oats are also eaten by humans. Family Poaceae/Gramineae; species *Avena sativa.*

Oates, Joyce Carol (1938–) US novelist, short-story writer, and poet. Oates' debut book of short stories was *By the North Gate* (1963). Her works, such as the trilogy *A Garden of Earthly Delights* (1967), *Expensive People* (1968) and *Them* (1969), are grim chronicles of violence and deprivation in modern America. Other novels include *The Assassins* (1975), *You Must Remember This* (1987), and *We Were the Mulvaneys* (1996).

Oates, Lawrence Edward Grace (1880–1912) English explorer and soldier. He accompanied Robert SCOTT on the Antarctic expedition (1910–12). They reached the South Pole but on the return journey became weatherbound. Captain Oates, crippled by frostbite, sacrificed his own life by crawling out into a blizzard rather than risk slowing the party down.

Oates, Titus (1649–1705) English author of the anti-Catholic Popish Plot (1678). He invented the story of a Jesuit plot to depose King CHARLES II. It provoked a hysterical reaction and encouraged efforts to exclude Charles' Catholic brother, the future JAMES II, from the succession.

Oaxaca (officially Oaxaca de Juárez) State capital of Oaxaca, S Mexico. Oaxaca is an agricultural state: coffee is the principal crop. Tourists use the city as a base for exploring archaeological sites, such as Monte Albán. The city is renowned for its jewellery and hand-woven textiles. Founded by the Aztecs, Spain captured Oaxaca in 1521. It played a major role in Mexico's struggle for independence. Pop. (2000) 256,848.

Ob River in W Siberia, central Russia. It flows NW then NE through the lowlands of W Siberia, before continuing N and then E to enter the Gulf of Ob, an arm of the Kara Sea within the Arctic Ocean. Length: 3,680km (2,300mi). With its principal tributary, the Irtysh, it is the seventh-longest river in the world: 5,410km (3,360mi).

obelisk Stone monolith, which usually has a tapering, square-based column with a pyramid-shaped point. Pairs of obelisks stood at the entrance to ancient Egyptian temples, such as Karnak (LUXOR). The two Cleopatra's needles in New York's Central Park and on London's Thames Embankment, date from 1500 BC, long before CLEOPATRA's reign.

Oberammergau Village in upper Bavaria, S Germany, famous for its PASSION PLAY. The performance takes place once every 10 years, in fulfilment of a vow made by the inhabitants in 1634 during an outbreak of the plague.

Oberon In medieval folklore, the king of the fairies and husband of TITANIA. Perhaps the most familiar use of the character is in SHAKESPEARE's *A Midsummer Night's Dream.*

Oberon, Merle (1911–79) Australian film actress. Her performance in *The Dark Angel* (1935) earned her an Oscar nomination. In 1939 she married Alexander KORDA, with whom she made *The Scarlet Pimpernel* (1934) and *The Divorce of Lady X* (1938).

obesity Condition of being overweight, generally defined as weighing 20% or more above the recommended norm for the person's sex, height, and build. People who are overweight are at increased risk of disease and have a shorter life expectancy than those of normal weight.

oboe WOODWIND musical instrument. It has a slightly flared bell and, like the BASSOON, is a double-reed instrument. The earliest true oboes were used in the mid-17th century and have been widely used since the 18th century.

Obote, (Apollo) Milton (1924–2005) Ugandan politician. He created the Uganda People's Congress in 1960, and became the first prime minister of independent Uganda (1962–66). In 1966, Obote drove out the king of the old kingdom of Buganda, and became president of a more centralized state. Ousted by his army chief, Idi AMIN, in 1971, Obote returned to power after Amin was overthrown in 1979. Obote was again overthrown by an army coup in 1985.

O'Brien, Edna (1932–) Irish novelist and short-story writer. Her novels, which include the trilogy *The Country Girls* (1960), *The Lonely Girl* (1962), and *Girls in Their Married Bliss* (1964), are distinguished by their frank depiction of female sexuality. O'Brien's short-story collections include *A Fanatic Heart* (1984).

O'Brien, Flann (1911–66) Irish novelist, b. Brian O'Nolan. His first and most ambitious novel was *At Swim-Two-Birds* (1939). He wrote three other novels in English – *The Hard Life* (1961), *The Dalkey Archive* (1964), and *The Third Policeman* (1967) – and one in Gaelic, *An Béal Bocht* (1941).

O'Brien, William Smith (1803–64) Irish nationalist leader. He entered Parliament as an Irish member in 1828, and supported Roman Catholic emancipation. In 1843, he joined Daniel O'CONNELL's Repeal Association against the Act of UNION (1800), but left in 1846 to set up the more militant Repeal League. Arrested after leading an ineffective insurrection in 1848, O'Brien was sentenced to death, later commuted to transportation.

observatory Location of TELESCOPES and other equipment for astronomical observations. Large optical telescopes are housed in domed buildings, usually sited well away from the smoke of cities. Radio observatories are open sites containing one or more large RADIO TELESCOPES. The largest radio-telescope dishes have been built in natural mountain hollows: the Arecibo Observatory in Puerto Rico is 300m (975ft) across.

obsidian Rare, grey to black, glassy volcanic rock. It is the uncrystallized equivalent of rhyolite and GRANITE. It makes an attractive semi-precious stone. Hardness 5.5; r.d. 2.4.

O'Casey, Sean (1880–1964) Irish playwright. His first play, *The Shadow of a Gunman* (1923), immediately made him famous. *Juno and the Paycock* (1924) was followed by *The Plough and the Stars* (1926). His later works, such as *The Silver Tassie* (1929), are in an expressionistic style, very different from the realism of his early plays.

Occam's razor *See* WILLIAM OF OCCAM

occupational therapy Development of practical skills to assist patients recovering from illness or injury. Therapists oversee a variety of pursuits, from the activities of daily living (ADLs), such as washing and dressing, to hobbies and crafts.

ocean Continuous body of salt water that surrounds the continents and fills the Earth's great depressions. Oceans cover *c.*71% of the Earth's surface (more than 80% of the Southern Hemisphere), and represent *c.*98% of all the water on the face of the Earth. There are five main oceans, the ATLANTIC, PACIFIC, INDIAN, ARCTIC, and Antarctic. The oceans are constantly moving in currents, TIDES, and WAVES, and they form an integral part of the Earth's HYDROLOGICAL CYCLE and CLIMATE. They are a rich source of fossils and minerals, such as oil and gas. Marine fauna, such as fish and plankton, are a vital part of the food chain. Total area: 360 million sq km (138 million sq mi). Total volume: *c.*1.4 billion cu km (322 million

INTERNET

observatory
▶ www.ifa.hawaii.edu/mko
▶ www.naic.edu
▶ www.eso.org

cu mi). Average depth: 3,500m (12,000ft). Average temperature: 3.9°C (39°F). *See also* CONTINENTAL DRIFT; DESALINATION; SEAFLOOR SPREADING; WATER POLLUTION; ANTARCTICA

Oceania Collective term applied to the islands in the central and s Pacific Ocean. It includes the islands of MELANESIA, MICRONESIA, and POLYNESIA and, sometimes, Australasia (Australia and New Zealand) and the Malay Archipelago.

Oceanic art Much art from OCEANIA involves objects used in religious rites. Among the most notable examples are the giant, stone, ancestor-cult figures of EASTER ISLAND, MAORI wood carvings, and the carved drums, masks, stools, and shields of NEW GUINEA.

oceanic current Movement of sea water between layers of varying temperature and density. OCEAN circulation is produced by CONVECTION, with warm currents travelling away from the Equator, cooler water moving from the poles. In the Southern Hemisphere the oceanic currents move in an anti-clockwise system, whereas in the Northern the system is clockwise, an effect caused by the Earth's rotation. There are *c.*50 major currents, including the GULF STREAM in the N Atlantic and the Humboldt (Peru) current off the w coast of South America. *See also* CORIOLIS EFFECT; EL NIÑO

Oceanic mythology Traditional beliefs of the native inhabitants of OCEANIA. The mythological traditions are varied and complex. Among the **Polynesians**, there are various accounts of the creation of the world by the celestial deity Tangaroa (Ta'aroa). Maui, the most famous of the Polynesian mythic heroes, often thought of as half god and half human, is known for his cunning deeds. In **Melanesian** creation myths, the beginning of the world is seen as a movement that brings order out of chaos. In the daily life of the Melanesians there are a vast number of unseen forces – benevolent spirits, demons, ghosts, and the souls of the departed – to be dealt with by means of elaborate rituals. In **Micronesian** creation myths, female deities play a prominent part. ANCESTOR WORSHIP is also an important part of social life. In most Oceanic mythology, the concept of *mana* plays a fundamental role. *Mana* is seen as an impersonal, supernatural force that resides in a person, a natural object, or a place.

oceanography Study of the OCEANS. The major subdisciplines of oceanography include marine geology (*see* PLATE TECTONICS), marine BIOLOGY, marine METEOROLOGY, and physical and chemical oceanography. The science of oceanography dates from the CHALLENGER EXPEDITION (1872–76). Jacques COUSTEAU's invention of the SCUBA aided human exploration of the seas. In 1948, August PICCARD invented the bathyscape to explore deep waters.

ocelot Small cat that lives in s USA, Central and South America. Its valuable fur is yellowish with elongated dark spots. It feeds on small birds, mammals and reptiles. Length: to 1.5m (4.9ft). Family Felidae; species *Felis pardalis*.

O'Connell, Daniel (1775–1847) Irish nationalist leader, known as 'the Liberator'. In 1823, he formed the Catholic Association. His election (1828) to Westminster as member for County Cork forced the Duke of WELLINGTON's government to pass the Act of CATHOLIC EMANCIPATION (1829). In 1840, O'Connell founded the Repeal Association to overturn the Act of UNION (1800). In 1844, he was arrested and briefly imprisoned for sedition. O'Connell's failure to deliver significant reforms and the potato famine led to the formation of the more radical Young Ireland.

octane number Indication of the anti-knock properties of a liquid motor fuel. The higher the number, the less likely the possibility of the fuel detonating.

octave In music, the interval between any given note and another one that is exactly twice (or half) the frequency of the first and thus, acoustically, a perfect consonance. In Western music, it encompasses the eight notes of the diatonic SCALE.

Octavian *See* AUGUSTUS

octopus Predatory, CEPHALOPOD mollusc with no external shell. Its sac-like body has eight powerful suckered tentacles. They feed mostly on crabs and other shellfish, paralysing their prey with poison. Many of the 150 species are small, but the common octopus (*Octopus vulgaris*) grows to 9m (30ft). Family Octopodidae.

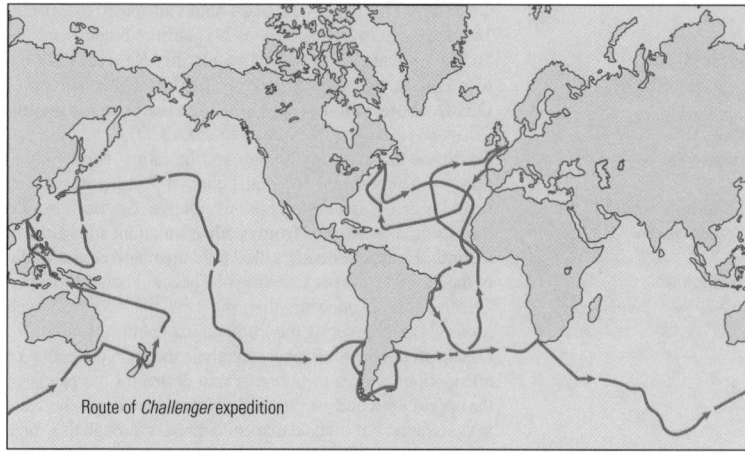

Route of *Challenger* expedition

ode Lyric poem of unspecific form but typically of heightened emotion or public address. The first great writer of odes was PINDAR, but more simple were the lyrical odes of HORACE and CATULLUS. In 17th-century England, it was taken up by JONSON, HERRICK, and MARVELL. Representative of the more personal type are the 19th-century odes of WORDSWORTH, SHELLEY, and KEATS.

Odense City and port in s central Denmark. Founded in the 10th century, Odense has a 13th-century Gothic cathedral and an 18th-century palace. Industries: shipbuilding, metalworking, engineering. Pop. (2000) 145,062.

Oder Second-longest river in the catchment basin of the Baltic Sea. It rises in the NE Czech Republic, flows N and w through sw Poland, before turning N, forming the Polish-German border and reaching the Baltic Sea. The Oder has many navigable tributaries, notably the rivers Neisse and Warta. Length: 886km (550mi).

Odessa City and port on the Black Sea, s Ukraine. The Tatars built a fortress here in the 14th century. It later passed to Poland-Lithuania and then to Turkey (1764). Brought under Russian control in 1791, it became a naval base. Odessa was the scene of the mutiny on the battleship *Potemkin* during the RUSSIAN REVOLUTION OF 1905. Industries: fishing, whaling, shipbuilding and repairing, oil refining, metalworking, chemicals, heavy machinery. Pop. (2001) 1,029,000.

Odin Principal god in Norse mythology. Identified with the Teutonic god Woden, he is considered to be the god of wisdom, culture, war and death. He lived with the Valkyries in VALHALLA, where he received the souls of dead warriors.

Odoacer (*c.*433–93) (Odovacar) Chief of the Germanic Heruli people and conqueror of the Western ROMAN EMPIRE. The Heruli were Roman mercenaries until 476, when they declared Odoacer king of Italy. After the Ostrogoths invaded in 489, Odoacer fled to Ravenna. King Theodoric of the Ostrogoths invited Odoacer to a banquet, where he was murdered.

odontology Study of the structure, development and diseases of the teeth. It is closely allied with DENTISTRY.

Odysseus (Ulysses) Greek hero of HOMER's EPIC poem, the ODYSSEY. King of the city-state of Ithaca, husband of the faithful PENELOPE, he was an astute and brave warrior. It was Odysseus who devised the wooden horse used to enter Troy during the TROJAN WAR.

▲ **oceanography** One of the most important scientific voyages ever made, the map shows the route of the *Challenger* expedition of 1872–76. The expedition lasted four years and laid the foundations for the modern science of oceanography. The *Challenger* covered a distance of 68,900 nautical miles. It established 362 observation stations, where measurements of ocean depth, temperature, and surface currents were made, and samples of water, fauna, and fishes collected. The ship held a cramped but very well-equipped laboratory.

0

◀ **ocelot** A member of the flesh-eating mammal order (Carnivora), the ocelot (*Felis pardalis*) is found in Central and South America, and sometimes as far N as Texas. It measures from 80 to 47cm (31–58in) long and is grouped with all other cats in the family Felidae.

OHIO
Statehood :
March 1, 1803
Nickname :
The Buckeye State
State bird :
Cardinal
State flower :
Scarlet carnation
State tree :
Buckeye
State motto :
With God, all things are possible

O

OKLAHOMA
Statehood :
November 16, 1907
Nickname :
The Sooner State
State bird :
Scissor-tailed flycatcher
State flower :
Mistletoe
State tree :
Redbud
State motto :
Labour conquers all things

Odyssey, The EPIC poem of 24 books attributed to HOMER. The story of ODYSSEUS tells of his journey home from the Trojan Wars after 10 years of wandering. He wins back his wife PENELOPE and his kingdom, after killing her suitors.

OECD Abbreviation of the ORGANIZATION FOR ECONOMIC COOPERATION AND DEVELOPMENT (OECD)

Oedipus In Greek mythology and literature, son of Laius (king of Thebes) and Jocasta; father of Antigone, Ismene, Eteocles and Polynices by his own mother. SOPHOCLES told how Oedipus was saved from death as an infant and raised in Corinth. He inadvertently killed his father, solved the riddle of the SPHINX, and became king of Thebes. There he married Queen Jocasta, unaware that she was his own widowed mother. On discovering the truth, he made himself blind.

Oedipus complex In psychoanalytic theory, a collection of unconscious wishes involving sexual desire for the parent of the opposite sex and jealous rivalry with the parent of the same sex. Sigmund FREUD held that children pass through this stage between the ages of three and five. The complex in females is sometimes known as the Electra complex, a term coined by C.G. JUNG. The theory has been considerably modified, if not totally rejected, by most modern practitioners.

Oersted, Hans Christian (1777–1851) Danish physicist and professor at Copenhagen University. He took the first steps in explaining the relationship between electricity and magnetism, thus founding the science of ELECTROMAGNETISM. The oersted unit of magnetic field strength is named after him.

oesophagus (gullet) Muscular tube, part of the ALIMENTARY CANAL (or gut), which carries swallowed food from the throat to the STOMACH. Food is moved down the lubricated channel by the wave-like movement known as PERISTALSIS.

oestrogen Female SEX HORMONE. First produced by a girl at PUBERTY, oestrogen leads to the development of the secondary sexual characteristics: breasts, body hair and redistributed fat. It regulates the MENSTRUAL CYCLE and prepares the UTERUS for pregnancy. It is also a constituent of the contraceptive PILL.

Offenbach, Jacques Levy (1819–80) French composer. His reputation was founded on the brilliance of his numerous operettas, notably *Orpheus in the Underworld* (1858). Offenbach also wrote one opera *Tales of Hoffmann* (1881), based on the stories of E.T.A. HOFFMANN.

Official Secrets Act (1989) Law passed by the British Parliament forbidding government employees to disclose information formally classified as secret. The Act, which replaced one passed in 1911, is aimed particularly at members of the national security and intelligence services.

offset Method of PRINTING widely used for high-volume publications. In the printing machine, a roller applies ink to the printing plate, which is mounted on a rotating cylinder. The image is then transferred (offset) to a cylinder with a rubber covering, called the blanket. This transfers the image to the paper. Usually, the plates are made by LITHOGRAPHY, and the process is called **offset lithography**. Separate plates are used for each colour of ink.

O'Flaherty, Liam (1897–1984) Irish novelist and short story writer. His novels, which often reflect contemporary Irish social conditions, include *The Informer* (1925), *The Puritan* (1931), *Famine* (1937), and *Insurrection* (1950). He also wrote three autobiographical works.

Ogdon, John (1937–89) English pianist and composer. He established his strong international reputation in 1962 when he was joint winner of the Tchaikovsky Competition in Moscow with Vladimir ASHKENAZY.

O'Higgins, Bernardo (1778–1842) South American revolutionary leader and ruler of Chile. A member of the revolutionary junta in colonial Chile, O'Higgins commanded the army against the Spanish. Defeated in 1814, he joined José de SAN MARTÍN in Argentina to defeat the Spanish at Chacabuco (1817). Appointed 'supreme director' of Chile, he declared independence in 1818 but resigned in 1823.

Ohio State in E central USA, bounded by Lake Erie in the N; the capital is COLUMBUS. Other cities include Toledo and CLEVELAND. Britain acquired the land in 1763, at the end of the Seven Years' War. It was ceded to the USA after the American Revolution, and in 1787 it became part of the

Northwest Territory. Ohio was accepted into the Union in 1803. Mostly low-lying, the state is drained chiefly by the OHIO, Scioto, Miami, and Muskingum rivers. Ohio's large farms produce hay, maize, wheat, soya beans and dairy foods, and cattle and pigs are raised. The state is highly industrialized. Ohio produces sandstone, oil, natural gas, clay, salt, lime and gravel. Its lake ports handle large amounts of iron and copper ore, coal and oil. Industries: vehicle and aircraft manufacture, transport equipment, primary and fabricated metals. Area: 106,764sq km (41,222sq mi). Pop. (2000) 11,353,140.

Ohio River in E central USA, formed at the confluence of the Allegheny and Monongahela rivers at Pittsburgh in W Pennsylvania. It flows W and then SW to join the Mississippi River at Cairo, Illinois. The Ohio River valley is a highly industrialized region. Length: 1,571km (976mi).

ohm (symbol Ω) SI unit of electrical RESISTANCE, equal to the resistance between two points on a conductor when a constant POTENTIAL DIFFERENCE of one VOLT between them produces a current of one AMPERE.

Ohm's law Statement that the amount of steady current through a material is proportional to the voltage across the material. For example, if the voltage doubles then the current also doubles. Proposed in 1827 by the German physicist Georg Ohm (1787–1854), Ohm's law is expressed mathematically as $V = IR$ (where V is the voltage in volts, I is the current in amperes, and R is the resistance in ohms).

oil General term to describe a variety of substances whose chief shared properties are viscosity at ordinary temperatures, a density less than that of water, inflammability, insolubility in water, and solubility in ether and alcohol. **Mineral** oils, most notably crude oil or PETROLEUM oil, are used as fuels. **Animal** and **vegetable** oils (fatty oils or FATS) are used as food, lubricants and as a major ingredient of soap. In addition, there are ESSENTIAL OILS from plants that, unlike fatty oils, are volatile. Fatty oils can be classified into two groups: drying, such as linseed and poppyseed oil, and non-drying, such as olive and castor oil.

oil palm Tree grown in humid tropical regions of W Africa and Madagascar, source of oil for margarine and soap. The long, feather-shaped fronds rise from a short trunk. Height: 9–15m (30–50ft). Family Arecaceae/Palmae.

Oistrakh, David (1908–74) Russian violinist. His interpretation of the violin repertoire earned him the reputation of being the greatest violinist of his day. His son and pupil, **Igor Oistrakh** (1931–), is also a virtuoso violinist.

Ojibwa (Chippewa) Group of Algonquian-speaking Native North Americans. In the 17th century, they were constantly at war with the Sioux, eventually driving them across the Mississippi River. Since then, they have lived on reservations in Michigan, Wisconsin, Minnesota and North Dakota. Today, *c*.90,000 live in the USA and Canada.

O'Keeffe, Georgia (1887–1986) US painter. O'Keeffe's first exhibition was in 1916, and in 1924 she married Alfred STIEGLITZ. Her early works were stylized, betraying the influence of ABSTRACT ART. She is, however, best known for her microscopically detailed paintings of flowers, such as *Black Iris* (1926). Her use of vibrant colour was combined with strong overtones of sexual symbolism.

Okhotsk, Sea of Arm of the N Pacific Ocean off the E coast of Russia, bounded E by the Kamchatka Peninsula and SE by the Kuril Islands. The chief ports are Magadan and Korsakov in Russia. Area: 1,528,000sq km (590,000sq mi).

Okinawa Largest island of the Okinawa archipelago, SW of mainland Japan, part of the RYUKYU ISLANDS group in the W Pacific Ocean; the major settlement is Naha. The N is mountainous, densely forested and sparsely populated. Economic activity, such as agriculture and fishing, is concentrated in the S. In April 1945, US troops landed, and met fierce Japanese resistance. Okinawa surrendered in June 1945 after many casualties. Area: 1,176sq km (454sq mi). Pop. (2000) 1,318,000.

Oklahoma State in central S USA; the capital is OKLAHOMA CITY. Other important cities are TULSA and Lawton. Much of the area was acquired by the USA from France in the LOUISIANA PURCHASE (1803). The Territory of Oklahoma was merged with the Indian Territory to form the state of Oklahoma in 1907. The w of the state is part of the GREAT PLAINS. The E is mountainous. Oklahoma is drained chiefly by the Arkansas and Red rivers. Wheat and cotton are the leading crops, but livestock is more important. There are many minerals, but oil and natural gas form the basis of Oklahoma's economic wealth. Area: 181,089sq km (69,918sq mi). Pop. (2000) 3,450,654.

Oklahoma City Capital and largest city of Oklahoma, USA, in the centre of the state on the North Canadian River. The area was settled in 1889. The city was made the state capital in 1910, and prospered with the discovery of rich oil deposits in 1928. It was the site of a terrorist bomb in April 1995, which killed 168 people and injured 400 others. Industries: oil refining, grain milling, cotton processing, steel products, electronic equipment, aircraft. Pop. (2000) 506,132.

okra (gumbo) Annual tropical plant with red-centred yellow flowers. The green fruit pods are edible. Height: 0.6–1.8m (2–6ft). Family Malvaceae; species *Hibiscus esculentus*

Okri, Ben (1959–) Nigerian novelist. The novels, *Flowers and Shadows* (1980) and *The Landscapes Within* (1981), built his reputation. He won the Booker Prize for *The Famished Road* (1991). Its sequel was *Songs of Enchantment* (1993).

Olaf II (Haraldsson), Saint (995–1030) Norwegian king (1015–30) and patron saint of Norway. He introduced Christianity, but this was unpopular with chiefs, who rebelled, backed by CANUTE II of Denmark. In 1028, Olaf was forced into exile and died in battle at Stikelstad. Following reports of miracles at his grave, he was canonized in 1164. His feast day is July 29.

Old Catholics Religious movement rejecting the dogma of PAPAL INFALLIBILITY, which had been announced by the First Vatican Council of 1870. The Old Catholics set up churches in German- and Dutch-speaking Europe, which later united in the Union of Utrecht in 1889. Since then the Archbishop of Utrecht has been head of the International Old Catholic Congress. Old Catholics have much affinity with Anglicans.

Oldenbarneveldt, Johan van (1547–1619) Dutch political leader in the Revolt of the Netherlands. With WILLIAM I (THE SILENT), he founded the Dutch Republic. He helped to arrange the union of the provinces at Utrecht (1579), and supported Maurice of Nassau as stadtholder when William was assassinated (1584). From 1586 he was the dominant figure in Holland and, with Maurice, practically the ruler of the United Provinces. He was instrumental in securing the truce with Spain (1609), which implied Dutch independence. He fell out with Maurice over religious differences and after an unjust trial was executed.

Oldenburg, Claes (1929–) US sculptor, a leading member of the POP ART movement. He is famous for his gigantic sculptures based on everyday objects, such as *Lipstick* (1969).

Old Testament First and older section of the BIBLE, originally written in Hebrew or Aramaic, and accepted as religiously inspired and sacred by both Jews and Christians. Among Jews it is known as the Hebrew Bible. It begins with the creation, but the main theme of the Old Testament is the history of the Hebrews. In addition, there are many examples of prophetic writing, poetry, and short narrative tales. It comprises the PENTATEUCH or TORAH (Genesis to Deuteronomy); the Historical Books (Joshua to I and II Kings); the Wisdom Books (Job, Proverbs, and Ecclesiastes); the Major Prophets (Isaiah, Jeremiah, and Ezekiel); the 12 Minor Prophets (Hosea to Malachi); and the miscellaneous collection known as the Writings (including Psalms and the Song of Songs). Sometimes included is a collection of books written in the final three centuries BC known as the APOCRYPHA. The number, order, and names of the books of the Old Testament vary between the Jewish and Christian traditions; texts for both are based mainly on the SEPTUAGINT. *See also* LAW AND THE PROPHETS

Olduvai Gorge Site in N Tanzania where remains of primitive humans have been found. Louis LEAKEY uncovered four layers of remains dating from *c.*2 million years ago to *c.*15,000 years ago. In 1964, he announced the discovery of *Homo habilis*, whom he believed to have been a direct ancestor of modern humans. The gorge, which is 40km (25mi) long and 100m (320ft) deep, runs through the Serengeti Plain.

Old Vic London theatre. Built in 1818 as the Royal Coburg Theatre, it was renamed the Royal Victoria in 1833, and soon became known as the Old Vic. Under the management of Lilian Baylis from 1898, it gained a reputation for its Shakespearean productions. From 1963 to 1976, it was the home of the National Theatre of Great Britain. The Young Vic opened in 1970.

oleander Evergreen shrubs of the genus *Nerium*, native to the Mediterranean region. They have milky poisonous sap, clusters of white, pink or purple flowers, and smooth leaves. The best-known is the rosebay (*N. oleander*). Family Apocynaceae.

oligarchy System of government in which power is concentrated in the hands of a few, who rule without the requirement of popular support and without external check on their authority. Oligarchs rule in their own interests.

Oligocene Extent of GEOLOGICAL TIME from *c.*38 to 25 million years ago. It is the third of five epochs of the TERTIARY period. In the Oligocene period, the climate cooled and many modern mammals evolved, including elephants and an ancestor of the modern horse.

olive Tree, shrub or vine and its fruit, especially the common olive tree, *Olea europaea*, native to the Mediterranean region. It has leathery, lance-shaped leaves, a gnarled and twisted trunk and may live for more than 1,000 years. The fruit is bitter and inedible before processing and is also used to make olive oil. Height: to 9m (30ft). Family Oleaceae.

Olivier, Laurence Kerr, Baron Olivier of Brighton (1907–89) English actor and director, the outstanding Shakespearean interpreter of his generation. He made his film debut in 1930, and established himself in films such as *Wuthering Heights* (1939) and *Pride and Prejudice* (1940). In 1944, Olivier and Ralph RICHARDSON became directors of the OLD VIC. He won a special Academy Award for his directorial debut, *Henry V* (1944). Olivier's second film, *Hamlet* (1948), earned him Oscars for best actor and best picture. He was director (1963–73) of the NATIONAL THEATRE of Great Britain. Olivier was the first actor to be made a life peer (1970). He was married to Jill Esmond (1930–40), Vivien LEIGH (1940–61), and Joan PLOWRIGHT (1961 until his death).

olivine Ferromagnesian mineral, $(MgFe)_2$

Olmec Early civilization of Central America, which flourished between the 12th and 4th centuries BC. Its heartland was the S coast of the Gulf of Mexico, but its influence spread more widely. From the 9th century BC the main Olmec centre was La Venta. Olmec art included high-quality carving of jade and stone, notably giant human heads in basalt. The Olmec heritage can be traced through later civilizations, including the MAYA.

Olympia Area in S Greece, the site of an ancient sanctuary and of the original OLYMPIC GAMES. Buried by earthquakes in the 6th century AD Olympia was not rediscovered until the 18th century. It contained some of the finest works of Classical art and architecture, including the huge temple of Zeus, which contained a giant statue of the god that was numbered among the SEVEN WONDERS OF THE WORLD.

Olympia State capital and port of entry for Washington State, USA, on the S tip of Puget Sound in the SW of the state. It was made capital of Washington Territory in 1853. Industries: agriculture, food canning, beer, oysters. Pop. (2000) 42,514.

Olympic Games World's major international athletic competition, held in two segments – the Summer Games and the Winter Games – since 1992 it has alternated so that there are two years between segments, but four years before a segment is repeated. In 776 BC the Games were first celebrated in OLYMPIA, Greece, and were held every four years until AD 393, when they were abolished by the Roman Emperor. The modern, summer Games were initiated by Baron Pierre de Coubertin, and were first held in Athens, Greece, in 1896. Women did not compete until 1912. The Games were cancelled during both world wars. Control of the Games is vested in the International Olympic Committee (IOC), which lays down the rules and chooses venues.

Olympus Mountain range in N Greece, on the border of Thessaly and Macedonia, *c.*40km (25mi) long. Its peak, Mount Olympus, is the highest point in Greece, at 2,917m (9,570ft). It was first climbed in 1913. In ancient Greek

▲ **okra** Originating in Africa and now widely cultivated throughout the tropics, the okra plant (*Hibiscus esculentus*) is related to the cotton plant. Its sticky green pods are picked ten weeks after planting, and are eaten as a vegetable.

▲ **Olivier** Perhaps the greatest classical actor of his generation, Laurence Olivier played all the great Shakespearean roles on stage and successfully transferred several of them to screen. He played a number of romantic leads, including that of Max de Winter in *Rebecca* (1940). Olivier produced, directed, and starred in *Henry V* (1944) and *Hamlet* (1948). In 1955, he directed and co-starred with Marilyn Monroe in *The Prince and the Showgirl*. Olivier's private life attracted a great deal of press attention, particularly his second marriage to actress Vivien Leigh.

O

INTERNET

Olympic Games
▶ www.olympic.org

mythology it was considered to be the home of the gods, (known as the Olympian gods) and closed to mortal eyes.

Om (Aum) Sacred mystical symbol representing a sound considered to have divine power by some Hindus, Buddhists, and other religious groups. The sound is chanted at the beginning and end of prayers, and is used as a mantra in meditation.

Omaha Port on the Missouri River, in E Nebraska, USA. The area was ceded to the US government in 1854. It was the capital of Nebraska Territory from 1854 to 1867. It is a leading livestock market and meat processing centre, and a major insurance centre. Pop. (2000) 390,007.

Oman Sultanate on the SE corner of the Arabian peninsula, SW Asia; the capital is MUSCAT. *See* country feature.

Omar (*c*.581–644) (Umar) Second CALIPH, or ruler, of ISLAM. He was converted to Islam in 618, and became a counsellor of MUHAMMAD. In 632, he chose the first caliph, ABU BAKR, and succeeded him in 634. Under his rule, Islam spread by conquest into Syria, Egypt, and Iran, and the foundations of an administrative empire were laid.

Omar Khayyám (active 11th century) Iranian poet, mathematician, and astronomer. He so impressed the Sultan that he was asked to reform the calendar. His fame in the West is due to a collection of quatrains freely translated by Edward Fitzgerald as *The Rubáiyát of Omar Khayyám* (1859).

Omayyads *See* UMAYYADS

ombudsman Official appointed to safeguard citizens' rights by investigating complaints of injustice made against the government or its employees. The office was created in Sweden in 1809. A number of other countries adopted the office from the mid-1950s onwards, including Britain in 1967, and companies may also use the system to deal with customer complaints.

omnivore Any creature, such as humans and pigs, that eat both animal and vegetable foods. Omnivorous animals have teeth adapted for cutting, tearing and pulping food.

Omsk City on the Irtysh and Om rivers, W Siberia, Russia. Founded as a fortress town in 1716, it became the administrative centre of W Siberia in 1824. From 1918–19 it was the headquarters of the anti-Bolshevik Kolchak government. It is

OMAN

The Sultanate of Oman is the oldest independent nation in the Arab world. It occupies the SE corner of the Arabian peninsula and includes the tip of the Musandam Peninsula which is separated from the rest of Oman by UAE territory. This peninsula overlooks the strategic Strait of Hormuz.

The Al Halar al Gharbi range, rising to 3,019m [9,904ft] above sea level, borders the narrow coastal plain in the N. This fertile plain along the Gulf of Oman is called Al Battinah. Inland are deserts, including part of the Rub' al Khali (Empty Quarter). Much of the land along the Arabian Sea is barren, but the province of Zufar (or Dhofar) in the southeast is a hilly, fertile region.

CLIMATE

Temperatures in Oman can reach 54°C [129°F] in summer, but winters are mild to warm. Rainfall in the N mountains can exceed 400mm [16in] per year, while in the SE it can be up to 630mm [25in], but for most of Oman the desert climate means less than 150 mm [6 in] per year. Sandstorms, duststorms and droughts feature and occasionally, tropical cyclones bring stormy weather.

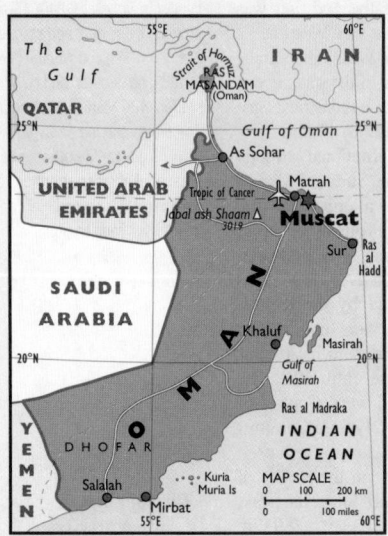

HISTORY

Oman first became a major trading region 5,000 years ago, on the main route between the Persian Gulf and the Indian Ocean. Islam was introduced into the area in the 7th century AD, and today 75% of the population follow the strict Ibadi Islam sect.

The Portuguese conquered several ports, including Muscat, in 1507. Portugal controlled maritime trade until expelled by the Ottomans in 1659. Oman set up trading posts in East Africa, including Zanzibar in 1698. Until the 1860s it was the dominant Arabian power. The Al Bu Said family came to power in the 1740s and have ruled the country ever since.

British influence dates back to the end of the 18th century, when the two countries entered into the first of several treaties. By 1850 most of Oman's overseas possessions were in British hands, and Oman's influence declined. During the early 20th century, the sultanate was often in conflict with religious leaders (imams) of the Ibahdi sect, who sought a more theocratic society. In 1920, Britain brokered an agreement whereby the interior was ruled by imams, with coastal areas under the control of the Sultan. Clashes between the two groups continued into the 1950s, but Sultan Said bin Taimur regained control of the whole country in 1959.

POLITICS

Under Sultan Said bin Taimur, Oman had been an isolated, feudal country. Its economy was backward compared to its oil-rich Gulf neighbours. Oman made substantial strides after Sultan Said bin Taimur was deposed by his son Sultan Qaboos ibn Said in 1970. With the help of soldiers from Iran and Jordan, he saw an end to war against Yemen-backed separatist guerrillas in the province of Zufar (1965–1975). He also led the way in developing an expanding economy based on oil. Production began in 1967 and reserves proved far larger than expected. Qaboos opened up Oman to the outside world, ending its long isolation. At home, he avoided the prestigious projects favoured by Arab leaders to concentrate on social programmes, including the education of girls. His leadership proved popular despite the lack of a democratic government.

AREA 309,500sq km [119,498sq mi]
POPULATION 3,205,000
CAPITAL (POPULATION) Muscat (41,000)
GOVERNMENT Monarchy with consultative council
ETHNIC GROUPS Arab, Baluchi, Indian, Pakistani
LANGUAGES Arabic (official), Baluchi, English
RELIGIONS Islam (mainly Ibadhi), Hinduism
CURRENCY Omani rial = 100 baizas

In 1991 Oman took part in the military campaign to liberate Kuwait. In 1997, Oman held its first direct elections to a Consultative Council. Unusually for the Gulf region, two women were elected. In 1999 Oman and the United Arab Emirates signed an agreement, confirming most of the borders between them. In 2001, while a military campaign was being launched in Afghanistan, Britain held military exercises in the Omani desert. This was an example of the long-standing political and military relationship between the two countries. In 2003 elections were held to the Consultative Council. For the first time, all citizens over 21 were allowed to vote although no parties are allowed. In 2004 the Sultan appointed the first woman minister with portfolio. In 2005 nearly 100 suspected Islamists were arrested and 31 were convicted of trying to overthrow the government, but they were later pardoned.

ECONOMY

The World Bank classifies Oman as an 'upper-middle-income' developing country. It has sizeable oil and natural gas deposits, a large trade surplus and low inflation. Oil accounts for more than 90% of Oman's export revenues. Huge natural gas deposits, equal to all the finds of the previous 20 years, were discovered in 1991. Although only about 0.3% of the land is cultivated, agriculture and fishing are the traditional economic activities. Major crops include alfalfa, bananas, coconuts, dates, tobacco and wheat. Water supply is a major problem. Oman depends on water from underground aquifers, which will eventually run dry. and also from desalination plants. Industries include copper smelting, cement, chemicals and food processing. Tourism is a growing activity.

now a major port. Industries: oil refining, chemicals, engineering, agricultural machinery, textiles. Pop. (1998) 1,137,900.

onager Fast-running animal related to the ASS, found in semi-desert areas of Iran and India. The onager is dun-coloured with a dorsal stripe that reaches the tip of the tail. Height at the shoulder: 0.9–1.5m (2.9–4.9ft). Family Equidae; species *Equus hemionus onager*.

Onassis, Jackie (1929–94) Widow of President John F. KENNEDY and Greek shipping tycoon Aristotle Onassis. She worked as a photo-journalist on the *Washington Times-Herald* before marrying Kennedy in 1953. During his presidential campaign, she became popular both at home and abroad. His assassination (1963) in Dallas signalled her withdrawal from the public arena. She was to give only two more interviews in her lifetime – both sealed until after her death. In 1968, she married Aristotle Onassis. The marriage was widely criticized and subsequently proved to be unhappy. When Onassis died (1975), she returned to New York and worked as an editor.

onchocerciasis (river blindness) Tropical disease of the skin and connective tissue, caused by infection with filarial worms; it may also affect the eyes, causing blindness. It is transmitted by blood-sucking blackflies found in Central and South America and Africa.

oncogene GENE that, by inducing a cell to divide abnormally, contributes to the development of CANCER. Oncogenes arise from gene mutations (proto-oncogenes), which are present in all normal cells and in some viruses. *See also* GENETICS

oncology In medicine, specialty concerned with the diagnosis and treatment of CANCER.

Onega, Lake (Onezhskoye Ozero) Lake in NW Russia, near the border with Finland; second-largest lake in Europe. It drains SW through the River Svir to Lake Ladoga, and has numerous inlets and islands along its N shore. The chief port is Petrozavodsk. Area: 9610sq km (3710sq mi).

O'Neill, Eugene Gladstone (1888–1953) US dramatist. His first full-length play, *Beyond the Horizon* (1920), won the Pulitzer Prize, as did *Anna Christie* (1921). *The Emperor Jones* (1920) was an experiment with EXPRESSIONISM. He won a third Pulitzer Prize for *Strange Interlude* (1928). His interest in Greek tragedy is evident in *Mourning Becomes Electra* (1931). In 1936, O'Neill was awarded the Nobel Prize for Literature. Suffering from Parkinson's disease, he did not produce another play until *The Iceman Cometh* (1946). He won a posthumous Pulitzer Prize for *Long Day's Journey into Night* (1956).

onion Hardy, bulb-forming, biennial plant of the lily family, native to central Asia, and cultivated worldwide for its strong-smelling, edible bulb. It has hollow leaves, white or lilac flowers. Height: to 130cm (50in). Family Alliaceae/Liliaceae.

on-line publishing Distribution of information for public access using COMPUTER networks. Access to on-line publications may be free or on a subscription basis. The content of on-line publications may be enhanced by the use of such features as hypertext, search facilities, and multimedia. The majority of on-line publishing takes place over the INTERNET, particularly the WORLD WIDE WEB (WWW).

Ontario Province in SE Canada, bounded to the S by four of the Great Lakes (Superior, Huron, Erie, and Ontario) and the USA; the capital is TORONTO. Other major cities include OTTAWA, HAMILTON, Windsor, and London. Ontario is Canada's most populous province. French explorers established trading posts in the region during the 17th century. The area became part of New France, but was ceded to Britain in 1763. Ontario was known as Upper Canada until 1841, when it joined with QUÉBEC to form the province of Canada. In 1867, the Dominion of Canada was created, and the province of Ontario was established. In the N is the forested Canadian Shield, with its lowlands bordering on the Hudson and James bays. To the E and S are the lowlands of the ST LAWRENCE River and the Great Lakes, where agriculture and industry are concentrated. Cattle, dairy produce, and pigs are important. The chief crops are tobacco, maize, wheat and vegetables. The Canadian Shield has many mineral deposits. Industries: motor vehicles, transport equipment, metallurgy, chemicals,

paper, machinery, electrical goods. Area: 1,068,587sq km (412,582sq mi). Pop. (2001) 11,410,046.

Ontario, Lake Smallest of the GREAT LAKES, bounded by New York state (S and E) and Ontario province, Canada (S, W, and N). Fed chiefly by the Niagara River, to the NE the St Lawrence River drains Lake Ontario. Forming part of the St Lawrence Seaway, it is a busy shipping route. The chief Canadian cities on Lake Ontario are TORONTO, HAMILTON and Kingston. On the US shore lie Rochester and Oswego. Area: 19,684sq km (7,600sq mi).

ontogeny Total biological development of an organism. It includes the embryonic stage, birth, growth, and death.

ontology Branch of METAPHYSICS that studies the basic nature of things; the essence of 'being' itself.

onyx Semi-precious variety of the mineral CHALCEDONY, a form of AGATE. It has straight parallel bands. White and red forms are called carnelian onyx; white and brown, sardonyx. It is found mostly in India and South America.

Oort, Jan Hendrik (1900–92) Dutch astronomer. He carried out research on the structure and dynamics of stellar systems, especially our GALAXY, whose rotation he confirmed in 1927. In 1950, he proposed the existence of what has come to be called the **Oort cloud** – a spherical region of space surrounding the SOLAR SYSTEM in which COMETS are thought to reside.

ooze Fine, deep-ocean deposit containing materials of more than 30% organic origin. Oozes divide into two main types: **calcareous** ooze, at depths of 2,000–3,900m (6,600–12,800ft), contains the skeletons of animals such as foraminifera and pteropods. **Siliceous** ooze, deeper than 3,900m (12,800ft), contains skeletons of radiolarians and diatoms.

opal Non-crystalline variety of QUARTZ, found in recent volcanoes, deposits from hot springs and sediments. Usually colourless or white with a rainbow play of colour in gem forms, it is the most valuable of quartz gems. Hardness 5.5–6.5; r.d. 2.0.

op art (optical art) US ABSTRACT ART movement, popular in the mid-1960s. It relies on optical phenomena to confuse the viewers' eye and to create a sense of movement on the surface of the picture. Leading exponents include Victor Vasarély, Kenneth Noland, and Bridget RILEY.

OPEC Acronym for ORGANIZATION OF PETROLEUM EXPORTING COUNTRIES

opencast mining Stripping surface layers from the Earth's crust to obtain coal, ores or other minerals. Dragline excavators strip away surface layers and mechanical shovels distribute minerals and spoil. Minerals are carried away for grading and processing. In some countries, owners of opencast mines are required to restore the environmental quality of the land after mining has ceased. See also MINE

open cluster (galactic cluster) Group of young stars in the spiral arms of our GALAXY, containing from a few tens of stars to a few thousand. They are usually several light-years across. One example is the PLEIADES.

Open Door US policy designed to preserve its commercial interests in China in the early 20th century. It originated (1899) in a pronouncement by US Secretary of State, John M. HAY. At that time, China was divided into spheres of interest among European powers and Japan. The 'Open Door' policy demanded that trade and traders from other countries should receive equal rights with other foreigners in China.

open-hearth process Method of producing STEEL in a furnace heated by overhead flames. The flames come from gas or oil burners, and oxygen may be blown through the furnace to increase its temperature. Pig iron, scrap steel and limestone are heated together. Various impurities form slag, which is removed from the surface of the molten metal. Other materials are added to the metal to produce steel of the required type.

opera Stage drama that is sung. It combines acting, singing, orchestral music, set and costume design, making spectacular entertainment. The best-known opera houses include LA SCALA (Milan), the Opéra (Paris), the ROYAL OPERA (London), the State Opera (Vienna), the Festspiele (Bayreuth), and the METROPOLITAN OPERA (New York City). Opera began in Italy in c.1600. The classical style evolved in c.1750; its greatest exponent was MOZART. VERDI and WAGNER dominated 19th-century opera. The

0

OPTICAL FIBRE

Optical fibres carry information as signals of light. The glass core (1) of a fibre optic cable is clad in glass of a different refractive index which confines the light pulses in the core. The light signal cannot leave the core because it always hits the edge of the core at too shallow an angle to escape. A sheath (2) provides physical protection and bundles of the sheathed cores are given strength by a central steel wire (3). Narrow cores (4) are now used because they allow signals to be sent across greater distances without blurring. In a wider cable (5) more reflections can occur, causing the pulse to spread out and merge with adjacent pulses. To prevent this, more space must be left between pulses in wider cables and that limits the volume of data that can be transmitted.

▼ **orchid** The bee orchid (*Ophrys apifera*) of Europe tempts its pollinators with sex rather than nectar. Its elaborate flowers imitate the colour, shape, texture, and scent of female bees of the genus *Eucera*. Male bees, which emerge before the females, alight on the flower's broad platform or labellum and attempt to mate with it. Structures containing thousands of pollen grains adhere to the bee's body. The bee transfers the pollen to other flowers, and cross-fertilization is followed by the formation of thousands of tiny seeds.

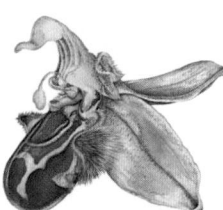

INTERNET

Oregon
▶ www.oregon.gov

Organization for Economic Cooperation and Development (OECD)
▶ www.oecd.org

Organization of American States (OAS)
▶ www.oas.org

Organization of Petroleum Exporting Countries (OPEC)
▶ www.opec.org

20th century brought a profusion of styles by composers as diverse as PUCCINI, STRAUSS, BERG, and BRITTEN.

opera buffa Style of Italian comic opera that developed in mid-18th-century Naples. Light and simple in style, it introduced the elaborate finale which influenced the subsequent development of opera. An early example of the style is *La Serva Padrona* (1733) by Giovanni Pergolesi.

opéra comique Style of French opera that began in the late 18th century. Its hallmarks are a witty plot involving some spoken dialogue, romantic subject matter, and simple engaging music. The genre can also include tragic works, such as Bizet's *Carmen* and Offenbach's *Tales of Hoffmann*.

opera seria Style of Italian opera in the 17th and early 18th centuries. The plots were usually heroic or tragic. Priority was given to virtuoso vocal display in elaborate arias. The formalism and stylization of such operas prompted a reaction that gave rise to the development of OPERA BUFFA.

operetta Type of light OPERA involving songs, dialogue, dancing and an engaging story. Operettas developed from attempts by composers to reach wider audiences. Among these composers were Johann STRAUSS, Arthur SULLIVAN (in association with W.S. GILBERT) and Jacques OFFENBACH.

ophthalmology Branch of medicine that specializes in the diagnosis and treatment of diseases of the eye.

ophthalmoscope Instrument for examining the interior of the eye, invented by Hermann von HELMHOLTZ in 1851.

Ophüls, Max (1902–57) German film director. His *mise-en-scène* style was superbly realized in two masterpieces, *Letter from an Unknown Woman* (1948) and *Reckless Moment* (1949). His son, **Marcel** (1927–), is a DOCUMENTARY film-maker. He often presents controversial issues, such as the Nuremberg trials in *The Memory of Justice* (1975).

opium Drug derived from the unripe seed-pods of the opium POPPY. Its components and derivatives have been used as NARCOTICS and ANALGESICS for many centuries. It produces drowsiness and euphoria and reduces pain. MORPHINE and CODEINE are opium derivatives.

Opium Wars (1839–42) Conflict between Britain and China. It arose because Chinese officials prevented the importation of opium. After a British victory, the Treaty of Nanking gave Britain trading rights in certain ports and the grant of Hong Kong. A second, similar war (1856–60) was fought by the British and French. When China refused to ratify the Treaty of Tientsin (1858), Anglo-French forces occupied Peking.

Oporto City and port on the River Douro, NW Portugal. A Roman settlement, it was occupied by the Visigoths (540–716)

and the Moors (716–997) and in 1092 gained Portuguese control. By the 17th century, it was a famous wine centre and its PORT is still exported. It is Portugal's second-largest city. Industries: textiles, fishing, fruit, olive oil. Pop. (2001) 262,928.

opossum (possum) New World MARSUPIAL animal. The only marsupial found outside Australasia. Omnivorous tree-dwellers, they have silky grey fur, and feign death when in danger. The common opossum, *Didelphis marsupialis*, grows up to 50cm (20in) long, plus a 30cm (12in) tail. Family Didelphidae.

Oppenheimer, (Julius) Robert (1904–67) US physicist. He was appointed director (1943–45) of the Los Alamos laboratory in New Mexico, where he headed the MANHATTAN PROJECT to develop the atomic bomb. In 1949, Oppenheimer opposed the construction of the HYDROGEN BOMB. In 1953, following investigations by Senator Joseph McCARTHY, Oppenheimer was suspended by the Atomic Energy Commission. In 1963, he was reinstated.

optical disk In computing, a high-density storage device consisting of a disk on which data is recorded and read by a laser. The most common type is a CD-ROM, although an audio COMPACT DISC (CD) is also a read-only device of this kind.

optical fibre Fine strand of glass, less than 1mm (0.04in) thick, that is able to transmit digital information in the form of pulses of light. More data can be transmitted (up to 10 billion bits of information a second) and there is less interference. Such transmission is possible because light entering an optical fibre is conducted, by reflection, from one end of the fibre to the other with very little loss of intensity. Initially used in ENDOSCOPES that examine the interior of the body, their application is spreading to many forms of mass communication.

optics Branch of physics concerned with the study of LIGHT and its behaviour. Fundamental aspects are the physical nature of light, both as a wave phenomenon and as particles (PHOTONS), and the REFLECTION, refraction (bending), and polarization (restricting vibrations in one direction) of light. Optics also involves the study of mirrors and LENS systems and of optically active chemicals and crystals that polarize light. *See also* POLARIZED LIGHT

optometry Testing of vision in order to prescribe corrective eyewear, such as spectacles or contact lenses. It is distinct from OPHTHALMOLOGY.

Opus Dei International Roman Catholic organization of *c.* 80,000 laymen and 1,000 priests, known for its highly conservative political and religious influence. It was founded (1928) in Spain by Escrivá de Balaguer (1902–75). Its members seek to promote conservative Catholic agendas through their professions. Pope John Paul II beatified de Balaguer in 1992.

oracle In ancient Greece, a priest or priestess who gave the answer of a god to questions put by individuals. The most famous was the oracle of Apollo at DELPHI. The god spoke through a priestess (Pythia), whose words were interpreted by priests. Answers tended to be ambiguous, so that the oracle could never be said to be wrong.

Oran (Wahran) City and seaport on the Gulf of Oran, NW Algeria. Founded in the 10th century, it was taken by Spain from its Arab rulers in 1509. Captured by Ottoman Turks in 1708, it was retaken by Spain in 1732. Under French rule from 1831 to 1962, it developed as a naval base. It is Algeria's second-largest city. Industries: iron ore, textiles, chemicals, cereals, wine, fruit. Pop. (1994) 692,516.

Orange Longest river of South Africa. It rises in the Drakensberg Mountains in N Lesotho and flows generally W, forming the boundary between FREE STATE and CAPE PROVINCE. It continues W through the Kalahari and Namib deserts, forming South Africa's border with Namibia. It empties into the Atlantic Ocean at Oranjemund. Length: *c.*2,100km (1,300mi).

orange Evergreen citrus tree and its fruit. The sweet orange (*Citrus sinensis*) is native to Asia and widely grown in the USA and Israel. The fruit develops without pollination and is often seedless. The sour orange (*C. aurantium*) is widely grown in Spain for the manufacture of marmalade. Related fruits include the mandarin, tangerine, and satsuma – all varieties of *C. reticulata*. Height: to 9m (30ft). Family Rutaceae; genus *Citrus*.

Orange, House of Royal dynasty of the Netherlands. Orange was a principality in S France, which was inherited by WILLIAM I (THE SILENT) in 1544. WILLIAM III became King of England in 1689. In 1815, the son of William V became WILLIAM I of the Netherlands.

Orange Free State Former name of FREE STATE province

Orangemen Members of the Orange Society, or Orange Order. It was founded (1795) in Ulster in response to the mainly Roman Catholic, nationalist United Irishmen, and was named for the Protestant hero, WILLIAM III (OF ORANGE). His victory against the Catholic JAMES II at the battle of the BOYNE (1690) is celebrated on its anniversary, July 12.

orang-utan (Malay, 'man of the forest') Stout-bodied great APE native to forests of Sumatra and Borneo. It has a bulging belly and a shaggy, reddish-brown coat. It swings by its arms when travelling through trees, but proceeds on all fours on the ground. Height: 1.5m (5ft); weight: to 100kg (220lb). Species *Pongo pygmaeus*. *See also* PRIMATES

oratorio Form of sacred musical composition for solo voices, chorus, and orchestra. The first of these compositions were presented in oratories (chapels) in 17th-century Italy. Outstanding examples are Handel's *Messiah* (1742) and Elgar's *Dream of Gerontius* (1900).

orbit Path of a celestial body in a gravitational field. The path is usually a closed one about the focus of the system to which it belongs, as with those of the planets around the Sun. Most celestial orbits are elliptical, although the ECCENTRICITY can vary greatly. It is rare for an orbit to be parabolic or hyperbolic.

orbital In PARTICLE PHYSICS, region around an atomic NUCLEUS in which ELECTRONS can move. There is a high probability of finding an electron in such an orbital, which can accommodate one or two electrons and has a shape and energy characterized by an atom's QUANTUM NUMBER.

orchestra Group of musicians who play together. During the 17th century, string orchestras developed out of viol consorts; in the 18th century, some wind instruments were added. The woodwind section was soon established and, by the end of the 19th century, the brass section was too. Modern orchestras consist of between 80 and 120 players divided into sections: STRINGS (violin, viola, cello, double bass, and harp); WOODWIND (flute, oboe, clarinet, and bassoon); BRASS (trumpet, trombone, French horn, and tuba) and PERCUSSION.

orchid Any plant of the family Orchidaceae, common in the tropics. There are *c*.35,000 species. All are perennials and grow in soil or as EPIPHYTES on other plants. Parasitic and saprophytic species are also known. All orchids have bilaterally symmetrical flower structures, each with three sepals. They range in diameter from *c*.2mm (0.1in) to 38cm (15in).

order In TAXONOMY (biological classification), a group of related plants or animals; order is one rank below CLASS and a rank above family. For example, the tiger is of the order Carnivora (CARNIVORES).

orders, holy In the Roman Catholic, Orthodox, and Anglican Churches, the duties of the clergy, and the grades of hierarchical rank as outlined in the office of ORDINATION. A person is ordained as a subdeacon, deacon, priest or bishop. These ranks are known as the major orders. The minor orders are those of porter, lector, exorcist, and acolyte.

orders of architecture In classical architecture, style and decoration of a column, its base, capital and entablature. Of the five orders, the Greeks developed the Doric, Ionic and Corinthian. The Tuscan and Composite orders were Roman adaptations. A typical **Doric** column has no base, a relatively short shaft with surface fluting meeting in a sharp edge and an unornamented capital. The **Ionic** order is characterized by slender columns with 24 flutes and prominent spiral scrolls on the capitals. The Corinthian is the most ornate of the Classical orders of architecture. A typical **Corinthian** column has a high base, sometimes with a pedestal, a slim, fluted column and a bell-shaped capital with acanthus-leaf ornament.

ordination Process of consecrating a person as a minister of religion. In Christian Churches organized along episcopal lines, ordination confirms the ordinand (the individual undergoing the process) as a priest or minister in holy ORDERS. In Roman Catholic and Orthodox Churches, the rite of ordination is a SACRAMENT. In Protestant Churches without episcopal organization, ordination is carried out by ministers, ruling

elders, or specially selected lay persons. In Christianity, the ban on women as full members of the clergy has persisted in some churches, notably the Roman Catholic Church. During the 20th century, however, many Protestant Churches began to admit women first as deacons and later as priests and ministers. The General Synod of the Church of England agreed that there was no theological objection to women priests in 1975; but the necessary Church legislation was not passed until 1992. The first women priests were ordained in 1994.

Ordovician Second-oldest period of the PALAEOZOIC era, 505 to 438 million years ago. All animal life was restricted to the sea. Numerous invertebrates flourished and included trilobites, brachiopods, corals, graptolites, molluscs, and echinoderms. Remains of jawless fish from this period are the first record of the vertebrates.

ore MINERAL or combination of minerals from which metals and non-metals can be extracted. It occurs in veins, beds or seams parallel to the enclosing rock or in irregular masses.

oregano (MARJORAM) Dried leaves and flowers of several perennial herbs of the genus *Oreganum*, native to Mediterranean lands and W Asia. It is a popular culinary herb. Family Lamiaceae/Labiatae; genus *Origanum*.

Oregon State of NW USA, on the Pacific coast; the capital is SALEM. Other major cities include PORTLAND and Eugene. Trading posts were set up in the 1790s, mainly by the HUDSON'S BAY COMPANY. From 1842, the OREGON TRAIL brought more settlers. Oregon Territory was formed in 1848, and was admitted to the Union in 1859. It is dominated by the forested slopes of the CASCADE RANGE and the Coast ranges. Between the two lies the fertile Willamette Valley. The COLUMBIA and the Willamette are the major rivers. Agriculture includes cattle, dairy produce, wheat, and market garden products. Oregon produces more than 20% of the nation's softwood timber. Area: 251,180sq km (96,981sq mi). Pop. (2000) 3,421,399.

Oregon Trail Main route of US pioneers to the West in the 1840s and 1850s. It ran 3200km (2000mi) from Independence, Missouri, to Fort Vancouver on the Columbia River in Oregon, and crossed the Rocky Mountains via South Pass. The journey took about six months. It was heavily used from 1843, when 'Oregon fever' attracted thousands of settlers. After 1848, when gold was discovered in California, numbers declined.

Orestes In Greek legend, the son of AGAMEMNON and CLYTEMNESTRA, and brother of ELECTRA. He killed his mother and her lover Aegisthus to avenge their murder of his father.

Orff, Carl (1895–1982) German composer. He deliberately used 'primitive' rhythms in his best-known works, *Carmina Burana* (1937) and *Catulli Carmina* (1943), and the opera *Trionfo di Afrodite* (1953).

organ In biology, group of TISSUES that form a functional and structural unit in a living organism. The major organs of the body include the brain, heart, lungs, skin, liver and kidneys.

organ KEYBOARD INSTRUMENT. The player sits at a console and regulates a flow of air to ranks of pipes, producing rich tones. The organ was in use in Christian churches in the 8th century. The modern organ dates from the BAROQUE period.

organic chemistry *See* CHEMISTRY

Organization for Economic Cooperation and Development (OECD) International consultative body set up in 1961 by the major Western trading nations. Its aims are to stimulate economic growth and world trade by raising the standard of living in member countries and by coordinating aid to less developed countries. Its headquarters are in Paris, and it has 26 member nations including all the world's major powers.

Organization of African Unity (OAU) Former name of the AFRICAN UNION (AU).

Organization of American States (OAS) Organization of 35 member states of the Americas that promotes peaceful settlements to disputes, regional cooperation in the limitation of weapons, and economic and cultural development. The successor to the Pan-American Union, the OAS emerged out of a conference in Colombia in 1948. It is an affiliate of the UNITED NATIONS (UN). Its headquarters are in Washington D.C.

Organization of Petroleum Exporting Countries (OPEC) Intergovernmental organization established in 1960 by many of the world's major oil producing states to

Doric

Ionic

Corinthian

Composite

Tuscan

▲ orders of architecture The five main orders of architecture were first presented by Sebastiano Serlio (1475–1554) in Book IV of his treatise on architecture (1537).

0

STATE OF OREGON

1859

OREGON
Statehood :
February 14, 1859
Nickname :
The Beaver State
State bird :
Western meadowlark
State flower :
Oregon grape
State tree :
Douglas fir
State motto :
She flies with her own wings

OSCILLOSCOPE

An oscilloscope displays an electronic signal on a display in analogue form. Usually time is represented on the *x* axis (horizontal), with the *y* axis (vertical) recording the incoming voltage – in this example, a heartbeat (1). The signal from the object being monitored is converted into an electrical voltage (2), which is shown in graphic form on the screen of a cathode-ray tube (3), similar to a black-and-white television. Deflector magnets (4) direct the stream of electrons from the electron gun (5). The magnets sweep the electron beam from left to right in a set period, while variations in the voltage of the external signal cause the wave pattern. The control box (6) allows the period of the *x* axis and the strength of the signal displayed to be changed.

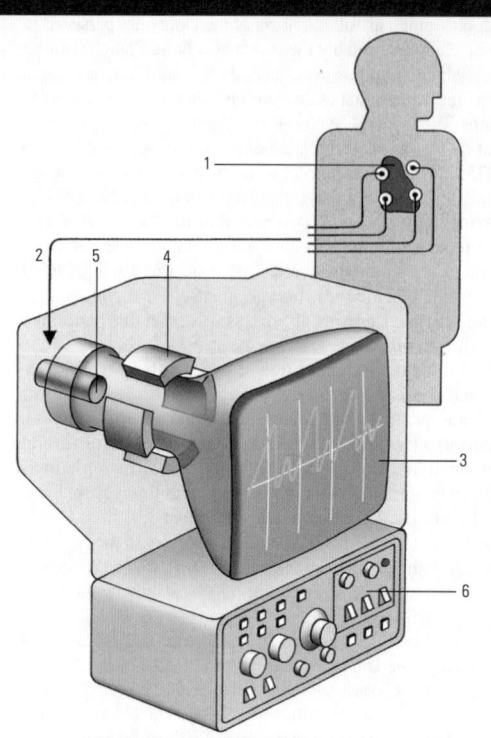

safeguard their interests. Its primary purpose is to set production quotas and co-ordinate prices among the 12 members. It was able to control oil prices in the 1970s, but its influence has waned since then, largely because of internal differences and the emergence of major oil-producing countries outside OPEC. Its headquarters are in Vienna, Austria.

orgasm Physiological culmination of sexual stimulation, marked by general release of muscular tension and waves of contractions causing climactic spasms of vaginal muscles in the female and ejaculation (the release of SEMEN) in the male.

orienteering Sport similar to cross-country running but requiring both athletic and navigational skills. Runners, leaving at timed intervals, carry a map and compass with which to locate control points around the usually 10km (6.2mi) course.

original sin In the Bible, the sin committed by ADAM and EVE when they ate from the tree of knowledge of good and evil, for which they were made mortal and expelled from the Garden of EDEN (Genesis 3). Their guilt was said to have been passed down to their descendants through all the generations.

Orinoco River in Venezuela. Rising in the Sierra Parima in S Venezuela, it flows NW to Colombia, then N, forming part of the Venezuela-Colombia border, and finally E into the Atlantic Ocean by a vast delta. Length: *c.*2062km (1281mi).

oriole Two unrelated types of songbirds. The Old World oriole (family Oriolidae) is brightly coloured and lays eggs in a cup-shaped nest. The New World oriole (family Icteridae) has similar colouring and builds hanging nests in trees.

Orion Prominent constellation, representing a hunter. Four young stars form a conspicuous quadrilateral containing a row of three other stars representing his belt.

Orion nebula Emission NEBULA visible to the naked eye in the constellation ORION. It is a mass of gas surrounding a quadrilateral grouping of four hot O-type stars (the trapezium).

Orissa State in NE India, on the Bay of Bengal; the capital is Bhubaneswar. After rule by Hindus, Afghans and Moguls, it was ceded to the Mahrattas in 1751. Occupied by the British in 1803, it became a constituent state of India in 1950. Industries: mining, fishing, rice, wheat, sugar cane, oilseeds, forestry. Area: 155,782sq km (60,147sq mi). Pop. (2001) 36,706,920.

Orkney Islands Archipelago of more than 70 islands off the N coast of Scotland. Mainland (Pomona) is the largest island, and is the seat of the regional capital (Kirkwall). Other principal islands include Hoy and South Ronaldsay. The land

is a low-lying, fertile plain and the climate is mild and wet. The islands were conquered in 875 by the Viking king Harald I. They remained Norwegian territory until 1231. In 1472, the islands were annexed by Scotland. Scapa Flow (between Mainland and Hoy) was the major British naval base in both World Wars. The local economy remains predominantly agricultural. Area: 974sq km (376sq mi). Pop. (2001) 19,220.

Orlando City in central Florida, USA. Orlando is one of the world's most popular tourist destinations, with the Disney World and Magic Kingdom theme parks. Established in 1827 as a trading post, Orlando was incorporated as a city in 1875 and expanded with the arrival of the railroad. Industries: citrus-growing, aerospace, electronics. Pop. (2000) 185,951.

Orlando, Vittorio Emanuele (1860–1952) Italian prime minister (1917–19). Orlando became prime minister after a series of Italian defeats in World War 1. He represented Italy at the Treaty of VERSAILLES. His early support for Benito MUSSOLINI turned to opposition in 1925. After World War 2 he rejoined the Senate and ran for president (1948).

Orléans City on the River Loire, N central France; capital of Loiret department. Besieged by the English during the HUNDRED YEARS' WAR, it was relieved by JOAN OF ARC in 1429. During the 16th-century Wars of RELIGION, the city was besieged by Catholic forces and held by them until the Edict of NANTES. Industries: tobacco, textiles, fruit and vegetables, chemicals. Pop. (1999) 113,126.

Orléans, Louis-Philippe, Duc d' (1747–93) French BOURBON prince. A liberal, he was elected to the National Convention (1792) and voted for the King's execution. When his son, the future King LOUIS PHILIPPE, defected (1793), he was arrested and executed during the so-called REIGN OF TERROR.

ornithology Study of birds. Included in general ornithological studies are classification, structure, function, evolution, distribution, migration, reproduction, ecology, and behaviour.

Orozco, José Clemente (1883–1949) Mexican painter. In his wash drawings *Mexico in Revolution* (1911–16), Orozco aimed to demonstrate the futility of war. His MURALS are grand in both scale and mood, none more so than *Katharsis* (1934). Orozco's final paintings became increasingly violent.

Orpheus In Greek mythology, the son of Calliope by APOLLO, and the finest of all poets and musicians. Orpheus married Eurydice, who died after being bitten by a snake. He descended into the Underworld to rescue her and was allowed to regain her if he did not look back at her until they emerged into the sunlight. He could not resist, and Eurydice vanished forever.

orphism (orphic CUBISM) Term invented in 1912 by APOLLINAIRE to describe a new art form combining elements of CUBISM, FUTURISM and FAUVISM. The style was first associated with the work of DELAUNAY, and its other exponents exerted considerable influence in Germany through the works of KLEE and KANDINSKY. *See also* BLAUE REITER

Ortega (Saavedra), Daniel (1945–) Nicaraguan statesman, president (1984–90, 2006–). He joined the SANDINISTAS (FSLN) in 1963, rising to become its leader in 1966. In 1979, Ortega led the revolution that toppled the SOMOZA regime and formed a socialist government. In 1984, he was elected president. The Sandinista government was destabilized by the US-backed CONTRA rebels. After two election defeats in the 1990s, Ortega was victorious in 2006 and returned to the presidency.

orthoclase Essential mineral in acidic IGNEOUS rocks and common in METAMORPHIC rocks. It is a potassium aluminium silicate, $KAlSi_3O_8$ with monoclinic system crystals. It is usually white but can be pink. Hardness 6–6.5; r.d. 2.5–2.6.

orthodontics *See* DENTISTRY

Orthodox Church, Eastern Community of *c.*130 million Christians living mainly in E and SE Europe, parts of Asia and a significant minority in the USA. The Church is a federation of groups that share forms of worship and episcopal organization, but each group has its own national head. The largest group is the Russian Orthodox Church. Although there is no central authority, member churches recognize the patriarch of Istanbul as titular head. Eastern Orthodox Christians reject the jurisdiction of the Roman pope. When Constantine moved his capital to Byzantium (Istanbul) in AD 330, a separate non-Roman culture developed. Conflicts grew between

0

the Eastern patriarchs and Rome. In the SCHISM (1054), Western and Eastern arms of Christendom excommunicated each other's followers. The split became irreparable when Crusaders invaded Constantinople (1204). Attempts at reconciliation in 1274 and 1439 failed. In 1962, Orthodox observers attended the Second Vatican Council. In 1963 Eastern Orthodox Churches opened dialogue with Rome.

orthopaedics Branch of medicine that deals with the diagnosis and treatment of diseases, disorders, and injuries of bones, muscles, tendons, and ligaments.

Orton, Joe (John Kingsley) (1933–67) English playwright who specialized in black satirical comedies. *Entertaining Mr Sloane* and *Loot* were staged in London in 1964 and 1965 respectively. *What the Butler Saw* was produced posthumously (1969) after Orton's murder by his lover, Kenneth Halliwell.

Orwell, George (1903–50) British novelist and essayist, b. Eric Arthur Blair in India. Early autobiographical works include *Down and Out in Paris and London* (1933), *The Road to Wigan Pier* (1937), and *Homage to Catalonia* (1938). Orwell is best-known, however, for his fictions on totalitarianism: the satirical fable *Animal Farm* (1945) and the dystopic novel *1984* (1949).

oryx (gemsbok) Any of four species of ANTELOPES. The male has a tuft of hair at the throat and adults have horns ringed at the base. Two species are almost extinct, but the other two survive in numbers in Africa. Height: 1.2m (4ft). Family Bovidae.

Osaka City on Osaka Bay, s Honshu island, Japan; capital of Osaka prefecture. Japan's third-largest city and its principal industrial port, Osaka was intensively bombed during World War 2. It was the imperial capital in the 4th-8th centuries. Pop. (2000) 2,599,000.

Osama bin Laden (1957–) Saudi dissident, leader of al-QAEDA (Arabic, 'the base'), a loose network of terrorist groups. He commanded a group of Arab *mujaheddin* against Soviet troops in Afghanistan. Expelled by the Saudi government in 1991, after denouncing the presence of US soldiers in Saudi Arabia during the Gulf War (1991), bin Laden went first to the Sudan and then to Afghanistan. In 1998, he was named as the architect of the bomb attacks on the US embassies in Kenya and Tanzania. The US responded with missile attacks against suspected bases in Sudan and Afghanistan. In 2001 evidence linked him to the terrorist attacks on the World Trade Center, NEW YORK CITY, and the Pentagon, Washington, D.C., which claimed *c.*2750 lives. The US declared war on al-Qaeda and the TALIBAN regime in Afghanistan.

Osborne, John James (1929–95) English dramatist whose play *Look Back in Anger* (1956) established his reputation as the 'ANGRY YOUNG MAN' of British theatre. His other successes included *The Entertainer* (1957) but later works such as *The Hotel in Amsterdam* (1968) provoked critical hostility.

Oscar (Academy Award) Prize awarded annually for services to the cinema by the US Academy of Motion Picture Arts and Sciences. The gold-plated bronze statuettes stand 25cm (13.5in) high.

oscillating universe theory Variant of the 'BIG BANG' theory in which it is suggested that the universe passes through successive cycles of expansion and contraction (or collapse). At the end of the collapse phase, with the universe packed into a small volume of great density, it is possible that a 'bounce' would occur. The universe would thus oscillate between Big Bang and 'Big Crunch' episodes, and so be infinite in age.

oscillator A device for producing electrical oscillations (vibrations), such as sound waves, as in SONAR or an ultrasonic generator. In electronics, an oscillator circuit converts direct current (DC) into high-frequency alternating current (AC).

oscilloscope (cathode-ray oscilloscope) Electronic instrument in which a CATHODE-RAY TUBE (CRT) system displays how quantities, such as voltage or current, vary over a period of time. The electron beam that traces the pattern on the screen is moved by a time-base generator within the oscilloscope. The result is generally a curve or graph on the screen.

Osiris In EGYPTIAN MYTHOLOGY, the god of the dead. He is generally depicted wearing a feathered crown and bearing the crook and flail of a king. In the myths, Osiris was killed by his brother SETH. His sister and wife, ISIS, retrieved the corpse, and Osiris' son HORUS avenged his death.

Oslo Capital of Norway, SE Norway. Founded in the mid-11th century and largely destroyed by fire in 1624, CHRISTIAN IV rebuilt the city, naming it Christiania. In 1905, it became the capital of independent Norway. It acquired the name Oslo in 1925. Industries: machinery, wood products, textiles, chemicals, shipbuilding. Pop. (2000) 507,467.

Osman I (1258–1326) Founder of the OTTOMAN EMPIRE. As ruler of the Osmanli (Ottoman) state in NW Anatolia (Turkey), he declared his independence of the SELJUK sultan in *c.*1290. He expanded his territory fighting the BYZANTINE EMPIRE.

osmium (symbol Os) Bluish-white, metallic element, one of the TRANSITION ELEMENTS. The densest of the elements, it is associated with PLATINUM; the chief source is as a by-product from smelting nickel. Osmium is used in producing hard alloys and to make electrical contacts and pen points. It was discovered in 1804 by English chemist Smithson Tennant (1761–1815) who named it. Properties: at.no. 76; r.a.m. 190.2; r.d. 22.57; m.p. 3,045°C (5,513°F); b.p. 5,027°C (9,081 °F); most common isotope Os^{192} (41.0%).

osmosis DIFFUSION of a SOLVENT (such as water) through a selectively permeable MEMBRANE (one which allows the passage of only certain dissolved substances) into a more concentrated solution. The solvent flows by diffusion to dilute the more concentrated solution until concentrations of solvent are equal on both side of the membrane. Osmosis is a vital cellular process to distribute water in animals and plants. *See also* TURGOR PRESSURE

Osnabrück City on the River Haase, Lower Saxony, NW Germany. It was the scene of the negotiations for the Peace of WESTPHALIA in 1648. Industries: metals, textiles, papermaking, chemicals, motor vehicles, machinery. Pop. (1999) 164,900.

osprey HAWK that lives beside lakes and in coastal regions of all continents except Antarctica. It has a short hooked bill, broad ragged wings, and a white head; it has brownish-black plumage on its back and a cream breast. Length: 51–61cm (20–24in). Family Pandionidae, species *Pandion haliaetus*.

Ossetia Region of the central Caucasus. The region is divided along the Terek River. **North Ossetia** is an autonomous republic in the Russian Federation: its capital is Vladikavkaz. **South Ossetia** is an autonomous region of GEORGIA, whose capital is Tshkinvali. Ossetia is a mountainous agricultural region. North Ossetia has rich mineral deposits. Ossetia became part of the Russian empire in the early 19th century. In 1861, it was annexed to Russia as the Terek region. In 1918, Ossetia became a republic of the Soviet Union and two years later was incorporated into a greater Mountain Autonomous Republic. In 1922, South Ossetia was made a region within the Republic of Georgia. In 1924, North Ossetia became part of the Russian republic, and in 1936 was made an autonomous republic. In 1990, Georgia abolished South Ossetia's autonomy, but it was restored in 1995. Area: North Ossetia, 8,000sq km (3,090sq mi); South Ossetia, 3,900sq km (1,505sq mi). Pop. North Ossetia (2000), 673,800; South Ossetia (2002 est.) 99,700.

ossification (osteogenesis) Process of BONE formation in vertebrates. Bone is formed through the action of special cells called osteoblasts, which secrete bone-forming minerals that combine with a network of tough protein COLLAGEN fibres.

osteomyelitis Infection of the BONE, sometimes spreading along the marrow cavity. Rare except in diabetics, it can arise from a compound fracture, where the bone breaks through the skin, or from infection elsewhere in the body. It is accompanied by fever, swelling, and pain. The condition may be treated with immobilization, ANTIBIOTICS, and surgical drainage.

osteopathy System of alternative medical treatment based on the use of physical manipulation to treat disease. US physician Andrew Still founded osteopathy in 1874.

osteoporosis Condition where there is loss of bone substance, resulting in brittle bones. It is common in older people, especially in women following the MENOPAUSE; it may also occur as a side-effect of prolonged treatment with corticosteroid drugs. There is no cure, but it may be treated with calcium supplements. HORMONE REPLACEMENT THERAPY (HRT) may help to prevent its occurence in post-menopausal women.

ostrich Largest living bird, from central Africa. It is flightless and has a small head and long neck. Plumage is black and

0

▲ **ostrich** Africa is the home of the ostrich, the largest living bird. It is the only member of the order Struthioniformes. Several large ground-dwelling birds, the ostrich, rhea, emu and cassowary, all resemble each other quite closely, but are thought to have arisen independently, and as such are examples of a phenomenon called convergent evolution.

0

▲ **Oswald** Lee Harvey Oswald assassinated US President John F. Kennedy in 1963, but was shot and killed while in police custody before he came to trial. Conspiracy theories claiming that more than one gunman carried out the assassination persist despite a lack of evidence.

white in males, brown and white in females. Eggs are laid in scrapes in the sand. Height: to 2.5m (8ft); weight: to 155kg (345lb). Family Struthionidae; species *Struthio camelus*.

Ostrogoths *See* GOTH

Ostrovsky, Alexsandr Nikolayevich (1823–86) Russian dramatist. He is an important figure in 20th-century Russian theatrical realism. Many of his plays deal with the life of the Russian merchant class. His plays include *Poverty is no Crime* (1854) and *The Thunderstorm* (1859).

Oswald, Lee Harvey (1939–63) Assassin of US President John F. KENNEDY, on November 22, 1963, in Dallas, Texas. Before he could stand trial he was murdered while in police custody by Jack Ruby. *See also* WARREN COMMISSION

Oswald, Saint (*c.*605–42) King of Northumbria (633–42). He became a Christian and converted his people with the help of St AIDAN. Oswald became King of Northumbria in 633 and was eventually killed in battle. His feast day is August 5.

Othman (Uthman) (574–656) Third CALIPH (644–56) A son-in-law of MUHAMMAD, he was a member of the UMAYYAD family of Mecca. He was blamed for widespread revolts and intrigues, culminating in his assassination.

O'Toole, Peter (1932–) Irish stage and film actor. He gained an Academy nomination for best actor in his film debut in *Lawrence of Arabia* (1962). Other Oscar nominations include *Becket* (1964), *The Lion in Winter* (1968), *Goodbye Mr Chips* (1969), and *The Ruling Class* (1972). O'Toole's career revived with further nominated performances in *The Stunt Man* (1980) and *My Favorite Year* (1982).

Ottawa Group of Algonquian-speaking Native North Americans. Hunter-farmers, they originally lived north of the Great Lakes. They allied with the French and HURONS, but were broken into five groups by the Iroquois and Anglo-Americans and now live in the Great Lakes area, Kansas, and Oklahoma.

Ottawa Capital of Canada, in SE Ontario, on the Ottawa River and the Rideau Canal. Founded in 1826 as Bytown, it acquired its present name in 1854. Queen Victoria chose it as capital of the United Provinces in 1858, and in 1867 it became the national capital of the Dominion of Canada. Industries: glass-making, printing, publishing, sawmilling, pulp-making, clocks and watches. Pop. (2001) 774,072.

otter Semi-aquatic carnivore of the WEASEL family found everywhere except Australia. They have narrow, pointed heads with bristly whiskers, sleek furry bodies and short legs with webbed hind feet. They feed mainly on fish. The river otter (genus *Lutra*) is small to medium-sized. Family Mustelidae.

Otto I (the Great) (912–73) King of the Germans (936–73) and Holy Roman Emperor (962–73). Otto succeeded his father, HENRY I, in Germany and defeated the rebellious princes and their ally, Louis IV of France. Royal power was further augmented by his close control of the Church. In 955, he crushed the MAGYARS at Lechfeld. He invaded Italy to aid Queen Adelaide of Lombardy, married Adelaide and became

king of Lombardy. In 962, he was crowned as Roman Emperor (the 'Holy', meaning 'Christian', was added later).

Otto IV (1174–1218) (Otto of Brunswick) Holy Roman Emperor (1198–1215). A member of the GUELPH family, Otto antagonized the powerful Pope INNOCENT III by his invasion of Italy against the HOHENSTAUFEN King Frederick I (later Emperor FREDERICK II). With Innocent's support, Frederick was elected king (1212) by the German princes, and supported by PHILIP II of France. Philip defeated Otto at Bouvines in 1214, forcing Otto to retire.

Otto, Nikolaus August (1832–91) German engineer. In 1861, he built a gas-fired engine which won a gold medal at the 1867 Paris Exhibition. He later built an INTERNAL COMBUSTION ENGINE based on a four-stroke cycle (also called the **Otto** cycle). *See also* FOUR-STROKE ENGINE

Ottoman Empire Former Turkish state that controlled much of SE Europe, the Middle East and North Africa between the 14th and 20th centuries. It was founded by Osman I (r.1290–1326). He ruled a small principality in Anatolia, which he greatly enlarged at the expense of the BYZANTINE EMPIRE. The contest with the Byzantines ended with the capture of Constantinople (now ISTANBUL), which became the Ottoman capital in 1453. Under SULEIMAN I (THE MAGNIFICENT) (r.1520–66), the Ottoman Empire included the Arab lands of the Middle East and North Africa, SE Europe, and the E Mediterranean. The decline of Ottoman power began before 1600, and thereafter, Ottoman territory was reduced in wars with its European neighbours, Austria and Russia. After World War 1, when Ottoman territory was reduced to roughly the present Turkish borders, nationalists led by ATATÜRK deposed the last sultan and created the modern Turkish republic (1923).

Ouagadougou Capital of Burkina Faso, West Africa. Founded in the late 11th century as capital of the Mossi empire, it remained the centre of Mossi power until captured by the French in 1896. Industries: handicrafts, textiles, food processing, groundnuts, vegetable oil. Pop. (2002 est.) 839,820.

Ouse (Great Ouse) River rising in Northamptonshire, central England, and flowing 256km (159mi) E through East Anglia before emptying into the Wash at King's Lynn.

ovary In biology, part of a multicellular animal or a flowering plant that produces egg cells (ova), the female reproductive cells. In vertebrates it also produces female sex hormones. In human women, there is an ovary on each side of the UTERUS. Controlled by the PITUITARY GLAND, each ovary produces OESTROGEN and PROGESTERONE, which control the female reproductive system. In flowering plants, the female sex cells are contained within structures called OVULES inside the ovary. After fertilization, the ovules develop into seeds and the ovary develops into fruit. *See also* HORMONES; MENSTRUAL CYCLE

overfishing Practice of catching too many marine creatures for an ecological balance to be maintained, resulting in the severe reduction in, or even disappearance of, food fishes, whales and other marine animals. It has become a worldwide concern, with falling catches in most of the world's major fisheries. It remains an international problem largely because of the inability of marine law to regulate FISHING and WHALING.

overture Instrumental prelude to an OPERA or OPERETTA; the term now also includes an orchestral composition in its own right, usually lively in character. Famous operatic overtures were composed by MOZART, ROSSINI, and WAGNER.

Ovid (43 BC–AD 18) (Publius Ovidius Naso) Roman poet. He was a great success in Rome until, aged 50, he was exiled by AUGUSTUS. His works include *Amores*, short love poems; *Ars Amatoria*, amusing instructions on how to seduce women; and *Metamorphoses*, a retelling of Greek myths.

ovule In seed-bearing plants, part of the reproductive organ that contains an egg cell or OVUM and develops into a seed after fertilization. In ANGIOSPERMS (having flowers), ovules develop inside an OVARY. In GYMNOSPERMS (without flowers), ovules are borne on the inner surface of the cone without any covering.

ovum (egg cell) Female GAMETE produced in an OVARY. After FERTILIZATION by SPERM it becomes a ZYGOTE, which is capable of developing into a new individual.

OVUM

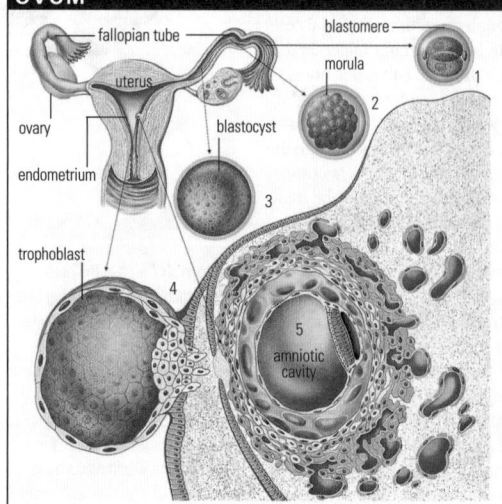

fallopian tube
uterus
ovary
endometrium
trophoblast
blastomere
morula
blastocyst
amniotic cavity

It takes about a week for the fertilized ovum to pass down the Fallopian tube and implant itself in the uterine lining, the endometrium. Within hours of conception, mitosis begins with the development of a sphere of an increasing number of cells; the sphere starts as the blastomere (1), develops into the morula (2) of about 64 cells. At this stage, it changes into a hollow, fluid-containing ball – blastocyst (3) – with the inner cell mass at one end. It can now begin implantation (4). By the ninth day after conception, the blastocyst has sunk deep into the endometrium (5) and is already receiving nutrition from the mother.

Owen, Wilfred (1893–1918) English poet. His World War 1 poems, including "Anthem for Doomed Youth" and "Dulce et Decorum Est", are a searing indictment of war. After his death in action, Siegfried SASSOON handled their publication. They are the basis of BRITTEN's *War Requiem* (1962).

Owens, Jesse (1913–80) US black athlete. Owens broke several world records for jumping, hurdling, and running (1935–36). He won four gold medals at the 1936 Olympics in Berlin, angering Adolf Hitler, who was keen to use the Games as a political demonstration of Aryan racial superiority.

owl Bird found worldwide, except at extreme latitudes. Owls have round heads, hooked bills, large eyes, and long, curved talons. Soundless in flight, most are nocturnal and feed on small birds and mammals. The order (Strigiformes) is divided into two families: barn owls (Tytonidae) and typical owls (Strigidae).

ox Domesticated cattle of the genus *Bos*. The term is specifically applied to castrated males used as draught animals. Many varieties of wild cattle are sometimes called wild oxen.

oxalic acid ($C_2H_2O_4$) Poisonous, colourless crystalline organic acid whose salts occur naturally in some plants, such as sorrel and rhubarb. It is used for metal and textile cleaning and in tanning. Properties: m.p. 101.5°C (214.7°F).

oxbow lake Crescent-shaped section of a RIVER channel that no longer carries the main discharge of water. It is formed by contact at the neck of a MEANDER, leaving the loop abandoned as stagnant water and silty marsh.

Oxfam British charity formed in 1948. It attempts to alleviate suffering due to poverty or natural disaster in all parts of the world. Nearly 75% of Oxfam's budget is devoted to long-term projects, including agriculture, family planning and medicine.

Oxford City and county district in s central England, on the River Thames; the county town of Oxfordshire. Established as a trading centre and fort, it was raided by the Danes in the 10th and 11th centuries. During the English Civil War the city was a Royalist stronghold. Industries: motor vehicles, steel products, electrical goods, printing and publishing. Pop. (2001) 134,248.

Oxford, University of Oldest university in Britain. It developed from a group of teachers and students who gathered in OXFORD in the 12th century. The first colleges, University, Balliol and Merton, were founded between 1249 and 1264. The colleges quickly increased in number and became almost autonomous. Women were not admitted until 1878.

Oxford Movement Attempt by some members of the CHURCH OF ENGLAND to restore the ideals of the pre-REFORMATION Church. It lasted from *c*.1833 to the first decades of the 20th century. Among the main proponents was John NEWMAN.

Oxfordshire County in s central England, bounded in the NW by the COTSWOLDS and in the SE by the Chilterns, and drained by the River THAMES. The county town is OXFORD. It lies mostly within the Thames basin. Its economy is based on agriculture, with sheep and arable farming, dairying and beef production. Industries: motor vehicles, pressed steel, light engineering. Area: 2,611sq km (1,008sq mi). Pop. (2001) 605,492.

oxidation Chemical reaction that involves a loss of one or more ELECTRONS by an atom or molecule (always part of an OXIDATION-REDUCTION reaction in which those electrons are gained by another atom or molecule). Previously, the term was more strictly applied to a reaction in which oxygen combines with another element or compound to form an oxide.

oxidation-reduction (redox) Chemical reaction involving simultaneous OXIDATION) loss of electrons) and reduction (a gain of those electrons by another atom or molecule). Many biochemical systems involve oxidation-reduction reactions.

oxide Any inorganic chemical compound in which OXYGEN is combined with another element. Oxides are often formed by burning the element in air or oxygen. Oxides are used to produce acids and manufacture glass.

oxygen (symbol O) Common gaseous element that is necessary for the RESPIRATION of plants and animals and for combustion. Oxygen is the most abundant element in the Earth's crust (49.2% by weight), and is a constituent of water and many rocks. It is also present in the atmosphere (23.14% by weight). Oxygen was discovered in 1772 by English chemist Joseph PRIESTLEY and independently that year by Swedish chemist Karl SCHEELE. It can be obtained by the ELECTROLYSIS of water or fractional distillation of liquid air. It is used in apparatus for breathing (oxygen masks) and resuscitation (oxygen tents); liquid oxygen is used in rocket fuels. It is chemically reactive, and forms compounds with most elements (especially by OXIDATION). Properties: at.no. 8; r.a.m. 15.9994; r.d. 1.429; m.p. −218.4°C (−361.1°F); b.p. −182.96°C; (−297.3°F); most common isotope O^{16} (99.759%). *See also* OXIDATION-REDUCTION; OZONE

oxygen debt Insufficient supply of oxygen in the muscles following vigorous exercise. This reduces the breakdown of food molecules that generate energy, causing the muscles to overproduce lactic acid creating a sensation of fatigue and sometimes muscular cramp.

oxytocin HORMONE produced by the PITUITARY GLAND in women during pregnancy. It stimulates the muscles of the UTERUS, initiating the onset of labour and maintaining contractions during childbirth. It also stimulates lactation.

oyster Edible BIVALVE mollusc found worldwide in temperate and warm seas. The European flat, or edible, oyster *Ostrea edulis* occurs throughout coastal waters. The pearl oyster (*Pinctada fucats*) produces cultured pearls.

oystercatcher Seashore bird with a strikingly marked black-and-white stocky body and bright orange legs and beak. Oystercatchers feed on molluscs, prying them open with their long thin beaks. Length: 43cm (17in). Family Haematopodidae; typical genus *Haematopus*.

Ozark plateau Mountainous upland region in s central USA, extending from sw Missouri across NW Arkansas into Oklahoma. The Boston Mountains contain the highest peaks, exceeding 610m (2000ft). The Ozarks are a source of lead and zinc. Noted for their scenery, forests and lakes, they are a popular tourist region. Area: *c*.129,500sq km (50,000sq mi).

ozone Unstable, pale-blue, gaseous allotrope of OXYGEN, formula (O^3). It has a characteristic pungent odour and decomposes into molecular oxygen. It is present in the atmosphere, mainly in the OZONE LAYER. Prepared commercially by passing a high-voltage discharge through oxygen, ozone is used as an oxidizing agent in bleaching, air-conditioning and purifying water. *See also* ALLOTROPY

ozone layer Region of Earth's atmosphere in which OZONE (O_3) is concentrated. It is most dense at altitudes of 21 to 26km (13 to 16mi). Produced by ultraviolet radiation in incoming sunlight, the ozone layer absorbs much of the ultraviolet, thereby shielding the Earth's surface. Aircraft, nuclear weapons, and some aerosol sprays and refrigerants yield chemical agents that can break down high-altitude ozone, which could lead to an increase in the amount of harmful ultraviolet radiation reaching the Earth's surface. *See also* CHLOROFLUOROCARBON (CFC)

▲ **Oxford** Dating from the mid-12th century, Oxford University is one of the most venerable institutions of higher learning in Europe. It is organized as a collection of self-contained, autonomous residential colleges, each employing its own teachers and enrolling its own students. The first three colleges were founded in the mid-13th century; Christ Church College, shown here, was established in 1546.

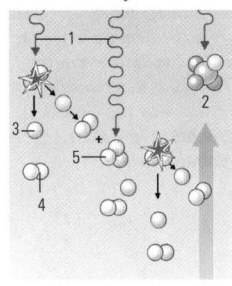

oxygen atom
oxygen molecule
ozone molecule

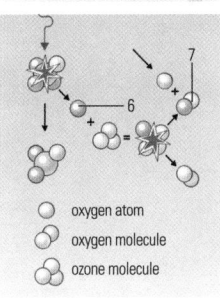

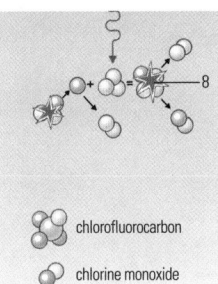

chlorofluorocarbon
chlorine monoxide

O

▲ **ozone** A naturally occurring substance, ozone acts as a sunscreen for the Earth because its molecules absorb the Sun's ultraviolet radiation (1). The presence of chlorofluorocarbon pollution (2) causes the ozone layer to break down allowing ultraviolet rays through. Ozone is created when ultraviolet rays split oxygen molecules. The lone oxygen atoms (3) bond with oxygen molecules (4) to make ozone (5). When, however, chlorofluorocarbons are present, they are split by the ultraviolet rays. The released chlorine atom (6) in turn splits ozone molecules to form a chlorine monoxide molecule (7) and oxygen. The process is continued as the chlorine monoxide absorbs the lone oxygen atoms that previously formed ozone. This frees the chlorine atom, which splits another ozone molecule (8) creating another chlorine monoxide molecule and oxygen.

P/p, 16th letter of the Roman alphabet, descends from the Semitic letter **pe**, *a word meaning mouth. The letter was modified in shape by the Greeks and taken into their alphabet as* **pi**.

paca (spotted cavy) Shy, nocturnal, tailless RODENT of South America; it is brown with rows of white spots and has a relatively large head. A burrow-dweller, the paca feeds mainly on leaves, roots and fruit. Length: to 76cm (30in). Family Dasyproctidae; species *Cuniculus paca*.

pacemaker (sino-atrial node) Specialized group of cells in the vertebrate heart that contract spontaneously, setting the pace for the heartbeat itself. If it fails, it can be replaced by an artificial pacemaker – an electronic unit that stimulates the heart by means of tiny electrical impulses.

Pacific Ocean Largest and deepest OCEAN in the world, covering *c.*33% of the Earth's surface and containing more than 50% of the Earth's seawater. The Pacific extends from the Arctic Circle to Antarctica, and from North and South America in the E to Asia and Australia in the W. The E Pacific region is connected with the Cordilleran mountain chain, and there is a narrow CONTINENTAL MARGIN. The ocean is ringed by numerous volcanoes, known as the 'Ring of Fire'. There are a number of large islands in the Pacific, mostly in the S and W. The major ones are New Zealand, and the Japan and Malay archipelagos. The principal rivers that drain into the ocean are the COLUMBIA in North America, and the HUANG HE and YANGTZE in Asia. The average depth of the Pacific is 4,300m (14,000ft). The greatest known depth is that of the Challenger Deep (SW of Guam in the Mariana Trench), at 11,033m (36,198ft). The current pattern of the Pacific is made up of two gyres: N of the Equator are the North Equatorial Current, the Kuroshio Current, the North Pacific Drift and the California Current; S of the Equator are the South Equatorial Current, the East Australian Current and the Humboldt Current. The Equatorial Counter-Current separates the two gyres. Most fishing in the Pacific is done on the continental margins. Crab, herring, cod, sardine and tuna form the main catch. Area: *c.*166,000,000sq km (64,000,000sq mi).

pacifism Philosophy opposing the use of war or violence as a means of settling disputes. Elements can be found in ancient Hebrew and early Christian theology, and in later Anabaptist and QUAKER beliefs. International pacifist groups were organized in the 19th century. The doctrine of 'Mahatma' GANDHI was based on pacifist philosophy. *See also* CAMPAIGN FOR NUCLEAR DISARMAMENT (CND)

Pacino, Al (Alberto) (1940–) US film actor. He studied method acting at Lee STRASBERG's Actors' Studio, and made his film debut in *Me, Natalie* (1969). Pacino appeared three times (1972, 1974, and 1990) in his famed role as Michael Corleone (in *The Godfather* and its two sequels), for which he received two of his several Academy Award nominations. He finally won a best actor Academy Award for *Scent of a Woman* (1992). Other films include *Serpico* (1973), *Dog Day Afternoon* (1975), *Scarface* (1983), and *Donnie Brasco* (1996). His directorial debut was *Looking for Richard* (1996).

paddlefish Primitive bony fish related to the sturgeon and found in the basins of the Mississippi and Yangtze rivers. Blue, green or grey, it has a cartilaginous skeleton and a long paddle-like snout. Length: 1.8m (6ft). Family Polyodontidae.

Paderewski, Ignacy Jan (1860–1941) Polish pianist, composer and statesman. He wrote a piano concerto (1888) and a symphony (1907), and his opera *Manru* was first produced in Dresden in 1901. He became prime minister and minister of foreign affairs of the newly created Polish state in 1919.

Padua (Pádova) City in Veneto region, NE Italy. The city is first mentioned (as Patavium) early in the 4th century BC. In the

Middle Ages it was a flourishing artistic centre. It came under Venetian control in 1405. In 1815 it passed to Austria, and took a leading part in the movement for Italian independence. The city is renowned for its art treasures. Industries: motor vehicles, textiles, machinery, electrical goods. Pop. (2000) 209,461.

paediatrics Medical speciality devoted to the diagnosis and treatment of disease and injury in children. Paediatricians require a knowledge not only of the wide range of conditions peculiar to children, but also of normal childhood development and the ways in which it may affect treatment and recovery.

Paganini, Niccolò (1782–1840) Italian violinist, the most famous virtuoso of his day. He enlarged the range of the violin by exploiting harmonics and mastered the art of playing double and triple stops (two or three notes at a time).

Pagnol, Marcel (1894–1974) French dramatist, film director, and writer. He first gained attention for the play *Topaze* (1928). Pagnol adapted for the screen his Marseilles trilogy – *Marius* (1929), *Fanny* (1931), and *César* (1937). In 1946, he became the first film-maker to be elected to the Académie Française. Readers rediscovered Pagnol via the film adpatations of his two-part novel *L'eau des collines* (1963): *Jean de Florette* and *Manon des Sources* (both 1986).

pagoda Eastern TEMPLE in the form of a multi-storeyed, tapering tower. The design is square or polygonal, and each storey is a smaller replica of the one beneath. The storeys often have wide, overhanging roofs. Pagodas originated in India and spread with BUDDHISM to China, Korea, and Japan.

Pahlavi, Muhammad Reza (1919–80) Shah of Iran (1941–79), son of Reza PAHLAVI. With the receipts from oil exports, Pahlavi encouraged rapid economic development and social reforms. The westernization of Iran, combined with a repressive regime and worsening social inequalities, aroused strong discontent among religious fundamentalists and others. In 1979, a theocratic revolution, led by Ayatollah KHOMEINI, forced him into exile. He died in Egypt.

Pahlavi, Reza (1878–1944) Shah of Iran and founder of the modern Iranian state. In 1921, he took part in a nationalist coup and built up a modern army as defence minister and prime minister. In 1925, Pahlavi deposed Ahmad Shah and assumed the crown. He enforced intensive social and legal reforms, crushed tribalism, and ended the influence in Iran of Britain and the Soviet Union. In 1941, when British and Soviet forces occupied Iran, he abdicated in favour of his son, Muhammad PAHLAVI.

pain Unpleasant sensation signalling actual or threatened tissue damage as a result of illness or injury; it can be **acute** (severe but short-lived) or **chronic** (persisting for a long time). Pain is felt when specific nerve endings are stimulated. Pain is treated in a number of ways, most commonly by drugs known as ANALGESICS.

Paine, Thomas (1737–1809) Anglo-American revolutionary political writer. He emigrated from England to Pennsylvania in 1754. His pamphlet *Common Sense* (1776) demanded independence for the North American colonies. He returned to England in 1787, and published *The Rights of Man* (1791–92), a defence of the French Revolution. Accused of treason, he fled to France in 1792. He became a French citizen and was elected to the National Convention, but later imprisoned (1793–94). He returned to the USA in 1802.

Painted Desert Barren high plateau region in N central Arizona, USA, E of the Colorado and Little Colorado rivers. Erosion and heat have exposed bands of red and yellow sediment and bentonite clay. Area: *c.*19,400sq km (7,500sq mi).

painting Art of creating pictures using pigment, usually suspended in water or oil and applied with a brush or other implement. Paintings are among the earliest of historical records. Painting in early civilizations, such as Egypt, was largely a matter of filling in with colour areas outlined by drawing. Little Greek painting survives (apart from that on pottery). The Romans were greatly influenced by Greek art, as the fine FRESCO paintings at Pompeii and Herculaneum demonstrate. In the early Christian and Byzantine periods, traditions in mural painting and manuscript ILLUMINATION were established that were to last throughout the Middle Ages. When the humanist ideals of the RENAISSANCE took root in S Europe, the range of subjects and techniques available to the artist widened enormously. The

▶ **paca** Found in tropical America, the paca (*Cuniculus paca*) is a shy rodent that lives in forests near water. It can reach a length of up to 76cm (30in) and an adult can weigh up to 10kg (20lb).

period also saw the first use of oil paint on canvas, the beginnings of GENRE PAINTING and pure portraiture. It was also the age of PERSPECTIVE and of a more natural approach to form and composition. The great painters of the BAROQUE period added an unrivalled bravura brushwork and drama of vision. North of the Alps, the Renaissance spread more gradually than in Italy. The 17th-century Dutch painters' choice of intimate, everyday subjects was the antithesis of the grand manner characteristic of the Italian masters. By the 18th century, British painters had become established in portraiture, animal, and landscape painting, although overshadowed by the great Venetian masters. The 19th century opened with the supremacy of NEO-CLASSICISM challenged by the new ROMANTICISM. Both schools were superseded, first by IMPRESSIONISM and then by a succession of new movements in the late 19th and early 20th centuries. Most of these movements – impressionism, POST-IMPRESSIONISM, SYMBOLISM, FAUVISM, CUBISM, DADA, and SURREALISM – originated in Paris. Germany was the cradle of EXPRESSIONISM and Russia contributed SUPREMATISM. In the latter half of the 20th century, the USA produced many original movements, such as ABSTRACT EXPRESSIONISM, POP ART, and OP ART.

Paisley, Ian (1926–) Northern Irish politician and clergyman. In 1951, he formed the Free Presbyterian Church of Ulster. Paisley was elected to Parliament in 1970. In 1972, he formed the Ulster Democratic Unionist Party. An outspoken defender of Protestant Unionism, Paisley briefly resigned over the ANGLO-IRISH AGREEMENT in 1985. He was elected to the European Parliament in 1979 and resigned in 2004. In 2007 he became First Minister of the Northern Ireland Assembly.

Pakistan Republic in S Asia. *See* country feature, page 574

palaeobotany Study of ancient plants and pollen that have been preserved by carbonization, waterlogging or freezing. Some plants have been preserved almost intact in frozen soils and in AMBER.

Palaeocene Geological epoch that extended from *c.*65 to 55 million years ago. It is the first epoch of the TERTIARY period, when the majority of the DINOSAURS had disappeared and the small early mammals were flourishing.

Palaeolithic (Old Stone Age) Earliest stage of human history, from *c.*2 million years ago until between 40,000 and 10,000 years ago. It was marked by the use of stone tools. It covers HUMAN EVOLUTION from *Homo habilis* to *Homo sapiens*.

Palaeolithic art Art from the PALAEOLITHIC period. Typical works are realistic cave paintings of bison, deer and hunting scenes. The best-known surviving examples are at ALTAMIRA and LASCAUX. Other forms include portable art, such as carved animals and figurines made from stone, bone, and antler.

palaeomagnetism Study of changes in the direction and intensity of Earth's MAGNETIC FIELD through GEOLOGICAL TIME. This is important in the investigation of the theory of CONTINENTAL DRIFT. Since the 'magnetic memory' of rocks is measurable, this determines their orientation in relation to magnetic north at the time they solidified. The EARTH's polarity reversed at least 20 times in the past 4 to 5 million years; earlier changes cannot at present be determined.

palaeontology Study of the fossil remains of plants and animals. Evidence from fossils is used in the reconstruction of ancient environments and in tracing the evolution of life.

Palaeozoic Second era of GEOLOGICAL TIME, after the PRECAMBRIAN era, lasting from 590 million to 248 million years ago. It is sub-divided into six periods: CAMBRIAN, ORDOVICIAN, SILURIAN, DEVONIAN, CARBONIFEROUS and PERMIAN. Invertebrate animals evolved hard skeletons capable of being preserved as fossils in the Cambrian; fish-like vertebrates appeared in the Ordovician; amphibians emerged in the Devonian; and reptiles in the Carboniferous.

palate Roof of the mouth, comprising the bony front part known as the **hard** palate, and the softer, fleshy part at the back, known as the **soft** palate.

Palatinate Historic state of the HOLY ROMAN EMPIRE, including the present German state of Rhineland-Palatinate and parts of adjacent states. It was ruled from 1156 by the Counts Palatine. It was a centre of the German Reformation and was a major battleground in the 17th century.

Palau Former name of BELAU.

Palermo City and seaport on the Tyrrhenian Sea, NW Sicily, Italy; capital of Sicily. It was founded by the Phoenicians in the 8th century BC and passed to the Romans in 254 BC and came under Byzantine control in the 6th century AD. From the 9th to 11th centuries it prospered under Arab rule. Captured by the Normans in 1072, it was briefly capital of the Kingdom of Sicily. It subsequently came under Spanish, then Austrian rule. It was the scene of the outbreak of the 1848 revolution in Italy, and was captured by Giuseppe GARIBALDI in 1860. Industries: shipbuilding, textiles, food processing, chemicals, tourism. Pop. (2000) 679,290.

Palestine Territory in the Middle East, on the E shore of the Mediterranean Sea; considered a Holy Land by Jews, Christians and Muslims. Palestine has been settled continuously since 4000 BC. The Jews moved into Palestine from Egypt *c.*2000 BC but were subjects of the Philistines until *c.*1020 BC when SAUL, DAVID, and SOLOMON established Hebrew kingdoms. The region was then under Assyrian and, later, Persian control before coming under Roman rule in 63 BC. In succeeding centuries, Palestine became a focus of Christian pilgrimage. Muslim Arabs conquered the region in 640. In 1099, Palestine fell to the Crusaders, but in 1291 they in turn were routed by the MAMLUKS. The area was part of the OTTOMAN EMPIRE from 1516 to 1918, when British forces defeated the Turks at Megiddo. The BALFOUR DECLARATION encouraged Jewish immigration. After World War 1, the British held a League of Nations mandate over the land W of the River JORDAN (once again called Palestine). Tension between Jews and the Arab majority led to an uprising in 1936. World War 2 and Nazi persecution brought many Jews to Palestine, and in 1947 Britain, unable to satisfy both Jewish and Arab aspirations, consigned the problem to the United Nations. The UN proposed a plan for separate Jewish and Arab states. This was rejected by the Arabs, and in 1948 (after the first ARAB-ISRAELI WAR) most of ancient Palestine became part of the new state of ISRAEL; the GAZA STRIP was controlled by Egypt and the WEST BANK by Jordan. After the 1967 Arab-Israeli war, both areas were occupied by Israel. The PALESTINE LIBERATION ORGANIZATION (PLO) led Palestinian opposition to Israeli rule, using terrorism and the INTIFADA. In 1993 Israel reached an agreement with the PLO, and in 1994 the Palestine National Authority took over nominal administration of the Gaza Strip and West Bank. Failure to find a peace settlement saw the resurgence of the Intifada in 2000. In 2005, Israel unilaterally withdrew from the Gaza Strip. The death of Yasir ARAFAT led to the election in January 2005 of Mahmoud Abbas as Palestinian leader. In 2006 the Islamist movement, Hamas, won general elections. Hamas' refusal to acknowledge Israel or renounce violence led the EU and US to cut off aid. In 2007, fighting between Hamas and the president's Fatah party split Palestine. The Gaza Strip fell entirely under Hamas control, while the West Bank remained in the hands of Fatah.

Palestine Liberation Organization (PLO) Organization of Palestinian parties and groups, widely recognized as the main representative of the Palestinian people. Founded in 1964, with the aim of dissolving the state of Israel and establishing a Palestinian state to enable Palestinian refugees to return to their ancestral land, many of its component guerrilla

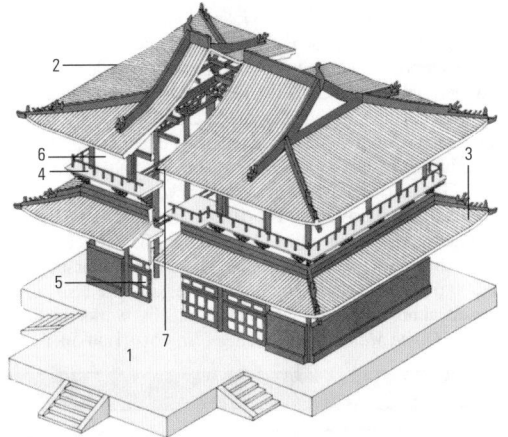

◄ **pagoda** A typical Chinese pagoda is built on a stone podium (1). The wooden hall has a two-storey elevation covered by a single hipped roof (2). The first storey is overhung by shallow eaves (3), which are supported by bracketing, as is the balcony (4). Divided into five bays, doors occupy the central three bays (5), which are left open on the upper storey (6). The fabric of the roof is wood; it is insulated with mud and tiled. The interior has a gallery (7) on each storey around the central wall, which is the full height of the temple.

P

groups engaged in political violence against Israel. In the 1970s, these guerrilla activities escalated into acts of international terrorism. Dominated by the al-Fatah group led by Yasir ARAFAT, in 1974 the United Nations and the Arab League recognized the PLO as a government-in-exile. In the early 1990s, PLO representatives conducted secret negotiations with Israel, culminating in the ISRAELI-PALESTINIAN ACCORD (1993). *See also* GAZA STRIP; PALESTINE; WEST BANK

Palestrina, Giovanni Pierluigi da (1525–94) Italian composer who spent most of his life in the service of the Church. Palestrina wrote masses, magnificats, litanies, and *c.*600 motets in four to eight or twelve parts. He also composed almost 100 secular madrigals. His works include *Missa Papae Marcelli* (1567). *See also* COUNTERPOINT

Palladianism Architectural style especially popular in England, derived from the work of Andrea PALLADIO. Based on Roman CLASSICISM, it emphasized symmetrical planning and harmonic proportions. Inigo JONES introduced Palladianism to England after visiting Italy. There was a revival of interest in Palladianism in the early 18th century. *See also* NEO-CLASSICISM

Palladio, Andrea (1508–80) Italian RENAISSANCE architect. He studied Roman architecture and published his own designs and drawings of Roman ruins in *Four Books of Architecture* (1570). *See also* PALLADIANISM

palladium (symbol Pd) Shiny silver-white metallic element of the TRANSITION ELEMENTS. It was discovered (1803) by the English chemist William Wollaston (1766–1828). Malleable and ductile, palladium is found in nickel ores associated with

PAKISTAN

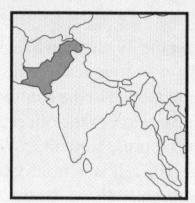

The Islamic Republic of Pakistan contains high mountains, fertile plains and rocky deserts. The KARAKORAM range contains K2, the world's second highest peak at 8,611m [28,251ft], and lies in the N of Jammu and Kashmir. The Thar (or Great Indian) Desert straddles the border with India in the SE. The arid BALUCHISTAN Plateau lies in the S.

CLIMATE

Most of Pakistan has hot summers and cool winters. Winters in the mountains are cold and snowy. Rainfall is sparse over much of the country.

HISTORY

The Indus Valley civilization, one of the world's earliest, was highly developed by *c.*2500 BC. It broke up *c.*1700 BC, possibly due to changes in the course of the Indus. Kushans conquered the region in the 2nd century AD. Arabs conquered Sind in 712 and introduced Islam. In 1211, Pakistan became part of the Delhi Sultanate. In 1526, the MOGUL EMPIRE supplanted the Sultanate and URDU began to develop. In the 18th century, Ranjit Singh conquered the Punjab and introduced SIKHISM.

In the early 19th century the British EAST INDIA COMPANY became a dominant force, and by the 1850s the region was conquered by Britain. The dominance of Hindus in British India led to the formation of the MUSLIM LEAGUE (1906). In the 1940s the League's leader, Muhammad Ali JINNAH, promoted the idea of a separate Muslim state, to be named Pakistan.

POLITICS

British India achieved independence in 1947 and was divided into Pakistan and India. Slaughter

AREA 796,095sq km [307,372sq mi]
POPULATION 164,742,000
CAPITAL (POPULATION) Islamabad (791,000)
GOVERNMENT Federal republic
ETHNIC GROUPS Punjabi, Sindhi, Pashtun (Pathan), Baluchi, Muhajir
LANGUAGES Urdu (official), many others
RELIGIONS Islam 97%, Christianity, Hinduism
CURRENCY Pakistani rupee = 100 paisa

ensued as Hindus and Sikhs fled Pakistan and Muslims fled India. Pakistan originally consisted of two parts, W and E, but following a civil war the E split in 1971 to become Bangladesh. In 1948–9 and 1965, Pakistan and India fought costly but inconclusive wars over KASHMIR.

Elections in 1988 led to Benazir BHUTTO becoming prime minister. She was removed from office in 1990 but returned from 1993 to 1996. Narwaz Sharif was elected prime minister in 1997. Rivalry with India continued, and in 1998 Pakistan responded in kind to a series of Indian nuclear weapon tests, provoking global controversy. In 1999 conflict in Kashmir flared up once again. Later that year, a military coup brought General Pervez Musharraf to power.

In 2001 Pakistan supported the US-led attack on Afghanistan, provoking a backlash by Islamists. Musharraf changed the constitution, increasing his powers. In 2003 India and Pakistan began to negotiate a peace settlement over Kashmir. In 2005 nearly 75,000 were killed in an earthquake. In 2006 Taliban and al-Qaeda forces operating from N Pakistan against Afghanistan became a major problem.

In 2007 Musharraf briefly imposed emergency rule before resigning as army chief and becoming a civilian president. Benazir Bhutto returned to contest forthcoming elections, but was assassinated. Musharraf's party lost control of parliament in 2008 elections.

ECONOMY

Pakistan is a poor country, although since 2000 the economy has begun to grow. The rapid growth of the population has led to problems of unemployment. Industries include motor vehicles and vehicle components, shipbuilding, cement, industrial chemicals, and textiles. IT and communications are rapidly growing sectors.

Agriculture employs over 40% of the workforce, and products include cotton, fruits, rice, sugar cane, vegetables, wheat, goats and sheep.

P

platinum, to which it is chemically similar. It does not tarnish or corrode and is used for electroplating, surgical instruments, dentistry, jewellery and in catalytic converters for cars. Properties: at.no. 46; r.a.m. 106.4; r.d. 12.02; m.p. 1,552°C (2,826°F); b.p. 3,140°C (5,684°F); most common isotope Pd[106] (27.3%).

palm MONOCOTYLEDON tree found in tropical and sub-tropical regions. Palms have a woody, unbranched trunk with a crown of large, stiff leaves. The leaves may be **palmate** (fanlike) or **pinnate** (feather-like). Fibres cover the trunks of palm trees. All palms produce DRUPES, as on the DATE and COCONUT palms. Palms are a source of wax, oil, fibre, and sugar. Height: 60m (200ft). Family Arecacae/Palmae. *See also* LIANA

Palma (Palma de Mallorca) City and seaport in Spain, in w Majorca Island; capital of the BALEARIC ISLANDS. Under Roman rule from the 2nd century BC Palma later became part of Byzantium before falling to the Arabs in the 8th century. Conquered by James I of Aragon in the 13th century, it finally united with Spain in 1469. Industries: tourism, pottery, glasswork, leather goods, jewellery and wine. Pop. (2000) 333,925.

Palmer, Arnold Daniel (1929–) US golfer. Palmer was the first player to win the US Masters four times (1958, 1960, 1962, 1964). He also won the British Open (1961, 1962) and the US Open (1960). In 1968, he became the first golfer to earn more than US$1 million in prize money.

Palmer, Samuel (1805–81) English Romantic landscape painter and graphic artist, the most important follower of William BLAKE. He enjoyed his most productive period at Shoreham, Kent (1826–35), where he was the focal point for a group of artists called 'the Ancients'.

Palmerston, Henry John Temple, 3rd Viscount (1784–1865) British statesman, prime minister (1855–58, 1859–65). He entered Parliament as a Tory in 1807, but defected to the Whigs in 1830. As foreign secretary (1830–34, 1835–41, 1846–51), Palmerston pursued 'gunboat diplomacy' in defence of British interests. As prime minister, he prosecuted the CRIMEAN WAR. In 1856, he initiated the second OPIUM WAR against China. In 1858, he ordered the suppression of the INDIAN MUTINY. Palmerston supported the Confederacy in the American Civil War, but maintained British neutrality. He died in office. John RUSSELL succeeded him as prime minister.

Palm Sunday In the Christian year, the Sunday before Easter. Palm Sunday commemorates JESUS CHRIST's triumphal entry into Jerusalem, when the people spread palm branches before him. It also marks the beginning of Holy Week, the period of days commemorating his betrayal, trial and crucifixion.

Palmyra (Tadmur, City of Palms) Ancient oasis city, in the Syrian Desert. By the 1st century BC it had become a city-state by controlling the trade routes between Mesopotamia and the Mediterranean. In *c*.AD 30, it became a Roman dependency. By the 2nd century AD Palmyra's influence had spread to Armenia. In 267, ZENOBIA became queen, the empire expanded, and she severed the state's links with Rome. In AD 273, Roman Emperor Aurelian laid waste to the city, which was afterwards largely forgotten. Today, tourists visit its extensive ruins.

Palomar, Mount Peak in s California, USA, 72km (45mi) NNE of San Diego. It is the site of the **Palomar Observatory**, which houses the 122–cm (48–in) Schmidt telescope and a 508–cm (200–in) reflecting telescope.

Pamirs Mountainous region in central Asia, lying mostly in Tajikistan and partly in Pakistan, Afghanistan, and China. The region forms a geological structural knot from which the TIAN SHAN, KARAKORAM, Kunlun, and HINDU KUSH mountain ranges radiate. The climate is cold during winter, and cool in summer; the terrain includes grasslands and sparse trees. The main activity is sheep herding, and some coal is mined. The highest peak is PIK ISMAIL SAMANI, at 7,495m (24,590ft).

pampas Large, treeless plains in s South America, situated mostly in Argentina. The humid pampas is extremely fertile; dairy farming is practised and cereals are grown. The larger dry pampas to the w, which includes the provinces of Buenos Aires, Santa Fe and Cordoba, supports mainly livestock grazing.

pampas grass Species of tall, reed-like GRASS native to South America and widely cultivated in warm parts of the world as a lawn ornamental. Female plants bear flower

clusters, 91cm (3ft) tall, which are silvery and plume-like. Family Poaceae/Gramineae; species *Cortaderia selloana*.

Pamplona City in N Spain; capital of Navarre province. Rebuilt by POMPEY in 68 BC CHARLEMAGNE conquered it in AD 778. In the 11th century, it became capital of Navarre. In 1512, control of Pamplona passed to Ferdinand of Aragon. In 1813, during the PENINSULAR WAR, the Duke of Wellington captured Pamplona from the French. Every July, in the fiesta of San Fermin, bulls are driven through the city streets. Industries: rope and pottery manufacture. Pop. (2000) 182,666.

Pan In Greek mythology, the god of woods and fields, shepherds and their flocks. He is depicted with the horns, legs and hoofs of a goat. A forest dweller, he pursued and loved the dryads (tree NYMPHS) and led their dances while playing the syrinx, the reed pipes that were his invention.

Pan-Africanism Historical political movement for the unification and independence of African nations. It began officially at the Pan-African Congress (1900) in London, organized by western black leaders such as W.E.B. DU BOIS. It met five times between 1900 and 1927, and worked to bring gradual self-government to African colonial states. In 1945, the Pan-African Federation convened the Sixth Congress, attended by future leaders of post-colonial Africa, such as Kwame NKRUMAH and Jomo KENYATTA. It demanded autonomy and independence for African states. As independence was gained, the movement broke up and was eventually replaced (1963) by the Organization of African Unity (now the African Union).

Panama Republic on the Isthmus of Panama; the capital is PANAMA CITY. *See* country feature page 576.

Panama Canal Waterway connecting the Atlantic and Pacific oceans across the Isthmus of Panama. A canal, begun in 1882 by Ferdinand de Lesseps, was subsequently abandoned because of bankruptcy. The US government decided to finance the project to provide a convenient route for its warships. The main construction took about ten years to complete, and the first ship passed through in 1914. The 82–km (51–mi) waterway reduces the sea voyage between San Francisco and New York by about 12,500km (7,800mi). Control of the canal passed from the USA to Panama at the end of 1999.

Panama City Capital of Panama, on the shore of the Gulf of Panama, near the Pacific end of the PANAMA CANAL. It was founded by Pedro Arias de Avila in 1519, and was destroyed and rebuilt in the 17th century. It became the capital of Panama in 1903. It developed rapidly after the construction of the Panama Canal in 1914. Industries: brewing, shoes, textile, oil-refining, plastics. Pop. (2000) 1,173,000.

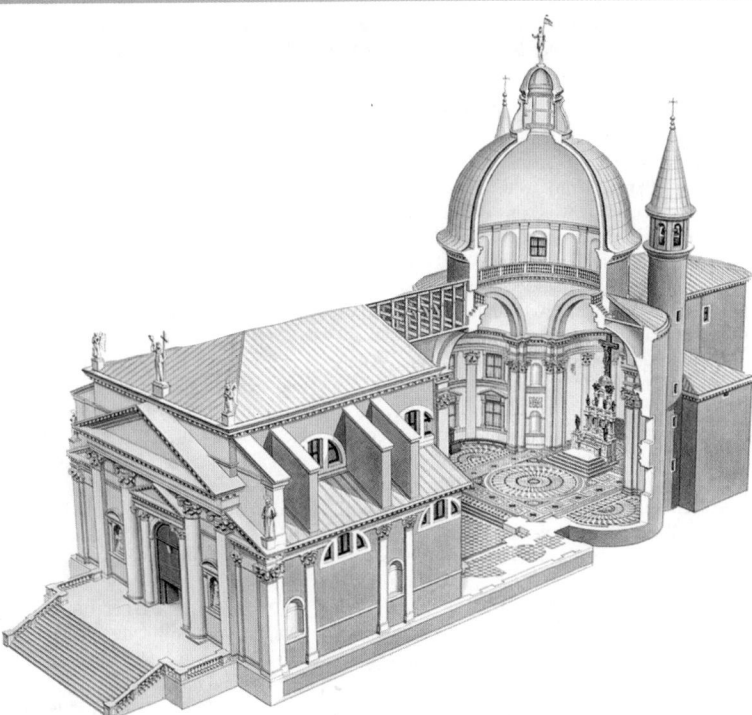

▲ **Palladio** The Redentore, Venice (1577–92), is a superb example of Italian architect Andrea Palladio's work. The whole church is raised on a podium, has a choir separated from the chancel (Palladio's innovation), an absolute minimum of non-architectural ornament, and a light, spacious interior. It was financed by the Venetian state, in fulfilment of a vow on deliverance of the city from the plague of 1575–76.

P

▲ **pampas grass** Native to Argentina, pampas grass (*Cortaderia argentea*) was originally grown to provide food for grazing animals. More recently, it has been grown extensively as an ornamental plant in gardens.

PANAMA

The Republic of Panama forms an isthmus linking Central America to South America. The narrowest part of Panama is less than 60km [37mi] wide. The PANAMA CANAL, which is 81.6km [50.7mi] long and cuts straight across the isthmus, has made the country a major transport centre. Most Panamanians live within 20km [12mi] of it. Much of the land between the Pacific and Caribbean coastal plains is mountainous, rising to 3,475m [11,400ft] at the volcano Barú.

Tropical forests cover approximately 50% of Panama. Mangrove swamps line the coast, though in recent years more than 400sq km [150sq mi] have been lost to agriculture, ranching and shrimp mariculture. Subtropical woodland grows on the mountains, while tropical savanna occurs along the Pacific coast.

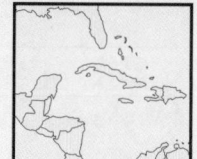

CLIMATE

Panama has a tropical climate, though the mountains are much cooler than the coastal plains. The rainy season is between May and December. The Caribbean side of the country has about twice as much rain as the Pacific side.

HISTORY

Christopher COLUMBUS landed in Panama in 1502. In 1510, Vasco Núñez de BALBOA became the first European to cross Panama and see the Pacific Ocean. Spain established control, and the indigenous population was soon wiped out by Spanish troops and exposure to European diseases. In 1821 Panama became a province of Colombia. The USA exerted great influence from the mid-19th century, and after a revolt in 1903 Panama declared independence from Colombia. In 1904 the USA began construction of the Panama Canal and established the Panama Canal Zone. The status of the canal has dominated Panamanian politics since it opened in 1914. American forces intervened in 1908, 1912, and 1918 to protect US interests.

POLITICS

Panama was politically unstable throughout the 20th century, with a series of dictatorial regimes and military coups.

Civil strife during the 1950s and 1960s led to negotiations with the USA for the transfer of the Canal Zone. In 1977 a treaty confirmed Panama's sovereignty over the canal, while providing for US bases in the Canal Zone. The USA agreed to hand over control of the canal on 31 December 1999. In 1979 the Canal Zone was disestablished and the canal was controlled jointly by Panama and the US.

In 1983 General Noriega took control of the National Guard and ruled Panama through a succession of puppet governments. In 1987 the USA withdrew its support for Noriega after he was accused of murder, electoral fraud and aid-

AREA 75,517sq km [29,157sq mi]
POPULATION 3,242,000
CAPITAL (POPULATION) Panamá (1,173,000)
GOVERNMENT Multiparty republic
ETHNIC GROUPS Mestizo 70%, Black and Mulatto 14%, White 10%, Amerindian 6%
LANGUAGES Spanish (official), English
RELIGIONS Roman Catholic 85%, Protestant 15%
CURRENCY US dollar; Balboa = 100 centésimos

ing drug smuggling. In 1988 the USA imposed sanctions. In 1989 Noriega annulled elections, made himself president, and declared war on the USA. On 20 December 1989, 25,000 US troops invaded Panama. Noriega was quickly captured and taken to the USA for trial.

Pérez Balladares became president in 1994 elections. He was succeeded in 1999 by Mireya Moscoso. Martin Torrijos, son of a former dictator, became president in 2004. Canal revenues rose in the early 21st century but the economy slowed, causing discontent. In 2006 the government announced major expansion of the canal.

ECONOMY

Panama is a 'lower-middle-income' developing country. The Panama Canal is a major source of revenue, generating jobs in commerce, trade, manufacturing and transport.

After the canal, the main activity is agriculture, which employs 27% of the workforce. Rice is the main food crop. Bananas, shrimps, sugar and coffee are exported. Tourism is also important. Many ships are registered under Panama's flag, because of its low taxes.

▶ **panda** The giant panda (*Ailuropoda melanoleuca*) is found in mountain forests in parts of Sichuan, central China, and on the slopes of the Tibetan plateau. It is a rare, solitary animal, which usually lives on the ground, but will climb trees if pursued. They spend about 12 hours a day feeding, mainly on bamboo stems and shoots. It is an endangered species, and pairs have been encouraged to breed in captivity.

Panchen Lama In TIBETAN BUDDHISM, religious leader who is second only in importance to the DALAI LAMA. In 1938, Bskal-bzang Tshe-brtan was born in China and later hailed by the Chinese government as the 10th Panchen Lama. In 1959, when the Dalai Lama fled to India, the Chinese government proclaimed the Panchen Lama the leader of Tibet. In 1964, he was stripped of power and died in 1989. In December 1995, another Tibetan, Gyaincain Norbu, was selected by the Chinese government and enthroned in Beijing as the 11th Panchen Lama. He is not recognized by the Tibetan government-in-exile nor by the majority of the international community.

pancreas Elongated gland lying behind the stomach, to the left of the mid-line. It secretes pancreatic juice into the SMALL INTESTINE to aid digestion. Pancreatic juice contains the enzymes AMYLASE, TRYPSIN, and lipase. The pancreas also contains a group of cells known as the islets of Langerhans, which secrete the hormones INSULIN and glucagon, concerned with the regulation of blood-sugar level. *See also* DIABETES

panda Two mainly nocturnal mammals of the family Ailuropodidae, related to raccoons and bears. The lesser or **red panda** (*Ailurus fulgens*) ranges from the Himalayas to w China. It has soft, thick, reddish brown fur, a white face and a bushy tail. It feeds mainly on fruit and leaves, as well as small birds, rodents and insects. Length: 115cm (46in) overall. The rare **giant panda** (*Ailuropoda melanoleuca*) inhabits bamboo forests in China (mainly Tibet). It has a short tail and a dense white coat with black fur on shoulders, limbs, ears and around the eyes. It eats plant material, particularly bamboo shoots. Length: 1.5m (5ft); weight: 160kg (350lb).

Pandora In Greek mythology, the first woman. She was created on ZEUS' orders as his revenge on PROMETHEUS. When she opened a jar that Zeus had ordered her not to look into, all the evils of the human race flew out. Hope alone remained inside the jar. In later tradition, the jar became a box.

Pangaea Name for the single supercontinent that formed about 240 million years ago, and which began to break up at the end of the Triassic period. Geologists have reconstructed existing land masses with continental shelves to form models of this supercontinent. *See also* GONDWANALAND

pangolin (scaly anteater) Any of several species of toothless insectivorous mammals, covered with horny overlapping plates, that live in Asia and Africa. It has short, powerful forelegs with which it climbs trees and tears open the nests of tree ants, on which it feeds. Length: to 175cm (70in). Family Manidae; genus *Manis*.

Pankhurst, Emily (Emmeline Goulden) (1858–1928) English leader of the SUFFRAGETTE MOVEMENT. In 1903 Pankhurst set up the Women's Social and Political Union, supported by her daughters, **Christabel** (1880–1958) and **Sylvia** (1882–1960). Their militant tactics courted prosecution, and they gained further publicity in prison by hunger strikes. After World War 1, she concentrated on the employment of women in industry. *See also* FEMINISM

panpipes (syrinx) Primitive musical wind instrument, probably originating in Asia. Several tubes of cane, reed, bamboo or clay, of different lengths, are joined together side by side. Blown across one end, each pipe produces one note of a scale. Panpipes are associated with the pastoral Greek god PAN.

pansy Common name for a cultivated hybrid VIOLET. An annual or short-lived perennial, it has velvety flowers, in various colour combinations, with five petals. Height: to about 15–30cm (6–12in). Family Violaceae; species *Viola tricolor.*

pantheism Religious system, contrasted with certain forms of DEISM, based on the belief that God (or gods) and the universe are identical. According to pantheism, all life is infused with divinity. It sees no distinction between the creator and creatures.

pantheon Ancient Greek and Roman TEMPLE for the worship of all the gods. The most famous is the Pantheon in Rome, originally built by Agrippa (27BC), rebuilt by Hadrian (c.AD 120), and converted into the church of Santa Maria AD Martyres in the 7th century. The term was later extended to apply to a building honouring illustrious public figures.

panther *See* LEOPARD

pantomime Theatrical spectacle with its modern origins in early 18th-century France. It has come to mean a Christmas extravaganza, with music and comic actors. Popular in England by the 19th century, the 'dame' figure was traditionally played by a male actor and the principal boy by a female. The once-central HARLEQUIN character now appears infrequently.

Paolozzi, Sir Eduardo (1924–2005) Scottish sculptor and graphic artist. He created box-like, chromium-plated sculptures evocative of jazz-age amusement arcades and picture palaces. Since the 1950s, he has worked mainly on large-scale ABSTRACT sculptures such as *City of the circle and the square* (1963–66).

papacy Office, status, or authority of the pope as head of both the ROMAN CATHOLIC CHURCH and the VATICAN CITY. The Pope is nominated Bishop of Rome and Christ's spiritual representative on Earth. He is elected by the College of Cardinals. There have been more than 265 holders of the office of pope from ST PETER to BENEDICT XVI. Until the REFORMATION the papacy claimed authority over all Western Christendom. Today, papal authority extends only over the members of the Roman Catholic Church. *See also* PAPAL INFALLIBILITY

papal bull Official letter from the Pope, written in solemn style and consisting of a formal announcement. Such a document usually contains a decree relating to doctrine, CANONIZATION, ecclesiastical discipline, promulgation of INDULGENCES or some other matter of general importance.

papal infallibility Roman Catholic doctrine according to which the Pope, under certain conditions, cannot make a mistake in formal statements on issues of faith or morals. It was defined in its present form, amid great controversy, at the First VATICAN COUNCIL (1869–70).

Papal States Territories of central Italy under the rule of the popes (756–1870). In the 15th century, the papal government displaced the feudal magnates who had ruled the Papal States in the Middle Ages and imposed direct control from Rome. The territory was lost during the Napoleonic period, restored to the papacy in 1815, and annexed by Italian nationalists during the RISORGIMENTO. The LATERAN TREATY (1929) restored the area comprising the VATICAN in Rome to papal rule.

Papandreou, Andreas (1919–96) Greek statesman, prime minister (1981–89, 1993–96). Papandreou founded the Pan-Hellenic Socialist Movement (PASOK) in the mid-1970s, becoming leader of the opposition in 1977. Elected as Greece's first socialist prime minister in 1981, he was re-elected in 1985. Implicated in a financial fraud, he was unable to form a government following the election of 1989 and resigned. Cleared of fraud, Papandreou was re-elected in 1993. Costas Simitis succeeded him as prime minister.

◄ **Pankhurst** The pioneers of the fight for women's suffrage in Britain, Emily Pankhurst (centre) and her daughter Christabel (left) were frequently arrested because of their use of militant protest tactics. They interrupted meetings of the cabinet, political parties, and even the House of Commons. Later they turned to even more violent methods of protest, including arson. The law granting full voting rights to women in Britain was passed a few weeks after Emily's death.

papaya (pawpaw) Palm-like tree widely cultivated in tropical America for its fleshy, melon-like, edible fruit. It produces the ENZYME papain, which breaks down proteins, and is used commercially. Height: to 6m (20ft). Family Caricaceae; species *Carica papaya. See* picture overleaf.

Papeete Capital and chief port of French Polynesia, in the s Pacific Ocean, on the NW coast of Tahiti. Papeete is a trade centre for the islands and a tourist resort. Its exports include copra, mother-of-pearl and vanilla. Pop. (1999) 25,553.

Papen, Franz von (1879–1969) German statesman, chancellor (1932). A member of the Catholic Centre Party, Papen resigned the chancellorship after only six months, and persuaded HINDENBURG to appoint Adolf HITLER as his successor. He served (1933–34) as Hitler's vice-chancellor. As ambassador to Austria (1936–38), he pressed for ANSCHLUSS. In 1946, he was acquitted of war crimes at the NUREMBERG TRIALS.

paper Sheet or roll of compacted cellulose fibres with a wide range of uses. The word 'paper' derives from PAPYRUS, the plant that the Egyptians used more than 5500 years ago to make sheets of writing material. The modern process of manufacture originated c.2,000 years ago in China, and consists of reducing wood fibre, straw, rags or grasses to a pulp by the action of an ALKALI, such as CAUSTIC SODA. The non-cellulose material is then extracted and the residue is bleached. After washing and the addition of a filler to provide a smooth and flat surface, the pulp is made into thin sheets and dried. These can be coated to produce a special surface, such as glossy paper for photographs.

papier-mâché (Fr. 'chewed paper') Method of moulding forms using paper strips soaked in a starch. The technique

▼ **papacy** Pope Innocent III (1198–1216) extended the power of the medieval papacy at the expense of Kings and Princes by intervening throughout Europe to combat any challenge, temporal or spiritual, to the authority of the Roman Catholic Church.

- ■ Papal States from 1213
- ■ Vassals of papacy
- ■ Intervention by papacy
- ■ New relations
- □ Sphere of papal influence
- □ Byzantine states
- □ Under Muslim rule
- — Holy Roman Empire

P

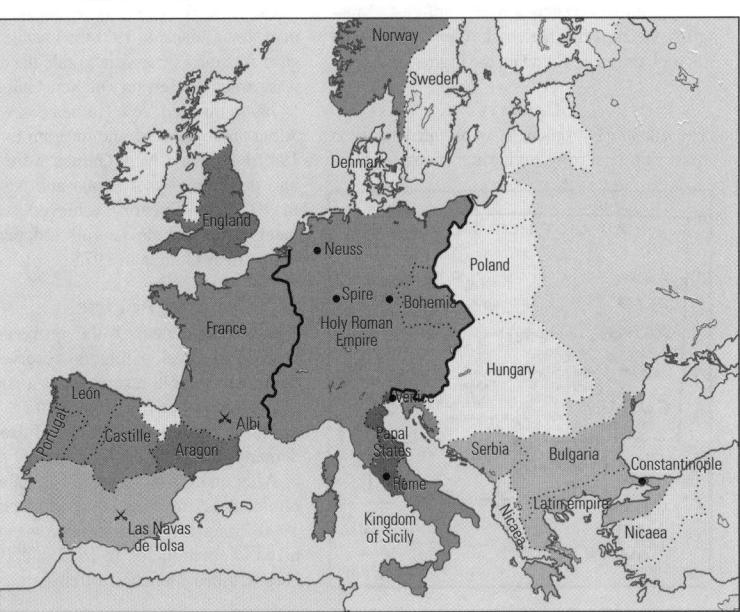

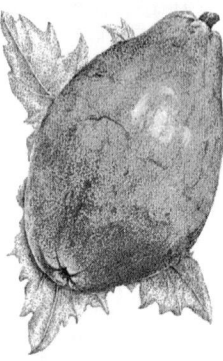

▲ **papaya** The skin of the papaya, or pawpaw, ripens from green to yellow or orange. Its succulent pulp encloses small, black/brown seeds in its centre. Papain, an enzyme contained in the leaves and unripe fruit, is used to tenderize meat.

originated in 18th-century France. The British adopted the technique to produce a thin paperboard to make trays and mouldings, which were popular in Victorian times. It is still widely used in the production of decorative objects.

Papineau, Louis Joseph (1786–1871) French-Canadian politician. He opposed the union of Upper and Lower Canada. His quarrels with Britain incited his followers to rebellion (1837). He escaped arrest by fleeing to the USA, then to France. Granted an amnesty (1847), he returned to Canada and was a member of the unified legislature (1848–54).

paprika Spicy condiment, a red powder ground from a sweet PEPPER (capsicum) native to C Europe. Family Solanaceae.

pap test *See* CERVICAL SMEAR

Papua New Guinea Independent Commonwealth island group in Melanesia, sw Pacific, 160km (100mi) NE of Australia; the capital is PORT MORESBY. *See* country feature.

papyrus Stout, perennial water plant, native to s Europe, N Africa, and the Middle East, used by the ancient Egyptians to make a PAPER-like writing material. Strips of the stem were arranged in layers, crushed and hammered to form a loosely textured, porous kind of paper. Height: to 4.5m (15ft). Family Cyperaceae; species *Cyperus papyrus*.

parable Short, simple story intended to convey a moral or religious message. The best-known parables are those attributed to Jesus Christ in the New Testament, including the Good Samaritan, the Prodigal Son, the Sower and the Seed, and the Pearl of Great Price.

parabola In mathematics, a curve formed by the intersection of a CONE by a plane parallel to the cone's sloping side. This conic section can be traced by a point that moves so that its distance from a fixed point, the **focus**, is equal to its distance from a fixed straight line, the **directrix**. The general equation of a parabola is $y = ax^2 + bx + c$, where a, b, and c are constants.

Paracelsus (1493–1541) Name meaning "Surpassing Celsus", taken by the Swiss physician and alchemist Philippus Aureolus Theophrastus Bombastus von Hohenheim. Paracelsus attempted to revolutionize European medicine using alchemical principles, and pioneered the use of metals such as mercury in medicine. While many of the treatments he devised were harmful, his ideas helped promote the use of experiment, evidence and testing in medicine.

paracetamol ANALGESIC drug that lessens pain and is also effective in reducing fever. It is used to treat mild to moderate pain, such as headaches, toothaches and rheumatic conditions, and is particularly effective against musculoskeletal pain.

parachute Lightweight fabric device for slowing movement through the air. Parachutes allow people to descend safely from aircraft or are used to drop cargo and supplies. The most common use is for the sport of SKYDIVING.

paradox In LOGIC, a self-contradictory or absurd statement that conflicts with preconceived notions of what is reasonable or possible, but which is significant when considered from the appropriate viewpoint. 'This statement is not true' appears to be true if false and false if true.

paraffin (kerosene) Common domestic fuel that is mainly a mixture of ALKANE hydrocarbons made by distilling PETROLEUM. Less volatile than petrol, paraffin is also used as jet aircraft fuel. Paraffin wax is a white, translucent mixture of solid alkanes obtained by solvent extraction; it is used to make candles, waxed paper, polishes and cosmetics.

Paraguay Landlocked republic in central South America; the capital is ASUNCIÓN. *See* country feature.

PAPUA NEW GUINEA

The Independent State of Papua New Guinea is part of a sw Pacific island region called Melanesia 160km [100mi] NE of Australia that includes the E part of New Guinea, Bismarck Archipelago, SOLOMON ISLANDS, New Hebrides, the Trobriand and D'Entrecasteaux Islands, the Louisiade Archipelago and the Tonga group.

The land is largely mountainous, rising to Mount Wilhelm, at 4,50m [14,790ft], eastern New Guinea. In 1995, two volcanoes erupted in Eastern New Britain. East New Guinea also has extensive coastal lowlands.

Forests cover more than 70% of the land. The dominant vegetation is rainforest. Mangrove swamps line the coast. 'Cloud' forest and tussock grass are found on the higher peaks.

CLIMATE

The climate is tropical. It is hot all year, with most rain occurring during the monsoon from

December to April when winds blow from the NE. Winds blow from the sw during the dry season.

HISTORY

The Portuguese made the first European sighting of the island in 1526, although no European settlements were established until the 19th century. The Dutch took w New Guinea (now IRIAN JAYA in Indonesia) in 1828, and in 1884 Germany took control of NE New Guinea as German New Guinea and Britain formed the protectorate of British New Guinea in SE New Guinea. In 1906 British New Guinea passed to Australia as the Territory of Papua. At the outbreak of World War 1 Australia occupied German New Guinea. In 1921 the League of Nations gave Australia a mandate to rule the area, which was named the Territory of New Guinea.

Japan invaded New Guinea in 1942, but the Allies reconquered the region in 1944. In 1949 Papua and New Guinea were combined into the Territory of Papua and New Guinea. In 1973 the Territory achieved self-government as a prelude to full independence as Papua New Guinea in 1975.

POLITICS

Since independence, the government has worked to develop mineral reserves. One of the most valuable reserves was a copper mine at Panguna on BOUGAINVILLE. Conflict developed when the people of Bougainville demanded a larger share in mining profits.

After an insurrection, the Bougainville Revolutionary Army proclaimed independence in 1990. Bougainville's secession was not recognized internationally. In 1992 and 1996 Papua New Guinea launched offensives against the

AREA 462,840sq km [178,703sq mi]
POPULATION 5,796,000
CAPITAL (POPULATION) Port Moresby (193,000)
GOVERNMENT Constitutional monarchy
ETHNIC GROUPS Papuan, Melanesian, Micronesian
LANGUAGES English (official), Melanesian Pidgin, more than 700 other indigenous languages
RELIGIONS Traditional beliefs 34%, Roman Catholic 22%, Lutheran 16%, others
CURRENCY Kina = 100 toea

rebels. The use of highly paid mercenaries created unrest in the army. In 1997 troops and civilians surrounded Parliament, forcing the resignation of Prime Minister Sir Julius Chan. He was succeeded by Bill Skate. In April 1998 a ceasefire was declared on Bougainville. An estimated 20,000 had been killed. Local autonomy was granted in 2000.

Michael Somare became president in 2002 elections. In 2004 Australia sent police to help fight rising crime. In 2005 the government began the evacuation of the Cartaret Islands due to rising sea levels. Somare won a second term in the 2007 elections. Crime, corruption and rising HIV infection rates remain problems.

ECONOMY

Papua New Guinea is a 'lower-middle-income' developing country. Agriculture employs 75% of the workforce, mostly at subsistence level. Minerals, notably copper and gold, are valuable exports. Unemployment is high; aid from Australia is a significant proportion of the economy.

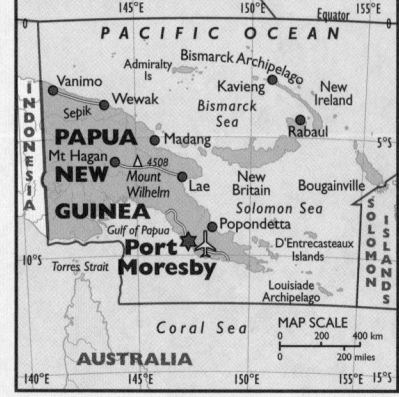

P

parakeet *See* PARROT

parallax Angular distance by which a celestial object appears to be displaced with respect to more distant objects, when viewed from opposite ends of a baseline. The parallax of a star (**annual** parallax) is the angle subtended at the star by the mean radius of the Earth's orbit (one astronomical unit); the smaller the angle, the more distant the star. *See also* PARSEC

parallelogram Quadrilateral (four-sided plane figure) having each pair of opposite sides parallel and equal. Both the opposite angles of a parallelogram are also equal. Its area is the product of one side and its perpendicular distance from the opposite side. A parallelogram with all four sides equal is a RHOMBUS.

Paralympic Games Sports meeting run every four years in parallel with the OLYMPIC GAMES, and in which all competitors are physically handicapped. Prosthetic limbs and other devices may be worn; many events are undertaken by competitors in wheelchairs.

paralysis Weakness or loss of muscle power; it can vary from a mild condition to complete loss of function and sensation in the affected part. It can be associated with almost any disorder of the NERVOUS SYSTEM, including brain or spinal cord injury, infection, stroke, poisoning, or progressive conditions such as a tumour or motor neurone disease. Paralysis is very rarely total.

Paramaribo Capital of Suriname, a port on the River Suriname. It was founded in the early 17th century by the French and became a British colony in 1651. It was held intermittently by the British and the Dutch until 1816, when the latter finally took control until independence. Industries: bauxite, timber, sugar cane, rice, rum, coffee, cacao. Pop. (2000 est.) 213,836.

Paramecium Genus of freshwater, ciliated PROTOZOANS characterized by their 'slipper' shape, defined front and rear ends, an oral groove for feeding, food vacuoles for digestion, an anal pore for elimination, and two nuclei. Its stiff outer covering is studded with short, hair-like CILIA. Order Holotricha; species include *Paramecium bursaria* and *P. aurelia*.

Paraná River in SE central South America. It rises in SE Brazil, flows s into Argentina, forming the SE and s border with Paraguay, and joins the River Uruguay to form the Río de la PLATA. It is an important route for inland communications. Combined length: Paraná/Plata *c.*4,000km (2,400mi).

paranoia Term in psychology for a psychotic disorder characterized by a systematically held, persistent delusion, usually of persecution or irrational jealousy. Paranoia can accompany SCHIZOPHRENIA, manic-depressive disorder, drug or alcohol abuse, and brain damage.

paraplegia PARALYSIS of both legs. It is usually due to spinal cord injury, and often accompanied by loss of sensation below the site of the damage.

parapsychology Research into phenomena that appear inexplicable by traditional science, such as EXTRASENSORY

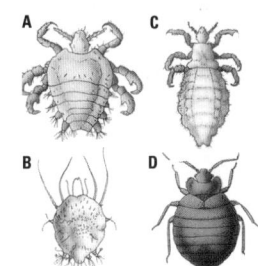

▲ **parasite** Some external parasites live on or near humans. The crab louse (A) lives on areas of the body with widely spaced coarse hair. The acarus mite (B), just visible to the human eye, can cause scabies. The body louse (C) is more dangerous, as a carrier of epidemic typhus. The common bedbug (D). found all over the world, is inactive by day. At night it finds humans and sucks their blood.

PARAGUAY

The Republic of Paraguay is a landlocked country in South America. Rivers form most of its borders. They include the PARANÁ in the s and the E, the Pilcomayo (Brazo Sur) in the sw, and the Paraguay in the NE. w of the River Paraguay is a region known as the GRAN CHACO, which extends into Bolivia and Argentina. The Gran Chaco is mostly flat, but the land rises in the NW. East of the Paraguay is a region of plains, hills and, in the east, the Paraná Plateau region.

CLIMATE

The N half of Paraguay lies in the tropics, while the s half is subtropical. Most of the country has a warm, humid climate. The Gran Chaco is the driest and hottest part of the country. Rainfall is higher on the Paraná Plateau in the SE.

HISTORY

The GUARANI, an Amerindian people, were the indigenous inhabitants of what is now Paraguay. Spanish and Portuguese explorers reached the area in the early 16th century. In

1537 a Spanish expedition built a fort at Asunción which later became the capital of Spain's colonies in SE South America. The Spaniards were attracted by the potential labour supply of the Guarani and the chance to find a short cut to the silver mines of Peru. From the late 16th century, Jesuit missionaries arrived to convert the Guarani to Christianity and to protect them against those who wanted to exploit them as cheap labour. Complaints against the Jesuits' power led to their expulsion by the King of Spain in 1767.

From 1776 Paraguay formed part of the Rio de la Plata Viceroyalty, ruled from its capital at Buenos Aires. This proved unpopular, and Paraguay overthrew the Spanish authorities in 1811, achieving independence.

Between 1865 and 1870, the disastrous War of the Triple Alliance against Brazil, Argentina and Uruguay cost the country more than half of its 600,000 population and much of its territory. Some territory was regained after the Chaco Wars against Bolivia between 1920 and 1935. A 1947 civil war was followed by a spell of political and economic stability, but while most other South American countries were attracting European settlers and foreign capital, Paraguay remained isolated.

POLITICS

In 1954 General Alfredo Stroessner seized power and assumed the presidency. During his dictatorship, there was considerable economic growth, with an emphasis on developing hydroelectricity. By 1976 Paraguay was self-sufficient in electrical energy due to the completion of the Aracay complex. A second hydroelectric project, the world's largest, started production in 1984, at Itaipu. This was a US$20 billion joint venture with Brazil to harness the Paraná, which allowed Paraguay to generate 99.9% of its electricity from water power. However, demand slackened and income declined, mak-

AREA 406,752sq km [157,047sq mi]
POPULATION 6,669,000
CAPITAL (POPULATION) Asunción (1,750,000)
GOVERNMENT Multiparty republic
ETHNIC GROUPS Mestizo 95%
LANGUAGES Spanish and Guarani (both official)
RELIGIONS Roman Catholic 90%, Protestant
CURRENCY Guarani = 100 céntimos

ing it difficult for Paraguay to repay foreign debts incurred on the projects. High inflation and balance of payments problems followed.

Stroessner's nepotistic regime was marked by torture, kidnappings and widespread corruption. His supporters deposed him in 1989 and he went into exile, dying in 2006. Elections were held in the 1990s but democracy was fragile. In 1998, newly elected president Raul Cubas Grau was threatened with impeachment after issuing a decree freeing his former running mate, General Lino Oviedo, who had been imprisoned for attempting a coup against the previous president. In March 1999 Paraguay's vice-president, an opponent of Cubas, was assassinated. Congress impeached Cubas, who resigned and fled to Argentina. In 2008 elections the conservative Colorado Party was defeated for the first time in 60 years, and Fernando Lugo became president.

ECONOMY

The World Bank classifies Paraguay as a 'lower-middle-income' developing country. Agriculture and forestry are the leading activities, employing 48% of the workforce. The country has very large cattle ranches, while crops are grown in the fertile soils of E Paraguay. Major exports include cotton, soya beans, timber, vegetable oils, coffee, tannin and meat products. The country has abundant hydroelectricity and exports power to Argentina and Brazil. Its factories produce cement, processed food, leather goods and textiles.

P

INTERNET

Parker, Dorothy
▶ www.americanpoems.com

PERCEPTION (ESP) and precognition (perceiving future events). Parapsychology has not produced any significant results.

parasite Organism that lives on or in another organism (the host) upon which it depends for its survival; this arrangement may be harmful to the host. Parasites occur in many groups of plants and in virtually all major animal groups. A parasite that lives in the host is called an **endoparasite**; a parasite that survives on the host's exterior is an **ectoparasite**. Many parasites, such as PROTOZOA, FLEAS and WORMS, carry disease or cause sores or lesions. The European CUCKOO and cowbird rely on other birds to rear their young, and are therefore considered 'brood parasites'. In **parasitoidism**, the relationship results in the death of the host. For example, various flying insects, such as the ichneumon flies, lay their eggs on or in a host that becomes the food for the insect larvae. A **hyperparasite** is one that parasitizes another parasite. See illustration page 579.

parathyroid glands Four small endocrine glands, usually embedded in the back of the THYROID GLAND, that secrete a HORMONE to control the level of calcium and phosphorus in the blood. Overproduction of parathyroid hormone causes loss of calcium from the bones to the blood; a deficiency causes tetany (involuntary muscle spasm). *See also* ENDOCRINE SYSTEM

Paré, Ambroise (1517–90) French physician regarded by some as the founder of modern surgery. In 1537, he was employed as an army surgeon, and in 1552 became surgeon to HENRY II. He introduced new methods of treating wounds, described in his book *The Method of Treating Wounds Made by Harquebuses and Other Guns* (1545), and revived the practice of tying arteries during surgery instead of cauterizing them.

Paris Capital of France, on the River SEINE. When the Romans took Paris in 52 BC it was a small village on the Ile de la Cité on the Seine. Under their rule it became an important administrative centre. Paris was the capital of the Merovingian Franks in the 5th century, but subsequently declined. In the 10th century, it was re-established as the French capital by the Capetian kings. In the 11th and 12th centuries, the city expanded rapidly. During the 14th century, Paris rebelled against the Crown and declared itself an independent commune. It suffered further civil disorder during the Hundred Years' War. In the 16th century, it underwent fresh expansion, its architecture strongly influenced by the Italian Renaissance. In the reign of LOUIS XIII, Cardinal RICHELIEU established Paris as the cultural and political centre of Europe. The FRENCH REVOLUTION began in Paris when the BASTILLE was stormed by crowds in 1789. Under Emperor NAPOLEON I the city began to assume its present-day form. The work of modernization was continued during the reign of NAPOLEON III, when Baron Haussmann was commissioned to plan the boulevards, bridges, and parks. Although occupied during the Franco-Prussian War (1870–71) and again in World War 2, Paris was not badly damaged. The city proper consists of the Paris department, Ville de Paris. Its suburbs lie in the departments of the Ile-de-France region. It has many famous buildings and landmarks popular with tourists. Sights include the EIFFEL TOWER, ARC DE TRIOMPHE, the LOUVRE, NOTRE-DAME, and the Pompidou Centre. Paris remains the hub of France despite attempts at decentralization, and retains its importance as a European cultural, commercial and communications centre. Paris is noted for its fashion industry and for the manufacture of luxury articles. Industries: motor vehicles, chemicals, textiles, clothing. Pop. (2000) 9,630,000.

Paris In Greek legend, the son of PRIAM and Hecuba. Paris chose APHRODITE as the victor in a competition among goddesses. Aphrodite helped Paris to abduct HELEN, wife of Menelaus, King of Sparta. This kidnapping sparked the TROJAN WAR, in which Paris slew ACHILLES.

Paris, Treaties of Name given to several international agreements made in Paris. The most notable include: the **Treaty of 1763**, which ended the SEVEN YEARS' WAR; the **Treaty of 1783**, which ended the AMERICAN REVOLUTION; the **Treaty of 1814**, which settled the affairs of France after the first abdication of NAPOLEON I; the **Treaty of 1815**, after Napoleon's final defeat; the **Treaty of 1856**, ending the CRIMEAN WAR; the **Treaty of 1898**, ending the

SPANISH-AMERICAN WAR and giving the Philippines to the USA; and the main international settlement (1919) after World War 1, more often called the Treaty of VERSAILLES. Also signed in Paris was the truce in the VIETNAM WAR (1973), in which the USA agreed to withdraw its forces.

Paris Commune (March 18–May 28, 1871) Revolutionary government in Paris. Anger with the national government after defeat in the FRANCO-PRUSSIAN WAR provoked Parisians into establishing an independent city government. Socialists and other radicals played an important part in the Commune. Besieged by the forces of the national government, the city fell and the Commune was violently suppressed. The slaughter of an estimated 30,000 Communards alienated many French workers and encouraged revolutionary doctrines.

parity (sympol P) In physics, term used to denote space-reflection symmetry. The principle of conservation of parity states that physical laws are the same in a left- and right-handed co-ordinate system. This was regarded as inviolable until 1956, when US physicists Chen Ning YANG and Tsung-Dao LEE showed that it was transgressed by certain interactions between ELEMENTARY PARTICLES. Parity is also used in information theory to denote a coding method employed in message transmission to detect errors.

Park, Mungo (1771–1806) Scottish explorer. The African Association (forerunner of the Royal Geographical Society) asked Park to investigate the course of the River Niger (1795). Approaching from the Gambia, he explored *c.*450km (280mi) of the Upper Niger, a journey described in his *Travels...* (1799). On a second, government-sponsored expedition (1805), he and his companions were ambushed and killed.

Park Chung Hee (1917–79) South Korean general and statesman, president (1963–79). In 1961, he seized power in a military coup. In 1963, Park was elected president. He was re-elected in 1967 and 1971. Park was assassinated by the head of the South Korean Central Intelligence Agency.

Parker, Alan (1944–) English film director. His debut feature, *Bugsy Malone* (1976), was followed by *Midnight Express* (1978), for which he received an Oscar nomination. *Mississippi Burning* (1988) earned him a second nomination. Other films include *Birdy* (1985), *The Commitments* (1991) and *Evita* (1997).

Parker, Charlie (Charles Christopher) (1920–55) ('Bird') US JAZZ alto saxophonist. In the 1940s, Parker, Dizzy GILLESPIE, Thelonious MONK, and Bud POWELL were the founders of BE-BOP, a revolutionary departure in jazz. Parker's powerful improvisations inspired a new generation of jazz musicians, such as Miles DAVIS.

Parker, Dorothy (1893–1967) US poet, short-story writer, and critic. She wrote three volumes of poetry, the first of which, *Enough Rope* (1926), was a best-seller. A large body of her short stories were collected in *Here Lies* (1939). Her gift for witty epigrams is evident throughout her work.

Parkinson's disease Degenerative BRAIN DISORDER characterized by tremor, muscular rigidity and poverty of movement and facial expression. It arises from a lack of the NEUROTRANSMITTER, dopamine. Slightly more common in men, it is rare before the age of 50. Foremost among the drugs used to control the disease is L-DOPA.

parliament Legislative assembly that includes elected members and acts as a debating forum for political affairs. Many parliamentary systems are based on the **British Parliament**, which emerged in the late 13th century as an extension of the King's Council, and has been housed at Westminster since that time. It is the supreme power in the UK. Parliament comprises the monarch, in whose name members of the government act, and two Houses: the HOUSE OF LORDS, an upper chamber of peers, bishops, and law lords; and the HOUSE OF COMMONS. There are 646 members of the Commons (known as 'members of Parliament' or MPs), elected in single-member constituencies by universal adult suffrage. The prime minister and cabinet members are almost always members of the Commons. There is a maximum of five years between elections. *See also* CONGRESS

Parma City in N Italy; capital of Parma province. Parma is famed for its food products, such as Parma ham and Parmesan cheese. It was founded by the Romans in 183 BC. In the 9th century AD it became a bishopric, and in 1513 was incorporated into the Papal States. In 1545, Pope Paul III established the duchy of Parma, and until 1731 it was controlled by the Farnese family. Despite suffering severe bombing in World War 2, the city retains many historic buildings. Pop. (2000) 170,031.

Parmigiano (1503–40) Northern Italian painter and graphic artist, b. Francesco Mazzola. He was a master of MANNERISM. Among Parmigiano's best-known works are *Madonna with St Zachary* (c.1530) and *Vision of St Jerome* (c.1527).

Parnassus Mountain peak in central Greece. In ancient times, it was considered sacred to APOLLO, DIONYSUS and the MUSES, and was the site of the equally sacred Castalian spring, which lies just above DELPHI, at the s foot of the mountain. Height: 2,457m (8,061ft).

Parnell, Charles Stewart (1846–91) Irish nationalist leader. In 1875, he entered the British Parliament. Parnell led the parliamentary movement for Irish HOME RULE. His filibustering tactics won the support of the FENIAN MOVEMENT. In 1879, Parnell became president of the National Land League. He was imprisoned in 1881–82. In 1886, he supported GLADSTONE's introduction of the Home Rule Bill. In 1889, his career collapsed when he was cited as co-respondent in the divorce of William O'Shea, whose wife, Kitty, he later married.

parody Work in which the characteristics of artists or their works are imitated and exaggerated for comic effect. While parody exists in music and the arts, it is most commonly associated with literature. The tendency of parody to follow hard on the heels of distinctive work means that it has often served to question, consolidate and extend original advances in form, style or subject. Among 20th-century writers who have employed parody are Max Beerbohm, James JOYCE, and Stephen Leacock.

parrot Common name for many tropical and subtropical birds. Parrots are brightly coloured and have thick, hooked bills. They include BUDGERIGARS, macaws, lories, lorikeets, parakeets, keas, kakapos, and others. In the wild they nest in tree holes, rock cracks or on the ground. Length: 7.5–90cm (3in-3ft). Family Psittacidae.

Parry, Sir (Charles) Hubert (Hastings) (1848–1918) English composer. His mastery of choral music is best shown in *Blest Pair of Sirens* (1887). He is well known for *Jerusalem* (1916). He also wrote many songs, five symphonies and an opera.

parsec (*pc*) Distance at which a star would have a PARALLAX of one second of arc; equivalent to 3.2616 light years, 206,265 astronomical units, or 3.0857×10^{13} km.

Parsi (Parsee) Modern descendant of a small number of ancient Persian Zoroastrians who emigrated to Gujarat in India from the 10th century onwards. Modern Parsis, concentrated in Bombay, follow a mixture of ZOROASTRIANISM and some Indian beliefs and practices.

parsley Branching biennial herb, native to the Mediterranean region and widely cultivated for its aromatic leaves used for flavouring and as a garnish. It has heads of small, greenish to yellow flowers. Height: to 0.9m (3ft). Family Apiaceae/Umbelliferae; species *Petroselinum crispum*.

parsnip Biennial vegetable native to Eurasia, widely cultivated for its edible white taproot. The plant has many leaves, deeply and finely lobed. The roots develop slowly until cool weather sets in, and then they mature quickly. Family Apiaceae/Umbelliferae; species *Pastinaca sativa*.

Pärt, Arvo (1935–) Estonian composer. His early works were written in a traditional 'Soviet' style. In the 1970s, he adopted a minimalist style of gradually shifting chords and note-patterns that he called 'tintinnabula'. Among his best-known works are *Tabula Rasa* (1977), *Cantus in memoriam Benjamin Britten* (1980), and the *St John Passion* (1981).

parthenogenesis Development of a female sex cell or GAMETE without fertilization. Since there is no involvement of a male gamete, it leads to the production of offspring genetically identical to the mother. This process occurs naturally among some plants and invertebrates, such as APHIDS.

Parthenon Temple to the goddess ATHENA erected (447–432BC) by PERICLES on the ACROPOLIS in Athens. The finest example of a DORIC ORDER temple, it was badly damaged by

an explosion in 1687. Most of the surviving sculptures were removed by Lord Elgin in 1801–03. *See* ELGIN MARBLES

Parthia Region in ancient Persia, corresponding approximately to the modern Iranian province of Khurasan, with part of s Turkmenistan. It was the seat of the Parthian Empire, founded after a successful revolt against the SELEUCIDS (238BC). Under the Arsacid dynasty, the Parthian Empire extended, at its peak, from Armenia to Afghanistan. In AD 224, the Parthians were defeated by the rising power of the SASSANIDS and the Empire rapidly crumbled.

particle accelerator *See* ACCELERATOR, PARTICLE

particle physics Branch of physics that studies SUBATOMIC PARTICLES and interactions between them. Physicists now recognize more than 300 different subatomic particles, which can be grouped in various ways, although they are all composed of a few basic building blocks. The indivisible, fundamental units of matter are known as ELEMENTARY PARTICLES. They are termed the gauge BOSON, LEPTON, and QUARK. Other subatomic particles, termed HADRONS, are made up of two or more elementary particles. For example, PROTONS and NEUTRONS are made up of three quarks, and MESONS are made up of two quarks. Most subatomic particles are unstable and decay into other particles.

partridge Any of several species of gamebirds found worldwide. True partridges of Europe belong to the pheasant family (Phasianidae), and include the common partridge *Perdix perdix*, which has been introduced to N America. It lives on heathland, scrub and farmland, and feeds on plants and insects.

Parvati In Hindu mythology, the wife of the god SHIVA in one of her more benevolent aspects as a mountain goddess. Parvati is also the mother of the elephant-headed god GANESH and his brother Skanda. She is generally depicted as a young woman.

Pascal, Blaise (1623–62) French scientist and mystic. With Pierre de FERMAT, he laid the foundations of the mathematical theory of probability. He also contributed to CALCULUS and hydrodynamics, devising **Pascal's law** in 1647. This states that the pressure applied to an enclosed fluid (liquid or gas) is transmitted equally in all directions and to all parts of the enclosing vessel. The SI unit of pressure is named after him.

Pashto (Pushto) One of the two major languages of Afghanistan, the other being Persian. Pashto is spoken by about 12 million people in E Afghanistan and N Pakistan. It is historically the language of the PATHAN tribes, and is written in an adapted Arabic alphabet. One of the Iranian languages, it forms part of the Indo-European family of languages.

Pasolini, Pier Paolo (1922–75) Italian poet, novelist, and film director. A Marxist, he wrote about urban poverty with great realism in novels such as *A Violent Life* (1959). His films include *The Gospel According to St Matthew* (1964), *Oedipus Rex* (1967), *The Decameron* (1970) and *Salo* (1975).

passion In Christian theology, the suffering of JESUS CHRIST from the time of his praying in the garden of Gethsemane until his death on the cross. Passion Sunday is the fifth Sunday in Lent; PALM SUNDAY and EASTER follow.

passion flower Any plant of the genus *Passiflora*, climbing tropical plants that probably originated in tropical America, especially the blue passion flower, *P. caerulea*. The flowers can be various colours; the outer petals ring a fringed centre. The leaves are lobed and some species produce edible fruits, such as granadilla and calabash. Family Passifloraceae.

passion play Dramatic presentation of Christ's PASSION, death and resurrection, originally developed in medieval

▲ **passion flower** A climbing woody plant, the passion flower, makes its way by means of twining tendrils. Some species produce large, edible fruits.

◀ **Parthenon** The ceremonial centrepiece of the Acropolis, Athens' hilltop temple complex, the Parthenon was constructed in the fifth century BC in honour of Athena, the city's patron goddess. It was designed by Athens' foremost architects and ornamented by its most gifted sculptors. A carved frieze, a section of which is shown here, ran around the top of the inner wall. It depicted the Panathenaia, the annual festival in honour of Athena.

P

INTERNET

Parthenon
▶ www.culture.gr
▶ www.thebritishmuseum.ac.uk

Europe. The best-known example of this tradition is still held every ten years in OBERAMMERGAU, Germany.

Passover (Pesach) Jewish festival lasting eight days, commemorating the Exodus from Egypt and the redemption of the Israelites. Symbolic dishes are prepared, including bitter herbs (*maror*) and unleavened bread (*matzot*), to remind the Jews of the haste with which they fled Egypt and, by extension, of their heritage. It is a family celebration, at which the HAGGADAH is read. Christ's 'Last Supper', at which he instituted the EUCHARIST, was a Passover meal.

Pasternak, Boris (1890–1960) Soviet poet, novelist, and translator. Before the Stalinist purges of the 1930s, he published works such as the poetry collection *My Sister, Life* (1922) and the autobiographical *Safe Conduct* (1931). After the death of Stalin, he began work on *Dr Zhivago* (1957). Its themes offended officials, and he was expelled from the Soviet Writers Union; the book was unpublished in the Soviet Union until the 1980s. He was also compelled by official pressure to retract his acceptance of the 1958 Nobel Prize in literature.

Pasteur, Louis (1822–95) French chemist, one of the founders of MICROBIOLOGY. His work on BACTERIA led to the 'germ theory' of infection. In 1862, Pasteur discovered that microorganisms can be destroyed by heat, a technique now known as PASTEURIZATION. He also found that he could weaken certain DISEASE-causing microorganisms, and then use the weakened culture to provide IMMUNITY against the disease. In 1881, Pasteur produced the first VACCINES against ANTHRAX. In 1885, he produced a vaccine against RABIES. In 1885, the **Pasteur Institute** was founded in Paris, France.

pasteurization Controlled heat treatment of food to kill bacteria and other microorganisms, discovered by French chemist Louis PASTEUR in 1862. Milk is pasteurized by heating it to 72°C (161.6°F), and holding it at that temperature for 16 seconds. Ultrapasteurization is now used to produce UHT (ultra-heat-treated) milk; it is heated to 132°C (270°F) for one second to provide a shelf-life of several months.

pastoral In literature, work portraying rural life in an idealized manner, especially to contrast its supposed innocence with the corruption of the city or royal court. In classical times, THEOCRITUS and VIRGIL wrote pastoral poems. The form was revived during the RENAISSANCE by such poets as DANTE, PETRARCH, BOCCACCIO, and SPENSER. MILTON and SHELLEY were noted for their pastoral elegies, and poets such as WORDSWORTH and FROST have been referred to as pastoral poets because their work has a characteristically rural setting.

pastoralism Form of subsistence agriculture that involves the herding of domesticated livestock. Societies practising this are small – restricted by the large amount of grazing land needed for each animal. Indigenous pastoralism is widespread in N Africa and central Asia, but in the Americas it is confined to the Andes. *See also* NOMAD

Patagonia Region in Argentina, E of the Andes Mountains, extending to the Strait of Magellan; the term is sometimes used to include part of S Chile. The area was first visited by MAGELLAN in the early 16th century. It was colonized in the 1880s, many of the settlers being Welsh or Scottish. The present boundaries were set in 1902. Most of Patagonia is arid, windswept plateau. Until recently, sheep rearing was the main source of income. Oil production is now important, and coal and iron ore are mined. Area: 805,490sq km (311,000sq mi).

patella (kneecap) Large, flattened, roughly triangular bone just in front of the joint where the FEMUR (thigh bone) and TIBIA (shinbone) are linked. It is surrounded by bursae (sacs of fluid) that cushion the joint.

patent (letters patent) Privilege granted to the inventor of a new product or process. A patent excludes others from producing or making use of an invention for a limited period, unless under license from the holder of the patent. *See also* COPYRIGHT

Pathans (Pashtuns) MUSLIM tribes of SE Afghanistan and NW Pakistan. They speak various dialects of an E Iranian language, PASHTO, and are composed of about 60 tribes, numbering in total *c.*10 million. Formerly, they were pastoralists inhabiting the mountainous border regions, but they are now mainly farmers and are more widely spread. In their clashes with the British in the 19th century, they gained a reputation as formidable warriors. Their way of life was disrupted by the Soviet occupation (1979–89) and the subsequent civil wars in Afghanistan.

Pathé, Charles (1863–1957) Pioneer French film producer. He produced many short films and is credited with having made one of the first long films, *Les Misérables* (1909). Through the Pathé newsreels, he can be closely identified with the development of the film DOCUMENTARY.

pathogen Microorganism that causes disease in plants or animals. Animal pathogens are most commonly BACTERIA and VIRUSES, while common plant pathogens also include FUNGI.

pathology Study of diseases, their causes and the changes they produce in the cells, tissues, and organs of the body.

Paton, Alan Stewart (1903–88) South African novelist and reformer. Strongly opposed to APARTHEID, he helped to found the South African Liberal Party, of which he was president (1958–68). His two best-known novels, *Cry, the Beloved Country* (1948) and *Too Late the Phalarope* (1953), raised awareness of injustices in South African society.

patriarch Head of a family or tribe, invested in certain circumstances with the status or authority of a religious leader. In the Old Testament, the term referred either to the ancestors of the human race who lived on Earth before the Flood (as recorded in Genesis 1–11) or more commonly to the ancestors of the ancient Israelites, namely: ABRAHAM, ISAAC, JACOB, and Jacob's 12 sons (Genesis 12–50). Since about the 4th century AD the word has also been used as an ecclesiastic title for a few exalted bishops in the Eastern Christian Church, who rule over large dioceses known as patriarchates.

patriarchy Social organization based on the authority of a senior male, usually the father, over a family.

patrician Aristocratic class in the ancient Roman Republic, members of the SENATE. In the early years of the Republic, the patricians controlled all aspects of government and society. Under the Empire, the division between patricians and PLEBEIANS disappeared.

Patrick, Saint (active 5th century AD) Patron saint of Ireland. What is known of him comes almost entirely from his autobiography, *Confessio*. He was born in Britain into a Romanized Christian family. Abducted by marauders at the age of 16, he was carried off to Ireland and sold to a local chief. After six years, he escaped back to Britain. He was sent to Ireland as a missionary by Pope Celestine I (432), and established an episcopal see at Armagh. His missionary work was so successful that Christianity was firmly established in Ireland before he died. His feast day is March 17.

Patten, Christopher Francis (1944–) British politician, last British governor of HONG KONG (1992–97). He held many ministerial portfolios during the 1980s and, as chairman of the Conservative Party (1990–92), he helped engineer a Conservative victory in the 1992 election, but lost his own seat. As governor of Hong Kong, Patten sought to preserve its political and economic institutions in the handover to China.

Patton, George Smith, Jr. (1885–1945) US general. In World War 1, he served with the American Expeditionary Force (AEF) in France. During World War 2, Patton commanded a tank corps in North Africa, and the 7th Army in Sicily. After the D-DAY invasion in 1944, he commanded the 3rd Army in its dash across France and into Germany. As military governor of Bavaria after the war, he was criticized for leniency to Nazis and was removed to command the US 15th Army.

Paul, Saint (active 1st century AD) Apostle of JESUS CHRIST, missionary, and early Christian theologian. His missionary journeys among the Gentiles form a large part of the ACTS OF THE APOSTLES. His many letters (epistles) to early Christian communities, recorded in the NEW TESTAMENT, represent the most important early formulations of Christian theology following the death of Jesus Christ. Named Saul at birth, he was both a Jew and a Roman citizen, brought up in the Roman colony of Tarsus. He saw the teachings of Jesus as a major threat to JUDAISM, and became a leading persecutor of early Christians. Travelling to Damascus to continue his persecution activities, he saw a bright light and heard the voice of Jesus addressing him. Having thus undergone his religious conversion, he adopted the name Paul and became an energetic evangelist and teacher of Christianity. In *c.*60,

▲ **Pavlov** During his study of the digestive process in dogs, the Russian physiologist Ivan Pavlov worked out a theory of conditioned reflexes. He established that dogs salivated when they were presented with food. This was a reflex action that the dog could not control. He then 'conditioned' a dog by ringing a bell every time he gave it food. Eventually the dog would salivate whenever it heard the bell. His work helped to establish the physiological basis of behaviour.

P

he was arrested and taken to Rome, where he died sometime between 62 and 68, probably suffering a martyr's execution.

Paul I (1754–1801) Emperor of Russia (1796–1801), son of CATHERINE II (THE GREAT). He re-established the principle of hereditary succession and instituted repressive measures to protect Russia from the influence of the French Revolution. Paul's erratic conduct and his hostility towards his son, Alexander, led to his murder by nobles and military officers.

Paul III (1468–1549) Pope (1534–49), b. Alessandro Farnese. As pope, he largely initiated the COUNTER-REFORMATION. Paul sponsored reform, established the JESUITS (1540) and summoned the Council of TRENT (1545). He commissioned MICHELANGELO to paint the ceiling of the Sistine Chapel.

Paul VI (1897–1978) Pope (1963–78), b. Giovanni Battista Montini. He earned a reputation as a reformer in the Vatican secretariat (1937–54) and as archbishop of Milan (1954–63). He continued the Second VATICAN COUNCIL, begun by John XXIII, but disappointed liberals by upholding the celibacy of priests, papal primacy, and condemning contraception.

Pauli, Wolfgang (1900–58) US physicist, b. Austria. His work on QUANTUM THEORY led him to formulate (1925) the EXCLUSION PRINCIPLE, which explains the behaviour of electrons in atoms. Pauli received the 1945 Nobel Prize in physics for the work. In 1931, he had predicted the existence of the NEUTRINO, and lived to see the prediction verified in 1956.

Pauling, Linus Carl (1901–94) US chemist. His work on the application of WAVE MECHANICS to molecular structure is detailed in *The Nature of the Chemical Bond* (1939). For this work, he won the Nobel Prize in chemistry in 1954. He also worked on the structure of PROTEINS. His work on DNA nearly anticipated the findings of Francis CRICK and James WATSON, when he suggested, in the 1950s, that its molecules were arranged in a helical structure. A keen advocate of nuclear disarmament, he received the 1962 Nobel Peace Prize.

Pavarotti, Luciano (1935–2007) Italian tenor. He made his operatic debut, as Rodolfo in Puccini's *La Bohème*, in 1961. He made his US début in 1968. His rich voice is well suited to the Italian repertoire and Mozart. Internationally famous, he later formed part of the popular concert in Rome called *The Three Tenors*, along with José CARRERAS and Placido DOMINGO.

Pavese, Cesare (1908–50) Italian poet, novelist, and translator. His translations of English and American novels had considerable influence on Italian literature of the time. His work with the Resistance during World War 2 influenced his own creative writing, which includes the poem *The Political Prisoner* (1949), the novel *The Moon and the Bonfire* (1950) and collections of poetry and essays.

Pavlov, Ivan Petrovich (1849–1936) Russian neurophysiologist. His early work centred on the PHYSIOLOGY and NEUROLOGY of digestion, for which he received the 1904 Nobel Prize in physiology or medicine. Pavlov is best known for his studies of CONDITIONING of behaviour in dogs. His major works include *Conditioned Reflexes* (1927).

Pavlova, Anna (1881–1931) Russian ballerina who made her debut in 1899. She toured in Europe and the USA, and left Russia in 1913 to tour with her own company. She excelled in *Giselle*, *The Dragonfly*, *Autumn Leaves*, and the *Dying Swan*, choreographed for her by Michel FOKINE in 1905.

Paxton, Sir Joseph (1803–65) English architect and landscape gardener. Noted for his greenhouses, he designed the CRYSTAL PALACE for the Great Exhibition of 1851.

Paz, Octavio (1914–98) Mexican poet and essayist. His work has gone through many phases, from Marxism to Surrealism and oriental philosophies. His poetry was collected in translation as *The Collected Poems of Octavio Paz, 1957–1987* (1987). He has also written essays and literary criticism, including *The Labyrinth of Solitude* (1950). He received the 1990 Nobel Prize in literature.

pea Climbing annual plant (*Pisum sativum*), probably native to W Asia. It has small oval leaves and white flowers that give rise to pods containing wrinkled or smooth seeds. It grows to 1.8m (6ft). Family Fabaceae/Leguminosae.

peach Small, fruit tree (*Prunus persica*) native to China and grown throughout temperate areas. The lance-shaped leaves appear after the pink flowers in spring. The fruit has a thin,

downy skin, white or yellow flesh, with a hard 'stone' in the middle. Height: to 6.5m (20ft). Family Rosaceae.

peacock (peafowl) Any of several species of birds of Asia and Africa. The male is called a peacock and the female a peahen. The male has a 150cm (60in) tail, which it can spread vertically as a semi-circular fan with a pattern of eye-like shapes. The body of the male may be metallic blue, green or bronze, depending on the species. Hens are almost as big as the males; they lack the tail and head ornaments, and are brown, red or green. In the wild, peafowl inhabit open, lowland forests, and roost in trees. Length of body: 75cm (30in). Family Phasianidae; genera *Pavo* and *Afropavo*.

Peacock, Thomas Love (1785–1866) English novelist and poet. Peacock is chiefly remembered for his idiosyncratic satirical romances, such as *Nightmare Abbey* (1818), *Crotchet Castle* (1831), and *Gryll Grange* (1860–61).

Peak District Plateau area at the S end of the PENNINES, Derbyshire, N central England. The Peak District National Park was established here in 1951. The highest point is Kinder Scout, at 636m (2088ft). Area: 1,404sq km (542sq mi).

Peale, Charles Willson (1741–1827) US painter, inventor, naturalist, and father of a family of artists. In 1782, Peale opened the USA's first art gallery, in Philadelphia, where he exhibited his own portraits. He later expanded the gallery into the country's first natural history museum. In 1795, he painted his most celebrated picture, *The Staircase Group*, a portrait of two of his sons.

peanut (groundnut) Annual, leguminous plant *Arachis hypogaea* of the PEA family. Native to South America, it is now grown in many temperate regions of the world. A versatile plant, in the 19th century, US scientist George Washington CARVER researched more than 300 uses for it. The seeds (peanuts) are a valuable source of protein and yield an oil used both in food and in industry. The body of the plant can be used as animal feed. Family: Fabaceae/Leguminosae.

pear Tree and its edible fruit, native to N Asia and S Europe and grown in temperate regions. The tree has white flowers and glossy, green leaves. The greenish-yellow, brownish or reddish fruit, picked unripe and allowed to mature, can beeaten fresh or preserved. Height: 15–23m (50–75ft). Family Rosaceae; species *Pyrus communis*.

pearl Hard, smooth, iridescent concretion of calcium carbonate produced by certain marine and freshwater bivalve MOLLUSCS. It is composed of nacre, or mother-of-pearl, which forms the inner layer of mollusc shells. A pearl results from an abnormal growth of nacre around minute particles of foreign matter, such as a grain of sand.

Pearl Harbor US naval base in Hawaii. On December 7, 1941, a Japanese naval taskforce, which approached within range of the islands unobserved, attacked Pearl Harbor, headquarters of the US Pacific fleet. The Japanese assault killed *c*.2,400 people and destroyed or damaged *c*.300 aircraft and 18 ships. The attack provoked US entry into WORLD WAR 2.

Pears, Sir Peter (1910–86) English tenor. A lifelong friend of Benjamin BRITTEN, he created many roles in Britten's operas, including the title roles of *Peter Grimes* (1945) and *Albert Herring* (1949), the Male Chorus in *The Rape of Lucretia* (1946), and Aschenbach in *Death in Venice* (1973).

Pearse, Patrick Henry (1879–1916) Irish writer and politician. He headed the revival of interest in Gaelic culture, writing poems, short stories and plays. Pearse led the insurgents in the EASTER RISING (1916), and was court-martialled and executed by British authorities.

Pearson, Lester Bowles (1897–1972) Canadian statesman and diplomat, prime minister (1963–68). A distinguished diplomatic career culminated in his appointment (1945) as head of Canada's delegation to the United Nations (UN). Pearson acted as President of the General Assembly (1952–53). In 1948, he entered the Canadian Parliament as a Liberal and was Secretary of State for External Affairs (1948–63). Pearson's efforts in resolving the Suez Crisis earned him the 1957 Nobel Peace Prize. In 1958, he became leader of the LIBERAL PARTY. He succeeded John Diefenbaker as prime minister. His term was marked by health and social welfare reforms.

▲ **peanut** The groundnut, or peanut (*Arachis hypogaea*), is the second most important source of vegetable oil after soya beans.

▲ **pear** A fruit from a plant of the rose family, pears thrive in warmer temperate regions. In Canada, Australia and South Africa, a large proportion of the crop is canned, whereas in Europe and the USA, canning is less significant.

P

INTERNET

Peel, Sir Robert
► www.number-10.gov.uk
► www.met.police.uk/history

Peloponnesian War
► classics.mit.edu/
Thucydides/pelopwar.html

Penn, William
► www.quaker.org/wmpenn.
html

Pennsylvania
► www.state.pa.us

▲ **pecan** Mottled brown shells of the pecan burst apart to release the ripe nut. The pecan, a relative of the walnut, grows on large trees, which are found in temperate parts of North America. Pecans make excellent dessert nuts.

P

▲ **Peel** Conservative politician Sir Robert Peel was known for his opposition to the Reform Act and the Corn Laws. He is perhaps best known for the establishment of the London police force (1828), hence the nickname 'peelers' or 'bobbies'.

Peary, Robert Edwin (1856–1920) US Arctic explorer. He made several expeditions to Greenland (1886–92), and in 1893 led the first of five expeditions towards the North Pole. He claimed to have reached the Pole in April 1909.

Peasants' Revolt (1381) Rebellion in England. The immediate provocation was a POLL TAX (1380). Fundamental causes were resentment at feudal restrictions and statutory control of wages, which were held down artificially despite the shortage of labour after the BLACK DEATH. Roused by a rebel priest, John Ball, and led by Wat TYLER, the men of Kent marched into London, where they were pacified by RICHARD II. Promises to grant their demands were broken after they dispersed.

Peasants' War (1524–25) Rebellion of German peasants, probably the largest popular uprising in European history. Sparked by anger against ever-increasing dues demanded by the princes, there was widespread pillaging in the countryside of s Germany. The peasants hoped for and needed the support of Martin LUTHER, but he rejected their *Charter of Liberties* and their rebellion was savagely suppressed.

peat Dark brown or black mass of partly decomposed plant material. It forms in bogs and areas of high rainfall, and contains a high proportion of water. It is thought to be similar to the first stage in the formation of coal, and its high carbon content makes it suitable for use as a fuel.

peat moss Decomposed organic matter (HUMUS) obtained from disintegrated sphagnum MOSS (bog moss). The most widely obtainable source of humus, it is dug into soil and added to compost to retain moisture. Its continuing use poses an ecological threat to peat bogs.

pecan North American nut tree whose nut, resembling a small, smooth-shelled WALNUT, is 70% fat. Family Juglandaceae; species *Carya illinoinensis*.

peccary Omnivorous, pig-like mammal native to sw USA and Central and South America. It has coarse, bristly hair, and scent glands on its back. Collared peccaries, or javelinas (*Tayassu taja*), have dark-grey hair with a whitish collar. White-lipped peccaries (*T. pecari*) have brown hair. Weight: 23–30kg (50–66lb). Family Tayassuidae.

Peck, (Eldred) Gregory (1916–2003) US film actor. Peck made his debut in *Days of Glory* (1943). He received Academy Award nominations for *The Keys of the Kingdom* (1945), *The Yearling* (1946), *Gentleman's Agreement* (1947), and *Twelve O'Clock High* (1950). In 1956, Peck won a best actor Oscar for his powerful performance in *To Kill a Mockingbird* (1962). Other films include *Spellbound* (1945), *The Gunfighter* (1950), *Moby Dick* (1956), *McKenna's Gold* (1968) and *The Omen* (1976). He starred in two versions of *Cape Fear* (1962, 1991).

Peckinpah, (David) Sam (Samuel) (1926–84) US film director. He first gained attention for *Ride The High Country* (1962). Peckinpah injected new life into the WESTERN genre with his depiction of the harsh and violent reality of the frontier. Other films include *The Wild Bunch* (1969), *Straw Dogs* (1971), *The Getaway* (1973) and *Bring Me the Head of Alfredo Garcia* (1975).

pectin Water-soluble POLYSACCHARIDE found in the cell walls and intercellular tissue of certain ripe fruits or vegetables. When fruit is cooked, it yields a gel that is the basis of jellies and jams.

pediment Low-pitched gable formed by the sloping eaves of a pitched roof and a horizontal cornice. The classic triangular pediment appeared in Greek temples such as the PARTHENON. Later architects developed more extravagant forms, featuring curved, broken and inverted styles over doors and windows.

Pedro I (1798–1834) Emperor of Brazil (1822–31). Son of the future JOHN VI of Portugal, he fled with the rest of the royal family to Brazil in 1807. When his father reclaimed the Portuguese Crown (1821), Pedro became Prince Regent of Brazil, soon declaring it an independent monarchy (1822). His reign was marked by opposition from right and left, military failure against Argentina (1825–28) and revolt in Rio de Janeiro (1831). He abdicated and returned to Portugal, where he secured the succession of his daughter, Maria II, to the Portuguese throne.

Pedro II (1825–91) Emperor of Brazil (1831–89). He reigned under a regency until 1840. His reign was marked by internal unrest and external threats from Argentina and Paraguay.

Slavery was abolished in 1888, and Pedro's policy was generally reformist, antagonizing the military and the rich planters. He was forced to resign in 1889 and Brazil became a republic.

Peel, Sir Robert (1788–1850) British statesman, prime minister (1834–35, 1841–46). As TORY PARTY home secretary, he created (1829) the first modern police force, the Metropolitan (London) Police. Peel was chiefly responsible for passage of the CATHOLIC EMANCIPATION Act (1829). Peel's Tamworth Manifesto (1834) was a founding text of the CONSERVATIVE PARTY. He became converted to the doctrine of FREE TRADE, and the Irish FAMINE convinced him of the need to repeal the CORN LAWS. The proposal split the Tory Party and Peel resigned. In his second term, he carried through the repeal before being finally forced from office.

peerage British nobility holding any of the following titles: Baron, Viscount, Earl, Marquess or Duke. Although all titles were originally hereditary, these are now rare, and non-hereditary life peerages are more usually granted. Peers constitute the Lords Temporal section of the HOUSE OF LORDS. In 2001, the number of hereditary peers reduced and the first list of so-called 'people's peers' introduced.

Pegasus (Winged Horse) Northern constellation between Andromeda and Cygnus. Three of its bright stars form the Giant Square in Pegasus with Alpha Andromedae; the brightest is Epsilon, with a magnitude of 2.30.

Pegasus In Greek mythology, winged horse. Born out of the blood of MEDUSA, it was tamed by Bellerophon and helped him in his battles. Later, it carried the thunderbolts of ZEUS.

Pei, Ieoh Ming (1917–) US architect, b. China. Some of his most important buildings include Mile High Center, Denver (1957), the National Airlines Terminal at Kennedy International Airport, New York (1971), the East Building to the National Gallery of Art, Washington, D.C. (1978) and the John F. Kennedy Library, Boston (1979). He designed the pyramid in front of the Louvre, Paris (1989).

Peirce, Charles Sanders (1839–1914) US scientist, philosopher, and logician, a leading exponent of PRAGMATISM. He explained pragmatism in a series of six articles published between 1877 and 1878. He also helped to develop SEMIOTICS, the study of the use of signs and symbols. Most of his work was published posthumously in eight volumes as *The Peirce Papers: Collected Papers* (1931–58).

Peking See BEIJING

Pelagius (*c.*360–*c.*420) Monk and theologian, probably born in Britain, who preached the heresy of Pelagianism. In *c.*380, he went to Rome and became the spiritual guide of many clerics and lay persons. After 410, he preached in Africa, where-Saint AUGUSTINE denounced his ideas, and later in Palestine. He maintained that man is master of his own salvation and rejected the idea of original sin. He countered criticisms from Augustine and Saint JEROME in his book *De Libero Arbitrio* in 416. He was excommunicated by Pope Innocent I in 417.

Pelé (1940–) Brazilian footballer, b. Edson Arantes do Nascimento. He scored 97 goals in 111 appearances for Brzail. Pelé led Brazil to three World Cup victories (1958, 1962, 1970). He made his last international appearance in 1971. Apart from 1975–77, when he played for the New York Cosmos, all his club games were played for Santos. Pelé scored a total of 1281 goals. In 1997, he became Brazil's minister for sport.

pelican Any of several species of inland water birds, with a characteristic distensible pouch under its bill for scooping up fish from shallow water. It is usually white or brown and has a long hooked bill, long wings, short thick legs and webbed feet. Length: to 1.8m (6ft). Family Pelecanidae; genus *Pelecanus*.

pellagra Disease caused by a deficiency of nicotinic acid, one of the B group of vitamins. Its symptoms are lesions of the skin and mucous membranes, diarrhoea and mental disturbance.

Peloponnesian War (431–404 BC) Conflict in ancient Greece between ATHENS and SPARTA. The underlying cause was Sparta's fear of Athenian hegemony. Athenian hostility towards CORINTH, Sparta's chief ally, provoked the Spartan declaration of war. Having a stronger army, Sparta regularly invaded Attica, while Athens, under PERICLES, avoided land battles and relied on its navy. The early stages were inconclusive. The Peace of Nicias (420 BC) proved temporary. In 415

BC Athens launched a disastrous attack on Syracuse, which encouraged Sparta to renew the war. With Persian help, Sparta built up a navy which, under LYSANDER, defeated Athens in 405 BC. Besieged and blockaded, Athens surrendered.

Pelopónnisos (Peloponnesos) Peninsula in S Greece, connected to the mainland by the Isthmus of Corinth. The chief cities are Patras, Corinth, Pirgos, and Sparta. A mountainous region, it included the ancient cities of Sparta, Corinth, Argos and Megalopolis. The peninsula was involved in the Persian Wars (500–449BC), and it was the site of many battles during the PELOPONNESIAN WAR (431–404 BC). In 146 BC the region fell to the Romans, who reduced it to the status of a province. Held by the Venetians from 1699 to 1718, then by the Ottoman Turks, it passed to Greece after independence. Industries: silk, fish, manganese, chromium, fruits, tobacco, wheat, tourism. Area: 21,756sq km (8,400sq mi). Pop. (2001) 632,955.

pelota Generic name for a range of games in which a small, hard ball is hit with gloved or bare hand, or with a scoop-shaped wicker racket known as a *cesta*. Enjoyed in the Basque regions of Spain and France, and in South America, pelota games can be played across a net or against a wall in a two- or three-sided court known as a *fronto*.

Peltier effect Phenomenon in the temperature changes at a junction where an electric current passes from one kind of metal to another. When a current passes through a thermocouple, the temperature at one junction increases while that at the other decreases. This has been used for refrigeration. French physicist Jean Charles Peltier discovered the phenomenon in 1834. It is the reverse of the SEEBECK EFFECT.

pelvis Dish-shaped bony structure that supports the internal organs of the lower abdomen in vertebrates. It serves as a point of attachment for muscles that move the limbs or fins.

penance Carrying out of a specified act as a mark of sincere regret following the commission of a sin or sins. The most common penance, prescribed by a priest after absolution, is to say a prayer at a special time.

Penang (Pulau Pinang) Island of MALAYSIA, off the NW coast of the Malay peninsula, which (together with a coastal strip on the mainland) forms a state of Malaysia; the capital is George Town. The island was Britain's first possession in Malaya (1786). In 1826, it united with Singapore and MALACCA, and in 1867 the group became the Straits Settlements colony. Penang joined the Federation of Malaya in 1948. Its products include rice, rubber, and tin. George Town is Malaysia's principal port. Area: 1,040sq km (400sq mi). Pop. (2000) 1,255,501.

penates Ancient Roman gods of the household, worshipped at home in association with the lares (spirits of ancestors). Originally the penates were the spirits of the store room.

Penderecki, Krzysztof (1933–) Polish composer. His reputation was established in 1960 with his *Threnody for the Victims of Hiroshima* for string orchestra. Other pieces include several operas, and two symphonies (1973 and 1980).

pendulum Any object suspended at a point so it swings in an arc. A **simple** pendulum consists of a small heavy mass attached to a string or light rigid rod. A **compound** pendulum has a supporting rod whose mass is not negligible. The pendulum was first used to regulate clocks in 1673 by the Dutch physicist Christiaan HUYGENS. Foucault's pendulum, devised by the French physicist Léon FOUCAULT, swings in all directions and was used to demonstrate the Earth's rotation.

Penelope In Greek mythology, wife of ODYSSEUS. As described in HOMER's *Odyssey*, she had been married for only a year when her husband left for ten years of war and ten of wandering. She remained faithful, putting off her many suitors with the promise that she would choose one when her weaving was done. By day she wove and by night she undid her work.

penguin Flightless sea bird that lives in the Southern Hemisphere and ranges from the Antarctic northwards to the Galápagos Islands. Their wings have been adapted to flippers and their webbed feet help to propel their sleek bodies through the water. Although they are awkward on land, they are fast and powerful swimmers, easily able to catch the fish and squid that they feed on. Height: to 1.22m (4ft). Family Spheniscidae.

penicillin ANTIBIOTIC agent derived from moulds of the genus *Penicillium*. Scottish bacteriologist Sir Alexander FLEMING dis-

covered penicillin, the first antibiotic, in 1928. It was synthesized and first became available in 1941. Penicillin was widely used for treating casualties in World War 2. It can produce allergic reactions, and some microorganisms have become resistant.

Peninsular War (1808–14) Campaign of the NAPOLEONIC WARS in Portugal and Spain. It began as a popular revolt in Spain against NAPOLEON I's imposition of his brother, Joseph BONAPARTE, as king of Spain. It flared into a bloody guerrilla war and British troops, led by the future Duke of WELLINGTON, landed in Portugal to support the expulsion of the French (August 1808). The major turning point was the repulsion of Massena's offensive against Lisbon (1810–11). Wellington's forces then gradually drove the French from the Iberian peninsula and, after the victory of Vitoria (1813), invaded S France. Napoleon's abdication (1814) brought the campaign to an end.

penis Male reproductive organ. It contains the URETHRA, the channel through which URINE and SEMEN pass to the exterior, and erectile tissue that, when engorged with blood, causes the penis to become erect. *See also* SEXUAL INTERCOURSE

Penn, William (1644–1718) English QUAKER leader and chief founder of what later became the US state of PENNSYLVANIA. Because of his advocacy of religious freedom, he was imprisoned four times. While in the Tower of London, he wrote *No Cross – No Crown* (1669), explaining Quaker-Puritan morality. He persuaded King CHARLES II to honour an unpaid debt by granting him wilderness land in America to be settled by the Quakers and others seeking refuge from religious persecution. The colony was named the Commonwealth of Pennsylvania in his honour.

Pennines Range of hills in N England, extending from the Tyne Gap and Eden Valley on the border with Scotland to the valley of the River Trent. The hills are a series of highland blocks dissected by rivers such as the Tees, Aire and Ribble. The rearing of sheep is the chief occupation. Tourism and limestone quarrying are also important. The highest peak is Cross Fell, at 893m (2,930ft). Length: c.260km (160mi).

Pennsylvania State in E USA; one of the Middle Atlantic states; the capital is HARRISBURG. The chief cities are PHILADELPHIA, PITTSBURGH, Scranton, Bethlehem, Wilkes-Barre and Erie. Swedish and Dutch settlements were made along the Delaware River in the mid-17th century. By 1664, the area was controlled by the English, and in 1681 William PENN received a charter from Charles II for what is now Pennsylvania. It was one of the 13 original states of the Union. The DECLARATION OF INDEPENDENCE was signed and the US Constitution was ratified in Philadelphia, which was also the national capital from 1790 to 1800. The Union victory at the Battle of GETTYSBURG in July 1863 was a turning point in the American CIVIL WAR. Apart from small low-lying areas in the NW and SE, the state is composed of mountain ridges and rolling hills with narrow valleys. Farming is concentrated in the SE; the principal crops are cereals, tobacco, potatoes and fruit, and dairy products are important. Pennsylvania has rich deposits of coal and iron ore. The State has long been a leading producer of steel, which today accounts for about 25% of the nation's output. Industries: chemicals, cement, electrical machinery, metal goods. Area: 117,412sq km (45,333sq mi). Pop. (2000) 11,881,643.

pension Money paid regularly to a retired person. Pension plans may be funded by the government, such as SOCIAL SECURITY, or by companies; both plans involve regular financial contributions by the individual for a qualifying period. *See also* NATIONAL INSURANCE (NI)

Pentagon Headquarters of the US Department of Defense in Arlington, Virginia. The complex consists of five concentric buildings in pentagonal form and covers 14ha (34 acres). It was completed in 1943. The Pentagon has come to signify the US military establishment. On September 11, 2001, terrorists piloted a passenger aircraft into the west wing of the Pentagon, killing 125 people in the building and all 64 passengers.

Pentateuch (Gk. Five scrolls) First five books of the Bible, traditionally attributed to MOSES, and in JUDAISM referred to collectively as the *Torah* (Law). The Pentateuch comprises the five Old Testament books of GENESIS, EXODUS,

▲ **pelican** The brown pelican (*Pelecanus occidentalis*) has a large bill with a distensible pouch that it uses to catch the fish on which it feeds. It lives on the coasts of tropical America.

PENNSYLVANIA
Statehood:
December 12, 1787
Nickname:
The Keystone State
State bird:
Ruffed grouse
State flower:
Mountain laurel
State tree:
Hemlock
State motto:
Virtue, liberty and independence

P

▲ **penguin** The royal penguin (*Eudyptes schlegeli*), like many other species of penguin, is a highly social bird. During the breeding season, colonies of up to 2 million royal penguins amass on Macquarie Island, SW of New Zealand.

▲ **pepper** Green peppers are used to flavour food. The strong flavour of some varieties of pepper is due to the presence of capsaicin, which is found in the walls of the fruit.

P

LEVITICUS, NUMBERS and DEUTERONOMY. Composed over a very long period (possibly 1,000 years or more), they were probably collected in their present form during the BABYLONIAN CAPTIVITY of the Jews during the 6th century BC.

pentathlon Athletic competition that originated in ancient Greece and consisting of five events. The modern pentathlon is an Olympic sport for women, consisting of the 100m hurdles, shot put, high jump, long jump and 200m.

Pentecost Important religious festival celebrated in May or June. In Judaism, it is a festival held seven weeks after the second day of the PASSOVER, commemorating the giving of the Law to MOSES. In the Christian calendar, it is also known as Whit Sunday, falling seven weeks after Easter.

Pentecostal Churches Fellowship of revivalist Christian sects, inspired by the belief that all Christians should seek to be baptized with the Holy Spirit, and experience events such as speaking in tongues. Pentecostalists believe in the literal truth of the Bible, and many abstain from alcohol and tobacco and disapprove of dancing, theatre, and other such pastimes. The Pentecostal movement began in the USA at Topeka, Kansas, in 1901. Today, there are *c.*100 million members worldwide. *See also* CHARISMATIC MOVEMENT

Penzias, Arno Allan (1933–) US astrophysicist, b. Germany. Penzias and Robert Wilson discovered the cosmic background radiation emanating from outer space. They detected a non-varying radio signal that is considered to be thermal energy left over from the BIG BANG. Penzias and Wilson shared the 1978 Nobel Prize in physics with Peter Kapitza.

peony Perennial plant native to Eurasia and North America. It has glossy, divided leaves and large white, pink or red flowers. Height: to 0.9m (3ft). Tree peonies grow in hot, dry areas and have brilliant blossoms of many colours. Height: to 1.8m (6ft). Family Paeoniaceae; genus *Paeonia*.

Pepin III (the Short) (*c.*714–68) First CAROLINGIAN king of the Franks (750–68). In 750, he deposed the last MEROVINGIAN king, Childeric III, and defeated the LOMBARDS in 754 and 756. He ceded the conquered territories (the future PAPAL STATES) to the papacy in what was known as the **Donation of Pepin**. He was suceeded by his son CHARLEMAGNE.

pepper (capsicum) Perennial woody shrub native to tropical America. The fruit is a many-seeded, pungent berry whose size depends on the species. Included are bell, red, cayenne and CHILLI peppers. They all belong to the NIGHTSHADE family, Solanaceae; genus *Capsicum*.

peppermint Common name for *Mentha piperita*, a perennial herb of the MINT family (Lamiaceae/Labiatae) grown for its ESSENTIAL OIL, distilled for use in medicine and as a flavouring.

pepsin Digestive ENZYME secreted by GLANDS of the STOMACH wall as part of the GASTRIC JUICE. In the presence of hydrochloric acid it catalyzes the splitting of PROTEINS in food into polypeptides. *See also* PEPTIDE

peptide Compound consisting of two or more linked AMINO ACID molecules. Peptides containing several amino acids are called polypeptides. PROTEINS consist of polypeptide chains with up to several hundred amino acids cross-linked to each other in various ways.

Pepys, Samuel (1633–1703) English diarist. His *Diary* (1660–69) describes his private life and the English society of his time. It includes a vivid account of the RESTORATION, the 1661 coronation ceremony, the PLAGUE, and the Great FIRE OF LONDON of 1666. Written in shorthand, it was not published until 1815, and not in complete form until 1983.

percentage Quantity expressed as the number of parts in 100 (considered to be a whole). Fractions can be expressed as a percentage by multiplying by 100, i.e. 3/4 becomes 75%.

perception Process by which the brain acquires and organizes incoming stimuli from the sensory nerves, translating them into meaningful information. *See also* EPISTEMOLOGY; MIND

perch One of two species of freshwater food fish. The European perch (*Perca fluviatilis*) is deep-bodied and greenish in colour with dark vertical banding. The North American yellow perch (*P. flavescens*) is gold-coloured with black sidebars. Weight: 1.0–2.7kg (2.2–6lb). Family Percidae.

percussion Term for any of several musical instruments that produce sound when struck with a beater or the hand. They are divided into two groups: **ideophones**, in which the whole object vibrates when struck (such as cymbals and XYLOPHONES); and **membranophones**, in which a stretched skin or membrane vibrates a column of air (this group includes all DRUMS).

Percy, Sir Henry (1364–1403) English noble, known as 'Hotspur' for his zeal in guarding the Scottish-English border. Son of the Earl of Northumberland, he supported the deposition of RICHARD II in 1299, but later quarrelled with the new king, HENRY IV. In 1403 Percy and his father, in alliance with Owain GLYN DŴR, launched a rebellion. They were defeated at Shrewsbury, W England, where Percy was killed.

peregrine falcon Crow-sized, grey, black and white BIRD OF PREY. It inhabits craggy open country or rocky coastlines and marshes or estuaries. The largest breeding FALCON in Britain, it flies swiftly with prolonged glides. Length: to 48cm (19in). Family Falconidae; species *Falco peregrinus*.

perennial Plant with a life cycle of more than two years. It is a common term for flowering herbaceous and woody plants, such as the LILY, DAISY, and all trees. *See also* ANNUAL; BIENNIAL

Peres, Shimon (1923–) Israeli statesman, prime minister (1986–88, 1995–96), president (2007–), b. Belarus. Elected to the Knesset in 1959, Peres was a founder (1968) of the Labour Party. He served in the cabinet under Golda MEIR, and became minister of defence under Yitzhak RABIN. In 1977, he succeeded Rabin as leader of the Labour Party, and led Labour to a narrow victory in 1984 elections. Unable to form a government, Peres entered a power-sharing arrangement with Yitzhak SHAMIR. In 1992, he lost the party leadership to Rabin, and subsequently served as foreign minister under him. Peres, Rabin and Yasir ARAFAT shared the 1994 Nobel Prize for peace for their roles in the ISRAELI-PALESTINIAN ACCORD. Peres returned as prime minister after Rabin's assassination (1995), but was narrowly defeated in 1996 elections by Binyamin NETANYAHU and stood down as Labour leader in favour of Ehud BARAK. Peres served as minister of regional cooperation (1999–2001) under Barak and foreign minister (2001–05), then vice premier (2005–7). In 2007 elections he became president.

perestroika (Rus. reconstruction) Adopted by Soviet President Mikhail GORBACHEV in 1986, *perestroika* was linked with GLASNOST. The restructuring included reform of government and the bureaucracy, decentralization and abolition of the COMMUNIST PARTY monopoly. Liberalization of the economic system included the introduction of limited private enterprise and freer movement of prices.

Pérez de Cuéllar, Javier (1920–) Peruvian diplomat, fifth secretary-general of the UNITED NATIONS (UN) (1982–91). He emerged as a successful compromise candidate following oppo-

PERISTALSIS

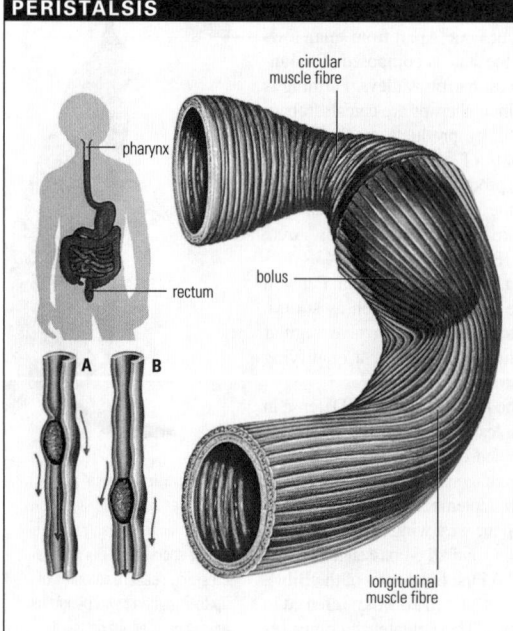

circular muscle fibre

pharynx

bolus

rectum

A   B

longitudinal muscle fibre

The digestive tract can be regarded as a long muscular tube, extending from the pharynx to the rectum. The walls of the tube bear an inner, circular muscle fibre coat and an outer, longitudinal muscle fibre coat. As the ball of food (bolus) formed in the mouth enters the pharynx, a reflex action begins. This produces slow, wave-like contractions of the walls of the oesophagus and later along the whole length of the tract. These peristaltic waves involve the contraction of the circular muscle fibres behind the bolus (A), and their relaxation in front of the bolus. Longitudinal muscles provide the wave-like action. The two functions combine to force the ball down the tract (B). The whole process of peristalsis is an involuntary response.

sition to the re-election of Kurt WALDHEIM. He earned a reputation for skillful diplomacy in the ceasefire agreements at the end of the FALKLANDS WAR (1982) and the IRAN-IRAQ WAR (1980–88). He was succeeded by Boutros BOUTROS-GHALI.

performance art Events that take place before an audience, but which defy the traditional definitions of DRAMA and MUSIC. Arguably originating in the USA in the 1960s, performance art is often visually oriented.

perfume Substance that produces a pleasing fragrance. The scents of such plants as rose, citrus, lavender, and sandalwood are obtained from their essential oils. These are blended with a fixative of animal origin, such as musk, ambergris or civet. Liquid perfumes are usually alcoholic solutions containing 10–25% of the perfume concentrate; colognes and toilet waters contain about 2–6% of the concentrate.

Pergamum Ancient city-state on the site of modern Bergama, W Turkey. It was founded by Greek colonists under licence from the Persian Emperors in the 4th century BC. At its peak in the 3rd-2nd centuries BC it controlled much of W Asia Minor. In 133 BC it was bequeathed to Rome by Attalus III.

Pergolesi, Giovanni Battista (1710–36) Italian composer. His intermezzo, *La Serva Padrona* (1733), became a model for Italian OPERA BUFFA. His *Stabat Mater* (1730) is one of the finest examples of religious music of the Baroque period.

Peri, Jacopo (1561–1633) Italian composer. His musical drama *Dafne* (1597) is generally regarded as the first opera. His next opera, *Euridice* (1600), is the earliest complete opera.

perianth Outer region of a flower. The perianth includes all the structures surrounding the reproductive organs and usually consists of an outer whorl of sepals (calyx) and an inner whorl of petals (corolla).

pericarp In seed plants, the wall of a ripened fruit that is derived from the ovary wall. The tissues of the pericarp may be fibrous, stony, or fleshy.

Pericles (*c*.490–*c*.429 BC) Athenian statesman. He dominated Athens from *c*.460 BC to his death, overseeing its golden age. He is associated with achievements in art and literature, including the building of the PARTHENON, while strengthening the Athenian Empire and the government. Believing war with Sparta to be inevitable, he initiated the PELOPONNESIAN WAR (431–404BC) but died of plague at the outset.

peridot Gem variety of transparent green OLIVINE, a silicate mineral. Large crystals are found on St John's Island in the Red Sea and in Burma (Myanmar).

peridotite Heavy IGNEOUS ROCK of coarse texture composed of olivine and pyroxene with small flecks of mica or hornblende. It alters readily into SERPENTINE.

perigee Point in the ORBIT about the Earth of the Moon or of an artificial satellite, at which the body is nearest to the Earth.

perihelion Point in the ORBIT of a planet, asteroid, comet or other body (such as a spacecraft) moving around the Sun at which the body is nearest the Sun.

periodic table Arrangement of the chemical elements in order of their ATOMIC NUMBERS in accordance with the periodic law first stated by chemist Dmitri MENDELEYEV in 1869. The metallic TRANSITION ELEMENTS are arranged in the middle of the table between groups II and III. ALKALI METALS are in group I, and ALKALINE-EARTH METALS in Group II. Metalloids and nonmetals are found from groups III to VII, with the HALOGENS in group VII and the NOBLE GASES (inert gases) collected into group 0. The elements in each group have the same number of VALENCE electrons and accordingly have similar chemical properties. Elements in the same horizontal period have the same number of electron shells. *See table below*

peripheral nervous system All parts of the nervous system that lie outside the CENTRAL NERVOUS SYSTEM. It comprises the 12 pairs of cranial nerves, which principally serve the head and neck region, and 31 pairs of spinal nerves with their fibres extending to the farthermost parts of the body.

periscope Optical instrument consisting of a series of mirrors or prisms that allows a person to view the surroundings from a concealed position by changing the direction of the observer's line of sight. Since World War 1, the periscope has been most commonly associated with SUBMARINES.

peristalsis Series of wave-like movements that propel food through the gut or digestive tract. It is caused by contractions of the smooth INVOLUNTARY MUSCLE of the gut wall. The reverse process, antiperistalsis, produces vomiting.

peritoneum Strong membrane of CONNECTIVE TISSUE that lines the body's abdominal wall and covers the abdominal organs. *See also* PERITONITIS

peritonitis Inflammation of the PERITONEUM, caused by bacterial infection or chemical irritation or it may arise spontaneously in certain diseases. Symptoms include fever, abdominal pain and distension and shock.

periwinkle Any of several species of trailing or erect evergreen plants that are cultivated as ground cover and for hanging baskets. Family Apocynaceae.

▲ **Peres** A co-recipient of the 1994 Nobel Peace Prize, Shimon Peres was actively involved in the Camp David Agreement and the Israeli-Palestinian Accord. He sought a truce in the conflict that followed Ariel Sharon's election as Israeli prime minister in 2001.

▼ **periodic table** Chemical elements are arranged according to their atomic number. The vertical columns, called groups, contain elements with similar chemical properties. The horizontal rows, called periods, are arranged in order of increasing atomic number and all elements in a row have the same number of electron shells. Elements coloured green in the table are non-metals; those coloured orange are metals; those coloured yellow are metalloid; those coloured blue, purple or pink are transition metals, the purple ones are the rare-earth elements, and the pink ones the transactinide elements.

PERIODIC TABLE

GROUP I	II													III	IV	V	VI	VII	0
1 **H** Hydrogen 1.00794																			2 **He** Helium 4.0026
3 **Li** Lithium 6.941	4 **Be** Beryllium 9.0122													5 **B** Boron 10.81	6 **C** Carbon 12.011	7 **N** Nitrogen 14.0067	8 **O** Oxygen 15.9994	9 **F** Fluorine 18.998	10 **Ne** Neon 20.179
11 **Na** Sodium 22.9898	12 **Mg** Magnesium 24.305													13 **Al** Aluminium 26.9815	14 **Si** Silicon 28.086	15 **P** Phosphorus 30.9738	16 **S** Sulphur 32.06	17 **Cl** Chlorine 35.453	18 **Ar** Argon 39.948
19 **K** Potassium 39.098	20 **Ca** Calcium 40.06	21 **Sc** Scandium 44.956	22 **Ti** Titanium 47.90	23 **V** Vanadium 50.941	24 **Cr** Chromium 51.996	25 **Mn** Manganese 54.9380	26 **Fe** Iron 55.847	27 **Co** Cobalt 58.9332	28 **Ni** Nickel 58.70	29 **Cu** Copper 63.546	30 **Zn** Zinc 65.38	31 **Ga** Gallium 69.72	32 **Ge** Germanium 72.59	33 **As** Arsenic 74.9216	34 **Se** Selenium 78.96	35 **Br** Bromine 79.904	36 **Kr** Krypton 83.80
37 **Rb** Rubidium 85.4678	38 **Sr** Strontium 87.62	39 **Y** Yttrium 88.906	40 **Zr** Zirconium 91.22	41 **Nb** Niobium 92.906	42 **Mo** Molybdenum 95.94	43 **Tc** Technetium [97]	44 **Ru** Ruthenium 101.07	45 **Rh** Rhodium 102.905	46 **Pd** Palladium 106.4	47 **Ag** Silver 107.868	48 **Cd** Cadmium 112.40	49 **In** Indium 114.82	50 **Sn** Tin 118.69	51 **Sb** Antimony 121.75	52 **Te** Tellurium 127.60	53 **I** Iodine 126.9045	54 **Xe** Xenon 131.30
55 **Cs** Caesium 132.905	56 **Ba** Barium 137.34	57–71 Lanthanide Series	72 **Hf** Hafnium 178.49	73 **Ta** Tantalum 180.948	74 **W** Tungsten 183.85	75 **Re** Rhenium 186.207	76 **Os** Osmium 190.2	77 **Ir** Iridium 192.22	78 **Pt** Platinum 195.09	79 **Au** Gold 196.9665	80 **Hg** Mercury 200.59	81 **Tl** Thallium 204.37	82 **Pb** Lead 207.2	83 **Bi** Bismuth 208.98	84 **Po** Polonium [209]	85 **At** Astatine [210]	86 **Rn** Radon [222]
87 **Fr** Francium [223]	88 **Ra** Radium [226]	89–103 Actinide Series	104 **Rf** Dubnium [261]	105 **Db**§ Hahnium [262]	106 **Rf** Rutherfordium [263]	107 **Uns** Unnilseptium [262]	108 **Uno** Unniloctium [265]	109 **Une** Unnilenium [266]											

KEY
atomic number — 43
atomic symbol — **Tc**
name of element — Technetium
relative atomic mass — [97]
(most stable isotope in brackets)

LANTHANIDE SERIES (rare earth elements)	57 **La** Lanthanum 138.9055	58 **Ce** Cerium 140.12	59 **Pr** Praseodymium 140.9077	60 **Nd** Neodymium 144.24	61 **Pm** Promethium [145]	62 **Sm** Samarium 150.36	63 **Eu** Europium 151.96	64 **Gd** Gadolinium 157.25	65 **Tb** Terbium 158.9254	66 **Dy** Dysprosium 162.50	67 **Ho** Holmium 164.9308	68 **Er** Erbium 167.26	69 **Tm** Thulium 168.9342	70 **Yb** Ytterbium 173.04	71 **Lu** Lutetium 174.97
ACTINIDE SERIES (radioactive rare earth elements)	89 **Ac** Actinium [227]	90 **Th** Thorium 232.0381	91 **Pa** Protactinium 231.0359	92 **U** Uranium 238.029	93 **Np** Neptunium 237.0482	94 **Pu** Plutonium [244]	95 **Am** Americium [243]	96 **Cm** Curium [247]	97 **Bk** Berkelium [247]	98 **Cf** Californium [251]	99 **Es** Einsteinium [254]	100 **Fm** Fermium [257]	101 **Md** Mendelevium [256]	102 **No** Nobelium [254]	103 **Lr** Lawrencium [256]

§Another proposed name is unnilpentium

periwinkle (winkle) Any of several marine snails, gastropod molluscs that live in clusters along marine shores. A herbivore, it nestles in cracks among rocks. Many are edible. Length: to 2.5cm (1in). Family Littorinidea; genus *Littorina*.

permafrost Land that is permanently frozen, often to a great depth. The top few centimetres generally thaw in the summer, but the meltwater is not able to sink into the ground because of the frozen subsoil. If the landscape is flat, surface water lies on the ground throughout the summer. Construction work is difficult, and many methods have been used in Russia, Canada and Alaska to overcome the problems. *See also* TUNDRA

permeability (symbol μ) In physics, ratio of the MAGNETIC FLUX density in a body to the external MAGNETIC FIELD inducing it. This means a magnetic field is related to, and altered by, the presence of a substance it surrounds. The permeability of free space is called the **magnetic constant** (symbol μ_0), and has the value $4\pi \times 10^{-7}$ henry per metre. The **relative** permeability of a substance (symbol μ_r) is the ratio of its permeability to the magnetic constant.

Permian Geological period of the PALAEOZOIC era lasting from 286 to 248 million years ago. There was widespread geologic uplift and mostly cool, dry climates with periods of glaciation in the southern continents. Many groups of marine invertebrate animals became extinct during the period.

Perón, Eva Duarte de (1919–52) Argentine dancer and politician, second wife of Juan PERÓN. Known as 'Evita', she administered Argentina's social welfare agencies and was the country's chief labour mediator. Eva's popularity contributed to the longevity of the Perónist regime.

Perón, Juan Domingo (1895–1974) Argentine statesman, president (1946–55, 1973–74). An army officer, he became the leading figure in the military junta (1943–46). Perón cultivated the trade unions and earned support from the poor by social reforms, greatly assisted by his wife 'Evita' PERÓN. He won the 1946 presidential election, and was re-elected in 1952. His populist programme was basically nationalist and totalitarian. Changing economic circumstances and the death of his wife reduced Perón's popularity, and he was overthrown in 1955. He retired to Spain, but returned to regain the presidency. Marred by violence, his second term was cut short by his death.

perpendicular style Final period of English GOTHIC architecture, from *c.*1330 to the mid-16th century. Named after the strong vertical lines of its window tracery and panelling, characteristic features are fan vaulting and flattened arches.

perpetual motion Hypothetical machine that continues to work without any energy being supplied. Such a machine would require either the complete elimination of FRICTION, or would have to violate the laws of THERMODYNAMICS.

Perrault, Charles (1628–1703) French poet and prose writer. A leading member of the Académie Française from 1671, he is best remembered for *Tales of Mother Goose* (1697).

Perry, Fred (Frederick John) (1909–95) English tennis and table-tennis player. World table-tennis champion in 1929, he won three successive Wimbledon tennis singles titles (1934–36). He also won the US, French and Australian titles.

Perry, Matthew Calbraith (1794–1858) US naval officer. In 1837, he commanded the first steam vessel in the US Navy, the *Fulton*. He also established the Navy's apprentice system in 1837, and organized the first naval engineer corps. He was responsible for opening up Japan to the West (1853–54).

Persephone In Greek mythology, goddess of spring. She was the daughter of ZEUS and the Earth goddess DEMETER. When HADES, king of the underworld, abducted Persephone to be his wife, famine spread over the Earth. To prevent catastrophe, Zeus commanded Hades to release her. He did so, and thus, each year, spring returns to the Earth. Persephone was known as Proserpine to the Romans.

Persepolis City of ancient Persia (Iran), *c.*60km (37mi) NE of SHIRAZ. As the capital (539–330BC) of the ACHAEMENID Empire, it was renowned for its splendour. It was destroyed by the forces of ALEXANDER THE GREAT in 330 BC.

Perseus In astronomy, a prominent northern constellation. Perseus is a rich constellation, crossed by the Milky Way.

Perseus In Greek mythology, son of Danaë and ZEUS. Perseus beheaded the snake-haired gorgon MEDUSA, turned

ATLAS to stone and rescued the princess ANDROMEDA from being sacrificed to a sea monster.

Pershing, John Joseph (1860–1948) US general. Pershing led a punitive expedition against Pancho VILLA in Mexico (1916) before being appointed to command the American Expeditionary Force (AEF) in World War 1 (1917–19). Returning a hero, he later served as army chief of staff (1921–24). A US surface-to-surface nuclear missile is named after him.

Persia Old, western name for IRAN, SW Asia. The earliest empire in the region was that of Media (*c.*700–549BC). CYRUS THE GREAT toppled Media and established the ACHAEMENID empire (549–330BC), in turn destroyed by ALEXANDER THE GREAT. In the 3rd century BC the Parthians supplanted his successors, the SELEUCIDS. In AD 224, Ardashir I established the SASSANID dynasty. Weakened by defeat by the Byzantines under HERACLIUS, it was overrun by Arabs in the 7th century.

Persian (Farsi, Iranian) Official language of IRAN. It is spoken by nearly all of Iran's population as a first or second language. It is also widely used in Afghanistan. Persian belongs to the Indo-Iranian family of INDO-EUROPEAN LANGUAGES. Persian has borrowed from ARABIC and is written in the Arabic script.

Persian art Earliest manifestations of art in Persia (Iran) prior to the 7th-century development of ISLAMIC ART AND ARCHITECTURE. The oldest pottery and engraved seals date back to *c.*3500 BC. The greatest achievements of Persian art occurred during the rule of the ACHAEMENID (*c.*550–330BC) and SASSANID (AD 224–642) dynasties. The former is best represented by the low relief carvings and massive gateway figures executed for the palace of Darius at PERSEPOLIS. The Sassanians excelled at metalwork and sculpture.

Persian Gulf (Arabian Gulf) Arm of the Arabian Sea between Arabia and the Asian mainland, and connected to it by the Strait of Hormuz and the Gulf of Oman. European powers began to move into the region in the 17th century. Britain had achieved supremacy in the Gulf by the mid-19th century. The discovery of oil in the 1930s increased its importance and, especially after the British withdrawal in the 1960s, both the USA and the Soviet Union sought to increase their influence in the region. Tension was heightened by the IRAN-IRAQ WAR in the 1980s, and the GULF WAR against Iraq in 1991. The Gulf remains a major shipping and oil supply route. Area: *c.*240,000sq km (93,000sq mi).

Persian mythology, ancient Beliefs of the ancient Persian (Iranian) people. The oldest Persian deity was Mithra, who was identified with the sun. He was a god of courage and enlightenment, and led the chariot of the sun across the sky on its daily journey. He was associated with Anahita, the goddess of water and of fertility. In the Zoroastrian period, Mithra became subordinate to AHURA MAZDAH, worshipped by the ACHAEMENID Kings of Persia as the creator and ruler of the world. Ahura Mazdah was engaged in an eternal conflict with Ahriman, the principle of evil. At a later period, both Ahura Mazdah and Ahriman (or Angra Mainyu) were regarded as the twin offspring of Zurvan (Time). Their cosmic struggle would end ultimately with the victory of Ahura Mazdah.

Persian Wars (499–479BC) Conflict between the ancient Greeks and Persians. In 499 BC the IONIAN cities of Asia Minor rebelled against Persian rule. Athens sent a fleet to aid them. Persian Emperor DARIUS I invaded Greece but suffered a defeat at MARATHON (490BC). In 480 BC his successor, XERXES, burned Athens but withdrew after defeats at Salamis and Plataea (479BC). Under Athenian leadership, the Greeks fought on, regaining territory in Thrace and Anatolia, until the outbreak of the PELOPONNESIAN WAR (431BC).

persimmon Any of several types of tree of the genus *Diospyros*. It produces reddish-orange fruit, which is sour and astringent until ripe. Species include the North American persimmon (*D. virginiana*) and the Japanese persimmon (*D. kaki*). Family Ebenaceae.

personality Emotional, attitudinal and behavioural characteristics that distinguish an individual. Psychologists use the term to refer to enduring, long-term characteristics of a person. Personality traits are assessed by a variety of methods, including personality tests and projective techniques. Influential theories of personality in psychology include

Sigmund FREUD'S PSYCHOANALYSIS, Carl JUNG's theories of personality types, and social theories, which examine the influence of the environment on personality.

perspective Method of showing three-dimensional objects and spatial relationships in a two-dimensional image. The linear perspective system is based on the idea that parallel lines converge at a vanishing point as they recede into the distance. It was outlined in the 15th century by BRUNELLESCHI, and developed by MASACCIO and UCCELLO.

Perth City on the Swan River, SW Australia; capital of Western Australia. Founded in 1829, the city grew rapidly after the discovery of gold at Coolgardie in the 1890s, the development of the port at Fremantle and the construction of railways to the E in the early 20th century. Industries: textiles, cement, food processing, motor vehicles. Pop. (2005) 1,484,000.

Peru Republic in W South America. *See* country feature

Perugia City on the Tiber River, central Italy; capital of Perugia province. A major Etruscan city, Perugia passed to Rome in 310 BC. The Lombards captured it in the 6th century AD and it became a duchy. Perugia was the scene of various power struggles, before subdued by the papacy in 1540. In 1860

Perugia joined a united Italy. The artistic centre of UMBRIA, tourism and commerce dominate Perugia's modern economy. Its chocolate is world-renowned. Pop. (1999) 156,673.

Perugino, Pietro Vannucci (1445–1523) Italian painter, an important figure in the art of the early Renaissance. He was a notable fresco painter. His *Christ Delivering the Keys to St Peter*, painted for the Sistine Chapel in Rome, did much to establish his reputation. He was also a skilled portraitist, and was well known for his altarpieces.

Peshawar City in NW Pakistan, 16km (9mi) E of the KHYBER PASS. An ancient settlement, it has always had great strategic importance. Brought under Muslim rule in the 10th century, it fell to the Afghans in the 16th century. Conquered by the Sikhs in 1834, it was annexed by Britain in 1849. In 1948, it became part of Pakistan. In the 1980s and 1990s, it was a base for rebel groups operating in Afghanistan. The city is famous for its handicrafts, carpets, and leather goods. Pop. (2005) 1,255,000.

Pestalozzi, Johann Heinrich (1746–1827) Swiss educational reformer whose theories formed the basis of modern elementary education. His books include *How Gertrude Teaches Her Children* (1801).

PERU

The Republic of Peru lies in the tropics in W South America. A narrow coastal plain borders the Pacific Ocean in the west. Inland are ranges of the ANDES Mountains, which rise to 6,768m [22,205ft] at Mount Huascarán, an extinct volcano. The Andes also contain active volcanoes, windswept plateaux, broad valleys and, in the far S, part of Lake TITICACA – the world's highest navigable lake. To the E the Andes descend to a hilly region and a huge plain. E Peru is part of the AMAZON basin.

CLIMATE

LIMA, on the coastal plain, has an arid climate. The coastal region is chilled by the cold offshore Humboldt Current. In the Andes, temperatures are moderated by altitude; many mountains are snow-capped. The E lowlands are hot and humid.

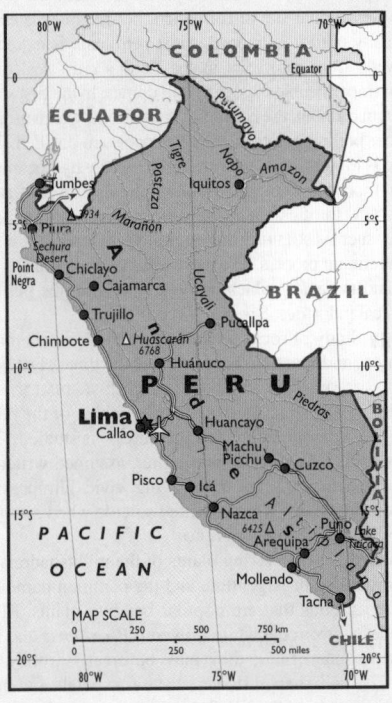

MAP SCALE

HISTORY

Native American civilizations developed more than 10,000 years ago. In *c.*AD 1200 the INCA established a capital at CUZCO. By 1500, their empire extended from Ecuador to Chile. The Spanish conquistador Francisco Pizarro visited Peru in the 1520s. Hearing of Inca riches, he returned in 1532 and captured the Inca ruler ATAHUALPA. By 1533 he had conquered most of Peru, and in 1535, he founded Lima. In 1544, Lima became capital of Spain's South American empire. Spain's rule caused frequent native revolts, such as that of Tupac Amaru.

In 1820 the Argentinian José de SAN MARTÍN led an army into Peru and declared the country to be independent. However, Spain still held large areas. In 1823, the Venezuelan Simón BOLÍVAR led another army into Peru and, in 1824, one of his generals defeated the Spaniards at Ayacucho. The Spaniards surrendered in 1826.

In 1836 Peru and Bolivia formed a short-lived confederation. In the War of the Pacific (1879–84) Peru lost some of its S provinces to Chile. The early 20th century was characterized by dictatorship and a growing gap between the wealthy oligarchy and an impoverished native population. From 1968 to 1980 a military junta blocked democratic reforms.

POLITICS

When civilian rule was restored in 1980, a Maoist group called the Shining Path began guerrilla warfare against the government. In 1990 Alberto Fujimori, son of Japanese immigrants, became president. In 1992 he suspended the constitution and dismissed the legislature. Shining Path leader Abimael Guzmán was arrested in 1992, but instability continued.

In 1993 a new constitution increased Fujimori's power. In 1996 Tupac Amaru (MRTA) rebels seized the Japanese ambassador's residence, taking hostages and demanding the release of guerrilla prisoners. The stalemate ended in April 1997 when Peruvian troops attacked and freed the remaining 72 hostages.

AREA 1,285,216sq km [496,222sq mi]
POPULATION 28,675,000
CAPITAL (POPULATION)
Lima (8,180,000)
GOVERNMENT Constitutional republic
ETHNIC GROUPS Mestizo (Spanish-Indian) 44%, Creole (mainly African American) 30%, Mayan Indian 11%, Garifuna (Black-Carib Indian) 7%, others 8%
LANGUAGES English (official), Creole, Spanish
RELIGIONS Roman Catholic 62%, Protestant 30%
CURRENCY Belize dollar = 100 cents

Fujimori began his third term as president in 2000, but in November the Congress declared him 'morally unfit' to govern. He resigned and sought sanctuary in Japan. In his absence he was banned from holding office until 2011. In 2005 the government began an attempt to extradite Fujimori and put him on trial for financial corruption and sanctioning death squads. In 2001 Alejandro Toledo became the first Peruvian of Amerindian descent to hold the office of president.

The years 2003–4 saw a resurgence of activity by Shining Path guerillas. By the time they were finally suppressed in 2005–6 *c.* 70,000 had been killed in their rebellion. Guzmán was sentenced to life imprisonment in 2006.

Toledo struggled to fight poverty, and was replaced by Alan Garcia in 2006 elections. In 2007 he claimed emergency powers, declaring them necessary to tackle organized crime.

ECONOMY

The World Bank classifies Peru as a 'lower-middle-income' developing country. Agriculture employs 35% of the workforce and major food crops include beans, maize, potatoes and rice. Coffee, cotton and sugar are the chief cash crops. Many farmers live at subsistence level. Other farms are co-operatives. Fishing is important.

Peru is one of the world's main producers of copper, silver and zinc. Iron ore, lead and oil are also produced, while gold is mined in the highlands. Most manufacturing is small-scale.

▲ **Pfeiffer** One of Hollywood's most popular leading actresses, Michelle Pfeiffer rose to stardom with her role in *The Witches of Eastwick* in 1987. Since then, she received three Academy Award nominations. A versatile actress, Pfeiffer played a wide range of roles, from a gangster's moll in *Married to the Mob* (1988), to the sheltered southerner who finds independence in *Love Field* (1992), and the seductive Catwoman in *Batman Returns* (1992).

pesticide Chemical substance that is used to kill insects, rodents, weeds and other pests. Among pesticides, a HERBICIDE is used for weeds, an insecticide for insects and a FUNGICIDE for fungal pests. Pesticides are usually harmful chemicals and an important factor in their manufacture is that they should decompose after they have performed their function. Some previously common pesticides, such as DDT, have been shown to be too toxic and long-lasting, so an international treaty to ban them was signed in 2001 in Stockholm, Sweden.

Pétain, Henri Philippe (1856–1951) French general and politician. In World War 1, his defence of VERDUN (1916) made him a national hero. He was appointed commander-in-chief in 1917, and held high positions between the world wars. With the defeat of France in 1940, he was recalled as prime minister. He signed the surrender and became head of the collaborationist VICHY regime. He was charged with treason after the liberation of France in 1945 and died in prison.

petal Part of a flower. The petals of a flower are together known as the corolla. Surrounded by SEPALS, flower petals are often brightly coloured and may secrete nectar and perfume to attract the insects and birds necessary for cross-pollination. Once fertilization occurs, the petals usually drop off.

Peter, Saint (d. *c*.64) APOSTLE of JESUS CHRIST. He was born Simon, son of Jonas. A fisherman on the Sea of Galilee, he and his brother ANDREW were called by Jesus to be disciples. Jesus gave Simon the name Peter (John 1:42). Peter was one of Jesus' closest and most loyal associates. With James and John, he witnessed the Transfiguration. While Jesus was on trial before the SANHEDRIN, Peter denied knowing him three times, just as Jesus had predicted. After Jesus' ascension, Peter was the first publicly to preach Christianity in Jerusalem. He took Christianity to Samaria. Imprisoned by King Herod, he was allegedly rescued by an angel and returned to Jerusalem. In his final years, he seems to have left Jerusalem and undertaken a missionary journey. Roman Catholic theology accepts him as the first head of the Church and the first bishop of Rome, from whom the popes claim succession. His feast day is June 29.

Peter I (the Great) (1672–1725) Russian Tsar (1682–1725), regarded as the founder of modern Russia. After ruling jointly with his half-brother Ivan (1682–89), he gained sole control in 1689. Peter employed foreign experts to modernize the army, transport, and technology. He compelled the aristocracy and the Church to serve the interests of the State, eliminating ancient tradition in favour of modernization. In the Great NORTHERN WAR, Russia replaced Sweden as the dominant power in N Europe, and gained lands on the Baltic, where Peter built his new capital, St Petersburg. In the E, he warred against Turks and Persians and initiated the exploration of Siberia.

Peter I (1844–1921) King of Serbia (1903–21), son of Alexander Karageorgevic. He was educated in France while the Obrenovic dynasty ruled Serbia. He was elected king after the assassination of Alexander Obrenovic. In 1918, he became the first king of the new kingdom of Serbs, Croats and Slovenes (later Yugoslavia). He was succeeded by his son, ALEXANDER I.

Peter II (1923–70) Last King of Yugoslavia (1934–41), son of ALEXANDER I. He acceded the throne (aged 12) on the assassination of his father. The actual ruler was his uncle, Prince Paul, deposed in 1941 by a military coup. Peter ruled for a month until the invasion of the AXIS POWERS, when he fled to London. After the monarchy was abolished in 1945, he lived in the USA.

Peterloo Massacre (August 16, 1819) Violent suppression of a political protest in Manchester, NW England. A large crowd, demonstrating for reform of Parliament, was dispersed by soldiers. Eleven people were killed and 500 injured.

Petipa, Marius (1819–1910) Russian dancer and choreographer. He rose to fame in 1847 as principal dancer at the Maryinski Theatre, St Petersburg, and was choreographer of the Imperial Russian Ballet (1862–1903). His *Don Quixote* (1869), *Sleeping Beauty* (1890), and *Raymonda* (1898) laid the foundations of classical ballet. *See also* KIROV BALLET

petition of right Means by which an English subject could sue the Crown; in particular, the statement of grievances against the Crown presented by Parliament to CHARLES I in 1628. It asserted that the Crown acted illegally in raising tax-ation without Parliament's consent, imprisoning people without charge, maintaining a standing army, and quartering soldiers on ordinary householders. It led to the dissolution of Parliament and Charles' period of untrammelled rule.

Petra Ancient city in what is now SW Jordan. It was the capital of the Nabataean kingdom from the 4th century BC. It was captured by the Romans in the 2nd century AD. The city, which was rediscovered in 1812 and is the scene of extensive excavation, can be reached only through narrow gorges. Many of its remarkable, ruined houses, temples, theatres and tombs were cut from the high, pinkish sandstone cliffs that protected it.

Petrarch, Francesco (1304–74) Italian lyric poet and scholar. Most of his lyric poems, *Rime sparse*, have as their subject 'Laura', a woman idealized in the style of earlier poets but seen in a more realistic and human light. Other works, which include an autobiography (1342–58), further illuminate his belief in the compatibility of classical and Christian traditions.

petrel Any of several small oceanic birds related to the ALBATROSS. Most nest in colonies and fly over open water, feeding on squid and small fish. They have webbed feet and tubular nostrils. Length: to 42cm (16in). Order Procellariiformes.

petrochemical Chemical substance derived from PETROLEUM or NATURAL GAS. The refining of petroleum is undertaken not only for fuels but also for a wide range of chemicals such as ALKANES (paraffins) and ALKENES (olefins), BENZENE, TOLUENE, NAPHTHALENE, and their derivatives. They are used to produce detergents and nitrogen fertilizers.

petrol (gasoline) Major HYDROCARBON fuel, a mixture consisting mainly of hexane, octane and heptane. One of the products of OIL refining, petrol is extracted from crude oil (PETROLEUM). Most modern cars have high-compression INTERNAL COMBUSTION ENGINES, and the mixture of air and petrol vapour supplied to it can explode too quickly, pushing against a rising instead of a descending piston. This effect is known as engine knock, and to eliminate it many petrol manufacturers add lead (IV) tetraethyl to slow the rate of combustion. However, this additive has been found to be implicated in atmospheric pollution and causes brain damage, and so many manufacturers omit the additive and instead improve the OCTANE NUMBER of the petrol by altering the mixture of hydrocarbons.

petrol engine *See* INTERNAL COMBUSTION ENGINE

petroleum (crude OIL) FOSSIL FUEL that is chemically a complex mixture of HYDROCARBONS. It accumulates in underground deposits and the chemical composition of petroleum strongly suggests that it originated from the bodies of dead organisms, particularly marine PLANKTON. Petroleum is rarely found at the original site of formation, but migrates laterally and vertically until it is trapped. Most petroleum is extracted via oil wells from reservoirs in the Earth's crust sealed by upfolds of impermeable rock or by salt domes. In the first stage of petroleum refining, the heavier hydrocarbons, which usually have higher boiling points than lighter ones, are distilled. The next stage is CRACKING, which breaks the heavy hydrocarbons down into more economically useful products, such as PETROL and PARAFFIN. Purification of the various products to remove impurities, such as SULPHUR and NITROGEN compounds, completes the refining process. The most versatile end products are ETHENE and PROPENE, which are widely used in the plastics and chemical industries. *See also* NATURAL GAS

petrology Study of rocks, including their origin, chemical composition, and location. Formation of the three classes of rocks – IGNEOUS (of volcanic origin); SEDIMENTARY (deposited by water); and METAMORPHIC (either of the other two changed by temperature and pressure) – is studied.

Petronius (d. *c*.AD 66) Roman writer, assumed writer of the *Satyricon*, a humorous tale giving vivid glimpses of contemporary society. He committed suicide when accused of plotting against Emperor NERO.

petunia Genus of flowering plants of the nightshade family that originated in Argentina, and the common name for the any of varieties that are popular bedding plants. Most varieties derive from the white flowered *P. axillaris* and the violet-red *P. integrifolia*; they may be erect, shrubby, or pendant. The bell-shaped flowers have five petals and may be almost any colour. Family Solanaceae.

Pevsner, Antoine (1886–1962) French sculptor, b. Russia, brother of Naum GABO. Initially influenced by CUBISM, he later became a leading exponent of CONSTRUCTIVISM, creating works in bronze and other materials. In the 1930s, Pevsner concentrated on NON-FIGURATIVE structures such as *Projections in Space*. Later works include *Monument Symbolizing the Liberation of the Spirit* (1956).

pewter Any of several silver-coloured, soft alloys that consist mainly of tin and lead. The most common form has about four parts of tin to one of lead, combined with small amounts of antimony and copper.

peyote (mescal) Either of two species of cactus of the genus *Laphophora* that grow in the USA. The soft-stemmed *L. williamsii* has pink or white flowers in summer and a blue-green stem. *L. diffusa* has white or yellow flowers. Peyote contains many ALKALOIDS, the principal one being **mescaline**, a hallucinogenic drug.

Pfeiffer, Michelle (1958–) US film actress. Pfeiffer first attracted attention in *Witches of Eastwick* (1987). She received an Academy nomination for best supporting actress in *Dangerous Liaisons* (1988), and gained further nominations for lead roles in *The Fabulous Baker Boys* (1989) and *Love Field* (1992). Other films include *Frankie and Johnny* (1991), *Batman Returns* (1992), and *The Age of Innocence* (1993).

pH Numerical scale that indicates the acidity or alkalinity of a solution. The pH value measures the concentration of hydrogen ions. The scale (introduced in 1909) runs from 0 to 14. A solution is acidic if the pH is less than 7 and alkaline if greater than 7. *See also* ACID; ALKALI; BASE

Phaedra In Greek mythology, the daughter of MINOS and the wife of THESEUS. She fell in love with her stepson HIPPOLYTUS. When Hippolytus spurned her advances, Phaedra accused him of raping her. Theseus condemend him to death and Phaedra hanged herself.

phaeophyte Any member of the phylum Phaeophyta, which consists of the brown ALGAE. Phaeophytes are part of the kingdom PROTOCTISTA. Classified by some biologists as plants, the organisms belonging to this group are mostly marine, found mainly in the intertidal zone of rocky shores. They include seaweeds such as *Fucus* (wracks) and *Ascophyllum* (bladderwrack). The largest, *Macrocystis*, grows to more than 100m (320ft) at up to 0.5m (18in) per day. *Sargassum* forms vast floating masses in the Sargasso Sea in the mid-Atlantic, with their own distinctive communities of animals and microorganisms.

Phaethon In Greek mythology, son of HELIOS, the Sun god. He drove his father's Sun chariot across the sky but lost control, setting the Earth on fire as he approached too close. To save the Earth, ZEUS struck him from the reins with a thunderbolt.

phagocyte Type of LEUCOCYTE (white blood cell) able to engulf other cells, such as bacteria. Part of the body's IMMUNE SYSTEM, it digests what it engulfs in the defence of the body against infection. Phagocytes also act as scavengers by clearing the bloodstream of the remains of the cells that die as part of the body's natural processes.

phalanger (possum) Any of around 45 species of mainly nocturnal, arboreal marsupials of Australasia. It has opposable digits for grasping branches and the tail is long and prehensile. Family Phalargeridae.

pharaoh Title of the rulers of ancient EGYPT. Though loosely applied to all Egyptian kings, the title was only adopted during the New Kingdom.

Pharisees Conservative Jewish religious group in ancient Palestine from the 2nd century BC to the time of the destruction of the second TEMPLE in Jerusalem (AD 70). For much of this period, they constituted a political party opposed to the pagan influences of their Greek and Roman conquerors, but by New Testament times they were largely non-political. They were the founders of orthodox JUDAISM and were often in conflict with the SADDUCEES.

pharmacology Study of the properties of DRUGS and their effects on the body. *See also* PHARMACOPOEIA

pharmacopoeia Reference book listing drugs and other preparations in medical use. Included are details of their formulae, dosages, routes of administration, known side-effects and precautions.

Pharos Island off the coast of N Egypt, in the Mediterranean, connected to the mainland by a causeway built by ALEXANDER THE GREAT. in *c*.280 BC Ptolemy II completed a lighthouse that was one of the SEVEN WONDERS OF THE WORLD. According to writers of the time, it was *c*.135m (450ft) tall, and its light could be seen 65km (40mi) away. In 1346 it was destroted by an earthquake. Pharos is now part of the city of ALEXANDRIA.

pharynx Cavity at the back of the nose and mouth that extends down towards the OESOPHAGUS and TRACHEA. It has muscles for swallowing and is part of the DIGESTIVE SYSTEM. Inflammation of the pharynx, usually caused by viral or bacterial infection, is known as pharyngitis.

phase Proportion of the illuminated hemisphere of a body in the Solar System (in particular the Moon or an inferior planet) as seen from Earth. The phase of a body changes as the Sun and the Earth change their relative positions. All the phases of the Moon (new, crescent, half, gibbous, and full) can be observed with the naked eye.

phase In physics, a stage or fraction in the cycle of an oscillation, such as the wave motion of light or sound waves. This is usually measured from an arbitrary starting point or compared with another motion of the same frequency. Two waves are said to be 'in phase' when their maximum and minimum values happen at the same time. If not, there is a 'phase difference', as seen in INTERFERENCE phenomenon. Phase can also refer to any one of the states of MATTER.

pheasant Gamebird of the genus *Phasianus* originally native to Asia, introduced into Europe and naturalized in North America. PEACOCKS and GUINEA FOWL belong to the same family. Males are showy, with brownish green, red and yellow feathers; females are smaller and brownish. Length: up to 89cm (35in). Family Phasianidae.

phenol Aromatic compound group whose members each have an attachment of a hydroxyl group to a carbon atom forming part of a BENZENE ring. The simplest of the family is also called phenol or **carbolic acid** (C_6H_5OH). Phenols are colourless liquids or white solids at room temperature. They are used by the chemical and pharmaceutical industries for such products as aspirin, dye, fungicide, explosive, and as a starting material for nylon and epoxy resin.

phenomenology Discipline in philosophy focusing on the study of human experience and consciousness. The term dates to the 18th century, although the idea is ancient. In the early 20th century, Edmund HUSSERL argued that phenomenology should be at the heart of philosophy. In contrast to EMPIRICISM, Husserl concentrated on the description of subjective experience. His ideas influenced the development of EXISTENTIALISM. *See also* HEIDEGGER, MARTIN; SARTRE, JEAN-PAUL

phenotype Physical characteristics of an organism resulting from HEREDITY. Phenotype is distinct from GENOTYPE, since not all aspects of genetic make-up manifest themselves. The phenotype also reflects the interaction of genotype and environment; for instance, a person inheriting a tallness gene may have growth restricted by poor nutrition or cigarette smoke.

pheromone Substance secreted externally by certain animals that influences the behaviour of members of the same species. Common in mammals and insects, these substances are often sexual attractants. They may be a component of body products such as urine, or secreted by specific glands.

Phidias (*c*.490–*c*.430 BC) Sculptor in ancient Greece. During his lifetime he was best known for two gigantic chryselephantine (gold and ivory) statues, one of Athena for the PARTHENON and the other of Zeus for the temple at Olympia. The Zeus was one of the SEVEN WONDERS OF THE WORLD.

◄ **pheasant** The golden pheasant (*Chrysolophus pictus*) is found in the highlands of central China. This pheasant is distinguished by its yellow head, rump and lower back, and by its golden collar edged in blue-black with red underparts. The golden pheasant is a member of a very diverse order (Galliformes), but all members have naked feet, no airsacs in the neck, and unfeathered nostrils.

P

Philadelphia City and port at the confluence of the Delaware and Schuylkill rivers, SE Pennsylvania, USA. The site was first settled by Swedes in the early 17th century. The city was founded by William PENN in 1681. By 1774, it was a major commercial, cultural and industrial centre of the American colonies and played an important part in the fight for independence. The CONTINENTAL CONGRESSES were held in the city, and the DECLARATION OF INDEPENDENCE was signed here in 1776. The CONSTITUTIONAL CONVENTION met in Philadelphia, and adopted the US Constitution in 1787. Philadelphia served as capital of the USA from 1790 to 1800. Industries: shipbuilding, textiles, chemicals, clothing, electrical equipment, vehicle parts, metal products, publishing and printing, oil refining, food processing. Pop. (2000) 5,149,000.

Philip, Saint (active 1st century AD) One of the 12 APOSTLES. Philip came from Bethsaida, on the Sea of Galilee. Tradition says he preached in Asia Minor and met a martyr's death. His feast day is May 3 (in the West) or November 14 (in the East). He appears to be different from **Philip the Evangelist**, one of the seven DEACONS who aided the apostles: the latter became Bishop of Tralles, now in Turkey. His feast day is June 9.

Philip II (Augustus) (1165–1223) King of France (1180–1223). Greatest of the French medieval kings, he increased the royal domain by marriage, by exploiting his feudal rights, and by war. His main rival was HENRY II of England. Philip supported the rebellions of Henry's sons, fought a long war against RICHARD I and, during the reign of JOHN, occupied Normandy and Anjou. English efforts to regain these lands were defeated at Bouvines in 1214. Philip persecuted Jews and Christian heretics, joined the Third CRUSADE but swiftly withdrew, and opened the Crusade against the ALBIGENSES in S France.

Philip II (382–336 BC) King of Macedonia (359–336BC). He conquered neighbouring tribes and gradually extended rule over the Greek states, defeating the Athenians at Chaeronea in 338 BC and gaining grudging acknowledgment as King of Greece. He was preparing to attack the Persian Empire when he was assassinated, leaving the task to his son, ALEXANDER THE GREAT.

Philip II (1527–98) King of Spain (1556–98), King of Portugal (1580–98). In 1554, he married MARY I of England. From his father, Emperor CHARLES V, Philip inherited Milan, Naples, Sicily, the Netherlands and Spain with its

PHILIPPINES

The Republic of the Philippines is an island country in SE Asia. It includes about 7,100 islands, of which 2,770 are named and about 1,000 are inhabited. LUZON and MINDANAO, the two largest islands, make up more than two-thirds of the country.

The land is mainly mountainous, unstable and prone to earthquakes. The islands also have several active volcanoes, one of which is the highest peak, Mount Apo, at 2,954m [9,692ft].

CLIMATE

The climate is tropical, with high temperatures all year. The dry season runs from December to April. The rest of the year is wet. Typhoons periodically strike the E coast bringing high rainfall.

MAP SCALE

HISTORY

Islam was introduced in the late 14th century. The first European to reach the Philippines was Ferdinand MAGELLAN in 1521. Spanish explorers claimed the region in 1565 when they established their first permanent settlement on Cebu. In 1571, the Spanish founded Manila, and named the archipelago *Filipinas*, after Philip II. The Spaniards regarded their new territory as a stepping stone to the Spice Islands to the south, and it became a vital trading centre subject to frequent attack from pirates. The Spanish also converted most of the population to Roman Catholicism, failing only with the Muslims on Mindanao and Sulu.

The economy grew from the late 18th century when the islands were opened up to foreign trade. In 1896 a secret revolutionary society called Katipunan launched a revolt against Spanish rule. The revolt was put down and the rebel leader Emilio Aguinaldo left the country. In 1898 the United States declared war on Spain, and the first major engagement of the SPANISH-AMERICAN WAR was the destruction of all the Spanish ships in Manila Bay. Aguinaldo returned to the Philippines and formed an army that fought alongside the Americans. He proclaimed the Philippines an independent nation, but the US gained control under the Treaty of Paris which ended their war with Spain. Aguinaldo led a fight for independence which continued until 1902.

The Philippines became a self-governing US Commonwealth in 1935 and was guaranteed full independence after a ten-year transitional period. During World War 2 Japanese troops occupied the islands, capturing Manila in 1942. US General MACARTHUR withdrew, and US forces retreated from BATAAN. In 1944 the USA began to reclaim the islands. The Philippines finally achieved independence on 4 July 1946, although the US was granted long leases on its military bases there.

POLITICS

From 1946 until 1971 the country was governed under a US-style constitution. In 1971 constitutional changes were proposed, but

AREA 300,000sq km [115,830sq mi]
POPULATION 91,077,000
CAPITAL (POPULATION) Manila (10,677,000)
GOVERNMENT Multiparty republic
ETHNIC GROUPS Christian Malay 92%, Muslim Malay 4%, Chinese and others
LANGUAGES Filipino (Tagalog) and English (both official), Spanish and many others
RELIGIONS Roman Catholic 83%, Protestant 9%, Islam 5%
CURRENCY Philippine peso = 100 centavos

President Ferdinand MARCOS declared martial law before they could be ratified. In 1977 the main opposition leader, Benigno Aquino, Jr, was sentenced to death but was allowed to escape to the US. Martial law was lifted in 1981, but Aquino was killed on his return to the Philippines in 1983. Marcos was proclaimed president again in 1986 after fraudulent elections. His opponent Corazon AQUINO, Benigno's widow, launched a campaign of civil disobedience. The US withdrew its support for Marcos and Aquino became president.

In 2001 Gloria Macapagal-Arroyo became president and set out to try to find peace in the southern Philippines. In 2003, the government put down military rebellion. Gloria Arroyo was re-elected president in 2004 despite corruption allegations. A ceasefire was agreed in the south with the Moro Islamic Liberation Front, but sporadic fighting continued. The years 2006–7 saw increased US assistance against Islamists, which helped suppress terrorist groups.

ECONOMY

The Philippines is a developing country with a 'lower-middle-income' economy. Agriculture employs 40% of the workforce. Rice and maize are the main food crops, along with bananas, cassava, coconuts, coffee, cocoa, fruits, sugar cane, sweet potatoes and tobacco. Farm animals include water buffalo, goats and pigs. Forests cover nearly half the land and forestry is a valuable industry. Sea fishing is also important and shellfish are obtained from inshore waters.

empire in the New World. War with France ended at Cateau-Cambrésis (1559), but the Revolt of the Netherlands began in 1566. A defender of Roman Catholicism, Philip launched the unsuccessful ARMADA of 1588 to crush the English who, as fellow Protestants, aided the Dutch.

Philip IV (the Fair) (1268–1314) King of France (1285–1314). Partly to pay for wars against Flanders and England, he expelled the Jews (1306), confiscating their property. Claiming the right to tax the clergy involved him in a long and bitter quarrel with Pope Boniface VIII. He used assemblies, later called the STATES-GENERAL, to popularize his case. After the death of Boniface (1303), Philip secured the election of a French pope, Clement V, based at Avignon.

Philip IV (1605–65) King of Spain, Naples and Sicily (1621–65), King of Portugal (as Philip III, 1621–40). Economic and social decline in Spain continued during Philip's reign. The THIRTY YEARS' WAR ended disastrously for Spain. Portugal threw off Spanish rule (1640), and maintained indepedence in the ensuing war. Philip supported the arts, and VELÁZQUEZ was his court painter.

Philip V (1683–1746) King of Spain (1700–46). Because he was a grandson and possible successor of LOUIS XIV of France, his accession to the Spanish throne provoked the War of the SPANISH SUCCESSION. Philip was the first BOURBON king of Spain. By the Treaty of UTRECHT (1713), he kept the Spanish throne by exclusion from the succession in France and the loss of Spanish territories in Italy and the Netherlands.

Philip VI (1293–1350) King of France (1328–50). First of the House of Valois, he was chosen to succeed his cousin, Charles IV, in preference to the rival claimant, EDWARD III of England. After the outbreak of the HUNDRED YEARS' WAR (1337), many of his vassals supported Edward. Philip suffered serious defeats in the naval battle of Sluys (1340) and at CRÉCY (1346).

Philip, Prince, Duke of Edinburgh (1921–) Husband of Queen ELIZABETH II of Britain and Prince Consort. He was born in Corfu, the son of Prince Andrew of Greece, and educated in Britain. He became a British citizen and took the surname Mountbatten. In 1947 he married Elizabeth after becoming the Duke of Edinburgh. He was created a Prince in 1957.

Philippines Republic in the SW Pacific Ocean, SE Asia. *See* country feature

Philistine Member of a non-Semitic people who lived on the S coast of modern Israel, known as Philistia, from *c.*1200 BC. They clashed frequently with the Hebrews, until decisively defeated by King DAVID. Today, the term philistine may be applied to a person indifferent to culture.

philodendron Genus of evergreen plants native to tropical America. Philodendrons have shiny, heart-shaped leaves that are sometimes split. They are popular houseplants. Height: 10cm-1.8m (4in-6ft). Family Araceae.

philology Study of both language and literature. In addition to PHONETICS, GRAMMAR and the structure of language, philology also includes textual criticism, ETYMOLOGY, and the study of art, archaeology, religion and any system related to ancient or classical languages.

philosophy Study of the nature of reality, knowledge, ETHICS and existence by means of rational inquiry. Western philosophy began among the Greeks with the work of THALES of Miletus. Later pre-Socratic philosophers included PYTHAGORAS, EMPEDOCLES, Anaxagoras, Parmenides, HERACLITUS, ZENO OF ELEA and DEMOCRITUS. Greek philosophy reached its high point with SOCRATES, who laid the foundations of ethics; PLATO, who developed a system of universal ideas; and ARISTOTLE, who founded the study of LOGIC. ZENO OF CITIUM evolved the influential school of STOICS, which contrasted with the system of EPICUREANISM, founded by EPICURUS. A dominant school of the early Christian era was NEOPLATONISM, founded by Plotinus in the 3rd century AD. The influence of Aristotle and other Greeks pervaded the thought of Muslim philosophers, such as AVICENNA and AVERRÖES, and the Spanish-born Jew, Moses Maimonides. In the work of scholastic philosophers, such as ABÉLARD, Albertus Magnus, Saint Thomas AQUINAS and WILLIAM OF OCCAM, philosophy became a branch of Christian theology. Modern scientific philosophy began in the 17th

century with the work of DESCARTES. His faith in mathematics was taken up by LEIBNIZ. In England, HOBBES integrated his materialist world view with a social philosophy. In the 18th century, EMPIRICISM was developed by BERKELEY and HUME. The achievements of KANT in Germany and the French Encyclopedists were also grounded in science. In the 19th century, a number of diverging movements emerged, among them the classical IDEALISM of HEGEL, the DIALECTICAL MATERIALISM of MARX and ENGELS, the POSITIVISM of COMTE, and the work of KIERKEGAARD and NIETZSCHE, which emphasized the freedom of the individual. In the 20th century, dominant philosophy movements included EXISTENTIALISM, LOGICAL POSITIVISM, PHENOMENOLOGY, and VITALISM. *See also* AESTHETICS; ENLIGHTENMENT; EPISTEMOLOGY; LOGIC; MATERIALISM; METAPHYSICS; PRAGMATISM; SCHOLASTICISM; UTILITARIANISM

phlebitis Inflammation of the wall of a vein. It may be caused by infection, trauma, underlying disease, or the presence of VARICOSE VEINS. Symptoms include localized swelling and redness. Treatment includes rest and anticoagulant therapy.

phloem Vascular tissue for distributing dissolved food materials in plants. Phloem tissue contains several types of cells. The most important are long, hollow cells called **sieve-tube** cells. Columns of sieve tubes are joined end to end, allowing passage of materials from cell to cell. The sieve tubes are closely associated with 'companion cells', which have dense cytoplasm and many MITOCHONDRIA, and are thought to produce the energy needed to transport the food substances (*see* ACTIVE TRANSPORT). Phloem may also contain fibres that help to support the tissue. *See also* XYLEM

phlogiston Odourless, colourless and weightless material believed by early scientists to be the source of all heat and fire. COMBUSTION was believed to involve the loss of phlogiston. The theory was proved erroneous when the true nature of combustion was explained by French chemist Antoine LAVOISIER.

Phnom Penh (Phnum Pénh) Capital of Cambodia, in the S of the country, a port at the confluence of the rivers Mekong and Tonle Sap. Founded in the 14th century, the city was the capital of the Khmers after 1434. In 1865, it became the capital of Cambodia. Occupied by the Japanese during World War 2, it was extensively damaged during the Cambodian civil war. After the KHMER ROUGE took power in 1975, the population was drastically reduced when many of its inhabitants were forcibly removed to work in the countryside. Industries: rice milling, brewing, distilling. Pop. (2005) 1,174,000.

phobia Irrational and uncontrollable fear that persists despite reassurance or contradictory evidence. Psychoanalytic theory suggests that phobias are actually symbolic subconscious fears and impulses.

Phobos Larger of the two SATELLITES of Mars. Discovered in 1877 by Asaph Hall, it is a dark, irregular body measuring 27 × 22 × 19km (17 × 14 × 12mi). It may well be a captured asteroid. It has two large craters, named Stickney and Hall.

Phoenicia Greek name for an ancient region bordering the E Mediterranean coast. The Phoenicians were related to the Canaanites. Famous as merchants and sailors, they never formed a single political unit, and Phoenicia was dominated by Egypt before *c.*1200 BC and by successive Near Eastern empires from the 9th century BC. The Phoenician city-states, such as TYRE, Sidon and BYBLOS, prospered in the intervening period, but the Phoenicians dominated trade in the Mediterranean throughout the Bronze Age. Expert navigators, they traded for tin in Britain, and sailed as far as West Africa. The Phoenicians founded colonies in Spain and North Africa, notably CARTHAGE. In 332 BC ALEXANDER THE GREAT captured Tyre and subsumed Phoenicia into the Hellenistic Empire.

Phoenician mythology Beliefs current in the Phoenician city-states of the E Mediterranean *c.*500 BC. The most ancient god was El, revered as the father of all gods and the creator of man. Closely related to the Hebrew YAHWEH, he was a remote, benevolent deity, usually depicted as an old man, but was also noted for his sexual powers. Baal, the storm god and the god of fertility, occupied an important place in the divine hierarchy. With lightning as his weapon, he defended the

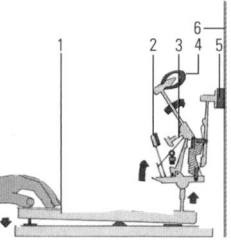

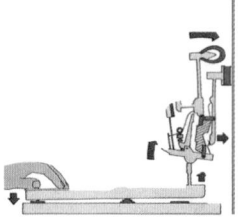

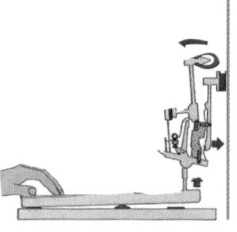

P

▲ **piano** Each key (1) of an upright piano controls a separate check (2), escapement (3), hammer (4), damper (5), and string (6). When a key is depressed, a felt-covered hammer is thrown against the strings for that particular pitch. At the same time, a felt-covered damper is lifted allowing the strings to vibrate. The hammer quickly bounces away from the strings, allowing a maximum vibration. When the key is released, the damper falls back onto the strings. The hammers connect to the keys via a series of levers, called the action, involving an escapement and a check, which catches the hammer as it returns.

INTERNET

photography
► www.geh.org

divine order against the ever-present menace of Chaos. Asherah was generally seen as a female counterpart to El. Anath, the goddess of love and war, was the consort of Baal; a ferocious figure in battle, she also helped Baal in his many conflicts. The goddess Astarte was subordinate to Anath.

Phoenix Capital of Arizona, USA, on the Salt River. Founded in 1870, the city expanded after agriculture was made possible by irrigation from the Salt River. It became the capital in 1889. Industries: computer parts, aircraft, fabricated metals, machinery, textiles, clothing, food products. Phoenix is a popular winter sports resort. Pop. (Phoenix-Mesa 2000) 2,907,000.

phoenix Mythological eagle-like bird linked with Sun-worship, especially in ancient Egypt. Of gold and scarlet plumage, only one phoenix could exist at a time, usually with a life span of c.500 years. When death approached, the phoenix built a nest of aromatic plant material and was then consumed by fire. From the ashes of the pyre rose a new phoenix.

pholidota Small order of mammals, containing only one genus, *Manis*, in the family Manidae; its members are called PANGOLINS. Some species are entirely toothless and feed almost exclusively on ants and termites.

phoneme Minimum unit of significant sound; a speech sound distinguishing meaning. The phonemes /p/ and /b/ distinguish 'tap' from 'tab'.

phonetics Study of the sounds of speech, divided into three main branches: **articulatory** phonetics (how the speech organs produce sounds); **acoustic** phonetics (the physical nature of sounds, mainly using instrumental techniques); and **auditory** phonetics (how sounds are received by the ear and processed). Linguists have devised notation systems to allow the full range of possible human speech sounds to be represented. *See also* LINGUISTICS

phosgene (carbonyl chloride, $COCl_2$) Colourless, toxic gas. It was used as a poison gas in World War 1 but is now used in the manufacture of various dyestuffs and resins. Properties: b.p. 8.2°C (46.8°F); m.p. -118°C (-180.5°F).

phosphate Chemical compounds derived from phosphoric acid (H_3PO_4). They are used to produce soaps, detergents, and glass. Their use as as FERTILIZERS can cause environmental damage.

phosphor Substance capable of **luminescence** (storing energy and later releasing it as light). They are used in coating inside cathode-ray tubes in television and computer screens and in fluorescent lamps.

phosphorescence Form of **luminescence** in which a substance emits light of one wavelength. Unlike FLUORESCENCE, it may persist for some time after the initial excitation. In biology, phosphorescence is the production of light by an organism without associated heat, as with a firefly. In warm climates, the sea often appears phosphorescent at night, as a result of the activities of millions of microscopic algae.

phosphoric acid Group of ACIDS. **Tetraoxophosphoric** acid (H_3PO_4, formerly orthophosphoric acid) is a colourless liquid obtained by the action of sulphuric acid on phosphate rock (calcium phosphate); it is used in dental adhesives, flavoured syrups, fertilizers, soaps, detergents, and anticorrosive coatings for metals. **Metaphosphoric** acid (HPO_3) is obtained by heating tetraoxophosphoric acid; it is used as a dehydrating agent. **Heptaoxodiphosphoric** ($H_4P_2O_7$, formerly pyrophosphoric acid) is formed by moderately heating tetraoxophosphoric acid or by reacting phosphorus pentoxide (P_2O_5) with water; it is used as a catalyst and in metallurgy.

phosphorus (symbol P) Common nonmetallic element of group V of the periodic table, discovered in 1669 by German alchemist Hennig Brand. It occurs (as PHOSPHATES) in many minerals; apatite being the chief source. The element is used in making PHOSPHORIC ACID for detergents and fertilizers. Small amounts are used in insecticides and in matches. Phosphorus exhibits ALLOTROPY. Properties: at.no. 15; r.a.m. 30.9738; r.d. 1.82 (white), 2.34 (red); m.p. 44.1°C (111.38°F) (white); b.p. 280°C (536°F) (white); most common isotope P^{31} (100%).

photocell *See* PHOTOELECTRIC CELL

photocopying Reproduction of photographs, words or illustrations by machine. In a photocopying machine, a light shines on the item to be copied, and an optical system

forms an image of it. Various techniques may be used to reproduce this image on paper. In a modern plain-paper copier, the image is projected onto an electrically charged **drum**, coated with the light-sensitive element SELENIUM. Light makes the selenium conduct electricity, so bright areas of the drum lose their charge. The dark areas, which usually correspond to image detail, retain their charge, and this attracts particles of a fine powder called **toner**. Electrically charged paper in contact with the drum picks up the pattern of toner powder. A heated **roller** fuses the powder so that it sticks to the paper and forms a permanent image.

photoelectric cell (photocell) Device that produces electricity when light shines on it. It used to be an electron tube with a photosensitive cathode, but nearly all modern photocells use two electrodes separated by light-sensitive semiconductor material. Photoelectric cells are used as switches (electric eyes), light detectors (burglar alarms), devices to measure light intensity (light meters), and power sources (solar cells).

photoelectric effect Liberation of ELECTRONS from the surface of a material when light, ultraviolet radiation, X-rays, or gamma rays fall on it. The effect can be explained only by the QUANTUM THEORY: PHOTONS in the radiation are absorbed by atoms in the substance and enable electrons to escape by transferring energy to them.

photography Process of obtaining a permanent chemical or electronic record of an image. A CAMERA is used to expose a light-sensitive medium to an image of the object to be photographed for a set time. In black-and-white photography, a film is covered on one side with an emulsion containing a SILVER halide (silver bromide or silver chloride). The silver compound is exposed, so that it reduces easily to metallic silver when treated with a **developer**. The action of the developer is to produce a black deposit of metallic silver particles on those parts of the film that were exposed to light, thus providing a 'negative' image. After fixing in 'hypo' (thiosulphate) and washing, the negative can be printed by placing it over a piece of sensitized paper and exposing it to light so that the silver salts in the paper are affected in the same way as those in the original film. The dark portions of the negative let through the least light, and the image on the paper is reversed back to a positive. Colour photography works on a similar, but more complex, process. Newer digital cameras have a built-in computer to record electronic images without using film. Incoming light is converted into electrical charges that may contain millions of photosensitive dots. Digital images are easily stored on computers. *See also* DAGUERRE, LOUIS JACQUES MANDE; TALBOT, WILLIAM HENRY FOX; individual photographers

photon Quantum of ELECTROMAGNETIC RADIATION, such as light; a 'particle' of LIGHT. The energy of a photon equals the frequency of the radiation multiplied by PLANCK's constant. Absorption of photons by atoms and molecules can cause excitation or ionization. A photon may be classified as a stable ELEMENTARY PARTICLE of zero rest mass, zero charge, SPIN 1, and travelling at the velocity of light. It is its own antiparticle. Virtual photons are thought to be continuously exchanged between charged particles and thus to be the carriers of ELECTROMAGNETIC FORCE (potential difference between terminals in a source of electric current). *See also* QUANTUM THEORY

photoperiodism Biological mechanism that governs the timing of certain activities in an organism by reacting to the length of its daily exposure to light and dark. For example, the start of flowering in plants and start of the breeding season in animals are determined by day length. *See also* BIOLOGICAL CLOCK

photosphere Visible surface of the SUN. It is a layer of highly luminous gas c.500km (300mi) thick and with a temperature of c.6,000K, falling to 4,000K at its upper level. It is the source of the Sun's visible spectrum. The lower, hotter gases produce the continuous emission spectrum, while the higher, cooler gases absorb certain wavelengths. Sunspots and other visible features of the Sun are situated in the photosphere.

photosynthesis Chemical process occurring in green plants, algae, and many bacteria, by which water and carbon dioxide convert into food and oxygen using energy absorbed from sunlight. The reactions take place in the CHLOROPLASTS, which are microscopic green sculptures. During the first part of the process, the green pigment CHLOROPHYLL absorbs light and splits water into hydrogen and oxygen. The hydrogen attaches to a carrier molecule and the oxygen is set free. The hydrogen and light energy build a supply of cellular chemical energy, **adenosine triphosphate** (ATP). Hydrogen and ATP convert the carbon dioxide into sugars, including glucose and starch.

phototropism Growth of a plant in response to the stimulus of light. Cell growth increases on the shaded side of the plant, resulting in curvature towards the source of light. Auxin hormones are involved in this process.

Phrygia Historic region of W central Anatolia. Early in the 1st millennium BC the Phrygians emigrated from SE Europe and established a kingdom with its capital at Gordium. MIDAS was a legendary Phrygian king. In the 6th century BC Phrygia was taken over by Lydia, then by Persia and later empires.

phylloxera Small, yellowish insect of the order Homoptera. It is a pest on grape plants in Europe and W USA. It attaches itself to the leaves and roots and sucks the plant's fluids, resulting in the eventual rotting of the plant. It destroyed all of France's native root stock of *vitis vinifera*. Family Phylloxeridae; species: *Phylloxera vitifoliae*.

phylogenetics Study of the evolutionary relationships between organisms. In **molecular phylogeny**, the evolutionary distances between organisms are analysed by comparing the DNA sequences of specific GENES. At the most fundamental level, molecular phylogeny revealed that all known organisms evolved from a common ancestor and can be grouped into five KINGDOMS, whose members are more closely related to each other than to members of other kingdoms.

phylum In the systematic categorization of living organisms, a major group within the animal KINGDOM. It comprises a diverse group of organisms with a common fundamental characteristic. In plant classification, the analogous category is sometimes called 'division'. *See also* TAXONOMY

physical chemistry Study of the physical changes associated with chemical reactions and the relationship between physical properties and chemical composition. The main branches are THERMODYNAMICS, concerned with the changes of energy in physical systems; chemical kinetics, concerned with rates of reaction; and molecular and atomic structure. Other topics include ELECTROCHEMISTRY, SPECTROSCOPY, and some aspects of NUCLEAR PHYSICS.

physical units Units used in measuring physical quantities. For example, the KILOGRAM unit of mass is defined as the mass of a specified block of platinum. Other masses are measured by weighing them and comparing them, directly or indirectly, with this. Units are of two types: **base** units that, like the kilogram, have fundamental definitions; and **derived** units that are defined in terms of these base units. Various systems of units exist, founded on certain base units. They include Imperial units (foot, pound, second), CGS units (centimetre, gram, second), and MKS units (metre, kilogram, second). For all scientific purposes, SI UNITS have been adopted.

physics Branch of science concerned with the study of MATTER and ENERGY. Physics seeks to identify and explain their many forms and relationships. Modern physics recognizes four FUNDAMENTAL FORCES in nature: GRAVITATION, which was first adequately described by Isaac NEWTON; ELECTROMAGNETIC FORCE, codified in the 19th century by MAXWELL's equations; WEAK NUCLEAR FORCE, which is responsible for the decay of some subatomic particles; and STRONG NUCLEAR FORCE, which binds together atomic nuclei. The latter is some 10^{12} times stronger than the weak force and is the least understood in physics. Branches of physics include PARTICLE PHYSICS, geophysics, BIOPHYSICS, ASTROPHYSICS and NUCLEAR PHYSICS. **Theoretical physics** involves devising theories to describe natural processes, while **experimental physics** conducts experiments that can prove or disprove theories. Physics may also be divided into six fundamental theories: Newtonian MECHANICS, THERMODYNAMICS, ELECTROMAGNETISM, STATISTICAL MECHANICS, RELATIVITY, and QUANTUM MECHANICS.

physiology Branch of biology concerned with the functions of living organisms, as opposed to their structure (anatomy).

physiotherapy (physical therapy) Use of various physical techniques to treat disease or injury. Its techniques include massage, manipulation, exercise, heat, hydrotherapy, the use of ultrasonics, and electrical stimulation.

pi (π) Symbol used for the ratio of the circumference of a circle to its diameter. It is an IRRATIONAL NUMBER, and an approximation to five decimal places is 3.14159. The ratio 22/7 is often used as a rougher approximation.

Piaf, Edith (1915–63) French cabaret singer, b. Edith Giovanna Gassion. Her small stature earned the nickname '*piaf*' (Fr. sparrow). Piaf's tragic life, which was ended prematurely by her addiction to drugs, is reflected in the emotional impact of songs such as "Non, je NE regrette rien" and "La vie en Rose".

Piaget, Jean (1896–1980) Swiss psychologist. In the 1920s and 1930s, he developed a comprehensive theory of the intellectual growth of children. He wrote several influential books, including *The Child's Conception of the World* (1926), *The Origin of Intelligence in Children* (1954), and *The Early Growth of Logic in the Child* (1964).

piano (pianoforte) Musical instrument whose sound is made with strings struck by hammers that are moved from a keyboard. Its invention (*c*.1709) is attributed to Bartolomeo Cristofori. Its name, from the Italian *piano* (soft) and *forte* (strong or loud), was adopted because its range of volume (as of tonal quality) far exceeded that of earlier instruments. The modern grand piano, much larger, louder, and more resonant than the 18th-century piano, developed in the early 19th century.

Picardy (Picardie) Region and former province of N France, on the English Channel; it includes Somme, and parts of Pas-de-Calais, Oise and Aisne departments. It was a French province from 1477 until the French Revolution, when it was replaced by a smaller department. Picardy was the scene of heavy fighting during WORLD WAR I. The area is made up of the plateau to the N of Paris, where wheat and sugar beet are grown; the valley of the Somme, where industrial centres such as Amiens are located; and the coast, where fishing is important. Area: 19,399sq km (7,488sq mi) Pop. (1999) 1,857,834.

picaresque (Sp. *pícaro*, rogue or knave) Term first applied to an early genre of prose fiction, such as Cervantes' *Don Quixote* (1615), in which a roguish hero has a series of adventures, providing the writer with a means for satirical comment. In a general sense, the term is often used to refer to fiction that is episodic in structure.

Picasso, Pablo (1881–1973) Spanish painter, sculptor, graphic artist, designer, and ceramicist. Art historians often divide his work into separate periods. During his 'Blue' and 'Rose' periods (1900–07), he turned from portrayals of poor and isolated people to representations of harlequins, acrobats and dancers in warmer colours. In 1904, he settled in Paris and

INTERNET

Picasso, Pablo
▸ www.spanisharts.com/reinasofia/reinasofia.htm
▸ www.moma.org
▸ www.ir-tmca.com
▸ www.nga.gov

P

◄ **Picasso** The most famous, prolific and versatile artist of the 20th century, Pablo Picasso was the driving force behind most of the radical art movements that occurred in the first half of the century. No single artist of the period had a greater expressive and emotional range. He produced remarkable paintings, sculptures, collages, lithographs and ceramics, and also designed stage sets and costumes for theatre and ballet.

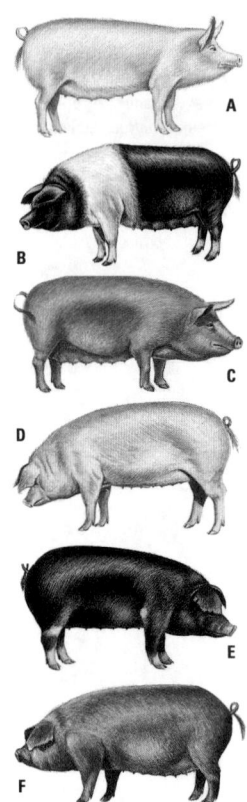

▲ **pig** Among nature's most efficient and omnivorous scavengers, there are a number of pure-bred pigs. The large white or Yorkshire (A) is the dominant breed in Britain. The saddlebacks (B) are popular free-range stocks in England, but are mainly used for cross breeding. The sandy-coloured Tamworth (C) was traditionally a forest pig. The China (D) and Chester White (E) are popular in the USA, along with the long red Duroc (F), but are uncommon in other countries.

P

▲ **pigeon** Homing pigeons successfully navigate their way home from hundreds of kilometres away, and from sites never previously visited. Scientists believe they use the stars to navigate at night, while during the day they rely on the position of the Sun. Experiments show that homing pigeons also possess a navigational back-up, using the Earth's magnetic fields.

became the centre of a group of progressive artists and writers. In 1906, Picasso began analysing and reducing forms. The result was his spectacular canvas, *Les Demoiselles d'Avignon* (completed 1907), which is now seen as a watershed in the development of contemporary art. The fragmentary forms in the painting also heralded CUBISM. In the 1920s, he produced solid, classical figures, but at the same time he was exploring SURREALISM. He started creating more violent and morbid works, which culminated in *Guernica* (1937). Picasso's sculpture ranks as highly as his painting. He was one of the first to use assembled rather than modelled or carved materials. The most famous example is his *Head of a Bull, Metamorphosis* (1943), which consists of a bicycle saddle and handlebars. He was also a printmaker and illustrated numerous books.

Piccard, Auguste (1884–1962) Swiss physicist who explored the STRATOSPHERE and deep seas. In 1931, a hydrogen balloon carried an airtight aluminium sphere containing Piccard and an assistant to an altitude of almost 15,800m (51,800ft). This was the first ascent into the stratosphere. From 1948, he experimented with designs for a diving vessel called a bathyscaphe. In 1953, Piccard and his son, **Jacques** (1922–), descended in the bathyscaphe *Trieste* to a depth of about 3,100m (10,000ft) in the Mediterranean Sea. In 1960, Jacques Piccard and a naval officer used the same craft in the Pacific Ocean to reach a record of 10,900m (35,800ft).

piccolo WOODWIND musical instrument of the FLUTE family. About half the size of the flute and pitched one octave higher, it is played in the same way.

Pickford, Mary (1893–1979) US film actress, b. Gladys Mary Smith. Her silent films include *Poor Little Rich Girl* (1917), *Pollyanna* (1919) and *Little Lord Fauntleroy* (1921). In 1919 she established the United Artists Corporation with Charlie CHAPLIN, Douglas FAIRBANKS and D.W. GRIFFITH.

Picts Ancient inhabitants of E and N Scotland. By the 8th century, they had a kingdom extending from Caithness to Fife, and had adopted Christianity. To the w and s of the Picts, invaders from Ireland established the kingdom of Dalriada; in 843 its king, Kenneth I, also became king of the Picts, uniting the two kingdoms into the kingdom of Scotland.

pidgin Simplified form of a language, differing from other LINGUA FRANCAS by comprising a very limited vocabulary and being used for communication between people who do not speak the same language. Most pidgins in use today are based on English, French, Spanish, or Portuguese, with a certain number of native words and structures added. The Pidgin English of Papua New Guinea (Tok Pisin) is an official national language.

Piedmont (Piemonte) Region of NW Italy, bounded to the N, w and s by mountains, and to the E by the Po Valley; it comprises the provinces of Alessandria, Asti, Cuneo, Novara, Torino, and Vercelli. Already an important region in Roman times, it was later subject to Lombard, then Frankish rule. Under the influence of Savoy from the early 15th century, it became part of the kingdom of Sardinia in 1720. In the early 19th century, it was the focus of the movement for Italian independence, joining a united Italy in 1861. The Po Valley has excellent farmland. Products: grain, vegetables, fruit, dairy. Industries: winemaking, motor vehicles, textiles, glass, chemicals. Area: 25,400sq km (9,807sq mi). Pop. (1999) 4,288,051.

Pierce, Franklin (1804–69) 14th US president (1853–57). He represented New Hampshire in the US House of Representatives (1833–37) and the Senate (1837–42), when he resigned. He remained politically active, with an interval of service in the Mexican War, and supported the COMPROMISE OF 1850. He gained the Democratic presidential nomination as a compromise candidate, and was elected in 1852. The most notable feature of his presidency was his endorsement of the Kansas-Nebraska Act (1854), which resulted in near-civil war in Kansas between pro- and anti-slavery settlers.

Piero della Francesca (1415–92) (Piero dei Franceschi) Italian painter. He was familiar with the innovations made by MASACCIO, DONATELLO, Filippo LIPPI and others. He drew their achievements together to create a deeply reflective style. His most important work is the FRESCO series depicting the *Legend of the True Cross* (*c.*1465) for the choir of San Francesco, Arezzo.

Pierre Capital of South Dakota, USA, on the Missouri River opposite Fort Pierre. Originally the capital of the Aricara Native Americans, it was a trading settlement in the early 19th century before becoming a railway terminus in 1880. It became the state capital in 1904. Government services and agriculture (grain, cattle) dominate the economy. Pop. (2000) 13,876.

Pietism Influential Christian spiritual movement within Protestantism, founded in the late 17th century by a German Lutheran minister, Philipp Spener (1635–1705). Its aim was to revitalize evangelical Christianity by emphasizing spiritual rather than theological or dogmatic issues.

piezoelectric effect Creation of positive ELECTRIC CHARGE on one side of a nonconducting crystal and negative charge on the other when the crystal is squeezed. The pressure results in an ELECTRIC FIELD that can be detected as voltage between the opposite crystal faces. The effect has been used in gramophone pickups, crystal microphones, and cigarette lighters.

pig Any of numerous species and varieties of domestic and wild swine of the family Suidae. The male is generally called a boar; the female, a sow. A castrated boar is usually known as a hog. It is generally a massive, short-legged omnivore with a thick skin. Wild pigs include the warthog, wild BOAR, bush pig and babirusa. The domestic pig (*Sus scrofa*) is reared for human consumption. For pork they are slaughtered at 70–90kg (155–200lb) and for bacon at 80–100kg (175–220kg).

pigeon (dove) Any of a large family of wild and domestic birds found throughout temperate and tropical parts of the world, but concentrated in s Asia and the Australian region. Pigeons have small heads, short necks, plump bodies, and scaly legs and feet. Plumage is loose but thick. Length: to 46cm (18in). Family Columbidae; typical genus, *Columba*.

Piggott, Lester Keith (1935–) English jockey. He rode his first winner at the age of 12. Piggott was champion jockey 11 times between 1960 and 1982. Among 30 victories in English classics, he rode a record nine winners of the Epsom Derby. Piggott won a career total of 4,493 races. He retired in 1996.

pigment Coloured, insoluble substance used to impart colour to an object and added for this purpose to paints, inks and plastics. They generally function by absorbing and reflecting light, although some luminescent pigments emit coloured light. Pigments also provide the natural colouring of animals and plants through PIGMENTATION.

pigmentation In biology, a natural chemical that gives colour to TISSUES. In humans, the skin, hair and iris are coloured by the pigments MELANIN and carotene, together with the HAEMOGLOBIN in ERYTHROCYTES (red blood cells), which also acts as a pigment.

pika Any of 12 species of short-haired relatives of the RABBIT. They live in cold regions of Europe, Asia, and w USA. Length: to 20cm (8in). Genus *Ochotona*.

pike Predatory, freshwater fish found in E North America and parts of Europe and Asia. It has a shovel-shaped mouth and a mottled, elongated body. Length: to 137.2cm (54in); weight: to 20.9kg (46lb) Family Esocidae; genus *Esox*.

pikeperch Freshwater food and game fish of Central Europe, where it includes the zander, and of North America, where it is related to the walleye and sauger. A dark olive, mottled fish, the pikeperch has an elongated body and large head and mouth. Length: to 91.4cm (3ft); weight: to 11.3kg (25lb). Family Percidae; species *Stizostedion vitreum*.

Pik Ismail Samani Mountain in the PAMIR range in SE Tajikistan, central Asia. The highest peak in the former Soviet Union, it was named Stalin Peak in 1932 and renamed Kommunizma Pik (Communism Peak) in 1962. It was given its present name in 1998. Height 7,495m (24,590ft).

Pilate, Pontius *See* PONTIUS PILATE

pilchard Marine food fish resembling a herring, found in shoals along most coasts except those of Asia. They are caught by the millions and support a huge canning industry. The young are sometimes called SARDINES. Length: less than 45.7cm (18in). Family Clupeidae; species *Sardina pilchardus*.

pilgrimage Religiously motivated journey to a shrine or other holy place in order to gain spiritual help or guidance, or for the purpose of thanksgiving. Pilgrimages are common to many religions, particularly in the East. A Muslim should make the pilgrimage to MECCA, where devotions last two weeks, at least once in his life. This pilgrimage is known as the HAJJ. Since the 2nd century AD Christians have made pilgrimages to Palestine, to the tomb of the Apostles Peter and Paul in Rome, and to that of James in Santiago de Compostela, NW Spain.

Pilgrims (Pilgrim Fathers) Group of English Puritans who emigrated to North America in 1620. After fleeing to Leiden, Netherlands, in 1608, seeking refuge from persecution in England, they decided to look for greater religious freedom by founding a religious society in America. They sailed from Plymouth, England, on the MAYFLOWER and founded the PLYMOUTH COLONY in present-day Massachusetts.

pill, the Popular term for oral contraceptives based on female reproductive hormones. They work by preventing ovulation. Two types of synthetic hormone, similar to OESTROGEN and PROGESTERONE, are generally used, although the former alone is effective in preventing ovulation; the latter helps to regulate the menstrual cycle. Possible side-effects include headache, HYPERTENSION, weight-gain, and a slightly increased risk of THROMBOSIS. *See* CONTRACEPTION

pilot fish Marine fish that lives in warm seas, often found swimming close to sharks, ships and other large objects. A blue fish with five to seven dark bar markings on the sides and a white tail, it feeds on smaller fish. Length: to 60cm (2ft). Family Carangidae; species *Naucrates ductor*.

Pilsen *See* PLZEN

Pilsudski, Józef (1867–1935) Polish general and statesman. He was instrumental in securing Poland's independence. During World War 1 he led Polish forces against Russia, hoping to establish a Polish state. After independence, he became head of state. His attempt to create a larger Polish state during the Russo-Polish War (1919–20) failed, although he inflicted a remarkable defeat on the invading Russians in 1920. He retired in 1923, but seized power again in 1926, establishing an authoritarian personal rule that lasted until his death.

pimpernel Small, trailing annual plant of the genus *Anagallis*, native to Britain and the USA. The single, small, five petalled flowers are scarlet, white or blue. The yellow pimpernel, a creeping European plant of shady areas, is *Lysimachia nemorum*. Family Primulaceae.

Pincus, Gregory Goodwin (1903–67) US biologist who helped to develop the contraceptive PILL using synthetic HORMONES. Pincus wrote several articles on hormones and a book, *The Eggs of Mammals* (1936).

Pindar (*c.*522–*c.*438 BC) Greek poet known for his choric lyrics and triumphal ODES. Of the 17 volumes of Pindar's works known to his contemporaries, only 44 odes survive, written to celebrate victories in athletic games.

pine Any of various EVERGREEN, cone-bearing trees of the genus *Pinus*, most of which are native to cooler temperate regions of the world. Many have two types of shoots, some with needle-like leaves and others with deciduous, scale-like leaves. The reproductive organs may be catkins or cones. Many species are valued for soft wood, wood pulp, oils and resins. Family: Pinaceae. *See also* GYMNOSPERM

pineal body (pineal gland) Small gland attached to the undersurface of the vertebrate brain. In human beings, it has an endocrine function, secreting the hormone melatonin, which is involved in daily rhythms. *See also* ENDOCRINE SYSTEM

pineapple Tropical, herbaceous, perennial plant, cultivated in the USA, South America, Asia, Africa and Australia; also its fruit. The fruit is formed from the flowers and bracts and grows on top of a short, stout stem bearing stiff, fleshy leaves. The fruit is eaten fresh, tinned, or made into juice. Height: to 1.2m (4ft). Family Bromeliaceae; species *Ananas comosus*.

Pinero, Sir Arthur Wing (1855–1934) English dramatist. His farces include *The Magistrate* (1885) and *Dandy Dick* (1887). Pinero is best-known for his 'problem play', *The Second Mrs Tanqueray* (1893), on the social discrimination against women. Other plays include *Trelawny of the 'Wells'* (1898).

ping pong *See* TABLE TENNIS

pink Common name for several genera of the pink family (Caryophyllaceae), especially the genus *Dianthus* of more than 300 species, most of which are native to the Mediterranean region. Short, herbaceous perennials, many are

hardy evergreens with showy, fragrant flowers. Leaves are simple and usually opposite, and the symmetrical flowers are usually bisexual. *See also* CARNATION

Pinkerton, Allan (1819–84) US detective, b. Scotland. He moved to the USA in 1842, and became a detective on the Chicago Police force, resigning in 1850 to establish his own agency, Pinkerton's National Detective Agency. He organized and headed a federal intelligence service (1861).

pinna Flap of skin and cartilage that comprises the visible, external part of the EAR. It helps to collect sound waves and direct them into the ear canal.

Pinochet (Ugarte), Augusto (1915–2006) Chilean general and statesman, president (1973–89). He led the military coup that overthrew Salvador ALLENDE. Pinochet established a military dictatorship that enforced social control through widespread torture and murder. In 1989, he was forced to permit democratic elections and was succeeded as president by Patricio Aylwin in 1990. Pinochet retained command of the armed forces until 1998. In 1998, British authorities arrested him for crimes of genocide and terrorism. In 2000, Pinochet returned to Chile on grounds of illness, only to face censure there. In 2001, a Chilean court ruled that Pinochet was unfit to stand trial.

Pinter, Harold (1930–) English dramatist. His elliptical dialogue and prolonged pauses induces a sense of unease and menace, often reinforced by a confined setting. His second play, *The Birthday Party* (1958), initially received adverse reviews. Pinter gained critical praise for his next play, *The Caretaker* (1960). Other major works include *The Homecoming* (1965), *Old Times* (1971), *No Man's Land* (1975), *Betrayal* (1978), and *A Kind of Alaska* (1982). Later plays, such as *Mountain Language* (1988) and *Moonlighting* (1993), are more explicitly political. His screenplays include *The Servant* (1963), *The Go-Between* (1969), and *The French Lieutenant's Woman* (1980).

Pinyin System of spelling used to transliterate ideographic Chinese characters into the Roman alphabet. It is a phonetic system (it represents the sounds of words) and was officially adopted by the People's Republic of China in 1958.

Pioneer program Series of unmanned interplanetary probes launched by the USA. In 1960, **Pioneer 5** measured distances within the SOLAR SYSTEM and studied magnetism and the SOLAR WIND. **Pioneer 10**, launched in 1972, reached Jupiter in 1973. It investigated the planet's atmosphere and magnetic field, and sent back more than 300 pictures of the planet. **Pioneer 11**, launched in 1973, reached Jupiter in 1974, and Saturn in 1979 – discovering two moons there. In 1978, **Pioneer Venus 1** and **Pioneer Venus 2** entered Venus' atmosphere. The first orbited the planet for 14 years before it ceased operations. The second mission impacted with the planet.

pipefish Any of numerous species of marine fish found in the shallow, warm and temperate waters of the Atlantic and Pacific oceans. Closely related to the seahorse, it has a pencil-like body covered with bony rings. Its mouth is at the end of a long snout. Length: to 58.4cm (23in). Family Syngnathidae.

Piper, John (1903–92) English painter. His early abstract phase gave way to a commitment to neo-Romanticism in the 1940s. As an official war artist (1940–42) during World War 2, Piper produced striking paintings of bomb-damaged

INTERNET

Pierce, Franklin
▶ www.whitehouse.gov/ history/presidents

Piero della Francesca
▶ www.nationalgallery.org.uk

Pioneer program
▶ spaceprojects.arc.nasa. gov/Space_Projects/ pioneer/PNhist.html

▲ **pine** The lodgepole pine (*Pinus contorta*) grows in w North America, reaching a height of 18m (60ft). It is a small, vigorous mountain tree that is hardy to an altitude of 3,500m (11,000ft).

◀ **pineapple** An important cash crop in some tropical regions, pineapples bear fleshy fruit. The fruit can be eaten fresh, but the majority is tinned or turned into pineapple juice.

▲ **piranha** The red piranha (*Serrasalmus natterei*) of South America is notorious for its ferocity. Its powerful jaws have sharp teeth, and it makes up for its relatively small size – 35cm (14in) – by swimming in large shoals. These represent a threat to larger fish, land animals, and even humans. They feed in bouts, rather than continuously, and use their sense of smell to locate their prey.

buildings. Queen Elizabeth II commissioned him to paint *Windsor Castle* (1941–42). Piper also designed the stage sets for Benjamin Britten's opera *Death in Venice* (1973) and the stained glass windows in Coventry Cathedral.

pipit (fieldlark, titlark) Any of more than 50 small, brown, inconspicuous birds that resemble LARKS in habits and appearance. They are found worldwide. The plumage of both sexes is streaked brown or greyish, with a long, white-edged 'wag' tail. Length: 15cm (6in). Family Motacillidae; genus *Anthus*.

Piraeus (Peiraías) Seaport city in SE Greece, 8km (5mi) sw of Athens; largest Greek port. Planned in *c*.490 BC Piraeus rapidly developed into a major sea outlet. In 86 BC Roman General SULLA destroyed the city, and it fell into decline. In the 19th century, following Greek independence, a process of reconstruction led to the creation of the modern naval and commercial port. It is the centre of a modern communications network with all the Greek islands. Industries: shipbuilding, oil-refining, textiles, chemicals. Pop. (2000 est.) 189,000.

Pirandello, Luigi (1867–1936) Italian dramatist, novelist, and short-story writer. Among his plays are *Six Characters in Search of an Author* (1921) and *As You Desire Me* (1930). His novels include *The Late Mattia Pascal* (1923). His work explores the boundaries between reality and illusion. He won the 1934 Nobel Prize in literature.

Piranesi, Giovanni Battista (1720–78) Italian engraver and architect. He lived in Rome where he became famous for his *Vedute*, 137 etchings of the ancient and modern city (1745). The one existing building that he designed is the Church of Santa Maria del Priorato, Rome (1764–65).

piranha (piraya) Tropical, freshwater, bony fish that lives in rivers in South America. It is a voracious predator, with formidable teeth and an aggressive temperament. Piranhas usually travel and attack in shoals and can pose a serious threat to much larger creatures. Length: to 24in (61cm). Family Characidae; genus *Serrasalmus*.

Pisa City on the River Arno, Tuscany, w central Italy. Already an important Etruscan town, Pisa prospered as a Roman colony from *c*.180 BC. In the Middle Ages, it was a powerful maritime republic but later came under Florentine domination. It is noted for its 12th-century 'Leaning Tower', an eight-storey circular campanile. The bell-tower is 54m (177ft) high, and is now *c*.6.5m (21ft) out of perpendicular. Industries: tourism, textiles, glass, machine tools. Pop. (1999) 91,977.

Pisanello (*c*.1395–*c*.1455) (Antonio Pisano) Italian painter and medallist. Working in the international gothic style, Pisanello drew detailed studies of birds, people, and costumes. His medals of important people of his time are of historic value.

Pisano, Nicola (*c*.1225–*c*.1278) Italian sculptor. His first masterpiece was the pulpit for the Baptistry in Pisa (1260). In his work on the cathedral pulpit in Siena (1265–68), Pisano was aided by his son, **Giovanni** (*c*.1250–*c*.1320), whose taste in decoration was influenced by the French Gothic style. Giovanni produced two other pulpits: Santa Andrea, Pistoia (1298–1301), and Pisa Cathedral (1302–10).

Piscator, Ervin Friedrich Max (1893–1966) German stage director. He developed the concept of epic theatre, which Bertolt BRECHT incorporated into the work of the Berliner Ensemble. Piscator shared the conviction that theatre should be a political medium. *See also* EXPRESSIONISM

Pisces (the Fishes) Inconspicuous equatorial constellation situated on the ecliptic between Aquarius and Aries; it is the 12th sign of the Zodiac.

Pisistratus (*c*.605–527 BC) Athenian ruler. He seized control by force in 560 BC but was overthrown in 554 BC and driven into exile. With support from Thebes and Argos, he regained power in 541 BC and ruled as "tyrant" until his death.

Pissarro, Camille (1830–1903) French painter who adopted IMPRESSIONISM and tried POINTILLISM. In the 1880s, he experimented with the pointillist theories of Georges SEURAT but abandoned them in the 1890s for a freer interpretation of nature. His works include *Louvre from Pont Neuf* (1902).

pistachio Deciduous tree native to the Mediterranean region and E Asia. It is grown commercially for the edible greenish seed (the pistachio nut) of its wrinkled red fruit. Height: to 6m (20ft). Family Anacardiaceae; species *Pistacia vera*.

pistil Female organ located in the centre of a flower. It consists of an OVARY, a slender STYLE and a STIGMA, which receives POLLEN.

pistol FIREARM held and fired in one hand. The first were matchlocks, in which a glowing fuse ignited the charge; by the end of the 16th century, wheel-locks and the cheaper flintlocks were also in use. The invention of the percussion cap in 1815 enabled pistol technology to advance rapidly, and Samuel Colt's revolver of 1835 was the first reliable repeating firearm. Since then pistols have become capable of automatic fire.

pit bull Any of several cross-breeds of bulldog and terrier. Examples include the American pit bull terrier, bull terrier, and Staffordshire bull terrier. The English bull terrier, measuring *c*.40cm (16in) at the shoulder, was originally developed for bull-baiting. The American pit bull terrier, not an official breed, is *c*.50cm (20in) at the shoulder and was bred as a aggressive watchdog. Weight: up to 23kg (50lb).

Pitcairn Island Volcanic island in the central s Pacific Ocean forming (together with the uninhabited islands of Henderson, Ducie and Oeno) a British crown colony. First sighted in 1767, mutineers from the British ship HMS *Bounty* settled Pitcairn in 1790. Some of their descendants still live on the island. The principal economic activity is the growing and exporting of fruit. Area: 4.6sq km (1.7sq mi). Pop. (1994) 50.

pitch Quality of sound that determines its position in a musical scale. It is measured in terms of the frequency of sound waves (measured in hertz) – the higher the frequency, the higher the pitch. It also depends to some extent on loudness and timbre: increasing the intensity decreases the pitch of a low note and increases the pitch of a high one.

pitchblende *See* URANINITE

pitcher plant Any of several species of INSECTIVOROUS PLANT of the tropics and sub-tropics. It traps insects in its vase-shaped leaves, which are lined with bristles. Trapped insects decompose and are absorbed as nutrients by plant cells. The flower is usually red. Height: 20–61cm (8–24in). Family Sarraceniacea; genera *Sarracenia* and *Nepenthes*.

Pitt (the Younger), William (1759–1806) British statesman, prime minister (1783–1801, 1804–06). The second son of William PITT, Earl of Chatham, he entered Parliament in 1781, became chancellor of the exchequer in 1782 and shortly after became Britain's youngest prime minister, aged 24. Pitt's reputation rests chiefly on his financial and commercial reforms in the 1780s that restored British prosperity and prestige after the disaster of the AMERICAN REVOLUTION. During his first administration, the India Act (1784), the Constitutional Act (1791) dividing Canada into French and English provinces, and the Act of UNION with Ireland (1800) were passed. Pitt resigned in the face of GEORGE III's refusal to consider CATHOLIC EMANCIPATION. In 1804, he returned to power and continued to hold office until his death. His second ministry was marked by coalition with Russia, Sweden and Austria against NAPOLEON I. Pitt stoutly defended his TORY views against his arch WHIG rival, Charles James FOX.

Pitt (the Elder), William, 1st Earl of Chatham (1708–78) British statesman, known as 'the Great Commoner'. He entered Parliament in 1735. Pitt was noted for his opposition to the foreign policies of prime ministers WALPOLE and Carteret and King GEORGE II. The crisis of the SEVEN YEARS' WAR (1756–63) made him effective head of the government. Widespread criticism of Pitt's dismissal (1757) brought about his reappointment as head of the government in coalition with the Duke of Newcastle. His ministry was a brilliant one, preserving and consolidating Britain's old empire and gaining a new one. Pitt placed his main efforts on successful attempts to conquer Canada and India. In 1761, he resigned after GEORGE III refused to declare war on Spain. After the war, he spoke out against the prosecution (1763) of John WILKES and the imposition of the STAMP ACT (1765) on the American colonies. The ministry he nominally headed from 1766 to 1768 was a confused and divided one. Created Earl Chatham in 1766, he retired to the House of Lords in 1768. There he spoke out against repression of the American colonies and in favour of any peace settlement that stopped short of granting independence.

Pittsburgh City and port at the confluence of the Allegheny and Monongahela rivers, sw Pennsylvania, USA. Fort Duquesne was founded on the site by the French in c.1750. The British captured the fort in 1758, renaming it Fort Pitt. Pittsburgh grew as a steel manufacturing centre in the 19th century (the industry is now in decline). Industries: glass, machinery, petroleum products, electrical equipment, publishing, coal mining, oil and natural gas extraction. Pop. (2000) 1,753,000.

pituitary gland Major gland of the ENDOCRINE SYSTEM, located at the base of the BRAIN. In human beings, it is about the size of a pea and connects to the HYPOTHALAMUS by a stalk. It produces many HORMONES, some of which regulate the activity of other endocrine glands, while others control growth.

Pius VII (1742–1823) Pope (1800–23), b. Barnaba Gregorio Chiaramonti. He secured the Concordat of 1801 with NAPOLEON I. After Napoleon seized Rome (1808) and annexed the PAPAL STATES (1809), Pius excommunicated him. Napoleon imprisoned Pius until 1814. On his restoration, he encouraged the reform of religious orders and education.

Pius IX (1792–1878) Pope (1846–78), b. Giovanni Maria Mastai-Ferretti. Pius fled from Rome (1848–50) in the REVOLUTIONS OF 1848 but was restored by NAPOLEON III. In 1860, the PAPAL STATES were seized by the Italian nationalists. Pius refused to acknowledge the new Kingdom of Italy, into which Rome was incorporated in 1870, and remained a voluntary 'prisoner' within the walls of the Vatican until his death. He defended German Catholics from persecution by BISMARCK and defined the dogma of the IMMACULATE CONCEPTION (1854). In 1869, Pius convened the First VATICAN COUNCIL, which proclaimed the principle of PAPAL INFALLIBILITY. His pontificate is the longest in papal history.

Pius XII (1876–1958) Pope (1939–58), b. Eugenio Pacelli. Fearing political reprisals, he failed to denounce the Nazis and the persecution of Jews during World War 2. He was more openly hostile to communism. He appointed local bishops in non-Western countries and created a non-Italian majority among the cardinals.

Pius V, Saint (1504–72) Pope (1568–72), b. Antonio Ghislieri. He was an energetic reformer of the Church and enemy of Protestantism. He excommunicated Queen ELIZABETH I of England in 1570. During his reign, he tightened the rules of INQUISITION and succeeded in eliminating Protestantism from Italy. He was canonized in 1712.

Pius X, Saint (1835–1914) Pope (1903–14), b. Giuseppe Melchiorre Sarto. He opposed religious modernism, placing several modernist books on the INDEX in 1907. Pius also condemned the separation of Church and state in France and recodified CANON LAW (a revision published posthumously in 1917). He was canonized in 1954. His feast day is August 21.

Pizarro, Francisco (1471–1541) Spanish *conquistador* of the INCA empire of Peru. He served under Hernán CORTÉS and led expeditions to South America (1522–28). Having gained royal support, he led 180 men to Peru in 1530. They captured and later murdered the Inca leader ATAHUALPA, and took Cuzco, the capital (1534). Pizarro acted as governor of the conquered territory, founding Lima in 1535.

placenta Organ in mammals (except MONOTREMES and MARSUPIALS) that connects the FETUS to the UTERUS of the mother. Part of the placenta contains tiny blood vessels through which oxygen and food are carried from the mother to the embryo via the umbilical cord and wastes are carried from the embryo to the mother's bloodstream to be excreted. The placenta secretes hormones that maintain pregnancy and is discharged from the mother's body as the afterbirth, immediately after delivery.

plagioclase Type of FELDSPAR. Plagioclase minerals occur in IGNEOUS and METAMORPHIC rocks. Off-white, or sometimes pink, green or brown, they are composed of varying proportions of the silicates of sodium and calcium with aluminium. They show an oblique cleavage and have triclinic system crystals. Hardness 6–6.5; r.d. 2.6.

plague Acute, infectious disease of humans and rodents caused by the bacillus *Yersinia pestis*. In humans, it occurs in three forms: **bubonic** plague, most common and characterized by vomiting, fever and swellings of the lymph nodes

called 'buboes'; **pneumonic** plague, in which the lungs are infected; and **septicaemic** plague, in which the bloodstream is invaded. Treatment is the administration of vaccines, bed rest, antibiotics and sulpha drugs. *See also* BLACK DEATH

plaice Marine flatfish found along the w European coast. An important food fish, it is brown or grey with orange spots. Length: to 90cm (3ft); weight: to 11.8kg (26lb). Family Pleuronectidae; species *Pleuronectes platessa*.

Plaid Cymru (Party of Wales) Welsh nationalist political party, founded in 1925 as Plaid Genedlaethol Cymru. A Plaid Cymru representative was first elected to the House of Commons in 1966. It advocates Welsh independence (from the United Kingdom) within the European Union.

plainsong (plainchant) Collection of unharmonized liturgical melodies of the Western Church, traditionally performed unaccompanied. Plainsong goes back to the beginning of the Christian era. The melodies use free rhythms, and the musical 'scales' they employ derive from the 'modes' of ancient Greek music. In the 6th century, plainsong was reformed, supposedly at the behest of Pope GREGORY I ('the Great'). In this reformed state (known as Gregorian chant), the range of a melody is not more than five notes.

Planck, Max Karl Ernst Ludwig (1858–1947) German theoretical physicist whose revolutionary QUANTUM THEORY helped to establish modern physics. In 1900, he came to the conclusion that the frequency distribution of BLACK-BODY radiation could only be accounted for if the radiation was emitted in separate "packets" called quanta, rather than continuously. His equation, relating the energy of a quantum to its frequency, is the basis of quantum theory. **Planck's constant** is a universal constant (symbol h) of value 6.626×10^{-34} joule seconds, equal to the energy of a quantum of ELECTROMAGNETIC RADIATION divided by the radiation frequency. Planck received the 1918 Nobel Prize in physics.

plane In mathematics, a flat surface such that a straight line joining any two points on it lies entirely within the surface. Its equation in the three-dimensional CARTESIAN CO-ORDINATES system is $ax + by + cz = d$, where a, b, c, and d are constants.

planet Large, non-stellar body in orbit around a star, shining only by reflecting the star's light. In our SOLAR SYSTEM there are eight major planets, as opposed to the many small bodies known as ASTEROIDS or minor planets. *See also* MERCURY; VENUS; EARTH; MARS; JUPITER; SATURN; URANUS; NEPTUNE.

planetarium Domed building in which a projector displays an artificial sky in order to demonstrate the positions and motions of the Sun, Moon, planets and stars relative to the Earth. Walter Bauersfeld of the Zeiss Optical Company invented the basis of the modern planetarium in 1923.

◀ **William Pitt (the Younger)** by John Hoppner (1758–1810). Pitt was born into a political family. His father, William Pitt (the Elder), was leading minister to George II, while his mother was the sister of George Grenville (1712–70), prime minister (1763–65). As prime minister himself, Pitt lacked the backing of a clearly defined party in Parliament, and was always dependent on royal patronage. His government faced a national debt of c.£250 million as a result of British defeat in the American Revolution (1775–81). Pitt imposed new taxes, reformed customs and excise duties, and created a sinking fund for the purpose of debt repayment.

plankton All the floating or drifting life of the ocean, especially that near the surface. The organisms are very small and move with the currents. There are two main kinds: **phytoplankton**, floating plants such as DIATOMS and dinoflagellates; and **zooplankton**, floating animals such as radiolarians, plus the larvae and eggs of larger marine animals. They are a vital part of the food chain.

plant Multicellular organism whose cells have cellulose cell walls and contain CHLOROPLASTS or similar structures (plastids). They develop from DIPLOID embryos, and have a regular alternation of HAPLOID and diploid generations in their life cycle. Most plants are green and make their own food by PHOTOSYNTHESIS. A few are colourless PARASITES or SAPROPHYTES. Simple plants reproduce by means of SPORES, while more advanced plants produce SEEDS and FRUITS. Plants show a wide range of biochemistry; some produce chemicals such as ALKALOIDS, NARCOTICS, and even cyanide; others secrete substances into the soil to prevent other plants growing near them. Many of these chemicals form the bases for the development of drugs. Plants are classified on the basis of their morphology (shape and structure). The most important phyla are: the Bryophyta (BRYOPHYTES), which include the mosses and liverworts; LYCOPODOPHYTA, or CLUB MOSSES; Sphenophyta (HORSETAILS); Filicinophyta (FERNS); Cycadophyta (CYCADS); Ginkgophyta (GINKGO); Coniferophyta (CONIFERS); and Angiospermophyta (ANGIOSPERMS). *See also* ALTERNATION OF GENERATIONS

Plantagenet English royal dynasty (1154–1485). The name encompasses the ANGEVINS (1154–1399) and the Houses of LANCASTER and YORK. They descended from Geoffrey of Anjou and Matilda, daughter of HENRY I. Richard, Duke of York and father of EDWARD IV, adopted the Plantagenet name during the Wars of the ROSES.

plantain Plant with a rosette of basal leaves and spikes of tiny, greenish-white flowers; it grows in temperate regions and was used for medicinal purposes. Family Plantaginaceae; genus *Plantago*. The name plantain also refers to a tropical banana plant believed to be native to SE Asia and now cultivated throughout the Tropics. It has fleshy stems, bright green leaves and green fruit that is larger and starchier than a banana. It is eaten cooked. Height: to 10m (33ft). Family Musaceae; species *Musa paradisiaca*.

plant classification System devised to group PLANTS according to relationships among them. Plants are known by common names that often vary from area to area, but have only one correct scientific name. *See* TAXONOMY

plant genetics Science of HEREDITY and VARIATION in plants. Research in GENETICS since 1900 supplied the principles of plant breeding, especially HYBRIDIZATION. The development of consistently reliable and healthy first-generation crosses (F1 hybrids) revolutionized the growing of food crops, ornamental annuals, and bedding plants. Genetic engineers grow cell and TISSUE CULTURES by the replication or cloning of sterile plant types. They also concentrate on isolating individual GENES with the aim of producing new colour varieties for traditional flowers, improving the flavour of food crops, breeding resistance to pests and herbicides, and lengthening the shelf life of harvested crops. These processes involve GENETIC ENGINEERING and produce GENETICALLY MODIFIED FOOD.

plaque Abnormal deposit building up on a body surface, especially the film of saliva and bacteria that accumulates on teeth. Fatty and fibrous plaque can also form in blood vessels. Dental plaque leads to tooth decay and gum disease.

plasma In physics, an ionized gas that contains about the same amount of positive and negative IONS. Plasma, often described as the fourth state of MATTER, occurs at extremely high temperatures, as in the interiors of the Sun and other stars and in fusion reactors.

plastic Synthetic material composed of organic molecules, often in long chains called POLYMERS, that can be shaped and then hardened. The weight and structure of the molecules determine the physical and chemical properties of a given compound. Plastics are synthesized from common materials, mostly from petroleum. CELLULOSE comes from cotton or wood pulp, CASEIN from skimmed milk, others from chemicals derived from plants. **Thermoset** plastics, such as BAKELITE, stay hard once set, while **thermoplastics**, such as POLYETHENE, can be resoftened by heat. New, biodegradable plastics are more expensive to produce but are environmentally friendly because they eventually decompose. US inventor John Hyatt (1837–1920) created the first plastic, which was CELLULOID in 1869. In 1908, US chemist Leo Baekeland produced the first mouldable industrial plastic.

plastic surgery Branch of surgery that involves the reconstruction of deformed, damaged or disfigured parts of the body. **Cosmetic surgery**, such as face-lifts, is performed solely to 'improve' appearance.

plastid Type of organelle (specialized structure) found in the cells of plants and green algae. CHLOROPLASTS and leucoplasts are two examples of plastids, which have a double membrane and contain DNA.

Plata, Río de la Estuary in SE South America formed by the junction of the PARANÁ and URUGUAY rivers at the border between Argentina and Uruguay. Europeans first explored the Río de la Plata in the early 16th century. The cities of BUENOS AIRES and MONTEVIDEO lie on its S and N shores respectively. It is 270km (170mi) long, and 190km (120mi) wide at its mouth. Area: *c*.35,000sq km (13,500sq mi).

platelet Colourless, usually spherical structures found in mammalian BLOOD. Chemicals in platelets, known as factors and co-factors, are essential to the mechanism of blood clotting. The normal platelet count is *c*.300,000 per cu mm of blood. Platelets are cell fragments from bone marrow cells.

plate tectonics Theory or model to explain the distribution, evolution, and causes of the Earth's crustal features. It proposes that the Earth's CRUST and part of the upper MANTLE (the LITHOSPHERE) consists of several separate, rigid slabs, termed plates, which move independently forming part of a cycle in the creation and destruction of crust. The plates collide or move apart at the margins, and these produce zones of earthquake and volcanic activity. Three types of plate boundary can be identified. At a **constructive** or divergent margin, new basaltic magma originating in the mantle injects into the plate. The crusts are forced to separate and an oceanic ridge is formed. At a **destructive** or convergent margin, plates collide and one plate moves under the other. This occurs along oceanic trenches. The recycling of crust by subduction results in the melting of some crustal material, and volcanic island arcs (such as the islands of Japan) are produced. Material that cannot be subducted is scraped up and fused onto the edge of plates. This can form a new continent or add to existing ones.

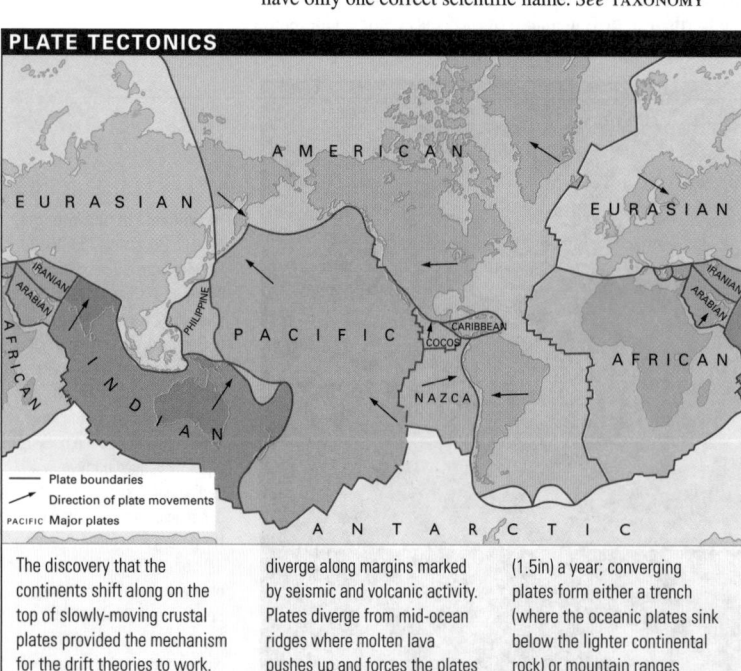

PLATE TECTONICS

AMERICAN — EURASIAN — EURASIAN — IRANIAN — ARABIAN — AFRICAN — PHILIPPINE — PACIFIC — CARIBBEAN — COCOS — INDIAN — NAZCA — IRANIAN — ARABIAN — AFRICAN — ANTARCTIC

— Plate boundaries
↗ Direction of plate movements
PACIFIC Major plates

The discovery that the continents shift along on the top of slowly-moving crustal plates provided the mechanism for the drift theories to work. The plates converge and diverge along margins marked by seismic and volcanic activity. Plates diverge from mid-ocean ridges where molten lava pushes up and forces the plates apart at a rate of up to 3.75cm (1.5in) a year; converging plates form either a trench (where the oceanic plates sink below the lighter continental rock) or mountain ranges (where two continents collide).

Mountain chains are explained as the sites of former subduction or continental collision. At a **conservative** margin, plates move past each other along a transform fault. Plate movement is thought to be driven by convection currents in the mantle. *See also* SEAFLOOR SPREADING

Plath, Sylvia (1932–63) US poet. Her verse includes *The Colossus* (1960) and *Ariel* (1965). The latter was published after her suicide, as were *Crossing the Water* (1971), *Winter Trees* (1971), *Johnny Panic and the Bible of Dreams* (1977), and *Collected Poems* (1981). She wrote one novel, *The Bell Jar* (1963). Deeply personal, confessional elements characterize her work. She was married (1956–62) to the English poet Ted HUGHES.

platinum (symbol Pt) Lustrous, silver-white metal, the first of the six metallic TRANSITION ELEMENTS Platinum was used for decorations by pre-Columbian South Americans. It was discovered in 1557 in Central America by the Italian-born French scientist Julius Scaliger (1484–1558) with the Spanish conquistadors and named 'little silver' in Spanish (*platina*). it is chiefly found in certain ores of nickel. Malleable and ductile, it is used in jewellery, dentistry, electrical-resistance wire, magnets, thermocouples, surgical tools, electrodes and other laboratory apparatus, and as a CATALYST in catalytic converters for car exhausts. It is chemically unreactive and resists tarnishing and CORROSION. Properties: at.no. 78; r.a.m. 195.09; r.d. 21.45; m.p. 1,772°C (3,222°F); b.p. 3,800°C (6,872°F); most common isotope Pt[195] (33.8%).

Plato (*c.*427–*c.*347 BC) Ancient Greek philosopher and writer who formulated an ethical and metaphysical system based upon philosophical IDEALISM. From *c.*407 BC he was a disciple of SOCRATES, from whom he may have derived many of his ideas about ethics. Following the trial and execution of Socrates in 399 BC Plato withdrew to Megara, after which he is believed to have travelled extensively in Egypt, Italy and Sicily. He visited Syracuse in Sicily three times, in about 388, 367, and 361–360 BC during the reigns of the tyrants Dionysius I and II. Plato sought to educate Dionysius II as a philosopherking and to set up an ideal political system under him, but the venture failed. Meanwhile, in Athens, Plato set up his famous ACADEMY (*c.*387BC). In the Academy he taught several young people, including ARISTOTLE. In addition to being a philosopher of great influence, Plato wrote in the form of dialogues, in which Socrates genially interrogates another person, demolishing their arguments. All of Plato's 36 works survive. His most famous dialogues include *Gorgias* (on rhetoric as an art of flattery), *Phaedo* (on death and the immortality of the soul) and the *Symposium* (a discussion on the nature of love). Plato's greatest work was the *Republic*, an extended dialogue on justice, in which he outlined his view of the ideal state.

platypus MONOTREME mammal of Australia and Tasmania. It is amphibious, lays eggs and has webbed feet, a broad tail and a soft duck-like bill. The male has a poison spur on the hind foot. It is 60cm (24in) long and eats small invertebrates. Family Ornithorhynchidae; species *Ornithorhynchus anatinus*.

Plautus, Titus Maccius (*c.*254–184 BC) Roman playwright. His works, such as *Miles Gloriosus* (*The Braggart Soldier*, *c.*211BC), were modelled on Greek originals. His plays typically combine farcical plots with amusing, low-life characters and witty dialogue. Shakespeare's *The Comedy of Errors* (1593) derives from Plautus' *Menaechmi* ('*The Two Menaechmuses*').

plebeian General body of Roman citizens, as distinct from the small PATRICIAN class. In the early years of the Republic, they were barred from public office and from marrying a patrician. By the 3rd century BC there was little legal distinction between them, although social differences remained.

Pléiade, La Group of seven 16th-century French poets. They were Pierre de RONSARD, the leader of the group, Joachim du Bellay (1522–60), Jean-Antoine de Baïf (1532–89), Rémy Belleau (1528–77), Estienne Jodelle (1532–73), Pontus de Tyard (1522–1605), and Jean Dorat (1508–88). Among the earliest writers of the French RENAISSANCE, they advocated French as a literary language instead of Latin and Greek.

Pleiades Young, OPEN CLUSTER in the constellation Taurus, popularly called the Seven Sisters. Although only six or seven stars are visible to the naked eye, there are in fact more than 1,000 embedded in a reflection NEBULA. The brightest member is Alcyone, which is more than 300 times as luminous as the Sun. The cluster lies slightly more than 400 light years away.

Pleistocene Geological epoch that began *c.*2 million years ago, during which humans and most forms of familiar mammalian life evolved. Episodes of climatic cooling in this epoch led to widespread glaciation in the Northern Hemisphere, and the Pleistocene is the best-known Ice Age in the Earth's history. It ended in *c.*8000 BC.

Plekhanov, Georgy Valentinovich (1857–1918) Russian revolutionary. After leading populist demonstrations, he was exiled in 1880 and adopted MARXISM. Plekhanov worked with LENIN until 1903 when, as leader of the MENSHEVIKS, he split with him. He returned to Russia in 1917, and died shortly after the RUSSIAN REVOLUTION.

pleura Double membrane that lines the space between the lungs and the walls of the chest. The fluid between the pleura lubricates the two surfaces to prevent friction during breathing movements. Inflammation of the pleura is called **pleurisy**.

Plimsoll, Samuel (1824–98) British social reformer. As a radical member of Parliament (1868–80), he was chiefly responsible for the Merchant Shipping Act (1876). This Act enforced government inspection of shipping and required merchant ships to have a line, subsequently known as the **Plimsoll line**, painted on their hulls to indicate safe loading limits.

Pliny (the Elder) (AD 23–79) (Gaius Plinius Secundus) Roman author of *Historia Naturalis* ('*Natural History*'). His one major surviving work, it covers a vast range of subjects, although it is an uncritical mixture of fact and fiction.

Pliny (the Younger) (*c.*AD 62–114) (Gaius Plinius Caecilius Secundus) Roman administrator. The nephew and adopted son of PLINY THE ELDER, he became a senator and governor of Bythnia in *c.*112. He is best known for his correspondence with the Emperor TRAJAN, which provides a unique record of the life of a Roman gentleman.

Pliocene Last era of the TERTIARY period. It lasted from 5 to 2 million years ago and preceded the PLEISTOCENE epoch. Animal and plant life was not unlike that of today.

PLO *See* PALESTINE LIBERATION ORGANIZATION

Plotinus (205–270) Ancient philosopher, the founder of NEOPLATONISM. In *c.*244, he opened a school in Rome. In essence, Plotinus conceived of the universe as a hierarchy proceeding from matter, through soul and reason, to God. God was pure existence, without form. His pupil and biographer, Porphyry, compiled and edited Plotinus' writings into six books of nine chapters each, known as the *Enneads*.

plover Any of several species of wading shorebirds, many of which migrate long distances over open seas from Arctic breeding grounds to Southern Hemisphere wintering areas. It has a large head, a plump grey, brown or golden speckled body, and short legs. Length: to 28cm (11in). Family Charadriidae; genera include *Charadrius* and *Pluvialis*.

Plowright, Joan Anne (1929–) British actress. She mainly performed at Chichester and the National Theatre, London, often with her husband Laurence OLIVIER. Plowright's modern roles included the first performances of John OSBORNE's *The Entertainer* (1957) and Arnold WESKER's *Roots* (1959).

plum Fruit tree, mostly native to Asia and naturalized in Europe and North America, cultivated for its fleshy, edible fruit, which has a hard 'stone' at the centre. The most common cultivated plum of Europe and Asia is *Prunus domestica*; in North America, the Japanese plum (*Prunus salicina*) is crossed with European varieties to give several strains. Family Rosaceae.

pluralism In politics, theory that a number of groups with conflicting interests, none of which has absolute authority, wield state power. In philosophy, pluralism is the name given to the theory that there are many ultimate substances, rather than one (as in MONISM). Pluralism can also mean the holding of more than one office at the same time, especially within the Church.

Plutarch (*c.*AD 46–120) Greek biographer and essayist. His best known work is *The Parallel Lives*, which consists of biographies of soldiers and statesmen.

Pluto Dwarf planet in the outer Solar System. Until 2006, it was considered to be the Solar System's smallest and most remote planet. Independently, William H. Pickering and Percival LOWELL calculated its possible existence, and

INTERNET

Plath, Sylvia
▶ www.plathonline.com

Pluto
▶ www.nineplanets.org/pluto.html

▲ **plum** A hybrid of two other fruits, the cherry plum and the sloe, the plum tree (*Prunus domestica*) is a hardy tree that thrives in temperate regions worldwide.

P

PLUTO: DATA

Diameter (equatorial): 2,324km (1,444mi)
Mass (Earth=1): 0.002
Volume (Earth=1): 0.01
Density (water=1): 2.03
Orbital period: 247.7 years
Rotation period: 6.375 days
Average surface temperature: 44 K

P

it was located in 1930 by Clyde Tombaugh within 5° of Lowell's predicted position. Pluto has a mottled surface with light and dark regions, and signs of polar caps. It is covered with icy deposits consisting of 98% nitrogen, with traces of methane, and also probably water, carbon dioxide and carbon monoxide. Pluto has three known moons: Charon, Nix and Hydra.

Pluto Roman god of the underworld, equivalent to the Greek god HADES. He ruled over the land of the dead and was also a god of wealth, since his realm contained all mineral riches.

plutonium (symbol Pu) Silver-white radioactive metallic element of the ACTINIDE SERIES. It was first synthesized in 1940 by US nuclear chemist Glenn Seaborg (1912–99) and associates at the University of California at Berkeley by deuteron (heavy hydrogen) bombardment of URANIUM. It is found naturally in small amounts in uranium ores. Pu^{239} (half-life 2.44×10^4 years) is made in large quantities in breeder reactors; it is a fissile element used in NUCLEAR REACTORS and nuclear weapons. Its production is closely monitored to prevent the illegal spread of such weapons. The element is very toxic and absorbed by bone, making it a dangerous radiological hazard. Properties: at.no. 94; r.d. 19.84; m.p. 641°C (1,186°F); b.p. 3,232°C (5,850°F); most stable isotope Pu^{244} (half-life 7.610^7 years). *See also* TRANSURANIC ELEMENTS

Plymouth City and port on the Tamar estuary, Devon, SW England. In 1588, Sir Francis DRAKE set out from Plymouth to attack the Spanish ARMADA, and the MAYFLOWER sailed for America from here in 1620. Plymouth was severely damaged by bombing in World War 2. It is an important naval base, and has ferry links with France and Spain. Industries: China clay, machine tools, precision instruments. Pop. (2001) 240,718.

Plymouth Brethren PURITAN sect of evangelical Christians, founded in Ireland in the late 1820s by J.N. Darby, an ordained Anglican. They are named for the sect's first centre at Plymouth (1831). In 1849 they split into two groups, the 'Open Brethren' and the 'Exclusive Brethren', and have since split further.

Plymouth Colony First colonial settlement in New England (1620). The settlers were a group of *c.*100 Puritan Separatist PILGRIMS, who sailed on the MAYFLOWER and settled on what is now CAPE COD bay, Massachusetts. They named the first town after their port of departure. Lacking a royal charter, government was established by the 'Mayflower Compact'. During the first winter nearly half of them died. Plymouth Colony became part of the province of Massachusetts in 1691.

Plzen (Pilsen) City in W Czech Republic. Founded in the 13th century by King Wenceslaus II, it was a focal point for Roman Catholic resistance during the HUSSITE Wars. It is a centre for heavy industry (machine tools, motor cars, armaments), and is internationally famous for its beer. Pop. (2001) 166,274.

pneumatic Device powered by compressed air normally used to produce rotary or a reciprocating (back and forth) motion to speed up operations such as sawing, grinding, digging, hammering and riveting. The pneumatic drill used in roadworks has a reciprocating, pounding motion.

pneumonia Inflammation of the LUNG tissue, most often caused by bacterial infection. Most at risk are the very young, the aged, and those whose immune systems have been undermined by disease or certain medical treatments. The most common form is pneumococcal pneumonia, caused by the bacterium *Streptococcus pneumoniae*. Symptoms include fever, chest pain, coughing and the production of rust-coloured sputum. Treatment is with ANTIBIOTICS.

Po Italy's longest river, in N Italy. It rises in the Cottian Alps near the French border, and flows E to empty into the Adriatic Sea. The Po valley is an important industrial and agricultural region, and water from the river is used extensively in irrigation schemes. Length: 650km (405mi).

Pocahontas (1595–1617) Native American princess and early colonial heroine. According to legend, she saved the life of John SMITH, leader of the JAMESTOWN colonists, when he was about to be killed by her father, POWHATAN. Captured by the colonists in 1613, she adopted their customs and in 1614 married John Rolfe. She died during a visit to England.

Po Chü-i (772–846) Chinese poet of the T'ANG period. He served in various administrative posts. He wrote poems of social protest in simple, everyday language. Among the best known is *The Everlasting Wrong* (or *Song of the Everlasting Sorrow*, 806).

podiatry Treatment and care of the foot. Podiatrists treat such conditions as corns and bunions and devise ways to accommodate foot deformities.

Poe, Edgar Allan (1809–49) US poet and short-story writer. Much of his finest poetry, such as *The Raven* (1845), deals with fear and horror in the tradition of the GOTHIC NOVEL. Other works include the poem *Annabel Lee* (1849), and the stories *The Fall of the House of Usher* (1839), *The Murders in the Rue Morgue* (1841) and *The Pit and the Pendulum* (1843).

poet laureate Title conferred by the British monarch on a poet whose duty is then to write commemorative verse on important occasions. Poet laureates include Robert SOUTHEY (1813–43), WORDSWORTH (1843–50), TENNYSON (1850–92), John MASEFIELD (1930–67), Cecil DAY-LEWIS (1968–72), Sir John BETJEMAN (1972–84), Ted HUGHES (1984–98) and Andrew Motion (1999–).

poetry Literary medium that employs the line as its formal unit, and in which the sound, rhythm and meaning of words are all equally important. Until the modern introduction of the concept of FREE VERSE, poetry was characteristically written in regular lines with carefully structured METRES, often with RHYMES. *See also* LITERATURE; PROSE

pogrom Russian term for a destructive riot, generally applied to attacks on Jews in Russia in the late 19th and early 20th centuries. They were usually carried out by anti-Semitic mobs, encouraged by the policies of the tsarist government and often instigated by local authorities.

poikilothermic (ectothermic) Any animal whose body temperature fluctuates with the temperature of its surroundings, often referred to as **cold-blooded**. Reptiles, amphibians, fish and invertebrates are poikilothermic. They can control their body temperature only by their behaviour – by moving in and out of the shade, or orientating themselves to absorb more or less sunlight. *See also* HOMEOTHERMIC

Poincaré, (Jules) Henri (1854–1912) French mathematician. He worked on CELESTIAL MECHANICS, winning an award for his contribution to the theory of orbits. In 1906, independently of Albert EINSTEIN, he obtained some of the results of the special theory of RELATIVITY. He attempted to make mathematics accessible to the general public in such works as *The Value of Science* (1905) and *Science and Method* (1908).

Poincaré, Raymond Nicolas Landry (1860–1934) French statesman. He served in several government posts and was prime minister (1912–13) before becoming president (1913–20). An ardent nationalist and conservative, he accepted his opponent Georges CLEMENCEAU as premier in 1917, for the sake of national unity. Poincaré was again prime minister in 1922–24 and 1926–29. In 1923, he ordered the occupation of the RUHR to force German payment of reparations.

poinsettia Ornamental shrub, native to Mexico. It has tapering leaves and tiny yellow flowers centred in leaf-like red, white or pink bracts. It is a popular house plant. In its natural environment, the tree grows to *c.*5m (16ft). Height: to 60cm (2ft) when potted. Family Euphorbiaceae; species *Euphorbia pulcherrima*.

pointer Smooth-coated, sporting and gun dog that developed in the 17th century for hunting. It can be trained to indicate the direction in which game lies by standing motionless, aligning its muzzle, body, and tail. It has a wide head with a solid muzzle. The strong, lean body is set on muscular legs. The short, dense coat can be white with black or brown markings. Height: to 63cm (25in); weight: to 27kg (60lb).

pointillism (Fr. *pointiller*, 'to dot') Technique of painting in regular dots or small dashes of pure colour, developed from NEO-IMPRESSIONISM by Georges SEURAT. When looked at from a distance, the dots create a vibrant optical effect.

poison ivy North American shrub that causes a severe, itchy rash on contact with human skin. It has greenish flowers and white berries. Species *Rhus radicans* and *R. toxicodendron*. Family Anarcardiaceae.

Poitier, Sidney (1927–) US actor and director. His first major role was in *No Way Out* (1950). Poitier received an Oscar nomination for best actor in *The Defiant Ones*

(1958). He was the first black actor to win a best actor Academy Award, for *Lilies of the Field* (1963). Other films include *Blackboard Jungle* (1955), *To Sir, with Love*, *In the Heat of the Night* and *Guess Who's Coming to Dinner* (all 1967). The films he directed include *Stir Crazy* (1980).

Poitiers City on the River Clain, w central France; capital of Vienne department and chief town of Poitou-Charentes region. Poitiers was the ancient capital of the Pictones (a Gallic tribe), and an important centre of early European monasticism. In the 5th century, the city fell to the Visigoths, who were in turn defeated by the Merovingian king Clovis I (507). In 732, the Franks halted the advance of the Muslim Saracens at Poitiers. The Battle of Poitiers (1356) was an important English victory in the HUNDRED YEARS' WAR. The modern city possesses many historical buildings. Industries: metallurgy, printing, chemicals, electrical equipment. Pop. (2000) 83,448.

POLAND

The Republic of Poland faces the Baltic Sea in N-central Europe. Behind the lagoon-fringed coast is a broad plain. The land rises to a plateau region in the SE of the country. The Sudeten Highlands straddle the border with the Czech Republic. Parts of the CARPATHIAN MOUNTAINS lie on the SE border with the Slovak Republic.

CLIMATE

Poland's climate is influenced by its geographical position. Warm, moist air masses come from the W, while cold air masses come from the N and E. Summers are warm, winters cold and snowy.

HISTORY

In the 9th century AD Slavic tribes unified the region and the Piast dynasty came to power. In 1025 Boleslav I became the first king of Poland, but the kingdom disintegrated in the 12th century. Ladislas I reunified Poland in 1320, but the dynasty collapsed under the might of the TEUTONIC KNIGHTS. The 16th-century rule of the JAGIELLO dynasty is regarded as Poland's 'golden age'. In 1569 Poland and Lithuania were united. In JOHN II's reign, Sweden, Russia and Turkey all plundered Poland. JOHN III SOBIESKI restored some prestige, but his death brought division. After the War of the Polish Succession (1733–35) Russia dominated Polish affairs. In 1772 and 1793 Austria, Prussia and Russia partitioned Poland. The defeat of a Polish revolt in 1795 led to further partition, and Poland ceased to exist. The Congress of Vienna (1814–15) partitioned the country between Austria, Prussia and Russia. Polish uprisings in 1848 and 1863 against Russian dominance led to more impositions.

In World War 1 Poland initially fought with Germany against Russia, but Germany later occupied Poland. Poland regained its independence in 1918 and, in 1920, recaptured Warsaw from Russia. In 1921, Poland became a republic. The 1920s and 1930s were a period of dictatorship and military rule.

In September 1939, following a secret pact between Hitler and Stalin, Germany invaded and Poland was partitioned between the Soviet Union and Germany. Following the German invasion of the Soviet Union, all of Poland fell under German rule. The Nazis established concentration camps, such as AUSCHWITZ, killing more than 6 million Poles. Only 100,000 Polish

AREA 323,250sq km [124,807sq mi]
POPULATION 38,518,000
CAPITAL (POPULATION) Warsaw (1,626,000)
GOVERNMENT Multiparty republic
ETHNIC GROUPS Polish 97%, Belarusian, Ukrainian, German
LANGUAGES Polish (official)
RELIGIONS Roman Catholic 95%, Eastern Orthodox
CURRENCY Zloty = 100 groszy

Jews, from a pre-war community of more than 3 million, survived the HOLOCAUST. Polish resistance intensified. In 1944, a provisional government was established. The Germans ruthlessly crushed the Warsaw Uprising (August–October 1944). The country again became independent in 1945, when it lost land and around 6 million people to the Soviet Union. In compensation it gained parts of Germany as far as the River Oder, an important industrial region in the W. Other gains were Silesia and Breslau (now Wroclaw) in the SW and the Baltic ports of Stettin (now Szczecin) and Danzig (now Gdánsk).

POLITICS

Communists took power in 1948. In the 1970s, economic difficulties heightened opposition to Communist rule. In 1980 Lech WALESA founded SOLIDARITY, an independent union which sought political reform. Despite repression, Solidarity weakened Communist power, and in 1989 a coalition government was formed between Solidarity and the Communists. In 1990 the Communist Party was dissolved and Walesa became president. He faced many problems in turning Poland towards a market economy. Solidarity divided in 1990 over the speed of reform.

In 1995, former Communist Aleksander Krasnicwski dcfcatcd Walcsa in prcsidcntial elections, but continued to follow westward-looking policies. Poland joined NATO in 1999 and the EU in 2004. Krasniewski lost in 1997 but was re-elected president in 2000. In 2005 a swing to the right elected Lech Kaczynski of the Law and Justice party as president, and in 2006 his twin brother Jaroslaw became prime minister, but in a 2007 snap election Jaroslaw lost to Civic Platform candidate Donald Tusk.

ECONOMY

The economy has grown rapidly, although unemployment remains a problem. Manufacturing is important, and products include chemicals, machinery, ships, steel, and textiles. Coal is mined on a large scale. The agricultural sector is large but inefficient. Crops include barley, potatoes, rye, sugar beet and wheat.

MAP SCALE
0 50 100 150 km
0   50   100 miles

P

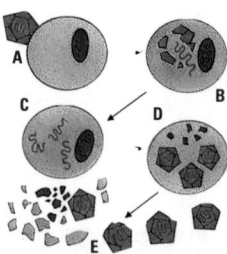

▲ **poliomyelitis** A viral disease that affects the human nervous system, poliomyelitis (polio) can often cause paralysis. Cells of the throat and intestines are the first to become infected. Virus absorption to the cell surface occurs (A), followed by penetration of the cell. Within the cell the virus protein coat is shed, releasing a coiled nucleic acid strand (B). Nucleic acid replication occurs (C), each new strand becoming surrounded by a protein coat (D). As many as 500 new infectious viruses are released as the cell bursts and dies (E).

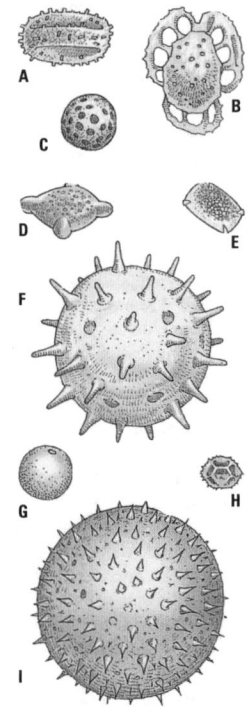

▲ **pollen** Pollen grains are found in pollen sacs, which are in the anthers (part of the stamens) of plants. Pollen grains are safe and effective storers of the male gametes (sex cells). They come in all shapes and sizes depending on the species of plant. The selection shows mistletoe (A), venus fly trap (B), spinach (C), honeysuckle (D), touch-me-not (E), cotton (F), rice (G), dandelion (H) and hollyhock (I).

poker Group of card games believed to have originated in Europe in the 16th century. All are gambling games in which the object is to win the pot (all the bets that are made after each card is dealt) either by holding the best combination of cards or by bluffing the other players into withdrawing. Many variants of different complexity exist.

Poland Republic in Europe. *See* country feature, page 603

Polanski, Roman (1933–) Polish director and actor. He established his reputation with the short film *Two Men and a Wardrobe* (1958). His first full-length film, *Knife in the Water* (1962), was followed by *Repulsion* (1965) and *Cul de-Sac* (1966). Later films include *Rosemary's Baby* (1968), *Macbeth* (1971), *Chinatown* (1974), and *The Tenant* (1976). He also achieved major successes with *Tess* (1980), *Bitter Moon* (1992) and *Death and the Maiden* (1994).

polar bear Large, white bear that lives on Arctic coasts and ice floes. It spends most of its time at sea on drifting ice, often swimming for many miles. It preys chiefly on seals and is hunted for fur and meat. Length: 2.3m (7.5ft); weight: to 400kg (900lb). Species *Thalarctos maritimus*.

Polaris *See* POLE STAR

polarized light Light waves that have electromagnetic vibrations in only one direction. (Ordinary light vibrates in all directions perpendicular to the direction of propagation.) Scientists distinguish between three types: plane-polarized, circularly polarized, and elliptical-polarized light – each depending on the net direction of the vibrations. Polarizing sunglasses use a Polaroid material to reduce the glare from light polarized by reflection from horizontal surfaces.

pole Generally either of the two points of intersection of the surface of a sphere and its axis of rotation. The Earth has four poles: the North and South geographic poles, where the Earth's imaginary axis meets its surface; and the north and south magnetic poles, where the Earth's MAGNETIC FIELD is most concentrated. A bar magnet has a north pole, where the magnetic flux leaves the magnet, and a south pole, where it enters. A pole is also one of the terminals (positive or negative) of a battery, electric machine or circuit.

Pole, Reginald (1500–58) English cardinal, the last Roman Catholic Archbishop of Canterbury. A grand-nephew of EDWARD IV, in 1527 he was made Dean of Exeter by HENRY VIII, who was his cousin. He opposed Henry's divorce of CATHERINE OF ARAGON and moved to Italy during the REFORMATION, returning to England in 1554 as papal legate to the MARY I. She made him Archbishop of Canterbury in 1556.

polecat Any of several species of small, carnivorous, nocturnal mammals that live in wooded areas of Eurasia and N Africa; especially *Mustela putorius*, the common polecat. It has a slender body, long bushy tail, anal scent glands, and brown to black fur known as fitch. It eats small animals, birds and eggs. Length: 45.7cm (18in). Family Mustelidae.

Pole Star (Polaris, North Star) Important navigational star, nearest to the N celestial star. It is in the constellation Ursa Minor and always marks due N.

police Body of people concerned with maintaining civil order and investigating breaches of the law. The first independent police force was established in Paris in 1667, becoming a uniformed force in 1829. Britain's first regular professional force was the Marine Police Establishment in 1800. The Metropolitan Police was created by Sir Robert PEEL in 1829. The first police force to be established in the USA was the New York City Police Department, formed in 1844.

poliomyelitis (polio) Acute viral infection of the nervous system affecting the nerves that activate muscles. Often a mild disease with effects limited to the throat and intestine, it is nonetheless potentially serious, with paralysis occurring in 1% of patients. It becomes life-threatening only if the breathing muscles are affected, in which case the person may need artificial ventilation. It has become rare in developed countries since the introduction of vaccination in the mid-1950s.

Polish National language of Poland, spoken by virtually all of the country's 39 million people. It belongs to the Slavonic family of INDO-EUROPEAN LANGUAGES. Polish is written in the Roman (Latin) alphabet, but with a large number of diacritical marks to represent the various Slavonic vowels and consonants.

Polish Corridor Strip of land along the River VISTULA, dividing East Prussia from the rest of Germany, and providing Poland with access (1919–39) to the Baltic Sea. It was created by the Treaty of VERSAILLES after World War 1, when Poland became independent. The city of GDANSK, near the mouth of the Vistula, was made a free city but, dominated by Germans, excluded Polish enterprise. The arrangement caused disputes between Germany and Poland, exploited by HITLER to justify his invasion of Poland in 1939.

Politburo (political bureau) Administrative and policy-making body of the COMMUNIST PARTY OF THE SOVIET UNION (CPSU). Formerly called the Presidium, it consisted of 11 or 12 full members and six to nine candidate members chosen by the party's Central Committee.

political party Group organized for the purpose of electing candidates to office and for promoting a particular set of political principles. *See individual articles*

politics Sphere of action in human society in which power is sought in order to regulate the ways in which people shall live together. For a society to engage in politics, it must conceive of society as being in a state of perpetual change.

Polk, James Knox (1795–1849) 11th US president (1845–49). During his administration, California and New Mexico were acquired as a result of the US victory in the MEXICAN WAR (1846–48), which Polk's aggressive policy had largely provoked. He also gained Oregon through the Oregon Treaty (1846). Other policy goals that he achieved included reduction of the tariff and restoration of an independent treasury.

polka Lively Bohemian folk dance. It became fashionable in Paris in the 1940s, and thereafter in Europe and the Americas. It is sometimes performed as a ballroom dance.

pollen Powder-like SPORES that give rise to the male sex cells in flowering plants. Pollen grains are produced in the anther chambers on the STAMEN. When the pollen lands on the STIGMA of a compatible plant, it germinates, sending a long pollen tube down through the STYLE to the OVARY. During this process, one of its nuclei divides, giving rise to two male nuclei (the equivalent of male sex cells or GAMETES), one of which fuses with a female sex cell in fertilization. The other sex cell fuses with two more of the female nuclei to form a special tissue, the endosperm. In many species, this tissue develops into a food store for the embryo in the seed. *See also* ALTERNATION OF GENERATIONS; POLLINATION

pollination Transfer of POLLEN from the STAMEN to the STIGMA of a flower. Self-pollination occurs on one flower and cross-pollination between two flowers on different plants. Incompatibility mechanisms in many flowers prevent self-pollination. Pollination occurs mainly by wind and insects. **Wind-pollinated** flowers are usually small and produce a large quantity of small, light, dry pollen grains. **Insect-pollinated** flowers are usually brightly coloured, strongly scented, contain nectar, and produce heavy, sticky pollen.

Pollock, Jackson (1912–56) US painter. A leading figure in ABSTRACT EXPRESSIONISM. He began experimenting with ABSTRACT ART in the 1940s. In 1947 he began pouring paint straight onto the canvas. Instead of brushes, he used sticks or knives to create the surface patterns. This method has been called ACTION PAINTING. His works include *The Blue Unconscious* (1946) and *Lavender Mist* (1950).

poll tax Tax of a fixed sum imposed on all liable individuals. Such taxes were occasionally levied by medieval governments: one provoked the PEASANTS' REVOLT (1381) in England. A poll tax called the **Community Charge**, introduced in Britain in 1989, was withdrawn after civil disobedience.

pollution Contamination of the natural environment, generally by industrialized society. Modern industrial and agricultural methods have polluted the Earth's air, land and water mainly through manufactured toxic chemicals (such as PESTICIDES and FERTILIZERS) or the over-production of naturally occurring chemicals (such as CARBON DIOXIDE). Pesticides, such as DDT, build up in the environment and can enter the FOOD CHAIN. The excessive use of nitrate fertilizers leaches the soil and causes WATER POLLUTION through concentrated run-off. The sulphur compounds produced by burning FOSSIL FUELS causes ACID RAIN. Carbon dioxide emissions from traffic exhausts contribute to the GREENHOUSE EFFECT. The use of CHLOROFLUOROCAR-BONS (CFCs) in AEROSOL propellants depletes the OZONE LAYER. A continuing problem is the storage of NUCLEAR WASTE. Pollution can also result from major disasters, such as CHERNOBYL, BHOPAL, or huge oil spillages from damaged tankers. *See also* CONSERVATION; ECOLOGY; EUTROPHICATION

Pollux (Beta Geminorum) Brightest star in the constellation Gemini; a red giant. Characteristics: apparent mag. 1.15; absolute mag. 0.7; spectral type KO; distance 35 light-years.

polo Field game played on horseback. Two teams of four players, on a field up to 182m (600ft) by 273m (900ft), each try to hit a small ball into a goal using flexible mallets. A game consists of four, six, or eight chukkas (periods), each 7.5 minutes long; additional chukkas may be played to decide a game if the scores are tied. Polo originated in Persia in ancient times and spread throughout Asia. It was revived in India in the 19th century and was taken up by British army officers there. It was first played in Britain in 1868, and is also played in the USA.

Polo, Marco (*c.*1254–1324) Venetian traveller. In 1271, he accompanied his father and uncle on a trading mission along the SILK ROAD, arriving at the court of KUBLAI KHAN, the MONGOL Emperor of China, in *c.*1275. According to his account, Marco became the confidant of the Emperor, travelling around s China and perhaps even visiting Burma. Captured by the Genoese navy in 1298, Marco recounted his tales to a fellow prisoner, a writer of romances named Rustichello. It was first published in English as *The Description of the World*. Although highly embellished, many of his descriptions and directions furnished European explorers with vital information.

polonium (symbol Po) Rare radioactive metallic element of group VI of the PERIODIC TABLE, discovered in 1898 by Polish-born French scientist Marie CURIE. Extremely toxic, it is found in trace amounts in uranium ores and may be synthesized. It is used in devices that remove static electricity and dust particles. Properties: at.no. 84; r.d. 9.40; m.p. 254°C (489°F); b.p. 962°C (1,764°F); most stable isotope Po209.

Pol Pot (1928–98) Cambodian ruler. In 1975, he led the communist KHMER ROUGE in the overthrow of the US-backed government of Lon Nol. Pol Pot instigated a reign of terror in CAMBODIA (renamed Kampuchea). Intellectuals were massacred and city-dwellers were driven into the countryside. Estimates suggest that *c.*2 million Cambodians were murdered. In 1979, a Vietnamese invasion overthrewn Pol Pot, but he continued to lead the Khmer Rouge in guerrilla warfare from a refuge in N Cambodia. In 1997, after a rift in the Khmer Rouge, it was reported that Pol Pot had been sentenced to life imprisonment. He died shortly afterwards, perhaps of heart failure. *See also* NORODOM SIHANOUK

polyanthus Any of a group of spring-flowering, PERENNIAL primroses of the genus *Primula*. Occurring mainly in the N temperate zone, they may be almost any colour. They have basal leaves and disc-shaped flowers, branching from a stalk to form a ball-like cluster. Height: to 15cm (6in). Family Primulaceae.

Polybius (*c.*200–*c.*120 BC) Greek historian. A leader in the Achaean Confederation, Polybius was deported as an honoured hostage to Rome in 168 BC. He became a friend of SCIPIO AFRICANUS MINOR, and accompanied him to Spain and Africa. He was present at the destruction of Carthage in 146 BC and later acted as intermediary between Rome and the Achaeans.

polychlorinated biphenyl (PCB) Any of several stable mixtures – liquid, resinous or crystalline – of organic compounds. They are fire-resistant and are used as lubricants and heat-transfer fluids. The use of PCBs has been restricted since 1973 because they are toxic and their resistance to decomposition in streams and soils poses a threat to wildlife.

polyester Class of organic substance composed of large molecules arranged in a chain or a network and formed from many smaller molecules through the establishment of ESTER linkages. Polyester fibres are resistant to chemicals and are made into ropes and textiles. Polyester plastics are used to make automobile parts, boats and bottles. Polyester films are used in sealing tapes and insulation wires.

polyethene (polythene, polyethylene) POLYMER of ETHENE. It is a partially crystalline, lightweight, thermoplastic RESIN with high resistance to chemicals, low moisture absorption and good

insulating properties. **Low-density** polyethene (LDPE) was first produced in the 1930s. It is mainly used in the manufacture of PLASTIC bags. **High-density** polyethene (HDPE), synthesized in the 1950s, is more flexible and is used for mouldings.

polygamy Marriage in which more than one spouse is permitted. The term is more often used to denote **polygyny** (several wives) than **polyandry** (several husbands). Polygamy is legal in some nations.

polygon Plane geometric figure having three or more sides intersecting at three or more points (vertices). They are named according to the number of sides or vertices: triangle (three-sided), quadrilateral (four-sided), hexagon (six-sided). A regular polygon is equilateral (has sides equal in length) and equiangular (has equal angles).

polygraph *See* LIE DETECTOR

polyhedron In geometry, three-dimensional solid figure whose surface is made up of POLYGONS. The polygons are called the faces of the polyhedron, and the points at which they meet are the vertices.

polymer Substance formed by the union of from two to several thousand simple MOLECULES (monomers) to form a large molecular structure. Some, such as CELLULOSE, occur in nature; others form the basis of PLASTICS and synthetic RESINS.

polymerase chain reaction (PCR) Chemical reaction, speeded up by an ENZYME, that is used to make large numbers of copies of a specific piece of DNA, starting from only one or few DNA molecules. It enables scientists to make large enough quantities of DNA to be able to analyze or manipulate it. PCR is extremely important in GENETIC ENGINEERING and GENETIC FINGERPRINTING.

Polynesia One of the three divisions of OCEANIA and the general term for the islands of the central Pacific Ocean; MICRONESIA and MELANESIA lie to the w. The principal islands in Polynesia are the Hawaiian Islands, Phoenix Islands, Tokelau Islands, the Samoa group, Easter Island, Cook Islands, and French Polynesia. Because of their Maori population, the two larger islands of New Zealand are also usually included. The islands are mostly coral or volcanic in origin. The inhabitants show physical similarities, and share common cultural and linguistic characteristics.

polynomial Sum of terms that are powers of a variable. For example, $8x^4 - 4x^3 + 7x^2 + x - 11$ is a polynomial of the fourth degree (the highest power is four). In general a polynomial has the form $a_0x^n + a_{1x}^{n-1} + a_2x^{n-2} + \ldots + a_{n-2}x^2 + a_{n-1}x + a_n$, although certain powers of x and the constant term a_n may be missing. The values a_n, a_{n-1}, etc., are the coefficients of the polynomial.

polyp Body type of various species of animal within the phylum Cnidaria. It has a mouth surrounded by extensible tentacles, and a lower end that is adapted for attachment to a surface. It is distinct from the free-swimming medusa. It may be solitary, as in the SEA ANEMONE, but is more often an individual of a colonial organism such as CORAL.

polyp In medicine, swollen mass projecting from the wall of a cavity lined with mucous membrane, such as the nose. Some growths can be cancerous.

polyphony Vocal or instrumental part music in which the compositional interest centres on the 'horizontal' aspect of each moving part rather than on the 'vertical' structure of chords. The golden age of polyphonic music was the 16th century, and masters included Giovanni PALESTRINA and William BYRD.

polysaccharide Any of a group of complex CARBOHY-DRATES made up of long chains of monosaccharide (simple-sugar) molecules. GLUCOSE is a monosaccharide, and the polysaccharides STARCH and CELLULOSE are both polymers of glucose. Higher carbohydrates are all polysaccharides and will decompose by HYDROLYSIS into a large number of monosaccharide units. Polysaccharides function both as food stores (starch in plants and GLYCOGEN in animals) and as structural materials (cellulose and PECTIN in the cell walls of plants, and CHITIN in the protective skeleton of insects).

polystyrene Synthetic, organic POLYMER, composed of long chains of the aromatic compound styrene. It is a strong thermoplastic RESIN, acid- and alkali-resistant, non-absorbent and an excellent electrical insulator.

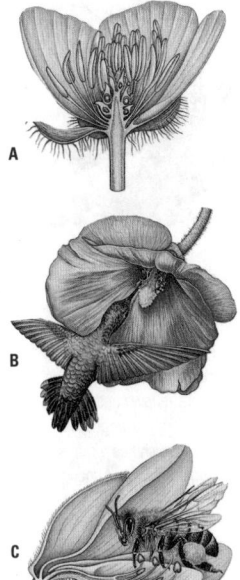
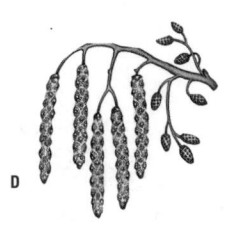

▲ **pollination** Flowers are adapted to different pollination methods. Non-specialized simple flowers, such as the buttercup (A), can be pollinated by a variety of means. Other flowers can only be pollinated by one method. There are bird-pollinated flowers, such as the hummingbird-pollinated hibiscus (B); bee-specialized flowers, including the gorse (C); and wind-pollinated flowers, such as the catkins found on the hazel (D).

P

▲ **pomegranate** The flesh of the pomegranate (*Punica granatum*), a fruit about the size of an apple, is densely packed with seeds that scatter when the fruit is burst. The pale yellow seeds are surrounded by a bright red, fleshy coating, which has a refreshing, astringent flavour. Although native to w Asia, it is now cultivated in warm regions throughout the world.

▲ **pondweed** The weedy, aquatic plant pondweed (*Potamogeton* sp.) is among the first flowering plants to colonize wetland areas. Over time, they encourage sediment to build up around the wetland edges, creating areas of shallower water where other species can take root. The run-off of agricultural chemicals, such as fertilizers, encourages the rapid growth of pondweed, accelerating the rate of evolution of wetland areas, often to a degree that can damage the habitat for other species of plants and animals.

P

INTERNET

Pontormo, Jacopo Carucci

▶ www.nationalgallery.org.uk
▶ www.nga.gov

polytetrafluoroethylene (PTFE) Chemically inert, solid plastic, known also by the trade names **Teflon** and **Fluon**. PTFE is used as a heat-resistant material for heat-shields on spacecraft, as a non-stick coating on cooking utensils and as a lubricant. PTFE is stable up to *c*.300°C (572°F).

polytheism Belief in or worship of many gods and goddesses. The ancient Egyptian, Babylonian, Greek and Roman religions were all polytheistic, as were the religions of the Americas before European settlement. HINDUISM is a modern polytheistic religion. *See also* ANIMISM; MONOTHEISM

polyunsaturate Type of FAT or OIL that has molecules of long CARBON chains with many double bonds. Polyunsaturated fats exist in fish oils and most vegetable oils. At room temperature, unsaturated oils are liquids and SATURATED FATS are solids. Polyunsaturates, which have low or no CHOLESTEROL content, are used in MARGARINES and cooking oils. They are considered healthier than saturated fats.

polyvinyl chloride (PVC) White, tough, solid thermoplastic that is a POLYMER of vinyl chloride. A PVC can be softened and made elastic with a plasticizer. Easily coloured and resistant to weather and fire, PVC is used to produce a variety of products, including fibres, windows, electrical insulation, pipes, vinyl flooring, audio discs, and coatings for raincoats and upholstery.

Pombal, Sebastião José de Carvalho e Mello, Marquês de (1699–1782) Portuguese statesman. His adept handling of the relief effort after a massive earthquake in Lisbon in 1755, led to his promotion to chief minister (1756–77) by King Joseph (r.1750–77). Virtual dictator of Portugal, Carvalho increased royal power at the expense of the old nobility, the Inquisition and the Jesuits, whom he expelled in 1759. His anti-clericalism and other reforms, such as the abolition of slavery in Portugal, led to him being classed as an 'enlightened despot'.

pomegranate Deciduous shrub or small tree native to w Asia. It has shiny, oval leaves and orange-red flowers. The round fruit has a red, leathery rind and numerous seeds coated with edible pulp. Family Punicaceae; species *Punica granatum*.

Pompadour, Jeanne-Antoinette Poisson, Marquise de (1721–64) Influential mistress and confidante of LOUIS XV after 1745. A strong influence on the court and on official appointments, she was a great patron of the arts, befriending DIDEROT and encouraging the publication of the *Encyclopédie*.

Pompeii Ancient Roman city in SE Italy, buried by a PYROCLASTIC volcanic eruption in AD 79. Pompeii was founded in the 8th century BC and ruled by Greeks, Etruscans and others before being conquered by Rome in 89 BC. The eruption of Mount VESUVIUS was so sudden and violent that *c*.2000 people were killed. The city was covered in volcanic ash, preserving houses intact until excavation began in the 18th century.

Pompey (106–48 BC) (Gnaeus Pompeius) Roman general. He fought for SULLA in 83 BC and campaigned in Sicily, Africa and Spain. He was named consul with CRASSUS in 70 BC and fought a notable campaign against MITHRIDATES VI of PONTUS in 66 BC. In 59 BC he formed the first triumvirate with Crassus and his great rival, Julius CAESAR. After the death of Crassus, Pompey joined Caesar's enemies, and civil war broke out in 49 BC. Driven out of Rome by Caesar's advance, Pompey was defeated at Pharsalus in 48 BC and fled to Egypt, where he was murdered.

Pompidou, Georges Jean Raymond (1911–74) French statesman. He served on DE GAULLE's staff from 1944 and was a member of the powerful council of state (1946–57), becoming premier in 1958. He was not reappointed when the Gaullists won the June election in 1968. After De Gaulle's resignation, he succeeded him as president (1969–74). He died in office.

Ponce de León, Juan (1460–1521) Spanish explorer. A veteran of COLUMBUS' second voyage, he conquered Puerto Rico for Spain (1508–09), and in 1513 led an expedition to explore rumoured islands north of Cuba. He reached land near what is now St Augustine, Florida, USA. In 1521, he returned with a colonizing expedition and received an arrow wound from which he later died.

pondweed Any of numerous species of a family of aquatic, perennial flowering plants of the genus *Potamogeton*, found mostly in temperate regions in freshwater lakes, but also in brackish and salt water. Most pondweeds have spike-like flowers that stick out of the water, and submerged or floating leaves. Family Potamogetonaceae.

Pontiac's Rebellion (1763–66) Native American rising against the British. Pontiac (d.1769) was an Ottawa chief who led a loose association of allies hostile to the British takeover of Québec (1760). A number of outposts in the Great Lakes region were overrun. News of the French withdrawal from North America fatally weakened the campaign, which soon collapsed.

Pontius Pilate (active 1st century AD) Roman prefect. In *c*.AD 26, Emperor Tiberius appointed him procurator (governor) of Judaea. The canonical gospels note his reluctance to execute JESUS CHRIST, although he eventually bowed to the crowd howling for his death. In *c*.AD 36, he was recalled to Rome after sanctioning the massacre of Samaritans.

Pontormo, Jacopo Carucci (1494–1557) Italian painter. He is thought to have painted *Vertumnus and Pomona* (1520–21), which shows qualities characteristic of MANNERISM. Other paintings include *The Madonna* (1518), *The Visitation* (1516), and *Deposition* (*c*.1527).

Pontus Ancient kingdom of NE Anatolia (Turkey). The coastal cities were colonized by Greeks in the 6th-5th centuries BC and retained virtual autonomy under the Persian Empire. The kingdom of Pontus reached the height of its power under MITHRIDATES VI (the Great), who conquered Asia Minor, gained control of the Crimea, and threatened Rome. After Mithridates' defeat by Pompey (65BC), Pontus was divided up under Roman rule, but it maintained its commercial prosperity.

pony Any of several breeds of small horses, usually solid and stocky. They are commonly used as children's saddle horses, for show and for draught. Types include the hardy Shetland pony; the Dartmoor and Exmoor ponies of Cornwall, Somerset and Devon; the grey Highland pony; the Welsh pony; and the Welsh Cob. Height: 115–145cm (45–57in) at the shoulder.

Pony Express (1860–61) US relay mail service between Saint Joseph, Missouri, and Sacramento, California. About 25 riders changed horses at 190 staging posts on the 3,200km (1,800mi) journey. The time for the journey was ten days, less than half the time taken by stagecoach. The service gradually petered out with the introduction of the telegraph system.

poodle Breed of dog believed to have originated in Germany. Bred originally to retrieve from water, its intelligence has made it a popular pet. It has a rounded skull and long, straight body, and a high-set tail, often docked. The thick, wiry coat is commonly clipped into an ornate style. The main sizes are standard, miniature and toy. Height: (standard) more than 38cm (15in) at the shoulder.

pool Form of billiards that originated in the USA. One version is played with eight single-colour balls and seven striped balls (numbered 1 to 15), plus a white cue ball, on a rectangular table with four corner pockets and two side pockets. The most popular version divides the striped balls and the single-colour balls, except the black ball (number 8), between the two players, so that the black is the last to be potted.

poor laws Legislation that was designed to relieve poverty in England. In 1601, the Poor Law Act required individual parishes to provide for the local poor via the levying of property rates. Three categories of poor were identified: vagabonds and beggars, the infirm and the 'deserving' unemployed. In 1795, the Speenhamland system provided levels of poor relief based on the price of bread and the size of families. In 1834, the Poor Law Amendment Act forbade the giving of assistance to the impoverished outside of the workhouse. In the 20th century, the poor laws were finally abolished by social security legislation and the creation of the WELFARE STATE.

pop art Movement inspired by consumerist images and popular culture that flourished in the USA and Britain from the late 1950s to the early 1970s. Pop art borrowed ideas from comic books, advertisements, packaging, television, and films. Techniques included SILK-SCREEN PRINTING and COLLAGE. Leading artists included Andy WARHOL, Roy LICHTENSTEIN, Claes OLDENBURG, Richard HAMILTON, and David HOCKNEY.

pope *See* PAPACY

Pope, Alexander (1688–1744) English poet. He first attracted attention for *Essay on Criticism* (1711), a poem in heroic couplets. Pope's reputation was established with the publication of his mock epic *The Rape of the Lock* (1712–14). The satire *The Dunciad* (1728–43) complemented his philosophical poem *Essay on Man* (1733–34). Pope also translated Homer's *Iliad* (1715–20) and *The Odyssey* (1726–26).

poplar Any of a number of deciduous, softwood trees of the genus *Populus*, native to cool and temperate regions. The oval leaves grow on stalks, and flowers take the form of catkins. Some species are called cottonwoods because of the cotton-like fluff on their seeds. Height: to 60m (200ft). Family Salicaceae. *See also* ASPEN

Popocatépetl Snow-capped, dormant volcano in central Mexico, 72km (45mi) SE of Mexico City. The crater contains sulphur deposits. Height: 5452m (17,887ft).

Popper, Sir Karl Raimund (1902–94) British philosopher of natural and social sciences, b. Austria. He proposed his theory of falsification in *The Logic of Scientific Discovery* (1934), saying scientific 'truth' cannot be absolutely confirmed. In *The Open Society and its Enemies* (1945), Popper attacked the historicism of MARXISM.

poppy Any annual or perennial plant of the genus *Papaver*, family Papaveraceae, or any related plant. About 100 species of the genus exist. They have bright red, orange or white flowers, often with dark centres, with four thin, overlapping petals and two thick sepals; all produce the milky sap, LATEX. The unripe capsules of the Asian opium poppy are used to produce the drug OPIUM. Plants closely related to the true poppy include the California poppy and the Welsh poppy.

popular front Alliance of left-wing political parties. In Europe, such alliances were formed in the 1930s partly in reaction to threats from the extreme right and with the encouragement of the Soviet Union. A popular-front government came to power in France, under Léon BLUM (1936–37), and in Spain (1936), where it provoked a military revolt and civil war. In more recent times, revolutionary parties in many African and Asian countries have adopted the name.

porcelain White, glass-like, non-porous, hard, translucent CERAMIC. Porcelain is used for tableware, decorative objects, laboratory equipment, and electrical insulators. It was developed by the Chinese in the 7th or 8th century. True or hard-paste porcelain is made of KAOLIN (white china clay) mixed with powdered petuntse (FELDSPAR) fired at about 1,400°C (2,550°F). Soft-paste porcelain is made of clay and powdered glass, fired at a low temperature, lead glazed, and refired.

porcupine Short-legged, mostly nocturnal, herbivorous RODENT with erectile, defensive quills in its back. Old World porcupines of the family **Hystricidae** have brown to black fur with white-banded quills and are terrestrial. New World porcupines of the family **Erethizontidae** are smaller with yellow to white quills and are arboreal. The largest European and African rodent, the African crested porcupine (*Hystrix cristata*), attains a length of *c*.80cm (31in).

pornography Visual or aural material presenting erotic behaviour that is intended to be sexually stimulating, and is lacking in artistic or other forms of merit. It is often considered to be demeaning to both sexuality and to the body. Although legal CENSORSHIP in most countries bans forms of pornography, the interpretation of the law is subjective.

porphyria Group of rare genetic disorders in which there is defective METABOLISM of one or more porphyrins, the breakdown products of haemoglobin. It can produce a wide range of effects, including intestinal upset, HYPERTENSION, weakness, abnormal skin reactions to sunlight, and mental disturbance. A key diagnostic indicator is that the patient's urine turns reddish-brown if it is left to stand.

porpoise Small, toothed whale with a blunt snout. Found in most oceans, the best known is the common porpoise of the Northern Hemisphere. Its body is black above and white below. Length: to 1.5m (5ft). Family Delphinidae; species *Phocaena phocaena*.

Porsche, Ferdinand (1875–1951) German car manufacturer who designed the Volkswagen Beetle. In 1934, Porsche produced plans for an affordable car that the Nazis named *Volkswagen* ('people's car') and promised to mass produce. Production did not start until 1945. Porsche also produced sports cars, for which the Porsche company is now famous.

port Fortified wine produced in the Douro Valley, N Portugal. It may be white, tawny (translucent brown) or red, and contains 17–20% alcohol. A vintage port ages in oak casks for 15 to 20 years. From the 17th to the early 20th centuries, manufacture relied on trade with Britain, using ships sailing from OPORTO on the Douro estuary.

Port-au-Prince Capital of Haiti, a port on the SE shore of the Gulf of Gonâve, on the W coast of Hispaniola. Founded by the French in 1749, Port-au-Prince became the capital of Haiti in 1770. Industries: tobacco, textiles, cement, coffee, sugar. Pop. (2005) 2,090,000.

Porter, Cole (1891–1964) US composer and lyricist. The majority of his many musicals for stage and film were vastly successful. They include *Gay Divorcee* (1932), *Anything Goes* (1934), *Kiss me Kate* (1948), and *High Society* (1956). Among his most popular songs are 'Night and Day', 'Let's Do It', 'Begin the Beguine', and 'In the Still of the Night'.

Porter, Katherine Anne (1890–1980) US short-story writer. She won acclaim with her first collection, *Flowering Judas* (1930). Later works include *Pale Horse, Pale Rider* (1939), *The Leaning Tower* (1944), and her best-known work, *Ship of Fools* (1962). Her *Collected Stories* won a Pulitzer Prize in 1966.

Portland City and port on the Willamette River, NW Oregon. First settled in 1845, it developed as a major port for exporting timber and grain after 1850. It was a supply station for the California goldfields and the Alaska gold rush (1897–1900). It is Oregon's largest city. Industries: shipbuilding, timber, wood products, textiles, metals, machinery. Pop. (2000) 1,583,000.

Portland Largest city and port in Maine, USA. Due to its deep natural harbour on Casco Bay, a settlement (Falmouth) was established here in 1632. The town grew rapidly under the MASSACHUSETTS BAY COMPANY. In 1775 it was devastated by the British during the American Revolution. From 1820 to 1832, it acted as state capital. The modern city is an oil terminus and shipping centre with important commercial links with MONTRÉAL. Pop. (2000) 64,249.

Portland, William Henry Cavendish Bentinck, 3rd Duke of (1738–1809) British statesman, prime minister (1783, 1807–09). He was briefly made prime minister at the end of the AMERICAN REVOLUTION. As home secretary (1794–1801), Portland helped William PITT (THE YOUNGER) draft the Act of UNION (1801). His second ministry ended in a feud between CANNING and CASTLEREAGH.

Port Louis Capital of Mauritius, a seaport in the NW of the island. It was founded by the French in 1735. Taken by the British during the Napoleonic Wars, it grew in importance as a trading port after the opening of the Suez Canal. The main export is sugar; other industries include electrical equipment and textiles. Pop. (1998) 147,100.

Port Moresby Capital of Papua New Guinea, on the SE coast of New Guinea. Settled by the British in the 1880s, its sheltered harbour was the site of an important Allied base in World War 2. It developed rapidly in the post-war period. Exports: gold, copper, rubber. Pop. (2000) 252,000.

Port of Spain Capital of Trinidad and Tobago, on the NW coast of Trinidad. Founded by the Spanish in the late 16th century, it was seized by Britain in 1797. From 1958 to 1962 it was the capital of the Federation of the West Indies. It is a major Caribbean tourist and shipping centre. Pop. (2002 est.) 45,200.

Porto-Novo Capital of Benin, West Africa, a port on the Gulf of Guinea near the border with Nigeria. Settled by 16th-century Portuguese traders, it later became a shipping point for slaves to America. It was made the country's capital at independence in

▲ **poppy** Cultivated since the Middle Ages, the opium poppy (*Papaver somniferum*) is the natural source of the drug opium and its derivatives, morphine and heroin. These are extracted from the latex of the seed pods. The seeds themselves are used as cattle food and as a source of oil. The dramatic flower makes the plant a popular garden ornamental.

P

◄ **porcupine** A coat of spines protects the porcupine (the Indian porcupine, *Hystrix indica*, is shown here). It erects these when danger threatens. The spines are loosely attached and may become embedded in predators.

INTERNET

Portugal
► www.portugal.org/
► www.portugal-info.net

1960, but Cotonou is assuming increasing importance. Today it is a market for the surrounding agricultural region. Exports: palm oil, cotton, kapok. Pop. (1992) 179,138.

Port Said (Bur Sa'id) City and seaport in NE Egypt, at the entrance to the SUEZ CANAL. Founded in 1859 with the start of the construction of the Suez Canal, it was a major coal-bunkering station. By the end of the 19th century it was Egypt's chief port after ALEXANDRIA. Although its harbour closed to shipping in 1967, after the war with Israel, it remained a fuelling station for ships using the canal. It reopened in 1974. Industries: fishing, tobacco, cotton, textiles. Pop. (1996) 469,533.

Portsmouth City and seaport in Hampshire, s England; Britain's principal naval base. The area was first settled in the late 12th century, and was already a base for warships when the naval dockyard was laid down in 1496. Industries: engineering, ship repairing, electronics. Pop. (2001) 186,704.

Portugal Republic in sw Europe. *See* country feature

Portuguese National language of both Portugal and Brazil, spoken by *c*.10 million people in Portugal and 100 million in Brazil. In addition, another 15 million people speak it in Angola, Mozambique, and other former Portuguese colonies. A ROMANCE LANGUAGE, it is closely related to Spanish.

Portuguese man-of-war Colonial CNIDARIAN animal found in marine subtropical and tropical waters. It has a bright blue gas float and long, trailing tentacles with highly poisonous stinging cells. It is not a true jellyfish: the tentacles are actually a cluster of several kinds of modified medusae and POLYPS. Length: to 18m (60ft). Class Hydrozoa; genus *Physalia*.

Poseidon In Greek mythology, god of all waters, and brother of Zeus and Pluto, identified with the Roman god NEPTUNE. Poseidon controlled the monsters of the deep, created the horse (he was the father of PEGASUS) and sired Orion and Polyphemus. He is always represented holding a trident.

positivism Philosophical doctrine asserting that 'positive' knowledge (definite or scientific facts) can be obtained

PORTUGAL

The Portuguese Republic shares the IBERIAN PENINSULA with Spain. It is the most westerly of Europe's mainland countries. The land rises from the coastal plains on the Atlantic Ocean to the w edge of the huge plateau, or Meseta, which occupies most of the Iberian Peninsula. In central Portugal, the Sera da Estrela contains Portugal's highest point at 1,993m [6,537ft]. Portugal also contains two autonomous regions, the AZORES and MADEIRA island groups.

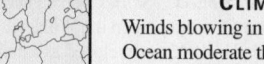

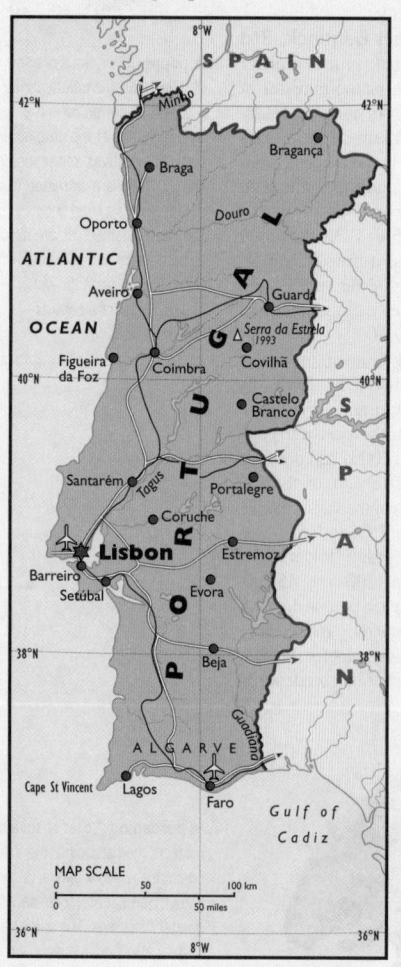

CLIMATE
Winds blowing in from the Atlantic Ocean moderate the climate. Portugal experiences cooler summers and milder winters than in other lands on the same latitude.

HISTORY
The Romans completed their conquest of the Iberian Peninsula around 2,000 years ago and Christianity was introduced in the 4th century AD. The Romans called Portugal Lusitania. Following the collapse of the Roman Empire in the 5th century, Portugal was conquered by the Christian Visigoths. In the early 8th century the entire Iberian Peninsula was conquered by Muslim Moors, who ejected the Visigoths in 711 AD. The Christians strove to drive out the Muslims and, in 1139, Alfonso I defeated the Moors. Spain recognized Portuguese independence in 1143. The reconquest ended when the Moors retreated from the Algarve in 1249.

JOHN I founded the Aviz dynasty in 1385 and launched Portugal's colonial and maritime expansion. His son, HENRY THE NAVIGATOR, captured the Azores and Madeira. In the 15th century the Portuguese led the 'Age of Exploration', and by 1510 had established colonies in Africa, Asia and South America. Portugal became wealthy through trade and the exploitation of its colonies, but its power began to decline in the 16th century when it could no longer defend its far-flung empire. The fall of the Aviz dynasty brought PHILIP II of Spain to the throne, and Spain ruled Portugal from 1580 until 1640. Portugal's independence was restored by John, Duke of Braganza, who took the title of JOHN IV. The BRAGANZA dynasty ruled until 1910.

In the 18th century, Marquês de POMBAL reformed Portugal's institutions and rebuilt Lisbon. England supported Portuguese independence and several times defended it from invasion or threats by Spain and its allies. JOHN VI fled to Brazil during the PENINSULAR WAR (1808–14) and his son, PEDRO I, declared Brazilian independence in 1822.

POLITICS
Portugal became a republic in 1910, but its first attempts at democracy led to great instability. Portugal fought alongside the Allies in World War 1. A coup in 1926 brought an army group

AREA 88,797sq km (34,285sq mi)
POPULATION 10,643,000
CAPITAL (POPULATION) Lisbon (1,977,000)
GOVERNMENT Multiparty republic
ETHNIC GROUPS Portuguese 99%
LANGUAGES Portuguese (official)
RELIGIONS Roman Catholic 94%, Protestant
CURRENCY Euro = 100 cents

to power. They abolished parliament and set up a dictatorial regime. In 1928 they selected António de Oliviera SALAZAR, an economist, as minister of finance. He became prime minister in 1932 and ruled as a dictator from 1933. After World War 2, when other European powers began to grant independence to their colonies, Salazar was determined to maintain his country's empire. Colonial wars flared up and weakened Portugal's economy. Salazar suffered a stroke in 1968 and died two years later. His successor, Marcello Caetano, was overthrown by another military coup in 1974 and the new military leaders set about granting independence to Portugal's colonies. Free elections were held in 1978 and full democracy was restored in 1982, when a new constitution abolished the military Council of the Revolution and reduced the powers of the president.

Portugal joined the European Community (now the EU) in 1986, and in 1999 became one of the 12 EU countries to adopt the euro, the single currency of the EU. In 2005 the Socialists, led by the moderate José Socrates, won a decisive victory in parliamentary elections.

ECONOMY
Although its economy was growing strongly in the late 1990s, Portugal remains one of the EU's poorer members. Agriculture and fishing were the mainstays of the economy until the mid-20th century, but manufacturing is now the most valuable sector. Textiles, processed food, paper products and machinery are important manufactures. Major crops include grapes for wine-making, olives, potatoes, rice, maize and wheat. Cattle and other livestock are raised and fishing catches include cod, sardines and tuna. Forest products including timber and cork are important, although forest fires often cause much damage.

P

through direct experience. Auguste COMTE first proposed positivism, and it was a dominant system of 19th-century philosophy. LOGICAL POSITIVISM developed in the 20th century, initially by the philosophers of the Vienna Circle, as an attempt to link 'positive knowledge' to the strict application of logic.

positron Particle that is identical to the ELECTRON, except that it is positively charged, making it the antiparticle of the electron. It was observed (1932) in COSMIC RADIATION by US physicist Carl ANDERSON. It is also emitted from certain radioactive nuclei. Electron-positron pairs can be produced when GAMMA RADIATION interacts with matter. *See also* ANTIMATTER; ELEMENTARY PARTICLE

positron emission tomography (PET) Medical imaging technique (used particularly on the brain) that produces three-dimensional images. Radioisotopes, injected into the bloodstream prior to imaging, are taken up by tissues where they emit POSITRONS that produce detectable photons.

possum Popular name for any of the PHALANGERS of Australasia. The term is also a US word for the OPOSSUM.

post-impressionism Various movements in painting that developed (c.1880–c.1905), especially in France, as a result of or reaction to IMPRESSIONISM. Roger Fry, the British painter and theorist, invented the term when he organized the exhibition *Manet and the post-impressionists* at the Grafton Gallery, London, in 1910. The show revolved around the work of MANET, CÉZANNE, GAUGUIN, and VAN GOGH, who are still considered to be the dominant figures in this phase of modern art. SEURAT was an important member of the post-impressionists, although his style is more accurately described as NEO-IMPRESSIONISM. The work of these artists varies stylistically but they are linked by their rejection of impressionist NATURALISM.

post-modernism Originally an architectural movement that started in the 1970s in reaction to the monotony of international MODERNISM. Its exponents sought new ways to merge anthropomorphic details or traditional design elements with 20th-century technology. The term is no longer restricted to architecture. In literature, post-modernism is characterized by works that refer to their own fictionality. In the early 1980s, the concept of post-modernism exploded into popular culture. The visual arts, television, and particularly advertising, were seen as producing the most exciting and creative work, again characterized by an anarchic, iconoclastic, parodic, and technically inventive approach. *See also* DECONSTRUCTION

post-mortem (autopsy) Dissection of a body to determine the cause of death. It is performed to confirm a diagnosis or to establish the cause of an unexpected death. Morbid anatomy (the examination of the dead) is a branch of PATHOLOGY.

post-natal depression Mood disorder, characterized by intense sadness, which may develop in a mother within a few days of childbirth. It ranges from mild cases of the 'baby blues', which are usually short-lived, to the severe depressive illness known as **puerperal psychosis**.

Post Office UK public corporation formed in 1969 from the General Post Office (GPO). Mail delivery, its sole function until the 19th century, was a Post Office monopoly until 2005. Private post, at rates related to distance, started in 1635; HILL's penny post of 1840 standardized the rate. The GPO set up a savings bank in 1861, a telegraph service in 1870, and nationalized existing private telephone companies in 1912.

post-traumatic stress disorder Anxiety condition that may develop in people who have been involved in or witnessed some horrific event. It is commonly seen in survivors of battles or major disasters. The condition is characterized by repeated flashbacks, hallucinations, nightmares, insomnia, edginess and depression. It usually recedes over time, but as many as 10% of sufferers are left with permanent psychological disability.

potash Any of several potassium compounds, especially potassium oxide (K_2O), potassium carbonate (K_2CO_3) and potassium hydroxide (KOH). Potash is mined for use as fertilizer because potassium is an essential element for plant growth. Potassium carbonate is used for making soap and glass, and potassium hydroxide for soap and detergents.

potassium (symbol K) Common metallic element first isolated in 1807 by English chemist Sir Humphry DAVY. Its chief ores are sylvite, carnallite and polyhalite. Chemically it resembles sodium. Potassium in the form of POTASH is used as a fertilizer. The natural element contains a radioisotope K^{40} (half-life 1.3×10^9 yr), which is used in the radioactive dating of rocks. Properties: at.no. 19; r.a.m. 39.102; density 0.86; m.p. 63.65°C (146.6°F); b.p. 774°C (1,425°F); most common isotope K^{39} (93.1%). *See also* ALKALI METALS

potato Plant native to Central and South America and introduced into Europe by the Spaniards in the 16th century. Best grown in a moist, cool climate, it has oval leaves and violet, pink or white flowers. The potato itself is an edible TUBER. The leaves and green potatoes contain the alkaloid solanine and are poisonous if eaten raw. Family Solanaceae; species *Solanum tuberosum*. *See also* SWEET POTATO

Potemkin, Grigori Aleksandrovich (1739–91) Russian soldier and politician. Involved in the coup that brought CATHERINE II (THE GREAT) to power in 1762, he became her lover for a time, and remained the most powerful man in Russia until his death.

potential, electric (symbol V) Energy required to transfer a unit positive electric charge from an infinite distance to a given point in an ELECTRIC FIELD. The unit of electric potential is the VOLT. The Earth's potential is taken by convention to be zero and a charged conductor has a higher potential. A battery's electric potential can make current flow in an external circuit. *See also* POTENTIAL DIFFERENCE

potential difference Difference in electric potential between two points in a circuit or ELECTRIC FIELD, usually expressed in volts. It is equal to the work done to move a unit electric charge from one of the points to the other. *See also* ELECTROMOTIVE FORCE (EMF)

potential energy Type of ENERGY an object possesses because of its vertical position in the Earth's gravitational field; also the energy stored in a system such as a compressed spring or in an oscillating system such as a pendulum. An object on a shelf has potential energy given by *mgh*, where *m* is its mass, g the acceleration due to gravity, and *h* the height of the shelf.

Potomac River in E USA. It rises in West Virginia at the confluence of the North and South Branch rivers, and flows E and SE to Chesapeake Bay on the Atlantic coast, forming the boundaries of Maryland-West Virginia and Maryland-Virginia. Length: 462km (287mi).

Potsdam City on the River Havel, E Germany; capital of Brandenburg state. During the 18th century it was a residence of the Prussian royal family. The 1805 Peace of Potsdam strengthened the alliance between Russia and Prussia against France. The POTSDAM CONFERENCE took place here in 1945. Industries: food processing, textiles, pharmaceuticals, electrical equipment. Pop. (1999) 129,500.

Potsdam Conference (July-August 1945) Summit meeting of Allied leaders in World War 2, held in Potsdam, Germany. The main participants were US President Harry S TRUMAN, Soviet leader Joseph STALIN and the British Prime Minister, at first CHURCHILL, later ATTLEE. It dealt with problems arising from Germany's defeat, including the arrangements for military occupation and the trial of war criminals, and issued an ultimatum to Japan demanding surrender.

Potter, (Helen) Beatrix (1866–1943) English children's writer and illustrator. Potter created the characters of Peter Rabbit, Jemima Puddleduck, Squirrel Nutkin and others. Her first animal stories were *The Tale of Peter Rabbit* (1901) and *The Tailor of Gloucester* (1902).

Potter, Dennis (1935–94) English playwright. He is best known for his television plays, notably *Brimstone and Treacle* (1976), *Pennies from Heaven* (1978), *Blue Remembered Hills* (1979) and *The Singing Detective* (1986). His unusual approach to dramatic form and his use of direct language often aroused controversy. He completed *Cold Lazarus* and *Karaoke* just before his death, and they were screened in 1996.

pottery Objects shaped of clay and hardened by fire or dried in the sun. The making of pottery is dependent on the plasticity and durability of clay after firing. The finished object can be divided into three categories: **earthenware**, the ordinary pottery dating from primitive times, baked at 700°C (1,292°F) or lower; **stoneware**, fired at up to 1,150°C (2,102°F), less

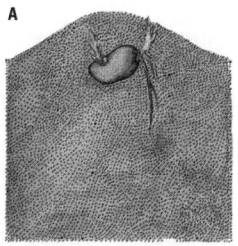

A

B

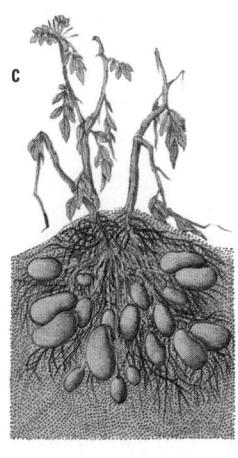

C

▲ **potato** The growth of the potato (*Solanum tuberosum*) takes three to seven months depending on variety. The tuber is covered with earth in fertile ground, and shoots its stems through 'eyes' in the skin surface (A). At six weeks, a large canopy of leaf growth develops and tubers grow (B) on underground shoots. Leaf growth can be dried chemically (C) to aid lifting.

P

porous, and until modern times produced more commonly in the Far East than in Europe; and PORCELAIN, fired at 1400°C (2552°F). After a clay pot is formed and dried, it is fired in a kiln; glaze is applied, and the pot is refired. *See also* CERAMIC

potto Slow-moving African PRIMATE with large eyes and a pointed face; it is nocturnal and arboreal. The common potto has sturdy limbs, a short tail and small spines formed by the neck vertebrae. Its woolly fur is grey-red. Length: 37cm (15in), excluding the tail. Species *Perodicticus potto*.

Poulenc, Francis (1899–1963) French composer and member of Les SIX. Spontaneity and melodiousness characterize his works, which include ballets, notably *Les Biches* (1923), orchestral works, chamber music, piano music and songs. Poulenc also wrote two operas: *Les Mamelles de Tirésias* (1944), and *Dialogues des Carmélites* (1957).

poultry Collective term for domestic fowl reared as a source of meat and eggs. Chickens are the most important domesticated bird in the world. They are the major source of eggs and an important meat source. These light-skeletoned birds have short, weak wings, strong legs, chin wattles and a head comb. Males are known as cocks; females as hens; and castrated males as capons. Some breeds, such as Rhode Island, Wyandotte and Plymouth Rock, are raised for meat and eggs. Others, such as White Plymouth Rock, Cornish and Rock Cornish, mainly supply meat. Species *Gallus domesticus*. Other forms of poultry are DUCK, GOOSE, GUINEA FOWL, and TURKEY.

pound Imperial unit of weight equal to 0.453kg. It has been replaced by the **kilogram**, the SI unit, but is retained in the USA for nonscientific measurements. It became a unit of currency when a pound (lb) weight of silver was divided into 240 penny units. The pound STERLING has been the main unit of English currency since the Middle Ages.

Pound, Ezra Loomis (1885–1972) US poet and literary critic. He was a leading figure in literary MODERNISM and a founder of IMAGISM and VORTICISM. In 1907, Pound emigrated to England. His early experimental works *Exultations* and *Personae* (both 1909) established him as a leading member of the avant-garde. In 1924, Pound moved to Italy, and during World War 2 he made pro-fascist, anti-Semitic broadcasts to the USA. In 1945, he was escorted back to the USA and indicted for treason. Pound was judged mentally unfit to stand trial and confined to a mental hospital (1946–58). He spent the rest of his life in Italy. Pound's masterpiece is the epic *Cantos* (1925–60), a reconstruction of Western civilization in free verse.

Poussin, Nicolas (1594–1665) French painter who worked mainly in Rome. At first inspired by MANNERISM, he later concentrated on antique art, specializing in mythological subjects. In the late 1630s, he turned to more elaborate Old Testament and historical themes. Among his notable works are *The Eucharist* (1644–48) and *The Seven Sacraments* (1648).

Powell, Anthony Dymoke (1905–2000) English novelist. He is best known for *A Dance to The Music of Time*, a series of 12 novels that portrays the snobbish world of the English upper classes after World War 1, beginning with *A Question of Upbringing* (1951) and ending with *Hearing Secret Harmonies* (1975). His later work includes the novel *The Fisher King* (1986) and four volumes of autobiography.

Powell, 'Bud' (Earl) (1924–66) US jazz pianist. A key figure in the development of BE-BOP, he gained a grounding with the Louis Armstrong All Stars (1953–66) and played with Charlie PARKER, Thelonius MONK, and Charlie MINGUS.

Powell, Cecil Frank (1903–69) English physicist. During the 1930s, he developed a technique to record SUB-ATOMIC PARTICLES directly onto film. In 1947, he used this method at high altitude to investigate COSMIC RADIATION and discovered a new particle, the pion (pi MESON). This discovery supported the theory of nuclear structure proposed by Hideki YUKAWA. Powell subsequently discovered the antiparticle of the pion and the decay process of kaons (K mesons). He received the 1950 Nobel Prize in physics.

Powell, Colin Luther (1937–) US statesman and general, secretary of state (2001–2004). He fought in the Vietnam War, and acted as national security adviser to Ronald REAGAN (1987–89). In 1989, aged 52, Powell became chairman

of the Joint Chiefs of Staff (1989–93), the youngest man and first African American to hold the highest ranking post in the US military. Powell and General Norman SCHWARZKOPF were the leading architects of the Allies' successful strategy in the GULF WAR (1991) against Iraq. Appointed secretary of state by President George W. BUSH, he was the first African American to hold such a prestigious political office.

Powell, (John) Enoch (1912–98) British politician. He entered Parliament as a Conservative in 1950, and was minister of health (1960–63). DOUGLAS-HOME dismissed Powell from the cabinet after his 'rivers of blood' speech (1968) against further UK immigration. He also opposed Britain's entry into the European Economic Community (EEC) and resigned (1974) from the Conservative Party over the issue. Powell later served as an Ulster Unionist MP (1974–89).

Powell, Michael (1905–90) and **Pressburger, Emeric** (1902–88) Powell and Pressburger were one of the most influential director/screenwriter partnerships in cinema history. Their collaboration began with *The Spy in Black* (1939). Their production company, The Archers, produced some of Britain's greatest film masterpieces. Their wartime films, such as *The Life and Death of Colonel Blimp* (1943), *A Canterbury Tale* (1944) and *A Matter of Life and Death* (1946), were intended as propaganda pieces. Other classics include *Black Narcissus* (1946) and *The Red Shoes* (1948).

power In mathematics, number of times a number is multiplied or divided by itself. If 2 is raised to the power 3 (written 2^3, called 2 cubed, or 2 to the 3rd power) it is $2 \times 2 \times 2$ or 8. A negative power indicates a fraction: e.g. 2^{-3} is $\frac{1}{2}^{-3}$, or 1/8. A fractional power indicates a root – the power $\frac{1}{2}$ is a square root ($\sqrt{}$), and the power $\frac{1}{3}$ is a cube root ($^3\sqrt{}$). Any number to the power 0 equals 1.

power In physics, rate of doing work or of producing or consuming energy. It is a measure of the output of an engine or other power source. The Scottish engineer James WATT was the first to measure power; he used the unit called HORSEPOWER. The modern unit of power is the WATT, named after him.

Powhatan (1550–1618) Chief of the Powhatan Confederacy of Native North Americans. This confederacy controlled the region around Jamestown, Virginia, at the time of the first English settlement (1607). The confederacy included *c*.30 peoples, with the capital at Werowocomoco. According to legend, the colonists' leader, John SMITH, was saved from execution by the intercession of POCAHONTAS, Powhatan's daughter.

Powys County in E central Wales; the county town is Llandrindod Wells. There are Iron Age and Roman remains. Offa's Dyke and the later Norman castles were built as border defences by the Welsh and English. During the Middle Ages, Powys was a powerful kingdom. The county includes fertile lowland valleys, highlands and plateau regions. It is drained by the Usk, Wye and Taff rivers. Agriculture and forestry are the main occupations. Area: 5,077sq km (1,960sq mi). Pop. (2001) 126,344.

Poznan City on the Warta River, w Poland. One of the oldest Polish cities, it became the seat of the first Polish bishopric in 968. It was the centre of Polish power in the 15th-17th centuries. In 1793 it passed to Prussia. The Grand Duchy of Poznan was created in 1815 as part of Prussia, but the area reverted to Poland in 1919. Industries: metallurgy, machinery, electrical equipment, chemicals, textiles. Pop. (1999) 578,235.

praetor Public official in ancient Rome, usually translated as 'magistrate'. From 242 BC two praetors were elected, serving a one-year term, usually followed by appointment as provincial governor. By the 1st century BC there were eight praetors. The office declined in importance under the emperors.

pragmatism Philosophical school holding the view that the truth of a proposition has no absolute standing but depends on its practical value or use. Primarily supported by US philosophers, C.S. PEIRCE first formulated pragmatism, and William JAMES and John DEWEY adopted and adapted it.

Prague (Praha) Capital of the Czech Republic, on the River Vltava. Founded in the 9th century, it grew rapidly after Wenceslaus I established a German settlement in 1232. In the 14th century it was the capital of BOHEMIA. It was the capital of the Czechoslovak republic (1918–93). It was occupied in

▲ **Pound** The US expatriate poet and critic Ezra Pound had a major impact on 20th-century Anglo-American literature, influencing writers such as Ernest Hemingway, T.S. Eliot and James Joyce.

P

World War 2 by the Germans and liberated by Soviet troops in 1945. Prague was the centre of Czech resistance to the Soviet invasion of the country in 1968. Sights include Hradcany Castle and Charles Bridge. It is an important commercial centre. Industries: engineering, iron and steel. Pop. (2005) 1,164,000.

Prague Spring (1968) Short-lived political and social reorganization in Czechoslovakia. From 1945, Czechoslovakia was subject to the hard-line communist policies of the Soviet Union. In January 1968, Alexander DUBČEK, a liberal communist, gained power and initiated reforms intended to create 'socialism with a human face'. Political prisoners were freed, censorship abolished, the power of central bureaucracy curbed and non-communist political parties legalized. In August, Soviet tanks rolled into Prague and imposed a Soviet occupation.

Praia Capital of CAPE VERDE, a port on the s shore of São Tiago Island. It is a key point in the Atlantic telegraph cable network. Praia exports castor oil, sugar cane, oranges and coffee. Industries: fishing, straw hats. Pop. (2000) 94,757.

prairie Region of treeless plain. The prairies of North America extend from Ohio through Indiana, Illinois, and Iowa to the Great Plains, and N into Canada. The pampas of s South America, the llanos of N South America and the steppes of central Europe and Asia correspond to the North American prairies.

prairie dog Squirrel-like rodent of w North America, named after its barking cry. It has a short tail and grizzled brown to buff fur. Active by day, it feeds on plants and insects, and lives in communal burrows interconnected to form colonies. Length: 30cm (12in). Genus *Cynomys*. *See also* GROUND SQUIRREL

praseodymium (symbol Pr) Silver-yellow metallic element of the LANTHANIDE SERIES (rare-earth metals). First isolated by Austrian chemist Carl von Welsbach in 1885, its chief ores are monazite and bastnasite. Soft, malleable and ductile, it is used in carbon electrodes for arc lamps, and its green salts are used in coloured glasses, ceramics, and enamels. Properties: at.no.59; r.a.m. 140.9077; r.d. 6.77; m.p. 931°C (1,708°F); b.p. 3,512°C (6,354°F); only one isotope Pr^{141} (100%).

prawn Any of numerous species of edible crustaceans in the order Decapoda; it is generally larger than a SHRIMP but smaller than a LOBSTER. Typical genera include *Penaeus*, *Pandalus*, *Crangon* and *Nephrops*, which includes the Dublin bay prawn or Norway lobster. Large prawns are called scampi.

Praxiteles (4th centuryBC) Greek sculptor whose graceful style epitomized the ancient Greek ideal. His most famous work was the *Aphrodite from Cnidus* (c.350BC).

prayer Act of thanking, adoring, conferring with or petitioning a divine power; also the form of words used for this purpose. Many religions have set forms for praying. Muslims recite prayers while facing in the direction of MECCA. In Christianity, the Roman Catholic missal contains regulated customary prayers. The Book of COMMON PRAYER plays the same role in the Anglican Communion. Prayer can also be the private devotional act of an individual using his or her own words.

praying mantis *See* MANTIS

Precambrian Oldest and longest era of Earth's history, lasting from the formation of the Earth c.4.6 billion years ago to the beginning of a good fossil record c.590 million years ago. Precambrian fossils are extremely rare, probably because the earliest life forms did not have hard parts suitable for preservation. Also, Precambrian rocks have been greatly deformed. Primitive bacteria and cyanobacteria have been identified in deposits that are more than 3 billion years old.

precession Wobble of the axis of a spinning object. It occurs as a result of the TORQUE on the spin axis, which increases as the angle of precession increases. The Earth precesses about a line through its centre and perpendicular to the plane of the ecliptic extremely slowly (a complete revolution taking 25,800 years) at an angle of 23.5°. The motion of a GYROSCOPE is another consequence of precession, because the entire ring containing the spinning wheel and its axle precesses around the support pivot.

precipitate Formation of an insoluble solid in a liquid either by direct reaction or by varying the liquid composition to diminish the solubility of a dissolved compound.

precipitation In meteorology, all forms of water particles, whether liquid or solid, that fall from the atmosphere to the

ground. Distinguished from cloud, fog, dew, and frost, precipitation includes RAIN, drizzle, SNOW and HAIL. Measured by rain and snow gauges, the amount of precipitation is expressed in millimetres or inches of liquid water depth. In chemistry, the formation of an insoluble solid in a liquid by a reaction in the liquid between two or more solubles. This is the opposite of dissolving. Precipitation is used to create insoluble salts; precipitation reactions are employed to recognize certain ions.

pre-Columbian art and architecture Arts of Mexico, Central America, and the Andean region of South America before colonization. In the MAYA period, beginning c.AD 200, many cities or ceremonial centres were built in Central America. The TEOTIHUACÁN, Zapotec, and Mixtec cultures also built pyramid temples. The TOLTEC and AZTEC civilizations succeeded these cultures in the post-classical period (AD 900–1300). The cultures constructed monuments without wheels or the use of the arch, and dazzling patterns decorated building surfaces. In the Andean region, the early Chavín sculptures were succeeded by the Mochica, the Tiahuanaco and, in the 14th century, by the rich temple architecture and sophisticated engineering of the INCA. Gold-working, weaving and sculpture were other important pre-Columbian arts.

predestination Christian doctrine that a person's ultimate spiritual salvation or condemnation by God has been ordained in advance. According to this doctrine, people are at birth committed to the events of life, and their fate at death is already mapped out for them. As possible solutions to the problem of how this doctrine affects free will, three propositions have been put forward: the first is to refute the doctrine altogether (**Pelagianism**); the second is to state that God never intended to save everybody (**Predestinarianism**); and the third is to qualify the premise by seeing God's prevision as conditional and subject to possible revision depending on the will and spirituality of the individual. This last position is the solution to which most Christians adhere. The concept of predestination is also found in ISLAM. *See also* PELAGIUS

pregnancy Period of time from conception until birth, in humans normally c.40 weeks (280 days). It is generally divided into three 3–month periods called trimesters. In the **first trimester**, the EMBRYO grows from a small ball of cells to a FETUS c.7.6cm (3in) in length. At the beginning of the **second trimester**, movements are first felt and the fetus grows to about 36cm (14in). In the **third trimester**, the fetus attains its full body weight. *See also* LABOUR

prehistory Period of human cultural development before the invention of writing. *See* BRONZE AGE; IRON AGE; MESOLITHIC; NEOLITHIC; PALAEOLITHIC; STONE AGE

prelude In music, a preliminary movement that serves to introduce a work of which it may or may not formally be a part. It was often used as the first movement of a SUITE. The popularity of CHOPIN's piano preludes led to its associations with a short piece of an imaginative nature.

premature birth Birth of a baby prior to 37 weeks' gestation or weighing less than 2.5kg (5.5lb). Premature babies are more at risk of death, illness or disability than those born at full term, and these problems worsen the more premature a baby is. Even if they survive, the most premature face serious and lasting health problems.

preposition Linguistic category or part of speech that shows the relationship (such as position or direction) between its complement and some other word in the sentence.

Pre-Raphaelite Brotherhood (PRB) Name adopted in 1848 by a group of young English painters who joined forces to revitalize British art. The most prominent members of the PRB were Dante Gabriel ROSSETTI, John Everett MILLAIS, and William Holman HUNT. They attracted fierce criticism for their rejection of RAPHAEL but were helped by the support of John RUSKIN. By 1853 the PRB had largely dissolved but Rossetti maintained the name, and under his influence a second wave of Pre-Raphaelite painting began in the 1860s, which lasted well into the 20th century. *See also* MORRIS, WILLIAM

Presbyterianism Major form of Protestant Christianity that became the national CHURCH OF SCOTLAND in 1690. It arose in the mid-16th century from the teachings of John CALVIN in Switzerland, and was taken to Britain by the Scottish religious

▲ **Prague** Hradčany Castle towers over the beautiful old city and the River Vltava. A large complex, most of it dates from the reign of Holy Roman Emperor Charles IV. Within the complex is St Vitus' Cathedral, which contains the tomb of Saint Wenceslas; the Royal Palace, which is the seat of the presidents; and many other important buildings.

▶ **primates** Because primates have large brains, they can learn complex skills and pass them down through the generations. Chimpanzees, for example, demonstrate high intelligence in their use of tools. They have been observed using sticks to 'fish' for termites. Young chimpanzees learn this by observing their parents – aged between two and three years, they manipulate sticks as a form of play, and by the time they are four years' old, they have mastered the use of the tool.

reformer John KNOX. Ministers, occasionally called pastors, are elected by their congregations and confirmed in their office by the Presbytery, a group of ministers from the local area. Members of the Presbytery are responsible for ordaining and installing (and removing) Church ministers. Once ordained, the minister carries out his work assisted by elders and trustees. Each presbytery sends delegates to a annual synod and to a General Assembly. In 1972, the Presbyterian Church of England (formed 1876) united with the CONGREGATIONAL Church of England and Wales. There are Presbyterian Churches all over the world, particularly in North America.

president Usual title for the head of a republic. In the USA, the president is elected by voters (through the ELECTORAL COLLEGE) for a term of four years and not exceeding two terms. The president is supreme military commander, appoints Supreme Court justices, ambassadors, and other high officials, has the authority to make treaties with foreign countries (with the advice and consent of two-thirds of the SENATE), grants pardons and vetoes legislation. A system of checks and balances limits presidential power.

Presley, Elvis Aaron (1935–77) US rock-and-roll singer. In 1953, he was signed to Sam Phillips' Sun Records in Memphis, Tennessee. In 1956, Presley took America by storm with his pelvic-thrusting performances of hits such as 'Heartbreak Hotel', 'Hound Dog', and 'Love Me Tender'. He starred in 33 highly successful films, including *Jailhouse Rock* (1957), *King Creole* (1958) and *G.I. Blues* (1960). Presley died at his Graceland mansion in Memphis, Tennessee, of a heart attack induced through drug dependence. He became a cult figure.

press *See* NEWSPAPER

pressure (symbol Pa) In physics, the force on an object's surface divided by the area of the surface. The SI unit is the pascal; 1 pascal is equal to the pressure exerted by a force of 1 newton on an area of $1m^2$. In meteorology, the millibar (symbol mb), which equals 100 pascals, is commonly used.

Prester John In Mediaeval legend, the supposed ruler of an undiscovered Christian kingdom in Asia or Africa. Stories of Prester (Priest) John and his miraculous kingdom, an early example of UTOPIANISM, first circulated in the 12th century. They placed him in India, perhaps a memory of earlier tales of Saint Thomas. 13th and 14th century accounts often claimed John's kingdom was in Africa, perhaps deriving from rumours of the COPTIC CHURCH in Ethiopia. European Christians hoped to make an alliance with Prester John against the Muslims in the age of the CRUSADES. Numerous expeditions tried and failed to find him and in the 16th century the legend faded into obscurity.

Pretoria Administrative capital of South Africa, Gauteng province. Founded in 1855, it was named after Andries PRETORIUS. It became the capital of the Transvaal in 1860, and of the South African Republic in 1881. The Peace of Vereeniging, which ended the SOUTH AFRICAN WARS, was signed here in 1902. In 1910, it became the capital of the Union of South Africa. Pretoria is an important communications centre. Industries: steel production, car assembly, diamond mining. Pop. (2000) 1,590,000.

Pretorius, Andries (1799–1853) AFRIKANER leader in the GREAT TREK (1835) to Natal. He defeated the ZULUS in 1838.

Pretorius was instrumental in establishing the independence of TRANSVAAL as the South African Republic (1852). His son, **Marthinus Wessel** Pretorius (1819–1901), served as first president of the new republic (1857–71) and of Orange Free State (1859–63). In 1881, Marthinus retired after victory in the first of the SOUTH AFRICAN WARS. *See also* KRUGER, PAUL

Previn, André George (1929–) US conductor, pianist, and composer, b. Germany. His early career was as a jazz pianist and musical director of Hollywood film scores, for which he won Academy Awards on four occasions. Previn was principal conductor of the London Symphony Orchestra (1968–79) and the Royal Philharmonic Orchestra (1988–91), and music director of the Los Angeles Philharmonic Orchestra (1985–89).

Prévost d'Exiles, Antoine François (1697–1763) (L'abbé Prévost) French novelist who lived as, alternately, a Jesuit novice, soldier, and forger. His most famous work, *Manon Lescaut* (1731), is the seventh novel of a series *Mémoires et aventures d'un homme de qualité* (1728–31).

Priam In Greek legend, the King of TROY at the time of the war with Greece. He had been installed as king in his youth by HERACLES, but by the time of the Ten Years' War was an old man. His sons HECTOR and PARIS were killed by the Greek forces. He was killed by Neoptolemus, the son of ACHILLES.

prickly heat Skin rash caused by blockage of the sweat glands in hot, humid weather. It occurs most often in infants and obese people. It disappears as the body cools.

prickly pear CACTUS with flat or cylindrical joints. It grows in North and South America and has been introduced into Europe, Africa and Australia. The jointed pads have tufts of bristles, and the edible fruit is red and pulpy. Family Cactaceae; genus *Opuntia*.

Pride's Purge (December 6, 1648) Expulsion of *c.*140 members from the English LONG PARLIAMENT. It was carried out by Colonel Thomas Pride (d.1658) on the orders of the army council. The aim was to rid Parliament of dissident members still anxious to negotiate with CHARLES I. The remnant, known as the RUMP PARLIAMENT, voted to put Charles on trial.

Priestley, J.B. (John Boynton) (1894–1984) English writer and literary critic. His literary criticism includes *The English Novel* (1927) and *Literature and Western Man* (1960). His novels include *The Good Companions* (1929), *Angel Pavement* (1930) and *Bright Day* (1946). Among his plays are *Time and the Conways* (1937) and *An Inspector Calls* (1945), both of which explore his notions of time.

Priestley, Joseph (1733–1804) English chemist and clergyman who discovered OXYGEN in 1774. He also discovered a number of other gases, including AMMONIA and oxides of NITROGEN. He studied the properties of CARBON DIOXIDE. Priestley advocated the later discredited PHLOGISTON theory.

primary Method used in the USA to select candidates for an election, in effect an election among the members of a political party. In a **direct** primary, the commonest type, any number of party members may stand and are voted for in a ballot of all the members. In an **open** primary, all the parties in an election are involved, and the voter votes for both the party and candidate of his or her choice. In a presidential election year, most US states select delegates to the national party convention in a **presidential** primary, the delegates having announced which presidential candidate they support.

primary school School providing elementary education for children. In the UK, primary school education starts at five, and children progress to SECONDARY SCHOOLS at 11 or 12. In the USA, primary education starts at first grade and continues through to the third or fourth year of elementary school.

primate Regional head of an episcopally structured church hierarchy. The term functions as a title. In the Church of England the term serves to describe the Archbishop of Canterbury, who is 'Primate of all England', and the Archbishop of York, who is 'Primate of England'.

primates Order of mammals that includes MONKEYS, APES, and HUMAN beings. Primates, native to most tropical and subtropical regions, are mostly herbivorous, diurnal (day-active), arboreal (tree-dwelling) animals. Their hands and feet, usually with flat nails instead of claws, are adapted for grasping. Most species have opposable thumbs, and all but humans have opposable big toes. They have a poor sense of smell, good hearing, and acute binocular vision. The outstanding feature of primates is a large complex brain and high intelligence. Primate characteristics are less pronounced in the relatively primitive prosimians (tree shrews, BUSHBABIES, LORISES, and TARSIERS) and are most pronounced in the more numerous and advanced anthropoids (monkeys, apes, and human beings).

prime minister Chief executive and head of government in a country with a parliamentary system. He or she is usually the leader of the largest political party in PARLIAMENT. The office evolved in Britain in the 18th century, along with the CABINET system and the shift of power away from the monarchy towards the HOUSE OF COMMONS.

prime number Positive or negative integer, excluding one and zero, that has no FACTORS other than itself or one. Examples are 2, 3, 5, 7, 11, 13, and 17. The integers 4, 6, 8, ... are not prime numbers since they can be expressed as the product of two or more integers.

primitivism Russian form of EXPRESSIONISM. It developed between c.1905 and c.1920, and was influenced by Russian folk art, FAUVISM, and CUBISM. It was characterized by simplified forms and powerful colour, used principally to depict scenes from working-class life. MALEVICH worked in the style early in his career; other exponents were Larionov and Gontcharova.

Primo de Rivera, Miguel (1870–1930) Spanish general. In 1923, he staged a coup with the support of King ALFONSO XIII. He dissolved Parliament, and established a military dictatorship modelled on the government of MUSSOLINI. He restored order and helped to end the revolt of Abd-el-Krim in Morocco (1926). The poor state of the economy forced him to resign in 1930. His son, **José Antonio** (1903–36) founded the FALANGE in 1933.

primrose Any of numerous species of herbaceous, generally perennial plants of the genus *Primula*, which grow in the cooler climates of Europe, Asia, Ethiopia, Java, and North America. It has a tuft of leaves rising from the rootstock and clustered flowers of pale yellow to deep crimson. In Britain, the name refers to *Primula vulgaris*. Family Primulaceae.

Prince (1960–) US singer-songwriter and guitarist, b. Prince Rogers Nelson. A prolific songwriter and recording artist, he first achieved major success with the album *Purple Rain* (1984). Other albums include *Sign o' the Times* (1988).

Prince Edward Island Province in E Canada, an island in the Gulf of St Lawrence off the coast of New Brunswick and Nova Scotia; the capital is Charlottetown. The island was visited by Jacques CARTIER in 1534 and colonized by French settlers as the Ile St Jean in 1720. Ceded to Britain in 1763, it was renamed in 1799 and became a province of Canada in 1873. Fishing and agriculture are the most important economic activities. Area: 5,,657sq km (2,184sq mi). Pop. (2001) 135,294.

Princeton Borough in W central New Jersey, USA; a leading academic and research centre. Princeton was settled in the late 17th century. An important battle in the American Revolution took place here in January 1777, when George Washington defeated the British forces. **Princeton University**, part of the Ivy League, opened in 1746. Pop. (2000) 14,203.

printed circuit Network of electrical conductors chemically etched from a layer of copper foil on a board of insulating material such as plastic, glass or ceramic. It interconnects components such as capacitors, resistors, and INTEGRATED CIRCUITS (SILICON chips). The printed circuit board (PCB) represents one stage in the miniaturization of electronic circuits. It was invented in 1948 by the Austrian scientist Paul Eisler.

printing Technique for multiple reproduction of images, such as text and pictures. In ancient China and Japan, carved wooden blocks were inked to print pictures. From the 10th century, the Chinese used separate pieces of type, so that each page could be printed from arrangements of standard characters. Metal type, made by casting, first appeared in Korea in c.1403. In Europe, GUTENBERG and CAXTON developed the use of letterpress in the 1400s. Printing expanded rapidly in the 1700s and 1800s. LITHOGRAPHY enabled printers to produce impressive colour prints. For text, stereotype printing plates were cast from the pages of type, so that the type could be re-used for setting other pages. Typesetting machines speeded up the process of setting up pages. The invention of

photography in the 1820s led to the development of new techniques for reproducing photographs in print, such as the halftone process. More recently, production speeds greatly increased with the application of photosetting, in which the type is set photographically on sheet film, and OFFSET printing. Today, many publications are produced using a WORD PROCESSOR to enter the text. DESKTOP PUBLISHING (DTP) programs allow images of the text and pictures to be assembled on standard computers. In the latest advances, computer files are transferred directly to printing plates.

prion Infective agent that appears to consist simply of a protein. Prions are thought to cause diseases such as CREUTZFELDT-JAKOB DISEASE (CJD) and kuru in humans, BOVINE SPONGIFORM ENCEPHALOPATHY (BSE) in cattle, and SCRAPIE in sheep. It is not yet understood how prions work; unlike viruses and bacteria, they do not contain DNA or RNA. A virus is a hundred times larger than a prion. The US neurologist Stanley Prusiner won the 1997 Nobel Prize for developing the prion theory in 1982.

prism In mathematics, a solid geometrical figure whose ends are congruent (most commonly triangles) and perpendicular to the length, with the other faces rectangles. The volume of a prism is equal to the area of the end multiplied by the length of the prism. In physics, a prism is a piece of transparent material, such as glass, plastic or quartz, in which a light beam is refracted (bent) and split into its component colours (spectrum).

prisoner of war (POW) In international law, military personnel captured by the enemy in an armed conflict between states. Their treatment is expected to be humane. The 1907 Hague Convention and the GENEVA CONVENTION of 1949 widened the scope of the first international convention on prisoners of war, signed at the Hague Peace Conference of 1899.

privateer Privately owned vessel with a government commission to capture enemy shipping. Government licences, called 'letters of marque', distinguished privateers from pirates. Crews were unpaid but were allowed to keep the booty. Privateering was at its height from the 16th to the 18th century. It was outlawed by most European powers in the Declaration of Paris (1856) and abolished by the Hague Conference of 1907.

privatization Transfer of state-run enterprises to private ownership. It is the opposite of NATIONALIZATION. In the 1980s, policy-makers in some European countries, as well as Canada, Japan, and New Zealand, maintained that economic growth would best be encouraged by governments selling nationalized industries to independent enterprises, which

P

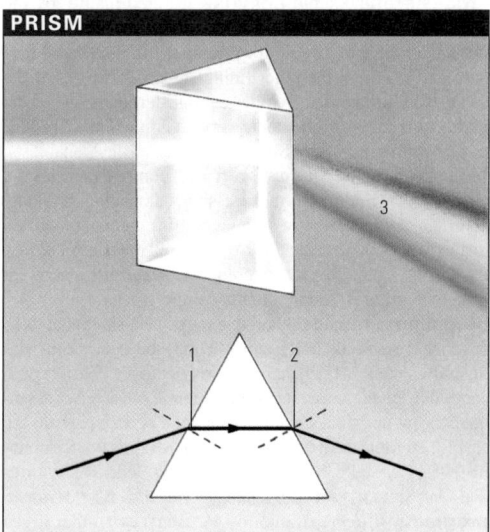

PRISM

When light hits a prism it is refracted by the two surfaces it hits (1, 2). White light splits into the spectrum (3) because each of the colours of spectrum have varying wavelengths. For example, the short wavelengths of blue and indigo are refracted more than colours further down the spectrum with longer wavelengths, such as orange and red.

were then free to respond to market forces and create a more efficient and competitive company. In the early 1990s, the trend was taken up by many former Soviet-bloc countries.

privy council Group of main advisers to the British monarch. It developed in the Middle Ages out of the King's Council (Curia Regis). As the CABINET system of government developed, the privy council's powers became increasingly restricted. Its judicial committee, established by legislation in 1833, is the final appeal court for most Commonwealth countries.

probability Number representing the likelihood of a given occurrence. The probability of a specified event is the number of ways that an event may occur divided by the total possible number of outcomes, assuming that each possibility is equally likely. For instance, in one throw of a six-sided die, there are six possible outcomes, and three of these are an even number: the probability of throwing an even number is thus 3/6, or 1/2. Blaise PASCAL and Pierre de FERMAT first developed the theory of probability c.1654.

probate Legal term for the certification by a court of law that a the will of a person who has died, or an official copy of one, is valid.

Procyon (Alpha Canis Minoris) Brightest star in the constellation of Canis Minor and one of the stars nearest to the Sun. The star, known as Procyon A, has a faint white dwarf companion, Procyon B. Characteristics: apparent mag. 0.34 (A), 10.8 (B); absolute mag. 2.6 (A), 13.1 (B); spectral type F5 (A), wF (B); distance 11.4 light-years.

Prodi, Romano (1939–) Italian statesman, prime minister of Italy (1996–98, 2006–), president of the EUROPEAN COMMISSION (1999–2004). He led the Olive Tree Alliance to a narrow victory in the 1996 elections in Italy. Prodi preserved a fragile coalition for 18 months, and his austerity measures enabled Italy to join the EURO in 1999. He served as head of the European Commission from 1999–2004, and sought to restore public confidence in the Commission and to prepare the EUROPEAN UNION (EU) for enlargement. In 2006 he led a broad centre-left coalition to victory in the Italian general elections. In 2007 he resigned over a foreign policy dispute but returned after a senate vote of confidence in his leadership.

Profumo, John Dennis (1915–2006) British politician. Profumo became a Conservative member of Parliament in 1940. In 1960, he joined Harold MACMILLAN as secretary of war. In 1963, Profumo was forced to resign after lying to the House of Commons about his affair with Christine Keeler, a call-girl who was also involved with a Soviet naval attaché.

progesterone Steroid HORMONE secreted mainly by the corpus luteum of the mammalian OVARY and by the PLACENTA during pregnancy. Its principal function is to prepare and maintain the inner lining (ENDOMETRIUM) of the UTERUS for pregnancy. Synthetic progesterone is one of the main components of the contraceptive PILL.

program (SOFTWARE) Set of instructions that enables a COMPUTER to carry out a task. A typical computer carries out many tasks including word processing, calculating, drawing, communicating, and providing games. Programs are written in a variety of COMPUTER LANGUAGES, and are usually stored on a HARD DISK. To make a computer perform a particular task, a program is loaded into the computer's RAM.

programme music (illustrative music) Music that aims to describe a scene or tell a story. It may be contrasted with **absolute music**, which has no direct references to experiences outside the music itself. Programme music is an essential concept in the music of the Romantic period; perhaps the earliest example from this time is BEETHOVEN's 6th Symphony ("The Pastoral"). Symphonic poems by Bedřich SMETANA and Jean SIBELIUS are later instances. *See also* ROMANTICISM

programming Preparation of a COMPUTER so that it can perform a specific task. Before being given DATA, a computer must be given a set of instructions, or a PROGRAM, telling it how to deal with the data. Each instruction is a single step, and all information must be in the form of binary numbers. For computer programmers, languages have been developed that make the task of programming increasingly intuitive.

Progressive Conservative Party (Fr. *Parti Progressiste-Conservateur du Canada*, formerly Liberal-Conservative Party) Canadian political party formed by John A. Macdonald in 1854. The party adopted its present name in 1942. Between 1948 and 1978, the Progressive Conservative Party held office only once (1957–63), under John Diefenbaker. Joe Clark formed a short-lived government (1979–80), but the Liberal Party soon returned to power. In the 1984 general elections, the Progressive Conservatives led by Brian MULRONEY won a landslide victory. In 1988, Mulroney was re-elected with a smaller majority. In 1993, Kim Campbell, Canada's first woman prime minister, succeeded Mulroney. Later the same year, Campbell was heavily defeated by a resurgent Liberal Party led by Jean CHRÉTIEN.

progressive education Movement that began in the late 19th century in Europe and the USA, as a reaction to formal traditional education. In Europe, FROEBEL, PESTALOZZI, and Maria Montessori were influential in the movement, which aimed to educate 'the whole child'. In the USA, the movement owed much to the philosophy of John DEWEY. It led in some cases to what critics termed laxness, and produced a backlash in the form of the 'back to basics' movement.

Prohibition (1919–33) Period in US history when the government prohibited the manufacture, sale, and transport of alcoholic drinks. The 18th Amendment to the US Constitution, confirmed by the Volstead Act (1919), brought in Prohibition. It failed due to smuggling, illicit manufacture, corruption of officials and police, and the growth of organized crime financed by BOOTLEGGING. The 21st Amendment (1933) repealed Prohibition.

projector Instrument with a lens system, used to cast images onto a screen from an illuminated flat object. An **episcope** is a projector for opaque objects such as a printed page; it uses light that is reflected from the object. A **diascope** is a projector for transparent objects such as photographic slides and films; it uses light transmitted through the object. An **epidiascope** can project images from both transparent and opaque objects. A motion-picture or **cine** projector produces moving images from many frames (pictures) on a transparent film.

prokaryote (formerly Monera) Any member of the biological KINGDOM (Prokaryotae); it includes BACTERIA and CYANOBACTERIA (formerly blue-green algae). They are simple celled organisms. DNA is not contained in chromosomes in the NUCLEUS, but lies in a distinct part of the CYTOPLASM, called the nucleoid. They have no distinct membrane-surrounded structures (organelles). Cell division is simple and, in the rare cases where SEXUAL REPRODUCTION occurs, genetic material is simply transferred from one partner to another; there are no separate sex cells. In photosynthetic prokaryotes, PHOTOSYNTHESIS takes place on the cell membrane. At present, two subkingdoms are recognized: ARCHAEBACTERIA and EUBACTERIA. *See also* ASEXUAL REPRODUCTION; EUKARYOTE; SYMBIOSIS

Prokhorov, Aleksandr Mikhailovich (1916–2002) Soviet physicist, b. Australia. He shared the 1964 Nobel Prize in physics with Nikolai BASOV and Charles H. TOWNES. Prokhorov's research in quantum electronics resulted in the development of the MASER and LASER.

Prokofiev, Sergei (1891–1953) Russian composer whose style is characterized by biting dissonances within rich harmony and brilliant orchestration. His most popular works include the ballets *Romeo and Juliet* (1935) and *Cinderella* (1944), the *Classical* (First) Symphony (1918), *Peter and the Wolf* (1936), and the comic opera *The Love for Three Oranges* (1921). He also composed film scores, notably *Lieutenant Kije* (1934), *Alexander Nevsky* (1938) and *Ivan the Terrible* (1942–45).

prolapse Displacement of an organ due to weakening of supporting tissues. It most often affects the rectum, due to bowel problems, or the UTERUS following repeated pregnancies.

proletariat Marxist term for those classes of an industrial society that have no source of income other than wages. According to MARX, the proletariat is the true creator of the objects produced by industry, and it would become an irresistible force when the internal contradictions of CAPITALISM weakened the authority of the factory-owning middle class.

promenade concerts Annual concert series organized by the BBC in the Royal Albert Hall, London, where

P

inexpensive standing room is available in the gallery and the stalls. Such concerts originated in Paris in 1833, and from 1838 were given at Drury Lane, Covent Garden and elsewhere. 'Proms' in their modern series began at the Queen's Hall, London, in 1895, under the baton of Sir Henry WOOD.

Prometheus In Greek mythology, the fire-giver. He created the human race, provided them with reason and stole fire from the gods. For this theft, ZEUS had him chained to a rock where an eagle consumed his liver for eternity. In some myths, he was rescued by HERACLES.

promethium (symbol Pm) Radioactive metallic element of the LANTHANIDE SERIES (rare-earth metals). It was made in 1941 by the particle bombardment of NEODYMIUM and PRASEODYMIUM. Promethium occurs in minute amounts in uranium ores. The isotope Pm^{147} is used in phosphorescent paints, X-rays, and in nuclear-powered batteries for space vehicles. Properties: at.no. 61; m.p. 1,080°C (1,976°F); b.p. 2,460°C (4,460°F); most stable isotope Pm^{145} (half-life 17.7 years).

pronghorn Only extant member of the family Antilocapridae, related to the ANTELOPE. It is a horned, hoofed, herbivorous animal of w USA and N Mexico. The swiftest North American mammal, it reaches speeds of 80km/h (50mph) over short distances. Height: 3ft (90cm); weight: 45kg (100lb).

pronoun Linguistic category (part of speech) that has no complete independent meaning and that derives some aspect of meaning from elsewhere. **Deictic** pronouns take some of their meaning from context, such as *you*, whose meaning changes according to who is speaking and who is addressed. **Anaphoric** pronouns take some of their meaning from a previous part of what is said or written: in the sentence *The piano stood where everyone could see it, 'it'* refers to the piano mentioned (its antecedent). Types of pronouns are: personal, relative, intensive, reflexive, interrogative, and demonstrative.

propaganda Systematic manipulation of public opinion through the media. Although examples are found in ancient and early modern writings, the most effective propagandists in the 20th century were totalitarian governments of industrialized states, which were able to control all means of public communication. Many political, economic and social organizations, and pressure groups employ some kind of propaganda.

propane Colourless, flammable gas (C_3H_8), the third member of the ALKANE series of HYDROCARBONS. It occurs in natural gas, from which it is obtained; it is also obtained during petroleum refining. Propane is used (as bottled gas) as a fuel, as a solvent and in the preparation of many chemicals. Properties: m.p. −190°C (−310°F); b.p. −42°C (−43.6°F).

propanol (propyl alcohol) Colourless ALCOHOL used as a solvent and in the manufacture of various chemicals. It exists as two ISOMERS. Normal propanol, $CH_3CH_2CH_2OH$, is a by-product of the synthesis of METHANOL (methyl alcohol). Isopropanol (isopropyl alcohol), $(CH_3)_2CHOH$, is a secondary alcohol that is easily oxidized into acetone.

propanone (acetone) Colourless flammable liquid (CH_3COCH_3) made by oxidizing isopropyl alcohol. It is a raw material for the manufacture of many organic chemicals and is a widely used solvent. Properties: r.d. 0.79; m.p. −94.8°C (−138.6°F); b.p. 56.2°C (133.2°F).

propene (propylene) Colourless HYDROCARBON, manufactured by the thermal CRACKING of ETHENE. It is used in the manufacture of a wide range of chemicals, including vinyl and acrylic resins. Properties: m.p. −185°C (−301°F); b.p. −48°C (−54.4°F).

prophet Individual who is thought to be a divinely inspired messenger from a god, or is believed to possess the power to foretell future events. The classic examples of prophets were the holy men and seers who preached by the authority of YAHWEH to the Jews of the Old Testament kingdoms of ISRAEL and JUDAH. Part of the Old Testament consists of books devoted to their preachings and predictions. The term 'prophet' also applied to ABRAHAM, MOSES, and SAMUEL. JOHN THE BAPTIST fulfilled the role of a New Testament prophet, predicting the coming of the Messiah. In ancient Greece and Rome, divinely inspired prophetesses made oracular pronouncements to those who consulted them. In Islam, MUHAMMAD is a prophet, the last of a long line of God's mes-

sengers, who included ADAM, Abraham, Moses, and JESUS CHRIST. In both Buddhist and Hindu literature predictions occur, and many prophetic reformers appear in HINDUISM.

proportion Mathematical relation of equality between two ratios, having the form a/b = c/d. A continued proportion is a group of three or more quantities, each bearing the same ratio to its successor, as in 1:3:9:27:81. The term is used to describe the relationship between two quantities having a constant ratio, such as between the radius and circumference of a circle.

proportional representation (PR) System of electoral representation in which the allocation of seats reflects the proportion of the vote commanded by each candidate or party. In the **single transferable vote** system, an elector ranks candidates in order of preference. In the **list system**, an elector votes for a party's entire list of candidates; the number of seats allocated to a party is determined by the number of votes for its list. The main contrast is with a majoritarian system in which representatives are elected for each of numerous single constituencies. Supporters of PR argue that it delivers more representative DEMOCRACY. Critics contend that it tends to produce coalition governments, and removes the bond between representatives and constituents.

propylene See PROPENE

proscenium In the THEATRE, the front part of the stage, especially the arch, first used in 17th-century Italian theatre to create a picture-frame effect.

prose In LITERATURE, a relatively unstructured form of language. Unlike the metrical discipline of POETRY, prose is more closely connected with the rhythms of everyday speech.

Proserpine Roman equivalent of PERSEPHONE

Prost, Alain (1955–) French motor racing driver. In 1985, racing for McLaren, he became the first Frenchman to win the Formula 1 world drivers' championship. He was champion twice more with McLaren (1986, 1989). He retired after winning a fourth title with Williams in 1993. Prost went on to develop his own Formula 1 team, which competed from 1998 to 2002, when it was declared bankrupt.

prostaglandin One of a series of related FATTY ACIDS, with hormone-like action, present in SEMEN and liver, brain and other tissues. Their biological effects include the lowering of blood pressure and the stimulation of contraction in a variety of smooth-muscle tissues, such as in the UTERUS.

prostate gland Gland in the male reproductive tract surrounding the URETHRA. It secretes specific chemicals that mix with sperm cells and other secretions to make up SEMEN.

prosthesis Artificial substitute for a missing organ or body part. Until the 17th century, artificial limbs were made of metal or wood, but innovations in metallurgy, plastics, and engineering enabled lighter, jointed limbs to be made. More recent devices include artificial heart valves made of silicone materials.

prostitution Provision of sexual services for reward, usually money. Most prostitutes are women. In Britain, prostitution is not strictly illegal, but soliciting, living off the earnings of prostitution, and brothel-keeping are all offences.

protactinium (symbol Pa) Rare radioactive metallic element of the ACTINIDE SERIES, first identified in 1913. Its chief source is URANINITE. Properties: at.no. 91; r.a.m. 231.0359; r.d. 15.4; m.p. 1,200°C (2,192°F); b.p. 4,000°C (7,232°F); most stable isotope Pa^{231} (half-life 3.25×10^4 yr).

Protectorate (1653–59) In 1653, BAREBONE'S PARLIAMENT passed the Instrument of Government that established Oliver Cromwell as lord protector. Cromwell established a state council of 11 major generals. The Humble Petition and Advice (1657) restored some power to Parliament. The Protectorate heavily depended on Oliver Cromwell's personal prestige and after his death (1658), his son, Richard, was lord protector for less than a year before the RESTORATION of CHARLES II.

protein Organic COMPOUND containing many AMINO ACIDS linked together by covalent, PEPTIDE bonds. Living CELLS use *c.*20 different amino acids, which are present in varying amounts. The GENETIC CODE, carried by the DNA of the CHROMOSOMES, determines which amino acids are used and in which order they are combined. The most important proteins are ENZYMES, which determine all the

P

▲ **Proust** Once a frequent visitor to the aristocratic salons of Paris at the turn of the century, the French novelist Marcel Proust became a recluse after the death of his mother when he was 34 years old. His 13-volume work, *Remembrance of Things Past*, is written in long, cascading sentences; it is founded on the effects of involuntary memory, the moment when a chance impression obliterates the present and propels one into the past.

chemical reactions in the cell, and ANTIBODIES, which combat infection. **Structural** proteins include KERATIN and COLLAGEN. **Gas transport** proteins include HAEMOGLOBIN. **Nutrient** proteins include CASEIN. protein HORMONES regulate METABOLISM. *See also* NUCLEIC ACID

Protestantism Branch of Christianity formed in protest against the practices and doctrines of the old ROMAN CATHOLIC CHURCH. Protestants sought a vernacular Bible to replace the Latin VULGATE, and to express individual elements of nationalism. According to tradition, the movement started when Martin LUTHER nailed his *95 Theses* to a church door in Wittenberg. His predecessors included John WYCLIFFE and Jan HUS. Later supporters included Ulrich ZWINGLI and John CALVIN, whose interpretation of the Bible and concept of PREDESTINATION had great influence. The Protestants held the EUCHARIST to be a symbolic celebration, as opposed to the Roman Catholic dogma of TRANSUBSTANTIATION, and claimed that because Christ is the sole medium between God and man, his function cannot be displaced by the priests of the Church. *See also* ANGLICAN COMMUNION

Proteus In Greek mythology, a sea god, son of Oceanus and Tethys. He is depicted as a little old man of the sea. Proteus possessed the gift of prophecy and the ability to alter his form at will; in an instant he could become fire, flood or a wild beast.

protoctist Any member of the kingdom Protoctista (formerly Protista), it includes such widely differing groups as ALGAE (including large SEAWEEDS), AMOEBAS and other PROTOZOA, SLIME MOULDS, and downy MILDEWS.

proton (symbol p) Stable ELEMENTARY PARTICLE with a positive charge equal in magnitude to the negative charge of the ELECTRON. The proton was discovered (1919) by Ernest RUTHERFORD. It forms the nucleus of the lightest isotope of HYDROGEN and, with the NEUTRON, is a constituent of the nuclei of all other elements. It is made up of three QUARKS. The proton is a BARYON with a mass $c.1836$ times heavier than the electron. The number of protons in the nucleus of an element is equal to its ATOMIC NUMBER. Protons also occur in primary COSMIC RADIATION. Beams of high-velocity protons, produced by particle ACCELERATORS, are used to study nuclear reactions. *See also* PARTICLE PHYSICS

protoplasm Living contents of a plant or animal CELL. It includes both the NUCLEUS and the CYTOPLASM of cells.

Protozoa Phylum of unicellular organisms found worldwide in marine or freshwater, free-living and as parasites. These microscopic animals move by CILIA or pseudopodia and have a nucleus, cytoplasm and cell wall; some contain CHLOROPHYLL. Reproduction is by FISSION or encystment. Length: 0.3mm (0.1in). The 30,000 species divide into four classes: Flagellata, Cnidospora, Ciliophora, and Sporozoa.

Proudhon, Pierre Joseph (1809–65) French political theorist. His anarchist theories of liberty, equality, and justice conflicted with the COMMUNISM of Karl MARX. In *What is Property?* (1840), Proudhon famously argued that 'property is theft'. His greatest work was *System of Economic Contradiction* (1846). *See also* ANARCHISM

Proust, Marcel (1871–1922) French novelist. Proust was involved in the DREYFUS AFFAIR, but asthma and his parents'

death led to his virtual seclusion from 1907. In 1912 he produced *Swann's Way*, the first part of a semi-autobiographical cyclical novel, collectively entitled *Remembrance of Things Past*. The next installment, *Within a Budding Grove* (1919), won the Prix Goncourt. Proust completed the series shortly before his death. Influenced by Henri BERGSON and Sigmund FREUD, *Remembrance of Things Past* offers an insight into the relationship between psyche and society, and the distortions of time and memory. *See also* FRENCH LITERATURE

Provençal Variety of the Occitan language, spoken in Provence, SE France. It is a ROMANCE LANGUAGE belonging to the family of INDO-EUROPEAN LANGUAGES. In the Middle Ages, it enjoyed a great literary flowering as the language of the TROUBADOURS. Provençal is now largely a spoken language.

Provence Region and former province of SE France, roughly corresponding to the present departments of Var, Vaucluse, and Bouches-du-Rhône, and parts of Alpes-de-Haute-Provence and Alpes-Maritimes. Greeks settled on the coast in *c.*600 BC and the Romans established colonies in the 2nd century BC. In the 6th century AD the region came under Frankish control. It passed to the Holy Roman Empire in the 11th century. Provence retained its distinctive identity and language (PROVENÇAL), and was the focus of a revival of secular literature and music in the Middle Ages. It finally united with France in 1481. Agriculture includes fruit and vegetable growing and stock raising. Tourism is the major industry.

Proverbs Book of the OLD TESTAMENT, probably the oldest existing example of Hebrew WISDOM LITERATURE. The book's subtitle attributes its authorship to King SOLOMON, but in fact scholars consider that it contains material from various periods later than Solomon's time.

Providence Capital of Rhode Island, USA, a port on Providence Bay in NE Rhode Island. The city founded in 1636 as a refuge for religious dissenters from Massachusetts. It later enjoyed great prosperity through trade with the West Indies. The city played an active role in the American Revolution. Industries: jewellery, electrical equipment, silverware, machine tools, rubber goods. Pop. (2000) 1,175,000.

Proxima Centauri Nearest star to the Sun, slightly closer than the nearby star ALPHA CENTAURI. Long thought to be part of the Alpha Centauri system, some astronomers now believe it to be an unrelated star making a close approach.

Prozac Trade name for one of a small group of antidepressants, known as selective SEROTONIN re-uptake inhibitors (SSRIs). They work by increasing levels of serotonin in the brain. Serotonin, or 5–hydroxytryptamine (5–HT), is a NEUROTRANSMITTER involved in a range of functions. Low levels of serotonin are associated with DEPRESSION. *See also* DRUG

Prud'hon, Pierre Paul (1758–1823) French painter who specialized in portraits and historical themes. A favourite of two French Empresses, JOSEPHINE and MARIE LOUISE, he bridged the gap between late 18th- and early 19th-century painting by creating work that was elegant and emotional.

Prussia Historic state of N Germany. The TEUTONIC KNIGHTS conquered the region in the 13th century. The Duchy of Prussia, founded in the 15th century, passed to the Electors of BRANDENBURG in 1618. They took the title of Kings of Prussia in 1701. In the 18th century, under FREDERICK WILLIAM I and FREDERICK II, Prussia became a strong military power, absorbing SILESIA and parts of Poland. After defeats in the NAPOLEONIC WARS, Prussia emerged again as a powerful state at the Congress of VIENNA (1815). In the 19th century, Prussia displaced Austria as the leading German power and, under Otto von BISMARCK, led the movement for German unity, accomplished in 1871. Comprising 65% of the new German Empire, it was the leading German state until World War 1. It ceased to exist as a political unit in 1945.

Przewalski's horse (Mongolian wild horse) Only surviving species of the original wild HORSE, found in Mongolia and Sinkiang. It is small and stocky with an erect black mane. Its red-brown coat has a darker line on the back and shoulders and leg stripes. Height: to 1.5m (4.8ft) at the shoulder. Family Equidae; species *Equus caballus przewalskii*.

psalm Musical hymn or sacred poem. The most famous are contained in the Old Testament Book of PSALMS.

▶ **Przewalski's horse** Because it is not descended from domestic horses, Przewalski's horse (*Equus przewalski*) is the last truly wild horse. They still exist in their natural state in a small area of SW Mongolia, although the species thrives in zoos. Numbers have fallen because they have to compete with livestock for grazing areas and water.

Psalms, Book of Book of the OLD TESTAMENT, consisting of 150 hymns, lyric poems, and prayers. The works were collected over a very long period, at least from the 10th to the 5th centuries BC and probably achieved their final form before the 2nd century BC. Most carry titles added afterwards, and 73 are stated to have been composed or collected by King DAVID.

Pseudepigrapha Jewish writings of the period 200BC– AD 200 that have been falsely attributed to a biblical author. They follow the style and content of authentic Old Testament works. The term refers more widely to almost all ancient Jewish texts that have not been accepted as canonical by the Christian Church. *See also* APOCRYPHA

psittacosis (parrot fever) Disorder usually affecting the respiratory system of birds. Caused by a bacterium, it can be transmitted to human beings, producing pneumonia-like symptoms. Treatment is with ANTIBIOTICS.

psoriasis Chronic recurring skin disease featuring raised, red, scaly patches. The lesions frequently appear on the chest, knees, elbows and scalp. Treatment is with tar preparations, steroids and ultraviolet light. Psoriasis is sometimes associated with a form of ARTHRITIS.

Psyche In Greek mythology, a beautiful mortal woman loved by EROS. She was also the personification of the soul.

psychiatry Analysis, diagnosis and treatment of mental illness and behavioural disorders. It includes research into the cause and prevention of MENTAL DISORDERS, and the administering of treatment, usually by physical means, such as drugs and electroconvulsive therapy. Some psychiatrists also use psychotherapeutic techniques.

psychoanalysis Therapy for treating behaviour disorders, particularly NEUROSIS, based on the work of Sigmund FREUD. Psychoanalysis emphasises UNCONSCIOUS mental processes and the determination of PERSONALITY by INSTINCT, chiefly sexual development in childhood. Psychoanalytic techniques include free association and the analysis and interpretation of dreams. The patient expresses repressed conflicts through transference to the analyst. *See also* ADLER, ALFRED; EGO; FROMM, ERICH; JUNG, CARL; KLEIN, MELANIE; OEDIPUS COMPLEX; REICH, WILHELM; REPRESSION; SUPEREGO

psychology Study of mental activity and behaviour. It includes the study of perception, thought, problem solving, personality, emotion, MENTAL DISORDER, and the adaptation of the individual to society. It overlaps with many other disciplines, including PHYSIOLOGY, PHILOSOPHY, ARTIFICIAL INTELLIGENCE, and social ANTHROPOLOGY. Central areas of psychology include neuropsychology, which relates experience and behaviour to BRAIN functioning; COGNITIVE PSYCHOLOGY, which studies thought processes; SOCIAL PSYCHOLOGY, which studies behaviour in its social context; and DEVELOPMENTAL PSYCHOLOGY, which studies the cognitive and emotional development of children. Applied psychology aims to use the discipline's insights into human behaviour in practical fields, such as education and industry. *See also* BEHAVIOURISM; ETHOLOGY; LEARNING; MEMORY

psychopathic personality (antisocial personality) Personality disorder that leads to antisocial behaviour. Such people's behaviour is impulsive, insensitive to the rights of others and often aggressive. There appears to be little anxiety, guilt or NEUROSIS, and psychoanalytic theory regards this disorder as stemming from an incompletely developed SUPEREGO.

psychopharmacology Study of how DRUGS affect behaviour. Drugs are classified according to their effect: sedative hypnotics, such as BARBITURATES; stimulants, such as AMPHETAMINES; opiate NARCOTICS, such as heroin; and psychedelics and HALLUCINOGENS, such as LSD.

psychosis Serious mental disorder in which the patient loses contact with reality, in contrast to NEUROSIS. It may feature extreme mood swings, delusions or hallucinations, distorted judgment, and inappropriate emotional responses. **Organic** psychoses may spring from brain damage, advanced SYPHILIS, senile DEMENTIA or advanced EPILEPSY. **Functional** psychoses, for which there is no known organic cause, include SCHIZOPHRENIA and MANIC DEPRESSION.

psychosomatic disorder Physical complaint thought to be rooted, at least in part, in psychological factors. The

◄ **pterodactyl** Living during the late Jurassic and early Cretaceous periods, the flying reptiles known as pterodactyls varied in size. The smallest specimen was the size of a sparrow (1), while the largest was the size of a hawk (2). Like the bats of today, it had a wing membrane (3) attached to an elongated fourth finger, and hind limbs and tail.

term has been applied to many complaints, including asthma, migraine, ulcers, and hypertension.

psychotherapy Treatment of a psychological disorder by nonphysical methods. It is carried out either with an individual or group, and usually involves some sort of 'talking cure' and the development of a rapport between patient and therapist. Psychotherapy is often based on PSYCHOANALYSIS, but also sometimes on behaviour therapy or other theories.

ptarmigan Any of three species of northern or alpine grouse, all of which have feathered legs. The wings and breast are white in colder months, but in the spring they become a mottled grey-brown. It inhabits high barren regions, feeding on leaves and lichens. Length: to 36cm (14in). Family Tetraonidae.

pteridophyte Former name for a phyla (Pteridophyta) of spore-bearing VASCULAR PLANTS. At one time, pteridophytes were taken to include CLUB MOSSES, HORSETAILS and FERNS. These plants have similar life cycles but in other respects are quite distinct and are now classified as separate phyla (divisions). *See also* TRACHEOPHYTE

pterodactyl Any of several species of small pterosaur. Now extinct, pterosaurs were flying reptiles distributed worldwide in Jurassic and Cretaceous times. Pterodactyls were almost tailless, with large toothed beaks and flimsy membranous wings. Fossil remains show a lack of muscular development and the absence of a breast keel. It is therefore believed that pterodactyls were gliders, incapable of sustained flapping flight.

PTFE *See* POLYTETRAFLUOROETHELENE

Ptolemy (AD 90–168) (Claudius Ptolemaeus) Greek astronomer and geographer. He worked at the library of Alexandria, Egypt. Ptolemy's chief astronomical work, the *Almagest*, drew heavily on the work of HIPPARCHUS. The **Ptolemaic system** is based on the geocentric world system of the ancient Greeks. His *Geography*, which provided the basis for a world map, was a definitive text until the Renaissance.

Ptolemy I (*c*.367–*c*.283 BC) (Ptolemy Soter) King of ancient Egypt, first ruler of the Ptolemaic dynasty. He was a leading Macedonian general of ALEXANDER THE GREAT, upon whose death in 323 BC Ptolemy received Egypt in the division of Alexander's empire. He assumed the title of king in 305 BC. He made Alexandria his capital where he created the famous library. He abdicated in 284 BC in favour of his son, PTOLEMY II.

Ptolemy II (*c*.308–246 BC) (Ptolemy Philadelphus) King of ancient EGYPT (284–246BC), son of PTOLEMY I. He built ALEXANDRIA into the cultural and commercial centre of the Greek world, attracting poets such as Callimachus and Theocritus, and greatly expanding the Library of Alexandria.

puberty Time in human development when sexual maturity is reached. The reproductive organs take on their adult form, and secondary sexual characteristics, such as the growth of pubic hair, start to become evident. Girls develop breasts and begin to menstruate; in boys there is deepening of the voice and the growth of facial hair. Puberty may begin at any time from about the age of ten, usually occurring earlier in girls than in boys. HORMONES known as gonadotrophins regulate the process.

P

▲ **Puccini** A performance of Verdi's *Aida* inspired the young Giacomo Puccini to enter a music conservatory and train as a composer. His gift for expressive melodies and harmonies, together with the drama of the libretti, have ensured his operas a permanent place in the world's opera houses. His best-known works are passionate love stories with tragic endings.

▲ **puffin** Feeding entirely on prey that they find underwater, puffins (*Fratercula artica*, shown here) can catch small or slow-moving fish for themselves or for their unfledged chicks. They carry as many as ten small fish at a time in their colourful beaks. Puffins nest in large colonies on cliffs by the sea.

P

INTERNET

Puccini, Giacomo
► www.classical.net

Puerto Rico
► welcome.topuertorico.org

public limited company (plc) Company with limited liability whose shares are quoted on a STOCK EXCHANGE. Most companies have limited liability, which means that their owners are responsible only for the money originally invested, and not for the whole of the company's debts. Unlike a private limited company, a plc may have any number of shareholders.

public sector borrowing requirement (PSBR) Amount a government needs to borrow to cover its expenditure. A government principally raises its money by taxes and excise duties. If it has to spend more than the amount covered by these sources, it must raise the rest by borrowing. To do this, it issues short-term and long-term stocks and BONDS, on which it pays INTEREST. These loans form part of the national debt.

Puccini, Giacomo (1858–1924) Italian composer of operas. Among his best-known works, which all combine dramatic libretti with magnificent music, are *La Bohème* (1896), *Tosca* (1900), *Madam Butterfly* (1904) and his last work, incomplete at his death, *Turandot* (1926).

Pueblo Generic name for the several Native American tribes inhabiting the Mesa and Rio Grande regions of Arizona and New Mexico. They belong to several language families, including Keresan, Tewa, Hopi, and Zuni. The multi-storeyed buildings of the Zuni gave rise to the legendary 'Seven Cities of Cíbola' eagerly sought by the Spaniards.

Puerto Rico Self-governing island commonwealth (in union with the USA) in the West Indies; the most easterly island of the Greater Antilles; the capital is San Juan. First visited by Columbus in 1493, the island remained a Spanish colony until 1898, when it was ceded to the USA. In 1952, it was proclaimed a semi-autonomous commonwealth. The decline in the sugar industry in the 1940s created considerable unemployment. Many Puerto Ricans emigrated to the USA. The island is of volcanic origin, and much of the land is mountainous and unsuitable for agriculture. The principal crops are sugar, tobacco, coffee, pineapples and maize. Industries: tourism, textiles, electronic equipment, petrochemicals. Area: 8875sq km (3427sq mi). Pop. (2000) 3,886,000. *See* WEST INDIES map

puff adder Widely distributed African VIPER. Its skin pattern varies, but it usually has yellow markings on brown. It hunts large rodents, and its poisonous bite can be fatal to humans. Up to 80 young are born at one time. Length: to 1.2m (4ft). Family Viperidae; species *Bitis arietans*.

puffball Any of a large order of MUSHROOMS (Lycoperdiales) whose SPORE masses become powdery at maturity

▲ **puma** A wild cat found in a variety of habitat types of the New World, the puma (*Felis concolor*) gives birth to between one and six cubs.

and are expelled in 'puffs' when the case is pressed. Puffballs are stemless, and some species, but not all, are edible.

puffin Small diving bird of the AUK family (Alcidae), found in large colonies in the Northern Hemisphere. The Atlantic puffin (*Fratercula arctica*) has a short neck, a triangular bill with red, yellow and blue stripes, and reddish legs and feet. The puffin lays a single egg in a burrow *c.*1–2m (3.3–6.6ft) deep on a cliff. Length: *c.*30cm (12in).

pug Small dog that probably originated in China. It has a large head and a wide-chested, short body. The short coat may be grey, light brown, or black with a characteristic black face. Height: to 28cm (11in) at the shoulder; weight: to 8kg (18lb).

Pugin, Augustus Welby Northmore (1812–52) English architect. With Sir Charles BARRY, he designed (1840–70) the HOUSES OF PARLIAMENT. Through his designs and writings, especially *True Principles of Pointed or Christian Architecture* (1841), he was a leading promoter of the GOTHIC REVIVAL.

Puglia (Apulia) Region in SE Italy, consisting of the provinces of Bari, Brindisi, Foggia, Lecce, and Taranto; the capital is Bari. Colonized by the Greeks, it was taken by the Romans in the 3rd century BC. Conquered in turn by Goths, Lombards and Byzantines, it later formed part of the Holy Roman Empire. The region became part of Italy in 1861. Products: wheat, almonds, figs, tobacco, wine, salt. Industries: petrochemicals, iron and steel. Area: 19,357sq km (7,472sq mi). Pop. (1999) 4,086,422.

Pulitzer Prize Annual US awards for outstanding achievement in journalism, letters and music. The cost is met by a trust fund left by newspaper publisher Joseph Pulitzer (1847–1911) to the trustees of Columbia University, New York City. The first prize was awarded in 1917. There are prizes for fiction, drama, US history, biography, poetry and musical composition.

pulley Simple machine used to multiply force or to change the direction of its application. A **simple** pulley consists of a wheel, often with a groove, attached to a fixed structure. The load is raised by a rope, chain or belt. A **compound** pulley consists of two or more such wheels, some movable, that allow a person to raise objects much heavier than he or she could lift unaided.

pulsar Object emitting radio waves in pulses of great regularity. English radio astronomer Jocelyn Bell first noticed pulsars in 1967. Pulsars are believed to be rapidly rotating NEUTRON STARS. A beam of radio waves emitted by the rotating pulsar sweeps past the Earth, and is received in the form of pulses. Pulsars are gradually slowing down, but some, such as the Vela Pulsar, occasionally increase their spin rate abruptly; such an event is called a glitch. More than 500 pulsars are now known, flashing at rates from *c.*4 seconds to 1 millisecond.

pulse Regular wave of raised pressure in arteries that results from the flow of blood pumped into them at each beat of the HEART. The pulse is usually taken at the wrist to measure the heart rate, although it may be observed at any point where an artery runs close to the body surface, such as the neck. The average pulse rate is *c.*70 per minute in adults.

pulse Any leguminous plant of the PEA family with edible seeds, such as the BEAN, LENTIL, pea, PEANUT and SOYA

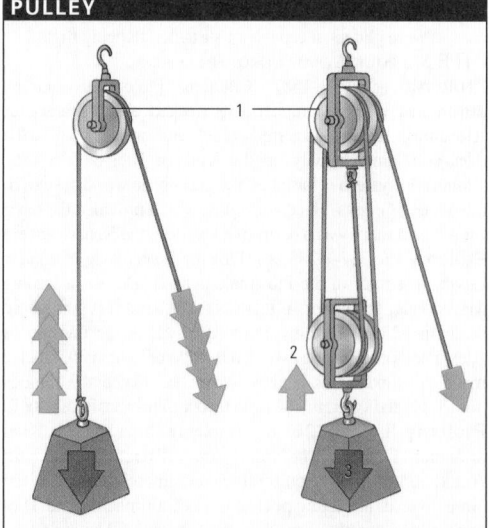

PULLEY

Pulleys (1) multiply the effect of a force applied. By passing the rope through four pulleys, the upward pulling force (2) is multiplied four times allowing a person to lift a weight (3) that they would not normally be able to lift. With four pulleys, however, the rope has to be pulled four times as far to move the weight the same distance. To move the weight up 1m (3.3ft), the rope must be pulled down 4m (13ft).

BEAN. The term may also refer to the seed alone. A valuable human food crop in developing countries where meat is in short supply (pulses are a good alternative source of protein), pulses are also used for oil production. Family Fabaceae/Leguminosae. *See also* LEGUME

puma (mountain lion, cougar) Large cat found in mountains, forests, swamps and jungles of the Americas. It has a small, round head, erect ears and a heavy tail. The coat is tawny with dark brown on the ears, nose and tail; the underparts are white. It preys mainly on deer and small animals. Length: to 2.3m (7.5ft), including the tail; height: to 75cm (30in) at the shoulder. Family Felidae; species *Felis concolor.*

pumice Light rock formed when molten LAVA is blown to a low-density rock froth by the sudden discharge of gases during a volcanic action. It is used as a light ABRASIVE.

pump Device for raising, compressing, propelling or transferring fluids. The **lift** pump, for raising water from a well, and the **bicycle** pump are reciprocating (to-and-fro) pumps. In many modern pumps, a rotating impeller (set of blades) causes the fluid to flow. Jet pumps move fluids by forcing a jet of liquid or gas through them.

pumpkin Orange, hard-rinded, edible garden fruit of a trailing annual VINE found in warm regions of the Old World and the USA; a variety of *Cucurbita pepo*. In the USA, the pumpkin is also called a squash, especially the winter pumpkin (or squash) *Cucurbita maxima* and *C. moschata.* Family Cucurbitaceae.

punctuated equilibrium Theory, expounded by US palaeontologists Stephen Jay GOULD and Niles Eldredge in 1972, that is strongly sceptical of the notion of gradual change in the EVOLUTION of the natural world, as advocated by Charles DARWIN. Fossil records rarely document the gradual development of a new SPECIES, rather showing its seemingly sudden appearance. Darwin argues that this is due to gaps in the fossil records. Punctuated equilibrium explains this by describing each species as in a steady state (equilibrium), which is punctuated by brief but intense periods of sudden change that give rise to new species.

Punic Wars (264–146BC) Series of wars between ROME and CARTHAGE. In the **First** Punic War (264–241BC), Carthage was forced to surrender Sicily and other territory. In the **Second** (218–201BC), the Carthaginians under HANNIBAL invaded Italy and won a series of victories. They were eventually forced to withdraw, whereupon the Romans invaded North Africa and defeated Hannibal. The **Third** Punic War (149–146BC) ended in the destruction of Carthage.

Punjab State in N India, bounded W and NW by Pakistan; the capital is CHANDIGARH. In the 18th century, Sikhs wrested part of the region from MOGUL rule and established a kingdom. In 1849, it was annexed by the British. In 1947, the Punjab split between the new countries of India and Pakistan, the smaller, E part going to India. In 1966, this further reorganized into two states HARYANA and Punjab, which is now the only Indian state with a Sikh majority. Apart from Chandigarh, other major cities include AMRITSAR and Jullundur. Punjab is mainly a flat plain. Much of the land is irrigated and agriculture is important. Industries: textiles, woollens, electrical goods, machine tools, fertilizers, cereals, cotton, sugar. Area: 50,376sq km (19,450sq mi). Pop. (2001) 24,289,296.

Punjab Province in NE Pakistan, bounded E and S by India; the capital is LAHORE. It was subject to a succession of foreign conquerors, including Aryans, Greeks and the British. The province was formed in 1947, acquiring its present boundaries in 1970. The area lies on an alluvial plain and most of the land under cultivation is irrigated. Agriculture is the chief source of income, with wheat and cotton the major crops. Industries: textiles, machinery, electrical appliances. It is Pakistan's most heavily populated province. Area: 206,432sq km (79,703sq mi). Pop. (1998) 72,585,000.

Punjabi (Panjabi) Language spoken by 50 million people in the PUNJAB. It belongs to the Indo-Iranian family of INDO-EUROPEAN LANGUAGES, and is one of the 15 languages recognized by the Indian Constitution. It has similarities to HINDI but possesses very few borrowings from Persian and Arabic.

punk Term used to describe music and fashion of the mid-1970s, characterized by raw energy and iconoclasm. Heavily

influenced by US bands, such as the New York Dolls, punk was pioneered in Britain by such as the Sex Pistols and The Clash. Often anti-establishment, the associated fashions in dress, hair and make-up were also designed to shock.

pupa Non-feeding, developmental stage during which an insect undergoes complete METAMORPHOSIS. It generally occurs as part of a four-stage life cycle from the egg, through LARVA (such as a caterpillar), to pupa, then IMAGO (winged adult). Most pupae consist of a protective outer casing, inside which the tissues of the insect undergo a drastic reorganization to form the adult body. Insects that undergo pupation include the many different kinds of BUTTERFLY and BEETLE and many kinds of FLY. The pupa is often called a CHRYSALIS in butterflies and moths.

pupil In the structure of the EYE, circular aperture through which light falls onto the LENS; it is located in the centre of the IRIS. Its diameter changes by reflex action of the iris to control the amount of light entering the eye.

puppet theatre Miniature stage for shows of glove puppets, marionettes, rod puppets, and flat and shadow figures. Such theatres existed in ancient Egypt and in Greece from the 5th century BC in China, Java and elsewhere in Asia, and were most popular in 18th-century Europe. They flourished in the PURITAN period in England when the live theatres were closed.

Purcell, Henry (1659–95) English composer and organist of the BAROQUE period. He is most famous for his church music, much of which is still frequently performed. His only opera, *Dido and Aeneas* (1689), was the first English opera and is regarded as an early masterpiece of the form. His many other stage works include *The Fairy Queen* (1692).

purgatory Place or state intermediate between HEAVEN and HELL where a soul that has died in a state of grace is purged of its sins before entering heaven. In the teachings of the Roman Catholic Church, souls that die with unforgiven venial and forgiven mortal sins go to purgatory.

Purim Ancient Jewish celebration of thanksgiving, held on the 14th day of the Jewish month of Adar (in February or March). It commemorates the deliverance of the Jews of Persia from a plot to destroy them. The story, which appears in the Old Testament Book of ESTHER, is read on this festival in all synagogue services. The gift of alms to the poor is obligatory, and the festival is associated with a carnival atmosphere.

Puritans British Protestants who were particularly influential during the 16th and 17th centuries. They originated in the reign of ELIZABETH I as a faction within the CHURCH OF ENGLAND; their chief aim was to make it a truly Protestant Church, rather than an Anglo-Catholic one. Following the teachings of CALVIN, they were initially opposed to Anglicanism because of its preoccupation with what they considered to be 'Popish' practice. However, they later demanded the establishment of PRESBYTERIANISM. In the 17th century, many of the parliamentary opponents of JAMES I and CHARLES I were Puritans. Among them were the PILGRIMS who emigrated to America. The English CIVIL WAR (1642–51) resulted in part from attempts by Puritan parliamentarians to block Charles I's policies on religious grounds. After the war, the Puritans reached their zenith in 1653, when Oliver CROMWELL established the Protectorate. In 1660, the authority of the Church of England as an Anglican institution was re-established, although 30

INTERNET

Purcell, Henry
► www.classical.net

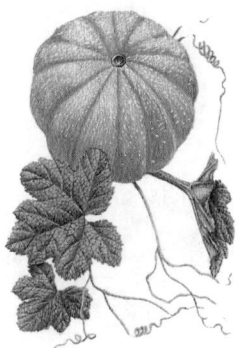

▲ **pumpkin** Related to cucumbers, pumpkins are soft-fleshed with a high water content. In pumpkin soup, the rind is removed and the flesh pulped. As well as food for humans, pumpkins also serve as livestock feed.

P

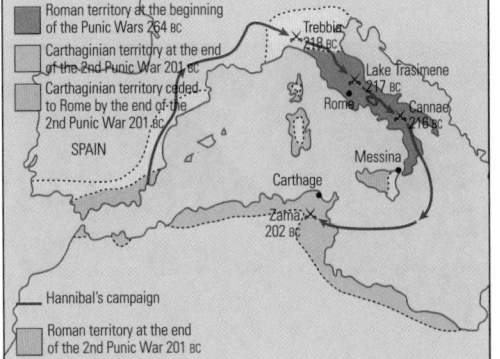

◄ **Punic Wars** To mount an effective challenge to Carthage's domination of the W Mediterranean, Rome became a naval power. It constructed a large fleet, equipped with boarding devices to allow for the hand-to-hand fighting at which the Romans excelled. As a result, after initial reverses, they inflicted naval defeat on Carthage in the First Punic War.

years later Presbyterianism was accepted as the state-supported form of Christianity in Scotland. In England, the Puritans lived on as Dissenters. *See also* NONCONFORMISM

pus Yellowish fluid forming as a result of bacterial infection. It comprises blood serum, LEUCOCYTES, dead tissue and living and dead BACTERIA. An ABSCESS is a pus-filled cavity.

Pusan City on the Korea Strait, SE South Korea. It thrives through its trading links with Japan. The Japanese modernized the city's harbour facilities during their occupation of Korea (1905–45). In the Korean War (1950–53), Pusan acted as the United Nations' supply port. An industrial and commercial centre, Pusan is the nation's leading port and second-largest city. Industries: shipbuilding, iron and steel. Pop. (2000) 3,830,000.

Pushkin, Alexander Sergeievich (1799–1837) Russian poet and novelist. He was exiled for his political beliefs in 1820, the year in which his folk poem *Ruslan and Lyudmila* published. *The Prisoner of the Caucasus* (1822) is his response to the beauty of the Crimea and the Caucasus; and the tragedy *Boris Godunov* (1826) reveals the influence of BYRON. Pushkin's masterpiece was the verse novel *Eugene Onegin* (1833). Other works include the short story *The Queen of Spades* (1834) and the historical novel *The Captain's Daughter* (1836). He was killed in a duel fought over his wife, Natalia.

Putin, Vladimir (1952–) Russian statesman, prime minister (1999–2000), president (2000–). He served for the KGB in East Germany until 1989, and became head of its successor organization in 1998. When Boris YELTSIN resigned in 1999, Putin became acting president. His strong support for the war in CHECHNYA earned him a comfortable victory in the ensuing presidential elections.

Pu Yi, Henry (1906–67) Last Emperor of China (1908–11). His reign name was Hsuan Tung. Deposed after the formation of the Chinese republic, he was temporarily rescued from obscurity to become President, later 'Emperor', of the Japanese puppet state of MANCHUKUO in 1932. Captured by Soviet forces (1945), he was delivered to Mao Zedong and imprisoned (1949–59). He later worked as a gardener in Beijing.

PVC *See* POLYVINYL CHLORIDE

pyelitis Inflammation of the pelvis of the KIDNEY, where urine collects before draining into the URETER. More common in women, it is usually caused by bacterial infection. Treatment is with ANTIBIOTICS and copious fluids.

Pym, John (1584–1643) English leader of the parliamentary opposition to King CHARLES I. In the LONG PARLIAMENT (1640) he initiated proceedings against Charles' advisers, STRAFFORD and LAUD, and helped draft the GRAND REMONSTRANCE (1641). Pym was one of five members whom Charles tried to arrest in the House of Commons (1642), and he helped to arrange the alliance with the Scots in the English CIVIL WAR.

Pynchon, Thomas (1937–) US novelist whose works are noted for their offbeat humour and inventiveness. His books include *V* (1963), *The Crying of Lot 49* (1966), *Vineland* (1990) and *Mason and Dixon* (1997). His best-known work, *Gravity's Rainbow* (1973), won the National Book Award.

Pyongyang Capital of North Korea, in the W of the country, on the River Taedong. An ancient city, it was the capital of the Choson, Koguryo and Koryo kingdoms. In the 16th and 17th centuries, it came under both Japanese and Chinese rule. Pyongyang's industry developed during the Japanese occupation from 1910–45. It became the capital of North Korea in 1948. During the KOREAN WAR (1950–53), it suffered

considerable damage. Industries: cement, iron and steel, chemicals, machinery, rubber, textiles. Pop. (2000) 3,124,000.

pyramid In geometry, solid figure having a POLYGON as one of its faces (the base), the other faces being triangles with a common vertex. Its volume is one third of the base area times the vertical height. Pyramids are described by the shape of their bases, such as a square pyramid or a triangular pyramid.

pyramids PYRAMID-shaped monuments. They are associated particularly with ancient EGYPT, where some of the largest survive almost intact. They served as burial chambers for pharaohs. The earliest Egyptian pyramid was a step pyramid, built *c*.2700 BC for Zoser, related to the Mesopotamian ZIGGURATS. Pyramid building in Egypt reached its peak during the 4th dynasty, the time of the Great Pyramid at GIZA. The largest pyramid in the world, it was built for Khufu *c*.2500 BC and stands 146m (480ft) high with sides 231m (758ft) long at the base. The largest New World pyramid was built at TEOTIHUACÁN, Mexico, in the 1st century AD; it was 66m (216ft) high.

Pyrenees Range of mountains in S France and N Spain, extending in an almost straight line E to W from the Mediterranean Sea to the Bay of Biscay. They formed in the Tertiary era. The Pyrenees contain deposits of marble, gypsum, and oil. There are extensive forests. Sheep and goat grazing is the chief farming activity. The highest point is Pico de Aneto, 3406m (11,168ft). Length: 435km (270mi).

Pyrenees, Peace of the (1659) Treaty between France and Spain after the THIRTY YEARS' WAR. France gained territory in Artois and Flanders, and Philip IV of Spain reluctantly agreed to his daughter's marriage to LOUIS XIV. She was to renounce her claim to the Spanish throne in exchange for a subsidy. Because Spain could not pay the subsidy, the renunciation became void, giving Louis a claim on the Spanish Netherlands and resulting in the War of Devolution.

pyrite (fool's gold) Widespread sulphide mineral, iron sulphide (FeS_2), occurring in all types of rocks and veins. It is a brass-yellow colour. It crystallizes as cubes and octahedra, and also as granules and globular masses. It is opaque, metallic, and brittle. Hardness 6.5; r.d. 5.0.

pyroclastic Fragment of rock thrown out by explosive volcanic activity. Pyroclasts normally include solidified lava left behind by a previous eruption of the volcano, as well as rocks from the crust, smaller pieces of cinders, ash, and dust.

pyroxene Group of rock-forming, silicate minerals, usually coloured dark green, brown, and black. Crystals are usually short prisms with good cleavages. Hardness 2.3–4; r.d. 5.5–6.

Pyrrho (*c*.360–*c*.270 BC) Greek philosopher, considered the founder of SCEPTICISM. His doctrine was that nothing can be known because every statement can be plausibly contradicted; therefore wisdom is in reserved judgement.

Pyrrhus (319–272 BC) King of Epirus (307–302, 295–272BC). An able general, he fought several battles against Rome. Although he won, the cost was so heavy that victory was useless, hence the term 'pyrrhic victory'.

Pythagoras (*c*.580–500 BC) Greek philosopher and founder of the Pythagorean school. The Pythagoreans were bound to their teacher by rigid vows and were ascetic in their way of life. They believed in the TRANSMIGRATION OF SOULS and that numbers and their interrelationships constitute the true nature of the universe. Pythagoras is credited with advances in mathematics and geometry, medicine and philosophy. The famous **theorem** that the square of the hypotenuse of a right-angled triangle equals the sum of the squares of the other two sides, is named after him; it had long been known to the Egyptians and Babylonians as a practical technique, but Pythagoras proved its truth as a general theorem. His school was suppressed at the end of the 6th century, but the Romans revived its doctrines *c*.500 years later.

python Name of more than 20 species of non-poisonous snakes of the BOA family (Boidae), found in tropical regions. Like boas, pythons kill their prey (birds and mammals) by squeezing them in their coils. Unlike boas, pythons lay eggs. The reticulated python (*Python reticulatus*) of SE Asia vies with the anaconda as the world's largest snake, reaching up to *c*.9m (30ft). Subfamily Pythoninae.

▲ **Pushkin** Often called the father of modern Russian literature, Alexander Pushkin demonstrated his talent for poetry while he was still a student in St Petersburg. Influenced by Byron, his masterpiece was *Eugene Onegin*, a romantic tale of unrequited love.

P

▶ **pyramids** The three large pyramids at Giza, N Egypt, are one of the Seven Wonders of the World, and the only to have survived virtually intact into the modern age. The largest was built for the Pharaoh Khufu, and vast pyramids were constructed at Giza for Khafre and Mankaure, also during the fourth dynasty. Although these are the best known of the Egyptian pyramids, many others were also constructed in the Nile Valley and elsewhere in the country, but they are not as well preserved.

Qaddafi, Muammar al- (1942–) Libyan de facto head of state. In 1969, he led the coup that toppled King Idris I. Qaddafi sought to remove all vestiges of LIBYA's colonial past. He supported attempts to bring Libya into union with other Arab countries and lent assistance to international terrorist groups, which led to USA bombing raids in 1986. Qaddafi survived, but one of his children died. During 2004 Quaddafi met foreign leaders to discuss improving Libya's international relations.

Qaeda, al- (Arabic, 'the base') A loose network of terrorist groups inspired by the Saudi dissident OSAMA BIN LADEN. Groups connected to al-Qaeda linked to a number of terrorist acts in the late 20th and early 21st century, including the devastating attacks on the World Trade Center in New York City, and the Pentagon, Washington, D.C., which killed *c.*2,750 people on September 11, 2001. Al-Qaeda targets western interests that it sees as a threat to Islam. *See also* JIHAD; TALIBAN

Qatar Sheikhdom on the Qatar peninsula in the Persian Gulf; the capital is DOHA. *See* country feature.

Qattara Depression Desert basin in the Libyan Desert, NW Egypt. It contains the lowest point in Africa, at 133m (4,36ft) below sea level. Area: *c.*18,130sq km (7,000sq mi).

Qin (formerly Ch'in) Imperial dynasty of China (221–206 BC) Originating in NW China, the Qin emerged after the collapse of the ZHOU dynasty; its founder was QIN SHIHUANGDI. They established the first centralized imperial administration, with the country divided into provinces, each under a governor. The GREAT WALL took permanent shape during this period.

Qing (formerly Ch'ing) Imperial Manchurian dynasty of China (1644–1911), established by NURHACHI following the collapse of the MING dynasty. The Qing extended their influence, until by 1800 they exercised control over an area stretching from Siam (Thailand) and Tibet to Mongolia and the River Amur. The dynasty weakened in the 19th century, following internal struggles, such as the TAIPING REBELLION, and with the increase of foreign influence, particularly after the OPIUM WARS. It ended with the abdication of PU YI in 1911.

Qinghai (Tsinghai) Province in NW China; the capital is Xining (Sining). Although parts of the region have long been under Chinese control, it was occupied mainly by Tibetan and Mongol nomads until recent times. It became a province of China in 1928. A mountainous region, it is the source of some of Asia's greatest rivers, including the HUANG HE, YANGTZE and MEKONG. There is farming of wheat, barley and potatoes and stock rearing. The province is famous for its horses. Iron ore, coal, oil, salt and potash are extracted. Area: 721,280sq km (278,486sq mi). Pop. (2000) 5,180,000.

Qin Shihuangdi (259–210 BC) Emperor of China (221–210 BC). The first QIN Emperor, he reformed the bureaucracy and consolidated the GREAT WALL. Excavations of his tomb on Mount Li (near XIAN) during the 1970s revealed, among other treasures, an 'army' of *c.*7,500 life-size terracotta guardians.

Qom City in W central Iran. The burial place of FATIMA, her shrine is a place of pilgrimage for SHI'ITE Muslims. Industries: textiles, rugs, pottery, glass, shoes. Pop. (2002) 893,500.

Q/q, 17th letter of the Roman alphabet, derived from the Semitic qoph, meaning monkey. It was taken into the Greek alphabet as **koppa***. It entered the Roman alphabet in c.ad 114 and assumed its current form c.1500.*

QATAR

The State of Qatar occupies a long, narrow peninsula jutting into the Persian Gulf. The peninsula is about 200km [12mi] long, with a greatest width of 90km [56mi]. The land is mostly flat desert covered by gravel and loose, wind-blown sand. Sand dunes occur in the SE. There are also some barren salt flats. The highest point, on a central limestone plateau, is only 98m [321ft] above sea level. Qatar also includes several offshore islands and coral reefs. Fresh water is scarce and much of the water supply comes from desalination plants.

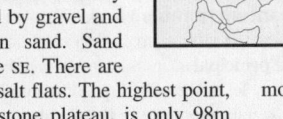

occupied a garrison on the peninsula. In 1916 Qatar agreed that Britain would take responsibility for the country's foreign affairs. Oil was struck in 1939, but exploitation was delayed by World War 2. Commercial exploitation began in 1949, leading to the rapid development and modernization of the country's infrastructure.

In 1968 Britain announced that it would withdraw its forces from the Gulf. Qatar negotiated with Bahrain and the United Arab Emirates concerning the formation of a federation.

AREA 11,437sq km [4,415sq mi]
POPULATION 907,000
CAPITAL (POPULATION) Doha (264,000)
GOVERNMENT Absolute monarchy
ETHNIC GROUPS Arab 40%, Pakistani 18%, Indian 18%, Iranian 10%
LANGUAGES Arabic (official), English
RELIGIONS Islam 95%
CURRENCY Rial = 100 dirham

CLIMATE

The weather from May to September is extremely hot and dry, with temperatures soaring to 49°C [120°F]. Sand and dust storms are common. Winters are mild to warm, with the weather generally sunny and pleasant. The total annual rainfall seldom exceeds 100mm [4in]. Most of the rain occurs in winter.

HISTORY

In the 18th century, three BEDOUIN tribes established trading settlements along the coast of the peninsula. Since the mid-19th century, members of the Al-Thani family have been the leaders of Qatar. Between 1871 and 1913 the Ottoman Turks, with Qatar's consent,

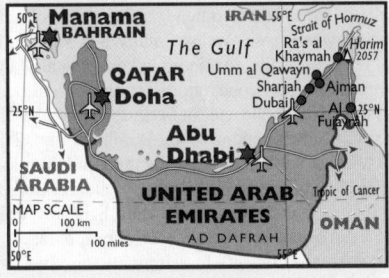

POLITICS

Qatar became fully independent on 3 September 1971. In 1972, because of rivalries in the ruling family, the deputy ruler Khalifa bin Hamad Al Thani seized power from his cousin Emir Ahmad in a coup. In 1982 Qatar, together with Bahrain, Kuwait, Oman, Saudi Arabia and the United Arab Emirates united to form the Gulf Co-operation Council.

In 1990, following Iraq's invasion of Kuwait, Qatar agreed to allow foreign troops on its soil. In 1991 Qatari troops were involved in the GULF WAR military campaign to free Kuwait. In 1995 Qatar signed a security pact with the United States. A bloodless coup occurred in 1995 when the heir apparent, Sheikh Hamad bin Khalifa Al-Thani, deposed his father. A counter-coup failed in 1996.

In 1996 the Al-Jazeera satellite television station was launched in Qatar. It soon won a worldwide reputation for tackling controversial issues, especially those connected with the Arab world. In 2001 it became famous when it became the first station to air recorded statements by the al Qaida leader Osama bin Laden and, from 2003, it covered the conflict in Iraq graphically.

Qatar is an emirate, ruled by the Emir and his appointed Council of Ministers. Municipal

elections in 1999 heralded moves towards democracy. A new constitution introduced in 2004 provided for a 45-member Consultative Council. This Council consisted of 45 members, two-thirds of whom would be elected by the public and one-third appointed by the Emir. The new constitution came into force in 2005 with elections expected by 2007. In foreign affairs, Qatar resolved long-standing boundary disputes with Bahrain and Saudi Arabia in 2001. In 2003, the US Central Command forward base on Qatar became the main centre for the US-led invasion of Iraq.

ECONOMY

The people of Qatar enjoy a high standard of living that derives from oil revenues. The country has a comprehensive welfare system, and many of its services are free or highly subsidized. Oil production has given Qatar one of the world's highest per capita incomes and accounts for more than 80% of the country's export revenues. Qatar has about 5% of the world's proven oil reserves and more than 15% of the world's proven natural gas reserves.

Besides oil refining, they produce ammonia, cement, fertilizers, petrochemicals and steel bars. Wells have been dug to develop agriculture and products include beef, dairy products, fruits, poultry and vegetables.

Q

Q

quadrant In plane geometry, a quarter of a circle, bounded by radii at right angles to each other and by the arc of the circle. In analytic geometry, it is one of the four sections of a plane divided by an x axis and a y axis. A quadrant is also a device for measuring angles, based on a 90° scale.

quadratic equation Algebraic equation in which the highest exponent of the variable is 2; an equation of the second degree. A quadratic equation has the general form $ax^2 + bx + c = 0$, where a, b and c are constants. It has, at most, two solutions (roots), given by the formula $x = [-b \pm \sqrt{(b^2 - 4ac)}]/2a$.

Quadruple Alliance Coalition between four states, in particular three alliances in Europe in the 18th and 19th centuries. The first was formed (1718) by Britain, France, the Holy Roman Empire, and the Netherlands against PHILIP V of Spain, after he seized Sicily and Sardinia. The second was formed (1814) by Austria, Britain, Prussia, and Russia against NAPOLEON I of France. After Napoleon's defeat the four partners created the CONGRESS SYSTEM. The third Quadruple Alliance (1834) consisted of Britain and France in support of Portugal and Spain, where liberal monarchies were threatened.

quail Any of a group of Old World gamebirds. The European quail (*Coturnix coturnix*), a small, short-tailed bird with white throat and brownish plumage, is found throughout Europe, Asia and Africa. The Australian quail (*Turnix velox*) is a stocky, brownish bird. Mainly ground-living birds, they scrape for seeds and nest on the ground. The Japanese quail (*C. coturnix japonica*) is used for meat and eggs in Europe and the USA.

Quakers (officially Society of Friends) Christian sect that arose in England in the 1650s, founded by George Fox. The name derived from the injunction given by early Quaker leaders that their followers tremble at the word of the Lord. Quakers rejected the episcopal organization of the CHURCH OF ENGLAND, believing in the priesthood of all believers and the direct relationship between man and the spiritual light of God. Quakers originally worshipped God in meditative silence unless someone was moved by the Holy Spirit. Since the mid-19th century, their meetings have included hymns and readings. There are *c.*200,000 Quakers worldwide.

qualitative analysis Identification of the chemical elements or ions in a substance or mixture. A QUANTITATIVE ANALYSIS identifies the amounts.

quantitative analysis Identification of the amount of chemical constituents in a substance or mixture. Chemical methods use reactions such as PRECIPITATION (the suspension of small particles in a liquid), NEUTRALIZATION, and OXIDATION, and measure volume (**volumetric** analysis) or weight (**gravimetric** analysis). Physical methods measure qualities such as density and refractive index (how much light is refracted by a medium).

quantum chromodynamics Study of the properties of QUARKS in which, to explain permissible combinations of quarks to form various ELEMENTARY PARTICLES, each is assigned a colour. Quarks are given one of the three primary colours: red, green, and blue. When three quarks combine to form BARYONS, the resulting colour is always white. Antiquarks are given one of the three complementary colours: cyan, magenta, and yellow. When a quark combines with an antiquark to form a MESON, the resulting colour is also white.

quantum electrodynamics (QED) Use of QUANTUM MECHANICS to study the properties of ELECTROMAGNETIC RADIATION and how it interacts with ELEMENTARY PARTICLES.

quantum mechanics Branch of physics that uses the QUANTUM THEORY to explain the behaviour of ELEMENTARY PARTICLES. According to quantum theory, all radiant energy emits and absorbs in multiples of tiny 'packets' or quanta. Atomic particles have wavelike properties and thereby exhibit a wave-particle duality. Sometimes the wave properties dominate, and other times the particle aspects dominate. The quantum theory uses four QUANTUM NUMBERS to classify ELECTRONS and their atomic states: energy level, angular momentum, energy in a magnetic field and SPIN. The EXCLUSION PRINCIPLE says any two electrons in an atom cannot have the same energy and spin. A change in an electron, atom or molecule from one quantum state to another, called a **quantum jump**, is accompanied by the absorption or emission of a quantum. The **quantum field theory** seeks to explain this exchange. The interactions between

QUARKS and between PROTONS and NEUTRONS are described by **quantum chromodynamics**. The idea that energy radiates and absorbs in packets was first proposed by German physicist Max PLANCK in 1900 to explain BLACK BODY radiation. Using Planck's work, German-born US physicist Albert EINSTEIN quantized light radiation, and in 1905 explained the PHOTO-ELECTRIC EFFECT. He chose the name of PHOTON for a quantum of light energy. In 1913, Danish physicist Niels BOHR used quantum theory to explain atomic structure and spectra, showing the relationship between the energy levels of an atom's electrons and the frequencies of radiation emitted or absorbed by the atom. In 1924, French physicist Louis de BROGLIE suggested that particles have wave properties, the converse having been postulated in 1905 by Einstein. In 1926, Austrian physicist Erwin SCHRÖDINGER used this hypothesis of WAVE MECHANICS to predict particle behaviour on the basis of wave properties, but a year earlier German physicist Werner HEISENBERG had produced a mathematical equivalent to Schrödinger's theory without using wave concepts. In 1928, English physicist Paul DIRAC unified these approaches while incorporating RELATIVITY into quantum mechanics. This predicted the existence of ANTIMATTER and helped develop the **quantum electrodynamics** theory of how charged subatomic particles interact within electric and magnetic fields. The SUPERSTRING THEORY provides a possible answer to gravitational interaction. The complete, modern theory of quantum mechanics is the quantum field theory of quantum electrodynamics, also known as the quantum theory of light. It was derived by US physicist Richard FEYNMAN in the 1940s. The theory predicts that a collision between an electron and a proton should result in the production of a photon of electromagnetic radiation, which is exchanged between the colliding particles. Quantum mechanics remains a difficult system because the UNCERTAINTY PRINCIPLE, formulated in 1927 by Heisenberg, states that nothing on the atomic scale can be measured or observed without disturbing it. This makes it impossible to know both the position and momentum of a particle.

quantum numbers In physics, a set of four numbers used in QUANTUM THEORY to classify electrons and their atomic states. The **principal** quantum number (symbol n) gives the electron's energy level; the orbital quantum number (symbol l) describes its angular momentum; the magnetic quantum number (symbol m) describes the energies of electrons in a magnetic field; and the SPIN quantum number (symbol m_s) gives the spin of the individual electrons. *See also* QUANTUM MECHANICS

quantum theory In physics, it concerns itself with the relationship between matter and energy at the elementary or subatomic level, and with the behaviour of ELEMENTARY PARTICLES. The theory is the basis of QUANTUM MECHANICS. *See also* QUANTUM NUMBERS

quark Any one of six particles and their antiparticles (antiquarks). Quarks are LEPTONS and occur in six 'flavours': up, down, top, bottom, charm, and strange. Antiquarks have corresponding flavours but their charge is opposite that of their corresponding quark. Quarks do not occur singly in nature, but exist in combination. A BARYON, such as a PROTON or NEUTRON, consists of three. Combinations of quarks, including baryons, are the constituents of the HADRON group of ELEMENTARY PARTICLES.

quartz Rock-forming mineral, the natural form of silicon dioxide (silica), SiO_2. It is widely distributed, occurring in igneous and metamorphic rocks, and in clastic sediments. It is also found in mineral veins. It forms six-sided crystals. Pure quartz is clear and colourless but the mineral may be coloured by impurities. The most common varieties are colourless quartz (rock crystal), rose, yellow, milky and smoky. The most usual cryptocrystalline varieties, whose crystals can be seen only under a microscope, are CHALCEDONY and FLINT. Quartz crystals exhibit the PIEZOELECTRIC EFFECT and are used in electronic clocks and watches. Hardness 7; r.d. 2.65.

quartzite METAMORPHIC ROCK usually produced from sandstone, in which the quartz grains have recrystallized. Quartzite is a hard and massive rock. It is usually white, light grey, yellow or buff, but it can be coloured green, blue, purple, or black.

quasar (quasi-stellar object) In astronomy, an object that appears to be a massive, highly compressed, extremely powerful source of radio and light waves, characterized by a large RED SHIFT. If such red shifts are due to the DOPPLER EFFECT, it can be deduced that quasars are more remote than any other objects previously identified; many are receding at velocities greater than half the speed of light. Their energy may result from the gravitational collapse of a GALAXY or from many SUPERNOVAS exploding in quick succession, although there seems to be no reason why such events should be occurring.

Quasimodo, Salvatore (1901–68) Italian poet. His first volume, *Waters and Land* (1930), established his reputation. He was imprisoned for anti-fascist conduct in World War 2. He received the 1959 Nobel Prize in literature.

Quaternary Most recent period of the CENOZOIC era, beginning *c.*2 million years ago and extending to the present. It is divided into the PLEISTOCENE epoch, characterized by a periodic succession of great Ice Ages, and the HOLOCENE epoch, which started some 10,000 years ago.

quattrocento (It. 'four hundred') In art history, the 15th-century period of the Italian RENAISSANCE. Leading figures included the painters, Fra ANGELICO, Fra Filippo LIPPI, MASACCIO, and UCCELLO; the architects, BRUNELLESCHI and ALBERTI; and the sculptors, DONATELLO and GHIBERTI.

Quayle, (James) Dan (Danforth) (1947–) US statesman, vice president (1989–93). He was a Republican congressman (1977–81) and senator (1981–88). In 1988, Quayle was chosen by George BUSH to act as his running mate.

Québec Province in E Canada; the second-largest province in area and population; the capital is QUÉBEC and the largest city is MONTRÉAL. Most of the province is on the Canadian Shield and is relatively uninhabited. In 1535, Jacques CARTIER landed on the Gaspé Peninsula of E Canada, and in 1536 he sailed up the ST LAWRENCE River. In 1608, Samuel de CHAMPLAIN established the first settlement on the present-day site of Québec City. It served as headquarters for the fur-traders' exploration of the interior. Following the FRENCH AND INDIAN WARS (1754–63), Britain gained French Canada in the Treaty of Paris (1763). The Constitution Act of 1791 separated off the area w of the Ottawa River as the colony of Upper Canada (now ONTARIO). Québec became the British colony of Lower Canada. The revolt (1837) led by Louis PAPINEAU saw the appointment of the Earl of DURHAM. With the establishment of the Dominion of Canada in 1867, Québec became a province. In the late 20th century, the Québec's French-speaking inhabitants intensified their demands for cultural recognition, including complete independence. In a 1995 referendum, a small majority of the population voted against independence. The lowlands by the St Lawrence River are the centre of industry and agriculture; the province's small farms provide vegetables, tobacco and dairy produce. Québec produces much hydroelectric power and timber. Copper, iron, zinc, asbestos and gold are mined. Area: 1,540,687sq km (594,860sq mi). Pop. (2001) 7,237,479.

Québec City and port at the confluence of the the St Lawrence and St Charles rivers, s QUÉBEC province, Canada. It is the capital of Québec province. Samuel de CHAMPLAIN established a French trading post here in 1608. Captured by the British in 1629, but retaken by France, it became the capital of New France in 1663. Britain took control at the end of the French and Indian Wars (1754–63). It was the capital of Lower Canada (1791–1841) and of the United Provinces of Canada (1851–55, 1859–65) before becoming capital of Québec province in 1867. In recent years, it became a focal point for Québec's French-speaking separatists. Industries: shipbuilding, paper, leather, textiles, machinery, canning, tobacco, chemicals. Pop. (2001) 169,076; 682,757 (metropolitan).

Quechua Most widely spoken of all Native South American languages, with *c.*5 million speakers in Peru, 1.5 million in Bolivia and 500,000 in Ecuador. Originally the language of the great INCA Empire, it is related to Aymará – the pair forming the Quechumaran family.

Queens Largest borough of NEW YORK CITY, on LONG ISLAND, SE New York State, USA. Settled by the Dutch in the early 17th century, the area came under English control in 1664. It became a borough of Greater New York in 1898. Its manufacturing industries produce consumer goods for New York City. Area: 280sq km (108sq mi). Pop. (2000) 2,229,379.

Queensland State in NE Australia; the capital is BRISBANE. Queensland was originally part of New South Wales and served as a penal colony (1824–40). It became a separate colony in 1859, and a state within the Commonwealth of Australia in 1901. Nearly 50% of Queensland lies N of the Tropic of Capricorn and there are rainforests in the N. The GREAT DIVIDING RANGE separates the fertile coastal strip from the interior plains. Its chief crops are sugar cane, wheat, cotton, and tropical fruits. Beef cattle are important. The main industry is mining, and there are are valuable mineral deposits. Area: 1,727,530sq km (667,000sq mi). Pop. (2001) 3,642,400.

quetzal Forest bird of Central America. The male is bright green above and crimson below with iridescent green tail plumes forming a 60cm (2ft) train. The Aztecs and Mayas regarded the quetzal as sacred and wore the tail plumes ceremonially. The duller female nests in a hole, often in a tree, and lays two eggs, which are incubated by both parents. Family Trogonidae; species *Pharomachrus mocinno.*

Quetzalcóatl God of CENTRAL AND SOUTH AMERICAN MYTHOLOGY, a principal deity of the TOLTECS, MAYA, and AZTECS. Quetzalcóatl (the Aztec name for the god) took the form of a feathered serpent. Essentially a creator, who made the human race by fertilizing bones with his own blood, he was associated with agriculture and the arts.

Quezon, Manuel Luis (1878–1944) Philippine statesman, first president of the Commonwealth of the Philippines (1935–44). Quezon was imprisoned for his part in the revolt against US rule in 1901. After his release, he became leader of the Nationalist Party and, as commissioner to the US (1909–16), secured the passage of the Tydings-McDuffie Bill (1934) that paved the way for independence. His strengthening of Philippine defences failed to prevent Japan's invasion, and Quezon formed a govenment-in-exile in the US.

Quezon City City on LUZON island, adjacent to MANILA, N Philippines. Second-largest city in the Philippines, it was named after Manuel Luis QUEZON and was capital of the Philippines from 1948 to 1976. It is mainly a residential area but has a thriving textile industry. Pop. (2000) 2,173,831.

Quiché Mayan group of Native South Americans located in the highlands of w Guatemala. Archeological remains show large pre-conquest population centres and an advanced civilization. Today, the Quiché are the most populous Native American group in Guatemala.

quince Shrub or small tree native to the Middle East and central Asia. Its greenish-yellow fruit is used in preserves. Height: to 6.1m (20ft). Family Rosaceae; species *Cydonia oblonga.*

Quine, Willard Van Orman (1908–2000) US philosopher. He was professor of philosophy at Harvard (1948–78). Quine regarded philosophy as a branch of natural science. In *Two Dogmas of Empiricism* (1951), he argued for a holistic approach to EMPIRICISM, abandoning the analytic synthetic distinction made by Immanuel KANT. In *Word and Object* (1960), Quine put forward the notion of the indeterminacy of translation. *See also* LOGICAL POSITIVISM

quinine White, crystalline substance isolated in 1820 from the bark of the cinchona tree. It was once widely used in the treatment of MALARIA but has been largely replaced by drugs that are less toxic and more effective.

Quisling, Vidkun (1887–1945) Norwegian fascist leader. A former minister of defence (1931–33), Quisling founded the National Union Party (1933), based on the German Nazi Party. In 1940 he collaborated with the invading Germans, and they set him up as a puppet ruler during their occupation of Norway. At the end of World War 2, he was shot as a traitor.

Quito Capital of Ecuador, at 2850m (9260ft), N central Ecudaor. Quito lies almost on the Equator. The site was first settled by Quito Native Americans, and was captured by the INCAS in 1487. It was taken by Spain in 1534, and liberated in 1822 by Antonio José de SUCRE. A cultural and political centre, it is the site of the Central University of Ecuador (1787). Products include textiles and handicrafts. Pop. (2002) 1,648,100.

Qumran Ancient village on the NW shore of the Dead Sea, in the Israeli-occupied West Bank. In 1947, the DEAD SEA SCROLLS (writings of a Jewish sect that settled in Qumran *c.*100 BC–AD 68) were found in nearby caves.

▲ **quetzal** The resplendent quetzal (*Pharomachrus mocinno*) is a rare, perching bird found in tropical rainforests from s Mexico to Costa Rica. The Aztec and Maya worshipped the bird, associating it with the god Quetzalcóatl. The quetzal is the national bird of Guatemala.

Q

INTERNET

Québec
▶ www.gouv.qc.ca

Queensland
▶ www.qld.gov.au

R/r, 18th letter of the English alphabet. It descends from the Semitic letter resh, *meaning head. It passed almost unchanged into the Greek alphabet as the letter* rho *and from there into the Roman alphabet.*

▲ **Rabin** Israeli Prime Minister Yitzhak Rabin shared the 1994 Nobel Peace Prize with Yasir Arafat and Shimon Peres for the diplomacy that led to the Israeli-Palestinian Accord (1993). In 1974, Rabin succeeded Golda Meir to become Israel's first native-born prime minister. The daring rescue of Israeli hostages at Entebbe Airport, Uganda, took place in his first term.

Ra (Re) In EGYPTIAN MYTHOLOGY, Sun god of Heliopolis and lord of the dead. He sailed his sun boat across the sky by day, and through the underworld by night. He is most often depicted as falcon-headed, with a solar disc on his head.

Rabat Capital of Morocco, on the Atlantic coast, N Morocco. Rabat dates from Phoenician times, but the fortified city was founded in the 12th century by the ALMOHAD ruler, Abd al-Mumin. Under French rule (from 1912), it was made the capital of the protectorate of Morocco. Sights include the 12th-century Hassan Tower. Industries: hand-woven rugs, textiles, food processing. Pop. (1999) 652,000; 2,227,000 (metropolitan).

rabbi Person qualified through study of the Hebrew Bible and the TALMUD to be the chief religious leader of a Jewish congregation and the person responsible for education and spiritual guidance. In some countries, such as the UK, Jews are led on a national basis by a chief rabbi. Modern Israel has a rabbinic council with two chief rabbis, one representing the SEPHARDIM tradition, the other representing the ASHKENAZIM.

rabbit Long-eared, herbivorous mammal of the family Leporidae, including the European common rabbit and the American cottontail. The common rabbit, *Oryctolagus cuniculus*, has thick, soft, greyish-brown fur. The wide variety of domesticated rabbits are also of this species. Length: 35–45cm (14–18in); weight: 1.4–2.3kg (3–5lb). *See also* HARE

Rabelais, François (1494–1553) French humanist and satirist. Rabelais is famed for his classic series of satires, now known collectively as *Gargantua and Pantagruel*. The series consists of *Pantagruel* (1532), *Gargantua* (1534), *Le Tiers Livre* (1546), *Le Quart Livre* (1552) and *Le Cinquième Livre* (1564).

rabies (hydrophobia) Viral disease of the central nervous system. It can occur in all warm-blooded animals, but is especially feared in dogs due to the risk of transmission to human beings. The incubation period varies from a week or two to more than a year. It is characterized by severe thirst, although attempting to drink causes painful spasms of the larynx; other symptoms include fever, muscle spasms, and delirium. Once the symptoms have appeared, death usually follows within a few days. Anyone bitten by a rabid animal may be saved by prompt injections of rabies vaccine and antiserum.

Rabin, Yitzhak (1922–95) Israeli statesman, prime minister (1974–77, 1992–95). As chief of staff (1964–68), he directed Israeli operations in the SIX-DAY WAR (1967). Rabin was ambassador to the USA (1968–73) before becoming prime minister. As minister of defence (1984–90), he directed operations against the Palestinian INTIFADA and, having regained leadership of the Labour Party from Shimon PERES, became prime minister again. In 1993, Rabin signed the ISRAELI-PALESTINIAN ACCORD with the PALESTINE LIBERATION ORGANIZATION (PLO), promising progress towards Palestinian autonomy in the occupied territories. On November 4, 1995, an Israeli extremist assassinated Rabin.

raccoon (racoon) Stout-bodied, omnivorous, mostly nocturnal mammal of North and Central American wooded areas. Raccoons have a black, mask-like marking across their eyes, and a long black-banded tail. They have agile and sensitive front paws and typically dip for food in water. The seven species include the North American *Procyon lotor*. Length: 40–61cm (16–24in); weight: 10–22kg (22–48lb). Family Procyonidae.

race Informal classification of the human species according to hereditary (genetic) differences. Different racial characteristics arose among geographically separated populations partly through adaptation to differing environments across many generations. However, as there is no evidence of genetic racial distinctions anthropologists reject the term.

Rachmaninov, Sergei (1873–1943) Russian composer and pianist. Rachmaninov's works include songs, four piano concertos, and three symphonies. His most popular works include Piano Concerto No. 2 (1901), *Rhapsody on a Theme of Paganini* (1934) and Symphony No. 2 (1907).

Racine, Jean Baptiste (1639–99) French classical dramatist whose early plays, such as *La Thebaïde* (1664) and *Alexandre le Grand* (1665), were influenced by contemporaries such as CORNEILLE. Racine's later plays, such as *Britannicus* (1669), *Bérénice* (1670), *Mithridate* (1673), and *Phèdre* (1677), are cornerstones of FRENCH LITERATURE.

racism Doctrine advocating the superiority of one human RACE. Racism has been the policy of certain regimes that, as a result, sanctioned SLAVERY and discriminatory practices, such as anti-Semitism in Nazi Germany and APARTHEID in South Africa. In 1967, UNESCO defined racism as 'anti-social beliefs and acts which are based on a fallacy that discriminatory inter-group relations are justifiable on biological grounds'.

racquets Game played by two or four people in an enclosed 18.3 × 9.1m (60 × 30ft) court. Each player uses a gut-strung racket with a circular head. On the front wall, a service line is painted at a height of 2.9m (9.6ft), and a fixed wooden board, extends 68.6cm (27in) up from the floor. These are the markers that determine when a ball is in play. A serve must be above the service line and must land behind a short line, 7.3m (24ft) from the back wall. Games are played to 15 points. *See also* SQUASH

radar (acronym for **ra**dio **d**etecting **a**nd **r**anging) Electronic system for determining the direction and distance of objects. Developed during World War 2, it works by the transmission of pulses of RADIO waves to an object. The object reflects the pulses, which are detected by an antenna. By measuring the time it takes for the reflected waves to return, the object's distance may be calculated, and its direction ascertained from the alignment of the receiving radar antenna.

radar astronomy Branch of ASTRONOMY in which radar pulses, reflected back to Earth from celestial bodies in our solar system, are studied for information concerning their distance from Earth, their orbital motion, and large surface features. Techniques developed for radar mapping of planetary surfaces have proved particularly important for cloud-covered VENUS.

Radhakrishnan, Sir Sarvepalli (1888–1975) Indian philosopher and statesman, president (1962–67). As professor of Eastern religions and ethics at Oxford (1936–52), Radhakrishnan did much to reconcile classical Hindu philosophy with contemporary social forces. Radhakrishnan served as vice president (1952–62) to Jawaharlal NEHRU.

radian Angle formed by the intersection of two radii at the centre of a circle, when the length of the arc cut off by the radii is equal to one radius in length. Thus, the radian is a unit of angle equal to c.57.295°, and there are 2π radians in 360°.

radiation Transmission of energy by SUBATOMIC PARTICLES or electromagnetic waves. See ELECTROMAGNETIC RADIATION

radiation, heat Energy given off from all solids, liquids or gases as a result of their temperature. The energy comes from the vibrations of atoms in an object and emits as ELECTROMAGNETIC RADIATION. Most objects in everyday life emit in the part of the spectrum known as INFRARED RADIATION, but exceptionally hot materials emit visible light and are seen to glow.

radiation, nuclear Particles or ELECTROMAGNETIC RADIATION emitted spontaneously and at high energies from atomic nuclei. Possible causes include RADIOACTIVE DECAY, which yields ALPHA PARTICLES, BETA PARTICLES, GAMMA RADIATION and, more rarely, POSITRONS. It also results from spontaneous FISSION of a nucleus, ejecting neutrons or gamma rays.

radiation sickness Illness resulting from exposure to sources of ionizing radiation, such as X-rays, gamma rays, or nuclear fallout. Diarrhoea, vomiting, fever and haemorrhaging are symptoms. Severity depends upon the degree of radiation, and treatment is effective in mild cases.

radio BROADCASTING or reception of ELECTROMAGNETIC RADIATION in the form of radio waves. A transmitter generates a radio signal of fixed FREQUENCY (the carrier wave). A MICROPHONE converts the sound to be broadcast into a varying electrical signal that combines with the carrier by means of MODULATION. FREQUENCY MODULATION (FM) minimizes interference and provides greater fidelity than AMPLITUDE MODULATION (AM) (varying the frequency or amplitude of the carrier). The modulated carrier wave passes to an AERIAL, which transmits it into the atmosphere. At the receiver, another aerial intercepts the signal, and it undergoes 'detection', the reverse of modulation, to retrieve the signal. Radio waves travel at the speed of light and are transmitted not only by line-of-sight (ground waves), but also by reflection from the IONOSPHERE (sky waves). Sky waves enable long-range transmission. The ULTRA HIGH FREQUENCY (UHF) and VERY HIGH FREQUENCY (VHF) radio waves used to send signals for TELEVISION penetrate the ionosphere with little reflection, and long-range broadcasting is made possible by means of artificial SATELLITES. The development of radio stems from the work of Scottish physicist James Clerk MAXWELL. German physicist Heinrich HERTZ devised an apparatus for the transmission and detection of radio waves. In 1895, Italian physicist Guglielmo MARCONI gave a demonstration of the first wireless TELEGRAPH, and in 1901 he sent the first transatlantic message using MORSE code. In 1904, English engineer Sir John FLEMING invented the **thermionic valve**. In 1906, US physicist Lee DE FOREST developed the **audion triode valve**, which was able to detect and amplify radio waves. It remained at the heart of radio and television manufacture until the invention (1948) of the TRANSISTOR.

radioactive decay Process by which a radioactive ISOTOPE (radioisotope) loses SUBATOMIC PARTICLES from its nucleus and so becomes a different element. The disintegration of the nuclei occurs with the emission of ALPHA PARTICLES (helium nuclei) or BETA PARTICLES (electrons), often accompanied by GAMMA RADIATION. The two processes of alpha or beta decay cause the radioisotope to transform into a different atom. **Alpha** decay results in the nucleus losing two PROTONS and two NEUTRONS; **beta** decay occurs when a neutron changes into a proton, with an ELECTRON (beta particle) emitted in the process. Thus, the ATOMIC NUMBER (total protons in the nucleus of an atom) changes in both types of decay, and an isotope of another element is produced that might also be radioactive. In a large collection of atoms, there is a characteristic time (the HALF-LIFE) after which one-half of the total number of nuclei would have decayed. This time varies from millionths of a second to millions of years, depending on the isotope concerned. The activity of any radioactive sample decreases exponentially with time. *See also* CARBON DATING

radioactivity Spontaneous change of the atomic nuclei of atoms, accompanied by the emission of RADIATION. The process by which a radioactive nucleus disintegrates is known as RADIOACTIVE DECAY.

radio astronomy Study of radio waves (ELECTROMAGNETIC RADIATION with wavelengths from c.1mm to many metres) that reach the Earth from objects in space. Observations can be made using a RADIO TELESCOPE. Karl JANSKY discovered radio noise from the Milky Way in 1931, and the subject grew rapidly after World War 2. The number of radio sources increases with distance, demonstrating that the universe evolves with time. This fact, combined with the discovery at radio wavelengths of the cosmic microwave background, is evidence in support of the BIG BANG theory of the origin of the universe.

radio galaxy GALAXY that emits strong ELECTROMAGNETIC RADIATION of radio frequency. These emissions seem to be produced by the high-speed motion of ELEMENTARY PARTICLES in strong magnetic fields.

radiography Use of X-RAYS to record the interiors of opaque bodies as images on a film or screen. Industrial X-ray photographs can show assembly faults and metal defects. In medicine and dentistry, radiography is invaluable for diagnosing bone damage, tooth decay and internal disease. Using modern scanning techniques, cross-sectional outlines of the body can be obtained showing organs, blood vessels, and diseased parts.

radiology Medical speciality concerned with the use of RADIATION and radioactive materials in the diagnosis and treatment of disease. *See also* RADIOGRAPHY; RADIOTHERAPY

radio telescope Instrument used to collect and record radio waves from space. The basic design is a large single dish or parabolic reflector, up to 100m (330ft) in diameter. The dish reflects radio waves via a secondary reflector to a focus, where they convert into electrical signals. The signals are amplified and sent to the control room and re-amplified before analysis and recording. *See also* RADIO ASTRONOMY; TELESCOPE

RADAR

A radar system locates flying objects by sending out a signal (1), and picking up any signal reflected back (2). The radar dish (3) reflects the outgoing signal in an arc (4), and focuses the return signal (5) onto the receiver (6). The radar array rotates (7) to cover 360°. A computer processes the signal (8), and planes in range (9) show up as blips (10) on an operator's screen (11).

radiotherapy In medicine, the use of RADIATION to treat tumours or other pathological conditions. It may be done either by implanting a pellet of a radioactive source in the part to be treated, or by dosing the patient with a radioactive isotope or by exposing the patient to precisely focused beams of radiation from a machine such as an X-ray machine or a particle accelerator. Cobalt-60 is often used as it produces highly penetrating gamma radiation. In the treatment of CANCERS, the radiation slows down the proliferation of the cancerous cells.

radish Annual garden vegetable developed from a wild plant native to the cooler regions of Asia. Its leaves are long and deeply lobed; the fleshy root, which may be red, white or black, is eaten raw. Family Brassicaceae; species *Raphanus sativus*.

radium (symbol Ra) White, radioactive, metallic element of the ALKALINE-EARTH METALS, first discovered (1898) in pitchblende by French physicists Pierre and Marie CURIE; the metal is present in uranium ores. It is used in RADIOTHERAPY to treat tumours. Radium has 16 isotopes, which emit alpha, beta and gamma radiation, as well as heat. RADON gas is a decay product. Properties: at.no. 88; r.a.m. 226.025; r.d. 5.0; m.p. 700°C (1,292°F); b.p. 1,140°C (2,084°F); most stable isotope Ra^{226} (half-life 1622 years).

radius In anatomy, one of the two forearm bones, extending from the elbow to the wrist. The radius rotates around the ULNA, permitting the hand to rotate and be flexible.

radon (symbol Rn) Radioactive gaseous element, a NOBLE GAS which is the densest gas known. It was first discovered (1899) by New Zealand-born British physicist Ernest RUTHERFORD. The 20 known isotopes, which are alpha particle emitters, are present in the Earth's atmosphere in trace amounts. Radon is mainly used in medical RADIOTHERAPY. Chemically, it is mostly inert but does form fluoride compounds. Properties: at.no. 86; r.d. 9.73; m.p. −71°C (−95.8°F); b.p. −61.8°C (−79.24 °F); most stable isotope Rn^{222} (half-life 3.8 days).

Raffles, Sir Thomas Stamford (1781–1826) British colonial administrator, founder of Singapore. When Java returned to Dutch rule (1816), Raffles bought the island of Singapore for the British East India Company (1819). Under his guidance, it developed rapidly into a prosperous free port.

rafflesia Parasitic plant native to Sumatra and Java. It grows as a PARASITE on the roots of jungle vines and has no stem or leaves. The foul-smelling, reddish-brown flowers are 1m (3.25ft) in diameter, the world's largest flowers. Family Rafflesiaceae; species *Rafflesia arnoldii*.

Rafsanjani, (Ali Akbar) Hashemi (1934–) Iranian statesman and cleric, president of Iran (1989–97). After Ayatollah KHOMEINI's triumphant return in 1979, Rafsanjani became

▲ **Rafsanjani** Former president of Iran, Hashemi Rafsanjani trained with Ruhollah Khomeini at Qom before Khomeini was forced into exile. Following the overthrow of Shah Pahlevi, Rafsanjani served in Khomeini's revolutionary government. After the conclusion of the Iran-Iraq War, Rafsanjani concentrated on the reconstruction of Iran. Muhammad Khatami succeeded him as president.

R

▲ **ragwort** There are around 1,200 species of ragwort (also known as groundsel) around the world. Some are cultivated as garden plants; others grow wild. Many species, including the common ragwort (*Senecio jacobaea*) are poisonous to livestock, but others have medicinal uses, helping to heal wounds and to bring on or increase menstrual flow.

R

▶ **rail** Native to marshes all around the world, rails are poor fliers that rely on their dull coloration for protective camouflage. Their strong legs allow them to run through dense undergrowth. The Ypecaha wood rail (*Aramides ypecaha*) shown here is found in Brazil, Paraguay, Uruguay and Argentina.

speaker of the Iranian parliament. A leading figure in the new theocracy, he was acting commander of the armed forces in the final stages of the IRAN-IRAQ WAR. Following Khomeini's death in 1989, Rafsanjani became president. His presidency witnessed a slight easing of tension in relations with the West.

raga (Sanskrit, colour) In Indian music, a sequence of five to seven notes that is used exclusively for the duration of a performance as a basis for improvisation. Its basic structure can be written in the form of a scale.

ragwort Any of several plants with daisy-like flowers, including the common ragwort (*Senecio jacobaea*), which bears flat-topped clusters of yellow flower heads. Height: to 1.3m (4ft). Family Asteraceae/Compositae.

rail Slender, long-legged marsh bird. Rails are shy, generally nocturnal, and often emit melodious calls. They lay 8–15 eggs in a reed-and-grass ground nest. Length: 10–45cm (4–18in). Family Rallidae. Typical genus *Rallus*.

railway (railroad) Form of transport in which carriages (wagons or bogies) run on a fixed track, usually steel rails. Railways date from the 1500s, when wagons used in mines were drawn by horses along tracks. English mining engineer Richard TREVITHICK built the first steam LOCOMOTIVE in 1804. In 1825, George STEPHENSON's *Locomotion* became the first steam locomotive to pull a passenger train, on the Stockton and Darlington Railway. The first full passenger-carrying railway, the Liverpool and Manchester Railway, opened in 1830, using Stephenson's *Rocket*. The growth of rail fed the Industrial Revolution. In the USA, *Tom Thumb* was the first domestically produced steam locomotive (1830). The first transcontinental railroad was completed in 1869, when the Union Pacific Railroad from Nebraska met the Central Pacific Railroad from California at Utah. The world's first deep-level UNDERGROUND RAILWAY to carry passengers was the City and South London Railway in 1890. Steam locomotives are still used in India, but most countries use electric, diesel, or diesel-electric locomotives. Modern developments include high-speed trains, such as the Japanese 'Bullet' train or the French TGV (**T**rain à **G**rande **V**itesse), that travel at an average speed of *c.*300km/h (185mph). **Maglev** (magnetic levitation) trains use magnetic forces to hold them above a guide rail. The decrease in friction permits even greater speeds. **Air** trains hover above the track by an air cushion. Trains that do not run on wheels are usually propelled by the magnetic forces of a linear electric motor, or by jet engine.

rain Water drops that fall from the Earth's atmosphere to its surface. Rain is one form of PRECIPITATION. Rain occurs when air carrying water vapour cools, which causes condensation of the vapour into drops. This most commonly happens when the air rises for one of three reasons: it passes over higher ground (relief rainfall), it is heated by warm ground (convectional rainfall), it meets colder air at a FRONT (frontal rainfall). *See also* HYDROLOGICAL CYCLE

rainbow Multicoloured band, usually seen as an arc opposite to the Sun or other light source. The primary bow is the one usually seen; in it the colours are arranged from red at the top to violet at the bottom. A secondary bow, in which the order of the colours is reversed, is sometimes seen beyond the primary bow. The colours are caused by reflection of light within raindrops, which cause white light to be dispersed into its constituent wavelengths. The colours seen are those of the visible SPECTRUM: red, orange, yellow, green, blue, indigo, and violet.

rainforest Dense forest of tall trees that grows in hot, wet regions near the Equator. The main rainforests are in Africa, central and s America, and SE Asia. They comprise 50% of the timber growing on Earth, and house 40% of the world's animal and plant species. There are many species of broad-leaved evergreen trees in rainforests, which grow up to 60m (180ft) tall. The crowns of other trees, up to 45m (135ft) tall, form the upper canopy of the forest. Smaller trees form the lower canopy. Climbing vines interconnect the various levels, providing habitats for many kinds of birds, mammals, and reptiles. Very little light penetrates to the forest floor, which consequently has few plants. Rainforest trees provide many kinds of food and other useful materials, such as fibrous kapok, and the drugs quinine and curare. The rainforests are being destroyed rapidly: up to 20 million ha are razed annually to provide timber and land for agriculture. This is cause for great concern, as clearing rainforest not only causes massive extinction of its species but also seriously contributes to the GREENHOUSE EFFECT and may lead to GLOBAL WARMING.

Rainier, Mount Peak in w central Washington, USA; the highest point in the Cascade Range. It was first climbed in 1870. The summit of this ancient volcano is the centre of the greatest single-peak glacier system in the United States. Height: 4,395m (14,410ft).

Rainier III (1923–2005) Prince of MONACO. He succeeded his grandfather Louis II in 1949, and married actress Grace KELLY in 1956. He was succeeded by Prince Albert.

raisin Dried, sweet, seedless GRAPE. Special varieties are grown, particularly in Australia and w USA.

Rajasthan State in NW India, on the border with Pakistan; the capital is JAIPUR. Other major cities include UDAIPUR, JODHPUR, and Jaisalmer. Rajasthan was the homeland of the RAJPUTS. The state formed in 1950, and enlarged in 1966. Pastoral nomads inhabit the THAR DESERT in the w. The E is part of the DECCAN plateau, where wheat, millet, and cotton grow with the aid of irrigation. There are coal, marble, mica, and gypsum mines. Industries: handicrafts, cotton milling. Area: 342,266sq km (132,149sq mi). Pop. (2001) 56,473,122.

Rajneesh, Shree (1931–90) (Chandra Mohan Jain) Indian religious leader who founded a religious movement in India based on what he called 'loving meditation'. Under Bhagwan Rajneesh's charismatic leadership, the movement spread to Europe and the USA.

Rajput Predominantly Hindi warrior caste from NW India. They became powerful in the 7th century AD gaining control of an historic region named Rajputana. They retained their independence despite the Muslim conquests in the 12th century, but by the early 17th century had submitted to the MOGUL EMPIRE. In the early 18th century, they extended their control. In the 19th century, they lost most of their territorial gains to the Marathas, Sikhs, and the British Empire. During the colonial period, much of Rajputana retained its independence under local princely rule. After Indian independence in 1947 most of the princes lost their powers. *See also* RAJASTHAN

Raleigh Capital of North Carolina, USA, in the E central part of the state. Founded in 1792 as state capital, it was named after Sir Walter Raleigh. It is a market centre for the cotton and tobacco trade. Industries: food processing, textiles, electronic equipment. Pop. (2000) 276,093.

Raleigh, Sir Walter (1552–1618) English soldier, explorer and writer. A favourite courtier of ELIZABETH I, he organized expeditions to North America, including the failed attempt to found a colony in Virginia (now North Carolina). He fought in France and against Spain and sat in Parliament. On JAMES I's ascension to the throne, he was imprisoned (1603–16) for treason, writing his *History of the World*. He was released in order to lead an expedition to Guiana in search of the gold of EL DORADO, but was betrayed to the Spanish. At Spanish insistence, Raleigh returned to prison and was executed for treason.

RAM (**r**andom **a**ccess **m**emory) INTEGRATED CIRCUITS (chips) that act as a temporary store for computer PROGRAM and DATA (information). To run a program on a COMPUTER, the program is first transferred from a HARD DISK, or other storage device, to RAM. RAM also holds documents produced when the program is used. Another part of RAM stores the images to be displayed on the screen. The contents of RAM are lost when the computer is switched off.

Rama Hero of the RAMAYANA. A chivalrous husband, obedient to sacred law, he was considered to be the seventh incarnation of VISHNU. His name became synonymous with God.

Ramadan Ninth month of the Islamic year. Throughout Ramadan, the faithful must abstain from food, drink, and sexual intercourse between sunrise and sunset. They are also encouraged to read the whole of the KORAN in remembrance of the 'Night of Power', when MUHAMMAD is said to have received his first revelation from ALLAH via the angel Gabriel.

Ramakrishna (1836–86) (Gadadhar Chatterji) Hindu teacher who taught that all religions were united in a common goal of union with the same God. His disciple, Swami Vivekananda, founded (1897) the Ramakrishna Mission in India.

Raman, Sir Chandrasekhara Venkata (1888–1970) Indian physicist. He greatly influenced the growth of science in India, and founded (1946) the Raman Institute. Raman received the 1930 Nobel Prize in physics for his research on the diffusion of light and his discovery of the **Raman effect**. This states that there is a slight change in the frequency of monochromatic (single-wavelength) light that has been scattered by passing through a transparent material. This effect appears as secondary spectral lines on each side of the primary spectral line. *See also* QUANTUM THEORY; SCATTERING

Ramayana (Romance of Rama) Epic poem of ancient India. Written in *c.*300 BC along with the MAHABHARATA, it is ascribed to the poet Valmiki and comprises 24,000 couplets in seven books. It concerns the life of RAMA and his wife Sita.

Rambert, Dame Marie (1888–1982) British ballet dancer, teacher and choreographer, b. Poland. She was a member (1912–13) of DIAGHILEV's BALLETS RUSSES, and was special adviser to NIJINSKY in the first performance of Stravinsky's *The Rite of Spring* (1913). She founded her own school in 1920, which became known as Ballet Rambert in 1935.

Ramsay, Allan (1713–84) Scottish portrait painter. The Scottish counterpart of Thomas GAINSBOROUGH and Joshua REYNOLDS, Ramsay settled in London where, in 1760, he was appointed painter to George III in preference to his rival, Reynolds. His style, graceful and Italianate, lent itself especially well to female portraiture, such as *The Artist's Wife* (1755).

Ramsay, Sir William (1852–1916) Scottish chemist. Working with Lord RAYLEIGH, he discovered ARGON in air. Later, he discovered HELIUM, NEON, and KRYPTON. He was knighted in 1902, and awarded the Nobel Prize in chemistry in 1904.

Ramses I Founder of the 19th dynasty of ancient EGYPT (r. *c.*1320–1318BC). He was a general under Horemheb, who chose him as his successor. The great hall of the temple at Karnak (LUXOR) was begun during his reign.

Ramses II Egyptian Pharaoh of the 19th dynasty (r.1290–1224BC). He reigned during a period of unprecedented prosperity and power. His efforts to confirm Egypt's dominant position in Palestine and to regain her possessions and influence in Syria, led to a major clash with the HITTITES at Kadesh in 1285 BC. A truce occurred in 1269 BC and Ramses later married a Hittite princess. He built many splendid monuments, including the temple at ABU SIMBEL.

Ramses III Egyptian Pharaoh of the 20th dynasty (r.*c.*1194–1163BC). He defended Egypt from attacks by Libya and the Sea Peoples. Later in his reign, however, Egypt withdrew into political and cultural isolation and the priesthood became the centre of power.

Ramsey, Sir Alf (Alfred) (1920–99) English football manager and player. Ramsay was a fullback for Southampton and Tottenham Hotspur, and made 32 appearances for England (1948–53). He began his managerial career with Ipswich Town, helping them win the League Championship (1962) before managing (1963–74) the national team. Ramsay created and guided England's only World Cup-winning side (1966).

Rand *See* WITWATERSRAND

Rangi In the creation myth of the Maoris, Rangi is the sky god who forms such a close embrace with the Earth goddess, Papa, that their unborn children cannot emerge. When they are finally separated, Light and Darkness make their first appearance in the world. Rangi also figures in other OCEANIC MYTHOLOGY.

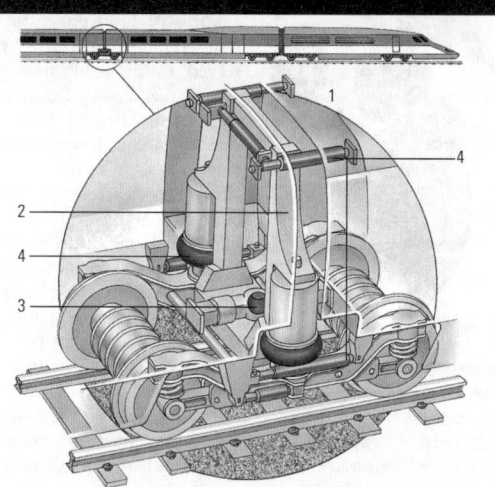

RAILWAY

Modern railways have trains, such as the Eurostar, with bogies that use an articulated air suspension system. This has great weight savings. The bogies (1) link the carriages, which attach to a metal frame (2) through a ball joint (3). Instead of each carriage having a bogie at either end, there is a single suspension unit between two carriages. Dampers (4) modify articulation to improve passenger comfort. The black rings between the frame and the wheel unit are the air suspension units.

Rangoon (Yangon) Capital of Burma (Myanmar), a seaport on the Rangoon River. The site of a Buddhist shrine, it became capital in 1886, when the British annexed the country. It was the scene of heavy fighting between British and Japanese forces in World War 2. It is the country's chief trade centre. Industries: oil refining, timber, rice, iron ore. Pop. (2002 est.) 4,016,000.

Ranjit Singh (1780–1839) Indian Maharaja, founder of the Sikh kingdom of the Punjab. At the age of 12, he became the ruler of a small territory in NW India. He absorbed neighbouring states, and in 1799 established his capital at Lahore. In 1803, he took possession of the Sikh holy city of Amritsar. He established the E boundary of his kingdom on the River Sutlej. Turning his attention to the W and N, he captured Peshawar and Kashmir. His kingdom collapsed after his death.

Rank, J. (Joseph) Arthur (1888–1972) English industrialist and film magnate, chairman of many film companies. Rank promoted the British film industry at a time when Hollywood and US film companies had a virtual monopoly.

Ransome, Arthur Mitchell (1884–1967) English writer and journalist. He is best-known for his popular children's novels, *Swallows and Amazons* (1930) and *Peter Duck* (1933).

rap Form of dance music that became popular during the early 1980s. Rap has its roots in the improvised street poetry of African-American and Hispanic teenagers in New York. The music places an emphasis on DJs who mix different tracks together, sometimes 'scratching' for increased effect.

rape Plant grown for animal fodder and for its small, black seeds, which yield rape oil, used industrially as a lubricant. It has curly, blue-green leaves, small yellow flowers, and slender seed pods. Family Brassicaceae; genus *Brassica*.

rape Crime of sexual intercourse without the victim's consent, often involving the use or threat of force. If the victim is considered incapable of giving consent (for example because s/he is below the age of consent) this is known as **statutory** rape, and evidence of lack of consent is not required. Usually applied to male use of force against women, though in some legal systems a man can prosecute for rape. **Marital** rape is now considered a crime in the UK and in many US states.

Raphael (1483–1520) (Raphael Sanzio or Raphael Santi) Italian painter, one of the finest artists of the High RENAISSANCE. Born in Urbino, Raphael absorbed HUMANISM as a child. One of his most important commissions was the decoration of the four *stanze* (rooms) in the Vatican. He only completed two of these but the first, the *Stanza della Segnatura*, gave him the chance to exercise his skills to the full. The room contains two large FRESCOS, the *School of Athens* and the *Disputà*, both of which show Raphael's mastery of PERSPECTIVE. After BRAMANTE's death, he became architect to St Peter's, Rome.

Raphael Biblical archangel who, with MICHAEL and GABRIEL, serves as a messenger of God. According to passages in the apocryphal Book of Tobit and the pseudographical Second Book of Enoch, he is one of the seven holy angels who present the prayers of the saints to God.

R

▲ **rape** Widely cultivated throughout China, India and Europe, rape (*Brassica napus*) produces seeds that have an oil content of 40–50%. Once extracted, the oil is used for cooking, lubrication, fuel, and the manufacture of soap and rubber. The seed residue is used for animal feed and fertilizer. Rape fields are easily identified by the bright yellow colour of the flowers.

▲ raspberry Popular as a wild fruit from ancient times, raspberries (*Rubus* sp.) have been cultivated since the early 17th century. The fruits grow on usually thorny bushes, although thornless varieties also exist. There are more than 200 varieties of raspberry in Asia, where the fruit is thought to have originated.

► rattlesnake Not normally aggressive, rattlesnakes try to avoid confrontation by warning of their presence. They produce their unmistakable and menacing rattle from 'bells' of hard skin on the end of the tail. The amount of venom they produce far exceeds that needed to kill the rodents that form their usual prey. They can also use the venom to protect themselves against large predators.

rare earth *See* LANTHANIDE SERIES

raspberry Fruit grown in Europe, North America, and Asia. The black, purple, or red fruit is eaten fresh or preserved. Canes, rising from perennial roots, bear fruit the second year. Family Rosaceae; species *Rubus idaeus*.

Rasputin, Grigori Yefimovich (1872–1916) Russian peasant mystic. Rasputin exercised great influence at the court of NICHOLAS II because of his apparent ability to cure Crown Prince Alexis' haemophilia. He attracted suspicion because of his advocacy of sexual ecstasy as a means of religious salvation. Rasputin was poisoned by a group of nobles in 1916, and when this failed, he was shot and drowned.

Rastafarianism West Indian religion focusing on veneration of Ras Tafari (HAILE SELASSIE I). The movement was started in Jamaica in the 1920s by Marcus GARVEY. He advocated a return to Africa in order to overcome black oppression. Followers of Rastafarianism follow a strict diet, and are forbidden various foods including pork, milk and coffee.

rat Any of numerous small RODENTS found worldwide. Most species are herbivorous. The best known are the black rat (*Rattus rattus*) and brown rat (*R. norvegicus*), both of the family Muridae. They carry diseases and destroy or contaminate property and food. Both live everywhere that humans live.

ratio Number relating two numbers or two quantities of the same kind, such as two prices or two lengths, that indicates their relative magnitude. Ratios, as of the numbers 3 and 4, can be written as a fraction $\frac{3}{4}$, or with a colon (3:4).

rationalism Philosophical theory that knowledge about the nature of the world can be obtained solely by reason, without recourse to experience. Rationalist philosophers, such as DESCARTES, LEIBNIZ, and SPINOZA, argued that reality could be logically deduced from 'self-evident' *a priori* premises. It contrasts with EMPIRICISM. In theology, rationalism holds that faith be explicable by human reason rather than divine revelation.

rational number Number representing the ratio of two integers, the second of which is not zero. Thus, $\frac{1}{2}$, $1\frac{8}{11}$, 0, $\frac{2}{3}$ and 12 are all rational numbers. Any rational number can be represented as a terminating decimal (such as 1.35) or a recurring decimal (such as $1\frac{8}{11} = 1.636363....$). *See also* IRRATIONAL NUMBER

ratite Group of large, usually flightless birds with flat breastbones instead of the keel-like prominences found in most flying birds. Ratites include the OSTRICH, RHEA, CASSOWARY, EMU, KIWI, and the unusual flying tinamou.

rattan Climbing PALM native to the East Indies and Africa. Its stems can grow to 150m (500ft). They are used for making ropes and furniture. Family Arecacae/Palmae; genus *Calamus*.

Rattigan, Sir Terence Mervyn (1911–77) English dramatist. He first attracted attention with the comedy *French Without Tears* (1936). His most popular plays include *The Winslow Boy* (1946), *The Browning Version* (1948), *Separate Tables* (1954), *Ross* (1960), and *In Praise of Love* (1973). He also wrote the screenplay for the musical *Goodbye Mr Chips* (1968).

Rattle, Sir Simon (1955–) English conductor. Rattle made his reputation as principal conductor (1980–98) and music director (1990–98) of the City of Birmingham Symphony Orchestra (CBSO). Known for his championing of new music and interpretations of Mahler, Rattle is chief conductor and artistic director of the Berlin Philharmonic Orchestra (2002–).

rattlesnake Any of *c*.30 species of venomous New World pit VIPERS characterized by a tail rattle of loosely connected segments of unshed skin. It ranges from Canada to South America, usually in arid regions. Most are blotched with dark diamonds, hexagons or spots on a lighter background. They feed mostly on rodents. Length: 30cm-2.5m (1–8ft). Family Viperidae. *See also* SNAKE

Rauschenberg, Robert (1925–2008) US painter and graphic artist. Influenced by Marcel DUCHAMP and Jasper JOHNS, Rauschenberg was a pioneer of POP ART in the 1950s. His works, such as *Bed* (1955) and *Monogram* (1959), combined the painting techniques of ABSTRACT EXPRESSIONISM with collages and assemblages of 'junk'.

Ravel, (Joseph) Maurice (1875–1937) French composer, a leading exponent of IMPRESSIONISM. Ravel's piano compositions include *Jeux d'eau* (1901), *Gaspard de la nuit* (1908), *Le Tombeau de Couperin* (1917), and two concertos. Among his orchestral works are *Rhapsodie espagnole* (1907) and *Boléro* (1927). He also composed the ballet *Daphnis and Chloe* (1912), and the song cycle *Shéhérazade* (1903).

raven Large bird of the crow family found in deserts, forests and mountainous areas of the Northern Hemisphere. It has a long, conical bill, shaggy throat feathers, a wedge-shaped tail and black plumage with a purple sheen. It eats carrion or any other animal food. Length: to 68cm (27in). Family Corvidae.

Ravenna City in Emilia-Romagna, NE Italy. It was the capital of the Western Roman Empire in the 5th century AD. It then became capital of the Ostrogothic kingdom and then the seat of the Byzantine government in Italy. An independent republic in the 13th century, it was under papal rule from the 16th to 19th centuries, becoming part of the Kingdom of Italy in 1860. Industries: petroleum, natural gas, furniture, cement, fertilizers, sugar refining. Pop. (2000) 139,771; 350,223 (metropolitan).

Rawalpindi City in Punjab province, NE Pakistan. It grew rapidly in the 18th century, and became a military base after Britain occupied the Punjab in 1849. It was interim capital of Pakistan from 1959 to 1969. Industries: iron, textiles, railway engineering, oil-refining, chemicals. Pop. (1998) 1,406,214.

ray Any of several species of cartilaginous, mostly marine fish related to the SKATE, SHARK and CHIMAERA. The ray is flattened dorso-ventrally; its body extends sideways into large, wing-like pectoral fins that are 'flapped' while swimming. The tail is narrow, and may be whip-like or bear poisonous spines. Electric (torpedo) rays stun their prey with electrical charges of up to 200 volts. Length: 1.5m (5ft).

Ray, Man (1890–1976) US photographer, painter, sculptor, and film-maker, the founder of the New York DADA movement with Marcel DUCHAMP and Francis Picabia. Ray is best known for photographs produced without a camera by placing objects on light-sensitive paper and exposing them to light.

Ray, Satyajit (1921–92) Indian film director. Ray introduced Indian cinema to the West. His 'Apu Trilogy' – *Pather Panchali* (1955), *The Unvanquished* (1956) and *The World of Apu* (1959) – is a beautiful, humanist series of films about life in post-colonial India. Other films include *The Big City* (1963), *The Hero* (1966), and *The Visitor* (1992).

Rayleigh, John William Strutt, Lord (1842–1919) English physicist. His work was chiefly concerned with various forms of wave motion. He received the 1904 Nobel Prize in physics for his discovery (with William RAMSAY) of the noble gas ARGON and for work on gas densities.

rayon Fine, smooth FIBRE made from solutions of CELLULOSE. It was the first synthetic textile fibre. **Viscose** rayon, the most common, is spun-dried and has a strength approaching NYLON. **Acetate** rayon is made of filaments of cellulose ACETATE. It was patented in 1884 by its inventor, the French chemist Hilaire Chardonnet (1839–1924), who named it 'artificial silk'.

razor-billed auk (razorbill) Stocky, penguin-like seabird that lives along coastlines in the cold parts of the Northern Hemisphere. It is black and white with a white-ringed, narrow bill. Length: 41cm (16in). Species *Alca torda*.

razor shell Bivalve MOLLUSC. Its long, hinged shells, each shaped like the blade of a cut-throat razor, are common on beaches of the Northern Hemisphere. Family Solenidae.

Reading City in S central England, at the confluence of the Thames and Kennet rivers; county town of BERKSHIRE. The area was occupied by the Danes in the 9th century. Industries: ironware, engineering, electronics. Pop. (2001) 143,124.

Reagan, Ronald Wilson (1911–2004) Fortieth US President (1981–89). A B-movie actor, he joined the Republican Party in 1962. Reagan won a landslide victory to become governor of California (1966–74). Nominated as presidential candidate at his third attempt in 1980, he defeated incumbent Jimmy CARTER. In 1981, Reagan survived an assassination attempt. As president, he introduced large tax cuts and reduced public spending, except on defence. By the end of Reagan's second term, budget and trade deficits reached record heights. Fiercely anti-communist, he adopted aggressive measures against opponents abroad – invading Grenada (1983), and undermining the SANDINISTA regime in Nicaragua. While pursuing his Strategic Defence Initiative (SDI, or 'Star Wars'), Reagan reached a historic nuclear DISARMAMENT treaty (1987) with Mikhail GORBACHEV that signalled an end to the COLD WAR. The IRAN-CONTRA AFFAIR overshadowed the final year of his presidency.

realism Broad term in art history, often interchangeable with NATURALISM. It is frequently used to define art that tries to represent objects accurately and without emotional bias. It also denotes a movement in 19th-century French art, led by Gustave COURBET, that revolted against conventional, historical or mythological subjects and focused on unidealized scenes of modern life. **Superrealism** is a 20th-century movement, in which real objects are depicted in very fine detail so that the overall effect appears unreal. *See also* SOCIALIST REALISM

realism Philosophical doctrine according to which universal concepts, as well as tangible things, exist in their own right, outside the human mind that recognizes or perceives them. The idea developed from a medieval view that 'universals' are real entities rather than simply names for things. Realism was thus opposed to NOMINALISM. Some philosophers rejected this view in favour of moderate realism, which held that 'universals' exist only in the mind of God. *See also* IDEALISM

real number Any number that is a RATIONAL NUMBER or an IRRATIONAL NUMBER. Real numbers exclude imaginary numbers (the square roots of negative quantities). *See also* COMPLEX NUMBER

real tennis (royal TENNIS, court tennis) Medieval game played with racket and ball on a rectangular indoor court surrounded by walls, three out of four of which are surmounted by a sloping roof; there are other hazards at each end. The game was first played during the 12th century in French monastic cloisters.

Rebellions of 1837 Risings in favour of self-rule in Upper and Lower Canada (ONTARIO and QUÉBEC). William Lyon Mackenzie led the first rising in Upper Canada. The revolt in Lower Canada, led by Louis PAPINEAU, was more serious, and was brutally suppressed. The outbreaks led to the Durham Report and the union of Upper and Lower Canada in 1841.

receptacle Biological structure that serves as a container for reproductive cells or organs in plants. In flowering plants, the receptacle is the enlarged end of a stalk to which the FLOWER is attached. In FERNS, it is the mass of tissue that forms the sporangium (the spore-bearing organ). In some seaweeds, it is the part that seasonally becomes swollen and carries the reproductive organs.

recession In economics, phase of the business cycle associated with a declining economy. Its manifestations are rising unemployment, contracting business activity, and decreasing purchasing power of consumers. Government policy, such as cuts in government spending or taxes, may be used to stimulate and expand the economy during a recession. If a recession is not checked, it can degenerate into a DEPRESSION.

reciprocal Quantity equal to the number 1 divided by a specified number. The reciprocal of 2 is $^1/_2$, and the reciprocal of $^1/_2$ is 2.

recombinant DNA research Branch of GENETIC ENGINEERING involving the transferral of a segment of DNA from a source organism into a host organism (typically a microbe). A RESTRICTION ENZYME is used to cut the DNA. The transferred segment is spliced into the host's overall DNA structure, thus altering the information contained in its GENETIC CODE. When the host undergoes asexual cell division, each product cell carries a replica of the new DNA. In this way, numerous clones of the new cell can be made.

Reconstruction In US history, the process of restoring the former Confederate states to the Union after the CIVIL WAR. It was the cause of fierce controversy within Congress. The pro-Southern approach of President Andrew JOHNSON led to his impeachment, which failed by one vote. The Republicans were determined to establish the CIVIL RIGHTS of African Americans, and they imposed the programme known as 'Radical Reconstruction' over presidential veto. It alienated many Southern whites, and growing violence in the 1870s required the presence of federal troops. When Rutherford B. HAYES became president (1877), he withdrew the troops. Southern Republican governments, and then Reconstruction itself, collapsed.

recorder Simple WOODWIND musical instrument, popular in Europe since the 15th century. It comprises an end-blown straight tube with eight finger-holes. Modern recorders include soprano, descant, tenor and bass instruments.

recording *See* SOUND RECORDING

rectangle Four-sided geometric figure (quadrilateral), the interior angles of which are right angles and each pair of opposite sides is of equal length and is parallel. It is a special case of a PARALLELOGRAM. A SQUARE is a rectangle with all sides of equal length.

rectifier Component of an electric CIRCUIT that converts alternating current (AC) into direct current (DC). The rectifier is usually a semiconductor DIODE (electronic device with two electrodes). *See also* ELECTRIC CURRENT

rectum In humans and many other vertebrates, last part of the large INTESTINE, where the faeces are stored prior to voiding.

recycling Natural and manufactured processes by which substances are broken down and reconstituted. In nature, elemental cycles include the CARBON CYCLE, NITROGEN CYCLE, and HYDROLOGICAL CYCLE. Natural cyclic chemical processes include the metabolic cycles in the bodies of living organisms. Manufactured recycling includes the use of bacteria to break down organic wastes to harmless, or even beneficial, substances. Large quantities of inorganic waste, such as metal scrap, glass bottles, and building spoil, are recycled.

red admiral Distinctive European butterfly with red bars on the wings and black wing-tips spotted with white. The caterpillar is dark with light side stripes and branching spikes. Family Nymphalidae; species *Vanessa atalanta*.

red algae Taxonomic group (PHYLUM) of reddish ALGAE, the Rhodophyta. They are numerous in tropical and subtropical seas. Most are slender, branching seaweeds that form shrub-like masses. Some become encrusted with calcium carbonate and are important in reef formation. Rhodophytes have red and purplish pigments, which absorb light for photosynthesis. They also have CHLOROPHYLL. They have complex life cycles with two or three stages, involving ALTERNATION OF GENERATIONS.

Red Army Army of the former Soviet Union. It was characterized by a high degree of political control, and was institutionalized at all levels with a system of commissars. During World War 2, the Red Army grew to more than 20 million men. It was renamed the Soviet Army in 1946. The Red Army was also the name of the Chinese revolutionary guard before it was formally renamed the People's Liberation Army.

red blood cell *See* ERYTHROCYTE

Red Cross International organization that seeks to alleviate human suffering, particularly through disaster relief and aid to war victims. It consists of more than 150 independent national societies in most countries, with central headquarters in Geneva, Switzerland. It is staffed largely by volunteers.

◀ **ray** Found in all oceans, the various species of electric ray (*Dasyatis* sp.) use the electric charge they can generate both for stunning prey and warding off predators – the shock of between 35 and 60 volts may be strong enough to stun humans. They feed on smaller animals and have specially adapted teeth for crushing shells.

INTERNET

Reagan, Ronald Wilson
▸ www.reaganfoundation.org
▸ www.whitehouse.gov/history/presidents

Red Cross
▸ www.icrc.org

▲ **Reagan** Appearing in more than 50 films from the time of his Hollywood debut in the 1930s, Ronald Reagan was a celebrity in the USA before he entered politics in the mid-1960s. Genial and optimistic, and highly skilled in televisual presentation, he was very popular, particularly with the right wing of the Republican Party. A few years after leaving office, he announced that he was suffering from Alzheimer's disease and received much public sympathy.

R

▲ **Redford** Although he is best known for his starring roles in films from *Butch Cassidy and the Sundance Kid* (1969) to *Indecent Proposal* (1993), Robert Redford began his acting career on the Broadway stage, where he starred in the 1963 production of *Barefoot in the Park*, which he later filmed. Always highly selective in choosing his film roles, he began to direct in the 1980s. Redford also established the Sundance Institute in Utah, a training centre for young, independent film-makers and the home of the annual Sundance Film Festival.

INTERNET

Redon, Odilon
▸ www.nga.gov
▸ www.metmuseum.org

R

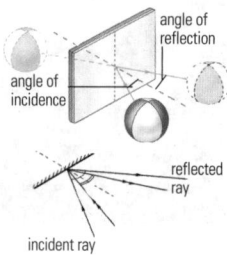

▲ **reflection** The top diagram shows the reflection of an image in a mirror. The image reflects back with an angle of reflection the same as the angle of incidence. The image, however, appears to the eye to be behind the mirror on an extension of the angle of reflection. The bottom line drawing illustrates that the angle of reflection is always the same as the angle of incidence, whatever its angle.

The name comes from its symbol: a red cross on a white background. The International Red Cross received the Nobel Peace Prize in 1917 and 1944. The organization is known as the **Red Crescent** in most Muslim countries.

redcurrant Widely cultivated shrub and its small, round, red, edible fruit; it is closely related to the blackcurrant. Family Grossulariaceae; species *Ribes silvestre*.

red dwarf STAR at the lower end of the main sequence. Red dwarfs have masses of between 0.8 and 0.08 of a solar mass. They are of small diameter, relatively low surface temperature (2,500–5,000K) and low absolute MAGNITUDE.

Redford, Robert (1937–) US film actor, director, and producer. Redford shot to fame appearing opposite Paul NEWMAN in *Butch Cassidy and the Sundance Kid* (1969). His popularity increased with films such as *The Candidate* (1982) and *All the President's Men* (1976). Redford won an Academy Award for his directorial debut *Ordinary People* (1980). Other films include *A River Runs Through It* (1992) and *Quiz Show* (1994).

Redgrave English acting family. **Sir Michael** (1908–85), also a director and writer, made major stage appearances in Shakespeare's *Hamlet*, *Macbeth*, and *As You Like It*. He appeared in many films, including *The Way to the Stars* (1945) and *The Browning Version* (1951). His children are actors. **Vanessa** (1937–) won an Academy Award as best supporting actress in *Julia* (1977). Her other films include *Howard's End* (1992). **Corin** (1939–) acts on stage and television and **Lynn** (1943–) received an Oscar nomination for *Georgy Girl* (1966).

Redgrave, Sir Steven (1962–) English oarsman. Redgrave won five gold medals at consecutive Olympic Games – the first athlete to achieve such a feat in an endurance event. He won gold medals for Britain in the coxed fours (1984), coxless pair (1998, 1992, 1996), and coxless fours (2000).

Red Guards Chinese youth movement active in the CULTURAL REVOLUTION (1966–68). They were named after the groups of armed workers who took part in the Russian Revolution (1917). The Chinese Red Guards attacked revisionists, Westerners and alleged bourgeois influences. Originally encouraged by MAO ZEDONG, they caused severe social disorder and were suppressed after 1968.

Red Jacket (1758–1830) (Otetiani) Native American chief of the SENECA. He was called Red Jacket from his association with the British colonial army during the AMERICAN REVOLUTION. He astutely exploited the differences between rival groups, and in the WAR OF 1812 supported the USA against the British.

Redon, Odilon (1840–1916) French painter and graphic artist. Redon was an influential exponent of SYMBOLISM. He worked mainly in black and white, creating a fantasy world of weird amorphous creatures, insects, and human heads with plant bodies. In the 1890s, he began painting mythological scenes and flower paintings in radiant colours.

Red Sea Narrow arm of the Indian Ocean between NE Africa and the Arabian Peninsula, connected to the Mediterranean Sea by the Gulf of Suez and the Suez Canal. With the building of vessels too large for the canal and the construction of pipelines, the Red Sea's importance as a trade route diminished. Max. width: *c.*320km (200mi). Area: 438,000sq km (169,000sq mi).

redshank Eurasian wading bird of the SANDPIPER family. It has a long slender bill, mottled grey, brown and white plumage, and characteristic slender red legs. Length: to 28cm (11in). Family Scolopacidae; species *Tringa totanus*.

red shift (*z*) Lengthening of the wavelength of light or other ELECTROMAGNETIC RADIATION from a source, caused either by the source moving away (the DOPPLER EFFECT) or by the expansion of the universe (cosmological red shifts). It is defined as the change in the wavelength of a particular spectral line, divided by the rest wavelength of that line. The Doppler effect results from motion through space; cosmological red shifts are caused by the expansion of space itself stretching the wavelengths of light travelling towards Earth.

reduction *See* OXIDATION-REDUCTION

redwood *See* SEQUOIA

reed Aquatic GRASS native to wetlands throughout the world. The common reed (*Phragmites communis*) has broad leaves, feathery flower clusters, and stiff smooth stems. Dry reed stems are used for thatching, construction and musical pipes. Height: to 3m (10ft). Family Poaceae/Gramineae.

Reed, Lou (1944–) US singer-songwriter and guitarist, b. Louis Firbank. Reed formed the cult rock band Velvet Underground in 1965. Following the group's demise in the 1970s, he pursued a solo career, achieving widespread popularity with *Transformer* (1972) and the single 'Perfect Day'.

Reed, Sir Carol (1906–76) English film director. He won an Academy Award for *Oliver* (1968). Other films include *Penny Paradise* (1938), *The Fallen Idol* (1948), *The Third Man* (1949), *Trapeze* (1956) and *The Agony and Ecstasy* (1965).

reed instrument Musical instrument that produces sound when an air current vibrates a fibre or metal tongue. In a CLARINET, a beating reed vibrates against a hole at the end of the tube. The OBOE and BASSOON have double-reed mouthpieces, the two tongues vibrating against each other when blown.

reef Rocky outcrop lying in shallow water, especially one built up by CORALS or other organisms.

referendum Political process in which legislation or constitutional proposals are put before all voters for approval or rejection. This direct form of voting was known in Greece and other early DEMOCRACIES. In the UK, referendums took place over membership of the EUROPEAN COMMUNITY (1975) and DEVOLUTION for Scotland and Wales (1979, 1998).

reflection Change in direction of part or all of a WAVE. When a wave, such as a light or sound wave, encounters a surface separating two different media, it bounces back into the original medium. The incident wave (striking the surface), reflected wave, and the normal (line perpendicular to the surface) all lie in the same plane; the incident wave and reflected wave make equal angles with the normal. *See also* REFRACTION

reflex action Rapid involuntary response to a particular stimulus – for example, the 'knee-jerk' reflex that occurs when the bent knee is tapped. It is controlled by the nervous system.

reflex camera CAMERA that allows the user to view and focus through the lens. A plane mirror and prism reflect the scene through the lens on to a ground glass screen. When the photographer presses the shutter on a **single-lens reflex** (SLR) camera, the mirror flips back and light reaches the film. The older **twin-lens reflex** (TLR) design has two sets of lenses, one for viewfinding, the other for passing light directly onto the film; the mirror does not need to move, so the camera is more stable. *See also* PHOTOGRAPHY

reflexology Complementary medicine based on the theory, which dates back to 3000 BC that the body is reflected in the foot and so foot massage clears blockages of energy flow in the body which are causing illness.

Reform Acts British Acts of Parliament extending the right to vote. The Great Reform Bill (1832) redistributed seats in the House of Commons to include large cities that were previously unrepresented. It also gave the vote to adult males occupying premises worth at least £10 a year. The second Reform Act (1867) extended the franchise to include better-off members of the working class. The Acts of 1884 and 1885 gave the vote to most adult males. Women age 30 and over gained the vote in 1918, and the Representation of the People Act (1928) introduced universal adult suffrage.

Reformation Sixteenth-century European movement that sought reform of the CATHOLIC CHURCH and resulted in the development of PROTESTANTISM. More than a revolt against the ecclesiastical and doctrinal authority of the Church, it also represented a protest by theologians and scholars against the interference of the Church in secular matters and the questionable activities of the contemporary clergy, notably the sale of INDULGENCES and holy relics. In the 14th and 15th centuries, the Catholic Church had been tested by the LOLLARDS, the HUSSITES, and HUMANISM. The Reformation started in 1517, when Martin LUTHER nailed his *Ninety-five Theses* to the Schlosskirche in Wittenburg, Germany. Luther's attack on the corruption of the Church and the doctrines of papal supremacy, TRANSUBSTANTIATION, and clerical celibacy won the support of several German princes. In Zurich, Switzerland, the Reformation was led first by Ulrich ZWINGLI, and then by John CALVIN. CALVINISM was adopted in France (*see* HUGUENOTS), the Netherlands, and Scandinavia. In England, the Reformation was more politically than religiously inspired. In 1534, Thomas CROMWELL drafted the Act of Supremacy that rejected papal authority, and made HENRY VIII the head of the English Church. Under EDWARD VI, Protestantism was established by the Book of COMMON PRAYER (1552). In 1559, in the reign of Elizabeth I, the CHURCH OF ENGLAND was formally established. In Scotland, the Reformation was led by John KNOX, and PRESBYTERIANISM was established as the state religion in 1560. *See also* COUNTER-REFORMATION

Reformed Church Any Christian denomination that came into being during the REFORMATION by separating, as a congregation, from the old universal Catholic Church (the Western Church). More specifically, Reformed Churches are those Churches that adopted CALVINISM in preference to LUTHERANISM. In the USA, the largest Reformed Churches, such as the Dutch Reformed Church and the Evangelical and Reformed Church, originated from N European countries, particularly Holland and Germany.

refraction Bending of a wave, such as a light or sound wave, when it crosses the boundary between two media, such as air and glass, and changes velocity. The incident wave (striking the surface), refracted wave and the normal (line perpendicular to the surface) all lie in the same plane. The incident wave and refracted wave make an angle of incidence, i, and an angle of refraction, r, with the normal. The index of refraction for a transparent medium is the ratio of the speed of light in a vacuum to its speed in the medium. **Snell's law** states that this ratio is constant for a given interface. *See also* REFLECTION

refrigeration Process by which heat is moved out of a container. In a domestic refrigerator, a gas, such as AMMONIA is first compressed by a pump and cooled in a condenser where it liquefies. It is then passed into an evaporator where it expands and boils, absorbing heat from its surroundings and thus cooling the refrigerator. It is then passed through the pump again to be compressed. CHLOROFLUOROCARBON (CFC), once the most common refrigerant, is being replaced because it damages the OZONE LAYER. Refrigeration is also used in air conditioning.

Regency style Style of art and architecture fashionable when the future George IV was Prince Regent (1811–20) and during his reign. A period of great variety, it generally denotes designs that are extremely elegant and refined.

regeneration Biological term for the ability of an organism to replace one of its parts if it is lost. An example is a lizard that can regrow a tail after the original one becomes detached. Regeneration also refers to a form of ASEXUAL REPRODUCTION in which a new individual grows from a detached portion of a parent organism.

Regensburg (Fr. Ratisbon) City and port at the confluence of the Danube and Regen rivers, Bavaria, s Germany. Founded by the Romans as Castra Regina, it was captured by Charlemagne in 788. During the 13th century, Regensburg flourished on the commercial trade with the Middle East and India and became an imperial free city. From 1663 to 1806, it was the seat of the Imperial Diet. In 1810, Bavaria annexed Regensburg, and in 1853 it became a free port. Pop. (1999) 125,200.

reggae Form of West Indian popular music. It first achieved prominence in the mid-1960s, growing out of rock-steady and ska. It is characterized by a repetitive back beat. Modern variations include ragga and lover's rock. Bob MARLEY was largely responsible for bringing reggae to a worldwide audience.

Reich, Steve (1936–) US composer. His works are characterized by shifting musical patterns. Many of his compositions were written for his percussion ensemble, Steve Reich and Musicians, who achieved fame with *Drumming* (1971).

Reich, Wilhelm (1897–1957) Austrian psychoanalyst, clinical assistant to Sigmund FREUD (1922–28). In the USA from 1939, he claimed to have discovered 'orgone' energy, a primal force in the atmosphere. The function of the sexual orgasm was to discharge orgone energy. In 1950, he was imprisoned for fraud and died in jail.

Reichstag German Parliament building. Erected 1884–94, the Reichstag is where the lower legislative assembly of Germany met until 1933, when it was severely damaged in a fire. After the reunification of Germany in 1990, it once again served as the meeting place of Germany's Parliament.

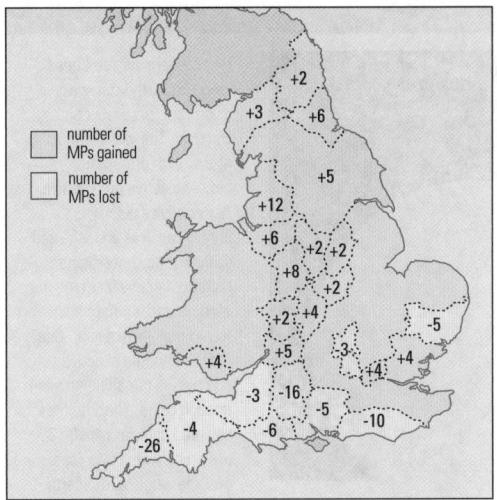

number of MPs gained
number of MPs lost

◄ **Reform Acts** In the early 19th century, many of the agricultural boroughs whose population had steadily declined still returned members to Parliament, whereas the new, densely populated industrial areas were unrepresented. Some of the seats taken away from the underpopulated boroughs by the Reform Bill were redistributed among these industrial centres, while others were used to increase county representation.

Reign of Terror (June 1793–July 1794) Phase of the FRENCH REVOLUTION. It began with the overthrow of the GIRONDINS and the ascendancy of the JACOBINS under ROBESPIERRE. Opponents were persecuted and *c.*1,400 executed. On July 27, 1794, the Terror ended with a coup in the National Convention. Robespierre and leading Jacobins were arrested and executed.

Reims City on the River Vesle, NE France; a port on the Aisne-Marne Canal. CLOVIS I was baptized and crowned here in 496, and it was the coronation place of later French kings. Reims is the centre of the champagne industry. Other industries: woollen goods, metallurgy, chemicals, glass. Pop. (1999) 191,325.

reincarnation Passage of the soul through successive bodies, causing the rebirth of an individual on Earth. In HINDUISM and BUDDHISM, an individual's KARMA (earthly conduct) determines the condition into which one is born in the next life.

reindeer (caribou) Large DEER of northern latitudes, which ranges from Scandinavia across Siberia to North America. It has thick fur and broad hoofs. It stands up to 1.4m (4.6ft) tall at the shoulders, and feeds on grasses and saplings in the summer and lichens it finds beneath the snow in the winter. Both sexes have antlers. Species *Rangifer tarandus*.

Reinhardt, 'Django' (Jean-Baptiste) (1910–53) Belgian jazz guitarist. Django blended folk music with jazz and swing styles, and is noted for his improvisations. In 1934, he formed a quintet with the violinist Stéphane Grappelli and played as the 'Hot Club'. He also played in the USA with Duke ELLINGTON.

relative atomic mass (r.a.m.) (formerly atomic weight) Mass of an atom of the naturally occurring form of an element divided by $\frac{1}{12}$ of the mass of an atom of carbon-12. The naturally occurring form may consist of two or more isotopes, and the calculation of the r.a.m. must take this into account.

relative density (r.d.) (formerly specific gravity) Ratio of the DENSITY of a substance to the density of water. Thus, the relative density of gold is 19.3: it is *c.*19 times denser than an equal volume of water.

relative molecular mass (formerly molecular weight) Mass of a molecule, the sum of the relative atomic masses

R

◄ **reindeer** Always found in herds, reindeer (*Rangifer tarandus*) migrate vast distances between summer and winter feeding grounds. They are adapted to two different environments: tundra and woodland. Their large hoofs spread when they walk on snow or soft ground.

REMOTE SENSING

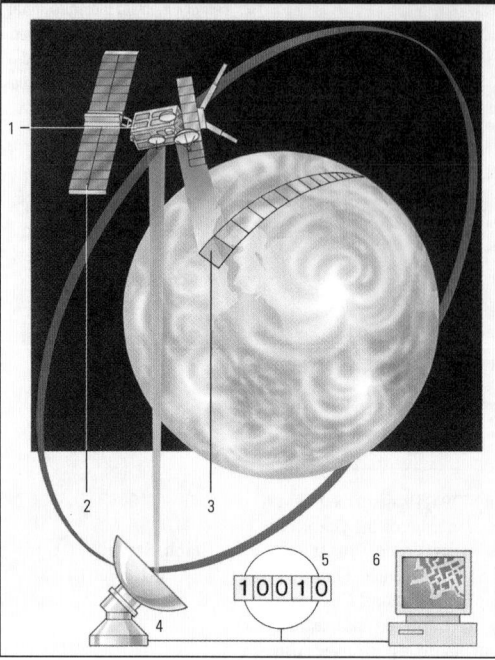

Remote sensing satellites (1) view the Earth from space using various sensors and cameras. The ways of looking at the Earth are divided between active and passive. Active devices, such as optical cameras and infra-red scanners, pick up reflected radiation. Active instruments send out radio pulses and record the return signal. One of the strengths of active scanning is the ability to see through cloud. The satellites, powered by solar panels (2), use orbits which take them over the whole of the Earth over a series of days (3). Images of the Earth's surfaces are beamed down to ground stations (4) in digital form (5), and are converted into pictures by computers (6).

of all its atoms. It is the ratio of the average mass per molecule of an element or compound to one twelfth of the mass of an atom of carbon-12. The molecular masses of reactants (elements or compounds) must be known in order to make calculations about yields in a chemical reaction.

relativity Theory, proposed by German-born US physicistAlbert EINSTEIN, based on the postulate that the motion of one body can be defined only with respect to that of a second body.Mass, space and time are interdependent. This theory led to the concept of a four-dimensional SPACE-TIME continuum in which the three space dimensions and time are treated on an equal footing. Einstein devised two theories concerning relativity. The **special theory**, put forward in 1905, is limited to the description of events as they appear to observers in a state of uniform relative motion. The more important consequences of the theory are: (1) that the velocity of light is absolute, that is, not relative to the velocity of the observer; (2) that the mass of a body increases with its velocity, although appreciably only at velocities approaching that of light; (3) that mass (m) and energy (E) are equivalent, that is, $E = mc^2$, where c is the velocity of light (this shows that when mass converts to energy, a small mass gives rise to large energy); (4) the LORENTZ-Fitzgerald contraction, that is, bodies contract as their velocity increases, again only appreciably near the velocity of light; and (5) an object's sense of elapsed time expands – 'time dilation'. The **general theory** of relativity, completed in 1915, is applicable to observers not in uniform relative motion. This showed the relation of space and GRAVITATION. The presence of matter in space causes space to 'curve', forming gravitational fields; thus gravitation becomes a property of space itself. The existence of BLACK HOLES, where not even light can escape extreme gravity, is postulated as a consequence of this.

relief (It. *rilievo*, 'projection') Three-dimensional sculpture projecting from a flat background. In *alto-rilievo* (high relief) the protrusion is great, *basso-rilievo* (low relief) protrudes only slightly, and *mezzo-rilievo* is between the two.

religion Code of beliefs and practices formulated in response to a spiritual awareness of existence. It may involve either faith in a state of existence after earthly death, or a desire for union with an omnipotent spiritual being, or a combination of the two. Polytheistic religions, such as those of ancient Egypt, Greece and Rome, entailed the worship of many distinct gods or personifications of nature. Many cultures classified their deities into hierarchies known as pantheons; some religions, such as HINDUISM, still have such pantheons. Other ancient

religions, some of which incorporated belief in a state of existence after death, were more of a system of ethical philosophy concentrating on metaphysical contemplation (for example, BUDDHISM and TAOISM). The ancient Hebrews were among the first people to worship a single omniscient and omnipotent being, YAHWEH. He gave them His protection in return for their total faith and obedience. Common to all religions dominated by a single omnipotent force (monotheistic religions such as JUDAISM, CHRISTIANITY, and ISLAM) is the idea that the power is all places at once, and that it is beyond the physical plane occupied by humans. In many religions, both monotheistic and polytheistic, sacrifice to an individual god or to God is an important element, either in propitiation, or to redeem the faithful from some wrongdoing, or in thanksgiving.

Religion, Wars of (1562–98) Series of religious conflicts in France. At stake was freedom of worship for HUGUENOTS (Protestants), but it was also a struggle between monarchy and nobility. The Huguenot leaders were, successively, Louis I de CONDÉ, Caspard de Coligny, and Henry of Navarre (later HENRY IV). The Catholic party was led by the House of GUISE. The monarchy, represented by CATHERINE DE' MEDICI and her sons, CHARLES IX and HENRY III, attempted to pursue a moderate Catholic line. The first three civil wars (1562–63, 1567–68, 1568–70) ended in the Treaty of St Germain (1570), which granted concessions to the Protestants. Hostilities recommenced with the SAINT BARTHOLOMEW'S DAY MASSACRE (1572). The fifth civil war (1574–76) resulted in the Edict of Beaulieu that granted freedom of worship to Huguenots. The Catholic party formed a Holy League and the Edict was revoked, prompting renewed conflict. Henry III's naming of Henry of Navarre as his heir led to the War of the Three Henrys (1585–89). Henry IV emerged victorious and the Edict of NANTES (1598) extended toleration to the Huguenots.

Remarque, Erich Maria (1898–1970) German novelist, b. Erich Paul Remark. A World War 1 veteran, his best-known novel, *All Quiet on the Western Front* (1929), is a savage indictment of war. The sequel, *The Road Back* (1931), concerns Germany's post-war collapse and readjustment.

Rembrandt Harmenszoon van Rijn (1606–69) Dutch painter and graphic artist. Between 1625 and 1631, he painted numerous self-portraits. Rembrandt settled in Amsterdam (1631–32), becoming highly regarded as a painter of group portraits such as the *Anatomy Lesson of Dr Tulp* (1632). By 1636 he was painting in the richly detailed BAROQUE style typified by the *Sacrifice of Abraham* (1636). In 1642 he finished his famous group portrait, *The Corporalship of Captain Frans Banning Cocq's Civic Guards* (or *The Night Watch*). By 1656 Rembrandt was so deeply in debt that he withdrew from society. During these later years, he produced some of his greatest works, such as *Jacob Blessing the Sons of Joseph* (1656) and *The Jewish Bride* (late 1660s). His works total more than 300 paintings, some 300 etchings, and 1,000 drawings.

Remembrance Sunday In the UK, annual commemoration of the dead in World War 1 and World War 2. After World War 1, the dead were remembered by a two-minute silence on Armistice Day, at the 11th hour on the 11th day of the 11th month, the time of the World War 1 ceasefire (1918). In 1945, it was renamed Remembrance Sunday, and has been observed on the second Sunday of November since 1956.

remote sensing Any method of obtaining and recording information from a distance. The most common sensor is the CAMERA; cameras are used in aircraft, satellites, and space probes to collect information and transmit it back to Earth (often by radio). The resulting photographs provide a variety of information, including archeological evidence and weather data. The images are also used in map-making. MICROWAVE sensors use radar signals that penetrate cloud. Infrared sensors measure temperature differences over an area.

Remus *See* ROMULUS AND REMUS

Renaissance (Fr. 'Rebirth') Period of European history lasting from the mid-l5th century to the end of the 16th century. Late 15th-century Italian scholars used the word to describe the revival of interest in classical learning. It was helped by the fall of Constantinople to the Ottoman Turks in 1453, resulting in the transport of classical texts to Italy. In Germany, the

R

INTERNET

Rembrandt Harmenszoon van Rijn
▶ www.rijksmuseum.nl
▶ www.nga.gov
▶ www.metmuseum.org
▶ www.nationalgallery.org.uk

invention of a printing press with moveable type aided the diffusion of the new scholarship. In religion, the spirit of questioning led to the REFORMATION. In politics, the era saw the rise of assertive sovereign states – Spain, Portugal, France and England – and the expansion of Europe beyond its own shores, with the building of trading empires in Africa, the East Indies and America. The growth of a wealthy urban merchant class led to a flowering of the arts. *See also* RENAISSANCE ARCHITECTURE; RENAISSANCE ART; RENAISSANCE MUSIC

Renaissance architecture Architectural style that began in Italy in the 15th century, and spread throughout Europe until the advent of MANNERISM and the BAROQUE in the 16th and 17th centuries. Revolting against GOTHIC ARCHITECTURE, it used Roman motifs. In Italy, BRUNELLESCHI and ALBERTI studied the Roman ruins. In France, the style was first employed by Lescot, who was commissioned by Francis I to work on the Louvre (1546). In other European countries, classical forms were integrated with medieval motifs.

Renaissance art Style that emerged in Italy in the 15th century, heavily influenced by classical Greek or Roman models and by HUMANISM. In painting, the differences between Gothic and Renaissance painting emerged in Florence in the early 15th century. These differences included: the development of PERSPECTIVE; a new interest in composition and colour harmonies; the increasing use of secular or pagan subject matter; the rise of portraiture; experimentation and a growing concern for the expression of the individual artist. The creators of High Renaissance painting were LEONARDO DA VINCI, MICHELANGELO, and RAPHAEL. The ideas of the Italian artists were taken to France and N Europe and emulated with national variations.

Renaissance literature found an early exponent in PETRARCH; other Italian Renaissance literary figures include DANTE. By the 16th century, the Renaissance literary movement reached N Europe, where it inspired much poetry and history writing and culminated, in England, in the dramas of SHAKESPEARE.

Renaissance music Music composed in Europe from *c*.1400–1600. It was mainly religious vocal POLYPHONY, usually masses and MOTETS. Non-religious music was mainly in the form of songs – Italian and English MADRIGALS, French *chansons*, German *Lieder* – and some instrumental music for organ, clavier, lute, or for small ensembles. Renaisssance composers include PALESTRINA, LASSO, BYRD, and GABRIELI.

renewable energy (alternative energy) ENERGY from a source that can be replenished or that replenishes itself, and is more environmentally safe than traditional energy forms such as COAL, GAS, or NUCLEAR ENERGY. SOLAR ENERGY harnesses the rays of the Sun. TIDAL POWER stations use the ocean's twice-daily motions. Wave power harnesses the natural movement of the sea. The power of rivers and lakes can be tapped by damming the flow and using turbines to generate HYDROELECTRICITY. WIND POWER has existed for centuries in the form of WINDMILLS. Another renewable source is the GEOTHERMAL ENERGY produced in the Earth's crust.

Reni, Guido (1575–1642) Italian painter who became the leading master of Bolognese art. Reni's most celebrated works include *Massacre of the Innocents* (1611), *Aurora* (1613), and *Atlanta and Hippoinenes* (*c*.1625).

Rennes City at the confluence of the Ille and Vilaine rivers, NW France; capital of Ille-et-Vilaine department. In the 16th century, Rennes became the seat of the parliament of Brittany. Rennes suffered heavy bombing in World War 2. Industries: leather, printing, textiles, electronic equipment, motor vehicles, oil refining. Pop. (1999) 212,494.

rennet Substance used to curdle milk in cheesemaking. Obtained as an extract from the inner lining of the fourth stomach of calves and other young ruminants, rennet is rich in rennin, an ENZYME that coagulates the casein (protein) of milk.

Renoir, (Pierre) Auguste (1841–1919) French Impressionist painter. In 1874, he contributed to the first exhibition of IMPRESSIONISM and masterpieces of this period include *La Loge* (1874) and *Bal au Moulin de la Galette* (1876). In the early 1880s, he became interested in the human figure with such works as *Bathers* (1884–87) and *After the Bath* (*c*.1895).

Renoir, Jean (1894–1979) French film director and actor, son of Auguste RENOIR. His best-known films are *La Grande*

Ilusion (1937), and *La Règle du Jeu* (1939). Renoir's work is noted for its lyric response to nature and humanity and its subtle style. Other films include *Nana* (1926), *Madame Bovary* (1934), *French Cancan* (1955) and *C'est la Revolution* (1967).

repetitive strain injury (RSI) Pain and reduced mobility in a limb, most often the wrist, caused by constant repetition of the same movements. The symptoms arise from inflammation of the tendon sheaths because of excessive use. RSI is an occupational disorder mostly seen in assembly-line workers and keyboard operators.

Representatives, House of *See* HOUSE OF REPRESENTATIVES

repression Process by which unacceptable thoughts or memories are kept in the UNCONSCIOUS so that they cannot cause guilt or distress. According to Sigmund FREUD, it is part of the function of the EGO, whereby it controls the primal and instinctual urges of the ID. Repressed desires find an outlet in dreams and are believed to be at the root of various neurotic disorders. *See also* PSYCHOANALYSIS

reproduction Process by which living organisms create new organisms similar to themselves. Reproduction may be sexual or asexual, the first being the fusion of two special reproductive cells from different parents, and the second being the generation of new organisms from a single organism. ASEXUAL REPRODUCTION is found mainly in PROTOZOA, SOME INVERTEBRATES and in many plants. By contrast, almost all living organisms have the capacity for SEXUAL REPRODUCTION. In most, the species has two kinds of individuals – male and female – with different sex functions. Male and female sex cells (in animals, sperm and egg) fuse to produce a new cell, the ZYGOTE, which contains genetic information from both parents, and from which a new individual develops. Some organisms are HERMAPHRODITES, each individual of the species having male and female functions, so that when two of them mate each individual fertilizes the other's eggs. Sexually reproducing plants (or generations) are called GAMETOPHYTE; ones which reproduce asexually, SPOROPHYTE. *See also* ALTERNATION OF GENERATIONS; POLLEN

reptile Any of *c*.6,000 species of VERTEBRATES distributed worldwide. Reptiles are cold-blooded. Most lay eggs on land. Some species – particularly SNAKES – carry eggs in the body and bear live young. The skin is dry with scales or embedded with bony plates. Limbs are poorly developed or non-existent. Those with limbs usually have five clawed toes on each foot. There are four orders: Chelonia (TURTLES); Rhynchocephalia (TUATARA); Squamata (scaly reptiles such as snakes and LIZARDS); and Crocodilia (ALLIGATORS and CROCODILES).

republic State in which sovereignty is vested in the people or their elected or nominated representatives. A republic may also be understood to be a state in which all segments of society are enfranchised and the power of the state is limited.

▼ **Renoir** *Bal au Moulin de la Gallete, Montmartre* (1876). The impressionist painter Auguste Renoir delighted in painting the human figure, particularly women. This painting clearly shows how he explored the effects of light and shadow on faces and bodies, which was typical of his early work. From the 1880s, influenced by a trip to Italy and study of the Old Masters, his style became more linear, moving away from the free brushwork of the 1070s.

R

R

Republican Party US political party. It was organized in 1854, as an amalgamation of the WHIG PARTY and Free-Soilers, with workers and professional people who had formerly been known as Independent Democrats, Know-Nothings, Barnburners, or Abolitionists. Its first successful presidential candidate was Abraham LINCOLN (elected 1860). During the early 20th century, the Republicans were generally the minority party to the DEMOCRATIC PARTY in CONGRESS, especially in the House of Representatives. Later, there was a reversal. There was a Republican president for all but four years between 1969 and 1993. Under Presidents Ronald REAGAN and George BUSH, the Republican Party seemed to have captured the popular vote until Bill CLINTON's charismatic campaign restored Democratic fortunes. In 1994 the Republicans regained control of the Senate and House of Representatives, and retained majorities in the 1998 elections. The Republicans recaptured the presidency in 2000 elections, when George W. BUSH defeated the Democrat candidate, Al GORE, by the narrowest of margins, but lost majority control of the Senate. Today, the Republican Party is considered to be more conservative than the Democratic Party.

requiem Solemn choral service for the dead sung in Roman Catholic Churches. Mozart, Verdi and Berlioz (among many others) composed requiems.

resin (rosin) Artificial or natural POLYMER that is generally viscous and sticky. **Artificial** resins include polyesters and epoxies and are used as adhesives and binders. **Natural** resins are secreted by various plants. Oleoresin, secreted by conifers, is distilled to produce turpentine; rosin remains after the oil of turpentine has been distilled off.

resistance (symbol R) Property of an electric CONDUCTOR, calculated as the ratio of the voltage applied to the conductor to the current passing through it. Conductors have low resistance. The SI unit of resistance is the OHM. It represents the opposition to the flow of ELECTRIC CURRENT. *See also* RESISTOR

resistivity (symbol ρ) Electrical property of materials. Its value is given by $\rho = AR/l$, where A is the cross-sectional area of a conductor, l is its length, and R is its RESISTANCE. Resistivity is generally expressed in units of ohm-metres and is a measure of the resistance of a piece of material of given size.

resistor Electrical CIRCUIT component with a specified RESISTANCE. Resistors limit the size of the current flowing. Those for electronic circuits usually consist of carbon particles mixed with a ceramic material and enclosed in an insulated tube. Resistors for carrying larger currents are coils of insulated wire.

resonance Increase in the amplitude of vibration of a mechanical or acoustic system when forced to vibrate by an external source. It occurs when the FREQUENCY of the applied force is equal to the natural vibrational frequency of the system. Large vibrations can cause damage to the system.

respiration Series of chemical reactions by which complex molecules are broken down to release energy in living organisms. ENZYMES control these reactions, which are an essential part of METABOLISM. There are two main types of respiration: AEROBIC and ANAEROBIC. In **aerobic** respiration, oxygen provided by BREATHING combines with the breakdown products and is necessary for the reactions to take place. Breathing is therefore different from respiration, though the terms are commonly interchanged. **Anaerobic** respiration takes place in the absence of oxygen, releasing energy through GLUCOSE and other foods. In most living organisms, the energy released by respiration is used to convert the compound **adenosine diphosphate** (ADP) to **adenosine triphosphate** (ATP), which transports energy around the cell. At the site where the energy is needed, ATP converts back to ADP with the aid of a special enzyme, a process that releases energy. The first stages of respiration take place in a cell's CYTOPLASM and the later stages, known as the KREBS CYCLE, in the cell's MITOCHONDRIA which contain enzymes. *See also* TRANSPIRATION

respiratory system System in air-breathing animals concerned with GAS EXCHANGE. The respiratory tract begins with the nose and mouth, through which air enters the body. Air then passes through the LARYNX and into the TRACHEA. At its lower end, the trachea branches into two bronchi, each BRONCHUS leads to a LUNG. The bronchi divide into many bronchioles, which lead in turn to bunches of tiny air sacs (ALVEOLI), where the exchange of gases between air and blood takes place. Exhaled air leaves along the same pathway.

response, conditioned Learned pairing of a response to an artificial stimulus. In his experiments, Ivan PAVLOV taught dogs to associate the ringing of a bell with receiving food, and they began to salivate just at the sound of the bell. The dog's salivation in these experiments was the conditioned response.

Restoration In English history, the re-establishment of the monarchy in 1660. After the death of Oliver CROMWELL, his son and successor, Richard, was unable to prevent growing conflict or restrain the increasing power of the army. He resigned (1659), and the crisis was resolved by the march of General George MONCK from Scotland. Army leaders backed down, and a new Parliament was elected. From exile, CHARLES II issued the Declaration of Breda (1660), promising an amnesty to opponents (except those directly responsible for the execution of CHARLES I), payment of the arrears in the army's wages and religious toleration. He was invited by a new Parliament to resume the throne. The term Restoration is often extended to the period following 1660, and is especially associated with a flowering of English literature, notably in RESTORATION DRAMA. In French history, it refers to the restoration of the BOURBONS (1814–30) after the defeat of Napoleon.

Restoration drama Plays and performances in the period following the restoration of CHARLES II, when the theatres reopened. The drama reflected the laxity of Court morals through broad satire, farce, wit, and bawdy comedy. Distinguished playwrights included DRYDEN and CONGREVE.

restriction enzyme ENZYME used in GENETIC ENGINEERING to cut a molecule of DNA at specific points, in order to insert or remove a piece of DNA. There are many different restriction enzymes; each cuts the DNA at a specific sequence of bases, allowing great precision in genetic engineering.

resurrection Rising of the dead to new life, in heaven or on Earth. JUDAISM, CHRISTIANITY and ISLAM hold that at the end of the world there will be a Day of Judgement: the worthy will draw near to God, while the unworthy will be cast out into darkness. The term also applies to the rising of JESUS CHRIST from the dead on the third day after his crucifixion.

resuscitation Measures taken to revive a person who is on the brink of death. The most successful technique available to the layman is **mouth-to-mouth** resuscitation. Medical staff receive instruction in **cardiopulmonary** resuscitation (CPR), which involves the use of specialized equipment and drugs to save patients whose breathing and/or heartbeat suddenly stop.

retail price index (RPI) Governmental measure of changing retail prices in Britain, from which the rate of INFLATION is calculated. It is based on a constant selection of goods, weighted according to their importance in a household's budget.

retina Inner layer of the EYE, composed mainly of different kinds of NEURONS, some of which are the visual receptors of the eye. Receptor cells (cones and rods) are sensitive to light. **Cones** respond to the spectrum of visible colours; **rods** respond to shades of grey and to movement. The rods and cones connect with sensory neurons, which in turn connect with the optic nerve, which carries the visual stimuli to the brain.

retriever Sporting dog originally used to kill or cripple downed game; today, it is also used to locate game and is a popular pet. Main breeds include the golden and Labrador retriever.

retrovirus Any of a large family of VIRUSES (Retroviridae) that, unlike other living organisms, contain the genetic material RNA (ribonucleic acid) rather than the customary DNA (deoxyribonucleic acid). In order to multiply, retroviruses make use of a special enzyme to convert their RNA into DNA, which then becomes integrated with the DNA in the cells of their hosts. Diseases caused by retroviruses include ACQUIRED IMMUNE DEFICIENCY SYNDROME (AIDS).

Réunion Volcanic island in the Indian Ocean, in the Mascarene group, c.700km (440mi) E of Madagascar, forming an overseas department (1948) of France; the capital is St Denis. Discovered in 1513 by the Portuguese, France claimed Réunion in 1638. The island became part of an administrative region in 1973. Exports: sugar, rum, maize, tobacco. Area: 2,510sq km (969sq mi). Pop. (2000)755,000.

Reuters News agency that transmits international news between cities worldwide. It originated as a service between Britain and continental Europe, using the telegraph. It is jointly owned by Australian, New Zealand, and British newspapers. It was founded (1851) by Paul Reuter (1816–99) in London.

Revelation (Apocalypse) Last book of the NEW TESTAMENT. It was written perhaps as late as AD 95 by St John the Divine. In highly allegorical and prophetic terms, it concentrates on depicting the end of Creation, the war between good and evil, the Day of Judgment, and the ultimate triumph of good.

Revere, Paul (1735–1818) American silversmith and patriot, who rode from Charlestown to Lexington, Massachusetts on the night of April 18, 1775 to warn the colonists of Massachusetts of the approach of British troops at the start of the AMERICAN REVOLUTION. It was commemorated in Henry LONGFELLOW's poem, 'Paul Revere's Ride' (1863).

reversible reaction Chemical reaction in which the products can change back into the reactants. Thus, nitrogen and hydrogen can be combined to give ammonia (as in the HABER PROCESS) and ammonia may be decomposed to nitrogen and hydrogen. Such processes yield an equilibrium mixture of reactants and products. *See also* CHEMICAL EQUILIBRIUM

revisionism Political theory derived from MARXISM. Eduard Bernstein, the first Marxist revisionist, asserted (1890) that CAPITALISM was not in crisis, and that the transition to SOCIALISM would be a peaceful evolution. This conflicted with orthodox Marxist belief in the inevitable collapse of capitalism. After 1945, the term was used by communist regimes to condemn political movements that threatened official party policy.

revolution Movement of a planet or other celestial object around its ORBIT, as distinct from ROTATION of the object on its axis. A single revolution is the planet's or satellite's 'year'.

revolution In a political sense, fundamental change in values, political institutions, social structure, and leadership brought about by a large-scale, successful revolt. The totality of change distinguishes it from coups, rebellions, and wars of independence, which seek to achieve only particular changes. The term is also used to indicate great economic and technical changes, such as the INDUSTRIAL REVOLUTION or the AGRICULTURAL REVOLUTION. *See also* AMERICAN REVOLUTION; FRENCH REVOLUTION; RUSSIAN REVOLUTION

Revolutions of 1848 Series of revolutions in European countries which broke out within a few months of each other. The general cause was the frustration of liberals and nationalists with the governing authorities, and a background of economic depression. The risings began with the FEBRUARY REVOLUTION against LOUIS PHILIPPE in France, which resulted in the foundation of the Second Republic. It inspired revolts in Vienna (forcing the resignation of Prince von METTERNICH), and among the national minorities under Austrian rule. In Germany, liberals forced FREDERICK WILLIAM IV to summon a constitutional assembly, while advocates of German unification hoped to achieve their aim in the Frankfurt Parliament.

Revolutions of 1989 Popular risings in East European states against communist governments. Long-suppressed opposition to Soviet-dominated rule erupted spontaneously in most of the Soviet satellite states. Within months, the communists were driven from power, and democratic systems installed. The risings were followed by the withdrawal of the constituent republics from the SOVIET UNION, which encountered little resistance.

revue Theatrical entertainment purporting to give a review, usually satirical, of current fashions, events and personalities.

Reykjavík Capital of Iceland, a port on the SW coast. Founded in c.870, it was the island's first permanent settlement. It expanded during the 18th century, and became the capital in 1918. During World War 2, it served as a British and US air base. Industries: food processing, fishing, textiles, metallurgy, printing and publishing, shipbuilding. Pop. (2000) 111,345.

Reynolds, Albert (1933–) Irish statesman, taoiseach (1992–94). In 1977, Reynolds entered the Dáil and soon joined the FIANNA FÁIL cabinet. In 1991, Reynolds was dismissed after trying to displace Charles HAUGHEY. Reynolds eventually succeeded Haughey as taoiseach. In ensuing elections, Fianna Fáil lost their majority and he was forced into coalition with the Labour Party. In 1993, Reynolds and British Prime Minister,

John MAJOR, issued the DOWNING STREET DECLARATION. In 1994, the Labour Party withdrew its support, and he was forced to resign. John BRUTON succeeded Reynolds as taoiseach.

Reynolds, Sir Joshua (1723–92) English portrait painter and writer on art. The first president (1768) of the ROYAL ACADEMY OF ARTS, he espoused the principles of the 'Grand Manner' style in his *Discourses*. These writings describe how painting, through allusions to classical, heroic figures, can be a scholarly activity. His portraits are remarkable for their individuality and sensitivity to the sitter's mood, many of whom are painted in classical poses.

rhapsody Musical term applied to orchestral works, usually performed in one continuous movement and most often inspired by a nationalist or romantic theme.

rhea Either of two species of large, brownish, flightless, fast-running South American birds resembling a small OSTRICH. They feed mostly on vegetation and insects. Height: to 1.5m (5ft). Family Rheidae.

Rhee, Syngman (1875–1965) Korean statesman, first president (1948–60) of South Korea. He was imprisoned (1898–1904) for his opposition to Japanese rule, before living (1912–45) in exile in the USA. In 1919, he formed a government-in-exile. After World War 2, he was leader of US-occupied South Korea. His presidency was marked by the KOREAN WAR. His regime became increasingly authoritarian and corrupt. Re-elected for a fourth time, accusations of vote-rigging sparked riots, and Rhee was forced to resign.

rhenium (symbol Re) Silver-white metallic element, one of the TRANSITION ELEMENTS, which have incomplete inner electron shells. Discovered in 1925, rhenium is found in molybdenite and PLATINUM ores from which it is obtained as a by-product. It is heavy and used in alloys in thermocouples, camera flash units and electronic filaments, and is also a useful catalyst. Properties: at.no. 75; r.a.m. 186.2; r.d. 21.0; m.p. 3,180°C (5,756°F); b.p. 5,627°C (10,160°F); most common isotope Re^{187} (62.93%).

rheostat Variable RESISTOR for regulating an ELECTRIC CURRENT. The resistance element may be a metal wire, carbon or a conducting liquid. Rheostats are used to adjust generators, to dim lights and to control the speed of electric motors.

rhesus Medium-sized, yellow-brown MACAQUE monkey of India. Short-tailed, it has a large head with a bare face, large ears and closely spaced, deep-set eyes. Height: 60cm (2ft). Species *Macaca mulatta*.

rhesus factor (Rh factor) Any of a group of ANTIGENS found on the surface of ERYTHROCYTES (red blood cells). Rh-negative (Rh−) blood lacks the rhesus factor. Rh factor is present in c.85% of humans (Rh+). Rh incompatibility (an Rh− pregnant woman with an Rh+ fetus) can give rise to ANAEMIA in newborn babies. The antigens were first identified in the blood of rhesus monkeys.

rhetoric Art of discourse and persuasive speaking; language, written or spoken, designed to impress or persuade. Rhetoric is valued in public speaking, but the sophistication of many of its modern techniques may have led rhetoricians – such as politicians – to be more distrusted by a better-informed public.

rheumatic fever Inflammatory disorder characterized by fever and painful swelling of the joints. Rare in the modern developed world, it mostly affects children and young adults. An important complication is possible damage to the heart valves, leading to rheumatic heart disease in later life.

rheumatism A group of disorders whose symptoms are pain, inflammation and stiffness in the bones, joints and surrounding tissues. Usually some form of ARTHRITIS is involved.

Rhine (Rhein, Rhin or Rijn) River in W Europe. It rises in the Swiss Alps and flows N, bordering on or passing through Switzerland, Austria, Liechtenstein, Germany, France, and the Netherlands to enter the North Sea at Rotterdam. The Rhine is navigable to ocean-going vessels as far as Basel in Switzerland and is a major transport route for some of W Europe's most industrialized areas. Length: c.1,320km (820mi).

Rhineland Region in W Germany along the W bank of the Rhine. It includes Saarland. Rhineland-Palatinate, and parts of Baden-Württemberg, Hesse and North Rhine-Westphalia. It saw heavy fighting in the later stages of World War 2.

R

▲ **rhea** The flightless rhea roams the pampas of South America in flocks of up to 30. Its height enables it to detect danger even in high grass, and it can run faster than a horse. The male rhea is responsible for incubation of eggs.

► **rhinoceros** The yellow-billed oxpecker (*Buphagus africanus*) and the African white rhino (*Ceratotherium simum*) have a symbiotic relationship. The oxpecker, a type of African starling, feeds by pulling ticks from the animal's hide and sipping blood that oozes from tick wounds. The rhino benefits from the removal of the parasites.

INTERNET

Rhode Island
► www.state.ri.us
► www.visitrhodeisland.com

Rhodes, Cecil John
► www.usyd.edu.au/su/
rhodes/Cecil_
John_Rhodes.html

rhinitis Inflammation of the mucous membrane of the nose. It may be an allergic reaction (such as HAY FEVER) or a symptom of a viral infection, such as the common cold.

rhinoceros (rhino) Massive, herbivorous mammal native to Africa and Asia. Rhinos are the second largest land mammals (after HIPPOPOTAMUSES). The largest of the five species, the central African white rhino *Ceratotherium simum*, reaches a height of 2m (1.5ft) at the shoulder. Rhinos have thick skin and poor eyesight, and are solitary grazers or browsers. They like to wallow in muddy pools in the heat. Now rare except in protected areas, rhinos are illegally hunted for their horns (believed to have aphrodisiac properties). Weight: 1–3.5 tonnes. Family Rhinocerotidae.

rhizoid Fine, hairlike growth used for attachment to a solid surface by some simple organisms, such as certain fungi and mosses. The rhizoid lacks the conducting TISSUES of a root.

rhizome Creeping, root-like underground stem of certain plants. It usually grows horizontally, is rich in accumulated starch, and can produce new roots and stems asexually. Rhizomes differ from roots in producing buds and leaves. *See also* ASEXUAL REPRODUCTION; TUBER

Rhode Island State in NE USA, on the Atlantic coast in New England; the smallest state in the USA; the capital is PROVIDENCE. Other major cities include Warwick, Pawtucket, and Cranston. The region was first settled in 1636 by people from Massachusetts seeking religious freedom. It received a royal charter in 1663. British troops occupied the area during the American Revolution. Much of the land is forested, but there is some dairy farming. Potatoes, hay, apples, oats, and maize are the chief crops, and fishing is significant. Other industries: textiles, metals, silverware, machinery, electronics, and tourism. Area: 3,144sq km (1,214sq mi). Pop. (2000) 1,048,319.

Rhodes (Ródhos) Greek island in the SE Aegean Sea; the largest of the Dodecanese archipelago. It was colonized by the Dorians in *c.*1000 BC and later conquered (at different times) by Persia, Sparta, Athens, Macedon, Rome, and the Byzantine Empire. In 1310 the KNIGHTS HOSPITALLERS captured Rhodes, and they defended it against the Turks for more than 200 years. It was finally seized by the Ottomans in 1522. Ceded to Italy in 1912, it became part of Greece in 1947. The chief city is Rhodes. Products: wheat, tobacco, cotton, olives, fruits, vegetables. Area: 1,400sq km (540sq mi). Pop. (2001) 90,963.

Rhodes, Cecil John (1853–1902) South African statesman, b. Britain. Rhodes emigrated to Natal in 1870, and made a fortune in the Kimberley diamond mines. In 1880, he founded the De Beers Mining Company. In 1885, he persuaded the British government to establish a protectorate over Bechuanaland. Rhodes founded (1889) the British South Africa Company, which occupied Mashonaland and Matabeleland, thus forming Rhodesia (now Zambia and Zimbabwe). Rhodes was prime minister (1890–96) of Cape Colony. The discovery of his role in Leander Jameson's attempt to overthrow Paul KRUGER in the TRANSVAAL led to his resignation.

Rhodesia Former name of a territory in s central Africa. Cecil RHODES developed the region. In 1923, Southern Rhodesia became a self-governing British colony, and in 1924 Northern Rhodesia was made a British Protectorate. In 1953,

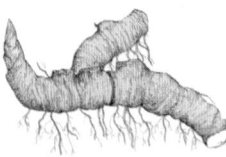

▲ **rhizome** Unlike other plant storage organs, rhizomes are not replaced annually. They grow continually, branching as they do so, and each growing tip produces aerial shoots. The oldest parts slowly die off. Shown here is the rhizome of Solomon's seal (*Polygonatum multiflorum*).

the two Rhodesias united with Nyasaland (now MALAWI) in the Central African Federation. When the Federation dissolved in 1963, Northern Rhodesia achieved independence as ZAMBIA. Southern Rhodesia continued to use the name Rhodesia until it gained independence as ZIMBABWE in 1980.

rhodium (symbol Rh) Silver-white metallic element, one of the TRANSITION ELEMENTS. Discovered in 1803 by English chemist William Wollaston (1766–1828), it is associated with PLATINUM, and its chief source is as a by-product of NICKEL smelting. It resists tarnish and corrosion, and is used in hard platinum alloys and jewellery. It is used to coat optical instruments because of its high reflectance. Properties: at. no. 45; r.a.m. 102.906; r.d. 12.4; m.p. 1,966°C (3,571°F); b.p. 3,727°C (6,741°F); most common isotope Rh^{103} (100%).

rhododendron Large genus of shrubs and small trees that grow in the acid soils of cool temperate regions in North America, Europe, and Asia. Primarily evergreen, they have leathery leaves and bell-shaped white, pink or purple flowers. Family Ericaceae. *See also* AZALEA

rhodophyte *See* RED ALGAE

rhombus Plane figure with all of its sides equal in length but no right angles. A rhombus is a type of PARALLELOGRAM whose diagonals bisect each other at right angles.

Rhône River in W Europe. It rises in the Rhône Glacier in s Switzerland, runs through the Bernese Oberland, flows w to Lake Geneva, and then crosses the French border. It continues s through LYON and AVIGNON to Arles, where it branches into the Grand Rhône and the Petit Rhône, which both enter the Mediterranean w of Marseilles. Length: 813km (505mi).

rhubarb Perennial herbaceous plant native to Asia and cultivated in cool climates throughout the world for its edible leaf stalks. It has large poisonous leaves and small white or red flowers. Height: to 1.2m (4ft). Genus *Rheum*.

rhyme Identity of similarity of final sounds in two or more words, such as keep/deep and baking/shaking. Rhyme is used in poetry to reinforce METRE. End rhymes establish verse lines, while internal rhymes emphasize rhythmic structures.

rhythm and blues Form of popular music. It developed as an urban form of the BLUES, and was influenced by JAZZ. Energetic and relatively simple, it was the basis of ROCK music.

rib Long, curved bones arranged in pairs, extending sideways from the backbone of vertebrates. In fish and some reptiles, they extend the length of the spine; in mammals, they form the framework of the chest, and protect the lungs and heart. There are 12 pairs of ribs in humans.

Ribbentrop, Joachim von (1893–1946) German diplomat and politician. Von Ribbentrop joined the Nazi Party in 1932, and became foreign affairs adviser to HITLER in 1933. He initiated the Nazi-Soviet Pact (1939), but steadily lost influence during World War 2. At the NUREMBERG TRIALS (1946), he was convicted of war crimes and hanged.

Ribera, José (1591–1652) Spanish painter and graphic artist. His early work, like that of CARAVAGGIO, used dark shadows, but Ribera was capable of expressing great tenderness. His late paintings, such as *The Clubfooted Boy* (1642), are richly coloured and softly modelled.

riboflavin VITAMIN B$_2$ of the B complex, lack of which impairs growth and causes skin disorders. It is a co-enzyme important in transferring energy within cells. Soluble in water, riboflavin is found in milk, eggs, liver and green vegetables.

ribonucleic acid *See* RNA

ribosome Structure in the CYTOPLASM of EUKARYOTE cells (having a membrane-bound nucleus), involved in synthesizing PROTEIN molecules. Segments of DNA, called GENES, contain the instructions for forming proteins, each of which has a specific sequence of AMINO ACIDS. The DNA molecule is too large to escape from the CELL nucleus into the cytoplasm, but a 'copy' is made in the form of **messenger** RNA, (mRNA) and this travels to the ribosomes. Ribosomes attach themselves to the mRNA, then assemble the amino acids in the correct sequence to form a particular protein. Ribosomes are made up of proteins and ribosomal RNA. *See also* GENETIC CODE

rice Plant native to SE Asia and Indonesia, cultivated in many warm humid regions, and the main grain food for Middle and Far East countries. Rice is a staple diet for half the world's population. It is an ANNUAL grass; the seed and husk is the edible portion. It usually grows in flooded, terraced paddies with hard subsoil to prevent seepage. Species *Oryza sativa*.

Rice, Condoleezza (1954–) US Secretary of State (2005–). Before joining the Bush administration Rice had a distinguished academic career, rising to become Professor of Political Science at Stamford University (1993). She was National Security Advisor to the first Bush government (2001–5) and a key proponent of the 2003 US invasion of Iraq. In 2005 she became US Secretary of State, the first African-American woman to do so.

Richard I (1157–99) King of England (1189–99), known as Richard the Lion-Heart, or *Coeur de Lion*. He was involved in rebellions against his father, HENRY II, before succeeding him. A leader of the Third CRUSADE (1189–92), he won several victories but failed to retake Jerusalem. He was a prisoner (1192–94) of Emperor HENRY VI. Meanwhile, his brother, JOHN, conspired against him in England, while in France PHILIP II invaded Richard's territories. The revolt in England was contained, and from 1194 until his death, Richard endeavoured to restore the ANGEVIN Empire in France.

Richard II (1367–1400) King of England (1377–99), son of EDWARD THE BLACK PRINCE. Richard succeeded his grandfather, EDWARD III, and soon faced the PEASANTS' REVOLT (1381). Conflict with the barons marked his reign. Richard's uncle, JOHN OF GAUNT, led a council of regency until 1381. On the orders of the 'Lords Appellant', the 'Merciless Parliament' (1388) executed many of Richard's supporters. Richard reasserted control and reigned ably until he began to assume authoritarian powers. In 1397–98, he exacted his revenge on the Lords Appellant by having the Duke of Gloucester murdered and the Duke of Hereford (son of John of Gaunt) banished. In 1399, Richard confiscated Gaunt's estates. Hereford led a successful revolt and was crowned HENRY IV. Richard was imprisoned and died in mysterious circumstances.

Richard III (1452–85) King of England (1483–85). As Duke of Gloucester, he ably supported his brother, EDWARD IV, in N England. When Edward died, Richard became protector and had the young King EDWARD V declared illegitimate and took the throne himself. Edward and his younger brother, the 'Princes in the Tower', subsequently disappeared. Richard's enemies supported the invasion of Henry Tudor (HENRY VII) in 1485. Richard's death at the Battle of BOSWORTH FIELD ended the Wars of the ROSES.

Richards, I.A. (Ivor Armstrong) (1893–1979) English literary critic and theorist. Richard's emphasis on close reading and verbal analysis of literary works is expounded in *The Principles of Literary Criticism* (1924) and *Practical Criticism* (1929). *See also* LITERARY CRITICISM

Richards, Sir Viv (Isaac Vivian Alexander) (1952–) West Indian cricketer, b. Antigua. Richards made his test debut in 1974, and was West Indies captain (1985–1991). He played county cricket in England for Somerset (1974–86) and Glamorgan (1990–93), and in Australia for Queensland (1976–77). Richards retired from test cricket in 1991. He scored 8540 runs in 121 test matches, including 24 centuries.

Richardson, Sir Ralph David (1902–83) English actor. Richardson's distinguished stage career included fine Shakespearean performances, yet he was equally at home in plays such as Harold PINTER's *No Man's Land* (1975). He received Oscar nominations for his film roles in *The Heiress* (1949) and *Greystoke: The Legend of Tarzan, Lord of the Apes* (1984).

Richardson, Samuel (1689–1761) English novelist and printer. His first work of fiction, *Pamela* (1740–41), was followed by two more NOVELS of letters, *Clarissa* (1747–48) and *Sir Charles Grandison* (1753–54). His work prompted FIELDING's parodies *An Apology for the Life of Shamela Andrews* (1741) and *Joseph Andrews* (1742).

Richelieu, Armand Jean du Plessis, Duc de (1585–1642) French cardinal and statesman. A protégé of MARIE DE MÉDICIS and a cardinal from 1622, Richelieu became chief of the royal council in 1624. He suppressed the military and political power of the HUGUENOTS, but tolerated Protestant religious practices. He alienated many powerful Catholics by his assertion of the primacy of state interests. He survived several aristocratic plots against him. In the THIRTY YEARS'

WAR, he formed alliances with Protestant powers against the HABSBURGS. His more scholarly interests resulted in the foundation of the ACADÉMIE FRANÇAISE (1635).

Richler, Mordecai (1931–2001) Canadian novelist. His satirical novels, such as *The Apprenticeship of Duddy Kravitz* (1959), explore the Jewish ghetto of his native Montréal, while the experience of North Americans in the UK is wryly observed in *Cocksure* (1968) and *St Urbain's Horseman* (1971). Later novels include *Joshua Then and Now* (1980) and *Solomon Gursky Was Here* (1989).

Richmond Capital of Virginia, USA, in E central Virginia, and a port on the James River. Settled in 1637, the city became state capital in 1779. During the Civil War, Richmond was capital (1861) of the CONFEDERATE STATES until it fell to Union forces in 1865. Industries: metal products, tobacco processing, textiles, clothing, chemicals, publishing. Pop. (2000) 197,790.

Richter, Burton (1931–) US physicist. Working with a very powerful particle ACCELERATOR, he discovered (1974) a new SUBATOMIC PARTICLE (which he named psi); it is a type of MESON. For this work, Richter shared the 1976 Nobel Prize in physics with Samuel Ting, who had discoverd the same particle during independent experiments.

Richter scale Classification of EARTHQUAKE magnitude set up in 1935 by the US geologist Charles Richter (1900–85). The scale is logarithmic – each INTEGER on the scale increases by a factor of ten, so an earthquake measuring 5 on the scale is ten times greater than one of 4. The scale is based on the total energy released by an earthquake, as opposed to a scale of intensity that measures the damage inflicted at a particular place.

rickets Disorder in which there is defective growth of bone in children; the bones fail to harden sufficiently and become bent. Due either to a lack of VITAMIN D in the diet or to insufficient sunlight to allow its synthesis in the skin, it results from the inability of the bones to calcify properly.

Ridley, Nicholas (1500–55) English bishop and Protestant martyr. He was made bishop of Rochester (1547) and of London (1550). As chaplain to Thomas CRANMER, Ridley helped to compile the BOOK OF COMMON PRAYER (1549). In 1553, he supported the Protestant Lady Jane GREY against the Catholic MARY I (MARY TUDOR). Convicted of heresy under Mary, he was burned at the stake.

Rie, Dame Lucie (1902–95) British potter, b. Lucie Marie Gomperz in Austria. She studied pottery in Vienna, but moved to England after Nazis occupation in 1938. She glazed principally in white, using a pin to incise a decorative grid of fine lines (*sgraffito*). In the 1960s, Rie began to throw pots in two different colour clays, producing a spiral effect.

Riefenstahl, Leni (1902–2003) German film director who was employed by Adolf Hitler to make propaganda films. Her films include *The Blue Light* (1932), *Triumph Of The Will* (1934), and *Olympische Spiele* (1936).

Riel, Louis (1844–85) French-Canadian revolutionary, leader of the *métis* (people of mixed French and native descent) in the Red River rebellion in MANITOBA (1869–70). When it collapsed, Riel fled to the USA. In 1884, he led resistance to Canada's western policies in Saskatchewan and set up a rebel government in 1885. He was captured and executed for treason.

Riemann, Georg Friedrich Bernhard (1826–66) German mathematician who laid the foundations for much of modern mathematics and physics. He worked on integration, functions of a complex variable, and differential and non-Euclidean geometry, which was later used in the general theory of RELATIVITY.

Rietveld, Gerrit Thomas (1888–1964) One of the leading 20th-century Dutch architects. His masterwork, the Schröder House, Utrecht (1924), was arguably the most modern European house of its time. He also designed De STIJL furniture.

rifle FIREARM with spiral grooves (rifling) along the inside of the barrel to make the bullet spin in flight, thereby increasing range and accuracy over that of a smooth bore weapon. Not until the adoption (1840s) of the Minié ball, which eased and speeded loading, were rifled weapons widely used. During the 19th century breech-loading and magazine rifles developed. After World War 2, rifles capable of fully automatic fire came into general use.

RHODE ISLAND
Statehood :
May 29, 1790
Nickname :
Ocean State
State bird :
Rhode Island Red
State flower :
Violet
State tree :
Red maple
State motto :
Hope

▲ **Richards** The greatest attacking batsman of his generation, Viv Richards became (1980) the first West Indies player to make 100 centuries in first-class cricket. He scored 8,540 runs in tests, at an average of 50.23.

R

RIFT VALLEY

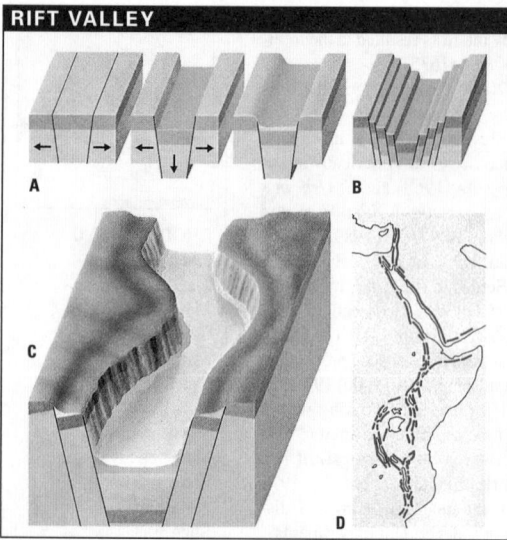

Rift valleys form through tension between two roughly parallel faults (A), causing downward earth movement resulting in the formation of a graben (trough of land between two faults). Sometimes a number of parallel faults result in land sinking in steps (B). A typical example of a step-faulted rift valley is shown (C). A series of block faults can occur on either side of a graben, sometimes tilting in the process of creating the block-faulted rift valley. The East African Rift Valley (D) is perhaps the world's best example of this type of geological formation.

R

▶ **Rio de Janeiro** Famous for its carnival, held annually before Lent, Rio de Janeiro is the second-largest city in Brazil. It has many remarkable buildings and monuments, ranging from 17th- and 18th-century churches to striking examples of modern architecture. Its Copacabana beach is world famous.

Rift Valley (Great Rift Valley) Steep-sided, flat-floored valley in sw Asia and e Africa. It runs from n Syria, through the Jordan Valley and the Dead Sea, and then continues as the trough of the Red Sea through e Africa to the lower valley of the Zambezi River in Mozambique. Dotted along its course are a number of significant lakes, including TANGANYIKA and Turkana. Length: c.6,400km (4,000mi).

Riga Capital of Latvia, on the River Daugava, on the Gulf of Riga. Founded at the beginning of the 13th century, it joined the Hanseatic League in 1282, growing into a major Baltic port. Tsar Peter I (the Great) took the city in 1710. In 1918, it became capital of independent Latvia. In 1940, when Latvia was incorporated into the Soviet Union, thousands of its citizens were deported or executed. Under German occupation from 1941, the city reverted to Soviet rule in 1944 and subsequently suffered further deportations and an influx of Russian immigrants. In 1991, it reassumed its status as capital of an independent Latvia. Industries: shipbuilding, engineering, electronic equipment, chemicals, textiles. Pop (2000) 826,000.

rigor mortis Stiffening of the body after death brought about by chemical changes in muscle tissue. Onset is gradual from minutes to hours, and it disappears within about 24 hours.

Riley, Bridget (1931–) English painter, a leading exponent of OP ART. Riley paints mostly black and white patterns, creating dazzling optical effects that cover the entire surface of the painting and create an illusion of constant movement and change. Examples include *Fall* (1963).

Rilke, Rainer Maria (1875–1926) German lyric poet, b. Prague. Rilke's first volume, *The Book of Hours* (1899–1903), was inspired by visits to Russia. During a 12–year sojourn in Paris, he developed the 'object poem' used in *New Poems* (1907–08); thereafter, he published little until 1922, when *Sonnets to Orpheus* and his existential masterpiece *Duino Elegies* both appeared.

Rimbaud, Arthur (1854–91) French anarchic poet, who influenced SYMBOLISM. Rimbaud had a stormy relationship with Paul VERLAINE, under whose tutelage he wrote *The Drunken Boat* (1871). In 1873, they separated and *A Season*

in Hell appeared. Rimbaud abandoned poetry to travel in Europe and North Africa, returning to Paris shortly before his death. In 1866, Verlaine published *Les Illuminations* as the work of the late Arthur Rimbaud.

Rimsky-Korsakov, Nikolai Andreievich (1844–1908) Russian composer, one of the RUSSIAN FIVE. His operas include *The Snow Maiden* (1881) and *The Golden Cockerel* (1907), and among his most popular orchestral works are *Sheherazade* (1888), *Capriccio espagnole* (1887) and 'The Flight of the Bumblebee' from the opera *Tsar Saltan* (1900).

ringworm Fungus infection of the skin, scalp or nails. The commonest type of ringworm is athlete's foot (*tinea pedis*). It is treated with antifungal preparations.

Rio de Janeiro City on Guanabara Bay, SE Brazil. Discovered by Europeans in 1502, it was later colonized by the French, then the Portuguese. By the 18th century, it was a major outlet for gold mined in the hinterland. In 1763, it became the seat of the viceroy and then Brazil's capital (1834–1960). The second-largest city in Brazil, Rio is its commercial and industrial centre. Its climate and beaches make it a popular tourist resort. There are large shanty towns surrounding the city. Industries: coffee, sugar refining, shipbuilding, pharmaceuticals, publishing and printing, engineering, textiles. Pop. (2000) 5,850,544; 10,894,156 (metropolitan).

Rio Grande (Rio Bravo del Norte) River in North America. It rises in the San Juan mountains of sw Colorado, USA, and flows s through New Mexico. It forms the border between Texas and Mexico, and empties into the Gulf of Mexico just e of Brownsville, Texas, and Matamoros, Mexico. One of North America's longest rivers, it is unnavigable and is used for irrigation and hydroelectricity. Length: c.3,035km (1,885mi).

Risorgimento (It. 'Resurgence') Nationalist movement (1859–70) resulting in the unification of Italy. With the restoration of Austrian and Bourbon rule in 1815, revolutionary groups formed, notably the Young Italy movement of MAZZINI, whose aim was a single, democratic republic. Mazzini's influence was at its peak in the REVOLUTIONS OF 1848. In Sardinia-Piedmont (the only independent Italian state), the aim of the chief minister, Conti di CAVOUR, was a parliamentary monarchy under the royal House of Savoy. Securing the support of France under Napoleon III in a war against Austria, Cavour acquired much of Austrian-dominated N Italy in 1859. In 1860, GARIBALDI conquered Sicily and Naples. Although Garibaldi belonged to the republican tradition of Mazzini, he cooperated with Cavour, and the Kingdom of Italy was proclaimed in 1861, under VICTOR EMMANUEL II of Savoy. Other regions were acquired later. Rome, the future capital, was seized when the French garrison withdrew in 1870.

river Large, natural channel containing water that flows downhill under gravity. A river system is a network of connecting channels. It can be divided into tributaries, which collect water and sediment, the main trunk river and the dispersing system at the river's mouth where much of the sediment is deposited. The **discharge** of a river is the volume of water flowing past a point in a given time. The **velocity** of a river is controlled by the slope, its depth, and the roughness of the river bed. Rivers carry sediment as they flow, by the processes of traction (rolling), saltation (jumping), suspension (carrying), and solution. Most river sediment is carried during flood conditions, but as a river returns to normal flow, it deposits sediment. This can result in the EROSION of a river channel or in the building up of flood-plains, sand and gravel banks. All rivers tend to flow in a twisting pattern, even if the slope is relatively steep, because water flow is naturally turbulent. Over time, on shallow slopes, small bends grow into large MEANDERS. The current flows faster on the outside of bends, thereby eroding the bank, while sedimentation occurs on the inside of bends where the current is slowest. This causes the curves to exaggerate forming loops. Rivers flood when their channels cannot contain the discharge. Flood risk can be reduced by straightening the channel, dredging sediment, or making the channel deeper by raising the banks. *See also* DELTA; LEVÉE; OXBOW

Rivera, Diego (1886–1957) Mexican painter, married to fellow artist Frida Kahlo. Rivera is one of Mexico's three great 20th-century muralists (with OROZCO and Siqueiros).

He often used symbolism and allegory to depict events in Mexico's history, and to express his hope for a Marxist future. His murals adorn public buildings in Mexico City.

Riviera Region of SE France and NW Italy, on the Mediterranean Sea, extending 370km (230mi) from CANNES, France, to La Spezia, Italy. Its spectacular scenery and mild climate make it a leading tourist centre. Resorts include NICE and Cannes in France, MONTE CARLO in Monaco, and San Remo and Alassio in Italy. Products: flowers, olives, grapes, and citrus fruits.

Riyadh Capital of Saudi Arabia, in the E central part of the country, *c.*380km (235mi) inland from the Persian Gulf. In the early 19th century, it was the domain of the Saudi dynasty, becoming capital of Saudi Arabia in 1932. The chief industry is oil refining. Pop. (2002) 3,627,700.

RNA (ribonucleic acid) Chemical (nucleic acid) that controls the synthesis of PROTEIN in a cell and is the genetic material in some viruses. The molecules of RNA in a cell are copied from DNA and consist of a single strand of nucleotides, each containing the sugar ribose, phosphoric acid, and one of four bases: adenine, guanine, cytosine or uracil. **Messenger RNA** (mRNA) carries the information for protein synthesis from DNA in the cell NUCLEUS to the RIBOSOMES in the CYTOPLASM. **Transfer RNA** (tRNA) brings amino acids to their correct position on the messenger RNA. Each AMINO ACID is specified by a sequence of three bases in mRNA.

roach European freshwater carp found in muddy or brackish waters. Colours include silver, white and green. Length: to 40cm (16in). Family Cyprinidae; species *Rutilus rutilus*.

Roach, Hal (1892–1992) US film producer. He is best remembered for his silent comedy shorts. Co-founder of The Rolin Film Company in 1915, he encouraged Harold LLOYD, LAUREL AND HARDY, and Will Rogers. In 1984 he received an honorary Academy Award.

road runner Fast-running, desert CUCKOO that lives in SW USA. It has a crested head, streaked brownish plumage, long, strong legs and long tail. It feeds on ground animals including snakes, which it kills with its long, pointed beak. Family Cuculidae; species *Geococcyx californianus*.

Robbe-Grillet, Alain (1922–2008) French novelist and theoretician, one of the originators of the NOUVEAU ROMAN in the 1950s. He later worked in films, writing the screenplay for *Last Year at Marienbad* (1961) and directing *Trans-Europe Express* (1966). His books include the novels *The Erasers* (1953), *Jealousy* (1957), *Topology of a Phantom City* (1976) and *Djinn* (1981), and the critical work *Towards a New Novel* (1963).

Robbins, Jerome (1918–98) US ballet choreographer and dancer. In 1940, he joined the American Ballet Theater. Robbins is celebrated for his choreography of Broadway musicals, including *The King and I* (1951, filmed 1956), *West Side Story* (1957, filmed 1961) and *Fiddler on the Roof* (1964, filmed 1971). From 1983 to 1990, he was joint ballet master of the New York City Ballet with Peter MARTINS.

Robert I (the Bruce) (1274–1329) King of Scotland (1306–29). He descended from a prominent Anglo-Norman family with a strong claim to the throne. He swore fealty to EDWARD I of England (1296), but joined a Scottish revolt in 1297. Robert later renewed his allegiance to Edward, but his divided loyalties made him suspect. After killing a powerful rival, John Comyn, he had himself crowned King of Scotland (1306) but, defeated at Methven (1306) by the English, he fled the kingdom. Returning on Edward's death (1307), the Bruce renewed the struggle with increasing support. In 1314, he won a famous victory over the English at BANNOCKBURN. The battle secured Scottish independence, which was finally recognized in the Treaty of Northampton (1328).

Robert II (1054–1134) (Robert Curthose) Duke of Normandy (1087–1106). The eldest son of WILLIAM I (THE CONQUEROR), he disputed Normandy and England with his younger brothers, WILLIAM II and HENRY I, and played a prominent part in the First CRUSADE (1096–99). In 1106, Robert was defeated and captured by Henry and imprisoned for life.

Roberts, Julia (1967–) US film actress. She was nominated for an Academy Award as best supporting actress in *Steel Magnolias* (1989). *Pretty Woman* (1990) was a massive box-office success. Roberts won an Academy Award

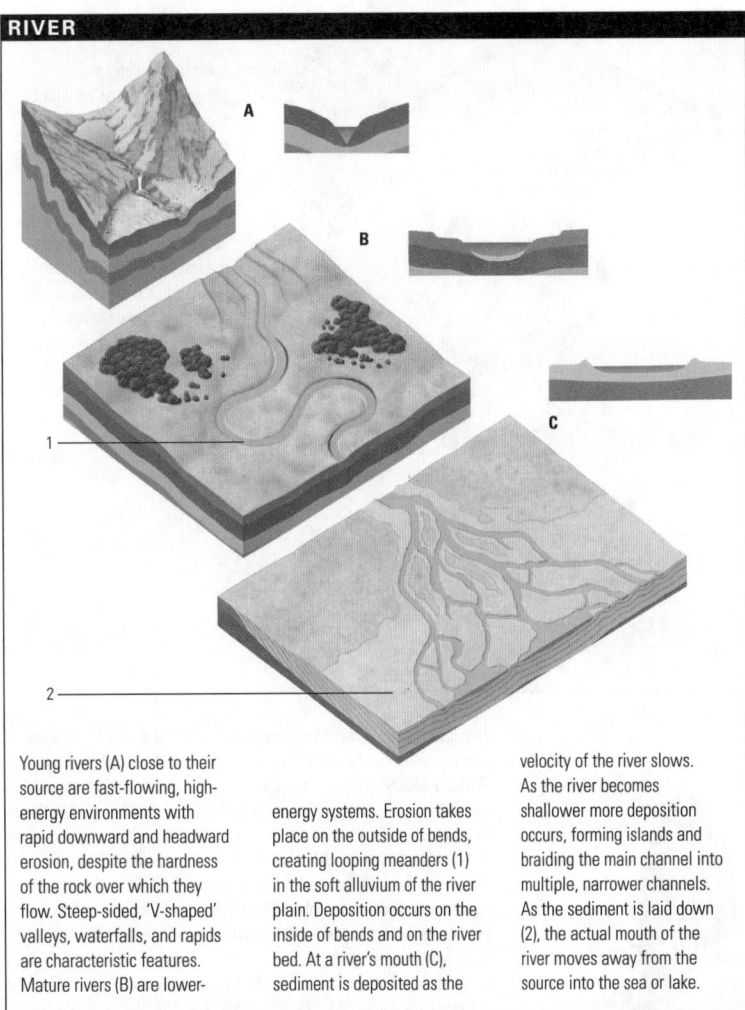

RIVER

Young rivers (A) close to their source are fast-flowing, high-energy environments with rapid downward and headward erosion, despite the hardness of the rock over which they flow. Steep-sided, 'V-shaped' valleys, waterfalls, and rapids are characteristic features. Mature rivers (B) are lower-energy systems. Erosion takes place on the outside of bends, creating looping meanders (1) in the soft alluvium of the river plain. Deposition occurs on the inside of bends and on the river bed. At a river's mouth (C), sediment is deposited as the velocity of the river slows. As the river becomes shallower more deposition occurs, forming islands and braiding the main channel into multiple, narrower channels. As the sediment is laid down (2), the actual mouth of the river moves away from the source into the sea or lake.

for best actress in *Erin Brockovich* (2000). Other credits include *The Pelican Brief* (1993) and *Notting Hill* (1999).

Robespierre, Maximilien François Marie Isidore de (1758–94) French revolutionary leader. Elected to the National Assembly in 1789, he advocated democracy and liberal reform. In 1791, he became leader of the JACOBINS, and gained credit when his opposition to war with Austria was justified by French defeats. With the King and the GIRONDINS discredited, Robespierre led the republican revolution of 1792, and was elected to the National Convention. His election to the Committee of Public Safety (June 1793) heralded the REIGN OF TERROR, in which hundreds died on the guillotine. Ruthless methods seemed less urgent after French victories in war, and Robespierre was arrested in the coup of 9th Thermidor (July 27, 1794) and executed.

robin Small Eurasian bird, with a characteristic red-orange breast. Length: to 14cm (5.5in). Family Turdidae; species

◀ **Rivera** *La Civilisation Tarasque: Dyeing Material* (1947). Despite being interested in cubism and influenced by the work of Henri Rousseau, Diego Rivera's work is rooted in the Mexican tradition. Characteristic of his style are simplified, flat geometric forms in expressive colours.

ROBOT

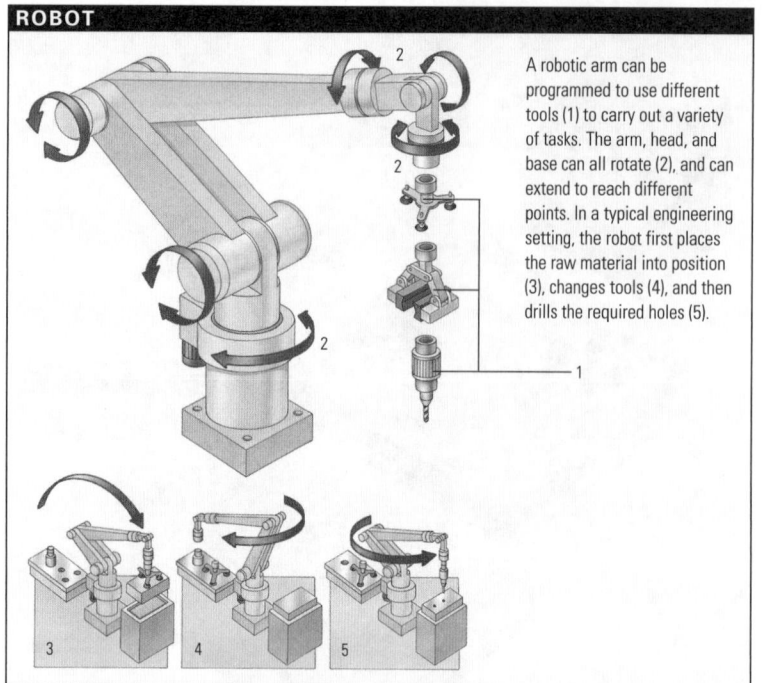

A robotic arm can be programmed to use different tools (1) to carry out a variety of tasks. The arm, head, and base can all rotate (2), and can extend to reach different points. In a typical engineering setting, the robot first places the raw material into position (3), changes tools (4), and then drills the required holes (5).

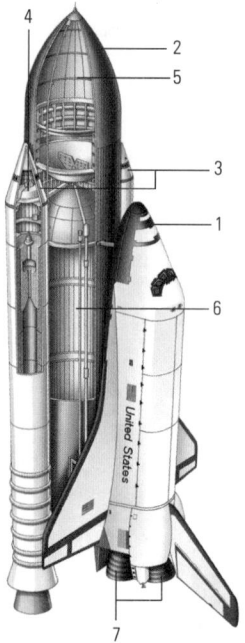

▲ **rocket** The space shuttle has three main components when launched. The orbiter (1) is attached to an external fuel tank (2), which is bracketed by booster rockets (3). The booster rockets are filled with solid fuel, and once the fuel has been burned, the boosters are jettisoned and return to Earth by parachute (4). The solid fuel is a mixture of an iron oxide catalyst, an oxidizer, and powdered aluminium. The liquid oxygen (5) and liquid hydrogen (6), contained in the external fuel tank, feed the shuttle's three main engines (7).

R

Erithacus rubecula. The American robin (*Turdus migratorius*) is a member of the thrush family and is *c.*25cm (10in) long.

Robin Hood Legendary English outlaw. Medieval tradition describes him as a displaced noble living with his outlaw band in Sherwood Forest, near Nottingham. He supposedly robbed the rich and gave to the poor, fighting a running battle with the Sheriff of Nottingham and the corrupt King JOHN. His 'merry men' included Little John, Friar Tuck and Maid Marian.

Robinson, Edwin Arlington (1869–1935) US poet. His first volume of poems, *The Torrent and The Night Before* (1896), was followed by *The Town down the River* (1910), *The Man against the Sky* (1916), and *The Three Taverns* (1920). He received the Pulitzer Prize in 1921, 1924, and 1927.

Robinson, (William) Heath (1872–1944) English cartoonist and illustrator. He is best-known for his drawings of 'Heath Robinson contraptions', absurdly complicated machines for performing simple, everyday tasks.

Robinson, Mary (1944–) Irish stateswoman, president (1990–97). She entered politics as a senator in 1969. Robinson became Ireland's first woman president. Her stand on human rights and support for the campaign to liberalize laws on abortion and divorce gave the office a high profile. She was UN Commissioner for Human Rights from 1997 to 2002.

Robinson, Sugar Ray (1920–89) US boxer, b. Walker Smith. Undefeated world welterweight champion from 1946 to 1950, he won the middleweight title five times in the 1950s. He fought the last of his 21 world title bouts in 1961.

robot Automated machine used to carry out various tasks. Robots are often COMPUTER-controlled, the most common type having a single arm that can move in any direction. Such robots are used in MASS PRODUCTION. *See also* ARTIFICIAL INTELLIGENCE (AI); AUTOMATION

Rob Roy (1671–1734) Scottish outlaw, b. Robert MacGregor. He took to banditry after the Duke of Montrose confiscated his lands. Rob Roy took part in the JACOBITE rising of 1715. Sir Walter SCOTT's novel *Rob Roy* (1817) romanticized his exploits.

rock Solid material that makes up the Earth's crust. Rocks are classified by origin into three major groups: IGNEOUS ROCKS, SEDIMENTARY ROCKS, and METAMORPHIC ROCKS.

rock (rock and roll) Form of popular music characterized by amplified guitars and singing, often with repetitive lyrics and driving rhythms. Rock music appealed largely to a white audience who found its forerunner, RHYTHM AND BLUES, inaccessible. It developed out of the BLUES and FOLK MUSIC of rural USA to become a major form of cultural

expression in the 1960s. Rock and roll was popularized by Bill Haley and the film *Rock Around the Clock* (1956). Its modern offshoots include heavy metal, grunge, and PUNK.

Rockefeller, John D. (Davison) (1839–1937) US industrialist and philanthropist. In 1863, Rockefeller built an oil refinery in Cleveland. In 1870, it incorporated into the Standard Oil Company of Ohio. On retirement, he devoted his attention to charitable corporations, donating *c.*US$550 million. In 1913, he founded the Rockefeller Foundation.

rocket Any vehicle powered by a rocket ENGINE. Most are used by the military as MISSILES. The largest rockets are capable of reaching SPACE, and are used to carry spacecraft into orbit. A typical rocket is slender, with a pointed nose to reduce DRAG. Most of its volume contains chemical fuel, which is burned in a COMBUSTION chamber and expelled at SUPERSONIC SPEED from the exhaust nozzle. They gain THRUST from the reaction (referred to in the third of NEWTON's LAWS of motion) produced by rapid, continuous output of exhaust gases. Unlike other engines this is not dependent on the atmosphere, allowing travel in space. **Liquid-fuelled** rockets usually use a fuel (such as liquid hydrogen) and a separate oxidizer (usually liquid oxygen), which burn together in the engine. **Solid-fuelled** rockets have both fuel and oxidizer in a solid mixture. A **single-stage** rocket has one fuel load, or several that are used simultaneously. A **multi-stage** rocket has several fuel loads, which are ignited singly in succession as the preceding one burns out.

Rockwell, Norman (1894–1978) US illustrator, a popular painter of rural and small-town life. He was best known for the covers he created for *The Saturday Evening Post* (1916–63).

Rocky Mountains Major mountain system in w North America. Extending from Mexico to the Bering Strait, N of the Arctic Circle, the mountains form the continental divide. The highest point is Mount ELBERT.

rococo Playful, light style of art, architecture and decoration that developed in early 18th-century France. It soon spread to Germany, Austria, Italy, and Britain. Rococo brought swirls, scrolls, shells, and arabesques to interior decoration. It was also applied to furniture, porcelain, and silverware.

Rodchenko, Alexander (1891–1956) Russian artist and photographer. Rodchenko studied traditional art before being inspired to produce abstract work by the paintings of MALEVICH in 1915. He became a pioneer of CONSTRUCTIVISM and, in the 1920s, abandoned painting for photography. Rodchenko pioneered constructivist photomontage and exerted enormous influence on 20th century graphic design. Criticism of modern art by Soviet officials drove him to abandon photography in the 1930s, but he was able to return to it in the 1950s.

rodent Any member of the vast order Rodentia, the most numerous and widespread of all mammals, characterized by a pair of gnawing incisor teeth in both the upper and lower jaws. Numbering close to 2,000 species, including rats, mice, squirrels, beaver, dormice, porcupines and guinea pigs, rodents live throughout the world. Most are small and light.

Rodgers, Richard Charles (1902–79) US composer of BROADWAY musicals. He worked first with Lorenz Hart and then with Oscar HAMMERSTEIN on successful musicals, including *Oklahoma!* (1943), *Carousel* (1945), *South Pacific* (1949), *The King and I* (1951), and *The Sound of Music* (1959).

Rodin, Auguste (1840–1917) French sculptor, one of the greatest European artists of his time. Rodin's first major work, *The Age of Bronze* (1878), caused a scandal because the naked figure was so naturalistic. His next great project was *The Gates of Hell*, unfinished studies for a bronze door for the Musée des arts décoratifs. It provided him with the subjects for further great sculptures, including *The Thinker* (1880), *The Kiss* (1886), and *Fugit Amor* (1897). Perhaps his most extraordinary work is the full-length bronze of Balzac, completed in 1897.

Roethke, Theodore (1908–63) US poet. His debut book of verse, *Open House*, appeared in 1941. He published other collections, including *The Waking: Poems 1933–53* (1953), which won both a Pulitzer Prize and the National Book Award.

Rogers, Ginger (1911–95) US actress and dancer. Rogers became famous in the 1930s for several film musicals co-starring Fred ASTAIRE, including *Flying Down To Rio* (1933) and *Top Hat* (1934). She also appeared on stage.

Rogers, Richard (1933–) British architect, b. Italy. He attracted international recognition with his designs for the Pompidou Centre, Paris (co-designed with Renzo Piano, 1971–77) and the Lloyds building, London (1978–80). Rogers designs his buildings 'inside-out' to allow for servicing without disrupting the interior. He designed the Millennium Dome, GREENWICH, London (1998–99).

Roget, Peter Mark (1779–1869) English scholar and physician. He helped to establish London University and is remembered for his *Thesaurus of English Words and Phrases* (1852).

roller Any of several species of Eurasian birds that roll over in flight. An occasional visitor to Britain, *Coracius garrulus*, has blue-green plumage and flies as far north as Sweden; it usually winters in Africa. Family Coraciidae.

roller skating Recreational activity in which a metal skate is attached to each foot, beneath which are free-running wheels. The traditional skate uses pairs of hard rubber rollers. An alternative form since the mid-1980s has three or more rubber wheels in line ('in-line skates' or 'rollerblades').

Rolling Stones, The British rock group, formed in 1962 around vocalist Mick Jagger (1943–), guitarist Keith Richards (1943–), bassist Bill Wyman (1941–) and drummer Charlie Watts (1942–). Their rebellious posturing courted great controversy and publicity. Both Jagger and Richards were convicted of drug offences, and a founder member, Brian Jones, died (1969) after a drugs overdose. Early hit singles included 'Satisfaction' (1965), 'Paint it Black' (1966), and 'Jumpin' Jack Flash' (1968). Million-selling albums include *Beggar's Banquet* (1968) and *Exile on Main Street* (1972). They continued to make world tours more than 40 years after their formation.

Rollins, 'Sonny' (Theodore Walter) (1930–) US jazz saxophonist. Influenced by Charlie PARKER, Rollins played with many of the BE-BOP greats, including Max Roach, 'Bud' POWELL, Thelonious MONK, and Miles DAVIS.

Rolls, Charles Stewart (1877–1910) English car manufacturer and aviator. In 1897, he helped found the Royal Automobile Club (RAC). In 1906, Rolls and Henry Royce formed Rolls-Royce Ltd., a major manufacturer of luxury automobiles and aircraft engines. In 1910, he became the first Englishman to fly across the English Channel. Rolls was the first Englishman to die in an air crash.

ROM Acronym for **R**ead-**O**nly **M**emory, INTEGRATED CIRCUITS that act as a permanent store for data required by a COMPUTER. The contents of ordinary ROM chips are set by the manufacturer and cannot be altered by the user.

Roman art and architecture Classical art and architecture of ancient ROME. Prior to 400 BC Roman art was largely ETRUSCAN art in the form of tomb decorations, after which Greek influence became dominant. Few examples of later Roman painting have survived: the best examples are found in the Italian towns of POMPEII and HERCULANEUM. Another common art form was the MOSAIC. Floors and walls were decorated mostly in elaborate geometric patterns, but mosaics were also created to depict everyday scenes, or gods and goddesses. In sculpture, the Romans excelled in portrait busts and reliefs. In architecture, notable features include the adoption of the ARCH, VAULT, and DOME. Fine examples include the PANTHEON and COLOSSEUM in Rome.

Roman Britain Period of British history from the Roman invasion (AD 43) in the reign of CLAUDIUS I until *c.*410. The occupation included Wales but not Ireland nor most of Caledonia (Scotland). From *c.*130, HADRIAN'S WALL marked its northern frontier. Only the English lowlands were thoroughly Romanized, and Roman rule brought this region a period of prosperity unmatched for more than 1,000 years. Britain was ruled as a province under Roman governors. Roman power disintegrated in the 3rd century. By 400, attacks from Ireland, Scotland, and the continental mainland were increasing and Roman troops were withdrawn to deal with enemies nearer home. In 410, Emperor Honorius warned the Britons to expect no further help. Local Romano-British kings held out for more than 100 years before the ANGLO-SAXONS overran lowland Britain.

Roman Catholic Church Christian denomination that acknowledges the supremacy of the Pope (*see* PAPACY;

◄ **Rolling Stones** Formed in 1962, the Rolling Stones remained one of the world's most successful rock and roll bands for more than 40 years. With their aggressive music and overtly sexual and political lyrics, they contrasted with the Beatles in the 1960s. In the 1970s, albums such as *Sticky Fingers* (1971) and their extravagantly staged worldwide tours increased their popularity. In 1993, bassist Bill Wyman left the group. He was replaced by Darryl Jones.

PAPAL INFALLIBILITY). An important aspect of doctrine is the primacy given to the Virgin MARY, whom Roman Catholics believe to be the only human being born without sin (IMMACULATE CONCEPTION). Before the REFORMATION in the 16th century, the 'CATHOLIC CHURCH' applied to the Western Church as a whole, as distinguished from the Eastern ORTHODOX CHURCH based at Constantinople. The Reformation led to a tendency for the Roman Catholic Church to be characterized by rigid adherence to doctrinal tradition from the 16th century. The government of the Church is episcopal, with archbishops and bishops responsible for provinces and dioceses. The priesthood is celibate. The centre of the Roman Catholic liturgical ritual is the MASS or EUCHARIST. Since the Second VATICAN COUNCIL (1962–65), the Roman Catholic Church has undergone marked changes, notably the replacement of Latin by the vernacular as the language of the liturgy. Today, there are *c.*600 million Roman Catholics worldwide, with large numbers in S Europe, Latin America and the Philippines.

romance (Old French *romanz*, 'vulgar tongue') Literary form, typically a heroic tale or ballad usually in verse. The form derives from the medieval narratives of TROUBADOURS. The romance spread throughout Europe during the 12th century, was used in English by CHAUCER, and remained popular through to the 16th century.

Romance languages Indo-European languages that evolved from LATIN. They include Italian, French, Spanish, Portuguese, Romanian, Catalan, Provençal, and Romansh (a language spoken in parts of Switzerland).

Roman Empire Mediterranean empire formed (*c.*27BC) by AUGUSTUS after the assassination (*c.*44BC) of Julius CAESAR. Its power centre was ancient ROME. The Romans adopted the culture of ancient GREECE, but their Empire was based on military power and ROMAN LAW. In terms of technology and (arguably) culture, Roman civilization was not surpassed in Europe until the RENAISSANCE. By the death of Augustus (AD 14), the Empire included most of Asia Minor, Syria, Egypt, and the whole North African coast. In the 1st and 2nd centuries, Britain was conquered; in the E, Roman rule extended to the Caspian Sea and the Persian Gulf, and further territory, including DACIA (Transylvania), was added in SE Europe. The Empire was at its greatest extent at the death of TRAJAN (AD 117), when it included all the lands around the Mediterranean and extended to N Britain, the Black Sea, and Mesopotamia. HADRIAN (r.117–138) called a halt to further expansion. Rome reached the height of its power during the first 150 years of imperial rule, becoming a city of grand, monumental buildings with *c.*1 million inhabitants. In the 3rd century, pressure from Germanic tribes and the Persians, plus economic difficulties, contributed to the breakdown of government. Armies in the provinces broke away from Rome. DIOCLETIAN restored order, and from his time the Empire tended to be split into E and W divisions. In 330, CONSTANTINE founded an E capital at CONSTANTINOPLE. Rome was increasingly challenged by different peoples, such as the GOTHS who sacked the city in 410. By 500, the Roman Empire in the west had ceased to exist. The Eastern or BYZANTINE EMPIRE survived until 1453.

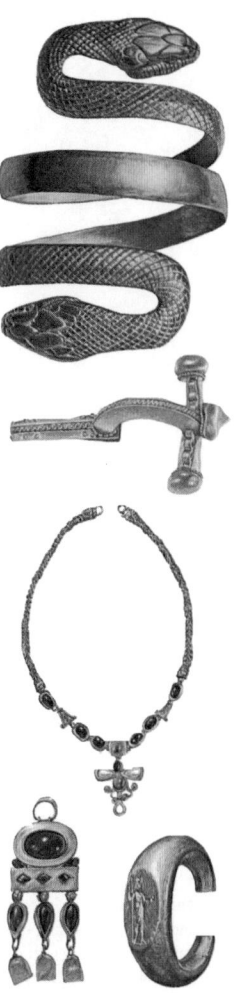

R

▲ **Roman art and architecture** During the imperial period of Roman art, from the 1st to the 3rd century AD, jewellery-making reached a level unsurpassed in Europe until the Renaissance in the 16th century. Early on, the snake motif was very popular, along with other decorative styles borrowed from Greek and Etruscan culture. Soon, however, Roman jewellery began to make greater use of gemstones and intricate, pierced decoration.

INTERNET

Robinson, Mary (page 640)
▶ www.eginitiative.org

Rodin, Auguste (page 640)
▶ www.musee-rodin.fr

Romania
▶ www.roembus.org

Romanesque Architectural and artistic style that spread throughout w Europe during the 11th and 12th centuries. English Romanesque architecture includes ANGLO-SAXON and NORMAN styles. *See also* ARCH; VAULT

Romania Balkan republic in SE Europe. *See* country feature
Romanian Official language of Romania, spoken by up to 25 million people in Romania, Macedonia, Albania, and N Greece. It is a language belonging to the Romance branch of the Indo-European family. Originally written in CYRILLIC characters, Romanian has used the Roman alphabet since 1860.

Roman law System of CIVIL LAW developed between 753 BC and the 5th century AD and which still forms the basis of the civil law in many parts of the world. Roman law was enacted originally by the PATRICIANS, then, increasingly after 287 BC by the PLEBEIAN assemblies. From 367 BC magistrates (PRAETORS) proclaimed the legal principles (*edicta*) which became an important source of law known as *jus honorium*. The Emperor could also enact laws, and by the mid-2nd century AD became the sole creator of laws. Roman law can be divided into two parts: *jus civile* (civil law), which applied only to Roman citizens and which was codified in the TWELVE TABLES of 450 BC; and *jus gentium*, which gradually merged into *jus civile*, originally applying to foreigners in Rome and to others within Roman lands who were not citizens. Roman law was codified by the Emperor JUSTINIAN I (r.527–64) and was adapted by many of the Barbarian invaders of the Empire.

Roman numeral Letter used by the ancient Romans and succeeding civilizations in Europe to represent numbers before the adoption of Arabic numerals. There were seven individual letters: I (1), V (5), X (10), L (50), C (100), D (500) and M (1,000). Combinations were used to represent the numbers. From one to ten they ran: I, II, III, IV, V, VI, VII, VIII, IX and X. The tens ran: X, XX, XXX, XL, L and so on up to XC, which represented 90. The ancients used Roman numerals for commerce and mathematics. Modern applications include numbering the preliminary pages of a book and numbering paragraphs or subparagraphs in a document.

Romanov Russian imperial dynasty (1613–1917). Michael, the first Romanov Tsar, was elected in 1613. His descendants, especially PETER I (THE GREAT) and CATHERINE II (THE GREAT), a Romanov only by marriage, transformed Russia into the largest empire in the world. The last Romanov Emperor, NICHOLAS II, abdicated in 1917 and was later murdered with his family by the BOLSHEVIKS.

Romans In the New Testament, a letter by Saint PAUL to the Christians of Rome. It was written in *c.*AD 57, probably while Paul was in Corinth. He declares the universality of the saving power of God realized in the life, death and resurrection of Jesus.

Romanticism Late 18th- and early 19th-century art movement. Its exponents valued individual experience and intuition, rather than the orderly, concrete universe of classical artists. For this reason, Romantics and classicists are often seen as opposites, but in fact they shared a belief in IDEALISM, as opposed to the exponents of REALISM and RATIONALISM. An emphasis on nature rather than science was also a characteristic. Leading

literary Romantics include GOETHE, SHELLEY, BYRON, KEATS, WORDSWORTH, and SCHILLER. William BLAKE was both a Romantic poet and artist. Other artists include DELACROIX, Caspar David FRIEDRICH, GÉRICAULT, TURNER, and the US artists of the HUDSON RIVER SCHOOL.

Romanticism Period of music history lasting from *c.*1800 to 1910. It is characterized by the importance given to emotional expression and imagination, in contrast to the restraint and strict forms of the CLASSICAL era. Orchestras expanded as composers experimented with unusual and colourful orchestration to express extra-musical influences. Leading Romantic composers include WAGNER, BERLIOZ, MENDELSSOHN, SCHUMANN, CHOPIN, and LISZT.

Romany (Gypsy) Nomadic people and their language. Romanies are believed to have originated in N India, and now inhabit Europe, Asia, America, Africa, and Australia. They first appeared in Europe in the 15th century. Their nomadic lifestyle aroused prejudice, often resulting in persecution. Their folklore is part of popular tradition. The Romany language originated in N India, and like HINDI and SANSKRIT to which it is related, it belongs to the Indo-Iranian branch of the family of INDO-EUROPEAN LANGUAGES. Many Romanies today speak it as a second language, but there is little written Romany.

Rome (Roma) Capital of Italy, on the River Tiber, w central Italy. Founded in the 8th century BC it was probably an Etruscan city-kingdom in the 6th century BC. The Roman Republic was founded in *c.*500 BC. By the 3rd century BC Rome ruled most of Italy and began to expand overseas. In the 1st century AD the city was transformed as successive emperors built temples, palaces, public baths, arches and columns. It remained the capital of the ROMAN EMPIRE until AD 330. In the 5th century, Rome was sacked during the Barbarian invasions, and its population (already in decline) fell rapidly. In the Middle Ages, Rome became the seat of the PAPACY. In 1527, it was sacked by the army of CHARLES V. The city began to flourish once more in the 16th and 17th centuries. Italian troops occupied it in 1870, and in 1871 it became the capital of a unified Italy. The 1922 Fascist march on Rome brought MUSSOLINI to power, and he did much to turn Rome into a modern capital city. It is also home to the VATICAN CITY. Industries: tourism, pharmaceuticals, chemicals, oil refining, engineering, textiles, films, printing and publishing, banking and finance. Pop. (2001) 2,656,000.

Rome, ancient Capital of the Roman republic and ROMAN EMPIRE. According to tradition, ROMULUS AND REMUS founded Rome in 753 BC. By 509 BC the Latin-speaking Romans had thrown off the rule of ETRUSCAN kings, and established an independent republic dominated by an aristocratic elite. Its history was one of continual expansion, and by 340 BC Rome controlled Italy s of the River Po. By the 3rd century BC the PLEBEIAN class had gained political recognition. The PUNIC WARS gave it dominance of the Mediterranean in the 2nd century BC when major eastward expansion began with the conquest of the Greek lands around the Aegean. Social division and military dictatorship placed strain on the republic. SPARTACUS' slave revolt was crushed by POMPEY, who emerged as SULLA's successor. Pompey and Julius CAESAR formed the First Triumverate (60BC). Caesar emerged as leader and greatly extended Rome's territory and influence. His assassination led to the formation of the Empire under AUGUSTUS (27BC).

Rome, Treaties of (1957) Two agreements establishing the European Economic Community, now the EUROPEAN UNION (EU), and the EUROPEAN ATOMIC ENERGY COMMISSION (EURATOM). The 1957 Treaty was extensively amended by the Single European Act (1986) and the MAASTRICHT TREATY (1992), but still forms the basis of the EU.

Rommel, Erwin (1891–1944) German general. Rommel commanded tanks in France in 1940, and later led the AFRIKA KORPS in a victorious campaign in North Africa – until defeated by the British at EL ALAMEIN (1942). Transferred to France in 1943, he was unable to repel the invasion of NORMANDY and was wounded. Implicated in a plot against Hitler in July 1944, he was forced to commit suicide.

Romulus and Remus In Roman mythology, twin brothers, said to be sons of Mars and the founders of ROME. Amulius,

R

▶ **Romanesque** The enduring monuments of Romanesque architecture are the churches and cathedrals of the period. Many regional differences in style existed. Dating from the 11th century, Monza Cathedral in Lombardy, shown here, is a prime example of a central Italian Romanesque building. The dominant feature of its façade is the striped pattern of facing material, a common motif of the Italian Romanesque – surface ornamentation was very important. The entrance is elaborated with columns, another popular design feature, with a rose window above.

who usurped the throne, ordered the babies to be drowned in the Tiber. They survived and were suckled by a wolf, before being found by a shepherd, Faustulus. They built a city on the site of their rescue. Romulus killed Remus during a quarrel.

Ronsard, Pierre de (1524–85) French poet and leader of the PLÉIADE. His *Odes* (1550) and *Les Amours* (1552) brought him fame and royal patronage. Other works include the incomplete national epic *La Franciade* (1572) and *Sonnets pour Hélène* (1578), some of his finest love poems.

röntgen (symbol R) Former unit used to measure X-RAY or gamma-ray RADIATION. One röntgen causes sufficient ionization to produce a total electric charge of 2.58×10^{-4} coulombs on all the positive (or negative) ions in one kilogram of air. The unit has been replaced by the SI unit, the GRAY (symbol Gy).

Röntgen, Wilhelm Konrad (1845–1923) German physicist. In 1895, Röntgen discovered X-RAYS. He also conducted important work on electricity, the specific heats of gases, and the heat CONDUCTIVITY of crystals. In 1901, Röntgen received the first Nobel Prize in physics.

rook Large gregarious European bird of the CROW family. It has glossy black plumage, but commonly loses the feathers from about its face. It feeds on grain and insects, and has a characteristic raucous cry. Family Corvidae; species *Corvus frugilegus*.

Roosevelt, (Anna) Eleanor (1884–1962) US reformer and humanitarian, wife of Franklin D. ROOSEVELT. She was a supporter of social causes, including civil rights. She served as US delegate to the UN (1945–52, 1961–62) and chairman of the UN Commission on Human Rights (1946–51).

ROMANIA

Romania is on the Black Sea in E Europe. E and S Romania form part of the Danube Basin. The delta region, where the river flows into the Black Sea, is one of Europe's finest wetlands. The S part of the coast contains several resorts.

The country is dominated by the CARPATHIAN MOUNTAINS, which curve around the plateaux of TRANSYLVANIA in central Romania. The S arm of the Carpathians, including Mount Moldoveanu (2,543m [8,341ft]), is known as the Transylvanian Alps. On the border with Serbia and Montenegro, the River DANUBE (Dunav/Dunărea) has cut a gorge, the Iron Gate (Portile de Fier), whose rapids have been tamed by a huge dam. Forests cover large areas in Transylvania and the Carpathians, while farmland dominates in the Danubian lowlands and the plateaux.

CLIMATE

Romania has hot summers and cold winters. Rainfall is heaviest in spring and early summer, when thundery showers are common.

HISTORY

Modern Romania roughly corresponds to ancient Dacia, conquered by the Romans in AD 106. The first step towards the creation of the modern state occurred in the 14th century when two principalities emerged: WALLACHIA (or Valachi) in the S and MOLDAVIA in the E. Both were conquered by the Ottoman Turks around 1500.

Russia captured Moldavia and Wallachia in the Russo-Turkish War (1828–29). Romanian nationalism intensified, and Wallachia and Moldavia united in 1861 to form modern Romania. The Congress of Berlin (1878) ratified Romania as an independent state, and in 1881 CAROL I became king.

Neutral at the start of World War 1, Romania joined the Allies in 1916. German forces occupied it in 1917. The Allied victory led to Romania acquiring large regions, such as Transylvania, almost doubling the country's size and population. MICHAEL became king in 1927, but surrendered the throne to his father, CAROL II, in 1930. Political instability and economic inequality led to the growth of fascism and anti-Semitism. In 1939 Romania lost territory to Bulgaria, Hungary and the Soviet Union. In 1940, Michael returned as king. Ion ANTONESCU became dictator, and in June 1941 Romania joined the German invasion of the Soviet Union. More than half of Romania's Jews were exterminated during the war.

Romania fought alongside Germany in World War 2 and was occupied by Soviet forces in 1944. Hungary returned N Transylvania to Romania in 1945, but Bulgaria and the Soviet Union kept former Romanian territory when King Michael was removed from the throne.

In 1945 a communist-dominated coalition assumed power, led by Gheorghe Gheorghiu-Dej. In 1947 Romania became a People's Republic, and in 1952 adopted a Soviet-style constitution. Industry was nationalized and agriculture collectivized. In 1949 Romania joined the Council of Mutual Economic Assistance (COMECON), and in 1955 it became a member of the Warsaw Pact. In the 1960s the Romanian government began to oppose Soviet control. In 1965 Gheorghiu-Dej was succeeded by Nicolae CEAUŞESCU.

Under Ceauşescu Romania developed industries based on its oil and natural gas reserves. His rule was corrupt and self-seeking, but he won plaudits from the West for his independent stance against Soviet control, including a knighthood from Queen Elizabeth II. However, he pursued a strict Stalinist approach and the remorseless industrialization and urbanization programmes of the 1970s caused severe debt. In the 1980s, he cut imports and diverted output to exports. Self-sufficiency turned to subsistence and shortages, with savage rationing of food and energy.

Ceauşescu's building schemes desecrated some of the country's finest architecture and demolished thousands of villages. In December 1989 mass anti-government demonstrations were held in Timisoara and there were protests across Romania. Security forces fired on crowds, causing many deaths. After army

AREA 238,391sq km [92,043sq mi]
POPULATION 22,276,000
CAPITAL (POPULATION) Bucharest (1,764,000)
GOVERNMENT Multiparty republic
ETHNIC GROUPS Romanian 89%, Hungarian 7%, Roma 2%, Ukrainian
LANGUAGES Romanian (official), Hungarian, German
RELIGIONS Eastern Orthodox 87%, Protestant 7%, Roman Catholic 5%
CURRENCY Leu = 100 bani

units joined the protests, Nicolae Ceauşescu and his wife Elena fled from Bucharest on 22 December. Both were executed on Christmas Day on charges of genocide and corruption. A provisional government of the National Salvation Front (NSF), took control, much of the old administrative apparatus was dismantled, and the Communist Party was dissolved.

POLITICS

In May 1990 the NSF under Ion Iliescu won Romania's first free elections since World War 2. A new constitution enshrining pluralist democracy and a market economy was passed by parliament in 1991. There were strikes and protests against the new authorities and also against the effects of the switch to a market economy, which caused food shortages, rampant inflation and increased unemployment. Foreign investment was sluggish, deterred by the political instability. Presidential elections in 1996 led to defeat for Iliescu and victory for the centre-right Emil Constantinescu. In 2000, Iliescu was re-elected president. His government continued privatization policies. In 2004 Traian Baiescu was elected to succeed him. Romania became a member of NATO in 2004 and joined the EU in 2007, though the country soon received EU criticism for failing to tackle corruption.

ECONOMY

According to the World Bank, Romania is a 'lower-middle-income' economy. Oil and natural gas are the chief mineral resources and the aluminium, copper, lead and zinc industries use domestic supplies. Manufactures include cement, processed food, petroleum products, textiles and wood. Agriculture employs nearly a third of the workforce. Crops include fruits, maize, potatoes, sugar beet and wheat. Sheep are the chief livestock.

R

▲ **rosemary** A strongly flavoured culinary herb, rosemary (*Rosmarius officinalis*) leaves are used as a seasoning for meat and fish. Its aromatic oil is used in perfumes and medicines. Since the earliest times, the plant has symbolized remembrance and faithfulness.

Roosevelt, Franklin Delano (1882–1945) Thirty-second US President (1933–45). Roosevelt served in the New York Senate as a Democrat, as assistant secretary (1913–20) of the navy under Woodrow WILSON, and was vice presidential candidate in 1920. In 1921, he lost the use of his legs as a result of polio. He was governor of New York (1928–32), and won the Democratic candidacy for president. He was elected in 1932. In response to the GREAT DEPRESSION, he embarked upon his NEW DEAL, designed to restore the economy through direct government intervention. He was re-elected in 1936, and won an unprecedented third term in 1940, and a fourth in 1944. When World War 2 broke out in Europe, Roosevelt gave as much support to Britain as a neutral government could until the Japanese attack on PEARL HARBOR ended US neutrality. He died in office and was succeeded by Harry S. TRUMAN.

Roosevelt, Theodore (1858–1919) Twenty-sixth US president (1901–09), fifth cousin of Franklin ROOSEVELT and uncle of Eleanor. Roosevelt gained national fame as the organizer of the Rough Riders in the SPANISH-AMERICAN WAR (1898). He became Republican governor of New York in 1899, and vice president in 1901. Roosevelt became president after the assassination of William MCKINLEY, and he was elected in 1904. A vigorous progressive, he moved to regulate monopolies through anti-trust legislation. Abroad, he expanded US power and prestige, gaining the PANAMA CANAL, and taking an increasing role in world affairs. His mediation after the RUSSO-JAPANESE WAR earned him the Nobel Peace Prize (1905). After retiring in 1909, he returned to challenge his successor, President William TAFT, for the presidency in 1912 as leader of the National Progressive Party (Bull Moose Party). The ensuing Republican split produced a Democratic victory.

root Underground portion of a VASCULAR PLANT that serves as an anchor, and absorbs water and minerals from the soil. Some plants, such as the dandelion, have taproots with smaller lateral branches. Other plants, such as grasses, develop fibrous roots with lateral branches.

root In mathematics, fractional POWER of a number. The SQUARE ROOT of a number, x, is written as either $\sqrt{x}$ or $x^{1/2}$. The fourth root of x may be written in radical form as $\sqrt[4]{x}$ or in power form as $x^{1/4}$. The fourth root of 16, for example, is 2 since $2 \times 2 \times 2 \times 2 = 16$.

root nodule Small swelling in the roots of various plants, such as LEGUMES, that contain nitrogen-fixing bacteria. *See also* NITROGEN CYCLE; NITROGEN FIXATION

Rorschach test (ink-blot test) In psychology, test used to analyse a person's motives and attitudes. The individual is presented with 10 standardized ink blots and interpretation is based on the description of them.

rosary Form of meditational prayer that contemplates the life of Jesus and the Blessed Virgin Mary within the Catholic and Orthodox churches. A rosary is also the string of beads on which a count may be kept of the number of prayers said.

Roscommon County in N central Republic of Ireland, in Connacht province; the county town is Roscommon. Part of the central plain of Ireland, Roscommon is generally low-lying. The Shannon is the principal river. Sheep and cattle rearing is the chief economic activity; coal-mining is important in the NE. Area: 2,463sq km (951sq mi). Pop. (2002) 53,803.

rose Wild or cultivated flowering shrub of the genus *Rosa*. Most are native to Asia, several to America, and a few to Europe and NW Africa. The stems are usually thorny, and flowers range in colour from white to yellow, pink, crimson and maroon; many are fragrant. There are *c*.250 species. Family Rosaceae.

Roseau Capital of Dominica, in the Windward Islands, a port on the SW coast at the mouth of the River Roseau. The city was burned by the French in 1805, and virtually destroyed by a hurricane in 1979. Tropical vegetables, oils, spices, limes and lime juice are exported. Pop. (2002) 19,700.

Rosebery, Archibald Philip Primrose, 5th Earl of (1847–1929) British statesman, Liberal prime minister (1894–95). Rosebery was foreign secretary (1886, 1892–94) under GLADSTONE. When Gladstone retired, Queen VICTORIA called on Rosebery to become prime minister. A controversial figure, his appointment caused a split in the LIBERAL PARTY and the Conservative Party won the ensuing election. Rosebery became leader of the imperialist wing of the Liberal Party.

rosemary Perennial evergreen herb of the mint family. It has small, needle-like leaf clusters of small pale-blue flowers. Sprigs of rosemary are commonly used as a flavouring. Family Lamiaceae/Labiatae; species *Rosmarinus officinalis*.

Rosenberg, Alfred (1893–1946) German Nazi leader, b. Estonia. He edited the newspaper of the National Socialist Party. Rosenberg's book *The Myth of the 20th Century* (1930) formed the basis of the anti-Semitism of NATIONAL SOCIALISM. In 1941, he became minister for the occupied E regions. Rosenberg was convicted of war crimes at the Nuremberg Trials and executed.

Roses, Wars of the (1455–85) English dynastic civil wars. They are named after the badges of the rival royal Houses of York (white rose) and Lancaster (red rose). Both Houses descended from EDWARD III. Richard, Duke of York, challenged the Lancastrian King HENRY VI, and gained brief ascendancy after the Battle of St Albans (1455). The Lancastrians recovered control, but in 1460 Richard, supported by the powerful Earl of WARWICK, forced Henry to recognize him as his heir. Richard was killed months later, but the Yorkist victory at Towton (1461) put his son on the throne as EDWARD IV. In 1469, Warwick changed sides and Edward was deposed, but he returned to win the decisive victory of Tewkesbury (1471). A final phase of the Wars began with the seizure of the throne by RICHARD III in 1483. He was defeated and killed at BOSWORTH FIELD, when Henry Tudor (HENRY VII) became King with support from both Houses.

Rosetta stone Slab of black basalt inscribed with the same text in Egyptian HIEROGLYPHICS, demotic (a simplified form of Egyptian hieroglyphs) and Greek script. By comparing the three versions, Thomas YOUNG (in 1818) and Jean-François Champollion (in 1822) deciphered the hieroglyphs, leading to a full understanding of hieroglyphic writing.

rosewood Any of several kinds of ornamental hardwoods derived from various tropical trees. The most important are Honduras rosewood, *Dalbergia stevensoni*, and Brazilian rosewood, *D. nigra*. It varies from a deep, ruddy brown to purplish and has a black grain. Family Fabiaceae/Leguminose.

Rosh Hashanah Jewish New Year and first day of the month of Tishri (generally in September). It is the day on which a ceremonial ram's horn, the *shophar* or *shofar*, is blown to call sinners to repentance – the Day of Judgment or of Remembrance. It begins the Ten Days of Penitence that culminate with the Day of Atonement, YOM KIPPUR.

Rosicrucians Esoteric, supposedly worldwide secret society of the 17th century, using supposedly magical knowledge drawn from ALCHEMY. The name comes from pamphlets published (*c*.1615) under the name Christian Rosenkreutz, of whom there is no other record.

Ross, Diana (1944–) US popular singer. Ross began a career with the vocal trio, The Supremes, whose Motown hits included 'Where Did Our Love Go?' (1964) and 'Baby Love' (1964). In 1969, she left to pursue a solo career. Her hits include 'Reach Out and Touch (Somebody's Hand)' (1970).

Ross Dependency Region of Antarctica that includes Ross Island, the coast along the Ross Sea and nearby islands. It has been under the jurisdiction of New Zealand since 1923. Area: land mass, *c*.415,000sq km (160,000sq mi); ice shelf, *c*.450,000sq km (174,000sq mi).

Rossellini, Roberto (1906–77) Italian film director and producer. His post-war films, such as *Open City* (1945), were landmarks in post-war Italian NEO-REALISM. During the 1950s he made a series of films with his wife, Ingrid BERGMAN, such as *Stromboli* (1949).

Rossetti, Christina Georgina (1830–94) English poet, sister of Dante Gabriel ROSSETTI. Her most enduring work is contained in *Goblin Market and Other Poems* (1862) and *The Prince's Progress and Other Poems* (1866).

Rossetti, Dante Gabriel (1828–82) English poet and painter. A founder of the PRE-RAPHAELITE BROTHERHOOD, he developed a style of medieval ROMANTICISM after the group dispersed. His lush style is evident in idealized portraits of women, such as *Beata Beatrix* (c.1863), which were often modelled on his wife, Elizabeth Siddal. Rossetti's poetry includes *Ballads and Sonnets* (1881). He died of drug and alcohol addiction.

Rossini, Gioacchino Antonio (1792–1868) Italian opera composer. Rossini's comic operas, including *The Barber of Seville* (1816) and *La Cenerentola* ('Cinderella', 1817), demonstrate his wit and sense of melody. His serious operas include *William Tell* (1829).

Rosso, Il (1495–1540) (Giovanni Battista Rosso) Italian painter and decorative artist. He collaborated with Primaticcio in decorating the royal palace at FONTAINEBLEAU and helped to found the FONTAINEBLEAU SCHOOL.

Rostand, Edmond (1868–1918) French poet and dramatist. His major verse plays include *Cyrano de Bergerac* (1897), *L'Aiglon* (1900), and *Chantecler* (1910).

Rostropovich, Mstislav Leopoldovich (1927–2007) Soviet musician, who established a reputation as one of the century's best cellists. Leading composers such as SHOSTAKOVICH, PROKOFIEV, and BRITTEN dedicated works to him.

rotation Turning of a body about its axis. In the Solar System, the Sun and all the planets, with the exception of Uranus and Venus, rotate from W to E.

Roth, Philip (1933–) US novelist and short-story writer. His works often draw on his Jewish background. Roth established his reputation with the short-story collection *Goodbye Columbus* (1959). His best-known novel is *Portnoy's Complaint* (1969). Other works include *Zuckerman Bound* (1985), *Operation Shylock* (1993), *Sabbath's Theater* (1995) and *American Pastoral* (1997).

Rothko, Mark (1903–70) US painter, b. Russia. A leader of the New York school, he developed a highly individual style featuring large, rectangular areas of thinly layered, pale colours arranged parallel to each other. Towards the end of his life, Rothko introduced darker colours, notably maroon and black. Examples of this phase can be seen in his nine paintings from the late 1950s, entitled *Black on Maroon* and *Red on Maroon*.

Rothschild, Meyer Amschel (1744–1812) German financier, founder of a banking dynasty. He made his fortune in Frankfurt during the Napoleonic Wars. His five sons established branches in the financial centres of Europe. The Rothschilds were one of the chief financial powers in the 19th century, but developments in state financing reduced their influence. The family continues to be active in banking and as wine-makers.

rotifer (wheel animacule) Microscopic metazoan found mainly in freshwater. Although it resembles ciliate PROTOZOA, it is many-celled with a general body structure similar to that of a simple WORM. Rotifers may be elongated or round, and are identified by a crown of cilia around the mouth. Class Rotifera.

Rotterdam City at the junction of the Rotte and the New Meuse rivers, W Netherlands; chief port and second-largest city in the Netherlands. Founded in the 14th century, it expanded with the construction of the New Waterway (1866–72), making it accessible to ocean-going vessels. In 1940, German bombs devastated the city centre. In 1966, the opening of the Europoort harbour made Rotterdam one of the world's largest ports. Industries: shipbuilding and ship repairing, petrochemicals, electronic goods, textiles, paper, motor vehicle assembly, clothing, brewing, oil refining, machinery. Pop. (2002) 599,048.

rottweiler German cattle dog. The short-backed, strong body is set on muscular, medium-length legs and the tail is commonly docked. The short, flat coat is black with brown markings. Height: to 68.5cm (27in) at the shoulder; 34–41kg (75–90lb).

Rouault, Georges (1871–1958) French painter, printmaker and designer. Studying under Gustave MOREAU with MATISSE, he embraced FAUVISM. A mental breakdown turned him toward more painful subjects. Rouault designed book illustrations, ceramics and tapestries, as well as the sets for DIAGHILEV's ballet, *The Prodigal Son* (1929). From the 1930s, he concentrated on religious art, such as *Christ Mocked by Soldiers* (1932).

Rouen City and port on the River Seine, NW France; capital of Seine-Maritime department. Already important in Roman times, by the 10th century Rouen was capital of Normandy and one of Europe's leading cities. Under English rule (1066–1204, 1419–49), it was the scene of Joan of Arc's trial and burning in 1431. Badly damaged in World War 2, it was later rebuilt. Industries: textiles, flour milling, iron foundries, petrochemicals, perfumes, leather goods. Pop. (1999) 108,758.

roulette Game of chance in which people gamble on which of 37 numbered slots (38 in the USA) in a spinning wheel a small white ball will end up in when the wheel stops. Gamblers place their bets on a table marked out with the numbers. The bank wins all stakes if the ball stops on 0 (and 00 in the USA).

Roundheads Name given to Puritans and other supporters of Parliament during the English CIVIL WAR. It was originally a derogatory nickname for Puritans who cut their hair short, in contrast to the ringlets of the CAVALIERS (Royalists).

roundworm Parasite of the class Nematoda, which inhabits the intestine of mammals. It breeds in the intestine. The larva bores through the intestinal wall, is carried to the lungs in the bloodstream and crawls to the mouth where it is swallowed. Length: 15–30cm (6–12in).

Rousseau, Henri (1844–1910) French painter, greatest of all naive painters. Rousseau is best known for his scenes from an imaginary tropical jungle, such as *Surprised! (Tropical Storm with Tiger)* (1891) and *The Dream* (1910).

Rousseau, Jean Jacques (1712–78) French philosopher of the Age of Reason, whose ideas about society helped to shape the political events that resulted in the FRENCH REVOLUTION. Rousseau was born a Protestant in Geneva, Switzerland, and became a Roman Catholic in the 1730s, but later in his life he reconverted to Protestantism in order to regain his citizenship rights in Geneva. In 1740, Rousseau moved to Paris and soon devoted himself to a career as a writer and composer. He contributed articles on music to the *Encyclopédie* of DIDEROT in the 1740s, and finally won fame for his essay, *Discourses on Science and the Arts* (1750). In *The Social Contract* (1762), he argued that man had been corrupted by civilization. His ideas on individual liberation from the constraints of society were developed in the novel *Émile* (1762). He described his early, wandering life in an autobiography, *Confessions*, published posthumously in 1782.

Rousseau, Théodore (1812–67) French painter, leading member of the BARBIZON SCHOOL. He was a pioneer of the

R

◀ **Rossetti** *Beata Beatrix* (c.1864–70). One of the founders of the Pre-Raphaelite Brotherhood, the artist and poet Dante Gabriel Rossetti had a lush and romantic painting style. Although his poetry was first published when he was 19, he remained virtually unknown as a poet until late in life. His paintings had a great influence on other artists, particularly the symbolists.

INTERNET

Rubens, Peter Paul
▶ www.nationalgallery.org.uk
▶ www.nga.gov
▶ www.metmuseum.org

Russell, John, 1st Earl
▶ www.number-10.gov.uk

open-air movement in landscape painting, and from 1836 worked in the Forest of Fontainebleau near Paris. His works include *Under the Birches, Evening* (1842–44).

rowing Using oars to propel a boat; a leisure activity and a sport. It was unofficially included in the Olympic Games in 1900, and became a full Olympic event in 1904. Modern racing boats hold crews of two, four or eight, each crew member using both hands to pull one oar (to use two oars is **sculling**). A coxswain steers for eights and directs the crew; pairs and fours may or may not have a coxswain.

Rowling, J.K. (Joanne Kathleen) (1965–) English writer. She is the author of a series of children's books about the adventures of Harry Potter, a young wizard, beginning with *Harry Potter and the Philosopher's Stone* (1997). The books smashed bestseller records.

Rowntree, Benjamin Seebohm (1871–1954) English businessman and sociologist. In 1889, he joined the family chocolate firm and introduced employees' pensions (1906), a five-day week (1919), and employee profit-sharing (1923).

Royal Academy of Arts (RA) British national academy of the arts, founded by George III in 1768, and based in London. Members aim to raise the status of the arts by establishing high standards of training and organizing annual summer exhibitions. The first president was Sir Joshua REYNOLDS.

Royal Greenwich Observatory UK national astronomical observatory, founded at GREENWICH, London, in 1675. After World War 2, the observatory moved to Herstmonceux in Sussex. In 1990, it relocated to Cambridge. It was dissolved in 1998.

Royal Marines British soldiers who serve at sea. The marines are also a mobile force, which can be put ashore at any time to operate as conventional soldiers. Their first success was the capture of Gibraltar in 1704. The Royal Marines played a significant role in both World Wars.

Royal Navy The oldest of Britain's armed forces, tasked with war at sea. The first naval fleet in Britain was built by ALFRED THE GREAT in 878 to fight off the Viking raids. In the 16th century, Henry VII built the first specialist naval ships and established the first dockyards. The following centuries saw a struggle for naval supremacy between Britain, France, and the Netherlands, culminating in the Battle of TRAFALGAR (1805). British victory confirmed the Royal Navy as the most powerful in the world, a state which lasted until the US navy surpassed it in the 20th century. During World War 2 it reached its largest size and served in many vital roles, including defending merchant shipping during the battle of the ATLANTIC. During the COLD WAR it re-equipped to fight Soviet submarines. After the fall of the Soviet Union the navy, now much smaller, was assigned to support British operations overseas.

Royal Opera House (originally Covent Garden Theatre) Home of the Royal Opera and, from 1946, of Sadler's Wells Ballet (now the Royal Ballet). The theatre first opened in 1732. A modernized and rebuilt Opera House was completed in 1999. The Royal Opera traditionally performs works in their original language. *See also* ENGLISH NATIONAL OPERA (ENO)

Royal Shakespeare Company (RSC) State-subsidized British theatrical repertory company, based in Stratford-upon-Avon. Originally known as the Shakespeare Memorial Company, it received a royal charter in 1961. In 1960, it established a second base in London and performed Shakespearean plays alongside other classical and contemporary pieces.

Royal Society British society founded in 1660, and incorporated two years later. Its aim was to accumulate experimental evidence on a wide range of scientific subjects, including medicine and botany as well as the physical sciences. In the 20th century, the Royal Society became an independent body.

RSI Abbreviation of REPETITIVE STRAIN INJURY

rubber Elastic solid obtained from the latex of the RUBBER TREE. **Natural** rubber consists of a POLYMER of cis-isoprene and is widely used for vehicle TYRES and other applications, especially after VULCANIZATION. **Synthetic** rubbers are polymers tailored for specific purposes.

rubber plant Evergreen FIG native to India and Malaysia. Tree-sized in the tropics, juvenile specimens are grown as houseplants in temperate regions. Once cultivated for its

white LATEX to make India rubber, it has large, glossy, leathery leaves and a stout, buttressed trunk. Height: to 30m (100ft). Family Moraceae; species *Ficus elastica*.

rubber tree Any of several South American trees whose exudations can be made into RUBBER; especially *Hevea brasiliensis* (family Euphorbiaceae), a tall softwood tree native to Brazil but introduced to Malaysia. The milky exudate, called LATEX, is obtained from the inner bark by tapping and then coagulated by smoking over fires or chemically.

rubella *See* GERMAN MEASLES

Rubens, Peter Paul (1577–1640) Flemish painter, engraver and designer, the most influential BAROQUE artist of N Europe. Rubens began to gain an international reputation with his huge, vigorous TRIPTYCHS, *Raising of the Cross* (1610–11) and *Descent from the Cross* (1611–14). He worked for many of the royal families of Europe, and his most notable commissions included 25 gigantic paintings of Marie de' Medici; a series of scenes depicting the life of James I for the Banqueting House, London; and a group of more than 100 mythological paintings for Philip IV of Spain.

Rubicon Ancient name for the River Fiumicino in N central Italy. It formed the border between Italy and Cisalpine Gaul. In 49 BC Julius CAESAR precipitated civil war by 'crossing the Rubicon' into Italy with his army, hence the modern phrase meaning to take an irrevocable step.

rubidium (symbol Rb) Silver-white metallic element of the ALKALI METALS (group I of the periodic table). It ignites spontaneously in air and can be liquid at room temperature. It was discovered in 1861 by the German chemist Robert BUNSEN and the German physicist Gustav KIRCHHOFF. The element has few commercial uses; small amounts are used in photoelectric cells, vacuum-tube filaments, and batteries. It chemically resembles SODIUM but is more reactive. Properties: at. no.37; r.a.m. 85.4678; r.d. 1.53; m.p. 38.89°C (102°F); b.p. 688°C (1,270°F); most common isotope Rb^{85} (72.15%).

Rubik, Ernö (1944–) Hungarian architect and designer. In 1975, he patented the Rubik's Cube – a mathematical puzzle with 26 small cubes in six colours.

Rubinstein, Artur (1887–1982) US pianist, b. Poland. He made his début with the Berlin Symphony Orchestra in 1901. Rubinstein first played in the USA in 1906 and became famous for his interpretations of CHOPIN and Spanish composers.

ruby Gem variety of the mineral CORUNDUM (aluminium oxide), whose characteristic red colour is due to impurities of chromium and iron oxides. The traditional source of rubies is Burma. Today, synthetic rubies are widely used in industry.

rudd (red eye) Fish related to the MINNOW. In the USA, it is called pearl ROACH. Found also in Europe, N and W Asia, the rudd is a large, full-bodied fish with reddish fins. Length: to 40.6cm (16in); weight: to 2kg (4.5lb). Family Cyprinidae; species *Scardinius erythrophthalmus*.

Rudolf I (1218–91) German King (1273–91). His election as King ended a period of anarchy (1250–73). He set out to restore the position of the monarchy, and won the Duchies of Austria, Styria, and Carniola from Ottokar II of Bohemia (1278). He was the first of the HABSBURG dynasty to become king. Rudolf was never crowned Emperor, and failed to persuade the Electors to confirm his son, Albert I, as his successor, though in 1298 Albert eventually succeeded to the German throne.

Rudolf II (1552–1612) Holy Roman Emperor (1576–1612). Son and successor of Emperor Maximilian II, he moved the imperial capital to Prague, which became a centre of the RENAISSANCE. His opposition to Protestantism caused conflict in Bohemia and Hungary. A Hungarian revolt was suppressed by his brother and eventual successor, Matthias, to whom he ceded Hungary, Austria, Moravia (1608), and Bohemia (1611).

ruff Bird of the SANDPIPER family (Scolopacidae). The male is noted for a collar of long feathers about its neck, and for its courtship performances. The female is called a reeve. The ruff migrates across N Europe and N Asia to Africa and India. Species *Philomachus pugnax*.

rugby Ball game for two teams in which an oval ball may be handled as well as kicked. There are two forms of the game, union and league, but the purpose in each is the same: to touch the ball down in the opposition in-goal area for a try,

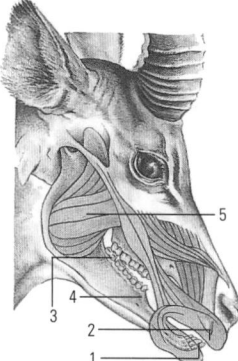

▲ **ruminant** Impalas are found in the grasslands of central and E Africa. Like other ruminants, they can regurgitate small amounts of food that have been partly digested, for chewing again, reswallowing, and further digestion. This enables them to obtain a lot of food in a short time, then retreat to a safe, sheltered place to digest it. When grazing, an impala grasps vegetation between its spade-like incisors (1) and a hard upper pad (2), and pulls it up rather than biting it off. The molars (3) are ideal for chewing. The gap between incisors and molars (4) allows the tongue to mix food with saliva. The powerful masseter muscle (5) moves the jaw up and down, while other facial muscles move it laterally for grinding.

which allows a kick at the H-shaped goal (a conversion). Kicks must pass over the crossbar between the line of the posts. Players may not pass the ball forwards or knock it forwards when attempting to catch it. The field of play is rectangular, 100m (330ft) long and 55–68m (180–225ft) wide. Play consists of two 40–minute halves. **Rugby union** is a 15–a-side game, which used to be restricted to amateurs. It is most popular in Britain, France, South Africa, New Zealand, and Australia. **Rugby league** is a 13–a-side game for professionals and amateurs, played mostly in England, Australia, New Zealand, and France. Recent development are bringing about a closer affinity between the two codes.

Ruhr River in Germany; its valley is Germany's manufacturing heartland. The River Ruhr rises in the Rothaargebirge Mountains, and flows w for 235km (146mi) to join the River RHINE at DUISBURG. Major cities on its banks include ESSEN, DORTMUND, and Mülheim. In the 19th century, the Krupp and Thyssen families intensively mined the region's high-quality coking coal and developed massive steelworks. Between 1923 and 1925, France and Belgium occupied the Ruhr in order to compel Germany to pay the agreed war reparations. During World War 2, its many armaments factories marked it out as a major Allied target, and more than 75% of the region was destroyed. The post-war decline in demand for coal led to a shift to light industry and the region regained prosperity.

Ruisdael, Jacob van (1628–82) Dutch landscape painter. Ruisdael brought to his paintings of the flat northern landscape an unusual breadth and accuracy. Among his many works are *Wooded Landscape* (c.1660) and *Windmill at Wijk* (c.1670).

rum Alcoholic spirit made by the fermentation of molasses and other sugar-cane products, which are then distilled. When distilled, rum is colourless, but storage in wooden casks and the addition of caramel give it a brown colour.

Rumi (1207–73) Persian poet, b. Jalal ad-Din ar-Rumi. A theologian and teacher whose huge body of work – some 30,000 couplets and numerous *rubaiyat* or quatrains – was inspired by SUFISM. Rumi is generally regarded as Persia's finest poet. His main work is the epic *Mathnawi* (or *Masnavi*).

ruminant Cud-chewing, even-toed, hoofed MAMMAL. They include the okapi, chevrotain, DEER, GIRAFFE, ANTELOPE, CATTLE, SHEEP, and GOAT. All except the chevrotain have four-chambered stomachs, and they are known for re-chewing food previously swallowed and stored in one of the chambers.

Rump Parliament (1648–53) Name given to the LONG PARLIAMENT in England after 140 members were expelled. Unrepresentative and quarrelsome, Oliver CROMWELL dissolved it in 1653. It was recalled after the collapse of the PROTECTORATE in 1659 and expelled members were reinstated.

Rumsfeld, Donald (1932–) US statesman, secretary of defense (1975–77, 2001–2006). He was first elected to Congress in 1962, resigning (1969) to serve under President Richard NIXON. After acting as Chief of Staff (1974–75) to President Gerald FORD, Rumsfeld became, at age 43, the youngest-ever secretary of defense. He returned to the Pentagon under President George W. BUSH.

Runcie, Robert Alexander Kennedy (1921–2000) English clergyman, Archbishop of Canterbury (1980–91). He was ordained in 1951, and became Bishop of St Albans in 1970. In 1982, during Pope JOHN PAUL II's historic trip to the UK, Runcie signed a pledge to move towards unity with the Roman Catholic Church. He was succeeded by George CAREY.

Rundstedt, Gerd von (1875–1953) German field marshal, one of Hitler's most successful army commanders. In 1939, he was called out of retirement to take a leading part in the Polish and French campaigns. He commanded an army group during the invasion of the Soviet Union, but was dismissed after being forced to retreat. Rundstedt later returned to active service as commander of the German forces in France. In September 1944, he directed the 'Battle of the Bulge', Germany's last-ditch attempt to halt the Allied advance in the west.

runes Angular characters or letters of an alphabet formerly used by Germanic peoples in early medieval times. Also called *futhark* after its first six letters (*f*, *u*, *th*, *a*, *r*, and *k*), the runic alphabet may have been developed by an unknown Germanic people from a N Italian alphabet.

runner In botany, a long, thin stem that extends along the surface of the soil from the axil of a plant's leaf and serves to propagate the plant. At points (nodes) along its length, a runner has small leaves with buds that develop shoots and roots and turn into small independent plants as the runner dies. Runners are produced by plants such as strawberries and creeping buttercups. *See also* ASEXUAL REPRODUCTION

Rupert, Prince (1619–82) British military commander, b. Bohemia and raised in the Netherlands. His uncle, CHARLES I, made him commander of the cavalry in the English CIVIL WAR. Rupert was undefeated until MARSTON MOOR (1644). He was dismissed after the Royalist defeat at NASEBY (1645). Rupert surrendered at Bristol. He led raids against English shipping during the PROTECTORATE period and, after the RESTORATION, he served as an admiral in the DUTCH WARS.

rupture *See* HERNIA

Rurik (d.c.879) Semi-legendary leader of the Varangians (VIKINGS) in Russia and first Prince of Novgorod. He established his rule in c.862, a date usually taken as marking the beginning of the first Russian state. The capital moved to KIEV under Rurik's successor, Oleg. Members of his dynasty ruled there, and later in Moscow, until the 16th century. They were eventually replaced by the ROMANOVS.

rush Any of c.700 species of perennial tufted bog plants found in temperate regions. It has long, narrow leaves and small flowers crowded into dense clusters. The most familiar rush is *Juncus effusus*, found in Europe, Asia, North America, Australia, and New Zealand. It has brown flowers and ridged stems. Height: 30–152cm (1–5ft). Family Juncaceae.

Rush-Bagot Convention (1817) British-US agreement providing for disarmament of the US-Canadian border. Besides ensuring an unfortified frontier, it agreed limits for ships of the two countries in the Great Lakes.

Rushdie, (Ahmed) Salman (1947–) British novelist, b. India. His early works, including the Booker Prize-winning *Midnight's Children* (1981), were eclipsed by *Satanic Verses* (1988). This novel incited the condemnation of Islamic extremists who perceived the book as BLASPHEMY, and he was sentenced to death by Ayatollah KHOMEINI of Iran. In hiding, he wrote a number of works, including a children's book, *Haroun and the Sea of Stories* (1990) and the novel *The Moor's Last Sigh* (1995). In 1998 the Iranian government revoked the death sentence and Rushdie returned to public life.

Ruskin, John (1819–1900) English writer, artist, and social reformer. A strong religious conviction was the basis for Ruskin's advocacy of Gothic naturalism as the best style through which to praise God. His ideas are outlined forcefully in his books on architecture: *The Seven Lamps of Architecture* (1849) and *The Stones of Venice* (three vols., 1851–53). His five-volume work *Modern Painters* (1834–60) championed the paintings of J.M.W. TURNER, and after 1851 he supported the PRE-RAPHAELITE BROTHERHOOD.

Russell, Bertrand Arthur William, 3rd Earl (1872–1970) Welsh philosopher, mathematician, and social reformer. A fellow at Trinity College, Cambridge, his pupils included Ludwig WITTGENSTEIN. Russell's most influential work, the monumental *Principia Mathematica* (1910–13), written in collaboration with A.N. WHITEHEAD, set out to show how mathematics was grounded in LOGIC. In *Our Knowledge of the External World* (1914), he developed a novel approach to problems in EPISTEMOLOGY. Russell's commitment to pacifism led to his imprisonment in 1918. He supported, however, the anti-fascist aims of World War 2. Russell's *History of Western Philosophy* (1946) was a popular bestseller. In 1950, he received the Nobel Prize in literature. In 1961, Russell was arrested in a demonstration on behalf of the CAMPAIGN FOR NUCLEAR DISARMAMENT (CND).

Russell, George William (1867–1935) Irish poet, essayist, journalist, and painter, who wrote under the pen name A.E. A leading figure of the Irish literary renaissance, he published many collections of romantic and often mystical poetry, among them *The Divine Vision* (1904) and *Midsummer Eve* (1928).

Russell, John, 1st Earl (1792–1878) British statesman, Liberal prime minister (1846–52, 1865–66). Russell

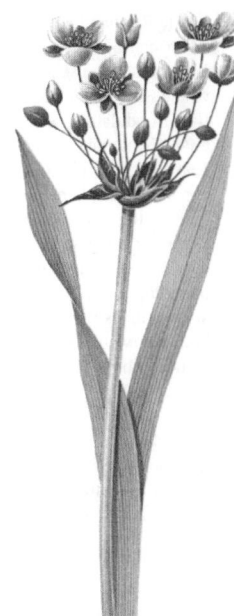

▲ **rush** A decorative aquatic plant, the flowering rush (*Butomus umbellatus*) has an attractive, three-petalled flower that grows above the surface of the water. The long leaves have parallel veins without a central vein or midrib.

▲ **Rushdie** After the publication of *Satanic Verses* (1988), Ayatollah Khomeini of Iran imposed a *fatwa* (death penalty) on Salman Rushdie. The death threats against him (and his publishers and translators) were serious enough to drive him into hiding under police protection and one of his translators was murdered. His subsequent works included the short story collection *East, West* (1994) and the novel *The Ground Beneath Her Feet* (1999).

R

The Russian Federation is the world's largest country. About 25% lies W of the URAL Mountains (Uralskie Gory) in European Russia, where 80% of the population lives. It is mostly flat or undulating, but the land rises to the CAUCASUS Mountains in the S, with Russia's highest peak, ELBRUS (5,633 m [18,481 ft]). SIBERIA contains vast plains and plateaux, with mountains in the E and S. The Kamchatka peninsula in the far E has many active volcanoes. Russia contains several of the world's longest rivers, including the YENISEI-Angara and OB-Irtysh. It also includes part of the world's largest inland body of water, the CASPIAN SEA, and Lake BAIKAL, the world's deepest lake.

CLIMATE

The Moscow climate is continental with cold and snowy winters and warm summers. Krasnoyarsk in s-central Siberia has a harsher, drier climate, but it is not as severe as parts of N Siberia.

HISTORY

The earliest inhabitants of European Russia were Slavic tribes. According to the earliest chronicles a Varangian king, RURIK, established a state in what is now Ukraine in AD 862. Rurik's successor Oleg made KIEV his capital, and the state became known as Kievan Rus. VLADIMIR I adopted Greek Orthodox Christianity as the state religion in 988. Kievan Rus expanded to the N into what is now Russia and grew in power and prestige, but in the second half of the 11th century it began to decline. Novgorod, VLADIMIR and Muscovy broke off and became powerful states in their own right.

In 1237 the Mongol TATARS invaded, and by 1240 they had conquered the Russian kingdoms. They established the GOLDEN HORDE, ruling from Sarai near modern VOLGOGRAD. The Horde exacted tribute but allowed the Russian states considerable independence, appointing ALEXANDER NEVSKI ruler of Kiev.

In the 14th century Muscovy grew in importance as the Grand Duchy of Moscow, which became strong enough to defeat the Golden Horde in 1380 and become an independent state. IVAN III (THE GREAT) greatly extended the power of Moscow, began the construction of the Kremlin, and completed the conquest of the Golden Horde in 1480.

In 1547 IVAN IV (THE TERRIBLE) was crowned Tsar of all Russia. Ivan the Terrible conquered the Tatar khanates of KAZAN (1552) and Astrakhan (1556), gaining control of the River Volga, and began the conquest of Siberia. Following the death of Boris GODUNOV (1605), Russia was subject to foreign incursions and ruled by a series of usurpers. In 1613 Ivan IV's great-nephew Michael founded the ROMANOV dynasty, which ruled Russia until 1917. In the 17th Century Russia rapidly expanded across Siberia, and the first Russian town on the Pacific – Okhotsk – was established in 1649. PETER I (THE GREAT), reigning from 1696 to 1725, fought against Sweden for access to the Baltic and took extensive territories, founding St. Petersburg in 1703. In 1712 he moved the capital there and embarked on a campaign to westernize and modernize Russia. Central governmental institutions emerged and

the Church became subordinate to the monarchy, but the number of serfs increased.

In 1762 CATHERINE II (THE GREAT) became Empress. Under her authoritarian government Russia became the greatest power in continental Europe, acquiring much of Poland, Belarus and Ukraine. ALEXANDER I's territorial gains led him into direct conflict with the imperial ambitions of Napoleon I. Napoleon invaded and captured Moscow in 1812, but the harsh Russian winter devastated his army and he was driven back.

The Decembrist Conspiracy (1825) unsuccessfully tried to prevent the accession of NICHOLAS I. Nicholas' reign was characterized by the battle against liberalization. At the end of his reign, Russia became embroiled in the disastrous CRIMEAN WAR (1853–56). ALEXANDER II undertook much-needed reforms, such as the emancipation of the serfs. ALEXANDER III's rule was more reactionary but continued Russia's industrialization, helped by the construction of the Trans-Siberian Railway. Alexander was succeeded by the last Romanov tsar, NICHOLAS II.

In the 1890s, drought caused famine in rural areas and there was much discontent in the cities. Defeat in the RUSSO-JAPANESE WAR (1904–05) precipitated the

RUSSIAN REVOLUTION OF 1905. Nicholas II was forced to adopt a new constitution and establish an elected Duma (parliament). Democratic reforms were soon reversed, revolutionary groups suppressed, and pogroms encouraged. The Russian Social Democratic Labor Party was secretly founded in 1898, supported primarily by industrial workers. In 1912, the Party split into BOLSHEVIK and MENSHEVIK factions. Russia's support of a Greater Slavic state contributed to the outbreak of World War 1, but Russia was ill-prepared for war and suffered great hardship.

The RUSSIAN REVOLUTION (1917) had two main phases. In March a provisional government was formed and Nicholas II was forced to abdicate; he and his family were executed in July 1918. In July KERENSKY became prime minister, but failed to satisfy the radical hunger of the SOVIETS. In November 1917 the Bolsheviks, led by LENIN, seized power and proclaimed Russia a Soviet Federated Socialist Republic. In 1918 the capital was transferred to Moscow. Under the terms of the Treaty of BREST-LITOVSK (1918) Russia withdrew from World War 1, but was forced to cede much territory to the Central Powers. For the next five years civil war raged between the Whites (monarchists and anti-communists) and Reds, complicated by foreign intervention. The Bolsheviks emerged victorious, but Russia was left devastated. In 1922 Russia united

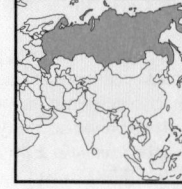

R

AREA 17,075,400sq km
[6,592,812sq mi]
POPULATION 141,378,000
CAPITAL (POPULATION)
Moscow (10,672,000)
GOVERNMENT Federal multiparty republic
ETHNIC GROUPS Russian 82%, Tatar 4%, Ukrainian
3%, Chuvash 1%, more than 100 others
LANGUAGES Russian (official), many others
RELIGIONS Russian Orthodox, Islam Judaism
CURRENCY Russian rouble = 100 kopeks

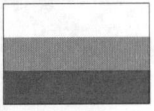

POLITICS

Despite Gorbachev's efforts at reform, his successor Boris Yeltsin inherited an economy in crisis. The abolition of price controls sent the cost of basic commodities rocketing, unemployment rose rapidly, and corruption and crime soared. Despite these difficulties, the government's programme of reforms was supported in a 1993 referendum and Yeltsin returned as president in 1996. Yeltsin resigned in 1999 due to poor health and appointed the prime minister Vladimir PUTIN as the acting president. Putin was elected president by a landslide in 2000.

Fighting began in the secessionist Chechnya during the 1990s and flared up into full-scale war in 1999. The conflict slowed in 2000, but Chechen terrorists began attacks on Russian cities. After the attacks on the United States on 11 September 2001, Putin supported US campaigns against terrorism and Afghanistan's Taliban, although relations soured when Russia opposed the 2003 attack on Iraq. The secessionist conflict in Chechnya had been largely suppressed by 2006, leaving the region devastated. In 2005 and 2006 high oil and gas prices boosted the economy, government funds and Russia's influence. The government has concentrated political power and media control in the president's hands. In 2008 Putin stepped down and Dmitry Medvedev became president.

ECONOMY

In the early 1990s the World Bank described Russia as a 'lower-middle-income' economy. In 1997 Russia was admitted to the Council of Europe; the same year, Russia attended the G7 summit, suggesting that it was now counted among the world's leading economies. Industry is the chief activity and light industries producing consumer goods are becoming important. Russia's resources include oil and natural gas, coal, timber, metal ores and hydroelectric power. Russia is a major agricultural producer. Principal crops include barley, flax, fruit, oats, rye, potatoes, sugar beet, sunflower seeds, vegetables and wheat.

with Ukraine, Belarus and Transcaucasia (Armenia, Azerbaijan and Georgia) to form the Union of Soviet Socialist Republics .

From 1924 Joseph STALIN introduced a socialist economic programme, suppressing all opposition both within the party and among the population. Five-year plans and collective farming transformed the USSR from a largely peasant society to a major world industrial power by the end of the 1930s. Collectivization was violently resisted by many peasants, and millions were killed by famine and mass repression.

The USSR joined WORLD WAR 2, referred to in Russia as the Great Patriotic War, in June 1941. Soviet troops brought about the downfall of Nazi Germany, but at enormous cost. After the war, deteriorating relations with the US led to a state of military tension known as the Cold War.

After Stalin's death Soviet leaders modified some policies but continued to adhere to Communist economics. Poor economic planning and the cost of the Cold War led to economic failure. In the 1980s Mikhail GORBACHEV sought to remedy this by political and economic reforms of *glasnost* (openness) and PERESTROIKA (restructuring). Despite his efforts Soviet power declined, and the Soviet Union broke up in December 1991. Russia maintained contact with 11 of the 15 former Soviet republics through a loose confederation called the COMMONWEALTH OF INDEPENDENT STATES (CIS). For a more detailed history 1922–91, see SOVIET UNION.

R

became a Whig MP in 1813. As paymaster general, he introduced the Great Reform Bill (1832). Russell was one of the founders of the LIBERAL PARTY. Conservative divisions over the repeal of the CORN LAWS helped Russell succeed Sir Robert PEEL as prime minister. His first administration collapsed following the resignation of his foreign secretary, Viscount PALMERSTON. Russell returned as foreign secretary (1852–55) in Aberdeen's coalition, but retired after accusations of incompetent handling of the CRIMEAN WAR. He returned as foreign secretary (1859–65) under Palmerston and became prime minister again on Palmerston's death. The defeat of a new Reform Bill (1866) curtailed his second term. *See also* REFORM ACTS

Russell, Ken (1927–) English film director. Russell's debut feature film was *French Dressing* (1963). His adaptation of *Women in Love* (1969) established his reputation for extravagance and controversy. *The Music Lovers* and *The Devils* (both 1971) reinforced this perception. Other films include *Tommy* (1975), *Altered States* (1980) and *Gothic* (1987).

Russia Federation in E Europe and N Asia. *See* country feature, pages 648–649

Russian Official language of the Russian Federation and several other republics that belonged to the former Soviet Union. It is the primary language of *c.*140 million people, and is a second language for millions more. It is the most

▲ **Ruth** Nicknamed 'the Bambino', Babe Ruth was one of the best baseball players of all time. A talented pitcher, his batting skills led him to achieve a career home-run record that lasted more than 25 years after his death. He spent the bulk of his career with the New York Yankees, and their stadium, built while he was on the team, was known as 'the house that Ruth built'. A physically large person, his colourful personality was even bigger, and he was a major US celebrity of the 1920s and 1930s.

R

important of the Slavic languages, which form a subdivision of the family of INDO-EUROPEAN LANGUAGES. It is written in the CYRILLIC alphabet.

Russian architecture Architectural style that began as a regional variety of BYZANTINE ARCHITECTURE in the 10th century with the Christianization of Russia. Important centres of architecture developed at Kiev, Novgorod, and Pskov. Early churches were built of wood. The Cathedral of Sancta Sophia in Kiev (1018–37) was the first stone construction. The distinctive onion-shaped dome was introduced in the 12th century at the Cathedral of Sancta Sophia, Novgorod. During the 15th century, Russia was subject to western European trends, and Italian architects built the KREMLIN in a Renaissance style. PETER I (THE GREAT) and CATHERINE II (THE GREAT) brought ROCOCO and NEO-CLASSICISM to St Petersburg. In the 19th century, there was a revival of medieval Russian architecture.

Russian art Paintings and sculpture produced in Russia after *c*.AD 1000, as distinct from the earlier SCYTHIAN art. In the Middle Ages, Russian art carried on BYZANTINE ART traditions, and was primarily religious. After the fall of Constantinople (1453), Russia regarded itself as the spiritual heir of Byzantium. Even so, its finest artworks were largely produced by foreigners. This began to change in the latter part of the 19th century, when Ilya Repin and the Wanderers breathed new life into Russian art. This led to an extraordinarily fruitful period in the early 20th century, when Russia was at the heart of new developments in MODERNISM, SUPREMATISM, and CONSTRUCTIVISM.

Russian Five Group of Russian composers, active in St Petersburg during the 1860s and 1870s, who hoped to create a truly Russian style of music. They were Mily BALAKIREV, Alexander BORODIN, César Cui, Modest MUSSORGSKY, and Nikolai RIMSKY-KORSAKOV.

Russian literature Literary works of Russia until 1917, then of the Soviet Union until 1991. Thereafter the literature properly belongs to the individual republics. Russian literature has its origins in religious works dating from *c*.AD 1000. They include biographies of saints, chronicles, hymns and sermons. After the 1600s, Western influences are found. ROMANTICISM beginning in the late 1700s – dominated by Nikolai Karamzin (*Letters of a Russian Traveller*, 1790) and Alexander PUSHKIN (*Boris Godunov*, 1825) – gave way to the realism of Leo TOLSTOY (*War and Peace*, 1869), Fyodor DOSTOEVSKY (*The Brothers Karamazov*, 1879–80), Anton CHEKHOV (*Uncle Vanya*, 1899), and Maxim GORKY (*The Lower Depths*, 1902). The revolutionary mood that dominated the early 20th century witnessed a literary revival. Major figures included the symbolist poet Alexsandr Blok (*The Twelve*, 1918) and the futurists, such as Vladimir Mayakovsky. After the Russian Revolution (1917), many writers fled overseas to escape censorship. The authors who remained could only depict favourable images of the Soviet Union. The major writers of this period were Boris PASTERNAK and Alexei TOLSTOY (*Road to Calvary*, 1941). Criticism of the regime was published, however, in works by novelists Alexander SOLZHENITSYN (*One Day in the Life of Ivan Denisovich*, 1962) and Yuri Trifonov (*Another Life*, 1975) and by Alexander Tvardovsky. *See also* SOCIALIST REALISM

Russian Orthodox Church *See* ORTHODOX CHURCH, EASTERN

Russian Revolution (1917) Events in Russia that resulted in the founding of a republic (March) and in the seizure of power by the BOLSHEVIKS (November). (In the calendar in use at the time, the two stages took place in February and October.) Widespread discontent, a strong revolutionary movement, and the hardships of World War 1 forced Tsar NICHOLAS II to abdicate in March. A provisional government was formed by liberals in the Duma (parliament), which represented the middle classes. Its aim was to make Russia into a liberal democracy and to defeat Germany. Workers and peasants had different desires: greater social and economic equality and an end to the war. The provisional government faced a challenge from the powerful, socialist SOVIET in Petrograd (St Petersburg), which in May formed a coalition government that included Alexander KERENSKY, prime minister from July, and

other socialists. The launching of a new military offensive, combined with disappointing reforms, discredited the government and the parties associated with it. Soviets sprang up in many cities; and in rural areas, peasants seized land, soldiers deserted the front. In the cities, the Bolsheviks secured growing support in the soviets. In November, at the order of LENIN, they carried out a successful coup in Petrograd. The Kerensky government folded, but a long civil war ensued before Lenin and his followers established their authority.

Russian Revolution of 1905 Series of violent strikes and protests against Tsarist rule in Russia. It was provoked mainly by defeat in the RUSSO-JAPANESE WAR (1904–05). It began on Bloody Sunday (January 22), when a peaceful demonstration in St Petersburg was fired on by troops. Strikes and peasant risings spread, culminating in a general strike in October, which forced the Tsar to institute a democratically elected Duma (parliament). By the time it met in 1906, the government had regained control. Severe repression followed.

Russo-Japanese War (1904–05) Conflict arising from the rivalry of Russia and Japan for control of Manchuria and Korea. The war opened with a Japanese attack on Port Arthur (Lüshun), Manchuria. Russian forces suffered a series of defeats on land and at sea, culminating in the Battle of Mukden (February-March 1905) and the annihilation of the Baltic fleet at Tsushima (May). Russia was forced to surrender Korea, the Liaotung Peninsula, and s Sakhalin to Japan.

rust In botany, group of FUNGI that live as PARASITES on many kinds of higher plants. Rusts damage cereal crops and several fruits and vegetables. They have complex life cycles that involve growth on more than one host plant.

rust Corrosion of IRON or its alloys by a combination of air and water. Carbon dioxide from the air dissolves in water to form an acid solution that attacks the iron to form iron (II) oxide. This is then oxidized by oxygen in the air to reddish-brown iron (III) oxide. Rusting may be prevented by GALVANIZING.

Ruth Eighth book of the Old Testament recounting the story of Ruth, a young Moabite widow. It tells of her devotion to Naomi, her Hebrew mother-in-law; her decision to leave her own land and settle in Israelite territory; and her eventual marriage to the wealthy Boaz, whereby she becomes the great-grandmother of Israel's greatest leader, King DAVID.

Ruth, 'Babe' (George Herman) (1895–1948) US baseball player. Ruth held the career home-run record (714) until surpassed (1974) by Hank Aaron. His record of 60 home runs in one season was not beaten until the season was extended from 154 to 162 games. He played for the Boston Red Sox (1914–19), New York Yankees (1920–34), and Boston Braves (1935). He was elected to the Baseball Hall of Fame in 1936.

ruthenium (symbol Ru) Silver-white metallic element, one of the TRANSITION ELEMENTS. It was discovered in 1844 by Russian chemist Karl Klaus (1796–1864). Ruthenium is found in PLATINUM ores. It is used as a catalyst to harden other metals, and its alloys are used in electrical contacts and to colour glass and ceramics. Properties: at.no. 44; r.a.m. 101.07; r.d. 12.41; m.p. 2,310°C (4,190°F); b.p. 3,900°C (7,052°F); most common isotope Ru^{102} (31.61%).

Rutherford, Ernest, Lord (1871–1937) British physicist, b. New Zealand, who pioneered modern NUCLEAR PHYSICS. He discovered and named alpha and beta radiation, named the NUCLEUS, and proposed a theory of the radioactive transformation of ATOMS for which he received the 1908 Nobel Prize in Chemistry. In Cambridge, England, under J.J. THOMSON, he discovered the uranium radiations. At McGill University, Canada, he formed the theory of atomic disintegration with Frederick Soddy (1877–1965). At Manchester, England, he devised (1907) the nuclear theory of the atom and, with Niels BOHR, the idea of orbital electrons. In 1919, at the Cavendish Laboratory, his research team became the first to split an atom's nucleus. He predicted the existence of the NEUTRON, later discovered by James CHADWICK.

rutherfordium (symbol Rf) Synthetic, radioactive, metallic element, first of the transactinide elements. The longest-lived of its ten ISOTOPES has a half-life of 70 seconds (the longest yet identified). It is named after the New Zealand-born British physicist Ernest RUTHERFORD. Properies: at.no. 104. It was first given the temporary name of unnilquadium until 1997.

rutile (titanium dioxide, TiO_2) Black to red-brown oxide mineral, found in igneous and metamorphic rocks and quartz veins. It occurs as long, prismatic crystals in the tetragonal system and as granular masses. It has a metallic lustre, is brittle and is used as a gemstone. Hardness 6–6.5; r.d. 4.2.

Ruwenzori Mountain range in central Africa on the Uganda-Zaïre border, between lakes Albert and Edward. The highest peak is Mount Margherita, 5,109m (16,763ft). Length of range: 121km (75mi).

Ruyter, Michiel de (1607–76) Dutch seaman, one of his country's greatest naval commanders. During the First Anglo-DUTCH WAR (1652–54) he reached the rank of vice admiral. In the Second Anglo-Dutch War (1665–67), he commanded the fleet that defeated the English off Dunkirk (1666). In 1667, he sailed up the Medway, destroying much of the English fleet. He was again victorious in the Third Anglo-Dutch War (1672–74), inflicting severe losses on an Anglo-French force.

Rwanda Republic in E central Africa. *See* country feature

Ryder Cup Biennial competition in which a team of professional male golfers from the USA plays a team from Europe. The event consists of eight 18–hole foursomes, eight 18–hole four-balls, and sixteen 18–hole singles.

rye Hardy, cereal grass originating in SW Asia and naturalized throughout the world. It grows in poor soils and colder climates than most other cereals can stand. It has flower spikelets that develop one-seeded grains. It is used for flour, as a forage crop and for making alcoholic drinks. Height: to 0.9m (3ft). Family Poaceae/Gramineae; species *Secale cereale*.

Ryle, Sir Martin (1918–84) English physicist and radio astronomer. After studying radar during World War 2, he pioneered RADIO ASTRONOMY at Cambridge University. He also catalogued radio sources, leading to his discovery of QUASARS.

Ryukyu Islands Japanese archipelago in the W Pacific Ocean, extending *c.*970km (600mi) between Kyushu and Taiwan; it separates the East China Sea (W) from the Philippine Sea (E). Inhabited since early times, China invaded the islands in the 14th century. Occupied by Japan in the 17th century, China relinquished them to Japan in 1879. After World War 2, they were administered by the USA, and restored to Japan in 1972. The group includes OKINAWA, Amami, and Sakishima. Agriculture and fishing are the main occupations. Area: *c.*2,200sq km (850sq mi). Pop. (2000) 1,318,281.

RWANDA

The Republic of Rwanda is Africa's most densely populated country. It is a small state in the heart of Africa. The W border is formed by Lake Kivu and the River Ruzizi. Rwanda has a rugged landscape, dominated by high, volcanic mountains, rising to Mount Karisimbi, at 4,507m [14,787ft]. The capital, KIGALI, stands on the central plateau. E Burundi consists of stepped plateaux, which descend to the lakes and marshland of the Kagera National Park on the Tanzania border.

The lush rainforests in the W are one of the last refuges for the mountain gorilla. Many of Rwanda's forests have been cleared and 35% of the land is now arable. The steep mountain slopes are intensively cultivated. Despite contour ploughing, heavy rains cause severe soil erosion.

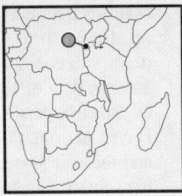

CLIMATE

Temperatures in Kigali are moderated by the altitude. Rainfall is abundant, but much heavier rain falls on the W mountains. The dry season is June–August. The floor of the Great Rift Valley is warmer and drier than the rest of the country.

HISTORY

The Twa, a pygmy people, were the first known people to live in Rwanda. About 1,000 years ago the Hutu, a farming people, settled in the area and gradually displaced the Twa. From the 15th century the Tutsi, a cattle-herding people, migrated from the north and began to dominate the Hutu. By the late 18th century Rwanda and Burundi formed a single Tutsi-dominated state, ruled by a King (*Mwami*).

In 1890 Germany conquered the area and subsumed it into German East Africa. Belgian forces occupied both Rwanda and Burundi during World War 1 in 1916. In 1919 the region became part of the Belgian League of Nations mandate territory of Ruanda-Urundi, which in 1946 became a UN Trust Territory. The Hutu majority intensified their demands for political representation. In 1959, the Tutsi Mwami died. The ensuing civil war between Hutus and Tutsis claimed more than 150,000 lives. Hutu victory led to a mass exodus of

Tutsis. The Hutu Emancipation Movement, led by Grégoire Kayibanda, won the 1960 elections. In 1961 Rwanda declared itself a republic. Belgium granted independence in 1962, and Kayibanda became president.

POLITICS

Rwanda was subject to continual Tutsi incursions from Burundi and Uganda. In 1973, Major General Habyarimana overthrew Kayibanda in a military coup. In 1978, Habyarimana became president. Drought and ethnic conflict devastated Rwanda in the 1980s, and large numbers were forced into exile as refugees. In 1990 the Tutsi-dominated Rwandan Patriotic Front (RPF) invaded Rwanda, forcing Habyarimana to adopt a multiparty constitution. In April 1994, Habyarimana and the president of Burundi died in a rocket attack. The Hutu army and militia launched an act of genocide against the Tutsi minority, massacring more than 800,000 Tutsis.

In July 1994, an RPF offensive toppled the government, creating 2 million Hutu refugees. A government of national unity, comprising Tutsis and Hutus, emerged. More than 50,000 people died in refugee camps in eastern Zaïre (now DR Congo). The flood of refugees into

AREA 26,338sq km [10,169sq mi]
POPULATION 9,908,000
CAPITAL (POPULATION) Kigali (234,000)
GOVERNMENT Republic
ETHNIC GROUPS Hutu 84%, Tutsi 15%, Twa 1%
LANGUAGES French, English and Kinyarwanda (all official)
RELIGIONS Roman Catholic 57%, Protestant 26%, Adventist 11%, Islam 5%
CURRENCY Rwandan franc = 100 centimes

neighbouring countries destabilized the region. In 1997, Rwandan troops supported Laurent Kabila's successful overthrow of President Mobutu in Zaïre. Kabila failed to expel the Hutu militia from Congo, and Rwanda switched to supporting rebel forces. In 1998, the UN International Criminal Tribunal sentenced Rwanda's former prime minister Jean Kambanda to life imprisonment for genocide. Paul Kagame, an RPF leader, became president in 2000. His government brought stability but suppressed opposition. He was re-elected in biased 2003 elections.

In the early 21st century, prosecutions began in both Belgium and Tanzania of people accused of genocide. Rwanda finally withdrew from DR Congo in late 2002 after signing a peace deal with Kinshasa.

ECONOMY

According to the World Bank, Rwanda is a 'low-income' developing country. Agriculture employs 90% of the workforce, but many farmers live at subsistence level. Chief food crops include bananas, beans, cassava, plantains, potatoes, sorghum and sweet potatoes. Some farmers raise cattle and other livestock. The chief cash crop is coffee, also the leading export, followed by tea and hides and skins. Rwanda also produces pyrethrum, which is used to make insecticide. The country produces some cassiterite (tin ore) and wolframite (tungsten ore). Manufacturing is small-scale and includes beverages, cement and sugar.

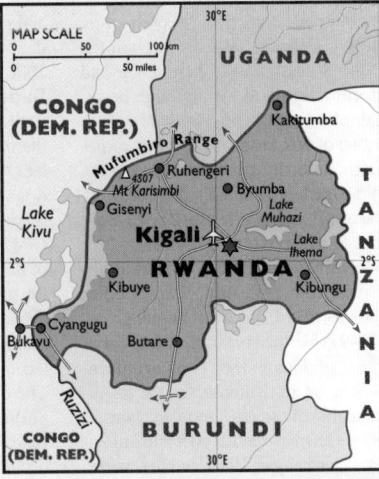

S/s, 19th letter of the Roman alphabet. It is descended from the Semitic letter sin *or* shin, *meaning tooth. It passed into the Greek alphabet primarily as the Greek letter* sigma.

▲ **Saddam Hussein** Despite a costly war with neighbouring Iran (1980–88), a crushing defeat by an Allied force following his invasion of Kuwait (1990), and an oil embargo which crippled Iraq's economy, Saddam Hussein managed to retain power until 2003. He was deposed when a coalition led by the United States invaded Iraq. In December 2003, Hussein was captured by US forces near his hometown of Tikrit.

▲ **sabre-toothed tiger** A fierce, carnivorous mammal, the sabre-toothed tiger (*Smilodon* sp.) lived in North and South America during the Pleistocene period. It possessed two long fangs and a wide-opening jaw structure that enabled it to kill its prey by stabbing and slashing at its throat. *Smilodon* was more powerfully built than a modern tiger, but is not thought to have been a fast runner, and probably ambushed its prey at waterholes.

Saarinen, Eero (1910–61) US architect and designer, b. Finland. His work provides a link between EXPRESSIONISM and the INTERNATIONAL STYLE. One of his most exciting buildings was the TWA terminal at New York's Kennedy Airport (1956–62). Other notable designs include the General Motors Technical Center in Warren, Michigan (1948–56), and the US Embassy, London (1955–61).

Saarland State in SW Germany on the borders with France (S) and Luxembourg (W); the capital is Saarbrücken. Belonging intermittently to France, the Saar was finally ceded to Prussia after the defeat of Napoleon I in 1815. France administered the region after World War 1 but in a 1935 plebiscite 90% of the people voted for German administration. French forces again occupied the Saar after World War 2. Saarland finally gained the status of a West German state in 1967. The valley of the River Saar includes many blast furnaces and steel works, which exploit local coal and nearby iron ore. There is little agriculture, and some market gardening. Area: 2,570sq km (992sq mi). Pop. (1999) 1,071,501.

Sabah (North Borneo) State of Malaysia and one of the four political subdivisions of the island of Borneo. The capital is Kota Kinabalu (2000 pop. 354,153). Ceded to the British in 1877, it remained the British Protectorate of North Borneo until 1963, when it became an independent state of the Malaysian Federation. The terrain is mountainous and forested. The main products include oil, timber, rubber, coconuts and rice. Area: 76,522sq km (29,545sq mi). Pop. (2000) 2,449,389.

Sabah, Sheikh Jabir al Ahmad al- (1926–2006) Emir of Kuwait (1977–2006). A member of the al-Sabah dynasty founded by Sheikh Sabah al-Awal (r.1756–72), he succeeded Sabah III al Salim as Jabir III. When Iraq invaded Kuwait (1990), Jabir took refuge in Saudia Arabia and set up a government in exile. He returned to Kuwait in 1991.

Sabbatarianism Religious doctrine of certain Protestants that Sunday, the Christian SABBATH, should be observed as a day of rest. Sabbatarianism began in Britain during the Puritan interregnum (1649–60). After the Sunday Entertainments Act of 1932, which empowered local authorities to license Sunday entertainment, Sabbatarianism lost much of its force in England, but remained strong in parts of Scotland and Wales.

Sabbath Seventh day of the week, set aside as a sacred day of rest. For Jews, the Sabbath runs from sunset on Friday to sunset on Saturday. Christians set aside Sunday for their Sabbath.

Sabin, Albert Bruce (1906–93) US virologist, b. Russia. In 1957, Sabin developed a live-VIRUS oral vaccine against POLIOMYELITIS (polio). It replaced Jonas SALK's inactivated virus VACCINE.

Sabines Ancient people of central Italy. They inhabited the Sabine Hills NE of Rome, and part of the early Roman population was Sabine in origin. After sporadic fighting, the Sabines were conquered in 290 BC and gradually Romanized.

sable MARTEN native to Siberia. It has been hunted almost to extinction for its thick, soft, durable fur, which is dark brown, sometimes flecked with white. Length: to 60cm (24in). Family Mustelidae; species *Martes zibellina*.

sabre-toothed tiger Popular name for a prehistoric member of the CAT family (Felidae) that existed from the OLIGOCENE period to the PLEISTOCENE period. It had extremely long canine teeth adapted to killing large herbivores. Subfamily Machairodontinae, genus *Smilodon*.

saccharide Organic COMPOUND based on SUGAR molecules. Monosaccharides include GLUCOSE and FRUCTOSE. Two sugar molecules join together to make a disaccharide, such as LACTOSE or SUCROSE. POLYSACCHARIDES have more than two sugar molecules. *See also* CARBOHYDRATE

saccharin ($C_7H_5NO_3S$) Synthetic substance used as a substitute for SUGAR. It derives from TOLUENE. Some studies have linked it with various forms of cancer in humans.

Sachs, Julius von (1832–97) German botanist. A founder of plant physiology, his *Textbook of Botany* (1868) was an influential synthesis of botanical data. Sachs demonstrated the importance of transpiration and the role of CHLOROPHYLL in plants.

Sachs, Nelly (1891–1970) German-Jewish poet and dramatist. She escaped from Nazi Germany in 1940, and her works, such as *In the Houses of Death* (1947) and *Later Poems*

(1965), bear witness to the suffering of European Jewry. Her best-known play is *Eli: A Mystery Play of the Sufferings of Israel* (1951). She shared the 1966 Nobel Prize in literature.

Sackville-West, Vita (Victoria Mary) (1892–1962) English poet and novelist. A friend of the writer Virginia WOOLF and a member of the BLOOMSBURY GROUP, her best-known works include *The Edwardians* (1930), *All Passion Spent* (1931) and the long poem 'The Land' (1926).

sacrament Symbolic action in which the central mysteries of a religious faith are enacted and which, on some accounts, confers divine grace upon those to whom it is given or administered. For Protestants, there are two sacraments: BAPTISM and the Lord's Supper (*see* LAST SUPPER). In the ROMAN CATHOLIC and EASTERN ORTHODOX CHURCHES, the sacraments are baptism, CONFIRMATION, the EUCHARIST, holy ORDERS, matrimony, PENANCE and the anointing of the sick.

Sacramento State capital and inland port of central California, USA, on the Sacramento River (which, at 560km/370mi, is the state's longest). It was the focal point of the 1848 gold rush, becoming the state capital in 1854. A 69km (43mi) long channel links it to an arm of San Francisco Bay. The city benefits from a large US Army depot and the McClellan Air Base. Industries: missile development, transport equipment, food processing, bricks. Pop. (2000) 1,393,000.

Sadat, (Muhammad) Anwar (al-) (1918–81) Egyptian statesman, president (1970–81). He was vice president (1964–66, 1969–70) to Gamal Abdel NASSER, and upon Nasser's death succeeded him as president. After the costly ARAB-ISRAELI WAR of 1973, he sought peace with ISRAEL and visited Israel in person in 1977. Sadat signed the historic CAMP DAVID ACCORD (1978) with Israeli leader Meanchem BEGIN, and the pair shared the 1978 Nobel Peace Prize. Under the terms of the agreement, the Sinai Peninsula returned to Egypt. Sadat's actions led to Egypt's temporary expulsion from the Arab League and he was assassinated by Islamic fundamentalists. Sadat was succeeded as president by Hosni MUBARAK.

Saddam Hussein (1937–2006) Iraqi statesman, president of IRAQ (1979–2003). In 1959, he was forced into exile for his part in an attempt to assassinate the Iraqi prime minister. In 1963 Saddam returned home, and he was imprisoned in 1964. After his release, he played a prominent role in the 1968 coup led by the BA'ATH PARTY. A Revolutionary Command Council (RCC) replaced the civilian government. In 1979, Saddam became chairman of the RCC. His invasion of Iran marked the beginning of the IRAN-IRAQ WAR (1980–88). At home, Saddam ruthlessly suppressed all internal opposition. His 1990 invasion of Kuwait provoked worldwide condemnation. In the GULF WAR (1991) a multinational force expelled the Iraqi forces from Kuwait. Further uprisings by KURDS and Iraqi SHI'ITES were ruthlessly suppressed and Saddam survived punitive economic sanctions. In April 2003, Saddam was deposed by US and British troops and disappeared into hiding. In December 2003 he was captured by US forces and placed under arrest. His trial for crimes against humanity (2004–6) by the Iraqi Interim Government frequently descended into farce and debates over the legitimacy of the court's authority. Saddam was found guilty and executed by hanging at the end of 2006, many of his crimes remaining untried.

Sadducees Jewish sect active in Judaea from *c.*200 BC until the fall of Jerusalem in AD 70. By the time of Jesus, the main difference between the Sadducees and the PHARISEES was the former's refusal to recognize the oral traditions surrounding the Scriptures as part of Hebrew Law.

Sade, Donatien Alphonse François, Marquis de (1740–1814) French novelist and playwright. De Sade is one of the founders of the modern French prose style. Imprisoned for sexual offences, he wrote many novels renowned for their licentiousness, among them *Justine* (1791) and *Juliette* (1797).

Safavid Iranian dynasty (1501–1722) that established the territorial and SHI'ITE theocratic principles of modern Iran. The dynastic founder, Shah ISMAIL, claimed descent from a Shi'ite SUFISM order, and the state adopted Shi'ism as the state religion. His successor, ABBAS I, accepted the Ottoman occupation of W Iran, and concentrated on subduing the threat to Iran's E borders. He captured Hormuz, Karbala, and

S

Najaf. His death created a power vacuum and Iran's borders contracted. Shah Husayn's fixation on the capture of Bahrain enabled Afghan troops to overrun the country. His forced abdication in 1722 marked the end of Safavid rule.

safety glass Form of GLASS that is less hazardous than ordinary glass when broken. One form of safety glass consists of two sheets of plate glass bonded to a thinner, central sheet of transparent plastic. If an impact breaks the glass, the plastic holds the fragments in place. **Bullet-proof** glass consists of several layers of glass and plastic.

safety lamp See DAVY, SIR HUMPHRY

safflower Annual plant with large red, orange or white flower heads that are used in making dyestuffs. The seeds yield oil, which is used in cooking and in the manufacture of MARGARINE. Family Asteraceae/Compositae; species *Carthamus tinctorius*.

saffron (autumn CROCUS) Perennial crocus, native to Asia Minor and cultivated in Europe. It has purple or white flowers. The golden, dried stigmas of the plant are used as a flavouring or dye. Family Iridaceae; species *Crocus sativus*.

saga In old NORSE LITERATURE (especially Icelandic), prose narrative that relates the lives of historical figures. The sagas were written between the 7th and 14th centuries. Notable examples include the *Gísla saga*, the *Njáls saga*, and the *Heimskringla* by SNORRI STURLUSON (1179–1241).

sage Common name for a number of plants of the MINT family (Lamiaceae/Labiatae) native to the Mediterranean region. The best-known is *Salvia officinalis*, an aromatic perennial herb used widely for seasoning. Height: 15–38cm (6–15in).

sagebrush Aromatic shrub common in arid areas of W North America. The common sagebrush has small, silvery-green leaves and bears clusters of tiny white flower heads. Height: to 2m (6.5ft). Family Asteraceae/Compositae; species *Artemisia tridentata*.

Sagittarius (archer) Southern constellation between Scorpio and Capricorn. Rich in stellar CLUSTERS, this region of the sky also contains much interstellar matter. The brightest star is Epsilon Sagittarii (*Kaus Australis*), magnitude 1.8.

sago palm (fern palm) Feather-leaved PALM tree native to swampy areas of Malaysia and Polynesia. Its thick trunk contains sago, a starch used in foodstuffs. It grows for 15 years, flowers once, then dies when the fruit ripens. Height: 1.2–9.1m (4–30ft). Family Arecaceae/Palmae; species *Metroxylon sagu*.

saguaro Large CACTUS native to Arizona, California, and Mexico. White, night-blooming flowers appear when the plant is 50 to 75 years old. Its red fruit is edible. Height: to 12m (40ft). Family Cactaceae; species *Carnegiea gigantea*.

Sahara World's largest DESERT, with an area of *c*.9,065,000sq km (3,500,000sq mi), covering nearly a third of Africa's total land area. It consists of Algeria, Niger, Libya, Egypt, and Mauritania, the S parts of Morocco and Tunisia, and the N parts of Senegal, Mali, Chad, and Sudan. It extends *c*.4,800km (3,000mi) W to E from the Atlantic Ocean to the Red Sea, and *c*.1,900km (1,200mi) N to S from the ATLAS Mountains to the SAHEL. The annual rainfall is usually less than 10cm (4in) and there is very little natural vegetation. Two-thirds of the Sahara is stony, and the topography ranges from the Tibesti Massif (N Chad) at 3,350m (11,000ft) to the Qattara Depression (Egypt) at 133m (436ft) below sea level. The numerous natural and man-made oases act as vital centres for water, crop farming and transport, and the Sahara's two million inhabitants are concentrated around them. The main ethnic groups are the Tuareg and the Tibu. Nomads continue to herd sheep and goats. Transportation is still primarily by camel and horse. Mineral deposits include salt, iron ore, phosphates, oil, and gas.

Sahel Band of semi-arid scrub and savanna grassland in Africa, S of the SAHARA. It extends through Senegal, S Mauritania, Mali, Burkina Faso, N Benin, S Niger, N Nigeria and S central Chad. Over the past 30 years, the Sahara has encroached on the N Sahel, causing severe DESERTIFICATION.

Saigon See HO CHI MINH CITY

sailing See YACHT

saint In the Roman Catholic and Eastern Orthodox Churches, individual saints are regarded as having a special relationship with God and are therefore venerated for their perceived role as intercessors. The Protestant reformers of the 16th century abolished the veneration of saints, saying that all believers have access to God through Christ. *See also* CANONIZATION

St Albans Historic cathedral city on the River Ver, Hertfordshire, England. The modern city is built amongst the ruins of the Roman city of Verulamium. St Albans developed around the abbey, built in 793 by King Offa to honour the martyrdom of St Alban in AD 304. The cathedral dates mostly from the 11th century. Industries: printing, clothing, tourism. Pop (2001) 128,982.

St Andrews Royal burgh and university town in Fife, on the NE coast of Scotland. It was the ecclesiastical capital of Scotland until the Reformation. The rules of golf were devised at the Royal and Ancient Golf Club. Pop. (2000 est.) 14,500.

Saint Bartholomew's Day Massacre (August 24, 1572) Mass murder of HUGUENOTS (French Protestants) on St Bartholomew's feast day. The Huguenot leaders gathered in Paris for the marriage of Henry of Navarre (later HENRY IV). On orders from CATHERINE DE' MÉDICI, a bungled attempt was made on the life of Gaspard de Coligny. The plot's failure led to a plan for a more widespread slaughter. With the support of the king, CHARLES IX, soldiers killed Coligny and other Huguenot leaders. The massacre spread and continued in the provinces until October 3. Modern estimates suggest that *c*.70,000 died.

St Bernard Swiss mountain and rescue dog with excellent scenting abilities; from the 17th century it has been used to find people lost in deep snow. It has a massive head with a short deep muzzle, and a dense white and red coat. Height: to 74cm (29in) at the shoulder; weight: to 77kg (170lb).

St Elmo's fire (corposant) Electrical discharge illuminating the tops of projecting objects or around aircraft. It usually occurs during a storm when the strongly charged atmosphere creates a bluish discharge between the air and an object.

Saint-Exupéry, Antoine de (1900–44) French novelist and aviator. His experiences as a pilot provided the material for his novels, which include *Southern Mail* (1928), *Night Flight* (1931), and *Flight to Arras* (1942). He is best known for his classic fable *The Little Prince* (1943). He died in an airplane crash during World War 2.

St George's Capital and port on the SW coast of GRENADA, West Indies. Founded in 1650 as a French settlement, it was capital (1885–1958) of the British WINDWARD ISLANDS. The town is built round a submerged volcanic crater that forms the horseshoe-shaped St George's Bay. Industries: rum distilling, sugar processing, tourism. Pop. (2002 est.) 4400.

St Germain, Treaty of (1919) Part of the peace settlement after World War 1. It established the new republic of Austria from the old AUSTRO-HUNGARIAN EMPIRE.

St Helena Rocky island in the S Atlantic, 1,920km (1,190mi) from the coast of W Africa; the capital is Jamestown.

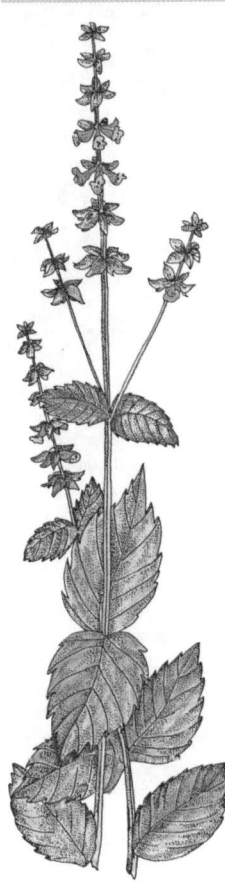

▲ **sage** Many culinary herbs, such as sage (*Salvia* sp.), are members of the Labiatae family. The medicinal uses for sage have been known for thousands of years. The word 'sage' (meaning wise) derives from the ancient belief that the herb enhanced people's memories.

◀ **sago palm** Flourishing in SE Asian freshwater swamps, the sago palm (*Metroxylon sagu*) is a primary source of carbohydrate in tropical regions. Just before flowering, the palm is cut, and the pith of the trunk is ground down to make sago flour.

The drum of St Paul's is an extremely complex structure. The huge outer dome was skilfully constructed above an inner, lower dome. Between the two, Wren placed a tall cone of bricks, reinforced by two iron chains; on this cone rests the lightweight timber dome covered in lead sheeting, which in turn carries the heavy stone lantern, globe and cross. Light falls on to the crossing through eight triple openings in the dome.

Thirty-two buttresses surround the drum, finishing in columns to create a classical effect.

The two Baroque towers, flanking the west front and framing the dome, are more than 60m (200ft) high. They were added in 1708.

The portico has a two-storey design of coupled Corinthian columns, echoing the theme of coupled pilasters, which is repeated around the exterior of the building.

▲ **St Paul's** The Gothic cathedral of old St Paul's (the portico of which was added by Inigo Jones) had to be pulled down following the Great Fire of London in 1666. The cathedral we see today was rebuilt (1675–1710) by Sir Christopher Wren. The plan is a Latin cross, 140m (460ft) long by 30m (100ft) wide. At the crossing, eight piers carry the dome, one of London's most famous landmarks. The wooden model for Wren's earlier design has been preserved.

Discovered by the Portuguese in 1502, it was captured by the Dutch in 1633. It passed to the British East India Company in 1659, and became a British crown colony in 1834. It is chiefly known as the place of NAPOLEON I's final exile. It is now a UK dependent territory and administrative centre for ASCENSION and TRISTAN DA CUNHA. It services ships and exports fish and handicrafts. Area: 122sq km (47sq mi). Pop. (2000) 5,000.

St Helens, Mount Volcanic peak in the Cascade Range, SW Washington state. Dormant since 1857, it erupted on May 18, 1980, killing 60 people. The 2,950m (9,578ft) summit was reduced to 2,560m (8,312ft) with a deep horseshoe crater. Two more eruptions occurred in the following two weeks, and it is predicted to erupt again in the early 21st century.

St John of Jerusalem, Knights Hospitallers of See KNIGHTS HOSPITALLERS

St John's Port and capital of Antigua, in the Leeward Islands, West Indies. During the 18th century, St John's was the headquarters of the Royal Navy in the West Indies. Industries: tourism, rum, sugar, cotton. Pop. (2002 est.) 23,400.

St John's Provincial capital and major port of Newfoundland, Canada, on the SE coast of Newfoundland Island. Founded in 1583, St John's is one of the oldest settlements in North America. Industries: fishing and fish processing, iron, shipbuilding, textiles, paper. Pop. (2001) 172,918.

St Kitts and Nevis Self-governing state in the Leeward Islands, West Indies. It includes the islands of St Kitts (St Christopher), Nevis, and Sombrero. Basseterre (on St Kitts) is the capital (2002 est. pop. 11,600). Christopher COLUMBUS discovered the islands in 1493. The English settled in 1623 and the French in 1624. The Treaty of Paris (1783) settled Anglo-French disputes over possession, and the islands gained self-government in 1967. Nevis held a referendum on independence in May 1998. Industries: tourism, sugar, cotton, salt, coconuts. Area: 261sq km (101sq mi). Pop. (2000) 39,000. See WEST INDIES map

Saint Laurent, Yves (1936–2008) French fashion designer, b. Algeria. He began by designing clothes for individual customers, but from 1962 established himself as a pioneer of ready-to-wear dresses, mass-produced in standard sizes.

St Lawrence Second-longest river in Canada, flowing from the NE end of Lake Ontario to the Gulf of St Lawrence, Québec. The river forms the boundary between the USA and Canada for c.180km (110mi) of its total length of 1,200km (750mi). Since the completion of the ST LAWRENCE SEAWAY in 1959, the river has been navigable to all but the very largest vessels. The St Lawrence system of canals, locks and dams generates much of the hydroelectric power used in Ontario and New York.

St Lawrence Seaway Waterway in Canada and the USA. Built in the 1950s, it connects the GREAT LAKES with the Atlantic Ocean. The St Lawrence Seaway extends about 750km (470mi) from N of Montréal down to the N shore of Lake Erie. The main part of the waterway consists of a series of canals and locks that bypass the rapids along the St Lawrence River. The waterway also includes the Welland Canal, which by-passes the Niagara Falls. The St Lawrence Seaway allows ocean-going vessels to reach industrial lakeside ports of central North America, such as Detroit, Chicago and Toronto.

St Louis US city and port in E Missouri, on the Mississippi River near its confluence with the Missouri. The second-largest city in Missouri, St Louis was founded (1763) by the French. It was held by Spain from 1770 to 1800, returned briefly to France, and then ceded to the USA in the LOUISIANA PURCHASE (1803). St Louis grew rapidly into one of the largest US river ports. Industries: mineral processing, brewing, chemicals, transport equipment. Pop. (2000) 2,078,000.

St Lucia Volcanic island in the Windward group, West Indies; the capital is Castries (2002 pop. 60,200). The island changed hands 14 times between France and Britain before being ceded to Britain in 1814. It finally achieved full self-government in 1979. Mountainous, lush and forested, its tourist income is growing rapidly, especially from cruise ships. The principal export crop is bananas. Area: 539sq km (208sq mi). Pop. (2000) 162,000. See WEST INDIES map

St Mark's BASILICA in Venice. Begun in 829, to enshrine the remains of the city's patron saint, St Mark, it was restored after a fire in 976. It was later demolished and rebuilt in the 11th century in the BYZANTINE style.

St Paul US state capital and port of entry, on the E bank of the MISSISSIPPI River, E MINNESOTA. In 1849, St Paul was made capital of Minnesota territory. When Minnesota was admitted to the Union in 1858, it became the state capital, developing rapidly as a river port and transportation centre. Today, it is a major manufacturing and distribution centre. Industries: computers, electronics, printing, automobiles. Pop. (2000) 287,151.

St Paul's Anglican cathedral in London, built (1675–1710) on the site of a medieval cathedral that had been destroyed in the Great FIRE OF LONDON in 1666. It was designed by Sir Christopher WREN in the classical style.

St Peter's Great Christian BASILICA in the VATICAN CITY. In 1506, Pope Julius II laid the foundation stone on the site of an earlier structure over the grave of St Peter. The church was completed in 1615, during the reign of Pope Paul V, under the architectural supervision of Carlo Maderno (1556–1629).

St Petersburg (formerly Petrograd and Leningrad) Second-largest city in RUSSIA and a major seaport at the E of the Gulf of Finland, on the delta of the River Neva. Founded in 1703 by PETER I (THE GREAT), the city was the capital of Russia from 1712 to 1918. It was the scene of the Decembrist revolt (1825), and the Bloody Sunday incident in the RUSSIAN REVOLUTION OF 1905. Renamed Petrograd in 1914, it was a centre of the political unrest that culminated in the RUSSIAN REVOLUTION. The city was renamed Leningrad in 1924. Damaged during World War 2, it has since been rebuilt. Renamed St Petersburg (1991), following the break-up of the Soviet Union, it has federal status within the Russian Republic. Industries: shipbuilding, engineering, electronics, chemicals. Pop. (2005) 5,315,000.

St Pierre and Miquelon Group of eight small islands in the Gulf of St Lawrence, SW of Newfoundland, Canada. The capital is St Pierre (1999 pop. 5618) on the island of the same name; Miquelon is the largest island. The group was claimed for France in 1535, and since 1985 has been a 'territorial collectivity', sending delegates to the French parliament. Fishing is the most important activity, and has led to disputes with Canada. Area: 242sq km (93sq mi). Pop. (1999) 6,316.

INTERNET

St Kitts and Nevis
► www.stkittsnevis.net

St Lucia
► www.stlucia.gov.lc
► www.stlucia.org

Saint-Saëns, Charles Camille
► www.classical.net

S

Saint-Saëns, Charles Camille (1835–1921) French composer, pianist, and organist. His conservative musical style is best represented by his third symphony (1886) and his sonatas. He also wrote descriptive works, such as *Danse Macabre* (1874) and *Carnival of the Animals* (1886). His operas include *Samson and Delilah* (1877).

St Sophia *See* HAGIA SOPHIA

St Valentine's Day Massacre (February 14, 1929) Gangland killings in Chicago, Illinois. The perpetrators, disguised as policemen, were gunmen of Al CAPONE and the seven victims were members of a rival gang in the profitable bootlegging business during the PROHIBITION era.

St Vincent and the Grenadines Island state of the Windward Islands, West Indies, situated between St Lucia and Grenada. The capital is Kingstown (2002 pop. 17,400). It comprises the volcanic island of St Vincent and five islands of the Grenadine group, the best known of which is Mustique. St Vincent remained uncolonized until British settlement in 1762. After wresting control from the French in 1783, the British deported most of the native Carib population, who were replaced by African slave labour. St Vincent was part of the British Windward Islands colony (1880–1958) and of the West Indies Federation (1958–62). It gained self-government in 1969, followed by full independence within the Commonwealth in 1979. Agriculture dominates the economy; major crops include arrowroot, bananas, and coconuts. Area: 388sq km (150sq mi). Pop. (2000) 117,000. *See* WEST INDIES map

Sakhalin (Jap. Karafuto) Island off the E coast of Russia, between the Sea of Okhotsk and the Sea of Japan. The capital is Yuzhno-Sakhalinsk (1994 pop. 162,000). Settled by Russians and Japanese in the 18th and 19th centuries, it came under Russian control in 1875. Japan regained the s in 1905, but was forced to cede it again in 1945. The island is mountainous and forested, with a harsh climate. Grains and potatoes grow in the s. Sakhalin's chief importance lies in its deposits of coal and iron ore; oil, extracted in the NE, is piped to the Russian mainland. Other industries: timber, fishing, canning. Area: 76,400sq km (29,500sq mi). Pop. (2000) 598,000.

Sakharov, Andrei Dimitrievich (1921–89) Soviet physicist and social critic. His work in nuclear FUSION was instrumental in the development of the Soviet HYDROGEN BOMB. An outspoken defender of civil liberties, he created the Human Rights Committee in 1970, and received the 1975 Nobel Peace Prize.

Saladin (1138–93) (Salah ad-din) Muslim general and founder of the Ayyubid dynasty. From 1152, he was a soldier and administrator in Egypt. Appointed grand vizier in 1169, he overthrew the FATIMIDS in 1171, and made himself Sultan of Egypt. After conquering most of Syria, he gathered widespread support for a JIHAD to drive the Christians from Palestine (1187). He reconquered Jerusalem, provoking the Third CRUSADE (1189). Saladin's rule restored Egypt as a major power and introduced a period of stability and growth.

Salam, Abdus (1926–96) Pakistani physicist who proposed (1967) a theory that unifies the electromagnetic and weak nuclear forces (*see* FUNDAMENTAL FORCES) within the NUCLEUS of an ATOM. Salam and Steven WEINBERG worked independently on the theory (now known as the **Weinberg-Salam** theory). After it was proved experimentally, the pair shared the 1979 Nobel Prize in physics with Sheldon Glashow.

Salamanca City on the River Tormes, W Spain, capital of Salamanca province. It was the site of a major British victory over the French in the Peninsular War (1812). Industries: pharmaceuticals, chemicals, tanning, brewing. Pop. (2001) 158,523.

salamander Any of 320 species of amphibians found worldwide, except in Australia and polar regions. It has an elongated body, a long tail and short legs. Most species lay eggs, but some give birth to live young. The largest European species, the fire salamander (*Salamandra salamandra*), may attain a length of 28cm (11in). Order Urodela.

Salazar, António de Oliveira (1889–1970) Dictator of Portugal (1932–68). In 1932 he became prime minister and assumed dictatorial powers. Imposing a fascist constitution (1933), Salazar held power through the army and secret police, enforcing order at the cost of economic progress. He was sym-

pathetic to FRANCO in Spain, remained neutral in World War 2, and subsequently sought good relations with the West.

Salem State capital of Oregon, USA, on the Willamette River. Founded in 1840 by Methodist missionaries, Salem was made territorial capital in 1851 and state capital in 1859. Industries: timber, paper, textiles, food canning, meat packing, high-technology equipment. Pop. (2000) 136,924.

Salem City on Massachusetts Bay, NE Massachusetts, USA, 22km (14mi) NE of Boston. First settled in 1626, Salem achieved notoriety for its witchcraft trials (1692), when 19 people were hanged. Industries: electrical products, leather goods, tourism. Pop. (2000) 40,407.

salicylic acid ($C_7H_6O_3$) Colourless, crystalline solid, derivatives of which are used as analgesics (including ASPIRIN, acetylsalicylic acid), antiseptics, dyes, and liniments. It occurs naturally in plants, including willow bark and oil of wintergreen.

Salieri, Antonio (1750–1825) Italian composer. As court composer in Vienna, he composed many operas (with which he made his reputation), much sacred music, and vocal and orchestral works. His pupils included Beethoven, Schubert, and Liszt.

Salinger, J.D. (Jerome David) (1919–) US novelist. He achieved fame with his first book and only novel, *Catcher in the Rye* (1951). The story of a tortured teenager, it is recounted in modern speech, and its style influenced a new generation of US writers. His other works are collections of short stories, including *Franny and Zooey* (1961).

Salisbury, Robert Arthur Talbot Gascoyne-Cecil, 3rd Marquess of (1830–1903) British statesman, prime minister (1885–86, 1886–92, 1895–1902). Salisbury entered Parliament as a Conservative in 1853, and served in Benjamin DISRAELI's administration (1874–80). On Disraeli's death (1881), he became leader of the opposition to GLADSTONE's government. In each of Salisbury's terms in office he also served as foreign secretary, guiding Britain's imperial and colonial affairs. Despite initial success, his diplomacy of 'splendid isolation' resulted in the SOUTH AFRICAN WARS (1899–1902). Salisbury was succeeded by his nephew, Arthur BALFOUR.

saliva Fluid secreted into the mouth by the SALIVARY GLANDS. In vertebrates, saliva consists of *c.*99% water with dissolved traces of sodium, potassium, calcium, and the ENZYME amylase. Saliva softens and lubricates food to aid swallowing, and amylase starts the digestion of starches.

salivary glands Three pairs of GLANDS located on each side of the mouth that form and secrete SALIVA. The **parotid** gland, just below and in front of each ear, is the largest of the salivary glands and the one that becomes enlarged in mumps; the **submaxillary** gland is near the angle of the lower jaw; and the **sublingual** gland is under the side of the tongue.

Salk, Jonas Edward (1914–95) US medical researcher. Salk developed the first vaccine against POLIOMYELITIS (polio) in 1952. It used an inactivated poliomyelitis virus.

salmon Marine and freshwater fish of the Northern Hemisphere. Most species are silvery and spotted until the spawning season when they turn dark or red. The **Pacific** salmon (*Oncorhynchus*) hatches, spawns, and dies in freshwater, but spends its adult life in the ocean. The **Atlantic** salmon (*Salmo salar*) is a marine trout that spawns in rivers on each side of the Atlantic Ocean and then returns to the sea. Weight: to 36kg (80lb). Family Salmonidae.

salmonella Several species of rod-shaped BACTERIA that cause intestinal infections in human beings and animals. *Salmonella typhi* causes TYPHOID FEVER; other species cause GASTROENTERITIS. The bacteria are transmitted by carriers, particularly flies, and in food and water.

Salome (active 1st century AD) Daughter of Herodias and stepdaughter of Herod Antipas. She conspired with her mother to have JOHN THE BAPTIST executed.

salsa Term first used in the early 1970s for the Cuban-inspired music being produced in New York. Salsa is a percussive and brass-led big-band music. It embraces dance forms, including rumba, mambo and guaracha.

salsify (oyster plant, vegetable oyster) Hardy biennial plant with a taproot. It is grown as a vegetable and prized for its oyster-like flavour. Height: to 1.2m (4ft). Family Asteraceae/Compositae; species *Tragopogon porrifolius*.

▲ **salamander** The fire salamander (*Salamandra salamandra*, top) is found in central, s and w Europe, NW Africa, and SW Asia. Its bright coloration acts as a warning to potential predators. Within the skin of the fire salamander are many glands that secrete a sticky, irritant fluid that wards off larger predators and can be fatal to smaller animals. Although the fire salamander obtains oxygen mainly through gas exchange on the surface of its body, it has a set of primitive lungs.

▲ **Salinger** US writer J.D. Salinger is famous for his depictions of lonely characters frustrated by a boring and conformist world. His only novel, *The Catcher in the Rye* (1951), is an enduringly popular tale of disaffected youth. He has been twice married and divorced, and now lives in rural seclusion.

S

salt Ionic COMPOUND formed, along with water, when an ACID is neutralized by a BASE. The hydrogen of the acid is replaced by a metal or ammonium ION. The most familiar salt is SODIUM CHLORIDE. Salts are typically crystalline compounds, usually soluble in water. They are formed of ions held together by electrostatic forces, and in solution they can conduct electricity. Salts are used to flavour food, preserve meat, keep roads ice-free, and manufacture soap.

Salt Lake City State capital in N central Utah, USA, 21km (13mi) E of Great Salt Lake. Founded in 1847 by the MORMONS led by Brigham YOUNG, it grew rapidly to become capital of the Territory of Utah (1856) and the State of Utah (1896). Zinc, gold, silver, lead, and copper are mined nearby. It hosted the 2002 Winter Olympics. Other industries: missiles, rocket engines, oil-refining, tourism, publishing. Pop. (2000) 888,000.

Salvador (Bahia) Seaport city in E central Brazil; capital of BAHIA state. Founded by the Portuguese in 1549, it was the capital of Brazil until 1763. Portuguese colonizers built vast sugar plantations using slave labour, and the city is noted for its African culture. Industries: oil refining, petrochemicals, tobacco, sugar, coffee, industrial diamonds. Pop. (2005) 3,331,000.

Salvador, El *See* EL SALVADOR

Salvation Army International Christian society devoted to the propagation of the gospel among the working classes. Its origin was the Christian Revival Association founded (1865) in London by William BOOTH. In 1878, it became the Salvation Army. Under the leadership of Booth's son, Bramwell, its work spread to other parts of the world.

Salween (Nu Chiang or Nu Jiang in China; Mae Nam Khong in Burma and Thailand) River in Southeast Asia. It rises in the Tibetan Plateau, E Tibet, and flows s through Yünnan province, cutting deep gorges through the terrain. It empties into Burma's Gulf of Martaban, an inlet of the Andaman Sea. It forms many rapids along its course and despite its length of *c.*2,800km (1,750mi) is navigable for only 120km (75mi) upstream.

Salzburg City on the River Salzach, NW Austria, capital of the alpine Salzburg state. It grew around a 7th-century monastery, and for more than 1,000 years was ruled by the Archbishops of Salzburg. It became part of Bavaria in 1809, but returned to Austria in the Congress of Vienna. The birthplace of Mozart and the home of several music festivals, its most important industry is tourism. Pop. (2001) 144,816.

Samaria Ancient region and town of central Palestine. It was built as the capital of the northern kingdom of Israel in the 9th century BC. Conquered by Shalmaneser in 722–721 BC Samaria was later destroyed by John Hyrcanus I and rebuilt by HEROD THE GREAT. *See also* SAMARITANS

Samaritans Descendants of those citizens of SAMARIA who escaped deportation after their kingdom was overrun by the Assyrians in 722 BC. The Jews to the south rejected them. The Samaritans call themselves 'Children of Israel' (Bene Yisreal), and their sole religious scripture is the TORAH.

samarium (symbol Sm) Grey-white, metallic element of the LANTHANIDE SERIES (rare-earth metals). First identified spectroscopically in 1879 by French chemist Paul Lacoq de Boisbaudran (1838–1912), its chief ores are monazite and bastnasite. Samarium is used in carbon-arc lamps, as a neutron absorber in NUCLEAR REACTORS, and as a CATALYST. Some samarium alloys are used in making powerful permanent magnets. Properties: at.no. 62; r.a.m. 150.35; r.d 7.52; m.p. 1,072°C (1,962°F); b.p. 1,791°C (3,256°F); most common isotope Sm^{152} (26.72%).

Samarkand City in the fertile Zeravshan valley, SE Uzbekistan. One of the oldest cities in Asia, it was conquered by ALEXANDER THE GREAT in 329 BC. A vital trading centre on the SILK ROAD, it flourished in the 8th century as part of the UMAYYAD Empire. Samarkand was destroyed in 1220 by GENGHIS KHAN, but became (1370) capital of the Mongol empire of TAMERLANE. Ruled by the Uzbeks from the 16th century, it was captured by Russia in 1868, though it remained a centre of Muslim culture. Products: cotton, silk, leather goods, wine, tea, carpets, canned fruit, motor vehicle parts. It is a major scientific research centre. Pop. (1997) 361,800.

Samoa Volcanic island group in the s Pacific, comprising the independent state of SAMOA and the US-administered AMERICAN SAMOA. Extending *c.*560km (350 mi), the islands are predominantly mountainous and fringed by coral reefs. The majority of the population are indigenous Polynesians. The first European discovery of the islands was in 1722.

Samoa (formerly Western Samoa) Independent island republic in the s Pacific Ocean, encompassing the w half of the SAMOA island chain. The capital, Apia (on Upolu), has 66% of the total population. Samoa comprises the two large, volcanic, mountainous islands of Savai'i and Upolu, the smaller islands of Manono and Apolima, and several uninhabited islets. Extensive lava flows on Savai'i have made much of the island uninhabitable. The cradle of Polynesian culture, the islands became a German Protectorate by an 1899 treaty. New Zealand seized them in 1914, and they were administered by New Zealand from 1920 to 1961. In 1962 Western Samoa became the first Polynesian nation to gain independence. In 1997 it changed its name to Samoa. Much of the workforce engages in subsistence agriculture. The chief exports are coconut oil, taro and copra. Area: 2,831sq km (1,093sq mi). Pop. (2000) 178,000.

Sampras, Pete (1971–) US tennis player. In 1990, Sampras became the youngest-ever winner of the US Open singles and also won the first Grand Slam Cup. He won Wimbledon seven times (1993–95, 1997–2000), the US Open three times (1993, 1995–96), and the Australian Open twice (1994, 1997).

Samson Israelite judge and Old Testament hero renowned for his great physical strength. Samson was a Nazarite, whose strength lay in his long hair. When his mistress, Delilah, discovered this, she had his hair cut off while he slept and handed him over to his enemies, the PHILISTINES. Samson regained his strength as his hair regrew, and when called upon to display his strength in the Philistine Temple of Dagon, he pulled down its pillars and roof, killing himself and thousands of his captors.

Samuel Ninth and tenth books of the OLD TESTAMENT. Through the stories of Samuel, the prophet and judge, and of SAUL and DAVID, Israel's first two kings, they describe the transition of ISRAEL from a collection of tribes under separate chiefs to a single nation ruled through a monarchy. Historically, the events belong roughly to the 11th century BC.

Samurai Member of the élite warrior class of feudal Japan. Beginning as military retainers in the 10th century, the samurai later emerged as an aristocratic ruling class. They conformed to a strict code of conduct, known as BUSHIDO ('the way of the warrior'). Under the TOKUGAWA shogunate in the 17th to 19th centuries, they divided into hereditary subclasses and increasingly became bureaucrats and scholars.

San (Bushmen) Khoisan-speaking people of s Africa. They have lived in the region for thousands of years and until recently had a hunting and gathering culture. About half still follow the traditional ways, mostly in the Kalahari region of Botswana and Namibia. Today, there are *c.*77,000 San.

► **Sampras** US tennis player Pete Sampras celebrates his 1995 Wimbledon singles title. Born in Washington D.C., Sampras dominated men's singles in the mid to late 1990s. He won a record seven Wimbledon singles titles. 'Pistol Pete' is renowned for his fast and devastatingly accurate serve and strong volleys.

S

Sana' (San'a) Capital and largest city of Yemen, 65km (40mi) NE of the Red Sea port of Hodeida. Situated on a high plateau at 2,286m (7,500ft), it claims to be the world's oldest city, founded by Shem, eldest son of Noah. During the 17th century and from 1872 to 1918, it was part of the Ottoman Empire. In 1918, it became capital of an independent Yemen Arab Republic, and in 1990 capital of the new, unified Yemen. It is noted for its handicrafts. Agriculture (grapes) and industry (iron) are also important. Pop. (2001) 1,590,624.

San Andreas fault Geological FAULT line extending more than 965km (600mi) through California. It lies on the boundary between the North American and the Eastern Pacific plates of the Earth's crust. PLATE TECTONIC movement causes several thousand EARTHQUAKES each year, although only a few are significant. SAN FRANCISCO lies close to the fault line, and is prone to earthquake damage. The most destructive earthquake occurred in 1906, when it horizontally displaced land around the fault by up to 6.4m (21ft) and killed 503 people. Notable tremors also occurred in 1989 and 1994.

San Antonio City on the San Antonio River, s central Texas, USA. It was founded on the site of the mission-fort San Antonio de Valero (the ALAMO), and was the scene of the legendary Mexico-Texas struggles in 1836. It adhered to five flags in its colourful history: Spain, Mexico, Republic of Texas, the Confederacy, and the USA. Industries: aircraft, meat packing, electronics, oil refining, chemicals, wood products, financial services and tourism. Pop. (2000) 1,328,000.

sanctions Punitive action taken by one or more states against another that can include the cessation of trade, severing of diplomatic relations, the use of a blockade, and the breaking of cultural and sporting contacts.

sand Mineral particles worn away from rocks by EROSION, individually large enough to be distinguished with the naked eye. Sand is composed mostly of QUARTZ, but black sand (containing volcanic rock) and coral sand also occur.

Sand, George (1804–76) French novelist, b. Amandine Aurore Lucie Dupin. Romantic novels such as *Lélia* (1833) and *Mauprat* (1837) advocate women's right to independence. Her later work includes *The Haunted Pool* (1846) and *The Master Bellringers* (1853). Her autobiographical works include *A Winter in Majorca* (1842). She is also remembered for her relationships with Musset and Chopin.

sandalwood Any of several species of Asian trees of the genus *Santalum*, many of which are PARASITES on the roots of other plants. The fragrant wood is used in carving and joss sticks. The distilled oil is used in perfumes and medicines. Height: to 10m (33ft). Family Santalaceae.

Sandburg, Carl (1878–1967) US poet and biographer. Strongly influenced by Walt WHITMAN, his first volume of poetry was *Chicago Poems* (1916). Other collections include *Cornhuskers* (Pulitzer Prize, 1918), *Smoke and Steel* (1920), *Good Morning, America* (1928) and *The People, Yes* (1936). He also won Pulitzer Prizes for his *Complete Poems* (1950) and for the biography *Abraham Lincoln: The War Years* (1939).

sand hopper (sand flea) Any of several species of small, terrestrial crustaceans. The nocturnal European sand hopper (*Talitrus saltator*) lives on beaches near the high tide mark, emerging to feed on organic debris. Length: to 1.5cm (0.6in). Order Amphipoda; family Talitridae.

San Diego City in s California, USA, almost adjoining Tijuana on the Mexican border. Located on a fine natural Pacific harbour, it was founded in 1769 as a mission. It has a huge naval base and is an important centre for scientific research (especially oceanography). Industries: aerospace, electronics, fishing and fish canning, shipbuilding, food processing, clothing, furniture, tourism. Pop. (2000) 2,674,000.

Sandinista (Sandinista National Liberation Front) Revolutionary group in Nicaragua. They took their name from Augusto César Sandino, who opposed the dominant SOMOZA family and was killed in 1934. The Sandinistas overthrew the Somoza regime in 1979, and formed a government led by Daniel ORTEGA. They were opposed by right-wing guerrillas, the CONTRA, supported by the USA. The conflict ended when the Sandinista agreed to free elections. They lost, but the Contra were disbanded and the Sandinista retain political influence.

sandpiper Wading bird that breeds in cold regions and migrates long distances to winter in warm areas, settling in grass or low bushes near water. It feeds on invertebrates, and nests in a grass-lined hole in the ground. Length: 15–60cm (6–24in). Family Scolopacidae.

sandstone SEDIMENTARY ROCK composed of sand grains cemented in such materials as SILICA or calcium carbonate. Most sand grains contain QUARTZ; other minerals in sandstone include FELDSPARS and MICAS. Iron also occurs, which gives sandstones a reddish or brownish colour. Most sandstones form through the accumulation of river sediments on the seabed. They are then compressed and uplifted to form new lands.

San Francisco City and port in w California, USA, on a peninsula bounded by the Pacific Ocean (W) and San Francisco Bay (E), which are connected by the Golden Gate Strait. Founded by the Spanish in 1776, it was captured (1846) by the USA in the MEXICAN WAR. A gold rush (1848) swelled the town's population. The Pony Express and the completion of the railroad (1869) brought more settlers, and saw the emergence of Chinatown. Devastated by an earthquake and fire in 1906, it was quickly rebuilt and prospered with the opening of the PANAMA CANAL. Industry developed rapidly and San Francisco became the leading commerical city on the West Coast. It was a major supply port for the war in the Pacific. Its mild climate and cosmopolitan air make it a major tourist centre. Other industries: finance, shipbuilding, food processing, oil refining, aircraft, fishing, printing and publishing. Pop. (2000) 3,229,000.

Sanger, Frederick (1918–) English biochemist who became the first person to receive two Nobel Prizes for chemistry. He gained the first in 1958 – for finding the structure of INSULIN. His second prize came in 1980 (shared with the US molecular biologists Walter Gilbert and Paul Berg) – for work on the chemical structure of NUCLEIC ACIDS.

Sanhedrin Ancient Jewish religious council, prominent in Jerusalem during the period of Roman rule in Palestine. The Great Sanhedrin is believed to have served as a legislative and judicial body on both religious and political issues. JESUS CHRIST appeared before the Sanhedrin after his arrest.

San José Capital and largest city of COSTA RICA, in central Costa Rica, capital of San José province. Founded in c.1736, it succeeded Cartago as capital in 1823, and soon became the centre of a prosperous coffee trade. Products: coffee, sugar cane, cacao, vegetables, fruit, tobacco. Pop. (2005) 1,145,000.

San Jose City in w California, USA, 64km (40mi) SE of San Francisco. Founded in 1777, it was California's capital from 1849–1851. San Jose is the centre of a rich fruit-growing region, but is best known as the focal point of "Silicon Valley", the hub of the US computer industry. Pop. (2000) 1,538,000.

San Juan Capital, largest city, and major port of PUERTO RICO, on the NE coast of the island. It has one of the finest harbours in the West Indies. Founded in 1508, the port prospered during the 18th and 19th centuries, and was captured (1898) by the USA during the SPANISH-AMERICAN WAR. The city is the commercial and financial centre of Puerto Rico. Exports: coffee, tobacco, fruit, sugar. Industries: cigars and cigarettes, sugar refining, rum distilling, metal products, pharmaceuticals, tourism. Pop. (2005) 2,357,000.

San Luis Potosí State in central Mexico, primarily on Mexico's N plateau; the capital is San Luis Potosí (2000 pop. 669,353). It is the chief mining state of Mexico, with mines yielding gold, copper, zinc, bismuth and (especially) silver since the 18th century. Arid conditions result in little farming, but the Pánuco River Valley produces coffee, tobacco, and sugar. Area: 62,848sq km (24,268sq mi). Pop. (2000) 2,296,363.

San Marino World's smallest republic and perhaps Europe's oldest state, in the Apennines, near the Adriatic Sea, NE Italy. According to legend, it was founded in the early 4th century AD. Its mountainous terrain enabled it to retain a separate status, becoming an independent commune in the 13th century. The economy is largely agricultural. Manufacturing is also important, but tourism is vital to the state's income. While San Marino has its own currency and stamps, Italian and Vatican City equivalents are widely used. It possesses its own legislative assembly, the

Great and General Council, which elects Captains Regent as heads of state. There are two towns: Serraville (2000 pop. 8,400), and the capital San Marino (2000 pop. 4,400). Area: 61sq km (24sq mi). Pop. (2000) 28,000.

San Martín, José de (1778–1850) South American revolutionary. He led revolutionary forces in Argentina, Chile, and Peru, gaining a reputation as a bold commander and imaginative strategist. After defeating the Spanish in Argentina, he gained the element of surprise in Chile (1817–18) by crossing the Andes, San Martín captured Peru (1821) after an unexpected naval attack. He surrendered his effective rule of Peru to Simón BOLÍVAR in 1822 and retired to Europe.

San Salvador Capital and largest city of El Salvador, in central El Salvador. Founded in 1524 – near the volcano of San Salvador, which rises to 1,885m (6,184ft) and last erupted in 1917 – the city has been frequently damaged by earthquakes. The main industry is the processing of coffee grown on the rich volcanic soils of the area. Other manufactures include beer, textiles, and tobacco. Pop. (2005) 1,472,000.

Sanskrit Classical language of India, the literary and sacred language of HINDUISM, and a forerunner of the modern Indo-Iranian languages spoken in N India, Pakistan, Nepal, and Bangladesh. Sanskrit was brought to India (c.1500BC) by immigrants from the NW. It was the language in which the VEDAS were written. This old form of the language (Vedic Sanskrit) gradually became simplified, achieving its classical form c.500 BC. Sanskrit is one of the INDO-EUROPEAN LANGUAGES. Although only c.3,000 Indians are able to speak Sanskrit today, it has been designated one of India's national languages.

Sanskrit literature Classical **Indian literature**. The two main periods in Sanskrit literature are the **Vedic** (c.1500–c.200BC) and the overlapping **Classical** (c.500BC–c.AD 1000). The Vedic period produced the VEDAS, the earliest works in Sanskrit literature and among the most important. Later Vedic literature included the UPANISHADS, which discuss the essence of the universe. The Early Classical period contributed the MAHABHARATA and the RAMAYANA. They are significant both as literature and as Hindu sacred works.

Santa Anna, Antonio López de (1794–1876) Mexican general and dictator. He was the dominant political figure in Mexico from 1823 to 1855, sometimes as president, sometimes unofficially as the result of a coup. In 1836, Santa Anna led the forces that captured the ALAMO but failed to subdue the rebellion in TEXAS. He regained power following gallant action against a French raid on Vera Cruz (1838). After his failure in the MEXICAN WAR (1846–48), he went into exile. He returned to power in 1853, but was overthrown in 1855.

Santa Claus Variant of the Dutch name *Sinte Klaas*, itself a version of the name Saint NICHOLAS, who was Bishop of Myra sometime during the 4th century. Santa Claus has become associated with the feast of Christmas and is identified with Father Christmas in North America, the UK, and some former Commonwealth countries.

Santa Cruz de Tenerife Capital of the CANARY ISLANDS and largest city in TENERIFE. Founded in 1494, it has a fine harbour and exports fruit, vegetables and sugar cane. Industries: oil refining, tourism. Pop. (2001) 214,153.

Santa Fe State capital of New Mexico, USA, at the foot of the Sangre de Cristo Mountains. The oldest US capital city, it was founded in c.1609 by the Spanish, and acted as a centre of Spanish-Native American trade for more than 200 years. Mexico's independence in 1821 opened trade with the USA. Santa Fe functioned as the W terminus of the Santa Fe Trail. In 1846, US troops captured the city, and in 1850 the region became US territory, achieving statehood in 1912. Today, it is primarily an administrative, tourist and resort centre. Pop. (2000) 62,203.

Santayana, George (1863–1952) US philosopher and poet, b. Spain. After 1939, Santayana withdrew from society – a seclusion reflected in the moral detachment of his writing. He stressed both the biological nature of the mind and its creative and rational powers. His works include *The Sense of Beauty* (1896), *The Life of Reason* (1905–06), *Skepticism and Animal Faith* (1923), and the popular novel *The Last Puritan* (1935).

Santer, Jacques (1937–) Luxembourg statesman, prime minister of Luxembourg (1984–94), president of the Euro-

pean Union (1994–99). Santer was a member of the Luxembourg Chamber of Deputies before being elected to the European Parliament, of which he was vice president (1975–77). In 1999, following charges of corruption, Santer and all the European commissioners resigned.

Santiago Capital of Chile, in central Chile on the River Mapocho, 90km (55mi) from the Atlantic coast. Founded in 1541, it was destroyed by an earthquake in 1647. Most of Santiago's architecture dates from after 1850. It is the nation's administrative, commercial, and cultural centre, accounting for nearly a third of the population. Industries: textiles, pharmaceuticals, clothing, footwear. Pop. (2005) 5,623,000.

Santo Domingo (formerly Ciudad Trujillo, 1936–61) Capital and chief port of the Dominican Republic, on the S coast of the island, on the River Ozama. Founded in 1496, the city is the oldest continuous European settlement in the Americas. It was the seat of the Spanish viceroys in the early 1500s, and base for the Spaniards' conquering expeditions until it was devastated by an earthquake in 1562. It houses more than a third of the country's population, many of whom work in the sugar industry. Pop. (2002 est.) 2,061,200; 2,799,600 (metro.).

São Paulo City on the River Tietê, SE Brazil, capital of São Paulo state, located almost exactly on the Tropic of Capricorn. Founded by the Jesuits in 1554, it grew as the base for expeditions into the interior in search of minerals. It expanded in the 17th century as a trading centre for a large coffee region. While its agricultural produce are now shipped through its port of Santos, São Paulo has become a major and diverse industrial centre attracting migrants from the interior. It is the world's fastest-growing metropolis. Pop. (2000) 10,406,166; (metropolitan) 17,878,703. São Paulo state houses up to 60% of Brazil's industry and most of its sugar production. Pop. (2005) 18,333,000.

São Tomé and Príncipe Country in the Gulf of Guinea, 300km (200mi) off the W coast of Africa. The capital is São Tomé. The republic consists of two main islands, São Tome (the largest) and Príncipe. The islands are volcanic and mountainous. The vegetation is mainly tropical rainforest. The islands were discovered in 1471 and, in 1483, a settlement was established at São Tomé. In 1522, the islands became a Portuguese colony. The Dutch controlled the islands from 1641 to 1740, but the Portuguese regained control and established plantations in the late 18th century. The official language is Portuguese and the major religion is Roman Catholicism. The islands became independent in 1975, ushering in 16 years of Marxist rule. In 1990, a new constitution introduced multi-party elections. In 2001, Fradique de Menezes was elected as president. In 2003 a military coup toppled the government but Menezes returned to power soon after. Cocoa, coffee, bananas, and coconuts are grown on plantations, and their export is the republic's major source of income. Area: 964sq km (372sq mi). Pop. (2000) 176,000.

sap Fluid that circulates water and nutrients through plants. Water is absorbed by the roots and carried, along with minerals, through the XYLEM to the leaves. Sap from the leaves is distributed throughout the plant.

sapphire Transparent to translucent gemstone variety of CORUNDUM. It has various colours produced by impurities of iron and titanium, the most valuable being deep blue.

Sappho Greek poet who was writing during the early 6th century BC. Her passionate love poetry, written on the island of Lesbos (from which the word 'lesbian' derives) was regarded by PLATO as the expression of 'the tenth MUSE'.

saprophyte Plant that obtains its food from dead or decaying plant or animal tissue. Generally, it has no CHLOROPHYLL. Included are most FUNGI and some flowering plants.

Saracens Name applied by the ancient Greeks and Romans to the Arab tribes who threatened their borders. The name was later extended to include all Arabs and eventually all Muslims. As a term similar to 'Moors', it was used particularly by medieval Christians to denote their Muslim enemies.

Sarajevo Capital of Bosnia-Herzegovina, on the River Miljacka. It fell to the Turks in 1429, and became a flourishing commercial centre in the Ottoman Empire. Passing to the

INTERNET

São Tomé and Príncipe
▶ www.sao-tome.com

Austro-Hungarian Empire in 1878, the city was a centre of Serb and Bosnian resistance to Austrian rule. On June 28, 1914, a Serbian nationalist assassinated the Austrian Archduke Franz Ferdinand and his wife in the city, an act that helped to precipitate World War 1. In 1991, Bosnia-Herzegovina declared independence from Yugoslavia, and a bloody civil war ensued among Croatian, Bosnian, and Serbian forces. Sarajevo became the focal point of the war between Bosnian-Serb troops and Bosnian government forces. The city lay under prolonged siege, often without water, electricity, or basic medical supplies. After the 1995 peace agreement (the **Dayton Accord**), it in effect became a Bosnian city, with the 1991 population figure of 526,000 drastically reduced as many Serbs fled. Pop. (2002 est.) 434,000.

Sarasvati In Hindu mythology, goddess of the arts, sciences, and eloquent speech. Depicted as a beautiful young woman, she is credited with the invention of the Sanskrit language. Sarasvati later became the consort of BRAHMA.

Saratoga, Battle of (October 7, 1777) First American victory in the AMERICAN REVOLUTION, fought in upper New York. In a series of battles, the Americans, led by Horatio GATES, prevented the British from linking up with other forces at Albany and taking the Hudson valley. The Americans eventually surrounded the British, forcing them to surrender. The victory persuaded the French to intervene against Britain.

Sarawak Largest state of Malaysia, in NW Borneo, comprising a highland interior and swampy coastal plain; the capital is Kuching City. Ruled as an independent state by Britain after 1841, it was made a British Protectorate in 1888 and a Crown Colony in 1946. Sarawak became a part of Malaysia in 1963, triggering a three-year dispute with Indonesia. Oil is an increasingly important product alongside the traditional coconuts, rice, rubber and sago. Area: 124,449sq km (48,050sq mi). Pop. (2000) 2,012,616.

sarcoma Cancerous growth or TUMOUR arising from muscle, fat, bone, blood or lymph vessels, and connective tissue. *See also* CANCER

sardine Small, marine food fish found throughout the world. It has a laterally compressed body, a large toothless mouth, and oily flesh. Length: to 30cm (1ft). Species include the Californian *Sardinops caerulea*, South American *S. sagax* and the European sardine, or PILCHARD, *S. pilchardus*. Family Clupeidae.

Sardinia (Sardegna) Mountainous island of Italy, 208km (130mi) W of the Italian mainland, separated by the Tyrrhenian Sea. The only large city is Cágliari, the capital. A trading centre for the Phoenicians, Greeks, Carthaginians, and Romans, Sardinia became a kingdom in 1720, and in 1861 its king, VICTOR EMMANUEL II, became the first king of Italy. Farming and fishing are the chief occupations of this sparsely vegetated island. Wheat, barley, grapes, olives, and tobacco are grown, and sheep and goats are reared. Salt extraction is important. Other minerals include coal, lead, magnesium, manganese, and zinc. Area: 24,090sq km (9,300sq mi). Pop. (1999) 1,654,470.

Sargasso Sea Area of calm, barely moving water in the N Atlantic between the West Indies and the Azores, which takes its name from the large quantities of floating seaweed (*Sargassum*) covering its surface.

Sargent, John Singer (1856–1925) US painter. Greatly influenced by Diego VELÁZQUEZ and Frans HALS, Sargent is best known for his glamorous and elegant portraits, such as *The Boit Children* (1882) and *Lord Ribblesdale* (1902).

Sargent, Sir (Harold) Malcolm (Watts) (1895–1967) English conductor. He conducted the Royal Choral Society from 1928, and the BBC Symphony Orchestra (1950–57). He was chief conductor (1948–67) of the PROMENADE CONCERTS.

Sargon (c.2334–c.2279 BC) King of Akkadia (c.2316–c.2279BC). One of the first of the great Mesopotamian conquerors, he was a usurper who founded his capital at Agade (Akkad), from which his kingdom took its name. Sargon conquered SUMERIA and Upper MESOPOTAMIA and extracted tribute from lands as far W as the Mediterranean.

Sargon (d. 705BC) King of ASSYRIA (721–705BC). He conquered SAMARIA in 721 BC and according to tradition dispersed those Israelites who became the 'lost tribes' of Israel.

He established an imperial administration and defeated his enemies before being killed in battle against the Cimmarians.

Sark One of the CHANNEL ISLANDS of the United Kingdom, divided into Great Sark and Little Sark, which are connected by a causeway. Sark is part of the Bailiwick of GUERNSEY with a feudal organization dating from the late 17th century. There are no cars and the residents pay no income tax. The population swells in the summer with an influx of tourists. Area: 5.5sq km (2.1sq mi). Pop. (1996) 550.

Saroyan, William (1908–81) US novelist, short-story writer, and dramatist. Saroyan followed the success of his first play, *My Heart's in the Highlands* (1939), with the Pulitzer Prize-winning *The Time of Your Life* (1939) and the autobiographical *My Name is Aram* (1940). His subsequent works were less successful, although *The Cave Dwellers* (1957) received some critical acclaim.

SARS *see* SEVERE ACUTE RESPIRATORY SYNDROME.

sarsaparilla Tropical perennial vine of the genus *Smilax*, native to Central and South America, whose roots are the source of a chemical used to give an aromatic flavour to medicines and drinks. The main species used are *S. aristolochiaefolia*, *S. regelii* and *S. febrifuga*. Family Liliaceae.

Sartre, Jean-Paul (1905–80) French philosopher and writer. Sartre was the leading advocate of EXISTENTIALISM. His debut novel, *Nausea* (1939), depicted man adrift in a godless universe, hostage to his own angst-ridden freedom. Sartre was a fighter in the French Resistance during World War 2. During the war, he began to write plays, such as *Huis Clos* (*No Exit*) (1944). His major philosophical work is *Being and Nothingness* (1943). After the war, Sartre wrote a trilogy of novels, *The Roads to Freedom* (1945–49), and founded (1945) the philosophy periodical *Modern Times*. His complex relationship with Marxism is explored in *Critique of Dialectical Reason* (1960). Sartre refused the 1964 Nobel Prize in literature on 'personal' grounds, but is later said to have accepted it. He had a long-term relationship with Simone de BEAUVOIR.

Saskatchewan Province in W central Canada, the southern half on the fertile Great Plains and the northern half in the lakestrewn Canadian Shield. The cultivation of wheat is the most important agricultural activity, but oats, barley, rye, flax and rapeseed are also grown. Rich mineral deposits include uranium, copper, zinc, gold, coal, oil, natural gas and the world's largest fields of potash. Most industries process raw materials; steel is also manufactured. The principal cities are Saskatoon (2001 pop. 225,927), Regina (capital, 192,800), Prince Albert (41,460) and Moose Jaw (33,519). The first permanent European settlement was in 1774; development was slow until the arrival of the Canadian Pacific Railroad in 1885. Saskatchewan was admitted to the Dominion of Canada in 1905. Area: 570,113sq km (251,700sq mi). Pop. (2001) 978,933.

sassafras Small E North American tree with furrowed bark, green twigs, yellow flowers and blue berries. Oil from the roots is used to flavour root beer. Family Lauraceae; species *Sassafras albidum*.

Sassanid (Sassanian) Royal dynasty of Persia (Iran) (AD 224–651). Founded by Ardashir I (r.224–241), the Sassanids revived the native Persian traditions of the ACHAEMENIDS, confirming ZOROASTRIANISM as the state religion. There were about 30 Sassanid rulers, the most important after Ardashir being Shapur II (309–379); Khoshru I (531–579), and Khoshru II (590–628), whose conquest of Syria, Palestine and Egypt marked the height of the dynasty's power. The Sassanids were finally overthrown by the Arabs.

Sassoon, Siegfried (1886–1967) English poet and novelist. His disillusionment with military service in World War 1 inspired some of his most memorable poetry. The semi-autobiographical trilogy *The Complete Memoirs of George Sherston* (1937) includes his most famous novel, *Memoirs of a Fox-hunting Man* (1928). His poetry was collected in 1961.

Satan Name for the DEVIL. Satan first appeared in the Old Testament as an individual angel, subordinate to God. Gradually, however, Satan took on a more sinister role. In the New Testament, he was the devil who tempted JESUS CHRIST. Satan emerged in medieval Christian theology as the chief devil, ruler of hell and source of all evil.

▲ **Sartre** French philosopher, playwright and novelist Jean-Paul Sartre studied at the Sorbonne in Paris with Simone De Beauvoir, who remained his close associate. He was influenced by German philosophers including Heidegger and Marx, and wrote several works of literary criticism. Outspoken against US involvement in Vietnam, he supported the student rebellion in Paris (1968).

S

INTERNET

Sardinia
▶ www.sardegna.net/docs/
cultura/storia_en.html

Sargent, John Singer
▶ www.mfa.org

Saskatchewan
▶ www.gov.sk.ca

INTERNET

Satie, Erik
▶ www.af.lu.se/~fogwall/
satie.html

Saturn
▶ www.nineplanets.org/
saturn.html

Saudi Arabia
▶ www.saudiembassy.net

SATURN: DATA

Diameter (equatorial):
120,536km (74,901mi)
Mass (Earth=1): 95.2
Volume (Earth=1): 744
Density (water=1): 0.71
Orbital period: 29.46 years
Rotation period: 10h 13m 59s
Temperature at cloud tops:
95K

satellite Body orbiting a planet or star. In the Solar System, planets with satellites are Earth (1), Mars (2), Jupiter (63), Saturn (60), Uranus (27), Neptune (13), and dwarf planet Pluto (3). There are probably more satellites of the giant planets awaiting discovery. They vary enormously in their size, orbit, surface features, and supposed origin.

satellite, artificial Artificial object placed in orbit around the Earth or other celestial body. Satellites can perform many tasks, including sending back data or pictures to the Earth. Hundreds of satellites of various types orbit the Earth. They may study the atmosphere, or photograph the surface for scientific or military purposes. **Communications** satellites relay radio, television, telephone, telegraph, and data signals from one part of the Earth to another. **Navigation** satellites transmit radio signals that enable navigators to determine their positions. The Global Positioning System (GPS) uses satellites in this way. **Geodetic satellites** are used to make accurate measurements of the Earth's size and shape. *Sputnik 1* was the first artificial satellite, launched on October 4, 1957.

satellite television TELEVISION services transmitted to viewers via communications SATELLITES in orbit around the Earth. These satellites orbit the Equator and keep in time with the Earth's spin. As a result, each one remains above a fixed point on the Equator. Television companies beam their signals to the satellites from ground stations. The satellites retransmit the signals back to viewers' dish-shaped receiving aerials. A fixed AERIAL receives many services from a single satellite.

Satie, Erik (1866–1925) French composer. Rebelling against Wagnerian ROMANTICISM, he developed a deceptively simple style in piano pieces such as *Trois Gymnopédies* (1888). He also composed the ballets *Parade* (1917) and *Relâche* (1924), and a choral work, *Socrate* (1918).

satire Literary work in which human foibles and institutions are mocked, ridiculed, and parodied. In Roman times, a satire was a poem in hexameters, a form established by the work of Lucilius, HORACE, and JUVENAL. In the Middle Ages, it often took the form of *fabliaux* or bestiaries, using animal characters to illustrate typical human failings. Since Thomas MORE's *Utopia* (1516), utopian or dystopian fiction, such as Zamyatin's *We* (1924) and SWIFT's *Gulliver's Travels* (1726), has frequently been used as a medium for satire. Dramatists have often employed the form, as in the plays of ARISTOPHANES, Ben JONSON, MOLIÈRE, Oscar WILDE, and Bertolt BRECHT.

SATELLITE, ARTIFICIAL

Four artificial satellite orbits around the globe are illustrated. Two are equatorial: one, a geostationary satellite, orbits at 35,900km (21,500mi) (1), another has a lower orbit (2). A polar orbit, as used by remote sensing satellites, is shown running vertically around the Earth (3) and the last is an angled elliptical orbit used by communications satellites for the high latitudes of the Earth (4). The diagrams above the orbital map show the launching of an Intelsat communication satellite by a NASA shuttle (5) and the two main types of satellites. To prevent them being knocked off course by fluctuations in the Earth's magnetic field, satellites are given centrifugal stability in one of two ways. The first is to rotate the whole satellite as is the case in 'spinners' such as the Intelsat satellite (6). The other method is to have gyroscopes placed within the satellite (7).

Sato, Eisaku (1901–75) Japanese statesman, prime minister (1964–72). Sato held a number of cabinet posts (1948–64) before becoming prime minister. His term in office is notable for its foreign policy successes, such as the restoration of relations with South Korea (1965). Sato negotiated the return (1972) of OKINAWA from the USA. A provision that US forces were allowed to remain on the island, however, inflamed public opinion. He received the 1974 Nobel Peace Prize.

saturated compound In organic chemistry, compounds in which CARBON atoms bond to one another by single COVALENT BONDS only, never by more reactive double or triple CHEMICAL BONDS. For this reason, they tend to be unreactive. A simple example is ETHANE (C_2H_6), in which each carbon atom is bonded to three hydrogen atoms and to the other carbon atom by single bonds. *See also* UNSATURATED COMPOUND

saturated fat Organic fatty compounds, the molecules of which contain only saturated FATTY ACIDS combined with GLYCEROL. These acids have long chains of carbon atoms which are bound together by single bonds only. *See also* SATURATED COMPOUNDS

saturated solution In chemistry, a SOLUTION containing so much of a dissolved compound (SOLUTE) that no more will dissolve at the same temperature.

Saturn Sixth planet from the Sun and second-largest in the SOLAR SYSTEM. Viewed through a telescope, it appears as a flattened golden yellow disk encircled by white rings. The rings are made up of particles ranging from dust to objects a few metres in size, all in individual orbits. The main rings are only a kilometre or so thick. **Voyager** space probes revealed the ring system to be made up of thousands of separate ringlets. Saturn has an internal heat source, which probably drives its weather systems. It is assumed to be composed predominantly of hydrogen, and to have an iron-silicate core about five times the Earth's mass, surrounded by an ice mantle of perhaps twenty Earth masses. The upper atmosphere contains 97% hydrogen and 3% helium, with traces of other gases.

satyr In Greek mythology, god of the woods and attendant of DIONYSUS. Sensual and lascivious, satyrs were later depicted by the Romans as goat-legged, goat-bearded men with budding horns. Satyr is also the common name for any butterfly of the Satyridae family.

Saud, Abdul Aziz ibn (1880–1953) Founder and first king of Saudi Arabia (1932–53). As leader of the Saudi dynasty, he was forced into exile (1891) by the rival Rashid family. He returned in 1902, and extended his authority, driving out the Turks and the Hashemites and founding the modern Saudi state in 1932. Ibn Saud was succeeded by his sons, **Ibn Abdul Aziz Saud** (r.1953–64) and **Faisal ibn Abd al Aziz** (r.1964–75). Saud (1902–69) acceded to the throne in 1953 but his fiscal mismanagement and personal extravagance caused a severe financial crisis in 1958. Soon afterwards his brother Faisal (1904–75) took over all administrative powers, formally replacing him as king in 1964.

Saudi Arabia Arabic kingdom on the Arabian Peninsula, sw Asia. *See country feature*

Saul (active late 11th centuryBC) First king of the Hebrew state of ancient ISRAEL (c.1020–c.1000BC). He was the son of Kish, a member of the tribe of Benjamin. Saul was anointed by the prophet SAMUEL, and acclaimed as king by all Israel. For much of his reign, he waged war against Israel's threatening neighbours, notably the PHILISTINES, the Ammonites, and the Amalekites. He and his sons eventually died in battle against the Philistines on Mount Gilboa. The story of Saul is contained in the First Book of SAMUEL, the ninth book of the Old Testament.

sauna Wood-lined room in which a wood-fired stove (or an electric heater) raises the temperature to between 60 and 95°C (140–203°F). It also refers to the activity of sitting in the heated room and sweating profusely, often leaving and returning to the heat several times. The sauna was originally a semi-religious exercise pioneered by the Finns.

Saussure, Ferdinand de (1857–1913) Swiss linguist, founder of modern linguistics. Saussure delivered (1907–11) a series of lectures at the University of Geneva, which were published posthumously (1916) as *Course in General Linguistics*.

For Saussure, language was a system of signs whose meaning is defined by their relationship to each other. His work laid the foundation for STRUCTURALISM and SEMIOTICS.

savanna Plain with coarse grass and scattered tree growth, particularly the wide plains of tropical and sub-tropical regions. An extensive example is the savanna of the East African tableland.

Savannah City and port on the Savannah River, E Georgia, USA. The oldest city in Georgia, it was founded in 1733, and became the seat of the colonial government in 1754. During the American Revolution, it was initially captured by the British in 1778, and resisted all attempts at invasion until 1782. The city prospered on the tobacco and cotton trade, despite a devastating fire in 1796. During the Civil War, it remained a Confederate stronghold until December 1864. Today, it is still a major port whose exports include tobacco, cotton and sugar. Industries: chemicals, petroleum, paper products, rubber, tourism. Pop. (2000) 131,510.

Savimbi, Jonas (1934–2002) Angolan politician. Prominent in the struggle for independence from Portugal, Savimbi formed (1966) the National Union for the Total Independence of Angola (UNITA). After liberation (1975), he began a guerrilla war against the MPLA government. In 1991, President DOS SANTOS and Savimbi signed a peace

SAUDI ARABIA

The Kingdom of Saudi Arabia occupies about three-quarters of the Arabian Peninsula in SW Asia. The land is mostly desert and includes the largest expanse of sand in the world, the Rub' al Khali (Empty Quarter), covering an area of 647,500sq km [250,000sq mi]. Mountains to the W border the RED SEA plains.

CLIMATE

Saudi Arabia has a hot, dry climate. In the summer, the temperatures are extremely high and often exceed 40°C [104°F], although the nights are cool.

HISTORY

Saudi Arabia contains the two holiest places in Islam. MECCA, the birthplace of the Prophet Muhammad in AD 570, is the site of the KAABA. MEDINA is the city in which Muhammad and his followers settled in AD 622.

In the mid-15th century, the Saud Dynasty established control over a small area near pre-sent-day Riyadh. In the mid-18th century an alliance was established with a religious leader, Muhammad Ibn Abd al-Wahhab, who wanted to restore strict observance of Islam. The Wahhabi movement swept across Arabia and the Saud family took over areas converted to the Wahhabi beliefs, establishing an independent state in the Najd. By the early 19th century, they had taken Mecca and Medina. The Ottoman governor of Egypt attacked to halt their expansion, and most of the Arabian Peninsula fell under the rule of Ottoman Turks.

In 1902 Abd al-Aziz Ibn SAUD led a force from Kuwait, where he had been living in exile, and captured Riyadh. By 1906 he captured the whole of the Najd, and in 1913 the Turkish province of Al Hasa also fell. In 1920, following the defeat of the Ottomans in World War 1, Ibn Saud seized the Asir. By 1925 he gained the whole of the Hejaz, and in 1932 the territories combined to form the Kingdom of Saudi Arabia. Ibn Saud became King, ruling in accordance with the *sharia* of Wahhabi Islam.

AREA 2,149,690sq km [829,995sq mi]
POPULATION 27,601,000
CAPITAL (POPULATION) Riyadh (5,514,000)
GOVERNMENT Absolute monarchy
ETHNIC GROUPS Arab 90%, Afro-Asian 10%
LANGUAGES Arabic (official)
RELIGIONS Islam 100%
CURRENCY Saudi riyal = 100 halalas

POLITICS

The first major oil discovery in the country was made in 1938, and full-scale production began after World War 2. Saudi Arabia eventually became the world's leading oil exporter and highly influential in the Arab world where it played a major role in supplying development aid.

Saudi Arabia supported Egypt, Jordan and Syria in the Six-Day War against Israel, in 1967. It did not send troops, but gave aid to the Arab combatants.

King Fahd suffered a stroke in 1995 and appointed his half-brother, Crown Prince Abdullah Ibn Abdulaziz, to act on his behalf. Fahd died in 2005 and Abdullah succeeded him as king.

Although assisted by a Consultative Council, the monarch holds executive and legislative powers and is also the imam (supreme religious ruler). Saudi Arabia is an absolute monarchy with no formal constitution.

Despite its support of Iraq in the IRAN-IRAQ WAR of the 1980s, Saudi Arabia asked for the protection of Western forces against possible Iraqi aggression during the invasion of Kuwait in 1990. In 1991 the country assisted in the quick victory over Iraq in the GULF WAR.

Relations between Saudi Arabia and the United States became strained following the terrorist attacks on the US on 11 September 2001, in part because Osama bin Laden and many of his followers were Saudi-born. Saudi authorities denounced the attacks and severed relations with Afghanistan's Taliban regime. In 2003 and 2004 Saudi Arabia was attacked by terrorists linked to al-QAEDA.

The government held nationwide municipal elections in 2005, its first exercise in democracy. However, political parties are banned and activists who publicly broach the subject of reform risk jail.

ECONOMY

Saudi Arabia is a wealthy country. It has about 25% of the world's known oil reserves, and oil and oil products make up 85–90% of its exports.

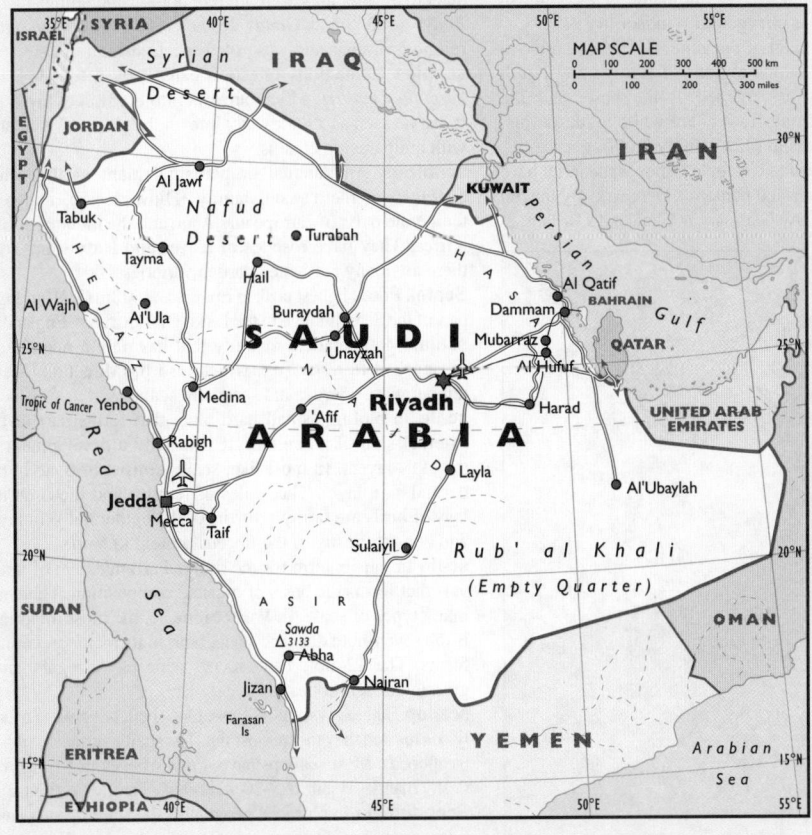

S

▲ **saxifrage** The rue-leaved saxifrage (*Saxifrage tridactylites*) thrives in dry conditions, and is capable of growing on rocks and walls. It is a member of the widespread family Saxifragaceae, whose name in Latin means 'breaker of rocks'.

S

▶ **Saxons** In the course of the 6th and 7th centuries, the once-unified Roman province of Britain split into a collection of petty kingdoms: barbarian Saxon in the s and E, Celtic in the w and N. Organized by family and clan, the Saxon kingdoms developed into seven stable entities. The frontiers, however, were not constant, kingship was personal rather than hereditary, and the balance of power was constantly changing.

agreement. Savimbi refused to recognize the 1992 re-election of Dos Santos, and civil war resumed. UNITA's dwindling support forced Savimbi to accept the **Lusaka Protocol** (1994). He refused the vice presidency, however, and fighting resumed as UNITA retained control in *c.*50% of Angola. In 1997, the UN imposed sanctions on UNITA. Savimbi was shot dead by government troops.

Savonarola, Girolamo (1452–98) Italian religious reformer. His sermons attacked the corruption of the PAPACY and the state of Florence. After the death of Lorenzo de' MEDICI (1494), Savonarola became spiritual and political leader of the city. His support for the invasion of Charles VIII of France infuriated Pope Alexander VI, and he was excommunicated in 1497. Public hostility to Savonarola's austere regime intensified. He was arrested and hanged for heresy.

Savoy European dynasty and ruling House of SAVOY and PIEDMONT from the 11th century, Sardinia from 1720 to 1861 and Italy from 1861 to 1946. The dynasty was founded by Humbert the White-handed (d. *c.*1047), the first Count of Savoy. Their seat was Chambéry, France, from 1232 to 1559, when Emmanuel Philibert relocated to Turin. The House of Savoy led the RISORGIMENTO movement, and Italy unified under VICTOR EMMANUEL II.

Savoy Area of SE France, bounded by Lake Geneva (N), the River Rhône (W), the Dauphiné (S), and the Alps of Italy and Switzerland (E); it includes the departments of Haute Savoie and Savoie. It was part of the first Burgundian kingdom, the kingdom of Arles and, in the 11th century, the Holy Roman Empire. In 1416 it became a duchy, incorporating parts of France, Switzerland, and Italy. An Italian state in the 16th century, it was part of the kingdom of SARDINIA after 1713. France annexed Savoy in 1792. It returned to Sardinia in 1815, who finally ceded to France by the Treaty of Turin (1860).

sawfly Any of 400 species of primitive, plant-feeding WASPS that lack a narrow waist between thorax and abdomen. Most typical sawflies are included in the family Tenthredinidae. Length: to 20mm (0.8in). Order Hymenoptera.

Saxe-Coburg-Gotha Duchy in Saxony, Germany, whose ruling dynasty intermarried with many royal families. After Prince Albert married the English Queen VICTORIA, Saxe-Coburg-Gotha became the name of the English royal House until it was changed to Windsor in 1917.

saxifrage Perennial plant of the genus *Saxifraga* native to temperate and mountainous regions of Europe and North America. The leaves are massed at the base, and the branched clusters of small flowers are white, pink, purple, or yellow. Height: to 61cm (2ft). Family Saxifragaceae.

Saxons Ancient Germanic people. They appear to have originated in N Germany and perhaps s Denmark. By the 5th century, they settled in NW Germany, N Gaul, and s Britain. In

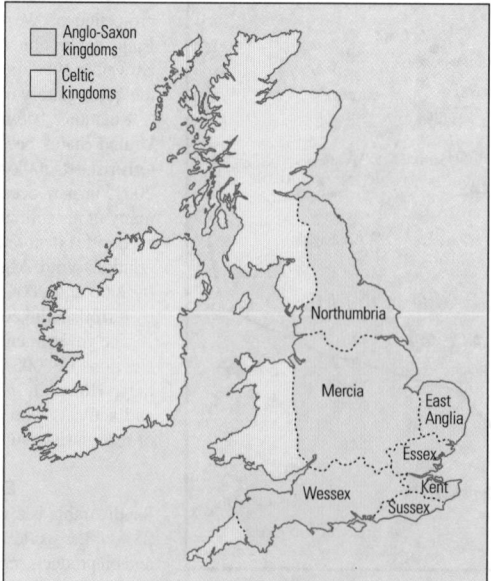

Anglo-Saxon kingdoms
Celtic kingdoms

Northumbria

Mercia

East Anglia

Essex

Kent

Wessex

Sussex

Germany, they were eventually subdued by CHARLEMAGNE. In Britain, together with other Germanic tribes, known collectively as ANGLO-SAXONS, they evolved into the English.

Saxony Federal state and historic region in E central Germany; the capital is DRESDEN. Initially it referred to the homeland of the SAXONS in NW Germany. It then successively became a Duchy, a collection of fiefdoms, an electoral region, a Duchy again, and finally (1815–71) comprised the Prussian Province of Saxony and the Kingdom of Saxony. After 1945, the Province of Saxony was united with Anhalt to form the state of SAXONY-ANHALT with MAGDEBURG as its capital. From 1871 to 1918, the Kingdom of Saxony was part of the German Empire. In the aftermath of World War 1, the kingdom was made a state of the WEIMAR REPUBLIC, with Dresden as its capital. After World War 2, it joined the German Democratic Republic (East Germany). Following German reunification in 1991, it became a state in the Federal Republic of Germany. Area: 18,409sq km (7106sq mi). Pop. (2001) 4,384,192.

Saxony-Anhalt Federal state in s Germany, with Lower Saxony to the NW and Saxony to the SE; the capital is MAGDEBURG. Other major cities include Halle and Dessau. The history of the region coincides with that of SAXONY until 1871, when it became a state of the German Empire. After World War 2, the Red Army briefly occupied the region and the district was abolished in 1952. Following German reunification in 1991, Saxony-Anhalt reformed as a Federal State of Germany. The region is mainly plains, with the Harz Mountains rising in the sw of the state. Predominantly an industrial region, its major manufacturing industries are machine and transport equipment. Area: 20,445sq km (7,892sq mi). Pop. (2001) 2,580,626.

saxophone Musical instrument with a single reed, conical metal tube and finger keys. It was invented by Adolphe Sax in the 1840s. Four members of the saxophone family are commonly used today; these are the soprano (in B^b), the alto (in E^b), the tenor (in B^b) and the baritone (in E^b).

Sayers, Dorothy L. (Leigh) (1893–1957) English novelist and playwright, best known for her detective fiction. Sayers' first novels featured Lord Peter Wimsey, a titled detective who appeared in ten books, including *Whose Body?* (1923) and *Gaudy Night* (1935). She later wrote religious dramas and was noted as a translator of DANTE.

scabies Contagious infection caused by a female mite, *Sarcoptes scabiei*, which burrows into the skin to lay eggs. It can be seen as a dark wavy line on the skin and is treated with antiparasitic creams.

scabious Any annual or perennial plant of the genus *Scabiosa* of the TEASEL family (Dipsacaceae), native to temperate parts of Europe and Asia, and the mountains of E Africa. They have rosettes of leaves and leafy stems, and there are many cultivated garden varieties.

Scafell Pike Highest peak in England, at 978m (3,210ft) high, part of the Scafell range in the LAKE DISTRICT, NW England.

scalar Mathematical quantity that has only a magnitude, as opposed to a VECTOR, which also has direction. Mass, temperature, energy, and speed are scalars.

scale In biology, small hard plate that forms part of the external skin of an animal. It is usually a development of the SKIN layers. In most fish, scales consist of bone in the dermal skin layer. The scales of reptiles and those on the legs of birds are horny growths of the epidermal skin layer and consist mostly of the fibrous protein KERATIN.

scale In music, term for the ordered arrangement of intervals that forms the basis of musical composition. There are many types of scale. In Western music, the most important is the seven-note diatonic scale, both in its major and minor forms. The 12–note CHROMATIC scale has a regular progression of semitones.

scallop Edible BIVALVE mollusc. One shell, or valve, is usually convex and the other almost flat. The shell's surface is ribbed (scalloped). Most scallops have a row of eyes that fringe the fleshy mantle. Width: 2.5–20cm (1–8in). Family Pectinidae.

Scandinavia In physical geography, the N European peninsular countries of SWEDEN and NORWAY. In a broader, cultural sense it also includes DENMARK, FINLAND, ICELAND and the FAROE ISLANDS. The climate ranges from subarctic in the N, to humid continental in the centre, and marine in the W and SW. The terrain is mountainous in the W with swift-flowing streams. In the E the land slopes more gently and there are thousands of lakes, notably in Finland. Part of the region lies within the Arctic Circle, where tundra predominates. Denmark and S Sweden have the best farmland. A large proportion of the land is forested, there are rich mineral deposits, particularly of iron ore and copper, and fishing is still important. The largest cities are STOCKHOLM and GOTHENBURG in Sweden; OSLO in Norway; COPENHAGEN in Denmark, and HELSINKI in Finland. Area: *c.*1.258 million sq km (485,250sq mi).

Scandinavian art Art in the Nordic countries dates back to the end of the Ice Age, when the first rock carvings were made. There was a tendency to use intricate interlacing patterns, which reached a peak in the stonework and wood-carving of the Viking period (*c.*800–*c.*1050). Overshadowed by other European cultures in the Middle Ages and beyond, it was only at the end of the 18th century that artists of international standing began to emerge. Chief among these was Edvard MUNCH.

scandium (symbol Sc) Silver-white, metallic element of group III of the periodic table discovered in 1879 by Swedish chemist Lars Nilson (1840–99) and named for Scandinavia where it was discovered. It is found in thortveitite and, in small amounts, in other minerals. Scandium is a soft metal used as a radioactive tracer and in nickel alkaline storage batteries. Scandium sulphate in a water solution is used to treat seeds for such crops as maize and peas. Chemically it resembles the rare-earth metals of the LANTHANIDE SERIES. Properties: at.no. 21; r.a.m. 44.956; r.d 2.99; m.p. 1,539°C (2,802°F); b.p. 2,832°C (5,130°F); most common isotope Sc^{45} (100%).

scanning In medicine, use of a non-invasive system to detect abnormalities of structure or function in the body. Detectable waves (X-rays, gamma rays, ultrasound) pass through the part of the body to be investigated and the computer-analysed results displayed as images on a viewing screen.

scarab beetle Any of several different species of broad beetles distributed worldwide. Most, including the June bug, Japanese beetle, and rhinoceros beetle, are leaf chafers. A smaller group, including the DUNG BEETLE, are scavengers. Family Scarabaeidae.

Scargill, Arthur (1938–) English trade union leader. In 1981, Scargill became president of the National Union of Mineworkers (NUM). His attempt to confront THATCHER's programme of pit closures and anti-union legislation led to a miner's strike (1984–85). The strike split the miners' and Labour movements.

Scarlatti, Alessandro (1660–1725) Italian BAROQUE composer who laid the foundations of the musical idioms that shaped music until Beethoven. The founder of Neopolitan opera, Scarlatti established the OPERA SERIA style. He wrote more than 100 operas, including *Mitridate Eupatore* (1707).

Scarlatti, (Giuseppe) Domenico (1685–1757) Italian composer, son of Alessandro SCARLATTI. He settled in Spain and is primarily known for his harpsichord sonatas, of which he composed more than 500. Scarlatti is considered the founder of modern keyboard technique.

scarlet fever (scarlatina) Acute infectious disease, usually affecting children, caused by BACTERIA in the *Streptococcus pyogenes* group. It is characterized by a bright red body rash, fever, vomiting and a sore throat. It is treated with ANTIBIOTICS.

scattering Deflection of ELECTROMAGNETIC RADIATION by particles. Where the particles are very much larger than the WAVELENGTH, scattering consists of a mixture of REFLECTION and DIFFRACTION, and the amount of scattering depends very little on wavelength. Where the particles are very much smaller than the wavelength, the amount of scattering is inversely proportional to the fourth power of the wavelength. Thus, small particles scatter blue LIGHT ten times as much as red light. ELEMENTARY PARTICLES can be scattered by atomic nuclei or other particles. It is the means by which the structure of ATOMS was discovered. Hans GEIGER and Ernest Marsden, students of Ernest RUTHERFORD, 'fired' ALPHA PARTICLES through thin metal films and noted their scattering. From the results, Rutherford deduced the existence of the atomic

NUCLEUS. Most knowledge of elementary particles and the discovery of new ones has been obtained by scattering experiments carried out in PARTICLE ACCELERATORS.

scepticism In philosophy, any position that in some way doubts our ability to gain knowledge about the world. Moral scepticism doubts aspects of reason, knowledge or fact in establishing moral values. Scientific scepticism, also called sceptical enquiry, questions claims (often those outside mainstream science) by examining empirical evidence and rejects claims that cannot be tested. More generally, the term can refer to doubts about particular propositions.

Scheele, Karl Wilhelm (1742–86) Swedish chemist who discovered OXYGEN. He discovered it in 1771, but publication of his discovery was delayed, and the credit went to Joseph PRIESTLEY. He made other important discoveries, including CHLORINE, GLYCEROL, and a number of organic acids.

Schelling, Friedrich Wilhelm Joseph von (1775–1854) German philosopher. His early work, *System of Transcendental Idealism* (1800), attempted to develop J.G. Fichte's science of knowledge alongside a philosophy of nature. His philosophy of IDEALISM, with its stress on the perfection of the Absolute, became the blueprint for ROMANTICISM.

Schiele, Egon (1890–1918) Austrian painter, one of the greatest exponents of EXPRESSIONISM. His characteristic paintings portray anguished or isolated naked figures whose distorted bodies reflect their mental pain. Schiele also produced landscapes and semi-allegorical pictures.

Schiller, Johann Christoph Friedrich von (1759–1805) German dramatist, historian, and philosopher. His early blank verse plays, such as *The Robbers* (1781) and *Don Carlos* (1787), are classics of the STURM UND DRANG period. Schiller's aesthetic and philosophical ideas were influenced by the IDEALISM of Kant. His masterpiece is the trilogy *Wallenstein* (1800). Other historical plays include *Mary Stuart* (1801), *Maid of Orleans* (1801), and *William Tell* (1804). Schiller's 'Ode to Joy' forms the finale of Beethoven's Ninth Symphony.

schism Split or division within a Church, sect, or other religious organization, or a breakaway from a Church. Before the Protestant REFORMATION, there were two other important schisms within Christianity. The first was the split between the Eastern ORTHODOX CHURCH and the Western (ROMAN CATHOLIC) Church, brought about by the two churches drifting apart over centuries, and by an escalating series of disputes culminating in a complete break in 1054. The so-called GREAT SCHISM occurred in the 14th and 15th centuries, and involved a split within the Roman Catholic Church itself. Various reasons, including civil war in Italy, led to the papacy transferring to AVIGNON, France, from 1309 to 1377. Rivalry grew between Avignon and Rome, with rival popes elected from 1378 to 1417. The schism was eventually resolved by the Council of CONSTANCE (1417).

schist Large group of METAMORPHIC ROCKS that have been made cleavable, causing the rocks to split into thin plates leaving a wavy, uneven surface.

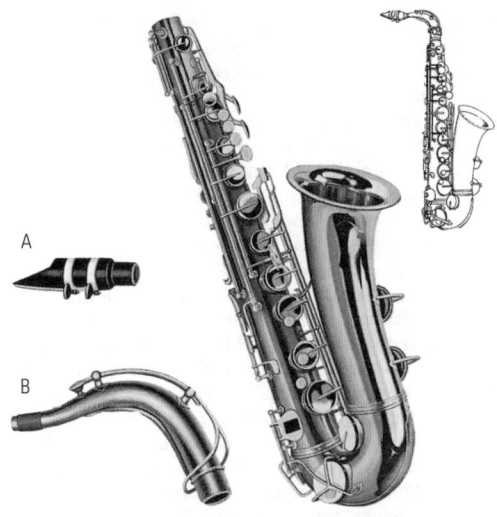

◄ **saxophone** Named after its 19th-century inventor, Adolphe Sax, the saxophone is a single reed instrument that combines features of the oboe and the clarinet, and is usually keyed in $E^{\flat}$ and $B^{\flat}$. It is shown here complete (top right) and with its mouthpiece (A) and neckpiece (B) separate.

▲ **scallop** The various scallops (*Pecten* sp.) are found in offshore waters in many parts of the world. The shell of the scallop has been used as decorative embellishment since Roman times, and was also used as an emblem by the pilgrims who travelled to the Cathedral of St James of Santiago de Compostela, Spain.

▲ **scarab beetle** The fierce-looking Hercules beetle (*Dynastes hercules*) is a type of scarab beetle. The male (shown here) can grow up to 20cm (8in) and possesses a large horn that grows up to 10cm (4in) from its head. Unlike the male, the female does not possess a horn, and its wing cases are covered in a layer of red hairs.

S

schizophrenia Severe MENTAL DISORDER marked by disturbances of cognitive functioning, particularly thinking. As well as the characteristic loss of contact with reality, symptoms can include HALLUCINATIONS and delusions, and muffled or inappropriate emotions. Research suggests that schizophrenia may be caused by high levels of dopamine, a NEUROTRANSMITTER.

Schlegel, August Wilhelm von (1767–1845) German poet, critic, and scholar. The founder and editor of the *Athenaeum*, Schlegel was one of the leading propagandists of German ROMANTICISM. His major work was *On the Language and Wisdom of India* (1808).

Schleswig-Holstein Federal state and historic region in NW Germany; the capital is KIEL. It occupies the S of the Jutland peninsula and extends from the Elbe to the border with Denmark. The land is mainly flat and fertile. The Kiel Canal links the North Sea with the Baltic. The region's principal economic activities of shipping and fishing are concentrated along the Baltic coast and its excellent natural harbours. The River Eider forms the historic border between Schleswig and Holstein. In the early 12th century, the Duchy of Holstein was created as part of the Holy Roman Empire, while Schleswig was made a fiefdom independent of Danish control. They were twice united under the Danish monarchy, but not incorporated into the Danish state. In 1848, Frederick VII proclaimed the complete union of Schleswig with Denmark, the predominantly German population of both Duchies rebelled, and the German Confederation occupied the two Duchies. The 1852 Treaty of London re-established the Duchies' personal union with Denmark. In 1863, Denmark again tried to incorporate Schleswig into the state proper, and Prussia and Austria declared war. In 1865, Schleswig was administered by Prussia, and Holstein by Austria. The resulting tension led to the AUSTRO-PRUSSIAN WAR (1866). Prussian victory created the state of Schleswig-Holstein. In 1920, following a plebiscite, the N part of Schleswig returned to Denmark. In 1937, the city of LÜBECK was incorporated into the German state of Schleswig-Holstein. Area: 15,738sq km (6,075sq mi). Pop. (2001) 2,804,249.

Schliemann, Heinrich (1822–90) German archaeologist. In 1871, he began excavations in Hisarlik, Turkey, which he believed to be the site of the Homeric city of TROY. He uncovered nine superimposed towns; later excavations indicated that the seventh layer was probably the Homeric Troy.

Schmidt, Helmut (1918–) Chancellor of West Germany (1974–82). He became chairman of the Social Democratic Party (SDP) in 1967, and was minister of defence (1969–72) and finance (1972–74) before succeeding Willy BRANDT. He was re-elected in 1976 and 1980, but was forced to resign.

Schnabel, Artur (1882–1951) Austrian pianist and composer who lived in the USA after 1939. He was best known as an interpreter of the classical repertoire, including Mozart and Beethoven, whose 32 piano sonatas he edited and recorded.

Schoenberg, Arnold Franz Walter (1874–1951) Austrian composer. In early works, such as *Verklärte Nacht* (1899), Schoenberg extended the chromaticism of ROMANTICISM. The song cycle *Das Buch der hängenden Gärten* (1908) and the expressionist opera *Erwartung* (1909) revolutionized modern music by abandoning TONALITY. Schoenberg's form of SERIAL MUSIC, known as TWELVE-TONE MUSIC, was first employed in *Suite for Piano* (1923). His operatic masterpiece, *Moses und Aron*, remained unfinished at his death.

scholasticism Medieval philosophy that attempted to join faith to reason by synthesizing theology with classical Greek and Roman thought. Scholasticism was first explored by John Scotus Erigena in the 9th century, and by ANSELM OF CANTERBURY in the 11th century. Its greatest thinkers were Albertus Magnus and Thomas AQUINAS in the 13th century, and DUNS SCOTUS at the turn of the 14th century.

school Place of education, usually at PRIMARY or SECONDARY level. In Western countries, there are usually two or three parallel school systems: one provided by the state and financed by taxpayers; one financed partly by the Church in conjunction with the state or parents; and a third, privately financed by parents. The term 'public school' is used of some private schools in the UK. *See also* COMPREHENSIVE SCHOOL

Schopenhauer, Arthur (1788–1860) German philosopher, whose exposition of the doctrine of the will opposed the IDEALISM of HEGEL and influenced, among others, NIETZSCHE and WAGNER. Schopenhauer's system, described in his main work, *The World as Will and Idea* (1819), was an intensely pessimistic one. The will to endure was an individual's prime motivation, and the negation of will and desire provided the possibility of escape from pain.

Schröder, Gerhard (1944–) German statesman, chancellor (1998–2005). Schröder built a reputation for moderation as Minister President of Lower Saxony for three terms. In 1998, he became the Social Democratic Party's candidate in the general election. His election victory ended Helmut KOHL's 16 years as chancellor. Schröder formed a coalition with the Greens. He was succeeded by Angela MERKEL.

Schrödinger, Erwin (1887–1961) Austrian physicist, who formulated a quantum mechanical wave equation. He went on to found the science of quantum WAVE MECHANICS and shared the 1933 Nobel Prize in physics with the English physicist Paul DIRAC. The wave equation was based on a suggestion by the French physicist Louis de BROGLIE that moving particles have a wave-like nature.

Schubert, Franz Peter (1797–1828) Austrian composer whose symphonies represent the final extension of the classical SONATA form, and whose lieder (songs) are the height of ROMANTICISM. Among his more popular works are symphonies such as the Eighth ('Unfinished', 1822), and the Ninth in C major (1825). Schubert wrote more than 600 songs to the lyrics of such poets as Heine and Schiller; these include the cycles *Die schöne Müllerin* (1823) and *Winterreise* (1827). In his tragically short lifetime, he also composed much chamber music, and his String Quintet (1828) is a masterpiece.

Schumacher, Michael (1969–) German racing driver. He began Formula 1 racing in 1991, and soon joined the Benetton team. He won his first Grand Prix in 1992. Schumacher won the world drivers' championship in 1994 and 1995. He switched to race for Ferrari in 1996. A supremely gifted driver, Schumacher narrowly failed to win the 1997 and 1998 world titles, but went on to win for Ferrari in 2000, 2001, 2002, 2003 and 2004.

Schumann, Clara Josephine Wieck (1819–96) German pianist and composer, wife of Robert SCHUMANN. She was an outstanding interpreter of the works of her husband and of their friend Brahms. She composed chamber works, piano pieces and songs, mainly for her own concerts.

Schumann, Robert Alexander (1810–56) German composer and leading figure of ROMANTICISM. Schumann's piano compositions include *Kinderszenen* (1838), *Carnaval* (1834–35), and *Waldscenen* (1848–49). Among his best song cycles is *Frauenliebe und Leben* (1840). His 'Spring' Symphony (1841) and Piano Concerto (1841–45) are among his best-known orchestral works.

Schwarzkopf, Dame Elisabeth (1915–2006) German soprano known for her versatility in recitals, oratorios, and operas. She sang with the Berlin State Opera from 1938 to 1942, and became principal soprano of the Vienna State Opera in 1944. She specialized in Richard Strauss, Mozart, Schubert, and Hugo Wolf, and made many fine recordings.

Schwarzkopf, H. Norman (1934–) US general. A Vietnam veteran, Schwarzkopf was deputy commander of the US forces that invaded Grenada in 1983. As supreme commander of Allied forces in the GULF WAR (1991), he liberated Kuwait

▶ **Schumacher** German racing driver Michael Schumacher is one of the greatest drivers in the history of Formula 1. After two successive world drivers' championships with Benetton, Schumacher switched to Ferrari. In 1997, he narrowly failed to become Ferrari's first world champion since Jody Scheckter (1979). In 1998, he finished second to Mika Hakkinen in the drivers' championship. In 1999, a broken leg forced him out of the championship. Schumacher regained his world title in 2000. His brother Ralf (1975–), a fellow Formula 1 driver, won his first grand prix in 2001 (San Marino).

S

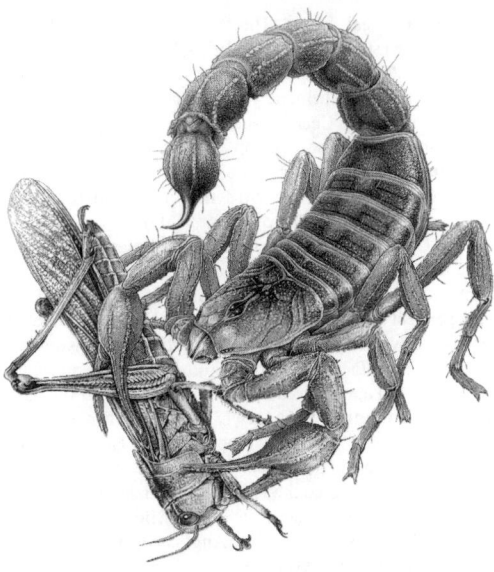

◄ **scorpion** The sting of the scorpion is worked by opposing muscles fixed to the base of the sting, which contract and relax, forcing the sharp tip into its prey's tissue. The poison, stored in the poison gland, is forced down and out of the tip of the sting by muscles located around the gland.

from Iraqi occupation. After retiring from the army, he published his memoirs, *It Doesn't Take a Hero* (1992).

Schweitzer, Albert (1875–1965) Theologian, musician, medical missionary, and philosopher. Schweitzer was born in Alsace, but spent most of his life in Gabon (then French Equatorial Africa), where he founded the Lambaréné Hospital in 1913. He was honoured as a scientist and humanitarian, and as an organist and an expert on J.S. Bach. He received the 1952 Nobel Peace Prize. His works include *Kant's Philosophy of Religion* (1899) and *Out of My Life and Thought* (1931).

Schwitters, Kurt (1887–1948) German DADA artist and writer. He is best known for his invention of *Merz* to denote art that was made from refuse. Schwitters constructed elaborate sculptures and even room interiors from such 'found objects' as old newspapers and tram tickets.

sciatica Severe pain in the back and radiating down one or other leg, along the course of the sciatic nerve. It is usually caused by inflammation of the sciatic nerve or by pressure on the spinal nerve roots.

science fiction Literary genre in which reality is subject to certain transformations in order to explore man's potential and his relation to his environment; these transformations are usually technological and the stories set in the future or in imaginary worlds. The birth of the modern genre is generally dated to the US comic strip *Amazing Stories* (1926). Until the 1960s, most science fiction involved adventure stories set in space. Some writers, such as Isaac ASIMOV, explored the paradoxes contained in purely scientific ideas; others, including Ray BRADBURY, stressed the moral implications of their stories.

Scientology Religion founded (1954) by L. Ron Hubbard in California, USA. It attracts criticism over its methods of recruiting and keeping members.

Scilly, Isles of Archipelago of more than 140 isles and islets in the Atlantic Ocean off the coast of Cornwall, sw England, 45km (28mi) sw of Land's End; the capital is Hugh Town (St Mary's). The terrain is mostly rocky, and many shipwrecks lie off the coasts. The combination of mild climate and heavy rainfall ensure a good environment for growing flowers and spring vegetables. Tourism is an increasingly important industry. Only five of the islands are inhabited: St Mary's (the largest), Tresco, St Martin's, St Agnes and Bryher. Total pop. (2001) 2153.

Scipio Africanus Major (236–183 BC) (Publius Cornelius Scipio) Roman general in the second of the PUNIC WARS. He defeated the Carthaginian forces in Spain in 209 BC. Elected consul in 205 BC he invaded North Africa with a volunteer army and defeated HANNIBAL at Zama in 202 BC earning the honorary surname Africanus. He was again elected consul in 194, but later retired from public life, disillusioned by attacks from opponents jealous of his popularity.

Scipio Africanus Minor (185–129 BC) (Publius Cornelius Scipio Aemilianus) Roman general of the third PUNIC WAR. He took his grandfather-by-adoption's name, SCIPIO AFRICANUS MAJOR. He destroyed Carthage in 146 BC ending the Punic Wars, and in 133 ended a long war in Spain by destroying the city of Numantia.

sclerosis Degenerative hardening of tissue, usually due to scarring following inflammation or as a result of ageing. It can affect the brain and spinal cord, causing neurological symptoms, or the walls of the arteries.

scorpion Any of numerous species of ARACHNIDS that live in warmer regions throughout the world. It has two main body sections, two eyes, a pair of pedipalps (pincers), and a long slender tail ending in a curved, poisonous sting. Length: to 17cm (7in). Class Arachnida; order Scorpionida.

Scorpius (Scorpio, scorpion) Constellation of the s sky, situated on the ecliptic between Libra and Sagittarius. The Milky Way passes through the region. The brightest star is the first-magnitude Alpha Scorpii (Antares).

Scorsese, Martin (1942–) US film director. His first major success was *Alice Doesn't Live Here Anymore* (1975). Scorsese often casts Robert DE NIRO in leading roles, such as in *Taxi Driver* (1976), *Raging Bull* (1980), *The King of Comedy* (1983) *Goodfellas* (1990) and *Cape Fear* (1991). Other films include *The Age of Innocence* (1993) and *Kundun* (1997).

Scotland Northern part of the main island of Great Britain, and a constituent of the United Kingdom of Great Britain and Northern Ireland; the capital is EDINBURGH. The largest city is GLASGOW. In 1996, Scotland divided into 29 new unitary authority areas and three island authority areas. Its jagged coastline features many islands (including the ORKNEY and SHETLAND ISLANDS), lochs (including LOMOND and NESS) and firths. Major Scottish rivers include the TAY, CLYDE, Dee, and Forth. Scotland broadly divides into three geographical regions: the Southern Uplands, immediately N of the English border, which are sparsely populated, hilly moorland; the Central Lowlands, where the majority of the population live; and the HIGHLANDS, including BEN NEVIS. In pre-history, Scotland was inhabited by the PICTS. In AD 843, Kenneth I united the lands of the Picts and the SCOTS. In 1174 Scotland became a fiefdom of England. Richard I granted Scottish freedom in 1189, but the enmity between England and Scotland continued. Edward I forced the Scots to submit, only for William WALLACE to lead a Scottish revolt. ROBERT I (THE BRUCE) recaptured much Scottish land and defeated the English at the Battle of Bannockburn (1314); this led to England's recognition of Scottish independence in 1328. Internal factionalism and weak government characterized the 15th century. JAMES IV and many Scottish nobles died at the Battle of Flodden (1513). The Protestant REFORMATION quickly took root in Scotland via the preaching of John KNOX. In 1538, JAMES V cemented the French alliance by marrying Mary of Guise, a French Catholic. When her daughter, MARY, QUEEN OF SCOTS, assumed the throne in 1561, England supported the Scottish Protestants, and France backed the Catholics. The Protestant faction forced Mary to relinquish the throne in 1567. Her son, James VI, assumed the Scottish crown, and in 1601 he was also crowned JAMES I of England, thereby uniting the English and Scottish thrones. The Scots opposed Charles I in the English CIVIL WAR, but the King's concessions to PRESBYTERIANISM won the support of the COVENANTERS. The GLORIOUS REVOLUTION (1688) re-established Presbyterianism as the Scottish national Church. The massacre of the Macdonald clan by WILLIAM III at Glencoe in 1692 tarnished his rule, and JACOBITE agitation prompted the constitutional union of the two crowns in the Act of UNION (1707). At CULLODEN Moor (1746), the Jacobite insurgency was finally suppressed with the defeat of the Highlanders led by Prince Charles Edward STUART. (*See* UNITED KINGDOM for subsequent history).

The principal agricultural activity is the rearing of livestock; oats and potatoes are the chief crops. Coal mining and heavy industry dominated the economy of the central lowlands by the end of the 19th century, but declined in the 1980s. The discovery of North Sea oil and natural gas in the 1970s benefited the Scottish economy. Other important industries include textiles,

▲ **Scott** Antarctic explorer Robert Falcon Scott and his four companions pulled heavy sledges by hand across the high polar plateau in their trek to the South Pole in 1910–12. All five men died. Their bodies were later recovered along with Scott's diaries, scientific collections, and letters to the widows of his companions. The story of Scott's tragic expedition entered into British folklore.

▲ **sea horse** Related to the pipe fishes – family *Syngnathidae* – the sea horse (*Hippocampus* sp.) is the only fish with a prehensile tail, which it uses to cling to seaweed. The sea horse swims weakly with an upright stance, and is carried along by ocean currents.

S

▶ **sea anemone** Having no rigid structures, the sea anemone supports itself by circulating water around its central cavity (1). Water is drawn down through siphonoglyphs (grooves) (2) at the side of the cavity, and is expelled up the centre. The tentacles (3) can be withdrawn by individual retractor muscles (4).

whisky, beer, and fishing. The SCOTTISH NATIONAL PARTY (SNP) gained support during the 1970s, but a 1979 referendum for a separate Scottish Assembly was defeated. A 1997 referendum voted overwhelmingly in favour of devolution. Scotland retains its own Church, education and legal system. Area: 77,167sq km (29,797sq mi). Pop. (2001) 5,062,011.

Scotland Yard Name given to the London headquarters of the Metropolitan Police and synonymous with the CRIMINAL INVESTIGATION DEPARTMENT (CID).

Scots Originally a Celtic people from N Ireland. They were Gaelic speaking. Their raids on the w coast of Roman Britain from the 3rd to the 5th century failed to establish independent settlements in Wales or NW England. In the 5th century, however, they were able to establish the Kingdom of Dalriada in Pictish territory. From the 11th century, the term has been applied to those people living in Scotland.

Scott, Sir George Gilbert (1811–78) English architect, prominent figure in the GOTHIC REVIVAL. He achieved a reputation with his design for the Church of St Nicholas, Hamburg. He designed the Albert Memorial (1862–70) and St Pancras Station, London. His son, **Giles Gilbert Scott** (1880–1960), designed the new Anglican Cathedral in Liverpool, the last major example of the Gothic revival.

Scott, Sir Ridley (1937–) English film director. *Alien* (1979) and *Blade Runner* (1982) were seminal science-fiction offerings. *Thelma and Louise* (1991) was another genre-breaking box-office success. Scott won an Academy Award for best picture for *Gladiator* (2000) and was knighted in 2003.

Scott, Robert Falcon (1868–1912) English Antarctic explorer. Scott's first expedition to the South Pole, in the *Discovery*, (1901–04) ended in failure. His second expedition (1910–12) reached the Pole, but found that Roald AMUNDSEN had got there first. Beset by blizzards on their return journey, Scott and his party perished within 18km (11mi) of safety. His diaries were published as *Scott's Last Expedition* (1913).

Scott, Sir Walter (1771–1832) Scottish novelist and poet. He began his career with a collection of old Scottish ballads, *Minstrelsy of the Scottish Border* (1802–03). The wider fame brought by *The Lay of the Last Minstrel* (1805) was consolidated by the poems *Marmion* (1808) and *The Lady of the Lake* (1810). In 1814, he turned to historical fiction. His first novel, the anonymously published *Waverley* (1814), was an immediate success and was followed by a series of Scottish novels, including *Rob Roy* (1818) and *The Heart of Midlothian* (1818). Among his later novels are *Ivanhoe* (1819), *Kenilworth* (1821) and *Quentin Durward* (1823).

Scottish (Scots) Dialect of English traditionally spoken in Scotland and regarded by some experts as a distinct GERMANIC language. It is also called Lowland Scots (or Lallans), to distinguish it from the Scots GAELIC (or broad Scots) spoken in the Scottish Highlands, and to differentiate it from the English of Scotland's middle class. It developed from the Northumbrian dialect of EARLY ENGLISH before AD 700. Over the following 600 or 700 years, it spread throughout Scotland.

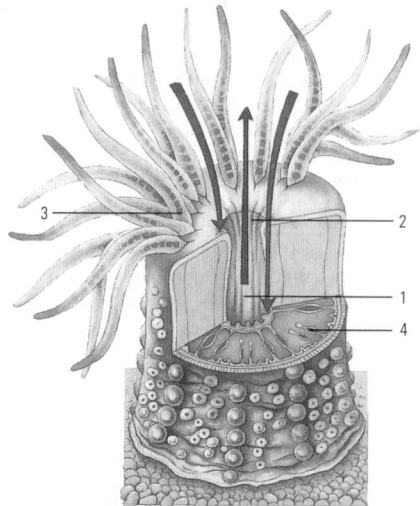

Before the union of the English and Scottish crowns in 1603, the Scottish language was both a national language and an official court language. The language continues as a spoken dialect in many areas, and as a vehicle for a vibrant literature.

Scottish National Party (SNP) UK political party, founded in 1928. The SNP grew out of the Scottish Home Rule Association, formed in 1886, and gained its first member of Parliament in 1945. During the 1960s, it significantly expanded its support base, gaining around 20% of the Scottish vote in most subsequent general elections. It advocates Scotland's independence (from the UK) within the European Union. The SNP won six seats in the 2005 general election under Alex Salmond, party leader (1990–2000, 2004–), and are the largest party in the Scottish Parliament.

scrapie Fatal disease of sheep and goats that affects the central nervous system, causing staggering and itching that makes an infected animal scrape itself against various objects. It is caused by a slow-acting, virus-like, microscopic particle called a PRION. The animal usually dies within six months of exhibiting the first symptoms. The disease is thought to be related to BOVINE SPONGIFORM ENCEPHALOPATHY (BSE) and CREUTZFELDT-JAKOB DISEASE (CJD).

scree (talus) Heap of rock waste lying at the bottom of a cliff. It is made up of particles that have been loosened from the cliff rock by weathering.

screening In medicine, a test applied either to an individual or to groups of people who, although apparently healthy, are known to be at risk of developing a particular disease. It is used to detect treatable diseases early in their development.

Scriabin, Alexander Nicolas (1872–1915) Russian composer and pianist. He wrote highly original piano music in which he used chords built in fourths instead of the conventional major and minor triads. His most significant works include ten piano sonatas, *The Poem of Ecstasy* (1908), three symphonies, and numerous short piano pieces.

scribe Court secretary in ancient times; in JUDAISM, member of a class of scholars expert in Jewish law. From the 6th century, the Scribes acted as teachers and interpreters of the TORAH.

scriptures Sacred writings of a RELIGION. In Christianity, they are the books of the OLD TESTAMENT and NEW TESTAMENT, with or without those of the APOCRYPHA. It is also possible to speak of the KORAN as the scripture of ISLAM, and the VEDAS as the scriptures of HINDUISM.

scuba diving Diving with the use of self-contained underwater breathing apparatus, or scuba. Initially developed by Jacques COUSTEAU, the equipment usually consists of tanks of compressed air connected to a demand regulator. This controls the air flow to the mouth. Other equipment includes a wet suit to insulate the diver, a weighted belt, a face mask, and flippers.

sculpture Art of creating forms in three dimensions, either in the round or in relief. Techniques employed include carving (in wood, stone, marble, ivory, etc.), modelling (in clay, wax, etc.), or casting (in bronze and other metals). The history of sculpture parallels that of PAINTING. The early civilizations of Egypt, Mesopotamia, India, and the Far East were rich in sculpture. The Greeks developed a style of relief and free-standing sculpture. Roman sculptors were profoundly influenced by the Greeks, but forsook the Greek ideal in portraiture, which they enriched with individual characterization. Medieval European sculpture was frequently a feature of ROMANESQUE and Gothic churches. Highly stylized in the Romanesque period, this architectural sculpture became more representative in the Gothic era. Prior to the RENAISSANCE, individual sculptors rarely achieved fame. The works of such masters as GHIBERTI, DONATELLO, and MICHELANGELO enriched the Florentine Renaissance. High BAROQUE sculpture is exemplified in the works of the architect-sculptor BERNINI in Rome. Pierre Puget was the movement's leading exponent in France where, in the 18th century, it was superseded by NEO-CLASSICISM. This extended into the 19th century, when it was rivalled and replaced by a movement of realist sculpture, such as that of RODIN. African, Aztec, and other ethnic and ancient sculpture stimulated modern sculptors such as PICASSO, MODIGLIANI, BRANCUSI and MOORE.

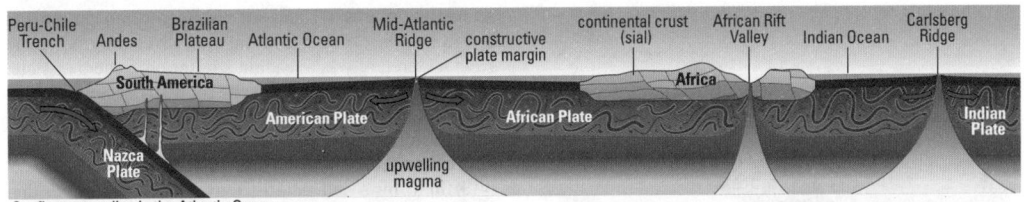

Seafloor spreading in the Atlantic Ocean

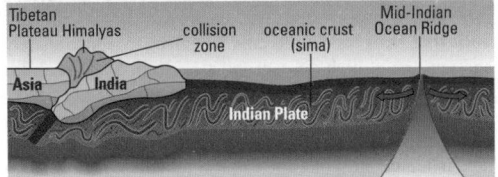

Seafloor spreading in the Indian Ocean and continental plate collision

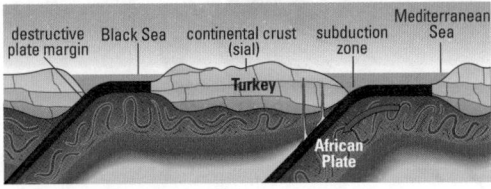

Oceanic and continental plate collision

◄ **seafloor spreading** The vast ridges that divide the Earth's crust beneath each of the world's oceans mark the boundaries between tectonic plates that are gradually moving in opposite directions. As the plates shift apart, molten magma rises from the mantle to seal the rift and the seafloor slowly spreads toward the continental landmasses. The rate of spreading, calculated by magnetic analysis of the rock, is c.3.75cm (1.5in) a year in the North Atlantic Ocean. Underwater volcanoes mark the line where the continental rise begins. As the plates meet, much of the denser ocean crust dips beneath the continental plate and melts back into the magma.

scurvy Disease caused by a deficiency of VITAMIN C (ascorbic acid), which is contained in fresh fruit and vegetables. It is characterized by weakness, painful joints, and bleeding gums.

Scylla In Greek mythology, a female sea monster. Once a beautiful nymph beloved of POSEIDON, changed by CIRCE into a long-necked, six-headed beast. She lived with CHARYBDIS by the Straits of Messina between Sicily and Italy and ate sailors.

Scythians Nomadic people who inhabited the steppes N of the Black Sea in the 1st millennium BC. In the 7th century BC their territory extended into Mesopotamia, the Balkans, and Greece. Powerful warriors, their elaborate tombs contain evidence of great wealth. Pressure from the Sarmatians confined them to the Crimea (c.300BC) and their culture disappeared.

SDLP Acronym for SOCIAL DEMOCRATIC LABOUR PARTY

SDP Acronym for SOCIAL DEMOCRATIC PARTY

sea anemone Sessile, polyp-type CNIDARIAN animal found in marine pools and along rocky shores. It has a cylindrical body with tentacles around its mouth; the colour varies according to species. Height: to 20cm (8in). Class Anthozoa; genera include *Tealia*, *Anemonia* and *Metridium*.

seaborgium (symbol Sg) Synthetic, radioactive, metallic ELEMENT of the transactinide series. It has a HALF-LIFE of less than a second. It was thought to have been discovered in 1974 by US nuclear scientist Albert Ghiorso (1915–) and colleagues at the University of California at Berkeley, but its existence was only proved in 1994. It was named in 1999 after US nuclear chemist Glenn Seaborg (1912–99), having first been temporarily named unnilhexium. Properties: at.no. 106.

sea cow See DUGONG

sea cucumber Marine ECHINODERM found in rocky areas. It is a cylindrical animal with a fleshy body in five parts around a central axis; it has branched tentacles around the mouth. Edible species are smoked and dried. Species include the cotton-spinners (*Holothuria* spp.). Class Holothuroidea.

seafloor Floor of the OCEANS. The major features of the seafloor are the continental shelf, the continental rise, the ABYSSAL floor, sea-mounts, oceanic trenches and mid-ocean ridges. The **abyssal** or deep ocean floor is c.3km (1.8mi) deep, and is mostly made of basaltic rock covered with fine-grained sediment consisting of dust and the shells of marine organisms. Oceanic **trenches** are up to 11km (7mi) deep, typically 50–100km (30–60mi) wide, and may be thousands of kilometres long. The slopes are usually asymmetrical with the steeper slope on the landward side and a more gentle slope on the side of the ocean basin. They are regarded as the site of plate subduction. Oceanic **ridges** are long, linear volcanic structures which tend to occupy the middle of seafloors; they are the sites of crustal spreading. *See also* SEAFLOOR SPREADING

seafloor spreading Theory that explains how CONTINENTAL DRIFT occurs. It proposes that the ocean floor is moved laterally as new basalt rock is injected along mid-ocean ridges, and so the ocean floor becomes older with increasing distance from the ridge. *See also* PLATE TECTONICS

sea horse Marine fish found in shallow tropical and temperate waters. It swims in an upright position, and has an outer bony skeleton of platelike rings, a mouth at the end of a long snout, and a curled, prehensile tail with which it clings

to seaweed. The male incubates the young in a brood pouch. Length: 3.8–30.5cm (1.5–12in). Family Syngnathidae.

seal Any of several species of carnivorous, primarily marine, aquatic mammals. It feeds on fish, crustaceans, and other marine animals; various species are hunted for meat, hides, oil, and fur. Species of true, earless seals such as the leopard seal (*Hydrurga leptonyx*), hooded seal (*Cystophora cristata*), and bearded seal (*Erignathus barbatus*) are included in the family Phocidae. They swim with powerful strokes of their hind flippers and sinuous body movements, but are clumsy on land and move by wriggling. Members of the eared family Otariidae have longer fore flippers used for propulsion, and use all four limbs when on land. They include fur seals (genera *Callorhinus* and *Arctocephalus*) and species of SEA LION. Order Pinnepedia.

sea lion Any of five species of SEALS that live in coastal waters of the Pacific and feed primarily on fish and squid. They have streamlined bodies and long fore flippers for propulsion. The males of all species, except the California sea lion (*Zalophus californianus*), have manes. The largest species is the Steller sea lion (*Eumetopias jubata*); it may reach 3.3m (11ft) in length. Order Pinnepedia; family Otariidae.

seaplane Aircraft that can land on and take off from water. The first practical seaplane was built in the USA by Glenn H. Curtiss, and flown in 1911. There are two main types of seaplane. **Floatplanes** have large floats that support the fuselage above the water. **Flying boats** float on their boat-shaped hulls, with small floats supporting the wings.

sea slug (nudibranch) Any of numerous species of marine gastropod molluscs, related to snails and found worldwide. They have no shells, quills or mantle cavities, frequent shallow water, and feed mainly on sea anemones. Order Nudibranchia.

seasonal affective disorder (SAD) Mental depression apparently linked to the seasonally changing amount of light. Sufferers experience depression during autumn and winter.

seasons Four periods of the year based on differential solar heating of the Earth as it makes its annual revolution of the Sun. The Northern Hemisphere receives more solar radiation when its Pole points towards the Sun in summer and less in winter when it points away. The opposite holds for the Southern Hemisphere. The seasons begin at the vernal (spring) and autumnal EQUINOXES and the winter and summer SOLSTICES.

SEATO Acronym for SOUTHEAST ASIA TREATY ORGANIZATION

Seattle City and seaport in w Washington, USA, on Elliott Bay between Lake Washington and Puget Sound. Settled in 1851, it developed rapidly after the arrival of the railway (1893). Seattle served as the gateway for the Alaska Gold Rush (1897). It has been the centre of the US aerospace industry since William Boeing opened his first factory here in 1916. Seattle's economy diversified in recent years. The computer company Microsoft has its headquarters here. Industries: shipbuilding, precision instruments, chemicals, lumber, fishing, tourism. Pop. (2000) 2,712,000.

sea urchin Spiny ECHINODERM animal found in marine tidal pools along rocky shores. Round with long, radiating (often poisonous) moveable spines, its skeletal plates fuse to form a perforated shell. Class Echinoidae.

▲ **seal** The harp seal (*Phoca groenlandica*, top) is a true seal. It breeds in the N Atlantic and Arctic oceans and migrates S in winter. They feed on large plankton and fish, and grow to a length of nearly 2m (6.5ft), and can weigh up to 180kg (400lb). The northern fur seal (*Callorhinus ursinus*, bottom), unlike the harp seal, is an eared seal. It migrates in winter from the Bering Sea to California and Japan. It feeds on squid, fish, and crustacea. They too grow to 2m (6.5ft), and an adult male can weigh between 180 and 300kg (400–650lb).

S

INTERNET

Scott, Sir Walter
▸ www.literatureclassics.com/authors/Scott

Scriabin, Alexander Nicolas
▸ www.karadar.net/Dictionary/scriabin.html

► **secretary bird** Found in sub-Saharan Africa, the secretary bird (*Sagittarius serpentarius*) gets its name from the feathers that protrude behind its head, resembling quill pens. It is a well-known snake killer and runs after its prey on foot in a zig-zag fashion. It kills the snake by a blow from its foot, followed by battering from the wings. The secretary bird is so unlike other members in the same order that it is in a separate family.

seaweed Any of numerous species of brown, green or red ALGAE, found in greatest profusion in shallow waters on rocky coasts. KELPS are the largest forms. Many species are important for the manufacture of fertilizers or food, or as a valuable source of chemicals such as iodine. Kingdom Protoctista.

sebaceous gland Gland in the skin producing the oily substance sebum, which secretes onto the skin and hair, making them water-repellent and supple.

Sebastian, Saint (d. *c.*AD 288) Roman Christian martyr. Legend says that he was a favourite of Emperor DIOCLETIAN who, on learning that Sebastian was a Christian, condemned him to be killed by arrows. He survived and later voluntarily appeared before Diocletian, who this time had him beaten to death. His feast day is January 20.

Sebastiano del Piombo (1485–1547) (Sebastiano Luciani) Italian painter of the VENETIAN SCHOOL. In 1511, he went to Rome, where he created a series of mythological FRESCOS at the Villa Farnese. Some of his best works are his portraits, including his portrayal of Pope Clement VII (1526).

seborrhoea Disorder of the SEBACEOUS GLANDS characterized by over-production of sebum that results in red, scaly patches on the skin and dandruff.

secant In TRIGONOMETRY, ratio of the length of the hypotenuse to the length of the side adjacent to an acute angle in a right-angled triangle. The secant of angle A is usually abbreviated to sec A, and is equal to the reciprocal of its COSINE.

secession Formal separation from an organized body. The term usually applies to the withdrawal of a political unit from the state of which it formed a part. An example is the secession of 11 Southern states from the USA to form the CONFEDERATE STATES OF AMERICA (1861).

second (symbol s) SI unit of time defined as the time taken for 9,192,631,770 periods of vibrations of the electromagnetic radiation emitted by a caesium-133 atom. It is commonly defined as $\frac{1}{60}$ of a minute. *See also* PHYSICAL UNITS

secondary school SCHOOLS providing education for pupils after PRIMARY SCHOOL. The ages at which pupils transfer from primary to secondary schools in the UK vary in different education authorities. It is usually at age 11. In some areas, with middle schools, transfer is at 12, and in independent schools it is usually at 13. Some secondary schools cater for the 11–16 age range, others for 11–18.

second coming Christian belief that JESUS CHRIST will one day return to Earth. He will sweep away the present world order, establish his kingdom, deal with his enemies, and reward those who have been faithful to him.

Second World War *See* WORLD WAR 2

secretary bird BIRD OF PREY found in Africa, s of the Sahara. It is pale grey with black markings, and has quill-like feathers behind its ears, large wings, and long legs and tail. It feeds on reptiles, eggs, and insects, and lays its eggs in a tree nest. Height: 1.2m (4ft). Species *Sagittarius serpentarius*.

secretary of state Name for several government officers in Britain. The office dates from the 14th century, when the King's secretary was a leading adviser on matters of state. There are now secretaries of state for many departments. In the USA, the name is given to the cabinet member responsible for formulating and implementing foreign policy.

secretion Production and discharge of a substance, usually a fluid, by a cell or a GLAND. The substance so discharged is also known as a secretion. Secretions include ENZYMES, HORMONES, SALIVA, and sweat.

sedative Drug used for its calming effect, to reduce anxiety and tension; at high doses it induces sleep. Sedative drugs include NARCOTICS, BARBITURATES, and BENZODIAZEPINES.

sedge Any of numerous species of grass-like perennial plants, especially those of the genus *Carex*, widely distributed in temperate, cold, and tropical mountain regions, usually on wet ground or in water. Cultivated as ornamental plants, they have narrow leaves and spikes of brown, green or greenish yellow flowers. Family Cyperaceae.

Sedgemoor, Battle of (July 16, 1685) Defeat of an English rebellion led by the Duke of MONMOUTH against JAMES II. An attempt to launch a surprise night attack by the untrained rebel forces ended in disaster.

sediment In geology, a general term used to describe any material (such as gravel, sand, and clay) that is transported and deposited by water, ice, wind, or gravity. The term includes material such as lime that is transported in solution and later precipitated, and organic deposits such as coal and coral reefs.

sedimentary rock Type of rock formed by deposition of SEDIMENT derived from pre-existing rocks, which may have been sedimentary, IGNEOUS or METAMORPHIC. Most sediment accumulates on the bed of the sea, having been dumped there by rivers, or having accumulated as dead sea creatures fall to the seafloor. This accumulated sediment is consolidated and compressed. Earth movements uplift the sediments, and they may be tilted, folded or faulted. The resulting rocks are sedimentary, and their type depends on their composition. Sedimentaries consisting of land sediment are **clastic** rocks, and are gravels, SANDS, SILTS or CLAYS, according to the size of the particles. Other types of sedimentary rock include: LIMESTONE, which consists of fragments of dead sea creatures; COAL, which is accumulated vegetation; coralline, which contains large quantities of CORAL; and CHALK, which is a pure form of limestone, with very little land sediment. *See also* FAULT; FOLD

Seebeck effect Thermoelectric effect important in the thermocouple for temperature measurement. If wires of two different metals are joined at their ends to form a circuit, a current flows if the junctions are maintained at differenttemperatures. It is named after German physicist Thomas Seebeck who made this discovery. *See also* PELTIER EFFECT

seed Part of a flowering plant that contains the embryo and food store. It is formed in the ovary by FERTILIZATION of the female GAMETE (*see* POLLEN). Food may be stored in a special tissue called the endosperm, or may be concentrated in swollen seed leaves (COTYLEDONS). Seeds are the unit of dispersal of ANGIOSPERMS and CONIFERS. *See also* FRUIT; GERMINATION

Segovia, Andrés (1893–1987) Spanish guitarist. Segovia helped establish the guitar as a concert instrument, adapting it to modern composers and transcribing early contrapuntal music.

Segrè, Emilio Gino (1905–89) US physicist, b. Italy. In 1937, Segrè discovered TECHNETIUM – the first ELEMENT to be artificially produced. In 1940, he helped to discover ASTATINE and PLUTONIUM-239. He is, however, chiefly remembered for his discovery of the anti-proton. In 1955, using a Bevatron particle ACCELERATOR, Segrè and US physicist Owen Chamberlain bombarded copper with high-energy PROTONS to produce the antiparticle of the proton. Chamberlain and Segrè shared the 1959 Nobel Prize in physics. *See also* ANTIMATTER

segregation Separation of a specific group from the rest of society on such grounds as race, religion, or sex. Such separation might be enshrined in law, as in the Southern states of the USA before the CIVIL RIGHTS movement or in South Africa in the era of APARTHEID.

Seine River in N central France. It rises in Langres Plateau near DIJON, and flows NW through PARIS to enter the English

S

Channel near LE HAVRE. It connects to the rivers LOIRE, RHÔNE, Meuse, Schelde, Saône, and Somme by a network of canals. With its main tributaries (Aube, Marne, Oise, Yonne, Loing, and Eure), the Seine drains the entire Paris Basin. The most important river of N France, it is navigable for most ocean-going vessels as far as ROUEN – 560km (350mi) of its full course of 776km (482mi).

seismology Study of seismic waves, the shock waves produced by EARTHQUAKES. The velocity of seismic waves varies according to the material through which they pass. Primary (P) and secondary (S) waves are transmitted by the solid earth. Only P waves are transmitted through fluid zones. Seismic waves are detected and recorded by **seismographs**.

Selassie, Haile *See* HAILE SELASSIE

Selene In Greek mythology, goddess of the Moon, daughter of Hyperion and sister of Helios (the Sun) and Eos (the Dawn). Each night, she drove her chariot across the sky, as her brother Helios, the Sun god, had done during the day.

selenium Grey METALLOID element of group VI of the periodic table, discovered (1817) by J.J. BERZELIUS. Its chief source is a by-product in the electrolytic refining of copper. It resembles sulphur. It is extensively used in PHOTOELECTRIC CELLS, SOLAR CELLS, XEROGRAPHY and red pigments. Properties: at.no. 34; r.a.m. 78.96; r.d. 4.79; m.p. 217°C (422.6°F); b.p. 684.9°C (1265°F); most common isotope Se^{80} (49.82%).

Seles, Monica (1973–) US tennis player, b. Yugoslavia. Seles won her first major championship (French Open, 1990) when only 16 years old. She also won the US Open (1991), and the Australian Open in three successive years (1991–93). Seles' career was briefly halted in 1993 when she was stabbed by a fan of her rival, Steffi GRAF. She resumed competitive play in 1995, and reclaimed her Australian title in 1996.

Seleucids Hellenistic dynastic empire founded by SELEUCUS I, a former general of ALEXANDER THE GREAT, between 306 and 281 BC. Centred on Syria, it included most of the Asian provinces of Alexander's empire, extending from the E Mediterranean to India. War with the Ptolemies of Egypt and, later, the Romans, steadily reduced its territory. In 63 BC its depleted territory became the Roman province of Syria.

Seleucus Name of two kings of Syria. **Seleucus I** (c.355–281BC) was a trusted general of ALEXANDER THE GREAT and founder of the SELEUCID dynasty. By 281 BC he secured control of Babylonia, Syria, and all of Asia Minor. He appeared to be on the brink of restoring the whole of Alexander's empire under his rule when he was murdered. **Seleucus II** (r.247–226BC) spent his reign fighting Ptolemy III of Egypt and Antiochus Hierax, his brother and rival, losing territory to both.

Seljuk Nomadic tribesmen from central Asia who adopted Islam in the 7th century, and founded the Baghdad sultanate in 1055. Their empire included Syria, Mesopotamia, and Persia. Under Alp Arslan, they defeated the Byzantines at Manzikert in 1071, which led to their occupation of Anatolia. They revived Sunni administration and religious institutions, checking the spread of Shi'ite Islam and laying the organizational basis for the future Ottoman administration. In the early 12th century, the Seljuk Empire began to disintegrate, and the MONGOLS conquered the Seljuk states in the 13th century.

Sellafield Site of a nuclear power station on the Irish Sea coast in Cumbria, NW England. It opened as Windscale in 1956. In 1957, a fire led to a serious radioactive emission. Between 1968 and 1979, it discharged more than 180kg (397lb) of plutonium into the Irish Sea, the world's largest discharge of nuclear waste. In 1979, the site was renamed as part of an effort to improve its image. In 1990, reports revealed that the children of Sellafield workers had an increased risk of leukemia due to radiation exposure levels at the site.

Sellers, Peter (1925–80) English comedy actor. His success began in radio with *The Goon Show* (1951–59). During the 1950s, he starred in various Ealing Studios black comedies such as *The Ladykillers* (1955) and *The Naked Truth* (1957). International recognition came in 1963 with *Dr. Strangelove* and the first of *The Pink Panther* series. Sellers won a best actor Academy Award for his final role in *Being There* (1979).

semantics Branch of LINGUISTICS and PHILOSOPHY concerned with the study of meaning. In historical linguistics,

it generally refers to the analysis of how the meanings of words change over time. In modern linguistics and philosophy, semantics seeks to assess the contribution of word-meaning to the meanings of phrases and sentences, and to comprehend the relationship among and between words and the things they refer to, or stand for.

semen Fluid in a male that contains SPERM from the TESTES and the secretions of various accessory sexual glands. In men, each ejaculate is normally c.3 to 6ml by volume, and contains c.200 to 300 million sperm. *See also* SEXUAL REPRODUCTION

semiconductor Substance with electrical CONDUCTIVITY between that of a CONDUCTOR and an insulator. The conductivity increases as temperature increases. A semiconductor consists of elements, such as GERMANIUM and SILICON, or compounds, such as aluminium phosphide, with a crystalline structure. At normal temperatures, some electrons break free giving rise to *n*-type (negative) conductivity with the electrons as the main carriers of the electric current. The holes (electron deficiencies) left by these electrons give rise to *p*-type (positive) conductivity with the holes as the main carriers. Impurities are usually added to the semiconductor material in controlled amounts to add more free electrons or create more holes. A semiconductor junction forms at an abrupt change along the length of the crystal from one type of impurity to the other. Such a *p-n* junction acts as a very efficient RECTIFIER, converting alternating current (AC) into direct current (DC), and is the basis of the semiconductor DIODE. Semiconductors are also used in TRANSISTORS and PHOTOELECTRIC CELLS.

Seminole Native North American band that separated from the main CREEK group in the late 18th century, and fled s into Florida under pressure of wars with white settlers. Seminole involvement in wars against the USA led to the **First Seminole War** (1817–18). In 1832, some Seminole leaders signed a treaty agreeing to move to Oklahoma. Others opposed the move, and the **Second Seminole War** (1835–42) began. The war claimed 1500 US troops before the Seminoles were forced to surrender. Today, c.12,000 Seminole live in Florida and Oklahoma.

semiotics (semiology) Study of signs and symbols, both visual and linguistic, and their function in communication. Pioneers of semiotics include Charles Sanders PEIRCE and Ferdinand de SAUSSURE. Roland BARTHES and Claude LÉVI-STRAUSS developed the principles of semiotics into STRUCTURALISM.

Semiramis In Assyrian mythology, a queen and goddess, wife of Ninus, founder of NINEVEH. Daughter of a fish goddess and the god of wisdom, Semiramis was reared by doves. After the death of Ninus she ruled alone, founded the city of BABYLON,

INTERNET

seismology
▶ neic.usgs.gov

S

◄ **Seles** US tennis player Monica Seles is renowned for her ruthless competitiveness, fast court speed and ferocious groundstrokes. Her long rivalry with Steffi Graf was interrupted in 1993 when Seles was stabbed by one of Graf's fans. Following a period of recovery, she returned to competitive play in 1995. She officially announced her retirement from tennis in 2008.

and led victorious armies against numerous enemies until, opposed by her son, she took the form of a dove and flew away.

Semites Peoples whose native tongue belongs to the group of SEMITIC LANGUAGES. They originally inhabited an area in Arabia and spoke a common language, Proto-Semitic, from which the Semitic languages descend. Among the modern Semites are Arabs, native Israelis, and many Ethiopians.

Semitic languages Group of languages spoken by peoples native to N Africa and the Middle East and forming one of the five branches of the Afro-Asiatic language family. The Semitic languages divide into three sub-branches: **North West Semitic** (including HEBREW, ARAMAIC, and Eblaite); **North East Semitic** (consisting of Akkadian); and **Central and Southern Semitic** (including ARABIC, South Arabian, and Ethiopic). Only Hebrew and Arabic survived to develop modern forms.

Senate Upper House of the US legislature, which together with the HOUSE OF REPRESENTATIVES forms the CONGRESS. It consists of two senators from each state, who are elected for six-year terms. Elections are held every other year, with about one third of the Senate elected at a time. There are usually 16 standing committees, and committee chairs retain their positions for as long as their party has a majority of the votes. The approval of a simple majority of the Senate is necessary for major presidential appointments, and a two-thirds majority for treaties. The Senate can initiate legislation except on fiscal matters. Officially, the presiding officer of the Senate is the vice president, but the position is often delegated.

Senate, Roman Chief governing body of the Roman republic. It originated as a royal council under the early kings. By the 2nd century BC it controlled all matters of policy. Senators were chosen for life by the CENSORS and at first were mainly former CONSULS. They numbered 300, raised to 600 under SULLA, to 900 by CAESAR, and reduced to 600 under AUGUSTUS. PLEBEIANS gained entry in the 4th century BC. Under the Empire, the Emperor's control of military and civil officials gradually restricted the Senate to judicial matters and to the city government in Rome. Under the late Empire, senatorial status was extended on a massive scale to the landowning élite.

Sendak, Maurice (1928–) US writer and illustrator of imaginative books for children. Sendak's *Where the Wild Things Are* received the Caldecott Medal in 1964. Other books he wrote and illustrated include *Higglety Pigglety Pop, or, There Must Be More To Life* (1967), *In the Night Kitchen* (1970) and *Outside Over There* (1981).

Seneca Most populous division of the IROQUOIS CONFEDERACY; a tribe of Native North Americans who inhabited N New York. In 1848, the Seneca Nation was formed by the peoples of the Allegany and Cattaraugus reservations. Other Seneca live in Oklahoma, Pennsylvania, and Ontario. Today, *c.*7000 Seneca live on reservations in W New York.

Seneca, Lucius Annaeus (AD 4–65) Roman STOIC philosopher, b. Spain. Based on Greek models, Seneca's nine tragedies, such as *Phaedra, Medea*, and *Oedipus*, had a lasting impact on European literature. His other works include 12 books of *Moral Essays* and many philosophical letters.

Senegal Republic in NW Africa. *See* country feature

Senghor, Léopold Sédar (1906–2001) Senegalese statesman and poet. He was the first president (1960–80) of the republic of Senegal. As president, he led (1974) Senegal into the West African Economic Community. His poetry, such as *Songs of the Shade* (1945), is intended for voice with musical accompaniment. Senghor was the first African to be elected to the Académie Française (1984).

senna Plants, shrubs, and trees of the genus *Senna*, native to warm and tropical regions; some species grow in temperate areas throughout the world. They have rectangular, feathery leaves and yellow flowers. Family Fabaceae/Leguminosae.

Senna, Ayrton (1960–94) Brazilian racing driver. Senna began Formula 1 racing in 1984. His first Grand Prix victory (Portugal) was in 1985. Senna won a total of 41 Grands Prix and three world drivers' championships (1988, 1990, 1991). Considered one of the greatest drivers of all time, he died in a crash at the San Marino Grand Prix.

Sennacherib (d.681BC) King of ASSYRIA (704–681BC). Son and successor of SARGON, he led expeditions to subdue

Phoenicia and Palestine in 701 BC and defeated the Elamite-Chaldean alliance in 691 BC. He destroyed Babylon in 689 BC and, with the peace of his empire thus assured, devoted himself to rebuilding his capital, NINEVEH. *See also* ASHURBANIPAL

Sennett, Mack (1884–1960) US film director, producer, and actor whose many short, slapstick comedies enlivened the age of silent films. Films made by his Keystone Company brought fame to Charlie CHAPLIN, Mabel Normand, Fatty Arbuckle, and the Keystone Kops.

senses Means by which animals gain information about their environment and physiological condition. The five senses (SIGHT, HEARING, TASTE, SMELL, and TOUCH) all rely on specialized receptors in sense organs on or near the external surface of the body. Internal sense organs are the HYPOTHALAMUS of the brain and muscle stretch receptors stimulated by muscle movements.

Seoul (Kyongsong) Capital of South Korea, on the River Han. The political, commercial, industrial and cultural centre of South Korea, it was founded in 1392 as the capital of the Yi dynasty. It developed rapidly under Japanese governorship (1910–45). After World War 2, Seoul was the headquarters for the US army of occupation. Following the 1948 partition, it became capital of South Korea. Seoul's capture by North Korean troops precipitated the beginning of the KOREAN WAR (1950–53), and the following months witnessed the city's virtual destruction. In March 1951, it became the headquarters of the UN command in Korea and a rebuilding programme commenced. By the 1970s, it was the hub of one of the most successful economies of Southeast Asia. In 1996, Seoul was the scene of violent student demonstrations for reunification with North Korea. Pop. (2000) 9,888,000.

sepal Modified leaf that makes up the outermost portion of a FLOWER bud. Although usually green and inconspicuous once the flower is open, in some species, the sepals look like the PETALS.

Sephardim Descendants of the Jews of medieval Spain and Portugal and others who follow their customs. Iberian Jews followed the Babylonian rather than the Palestinian Jewish tradition and developed their own language, Ladino. After the expulsion of the Jews from Spain (1492), many settled in parts of the Middle East and North Africa under the Ottoman Empire. Continuing persecution led many of them to form colonies in Amsterdam and other cities of NW Europe.

Sepoy Rebellion Alternative name for the INDIAN MUTINY

sepsis Destruction of body tissue by disease-causing (pathogenic) bacteria or their toxins. Local or widespread inflammation may occur, possibly followed by necrosis, the death of tissue. Treatment is with ANTIBIOTICS.

septicaemia Term for severe SEPSIS or BLOOD POISONING

Septuagint Earliest surviving Greek translation of the Hebrew Bible (the OLD TESTAMENT), made for the Greek-speaking Jewish community in Egypt in the 3rd and 2nd centuries BC. It contains the entire Jewish CANON plus the APOCRYPHA. It divides into four sections: the law, history, poetry, and prophets. It is still used by the Greek Orthodox Church.

sequoia Two species of giant evergreen conifer trees native to California and S Oregon: the giant sequoia (*Sequoiadendron giganteum*) and the Californian redwood (*Sequoia sempervirens*). Their height, up to 100m (330ft), has made them a natural wonder of the USA. Family Taxodiaceae.

Serbia *See* country feature, page 672

Serbs Slavic people who settled in the Balkans in the 7th century, and who became Christians in the 9th century. They were distinguished from Croats and Slovenes by their use of the Cyrillic, not the Roman, alphabet. Most of them now live in Serbia but there are Serb minorities in Bosnia and Croatia.

serf Person legally bound to a lord. In Europe, under the FEUDAL SYSTEM, serfs had to provide labour and other services and were usually bound to the land. Gone from W Europe by the end of the Middle Ages, serfdom persisted in Russia and parts of E Europe into the mid-19th century.

serial music Technique of musical composition in which a work is structured on a fixed series of notes; the series repeats in various permutations for the duration of the work. The TWELVE-TONE MUSIC of Arnold SCHOENBERG is a form of serial music.

series In mathematics, the summation (adding up) of a list or sequence of numbers. Thus, the series $1 + 4 + 9 + 16 + ...$ is formed from the sequence 1, 4, 9, 16 .... Series (like number sequences) may be finite or infinite. A series formed from increasing powers of a number is a power series.

Sermon on the Mount Address given by JESUS CHRIST to his disciples and a huge crowd of other listeners on one of the hills above GALILEE. It presents many of the now familiar Christian teachings. *See also* BEATITUDES

serotonin (5–hydroxytryptamine) Chemical found in cells of the gastrointestinal tract, blood platelets, and brain tissue, concentrated in the midbrain and HYPOTHALAMUS. It is a VASO-CONSTRICTOR and has an important role in the functioning of the nervous system and in the stimulation of smooth MUSCLES.

serpentine Group of sheet silicate minerals, hydrated magnesium silicate ($Mg_3Si_2O_5(OH)_4$). Serpentine minerals come in various colours, usually green, although sometimes brownish, with green mottling. They have monoclinic system crystals. They are commonly used in decorative carving; fibrous varieties are used in asbestos cloth. Hardness 2.5–4; r.d. 2.5–2.6.

serum Clear fluid that separates out if blood is left to clot. It is essentially of the same composition as plasma, but without fibrinogen and clotting factors.

serval (bush cat) Orange and black spotted, dog-like cat found in grassy areas of sub-Saharan Africa. Length: body 70–100cm (30–40in). Family Felidae; species *Felis serval*.

Servetus, Michael (1511–53) Spanish physician and theologian. Servetus published (1531–32) his unorthodox opinions concerning the TRINITY and discovered that blood circulates through the lungs. Forced to flee from the INQUISITION, he was equally unwelcome among Reformation theologians. He was arrested and tried in Geneva and burned as a heretic.

servomechanism Device that provides remote control of a mechanism. An input signal, such as a radio impulse or mechanical movement, converts into a mechanical output. The device is usually part of a control system. Some servomechanisms, such aircraft autopilots, incorporate a feedback mechanism that makes them independent of human control.

sesame Tropical plant native to Asia and Africa. It is also cultivated in Mexico and sw USA for its oil and seeds, both used in cooking. An annual, it has oval leaves, small pink or white flowers, and seed capsules along the stem. Height: 61cm (2ft). Family Pedaliaceae; species *Sesamum indicum*.

sessile In zoology, describing animals that mostly remain fixed in one place, such as barnacles, limpets and mussels. In general biology, describing a structure that has no stalk where one might be expected.

Sessions, Roger (1896–1985) US composer whose complex and highly individual works include a Violin Concerto (1935), eight symphonies, and various piano and organ works.

set In mathematics, a defined collection of objects. The objects are called the elements or members of the set. The

SENEGAL

The Republic of Senegal is situated on the NW coast of Africa. The volcanic Cape Verde (Cap Vert), on which DAKAR stands, is the most w point in Africa. The country entirely surrounds Gambia. The Atlantic coastline from St Louis to Dakar is sandy. Plains cover most of Senegal, although the land rises gently in the SE. The N forms part of the SAHEL. The main rivers are the Sénégal, which forms the N border, and the Casamance in the s. The River Gambia flows into the Gambia.

Desert and semi-desert cover NE Senegal. In central Senegal, dry grasslands and scrub predominate. Mangrove swamps border parts of the s coast. The far s is a region of tropical savanna, though large areas have been cleared for farming. Senegal has several protected parks, of which the largest is the Niokolo-Kobo Wildlife Park.

CLIMATE
Dakar has a tropical climate, with a short rainy season between June and September when moist winds blow from the sw. Temperatures are higher inland. Rainfall is greatest in the s.

HISTORY
From the 6th to 10th century, Senegal formed part of the Empire of ancient Ghana. Between the 10th and 14th centuries the Tukolor state of Tekrur dominated the Sénégal valley. The ALMORAVID dynasty of Zenega Berbers introduced Islam, and it is from the Zenega that Senegal got its name. In the 14th century, the Mali Empire conquered Tekrur. In the early 15th century the WOLOF established the Jolof Empire. The SONGHAI Empire then began to dominate the region.

In 1444, Portuguese sailors became the first Europeans to reach Cape Verde. Trading stations were rapidly established in the area. In the 17th century, France and the Netherlands replaced Portuguese influence. France gradually gained control of the valuable slave trade,

and founded St Louis in 1658. By 1763 Britain expelled the French from Senegal and, in 1765, set up Senegambia, the first British colony in Africa. In 1783 France regained control and in the mid-19th century, battled for control of the interior. The French founded Dakar in 1857.

In 1895 Senegal became a colony within the Federation of French West Africa. In 1902 the capital of this huge empire transferred from St Louis to Dakar. Dakar became a major trading centre. In 1946 Senegal joined the French Union.

POLITICS
In 1959 Senegal joined French Sudan (now Mali) to form the Federation of Mali. Senegal withdrew in 1960 to become the separate Republic of Senegal, within the French community. Its first post-colonial president, Léopold Sédar SENGHOR, was a noted African poet.

Following an unsuccessful coup in 1962, Senghor gradually assumed wider powers. During the 1960s Senegal's economy deteriorated amid drought, starvation and civil unrest.

During the 1970s s Senegal was a base for guerrilla movements in Guinea and Portuguese Guinea (now Guinea-Bissau). In

MAP SCALE

AREA 196,722sq km [75,954sq mi]
POPULATION 12,522,000
CAPITAL (POPULATION) Dakar (2,313,000)
GOVERNMENT Multiparty republic
ETHNIC GROUPS Wolof 44%, Pular 24%, Serer 15%
LANGUAGES French (official), tribal languages
RELIGIONS Islam 94%, Christianity (mainly Roman Catholic) 5%, traditional beliefs 1%
CURRENCY CFA franc = 100 centimes

1974, Senegal was a founding member of the West African Economic Community.

Senghor continued in office until 1981, when he was succeeded by the prime minister, Abdou Diouf. That year, Senegalese troops suppressed a coup in the Gambia. In 1982 the two countries joined to form the Confederation of Senegambia, but the union collapsed in 1989. From 1989 to 1992, Senegal was at war with Mauritania.

In 2000, Diouf was surprisingly beaten in presidential elections by opposition leader Abdoulaye Wade, ending 40 years of Socialist Party rule. In 2004 a peace treaty with separatist rebels in the s Casamance province was reached. The 2007 elections gave Wade a second term, although the opposition claimed they were unfair and later boycotted parliamentary elections.

ECONOMY
According to the World Bank, Senegal is a 'lower-middle-income' developing country. Agriculture still employs 65% of the population, though many farmers produce little more than they need to feed their families. Food crops grown include cassava, millet and rice. Senegal is also the world's sixth largest producer of peanuts. Phosphates are the chief resource, and Senegal also refines oil imported from Gabon and Nigeria. Fishing is an important industry.

S

number of members can be finite or infinite, or even be zero (the **null set**). Various relations can exist between two sets, *A* and *B*: *A* equals *B* if both sets contain exactly the same members; *A* is included in, or is a subset of, *B* if all members of *A* are members of *B*; disjoint sets have no members in common; overlapping sets have one or more common members. Operations on sets produce new sets: the union of *A* and *B* contains the members of both *A* and *B*; the intersection of *A* and *B* contains only those members common to both sets.

Seth Egyptian god. Although a beneficent god in predynastic Egypt, Seth became associated with darkness and was later identified as a god of evil and the antagonist of HORUS.

Seth, Vikram (1952–) Indian novelist. He came to attention with his award-winning 1983 travelogue, *From Heaven Lake*. His epic *A Suitable Boy* (1993) is one of the longest novels in English. Other novels include *An Equal Music* (1999).

setter Long-haired hunting dog used to locate game and stand until the hunter arrives. They were first bred in 16th-century England. Types include English, Irish (red), and Gordon.

set theory Branch of mathematics developed by German mathematician Georg Cantor in the late 19th century. It is based on George BOOLE's work on mathematical logic, but it manipulates sets of abstract or real objects rather than log-ical propositions. It is concerned with the properties of SETS and can be applied to most other branches of mathematics.

Settlement, Act of (1701) English parliamentary statute regulating the succession to the throne. The purpose of the Act was to prevent the restoration of the Catholic STUART monarchy. It settled the succession on SOPHIA of Hanover, granddaughter of JAMES I, and her heirs, providing they were Protestants. The throne was inherited (1714) by Sophia's son, later GEORGE I.

Seurat, Georges Pierre (1859–91) French painter and founder of NEO-IMPRESSIONISM. From 1876 to 1884, he developed his theory of colour vision known as POINTILLISM, which was based on the juxtaposition of pure colour dots. His paintings include *Bathing at Asnières* (1883–84) and *Sunday in Summer on the Island of La Grande-Jatte* (1886).

Sevastopol (Sebastopol) Black Sea port on the SW of the Crimean Peninsula, Ukraine. Founded in 1783 by Catherine II, it was fortified in 1804. Sevastopol became home to the Russian Black Sea fleet and was the major strategic objective of the CRIMEAN WAR. The Russians sank their own fleet to block the harbour entrance, and inflicted heavy Allied casualties. The fortifications were destroyed, only to be raised again after 1871. By 1890, the city was again a naval base. During World War 2 the German army besieged Sevastopol for eight months

---

SERBIA

Serbia is a landlocked country in E Europe, formerly part of YUGOSLAVIA. When Yugoslavia broke up in the early 1990s Serbia included Montenegro, and in 2003 it adopted the name of the Union of Serbia and Montenegro. In 2006 they divided into separate countries.

Serbia contains a mountainous region including the DINARIC ALPS and part of the BALKAN MOUNTAINS. The Pannonian Plains, which are drained by the River DANUBE, are in the N.

BYZANTINE rule. Serbia was the leading Balkan power until its defeat by the Ottoman Turks in 1389. In 1459, it became a province of the OTTOMAN EMPIRE.

In 1829, Serbia gained autonomy under Russian protection. In 1867, Milan Obrenović began a war in support of a rebellion against Turkish rule in Bosnia and Herzegovina. Russia intervened to aid Serbia and, in 1878, Turkey finally granted Serbia independence.

In 1908, Serbia formed the Balkan League with Bosnia and Herzegovina. The alliance defeated the Turks in 1912 but disintegrated into feuding factions. In 1913, Serbia defeated Bulgaria in the second Balkan War. The expansion of Serbia in the BALKAN WARS antagonized Austria and was a major contributing factor to the outbreak of WORLD WAR I.

In 1918 the South Slavs united in the Kingdom of the Serbs, Croats and Slovenes, ruled by PETER I of Serbia. ALEXANDER I succeeded Peter I in 1921, and in 1929 abolished the constitution and renamed the country Yugoslavia. Ruling as a dictator, Alexander sought to enforce the use of Serbo-Croatian as the sole language. After the Germans invaded in 1941, abruptly halting PETER II's reign, the Communist-led partisans of Josip Broz Tito and the royalist *chetniks* fought both the Germans and each other.

AREA 88,361sq km [34,118sq mi]
POPULATION 8,024,000
CAPITAL (POPULATION) Belgrade (1,116,000)
GOVERNMENT Federal republic
ETHNIC GROUPS Serb 66%, Albanian 17%, Hungarian 3%, others
LANGUAGES Serbian (official), Albanian
RELIGIONS Orthodox 65%, Islam 19%, others
CURRENCY New dinar = 100 paras

CLIMATE

The country is mostly composed of upland areas with a continental climate. The highlands have cold, snowy winters while the Pannonian Plains have hot, arid summers, and heavy rains in the spring and autumn.

HISTORY

South Slavs moved into the region *c.*1,500 years ago. They adopted Orthodox Christianity under

POLITICS

From 1991 Yugoslavia split up, as Bosnia-Herzegovina, Croatia, Macedonia and Slovenia each proclaimed independence. Serbia and Montenegro were all that remained of Yugoslavia.

Fighting broke out in Croatia and Bosnia as rival groups struggled for power. In 1992 the United Nations withdrew recognition of Yugoslavia because of its failure to halt atrocities committed by Serbs living in Croatia and Bosnia. International sanctions and the region's wars heavily damaged the economy. In 1995 Yugoslavia took part in the Dayton Peace Accord talks, but the region remained fragile.

In 1998 further conflict arose in Kosovo, a former autonomous region of Albanian-speak-ing Muslims in S Serbia. Serbians forced Muslims to leave their homes, but were opposed by the Kosovo Liberation Army (KLA). In 1999, after failed attempts to find an agreement, NATO forces launched aerial attacks on Serbian targets. Serbian forces stepped up attacks on Albanian-speaking villages, forcibly expelling the people, who fled into Albania and Macedonia. The NATO offensive ended when Serbian forces withdrew from Kosovo and the KLA was disbanded. In 2000, the Yugoslav leader Slobodan MILOŠEVIĆ was defeated in presidential elections. From 2002 he faced charges at the UN War Crimes Tribunal in The Hague, but he died in 2006 before his trial could be completed.

Serbia and Montenegro made their first steps towards separation in 2003, making both semi-independent. Montenegro voted for full independence in a 2006 referendum which Serbia accepted. In 2007 the UN unveiled a draft plan for an independent Kosovo, which had remained under UN and NATO occupation since the Serbian withdrawal. Serbia rejected the plan and talks collapsed. In 2008 Kosovo unilaterally declared its independence. The EU and US accepted it as a new country, but Serbia, Russia and others refused to acknowledge the declaration.

ECONOMY

Resources include bauxite, coal, copper and other metals, together with oil and natural gas. Manufactures include aluminium, machinery, plastics, steel, textiles and vehicles. Agriculture remains important.

before it capitulated in July 1942. It was recaptured in 1944, and again reconstructed. In 1995 Ukraine agreed to allow the Russian fleet to maintain its base in return for Ukrainian ownership of 19% of the fleet. Pop. (2001) 341,000.

Seventh-Day Adventists Christian denomination whose members expect JESUS CHRIST to return to Earth in person. They hold the SABBATH on Saturday, and accept the BIBLE literally as their guide for living. The sect was formally organized in the USA in 1863, and today it is the largest ADVENTIST denomination, with followers in many countries.

Seven Weeks' War *See* AUSTRO-PRUSSIAN WAR

Seven Wonders of the World Group of fabled sights that evolved from various ancient Greek lists. They were, in chronological order: the PYRAMIDS of Egypt, the HANGING GARDENS OF BABYLON, the statue of ZEUS by PHIDIAS at OLYMPIA, the temple of ARTEMIS at EPHESUS, the mausoleum at HALICARNASSUS, the COLOSSUS OF RHODES and the Pharos (lighthouse) at ALEXANDRIA.

Seven Years' War (1756–63) Major European conflict that established Britain as the foremost maritime and colonial power and ensured the survival of Prussia as a major power in central Europe. The war was a continuation of the rivalries involved in the War of the AUSTRIAN SUCCESSION (1740–48). Britain and Prussia were allied, with Prussia undertaking nearly all the fighting in Europe against Austria, Russia, France and Sweden. FREDERICK II (THE GREAT) of Prussia fought a defensive war against superior forces. Only his brilliant generalship and the withdrawal of Russia from the war in 1762 saved Prussia from being overrun. Overseas, Britain and France fought in North America (FRENCH AND INDIAN WARS), India, and West Africa, with the British gaining major victories. At the end of the war, the Treaty of PARIS (1763) confirmed British supremacy in North America and India, while the Treaty of Hubertusberg left Prussia in control of Silesia.

severe acute respiratory syndrome (SARS) Viral respiratory illness causing a condition similar to PNEUMONIA combined with INFLUENZA-like symptoms. SARS is fatal in about one in ten cases. It is thought to be transmitted most readily through respiratory droplets, but may also be spread more widely through the air. SARS was first recognized in southern China in 2002 and caused worldwide concern in 2003.

Severn Longest river in the UK, flowing 290km (180mi) through Wales and W England. It rises on Mount Plynlimon in W Wales, flows NE to Shrewsbury, turns SE and then SW to enter the Bristol Channel through a wide estuary. The Severn Road Bridge (1966) is one of the world's longest suspension bridges.

Severus, Lucius Septimius (146–211) Roman Emperor (193–211). Severus was proclaimed emperor by his troops, who marched on Rome and persuaded the Senate to confirm him. He dissolved the Praetorian Guard and proclaimed himself posthumously adopted by the Emperor MARCUS AURELIUS (d.180). He divided (208) Britain into two provinces and launched a campaign to conquer Scotland. Repulsed, he died at York.

Seville River port on the River Guadalquivir, capital of Seville province, SW Spain. Ruled by the Romans from the 2nd century BC to the 5th century AD it was taken by the Moors in 712, and conquered by Ferdinand III in 1248. The port exports fruit (notably oranges) and wine from the fertile area. Industries: agricultural machinery, shipbuilding, chemicals, textiles, spirits, porcelain, shipping, tourism. Pop. (2001) 702,520.

Sèvres, Treaty of (1920) Peace treaty between Turkey and its European opponents in World War 1 that imposed harsh terms on the Ottoman Sultan. It was not accepted by the Turkish nationalists led by ATATÜRK, who fought a war for Turkish independence (1919–22). The treaty, never ratified, was superseded by the Treaty of LAUSANNE (1923).

Seward, William H. (1801–72) US statesman. Seward lost the Republican nomination for president (1860) to Abraham LINCOLN, who appointed him secretary of state. He succeeded in maintaining good relations with Europe during the Civil War, and his handling of the TRENT AFFAIR averted British recognition of the Confederacy. Seward was wounded in the shooting that killed Lincoln, but continued in office under Andrew JOHNSON, negotiating (1867) the purchase of Alaska.

sex Classification of an organism into male or female, denoting the reproductive function of the individual. In mammals, the presence of sex organs (OVARIES in the female, TESTES in the male) are **primary** sexual characteristics. **Secondary** sexual characteristics, such as size, coloration, and hair growth, are governed by the secretion of SEX HORMONES. In flowering plants, the female sex organs are the CARPEL, including the OVARY, STYLE and STIGMA, and the male organs the STAMENS. Male and female organs may occur in the same flower or on separate flowers or plants. *See also* SEXUAL REPRODUCTION

sex hormones Chemical 'messengers' secreted by the gonads (TESTES and OVARIES). They regulate sexual development and reproductive activity and influence sexual behaviour. In males, they include TESTOSTERONE, made by the testes; in females, the sex hormones OESTROGEN and PROGESTERONE are produced by the ovaries.

sexism Discrimination against and subordination of people on the basis of their SEX. It may result from prejudice, stereotyping, or social pressure. *See also* WOMEN'S RIGHTS MOVEMENT

sextant Optical instrument for finding LATITUDE (angular distance N or S of the Equator). A sextant consists of a frame with a curved scale marked in degrees, a movable arm with a mirror at the pivot, a half-silvered glass and a telescope. The instrument measures the angle of a heavenly body above the horizon, which depends on the observer's latitude. A set of tables gives the corresponding latitude for various angles measured.

sexual intercourse Term used to describe physical sexual relations between people. The term may be used specifically to describe the insertion of a man's penis into a woman's vagina. *See also* CONTRACEPTION; HOMOSEXUALITY; ORGASM; SEXUAL REPRODUCTION

sexually transmitted disease (STD) Any disease that is transmitted by sexual activity. It encompasses a range of conditions that are spread primarily by sexual contact, although some may also be transmitted in other ways also. These include ACQUIRED IMMUNE DEFICIENCY SYNDROME (AIDS), SYPHILIS, GONORRHOEA, CHLAMYDIA, cervical CANCER and viral HEPATITIS. STDs are a significant public health problem.

sexual reproduction Biological process of reproduction involving the combination of genetic material from two parents. It occurs in different forms throughout the plant and animal kingdoms. This process gives rise to variations of the GENOTYPE (genetic makeup) and PHENOTYPE (physical characteristics) within a species. GAMETES, HAPLOID sex cells produced by MEIOSIS, contain only half the number of CHROMOSOMES of their parent cells (which are DIPLOID). At FERTILIZATION, the gametes, generally one from each parent, fuse to form a ZYGOTE with the diploid number of chromosomes.

◀ **Seville** A Moorish watchtower in Seville, S Spain. Seville was the centre of the Moorish kingdom in Spain from 712 to 1248, and was also the major port in Spanish colonial history. Its cathedral, built around an existing mosque, is the world's largest Gothic church. Seville's April fair is famous for its flamenco dancing.

S

The zygote divides repeatedly and the cells differentiate to give rise to an EMBRYO and, finally, a fully formed organism.

Seychelles Republic consisting of more than 100 islands in the Indian Ocean, *c.*970km (600mi) N of Madagascar. Seychelles comprises two geologically distinct island groups: the volcanic, **Granitic** group are to the NE, and include the three main islands of Mahé, Praslin and La Digue. Mahé is home to more than 80% of the republic's people; Seychelles' capital, Victoria, lies on its NE coast. To the SW lie the **Outer** group of coral islands. In 1502, Vasco da GAMA explored the islands and named them the 'Seven Sisters'. The French colonized the islands in 1756, establishing plantations worked by slaves from Mauritius. The British captured the archipelago (1794) during the Napoleonic Wars and, in 1814, it became a dependency of Mauritius. In 1903, the Seychelles became a Crown Colony. In 1976, they achieved full independence. In 1977, a coup established Albert René as president. In 1981, South African mercenaries attempted to overthrow the government. Continued civil unrest and another failed coup in 1987, led to the first multi-party elections in 1991. In 1998 elections, Albert René secured a fifth consecutive term. He stood down in 2004 and was succeeded by James Michel. Exports include coconuts and tuna. Area: 455sq km (176sq mi). Pop. (2000) 80,000.

Seyfert galaxy Class of GALAXIES that have extremely bright, compact nuclei and whose spectra show strong emission lines. Most are spiral galaxies. About 1% of all galaxies are Seyferts. They emit strongly at ultraviolet and infrared wavelengths, and exhibit a degree of short-term variability.

Sezession Radical movement (formed 1897) of young Austrian artists who organized their own exhibitions in defiance of the traditional organizations and aligned themselves with progressive European contemporaries. The first president was Gustav KLIMT. Other members included Oskar KOKOSCHKA and, later, Egon SCHIELE.

Sforza, Ludovico (*c.*1451–1508) Duke of Milan (1494–99). Sforza was in effective control of the city-state from 1480. Sforza's alliance (1494) with CHARLES VIII of France marked the start of the Italian Wars. He reneged on the agreement, however, and LOUIS XII invaded Milan and dispossessed Sforza. He died a prisoner in France. He is mainly remembered for his patronage of LEONARDO DA VINCI and BRAMANTE.

Shackleton, Sir Ernest Henry (1874–1922) Irish Antarctic explorer. He led an expedition (1907–09) which got to within 155km (97mi) of the South Pole. On his second expedition (1914–16), his ship was crushed by ice and his men marooned on an island. Shackleton's successful rescue mission, described in *South* (1919), is one of the epics of polar exploration.

shad Saltwater food fish of the HERRING family that swims upriver to spawn. Shads are prized for their roe. Deep-bodied, they have a notch in the upper jaw for the tip of the lower jaw. Length: to 75cm (30in). Family Clupeidae.

shadow Area screened from a light source and therefore relatively dark. It differs in size depending on the distance between the light source and the screening object. When the light source is extended, the outline of the shadow is blurred; where the source is partly visible, there is an area of mid-shadow (**penumbra**) lying outside the darker shadow itself (**umbra**).

Shaffer, Peter (1926–) English dramatist. Following the success of *Five Finger Exercise* (1960), he wrote *The Private Ear and The Public Eye* (1962). Schaffer's plays *Equus* (1973) and *Amadeus* (1979) were both made into films.

Shaftesbury, Anthony Ashley Cooper, 1st Earl of (1621–83) British statesman. Shaftesbury was a member of the COMMONWEALTH council of state under Oliver CROMWELL. Dismayed by the autocracy of the PROTECTORATE, he supported the RESTORATION of CHARLES II (1660), and was rewarded with the chancellorship. Opposed to the Earl of CLARENDON, Shaftesbury became lord chancellor (1672) but was soon dismissed. His determination to prevent the succession of the Catholic JAMES II drove him to found (1673) the WHIGS in opposition to the Earl of Danby. Shaftesbury's support for the Duke of MONMOUTH led to his exile (1682) in Holland.

Shaftesbury, Anthony Ashley Cooper, 7th Earl of (1801–85) English social reformer. Shaftesbury was the

SEXUAL REPRODUCTION

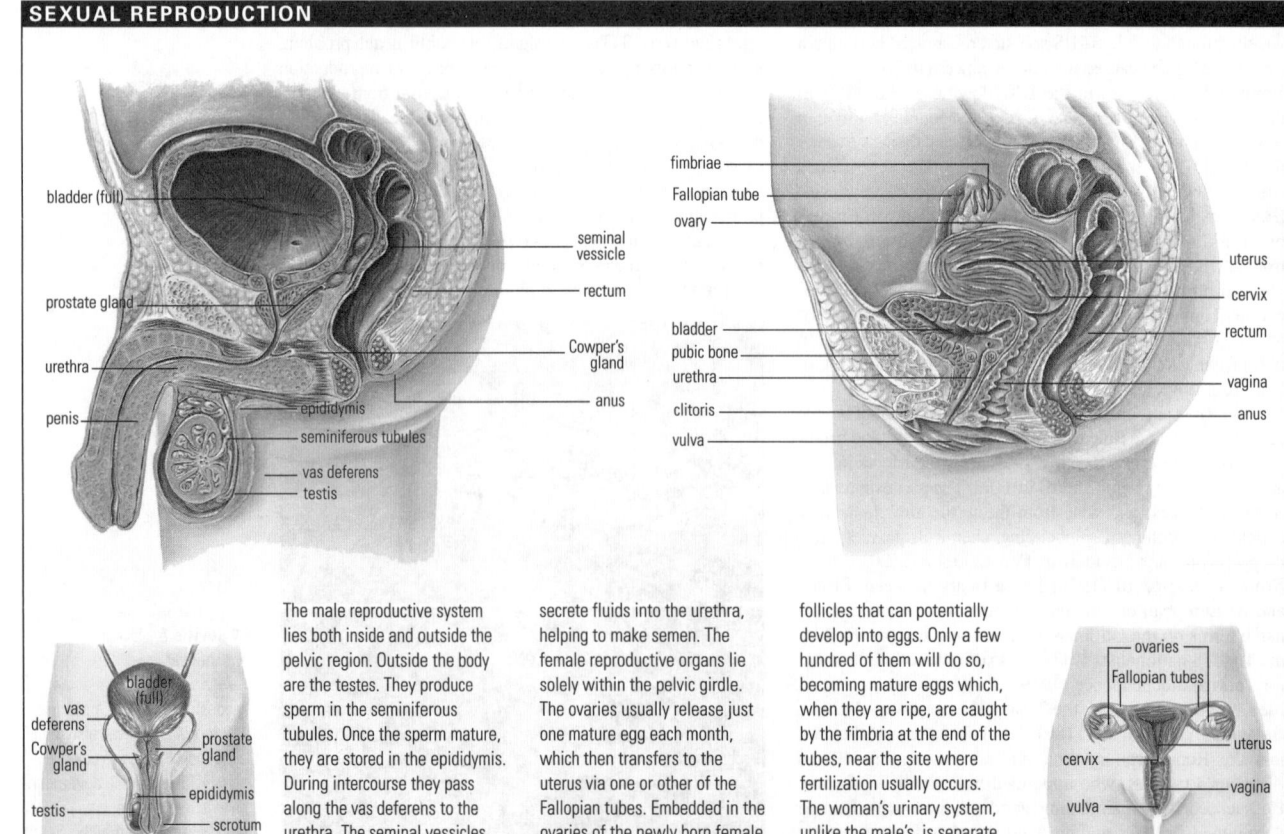

The male reproductive system lies both inside and outside the pelvic region. Outside the body are the testes. They produce sperm in the seminiferous tubules. Once the sperm mature, they are stored in the epididymis. During intercourse they pass along the vas deferens to the urethra. The seminal vessicles, prostate, and Cowper's glands all secrete fluids into the urethra, helping to make semen. The female reproductive organs lie solely within the pelvic girdle. The ovaries usually release just one mature egg each month, which then transfers to the uterus via one or other of the Fallopian tubes. Embedded in the ovaries of the newly born female are several hundred thousand follicles that can potentially develop into eggs. Only a few hundred of them will do so, becoming mature eggs which, when they are ripe, are caught by the fimbria at the end of the tubes, near the site where fertilization usually occurs. The woman's urinary system, unlike the male's, is separate from the genitals.

chief driving force behind the Acts that prohibited employment of women and young children in mines (1842) and restricted the working day to ten hours (1847).

Shah Jahan (1592–1666) MOGUL Emperor of India (1628–58). Third son of JAHANGIR, he secured his succession by killing most of his male relatives. His campaigns expanded the Mogul dominions. Although relatively tolerant of Hinduism, he made Islam the state religion. Shah Jahan was responsible for building the TAJ MAHAL and the vast chambers of the Red Fort at DELHI, which became his capital.

Shahn, Ben (1898–1969) US painter, lithographer and photographer, b. Lithuania. Shahn's work reflected his concern for social and political justice, notably the DREYFUS AFFAIR. In the 1930s he worked with Diego RIVERA on murals for the Rockefeller Center, New York. He was involved with the Farm Security Administration, painting and photographing rural poverty.

Shaka (1787–1828) King of the ZULU. He claimed the throne in c.1816 and reorganized the Zulu, forming a powerful army and extending his control over all of what is now Kwazulu-Natal. He remained on good terms with the white government in the Cape, but his cruel and arbitrary rule provoked opposition at home and he was murdered by his half brothers.

Shakers (officially United Society of Believers in Christ's Second Appearing) US religious sect. Originally an offshoot of the English QUAKERS, the nickname derived from the fervour of their religious ceremonies. In 1774, Ann Lee and eight of her followers emigrated to New York. 'Mother Ann' believed she was the female reincarnation of Jesus Christ. After her death (1784), the movement spread, and by c.1850 they numbered c.6000 in more than 18 communes. One of the central beliefs of Shakers is the dual (male and female) nature of the Deity. They are noted for their crafts.

Shakespeare, William (1564–1616) English poet and dramatist. By 1592 he was established in London, having already written the three parts of *Henry VI*. By 1594, Shakespeare was a member of the Lord Chamberlain's Men, and in 1599 a partner in the GLOBE THEATRE, where many of his plays were presented. He retired to STRATFORD UPON AVON around 1613. His 154 *Sonnets*, which were first published in 1609, stand among the finest works in ENGLISH LITERATURE. The plays are usually divided into four groups – historical plays, comedies, tragedies, and late romances. Shakespeare's plots are generally drawn from existing sources, such as Holinshed.

shale Common SEDIMENTARY ROCK formed from mud or clay. Characterized by very fine layering, it may contain various materials such as fossils, carbonaceous matter and oil.

shallot Perennial plant native to W Asia and cultivated in temperate climates. It has thin leaves and clustered bulbs, with an onion-like flavour. Family Liliaceae; species *Allium cepa*.

shaman Tribal witch doctor or medicine man believed to be in contact with spirits or the supernatural world, and thought to have magical powers. Shamanism is found among the ESKIMOS and NATIVE AMERICANS and in Siberia, where the term originated. African equivalents also exist. *See also* ANIMISM

Shamir, Yitzhak (1915–) Israeli statesman, prime minister (1983–84, 1986–92). He was the leader (1940–48) of the Stern Gang of Zionist guerrillas against the British mandate in Palestine. Shamir became head (1955–65) of Mossad, the Israeli secret service. He was foreign minister (1980–83) under Menachim BEGIN and succeeded him as prime minister and head of the right-wing Likud Party. In 1986, he succeeded Shimon PERES as head of a coalition government. Shamir oversaw the Jewish settlement of the WEST BANK and GAZA STRIP. Defeated by Yitzhak RABIN in 1992 elections, Binyamin NETANYAHU replaced Shamir as leader of Likud.

shamrock Plant with three-part leaves, usually taken to be *Trifolium repens* or *T. dubium*, the national emblem of Ireland. Legend tells that St Patrick used it to symbolize the Trinity. Other plants called shamrock include *Oxalis acetosella* and *Medicago lupulina*. Family Fabiaceae/Leguminosae.

Shandong (Shantung) Province in E China. Jinan is the capital. The E part of the province is a peninsula between the Po Hai and the Huang Hai; the W is part of the HUANG HE delta. Much of the land has been reclaimed. Oil, coal, iron ore, salt, and gold are all extracted. Fishing and silk are important industries. It is the birthplace of Confucius. Area: 153,600sq km (59,304sq mi). Pop. (2000) 90,790,000.

Shang (Yin) Early Chinese dynasty (c.1523–c.1030BC). Successors to the Hsia (Xia) dynasty, the Shang was based in the valley of the Huang He (Yellow) River. During the Shang period, the Chinese written language was perfected, techniques of flood control and irrigation were practised, and artefacts were made in cast bronze.

Shanghai City-port in SE China, 22km (13mi) from the Yangtze (Changjiang) delta, the largest city in China. By the Treaty of Nanking (1842), Shanghai opened to foreign trade, stimulating economic growth. The USA, Britain, France, and Japan all held their own areas of the city. Occupied by the Japanese in 1937, it returned to China at the end of World War 2, and fell to the communists in 1949. Industries: textiles, steel, chemicals, publishing, rubber products, farm machinery, shipbuilding, financial services. Pop. (2005) 12,665,000.

Shankar, Ravi (1920–) Indian musician. He was responsible for popularizing the SITAR and Indian music in general in the West. Shankar founded the National Orchestra of India and was music director of All-India Radio (1948–56). He toured Europe and the USA extensively during the 1960s and 1970s.

Shannon Longest river in the Republic of Ireland and the British Isles. It rises on Cuilcagh Mountain in NW County Cavan and flows S through loughs Allen, Ree, and Derg, then S across the central plain of Ireland to Limerick, and W to enter the Atlantic Ocean. The Shannon separates Connacht from the provinces of Leinster and Munster. Length: 370km (230mi).

Shapley, Harlow (1885–1972) US astronomer who provided the first accurate model of the MILKY WAY. By observing CEPHEID VARIABLE stars in globular clusters, Shapley calculated the distance to each cluster in the galaxy, obtaining a picture of its shape and size.

share index Indicator used to show the movement of the prices of SHARES on a STOCK EXCHANGE. Indices usually take a price or capitalization-weighted sample of the share prices of a top rated group of companies on a given stock exchange. Examples include the Nikkei Dow in Tokyo, the FTSE-100 in London, and the Dow Jones in New York.

shares Documents representing money invested in a company in return for membership rights in the ownership of that company. Shares are expressed in monetary units. Shareholders regularly receive payment of dividends that depend on the net profit of the company. In the UK, although the definitions have become blurred, **stocks** usually mean fixed-interest securities such as those issued by government.

sharia Traditional law of ISLAM, believed by Muslims to be the result of divine revelation. It derives from a number of sources, including the KORAN and a collection of teachings and legends about the life of MUHAMMAD known as the *Hadith*.

Sharjah Capital of the Sheikdom of Sharjah, third largest of the UNITED ARAB EMIRATES, on the Persian Gulf, E Arabia. A British Protectorate until 1971, the sheikdom is part of a prosperous oil- and gas-producing area. Pop. (2002 est.) 417,400.

shark Torpedo-shaped, cartilaginous fish found in subpolar to tropical marine waters. They have well-developed jaws, bony teeth, usually five gill slits on each side of the head, and a lobe-shaped tail with a longer top lobe. Sharks are carnivorous, and at least ten species are known to attack humans. There are c.250 living species. Order Selachii. *See also* DOGFISH; HAMMERHEAD; WHALE SHARK; WHITE SHARK

S

▼ **shark** The mako shark (*Isurus oxyrhyncus*) belongs to the mackerel shark family, the same family to which the great white belongs. A ferocious predator, the mako's streamlined body enables it to swim at speeds of more than 65km/h (40mph). Makos are found in the Atlantic, Pacific and Indian Oceans, and like the great white, have been known to attack humans. Adults grow to more than 3.7m (12ft), and weigh up to 400kg (880lb).

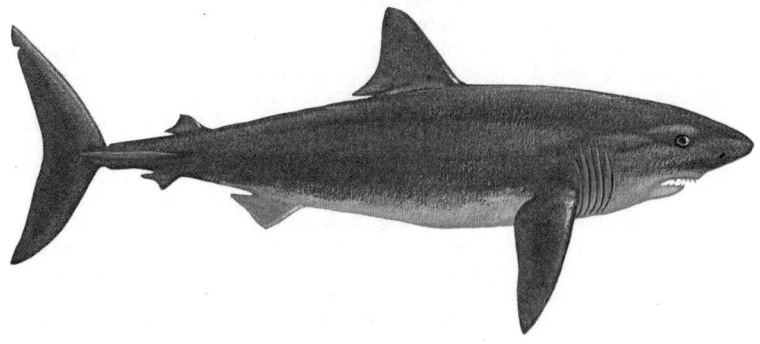

INTERNET

Sharon, Ariel
► www.mfa.gov.il/mfa/go.
  asp?MFAH00ge0

Shepard, Alan Bartlett, Jr
► history.nasa.gov/
  40thmerc7/shepard.htm

**Sherman, William
Tecumseh**
► ngeorgia.com/people/
  shermanwt.html

Sharon, Ariel (1928–) Israeli statesman and general, prime minister (2001–2006). A commander in the first of the ARAB-ISRAELI WARS (1948) and the SIX-DAY WAR (1967), he was a founder of the right-wing Likud Party. As minister of defence (1981–83) under Menachem BEGIN, Sharon masterminded Israel's invasion of Lebanon. He served as minister of foreign affairs (1999) under Binyamin NETANYAHU, supporting further Jewish settlements in the Occupied Territories. In 2000, Sharon succeeded Netanyahu as leader of Likud and led the party to a landslide victory over Ehud BARAK. In 2006 a severe stroke left him in a coma.

sharp In musical notation, an accidental sign placed before a note or immediately after the clef to indicate that the note should be sounded a semitone higher. It is designated by the sign #.

Sharpeville Black township, N of Vereeniging, South Africa, scene of a massacre by security forces in March 1960. A large gathering of local people demonstrating against the pass laws failed to obey orders to disperse. The police opened fire, killing 67 people and wounding 186. The massacre led to greater militancy in the struggle against APARTHEID.

Shatt al Arab Channel in SE Iraq, formed by the confluence of the rivers TIGRIS and EUPHRATES. It flows SE to the Persian Gulf through a wide delta. Forming the Iraq-Iran border, its lower course was the scene of bitter fighting between the two countries during the IRAN-IRAQ WAR (1980–88).

Shaw, George Bernard (1856–1950) Irish dramatist, critic, and member of the FABIAN SOCIETY. Shaw transformed Victorian theatre, rejecting melodrama in favour of socially conscious drama. Although many of his plays were comedies, they expressed his often radical political and philosophical ideas. His first play was *Widower's Houses* (1892). *Mrs Warren's Profession* (1893) was considered immoral and banned from performance. *Arms and the Man* (1894) was Shaw's first publicly performed play. Plays such as *Man and Superman* (1905) and *Major Barbara* (1905) were first performed at the Royal Court, London. *Pygmalion* (1913) was turned later into the musical *My Fair Lady* (1956). Other major plays include *Heartbreak House* (1920), *Back to Methuselah* (1922) and *Saint Joan* (1923). In 1925, Shaw received the Nobel Prize in literature.

Shearer, Alan (1970–) English footballer. Shearer began his professional career with Southampton in 1988. He joined Blackburn Rovers in 1992. In 1996, he was the leading scorer in the European Championship and moved to Newcastle United for a world-record transfer fee of £15 million. In 1998, he captained England's World Cup team. In 2002, Shearer became the first player to score 100 goals in the Premier League.

shearwater Seabird related to the ALBATROSS and PETREL. Most species are brown or black with pale underparts. Shearwaters live most of their lives on the ocean; they feed on fish and squid, and burrow nests in coastal cliffs. Length: 19–56cm (7.5–22in). Family Procellariidae.

Sheba Legendary ancient kingdom celebrated for its trade in gold, spices and precious stones. In the 10th century BC according to the Bible, the Queen of Sheba visited Jerusalem to hear the wisdom of SOLOMON. Sheba may have been the historically recorded state of Saba or Sabaea in s Arabia.

sheep Ruminants of the genus *Ovis*, and those of the less numerous genera *Pseudois* and *Ammotragus*. Domestic sheep, *O. aries*, are now bred for WOOL, fur (karakul), and meat. Wild species are found in the mountains of Europe, Asia, Africa and North America. All are of the Family Bovidae.

sheepdog Any of several breeds of dog that were originally bred to herd and guard sheep. The term includes such breeds as the Old English sheepdog, Shetland sheepdog, COLLIE, border collie and GERMAN SHEPHERD.

Sheffield City and county district in South Yorkshire, N England. A hilly city, it lies at the confluence of the River Don and its tributaries, the Sheaf, Rivelin, and Lordey. It is a major industrial centre, noted for its steel. Pop. (2001) 513,234.

shell In biology, the hard protective case of various MOLLUSCS or eggs of animals, such as birds, tortoises, turtles, or snakes. The case is secreted by the epidermis of the mollusc and consists of a protein matrix strengthened by calcium carbonate. The shell of a bird's egg is also mostly composed of calcium.

Shelley, Mary Wollstonecraft (1797–1851) English novelist, daughter of Mary WOLLSTONECRAFT. She eloped with Percy SHELLEY in 1814, and married him in 1816. Her later works of fiction, which include *The Last Man* (1826) and *Lodore* (1835), have been eclipsed by her first novel, *Frankenstein* (1818).

Shelley, Percy Bysshe (1792–1822) English poet. A committed atheist, Shelley was expelled (1811) from Oxford University for his beliefs. His radical pamphlets forced him into hiding in Wales, where he wrote *Queen Mab* (1813). *Alastor* (1816) reflects his political idealism. From 1818, he lived in Italy with his second wife, Mary SHELLEY. *The Cenci* (1819) is a five-act tragedy. The Peterloo Massacre (1819) prompted *The Mask of Anarchy*. *Prometheus Unbound* (1820), a four-act lyrical drama, is a masterpiece of ROMANTICISM. *Julian and Maddalo* (1924) explores his friendship with Lord BYRON. Smaller poems include 'Ode to the West Wind' (1819), and 'To a Skylark' (1820). The death of John KEATS inspired *Adonais* (1821). Shelley drowned in a boating accident.

shellfish Common name for edible, shelled MOLLUSCS and CRUSTACEA. Shelled molluscs include CLAMS, MUSSELS, OYSTERS and SCALLOPS; crustaceans include LOBSTERS, and CRABS.

Shenyang Capital of Liaoning province, NE China. Once capital of the QING dynasty, it is the centre of a group of communes that grow rice, cereals and vegetables under intensive cultivation. Industries: aircraft, machine tools, heavy machinery, cables, cement. Pop. (2005) 1,285,000.

Shepard, Alan Bartlett, Jr (1923–98) US astronaut. In 1961, he became the first American to be launched into space. Shepard commanded *Apollo 14* on its flight to the Moon in 1971 and was the fifth man to walk on the lunar surface.

Shepard, Sam (1943–) US playwright and actor. His plays include *Icarus's Mother* (1965), *The Tooth of Crime* (1972), *Buried Child* (1978), for which he won a Pulitzer Prize, and *True West* (1983). He has acted in films of his own screenplays, including *Paris, Texas* (1984) and *Fool for Love* (1985).

Sheridan, Philip Henry (1831–88) US general. An aggressive Union commander in the American CIVIL WAR, he reorganized and led the cavalry of the Army of the Potomac (1864). Commanding the Army of the Shenandoah, he devastated the Shenandoah valley. In the final campaign, he forced Robert E. LEE's surrender at Appomattox (1865).

Sheridan, Richard Brinsley (1751–1816) English dramatist and politician. He excelled in comedies of manners, such as *The Rivals* (1775) and *The School for Scandal* (1777). Entering Parliament as a member of the Whigs in 1780, he became one of the most brilliant orators of his generation.

Sherman, William Tecumseh (1820–91) Union general in the American CIVIL WAR (1861–65). He took part in the first battle of BULL RUN, and in the capture of Vicksburg. He won the battle of ATLANTA, and led the 'March to the Sea' from Atlanta to Savannah in 1864.

Sherpa Buddhist people who inhabit the Khumba Valley, NE Nepal. Of Tibetan origin, they are renowned for their portering of Himalayan expeditions.

sherry Fortified wine with a characteristic raisiny flavour produced by a special method of vinification and expert blending. Drier apéritif sherries include fino, manzanilla and amontillado; sweeter, dessert sherries include oloroso, amoroso, golden and cream. True sherry comes from Jerez, s Spain.

Sherwood, Robert Emmet (1896–1955) US dramatist. Sherwood won four Pulitzer Prizes: *Idiot's Delight* (1936), *Abe Lincoln in Illinois* (1938), *There Shall be No Night* (1940) and his memoir *Roosevelt and Hopkins* (1948). He was a speechwriter for President Franklin D. Roosevelt. He won an Oscar for best screenplay for *The Best Years of Our Lives* (1946).

Sherwood Forest Ancient royal hunting ground in Nottinghamshire, central England. Famous as the home of the legendary ROBIN HOOD, some of the original forest remains and is protected in a country park.

Shetland Islands Group of c.100 islands NE of the Orkneys, 210km (130mi) off the N coast of Scotland, constituting an administrative region. The principal islands are Mainland (which has the main town of Lerwick), Yell, Unst, Whalsay

▲ **Shaw** George Bernard Shaw, here pictured aged 90, was one of the most prolific dramatists of the 20th century. He first came to public attention as a journalist and critic. Many of Shaw's plays reflect his political commitment to socialism and pacifism, and expose the iniquities of the English class system. *Heartbreak House* (1920) is a witty indictment of the aristocracy in World War 1.

S

and Bressay. Settled by Norse invaders in the 9th century, Scotland sezied the islands in 1472. The islands are famous for SHETLAND PONIES. Oil and tourism have become major industries. Area: 1433sq km (553sq mi) Pop. (2001) 21,960.

Shetland pony One of the smallest types of light horse. Originating in the SHETLAND ISLANDS, it has been introduced to most parts of the world. Used for draught or road work, it also makes an ideal child's mount. Height: typically 71cm (28in) at the shoulder; weight: 169kg (350lb).

Shevardnadze, Eduard Amvrosiyevich (1928–) Georgian statesman, president (1992–2003). A close ally of Mikhail GORBACHEV, he was Soviet foreign minister (1985–90). He oversaw the Soviet withdrawal from Afghanistan, and worked on détente with the West. In 1990, warning of impending dictatorship, Shevardnadze resigned and formed the Democratic Reform Movement. As president of Georgia, he sought Russian help to overcome supporters of the deposed leader, Zviad Gamsakhurdia. Shevardnadze survived assassination attempts in 1995 and 1998 but was removed from power in 2003 during protests over vote rigging.

Shi'ite Follower of Shi'a, the second-largest branch of ISLAM. Shi'ites believe that the true successor of MUHAMMAD was ALI, whose claim to be CALIPH was not recognized by SUNNI Muslims. It rejects the *Sunna* (the collection of teachings outside the KORAN) and relies instead on the pronouncements of a succession of holy men called IMAMS. The SAFAVID dynasty in Iran was the first to adopt Shi'a as a state religion. One of the principal causes of the Iranian Revolution was Shah PAHLAVI's attempt to reduce clerical influence on government. Ayatollah KHOMEINI's Shi'ite theocracy stressed the role of Islamic activism in liberation struggles. The largest Shi'ite group is the Twelve-Imam Shi'ites; the other major group is the ISMAILIS.

Shikoku Smallest of the four main islands of Japan, S of Honshu and E of Kyushu. The interior is mountainous and extensively forested, and most settlements are on the coast. Products: rice, tea, wheat, fish, tobacco, soya beans, camphor, copper. Area: 18,798sq km (7,258sq mi). Pop. (1999 est.) 4,166,000.

shingles (herpes zoster) Acute viral infection of sensory nerves. Groups of small blisters appear along the course of the affected nerves and the condition is very painful.

Shinto (Jap. 'way to the gods') Indigenous religion of Japan. Originating as a primitive cult of nature worship, it was shaped by the influence of CONFUCIUS and, from the 5th century, BUDDHISM. A revival of the ancient Shinto rites began in the 17th century, and contributed to the rise of Japanese nationalism in the late 19th century. Shinto has many deities in the form of spirits, souls, and forces of nature.

ship Vessel for conveying passengers and freight by sea. The earliest sea-going ships were probably Egyptian, making voyages to the E coast of Africa in c.1500 BC. In China, extensive sea voyages were being made by ships that carried more than one mast and featured a rudder by c.AD 200, some 1200 years before such ships appeared in Europe. In the Mediterranean region, the galleys of the Greek, Phoenician and Roman navies combined rows of oars with a single square sail, as did the Viking longboats, which were capable of withstanding violent seas. By the 14th and 15th centuries, carracks and galleons were being developed to fulfil the exploration of the New World. Fighting ships of the 17th and 18th centuries included frigates of various designs. Sailing freighters culminated in the great clippers of the late 19th century, some of which had iron hulls. A century or so earlier, the first steamships had been built. They were powered by wood or coal-burning steam engines that drove large paddle wheels. In 1819, the first Atlantic crossing was made by 'steam-assisted sail', and this crossing soon became a regular service. By the mid-19th century, steamships, such as Brunel's *Great Britain* (1844), were driven by propellers or screws. Marine steam TURBINES developed at the turn of the 19th century, and gradually replaced reciprocating (back-and-forth cranking) steam ENGINES for large vessels, early examples being the ocean liners of the 1900s. Oil, rather than coal, soon became the favoured fuel for large engines. Diesel engines developed in the early 1900s, but were considered unreliable and, although less expensive to run, they did not replace steam turbines until

the 1970s. Some of the newest military ships and icebreakers are fitted with nuclear engines in which heat from a NUCLEAR REACTOR raises steam in boilers to drive steam turbines. *See also* AIRCRAFT CARRIER; BOAT; SUBMARINE

Shiraz Capital of Fars province, in the Zagros Mountains, SW Iran. An ancient city established near PERSEPOLIS, Shiraz was an artistic centre from the 4th century. From the 7th century it was a trade centre, and in the 9th century it developed into a place of Muslim pilgrimage. Shiraz was the capital (1750–94) of Persia, and many buildings date from that period. Still noted for its wine and carpets; other products include metalwork, textiles, cement and sugar. Pop. (1994) 1,053,025.

Shiva (Siva) Major god of HINDUISM. A complex god who transcends the concepts of good and evil, Shiva represents both reproduction and destruction (a combination of seemingly contradictory qualities is not uncommon in Hinduism). He periodically destroys the world in order to create it once more. He takes little part in the affairs of humanity, although his wife, KALI, is actively involved in them.

shock Acute, circulatory failure, possibly with collapse. Caused by disease, injury, or emotional trauma, it is characterized by weakness, pallor, sweating, and a rapid shallow pulse. In shock, blood pressure drops to a level below that needed to oxygenate the tissues.

Shockley, William Bradford (1910–89) US physicist who, with his colleagues, John BARDEEN and Walter BRATTAIN, invented the TRANSISTOR. They shared the 1956 Nobel Prize in physics. In 1947, they produced a point-contact transistor and a junction transistor.

shoebill stork (whale-headed stork) Tall, wading bird found in papyrus marshes of tropical NE Africa. It has a shoe-shaped bill with a sharp hook, dark plumage, and long legs. It feeds at

◀ **Shearer** English striker Alan Shearer was England captain for the 1996 European Championship. His striking partnership with Chris Sutton enabled Blackburn Rovers to win the 1994–95 Premier League title, and Shearer equalled the Premiership scoring record with 34 goals. In 1996, he moved from Blackburn to Newcastle United. Injury forced him to miss much of the 1997–98 season. Shearer recovered in time for the 1998 World Cup. Shearer retired from international football after the 2000 European Championships. In 2002, he helped Newcastle qualify for the European Champions League.

INTERNET

Shetland Islands
▶ www.shetland.gov.uk
▶ www.visitshetland.com

◀ **ship** Worldwide expansion of Europe's trading empire during the 18th century was made possible by ships, such as the heavily armed Dutch East Indiaman shown here.

S

INTERNET

Shostakovich, Dmitri Dmitrievich
▶ www.classical.net

Sibelius, Jean Julius Christian
▶ www.classical.net

S

night on small animals, including frogs and turtles. Height: to 1.4m (4.6ft). Family Balaenicipitidae; species *Balaeniceps rex*.

shogun Title of the military ruler of Japan, first conferred upon Yoritomo in 1192. The Minamoto (1192–1333), Ashikaga (1338–1568), and TOKUGAWA (1603–1868) shogunates in effect ruled feudal Japan, although the Emperor retained ceremonial and religious duties. The Shogunate ended with the MEIJI RESTORATION in 1868.

Sholokhov, Mikhail Alexandrovich (1905–84) Soviet novelist. Sholokhov became famous for his novel about his native land, *Tikhy Don* (1928–40); translated as *And Quiet Flows the Don* (1934) and *The Don Flows Home to the Sea* (1940). He received the 1965 Nobel Prize in literature.

Shona Bantu-speaking people of E Zimbabwe. Shona society is based on subsistence agriculture and is centred on small villages, abandoned when local resources are exhausted. Their culture is noted for its pottery, music, and dance.

shooting Competitive sport involving firearms, in which a competitor, or team of competitors, fires at stationary or moving targets. The three main types of shooting are rifle, pistol, and clay-pigeon shooting. Within **rifle** shooting, the three basic classes of competition are for air rifle, small-bore, and large-bore rifle; all but air rifle shooting are Olympic sports. The two main forms of **pistol** shooting, rapid-fire (or silhouette) and free shooting, are both Olympic sports. There are three disciplines of **clay-pigeon** shooting – Olympic trench, skeet, and down-the-line shooting. The first two types are Olympic sports.

shorthand System of writing, used to record speech quickly. Phonetic shorthand systems first appeared during the 18th century, and the most famous system, **Pitman's** shorthand, was published in 1837. All the sounds of the English language are represented by 49 signs for consonants and 16 signs to indicate vowels. The Gregg system of phonetic shorthand, widely taught in the USA, has a script based on ordinary writing.

Short Parliament (1640) English Parliament that ended 11 years of personal rule by CHARLES I. Charles was forced to summon Parliament to raise revenue through taxation for war against Scotland. When it refused his demands, he dissolved it, but had to summon the LONG PARLIAMENT a few months later.

Shoshone (Shoshoni) Native North Americans of the UTO-AZTECAN LANGUAGE group. They occupy reservations in California, Idaho, Nevada, Utah, and Wyoming. They comprise the COMANCHE, the Northern, the Western, and the Wind River Shoshone. Today, there are *c*.9,500 Shoshone.

Shostakovich, Dmitri Dmitrievich (1906–75) Russian composer. Shostakovich's use of contemporary western musical developments in his compositions did not conform with Soviet SOCIALIST REALISM. His opera *The Lady Macbeth of the Mtsenk District* (1934) received international acclaim but was later criticized in *Pravda*. Other works were deliberately more conventional. He composed 15 symphonies, 13 string quartets, ballets, concertos, piano music, film music, and vocal works.

shot put Field event in which an athlete throws a heavy metal ball from a position close to the neck by means of a swift extension of the arm. The athlete must remain inside the throwing circle. Men throw a 7.3kg (16lb) shot; women a 4kg (8lb 13oz) shot. The shot put has been an Olympic event since 1909.

shoulder In human anatomy, mobile joint at the top of the arm. It consists of the ball-and-socket joint between the upper arm bone (HUMERUS) and the SHOULDER BLADE (scapula).

shoulder blade (scapula) In vertebrates, either of two large, roughly triangular, flat bones found one on either side of the upper back. They provide for the attachment of muscles that move the forelimbs. *See also* SHOULDER.

shrew Smallest mammal, found throughout the world. It is an active, voracious insectivore that eats more than its own weight daily. Family Soricidae.

shrike (butcherbird) Small, perching bird found worldwide, except in South America and Australia. It dives at its prey, hitting them with its strong, hooked bill and then impaling them on a sharp fence post, twig or thorn. Family Laniidae.

shrimp Mostly marine, swimming crustacean. Its compressed body has long antennae, stalked eyes, a beak-like prolongation, segmented abdomen with five pairs of swimming legs, and a terminal spine. There are true, sand, and pistol shrimps. Large edible shrimps are often called PRAWNS or scampi. Length: 5–7.5cm (2–3in).

Shropshire (Salop) County in W England; the county town is Shrewsbury. Shropshire is crossed by the River SEVERN. To the N of the river the land is generally low-lying, while to the S it rises to the Welsh hills. Part of Mercia in Anglo-Saxon history, after the Norman Conquest it became part of the Welsh Marches. The economy is primarily agricultural. Mineral deposits include coal, and industries include metal products. Area: 3,197sq km (1,235sq mi). Pop. (2001) 283,240.

Shrove Tuesday Day before Ash Wednesday, which is the first day of LENT. *See also* MARDI GRAS

shrub (bush) Woody, perennial plant that is smaller than a TREE. Instead of having a main stem, a shrub branches at, or slightly above, ground level into several stems. Its hard stem distinguishes it from an HERB.

sial In geology, uppermost of the two main rock-classes in the Earth's crust. Sial rocks are so called because their main constituents are silicon and aluminium. They make up the material of the continents and overlay the SIMA.

Siamese twins Identical twins who are born physically joined together, sometimes with sharing of organs. Surgical separation is usually possible.

Sibelius, Jean Julius Christian (1865–1957) Finnish composer whose work represents the culmination of nationalism in Finnish music. He wrote chamber music and works for piano and organ, but is best known for his orchestral works, including seven symphonies, a violin concerto (1903–35), and the tone poems *En Saga* (1892) and *Finlandia* (1899).

Siberia (Sibir) Extensive region of Asian Russia, extending E to W from the Ural Mountains to the Pacific Ocean, and N to S from the Arctic Ocean to the steppes of Kazakhstan and the Mongolian border. The region includes areas of tundra, taiga, and steppe, almost half of it is forested. Drained chiefly by vast rivers, OB, YENISEI, and LENA and their tributaries, Siberia divides into five geographical areas: (1) the W Siberian plain, between the URALS and the Central Plateau, favours dairy farming, but wheat, oats, flax, potatoes, rye, and sugar beet are also grown. Two-thirds of the population live in the SW, where industry concentrates in cities such as NOVOSIBIRSK and OMSK, and in the Kuznetz Basin, which has large coal deposits; (2) the Central Siberian plateau, between the Yenisei and Lena rivers. KRASNOYARSK lies on the Yenisei and the city of Yakutsk on the Lena. The region is Russia's chief producer of gold, mica, diamonds, and aluminium, and forestry is important; (3) the NE Siberian mountains lie to the E of the Lena. The region is sparsely populated due to the Arctic climate. Verkhoyansk is the world's coldest permanent settlement. The breeding of reindeer, fishing, and seal-hunting are the chief occupations; (4) the mountains of the S Trans-Baikal region form the watershed between the Pacific and the Arctic. The major city is Irkutsk, close to Lake BAIKAL; (5) the volcanic KAMCHATKA peninsula. The Russian Cossacks conquered Siberia between 1581 and 1644, although the Far Eastern territory was held by the Chinese until 1860. Mining developed in the 19th century, and the region became a penal colony for political prisoners of the Russian Empire and its Soviet successors. Large scale settlement came only after the construction of the TRANS-SIBERIAN RAILWAY between 1881 and 1905; Siberia's population doubled between 1914 and 1946. The importance of Siberian grain to Russian agriculture was emphasized during World War 2, and during the 1950s Khrushchev encouraged the cultivation of land in the SW. The 1960s witnessed the development of vast hydroelectric schemes in the Trans-Baikal region. Area: 13,807,000sq km (5,331,000sq mi). Pop. (2000 est.) 20,792,500.

Sibyl Prophetess of Greek and Roman mythology. The Sibyl of Cumae offered nine books of her prophecies to Tarquinius Superbus of Rome. He refused her price, so she began burning them until he bought the remaining three for the price she had asked for all nine. They were consulted in times of emergency.

Sichuan (Szechwan) Province in SW China, almost completely surrounded by mountains, and the most populous in

▲ **shoebill stork** Although it displays some behavioural similarities to pelicans and herons, the shoebill stork (*Balaeniceps rex*) is the sole member of a separate bird family, Balaenicipidae. It uses its distinctive, shovel-like bill to dig in the mud to find the fish and aquatic animals on which it feeds. Despite its large size and clumsy, sluggish appearance on land, it is a graceful flyer with broad wings. Silent and solitary birds, shoebills have unwebbed feet that are specially adapted to walking on marshy land.

the country; the capital is Chengdu. The E part of the region comprises the heavily populated Red Basin, the most prosperous area of China. Sichuan is China's leading producer of rice, maize and sweet potatoes, while soya beans, barley, and fruit are also grown. Livestock, including cattle, pigs, horses and oxen, are reared, particularly in the w. Salt, coal, and iron are mined; other products include rapeseed oil, and silk – for which Sichuan was once world famous. Area: 569,215sq km (219,774sq mi). Pop. (2000) 83,290,000.

Sicily Largest and most populous island in the Mediterranean Sea, off the sw tip of the Italian peninsula, comprising (with nearby islands) an autonomous region of Italy. The capital is PALERMO; other major cities include MESSINA. The narrow Strait of Messina separates Sicily from the rest of Italy. Mostly mountainous, Mount ETNA, at 3323m (10,902ft), is the highest volcano in Europe. There are fertile valleys in the central plateau, and agriculture is the economic mainstay. Situated between Europe and Africa, from the 5th to 3rd century BC it was a battleground for the rival Roman and Carthaginian empires and, following the first PUNIC WAR in 241 BC became a Roman province. At the end of the 11th century AD the Normans conquered the island and s Italy. In 1266, the throne passed to Charles of Anjou, whose unpopular government caused the Sicilian Vespers revolt of 1282 and the election of an Aragónese king. In 1302, peace terms led to Aragón keeping Sicily, while s Italy became the Angevin kingdom of Naples. In 1735, the two regions reunified under the rule of the Bourbon Don Carlos (Charles III of Spain). Ferdinand I was crowned as King of Two Sicilies in 1816. Sicilian revolts of 1820 and 1848–49 were ruthlessly suppressed. In 1860, Garibaldi liberated the island, and it became part of the new, unified kingdom of Italy. Grain, olives, wine, and citrus fruits are the principal products; tourism is also important. Area: 25,706sq km (9,925sq mi). Pop. (2001) 5,076,700.

Sickert, Walter Richard (1860–1942) English painter. Sickert attracted a circle of progressive painters to his studio, and inspired them to form the Camden Town Group and later the London Group. He was a precursor of the 1950s 'kitchen sink' school of drama in his rejection of 'nice' subjects in favour of drab domestic interiors, sordid bedroom scenes, and a spirit of desperate boredom, as in *Ennui* (*c*.1914).

sickle-cell disease Inherited blood disorder featuring an abnormality of HAEMOGLOBIN. The haemoglobin is sensitive to a deficiency of oxygen and it distorts ERYTHROCYTES, causing them to become rigid and sickle shaped. Sickle cells are rapidly lost from the circulation, giving rise to anaemia and jaundice.

sidereal period Orbital period of a planet or other celestial body with respect to a background star. It is the true orbital period. **Sidereal time** is local time reckoned according to the rotation of the Earth with respect to the stars. The sidereal day is 23 hours, 56 minutes and 4 seconds of mean solar time, nearly 4 minutes shorter than the mean solar day. The sidereal year is equal to 365.25636 mean solar days.

sidewinder (horned rattlesnake) Nocturnal RATTLESNAKE found in deserts of sw USA and Mexico. It has horn-like scales over the eyes and is usually tan with a light pattern. It loops obliquely across the sand, leaving a J-shaped trail. Length: to 75cm (30in). Family Viperidae; species *Crotalus cerastes*. The term is also used to describe desert-dwelling snakes of the Old World that move in a similar way.

Sidney, Sir Philip (1554–86) English poet, diplomat, and courtier. Sidney's intricate romance *Arcadia* (1590) is the earliest example of PASTORAL in English. His love for Penelope Devereux inspired *Astrophel and Stella* (1591), the first English SONNET sequence. *An Apology for Poetry* (1595) is the most important critical work of the Elizabethan era.

Siemens German brothers, who were associated with the electrical engineering industry. **Ernst Werner** von Siemens (1816–92), developed an electric telegraph system in 1849. Ernst and **Karl** (1829–1906) set up subsidiaries of the family firm in London, Vienna, and Paris. **Frederich** (1826–1904) and **Karl Wilhelm** (later William) (1823–83) developed a regenerative furnace that was used extensively in industry. Karl Wilhelm introduced (1843) an ELECTROPLATING process to Britain.

Siena Capital of Siena province, Tuscany, central Italy. It is one of Italy's foremost tourist attractions. The town lends its name to the yellow-brown pigment sienna, present in the region's soil, and the area is famous for its orange marble. Founded by the Etruscans, Siena became a commune in the 12th century. During the 13th century, it rapidly expanded to rival Florence, and was the centre of the Ghibelline faction. In the mid-16th century, it fell under the control of the Medici. In art history, it is especially famed for its Sienese School of painting (13th-14th centuries). Pop. (2001) 54,366.

Sienkiewicz, Henryk (1846–1916) Polish novelist and short-story writer. He gained international recognition with *Quo Vadis?* (1896), and received the 1905 Nobel Prize in literature. He glorified his country's struggle for nationhood in the trilogy *With Fire and Sword* (1884), *The Deluge* (1886), and *Pan Michael* (1887–88).

Sierra Leone Republic on the w coast of Africa; the capital is FREETOWN. *See* country feature, page 680

Sierra Madre Mountain range in Mexico, from the US border to SE Mexico and extending s into Guatemala. It comprises the Sierra Madre Occidental, Sierra Madre Oriental, Sierra Madre del Sur, and the sub-range Sierra Madre del Guatemala. The ranges enclose the central Mexican plateau, and have long been a barrier to E-W travel. The main range is 2,400km (1,500mi) long and *c*.16–480km (10–300mi) wide. The highest peak is Orizaba (Giltaltepetl) at 5,700m (18,700ft).

Sierra Nevada Mountain system in E California, USA. In the E it rises steeply from the Great Basin, while the w edge slopes gently down to the Central Valley of California. The snow-fed rivers are used to irrigate the Central Valley and also to provide hydroelectric power. Mount WHITNEY, 4,418m (14,494ft), is the highest peak. The range is 650km (400mi) long.

sight Sense by which form, colour, size, movement, and distance of objects are perceived. Essentially, it is the detection of light by the EYE, enabling the formation of visual images.

Sigismund (1368–1437) Holy Roman Emperor (1433–37), and King of Germany (1411–37), Hungary (1387–1437) and Bohemia (1419–37). As King of Hungary, he was defeated by the OTTOMAN EMPIRE in 1396 and 1427. In Bohemia, he was challenged by the HUSSITES revolt. As Emperor (crowned 1433), he was partly responsible for ending the GREAT SCHISM (1415). He secured the succession for Albert II, his son-in-law, the first ruler of the HABSBURG dynasty.

Signac, Paul (1863–1935) French painter. Signac was the main writer of NEO-IMPRESSIONISM, especially in *D'Eugène Delacroix au néo-impressionisme* (1899). Towards the second half of his life, his painting became much freer and his colour more brilliant, such as *View of the Port of Marseille* (1905).

sign language Non-phonetic communication using hand symbols, movements and gestures. It is used as a primary means of communication among many deaf people.

Sikhism Indian religion founded in the 16th century by NANAK, the first Sikh GURU. Combining HINDU and MUSLIM teachings, it is a MONOTHEISTIC religion whose adherents believe that their one God is the immortal creator of the universe. All human beings are equal, and Sikhs oppose any CASTE system. The path to God is through prayer and meditation, but nearness to God is achievable only through divine grace. Sikhs believe in REINCARNATION, and are taught to seek

◄ shrew Among the smallest of the mammals, shrews inhabit forests all around the world: two examples are tree shrews (*Tupaia glis*, top), which live in SE Asia, and forest elephant shrews (*Petrodromus tetradactylus*, bottom), found in Kenya and SW Africa. Because they are extremely active with very high metabolic rates, shrews must eat constantly just to stay alive: they will die of starvation if they are deprived of food for even a few hours. Although they have poor vision, they have keen senses of smell and hearing, and loud noises can cause them to faint or even to drop dead. They produce a foul-smelling secretion from special glands on their backs, which protects them from most mammalian predators, but this does not deter many birds of prey, including hawks and owls.

S

INTERNET

Sicily
▸ www.bestofsicily.com

Sickert, Walter Richard
▸ www.tate.org.uk

Sierra Leone
▸ www.sierra-leone.org

Signac, Paul
▸ www.famsf.org
▸ www.artsmia.org

spiritual guidance from their leader. Begun in PUNJAB as a pacifist religion, Sikhism (under Nanak's successors) became an activist military brotherhood and political force. Sikh men adopt the surname Singh ('lion'). After Indian independence, Sikh extremists periodically agitated for an independent Sikh state (Khalistan). In 1984, government forces killed Sant Jarnail Singh Bhindranwale (1947–84), the leader of a Sikh fundamentalist revival, at the Golden Temple of AMRITSAR. In retaliation, Indira GANDHI was assassinated by her Sikh bodyguard. More than 1,000 Sikhs died in the ensuing riots.

Sikh Wars (1845–46, 1848–49) Two conflicts between the SIKHS and the British in NW India. After the death of RANJIT SINGH in 1839, disorder affected the Sikh state in the PUNJAB. When Sikh forces, including many non-Sikhs, crossed the frontier on the River Sutlej, the British declared war. After several battles involving heavy casualties on both sides, the British advanced to Lahore where peace was agreed (1846). The conflict renewed two years later, but superior British artillery led to a heavy Sikh defeat at Gujarat (1849). The Sikhs surrendered and the Punjab became part of British India.

Sikkim State in N India, bounded by Tibet, China (N and NE), Bhutan (SE), India (S), and Nepal (W); the capital is Gangtok (1991 pop. 25,024). The terrain is mountainous, rising to Mount Kanchenjunga, at 8,591m (28,185ft), the world's third-highest peak. The original inhabitants were the Lepcha, but after the 17th century the Rajas of Tibet ruled Sikkim. By 1816 it fell under British influence, and after British withdrawal from India in 1947, Sikkim gained independence. Political unrest led to the country becoming an Indian Protectorate in 1950, and it was made an associate state in 1975. Agriculture is the main source of income, with maize, rice, barley, fruits, tea, and cardamom among the main crops; the tourist industry is growing. Area: 7,096sq km (2,734sq mi). Pop. (2001) 540,493.

Sikorsky, Igor Ivanovich (1889–1972) US aeronautical engineer, b. Russia. In 1913, he built and piloted the world's first multi-motored aircraft. He also developed the HELICOPTER.

Silesia Historic region in E central Europe, now mostly lying in SW Poland, with the remainder in N Czech Republic and SE Germany. A former Polish province, it passed from Poland to Bohemia in the 14th century, became part of the Habsburg empire, and was seized by Prussia from Austria in 1742. In World War 2, it was invaded by the Soviet Union, but in 1945 a greater part of the land returned to Poland by the terms of the POTSDAM CONFERENCE. Upper Silesia is primarily an industrial region of mining and metals, based around KATOWICE; Lower Silesia, with a milder climate, is more agricultural.

silica (silicon dioxide, SiO_2) Compound of SILICON and oxygen. It occurs as QUARTZ and chert (which includes FLINT). Silica is used in the manufacture of glass, ceramics, and SILICONE.

silicon (symbol Si) Common, grey, nonmetallic element of group IV of the periodic table. Silicon is found only in combinations, such as SILICA and silicate. It is the second most abundant element in the Earth's crust (27.7% by weight) and was discovered in 1823 by Swedish chemist J.J. BERZELIUS. Microprocessors make extensive use of SILICON CHIPS. Properties: at.no. 14; r.a.m. 28.086; r.d. 2.33; m.p. 1,410°C (2,570°F); b.p. 2,355°C (4,271°F); most common isotope Si^{28} (98.21%).

silicon chip Small piece of SILICON etched to carry many tiny electric circuits. Silicon chips are at the heart of most electronic equipment. Chips are etched, layer by layer, onto slivers of pure silicon. Each layer is 'doped' to give it particular electrical properties, and the combination of different layers form components such as TRANSISTORS and DIODES. *See also* CHARGE-COUPLED DEVICE (CCD); INTEGRATED CIRCUIT (IC); PRINTED CIRCUIT; SEMICONDUCTOR

silicone Odourless and colourless polymer based on SILICON. Silicones are inert and stable at high temperatures,

---

SIERRA LEONE

The Republic of Sierra Leone on the W coast of Africa is about the same size as the Republic of Ireland. The coast contains several deep estuaries in the N, with lagoons in the S. The most prominent feature is the mountainous Freetown (or Sierra Leone) peninsula. N of the peninsula is the River Rokel estuary, W Africa's best natural harbour. Behind the coastal plain the land rises to mountains, with the highest peak, Loma Mansa, reaching 1,948m [6,391ft].

Swamps cover large areas of the country near the coast. Inland, much of the rainforest has

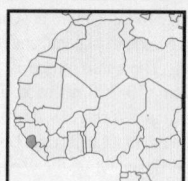

been destroyed. The N is largely covered by tropical savanna.

CLIMATE

The climate is tropical, with heavy rainfall. In the N it is dry between December and March. In the S it is dry in January and February.

HISTORY

Portuguese sailors reached the coast in 1460. In the 16th century the area became a source of slaves. Freetown was founded in 1787 as a home for freed slaves, and in 1808 the settlement became a British Crown Colony. In 1896 the interior was made a Protectorate, and in 1951 the Protectorate and Colony united. In 1961 Sierra Leone gained independence. In 1971 it became a republic, but in 1978 the All People's Congress declared itself the sole political party

POLITICS

A 1991 referendum voted for the restoration of multi-party democracy, but the military seized power in 1992. A civil war raged between government forces and the Revolutionary United Front (RUF). The RUF fought to end foreign interference and to nationalize the diamond mines. After 1996 elections, Ahmad Tejan Kabbah led a civilian government. In 1997, Major Johnny Paul Koroma seized power in a military coup. The Economic Community of West African States (ECOWAS) imposed sanctions, and Nigeria led an intervention force that restored Kabbah as president in 1998.

A 1999 peace treaty and the arrival of UN peace-keeping forces seemed to signal an end to

AREA 71,740sq km [27,699sq mi]
POPULATION 6,145,000
CAPITAL (POPULATION) Freetown (1,007,000)
GOVERNMENT Single-party republic
ETHNIC GROUPS Native African tribes 90%
LANGUAGES English (official), Mende, Temne, Krio
RELIGIONS Islam 60%, traditional beliefs 30%, Christianity 10%
CURRENCY Leone = 100 cents

the civil war, but in 2000 RUF rebels, led by Foday Sankoh and backed by Liberia, abducted UN troops and renewed the war. British soldiers arrived to bolster the UN peace-keeping effort. Disarmament continued throughout 2001 through a UN-brokered peace plan. Sankoh was captured and, in 2002, the war appeared to be over. About 50,000 people had been killed. Rebel raids from Liberia in 2003 failed to disturb the country's fragile peace. Stability was gradually restored and, in late 2005, the last UN soldiers left the country. Ernest Bai Koroma was elected president in 2007.

ECONOMY

The World Bank classifies Sierra Leone among the 'low-income' economies. Agriculture provides a living for 70% of the workforce, though farming is mostly at subsistence level. Food crops include cassava, maize and rice, the staple food and export crops include cocoa and coffee. The most valuable exports include diamonds, bauxite and rutile (titanium ore).

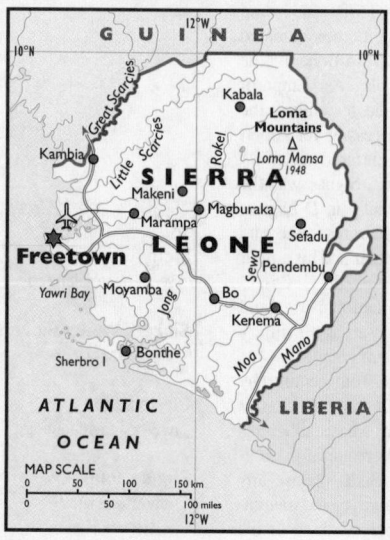

and are used in lubricants, varnishes, adhesives, water repellents, hydraulic fluids, and artificial heart valves.

silk Natural fibre produced by many creatures, notably the SILKWORM. The many kinds of silk include crêpe, satin, taffeta, and velvet. Almost all silk comes from silkworms reared commercially; a single cocoon can provide between 600 and 900m (2,000–3,000ft) of filament. When the cocoons have been spun, the farmer heats them to kill the insects. The cocoons are then soaked to unstick the fibres, and the strands are unwound together to form a single thread of yarn. The Chinese were the first to use silk. Silk manufacturing developed in England in the 17th century. China is the largest producer of raw silk.

Silk Road Ancient trade route linking China with Europe, the major artery of all Asian land exploration before AD 1500. For 3000 years, the secret of SILK was closely guarded by the Chinese. Silk fetched extravagant prices in Greece and Rome, and the trade became the major source of income for the Chinese ruling dynasties. By 100 BC the tax on the trade provided a third of all the HAN dynasty's revenue. The silk trade began to decline in the 6th century, when the SILKWORM's eggs were smuggled to Constantinople and the secret exposed. During the 13th century, European merchants (including Marco POLO in 1271) travelled along the Silk Road. In the 14th century, trade became possible via a sea route to the Far East.

silk-screen printing (serigraphy) In PRINTING, a means of producing a print, generally on paper. A screen composed of a mesh of silk or man-made fibres is stretched over a wooden frame; a design is 'stopped out' (painted) on the mesh, using glue, varnish, gelatin, or a paper stencil. To make the print, ink is taken across the screen with a squeegee; the pressure of this pushes the ink through the unstopped areas of the mesh. Several screens may be used to build up a multi-coloured print.

silkworm Moth CATERPILLAR that feeds chiefly on MULBERRY leaves. The common domesticated *Bombyx mori* is raised commercially for its SILK cocoon. Length: 7.5 cm (3in). Family Bombycidae.

sill Sheet-like intrusion of IGNEOUS ROCK that is parallel to the bedding or structure of the surrounding rock. Sill rock is medium-grained; basic sills (**dolerites**) are the commonest.

Sillitoe, Alan (1928–) English novelist and short story writer. Sillitoe's best-known novel was *Saturday Night and Sunday Morning* (1958, filmed 1960). *The Loneliness of the Long-distance Runner* (1959) is his most celebrated novella. More recent novels include *The Flame of Life* (1974), *The Open Door* (1989), *Leonard's War* (1991) and *Snowdrops* (1993).

silt Mineral particles produced by the weathering of rock. These particles, varying in size between grains of sand and clay, are carried along in streams and rivers, to be deposited in the gently flowing lower reaches of rivers. When the river overflows its bank, the silt deposit forms fertile land.

Silurian Third oldest period of the PALAEOZOIC era, 438–408 million years ago. Marine invertebrates resembled those of ORDOVICIAN times, and fragmentary remains show that jawless fish began to evolve. The earliest land plants (psilopsids) and first land animals (archaic mites and millipedes) developed. Mountains formed in NW Europe and Greenland.

silver (symbol Ag) White, metallic element in the second series of TRANSITION ELEMENTS in the periodic table. It occurs in argentite (a sulphide) and horn silver (a chloride), and is also obtained as a by-product in the refining of copper and lead. Silver ores are scattered throughout the world, Mexico being the major producer. Silver is used for some electrical contacts and on some PRINTED CIRCUITS. Other uses include jewellery, ornaments, coinage, mirrors, and silver salts for light-sensitive materials used in photography. The metal does not oxidize in air, but tarnishes if sulphur compounds are present. Properties: at.no. 47; r.a.m. 107.868; r.d. 10.5; m.p. 961.93°C (1,763°F), b.p. 2,212°C (4,104 °F); most common isotope Ag[107] (51.82%).

silverfish (bristletail) Primitive, grey, wingless insect found throughout the world. It lives in cool, damp places, feeding on starchy materials such as food scraps and paper. It gets its name from the silvery scales that cover its body. Length: 13mm (0.5in). Family Lepismatidae; species *Lepisma saccharina*.

silver nitrate (AgNo₃) Colourless, solid compound. It is the most important salt of silver because it is very soluble

SILICON CHIP

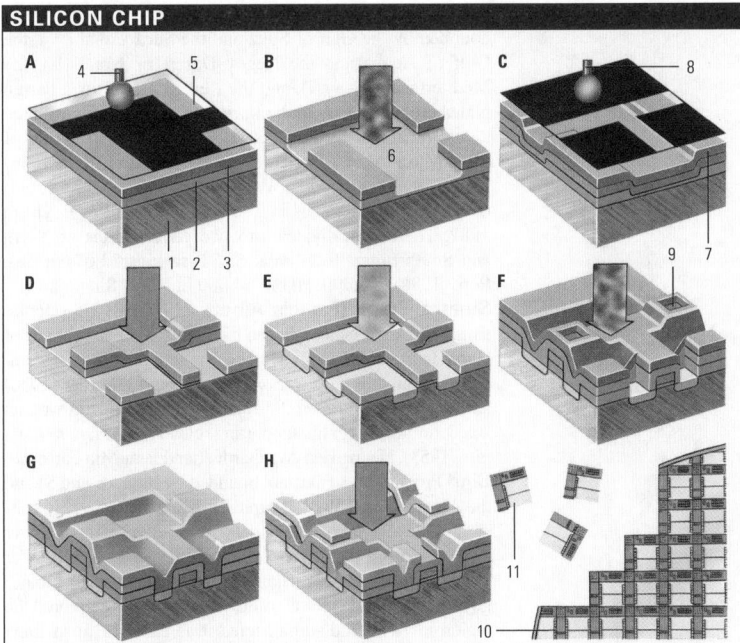

A silicon chip is manufactured by building up layers on top of a wafer of silicon (1). (A) First a layer of silicon dioxide (2), an insulator, is laid down followed by photo-sensitive photoresist (3). Photoresist hardens when hit by ultraviolet light (4). By using a mask (5), the area to be hardened can be controlled. (B) The unhardened area shielded by the mask can then be rinsed out with a solvent (6). The photoresist is then removed by hot gases. (C) The same process is used to apply a conducting polysilicon (7). Again ultraviolet light fixes the photoresist (8) in the unmasked area. (D) A solvent removes the photoresist. (E) N-type silicon, which only carries a negative charge, is then created by doping of the silicon base. (F) A third masking process creates shafts (9) to the n-type silicon. (G) An aluminium layer is then applied. (H) A fourth masking forms electrical contacts connecting the layers of silicon. Hundreds of chips are simultaneously made on a single wafer of silicon (10) before they are eventually separated (11) and mounted individually for use.

in water. Silver nitrate is used in PHOTOGRAPHY, chemical analysis, silverplating, mirrors, inks, and dyes.

sima In geology, undermost of the two main rock-classes that make up the Earth's crust, so called because its main constituents are silicon and magnesium. It underlies the SIAL of the continents.

Simenon, Georges (1903–89) Belgian novelist. He published more than 500 novels and many more short stories. His character Maigret, a Parisian police inspector, is one of the best-known creations in 20th-century detective fiction.

simile Figure of speech comparing two things. It differs from ordinary comparisons in that it compares, for effect, things usually considered dissimilar and sharing only one common characteristic, as, for example, in the phrase 'its fleece was white as snow'. *See also* METAPHOR

Simon, Neil (1927–) US playwright. Simon's plays include *Come Blow Your Horn* (1961), *The Odd Couple* (1965), the musical *Sweet Charity* (1966) and *Little Me* (1982). His films include *California Suite* (1978), *I Ought to Be in Pictures* (1982) and *Brighton Beach Memoirs* (1986).

Simpson, Wallis Warfield Spencer, Duchess of Windsor (1896–1986) Wife of the Duke of Windsor, the former King EDWARD VIII of England. A US divorcee, she began her association with Edward when he was Prince of Wales. Their relationship caused controversy and was the pretext for Edward's abdication in 1936. She married Edward in 1937.

simultaneous equations Two or more equations that can be manipulated to give common solutions. In the simultaneous equations $x + 10y = 25$ and $x + y = 7$, the problem is to find values of x and y, such that those values are solutions of both the equations simultaneously. This can be done by subtracting the two equations to give a single equation in y, which can then be solved. Substituting the value of y in either equation gives the value of x.

S

▲ **silverfish** Because they feed on starchy materials, including paste, paper, fabric and wallpaper, silverfish (*Lepisma saccharina*) can be highly destructive in cool, damp, dark interiors such as basements, archives and other storage facilities. However, they can be controlled with the use of insecticides or poisonous baits.

Sinai Peninsula constituting a protectorate of Egypt, bounded by the Gulf of Suez and the Suez Canal (W), the Gulf of Aqaba and the Negev Desert of Israel (E), the Mediterranean Sea (N), and the Red Sea (S). It is a barren plateau region, sandy in the N, rising to granite ridges in the S, and inhabited by nomads. The peninsula is the site of Jabal Musa (Mount Sinai). It was the scene of fierce fighting in the ARAB-ISRAELI WARS (1956, 1967, 1973). It was occupied by the Israelis in 1967, and returned to Egypt in 1982. The region divides into two governorates of North and South Sinai. Total area: 58,714sq km (22,671sq mi). Pop. (1996) 307,300, all but 54,000 in North Sinai.

Sinatra, Frank (Francis Albert) (1915–98) US popular singer and actor. Sinatra began his career in the jazz bands of Harry James and Tommy Dorsey. His interpretations of standards, on albums such as *Songs for Swinging Lovers* (1956) and *Come Fly with Me* (1958) are definitive. Sinatra won an Academy Award for his supporting role in *From Here to Eternity* (1953). He married Ava Gardner and later Mia Farrow.

Sind Province in S Pakistan, bounded by India (E and S) and the Arabian Sea (SW); the capital is KARACHI. It largely consists of the alluvial plain and delta of the River INDUS. Under Arab rule from the 7th to 11th centuries, it then fell under Turkish Muslim control. Islam has historically been the major governmental and cultural influence. The British captured the region in 1843, and administered it as part of British India until 1937. An autonomous province from 1937 until partition in 1947, Sind received many Muslim refugees after the creation of Pakistan. The major economic activity is agriculture. Products: grain, cotton, sugar cane, fruits, tobacco. Area: 140,914sq km (54,428sq mi). Pop. (1998) 29,991,000.

Sindhi Language of Pakistan and India, spoken by *c.*15 million people in the province of Sind, S Pakistan, and across the border in India. Related to Sanskrit and Hindi, Sindhi belongs to the Indic branch of the INDO-EUROPEAN LANGUAGES.

sine In a right-angled triangle, ratio of the length of the side opposite an acute angle to the length of the hypotenuse. The sine of angle *A* is usually abbreviated to sin *A*.

Singapore Island republic in SE Asia. *See* country feature

Sinhalese People who make up the largest ethnic group of Sri Lanka. They speak an INDO-EUROPEAN LANGUAGE and practise THERAVADA Buddhism.

Sinn Féin (Gaelic, 'Ourselves Alone') Irish republican, nationalist party founded in 1905 by Arthur GRIFFITH. It seeks to bring about a united IRELAND. Sinn Féin became a mass party after the EASTER RISING (1916). It won 75% of the vote in the last all-Ireland election (1918), and formed an Irish assembly (the Dáil Éireann) led by Éamon DE VALERA. A two-year war of independence was fought between Britain and the IRISH REPUBLICAN ARMY (IRA), led by Michael COLLINS. The Anglo-Irish Treaty (1921) partitioned Ireland into the Irish Free State and Northern Ireland. Sinn Féin was split and the country plunged into civil war. The pro-treaty wing (FINE GAEL), led by William COSGRAVE, formed a government. De Valera, leader of the anti-treaty wing, withdrew from Sinn Féin and formed FIANNA FÁIL (1926). In 1938, the remaining republican intransigents joined the outlawed IRA. In 1969, two groups emerged that mirrored the

SINGAPORE

The Republic of Singapore is an island country at the S tip of the MALAY PENINSULA. It consists of the large Singapore Island and 59 small islands, 20 of which are inhabited.

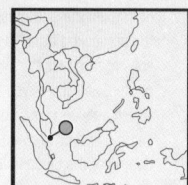

Singapore Island is just 42km [26mi] wide and 28km [14mi] across. It is linked to the peninsula by a 1,056m [3,465ft] long causeway. The land is mostly low-lying; the highest point, Bukit Timah, is only 176m [577ft] above sea level. Its strategic position at the convergence of some of the world's most vital shipping lanes ensured its growth.

Rainforest once covered Singapore, but forests now grow on only 5% of the land. Today, about 50% of Singapore is built-up. The distinction between island and city has all but disappeared. Most of the rest consists of open spaces, including parks, granite quarries and inland waters. Farmland covers 4% of the land and plantations of permanent crops make up 7%.

CLIMATE
Singapore has a hot, humid equatorial climate. Temperatures average 30°C [86°F]. Mean yearly

rainfall exceeds 2,400mm [95in], over an average of 180 days a year.

HISTORY
According to legend, Singapore was founded in 1299. It was first called Temasak, but was renamed Singapura (city of the lion). Singapore soon became a busy trading centre within the Sumatran Srivijaya kingdom. Javanese raiders destroyed it in 1377. Subsumed into Johor, Singapore became part of the powerful MALACCA sultanate. In 1819, Sir Thomas Stamford RAFFLES of the British EAST INDIA COMPANY leased the island from Johor, and the Company founded the city of Singapore. In 1826 Singapore, Pinang, and Malacca formed the Straits Settlement, and Singapore soon became the most important British trading centre in Southeast Asia. The Straits Settlement became a Crown Colony in 1867. Despite British defensive reinforcements in the early 20th century, Japanese forces seized the island in 1942.

POLITICS
British rule returned in 1945. The Straits Settlement dissolved and Singapore became a separate colony in 1946, achieving self-government in 1959. Following a referendum in 1963 Singapore merged with Malaya, SABAH and SARAWAK to form the Federation of Malaysia. In 1965 Singapore broke away to become an independent republic within the Commonwealth.

The People's Action Party (PAP) has ruled Singapore since 1959. Its leader, Lee Kuan Yew, served as prime minister from 1959 until 1990, when he resigned and was succeeded by GOH CHOK TONG. The efficient PAP government has rapidly grown the economy, although it has been accused of dictatorial rule and oversensitivity to criticism. In 2004 Lee Hsien Loong, eldest son of Lee Kuan Yew, succeed-

AREA 683sq km [264sq mi]
POPULATION 4,553,000
CAPITAL (POPULATION) Singapore City (4,372,000)
GOVERNMENT Multiparty republic
ETHNIC GROUPS Chinese 77%, Malay 14%, Indian 8%
LANGUAGES Chinese, Malay, Tamil and English (all official)
RELIGIONS Buddhism, Islam, Hinduism, Christianity
CURRENCY Singaporean dollar = 100 cents

ed Goh Chok Tong as prime minister. Support for political opposition groups has slowly increased, but the electoral system remains heavily in favour of the PAP.

ECONOMY
The World Bank classifies Singapore as a 'high-income' economy. It is one of the world's fastest growing 'tiger' economies. Historically Singapore's economy has been based on trans-shipment, which remains a vital component; it is one of the world's busiest ports, annually handling more than 290 million tonnes of cargo. After 1945 the economy diversified, and Singapore has a highly skilled and productive workforce. The service sector employs 65% of the workforce; banking and insurance provide many jobs.

Manufacturing is the largest export sector. Industries include computers and electronics, telecommunications, chemicals, machinery, scientific instruments, ships and textiles. It has a large oil refinery. Agriculture is relatively unimportant. Most farming is highly intensive, and farmers use the latest technology and industrial methods.

S

factions of the Provisional and Official IRA. 'Official' Sinn Féin became the Workers Party. The Provisionals refused to recognize the authority of Dublin or Westminster. The President of Sinn Féin, Gerry ADAMS, was elected to Westminster five times (1983, 1987, 1997, 2001, 2005).

Sino-Japanese Wars Two wars between China and Japan, marking the beginning and end of Japanese imperial expansion in Asia. The first (1894–95) arose from rivalry for control of Korea. In 1894, Japan helped to provoke a rebellion in Korea. Both states intervened, and Japanese troops swiftly defeated the Chinese. China was forced to accept Korean independence, and ceded territory including Taiwan and the Liaotung peninsula. The latter was returned. The second war (1937–45) developed from Japan's seizure of Manchuria (1931), where it set up the puppet state of MANCHUKUO. Further Japanese aggression led to war, in which Japan conquered E China, driving the government out of Peking (Beijing). The US and UK despatched aid to China (1938), and the conflict merged into World War 2, ending with the defeat of Japan in 1945.

Sino-Tibetan languages Large family of languages. It includes Chinese, Tibeto-Burman, Tai, and possibly Miao (Meo) and Yao, spoken in S China and SE Asia.

sinus Hollow space or cavity, usually in bone. Most often the term refers to the paranasal sinuses, any of the four sets of air-filled cavities in the skull near the nose.

Sioux (Dakota) Group of seven NATIVE AMERICAN tribes inhabiting Minnesota, Nebraska, North and South Dakota, and Montana. The tribes concluded several treaties with the US government during the 19th century, and finally agreed in 1867 to settle on a reservation in sw Dakota. The discovery of gold in the Black Hills and the rush of prospectors brought resistance. The last confrontation resulted in the massacre of more than 200 Sioux at WOUNDED KNEE (1890). The Sioux culture was typical of the tribes of the GREAT PLAINS. Today, there are more than 50,000 Sioux. *See also* SITTING BULL

siren Aquatic, tailed AMPHIBIAN of North America. The adult is neotenic. These eel-like animals have external gills, tiny forelegs, and minute eyes. They have no hind legs. Length: to 92cm (36in). Family Sirenidae. *See also* SALAMANDER

Sirens In Greek mythology, three sea nymphs with women's heads and birds' bodies. They lived on a rocky island near the straits of Messina, home to SCYLLA and CHARYBDIS, and their beautiful singing was said to attract sailors onto the rocks.

Sirius (Alpha Canis Majoris) Brightest star visible from Earth, in the northern constellation of Canis Major. Its luminosity is 23 times that of the Sun.

sirocco Wind often arising over the Sahara Desert in North Africa, picking up moisture from the Mediterranean Sea, and bringing hot, rainy weather to the Mediterranean coast of Europe. This occurs mainly in spring.

sisal (sisal hemp) Plant native to Central America and cultivated in Mexico, Java, E Africa, and the Bahamas. Fibres from the leaves are used for rope, matting, and twine. Family Agavaceae; species *Agave sisalana*. *See also* AGAVE

Sistine Chapel Private chapel of the Popes in the VATICAN CITY, painted by some of the greatest artists of RENAISSANCE Italy. It was built between 1473 and 1481 for Pope Sixtus IV. Frescos painted by PERUGINO, Pinturicchio, BOTTICELLI, GHIRLANDAIO, and Signorelli adorned its side walls. Its most celebrated features are the ceiling, window lunettes, and altar wall, painted by MICHELANGELO between 1508 and 1541.

Sisulu, Walter (1912–2003) South African civil-rights activist, a fierce opponent of APARTHEID. Sisulu became secretary general of the AFRICAN NATIONAL CONGRESS (ANC) in 1949. The ANC was declared illegal in 1961, and Sisulu, Nelson MANDELA, and six others were sentenced (1964) to life imprisonment. Sisulu was released in 1989 and, after the legalization of the ANC, became its deputy president (1991–94).

Sisyphus In Greek mythology, king of CORINTH. He was punished for trying to trick Thanatos (Death) and condemned to the underworld to work for eternity, pushing a rock to the top of a hill. The rock rolled back as soon as he reached the summit.

sitar Indian stringed musical instrument with a gourd-like body and long neck. It has three to seven strings, tuned in fourths or fifths, and a lower course of 12 strings.

Sitting Bull (1831–90) North American SIOUX leader. With others, he led the attack on CUSTER's US cavalry at the Battle of LITTLE BIGHORN (1876). He was captured in 1881, and imprisoned for two years. Later, he joined the Wild West Show of Buffalo Bill. Accused of anti-white activities, he was arrested again in 1890, and killed in the ensuing skirmish.

Sitwell, Dame Edith (1887–1964) English poet. Sitwell's anthology *Wheels* (1916) encouraged experimentalism in British verse. She contributed the words to William WALTON's *Façade* (1922). Sitwell also wrote a biography of Alexander POPE (1930) and the *English Eccentrics* (1933).

Sitwell, Sir Osbert (1892–1969) English writer, brother of Dame Edith SITWELL. He wrote the words for William WALTON's oratorio *Belshazzar's Feast* (1931). He is chiefly remembered for his five volumes of family reminiscences, including *Left Hand, Right Hand* (1945) and *Noble Essences* (1950).

SI units (*Système International d'Unites*) Internationally agreed system of units, derived from the mks (metre, kilogram, and second) system. SI units are now used for many scientific purposes, and have replaced the fps (foot, pound, and second) and cgs (centimetre, gram, and second) systems. The seven basic units are: the METRE (m) for length, KILOGRAM (kg) for mass, SECOND (s) for time, AMPERE (A) for electrical current, KELVIN (K) for temperature, MOLE (mol) for amount of substance, and CANDELA (cd) for luminous intensity.

Six, Les Collective name for six French composers who were organized as a group by Jean Cocteau in 1917. The members were Georges Auric, Louis Durey, Arthur HONEGGER, Darius MILHAUD, Francis POULENC, and Germaine Tailleferre.

Six-Day War ('June War', 1967) Third of the ARAB-ISRAELI WARS. Israeli forces, led by Moshe DAYAN, rapidly defeated the four Arab states (Egypt, Jordan, Syria, and Iraq). Israel gained control of the old city of JERUSALEM, Jordanian territory on the WEST BANK (of the River Jordan), the GOLAN HEIGHTS and the SINAI peninsula, including the GAZA STRIP.

skate Flattened, food fish belonging to the RAY family, living mainly in shallow temperate and tropical waters. The pectoral fins are greatly expanded to form wing-like flaps. Length: to about 2.5m (8ft). Family Rajidae.

skating *See* ICE SKATING; ROLLER SKATING

skeletal muscle *See* VOLUNTARY MUSCLE

skeleton Bony framework of the body of a VERTEBRATE. It supports and protects the internal organs, provides sites of attachment for muscles and a system of levers to aid locomotion. *See also* EXOSKELETON. *See* illustration on page 684

Skelton, John (1460–1529) English poet. Skelton was tutor to the young Henry VIII, and took holy orders in 1498. He wrote satires on the court, the clergy, and Cardinal Thomas WOLSEY. His work includes *Speak, Parrot*, *Colin Clout*, *Why Came Ye Not to Court?* and the long secular morality play *Magnyfycence* (c.1516). *Philip Sparrow* (c.1505), an elegy for a court pet bird, is his most widely known poem.

skiing A number of winter sports based on the use of flat runners (skis) to slide over snowy ground. The principal forms of competitive skiing are Alpine skiing, ski jumping, cross-country skiing and freestyle skiing. Freestyle skiing

◀ **sitar** Originally developed in India in the 14th century, the sitar is either played solo, or in an ensemble with tabla (small kettle-drums) and a tambura (a lute-like instrument that produces a droning sound). Popularized by Ravi Shankar, it has also been used in Western music since the 1960s.

was added to the Winter Olympic schedule in 1994; the other disciplines have been Olympic sports since 1924.

skin Tough, elastic outer covering of invertebrates. In mammals, it is the largest organ of the body and serves many functions. It protects the body from injury and from the entry of some microorganisms and prevents dehydration. Nerve endings in the skin provide the sensations of touch, warmth, cold, and pain. It helps to regulate body temperature through sweating, regulates moisture loss, and keeps itself smooth and pliable with an oily secretion from the SEBACEOUS GLANDS. Structurally the skin consists of two main layers: an outer layer (EPIDERMIS) and an inner layer (DERMIS). The top layer of epidermis is made of closely packed dead cells constantly shed as microscopic scales. Below this is a layer of living cells that contain pigment and nerve fibres, and that divide to replace outer layers. The dermis contains dense networks of connective tissue, blood vessels, nerves, glands, and hair follicles.

skink Common name for any of more than 600 species of LIZARDS of tropical and temperate regions. They have cylindrical bodies, cone-shaped heads, and tapering tails. They live in various habitats and eat vegetation, insects, and small invertebrates. Length: to 66cm (26in). Family Scincidae.

Skopje Capital of Macedonia, on the River Vardar. Founded in Roman times, it became capital of the Serbian Empire in the 14th century, fell to the Ottoman Turks in 1392, and incorporated into Yugoslavia in 1918. In 1963 an earthquake destroyed most of the city. Industries: metals, textiles, chemicals, glassware. Pop. (2002 est.) 448,600.

skull (cranium) In vertebrates, brain case that supports and protects the brain, eyes, ears, nose, and mouth.

SKELETON

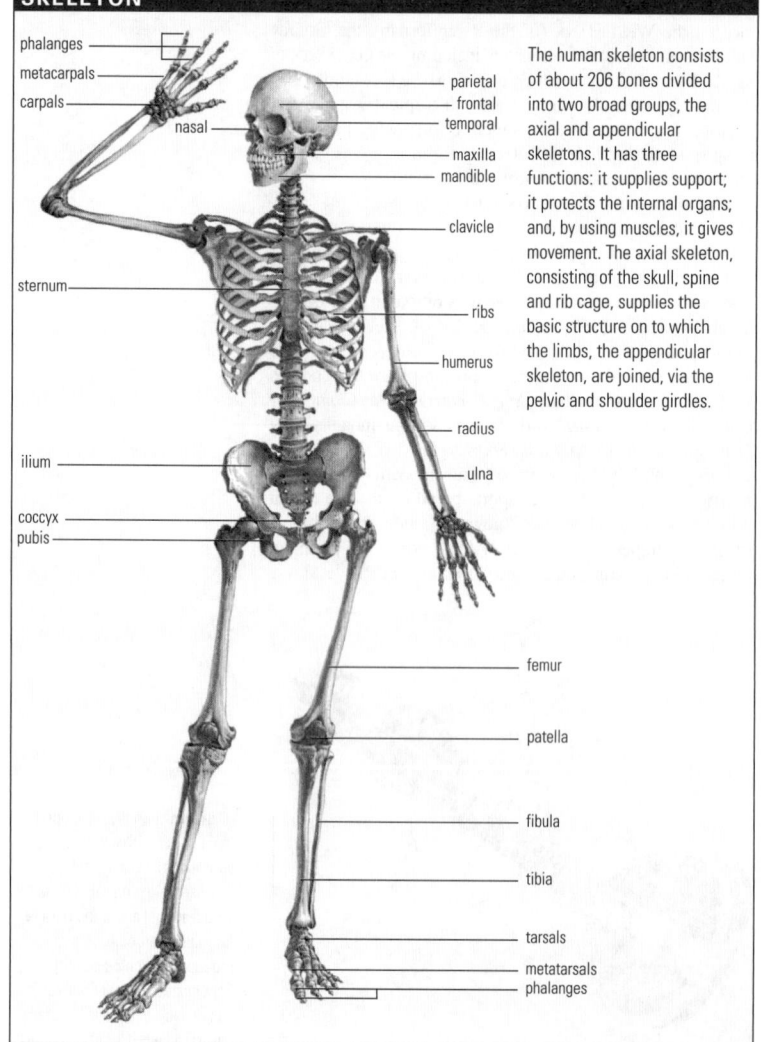

phalanges
metacarpals
carpals
nasal
parietal
frontal
temporal
maxilla
mandible
clavicle
sternum
ribs
humerus
radius
ilium
ulna
coccyx
pubis
femur
patella
fibula
tibia
tarsals
metatarsals
phalanges

The human skeleton consists of about 206 bones divided into two broad groups, the axial and appendicular skeletons. It has three functions: it supplies support; it protects the internal organs; and, by using muscles, it gives movement. The axial skeleton, consisting of the skull, spine and rib cage, supplies the basic structure on to which the limbs, the appendicular skeleton, are joined, via the pelvic and shoulder girdles.

skunk Nocturnal, omnivorous mammal that lives in the USA, Central and South America. It has powerful anal scent glands, which eject a foul-smelling liquid, used in defence. It has a small head, and a slender, thickly furred body with short legs and a large bushy tail. The coat is black with bold white warning markings along the back. The most common species is the striped skunk, *Mephitis mephitis*. Length: to 38cm (15in); weight: 4.5kg (10lb). Family Mustelidae.

skydiving Sport in which parachutists jump from 3,500m (12,000ft) and free-fall to *c.*650m (2,000ft) before opening their PARACHUTES. Competition skydiving has events based on accuracy, in which the parachutist aims for a target area, and events based on style, in which a series of manoeuvres are performed by one or more parachutists.

Skye Largest island in the Inner Hebrides, off the NW coast of Scotland, with the chief town of Portree. Its scenery makes it a popular holiday attraction. A bridge to the mainland opened in 1996. Occupations include rearing livestock, weaving, fishing. Area: 1,735sq km (670sq mi). Pop. (2002) 11,750.

skyscraper Very tall building. True skyscraper construction, in which the metal skeleton supports both floors and walls, was introduced (1885) in Chicago by William Le Baron Jenney. Competition arose between companies, cities, and eventually countries to construct the tallest skyscraper, and continues to the present day. By the early 2000s the tallest reached *c.*500m (1,600ft) tall, but buildings over 800m (2,600ft) were planned.

slander In law, oral defamation of a person's character made in the presence of one or more witnesses. *See also* LIBEL

slang Non-standard, colloquial form of idiom or vocabulary that is highly informal and often full of obscure or colourful imagery. Slang may be restricted to certain social, ethnic, occupational, hobby, special-interest, or age groups.

slate Grey to blue, fine-grained, homogeneous METAMORPHIC ROCK, which splits into smooth, thin layers. It forms by the metamorphosis of SHALE, and is valuable as a roofing material.

Slav Largest ethnic and linguistic group of peoples in Europe. Slavs are generally classified in three main divisions: the East Slavs (the largest division) include the Ukrainians, Russians, and Belorussians; the South Slavs include the Serbs, Croats, Macedonians, and Slovenes (and frequently also the Bulgarians); the West Slavs comprise chiefly the Poles, Czechs, Slovaks, and Wends.

slavery Social system in which people are the property of their owner, and are compelled to work without pay. Slavery of some kind was common to practically all ancient societies, including the ancient Egyptians, Romans, and Greeks, and to most modern societies until the 19th century. An extreme form of slavery also existed in the Americas from the 16th century, where the need for cheap labour in European colonies was not satisfied by enslaving Native Americans or by acquiring poor Europeans as servants. This situation gave rise to the highly organized and profitable **Atlantic triangular slave trade**. Ships sailed from ports such as Liverpool with guns and other goods that were exchanged for slaves in states on West African coasts. The slaves were sold in markets in the Caribbean, Brazil, and North America to work on plantations. On the return journey, the ships carried colonial produce from the Americas to Europe. An estimated 15 million Africans were sold into slavery and millions more died on the voyage across the Atlantic. By the early 19th century slavery had been abolished throughout much of Europe; it was declared illegal in Britain in 1807, and outlawed in 1833. Most South American states abolished it soon after gaining independence. In the USA, slavery was one cause of the CIVIL WAR, and was formally ended when the aims of the EMANCIPATION PROCLAMATION (1863) were incorporated in the 13th Amendment to the US Constitution (1865). Some forms of slavery persisted into the 21st century in the developing world, particularly in Africa.

Slavic languages (Slavonic languages) Group of languages spoken in E Europe and the former Soviet Union, constituting a major subdivision of the family of INDO-EUROPEAN LANGUAGES. The main ones in use today are East Slavic (Russian, Ukrainian, Belorussian); West Slavic (Polish, Czech, Slovak, Sorbian or Lusatian – a language spoken

S

in parts of E Germany); and South Slavic (Bulgarian, Serbo-Croat, Slovenian, Macedonian). Some Slavic languages are written in the Cyrillic alphabet, others in the Roman.

sleep Periodic state of unconsciousness from which a person or animal can be roused. During an ordinary night's sleep there are intervals of deep sleep associated with rapid eye movement (REM) sleep. It is during this REM sleep that dreaming occurs. Studies have shown that people deprived of sleep become grossly disturbed. Sleep requirement falls sharply in old age. Difficulty in sleeping is called **insomnia**.

sleeping sickness Popular name of two diseases. **Trypanosomiasis** is a disease of tropical Africa caused by a parasite transmitted by the TSETSE FLY. It is characterized by fever, headache, joint pains, and anaemia. Ultimately, it may affect the brain and spinal cord, leading to profound lethargy and sometimes death. **Encephalitis lethargica** is a rare, viral disease of the brain characterized by headache and drowsiness progressing to coma. It occurs in epidemic and sporadic forms and, most notoriously, was the cause of an epidemic that followed World War 1, leaving many helpless survivors.

slime mould Any of a small group of strange, basically single-celled organisms that are intermediate between the plant and animal kingdoms. During their complex life cycle, they pass through several stages. These include a flagellated swimming stage, an amoeba-like stage, a stage consisting of a slimy mass of protoplasm with many nuclei, and a flowering, sporangium stage.

slipped disc (prolapsed intervertebral disc) Protrusion of the soft, inner core of an intervertebral disc through its covering, causing pressure on the spinal nerve roots. It is caused by a sudden mechanical force on the spine. It causes stiffness and SCIATICA. There are various treatments available.

sloe See BLACKTHORN

sloth Any of several species of slow-moving, herbivorous Central and South American mammals. It has long limbs with long claws, and spends most of its life climbing in trees, where it generally hangs upside down. Length: to 60cm (2ft); weight: to 5.5kg (12lb). Family Brachipodidae.

Slovak Official language of the Slovak Republic, spoken by about 5 million people. It is closely related to Czech, and is considered distinct largely for political reasons.

Slovak Republic Republic in Europe. See country feature, page 686

Slovenia Mountainous republic in SE Europe; the capital is LJUBLJANA. See country feature, page 687

slow-worm (blind-worm) European snake-like, legless lizard of grassy areas and woodlands. It is generally brownish; the female has a black underside. It has pointed teeth and feeds primarily on slugs and snails. Length: to 30cm (12in). Family Anguidae; species *Anguis fragilis*.

slug Mostly terrestrial gastropod MOLLUSC, identified by the lack of shell and uncoiled viscera. It secretes a protective slime, used to aid movement. Length: to 20cm (8in). Class Gastropoda; subclass Pulmonata; genera *Arion, Limax*. See SEA SLUG

small intestine Part of the DIGESTIVE SYSTEM that, in humans, extends – about 6m (20ft) coiled and looped – from the STOMACH to the large INTESTINE, or colon. Its function is the digestion and absorption of food. See also DUODENUM; ILEUM

smallpox Formerly a highly contagious viral disease characterized by fever, vomiting, and skin eruptions. It remained endemic in many countries until the World Health Organization (WHO) campaign, launched in the late 1960s; global eradication was achieved by the early 1980s.

smell (olfaction) Sense that responds to airborne molecules. The **olfactory receptors** in the NOSE can detect even a few molecules per million parts of air.

smelt Small, silvery food fish related to SALMON and TROUT. It lives in the N Atlantic and Pacific Oceans, and in North American inland waters. Family Osmeridae.

smelting Heat treatment for separating metals from their ORES. The ore, often with other ingredients, is heated in a furnace to remove non-metallic constituents. The metal produced is later purified.

Smetana, Bedřich (1824–84) Czech composer. His masterpiece, *The Bartered Bride* (1866), is one of the greatest

SKIN

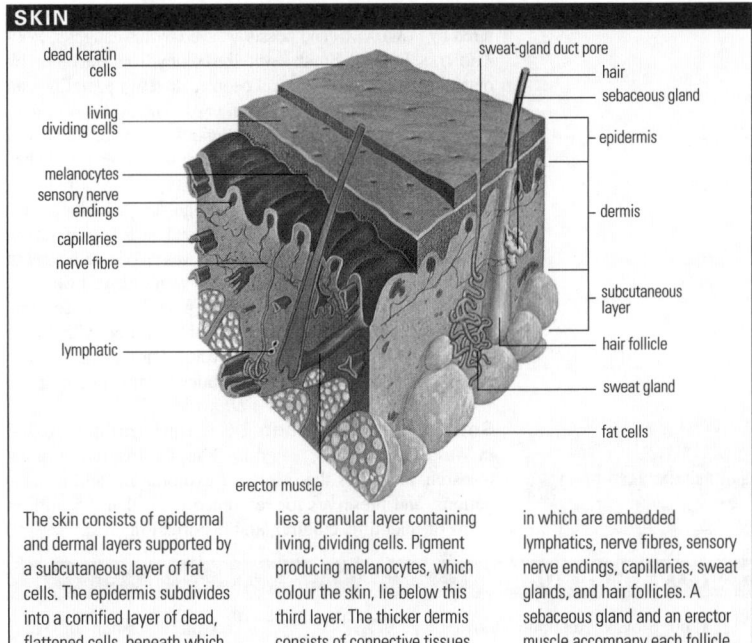

The skin consists of epidermal and dermal layers supported by a subcutaneous layer of fat cells. The epidermis subdivides into a cornified layer of dead, flattened cells, beneath which lies a granular layer containing living, dividing cells. Pigment producing melanocytes, which colour the skin, lie below this third layer. The thicker dermis consists of connective tissues in which are embedded lymphatics, nerve fibres, sensory nerve endings, capillaries, sweat glands, and hair follicles. A sebaceous gland and an erector muscle accompany each follicle.

folk operas. Among other popular works by Smetana is the cycle of symphonic poems *Má Vlast* (*My Country*, 1874–79).

Smirke, Robert (1781–1867) English neo-classical architect, a major promoter of the Greek revival in British architecture. Smirke's most famous building is the British Museum, London (begun 1823), with its impressive Ionic façade. He also built the Covent Garden Theatre (1808–09). See also NEO-CLASSICISM

Smith, Adam (1723–90) Scottish philosopher, regarded as the founder of modern economics. His book *The Wealth of Nations* (1776) was enormously influential in the development of Western CAPITALISM. It outlined the theory of the **division of labour**. In place of MERCANTILISM, Smith proposed the doctrine of LAISSEZ-FAIRE: that governments should not interfere in economic affairs and that free trade increases wealth.

Smith, Ian Douglas (1919–2007) Rhodesian statesman, prime minister (1964–78). Smith entered Parliament in 1948. He founded (1961) the Rhodesia Front Party, and sought independence from Britain. In 1965, Smith's white minority regime issued a Unilateral Declaration of Independence (UDI). Persistent international sanctions and guerrilla warfare forced his government to accept free elections in 1980. Smith was defeated by Robert MUGABE's Zimbabwe African National Union (ZANU). Smith continued to lead white opposition to Mugabe until 1987.

Smith, John (1580–1631) English soldier and colonist. Smith established the first English colony in North America, at

▲ **sloth** The sloth is an unusual herbivore in that it can survive on a particularly poor diet of tough leaves by means of a lifestyle that involves very little expenditure of energy. They sleep a lot and move extremely slowly. In fact, they have only half the musculature of most mammals, and their food may take a whole week to pass through the digestive system. There are two species of two-toed sloth (*Choloepus*). The one shown here has two toes on its front legs and three on its back legs.

S

SLIME MOULD

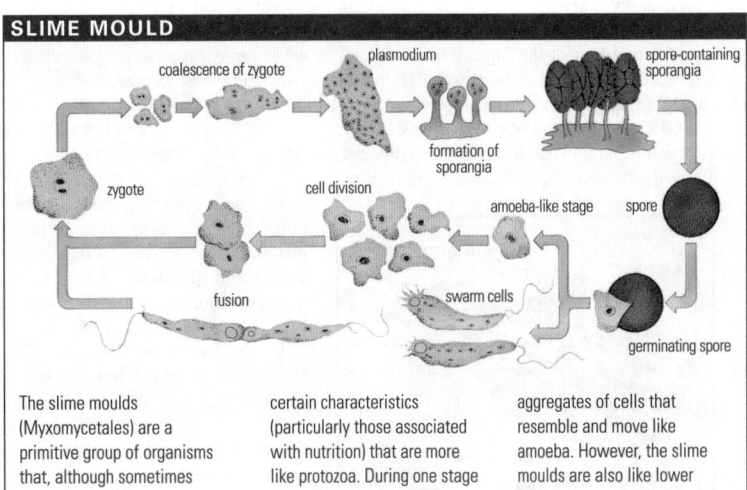

The slime moulds (Myxomycetales) are a primitive group of organisms that, although sometimes classed as fungus, have certain characteristics (particularly those associated with nutrition) that are more like protozoa. During one stage of their life cycle, they form aggregates of cells that resemble and move like amoeba. However, the slime moulds are also like lower plants in spore formation.

S

JAMESTOWN (1607). Exploring Chesapeake Bay, he was captured by POWHATAN and possibly saved by his daughter, POCAHONTAS. In 1608, Smith saved the colony from starvation by obtaining maize from the local people. He returned to England in 1609, later writing his *Description of New England* (1616).

Smith, Joseph (1805–44) US religious leader and founder of the MORMON Church of Jesus Christ of the Latter Day Saints (1830). His *Book of Mormon* (1830) was based on sacred writings he claimed were given to him on golden plates by a messenger named Moroni. In 1830, Smith and his followers set out to found the New Zion. In 1844, Smith was jailed on a charge of treason at Carthage, Illinois, where he was murdered by a mob.

Smith, Stevie (1902–71) English poet, b. Florence Margaret Smith. Smith first came to public notice with *Novel on Yellow Paper* (1936). Her witty and often pathetic poetry was collected in 1975, and includes the title poem of her 1957 volume *Not Waving But Drowning*.

Smithsonian Institution US independent trust, based in Washington, D.C. Created in 1846, the Institution funds research, publishes the results of explorations and investigations, and preserves for reference more than 65 million items of scientific, cultural, and historical interest.

INTERNET

Smithsonian Institution
► www.si.edu

smog Dense atmospheric mixture of smoke and fog or chemical fumes, commonly occurring in urban or industrial areas. Smog can cause illnesses and in some cases deaths.

Smolensk City on the upper reaches of the River Dnieper, near the Belarus border, E Russia; capital of Smolensk oblast. First mentioned in 882 BC it was an important medieval commercial centre on the routes from Byzantium to the Baltic, and from Moscow to Warsaw. The capital of Belorussia in the 12th century, it was sacked (1238–1240) by the Mongols. In the 15th and 16th centuries, it was a battleground for Polish and Russian forces. In 1812, Napoleon I seized the city and burned it in retreat from the Russian Army. Occupied (1941–43) by German forces, it was the scene of some of the fiercest fighting in World War 2. It remains an important transport and distribution centre. Industries: linen, textile machines, timber, electrical goods, flour milling, distilling, brewing. Pop. (2000) 353,400.

Smollett, Tobias George (1721–71) Scottish novelist and surgeon. Smollett's debut novel, *The Adventures of Roderick Random* (1748), drew on his naval experience. *The Adventures of Peregrine Pickle* (1751) was in the same bawdy, PICARESQUE vein. His masterpiece is *The Expedition of Humphrey Clinker*

SLOVAK REPUBLIC

The Slovak Republic (Slovakia) is a predominantly mountainous country. Part of the CARPATHIAN MOUNTAINS system that divides the Slovak Republic from Poland is found in the N. The highest peak, Gerlachovka (at 2,655m [8,711ft]), is in the scenic Tatra (Tatry) Mountains on the Polish border.

Forests cover much of the mountain slopes and there is also extensive pasture. The SW Danubian lowlands form a fertile lowland region. The DANUBE forms part of the S border with Hungary.

quered much of Hungary, and the Turks and the Austrians divided up Slovakia between them. From 1541 to 1784 Bratislava served as the Habsburg capital. The joint rule of MARIA THERESA and JOSEPH II pursued a policy of Magyarization, which increased nationalist sentiment. The AUSTRO-HUNGARIAN EMPIRE emerged in 1867 and continued the suppression of native culture. Many Slovaks fled to the USA. During World War 1, Slovak patriots fought on the side of the Allies. After the defeat of Austro-Hungary in 1918, Slovakia incorporated into Czechoslovakia as an autonomous region (for 1918–93 history, see CZECHOSLOVAKIA).

The Czechs dominated the union, and many Slovaks grew dissatisfied. Following the MUNICH AGREEMENT (1938), part of Slovakia became an independent state, while much of southern Slovakia (including Kosice) was ceded to Hungary. In March 1939 Slovakia gained nominal independence as a German Protectorate. In August 1939 Hitler invaded Czechoslovakia, and Slovakia became a Nazi puppet state. In 1944 Soviet troops liberated Slovakia, and in 1945 it returned to Czechoslovakia. The PRAGUE SPRING (1968) attempted to reform the Communist system, but was crushed by a Soviet invasion.

AREA 49,012sq km [18,924sq mi]
POPULATION 5,448,000
CAPITAL (POPULATION) Bratislava (449,000)
GOVERNMENT Multiparty republic
ETHNIC GROUPS Slovak 86%, Hungarian 11%
LANGUAGES Slovak (official), Hungarian
RELIGIONS Roman Catholic 60%, Protestant 8%, Orthodox 4%, others
CURRENCY Slovak koruna = 100 halierov

CLIMATE

Slovakia has a transitional climate, in between the mild conditions of W Europe and the continental conditions of Russia to the E. The conditions in Kosice, E Slovakia, are fairly typical. Temperatures can range from –3°C [27°F] in January to 20°C [68°F] in July. Kosice has an average annual rainfall of 600mm [24in]. The mountains have a more extreme climate, with snow or rain throughout the year.

HISTORY

Slavic peoples settled in the region in the 5th and 6th centuries AD. In the 9th century the area formed part of the Empire of MORAVIA. Conquered by the MAGYARS in the 10th century, Hungary dominated the region for nearly 900 years. At the end of the 11th century, it became part of the Kingdom of Hungary. In the 16th century the Ottoman Empire con-

POLITICS

At the end of November 1989 Czechoslovakia's parliament abolished the Communist Party's sole right to govern. In December the head of the Communists, Gustáv Husak, resigned. Non-Communists led by the playwright and dissident Václav Havel formed a new government, which then won a majority in the elections of June 1990.

In the elections of 1992 the Movement for Democratic Slovakia, led by Vladimir Mečiar, campaigned for Slovak independence and won a majority in Slovakia's parliament. The Slovak National Council then approved a new constitution for the Slovak Republic, which came into existence on 1 January 1993.

The Slovak Republic became a member of the OECD in 1997 and maintained close contacts with its former partner. Slovak independence raised national aspirations among the Magyar-speaking community. Relations with Hungary worsened in 1996 when the Slovak government initiated new administrative regions which the Hungarian minority claimed under-represented them politically. The government made Slovak the only official language. The government's autocratic rule and apparent tolerance of organized crime led to mounting international criticism. In 1998, Mečiar's party was defeated in a general election by a four-party coalition and Mikuláš Dzurinda, leader of the centre-right Slovak Democratic Coalition, became prime minister. Dzurinda won 2002 parliamentary elections and his government continued to strengthen ties with the West. Slovakia became a member of both NATO and the EU in 2004. In 2006 elections Dzurinda was replaced by Robert Fico.

ECONOMY

Communist governments developed manufacturing industries, producing chemicals, machinery, steel and weapons. Since the late 1980s many state-run businesses have been handed over to private owners. Manufacturing employs around 33% of workers. Bratislava and Kosice are the chief industrial cities. Products include ceramics, machinery and steel. The armaments industry is based at Martin, in the NW.

Farming employs about 12% of the workforce. Major crops include barley, grapes for wine-making, maize, sugar beet and wheat.

(1771), a comic, epistolary novel. Smollett also translated Voltaire and Cervantes and edited several periodicals.

smooth muscle *See* INVOLUNTARY MUSCLE

Smuts, Jan Christiaan (1870–1950) South African statesman, prime minister (1919–24, 1939–48). He was a guerrilla commander during the SOUTH AFRICAN WARS (1899–1902), but afterwards worked with Louis BOTHA to establish the Union of South Africa (1910). During World War 1, he suppressed a pro-German revolt, commanded British forces in East Africa, and became a member of the British war cabinet. Upon Botha's death, Smuts succeeded as prime minister. He formed a second administration after James HERTZOG opposed entry into World War 2. After the war, Smuts was defeated by the APARTHEID policies of the Nationalist Party.

Smyrna *See* IZMIR

snail Terrestrial, marine or freshwater gastropod mollusc. It has a large fleshy foot, antennae on its head, and a coiled protective shell encasing an asymmetric visceral mass. It may breathe through gills (aquatic species) or through a kind of air-breathing lung (terrestrial species), and has a radula – a rasping organ in its mouth. Some species, such as the Roman snail (*Helix pomatia*), are edible. Length: to 35cm (14in). Class Gastropoda. *See* illustration page 688

snake Any of *c.*2,700 species of legless, elongated REPTILES forming the suborder Serpentes of the order Squamata (which also includes LIZARDS). There are 11 families. They range in length from *c.*10cm (4in) to more than 9m (30ft). They are terrestrial, arboreal (tree-dwelling), semi-aquatic and aquatic species; one group is entirely marine; many are poisonous. They have no external ear openings, eardrums or middle ears; sound vibrations are detected through the ground. Their eyelids are immovable and their eyes covered by a transparent protective cover. The long, forked, protractile tongue is used to detect odours. Their bodies are covered with scales. Poisonous snakes have hollow or grooved fangs through which they inject venom. *See* individual species. *See* illustration page 689

snakebite Result of an injection of potentially lethal SNAKE venom into the bloodstream. There are three types of venomous snake: the **Viperidae**, subdivided into true VIPERS and pit vipers, whose venom causes internal haemorrhage; the **Elapidae** (including COBRAS, MAMBAS, kraits), whose venom paralyzes the nervous system; and the **Hydrophidae**, Pacific sea snakes with venom that disables the muscles. Treatment for all three types is with anti-venoms.

snapdragon Any of several species of PERENNIAL plants of the genus *Antirrhinum*, with sac-like, two-lipped, purple,

---

SLOVENIA

The Republic of Slovenia was one of the six republics which made up Yugoslavia. Much of the land is mountainous and forested. The highest peak is Mount Triglav (2,863m [9,393ft]) in the Julian Alps (Julijske Alpe), an extension of the main Alpine ranges in the NW. Much of central and E Slovenia is hilly. The River Sava which flows through central Slovenia is a tributary of the Danube, as is the Drava in the NE.

Central Slovenia contains the limestone Karst region, with numerous underground streams and cave networks. The Postojna Caves, SW of LJUBLJANA, are among the largest in Europe. The country has a short coastline on the Adriatic Sea.

Forests cover about half of Slovenia. Mountain pines grow on higher slopes, with beech, oak and hornbeam at lower levels. The Karst region is largely bare of vegetation because of the lack of surface water. Farmland covers about a third of Slovenia.

CLIMATE

The Slovenian coast has a mild Mediterranean climate. The climate inland is more continental, with snow capping the mountains in winter. Eastern Slovenia has cold winters and hot summers. Rain occurs in every month in Ljubljana, late summer being the rainiest.

HISTORY

The ancestors of the Slovenes, the W branch of a group of people called the South Slavs, settled in the area around 1,400 years ago. An independent Slovene state was formed in AD 623, but the area came under Bavarian-Frankish rule in 748. The Austrian royal family, the HABSBURGS, took control of the region in 1278. Apart from a short period of French rule between 1809 and 1815 it remained under Austrian control until 1918, when the dual monarchy of Austria-Hungary collapsed.

At the end of World War 1, Slovenia became part of a new country called the Kingdom of the Serbs, Croats and Slovenes, renamed Yugoslavia in 1929. Slovenia was invaded by Germany and Italy in 1941 and was partitioned between them and Hungary. At the end of the war, Slovenia again became one of the six republics of Yugoslavia.

In the late 1960s and early 1970s some Slovenes called for the secession of their federal republic from Yugoslavia, but the dissidents were removed from the Communist Party by President Josip Broz Tito, whose strong rule maintained the unity of his country.

POLITICS

After Tito's death in 1980, the federal government in Belgrade found it increasingly difficult to maintain the unity of the disparate elements of the population. It was also weakened by the fact that Communism was increasingly seen to have failed in Eastern Europe and the Soviet Union. In 1990, Slovenia held multiparty elections and a non-Communist coalition was formed to rule the country.

Slovenia and neighbouring Croatia proclaimed their independence in June 1991, but these acts were not accepted by the central government. After a few days of fighting between the Slovene militia and Yugoslav forces, Slovenia, the most ethnically homogenous of Yugoslavia's six component parts, found ready support from Italy and Austria (which had

AREA 20,256sq km [7,821sq mi]
POPULATION 2,009,000
CAPITAL (POPULATION) Ljubljana (264,000)
GOVERNMENT Multiparty republic
ETHNIC GROUPS Slovene 92%, Croat 1%, Serb, Hungarian, Bosniak
LANGUAGES Slovenian (official), Serbo-Croatian
RELIGIONS Mainly Roman Catholic
CURRENCY Euro = 100 cents

Slovene minorities of about 100,000 and 80,000, respectively), as well as Germany (an early supporter of Slovene independence). After a three-month moratorium, during which there was a negotiated, peaceful withdrawal, Slovenia became independent on 8 October 1991, avoiding the conflict that was to plague other former Yugoslav states.

Slovenia's independence was recognized by the EC in 1992. Multiparty elections were held and Milan Kučan, a former Communist, became president. Janez Drnovšek, of the centre-left Liberal Democratic Party, became prime minister, heading a coalition government. The Liberal Democrat coalition government was returned again in 1996 and 2000. Slovenia became a member of NATO and the EU in 2004. In 2004 elections a centre-right coalition was formed. In January 2007 Slovenia adopted the euro as sole currency.

In 2007 elections left-wing candidate Danilo Türk, former UN ambassador, became president.

ECONOMY

The reform of the formerly state-run economy and fighting in areas to the s caused problems for Slovenia. It remains one of the fastest growing economies in Europe.

Manufacturing is the principal activity and manufactures include chemicals, machinery and transport equipment, metal goods and textiles. Slovenia mines some iron ore, lead, lignite and mercury. The leading crops are maize, potatoes and wheat.

S

red, yellow or white flowers. The common snapdragon (*A. majus*) is a popular garden plant. Height: 15–91cm (0.5–3ft). Family Scrophulariaceae.

snapper Marine food fish found in tropical waters of the Indo-Pacific and Atlantic Oceans. Length: to 90cm (3ft); weight: 50kg (110lb). The 250 species include the red snapper (*Lutianus campechanus*), yellowtail (*Ocyurus chrysurus*) and Atlantic grey (*L. griseus*). Family Lutjanidae.

snipe Any of several species of migratory, long-billed, wading shorebirds found in swampy grasslands and coastal areas throughout the world. It is generally mottled brown and buff. Length: 30cm (12in). Family Scolopacidae; genus *Gallinago*.

Snorri Sturluson (1179–1241) Icelandic poet and historian. *Prose Edda* is a collection of Norse mythology and a discussion of the art of poetry. *Heimskringla*, SAGAS of the Norwegian kings to 1184, mingles NORSE LITERATURE, history and legend.

snow Flakes of frozen water that fall from clouds to the Earth's surface. Snowflakes are symmetric (usually hexagonal) crystalline structures that show an infinite variety of forms. *See also* PRECIPITATION

Snow, C.P. (Charles Percy), Baron (1905–80) English novelist, scientist, and civil servant. He is especially celebrated for his lecture *The Two Cultures and the Scientific Revolution* (1959), which diagnosed a radical divide between scientists and literary intellectuals, and for his 11–volume novel sequence, known collectively as *Strangers and Brothers* (1940–70), which includes *The Corridors of Power* (1963).

Snowdon Mountain in Gwynedd, NW Wales. Much of the area is included in the Snowdonia National Park, established in 1951. Snowdon has five peaks, one of which, at 1085m (3560ft), is the highest in England and Wales.

snowdrop Low-growing, perennial plant of the Mediterranean region, widely cultivated as a garden ornamental. The drooping, green and white, fragrant flowers appear early in spring. The common snowdrop (*Galanthus nivalis*) has narrow leaves; height: to 15cm (6in). Family Amaryllidaceae.

Soane, Sir John (1753–1837) English architect. One of the most original of all British architects, Soane developed his own personal style of CLASSICISM. He designed (1795–1827) the Bank of England, London.

soap Cleansing agent made of salts of fatty acids, used to remove dirt and grease. Common soaps are produced by heating fats and oils with an alkali, such as sodium hydroxide or potassium hydroxide. Soap consists of long-chain molecules; one end of the chain attaches to grease while the other dissolves in the water, causing the grease to loosen. *See also* DETERGENT

soap opera Ongoing, episodic work of fiction in radio or television media. Open-ended narratives run continuously, usually focusing on personal and domestic situations, and no single episode closes all plot threads. The term was coined in the 1930s to describe programmes sponsored by soap powder manufacturers, dismissing soaps' claims to naturalism by comparing them to sensationalist melodrama.

Sobers, Sir Gary (Garfield St Aubrun) (1936–) Barbadian cricketer, perhaps the game's greatest all-rounder. Sobers played county cricket for Nottinghamshire and 93 tests for West Indies, 39 as captain. In 1968, against Glamorgan, he was the first to score six sixes in an over in first-class cricket.

soccer *See* FOOTBALL, ASSOCIATION

Social and Liberal Democrats (SLDP) Official name of the LIBERAL DEMOCRATS

social contract Concept that society is based on the surrender of natural freedoms by the individual to the organized group or state in exchange for personal security. It can be traced back to the ancient Greeks and was developed by HOBBES, LOCKE, and by ROUSSEAU in *The Social Contract* (1762).

social democracy Political ideology concerning the introduction of socialist ideals without an immediate overhaul of the prevailing political system. Before 1914, MARXIST parties of central and eastern Europe termed themselves social democrats. Contemporary social democracy, however, has been invoked by those wishing to distinguish their socialist beliefs from the those of Marxist parties. *See also* SOCIALISM

Social Democratic Labour Party (SDLP) Political party in Northern Ireland. It favours unification with the Republic of Ireland by non-violent, constitutional methods. Founded in 1970, its leader until 2001 was John HUME.

Social Democratic Party (SDP) Political party in Britain (1981–90), centrist in political outlook. At the general elections of 1983 and 1987 the party joined forces with the Liberal Party, and by 1987 the two parties were in the process of merging to form the LIBERAL DEMOCRATS.

social history Branch of HISTORY that focuses on the ordinary lifestyles of people in communities of all types and sizes at specific times and places. *See also* ETHNOLOGY

socialism System of social and economic organization in which the means of production are owned not by private individuals but by the community, in order that all may share more fairly in the wealth produced. Modern socialism dates from the late 18th-early 19th centuries. With the REVOLUTIONS OF 1848, socialism became a significant political doctrine in Europe. Karl MARX, whose *Communist Manifesto* was published in that year, believed that socialism was to be achieved only through the class struggle. Thereafter, a division appeared between the revolutionary socialism of Marx and his followers, later called COMMUNISM or Marxism-Leninism, and more moderate doctrines that argued socialism could be achieved through education and the democratic process. In Russia, the revolutionary tradition culminated in the RUSSIAN REVOLUTION of 1917. From the moderate wing, social democratic parties, such as the British LABOUR PARTY, emerged. They were instrumental in mitigating the effects of the market economy in w Europe through political measures and for securing social justice and welfare.

socialist realism State policy on the arts promoted by the Soviet Union from the 1930s to the 1980s. It asserted that all the arts should appeal to ordinary workers, and should be inspiring and optimistic in spirit. Art that did not fulfill these precepts was effectively banned, and most serious writers, artists and composers were forced underground or into exile.

social psychology Field that studies individuals interacting with others in groups and with society. Topics include attitudes and how they change, prejudice, rumours, aggression, altruism, group behaviour, conformity, and social conflict. There is some overlap with SOCIOLOGY.

social security Public provision of economic aid to help alleviate poverty and deprivation. In 1883, Germany became the first country to adopt social security legislation, in the form of health insurance. By the end of the 1920s, public social security provisions had been adopted throughout Europe. In 1909, the UK adopted an old-age pension scheme, and in 1911 LLOYD GEORGE drafted the National Insurance Act to provide health and unemployment insurance. In 1946, the National Insurance Act and the National Health Service Act were passed. In 1948, the National Assistance Act complemented these, and the WELFARE STATE and the NATIONAL HEALTH SERVICE (NHS) were born. In the USA, as part of the NEW DEAL, the Social Security Act (1935) was adopted. It provided unemployment compensation, old-age pensions, and federal grants for state welfare programs. In 1965, Congress enacted the Medicare programme, which provided medical benefits for persons over 65 and the Medicaid programme for the poor.

Social Security, UK Department of *See* WORK AND PENSIONS, DEPARTMENT FOR

social work Community assistance and/or care. Social workers monitor the well-being of families known to have problems and sometimes have the power to remove children from parents deemed to be dangerously violent or abusive. They may be asked to assist the police in dealing with juvenile suspects. They also help various handicapped, homeless, or unemployed people.

▶ **snail** Remarkably adept at exploring new habitats, snails originated in the sea, but gradually the *c*.22,000 species adapted to life on dry land, losing their gills and evolving air-breathing lungs. Most species of land snail, such as *Helix pomatia*, shown here, live on the ground and are dull in coloration. A few species are arboreal: these tend to be brightly coloured. Others have returned to aquatic environments and must surface periodically to breathe.

S

Society Islands South Pacific archipelago, part of FRENCH POLYNESIA; the capital is PAPEETE on TAHITI. The archipelago divides into two groups of mountainous, volcanic and coral islands. Only eight are inhabited. The larger **Windward** group includes the islands of Tahiti, Moorea, Maio, and the smaller Mehetia, and Tetiaroa. The **Leeward** group includes Raiatéa (the largest and site of the chief town, Uturoa), Tahaa, Huahine, Bora-Bora, and Maupiti. Tourism is the most important industry. The economy is primarily agricultural, and the major crop is copra, with coconut trees dominating the coastal plains. The islands were first sighted by Europeans in 1607. The French claimed the islands in 1768. In 1769, the islands were visited by James COOK, who named them after the Royal Society. In 1843, they were made a French Protectorate, and in 1880 became a French colony. In 1946, they became a French overseas territory. The principal language is Tahitian. Area: 1,446sq km (558sq mi). Pop. (2002) 214,445.

Society of Friends See QUAKERS

Society of Jesus See JESUITS

sociobiology Study of how GENES can influence social behaviour. A basic tenet of biology is that physical characteristics, such as structure and physiology, evolve through NATURAL SELECTION of those traits that are most likely to guarantee an organism's survival. Sociobiologists hold the controversial view that this selection process also applies to social behaviour.

sociology Scientific study of society, its institutions and processes. It examines areas such as social change and mobility, and underlying cultural and economic factors. Auguste COMTE invented the term 'sociology' in 1843, and since the 19th century numerous complex and sophisticated theories have been expounded by Herbert Spencer, Karl MARX, Emile DURKHEIM, Max WEBER, and others.

Socotra Island territory in the Indian Ocean, s of the Arabian Peninsula, with the capital at Tamridah. Strategically placed at the entrance to the Red Sea, it became a British Protectorate in 1866. In 1967, it joined South Yemen and is now administered by Yemen. The mountain terrain includes peaks rising to *c.*1,520m (5,000ft). The economy is based on stock-rearing, but exports include tobacco, ghee, dates, myrrh, aloes and pearls. Area: 3,100sq km (1,200sq mi). Pop. (2000 est.) 44,000.

Socrates (*c.*470–399 BC) Greek philosopher, who laid the foundation for an ethical philosophy based on the analysis of human character and motives. None of Socrates writings survive. Information about his life and philosophy is found in the dialogues of his pupil, PLATO, and the *Memorabilia* of XENOPHON. The son of a sculptor, he fought in the PELOPONNESIAN WAR. In 429 BC according to Plato's *Apology*, the ORACLE at DELPHI pronounced Socrates the wisest man in Greece. Socrates' methodology was based on the DIALECTIC. Unlike the SOPHISTS, he believed that moral excellence is attained through self-knowledge. For Socrates, knowledge and virtue were synonymous; immorality was founded on ignorance. Socrates' criticism of tyranny attracted powerful enemies and he was charged with impiety and corrupting the young. Condemned to death, he drank the hemlock required by law.

soda Any of several sodium compounds, especially sodium carbonate (Na_2CO_3), usually manufactured from common salt (sodium chloride, NaCl) and ammonia by the Solvay process. The anhydrous (lacking water) form is known as soda ash; washing soda is hydrated sodium carbonate ($Na_2CO_3.10H_2O$)

Soddy, Frederick (1877–1956) English chemist who received the 1921 Nobel Prize in chemistry for his studies of radioactive ISOTOPES. In 1920, Soddy revealed the value of isotopes in computing geological age. With Ernest RUTHERFORD, he worked out an explanation of RADIOACTIVE DECAY and later, with William RAMSAY, found HELIUM to be a product of URANIUM decay.

sodium (symbol Na) Common, silvery-white metallic element, one of the ALKALI METALS, first isolated (1807) by English chemist Sir Humphry DAVY. It occurs in the sea as salt (sodium chloride) and in many minerals. Its chief source is sodium chloride, from which it is extracted by electrolysis. The soft reactive metal is used in petrol additives and as a heat-transfer medium in nuclear reactors.

Properties: at.no. 11; r.a.m. 22.9898; r.d. 0.97; m.p. 97.81°C (208.05°F); b.p. 882°C (1,620°F).

sodium bicarbonate (sodium hydrogen carbonate, $NaHCO_3$, popularly known as bicarbonate of soda) White, crystalline salt that decomposes in acid or on heating to release carbon dioxide gas. It has a slightly alkaline reaction and is an ingredient of indigestion medicines.

sodium carbonate See SODA

sodium chloride (NaCl) Common salt. It is the major mineral component of seawater, making up 80% of its dissolved material. Sodium chloride is also the major ELECTROLYTE of living cells, and the loss of too much salt, through evaporation from the skin or through illness, is dangerous. It is used as a seasoning, to cure and preserve foods, and in the chemical industry.

Sofia (Sofija) Capital of Bulgaria and Sofia province, in W central Bulgaria, at the foot of the Vitosha Mountains. Known for its hot mineral springs, Sofia was founded by the Romans in the 2nd century AD. From 1018 to 1185, it was ruled by the Byzantine Empire (as Triaditsa). Sofia passed to the second Bulgarian Empire (1186–1382), and then to the Ottoman Empire (1382–1878). In 1877, Sofia was captured by Russia and chosen as the capital of Bulgaria by the Congress of Berlin. Industries: steel, machinery, textiles, rubber, chemicals, metallurgy, leather goods, food processing. Pop. (2005) 1,045,000.

softball Game similar to BASEBALL in which a lighter bat, a larger and softer ball, and a smaller field are used. It is played by two teams of nine or ten people. The rules are close to those of baseball, except for the pitching delivery (underhand) and the number of innings (seven instead of nine). Softball was originally invented (1888) as an indoor game in Chicago. The sport is governed by the Amateur Softball Association (founded 1934). The International Softball Federation co-ordinates competition in more than 20 nations.

software Alternative term for a COMPUTER PROGRAM. The term software is used to distinguish the program itself, existing only as stored data, from computer HARDWARE or equipment. *See also* PROGRAM

soil Surface layer of loose material resting on top of the rock which makes up the surface of the Earth. It consists of undissolved minerals produced by the WEATHERING and breakdown of surface rocks, organic matter, water, and gases. The organic remains provide the HUMUS and the inorganic particles provide vital minerals. Soils are classified by structure and texture. The structure is determined by the aggregation of particles (peds). The four main textures of soil are SAND, SILT, CLAY, and loam. Loam soils are best for cultivation, since they are able to retain more water and nutrients. EROSION and mismanagement are the chief causes of soil infertility.

solar cell Device that converts sunlight directly to electricity. It normally consists of a *p*-type (positive) silicon SEMICONDUCTOR coated with an *n*-type (negative) one. Light radiation causes electrons to be released and creates a POTENTIAL DIFFERENCE so that current can flow between electrodes connected to the two crystals. The cells are about 10% efficient. Solar cells are often used to power small electronic devices, such as pocket calculators. Several thousand cells may be used in panels to provide power of a few hundred watts. Panels have been used to power space vehicles and satellites. *See* illustration page 690

solar constant Steady rate at which energy from the Sun is received from just outside the Earth's atmosphere. Its value is *c.*1.353 kilowatts per square metre (perpendicular to the Sun's rays).

solar energy Heat and light from the Sun consisting of ELECTROMAGNETIC RADIATION, including heat (infrared rays), light and radio waves. About 35% of the energy reaching the Earth is absorbed; most is spent evaporating moisture into clouds, and some is converted into organic chemical energy by PHOTOSYNTHESIS in plants. All forms of energy (except NUCLEAR ENERGY) on Earth come ultimately from the Sun. SOLAR CELLS are used to power instruments on spacecraft, and experiments are being conducted to store solar energy in liquids from which electricity can be generated.

solar flare Sudden and violent release of matter and energy from the Sun's surface, usually from the region of an

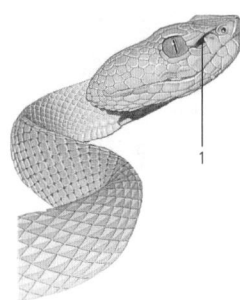

▲ **snake** Many snakes feed on small nocturnal mammals, and must find their prey in the semi-darkness. They do so with the aid of heat-sensitive organs located in pits on the upper jaw (1). The heat sensors feed the information to the same part of the brain as the eyes. In this way, snakes can see a thermal image of their prey superimposed on the visual image.

▲ **Sobers** West Indian cricketer Sir Gary Sobers was perhaps cricket's greatest all-rounder. A talented left-handed batsmen and fine fast-medium and spin bowlor, Sobers is the only player to score more than 8000 test runs and take more than 200 test wickets. He held the record for the highest test innings (365 not out) from 1958 to 1994. Sobers was knighted in 1975.

S

INTERNET

Solomon Islands
▶ www.commerce.gov.sb

Solzhenitsyn, Alexander
▶ www.kirjasto.sci.fi/alesol.
htm

active group of SUNSPOTS. Flares emit radiation right across the electromagnetic spectrum. Particles are emitted, mostly electrons and protons and smaller numbers of neutrons and atomic nuclei. A flare can cause material to be ejected in bulk in the form of prominences. When energetic particles from flares reach the Earth, they may cause radio interference, magnetic storms and more intense AURORAE.

Solar System SUN and all the celestial bodies that revolve around it: the eight PLANETS, together with their SATELLITES and ring systems, the dwarf planets, the thousands of ASTEROIDS and COMETS, meteoroids, and other interplanetary material. The boundaries of the Solar System lie beyond the orbit of Pluto to include the **Kuiper Belt** and the **Oort Cloud** of comets. The Solar System came into being nearly 5000 million years ago, probably as the end-product of a contracting cloud of interstellar gas and dust. *See also* BIG BANG

solar wind Particles, mostly PROTONS and ELECTRONS, accelerated by high temperatures of the solar CORONA to velocities great enough to allow them to escape from the Sun's gravity. The solar wind deflects the tail of the Earth's magnetosphere and the tails of comets away from the Sun.

sole Marine flatfish found in the Atlantic Ocean from NW Africa to Norway, especially *Solea solea*. A food fish, which is farmed in some countries, it is green-grey or black-brown with dark spots. Length: to 60cm (24in). Family Soleidae.

Solemn League and Covenant (September 1643) Agreement between the LONG PARLIAMENT and the Scots during the English CIVIL WAR. In return for Parliament's promise to reorganize the established Church on a PRESBYTERIAN basis, the Scots agreed to raise an army in the North of England against CHARLES I. The Scottish help led directly to the Parliamentary victory over the Royalists at MARSTON MOOR.

solid State of matter in which a substance has a relatively fixed shape and size. The forces between atoms or molecules are strong enough to hold them in definite locations (about which they can vibrate) and to resist compression. *See also* CRYSTAL; GAS; LIQUID

Solidarity Polish organization that provided the chief opposition to the communist regime during the 1980s. The National Committee of Solidarity, led by Lech WALESA, was founded in 1980 among dockworkers in GDANSK. Solidarity organized strikes and demanded economic reform, but soon acquired a political, revolutionary character. Banned from 1981, it re-emerged as a national party, winning the free elections of 1989, and forming the core of a new democratic government.

solid-state physics Physics of SOLID materials. From the study of the structure, binding forces, electrical, magnetic and thermal properties of solids has come the development of the SEMICONDUCTOR, MASER, LASER and SOLAR CELL.

solipsism Philosophical theory that the mind knows nothing other than itself and that the outside world only exists in the mind of the observer. It is a form of IDEALISM.

Solomon (d. 922BC) King of Israel (*c.*972–922BC), son of DAVID and Bathsheba. His kingdom prospered thanks partly to economic relations with the Egyptians and Phoenicians, enabling Solomon to build the Jerusalem TEMPLE. His reputation for wisdom reflected his interest in literature, although the works attributed to him, including the **Song of Solomon**, were probably written by others.

Solomon Islands Melanesian archipelago and nation in the SW Pacific Ocean, SE of New Guinea; the capital is Honiara (on GUADALCANAL). Solomon Islands include several hundred islands scattered over 1,400km (900mi) of the Pacific Ocean. The principal islands are volcanic, mountainous, and densely covered by equatorial rainforest. The N Solomons have a tropical, oceanic climate, but further S there is a longer cool season. The largest island is Guadalcanal, and other inhabited islands include Choiseul, Malaita, New Georgia, San Cristobal (Makira), Santa Isabel (Ysabel), and the Shortland Islands. The coastal plains support *c.*90% of the population and are used for subsistence farming. The majority of the population are indigenous Melanesians. The main languages are Melanesian dialects, but English is the official tongue. The first European discovery of the islands was by the Spanish in 1568. The islands resisted colonization until the late 19th century. In 1893, the S islands became a British Protectorate, while the Germans controlled the N from 1895. In 1900, Germany ceded its territory to Britain. During World War 1, Australian troops occupied Bougainville and Buka (now in PAPUA NEW GUINEA) and the League of Nations mandated them to Australia in 1920. In 1942, the Japanese occupied the S islands. After heavy fighting, particularly on Guadalcanal, US troops liberated the islands in 1944. In 1976, the Solomons became self-governing and in 1978 achieved independence within the Commonwealth. Ethnic conflict from 1998 led to economic collapse and the presence of Australian peacekeepers. Coconuts (providing copra and palm oil) are the major products, but tuna is the biggest export earner and lumber the main industry. Area: *c.*28,896sq km (11,157sq mi). Pop. (2000) 509,000.

solstice Either of the two days each year when the Sun is at its greatest angular distance from the celestial equator, leading to the longest day and shortest night (**summer** solstice) in one hemisphere of the Earth, and the shortest day and longest night (**winter** solstice) in the other hemisphere. In the Northern Hemisphere, the summer solstice occurs around June 21, and the winter solstice around December 22.

Solti, Sir Georg (1912–97) British conductor, b. Hungary. He was music director of Covent Garden Opera (now ROYAL OPERA), London (1961–71); Orchestre de Paris (1971–75); and the Chicago Symphony Orchestra (1969–91). An outstanding operatic music director, Solti was the first conductor to record (1965) Wagner's entire *Ring* cycle.

solubility Measure of mass (grams) of a SOLUTE that will saturate 100 grams of SOLVENT under given conditions to give a SATURATED SOLUTION. This is normally measured in grams of solute per 100 grams of solvent or, for a gas, in parts per million of solvent. Solubility generally rises with temperature, but for a few solutes, such as calcium sulphate, increasing temperature decreases solubility in water.

solute Gaseous, liquid or solid substance that dissolves in a SOLVENT to form a SOLUTION. Many solids dissolve in water. Liquids can dissolve in liquids, and some gases, such as hydrogen chloride (HCl), are soluble in water.

solution Liquid (the SOLVENT) into which another substance (the SOLUTE) is dissolved, or a liquid consisting of two or more chemically distinct compounds, inseparable by filtering. The amount of a solute dissolved in a solvent is called the concentration. *See also* MIXTURE; SATURATED SOLUTION

solvent Liquid that dissolves a substance (the SOLUTE) without changing its composition. Water is the most universal solvent, and many inorganic compounds dissolve in it. Ethanol, ether, acetone, and carbon tetrachloride are common solvents for organic substances. *See also* SOLUTION

Solzhenitsyn, Alexander (1918–2008) Russian novelist. Sentenced to a forced labour camp in 1945 for criticizing

S

SOLAR CELL

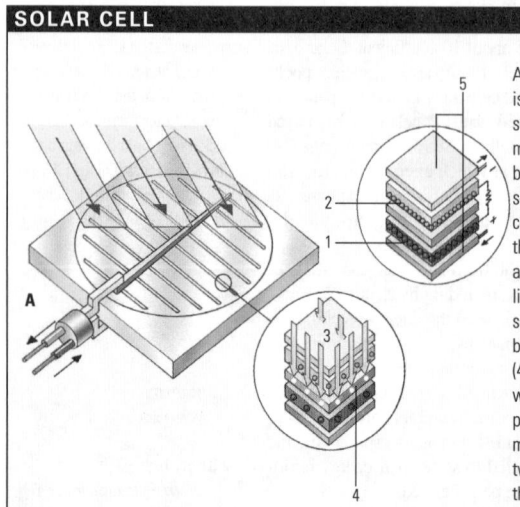

A solar (photovoltaic) cell (A) is made up of two silicon semiconductors between metal contacts protected by a grid. One of the silicon semiconductors tends to collect positive charge (1), the other negative (2), creating a potential difference. As light photons (3) hit the p-n semiconductor junction between the semiconductors (4) they displace electrons which are attracted to the positive semiconductor. The metal contacts (5) connect the two charged areas, exploiting the potential difference and creating a current.

Stalin, he was subsequently exiled to Ryazan but was officially rehabilitated in 1956. His novels include *One Day in the Life of Ivan Denisovich* (1962), *The First Circle* (1968) and *Cancer Ward* (1968). He received the 1970 Nobel Prize in literature. Criticism of the Soviet regime in *The Gulag Archipelago* (1974) led to his forced exile to the West until 1994.

Somalia Republic in E Africa. *See* country feature, page 692

Somerset County on the Bristol Channel, SW England. Somerset is divided into five districts, with the administrative centre at Taunton (2000 pop. 60,700). Other major towns include Yeovil and Bridgewater. The region is generally low-lying in the centre, and is drained by the rivers Avon, Exe, and Parrett. Much land is given over to agriculture. Dairy farming and fruit growing are the most important economic activities and the region is noted for Cheddar cheese and cider. Limestone is mined. Area: 3,452sq km (1,332sq mi). Pop. (2001) 498,093.

Somerset, Edward Seymour, 1st Duke of (1500–52) Regent for EDWARD VI. HENRY VIII appointed him to a Council of Regents for Edward VI (r.1547–53), but he assumed supreme authority and the title of Protector on Henry's death.

Somme, Battle of the Major WORLD WAR I engagement along the River Somme, N France. It was launched by the British Commander Douglas HAIG on July 1, 1916. On the first day, the British suffered more than 60,000 casualties in a futile attempt to break through the German lines. A desperate trench war of attrition continued until the offensive was abandoned on November 19, 1916. Total casualties were more than one million, and the British advanced a mere 16km (10mi). A second battle around St Quentin (March-April 1918) is sometimes referred to as the Second Battle of the Somme. A German offensive, designed to secure a victory before the arrival of US troops, was halted by Anglo-French forces.

Somoza García, Anastasio (1896–1956) Nicaraguan dictator. In 1934, as director of the National Guard, Somoza had Augusto César Sandino killed. In 1937, he ousted President Sacasa and assumed the presidency. Somoza created both a dictatorship and a political dynasty; he was succeeded in office by his two sons, Luis and Anastasio. The Somoza regime was overthrown in the SANDINISTA revolution (1979).

sonar (acronym for **so**und **n**avigation **a**nd **r**anging) Underwater detection and navigation system. The system emits high-frequency sound that is reflected by underwater objects and detected on its return.

sonata Musical composition in several movements. In the BAROQUE era, sonatas were usually written for two melodic parts and a continuo. In the CLASSICAL period, the sonata became a more defined form for one or two instruments. The movements, usually three or four in number, are in related keys. The first movement of a sonata is usually in sonata form, a widely used MUSICAL FORM. The second movement is generally slow in tempo and the third and fourth movements are faster.

Sondheim, Stephen (1930–) US composer and lyricist. Sondheim made his mark on Broadway in 1957 with the lyrics for Leonard BERNSTEIN's *West Side Story*. His first success as a lyricist-composer was *A Funny Thing Happened on the Way to the Forum* (1962). Sondheim's reputation was enhanced by works such as *A Little Night Music* (1972), *Sunday in the Park with George* (1984) and *Assassins* (1991).

Song (960–1279) (Sung) Chinese imperial dynasty (960–1279). The period divides into the Northern (960–1126) and, after the Jurchen tribes overran the N, the Southern (1127–1279) Song. After the initial conquests of Zhao Kuang-ying, the Song dynasty was notable for a deliberate reduction in military might. The Song established a powerful civil service. The Mongols conquered the Southern Song, including its capital Hangzhou.

Songhai West African empire, founded c.AD 700. In 1468, Sonni Ali captured the market city of TIMBUKTU, and the Songhai Empire acquired control of most of the trade in W Africa. Askia Muhammad I succeeded Sonni, and further increased the stranglehold on trade routes. The Empire began to disintegrate because of factional in-fighting. The Songhai peoples still control much of the trans-Saharan trade.

sonic boom Sudden noise produced by shock waves from an aircraft flying at SUPERSONIC SPEED. The shock waves form at the front and back of the aircraft as air is forced apart and then refills the space left by the aircraft. The waves spread out and sweep across the ground behind the aircraft, often causing a double bang. *See also* SOUND BARRIER

sonnet Poem of 14 lines, most often in iambic pentameter and usually employing Petrarchan or Shakespearean rhyme schemes. The **Petrarchan** consists of an octet and a sextet, usually with an *abbaabbacdecde* rhyme scheme. The **Shakespearean**, having a final rhyming couplet, is *ababcdcdefefgg*.

Sontag, Susan (1933–2004) US writer, critic, and essayist. Sontag is perhaps best-known for her cultural criticism, such as *Against Interpretation* (1966). She has also written novels and short stories, including *The Benefactor* (1963), *Death Kit* (1967), and *In America* (1999). The influence of Roland BARTHES and STRUCTURALISM are particularly evident in her *Illness as Metaphor* (1978) and *Aids and its Metaphors* (1986).

Sophia (1630–1714) Electress of Hanover, granddaughter of James I and widow of the Elector of Hanover. Sophia was recognized as heir to the English throne by the Act of SETTLEMENT (1701), to ensure a Protestant succession and prevent the return of the Catholic Stuarts. When she died, her son, the current Elector, became king as GEORGE I.

sophists Professional Greek teachers of the 5th-4th centuries BC. Although not a formal school, they emphasized the intellectual and rhetorical skills needed to succeed in ancient Greek society, and regarded law and ethics as convenient human inventions with no basis in natural law. Serious philosophers, such as SOCRATES and PLATO, disapproved of them.

Sophocles (c.496–406 BC) Greek playwright. Of his 100 plays, only seven TRAGEDIES and part of a Satyr play remain. These include *Ajax*, *Antigone* (c.442–441 BC), *Electra* (409 BC), *Oedipus Rex* (c.429 BC), and *Oedipus at Colonus* (produced posthumously). Sophocles introduced a third speaking actor and increased the members of the chorus from 12 to 15.

soprano Highest singing range of the human voice. The normal range may be given as two octaves upwards from middle C, although exceptional voices may reach notes considerably higher. Sopranos have always been important in opera, with various types of soprano (dramatic, lyric, or coloratura) taking different types of roles.

Sorbonne Building in the Latin Quarter of Paris that houses the rectorate of the Paris universities and a number of university faculties. It was built for a theological college founded in 1253 by Robert de Sorbon (1201–74). The name was used in the 19th century to describe the University of Paris and is now a part of the names of three Paris universities.

sorghum Tropical cereal grass native to Africa and cultivated worldwide. Types raised for grain are varieties of *Sorghum vulgare* that have leaves coated with white waxy blooms and flower heads that bear up to 3,000 seeds. It yields meal, oil, starch and dextrose (a sugar). Height: 0.5–2.5m (2–8ft). Family Poaceae/Gramineae. See picture page 693

sorrel (dock) Herbaceous perennial plant native to temperate regions. It has large leaves that can be cooked as a vegetable, and small green or brown flowers. Height: to 2m (6ft). Family Polygonaceae; genus *Rumex*, especially *Rumex acetosa*.

Sosnowiec See KATOWICE

Sotho Major cultural and linguistic group of S Africa. It includes the Northern Sotho of TRANSVAAL, South Africa, the Western Sotho (better known as the Tswana) of BOTSWANA, and the Southern Sotho (Basotho or Basuto) of LESOTHO. Although dominating the rural territories they inhabit, the c.4 million Sotho share those areas with people of other Bantu-speaking tribes. Many work and live in the urban areas and surrounding townships.

Soto, Hernando de See DE SOTO, HERNANDO

soul Non-material or non-tangible part of a person that is the central location of his/her personality, intellect, emotions and will; the human spirit. Most religions teach that the soul lives on after the death of the body.

soul music Form of popular music. The term designates black music that developed in the USA in the 1960s from RHYTHM AND BLUES. Soul is also used generically to describe music that possesses a certain 'soulful' quality. Its influence extends into many popular musical styles.

▲ **Solzhenitsyn** Russian writer Alexander Solzhenitsyn served with distinction in the Red Army in World War 2, but his criticism of strict censorship in Russia led to the banning of all his novels, except the first. His works were mostly semi-autobiographical and exposed corruption in Russian society while supporting socialism.

sound Waves of vibration or pressure change passing through a physical medium at frequencies that can be percieved by the human ear. The speed at which a sound wave travels through a medium depends on the ELASTICITY of the medium and its DENSITY. If the medium is a gas, such as air, the speed depends on the gas's temperature and pressure. The speed of sound in dry air at STANDARD TEMPERATURE AND PRESSURE (STP) is 331m/s (1,087ft/s) or 1,193km/h (741mph). Sounds may be characterized by PITCH (highness or lowness), TIMBRE (mixture of frequencies within a sound), and intensity or loudness (the rate of flow of sound energy).

sound barrier Name for the technical difficulties in accelerating an aircraft to a speed faster than that of SOUND. When an aircraft approaches the speed of sound, various problematic aerodynamic factors come into effect. These were discovered during World War 2 and can cause conventional aircraft to lose control or suffer serious damage. They are caused by the buildup of shock waves, particularly at the front and rear of the aircraft. In the late 1940s and the 1950s aircraft designers developed shapes designed to minimize and control these shocks, using thinner swept-back wings and refined streamlining, which allowed the speed of sound to be exceeded. *See also* SONIC BOOM

sound recording Conversion of sound waves into a form that can be stored and reproduced. Thomas EDISON's phonograph (1877) recorded sound vibrations as indentations made by a stylus on a revolving cylinder wrapped in tinfoil. Another US inventor, German-born Emile Berliner produced a gramophone that improved the process by using a zinc disc instead of a cylinder. The volume was amplified by the addition of acoustical horns, which were replaced before World War 1 by valve amplifiers. Moulded thermoplastic records were introduced in 1901. In 1927 and 1928 patents were issued in the USA and Germany for MAGNETIC RECORDING processes. Later innovations include high-fidelity (hi-fi), stereophonic and quadrophonic reproduction. Modern recordings on COMPACT DISC (CD) usually employ laser-scanned digital signals.

Sousa, John Philip (1854–1932) US composer and bandmaster. He composed *c*.100 marches, including *Semper Fidelis* (1888) and *The Stars and Stripes Forever* (1896). His operettas include *El Capitan* (1896). He introduced the sousaphone (a large member of the tuba family) to US military bands.

South Africa Republic in s Africa. *See* country feature, p.694

South African Wars Two wars between the Afrikaners (Boers) and the British in South Africa. The **first** (1880–81) arose from the British annexation of the TRANSVAAL in 1877. Under Paul KRUGER, the Transvaal regained autonomy, but further disputes, arising largely from the discovery of gold and diamonds, provoked the **second**, greater conflict (1899–1902), known to Afrikaners as the Second War of Freedom and to the British as the Boer War. It was also a civil war between whites;

SOMALIA

Somalia is in a region known as the 'Horn of Africa'. A narrow, mostly barren, coastal plain borders the Indian Ocean and the Gulf of Aden. In the interior, the land rises to a plateau at 1,000m [3,300ft]. In the N is a highland region. The s contains the only rivers, the Juba and the Scebeli.

Much of Somalia is dry grassland or semi-desert. There are areas of wooded grassland, with trees such as acacia and baobab. Plants are most abundant in the the lower Juba valley.

CLIMATE
Rainfall is light throughout, the wettest regions being in the s and the N mountains. The country is prone to droughts, and temperatures on the plateaux and the plains often reach 32°C [90°F].

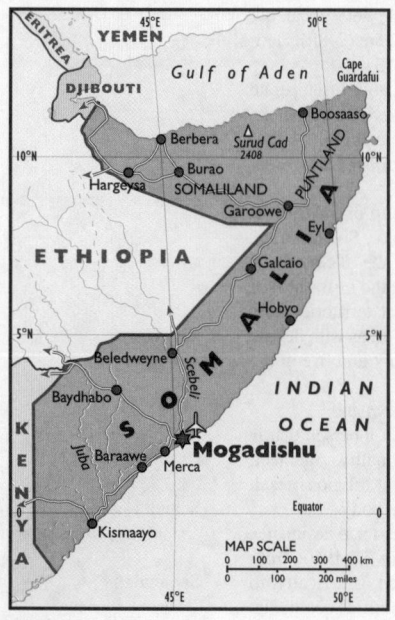

MAP SCALE

HISTORY
In the 7th century, Arab traders established coastal settlements and introduced Islam. Around AD 900 MOGADISHU was founded as a trading centre. The interest of the European imperial powers increased after the opening of the Suez Canal in 1869, and in 1887 Britain established a Protectorate in what is now N Somalia. In 1889 Italy formed a Protectorate in the central region, and extended its power to the s by 1905. In 1896 France established a colony in what is now Djibouti.The new boundaries divided the Somalis into five areas: the two Somalilands, Djibouti, Ethiopia and Kenya. In 1936 Italian Somaliland united with the Somali regions of Ethiopia to form Italian East Africa. During World War 2 in 1940 Italy invaded British Somaliland. British forces conquered the region in 1941 and ruled both Somalilands until 1950, when Italian Somaliland returned to Italy as a UN Trust Territory. In 1960 both Somalilands gained independence and joined to form the United Republic of Somalia.

POLITICS
In 1969 the army, led by Siad Barre, seized power and formed a socialist Islamic republic. During the 1970s Somalia and Ethiopia fought for control of the Ogaden Desert, inhabited mainly by Somali nomads. In 1978 Ethiopia forced Somalia to withdraw but resistance continued, forcing one million refugees to flee to Somalia. In 1991 Barre was overthrown and the United Somali Congress, led by Ali Mahdi Muhammad, gained power. Somalia disintegrated into civil war between rival clans. The Ethiopia-backed Somali National Movement gained control of the NW and seceded as the Somaliland Republic. An attack from the Somali National Alliance, led by General Muhammad Aideed, shattered Mogadishu. War and drought resulted in a devastating famine. The UN was slow to provide relief; US marines led a taskforce

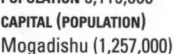

AREA 637,657sq km [246,199sq mi]

POPULATION 9,119,000

CAPITAL (POPULATION) Mogadishu (1,257,000)

GOVERNMENT Transitional, parliamentary federal government

ETHNIC GROUPS Somali 85%, Bantu, Arab, others

LANGUAGES Somali (official), Arabic, English, Italian

RELIGIONS Islam (Sunni Muslim)

CURRENCY CFA franc = 100 centimes

to aid food distribution, but became embroiled in conflict with Somali warlords.

In 1994, 30 US marines died in the fighting and US forces withdrew. Civil strife continued, and in 1996 Aideed was killed. In 2004 an interim government was set up, but withdrew to Kenya for safety. In mid 2006 the Union of Islamic Courts defeated the warlords and took power in Mogadishu, with public support.

In late 2006 the transitional government, backed by Ethiopian forces, captured Mogadishu and claimed the country. Fighting continued in the sw. The transitional government struggled to control the capital and prevent a return to warlord rule. The Ethiopian force supporting them is unpopular, but the African Union has failed to send peacekeeping troops to replace them.

ECONOMY
Somalia is a developing country whose economy has been shattered by drought and war. Catastrophic flooding in late 1997 displaced tens of thousands of people, further damaging the infrastrucure and hopes of economic recovery.

Many Somalis are nomads who raise livestock. Live animals, meat and hides are major exports, plus bananas grown in the wetter south. Other crops include citrus fruits, cotton, maize and sugar cane.

S

black Africans played little part on either side. In 1900, the British gained the upper hand, defeating the Boer armies and capturing Bloemfontein and Pretoria. Boer commandos fought a determined guerrilla campaign but were forced to accept British rule in the peace treaty signed at Vereeniging (1902).

South America Fourth-largest continent, the southern of the two continents of America, in the Western Hemisphere, connected to North America by the isthmus of PANAMA. **Land** South America is surrounded by the Caribbean Sea (N), the Atlantic Ocean (E), and the Pacific Ocean (W). Politically, it divides into 12 independent nations: BRAZIL and ARGENTINA (the two largest), BOLIVIA, CHILE, COLOMBIA, ECUADOR, GUYANA, PARAGUAY, PERU, SURINAME, URUGUAY and VENEZUELA, plus the French overseas department of FRENCH GUIANA. It is *c*.7,650km (4,750mi) long (Punta Gallinas, Colombia to Cape Horn, Chile), and at its widest (near the Equator) *c*.5,300km (3,000mi). **Structure and geology** South America's w edge towers above the rest of the continent, which slopes downwards towards the Atlantic Ocean, except for the Guiana and Brazilian Highlands which form the continental shield. The ANDES, which stretch from Colombia to Chile, contain the highest peaks of the Americas, and ACONCAGUA (Argentina) is the tallest mountain outside Asia. PATAGONIA, a semi-arid plateau composed of rocky terraces, lies to the E of the Andes. A series of lowlands, including the GRAN CHACO, marks the middle of the continent. The ATACAMA DESERT, a coastal strip in N Chile, is the driest place on Earth. Major islands include the FALKLAND ISLANDS (a British Crown Colony) and the GALÁPAGOS (a territory of Ecuador). **Lakes and rivers** Excluding Lake MARACAIBO (13,512sq km/5,217sq mi) as an extension of the Gulf of Venezuela, the largest lake in South America is Lake TITICACA, on the Peru-Bolivia border, covering 8,290sq km (3,200sq mi). Lengthy rivers combine to form three major systems that reach the Atlantic. The AMAZON is the world's second-longest river (after the NILE). Flowing s is the Paraguay-PARANÁ system, and NE is the ORINOCO. **Climate and vegetation** Except in the mountains and the s, the climate remains generally warm and humid. Much of the N supports tropical RAINFOREST, while lowlands in the extreme N and the central region have a cover of tropical grass. The Pampas, s of the Tropic of Capricorn, are temperate grasslands, but vegetation is scarce to the far SE of the mountains. Pine and other temperate forests grow along the SW coast. **People** Some Incas (Quechuas) still remain in the Andes, as do some Mapucho (Araucanians) in Chile. But the majority of the population is *mestizo* (of dual Indian and European descent), except in Argentina, s Brazil, Chile and Uruguay, whose population is primarily European. Since the early 19th century, many Europeans (especially Italians) and Asians (particularly Japanese) migrated to Argentina and Brazil. Sizeable black populations exist in Brazil, Colombia, French Guiana, and Venezuela – descendants of slaves brought from Africa to work in the sugar cane, coffee, rubber and cotton plantations. The majority of South Americans live in urban areas close to the coast. SÃO PAULO is the world's fastest-growing city. Latin American Spanish and Portuguese are the dominant languages and Roman Catholicism is the major religion. **Recent history** The early 1900s saw a number of conflicts within and between countries of the region. Notable among these were the territorial Chaco Wars (1928–30, 1932–35) between Bolivia and Paraguay. South American republics only became world powers after World War 2, helped by the formation of the United Nations in 1945, and the ORGANIZATION OF AMERICAN STATES (OAS) in 1948. Many countries swung between military dictatorships and democratic governments, mainly caused by wildly fluctuating economic fortunes, which in turn brought about extremes of wealth and poverty, leading to unrest and instability. The periodic repressive regimes have been the focus for international condemnation of human rights abuses. In the 1980s and 1990s, international pressure, particularly from the USA, was brought to bear on those governments, notably Bolivia and Colombia, who were either unwilling or unable to control the production and export of vast quantities of cocaine. **Economy** Subsistence farming is important, with *c*.30% of the workforce working 15% of the land, most of

which is owned by Europeans. Chief exports include cash crops, such as coffee, bananas, sugar cane, and tobacco. The drugs industry is also important: Peru and Colombia are major cultivators of coca leaves, and Colombia supplies more than 50% of the world's illegal trade in cocaine. Historically, Europe and the USA dominated industrial development and mineral exploitation. Since 1945, South American countries sought greater economic independence, yet reliance on banking finance often led to a burden of debt. Another drawback is the scarcity of continental coal reserves and the overdependence on petroleum, especially from Venezuela's Maracaibo region. The Guiana and Brazilian highlands have large deposits of iron ore, and the Andes range has many copper reserves. Bolivia has large tin mines, and Brazil has reserves of manganese. However, despite the industrialization of some countries, particularly Brazil, Venezuela and Argentina, most countries remain industrially underdeveloped. In the 1970s and 1980s, the rush for economic growth and industrialization was often at the expense of the continent's rainforests. Worldwide treaties in the 1990s attempted to slow down the deforestation, but with little success. Also, industrialization exacerbated South America's high inflation and huge debt crises. Total area: *c*.17,793,000sq km (6,868,000sq mi); *Highest mountain* Aconcagua 6,960m (22,834ft) *Longest river* Amazon 6,450km (4,010mi) *Population* (2001) 351,000,000 *Largest cities population* (metropolitan area) São Paulo 17,878,703; Buenos Aires 13,755,993; Rio de Janeiro 10,894,156. *See* map page 696.

Southampton Port and county district in Hampshire, s England. At the head of Southampton Water, and a port since Roman times, it is Britain's principal passenger port and a major commercial port, now heavily containerized. Industries: shipbuilding, engineering, oil refining. Pop. (2001) 217,478.

South Australia State on the Southern Ocean, s central Australia. The capital is ADELAIDE, home to 73% of the state's population. Inland is arid, mostly covered by sand and gibber desert and plains. It is the driest state in Australia (average rainfall 528mm) and most of the population live along the coast which has a Mediterranean climate. The Mount Lofty-Flinders Ranges in the E are the main mountain system. Part of the Nullarbor Plain is in the W. The MURRAY, in the SE, is the only important river. Lake EYRE is part of a series of vast salt lakes in the N. Barley, wheat, fruit and grapes (notably in the Barossa Valley) are the chief crops. Commercial fisheries are important. Mineral deposits include iron ore, uranium, silver, lead, salt, gypsum, opals, coal and natural gas. Industries: motor vehicle assembly, wine production, electrical goods. The s coast was visited by the Dutch in 1627, the first English colonists arrived in 1836, and the region was federated as a state in 1901. Area: 984,380sq km (379,760sq mi). Pop. (1999) 1,493,074.

South Carolina State on the Atlantic Ocean, SE USA; the capital and largest city is COLUMBIA. The main port is CHARLESTON. The land rises from the coastal plain to the Piedmont plateau and the BLUE RIDGE MOUNTAINS in the NW. The region is drained by many rivers, including the Savannah, which forms most of the Georgia border. Major crops include tobacco, soya beans, maize, sweet potatoes and peanuts. Timber and fishing are important, but tourism is now the state's next source of income after textiles and clothing. The English built the first permanent settlements in the area from 1663. South Carolina became a royal province in 1729, and a plantation society evolved based on rice, indigo and cotton. One of the original 13 US states (1789), it was the first to secede from the Union and the first shots of the Civil War were fired at FORT SUMTER. Union troops devastated the state in 1865. Area: 80,432sq km (31,055sq mi). Pop. (2000) 4,012,012.

South China Sea Part of the Pacific Ocean, surrounded by SE China, Indochina, the Malay Peninsula, Borneo, the Philippines, and Taiwan; connected to the East China Sea by the Formosa Strait. The world's largest sea, its chief arms are the Gulf of Tonkin and Gulf of Thailand. The Si, Red, Mekong, and Chao Phraya rivers flow into it. Area: 2.3 million sq km (848,000sq mi). Average depth: 1,140m (3,740ft).

South Dakota State in the N central USA, on the GREAT PLAINS. The capital is PIERRE; the largest cities are Sioux Falls

▲ **sorghum** The most widely cultivated grain in Africa, sorghum is also commonly grown in Asia and the USA. It is more tolerant of a hot climate than corn and many other grains, and is extremely resistant to drought. High in carbohydrates, it is usually eaten after being ground into a paste and made into bread, cakes, or porridges. It is also used extensively in the manufacture of beer.

SOUTH CAROLINA
Statehood:
May 23, 1788
Nickname:
The Palmetto State
State bird:
Carolina wren
State flower:
Carolina jessamine
State tree:
Palmetto
State motto:
Prepared in mind and resources

S

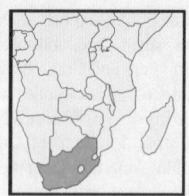

The Republic of South Africa is geologically very ancient, with few deposits less than 600 million years old. The country can be divided into two main regions: the interior plateau – the s part of the huge plateau that makes up most of s Africa – and the coastal fringes.

The interior consists of two main parts. Most of Northern Cape Province and Free State are drained by the ORANGE River and its right-bank tributaries that flow over level plateaux, varying in height from 1,200 to 2,000m [4,000–6,000ft]. The Northern Province is occupied by the Bushveld, an area of granites and igneous intrusions.

The Fringing Escarpment divides the interior from the coastal fringe. In the E the massive basalt-capped wall of the Drakensberg range, at its most majestic near Mont-aux-Sources, rises to more than 3,000m [10,000ft]. It overlooks KwaZulu-Natal and the Eastern Cape coastlands.

In the w there is a similar, but less well developed, divide between the interior plateau and the coastlands. The Fringing Escarpment parallels the s coast, where it is fronted by a series of mountain ranges including the Cape Ranges.

CLIMATE

Most of South Africa has a mild, sunny climate. Much of the coastal strip, including the city of Cape Town, has warm, dry summers and mild, rainy winters, just like the Mediterranean lands in northern Africa. Inland, large areas are arid.

HISTORY

Early inhabitants were the Khoisan or SAN (Hottentots and Bushmen). However, the majority of the people today are Bantu-speakers from the N, who entered the country and introduced a cattle-keeping, grain-growing culture. Arriving via the plateaux of the NE, they continued s into the well-watered zones below the Fringing Escarpment of KwaZulu-Natal and Eastern Cape. By the 18th century, these people had reached the SE. They formed large groups, including the ZULU, XHOSA, Sotho and Tswana.

The first European settlement was led by Jan van Riebeeck, who founded a supply base for the Dutch EAST INDIA COMPANY in 1652 on the site of present-day Cape Town. Some Company employees set up their own farms using native slaves, and became known as Boers (farmers).

Britain took over the Cape Town settlement in the early 19th century. Following Britain's abolition of slavery in 1833 many Boers, resenting British rule, began to move inland in the GREAT TREK. They met with fierce resistance, particularly from the Zulu kingdom. The Boer republics of TRANSVAAL and Orange FREE STATE were established in 1852 and 1854.

In 1870 diamonds were found near where Kimberley now stands. Both the British and the Boers claimed the area, but Britain annexed it in 1871. The discovery quickened the pace of colonization, increasing conflict with the Zulu. Britain sought control of Boer- and Zulu-held areas, and defeated the Zulu in the ZULU WAR (1879). In 1880 the Boers rebelled and defeated the British in the first of the SOUTH AFRICAN WARS, also known as Boer Wars.

In 1886 gold was discovered in the WITWATERSRAND in what is now Gauteng. Many immigrants flooded to the area. Most were British and, to maintain control, the Boers restricted their freedom. Tension developed, culminating in the Second Boer War (1899–1902). The defeated Boer republics of Orange Free State and Transvaal became British colonies.

AREA 1,221,037sq km [471,442sq mi]
POPULATION 43,998,000
CAPITAL (POPULATION)
Cape Town (legislative, 2,930,000); Tshwane/Pretoria (administrative, 1,590,000); Bloemfontein (judiciary, 350,000)
GOVERNMENT Multiparty republic
ETHNIC GROUPS Black 76%, White 13%, Coloured 9%, Asian 2%
LANGUAGES Afrikaans, English, Ndebele, Pedi, Sotho, Swazi, Tsonga, Tswana, Venda, Xhosa and Zulu (all official)
RELIGIONS Christianity 68%, Islam 2%, Hinduism 1%
CURRENCY Rand = 100 cents

POLITICS

In 1906 Transvaal was granted self-rule, followed by Orange Free State in 1907. The other two parts of the country, Cape Colony and Natal, already had self-rule. In 1910 the entire country was united as the Union of South Africa, a self-governing country within the British Empire. During World War 1, two Boer generals led South African forces against Germany. In German South West Africa (now Namibia) General Louis BOTHA conquered the Germans, while General Jan Christiaan Smuts led Allied forces in German East Africa (now Tanzania). In 1920 the League of Nations gave South Africa control over South West Africa under a trusteeship agreement. In 1931 Britain granted South Africa full independence as a member of the Commonwealth of Nations.

The development of minerals and urban complexes in South Africa caused an even greater divergence between black and white. The African farmers gained little from the mineral boom. With taxes to pay, they had little alternative but to seek employment in the mines or on European-owned farms. Migrant labour became the normal way of life for many men, while agriculture in black areas stagnated. Groups of Africans took up urban life, living in communities set apart from the white settlements. These townships, with their rudimentary housing often supplemented by shanty dwellings and without any real services, mushroomed during World War 2 and left South Africa with a major housing problem in the late 1940s. Nowhere was this problem greater than in Johannesburg, where a vast complex of brick boxes called SOWETO (South-Western Townships) was built. The contrast between the living standards of blacks and whites increased rapidly.

At the start of World War 2 opinion was divided as to whether South Africa should remain neutral or support Britain. The pro-British General Smuts triumphed. He became prime minister and South African forces served in Ethiopia, N Africa and Europe. During the war Daniel Malan, a supporter of AFRIKANER nationalism, reorganized the National Party. They came to power in 1948, with Malan as prime minister, and introduced APARTHEID. The AFRICAN NATIONAL CONGRESS, which had been founded in 1912, became the leading black opposition group. Opposition to South Africa's segregationist policies mounted around the world. Stung by criticism from Britain and Commonwealth members, South Africa became a republic and

SOUTH AFRICA

withdrew from the Commonwealth in 1961. In 1966 the UN voted to end South Africa's control over South West Africa. In 1990 the territory finally became independent as Namibia.

In response to continuing opposition South Africa repealed some apartheid laws. In 1984, a new three-house parliament was set up. The three houses were for whites, Asians, and the so-called "Coloured" non-white minority, but the black majority were still unrepresented. In 1986 the European Community (now the European Union), the Commonwealth and the United States applied sanctions on South Africa, banning trade in certain areas. In 1989 F. W. DE KLERK was elected president, and in 1990 he released the banned ANC leader Nelson MANDELA from prison.

In the early 1990s, more apartheid laws were repealed. The country began to prepare a new constitution giving all non-whites the right to vote, though progress towards majority rule was marred by fighting between the Zulu-dominated Inkatha Freedom Party and the ANC.

Elections held in 1994 resulted in victory for the ANC, and Mandela became president. He advocated reconciliation between whites and non-whites, and his government sought to alleviate the poverty of Africans in the townships. The slow rate of progress disappointed many, as did an increase in crime and the continuing massive gap in living standards between races. However, in 1999, following the retirement of Nelson Mandela, his successor, Thabo MBEKI, led the African National Congress to an overwhelming electoral victory. Besides poverty, one of the biggest problems facing the country is the high HIV rate; government studies estimate that one in five South Africans is infected with the HIV virus. The ANC government has been criticized for its poor response to the crisis.

ECONOMY

South Africa is Africa's most developed country. However, most of the black people – rural and urban – are poor, with low standards of living. Natural resources include diamonds and gold, which formed the basis of its economy from the late 19th century. Today, South Africa ranks first in the world in gold production and fifth in diamond production. South Africa also produces coal, chromite, copper, iron ore, manga- nese, platinum, phosphate rock, silver, uranium and vanadium. Mining and manufacturing are the most valuable economic activities and gold, metals and metal products, and gem diamonds are the chief exports.

Manufactures include chemicals, processed food, iron and steel, machinery, motor vehicles and textiles. The main industrial areas lie in and around the cities of Cape Town, Durban, Johannesburg, Port Elizabeth and Pretoria. Investment in South African mining and manufacturing declined in the 1980s, but foreign companies began to invest again following the abolition of apartheid.

Farmland is limited by the aridity of many areas, but the country produces most of the food it needs and food products make up around 7% of South Africa's exports. Major crops include apples, grapes (for wine-making), maize, oranges, pineapples, sugar cane, tobacco and wheat. Sheep-rearing is important on land which is unfit for arable farming. Other livestock products include beef, dairy products, eggs and milk.

---

and Rapid City. The land rises gradually from the E to the Black Hills (featuring Mount Rushmore) in the W and the Badlands in the SW, with the Missouri River bisecting the state. One fifth of the area W of the river is semi-arid plain, inhabited mainly by Native Americans, and the rest is divided into large cattle and sheep ranches. French trappers claimed the region for France in the 1740s, and the USA acquired part of it in the LOUISIANA PURCHASE of 1803. Dakota Territory formed in 1861. In 1874, the discovery of gold in the Black Hills led to an increase in population, and the territory divided into the states of North and South Dakota, both of which joined the Union in 1889. Agriculture is important, with livestock rearing E of the Missouri; major crops include wheat, maize, oats, and soya beans. South Dakota is the largest producer of gold in the USA, but tin, beryllium, stone, sand, and gravel are also mined. Industries: meat packing, food processing. Area: 199,551sq km (77,047sq mi). Pop. (2000) 754,844.

Southeast Asia Region bounded by India, China, and the Pacific Ocean, and comprising BURMA, THAILAND, MALAYSIA, CAMBODIA, LAOS, VIETNAM, PHILIPPINES, SINGAPORE, and INDONESIA. Area: c.4.5 million sq km (1.75 million sq mi).

Southeast Asia Treaty Organization (SEATO) Regional defence agreement signed by Australia, New Zealand, France, Pakistan, the Philippines, Thailand, Britain and the USA in Manila in 1954. It was formed in response to communist expansion in Southeast Asia. With administrative headquarters in Bangkok, SEATO had no standing forces. Some members were unwilling to support the USA in the VIETNAM WAR and SEATO was abandoned in 1977. The ASSOCIATION OF SOUTHEAST ASIAN NATIONS (ASEAN) replaced the non-military aspects of the treaty.

Southey, Robert (1774–1843) English poet and prose writer, poet laureate (1813–43). His long, epic poems include *Thalaba the Destroyer* (1801), *Madoc* (1805), *The Curse of Kehama* (1810), and *Roderick the Last of the Goths* (1814).

South Georgia Island in the S Atlantic Ocean, c.1,750km (1,100mi) E of Tierra del Fuego. Mountainous and barren, it rises to 2,934m (9,626ft). A British dependency administered from the FALKLAND ISLANDS, the island has a research station and garrison but no permanent population.

South Glamorgan County on the Bristol Channel, S Wales; the capital is CARDIFF. It is divided into two districts – Cardiff and the Vale of Glamorgan. The Vale of Glamorgan is agricultural land, and the major economic activity is dairy farming. Cardiff is an industrial district. Industries: engineering, steel. Area: 416sq km (161sq mi). Pop. (2000 est.) 450,400.

South Island Larger of the two principal islands that comprise NEW ZEALAND. Its chief cities are CHRISTCHURCH, DUNEDIN, and Invercarguill. The Southern Alps extend the length of the island, and separate the thickly forested W coast from the broad Canterbury Plains in the E. Cereal growing, sheep and cattle rearing, and dairying are important on the plains, and tourism is a valuable source of income in almost all parts. Area: 150,461sq km (58,093sq mi). Pop. (2001) 942,213.

South Pole Southernmost geographical point on the Earth's surface. The magnetic south pole is located c.2,400km (1,500mi) from the geographical South Pole c.500km (300mi) S of the Ross Ice Shelf. It was first reached (1911) by Roald AMUNDSEN.

South Sea Bubble (1720) Speculation in the shares of the English South Sea Company ending in financial collapse. The South Sea Company was founded (1711) for trade in the Pacific. Shares sold so well, and interest was so high, that in 1720 the company volunteered to finance the national debt. The result was intensive speculation with a 900% rise in the price of shares, until the bubble burst in September 1720, bankrupting investors and closing banks. Credit for saving the company and the government was given to Robert WALPOLE.

South West Africa *See* NAMIBIA

South West Africa People's Organization (SWAPO) Political organization formed (1960) in South West Africa (now NAMIBIA). SWAPO's aim was independence for Namibia, and declared itself at war with South Africa. After ANGOLA gained independence in 1975, SWAPO established guerrilla bases there, which in 1978 were attacked by South Africa. In 1981, truce talks in Geneva failed and in 1984 SWAPO refused to cooperate with the rival Multi-Party Conference (MCP) in drawing up a timetable for independence. When independence was achieved, SWAPO fought a general election in 1989, and gained 57% of the votes and 75% of the seats in the constituent assembly. In 1990, SWAPO leader Sam NUJOMA became president of Namibia. He was re-elected in 1994 and 1999.

South Yorkshire Metropolitan county in N central England. The county divides into four districts, with Barnsley its administrative centre. South Yorkshire's only city is SHEFFIELD, but other major towns include Doncaster and Rotherham. The area includes the PEAK DISTRICT National Forest and the western Pennine moors. The River Don flows E across the county. Following the Industrial Revolution, the county's prosperity depended on its heavy industry, and its major industries still include iron, steel and coal mining. Area: 1,561sq km (603sq mi). Pop. (2001) 1,266,337.

S

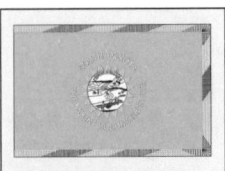

SOUTH DAKOTA
Statehood :
November 2, 1889
Nickname :
The Sunshine State
State bird :
Ring-necked pheasant
State flower :
American pasqueflower
State tree :
Black Hills spruce
State motto :
Under God the people rule

sovereignty Ultimate authority, held by a person or institution, against which there is no appeal. In early modern Europe, sovereignty came to be ascribed to the absolute monarchs of the new nation-states. In Britain, sovereignty resides in Parliament. In most countries, it now resides in 'the people'. Since 1945 states agreed to pool sovereignty in certain intergovernmental organizations, such as the NORTH ATLANTIC TREATY ORGANIZATION (NATO) and the EUROPEAN UNION (EU).

soviet Russian revolutionary workers' council. Soviets appeared briefly in the 1905 Revolution, and again in 1917. The Petrograd (St Petersburg) Soviet, led by Leon TROTSKY, was the leading organization in the BOLSHEVIK Revolution of November 1917. In the Soviet Union, soviets were organized at every level from village upwards. At the top was the Supreme Soviet, the chief legislative body.

Soviet Union (Union of Soviet Socialist Republics, USSR) Former federal republic, successor to the Russian Empire and the world's first communist state. The Soviet Union formed on December 30, 1922 and, when dissolved on December 31, 1991, was the largest country in the world. The BOLSHEVIK regime, led by LENIN, came to power in the RUSSIAN REVOLUTION (1917). Lenin's government survived civil war (1918–22) and famine by instituting a centralized command economy. In 1921, the New Economic Policy (NEP) marked a return to a mixed economy. In 1922, the republics of Russia, Ukraine, Belorussia and TRANSCAUCASIA signed a treaty of union. In 1923, a new constitution was adopted establishing the supremacy of the COMMUNIST PARTY OF THE SOVIET UNION (CPSU), and the Supreme Soviet as the highest legislative body. Lenin died in January 1924, and a power struggle ensued between Leon TROTSKY and Joseph STALIN. Stalin emerged the victor, and Trotsky was expelled in 1927.

In 1928, the first five-year plan was introduced. It transformed Soviet agriculture and industry: collective and state

► **South America** In the N of South America is the Amazonian rainforest, the world's largest area of tropical rainforest. Its rapid deforestation is a major cause of environmental concern. The Atacama Desert, in N Chile, is the driest place on Earth. The imposing Andes ranges run parallel to the w, Pacific coast. In the far s of the continent lies Cape Horn, a cold, isolated region notorious for its violent storms. Spanish and Portuguese colonization of South America began in the 16th century. Native cultures, such as the Inca, were conquered or converted to Roman Catholicism. In the early 19th century, much of the continent gained independence. The descendants of European settlers, however, continued to dominate South American politics and economics. The inequitable distribution of land and power has been a major cause of political instability.

farms were imposed, and industrialization was accelerated. The urban population rapidly doubled. The collectivization schemes led directly to the Ukraine famine (1932–34), which claimed more than seven million lives. State control infiltrated all areas of society, and was sometimes brutally imposed by the secret police. The systems of control led to the creation of a massive bureaucratic administration. The murder (1934) of Sergei Kirov led to the Stalinist purges, and a wave of terror in 1936–38. Supposed dissidents within the government, party and army were sentenced to death, or exiled to the Siberian gulags. The purges also targeted Soviet Jews and other ethnic groups. In 1936, Transcaucasia divided into the republics of Georgia, Armenia, and Azerbaijan.

In August 1939, Stalin concluded a non-aggression pact with Hitler. Germany and the USSR invaded Poland and divided up the country. In 1940, Soviet expansion incorporated the Baltic states of Lithuania, Latvia and Estonia into the Union. War with Finland led to the formation of the Karelo-Finnish republic. On June 22, 1941, Germany invaded Russia. The failure of the siege of Stalingrad (1943) led to the surrender of 330,000 Axis troops and was a decisive turning-point in World War 2. The Red Army's counter-offensive liberated much of e Europe. World War 2 devastated the Soviet Union, with an estimated 25 million Soviet lives lost. The Soviet Union and the USA emerged as the two post-war superpowers. Their antagonistic ideologies and ambitions led to the Cold War. Not only had Soviet territory increased, but its European sphere of influence extended into Albania, Bulgaria, Czechoslovakia, East Germany, Hungary, Poland and Romania. The importance of the military-industrial sector in Soviet politics was greatly enhanced. In 1948, the Soviet army attempted to blockade the western sectors of Berlin. In 1949, when NATO was formed, the Soviet Union exploded its first atomic bomb. In March 1953, Stalin died and a collective leadership was installed. In 1955, the Warsaw Pact was established as the communist counterpart to NATO.

In 1956, at the 20th CPSU Congress, Nikita Khrushchev made his famous secret speech denouncing Stalin as a dictator. In October 1956, Soviet troops crushed a Hungarian uprising against Moscow's domination. In 1958, Khrushchev won the battle for succession. He began a policy of liberalization. Economic decentralization entailed a reduction in the bureaucracy. Huge areas of 'virgin land' were opened to grain cultivation in order to prevent further famine. Khrushchev forged new alliances with anti-colonial movements worldwide, and formulated a policy of peaceful coexistence with the West. The Cold War shifted into a technological battle to produce more powerful weapons of mass destruction, and a 'Space Race'. In 1957, the Soviet Union launched Sputnik 1, the world's first artificial satellite, and in 1961 Yuri Gagarin became the first man in space. Also in 1961, the Berlin Wall was built to divide East Berlin from West. In 1962, the Cuban missile crisis shattered the Cold War stand-off, and nuclear war threatened. Khrushchev agreed to remove Soviet missiles and catastrophe was avoided. In October 1964, a conservative collective leadership, headed by Leonid Brezhnev and Aleksei Kosygin, removed Khrushchev from office and began reversing his reforms.

Brezhnev ruled by consensus and brought close political associates such as Yuri Andropov (KGB chief) and Andrei Gromyko (foreign minister) into his politburo. He instituted cautious economic reforms and agricultural production increased dramatically. In foreign affairs, the 'Brezhnev doctrine' preserved the right of the Soviet Union to intervene in communist states to preserve international communism. The doctrine was invoked to stem the liberalization of Czechoslovakia, and on August 21, 1968, Warsaw Pact troops invaded to crush the Prague Spring. Internal dissent was not tolerated. Leading dissident scientists and intellectuals, such as Alexander Solzhenitsyn and Andrei Sakharov, were sent to prison or forced exile. Many Soviet Jews emigrated in the early 1970s. In 1969, an era of superpower détente began with a series of strategic arms limitation talks (SALT) resulting in the signing of SALT I by Brezhnev and Nixon in 1972. In 1975, the Helsinki Accords recognized the post-war European borders. In 1977, Brezhnev became president and a new constitution adopted. In 1979, SALT II was signed, but the Soviet invasion of Afghanistan ended the period of détente and the USA never ratified the treaty. In 1980, the USA led a boycott of the Moscow Olympics, and placed new, intermediate-range Pershing II missiles on European soil. The Soviet economy stagnated with the stabilization of world oil prices and its outdated manufacturing technology.

After Brezhnev's death in 1982, Andropov became leader. He began a series of far-reaching economic reforms targeting centralization, corruption, inefficiency, and alcoholism. He promoted a series of advisers, including Mikhail Gorbachev, to implement the reforms but Andropov died after only 15 months in office. He was replaced by a hardline Brezhnevite, Konstantin Chernenko. Chernenko died 13 months later, and (in March 1985) Gorbachev became general secretary.

Gorbachev began a process of economic restructuring (perestroika) and political openness (glasnost). Dissidents were released and restraints on emigration were lifted, but the Chernobyl disaster (1986) provided the first real test of glasnost. Gorbachev began a new détente initiative, focusing on nuclear disarmament. A series of meetings with Ronald Reagan led to the Intermediate Nuclear Forces (INF) Treaty, which resolved to scrap intermediate-range nuclear missiles. The Soviet Union agreed to halt the war in Afghanistan, and all its troops withdrew by February 1989. Perestroika continued Andropov's reduction of bureaucracy, and allowed a more mixed economy. Restructuring was hampered, however, by opposition from conservatives and radicals led by Boris Yeltsin, who urged more far-reaching policy shifts. In 1988, Gorbachev convened a conference of the CPSU (the first since 1941) at which parliamentary elections were approved. In March 1989, the first pluralist elections since 1917 were held. Gorbachev was elected state president.

A tide of reform swept over Eastern Europe; by the end of 1989 every communist leader in the Warsaw Pact had been overthrown. The constituent republics of the Soviet Union began to clamour for secession. In 1989, Gorbachev and Bush declared an end to the Cold War. The Baltic republics, Kazakhstan, and Georgia demanded independence. Armenia and Azerbaijan fought for control of Nagorno-Karabakh. In March 1990, the newly elected Soviet parliament authorized private ownership of the means of production: the central economic principle of Marxism had been removed. The CPSU fractured, and Boris Yeltsin resigned from the party. Amid the breakdown in federal government structures, the economy declined by 4%. In December 1990, Gorbachev gained emergency presidential powers and the conservatives demanded action to prevent the disintegration of the Union of Soviets. Soviet paratroopers fought to prevent secession in Latvia and Lithuania. Miners went on strike, calling for Gorbachev's resignation. Eduard Shevardnadze resigned and formed the Democratic Reform Movement. In June 1991, a new Union Treaty that devolved power to the republics and reconstituted the federal government was drafted. It was approved by nine republics, but Armenia, the Baltic states, Georgia and Moldova refused to cooperate. In the same month, Boris Yeltsin was elected president of the Russian Republic. In July 1991, Gorbachev attended the Group of Seven (G7) summit and signed the Strategic Arms Reduction Treaty (START), reducing the number of long-range missiles. On August 18, 1991, hardliners Vice President Yanayev and Defence Minister Dmitri Yazov mounted a coup against Gorbachev, who was kept under house arrest in the Crimea while the coup leaders assumed control of the media and sent tanks into Moscow to capture the Russian Parliament and Boris Yeltsin. The coup failed and Gorbachev was reinstated on August 22, 1991. The republics declared their independence from federal control. Yeltsin emerged as the new political power-broker. He banned the CPSU, took control of the Russian Army, and forced Gorbachev to suspend the Russian Communist Party. Gorbachev resigned as general secretary of the CPSU. In September 1991, the Baltic states of Estonia, Latvia, and Lithuania gained independence. On December 8, 1991, Russia, Ukraine, and Belarus formed the Commonwealth of Independent States

▲ **Soviet Union** St Isaac's Cathedral, St Petersburg. In the early years of the Soviet era, religious bodies were persecuted. Many priests and bishops were killed during the unrest following the Russian Revolution of 1917 and churches were plundered of their valuable relics. It was not until Gorbachev came to power that relations with the Russian Orthodox Church began to improve. The State returned confiscated relics, granted legal status to the Church, and lifted restrictions on worship.

S

▲ **soya bean** Now grown extensively throughout the world, soya beans are native to China where they were first cultivated *c.*4000 years ago. Introduced into North America in 1880, their flowers vary from pure white to light purple. The beans themselves are yellow, brown or black, depending on the variety. Cultivation spread in response to the increasing worldwide demand for protein. The main areas of cultivation are the USA, with more than half of world production, and the Far East, notably China, Japan, and Korea. The crop also spread into parts of South America, especially Brazil and Africa.

S

(CIS). By the end of December, the republics of Armenia, Azerbaijan, Kazakhstan, Kyrgyzstan, Moldova, Tajikistan, Turkmenistan and Uzbekistan had all joined the CIS. On December 25, 1991, Gorbachev resigned as president of the USSR, and a week later the Soviet Union officially dissolved.

Soweto (South-West Township) Group of black townships of more than a million people on the outskirts of JOHANNESBURG, South Africa. In June 1976, Soweto attracted international attention, when a student demonstration against the compulsory teaching of Afrikaans in Bantu schools sparked a series of riots against the APARTHEID regime. The police brutally suppressed the disturbances, killing 618 people. Comprising mostly sub-standard government housing, it remained a focus of protest. Pop. (2000) 992,100.

soya bean ANNUAL plant native to China and Japan. It has oval, three-part leaves, and small lilac flowers. Grown internationally for food, forage, green manure, and oil, its seed is an important source of PROTEIN. Height: 60cm (24in). Family Fabaceae/Leguminosae; species *Glycine max*.

Soyinka, Wole (1934–) Nigerian playwright, novelist, and poet. Soyinka's plays include *The Lion and the Jewel* (1963), *Madmen and Specialists* (1970), and *A Play of Giants* (1984). *The Road* (1965), *Season of Anomy* (1973), and *Death and the King's Horseman* (1975) are among his most powerful novels. Detained (1967–69) without trial during the Nigerian civil war, Soyinka remains a vocal opponent of the military regime. He received the 1986 Nobel Prize in literature.

space Boundless three-dimensional expanse in which objects are located. RELATIVITY states space and time are aspects of one thing, known as SPACE-TIME. Also, space has a non-Euclidean GEOMETRY wherever there is a gravitational field. In another sense, space, sometimes referred to as outer space, is taken to mean the rest of the Universe beyond the Earth's atmosphere.

space exploration Using spacecraft to investigate outer space and heavenly bodies. The early stages of space exploration were dominated by competition between the Soviet Union and the United States. The Soviet Union launched the first artificial satellite, **Sputnik 1**, into Earth orbit on October 4, 1957, the first probe to land on the Moon, **Luna 2**, on September 13, 1959, and the first manned space flight, with Yuri GAGARIN aboard, on April 12, 1961. The first US citizen to reach Earth orbit was John GLENN on February 20, 1962. The first close-up pictures of Mars were taken by the US **Mariner 4** probe and received on July 14, 1965. The Soviet **Venera 3**, was the first to crash-land on another planet, Venus, on March 1, 1966; Venera 7 landed without crashing on December 15, 1970. In 1969, the US **Apollo 11** mission was the first to place a man on the Moon, with Neil ARMSTRONG stepping onto the surface on July 20, 1969. From the mid-1970s, there was more cooperation between the US and Soviet Union, and Europe and China become increasingly involved in space exploration. Many more important missions have been launched, such as: the first probes to land on Mars (July 1976) were **Viking 1 and 2**; **Voyager 2** flew by Jupiter (1979), Saturn (1981), Uranus (1986), and Neptune (1989); **Gallileo** (launched 1989) reached Jupiter in 1995 and returned data for eight years; **Cassini-Huygens** (launched 1997) reached Saturn in 2004. The use of re-usable vehicles began with the first SPACE SHUTTLE, *Columbia*, launched on April 12, 1981. On June 21, 2004, SpaceShipOne was the first privately developed spacecraft to take people into sub-orbital space.

space research Scientific and technological investigations that gather knowledge through SPACE EXPLORATION. Optical and radio telescopes and the orbiting HUBBLE SPACE TELESCOPE launched by NASA in 1990, determined the physical make-up and behaviour of stars, planets, and other astronomical objects. Artificial SATELLITES, the SPACE SHUTTLE, space stations and space probes have all carried research projects into space. The results have been used in many fields.

space shuttle Re-usable rocket-powered US spacecraft. It ferries people and equipment between the ground and Earth orbit. The main part of the shuttle, the orbiter, looks like a bulky jet aircraft with swept-back wings. It takes off attached to a large fuel tank, using its own three rocket engines, assisted by two booster rockets. The boosters are jettisoned about

two minutes after launch and are later recovered for re-use. Six minutes later, the orbiter's main engines cut off and the external fuel tank is dumped. Manoeuvring engines then put the craft into orbit. When returning to Earth, these engines provide reverse thrust to slow the craft down for descent into the atmosphere. It glides down and lands on a runway. The first space shuttle, *Columbia*, was launched into orbit on April 12, 1981. The orbiter had a large payload bay in which it carried satellites for release into orbit. On mission 25 in January 1986, the shuttle *Challenger* exploded soon after launch, killing all seven people on board. A leak enabled burning gases from a booster rocket to ignite the fuel in the main tank. On mission STS-107, in February 2003, shuttle *Columbia* exploded minutes before it was due to return to Earth. All seven crew members died. Three shuttles, *Atlantis*, *Discovery*, and *Endeavour*, remain in use and will be retired in *c.*2010.

space station Orbiting structure in space for use by astronauts and scientists. Space stations are more spacious than most space craft as the occupants may live there for several months before returning to Earth. Space laboratories, such as the American *Skylab* (launched 1972) and the Russian MIR (launched 1986), are space stations built for scientists to carry out experiments, study the Solar System, and observe distant parts of the Universe, their view undistorted by the Earth's atmosphere. The International Space Station (ISS) became operational in 2000.

space-time In RELATIVITY theory, a central concept that unifies the three space dimensions (length, breadth, and height) with time to form a four-dimensional frame of reference. Durations and rates of processes depend on the relative state of motion of the observer and the system observed. In 1907, Hermann Minkowski clarified relativity theory by describing space-time in terms of a four-dimensional geometry. Three co-ordinates of space and a time co-ordinate specify an event in space-time. A line drawn in this space represents a particle's path both in space and time. Albert EINSTEIN incorporated this viewpoint into his theory of relativity: in the General Theory, gravity is a distortion of space-time by matter.

spadix In some flowering plants, a spike of small flowers; it is generally enclosed in a sheath called a SPATHE. A familiar example is the CUCKOOPINT (*Arum maculatum*).

Spain *See* country feature, page 700

spaniel Any of several breeds of sporting dogs that may be trained to locate and flush game, and sometimes to retrieve on command. Land spaniels include the springer, cocker, and toy breeds. Water spaniels are usually RETRIEVERS.

Spanish Major world language, spoken as an official language in Spain, South America (except Brazil, French Guiana, Guyana, and Surinam), all of Central America, Mexico, Cuba, the Dominican Republic, and Puerto Rico. It is also spoken in a number of other countries, notably the USA and former Spanish dependencies such as the Philippines. Spanish is a member of the Romance group of INDO-EUROPEAN LANGUAGES but its vocabulary contains a large number of words of Arabic origin, the result of Moorish domination of Spain for many centuries. There are more than 200 million Spanish speakers worldwide.

Spanish-American War (1898) Conflict fought in the Caribbean and the Pacific, between Spain and the USA. The immediate cause was the sinking of the US battleship *Maine* at Havana. Fighting lasted ten weeks (April-July). The US Navy destroyed Spanish fleets in the Philippines and Cuba. Spanish troops in Cuba surrendered after defeat at San Juan Hill, where Theodore ROOSEVELT led the 'Rough Riders'. The USA also seized Guam and Wake Island, annexed Hawaii and the Philippines. The Treaty of Paris forced Spain to cede Puerto Rico.

Spanish Armada *See* ARMADA, SPANISH

Spanish art Artistic tradition beginning with the Palaeolithic cave paintings at ALTAMIRA, N Spain. Successively occupied by the Romans, Visigoths and Moors, Spain's earliest native traditions were the Mozarabic and Mudéjar styles, which blended Moorish and Christian elements. As the Moors retreated from Spain, the country drew closer to artistic developments in the rest of Europe. By the 16th century, it was the most powerful force on the continent, and this period coincided with the career of its first true genius, El GRECO. The golden era of Spanish art was the 17th century. Leading figures from this epoch include Diego VELÁZQUEZ, José RIBERA, and Francisco de Zurbarán. In later years, Francisco GOYA was a master of ROMANTICISM, and Pablo PICASSO was the dominant figure in 20th-century art.

Spanish literature One of the major early works is the epic poem *Cantar de Mío Cid* (*c*.1140). Major figures of the 14th and 15th centuries include the poet Juan Ruiz (*c*.1283–1350). The most important work of fiction of the 15th century was the novel *La Celestina* (1499). French and Italian influences predominate until the 16th century, when a truly Spanish literature emerged. The late 16th and 17th centuries are known as the 'Golden Age'. Miguel de CERVANTES' *Don Quixote de la Mancha* (1605–15) is a masterpiece of European literature. Other major figures include Luis de Góngora y Argote, Lope de VEGA CARPIO, and Pedro Calderón de la Barca. The 18th century witnessed a decline in Spanish writing, saved by the rise of ROMANTICISM. *Costumbrismo* (sketches of Spanish life and customs) flourished in the 19th century. In the early 20th century, the writers of the Generation of '98 re-examined Spanish traditions. The Spanish Civil War (1936–39) drove many Spanish writers into hiding, and its reverberations can be seen in the grim realism of much of the work that followed. MODERNISM exerted an influence on formal technique and narrative style; SURREALISM also inspired the 'Generation of 1927' group of poets. Probably the most important Spanish writer of the 20th century was Federico GARCÍA LORCA.

Spanish Sahara Former name of WESTERN SAHARA

Spanish Succession, War of the (1701–14) Last of the series of wars fought by European coalitions to contain the expansion of France under LOUIS XIV. It was precipitated by the death of the Spanish king, Charles II, without an heir. He willed his kingdom to Philip of Anjou, Louis' grandson. England and the Netherlands supported the Austrian claimant to the Spanish throne, the Archduke (later Emperor) Charles. The ensuing war marked the emergence of Britain as a maritime and colonial power. The compromise deal in the Peace of UTRECHT settled the Spanish succession, with Philip attaining the Spanish throne on condition that he renounced any claim to France, and Britain and Austria receiving substantial territorial gains. Exhaustion of the participants, especially France, ensured general peace in Europe until the outbreak of the War of the AUSTRIAN SUCCESSION in 1740.

Spark, Dame Muriel (1918–2006) Scottish novelist, short-story writer, and poet. Spark's collected poems and short stories were published in 1967, but she is best known for her novels, which include *Memento Mori* (1959), *The Ballad of Peckham Rye* (1960), *The Prime of Miss Jean Brodie* (1961), *Girls of Slender Means* (1963), *The Mandelbaum Gate* (1965) and *Symposium* (1990).

sparrow Any of a number of small FINCH-like birds that live in or around human settlements. The male has a chestnut mantle, grey crown and rump, and black bib. The female is duller and lacks the bib and grey rump. Sparrows feed, roost, and dust-bathe in noisy, twittering flocks. Basically seed-eaters, with a preference for grain, they are widely regarded as pests. They also eat fruit, worms and household scraps. Length: 14.5cm (5.75in). Family Ploceidae; species *Passer domesticus*.

Sparta City-state of ancient Greece, near the modern city of Spárti. Founded by Dorians after *c*.1100 BC Sparta conquered Laconia (SE Peloponnese) by the 8th century BC and headed the Peloponnesian League against Persia in 480 BC. In the PELOPONNESIAN WAR (431–404BC), it defeated its great rival, ATHENS, but was defeated by THEBES in 371 BC and failed to withstand the invasion of PHILIP II of Macedon. In the 3rd century BC Sparta struggled against the Achaean League (a confederation of city-states), subsequently joining it but coming under Roman dominance after 146 BC. In AD 395 the GOTHS, led by ALARIC, destroyed the ancient city.

Spartacists Members of the German political party called the **Spartacus League**, which broke away from the Social Democrats during World War 1. Led by Karl LIEBKNECHT and Rosa LUXEMBURG, they refused to support the war and rejected any part in the post-Versailles republican government. They instigated a number of uprisings, including one in Berlin (1919), after which they were repressed and the leaders murdered.

Spartacus (d.71BC) Thracian gladiator in Rome who led a slave revolt known as the Third Servile (Gladiatorial) War (73–71BC). His soldiers devastated the land and then moved south towards Sicily, where they were eventually defeated by CRASSUS with POMPEY's aid. Spartacus died in battle.

spathe Broad leaf-like organ that spreads from the base of, or enfolds, the SPADIX of certain plants.

▲ **spaniel** Although now very popular as pets, spaniels were originally bred to frighten game birds from undergrowth, much as beaters do today. Other spaniels can be trained to retrieve downed fowl. Originating in Spain, they were bred extensively in Britain.

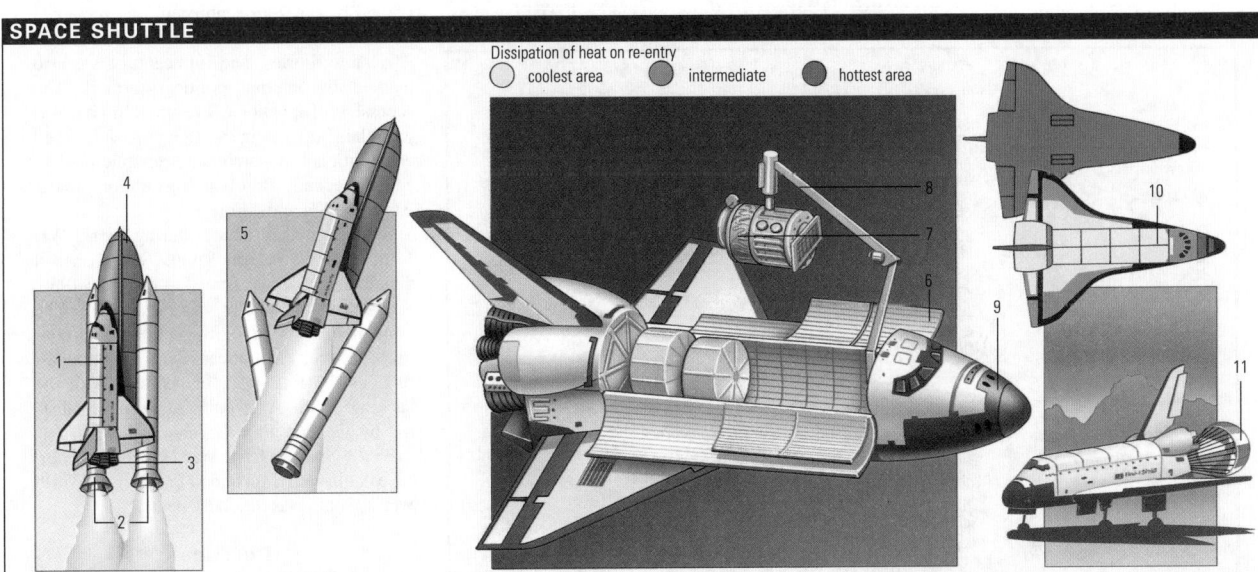

SPACE SHUTTLE

A space shuttle flight has three distinct phases. The first is reaching orbit. Two solid fuel boosters (2) and the shuttle's three engines (3), fed with liquid oxygen and liquid hydrogen fuel from the external tank (4), propel the orbiter (1) upward from the launch platform. After the boosters burn out they detach (5), and float back to the surface of the Earth by parachute. The external tank detaches later and burns up in the Earth's upper atmosphere. The second phase now commences. Once in orbit, the shuttle floats upside down above the Earth, with its cargo bay doors (6) open to dispel heat. Satellites (7) launch from the cargo bay, and can be retrieved with the use of a motorized arm (8). While in orbit, the shuttle manoeuvres using helium-fuelled thrusters in the nose (9). Finally, the shuttle returns to land unpowered. Ceramic tiles (10) on the orbiter's outer surface shield it from the enormous heat generated on re-entering the Earth's atmosphere. A parachute (11) acts as a brake, slowing the orbiter after touchdown on the runway.

The Kingdom of Spain is the second largest country in W Europe after France. It shares the Iberian Peninsula with Portugal. A plateau, called the *Meseta*, covers most of Spain. Much of it is flat, but crossed by several mountain ranges (*sierras*).

The N highlands include the Cantabrian Mountains (Cordillera Cantabrica) and the high PYRENEES, which form Spain's border with France. Mulhacén, the highest peak on the Spanish mainland, is in the Sierra Nevada in the SE. Spain also contains fertile coastal plains. Other lowlands are the EBRO River Basin in the NE and the Guadalquivir River Basin in the SW.

Spain also includes the BALEARIC ISLANDS (Islas Baleares) in the Mediterranean Sea and the Canary Islands off the NW coast of Africa. Tenerife in the Canary Islands contains Pico de Teide, Spain's highest peak (3,718m [12,918ft]).

Forests lie to the rainier N and NW, with beech and deciduous oak being common. Towards the drier S and E Mediterranean pines and evergreen oaks take over, and the forests resemble open parkland. Large areas are *matorral*, a Mediterranean scrub. Where soils are thin and drought is prevalent, matorral gives way to steppe.

CLIMATE

Spain has the widest range of climate in W Europe. One of the most striking contrasts is between the humid N and NW, where winds from the Atlantic bring mild, wet weather throughout the year, and the mainly arid remainder of the country. Droughts are common in much of Spain, although these are occasionally interrupted by thunderstorms.

The *Meseta*, removed from the influence of the sea, has a continental climate, with hot summers and cold winters. In winter frosts often occur, and snow blankets the mountain ranges that rise above the plateau surface. By contrast, the Mediterranean coastlands and the Balearic Islands have mild, moist winters. Summers along the Mediterranean coast are hot and dry. The Canary Islands have mild to warm weather throughout the year.

HISTORY

5,000 years ago Spain was inhabited by farming peoples called Iberians. Some historians believe the BASQUES of northern Spain may be descendants of these people. In the 9th century BC Phoenicians from the eastern Mediterranean reached the Iberian Peninsula and began to establish trading colonies on the S coast, some on the sites of modern cities such as Cádiz and MÁLAGA. Celtic peoples arrived later from the N, while Greek merchants reached the E coast of Spain around 600 BC.

In the 5th century BC the Carthaginians conquered much of Spain, but after the Second Punic War (218–201 BC) the Iberian Peninsula gradually came under Roman rule. The Romans made Iberia a Roman province called Hispania.

By 573 the Visigoths had conquered the entire peninsula, including what is now Portugal. They ruled until the early 8th century when the MOORS invaded from North Africa. The Moors founded an independent Muslim state in 756 and introduced their culture and scholarship, building superb mosques and palaces. In the 11th century, the country began to divide into many small Moorish kingdoms, leaving them open to attack by the Christian kingdoms in the north. Portugal broke away from Spain in the 11th–12th centuries. By the late 13th century, Muslim power was confined to the southern Kingdom of GRANADA.

The rest of Spain was ruled by the Christian kingdoms of ARAGON, NAVARRE and, most powerful of all, CASTILE. In 1469 Castile and Aragón were united by the marriage of FERDINAND V and ISABELLA I. The conquest of Granada (1492) and Navarre (1512) saw Ferdinand and Isabella become rulers of all Spain. The INQUISITION ensured Catholic supremacy through persecution and conversion. Christopher Columbus' discovery of America in 1492 allowed the Spanish to conquer much of South America, and by the mid-16th century Spain was a great world power controlling much of Central and South America, parts of Africa and the Philippines in Asia. In 1519 King Charles I became Holy Roman Emperor as CHARLES V, and the supremacy of the HABSBURGS was established. PHILIP II continued the extension and centralization of power, gaining Portugal in 1580. The defeat of the Spanish ARMADA in 1588 dented Spanish naval domination, and during the 17th century Spain's political and economic power went into decline.

The War of the SPANISH SUCCESSION (1701–14) resulted in the accession of PHILIP V and the establishment of the BOURBON dynasty. CHARLES III brought the Church under state control. CHARLES IV's reign ended in French occupation and the appointment of Joseph BONAPARTE as king. Spanish resistance led to the restoration of the Bourbons in 1813.

Many of Spain's New World colonies gained independence in the early 19th century, and by the 20th century all that remained of the Spanish empire were a few small African territories. The 19th century was also marked by internal political turmoil. The accession of ISABELLA II resulted in civil war with the CARLISTS in the 1830s. A short-lived constitutional monarchy and republic preceded a second Bourbon restoration under ALFONSO XII and Alfonso XIII.

Spain remained neutral during World War 1. In 1923 PRIMO DE RIVERA established a dictatorship. He was forced to resign in 1930, and a second republic was proclaimed. The Popular Front won 1936 elections, and conflict between republicans and nationalists, such as the FALANGE, intensified. With the backing of the Axis powers, the nationalists led by General FRANCO emerged victorious from the Spanish Civil War (1936–39). Franco established a dictatorship. During World War 2, Spain was officially neutral.

POLITICS

The revival of Spain's shattered economy began in the 1950s through the growth of manufacturing industries and tourism. As standards of living rose, people began to demand more freedom. After Franco died in 1975 the monarchy was restored and JUAN CARLOS, grandson of Alfonso XIII, became king. The ban on political parties was lifted and, in 1977, elections

AREA 497,548sq km [192,103sq mi]
POPULATION 40,448,000
CAPITAL (POPULATION)
Madrid (3,017,000)
GOVERNMENT Constitutional monarchy
ETHNIC GROUPS Mediterranean and Nordic types
LANGUAGES Castillian Spanish (official) 74%, Catalan 17%, Galician 7%, Basque 2%
RELIGIONS Roman Catholic 94%, others
CURRENCY Euro = 100 cents

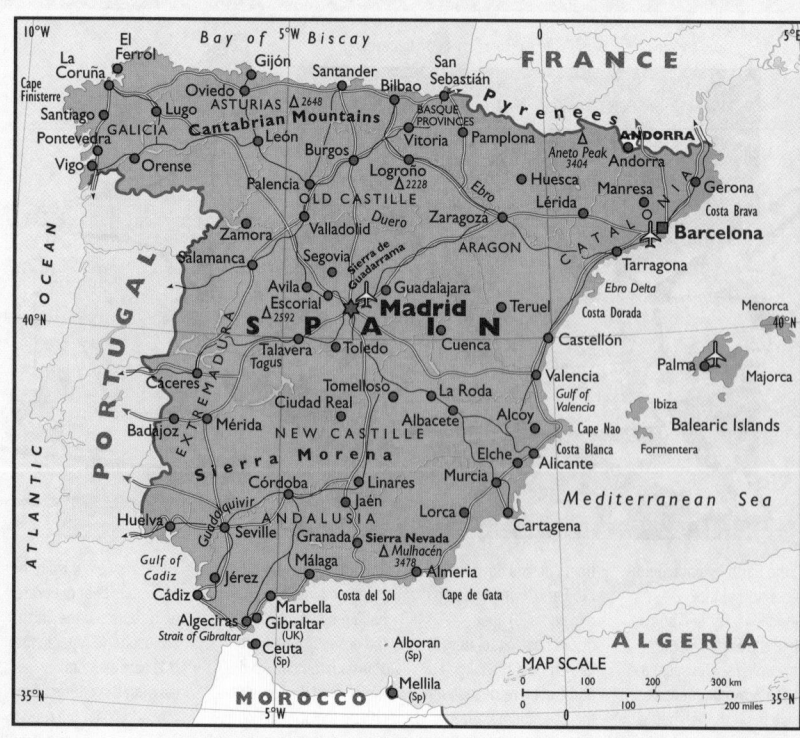

SPAIN

were held. A new constitution making Spain a parliamentary democracy, with the king as head of state, came into effect in December 1978.

From the late 1970s Spain began to tackle the problem of its regions. In 1980, a regional parliament was set up in the BASQUE COUNTRY (*Euskadi* in Basque and *Pais Vasco* in Spanish). Similar parliaments were initiated in Catalonia (Cataluña) in the NE and Galicia in the NW. While regional devolution was welcomed in Catalonia and Galicia, it did not end the terrorist campaign of the Basque separatist movement, Euskadi Ta Askatasuna (ETA). ETA announced an indefinite ceasefire in September 1998, but

the truce was ended in December 1999 and the conflict continued. The Supreme Court voted in 2003 to ban Batasuna, the Basque separatist party deemed to be the political wing of ETA.

In March 2004 terrorist bombs exploded in Madrid killing 191 people. Although the government sought to blame ETA, the bombings proved to be linked to al-QAEDA. In elections days later, the right-wing government was voted out, as the people blamed the bombings on government support for the US-led invasion of Iraq. The new Socialist prime minister, Jose Zapatero, immediately withdrew all troops from Iraq. From 2006 ETA resumed its own terror campaign.

ECONOMY

Spain has the fifth largest economy in the EU. By the early 2000s agriculture employed only 6% of the workforce, as compared with industry at 17% and services including tourism employing 77%. Farmland makes up two-thirds of the land, and forest most of the rest. Major crops include barley, citrus fruits, grapes for wine-making, olives, potatoes and wheat. The raising of sheep is also important.

There is some high-grade iron ore in the N. Spain's many manufacturing industries include cars, chemicals, clothing, electronics, processed food, metal goods, steel and textiles.

Speaker Presiding officer who ensures procedures are adhered to in a legislature. In the UK, the Speaker of the House of Commons presides over debates but has no other formal powers. In the USA, the Speaker of the House of Representatives is elected from the majority party by the House. Powers include the recognition of members for debate, the appointment of select and conference committees, the referral of bills to committees, and the signing of documents on behalf of the House.

spearmint Common name of *Mentha spicata*, a hardy PERENNIAL herb of the MINT family (Lamiaceae/Labiatae). Its leaves are used for flavouring, especially in sweets. Oil distilled from spearmint is used as a medicine. The plant has pink or lilac flowers that grow in spikes.

Special Branch Department within every British police force that is technically affiliated to MI5, the intelligence bureau within the Home Office. Its duties are to investigate and deter all activities against the interests of the state, to protect visiting foreign rulers and dignitaries, and to monitor the immigration and naturalization of foreign nationals.

species Group of physically and genetically similar individuals that interbreed to produce fertile offspring under natural conditions. In biological classification, species is the lowest level. Each species has a unique two-part Latin name, the first part being the capitalized GENUS name and the second part, the species. So far, more than 1.5 million plant and animal species have been identified. *See also* BINOMIAL NOMENCLATURE; TAXONOMY

specific gravity (sp. gr.) *See* RELATIVE DENSITY (R.D.)

specific heat capacity Heat necessary to raise the temperature of one kilogram (1kg) of a substance by one kelvin (1°C). It is measured in J/kgK (J equals joule).

spectroscopy Branch of OPTICS dealing with the measurement of the wavelength and intensity of a SPECTRUM. The main tool is the **spectroscope**. It produces a spectrum and a **spectrograph** photographs it. An analysis of the spectrogram can reveal the substances causing the spectrum by the position of emission and absorption lines and bands. Analyses are used for determining the composition and motion of stars and other celestial bodies. A **spectrometer** is a calibrated spectroscope capable of precise measurements.

spectrum Arrangement of ELECTROMAGNETIC RADIATIONS ordered by wavelength or frequency. The visible light spectrum is a series of colours: red, orange, yellow, green, blue, indigo, and violet. Each colour corresponds to a different wavelength of light. This was first noted in 1666 by English physicist Isaac NEWTON. A spectrum is seen in a RAINBOW or when white light passes through a PRISM. This effect, also seen when visible light passes through a DIFFRACTION grating, produces a continuous spectrum in which all wavelengths (between certain limits) are present. Spectra formed from objects emitting radiations are called **emission** spectra. These occur when a substance is heated or bombarded by electrons. An **absorption** spectrum, consisting of dark regions on a bright background, is obtained when white light passes through a semi-transparent medium that absorbs certain frequencies. A line spectrum is one in which only certain wavelengths or 'lines' appear. *See* SPECTROSCOPY

speed Rate of motion of a body. Speed is a SCALAR (magnitude only) which does not specify direction, whereas VELOCITY is a VECTOR (magnitude and direction). An object's speed is calculated by dividing the distance *s* it has travelled by the time *t* taken, and this is expressed as $v=s/t$ and given in metres per second (ms^{-1}) or kilometres/miles per hour.

speedwell Common name applied to herbaceous plants of many species of the genus *Veronica* found throughout the world. Germander speedwell, *V. chamaedrys*, is a common British wild flower. Family Scrophulariaceae.

Speer, Albert (1905–81) German architect and NAZI official. A close associate of Adolf HITLER, he drew up the plans for Germany's autobahns and the stadium at Nuremberg. By 1943, his authority over the war economy was second only to that of GOERING. In 1946, Speer was tried by the NUREMBERG war crimes tribunal, and sentenced to 20 years in Spandau Prison.

Speke, John Hanning (1827–64) English explorer of E Africa. After service in India, Speke joined Richard BURTON in an expedition to Somalia (1854) and, on behalf of the Royal Geographical Society, to the E African lakes (1856). In Burton's absence, he reached Lake Victoria, which he identified as the source of the Nile.

speleology Scientific study of CAVES and cave systems. Included also are the hydrological and geological studies of the formation of STALAGMITES and STALACTITES, and the influence of GROUNDWATER conditions on cave formation.

Spence, Sir Basil (1907–76) English architect. Spence is best-known for his modernist design of the new Coventry Cathedral (1951, consecrated in 1962). Other works include the British Embassy, Rome (1971).

Spencer, Sir Stanley (1891–1959) English painter. During World War 2, he was a war artist and painted a series of large pictures showing shipbuilding on the Clyde. He is also known for his nude paintings, such as the *Leg of Mutton Nude* (1937).

Spender, Sir Stephen Harold (1909–95) English poet. Spender was a member of the AUDEN circle in the 1930s, and his autobiography, *World within World* (1951), is a powerful evocation of the generation. His best verse, such as 'I Think Continually of Those Who Were Truly Great', is a combination of lyricism and political commitment. His *Collected Poems 1928–1985* appeared in 1985. Spender was knighted in 1983.

Spenser, Edmund (1552–99) English poet. Spenser's debut volume was the pastoral *The Shepheardes Calender* (1579), dedicated to Sir Philip SIDNEY. His masterpiece is *The Faerie Queene* (1589–96), a romance and moral allegory.

sperm (spermatozoon) Motile male sex cell (GAMETE) in sexually reproducing organisms. It corresponds to the female OVUM. Sperm are produced in the testes of male animals. The head of the sperm contains the genetic material of the male parent, while its tail or other motile structure provides the means of moving to the ovum to carry out FERTILIZATION. Up to 500 million sperm together may attempt to reach the egg, but only one will fertilize it. *See also* SEXUAL REPRODUCTION

spermatophyte Seed-bearing plant, including most trees, shrubs, and herbaceous plants. It has a stem, leaves, roots, and a well-developed vascular system. The dominant generation is the SPOROPHYTE. Divisions are the Angiospermophyta

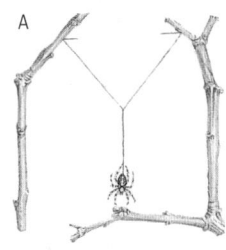
A

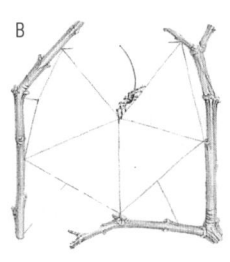
B

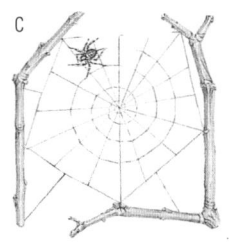
C

▲ **spider** When spinning a web to catch prey, spiders first cast out a thread of silk to form a horizontal strut. A second, drooping thread trails across below the bridge-line. Halfway along the second thread, the spider drops down on a vertical thread until it reaches a fixed object (A). It pulls the silk taut and anchors it, forming a 'Y' shape, the centre of which forms the hub of the web. The spider then spins the framework threads and the radials, which are linked together at the hub (B). After spinning the remainder of the radials, a wide, temporary spiral of dry silk is laid down, working from the inside of the web outwards (C). This holds the web together while the spider lays down the sticky spiral. This time the spider starts from the outside of the web, attaching the spiral successively to each radial thread.

S

▲ **Spielberg** Steven Spielberg's first feature film was *Sugarland Express* (1974). With his friend George Lucas, Spielberg dominated Hollywood in the 1980s with a series of commercial blockbusters such as *E.T. The Extra-Terrestrial* (1982). In 1984, he founded his own production company, responsible for *Back to the Future* (1985) and *Who Framed Roger Rabbit* (1988). Famous for his ability to convey a magical sense of childlike wonder in his 'entertainments', Spielberg revealed his ability to tackle serious historical and social events in films such as *Schindler's List* (1993) – a story of the Holocaust – and *Amistad* (1997), on slavery in US history. He won a second Academy Award for best director for the World War 2 drama *Saving Private Ryan* (1998).

S

▶ **sponge** Classified according to the substance that makes up the supporting skeleton, the sponges include the breadcrumb sponge *Halichondria panica* (A), with a skeleton (B) composed of spicules of silicon. The purse sponge *Grantia compressa* (C) has a skeleton of calcium carbonate spicules and is in a group called calareous sponges. Two commercial sponges, *Hippospongia equina* (D) and *Euspongia officinalis* (E), have skeletons of a horny, elastic substance called spongin. After harvesting from the seabed, they are dried, beaten, and washed to remove hard debris so that the only part remaining is the skeleton.

(flowering plants), Coniferophyta (conifers), Ginkgophyta (ginkgo or maidenhair tree), Cycadophyta (cycads), and Gnetophyta (a group of cone-bearing desert plants).

sperm whale Largest of the toothed WHALES. It has a squarish head and feeds on squid and cuttlefish. Species *Physeter catodon*.

sphalerite (blende) Sulphide mineral composed of zinc sulphide (ZnS), an important source of ZINC. It has cubic system tetrahedral crystals or granular masses. It is white when pure, but more commonly yellow, black, or brown with a resinous lustre. Hardness 3.5–4; r.d. 4.

sphere Solid round figure or its surface. It is a three-dimensional geometric figure formed by the locus in space of points equidistant from a given point (the centre). The distance from the centre to the surface is the radius, r. The volume is $(4/3)\pi r^3$ and the surface area is $4\pi r^2$.

sphinx Mythical beast of the ancient world, usually represented with the head of a person and the body of a lion. In Greek mythology, OEDIPUS solved the riddle of the Sphinx of Thebes, so destroying the Spinx's evil power. Although found throughout the Middle East, images of sphinxes were especially popular in Egypt, where thousands were built. The most famous is the Great Sphinx near the PYRAMIDS at GIZA.

sphygmomanometer Instrument used to measure blood pressure. The device incorporates an inflatable rubber cuff connected to a column of mercury with a graduated scale. The cuff wraps around the upper arm and inflates to apply tension to a major artery. When the air slowly releases, blood pressure readings can be ascertained from the scale.

spice Food flavouring consisting of the dried form of various plants. Spices were used in medieval times to disguise the taste of food that was overripe or decaying, and as preservatives. They also had medicinal and religious functions.

spider Any of numerous species of terrestrial, invertebrate, ARACHNID arthropods found throughout the world in a wide variety of habitats. Spiders have an unsegmented **abdomen** attached to a **cephalothorax** by a slender **pedicel**. There are no antennae; sensory hairs are found on the appendages (four pairs of walking legs). Most species have spinnerets on the abdomen for spinning silk to make egg cases and webs. *See* illustration page 701

spider monkey Medium-sized, arboreal (tree-dwelling) MONKEY found from s Mexico to SE Brazil. It has long, spidery legs, a fully prehensile tail, and is an agile climber, using the tail as a fifth limb. It eats mainly fruit and nuts. Genera *Ateles* and *Brachyteles*.

Spielberg, Steven (1947–) US film director and producer. The success of *Jaws* (1975) established his reputation. *Close Encounters of the Third Kind* (1977) earned him an Academy Award nomination. The 'Indiana Jones' series began with *Raiders of the Lost Ark* (1981). *E.T. The Extra-Terrestrial* (1982) confirmed Spielberg's mastery of special effects. In 1984, he founded an independent production company. *Jurassic Park* (1993) is one of the highest grossing

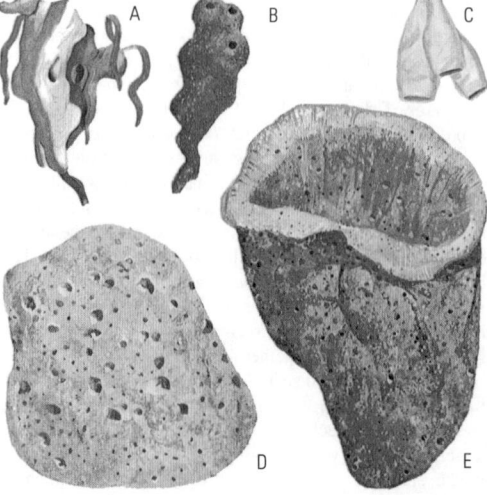

films of all time. He won a best director Academy Award for *Schindler's List* (1993), a harrowing document of the Holocaust, and another for *Saving Private Ryan* (1998).

spin (symbol *s*) In QUANTUM MECHANICS, intrinsic angular momentum possessed by some SUBATOMIC PARTICLES, atoms, and nuclei. This may be regarded by analogy as the spinning of the particle about an axis within itself. Spin is one of the quantum numbers by which a particle is specified.

spina bifida Congenital disorder in which the bones of the SPINE do not develop properly to enclose the SPINAL CORD. Surgery to close the defect is usually performed soon after birth, but this may not cure disabilities caused by the condition.

spinach Herbaceous, annual plant cultivated in areas with cool summers. Spinach is used as a culinary herb and as a vegetable. Family Chenopodiaceae; species *Spinacia oleracea*.

spinal cord Tubular, central nerve cord, lying within the SPINE. It carries sensory information to the brain. With the brain, it makes up the CENTRAL NERVOUS SYSTEM. It gives rise to the 31 pairs of spinal nerves, each of which has sensory and motor fibres, and these connect to various parts of the body.

spinal tap (lumbar puncture) Procedure for withdrawing CEREBROSPINAL FLUID from the lumbar (lower back) portion of the spinal cord for laboratory examination to aid diagnosis.

spine (vertebral column) Backbone of VERTEBRATES, extending from the skull to the tip of the tail and enclosing the SPINAL CORD. The human spine consists of 26 vertebrae, interspersed with discs of CARTILAGE. It articulates with the SKULL, ribs, and hip bones, and provides attachment points for the back muscles.

spinet Early musical instrument of the HARPSICHORD family with one keyboard and one string to each note. The musician plucked the strings with a quill or leather plectrum.

spinning Process of making thread or yarn by twisting fibres together. The fibres may be of animal, vegetable or synthetic origin. Machines developed for mechanizing the spinning process include the spinning wheel, spinning frame (invented by Richard ARKWRIGHT), spinning jenny (invented by James HARGREAVES), and spinning mule (invented by Samuel CROMPTON). Today, large machines carry out the same basic process, but at much increased speeds.

Spinoza, Baruch (1632–77) Dutch-Jewish rationalist philosopher, also known as Benedict de Spinoza. He was the son of Portuguese Jews, forced by the INQUISITION to adopt Christianity and eventually flee to the relative religious freedom of the Netherlands. Spinoza argued that all mind and matter were modes of the one key substance, which he called either God or Nature. In *Ethics* (1677), he held that free will was an illusion that would be dispelled by man's recognition that every event has a cause.

spiny anteater *See* ECHIDNA

spiritualism Belief that, at death, the personality of an individual is transferred to another plane of existence, with which communication from this world is possible. The channel of such communication is a receptive person called a **medium**. Spiritualism as a movement began in the USA in 1848.

spleen Dark-red organ located on the left side of the abdomen, behind and slightly below the stomach. It is important in both the lymphatic and blood systems, helping to process LYMPHOCYTES (white blood cells), destroying worn out or damaged ERYTHROCYTES (red blood cells) and storing iron. Removal of the spleen (splenectomy) is sometimes necessary following trauma or in the treatment of some blood disorders.

Split Major port on the Dalmatian coast of the Adriatic Sea, Croatia. Venice held Split from 1420 to 1797, when it passed to Austria. It became part of Yugoslavia in 1918. Split's industries include shipbuilding, textiles, chemicals, and cement. The conflict that followed the breakup of Yugoslavia severely disrupted the tourist industry. Pop. (2001) 173,700.

Spock, Dr Benjamin McLane (1903–98) US writer and paediatrician. Spock bestselling work *The Common Sense Book of Baby and Child Care* (1946) called on parents to trust their instincts and show their child warmth and understanding.

Spode, Josiah (1754–1827) English potter. He gave his name to Spode PORCELAIN, which became the standard English bone china. For this hybrid porcelain, he used bone ash and feldspar in the paste as well as china clay and china stone.

spoils system Form of US political patronage. The practice of appointing loyal members of the party in power to public offices was first referred to as the spoils system under Andrew JACKSON. It reached its height between c.1860 and c.1880, and declined after the Civil Service Act of 1883.

sponge Primitive, multicellular aquatic animal. A skeleton of lime, silica or spongin supports its extremely simple structure. There is no mouth, nervous system or cellular coordination, nor are there any internal organs. Sponges reproduce sexually and by asexual budding. There are c.5,000 species, including the simple sponge genus *Leucosolenia*. Length: 1mm-2m (0.4in-6ft). Phylum: Porifera.

spontaneous combustion Outbreak of fire without external application of heat. Phosphorous, for example, ignites spontaneously in air. When combustible material, such as damp hay, paper or rags, is slowly oxidized by bacteria or air, the temperature may rise to the ignition point.

spoonbill Any of several species of wading birds, each with a long bill that is flat and rounded at the tip; species are found in tropical climates. It has large wings, long legs, a short tail, and white or pinkish plumage; it feeds on small plant and animal matter. Length: 90cm (3ft). Family: Threskiornithidae.

spore Small, reproductive body that detaches from the parent organism to produce new offspring. Mostly microscopic, spores may consist of one or several cells (but do not contain an EMBRYO) and are produced in large numbers. Some germinate rapidly, others 'rest', surviving unfavourable environmental conditions. Spores are formed by FERNS, HORSETAILS, MOSSES, FUNGI, and BACTERIA.

sporophyte DIPLOID stage in the life cycle of a plant or alga. Usually, the sporophyte gives rise to HAPLOID spores which germinate to produce a haploid generation (the GAMETOPHYTE stage) that will produce the GAMETES. In FERNS, HORSETAILS, CONIFERS and ANGIOSPERMS, the diploid sporophyte is the dominant phase of the life cycle, the plant body we usually see. In mosses and liverworts, the main plant body is the gametophyte. *See also* ALTERNATION OF GENERATIONS

sprain Injury to one or more ligaments of a joint caused by sudden over-stretching. Symptoms include pain, stiffness, bruising and swelling. Treatment includes resting and supporting the affected part before gentle mobilization.

sprat (brisling) Small, herring-like commercial fish found in the N Atlantic Ocean. It is slender and silvery. Length: to 12.5cm (5in). Family Clupeidae; species *Clupea sprattus*.

spring Mechanical device designed to be elastically compressed, extended or deflected. It may be used to store energy, absorb shock, or maintain contact between two surfaces.

springbok (springbuck) Small, horned ANTELOPE native to S Africa; the national emblem of South Africa. The reddish-brown colour on the back, shades into a dark horizontal band just above the white underside. Height: to 90cm (3ft) at the shoulder. Family Bovidae; species *Antidorcas marsupialis*.

Springfield State capital of Illinois, 298km (185mi) SW of Chicago. Founded in 1818, it became state capital in 1837. The centre of a fertile farming area, Springfield's industries include machinery, electronics and fertilizers. Pop. (2000) 111,454.

spruce Various evergreen trees, related to firs, native to mountainous or cooler temperate regions of the Northern Hemisphere. Pyramid-shaped and dense, they have angular rather than flattened needles and pendulous cones. The timber is used in cabinet-making, and some species yield turpentine. Height: to 52m (170ft). Family Pinaceae; genus *Picea*.

Sputnik World's first artificial satellite, launched by the Soviet Union on October 4, 1957. Weighing 83.5kg (184lb) and with a radio transmitter, *Sputnik 1* circled the Earth for several months.

square In geometry, RECTANGLE with four sides of the same length. In arithmetic or algebra, a square is the result of multiplying a quantity by itself: the square of 3 is 9, and the square of x is x^2.

square root (symbol $\sqrt{}$) Number or quantity that must be multiplied by itself to give a specified number or quantity. The square root of 4 is 2, often written as. $\sqrt{4} = 2$. A negative number has imaginary square roots. *See also* IMAGINARY NUMBER

squash Any of several species of vine fruits of various shapes, all of which belong to the genus *Cucurbita*.

Squashes are native to the Americas, and are cultivated as vegetables. Family Cucurbitaceae.

squash Ball game played with small, round-headed rackets by two people on an enclosed, rectangular, four-walled court. The wall at the front of the court is marked with three horizontal lines at different heights. The bottom section (the telltale) up to the first line is covered with tin to make a noise when hit by the ball. When hit, the ball is out. The serve must land above the middle line (cut line). Balls hitting the wall above the third line are out. The hollow rubber ball may bounce off front, side, and back walls, but may bounce only once on the floor before it is struck. The object of each point is to make it impossible for the opponent to return the ball. Only the server scores, and the first player to reach 9 points wins the game.

squid Any of numerous species of marine CEPHALOPOD molluscs that have a cylindrical body with an internal horny plate (the **pen**) that serves as a skeleton. It has eight short, suckered tentacles surrounding the mouth, in addition to which there are two longer, arm-like tentacles that can be shot out to seize moving prey. Several species of giant squid (genus *Architeuthis*) may reach 20m (65ft) in length. Class Cephalopoda; order Teuthoidea.

squirrel Any of numerous species of primarily arboreal, diurnal rodents found throughout the world. Species of Eurasia and the Americas, such as the common grey squirrel, red squirrel, and flying squirrels, are the best known. Most species feed on nuts, seeds, fruit, insects. Most have short fur and characteristically bushy tails. Family Sciuridae.

squirrel monkey Either of at least two species of small, diurnal, arboreal MONKEYS of tropical South America; it has thick, dark fur and a long, heavy tail. *Saimiri sciureus* has a cap of greyish fur; *S. oerstedi* has a black cap and reddish fur on its back. Both are gregarious and live primarily on fruit. Length: to 40cm (16in); tail: 47cm (19in). Family Cebidae.

Sri Lanka Republic in the Indian Ocean. *See* country feature, page 704.

SS (*Schutzstaffeln*, guards unit) Chief paramilitary force of Nazi Germany. It was originally Adolf HITLER's bodyguard but expanded after 1928, under Heinrich HIMMLER, to become the Nazi Party militia and internal police force. With its distinctive black uniform, the SS controlled the GESTAPO and the SD (security organization). It ran the CONCENTRATION CAMPS and, from 1936, controlled the police. After the outbreak of war it formed its own fighting units, notorious for their ferocity, known as the Waffen SS.

Staël, (Anne-Louise-Germaine), Madame de (1766–1817) French writer. One of the most influential intellectual figures of her time, she published two proto-feminist novels, *Delphine* (1802) and *Corinne* (1807), but is best known for her works of social and aesthetic philosophy. They include *A Treatise on the Influence of the Passions upon the Happiness of Individuals and of Nations* (1796), a key text of ROMANTICISM.

Staffordshire County in W central England. The terrain consists of rolling hills with moorlands in the N. The region is drained chiefly by the River Trent. The county is largely industrial. It includes the Potteries around STOKE ON TRENT and the Black Country, one of the great industrial hubs of England. Stafford (2001 pop. 120,653) is the county town. Area: 2,716sq km (1,049sq mi). Pop. (2001) 806,737.

stag beetle Large, brown or black BEETLE of Eurasian oak forests; the male bears large antler-like mandibles. The larvae feed on rotten wood. Length: to 8cm (3in). Family Lucanidae; species *Lucanus cervus*.

stained glass Coloured glass used for decorative, often pictorial effect in windows. In its purest form, stained glass is made by adding metal-oxide colouring agents during the manufacture of glass. Shapes cut from the resulting sheets are then arranged to form patterns or images. These shapes are joined and supported by flexible strips of lead that form dark, emphatic contours. Details are painted onto the glass surfaces in liquid enamel and fused on by heat.

stainless steel Group of iron alloys that resist corrosion. Besides carbon, found in all steels, stainless steels contain from 12% to 25% chromium. This makes the steel stainless by forming a thin, protective oxide coating on the surface.

▲ **squash** Cultivated since prehistoric times, the many varieties of edible squash include the winter squash (*Cucurbita maxima*) shown here. Squash grow in a wide range of colours and shapes. There are also several varieties of inedible squash, which can be dried and put to different uses, serving, for example, as bowls or cups.

▲ **squirrel monkey** Found in many forested areas of South America, common squirrel monkeys (*Saimiri sciureus*) spend most of their time in the treetops, feeding on fruit and nuts as well as insects, eggs and young birds. However, they are also known to feed on the ground and to make bold raids on areas of cultivated fruit. Lively and friendly, they commonly live in groups of up to 30 individuals and sleep huddled together on large tree branches. Sometimes they join into large bands numbering several hundred.

S

INTERNET

Sputnik
▶ www.hq.nasa.gov/office/
pao/History/sputnik

Sri Lanka
▶ www.lanka.net/home/

Most also contain nickel. Other metals and non-metals may be added to give the steel particular properties.

stalactite Icicle-like formation of CALCIUM CARBONATE found hanging from the roofs of CAVES. It is made by the precipitation of LIMESTONE from water that seeps into limestone caves.

stalagmite Deposit of crystalline CALCIUM CARBONATE rising from the floor of a cavern, and formed by dripping water that seeps into limestone CAVES.

Stalin, Joseph (1879–1953) (Joseph Vissarionovich Dzhugashvili) Leader of the Soviet Union (1924–53). He supported LENIN and the BOLSHEVIKS from 1903, adopting the name Stalin ('man of steel') while editing *Pravda*, the party newspaper. Exiled to Siberia (1913–17), Stalin returned to join the RUSSIAN REVOLUTION (1917), and became secretary of the central committee of the party in 1922. On Lenin's death in 1924, he achieved supreme power through his control of the party organization. Stalin outmanoeuvred rivals such as TROTSKY and BUKHARIN and drove them from power. From 1929, he was virtually dictator. Stalin enforced collectivization of agriculture and intensive industrialization, suppressing all opposition and, in the

1930s, he exterminated all possible opponents in a series of purges of political and military leaders. During World War 2, Stalin controlled the armed forces and negotiated skilfully with the Allied leaders, CHURCHILL and ROOSEVELT. After the war he reimposed severe repression and forced puppet communist governments on the states of Eastern Europe.

Stalingrad *See* VOLGOGRAD

Stalingrad, Battle of (1942–43) Decisive conflict marking the failure of the German invasion of the Soviet Union during World War 2. The city (now VOLGOGRAD) withstood a German siege from August 1942 to February 1943, when the German 6th Army under Friedrich von Paulus, with no prospect of relief, surrendered to the Russian General ZHUKOV. Total casualties at Stalingrad exceeded 1.5 million.

stamen Pollen-producing male organ of a FLOWER. It consists of an ANTHER, in which POLLEN is produced, on the end of a stalk-like **filament**. The arrangement and number of stamens is important in the classification of flowering plants.

Stamp Act (1765) First direct tax levied on the American colonies by the British government. Introduced to raise revenue for the defence of the colonies, it required a special

---

SRI LANKA

The Democratic Socialist Republic of Sri Lanka is an island nation, sometimes called the 'pearl of the Indian Ocean'. It lies on the same continental shelf as India, separated by the shallow Palk Strait. Most of the land is low-lying but, in the s-central part of Sri Lanka, the land rises to a mountain massif. The nation's highest peak is Pidurutalagala (2,524m [8,281ft]). The nearby Adam's Peak, at 2,243m [7,359ft], is a place of pilgrimage. The sw is also mountainous, with long ridges.

Around the s-central highlands are broad plains, while the Jaffna Peninsula in the far north is made of limestone. Cliffs overlook the sea in the sw, while elsewhere lagoons line the coast. Forests cover nearly two-fifths of the land, with open grasslands in the E highlands. Farmland, including pasture, covers another two-fifths of the country.

CLIMATE

The w part of Sri Lanka has a wet equatorial climate. Temperatures are high and the rainfall is heavy. The wettest months are May and October – the advance and the retreat of the summer monsoon. E Sri Lanka is drier.

HISTORY

The ancestors of the SINHALESE people settled on the island around 2,400 years ago. They pushed the Veddahs, descendants of the earliest inhabitants, into the interior. The Sinhalese founded the city of Anuradhapura in 437 BC; it acted as their capital and a centre of THERAVADA Buddhism until the arrival of the Tamils in the 8th century AD. The Sinhalese and Tamils fought until the 11th century, when the Tamil CHOLA dynasty conquered the island and the Sinhalese were gradually forced south.

The Portuguese landed in 1505 and formed coastal settlements. In 1658 Portuguese lands passed to the Dutch EAST INDIA COMPANY. In 1796 the British captured the Dutch colonies, and in 1802 Ceylon became a Crown Colony. In 1815 Britain captured KANDY. Colonial settlers developed plantations. In 1948 Ceylon achieved self-government within the Commonwealth.

POLITICS

In the late 1950s, following the declaration of Sinhalese as the official language, communal violence flared between Tamils and Sinhalese. In 1958 Prime Minister Solomon BANDARANAIKE was assassinated. In 1960 his widow, Sirimavo BANDARANAIKE, became the world's first woman prime minister. Following a brief period in opposition, she was re-elected in 1970. In 1972 Ceylon became the independent republic of Sri Lanka ('Resplendent Island')

Conflict between Tamils and Sinhalese continued in the 1970s and 1980s. In 1987, India helped to engineer a ceasefire. Indian troops arrived to enforce the agreement. They withdrew in 1990 after failing to subdue the main guerrilla group, the TAMIL TIGERS, who wanted an independent Tamil homeland in northern Sri Lanka. In 1993, the country's president, Ranasinghe

AREA 65,610sq km
[25,332sq mi]
POPULATION 20,926,000
CAPITAL (POPULATION)
Colombo (642,000)
GOVERNMENT Multiparty republic
ETHNIC GROUPS Sinhalese 74%, Tamil 18%,
Moor 7%
LANGUAGES Sinhala and Tamil (both official)
RELIGIONS Buddhism 70%, Hinduism 15%,
Christianity 8%, Islam 7%
CURRENCY Sri Lankan rupee = 100 cents

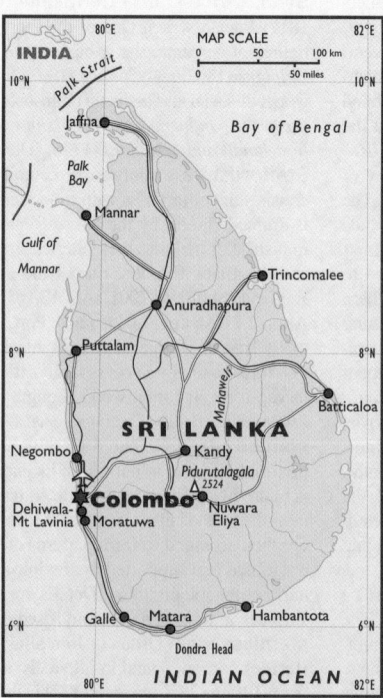

Premadasa, was assassinated by a suspected Tamil separatist. A ceasefire was signed in May 1993, but fighting soon broke out. In 1995, government forces captured Jaffna, stronghold of the 'Liberation Tigers of the Tamil Eelam' (LTTE).

The 1998 bombing of the Temple of the Tooth in Kandy created outrage among Sinhalese Buddhists, who believe that the temple's treasured tooth belonged to Buddha. This led to rioting, provoked President Chandrika Kumaratunga to ban the LTTE, and led to some of the fiercest fighting in the civil war including several suicide bombings. The government lost most of the gains it had made in the mid-1990s. A long-term ceasefire agreement was signed in 2002.

In 2004 Sri Lanka was hit by a TSUNAMI, which killed more than 30,000 people. In 2005 elections Mahinda Rajapakse became president and promised to end the Tamil conflict. Violence intensified in 2006-7 as both sides openly violated the ceasefire. In 2008 the government formally abandoned the ceasefire agreement.

ECONOMY

The World Bank classifies Sri Lanka as a 'low-income' developing country. Agriculture employs around a third of the workforce, coconuts, rubber and tea are the cash crops. Rice is the chief food crop. Cattle, water buffalo and goats are the chief farm animals, while fish provide another source of protein. Manufacturing is mainly the processing of agricultural products and textile production. The leading exports are clothing and accessories, gemstones, tea and rubber.

S

stamp on all printed material, including newspapers and legal documents. It roused widespread opposition and led to the Stamp Act Congress (1765), at which representatives of nine colonies met in New York City, and resolved that only the colonies could tax themselves. It was repealed in 1766.

standard deviation (symbol σ or *s*) In statistics, a measure of deviation of observed data or scores from the MEAN. A small standard deviation indicates that observations cluster around the mean, while a large one indicates that the data are spread far from the mean. The standard deviation is equal to the SQUARE ROOT of the **variance** (the mean of the sum of the squared differences of the data points from the mean).

standard temperature and pressure (STP) (normal temperature and pressure) In chemistry and physics, normal conditions for measurements, especially when comparing the volumes of gases. It is a temperature of 273K or 0°C (32°F), and a pressure: 1 standard atmosphere (101,325 pascals).

standing wave In physics, a wave in which the points of maximum vibration (the **antinodes**) and the points of no vibration (the **nodes**) do not move. A standing wave forms by the interference of waves of equal frequency and intensity travelling in opposite directions.

Stanford-Binet scale Most commonly used English-language APTITUDE TEST for measuring children's IQ. It was formulated (1916) at Stanford University, California.

Stanislavsky, Konstantin (1863–1938) (Konstantin Sergeievich Alekseiev) Russian actor, director, and teacher. Stanislavsky's theory of drama, as described in *My Life In Art* (1924), stressed the value of the ensemble and a naturalistic approach, with each actor making emotional contact with their character. *See also* ACTORS' STUDIO

Stanley (Port Stanley) Capital and chief port of the FALKLAND ISLANDS, on East Falkland. Originally called Port William, it became capital of the Falkland Islands in 1843. In 1982, it was captured by the Argentinians, precipitating the FALKLANDS WAR. The British Army have maintained a base here since 1983. Pop. (2001) 1989.

Stanley, Sir Henry Morton (1841–1904) British-US explorer of Africa, b. Wales. He emigrated to the USA at the age of 16. He became a journalist and was commissioned by the *New York Herald* to lead an expedition in search of David LIVINGSTONE in E Africa. The pair met in 1871. On a second expedition, Stanley led a large party from the E African lakes down the River Congo to the W coast. He returned to the area (1880) as an agent for King LEOPOLD II, and in 1887–89 led an expedition supposedly to rescue Emin Pasha from the Sudan and pressed on, with heavy losses, to the Indian Ocean.

staphylococcus Spherical bacterium that grows in grape-like clusters and is found on the skin and mucous membranes of human beings and other animals. Pathogenic staphylococci cause a range of local or generalized infections, including PNEUMONIA and SEPTICAEMIA. They may be destroyed by ANTIBIOTICS, although some strains have become resistant.

star Self-luminous ball of gas, the radiant energy of which is produced by fusion reactions, mainly the conversion of hydrogen into helium. The temperatures and luminosities of stars are prescribed by their masses. The most massive stars are about 100 solar masses (a mass a hundred times greater than the Sun). Large stars are luminous and hot, and therefore appear blue. Medium-sized stars are yellow, while small stars are a dull red. The smallest stars contain less than one-twentieth of a solar mass. Stars form when a cloud of gas and dust collapses under its own gravity. As the cloud collapses, atoms collide and generate heat. This process continues until the heat generated causes nuclear FUSION reactions, converting hydrogen to helium. The reactions from the core throw out radiation, which prevents further collapse. This stage (the **main sequence** phase) is the longest in a star's lifetime. Eventually the mainly hydrogen core of the star is depleted, and fusion can no longer occur. With the central energy source removed, the core collapses under gravity, and heats itself further until hydrogen fusion is able to occur in a spherical shell surrounding the core. As this change takes place, the outer layers of the star expand considerably, and the star becomes either a **red giant**, or in the most massive stars, a **supergiant**. During this phase, the core

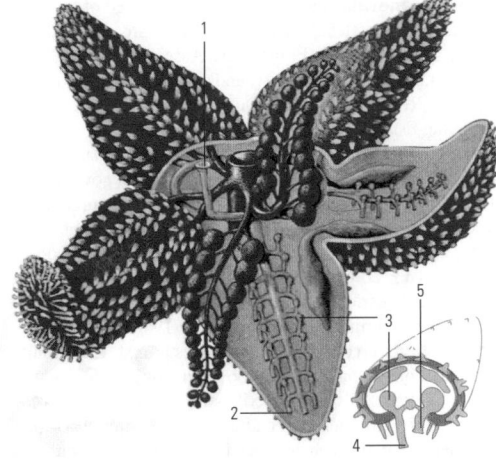

can reach temperatures of 100 million K, hot enough for fusion of helium to carbon. When this second process of fusion finishes, the core collapses again and heats up. In low-mass stars, the temperature will not rise sufficiently for carbon fusion to take place and the red giant loses its outer layers, leaving a WHITE DWARF. In high-mass stars, carbon fusion is initiated, converting the carbon into elements with relative atomic masses close to that of iron. At this stage, no further fusion is possible and the core collapses explosively, throwing off outer layers in a SUPERNOVA explosion. The resulting super-dense core forms either a NEUTRON STAR or BLACK HOLE. *See also* BINARY STAR

starch CARBOHYDRATE stored in many plants and providing about 70% of human food in such forms as rice, potatoes, and cereals. Animals and plants convert it to GLUCOSE for energy (RESPIRATION). Consisting of linked glucose units, starch exists in two forms: **amylose**, in which the glucose chains are unbranched; and **amylopectin**, in which they are branched. It is made commercially from cereals, maize, potatoes, and other plants, and used in the manufacture of adhesives and foods.

Star Chamber English court of the 15th to 17th centuries, named after its meeting place in Westminster. It arose as a judicial branch of the Royal Council, which received petitions from subjects and tried offences against the Crown. It was efficient and well regarded under the early TUDORS, but lacked mechanisms to prevent abuses. Court sessions were held in secret, without juries or witnesses, and their decision was final. Later monarchs abused its powers in an increasingly arbitrary and oppressive fashion, and it was used by CHARLES I simply to attack his political opponents. It was dissolved in 1641.

starfish Any marine ECHINODERMS with a central disc body and a five-rayed symmetry resulting in five to 40 radiating arms. The mouth is on the underside of the disc and the stomach can be extruded to digest other echinoderms and shellfish. Calcareous spines are embedded in the skin. Starfish move by means of tube feet. Class Asteroidea.

Stark, Dame Freya Madeline (1893–1993) British explorer and writer, b. France. Stark travelled widely in the Middle East, especially Arabia, and gained fame with her classics of travel literature. *The Valley of the Assassins* (1934) describes her journeys in Iran. Stark's travels in the Hadramaut (Yemen) were recorded in *The Southern Gates of Arabia* (1936).

starling Any of several species of small, aggressive birds found throughout the world. The common Eurasian starling, *Sturnus vulgaris*, is mottled black and brown. It feeds on the ground on insects and fruit, often damaging crops. Length: to 36cm (14in). Family Sturnidae.

Star of David (Shield of David) Six-pointed device formed by opposing two equilateral triangles. Known in Hebrew as *Magen David* or *Mogen David*, it was used as an emblem or magic sign by pagans, Christians, Muslims, and gradually found its way into JUDAISM as a cabbalistic sign. It appears on the flag of the modern state of ISRAEL.

State, US Department of US government department that conducts foreign policy. It is the oldest federal government department, created in 1789, and the Secretary of State (foreign minister) is a senior member of the Cabinet.

◀ **starfish** A starfish feeds by surrounding its prey, eventing its stomach through its mouth and partially digesting the food, which is then taken back into the stomach extensions (red). It moves by means of a water-vascular system (blue) unique to echinoderms. Water enters through the sieve plate (1), and is drawn by tiny hairs through the five radial canals into the many pairs of tube feet (2), armed with suckers. When the ampulla (3) of each tube foot contracts, water is forced into the foot (illustrated in cross-section), which extends (4) and allows attachment to the hard rock. Muscles in the foot then shorten it (5), forcing water back into the ampulla and drawing the starfish forward.

S

▲ **starling** With the brightest plumage of its family, the superb starling (*Spreo superbus*) lives in East Africa. Like the other starlings, it is noisy and bold and lives in large colonies, often near villages and towns. In general, the starling family (Sturnidae) is highly adaptable – the common starling spread throughout North America within 80 years of its arrival (1890).

▲ **Statue of Liberty** A huge copper monument at the mouth of New York City harbour, the Statue of Liberty has become a symbol of the United States. From the base of the pedestal to the top of the torch, it is 93m (300ft) high. In the crown is an observation deck. The statue is inscribed with *The New Colossus*, a sonnet by Emma Lazarus: 'Give me your tired, your poor, your huddled masses, yearning to breathe free...' Lazarus called the statue 'The Mother of Exiles'.

S

States-General National assembly composed of separate divisions, or 'estates', each historically representing a different social class. In France, the Assembly divided into three estates – clergy, nobility, and commoners – before the FRENCH REVOLUTION. The Dutch parliament still retains the name Estates-General.

states' rights In the USA, the doctrine that the states have authority in matters not delegated to the federal government. The controversy between federal and state jurisdiction reached a peak with John C. CALHOUN's interpretation that a state could refuse to obey a federal law it deemed unconstitutional. This led to the Nullification Crisis (1832) and contributed to secession and the CIVIL WAR. It was also an issue during the civil rights' movement of the 1950s and 1960s.

static electricity ELECTRIC CHARGES at rest. Electrically charged objects have either too many or too few ELECTRONS. COULOMB's law describes the forces that charged objects have on each other and relates the force to their charge and the distance between them. Static electricity can be produced by friction. Electrons may then jump off as a spark, shocking anyone touching the object. Static electricity is used in xerography, the most common form of photocopying. Lightning is a larger result of static electricity. This form of electricity is studied in **electrostatics**.

statics Branch of MECHANICS that deals with the action of forces on objects at rest. Its topics include: finding the resultant (net) of two or more forces, centres of gravity, moments, and stresses and strains. *See also* DYNAMICS

statistical mechanics Branch of physics that studies large-scale properties of matter based on the statistical laws of large numbers. The large number of molecules in such a system allows the use of statistics to predict the probability of finding the system in any state. The ENTROPY (disorder or randomness) of the system relates to its number of possible states; a system left to itself will tend to approach the most probable distribution of energy states. *See also* THERMODYNAMICS

statistics Science of collecting and classifying numerical data. Statistics can be **descriptive** (summarizing the data obtained) or **inferential** (leading to conclusions or inferences about larger numbers of which the data obtained are a sample). Inferential statistics are used to give a greater degree of confidence to conclusions, since statistics make it possible to calculate the probability that a conclusion is in error.

Statue of Liberty Large, copper statue of a woman, standing on Liberty Island, New York City harbour. A symbol of US democracy, it was a gift from France, and was built (1876) to commemorate the centenary of US independence. It was designed by BARTHOLDI on an iron framework designed and built by Gustave Eiffel. The statue's official name is *Liberty Enlightening the World*. It stands 45m (150ft) tall to the top of the torch in the goddess's raised right hand.

status In western sociology, a person's social position in a hierarchically arranged society, based on factors including lifestyle, prestige, income, and education. Status can be inherited (**ascribed** status) or achieved by the acquisition of socially enviable possessions (**status symbols**), which is termed **achieved** status.

steady-state theory Cosmological theory proposed (1948) by Austrian astronomers Hermann Bondi and Thomas Gold, and further developed by Fred HOYLE and others. According to this theory, the UNIVERSE has always existed; it had no beginning and will continue forever. Although the universe is expanding, it maintains its average density – steady-state – through the continuous creation of new matter. Most cosmologists now reject the theory because it cannot explain BACKGROUND RADIATION or the observation that the appearance of the universe changes with time.

stealth technology Methods used to render an aircraft nearly invisible, primarily to radar or heat detection. To achieve 'invisibility', a stealth aircraft must have sympathetic airframe design (all radar-reflecting 'hard' edges smoothed away), engine exhaust-dampers that mask and disperse jet efflux, and radar absorbent material that 'holds' electronic emissions rather than reflecting them. This coating has to be regularly applied, since it is sensitive to water and wear. The US Lock-

heed F-117A was the first 'stealth' aircraft to enter frontline service (1983), followed a decade later by the Northrop B-2.

steam engine ENGINE powered by steam. Steam, generated by heating water, is used to produce movement. In some engines, the steam forces pistons to move along cylinders. This results in a reciprocating (back-and-forth) motion. A mechanism usually changes this into rotary motion. Steam LOCOMOTIVES use reciprocating engines. Steam TURBINES are engines that produce rotary motion directly by using the steam to turn sets of fan-like wheels. In any steam engine, some of the HEAT used to turn water into steam in a boiler converts into energy of motion. The heat may be produced by burning fuel in a FURNACE, or may come from a NUCLEAR REACTOR. The first steam engine, invented by Thomas Savery in 1689, was a form of pump, used to remove water from mines. In 1712, Thomas Newcomen invented a steam-operated pump with pistons. From the 1760s, James WATT improved on Newcomen's ideas and produced more efficient steam engines. This led to the use of steam engines to power machinery in factories. In 1884, English engineer Charles Parsons invented the first practical steam turbine. His machines were so efficient that turbines soon started to replace reciprocating steam engines in power stations.

stearic acid (octadecanoic acid) Common saturated fatty acid ($C_{18}H_{36}O_2$) often found as glyceride in animal and vegetable fats. It is used in ointments, lubricants, creams, candles, and soap. Properties: r.d. 0.85; m.p. 70°C (158°F).

steel Group of iron alloys containing a little CARBON. The great strength of steel makes it an extremely important material in construction and manufacturing. The most common type is called **plain carbon** steel, because carbon is the main alloying material. This kind of steel usually contains less than 1% of carbon by weight. **Alloy** steels contain some carbon, but owe their special properties to the presence of manganese, nickel, chromium, vanadium, or molybdenum. **Low-alloy** steels, with less than 5% of alloying metals, are exceptionally strong, and are used in buildings, bridges, and machine parts. **High-alloy** steels contain more than 5% of alloying metals. This groups includes various forms of STAINLESS STEEL

Steel, Sir David Martin Scott (1938–) British politician, leader of the Liberal Party (1976–88). Steel entered Parliament in 1965, and sponsored the bill that became the 1967 Abortion Act. In 1981, he took the Liberal Party into an electoral alliance with the newly-formed SOCIAL DEMOCRATIC PARTY (SDP). In 1988, the two parties merged to form the LIBERAL DEMOCRATS, and Steel stood down in favour of Paddy ASHDOWN. He served (1999–2003) as Presiding Officer of the Scottish Parliament.

Steele, Sir Richard (1672–1729) English essayist and dramatist. He helped set the tone of public debate in his various publications, including most notably *The Tatler* (1709–11) and *The Spectator* (1711–12), which he co-founded with Joseph ADDISON. Of his plays, only *The Conscious Lovers* (1722) has won lasting acclaim.

Stein, Gertrude (1874–1946) US writer and critic. Stein was influential in the US expatriate community in Paris. Her prodigious, experimental output includes the novel *Three Lives* (1909) and *The Autobiography of Alice B. Toklas* (1933), a fictionalized account of her life from her lover's point of view.

Steinbeck, John (1902–68) US novelist. Steinbeck first came to notice with *Tortilla Flat* (1935), the success of which was consolidated by the novella *Of Mice and Men* (1937). Later novels include *Cannery Row* (1945), *East of Eden* (1952) and his masterpiece *The Grapes of Wrath* (1939), which earned him a Pulitzer Prize and a National Book Award. He received the 1962 Nobel Prize in literature.

Steiner, Rudolf (1861–1925) Austrian philosopher and educator who helped to found the German THEOSOPHY movement. He later developed a philosophy of his own, called **anthroposophy**, which sought to explain the world in terms of people's spiritual nature or thinking independent of the senses.

stem Main, upward-growing part of a plant that bears leaves, buds and flowers, or other reproductive structures. In VASCULAR PLANTS, the stem contains conducting tissues (XYLEM and PHLOEM). In flowering plants, this vascular tissue is arranged in a ring (in DICOTYLEDONS) or scattered (in MONOCOTYLEDONS).

They may be modified into underground structures (RHIZOMES, TUBERS, CORMS, BULBS). Stems vary in shape and size from the thread-like stalks of aquatic plants to tree-trunks.

Stendhal (1783–1842) (Marie Henri Beyle) French novelist, whose debut work, *Armance*, appeared to critical scorn in 1827. Today, Stendhal is regarded as a major precursor of psychological realism. His masterpiece, *Scarlet and Black* (1830), focuses on Julian Sorel, an anti-hero whose ironic detachment from Parisian society satirizes 19th-century bourgeois morality. His other great work is *Charterhouse of Parma* (1839).

Stephen (1097–1154) King of England (1135–54), nephew of HENRY I. Stephen usurped the throne on Henry's death, despite an earlier oath of loyalty to Henry's daughter, Matilda. A long civil war (1139–48) began when Matilda's forces invaded. He received support from most of the English barons, who were unwilling to accept a female sovereign. Stephen was captured in 1141, but exchanged for the Duke of Gloucester. After the death of his son, Eustace, in 1153, Stephen accepted Matilda's son, the future HENRY II, as heir to the throne.

Stephen, Saint (977–1038) Stephen I of Hungary (r.1000–38), the first king of the Árpád dynasty. His chief work was to continue the Christianization of Hungary begun by his father. He was canonized in 1083.

Stephenson, George (1781–1848) English engineer, regarded as the father of the locomotive. Stephenson built his first locomotive, *Blucher*, in 1814. This locomotive, the first to have flanged wheels, ran on a tramway. His most famous locomotive, *Rocket*, was built in 1829. Reaching a top speed of 47km/h (29mph), it ran on the Liverpool to Manchester line, one of the many railway lines that he engineered.

Stephenson, Robert (1803–59) English engineer, son of George STEPHENSON. From 1827, Robert Stephenson managed his father's locomotive works. He built several railway lines and tubular bridges, including the Britannia Bridge across the Menai Strait, Wales. He served as an MP from 1847.

steppe Extensive, semi-arid plains of central Eurasia. The landscape is usually flat and open with few trees. Steppes have very cold winters and warm summers, with light rainfall in the summer and little rain in the winter. The steppe comprises three zones of vegetation: the forest steppe; the grassland prairie, which is now usually cultivated; and the non-tillable steppe, which is semi-desert and fertile only after irrigation.

stereochemistry Study of the chemical and physical properties of compounds as affected by the ways in which the atoms of their molecules are arranged in space. Such arrangements can result in two or more compounds having the same numbers and kinds of atoms but differently shaped molecules, which are called **stereoisomers**. Stereochemistry also deals with optical isomerism, in which the configuration of one molecule is the mirror image of another.

stereoscope Optical device that produces an apparently three-dimensional image by presenting two slightly different plane images, usually photographs, to each eye. Some modern stereoscopes use POLARIZED LIGHT (light waves with electromagnetic vibrations in only one direction) to project images that are viewed through polarized filters.

sterility Inability to reproduce. It may be due to INFERTILITY or, in humans and other animals, to STERILIZATION.

sterilization Surgical intervention that terminates the ability of a human or other animal to reproduce. In women, the usual procedure is tubal ligation: sealing or tying off the FALLOPIAN TUBES so that fertilization can no longer take place. In men, a VASECTOMY is performed to block the release of sperm. The term is also applied to the practice of destroying microorganisms in order to prevent the spread of infection. Techniques include heat treatment, irradiation, and the use of disinfecting agents. *See also* SEXUAL REPRODUCTION

sterling Term for British currency. It is used to distinguish the UK pound from those of other currencies and can also be used to describe the quality and standard weight of coins. The sterling silver mark on silver (the stamp of a lion *passant*) represents a purity of more than 90%.

Sterne, Laurence (1713–68) British novelist, b. Ireland. Sterne achieved immediate acclaim following the publication of the first two volumes of the novel *Tristram Shandy* (1760). Sterne's playful, anarchic experiments with form foreshadowed MODERNISM. He adopted the persona of the parson in *Tristram Shandy* for *The Sermons of Mr Yorick* (1760–69) and his second novel, *A Sentimental Journey* (1768).

sternum (breastbone) Flat, narrow bone extending from the base of the front of the neck to just below the diaphragm in the centre of the chest. The top attaches by ligaments to the collarbones and the centre part joins to the ribs by seven pairs of costal cartilages.

steroid Class of organic compounds with a basic molecular structure of 17 carbon atoms arranged in four rings. Steroids are widely distributed in animals and plants, the most abundant being the sterols, such as cholesterol. Another important group are the steroid HORMONES, including the corticosteroids, secreted by the adrenal cortex, and the sex hormones (OESTROGEN, PROGESTERONE, and TESTOSTERONE). Synthetic steroids are widely used in medicine. Athletes sometimes abuse steroids to increase their muscle mass, strength, and stamina, but there are harmful side effects. Taking steroids is illegal in sports.

stethoscope Instrument that enables an examiner to listen to the action of various parts of the body, principally the heart and lungs. It consists of two earpieces attached to flexible rubber tubes that lead to either a disc or a cone.

Stevens, Wallace (1879–1955) US poet. A lawyer and insurance company executive, his first collection of poems, *Harmonium*, appeared in 1923. His work is rich in metaphors, and he contemplates nature and society. Stevens' early poems are often set in the tropics and reflect the lushness of their location. *Collected Poems* (1954) won a Pulitzer Prize.

Stevenson, Robert Louis (1850–94) Scottish novelist, essayist, and poet. He is celebrated for his classic children's adventure stories, such as *Treasure Island* (1883) and *Kidnapped* (1886). His later work includes historical novels, such as *The Black Arrow* (1888) and *The Master of Ballantrae* (1889), as well as the psychological novel *The Strange Case of Dr Jekyll and Mr Hyde* (1886). Stevenson spent the last years of his life in Samoa, where he wrote *The Ebb-Tide* (1894).

Stewart, Jackie (John Young) (1939–) Scottish Formula 1 motor racing driver. Stewart retired from racing in 1973 after winning what was then a record 27 Grands Prix. In 1997, he established his own Formula 1 racing team.

Stewart, James Maitland (1908–97) US film actor. Stewart's roles in the Frank CAPRA comedies *You Can't Take It With You* (1938) and *Mr Smith Goes to Washington* (1939) gained plaudits and awards. Further praise followed for his performance in *It's a Wonderful Life* (1939). Stewart won a best actor Academy Award for the classic *The Philadelphia Story* (1940). He starred in three Hitchcock films: *Rope* (1948), *Rear Window* (1954) and *Vertigo* (1958). Other films include *Anatomy of A Murder* (1959), *The Man who Shot Liberty Valance* (1962), *Shenandoah* (1965) and *The Shootist* (1976).

stick insect Any of numerous species of herbivorous insects of the order Phasmida, which resemble the shape and colour of the twigs upon which they rest; known in North America as walking stick. Some lay eggs that resemble seeds. Length: to 32cm (11in). *See also* LEAF INSECT

stickleback Small fish found in fresh, brackish, and salt water. It is usually brown and green, and may be identified by the number of spines along its sides and back. The male builds a nest of water plants, and drives the female into it. He then watches the eggs and cares for the young. Length: 8–11cm (3–4.5in). The 12 or so species include the three-spined *Gasterosteus aculeatus*. Family Gasterosteidae.

Stieglitz, Alfred (1864–1946) US photographer, editor, and promoter of modern art. In 1902, Stieglitz founded the

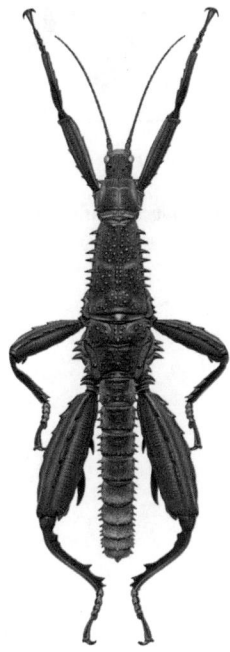

▲ **stick insect** Highly modified for the purposes of camouflage, the stick insects of New Guinea, such as *Euryacantha horrida* shown here, mimic the plants on which they live. Because they look like twigs, which are inedible, they are protected from predators. Their spindly legs are barely noticeable at rest. Some stick insects may remain motionless for hours; others sway backwards and forwards as if moving in the breeze.

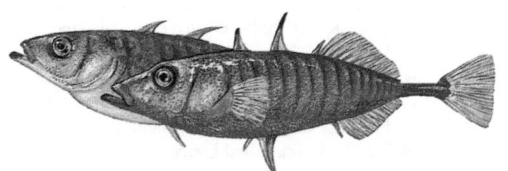

◄ **stickleback** Often found in estuaries, the males of the three-spined stickleback (*Gasterosteus aculeatus*) lure females by adopting a bright-red belly colouring and performing a complex mating dance. They also use their colouring to defend territory against other males: they adopt a threatening head-down position that displays the red belly and the iridescent blue head at the same time.

STOMACH

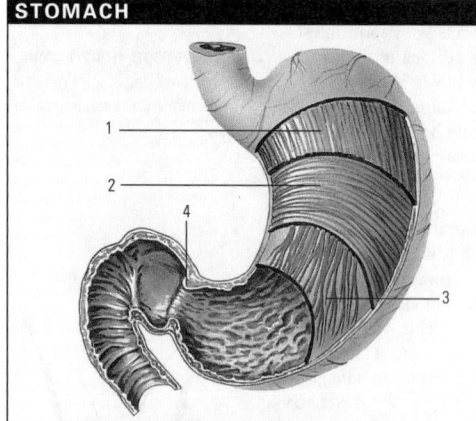

The stomach, like most of the digestive tract, is walled with involuntary (smooth) muscle. The fibres of the stomach wall are built up in three layers: longitudinal (1), circular (2) and oblique (3). These muscular layers contract in turn, producing a wave-like movement (peristalsis) and forcing food through the stomach, past the circular muscle valve sphincter (4) at the base and into the adjoining duodenum.

Photo-Secession Group. His photographs include classic portraits of his wife, Georgia O'KEEFFE, studies of Manhattan, and the cloud images known as 'equivalents'.

stigma In botany, the free upper part of the STYLE of the female organs of a flower, to which pollen grains adhere before FERTILIZATION.

Stijl, De (Dutch, 'The Style') Group of modern artists that originated in the Netherlands in 1917. They were associated with the eponymous art periodical co-founded by Piet MONDRIAN and Theo van Doesburg. De Stijl's aesthetic was an austere use of bold, vertical and horizontal lines, often breaking up primary colours. It was especially influential in architecture, informing the work of Gerrit RIETVELD.

stimulant Substance that increases mental alertness and activity. There are a number of stimulants that act on the CENTRAL NERVOUS SYSTEM, notably drugs in the amphetamine group. Many common beverages, including tea and coffee, contain small quantities of the stimulant caffeine.

stingray Any of several species of bottom-dwelling elasmobranch fish that live in marine waters and in some rivers in South America. It has a flattened body, with wing-like fins around the head. It has a long, slender tail which can inflict a venomous sting to stun prey, and can cause injury to human beings. Width: to 2.1m (7ft). Family Dasyatidae.

stinkhorn Any of several species of foul-smelling Basidiomycete fungi. At first, it resembles a small, whitish 'egg', which contains the unripe fruit body (receptacle). When ripe, the receptacle elongates to 10–20cm (4–8in) in height, rupturing the egg. It carries with it a glutinous brownish spore mass that attracts the flies that disperse the spores. Genus *Phallus*.

Stirling, James (1926–92) Scottish architect. Stirling was known for his post-modernist designs, such as the Cambridge University History Faculty building (1964–67) and the Clore Gallery extension to the TATE GALLERY, London (1987).

stoat Carnivorous mammal of the WEASEL family. Its slim body is *c*.30cm (12in) long, including the tail, and it has short legs and moves sinuously. It preys upon rabbits and smaller animals in many temperate and northern parts of the world. In the latter regions, its fur turns from red-brown and white to white in winter, when it is known as ermine. Family Mustelidae; species *Mustela ermina*.

stock (gilliflower) Annual plant native to s Europe, South Africa, and parts of Asia. Cultivated as a garden flower, it has oblong leaves and pink, purple, or white flower clusters. Height: to 80cm (30in). Family Brassicaceae/Cruciferae

stock *See* SHARES

stock exchange (stock market, securities exchange) Organized market for the buying and selling of stocks and SHARES issued by corporations. The stock exchange allows for the speculative purchase of stock in the hope that the price will increase, and thus yield a profit to the investor, or provide dividend payment giving a fair rate of return on the investment. Stockbrokers act as the agents in the purchase and selling of stocks and shares. There are exchanges in major cities throughout the world, with the largest in New York, Tokyo and London.

Stockhausen, Karlheinz (1928–2007) German composer and theorist, the most successful exponent of ELECTRONIC MUSIC. An example of his work is *Kontakte* (1960), which uses instruments with tape. His seven-part opera, *Licht,* was begun in 1977 and completed in 2003.

Stockholm Port and capital of Sweden, on Lake Mälar's outlet to the Baltic Sea. Founded in the mid-13th century, it became a trade centre dominated by the HANSEATIC LEAGUE. GUSTAVUS I (VASA) made it the centre of his kingdom, and ended the privileges of Hanseatic merchants. Stockholm became the capital of Sweden in 1436, and developed as an intellectual centre in the 17th century. Industrial development dates from the mid-19th century. Industries: textiles, clothing, paper and printing, rubber, chemicals, shipbuilding, beer, electronics, metal, machine manufacturing. Pop. (2005) 1,729,000.

Stockton-on-Tees Industrial town and unitary authority on the River Tees, NE England. The town developed around the world's first passenger rail service, the Stockton and Darlington Railway (1825). Industries: iron, engineering, chemicals. Pop. (2001) 178,405.

Stoics Followers of the school of philosophy founded (*c*.300BC) by ZENO OF CITIUM. Founded on the premise that virtue is attainable only by living in harmony with nature, stoicism stressed the importance of self-sufficiency and of equanimity in adversity. The philosophy was first expressed by Chrysippus in the 3rd century BC. It was introduced into Rome in the 2nd century BC where it found its greatest adherents: SENECA in the 1st century AD; Epictetus in the 1st and 2nd centuries; and the 2nd-century Emperor Marcus AURELIUS.

Stoke-on-Trent City and county district on the River Trent, NW STAFFORDSHIRE, W central England. Stoke is the centre of the Potteries and is noted for its manufacture of china and porcelain. Pop. (2001) 240,643.

Stoker, Bram (Abraham) (1847–1912) Irish novelist. Stoker wrote several novels and a memoir of the actor Henry Irving (1906), but he is best-remembered for the classic, gothic horror novel *Dracula* (1897).

Stokowski, Leopold (Antoni Stanislaw) (1882–1977) US conductor, b. Britain. Stokowski was director (1909–12) of the Cincinnati Symphony and conductor (1912–36) of the Philadelphia Orchestra. He became known for his individual interpretations and flexibility of approach.

stolon Modified, horizontal, underground or aerial stem growing from the basal node of a plant. Aerial stolons, also called runners, may be slender, as in a strawberry, or stiff and arching, as bramble. The stolon produces a new plant at its tip, which puts out adventitious roots to anchor itself. *See also* TUBER; VEGETATIVE REPRODUCTION

stoma In botany, pores found mostly on the undersides of leaves that allow atmospheric gases to pass in and out for RESPIRATION and PHOTOSYNTHESIS. Surrounding each stoma are two guard cells that can close to prevent excessive loss of water vapour. *See also* GAS EXCHANGE; TRANSPIRATION

stomach J-shaped organ, lying to the left and slightly below the DIAPHRAGM in human beings; one of the organs of the DIGESTIVE SYSTEM. At its upper end, it connects to the gullet (OESOPHAGUS), and at the lower end to the SMALL INTESTINE. The stomach itself is lined by three layers of muscle and a folded mucous layer that contains gastric glands. These GLANDS secrete hydrochloric acid that destroys some food bacteria and makes possible the action of pepsin, the ENZYME that digests PROTEINS. Gastric gland secretion is controlled by the sight, smell, and taste of food, and by hormonal stimuli, chiefly the HORMONE gastrin. As the food digests, it is churned by muscular action into a thick liquid state called chyme, at which point it passes into the small intestine.

stomata In botany, pores found mostly on the undersides of leaves that allow atmospheric gases to pass in and out for RESPIRATION and PHOTOSYNTHESIS. Surrounding each stoma are two guard cells that can close to prevent excessive loss of water vapour. *See also* GAS EXCHANGE; TRANSPIRATION

Stone, Oliver (1946–) US film director and screenwriter. Stone achieved commercial success with his film about the Vietnam War, *Platoon* (1987), for which he won an Academy Award for best director. Other films include *Salvador* (1986),

S

Wall Street (1987), *Talk Radio* (1988), *Born on the Fourth of July* (1989), *JFK* (1991) and *Natural Born Killers* (1994).

Stone Age Period of human evolution defined by the use of stone tools. The Stone Age dates from the earliest identifiable broken-pebble tools made by human ancestors *c.*2.5 million years ago. The period is generally considered to have ended when metal tools first became widespread during the BRONZE AGE. The Stone Age usually subdivides into the PALAEOLITHIC, MESOLITHIC, and NEOLITHIC.

stonechat Small thrush found in open heath and scrubland of Europe, Africa, and Asia. The plumage of the male is black, white, and rust-brown. Stonechats feed on the ground on insects. Species *Saxicola torquata*.

stonecrop Any plant of the genus *Sedum* of the family Crassulaceae, especially creeping sedum (*S. acre*), a succulent, low-growing plant of European origin with pungent, fleshy leaves and yellow flowers found in rocky areas.

stonefish Bottom-dwelling, marine fish that lives in tropical waters of the Indo-Pacific Ocean. It has a warty, slime-covered body and sharp dorsal spines with which it can inflict a painful, sometimes deadly, sting to human beings. Length: to 33cm (13in). Family Synancejidae; species *Synanceja verrucosa*.

stonefly (salmon fly) Soft-bodied insect with long, narrow front wings and chewing mouthparts, found throughout the world. The aquatic nymphs have branched gills, and the adults, used as bait by anglers, are brown to black. Length: 5–60mm (0.2–2.5in). Order Plecoptera.

Stonehenge Circular group of prehistoric standing stones within a circular earthwork on Salisbury Plain, S England, 13km (8mi) N of Salisbury. The largest and most precisely constructed MEGALITH in Europe, Stonehenge dates from the early 3rd millennium BC although the main stones were erected *c.*2000–1500 BC. The large standing bluestones were brought from SW Wales in *c.*2100 BC. The significance of the structure is unknown.

Stopes, Marie Charlotte Carmichael (1880–1958) English pioneer of birth control. Stopes campaigned for a more rational and open approach to contraception, establishing the first birth control clinic in Britain in 1921. She wrote *Wise Parenthood* (1918) and *Contraception: Its Theory, History and Practice* (1923, 1931).

Stoppard, Tom (1937–) English dramatist, b. Thomas Straussler. His reputation was established with *Rosencrantz and Guildenstern are Dead* (1966). Plays such as *The Real Inspector Hound* (1968) and *Jumpers* (1972) confirmed his ability to combine philosophical speculation with humour. Stoppard wrote plays for radio (*Artist Descending a Staircase*, 1973) and television (*Professional Foul*, 1977). Other plays include *Arcadia* (1993) and *The Invention of Love* (1997). Stoppard won an Academy Award for best screenplay for *Shakespeare in Love* (1998).

Storey, David (1933–) English novelist and dramatist. Storey's debut novel, *This Sporting Life* (1960), explored his favourite themes of class conflict and alienation. *Radcliffe* (1963) is perhaps his best-known work. Storey won the Booker Prize for *Saville* (1976). His plays include *Home* (1970).

stork Long-legged wading bird that lives along rivers, lakes, and marshes in temperate and tropical regions, often nesting in colonies in trees. Usually black, white and grey, storks have straight bills, long necks, robust bodies and long broad wings. They are diurnal and feed on small animals and sometimes carrion. Length: 0.8–1.5m (2.5–5ft). Family Ciconiidae.

Stowe, Harriet Beecher (1811–96) US novelist. A prolific writer, Stowe is best known for *Uncle Tom's Cabin* (1851–52), a powerful and influential anti-slavery novel.

STP *See* STANDARD TEMPERATURE AND PRESSURE

strabismus (squint) Condition in which the eyes do not look in the same direction. It may result from either disease of or damage to the eye muscles or their nerve supply, or an error of refraction within the eye.

Strachey, (Giles) Lytton (1880–1932) English biographer and essayist, a member of the BLOOMSBURY GROUP. His works include *Eminent Victorians* (1918), *Queen Victoria* (1921), and *Elizabeth and Essex* (1928). He is often credited with adding the psychological dimension to modern BIOGRAPHY.

Stradivari, Antonio (1644–1737) Italian violin-maker. Originally an apprentice to Nicolò AMATI, Stradivari perfected violin design. His instruments remain unsurpassed in brilliance of tone.

Strafford, Thomas Wentworth, 1st Earl of (1593–1641) English minister of CHARLES I. Strafford became the King's chief adviser after the death of the Duke of BUCKINGHAM and proved an extremely capable administrator as Lord President of the North (1628–33) and Lord Deputy of Ireland (1633–39). In 1639, Charles made him an Earl, but he failed to quell a Scottish rebellion (1640). Strafford was impeached by the LONG PARLIAMENT and he was executed.

Strasberg, Lee (1901–82) US theatrical director. One of the founders of the Group Theatre (1931), he began teaching a 'method' approach, based on the the teachings of STANISLAVSKY. In 1947, Strasberg and Elia KAZAN founded the ACTORS' STUDIO. As the Studio's artistic director, he was influential in shaping the careers of many leading Hollywood actors, such as Marilyn MONROE and Al PACINO.

Strasbourg City on the River Ill, capital of Bas-Rhin department and commercial capital of the Alsace region, E France. Known in Roman times as Argentoratum, the Huns destroyed the city in the 5th century. In 923, it became part of the HOLY ROMAN EMPIRE and developed into an important commercial centre, becoming a free imperial city in 1262. Strasbourg was a centre of medieval German literature, and of 16th-century Protestantism. France seized the city in 1681, Germany regained it after the FRANCO-PRUSSIAN WAR (1870–71), but France recovered it at the end of World War 1. German troops occupied the city during World War 2. The European Parliament sits in Strasbourg's Palais de l'Europe. Industries: metallurgy, oil and gas refining, machinery. Its port, on the Rhine, is France's chief grain outlet. Pop. (1999) 267,051.

Strategic Arms Limitation Talks (SALT) Two phases of talks between the USA and the Soviet Union to limit the expansion of nuclear weapons. The talks began in 1969 between Lyndon B. JOHNSON and Leonid BREZHNEV. In 1972, Richard NIXON and Brezhnev signed SALT I. This agreement limited anti-ballistic missile systems and produced an interim accord on intercontinental ballistic missiles (ICBMs). A second phase of meetings between Gerald FORD and Brezhnev resulted in an agreement (1974) to limit ballistic missile launchers. SALT II, signed in Vienna between Jimmy CARTER and Brezhnev, banned new ICBMs and limited other launchers. The Soviet invasion of Afghanistan meant the US Senate never ratified the treaty. Nevertheless, the two superpowers observed its terms until Ronald REAGAN began to increase the US nuclear arsenal. In 1986 START (Strategic Arms Reduction Talks) between Mikhail GORBACHEV and Reagan superseded SALT. START ushered in a new era of DISARMAMENT.

Stratford upon Avon Town in Warwickshire, central England. Stratford upon Avon is the birthplace of William SHAKESPEARE and home of the ROYAL SHAKESPEARE COMPANY (RSC). Industries: tourism, engineering, boatbuilding, textiles. Pop. (2001) 111,474.

Strathclyde Region in W Scotland, bounded N by the Highlands, S by the Southern Uplands, and W by the Atlantic Ocean. The capital is GLASGOW; other major towns include Paisley, Kilmarnock, Clydebank and Motherwell. The industrial heartland of Scotland, it contains half of

◄ **Stonehenge** Surrounded by a circular ditch and bank, the stones at Stonehenge, SW England, were arranged in three concentric series: the outermost is a circle of 30 upright stones linked at the top by lintel stones; the second is a circle of singular menhirs; the third is a horseshoe formed by five trilithons (two upright stones joined by a lintel) with a single upright stone (the altar stone) at the open end, facing the rising sun. It has been proposed that Stonehenge might have been an astronomical observatory or a temple, but its actual use remains uncertain.

S

INTERNET

Strauss, Johann (the Younger)
▶ www.classical.net

Strauss, Richard
▶ www.classical.net

Stravinsky, Igor Feodorovich
▶ www.ipl.org/div/mushist/twen/stravinsky.htm

S

▲ **strawberry** Intensively cultivated since the 15th century, the strawberry was brought to Europe by early explorers of the New World. The entire French strawberry industry originates from one common strawberry plant. The fruiting season is short and the fruit is easily perishable once it is picked.

Scotland's population. Sites include Loch LOMOND, Glencoe, and the islands of Mull, Arran, and Bute. The ancient British or Welsh kingdom of Strathclyde existed from the 5th to 10th centuries. Its capital was at Dumbarton. In the late 9th century, Norse raiders devastated the kingdom, and the native Welsh dynasty died out. Awarded to Scotland in 945, it was only incorporated into the Scottish kingdom in the 11th century. Industries: shipbuilding, engineering. Area: 13,529sq km (5,222sq mi) Pop. (1991) 2,248,700.

stratigraphy Branch of geology concerned with stratified or layered rocks. It deals with the correlation of rocks from different localities using fossils and distinct rock types.

stratosphere Section of the Earth's ATMOSPHERE between the troposphere and the higher mesosphere. It is *c*.40km (25mi) thick, fairly stable, and the temperature generally increases with greater height. The stratosphere contains most of the OZONE LAYER.

Strauss, Johann (the Younger) (1825–99) Austrian composer and conductor, son of Johann (1804–49), who was also a conductor and composer. He became popular for his waltzes, such as *The Blue Danube*, *Tales from the Vienna Woods* and *Wine, Women and Song*. He composed two popular operettas, *Die Fledermaus* (1874) and *The Gypsy Baron* (1885).

Strauss, Richard (1864–1949) German composer and conductor. Strauss' SYMPHONIC POEMS, such as *Don Juan* (1888), *Till Eulenspiegel* (1895), and *Also sprach Zarathustra* (1896), use brilliantly coloured orchestration for characterization. His early operas, *Salome* (1905) and *Elektra* (1909), deal with female obsession. *Der Rosenkavalier* (1911) also used the dramatic range of the female voice, but in a comic setting.

Stravinsky, Igor Feodorovich (1882–1971) Russian composer who revolutionized 20th-century music. Stravinsky studied (1907–08) with Rimsky-Korsakov. His early ballets, *The Firebird* (1910) and *Petrushka* (1911), were commissioned by Sergei DIAGHILEV for his BALLETS RUSSES. The première of the ballet *The Rite of Spring* (1913) caused a riot because of its dissonance and unfamiliar rhythms. Stravinsky turned to Russian folk themes for *The Wedding* (1923) and neo-classicism in *Pulcinella* (1920). In 1939, he moved to the USA, collaborating with George BALANCHINE on the abstract ballet *Agon* (1957). After composing *The Rake's Progress* (1951), Stravinsky experimented with serial music and TWELVE-TONE MUSIC.

strawberry Fruit-bearing plant of the rose family, common in America, Europe, and Asia. It has three-lobed leaves and clusters of white or reddish flowers. The large, fleshy fruit is dotted with seeds (pips). Family Rosaceae; genus *Fragaria*.

stream of consciousness Literary style in which the thought processes of characters are presented in the disconnected, illogical, chaotic or seemingly random way they might come to them, without the usual literary regard for narrative continuity or linear sequence. Edouard Dujardin's novel *Les Lauriers Sont Coupes* (1888) is generally regarded as the first example of the style in literature. Generally, it is associated stylistically with early MODERNISM, and in particular the writings of James JOYCE, Virginia WOOLF and William FAULKNER.

Streep, Meryl (1949–) US film actress. She is renowned for her attention to realistic characterization. After an Academy Award nomination for *The Deer Hunter* (1978), Streep won a best supporting actress Oscar for *Kramer vs. Kramer* (1979). Her performance as a Holocaust victim in *Sophie's Choice* (1982) earned her an Academy Award for best actress. She later gained Academy Award nominations for *Postcards from the Edge* (1990) and *The Bridges of Madison County* (1995).

Streisand, Barbra (1942–) US singer and actress. Streisland achieved fame with her Broadway performance in *Funny Girl* (1964, filmed 1968). She made numerous recordings and starred in such films as *Hello Dolly* (1969) and *A Star is Born* (1976). Streisland directed, produced, and starred in *Yentl* (1983) and *The Prince of Tides* (1993).

streptococcus Genus of gram-positive spherical or oval BACTERIA that grow in pairs or bead-like chains. They live mainly as parasites in the mouth, respiratory tract and intestine. Some are harmless but others are pathogenic, causing SCARLET FEVER and other infections. Treatment is with ANTIBIOTICS.

Stresemann, Gustav (1878–1929) German statesman. Stresemann was the outstanding politician of the WEIMAR REPUBLIC. He concluded the LOCARNO PACT (1925) and worked to achieve a practicable postwar settlement with Germany's former opponents under the disadvantageous terms imposed by the Treaty of VERSAILLES. Stresemann negotiated Germany's entry into the LEAGUE OF NATIONS (1926) and shared the 1926 Nobel Peace Prize with Aristide BRIAND.

stress In physics, internal tension in a material. **Tensile** stress stretches an object, **compressive** stress squeezes it and **shearing** stress twists it. Fluid stresses are called PRESSURE.

Strindberg, (Johan) August (1849–1912) Swedish dramatist and novelist. Strindberg focused on subjective, psychological experience as the location for his plays. Drawing on the insights of Henrik IBSEN and the NATURALISM of Emile ZOLA, plays such as *The Father* (1887) and *Miss Julie* (1888) take a characteristically pessimistic view of gender relations. After suffering a mental breakdown, he produced *A Dream Play* (1902) and *The Ghost Sonata* (1907), both of which prefigure the Theatre of the ABSURD and German EXPRESSIONISM.

stringed instrument Musical instrument sounded by the vibration of strings. Instruments fall into different classes, according to the action used to set the strings in motion: bowed, chiefly those of the VIOLIN family; plucked, chiefly the HARP, LUTE, and GUITAR; and plucked and struck, such as the cittern and DULCIMER.

stroboscope (strobe) Device that emits regular flashes of light. Stroboscopes usually have a calibrated scale from which the number of flashes per minute can be read. They are used in photography to make multiple exposures of moving subjects and in engineering to apparently 'slow down' or 'stop' moving objects for observation.

stroke (apoplexy) Interruption of the flow of blood to the brain. It is caused by blockage or rupture of an artery and may produce a range of effects from mild impairment to death. Conditions that predispose to stroke include atherosclerosis and HYPERTENSION. Many major strokes are prevented by treatment of risk factors, including surgery and the use of anticoagulant drugs. Transient ischaemic attacks (TIAs), or 'mini-strokes', which last less than 24 hours, are investigated to try to prevent the occurrence of a more damaging stroke.

strong nuclear force One of four FUNDAMENTAL FORCES in nature. The strongest of these forces, it binds together protons and neutrons within the NUCLEUS of an atom. Like the WEAK NUCLEAR FORCE, it operates at very short distances (a millionth of a millionth of a centimetre), and therefore occurs only within the nucleus. *See also* GRAND UNIFIED THEORY (GUT)

strontianite Carbonate mineral, strontium carbonate ($SrCO_3$). It has an orthorhombic system, massive or columnar aggregates, or hexagonal twinned crystals. It can be pale green, white, grey, yellow, or brown. It is found in veins, often in limestone. Hardness 3.5–4; r.d. 3.7.

strontium (symbol Sr) Silvery-white, metallic element of the alkaline-earth metals in Group II of the periodic table. Resembling CALCIUM physically and chemically, it occurs naturally in strontianite and celestite and is extracted by ELECTROLYSIS. It was isolated in 1808 by English chemist Sir Humphry DAVY. Strontium salts are used to colour flares and fireworks red. The isotope Sr^{90} (half-life 28 years) is a radioactive element present in fallout, from which it is absorbed into milk and bones; it is used in NUCLEAR REACTORS. Strontium salts are used in fireworks and signal flares. Properties: at.no. 38; r.a.m. 87.62; r.d. 2.554; m.p. 769°C (1,416°F); b.p. 1384°C (2,523°F).

structuralism Twentieth-century school of critical thought. Ferdinand de SAUSSURE argued that underlying the everyday use of language is a language system (*langue*), based on relationships of difference. He stressed the arbitrary nature of the relationship between the **signifier** (sound or image) and the **signified** (concept). Initially a linguistic theory, Claude LÉVI-STRAUSS and Roland BARTHES developed structuralism into a mode of critical analysis of cultural institutions and products. It is associated especially with the notion of a literary text as a system of signs. *See also* DECONSTRUCTION; SEMIOTICS

strychnine Poisonous ALKALOID obtained from the plant *Strychnos nux-vomica*. In the past, it was believed to have therapeutic value in small doses as a tonic. Strychnine poisoning causes symptoms similar to those of TETANUS, with death occurring due to spasm of the breathing muscles.

Stuart, Charles Edward (1720–88) Scottish Prince, known as 'Bonnie Prince Charlie' or the 'Young Pretender'. A grandson of the deposed JAMES II, he led the JACOBITES in the rebellion of 1745 ('the '45') on behalf of his father, James, the 'Old Pretender'. Landing in the Scottish Highlands without the hoped-for backing of France, Bonnie Prince Charlie gained the support of many clan chiefs, defeated government troops at Prestonpans, E central Scotland, and marched on London. Lacking widespread support in England, he turned back at Derby. The following year, his largely Highland force was decimated in the Battle of CULLODEN. He escaped to the continent and lived in exile until his death.

Stuart, Gilbert Charles (1755–1828) One of the foremost US portraitists of the late 18th and early 19th century. He is famous for three portraits of George WASHINGTON. These paintings are known as the 'Vaughan' type (1795), the 'Lansdowne' type (1796), and the 'Athenaeum' type (1796). The last is the model for Washington's face on the one-dollar bill.

Stuart, James Francis Edward (1688–1766) British claimant to the throne, called the 'Old Pretender'. The only son of JAMES II, his birth precipitated the GLORIOUS REVOLUTION (1688), and he was brought up in exile. On the death of his father in 1701, the JACOBITES proclaimed James king. After an abortive attempt to depose ANNE (1708) by invading from Scotland (where support for the Stuart cause was greatest), James served in the French army. The accession of GEORGE I (1714) prompted James to attempt a further unsuccessful uprising. His son was Charles STUART.

Stuart, Mary *See* MARY II

Stuarts (Stewarts) Scottish royal House, which inherited the Scottish throne in 1371 and the English throne in 1603. The Stuarts descended from Alan, whose descendants held the hereditary office of steward in the royal household. Walter (d.1326), the sixth steward, married a daughter of King Robert I, and their son, Robert II, became (1371) the first Stuart king. The throne descended in the direct male line until the death of James V (1542), who was succeeded by his infant daughter, MARY, QUEEN OF SCOTS. In 1603, her son, James VI, succeeded ELIZABETH I of England as JAMES I. His son, CHARLES I, was executed in 1649 following the English CIVIL WAR, but the dynasty recovered with the RESTORATION of Charles II in 1660. His brother, JAMES II, lost the throne in the GLORIOUS REVOLUTION (1688) and was replaced by the joint monarchy of WILLIAM III and MARY II, James' daughter. On the death (1714) of ANNE, the House of HANOVER succeeded. James STUART and Charles STUART made several unsuccessful attempts to regain the throne. *See also* JACOBITES

Stubbs, George (1724–1806) English painter and engraver. Stubbs is best-known for the book *The Anatomy of the Horse* (1766), illustrated with his own engravings. *Horses attacked by a lion* (1770) reveals a more Romantic approach.

sturgeon Large, primitive, bony fish found in temperate fresh and marine waters of the Northern Hemisphere. The ovaries of the female are the source of CAVIAR. It has five series of sharp-pointed scales along its sides, fleshy whiskers and a tapering, snout-like head. Family Acipenseridae; species Atlantic sturgeon (*Acipenser sturio*) length: to 3.3m (11ft), weight: to 272kg (600lb). The Eurasian freshwater sturgeon is also called beluga.

Sturm und Drang ('Storm and Stress') German literary movement that takes its name from a play (1776) by F.M. von Klinger. Sturm and Drang rejected the prevailing neoclassicism in favour of subjectivity, artistic creativity, and the beauty of nature. Associated principally with the early works of Johann Wolfgang von GOETHE, Friedrich SCHILLER, and Johann Gottfried von HERDER, it is seen as a precursor of ROMANTICISM. The movement influenced HAYDN's group of minor-key symphonies.

Stuttgart Capital of Baden Württemberg, SW Germany, on the River Neckar. It was founded in *c*.950 when a German Duke, Liutolf, set up a *stuttgarten* (stud farm). The capital of the kingdom of Württemberg (1495–1806), Stuttgart's industrial base expanded rapidly during the 19th century. Historically, it is associated with motor vehicle construction; the Daimler-Benz factory is the world's oldest car-plant (1890). Other industries: electronics, photographic equipment, publishing, wine and beer. Although bombed during World War 2, much of Stuttgart's famous architecture has survived. Pop. (1999) 581,200.

Stuyvesant, Peter (1610–72) Dutch colonial administrator. Stuyvesant became governor of the Caribbean islands of Curaçao, Bonaire, and Aruba in 1643, and in 1647 he became director-general of all the Dutch territories, including New Amsterdam (later New York City). He ended Swedish influence in Delaware in 1655, and ruled until the colony was taken over by the English in 1664 and renamed New York.

style In botany, part of a flower – the tube that connects the pollen-receiving STIGMA at its tip to the ovary at its base.

Styx In Greek mythology, the river across which Charon ferried the souls of the dead on their journey from the world of the living to the underworld.

subatomic particles Particles smaller than ATOMS or are of the types that make up atoms. They can be divided into two groups: the HADRONS, such as PROTONS and NEUTRONS, which can be further subdivided; and ELEMENTARY PARTICLES, such as QUARKS and ELECTRONS, which cannot be further divided.

sublimation Direct change from solid to gas, without an intervening liquid phase. Most substances can sublimate at certain pressures, but usually not at atmospheric pressure. *See also* CONDENSATION; EVAPORATION

submarine Seagoing warship capable of travelling both on and under the water. Experimental submarines were used in warfare from the late 18th century. Technical advances in the late 19th century led to the adoption of underwater craft by the world's navies. Early submarines were essentially surface ships with a limited ability to remain submerged. Once underwater, they used battery-powered electric motors for propulsion and, with a limited air supply, were soon forced to surface. Submerging is accomplished by letting air out of internal ballast tanks; trimming underwater is done by regulating the amount of water in the ballast tanks with pumps; and surfacing is accomplished by pumping ('blowing') the water out of the tanks. The most modern submarines use nuclear power, which eliminates the need to surface while on operations.

submersible Small craft for underwater exploration, research, or engineering. The **bathyscape**, invented in the 1940s by Swiss scientist Auguste Piccard, had a spherical chamber attached to a much larger hull, which functioned as a buoyancy control device. From the late 1950s, a new generation of submersibles evolved for engineering and research work. A typical craft has a spherical passenger capsule capable of withstanding water pressure down to *c*.3,600m (12,000ft). Attached to this is a structure containing batteries, an electric motor with propeller, lighting, a mechanical arm for gathering samples, and other technical equipment.

subpoena (Lat. 'under penalty') In law, an order that commands a person to appear before a court or judicial officer to give evidence at a specific time and place.

subsidies Government assistance to individuals or organizations to benefit the public. Subsidies are usually intended to promote growth or stability, generating higher outputs of certain products, or maintaining or reducing prices. They can be **direct** (for example, cash payments) or **indirect** (for example, when the government buys goods at artificially high prices or grants tax concessions). They are often used to protect industries by enabling them to offer more competitive prices. Commonly subsidized enterprises include agriculture, business expansion, housing, and regional development.

substitution reaction Chemical reaction in which one atom or group of atoms replaces (usually in the same structural position) another group in a molecule or ion.

succession Orderly change in plant and animal life in a biotic community over a long time period. It is the result of modifications in the community environment. The process ends in establishment of a stable ECOSYSTEM (**climax community**).

▲ **Strauss** Richard Strauss began composing at the age of six. He devoted the early part of his career to the development of the symphonic poem. Pieces such as *Tod und Verklärung* (1889) betray the Romantic influences of Wagner and Liszt. In the early 20th century, Strauss concentrated on opera. With the help of the poet Hugo von Hofmannsthal, operas such as *Ariadne auf Naxos* (1912) expanded the emotional range of operatic drama.

INTERNET

Stuart, Gilbert Charles
▶ www.nga.gov

Stubbs, George
▶ www.tate.org.uk
▶ www.nationalgallery.org.uk

succulent Plant that stores water in its tissues to resist periods of drought. Usually PERENNIAL and evergreen, they have bodies made up of water storage cells, which give them a fleshy appearance. A well-developed CUTICLE and low rate of daytime TRANSPIRATION also conserve water. Succulent plants include CACTUS, LILY, and STONECROP.

sucker Any of several species of freshwater fish found from N Canada to Mexico. A bottom-grubber similar to a minnow, it has a thick-lipped mouth for feeding by suction. Length: to 66cm (26in); weight: to 5.4kg (12lb). Family Catostomidae.

Sucre City in s central Bolivia and the legal capital of BOLIVIA, the seat of government being LA PAZ. Known successively as La Plata, Chuguisaca, and Charcas, Sucre was renamed in 1839 after the revolutionary leader and first president of Bolivia, Antonio José de SUCRE. It is a commercial and distribution centre for the surrounding farming region. Industries: cement, oil refining. Pop. (2001 est.) 202,700.

Sucre, Antonio José de (1795–1830) South American revolutionary leader, first president of Bolivia (1826–28). De Sucre joined the fight for independence in 1811, and played a key role in the liberation of Ecuador, Peru, and Bolivia, winning the final, decisive Battle of Ayacucho (1824). With Simon BOLÍVAR's support, he became president of Bolivia.

Native opposition forced his resignation and he was assassinated while working to preserve the unity of Colombia.

sucrose ($C_{12}H_{22}O_{11}$) Common, white, crystalline SUGAR, a disaccharide sugar consisting of linked GLUCOSE and FRUCTOSE molecules. It occurs in many plants, but its principal commercial sources are SUGAR CANE and SUGAR BEET. It is widely used for food sweetening and making preserves.

Sudan Republic in NE Africa. See country feature

sudden infant death syndrome See COT DEATH

Sudetenland Border region of N Bohemia (Czech Republic), including part of the Sudeten Mountains. Largely populated by Germans, Nazi-inspired agitation in the 1930s demanded its inclusion in Germany. Britain and France gave approval for its annexation in the MUNICH AGREEMENT (1938). After World War 2, it was restored to Czechoslovakia, and the German population was expelled.

Suez Canal Waterway in Egypt linking Port Said on the Mediterranean Sea with the Gulf of Suez and the Red Sea. The 169km (105mi) long canal was planned and built (1859–69) by the Suez Canal Company under the supervision of French canal builder Ferdinand de LESSEPS. In 1875, the British government became the major shareholder in the company. In 1955, more than 120 million tonnes of merchandise

SUDAN

The Republic of the Sudan is the largest country in Africa. It extends from the arid SAHARA in the N to an equatorial swamp region (the *Sudd*) in the s.

Much of the land is flat, but there are mountains in the north east and south east; the highest point is Kinyeti, at 3,187m [10,456ft]. The River Nile (*Bahr el Jebel*) runs s to N, entering Sudan as the White Nile, converging with the Blue Nile at KHARTOUM, and flowing north to Egypt.

Khartoum is prone to summer dust storms (*haboobs*). From the bare deserts of the N, the land merges into dry grasslands and savanna. Dense rainforests grow in the s.

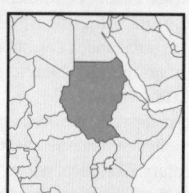

CLIMATE

N Sudan is hot and arid. The centre has an average annual rainfall of 100 to 510mm [4–32in], while the tropical s has between 810 and 1,400mm [32–55in] of rain per year.

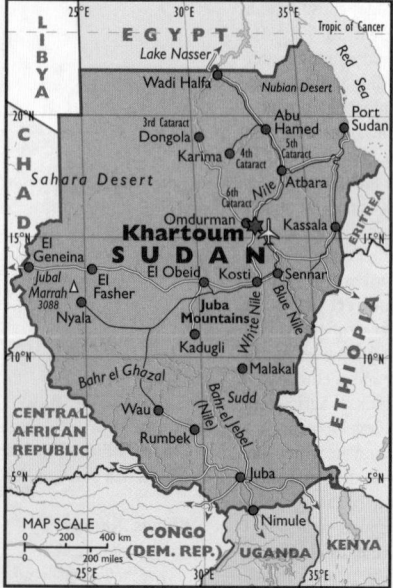

HISTORY

One of the earliest civilizations in the Nile region of N Sudan was Nubia, which came under the rule of Ancient EGYPT around 4,000 years ago. Another Nubian civilization, called KUSH, developed from *c*.1000 BC and survived until *c*.AD 350. At its height Kush took control of Egypt, and some of the later dynasties of Pharaohs were Nubian. Christianity was introduced to northern Sudan in the 6th century AD. From the 13th to 15th centuries, northern Sudan came under Muslim control, and Islam became the dominant religion.

In 1821 MUHAMMAD ALI's forces occupied Sudan. Anglo-Egyptian forces, led by General GORDON, attempted to extend Egypt's influence into the s. Muhammad Ahmad led the MAHDI uprising, which briefly freed Sudan from Anglo-Egyptian influence. In 1898 General KITCHENER's forces defeated the Mahdists, and in 1899 Sudan became Anglo-Egyptian Sudan, governed jointly by Britain and Egypt.

POLITICS

After Sudan's independence in 1952 the s Sudanese, who are predominantly Christians or followers of traditional beliefs, revolted against the dominance of the Muslim north, and civil war broke out. In 1958, the military seized power. Civilian rule was re-established in 1964 but overthrown again in 1969, when Gaafar Muhammad Nimeri seized control. In 1972 s Sudan received considerable autonomy, but unrest persisted.

In 1983 the imposition of strict Islamic law sparked off further conflict between the government and the Sudan People's Liberation Army (SPLA) in the s. In 1985 Nimeri was deposed and a civilian government installed. In 1989 the military, led by Omar Hassan Ahmed al-Bashir, established a Revolutionary Command Council. Civil war continued in the s. In 1996 Bashir became president after rigged elections. The National Islamic Front (NIF) dominated the government and was believed to have strong links with Iranian terrorist groups.

AREA 2,505, 813sq km [967,494sq mi]
POPULATION 39,379,000
CAPITAL (POPULATION)
Khartoum (2,742,000)
GOVERNMENT Military regime
ETHNIC GROUPS
Black 52%, Arab 39%, Beja 6%, others
LANGUAGES Arabic (official), Nubian, Ta Bedawie
RELIGIONS Islam 70%, traditional beliefs
CURRENCY Sudanese dinar = 10 Sudanese pounds

In 1996 the UN imposed sanctions on Sudan. A South African peace initiative in 1997 led to the formation of a Southern States' Co-ordination Council. The US imposed sanctions on Bashir's regime, and US Secretary of State Madeleine Albright met with rebel leaders. In 1998, the US bombed a pharmaceuticals factory in Khartoum in the mistaken belief that it produced chemical weapons.

In 2003 conflict broke out in the Darfur region in the w, primarily between rebels and Arab militias, and a severe humanitarian crisis developed. In the s, government and rebels signed a peace deal in 2005, but the Darfur conflict worsened. By mid-2006 over 200,000 had died, most killed by the government-backed militias, and 2 million had become refugees. The militias were accused of ethnic cleansing. The government of Sudan refused to accept a UN peacekeeping force. In 2006–8 the fighting spilled over into neighbouring countries as UN and African Union peacekeeping efforts proved ineffective.

ECONOMY

The World Bank classifies Sudan as a 'low-income' economy. Food shortages and a refugee crisis worsened its economic plight. 80% of the population are farmers or herders, most at a subsistence level. Ongoing conflict has hindered food aid.

Industries include processed foods, cement, fertilizers and textiles. Exports include oil, cotton, gum arabic and sesame seeds.

S

passed through the canal, much of it oil. In 1956, President NASSER of Egypt nationalized the canal. Israel, Britain and France launched a disastrous attack on Egypt. The canal shut (1956–57) while repairs were carried out. It was again closed during the SIX-DAY WAR (1967). The canal reopened in 1975. In the intervening years, many new ships, especially oil tankers, had became too large to pass through the canal. Loss of revenue forced Egypt to clear and widen the waterway.

Suffolk County in E England, on the North Sea coast; the county town is IPSWICH. The land is mainly low-lying and flat, rising in the SW. The principal rivers are the Orwell, Stour and Waveney. The economy is mainly agricultural, growing cereal crops and sugar beet, and rearing sheep, pigs, and poultry. Fishing along the coast is in decline. Industries: food processing, farm machinery, fertilizers, finance. Area: 3807sq km (1470sq mi). Pop. (2001) 668,548.

suffragette movement Women's campaign in Britain in the late 19th and early 20th centuries to gain the right to vote. It began in the 1860s, and developed until the founding of the National Union of Women's Suffrage Societies in 1897. Emmeline PANKHURST founded the Women's Social and Political Union in 1903. By 1910 the movement split into several factions, including the Women's Freedom League (founded 1908). In 1913, Sylvia Pankhurst founded the East London Federation, which organized marches in London. Women age 30 and over were given the vote in 1918.

Sufism Mystic philosophical movement within ISLAM that developed among the SHI'ITE communities in the 10th and 11th centuries. Sufis stress the capability of the soul to attain personal union with God. *See also* DERVISH

sugar Sweet-tasting, soluble, crystalline monosaccharide or disaccharide CARBOHYDRATE. The common sugar in food and beverages is SUCROSE. This is also the main sugar transported in plant tissues. The main sugar transported around the bodies of animals to provide energy is GLUCOSE. *See also* SACCHARIDE

sugar beet Variety of BEET grown commercially for its high SUGAR content, which is stored in its thick white roots. Family Chenopdiaceae; species *Beta vulgaris*.

sugar cane Perennial GRASS cultivated in tropical and subtropical regions throughout the world. The main source of SUGAR, most cultivated canes are *Saccharum officinarum*. Height: to 4.5m (15ft). Family Poaceae/Gramineae.

Suharto, Raden (1921–2008) Indonesian general and statesman, president (1967–98). In 1966, Suharto seized power from President SUKARNO, averting an alleged communist coup. He was formally elected president in 1968, and re-elected (unopposed) five times. In 1975, Suharto ordered the invasion of East Timor. Under Suharto, INDONESIA experienced rapid economic development, but his autocratic rule was criticized for frequent abuses of human rights. In 1997, economic collapse destabilized Suharto's government, and in 1998 he was ousted after widespread student rioting.

Suhrawardi, as- (1155–91) Islamic philosopher and theologian, b. Iran. He was the founder of the *Ishraqi* (Illuminationist) school of thought, which embraced elements of ORPHISM, HELLENISM, ZOROASTRIANISM, SUFISM and SHI'ITE Islam. His thinking is still in evidence among Iranian mystical sects, such as the Nuyah. His principal work is *Kitab Hikmat al-ishraq* (*The Wisdom of Illumination*). He was put to death by Malikaz-Zahir, the son of SALADIN.

suite Musical form, popular in the BAROQUE period, comprising a number of instrumental dances, which differ in metre, tempo and rhythm but are generally all in the same key. The earliest suites date from the 16th century, and usually involved only two dances, the pavane and galliard. By the 18th century, the dances had become standardized: a prelude, allemande, courante, saraband, and gigue. There was some flexibility, and the minuet, gavotte, bourrée and rondeau were often added.

Sukarno, Achmad (1901–70) Indonesian statesman, first president of independent Indonesia (1947–67). Founder of the Indonesian Nationalist Party (1927), he led opposition to Dutch rule and was frequently imprisoned or exiled (1933–42). At the end of World War 2, he declared Indonesian independence and became president of the new republic. In the 1950s, his rule

became increasingly dictatorial. In 1963, he dissolved parliament, declared himself president for life, and aligned himself with the communists. The failure of a communist coup against the leaders of the army in 1965 weakened Sukarno's position. He was forced out of power by the generals, led by SUHARTO, who eventually replaced him as president.

Sukkoth (Sukkat) Jewish Feast of TABERNACLES, or Feast of Booths, an autumn festival that lasts for seven days. It commemorates the wandering of the Jews in the desert and their salvation through God. A *sukkat*, or simple tent of branches, is raised in the synagogue.

Sukkur City on the River Indus, SIND province, W Pakistan. It is the site of the Sukkur Barrage across the Indus, controlling one of the largest irrigation schemes in the world with canals watering more than 12 million hectares (5 million acres) of the Indus valley. Completed in 1932, the dam is 58m (190ft) high, and *c.*1500m (5000ft) long. Industries: textiles, foodstuffs. Pop. (1998) 329,176.

Sulawesi (formerly Celebes) Large island in E Indonesia, separated from Borneo by the Makasar Strait. Made up of four separate provinces: Utara, Tengah, Selatan, and Tenggara; Ujung Pandang is the largest city and main port. A largely mountainous and volcanic island, the highest peak is Mount Rantekombola, at 3455m (11,335ft). The first European discovery was by the Portuguese in 1512. The Dutch assumed control in the early 17th century, and successfully suppressed the native population in the Makasar War (1666–69). In 1950, it became a province of the Republic of Indonesia. The population is primarily Malayan. Industries: fishing, agriculture. Area: 189,216sq km (73,031sq mi). Pop. (2000) 14,446,483

Suleiman I (the Magnificent) (1494–1566) Ottoman Sultan (1520–66). He succeeded his father, Selim I. Suleiman captured Rhodes from the KNIGHTS HOSPITALLERS and launched a series of campaigns against the Austrian HABSBURGS, defeating the Hungarians at Mohács (1526), and subsequently controlling most of Hungary. In 1529, his troops besieged Vienna. Suleiman's admiral, BARBAROSSA, created a navy that dominated the Mediterranean and ensured Ottoman control of much of the North African coastal region. In the E, Suleiman won victories against the Safavids of Persia and conquered Mesopotamia. *See also* OTTOMAN EMPIRE

Sulla, Lucius Cornelius (138–78 BC) Roman dictator (82–81BC). Elected consul in 88 BC he defeated MITHRIDATES VI in spite of the opposition of MARIUS, Cinna, and their supporters in Rome. Invading Italy, he captured Rome in 82 BC and massacred his anti-patrician enemies.

Sullivan, Sir Arthur Seymour (1842–1900) English composer, famous for a series of operettas written with the librettist W.S. GILBERT. They included *HMS Pinafore* (1878), *The Pirates of Penzance* (1879), and *The Mikado* (1885). Sullivan also composed one opera, *Ivanhoe* (1881), and oratorios, cantatas and church music, including many hymns, such as 'Onward, Christian Soldiers'.

Sullivan, Louis Henry (1856–1924) US architect. Sullivan was a pioneer of the SKYSCRAPER. His dictum that 'form follows function' became a guiding principle in the development of architectural MODERNISM. Sullivan's designs placed emphasis on structure rather than ornamentation. Examples include Wainwright Building, St Louis (1890), and the Carson, Pirie, Scott Department Store, Chicago (1904).

sulphate Salt of SULPHURIC ACID (H_2SO_4). Common sulphates include copper(II) sulphate ($CuSO_4$) and iron(II) sulphate ($FeSO_4$).

sulphonamide drug Any of a group of DRUGS derived from sulphanilamide, a red textile dye, that prevent the growth of bacteria. Introduced in the 1930s, they were the first antibacterials, prescribed to treat a range of infections. They were replaced by less toxic and more effective ANTIBIOTICS.

sulphur (symbol S) Nonmetallic element in group VI of the periodic table, known since pre-history (the biblical **brimstone**). Essential to animal and plant life, it may occur naturally as a free element or in sulphide minerals such as GALENA and iron pyrites, or in sulphate minerals such as GYPSUM. The main commercial source is native (free) sulphur, extracted by the Frasch process. It is used in the VULCANIZATION of rubber

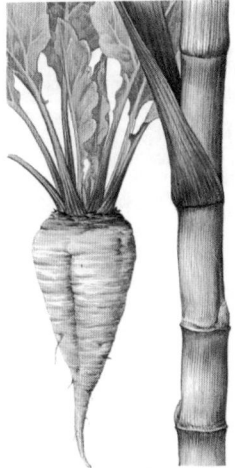

▲ **sugar** Sugar beet (left) and sugar cane (right) produce the same sugar – sucrose – but require completely different climatic conditions. Sugar cane is grown as a single crop in tropical regions, while sugar beet forms part of regular crop rotation in Europe, North and South America. Although sugar is extracted by the same method from both sources, the yield of sugar cane is higher.

S

INTERNET

Sumatra
▶ www.tourismindonesia.com

Sun
▶ www.nineplanets.org/
sol.html

and in the manufacture of drugs, matches, dyes, fungicides, insecticides, and fertilizers. Properties: at.no. 16; r.a.m. 32.064; r.d. 2.07; m.p. 112.8°C (235°F); b.p. 444.7°C (832.5°F). Most common isotope S^{32} (95.1%).

sulphuric acid (H_2SO_4) Colourless, odourless liquid, one of the strongest acids known. It is produced by the oxidation of sulphur dioxide (SO_2). Sulphuric acid is a major industrial chemical, used in the manufacture of many acids, fertilizers, detergents, drugs and a wide range of chemicals. Properties: r.d. 1.84; m.p. 10.3°C (50.5°F); b.p. 330°C (626°F).

Sumatra (Sumatera) World's sixth largest island, in W Indonesia. The largest cities (pop. 1990) are Medan (1,685,972), Palembang (1,084,483), and Padang (477,344). Sumatra's W coast is rugged and mountainous, the Barisan Mountains rising to 3810m (12,500ft), and nearly 60% of the lowland area is jungle. By the 7th century, India established two states in Sumatra: Melayu and Srivijaya. The Portuguese landed on the island in the 16th century, and the Dutch followed a century later. Britain briefly held certain parts of Sumatra in the 18th and 19th centuries. In 1950, Sumatra became part of newly independent Indonesia. The main products are oil (the greatest earner), timber, rubber, tin, tobacco, palm oil, tea, coffee, sisal, and rice. Mining and farming were the chief occupations, but the N is being rapidly industrialized, and Sumatra now accounts for c.75% of Indonesia's total income. Area: 425,000sq km (164,000sq mi). Pop. (2000) 42,666,048.

Sumeria World's first civilization, dating from before 3000 BC in S MESOPOTAMIA. The Sumerians are credited with inventing cuneiform writing, the first basic socio-political institutions, and a money-based economy. Major cities were UR, Kish and Lagash. During the third millennium BC Sumeria developed into an imperial power. In c.2340 BC the Semitic peoples of Akkadia conquered Mesopotamia, and by c.1950 BC the ancient civilization had disintegrated.

summer time (daylight saving time) System by which clocks in Britain are kept one hour ahead of GMT (Greenwich mean time) throughout the summer. Some other countries have similar daylight saving schemes.

sumo wrestling Traditional and popular sport of Japan. Pairs of wrestlers, who usually weigh more than 160kg (350lb), attempt to force each other out of a ring. The technique employs holds, trips, pushes, and falls. A referee monitors the brief bout and keeps score.

Sun STAR at the centre of our SOLAR SYSTEM, around which all other Solar System bodies revolve in their orbits. The Sun is a typical, average star. It consists of c.70% hydrogen (by weight) and 28% helium, with the remainder mostly oxygen and carbon. Its temperature, pressure, and density increase towards the centre. Like all stars, the Sun's energy generates by nuclear fusion reactions taking place under the extreme conditions in the core. This core is c.400,000km (250,000mi) across. Energy released from the core passes up through the radiative zone, which is c.300,000km (200,000mi) thick, then passes through the 200,000km (125,000mi) thick convective zone to the surface, the PHOTOSPHERE, from where it radiates into space. Most of the Sun's visible activity takes place in this 500km (300mi) thick photosphere. Above the photosphere lies the chromosphere, which consists of hot gases and extends for thousands of kilometres. Extending outwards from the chromosphere for millions of kilometres is the CORONA, which emits the SOLAR WIND. The solar wind and the Sun's magnetic field dominate a region of space called the heliosphere, which extends to the boundaries of the Solar System.

sunbird Tropical, nectar-feeding songbird of the Old World, often considered a counterpart of the New World hummingbird. The males are usually brightly coloured. Length: 9–15cm (3.5–6in). Family Nectariniidae.

sunburn Damage to skin caused by prolonged or unaccustomed exposure to sunlight. It varies in severity from redness and soreness to the formation of large blisters. Excessive exposure to sunlight is associated with the skin cancer known as **melanoma**.

sun dance Important and spectacular religious rite of the North American Plains Indians. It was usually held annually in early summer, and performed around a TOTEM POLE. The sun dance was part of elaborate ceremonies held to reaffirm a tribe's affinity with nature and the universe.

Sunderland County district at the mouth of the River Wear, SE TYNE AND WEAR, NE England. Once renowned for coal-mining and the biggest shipbuilding centre in the world, industries now include chemicals, vehicles, glass, electronics, and furniture. Pop. (2001) 280,807.

sundew Any INSECTIVOROUS PLANT of the genus *Drosera*, native to temperate swamps and bogs. Sundews have hairy, basal leaves that glisten with a sticky, dew-like substance that attracts and traps insects. The leaves then fold over the insect, and secrete ENZYMES to digest it. Family Droseraceae.

sunfish North American freshwater fish. A popular angler's fish, similar in appearance to PERCH, it has a continuous dorsal fin containing spiny and soft rays. The 30 species range in size from the blue-spotted *Enneacanthus gloriosus* (length: 8.9cm; 3.5in) to the large-mouth bass *Micropterus salmoides* (length: 81.3cm; 32in; weight: 10kg; 22lb). Family Centrarchidae.

sunflower Any of several ANNUAL and PERENNIAL plants of the genus *Helianthus*, native to North and South America. The flower heads resemble huge daisies with yellow ray flowers and a centre disc of yellow, brown, or purple. The seeds yield a useful oil. The common sunflower (*H. annuus*) has 30cm (1ft) leaves and flower heads more than 30cm (1ft) across; height: to 3.5m (12ft). Family Asteraceae/Compositae.

Sung *See* SONG

Sunni Traditionalist, orthodox branch of ISLAM, whose followers are called *Ahl as-Sunnah* ('People of the Path'). It is followed by 90% of Muslims. Sunnis accept the *Hadith*, the body of orthodox teachings based on Muhammad's spoken words outside the KORAN. The Sunni differ from the SHI'ITE sect in that they accept the first four caliphs (religious leaders) as the true successors of MUHAMMAD.

sunspot Region in the Sun's PHOTOSPHERE which is cooler than its surroundings and appears darker. Sunspots vary in size from c.1,000 to 50,000km (600 to 30,000mi), and occasionally up to c.200,000km (125,000mi). Their duration varies from a few hours to a few weeks, or months for the very biggest. Sunspots occur where there is a local strengthening of the Sun's magnetic field.

sunstroke Potentially fatal condition caused by overexposure to direct sunlight, in which the body temperature rises to 40.5°C (105°F) or more. Symptoms include hot, dry skin, exhaustion, vomiting, delirium and coma. Urgent medical treatment is required, possibly in an intensive care unit. Recovery is usual within a day or two.

Sun Yat-sen (1866–1925) Chinese nationalist leader, first president of the Chinese Republic (1911–12). In exile (1895–1911), he adopted his "three principles of the people": nationalism, democracy, and prosperity. After the Revolution of 1911, he became provisional president, but soon resigned in favour of the militarily powerful Yuan Shikai. When Yuan turned autocratic, Sun gave his support to the KUOMINTANG, or Nationalist Party, formed to oppose Yuan.

supercluster *See* GALAXY CLUSTER

superconductivity Electrical behaviour in metals and alloys that are cooled to very low temperatures. In a superconducting circuit, an electric current flows indefinitely because there is no electrical resistance. This results from electrons becoming paired to move through the material. Otherwise, one passing electron can create a distortion that can effect the passage of the next electron. Research continues to develop superconductors that function at higher temperatures. This electrical behaviour was discovered in 1911 by the Dutch physicist Heike KAMERLINGH-ONNES.

superego In PSYCHOANALYSIS, level of personality that acts as a conscience or censor. It develops as a child internalizes the standards of behaviour defined by the rewards and punishments of parents and society. *See also* EGO; ID

superfluidity Property of a liquid that has no viscosity and therefore no resistance to flow. HELIUM II – liquid helium at temperatures less than 2K (−271°C/−456°F) – was the first known superfluid. Superfluids have remarkable thermal

▲ **Sumeria** This Sumerian vessel dates from c.3500 BC. Clay was one of the few raw materials available to the Sumerians, and the quality of their pottery was very advanced. The Sumerians were also renowned for their architecture, notably the stepped-pyramid structures called ziggurats.

S

properties which cause them to behave unlike other fluids, sometimes flowing up slopes or rising up the walls of a container in a layer an atom thick. *See also* CRYOGENICS

Superior, Lake Lake in the USA and Canada, the largest freshwater lake in the world, bordered on the w by Minnesota, on the N and E by Ontario, and on the s by Michigan and Wisconsin. The most westerly of the five GREAT LAKES, it connects to Lake HURON and the ST LAWRENCE SEAWAY by the St Mary's River and the Soo (Sault Ste Marie) canals. A centre for commercial and recreational fishing, the lake is also a major commercial transport route, particularly for grain and iron ore from Duluth, Michigan, and Thunder Bay, Ontario. Area: 82,413sq km (31,820sq mi). Max. depth: *c.*1,300ft (400m).

supernova Stellar explosion in which virtually an entire STAR is disrupted. For a week or so, a supernova may outshine all the other stars in its galaxy. After a couple of years, the outer layers of the supernova expands so much it becomes thin and transparent. For hundreds or thousands of years, the ejected material remains visible as a supernova remnant. A supernova is *c.*1,000 times brighter than a NOVA.

superposition, law of In geology, law that states that in undisturbed layers of sedimentary deposits, younger beds overlie older ones.

supersonic speed Speed greater than that of the speed of SOUND. Supersonic speed is usually given as a MACH NUMBER, with Mach 1 being the speed of sound. Speeds below Mach 1 are described as **subsonic**, and those around Mach 1 (close to the SOUND BARRIER) as **transonic**. A speed in excess of Mach 5 is said to be **hypersonic**. An aircraft travelling at supersonic speed creates a shock wave that a ground observer may hear as a SONIC BOOM.

superstring theory Theory that attempts to explain the properties of ELEMENTARY PARTICLES and the interactions between them. It combines QUANTUM THEORY and RELATIVITY, especially to explain nuclear forces and the force of GRAVITATION (*see* FUNDAMENTAL FORCES). Superstrings are hypothetical one-dimensional objects about 10^{-35}m long that require a 10–dimensional universe to accommodate them. Their use in quantum calculations predicts the existence of gravitons, the particles believed to be involved in gravitational interaction. Some scientists believe this theory could explain everything in the universe. *See also* UNIFIED FIELD THEORY

supply and demand, law of Economic balance between goods required and produced. The law of supply indicates that, other things being equal, as the price of an item increases, suppliers are willing to produce more, and as the price decreases producers are willing to produce less. Thus, price and quantity supplied are directly related. The law of demand states the reverse: as prices increase, consumers demand less, and as prices decrease, consumers demand more. Thus, prices and quantity demanded are inversely related.

supply-side economics Policies designed to reduce the role of governments in economic matters. The theory of supply-side economics is that production of goods and services can be stimulated by reducing taxes, thereby increasing the supply of money for investment. It also promotes government expenditure to generate industrial activity.

suprematism Abstract art movement launched (1915) in Russia by Kasimir MALEVICH. Epitomized by the stark geometrical forms of Malevich's painting *White on White* (1919), suprematism had a profound influence on the future development of geometrical ABSTRACT ART and CONSTRUCTIVISM.

Supreme Court, Canadian Highest court of appeal in Canada, established in 1875. Its judgement became final when appeals to the Judicial Committee of the Privy Council in London ended: for criminal cases in 1933, for civil cases in 1949. It sits in Ottawa, and consists of a chief justice and eight judges.

Supreme Court of the United States US court of final appeal, the highest in the nation. Its duty is to decide and interpret the constitutionality of state and federal legislation and of executive acts. Once the Supreme Court arrives at a decision, all lower courts must follow it in similar cases. Cases are decided by majority vote. Created by the Constitution of 1787, the Supreme Court consists of nine justices appointed for life by the president with the advice and consent of the Senate.

Surabaja Port in NE Java, second-largest city in Indonesia, and capital of East Java province. An important naval base occupied by Japan in World War 2, the city remains Indonesia's primary naval centre. A fishing and industrial port with shipyards, textile mills, car-assembly plants and oil refining, it exports rice, sugar cane, spices, tobacco, maize, tapioca, coffee, cocoa, rubber and copra. Pop. (2000) 2,701,300.

surfing Water sport in which a person stands on a specially designed fibreglass board, usually 1.22–1.83m (4–6ft) long, and is propelled by the crest of a wave towards the shore.

surgery Branch of medical practice concerned with treatment by operation. Traditionally, it has mainly involved open surgery: gaining access to the operative site by way of an incision. However, the practice of using ENDOSCOPES enabled the development of 'keyhole surgery', using minimally invasive techniques. Surgeons perform operations under sterile conditions, using local or general ANAESTHESIA.

Suriname (formerly Dutch Guiana) Nation in NE South America. Its capital is PARAMARIBO. *See* country feature, page 716

surrealism Twentieth-century artistic movement that evolved out of DADA. André BRETON's *Surrealist Manifesto* (1924) set out the key features of the movement. Taking inspiration from Sigmund FREUD's theories of the unconscious, the surrealists used the techniques of 'free association' to produce imagery to surprise and shock viewers. Important surrealist writers include Paul Éluard, Louis Aragon, Georges Bataille, and Benjamin Peret, while painters include Jean ARP, Max ERNST, René MAGRITTE, Salvador DALÍ, Joan MIRÓ and Paul KLEE. Jean COCTEAU and Luis BUÑUEL directed surrealist films.

Surrey County in SE England, bordering Greater London. From E to W are the North Downs, which slope down to the Thames Valley. The Wey and the Mole are the principal rivers. Much of the land in the w is devoted to farming, with dairy and market-garden produce, wheat and oats the chief products. Guildford (1999 pop. 129,200) is the county town, but the county council is sited in Kingston-upon-Thames (pop. 146,615), a Greater London borough no longer in Surrey. Area: 1,679sq km (6,48sq mi). Pop. (2001) 1,059,015.

Surrey, Henry Howard, Earl of (1517–47) English poet. Like his cousin Catherine HOWARD, he died on the scaffold – a victim of the bloody power politics of HENRY VIII's court. Surrey wrote some of the earliest English SONNETS and, with his translation of two books of the *Aeneid* by VIRGIL, introduced BLANK VERSE into English poetry.

surveying Accurate measurement of the Earth's surface. It is used in establishing land boundaries, the topography of land forms, and for major construction and civil engineering work. For smaller areas, the land is treated as a horizontal plane. Large areas involve considerations of the Earth's curved shape and are referred to as geodetic surveys.

Susa Ancient city in SW Iran, capital of the Elamites. It became an important centre under the ACHAEMENID Kings of Persia, containing a palace of DARIUS I. After the conquests of ALEXANDER THE GREAT, it became the capital of a small Greek state. Among archaeological finds at Susa was the stele (stone slab) of HAMMURABI, inscribed with his code of law.

suspension Liquid (or gas) medium in which small solid (or liquid) particles are uniformly dispersed. The particles are larger than those found in a COLLOID and will settle if the suspension stands undisturbed.

Sussex Former county in SE England, on the English Channel, since 1974 divided into the counties of EAST SUSSEX and WEST SUSSEX. Area: 3,773sq km (1,457sq mi).

Sussex Kingdom of Anglo-Saxon England, settled by the South Saxons under Aelle (*c.*AD 477). It was allegedly the last Anglo-Saxon kingdom to adopt Christianity (*c.*680). A number of Kings of Sussex are known from the 7th and 8th centuries, but at various times they were under the dominance of Mercia. WESSEX absorbed Sussex in the early 9th century. *See* EAST SUSSEX; WEST SUSSEX

Sutherland, Graham (1903–80) English painter, draughtsman, and printmaker. During World War 2, Sutherland was employed as an official artist to record bomb damage. After the war, he concentrated on religious themes, and created the celebrated tapestry *Christ in Glory* (1962) for Coventry Cathedral.

S

▲ **sunflower** Widely cultivated throughout Europe and North America, the common sunflower (*Helianthus annus*) produces seeds from which a light, high-quality oil is yielded. This oil is used in cooking, margarine, shortening, and confectionery. The nutritious seeds can also be eaten whole or used in breads and cereals for human consumption, or in poultry feed.

▲ **Suzman** Helen Suzman became a member of the South African parliament in 1953. An opponent of apartheid, she gained the respect of the black community. She was a key figure in the South African Institute of Race Relations, and received the UN Human Rights Award in 1978.

INTERNET

Sutton Hoo
► www.suttonhoo.org

Lady Churchill destroyed his controversial portrait of Winston Churchill (1954) on her husband's behalf.

Sutherland, Dame Joan (1926–) Australian coloratura soprano. Sutherland made her London début in *Die Zauber-flöte* (1952), but it was her performance in the title role of Donizetti's *Lucia di Lammermoor* (1959) that earned her worldwide acclaim. She went on to perform in all the world's major opera houses before her retirement in 1990.

sutra Sacred or authoritative text in Indian philosophy or religion. In HINDUISM, it is a concise work for use within an oral tradition. Most philosophical traditions had their own sutras, which were written down in the first few centuries of the Christian era. In Buddhism, a sutra was often a lengthy sacred text dealing with a specific point of doctrine.

suttee Former Indian custom of a widow throwing herself alive on to her husband's funeral pyre. Originally confined to royalty, it was forbidden (1829) under British rule.

Sutton Hoo Archaeological site in Suffolk, SE England. In 1939, the excavation of an Anglo-Saxon burial mound – perhaps that of Raedwald, King of East Anglia (d.625), revealed a Saxon oared longship, 27m (90ft) long. In the centre of the boat lay a wooden funeral chamber, containing silver plate, gold jewellery and coins, and bronze armour. It is one of Britain's most spectacular archaeological finds.

Suva Seaport on the SE coast of Viti Levu Island, in the SW Pacific Ocean, capital of FIJI. It is the manufacturing and trade centre of the islands, with an excellent harbour. Exports include tropical fruits, copra, and gold. Pop. (1996) 77,366.

Suzhou (Soochow, Su-chow) City on the Grand Canal, Jiangsu province, E central China. Capital of the Wu kingdom in the 5th century BC its famous silk industry developed under the Sung dynasty in the 12th century. Since 100 BC it has been noted for its many gardens, temples, and canals. Industries: silk, cotton, embroidery, chemicals. Pop. (2005) 1,201,000.

Suzman, Helen (1917–) South African politician. Suzman was an outspoken opponent of South Africa's APARTHEID regime. Elected to Parliament in 1953, she formed the Progressive Party in 1959, and for the next 12 years was the party's only member. Suzman retired from Parliament shortly after the election of Nelson MANDELA as president.

Svalbard Archipelago in the Arctic Ocean, *c.*640km (400mi) N of Norway, to which it has officially belonged since 1925. There are nine main islands, of which by far the largest is Spitsbergen. The administrative centre and largest settlement is Longyearbyen on Spitsbergen. Ice fields and glaciers cover more than half the land mass, although the w edge of the islands is ice-free for most of the year. The area abounds in Arctic flora and fauna. The islands are an important wildlife refuge, and protective measures have saved certain mammals from extinction. Animals include polar bear, walrus, and whale. Although the Vikings discovered Svalbard in 1194, the islands remained neglected until Willem Barents rediscovered them in 1596. In the 17th century, they were an important whaling centre, and in the 18th century, Russian and Scandinavian fur traders hunted the lands. Large coal deposits were found on Spitsbergen at the end of the 19th century, and Norway, Russia and Sweden mined the area. In 1925, the islands became a sovereign territory of Norway (although more than half the population is Russian), in return for allowing mining concessions to other nations. Area: 62,000sq km (24,000sq mi). Pop. (2000) 2400.

Swahili BANTU language of the Niger-Congo family of African languages. It developed as a *lingua franca* and trad-

---

SURINAME

The Republic of Suriname is on the Atlantic Ocean in NE South America bordered by Brazil to the S, French Guiana to the E and Guyana to the w. Suriname is made up of the Guiana Highlands plateau, a flat coastal plain, and a forested inland region. Its many rivers serve as a source of hydroelectric power. The narrow coastal plain was once swampy, but it has been drained and now consists mainly of farmland. Inland lie hills and low mountains which rise to 1,280m [4,199ft].

CLIMATE
Suriname has a hot, wet and humid climate. Temperatures are high throughout the year.

HISTORY
Spanish explorer Alfonso de Ojeda discovered what is now Suriname in 1499, but it was the British who founded the first colony in 1651. In 1667 Britain handed Suriname to the Dutch in return for New Amsterdam, an area that is now the state of New York. Slave revolts and Dutch neglect hampered development.

In the early 19th century Britain and the Netherlands disputed the ownership of the area. The British gave up their claims in 1813, and in 1815 the Congress of Vienna gave the Guyana region to Britain and reaffirmed Dutch control of 'Dutch Guiana'. Slavery was abolished in 1863 and soon afterwards Indian and Indonesian labourers were introduced to work on plantations. Dutch Guiana gained autonomy in 1954.

POLITICS
The country became fully independent from the Netherlands as Suriname in 1975 and gained membership of the United Nations, but the economy was weakened when thousands of skilled people emigrated to the Netherlands.

Following a coup in 1980 Suriname was ruled by a military dictator, Dési Bouterse, who banned all political parties. Guerrilla warfare disrupted the economy. In 1987 a new constitution provided for a 51-member National Assembly, with powers to elect the president. Rameswak Shankar became president in 1988 elections, but he was overthrown by a military coup in 1990.

In 1991 Ronald Venetiaan, leader of the New Front for Democracy and Development, became president. In 1992 the government negotiated a peace agreement with the bosch-

AREA 163,265sq km [63,037sq mi]
POPULATION 471,000
CAPITAL (POPULATION) Paramaribo (216,000)
GOVERNMENT Multiparty republic
ETHNIC GROUPS Hindustani/East Indian 37%, Creole (mixed White and Black) 31%, Javanese 15%, Black 10%, Amerindian 2%, Chinese 2%, others
LANGUAGES Dutch (official), Sranang Tonga
RELIGIONS Hinduism 27%, Protestant 25%, Roman Catholic 23%, Islam 20%
CURRENCY Surinamese dollar = 100 cents

neger, descendants of African slaves, who had launched a struggle against the government. That same year, the constitution was amended in order to limit the power of the military and a peace agreement was reached with the rebels. Elections were held in 1996 and again in 2000.

In 1999 Bouterse was convicted in absentia in the Netherlands of having led a cocaine-trafficking ring during and after his tenure in office. In 2004 the government announced that he and others would face trial over the killings of 15 people in 1982.

ECONOMY
The World Bank classifies Suriname as an 'upper-middle-income' developing country. Its economy is based on mining and metal processing. Suriname is a leading producer of bauxite, from which aluminium is made.

The chief agricultural products are rice, bananas, sugar cane, coffee, coconuts, timber and citrus fruits.

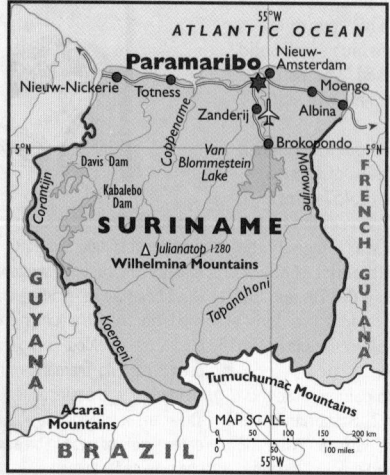

ing language in most of E Africa, becoming the official language of Tanzania in 1967, and of Kenya in 1973. It is also in use in parts of central Africa. It has a large body of literature.

swallow Any of 75 species of graceful and agile birds with long, tapering wings and a long, forked tail. The common swallow (*Hirundo rustica*), known as the barn swallow in North America, is grey-blue with a light brown underside and red throat markings; it feeds primarily on insects, which it catches in flight. Length: 20cm (8in). Family Hirundinidae.

swamp Low-lying wetland area, near large body of open water. They are characterized by numerous animals and plants, including rushes and sedge in cool regions, and species of trees, such as the swamp cypress, in warmer areas. They can prevent flooding by absorbing flood waters from rivers and coastal regions. *See also* BOG; MARSH

swan Any of several species of graceful, white or black waterfowl that nest in N Northern Hemisphere and migrate s for winter. Most have broad, flat bills, long necks, plump bodies, and dense plumage. They dip their heads under water to feed on plant matter. Length: to 2m (6.5ft). Family Anatidae; genus *Cygnus*.

Swansea (Abertawe) City and county district on Swansea Bay at the mouth of the River Tawe, West Glamorgan, s Wales. The second-largest Welsh city, it is the administrative centre of West Glamorgan. Swansea grew with the export of coal in the 19th century. Formerly noted for its production of steel, it is now dominated by light industry. Pop. (2001) 223,293.

SWAPO Acronym for the Namibian SOUTH WEST AFRICA PEOPLE'S ORGANIZATION

Swaziland Small, landlocked, and mountainous kingdom in s Africa; the capital is MBABANE. *See* country feature.

sweating (perspiring) Loss of water, salts, and urea from the body surface of many mammals as a result of the action of certain glands (sweat glands). Sweat glands lie in the dermis (inner layer) of the skin, and open onto the surface through tiny pores. In humans, they are found all over the body, but in some mammals they are found only on the soles of the feet. The nervous system controls sweating, which forms an important part of the body's temperature control mechanism. The evaporation of sweat cools the skin and the blood passing through capillaries close to the skin surface. Excessive sweating must be compensated for by increased intake of water and salt.

swede Root vegetable belonging to the mustard family (Brassicaceae/Cruciferae). The large, swollen taproot may be eaten cooked as a vegetable or fed to animals as fodder. Height: *c.*30cm (12in). Species *B. napus napobrassica*.

Sweden Kingdom on the E half of the Scandinavian peninsula, N Europe. *See* country feature, page 718

Swedenborg, Emanuel (1688–1772) Swedish scientist, philosopher, theologian, and mystic. In 1745, after a glittering scientific career in which he wrote many books (notably on metallurgy and metaphysics), Swedenborg gave up worldly learning to concentrate on religious affairs. His religious writings include *Heavenly Arcana* (1749–56), *The New Jerusalem* (1758), and *True Christian Religion* (1771). After his death, the Church of the New Jerusalem carried forward his theology.

Swedish National language of Sweden, spoken by virtually all of its 8.7 million people. It is also spoken by many people in Finland. Closely related to Norwegian and Danish, it is a member of the northern branch of the Germanic family of INDO-EUROPEAN LANGUAGES.

▲ **swallow** Extremely agile fliers, swallows spend most of their time in the air and feed on the wing. They migrate very long distances: in North America, the common, or barn, swallow (*Hirundo rustica*, above) may summer in Canada and winter in South America.

SWAZILAND

The Kingdom of Swaziland is a small, landlocked country in s Africa bounded by South Africa to the N, W and s and by Mozambique to the E. The country has four regions which run N–S.

In the W of the country the Highveld, with an average height of 1,200 [3,937ft], makes up 30% of Swaziland. The Middleveld, between 350 and 1,000m [1,148–3,281ft], covers 28% of the country. The Lowveld, with an average height of 270m [886ft], covers another 33%. The

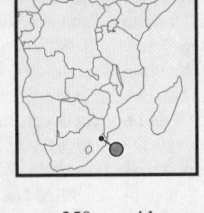

Lebombo Mountains reach 800m [2,600ft] along the E border.

Meadows and pasture cover 65% of Swaziland. Arable farming covers 8% of the land, and forests only 6%.

CLIMATE
The Lowveld is almost tropical, with an average temperature of 22°C [72°F] and a low rainfall of 500mm [20in] a year. The altitude moderates the climate in the W of the country. Mbabane has a climate typical of the Highveld with warm summers and cool winters.

HISTORY
In the 18th century, according to tradition, a group of Bantu-speaking people under the Swazi Chief Ngwane II crossed the Lebombo range and united with local African groups to form the Swazi nation. In the 1840s, under attack from the Zulu, the Swazi sought British protection. Gold was discovered in the 1880s, and many Europeans sought land concessions from the king, who did not realize that in acceding to their demands he lost control of the land. In 1894, Britain and the Boers of South Africa agreed to put Swaziland under the control of the South African Republic (the TRANSVAAL). Britain took control at the end of the second SOUTH AFRICAN WAR (1899–1902).

POLITICS
In 1968, when Swaziland became fully independent as a constitutional monarchy, the head of state was King Sobhuza II. In 1973 Sobhuza suspended the constitution and assumed supreme power. In 1978 he banned all political parties. Sobhuza died in 1982 after a reign of 82 years.

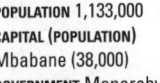

AREA 17,364sq km [6,704sq mi]
POPULATION 1,133,000
CAPITAL (POPULATION) Mbabane (38,000)
GOVERNMENT Monarchy
ETHNIC GROUPS African 97%, European 3%
LANGUAGES Siswati and English (both official)
RELIGIONS Zionist (a mixture of Christianity and traditional beliefs) 40%, Roman Catholic 20%, Islam 10%
CURRENCY Lilangeni = 100 cents

In 1986 his son, Prince Makhosetive, became King Mswati III. Elections in 1993 and 1998, in which political parties were banned, failed to satisfy protesters who opposed the absolute monarchy. Mswati continued to rule by decree and in 2004 he announced plans to build palaces for each of his 11 wives. At the same time the government appealed for aid in the face of a national disaster caused by the spread of HIV and a severe drought. In 2006 Mswati announced a new constitution reinforcing his authority.

ECONOMY
The World Bank classifies Swaziland as a 'lower-middle-income' developing country. Agriculture employs 50% of the workforce, with many farmers living at subsistence level. Farm products and processed foods, including sugar, wood pulp, citrus fruits and canned fruit, are the leading exports. Swaziland exhausted its high-grade iron ore reserves in 1978, while the world demand for its asbestos fell. Swaziland is heavily dependent on South Africa and the two countries are linked through a customs union.

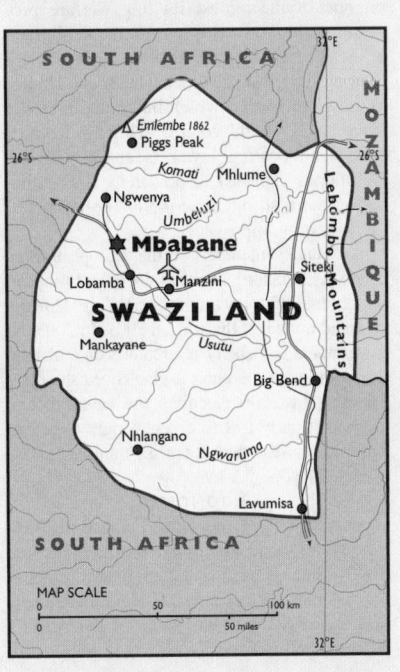

SOUTH AFRICA
32°E
Emlembe 1862
Piggs Peak
26°S
Komati
Mhlume
Ngwenya
Umbeluzi
Mbabane
Lobamba
Manzini
Siteki
SWAZILAND
Mankayane
Usutu
Big Bend
Nhlangano
Ngwaruma
Lavumisa
SOUTH AFRICA
MAP SCALE
0   50   100 km
0   50 miles
32°E
MOZAMBIQUE
Lebombo Mountains

S

INTERNET

Swift, Jonathan
▸ etext.library.adelaide.edu.
au/aut

Switzerland
▸ www.gov.ch/govchen.nsf
▸ www.about.ch

sweet pea Climbing annual plant native to Italy. Widely cultivated as an ornamental, it has fragrant, butterfly-shaped flowers of white, pink, purple, red or orange. Height: to 1.8m (6ft). Family Fabaceae/Leguminosae; species *Lathyrus odoratus*.

sweet potato Trailing plant native to South America and cultivated as a vegetable in Japan, Russia, USA, and the Pacific. Its flowers are pink or violet. The orange or yellow, tuber-like root is edible. Family Convolvulaceae; species *Ipomoea batatas*.

sweet william Common name for a flowering plant native to Europe. Introduced as a garden plant, it is now a wildflower in the USA. Its flower heads are pink, red, or white. Height: to 60cm (24in). Family Caryophyllaceae; species *Dianthus barbatus*.

swift Any of several species of fast-flying, widely distributed birds. They have hooked bills, wide mouths, long narrow wings, and darkish plumage. They typically feed on insects, which they catch in flight, and build nests of plant matter held together with saliva. Length: to 23cm (9in). Family Apodidae.

Swift, Jonathan (1667–1745) Irish satirist and poet. Ordained an Anglican priest in 1694, in 1713 he became Dean of St Patrick's Cathedral, Dublin. Swift's early works include

SWEDEN

The Kingdom of Sweden is the largest of the countries of SCANDINAVIA in both area and population. It shares the Scandinavian Peninsula with Norway. The w part of the country, along the border with Norway, is mountainous. The highest point is Kebnekaise, which reaches 2,117m [6,946ft], in the NW.

CLIMATE

The N latitude and high mountains and plateaux of Norway cut Sweden off from the mild influences of the Atlantic in the w. The Gulf Stream warms the s coastlands. The February temperature in the central lowlands is just below freezing, but in the north it is –15°C [5°F].

Precipitation is low throughout Sweden, but lies as snow for more than six months in the north. In summer there is little difference between the N and s. Most areas have an average temperature range between 15°C and 20°C [59–68°F].

HISTORY

The settlement of Sweden began at the close of the last Ice age, *c.*8,000 years ago. In prehistoric times it was a centre of the Nordic Bronze Age (*c.*1800-600 BC). A succession of wealthy cultures developed advanced bronze-smithing and were influential across N Europe. The end of the Bronze Age was marked by worsening climate and declining population, and the region did not rise to prominence again until the VIKING age. The earliest historically known tribe in the region were the Svear, recorded in the early first millennium AD, who gave their name to the country.

In the second half of the first millennium Viking culture became dominant, but the Swedes' energies were directed to the s and E rather than towards NW Europe. Between the 9th and 11th centuries AD Swedes known as Varangians explored Russia, trading, establishing colonies and conquering local kingdoms. They travelled the region's rivers to the Black Sea, and from there raided s and E Europe before becoming mercenaries in the service of the Byzantine Empire.

In the 11th century Sweden, Norway and Denmark were separate kingdoms. In 1319 Sweden and Norway united under Magnus VII, and in 1389 the Danish Queen Margaret united Sweden, Denmark, and Norway in the Kalmar Union. Her successors failed to control Sweden, and in 1520 Gustavus Vasa led a successful rebellion. In 1523 he was crowned GUSTAVUS I, king of an independent Sweden. Southern Sweden remained under Danish control until 1660. Gustavus made the monarchy hereditary within the Vasa dynasty and made Lutheranism the state religion.

John III's marriage to the King of Poland's sister strengthened Sweden's power. Their son Sigismund III, a Roman Catholic, came to the throne in 1592 but was deposed by Charles IX in 1599 on account of his religion. Charles' son, GUSTAVUS II, won territory in Russia and Poland. Further victories in the THIRTY YEARS' WAR established Sweden as a great European power. CHARLES XII fought brilliant campaigns in Denmark, Poland, Saxony and Russia, but his eventual defeat in Russia at the hands of Peter I (the Great) in 1709 seriously weakened Sweden.

AREA 449,964sq km [173,731sq mi]
POPULATION 9,031,000
CAPITAL (POPULATION) Stockholm (1,729,000)
GOVERNMENT Constitutional monarchy
ETHNIC GROUPS Swedish 91%, Finnish, Sami
LANGUAGES Swedish (official), Finnish, Sami
RELIGIONS Lutheran 87%, Roman Catholic, Orthodox
CURRENCY Swedish krona = 100 öre

Internal friction marred the 18th century. Gustavus IV (r.1792–1809) took Sweden into the NAPOLEONIC WARS. Charles XIII (r. 1809–18) lost Finland to Russia in 1809, but the Congress of VIENNA granted Norway to Sweden as compensation.By the late 19th century Sweden was a major industrial nation, and the Social Democratic Party was set up in 1889 to improve the conditions of workers.

In 1905 Norway's parliament voted for independence from Sweden, and the union between the two was dissolved. Under Gustavus V (r.1907–50) Sweden remained neutral in both World Wars. In 1946 it joined the United Nations.

POLITICS

Sweden has a high standard of living, and more than 70% of the national budget is spent on one of the widest ranging welfare programmes in the world. In turn, the tax burden is the world's highest. The elections of September 1991 saw the end of the Social Democratic government, which had been in power since 1932, with voters swinging towards parties advocating lower taxes. The Social Democrats returned to power in 1994 advocating more stringent economic policies, and the economy improved.

A founder member of the European Free Trade Association, Sweden joined the European Union in 1985 following a referendum. However, it did not adopt the euro in 2001. In 2003 the government launched a referendum on replacing the krona with the euro, a plan Swedish voters rejected. In 2006 elections the ruling Social Democrat party lost to a centre-right coalition. Fredrik Reinfeldt became prime minister.

ECONOMY

Sweden is a highly developed industrial country. Major products include iron and steel goods. Steel is used in the engineering industry to manufacture aircraft, cars machinery and ships. Sweden has some of the world's richest iron ore deposits.

S

The Battle of the Books (1704) and *A Tale of a Tub* (1704). His best-known work, *Gulliver's Travels* (1726), is a satire on human follies. He wrote numerous works criticizing England's treatment of Ireland, including *A Modest Proposal* (1729). His poetry includes *Verses on the Death of Dr Swift* (1739).

swimming Water-borne leisure activity or competitive sport. Formal competition was first introduced (1603) in Japan. In 1837, the National Swimming Association formed in England; the *Fédération Internationale de Natation Amateur* (FINA), the world governing body, formed by 1908. There are four main strokes – breaststroke, front crawl, backstroke, and butterfly. Recognized race distances for men and women, established by the Federation in 1968, range from 100m to 1500m; there are also relay and medley races. Synchronized swimming also features at the Olympic Games and at the four-yearly World Championships, as does DIVING. Swimming is one of the disciplines of the triathlon and the modern PENTATHLON.

Swinburne, Algernon Charles (1837–1909) English poet and critic. A play, *Atalanta in Calydon* (1865), brought him fame, and his *Poems and Ballads* (1866) also won praise. Some of the poems in the collection, including 'The Garden of Proserpine', are among his finest. Two further series of *Poems and Ballads* appeared in 1876 and 1889.

swing Form of JAZZ prevalent in the USA during the 1930s and 1940s. It originated in the music of small groups who played a rhythm of four even beats to the bar, as opposed to the two beats to the bar of the New Orleans' style. The groups also made more use of soloists, particularly saxophonists. Larger groups, such as those of Duke ELLINGTON and Count Basie, made great use of the new possibilities. Their innovations were taken up by white musicians such as Benny Goodman and Glenn MILLER.

Swithin, Saint (d.862) Anglo-Saxon bishop of WINCHESTER (852–62). Details of his life are sketchy, it is known that he was an adviser to the West Saxon kings Egbert and Ethelwulf. His feast day is July 15. According to superstition, the weather on St Swithin's Day will last for the next 40 days.

Switzerland Small, landlocked republic in central Europe. *See country feature, page 720*

swordfish (broadbill) Marine fish found worldwide in temperate and tropical seas. A popular food fish, it is silvery-black, dark purple, or blue. Its long, flattened upper jaw, in the shape of a sword, is one-third of its length and used to strike at prey. Length: to 4.5m (15ft); weight: 530kg (1,180lb). Family Xiphiidae; species *Xiphias gladius*.

sycamore (great MAPLE or false plane) Deciduous tree of the family, native to central Europe and w Asia but widely naturalized. It has deeply toothed, five-lobed leaves, greenish yellow flowers, and winged brown fruit. Height: to 33m (110ft). Family Aceraceae; species *Acer pseudoplatanus*.

Sydenham, Thomas (1624–89) English physician, often called the 'English Hippocrates'. Sydenham initiated the cooling method of treating SMALLPOX, made a thorough study of epidemics, and wrote descriptions of MALARIA and GOUT.

Sydney State capital of New South Wales, SE Australia, on Port Jackson, an inlet on the Pacific Ocean. Sydney is Australia's oldest and largest city, and its most important financial, industrial and cultural centre, and principal port. The city was founded (1788) on a natural harbour as the first British penal colony in Australia. Industries: shipbuilding, textiles, motor vehicles, oil refining, building materials, chemicals, brewing, tourism, clothing, paper, electronics. In 2000, Sydney hosted the Summer Olympic Games. Pop. (2005) 4,388,000.

syllogism Logical argument consisting of three categorical propositions: two premises and a conclusion. It was devised by ARISTOTLE to establish the conditions under which the conclusion of a deductive inference is valid or not valid. A valid conclusion can only come from premises that are logically related. Examples of syllogisms are: All men are mortal; John is a man; therefore John is mortal (valid); All trees have leaves; a daffodil has leaves; therefore a daffodil is a tree (invalid).

symbiosis Relationship between two or more different organisms that is generally mutually advantageous. It is more accurately referred to as MUTUALISM. If only one partner benefits, this is called COMMENSALISM. *See also* PARASITE

symbolism European art and literary movement. Symbolism has its origins in France in the 1880s, where it arose as a reaction against the pragmatic REALISM of COURBET and IMPRESSIONISM. Its exponents wanted to express ideas or abstractions, rather than simply imitate the visible world. The most powerful tendency in the movement stemmed from GAUGUIN and Émile Bernard (*c.*1888). Another less dynamic trend introduced formal innovations into traditional painting. Its chief exponents were Gustave MOREAU, Odilon REDON, and Puvis de Chavannes. Outside France, BURNE-JONES and MUNCH are considered as symbolists. In literature, the movement included a group of poets active in the 19th century, who were followers of VERLAINE and BAUDELAIRE, such as MALLARMÉ and RIMBAUD in France, and POE and SWINBURNE in the US and Britain.

symbolists Group of French poets active in the latter part of the 19th century, of whom the most famous were MALLARMÉ, VERLAINE, RIMBAUD, Corbière, and Laforgue. Influenced by BAUDELAIRE, they sought to transcend reality as portrayed in the realist novel and to create poetic impressions through suggestion rather than statement. *See also* SYMBOLISM

symmetry In biology, anatomical description of body form or geometrical pattern of a plant or animal. It is used in the classification of living things (TAXONOMY), and to clarify relationships. In mathematics, a symmetrical figure is one that has an exact correspondence of shape about a point, line, or plane.

symphonic poem (tone poem) Orchestral piece of the late-Romantic period that describes in music a poem, story, or other extra-musical programme. The term was first used by Franz LISZT. *Till Eulenspiegel* and *Also sprach Zarathustra* by Richard STRAUSS are perhaps the best-known examples of the genre. *See also* PROGRAMME MUSIC

symphony Large-scale, musical work for orchestra. It evolved from the 18th century, when it received its first classical definition in the works of HAYDN and MOZART. They usually have four movements and, in the classical tradition, a first movement in SONATA form. The first symphonies were scored almost exclusively for instruments of the violin family, but in the early 19th century, brass and woodwind sections became more common. Later composers of symphonies include BEETHOVEN, SCHUBERT, SCHUMANN, BRAHMS, BRUCKNER, TCHAIKOVSKY, MAHLER, SIBELIUS and SHOSTAKOVICH.

synagogue Place of assembly for Jewish worship, education and cultural development. Synagogues serve as communal centres, under the leadership of a RABBI, and house the ARK OF THE COVENANT. The first synagogue buildings

▲ **Swift** Irish satirist and poet Jonathan Swift also wrote numerous political pamphlets, such as *The Conduct of The Allies* (1711). He left Ireland in 1689, but returned in 1714, and became a champion of Irish rights. His satirical masterpiece, *Gulliver's Travels* (1726), describes the travels of Lemuel Gulliver in imaginary lands, such as Lilliput, where he meets the Houyhnhnms and the Yahoos. It skilfully lampoons politicians, religious dissenters, philosophers, and scientists, as well as being a parody of travel literature. *Journal to Stella* (1768) was a collection of letters to a former pupil and close friend. Swift suffered from Ménière's syndrome, and was pronounced insane in 1742.

S

SYMBIOSIS

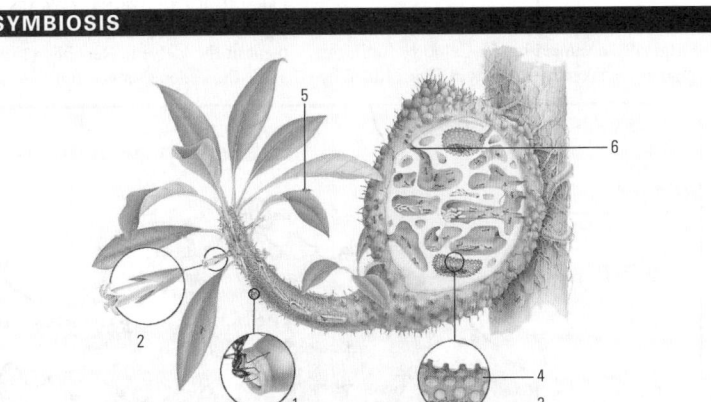

Iridomyrmex ants and the Myrmecodia (ant plant) benefit from a symbiotic relationship. The ants feed on the sugary nectar of the plant. This is produced in nectaries (1), which develop at the base of the flower (2) after the petals and sepals have fallen off. The plant benefits from the vital minerals in the ants' faeces and waste materials (3), which it absorbs through the warty inner surface of its chambers (4). The ant plant is epiphytic, growing suspended from trees in upland rainforests, where the soils are often lacking in nutrients. The mineral nutrients provided by the ants supplement the plant's poor diet. As the plant grows, its stem enlarges and develops cavities that are invaded by the ants (5). These chambers do not interconnect, but have separate passages to the outside (6). A complete ant colony soon becomes established in the plant.

date from the 3rd century BC but may go back to the destruction (586 BC) of Solomon's TEMPLE in Jerusalem.

synapse Connection between the end of one nerve cell (NEURON) and the next, or between a nerve cell and a muscle, where nerve impulses are transmitted by NEUROTRANSMITTERS.

syncline Downward FOLD in rocks. When rock layers fold down into a trough-like form, it is called a syncline.

syncope See FAINTING

syndicalism Early 20th-century form of SOCIALISM originating in France, but also influential in Spain and Italy. It proposed public ownership of the means of production by small worker groups and called for the elimination of central government.

Synge, John Millington (1871–1909) Irish dramatist who was important in the renaissance of IRISH LITERATURE. Synge was one of the organizers of the ABBEY THEATRE in 1904, and his comedy *The Playboy of the Western World* (1907) caused a riot when first performed. *Riders to the Sea* (1904) is a paean to the spirit of the Aran islanders. Other works include *The Well of the Saints* (1905), and *Deidre of the Sorrows* (1910).

Synoptic Gospels Three of the GOSPELS of the New Testament (Saint MATTHEW, Saint MARK, Saint LUKE), which present a common account of the life of JESUS CHRIST. Saint Mark's Gospel is generally held to have been the model for Saint Matthew's and Saint Luke's, although most scholars believe that the latter two have gathered some material from a common source known as 'Q', which no longer exists.

synovial fluid Viscous, fluid that lubricates the movable joints between bones. It is secreted by the synovial membrane. It is also in **bursae**, the membranous sacs that help to reduce friction in major joints such as the shoulder, hip or knee.

syntax Branch of grammar that encompasses the body of rules governing the ways in which words are used to form phrases, clauses and sentences. Syntax also describes the sentence structure of an utterance produced by a writer or speaker.

synthesizer In music, an electronic instrument capable of producing a wide variety of different sounds, pitches and timbres. The instrument was devised (1964) by the US inventor Robert Moog. Computer technology is now used to control the instrument's different functions, enabling synthesizers to replicate non-electronic sounds.

syphilis Sexually transmitted disease caused by the spiral-shaped bacterium (spirochete) *Treponema pallidum*. Untreated, it runs its course in three stages. The first symptom is often a hard, painless sore on the genitals, appearing usually within a month of infection. Months later, the second stage features a skin rash and fever. The third stage, often many years later, brings the formation of growths and serious involvement of the heart, brain and spinal cord, leading eventually to blindness, insanity and death. The disease is treated with ANTIBIOTICS.

Syracuse (Siracusa) Italian seaport city in Sicily, on the Ionian Sea, capital of Syracuse province. Founded in 734 BC by Corinthian Greek colonists, it prospered and established its

---

SWITZERLAND

The Swiss Confederation is a landlocked country in W Europe. Much of the land is mountainous. The JURA MOUNTAINS lie along Switzerland's W border with France, while the Swiss ALPS make up about 60% of the country in the S and E. Four-fifths of the people of Switzerland live on the fertile Swiss Plateau, which contains most of Switzerland's large cities.

CLIMATE
The climate varies greatly according to the height of the land. The plateau region has a central European climate with warm summers, but cold and snowy winters.

HISTORY
Originally occupied by the Celtic Helvetii, the region was taken by Romans in 58 BC. Ruled by

FRANKS in the 6th century AD, it was later divided between Swabia and Burgundy. United within the HOLY ROMAN EMPIRE, it came under HABSBURG rule in the 13th century. In 1291 the CANTONS, Schwyz, Uri, and Unterwalden, united against the Habsburgs. Traditionally led by William TELL, the Swiss League expanded and defeated the Habsburgs in 1386 and 1388. In 1499, victory over MAXIMILIAN brought partial independence. Defeated by the French in 1515, the Swiss adopted a policy of neutrality which is still followed today. The REFORMATION caused religious divisions, but the Confederation survived to achieve independence in 1648. The FRENCH REVOLUTIONARY WARS led to the overthrow of the oligarchy and the establishment of the Helvetic Republic (1798–1803). In 1815, the Federation was fully re-established.

AREA 41,284sq km [15,940sq mi]
POPULATION 7,555,000
CAPITAL (POPULATION) Bern (124,000)
GOVERNMENT Federal republic
ETHNIC GROUPS German 65%, French 18%, Italian 10%, Romansch 1%, others
LANGUAGES French, German, Italian and Romansch (all official)
RELIGIONS Roman Catholic 46%, Protestant 40%
CURRENCY Swiss franc = 100 centimes

The Congress of VIENNA expanded it to 22 cantons and guaranteed its neutrality. A brief civil war led to the constitution of 1848, turning Switzerland into a federal state. In 1979 Jura became the 23rd canton. A referendum in 1986 rejected Swiss membership of the UN to avoid compromising its neutrality.

POLITICS
In 1993 the Swiss voted against joining the European Union. However, in 2002, the Swiss voted by a narrow majority to weaken isolationism and join the United Nations. In 2007 elections, the right-wing Swiss People's Party rose to dominate the government. All four major parties are represented in Switzerland's consensus-based system.

ECONOMY
Although lacking in natural resources, Switzerland is a wealthy, industrialized country with many highly skilled workers. Major products include chemicals, electrical equipment, machinery and machine tools, precision instruments, processed food, watches and textiles. The country produces about 60% of its food, the rest being imported. Dairy farming is the chief agricultural activity. Crops include fruits, potatoes and wheat. Tourism and banking are also important. Swiss banks attract investors from all over the world.

S

own colonies, triumphing over the Carthaginians in 480 BC. It grew to become the most important Hellenic city outside Greece, and at one time was probably the world's largest city. Industries: tourism, petrochemicals. Pop. (2001) 125,673.

Syria Arab republic in the N Middle East. *See* country feature

Syriac Semitic language belonging to the eastern ARAMAIC group. In ancient times it was spoken in Edessa, now Urfa in SE Turkey. Because of the importance of Edessa as a centre of Christianity in the 2nd century, the neighbouring Aramaic Christians adopted Syriac and it has been used ever since as a liturgical language by Oriental Christians of the Syrian rite. Syriac literature preserves many translations of Greek Christian texts that have not survived in the original Greek.

Szczecin (Stettin) City in NW Poland near the mouth of the River Oder, only 10km (6mi) from the German border. From 1720, Szczecin acted as the main port for BERLIN. The city returned to Poland by the Potsdam Conference in 1945. Industries: shipbuilding, ironworks, chemicals. Pop. (1999) 416,988.

Szechwan *See* SICHUAN

Szell, George (1897–1970) US conductor and pianist, b. Hungary. He assisted Richard Strauss at the Berlin State Opera and became its director (1924–30). In 1939, he moved to the USA to conduct (1942–46) the Metropolitan Opera, New York, then direct (1946–70) the Cleveland Orchestra.

Szent-Györgyi, Albert von (1893–1986) US biochemist, b. Hungary. He received the 1937 Nobel Prize in physiology or medicine for his work on biological oxidation processes and the isolation of vitamin C. He also studied the biochemistry of MUSCLE, discovering the muscle protein actin.

Szilard, Leo (1898–1964) US physicist, b. Hungary. Szilard's early work established the relation between information transfer and ENTROPY. He devised a means of separating radioactive ISOTOPES. He was a key figure in the MANHATTAN PROJECT to develop the nuclear bomb and, with Enrico FERMI, created the first sustained nuclear chain reaction based on uranium FISSION. He led the 'Szilard Petition' of scientists opposing the use of the bomb against Japan.

Szymanowski, Karol (1882–1937) Polish post-Romantic composer who did much to promote the nationalist cause in Poland. Szymanowski studied (1906–08) the works of Wagner and Richard Strauss in Germany. His works include two violin concertos (1917, 1933) and the opera *King Roger* (1926).

SYRIA

The Syrian Arab Republic is in SW Asia. The narrow coastal plain is overlooked by a low mountain range which runs N–S. Another range, the Jabal ash Sharqi, runs along the border with Lebanon. S of this range are the Golan Heights, which Israel has occupied since 1967. E of the mountains, the bulk of Syria consists of fertile valleys, grassy plains and large sandy deserts. This region contains the valley of the River EUPHRATES (*Nahr al Furat*).

CLIMATE
The coast has a Mediterranean climate, with dry, warm summers and wet, mild winters. The low mountains cut off Damascus from the sea. It has less rainfall than the coastal areas and becomes drier to the east.

HISTORY
The earliest known settlers were Semitic peoples who set up city-states such as Ebla, which existed between about 2700 and 2200 BC. The people of Ebla used clay tablets inscribed in cuneiform, an ancient system of writing developed by the Sumer people of Mesopotamia, to write one of the earliest recorded Semitic languages. Syria's location on the trade routes between Europe, Africa, and Asia made it a desired possession of many rulers. The area,

including what is now Lebanon and some of modern-day Jordan, Israel, Saudi Arabia and Iraq, was ruled by the HITTITES and by EGYPT during the 15th–13th centuries BC. Under the PHOENICIANS (13th–10th centuries BC) trading cities flourished on the Mediterranean coast. From the 10th century BC Syria suffered invasions by ASSYRIANS and Egyptians. The ACHAEMENID Empire provided stability until destroyed by ALEXANDER THE GREAT. From the 3rd century BC the Hellenistic SELEUCIDS controlled Syria, often challenged by Egypt. PALMYRA flourished as a city-state. The Romans took over in 64 BC, and Syria remained under Roman law for nearly 700 years.

Christianity became the state religion of Syria in the 4th century AD. When the ROMAN EMPIRE split in the 4th century Syria came under BYZANTINE rule, but in 636 AD Muslims from Arabia invaded the region. Islam gradually replaced Christianity as the main religion, and Arabic became the chief language. From 661 Damascus became the capital of a vast Muslim empire which was ruled by the UMMAYAD Dynasty. When the ABBASID Dynasty took over in 750 the centre of power passed to Baghdad.

From the 11th century Syria was a target of the CRUSADES. At the end of the 12th century SALADIN, a Muslim ruler of Egypt, triumphed over the Crusaders and took control of an extended empire. Egypt's MAMLUK Dynasty ruled Syria from 1260–1516, when the region became part of the Turkish OTTOMAN EMPIRE. European interest intensified in the 19th century. During World War 1, Syrian nationalists revolted and, fighting alongside British forces, helped Britain defeat the Turks and end Ottoman rule.

POLITICS
After the collapse of the Turkish Ottoman empire in World War 1, Syria was ruled by France. Syria became fully independent from France in 1946. The partition of Palestine and the creation of Israel in 1947 led to the first ARAB-ISRAELI WAR, when Syria and other Arab nations failed to defeat Israeli forces. In

AREA 185,180sq km [71,498sq mi]
POPULATION 19,315,000
CAPITAL (POPULATION)
Damascus (2,317,000)
GOVERNMENT Multiparty republic
ETHNIC GROUPS
Arab 90%, Kurdish, Armenian, others
LANGUAGES Arabic (official), Kurdish, Armenian
RELIGIONS Sunni Muslim 74%, other Islam 16%
CURRENCY Syrian pound = 100 piastres

1949, a military coup established a military regime, starting a long period of revolts and changes of government. In 1967, in the third Arab-Israeli war (known as the Six-Day War), Syria lost the strategically important GOLAN HEIGHTS to Israel.

In 1970 Lieutenant-General Hafez al ASSAD led a military revolt, becoming Syria's president in 1971. His repressive but stable regime attracted much Western criticism and was heavily reliant on Arab aid. Syria's anti-Iraq stance in the 1991 GULF WAR, and the involvement of about 20,000 Syrian troops in the conflict, greatly improved its standing in the West. In the mid-1990s Syria held talks with Israel over the future of the Golan Heights. These negotiations were suspended after the election of Binyamin NETANYAHU's right-wing government in Israel in 1996. Assad died in 2000 and was succeeded by his son, Bashar al Assad.

Syria has been criticized for supporting Palestinian terrorist groups and for its long occupation of Lebanon. In 2005, following demonstrations in Lebanon, Syria announced the phased withdrawal of its troops. However, it has been accused of continued interference in Lebanese politics.

ECONOMY
The World Bank classifies Syria as a 'lower-middle-income' developing country. Its main resources are oil, hydroelectricity and fertile land. Agriculture employs about 26% of the population. Oil is the chief mineral product, and phosphates are mined to make fertilizers.

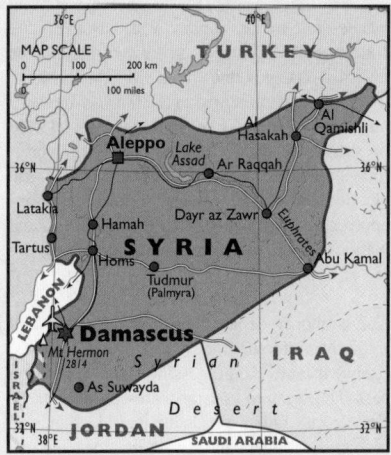

MAP SCALE
0   100   200 km
0   100 miles

TURKEY

Al Qamishli
Al Hasakah
Aleppo
Lake Assad
Ar Raqqah
Latakia
Hamah
Dayr az Zawr
Euphrates
Tartus
SYRIA
Homs
Abu Kamal
Tudmur (Palmyra)
LEBANON
Mt Hermon 2814
Damascus
Syrian Desert
IRAQ
As Suwayda
ISRAEL
JORDAN
SAUDI ARABIA

S

T/t, 20th letter of the alphabet, is derived from the Semitic letter taw *(meaning mark) and the Greek letter* tau. *The Roman letter had the same form as the modern T.*

Tabernacle Portable shrine used by the Hebrews for worship during their wanderings in Sinai. It was a rectangular tent covered with a curtain of goat's hair and a layer of animal skins and roofed with a ceiling of linen tapestry. Inside the Tabernacle, the space divided into two rooms: the **outer** room was the Holy Place, and the **inner** was the Holy of Holies, where God was believed to be present. The Holy of Holies contained the ARK OF THE COVENANT, above which was a slab of gold believed to be the throne of God. After the Hebrews settled CANAAN, there was no further need for the Tabernacle. Eventually its relics transferred to the TEMPLE built by Solomon in Jerusalem. In the Christian Church, a tabernacle is a receptacle in which the Blessed Sacrament is reserved for the EUCHARIST, or a recess used for spiritual contemplation.

table tennis (Ping Pong™) Table sport played by two or four people, who use a rubber-covered, wooden bat to hit a small, celluloid ball back and forth across a net 15.2cm (6in) high. The table is 2.7m (9ft) long and 1.5m (5ft) wide. After the serve, the ball must bounce only on the far side of the net. If the ball misses the table or fails to clear the net, a point is scored by the opponent. The winner is the first player to score 21 points, while leading by at least two points.

taboo (tabu) Prohibition of a form of behaviour, object, or word. A thing may be regarded as taboo if it is unclean or if it is sacred. Breaking a taboo is believed to bring supernatural retribution and often brings social ostracism or other punishment. The term originates in Tonga.

Tabriz (formerly Tauris) Capital of East Azerbaijan province, NW Iran, in the foothills of Mount Sahand. It is Iran's fourth-largest city. From 1295, it was the chief administrative centre for the Iranian Empire. It was occupied by the Ottoman Turks, and later held by the Russians. Tabriz's proximity to Turkey and the Commonwealth of Independent States makes it an important trading centre. Manufactures: carpets, shoes, soap, textiles. Pop. (1996) 1,191,043.

tachycardia Increase in heart rate beyond the normal. It may occur after exertion or because of excitement or illness, particularly during fever; or it may result from a heart condition.

Tacitus, Cornelius (*c*.AD 55–120) Roman historian. His crisp style and reliability make him one of the greatest of

TAIWAN

Taiwan, formerly Formosa, is an island *c*.140km [87mi] off the S coast of mainland China. The country administers a number of nearby islands, including Quemoy (Jinmen) and Matsu (Mazu).

High mountain ranges, extending the length of the island, occupy the central and E regions. Only a quarter of the island's surface is used for agriculture. The highest peak is Yü Shan (Morrison Mountain), 3,952m [12,966ft] above sea level. Several peaks in the central ranges rise to more than 3,000m [10,000ft] and carry dense forests of broadleaved evergreen trees, such as camphor and Chinese cork oak. Above 1,500m [5,000ft] conifers, such as pine, larch and cedar, dominate. In the E, where the mountains often drop steeply down to the sea, the short rivers have cut deep gorges. The W slopes are more gentle.

CLIMATE

Taiwan has a tropical monsoon climate. The annual rainfall exceeds 2,000mm [79in] in almost all areas. From July to September the island is often hit by typhoons. When humidity is high, the heat can be oppressive.

HISTORY

Chinese settlers arrived in Taiwan from the 7th century AD, displacing the native population, but large settlements were not established until the 17th century. When the Portuguese first reached the island in 1590 they named it Formosa – meaning 'beautiful island' – but chose not to settle there. The Dutch occupied a trading port in 1624, but were driven out in 1661 by refugees from the deposed MING Dynasty on the mainland. A Ming official tried to use the island as a base for attacking the Manchu QING Dynasty, but without success. The Manchus took the island in 1683 and incorporated it into what is now Fujian province.

The Manchus settled the island in the late 18th century and, by the mid 19th century, population had increased to about 2,500,000. The island was a major producer of sugar and rice, which were exported to the mainland. In 1886 the island became a Chinese province, and Taipei became its capital in 1894. However, in 1895, Taiwan was ceded to Japan following the SINO-JAPANESE WAR. Japan used the island as a source of food crops and, from the 1930s, developed manufacturing industries based on hydroelectricity.

POLITICS

In 1945, the Japanese army surrendered Taiwan to General CHIANG KAI-SHEK's KUOMINTANG nationalist government. Following victories by Mao Zedong's Communists, about 2 million Nationalists, together with their leader, fled the mainland to Taiwan in the two years before 1949, when the People's Republic of China was proclaimed. The influx was met with hostility by the 8 million Taiwanese and the new regime, the 'Republic of China', was imposed with force. Boosted by help from the United States, Chiang's government set about ambitious programmes for land reform and industrial expansion and, by 1980, Taiwan had become one of the top 20 industrial nations.

AREA 13,900sq km [36,000sq mi]	
POPULATION 22,859,000	
CAPITAL (POPULATION) Taipei (2,473,000)	
GOVERNMENT Unitary multiparty republic	
ETHNIC GROUPS Taiwanese 84%, mainland Chinese 14%	
LANGUAGES Mandarin Chinese (official), Min, Hakka	
RELIGIONS Buddhism, Taoism, Confucianism	
CURRENCY New Taiwan dollar = 100 cents	

Economic development was accompanied by a marked rise in living standards.

Nevertheless, Taiwan remained politically isolated and it lost its seat in the United Nations to Communist China in 1971. It was then abandoned diplomatically by the United States in 1979, when the US switched its recognition to mainland China. However, in 1987 with continuing progress in the economy, martial law was lifted. In 1988, a native Taiwanese became president and in 1991 the country's first general election was held.

China continued to regard Taiwan as a Chinese province. In 1999, tension developed when the Taiwanese President Lee Teng-hui stated that relations between China and Taiwan should be on a 'special state-by-state' basis. This angered the Chinese President Jiang Zemin, whose 'one-nation' policy was based on the concept that China and Taiwan should be regarded as one country with two equal governments. Tension mounted in 2000 when Taiwan's opposition leader, Chen Shui-bian, was elected president, because Chen had adopted a pro-independence stance. However, after the elections, Chen adopted a more conciliatory approach to mainland China. In 2007 the United Nations rejected Taiwan's bid for membership.

ECONOMY

The economy depends on manufacturing and trade. Manufactures include electronic goods, footwear and clothing, ships and television sets. The western coastal plains produce large rice crops. Other products include bananas, pineapples, sugar cane, sweet potatoes and tea.

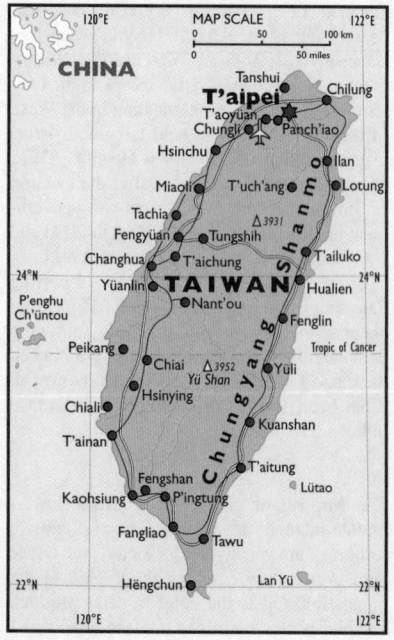

Roman historians. His books include a eulogy for his father-in-law, Agricola, governor of Britain. His major works, the *Annals* and *Histories*, exist only in fragmentary form.

tadpole Aquatic larva of a TOAD or FROG; it has feathery gills and a finned tail, and lacks lungs and legs. The tadpoles of most species are herbivores, feeding on algae and other aquatic plants. During METAMORPHOSIS legs grow, the tail reabsorbs, and internal lungs replace gills.

Taegu City in s central South Korea; capital of North Kyongsang province and the country's third-largest city. Successfully defended by United Nations' (UN) troops during the KOREAN WAR, it is the trading centre for a large apple-growing area. The main industries are textiles, including silk and synthetic fabrics. Pop. (2000) 2,480,000.

tae kwon do Korean martial art. It is a form of unarmed combat developed over 2000 years in Korea, and is characterized by high standing and jump kicks as well as punches. It is practised both for sport and for spiritual development.

Taft, Robert Alphonso (1889–1953) US politician, son of William Howard TAFT. He was a US senator (1938–53). A conservative Republican, he sponsored the Taft-Hartley Act (1947), which restricted trade unions.

Taft, William Howard (1857–1930) Twenty-seventh US President (1909–13) and Chief Justice of the Supreme Court (1921–30). Governor of the Philippines (1901–04), he entered the cabinet of Theodore ROOSEVELT. Taft won the Republican nomination for President and was elected in 1908. His lack of political experience caused increasing dissension. In 1912, Roosevelt, having failed to regain the presidential nomination, set up his own Progressive Party and split the Republican vote. The Democrat, Woodrow WILSON, won the election. As Chief Justice, Taft streamlined the operations of the federal judiciary.

Tagore, Rabindranath (1861–1941) Indian poet and philosopher. He wrote novels, essays, plays, and poetic works in colloquial Bengali. His best-known work is *Gitanjali* (1912), a volume of spiritual poetry. In 1913, Tagore became the first Asian writer to receive the Nobel Prize in literature. He was knighted in 1915, but renounced the honour after the AMRITSAR Massacre (1919).

Tagus (Tajo, Tejo) Longest river on the Iberian peninsula, flowing *c.*1,000km (620mi). The Tagus rises in the Sierra de Albarracin, Teruel, E central Spain. It flows generally sw for 785km (488mi), passing through Toledo, to the Spain-Portugal border. It then winds s to drain into the Atlantic at Lisbon. The Tagus estuary is one of the world's finest natural harbours.

Tahiti Island in the s Pacific Ocean, in the Windward group of the SOCIETY ISLANDS, the largest in FRENCH POLYNESIA and accounting for more than half its population. Tahiti is mountainous, rising to 2,237m (7,339ft), but also fertile – producing tropical fruits, copra, sugar cane, and vanilla. Charted in 1767 by the British navigator Samuel Wallis and explored by Captain COOK, France colonized it in 1880. Paul GAUGUIN lived and painted here. Industries: tourism, pearl-fishing, phosphates. Area: 1,058sq km (408sq mi). Pop. (1996) 150,000.

TAJIKISTAN

The Republic of Tajikistan is one of the five central Asian republics that formed part of the former Soviet Union. Only 7% of the land is below 1,000m [3,280ft], while almost all of eastern Tajikistan is above 3,000m [9,840ft]. The highest point is Pik Ismail Samani, formerly known as Communism Peak (Pik Kommunizma), which reaches 7,495m [24,590ft]. The main ranges are the w extension of the TIAN SHAN Range in the N and the snow-capped PAMIRS in the SE. Earthquakes are common throughout the country.

Vegetation varies greatly according to altitude. Much of Tajikistan consists of desert or rocky mountain landscapes capped by snow and ice.

CLIMATE
Tajikistan has an extreme continental climate. Summers are hot and dry in the lower valleys, and winters are long and bitterly cold in the mountains. Much of the country is arid, but the SE has heavy snowfalls.

HISTORY
The ancestors of the people of Tajikistan were Persians who had settled in the area about 2,500 years ago. Macedonian Greeks led by Alexander the Great conquered the region in 331 BC. From 323 BC the area was split into several independent states. Arab armies conquered the area in the mid-7th century and introduced Islam, which remains the chief religion today. In the 9th century it fell to the Iranian Empire. The Tajik cities of BUKHARA and SAMARKAND were vital centres of trade and Islamic learning. In the 13th century, Tajikistan was overrun by the Mongol hordes of Genghis Khan. Uzbeks, a Turkic people, ruled the area as the Khanate of Bukhara from the 16th to the 19th centuries.

The fragmentation of the region aided Russian conquest from 1868. Following the RUSSIAN REVOLUTION (1917), Tajikistan rebelled against Russian rule. Although Soviet troops annexed northern Tajikistan into Turkistan in 1918, the Bukhara Emirate held out against the Red Army until 1921. In 1924 Tajikistan became an autonomous part of the Republic of Uzbekistan. In 1929 Tajikistan achieved full republic status, but Bukhara and Samarkand remained in the Republic of Uzbekistan. During the 1930s vast irrigation schemes increased agricultural land. Many Russians and Uzbeks were settled in Tajikistan.

POLITICS
While the Soviet Union began to introduce reforms in the 1980s, many Tajiks demanded freedom. In 1989, the Tajik government made Tajik the official language instead of Russian and, in 1990, it stated that its local laws overruled Soviet laws. Tajikistan became fully independent in 1991, following the break-up of the Soviet Union. As the poorest of the ex-Soviet republics, Tajikistan faced many problems in trying to introduce a free-market system.

In 1992, civil war broke out between the government, which was run by former Com-

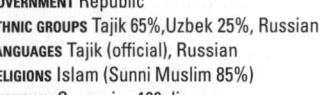

AREA 143,100sq km [55,521sq mi]
POPULATION 7,077,000
CAPITAL (POPULATION) Dushanbe (529,000)
GOVERNMENT Republic
ETHNIC GROUPS Tajik 65%, Uzbek 25%, Russian
LANGUAGES Tajik (official), Russian
RELIGIONS Islam (Sunni Muslim 85%)
CURRENCY Somoni = 100 dirams

munists, and an alliance of democrats and Islamic forces. The government maintained control, but it relied heavily on aid from the COMMONWEALTH OF INDEPENDENT STATES, the organization through which most of the former Soviet republics kept in touch. Presidential elections in 1994 resulted in victory for Imomali Rakhmonov, though the Islamic opposition did not recognize the result.

A ceasefire was signed in December 1996. Further agreements in 1997 provided for the opposition to have 30% of the ministerial posts in government, but many small groups excluded from the process continued to undermine the peace through killings and military action. In 1999, Rakhmonov was re-elected president. Changes to the constitution in 2003 enabled him to serve two more seven-year terms. In 2006 Rakhmonov was again reappointed president after elections in which opposition parties were heavily restricted. International observers criticized the polls as neither free nor fair.

ECONOMY
The World Bank classifies Tajikistan as a 'low-income' developing country. Agriculture, mainly on irrigated land, is the main activity and cotton is the chief product. Other crops include fruits, grains and vegetables. The country has large hydroelectric power resources, and produces aluminium.

tai chi Neo-Confucian concept of the intrinsic energy of the universe (*chi*). *Tai chi* also refers to a popular form of exercise, a martial arts-based series of slow, flowing movements.

Taipei Capital and largest city of Taiwan, at the N end of the island. A major trade centre for tea in the 19th century, the city enlarged under Japanese rule (1895–1945), and became the seat of the Chinese Nationalist government in 1949. Industries: textiles, chemicals, fertilizers, metals, machinery. From 1945, the city expanded rapidly from a population of just 335,000 people. Pop. (2005) 2,473,000.

Taiping Rebellion (1851–64) Revolt in China against the Manchurian QING dynasty, led by a Hakka fanatic, Hung Hsiu-ch'uan. The fighting laid waste to 17 provinces of China and resulted in more than 20 million deaths. The Qing never fully recovered their ability to govern all of China.

Taiwan (officially the Republic of China) Pacific island, separated from the SE coast of the Chinese mainland by the 160km (100mi) Taiwan Strait. *See* country feature page 722.

Taiyuan City in NE China; capital of Shanxi province. The region has rich coal and iron ore deposits. Taiyuan is a major industrial city with iron and steel, chemical and engineering plants and textile industries. Pop. (1998 est.) 2,956,900.

Tajik Native speaker of Tajiki, an Iranian language spoken in Tajikistan and (with some TURKIC elements) in Afghanistan, S Russia and much of central Asia.

Tajikistan Republic in central Asia. *See* country feature page 723.

Taj Mahal Mausoleum near Agra, N India, built (1632–54) by Mogul Emperor SHAH JAHAN for his favourite wife, Mumtaz Mahal. By far the largest Islamic tomb ever destined for a woman, the Taj stands in a Persian water garden that represents Paradise. With its bulb-shaped dome, intricate inlays of semiprecious stones, and rectangular reflecting pool, it is one of the world's most beautiful buildings.

takahe Rare, flightless New Zealand bird, related to the RAIL and gallinule. Turkey-sized, it has a heavy, curved bill, a reddish shield on the forehead and bright, blue-green plumage. Family Rallidae; species *Notornis mantelli*.

Talbot, William Henry Fox (1800–77) English scientist. Talbot improved on the work of DAGUERRE by inventing the first photographic process capable of producing any number of positive prints from an original negative. *See also* PHOTOGRAPHY

TANZANIA

The United Republic of Tanzania consists of the former mainland country of Tanganyika and the island nation of ZANZIBAR, which also includes the island of Pemba.

Behind a narrow coastal plain, the majority of Tanzania is a plateau lying between 900 and 1,500m [2,950–4,920ft] above sea level. The plateau is broken by arms of the Great African RIFT VALLEY. The W arm contains lakes Nyasa (also called MALAWI) and TANGANYIKA, while the E arm contains the strongly alkaline Lake Natron, together with lakes Eyasi and Manyara. Lake VICTORIA occupies a shallow depression in the plateau and is not situated within the Rift Valley.

KILIMANJARO, the highest peak, is an extinct volcano. At 5,895m [19,340ft], it is also Africa's highest mountain. Zanzibar and Pemba are coral islands.

CLIMATE

The coast has a hot, humid climate. The greatest rainfall is in April and May. Inland mountains and plateaux are cooler and less humid. The Rift Valley is hot. Mount Kilimanjaro was until recently permanently snow and ice covered, but is now almost bare, partly due to the effects of climate change.

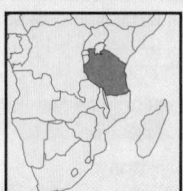

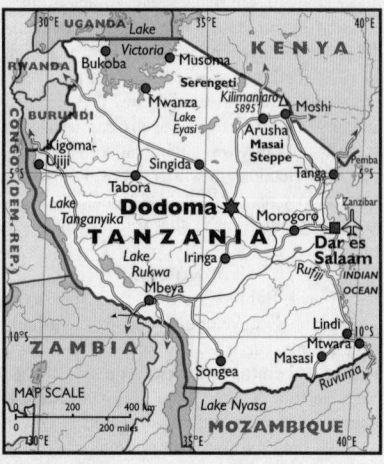

HISTORY

Around 2,000 years ago Arabs, Persians and Chinese traded along the Tanzanian coast. Arabic traders often intermarried with local people and the Arab-African people produced the distinctive Arab-Swahili culture. In 1498, Vasco da Gama became the first European to land on the Tanzanian coast. The Portuguese took control of coastal trade in the early 16th century.

In 1698 Arabs from Oman took control of Zanzibar, driving out the Portuguese. From this base they developed inland trade, bringing gold, ivory and slaves from the interior. In 1841, the Sultan moved his capital to Zanzibar. The interior of Tanganyika was opened up by new caravan routes bringing slaves and ivory to the coast for transshipment.

During the 19th century European explorers and missionaries were active, mapping the country and striving to stop the slave trade. In the 1880s the country was carved up between European powers as part of the Scramble for Africa.

POLITICS

Mainland Tanganyika became a German territory in 1887, while Zanzibar (including Pemba) became a British protectorate in 1890. The Germans introduced a system of forced labour to develop plantations. This led to a major rebellion in 1905, which was put down with great brutality.

Following Germany's defeat in World War 1, Britain gained control of Tanganyika and was granted a mandate to rule it by the League of Nations. Tanganyika remained a Briish territory until winning its independence in 1961, followed by Zanzibar in 1963. Tanganyika and Zanzibar united to form the United Republic of Tanzania in 1964.

The country's first president, Julius NYERERE, pursued socialist policies of self-help (called *ujamaa* in Swahili) and egalitarianism. While many of its social reforms were successful, the country failed to make economic progress. Nyerere resigned as president in 1985, though he remained influential until his death in 1999. His successors, Ali Hassan Mwinyi, who

AREA 945,090sq km [364,899sq mi]
POPULATION 39,384,000
CAPITAL (POPULATION) Dodoma (204,000)
GOVERNMENT Multiparty republic
ETHNIC GROUPS Native African 99% (Bantu 95%)
LANGUAGES Swahili (Kiswahili) and English (both official)
RELIGIONS Islam 35% (99% in Zanzibar), traditional beliefs 35%, Christianity 30%
CURRENCY Tanzanian shilling = 100 cents

served from 1985 until 1995, and Benjamin Mkapa, who was re-elected in 2000, pursued more liberal economic policies. In 2005, Mkapa was succeeded by Jakaya Kikwete, another CCM (Chama Cha Mapinduzi) candidate.

ECONOMY

Tanzania is one of the world's poorest countries. Although crops are grown on only 5% of the land, agriculture employs 85% of the people. Most farmers grow only enough to feed their families. Food crops include bananas, cassava, maize, millet, rice and vegetables. Export crops include coffee, cotton, cashew nuts, tea and tobacco. Other crops grown for export include cloves, coconuts and sisal. Some farmers raise animals, but sleeping sickness and drought restrict the areas for livestock farming.

Diamonds and other gems are mined, together with some coal and gold. Industry is mostly small-scale. Manufactures include processed food, fertilizers, refined petroleum products and textiles.

Tourism is increasing. Tanzania has beautiful beaches, but its main attractions are its magnificent national parks and reserves, including the celebrated Serengeti and the Ngorongoro Crater. These are renowned for their wildlife and are among the world's finest.

Tanzania also contains a major archaeological site, OLDUVAI GORGE, west of the Serengeti. The British archaeologist and anthropologist Dr Louis LEAKEY discovered 1.75 million year-old fossils of *Homo habilis* at Olduvai in 1964.

T

talc (hydrous magnesium silicate, $Mg_3Si_4O_{10}(OH)_2$). It occurs as rare tabulate crystals in a monoclinic system and as masses. It is used in talcum powder and in ceramics. Hardness 1; r.d. 2.6.

Taliban Radical SUNNI political movement in AFGHANISTAN. In 1996, from their headquarters in Kandahar, sw Afghanistan, Taliban militia launched themselves on Afghan society, vowing to spread SHARIA (Islamic law) throughout the country. They soon captured Kabul. They were driven from power by Northern Alliance and US forces in 2001 and mounted a lengthy and brutal insurgency from the border with Pakistan.

Tallahassee State capital of Florida, USA. First discovered by Europeans in 1539, it was the site of a Spanish mission. Tallahassee became the capital of Florida Territory in 1824. Industries: chemicals, timber, paper, tourism. Pop. (2000) 150,624.

Talleyrand (-Périgord), Charles Maurice de (1754–1838) French statesman and diplomat. As foreign minister under the Directory (1797–99), he participated in the coup that brought NAPOLEON to power. In 1807, concerned about the latter's growing power, Talleyrand resigned as foreign minister. In 1814, he negotiated the restoration of the BOURBON monarchy. As foreign minister to LOUIS XVIII, Talleyrand represented France at the Congress of VIENNA (1814–15). He was LOUIS PHILIPPE's chief adviser in the July Revolution (1830) and served (1830–34) as his ambassador to Britain.

Tallinn (Talin) Capital and largest city of Estonia, on the Gulf of Finland, opposite Helsinki. Founded (1219) by the Danes, it became a member of the Hanseatic League in 1285. It passed to Sweden in 1561, and was ceded to Russia in 1721. Developed in the 19th century for Russia's Baltic Fleet, it remains a major port and industrial centre. It was badly damaged in World War 2. Industries: machinery, cables, paper. Pop. (2000) 404,000.

Tallis, Thomas (c.1505–85) English composer of church music. In 1575, Elizabeth I granted Tallis and William BYRD a licence to print and publish music; they published the *Cantiones Sacrae*, a set of motets. His church music includes a setting of Lamentations, two masses, and a number of anthems, and the 40-part motet, *Spem in alium* (c.1573).

Talmud Body of Jewish religious and civil laws and learned interpretations of their meanings. Study of the Talmud is central to Orthodox JUDAISM. The Talmud consists of two elements: the MISHNA and the *Gemara*. The *Mishna* is the written version of a set of oral laws that were handed down from the time of MOSES (c.1200BC); the written version was completed by c.AD 200. The **Gemara**, the interpretation and commentary on the Mishna, was completed by c.500. The Talmud consists of short passages from the Mishna followed by the relevant and extensive part of the Gemara.

tamarind Tropical tree native to Asia and Africa. It has divided (feather-like) leaves and pale yellow flowers, streaked with red. The fruit pulp is used in beverages, food, and medicines. Height: 12–24m (40–80ft). Family Fabaceae/Leguminosae; species *Tamarindus indica*.

tamarisk Any of a group of shrubs usually found in semi-arid areas. They are DECIDUOUS and have slender branches covered with blue-green, scale-like leaves and clusters of small, white or pink flowers. Height: to 9m (30ft). Family Tamaricaceae; genus *Tamarix*.

Tambo, Oliver (1917–93) South African politician, president (1977–90) of the AFRICAN NATIONAL CONGRESS (ANC). He joined the ANC in 1944. In 1960, Tambo left South Africa to organize the external activities of the ANC. During Nelson MANDELA's long imprisonment, Tambo served first as acting president (1967–76) then full president of the ANC. On Mandela's release, he relinquished the post. *See also* APARTHEID

tambourine PERCUSSION musical instrument much used by wandering musicians in Europe in the Middle Ages. It comprises a narrow circular frame, made of wood, with a single parchment drumhead and metal jangles attached to the sides.

Tamerlane (1336–1405) (Turkish *Timur Leng*, 'Timur the Lame') Mongol conqueror, b. Uzbekistan. He claimed descent from GENGHIS KHAN. By 1369, Tamerlane conquered present-day Turkistan and established SAMARKAND as his capital. He extended his conquests to the region of the GOLDEN HORDE between the Caspian and Black Seas. In 1398, Tamerlane invaded NW India and defeated the Delhi Sultanate. He

then turned towards the MAMLUK Empire, capturing Syria and Damascus. In 1402, he captured the Ottoman Sultan Beyazid I at Angora. His death, at the head of a 200,000-strong invasion force of China, enabled the reopening of the SILK ROAD. His vast empire was divided among the Timurid dynasty.

Tamil Language spoken in s India, chiefly in the state of Tamil Nadu, by up to 50 million people. In addition, there are c.3 million speakers in N SRI LANKA and c.1 million distributed throughout Malaysia, Singapore, Fiji, Mauritius and Guyana.

Tamil Tigers Militant TAMIL group in Sri Lanka seeking independence for the 3 million Hindu Tamils N and E of the island from the Buddhist SINHALESE majority. From the 1980s, the Tamil Tigers waged a campaign of civil disobedience and terrorism. In 1986, autonomy for the Tamils was agreed by India and Sri Lanka, but no date was fixed. In 1987, the Indian Army was sent to restore order but withdrew in 1990, having failed to stop the violence. A 2002 ceasefire led to hopes for peace, but violence continued sporadically.

tanager Small, brightly coloured, American forest bird with a cone-shaped bill. Tanagers feed on insects and fruit. The scarlet tanager (*Piranga olivacea*) of E North America has black on its wings and tail. Family Emberizidae.

T'ang Chinese imperial dynasty (618–907). The early period was a golden age of China, when it was the largest, richest and culturally most accomplished society in the world. T'ang armies carried Chinese authority to Afghanistan, Tibet, and Korea. Towns grew as trade expanded, new ideas and foreign influences were freely admitted, and the arts flourished. During the 8th century, the dynasty was submerged in civil conflicts.

Tanganyika, Lake Second-largest lake in Africa and the second-deepest freshwater lake in the world. It lies in E central Africa on the borders of Tanzania, Congo, Zambia, and Burundi, in the RIFT VALLEY. Area: 32,893sq km (12,700sq mi). Depth: 1,437m (4715ft).

tangent In TRIGONOMETRY, ratio of the length of the side opposite an acute angle to the length of the side adjacent to it within a right-angle triangle. The term is also used for a line that contacts a circle or curve at one point, at the angle of the slope of the curve. For a circle this is at a right angle to the radius at the point of contact.

Tangier (Tanger) Port on the Strait of Gibraltar, N Morocco. An ancient Greek, Phoenician, and then Roman port, it was later occupied by Moors and taken by the Portuguese in 1471. Tangier passed to England in 1662, but the English abandoned the city to the Sultan of Morocco in 1684. Under international control from 1904 to 1956 (except during World War 2), it became part of Morocco in 1956. Industries: rugs, pottery, shipping, fishing, tourism. Pop. (2002 est.) 591,300.

tango Ballroom dance that originated in Buenos Aires, Argentina, in the late 19th century. Developed from Argentinian *milonga*, it was a ballroom favourite in Europe and the USA by 1915. It is characterized by quick, long strides and rapid reversals of direction on the balls of the feet.

Tanizaki, Junichiro (1886–1965) Japanese novelist and dramatist. Influenced by classical JAPANESE LITERATURE and by Charles BAUDELAIRE, Tanizaki's writing include *Some Prefer Nettles* (1928–29) and *The Makioka Sisters* (1943–48).

tank Tracked, armoured vehicle mounting a single primary weapon, usually an artillery piece, and one or more machine guns. Modern tanks have an enclosed, fully revolving turret and are heavily armoured; main battle tanks weigh from 35 to 50 tonnes and usually have a crew of four. Developed in great secrecy by the British during World War 1, tanks were first employed at the Battle of the Somme (1916).

tannin (tannic acid) Any of a group of complex organic compounds derived from tree bark, roots and galls, unripe fruit, tea and coffee. Tannin is used in tanning to cure hides and make leather, in inks and dyes, and as an astringent in medicine.

tansy Any of several mostly perennial plants characterized by fern-like, aromatic leaves and clusters of yellow, button-like flower heads. *Tanacetum vulgare*, native to Eurasia, is a common weed in North America. Height: to 91cm (3ft). Family Asteraceae/Compositae.

tantalum (symbol Ta) Rare, lustrous, blue-grey metallic element. Its chief ore is columbite-tantalite. Hard but malleable,

▲ **Taj Mahal** It took more than 20,000 skilled workmen drawn from all over India and Asia more than ten years to complete the mausoleum of the Taj Mahal. A masterpiece of Islamic architecture, the building symbolizes the throne of Allah.

T

▶ **tapestry** By the Middle Ages, one of the most common ways of creating tapestries was by using a low-warp loom (A). It had a back roller (1) to carry the unused warp threads, and a front roller (2) to carry the woven tapestry. These, and the drawing board (3), to which the cartoon (4) is pinned, are supported by sturdy side beams (5). A slide block (6) enables the back roller to be moved to tauten the warp threads (7). The treadles (8), connected to heddle bars, are used to cross even and uneven warp threads. The weaver's tools are the bobbins, which carry the colour threads (9), a box-wood comb and scraper (10) to pack down the threads, and a mirror (11) to check the underside (the side that will be seen) of the tapestry during weaving.

INTERNET

Tasmania
▶ www.tas.gov.au
▶ www.discovertasmania. com.au

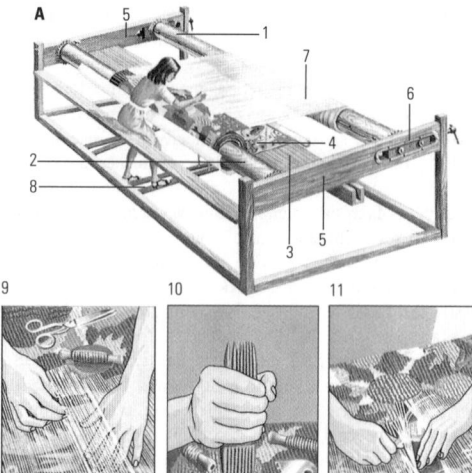

A

▲ **tarantula** The bite of the tarantula (*Aphonopelma* sp.) is not deadly to humans, although it is powerful enough to kill small birds, amphibians, and mice. Found in sw USA and Central America, the body can be up to 7.5cm (3in) long and, including the legs, up to 25cm (10in) across.

▶ **tapir** The Brazilian tapir (*Tapirus terrestris*) lives in South America – from Venezuela to Paraguay. It inhabits wooded or grassy habitats near water, and feeds on grass, small shrubs, and aquatic plants. Its dark brown colour identifies it as a New World tapir, in contrast to the black-and-white Malayan tapir.

tantalum is used as a wire and in electrical components, mobile phone capacitors, chemical equipment and medical instruments. It was discovered in 1802 by Swedish chemist Anders Ekeberg (1767–1813). Properties: at.no. 73; r.a.m. 180.948; r.d. 16.6; m.p. 2,996°C (5,425°F); b.p. 5,425°C (9,797°F); most common isotope Ta[181] (99.988%).

tantrism Term for religious systems within BUDDHISM, JAINISM, and HINDUISM that are based on esoteric practices recorded in sacred texts called Tantras. For Hindus and Jains, the Tantras are post-Vedic (VEDAS) texts telling how to fulfil sexual desires and attain spiritual experiences. They contain spells and MANTRAS and give instructions on YOGA and meditative techniques for purifying and controlling the body and mind. For Buddhists, the Tantras are writings attributed to BUDDHA explaining how the believer may attain enlightenment.

Tanzania Republic in E Africa. *See* country feature page 724

Tao Ch'ien (365–427) Chinese poet. He developed a simple style that distinguished his work from the ornateness of his contemporaries. His verse, which has a predominantly Taoist outlook, often extols the pleasures of nature and wine.

Taoism Chinese philosophy and religion considered as being next to CONFUCIANISM in importance. Taoist philosophy is traced to a 6th-century BC classic of LAO TZU, the *Tao Te Ching*. The recurrent theme of this work is the *Tao* (way or path). To follow the *Tao* is to follow the path leading to self-realization. *Te* (virtue) and *ch'i* (energy) represent the goal of effortless action. Taoist ethics emphasize patience, simplicity, and the harmony of nature, achieved through the proper balance of YIN AND YANG (male and female principles). As a religion, Taoism dates from the time of Chang Tao-ling, who organized a group of followers in AD 142. *See also* BOOK OF CHANGES; TAI CHI

tape, magnetic Thin strip of plastic, coated on one side with a layer of iron or chromium oxide, used in audio and video TAPE RECORDERS. During SOUND RECORDING, a recording head magnetizes the oxide layer in a pattern corresponding to the input signal. During playback, the magnetized oxide particles induce an electric current almost identical to the one that produced them. *See also* DIGITAL AUDIO TAPE (DAT)

tape recorder Device which records and plays back sound or video on magnetic TAPE. Sound transforms into electric current and feeds to a TRANSDUCER, which converts it into the magnetic variations that are recorded on the tape. *See also* DIGITAL AUDIO TAPE (DAT); MICROPHONE; SOUND RECORDING

tapestry Hand-woven, plain-weave fabric. Used for wall decoration and hangings, tapestry design is a very ancient craft and a few fragments survive from 15th-century BC Egypt. The first great French woollen tapestry came from Arras in the 14th century AD. The most famous designs originated from the GOBELINS factory, Paris. Some 20th-century textile artists use tapestry techniques in their work.

tapeworm Parasite of the genus *Taenia*, which colonizes the intestines of vertebrates, including human beings. Caught from eating raw or under-cooked meat, it may cause serious disease.

tapioca *See* CASSAVA

tapir Any of several species of nocturnal, plant-eating, hoofed mammals native to forests of tropical South America and Malaysia. The tapir has a large head, a long, flexible snout, a heavy body, short legs, and a tiny tail. Length: to 2.5m (7.5ft). Family Tapiridae; genus *Tapirus*.

tar Black or dark brown, complex liquid mixture of HYDROCARBON compounds, derived from wood, coal, and other organic materials. Tar from PETROLEUM oil is a major source of hydrocarbons for the synthesis of pharmaceuticals, pesticides, and plastics; cruder tar compounds, such as pitch, are used for road surfacing and protecting timber against rot and pests. Wood tar yields creosote and paraffin.

Tarantino, Quentin (1963–) US film director, screenwriter, and actor. His debut feature, *Reservoir Dogs* (1991), established his reputation for controversial, violent, and discursive films. *Pulp Fiction* (1994) was a cult hit, featuring many references to pop culture and film classics.

tarantula Large, hairy wolf-spider of s Europe. It spins no web, but chases and pounces on its prey. Length of body: to 2.5cm (1in). Family Lycosidae; species *Lycosa tarentula*. The name is also applied to the sluggish, dark, hairy spiders of sw USA, Mexico, and South America. Many species burrow and feed on insects. Length of body: to 7.5cm (3in). Family Theraphosidae; genera *Aphonopelma* and *Eurypelma*.

Tarawa Town on an atoll of the same name in the w Pacific Ocean, capital of KIRIBATI. Located in the N central part of the group, it is the main trade centre for the islands. Copra, fish and fish products are its principal exports. Pop. (2002 est.) 39,000.

tariff Tax placed on imports, calculated either as a percentage of the value of the item (AD valorem tariff) or per unit (specific duty). Tariffs may be used to discourage the import of certain types of goods or to adjust for price differentials in order to allow the home country's products to be competitive.

Tarim Basin Basin in XINJIANG region, NW China, between the TIAN SHAN and Kunlun mountain ranges. Taklamakan Desert covers most of the region. The Turfan Depression, China's lowest point, at 154m (505ft), is in the extreme E. The River Tarim, 2,027km (1,260mi) long, is formed by the confluence of the Kashgar and Yarkand rivers. It flows E then SE into the basin.

taro Large, tropical plant native to the Pacific islands and SE Asia and cultivated in other parts of the world for its edible tuberous root. Family Araceae; species *Colocasia esculenta*.

tarpon Tropical, marine game fish. Blue and bright silver, it has a long, forked tail. Length: to 1.8m (6ft); weight: to 150kg (300lb). Species include the small Pacific *Megalops cyprinoides* and the large Atlantic *M. atlanticus*. Family Elopidae.

tarragon Perennial plant with liquorice-flavoured leaves used as a culinary HERB. Family Asteraceae/Compositae; species *Artemisia dracunculus*.

tarsier Any of several species of nocturnal primates of Indonesia. They are small, squat animals with large eyes, long tails and monkey-like hands and feet. Family Tarsiidae; genus *Tarsius*.

tartan Cloth, usually woollen, with a pattern of stripes crossing at right angles. The cross-bars are of different colours and widths, usually on a red or green background. The patterned cloth is now associated mainly with the Highlands of Scotland. Many Scottish clans have their own, unique tartan patterns.

Tartars *See* TATARS

Tasaday Small group of isolated aboriginal people of the rainforests of s Mindanao in the Philippines. They are food-gathering cave dwellers with a STONE AGE culture.

Tashkent Largest city and capital of UZBEKISTAN, in the Tashkent oasis in the foothills of the TIAN SHAN mountains, watered by the River Chirchik. It was ruled by the Arabs from the 8th until the 11th century. The city was captured by TAMERLANE in 1361, and by the Russians in 1865. The modern city is a transport and economic centre of the region. Industries: textiles, chemicals, food processing, mining machinery, paper, porcelain, clothing, leather, furniture. Pop. (2005) 2,160,000.

Tasman, Abel Janszoon (1603–59) Dutch maritime explorer who made many discoveries in the Pacific. On his voyage of 1642–43, he discovered what is now called Tasmania. Tasman reached New Zealand, but was attacked by Maoris in Golden Bay. He landed on Tonga and Fiji, and sailed along the N coast of New Ireland. Although he circumnavigated Australia, he never sighted the mainland coast.

Tasmania Island state of Australia, separated from Victoria by the Bass Strait. The chief cities are HOBART, the state capital in the s, and Launceston in the N. Tasmania is mountainous and forested, with a temperate maritime climate. The first European discovery was made by Abel TASMAN in 1642, and it was named Van Diemen's Land. In 1777, Captain COOK visited it and claimed it for the British, who established a penal colony. In 1825, Tasmania became a separate colony and it was federated as a state of the Commonwealth of Australia in 1901. Mineral deposits include copper, tin and zinc. The development of hydroelectric power has stimulated the growth of manufacturing. Industries: metallurgy, textiles. Area: 68,332sq km (26,383sq mi). Pop. (2000 est.) 470,100.

Tasmanian devil Carnivorous marsupial with a bear-like appearance; it is found only in the forest and scrub of Tasmania. It feeds on a wide variety of animal food, including carrion. Length: to 80cm (31in). Species *Sarcophilus harrisii*.

Tasmanian wolf (thylacine) Largest carnivorous marsupial. It became extinct on mainland Australia because of relentless hunting; a few specimens are rumoured to have survived in forested areas of Tasmania. It has a wolflike appearance, but its coat is marked with transverse dark stripes on the back, hindquarters and tail. Species *Thylacinus cynocephalus*.

TASS (acronym for **T**elegrafnoye **A**gentsvo **S**ovyetskovo **S**oyuza) News agency of the former Soviet Union. Affiliated with press agencies around the world, it was one of the major news services used by the Western press.

Tasso, Torquato (1544–95) Italian poet and prose writer. He was a member of the Court at Ferrara from 1565. His masterpiece, *Jerusalem Delivered* (1575), an epic on the First Crusade, became a model for later writers.

taste One of the five SENSES. It responds to the chemical constituents of anything placed in the mouth. In human beings, the taste buds of the TONGUE differentiate four qualities: sweetness, saltiness, bitterness and sourness.

Tatars (Tartars) Turkic-speaking people of central Asia. In medieval Europe, the name Tatar referred to many different Asiatic invaders. True Tatars originated in E Siberia, and converted to Islam in the 14th century. They divided into two groups: one in s Siberia, who came under Russian rule; the other in the Crimea, which was part of the Ottoman Empire until annexed by Russia in 1783.

Tatarstan Autonomous region in the Russian Federation populated mainly by the TATARS. Tatar nationalism has its origins in the Crimean Autonomous Socialist Republic, founded in 1921. The Republic was dissolved and the entire population deported by Stalin in 1945. After the break-up of the Soviet Union in 1991, many of the 300,000 to 400,000 exiled Tatars began to return to the Crimea. Pop. (2000) 3,778,600.

Tate Gallery UK national collection of modern art. The main building at Millbank opened in 1897 as a collection of British painting and sculpture, which ranges from the mid-16th century to the present day. An extension was added in 1979. In 1987 the Clore Gallery opened, containing the TURNER bequest. There are Tate Galleries in Liverpool and St Ives, Cornwall. Tate Modern (2000) is in the former Bankside Power Station and houses the modern, international art collection.

◀ **Tasmanian devil** The Tasmanian devil (*Sarcophilus harrisii*) was once found on the mainland of s Australia, but is now confined to remote parts of the island of Tasmania. A nocturnal marsupial, it preys on a variety of animals as well as scavenging. Very strong for its size, its prey is sometimes much larger than itself.

Tati, Jacques (1908–82) French film director and actor , b. Jacques Tatischeff. His debut feature was *Jour de Fête* (1949). Tati's distinctive style of whimsical, visual humour is most apparent in *Monsieur Hulot's Holiday* (1953). He won an Academy Award for best foreign language film for *Mon Oncle* (1958). Other films include *Playtime* (1968) and *Traffic* (1971).

Tatlin, Vladimir Evgrafovitch (1885–1953) Russian sculptor. In 1913, influenced by CUBISM and FUTURISM, he instigated the ABSTRACT ART style known as CONSTRUCTIVISM. Tatlin used industrial materials such as metal, tin, and glass. He is chiefly celebrated for his *Reliefs*: innovative, three-dimensional constructions that removed pictorial illusion.

Tatum, Art (1909–56) (Arthur Tatum) US jazz pianist. Almost blind since birth, Tatum established a standard for solo jazz piano technique. He made his first recording in 1932. His reputation for technical virtuosity endures.

Taurus (the Bull) In astronomy, northern constellation on the ecliptic between Aries and Gemini. It contains the Pleiades and Hyades stellar clusters, and the Crab Nebula. The brightest star is the first-magnitude Alpha Tauri (Aldebaran).

Tavener, John Kenneth (1944–) English composer. He achieved early success with his biblical cantata *The Whale* (1966) and has continued to compose works that are religious in character and inspiration. The opera *Thérèse* (1973–76) is a fine example of his early style. His conversion (1977) to the Eastern Orthodox Church accompanied a move towards a more austere musical style. A feast of the Orthodox Church inspired *The Protecting Veil* (1987), for cello and orchestra.

Taverner, John (*c.*1490–1545) English composer. Most of his surviving works date from 1526–30. He composed mostly church music, notably masses and motets. His six-voice masses are complex contrapuntal structures; the smaller-scale masses are in a simpler, more restrained style.

taxation Compulsory payments of various kinds made by members of a society. Taxes are levied both on individuals and corporations and are of two chief kinds, direct and indirect. **Direct** taxes are levied on income. **Indirect** taxes, such as VALUE-ADDED TAX (VAT), are levied on commodities and services. Taxation funds government expenditure on defence, social services, administration and the repayment of public debt. It may also be used to reduce the inequality of income and wealth in a community; changing the rate of income tax can either reduce or increase the purchasing power of consumers by altering the level of disposable income. Indirect taxes can check the flow of imports or exports to alter the balance of trade.

taxonomy Organization of plants, animals, and other organisms into categories based on similarities of genetic sequences, appearance, structure or evolution. The categories, from the most inclusive to the exclusive, are: KINGDOM, phylum, class, order, family, GENUS, SPECIES (the last two of which appear in *italics*), and sometimes variety. In some categories, there are also subphyla, subfamilies, and so on. Ancient and extinct animals and plants are included in detailed classifications. *See also* PHYLOGENETICS; PLANT CLASSIFICATION

Tay River in central Scotland, rising in the Grampians and flowing SE to enter the North Sea through the Firth of Tay near Dundee. At 193km (120mi), it is the longest river in Scotland and has the largest drainage basin, 6,200sq km (2,400sq mi) in area. The Tay Bridge (1883–88) crosses the firth at Dundee.

Taylor, Elizabeth (1932–) US film actress, b. England. She became a child star in *National Velvet* (1944). Taylor's early mature roles include *A Place in the Sun* (1951) and *Cat on a Hot Tin Roof* (1958). She won two Academy Awards, for *Butterfield 8* (1960) and *Who's Afraid of Virginia Woolf?* (1966).

▲ **Taylor** Discovered by talent scouts in Los Angeles, Elizabeth Taylor made her film debut at the age of 10 in *There's One Born Every Minute* (1942). Her first major adult role was in *Father of the Bride* (1950). A striking beauty with violet eyes, Taylor was married a total of eight times. Her husbands include Michael Wilding, Mike Todd, and Richard Burton (twice). Taylor has undergone treatment for drug and alcohol abuse, and surgery for a brain tumour. She performed the voice-over for Baby Maggie in the US animated television series *The Simpsons*.

T

INTERNET

Tate Gallery
▸ www.tate.org.uk

Taverner, John
▸ www.classical.net

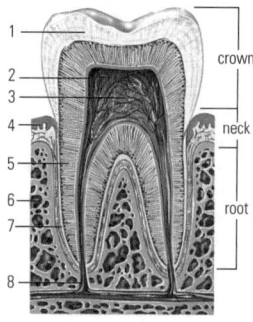

Key:
1 enamel
2 capillaries, nerves, lymphatics
3 pulp
4 gum
5 dentine
6 jaw
7 cementum
8 root canal

▲ **teeth** A human tooth consists of the crown, neck, and root. The crown is made up of a dense mineral, enamel, surrounding the hard dentine, which has a soft centre – the pulp. The pulp is filled with blood vessels, lymphatics and the nerve, which reach the tooth through the root canal. The neck adheres to the gum, and the root penetrates the bone, where it is held in place by a ligament and cementum.

Taylor, Zachary (1784–1850) Twelfth US president (1849–50). A soldier with little formal education, he fought in the WAR OF 1812. In 1845, Taylor was ordered to occupy the recently annexed land of Texas – an act which set off the MEXICAN WAR. He emerged from the war a popular hero. Taylor won the Whig nomination for president and the subsequent election (1848), but died after only 16 months in office.

Tayside Region in E Scotland, bounded N and W by the Grampians and E by the North Sea. The capital is DUNDEE, and other major cities include Perth, Arbroath, and Montrose. The N of the region is mountainous and the s is low-lying farmland. It is drained by the rivers Tay, Isla, Earn, South Esk, and Ericht. The economy is primarily agricultural, the major products being beef and dairy products. Area: 7,502sq km (2,896sq mi). Pop. (1998 est.) 389,800.

Tbilisi (Tiflis) Largest city and capital of Georgia, on the upper River Kura. It was founded in the 5th century AD and ruled successively by the Iranians, Byzantines, Arabs, Mongols, and Turks, before coming under Russian rule in 1801. Tbilisi's importance lies in its location on the trade route between the Black Sea and Caspian Sea. It is now the administrative and economic focus of modern Transcaucasia. Industries: chemicals, petroleum products, locomotives, electrical equipment, beer, wine, spirits. Pop. (2000) 1,406,000.

T-cell (Thymus-cell or T-lymphocyte) Type of LYMPHOCYTE (white blood cell) that is the key to the defence mechanism of the IMMUNE SYSTEM. There are three main kinds of T-cells: **Th** (helper T-cells), **Ts** (suppressor T-cells), and **Tc** (cytotoxic T-cells). **Helper** T-cells recognize foreign ANTIGENS and help other immune cells to act; **suppressor** T-cells prevent specific immune reactions; and **cytotoxic** T-cells, or effector T-cells, kill cancerous cells or cells infected with a virus. T-cells are produced in the bone marrow and then go to the THYMUS GLAND. *See also* ACQUIRED IMMUNE DEFICIENCY SYNDROME (AIDS)

Tchaikovsky, Peter Ilyich (1840–93) Russian composer. His gift for melody and expressiveness is apparent in all his works, which include nine operas, four concertos, six symphonies, three ballets, and overtures. Tchaikovsky's popular ballets include *Swan Lake* (1876), *The Sleeping Beauty* (1889), and *The Nutcracker* (1892). His operas include *Eugene Onegin* (1879) and *The Queen of Spades* (1890). Other famous works include the First Piano Concerto (1875), the *1812* overture (1880), and the sixth (*Pathétique*) symphony (1893).

tea Family of trees and shrubs with leathery, undivided leaves and five-petalled blossoms. Among 500 species is *Camellia sinensis*, the commercial source of tea. Cultivated in moist, tropical regions, tea plants can reach 9m (30ft) in height, but are kept low by frequent picking of the young shoots for tea leaves. The leaves are dried immediately to produce green tea and are fermented before drying for black tea. Family Theaceae.

teak Tree, native to s India, Burma, and Indonesia, valued for its hard, yellowish-brown wood. Teak wood is water-resistant and takes a high polish; it is widely used for furniture and in shipbuilding. Height: 45m (150ft). Family Verbenaceae; species *Tectona grandis*.

teal Small, widely distributed river DUCK; many species have bright plumage. Teal dabble for food from the surface of the water. Family Anatidae, genus *Anas*.

tear Salty fluid secreted by glands that moistens the surface of the eye. It cleanses and disinfects the surface of the eye and also brings nutrients to the CORNEA.

tear gas Chemical compound known as a lachrymator, a gas or aerosol that causes an excessive flow of TEARS. It blinds and incapacitates temporarily without causing permanent injury.

teasel Any of several species of plants that grow in Europe, the Middle East, and the USA. They are prickly, with cup-like leaf bases that trap water. Species include fuller's teasel, whose purple heads were used for carding wool. Family Dipsacaceae.

technetium (symbol Tc) Silver-grey, radioactive, metallic element, one of the TRANSITION ELEMENTS. It was the first element artificially produced, its name taken from the Greek *tekhnetos* meaning 'artificial'. It was synthesized in 1937 by Italian physicist Carlo Perrier and Italian-born US physicist Emilio Segrè. Technetium is found in the FISSION products of URANIUM, and is present in some stars. It is used in radioactive tracer studies. There are 16 known isotopes. Properties: at.no. 43; r.a.m. 98.9062; r.d. 11.5; m.p. 2,172°C (3,942°F); b.p. 4,877°C (8,811°F); most stable isotope Tc^{99} (half-life 2.6×10^6 years).

Technicolor Trade name of the colour film process invented by Herbert T. Calmus and Daniel F. Comstock, still used in the majority of motion pictures. A primitive Technicolor first appeared in 1917, and in 1933 Walt DISNEY used three-colour Technicolor for the animated film *Flowers and Trees*.

technology Systematic study of the methods and techniques employed in industry, research, agriculture, and commerce. More often the term is used to describe the practical application of scientific discoveries to industry.

tectonics Deformation within the Earth's CRUST and the geological structures produced by deformation, including folds, FAULTS and mountain chains. *See also* PLATE TECTONICS

Tecumseh (1768–1813) Native American leader. A Shawnee chief, he worked with his brother, known as 'the Prophet', to unite the Native Americans of the West and resist white expansion. After the Prophet's defeat, Tecumseh joined the British in the WAR OF 1812. He led 2000 warriors in several battles and died fighting in Upper Canada.

teeth Hard, bone-like structures embedded in the jaws of vertebrates, used for chewing food, defence, or other purposes. Mammalian teeth have an outer layer of hard enamel. A middle layer consists of dentine, a bone-like substance that is capable of regeneration. The core of a tooth contains pulp, which is softer and has a blood supply and nerves. *See also* DENTITION

Teflon Trade name for POLYTETRAFLUOROETHYLENE (PTFE).

Tegucigalpa Capital and largest city of HONDURAS, located in the mountainous central Cordilleras. Founded in the 16th century by the Spanish as a mining town, it became the national capital in 1880. Industries: sugar, textiles, chemicals, cigarettes. Pop. (2005) 1,061,000.

Tehran Capital of Iran, 105km (65mi) s of the Caspian Sea, in a strategic position on the edge of the plains and in the foothills of the country's highest mountains. In 1788, it replaced

TELEPHONE

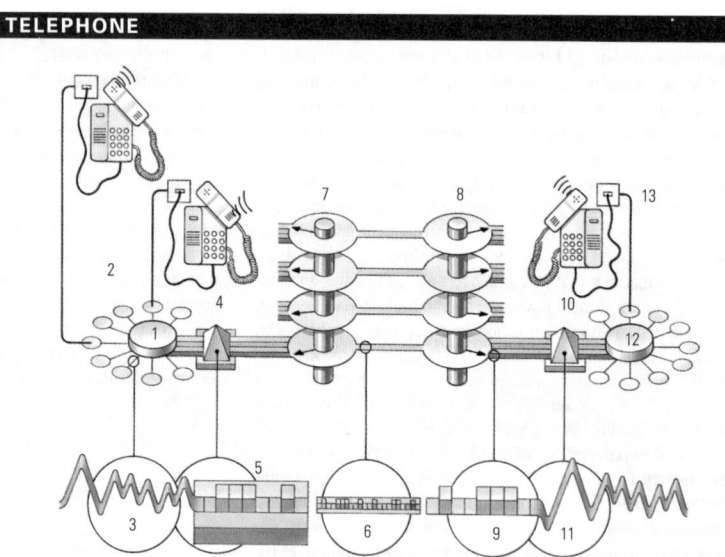

Local telephone exchanges (1) connect local calls (2), which are analogue signals (3). Long-distance calls are routed to the long-distance exchange (4), where they are converted from analogue to digital. Digital snapshots are taken of the analogue signal 8000 times a second (every 125 microseconds) – enough information to recreate the analogue signal accurately enough for the human ear. This whole process is called pulse-code modulation. Each eight-bit sample (5) is only 4 microseconds long, which leaves 121 microseconds between each one on the telephone line. To increase capacity, multiplexing combines the samples of up to 25 calls going to the same destination on the same line (6). This is done by feeding all the calls into a memory buffer (7) and then feeding them onto the long distance line in turn. At the receiving end, the process is reversed and the combined call is again fed into a memory buffer (8), separated (9), passed to the long-distance exchange (10) where it is turned back into an analogue signal (11), and sent to the local exchange (12). From there it is routed to its final destination (13). The process happens so fast that the human ear hears a continuous voice.

T

ISFAHAN as the capital of Persia. In the early 20th century, Muhammad Reza PAHLAVI demolished the old fortifications and established a planned city. Tehran is now the industrial, commercial, administrative and cultural centre of Iran. Industries: carpets, cement, textiles. Pop. (2005) 7,352,000.

Tehran Conference (1943) Meeting in Tehran of the British, Soviet, and US leaders (Winston CHURCHILL, Joseph STALIN, and Franklin D. ROOSEVELT) during World War 2. It was the first meeting of the 'Big Three'.

Teilhard de Chardin, Pierre (1881–1955) French JESUIT philosopher and palaeontologist. He worked in China (1923–46), and shared in the discovery of 'Peking Man' (a fossilized Stone-Age human). His philosophical works, such as *The Phenomenon of Man* (1955), attempt to reconcile scientific views of evolution with Christian faith. His ideas were deemed unorthodox by the Church and were published posthumously.

Te Kanawa, Dame Kiri (1948–) New Zealand opera singer of Maori origin. She first attracted attention in the role of the Countess in Mozart's *The Marriage of Figaro* at the Royal Opera House, London (1970). In 1981, Te Kanawa sang at the wedding of Prince Charles and Lady Diana Spencer. She became a dame in 1982.

Tel Aviv (Tel Aviv-Yafo) City and port in Israel, on the Mediterranean Sea, *c*.50km (30mi) w of Jerusalem. The business, cultural, communications and tourist centre of Israel, it was founded (1909) as a suburb of the port of Jaffa. During the British administration of Palestine (1923–48), the town grew rapidly as Jews fled persecution in Europe. It served as the seat of the transitional government and legislature of the new state of Israel (1948–49), until the capital moved to JERUSALEM. In 1950, it merged with Jaffa. Industries: construction, textiles, clothing. Pop. (2005) 3,025,000.

telecommunications Technology involved in the sending of information over a distance. The information comes in a variety of forms, such as digital signals, sounds, printed words or images. The sending is achieved through TELEGRAPH, TELEPHONE or RADIO, and the medium may be wires or electromagnetic (radio) waves, or a combination of the two. There are two basic types of message: DIGITAL SIGNALS, in which the message is converted into simple, coded pulses and then sent (as in MORSE code); and ANALOGUE SIGNALS, in which the message – for example, a human voice – is converted into a series of electrical pulses that are similar in wave form to the MODULATIONS of the original message. *See also* FAX; SATELLITE, ARTIFICIAL

telegraph Any communications system that transmits and receives visible or audible coded signals over a distance. The first, optical, telegraphs were forms of semaphore. Credit for the electric telegraph and its code is generally given to Samuel MORSE, who inaugurated (1844) the first public line – between Washington and Baltimore. In 1866, the first permanently successful telegraph cable was laid across the Atlantic. In 1875, Thomas EDISON invented a method of transmitting several messages simultaneously over the same wire.

Telemann, Georg Philipp (1681–1767) German composer. He wrote more than 40 operas, 600 overtures, and 44 settings of the Passion. His church music, of more historical importance than his operas, shows his technical mastery.

teleology Explanation by reference to an end or purpose achieved (or thought to be achieved) by the thing being explained. Since the advent of modern science in the 17th century, things tend to be explained as having been caused by earlier events. This cause-and-effect approach is known as **efficient causation**. In teleology, this way of thinking is reversed in an approach called **final causation**, which explains that things have developed the way they have in order to achieve the effect we now perceive or experience. In the later 18th century, William Paley (1743–1805) applied a form of teleology to biological processes, explaining biological organisms as complex and ingenious machines devised by an intelligent being specifically to act in the way that they do. As a theory of morality, teleological ETHICS derives the concept of moral duty or obligation from what is good as a goal or aim to be achieved.

telepathy Form of EXTRASENSORY PERCEPTION (ESP) involving the transmission and reception of thoughts without using the usual sensory channels. No claims of telepathy have ever been proven, despite extensive investigations.

telephone Instrument that communicates speech sounds over a distance by means of wires or microwaves. In 1876, Alexander Graham BELL invented a prototype, which employed a diaphragm of soft iron that vibrated to sound waves. These vibrations caused disturbances in the MAGNETIC FIELD of a bar magnet, causing an electric current of fluctuating intensity in the thin copper wire wrapped around the magnet. This current could be transmitted along wires to a distant device that reversed the process to reproduce audible sound. Later changes separated the transmitter from the receiver, and replaced the magnet with a powered microphone. *See also* MOBILE TELEPHONE

telephoto lens CAMERA lens with a long focal length. A true telephoto LENS has a focal length longer than the physical length of the lens, as opposed to a long-focus lens, in which the focal length is equal to the physical length. For a 35mm camera, any lens with a focal length of more than *c*.80mm may be regarded as a telephoto lens. For larger-format cameras, the focal length may be as much as 1,000mm. *See also* PHOTOGRAPHY

telescope Instrument for enlarging a distant object or studying ELECTROMAGNETIC RADIATION from a distant source. **Optical** telescopes can use lenses (refracting telescopes) or mirrors (reflecting telescopes); **catadioptric** telescopes use both in combination. The lens or mirror is the telescope's main light-gathering part (**objective**), and its diameter, known as the APERTURE of the telescope, determines its magnifying power. The point at which the objective concentrates the light from the source is its **focus**, and the distance from the focus to the objective is its FOCAL LENGTH. **Refracting** telescopes were invented by Dutch optician Hans Lippershey (1608) and Italian astronomer GALILEO (1609). The main disadvantage with refracting telescopes was chromatic ABERRATION. This problem was solved in **reflecting** telescopes by combining lenses so their aberrations cancelled each other out. In 1668, English scientist Sir Isaac NEWTON built an early astronomical reflector. Modern observatories are built on mountain peaks in order to improve 'seeing' and to observe INFRARED RADIATION from celestial bodies. Earth-bound telescopes have limitations because the incoming radiation has to pass through the Earth's atmosphere. This ceases to be a problem with telescopes in Earth orbit, such as the HUBBLE SPACE TELESCOPE. Orbiting telescopes can also detect other types of electromagnetic radiation more easily, such as ULTRAVIOLET RADIATION, X-RAYS and GAMMA RADIATION. RADIO TELESCOPES are complex electronic systems that detect and analyse radio waves from beyond the Earth. In 1937, the first radio telescope was built by US radio engineer Grote Reber. Radio interferometers are arrays of smaller dishes that permit the investigation of even more distant radio sources.

teletext System for transmitting text so that it can be displayed on TELEVISION receivers. Television companies transmit the text in coded form along with the sound and vision signals. Sets are equipped to receive teletext separately and decode the text signals so that they can be displayed on the screen.

television System that transmits and receives visual images by RADIO waves or cable. A television CAMERA converts the images from light rays into electrical signals. The basis of most television cameras is an image orthicon tube. The electrical signals are amplified and transmitted as VERY HIGH FREQUENCY (VHF) or ULTRA HIGH FREQUENCY (UHF) radio waves. Typically, a television channel has a bandwidth of 5MHz (5 million cycles per second). The television set operates in reverse to the camera. On reception, a CATHODE-RAY TUBE amplifies the signals and reconverts it to light. Colour television has three synchronized image orthicon tubes in the camera, one for each of the three primary colours – red, blue, and green. The tube of the receiver has three electron guns and the face of the tube is covered with a mosaic of fine phosphors in groups of three, each emitting only red, blue, or green light when struck by a beam.

T

INTERNET

Telstar
▶ roland.lerc.nasa.gov/
~dglover/sat/telstar.html

These primary colours merge on the face of the screen to reconstitute the originally transmitted image. *See also* BROADCASTING; CABLE TELEVISION; SATELLITE TELEVISION

Telford, Thomas (1757–1834) Scottish civil engineer who built roads, bridges, canals, docks, and harbours. His most notable achievements were the Caledonian Canal in Scotland, and the 177m (580ft) Menai Strait suspension bridge, connecting Anglesey with mainland Wales.

Tell, William Legendary Swiss hero, leader in the 14th-century war of liberation against Austria. For refusing to salute Albert I's steward, Gessler, he was made to shoot an arrow through an apple placed on his son's head.

Teller, Edward (1908–2003) US physicist, b. Hungary. Often referred to as the 'father of the HYDROGEN BOMB', in 1935 Teller left Europe and settled in the USA, where he conducted research on solar energy. During World War 2, he contributed to NUCLEAR WEAPONS research with Enrico FERMI. He was involved in the MANHATTAN PROJECT that produced the first atomic bomb and was a central figure in developing and testing (1952) the hydrogen bomb.

tellurium (symbol Te) Silver-white, metalloid element. It occurs naturally, combined with gold in sylvanite. Its chief source is as a by-product in the electrolytic refining of copper. The brittle element is used in semiconductor devices, as a catalyst in petroleum cracking, and as an additive to increase the ductility of steel. It was discovered in 1782 by the Austrian mineralogist Franz Müller. Properties: at.no. 52; r.a.m. 127.60; r.d. 6.24; m.p. 449.5°C (841.1°F); b.p. 989.8°C (1,814°F).

Telstar First active communications satellite, launched by the USA on July 10, 1962. It contained a microwave radio receiver, amplifier and transmitter for relaying telephone and television signals. It operated for about 18 weeks, failed for five weeks, and then worked again for a further seven weeks before failing for good.

tempera PAINTING medium used extensively during the Middle Ages, made of powdered pigments mixed with an organic gum or glue, usually of egg white or egg yolk. Tempera dries quickly and is applied with a sable brush, one thin layer on another, so that the finished effect is semi-opaque and luminous. During the 15th century, the more flexible medium of oil painting began to replace tempera.

temperance movement Organized effort to promote moderation in, or abstinence from, the consumption of alcohol. It probably began in the USA in the early 19th century and spread to Britain and continental Europe. The US crusade reached its peak with the ratification of the 18th Amendment (1919) that brought in PROHIBITION.

temperature In biology, intensity of heat. In warm-blooded (HOMEOTHERMIC) animals, body temperature is maintained within narrow limits regardless of the temperature of their surroundings. This is accomplished by muscular activity, the operation of cooling mechanisms, such as vasodilation, vasoconstriction and sweating, and metabolic activity. In humans, normal body temperature is c.36.9°C (98.4°F), but this varies with degree of activity. In so-called cold-blooded (POIKILO-THERMIC) animals, body temperature varies between wider limits, depending on the temperature of the surroundings.

temperature In physics, measure of the hotness or coldness of an object. Strictly, it describes the number of ENERGY states available to a substance or system. Two objects in thermal contact initially exchange HEAT energy but eventually arrive at thermal EQUILIBRIUM. At equilibrium, the most probable distribution of energy states among the atoms and molecules of the objects has been attained. At high temperatures, the number of energy states available to the atoms and molecules of a system is large; at lower temperatures, fewer states are available. At a sufficiently low temperature, all parts of the system are at their lowest energy levels, the ABSOLUTE ZERO of temperature.

tempering HEAT treatment to alter the HARDNESS of an ALLOY. The effect produced depends on the composition of the alloy, the temperature to which it is heated, and the rate at which it is cooled. Usually, the metal is heated slowly to a specific temperature, then cooled rapidly.

temple Place of worship for Jews and members of many other religions. Temples were a grand architectural focal point in the religion and culture of ancient Egypt and the Near East. In Mesopotamia, they took the form of elaborate towers called ZIGGURATS. Greek and Roman temples, with beautifully carved statues and columns, were houses fit for the gods. In Judaism, the term refers specifically to the first and second TEMPLES built in Jerusalem. Today, Jews worship in a local SYNAGOGUE. Temples also exist as places of worship for Muslims, Hindus, Buddhists and Sikhs. Some Evangelical Christian sects and the Mormon Church use the term.

Temple, Jerusalem Most significant shrine of the Jews, originally located on a hilltop known as Temple Mount in what is now East Jerusalem. There have been three temples on the site. The first was built (10th centuryBC) by order of SOLOMON as a repository for the ARK OF THE COVENANT. In c.587 BC it was destroyed by NEBUCHADNEZZAR, King of Babylon. In c.515 BC a second temple was erected by the Jewish exiles who had returned from Babylon in 537 BC. Between 19 and 9 BC this second temple was replaced by a more elaborate structure on the orders of HEROD THE GREAT; it was destroyed by the Romans during the Jewish rebellion of AD 70. It has never been rebuilt, but part of its ruins remain as a place of pilgrimage and prayer, known as the WESTERN WALL. Part of the ancient temple site is occupied by the DOME OF THE ROCK and al-Aqsa Mosque, both built in the late 7th century.

Temple, Shirley (1928–) US film actress. She became a child star in films such as *Bright Eyes* (1934) and *The Little Princess* (1939). Temple continued to make films as a young adult, but could never recapture her early success. As Shirley Temple Black, she went into politics, serving as a US delegate to the UN (1969–70), then as US Ambassador to Ghana (1974–76) and to Czechoslovakia (1989–93).

tempo Speed at which a piece of music should be performed, usually indicated on a score, in western music, by Italian words, such as *allegro* (fast) and *adagio* (slow).

tench Freshwater food and sport fish of Europe and Asia, belonging to the carp family Cyprinidae. It has a stout, golden yellow body with small scales. Length: to 71cm (28in). Species *Tinca tinca*.

Ten Commandments (Decalogue) Code of ethical conduct held in Judaeo-Christian tradition to have been revealed by God to MOSES on Mount Sinai during the Hebrew exodus from Egypt (c.1200BC). They represent the moral basis of the Covenant made by Yahweh (God) with Israel.

tendon Strong, flexible band of CONNECTIVE TISSUE of the protein COLLAGEN that joins muscle to bone.

tendril Coiling part of stem or leaf, a slender, thread-like structure used by climbing plants for support.

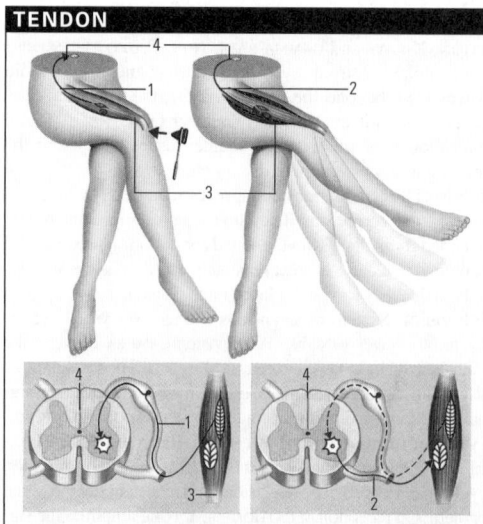

TENDON

The tendon jerk is the simplest reflex action, involving only a sensory receptor neuron (1) and a motor neuron (2). Impulses, such as those created by a hammer tapping a knee, run to and from the muscles (3) and traverse only one segment of the spinal cord (4). This reflex is independent of the brain.

Tenerife Largest of the CANARY ISLANDS, Spain, in the Atlantic Ocean, 64km (40mi) WNW of Grand Canary Island. It is a mountainous island, rising to Pico de Teide at 3718m (12,198ft). Products include dates, sugar cane, palms, and cotton. Tourism is important. The main town is SANTA CRUZ DE TENERIFE. Area: 2,059sq km (795sq mi). Pop. (2001) 856,808.

Tennessee State in SE central USA between the Appalachian Mountains and the MISSISSIPPI River. The capital is NASHVILLE. Other cities include MEMPHIS, CHATTANOOGA, and Knoxville. In the E are the GREAT SMOKY MOUNTAINS and the Cumberland Plateau. Central Tennessee is a BLUEGRASS region famed for its horse-breeding and livestock rearing; West Tennessee has fertile floodplains, drained by the TENNESSEE River, which produce cotton, tobacco, and soybeans. The first European discovery was by Hernando DE SOTO in 1540. The French followed a century later, but their claim was ceded to Britain in 1763, and the first permanent settlement was established in 1769. In 1796, Tennessee became the 16th State of the Union. Tennessee's enthusiastic response to the request for volunteers during the MEXICAN WAR (1846–48) earned it the nickname of the Volunteer State. During the American CIVIL WAR, the State was the site of some of the bloodiest battles, including Shiloh (1862) and Chattanooga (1863). In 1866, it became the first southern state to be readmitted to the Union. Christian fundamentalism exerts a powerful influence, and the teaching of evolution was banned from 1925 to 1967. Industries: chemicals, electrical equipment, foods, tourism. Area: 109,411sq km (42,244sq mi). Pop. (2001) 5,740,021.

Tennessee River in Tennessee, N Alabama, and W Kentucky. Formed by the confluence of the Holston and French Broad rivers, it joins the Ohio at Paducah, Kentucky, and forms part of the Alabama-Mississippi border. From 1933, the Tennessee Valley Authority (TVA) developed the river's hydroelectric potential (nine major dams) and transport facilities, along with irrigation and flood control. Length: 1,050km (652mi).

tennis Racket and ball game played either by two (singles) or four (doubles) players. It is sometimes known as **lawn tennis**, despite being played on concrete, clay, shale, and wood as well as grass. The game is played on a court, 23.8m (78ft) by 8.2m (27ft) for singles. For doubles play, the court widens to 11m (36ft). A net, 0.9m (3ft) high at the centre, bisects the court. On each side of the net there are two service areas marked by rectangular lines. The ball is put into play by the server, who is allowed two attempts to hit it into the opposite service court. One player serves for a complete game. If the opponent returns the ball in court, play continues until one player fails to hit the ball, hits it into the net, or hits it outside the confines of the court; his opponent then wins the point. A minimum of four points are required to win a game, which must be won by two clear points. A minimum of six games must be won to WIN a set, which must be won by either two clear games or by winning the tie-break game, which is played at six games all. Modern tennis evolved from REAL TENNIS in England in the 1860s.

Tennyson, Alfred, 1st Baron (1809–92) English poet. He became Poet Laureate in 1850. His massive oeuvre includes such patriotic classics as 'Ode on the Death of the Duke of Wellington' (1852) and 'The Charge of the Light Brigade' (1855). Tennyson also wrote deeply personal utterances, such as 'Crossing the Bar' (1889) and *In Memoriam* (1850) – an extended elegy for his friend Arthur Henry Hallam that is often regarded as his masterpiece. Other works include ;The Lady of Shalott; (1832), *Maud* (1855) and *Idylls of the King* (1872–73).

tenor Range of the human voice, falling below CONTRALTO and above BARITONE. It is the highest natural male voice apart from the COUNTERTENOR.

tension Molecular forces associated with the boundary layer of a liquid. It makes a liquid behave as if there were a 'skin' on the surface. Attractive forces in this skin can resist disruption, so that a needle or razor blade placed carefully on the surface floats, even though its density is many times that of the liquid.

Teotihuacán Ancient AZTEC city of Mexico, *c.*48km (30mi) N of Mexico City. It flourished between *c.*100 BC and *c.*AD 700. It contained huge and impressive buildings, notably the Pyra-

mid of the Sun. At its greatest extent, *c.*AD 600, the city housed at least 100,000 people and was the centre of a large empire.

tequila Mexican alcoholic drink distilled from the fermented juice of the AGAVE plant. It is 40–50% alcohol by volume.

terbium (symbol Tb) Silver-grey, metallic element of the LANTHANIDE SERIES (rare-earth metals). It is found in such minerals as monazite, gladolinite, and apatite. The soft element is used in semiconductors; sodium terbium borate is used in lasers. It was discovered in 1843 by the Swedish chemist Carl Mosander. Properties: at.no. 65; r.a.m. 158.9254; r.d. 8.234; m.p. 1,360°C (2,480°F); b.p. 3,041°C (5,506°F). Single isotope Tb[159].

Teresa, Mother (1910–97) (Agnes Gonxha Bojaxhiu) Macedonian Roman Catholic missionary. She began her missionary work as a teacher in Calcutta (now KOLKATA), India. In 1948 the Vatican granted her permission to leave her convent in order to tend the homeless, starving, and sick in Calcutta's slums. In 1950 she established the Order of the Missionaries of Charity, which then extended to other countries. She received the first Pope John XXIII Peace Prize in 1971, and the Nobel Peace Prize in 1979. In 2003, Mother Teresa was beatified by Pope John Paul II.

Teresa of Ávila, Saint (1515–82) (Teresa de Cepeda y Ahumada) Spanish CARMELITE nun and mystic. In 1529 she entered the Convent of the Incarnation at Ávila, central Spain. From 1558 she reformed the Carmelite Order for women. Under her influence, St JOHN OF THE CROSS introduced a Carmelite Order for men. Her literary works, including the meditative *Interior Castle* (1577), as well as her monastic reforms, led to her canonization in 1622. Her feast day is October 15.

terminal velocity Maximum velocity attainable by a falling body or powered AIRCRAFT. It is dependent upon the shape of the body, the resistance of the air through which it is moving, and (in the case of aircraft) the THRUST of the engines.

termite Social insect found worldwide in subterranean nests and above-ground mounds. The king and queen are guarded and tended by soldiers, workers and nymphs in a caste system. Wood is a common component of their diet, which is digested with the help of symbiotic protozoa or bacteria that live in the termites' intestines. Length: 0.2–2.25mm (0.08–0.9in); queens: to 10cm (4in). Order Isoptera. *See* illustration page 732

tern (sea swallow) Any of several species of graceful seabirds that live throughout the world. The tern is usually white and grey, and has a pointed bill, long pointed wings, a forked tail and webbed feet; it dives for fish and crustaceans. Length: to 55cm (22in). Family Laridae; genus *Sterna*.

terracotta Hard, porous, usually unglazed, yellow, brown or red earthenware (fired CLAY). Terracotta is used in building, sculpture and POTTERY. *See also* CERAMIC

terrapin Any of several species of aquatic TURTLES that live in fresh or brackish water in the USA and South America, especially the diamondback terrapin (*Malaclemys terrapin*). Length: to 23cm (9in). Family Emydidae.

terrier Any of several breeds of DOG. Originally trained to dig out game, they have been used to hunt badgers, foxes, weasels, and rats. When the quarry is located, the terrier(s) is sent down to dig it out of its burrow. Breeds include the Sealyham terrier, fox terrier, and Manchester terrier. Larger breeds, such as the Airedale terrier and Irish terrier, are often used as guard and police dogs.

territory In ecology, the restricted life space of an organism. An area selected for mating, nesting, roosting, hunting, or feeding, it may be occupied by one or more organisms and defended against others of the same, or a different, species.

terrorism Use of violence, sometimes indiscriminately, against persons and property for the nominal purpose of making a political statement. Intending to inspire terror, terrorists act principally in the name of empowering political minorities, and to publicize perceived political grievances.

Tertiary Informal term for a sub-era of the CENOZOIC era, lasting from 65 million to *c.*2 million years ago. It divides into five epochs, starting with the PALAEOCENE and followed by the EOCENE, OLIGOCENE, MIOCENE, and PLIOCENE. Early Tertiary times were marked by great mountain-building activity. Both marsupial and placental mammals diversified greatly. Archaic forms of carnivores and herbivores flourished, along with primitive primates, bats, rodents, and early whales.

TENNESSEE
Statehood:
June 1, 1796
Nickname:
The Volunteer State
State bird:
Mockingbird
State flower:
Iris
State tree:
Tulip-poplar
State motto:
Agriculture and commerce

▲ **Mother Teresa** Recognized throughout the world for her charitable work in the slums of Calcutta, Mother Teresa worked not only with orphaned and handicapped children but also with lepers and other people with disfiguring diseases. There are more than 2,000 nuns in the order she founded, the Missionaries of Charity, who care for the ill and the dying throughout the world.

T

INTERNET

Tennessee
▶ www.tennesseeanytime. org

Tennyson, Alfred, 1st Baron
▶ eir.library.utoronto.ca/rpo/ display/poet323.html

termite Built of saliva and soil particles, termite mounds (A) dominate the African savanna. Most termites prefer to eat dead plant material that has been partly softened by fungus. This food supply is limited in dry conditions because fungi need moisture. For this reason *Macrotermes* termites create fungus chambers (1). These are combs of carton (a mixture of saliva and faecal pellets), which provide a large surface area on which the fungus grows. The fungus flourishes in the humid atmosphere of the nest as it breaks down the faeces in the carton walls. Some termite species dig deep tunnels (2) to find underground water to ensure that the nest is moist enough for the fungus to thrive. The peaks of the mound (3) act as lungs. Air seeps into the main nest from an air cellar below (4). As the fungus breaks down the faecal comb, heat is generated. The hot air rises, via a large central air space (5) into the chimneys (6). The walls of the nest are porous, so carbon dioxide diffuses into the chimneys. The newly oxygenated air loses heat to the air outside and cools, sinking back to the cellar. The royal cell (7) lies at the heart of the nest, where the king (8) and the queen (9) can be protected. The workers, as well as feeding the royal couple, also remove the eggs to the brood chambers (10). There the workers lick the eggs to keep them clean. Most termite species have a variety of castes (B) or types. There are the temporarily winged reproductives (male and female) called alates (1), responsible for setting up colonies, the queen (2), whose enlarged abdomen contain thousands of eggs, the soldier termites (3), which protect the colony, and the workers (4), which collect food, care for the queen and serve as builders.

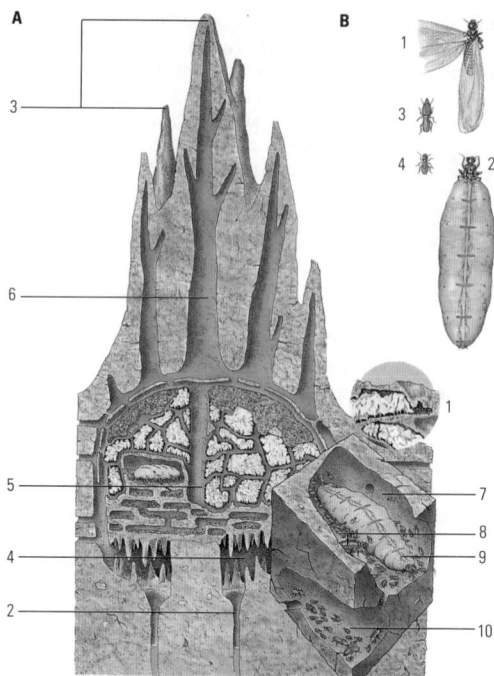

INTERNET

Texas
www.state.tx.us

Thackeray, William Makepeace
www.victorianweb.org/authors/wmt/wmtov.html

Thailand
www.tourismthailand.org
sunsite.au.ac.th/thailand/thai_his

tesla (symbol T) SI unit of MAGNETIC FLUX density (the strength and extent of a magnetic field). It is equal to one WEBER of magnetic flux per square metre, and is named after the Croatian-born US electrical engineer Nikola TESLA.

Tesla, Nikola (1856–1943) US electrical engineer and inventor, b. Croatia, who pioneered the applications of high-voltage electricity. He developed arc lighting, the first generator of alternating current (AC), and the high-frequency Tesla coil.

Test Ban Treaty (1963) Agreement signed in Moscow by the Soviet Union, the USA, and Britain to cease most tests of nuclear weapons. Nearly 100 other states eventually signed the treaty, although France and China continued to conduct tests in the atmosphere and underwater.

testis (pl. testes) Male sex GLAND, found as a pair located in a pouch, the scrotum, external to the body. The testes are made up of seminiferous tubules in which SPERM are formed and mature, after which they drain into ducts and are stored in the epididymis prior to being discharged.

testosterone Steroid HORMONE secreted mainly by the mammalian TESTIS. It is responsible for the growth and development of male sex organs and male secondary sexual characteristics, such as voice change and facial hair.

tetanus (lockjaw) Life-threatening disease caused by the toxin secreted by the anaerobic bacterium *Clostridium tetani*. The symptoms are muscular spasms and rigidity of the jaw, which then spreads to other parts of the body, culminating in convulsions and death. The disease is treated with anti-tetanus toxin and ANTIBIOTICS.

Tet Offensive (1968) Campaign in the VIETNAM WAR. North Vietnamese and VIET CONG troops launched attacks on numerous towns and cities of South Vietnam. Although of little strategic effect, the offensive discredited US military reports that victory over North Vietnam was imminent.

tetracycline One of a group of broad-spectrum ANTIBIOTICS that are effective against a wide range of bacterial infections.

Teutonic Knights German military and religious order, founded in 1190. Its members, of aristocratic class, took monastic vows of poverty and chastity. During the 13th century, the Knights waged war on non-Christians, particularly those in Prussia, whom they defeated, annexing their land. In 1242, they were defeated by ALEXANDER NEVSKI. In 1410, the Poles and Lithuanians crushed the Knights at Tannenberg, NE Poland.

Teutonic mythology Traditional beliefs of the Germanic peoples. Much of the mythology of pre-Christian Germany and Scandinavia is preserved in two Icelandic works, the Eddas. According to the Eddas, before the creation of the world there existed a land of ice and shadows called Niflheim

and a land of fire known as Muspellsheim. The two lands together created the first giant, Ymir. ODIN and his brothers killed Ymir and founded the race of gods. They then created the world from parts of Ymir's body, and made the first man and woman from pieces of trees. At the centre of the worlds of gods and men stood a giant ash tree, Yggdrasil. Odin, the head of the AESIR (heroic gods), was the god of poetry and of battle. VALHALLA, a great hall in Asgard, was the resting place of warriors slain in battle. Next in line to Odin was THOR, the god of thunder, rain, and fertility. Other members of the Teutonic pantheon included the handsome Balder and Loki, the son of a giant. The Vanir gods, regarded as less important than the Aesir, included Njörd, the sea-god, his son Freyr, a god of fertility, his daughter Freya, the goddess of love and magic, and Hel, the goddess of death and the underworld.

Texas State in central S USA, bounded by the Gulf of Mexico (SE) and the Rio Grande (SW). The state capital is AUSTIN. Other major cities include HOUSTON, DALLAS, SAN ANTONIO, and FORT WORTH. Texas has pine-covered hills and cypress swamps; cotton and rice are the main crops and the timber industry is important. Cattle are raised on the plains of the Rio Grande valley, from where the land rises to the Guadalupe Mountains of W Texas and the Great Plains area of the Texas Panhandle in the N. The Spaniards explored the region in the early 16th century, and it became part of the Spanish colony of Mexico. By the time Mexico attained independence in 1821, many Americans had begun to settle in Texas. They rebelled against Mexican rule and in 1836, after defeating the Mexican Army, established the Republic of Texas, recognized by the USA in 1837. Eight years later, Texas joined the Union. Rich oilfields are the mainstay of the state's economy. Industries: oil refining, food processing, aircraft, electronics. Area: 692,405sq km (267,338sq mi). Pop. (2000) 20,851,830.

textile Fabric, especially those produced by WEAVING yarn. The yarn is made by SPINNING natural or artificial FIBRES. Textiles are used to make clothing, curtains, carpets, and many other products. Powered LOOMS for spinning and weaving were introduced in the 18th century. *See also* ACRYLIC; COTTON; FLAX; LINEN; NYLON; POLYESTER; RAYON; SILK; WOOL

Tezcatlipoca One of the great gods of the AZTECS. He appears in many different forms but is best known as the god of the night sky and summer sun. He was a protector, a creator, and a harmful wizard. His cult required human sacrifice.

Thackeray, William Makepeace (1811–63) British novelist, b. India. The *Book of Snobs* (1846–47) established his reputation. Thackeray's best-known novel is *Vanity Fair* (1847–48), a satire on early 19th-century upper-class London society. Other novels include *Barry Lyndon* (1844), *Pendennis* (1848–50), *Henry Esmond* (1852), *The Newcomes* (1853–55), and *The Virginians* (1857–59). Thackeray was the founding editor (1860–75) of the *Cornhill Magazine*.

Thai National language of Thailand, spoken by most of the population. It is closely related to Lao, spoken across the border in Laos. It belongs to the Tai family, possibly a subfamily of the SINO-TIBETAN LANGUAGES group.

Thailand Kingdom in SE Asia. *See* country feature

thalamus One of two ovoid masses of grey matter located deep on each side of the forebrain. Sometimes called the sensory-motor receiving areas, they fulfil relay and integration functions in respect of sensory messages reaching the BRAIN.

thalassemia (Cooley's anaemia) Group of hereditary disorders characterized by abnormal bone marrow and ERYTHROCYTES (red blood cells). The predominant symptom is ANAEMIA, requiring frequent blood transfusions.

Thales (*c*.636–*c*.546 BC) First Greek scientist and philosopher of whom we have any knowledge. He made discoveries in geometry, such as the angles at the base of an isosceles triangle are equal. Thales predicted the eclipse of the Sun that took place in 585 BC.

thalidomide Drug originally developed as a mild hypnotic, but whose use by women in early pregnancy until the early 1960s came to be associated with serious birth deformities. It is still manufactured for occasional use in the treatment of LEPROSY and ACQUIRED IMMUNE DEFICIENCY SYNDROME (AIDS).

thallium (symbol Tl) Shiny, metallic element of group III of the periodic table. Soft and malleable, it is obtained as a by-product of processing zinc or lead sulphide ores. It is used in electronic components, infrared detectors and optical and infrared glasses. Thallium is a toxic compound, and thallium sulphide is used as a rodent and ant poison. It was discovered in 1861 by English chemist and physicist Sir William CROOKES. Properties: at.no. 81; r.a.m. 204.37; r.d. 11.85; m.p. 303.5°C (578.3°F); b.p. 1,457°C (2,655°F); most common isotope Tl²⁰⁵ (70.5%).

Thames Longest river in England. It rises in the Cotswold Hills, E Gloucestershire, then flows E across S England and through London to enter the North Sea at The Nore. It is tidal up to Teddington. The Thames Conservancy Board controls the freshwater river; the Port of London Authority administers the river below Teddington. The river is navigable for ocean-going vessels below Tilbury. The Thames Barrier (completed 1982) at Woolwich, London, controls the river's tidal system. Length: 338km (210mi).

Thant, U (1909–74) Burmese diplomat, third secretary general (1962–72) of the United Nations (UN). He was acting secretary general from 1961 before being elected in his own right. Thant helped to settle several major disputes, including the civil wars in the Congo (1963) and Cyprus (1964).

Thar Desert (Great Indian Desert) Region in NW India and SE Pakistan, between the Aravalli Mountains (E) and the River Indus (W). The region covers parts of RAJASTHAN, GUJARAT, PUNJAB, and SIND. The desert areas of Rajasthan now benefit from the Indira Gandhi Canal, c.650km (400mi) long, bringing water from the rivers of HIMACHAL PRADESH. Area: c.200,000sq km (77,000sq mi).

Thatcher, Margaret Hilda, Baroness (1925–) British stateswoman, prime minister (1979–90). She was perhaps the most influential British political leader since CHURCHILL. Thatcher was Secretary of State for education and science (1970–74) under Edward HEATH, whom she succeeded as Conservative Party leader in 1975. In 1979, she defeated James CALLAGHAN to become Britain's first woman Prime Minister. Her government embarked on a radical free-market programme that became known as 'Thatcherism'. Her monetarist policies, especially cuts in public spending, provoked criticism and contributed to a recession, but her popularity was restored by victory in the FALKLANDS WAR (1982). Thatcher's determination to curb the power of trade unions provoked a bitter miners' strike (1983–84). Controversial PRIVATIZATION of national utilities boosted government revenue in a period of rapidly rising incomes, except among the poor. In 1987, Thatcher won a third term, but clashed with cabinet

TEXAS
Statehood :
December 29, 1845
Nickname :
The Lone Star State
State bird :
Mockingbird
State flower :
Bluebonnet
State tree :
Pecan
State motto :
Friendship

THAILAND

The Kingdom of Thailand is one of ten nations in SE Asia. Central Thailand is a fertile plain drained mainly by the Chao Phraya. A densely populated region, it includes the capital, BANGKOK. The highest land occurs in the N and includes the second largest city CHIANGMAI and Doi Inthanon, the highest peak, which reaches 2,595m [8,514ft].

The Khorat Plateau, in the NE, makes up about 30% of the country and extends to the River MEKONG border with Laos. In the S, Thailand shares the finger-like MALAY PENINSULA with Burma and Malaysia.

The vegetation of Thailand includes many hardwood trees to the N. The S has rubber plantations. Grass, shrub and swamp make up 20% of land. 33% of the land is arable, mainly comprising rice fields.

AREA 513,115sq km [198,114sq mi]
POPULATION 65,068,000
CAPITAL (POPULATION)
Bangkok (6,604,000)
GOVERNMENT Constitutional monarchy
ETHNIC GROUPS Thai 75%, Chinese 14%, others
LANGUAGES Thai (official), English, ethnic and regional dialects
RELIGIONS Buddhism 95%, Islam, Christianity
CURRENCY Baht = 100 satang

CLIMATE

Thailand has a tropical climate. Monsoon winds from the south-west bring heavy rains between May and October. Bangkok is drier than many parts of SE Asia because mountains shelter the central plains from the rain-bearing winds.

HISTORY

The Mongol capture in 1253 of a Thai kingdom in SW China forced the Thai people to move S to settle around Sukothai. In the 14th century the kingdom expanded and the capital moved to Ayutthaya. European contact began in the 16th century. In the 17th century the Thais, fearing interference in their affairs, forced all Europeans to leave. This policy continued for 150 years, and Thailand remained the only SE Asian nation to resist colonization. In the late 17th century the kingdom was briefly held by the Burmese.

In 1782 a Thai General, Chao Phraya Chakkri, became king as Rama I. His dynasty continues today. The country became known as Siam, and Bangkok became its capital. From the mid 19th century, contacts with the West were restored. In World War 1 Siam supported the Allies. In 1932 the country became a constitutional monarchy.

POLITICS

In 1938 Pibul Songkhram became premier and changed the country's name to Thailand. Pibul was overthrown in a military coup in 1957, and the military governed until 1973. Thailand became a member of the ASSOCIATION OF SOUTH-EAST ASIAN NATIONS in 1967 and its economy grew rapidly. In 1997 it suffered recession along with other E Asian countries.

A military group seized power in 1991, but democracy returned in 1992. In 2004 Thailand was rocked by sectarian violence in the S, where a Muslim minority claim to suffer discrimination by the central government. In 2006 the government of Thaksin Shinawatra, accused of corruption, called elections. These were annulled as illegitimate and the King approved a re-run, but a military coup took place before it could be carried out. Retired general Surayat Chulanont became prime minister. In 2007 the military banned the former ruling party and changed the constitution to limit the powers of the prime minister before calling elections. The People's Power Party, allied to Shinawatra, won elections and Samak Sundaravej became prime minister.

ECONOMY

Despite its rapid progress, the World Bank classifies the country as a 'lower-middle-income' developing country. Manufactures, including commercial vehicles, food products, machinery, timber products and textiles, are exported.

Agriculture employs two-thirds of the workforce. Rice is the chief crop, while other major crops include cassava, cotton, maize, pineapples, rubber, sugar cane and tobacco. Tin and other minerals are mined. Tourism is a major source of income, though the 2004 tsunami killed over 5,000 and cast a shadow over its future growth.

T

▲ **Thatcher** Trained as a research chemist and a barrister specializing in tax law, Margaret Thatcher was first elected to Parliament in 1959, as an MP for Finchley, N London. She quickly rose to prominence, joining the shadow cabinet in 1967, and succeeding Edward Heath as leader of the Conservative Party in 1975. Thatcher became prime minister in 1979 elections. Her forceful personality and determination to radically reform the British economy and society created considerable worldwide impact. The Russians called her the 'Iron Lady'. She formed a good relationship with US President Ronald Reagan. After her resignation as prime minister in 1990, she travelled and lectured internationally, remaining as outspoken as ever. In 2002, after suffering a stroke, she retired from public speaking.

colleagues over economic and social policy, and her hostile attitude to the EUROPEAN UNION (EU). A poll tax (1989) was widely seen as unfair, and she was forced to resign. John MAJOR succeeded her as prime minister.

theatre Building where DRAMA is staged. Its architecture evolved gradually from early times, when ritual was most often performed in the open air. In medieval Europe, churches were used as dramatic venues. Renaissance architects such as PALLADIO were commissioned to design private theatres with acoustics and perspective in mind. At the same time, popular open stages had evolved in Shakespearean England. By the Restoration, the PROSCENIUM arch stage had become established as the only viable form of theatre. Since World War 2, theatrical architecture has again stressed adaptability.

theatre-in-the-round Form of theatrical presentation derived from the ancient arena stage. The audience is seated on all sides of the players, thus creating a sense of informality between the actors and the audience. *See also* DRAMA

Theatre Workshop Drama company founded (1945) in London, England, by Joan Littlewood (1914–2002). It staged many experimental and politically contentious plays. Several of its productions transferred to the West End, including *The Quare Fellow* (1956), and *Oh! What a Lovely War* (1963).

Thebes City-state of ancient Greece, the dominant power in Boeotia. It allied with Persia during the PERSIAN WARS, and during the 5th century BC was continually in conflict with Athens. It reached the peak of its power under Epaminondas in the 4th century BC defeating the Spartans at Leuctra in 371 BC and invading the Peloponnese. In 336 BC the city was largely destroyed after a rising against ALEXANDER THE GREAT.

Thebes Greek name for the ancient capital of Upper Egypt, roughly corresponding to the present-day town of LUXOR.

theism Any of various philosophical and theological systems that profess belief in the existence of one supreme being, who is the creator of the universe. In most theistic systems, human beings have free will, and religious doctrines are usually based on divine revelation. *See also* MONOTHEISM; POLYTHEISM

theocracy Government by religious leaders in accordance with divine law. Theocracies were common in non-literate societies and existed in ancient Egypt and the Orient.

Theocritus (*c.*310–250 BC) Greek poet, regarded as the father of pastoral poetry. His work, which influenced generations of later writers from VIRGIL to Matthew ARNOLD, is noted for its vivid expression and perceptive portrayal of rural life.

Theodora Name of three empresses of the BYZANTINE EMPIRE. The most famous **Theodora** (*c.*AD 500–48) was the wife of JUSTINIAN I. A courtesan before her marriage, she had such influence that she was virtually a joint ruler. The second **Theodora** (d.867) ruled as regent for her young son Michael III (842–856). She expelled the iconoclasts and restored the worship of images. The third **Theodora** (980–1056) was co-ruler from 1042 and was briefly sole empress after the death of Constantine IX Monomachus in 1055.

Theodoric the Great (*c.*454–526) King of the Ostrogoths and ruler of Italy. He drove ODOACER from Italy (488) and attempted to recreate the Western Roman Empire with himself as emperor. His kingdom was destroyed by JUSTINIAN I after his death.

Theodosius II (401–50) Eastern Roman (Byzantine) Emperor (408–50). Theodosius' armies repelled Persian invasions, and the fortifications of Constantinople were strengthened. He promulgated the **Theodosian Code** of laws (438).

theology Systematic study of God or gods. In its narrowest sense, it is the investigation or expression of the beliefs and precepts of a RELIGION. In a much broader sense, theology is intricately related to philosophical and historical studies and strives to achieve an understanding of various beliefs. Such preoccupations exercise the minds of theologians of Islam, Hinduism and most other religions, including Christianity.

theosophy 19th and early 20th century religious movement which incorporated some elements of Indian mysticism. It was founded by Helena Blavatsky (b. Russia) in 1875 and was a strong influence on a number of poets, writers and artists.

Theravada ('Doctrine of the Elders') Older of the two major schools of BUDDHISM. The doctrine originated early in the history of Buddhism as a contrast to MAHAYANA ('greater vehicle'). Theravada Buddhism stresses that sorrow and suffering can be conquered only by the suppression of desire. Desire can be suppressed only if the individual realizes that everything is always in a state of flux and the only stable condition is NIRVANA, an indefinable state of rest. This type of Buddhism is widespread in Sri Lanka and SE Asia.

Thérèse of Lisieux, Saint (1873–97) (Marie Françoise Thérèse Martin) French CARMELITE nun. She entered the convent at Lisieux, N France, at the age of 15. She chronicled her spiritual struggle in a series of letters, *Story of a Soul* (1898). She was canonized in 1925. Her feast day is October 1.

thermal Small-scale, rising current of air produced by local heating of the Earth's surface. Thermals are often used by GLIDING birds and human-built gliders.

thermionics Study of the emission of ELECTRONS or IONS from a heated CONDUCTOR. This is the principle on which electron tubes (valves) work. The heated conductor is the CATHODE and the emitted electrons are attracted to the ANODE. A more modern aim for thermionics is the design and construction of thermionic power generators.

thermodynamics Branch of physics that studies HEAT and how it is transformed to and from other forms of ENERGY. The original laws of thermodynamics were conceived by observing large-scale properties of systems and with no understanding of the underlying atomic structure. The KINETIC THEORY of gases developed in the mid-19th century. In general, the TEMPERATURE of a body is a measure of its internal energy. The three existing laws are now calculated using statistics and QUANTUM MECHANICS. The **first law** of thermodynamics, basically a restatement of the CONSERVATION law of energy, is that the change in a system's internal energy is equal to the heat that flows into the system plus the work done on the system. The two main forms of change are adiabatic (without heat entering or leaving a system) and isothermal (at constant temperature). The **second law** says that if a system is left alone, its ENTROPY (measure of thermal energy unavailable for work) tends to increase. This rules out the possibility of PERPETUAL MOTION. The **third law** states that a system at ABSOLUTE ZERO would effectively have an entropy of zero. *See also* CARNOT CYCLE; CLAUSIUS, RUDOLF; KELVIN, WILLIAM THOMSON, 1ST BARON

thermometer Instrument for measuring TEMPERATURE. A MERCURY thermometer depends on the expansion of the metal mercury, which is held in a glass bulb connected to a narrow, graduated tube. Temperatures can also be measured by a gas thermometer and by a resistance thermometer that measures resistance of a conductor, such as a platinum wire. Common scales are the CELSIUS, FAHRENHEIT, and KELVIN.

Thermopylae Strategic mountain pass in E central Greece, site of several battles in ancient times. The most famous was the defence of the pass by Leonidas of SPARTA against the Persian invasion of XERXES I in 480 BC.

thermostat Device for maintaining a constant TEMPERATURE. A common type contains a strip of two metals, one of which expands and contracts more than the other. At a set temperature, the strip bends and breaks the circuit. As it cools, the strip straightens, makes contact, and the heating begins again once the circuit is complete. Thermostats are used in air-conditioning systems and in refrigerators, ovens and water heaters.

Theroux, Paul (1941–) US novelist and travel writer. Long-time resident in Britain, he has written short stories and a number of novels, including *Girls at Play* (1969), *The Family Arsenal* (1976), *The Mosquito Coast* (1981), *My Secret History* (1989), and *My Other Life* (1996). His fiction has been overshadowed by his travel writing, which includes *The Great Railway Bazaar* (1975) and *Riding the Iron Rooster* (1988).

Theseus In Greek mythology, a great hero of many adventures, the son of Aethra by Aegeus, King of Athens, or by the sea god POSEIDON. His most famous exploit was the vanquishing of the MINOTAUR of Crete.

Thespis (6th centuryBC) Greek writer, according to tradition, the inventor of tragedy. He is also said to have introduced a character separate from the chorus, who provided dialogue by responding to the chorus' comments.

Thessalonians, Epistles to the Two of Saint Paul's earliest letters, forming the 13th and 14th books of the New Testament. The first letter was written in *c.*AD 50, and the second followed shortly afterwards. The letters contained encouragement and pastoral guidance for the Thessalonians and neighbouring Christian communities.

Thessaloníki (Salonica) Port on the Gulf of Thessaloníki, Greece, the country's second-largest city and capital of Greek Macedonia. Founded in *c.*315 BC it flourished as the capital of Macedonia under the Romans after 148 BC. The city was part of the Ottoman Empire until 1913, when it was conquered by Greece. Industries: oil refining, textiles, metals, engineering, chemicals, cement, soap. Pop. (2005) 824,000.

thiamine Vitamin B$_1$ of the B complex, required for carbohydrate metabolism. Its deficiency causes beriberi. Thiamine is found in grains, nuts, liver, yeast, and legumes.

Third Reich Official name of Nazi Germany (1933–45). The first *Reich* (Ger. 'Empire') was the Holy Roman Empire, the second the German Empire of 1871–1918.

Third World Former term for less-developed countries. 'First' and 'Second' World countries were those of the Western and Eastern blocs respectively.

Thirteen Colonies English colonies in North America that jointly declared independence from Britain (1776) and became the USA. They were: Connecticut, Delaware, Georgia, Maryland, Massachusetts, New Hampshire, New Jersey, New York, North Carolina, Pennsylvania, Rhode Island, South Carolina, and Virginia. *See also* American Revolution

Thirty Years' War (1618–48) Conflict fought mainly in Germany, arising out of religious differences and developing into a struggle for power in Europe. It began with a Protestant revolt in Bohemia against the Habsburg Emperor, Ferdinand II. Both sides sought allies and the war spread to much of Europe. The Habsburg generals Tilly and Wallenstein registered early victories and drove the Protestant champion, Christian IV of Denmark, out of the war (1629). A greater champion appeared in Gustavus II (Adolphus) of Sweden, who waged a series of victorious campaigns before being killed in 1632. In 1635, France, fearing Habsburg dominance, declared war on Habsburg Spain. Negotiations for peace were not successful until the Peace of Westphalia was concluded in 1648. War between France and Spain continued until the Peace of the Pyrenees (1659), and other associated conflicts continued for several years. The chief loser in the war was Emperor Ferdinand III, who lost control of Germany. Sweden was established as the dominant state in N Europe, while France replaced Spain as the greatest power in Europe.

thistle Any of numerous species of plants with thorny leaves and yellow, white, pink, or purple flower heads with prickly bracts. The field thistle, *Cirsium discolor*, resembles the heraldic thistle, which is the national emblem of Scotland. Family Asteraceae/Compositae.

Thomas, Dylan Marlais (1914–53) Welsh poet and short-story writer. A self-styled *enfant terrible*, whose flamboyant alcoholic lifestyle led to his early death in New York, Thomas was a resonant reader of his own and others' poetry, his public persona contributing to the popularity of his meticulously crafted, often wilfully obscure verse. His *Collected Poems* was published in 1953. Many of his best short stories appear in *Portrait of the Artist as a Young Dog* (1940) and *Adventures in the Skin Trade* (1955). The 'play for voices' *Under Milk Wood*, written in 1952, is perhaps his best-known work.

Thomas, R.S. (Ronald Stuart) (1913–2000) Welsh poet. He was a clergyman for more than 40 years. Thomas' early verse is collected in *Song at the Year's Turning* (1955); it embodies his characteristic concerns with Wales and its people, and with the implications of his faith. His later work evinces a fierce distrust of the modern world.

Thomas, Saint One of the original 12 apostles or disciples of Jesus Christ. He has been called 'Doubting Thomas' because, after the resurrection of Christ, he refused to believe that the risen Lord had appeared to the other disciples (John 20). Only when Jesus appeared to him and allowed him to touch his wounds did he then believe. According to Christian tradition, he took Christianity to India. His feast day is July 3.

Thomas à Kempis *See* Kempis, Thomas à
Thomas Aquinas, Saint *See* Aquinas, Saint Thomas
Thomism Philosophy of Saint Thomas Aquinas, one of the major systems in scholasticism. Aquinas blended the philosophy of Aristotle with Christian theology. Using Aristotle's concept of matter and form, he conceived a hierarchy in which spirit is higher than matter, soul higher than body, and theology above philosophy.

Thompson, Emma (1959–) English actress and screenwriter. She was married (1989–95) to Kenneth Branagh, and acted in his film adaptations of Shakespeare's *Henry V* (1989) and *Much Ado Nothing* (1993). Thompson won Academy Awards for best actress in *Howard's End* (1991) and for best screenplay for *Sense and Sensibility* (1995). Other films include *Remains of the Day* (1993) and *Love Actually* (2003).

Thomson, Sir George Paget (1892–1975) English physicist, son of Sir Joseph John Thomson. He shared the 1937 Nobel Prize in physics with Clinton Davisson for their independent work in diffracting electrons (1927). This work confirmed the wave nature of particles first predicted (1923) by Louis de Broglie.

Thomson, James (1700–48) Scottish poet. A precursor of romanticism, Thomson's best-known work is the four-part nature poem *The Seasons* (1730). It was used by Haydn as the basis for his oratorio (1801). Other works include the song 'Rule Britannia' (1740), and the Spenserian allegory *The Castle of Indolence* (1748).

Thomson, Sir Joseph John (1856–1940) British physicist, father of George Thomson, b. Belfast. He succeeded James Clerk Maxwell as professor of experimental physics (1884–1919) at Cambridge. Thomson's discovery (1897) of the electron is regarded as the birth of particle physics. He received the 1906 Nobel Prize in physics for his investigations into the electrical conductivity of gases. Thomson and Francis Aston produced evidence of isotopes of neon. He transformed the Cavendish Laboratory into a major centre for atomic research, attracting scientists like Ernest Rutherford. Thomson served as president (1915–20) of the Royal Society.

Thor In Teutonic mythology, god of thunder and lightning, corresponding to Jupiter. The eldest and strongest of Odin's sons, he was represented as a handsome, red-bearded warrior, benevolent towards humans but a mighty foe of evil.

thorax In animal anatomy, part between the neck and the abdomen. In mammals, it is formed by the rib cage and contains the lungs, heart and oesophagus. In insects, it consists of several segments to which legs and other appendages are attached.

Thoreau, Henry David (1817–62) US writer and naturalist. He was a friend of fellow transcendentalist Ralph Waldo Emerson, who encouraged him to keep the journals from which he quarried much of his later work. An ardent individualist, he experimented in living a near-solitary life, rejecting materialism and finding fulfilment in observing plant and animal life. His essay *Civil Disobedience* (1849) influenced many passive resistance movements. *See also* transcendentalism

thorium (symbol Th) Radioactive, metallic element of the actinide series, first discovered in 1828 by Swedish chemist J.J. Berzelius who named it after the Norse god Thor. The chief ore is monazite. The metal is used in photoelectric and thermionic emitters. One decay product is radon-220. Thorium is sometimes used in radiotherapy, and is increasingly used for conversion into uranium-233 for nuclear fission. Chemically reactive, it burns in air but reacts slowly in water. Properties: at.no. 90; r.a.m. 232.0381; r.d. 11.72; m.p. 1,750°C (3,182°F); b.p. 4,790°C (8,654°F); most stable isotope Th^{232} (1.41 × 10^{10} yrs).

thorn apple Plant of the genus *Datura*, especially Jimson weed (*D. stramonium*), a poisonous, annual weed of tropical American origin. It has foul-smelling leaves and large white or violet trumpet-shaped flowers that are succeeded by round prickly fruits. Family Solanaceae.

Thoth In Egyptian mythology, the scribe of the gods. He appears as the record-keeper of the dead, patron of the arts and learning, inventor of writing, and as creator of the universe. Thoth is depicted as a man with the head of an ibis or of an ape, bearing pen and ink, or the lunar disc and crescent.

▲ **thistle** The creeping thistle is a weed, which is common on waste and cultivated land. Like the dandelion, it is a composite. There are about 150 species of *Cirsium* whose flowers may be violet, mauve, pink, yellow, or white.

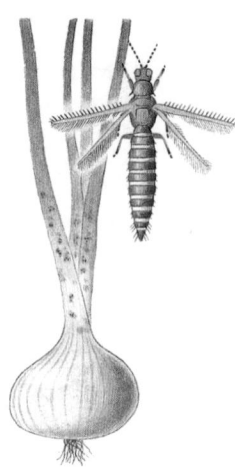

▲ **thrip** A tiny pest, thrips (order Thysanoptera) are significant for the damage they do to crops and for carrying disease. They have simple, fringed wings – or none at all – and unusual mouthparts with which they suck up plant juices. The onion thrips in both adult and nymphal stages infest a number of hosts to which they may transmit the tomato spotted wilt virus.

Thrace (Thráki) Ancient SE European country, now divided between Bulgaria, Greece and European Turkey. From 1300 to 600 BC the Thracian lands extended W to the Adriatic and N to the Danube. By *c.*600 BC Thrace lost much of its E lands to the Illyrians and Macedonians, and the Greeks established the colony of Byzantium. In 342 BC Philip II of Macedon conquered the country. After 100 BC it became part of the Roman Empire. In the 7th century AD the Bulgarians conquered the N of the region, and by 1300 they controlled all Thrace. From 1361 to 1453, the Bulgarians and the emerging Ottoman Empire disputed the region, which eventually fell to the Ottoman Turks. In 1885, Bulgaria annexed N Thrace. The regions either side of the River Maritsa became known as Eastern Thrace (Bulgaria) and Western Thrace (Turkey). After World War 1, Bulgaria ceded S and most of E Thrace to Greece. The Treaty of Lausanne (1923) restored E Thrace to Turkey, and the region retains these boundaries. A fertile region, its main economic activity is agriculture.

threadworm (pinworm) Small ROUNDWORM of the phylum Aschelminthes. It is most common in moist tropical regions and resembles a short length of hair or thread. It may inhabit the intestines of human beings and other animals, but can live and breed freely in soil. Species *Oxyurus vermicularis*.

Three Mile Island Island on the River Susquehanna near Harrisburg, Pennsylvania, USA. It is the site of a nuclear power-generating plant where a near-disastrous accident took place in March 1979. The accident involved the failure of the feedwater system, which picks up heat from the system that has circulated through the reactor core. The accident released radioactive water and gases into the environment.

thrip Any of numerous species of slender, sucking insects found throughout the world. Most feed on plants and some carry plant diseases. Length: to 8mm (0.3in). Order Thysanoptera.

throat *See* PHARYNX

thrombophlebitis Inflammation of the walls of veins associated with THROMBOSIS. It can occur in the legs during a woman's pregnancy.

thrombosis Formation of a blood clot in an artery or vein. Besides causing loss of circulation to the area supplied by the blocked vessel, it carries the risk of EMBOLISM.

thrush (candidiasis) Fungal infection of the mucous membranes, usually of the mouth but also sometimes of the vagina. Caused by the fungus *Candida albicans*, it is sometimes seen in people taking broad-spectrum ANTIBIOTICS.

thrush Any of numerous species of small songbirds of the family Turdidae. The European song thrush (*Turdus philomelos*) is mottled brown with a lighter, speckled breast. North American species include the (North American) robin, bluebird, and bluethroat. Length: to 30cm (12in).

thrust Driving force resulting from operation of a propeller, jet engine or rocket engine. An aircraft propeller forces air backwards, and jet and rocket engines expel gases backwards. Thrust occurs in the forward direction in accordance with the third of NEWTON'S LAWS of motion. *See also* AERODYNAMICS

Thucydides (*c.*460–*c.*400 BC) Greek historian. A commander in the PELOPONNESIAN WAR, his *History of the Peloponnesian War* is a determined attempt to write objective history, and it displays a profound understanding of human motives.

thugs Murderous gangs in India who preyed on travellers. They were members of a secret society, who killed their victims by ritual strangulation (*thuggee*) in honour of KALI, the Hindu goddess of destruction. The British suppressed the thugs in the 1830s.

thulium (symbol Tm) Lustrous, silver-white, metallic element of the LANTHANIDE SERIES (rare-earth metals). Its chief ore is monazite but thulium is as rare as gold. Soft, malleable and ductile, it combines with OXYGEN and the HALOGENS. It is used in arc lighting and portable X-ray units. It is used in arc lighting and portable X-ray units. It was discovered in 1879 by Swedish chemist Per Cleve (1840–1905). Properties: at.no. 69; r.a.m. 168.9342; r.d. 9.31 (25°C); m.p. 1,545°C (2,813°F); b.p. 1,947°C (3,537°F); most stable isotope Tm[169] (100%).

thunderstorm Electrical storm caused by the separation of electrical charges in clouds. Water drops are carried by updraughts to the top of a CLOUD, where they become ionized and accumulate into positive charges – the base of the cloud being negatively charged. An electrical discharge (a spark) between clouds, or between a cloud and the ground, is accompanied by light (seen as a LIGHTNING stroke) and heat. The heat expands the air explosively and causes it to reverberate and produce sounds and echoes called thunder.

Thurber, James Grover (1894–1961) US humorist and cartoonist. From 1923, he was a regular contributor of essays, short stories and cartoons to the *New Yorker*. Collections of Thurber's essays and stories include *My Life and Hard Times* (1933), and *My World and Welcome to It* (1942), which includes his best-known short story, 'The Secret Life of Walter Mitty' (1932).

Thuringia Historic region of central Germany. Its rulers became powerful princes with the HOLY ROMAN EMPIRE in the 11th century. Thuringia was reconstituted as a state (*Land*) in 1920 under the WEIMAR REPUBLIC, but lost its separate identity in 1952. The main industries are manufacturing and cereal cropping. Area: 16,176sq km (6,244sq mi). Pop. (1999) 2,449,082.

Thutmose Name of four kings of the 18th dynasty in ancient EGYPT. **Thutmose I** (r. *c.*1525–*c.*1512BC) extended his kingdom S into NUBIA, and campaigned successfully in the Near East. He was succeeded by his son, **Thutmose II** (r. *c.*1512– *c.*1504BC), who married his half-sister, HATSHEPSUT. She ruled as regent for his son, **Thutmose III** (r. *c.*1504– 1450BC). Thutmose III expanded the kingdom to its greatest extent. His grandson, **Thutmose IV** (r. *c.*1425– *c.*1416BC), continued an expansive policy but also sought to strengthen the empire by peaceful means, marrying a Mitanni princess.

thyme Aromatic garden herb of the MINT family (Lamiaceae/Labiatae), used as an ornamental plant and in cooking. It yields an oil from which the drug thymol is prepared. It has purple flowers. Height: 15–20cm (6–8in). Genus *Thymus*.

thymus gland One of the endocrine GLANDS, located in the upper chest in mammals. In childhood, it controls the development of lymphoid tissue and the immune response to infection. Disorder of the thymus may be associated with AUTOIMMUNE DISEASES (those caused by the body's own antibodies). *See also* ENDOCRINE SYSTEM

thyroid gland H-shaped gland of the ENDOCRINE SYSTEM. It lies in the base of the neck, straddling the trachea below the Adam's apple. It secretes hormones, principally THYROXINE that regulates growth and development. The enlargement of the thyroid gland, usually due to a lack of iodine in the diet, causes a swelling of the neck called a **goitre**.

thyroxine Hormone secreted by the THYROID GLAND. It contains IODINE and helps regulate the rate of metabolism; it is essential for normal growth and development.

Tiananmen Square World's largest public square, covering 40ha (98 acres) in BEIJING, China. On the S side, a marble monument is dedicated to the heroes of the revolution. A gate on the the N side leads into the Forbidden City. A huge portrait of Mao adorns the side of the MAO ZEDONG Memorial Hall. On May 4, 1919, China's first mass public rally was held in the square, and on October 1, 1949, Mao Zedong proclaimed the establishment of the People's Republic of China. In 1966, Mao made his pronouncements on the CULTURAL REVOLUTION to more than one million Red Guards assembled in the square. In April 1989, a series of nationwide pro-democracy demonstrations culminated in the occupation of the square by protesters. Hundreds of thousands of citizens joined in the demonstrations. On June 4, 1989, tanks and troops stormed the square. Official casualties were put at more than 200 demonstrators and dozens of soldiers. Eyewitness reports suggest thousands of deaths. The government imposed a year-long martial law and executed several student leaders.

Tianjin (Tientsin) Port and industrial city on the River Hai, NE China. It is China's third-largest city and the most important international port in N China. Founded in *c.*300 BC it became prominent in the late 18th century because of its strategic position en route to Manchuria. In 1860, the British and French obtained the right to use Tianjin as a treaty port. In 1900, the city came under European occupation. Because of its excellent transport links, it remains N

China's main trading centre. The city is administered as a special economic zone to encourage inward investment. Industries: iron, steel, heavy machinery, transport equipment, textiles, carpets. Pop. (2005) 9,346,000.

Tian Shan (Tien Shan) Mountain range in C Asia, 2,400km (1,500mi) long, forming the border between Kyrgyzstan and Xinjiang, NW China. At their W edge, the Tian Shan ('Celestial Mountains') divide the Tarim and Junggar Basins. The range rises to 7,439m (24,406ft) at Peak Pobeda, on the Chinese border with Kazakhstan and Kyrgyzstan. The Issyk Kul in Kyrgyzstan is one of the world's largest mountain lakes.

Tiber (Tevere) River in central Italy. It rises in the Etruscan Apennines, flows S then SW through Rome, and empties into the Tyrrhenian Sea at Ostia. The silting of the river closed Fiumara, one of its two mouths, and its delta continues to expand; the ancient coastal port of Ostia Antica now lies 6km (4mi) inland. Length: 404km (251mi).

Tiberius, Julius Caesar (42 BC–AD 37) Roman Emperor (AD 14–37). He was the stepson of AUGUSTUS, who adopted him as his heir (AD 4). Initially, his administration was just and moderate, but he became increasingly fearful of conspiracy and had many people executed for alleged treason. Tiberius left Rome and spent his last years in seclusion on Capri.

Tibet (Xizang) Autonomous region in SW China. The capital and largest city is LHASA. Tibet is the highest region on earth, with an average altitude of 4,875m (16,000ft). An historically inaccessible area, surrounded by mountains on three sides. The Tibetan HIMALAYAS include the world's highest mountain, EVEREST. Nam Co is the world's largest natural salt lake. Many of Asia's greatest rivers (including the YANGTZE, MEKONG, HUANG HE, INDUS, and GANGES) have their source in Tibet, although its major river is the BRAHMAPUTRA. The area has scant rainfall, and the Brahmaputra valley is the only agricultural area and the location of the major cities. Many of the people remain nomadic pastoralists. Tibet is rich in mineral resources, such as gold, copper, and uranium. The Chinese government built internal highways and links to the Chinese provinces. The principal religion is TIBETAN BUDDHISM. Until 1959, a large percentage of the urban male population were Buddhist monks (lamas). Tibet flourished as an independent kingdom in the 7th century, and in the 8th century Padmasambhava developed the principles of MAHAYANA Buddhism and founded Lamaism. The spiritual leaders of Lamaism (the DALAI LAMA and PANCHEN LAMA) also acted as the country's temporal rulers. In 1206, Genghis Khan conquered the region, and it remained under nominal Mongol rule until 1720, when the Chinese QING dynasty claimed sovereignty. At the close of the 19th century, the Tibetan areas of Ladakh and SIKKIM became part of British India, and in 1906 Britain recognized Chinese sovereignty over Tibet. In 1912, the fall of the Qing dynasty prompted the Tibetans to reassert their independence. China, however, maintained its right to govern, and in 1950 the new communist regime invaded. In 1951, Tibet was declared an autonomous region of China, nominally governed by the Dalai Lama. The Chinese government began a series of repressive measures, principally targeting the Buddhist monasteries. In March 1959, a full-scale revolt was suppressed by the Chinese Army. On December 25, 1959, the Dalai Lama fled to N India, and established a government-in-exile at Dharamsala. In 1965, China formally annexed Tibet as an autonomous region. The CULTURAL REVOLUTION banned religious practice and destroyed 4000 monasteries. Many thousands of Tibetans fled into exile to escape the brutality of the communist regime. Despite the restoration of some of the desecrated monasteries and the reinstatement of Tibetan as an official language, human rights violations continued. Pro-independence rallies between 1987–89 were violently suppressed by the Chinese army. Area: 1,222,070sq km (471,841sq mi). Pop. (2000) 2,620,000.

Tibetan art Virtually all art in Tibet is religious in character, designed to serve the elaborate rituals of TIBETAN BUDDHISM. All artworks are anonymous and most are undated. Paintings come in two forms – wall-paintings and *thangkas*, which are banners, usually displayed in temples or carried in processions. *Thangkas* generally depict scenes from the life of a deity or *mandalas* (patterns used for meditation).

Tibetan Buddhism Distinctive blend of Mahayana BUDDHISM and Bonism (a pre-Buddhist shamanism). It mixes meditative monasticism with indigenous folk-religion and involves a system of reincarnating lamas (monks). Both spiritual and temporal authority reside in the person and office of the DALAI LAMA. King Srong-tsan-gampo (b.617 or 629) sought to bring Buddhist teachers from China and India to Tibet. The Bon priests opposed the new Buddhist ways, and Buddhism was not thoroughly introduced into Tibet until the 8th century. Following reforms initiated by the 11th-century Indian master Atisha, four major sects emerged in Tibetan Buddhism. Of these, the Gelugpa order, to which the Dalai and PANCHEN LAMAS belong, was politically dominant from the 17th century. There are now two Gelugpa sects, the Red and Yellow monks. The Dalai Lama, a member of the latter, became revered as the 'Living Buddha' and the spiritual and temporal ruler of Tibet. Each new Dalai Lama is believed to be a reincarnation of AVALOKITESVARA. The Panchen Lama heads the Red monks.

tibia (shinbone) Inner and larger of the two lower leg bones. It articulates with the FEMUR, or upper leg bone, at the knee and extends to the ankle, where its lower end forms the projecting ankle bone on the inside of the leg. *See also* FIBULA

tic Sudden and rapidly repeated muscular contraction, limited to one part of the body, especially the face.

tick Any of numerous species of wingless, bloodsucking ARACHNIDS, the most notable of which are ectoparasites of vertebrates and invertebrates. Many species carry diseases (some fatal) in wild and domesticated animals, and in humans. Length: to 3mm (0.1in). Class Arachnida; order Acarina.

tidal power Energy harnessed from tidal movement of the Earth's OCEANS and used by humans. It is economic only where the tidal range is greater than *c*.4.6m (15ft). Modern schemes involve the use of turbo-generators driven by the passage of water through a tidal barrage. *See* illustration page 738

tide Periodic rise and fall of the surface level of the OCEANS caused by the gravitational attraction of the Moon and Sun. Tides follow the Moon's cycle of 28 days, so they arrive at a given spot 50 minutes later each day. When the Sun and Moon are in conjunction or opposition, the greatest tidal range occurs, called spring tides. When they are in quadrature, when the Moon is half-full, tidal ranges are lowest and are called neap tides. *See* illustration page 739

Tiepolo, Giovanni Battista (1696–1770) Italian painter. His ROCOCO pictures are full of action, using light, sunny colours, with figures and objects seen in a deep, theatrical PERSPECTIVE. The peak of his career came in the 1750s, when he decorated the Kaisersaal and the grand staircase of the Prince Archbishop's Palace, Würzburg.

Tierra del Fuego (Sp. 'Land of Fire') Archipelago separated from mainland S South America by the Magellan Strait. It consists of one large island and other smaller islands. At the S extremity of the islands lies Cape Horn. The main island is politically divided between Argentina and Chile. The islands remained undiscovered by Europeans until Ferdinand MAGELLAN landed in 1520. The Tierra del Fuego were not settled until the 1880s, when the discovery of gold (and later oil) attracted many Europeans, Argentinians, and Chileans to the area. The indigenous population was killed by diseases brought by settlers. The mountainous terrain and harsh climate limit economic activity to sheep rearing and oil exploration. Area: 73,746sq km (28,473sq mi). Pop. (2000) 139,945.

Tiffany, Louis Comfort (1848–1933) US painter and designer, leader of the ART NOUVEAU style in the USA. In 1878, he formed an interior decorating firm, which by 1900 was known as Tiffany Studios. It specialized in what he termed 'favrile' glass – freely shaped iridescent glasswork, sometimes combined with various metals.

tiger Large, powerful CAT found (in decreasing numbers) throughout Asia, mainly in forested areas. It has a characteristic striped coat of yellow, orange, white and black,

T

▲ **thyme** Thyme (*Thymus vulgaris*) has a pungent aroma, and retains much of its flavour when dried. It is a favourite herb for Mediterranean cooking and is an essential ingredient of bouquet garni.

with the chin and underparts white. Relying on keen hearing, it hunts for birds, deer, cattle, and reptiles. An adult tiger will eat up to 25kg (50lb) of meat in one meal. The largest tiger is the endangered Siberian race. Length: to 4m (13ft) overall; weight: to 230kg (500lb). Family Felidae; species *Panthera tigris*.

Tigris River in SW Asia. It rises in the Taurus Mountains of E Turkey and flows SE through Iraq, joining the River EUPHRATES to form the SHATT AL ARAB waterway. The river is liable to sudden flooding, but there are flood-control schemes and the river irrigates more than 300,000ha (750,000 acres). The Tigris is navigable for shallow-draught vessels as far as BAGHDAD. Length: *c*.1,900km (1,180mi).

till In geology, sediment consisting of an unsorted mixture of clay, sand, gravel, and boulders that is deposited directly by the ice of GLACIERS.

timber *See* WOOD

timbre Characteristic of a musical sound determined by the number and intensity of the overtones (HARMONICS) produced as well as the principal (fundamental) note. Musical instruments of different types make characteristic sounds because of the different harmonics produced.

Timbuktu Town in N Mali, W Africa. It was founded by the Tuareg people in the 11th century, and soon became a centre of Muslim learning. The southern terminus of a Saharan caravan route, it later became famous throughout Europe as a market for slaves and gold. Sacked by the Moroccans in 1591, and seized by the French in 1893, its most important trading commodity today is salt. Pop. (2002 est.) 34,600.

time Perception of a sequential order in all experience; also the interval perceived between two events. A consideration of time falls within the disciplines of physics, psychology, philosophy, and biology. Until the theory of RELATIVITY was devised by Albert EINSTEIN, time was conceived of as absolute – a constant one-direction (past to future) flow. Since then the concept of time linked with distance in SPACE ('space-time') has connected time with the relative velocities of those perceiving it. For clocks at velocities approaching that of light, time expands from the point of view of a stationary observer, but it still flows in the same direction.

time scale *See* GEOLOGICAL TIME

time zone One of 24 divisions of the Earth's surface, each 15° of longitude wide, within which the time of day is reckoned to be the same. At a conference held in Washington, D.C., in 1884, the meridian of Greenwich was adopted as the zero of longitude, and zones of longitude were established. Standard time in each successive zone westwards is one hour behind that in the preceding zone. *See also* GREENWICH MEAN TIME (GMT)

Timişoara City in W Romania, on the River Bega and Canal. An ancient Roman settlement, it was ruled by the MAGYARS from 896, annexed to Hungary in 1010, and ruled by the Turks from 1552 to 1716. It was returned to Austria-Hungary in 1716, and passed to Romania in 1920. Events here in 1989 triggered the fall of CEAUŞESCU's regime. Industries: engineering, tobacco, chemicals, textiles, machinery. Pop. (1998 est.) 324,304.

Timor Largest of the Lesser Sunda Islands in the Malay archipelago. The chief towns are Kupang in the W and Dili in the E. From *c*.1520, Portuguese spice traders began to settle on Timor. When the Dutch landed in 1620, they settled on the W side. Japan occupied the island during World War 2. In 1950, West Timor became part of the Nusa Tenggara Timur province of the newly created Republic of INDONESIA. In 1975, Portugal abandoned East Timor and the colony declared independence. Indonesia immediately invaded, and in 1976 annexed East Timor. After decades of violence East Timor regained independence in 2002; *see* country feature, p. 290.

timpani (kettledrums) Main percussion instruments in a symphony orchestra. They are hemispherical vessels of copper or brass with single skins, tuned by pedals or screws, and struck with sticks with hard felt heads. Military kettledrums, played on horseback, were introduced to Europe by the Crusaders *c*.1100.

Timur *See* TAMERLANE

tin (symbol Sn) Metalloid element of group IV of the periodic table, known from ancient times. Its chief ore is cassiterite (an oxide). Soft, malleable and resistant to corrosion, tin is used as a protective coating for iron, steel, copper and other metals, and in such alloys as solder, pewter, bronze and type metal. Properties: at.no. 50; r.a.m. 118.69; r.d. 7.29; m.p. 232°C (449.6°F); b.p. 2,270°C (4,118°F); most common isotope Sn^{118} (24.03%).

Tinbergen, Nikolaas (1907–88) Dutch ethologist. He shared (with Konrad LORENZ and Karl von FRISCH) the 1973 Nobel Prize in physiology or medicine for his pioneering work in ETHOLOGY. Tinbergen studied how certain stimuli evoke specific responses in animals.

Tintoretto (1518–94) Italian painter, b. Jacopo Robusti. Tintoretto was the outstanding Venetian painter in the generation that succeeded TITIAN. Among his notable works are *The Finding of the Body of St Mark* (1562), *The Last Supper* (1592–94), and the huge *Paradiso* (1588–90) in the Doge's Palace, Venice. Some of Tintoretto's finest paintings are in the series of the life of Christ (1565–87).

Tipperary County in Munster province, central s Republic of Ireland. The county town is Clonmel. The region is part of the central plain of Ireland, but there are hills in the S; the Suir and Shannon are the principal rivers. The soil is fertile and Tipperary is one of the country's best farming regions. Area: 4,255sq km (1,643sq mi). Pop. (2002) 140,281.

TIDAL POWER

The power of the sea can be harnessed to generate electricity. Tidal power uses a barrage (1) across an estuary or bay. The barrage contains turbines that can spin with a flow of water in either direction. As the tide comes in, gates on the barrage remain closed until a head of water has built up on the sea side of the structure (2). The gates are then opened (3), and the incoming tide flows through the barrage driving the turbines (4). As the tide falls, the process is reversed – with the gates closed until the sea has fallen below the level of water retained in the estuary (5). A second method of utilizing the power of the sea involves harnessing wave power (6). The key difference is that the turbine (7) is air driven, not turned by water. As a wave hits the shore, the force of the water (8) drives air (9) through the turbine blades (10). When the water level drops, air is sucked back down through the turbine, spinning it again.

Tippett, Sir Michael Kemp (1905–98) English composer. His music incorporates apparently disparate musical forms and social themes of justice, pacifism, and humanism. Tippett's oratorio *A Child of our Time* (1941) was a response to the 'Kristallnacht' in Nazi Germany in 1938. His operas include *The Midsummer Marriage* (1952), *King Priam* (1962), and *New Year* (1988). Other works include the oratorio *The Mask of Time* (1982), *String Quartet No.1* (1934), and four symphonies (1945, 1957, 1972, 1977). He was knighted in 1966.

Tirana (Tiranë) Capital of Albania, on the River Ishm, central Albania. Tirana was founded in the early 17th century by the Ottoman Turks, and became Albania's capital in 1920. In 1946, the communists came to power and the industrial sector of the city was developed. Industries: metal goods, agricultural machinery, textiles. Pop. (2000) 288,217.

Tirol (Tyrol) Federal state in w Austria, bordered N by Germany and S by Italy. The capital is INNSBRUCK. The Romans conquered the region in 15 BC and the Franks held it during the 8th century. In 1363, the province was taken by the Habsburgs. In 1805, Napoleon I awarded Tirol to Bavaria in return for its support. In 1810, Napoleon gave S Tirol to the Italians, but the Congress of Vienna (1815) reunited Tirol with Austria. After World War 1, when S Tirol was awarded to Italy, a process of Italianization was resisted by the German-speaking inhabitants. After World War 2, S Tirol was made an autonomous Italian region. Tourists are attracted by the good skiing conditions in the Tirolean Alps. Other economic activities are mainly agricultural. Area: 12,647sq km (4882sq mi). Pop. (2001) 675,063.

Tirpitz, Alfred von (1849–1930) German admiral. Tirpitz was chiefly responsible for the build-up of the German navy before World War 1. Frustrated by government cut-backs and restrictions on submarine warfare, he resigned in 1916. He later sat in the Reichstag during the WEIMAR REPUBLIC.

tissue Material of a living body consisting of a group of similar and often interconnected cells, usually supporting a similar function. Tissues vary greatly in structure and complexity. In animals, they may be loosely classified according to function into epithelial, connective, skeletal, muscular, nervous, and glandular tissues.

tissue culture In biology, artificial cultivation of living TISSUE. Tissue culture in laboratories is used for biological research or to help in the diagnosis of diseases. It is also used as a means of propagating plant CLONES. *See also* GENETIC ENGINEERING

Titan Largest SATELLITE of Saturn, and the second largest in the Solar System, discovered (1655) by Christiaan Huygens. It is unique among planetary satellites in having a substantial atmosphere. It is composed of rock and water-ice in roughly equal proportions. The space probe Voyager 1 found no gaps in an opaque, reddish cloud layer *c*.200km (125mi) above the surface. The atmosphere is mostly nitrogen, with some methane and other hydrocarbon compounds. The surface temperature is 95K, at which METHANE can exist as solid, liquid or gas, forming clouds, rain, rivers and lakes. In 2005 the Huygens probe landed on Titan and sent back large amounts of data.

Titan In Greek mythology, one of 12 gods and goddesses who were the sons and daughters of URANUS and GAIA. They preceded the Olympians who, led by ZEUS, overthrew them.

Titania In folklore, queen of the fairies and wife of OBERON. In the writings of OVID, she represents DIANA at the head of her nymphs. In Shakespeare's *A Midsummer Night's Dream* (1595), she quarrels with her husband over a changeling boy.

Titanic British passenger liner that sank on her maiden voyage (April 14–15, 1912). The largest vessel of her time, she was sailing from Southampton to New York when she struck an iceberg in the N Atlantic. About 1500 people were drowned. The disaster resulted in international agreements on greater safety precautions at sea. In 1985, the wreck of the *Titanic* was located on the ocean floor.

titanium (symbol Ti) Lustrous, silver-grey, metallic element, one of the TRANSITION ELEMENTS. A common element, it is found in many minerals, chief sources being ilmenite and RUTILE. Resistant to corrosion and heat, it is used in steels and other alloys, especially in aircraft, spacecraft and guided missiles where strength must be combined

◀ **tiger** Once common throughout Asia, hunting and the reduction of habitat drastically reduced the tiger population. Reserves have been established in India for the protection of the tiger. It can leap 4m (15ft) in one bound.

with lightness. It was discovered in 1791 by the English mineralogist William Gregor (1761–1817). Properties: at.no. 22; r.a.m. 47.90; r.d. 4.54; m.p. 1,660°C (3,020°F); b.p. 3,287°C (5,949°F); most common isotope Ti^{48} (73.94%).

tithe Tax of one-tenth of income levied to support a religious institution. Tithes were prescribed in the Old Testament and were a major source of Church income in medieval Europe. They were largely abandoned in the 19th century.

Titian (1485–1576) Venetian painter, b. Tiziano Vecellio. He trained first with Giovanni BELLINI, and then with GIORGIONE. His reputation was established with the monumental *The Assumption of the Virgin* (1516–18). Titian combined the balance of High RENAISSANCE composition with a new dynamism, which heralded the BAROQUE. He favoured vivid, simple colours, and often silhouetted dark forms against a light background. His finest mythological paintings include *Bacchanal* (*c*.1518) and the earthy *Bacchus and Ariadne* (1522–23). In 1533, Emperor Charles V appointed Titian as court painter, and his *Charles V at Mühlberg* (1548) is one of the earliest equestrian portraits. From 1550, Titian produced erotic mythologies for Philip II of Spain, such as *The Rape of Europa* (1562). His last work was the astonishingly powerful *Pietà*, which he designed for his own tomb. Titian's oil technique was freer and more expressive than any earlier style, and he had a revolutionary influence on later artists.

Titicaca Lake in the Andes on the Peru-Bolivia border, draining S through the River Desaguader into Lake Poopó. At an altitude of 3,810m (12,500ft), it is the world's highest navigable body of water. The constant supply of water has enabled the region to grow crops since ancient times. The lake is home to giant edible frogs, and is famed for its totora reeds, from which the Uru make their floating island homes and fishing rafts. Area: 8,290sq km (3,200sq mi); max. depth 280m (920ft).

titmouse (tit, chickadee) Small, stubby-bodied and large-headed bird of open woodlands and wooded parks of the Northern Hemisphere and Africa. Most true titmice nest in self-drilled holes or abandoned woodpecker holes. Family Paridae; genus *Parus*. The long-tailed titmice and bush tits of Eurasia and w North America are larger and build closed, often hanging, nests. Subfamily Aegithalinae.

Tito (1892–1980) Yugoslav statesman, b. Croatia as Josip Broz. As a soldier in the Austro-Hungarian army, he was captured by the Russians (1915), but released by the Bolsheviks in 1917. He helped to organize the Yugoslav Communist Party, and adopted the name Tito in 1934. He led the Partisans' successful campaign against the Germans in YUGOSLAVIA during WORLD WAR 2. In 1945, Tito established a communist government and was prime minister (1945–53), and thereafter president, although virtually a dictator. Soviet efforts to control Yugoslavia led to a split between the two countries in 1948. At home, Tito sought to balance the ethnic and religious divisions in Yugoslavia and to develop an eco-

▲ **Tito** A forceful and charismatic personality, Tito ruled Yugoslavia from 1945 until his death in 1980. By maintaining tight, dictatorial control domestically, he was able to hold the country's various nationalist groups in check. He encouraged decentralization and worker participation in the economy, and fairly liberal social policies. Internationally, he pursued an independent foreign policy, keeping his distance from the Soviet Union.

▼ **tides** The daily rise and fall of the ocean's tides are the result of the gravitational pull of the Moon and that of the Sun, although the effect of the latter is less than half as strong as that of the Moon. The effect is greatest on the hemisphere facing the Moon and causes a tidal 'bulge'. When the Sun, Earth, and Moon are in line, tide-raising forces are at a maximum, and spring tides occur; high tide reaches the highest values, and low tide falls to low levels. When lunar and solar forces are least coincidental, with the Sun and Moon at an angle (near the Moon's first and third quarters), neap tides occur, which have a small tidal range.

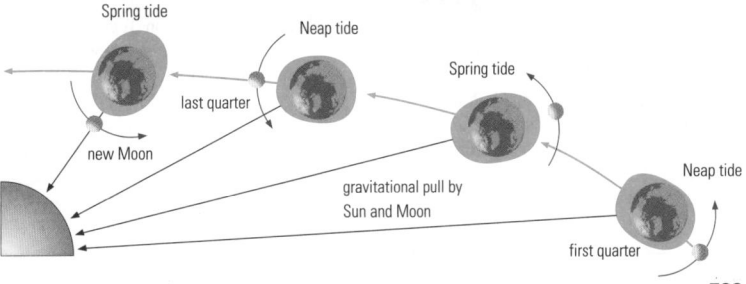

Spring tide
Neap tide
Spring tide
last quarter
new Moon
gravitational pull by Sun and Moon
Neap tide
first quarter

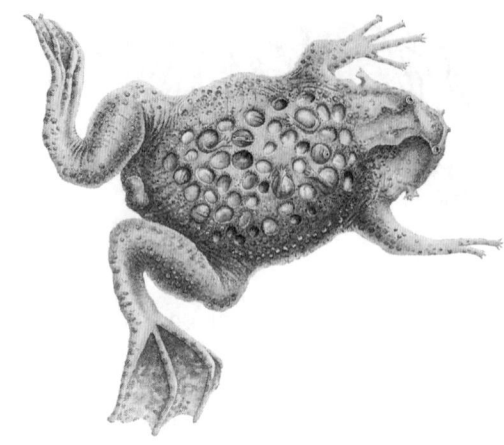

▶ **toad** The Suriname toad (*Pipa pipa*) lays three to ten eggs, which the male fertilizes and presses into the back of the female; her skin swells up, enveloping the eggs within cysts. After carrying her offspring for about 80 days, the female moults, and the young toads are released into the water.

nomic model of communist 'self-management'. Abroad, he became an influential leader of the Non-Aligned Movement. Tito's greatest achievement was to hold Yugoslavia together.

titration Method used in analytical chemistry to determine the concentration of a compound in a solution by measuring the amount needed to complete a reaction with another compound. A solution of known concentration is added in measured amounts to a liquid of unknown concentration until the reaction is complete. The volume added enables the unknown concentration to be calculated.

Titus (AD 39–81) Roman Emperor (r.79–81), eldest son of VESPASIAN. In AD 70, he destroyed Jerusalem after a Jewish revolt. As Emperor, he stopped persecutions for treason, completed the COLOSSEUM and aided for the survivors after the eruption of VESUVIUS (79). He was succeeded by DOMITIAN.

Tlingit NATIVE AMERICANS of the SE coast of Alaska. Famous for their TOTEM POLES (featuring stylized forms of local wildlife), they rely on fishing, tourism, and government aid.

TNT (2,4,6–trinitrotoluene) Explosive organic compound ($C_7H_5N_3O_6$) made from TOLUENE by using sulphuric and nitric acids. Its resistance to shock (requiring a detonator to set it off) makes it one of the safest high explosives.

toad Any of numerous species of tailless amphibians found throughout the world, except Antarctica. Most are short and

TOGO

The Republic of Togo is a long, narrow country in W Africa. From N to S, it extends about 500km [311mi]. Its coastline on the Gulf of Guinea is only 64km [40mi] long, and it is only 145km [90mi] wide at its widest point. The coastal plain is sandy. N of the coast is an area of fertile, clay soil. N of that lies the Mono Tableland, which reaches an altitude of 450m [1,500ft] and is drained by the River Mono. The Atakora Mountains are the fourth region. The vegetation is mainly open grassland.

CLIMATE

Togo has year-round high temperatures. The main wet season runs from March to July, with a minor wet season in October and November.

HISTORY

The historic region of Togoland comprised what is now the Republic of Togo and W Ghana. From the 17th to the 19th century the ASHANTI raided Togoland and sold the indigenous inhabitants, the Ewe, to Europeans as slaves.

Togo became a German protectorate in 1884; it developed economically and Lomé was built. At the beginning of World War 1, Britain and France captured Togoland from Germany. In 1922 it divided into two mandates, which became UN Trust Territories in 1946. In 1956 the people of British Togoland voted to join Ghana, while French Togoland gained independence as the Republic of Togo in 1960.

AREA 56,785sq km [21,925sq mi]
POPULATION 5,702,000
CAPITAL (POPULATION) Lomé (658,000)
GOVERNMENT Multiparty republic
ETHNIC GROUPS Native African 99% (largest tribes are Ewe, Mina and Kabre)
LANGUAGES French (official), African languages
RELIGIONS Traditional beliefs 51%, Christianity 29%, Islam 20%
CURRENCY CFA franc = 100 centimes

In 1961 Sylvanus Olympio became the first president, but was assassinated in 1963. Nicolas Grunitzky became president, but he was overthrown in a military coup of 1967. The head of the armed forces, General Gnassingbé Eyadéma, then became president. In 1969 a new constitution confirmed Togo as a single-party state, the sole legal party being the *Rassemblement du Peuple Togolais* (RPT).

Re-elected in 1972 and 1986, Eyadéma was forced to resign in 1991 after pro-democracy riots. Kokou Koffigoh led an interim government. Unrest continued with troops loyal to Eyadéma attempting to overthrow Koffigoh.

POLITICS

A new constitution was adopted in 1992. In 1993 Eyadéma won rigged elections, and the EU cut off aid in response to the country's poor human rights record. Multiparty elections were held in 1994 and these were won by an opposition alliance, but Eyadéma formed a coalition government. In 1998 paramilitary police prevented the completion of the count in presidential elections when it became clear that Eyadéma had been defeated. Eyadéma continued in office and the main opposition parties boycotted the general elections in 1999. In late 2002 the constitution was changed to allow Eyadéma to stand for re-election. He won the subsequent elections in 2003.

Eyadéma died in 2005 and his son, Faure, became president. After international pressure, he stepped down and called elections. Faure won these two months later amid claims by the opposition that the vote was rigged. In addition, the political violence surrounding the presidential poll was such that around 40,000 Togolese fled to neighbouring countries. These events called into question Togo's 2004 declaration of commitment to democracy, which aimed to normalize ties with the EU and restore access to aid.

ECONOMY

Togo is a poor developing country. Farming employs 65% of the people, but most farmers grow little more than they need to feed their families. Major food crops include cassava, maize,

millet and yams. The chief cash crops are cocoa, coffee and cotton. The leading exports are phosphate rock, which is used to make fertilizers, and palm oil. Togo's small-scale manufacturing and mining industries employ about 6% of the people.

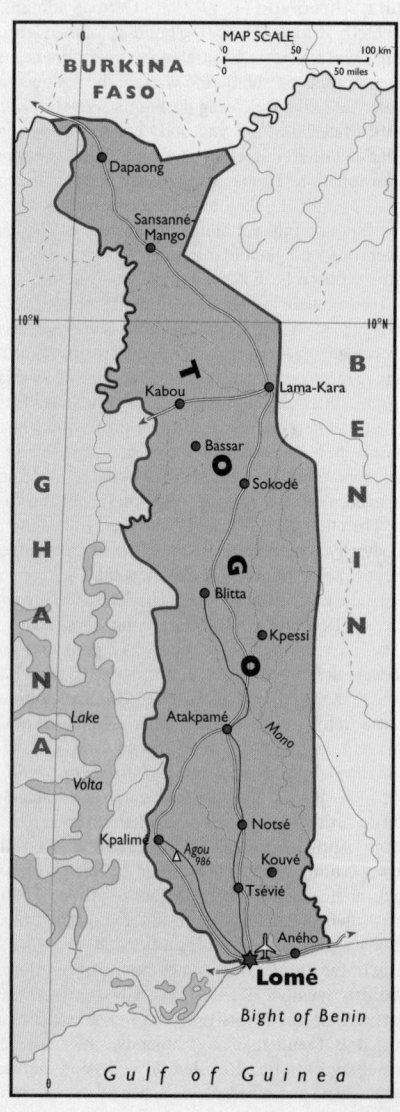

T

rotund, and move with a crawling or hopping gait. Toads are differentiated from FROGS by having a rougher, bumpier skin and a rounder body with shorter legs. Length: 2–25cm (1–10in). Order Anura; family Bufonidae. *See also* TADPOLE

toadstool Popular name for the fruiting body of a FUNGUS of the class Basidiomycetae. The name usually refers to inedible species and describes the somewhat stool-like appearance of the stem and a cap.

tobacco Herb native to the Americas but cultivated throughout the world for its leaves, which are dried and smoked. It has large leaves with no stalk, and white, pink or red, star-shaped flowers. *Nicotiana tabacum* is the principal cultivated species. Seeds were brought to Europe in *c.*1520–30. Settlers in Virginia obtained seeds from the Spanish colonies (1612) and soon tobacco was the major crop of the Virginia colony and America's first export. Leaves are prepared for smoking by curing (drying) and then ageing. Family Solanaceae (NIGHTSHADE family). Height: 0.6–2m (2–6ft). *See also* NICOTINE

Tobago *See* TRINIDAD AND TOBAGO

Tocqueville, Alexis de (1805–59) French historian. Sent on a fact-finding tour to the USA by the French government, he produced *Of Democracy in America* (1835), the first in-depth study of the US political system. His later work includes *L'Ancien Régime et la Révolution* (1856).

Togo Small republic in W Africa, the capital is LOMÉ. *See* country feature

Tojo, Hideki (1885–1948) Japanese statesman and general, prime minister (1941–44). He was chief of staff (1937–40) in Manchuria, and minister of war (1940–41). As prime minister, Tojo approved the attack on PEARL HARBOR and was responsible for all aspects of the war effort. In July 1944, he resigned after Japan lost Saipan. In 1945, Tojo was arrested by the Allies, tried for war crimes, found guilty, and hanged.

Tokugawa Japanese family that controlled Japan through the SHOGUN (1603–1867). The Tokugawa shogunate was established by Ieyasu Tokugawa (1543–1616) who completed the unification of Japan. The Tokugawa ruled through the provincial nobility (*daimyo*), and they controlled much of Japan's wealth and farmland as well as controlling the emperor and priests. They banned Christianity and Western trade and isolated Japan from the rest of the world. The regime declined during the 19th century as their isolationist policy began to crack under Western pressure. The last Tokugawa shogun was toppled before the MEIJI RESTORATION (1867).

Tokyo (Jap. 'Eastern capital') Capital of Japan, on E central Honshu, at the head of Tokyo Bay. The modern city divides into distinct districts: Kasumigaseki, Japan's administrative centre; Marunouchi, its commercial centre; Ginza, its shopping and cultural centre; the W shore of Tokyo Bay, its industrial centre. Modern Tokyo also serves as the country's educational centre with more than 100 universities. Founded in the 12th century as EDO, it became capital of the TOKUGAWA shogunate in 1603. In 1868, the Japanese Reformation re-established imperial power, and the last SHOGUN surrendered Edo Castle. Emperor MEIJI renamed the city Tokyo, and it replaced KYOTO as the capital of Japan. In 1923, an earthquake and subsequent fire claimed more than 150,000 lives and necessitated the city's reconstruction. In 1944–45, intensive US bombing destroyed more than half of Tokyo, and another modernization and restoration programme began. Industries: electronics, cameras, car manufacture, metals, chemicals, textiles. Pop. (2005) 12,046,000.

Toledo Capital of Toledo province, on the River Tagus, Castilla-La Mancha, central Spain. In 1031, the Moors made it the capital of an independent kingdom. The city was fortified, and acquired its enduring reputation for quality swordmaking. Toledo flourished as a multi-denominational city, with Mudéjar-style synagogues, mosques, and churches. In the 16th century, it became the spiritual capital of Catholic Spain and the headquarters of the Spanish Inquisition; Jews and Muslims suffered persecution and the synagogues were converted to churches. In 1936, during the Spanish CIVIL WAR, the city was under a Loyalist siege. Pop. (2001) 68,382.

Tolkien, J.R.R. (John Ronald Reuel) (1892–1973) British novelist and academic, b. South Africa. He was professor of Anglo-Saxon (1925–45) and English language and literature (1945–59) at Oxford University. Tolkien is chiefly celebrated for his novel *The Hobbit* (1937), the epic trilogy *The Lord of the Rings* (1954–55), and *The Silmarillion* (1977). These popular adventure stories are set in the fantasy world of Middle Earth.

Tolpuddle Martyrs Name given to six British farm labourers in Dorset, S England, who were sentenced to transportation for forming a TRADE UNION (1834). The government was worried by the growth of organized labour, but as unions were not illegal, the Dorset men were charged with taking a seditious oath. After a public outcry, they were pardoned in 1836.

Tolstoy, Leo Nikolaievich, Count (1828–1910) Russian novelist, moralist, and mystic. He took part in the defence of Sebastopol during the CRIMEAN WAR (1853–56). In 1862, Tolstoy married and settled down on his Volga estate, where he wrote the masterpiece *War and Peace* (1865–69) – an epic account of the Napeolonic Wars. Tolstoy's most popular work, *Anna Karenina* (1875–77), is a tragic love story. In his *Confession* (1879), Tolstoy outlines his conversion to an extreme form of Christian anarchism. He renounced all property and possessions and espoused total pacifism. Tolstoy's later moral works include the story 'The Death of Ivan Ilyich' and the novel *The Kreutzer Sonata* (1889). *See also* RUSSIAN LITERATURE

Toltec (Nuhuatl, master-builder) Ancient Native American civilization, whose capital was Tollán (Tula), Mexico. The Toltec were the dominant people in the region from AD 900 to 1200. Their architecture is characterized by PYRAMID building. Although theirs was considered a polytheistic culture, images of QUETZALCÓATL predominate. In the 12th century, the civilization was gradually supplanted by the AZTEC.

toluene (methylbenzene) Aromatic hydrocarbon ($C_6H_5CH_3$) derived from coal tar and petroleum. It is a colourless, flammable liquid used as an industrial solvent and in aircraft and motor fuels. Toluene is also used to make TNT. Properties: r.d. 0.87; m.p. $-94.5°C$ ($-138.1°F$); b.p. $110.7°C$ ($231.3°F$).

tomato FRUIT plant native to the Americas. The plant was cultivated in Europe as early as 1544. It was not eaten until the 16th century because it was believed to be poisonous. Species *Lycopersicum esculentum*. The small, cherry tomato is a variety (*L.e. cerasiforme*). Family Solanaceae.

tomography Technique of X-RAY photography in which details of only a single slice or plane of body tissue are shown.

tonality Harmonic system that underpins most Western music from the 17th century to the 20th century, using the twelve major and minor SCALES. The notes of the scale, and their corresponding chords and HARMONIES, have their own hierarchy around the central KEY note. *See also* ATONALITY

tone poem *See* SYMPHONIC POEM

Tonga (Friendly Islands) South Pacific island kingdom, *c.*2,200km (1,370mi) NE of New Zealand. The archipelago consists of *c.*170 islands in five administrative groups. Only 36 of the islands are inhabited. They are mainly coral atolls, but the W group are volcanic, with some active craters. The largest island is Tongatapu, the seat of the capital, NUKUALOFA, and home to 66% of the population. The N islands were discovered by Europeans in 1616, and the rest by Abel TASMAN in 1643. During the 19th century, British missionaries converted the indigenous population to Christianity. In 1900, Tonga became a British Protectorate. In 1970, the country achieved independence. The economy is dominated by agriculture, the chief crops are yams, tapioca and fish. Area: 650sq km (251sq mi). Pop. (1996) 108,000.

tongue Muscular organ usually rooted to the floor of the mouth. The tongue contains the TASTE buds and helps to move food around the mouth for chewing and swallowing; animals also use it for lapping fluids and for grooming. In human beings, the tongue is vital for the production of speech. *See also* SENSES

Tonkin (Tongking) Historical region of N VIETNAM; the capital was HANOI. It was ruled by the Chinese (111 BC–AD 939), later becoming independent. In 1801, it united with ANNAM. In 1883, it became part of the French Protectorate of INDOCHINA. The Japanese occupied it during World War 2. After the war, France tried to re-establish control but were defeated at DIEN BIEN PHU (1954). Tonkin became part of North Vietnam.

▲ **Tolstoy** His first work was an autobiographical trilogy: *Childhood* (1852), *Boyhood* (1854), and *Youth* (1857). Tolstoy's realistic account of his life as a soldier in the Crimean War appeared in the journal *Contemporary* (1854). From 1879, he devoted his life to preaching his Christian faith. Tolstoy propagated the principle of nonviolence and the abandonment of materialism. He renounced his previous work.

▲ **tobacco** Tobacco is produced mainly from the plant *Nicotiana tabacum*, which is cultivated throughout the world. The leaves are removed from the plant and dried. Native Americans smoked tobacco leaves and used them medicinally long before Europeans arrived in the New World.

tonsillitis Acute or chronic inflammation of the TONSILS caused by bacterial or viral infection. It is signalled by fever, sore throat, and difficulty in swallowing. Chronic tonsillitis is often treated by surgical removal of the tonsils (tonsillectomy).

tonsils Two masses of oval-shaped LYMPH tissue located at the back of the throat (palatine tonsils) or on the rear of the tongue (lingual tonsils). They filter disease organisms. Their pitted surface easily becomes infected (TONSILLITIS).

tooth *See* TEETH

topaz Transparent, glassy mineral, aluminium fluosilicate, $Al_2SiO_4(F,OH)_2$, found in pegmatites. Its crystals are orthorhombic system columnar prisms. Topaz is colourless, white, blue or yellow; some large crystals are of gem quality. Hardness 8; r.d. 3.5.

tope Small SHARK that lives in British waters. It has a greybrown body and feeds near the bottom on small fish. Length: to 2m (6.5ft). Family Carcharinidae; species *Galeorhinus galeus*.

Topeka State capital of Kansas, USA, on the River Kansas, 90km (55mi) w of Kansas City. Founded by settlers from New England in 1854, it became the state capital in 1861. Topeka is a major transport centre for cattle and wheat. Industries: printing, rubber goods, steel products, footwear. Pop. (2000) 122,377.

topiary Practice of trimming densely leaved evergreen shrubs and trees into decorative artificial shapes.

topology Branch of mathematics concerned with those properties of geometric figures that remain unchanged after a continuous deformation process, such as squeezing, stretching, or twisting. The number of boundaries of a surface is such a property. Any plane-closed shape (i.e. any line that eventually comes back to its beginning, all on a single plane) is topologically equivalent to a circle; a cube, a solid cone, and a solid cylinder are topologically equivalent to a sphere. *See also* MÖBIUS STRIP

Torah (Hebrew, law) Hebrew name for the PENTATEUCH, the first five books of the Old Testament. The Torah is the body of written Jewish laws contained within these five books. The Torah also describes the complete Jewish Bible.

tornado Funnel-shaped, violently rotating storm extending downwards from the cumulonimbus cloud in which it forms. At the ground its diameter may be only *c*.100m (300ft). Rotational wind speeds range from 150 to 500km/h (100 to 300mph). Tornadoes occur in deep low pressure areas. They are most frequent in the Midwest and the s USA, where the names 'CYCLONE' or the informal 'twister' are also used..

Toronto Capital of Ontario province and Canada's largest city, on the N shore of Lake Ontario. An inland port at the mouth of the River Don, it is Canada's main financial and manufacturing centre. The site was first visited (1615) by the French explorer Étienne Brulé. In 1787, the British purchased the site from Native Americans, and the settlement of York was founded in 1793. US troops twice captured the city during the WAR OF 1812. In 1834, it was renamed Toronto (Huron, 'meeting place'), and it became the capital of Ontario province in 1867. Its development as a major distribution centre was spurred by the opening (1959) of the ST LAWRENCE SEAWAY. Toronto produces more than half of all Canada's manufacturing products. Industries: electrical equipment, brewing, printing and publishing, iron and steel, meat packing, aircraft and motor vehicle manufacture. Pop. (2005) 5,060,000.

▶ **toucan** The New World counterparts of the hornbills, there are some 35 species of toucans in the forests of tropical America. The large, bright bill of the Toco toucan (*Ramphastos toco*) is typical of the family. It uses its bill to reach fruit.

torpedo Self-propelled underwater MISSILE used by submarines, small surface warships, and aircraft to destroy enemy vessels. Modern torpedoes may be launched by rocket boosters, and often have internal electronic equipment for guiding the missile to the target. *See also* GUIDED MISSILE

torpedo ray *See* RAY

torque Turning effect of a force. A TURBINE produces a torque on its rotating shaft to turn a generator. The output of a rotary ENGINE, such as the familiar FOUR-STROKE ENGINE or an electric motor, is rated by the torque it can develop. A measurement is made by multiplying the force by its perpendicular distance from the turning point. The unit of measurement is the newton metre (Nm).

Torquemada, Tomás de (1420–98) Spanish cleric and grand inquisitor. A DOMINICAN priest and confessor to King FERDINAND V and Queen ISABELLA I, who appointed him head of the Spanish INQUISITION in 1483, Torquemada was noted for the severity of his judgments and punishments. He was responsible for *c*.2,000 burnings.

Torricelli, Evangelista (1608–47) Italian physicist. Assistant and secretary to GALILEO, he is credited with the first man-made VACUUM (the Torricellian vacuum) and the invention of the mercury BAROMETER (1643).

tort In British law, wrongful act or omission that can give rise to a civil action at law, other than concerning breach of contract. The law of tort includes negligence, libel, slander, trespass, false imprisonment, and nuisance.

Tortelier, Paul (1914–90) French cellist. He made his concert debut in 1931. Tortelier is celebrated for his interpretations of Bach and Elgar. In 1957, he became professor at the Paris Conservatoire, where his pupils included Jacqueline DU PRÉ. His son, **Yan Pascal** Tortelier (1947–), is a noted conductor.

tortoise Terrestrial or freshwater reptile of the order Chelonia. They live in tropical and subtropical regions, and hibernate in temperate countries. All tortoises are heavily armoured and enclosed within a high, domed, bony, box-like structure called a carapace (commonly shell). When disturbed, tortoises pull their scaly legs, head and tail into the shelter of the shell. They are slow movers, feed almost entirely on plants, and live to a great age. Length: usually to 30cm (1ft). A giant species, up to 1.9m (5ft) long, lives in the GALÁPAGOS ISLANDS. *See also* TURTLE

Tory Party British political party traditionally opposed to the WHIGS. In 1670, the supporters of the STUART monarchy were called Tories (Irish bandits) by their opponents. Under JAMES II, the Tories represented the interests of landowners, supported the royal prerogative, maintained close links to the CHURCH OF ENGLAND and favoured an isolationist foreign policy. The Tories, led by Robert Harley, were at their most powerful in the reign of Queen ANNE. They were discredited by association with the JACOBITES, and were excluded from power when GEORGE I acceded to the throne. In the late 18th century, accusations of Toryism were levelled at independent Whigs, such as William PITT (THE YOUNGER). The Reform Bill of 1832 split the party, and the CONSERVATIVE PARTY was formed from its remnants. *See also* PEEL, SIR ROBERT; REFORM ACTS

Toscanini, Arturo (1867–1957) Italian conductor. He was musical director (1898–1903, 1906–08) at La Scala, Milan, before becoming conductor (1908–21) of the Metropolitan Opera, New York. Toscanani conducted the New York Philharmonic Orchestra (1928–36). In 1937 he founded the NBC Symphony Orchestra in New York. Toscanini returned to La Scala (1921–29), where he premiered Puccini's *Turandot* (1926).

totalitarianism Form of government in which the state tries to acquire total control of every aspect of social and individual activity or thought, by means of controlling the mass media, suppression of opposition, and the often violent use of the police or army. The term arose in the 1920s to describe Italian FASCISM and has since been applied to Nazi Germany, the Soviet Union, and many other states. *See also* AUTHORITARIANISM

totemism Complex collection of ideas held by certain primitive societies about the relationships between human beings and the animals or plants around them. The natural objects or people with which many tribal societies believe they have a kinship or mystical relationship are called totems. Members of a totem group are prohibited from marrying others of the same group, and from killing or eating their totem. Elaborate, often secret, rituals form an important part of totemistic behaviour.

totem pole Carved and painted wooden column erected by the Native Americans of the Pacific Coast of the USA and Canada. They are carved with stylized representations of real and mythical animals and men. Their function is closer to that of heraldic crests than of religious symbols. They are usually erected as roof supports, as doorways, as symbols of greeting, as mortuary poles, or grave-markers.

toucan Any of 35 species of colourful, gregarious birds of the forests of tropical America, characterized by a large, colourful bill. The plumage is generally red, yellow, blue, black, or orange. It feeds on fruit and berries, which may be regurgitated to feed the young. Length: 60cm (2ft). Family Ramphastidae.

touch One of the five SENSES, functioning by means of specialized nerve receptors in the skin. The stimulated receptors activate nerve impulses that are sent to the brain.

Toulon Capital of Var department, on the Mediterranean coast, SE France. Toulon is France's leading naval base and its second-largest Mediterranean port after MARSEILLES. Originally known as Telo Martius, the city was a Roman naval base and an important port of embarkation for the Crusaders. During the 17th century the port's fortifications were improved. In 1942, the French navy was scuttled here to prevent German capture. Industries: shipbuilding and naval repairs. Pop. (1999) 160,639.

Toulouse City on the River Garonne, S France, capital of Haute-Garonne department. Canals connect the city, the fourth largest in France, to both the Mediterranean Sea and the Atlantic Ocean. The capital of the Visigoths in the 5th century, it became part of the French crown lands in 1271. It is the centre of France's aviation industry. Other industries: paper, textiles, chemicals, fertilizers, armaments. Pop. (2000) 761,000.

Toulouse-Lautrec, Henri Marie Raymond de (1864–1901) French painter and lithographer. He chose a career in painting after an accident left his legs permanently deformed. In c.1888, he began to illustrate the theatres, cabarets, music halls, cafés, and brothels of the Montmartre district of Paris, such as the *Moulin Rouge* series (1894). He was profoundly influenced by DEGAS and drew inspiration from GAUGUIN and Japanese wood-block prints. The impact of his prints helped to establish the poster as a respected art form.

Tour de France Premier professional road CYCLING race in Europe. Raced over three weeks from the end of June, it travels across all types of terrain in a series of timed stages. It mostly circles France, occasionally venturing into neighbouring countries, and ends in Paris. The first Tour was in 1903.

Tourette's syndrome (Gilles de la Tourette's syndrome) Rare disorder of movement. It is a lifelong affliction that starts in childhood with tics and involuntary grimaces. Involuntary sounds also frequently occur. Its cause is unknown.

tourmaline Silicate mineral, sodium or calcium aluminium borosilicate, found in IGNEOUS and METAMORPHIC rocks. Its crystals are hexagonal system and glassy, either opaque or transparent. Some are prized as gems. Hardness 7.5; r.d. 3.1.

Tours City on a triangle of land between the rivers Loire and Cher, W central France, capital of Indre-et-Loire department. It was the seat of the French government during the siege of Paris in 1870. A large wine market, Tours has food processing, electronic, and pharmaceutical industries. Pop. (1999) 132,820.

Tower Bridge Bascule bridge over the River Thames in LONDON, built by Sir Horace Jones between 1886 and 1894. The bridge has a pseudo-Gothic tower at each end, and a double-leaf mechanism that opens to provide a 76m (250ft) gap.

Tower of London English royal castle in LONDON. Begun by William the Conqueror in 1078, later monarchs added and extended the Tower. It has served various functions throughout the centuries – residence, arsenal, prison and museum. It is associated especially with the imprisonment and execution (on Tower Hill) of traitors. The crown jewels are held here.

Townes, Charles Hard (1915–95) US physicist. In 1953, he invented the first operational MASER and shared the 1964 Nobel Prize in physics with Alexsandr PROKHOROV and Nikolai BASOV.

Townshend, Charles, 2nd Viscount (1674–1738) British Whig statesman, known as 'Turnip Townshend'.

Robert WALPOLE's brother-in-law, he helped to arrange GEORGE I's accession to the throne in 1714 and, as Secretary for the Northern Department, suppressed the JACOBITE rebellion of 1715. He was forced to resign in 1730, and devoted his retirement to agricultural improvements.

toxic shock syndrome Potentially fatal condition in which there is a dangerous drop in blood pressure and rapid onset of fever, diarrhoea, vomiting, and muscular pains. It is caused by BLOOD POISONING (septicaemia) arising from toxins put out by bacteria that normally reside in the body without causing harm.

toxin Poisonous substance produced by a living organism. The unpleasant symptoms of many bacterial diseases are due to the release of toxins into the body by BACTERIA. Many MOULDS, some larger FUNGI, and seeds of some higher plants produce toxins. The venom of many snakes contains powerful toxins. *See also* SNAKEBITE

toxoplasmosis Disease caused by the protozoan *Toxoplasma gondii*, transmitted from animals to human beings. It produces symptoms that are generally mild and flu-like in adults, but it can damage the nervous system, eyes and internal organs.

trace elements Chemical elements that are essential to life but normally obtainable from the diet only in small quantities. An example in mammals is iodine needed in the thyroid gland to produce hormones controlling growth. They are essential to the reactions of ENZYMES and HORMONES.

trachea (windpipe) Airway that extends from the larynx to about the middle of the sternum (breastbone). Reinforced with rings of CARTILAGE, it is lined with hair-like CILIA that prevent dirt and other substances from entering the lungs.

tracheophyte In certain classification systems, any VASCULAR PLANT of the phylum Tracheophyta. Within this phylum are: psilopsids (leafless, rootless primitive forms, such as whisk fern); sphenopsids (such as HORSETAIL); lycopsids (such as CLUB MOSS); pteropsids (such as FERN); GYMNOSPERMS and ANGIOSPERMS.

tracheotomy (tracheostomy) Surgical procedure in which an incision is made into the TRACHEA to allow insertion of a tube to facilitate breathing. It is done to bypass disease or damage in the trachea or to safeguard the airway if a patient has to spend a long time on a mechanical ventilator.

trachoma Chronic eye infection caused by the microorganism *Chlamydia trachomatis*, characterized by inflammation of the cornea, and pus. A disease of dry, tropical regions, it is the major cause of blindness in the developing world.

Tractarianism *See* OXFORD MOVEMENT

tractor Four-wheeled or tracked vehicle for moving and operating heavy implements. Tractors are used mostly in farming and construction. The first tractors were built in the 1870s. Modern tractors have petrol or diesel engines, and can haul and power a wide range of implements, including hay balers, crop sprayers, and mowing machines.

Tracy, Spencer (1900–67) US film actor, renowned for his intelligent, sincere character portrayals. Making his debut in

▲ **Tower Bridge** Tower Bridge in London has two bascule arms, each weighing more than 1,100 tonnes, that pivot. Despite their weight, they can be entirely raised in less than one minute. Famous throughout the world, it is one of the city's most popular tourist attractions. There is a museum dedicated to the bridge in the top gallery.

T

T

1930, Tracy soon became a leading Hollywood actor, appearing in nearly 80 films, of which nine, including *Adam's Rib* (1949), *Pat and Mike* (1957), and his last film, *Guess Who's Coming to Dinner* (1967), were with his on- and off-screen partner, Katharine HEPBURN. He won Academy Awards for *Captains Courageous* (1937) and *Boys Town* (1938).

trademark Distinguishing mark, such as a name, symbol, or word, attached to goods, which identifies them as made or sold by a particular manufacturer. A trademark must be registered at a PATENT office to establish an exclusive right to it.

Trades Union Congress (TUC) Permanent association of UK TRADE UNIONS. The TUC was founded (1868) to promote trade union principles. Each year, it holds an annual assembly of delegates who discuss common problems. Today, the TUC has *c.*8 million members.

trade union Group of workers organized for the purpose of improving wages and conditions of work. The first trade unions were founded in Britain around the time of the INDUSTRIAL REVOLUTION. Although some craft and agricultural unions developed before industrialization, the growth of trade unionism paralleled the growth of industry. In 1825, trade unions were given restricted legality in Britain. In 1871, the Trades Union Act put the unions on a firm legal basis and, over the next 150 years, the movement grew steadily. Their rights were progressively curbed in the 1980s through Conservative legislation under Margaret THATCHER. In the USA, the movement was firmly established by 1886 with the founding of the American Federation of Labor (AFL). The AFL primarily represented skilled workers, and it was not until the creation (1930) of the Congress of Industrial Organizations (CIO) that unskilled labour gained some form of representation. In 1955, the two organizations merged to form the AMERICAN FEDERATION OF LABOR AND CONGRESS OF INDUSTRIAL ORGANIZATIONS (AFL-CIO). *See also* TOLPUDDLE MARTYRS

trade winds Steady warm moist winds that blow westwards towards the Equator from subtropical high-pressure zones between 30° and 40° N and s. The winds, which are stronger in the winter, converge at the calm area of the DOLDRUMS.

Trafalgar, Battle of (October 21, 1805) British naval victory over the French and Spanish fleets off Cape Trafalgar, Spain. It ended NAPOLEON I's plans for an invasion of England. The victory was secured by the skill of Lord NELSON.

tragedy Form of drama in which a noble hero (the protagonist) meets a fate inherent in the drama's action. *Oedipus Rex* by SOPHOCLES is an early example, which was unmatched until the tragedies of Christopher MARLOWE. ARISTOTLE's *Poetics* systematized tragedy and introduced such ideas as *anagnorisis* (recognition) and *catharsis* (purging of pity). *See also* AESCHYLUS; EURIPIDES; GREEK DRAMA; SHAKESPEARE, WILLIAM

Trajan (AD 53–117) Roman Emperor (98–117), b. Spain. He was a skilled general and administrator and was made junior co-emperor by Nerva in 97, on whose death, he became Emperor. He conducted major campaigns in DACIA (101–

102, 105–106) and against the people of PARTHIA (113–117), enlarging the ROMAN EMPIRE to its greatest extent.

tram Passenger carriage that runs on rails. Horse-drawn trams first appeared in New York in 1832. Some later trams were powered by steam locomotives. Trams with electric motors, supplied by overhead cables, became common in the early 1900s. Many European cities retain tramway systems and electric trams are attracting renewed interest.

tranquillizer Drugs prescribed to reduce anxiety or tension and generally for their calming effect. They are used to control the symptoms of mental disturbance, such as schizophrenia or manic depression. They are also prescribed to relieve depression. Prolonged use of tranquillizers can produce dependence and a range of unwanted side-effects.

Transcaucasia Former Soviet republic, corresponding to the three constituent republics ARMENIA, AZERBAIJAN, and GEORGIA. Created in 1918, after the RUSSIAN REVOLUTION, it re-emerged in 1922, and gained full republic status in 1924. Georgia, Azerbaijan, and Armenia were re-established as separate republics in 1936, and became independent nations on the break-up of the SOVIET UNION in 1990.

transcendentalism School of philosophy that traced its origin to the IDEALISM of Immanuel KANT. It concerned itself not with objects, but with our mode of knowing objects. It spread from Germany to England, where Samuel COLERIDGE and Thomas CARLYLE came under its influence. In the mid-19th century, it spread to the USA, where its proponents included Ralph Waldo EMERSON and Henry David THOREAU. In general, it emphasized individual (as opposed to collective) moral and spiritual responsibilities and rejected materialism, returning to nature for spiritual guidance.

transducer Device for converting any nonelectrical signal, such as sound or light, into an electrical signal, and vice versa. Examples include MICROPHONES, LOUDSPEAKERS, and various measuring instruments used in ACOUSTICS.

transformer Device for converting alternating current at one voltage to another voltage at the same frequency. It consists of two coils of wire coupled together magnetically. The input current is fed to one coil (the primary), the output being taken from the other coil (the secondary).

transfusion, blood *See* BLOOD TRANSFUSION

transhumance Seasonal moving of livestock from one region to another. It occurs in societies that live in zones with extensive climatic changes, such as in the mountainous terrain of the Arctic regions or the deserts of Central Africa. *See also* NOMAD

transistor Electronic device made of SEMICONDUCTOR material that can amplify electrical signals. The material, such as SILICON or GERMANIUM, is 'doped' with minute amounts of PHOSPHORUS, ARSENIC or ANTIMONY to produce *n*-type material, in which negative charges (ELECTRONS) carry current; or with ALUMINIUM, GALLIUM or INDIUM to give a *p*-type material. Joining together a piece of each produces a DIODE. Sandwiching one type between two of the other produces a transistor. Transistors were first developed (1948) by US physicists John BARDEEN, Walter BRATTAIN, and William SHOCKLEY, making possible many advances in technology, especially in computers, portable radios and televisions, satellites, and control systems.

transition element Metallic element that has an incomplete inner electron shell. These include copper, iron, and cobalt. Transition elements are characterized by variable VALENCIES (combining power) and the formation of coloured ions. They are especially good conductors of electricity and often used for alloys. *See also* PERIODIC TABLE

translocation In VASCULAR PLANTS, the movement of food materials in solution through the tissues from one part of the plant to another.

transmigration of souls Belief that the soul is reborn in one or more successive mortal bodies; a form of REINCARNATION. A tenet of Asian religions such as BUDDHISM, it was also accepted by the followers of PYTHAGORAS and Orphism in Greece during the 6th century BC.

transmutation In physics, formation of one element or ISOTOPE from another by RADIOACTIVE DECAY or by bombardment

▼ **trade winds** The map shows the direction of the prevailing trade winds in July, and the routes of various explorers who made use of the July winds. Sailors exploring in the 15th and 16th centuries had to find out for themselves how the winds in different zones of the sea change with the season, and chart their course accordingly.

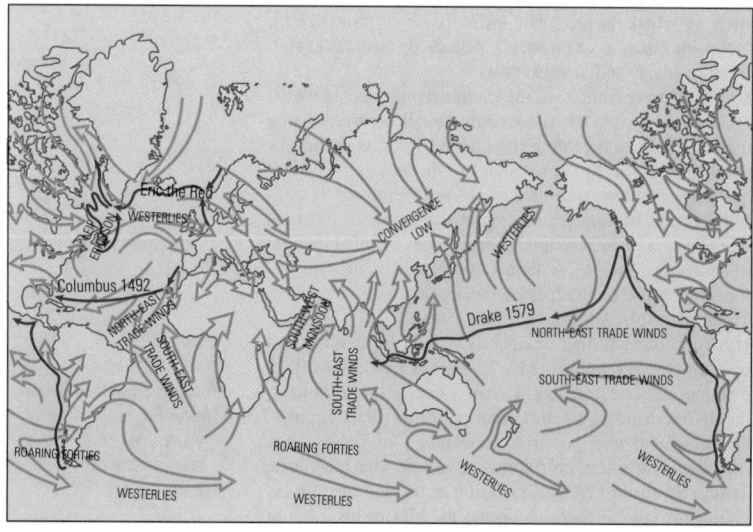

with energetic particles. The term was formerly applied to alchemists' attempts to convert base metals into gold.

transpiration In plants, the loss of moisture as water vapour from leaf surfaces or other plant parts. Most of the water entering plant roots is lost by transpiration. The process is speeded up in light, warm, and dry conditions. The flow of water from the roots to the STOMATA is called the transpiration stream. *See also* PHOTOSYNTHESIS; RESPIRATION

transplant Surgical operation to introduce organ or tissue from one person (the donor) to another (the recipient); it may also refer to the transfer of tissues from one part of the body to another, as in grafting of skin or bone. Major transplants are performed to save the lives of patients facing death from end-stage organ disease. Organs routinely transplanted include the heart, kidneys, lungs, liver, and pancreas. Experimental work continues on some other procedures, including small bowel and face grafting. Many other tissues are commonly grafted, including heart valves, bone and bone marrow. The oldest transplant procedure is corneal grafting, undertaken to restore the sight of one or both eyes. In 1967, Christiaan BARNARD performed the first successful heart transplant. Most transplant material is acquired from dead people, although kidneys, part of the liver, bone marrow and corneas may be taken from living donors.

transport *See* AIRCRAFT; AIR-CUSHION VEHICLE (ACV); AIRSHIP; AUTOMOBILE; BICYCLE; HELICOPTER; MOTORCYCLE; SHIP; SPACE SHUTTLE; UNDERGROUND RAILWAY

Trans-Siberian Railway Russian railway from Moscow to Vladivostok. The world's longest railway, the major part, is from Chelyabinsk, was built between 1891 and 1905, giving Russia access to the Pacific via a link with the Chinese Eastern Railway in Manchuria. Total length: *c.*9,000km (5,750mi).

transubstantiation Belief accepted by the Roman Catholic Church that, during the prayer of consecration at the MASS (the EUCHARIST), the 'substance' of the bread and wine is changed into the 'substance' of the body and blood of JESUS CHRIST, while the 'accidents' (the outward forms of bread and wine) remain unchanged. The doctrine was defined at the LATERAN COUNCIL of 1215. The definition involving 'substance' and 'accidents' was rejected by the architects of the REFORMATION.

transuranic elements (transuranium element) Elements with atomic numbers higher than that of URANIUM (92), the best known of which are members of the ACTINIDE SERIES (atomic numbers 89 to 103). All transuranic elements are radioactive. Only NEPTUNIUM and PLUTONIUM occur naturally (in minute amounts) but all can be synthesized. The only commercially important transuranic element is plutonium, which is used in NUCLEAR WEAPONS and as a fuel for NUCLEAR REACTORS.

Transvaal Former province of South Africa. In 1994–95, Transvaal divided into Northern Province (now LIMPOPO), Mpumalanga, GAUTENG, and NORTH-WEST PROVINCE. The indigenous population are the Bantu-speaking Venda and Sotho peoples. In the GREAT TREK (1836), the BOERS crossed the River Vaal and began to settle the region. In 1857, the South African Republic was formed. In 1877, the British annexed the republic. In 1881, after a Boer revolt, the Transvaal again gained self-government under Paul KRUGER. The 1886 discovery of gold in WITWATERSRAND attracted vast numbers of Britons and Germans. The Boers imposed heavy taxation and denied political rights to the newcomers. In 1895, Leander Starr Jameson launched an incursion into the Transvaal. The 'Jameson Raid' failed to ignite a full-scale rebellion, but the resultant tension between the Boers and the British led to the SOUTH AFRICAN WARS. By the Treaty of Vereeniging (1902), the Transvaal became a British Crown Colony. In 1907, the region was again allowed self-government, and in 1910 it became a founding province in the Union of South Africa. During the 1960s, the apartheid government created separate tribal 'homelands' (Bantustans). In 1995, Transvaal ceased to exist as a political entity and was split into four of South Africa's nine new provinces.

Transylvania (Romanian, 'Beyond the Forest') High plateau region in central and NW Romania, separated from the rest of Romania by the CARPATHIAN MOUNTAINS and the Transylvanian Alps. Its major cities are Cluj-Napoca, Braşov and

Sibiu. In AD 107, it became part of the Roman province of DACIA. Hungary conquered it at the beginning of the 11th century. In 1526, the ruler of Transylvania, John Zapolya, defeated the Hungarian army, and claimed the Hungarian throne as John I. The Ottoman Turks supported his claim and, following Zapolya's death in 1540, occupied Transylvania on the pretext of ensuring his son's succession. For the next two centuries, Transylvania retained its semi-independent status by playing off the competing imperial claims of Turkey and Austria. During the 17th century, it flourished as Hungary's intellectual and cultural centre, but in 1765 it became an Austrian province. In 1867, Hungary reasserted its authority. After World War 1, Hungary ceded the territory to Romania, which embarked on a wholesale process of land redistribution and forced assimilation of other nationalities. Hungary annexed part of Transylvania in World War 2, but was forced to return it in 1947.

Trappists Popular name for the CISTERCIANS of the Strict Observance, a religious order of monks and nuns. The order originated (1664) in La Trappe Abbey, France. They maintain complete silence and practise vegetarianism.

trauma Any injury or physical damage caused by some external event such as an accident or assault. In psychiatry, the term is applied to an emotional shock or harrowing experience.

treason Any act the intention of which is to overthrow the recognized government or harm the head of state. Treason is an extremely serious criminal offence and is punishable by death in many countries. In Britain, treason is defined to include the infliction of death or injury on the monarch, violation of members of the royal family, levying war against the government, or giving assistance to the enemy.

Treasury Government department responsible for national finance and monetary policy. Dating from the Norman Conquest in the UK, when the chancellor and barons exercised control of royal revenues, the Treasury developed from the office of the CHANCELLOR OF THE EXCHEQUER. It became a separate ministry in the 19th century.

tree Woody, PERENNIAL plant with one main stem or trunk and smaller branches. The trunk increases in diameter each year, and the leaves may be evergreen or DECIDUOUS. The largest trees, SEQUOIAS, grow more than 110m (420ft) tall; the bristlecone pine can live for more than 5,000 years. *See* illustrations page 746

treecreeper Brownish, agile bird that scurries up and down trees in cooler areas of the Northern Hemisphere. It uses its long, slightly down-curved bill to probe for insects under the bark. Length: 13cm (5in). Species *Certhia familiaris*.

tree fern Tree-like FERN of the family Cyatheaceae. Tree ferns grow in tropical and sub-tropical regions, particularly moist mountainous areas. Height: 3–25m (10–80ft). There are 600 species. Phylum Filicinophyta; genus *Cyathea*.

trefoil Any of numerous plants, such as CLOVER, with leaves divided into three parts. Bird's-foot trefoil (*Lotus corniculatus*) is used as hay and forage. Family Fabaceae/Leguminosae.

Trent River in central England, at 274km (170mi) the country's third-longest. It rises on Biddulph Moor, Staffordshire, and flows SE through the Potteries, and then NE across central England to join the River Ouse and form the Humber estuary. Linked by canals to many industrial towns, its major modern use is the provision of water for the cooling of power stations.

Trent, Council of (1545–63) Nineteenth ecumenical council of the Roman Catholic Church, which provided the main impetus of the COUNTER-REFORMATION in Europe. It met at Trent, N Italy, in three sessions under three popes (PAUL III, Julius III, Pius IV). It clarified Catholic doctrine and refused concessions to the Protestants, while also instituting reform of many of the abuses that had provoked the REFORMATION.

Trent Affair (1861) Diplomatic incident between the UK and the USA during the US CIVIL WAR. Union officers seized two Confederate commissioners from the British ship *Trent*. Britain claimed its neutrality had been violated. President Abraham LINCOLN, wishing to avoid war with Britain, released the men.

Trenton State capital of New Jersey, USA, on the Delaware River. It was first settled by English Quakers in the 1670s. A city monument commemorates the 1776 battle in which George WASHINGTON crossed the frozen Delaware River to

T

► **tree** Trees increase in girth by rings of new wood produced annually in temperate zones but less often in the tropics. The cambium (1) produces xylem (2) and phloem (3). These sections are alive but the heartwood (4) is dead. The medullary rays (5) allow the transport of food across the trunk. Bark (6) is a protective outer coating.

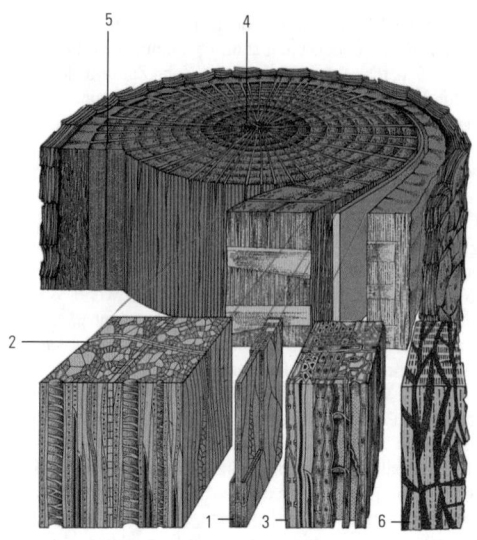

► **tree** Trees grow taller than any other living thing but can still survive in miniature form. If the roots are restricted either artificially, such as the cultivation of bonsai in Japan, or by natural means, as when a seed germinates in very thin soil on a mountain, a fully formed tree only a few centimetres high will result. The California redwood, the world's tallest tree, is closely rivalled by a eucalyptus, such as the mountain ash of Australia. The coconut palm reaches its height of 27m (90ft) in a few years. The English oak is one of 450 species of oak that grow as trees, bushes, and shrubs. It enlarges slowly – c.4.5m (15ft) – in ten years, but produces wood of prodigious strength. *Espeletia* grows on snowy ledges above 400m (1300ft) in the Sierra Nevada.

defeat Hessian troops during the AMERICAN REVOLUTION. Industries: ceramics, automobile parts, plastics, metal products, rubber goods, steel cables, textiles. Pop. (2000) 85,403.

Trevithick, Richard (1771–1833) English engineer. In 1801, he built a steam-powered road vehicle. In 1802, Trevithick patented a high-pressure STEAM ENGINE, his most important invention. In 1803, he built the first steam railway LOCOMOTIVE. In 1816, he went to Peru to install his steam engines in mines.

trial In law, judicial examination or hearing of the facts and passing of sentence in a civil or criminal case. A jury may or may not be present. *See also* TRIAL BY JURY

trial by jury TRIAL by a number of people (usually 12), who are sworn to deliver a verdict in a court of law. As a method of trial, it developed from an Anglo-Saxon judicial custom. It is now the main method of trying criminal and some civil cases at common law in the West.

Triassic First period of the MESOZOIC era, lasting from 248 to 213 million years ago. Many new kinds of animals developed. On land, the first DINOSAURS roamed. Mammal-like reptiles were common, and by the end of the period, the first true MAMMALS existed. In the seas lived the first ichthyosaurs, placodonts, and nothosaurs. The first frogs, turtles, crocodilians, and lizards also appeared. Plant life consisted mainly of primitive gymnosperms.

tribune Official of ancient Rome. Of the various kinds of tribune, some had military functions, some political. The tribunes of the PLEBEIANS, generally ten in number, who were elected annually, gained an important role under the republic. In the 2nd century BC the Gracchi brothers used the office of tribune to pursue radical social reforms. *See also* GRACCHUS

triceratops Large, horned, ornithischian DINOSAUR of the late CRETACEOUS period of w North America. The 2.4–m (8–ft) skull carried two 102–cm (40–in) horns above its eyes and a smaller horn at the tip of its snout. Length: 6.1–7.6m (20–25ft); height: 2.4m (8ft); weight: 10 tonnes.

Trieste City on the Gulf of Trieste, at the head of the Adriatic Sea, NE Italy. It was an imperial free port from 1719 to 1891, and became an Austrian crown land in 1867. It was ceded to Italy in 1919, occupied by Yugoslavia in 1945 and returned to Italy in 1954. It is an important industrial and commercial centre with large shipyards. Industries: steel, textiles and petroleum. Pop. (2000) 215,096.

triggerfish Any of several tropical marine fish found in warm, shallow Pacific waters, identified by a dorsal fin spine that can be erected to lodge it in a coral cavity, as a protection against predators. Length: to 60cm (24in). Family Balistidae; typical genus *Balistoides*.

triglyceride *See* LIPID

trigonometric function Six ratios of the sides of a right-angled triangle containing a given acute angle – they are the SINE, COSINE, TANGENT, COTANGENT, SECANT, and COSECANT of the angle. These functions can be extended to cover angles of any size by the use of a system of rectangular co-ordinates.

trigonometry Use of ratios of the sides of a right-angled triangle to calculate lengths and angles in geometrical figures. If three sides, or two sides and the included angle, or one side and two angles of a triangle are known, then all the other sides and angles may be found.

trilobite Any of an extinct group of ARTHROPODS found as fossils in marine deposits, dating from the CAMBRIAN to the PERMIAN period. The body was oval, tapering towards the rear, and covered by a chitinous skeleton. Transverse divisions show segmentation, with each segment bearing a pair of jointed limbs. Most species were bottom-crawling, shallow-water forms, and ranged in size from 6mm (0.25in) to 75cm (30in).

Trimble, David William, Baron Trimble (1944–) Northern Irish statesman, first minister of Northern IRELAND (1998–2005). He entered the British Parliament in 1990. In 1995, he succeeded James Molyneaux as leader of the ULSTER UNIONIST PARTY. He became first minister after the GOOD FRIDAY AGREEMENT (1998), when he and John HUME shared the Nobel Peace Prize for their efforts to find a peaceful solution to the conflict in Northern Ireland. After poor election results in 2005 he was succeeded as leader of the UUP by Sir Reg Empey and joined the House of Lords in 2006.

Trinidad and Tobago Republic composed of the two southernmost islands of the LESSER ANTILLE; the capital is PORT OF SPAIN. *See* country feature.

Trinity Central doctrine of Christianity, according to which God is three persons: the Father, the Son, and the HOLY SPIRIT or Holy Ghost. There is only one God, but he exists as 'three in one and one in three'. The nature of the Trinity is held to be a mystery that cannot be fully comprehended. The doctrine of the Trinity was stated in early Christian creeds to counter heresies such as GNOSTICISM. *See also* APOSTLES' CREED; ATHANASIAN CREED; JESUS CHRIST; NICENE CREED

Triple Alliance International coalitions involving three states. They included the anti-French alliance of Britain, the Netherlands and Sweden of 1668, and the alliance of Britain, France and the Netherlands of 1717, directed against Spanish ambitions in Italy. The most recent was the Triple Alliance of 1882, when Italy joined the Dual Alliance of Austria-Hungary and Germany. In South America, Argentina, Brazil, and Uruguay formed a triple alliance in the war against Paraguay (1865–70).

Triple Entente Alliance of Britain, France, and Russia before World War 1. It developed from the Franco-Russian Alliance (1894) formed to counterbalance the threat posed by the TRIPLE ALLIANCE of Germany, Austria, and Italy. In 1904, Britain allied with France in the ENTENTE CORDIALE, and the Anglo-Russian Convention of 1907 completed the Triple Entente.

triple jump In athletics, similar to the LONG JUMP with the exception that, from the take-off line, a contestant takes two extended leaps on alternate legs to launch into the final jump.

Tripoli (Tarabulus) Capital and chief port of LIBYA, on the Mediterranean Sea. It was founded as Oea in the 7th century BC

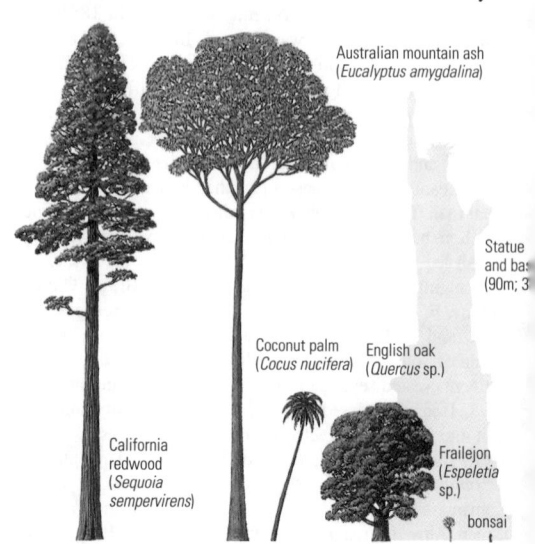

Australian mountain ash (*Eucalyptus amygdalina*)

Statue and bas (90m; 3

Coconut palm (*Cocus nucifera*)

English oak (*Quercus* sp.)

California redwood (*Sequoia sempervirens*)

Frailejon (*Espeletia* sp.)

bonsai

by the Phoenicians and developed by the Romans. From the 7th century AD the Arabs developed Tripoli as a market centre for the trans-Saharan caravans. In 1551, it was captured by the Ottoman Turks. In the 17th century, Tripoli was a notorious base for pirates. In 1911, it was made capital of the Italian colony of Libya, and during World War 2 it was an important base for Axis forces. After intensive Allied bombing in 1941–42, Britain captured the city in 1943. In 1986, the US Air Force bombed it in retaliation for Libya's alleged support of terrorism. The city is the commercial, industrial, transport and communications centre of Libya. The oases comprise the most fertile agricultural area in N Africa. Pop. (2002 est.) 1,223,300.

Tripoli (Tarabulus) Mediterranean port and second-largest city in LEBANON. Tripoli was an important city of the SELEUCID and ROMAN EMPIRES. In AD 638, it was captured by the Arabs. In 1109, the city was conquered by the Crusaders, who developed the city's fortifications. In 1289, Tripoli returned to Islamic rule under the Egyptian Mamelukes. The Turks held the city until the arrival of the British in 1918, and in 1920 it became a Lebanese city. It suffered severe damage during the 1975–76 Lebanese civil war. The city remains an important centre for trade between Syria and Lebanon, and is the terminus of the oil pipeline from Iraq. Industries: oil refining, textiles, food processing. Pop. (2000) 1,733,000.

triptych Three panelled painting or carving, used as an altarpiece. The panels may form one picture, or the outer panels may be separate and subordinate to the central picture.

Tristan (Tristram) Hero of many medieval romances, most commonly as a knight of the Round Table in the Arthurian romances. His fatal love for the Irish Princess Isolde (or Iseult) is the subject of Richard Wagner's opera *Tristan and Isolde* (1865). *See also* ARTHUR

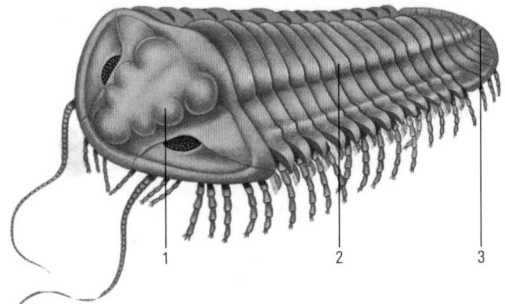

◄ **trilobite** The trilobite looked rather like today's woodlouse, being covered by a chitinous skeleton. This was divided into: (1) the cephalon or headshield, which carried sensory organs and the glabella, a bump that housed the stomach; (2) the thorax, a region of articulated segments below each of which was a pair of legs; and (3) the pygidium or tail shield. Each limb consisted of a jointed organ for walking, a swimming and breathing organ, and a paddle that swept food particles towards the mouth.

Tristan da Cunha Group of four islands in the S Atlantic Ocean, located midway between S Africa and South America. The group was discovered (1506) by the Portuguese and annexed by Britain in 1816. In 1961, Tristan suffered a volcanic eruption. A British overseas territory, it is administered from ST HELENA. Area of Tristan: 98sq km (38sq mi). Pop. (2000) 283, all of whom live in the settlement of Edinburgh.

Triton In Greek mythology, a sea god, son of Poseidon and Amphitrite. He was half man and half fish, with a scaled body, sharp teeth and claws, and a forked fish tail. He had power over the waves and possessed the gift of prophecy.

triumphal arch Massive masonry structure, containing one, two or three ARCHES covered with a flat, oblong attic. Triumphal arches were originally built by the Romans to commemorate specific victories, and in imperial times only emperors could pass through them. They were decorated with bronze statuary and carved scenes. *See also* ARC DE TRIOMPHE

Trivandrum (Triruvananthapuram) Seaport on the Malabar Coast, SW India; largest city and capital of Kerala state. It

INTERNET

Trinidad and Tobago
▶ www.gov.tt
▶ www.visittnt.com

TRINIDAD & TOBAGO

The Republic of Trinidad and Tobago consists of two main islands and is the most southerly in the LESSER ANTILLES. The largest island, Trinidad, is just 16km [10mi] off Venezuela's Orinoco delta. Tobago, which is a detached extension of Trinidad's hilly Northern Range, lies 34km [21mi] to the N. The country's highest point is Mount Aripo (940m [3,085ft]) in Trinidad's rugged and forested Northern Range. Fertile plains cover much of the country.

CLIMATE

Temperatures are high throughout the year, ranging from 18 to 33°C [64–92°F]. Rainfall is heavy, with the wettest months from June to November. Annual rainfall ranges from 1,270mm [50in] on SW Trinidad to more than 2,540mm [100in] on the highlands of Tobago.

HISTORY

Christopher Columbus visited the islands, then populated by Arawak and Carib Amerindians, in 1498. He named Trinidad after three peaks at its southern tip; the name Tobago, formed later, probably derives from tobacco. Spain

colonized Trinidad in 1532, while Dutch settlers planted sugar on plantations in Tobago in the 1630s. In 1781 France colonized Tobago and further developed its plantation economy. The British captured Trinidad from Spain in 1797 and, in 1802, Spain formally ceded the island to Britain. In 1814, France also ceded Tobago to Britain, and in 1869 the two islands were combined into one colony. Black slaves worked on the plantations until slavery was abolished in 1834. To meet the problem of labour shortages, the British recruited Indian and Chinese indentured labourers. The presence of people of African, Asian and European origin has resulted in a complex cultural mix in present-day Trinidad and Tobago.

POLITICS

Independence was achieved in 1962. Eric Williams, moderate leader of the People's National Movement (PNP) which he had founded in 1956, became prime minister. In 1970, the government declared a state of emergency following violence by black power supporters, who called for an end to foreign influence and unemployment. The emergency was lifted in 1972, but strikes caused problems in 1975. Trinidad and Tobago became a republic in 1976, with Williams continuing as prime minister. In 1986, after 30 years in office, the PNP was defeated in elections. The National Alliance for Reconstruction (NAR) coalition took office under Arthur Robinson. In 1990, Islamists seized parliament and held Robinson and other officials hostage for several days. In 1991, Patrick Manning became prime minister

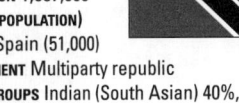

AREA 5,130sq km [1,981sq mi]
POPULATION 1,057,000
CAPITAL (POPULATION) Port of Spain (51,000)
GOVERNMENT Multiparty republic
ETHNIC GROUPS Indian (South Asian) 40%, African 38%, mixed 21%, others
LANGUAGES English (official), Hindi, French, Spanish, Chinese
RELIGIONS Roman Catholic 26%, Hindu 23%, Anglican 8%, Baptist 7%, Pentecostal 7%, others
CURRENCY Trinidad and Tobago dollar = 100 cents

following an election victory for the PNP, but, in 1994, Baseo Panday, leader of the Indian-based United National Congress (UNC), became prime minister, leading a coalition with the NAR. In the 2002 elections, the PNP was victorious and Patrick Manning returned as prime minister. He was re-elected in 2007.

Trinidad and Tobago is a major transshipment point for cocaine being moved from South America to North America and Europe. Cannabis is also produced in the country. The drug trade has fuelled gang violence and corruption. The death penalty was reintroduced in 1999, despite strong international pressure. In 2005, a Caribbean Court of Justice was set up in Trinidad as a final court of appeal to replace the British Privy Council.

ECONOMY

Oil is vital to the economy. Chief exports include refined and crude petroleum, anhydrous ammonia, and iron and steel.

T

served as capital of Travancore kingdom from 1745 and has an 18th-century fort that contains palaces and fine Hindu temples. Industries: tyres, tiles, plywood, titanium products, textiles, soap, sand and ivory products. Pop. (2005) 918,000.

trogon Brilliantly coloured bird of dark tropical forests in America, Africa and Asia. Trogons nest in holes in trees and feed on fruit and some insect larvae. Length: about 30cm (12in). Family Trogonidae; typical genus *Trogon*.

Trojan War War between the Greeks and Trojans, lasting 10 years. It began when PARIS, son of King Priam of TROY, kidnapped HELEN, wife of King Menelaus of Sparta. When the Trojans refused to return her, the Greeks formed an army, led by AGAMEMNON, including ACHILLES, ODYSSEUS and the two AJAXES. After nine years of fighting, the Greeks pretended to sail for home, leaving behind a large, hollow, wooden horse in which they concealed some warriors. Sinon persuaded the Trojans to bring the horse within the fortified city walls of Troy, despite the warnings of CASSANDRA. That night the Greeks returned, and when the concealed warriors opened the city gates, they destroyed the city. HOMER wrote about the events of the war in his epic, the *Iliad*. Historians continue to dispute the extent to which the Trojan War reflects historical events. *See also* TROY

Trollope, Anthony (1815–82) English novelist. He spent most of his life working for the Post Office and was responsible for the introduction of the pillar-box. Trollope's reputation as a writer is founded chiefly on a series of six novels, chronicling rural Victorian life in the imaginary county of Barsetshire. The series included *The Warden* (1855), *Barchester Towers* (1857) and *The Last Chronicle of Barset* (1858). His novels of the Palliser family include *Can You Forgive Her?* (1864–65) and *The Way We Live Now* (1874–75).

trombone BRASS musical instrument with a cylindrical bore, cupped mouthpiece and flaring bell. It is usually played with a slide, except for a variant which has three or four valves. The tenor and bass trombones have a range of three and a half octaves.

Trondheim City on the s shore of Trondheim fjord, central Norway, the third-largest city in Norway. Founded as Nidaros in 997, the city was the political and religious capital of medieval Norway. Until 1906, the kings of Norway were crowned in its 12th-century cathedral. The city exports wood and metal products. Industries: fish canning, brewing, electronics, shipbuilding, clothing, hardware. Pop. (2000) 148,859.

tropical disease Any of a number of diseases predominantly associated with tropical climates. Major ones are MALARIA, leishmaniasis, SLEEPING SICKNESS, FILARIASIS and schistosomiasis (bilharzia). The infectious agents of tropical diseases include viruses, bacteria, protozoa, fungi and worms of various kinds. Many of these disease microbes are spread by insect vectors such as MOSQUITOES.

tropics *See* CANCER, TROPIC OF; CAPRICORN, TROPIC OF

tropism (tropic response) Response in growth and orientation of a plant or a part of it in relation to a directional, external stimulus, such as light or water.

Trotsky, Leon (1879–1940) Russian revolutionary leader and theoretician, b. Lev Davidovich Bronstein. A Marxist revolutionary from 1897, he headed the workers' soviet (revolutionary council) in St Petersburg in the RUSSIAN REVOLUTION OF 1905. Arrested, he escaped abroad and embarked on the work that made him, with LENIN, the leading architect of the RUSSIAN REVOLUTION of 1917. He returned to Russia after the March revolution (1917) and joined the BOLSHEVIKS. As chairman of the Petrograd (St Petersburg) Soviet, he set up the Military Revolutionary Committee to seize power, ostensibly for the Soviet, actually for the Bolsheviks. After the Bolshevik success, he negotiated the peace of BREST-LITOVSK, withdrawing Russia from World War 1. As commissar of war (1918–25), he created the Red Army, which won the Civil War and made the Bolshevik revolution safe. However, he criticized the growth of bureaucracy in the party, the lack of democracy and the failure to expand industrialization. He also disapproved of Lenin's dictatorial tendencies in power and fiercely objected to STALIN's adoption of a policy of 'socialism in one country', rather than the world revolution

in which Trotsky believed. He was driven from power, from the party and eventually from the country. In exile, he continued to write prolifically on many subjects. His ideas, though rejected in the Soviet Union, were extremely influential internationally, especially in Third World countries. He was assassinated in Mexico by a Stalinist agent.

troubadour Poet in the s of France from the 11th to the 14th century who wrote about love and chivalry. Troubadors' poems were sung by wandering minstrels called jongleurs. They wrote in the Provençal tongue, the *langue d'oc*, and much of their work, which was highly influential in the development of European lyric poetry, survives in songbooks.

trough In meteorology, area of low atmospheric pressure, usually an extension to a DEPRESSION.

trout Any fish of the SALMON family (Salmonidae). There are three types of the single species of European trout (*Salmo trutta*). The brown or river trout is small and dark, and does not migrate. The lake trout, of rivers and lakes, is a larger, paler version, and is sometimes migratory. The large, silvery sea trout is definitely migratory and is sometimes confused with the salmon. Length: to 1m (3ft); weight: to 13.5kg (30lb).

Troy (Ilium) Ancient city at what is now Hissarlik, Turkey, familiar chiefly through HOMER's *Iliad*. Archaeological excavation, begun by Heinrich SCHLIEMANN in the 1870s, suggests that the legend of the TROJAN WAR may be based on an actual episode. Nine cities have been detected in the archaeological strata, dating from *c*.3000 BC and reaching a peak in Troy VI (*c*.1800–1300BC). Troy VI was ruined by an earthquake. Its successor, Troy VIIA, was destroyed, apparently by enemy attack, *c*.1200 BC close to the legendary date of the fall of Troy.

Troyes, Chrétien de (active late 12th century) French poet. He was the author of the earliest extant Arthurian romances. Troyes' work includes translations of OVID and the romances *Erec* (after 1155), *Cligès* (*c*.1176) and the unfinished *Perceval (Le Conte du Graal)*, which contains the earliest known reference to the legend of the Holy Grail. *See also* ARTHUR

Trudeau, Pierre Elliott (1919–2000) Canadian statesman, prime minister (1968–79, 1980–84). He was minister of justice before succeeding Lester PEARSON as prime minister. He promoted the economic and diplomatic independence of Canada, reducing US influence. Aided by his French-Canadian origins, he resisted QUÉBEC separatism. Defeated in the elections of 1979, he returned to power in 1980. Autonomy for Québec was rejected in a referendum (1980) and he succeeded in winning agreement for a revised constitution (1981).

True Levellers *See* DIGGERS

Truffaut, François (1932–84) French film director. His first feature film was *The 400 Blows* (1959). Other films include *Shoot the Pianist* (1960), *Jules et Jim* (1961), and *Pocket Money* (1976). Truffaut won an Academy Award for best foreign language film for *Day for Night* (1973). Deeply influenced by Alfred HITCHCOCK and Jean RENOIR, and a leading member of the nouvelle vague, Truffaut scripted or co-scripted all of his films.

truffle Any of several species of ascomycete FUNGI that grow underground, often among tree roots. Most are edible and are highly prized delicacies. Found in Europe, particularly France, and in parts of the USA, they are hunted with trained pigs and dogs that can scent them out. Family Tuberaceae.

Truman, Harry S. (1884–1972) 33rd US President (1945–53). He was elected to the Senate in 1934. In 1944, he was Franklin D. ROOSEVELT's running mate. Truman became president on FDR's death and faced many difficulties abroad. He approved the use of the atomic bomb to force Japanese surrender (1945) at the end of WORLD WAR 2, and adopted a robust policy toward the Soviet Union in the COLD WAR. Truman approved the MARSHALL PLAN (1947) and the creation (1949) of the NORTH ATLANTIC TREATY ORGANIZATION (NATO). In the KOREAN WAR (1950–53), he was forced to dismiss US commander, General MACARTHUR. He declined renomination in 1952. Dwight D. EISENHOWER succeeded him.

Truman Doctrine Principle of US foreign policy under President Harry S. TRUMAN. It promised US support for any democratic country threatened by foreign domination. In practice, application of the Truman Doctrine was limited.

INTERNET

Trotsky, Leon
▶ www.marxists.org

Trudeau, Pierre Elliott
▶ www.clevernet.on.ca/
pierre_trudeau

Truman, Harry S.
▶ www.trumanlibrary.org
▶ www.whitehouse.gov/
history/presidents

The USA did not act against communist takeovers in Eastern Europe, although it did resist the invasion of South Korea.

trumpet BRASS instrument of ancient origin. It has a cylindrical bore in the shape of a flattened loop and three piston valves. It became an important ceremonial instrument in the 15th century, and by the late 17th century had become standard in the orchestra.

trunkfish (boxfish) Temperate and tropical marine fish. It is almost triangular when seen from the front, with a broad flat ventral region tapering to a narrow dorsal region. Length: to 50cm (20in). Family Ostraciontidae; genus *Lactophrys*.

truth State or condition of being true. A 'truth' is something that is deemed to be genuine, an accurate representation of reality or a statement that accords with proven, provable, or observable facts. Two famous theories for determining the meaning of truth are the **correspondence** theory, which defines it as 'that which corresponds with facts', and the **coherence** theory, which defines it as 'that which conforms with what we have come to accept'. Other theories, espoused by pragmatists, take a utilitarian view of truth, defining it as 'that which it is good, useful, or helpful to believe'. This evaluative concept is also important in LOGIC, where either of two truth-values can be assigned to a statement, describing it as either true or false. *See also* EPISTEMOLOGY; ONTOLOGY; PRAGMATISM

Truth, Sojourner (1797–1883) US abolitionist. Born a slave in New York and unable to read or write, she was freed by the New York Emancipation Act (1827). Inspired by a religious calling, Truth became a leading propagandist for abolition of SLAVERY and votes for women. The 'micro-rover' on NASA's Mars Pathfinder mission was named after her.

trypsin Digestive ENZYME secreted by the PANCREAS. It is secreted in an inactive form that is converted into active trypsin by an enzyme in the small intestine. It breaks down peptide bonds on the amino acids lysine and arginine. *See also* ALIMENTARY CANAL; DIGESTION; DIGESTIVE SYSTEM

tsetse fly Any of several species of blood-sucking flies that live in Africa. Larger than a housefly, it has a grey thorax and a yellow to brown abdomen. Females transmit a cattle disease. Almost 80% of flies that bite humans are males, which carry SLEEPING SICKNESS. Length: to 16mm (0.6in). Order Diptera; family Muscidae; genus *Glossina*.

Tsiolkovsky, Konstantin Eduardovich (1857–1935) Russian aeronautical engineer. In 1898, he became the first person to stress the importance of liquid propellants in ROCKETS. Tsiolkovsky also proposed the idea of using multi-stage rockets to overcome GRAVITATION and achieve space travel.

tsunami (seismic sea wave) Ocean wave caused by a submarine EARTHQUAKE, subsidence or volcanic eruption. Erroneously called a tidal wave, tsunamis spread radially from their source in ever-widening circles. Tsunamis travel across oceans at speeds up to 400km/h (250mph) and can reach heights of about 10m (30ft). On December 26, 2004, a massive tsunami, resulting from an earthquake in the Indian Ocean near to Sumatra, killed more than 250,000 people, mostly in Indonesia (particularly western Sumatra), Sri Lanka, India and Thailand.

Tuareg Fiercely independent BERBERS of Islamic faith, who inhabit the desert regions of N Africa. Their matrilineal, feudal society is based on nomadic pastoralism; it traditionally maintained a class of black, non-Tuareg servants. Tuareg males wear blue veils, while the women are unveiled.

tuatara Nocturnal, lizard-like reptile of New Zealand; remarkable for being active at quite low temperatures for a reptile (7°C/45°F) and for being the sole surviving member of the primitive order Rhynchocephalia. It is brownish in colour and has an exceptionally well-developed PINEAL BODY on its head, thought to be a vestigial third eye. Length: to 70cm (2.3ft). Species *Sphenodon punctatus*.

tuba Family of BRASS musical instruments, the lowest of the orchestral brass instruments. The tuba has a conical bore and a cupped mouthpiece and usually has four or five valves.

tuber In plants, the short, swollen, sometimes edible underground stem, modified for the storage of food, as in the potato, or as a swollen root (for example, dahlia). They enable the plant to survive an adverse season (winter or dry season), providing food for the later development of new shoots and roots.

tuberculosis (TB) Infectious disease caused by the bacillus *Mycobacterium tuberculosis*. It affects the lungs (pulmonary tuberculosis), but may involve the bones and joints, skin, lymph nodes, intestines and kidneys. One-third of the world's population is infected, and up to 5% of those infected eventually develop TB. Poor urban living conditions have led to a resurgence of the disease in the USA and Europe, where it had been in decline. The BCG vaccine against tuberculosis developed in the 1920s and the first effective treatment drug, streptomycin, became available in 1944. The bacillus shows increasing resistance to drugs and some strains are multi-resistant.

Tubman, Harriet (1820–1913) US abolitionist. Born a slave, she escaped to the North by following the Underground Railroad. Tubman then led *c.*300 fugitive slaves, including her parents, to freedom during the 1850s and became a prominent spokesperson for abolition.

Tubman, William Vacanarat Shadrach (1895–1971) Liberian statesman, president (1944–71). A descendant of US freed slaves who settled the country during the 19th century, he preserved Liberia's close connections with the USA, maintained prosperity, and showed respect for the customs of the non-Westernized people of the interior.

TUC *See* TRADES UNION CONGRESS

Tucana (Toucan) Far southern constellation representing a toucan. Its overall faintness is redeemed by the presence of the small MAGELLANIC CLOUD and a superb globular cluster. It lies 15,000 light years away

Tucson City on the Santa Cruz River, S Arizona, USA. The Spanish built the presidio fort of Tucson in 1776, and the city was state capital from 1867 to 1877. Today, it is a foothills resort with a dry, sunny climate. It is a port for cotton and cattle. Industries: textiles, meat packing, copper smelting, aircraft parts, electronics, optical instruments. Pop. (2000) 486,699.

Tudjman, Franjo (1922–99) Croatian president (1990–99). He was imprisoned twice by the Yugoslavian government for nationalist activities. In 1989, Tudjman founded the ultra-nationalist Croatian Democratic Union (HDZ) party, which helped form a coalition government in Bosnia-Herzegovina (1990). Elected president of CROATIA, he retained the position during the ensuing civil war and led the country to independence. Tudjman was re-elected in 1997. An authoritarian figure, he died in office.

▲ **trout** The brown trout (*Salmo trutta fario*) is found throughout Asia Minor, Europe, and Iceland. Brown trout show great variety in shape, colour and markings, and these are dictated by the nature and quality of the water and not, as in some flatfish and Perciformes, in response to visual stimuli.

INTERNET

Truth, Sojourner
➤ www.lkwdpl.org/wihohio/trut-soj.htm

Tubman, Harriet
➤ www.nyhistory.com/harriettubman

Tudjman, Franjo
➤ www.croatiaemb.org/tudjman/biography.html

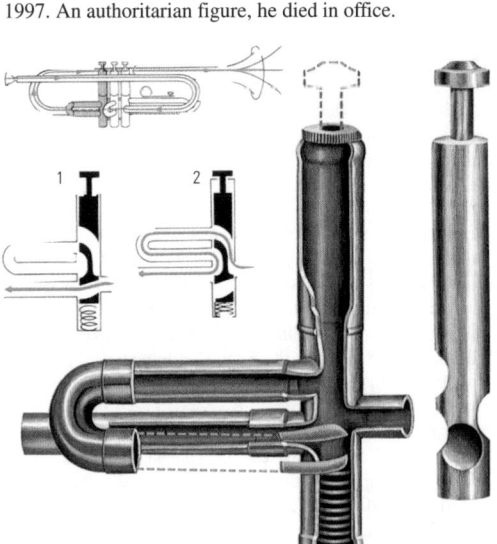

◄ **trumpet** A modern trumpet is fitted with three valves, which lower the pitch of the instrument by increasing its length; this is done by means of 'crooks', which are brought into play when the valves are depressed. A raised valve lets the air pass directly through (1); when the valve is depressed, the air flows through the crook (2) The first valve, nearest the mouthpiece, lowers the pitch by two semitones; the middle valve lowers it by one semitone; and the third valve, furthest from the mouthpiece, lowers it by three semitones.

T

TURBOCHARGER

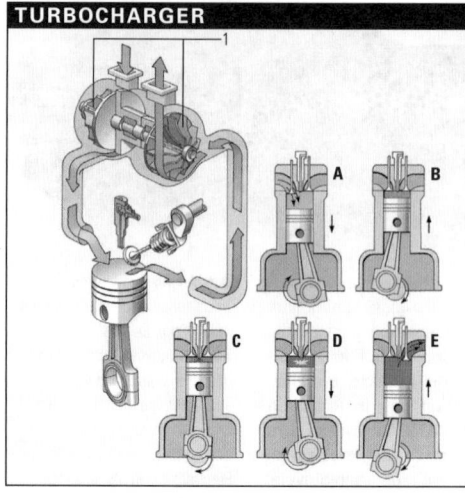

A diesel turbocharger uses the energy of the exhaust gases to force air into the cylinder via linked impellers (1). First air is sucked into the engine (A). The air is compressed into a space 22 times smaller (B). The compression heats the air. Diesel fuel is then injected in a swirling manner to maximize mixing, accentuated by the shape of the piston head (C). Combustion occurs spontaneously, without the need of a spark plug, pushing the piston down (D). The rotation of the crankshaft pushes the piston up, expelling the waste gases (E).

Tudors English royal dynasty (1485–1603). Of Welsh origin, they were descended from Owen Tudor (d.1461), who married the widow of HENRY V. In 1485, Owen Tudor's grandson defeated RICHARD III at Bosworth to win the English throne as HENRY VII. The dynasty ended with the death of ELIZABETH I in 1603. *See also* HENRY VIII; EDWARD VI; MARY I; STUART

Tu Fu (712–70) Chinese poet of the T'ANG dynasty. He wrote about such topics as war, corruption, and patriotism. His poetry reflects his troubled personal life and laments the corruption and cruelty that prevailed at court.

tulip Hardy, bulb-forming plant of the genus *Tulipa*, native to Europe, Asia and North Africa. Tulips have long, pointed leaves growing from the base and elongated, cup-shaped flowers that can be almost any colour or combination of colours. Family Liliaceae; genus *Tulipa*.

Tull, Jethro (1674–1741) English agriculturalist. He influenced agricultural methods through his invention (1701) of a mechanical seed drill. The drill sowed seeds in straight lines, reducing the labour involved in weeding.

Tulsa Port on the Arkansas River, NE Oklahoma, the state's second-largest city. It developed with the 1882 arrival of the Atlantic and Pacific Railroad; the 1901 discovery of oil further accelerated development. Industries: oil refining and research, petroleum products, oilfield machinery, mining, metal goods, aerospace. Pop. (2000) 393,049.

tumbleweed Plant that characteristically breaks off near the ground in autumn and is rolled along by the wind. Height: to 51cm (20in). Family Amaranthaceae; genus *Amaranthus*.

tumour Any uncontrolled, abnormal proliferation of cells, often leading to the formation of a lump. Tumours are classified as either benign (non-cancerous) or malignant.

tuna (tunny) Marine fish related to MACKEREL, found in tropical and temperate seas. An important commercial fish, it has a blue-black and silvery streamlined body with a large, deeply divided tail. Length: to 4.3m (14ft); weight: to 810kg (1800lb).

tundra Treeless, level, or gently undulating plain characteristic of arctic and subarctic regions. It is marshy with dark soil that supports mosses, lichens, and low shrubs. It has a permanently frozen subsoil known as PERMAFROST.

tungsten (wolfram, symbol W) Silvery-grey, hard, metallic element, one of the TRANSITION ELEMENTS. Tungsten has the highest melting point of all metals and is used for lamp filaments and in special alloys. Tungsten carbide is used in high-speed cutting tools. Chemically, tungsten is fairly unreactive; it oxidizes only at high temperatures. It was isolated in 1783 by the Spanish chemists and brothers Fausto and Juan José de Elhuyar. Properties: at.no. 74; r.a.m. 183.85; r.d. 19.3; m.p. 3,410°C (6,170°F); b.p. 5,660°C (10,220°F); most common isotope W^{184} (30.64%).

Tunis Capital and largest city of Tunisia, N Africa. Tunis became the capital in the 13th century under the Hafsid dynasty. Seized by BARBAROSSA in 1534 and controlled by Turkey, it attained infamy as a haven for pirates. The French assumed control in 1881. Tunis gained independence in 1956.

Products include olive oil, carpets, textiles and handicrafts. The ruins of CARTHAGE are nearby. Pop. (2005) 2,063,000.

Tunisia Republic in N Africa. *See* country feature

Tupí-Guaraní Combination of two major tribes that now represents the major native cultural population in rural Brazil, Paraguay, and parts of Argentina. The Tupí traditionally inhabit the banks of the lower Amazon and much of coastal Brazil south to Uruguay. The Guaraní, a more scattered grouping, once lived mainly in what is now Paraguay, but migrated into Brazil and Argentina.

turbidity current Dense current in air, water or other fluid caused by different amounts of matter in suspension. In the ocean, when sediment along the continental shelves breaks off and rushes down slope, the resulting turbidity current carves out submarine canyons and deposits distinctively bedded layers on the ocean floor.

turbine Rotary device turned by a moving liquid or gas. A modern water turbine is like a many-bladed propeller and is used to generate HYDROELECTRICITY. In power stations that burn fuels to produce electricity, the energy released by the burning is harnessed by the blades of jet engine-like steam turbines. As they spin, the turbines turn GENERATORS to produce ELECTRICITY. Modern wind generators produce electricity as the wind turns their rotors. In gas turbines, hot gases from burning fuel turn turbines to operate generators or other machinery.

turbocharger Device that boosts the performance of an INTERNAL COMBUSTION ENGINE. A TURBINE driven by exhaust gases compresses the fuel/air mixture before it passes through the inlet valve.

turbot Scaleless, bottom-dwelling, European marine FLATFISH. It has a broad flat body with both eyes on its grey-brown, mottled upper surface, which may also be covered in bony knobs. Length: to 1m (3.3ft). Family Scophthalmidae; species *Scophthalmus maximus*.

Turgenev, Ivan Sergeievich (1818–83) Russian novelist, playwright, and short-story writer. His novels often opposed social and political evils and attracted official disapproval. The play *A Month in the Country* (1855) is often considered the first psychological drama of the Russian theatre. After the appearance of Turgenev's masterpiece *Fathers and Sons* (1862), he left Russia permanently.

turgor pressure Hydrostatic pressure generated in cells of plants and bacteria as a result of the uptake of water by OSMOSIS. Water diffuses through the semi-permeable membrane of the cell, causing the cell to swell; the increase in volume is resisted by the limited elasticity of the cell wall. When water is lost, a plant's cells collapse and it wilts.

Turin (Torino) City on the River Po, NW Italy, the country's fourth-largest city and capital of Piedmont (Piemonte). A Roman town under Augustus, it was a Lombard Duchy between 590 and 636. From 1720 to 1861, it was capital of the Kingdom of Sardinia and a centre of the RISORGIMENTO. Turin remains an important centre of industry. Industries: electronic equipment, chemicals, machinery, rubber, paper, leather goods, pharmaceuticals. Pop. (2000) 857,000.

Turing, Alan Mathison (1912–54) English mathematician. In 1937, he invented the **Turing machine**, a hypothetical machine that could modify a set of input instructions. It was the forerunner of the modern COMPUTER. During World War 2, Turing played a major role in deciphering the German 'Enigma' code. In 1950, he devised the **Turing test**, which paved the way for the foundation of ARTIFICIAL INTELLIGENCE (AI). He committed suicide after being prosecuted for homosexuality.

Turin shroud Sheet of very old linen kept in Turin Cathedral, NW Italy, by tradition the cloth in which the body of Christ was wrapped after the Crucifixion. When photographed in 1898, negatives appeared to show the outline of a human figure. In 1988, results of carbon dating tests revealed that the shroud had in fact been made sometime in the middle ages, more than a millennium after the death of Christ.

Turkey Republic in SE Europe and Asia. *See* country feature, page 752

turkey North American gamebird now widely domesticated throughout the world. The common wild turkey (*Meleagris gallopavo*), once abundant in North America, was over-hunted and is now protected. The male, or gobbler, is often bearded. Length: 125cm (50in). Family Meleagrididae.

Turkic languages Branch of the ALTAIC family of languages. Divided into six or seven separate subclasses, Turkish is the most important. The languages are remarkable for their grammatical uniformity and structural inter-resemblances, and their relative lack of linguistic change over the centuries.

Turkistan (Turkestan) Historic region of central Asia, inhabited by Turkic-speaking peoples. **Western** (Russian) Turkistan now consists of the republics of Turkmenistan, Uzbekistan, Tajikistan, Kyrgyzstan, and S Kazakhstan. It mainly comprises the deserts of KYZYL KUM and Kara Kum. **Eastern** (Chinese) Turkistan comprises the Chinese region of XINJIANG and includes the TIAN SHAN mountains. Southern Turkistan consisted of part of N Afghanistan. For nearly two centuries, Turkistan was the geographical bridge for trade between East and West. The first imperial power to control the region was PERSIA (Iran) in 500 BC. In c.330 BC ALEXANDER THE GREAT defeated the Iranians and for the next few centuries, Bactria,

PARTHIA, and China disputed the region. Market towns developed around the oases, becoming centres for trade and religion. In the 8th century, the Arabs conquered the region and converted the local population to Islam. During the 13th century, the Mongols controlled the region, but then it fractured into small, independent khanates. In 1867, the Russian Empire imposed military rule over the area, and in 1918 Turkistan became an autonomous region within the SOVIET UNION. In 1924, the S part of Turkistan divided into the republics of Uzbekistan and Turkmenistan. In 1929, Tajikistan became a republic and Kyrgyzstan followed in 1936. The N part of Russian Turkistan was incorporated into the Kazak republic, and Russian Turkistan became known as **Soviet Central Asia**.

Turkmenistan Republic in central Asia. The capital is ASHGABAT. *See* country feature page 753.

Turks and Caicos Islands Two island groups of the British West Indies, including more than 40 islands, eight of them inhabited. The capital is Cockburn Town on Grand Turk Island. Discovered (1512) by PONCE DE LEÓN, the

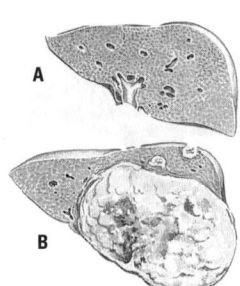

▲ **tumour** A tumour is a swelling composed of cells independent of the body's control mechanism, so that they rapidly divide, invade, and kill surrounding tissue. Cross-sections of a healthy (A) and a diseased liver (B) are shown.

TUNISIA

The Republic of Tunisia is the smallest country in North Africa. The mountains in the N are an E and comparatively low extension of the ATLAS Mountains. N and E of the mountains lie fertile plains, especially between Sfax, Tunis and Bizerte. S of the mountains lie broad plateaux which descend towards the S. This low-lying region contains a large salt pan, called the Chott Djerid, and part of the SAHARA.

the new parliament abolished the monarchy and declared Tunisia to be a republic in 1957. The nationalist leader, Habib Bourguiba, became president. The NDP became the foundation of all subsequent Tunisian government; it was renamed the Socialist Destour Party in 1964, and is now known as the Constitutional Assembly.

POLITICS
In 1975, Bourguiba was elected president for life. His government introduced many reforms, including votes for women. The pace of reform brought its own problems. A national school sys-

AREA 163,610sq km [63,170sq mi]
POPULATION 10,276,000
CAPITAL (POPULATION) Tunis (2,063,000)
GOVERNMENT Multiparty republic
ETHNIC GROUPS Arab 98%, European 1%
LANGUAGES Arabic (official), French
RELIGIONS Islam 98%, Christianity 1%, others
CURRENCY Tunisian dinar = 1,000 millimes

CLIMATE
Northern Tunisia has a Mediterranean climate, with dry summers, and mild winters with a moderate rainfall. The average yearly rainfall decreases towards the S, which forms part of the Sahara desert.

HISTORY
The Phoenicians began the Carthaginian Empire in Tunisia around 1100 BC and, according to legend, the colony of Carthage was established by Queen Dido in 814 BC on a site near present-day Tunis. At their peak the Carthaginians controlled large areas in the eastern Mediterranean but, following the three Punic Wars with Rome, Carthage was destroyed in 146 BC. The Romans ruled the area for 600 years, until they were defeated by the Vandals in AD 439. The Vandals were conquered by the Byzantines, but in AD 640 an Arabian invasion ended Byzantine rule. The BERBERS slowly converted to Islam, and Arabic became the pricipal language.

In 1159 the ALMOHAD dynasty conquered Tunisia. From 1230 to 1574, Tunisia was ruled by the Hafsids. In the 16th century, Tunisia's ports were a haven for pirates. Spanish forces invaded and captured much of the coast; the Ottoman Empire intervened and drove them out, and in 1574 Tunisia came under Turkish rule.

In 1881 the French invaded, establishing a protectorate over Tunisia. French rule aroused nationalist sentiment, and Habib BOURGUIBA formed the the Neo-Destour (New Constitution) Party, the first effective opposition group.

Tunisia was a major battleground of the North African campaigns in World War 2. After the war opposition to French rule intensified, and it ended in 1956. Following independence,

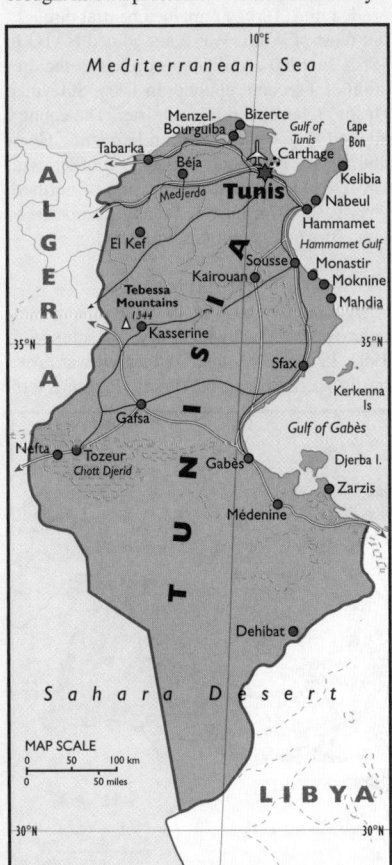

tem was established, although its success was not matched by the economy, leading to a rapid increase in the number of educated young people unable to find jobs that measured up to their qualifications. The growth of tourism, which provided a valuable source of foreign currency, led conservatives to fear that Western influences might undermine Muslim values.

The prime minister, Zine el Abidine Ben Ali, removed Bourguiba from office in 1987 and succeeded him as president. He regularly claimed election victories, most recently in 2004, and his party dominated the government. Some seats were reserved for opposition parties whatever their proportion of the popular vote, but much of the opposition boycotted the flawed elections. Occasional violence and suppression of human rights marred his presidency. He faced opposition from Islamic fundamentalists, and responded by banning al-Nahda, the main Islamic party. Fundamentalism was suppressed effectively, in contrast to neighbouring Algeria.

ECONOMY
The World Bank classifies Tunisia as a 'middle-income' developing country. Its main natural resources are oil and phosphates. Agriculture employs 22% of the people. Chief crops are barley, citrus fruits, dates, grapes, olives, sugar beet, tomatoes and wheat. Sheep are the most important livestock.

Since independence, new industries have arisen. Major manufactures include cement, flour, phosphoric acid, processed food and steel. An important stimulus was the signing of a free-trade agreement with the EU in 1995. Tunisia was the first Arab country on the Mediterranean to sign such an agreement. Tourism has become a substantial sector of the economy.

T

▲ **turtle** The North American box turtle (*Terrapene carolina*) spends most of its time on land. As with other turtles, it has a massive bony shell made of plates of keratin that are fused to the backbone and ribs. It can pull back its head under the shell when danger threatens.

islands were British from 1766, administered via Jamaica from 1873 to 1959, and a separate Crown Colony from 1973. Exports include salt, sponges, and shellfish. The islands' main sources of income are tourism and offshore banking. Area: 430sq km (166sq mi). Pop. (2000) 19,000.

Turku (Åbo) Finland's largest port, at the mouth of the Aurajoki River on the Baltic Sea. A Swedish settlement was established in 1157, and in 1220 it became the seat of the first Finnish diocese. It was the national capital until 1812. Industries: steel, shipbuilding, engineering, textiles. Pop. (1999) 172,107.

turmeric Herbaceous, perennial plant originally native to India and cultivated in SE Asia. The dried RHIZOME is powdered for use as seasoning, a yellow dye and in medicines. Family Zingiberaceae; species *Curcuma longa*.

Turner, Joseph Mallord William (1775–1851) English landscape painter. He was an associate of the Royal Academy (RA) by the age of 24, and professor of perspective at the RA from 1807 to 1838. Turner's paintings were revolutionary in their representation of light, especially on water. His style

changed dramatically in his late works, such as *The Slave Ship* (1840) and *Rain, Steam and Speed* (1844), in which the original subjects are almost obscured in a hazy interplay of light and colour. His work had a profound influence on IMPRESSIONISM.

Turner, Nat (1800–31) US African-American revolutionary. Born a slave, he believed that he was called by God to take violent revenge on whites and win freedom for blacks. With *c.*70 followers, he took a solar eclipse as a sign to begin his insurrection. More than 50 whites were killed before the revolt was crushed. Turner was later captured and hanged.

Turner's syndrome Hereditary condition in females, in which there is only one X-CHROMOSOME instead of two. It results in short stature, infertility, and developmental defects.

turnip Garden vegetable best grown in cool climates. The edible leaves are large and toothed with thick midribs; the young leaves are eaten as 'spring greens'. A biennial, it has a large, bulbous, white or yellow, fleshy root, which is cooked and eaten. Diameter: 8–15cm (3–6in). Height: to 55cm (20in). Family Brassicaceae/Cruciferae; species *Brassica rapa*.

TURKEY

The Republic of Turkey lies in two continents. The European section (THRACE) lies w of a waterway between the Black and Mediterranean seas. This consists of the BOSPORUS, the Sea of Marmara, and a narrow strait called the DARDANELLES.

Most of the Asian part, Anatolia or ASIA MINOR, consists of plateaux and mountains. These rise to 5,165m [16,945ft] at Mount ARARAT (Agri Dagi) near the border with Armenia. Earthquakes are common. Deciduous forests grow inland with conifers on the mountains. The plateau is mainly dry steppe.

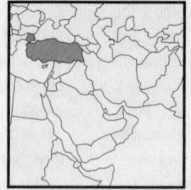

CLIMATE
Central Turkey has a dry climate, with hot, sunny summers and cold winters. The driest part of the central plateau lies s of ANKARA, around Lake Tuz. w Turkey has a Mediterranean climate, while the Black Sea coast has cooler summers.

HISTORY
In AD 330 the Roman Empire moved its capital to Byzantium, renaming it Constantinople. Constantinople became the capital of the East Roman (or BYZANTINE) Empire in 395. SELJUK Turks from central Asia invaded Anatolia in the 11th century, introducing Islam, and made KONYA their capital. In the 14th century another group of Turks, the Ottomans,

conquered the area. In 1453 the Ottoman Turks under MUHAMMAD II took Constantinople, ending the Byzantine Empire. They made the city their capital, renamed it Istanbul and built up the massive OTTOMAN EMPIRE, which lasted until the 20th century but finally collapsed after World War 1 with the punitive Treaty of SÈVRES of 1920. Nationalists, led by Mustafa Kemal (ATATÜRK), launched a war of independence. In 1923 Turkey became a republic, with Kemal as its president. Atatürk's 14-year dictatorship created a secular, Westernized state.

In 1938 Atatürk died, and Ismet INÖNÜ succeeded him. Turkey remained neutral throughout most of World War 2 and joined NATO in 1952. In 1960 a military coup led to the creation of a second republic. In 1965, Süleyman DEMIREL became prime minister. The country applied to join the European Economic Community in 1987 but Turkey's conflict with Greece, together with its invasion of northern Cyprus in 1974, have led many Europeans to treat Turkey's aspirations with caution.

POLITICS
After a military coup in 1980, civilian government was restored with a new constitution in 1982. In the 1980s and 1990s civil war broke out in the E and SE of Turkey. Fighting took

AREA 774,815sq km [299,156sq mi]
POPULATION 71,159,000
CAPITAL (POPULATION) Ankara (3,203,000)
GOVERNMENT Multiparty republic
ETHNIC GROUPS Turkish 80%, Kurdish 20%
LANGUAGES Turkish (official), Kurdish, Arabic
RELIGIONS Islam (mainly Sunni Muslim) 99%
CURRENCY New Turkish lira = 100 kurus

place between Turkish forces and those of the secessionist Kurdistan Workers' Party (PKK). Over 30,000 people were killed and the Turkish government has frequently been accused of violating the human rights of the KURDS.

In 1998, the government banned the Islamist Welfare Party for violating secular principles. In 1999 a ceasefire with the PKK was reached, although by 2004 it had broken down and violence resumed. In 2001 the Turkish parliament adopted reforms to ease the country's entry into the European Union, including formally recognizing men and women as equals. In 2002 elections the moderate Islamic Justice and Development Party won a majority in parliament, sparking fierce debate about the country's secularist tradition, while the parties in the former ruling coalition lost almost all their seats. Turkey finally agreed to recognize Cyprus as an EU member, and this led to EU membership talks being formally launched in 2005 with negotiations expected to take about 10 years. In 2006, however, the talks were partially suspended over failures to put the recognition of Cyprus into practice. In 2007 military action against the PKK spilled over into neighbouring Iraq.

ECONOMY
Turkey is a 'lower-middle-income' developing country. Agriculture employs 40% of the people, and barley, cotton, fruits, maize, tobacco and wheat are major crops. Livestock farming is important and wool is a leading product. Manufacturing is the chief activity, including processed farm products and textiles, cars, fertilizers, iron and steel, machinery, metal products and paper products. Tourism is a vital sector of the economy, and the country receives more than 9 million tourists a year.

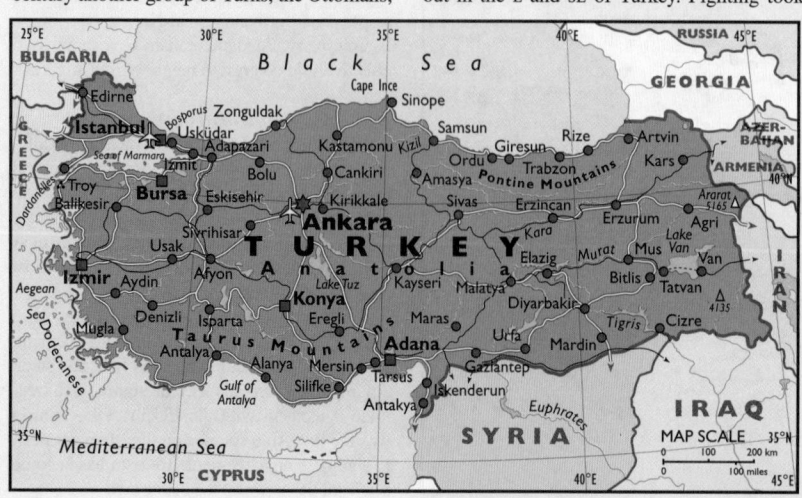

TURKMENISTAN

The Republic of Turkmenistan is one of five central Asian republics that once formed part of the Soviet Union. Most of the land is low-lying, with mountains on the s and sw borders.

In the w lies the salty Caspian Sea. A depression called the Kara Bogaz Gol Bay contains the country's lowest point. Most of the country is arid and Asia's largest sand desert, the Garagum, covers 80% of the country, though parts of it are irrigated by the Garagum Canal.

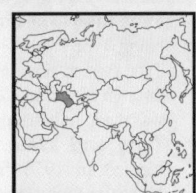

CLIMATE

Turkmenistan has a continental climate, with average annual rainfall varying from 80 mm [3 in] in the desert to 300 mm [12 in] in the mountains. Summers are very hot, but temperatures during winter drop below freezing.

HISTORY

Turkmenistan was originally part of the Persian Parthian Empire, but was overrun by Arabs in the 8th century AD. At the end of the first millennium AD Turkic peoples settled in the lands east of the Caspian Sea, and the name 'Turkmen' comes from this time. GENGHIS KHAN and his Mongol armies conquered the area in the 13th century and it subsequently became part of TAMERLANE's vast empire. With the break up of the Timurid dynasty, Turkmenistan came under Uzbek control. Islam became the dominant religion in the 14th century.

Russia took over the region during the 1870s and 1880s. In 1899, despite fierce resistance, Turkmenistan became part of Russian Turkistan. After the Russian Revolution of 1917, the area came under Communist rule and, in 1924, it joined the SOVIET UNION as part of the Turkistan Autonomous Soviet Socialist Republic. The Communists strictly controlled all aspects of life and, in particular, they discouraged religious worship. But they also improved such services as education, health, housing and transport.

POLITICS

During the 1980s the Soviet Union introduced reforms, and the Turkmen began to demand more freedom. In 1990 the Turkmen government stated that its laws overruled Soviet laws. In 1991 Turkmenistan became fully independent after the break-up of the Soviet Union, but kept ties with Russia through the Commonwealth of Independent States (CIS).

In 1992 Turkmenistan adopted a new constitution, allowing for political parties providing that they were not ethnic or religious in character, but effectively Turkmenistan remained a one-party state. In 1992 Saparmurad Niyazov, the former Communist leader, was the only candidate. In 1999 parliament declared him president for life. 2004 parliamentary elections were described as a 'sham' because all the candidates supported the president. In 2005 he surprised observers by calling for contested presidential elections to take place in 2009.

Niyazov sought to influence every aspect of his people's lives. He passed laws requiring all Turkmen to take 'spiritual guidance' from a book he published, called Ruhnama, and imposed bans on everything from opera and ballet to young men wearing beards and long hair. He spent the country's oil wealth on grandiose projects while heavily damaging the country's education, health and welfare systems. Inequality rose steeply.

Niyazov died at the end of 2006. In early 2007 one of his aides, Gurbanguly Berdimuhammedov, became president after elections widely condemned as unfair.

ECONOMY

The World Bank classifies Turkmenistan as a 'lower middle income' country. Turkmenistan joined the Economic Co-operation Organization which was set up in 1985 by Iran, Pakistan and Turkey. In 1996 a rail link from Turkmenistan to the Iranian coast improved communications. Agriculture is important. The chief cash crop, grown on irrigated land, is cotton. Manufactures include cement, glass, petrochemicals and textiles. Turkmenistan's extensive hydrocarbon and natural gas reserves have brought wealth, but limited export routes restrict growth. In 2006 a dispute with Russia's Gazprom, the main customer, ended with Turkmenistan obtaining a larger share of oil and gas profits.

AREA 488,100sq km [188,455sq mi]
POPULATION 5,097,000
CAPITAL (POPULATION) Ashkhabad (521,000)
GOVERNMENT Single-party republic
ETHNIC GROUPS Turkmen 85%, Uzbek 5%, Russian 4%, others
LANGUAGES Turkmen (official), Russian, Uzbek
RELIGIONS Islam 89%, Eastern Orthodox 9%
CURRENCY Turkmen manat = 100 tenesi

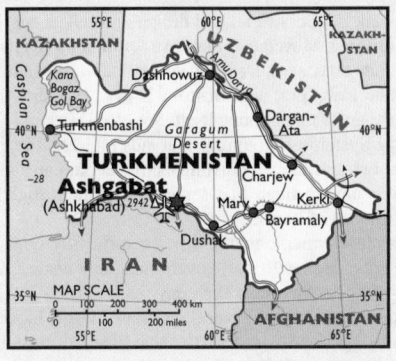

---

turnstone Two species of migratory shore birds that use their curved bills to turn over pebbles in search of food; they nest on the Arctic TUNDRA. The ruddy turnstone (*Arenaria interpres*) ranges widely in winter. Family Scolopacidae.

turquoise Blue mineral, hydrated copper aluminium phosphate, found in aluminium-rich rocks in deserts. Its crystal system is triclinic and it occurs as tiny crystals and dense masses. Its colour ranges from sky-blue and blue-green to a greenish grey and it is a popular gemstone. Hardness 6; r.d. 2.7.

turtle REPTILE found on land or in marine and fresh waters. Turtles have the most ancient lineage of all reptiles, preceding even the dinosaurs. They have a bony, horn-covered, boxlike shell (carapace) that encloses shoulder and hip girdles and all internal organs. All lay eggs on land. Terrestrial turtles are usually called TORTOISES, and some edible species found in brackish waters are called TERRAPINS. Marine turtles have smaller, lighter shells. Length: 10cm-2m (4in-7ft). Order Chelonia.

Tuscany (Toscana) Region in central Italy between the Mediterranean coast and the Apennine Mountains; the capital is FLORENCE. Other cities include SIENA and PISA. Tuscany is mostly mountainous with fertile valleys. Agriculture is the most important activity, with cereals, olives, and grapes among the main products. Carrara marble is quarried in the NW, and there is mining for lead, zinc, antimony and copper in the SW. Industries: tourism, wine, woollens, chemicals, steel, motor scooters, artisan industries. Area: 22,992sq km (8,877sq mi). Pop. (2001) 3,460,835.

Tussaud, Madame Marie (1761–1850) French modeller, b. Marie Grosholtz. She produced wax figures in Paris, and in 1802 to her collection to London. In 1835, she founded a permanent waxworks museum on Baker Street, London. It has been at its present site on Marylebone Road since 1884.

Tutankhamen (*c.*1341–1323 BC) Egyptian pharaoh (r.1333–1323 BC) of the New Kingdom's 18th dynasty (1550–1307 BC). The revolutionary changes made by his predecessor, AKHNATEN, were reversed during his reign. The capital was re-established at Thebes (LUXOR) and worship of AMUN reinstated. Tutankhamen's fame is due to the discovery of his tomb by Howard Carter in 1922. The only royal tomb of ancient EGYPT not completely stripped by robbers, it contained magnificent treasures, which are now on display in Cairo.

Tutu, Desmond Mpilo (1931–) South African Anglican cleric. A prominent anti-APARTHEID campaigner, he trained as a teacher before becoming an Anglican priest in 1960. Tutu was Archbishop of Cape Town (1986–96). In 1984, he received the Nobel Peace Prize. Tutu acted as chairman (1995–98) of the Truth and Reconciliation Committee.

Tutuola, Amos (1920–97) Nigerian writer. A visionary who drew on traditional tales of the YORUBA people to create a world of mixed fantasy and reality. His works include *The Palm Wine Drinkard* (1952).

Tuvalu (formerly Ellice Islands) Independent republic in w Pacific Ocean, s of the Equator and w of the International Date Line. None of the cluster of nine low-lying coral islands

▲ **Tutu** An outspoken critic of the apartheid system, Archbishop Tutu advocated the use of international economic sanctions to force the South African government towards reform. He abhorred the use of violence, even by opponents of apartheid, always working for a peaceful settlement of the country's problems.

T

INTERNET

Tutu, Desmond Mpilo
(page 753)
▶ www.tutu.org

Tuvalu
▶ www.tuvaluislands.com

Tyler, John
▶ www.whitehouse.gov/
history/presidents

rises more than 4.6m (15ft) out of the Pacific, making them vulnerable to rising sea levels. Poor soil restricts vegetation to coconut palms, breadfruit and bush. The population survive by subsistence farming, raising pigs and poultry, and by fishing. Copra is the only significant export crop, but more foreign exchange is derived from the sale of elaborate postage stamps. The first European to discover the islands (1568) was the Spanish navigator Alvaro de Mendaña. Between 1850 and 1880, the population was reduced from c.20,000 to just 3,000 by Europeans abducting workers. In 1892, the British assumed control, and it was subsequently administered with the nearby Gilbert Islands (now KIRIBATI). In 1978, Tuvalu became a separate self-governing colony within the Commonwealth. Area: 26sq km (10sq mi). Pop. (2000) 11,000.

Twain, Mark (1835–1910) US writer, journalist, and lecturer, b. Samuel Langhorne Clemens. He took his pseudonym from the sounding calls of steamboatmen on the Mississippi, on the banks of which he was brought up. Twain was among the first to write novels in the American vernacular, such as *The Adventures of Tom Sawyer* (1876) and *The Adventures of Huckleberry Finn* (1884), which is seen as one of the great works of US fiction. His later books, such as *The Mysterious Stranger* (1916), are often bitter and pessimistic.

Twelve Tables Laws engraved on wooden tables representing the earliest codification of Roman law, traditionally dated 451–450 BC. They were written by *decemviri* (committee of 10) at the probable instigation of the PLEBEIANS. They codified the existing laws and customs of ancient Rome thereby providing a measure of certainty in the administration of the law.

twelve-tone music (twelve-note music) SERIAL MUSIC in which the series contains all twelve notes of the CHROMATIC scale. Its introduction, in the early 20th century, is credited to Arnold SCHOENBERG. This method of composition relies not on the principle of TONALITY, in which the tonic or keynote is the focal centre, but on the relationship between the twelve notes of the chromatic scale. The composer selects the order in which the notes are to be played and the resultant sequence is manipulated throughout the composition. Many composers have experimented with twelve-note music; these include Anton WEBERN, Alban BERG, and Hans Werner HENZE.

two-stroke engine INTERNAL COMBUSTION ENGINE in which the operation of each piston is in two stages. In the two-stroke cycle, a piston moves up a cylinder to compress a fuel-air mixture in the top. At the same time, more of the mixture is sucked in below the piston. A spark ignites the compressed mixture, causing an explosion. This sends the piston back down the cylinder. The piston forces the fresh fuel-air mixture out from beneath it, and along a transfer port leading to the top part of the cylinder. The mixture forces the exhaust gases out from the top of the cylinder. The process then repeats. *See also* FOUR-STROKE ENGINE

Tyler, John (1790–1862) Tenth US President (1841–45). He served in Congress (1811–16) and as governor of Virginia (1825–27). Tyler was a supporter of STATES' RIGHTS. The WHIG PARTY chose him as vice presidential candidate with William H. HARRISON, and he succeeded to the presidency on Harrison's death (1841). He came into conflict with the nationalistic Whigs in Congress, repeatedly vetoing legislation to create a national bank. His determination to annex TEXAS was realized only after he had left office.

Tyler, Wat (d.1381) English leader of the PEASANTS' REVOLT. He was chosen as leader of the rebels in Kent, SE England, and led their march on London. Tyler was killed by the Lord Mayor of London while parleying with RICHARD II.

Tyndale, William (c.1494–1536) English translator and religious reformer. In 1525, he started printing an English version of the New Testament in Cologne, Germany. Tyndale then began translating the Old Testament. He also wrote numerous Protestant tracts and was captured by the Church authorities and burned at the stake. His translation later provided a basis for the Authorized Version of the English BIBLE.

Tyndall, John (1820–1893) Irish physicist, who correctly suggested that the blue colour of the sky is due to the scattering of light by particles of dust and other colloidal particles. By 1881, Tyndall helped disprove the theory of spontaneous generation by showing that food does not decay in germ-free air.

Tyne River in NE England. It is formed at the confluence of the North Tyne (which rises in the S Cheviot Hills) and the South Tyne (which rises in Cumbria) and flows E for 48km (30mi) through Newcastle to enter the North Sea near Tynemouth. It was made fully navigable at the end of the 19th century.

Tyne and Wear Metropolitan council in NE England, formed in 1974 from parts of the former counties of NORTHUMBERLAND and DURHAM, and including the former county borough of NEWCASTLE UPON TYNE, which is its administrative centre. A highly industrialized area, its staple industries of coal-mining, iron and steel production, and shipbuilding declined after the 1920s. There were signs of a recovery in the 1990s, based on various light industries. Area: 537sq km (207sq mi). Pop. (2001) 1,075,979.

typhoid fever Acute, sometimes epidemic communicable disease of the DIGESTIVE SYSTEM. Caused by *Salmonella typhi*, which is transmitted in contaminated water or food, it is characterized by bleeding from the bowel and enlargement of the spleen. Symptoms include fever, headache, constipation, sore throat, cough and skin rash.

typhoon Name given in the Pacific Ocean to a HURRICANE, a violent tropical cyclonic storm.

typhus Any of a group of infectious diseases caused by rickettsiae (small bacteria) and spread by parasites of the human body such as lice, fleas, ticks and mites. **Epidemic** typhus, the result of infection by *Rickettsia prowazekii*, is the most serious manifestation. Associated with dirty, overcrowded conditions, it is mainly seen during times of war or famine.

typography Practice of designing typefaces and type styles mainly for use in printed texts. Typography is widely used in experimental, progressive art and design, as well as conventional publishing. Movements that have revolutionized typography include FUTURISM, Dadaism, and SURREALISM. Individuals include Eric GILL and MOHOLY-NAGY. The term also refers to the art of fine printing itself. *See also* DADA

typology System of groupings that aids understanding of the things being studied by distinguishing certain attributes or qualities among them that serve to link them together into a closed set of items.

Tyr (Tiw) In Germanic mythology, powerful sky god. He was also associated with war, government, and justice. The word Tuesday derives from Tyr's day.

tyrannosaurus Any of several species of large, bipedal, carnivorous, theropod DINOSAURS that lived during late CRETACEOUS times. Its head, 1.2m (4ft) long, was armed with a series of dagger-like teeth. The hind legs were stout and well developed, but the forelegs were small and may have been of limited use. The best-known species is *T. rex*. Length: 14m (47ft); height: 6.5m (20ft).

Tyre (Sur) Historic city on the coast of modern Lebanon. Built on an island, it was a major commercial port of ancient PHOENICIA. It supplied craftsmen and raw materials, especially cedarwood, for the building of the TEMPLE in Jerusalem in the 10th century BC. It established colonies, including CARTHAGE, around the Mediterranean. It was defeated when ALEXANDER THE GREAT built a causeway linking the island to the mainland (332 BC). Ruled by successive empires, including the Romans, it was captured by the Arabs in AD 638, and destroyed by the Mamelukes in 1291. Pop. (2002 est.) 114,800.

tyre Air-filled RUBBER and fabric cushion that fits over the wheels of vehicles to grip the road and absorb shock. The pneumatic tyre was invented in 1845, but was not commonly used until the end of the 19th century. It consists of a layer of fabric surrounded by a thick layer of rubber treated with chemicals to harden it and decrease wear and tear.

Tyrol *See* TIROL

Tyrone Largest of the six counties of Northern Ireland, in the SW of the country. The county town is Omagh. Mainly hilly with the Sperrin Mountains in the N, and Bessy Bell and Mary Gray in the S, the region is drained by the Blackwater and Mourne rivers. Cereals and root crops are grown and dairy cattle are raised. Industries: linen, whiskey, processed food. Area: 3,263sq km (1,260sq mi). Pop. (1996) 161,800.

Uccello, Paolo (1397–1475) Florentine painter. Celebrated as an early master of PERSPECTIVE, his works include *The Flood* (*c*.1450) and *The Rout of San Romano* (1454–57).

Udaipur City on Lake Pichola, Rajasthan, NW India. In 1586 it was made capital of the princely state of Udaipur by Udai Singh. The walled city has three palaces. It is an agricultural market and a centre for textiles. Pop. (2001) 389,317.

Uffizi (It. 'offices') Chief public gallery in Florence, Italy, housing one of the best collections of Italian paintings. Giorgio VASARI built the palace in the 16th century for Grand Duke Cosimo I de' Medici, and it once housed government offices.

UFO Abbreviation of UNIDENTIFIED FLYING OBJECT

Uganda Landlocked republic in E Africa. *See* country feature.

Ugarit Ancient city in NW Syria. Inhabited as early as the 7th millennium BC it was a great commercial power, trading with Mesopotamia and Egypt. Excavations have revealed a vast palace from the 14th century BC and many large houses filled with treasures and artefacts.

UHF Abbreviation of ULTRA HIGH FREQUENCY

Ujjain City on the River Sipra, Madhya Pradesh, W central India. Ujjain is one of the seven holy cities of India, and a Hindu pilgrimage centre. Nearby are the ruins of an ancient city dating from the 2nd millennium BC. Pop. (2001) 429,933.

ukiyo-e Japanese paintings and woodblock prints that were prevalent in the Edo period (1615–1867). Their subject matter included people engaged in everyday activities as well as Kabuki actors. Moronobu (*c*.1625–95) is generally considered the originator of the true *ukiyo-e* print; he gained renown for his woodcut illustrations for popular literature. Other famous *ukiyo-e* printmakers were Harunobu, HIROSHIGE, HOKUSAI, Kiyonaga, Sharaku, and UTAMARO.

Ukraine Independent state in E Europe. *See* country feature, page 756

Ukrainian Language spoken by *c*.40–45 million people in Ukraine. Significant Ukrainian-speaking communities are to be found in Kazakhstan, Poland, Romania, Slovak Republic, and Siberian Russia. Like Russian and Belorussian, Ukrainian belongs to the E branch of the Slavic family of INDO-EUROPEAN LANGUAGES.

ukulele Small guitar, which developed in Hawaii from the Portuguese guitar. It is shaped like a classical guitar with a wooden body, round sound-hole and fretted fingerboard.

Ulan Bator (Ulaanbaatar, formerly Urga) Capital of Mongolia, on the River Tola. Ulan Bator dates back to the founding of the Lamaistic Temple of the Living Buddha in 1639. It grew as a stop for caravans between Russia and China. It was later a

U/u, 21st letter of the Roman alphabet. Like some other letters in the alphabet it is derived from the Semitic letter vaw, meaning hook. It was adopted by the Greeks before moving into the Roman alphabet.

UGANDA

The Republic of Uganda is landlocked on the East African Plateau. It contains part of Lake VICTORIA, which occupies a shallow depression in the plateau.

The plateau varies in height from *c*.1,500m [4,921ft] in the S to 900m [2,953ft] in the N. The highest mountain is Margherita Peak, at 5,109m [16,762ft] in the Ruwenzori Range in the SW. Other mountains, including Mount Elgon at 4,321m [14,177ft], rise along Uganda's E border.

Part of the Great African RIFT VALLEY, which contains lakes Edward and ALBERT, lies in W Uganda. The landscape ranges from rainforests in the S, through savanna in the centre, to semi-desert in the N.

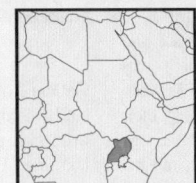

CLIMATE

The Equator runs through Uganda and the country is warm throughout the year, though the high altitude moderates the temperature. The lands to the N of Lake Victoria and the W mountains, especially the high Ruwenzori Range, are the wettest regions. Much of Uganda has two rainy seasons from April to May and October to December. In the centre

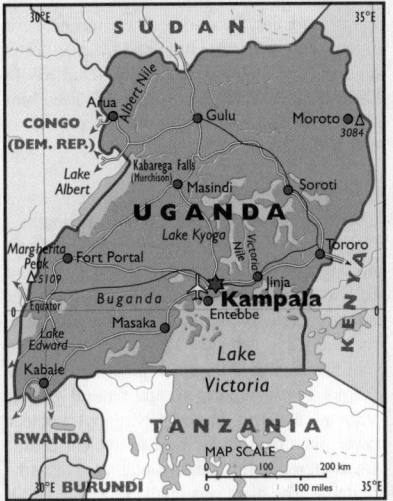

and the N these merge into one, with a distinct dry season.

HISTORY

In around 1500 the Nilotic-speaking Lwo people formced various kingdoms in SW Uganda, including Buganda (kingdom of the Ganda) and Bunyoro. During the 18th century the Buganda kingdom expanded and trade flourished. In 1862 a British explorer, John Speke, became the first European to reach Buganda. He was closely followed in 1875 by Sir Henry STANLEY. The conversion activities of Christian missionaries led to conflict with Muslims. The Kabaka (king) came to depend on Christian support. In 1892 Britain dispatched troops to Buganda, and in 1894 Uganda became a British Protectorate. Unusually, the colonial administration encouraged Asian, rather than European, settlers. African political representation remained minimal until after World War 2.

In 1962 Uganda gained independence with Buganda's Kabaka, Sir Edward Mutesa II, as president and Milton Obote as prime minister. In 1966 Mutesa II was forced into exile. Obote also abolished the traditional kingdoms, including Buganda. Obote was overthrown in 1971 in a military coup led by General Idi Amin Dada. Amin quickly established a personal dictatorship and launched a war against foreign interference that resulted in the mass expulsion of Asians. Amin's regime was responsible for the murder of more than 250,000 Ugandans. Obote loyalists resisted the regime from neighbouring Tanzania. In 1976 Amin declared himself president for life and Israel launched a successful raid on Entebbe Airport to end the hijack of one of its passenger planes. In 1978 Uganda annexed the Kagera region of NW Tanzania.

POLITICS

In 1979 Tanzania helped the Uganda National Liberation Front (UNLF) overthrow Amin and capture Kampala. In 1980 Apollo Milton Obote won national elections. After charges of fraud Obote's opponents, the National Resistance Movement (NRA), began guerrilla warfare.

AREA 241,038sq km [93,065sq mi]
POPULATION 30,263,000
CAPITAL (POPULATION) Kampala (1,345,000)
GOVERNMENT Republic
ETHNIC GROUPS Baganda 17%, Ankole 8%, Basogo 8%, Iteso 8%, Bakiga 7%, Langi 6%, Rwanda 6%, Bagisu 5%, Acholi 4%, Lugbara 4% and others
LANGUAGES English and Swahili (both official), Ganda
RELIGIONS Roman Catholic 33%, Protestant 33%, traditional beliefs 18%, Islam 16%
CURRENCY Ugandan shilling = 100 cents

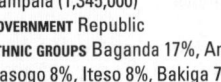

More than 200,000 Ugandans sought refuge in Rwanda and Zaïre. A military coup overthrew Obote in 1985. Strife continued until 1986, when the NRA captured Kampala and Yoweri Museveni became president. Museveni began to rebuild the economy and improve foreign relations.

In 1987 the Lord's Resistance Army (LRA) began a rebellion in the N. The government failed to suppress them or protect civilians from massacres and mutilations. The LRA abducted many children and forced them to serve as soldiers.

In 1996 Museveni claimed victory in Uganda's first direct presidential elections, though opposition groups were suppressed in this and subsequent polls. In 2005 the people voted to restore multiparty politics, but attacks on the opposition continued. LRA attacks spread to the E of the country. The year 2006 saw a ceasefire with the LRA, but a peace deal proved elusive.

ECONOMY

Stability was restored to the economy under President Museveni and it finally expanded. Agriculture dominates, employing 80% of the people. Food crops include bananas, cassava, maize, millet, sorghum and sweet potatoes, while the chief cash crops are coffee, cotton, sugar cane and tea. The only important metal is copper. The Owen Falls Dam, at Jinja on the outlet of Lake Victoria, produces cheap electricity.

focus for the Mongolian autonomy movement. It became the capital in 1921. It is the political, cultural and economic centre of Mongolia. Industries: textiles, building materials, leather, paper, alcohol, carpets, glassware. Pop. (2005) 842,000.

Ulanova, Galina (1910–98) Russian ballerina. In 1944, she became the prima ballerina of the BOLSHOI BALLET. Her skill in lyrical-dramatic interpretation and the purity and lightness of her classical style earned her international recognition. Her major roles include Lavrovsky's productions of *The Red Poppy*, *Giselle*, and *Romeo and Juliet*. In 1962, Ulanova retired and became a coach for the new generation of Bolshoi ballerinas.

Ulbricht, Walter (1893–1973) East German statesman, leader of East GERMANY (1950–71). A founder of the German Communist Party, Ulbricht was forced into exile by the rise of fascism, and he spent World War 2 in the Soviet Union. In 1949, he became deputy premier of the newly created German Democratic Republic (East Germany). In 1950, he became general secretary of the Communist Party. Ulbricht established close links with the Soviet Union. The repressive nature of his regime led to a rebellion in 1953; the BERLIN WALL was built (1961) to prevent further defections to the West. In 1971, he was replaced as general secretary by Erich HONECKER.

UKRAINE

Ukraine is the second largest country in Europe. The mostly flat country faces the Black Sea in the s. The Crimean Peninsula includes a highland region overlooking Yalta. The highest point of the country is in the E CARPATHIAN MOUNTAINS. The most extensive land region is the central plateau, which descends in the north to the Dnipro-Pripet Lowlands. A low plateau occupies the NE.

The enserfment of the peasantry and persecution of the Ukrainian Orthodox Church marked Polish rule. In 1648 refugees from Polish rule, the COSSACKS, completed Ukraine's liberation. Independence was short-lived due to the emerging power of Russia. A succession of wars resulted in the division of Ukraine into three Russian provinces in 1775. The nationalist movement was barely suppressed and found an outlet in GALICIA. Ukraine's industry developed from the 1860s.

In 1918, Ukraine declared independence and was invaded by the Red Army, which was repulsed with the support of the Central Powers, but the World War 1 armistice prompted their withdrawal. A unified, independent Ukraine was once more proclaimed. The Red Army invaded again, with greater success. In 1921 Poland took control of w Ukraine, and in 1922 E Ukraine became a constituent republic of the Soviet Union. In the 1930s Stalin's autocratic rule and agricultural collectivization caused between 3 and 6 million Ukrainians to die of famine. The 1939 Nazi-Soviet partition of Poland reunified the Ukraine. In 1940 it also acquired Northern Bukovina and part of Bessarabia from Romania.

In World War 2 the Ukraine was conquered by the Nazis, resulting in millions of deaths. It was recaptured by the Soviet Union in 1945 and gained Ruthenia from Hungary and E

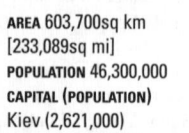

AREA 603,700sq km [233,089sq mi]
POPULATION 46,300,000
CAPITAL (POPULATION)
Kiev (2,621,000)
GOVERNMENT Multiparty republic
ETHNIC GROUPS Ukrainian 78%, Russian 17%, Belarusian, Moldovan, Bulgarian, Hungarian, Polish
LANGUAGES Ukrainian (official), Russian
RELIGIONS Mainly Ukrainian Orthodox
CURRENCY Hryvnia = 100 kopiykas

CLIMATE

Ukraine has warm summers, but the winters are cold, becoming more severe from w to E. In the summer, the E of the country is often warmer than the w. The heaviest rainfall occurs in the summer.

HISTORY

In ancient history the area was successively inhabited by Scythians and Sarmatians before invasions by the Goths, Huns, Avars, and Khazars. In the 9th century the Varangians united the N regions as Kievan Rus, with its capital at Kiev In the 13th century the empire disintegrated under the onslaught of the Mongol hordes. In the late 14th century, Ukraine became part of Lithuania. In 1478 the Black Sea region was absorbed into the Ottoman Empire. In 1569 the Lithuanian sector passed to Poland following the union of Poland with Lithuania.

Galicia from Poland. After 1945, all Ukrainian land was unified into a single Soviet republic. In 1954 the Crimea was annexed to the Ukraine. Ukraine became one of the most powerful republics in the Soviet Union, contributing 30% of total Soviet industrial output.

POLITICS

The country became independent when the Soviet Union broke up in 1991. Ukraine continued to work with Russia through the COMMONWEALTH OF INDEPENDENT STATES but differed with Russia on some issues, including control over Crimea. In 1999 Russia rejected a treaty confirming Ukraine's present boundaries.

Leonid Kuchma, who became president in 1994, came under fire in the 2000s for corruption and alleged involvement in a journalist's murder. In 2004 prime minister Victor Yanukovich, a supporter of Kuchma, was declared winner in presidential elections. After massive demonstrations, the election was declared invalid and re-run. Pro-Western opposition leader Victor Yuschenko was elected president, leading to tensions with Russia. Disputes with Russia over energy supplies followed. After inconclusive 2006 elections Yanukovich again became prime minister, and political instability returned. In 2007 elections Yulia Timoshenko replaced him as PM at the head of a pro-Western coalition.

ECONOMY

The World Bank classifies Ukraine as a 'lower-middle-income' economy. Agriculture is important, the major export crops are wheat and sugar beet. Livestock rearing and fishing are also important. Manufacturing is the chief economic activity and includes iron and steel, machinery and vehicles. The country has large coalfields and hydroelectric and nuclear power stations, but it imports oil and natural gas. In 1986 an accident at the Chernobyl nuclear power plant caused widespread nuclear contamination, rendering the surrounding area uninhabitable. The plant was finally closed in 2000.

ulcer Any persistent sore or lesion on the skin or on a mucous membrane, often associated with inflammation. Ulcers may be caused by infection, chemical irritation or mechanical pressure.

Ulm Industrial city on the River DANUBE, BADEN-WÜRT-TEMBERG, S Germany. Founded before 800, Ulm was an important political and commercial centre of medieval Europe. Industries: car manufacture, electrical goods, textiles, food products. Pop. (1999) 116,000.

ulna Long bone of the inner side of the forearm. At its upper end it articulates with the HUMERUS in the upper arm and with the RADIUS in the forearm.

Ulster Most northerly of Ireland's four ancient provinces, consisting of nine counties. Since 1922, six of these counties have been in Northern IRELAND, while Cavan, Donegal, and Monaghan form Ulster province in the Republic of IRELAND. Area: 8,012sq km (3,092sq mi). Pop. (2002) 246,571 (Republic).

Ulster Unionist Party Loyalist party in Northern IRELAND. It developed in the late 19th century to defend the six northern provinces of ULSTER from Irish home rule and to maintain the union with Britain. Almost exclusively Protestant, it was the ruling party in Northern Ireland from 1922 until the imposition of direct rule from Westminster in 1972.

ultra high frequency (UHF) RADIO waves in the frequency band 300–3,000MHz. UHF waves have a wavelength of *c.*1m (3ft) or less, and are used for television BROADCASTING.

ultrasonics Study of sound waves with frequencies beyond the upper limit of human hearing (above 20,000Hz). In medicine, ultrasonics are used to locate a tumour, to scan a pregnant woman's abdomen in order to produce a 'picture' of the fetus, and to treat certain neurological disorders. Other applications of ultrasonics include the agitation of liquids to form emulsions, detection of flaws in metals (the ultrasonic wave passed through a metal is reflected by a hairline crack), cleaning small objects by vibrating them ultrasonically in a solvent, echo sounding in deep water, and soldering aluminium.

ultraviolet radiation Type of ELECTROMAGNETIC RADIATION of shorter wavelength and higher frequency than visible light. Wavelengths range from four to 400nm (nanometres). Sunlight contains ultraviolet rays, most of which are filtered by the OZONE LAYER. If the ozone layer is weakened, enough ultraviolet can reach the ground to harm living things. Excessive exposure to sunlight can cause sunburn and skin cancer in people with fair skins. Ultraviolet is used medically to sterilize equipment. *See also* LIGHT; RADIATION

Ulysses *See* ODYSSEUS

Umayyads (Omayyads) Dynasty of Arabian Muslim caliphs (661–750). From their capital at DAMASCUS, the Umayyads ruled a basically Arab empire, which stretched from Spain to India. They made little effort to convert conquered peoples to Islam, but there was great cultural exchange, and Arabic became established as the language of Islam. They were overthrown by the ABBASIDS.

umbelliferae Family of flowering plants, all of which have many small flowers borne in umbrella-like clusters (umbels) at the ends of stalks. Umbellifers are mainly herbs and shrubs. Many species are edible, including CARROT, PARSLEY, CELERY, PARSNIP, FENNEL, and DILL.

umbilical cord Long cord that connects a developing FETUS with the PLACENTA. At birth, the cord is cut from the placenta, leaving a scar on the baby's abdomen known as the navel.

umbrella bird Any of three species of large tropical American birds, each with a retractile, black, umbrella-like crest, and a long, often tubular-shaped, feathered lappet (tuft) on the throat. The ornate umbrella bird (*Cephalopterus ornatus*) lives in trees and feeds on fruits. Family Cotingidae.

Umbria Region in central Italy comprising the provinces of Perugia and Terni; the capital is PERUGIA. The only landlocked region of Italy, it is traversed by the APENNINES and drained by the River TIBER. Cereal crops, grapes, and olives are grown, and cattle and pigs are raised. The medieval hilltowns scattered across the region attract tourists. Industries: iron and steel, chemicals, textiles, confectionery. Area: 8,456sq km (3,265sq mi). Pop. (1999) 832,675.

UN Abbreviation of the UNITED NATIONS

uncertainty principle In particle physics, principle stating that it is not possible to know both the position and the momentum of a particle at the same time, because the act of measuring would disturb the system. German physicist Werner HEISENBERG established the principle.

unconformity In geology, break in the time sequence of rocks layered one above the other. The gap may be caused by interruptions in the deposition of sediment, ancient erosion, earth movements, or other activity.

unconscious Term in psychology for that part of mental life believed to operate without the individual's immediate awareness or control. It includes memories that the person is not actually thinking about, and the organizing processes underlying speech and reading. In FREUD's analysis, it is the area containing the desires and conflicts of the ID. JUNG believed that part of the unconscious (the collective unconscious) contains inherited concepts, shared by all other human beings.

underground railway Transport system used in urban areas. The first underground railway opened in London in 1863. It was steam-powered and carried passengers between Farringdon and Paddington. Today, many cities throughout the world have underground, electrically powered railway systems for mass passenger transport.

unemployment Inability of workers who are ready, able and willing to work to find employment. Unemployment is usually expressed as a percentage of the labour force. **Cyclical** unemployment exists when the level of aggregate demand in the economy is less than that required to maintain full employment. **Structural** unemployment exists when jobs are available and workers are seeking jobs, but they cannot fill vacancies. **Technological** unemployment exists when workers are replaced by machines faster than they can find alternative employment. **Seasonal** unemployment occurs when workers are unable to find jobs at certain seasons of the year. **Underemployment** is inefficient use of labour (for example, an employer may keep unneeded workers on the payroll in order to have experienced help available when demand increases).

UNESCO Acronym for UNITED NATIONS EDUCATIONAL, SCIENTIFIC AND CULTURAL ORGANIZATION

ungulate MAMMAL with hoofed feet. Most ungulates, including cattle, sheep, pigs and deer, are members of the order Artiodactyla (with an even number of toes). The order Perissodactyla (ungulates with an odd number of toes) consists of horses, tapirs, and rhinoceroses. The orders Proboscidea and Hyracoidea, collectively known as sub-ungulates, contain elephants and hyraxes.

UNICEF Acronym for UNITED NATIONS CHILDREN'S FUND

unicorn In mythology and heraldry, a magical animal usually resembling a graceful horse with one thin conical or helical horn on its forehead.

unidentified flying object (UFO) Any flying object that observers fail to identify as either a man-made aircraft or a natural phenomenon. The majority of supposed UFO sightings are later shown to have mundane causes, such as spy planes, the planet Venus, optical floaters in the observer's eye, weather balloons, and artificial satellites. Despite a lack of evidence, the belief that UFOs represent visitors from space remains popular.

Unification Church International religious movement founded (1954) in South Korea by Sun Myung Moon. Its adherents are popularly known as Moonies. The movement's teachings are based on Moon's book *Divine Principle* (1952), which interprets the Bible. The movement aims to re-establish God's rule on Earth through the restoration of the family. The Unification Church is famous for its mass weddings and has been accused of CULT-like practices, such as brainwashing.

unified field theory Attempt to extend general RELATIVITY to give a simultaneous representation of both gravitational and electromagnetic fields. A more comprehensive theory would also include the STRONG and WEAK NUCLEAR FORCES. Although some success has been achieved in unifying the ELECTROMAGNETIC and weak nuclear forces, the general problem is still unsolved. *See also* GRAND UNIFIED THEORY (GUT)

Uniformity, Act of (1662) English Act of Parliament regulating the form of worship in the CHURCH OF ENGLAND after

INTERNET

Uccello, Paolo (page 755)
▸ musa.uffizi.firenze.it
▸ www.nationalgallery.org.uk
▸ www.louvre.fr

Uganda (page 755)
▸ www.government.go.ug
▸ www.myuganda.co.ug

Ukraine
▸ www.ukremb.com

U

the RESTORATION of the monarchy. It required all ordained clergy to follow the Book of COMMON PRAYER. The Act also required the clergy to repudiate the SOLEMN LEAGUE AND COVENANT, to forswear the taking up of arms against the Crown, and to adopt the liturgy of the Church of England.

Union, Acts of Series of acts uniting ENGLAND with WALES (1536) and SCOTLAND (1707), and Britain with IRELAND (1800). In addition, the 1841 Act of Union united French-speaking Lower CANADA and English-speaking Upper Canada. The Welsh Acts incorporated Wales within the kingdom of England, provided Welsh parliamentary representation and made English the official language. The Scottish Act united the Kingdoms of England and Scotland to form Great Britain. Scotland retained its legal system and Presbyterian Church. In accordance with the Irish Act, the Irish legislature was abolished, and Ireland was given 32 peers and 100 seats in the British Parliament. The established Churches of the two countries were united, and free trade was introduced. The Canadian Act led to the establishment of a Parliament for the province.

Union of Soviet Socialist Republics Official name for the SOVIET UNION

Unitarianism Version of CHRISTIANITY that denies the TRINITY, accepts God as the father, and rejects the divinity of JESUS CHRIST. Originally considered a heresy, it flourished in Poland in the 16th century. John Biddle (1615–62) first preached Unitarianism in England in the 1640s. Unitarianism in the 20th century has been identified with liberal politics and the movement for world peace; it has taken an increasingly humanist point of view.

United Arab Emirates (UAE) Federation of seven independent sheikhdoms on the Arabian peninsula. *See* country feature

United Kingdom (UK) Kingdom in w Europe. *See* country feature, pages 760–761

United Nations (UN) International organization set up to enable countries to work together for peace and mutual development. It was established (June 1945) by a charter signed in San Francisco by 50 countries. By 2000, the UN had 188 members, essentially all the world's sovereign states except for North and South Korea and Switzerland.

United Nations agencies Executive bodies operating on behalf of and responsible to the UNITED NATIONS (UN). They include: the FOOD AND AGRICULTURE ORGANIZATION (FAO, Rome); INTERNATIONAL ATOMIC ENERGY AGENCY (IAEA, Vienna); the International Civil Aviation Organization (ICAO, Montreal); INTERNATIONAL LABOUR ORGANIZATION (ILO, Geneva); International Maritime Organization (IMO) (IMO, London); INTERNATIONAL MONETARY FUND (IMF, Washington, D.C.); International Telecommunication Union (ITU, Geneva); United Nations' Conference on Trade and Development (UNCTAD, Geneva); UNITED NATIONS EDUCATIONAL, SCIENTIFIC AND CULTURAL ORGANIZATION (UNESCO, Paris); United Nations High Commission for Refugees (UNHCR, Geneva); UNITED NATIONS CHILDREN'S FUND (UNICEF, New York); Universal Postal Union (UPU, Bern); WORLD BANK (International Bank for Reconstruction and Development or IBRD, New York) and its own agencies – the International Development Association (IDA) and the International Finance Corporation (IFC); World Food Council (WFC, Rome); World Food Programme (WFP, Rome); WORLD HEALTH ORGANIZATION (WHO, Geneva); and the WORLD TRADE ORGANIZATION (WTO, Geneva). For internal administration in its main offices in New York, the United Nations has a Secretariat staffed by international personnel.

United Nations Children's Fund (UNICEF) Intergovernmental organization, agency of the UNITED NATIONS (UN). Founded in 1946 (as the United Nations International Children's Emergency Fund), its aim is to assist children and adolescents worldwide, particularly in war-devastated areas and developing countries.

United Nations Educational, Scientific and Cultural Organization (UNESCO) Intergovernmental organization, agency of the UNITED NATIONS (UN). Founded in 1945, it aims to promote peace by improving the world's standard

of education, and by bringing together nations in cultural and scientific projects. It also gives aid to developing countries.

United Nations peace-keeping force Military personnel and their equipment placed at the UNITED NATIONS' disposal by member states. The function of the force is to keep the peace between warring factions anywhere in the world, as requested by the UNITED NATIONS SECURITY COUNCIL. The first UN peace-keeping forces deployed in the Sinai Peninsula and Beirut in June 1948. The greatest deployment of UN peace-keeping forces was in Bosnia during the mid-1990s.

United Nations Security Council Council responsible for taking action against any nation or faction considered to be a threat to the security or continued wellbeing of a member state. Such action can be political, economic or, as a last resort, military. The Council also has the power to hold a formal investigation into matters of common concern. There are five permanent member states: the USA, UK, France, Russia, and China.

United States of America (USA) Federal republic of North America. *See* country feature, pages 762–763

units *See* WEIGHTS AND MEASURES

unit trust (mutual fund) Pooled form of investment, usually in the form of a portfolio of shares. The trust chooses and manages, through fund managers, a diverse range of securities. *See also* STOCK EXCHANGE

universal time System of time reckoning based on the mean solar day, the average interval between two successive transits of the Sun across the GREENWICH (0°) meridian.

universe Aggregate of all matter, energy, and space. On a large scale, the universe is uniform: it is identical in every part. It is believed to be expanding at a uniform rate, the GALAXIES all receding from one other. The origin, evolution, and future characteristics of the universe are considered in several cosmological theories. Recent developments in astronomy imply a finite universe, as postulated in the BIG BANG theory. In 1998 scientists discovered evidence that the Universe is expanding at an accelerating rate. *See also* COSMOLOGY; STEADY-STATE THEORY

university Institution of higher learning. Universities grew from the *studia generalia* of the 12th century, which provided education for priests and monks. In the 11th century, Bologna became an important centre of legal studies. Other great *studia generalia* were founded in the mid-12th century at Paris, OXFORD, and CAMBRIDGE. The first Scottish university was founded at St Andrews in *c.*1412; the first Irish university at Dublin (Trinity College) in 1591. The oldest US university is HARVARD, founded in 1636.

unnilquadium *See* DUBNIUM

unsaturated compound In organic chemistry, compound in which two or more carbon atoms are linked, or bonded together, with double or triple bonds. Simple examples are ETHENE and ETHYNE.

untouchables Fifth and lowest *varna* (class) of the Indian CASTE system, making up *c.*20% of India's population. The term arises from the belief among higher castes, such as BRAHMIN, that to touch *panchamas* amounts to ritual pollution or defilement. Although their pariah status and the resultant social injustice were legally abolished in India (1949) and Pakistan (1953), much discrimination remains. *See also* HINDUISM

Upanishads (Sanskrit, 'session') Texts of HINDUISM, constituting the final stage of Vedic literature. Written in prose and verse, they take the form of dialogues between teacher and pupil. They are of uncertain authorship and date from *c.*650 BC or earlier. Often referred to as the VEDANTA, the Upanishads speculate on reality and man's salvation. *See also* BRAHMANISM

Updike, John Hoyer (1932–) US writer. Updike is best known for his lyrical chronicles of Rabbit Angstrom, whose relationship crises often reflect contemporary social pressures. The tetralogy began with *Rabbit Run* (1960) and *Rabbit Redux* (1971). *Rabbit is Rich* (1981) won a Pulitzer Prize. *Rabbit at Rest* (1990) completed the series. Other novels, which explore sexuality and morality, include *Couples* (1968) and *The Witches of Eastwick* (1984, filmed 1987). A regular contributor to *New Yorker* magazine since 1955, Updike is a master of shorter prose, such as the essay collection *Hugging the Shore* (1984) and the short-story collection *Forty Stories* (1987).

U

Upper Volta Former name (until 1984) of BURKINA FASO

Uppsala (Upsala) Medieval city in E Sweden. Its university was founded in 1477. King Gustavus I (Vasa) is buried in the 15th-century Gothic cathedral. Industries: machinery, building materials, pharmaceuticals, printing, metal goods. Pop. (2000) 189,559.

Ur (Ur of the Chaldees) Ancient city of SUMERIA, S MESOPOTAMIA. Ur flourished in the 3rd millennium BC but SARGON I conquered it in c.2340 BC. The Akkadian period witnessed the integration of Semitic and Sumerian cultures. In c.2060 BC the great ziggurat was built by King Ur-Nammu. In c.2000 BC the invading Elamites destroyed much of the city. In the 6th century BC NEBUCHADNEZZAR briefly restored Ur as a centre of Mesopotamian civilization, but by the 5th century BC it was in terminal decline.

Urals Range of mountains in Russia, traditionally marking the boundary between Europe and Asia. The range extends 2,400km (1,500mi) from the Arctic in the N to the River Ural and the Kazakhstan frontier in the S. The mountains are extensively forested and the timber industry is important. The Urals' chief importance lies in their mineral deposits, which include iron ore, oil, coal, copper, nickel, gold, silver, zinc, and many precious stones. These resources have given rise to the Urals industrial region. Industrial development was increased under the first two Soviet five-year plans (1929–39) and during World War 2, when many industries were moved there from W Soviet Union. The highest peak is Mount Narodnaya, rising to 1894m (6214ft).

uraninite (pitchblende) Dense radioactive mineral form of uranium oxide, UO_2, the chief ore of URANIUM and the most important source for uranium and radium. The blackish, lustrous ore occurs in quartz veins. Hardness 5–6; r.d. 6.5–8.5.

uranium (symbol U) Radioactive, metallic element, one of the ACTINIDE SERIES. Discovered in 1789 by the German chemist Martin Klaproth, it is used in nuclear reactors and bombs. The isotope U^{238} makes up more than 99% of natural uranium. Chemically, uranium is a reactive metal; it oxidizes in air and reacts with cold water. Uranium-235 is fissionable and will sustain a neutron chain reaction as a fuel for reactors. Uranium is used to synthesize the TRANSURANIC ELEMENTS. Properties: at.no. 92; r.a.m. 238.029; r.d. 19.05; m.p. 1,132°C (2,070°F); b.p. 3,818°C (6,904°F); most stable isotope U^{238} (half-life 4.5110^9 years).

Uranus Seventh planet from the Sun, discovered (1781) by Sir William HERSCHEL. Uranus is visible to the naked eye under good conditions. Through a telescope it appears as a small, featureless, greenish-blue disc. Like all the giant planets, it possesses a ring system and a retinue of satellites. Like PLUTO, Uranus' axis of rotation is steeply inclined, and its poles spend 42 years in sunlight, followed by 42 years in darkness. Highly exaggerated seasonal variations are experienced by the planet and its satellites. The fly-by of the VOYAGER 2 probe in 1986 provides most of our knowledge of the planet. The upper atmosphere is about 83% molecular hydrogen, 15% helium, and the other 2% mostly methane. The five largest satellites were known before the Voyager encounter, which led to the discovery of 11 more. Nineteen of its 27 moons are regular satellites, orbiting in or close to Uranus' equatorial plane. They are all darkish bodies composed of ice and rock. The main components of Uranus' ring system were discovered in 1977, and others were imaged by Voyager.

Uranus In Greek mythology, the original god of the sky, and the husband and son of GAIA, with whom he was father to the TITANS and the CYCLOPES.

Urban II (c.1035–99) Pope (1088–99), b. Odo of Châtillon-sur-Marne. Urban carried on the reforms begun by GREGORY VII. In 1095, at the Council of Clermont, he proposed the First CRUSADE. His work as a reformer led to the development of the Curia Romana and the formation of the College of Cardinals.

URANUS: DATA

Diameter (equatorial): 51,118km (31,765mi)
Mass (Earth = 1): 14.6
Volume (Earth = 1): 67
Density (water = 1): 1.27
Orbital period: 84.01 years
Rotation period: 17h 14m 0s
Temperature at cloud tops: 55K
Surface gravity (Earth = 1): 0.79

UNITED ARAB EMIRATES

The United Arab Emirates (UAE) is a union of seven small Arab emirates (or sheikhdoms). Swamps and salt marshes border much of the coast in the N. The land is a flat, stony desert with occasional oases. Sand dunes occur in the E. Highlands rise in the E near the border with Oman. In the S the land merges into the bleak Rub' al Khali (Empty Quarter) of Saudi Arabia.

CLIMATE

In most of the country, the average annual rainfall is less than 130 mm [5 in], most of it occurring between November and March. In summer (May to September) temperatures can soar to 49°C [120°F], with high humidity along the coast where conditions can become unpleasant. Winters are warm to mild. The E highlands are generally cooler and rainier than the rest of the country. Sandstorms and duststorms are common.

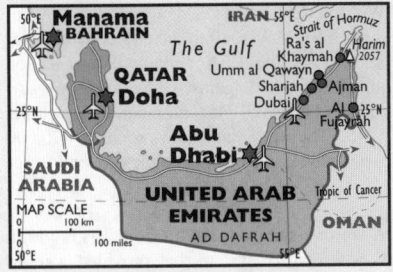

HISTORY

The area has its roots as a trading centre between the Mesopotamian and Indus Valley civilizations, later coming under Persian control and, in the 7th century AD, embracing Islam. In the 16th century various European nations set up coastal trading posts. The emirates of today began to develop in the 18th century. Their economies were based on pearl fishing and trading. In 1820 conflict between local rulers and piracy along the coast led Britain to force the states to sign a series of truces. Britain took control of the foreign affairs of the states, while promising protection from attack by outsiders. The states retained control over internal affairs. Because of these truces the region became known as the Trucial States. In 1952 the emirates set up a Trucial Council to increase co-operation between them. Oil was discovered in 1958 and first exported in 1962. In 1968 Britain announced the withdrawal of its forces.

POLITICS

The country became independent in 1971 when six of its seven states, Abu Zaby (ABU DHABI), Ajman, Dubayy (DUBAI), Al Fujayrah, Ash Shariqah (SHARJAH), and Umm-al-Qaywayn agreed to form a single country – the United Arab Emirates. A seventh state, Ras al Khaymah, joined the country in 1972. Each of the seven Emirates has its own Emir, who controls internal affairs. The federal government controls foreign affairs and defence and plays a leading role in the social and economic development of the country. The seven Emirs form a Federal Supreme Council, which elects the federation's president and vice-president who serve five-year terms. The president appoints the prime minister. The only elections, introduced in 2006, are for half the members of an advisory council with no direct powers. Despite this, the country is one of the most liberal and tolerant of the Persian Gulf countries. The UAE joined the allied force against Iraq in 1991 following the invasion of Kuwait, and the United States stationed forces there during the 2003 invasion of Iraq.

ECONOMY

The wealthy economy is based on oil production, and the country is a major oil exporter. In the 1990s and 2000s, oil revenues were invested in diversifying the economy. Dubai has become a tourist and financial centre, with many extravagant architectural landmarks.

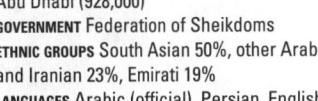

AREA 83,600sq km [32,278sq mi]
POPULATION 4,444,000
CAPITAL (POPULATION) Abu Dhabi (928,000)
GOVERNMENT Federation of Sheikdoms
ETHNIC GROUPS South Asian 50%, other Arab and Iranian 23%, Emirati 19%
LANGUAGES Arabic (official), Persian, English, Hindi, Urdu
RELIGIONS Muslim 96% (Shi'a 16%), others
CURRENCY Emirati dirham = 100 fils

U

The United Kingdom of Great Britain and Northern IRELAND is a union of four countries. Three of them – ENGLAND, SCOTLAND and WALES – make up Great Britain. The Isle of MAN and the CHANNEL ISLANDS, including Jersey and Guernsey, are not part of the UK but are instead self-governing British dependencies.

Much of Scotland and Wales is mountainous, and the highest peak is Scotland's Ben Nevis at 1,342m [4,404ft]. England has some highland areas, including the Cumbrian Mountains (Lake District) and the Pennine range in the N. England also has large areas of fertile lowland. Northern Ireland is a mixture of lowlands and uplands and contains the UK's largest lake, Lough Neagh.

CLIMATE

The UK has a mild climate, influenced by the warm Gulf Stream flowing across the Atlantic. Moist winds from the SW bring rain, which diminishes W to E. Winds from the E and N bring cold conditions in winter. The weather is markedly changeable, as low pressure systems over the Atlantic form weather fronts which pass rapidly over the country.

HISTORY

For early history, see separate country articles. In the late 17th century England's development of empire coincided with a financial revolution, which included the founding of the BANK OF ENGLAND (1694). Scotland was joined to England by the Act of Union in 1707, creating Great Britain. Sir Robert WALPOLE's prime ministership (1721–42) marked the beginnings of CABINET government. Great Britain emerged from the SEVEN YEARS' WAR (1756–63) as the world's leading imperial power. GEORGE III's conception of absolute monarchy and resistance to colonial reform led to conflict with Parliament and contributed to the AMERICAN REVOLUTION (1775–83). William PITT (THE YOUNGER) oversaw the creation of the United Kingdom of Great Britain and Ireland in 1801.

AREA 241,857sq km [93,381sq mi]
POPULATION 60,776,000
CAPITAL (POPULATION)
London (8,089,000)
GOVERNMENT Constitutional monarchy
ETHNIC GROUPS English 82%, Scottish 10%, Irish 2%, Welsh 2%, Ulster 2%, West Indian, Indian, Pakistani, others
LANGUAGES English (official), Welsh, Gaelic
RELIGIONS Christianity, Islam, Sikhism, Hinduism, Judaism
CURRENCY Pound sterling = 100 pence

The AGRICULTURAL REVOLUTION was both a cause and effect of the doubling of the population between 1801 and 1861, while the INDUSTRIAL REVOLUTION brought profound socioeconomic changes. The 1820s and 1830s saw new reform legislation, including the Act of CATHOLIC EMANCIPATION (1829), the abolition of SLAVERY (1833), harsh new POOR LAWS (1834) and the extension of the franchise to the middle classes in the REFORM ACTS. Sir Robert PEEL's repeal of the CORN LAWS (1846) marked the birth of FREE-TRADE and the emergence of the CONSERVATIVE PARTY from the old TORY PARTY. The LIBERAL PARTY similarly evolved out of the WHIG PARTY. CHARTISM marked the birth of a working-class movement.

The reign of VICTORIA saw the emergence of a second British Empire, spurred on by the imperial ambitions of Lord PALMERSTON. The importance of trade to the UK economy was firmly established. Between 1868 and 1880 Benjamin DISRAELI and William GLADSTONE dominated British politics, but the defeat of Gladstone's Home Rule Bill for Ireland in 1886 split the Liberal Party. Between 1908 and 1916 Herbert ASQUITH and David LLOYD GEORGE enacted a range of progressive social welfare policies, such as NATIONAL INSURANCE and state pensions. The growing power of Germany led the country into World War 1. GEORGE V changed the name of the British royal family from Saxe-Coburg to Windsor. The Allied victory cost more than 750,000 British lives. The UK faced rebellion in Ireland, and the Anglo-Irish Treaty (1921) confirmed the partition of Ireland. The Irish Free State emerged in 1922 and the UK officially became known as the United Kingdom of Great Britain and Northern Ireland. In 1924 Ramsay MACDONALD formed the first LABOUR PARTY government. The COMMONWEALTH OF NATIONS was founded in 1931. In 1936 EDWARD VIII abdicated in favour of GEORGE VI. Neville CHAMBERLAIN's policy of APPEASEMENT towards Nazi Germany ended in failure. On September 3 1939, after the German invasion of Poland, Britain declared war. Winston CHURCHILL led a coalition government from May 1940 to the end of World War 2. In 1941 the USA and the Soviet Union joined the battle against Hitler. Germany surrendered in May 1945, and Japan in September 1945. The war claimed more than 420,000 British lives, and devastated the economy.

POLITICS

A welfare state was set up from 1945, with a social security system that provided welfare

UNITED KINGDOM

for people 'from the cradle to the grave'. In 1960 the UK helped to set up the EUROPEAN FREE TRADE ASSOCIATION with six other nations. In 1963 Britain's request to join the EEC was rejected. The UK finally joined the EEC in 1973, although a strong body of opinion still feared that the development of a federal Europe would jeopardize British sovereignty. Membership was endorsed by a referendum in 1975 but, at the turn of the century, Britons were still debating whether it was advisable for Britain to adopt the euro – the single European currency adopted by 12 of the 15 European Union members in 1999.

Since the 1960s Northern Ireland has been the scene of conflict between the Protestant majority, who favour continuing union with the UK, and the Roman Catholic minority, many of whom are republicans who would like to see Ireland reunified. British troops were sent to the province in 1969 to control violence between the communities and, at various times, Britain has imposed direct rule. In 1998 the 'GOOD FRIDAY' AGREEMENT held out hope for the future, when unionists and nationalists agreed that Northern Ireland would remain part of the United Kingdom until a

majority of its people voted in favour of a change. The agreement also allowed the Republic of Ireland to play a consulting role in Northern Ireland, and the Republic amended its constitution to remove all claims to Northern Ireland. A Northern Ireland Assembly was set up to handle local affairs. In July 2005 the IRA declared that it had fully disarmed. Negotiations led, in 2007, to full power-sharing in the Northern Ireland Assembly.

Before 1999, Scotland and Wales were directly ruled by the British parliament in London. In 1997, following the landslide victory of the Labour Party under Tony BLAIR, 74% of voters in Scotland and 50.3% of voters in Wales opted for the set-up of local assemblies. The Scottish parliament is responsible for local affairs, with limited powers to raise or reduce taxes. The Welsh Assembly has no powers over taxation. Both met for the first time in 1999. DEVOLUTION has caused concern among those who fear that it might lead to the break-up of the UK. Regional elections in 2007 saw successes for pro-independence nationalists in both countries.

After the terrorist attacks on the United States in 2001 Britain was prominent in its

support for the US, joining the alliance that attacked the Taliban government of Afghanistan. Britain also joined the 2003 invasion of Iraq and subsequent occupation, despite public opposition. In July 2005 four suicide bombers struck in central London, killing 52 and injuring hundreds. In 2007 Tony Blair stepped down as Prime Minister and was succeeded by Gordon Brown.

ECONOMY

The UK is a major industrial and trading nation. Its natural resources are coal, iron ore, oil and natural gas, but it has to import most of the materials it needs for industry. It also has to import food. Since the 1980s traditional manufacturing has declined, while service industries have grown to dominate the economy. The rapid change has caused imbalances in employment. London is one of the world's leading centres of financial services. Tourism is an important sector.

Agriculture employs only 1% of the workforce. Production is high. Major crops include barley, potatoes, sugar beet and wheat. Sheep are the leading livestock, beef and dairy cattle, pigs and poultry are also important, as is fishing.

Urban V (*c*.1310–70) Pope (1362–70), b. Guillaume de Grimoard. Crowned at AVIGNON, he tried (in 1367) to return the papacy from Avignon to Rome. Insurrections at Rome and the Papal States forced him back to Avignon in 1370. As pope, he attempted to unite the Roman and Orthodox Churches.

Urban VI (1318–89) Pope (1378–89), b. Bartolomeo Prignano. The College of Cardinals declared his election invalid and appointed an ANTIPOPE, CLEMENT VII, thus beginning the GREAT SCHISM. Urban VI's papacy was marked by confusion and financial losses in the PAPAL STATES.

Urban VIII (1568–1644) Pope (1623–44), b. Maffeo Barberini. His reign coincided with much of the THIRTY YEARS' WAR. Fearing possible domination of the papacy by the HABSBURGS, he supported France and gave little help to German Roman Catholics. An active and knowledgeable patron of the arts, he also approved the establishment of new orders.

Urdu Language belonging to the Indic group of the Indo-Iranian sub-family of INDO-EUROPEAN LANGUAGES. It is the official language of Pakistan but is used as a first language by less than 10% of the population. It is also spoken by most Muslims in India. Urdu has virtually the same grammar as HINDI, the chief difference being that Urdu is written in the ARABIC script. Both derive from SANSKRIT.

urea (CO(NH$_2$)$_2$) Organic compound, a white, crystalline solid excreted in URINE. Most vertebrates excrete their nitrogen wastes as urea; human urine contains *c*.25 grams of urea to a litre. Because it is so high in nitrogen, urea is a good fertilizer.

ureter In vertebrates, the long, narrow duct that connects the KIDNEY to the urinary BLADDER. It transports URINE from the kidney to the bladder.

urethra Duct through which URINE is discharged from the bladder in MAMMALS. In males, the urethra is also the tube through which SEMEN is ejaculated.

urethritis Inflammation of the URETHRA. It is usually due to a SEXUALLY TRANSMITTED DISEASE but may also arise from infection.

Urey, Harold Clayton (1893–1981) US chemist. He received the 1934 Nobel Prize in chemistry for his isolation of DEUTERIUM, an isotope of hydrogen. Urey later isolated isotopes of oxygen, nitrogen, carbon, and sulphur. During World War 2, he helped in the research that led to the production of the atomic bomb. Urey then turned to GEOPHYSICS and worked on recreating the atmospheric conditions of the primeval Earth to elucidate the origin of life.

urine Fluid filtered out from the bloodstream by the KIDNEY. It consists mainly of water, salts, and waste products such as UREA. From the kidneys it passes through the URETERS to the BLADDER for voiding by way of the URETHRA.

urogenital system Organs comprising the body's urinary and reproductive systems. The urinary system consists of the KIDNEYS, URETERS, the BLADDER, and URETHRA. In males, the reproductive system consists of: paired TESTES located in the scrotum; accessory glands; and the PENIS. In females, the reproductive system consists of: paired OVARIES; Fallopian tubes, which provide a passage from the ovaries to the UTERUS; the CERVIX; and the VAGINA.

urology Medical speciality concerned with the diagnosis and treatment of diseases of the urinary tract in women and of the urinary and reproductive systems in men.

Ursa Major (Great Bear) Northern constellation, whose main pattern, consisting of seven stars, is known as the **Plough** or **Big Dipper**. Five of the Plough stars make up a CLUSTER.

Ursa Minor Constellation that contains the north celestial pole. Its brightest star is Alpha, the POLE STAR. The constellation's seven main stars make a pattern resembling a faint and distorted plough.

Ursula, Saint (active 4th century AD) Legendary virgin and martyr who, according to some traditions, was a British princess. She was especially honoured at Cologne, where she is said to have been slain by the HUNS with her 11 (or in some reports 11,000) virgins on their return from a pilgrimage to Rome. She became the patron Saint of many educational establishments, including the Ursuline order.

Uruguay Republic in South America; the capital is MONTEVIDEO. *See* country feature page 764.

Uruguay River in SE South America. Rising in S Brazil and forming part of the boundary between Rio Grande do Sul and Santa Catarina states, it flows SW to form the boundary between Argentina and S Brazil, and then Argentina and Uruguay. It empties into the Río de la PLATA. Length: *c*.1,600km (1,000mi).

USA Abbreviation of UNITED STATES OF AMERICA

USSR Abbreviation of Union of Soviet Socialist Republics, *see* SOVIET UNION

Ustinov, Peter Alexander (1921–2004) British actor and dramatist. His plays include *The Love of Four Colonels* (1951) and *Romanoff and Juliet* (1956). He acted in many films, including *Billy Budd* (1962), which he also directed. In later years, Ustinov won a reputation as an entertaining raconteur.

▲ **Ustinov** Of French and Russian parentage, Peter Ustinov was born in London. A successful actor and playwright, in later years he became best known for his one-man shows, which provided him with the opportunity to portray a variety of characters.

U

The United States of America is the world's fourth largest country in area and the third largest in population. It contains 50 states, 48 of which lie between Canada and Mexico. The other two are ALASKA, in NW North America, and HAWAII, a group of volcanic islands in the N Pacific Ocean.

Densely populated coastal plains lie toe the E and S of the Appalachian Mountains. The central lowlands drained by the Mississippi-Missouri rivers stretch from the Appalachians to the Rocky Mountains in the W. The Pacific region contains fertile valleys separated by mountain ranges.

CLIMATE

The climates of the United States vary greatly, ranging from the Arctic conditions in northern Alaska, where average temperatures plummet to –13°C [9°F], to the intense heat of DEATH VALLEY. which holds the record for the highest shade temperature ever recorded in the United States at 57°C [134°F].

The Midwest, New England and the Middle Atlantic States experience cold winters and warm summers. By contrast, the southern states have long, hot summers and mild, wet winters. In the central United States a lack of topographical features allows the N movement of hot, moist air from the Gulf of Mexico, and in winter the S movement of dry, cold air from the Arctic. These air masses produce contrasts of climate, exacerbated by storms, blizzards and tornadoes. Parts of California have a pleasant Mediterranean-type climate, but the mountains of the W are much cooler and wetter. The central plains are arid, while deserts occur in parts of the W and SW.

HISTORY

NATIVE AMERICANS arrived from Asia more than 10,000 years ago. VIKINGS, led by LEIF ERICSSON, probably reached North America c.1000 AD but did not settle. European exploration did not begin until the discovery of the New World by Christopher COLUMBUS in 1492. In 1565, Spain built the first permanent European settlement at St Augustine, Florida. The French also formed settlements in LOUISIANA, but the first major colonists were the British, who founded JAMESTOWN, Virginia, in 1607. In 1620 PURITANS landed at Cape Cod, Massachusetts, and founded the PLYMOUTH COLONY. The economic success of Massachusetts encouraged further colonization along the E coast; the S colonies developed a plantation economy based on SLAVERY. In the 18th century, British MERCANTILISM (especially the NAVIGATION ACTS) restricted commercial growth. The defeat of the French in the FRENCH AND INDIAN WARS (1754–63) encouraged independence movements. Benjamin FRANKLIN's failure to win concessions from the British led to the AMERICAN REVOLUTION (1775–83), which ended British rule in the THIRTEEN COLONIES.

George WASHINGTON became the first president. The ARTICLES OF CONFEDERATION (1777) produced weak central government, and were superseded by the CONSTITUTION OF THE UNITED STATES (1787). The BANK OF THE UNITED STATES opened in 1791. US politics became divided between the FEDERALIST PARTY and the DEMOCRATIC REPUBLICAN PARTY. Federalist

President John ADAMS passed the ALIEN AND SEDITION ACTS (1798) and the XYZ AFFAIR saw armed confrontation with France.

In 1801, the Democratic-Republican Thomas JEFFERSON became president. He negotiated the LOUISIANA PURCHASE (1803). James MADISON led the USA into the WAR OF 1812, which cemented the nation's independence and culminated in the MONROE Doctrine (1823) to protect the Western Hemisphere from European interference. The MISSOURI COMPROMISE (1820) papered over the growing conflict between North and South over slavery. The Democratic-Republican Party became simply the DEMOCRATIC PARTY. Andrew JACKSON furthered the westward expansion of the FRONTIER. In 1841 William HARRISON became the first WHIG president. Texas and Oregon Territory were acquired in 1845-6. The MEXICAN WAR (1846–48) confirmed US acquisitions. The 1848 discovery of gold in Californi led to a rush of settlers. Territorial expansion was achieved at the expense of Native Americans, who were forced onto reservations.

The addition of states to the Union intensified the conflict between free and slave states. The repeal of the Missouri Compromise led to the founding of the anti-slavery REPUBLICAN PARTY (1854). In 1861, Abraham LINCOLN became the first Republican president. The southern states seceded as the CONFEDERATE STATES OF AMERICA. The American CIVIL WAR (1861–65) claimed more than 600,000 lives and devastated the country. Union victory resulted in the abolition of slavery. The RECONSTRUCTION of the South was unpopular, and corruption plagued the administration of Ulysses S. GRANT. In 1867 the USA bought Alaska from Russia. The late 19th century was the era of the railroad, which sped industrialization and urban development. Millions of European immigrants flocked to the USA.

The SPANISH-AMERICAN WAR (1898) heralded the emergence of the USA as a major world power. Construction of the PANAMA CANAL began in 1902. In 1917 Woodrow WILSON led the USA into World War 1. Economic boom and PROHIBITION preceded the GREAT DEPRESSION of the 1930s. Franklin D. ROOSEVELT's NEW DEAL attempted to restore prosperity. Japan's bombing of PEARL HARBOR on December 7,

The highest mountain in the USA is Mount McKinley (6194m) in Alaska.

MAP SCALE

| 0 | 250 | 500 km |

| 0 | 250 miles | |

Alaska and Hawaii are states of the USA.

U

1941, brought the USA into World War 2. Rearmament fuelled economic recovery. Harry S. TRUMAN became president on Roosevelt's death in 1945. The use of atomic bombs led to Japan's surrender. The USA was a founder member of NATO. Post-war tension with the Soviet Union led to the COLD WAR and spurred the space race.

POLITICS

The United States has long played a leading role in industrial, economic, social and technological innovation, and the majority of Americans continue to enjoy one of the world's highest material standards of living. At the same time, the country faces many problems. One concerns the maintenance of social cohesion as the composition of American society changes. Another is the issue of poverty and the low standards of living of a sizeable underclass of poor and inadequately educated people, many of whom are members of ethnic minorities. Associated problems include crime, drug addiction and racial conflict.

The United States has one of the most diverse populations of any country in the world. Until about 1860, the population, with the exception of the Native Americans and African slaves, was made up largely of immigrants of British and Irish origin. However, after the Civil War, increasing numbers of immigrants arrived from the countries of central and south-eastern Europe. This vast influx of Europeans, c.30 million between 1860 and 1920, was vastly different in culture and language from the established population. More recently, the country has received lesser influxes of Japanese, Chinese, Filipinos, Cubans, Puerto Ricans, and large numbers of Mexicans. The English language was readily adopted by most immigrants in the late 19th and early 20th century, because they sought acceptance in the 'melting pot' that makes up the United States; however, many of the recent Hispanic immigrants persist in speaking Spanish, which has become the country's second language. Many Americans are concerned about this trend towards 'cultural pluralism'.

From the 1890s, the United States developed into a world power, and played a leading role in international affairs throughout the 20th century. It played a key role in both World Wars; after the second, the US and Soviet Union had become the world's sole superpowers. After World War 2, the US led the West into the COLD WAR with

AREA 9,629,091sq km
[3,717,792sq mi]
POPULATION 301,140,000
CAPITAL (POPULATION)
Washington, DC (3,934,000)
GOVERNMENT Federal republic
ETHNIC GROUPS White 77%, African American 13%, Asian 4%, Amerindian 2%, others
LANGUAGES English (official), Spanish, more than 30 others
RELIGIONS Protestant 56%, Roman Catholic 28%, Islam 2%, Judaism 2%
CURRENCY US dollar = 100 cents

the Soviet Union. After the fall of communism in 1991, the United States faced new threats from terrorism. Disputed 2000 elections made the Republicans' George Walker BUSH president, though with little popular support.

September 2001 saw terrorist attacks on New York City and Washington, DC. Al-QAEDA terrorists claimed responsibility, and the US led a coalition force to depose the Taliban regime in Afghanistan, which it accused of protecting them. In 2003 the US led another coalition force to swiftly overthrow the repressive regime of Saddam Hussein in Iraq, but the subsequent occupation proved troubled and costly. George W. Bush was re-elected in 2004. Discontent with the occupation of Iraq led to the opposition Democrats gaining control of both Congress and the House of Representatives in 2006 elections.

ECONOMY

The spread of prosperity generated new consumer industries to satisfy demands of a large middle class for ever-increasing standards of comfort. The United States was a pioneer of large-scale industrial production. With almost every raw material available within its own boundaries, or readily gained through trading, its mining and extractive industries have been heavily exploited. Brown coal from eastern Pennsylvania and bituminous and coking coals from the Appalachians, Indiana, Illinois, Colorado and Utah are still in demand, and vast reserves remain.

Oil, first drilled in Pennsylvania in 1859, was subsequently found in several major fields underlying the Midwest, the E and central mountain states, the Gulf of Mexico, California and Alaska. Home consumption of petroleum products has grown steadily. Although the United States is a major producer, it is also by far the world's greatest consumer and has long been a net importer of oil. In the Gulf Coast states, the exploitation of oil in Oklahoma, Texas and Louisiana has shifted the former dependence on agriculture to the refining and petrochemical industries. Oil has transformed Dallas-Fort Worth into a major conurbation, while Denver has changed from a small railhead town into a wealthy state capital. Natural gas is also found in abundance, usually associated with oil.

Agriculture employs only 2.4% of the labour force. The US has become a leading producer of meat, dairy products, soya beans, maize, oats, wheat, barley, cotton, sugar and many other crops. The W plains are the main centres of production. Much of the land farmed by the Pilgrim Fathers and other settlers is now built over, or has reverted to forest.

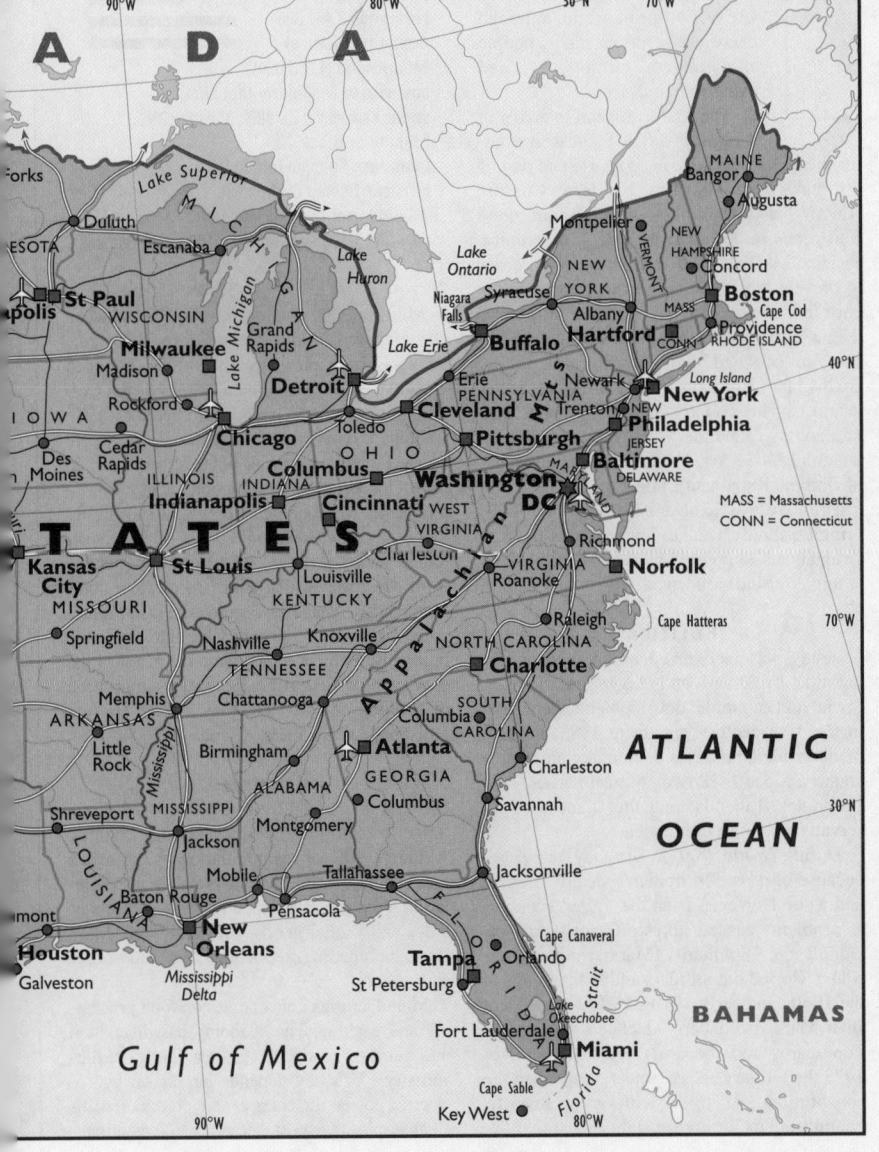

usury Lending of money at an excessive or unlawful rate of interest. Before the Middle Ages, any payment for the borrowing of money was regarded as usury by Christians. In the late Middle Ages, reasonable interest on a loan became acceptable when the lender risked capital.

Utah State in the w USA in the ROCKY MOUNTAINS; the state capital is SALT LAKE CITY, other cities include Provo and Ogden. The region was ceded to the USA at the end of the MEXICAN WAR in 1848, and Utah was admitted to the Union in 1896. The influence of the MORMON Church is strong in the state, and in 1857–58 there were conflicts between federal troops and the Mormons. In the N the Wasatch Range separates the mountainous E from the Great Basin, which includes the GREAT SALT LAKE. The arid climate hinders agriculture, but hay, barley, wheat, beans, and sugar beet grow with the aid of irrigation. The chief farming activity is stock raising. Mining is also important: there are rich deposits of copper, petroleum, coal, molybdenum, silver, lead, and gold. With many national parks and monuments, tourism is vital to the economy. Area: 219,931sq km (84,915sq mi). Pop. (2000) 2,233,169.

Utamaro, Kitagawa (1753–1806) Japanese master of the UKIYO-E woodblock colour print, the first Japanese artist to become famous in the West. Utamaro excelled in depicting birds, flowers, and feminine beauty. His works were strongly erotic, precise, graceful, and immensely popular.

Ute Shoshonean-speaking tribe of Native North Americans. They were fierce, nomadic warriors, who engaged in warfare with other Native American tribes and hunted bison. Today, c.4,000 live on reservations in Colorado and Utah.

uterus (womb) Hollow muscular organ located in the pelvis of female mammals. It protects and nourishes the growing FETUS until birth. The upper part is broad and branches out on each side into the FALLOPIAN TUBES. The lower uterus narrows into the CERVIX, which leads to the VAGINA. Its muscular walls are lined with ENDOMETRIUM (mucous membrane), to which the fertilized egg attaches itself. *See also* MENSTRUAL CYCLE

utilitarianism Branch of ethical philosophy. It holds that actions are to be judged good or bad according to their consequences. An action is deemed to be morally right if it produces good results. English philosophers Jeremy BENTHAM, James MILL, and J.S. MILL developed the philiosophy of utilitarianism during the late-18th and 19th centuries.

Uto-Aztecan languages Family of NATIVE AMERICAN languages spoken in sw USA and Mexico. It includes

URUGUAY

The Oriental Republic of Uruguay, as Uruguay is officially known, is South America's second smallest independent nation after Suriname. The River URUGUAY, which forms the country's w border, flows into the Río de la PLATA (River Plate), a large estuary fringed with lagoons and sand dunes which leads into the South Atlantic Ocean.

The land consists mainly of low-lying plains and hills. The highest point lies s of Minas and is only 501m [1,644ft] above sea level. The main river in the interior is the Rio Negro.

CLIMATE

Uruguay has a mild climate, with rain throughout the year, though droughts sometimes occur. The summer is pleasantly warm, especially near the coast. The weather remains relatively mild in winter.

HISTORY

The first people of Uruguay were Amerindians, but the Amerindian population has largely disappeared. Most were killed by Spanish

settlers or died of imported diseases to which they had no resistance. Most Uruguayans today are of European origin, although there are some *mestizos*, people of mixed European and Amerindian descent.

The first European to arrive in Uruguay was a Spanish navigator, Juan Diaz de Solis, in 1516. He and part of his crew were killed by the local Charrúa Amerindians when they went ashore. Few Europeans settled until the late 17th century. Spanish settlers founded Montevideo in order to prevent the Portuguese from gaining influence in the area. Uruguay was then little more than a buffer zone between the Portuguese territory to the N and Spanish territories to the w. By the late 18th century, Spaniards had settled in most of the country. Uruguay became part of a colony called the Viceroyalty of La Plata, which included Argentina, Paraguay, and parts of Bolivia, Brazil and Chile.

Uruguay was annexed by Brazil in 1820, bringing about an end to Spanish rule. In 1825 Uruguayans, supported by Argentina, began a struggle for independence.

POLITICS

Uruguay was recognized as an independent republic by Brazil and Argentina in 1828. Social and economic developments were slow in the 19th century but, from 1903, governments made Uruguay a democratic and stable country. Since 1828 two political parties – the Colorados (Liberals) and the Blancos (Conservatives) – have dominated.

During World War 2 Uruguay prospered because of its export trade, especially in meat and wool. However, from the 1950s, economic problems caused unrest. Terrorist groups, notably the Tupumaros (Marxist urban guerrillas), carried out murders and kidnappings in the 1960s and early 1970s. In 1972 President Juan Maria Bordaberry declared war on the Tupumaros and the army crushed them. In 1973 the military seized power, suspended the constitution and ruled with great severity, committing major human rights abuses.

AREA 175,016sq km [67,574sq mi]
POPULATION 3,461,000
CAPITAL (POPULATION) Montevideo (1,353,000)
GOVERNMENT Multiparty republic
ETHNIC GROUPS White 88%, Mestizo 8%, Mulatto or Black 4%
LANGUAGES Spanish (official)
RELIGIONS Roman Catholic 66%, Protestant 2%, Judaism 1%
CURRENCY Uruguayan peso = 100 centésimos

Military rule continued until 1984, when elections were held. General Gregorio Alvarez, who had been president since 1981, resigned and Julio Maria Sanguinetti, leader of the Colorado Party, became president in February 1985 leading a government of National Unity. He ordered the release of all political prisoners. In the 1990s Uruguay faced problems in trying to rebuild its weakened economy and shoring up its democratic traditions. In 1991 Uruguay joined with Argentina, Brazil and Paraguay to form Mercosur, which aimed to create a common market. Mercosur's secretariat is in Montevideo. The early 21st century brought economic problems, many of which were the result of the economic crisis in Argentina and its imposition of banking controls. Uruguay elected its first leftist president, Tabare Vasquez, in 2004.

ECONOMY

Uruguay is classed by the World Bank as an 'upper-middle-income' developing country. Although 90% of the population live in urban areas and agriculture employs 3% of the population, the economy depends on the exports of hides and leather goods, beef and wool. Main crops include maize, potatoes, rice, sugar beet and wheat.

Manufacturing concentrates on food processing and packing. The economy has diversified into cement, chemicals, leather goods, textiles and steel. Uruguay depends largely on hydroelectric power for energy, and produces sufficient surplus to export electricity to Argentina.

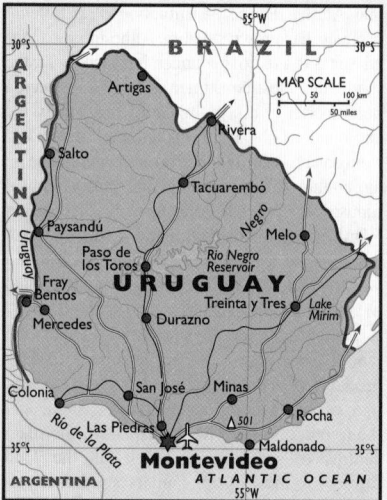

COMANCHE (Oklahoma) and SHOSHONE, spoken in some w states. In Mexico, it includes NAHUATL (the language of the Aztecs), Tarahumara, and Mayo.

utopianism (Gk. 'no place') Projection of ideal states or alternative worlds, ordered for the benefit of all and where there exist no social ills. Sir Thomas MORE's *Utopia* (1516) outlines his notion of an ideal commonwealth based entirely on reason. It critically describes contemporary social existence, while prescribing a transcendent, imaginative vision of the best of all possible worlds. ENLIGHTENMENT philosophers, such as Jean Jacques ROUSSEAU, portrayed a vision of a pre-feudal European 'golden age'. Other writers, such as Saint-Simon, Charles Fourier, and Robert Owen, outlined ideal communities based on cooperation and economic self-sufficiency. Karl MARX and Friedrich ENGELS valued the satirical social insights of utopianism but rejected its unscientific analysis of political and economic realities. By the late 19th century, the utopian novel was an established literary genre. Works such as *Erewhon* (1872) by Samuel BUTLER were popular and influential. The spread of totalitarianism in Europe during the 1930s encouraged **dystopian** novels, such as *Brave New World* (1932) by Aldous HUXLEY and *1984* (1949) by George ORWELL.

Utrecht City on the Oude Rijn River, central Netherlands. Utrecht is the fourth-largest city in the Netherlands. It has been a trading centre since medieval times. It was the scene of the Peace of UTRECHT (1713). The old city includes the 14th-century St Martin's Cathedral. Utrecht is a major cultural, financial and rail centre. Industries: steel, machinery, textiles, electrical equipment. Pop. (2001) 256,202.

Utrecht, Peace of (1713–14) Series of treaties that ended the War of the SPANISH SUCCESSION. It confirmed the BOURBON King PHILIP V on the Spanish throne, on condition that he renounced any claim to the throne of France. Austria received the Spanish Netherlands and extensive Italian territories; Britain gained Gibraltar, Minorca, and provinces of E Canada.

Uttar Pradesh State in N India, bordering Nepal and Tibet; the capital is LUCKNOW. The heartland of early HINDUISM, it is the hub of India's Hindi-speaking region and is by far the most populous Indian state. The region has the foothills of the Himalayas to the N and hills in the S, enclosing a low-lying plain drained by the GANGES and its tributaries. In 2000 the state of Uttaranchal was created out of part of Uttar Pradesh. The economy is based on agriculture, mainly cereals, sugar cane, rice and pulses, and the mining of coal, copper, bauxite and limestone. Industries: cotton and sugar processing. Area: 240,928sq km (93,022sq mi). Pop. (2001) 166,052,859.

Uzbekistan Republic in central Asia; the capital is TASHKENT. *See* country feature.

Uzbeks Turkic-speaking people, originally of Iranian culture, who form 71% of the population of UZBEKISTAN. They took their name from Uzbeg Khan (d.1340), a chief of the GOLDEN HORDE. By the end of the 16th century, the Uzbeks had extended their rule to parts of Persia, Afghanistan and Chinese Turkistan. Their empire was never united, and in the 19th century its states were absorbed by Russia.

UTAH
Statehood :
January 4, 1896
Nickname :
The Beehive State
State bird :
Sea gull
State flower :
Sego lily
State tree :
Blue spruce
State motto :
Industry

UZBEKISTAN

The Republic of Uzbekistan is one of five republics in Central Asia which were once part of the Soviet Union. Plains cover most of w Uzbekistan, with highlands in the east. The main rivers, the Amu (or Amu Darya) and Syr (or Syr Darya), drain into the ARAL SEA. So much water has been taken from these rivers for irrigation that the Aral Sea is now only a quarter of its size in 1960. Much of the former sea is now desert.

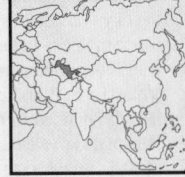

AREA 447,400sq km [172,741sq mi]
POPULATION 27,780,000
CAPITAL (POPULATION)
Tashkent (2,160,000)
GOVERNMENT Socialist republic
ETHNIC GROUPS Uzbek 80%, Russian 5%, Tajik 5%, Kazakh 3%, Tatar 2%, Kara-Kalpak 2%
LANGUAGES Uzbek (official), Russian
RELIGIONS Islam 88%, Eastern Orthodox 9%
CURRENCY Uzbekistani sum = 100 tiyin

century. Following the RUSSIAN REVOLUTION (1917), the communists took over, establishing the Uzbek Soviet Socialist Republic in 1924. Under communism, all aspects of Uzbek life were regulated; religious worship was discouraged, but education, health, housing and transport services improved. In the 1980s, when the Soviet Union introduced reforms, Uzbeks demanded greater freedoms. In 1990 the Uzbek government declared that its laws overruled those of the Soviet Union.

CLIMATE

Uzbekistan has a continental climate. Winters are cold, but temperatures soar in the summer. In the w conditions are extremely arid, with an average annual rainfall of about 200mm [8in].

HISTORY

Uzbekistan lies on the ancient Silk Road between Europe and Asia. Turkic people first settled in the area c.1500 years ago. Islam was introduced in the 7th century AD. MONGOLS invaded in the 13th century, and in the late 14th century TAMERLANE ruled a great empire from SAMARKAND. Turkic Uzbek people conquered the region in the 16th century, and gradually the area divided into states known as khanates. Russia took control of the area in the 19th

POLITICS

Uzbekistan became independent in 1991 with the break-up of the Soviet Union, but retained links with Russia through the COMMONWEALTH OF INDEPENDENT STATES. It subsequently pulled out, as it opposed closer integration on post-Soviet territory.

Islam Karimov, leader of the People's Democratic Party (formerly the Communist Party), was elected president in December 1991. In 1992–3 many opposition leaders were arrested, the government claiming that they threatened national stability. In 1994-5 the PDP claimed victory in flawed national elections, and in 1995 a referendum extended Karimov's term in office until 2000. In 2000 he again claimed victory in unfair elections.

In 2001 Karimov declared Uzbekistan's support for the United States in its campaign against the terrorist al-QAEDA bases in Afghanistan. He sought US favour by allowing American forces to construct a base on Uzbek territory. Due to the country's poor record on human rights the European Bank for Reconstruction and Development announced in 2004 that it would cut aid to Uzbekistan.

Recent years have seen bombings and shootings, which the authorities have blamed on Islamic extremists. In 2005 protests against the jailing of several people charged with Islamic extremism in the city of Andijan turned to violence, with troops opening fire. Several hundred civilians were killed.

Karimov accused fundamentalists of aiming to destabilize the country, but his opponents blamed Karimov's determination to crush all dissent and maintain a repressive state. There were calls for an international inquiry which the government rejected, as a result of which the US reduced aid. Uzbekistan reacted by ordering US forces to leave their base in the country. A sham election in 2007 extended Karimov's term in office beyond the constitutional maximum.

ECONOMY

The World Bank classifies Uzbekistan as a 'lower-middle-income' developing country. The government still controls most economic activity and economic reform has been very slow. Uzbekistan produces coal, copper, gold, oil and natual gas, while manufacturing industries include agricultural machinery, chemicals and textiles. Agriculture is important, with cotton the main cash crop. Soviet-era drives to increase production resulted in widespread environmental damage. Other crops include fruits, rice and vegetables; cattle, sheep and goats are raised.

U

V/v, 22nd letter of the Roman alphabet, derived (as were f, u and y) from the Semitic letter vaw, meaning hook. It was identical to u in the Greek and Roman alphabets, and was not differentiated from u in English until the Middle Ages.

V-weapons (abbreviation for *Vergeltungswaffen*, vengeance weapons) Series of early guided missiles used by Germany in the closing stages of World War 2. V-1s, popularly known as **flying bombs**, were pilotless aircraft, powered by a pulse-jet engine and were the precursors of modern CRUISE MISSILES. Launched by the LUFTWAFFE against SE England in June 1944, they carried about one tonne of high explosive but were inaccurate and could be intercepted by British fighters. The V-2 rocket was a technological revolution, a long-range liquid-fuelled rocket carrying a one-tonne warhead to a range of 320km (200mi). Reaching 95–110km (60–70mi), they were the first man-made objects to enter space and were the ancestors of all modern ballistic MISSILES and space rockets.

vaccination Injection of a VACCINE in order to produce IMMUNITY against a disease. In many countries, children are routinely vaccinated against infectious diseases.

vaccine Agent used to give IMMUNITY against various diseases without producing symptoms. A vaccine consists of modified disease organisms, such as live, weakened VIRUSES, or dead ones that are still able to induce the production of specific ANTIBODIES within the blood. *See also* IMMUNE SYSTEM

vacuole Membrane-bound, fluid-filled cavity within the CYTOPLASM of a CELL. Vacuoles perform various functions including the discharge of wastes from cell metabolism.

vacuum Region of extremely low pressure. Interstellar space is a high vacuum, with an average density of less than 1 molecule per cubic centimetre; the highest man-made vacuums contain less than 100,000 molecules per cubic centimetre. The common laboratory device for reducing pressure in a container is a **vacuum pump**. Italian physicist Evangelista Torricelli is credited with developing (1643) the first man-made vacuum in a mercury BAROMETER.

vacuum flask Container for keeping things (usually liquids) hot or cold. A vacuum flask consists of double, silvered glass walls, separated by a near VACUUM. This vessel is held in an insulated metal or plastic case. The vacuum reduces heat transfer by CONDUCTION of CONVECTION between the contents and the surroundings. The silvering on the glass minimizes heat transfer by radiation. James DEWAR invented the vacuum flask in 1892.

vagina Portion of the female reproductive tract, running from the CERVIX of the UTERUS to the exterior of the body. Tube-like in shape, it receives the PENIS during sexual intercourse. Its muscular walls enable it to dilate during LABOUR.

valence (valency) Measure of the 'combining power' of a particular element, equal to the number of single CHEMICAL BONDS one atom can form, or the number of electrons it gives up or accepts when forming a compound. Hydrogen has a valency of 1, carbon 4, and sulphur 2, as seen in compounds such as methane (CH_4), carbon disulphide (CS_2), and hydrogen sulphide (H_2S). *See also* ATOMIC NUMBER; COVALENT BOND; IONIC BOND

Valencia City in E Spain, capital of the province of Valencia, situated on the River Turia. The region of Valencia comprises the provinces of Alicante, Castellón, and Valencia. Originally settled by the Romans, the city was conquered by the MOORS in the 8th century, eventually becoming capital of the independent Moorish kingdom of Valencia. In the Spanish CIVIL WAR (1936–39), it was the last Republican city to fall to Nationalist forces. It is an agricultural, industrial and communications centre. Tourists are drawn by the city's many fine buildings. Industries: electrical equipment, chemicals, textiles, shipbuilding, vehicles, machinery, fruit, wine. Pop. (2005) 2,330,000.

Valencia City in N Venezuela, capital of Carabobo state. Valencia was the capital of Venezuela in 1830, when the country gained independence from Greater Colombia. It is an industrial and transport centre. Industries: textiles, paper, cement, glass, soap, furniture vehicles, brewing. Pop. (2000) 1,338,833.

Valentine, Saint Name traditionally associated with two legendary saints of the 3rd century: Valentine of Rome and Valentine of Interamna (modern Terni). The former was a Roman priest and physician; the latter, the Bishop of Terni. Little is known about either of them. The martyrdom of both is commemorated on February 14. The custom of lovers exchanging cards on St Valentine's Day possibly has its roots in the pagan Roman festival of Lupercalia, an ancient fertility rite celebrated in Rome on February 15.

Valentino, Rudolph (1895–1926) US silent-film star, b. Italy. His smouldering blend of passion and melancholy wooed female audiences in the 1920s. Valentino's films include *Four Horseman of the Apocalypse* (1921), *The Sheik* (1921), *Blood and Sand* (1922) and *The Eagle* (1925). His early death caused hysteria among his fans.

valerian (garden heliotrope) Plant native to Europe and N Asia and naturalized in the USA. It has pinkish or pale purple flower clusters. Height: to 1.2m (4ft). Family Valerianaceae; species *Valeriana officinalis*.

Valéry, Paul (1871–1945) French poet and critic. Influenced by SYMBOLISM and Stephane MALLARMÉ in particular, Valéry's masterpiece is *La Jeune Parque* (1917). Other works, such as *Le Cimetière marin* (1920) and *Charmes* (1922), cemented his lyrical, abstract style. Valéry's *Cahiers* (1957–60) record his thoughts on a wide range of issues. He was elected to the Académie Française in 1925.

Valhalla In Norse mythology, the Hall of the Slain, where chosen warriors enjoyed feasts with the god ODIN. It is depicted as a glittering palace, with golden walls and a ceiling of shields.

Valium Proprietary name for diazepam, a sedative drug in the BENZODIAZEPINE group. It is used in the treatment of anxiety, muscle spasms and epilepsy.

Valkyries In Norse mythology, warlike handmaidens of the god ODIN, who selected and conducted to VALHALLA those slain heroes who merited a place with him.

Valladolid City on the River Pisuerga, NW central Spain, capital of Valladolid province. There is a 12th-century Romanesque church and a monument to Christopher Columbus, who died in the city. Valladolid's university, founded in 1346, is one of the oldest in Spain. Industries: vehicles, railway engineering, chemicals, flour milling, metalwork, textiles. Pop. (2001) 318,293.

Valletta Port and capital of MALTA, on the NE coast of the island. Founded in the 16th century, it was named after Jean Parisot de la Valette, Grand Master of the Order of the Knights of St John, who organized the reconstruction of the city after repelling the Turks' Great Siege of 1565. Notable sights include the Royal University of Malta (1592) and the Cathedral of San Giovanni (1576). Industries: shipbuilding and repairs, transshipment, tourism. Pop. (1995) 7,100; 195,500 (metro.).

valley Elongated, gently sloping depression of the Earth's surface. It often contains a stream or RIVER that receives the drainage from the surrounding heights. A U-shaped valley was probably formed by a GLACIER, a V-shaped one by a stream. The term may also be applied to a broad, generally flat area that is drained by a large river.

Valois Royal dynasty that ruled France from the accession (1328) of PHILIP VI to the death (1589) of HENRY III, when the throne passed to the BOURBONS. *See also* CHARLES VIII; FRANCIS I; LOUIS XI; LOUIS XII

Valois, Dame Ninette de (1898–2001) Irish ballerina and choreographer, b. Edris Stannus. She danced with Diaghilev's BALLETS RUSSES (1923–26). In 1931, de Valois founded the Sadler's Wells Ballet School, which later became the Royal Ballet. She acted as its director (1931–63).

Valparaíso Main port of Chile and capital of Valparaíso region, 100km (60mi) W of Santiago. Founded in 1536, Valparaíso is vulnerable to earthquakes. As well as Chile's chief port, it is also a cultural centre, with two universities and museums of fine arts and natural history. Industries: chemicals, textiles, sugar refining, vegetable oils, paint. Pop. (1999) 285,000.

value-added tax (VAT) Indirect tax imposed in most European countries. Introduced in Britain in 1971, it consists of a series of taxes (calculated as a percentage) levied on goods (or services) in the various stages of their manufacture until the point of sale. *See also* TAXATION

valves In anatomy, structures that prevent the backflow of blood in the HEART and VEINS. Heart valves separate and connect the two atria and ventricles, the right ventricle and the pulmonary artery, and the left ventricle and the aorta.

vampire bat Small, brown BAT that lives in tropical and subtropical America. It uses its sharp teeth to slice the skin of resting animals (including human beings) and then laps up their blood. Length: 7.6cm (3in). Wingspan: 30cm (12in). Family Desmodontidae; species *Desmodus rotundus*.

vanadium (symbol V) Silver-white, metallic element, one of the TRANSITION ELEMENTS. Discovered in 1801, the malleable and ductile metal is found in iron, lead, and uranium ores, and in coal and petroleum. It is used in steel alloys to add strength and heat resistance. Chemically, vanadium reacts with oxygen and other nonmetals at high temperature. Properties: at.no. 23; r.a.m. 50.9414; r.d. 6.1 at 18.7°C; m.p. 1,890°C (3,434°F); b.p. 3,380°C (6,116°F); most common isotope V^{51} (99.76%).

Van Allen radiation belts Two rings of radiation trapped by the Earth's magnetic field in the upper atmosphere. The belts contain high-energy, charged particles. The inner belt (of ELECTRONS and PROTONS) extends from *c*.1,000 to 4,000km (600–2,500mi) above the Equator. The outer belt (of electrons) extends from *c*.15,000 to 25,000km (9,000–15,000mi). It is thought that the particles come from SOLAR FLARES carried by the SOLAR WIND. The belts were discovered in 1958 by the US physicist James Van Allen.

Vanbrugh, Sir John (1664–1726) English BAROQUE architect and dramatist, who worked with and was influenced by Sir Christopher WREN. Vanbrugh took London by storm with his witty RESTORATION comedies, *The Relapse* (1696) and *The Provok'd Wife* (1697), before turning to architecture. Blenheim Palace (1705–20) and Castle Howard (1699–1726) are among his architectural masterpieces.

Van Buren, Martin (1782–1862) Eighth US President (1837–41). Van Buren served (1921–28) in the US Senate. As Andrew JACKSON's secretary of state, his opposition to John C. CALHOUN's idea of nullification earned him the vice-presidency (1832–36) and the Democratic nomination. An advocate of STATES' RIGHTS, his presidency plunged into crisis with the lack of federal intervention in the economic depression (1837). In foreign affairs, Van Buren sought conciliation with Great Britain over the AROOSTOOK WAR. He was heavily defeated by William Henry HARRISON in the 1840 presidential elections. Van Buren's rejection of the annexation of Texas and extension of SLAVERY lost him the Democratic nomination in 1844.

Vancouver City on the S shore of Burrard Inlet, S British Columbia, Canada. It is Canada's third-largest city and principal Pacific port. The area was first explored (1792) by British Captain George Vancouver. The building of the Canadian Pacific Railway allowed it to grow into the largest city on Canada's W coast. Its excellent sea and air links make it one of North America's leading centres for transport and communication with countries of the Pacific Rim. Vancouver's beautiful harbour setting, pleasant climate, and terminus of both trans-Canadian railroads make it a magnet for tourists. The city has two universities: British Columbia (1908) and Simon Fraser University (1963). Industries: tourism, timber, oil refining, shipbuilding, fish-processing. Pop. (2005) 2,125,000.

Vancouver Island Island off the Pacific coast of British Columbia, Canada. Captain Cook visited it in 1778, it became a British Crown Colony in 1849, and part of British Columbia in 1866. The largest island off the W coast of N America, the interior is rugged and forested. The main city, VICTORIA, is the province's capital. Industries: timber, fishing, copper, coal-mining, tourism. Area: 32,137sq km (12,408sq mi).

Vandals Germanic tribe who attacked the Roman Empire in the 5th century AD. In 409, they looted Roman Gaul and invaded Spain. Defeated by the GOTHS, they moved further south and invaded North Africa (429), establishing a kingdom from which they controlled the W Mediterranean. They sacked Rome in 455. In 533–534, Byzantine General Belisarius destroyed the Vandal kingdom.

Van de Graaff generator Machine that generates high voltages by concentrating electrical charges on the outside of a hollow conductor. Positive or negative charges are sprayed onto a vertically moving belt that carries them up to a large hollow metal sphere where voltage builds up. An applied voltage of *c*.50,000 volts can generate up to 10 million volts. The generator was invented by US physicist Robert J. Van de Graaf.

Van der Waals, Johannes Diderik (1837–1923) Dutch physicist. In 1910, he received the Nobel Prize in physics for his work on gases. The Van der Waals gas equation takes into account intermolecular attraction and repulsion, ignored by the previous KINETIC THEORY of gases.

Van der Waals forces Weak forces of mutual attraction that contribute towards cohesion between neighbouring ATOMS or MOLECULES. They are named after Johannes VAN DER WAALS.

Van Diemen's Land Original name of TASMANIA. Discovered (1642) by Abel TASMAN, it was named in honour of the governor general of the Dutch East Indies. It became part of New South Wales in 1803, was made a separate colony in 1825, given self-government in 1850, and named Tasmania in 1855.

Van Dyck, Sir Anthony (1599–1641) Flemish portrait and religious painter. Van Dyck worked in RUBENS' studio before travelling abroad. His portraits of the aristocracy, such as *Marchesa Elena Grimaldi* (*c*.1625), were widely copied. In 1632, Van Dyck was invited to England by Charles I, who made him court painter and a knight. The elegance and sophistication of his depictions of the English aristocracy was the model for portraiture until John Singer SARGENT.

Vane, Sir Henry (1613–62) English statesman. A Puritan, he was briefly governor (1636–37) of Massachusetts, before returning to domestic politics. A proponent of the abolition of episcopacy in the LONG PARLIAMENT, Vane was dismissed by CHARLES I. During the English CIVIL WAR, he secured the SOLEMN LEAGUE AND COVENANT (1643) with Scotland. He was a member of the COMMONWEALTH council of state, but fell out with Oliver CROMWELL. After the RESTORATION (1660), Vane was convicted of treason and executed.

Van Gogh, Vincent (1853–90) Dutch painter, a leading exponent of EXPRESSIONISM. He was a lay preacher to Belgian coal miners before suffering a psychological crisis. Virtually self-taught, Van Gogh's early works, such as *The Potato Eaters* (1885), are MILLET-influenced studies of working-class life. In 1886, he left Holland for Paris, where his palette was transformed by POST-IMPRESSIONISM, experimenting briefly with POINTILLISM. In 1888, Van Gogh moved to Arles, Provence, where he was joined by GAUGUIN. Suffering from mental illness and depression, he cut

◀ **Van Dyck** *Portrait of King Charles I wearing the Order of the Garter*. Born in Antwerp, Belgium, Sir Anthony Van Dyck was one of the great masters of 17th-century portraiture. In 1632, Charles I invited van Dyck to become his court painter in England. Van Dyck completed a vast number of commissions, often using assistants to paint the backdrop. His refined and restrained style perfectly suited the dignified and patriarchal sensibilities of the European aristocracy.

V

INTERNET

Vanuatu
▶ www.vanuatu.net.vu

Vatican City
▶ www.vatican.va

off part of his left ear after a quarrel with Gauguin. Van Gogh's paintings from this period include the *Sunflower* series (1888), and the *Night Café* (1888). He entered an asylum at Saint Rémy, where he painted a series of landscapes, such as *Starry Night* (1889). These paintings are executed with heavy brushwork in flame-like colour, with passionate expression of light and emotion. Van Gogh committed suicide in Auvers. In a brief and turbulent life, he sold only one painting and was supported by his younger brother Théo.

vanilla Climbing ORCHID native to Mexico. The vines bear greenish-yellow flowers that produce seed-pods 20cm (8in) long, which are the source of the flavouring vanilla. Family Orchidaceae; species *Vanilla planifolia*.

Vanuatu Volcanic island group in the sw Pacific Ocean, *c*.2,300km (1,430mi) E of Australia. The group consists of 13 large islands and 70 islets, the majority of them mountainous, which form a chain *c*.725km (450mi) in length. The main islands are Espiritu Santo, Efate (which has the capital Vila, 2002 pop. 33,900), Malekula, Pentecost, Malo, and Tanna. Europeans first visited in 1606. The English and French settled the group in the early 1800s. Governed jointly by France and Britain as the New Hebrides from 1906, the islands became a republic in 1980. Industries: fishing, farming, mining. Copra accounts for almost half of export earnings. Area: 12,189sq km (4,706sq mi). Pop. (2000)199,000.

Van Vleck, John (Hasbrouck) (1899–1980) US mathematician and physicist. He studied the behaviour of electrons in non-crystalline, magnetic materials. In the 1930s, Van Vleck became the first scientist to use QUANTUM MECHANICS to explain the phenomenon of MAGNETISM. He shared the 1977 Nobel Prize in physics.

vaporization (volatilization) Conversion of a liquid or solid into its vapour, such as water into steam. Some solids (such as ammonium chloride), when heated, pass directly into the vapour state, a process known as SUBLIMATION.

vapour pressure Pressure exerted by a vapour when it evaporates from a liquid or solid. When as many molecules leave to form vapour as return (in an enclosed space), this equilibrium is called a saturated vapour pressure. When a solid is dissolved in a liquid, the vapour pressure of the liquid is reduced by an amount proportional to the solid's relative molecular mass.

Varanasi (Benares, Banoras) City on the River Ganges, Uttar Pradesh, N India. Hindus consider Varanasi to be the most holy city. Each year, it attracts millions of pilgrims who bathe in the Ganges. BUDDHA reputedly preached his first sermon nearby. Silk brocade, brassware, and jewellery are among the city's specialist industries. Pop. (2000) 1,300,000.

Varèse, Edgard (1885–1965) French composer, a leading advocate of 20th-century experimental music. Varèse experimented with new rhythms and timbres and dissonant harmonies in works such as *Hyperprism* (1923) for wind instruments and percussion, and *Déserts* (1954) for tape-recorded sound. He concentrated on ELECTRONIC MUSIC after the early 1950s.

▼ **Varanasi** The holiest of Hindu cities, Varanasi is located close to the confluence of two holy rivers, the Ganges and the Yamuna. The water of the Ganges is considered to be purifying by Hindus, and multitudes of pilgrims descend the ghats (flights of steps) down to the river each day to bathe. The ghats are also the site of open funeral pyres, where bodies are burned and the ashes washed into the Ganges in the belief that the dead will be released from the earthly cycle of rebirths and enter nirvana.

Vargas, Getúlio Dornelles (1883–1954) Brazilian statesman, president (1930–45, 1951–54). He led a revolt after being defeated in presidential elections. Vargas' autocratic regime was bolstered by the army. He established a corporative state, but there were few signs of economic improvement. His refusal to grant elections led to a military coup. Opposition from the right wing increased until, rather than resign, he committed suicide.

variable In mathematics, symbol used to represent an unspecified quantity. Variables are used to express a range of possible values. For example, in the expression $x^2 + x + 1$, the quantity x may be assigned the value of any real number; here x is said to be an independent variable. If y is defined by $y = x^2 + x + 1$, then y is a dependent variable because its value depends on the value of x.

variable star Star whose brightness varies with time. **Intrinsic** variables are stars that vary because of some inherent feature. In **extrinsic** variables, external factors, such as eclipses or dust, affect the amount of light reaching us from the star. *See also* MAGNITUDE

variation In biology, differences between members of the same SPECIES. Variation occurs naturally due to HEREDITY and to differences in the environment during development. *See also* ADAPTATION; EVOLUTION

variation In music, a variety of treatments upon a single theme. Successive statements of the theme are altered by such means as simple elaboration, change of key, or change of time signature.

varicose vein Condition where a VEIN becomes swollen and distorted. Varicose veins can occur anywhere in the body, but are commonly found in the legs.

varnish Solution of a RESIN or a PLASTIC that dries to form a hard, transparent, protective and often decorative coating. Varnishes may have a matt or glossy finish. Pigments are often added to colour the varnish.

Varuna In ancient Hindu mythology, the supreme ruler and possessor of universal power. He is worshipped as the upholder of moral order, and is closely identified with the Moon.

Vasari, Giorgio (1511–74) Italian painter, architect, and biographer. Vasari's fame now rests on his history of Italian art, *The Lives of the most excellent Painters, Sculptors and Architects* (1550). This lively account is the single most important document of Italian RENAISSANCE art. In architecture, he is noted for his design for the UFFIZI.

Vasco da Gama *See* GAMA, VASCO DA

vascular bundle Strand of conductive tissue that transports water and dissolved mineral salts and nutrients in a VASCULAR PLANT. They extend from the roots, through the stem, and out to the leaves. They consist of two types of tissue: XYLEM, which conducts water from the roots to the shoot and is located towards the centre of the bundle; and PHLOEM, which conducts salts and nutrients and forms the outer regions of the bundle.

vascular plant Plant with vessels to carry water and nutrients within it. All higher plants – FERNS, CONIFERS, and FLOWERING PLANTS – have a vascular system (XYLEM and PHLOEM).

vasectomy Operation to induce male sterility, in which the tube (*vas deferens*) carrying sperm from the testes to the penis is cut. A vasectomy is a form of permanent CONTRACEPTION, although in some cases the operation is reversible.

vasoconstrictor Any substance that causes constriction of blood vessels and, therefore, decreased blood flow. Examples include NORADRENALINE, angiotensin, and the HORMONE vasopressin (also known as anti-diuretic hormone).

vasodilator Any substance that causes widening of the blood vessels, permitting freer flow of blood. Vasodilator drugs are mostly used to treat HYPERTENSION and ANGINA.

VAT *See* VALUE-ADDED TAX

Vatican City Independent sovereign state, existing as a walled enclave on the w bank of the River TIBER, within the city of ROME. It is the official home of the PAPACY and an independent base for the Holy See (governing body of the ROMAN CATHOLIC CHURCH). The first papal residence was established in the 5th century, and it has been the papal home ever since (apart from a brief spell at AVIGNON in the 14th century). Vatican City did not achieve full independence until 1929.

V

The world's smallest nation, its population of *c*.1,000 (mostly unmarried males) includes the Pope's traditional Swiss Guard of 100. The Commission, appointed to administer the Vatican's affairs, has its own radio service, police and railway station and issues its own stamps and coins. The treasures of the Vatican, notably Michelangelo's frescos in the SISTINE CHAPEL and ST PETER'S, attract huge numbers of tourists and pilgrims. The official language is Latin. Area: 0.44sq km (0.17sq mi).

Vatican Council, First (1869–70) Twentieth ecumenical council of the Roman Catholic Church. Convened by Pope PIUS IX to refute various contemporary ideas associated with the rise of liberalism and materialism, it is chiefly remembered for its declaration of PAPAL INFALLIBILITY.

Vatican Council, Second (1962–65) Twenty-first ecumenical council of the Roman Catholic Church. It was convened by Pope JOHN XXIII to revive and renew Christian faith and move the Church into closer touch with ordinary people. Among the most significant results were the introduction of the MASS in the vernacular, a greater role for lay people and a greater tolerance for other sects and other religions.

Vatican Palace Residence of the pope within the VATICAN CITY. A complex of more than 1,000 rooms clustered around a number of courtyards, it contains the papal apartments, the offices of the Vatican City state secretariat, state reception rooms, the Vatican Museums, the Vatican Archive, and the Vatican Library.

vaudeville US equivalent of the British MUSIC HALL.

Vaughan, Henry (1622–95) Welsh poet. His METAPHYSICAL POETRY was inspired by the religious verse of George HERBERT. Vaughan's masterpiece, *Silex Scintillans* (1650, revised 1655), meditates on man and nature.

Vaughan, Sarah (1924–90) US singer. Vaughan's operatic style contrasted with the naturalism of Ella FITZGERALD. Her early work with Billy Eckstine led to the recording of 'Lover Man' with Dizzy GILLESPIE. Often with full orchestral accompaniment, Vaughan sang with the bands of Duke ELLINGTON and Count BASIE. Albums include *After Hours* (1961).

Vaughan Williams, Ralph (1872–1958) English composer. His interest in English folk music is apparent in his three *Norfolk Rhapsodies* (1905–07) and *The Lark Ascending* (1914). Vaughan Williams' modal style, based on Tudor music, found its fullest expression in *Fantasia on a theme by Thomas Tallis* (1910) and *A Sea Symphony* (1909). Works such as The *Pilgrim's Progress* (1951) and *Mass in G Minor* (1923) show the influence of the English visionary tradition.

vault Curved roof or ceiling usually made of stone, brick or concrete. The simple **barrel** vault is semi-cylindrical; the **groin** vault consists of two barrel vaults intersected at right-angles; the **ribbed groin** is the same as the groin vault except that it has ribs to give the edges extra support; the so-called **Gothic** vault has four pointed compartments; the **fan** vault has a delicate, fan-like appearance. In the 15th century, English masons developed the fan vault, using tracery to make it more elaborate, as in King's College Chapel, Cambridge.

Veblen, Thorstein Bunde (1857–1929) US sociologist and economist. Veblen wrote *The Theory of the Leisure Class* (1899), in which he introduced the idea of conspicuous consumption. He founded the institutionalist school, believing that economics must be studied in the context of social change.

vector In mathematics, a quantity that has both a magnitude and a direction, as contrasted with a SCALAR, which has magnitude only. For example, the VELOCITY of an object is specified by its speed and the direction in which it is moving; similarly, a FORCE has both magnitude and direction. Mass is a scalar quantity, but WEIGHT (the force of gravity on a body) is a vector.

Vedanta (Sanskrit, 'conclusion of the VEDAS') Best known and most popular form of Indian philosophy; it forms the foundation for most modern schools of thought in HINDUISM. One of the most influential Vedanta schools was that expounded by the 7th-8th-century philosopher Sankara. This school holds that the natural world is an illusion. There is only one self, BRAHMAN-ATMAN; ignorance of the oneness of the self with Brahman is the cause of rebirth. The system includes a belief in the TRANSMIGRATION OF SOULS and the desirability of release from the cycle of rebirth. *See also* UPANISHADS

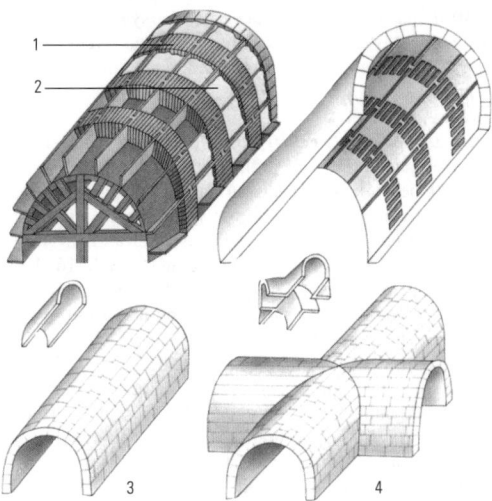

Vedas Ancient and most sacred writings of HINDUISM. They consist of series of hymns and formulaic chants that constituted a Hindu LITURGY. There are four Vedas: **Rig Veda**, containing a priestly tradition originally brought to India by ARYANS; **Yajur Veda**, consisting of prayers and sacred formulas; **Sama Veda**, containing melodies and chants; and **Atharva Veda**, a collection of popular hymns, incantations and magic spells. The Vedas were composed between *c*.1500 and 1200 BC.

Vega (Alpha Lyrae) White, main-sequence star in the constellation of Lyra; the fifth-brightest star in the sky. Its luminosity is 50 times that of the Sun.

Vega Carpio, Félix, Lope de (1562–1635) Spanish poet and dramatist. A prolific writer, only *c*.300 of his major works survive, including the plays *Peribáñez and the Commander of Ocaña* (*c*.1610), and *All Citizens Are Soldiers* (*c*.1613).

vegetable As opposed to an ANIMAL, a form of life that builds up its tissues by means of growth using the energy of sunlight, carbon dioxide from the air, and the green pigment CHLOROPHYLL. This process is known as PHOTOSYNTHESIS. Vegetables, or green plants, need also to be supplied with water and mineral salts, which are usually present in the soil.

vegetarianism Practice of abstaining from eating meat and fish. A minority of vegetarians, known as vegans, further exclude from their diet all products of animal origin, such as butter, eggs, milk and cheese. Some eastern religions, particularly Jains, Hindus, and Buddhists, encourage vegetarianism; in the west, most vegetarianism has a secular basis.

vegetative reproduction Form of ASEXUAL REPRODUCTION in higher plants. It involves an offshoot or a piece of the original plant (from leaf, stem or root) separating and giving rise to an entire new plant. It may occur naturally, as in strawberries reproducing by runners, or artificially, as in a houseplant-cutting yielding a new plant.

◀ **vault** Concrete enabled the Romans to build vaults of a size unequalled until the introduction of steel construction. Concrete vaults were supported on timber centring, which was removed after the concrete set. In some cases, vaults were built of brick ribs (1), filled with concrete (2) to lighten the weight on the centring and avoid cracking. The simplest vault was the barrel, wagon or tunnel (3) – basically a prolonged rounded arch – which was used for small spans and simple oblong structures with parallel sides. The groin vault (4), formed by two barrels intersecting at right angles, was used over square apartments, or over long corridors divided by piers into square bays, each covered with a groin vault.

INTERNET

Vaughan Williams, Ralph
▶ www.rvwsociety.com

VEIN

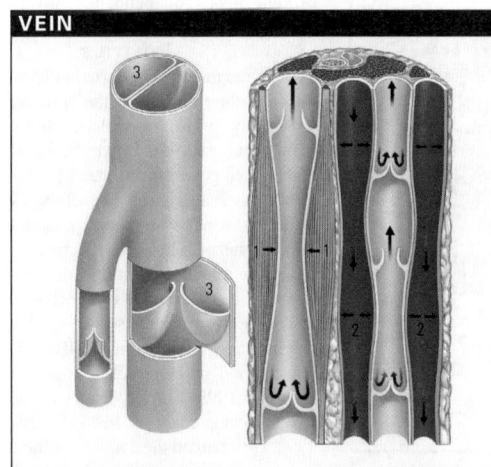

Veins carry blood to the heart. The returning venous blood moves slowly due to low pressure, and the veins can collapse or expand to accommodate variations in blood flow. Movement relies on the surrounding muscles, which contract (1) and compress the vein. Pulsation of adjacent arteries (2) has a regular pumping effect. Semi-lunar valves (3) appear at regular intervals throughout the larger veins and these allow the blood to move only in one direction.

V

vein In mammals, vessel that carries deoxygenated BLOOD to the heart. An exception is the pulmonary vein, which carries **oxygenated** blood from the lungs to the left upper chamber of the heart. *See* illustration page 769. *See also* ARTERY; VENA CAVA

Velázquez, Diego Rodriguez de Silva y (1599–1660) Spanish painter. He was strongly influenced by MANNER-ISM and the work of CARAVAGGIO, but developed a personal style that combined NATURALISM with a deep spirituality. Velázquez painted religious works and GENRE PAINTINGS, notably *The Old Woman Cooking Eggs* (1618). In 1623, he became court painter to King Philip IV of Spain. During the 1630s and 1640s, he produced a striking series of royal and equestrian portraits. A trip to Italy resulted in the superb portrait of *Pope Innocent X* (1650). Towards the end of his life, Velázquez continued to paint with dazzling brushwork, culminating in *The Maids of Honour* (*c*.1656). Unknown outside Spain until the early 19th century, he influenced many European artists, especially MANET.

velocity (symbol *v*) Rate of motion of a body in a certain direction. Velocity is a VECTOR (magnitude and direction), whereas SPEED, which does not specify direction, is a SCALAR. Velocity can also be a measurement of how quickly an object changes its position in a given direction. An object's velocity can be found in the same manner as speed,

by dividing the distance *s* it has travelled by the time *t* taken, and this is expressed as $v=s/t$ and given in metres per second (ms^{-1}) or kilometres/miles per hour. Velocity is then stated, for example, as '60kph/37mph eastward'. Positive and negative values to represent movement in opposite directions can be shown on both a velocity-time graph and a displacement-time graph (movement from a fixed position).

vena cava Main VEIN of vertebrates. It supplies the HEART with deoxygenated blood, emptying into its right atrium.

veneer Extremely thin sheet of wood, or a thin sheet of a precious material such as ivory or tortoise-shell, which gives furniture or other objects the appearance of being more valuable than they are. Veneers may also be used as decorative shapes inlaid into a surface.

venereal disease (VD) Outmoded term for SEXUALLY TRANSMITTED DISEASE (STD)

Venetian school School of Italian painting that flourished in the 15th, 16th, and 18th centuries. It was noted for the sumptuousness and radiance of its colour. Early Venetian masters included the BELLINI and Vivarini families, who were followed by its greatest exponents, TITIAN and GIORGIONE. TINTORETTO and VERONESE represent the transition from RENAISSANCE to BAROQUE, while TIEPOLO, CANALETTO, and GUARDI revived Venetian painting in the 18th century.

VENEZUELA

The Bolivarian Republic of Venezuela, in N South America, contains the Maracaibo Lowlands in the W. The lowlands surround the oil-rich Lake Maracaibo (Lago de Maracaibo). Arms of the ANDES Mountains enclose the lowlands and extend across most of N Venezuela. Between the N mountains and the scenic Guiana Highlands in the SE, where the ANGEL FALLS are found, lie the *llanos* (tropical grasslands), a low-lying region drained by the River ORINOCO and its tributaries. The Orinoco is Venezuela's longest river.

CLIMATE
Venezuela has a tropical climate. Temperatures are high throughout the year on the lowlands, though far cooler in the mountains. There is a marked dry season in much of the country that falls between December and April. Most rainfall is in the mountains.

HISTORY
The original inhabitants of Venezuela were the Arawak and Carib Native Americans. The first

European to arrive was Christopher COLUMBUS, who sighted the area in 1498. In 1499 Amerigo VESPUCCI explored the coastline and nicknamed the country Venezuela (Spanish for 'little Venice'). Spaniards began to settle in the early 16th century, but economic development was slow.

In the early 19th century, Spain's colonies in South America began their struggle for independence. The Venezuelan patriots Simón BOLÍVAR and Francisco de Miranda were prominent in the struggle. Venezuela was the first South American country to demand freedom and, in July 1811, it declared its independence, although Spaniards still held most of the country. In 1819 Venezuela became part of Gran Colombia, a republic led by Simón Bolívar that also included Colombia, Ecuador and Panama.

The country became fully independent in 1821, after the Venezuelans had defeated the Spanish in a battle at Carabobo, near Valencia. Venezuela broke away from Gran Colombia in 1829 and in 1830 a new constitution was drafted. The country's first president was General José Antonio Páez, one of the leaders of Venezuela's independence movement.

POLITICS
The development of Venezuela in the 19th century and the first half of the 20th century was marred by instability, violence and periods of harsh dictatorial rule. However, the country has had elected governments since 1958.

Venezuela has greatly benefited from its oil resources, which were first exploited in 1917. In 1960, Venezuela helped to form the Organization of Petroleum Exporting Countries (OPEC). In 1976, the government of Venezuela took control of the entire oil industry.

Financial problems in the late 1990s led to the election of Hugo Chávez as president in February 1999. Chávez, leader of the Patriotic Pole left-wing coalition, had led a failed coup in 1992. He changed the country's official name to

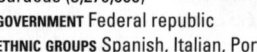

AREA 912,050sq km [352,143sq mi]
POPULATION 26,024,000
CAPITAL (POPULATION) Caracas (3,276,000)
GOVERNMENT Federal republic
ETHNIC GROUPS Spanish, Italian, Portuguese, Arab, German, African, indigenous peoples
LANGUAGES Spanish (official), indigenous dialects
RELIGIONS Roman Catholic 96%
CURRENCY Bolivar = 100 céntimos

the Bolivarian Republic of Venezuela and changed the constitution, giving himself increased powers over military and civilian institutions which he claimed to need to counter corruption. In 2002 Chávez himself survived a coup attempt, and in 2004 he won a majority in a referendum which the opposition had intended would remove him from office. He was re-elected in 2006. In 2007 he granted himself extensive 'emergency powers' and withdrew from the World Bank and IMF.

ECONOMY
The World Bank classifies Venezuela as an 'upper-middle-income' developing country. Oil accounts for 80% of the exports. Oil money has helped Venezuela raise living standards, but the country has failed to diversify the economy. Other exports include aluminium, iron ore, and farm products.

Agriculture employs 9% of the people. Cattle ranching is important. Major crops include bananas, cassava, citrus fruits, coffee, maize, plantains, rice and sorghum. Commercial crops are grown on large farms, but many people farm small plots at subsistence level.

Manufacturing industries now employ 21% of the population. The leading industry is petroleum refining, centred on Maracaibo. Other manufactures include aluminium, cement, processed food, steel and textiles.

Venezuela Republic in N South America. *See* country feature

Venice (Venézia) City on the Gulf of Venice, at the head of the Adriatic Sea, N Italy, capital of Venetia region. Built on 118 islands, separated by narrow canals, in the Lagoon of Venice, and joined by causeway to the mainland. Settled in the 5th century, it was a vassal of the Byzantine Empire until the 10th century. After defeating Genoa in 1381, Venice became the leading European sea-power, trading with the Mediterranean and Asia. It declined in the 16th century, and was ceded to Austria in 1797, becoming part of Italy in 1866. Venice has many churches, palaces and historic buildings, and is one of Europe's major attractions, drawing more than 2 million tourists a year. Tourism imposes a massive strain on a city already suffering from erosion, subsidence, and pollution. Industries: glass-blowing, textiles, petrochemicals. Pop. (2000) 275,368.

Venn diagram In mathematics, diagrammatical representation of the relations between mathematical SETS or logical statements, named after the English logician John Venn (1834–1923). The sets are usually drawn as circles or ovals that overlap whenever different sets share some elements.

ventilation In biology, the process by which air or water is taken into and expelled from the body of an animal and passed over a surface across which GAS EXCHANGE takes place. Ventilation mechanisms include BREATHING, by which air is drawn into the LUNGS for gas exchange across the wall of the ALVEOLI, and the movements of the floor of a fish's mouth, coupled with those of its GILL covers, which draw water across the gills.

ventricle Either of the two lower chambers of the HEART. Blood is pumped from the right ventricle to the lungs and from the left ventricle throughout the body.

venture capital Outside CAPITAL provided for a business. Venture capital is often needed to start up new businesses or to expand existing businesses. It is provided by MERCHANT BANKS or investment and private investors.

Venturi, Robert (1925–) US architect. Venturi's stress on the importance of 'vernacular' or contextual architecture heralded POST-MODERNISM. His publications include *Complexity and Contradiction in Architecture* (1966), and *Learning from Las Vegas* (1972). His buildings include Gordon Wu Hall, Princeton University, USA (1984) and the Sainsbury Wing of the National Gallery, London, UK (1991).

Venus Second planet from the Sun, it is almost as large as the Earth. Visible around dawn or dusk as the so-called **morning star** or **evening star**, it is the most conspicuous celestial object after the Sun and Moon. A telescope shows the planet's dazzling, yellowish-white cloud cover, with faint markings. In 1958 measurements at radio wavelengths indicated the very high surface temperature of Venus. Space probes revealed more about the surface. A gently undulating plain covers two-thirds of Venus. Highlands account for a further quarter, and depressions and chasms the remainder. Most of the surface features are volcanic in origin. The atmosphere consists of 96% carbon dioxide and 3.5% nitrogen, with traces of helium, argon, neon, and krypton. Venus has no satellites.

Venus Roman goddess originally associated with gardens and cultivation, but also with the ideas of charm, grace, and beauty. She became identified with the Greek goddess APHRODITE, and hence also personified love and fertility.

verb Linguistic category (part of speech) found in all languages, consisting of words typically denoting an action, an event or a state (for example, in English, *to run, to snow, to depend*). Typical verbs are associated with one or more 'arguments', such as subject and direct object. In English, verbs may be intransitive or transitive; intransitives have one argument (*she sneezed*), and transitives two or (rarely) more (*she played snooker, she taught him Russian*). Verbs may carry grammatical information, including: person (as grammatical agreement with the subject); tense (relating to when the verb took place); aspect (whether what is meant is complete or incomplete at some reference time); number (whether any of the arguments are singular or plural); and voice (which argument serves as subject). In other languages, verbs may encode different information. A list of all forms of a verb is called its **paradigm**, and this may be regular (predictable by a rule) or irregular. The most irregular verbs in a language are often those in most frequent use and with the most general meaning.

verbena Genus of annual and perennial trees, shrubs and herbs, native to the Western Hemisphere. Some species are popular garden plants and have pink, red, white, or purple flowers. Family Verbenaceae; there are *c.*250 species.

Verdi, Giuseppe (1813–1901) Italian composer. His early operas displayed an original and lively talent and a promising sense of the dramatic. Up to 1853, his masterpieces were *Rigoletto* (1851), *Il trovatore* (1853) and *La traviata* (1853). *Aïda* (1867) shows a development in style, with richer and more imaginative orchestration. With Verdi's last three operas, *Don Carlos* (1884), *Otello* (1887) and *Falstaff* (1893), Italian opera reached its greatest heights. Among other compositions are several sacred choral works, including the *Requiem* (1874).

verdict Conclusive pronouncement of a COURT OF LAW. The verdict at most courts is either 'guilty' or 'not guilty' of the charge, although in some countries (including Scotland) there is the third alternative of 'not proven'. Whether the verdict is delivered by court authorities or by a panel of jurors depends on the type of court. Verdicts may be subject to appeal, if permission is granted, and may be overturned altogether if new and conclusive evidence appears at a later stage.

Verdun, Battle of (February-December 1916) Campaign of WORLD WAR I. A German offensive in the region of Verdun, NW France, made initial advances, but was checked by the French under Marshal PÉTAIN. After a series of renewed German assaults, the Allied offensive on the SOMME drew off German troops and the French regained the lost territory. Total casualties are estimated at one million.

Verlaine, Paul (1844–96) French poet. His early poetry, *Poèmes Saturniens* (1866) and *Fêtes Galantes* (1869), was influenced by BAUDELAIRE, with whom he is grouped as one of the *fin de siècle* decadents (an appellation amply fulfilled by his lifestyle). An intense relationship with RIMBAUD ended violently. While in jail (1874–75), Verlaine wrote *Songs Without Words* (1874), an early work of SYMBOLISM. Returning to Catholicism, his later poetry deals with the conflict between the spiritual and the carnal. His critical work includes the famous study *The Accursed Poets* (1884).

Vermeer, Jan (1632–75) Dutch painter, one of the most celebrated of all 17th-century Dutch painters. Early mythological and religious works gave way to a middle period featuring the serene and contemplative domestic scenes for which he is best known. The compositions are extremely simple and powerful, and the colours are usually muted blues, greys, and yellows. He treated light and colour with enormous delicacy, as in the superb landscape, *View of Delft* (*c.*1660). Towards the end of his life, Vermeer began to paint in a heavier manner and his work lost some of its mysterious charm.

Vermont State in New England, NE USA, on the Canadian border. The state capital is MONTPELIER; other major cities include Burlington. The Green Mountains range N-S and dominate the terrain; most of the W border of the state is formed by Lake Champlain. In 1609, Samuel de CHAMPLAIN discovered the lake, but the region was not settled permanently until 1724. Land grant disputes with New Hampshire and New York persisted for many years. In 1777, Vermont declared its independence, retaining this unrecognized status until it was admitted to the Union in 1791. The region is heavily forested and arable land is limited. Dairy farming is by far the most important farming activity. Mineral resources include granite, slate, marble and asbestos. Industries: pulp and paper, food processing, computer components, machine tools. Area: 24,887sq km (9,609sq mi). Pop. (2000) 608,827.

Verne, Jules (1828–1905) French novelist. He is often considered one of the founding fathers of SCIENCE FICTION. Verne's imaginative adventure novels include *Journey to the Centre of the Earth* (1864), *Twenty Thousand Leagues Under the Sea* (1869) and *Around the World in Eighty Days* (1873).

VENUS: DATA

Diameter (equatorial): 12,104km (7521mi)
Mass (Earth = 1): 0.815
Volume (Earth = 1) 0.86
Density (water = 1): 5.25
Orbital period: 224.7 days
Rotation period: 243.16 days
Average surface temperature: 750K
Surface gravity (Earth = 1): 0.90

V

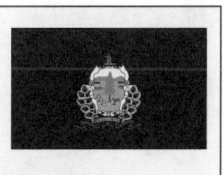

VERMONT
Statehood :
March 4, 1791
Nickname :
The Green Mountain State
State bird :
Hermit thrush
State flower :
Red clover
State tree :
Sugar maple
State motto :
Freedom and unity

INTERNET

Veronese, Paolo Caliari
▶ www.nationalgallery.org.uk
▶ www.nga.gov

Versailles
▶ www.chateauversailles.fr

Versailles, Treaty of
▶ www.yale.edu/lawweb/
avalon/imt/menu.htm

Vesuvius
▶ www.vesuvioinrete.it/
e_webcam.htm

Verona City on the River Adige, NE Italy, capital of Verona province. The city was captured by Rome in 89 BC and still has a Roman amphitheatre. It prospered under the Della Scala family in the 13th and 14th centuries, and was held by Austria from 1797 to 1866, when it joined Italy. Industries: textiles, chemicals, paper, printing, wine. Pop. (2000) 257,477.

Veronese, Paolo Caliari (1528–88) Italian painter and decorative artist. A prominent member of the VENETIAN SCHOOL, he excelled at painting large scenes featuring flamboyant pageants. Veronese also painted religious and mythological themes. He ran into trouble with the Inquisition for his irreverent treatment of *The Last Supper* (1573) and had to rename it *The Feast in the House of Levi*. Other celebrated works are his decorative frescos for the Villa Barbaro near Treviso (1561) and his ceiling, *Triumph of Venice* (1553), for the Doge's Palace.

veronica (speedwell) Widely distributed genus of annual and perennial plants of the figwort family. The small flowers are white, blue, or pink. Height: 7.5–153cm (3in-5ft). Family Scrophulariaceae; the genus includes about 250 species.

verruca In medicine, form of WART on the sole of the foot, which is painful because it is forced to grow inwards. Like other warts, it is due to infection with the human papillomavirus.

Versailles City in N France, 16km (10mi) WSW of Paris, capital of Yvelines department. It is famous for its former royal palace, now a world heritage site visited by two million tourists a year. Louis XIII built his hunting lodge at Versailles. In 1682, Louis XIV made Versailles his royal seat and transformed the lodge into a palace with extensive gardens. The architects Louis LE VAU, Jules HARDOUIN-MANSART, and Robert de Cotte built the monumental palace in a French classical style. Charles Lebrun designed the interior, which includes the Royal Apartments and the Hall of Mirrors. André LE NÔTRE landscaped the magnificent gardens. The park also contains the Grand and Petit Trianon Palaces. Versailles was a royal residence until the French Revolution (1789). It was the scene of the signing of several peace treaties, notably at the conclusion of the Franco-Prussian War and World War 1. Pop. (1999) 85,726.

Versailles, Treaty of (1919) Peace agreement concluding WORLD WAR I, signed at VERSAILLES. The treaty represented a compromise between US President Woodrow Wilson's FOURTEEN POINTS and the demands of the European allies for heavy penalties against Germany. German territorial concessions included Alsace-Lorraine to France, and smaller areas to other neighbouring states, as well as the loss of its colonies. The RHINELAND was demilitarized, strict limits were placed on German armed forces, and extensive reparations for war damage were imposed. The treaty also established the LEAGUE OF NATIONS. The USA never ratified it, and signed a separate treaty with Germany in 1921.

versification Art or practice of composing metrical lines. The terms 'verse' and 'POETRY' often appear interchangeable. When distinctions arise, verse is characterized by structure and form, and poetry by intensity of feeling and imaginative power.

vertebra One of the bones making up the SPINE (backbone), or vertebral column. Each vertebra consists of a large solid body from the top of which wing-like processes project to either side. It has a hollow centre through which the SPINAL CORD passes. The human backbone consists of 26 vertebrae (the five sacral and four vertebrae of the coccyx fuse together to form two solid bones), which are held together by ligaments and intervertebral discs.

vertebrate Animal with individual discs of bone or cartilage called VERTEBRA, which surround or replace the embryonic NOTOCHORD to form a jointed backbone enclosing the spinal column. The principal division within vertebrates is between FISH and partly land-adapted forms (AMPHIBIANS), and the wholly land-adapted forms (REPTILES, BIRDS, and MAMMALS, although some mammals, such as whales, adapted to a totally aquatic existence). Phylum CHORDATA; subphylum VERTEBRATA.

vertigo Dizziness, often accompanied by nausea. Due to disruption of the sense of balance, it may be produced by ear disorder, reduced flow of blood to the brain caused by altitude, emotional upset, or spinning rapidly.

vervet monkey *See* GUENON

Verwoerd, Hendrik Frensch (1901–66) South African statesman, prime minister (1958–66), b. Holland. A vocal advocate of APARTHEID, he promoted the policy of "separate development" (physical separation) of the races. In 1961, Verwoerd led South Africa out of the Commonwealth of Nations. He was assassinated by a white extremist. Verwoerd was succeeded as prime minister by Johannes VORSTER.

very high frequency (VHF) Range or band of RADIO waves with frequencies between 30 and 300MHz and wavelengths between one and 10m (3–33ft). This band provides high-quality reception for TELEVISION and FREQUENCY MODULATION (FM) radio broadcasts. *See also* BROADCASTING

Vespasian (AD 9–79) (Titus Flavius Vespasianus) Roman Emperor (69–79). A successful general and administrator, he was leading the campaign against the Jews in Palestine when he was proclaimed Emperor by his soldiers. Vespasian proved a capable ruler, extending and strengthening the Empire, rectifying the budget deficit, widening qualifications for Roman citizenship and adding to the monumental buildings of Rome.

vespers Evening office of the Western Church. It is a service of thanksgiving and praise, in which the liturgy consists of psalms, a reading from the Bible, the Magnificat canticle, a hymn, and a collect. Celebrated in the late afternoon, it is the basis of the Anglican service of evensong.

Vespucci, Amerigo (1454–1512) Italian maritime explorer. He was possibly the first to realize that the Americas constituted new continents, which were named after him by the German cartographer Martin Waldseemüller in 1507. Vespucci made at least two transatlantic voyages (1497–1504).

Vesta In Roman religion, goddess of fire and purity, supreme in the conduct of religious ceremonies. Her priestesses were the VESTAL VIRGINS. Vesta was the guardian of the hearth and the patron goddess of bakers.

vestal virgin In ancient Rome, priestess of the cult of VESTA, who tended the sacred fire in the Temple of Vesta and officiated at ceremonies in her honour. The vestals remained in the service of the temple for up to 30 years under vows of chastity, violation of which was punishable by being buried alive.

Vesuvius (Vesuvio) Active volcano on the Bay of Naples, S Italy. The earliest recorded eruption was in AD 79, when POMPEII and HERCULANEUM were destroyed. The height of the volcano has changed with each of the 30 or so eruptions recorded since Roman times.

veterinary medicine Medical science that deals with diseases of animals. It was practised by the Babylonians and Egyptians some 4000 years ago. In the late 18th century, schools of veterinary medicine were established in Europe.

VHF Abbreviation of VERY HIGH FREQUENCY (VHF)

vibraphone PERCUSSION musical instrument with metal bars of different lengths that are struck with sticks or mallets to produce various notes. Tubes beneath the bars vibrate at the same frequency as the bar above and magnify the sound.

viburnum Genus of flowering shrubs and small trees, native to North America and Eurasia. All have small, fleshy fruits containing single flat seeds. There are c.120 species. Family Caprifoliaceae.

vicar Priest in the CHURCH OF ENGLAND who is in charge of a parish. In the ROMAN CATHOLIC CHURCH, the term 'vicar' is used to mean 'representative'. The Pope is called the Vicar of Christ. A **Vicar Apostolic** was originally a BISHOP representing the Pope. Today, a Vicar Apostolic is appointed to govern territories that have not yet been organized into dioceses. A **Vicar General** is appointed by and represents a Bishop in the administration of a diocese. *See also* PAPACY

Vicenza Industrial city in NE Italy, 64km (40mi) W of Venice. Founded as a Ligurian settlement, Venice captured it in 1404, and Austria held it from 1797 until 1866, when it united with Italy. An important rail junction, its industries include steel, machinery, chemicals, textiles, printing, glass, and gold jewellery. Pop. (2000) 110,454.

Vichy government (1940–45) Regime established in France after the defeat by Germany in June 1940. Its capital was the town of Vichy, Auvergne, central France. It held authority over French overseas possessions as well as the unoccupied part of France. After German forces occupied Vichy

▲ **vicuña** Native to the high Andes, the vicuña (*Vicugna vicugna*) lives in small herds of six to 12 females with a single male. Prized for its expensive, fine fur, the vicuña was hunted to near extinction in the 1970s. Reserves subsequently were established to protect the species. It is specially adapted to living at high altitudes, with an extremely high concentration of very efficient red blood cells that allow it to absorb oxygen quickly from the thin air.

V

France in November 1942, it became little more than a puppet government. *See also* LAVAL, PIERRE; PÉTAIN, HENRI PHILIPPE

Vicksburg, Siege of (1863) Fourteenth-month assault by Union forces under General Ulysses S. GRANT during the American CIVIL WAR. The capture of Vicksburg, Mississippi, on July 4, 1863, gave the Union control of the Mississippi River and split the Confederacy in two.

Vico, Giambattista (1668–1744) Italian philosophical historian. In his *New Science* (1725, revised 1730 and 1744), Vico advanced the arguments of historicism: that all aspects of society and culture are relevant to the study of history, and that the history of any period should be judged according to the standards and customs of that time and place. Overlooked until the late 19th century, he is now regarded as one of the greatest philosophers of history.

Victor Emmanuel II (1820–78) King of Italy (1861–78). In 1849, he succeeded his father, Charles Albert, as King of Piedmont-Sardinia. From 1852, guided by his able minister, Conti di CAVOUR, he strengthened his kingdom, formed a French alliance, and consequently defeated Austria (1859–61). In 1861, he assumed the title of King of Italy. Rome became his new capital after French troops withdrew (1870).

Victor Emmanuel III (1869–1947) King of Italy (1900–46). In 1922, he appointed Benito MUSSOLINI as prime minister. Although Mussolini established a dictatorship, the king retained the power to dismiss him, and eventually did so in 1943. Victor Emmanuel abdicated in 1946.

Victoria (1819–1901) Queen of Great Britain and Ireland (1837–1901), Empress of India (1876–1901). A granddaughter of GEORGE III, she succeeded her uncle, WILLIAM IV. In 1840, she married her first cousin, Prince Albert of SAXE-COBURG-GOTHA. During her reign, the longest in English history, the role of the monarchy was established as a ceremonial, symbolic institution, with virtually no power but much influence. Victoria learned statecraft from her first prime minister, Lord MELBOURNE, and was greatly influenced by the hard-working Prince Albert. After Albert's death in 1861, Victoria went into lengthy seclusion and her neglect of public duties aroused republican sentiments. Her domestic popularity returned when she became Empress of India and with the golden (1887) and diamond (1897) jubilee celebrations. Among later prime ministers, she maintained excellent terms with Benjamin DISRAELI (who astutely flattered her) but was on frosty terms with William GLADSTONE (who lectured her). She reigned over an Empire containing 25% of the world's people and 30% of its land. Britain's trade and industry made it the world's richest country.

Victoria State in SE Australia, bounded by the Indian Ocean, the Bass Strait and the Tasman Sea. The capital is MELBOURNE (home to more than 66% of the state population); other major cities are Geelong, Ballarat, and Bendigo. The region was part of NEW SOUTH WALES until 1851, when it became a separate colony. The population increased rapidly after 1851, when prospectors discovered gold at Ballarat and Bendigo. In 1901, Victoria became part of the Commonwealth of Australia. The area is crossed by the Australian Alps and other ranges of the Eastern Highlands. Irrigation is used extensively to grow wheat, oats, barley, fruit, and vegetables, while sheep and dairy cattle are also important. Brown coal, natural gas, and oil are the chief mineral resources. Industries: motor vehicles, textiles, food processing. Area: 227,620sq km (87,813sq mi). Pop. (2000 est.) 4,197,400.

Victoria City on SE VANCOUVER ISLAND, capital of BRITISH COLUMBIA province, SW Canada. Founded in 1843, Victoria developed during the 1858 gold rush as a supply base for prospectors. Industries: timber, paper, shipbuilding, fishing, tourism. It also has a large naval base. Pop. (2001) 74,125.

Victoria (Victoria Nyanza) Lake in E central Africa, bordered by Uganda, Kenya and Tanzania. The second-largest freshwater lake in the world, it is the chief reservoir of the River Nile. Its long coastline provides harbours for coastal towns, notably KAMPALA, KISUMU, and MWANZA. Area: 68,000sq km (26,000sq mi).

Victoria Falls Waterfalls on the River Zambezi, on the border of Zimbabwe and Zambia. Formed by water erosion

along a fracture in the Earth's crust, islets divide the falls into five main sections. David LIVINGSTONE made the first European discovery in 1855. Maximum drop: 108m (355ft); Minimum width: 1,700m (5,580ft).

vicuña Graceful, even-toed, hoofed South American mammal. The smallest member of the CAMEL family, it is humpless and resembles the LLAMA. Its silky coat is tawny brown with a yellowish bib under the neck. Vicuña wool was used by the Inca kings and is still expensive and rare. Height: 86cm (34in) at the shoulder; weight: 45kg (100lb). Family Camelidae; species *Vicugna vicugna*.

Vidal, Gore (1925–) US novelist, playwright, and essayist, b. Eugene Luther Vidal. His debut novel, *Williwaw* (1946), drew on his experiences in World War 2. *The City and the Pillar* (1948), a frank account of homosexuality, was a bestseller. Vidal's satires include *Myra Breckinridge* (1968), and its sequel *Myron* (1974). Political novels include *Washington D.C.* (1967), and the trilogy *Burr* (1976), *1876* (1976), and *Lincoln* (1984). Vidal also wrote the screenplay for *Suddenly Last Summer* (1958). Other works include *Hollywood* (1990) and *Live from Golgotha* (1992).

video Term used in TELEVISION and computing to refer to electronic vision signals, and to equipment and software associated with visual displays. The picture component of a television signal is often referred to as video. *See also* VIDEOTAPE RECORDING

video disc Vinyl disc coated with a reflective, metallic surfacing. On one side of the reflective surface is etched a spiral of microscopic pits corresponding to digital information that can be picked up by a laser scanner and converted electronically to video pictures and sound. Since the late 1980s, video discs have been almost entirely superseded by the smaller, more comprehensive type of COMPACT DISC (CD) called a CD-ROM.

video game Game using electronically generated images displayed on a screen. High-quality graphics increasingly resemble the real world or stylized fantastical environments. Some video games test the skill of a single player, whilst other games allow two or more players to compete. *See also* VIRTUAL REALITY

videotape recording Recording and reproducing sound and moving pictures using magnetic tape. The video

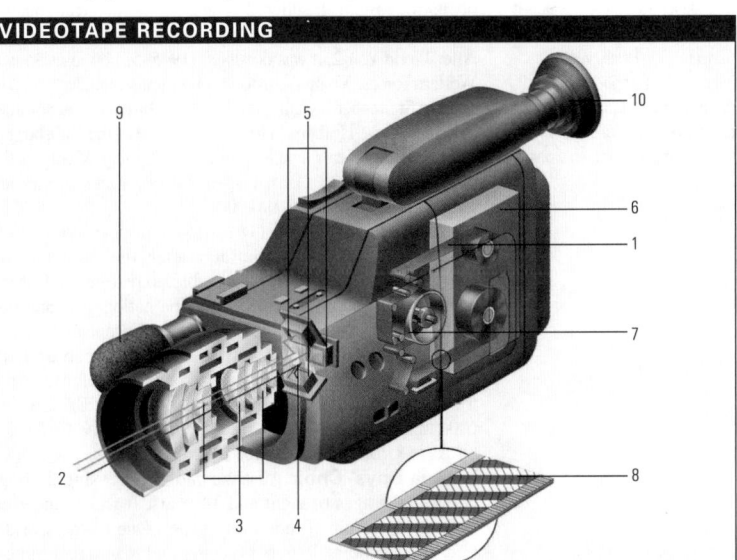

VIDEOTAPE RECORDING

A videotape recorder (camcorder) converts an image into an electrical signal, which can then be stored on magnetic tape (1). Light from an image (2) is focused by a series of lenses (3), and then split into its component colours by a prism (4). The red, green, and blue light strikes separate light-sensitive chips (5) that reproduce them in electronic form. The magnetic tape is housed in a protective case (6), which opens when inserted into the camcorder. The recording head (7) is angled and records information onto the tape in diagonal bands of magnetic particles (8). The helical scanning allows more information to be stored on a length of tape. A microphone (9) picks up sound, which is laid down in parallel to the visual information. Camcorders have a small television screen in the eyepiece (10) that allows the operator to play back and review the pictures taken. The camcorder can also be plugged directly into the television and the images played back.

V

773

▶ **Vikings** The Vikings were those Scandinavians who left their homelands between *c.*AD 800 and 1050, intent on trade, piracy, or settlement. Those from present-day Norway began their expansion by settling in the Orkneys and Shetland, fulfilling a need for land. It is believed that there may have been overpopulation and land shortage in Norway at this time; an additional reason may have been the growth of an absolutist monarchy in Norway. From the Orkneys and Shetland, the Vikings moved to N England, Ireland, the Faroe Islands, and the Isle of Man, where the chiefs founded towns to further trade and act as bases for pirate attacks. Across the Atlantic, the Norsemen discovered new lands – Iceland, Greenland, and North America. However, settlement of America was impossible due to overly long lines of communication. Danes settled in the E lowlands of England, and concentrated their activities along the coasts of the North Sea and the English Channel – in France and Friesia. Some ventured further afield to Spain and the Mediterranean. The Swedes journeyed into Russia, and acquired considerable wealth. The Vikings were extremely fine seamen and skilful shipbuilders; they also developed fairly sophisticated means of land transport. They were vitally important in Europe's trade, and there is evidence that they had commercial connections with all the contemporary known world.

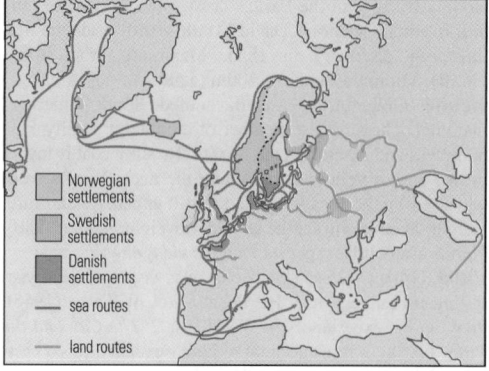

Norwegian settlements
Swedish settlements
Danish settlements
sea routes
land routes

recorder developed from the audio magnetic tape recorder, from which it differs significantly in two respects: videotape is wider to accommodate the picture signals; and the relative speed at which the tape passes the magnetic head is greater in order to deal with the larger amount of information necessary for recording and reproducing pictures. *See also* MAGNETIC RECORDING; SOUND RECORDING

videotext General term for the methods by which information can be brought to a TELEVISION screen. Information that is transmitted by the BROADCASTING authority in parallel with the ordinary TV signals, and that may be screened simultaneously with or independently from other channels, is known as **teletext**. The system that brings information to the screen from a computer databank via a telephone landline is called **videotex**.

Vienna (Wien) Capital of Austria, on the River DANUBE. Vienna became an important town under the Romans, but after their withdrawal in the 5th century it fell to a succession of invaders from E Europe. The first HABSBURG ruler was installed in 1276, and the city was the seat of the HOLY ROMAN EMPIRE from 1558 to 1806. Occupied by the French during the NAPOLEONIC WARS, it was later chosen as the site of the Congress of VIENNA. As the capital of the AUSTRO-HUNGARIAN EMPIRE, it was the cultural and social centre of 19th-century Europe under Emperor FRANZ JOSEPH. It suffered economic and political collapse following the defeat of the Central Powers in World War 1. After World War 2, it was occupied (1945–55) by joint Soviet-Western forces. Vienna's historical buildings include the 12th-century St Stephen's Cathedral, the Schönbrunn (royal summer palace), and the Hofburg (a former residence of the Habsburgs). Industries: chemicals, textiles, furniture, clothing. Vienna is the world's third-largest German-speaking city (after Berlin and Hamburg). Pop. (2000) 2,190,000.

Vienna, Congress of (1814–15) European conference that settled international affairs after the NAPOLEONIC WARS. It attempted, as far as possible, to restore the Europe of pre-1789, and thus disappointed the nationalists and liberals. Among steps to prevent future European wars, it established the CONGRESS SYSTEM and the German Confederation, a loose association for purposes of defence. Austria was represented by METTERNICH; Britain by CASTLEREAGH; Prussia by FREDERICK WILLIAM II; Russia by ALEXANDER I; and France by TALLEYRAND.

Vienna Boys' Choir Austrian choir comprising 22 boys between the ages of eight and 14 years. It was founded in 1498 as the choir of the court chapel. One of the world's best-known choirs, it tours regularly and makes recordings.

Vientiane (Viangchan) Capital and chief port of Laos, on the River Mekong, close to the Thai border, N central Laos. It was the capital of the Lao kingdom (1707–1828). The city became part of French INDOCHINA in 1893, and in 1899 became the capital of the French Protectorate. It is a major source of opium for world markets. Industries: textiles, brewing, cigarettes, hides, wood products. Pop. (1996) 189,600.

Viet Cong Nickname for the Vietnamese communist guerrillas who fought against the US-supported regime in South Vietnam during the VIETNAM WAR. After earlier, isolated revolts against the government of Ngo Dinh DIEM, the movement unified (1960) as the National Liberation Front (NLF), modelled on the VIET MINH.

Viet Minh Vietnamese organization that fought for independence from the French (1946–54). It resisted Japan's occupation of French INDOCHINA during World War 2. After the war, when the French refused to recognize it as a provisional government, it began operations against the colonial forces. The French withdrew after defeat at DIEN BIEN PHU (1954).

Vietnam Republic in SE Asia. *See* country feature

Vietnamese National language of VIETNAM, spoken by *c.*70 million people. It is part of the Muong branch of the Mon-Khmer sub-family of Asiatic languages, and derives much of its vocabulary from Mandarin Chinese.

Vietnam War (1954–75) Conflict between US-backed South Vietnam and the VIET CONG, who had the support of communist North Vietnam. It followed the defeat of the French at DIEN BIEN PHU (1954) and the partition of Vietnam. In 1956, President Ngo Dinh DIEM cancelled elections in South Vietnam. HO CHI MINH denounced the action and the Viet Cong launched an insurgency. Fuelled by fear of the spread of communism, the USA supported the Diem government and sent its first troops in 1961. The USA received token support from its allies in the Pacific region, while China and the Soviet Union supplied North Vietnam. In 1963, Diem was overthrown and executed. In 1965, the USA began bombing North Vietnam. As fighting intensified, the USA committed troops in greater numbers: by 1968 there were more than 500,000. In spite of US technological superiority and air supremacy, military stalemate ensued. The unrepresentative South Vietnamese government, US involvement in war crimes, heavy casualties, and daily TV coverage made the war highly unpopular in the USA. In 1973, a peace agreement, negotiated by Henry KISSINGER and Le Duc Tho, was signed in Paris. In 1975, North Vietnamese forces overran South Vietnam, and the country united under communist rule. The war claimed 50,000 American lives, 400,000 South Vietnamese, and 1 million Viet Cong and North Vietnamese.

Vignola, Giacomo Barozzi da (1507–73) Italian architect, who succeeded MICHELANGELO as architect of ST PETER'S (1567–73). His Gesú Church, Rome (1568), with its revolutionary design uniting clergy and congregation more closely, has been widely copied. Other major works include the Palazzo Farnese, Caprarola (1559) and the Tempieto di San Andrea, Rome (1550).

Vigny, Alfred de (1797–1863) French poet, dramatist, and novelist. Pessimistic in tone, his work often emphasizes the lonely struggle of the individual in a hostile universe, as in the quintessential Romantic drama *Chatterton* (1853). Vigny's best poems are contained in *Poems Ancient and Modern* (1826). His fiction includes the pioneering French historical novel *Cinq-Mars* (1826). *See also* ROMANTICISM

Vigo Seaport city on Vigo Bay, Galicia, NW Spain, near the Portuguese border. It was the scene of a naval battle in 1702, when an Anglo-Dutch fleet attacked Spanish galleons carrying a cargo of gold from the New World. Industries: fishing, fish processing and canning, boat-building. Pop. (2000) 285,526.

Vigo, Jean (1905–34) French film director. He died tragically young of leukaemia. Vigo's anarchic debut feature, *Zéro de Conduite* (1933), was banned in France until 1945. *Atalante* (1934), his second and last feature, is an elegant amalgam of social realism and poetic lyricism, set in a dream-like Parisian landscape.

Vikings Scandinavian seaborne marauders, traders and settlers, who spread throughout much of Europe and the North Atlantic region in the 9th to 11th centuries. The Viking expansion seems to have been caused by rapid population growth, and consequent scarcity of good farming land, as well as the desire for new sources of wealth. It was made possible by their advanced maritime technology, which enabled them to cross N European waters in a period when other sailors feared to venture out of sight of land. They were in many respects more advanced than other European peoples, notably in metalwork. Although they first appeared in their 'longships' as raiders on the coasts of NW Europe, later groups came to settle. Swedes, known as Varangians, founded the first Russian state at NOVGOROD, and traded via

INTERNET

Vietnam
▶ www.vietnamembassy-usa.org

Vietnam War
▶ www.vwip.org

the River Volga in Byzantium and Persia. Danes conquered much of N and E England. Norwegians created kingdoms in N Britain and Ireland, founding Dublin (c.840) and other cities; they also colonized Iceland and established settlements in Greenland. A short-lived settlement, VINLAND, was established in North America by LEIF ERICSSON in c.1003. In the early 10th century, the Vikings settled in NORMANDY. Anarchic conditions in 10th-century Scandinavia resulted in the formation of larger, more powerful kingdoms, and Viking expansion declined. It renewed in a different form with the conquest of England by King Sweyn of Denmark in 1013 and the NORMAN CONQUEST of 1066.

Viking space mission (1976) US space project to investigate conditions on MARS. Two spacecraft, Viking 1 and Viking 2, each attached to separate vehicles that orbited the planet, made the first successful landings on Mars. They transmitted much information back to Earth, including dramatic photographs of the surface. *See also* SPACE EXPLORATION

villa Large country house of the ROMAN EMPIRE and post-Roman period. In ancient Rome, they were the private residences of important citizens. They had spacious reception rooms, often with MOSAIC floors and sometimes even underfloor heating.

Villa, 'Pancho' (Francisco) (1877–1923) Mexican revolutionary leader. An outlaw, he later joined the forces of Francisco MADERO (1909) during the MEXICAN REVOLUTION. Villa

sided with Venustiano CARRANZA for some time but later supported Emiliano ZAPATA. Angered by US recognition of Carranza's government, he murdered US citizens in N Mexico and New Mexico. In 1920, Villa was pardoned in return for agreeing to retire from politics. He was later assassinated.

Villa-Lobos, Heitor (1887–1959) Brazilian composer and conductor. Villa-Lobos' *Chôros* compositions were influenced by Brazilian folk music and the music of Claude Debussy. His range of works includes operas, ballets, symphonies, religious and chamber music. His nine *Bachianas Brasileiras* are a Brazilian transcription of the music of J.S. Bach.

Villehardouin, Geoffroi de (1150–1213) French historian. He was a leader of the Fourth CRUSADE. Villehardouin's incomplete account of the Crusade, *Conquest of Constantinople*, was the first historical chronicle written in French.

villi In anatomy, small, finger-like projections of a MUCOUS MEMBRANE such as that which lines the inner walls of the SMALL INTESTINE. They increase the absorptive surface area of the gut. In digestion, intestinal villi absorb most of the products of food broken down in the STOMACH, DUODENUM, and ILEUM.

Villon, François (1430–63?) French lyric poet, b. François de Montcorbier or François des Loges. He led a troubled life after killing a priest in 1455. Villon wrote the famous *Ballad of a Hanged Man* while awaiting execution in 1462 (the sentence was later commuted to banishment). Among his other major

---

VIETNAM

The Socialist Republic of Vietnam occupies an S-shaped strip of land facing the South China Sea in SE Asia. The coastal plains include two densely populated, fertile river delta areas. The Red (Hong) Delta faces the Gulf of Tonkin in the N, while the MEKONG Delta is in the S.

Inland are thinly populated highland regions, including the Annam Cordillera (Chaîne Annamitique), which forms much of the boundary with Cambodia. The highlands in the NW extend into Laos and China.

CLIMATE

Vietnam has a tropical climate, although the drier months of January to March are cooler than the wet, hot summer months, when monsoon winds blow from the SW. Typhoons sometimes hit the coast, causing much damage.

HISTORY

In 111 BC China seized Vietnam, naming it ANNAM. In 939 AD it became independent. In 1558 it split into two parts: TONKIN in the north, ruled from Hanoi, and Annam in the south, ruled from Hué. In 1802, with French support, Vietnam was united as the Empire of Vietnam

AREA 331,689sq km [128,065sq mi]
POPULATION 85,262,000
CAPITAL (POPULATION)
Hanoi (4,147,000)
GOVERNMENT Socialist republic
ETHNIC GROUPS Vietnamese 87%, Chinese, Hmong, Thai, Khmer, Cham, mountain groups
LANGUAGES Vietnamese (official), English, French, Chinese, Khmer, mountain languages
RELIGIONS Buddhism, Christianity, indigenous beliefs
CURRENCY Dong = 10 hao = 100 xu

under Nguyen Anh. The French seized Saigon in 1859, and by 1887 had formed INDOCHINA from the union of Tonkin, Annam, and Cochin China.

Japan conquered Vietnam during World War 2, and established a Vietnamese state under Emperor Bao Dai. After the war Bao Dai's government collapsed, and the nationalist VIET MINH, led by HO CHI MINH, set up a Vietnamese republic. In 1946 the French tried to reassert control and war broke out. Despite aid from the USA, the Viet Minh defeated the French at DIEN BIEN PHU.

POLITICS

In 1954, Vietnam divided along the 17th Parallel into North Vietnam under the communist government of Ho Chi Minh and South Vietnam under the French-supported Bao Dai. In 1955 Bao Dai was deposed and Ngo Dinh Diem was elected president. The west recognized Diem as legal ruler despite his authoritarian regime. North Vietnam, supported by China and the Soviet Union, extended its influence into South Vietnam mainly through the VIET CONG. The USA became involved in what they perceived to be a fight against communism, and the conflict escalated into the VIETNAM WAR (1954–75). In 1975, after the withdrawal of US troops, Ho Chi Minh's forces overran South Vietnam and it surrendered.

In 1979 Vietnam helped overthrow the KHMER ROUGE government in Cambodia, only withdrawing in 1989. The United States opened an embassy in Hanoi in 1995, and in 2002 a trade agreement opened access to US markets. The early 2000s saw economic liberalization and rapid development, and the country joined the World Trade Organization in 2007.

ECONOMY

The World Bank classifies Vietnam as a 'low-income' developing country. Agriculture

employs 67% of the workforce. The main food crop is rice. Other products include maize and sweet potatoes; commercial crops include bananas, coffee, peanuts, rubber, soya beans and tea. Fishing is also important.

N Vietnam has most of the country's natural resources, including coal. The country also produces chromium, oil, phosphates and tin. Manufactures include cement, fertilizers, processed food, machinery, steel and textiles.

V

V

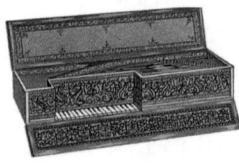

▲ **violin** Late 17th-century violin. The violin was perfected in Italy by the Amati, Stradivari, and Guarneri families from 1650 to 1740. The brilliance of violin tone soon overwhelmed the softer tones of the viols, which died out.

▲ **virginal** Related to the harpsichord, and producing a similar plucked sound, the virginal was a small keyboard instrument without legs. The best collection of virginal music is the Fitzwilliam Virginal Book (1606–16), consisting of pieces by English composers such as John Bull, William Byrd, and Giles Farnaby.

VIRGINIA
Statehood :
June 25, 1788
Nickname :
Old Dominion
State bird :
Cardinal
State flower :
Flowering dogwood
State tree :
Flowering dogwood
State motto :
Thus always to tyrants

---

works are *Le Petit Testament* (1456), a satirical will in verse, and *Le Grand Testament* (1461), in part a lament for lost youth.

Vilnius Capital of LITHUANIA, on the River Nerisr. Founded in 1323 as the capital of the Grand Duchy of Lithuania, the city declined after the union of Lithuania-Poland. Vilnius was captured by Russia in 1795. After World War 1, it was made capital of an independent Lithuania. In 1939, Soviet troops occupied the city and, in 1940, Lithuania became a Soviet republic. During World War 2, the city was occupied by German troops, and its Jewish population was all but exterminated. In 1944, it reverted to its Soviet status. In 1990, Lithuania unilaterally declared independence, leading to clashes with Soviet troops and pitched battles on the streets of Vilnius. In 1991, the Soviet Union recognized Lithuanian independence. Despite bombing in World War 2, the old city retains many historic synagogues, churches, and civic buildings, as well as remnants of its 14th-century castle and fortifications. Industries: engineering, chemicals, textiles, food processing. Pop. (2001) 553,000.

Vincent de Paul, Saint (1581–1660) French priest. As a young man he was said to have been captured by Barbary pirates and to have spent two years as a slave in Tunisia. After his return to Paris, Vincent de Paul began a mission to the peasantry, founding the Congregation of the Mission (or Lazarists). In 1633 he helped to found the Sisters of Charity of St Vincent de Paul to minister to the sick, the old and orphans. He was canonized in 1737.

vine Plant with a long, thin stem that climbs rocks, plants and supports. To aid their climb, vines develop modifications such as tendrils, disc-like holdfasts, adventitious roots and runners. Examples are tropical LIANA, wild GRAPE, and morning glory.

vinegar Any of various types of liquid condiment and preservative based on a weak solution of ETHANOIC ACID. It is produced commercially by the fermentation of alcohol. The major type of vinegar is known as malt vinegar which, when distilled, becomes white (or clear) vinegar. Vinegar can also be processed from cider or wine.

Vinland Region of North America settled (*c.*1003) by VIKINGS from Greenland led by LEIF ERICSSON. The existence of land w of Greenland had been reported a few years earlier. Leif stayed for one season only, but at least two other expeditions settled there briefly. Vinland was soon abandoned, apparently because of the hostility of local people.

viol Fretted STRINGED INSTRUMENT, played with a bow. It is held on or between the knees and, in its most usual shape, has sloping shoulders and a flat back. The six strings are tuned in fourths, in the same manner as the LUTE. A possible derivative, the modern DOUBLE BASS, is perhaps the only type of viol to survive; it shows its ancestry by being tuned in fourths (unlike members of the violin family, which are tuned in fifths).

viola STRINGED INSTRUMENT of the VIOLIN family. It is slightly larger than the violin and its four strings are tuned a fifth lower. It is the tenor member of a string quartet.

violet Any of *c.*400 species of herbs and shrublets of the genus *Viola*, found worldwide. Violets may be annual or perennial, with five-petalled flowers that grow singly on stalks; usually blue, violet, lilac, yellow, or white. Family Violaceae.

violin STRINGED INSTRUMENT. It is thought to have derived from the *lira da braccio*, a Renaissance bowed instrument, and the rebec. It was perfected in Italy by the AMATI, STRADIVARI, and Guarneri families between 1650 and 1740. The body is assembled from curved, wooden panels, the front pierced by two *f*-shaped sound-holes. Four taut strings are played by drawing a bow across them, or sometimes by plucking them with the fingers (pizzicato).

violoncello *See* CELLO

viper Any of 150 species of poisonous SNAKES characterized by a pair of long, hollow, venom-injecting fangs in the front of the upper jaw. The fangs can be folded back when not in use. The common adder (*Vipera berus*) of Europe and E Asia has a dark, zigzag band along its back. Length: to 3m (10ft). Family Viperidae.

Virgil (70–19 BC) (Publius Vergilius Maro) Roman poet. Virgil gained a high literary reputation in Rome with the *Eclogues* (42–37BC) and the *Georgics* (37–30BC), a pastoral but instruc-

tive work on farming and country life. His greatest work was the *Aeneid*, which established him as an epic poet. It relates the adventures of the Trojan hero AENEAS, and echoes the themes of Homer's *Odyssey* and *Iliad*. Unfinished at his death, it was published at the command of Emperor AUGUSTUS.

virginal Musical instrument of the HARPSICHORD family. The strings, a single set running nearly parallel to the keyboard, are plucked by quills. Two keyboards, differing in size and pitch, were sometimes incorporated into the same case. Virginals were particularly popular in 16th- and 17th-century England.

virgin birth Christian doctrine teaching that the Blessed Virgin MARY conceived JESUS CHRIST through the power of the HOLY SPIRIT and without the involvement of a human male. That Jesus had no earthly father is a basic tenet of Roman Catholicism, all the Eastern Orthodox Churches, and most Protestant Churches.

Virginia State in E USA, on the Atlantic coast, the most northerly of the 'southern states'; the capital is RICHMOND. The coastal plain is low-lying. In the w, the Piedmont Plateau rises to the BLUE RIDGE MOUNTAINS, and there are extensive forests. The first permanent British settlement in North America was at JAMESTOWN (1607). Virginia evolved an aristocratic plantation society based on vast tobacco holdings. Virginia's leaders were in the forefront of the AMERICAN REVOLUTION. During the CIVIL WAR, Richmond acted as the Confederate capital, and Virginia was the main battleground of the war. In 1870, Virginia rejoined to the Union. Farming is a vital part of Virginia's economy, and the chief crops include tobacco, peanuts, grain, vegetables, and fruits. Dairying and poultry are also widespread. Industries: chemicals, shipbuilding, fishing, transport equipment. Coal is the most important mineral deposit. Stone, sand, and gravel are quarried. Area: 105,710sq km (40,814sq mi). Pop. (2000) 7,078,515.

Virginia Beach City on the Atlantic Ocean, SE Virginia. Site of the Cape Henry Memorial Cross (commemorating the first landing of English colonists, 1607), and of the oldest brick house in the USA, it is a rapidly expanding tourist centre with good beaches and recreational facilities. Its economy is helped by market gardening and nearby military complexes. The population increased by nearly 60% between 1980 and 1992, making it the state's largest city. Pop. (2000) 425,527.

Virgin Islands, British British colony in the West Indies. It is a group of 36 islands, which form part of the ANTILLES group between the Caribbean Sea and the Atlantic Ocean; the capital is Road Town (on Tortola, the main island). First settled in the 17th century, the islands formed part of the LEEWARD ISLANDS colony until 1956. The chief economic activity is tourism. Area: 1151sq km (58sq mi). Pop. (2000) 22,000. *See* WEST INDIES map

Virgin Islands, US Group of 68 islands in the Lesser ANTILLES, West Indies. They are administered by the USA with the status of an 'unincorporated territory'. The chief islands are St Croix and St Thomas – the latter includes the capital Charlotte Amalie (2000 pop. 11,044). Spanish from 1553, the islands were Danish until 1917, when the USA bought them for US$25 million, in order to protect the northern approaches to the newly completed PANAMA CANAL. Tourism is the biggest money earner. Industries: oil refining, aluminium, textiles, rum, pharmaceuticals, perfumes. Area: 347sq km (134sq mi). Pop. (2000) 125,000. *See* WEST INDIES map

Virgin Mary *See* MARY; VIRGIN BIRTH

Virgo (Virgin) Equatorial constellation on the ecliptic between Leo and Libra. It lies in a region of the sky that has many galaxies and galaxy clusters. The brightest star is the first-magnitude Alpha Virginis, or Spica.

virology Study of VIRUSES. The existence of viruses was established (1892) by D. Ivanovski, a Russian botanist, who found that the causative agent of tobacco mosaic disease could pass through a porcelain filter impermeable to BACTERIA. The introduction of the electron microscope in the 1940s made it possible to view viruses.

virtual reality Term that has been used for computer graphics that simulate a three-dimensional environment that users can explore as if it were real. A virtual reality system can allow an architect to see what the inside of a building will look like before construction begins. Computer images are produced using an architect's drawings of the building. Virtual reality technology has influenced the development of the VIDEO GAME industry.

virus Submicroscopic infectious organism. Viruses vary in size from ten to 300 nanometres, and contain only genetic material in the form of DNA or RNA. Viruses are incapable of independent existence: they can grow and reproduce only when they enter another cell, such as a bacterium or animal cell, because they lack energy-producing and protein-synthesizing functions. When they enter a cell, viruses subvert the host's metabolism so that viral reproduction is favoured. Control of viruses is difficult because harsh measures are required to kill them. The animal body has, however, evolved some protective measures, such as production of INTERFERON and of ANTIBODIES directed against specific viruses. Where the specific agent can be isolated, VACCINES can be developed, but some viruses change so rapidly that vaccines become ineffective. *See also* IMMUNE SYSTEM

Visconti Italian family that ruled Milan from the 13th century until 1447. Ottone Visconti (*c.*1207–95) was appointed Archbishop of Milan in 1262, and used his position to become the first Visconti *Signore* (It. 'Lord') of Milan. Supporters of the anti-papal GHIBELLINES, the Visconti established control over Lombardy in the 14th century, and in 1349 the title of *Signore* became hereditary. Visconti lordship of Milan passed to the Sforza family in 1447.

Visconti, Luchino (1906–76) Italian film director, b. Count Don Luchino Visconti di Modrone. His debut film, *Ossessione* (1942), was a pioneering work of Italian NEO-REALISM. Other films include *Senso* (1953), *Rocco and His Brothers* (1960), *The Leopard* (1963), *Death in Venice* (1971), and *Conversation Piece* (1975). A more opulent style characterizes Visconti's later work. He was also acclaimed for his theatre and opera work, and greatly helped the career of Maria CALLAS.

viscosity Resistance to flow of a FLUID because of internal friction. The more viscous the fluid, the slower it flows. Viscosity is large for liquids and extremely small for gases. It is measured in the SI unit of pascal seconds.

Vishnu Major god of HINDUISM; one of the supreme triad of gods, along with BRAHMA and SHIVA. Vishnu was mentioned as a sun god in the VEDAS (*c.*1500–*c.*1200BC). Over the next 1,000 years or more, his importance grew and he became an amalgam of local cultic gods and heroes. In mythology, Vishnu is worshipped as a preserver and restorer. According to Hindu tradition, he reigns in heaven with his wife, LAKSHMI, the goddess of wealth. On occasion, he comes into the world to fight evil, assuming a different incarnation each time. His incarnations have included RAMA and KRISHNA. In art, Vishnu is depicted as a man with four hands holding a shell, discus, mace, and lotus.

Visigoths *See* GOTH

vision *See* SIGHT

Vistula (Wisla) Longest river in Poland. It rises in the Carpathian Mountains of W Poland and flows NW through Warsaw, then NW through Torun to enter the Gulf of Danzig at Gdansk. The major waterway of Poland, it serves a large area through a tributary system. Canals link it with other important rivers both E and W. Length: 1,090km (675mi).

vitalism Philosophical theory that all living organisms derive their characteristic qualities from a universal life force. Vitalists hold that the force operating on living matter is peculiar to such matter and is quite different from any forces of inanimate bodies. In the late 20th century, few scientists give vitalism much credence, but it has influenced many forms of alternative medicine.

vitamin Organic compound that is essential in small amounts to the maintenance and healthy growth of all animals. Vitamins are classified as either water-soluble (B and C) or fat-soluble (A, D, E, and K). They are usually taken in the diet, but today most can be made synthetically. A danger exists in taking too many vitamin supplements. Some are synthesized in the body. Many vitamins act as coenzymes, helping ENZYMES in RESPIRATION and other metabolic processes. Lack of a particular vitamin can lead to a deficiency disease.

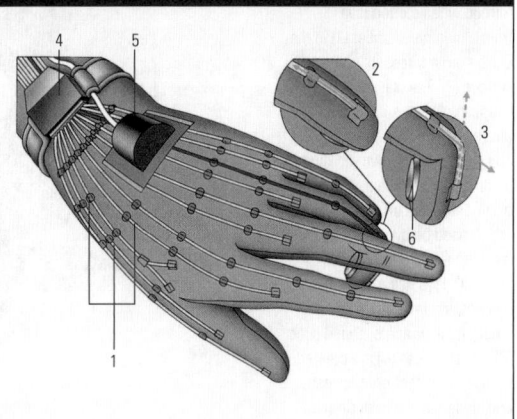

A data glove measures the movements of the wearer's hand and allows the user to manipulate objects in virtual reality. Fibre optic cables (1) on the glove detect the flexing of the hand. Light travels up and down the cables (2). When the cables bend (3), they no longer reflect light back to the interface board (4). A position sensor (5) detects the movement of the glove in three dimensions. Fingertip padding (6) convinces the user they are touching an actual object.

Vitamin E is important in reproduction and many other biological processes. **Vitamin D** helps the body absorb phosphorus and calcium. It is essential for the normal growth of bone and teeth. Existing in human skin (activated by sunlight), vitamin D is also found in fish-liver oil, yeast, and egg yolk. **Vitamin C** (ascorbic acid) is commonly found in many fruits and vegetables. It helps the body resist infection and stress, and is essential to normal metabolism. **Vitamin B** is actually a group of 12 vitamins, important in assisting the process by which energy is produced in the body (respiration). Vitamin B_1 (THIAMINE) occurs in yeast and cereals. Another B vitamin is niacin (nicotinic acid) found in milk, meat, and green vegetables. Vitamin B_{12} is needed for the formation of blood cells. It is found especially in meat, liver and eggs. **Vitamin A** (retinol), found in fish liver oil, is important for healthy eyes. *See also* RIBOFLAVIN

Vitruvius (active early 1st century AD) Roman architect and engineer. His encyclopedic *De Architectura* (before AD 27) covers almost every aspect of ancient architecture, including town planning, types of buildings, and materials. It is the only work of its type to survive from the ancient world.

Vitus, Saint (active 4th century) Italian martyr. Secretly raised as a Christian by his nurse, he was put to death during the persecutions of DIOCLETIAN. He is the patron saint of actors.

Vivaldi, Antonio (1675–1741) Italian composer. A master of the CONCERTO and a virtuoso violinist, Vivaldi helped to standardize the three-movement concerto form and to develop the *concerto grosso* (a concerto for two or more solo instruments). His best-known work is *The Four Seasons* (1725). He also composed sacred vocal music and *c.*50 operas, of which 20 survive.

viviparity (VIVIPARY) Process or trait among animals of giving birth to live young. Placental mammals show the highest development of viviparity, in which the offspring develops inside the body, within the mother's UTERUS.

vivisection Dissection of living bodies for experimental purposes. Work with laboratory animals in testing drugs, vaccines and pharmaceuticals frequently involves such dissections. The ethical issue of experimenting on living animals is a matter of controversy. *See also* ANIMAL RIGHTS

Vladimir City on the N bank of the River Klyazma, Russia. Founded early in the 12th century by Vladimir II of Kiev, it is one of Russia's oldest cities. The grand dukes of Moscow were crowned here in the 14th century. Tourists are drawn partly by three 12th-century buildings – the two cathedrals and the Golden Gate (a fortified city gate). Industries: chemicals, cotton textiles, plastics, tractors, machine tools, electrical goods. Pop. (1999) 339,200.

Vladimir I (the Great) (956–1015) Grand Duke of Kiev and first Christian ruler of Russia (980–1015). Vladimir raised an army of VIKING mercenaries in 979, and conquered Polotsk and Kiev. Proclaimed Prince of all Russia, he extended Russian territories, conquering parts of Poland and Lithuania. Impressed by accounts of Constantinople, he became a Christian and married a Byzantine princess (988). St Vladimir, as he is also called, established the Greek Orthodox faith in Russia.

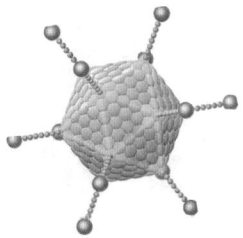

▲ **virus** The human adenovirus is of the type responsible for colds and sore throats. The casing consists of 252 protein molecules (capsomeres) arranged into a regular icosahedron (20 faces). This structure, here shown color coded for ease of identification, occurs in many viruses,. It is the most economical packing arrangement around the DNA inside. Twelve of the capsomeres, located at the points of the icosahedron, are five-sided pentagon bases (yellow). The remaining 240 are six-sided hexons (green). Five of these (green-yellow) adjoin each penton base, from which extends a single fibre (red) tipped with a terminal structure (blue) that begins cell entry.

V

▶▼ volcano Volcanoes (A) are formed when molten lava (1) from a magma chamber (2) in the Earth's crust forces its way to the surface (3). The classic cone-shaped volcano is formed of alternating layers of cooled lava and cinders (4) thrown out during an eruption. Side vents (5) can occur and when offshoots of lava are trapped below the surface, laccoliths (6) are formed. When a volcano's lava has a low silica content, the lava flows easily creating a low-angle, shield cone (B). Cinder cones (C) are created by volcanoes that produce ash and cinders not lava during eruptions. The layers of ash and cinders do not have the stability to create the classic cone-shaped volcano. When a magma chamber collapses, a caldera (D) is formed as the centre of the volcanic cone follows suit. Lakes (1) often fill the resulting crater and subsequent upsurges of lava can create islands (2).

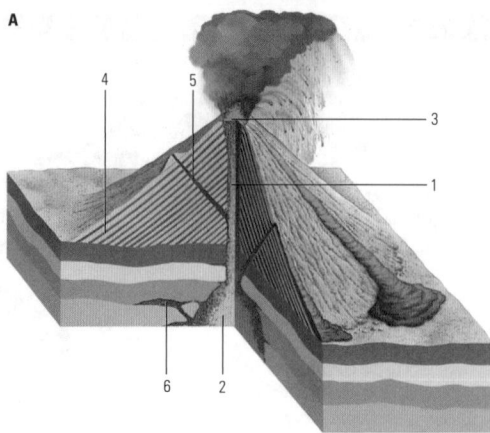

A

B

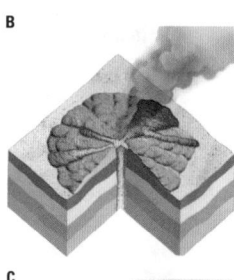

C

D

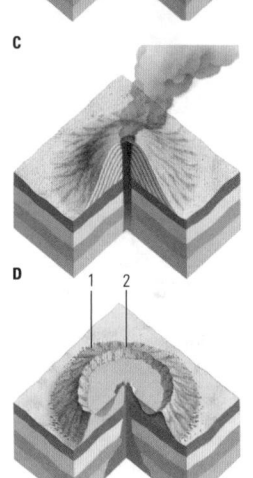

Vladivostok Main port, naval base, and cultural centre of SIBERIA, Russia. It is located around a sheltered harbour on the Pacific coast, 50km (30mi) from the Chinese border. Founded in 1860 as a military post, the city developed as a naval base after 1872. Vladivostok is the main E terminus of the TRANS-SIBERIAN RAILWAY. The harbour is kept open in winter by ice-breakers, and is a major base for fishing fleets. Industries: ship repairing, oil refining, metal-working, timber products, food processing. Pop. (1999) 613,100.

Vlaminck, Maurice (1876–1958) French painter, graphic artist, and writer. One of the leading exponents of FAUVISM, Vlaminck painted with colours squirted straight from the tube, producing exuberant landscapes that were partly inspired by the work of Vincent VAN GOGH. In 1908, he began using darker colours and studied Paul CÉZANNE in an attempt to give his painting more weight.

vocal cords *See* LARYNX

vocational education Instruction in industrial or commercial skills. A range of levels of vocational training and qualification are available from schools and colleges, often in collaboration with organizations concerned to improve training and quality standards in particular areas of employment.

Voice of America (VOA) Radio station subsidized by the US government. It presents news, other generally factual information, and cultural programmes aimed at both English-speaking citizens of foreign countries and US troops serving abroad. VOA was originally set up by the US Office of War Information in 1943–44 to broadcast war news and propaganda. *See also* WORLD SERVICE

Vojvodina Autonomous province in N SERBIA, bordered by Croatia, Hungary, and Romania. The capital is Novi Sad. From 1849 to 1860, it was the independent crown land of Vojvodina, but it was ceded to Yugoslavia in 1920. Given nominal autonomy by Belgrade in 1946, it remains firmly part of Serbia. Only around 50% of the population are Serbs: the rest are Hungarian (19%), Croats, Slovaks, and Romanians. The province is densely populated with a fertile agricultural plain. Industries: fruit, cattle, food processing. Area: 21,500sq km (8301sq mi). Pop. (2000) 1,946,000.

volcanism (vulcanism) Volcanic activity. The term includes all aspects of the process: the eruption of molten and gaseous matter from VOLCANOES, the building up of cones and mountains, and the formation of LAVA flows, GEYSERS and hot springs.

volcano Vent from which molten rock or LAVA, solid rock debris, and gases issue. Volcanoes may be of the **central vent** type, where the material erupts from a single pipe, or of the **fissure** type, where material is extruded along an extensive fracture. Volcanoes are usually classed as active, dormant or extinct. *See also* VOLCANISM

vole Short-tailed, small-eared, prolific RODENT that lives in the Northern Hemisphere. Most voles are greyish-brown, herbivorous ground-dwellers and are small. The semi-aquatic water vole is the largest. Length: to 18cm (7in). Family Cricetidae.

Volga Europe's longest river, at 3750km (2330mi), in E European Russia. The river rises in the Valdai Hills, then flows E past Rzhev to Kazan, where it turns S. It continues SW to Volgograd, and then SE to enter the Caspian Sea below

Astrakhan. The Volga connects to the Baltic Sea by the Volga-Baltic Waterway, to Moscow by the Moscow Canal, and to the Sea of Azov (and the Black Sea) by the Volga-Don Canal. Many dams and hydroelectric power stations lie along its course. Navigable for c.3,550km (2,200mi), it carries about two-thirds of Russia's river freight traffic.

Volgograd Major Russian inland port on the River VOLGA, the E terminus of the Volga-Don Canal. During the Civil War that followed the Russian Revolution, it was defended by Bolshevik troops under STALIN (1918–20), and was renamed Stalingrad in his honour (1925). In the winter of 1942–43, it was almost completely destroyed in a fierce battle that halted the German advance. Rebuilt after World War 2 and renamed Volgograd in 1961, it is a major rail and industrial centre. Industries: oil-refining, shipbuilding, chemicals, aluminium, steel, farm vehicles. Pop. (1999) 1,000,000.

volleyball Game in which a ball is volleyed by hand over a net across the centre of a court by two six-a-side teams. The court is 18m (59ft) long by 9m (29ft 6in) wide; the top of the net is 2.4m (8ft) high. The object of the game is to get the ball to touch the ground within the opponents' half of the court, or to oblige an opponent to touch the ball before it goes directly out of court. Only the serving team can score, and failure to score loses service; 15 points wins a set, and a game is the best of five sets. Volleyball has been included in the Olympic Games since 1964.

volt (symbol V) SI unit of electric potential and ELECTROMOTIVE FORCE (EMF). It is the POTENTIAL DIFFERENCE between two points on a conducting wire carrying a current of one ampere when the power dissipated is one watt. It is named after the Italian physicist Alessandro Volta.

Volta West African river, c.470km (290mi) long, formed by the confluence of the Black Volta and White Volta rivers at New Tamale, central Ghana. The river flows S into the Gulf of Guinea at Ada. In 1965, it was dammed at Akosombo to form Lake Volta.

Voltaire (1694–1778) French philosopher, historian, playwright, and poet, b. François Marie Arouet. He is the outstanding figure of the French ENLIGHTENMENT. Voltaire spent much of his life combating intolerance and injustice, and attacking institutions such as the Church. While in the Bastille (1717), he wrote his first tragedy *Oedipe* (1718). In 1726, Voltaire was beaten and returned to the Bastille for insulting a nobleman. While in exile in England (1726–29), he was strongly influenced by John LOCKE and Isaac NEWTON and wrote a classic biography of Charles XII of Sweden. Back in France, Voltaire wrote several tragedies and the eulogistic *Philosophical Letters* (1734), which provoked official censure. Voltaire corresponded for many years with FREDERICK II (THE GREAT) and contributed to DIDEROT's *Encyclopédie*. His best-known work, the philosophical romance *Candide* (1759), published anonymously. Other works that express his philosophy of RATIONALISM include *Jeannot et Colin* (1764), and *Essay on Morals* (1756). The *Dictionnaire philosophique* (1764) is a collection of his thoughts on contemporary matters.

voltmeter Instrument for measuring the voltage (POTENTIAL DIFFERENCE) between two points in an electrical CIRCUIT. Voltmeters are always connected in parallel with the components whose voltages are being measured. A voltmeter has a high internal resistance compared with the resistance across which it is connected. *See also* AMMETER

volume Amount of space taken up by a body. Volume is measured in cubic units, such as cm^3 (cubic centimetres).

voluntary muscle (skeletal MUSCLE) In human beings and other mammals, the most plentiful of the three types of muscle comprising the bulk of the body. It is under conscious control and has a striped appearance under a microscope. *See also* INVOLUNTARY MUSCLE

vomiting Act of bringing up the contents of the stomach by way of the mouth. Vomiting is a reflex mechanism that may be activated by any of a number of stimuli, including dizziness, pain, gastric irritation, or shock. It may also be a symptom of serious disease.

Von Braun, Wernher (1912–77) US aeronautical engineer, b. Germany. In World War 2, he was responsible for building the V-2 rocket (see V-WEAPONS). In 1945, Von Braun went to the USA, where he developed the Jupiter ROCKET that took the first US satellite, Explorer 1, into space in 1958. In 1960, he joined the NATIONAL AERONAUTICS AND SPACE ADMINISTRATION (NASA) and developed the Saturn rocket that took astronauts to the Moon. *See also* SPACE EXPLORATION

Vondel, Joost von den (1587–1679) Dutch poet and dramatist. Vondel struggled against the handicaps of humble birth, limited education, and religious persecution to produce outstanding work based on biblical and classical sources. Of his trilogy of plays, *Lucifer* (1654), *Adam in Exile* (1664) and *Noah* (1667), the first -a tragedy – is generally regarded as his masterpiece. He also wrote in various poetic genres.

Vonnegut, Kurt, Jr (1922–2007) US novelist. He often draws on the conventions of fantasy to satirize the horrors of the 20th century. Vonnegut's novels, which experiment with time and narrative structure, include *Player Piano* (1952), *Slaughterhouse-Five* (1969), and *Hocus Pocus* (1991). His short stories were collected in *Welcome to the Monkey House* (1968). Other works include *Three Complete Novels* (1995).

Von Neumann, John (1903–57) US mathematician, b. Budapest. He left Hungary to teach at Princeton University (1930–33), and then at the Institute of Advanced Studies. In mathematics, Von Neumann helped to develop GAME THEORY. His early contribution to QUANTUM THEORY was followed by work on the atomic bomb at Los Alamos. Von Neumann is chiefly celebrated for his role in the early development of COMPUTERS. One of his first designs was used to test (1952) the first hydrogen bomb.

voodoo Religious belief of African origin. It is prevalent in parts of Africa, but is better known as the national religion of Haiti. Adherents believe in the reincarnate qualities of **Loa**, which include deified ancestors, local gods and Roman Catholic saints. Loa possesses the believers during dreams or ceremonies, which include dancing and hypnotic trances.

Voronezh Industrial port on the River Voronezh, w central Russia, capital of Voronezh province. Founded as a fortress in 1586, it became a shipbuilding centre under Peter I. During World War 2, the city was almost totally destroyed and most of it has been rebuilt. Industries: locomotives, machinery, synthetic rubber, oil, chemicals, food processing, cigarettes, television sets. Pop. (2000) 918,000.

Voroshilov, Kliment Yefremovich (1881–1969) Soviet statesman, president (1953–60). He joined the Bolsheviks in 1903, and took an military role in the RUSSIAN REVOLUTION (1917). Voroshilov was a Red Army commander in the civil war (1918–20) before becoming commissar for defence (1925–40). He commanded the Red Army on the NW front in World War 2. Voroshilov became president on the death of STALIN, but was implicated in a plot against Nikita KHRUSHCHEV and resigned.

Vorster, Balthazar Johannes (1915–83) South African statesman, prime minister (1966–78). Imprisoned during World War 2 as a Nazi sympathizer, he was a staunch advocate of APARTHEID under Hendrik VERWOERD and succeeded him as prime minister and Nationalist Party leader. Vorster established Transkei as a 'bantustan' and suppressed the SOWETO rising (1976). He invaded Angola to try and prevent Namibian independence. In 1978, Vorster became president but corruption charges forced his resignation in 1979. He was succeeded by P.W. BOTHA.

vortex Eddy or whirlpool observed in fluid motion. Vortices cannot occur in ideal (nonviscous) fluid motion, but they are important in the study of real fluids. In particular, the vortices occurring behind aerofoils are of great interest in aerodynamic design.

vorticism British art movement. Derived from CUBISM and Italian FUTURISM, it originated (1913) with Wyndham LEWIS' attempt to express the spirit of the time in harsh angular forms derived from machinery. David Bomberg, Ezra Loomis

POUND, Henri GAUDIER-BRZESKA, and Jacob EPSTEIN were also members. The term was coined by Ezra POUND.

voting Process employed to choose candidates for public office or to decide controversial issues. Early forms were by voice or sign, but the secret ballot became popular in order to eliminate the possibility of intimidation and corruption. Voters usually mark a piece of paper and deposit it in a ballot box, but in the USA voting machines, operated by polling levers, are commonly in use. *See also* DEMOCRACY

Voting Rights Act (1965) US legislation authorizing federal authorities to check registration and voting procedures in order to protect the rights of black voters in nine southern states. Within a year of its passage, the number of blacks registered in five 'Deep South' states increased by almost 50%.

Voyager program SPACE EXPLORATION project to study JUPITER, SATURN, URANUS, and NEPTUNE, using two unmanned craft. In 1977, the two Voyager probes were launched (16 days apart) from Kennedy Space Center at CAPE CANAVERAL, Florida, USA. In 1979, they beamed back the first close-up pictures of Jupiter. The probes then passed Saturn, and showed the structure of the planet's rings. Voyager 2 went on to study Uranus in 1986, and Neptune in 1989. Both probes have now left the Solar System.

Vulcan (Volcanus) Roman god of fire and volcanoes, identified with the Greek god HEPHAESTUS. His temples were prudently sited outside city walls. Often invoked to avert fires, he was associated with thunderbolts and the Sun.

vulcanization Chemical process, discovered in 1839 by Charles Goodyear, of heating SULPHUR or its compounds with natural or synthetic RUBBER in order to improve the rubber's durability and resilience.

Vulgate Oldest surviving version of the complete BIBLE, compiled and translated, mostly from Greek, into Latin by Saint JEROME from 382. The text was revised several times, and was used universally in the Middle Ages. In 1546, the Council of TRENT promoted it as the official Latin translation.

vulture Large, keen-sighted, strong-flying bird that feeds on carrion. **New World** vultures, found throughout the Americas, include the CONDOR, turkey BUZZARD, and king vulture; family Cathartidae. **Old World** vultures, related to eagles, are found in Africa, Europe, and Asia, and include the Egyptian vulture and the griffon vulture; family Accipitridae.

vulva In human females, the external genitalia. Extending downwards from the clitoris (a small, sensitive, elongated, erectile organ), a pair of fleshy lips (labia majora) surround the vulvar orifice. Within the labia majora, two smaller folds of skin (labia minora) surround a depression called the vestibule, within which are the urethral and vaginal openings.

Vyatka (formerly Kirov) City and river port on the w bank of the River Vyatka, w Russia; capital of Kirov region. Founded as Khlynov in 1174, it was annexed by Ivan III in 1489. The city was renamed Vyatka in 1780, and then known as Kirov from 1934 to 1992. It has a 17th-century cathedral. Industries: metal products, agricultural machinery, meat processing, timber, leather, furs. Pop. (1999) 466,100.

▲ **vulture** The red-headed turkey vulture (*Cathartes aura*) is a New World vulture, found in mountainous regions from Canada to the Magellan Strait. It has a sharply hooked bill, with fleshy seres across the top, through which the nostrils open. A scavenger, it is not as strong as other birds of prey and relies on its keen sight to spot carrion.

V

W/w, 23rd letter of the Roman alphabet, and like f, u, v, and y, derived from the Semitic letter waw, *meaning hook. The Greeks adopted waw into their alphabet as the letter upsilon. In Anglo-Saxon times, it appeared as VV.*

▶ **wallaby** The pretty-faced wallaby (*wallabia pattyi*) inhabits the grassy hills and woodlands of Queensland and New South Wales. Its hopping gait is very efficient at high speeds, but at low speeds it is clumsy, using its forelegs and tail for support.

Waco City on the River Brazos, central Texas. Settled as a ferry-crossing in 1849 on a former Waco (Huaco) Indian colony, it became a major transport and agricultural centre. In 1993, FBI agents stormed the nearby headquarters of the BRANCH DAVIDIANS religious sect, resulting in a fire in which 80 cult members died. Industries: cotton, grain, tyres, paper, furniture, clothing, glass, aircraft parts. Pop. (2000) 113,726.

Wagner, Richard (1813–83) German composer. His works consist almost entirely of operas, for which he provided his own libretti. His early operas include *Der fliegende Holländer* (1843), *Tannhäuser* (1845) and *Lohengrin* (1850). With *Tristan and Isolde* (1865) and the four-part *The Ring of the Nibelung* (1851–76), the genius of Wagner is fully displayed. His rich, chromatic style gives the music great emotional depth, and the complex, ever-developing web of leitmotifs, which are heard in the voices and in the orchestra, propel the drama. Other operas include *The Mastersingers of Nuremberg* (1868) and the sacred stage drama *Parsifal* (1882).

wagtail Any of several species of mainly Old World birds that live near streams; it wags its long tail while foraging for insects. Family Motacillidae.

Waikato Longest river in New Zealand, in central and NW North Island. It rises from Lake Taupo in the central highlands, and flows NNW into the Tasman Sea. Hydroelectric schemes from eight dams along the river provide power for most of North Island. The river is navigable for 129km (80mi) of its 425km (264mi) course.

Wailing Wall *See* WESTERN WALL

Waitangi, Treaty of (1840) Pact between Britain and several New Zealand MAORI tribes. The agreement protected and provided rights for Maoris, guaranteeing them possession of certain tracts of land, while permitting Britain formally to annex the islands and purchase other land areas.

Wake Island Largest of three small coral islands, known collectively as Wake Island, enclosing a lagoon in the W Pacific Ocean. The Spanish discovered the island in 1568, and the British named it in 1796. Annexed by the USA in 1898, Wake Island became a US naval base. It was captured by the Japanese in 1941, and recaptured by the USA in 1945.

Waksman, Selman Abraham (1888–1973) US microbiologist, b. Russia. He received the 1952 Nobel Prize in physiology or medicine for his discovery (1943) of the antibiotic streptomycin. He developed techniques for extracting antibiotics from various microorganisms and discovered new ones, including neomycin.

Walcott, Derek (1930–) Caribbean poet and playwright. His numerous plays include *Henri Christophe* (1950), *Drums and Colours* (1961), *O Babylon* (1978) and *Viva Detroit* (1992), but he is perhaps best known as a poet. His verse, the first volume of which was published in 1948, was collected in 1986. He received the 1992 Nobel Prize in literature.

Waldemar IV (1320–75) (Waldemar Atterday) King of Denmark (1340–75). After a century of disintegration, he restored the Danish kingdom by a mixture of force, diplomacy, and persuasion. In 1367, his enemies, including the HANSEATIC LEAGUE, combined to drive him from the country. He regained the throne after the Peace of Stralsund (1370).

Waldenses Small Christian sect founded in the 12th century. It had its origins in the 'Poor Men of Lyons', the followers of Peter WALDO of Lyons. The Waldenses renounced private property and led an ascetic life. They repudiated many Roman Catholic doctrines and practices, such as INDULGENCES, PURGATORY and MASS for the dead,

and denied the validity of SACRAMENTS administered by unworthy priests. The movement flourished briefly in the 13th century, but active persecution extinguished it except in the French and Italian Alps. Persecution continued until the Waldenses received full civil rights in 1848. In the later 19th century, many Waldenses emigrated to the Americas.

Waldheim, Kurt (1918–) Fourth secretary general of the UNITED NATIONS (UN) (1972–81) and Austrian President (1986–1992). He succeeded U THANT as secretary general, and was replaced by PÉREZ DE CUÉLLAR. Questions over his World War 2 record caused much controversy and tainted the end of his time at the UN and as President.

Waldo, Peter (1140–1218) French religious reformer after whom the WALDENSES are named. He sent out disciples, known as Poor Men, to read to the common people from the Bible. He preached without ecclesiastical authorization and was excommunicated.

Wales Principality of the UNITED KINGDOM, occupying a broad peninsula in W Great Britain; the capital is CARDIFF. Other major cities include SWANSEA. **Land and climate** In the N lies Wales' highest peak, SNOWDON, at 1,085m (3,560ft). ANGLESEY lies off the NW coast. The Black Mountains lie in the SE. The border regions and coastal plains are lowlands. The principal rivers are the SEVERN and Dee. On average, Cardiff experiences twice as much annual rainfall as London. Winter sees the heaviest rains. **History** The Celtic-speaking Welsh stoutly resisted Roman invasion in the first centuries AD. In the 5th century, Saint DAVID introduced Christianity. In the 10th century, political power was centralized. In the 11th century, the English conquered the border counties and established the Welsh Marches. In 1284, the Welsh were forced to relinquish their independence, and in 1301 Prince Edward (later EDWARD II) became Prince of Wales. In the early 15th century, Owain GLYN DŴR led spirited resistance to English rule. The accession of the Welsh TUDOR dynasty to the English throne paved the way for the Act of UNION (1536) of England and Wales. Wales supported the Royalist cause in the English Civil Wars. In the late 19th century, Wales became the world's leading producer of coal. Rapid industrialization brought large social problems, such as unemployment and poverty. From the 18th century, Wales had been a centre of Nonconformism, and Calvinism injected new life into Welsh nationalism. In 1914, the Church of England disestablished in Wales. The Welsh nationalist party (PLAID CYMRU) was founded in 1926. The post-war Labour government, consisting of many Welsh members, nationalized industry and began to deal with regional inequality. In 1966, Plaid Cymru gained its first seat in the House of Commons. A 1979 referendum voted against devolution. The maintenance of a distinct Welsh culture has been strengthened by the teaching of Welsh in schools and a separate Welsh-language television channel (1982). A 1997 referendum approved, by the narrowest of margins, the establishment of a separate Welsh Assembly in Cardiff. **Economy** North Wales is predominantly agricultural, with the world's greatest density of sheep. Dairy farming is also important. Tourism is important in the coastal region of GWYNEDD. The S valleys and coastal plain are Wales' industrial heartland. The late 20th-century decline of its traditional heavy industries of coal and steel has been only partly offset by investment in light industries, such as electronics. Area: 20,761sq km (8,016sq mi). Pop. (2001) 2,903,085.

Wałesa, Lech (1943–) Polish labour leader and president (1990–95). In August 1980, he organized SOLIDARITY, an independent self-governing trade union. Wal-esa became a symbol of the Polish workers' determination to have a greater voice in government affairs. In 1981, the government outlawed Solidarity; Wałesa was interned until late 1982 as part of the government's effort to silence opposition. In 1983, he received the Nobel Peace Prize. Following reforms in the Soviet Union, Solidarity was legalized and won free elections in 1989. In 1990, the Communist Party was disbanded and Wałesa became president. He was defeated in 1995 elections.

Walker, Alice (1944–) African-American writer. Her volumes of poetry include *Revolutionary Petunias and Other*

Poems (1973). Walker won a Pulitzer Prize for her epistolary novel *The Color Purple* (1982). Other works include *In Search of My Mother's Garden* (1983).

wallaby Any of various medium-sized members of the KANGAROO family of MARSUPIAL mammals, occurring chiefly in Australia. All species are herbivorous, feeding in open grassland at night. They move fast in a series of leaps, using both strong hind legs simultaneously, balanced by the tail. Length: head and body 45–105cm (18–41in); tail 33–75cm (13–30in). Family Macropodidae.

Wallace, Alfred Russel (1823–1913) English naturalist and evolutionist. Wallace developed a theory of NATURAL SELECTION independently of (but at the same time as) Charles DARWIN. He wrote *Contributions to the Theory of Natural Selection* (1870), explaining the theory of EVOLUTION.

Wallace, Sir William (1270–1305) Scottish nationalist leader. In 1297–98, he led resistance to King EDWARD I of England. He defeated an English army at Stirling Bridge (1297) and pursued them over the border. In 1298, confronted by Edward with a large army at Falkirk, he was defeated. He went into hiding, but was eventually captured (1305) and executed.

Wallachia (Walachia, Valahia) Historic region in Romania, formerly the principality between the River Danube and the Transylvanian Alps. It is said to have been established (1290) by Ralph the Black, vassal of the King of Hungary, from whom the region secured temporary independence in 1330. It gradually came under the domination of the Turks, whose suzerainty was acknowledged in 1417. Wallachia and MOLDAVIA became Protectorates of Russia under the Treaty of Adrianople (1829) and by their union formed the state of ROMANIA in 1859. An important agricultural region, it has been developed industrially since World War 2. Industries: chemicals, heavy machinery. Area: 76,599sq km (29,575sq mi).

Wallenstein, Albrecht Eusebius Wenzel von (1583–1634) German general. During the THIRTY YEARS' WAR (1618–48), he was commander of the armies of the Holy Roman Empire. He won a series of victories in the late 1620s, but lost the Battle of Lützen in 1632. He was later convicted of treason, dismissed, and then assassinated.

Waller, Fats (1904–43) US jazz and blues pianist and composer, b. Thomas Waller. He wrote many successful tunes, including 'Honeysuckle Rose' and 'Ain't Misbehavin''.

wallflower Any of several species of perennial plants of the genera *Cheiranthus* and *Erysimum*, commonly cultivated in Europe and USA. The European wallflower, *C. cheiri*, has lance-shaped leaves and red, orange, yellow or purple flowers. Height: to 90cm (36in). Family Brassicaceae/Cruciferae.

Wallis, Sir Barnes Neville (1887–1979) English aeronautical engineer and inventor, best known for his invention of the bouncing bomb during World War 2. In the 1920s, he designed the airship R100, and in the 1950s the first swing-wing aircraft.

Wallis and Futuna French territory in the s Pacific Ocean, w of Samoa. It comprises two small groups of volcanic islands: the Wallis Islands and the Hoorn Islands. The principal islands are Uvea, Futuna, and Alofi. Uvea contains 60% of the population and includes the capital of Mata-Utu (2002 est. pop. 1500). Timber is the main export. The French took the islands in 1842, and in 1959 they became an overseas territory. The islands' economy is based on subsistence agriculture of copra, cassava, yams, taro, and bananas. Pop. (2002 est.) 16,000.

Walloons French-speaking people of s Belgium, as opposed to the Flemish-speaking people of the N. They inhabit chiefly the provinces of Hainaut, Liège, Namur, and s Brabant. Today, they number *c*.3 million.

walnut Deciduous tree native to North and South America, Europe and Asia. It has smoother bark than HICKORY, to which it is related, and is grown for timber, ornament, and nuts. Height: to 50m (165ft). Family Juglandaceae; genus *Juglans*.

Walpole, Horace, 4th Earl of Orford (1717–97) English writer. The Gothicization of his house near London represents a milestone in architectural taste; his bizarre novel *The Castle of Otranto* (1764) established a parallel fashion for the Gothic in literature. Walpole's lasting reputation, however, rests on his letters, which provide a portrait of life in Georgian England.

Walpole, Sir Robert, 1st Earl of Orford (1676–1745) British statesman, widely acknowledged as the first prime minister (1721–42). After the Tory victory in the general election of 1710, Walpole was impeached for corruption, expelled from Parliament and sent to the Tower of London (1712). A Whig martyr, he was reinstated on the accession of GEORGE I. He resigned as chancellor of the exchequer (1715–17) out of sympathy for his brother-in-law Charles TOWNSHEND, but returned to restore order after the SOUTH SEA BUBBLE crisis (1720). Patronage from George I and GEORGE II enabled him to unite the House of Commons and grasp of economic issues, ushered in a period of relative peace and prosperity in Britain.

walrus Arctic seal-like mammal; it has a massive body and a large head. Its tusks, developed from upper canine teeth, can reach 1m (39in) in length and are used to rake up the sea-bed in search of molluscs and to climb up onto ice floes. Length: to 3.7m (12ft). Family Odobenidae; species *Odobenus rosmarus*.

Walsingham, Sir Francis (1532–90) English statesman, a leading minister of ELIZABETH I. He was a zealous Protestant, who set up an efficient intelligence system, based on bribery, to detect Catholic conspiracies. He produced the evidence that led to the conviction and execution of MARY, QUEEN OF SCOTS.

Walter, Bruno (1876–1962) German conductor, b. Bruno Walter Schlesinger. After a series of posts in Europe, he went to the USA in 1939. From 1941 to 1957, he worked with the METROPOLITAN OPERA COMPANY, New York. He was highly regarded for his interpretations of Richard Strauss and Mahler.

Walter, Hubert (d.1205) English statesman. As Bishop of Salisbury, he joined RICHARD I on the Third CRUSADE and later negotiated his ransom. Appointed Archbishop of Canterbury and Chief Justiciar (1193), he was virtual ruler of England during Richard's absence.

Walther von der Vogelweide (1170–1230) German poet, considered the greatest MINNESINGER of the Middle Ages. He produced poems of enduring immediacy, such as the popular 'Unter den Linden'.

Walton, Ernest Thomas Sinton (1903–95) Irish physicist. Walton shared the 1951 Nobel Prize in physics with John COCKCROFT for their development (1929) of the first nuclear particle ACCELERATOR. In 1931, they produced the first artificial nuclear reaction without radioactive isotopes, using high-energy protons to bombard lithium nuclei.

Walton, Izaak (1593–1683) English biographer and writer. His lives of Donne (1640), Sir Henry Wotton (1651), Richard Hooker (1665), George Herbert (1670), and Bishop Sanderson (1678) are the first truly biographical works in English literature. His most famous work is *The Compleat Angler* (1653).

Walton, Sir William Turner (1902–83) English composer. His best-known works, all of which are characterized by colourful harmony and orchestration, include the jazz-oriented *Façade* (1923), the oratorio *Belshazzar's Feast* (1931), and the viola concerto (1929). He composed the opera *Troilus and Cressida* (1954), and the coronation marches for George VI and Elizabeth II – *Crown Imperial* (1937) and *Orb and Sceptre* (1953).

waltz Dance performed by couples to music in triple time. This graceful ballroom dance came into fashion in the early 19th century, having developed during the previous century from south-German folk dances, such as the *Ländler*.

Wang Mang (33 BC–AD 23) Emperor of China. A usurper, he overthrew the HAN dynasty and proclaimed the Hsin (New) dynasty in AD 8. Opposition from landowners and officials forced him to withdraw reforms and the dynasty, which divides the Early Han from the Later Han, ended with his assassination.

INTERNET

Walpole, Sir Robert, 1st Earl of Orford
▶ www.number-10.gov.uk

Walton, Sir William Turner
▶ www.williamwalton.net

▲ **walnut** Walnut trees are commercially valuable for their wood and nuts. Before the fruits harden into nuts they can be used for pickling, but once mature, they burst from their green casing and the edible nuts can be removed from the hard outer shell.

▼ **walrus** A unique relative of the seal, the walrus (*Odobenus rosmarus*) is in a family of its own. It is a gregarious animal, and has a tough hide and a thick fat layer, which helps protect against cold as well as the tusks of other walruses.

W

WANKEL ROTARY ENGINE

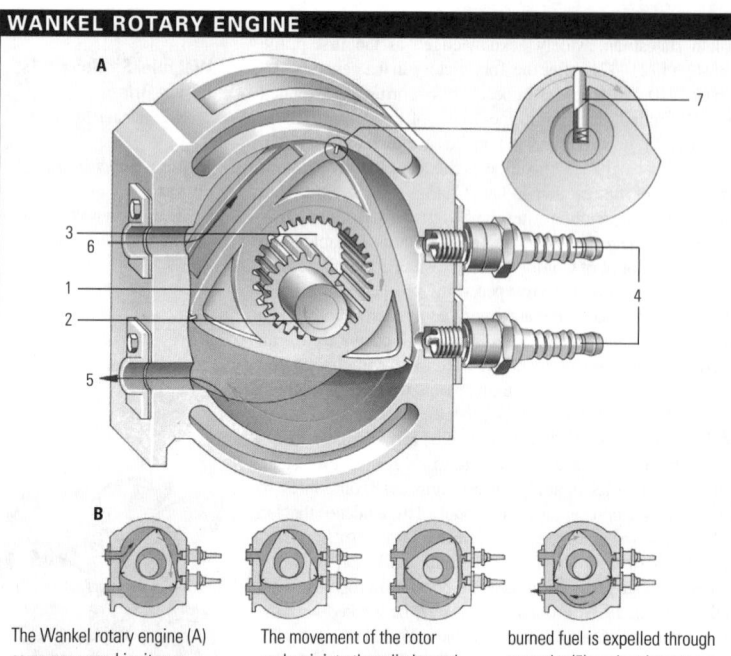

The Wankel rotary engine (A) compresses and ignites a petrol/air mixture with a spark plug like a normal combustion engine, but does so with a rotating three-sided rotor (1) not an in-line action. The explosion of the fuel/air mixture drives a crankshaft (2) passing through the centre of the cylinder. (3)

The movement of the rotor sucks air into the cylinder and, as it continues to rotate, seals the inlet (so valves are not needed), and then compresses the mixture as it continues to turn. The spark plugs (4) then ignite the mixture, which expands, rotating the piston and driving the crankshaft. The

burned fuel is expelled through an outlet (5) as the piston turns, pulling in more air to repeat the process (6). The seals (7) at the edge of the piston's faces are very important in creating the vacuum needed to pull in the fuel/air mixture and in compressing the mixture. A complete cycle is shown (B).

▶ **Warhol** Born in Pittsburgh, Pennsylvania, Andy Warhol was a successful commercial artist in New York before becoming a leading exponent of pop art. In 1966, he collaborated with Lou Reed and his band the Velvet Underground on a pioneering tour of multi-media shows. In 1968, he was shot and almost killed by Valerie Solanas, a radical feminist. In the 1970s and 1980s, he remained active, producing improvisational and experimental films as well as a magazine and portraits.

Wankel rotary engine INTERNAL COMBUSTION ENGINE with rotors instead of pistons, invented in the 1950s by German engineer Felix Wankel (1902–88). Each triangular rotor turns inside a close-fitting casing. Gaps between the casing and rotor form three crescent-shaped combustion chambers. Each chamber goes through a sequence of events similar to those in a FOUR-STROKE ENGINE with pistons.

wapiti Large deer of North America, closely related to the Old World red deer, second only to the ELK in size. It is grey-brown with a whitish rump and dark, brown-black legs, head and neck; its antlers may reach a span of 1.5m (5ft). Height: to 1.5m (5ft); length: to 2.5m (7.5ft). Family Cervidae; species *Cervus canadensis*.

war Military combat between large communities, nations, and/or groups of nations. All-out (nuclear) war between major powers using modern weapons would undoubtedly result in what is known as 'mutually assured destruction' (MAD). Other forms of war include civil war, in which factions within one state or community struggle between themselves for supremacy, and guerrilla war, in which par-

tisan forces harass occupying or government troops by surprise attacks. *See also* DISARMAMENT

warbler Numerous birds of two families, one in the Old World (Sylviidae) and the other in the New World (Parulidae). Old World warblers include the hedge sparrow and tailorbird. Most New World warblers have brighter plumage.

war crimes Violations of international laws of war. The modern conception of war crimes followed the atrocities committed in the era of World War 2, which was followed by the NUREMBERG TRIALS, the first trials of war criminals. Atrocities marked the civil wars in BOSNIA-HERZEGOVINA, RWANDA, and KOSOVO. *See also* GENEVA CONVENTION

Warhol, Andy (1928–87) US painter, printmaker, and filmmaker, innovator of POP ART. Warhol achieved immediate fame with his stencil pictures of Campbell's soup cans and his sculptures of Brillo soap pad boxes (1962). In 1965, he gave up art to manage the rock group *The Velvet Underground*. He continued to make films, which often have a voyeuristic quality.

warm-blooded *See* HOMEOTHERMIC

War of 1812 (1812–15) Conflict between the USA and Britain. The main source of friction was British maritime policy in the NAPOLEONIC WARS, including the impressment of sailors from US vessels and the interception of US merchant ships. Border disputes with Canada also contributed. In 1811, President James MADISON reimposed the Nonintercourse Act on trade with the British. The USA was ill-prepared for war and an invasion of Canada failed. Stephen Decatur restored US pride. Victory on Lake Erie (September 1813) enabled US forces, led by William H. HARRISON, to force British troops back across the Canadian border. The HARTFORD CONVENTION raised the possibility of New England secession, while the end of the NAPOLEONIC WARS (1814) freed more British forces. The British imposed a naval blockade and captured Washington, D.C., burning the White House. A US naval victory on Lake Champlain, however, ended the British threat to New York. With the war at stalemate, John Quincy ADAMS and Henry CLAY led US negotiations that resulted in the Treaty of Ghent (December 24, 1814). Andrew JACKSON's victory at New Orleans occurred after the signing of the treaty.

Warren, Earl (1891–1974) US politician and jurist. Appointed by President Dwight D. Eisenhower as Chief Justice of the SUPREME COURT (1953–69), he began the 'Warren revolution' that lasted until his retirement. Some of the Warren Court's noteworthy cases include: *Brown* v. *Board of Education of Topeka* (1954), which made segregation in the public schools unconstitutional; *Engel* v. *Vitale* (1962), which prohibited prayers in public schools; and *Miranda* v. *Arizona* (1966), which made it obligatory that a suspect be informed of his rights, be provided with free state counsel, and be given the right to remain silent. *See also* WARREN COMMISSION

Warren, Robert Penn (1905–89) US poet, novelist, and critic. In his fiction, which includes the Pulitzer Prize-winning novel *All the King's Men* (1946), Warren concentrated on Southern themes and characters. He received the Pulitzer Prize twice more, for the poetry collections *Promises* (1957) and *Now and Then* (1978). He became the first American poet laureate in 1986.

Warren Commission (1963–64) US presidential commission that investigated the assassination of President John F. KENNEDY. It was headed by Earl WARREN. After taking evidence from 552 witnesses, it concluded that the act had been committed by Lee Harvey OSWALD, acting alone. Its denial of a conspiracy was not universally accepted.

Warsaw Capital and largest city of Poland, on the River VISTULA. Its first settlement dates from the 11th century. In 1596 it became Poland's capital and developed into the country's main trading centre. Controlled by Russia from 1813 to 1915, German troops occupied it during World War 1. In 1918, Polish troops liberated the city. The 1939 German invasion and occupation of Warsaw marked the beginning of World War 2. In 1940, the Germans isolated the Jewish ghetto, which contained 500,000 people, and following a brutal suppression of a Jewish uprising in February 1943, they killed more than 40,000 survivors. In January 1945, when the Red Army liberated Warsaw, they found only 200 surviving Jews. After

World War 2, the old town was painstakingly reconstructed. Warsaw is a major transport and industrial centre. Industries: steel, cars, cement, machinery. Pop. (2000) 1,626,000.

Warsaw Pact Agreement creating the Warsaw Treaty Organization (1955), a defensive alliance of the SOVIET UNION and its communist allies in Eastern Europe. It was founded after the admission of West Germany to the NORTH ATLANTIC TREATY ORGANIZATION (NATO), the equivalent organization of Western Europe. Its headquarters were in Moscow, and it was effectively controlled by the Soviet Union. Attempts to withdraw by Hungary (1956) and Czechoslovakia (1968) were forcibly denied. It was officially dissolved in 1991 after the collapse of the Soviet Union.

wart Raised and well-defined small growth on the outermost surface of the skin, caused by the human papillomavirus. It is usually painless unless in a pressure area, as with a VERRUCA.

wart hog Wild, tusked PIG native to Africa. It has a brownish-black skin with a crest of thin hair along the back. Height: about 76cm (2.5ft) at shoulder; weight: 90kg (200lb). Family Suidae; species *Phacochoerus aethiopicus*.

Warwick, Richard Neville, Earl of (1428–71) English magnate known as 'the Kingmaker', who held the balance of power during the Wars of the ROSES. After the death of Richard of York, he was the chief power in the kingdom (1461–64). Breaking with Richard's son, EDWARD IV, Warwick changed sides, and restored HENRY VI to the throne in 1470. Edward returned with fresh troops and Warwick was defeated and killed at the Battle of Barnet.

Warwickshire County in central England. The land is gently rolling, rising to the Cotswold Hills in the s, and is drained chiefly by the River Avon. Cereals are the principal crops, and dairy cattle and sheep are raised. There is growing light industry, especially near Nuneaton, Rugby, and Leamington. The county town of Warwick (2001 pop. 125,962), Kenilworth and STRATFORD UPON AVON all draw considerable numbers of tourists. Area: 1,981sq km (765sq mi). Pop. (2001) 505,885.

Washington State in the extreme NW USA. The state capital is OLYMPIA and the largest city is SEATTLE. In the NW is the navigable Puget Sound, along which lie Washington's major industrial and commercial cities. The CASCADE RANGE, including Mount RAINIER and Mount ST HELENS, dominates the state. The coastal region to the W of the range is one of the wettest areas of the USA and has dense forest; the region to the E of the Cascades is mostly treeless plain with low rainfall. An important wheat-producing area, the plateau depends on irrigation schemes. The COLUMBIA River is one of the world's best sources of hydroelectricity, and is also used for irrigation. The Spanish discovered the mouth of the Columbia river in 1775. In 1792, George Vancouver mapped the Puget Sound, and Robert Gray sailed down the Sound to establish the US claim to the region. The claim was strengthened by the LEWIS AND CLARK EXPEDITION (1805) and the establishment (1811) of an American Fur Company trading post by John Jacob ASTOR. From 1821 to 1846, the HUDSON'S BAY COMPANY administered the region. In 1846, a treaty with the British fixed the boundary with Canada, and in 1847 most of present-day Washington state became Oregon Territory. In 1853, Washington Territory was created. It is the leading producer of apples in the USA. Industries: food processing, timber, aluminium, aerospace, computer technology. Area: 172,431sq km (66,581sq mi). Pop. (2000) 5,142,746.

Washington, Booker T. (Taliaferro) (1856–1915) US educator and African American leader. Born a slave, he gained an education after the Civil War and became a teacher. Washington advocated self-help, education, and economic improvement as preliminaries to the achievement of equality for blacks, and believed in compromise with white segregationists. He had considerable influence among whites as a spokesman for African-American causes.

Washington, D.C. Capital of the USA, on the E bank of the POTOMAC River, covering the District of Columbia and extending into the neighbouring states of Maryland and Virginia. The site was chosen as the seat of government in 1790, and French engineer Pierre Charles L'Enfant planned the city. Construction of the WHITE HOUSE began in 1793, and the building of the CAPITOL the following year. In 1800, Congress moved from Philadelphia to Washington. During the WAR OF 1812, the British occupied the city and many public buildings were burned (1814), including the White House and the Capitol. Washington is the legislative, judicial, and administrative centre of the USA. The main governmental buildings are the Library of Congress, the PENTAGON, the SUPREME COURT, the SENATE, the HOUSE OF REPRESENTATIVES, and Constitution Hall. Despite its role, Washington has severe social problems; many of its large African-American population live in slum housing. Pop. (2000) 3,934,000.

Washington, Denzel (1954–) US film actor. His first major film role was as Steve Biko, in the anti-apartheid film *Cry Freedom* (1987). Spike LEE chose him to play the leads in *Mo' Better Blues* (1990) and *Malcolm X* (1992). Other credits include *Philadelphia* (1993), and *Devil in a Blue Dress* (1995). He won the Oscar for best actor for *Training Day* (2001).

Washington, George (1732–99) American general and statesman, commander in chief of the Continental Army during the AMERICAN REVOLUTION (1775–83), and first president of the UNITED STATES (1789–97). A wealthy Virginian, Washington fought with distinction in the last of the FRENCH AND INDIAN WARS (1754–63). He served in both CONTINENTAL CONGRESSES (1774, 1775), the latter appointing him commander in chief. Washington retired after securing victory over the British, but was recalled to preside over the CONSTITUTIONAL CONVENTION at Philadelphia (1787). In 1789, he was elected (unopposed) as president of the new republic. Washington was unable to heal the divisions between Thomas JEFFERSON and Alexander HAMILTON that resulted in the creation of the FEDERALIST PARTY and the DEMOCRATIC REPUBLICAN PARTY. Re-elected in 1793, the Federalists dominated his second administration, and the Jeffersonians criticized what they saw as his pro-British policy during the FRENCH REVOLUTIONARY WARS. Washington declined a third term as president, and retired to his family estate at Mount Vernon.

Washington, Treaty of (1871) Agreement settling a number of disputes involving the USA, Britain, and Canada. The most serious was the question of the ALABAMA CLAIMS, which was submitted to international arbitration. US-Canadian disputes over fisheries and the border were also resolved.

wasp Any insect of the stinging Hymenoptera that is neither a bee nor an ant. The common wasp (*Vespa vulgaris*) has a yellow body ringed with black. Adults feed on nectar, tree sap, and fruit. Length: to 3cm (1.2in). Family Vespidae.

water (H₂O) Odourless, colourless liquid that covers about 70% of the Earth's surface and is the most widely used solvent. Essential to life, it makes up 60–70% of the human body. It is a compound of hydrogen and oxygen, with the two H-O links of the molecule forming an angle of 105°. This asymmetry results in polar properties and a force of attraction (hydrogen bond) between opposite ends of neighbouring water molecules. These forces maintain the substance as a liquid, in spite of its low molecular weight, and account for its unusual property of having its maximum density at 4°C (39.2°F). Besides its everyday uses, water is used to manufacture sulphuric acid, nitric acid, sodium carbonate, and ammonia; it is also employed to extract oil and sulphur from the ground. Properties: r.d. 1.000; m.p. 0°C (32°F); b.p. 100°C (212°F).

water beetle Aquatic BEETLE. WHIRLIGIG BEETLES (family Gyrinidae) skim around the surface of water, feeding on small insects. **Water scavenger** beetles (family Hydrophilidae) feed on water plants. Their larvae are fierce predators. **Predaceous diving beetles** are the most numerous water beetles. They are black, brown, or greenish and can remain underwater for long periods. They prey on snails and fish.

water boatman Aquatic insect found worldwide. Its body is grey to black, oval and flat, with fringed, oar-like hind legs. Length: about 15mm (0.6in). Order Hemiptera; family Corixidae. The carnivorous 'backswimmers' of the family Notonectidae are also sometimes called water boatmen.

waterbuck (waterbok) Six species of large, gregarious, coarse-haired ANTELOPE native to sub-Saharan Africa and the Nile Valley. Length: 1.4–2.1m (4.5–7ft); height: 1.1–1.5m (3.6–4.9ft) at the shoulder. Family Bovidae; genus *Kobus*.

▲ **Washington** George Washington was an outstanding general and statesman. At the start of the Revolution, he expelled the British from Boston (March 1775), but narrowly avoided capture in the unsuccessful defence of New York. Washington surprised the British by crossing the Delaware River and defeating them at Trenton (December 1776). His defeat at Brandywine (September 1777) enabled the British to capture Philadelphia and, wintering at Valley Forge, Washington faced the Conway Cabal. He was robbed of victory at Monmouth (June 1778) largely because of Charles Lee's treachery, but his defeat of Charles Cornwallis at Yorktown (October 1781) was decisive. After the war, Washington was instrumental in the adoption of the Constitution at the Constitutional Convention in Philadelphia (1787). In his *Farewell Address* (September 17, 1796), Washington warned against forming 'permanent alliances' with foreign powers.

WASHINGTON
Statehood :
November 11, 1889
Nickname :
The Evergreen State
State bird :
Willow goldfinch
State flower :
Coast rhododendron
State tree :
Western hemlock
State motto :
Alki (Native American for 'by and by')

W

▶ **water buffalo** The Asiatic water buffalo (*Bubalus bubalis*) feeds on river and lakeside vegetation. Both sexes carry large horns, but the males are generally larger and can weigh almost one tonne. Wild water buffalo are extremely fierce and have been known to kill fully grown tigers. The domesticated animals are used to pull ploughs and carts, but produce little milk.

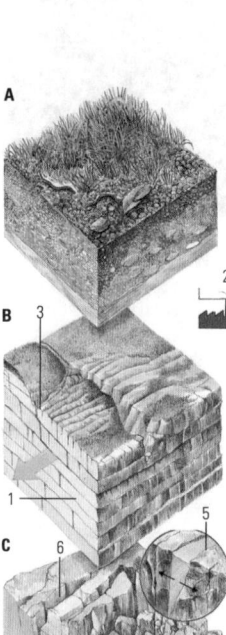

▲ **weathering** Weathering is the breakdown of rock in situ. It occurs in two main ways: physical (A and C) and chemical (B) – usually in combination. At the surface, plant roots and animals such as worms break down rock turning it into soil (A). In chemical weathering (B), soluble rocks such as limestone (1) are dissolved by ground water, which is a very mild solution of carbonic acid. Acid rain caused by sulphate pollution (2) also attacks the rock. The water can create cave systems deep below the surface. Both heat and cold can cause physical weathering (C). When temperatures drop below freezing, freeze-thaw weathering can split even the hardest rocks such as granite (4). Water that settles in cracks and joints during the day expands as it freezes at night (5). The expansion cleaves the rock along the naturally occurring joints (6). In deserts, rock expands and contracts due to the extremes of cooling and heating, resulting in layers of rock splitting off.

W

water buffalo (caraboa) Large OX, domesticated in much of the tropical world; it is feral in parts of India. Height: to 1.8m (6ft) at the shoulder. Family Bovidae; species *Bubalus bubalis*.

watercress Floating or creeping plant found in running or spring waters. The succulent leaves, divided into small, oval leaflets, have a pungent flavour and are used in salads and soups. The clustered flowers are white. Height: 25cm (10in). Family Brassicaceae/Cruciferae; species *Nasturtium officinale*.

water cycle *See* HYDROLOGICAL CYCLE

waterfall Point in the course of a river at which the water drops perpendicularly. The site usually indicates an outcrop of rock that is particularly resistant to erosion. Spectacular falls include ANGEL FALLS, NIAGARA FALLS, and VICTORIA FALLS.

water flea Any of numerous species of small, chiefly freshwater branchiopod crustaceans, especially those within the genus *Daphnia*, which are common throughout the world. Order Cladocera. *See also* CRUSTACEA

Waterford County in Munster province, on the Atlantic Ocean, s Republic of Ireland. It is a mountainous region, drained chiefly by the rivers Blackwater and Suir. The raising of beef and dairy cattle and sheep is the chief agricultural activity. Industries: fishing, food processing, tanning and glassware. The county town of Waterford (2002 pop. 44,564) is an important port. Area: 1,838sq km (710sq mi). Pop. (2002) 101,518.

waterfowl Birds, including species of DUCK, GOOSE, and SWAN, found throughout most of the world. Flocks migrate from cool nesting grounds to warm winter homes. All have short bills, short legs, and dense plumage. Undomesticated species are known as wildfowl in Britain. Order Anseriformes.

Watergate affair (1972–74) US political scandal that led to the resignation of President Richard NIXON. It arose from an attempted burglary of the Democratic Party's headquarters in the Watergate building, Washington D.C., organized by members of Nixon's re-election committee. Evidence of the administration's involvement provoked investigations by the Senate and the Justice Department, which implicated Nixon. He was pardoned by his successor, Gerald FORD, but his close advisers (Halderman, Erlichman and Mitchell) were convicted.

water hyacinth Aquatic herb native to the American tropics. It has swollen petioles that float in water and spikes of violet flowers. Family Pontederiaceae; species *Eichhornia crassipes*.

water lily Any of *c*.90 species of freshwater plants widely distributed in temperate and tropical regions. They have leaves that float at the surface, and showy flowers of white, pink, red, blue, or yellow. Family Nymphaeaceae; genera *Nymphaea*, *Nuphar*, *Nelumbo*, and *Victoria*.

Waterloo, Battle of (June 18, 1815) Final engagement of the NAPOLEONIC WARS, fought *c*.20km (12mi) from Brussels, Belgium. The Duke of WELLINGTON commanded Allied troops against NAPOLEON's slightly larger French forces. The conflict was stalemated until the Prussians, under Marshal Blücher, arrived to overwhelm the French flank, whereupon Wellington broke through the centre. The battle ended Napoleon's HUNDRED DAYS and resulted in his second and final abdication.

watermelon Trailing, annual VINE native to tropical Africa and Asia and cultivated in warm areas worldwide. Its edible fruit has a greenish rind, red flesh and many seeds. Family Cucurbitaceae; species *Citrullus lanatus*. *See also* GOURD

water moccasin (cottonmouth) Venomous semi-aquatic SNAKE of SE USA. It is a pit VIPER, closely related to the COPPERHEAD. When threatened, it vibrates its tail and holds its white mouth open. Length: to 1.2m (4ft). Family Viperidae; species *Agkistrodon piscivorus*.

water pollution Contamination of water by harmful wastes. The chief source of water POLLUTION is **industrial waste**. Toxic chemicals, such as POLYCHLORINATED BIPHENYL (PCB), discharge as effluent and cannot be disinfected with CHLORINE. In addition, the burning of fossil fuels causes ACID RAIN. Untreated or partially treated **sewage** is another source of water pollution. Sewage treatment is unable to prevent the spread of viruses and some phosphorus-based detergents that cause EUTROPHICATION. Agricultural chemicals and wastes, such as PESTICIDES and FERTILIZERS, are another major cause. Once pollution has affected GROUNDWATER it spreads rapidly. Oil spills and ocean dumping are major causes of marine pollution.

water polo Sport devised as an aquatic form of FOOTBALL, played by two teams of seven people in a pool. At each end of the pool is a net-enclosed goal defended by one player per team. Water polo has been an Olympic event since 1900.

water power *See* HYDROELECTRICITY

water skiing Leisure activity and competitive sport in which a person skis across the surface of water while being towed by a motor-boat. Competition skiing comprises three disciplines: slalom, jumping, and tricks. In slalom, skiers are towed several times through a series of staggered buoys. In jumping, each skier must ski up and over a wooden ramp. For tricks, skiers devise their own 20–second routines of complex manoeuvres.

water table In geology, level below which the ground is saturated. The height of the water table gradually changes, moving up or down depending on the recent rainfall. Water located below the water table is called GROUNDWATER.

Watson, James Dewey (1928–) US geneticist and biophysicist. Watson is known for his role in the discovery of the molecular structure of deoxyribonucleic acid (DNA), and he shared the 1962 Nobel Prize in physiology or medicine with Francis CRICK and Maurice Wilkins. Watson later helped to break the GENETIC CODE of the DNA base sequences and found the ribonucleic acid (RNA) messenger that carries the DNA code to the cell's protein-forming structures.

Watson, John Broadus (1878–1958) US psychologist, the founder of BEHAVIOURISM in the USA. His point of view was continued in the work of B.F. Skinner.

Watson-Watt, Sir Robert Alexander (1892–1973) Scottish physicist. He was a major influence on the rapid development of RADAR in World War 2. In 1941 he helped to establish the US radar system.

watt Unit of power in the SI system of units. A machine consuming one JOULE of energy per second has a power output of one watt. One horsepower corresponds to 746 watts. A watt is also a unit of electrical power, equal to the product of voltage and current. It is named after the Scottish engineer James WATT.

Watt, James (1736–1819) Scottish engineer. In 1765, Watt invented the condensing steam engine. In 1782, he invented the double-acting engine, in which steam pressure acted alternately on each side of a piston. With Matthew Boulton, Watt coined the term 'horsepower'. The unit of power, the WATT, is named after him.

Watteau, Jean-Antoine (1684–1721) French painter. Watteau's early work was influenced by the Flemish genre painter David Teniers (1610–90), as seen in his early painting *La Marmotte*. He is best known for his *fêtes galantes*, notably his masterpiece *Departure for the Islands of Cythera* (1717), which is an early example of ROCOCO.

Watts, George Frederick (1817–1904) English painter and sculptor. He produced complicated, moralistic allegories such as *Hope* (1886). Watts' best-known sculpture is an equestrian statue called *Physical Energy* (1904).

Waugh, Evelyn Arthur St John (1903–66) English novelist. He established his reputation with *Decline and Fall* (1928). *Vile Bodies* (1930), *A Handful of Dust* (1934) and *Put Out More Flags* (1942) reflect inter-war British upper-class life, while *Brideshead Revisited* (1945) is informed by the Roman Catholicism to which he converted in 1928.

Among his other major works are *The Loved One* (1948) and the *Sword of Honour* trilogy – *Men at Arms* (1952), *Officers and Gentlemen* (1955) and *Unconditional Surrender* (1961).

wave In oceanography, moving disturbance travelling on or through water, but that does not move the water itself. Wind causes waves by frictional drag. Waves not under pressure from strong winds are called swells. Waves begin to break on shore or 'feel bottom' when they reach a depth shallower than half the wave's length. When the water depth is about 1.3 times the wave height, the wave front is so steep that the top falls over and the wave breaks.

wave In physics, carriers of energy from place to place. Waves are caused by disturbances that result in some sort of oscillation. These oscillations then spread out (propagate) as waves. The velocity depends on the type of wave and on the medium. **Electromagnetic** waves, such as light, consist of varying magnetic and electric fields vibrating at right angles to each other and to the direction of motion; they are **transverse** waves. Sound waves are transmitted by the vibrations of the particles of the medium itself, the vibrations being in the direction of wave motion; they are **longitudinal** waves. **Sound** waves, unlike electromagnetic waves, cannot travel through a vacuum or undergo polarization. Both types of waves can undergo REFLECTION and REFRACTION, and give rise to INTERFERENCE phenomena. A wave is characterized by its WAVELENGTH and FREQUENCY, the VELOCITY of wave motion being the product of wavelength and frequency. *See also* ELECTROMAGNETIC RADIATION; POLARIZED LIGHT; WAVE AMPLITUDE; WAVE FREQUENCY

wave amplitude (symbol a) Peak value of a periodically varying quantity. This peak value may be either positive or negative, as the quantity varies either above or below its zero value. Wave amplitude, for example, can be measured on electromagnetic radiation.

wave dispersion Alteration of the refractive index (measurement of bending) of a medium with wavelength, such as light. It occurs with all electromagnetic waves but is most obvious at visible wavelengths, causing light to be separated into its component colours. Dispersion is seen when a beam of light passes through a refracting medium, such as a glass PRISM, and forms a SPECTRUM. Each colour has a different wavelength, and so the prism bends each colour in the light a different amount. *See also* REFRACTION

wave frequency Number of complete oscillations or wave cycles produced in one second, measured in HERTZ. It can be calculated from the wave velocity divided by wavelength. By QUANTUM THEORY, the frequency of any ELECTROMAGNETIC RADIATION (such as light, radio waves, and X-rays) is proportional to the energy of the component PHOTONS.

wavelength (symbol Λ) Distance in metres between successive points of equal phase of a WAVE. The wavelength of water waves could be measured as the distance from crest to crest. The wavelength of a light wave determines its colour. Wavelength is equal to the wave VELOCITY divided by the WAVE FREQUENCY.

wave mechanics Version of QUANTUM MECHANICS developed (1926) by Austrian physicist Erwin SCHRÖDINGER. It explains the behaviour of ELECTRONS in terms of their wave properties. Although quickly superseded by a more complex formulation by English physicist Paul DIRAC, it is still widely used in calculations.

wax Solid, insoluble substance of low melting point that is malleable and water-repellent. There are four types: animal, vegetable, mineral, and synthetic. The first two are simple lipids consisting of esters of fatty acids; mineral waxes include paraffin wax made from petroleum. Synthetic waxes are of diverse origins and include POLYETHENES. Waxes are used in the manufacture of lubricants, polishes, cosmetics, and candles, and to waterproof leather and coat paper.

waxwing Any of a few species of small, grey-brown birds with distinctive black markings on the head, a small crest, and characteristic red or red-and-yellow waxy tips on the secondary wing feathers. They are found in the forests of Eurasia and North America and feed on berries and fruit. Length: to 20cm (8in). Family Bombycillidae; genus *Bombycilla*.

Wayne, John (1907–79) US film actor, b. Marion Michael Morrison. His first major success was in *Stagecoach* (1939). He made many more films, including *She Wore a Yellow Ribbon* (1949), *The Man Who Shot Liberty Valance* (1962), *True Grit* (1969) – for which he received an Academy Award for best actor – and *The Shootist* (1976).

Waziristan Arid and mountainous region in North-West Frontier province, NW Pakistan, on the Afghanistan border. In 1893, Waziristan became an independent territory. In 1947, it was incorporated into Pakistan, but with the support of Afghanistan it struggled to create an independent Pushtu state. Area: 11,585sq km (4,473sq mi). Pop. (1998 est.) 865,000.

weak nuclear force (weak interaction) One of the four FUNDAMENTAL FORCES in physics. It causes radioactive beta decay of particles. This weak force is carried by **intermediate vector bosons**, elementary particles that are also called weakons. Being of very short range, the weak nuclear force can be observed only in the subatomic realm. It is weaker than the ELECTROMAGNETIC FORCE and the STRONG NUCLEAR FORCE (the strongest of the forces) but stronger than GRAVITATION.

weasel Any of several species of small, carnivorous, mostly terrestrial mammals of Eurasia, N Africa, and North and South America. Most species have small heads, long necks, slender bodies, and long tails. Reddish-brown with light coloured underparts, some species turn completely white in winter. Weasels are fierce predators, eating eggs and rodents. Length: 50cm (20in) overall. Family Mustelidae; Genus *Mustela*.

weather State of the atmosphere at a given locality or over a broad area, particularly as it affects human activity. Weather refers to short-term states (days or weeks) as opposed to long-term CLIMATE conditions. METEOROLOGY is the study of weather conditions.

weather forecasting *See* METEOROLOGY

weathering Breakdown and chemical disintegration of rocks and minerals at the Earth's surface by physical and chemical processes. In **physical weathering** in cold, wet climates, water seeping into cracks in the rock expands on freezing, so causing the rock to crack further and to crumble. Extreme temperature changes in drier regions, such as deserts, also cause rocks to fragment. **Chemical weathering** can lead to a weakening of the rock structure by altering the minerals of a rock and changing their size, volume, and ability to hold shape. Unlike EROSION, weathering does not involve transportation.

weaverbird Any of several species of short-billed, often yellow-and-black, finch-like birds that weave complex nests from grass and leaves. The weaverbirds are gregarious insect-eaters of hot, dry areas. The African *Ploceus cucullatus* knots strands of grass together. Length: to 22cm (7.5in). Family Ploceidae.

weaving Process of making fabric by intertwining two sets of threads. A loom is threaded with a set of warp threads. The weft thread winds round a shuttle and passes between the warp threads, which are separated according to the desired pattern. A reed keeps the woven rows tightly packed.

Webb, Beatrice (née Potter) (1858–1943) and **Sidney** (1859–1947) British social historians and politicians. Sidney Webb was one of the founders of the FABIAN SOCIETY. The Webbs founded the London School of Economics (1895) and helped to found the *New Statesman* magazine (1913).

weber (symbol Wb) SI unit of magnetic flux (the strength and extent of a magnetic field). In a circuit of one turn, one weber produces an ELECTROMOTIVE FORCE (EMF) of one volt as it is reduced to zero in one second. It is named after the German physicist Wilhelm Weber (1804–91).

Weber, Carl Maria von (1786–1826) German composer, conductor, and pianist. He helped to establish a German national style in his operas *Der Freischütz* (1821) and *Euryanthe* (1823). He also composed piano and chamber music, concertos and the popular *Invitation to the Dance* (1819).

Weber, Max (1864–1920) German sociologist. He advanced the concept of 'ideal types', generalized models of social situations, as a method of analysis. In his book *The Protestant Ethic and the Spirit of Capitalism* (1904–05), he put forward the idea that CALVINISM was influential in the rise of CAPITALISM.

Webern, Anton von (1883–1945) Austrian composer. His *Passacaglia* was written using late-Romantic tonality.

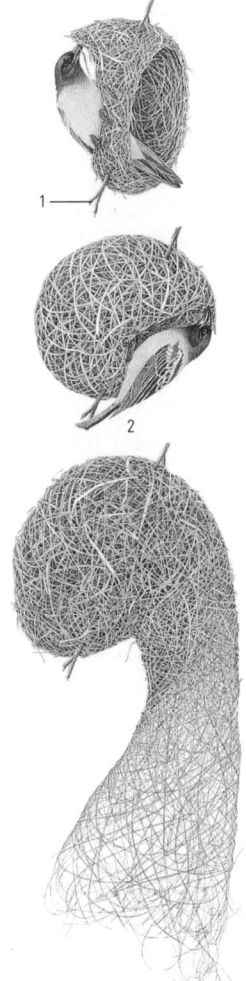

▲ **weaverbird** The weaverbird's nest is built by the male. Using no adhesive, he loops, twists, and knots strips of leaves to make an enclosed hanging structure. Starting with a ring attached to a forked twig (1), he gradually adds a roof and entrance (2). When the female accepts the finished nest, she inserts soft, feathery grass tops or feathers to make a thick, soft lining around the base of the egg chamber. Young male birds' first nests are untidy; gradually, however, they learn how to make neater and better nests, using good vision and well-coordinated head movements to direct claws and beak to manipulate the nest material.

W

INTERNET

Watergate affair
(see page 784)
▶ www.watergate.info

Watteau, Jean-Antoine
(see page 784)
▶ www.hermitagemuseum.org

Weber, Carl Maria von
(see page 785)
▶ www.classical.net

Weill, Kurt
▶ www.kwf.org

Influenced by his teacher, SCHOENBERG, Webern adopted atonality, as in the *Six Bagatelles* (1913), and then TWELVE-TONE MUSIC, notably in his symphony (1928).

Webster, John (1580–1634) English dramatist whose reputation rests upon his two great tragedies: *The White Devil* (c.1612) and *The Duchess of Malfi* (1614). Both plays explore the theme of revenge using macabre language.

Wedekind, 'Frank' (Benjamin Franklin) (1864–1918) German dramatist whose use of theatre anticipated that of EXPRESSIONISM and influenced Bertolt BRECHT. His plays include *Spring Awakening* (1906) and *Lulu*, which appeared in two parts: *Earth-Spirit* (1902) and *Pandora's Box* (1905).

wedge In mechanics, an example of the inclined plane. It is used to multiply an applied force while changing its direction of action. For example, if a metal or wooden wedge is driven into a block of wood then a force is exerted by the wedge at right angles to the applied force and greater than it.

Wedgwood, Josiah (1730–95) English potter. He pioneered the mass production of pottery at his Etruria works near Stoke-on-Trent, and became famous for his creamware. He is best known for his jasper ware, which gave expression to the contemporary interest in the revival of classical art.

weed Uncultivated or unwanted plant. Weeds are a threat to commercial crops because they compete for water and sunlight, and harbour pests and diseases. *See also* HERBICIDE

Weelkes, Thomas (c.1575–1623) English madrigal composer and organist. Almost 100 of his madrigals have survived, the finest being sets of five- and six-part madrigals.

weever Any of four species of small fish that commonly bury themselves in sand in European and Mediterranean coastal waters. Poison spines on the dorsal fin and gill covers can inflict a painful sting. Family Trachinidae; genus *Trachinus*.

weevil Any of numerous species of beetle that are pests to crops, especially the numerous snout beetles (time weevils), with long, down-curved beaks for boring into plants. Family Curculionidae, the largest in the animal kingdom.

Wegener, Alfred Lothar (1880–1930) German geologist, meteorologist, and Arctic explorer. In *The Origin of Continents and Oceans* (1915), Wegener was the first to use scientific argument in support of a theory of CONTINENTAL DRIFT.

weight (symbol W) Force of attraction on a body due to GRAVITATION. It is measured in NEWTONS. An object's weight is the product of its MASS and the gravitational field strength at that point. Mass remains constant, but weight depends on the object's position on the Earth's surface, decreasing with increasing altitude.

weightlessness Condition experienced by an object on which the force due to GRAVITATION is neutralized. Such an object is said to have zero gravity and no weight; it floats and cannot fall. Weightlessness can be experienced in space and during free fall. The adverse effects on the human body of prolonged weightlessness (called hydrogravics) include decreased circulation of blood, less water retention in tissues and the bloodstream, and loss of muscle tone.

weightlifting Sport in which weights at the end of a bar are lifted over the head. Competitions are conducted according to weight classes that range from bantamweight to heavyweight. In a weightlifting competition, each participant uses three standard lifts known as two-hand press, clean-and-jerk, and snatch. The competitor who lifts the greatest combined total of weights wins. It has been an Olympic event since 1920.

weights and measures Agreed units for expressing the amount of some quantity, such as capacity, length or weight. Early measurements were based on body measurements and on plant grains. The French introduced the metric system in 1799, in which the unit of length, the metre, was taken as one ten millionth of the distance from the Equator to the North Pole. A litre was the volume occupied by one kilogram of water. SI UNITS, proposed in 1960, have expanded and replaced the metric system for scientific purposes. The British IMPERIAL SYSTEM, has been partly replaced by the metric system for everyday measurements, but not in the USA.

Weil, Simone (1909–1943) French philosopher and writer. In the late 1930s, she had the first of several mystical experiences that drew her to the ROMAN CATHOLIC CHURCH. During World War 2, she became an activist in the French Resistance. Most of Weil's works appeared after her death, and include *Gravity and Grace* (1947) and *Waiting for God* (1951).

Weill, Kurt (1900–50) German composer. He is best known for his satirical operas, which include *Der Protagonist* (1926) and *Rise and Fall of the City of Mahagonny* (1927), the latter with a libretto by Bertolt BRECHT. Weill parodied commercial music as a means of social criticism. *The Threepenny Opera* (1928) was a modern version of John Gay's *Beggar's Opera*, again with a libretto by Brecht. After moving to the USA in 1935, Weill composed musicals for Broadway. His wife, Lotte LENYA, was a respected interpreter of his work.

Weimar City in the state of Thuringia, E central Germany. Founded in 975 and chartered in 1348, the city was capital of the Duchy of Saxe-Weimar from 1547 to 1918. It reached its zenith in the 18th century as the literary capital of Europe. The 19th century witnessed a gradual artistic decline. In 1919, the German National Assembly convened here to establish the WEIMAR REPUBLIC, and Walter GROPIUS founded the BAUHAUS school of art. Pop. (1998) 62,176.

Weimar Republic (1919–33) Popular name for the republic of Germany created after World War 1. It was named after the city of WEIMAR where the constitution was drawn up in 1919. It was hampered by severe economic difficulties. The Weimar constitution was suspended after Adolf HITLER became chancellor and the republic was superseded by the THIRD REICH.

Weinberg, Steven (1933–) US physicist who in 1967, independently of Pakistani physicist Abdus SALAM, proposed a theory that unified the ELECTROMAGNETIC and WEAK NUCLEAR FORCES between subatomic particles – now known as the electroweak force. Later experiments proved the Salam-Weinberg hypothesis to be true. In 1979, they shared the Nobel Prize in physics with Sheldon Glashow, who had earlier proposed a similar theory. *See also* GRAND UNIFIED THEORY (GUT)

Weismann, August (1834–1914) German biologist. His essay discussing the germ plasm theory, *The Continuity of the Germ Plasm* (1885), proposed the immortality of the germ line cells as opposed to body cells. It was influential in the development of modern genetic study.

Weiss, Peter (1916–82) Swedish dramatist, b. Germany. His reputation was established with *The Persecution and Assassination of Jean-Paul Marat as Performed by the Inmates of the Asylum of Charenton Under the Direction of the Marquis de Sade* (1964), more commonly known as *Marat/Sade*. Other plays include *The Investigation* (1965) and *Trotsky in Exile* (1970). His final play was *The New Investigation* (1981).

Weissmüller, Johnny (1904–84) US swimmer and actor. He won gold medals at the 1924 and 1928 Olympics, and later played Tarzan in a series of successful Hollywood films.

Weizmann, Chaim (1874–1952) Zionist leader, first president of Israel (1948–52). Born in Belarus, he became a naturalized British subject in 1910. He played the major role in securing the BALFOUR DECLARATION (1917). He was president of the World Zionist Organization (1920–31,1935–46), provisional president of Israel (1948) and elected president from 1949.

Weld, Theodore Dwight (1803–95) US campaigner for the abolition of slavery. He was leader of the more moderate wing of the ABOLITIONIST movement. In 1839 he and his wife, Angelina Grimké, published *American Slavery As It Is*.

welding Technique for joining metal parts, usually by controlled melting. In **fusion** welding, the parts to be joined are heated together until the metal starts to melt. On cooling, the molten metal solidifies to form a permanent bond between the parts. Such welds are usually strengthened with filler metal from a welding rod or wire. In **arc** welding, an electric arc heats the work and filler metal. In **oxyacetylene** welding, heat is provided by burning ethyne gas in oxygen. In resistance or **spot** welding, heat is generated by passing an electric current through the joint. In brazing and soldering, the heat is sufficient to melt the filler metal, but not the parts that it joins.

welfare state Description of a state that takes responsibility for the health and subsistence of its citizens. Limited forms of welfare were introduced by Western governments, such as that of Otto von BISMARCK in Germany, in the late 19th century. Comprehensive policies covering the whole of society were introduced after World War 2, particularly in Scandinavian countries and the UK, an influential example being the NATIONAL HEALTH SERVICE (NHS) *See also* SOCIAL SECURITY

well Shaft sunk vertically in the Earth's CRUST through which water, oil, natural gas, brine, sulphur or other mineral substances can be extracted. Artesian wells are sunk into water-bearing rock strata, the AQUIFERS, from which water rises under pressure in the wells to the surface.

Welles, (George) Orson (1915–85) US actor and director. His first publicly shown film, *Citizen Kane* (1940), was a great critical success and won an Oscar for its screenplay. As an actor, he starred in the classic *The Third Man* (1949) and acted in and directed *Touch of Evil* (1958). Disenchanted with Hollywood, Welles went into self-imposed exile from the USA, directing European productions, including *The Trial* (1963), *Chimes at Midnight* (1966) and *The Immortal Story* (1968).

Wellington Capital and region of New Zealand, in the extreme s of North Island, on Port Nicholson, an inlet of Cook Strait. First visited by Europeans in 1826, it was founded in 1840. In 1865 it replaced Auckland as capital. Wellington's excellent harbour furthered its development as a transport and trading centre. Industries: textiles, clothing, transport equipment, machinery. Pop. (2001) 163,824; 423,765 (region).

Wellington, Arthur Wellesley, Duke of (1769–1852) British general and politician, prime minister (1828–30). He commanded Allied forces in the PENINSULAR WAR (1808–14) against Napoleon, driving the French back over the Pyrenees. He represented Britain at the Congress of VIENNA (1814–15). Together with the Prussian General von Blücher, he defeated Napoleon at the Battle of WATERLOO in 1815. He became a Tory cabinet minister in 1818 and prime minister in 1828.

Wells, H.G. (Herbert George) (1866–1946) English writer. His reputation was established by the science fiction novels *The Time Machine* (1895), *The Invisible Man* (1897) and *The War of the Worlds* (1898). Later novels, including *Love and Mr Lewisham* (1900), *Kipps* (1905), *Tono-Bungay* (1909) and *The History of Mr Polly* (1910), draw on the experiences more directly related in his *Experiment in Autobiography* (1934). *Ann Veronica* (1909) and *The New Machiavelli* (1911) reflect his strong interest in sociology and politics.

Welsh (*Cymraeg*) Language of Wales. It is spoken natively by less than 19% of the Welsh population, chiefly in the rural north and west of the country. It belongs to the Brittonic sub-branch of the Celtic family of INDO-EUROPEAN LANGUAGES, and is closely related to BRETON and Cornish. It survives more strongly than most other CELTIC LANGUAGES.

Welsh National Party *See* PLAID CYMRU

Welsh pony Light saddle-horse of a breed known in Wales since Saxon times. It has a short, muscular body and great endurance. Its coat may be grey, bay, chestnut or black. Height: to 1.2m (48in) at the shoulder; weight: to *c*.225kg (500lb).

Welty, Eudora (1909–2001) US short-story writer and novelist. Welty's works are often set in her native Mississippi. Her short-story collections include *A Curtain of Green* (1941) and *The Golden Apples* (1949). Her novels include the Pulitzer Prize-winning *The Optimist's Daughter* (1972). Her autobiography is *One Writer's Beginnings* (1984).

welwitschia (tumboa) Plant that grows in the sandy regions of sw Africa. It produces only two leathery leaves that split into many ribbon-like strands up to 1.2–1.8m (4–6ft) long. It may live up to 2,000 years. Cone clusters – actually small flower spikes – are borne each year on both male and female plants. Division Gnetophyta; species *Welwitschia mirabilis*.

Wembley Complex of sports stadiums in Wembley, NW London. The outdoor Empire Stadium, with its twin towers, built for the 1924 Empire Exhibition, was used for the finals of the FA Cup, Football League Cup, and Rugby League Cup, as well as England's home international football matches. In the nearby covered Wembley Arena, ice shows and pop concerts share the facilities with boxing, showjumping and other sports. Major redevelopment was plagued by design changes and legal disputes, leading to late completion of the new stadium in 2007.

Wenceslas, Saint (907–29) Prince of Bohemia and patron saint of the Czechs. In *c*.925, he overthrew his mother who, as regent, had persecuted Christians. Wenceslas

continued the Christianization of the country, which, together with his submission to the Germans, aroused opposition. He was killed by his brother and successor, Bolesław I.

Wenceslas (1361–1419) King of the Germans (1378–1400) and King of Bohemia (1378–1419) as Wenceslaus IV. He succeeded his father, the Emperor CHARLES IV, but was never crowned Emperor and was deposed in 1400.

Wentworth, William Charles (1793–1872) Australian journalist and politician. In 1824, he founded *The Australian* newspaper, which he used to promote the cause of self-government for the Australian colonies. His activism was the most important factor leading to the granting of self-government by the British Parliament in 1842.

werewolf In folklore, a person who metamorphoses into a wolf at night but reverts to human form by day. Some werewolves can change form at will; in others the change occurs involuntarily, under the influence of a full moon.

Werfel, Franz (1890–1945) Austrian dramatist, novelist, and poet. His religious, historical, and modernist dramas include *The Trojan Women* (1915), *Paulus Among the Jews* (1926) and *Jacobowsky and the Colonel* (1943). *The Forty Days of Musa Dagh* (1933), *Embezzled Heaven* (1939), *The Song of Bernadette* (1941) and *Star of the Unborn* (1946) are among Werfel's most famous novels. His popular expressionist poetry, found in *The Friend of the World* (1911) and *Each Other* (1915), expressed his love for mankind.

Wergeland, Henrik Arnold (1808–45) Norwegian poet and patriot. Such works as *Jan van Huysum's Flowerpiece* (1840) and *The English Pilot* (1844) helped to establish his reputation as Norway's national poet.

Werner, Alfred (1866–1919) Swiss chemist. He received the 1913 Nobel Prize in chemistry for his co-ordination theory of VALENCE. This theory correctly suggested that metals have co-ordinate bonds that would make ISOMERS possible in inorganic compounds.

Wertheimer, Max (1880–1943) German psychologist. Wertheimer was a founder of GESTALT PSYCHOLOGY. His early work concerned visual perception. Later, he attempted to apply Gestalt principles to cognitive and educational problems.

Wesker, Arnold (1932–) English playwright and director. His plays have socialist themes, and his reputation was established with the trilogy *Chicken Soup with Barley* (1958), *Roots* (1959) and *I'm Talking about Jerusalem* (1960). Other works include *Chips with Everything* (1962), *The Friends* (1970), *The Old Ones* (1972) and *Love Letters on Blue Paper* (1978).

Wesley, Charles (1707–88) English evangelist and hymn-writer, brother of John WESLEY. He was ordained in 1735, and in 1738 underwent a evangelical conversion. Wesley wrote nearly 6000 hymns, including 'Hark! the herald angels sing" and 'Love divine, all loves excelling'.

Wesley, John (1703–91) English theologian and evangelist who founded METHODISM. In 1729, with his brother Charles WESLEY, he founded the Holy Club at Oxford. In 1738, he underwent a personal, religious experience during a Moravian meeting and this laid the foundation upon which he built the Methodist movement. Wesley's *Journal* (1735–90) records the great extent of his itinerant preaching.

Wessex Anglo-Saxon kingdom established in Hampshire, sw England. Traditionally founded by Cerdic (r.519–534), by the beginning of the 9th century it had extended its territory to include much of s England. Egbert (r.802–39) became overlord of all England, but his successors relinquished much of their kingdom to the invading Danes. ALFRED THE GREAT managed to resist further Danish encroachment, and Wessex was the only English kingdom to escape Danish conquest.

West, Benjamin (1738–1820) US painter. He settled in Britain, where he became historical painter to George III and a leader of NEO-CLASSICISM. His best-known paintings are *Death of Wolfe* (1771) and *Penn's Treaty with the Indians* (1772).

West, Mae (1893–1980) US stage and film actress. She began her career in burlesque. Her first film was *Night After Night* (1932). Her overt sexuality and use of double entendre in *She Done Him Wrong* and *I'm No Angel* (1933) led to increased censorship in the movie industry. Other films include *Go West, Young Man* (1936) and *My Little Chickadee* (1940).

▲ **Welles** Film director Orson Welles' reputation was established by *Citizen Kane* (1940), which he directed, produced and starred in. Widely acknowledged as one of the greatest films of all time, it was certainly one of the most influential. Welles earned notoriety with his dramatization for radio of H.G. Wells' *War of the Worlds* (1938), which was so vivid that thousands of listeners believed the broadcast real and reacted with panic and hysteria.

W

West, Nathanael (1903–40) US novelist and scriptwriter, b. Nathan Wallenstein Weinstein. He wrote just four novels: *The Dream Life of Balso Snell* (1931), *Miss Lonelyhearts* (1933), *A Cool Million* (1934) and *The Day of the Locust* (1939) – all of which are concerned with the barrenness of contemporary life.

West, Dame Rebecca (1892–1983) English novelist and critic, b. Cicily Isabel Fairfield. She is best known for her first novel, *The Return of the Soldier* (1918) – the story of a shell-shock victim. Her political works include *The Meaning of Treason* (1949) and *A Train of Powder* (1955). She also wrote perceptive psychological novels such as *The Thinking Reed* (1936) and *Birds Fall Down* (1966). She published her last book, *1900*, a year before her death at age 91.

West Bank Region w of the River JORDAN and NW of the Dead Sea. It was designated an Arab district in the United Nations' (UN) plan for the partition of PALESTINE (1947). It was administered by Jordan after the first ARAB-ISRAELI WAR (1948), but captured by Israel in the SIX-DAY WAR (1967). In 1988, Jordan surrendered its claim to the Israeli-occupied West Bank to the PALESTINE LIBERATION ORGANIZATION (PLO) led by Yasir ARAFAT. The Palestinian National Authority (PNA) gained limited autonomy in the West Bank by the ISRAELI-PALESTINIAN ACCORD (1994). Difficulties created by the growth of Israeli settlements, security disputes, and less conciliatory governments in Israel halted progress towards total Israeli withdrawal. *See also* BARAK, EHUD; NETANYAHU, BINYAMIN; PERES, SHIMON; RABIN, YITZHAK; SHARON, ARIEL

West Bengal State in NE India bordering Nepal, Bhutan and Sikkim (N), Bangladesh, and Assam state (E), the Bay of Bengal (S) and Bihar and Orissa states (W). The state capital is KOLKATA. It was formed (1947) after the independence of India and Pakistan, and the partitioning of the former British province of BENGAL into Hindu West Bengal (India) and Muslim East Bengal (East Pakistan). In 1950, West Bengal absorbed the state of Cooch Bihar. In the 1970s, political instability was caused by Muslim-Hindu disputes, large refugee immigration from newly created BANGLADESH, and Maoist Naxalite disturbances. The state is highly industrialized, its cities attracting vast numbers of male migrants from neighbouring agrarian states. Industries: vehicles, steel, fertilizers, chemicals. Agricultural products: rice, fish, jute, oilseeds, tea, tobacco. Area: 88,752sq km (34,258sq mi). Pop. (2001) 80,221,171.

western Popular fiction and film genre, native to the USA, featuring 'cowboys' and 'Indians' in a Wild West setting. It first appeared in the form of short stories and novels in the 'pulp' magazines of the late 19th century. Owen Wister's *The Virginian* (1902) is perhaps the most defining influence and Zane Grey its most prolific exponent. *The Squaw Man* (1914), an early Hollywood westerns, set a trend for a whole new breed of movie cowboy, such as Tom Mix, Roy Rogers and 'Hopalong Cassidy'. More recent examples of the genre re-evaluated the treatment of Native Americans by settlers.

Western Australia State in Australia, bordered by the Timor Sea (N), the Indian Ocean (W and S), South Australia state and the Northern Territory (E). The capital is PERTH; other major cities are Mandurah, Kalgoorlie, Bunbury, and Fremantle – Perth's main port. Western Australia was first visited by Dirck Hartog in 1616, but settlement did not begin until 1826, when a penal colony was founded. The first free settlement was in 1829. The largest state in Australia, it was governed by New South Wales until 1831, becoming a state of the Commonwealth of Australia in 1901. The climate is mainly tropical or sub-tropical and more than 90% of the land is desert or semi-desert. Most settlements are in the sw, which has a temperate climate. The Swan River, the only significant water source, drains this sw region. The raising of sheep and cattle is the main agricultural activity, but cereals, fishing and forestry are also important. Western Australia is the country's major gold-producing state; there is also mining for iron ore, coal, nickel, uranium, bauxite, phosphates, mineral sands, oil, and natural gas. Winemaking is also important. Area: 2,525,500sq km (975,095sq mi). Pop. (2000 est.) 1,897,400.

Western Cape Province in sw South Africa, bounded by the Indian Ocean to the s and Atlantic Ocean to the w. The capital is CAPE TOWN; other major towns include Simonstown and Stellenbosch. Formerly part of Cape Province, Western Cape was formed in 1994. Its chief physical features are Table Mountain (1,087m) and the rugged Swartberg Range (up to 2,325m). Robben Island was the site of a prison used to house political prisoners during the APARTHEID era. The main economic activity is agriculture, with fruit and tobacco growing, dairy farming and sheep rearing. There is an important fishing industry, and an offshore gas field is exploited in Mossel Bay. Industries: chemicals, machinery, metal goods, textiles. Area: 129,390sq km (50,500sq mi). Pop. (2000 est.) 4,178,600.

W

▶ **West Indies** Stretching for 3200km (2000mi), the island chain of the West Indies divides the Atlantic Ocean from the Caribbean. The region is famed for its great natural beauty, while its thousands of kilometres of sandy, secluded beaches make the West Indies a popular holiday destination.

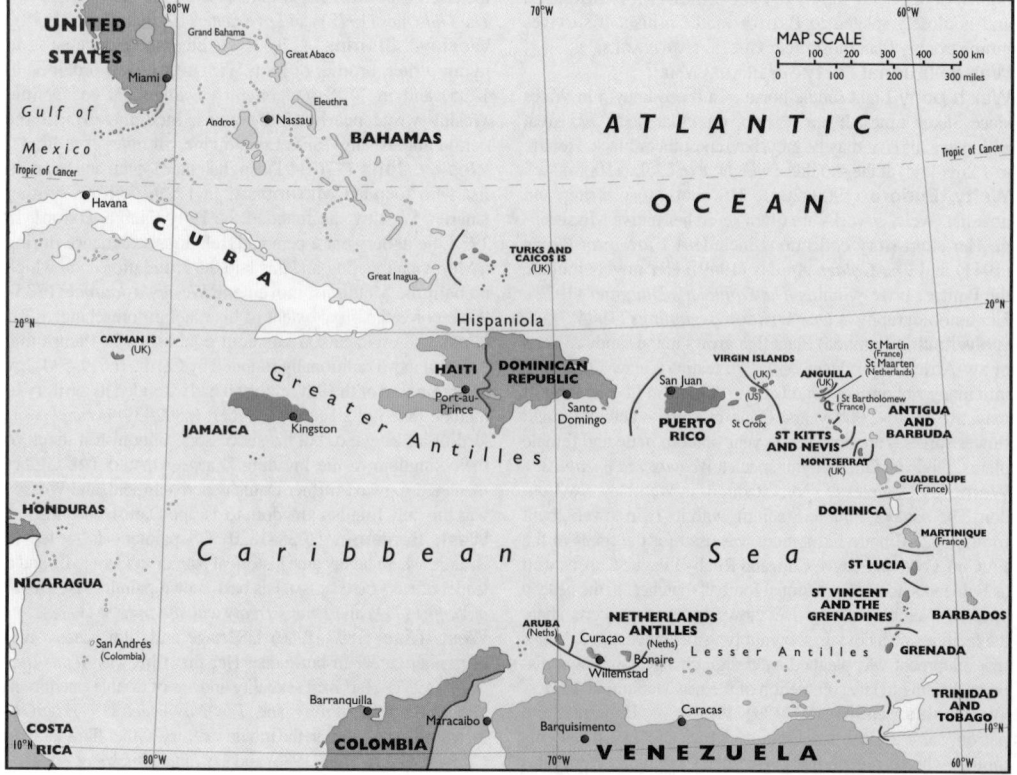

Western European Union (WEU) Defence alliance consisting of most of the European members of the NORTH ATLANTIC TREATY ORGANIZATION (NATO).

Western Isles *See* HEBRIDES

Western Sahara (formerly Spanish Sahara) Desert territory on the Atlantic coast of NW Africa, bordering N with Morocco, NE with Algeria, and E and S with Mauritania; the capital is El Aaiún. The territory comprises two districts: Saguia el Hamra in the N, and Río de Oro in the S. The population consists of Arabs, Berbers, and pastoral nomads, most of whom are Sunni Muslims. Livestock-rearing dominates agriculture. The first European arrival was in 1434, but the area remained unexploited until the 19th century, and even then Spain controlled only the coastal area. In 1957, a nationalist movement temporarily overthrew the Spanish. In 1958 the Spanish regained control of the region, and merged Saguia el Hamra and Río de Oro to form the province of Spanish Sahara. In 1963, large phosphate deposits were discovered. In 1973, the Polisario Front began a guerrilla war, which eventually forced a Spanish withdrawal in 1976. Within a month, Morocco and Mauritania partitioned the country. Polisario (backed by Algeria) continued to fight for independence, unilaterally renaming the country the Saharawi Arab Democratic Republic. In 1979, Mauritania withdrew and Morocco assumed full control. In 1982, the Saharawi Republic became a member of the Organization of African Unity (OAU). By 1988 it controlled most of the desert up to the Moroccan defensive line. Fragile ceasefires were agreed in 1988 and 1991. A promised referendum failed to materialize and *c.*200,000 Saharawis continue to live in refugee camps, mostly in Algeria. Talks between Moroccan and Western Saharan government delegations began in 1997 and have been inconclusive. Area: 266,769sq km (102,680sq mi). Pop. (2000) 228,000. *See* MOROCCO map page 526.

Western Wall (Wailing Wall) Place in S Wales on the Bristol Channel; Jews. It is a remnant of a wall of the great TEMPLE destroyed by the Romans in AD 70. It is the focus of many pilgrimages.

West Glamorgan County in S Wales on the Bristol Channel; the administrative centre is SWANSEA. Now divided into four districts (Lliw Valley, Neath, Port Talbot, and Swansea), the area has been renowned for its metallurgical industry since the 18th century. Anthracite mining and oil refining are important industries, while tourists are attracted by the Gower Peninsula. Area: 820sq km (317sq mi). Pop. (2000 est.) 443,274.

West Indies Chain of islands encircling the Caribbean Sea and separating it from the Atlantic Ocean, extending from Florida to Venezuela. Geographically they divide into three main groups: the BAHAMAS, and the Greater and Lesser ANTILLES. Most islands are now independent, but were formerly British, Spanish, French, or Dutch possessions. The indigenous population was killed by the colonial powers, who fought for possession of the islands. They were transformed by the introduction of sugar cane in the 17th century, fuelling the slave trade from Africa. *See* individual country articles

Westinghouse, George (1846–1914) US engineer and inventor. The best known of his hundreds of inventions was the air brake, which made high-speed rail travel safe. He formed the Westinghouse Electric Company in 1886.

Westmeath County in Leinster province, N central Republic of Ireland, bounded by the counties of Meath, Cavan, Roscommon, and Offaly. The county town is Mullingar. It is mainly low-lying with many lakes or loughs, including Sheelin and Rees, and is drained by the rivers SHANNON, Inny, and Brosna. The main economic activity is cattle raising. Area: 1,763sq km (681sq mi). Pop. (2002) 72,027.

West Midlands Metropolitan county in central England. It is divided into seven council districts: BIRMINGHAM (the administrative centre), COVENTRY, Dudley, Sandwell, Solihull, Walsall, and Wolverhampton. The other major town is West Bromwich. Area: 899sq km (347sq mi). Pop. (2001) 5,267,337.

Westminster, City of Part of the LONDON borough of Westminster since 1965. Westminster was the site of a monastery from 785, and is where EDWARD THE CONFESSOR built WESTMINSTER ABBEY. Parliament met in Westminster Palace until a fire (1834) led to the building of the Houses of Parliament (1840–67). Pop. (2001) 181,279.

Westminster, Statutes of English Acts in the reign of EDWARD I. The First (1275) and Second (1285) Statutes enshrined Edward's extensive overhaul of medieval English law. A further statute of 1290 is sometimes called the Third Statute of Westminster. The Statute of Westminster of 1931 granted autonomy to the dominions in the British Empire.

Westminster Abbey Gothic church in London, originally the abbey church of a Benedictine monastery (closed 1539). In 1050, EDWARD THE CONFESSOR began to build a Norman church on the site. In 1245, Henry III began work on the present structure. The Lady Chapel, dedicated to Henry VII, is a fine example of the PERPENDICULAR STYLE. The two western towers were built (1722–45) by Sir Christopher WREN and Nicholas HAWKSMOOR. The 19th-century restoration was managed by Sir George Gilbert SCOTT. The Abbey is cruciform in plan. Since William the Conqueror, most English monarchs have been crowned in the Abbey. It is the burial place of 18 monarchs. Poets' Corner lies in the S transept.

Weston, Edward (1886–1958) US photographer. He developed his style in the 1920s, influenced by Alfred STIEGLITZ. His aim was to give new meaning to mundane objects.

Westphalia Historic region of W Germany between the rivers Rhine and Weser. From 1180, it was a Duchy under the Archbishops of Cologne. Briefly a kingdom during the NAPOLEONIC WARS, it became a province of Prussia in 1816.

Westphalia, Peace of (1648) Series of treaties among the states involved in the THIRTY YEARS' WAR. In 1642, peace negotiations began in the cities of Westphalia, leading to the final settlement. In Germany, the peace established the virtual autonomy of the German states, which diminished the authority of the Holy Roman Emperor. The peace also established the ascendancy of France, the power of Sweden in N Europe, and the decline of Spain.

West Sussex Non-metropolitan county in SE England. It is divided into seven districts: Chichester (the county town), Adur, Arun, Crawley, Horsham, Mid-Sussex, and Worthing. Area: 2016sq km (778sq mi). Pop. (2001) 753,612.

West Virginia State in the Appalachian Mountain region, E central USA. The capital is CHARLESTON. The land is mountainous and rugged. West Virginia has two narrow projections: the Northern Panhandle extends N between Ohio and Pennsylvania; and the Eastern Panhandle cuts E between Maryland and Virginia. Harpers Ferry lies on the bank of the Potomac River, which forms much of the state's E border. The Ohio River forms most of its W border. In 1727, Germans established the first settlement at New Mecklenburg (Shepherdstown). Settlers crossing the Appalachian and Allegheny mountains led to the last of the FRENCH AND INDIAN WARS (1754–63). The region was then part of Virginia, but political and economic disagreements, especially on slavery, arose between western Virginians and the dominant E. When Virginia seceded from the Union in May 1861, there was much opposition in the W, and it was admitted to the Union as West Virginia in 1863. Hay, tobacco, maize, and apples are the principal crops, but West Virginia also has rich mineral deposits, and is the leading US producer of bituminous coal. Some 65% of the land is forested. Industries: glass, chemicals, steel, machinery, tourism. Area: 62,629sq km (24,181sq mi). Pop. (2000) 1,825,754.

West Yorkshire Metropolitan county in N central England. It divides into five districts: BRADFORD, Calderdale, Kirklees, LEEDS, and Wakefield (the county town). Area: 2,036sq km (7,86sq mi). Pop. (2001) 2,079,217.

wetland Ecosystem where the WATER TABLE lies close to the surface for much of the year. Wetlands include bogs, marshes, swamps and fens. There are both saltwater and freshwater wetlands. Coastal wetlands are said to contain a greater concentration of flora and fauna than any other ecosystem. They are also ecologically valuable as regulators of flooding and the water cycle. Many of the world's wetlands have been drained for farming or housing.

Wexford County in Leinster province, SE Republic of Ireland. The county town is Wexford (1996 pop. 15,862). The land is mostly low-lying but rises to the Blackstairs Mountains in the W. The chief river is the Slaney. Wexford is primarily an

WEST VIRGINIA
Statehood :
June 20, 1863
Nickname :
The Mountain State
State bird :
Cardinal
State flower :
Rhododendron
State tree :
Sugar maple
State motto :
Mountaineers are always free

W

▶ **whale** Among the largest and most intelligent animals that have ever lived, whales all belong to the order Cetacea. The beluga whale (*Delphinapterus leucas*, A) is an Arctic species, and travels in schools of many hundreds. It grows to 4.25m (17ft). The pilot whale (*Globicephala* sp., B) is found in most oceans except the polar seas. They migrate between cold and warm waters depending on the season. The Californian grey whale (*Eschrichtius glaucus*, C) is confined to the North Pacific. From the N seas, they migrate S in winter to breed in the shallow, warmer seas off Baja California and South Korea. They feed on plankton, which they strain from the water by means of baleen plates (1). They grow to 9m (30ft).

▲ **wheat** Along with rice, wheat is the world's most important food crop. The kernels of the plant are ground into flour, which can then be used to make a variety of foods. Wheat remains green in colour until it ripens, becoming golden-brown.

W

A

B

C

1

agricultural county; wheat is the chief crop, and cattle raising is important. Area: 2,351sq km (908sq mi). Pop. (2002) 116,543.

Weyden, Rogier van der (1400–64) Netherlandish painter. In 1436, he became official painter to the city of Brussels, where he lived for the rest of his life. His finest works include *Deposition* (before 1443). He excelled at inventive compositions.

whale Any of several species of large aquatic mammals; it has a fish-like body with paddle-like flippers, and a tail flattened horizontally into flukes for locomotion. It spends its whole life in water. Two main groups exist: toothed whales and baleen whales. Toothed whales (Odontoceti) have simple teeth and feed primarily on fish and squid. They include the bottle-nosed whale, SPERM WHALE, and BELUGA. Baleen whales (Mysticeti), including the right whale, BLUE WHALE, and California grey whale, have no teeth but carry comb-like plates of horny material (baleen or whalebone) in the roof of the mouth. These form a sieve, through which the whales strain KRILL on which they feed. Order Cetacea. The order also includes DOLPHINS and PORPOISES. *See also* WHALING

whale shark Largest species of shark; it lives in tropical waters worldwide. Brownish to dark grey with white or yellow spots and stripes, this docile, egg-laying fish often travels near the surface. Length: 9m (30ft). Family Rhincodontidae; species *Rhincodon typus*.

whaling Industry involved in the pursuing and catching of whales for their oil and flesh. Originating in the Middle Ages, the modern whaling era began in the 1850s with the development of harpoons with explosive heads. After 1925, ocean-going factory ships were sent to the Antarctic. Since that time most larger whale species have been hunted to near-extinction. In 1986, the International Whaling Commission (IWC) agreed a moratorium on commercial whaling. Whaling for 'scientific purposes' by Japan, Iceland, and Norway continued. In 1990, Norway claimed that whale numbers were high enough to sustain hunting; however, public opposition remains strong.

Wharton, Edith Newbold (1862–1937) US novelist. She is best known for *Ethan Frome* (1911), a grim portrait of New England farm life, and her polished anatomies of New York society, *The House of Mirth* (1905) and *The Age of Innocence* (1920), for which she became the first woman to receive a Pulitzer Prize.

wheat CEREAL grass originating in the Middle East. Cultivated there since 7000 BC it is now grown worldwide. It is used for BREAD, pasta, cake, and pastry flour. Wheat is also used in the preparation of MALT, dextrose and ALCOHOL. Family Poaceae/Gramineae.

Wheatstone, Sir Charles (1802–75) English physicist and inventor. In 1843, with William Cooke, he improved the Wheatstone bridge, a device for measuring electrical resistance. In 1837, they patented an electric TELEGRAPH. Wheatstone also invented the harmonica and concertina.

wheel Circular structure that revolves around a central axis. Before the wheel was invented, heavy loads were sometimes moved by rolling them on logs or on rounded stones. More than 5,000 years ago, sections of tree trunks were cut to form the first wheels for carts. Spoked wheels were introduced several hundred years later. Eventually, the wheel was used in simple machines, such as the waterwheel and potter's wheel.

wheel and axle Machine based on the principle that a small force applied to the rim of a wheel will exert a larger force on

an object attached to the axle. The MECHANICAL ADVANTAGE is the ratio of the radius of the wheel to that of the axle.

whelk Edible, marine GASTROPOD distributed worldwide on seashores. It has a coiled shell, with a smooth rim and a notch at the end. Family Buccinidae. Length: 13–18cm (5–7in).

Whig Party One of the two major US political parties from 1834 to 1854. It was a coalition party, garnering the support of eastern capitalists, western farmers, and southern plantation owners. The party elected two presidents: William Henry HARRISON in 1840 and Zachary TAYLOR in 1848. The issue of slavery split the Whigs, however, and the REPUBLICAN PARTY emerged from its disintegration in 1854.

Whigs Semi-formal parliamentary grouping in the UK from the late-17th to the mid-19th centuries. The word Whig was used by the TORY supporters of JAMES II for politicians who wished to exclude the Duke of York from the throne. The Whig Party thus became those people who promoted the GLORIOUS REVOLUTION (1688) and who applauded the Hanoverian succession of 1714. Between 1714 and the accession of GEORGE III in 1760, the Tories were so discredited by association with the JACOBITES that most politicians became Hanoverian Whigs, even in opposition to a Whig ministry. In the reign of GEORGE III, Toryism gradually reasserted itself. Whiggism became the party of religious toleration, parliamentary reform, and opposition to slavery. From the appointment of William PITT (THE YOUNGER) as prime minister in 1783 until 1830, the Whigs remained in opposition (with one brief exception). They returned to office under Lord GREY, who passed the Great Reform Act of 1832. By the mid-19th century, they had come to be replaced by, or known as, the LIBERAL PARTY.

whinchat Small Eurasian THRUSH that commonly inhabits grassy coastal areas in England. It has a brown, mottled back with a white rump and distinctive red breast. The dark head is clearly marked by a white eye-stripe. Length: to 13cm (5in). Species *Saxicola rubetra*.

whip UK government officer whose duty is to see that government supporters attend debates and vote in divisions. It is also the name for the notices that they send to members of Parliament. There are also opposition whips.

whippet Sporting dog that was originally bred in England for racing and hare coursing. It is capable of running at speeds of 56.5km/h (35mph). It resembles a small GREYHOUND. Height: to 56cm (22in) at the shoulder; weight: to 11kg (24lb).

whippoorwill *See* NIGHTJAR

whirligig beetle Medium-sized, dark-coloured WATER BEETLE often seen resting or gyrating on the surface of a still pool. They prey on small insects. Family Gyrinidae.

whirling dervish *See* DERVISH

whirlpool Circular motion of a fluid. Whirlpools in rivers occur in regions where waterfalls or sharp breaks in topographic continuity make steady flow impossible. Also, in rivers and seas they can occur where two currents meet. *See also* VORTEX

whisky (Irish or US whiskey) Alcoholic spirit made by distilling fermented cereal grains. Scotch whisky and Irish whiskey are both distilled from barley that has been allowed to sprout. It is then roasted, 'mashed', and distilled. In the USA, maize and rye are used to produce bourbon whiskey (corn) and rye whiskey. After distillation, refined whisky spirit is 70–85% alcohol by volume; all whiskies are therefore heavily diluted. Most whiskies are blended.

whist Card game for four people playing as two pairs of partners. The aim is to accumulate 'tricks' – sets of cards, one from each player, in which the player of the highest-value card 'takes the trick'. The object of ordinary whist is to amass more tricks than any other player. Other whist games include contract whist, in which players specify how many tricks they will make; and solo whist, in which one player contracts to make tricks and all the others conspire to thwart him or her.

Whistler, James Abbott McNeill (1834–1903) US painter and etcher who lived and worked in England from 1859. He was a precursor of ABSTRACT ART. For Whistler, the artist's duty was to select elements from nature to create a harmonious composition that, like music, existed for its own sake. His most famous painting is the portrait of his mother, entitled *Arrangement in Gray and Black* (1872).

Other works include *Chelsea: Nocturne in Blue and Green* (c.1870). He also produced some 400 plates of etchings.

Whitby Coastal town in N Yorkshire, England. Saint Hilda founded an abbey here in 657, which was destroyed by the Danes in the 9th century. In c.663, the **Synod of Whitby** was held at the abbey. The subsequent break with the Celtic Church placed the English Church in line with mainstream European Christian theology.

White, Gilbert (1720–93) English naturalist. White held curacies at Selborne in Hampshire, devoting himself to the study of natural history around his parish. His famous work *The Natural History and Antiquities of Selborne* (1789) consists of letters to his fellow naturalists.

White, Patrick Victor Martin Sale (1912–90) Australian novelist, b. Britain. His novels, concerned with the nature of the Australian experience, include *The Tree of Man* (1955), *Voss* (1957), *Riders in the Chariot* (1961), *The Vivisector* (1970), *The Eye of the Storm* (1973), *A Fringe of Leaves* (1976) and *The Twyborn Affair* (1979). In 1973, he became the first Australian to win a Nobel Prize in literature.

White, T.H. (Terence Hanbury) (1906–64) English writer. His autobiographical *England Have My Bones* attracted notice in 1936, but he is best known for his Arthurian tetralogy *The Once and Future King*, collectively published in 1958.

White, Walter (1893–1955) US civil rights leader. As an officer of the NATIONAL ASSOCIATION FOR THE ADVANCEMENT OF COLORED PEOPLE (NAACP), he campaigned for desegregation, voting rights, and prevention of lynching. He also wrote several books in the cause of justice for blacks, including his autobiography *A Man Called White* (1948).

white ant *See* TERMITE

whitebait Young of several types of European HERRING. Length: to 5cm (2in). The name is also given to a tropical marine fish found in Australian waters. This fish, *Galaxias attenuatus*, is elongated with its dorsal fin set far back. Family Galaxiidae. Length: to 10cm (5in).

white blood cell *See* LEUCOCYTE

white dwarf High-density type of STAR about the size of the Earth, but with a mass about that of the Sun. White dwarfs are of low LUMINOSITY and gradually cool down to become cold, dark objects.

white-eye Common name for a group of arboreal songbirds found mainly in tropical forests in Africa, Asia, and Australasia. They are usually small and green with a prominent ring of white feathers around the eyes. They have pointed bills and extensible tongues for feeding on fruits. Length: to 12.5cm (5in). Family Zosteropidae.

Whitefield, George (1714–70) English evangelical preacher, an important figure in early METHODISM. In 1738, he made his first visit to America. Whitefield's stirring, open-air sermons contributed to the GREAT AWAKENING. He broke from John WESLEY to form the Calvinistic Methodist Church.

whitefish (cisco or lake herring) Any of several species of freshwater food fish that live in Eurasia and the USA. It is silvery, with large scales and a small mouth. Length: to 150cm (59in); weight: to 29kg (63lb). Family Salmonidae.

White Friars *See* CARMELITES

Whitehead, A.N. (Alfred North) (1861–1947) English philosopher and mathematician. In his 'philosophy of organism', Whitehead attempted a synthesis of modern science and metaphysics. The system is presented in his *Process and Reality* (1929). His three-volume *Principia Mathematica* (1910–13), written in collaboration with Bertrand RUSSELL, is an important work in the study of LOGIC.

White House Official residence of the US President in WASHINGTON, D.C. It was designed in the neo-classical style by James Hoban in 1792, and completed in 1800. After being burned down during the British invasion in 1814, it was rebuilt and the porticoes were added in the 1820s.

white shark (great white shark) Aggressive shark found in tropical and subtropical waters worldwide. It has a heavy body, a crescent-shaped tail, and saw-edged triangular teeth; it is grey, blue or brown with a white belly. Length: to 11m (36ft); weight: to 2,200kg (7,000lb). Family Isuridae; species *Carcharodon carcharias*.

whitethroat Small bird of the Old World WARBLER family (Sylviidae). It has drab brown plumage with red-brown wing patches, a long white-edged tail, and a white throat. Length: 13cm (5in). Genus *Sylvia*.

white whale *See* BELUGA

whiting Several unrelated food fish. The European whiting (*Merlangus merlangus*) is a haddock-like fish of the COD family, Gadidae. It is found primarily in the North Sea, where it feeds on invertebrates and small fish. It is silver with distinctive black markings at the base of the pectoral fin. Length: to 70cm (28in). Other fish commonly called whitings include the kingfish, *Menticirrhus saxatilis*, and the freshwater WHITEFISH, *Coregonus clupeaformis*.

Whitlam, (Edward) Gough (1916–) Australian statesman, prime minister (1972–75). In 1967, Whitlam became leader of the Australian LABOR PARTY. His government ended compulsory conscription and relaxed Australia's stringent immigration laws. In 1975, the governor general dismissed Whitlam, an action that highlighted Australia's constitutional relationship with the UK. In December 1977, after a crushing defeat in the general election, Whitlam resigned as party leader.

Whitman, Walt (Walter) (1819–92) US poet. In 1855 he published, at his own expense, *Leaves of Grass* - a volume of 12 poems that included 'Song of Myself'. In 1856 and 1860, Whitman produced enlarged editions of the work. *Drum-Taps* (1865), which draws on his experience of medical service in the Civil War, and *Sequel to Drum-Taps* (1865–66), which includes his famous elegies to Abraham Lincoln, 'When Lilacs Last in the Dooryard Bloom'd' and 'O Captain! My Captain!', were both incorporated into a much-expanded 1867 edition of *Leaves of Grass*. Whitman's use of free verse, symbolic association and colloquial language represents a major transition in AMERICAN LITERATURE.

Whitney, Eli (1765–1825) US inventor and manufacturer. He invented the COTTON GIN (1793), which revolutionized cotton picking in the South and turned cotton into a profitable export. After 1798, he manufactured muskets at a factory in New Haven, Connecticut, which was one of the first to use mass-production methods.

Whitney, Mount Second-highest peak in the USA (after Mount MCKINLEY), at 4,418m (14,495ft). Situated on the E edge of Sequoia National Park, it is part of the Sierra Nevada range in E California.

Whitsun *See* PENTECOST

Whittington, Dick (Richard) (1358–1423) English merchant, Lord Mayor of London on several occasions between 1397 and 1420. The son of a knight, he became wealthy dealing in fine cloths. He made loans to Henry IV and Henry V, and endowed many charitable institutions. He is, however, best known as the subject of a legend about a poor boy and his cat, who come to London to make their fortune.

Whittle, Sir Frank (1907–96) English inventor. In 1930, he patented the first turbojet (gas turbine) engine for aircraft. He developed the engine while a test pilot in the Royal Air Force (RAF), but was refused government support until the outbreak of World War 2. By 1941, his first jet plane was flying. The first jets entered service with the RAF in 1944. *See also* JET ENGINE

whooping cough (pertussis) Acute, highly contagious childhood respiratory disease. It is caused by the bacterium *Bordetella pertussis* and is marked by spasms of coughing, followed by a long-drawn intake of air, or 'whoop'. It is frequently associated with vomiting and severe nose bleeds. Immunization reduces the number and severity of attacks.

Whorf, Benjamin Lee (1897–1941) US structural linguist. He formed the Whorf hypothesis (or Sapir-Whorf hypothesis), which states that "the structure of language influences thought processes and our perception of the world around us."

whortleberry *See* BILBERRY

▲ **whelk** Found in temperate waters, the whelk (*Baccinum* sp.) can be eaten or used as bait. Whelks are scavengers and carnivores. They hold on to their victim, usually a crab or lobster, using their large, muscular foot. They then bore a hole through the shell using an extensible proboscis tipped with an abrasive radula, through which they feed.

W

◀ **whiting** The European whiting (*Merlangus merlangus*) is found primarily in the North Sea, where it feeds on invertebrates and small fish. It is an important commercial fish and congregates in large shoals.

W

Wichita City at the confluence of the Arkansas and Little Arkansas rivers, s central Kansas. Established in 1864 as a trading post, Wichita developed with the arrivals of the Chisholm Trail and the railroad (1872). A cattle town and later a wheat centre, its commercial growth was spurred by the discovery of oil (1915) and by the development of its aircraft industry (1920). It is by far the largest city in Kansas. Industries: aviation, railroad workshops, oil refining, grain processing, meat-packing. Pop. (2000) 344,284.

Wicklow County in Leinster province, E Republic of Ireland; the county town is Wicklow. The Wicklow Mountains dominate the county. The Liffey, Slaney, and Avoca are the chief rivers. Farmers rear sheep and cattle and grow cereals. Wicklow's beautiful scenery attracts many tourists. Area: 2,025sq km (782sq mi). Pop. (2002) 114,719.

widgeon River duck with mainly brownish plumage. It feeds on the surface of the water and engages in complex courtship displays. Species include the North American *Mareca americana* and European *Mareca penelope*.

Wieland, Christoph Martin (1733–1813) German novelist and poet. His works include prose translations of 22 of Shakespeare's plays – the first to be made in German – and the novels *Agathon* (1766–67); *Peregrinus Proteus* (1791) and *Aristipp* (1800–01). He also wrote the verse epic *Oberon* (1780).

Wieland, Heinrich Otto (1877–1957) German chemist. Wieland received the 1927 Nobel Prize in chemistry for his research into BILE acids. He showed them to have a STEROID skeleton, and thus found that they were structurally related to CHOLESTEROL. He also did research into oxidation reactions occurring in living tissues and discovered that they involved the removal of hydrogen, not the addition of oxygen.

Wiener, Norbert (1894–1964) US mathematician and originator of CYBERNETICS. He contributed to the study and development of the COMPUTER and to the understanding of feedback systems that control the behaviour of humans and machines.

Wiesbaden City on the River Rhine at the foot of the Taunus Mountains, W central Germany; state capital of Hessen. Founded in the 3rd century BC and later a Roman spa town, Wiesbaden remains famous for its mineral springs. It became a free imperial city in *c.*1241, and served as capital of the Duchy of Nassau from 1806 to 1866, when it passed to Prussia. Industries: wine-making, metal goods, chemicals, cement, publishing, tourism. Pop. (1999) 268,200.

Wiesel, Elie (1928–) US writer, b. Romania. The sole family survivor from the Nazi concentration camp at AUSCHWITZ, Wiesel became a US citizen in 1963. In 1986, he won the Nobel Peace Prize for his work on behalf of oppressed peoples. His first three accounts of concentration camp survivors, *Night*

(1958), *Dawn* (1960) and *The Accident* (1961), are known in collected form as the *Night Trilogy*. Other novels include *The Town Beyond the Wall* (1962), *A Beggar in Jerusalem* (1968), *The Fifth Son* (1985) and *The Forgotten* (1989).

Wight, Isle of Island and non-metropolitan county off the s coast of England, separated from the mainland (Hampshire) by the Solent. Newport is the county town. The island's mild climate and attractive scenery make it a popular tourist destination. It is divided into two administrative districts: South Wight and Medina (also the principal river). Cowes is a famous yachting centre. Area: 318sq km (147sq mi). Pop. (2002) 132,719.

Wigner, Eugene Paul (1902–95) US physicist, b. Hungary. During World War 2, Wigner worked on the MANHATTAN PROJECT. He was the first physicist to apply group theory to QUANTUM MECHANICS. With this technique, he discovered the law of conservation of parity. For his work on the structure of the atomic nucleus, Wigner shared the 1963 Nobel Prize in physics with Hans Jensen and Maria Goeppert-Mayer.

wigwam Shelter used by Native North Americans of the Eastern Woodlands culture. Wigwams were made from bark, reed mats or thatch, spread over a pole frame. They should not be confused with the conical, skin-covered tepees of the Native Americans of the Plains.

Wilberforce, William (1759–1833) English social reformer. He was elected to Parliament in 1780. In 1785, he converted to evangelicalism. Wilberforce led the ABOLITIONIST cause in Parliament for more than 20 years. His campaign led to the abolition of the slave trade in 1807, but Wilberforce continued to work for abolition throughout the British Empire. His works include *A Practical View* (1797).

wild boar Tusked, cloven-hoofed mammal of the PIG family that lives wild in forested areas of Eurasia and Africa. Length: to 1.8m (6ft); weight: to 200kg (450lb). Family Suidae; species *Sus scrofa*.

Wilde, Oscar (1854–1900) (Oscar Fingal O'Flahertie Wills) Irish dramatist, poet, prose writer, and wit. He wrote one novel, *The Picture of Dorian Gray* (1891), but most characteristic of his gift for dramatizing serious issues with epigrammatic wit are his plays, which include *Lady Windermere's Fan* (1892), *A Woman of No Importance* (1893), *An Ideal Husband* (1895) and his masterpiece *The Importance of Being Earnest* (1895). He was convicted of homosexual practices in 1895, and sentenced to two years' hard labour. While in prison he wrote *The Ballad of Reading Gaol* (1898).

wildebeest *See* GNU

Wilder, Billy (1906–2002) US film director and screenwriter, b. Germany. His creative partnership with Charles Brackett began with comedy scripts, such as *Ninotchka* (1939). *Double Indemnity* (1944) is a classic FILM NOIR. Wilder won Academy Awards for best director, best picture and shared the best screenplay prize with Brackett for *The Lost Weekend* (1945). Their last collaboration, *Sunset Boulevard* (1950), also earned them a best screenplay Oscar. Wilder's solo career proved just as successful with films such as *The Seven Year Itch* (1955) and *Some Like it Hot* (1959). He won further Academy Awards for best picture and best director for *The Apartment* (1960).

Wilder, Thornton Niven (1897–1975) US novelist and playwright. Wilder received the Pulitzer Prize for his novel *The Bridge of San Luis Rey* (1927). He is perhaps best known for his plays, which include *Our Town* (1938), and *The Skin of Our Teeth* (1942), both of which also won Pulitzer Prizes.

Wilhelmina (1880–1962) Queen of the Netherlands (1890–1948). She helped to keep the country neutral in World War 1 and often intervened in political affairs. During World War 2, she led a government-in-exile in England and became a symbol of Dutch independence. In 1948 Wilhelmina abdicated in favour of her daughter, Juliana.

Wilkes, John (1727–97) British radical politician and journalist. He was expelled from Parliament for his savage criticism of GEORGE III and his government in the political journal *North Briton* (1763). His prosecution under a general warrant was condemned in the courts, a landmark in civil liberties. The refusal of Parliament to readmit him as member for Middlesex after he had been elected three times encouraged the movement towards parliamentary reform.

▶ **Wilde** A supporter of the Aesthetic movement, Oscar Wilde shocked and enthralled London society with his flamboyant style and caustic wit. He gave an acclaimed lecture tour in the USA, where, when asked on his arrival at customs if he had anything to declare, Wilde reputedly replied, 'Only my genius'. He married in 1884 and had two sons. Wilde was financially ruined by bringing an unsuccessful court case for libel, and was himself then prosecuted and convicted for homosexuality. He spent his final years living in self-imposed exile in France.

Wilkinson, Sir Geoffrey (1921–96) English chemist. His work on organometallic sandwich compounds earned him a Nobel Prize in chemistry in 1973, which he shared with Ernst Fischer, who worked independently on the same subject.

Wilkinson, James (1757–1825) American general. He served in the AMERICAN REVOLUTION, but was forced to resign (1778) because of his part in the Conway Cabal. In 1784, Wilkinson moved to Kentucky and joined a conspiracy with the Spanish governor of Louisiana to gain trade monopolies and to give Kentucky to Spain. Returning to the army, he was dismissed after failing to capture Montréal in the WAR OF 1812.

will In law, a clear expression of intent by a person (the testator) concerning the disposal of his or her effects after death. The testator must be of sound mind and legal age, and the will must be witnessed by two competant people who are not beneficiaries. It may be altered or revoked by the testator, with due legal process.

Willemstadt Capital of NETHERLANDS ANTILLES, on Curaçao Island, West Indies. Willemstadt is a free port, exporting oil and coffee. Oil refining and tourism are major industries. It has the largest dry dock in the Americas. Pop. (1995) 119,000.

William I (1797–1888) King of Prussia (1861–88) and Emperor of Germany (1871–88). From 1858, He served as regent for his brother, FREDERICK WILLIAM IV. His suppression of revolution in 1848–49 earned him a reputation as a reactionary, but as King he displayed sensible pragmatism and followed the advice of his minister, BISMARCK. He supported the unification of Germany, but accepted his proclamation as Emperor reluctantly, fearing a reduction in Prussia's status.

William I (the Conqueror) (1027–87) King of England (1066–87) and Duke of Normandy (1035–87). Supported initially by Henry I of France, he consolidated his position in Normandy against hostile neighbours. On the death of EDWARD THE CONFESSOR, he claimed the English throne, having allegedly gained the agreement of King HAROLD in 1064. William defeated and killed Harold at the Battle of HASTINGS (1066), and enforced his rule over the kingdom. He rewarded his followers by land grants, eventually replacing almost the entire feudal ruling class, and intimidated potential rebels by rapid construction of castles. He invaded Scotland (1072) – extracting an oath of loyalty from Malcolm III Canmore – and Wales (1081), although he spent much of his reign in France. He ordered the survey known as the DOMESDAY BOOK (1086).

William I (1772–1843) King of the Netherlands (1815–40) whose kingdom included Belgium and Luxembourg. He fought in the French Revolutionary Wars and Napoleonic Wars. His forceful government offended liberals and Roman Catholics, and a revolution in Belgium (1830) was followed by independence (1839). Compelled to accept a more liberal constitution, he abdicated in favour of his son, William II.

William I (the Lion) (1143–1214) King of Scotland (1165–1214). He succeeded his brother Malcolm IV and forged what was later called the 'Auld Alliance' with France. Captured by the English during an attempt to regain Northumbria, he was forced to swear fealty to HENRY II (1174). He bought back his kingdom's independence from RICHARD I in return for a cash payment towards the Third Crusade in 1189. William the Lion established the independence of the Church (under the Pope) and strengthened royal authority in the north.

William I (the Silent) (1533–84) Prince of Orange, leader of the revolt of the Netherlands against Spanish rule. In 1572, he became the leader of a broad coalition in the Low Countries that opposed Spanish rule on the principle of religious tolerance. It broke down in 1579, when the Catholic s provinces, seeking reconciliation with Spain, broke away. William continued as leader of the N provinces until he was assassinated in Delft.

William II (1859–1941) Emperor of Germany (1888–1918). He modelled himself on his grandfather, WILLIAM I, but lacked his good sense. Clashing with BISMARCK, he dismissed him in 1890, and assumed leadership of the government himself. His aggressive foreign policy, including the construction of a navy to challenge the British, antagonized Britain, France, and Russia. Many historians regard his policies as largely responsible for the outbreak of WORLD WAR 1 (1914). During the war, William was exclusively concerned with military matters. He abdicated after the armistice (November 1918).

William II (Rufus) (1056–1100) King of England (1087–1100). The second surviving son of WILLIAM I (THE CONQUEROR). His elder brother, Robert Curthose (Robert II), was Duke of Normandy, and William had to crush revolts by Anglo-Norman lords in Robert's favour. He invaded the Duchy twice, and in 1096 Robert mortgaged it to him to raise cash for the First Crusade. He invaded Scotland, later killing MALCOLM III (1093), annexed Cumbria, and subdued Wales (1097). He was killed hunting in the New Forest allegedly by accident.

William III (of Orange) (1650–1702) Prince of Orange and King of England, Scotland, and Ireland (1689–1702). He was born after the death of his father, William II, and succeeded him as the ruler of the United Provinces (Netherlands) in 1672. In 1677, he married Mary (later MARY II), daughter of JAMES II of England. Following the GLORIOUS REVOLUTION (1688), he and Mary, strong Protestants, replaced the Catholic James II. They ruled jointly until her death in 1694. After crushing a JACOBITE revolt in Scotland and Ireland (1690), William devoted himself to his lifelong task of resisting the forces of LOUIS XIV of France. In 1697 he forced the French to sign the Peace of Ryswick (1697). In 1699, he organized the alliance that was to defeat the French in the War of the SPANISH SUCCESSION. William approved the BILL OF RIGHTS (1689) and other measures that diminished the royal prerogative.

William IV (1765–1837) King of Great Britain and Ireland and Elector of HANOVER (1830–37). Third son of GEORGE III, he succeeded unexpectedly at the age of 65, after a long career in the navy. Nicknamed 'Silly Billy', he was well-meaning though unkingly. He assisted the passage of the Great Reform Bill (1832), by creating new peers to give the government a majority in the House of Lords.

William of Occam (1285–1349) English scholastic philosopher and theologian. Contributing to the development of formal logic, he employed the principle of economy known as **Occam's Razor**; that is, a problem should be stated in its most basic terms. As a Franciscan monk, he upheld Franciscan ideas of poverty against Pope John XXII and was excommunicated. In 1328, he was imprisoned in Avignon, France, but he escaped and fled to Munich, where he later died.

William of Wykeham (1324–1404) English bishop and political leader. As Bishop of Winchester from 1367, he was prominent in royal counsels. He served as chancellor (1367–71) under EDWARD III and (1389–91) under RICHARD II. He founded Winchester College, Winchester, and New College, Oxford.

Williams, Ralph Vaughan *See* VAUGHAN WILLIAMS, RALPH

Williams, Roger (1603–83) US PURITAN minister, b. England. He emigrated to Boston in 1631, but his liberal notions and support for Native Americans antagonized the Puritans. He was expelled from the Massachusetts Colony in 1635, and sought shelter with the Narragansett. In 1636 he founded PROVIDENCE, the first settlement in Rhode Island.

Williams, Rowan Douglas (1950–) Anglican Archbishop of Canterbury and Primate of all England (2002–). Dr Williams was Professor of Theology at Oxford University from 1986–1992. He was enthroned as Bishop of Monmouth in 1992 and Archbishop of Wales in 2000. His sympathetic stance towards single-sex marriage and outspoken response to post-September 11th military aggression earned him a reputation as a radical among some sections of the Anglican church.

Williams, Tennessee (Thomas Lanier) (1911–83) US playwright. His first Broadway play, *The Glass Menagerie* (1945), received the New York Drama Critics' Circle Award. He received Pulitzer Prizes for *A Streetcar Named Desire* (1947) and *Cat on a Hot Tin Roof* (1955). His other plays include *Suddenly Last Summer* (1958), *Sweet Bird of Youth* (1959) and *The Night of the Iguana* (1961). Many of his plays were set in the South, in a cloying and repressive environment that reflected the plight of the characters.

Williams, Venus (1980–) Elder of two professional tennis playing sisters. Venus and Serena (1981–) shot to fame in the 1990s with a series of high-profile wins. In 1997, Venus became the first unseeded woman to reach the final of the US Open, and the first African-American woman to do so since Althea Gibson in 1958. Venus won Wimbledon

W

▲ **Wilson** US President Woodrow Wilson strove to keep the USA neutral during World War 1, but was forced to declare war by unrestricted German submarine attacks on US ships. In his war message to Congress, he stated that "the world must be made safe for democracy". His subsequent public speeches did much to consolidate national support behind the war effort. Domestically, his 'New Freedom' initiative brought constitutional amendments, including the introduction of prohibition and giving women the right to vote.

▲ **willow** Willows (family Salicaceae) are fairly small trees – the European willow grows to a maximum height of 10m (35ft). The seeds are light, wind dispersed, and contain little food. Willows often grow near water, facilitating rapid germination.

five times (2000, 2001, 2005, 2007, 2008) and the US Open twice (2000, 2001). Serena Williams won twice at the US Open (1999, 2002), and twice at Wimbledon (2002, 2003).

Williams, William Carlos (1883–1963) US poet. His deceptively simple style incorporates colloquial American. Williams' early work shows the influence of IMAGISM. His most monumental achievement was *Paterson* (1946–58), a five-volume epic of American life as seen in the microcosm of a New Jersey city. His *Pictures from Brueghel* (1962) won a posthumous Pulitzer Prize and his *Collected Poems* appeared in 1986–88.

Williamsburg Historic city in SE Virginia, USA. Founded in 1633, Williamsburg was capital of Virginia from 1699 to 1779. The Virginia Resolution for American Independence was passed in the city in 1776. The Battle of Williamsburg (1862) was part of the Peninsular campaign in the Civil War. In 1926, John D. Rockefeller Jr. provided for the restoration of the colonial city. Today, it is a major tourist site. Pop. (2000) 11,998.

Williamson, Malcolm (1931–2003) Australian composer, he was made Master of the Queen's Music in 1975. Williamson composed symphonies, concertos, choral works, and operas, of which the best known is *Our Man in Havana* (1963).

will-o'-the-wisp (jack-o'-lantern) Mysterious light sometimes seen at night in marshy areas. It is thought to be due to the spontaneous combustion of marsh gas (METHANE).

willow DECIDUOUS shrub and tree native to cool or mountainous temperate regions. It has long, pointed leaves, and flowers borne on catkins. Familiar species include the weeping willow (*Salix babylonica*) with drooping branches, and pussy willow (*S. caprea*) with fuzzy catkins. Family Salicaceae.

willow herb Any of several species of perennial plants with willow-like leaves, especially *Epilobium angustifolium*, the fireweed or rosebay willowherb. It has a long, unbranched stem with narrow leaves and purple-red flowers. Height: to 1m (3.3ft). Family Onagraceae; genus *Epilobium*.

Wilmington City in N Delaware, USA, at the junction of the Delaware and Christina rivers and Brandywine Creek. The first settlement in Delaware (1638), Wilmington was founded by Swedes. It was later enlarged by Dutch and British settlers and became the state's largest city. It is an important industrial centre with shipyards, railway shops and chemical manufacturing plants. Pop. (2000) 72,664.

Wilson, August (1945–2005) US playwright. His plays, the most well known including *Joe Turner's Come and Gone* (1986) and *The Piano Lesson* (1988), draw on African-American history and culture. *Fences* won the Pulitzer Prize in 1987.

Wilson, Charles Thomson Rees (1869–1959) English physicist. He invented the Wilson cloud chamber used to study radioactivity, X-rays, and cosmic rays. It uses water droplets to track ions left by passing radiation. For this invention, he shared the 1927 Nobel Prize in physics with Arthur COMPTON.

Wilson, Edmund (1895–1972) US journalist and critic. He was editor of *Vanity Fair* (1920–21) and literary editor of *The New Republic* (1926–31). His influential critical work includes *Axel's Castle* (1931) on SYMBOLISM; *To the Finland Station* (1940) on European revolutionary traditions; and *Patriotic Gore* (1962) on the literature of the American Civil War.

Wilson, Edward O. (Osborne) (1929–) US entomologist, ecologist and sociobiologist. In 1956, a year after obtaining his Ph.D. from Harvard University, Wilson and William L. Brown introduced the concept of 'character displacement' to describe how closely related species undergo rapid evolutionary differentiation after first coming into contact with each other. In *Theory of Island Biogeography* (1967), Wilson and Robert MacArthur developed the notion that 'a dynamic equilibrium number of species exists for any island.' In *Sociobiology: The New Synthesis* (1975), Wilson presented his controversial theories about the biological basis of human social behaviour. Wilson won a Pulitzer Prize for *On Human Nature* (1978), in which he explored the contribution of sociobiology to the understanding of human aggression and sexuality. He received a second Pulitzer Prize for *The Ants* (1988, written with Bert Hôlldobler). In *The Diversity of Life* (1992) and *The Future of Life* (2001), Wilson examined the threat to biodiversity posed by human activity. Other works include the autobiography *Naturalist* (1994). *See also* EVOLUTION

Wilson, Sir (James) Harold (1916–95) British statesman, prime minister (1964–70, 1974–76). Wilson entered Parliament in 1945 and, as President of the Board of Trade (1945–51) under Clement ATTLEE, was Britain's youngest Cabinet member since William Pitt (the Younger). In 1951, he resigned over the imposition of medical prescription charges. In 1963, he succeeded Hugh GAITSKELL as Labour leader. Wilson narrowly defeated Harold MACMILLAN in the 1964 general election. His government faced a foreign policy dilemma when Rhodesia's white-minority government declared independence in 1965. Challenged by a domestic economic crisis, Wilson imposed strict price and income controls and devalued the pound in 1967. Rising unemployment and labour disputes contributed to defeat by Ted HEATH in the 1970 general election. Disagreements over nationalization and membership of the European Economic Community (EEC) threatened to divide the LABOUR PARTY. Nevertheless, in 1974 Wilson returned as leader of a minority Labour government. In 1976, he unexpectedly resigned and Jim CALLAGHAN succeeded him.

Wilson, (Thomas) Woodrow (1856–1924) 28th US president (1913–21). As governor of New Jersey (1910–12), he was a progressive Democrat. In 1912, he unexpectedly gained the Democratic nomination. The split in the Republican vote between William TAFT's REPUBLICAN PARTY and Theodore ROOSEVELT's Progressive Party handed Wilson the presidency. His 'New Freedom' reforms included the establishment of the FEDERAL RESERVE SYSTEM (1913). Several amendments to the US CONSTITUTION were introduced, including PROHIBITION (18th, 1919) and the extension of voting rights to women (19th, 1920). The MEXICAN REVOLUTION brought instability to the s border and Wilson ordered John PERSHING's intervention. His efforts to maintain US neutrality at the start of WORLD WAR 1 aided his re-election in 1916. The failure of diplomacy and continuing attacks on US shipping forced Wilson to declare war on Germany (April 1917). His FOURTEEN POINTS (January 1918) represented US war aims and became the basis of the peace negotiations at the VERSAILLES peace conference (1919). He was forced to compromise in the final settlement, but succeeded in establishing a LEAGUE OF NATIONS. Domestic opposition to the League was led by Henry Cabot Lodge and the Republican-dominated Senate rejected it. In October 1919, he suffered a stroke and became an increasingly marginal figure for the remainder of his term.

wilt Any of a group of plant diseases characterized by yellowing and wilting of leaves and young stems, often followed by death of the plant. Wilt diseases are caused by bacteria or fungi that grow in the sapwood and plug water-conducting tissues or disrupt the plant's water balance in some other way.

Wiltshire County in s England; the county town is Trowbridge. Dominated by Salisbury Plain and the Marlborough Downs, the county's historic sites attract many tourists. STONEHENGE and Avebury Hill are England's oldest monuments, built more than 4,000 years ago. Wiltshire was an important centre of SAXON culture. Much of this rural county is given over to agriculture, but industry is becoming increasingly important to the local economy. Swindon, the principal manufacturing town, is one of the fastest-growing urban areas of England. Industries: textiles, farm machinery, food processing, electrical goods. Area: 3,481sq km (1,344sq mi). Pop. (2001) 432,973.

Wimbledon Popular name for the All England Lawn Tennis Championships played annually at the All England Club, Wimbledon, a suburb in sw London. It is the world's foremost championship played on grass. It was first held in 1877, and was open only to amateurs until 1968. The championships have been held at the present venue since 1922.

winch Drum that turns to pull or release a rope, cable or chain. A winch is used to raise, lower or pull heavy loads. The device may be motor-driven or operated by hand.

Winchester County town of Hampshire, on the River Itchen, s central England. Known as Venta Belgarum by the Romans, it became capital of the Anglo-Saxon kingdom of WESSEX in AD 519. During the reign of ALFRED THE GREAT, it was capital of England. Despite the increasing influence of London, Winchester retained its importance as a centre of learning and religion throughout the medieval period. Much of the old city remains, including a 14th-century Gothic cathedral and the ruins of a Norman castle. Pop. (2001) 107,213.

wind Air current that moves rapidly parallel to the Earth's surface. (Air currents in vertical motion are called updraughts or downdraughts.) Wind direction is indicated by wind or weather vanes, wind speed by ANEMOMETERS and wind force by the BEAUFORT WIND SCALE. Steady winds in the tropics are called TRADE WINDS. MONSOONS are seasonal winds that bring predictable rains in Asia. **Föhns** (foehns) are warm, dry winds produced by compression, accompanied by temperature rise as air descends the lee of mountainous areas in the Alps; a similar wind, called a **chinook**, occurs in the Rockies. SIROCCOS are hot, humid Mediterranean winds. Dangerous circular (cyclone) storm winds include HURRICANES and TORNADOES.

Windermere Largest lake in England, in the LAKE DISTRICT, Cumbria. It is linked to Morecambe Bay by the River Leven; the town of Windermere lies on the E shore of the lake. Length: *c.*17km (10mi); Max. width 1.6km (1mi).

Windhoek Capital and largest city of Namibia, situated some 300km (190mi) inland from the Atlantic at a height of 1650m (5410ft). Originally serving as the headquarters of a Nama chief, in 1892 it was made the capital of the new German colony of South-West Africa. It was taken by South African troops in World War 1. In 1990, it became capital of independent Namibia. An important world trade market for karakul sheepskins, its industries include diamonds, copper and meat-packing. Pop. (2002 est.) 194,300.

wind instrument Musical instrument that is sounded by blowing, which sets the air inside it vibrating. Wind instruments may be classified into two types: WOODWIND and BRASS.

windmill Machine powered by the wind acting on sails or vanes. The earliest windmills were built in the Middle East in the 7th century. They spread to Europe in the Middle Ages. Their use was widespread during the early years of the INDUSTRIAL REVOLUTION, but declined with the development of the STEAM ENGINE. A new version, the wind turbine, is used to harness WIND POWER. *See also* RENEWABLE ENERGY

window In computing, a rectangle displayed on a COMPUTER screen that shows what is stored in one part of the machine's memory or in some other storage device, such as a disk. A window may display information using text or graphics.

windpipe *See* TRACHEA

wind power Harnessing of wind energy to produce power. Since the 1970s, advanced aerodynamic designs have been used to build wind turbines that generate electricity. The largest of these, on Hawaii, has two blades, each 50m (160ft) long, attached to a 20–storey high tower. Individual turbines are often grouped in strategic locations (wind farms) to maximize the generating potential. Wind power is a cheap form of RENEWABLE ENERGY, but cannot as yet produce sufficiently large amounts of electricity to provide a realistic alternative to fossil fuel and nuclear power stations. *See also* WINDMILL

Windsor, Duke of *See* EDWARD VIII

Windsor Castle English royal residence, 32km (20mi) W of London. It was founded by WILLIAM I to defend the Thames valley. It was occupied by parliamentary forces during the CIVIL WAR. Windsor Castle has been extended, reconstructed, and restored, but retains the appearance of a medieval fortress. In 1992, it was damaged by fire.

wind tunnel Chamber in which scale models and even full-size aircraft and road vehicles are tested in a controlled airflow. Some wind tunnels can reproduce extreme conditions of wind speed, temperature, and pressure. Models of bridges and other structures are tested in wind tunnels to check that winds cannot set up destructive vibrations.

Windward Islands Southern group of the Lesser Antilles islands, SE West Indies. They extend from the Leeward Islands to the NE coast of Venezuela. The principal islands are MARTINIQUE, GRENADA, DOMINICA, ST LUCIA, and ST VINCENT AND THE GRENADINES group. The islands, volcanic in origin, are mountainous and forested. Tropical crops are grown, including bananas, spices, limes and cacao, but tourism is the leading industry. The islands were inhabited by the indigenous Carib until colonization began in the 17th century. The next two centuries witnessed a struggle for control between France

and Britain. Britain eventually controlled all the islands, with the exception of Martinique. *See* WEST INDIES map

wine Alcoholic beverage made from the fermented juice (and some solid extracts) of fruits, herbs, and flowers – but classically from the juice and skins of grapes. The three standard grape wine colorations are white, red and rosé, depending on the grape used and whether, and for how long, the grape skins are left on. For **white** wine, the grapes are fermented without the skin; for **red** wine, the whole grape is used; for **rosé** wine, the skins are removed after fermentation has begun. Dry wines are fermented until the sugar has turned to alcohol; sweet wines are fermented for less time so some sugar remains. Champagne is bottled while it is still fermenting. Table wines contain 7–15% alcohol by volume; fortified wines, such as SHERRY, contain added brandy, giving a 16–23% alcohol content.

wings In biology, specialized organs for flight that are possessed by most birds, many insects, and certain mammals and reptiles. The forelimbs of a bird developed into such structures. Bats have membranous tissue supported by the digits ('fingers') of the forelimbs. Insects may have one or two pairs of veined or membranous wings.

Winnipeg Capital of Manitoba, Canada, at the confluence of the Assiniboine and Red rivers, in the S of the province. Founded (1812) by the HUDSON'S BAY COMPANY, the town came under the control of the Canadian government in 1870. It grew after the completion of the Canadian Pacific Railroad (1882), and is now the major city of the Canadian prairies. It has one of the world's largest wheat markets and vast flour mills, grain elevators and food-processing plants. Pop. (2001) 626,685.

Winnipeg, Lake Resort lake in S central Manitoba province, the third-largest in Canada. It was used extensively by early fur traders and explorers in the 18th century. Fed by the Red, Saskatchewan and Winnipeg rivers, and drained by the Nelson River to Hudson Bay, it is believed to be a remnant of the glacial Lake Agassiz. Area: 24,514sq km (9,465sq mi).

wire Strand of metal made by drawing a rod through progressively smaller holes in metal dies. The process toughens STEEL, so that a CABLE made from steel wire is much stronger than an undrawn steel rod of the same diameter. Electric cables consist of copper and aluminium wires. If flexibility is important, each conductor consists of fine strands of wire.

wireworm Long, cylindrical larva of a click beetle of N temperate woodlands. It is generally brown or yellow and is distinctly segmented. Most species live in the soil, and may cause serious damage to the roots of cultivated crops. Family Elateridae. The name also refers to any of the smooth-bodied MILLIPEDES of the family Paraiulidae.

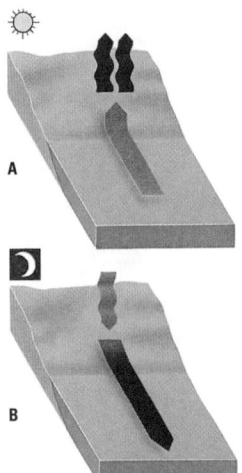

▲ **wind** Onshore winds (A) generally occur during the day. The Sun land heats the Sun, causing the air over it to rise. As the warm air rises, it is replaced by cooler air overlying the sea. At night, because the land loses heat quicker than the sea, air flows down hillsides out to sea, where the air is relatively warmer, generating offshore breezes (B).

WIND POWER

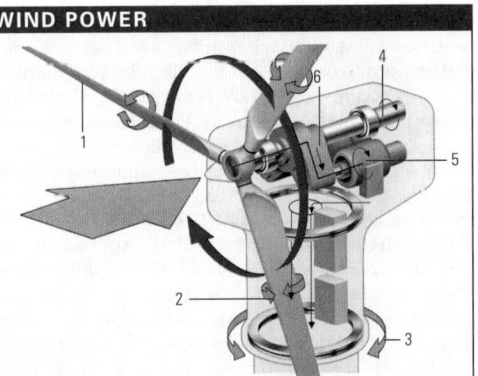

A wind generator converts the energy of the wind into electricity. Three-bladed, variable-pitch designs are the most efficient. Variable pitch means the attitude of the blades (1) can be changed. By altering the pitch (2) of the blades, they can generate at maximum efficiency in varying wind conditions. The whole rotor assembly rotates (3) into the wind. The blades turn a prop shaft (4), which links to a generator (5) through gearing (6). The largest wind farms have thousands of linked turbines and can produce the same power as a fossil-fuel power station.

W

WISCONSIN
Statehood :
May 29, 1848
Nickname :
The Badger State
State bird :
Robin
State flower :
Wood violet
State tree :
Sugar maple
State motto :
Forward

Wisconsin State in N central USA, SW of the GREAT LAKES and E of the River Mississippi. MADISON is the state capital and MILWAUKEE the largest city. The land is rolling plain that slopes gradually down from the N. There are numerous glacial lakes. The French claimed the region in 1634, but Britain seized it in 1763, and it was ceded to the USA in 1783. Settlement of the region was slow. The Territory of Wisconsin was established in 1836. Wisconsin is the leading US producer of milk, butter, and cheese. The chief crops are hay, maize, oats, fruit, and vegetables. Wisconsin's most valuable resource is timber: 45% of the land is forested. Mineral deposits include zinc, lead, copper, iron, sand, and gravel. Industries: food processing, farm machinery, brewing, tourism. Area: 145,438sq km (56,154sq mi). Pop. (2000) 5,363,675.

wisdom literature Collection of writings and sayings in the Hebrew Bible. In the Old Testament, it includes the Books of Proverbs, Ecclesiastes, Job, and the Song of Solomon. From the Apocrypha, it includes the Books of Ecclesiasticus, and the Wisdom of Solomon.

wisent *See* BISON

wisteria Genus of hardy, woody vines, native to North America, Japan, and China. They have showy, fragrant, pendulous flower clusters of purplish-white, pink or blue. Family Fabaceae/Leguminosae.

witchcraft Exercise of supernatural occult powers, usually due to some inherent power rather than to an acquired skill, such as sorcery. In Europe, it originated in pagan cults and in mystical philosophies such as GNOSTICISM, which believed in the potency of both good and evil in the universe. In some societies, the belief in spirits is associated with attempts to control them through witchcraft for harmful or beneficial ends.

witch doctor *See* SHAMAN

witch hazel Shrubs and small trees of the genus *Hamamelis*, native to temperate regions, mostly in Asia. They bloom in late autumn or early spring. The common witch hazel (*Hamamelis virginiana*) has yellow flowers. Family Hamamelidaceae.

witness Legal term referring to a person who testifies in court to facts within his/her knowledge. In most western legal systems, a witness is usually required to take an oath swearing truthfulness prior to testifying, and he/she is then first examined (questioned) by the party who offers him/her and then cross-examined by the opposing party.

Witt, Jan de (1625–72) Dutch politician. A republican and opponent of the House of Orange, he became Grand Pensionary and effectively head of government in 1653. He defeated the English in the second of the DUTCH WARS (1665–67). In 1672 he resigned after a French invasion, the accession of WILLIAM OF ORANGE as stadholder (which he had long resisted), and an attempt on his life. He and his brother, Cornelis, were killed by Orangist partisans a few months later.

Wittenberg Town on the River Elbe, Sachsen-Anhalt, E central Germany. Founded by Frederick III, Wittenberg's university became the cradle of the Protestant REFORMATION during the time Martin LUTHER and Philipp MELANCHTHON were teaching there. Today, Wittenberg is primarily a mining and industrial centre, producing chemicals, rubber goods, machinery, and foodstuffs. Pop. (1998) 50,950.

Wittgenstein, Ludwig (1889–1951) Austrian philosopher. His masterwork, *Tractatus Logico-philosophicus* (1921), influenced LOGICAL POSITIVISM, arguing the strict relationships between language and the physical world. After 1929, he criticized this hypothesis in his Cambridge lectures, published posthumously as *Philosophical Investigations* (1953). He claimed language was a conventional 'game', where meaning was affected more by context than formal relationships to reality.

Witwatersrand (Rand) Series of parallel mountain ranges more than 1,500m (5,000ft) high, forming a watershed between the Vaal and Olifant rivers, in former TRANSVAAL, NE South Africa. The region extends *c.*100km (62mi) E and W of Johannesburg. Gold was first discovered in 1884 and mining began two years later. Witwatersrand still produces *c.*30% of the world's total output of gold. Silver is recovered as a by-product of gold refining. Coal and manganese are also mined, and there are many ancillary industries in the region.

woad (dyerswoad) BIENNIAL or PERENNIAL herb once grown as a source of blue dye. It was probably introduced by the early Britons to dye clothing and paint their bodies. A native of Eurasia, it bears small four-petalled, yellow flowers. Height: 90cm (3ft). Family Brassicaceae/Cruciferae; species *Isatis tinctoria*.

Wodehouse, P.G. (Sir Pelham Grenville) (1881–1975) British novelist, short-story writer, playwright, and lyricist. He began his writing career in 1902, and wrote more than 100 humorous books. His best-known creations are Bertie Wooster and his valet Jeeves, who feature in a number of books from 1917 to 1971. During World War 2, Wodehouse's ill-advised radio broadcasts from Berlin outraged British public opinion, and he became an American citizen in 1955.

Woden *See* ODIN

Wöhler, Friedrich (1800–82) German chemist who first isolated ALUMINIUM and BERYLLIUM, and discovered calcium carbide. In 1828, his synthesis of UREA (from ammonium cyanate) was the first synthesis of an organic chemical compound from an inorganic one; it contributed to the foundation of modern organic chemistry.

wolf Wild, dog-like carnivorous mammal, once widespread in the USA and Eurasia, especially the grey wolf (*Canis lupus*), which is now restricted to the USA and Asia. It is powerfully built, with a deep-chested body and a long, bushy tail. It has earned a reputation for savagery and cunning from occasional attacks on livestock and human beings. Length: to 2m (6.6ft), including the tail. Family Canidae.

Wolf, Hugo (1860–1903) Austrian composer, regarded as one of the finest exponents of Lieder. He produced in rapid succession five 'songbooks'. He set poems by Mörike (1888), Eichendorff (1888–89), Goethe (1888–89), Spanish writers (1889–90), and Italian poets (1891, 1896). *See also* LIED

Wolfe, James (1727–59) British general. He commanded the force that captured Québec by scaling the cliffs above the St Lawrence River and defeating the French, under Montcalm, on the Plains of Abraham (1759). This victory resulted in Britain's acquisition of Canada. Wolfe's death in action made him an almost legendary hero.

Wolfe, Thomas Clayton (1900–38) US writer. His reputation rests on his sequence of four sprawling autobiographical novels, *Look Homeward, Angel* (1929), *Of Time and the River* (1935), *The Web and the Rock* (1939) and *You Can't Go Home Again* (1940).

Wolfe, Tom (Thomas Kennerley) (1931–) US journalist and novelist. Wolfe established his reputation with essays on American counter-culture such as *The Electric Kool-Aid Acid-Test* (1968). His novel *The Bonfire of the Vanities* (1987) is a sharply observed satire on the materialist ethos of the 1980s. Other works include *A Man in Full* (1998).

wolffish Voracious fish that lives in the N waters of the Atlantic Ocean. It is brown or grey with long fins along its back and belly, and powerful jaws and teeth. It is valued as a food fish in Iceland, where its skin is made into leather. Length: 91cm (3ft). Family Anarhichadidae; species *Anarhichas lupus*.

wolfram *See* TUNGSTEN

wolframite (iron-manganese tungstate) Black to brown mineral, $(Fe,Mn)WO_4$. It is the chief ore of the metal TUNGSTEN. It occurs as crystals in the monoclinic system or as granular masses. It is found in quartz veins and pegmatites associated with granitic rocks and also in hydrothermal veins. Hardness 5–5.5; r.d. 7–7.5.

Wolfram von Eschenbach (1170–1220) German poet. His only complete work is the Middle High German epic *Parzival*. A masterpiece of medieval literature, it introduced the Grail legend into German.

Wollongong City and port in New South Wales, Australia, 65km (40mi) S of Sydney. Settled in 1815, Wollongong became a major exporter of grain and coal, and a large iron and steel centre. Port Kembla has Australia's biggest steelworks. Other industries: chemicals, textiles, copper. Pop. (1999 est.) 262,600.

Wollstonecraft, Mary (1759–97) English writer. Her *Vindication of the Rights of Women* (1792) was FEMINISM's first great work. She was the mother of Mary Wollstonecraft SHELLEY.

Wolof People of Senegal who speak a language belonging to the NIGER-CONGO family. In the 15th century, a Wolof

W

▲ **wolf** The shy, nocturnal maned wolf (*Chrysocyon brachyurus*) is found in deciduous forests and plains of South America. As with other plains' predators, it feeds on almost anything from small animals to fruit. It is the largest South American canid, with a head and body length up to 132cm (52in).

Empire dominated West Africa and traded in slaves with the Portuguese. They converted to ISLAM in the 18th century.

Wolsey, Thomas (1475–1530) English cardinal and statesman, lord chancellor (1515–29). After the accession of HENRY VIII in 1509, Wolsey acquired major offices of Church and State. He became archbishop of York (1514), and then cardinal and lord chancellor. As chancellor, Cardinal Wolsey controlled virtually all state business. His attempts to place England at the centre of European diplomacy ended in failure. Despite becoming papal legate (1518), Wolsey's ambition to become Pope was never realized. Domestically, he made powerful enemies through his method of raising taxes by forced loans, his conspicuous wealth, and his pluralism. Wolsey gave HAMPTON COURT PALACE to Henry VIII, but his failure to obtain the King a divorce from CATHERINE OF ARAGON brought about his ruin. Thomas MORE replaced him as chancellor. Charged with high treason, Wolsey died before his trial.

wolverine Solitary, ferocious mammal native to pine forests of the USA and Eurasia, the largest member of the WEASEL family. Dark brown, with lighter bands along the sides and neck, it has a bushy tail and large feet. Length: 91cm (36in); weight: 30kg (66lb). Species *Gulo gulo*.

womb *See* UTERUS

wombat Either of two species of large, rodent-like marsupial mammals of SE Australia and Tasmania. Both species are herbivorous, primarily nocturnal, and live in extensive burrows. The common wombat (*Vombatus ursinus*) has coarse black hair and small ears. The hairy-nosed wombat (*Lasiorhinus latifrons*) has finer, grey fur and large ears. Length: to 1.2m (3.9ft). Family Vombatidae.

women's rights movement Broad term for the international movement that began in the early 19th century to promote the equality of women. Originally concentrating on women's suffrage, the movement has since worked for equality of employment opportunity and pay. *See also* FEMINISM; SUFFRAGETTE MOVEMENT

Wonder, Stevie (1950–) US SOUL singer and songwriter, b. Steveland Judkins Morris. Blind from birth, Wonder was a precocious polymath, playing the harmonica, keyboard, guitar, and drums. In 1961, he joined MOTOWN Records. His first album, *Little Stevie Wonder: A 12–year-old Musical Genius*, was an instant hit. Consistently successful, his albums include *Talking Book* (1972), *Innervisions* (1973), *Songs in the Key of Life* (1976) and *Hotter Than July* (1980).

wood Hard substance that forms the trunks of trees; it is the XYLEM which comprises the bulk of the stems and roots, supporting the plant. Wood consists of fine, cellular tubes arranged vertically within the trunk, which accounts for its grain. The relatively soft, light-coloured wood is called **sapwood**. The non-conducting, older, darker wood is called **heartwood**, and

is generally filled with RESIN, gums, mineral salts, and TANNIN. The two chief types are softwoods from CONIFERS, such as PINE, and hardwoods from deciduous species, such as OAK. Wood is commonly used as a building material, fuel, to make some types of PAPER, and as a source of CHARCOAL, CELLULOSE, ESSENTIAL OIL, LIGNIN, tannins, dyes, and SUGAR.

Wood, Sir Henry Joseph (1869–1944) English conductor. He conducted the London PROMENADE CONCERTS from 1895 to 1944. The concerts are now named after him.

woodcock Any of five species of reddish-brown shorebirds that nest in cool parts of the Northern Hemisphere and winter in warm areas. Both the Eurasian *Scolopax rusticola* and American *Philohela minor* use their long, flexible bills to find worms in swamps. Length: to 34cm (14in). Family Scolopacidae.

woodcut One of the simplest methods of printing, using designs carved into wood. The carving produces a negative image: the carved areas representing blank spaces while the flat areas retain the ink. Woodcuts were invented in China in the 5th century AD and became popular in Europe in the Middle Ages.

wood engraving Print made by incising a design on the flat, polished transverse section of a block of hardwood. Textural and linear effects can be achieved by varying the pressure and direction of the cutting strokes. This technique developed from the less-sophisticated WOODCUT in 18th-century England.

woodlouse (sowbug) Terrestrial, isopod crustacean found worldwide, living under damp logs and stones, and in houses. It has an oval, segmented body, feeds mainly on vegetable matter, and retains its eggs in a brood pouch. Length: 20mm (0.75in). Order Isopoda; Genus *Oniscus*.

woodpecker Tree-climbing bird found almost worldwide. Woodpeckers have strong, pointed beaks and long, protrudable tongues, which in some species have harpoon-like tips for extracting insect larvae. They have two toes pointing forward, and black, red, white, yellow, brown, or green plumage; some are crested. The tail is stiff and helps to support the bird's body when pressed against a tree trunk. Family Picidae.

Woods, 'Tiger' (Eldrick) (1975–) US golfer. Woods won the US amateur championship three times (1994, 1995, 1996) before turning professional. In 1997, Woods became the youngest-ever player to win the US Masters. In 1999, he won the US PGA title. In 2000, he held the PGA title and won the British and US Opens. In 2001, he won the US Masters for a second time and became the first golfer to hold all four major titles at once. In 2002 he won the US Open and the US Masters again, becoming the third person, after Jack Nicklaus and Nick FALDO, to win it back to back. In 2005 he won the US Masters and the British Open.

Woodstock Music festival held between August 15 and 17, 1969, near Bethel, SW of Woodstock, New York, USA. Forced to shift from the original Woodstock location because of residents' protests, *c*.450,000 people arrived for the free, outdoor concert. The event was a celebration of both the music and aspirations of the hippie generation.

woodwind Family of musical WIND instruments that are traditionally made of wood but now often metal. They are played by means of a mouthpiece containing one or two reeds. The FLUTE and PICCOLO, however, are exceptional in that they are played by blowing across a hole. Other woodwind instruments include the CLARINET, SAXOPHONE (both single reed) and the OBOE, COR ANGLAIS, and BASSOON (all double reed).

woodworm (furniture beetle) Larva of various species of beetles that burrow in wood. When present in large numbers woodworms can cause extensive damage. Their presence

◄ **woodpecker** The ivory-billed woodpecker (*Campephilus principalis*) is the largest of the North American woodpeckers, and is one of the rarest birds in the world. It is believed to be nearly extinct now; any that remain are thought to inhabit swamp forests in SE USA and Cuba. Native American chiefs once adorned their belts with its bill and plumes, but tree felling has now removed most of the big trees in which it breeds.

A B C D E

▲ **woodwind** The woodwind family of musical instruments is an important grouping in the modern orchestra. Shown above are the reed instruments: the bassoon (A), oboe (B), cor anglais (C), clarinet (D), and bass clarinet (E). The saxophone is sometimes included in this group. Sound is produced by the vibration of an air column, which is set in motion by the movement of the reed. Altering the length of the vibrating column, by closing or opening holes on the body of the instrument, produces different notes.

W

WOODCUT

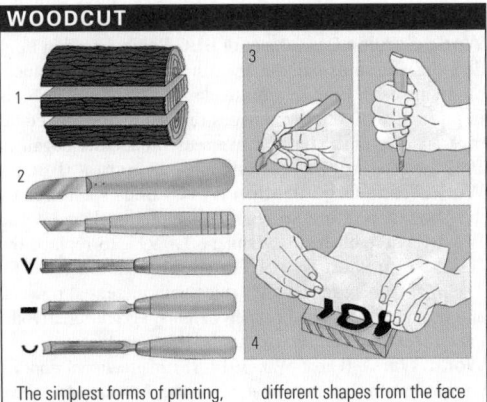

The simplest forms of printing, woodcuts are produced by carving a design in relief on wood. A flat piece of wood is needed from the centre of a log (1). Various different tools (2) are then used to cut different shapes from the face of the wood (3) to achieve the desired design. The wood is then rolled with ink, and pressed against paper (4). The resulting print appears as a negative image of the carving.

can be detected by holes in the wood from which the adult beetles have emerged. Genera include *Anobium* and *Lyctus*.

wool Soft, generally white, brown or black animal fibre that forms the fleece of sheep. Wool is also the name of the yarns and textiles made from the fibres after spinning, dyeing and weaving. The fibres, composed chiefly of KERATIN, are treated to remove a fat called lanolin, which is used in some ointments.

Woolf, Virginia (1882–1941) English novelist and critic. Her novels, which often use the STREAM OF CONSCIOUSNESS style associated with MODERNISM, include *Mrs Dalloway* (1925), *To the Lighthouse* (1927), *Orlando* (1928) and *The Waves* (1931). *Between the Acts*, her final novel, was published posthumously. A member of the BLOOMSBURY GROUP, her long essay *A Room of One's Own* (1929) is a key text of feminist criticism. Her critical essays, including *Modern Novels* (1919) and *The Common Reader* (1925), are integral to modernist literary theory.

Worcester County town of Worcestershire, on the River SEVERN, W central England. Worcester was founded in *c.*680. Its 13th-14th century cathedral is the burial place of King John. King Charles II's defeat by Oliver Cromwell at Worcester (1651) was the final battle in the English Civil War. Industries: Royal Worcester porcelain (manufactured here since 1751) and Worcestershire sauce. Pop. (2001) 93,358.

word processor COMPUTER system used for writing and printing text. The system may be designed just for this purpose, in which case it is called a **dedicated word processor**. More common is a general-purpose personal computer running a **word processing program**. Text typed on the computer keyboard displays on the screen. Any errors are easily corrected before a 'printout' or 'hard copy' is produced on a printer connected to the computer. If required, the text can be stored in code on a magnetic disk for future use.

Wordsworth, William (1770–1850) English poet, a leading figure of ROMANTICISM. He collaborated with Samuel Taylor COLERIDGE on *Lyrical Ballads* (1798). The collection concluded with Wordsworth's 'Tintern Abbey'. His preface to the second edition (1800) outlined the aims of English Romanticism, which through the use of everyday language enabled 'the spontaneous overflow of powerful feelings'. Critics derided his style. In 1799, he and his sister Dorothy moved to the Lake District; his poetry always bound up with nature. *The Prelude*, a long autobiographical poem, was completed in 1805, but only published posthumously in 1850. After *Poems in Two Volumes* (1807), which includes 'Ode: Intimations of Immortality', it is generally recognized that his creativity declined. In 1843, he succeeded Robert SOUTHEY as POET LAUREATE.

work In physics, ENERGY transferred in moving a force. Measured in JOULES, it equals the magnitude of the force multiplied by the distance moved in the direction of the force. If the force opposing movement is the object's weight mg (where m is the object's mass and g is the acceleration due to gravity), the work done in raising it a height h is mgh. This work transfers to the object in the form of POTENTIAL ENERGY; if the object falls a distance x, the KINETIC ENERGY at the bottom of the fall equals the work done in raising it through the height x. ENERGY is the capacity to do work, and POWER is the rate of doing work.

Work and Pensions, Department for UK government department responsible for the payment of universal benefits, the means-testing of other benefits, and collection of national

▶ **World War 1** The infantry of the 15th Brigade on July 9, 1918, under direct observation of the enemy near Morlancourt, Belgium, keep low down in the trenches. The soldiers are in a bomb crater, so close to the enemy lines that they could hear the Germans talking while the picture was being taken.

insurance contributions. It also administers the social fund and the legal aid scheme. *See also* SOCIAL SECURITY

workhouse Institution in England for the unemployed. Workhouses originated from the houses of correction for vagabonds by the POOR LAWS of 1601, but officially they date from 1696, when they were established by the Bristol Corporation. An Act permitting workhouses in all parishes was passed in 1723. The Act denied relief to those people who refused to enter a workhouse. Workhouses declined in the late 18th and early 19th centuries, but were revived by the Poor Law of 1834. Workhouses fell into disuse by the early 20th century.

World Bank (International Bank for Reconstruction and Development, IBRD) Intergovernmental organization, a specialized agency of the UNITED NATIONS since 1945. Its role is to make long-term loans to member governments to aid their economic development. The major part of the bank's resources are derived from the world's capital markets. Its headquarters are in Washington, D.C.

World Council of Churches International fellowship of Christian Churches formed in Amsterdam, the Netherlands, in 1948. Its aim is to work for the reunion of all Christian Churches and to establish a united Christian presence in the world. Its membership consists of some 300 churches. Its headquarters are in Geneva, Switzerland.

World Cup Worldwide competition for national association FOOTBALL teams, held every four years. The winner receives the Jules Rimet trophy. Qualifying rounds take place over the previous two years on a geographical league basis. The finals are organized by the Fédération Internationale de Football Associations (FIFA), football's governing body. Only the winners of each group, the host nation, and the previous winner automatically qualify for the finals. There are also world cup competitions in other sports, notably rugby, cricket and hockey.

World Health Organization (WHO) Intergovernmental organization, a specialized agency of the UNITED NATIONS. Founded in 1948, it collects and shares medical and scientific information and promotes the establishment of international standards for drugs and vaccines. WHO has made major contributions to the prevention of diseases such as malaria, polio, leprosy and tuberculosis, and the eradication of smallpox. Its headquarters are in Geneva, Switzerland.

World Meteorological Organization (WMO) Intergovernmental organization, a specialized agency of the UNITED NATIONS since 1950. It promotes cooperation in meteorology through the establishment of a network of meteorological stations worldwide, and by the mutual exchange of weather information. Its headquarters are in Geneva, Switzerland.

world music Generic term used to describe ethnic or ethnically influenced music. As part of a growing interest during the 1980s in non-Western music, many Western artists, such as Peter Gabriel and Paul Simon, began to draw particularly on the traditions of African culture, bringing together a variety of diverse styles and musicians.

World Service Department of BBC Radio, based in London, that transmits daily news, cultural, and entertainment programmes in English worldwide, and on a regular basis in more than 30 other languages relayed to specific countries and regions. The first overseas broadcasts began in 1932. *See* BRITISH BROADCASTING CORPORATION (BBC)

World Trade Organization (WTO) Body sponsored by the UNITED NATIONS to regulate international trade. The WTO was established on January 1, 1995, to replace the GENERAL AGREEMENT ON TARIFFS AND TRADE (GATT). The WTO took over GATT's rules with increased powers, and brought intellectual property rights, agriculture, clothing and textiles, and services under its control.

World War 1 (Great War, 1914–18) International conflict precipitated by the assassination of the Austrian Archduke FRANZ FERDINAND by Serbs in Sarajevo (June 28, 1914). Austria declared war on Serbia (July 28), Russia mobilized in support of Serbia (from July 29), Germany declared war on Russia (August 1) and France (August 3), and Britain declared war on Germany (August 4). World War 1 resulted from growing tensions in Europe exacerbated by the rise of the German Empire since 1871 and the decline of Ottoman power in the Balkans.

W

The chief contestants were the Central Powers (Germany and Austria) and the Triple Entente (Britain, France and Russia). Many other countries were drawn in: Ottoman Turkey joined the Central Powers in 1914, Bulgaria in 1915. Italy joined the Western Allies in 1915, Romania in 1916 and, decisively, the USA in 1917. Russia withdrew following the RUSSIAN REVOLUTION (1917). In Europe, the Allies checked the initial German advance through Belgium at the MARNE and the Western Front settled into a war of attrition with huge losses but little progress. On the Eastern Front, the Germans checked the initial Russian advance and overran Poland before stagnating. An Anglo-French effort to relieve the Russians by attacking GALLIPOLI (1916) failed. Italy and Austria became bogged down on the Isonzo Front. Campaigns were also fought outside Europe – against the Turks in the Middle East, and the German colonies in Africa and the Pacific. The only major naval battle was at JUTLAND (1916). The naval blockade of Germany caused food shortages and helped to end the war. An armistice was agreed in November 1918 and peace treaties were signed at VERSAILLES (1919). Some 10 million people died in the war.

World War 2 (1939–45) International conflict arising from disputes provoked by the expansionist policies of Germany in Europe and Japan in the Far East. During the 1930s, APPEASEMENT failed to check the ambitions of Adolf HITLER's regime. Having made a defensive pact with the Soviet Union (August 1939), Germany invaded Poland and Britain and France declared war (September 3). In 1940, German *Blitzkrieg* tactics resulted in the rapid conquest of Denmark, Norway, the Low Countries and France (June). Inability to gain command of the air prevented a German invasion of Britain, although bombing (*see* BLITZ, THE) devastated British cities. German submarines also took a heavy toll of Britain's merchant fleets. Italy, under MUSSOLINI, having annexed Albania (1939) and invaded Greece (1940), joined Germany in 1941. Germany invaded Greece, where the Italians had been checked, and Yugoslavia. In June 1941, the Germans, violating the pact of 1939, invaded the Soviet Union, advancing to the outskirts of Moscow and Leningrad (now St Petersburg). Italian defeats by the British in North Africa also drew in German troops, who forced a British retreat. In the Pacific, the Japanese attack on PEARL HARBOR (December 7, 1941) drew the USA into the war. Japan rapidly overran SE Asia and Burma, but the Battle of Midway (June 1942) indicated growing US naval and air superiority. From 1942, the tide in Europe turned against Germany. Defeat at STALINGRAD (January 1943) was followed by a Soviet advance that drove the Germans out of the Soviet Union by August 1944. Defeats in North Africa in 1942–43 led to the Allied invasion of Italy, forcing the Italians to make peace (September 1943). German troops then occupied Italy, where they resisted the Allied advance until 1945. In June 1944, Allied forces invaded NORMANDY. They liberated France and advanced into Germany, linking up with the Soviets beside the River Elbe in April 1945. Germany surrendered in May. Japan continued to resist, but surrendered in August after atomic bombs were dropped on Hiroshima and Nagasaki. Estimates of the numbers killed in World War 2 exceed 50 million. The great majority of the dead were civilians, many murdered in Nazi CONCENTRATION CAMPS. Politically, two former allies, the USA and the Soviet Union, emerged as dominant world powers, with antagonistic ideologies. *See also* COLD WAR

Worldwide Fund for Nature (WWF) International organization, established (1961) in Britain. Its headquarters are in Gland, Switzerland. It raises voluntary funds for the conservation of endangered wild animals, plants and places.

world wide web (www) Name given to a series of COMPUTER NETWORKS that can be accessed via local servers, which in turn are serviced by telephone lines. It consists of a network of sites that users can access via the INTERNET to retrieve or post data. Web documents may include text, graphics, and sound, and have hypertext that the user can click on to access further related information from other Web documents.

worm Any of a large variety of wriggling, limbless creatures with soft bodies. Most worms belong to one or other of four main groups: ANNELIDS, FLATWORMS, nematodes (ROUNDWORMS), and ribbon worms.

Worms Industrial town on the River Rhine, Rhineland Palatinate, w Germany. In the 5th century, it became the capital of the Kingdom of Burgundy. In 1156, Worms was made a free imperial city. It was annexed to France in 1797, but passed to Hesse-Darmstadt state in 1815. The French occupied the city from 1918 to 1930, and much of it was destroyed during World War 2. Today, it is a centre of the wine industry. Pop. (1998) 80,622.

Worms, Concordat of (1122) Agreement between Holy Roman Emperor Henry V and Pope Calixtus II settling the investiture conflict, a struggle between the Empire and the papacy over control of Church offices. The Emperor agreed to the free election of Bishops and Abbots, and surrendered his claim to invest them with the spiritual symbols of ring and staff. They were, however, obliged to pay homage to him as feudal overlord for their temporal possessions.

Worms, Diet of (1521) Conference of the Holy Roman Empire presided over by Emperor CHARLES V. Martin LUTHER was summoned to appear before the Diet to retract his teachings, which had been condemned by Pope LEO X. Luther refused to retract them, and the Edict of Worms (May 25, 1521) declared him an outlaw. The Diet was one of the most important confrontations of the early REFORMATION.

wormwood Genus (*Artemisia*) of aromatic bitter shrubs and herbs, including common wormwood (*A. absinthium*), a European shrub that yields a bitter, dark green oil used to make absinthe. Family Asteraceae/Compositae.

Wounded Knee, Massacre at (December 29, 1890) Last stage in the conflict between Native Americans and US forces. Fearing a rising by the SIOUX, US troops arrested several leaders. SITTING BULL was killed resisting arrest. Another group was arrested a few days later and brought to Wounded Knee, South Dakota. A shot was fired and the troops opened fire. About 300 people, including women and children, were killed.

wren Small, insect-eating songbird of temperate regions of Europe, Asia, and most of the New World. Many species have white facial lines. The typical winter wren (*Troglodytes troglodytes*) has a slender bill, upright tail, and dark brownish plumage; length: to 10cm (4in). Family Troglodytidae.

Wren, Sir Christopher (1632–1723) English architect, mathematician, and astronomer. After the FIRE OF LONDON (1666), Wren designed more than 50 new churches in the City of London based on syntheses of CLASSICAL, RENAISSANCE, and BAROQUE ideas; the greatest of these is ST PAUL'S Cathedral. Other works include Chelsea and Greenwich Hospitals, London, and the Sheldonian Theatre, Oxford.

wrestling Sport in which two unarmed opponents try to throw each other to the ground or to secure each other in an unbreakable hold, by means of body grips, strength, and adroitness. The two major competitive styles are **Greco-Roman** (most popular in continental Europe), which permits no tripping or holds below the waist, and **freestyle**, which permits tackling, leg holds and tripping (most popular in Britain and the USA). A match consists of three periods of three minutes each; points are awarded for falls and other manoeuvres. Competitive wrestling originated in ancient Greece, where it was regarded as the next most important event after discus-throwing in the Olympic Games. Wrestling has been an Olympic event since 1904. *See also* SUMO WRESTLING

Wright, Frank Lloyd (1869–1959) US architect, regarded as the leading modernist designer of private housing. He worked with Louis SULLIVAN in the Chicago School of architecture, before his first independent design in 1893. His distinctive 'organic' style of low-built, prairie-style houses was designed to blend in with natural features. Influenced by JAPANESE ART AND ARCHITECTURE, Wright's open-plan approach to interiors was highly influential. His use of materials and construction techniques was radical. Buildings include: Robie House, Chicago (1909); 'Falling Water', Bear Run, Pennsylvania (1936–37); and the Guggenheim Museum, New York (1946–59).

Wright, Joseph (1734–97) English painter. He made a speciality of industrial and scientific subjects, most notably in *An Experiment on a Bird in the Air Pump* (1768). Returning from time spent in Italy, Wright moved to Bath in 1775, hoping to emulate the success of GAINSBOROUGH. Disappointed in this, he settled in Derby, concentrating on poetic landscapes.

W

▲ **wren** Wrens are songbirds, and the winter wren (*Troglodytes troglodytes*) shown here is one of the best singers. It is the only species of wren native to the Old World, but is also found in N Asia and North America.

▲ **Wright brothers** On December 17, 1903, Wilbur and Orville Wright made the world's first flights in a power-driven, heavier-than-air machine. The aircraft cost less than US$1000 to construct. The first flight, by Orville, lasted only 12 seconds; the fourth flight, by Wilbur, lasted 59 seconds. In 1909, after further tests and improvements, the brothers established the Wright Company in New York City to manufacture aircraft.

WYOMING
Statehood :
July 10, 1890
Nickname :
The Equality State
State bird :
Meadowlark
State flower :
Indian paintbrush
State tree :
Cottonwood
State motto :
Equal rights

W

Wright, Richard (1908–60) US novelist. He is best known for the novel *Native Son* (1940), which describes the life of an African-American youth in white-dominated Chicago, and *Black Boy* (1945), an account of the author's boyhood in the South. He also wrote short stories and non-fiction.

Wright brothers Wilbur (1867–1912) and **Orville** (1871–1948), US aviation pioneers. They assembled their first aircraft in their bicycle factory. In 1903, Orville made the first piloted flight in a power-driven plane at Kitty Hawk, North Carolina. This flight lasted just 12 seconds, and attracted little attention. In 1908, Wilbur made longer and higher flights in France, and Orville was equally successful in the USA. The brothers eventually convinced military authorities and manufacturers to invest in powered aircraft.

writing Process or result of making a visual record for the purpose of communication by using symbols to represent the sounds or words of a language. Writing systems fall into the following categories: **ideographic** (using signs or symbols that represent concepts or ideas directly rather than the sound of words for them); **pictographic** (in which a picture or sign represents the meaning of a word or phrase); **syllabic** (in which signs represent groups of consonants and vowels); and **alphabetic** (in which symbols stand for individual speech sounds or certain combinations of sounds). The Chinese dialects have long made use of ideographic symbols. Ancient Egyptian HIEROGLYPHICS and CUNEIFORM scripts from Mesopotamia and other regions of the ancient Middle East are originally pictographic, although later examples are syllabic. The LINEAR SCRIPTS of ancient Crete and Greece are syllabic, as is the modern Japanese Katakana. The Phoenicians were the first to use a phonetic system, with an ALPHABET of signs representing speech sounds. The Greek and Roman alphabets in use for most modern non-Asiatic languages descend from the Phoenician alphabet.

Wrocław (formerly Breslau) Industrial city and port on the River Oder, sw Poland; capital of lower Silesia. Originally a Slavic settlement, it was destroyed by the MONGOLS in 1241. Rebuilt by the Austrians from 1526, it was ceded to Prussia in 1741. It developed as a trade centre in the 19th century, and was badly damaged in World War 2. It became part of Poland under the terms of the Potsdam Conference (1945). Industries: heavy machinery, processed food, electrical equipment, textiles, paper, timber, chemicals. Pop. (1999) 637,877.

wrought iron Commercial form of smelted IRON (the other is cast iron), containing less than 0.3% carbon with 1 or 2% slag mixed with it. Wrought iron replaced bronze in Asia Minor (*c.*2000BC) at the beginning of the Iron Age. In the 19th century AD it began to be used in building construction, but was replaced by STEEL after the invention of the BESSEMER PROCESS and OPEN-HEARTH PROCESS. Today, wrought iron is used principally for decoration, as in ornamental gates and railings.

Wuhan City and river port at the confluence of the Han and Yangtze rivers; capital of Hubei province, central China. Wuhan developed after being declared a treaty port following the OPIUM WARS of the 19th century. It grew further with the arrival of the railway and China's first modern iron and steel plants in 1891. Wuhan itself was formed in 1950, by the merger of Hankow, Hanyang, and Wuchang. It is now the industrial and commercial hub of central China. Despite being 970km (600mi) from the sea, the port handles many ocean-going vessels. Industries: cotton and textiles, iron, steel, heavy machinery, cement, soap. Pop. (2005) 6,003,000.

Wundt, Wilhelm (1832–1920) German psychologist. In 1879, Wundt established the first laboratory for experimental psychology at Leipzig. He did much to convince early psychologists that the mind could be studied with objective, scientific methods. His major publication is *Principles of Physiological Psychology* (1873–74).

Würzburg Capital of Lower Franconia, Bavaria, on the River Main, w central Germany. Made an episcopal see by St Boniface in 741, the city was secularized by the Treaty of Lunéville in 1801, and annexed to Bavaria two years later. It is the heart of a wine-producing region. Pop. (1998) 126,392.

Wyatt, Sir Thomas (1503–42) English poet and courtier, a pioneer of the English SONNET. He was popular at HENRY

VIII's court although, as an alleged former lover of Anne BOLEYN and friend of Thomas CROMWELL, he was briefly imprisoned in 1536 and 1541. His son, also Thomas Wyatt, led Wyatt's Rebellion (1554), an attempt to prevent the marriage of Mary I to the Catholic Philip II of Spain.

Wycliffe, John (1330–84) English religious reformer. Under the patronage of JOHN OF GAUNT, he attacked corrupt practices in the Church and the authority of the Pope, condemning in particular the Church's landed wealth. His criticism became increasingly radical, questioning the authority of the Pope and insisting on the primacy of scripture, but he escaped condemnation until after his death. His ideas were continued by the LOLLARDS in England and influenced Jan HUS in Bohemia.

Wyeth, Andrew Newell (1917–) US painter. His best-known painting is *Christina's World* (1948). He was trained by his father, the illustrator N.C. Wyeth, and is known for his naturalistic portraits. His son, James (1946–), is also a noted painter and artist.

Wyler, William (1902–81) US film director, famous for his long, meticulously crafted, single takes. Wyler won three best director and best picture Academy Awards: *Mrs Miniver* (1942), *The Best Years of Our Lives* (1946), and *Ben-Hur* (1959). Other credits include *Jezebel* (1938), *Wuthering Heights* (1939), *The Little Foxes* (1941) and *Roman Holiday* (1953).

Wyndham, John (1903–69) English novelist. Wyndham is known for science-fiction 'disaster' novels, of which his first, *The Day of the Triffids* (1951), is best-known. Other works include *The Kraken Wakes* (1953), *The Chrysalids* (1955) and *The Midwych Cuckoos* (1957).

Wyoming State in NW USA, bounded N by Montana, E by South Dakota, s by Colorado, sw by Utah, and w by Idaho; the state capital is CHEYENNE. Other major cities are Jasper and Laramie. Wyoming has the nation's smallest state population. The landscape is dominated by mountains and four million hectares (10 million acres) of forest. The ROCKY MOUNTAINS cross the state from NW to SE. To the E of the Rockies lie the rolling grasslands of the GREAT PLAINS, and the centre of the state is also high plains country. The N of the state is primarily tall grass plain, where buffalo roamed and were hunted by the CROW and then the SIOUX. Today, it is fertile farmland and cattle ranch country. YELLOWSTONE NATIONAL PARK is the oldest and largest US National Park, occupying the entire NW corner of Wyoming. Many rivers flow down from the mountains, including the North Platte and the Snake. Following the LOUISIANA PURCHASE (1803), the USA had, by 1846, acquired the entire territory of Wyoming through treaties. Nineteenth-century development was linked to the fur trade and westward migration along the Oregon Trail. The 1860s marked the first dramatic arrival of new settlers: the Bozeman Trail opened in 1864, and the railway arrived in 1868. By the end of the 1870s, the Native American population had been placed on reservations. The next 20 years were marked by a rise of vigilante groups to deal with cattle rustlers and outlaws, and in 1890 Wyoming became the 44th state of the Union. Tourism is a vital industry, with the state's natural beauty attracting more than seven million annual visitors. While cattle ranching, sheep and wheat farming remain important to the economy, Wyoming is primarily an oil-producing state. Oil was discovered in the 1860s, and in 1993 output totalled 87.7 million barrels. Other important mineral resources include coal and uranium. Area: 253,596sq km (97,913sq mi). Pop. (2000) 493,782.

Wyszynski, Cardinal Stefan (1901–81) Polish Roman Catholic cardinal. As Archbishop of Gniezno and Warsaw and Primate of Poland from 1948, he protested to communist authorities against the accusations launched against the Church during the trial of Bishop Kaczmarek of Kielce. In 1952, Pope Pius XII appointed him Cardinal. Wyszynski was imprisoned from 1953 to 1956. In 1957, he was allowed to go to Rome to receive the honour of a cardinal's hat. In the late 1970s and early 1980s, as leader of Poland's Roman Catholics, he played an active mediating role between the workers and government authorities.

x-chromosome One of the two kinds of sex-determining CHROMOSOME; the other is the Y-CHROMOSOME. In many organisms, including humans, females carry two x-chromosomes in their DIPLOID cell nuclei, while males carry one x- and one y-chromosome. Non-sexual characteristics are also carried on the x-chromosome: for example, the genes for one form of colour blindness and for haemophilia. *See also* GENETICS; HEREDITY

Xenakis, Yannis (1922–2001) Greek composer. Xenakis studied music under Arthur Honegger and Olivier Messiaen and architecture under Le Corbusier. His first composition, *Metastasis* (1954), was based on an architectural design. Some of Xenakis' work is TWELVE-TONE MUSIC and he has been a pioneer of the use of computers and mathematical models in the compositional process. Other works include *Stratégie* (1962).

xenon (symbol Xe) Gaseous nonmetallic element, one of the NOBLE GASES. It was discovered in 1898 by Scottish chemist William Ramsey and English chemist Morris Travers (1872–1961). Xenon is present in the Earth's atmosphere (about one part in 20 million) and is obtained by fractionation of liquid air. Colourless and odourless, it is used in light bulbs, lasers and arc lamps for cinema projection. The element, which has nine stable isotopes, forms some compounds, mostly with FLUORINE. Properties: at.no. 54; r.a.m. 131.30; r.d. 5.88; m.p. −111.9°C (−169.42°F); b.p. −107.1°C (−160.8°F); most common isotope Xe^{132} (26.89%).

Xenophanes of Colophon (*c.*560–478 BC) Travelling Greek poet and philosopher. Xenophanes proposed a version of pantheism, holding that all living creatures have a common natural origin. His work survives only in fragmentary form.

Xenophon (*c.*430–354 BC) Greek historian. Xenophon studied with SOCRATES, whose teaching he described in *Memorabilia*. His best-known work is *Anabasis*, an account of his march with a Greek mercenary army across Asia Minor in 401–399 BC in support of a pretender to the Persian throne. Other works include a history of Greece from 411 to 362 BC.

xerography Most common process used for PHOTOCOPYING.

xerophyte Any plant that evolved to survive in dry conditions, in areas subject to drought, or in physiologically dry areas (such as salt marshes and acid bogs) where saline or acid conditions make the uptake of water difficult. A succulent, such as a CACTUS, has thick fleshy leaves and a stem for storing water. Other adaptations include the ability to reduce water loss by shedding leaves during drought, or having waxy or hairy leaf coatings or reduced leaf area.

Xerxes I (*c.*519–465 BC) King of Persia (486–465 BC). Succeeding his father, DARIUS I, Xerxes regained Egypt and crushed a rebellion in Babylon before launching his invasion of Greece (480 BC). After his fleet was destroyed at the Battle of Salamis he retired, and the defeat of the Persian army in Greece at the Battle of Plataea ended his plans for conquest. He was assassinated by one of his own men. *See also* PERSIAN WARS.

Xhosa (Xosa) Group of related BANTU tribes. The Xhosa moved from E to the vicinity of the River Great Fish, s Africa, in the 17th and 18th centuries. They were defeated and subjected by Europeans in 1835. In culture, they are closely related to the ZULU. Today, the 2.5 million Xhosa live in the EASTERN CAPE and form an important part of South Africa's industrial and mining workforce. Xhosa is the most widely spoken African language in South Africa.

Xiamen Seaport city in Fujian province, SE China. As Amoy, it flourished in the 19th century after being declared an open port by the Treaty of Nanking (1842). Xiamen gained extra strategic importance after the communists took control of the Chinese mainland (1949), and in 1981 was granted the status of a 'special economic zone', accelerating its role as the centre of growing trade between China and Taiwan. Pop. (1999) 593,401.

Xian (Sian, formerly Changan) Capital of Shaanxi province, at the confluence of the Wei and Huang He rivers, NW China. Inhabited since 6000 BC from 255 to 206 BC it was the site of Xianyang, the capital of the QIN dynasty. The elaborate tomb of the dynastic founder, Emperor QIN SHIHUANGDI, is a world heritage site and major tourist attraction. Changan was the focus for the introduction of BUDDHISM to China, and in 652 the Big Wild Goose pagoda was built here. In the following centuries it became a major centre for other religious missionaries. The

Great Mosque was built in 742. At the start of the 10th century, Changan was the world's largest city. Known as Xian since the MING dynasty (1368–1644), extant monuments from this period include the 14th-century Drum and Bell towers. The Hua Qing curative hot springs were the site of the 1936 Xian Incident, when CHIANG KAI-SHEK was held hostage until he agreed to a united Nationalist-Communist Chinese front against the Japanese. It is an important commercial centre of a grain-growing region. Industries: cotton, textiles, steel, chemicals. Pop. (2005) 3,256,000.

Xingu Brazilian river, rising in central Mato Grosso state. It flows N for 1,979km (1,230mi) and empties into the River Amazon at its delta. It courses through rainforest and is navigable only in its lower reaches. The area focused international attention on the plight of Native Americans when a government proposal to dam the Xingu meant the flooding of tribal land. The dam and hydroelectric scheme, costing US$3.2 billion, finished in December 1994.

Xinjiang (Mandarin, 'new frontier'; Sinkiang or Chinese Turkistan) Autonomous region in NW China, bordered by Tajikistan, Kyrgyzstan, and Kazakhstan (N and W), Mongolia (E) and Kashmir and Tibet (S); the capital is Ürümqi. Xinjiang includes the Dzungarian Basin to the E and the Tarim Basin to the W. The ALTAI, TIAN SHAN, and Kunlun mountains frame the region to the N, W, and S respectively. First conquered by the Chinese in the 1st century BC Xinjiang changed hands many times in the following centuries. From the 13th to 18th centuries, the MONGOLS loosely controlled the area. In 1756, the QING dynasty assumed control of the region. It became a Chinese province in 1881. It is a mainly agricultural region growing wheat, cotton, maize, rice, millet, vegetables, and fruit. Livestock rearing (particularly sheep) is also important. The area is rich in minerals including oil, copper, zinc, gold and silver. Industries: iron and steel, chemicals, textiles. Area: 1,647,435sq km (636,075sq mi). Pop. (2000) 19,250,000.

X-ray ELECTROMAGNETIC RADIATION of shorter wavelength (or higher frequency) than visible light, produced when a beam of ELECTRONS hits a solid target. German physicist Wilhelm RÖNTGEN discovered X-rays in 1895. They are normally produced for scientific use in X-ray tubes. Because they are able to penetrate matter that is opaque to light, X-rays are used to investigate inaccessible areas, especially of the body. They pose a danger and can cause cancer. *See also* RADIOGRAPHY

X-ray astronomy *See* ASTRONOMY

X-ray crystallography Use of X-RAYS to discover the molecular structure of CRYSTALS. It uses the phenomenon of X-ray diffraction, the scattering of an X-ray beam by the atomic structure of a crystal, and has been used to show that DNA can produce crystals.

xylem Transport TISSUE of a PLANT, which conducts water and minerals from the ROOTS to the rest of the plant and provides support. The most important cells are long, thin tapering cells called **xylem vessels**. These cells are dead and have no cross-walls; they are arranged in columns to form long tubes, up which water is drawn. As water evaporates from the leaves (TRANSPIRATION), water is drawn across the leaf by OSMOSIS to replace it, drawing water out of the xylem. This suction creates a tension in the xylem vessels, and the side walls are reinforced with rings or spirals of LIGNIN, a rigid substance, to prevent them collapsing. Tiny holes in the walls of the xylem vessels (pits) allow water to cross from one tube to another. In trees, the xylem becomes blocked with age, and new xylem forms towards the outside of the trunk to replace it. The core of dead, non-functioning xylem remains an essential part of the support system. *See also* PHLOEM; VASCULAR BUNDLE

xylene ($C_6H_4(CH_3)_2$) Organic chemical compound obtained from the distillates of coal tar and petroleum, and important as a solvent. Chemically it is dimethyl benzene which exists in three isomeric forms: ortho-, meta-, and para-xylene. The ISOMERS have different physical properties.

xylophone Tuned PERCUSSION instrument. It is made of hardwood bars arranged as in a piano keyboard and played with mallets. The modern xylophone normally has a range of four octaves, extending from middle C upwards.

X/x, 24th letter of the Roman alphabet. It is believed to have developed from the Semitic character, samekh. Chi in the Greek alphabet resembled the modern X.

▲ **xerophyte** Plant species evolved to survive in arid conditions. Xerophytes have a number of ways of increasing water aquisition and reducing water loss. Their external surfaces generally have a thick cutinized layer, and the number of stomata is greatly reduced. In many cases, leaves are reduced to spines. Deep roots seek water, and succulence – in which the interior of the plant is adapted for water storage – occurs.

Y/y, 25th letter of the Roman alphabet. It was derived (as were f, u, v and w) from the Semitic letter vaw. It was adopted by the Greeks as upsilon. The Romans made two letters out of upsilon – Y and V. They only employed Y when writing.

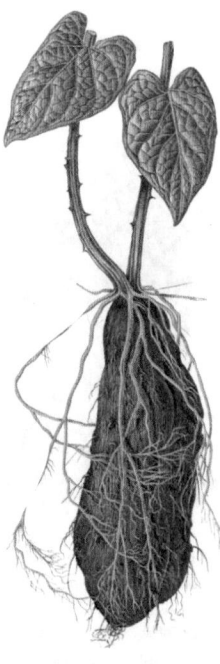

▲ **yam** Commercially important in E Asia and in tropical America, the yam (*Dioscorea* sp.) produces thick, starchy rhizomes, often weighing up to 30lb (13.6kg). These are a valuable food source and form part of the staple diet of many people worldwide, especially in Africa.

yacht Boat used for sport and recreation, powered by sail or motor. Sailing yachts, which are usually fore and aft rigged, vary from 6m (20ft) to more than 30m (98ft) long and include cutters, schooners, ketches, sloops, and yawls, Those fitted with diesel or petrol engines are usually classified as cruising (or motor) yachts. Although most yachts are used for vacationing and cruising, it has been an international sport since 1851, when the Royal Yacht Squadron (formed at Cowes, England, in 1812) offered a silver cup as a prize for a race of 97km (60mi) around the Isle of Wight. The race was won by the schooner *America*, owned by the members of the New York Yacht Club (established 1844), and has since been known as the AMERICA'S CUP. The Admiral's Cup is an international race held biennially since 1957 at Cowes. *The Observer* Single-Handed Transatlantic Race has been held every four years since 1960. The Olympics have competitions in seven yachting categories.

Yahweh (latinized form: Jehovah) Personal name of the God of the ancient Israelites of the OLD TESTAMENT. God revealed His name to MOSES when He called to him out of the burning bush at Mount Horeb (Sinai) (Exodus 3:14). In Hebrew, it was made up of four consonants, YHWH, and was apparently related to the Hebrew verb 'to be'. Most English translations render it as 'I am'.

yak Large, powerful, long-haired ox, native to Tibet, with domesticated varieties throughout central Asia; it inhabits barren heights up to 6,000m (20,000ft). Domesticated varieties are generally smaller and varied in colour; they breed freely with domestic cattle. Wild yaks have coarse, black hair, except on the tail and flanks, where it hangs as a long fringe. The horns curve upward and outward. Height: to 1.8m (6ft) at the shoulder. Family Bovidae; species *Bos grunniens*.

Yakutia (officially Republic of Sakha) Constituent republic of the Russian Federation, in NE Siberia; the capital is Yakutsk. The region is bounded by the Laptev and East Siberian Seas (N) and the Stanovoy Range (S). It is the largest Russian republic and one of the coldest inhabited regions, with more than 40% of the territory within the Arctic Circle. The principal rivers are the LENA, Yana, Indirka, and Kolyma. A third of the population is Yakut, a Turkic-speaking people who settled in the Lena basin from the 13th to 15th century. They are noted bone-carvers, iron-workers, and potters. The area was colonized by Russia during the 17th century, and many of the Yakuts were forcibly converted from SHAMANISM to Christianity. A republic of the former Soviet Union (1922–91), Yakutia became a member of the new Russian Federation in 1992. Agriculture is only possible in the S. The major industry is diamond mining and processing. Other important minerals include gold, silver, lead and coal. Timber is an important industry in the taiga regions. Area: 3,103,200sq km (1,200,000sq mi) Pop. (2000) 976,400.

Yale University Institute of higher education, in New Haven, Connecticut, USA. Founded in 1701, its current charter dates from 1745. It is a member of the Ivy League.

Yalow, Rosalyn (1921–) US biochemist. In the 1950s, she found that some people who received INSULIN injections developed ANTIBODIES against the hormone. Yalow discovered that insulin, labelled with radioactive iodine, combined with the antibodies; from this she developed radio-immunological tests to detect and measure the amount of insulin present. Yalow shared the 1977 Nobel Prize in physiology or medicine for her development of a method of detecting peptide HORMONES in the blood.

Yalta Conference (February 1945) Meeting of the chief Allied leaders of WORLD WAR 2 at Yalta in the Crimea, S Ukraine. With victory over Germany imminent, ROOSEVELT, CHURCHILL, and STALIN met to discuss the final campaigns of the war and the post-war settlement. Agreements were reached on the foundation of the UNITED NATIONS (UN); the territorial division of Europe into 'spheres of interest'; the occupation of Germany; and support for democracy in liberated countries. Concessions were made to Stalin in the Far East in order to gain Soviet support against Japan.

yam Any of several species of herbaceous vines that grow in warm and tropical regions; also the large, tuberous roots of several tropical species, which are edible. The plant is an annual, with a long, climbing stem, lobed or unlobed leaves and small clusters of greenish, bell-shaped flowers. The SWEET POTATO is also sometimes called a yam. Family Dioscoreaceae; genus *Dioscorea*.

Yamoussoukro Capital of Ivory Coast since 1983. Originally a small Baouké tribal village and birthplace of Ivory Coast's first president, Felix HOUPHOUËT-BOIGNY, it developed rapidly into the administrative and transport centre of Ivory Coast. Yamoussoukro's Our Lady of Peace Cathedral (consecrated by Pope John Paul II in 1990) is the world's largest Christian church. Pop. (2002 est.) 195,500.

Yamuna (Jumna) River in N central India. It rises in the Himalayas and flows S and SE. The Yamuna's confluence with the GANGES at ALLAHABAD is one of the most sacred Hindu sites. The TAJ MAHAL at AGRA lies on its bank. Navigable for almost its entire length, the Yamuna was once an important trade route, but is now primarily used for irrigation. Length: *c.*1380km (860mi).

Yang, Chen Ning (1922–) US physicist, b. China. With T.D. Lee, he studied the decay of K MESONS, which seemed to break down in two different ways. In 1956, they concluded that in these weak interactions PARITY need not be conserved. Yang and Lee shared the 1957 Nobel Prize in physics.

Yangtze (Chang Jiang) River in China, the longest in Asia and third-longest in the world. Rising in the Kunlun Mountains in NE Tibet, it flows 6,300km (3,900mi) through the central Chinese provinces to the East China Sea near Shanghai. It was joined to the HUANG HE by the Grand Canal in 610. The Yangtze and its main tributaries traverse one of the world's most populated areas, providing water for irrigation and hydroelectricity. It is China's most economically important waterway. The government's controversial 'Three Gorges Dam' scheme at Yichang, structurally completed in 2006, eased navigation by creating a reservoir *c.*600km (375mi) long. When all generators are installed it could produce up to 18,000 megawatts of electric power, but its construction has displaced *c.*1.2–1.9 million people and is causing massive damage to wildlife, habitats and the region's ecology.

Yanomami Native American tribal group living chiefly in the rainforests of N Brazil and S Venezuela. Traditionally semi-nomadic hunter-gatherers, during the 1980s and 1990s much of their land was lost to road-builders, logging companies and gold prospectors, causing the population to fall to *c.*18,000. Their plight raised international concern.

Yaoundé Capital of Cameroon, W Africa. Located in beautiful hills on the edge of dense jungle, German traders founded it in 1888. In World War 1, it was occupied by Belgian troops, and later acted as capital (1921–60) of French Cameroon. Since independence, it has grown rapidly as a financial and administrative centre with strong Western influences. It is the site of the University of Cameroon (1962). The city also serves as a market for the surrounding region, notably in coffee, cacao, and sugar. Pop. (2005) 1,727,000.

yard Imperial unit of length equal to 3 feet (ft). One yard (yd) equals 0.9144 metres (m).

Yaroslavl (Jaroslavl') City and river port on the Volga, W central Russia; capital of Yaroslavl oblast. The oldest town on the Volga (founded 1010 by Yaroslavl the Great), it was capital of Yaroslavl principality when absorbed by MOSCOW in 1463. From March to July 1612 it served as Russia's capital. It boasts many historic buildings. Yaroslavl is a major rail junction. Industries: linen, diesel engines, construction equipment, oil refining, petrochemicals, plastics. Pop. (2002 est.) 611,300.

yaws (framboesia) Contagious skin disease found in the humid tropics. It is caused by a spirochete (*Treponema pertenue*), related to the organism causing SYPHILIS. Yaws, however, is not a SEXUALLY TRANSMITTED DISEASE (STD), but is transmitted by flies and by direct skin contact with the sores. It may go on to cause disfiguring bone lesions.

y-chromosome One of the two kinds of sex-determining CHROMOSOME; the other is the X-CHROMOSOME. Many male organisms have one x- and one y-chromosome in their DIPLOID cell nuclei. SPERM cells contain either an x- or y-chromosome, and since female ova (egg cells) always contain an x-chromosome, the resulting offspring is either XY (male)

Y

or XX (female). The y-chromosome is smaller than the x- and contains fewer GENES. *See also* GENETICS; HEREDITY

year Length of time taken by the Earth to circle once round the Sun in its orbit. It is defined in various ways, such as the sidereal year, which is timed with reference to the fixed stars.

yeast Any of a group of single-celled microscopic FUNGI found in all parts of the world in the soil and in organic matter. Yeasts reproduce asexually by BUDDING or FISSION. Yeasts are also produced commercially for use in baking, BREWING and WINE-making. They occur naturally as a bloom (white covering) on grapes and other fruit.

Yeats, W.B. (William Butler) (1865–1939) Irish poet and dramatist, often cited as the greatest English language poet of the 20th century. In 1904, he and Lady Gregory founded the ABBEY THEATRE, Dublin, as an Irish national theatre. Yeats' plays *On Baile's Strand* (1905) and *Cathleen Ni Houlihan* (1902) were on the first bill, the latter often regarded as the beginning of the renaissance in IRISH LITERATURE. His early poetry, collected in *The Wanderings of Oisin, and Other Poems* (1889), shows the influence of mysticism. Yeats' unrequited love for Maud Gonne inspired him into more directly nationalist statements. The poetry in *Responsibilities* (1914) acted as contemporary social commentary. Following the creation of the Irish Free State, he served (1922–28) as a senator. Yeats' mature, symbolist poetry, such as *A Vision* (1925), often adopted dramatic voices. Works from this second phase include *Michael Robartes and the Dancer* (1921, which contains 'The Second Coming' and 'Easter 1916') and *The Tower* (1928, which contains 'Sailing to Byzantium'). Yeats received the 1923 Nobel Prize in literature.

yellow fever Acute, infectious disease marked by sudden onset of headaches, fever, muscle and joint pain, jaundice and vomiting; the kidneys and heart may also be affected. It is caused by a VIRUS transmitted by mosquitoes in tropical and subtropical regions. It may be prevented by vaccination.

Yellowstone National Park Park in NW Wyoming and reaching into Montana and Idaho, USA. Established in 1872, it is the oldest and one of the largest US national parks. Formed by volcanic activity, the park contains *c*.10,000 hot springs (including the giant Hot Springs) and 200 geysers (the most famous of which is "Old Faithful"). Other scenic attractions include Yellowstone River and the petrified forests. It is one of the world's greatest wildlife sanctuaries. In 1988 large-scale forest fires devastated much of the park. Area: 900,000ha (2.22 million acres).

Yeltsin, Boris Nikolayevich (1931–2007) Russian statesman, first democratically elected president of the Russian Federation (1991–99). He was Communist Party leader in Sverdlovsk (now Ekaterinburg) before joining (1985) the reforming government of Mikhail GORBACHEV, becoming party chief in Moscow. Yeltsin's blunt criticism of the slow pace of PERESTROIKA led to demotion in 1987, but his popularity saw him elected as president of the Russian Republic in 1990. His prompt denunciation of the attempted coup against Gorbachev (August 1991) established his political supremacy. Elected president of the Russian Federation, Yeltsin presided over the dissolution of the SOVIET UNION and the end of Communist Party rule. Economic disintegration, rising crime, and internal conflicts – notably in CHECHNYA – damaged his popularity, and failing health reduced his effectiveness. Nevertheless, he was re-elected in 1996. In 1998, in the face of economic crisis in Russia, Yeltsin twice sacked the entire cabinet. In 1999, Yeltsin resigned as president in favour of Vladimir PUTIN.

Yemen Republic on the s tip of the Arabian peninsula. *See* country feature, page 804.

Yenisei (Yenesey) River in central Siberia, Russia. Formed by the confluence of the Bolshoi Yenisei and the Maly Yenisei at Kyzyl, it flows for 4,090km (2,540mi) w then N through the Sayan Mountains and across Siberia, forming the w border of the central Siberian plateau, emptying into the Yenisei Gulf on the Kara Sea. A large hydroelectric station has been built at Krasnoyarsk. The Yenisei is a source of sturgeon and salmon. A shipping route, some

of its sections are frozen in winter. When combined with the Angara (its major tributary), the Yenisei is the world's fifth-longest river, at 5,550km (3,445mi).

Yerevan Capital of Armenia, on the River Razdan, s CAUCASUS. One of the world's oldest cities, it was capital of Armenia from as early as the 7th century (though under Persian control). A crucial crossroads for caravan routes between India and Transcaucasia, it is the site of a 16th-century Turkish fortress. It is a traditional wine-making centre. Industries: chemicals, plastics, cables, tyres, metals, electrical appliances, vodka. Pop. (2001 est.) 1,247,200.

Yerkes Observatory Observatory of the University of Chicago, at Williams Bay, Wisconsin, USA. Founded by George Ellery HALE in 1897, Yerkes' main instrument is a 1m (40in) refractor, still the largest in the world.

Yevtushenko, Yevgeny (1933–) Russian writer. During the 1960s, he headed a new wave of nonconformist, modern Soviet poetry. Explicitly rejecting SOCIALIST REALISM, Yevtushenko's rhetorical poetry anticipated GLASNOST in its examination of Soviet history. His most famous work, *Babi Yar* (1961), was a direct indictment of Soviet anti-Semitism. Other works include *Precocious Autobiography* (1963) and *The Bratsk Station* (1965). His *Collected Poems* appeared in 1991.

yew Any of a number of evergreen shrubs and trees of the genus *Taxus*, native to temperate regions of the Northern Hemisphere. They have stiff, narrow, dark green needles, often with pale undersides, and red, berry-like fruits. Height: to 25m (80ft). Family Taxaceae.

Yiddish Language spoken by Jews living in central and E Europe and other countries (including the USA) with Jewish communities. It first developed in w Europe in the 10th and 11th centuries, and was taken E with migrating Jews. It is basically a variety of German, with many HEBREW, Aramaic, French, Italian, and Slavic words added. Written using the Hebrew alphabet, it contains many English borrowings. Many words and expressions have passed into American English.

Yin Alternative transliteration of the SHANG dynasty

yin and yang In the Chinese philosophy of TAOISM, two interacting, complementary forces in the universe. *Yin* and *yang* are cosmic energy modes comprising the *Tao* or the eternal, dynamic way of the universe. Earth is *yin,* the passive, dark, female principle; heaven is *yang,* the active, bright, male principle. All the things of nature and society are composed of combinations of these two principles of polarity, which maintain the balance of all things. The hexagrams of the BOOK OF CHANGES embody *yin* and *yang.*

YMCA *See* YOUNG MEN'S CHRISTIAN ASSOCIATION

yoga (Sanskrit, 'union') Term used for a number of Hindu disciplines to aid the union of the soul with God. Based on the *Yoga sutras* of Patañjali (active 2nd century BC), the practice of yoga generally involves moral restraints, meditation, and the awakening of physical energy centres through specific postures (*asanas*) or exercises. Devoted to freeing the soul or self from earthly cares by isolating it from the body and the mind, these ancient practices became popular in the West during the second half of the 20th century as a means of relaxation, self-control, and enlightenment.

Yogyakarta (Jogjakarta) City in s Java, Indonesia. Founded in 1749, it is the cultural and artistic centre of Java. Capital of a Dutch-controlled Sultanate from 1755, it was the scene of a revolt (1825–30) against colonial exploitation. During the 1940s, it was the centre of the Indonesian independence movement and, in 1949, acted as the provisional capital of Indonesia. Its many visitors are drawn by the 18th-century palace, the Grand Mosque, the religious and arts festivals, and its proximity to the BOROBUDUR temple. The major industry is handicrafts. Pop. (1995) 418,944.

Yokohama Port and major industrial city on the w shore of Tokyo Bay, SE HONSHU, Japan. The country's main port for many years, it is now the second-largest city. Yokohama grew from a small fishing village to a major port after opening to foreign trade in 1859. It served as Tokyo's deep-water harbour and was a vital silk-exporting centre. The city has been rebuilt twice: once after the devastating earthquake in 1923, and again following intensive Allied bombing during World War 2. Many

INTERNET

Yemen
▶ www.yemenembassy.org

Yerkes Observatory
▶ astro.uchicago.edu/yerkes

▲ **Yeats** One of the greatest figures in 20th-century literature, W.B. Yeats was born in a suburb of Dublin, Ireland. At art school he developed an interest in mysticism, the occult, and Irish mythology, These interests provided the inspiration for much of his poetry. Yeats played a major role in the Irish cultural renaissance and produced powerful nationalist works.

▲ **Yeltsin** Educated at Urals Polytechnic, Russian Federation former President Boris Yeltsin began his career in the construction industry. He gained a reputation as an outspoken, hands-on reformer, and passed in and out of favour with the Politburo during the *perestroika* reforms of the 1980s. As president of Russia, he was a progressive advocate of price deregulation, privatization, and nuclear disarmament.

of the modern port and industrial facilities were built on land reclaimed from the sea. It hosted the 2002 World Cup final. Industries: iron, steel, shipbuilding. Pop. (2000) 6,427,000.

yolk Rich substance found in the eggs or ova of most animals except those of placental mammals. It consists of fats and proteins and serves as a store of food for the developing EMBRYO.

yolk sac Membranous sac-like structure in the eggs of most animals. It attaches directly to the ventral surface or gut of the developing EMBRYO in the eggs of birds, reptiles, and some fish, and contains YOLK. The term also refers to an analogous sac-like membrane that develops below the mammalian embryo. It contains no yolk but is connected to the umbilical cord.

Yom Kippur (Day of Atonement) Most solemn of Jewish feasts. It is the last of the Ten Days of Penitence that begin the New Year. On this day, set aside for prayer and fasting, humanity is called to account for its sins and to seek reconciliation with God. Yom Kippur is described as the SABBATH of Sabbaths, because the break from work is almost complete, and Jews must abstain from food, drink, and sex. *See also* ROSH HASHANAH

Yonkers City on the Hudson River, SE New York state, USA. Land was originally purchased from Native Americans in 1639 by the Dutch West India Company. The acquittal of John Peter Zenger here in 1735 helped set up freedom of the press in the USA. Yonkers has various museums (including the Hudson River Museum) and research institutions. Industries: lifts (since 1852), chemicals, cables. Pop. (2000) 196,086.

York City and county district in NORTH YORKSHIRE, N England. Located at the confluence of the Ouse and Foss rivers, it was an important Roman military post, an Anglo-Saxon capital, a Dan-

ish settlement and then the ecclesiastical centre of the North of England. York Minster cathedral dates from the 13th century. Industries: tourism, engineering (including rail workshops), confectionery, precision instruments. Pop. (2001) 181,131.

York, Archbishop of Second-highest office of the CHURCH OF ENGLAND. The Acts of the Council of Arles (314) mention a Bishop of York, but the early Christian community in York was destroyed by Saxon invaders. The uninterrupted history of the present see began with the consecration of Wilfrid as Bishop of York in 664. In 735, York was raised to the dignity of an archbishopric, when Egbert was given the title PRIMATE of the Northern Province. The Archbishop is now Primate of England (the Archbishop of CANTERBURY is Primate of all England).

York, House of English royal House, a branch of the PLANTAGENETS. During the Wars of the ROSES, rival claimants from the Houses of York and LANCASTER contended for the throne. The Yorkist claimant, Richard, Duke of York, was a greatgrandson of EDWARD III. His son was crowned as EDWARD IV. In 1485, the defeat of Edward's brother, RICHARD III, by HENRY VII brought the Yorkist line to a close. *See also* TUDORS

Yorkshire *See* NORTH YORKSHIRE, SOUTH YORKSHIRE, and WEST YORKSHIRE

Yorkshire terrier Small, long-haired dog originally bred in Lancashire and Yorkshire, England, in the 19th century. It has a compact body and short legs. The tail is commonly docked. The silky coat is generally blue-grey and tan. Height: to 20cm (8in) at the shoulder; weight to 3kg (7lb).

Yorktown, Siege of (1781) Last major military campaign of the AMERICAN REVOLUTION. Trapped on the

---

YEMEN

The Republic of Yemen faces the Red Sea and the Gulf of Aden in the SW corner of the Arabian Peninsula. Behind the narrow coastal plain along the Red Sea, the land rises to a mountain region called High Yemen. Beyond the mountains, the land slopes down towards the Rub' al Khali Desert. Other mountains rise behind the coastal plain along the Gulf of Aden. To the E lies a fertile valley called the Hadramaut and also the deserts of the Arabian Empty Quarter.

Palm trees grow along the coast. Plants such as acacia and eucalyptus flourish in the interior. Thorn shrubs and mountain pasture are found in the highlands.

CLIMATE

The climate in SAN'A is moderated by its altitude. Temperatures are much lower than in ADEN (Al' Adan), which is at sea level. In summer, SW monsoon winds bring thunderstorms, but most of Yemen is arid. The S coasts are particularly hot and humid, especially from June to September. There are two seasonal rainfalls,

during March to May and during July to September. The average rainfall is about 50mm [2in] on most parts of the plateaux, but may rise to 1,000mm [40in] in the highlands, while the coastal lowlands may have only 12mm [0.5in].

HISTORY

The ancient kingdom of Saba or Sabaea flourished in present-day S Yemen between *c.*750 BC and 100 BC and could possibly be identified with the biblical SHEBA. The kingdom was renowned for its advanced technology and wealth, gained through its strategic location on important spice trade routes.

Islam was introduced in AD 628. The Rassite dynasty of the Zaidi sect established a theocratic state. In *c.* 1000, the FATIMIDS conquered Yemen. In 1517 the area became part of the Ottoman Empire, and remained under Turkish control until 1918. In the 19th century the Saudi Wahhabi sect ousted the Zaidi imams, but were in turn expelled by Ibrahim Pasha. In 1839 the British captured Aden. During the 19th century it became a British protectorate.

POLITICS

After World War 1 N Yemen, which had been ruled by Turkey, began to evolve into a separate state from the S, where Britain was in control. Britain withdrew in 1967 and a leftwing regime took power in the S. North Yemen became a republic in 1962 when the monarchy was abolished.

Clashes occurred between the traditionalist Yemen Arab Republic in the N and the Marxist People's Democratic Republic of Yemen in the S. In 1990 they were resolved when the two Yemens merged to form one country. Marrying the needs of the two parts of Yemen has proved difficult. In 1994 civil war erupted when Presi-

AREA 527,968sq km [203,848sq mi]
POPULATION 22,231,000
CAPITAL (POPULATION) San'a (1,621,000)
GOVERNMENT Multiparty republic
ETHNIC GROUPS Predominantly Arab
LANGUAGES Arabic (official)
RELIGIONS Islam
CURRENCY Yemeni rial = 100 fils

dent Saleh, a northerner, attempted to remove the vice-president, a southerner. The war ended when Aden was captured by government forces. In 1995 Yemen resolved border disputes with Oman and Saudi Arabia, but clashed with Eritrea over uninhabited islands in the Red Sea. In 1998–9, militants in the Aden-Abyan Islamic Army sought to destabilize the country. The 1999 elections made Saleh president once again, though opposition was forbidden. In 2000 a suicide bomb attack on the USS *Cole* in Aden killed 17 US personnel. In 2001 President Saleh offered support to the USA in its 'war on terrorism'. President Saleh was reappointed in 2006 elections, the first in which an opposition candidate was permitted. The year 2007 saw clashes between government forces and Islamist rebels.

ECONOMY

The World Bank classifies Yemen as a 'lowincome' developing country. Agriculture employs up to 63% of the people. Herders raise sheep and other animals, while farmers grow such crops as barley, fruits, wheat and vegetables in highland valleys and around oases. Cash crops include coffee and cotton. Imported oil is refined at Aden and petroleum extraction began in the NW in the 1980s. Handicrafts, leather goods and textiles are manufactured.

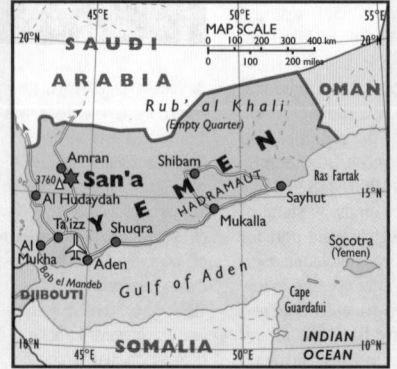

Y

peninsula of Yorktown, Virginia, 7000 British troops under Lord Cornwallis surrendered to superior US and French forces, after attempts to relieve them failed.

Yoruba People of sw Nigeria of basically Christian or Islamic faith. Most are farmers, growing crops that include yams, maize, and cocoa. Many live in towns built around the palace of an *oba* (chief) and travel daily to their outlying farms.

Yosemite National Park Spectacular national park, established 1890, in the SIERRA NEVADA range of central California, USA. Yosemite means 'grizzly bear', and the park was named after the river that runs through it. It is a mountainous area of glacial gorges and granite cliffs rising to the 3,990m (13,090ft) of Mount Lyell. Yosemite Falls, the highest waterfall in North America, drops 739m (2,425ft) in two stages. Other features include Half Dome Mountain and the vertical rock-face of El Capitan. Area: 308,335ha (761320 acres).

Young, Brigham (1801–77) US religious leader, founder of SALT LAKE CITY. An early convert to the Church of Jesus Christ of Latter-Day Saints (MORMONS), Young took over the leadership when Joseph SMITH, the founder, was killed by a mob in 1844. Young held the group together through persecutions and led their westward migration (1846–47) to UTAH, where he organized the settlement that became Salt Lake City. He was governor of Utah Territory (1850–57).

Young, Lester Willis (1909–59) US jazz saxophonist. A major influence on BE-BOP music, with his characteristically cool and melodious improvisations, 'Prez' made his name playing tenor saxophone with Count BASIE. He also played with Benny Goodman and Dizzy GILLESPIE. Charlie MINGUS wrote 'Goodbye, Pork Pie Ha' in memory of Young.

Young, Thomas (1773–1829) English physicist and physician. He revived the wave theory of light first put forward in the 17th century by Christiaan HUYGENS. He helped present the Young-Helmholtz theory of colour vision and detailed the cause of ASTIGMATISM. He studied elasticity, giving his name to the tensile elastic (Young's) modulus. Young was also an Egyptologist who helped decipher the ROSETTA STONE.

Young Men's Christian Association (YMCA) Christian association for young men established (1844) in London by George Williams. Its aim is to develop Christian morals and leadership qualities in young people. Clubs were soon formed in the USA and Australia, and the World Alliance of the YMCA was formed in Geneva in 1855. Women were accepted as members in 1971. *See also* YOUNG WOMEN'S CHRISTIAN ASSOCIATION (YWCA)

Young Turks Group of Turks who wished to remodel the OTTOMAN EMPIRE and make it a modern European state with a liberal constitution. Their movement began in the 1880s with unrest in the army and universities. In 1908, a Young Turk rising, led by ENVER PASHA and his chief of staff Mustafa Kemal (ATATÜRK), deposed Sultan Abdul Hamid II and replaced him with his brother, Muhammad V. Following a 1913 *coup d'etat*, Enver Pasha became a virtual dictator. Under Atatürk, the Young Turks merged into the Turkish Nationalist Party.

Young Women's Christian Association (YWCA) Christian association for young women; the counterpart of the YOUNG MEN'S CHRISTIAN ASSOCIATION (YMCA). Two YWCA groups founded simultaneously (1855) in different parts of England, and the associations merged in 1877. The YWCA provides accommodation, education, recreation facilities, and welfare services to young women. It has local branches in more than 80 countries.

Ypres, Battles of Several battles of World War 1 fought around the Belgian town of Ypres. The first (October-November 1914) stopped the German 'race to the sea' to capture the Channel ports, but resulted in the near destruction of the British Expeditionary Force. The second (April–May 1915), the first battle in which poison gas was used, resulted in even greater casualties, without victory to either side. The third (summer 1917) was a predominantly British offensive. It culminated in the Passchendaele campaign, the costliest campaign in British military history, which continued until November.

ytterbium (symbol Yb) Silver-white, metallic element of the LANTHANIDE SERIES (rare-earth metals). First isolated in 1828, ytterbium's chief ore is monazite. The shiny, soft element is malleable and ductile and is used to produce steel and other alloys. Properties: at.no. 70: r.a.m. 173.04; r.d. 6.97; m.p. 824°C (1,515°F); b.p. 1,193°C (2,179°F); most common isotope Yb^{174} (31.84%).

yttrium (symbol Y) Silver-grey, metallic element in group III of the periodic table. First isolated in 1828 by German chemist Friedrich WÖHLER, it is found with LANTHANIDE elements (rare-earth metals) in monazite sand, bastnasite, and gadolinite. It resembles the lanthanides in its chemistry. Yttrium was found in lunar rock samples collected by the Apollo 11 space mission. Its compounds are used in phosphors and communications devices, such as colour television picture tubes and superconducting ceramics. Properties: at.no. 39; r.a.m. 88.9059; r.d. 4.47; m.p. 1,523°C (2,773°F); b.p. 3,337°C (6,039°F); most common isotope Y^{89} (100%).

Yüan (1246–1368) MONGOL dynasty in China. Continuing the conquests of GENGHIS KHAN, KUBLAI KHAN established his rule over China, eliminating the last SUNG claimant in 1279. Kublai Khan returned the capital to Beijing and promoted construction and commerce. CHINESE LITERATURE took new forms during the Mongol period. Native Chinese were excluded from government, and foreign visitors, including merchants such as Marco POLO, were encouraged. Among the Chinese, resentment of alien rule was aggravated by economic problems, including runaway inflation. The less competent successors of Kublai were increasingly challenged by rebellion, culminating in the victory of the MING.

Yucatán State in the N part of the Yucatán Peninsula, SE Mexico; the capital is Mérida. The terrain is low-lying, covered in places with scrub and cactus thickets. Once the centre of the MAYA civilization, the Spanish conquered Yucatán in the 1540s. The region is a major producer of henequen (sisal hemp used for cordage). Other products: tobacco, sugar, cotton, tropical fruits. Fishing is an important industry. Area: 38,508sq km (14,868sq mi). Pop. (2000) 1,655,707.

yucca Genus of *c.*40 species of SUCCULENT plants native to s USA, Mexico, and the West Indies. Most species are stemless, forming a rosette of leaves, or have a trunk. The flowers grow in clusters and are white, tinged with yellow or purple. The leaves are poisonous. Height: to 10m (33ft). Family Liliaceae.

Yugoslavia Former state in Eastern Europe. Serbian-led demands for the unification of South Slavic lands contributed to the outbreak of WORLD WAR I. After the war, a 'Kingdom of the Serbs, Croats and Slovenes' was formed under the Serbian king PETER I. In 1929 his successor, ALEXANDER I, renamed the country Yugoslavia. The name means 'Land of the South Slavs'. The country was dissolved when it was conquered by the Axis powers in WORLD WAR 2, but reformed at the war's end. In 1945 it became a COMMUNIST state under the leadership of TITO, who kept the country stable but had to allow the country's constituent regions more independence in the 1970s. After his death in 1980 the economy declined and the regions' demands for autonomy grew. In the early 1990s, with the downfall of communism, Yugoslavia fragmented; SLOVENIA, CROATIA, MACEDONIA and BOSNIA-HERZEGOVINA declared their independence and the region fell into civil war. The remainder retained the name Yugoslavia until 2003, when it became the Union of Serbia and Montenegro. Montenegro became independent from Serbia in 2006; *see also* MONTENEGRO and SERBIA.

Yukawa, Hideki (1907–81) Japanese physicist. In the 1930s, he proposed that there was a nuclear force of very short range (less than 10^{-15}m) strong enough to overcome the repulsive force of protons and that diminished rapidly with distance. Yukawa predicted that this force manifested itself by the transfer of particles between NEUTRONS and PROTONS. In 1947 Cecil POWELL discovered the pion (pi MESON), thus confirming Yukawa's theory. In 1949, he received the Nobel Prize in physics for his prediction of the existence of the meson.

Yukon Fourth-longest river in North America, deriving its name from a Native American word for 'great'. It rises at Lake Tagish on the border of British Columbia, Canada, and flows N and NW through Yukon Territory across the border into Alaska. It then flows SW to enter the Bering

Y

INTERNET

Yukon Territory
▶ www.gov.yk.ca

Sea. The Russians explored the lower course of the river in 1836–37; Robert Campbell explored the upper course in 1843. It was a major transportation route during the KLONDIKE GOLD RUSH. It is navigable for *c.*2,858km (1,775mi) of its 3,185km (1,980mi) course, but is ice-bound from October to June. The river teems with salmon.

Yukon Territory Small territory in the extreme NW of Canada, bounded by the Arctic Ocean (N), Northwest Territories (E), British Columbia (S), and Alaska (W); the capital and largest town is Whitehorse. The N consists of Arctic waste and is virtually uninhabited. Further S there is spectacular mountain scenery with lakes and coniferous forests. The region is drained by the YUKON and MACKENZIE rivers. The climate is harsh, with freezing winters and short summers. The region was first explored by fur traders from the HUDSON'S BAY COMPANY after 1840. The KLONDIKE GOLD RUSH brought over 30,000 prospectors in the 1890s. In 1991 the Canadian government recognized the land claims of the indigenous Yukon (First Nation) Native Americans. Farming is extremely limited, but a few cereal crops and vegetables are grown in the valleys. The principal activity is mining, with deposits including lead, zinc and gold.

Forestry and tourism are economically important. Area: 483,450sq km (186,675sq mi). Pop. (2001) 28,674.

Yunnan ('South of the Clouds') Province in S central China, bounded by Laos and Vietnam (S) and Burma (W); the capital is Kunming. Its remote mountain location enabled Yunnan to retain an independent status until conquered by the MONGOLS in 1253. In 1659 it became a province of China. Chinese communist forces captured it in 1950. Yunnan divides (along ethnic lines) into eight autonomous districts, which are home to many of China's minority nationalities. It is renowned for the rich diversity of its wildlife, particularly rare plant species. Agriculture is restricted to a few plains, with rice the major crop. Its valuable mineral resources include deposits of tin, tungsten, copper, gold, silver. Mining and timber are the main industries. Area: 436,200sq km (168,482sq mi). Pop. (2000) 42,880,000.

Yurok Native American tribe formerly living around the estuary of the Klamath River, California, USA, and speaking an Algonquian language. Reduced in number to fewer than 1,000, the Yurok are now scattered along the N Californian coast.

YWCA Abbreviation of YOUNG WOMEN'S CHRISTIAN ASSOCIATION

Zacharias Variant spelling of ZECHARIAH
Zacharias, Saint (d.752) (Zachary) Pope (741–52). He strengthened the Holy See, and during his papacy he achieved a 20–year truce with the LOMBARDS. Along with St BONIFACE, he established cordial relations with the FRANKS by supporting the accession of PEPIN III (THE SHORT) to the Frankish throne.
Zagreb Capital of Croatia, on the River Sava. Founded in the 11th century, it became capital of the Hungarian province of Croatia and Slavonia during the 14th century. The city was an important centre of the 19th-century Croatian nationalist movement. In 1918 it was the meeting place of the Croatian Diet (parliament), which severed all ties with Austria-Hungary. It later joined a new union with Serbia in what was to become Yugoslavia. In World War 2, Zagreb was the capital of the Axis-controlled, puppet Croatian state. It was wrested from Axis control in 1945, and became capital of the Croatian Republic of Yugoslavia. Following the break-up of Yugoslavia in 1992, Zagreb remained capital of the newly independent state of Croatia. The old city has many places of historical interest, including a Gothic cathedral and a Baroque archiepiscopal palace. Zagreb has a university (founded 1669) and an Academy of Arts and Sciences (1861). It is also the industrial and manufacturing heart of Croatia. Industries: steel, cement, machinery, chemicals. Pop. (2000) 1,067,000.
Zagros Mountain range in s and sw Iran, extending c.900km (560mi) from the borders with Turkey and Armenia almost to the Persian Gulf. The topography varies from rugged peaks in the N to ridges and fertile valleys in the central region (producing cotton, tobacco, and fruits) and lowland marshes and rock in the s. One of the world's most productive oilfields is located in the w foothills. Zard Kuh is the highest peak, at 4,548m (14,921ft).
zaibatsu Large industrial conglomerates in Japan formed after the MEIJI RESTORATION (1868). Headed by powerful families such as Mitsui, they dominated the Japanese economy in the early 20th century. Although broken up during the US occupation after 1945, they subsequently reformed and reclaimed their dominant position.
Zaïre See CONGO, DEMOCRATIC REPUBLIC
Zaïre River See CONGO
Zambezi River in s Africa. Rising in NW Zambia, it flows in a rough 'S' shape through E Angola and w Zambia before turning E to form part of the Zambian border with Namibia and the entire border with Zimbabwe (including the VICTORIA FALLS). It crosses the widest part of Mozambique and turns SE to empty into the Indian Ocean. There is great potential for the generation of hydroelectricity along the river's course, and it has two of Africa's biggest dams: Kariba (Zambia-Zimbabwe) and Cabora Bassa (Mozambique). Length: 2,740km (1,700mi).
Zambia Landlocked republic in s central Africa. See country feature, page 809
Zamyatin, Yevgeni Ivanovich (1884–1939) Russian novelist and dramatist. He was censored both by the pre-revolutionary Tsarist authorities and by their revolutionary Bolshevik successors. Zamyatin was an early exponent of the dystopian novel in the form of his most famous work, *We*, an attack on Soviet society and politics, written in 1924 but not published in the Soviet Union until 1989. He emigrated in 1931, and died in Paris.
Zanzibar Island region of TANZANIA, in the Indian Ocean, off the E coast of Africa; the capital is Zanzibar. The first European discovery was by Vasco da Gama in 1499, and the Portuguese quickly established colonial rule. In the late 17th century, it came under the control of the Omani Arabs, who developed into the major centre of the East African ivory and slave trade. The slave trade halted in 1873, and in 1890 the Sultanate of Zanzibar became a British Protectorate. In 1963, it became an independent state and a member of the Commonwealth. Tension between the Arab ruling class and indigenous Africans (the majority of the population) led to the overthrow of the Sultanate. In 1964, Zanzibar and Tanganyika merged to form the United Republic of Tanzania. Zanzibar retained control over domestic affairs. During the

1980s and 1990s, conflict developed between secessionist and mainland centralist forces. In 1993, a regional parliament for Zanzibar was established. Violence erupted on the islands after 2000 elections. The two largest population groups are the Hadimu and Tumbatu. The major religion is Sunni Muslim, and the main language is Swahili. The chief export is cloves, and the biggest industry is fishing. Area: 1,660sq km (641sq mi). Pop. (2002 est.) 934,400 (with Pemba).
Zapata, Emiliano (1880–1919) Mexican revolutionary leader. His Indian peasant army supported Francisco MADERO's successful coup (1910) against Porfirio DÍAZ. Madero's failure to meet his demands for radical agrarian reform, such as the return of *haciendas* (great estates) to native Mexican communal ownership, led to the MEXICAN REVOLUTION. In pursuit of 'land and liberty', Zapata captured much of s Mexico. Allied with 'Pancho' Villa, he opposed the regimes of Victoriano HUERTA and Venustiano CARRANZA and captured Mexico City (1914–15). Zapata was murdered by an agent of Carranza.
Zaporizhzhya (Ukrainian, 'Beyond the Rapids') City on the River DNIEPER, SE Ukraine. Zaporozhye Cossacks, leaders of the Ukrainian nationalist movement, settled the area in the 16th century. In 1770, Zaporizhzhya was founded as a fortress, and in 1775 the Russian army of Catherine II forcibly ejected the Cossacks. In the early 19th century, the fortress became a town, known as Aleksandrovsk until 1921. Zaporizhzhya consists of the old city and the new industrial area, development of which began in the 1930s with the construction of the Dneproges dam and a large hydroelectric plant. It is now one of the Ukraine's leading industrial complexes, producing aluminium, iron and steel, motor vehicles and chemicals. Pop. (2000) 863,000.
Zaragoza (Saragossa) City on the River Ebro, NE Spain; capital of Zaragoza province and Aragón region. The city was taken by the Romans in the 1st century BC and by Moors in the 8th century. In 1118, it was captured by Alfonso I of Aragón, who made it his capital. It was the scene of heroic resistance against the French in the Peninsular War (1808–09). Its main landmark is the Moorish palace of Aljafarería. Other sites include the cathedrals of La Seo and El Pilar. The city is an important commercial and communications centre. At the heart of an agricultural region, it acts as a distribution point for wine, olives and cereal. Industries: heavy machinery, textiles. Pop. (2001) 614,905.
Zarathustra See ZOROASTER
Zatopek, Emil (1922–2000) Czech athlete. He won a gold medal in the 10,000m at the 1948 Olympics and three gold medals (5,000m, 10,000m and the marathon) at the 1952 Olympics. From 1948 to 1954, he was unbeaten at 10,000m.
Zealots Jewish sect, active in opposition to Roman rule at the time of JESUS CHRIST and after. They refused to agree that Jews could be ruled by pagans, led resistance to the Roman census of AD 6, pursued a terrorist campaign, and played an important role in the rising of AD 66. Their activities continued into the 2nd century.
zebra Any of three species of strikingly patterned, striped, black-and-white, equine mammals of the grasslands of Africa; the stripes are arranged in various patterns, according to species. It has long ears, a tufted tail, and narrow hooves. Height: to 140cm (55in) at the shoulder. Family Equidae; genus *Equus*.
zebu (Brahman cattle) Numerous, domestic varieties of a single species of ox, native to India. Zebu have been used extensively in Asia and Africa, and have been introduced to the New World as livestock. Species *Bos indicus*.
Zechariah (Zachariah) Any of several biblical personalities. One of the most significant was a Jewish prophet of the late 6th century BC. He prophesied the rebuilding of the TEMPLE in JERUSALEM by the Jews who had returned from exile in BABYLON. In the Book of Zechariah, the 11th book of the 12 minor prophets of the OLD TESTAMENT, he described visions of four horsemen patrolling God's world, four horns symbolizing the destruction of Israel's enemies, and six other night visions prefiguring the coming of God in judgment. Many of Zechariah's images were taken up in the REVELATION of St John the Divine. The other important Zechariah was the priest

Z/z, 26th and last letter of the Roman alphabet. It is derived from the Semitic letter, zayin, which then passed into Greek as the letter zeta where it assumed its present form.

mentioned in the GOSPEL According to St LUKE as the father of Saint JOHN THE BAPTIST. In the New Testament account (Luke 1), Zechariah was visited by the angel Gabriel, who foretold the birth of John to Zechariah's wife Elizabeth. For doubting Gabriel's prophecy, Zechariah was struck dumb until the time of John's circumcision.

Zedillo, Ernesto (1951–) Mexican statesman, president (1994–2000). Zedillo joined the Institutional Revolutionary Party (PRI) in 1971, and entered the presidential race after the PRI's candidate Luis Colosio was assassinated (1994). He received just over 50% of the vote. Zedillo promised to combat unemployment and tackle the failing economy. Within a few months, however, he was forced to devalue the peso. Vicente Fox won presidential elections in 2000, the first time in Mexico's history that the PRI were out of power.

Zeeman, Pieter (1865–1943) Dutch physicist. He shared the 1902 Nobel Prize in physics with Hendrik LORENTZ for their discovery (1896) of the ZEEMAN EFFECT. Zeeman also detected the magnetic fields at the surface of the Sun.

Zeeman effect In physics, effect produced by a strong magnetic field on the light emitted by a radiant body; it is observed as a splitting of its spectral lines. It was first observed (1896) by Pieter Zeeman. The effect has been useful in investigating the charge/mass ratio and magnetic moment of an ELECTRON.

Zeffirelli, Franco (1923–) Italian theatre, opera, and film director. Zeffirelli worked at Covent Garden on *Cavalleria rusticana*, at Stratford-upon-Avon on *Othello*, and on Broadway on *The Lady of the Camellias*. Renowned for his sumptuous and rich production, his films include *The Taming of the Shrew* (1966), *Romeo and Juliet* (1968) and *Brother Sun and Sister Moon* (1973). His major success, *Jesus of Nazareth* (1978), was originally made for television.

Zeiss, Carl (1816–88) German manufacturer of optical instruments. In 1846, Zeiss established a factory at Jena and made various optical components, including lenses, binoculars and microscopes.

Zemin, Jiang *See* JIANG ZEMIN

Zen Japanese school of BUDDHISM, initially developed in China, where it is known as Ch'an. Instead of doctrines and scriptures, Zen stresses mind-to-mind instruction from master to disciple in order to achieve *satori* (awakening of Buddha-nature). There are two major Zen sects. **Rinzai** (introduced to Japan from China in 1191) emphasizes sudden enlightenment and meditation on paradoxical statements. The **Soto** sect (also brought from China, in 1227) advocates quiet meditation. In its secondary emphasis on mental tranquillity, fearlessness, and spontaneity, Zen influenced JAPANESE ART AND ARCHITECTURE and some forms of JAPANESE LITERATURE.

Zend-Avesta *See* AVESTA; ZOROASTRIANISM

zenith In astronomy, point on the CELESTIAL SPHERE that is directly overhead. The zenith distance of a heavenly body is the angle it makes with the zenith. It is diametrically opposite the NADIR.

Zenobia Queen of PALMYRA (r. *c*.AD 267–72). She ruled as regent for her young son after the death of her husband. Palmyra was an ally of Rome, but Zenobia made it so powerful, conquering Egypt in 269, that the Romans resolved to crush her. AURELIAN defeated her in Syria, and captured Palmyra in 272.

Zeno of Citium (*c*.334–*c*.262 BC) Greek philosopher and founder of the STOICS. Zeno attended lectures by various philosophers before formulating his own philosophy. Proceeding from the CYNICS' concept of self-sufficiency, he stressed the unity of the universe and the brotherhood of men living in harmony with the cosmos. Zeno claimed virtue to be the only good, and wealth, illness and death to be of no human concern.

Zeno of Elea (*c*.495–*c*.430 BC) Greek philosopher, a disciple of Parmenides. He is best known for the use of paradoxical arguments to reveal logical absurdities. In particular, his paradoxes of motion provoked much constructive debate. His work does not survive, but is known through other authors such as Aristotle.

zeolite Group of alumino-silicates that contain sodium, calcium or barium, and loosely held water that can be continuously expelled on heating. Some zeolites occur as fibrous aggregates, while others form robust, non-fibrous crystals. Zeolites vary in hardness from 3 to 5 and in specific gravity from 2 to 2.4. They include analcime, $NaAlSi_2O_6.H_2O$, stilbite, $NaCa_2(Al_5Si_{13})O_{36}.14H_2O$, and natrolite, $Na_2Al_2Si_3O_{10}.2H_2O$.

Zephaniah (active *c*.630BC) OLD TESTAMENT prophet. Zephaniah was named as the author of the Book of Zephaniah, the ninth of the 12 books of the Minor Prophets. He condemned Israel's religious and political corruption and stressed the certainty of God's judgment against Israel.

Zeppelin, Ferdinand, Count von (1838–1917) German army officer and inventor. Zeppelin served in the armies of Württemburg and Prussia. While an observer with the Union Army during the US Civil War (1861–65), he made his first balloon ascent. In 1900, he invented the first rigid airship, which was called Zeppelin after him.

Zernike, Frits (1888–1966) Dutch physicist. In 1935, Zernike developed the phase contrast microscope, in which objects being viewed (often living-cell biological specimens) take on a different colour from their surroundings. For this work, he received the 1953 Nobel Prize in physics.

Zeus In Greek mythology, the sky god, lord of the wind, clouds, rain, and thunder. He is identified with the Roman god, JUPITER. Zeus was the son of Rhea and Cronus, whom he deposed. Zeus was the supreme deity of the Olympians. He fathered huge numbers of children by his wives and others, often seducing goddesses, nymphs, and mortal women by taking the form of an animal.

Zhao Ziyang (1919–2005) Chinese statesman, who played a leading part in China's economic modernization. Zhao joined the Chinese COMMUNIST PARTY in 1938, and during the 1960s acted as party secretary of Guangdong province. He was dismissed by MAO ZEDONG during the CULTURAL REVOLUTION, but rehabilitated and restored to his post in 1971. In 1975, he was appointed party secretary of Sichuan province. Zhao introduced radical economic reforms, which vastly improved industrial and agricultural production. He became premier in 1980. In 1987, LI PENG replaced him as premier and Zhao became general secretary. With the support of DENG XIAOPING, his liberal economic reforms moved China towards a market economy. In 1989, Zhao was dismissed from office and placed under house arrest for advocating negotiation with the pro-democracy demonstrators in TIANANMEN SQUARE.

Zhejiang (Chekiang) Province in SE China, S of the River Yangtze and on the East China Sea; the capital is Hangzhou. It was the centre of the Sung dynasty in the 12th and 13th centuries. Many of Zhejiang's cities were razed during the Taiping Rebellion (1850–65). A mountainous region, it is one of China's most populous areas and includes the Zhoushan Archipelago. To encourage inward capital investment, it is part of the special economic zone of SHANGHAI. The major river is the Qiantang. Mount Tianmu is on the tourist and pilgrimage trails. More than one-third of the region is pine or bamboo forest. The chief crops are rice and tea. Major industries include silk production and fishing. Area: 101,830sq km (39,300sq mi). Pop. (2000) 46,770,000.

Zheng Ho (1371–1435) Chinese admiral, explorer, and diplomat, known as the 'three-jewelled eunuch'. Between 1405 and 1433, Zheng Ho led seven naval expeditions across the China Sea and the Indian Ocean to gather treasures and unusual tributes for the Imperial court. His voyages reached as far W as the Persian Gulf, visiting ports in SE Asia, India, East Africa, and Egypt. His voyages prepared the way for Chinese colonization of SE Asia.

Zhengzhou (Chengchow) City in E central China, 16km (10mi) S of the Huang He ('Yellow') River; capital of Henan province. Capital of the Shang dynasty before 2000 BC it has been a walled city from that time. The modern city grew with the railway (1898) to become the main rail junction of E China. Industries: cotton, food processing, agricultural tools, thermal power. Pop. (2005) 2,250,000.

Zhou Chinese dynasty (1030–221BC). After the nomadic Zhou overthrew the SHANG dynasty, Chinese civilization spread to most of modern China, although the dynasty never established effective control over the regions. The Late Zhou, from 772 BC was a cultural golden age, marked by the writings of CONFUCIUS and LAO TZU, and a period of prosperity. As the provincial states gained power, the Zhou dynasty disintegrated.

Zhou Enlai (1898–1976) Chinese statesman. Zhou was a founder of the Chinese COMMUNIST PARTY. As a member of the Communist-KUOMINTANG alliance (1924–27), he directed the general strike (1927) in Shanghai. When CHIANG KAI-SHEK broke the alliance, Zhou joined the LONG MARCH (1934–35). He was the chief negotiator of a renewed peace (1936–46) with nationalist forces. After the establishment of a communist republic, Zhou became prime minister (1949–76) and foreign minister (1949–58). Although publicly supportive of the CULTURAL REVOLUTION, he protected many of its intended victims.

Zhu De (1886–1976) Chinese communist military leader. Zhu helped to overthrow (1912) the MANCHU dynasty. In 1922, he met ZHOU ENLAI and joined the Chinese Communist Party. In 1928, Zhu joined forces with MAO ZEDONG, and led his section of the Fourth Red Army on the LONG MARCH (1934–35). Commander in chief during the Second Sino-Japanese War, he retained the post after the establishment of a communist republic (1949). Zhu held several important party posts before being denounced during the CULTURAL REVOLUTION.

Zhukov, Georgi Konstantinovich (1896–1974) Soviet military commander and politician. Zhukov fought in the Russian Revolution (1917), and in the ensuing civil war (1918–20). During World War 2, he led the defence of Moscow (1941), and defeated the German siege of Stalingrad and Leningrad (1943). In 1945, Zhukov led the final assault on Berlin. After STALIN's death, he became defence minister (1955). Although supportive of Nikita KHRUSHCHEV's reforms, he was removed from office in 1957. He was rehabilitated in the 1960s, receiving the Order of Lenin in 1966.

Ziegler, Karl (1898–1973) German chemist. Ziegler shared the 1963 Nobel Prize in chemistry with Giulio Natta for research into POLYMERS. He discovered a technique that used a resin with metal ions attached as a catalyst in the production of POLYETHENE. He also conducted research into aromatic compounds and organometallic compounds.

ziggurat Religious monument originating in BABYLON and ASSYRIA. It was constructed as a truncated, stepped PYRAMID, rising in diminishing tiers, usually square or rectangular. The shrine at the top was reached by a series of ramps. Ziggurats date from 3000 to 600 BC and the one at UR still stands.

INTERNET

Zhou Enlai
▶ www.marxists.org

ZAMBIA

The Republic of Zambia is a landlocked country in S Africa. The country lies on the plateau that makes up most of S Africa. Much of the land is between 900 and 1,500m [2,950–4,920ft] above sea level. The Muchinga Mountains in the NE rise above this flat land.

Lakes include Bangweulu, which is entirely within Zambia, together with parts of lakes Mweru and TANGANYIKA in the N. Most of the land is drained by the ZAMBEZI – from which the country takes its name – and its two main tributaries, the Kafue and Luangwa. Occupying part of the Zambezi Valley and stretching along the southern border, Lake Kariba, which was dammed in 1961, is the largest artificial lake in Africa and the second largest in the world. It is 280km long, and 40km across at its widest point. Zambia shares Lake Kariba and the VICTORIA FALLS with Zimbabwe.

Grassland and wooded savanna cover much of Zambia. There are also swamps. Evergreen forests exist in the drier SW.

CLIMATE

Zambia lies in the tropics, although temperatures are moderated by the altitude. The rainy season runs between November and March, when the

rivers sometimes flood. N Zambia is the wettest region of the country. The average annual rainfall ranges from about 1,300mm [51in] in the N down to between 510 and 760mm [20–30in] in the S.

HISTORY

In c. AD 800, Bantu-speakers migrated to the area. By the late 18th century, Zambia was part of the copper and slave trade. European contact with Zambia began in the 19th century, when the explorer David LIVINGSTONE crossed the River Zambezi. In the 1890s the British South Africa Company, set up by the British financier and statesman Cecil RHODES (1853–1902), made treaties with local chiefs and gradually took over the area. In 1911 the company named the area Northern Rhodesia. In 1924 Britain took over the government of the country, and the discovery of large copper deposits led to an influx of Europeans in the late 1920s.

Following World War 2, the majority of Europeans living in Zambia wanted greater control of their government. Some favoured a merger with their southern neighbour, Southern Rhodesia (now Zimbabwe). In 1953 Britain set up a federation of Northern Rhodesia, Southern Rhodesia and Nyasaland (now Malawi). Local Africans opposed the federation, arguing that it concentrated power in the hands of the white minority in Southern Rhodesia. Their opposition proved effective and the federation was dissolved in 1963. In 1964 Northern Rhodesia became an independent nation called Zambia.

POLITICS

The leading opponent of British rule, Kenneth KAUNDA, became president in 1964. His government enjoyed reasonable income until copper prices crashed in the mid-1970s, but his collectivist policies failed to diversify the economy. In 1972 he declared the United Nationalist Independence Party (UNIP) the only legal party, and ended democratic rule.

Under a new constitution, adopted in 1990, elections were held in 1991 in which Kaunda was trounced by Frederick Chiluba of the

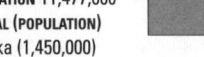

AREA 752,618sq km [290,586sq mi]
POPULATION 11,477,000
CAPITAL (POPULATION) Lusaka (1,450,000)
GOVERNMENT Multiparty republic
ETHNIC GROUPS Native African (Bemba, Tonga, Maravi/Nyanja)
LANGUAGES English (official), Bemba, Kaonda
RELIGIONS Christianity 70%, Islam, Hinduism
CURRENCY Zambian kwacha = 100 ngwee

Movement for Multiparty Democracy (MMD). Chiluba was re-elected in 1996, but he stood down in 2001 after an MMD proposal to amend the constitution to allow Chiluba to stand for a third term met with substantial popular and parliamentary opposition. In the 2001 elections the MMD candidate, Levy Mwanawasa, was elected president. In 2005 the Supreme Court rejected a challenge to his election, but stated that the 2001 ballot had been flawed. In 2006 Mwanawasa was re-elected, though opposition allegations of fraud led to violent unrest.

ECONOMY

Zambia holds 6% of the world's copper reserves and copper is the leading export, accounting for 49% of Zambia's total exports. Zambia also produces cobalt, lead, zinc, and various gemstones. The country's dependence on minerals has created problems, especially when prices fluctuate. Agriculture employs 69% of the workforce, compared with 4% in mining and manufacturing. Major food crops include cassava, fruits and vegetables, maize, millet and sorghum, while cash crops include coffee, sugar cane and tobacco.

The Copperbelt, centred on Kitwe, is the main urban region, while Lusaka provides the other major growth pole. Rural to urban migration has increased since 1964, but work is scarce. The production of copper products is the leading industrial activity. Other manufactures include beverages, processed food, iron and steel, textiles, and tobacco.

Z

Zimbabwe Republic in s central Africa. *See country feature*

zinc (symbol Zn) Bluish-white, metallic element of group II of the periodic table. Chief ores are SPHALERITE, smithsonite, and calamine. The German chemist Andreas Marggraf (1709–82) isolated it in 1746. Zinc is a vital trace element, found in ERYTHROCYTES (red bood cells), and is essential for growth in humans and animals. It is used in many alloys, including brass, bronze, nickel and soft solder. It is corrosive-resistant and used in galvanizing iron. Zinc oxide is used in cosmetics, pharmaceuticals, paints, inks, pigments, and plastics. Zinc chloride is used in dentistry and to manufacture batteries and fungicides. Properties: at.no. 30; r.a.m. 65.38; r.d. 7.133; m.p. 419.6°C (787.3°F); b.p. 907°C (1,665°F); most common isotope Zn^{64} (48.89%).

Zinnemann, Fred (1907–97) US film director, b. Austria. Zinnemann won his first Academy Award for the short film *That Mothers Might Live* (1938). He moved into commercial features, and won his second Oscar for the western *High Noon* (1952). Zinneman won a third award for *A Man For All Seasons* (1966). Other films include *From Here to Eternity* (1953) and *Julia* (1978). His autobiography *A Life in the Movies* was published in 1992.

zinnia Genus of chiefly annual plants native to North and South America. Most garden zinnias are varieties of *Zinnia elegans*, which has flower heads of all colours but blue and green. Height: to 91cm (3ft). Family Compositae.

Zinoviev, Grigori Evseyevich (1883–1936) Russian revolutionary. A self-educated lawyer, Zinoviev joined the BOLSHEVIKS in 1903, and was active in the RUSSIAN REVOLUTION OF 1905. He was a close collaborator of LENIN in exile (1908–17). In the RUSSIAN REVOLUTION (1917), Zinoviev voted against seizing power but remained a powerful figure in ST PETERSBURG and was appointed head of the COMMUNIST INTERNATIONAL in 1919. Although he sided with STALIN against TROTSKY in 1922, Zinoviev was later expelled from the party and eventually executed. The 'Zinoviev letter' (1924), urging the British Communist Party to revolt, may have contributed to the subsequent electoral defeat of the Labour government, but has since proved to be a forgery.

Zion Hill in E Jerusalem, Israel. Zion was originally the hill on which a Jebusite fortress was built. It now refers to the hill on which the TEMPLE was built. It is a centre of Jewish spiritual life and symbolic of the Promised Land.

Zionism Jewish nationalist movement advocating the return of Jews to the land of Zion (Palestine). Although it represents a desire expressed since the Jewish DIASPORA began in the 6th century BC the modern Zionist movement dates from 1897, when Theodor HERZL established the World Zionist Congress at Basel, Switzerland. In 1917, it secured British approval for its objective in the BALFOUR DECLARATION, and Jewish emigration to Palestine increased in the 1920s and 1930s. In 1947, the United Nations voted to partition Palestine between Jews and Arabs, leading to the foundation of the state of ISRAEL.

zircon Orthosilicate mineral, zirconium silicate ($ZrSiO_4$), found in IGNEOUS and METAMORPHIC rocks and in sand and gravel. It displays prismatic crystals. It is usually light or reddish brown, but can be colourless, grey, yellow or green. It is used widely as a gemstone because of its hardness and high refractive index. Hardness 7.5; r.d. 4.6.

zirconium (symbol Zr) Greyish-white, metallic element, one of the TRANSITION ELEMENTS. Zirconium was first discovered (1789) by the German chemist Martin Klaproth, and its chief source is ZIRCON. Lunar rocks collected during the Apollo space missions show a higher content of zirconium than Earth ones, and zirconium exists in meteorites and stars, including the Sun. Chemically similar to titanium, it is used in ceramics, and in alloys for wire and absorption of neutrons in nuclear reactors. Properties: at.no. 40; r.a.m. 91.22; r.d. 6.51; m.p. 1,852°C (3,366°F); b.p. 4,377°C (7,911°F); most common isotope Zr^{90} (51.46%).

zither STRINGED INSTRUMENT. It consists of a resonator in the form of a wooden box with 30 to 45 strings stretched over it. A few of the strings are stretched over a fretted board for melody; the rest are used for accompaniment. The melody strings are plucked with the fingers or a plectrum.

zodiac (Gk. 'circle of animals') Belt on the celestial sphere that forms the background for the motions of the Sun, Moon, and planets (except Pluto). The zodiac is divided into twelve **signs**, which are named after the constellations they contained at the time of the ancient Greeks: Aries, Taurus, Gemini, Cancer, Leo, Virgo, Libra, Scorpio, Sagittarius, Capricorn, Aquarius, and Pisces. The constellations inside the Zodiac do not now correspond to those named by the ancients, because precession of the Earth's axis has meanwhile tilted the Earth in a different direction. To modern astronomers, the zodiac has only historical significance. *See also* ASTROLOGY; ASTRONOMY

Zola, Émile Edouard Charles Antoine (1840–1902) French novelist. Zola became widely known following the publication of his third book, the novel *Thérèse Raquin* (1867). For the next quarter of a century, he worked on what became the Rougon-Macquart sequence (1871–93) – a 20–novel cycle telling the story of a family during the Second Empire; it established Zola's reputation as the foremost exponent of NATURALISM in fiction. The sequence includes his famous novels *The Drunkard* (1877), *Nana* (1880), *Germinal* (1885) and *The Human Animal* (1890). In 1898, he wrote a famous letter, beginning 'J'Accuse', which denounced the punishment of Alfred Dreyfus. This led to a brief exile in England and, after the vindication of Dreyfus, a hero's return. *See also* DREYFUS AFFAIR

Zollverein German customs union formed (1834) by 18 German states under Prussian leadership. By reducing tariffs and improving transport, it promoted economic prosperity. Nearly all other German states joined the Zollverein by 1867, despite Austrian opposition. It represented the first major step towards the creation of the German Empire (1871).

zoo (zoological gardens) Public or private institution in which living animals are kept and exhibited. Wild animals have been kept in captivity since the beginning of recorded history. Organized public zoos, sometimes called menageries or aquariums (for fish), have been operating for more than 500 years in Europe. Today, non-profit-making organizations or zoological societies run most zoos in a scientific manner. They are organized for public recreation as well as for scientific and educational purposes. The emphasis is on conservation of endangered species and exhibiting animals in natural settings.

zoology Study of animals; combined with BOTANY, it comprises the science of BIOLOGY. It is concerned with the structure of the animal and the way in which animals behave, reproduce and function, their evolution, and their role in interactions with humankind and their environment. There are various subdivisions of the discipline, including TAXONOMY, ECOLOGY, PALAEONTOLOGY, ANATOMY, and zoogeography (the distribution of animals). ANTHROPOLOGY is an extension of zoology. *See also* GENETICS; MORPHOLOGY

zoonosis Any infection or infestation usually found in VERTEBRATES that is capable of transmission to human beings.

zooplankton Animal portion of the PLANKTON. It consists of a wide variety of micro-organisms, including small CRUSTACEANS and larval forms of higher animals. It is an important constituent of the ocean's food chain. There are few levels or areas of the ocean that have no zooplankton.

Zoroaster (*c.*628–*c.*551 BC) (Zarathustra) Ancient Persian (Iranian) religious reformer and founder of ZOROASTRIANISM. At the age of 30, he saw the divine being AHURA MAZDAH in the first of many visions. Unable to convert the petty chieftains of his native region, Zoroaster travelled to E Persia, where in Chorasmia (now in Khorasan province, NE Iran) he converted the royal family. By the time of Zoroaster's death (tradition says that he was murdered while at prayer), his new religion had spread to a large part of Persia. Parts of the AVESTA, the holy scripture of Zoroastrianism, are believed to have been written by Zoroaster himself.

Zoroastrianism Religion founded by ZOROASTER in the 6th century BC. It was the state religion of PERSIA from the middle of the 3rd century AD until the mid-7th century. Viewing the world as divided between the spirits of good and evil, Zoroastrians worship AHURA MAZDAH as the

▲ **Zola** Born in Paris, the son of an Italian engineer, Émile Zola worked as a journalist before becoming a short-story writer and novelist. With Flaubert, the Goncourts, and Turgenev, he helped develop the 'naturalist school', which held that the novel should be strictly scientific. To this end, Zola employed scientific techniques and observations in his novels, often describing professions and lifestyles in minute, and sometimes sordid, detail. He died by accidentally inhaling charcoal fumes from a blocked chimney.

supreme deity, who is forever in conflict with Ahriman, the spirit of evil. They also consider fire sacred. The rise of Islam in the 7th century led to the decline and near disappearance of Zoroastrianism in Persia. Today, the PARSI comprise most of the adherents of Zoroastrianism, which has its main centre in MUMBAI, India.

Zsigmondy, Richard Adolf (1865–1929) Austrian chemist who received the 1925 Nobel Prize in chemistry for his work on COLLOIDS. While employed at a glass manufacturing company (1897–1900), Zsigmondy discovered a water suspension of gold, and proposed that the shape and size of colloids could be deduced from the way in which the particles scatter light. To aid such studies, he developed the ultra-microscope with Heinrich Siedentopf in 1903.

Zulu BANTU people of South Africa, most of whom live in KWAZULU-NATAL. They are closely related to the Swazi and the XHOSA. The Zulus have a patriarchal, polygamous society with a strong militaristic tradition. Traditionally cereal farmers, they possessed large herds of cattle, considered to be status symbols. Under their leader SHAKA, they fiercely resisted 19th-century colonialism. The predominant religion is now Christianity, although ethnic religions are still common. They are organized politically into the INKATHA movement under Chief Mangosutho BUTHELEZI.

Zululand Historic region of South Africa, now part of KWAZULU-NATAL

Zulu War (1879) Conflict in South Africa between the British and the ZULU. Fearing a Zulu attack, the Afrikaners of Transvaal requested British protection. The British High Commissioner demanded that the Zulu king, Cetewayo, disband his army. He refused, and the Zulu made a surprise attack at Isandhlwana, killing 800 British soldiers. Lacking modern weapons, the Zulu were checked at Rorke's Drift and decisively defeated at Ulundi.

ZIMBABWE

The Republic of Zimbabwe is a landlocked country in S Africa. Most of the country lies on a high plateau between the ZAMBEZI and LIMPOPO Rivers, between 900 and 1,500m [2,950–4,920ft] above sea level.

The principal land feature is the High Veld, a ridge that crosses Zimbabwe from NE to SW. HARARE lies on the north E edge, BULAWAYO on the SW edge. Bordering the High Veld is the Middle Veld, the country's largest region and the site of many large ranches. Below 900m [2,950ft] is the Low Veld. The country's highest point is Mount Inyangani, which reaches 2,593m [8,507ft] near the Mozambique border. Zimbabwe's best-known physical feature, Victoria Falls, is in the NE. The Falls are shared with Zambia, as too is the artificial Lake Kariba which is also on the River Zambezi.

Wooded savanna covers much of Zimbabwe. The Eastern Highlands and river valleys are forested. There are many tobacco plantations.

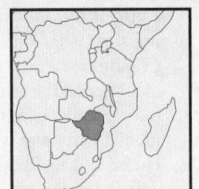

CLIMATE
The subtropical climate varies greatly according to altitude. The Low Veld is much warmer and drier than the High Veld. November to March is mainly hot and wet. Winter in Harare is dry but cold. Frosts have been recorded between June and August.

HISTORY
Bantu-speakers migrated to the region in AD 300. By 1200 the SHONA established a kingdom in

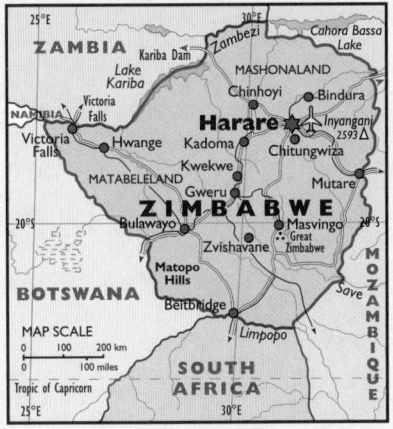

Mashonaland, E Zimbabwe. GREAT ZIMBABWE was the capital of this advanced culture. Portugal formed trading links in the early 16th century. In 1837 the Ndebele displaced the Shona from W Zimbabwe and formed Matabeleland. In 1855 David LIVINGSTONE made the first European discovery of VICTORIA FALLS. In 1888 Matabeleland became a British Protectorate. In 1889 the British South Africa Company, under Cecil RHODES, received a charter to exploit the region's mineral wealth. In 1896 the area became Southern Rhodesia. In 1923 it became a British Crown Colony. European settlers excluded Africans from the government and economy. In 1953 Southern Rhodesia, Northern Rhodesia (now Zambia), and Nyasaland (Malawi) were joined as the Central African Federation. In 1961 Joshua Nkomo formed the Zimbabwe African People's Union (ZAPU). In 1963 the federation dissolved and Zambia and Malawi acquired African majority governments. Southern Rhodesia became simply Rhodesia. Robert Mugabe formed the Zimbabwe African National Union (ZANU). In 1964 the white nationalist leader Ian Smith became prime minister. Nkomo and Mugabe were imprisoned.

POLITICS
In 1965 the European government of Southern Rhodesia (then known as Rhodesia) declared their country independent. However, Britain refused to accept this declaration. Finally, after a civil war, the country became legally independent in 1980.

After independence, rivalries between the Shona and Ndebele people threatened its stability. Order was restored when the Shona prime minister, Robert MUGABE, brought his Ndebele rivals into his government. In 1987 Mugabe became the country's executive president and, in 1991, the government renounced its Marxist ideology. In 1990 the state of emergency that had lasted since 1965 was allowed to lapse – three months after Mugabe had secured a landslide election victory. Mugabe was re-elected in 1996. In the late 1990s Mugabe began to seize white-owned farms without paying compensation to owners. His announcement caused much disquiet among white farmers. The situation worsened in the early 2000s when landless 'war veterans' began to occupy white-owned farms, resulting in violence and deaths. Food shortages

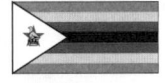

AREA 390,757sq km [150,871sq mi]
POPULATION 12,311,000
CAPITAL (POPULATION) Harare (1,527,000)
GOVERNMENT Multiparty republic
ETHNIC GROUPS Shona 82%, Ndebele 14%, other African groups 2%, mixed and Asian 1%
LANGUAGES English (official), Shona, Ndebele
RELIGIONS Christianity, traditional beliefs
CURRENCY Zimbabwean dollar= 100 cents

have become a major problem, with aid agencies blaming the land reform programme while the government blames drought.

In 2002, amid accusations of electoral irregularities, Mugabe was re-elected president. Mounting criticism of Mugabe led the Commonwealth to suspend Zimbabwe's membership. Zimbabwe declared that it had pulled out of the Commonwealth permanently. In 2004 the European Union renewed sanctions against the country. In 2006–7 the country's problems worsened as economic mismanagement led to crippling hyperinflation, and rising political opposition was brutally suppressed. In 2008 elections Mugabe and his party failed to gain a majority despite committing widespread fraud, but he refused to relinquish his hold on power.

ECONOMY
The World Bank classifies Zimbabwe as a 'low-income' economy. Its economy became significantly more diverse after the 1960s, having evolved to virtual self-sufficiency during the days of international sanctions between 1965 and 1980. After independence the economy underwent a surge in most sectors, with successful agrarian policies and the exploitation of the country's mineral resources. However, in the 2000s the economy collapsed and many people faced starvation.

Agriculture employs approximately 56% of the people. Maize is the chief food crop, while cash crops include cotton, sugar and tobacco. Cattle ranching is another important activity. Gold, asbestos, chromium and nickel are mined and the country also has some coal and iron ore. Manufactures include beverages, chemicals, iron and steel, metal products, processed food, textiles and tobacco. The principal exports include tobacco, gold, other metals, cotton and asbestos.

Z

Zuni PUEBLO Native Americans who live on the Zuni reservation in w New Mexico, USA. The present pueblo is on the site of one of the seven Zuni villages discovered by Marcos de Niza in the early 16th century and identified as the mythical Seven Cities of Cibola. In 1540, the CONQUISTADOR Coronado sacked the villages, and following a revolt in 1680 the Pueblo abandoned the site for fear of reprisal from the Spanish. Modern Zuni maintain their tradition and skills.

Zürich City on the River Limmat, at the NW end of Lake Zürich, in the foothills of the Alps, N Switzerland; the country's largest city. Conquered by the Romans in 58 BC the city later came under Alemanni and then Frankish rule. It became a free imperial city in 1218, and joined the Swiss Confederation in 1351. In the 16th century, it was a focal point of the Swiss REFORMATION. Ulrich ZWINGLI founded Swiss Protestantism at Zürich's cathedral in 1523. In the 18th and 19th centuries, the city developed as a cultural and scientific centre. It has the Swiss National Museum and many old churches. Zürich is the commercial hub of Switzerland and has numerous banking and financial institutions. Industries: motor vehicles, machinery, paper, textiles, electrical products, printing and publishing, tourism. Pop. (2005) 984,000.

Zwingli, Ulrich (1484–1531) Swiss Protestant theologian and reformer. Zwingli was ordained as a Roman Catholic priest in 1506, but his studies of the New Testament in ERASMUS' editions led him to become a reformer. By 1522, he was preaching reformed doctrine in ZÜRICH, a centre for the REFORMATION. More radical than Martin LUTHER, Zwingli regarded communion as mainly symbolic and commemorative. He died while serving as a military chaplain with the army of Zürich during a battle against the Catholic cantons at Kappel.

Zworykin, Vladimir Kosma (1889–1982) US physicist and inventor, b. Russia. A pioneer of TELEVISION, in 1929 Zworykin joined the Radio Corporation of America (RCA), becoming its director of electronic development and (in 1947) a vice president. Zworykin and his colleagues developed the iconoscope, the forerunner of the modern television camera tube, and the kinescope, a CATHODE-RAY TUBE for TV sets. In 1928, he patented a colour television system. He also invented the ELECTRON MICROSCOPE and developed a secondary emission multiplier for a sensitive radiation detector. In 1967, Zworykin received the National Medal of Science for his inventions and contributions to medical research.

zygote In sexual reproduction, a cell formed by fusion of a male and a female GAMETE. It contains a DIPLOID (two sets) number of CHROMOSOMES, half contributed by the SPERM, half by the OVUM. Through successive cell divisions, the zygote will develop into an EMBRYO.

Zyuganov, Gennady (1944–) Russian politician. During the 1970s and 1980s, Zyuganov moved up the Soviet Communist Party hierarchy, taking positions focused on ideology and propaganda. In 1993, he became chairman of the executive committee of the reconstituted Russian Communist Party and was elected to the State Duma (the lower House of the Russian Parliament). The Communist Party gained the largest number of votes in 1995 elections, and Zyuganov mounted a strong challenge in the 1996 presidential elections. He was defeated by a coalition of Boris YELTSIN and Aleksander LEBED.

Z

HISTORY
of the
WORLD

In creating this History of the World, every care has been taken to use accurate and informative dates. However, it is impossible to achieve 'definitive' dates when referring to events that occurred many thousands of years ago. Many early dates are derived from unreliable documents or based on archaeology, which can rarely give exact calendar years. Because of the uncertainties, many dates are prefixed by the abbreviation *c*. (*circa*) to indicate a date-range. Broadly speaking, the size of the date-range indicated by *c*. depends on the nature of the date: *c*.5500 BC means 6000 BC to 5000 BC; *c*.2500 BC means 2750 BC to 2250 BC. In more recent times, *c*. indicates a degree of uncertainty owing to the lack of definitive written records, hence *c*.1500 BC means 1600 BC to 1400 BC; *c*.1000 BC means 1050 BC to 950 BC; *c*.500 BC means 525 BC to 485 BC; *c*.250 BC means 255 BC to 245 BC; *c*.1281 means 1280 to 1282.

Other complications arise from the use of different dating systems by various peoples at different times in the past. Roman emperors measured their rule In regnal years that straddle our years, which can produce a plethora of unsatisfactory dates, such as 68/69, 138/139, 257/258, and so on, unless a firm hand is applied. Chinese emperors divided their reigns into named periods which could vary in length from 3 to 30 years, and many events are dated accordingly.

Even recent centuries are beset by chronological problems. The Russian Revolution of 1917, often called the 'October Revolution', occurred in November in the Gregorian (New Style) Calendar.

► *Acheulian* The Acheulian hand axe, which replaced the primitive chopper more than 1.5 million years ago, represented a fundamental advance in human technology. It was a general purpose tool, probably used to cut plant materials as well as butcher animals, and may also have carried symbolic social significance.

PREHISTORY

15,000 mya (million years ago)
According to the Big Bang theory, the Universe is formed.

4600 mya
The Earth is formed.

3800 mya
Simple single-celled life (bacteria) appears.

1200 mya
Complex single-celled plants and animals appear.

600 mya
Multi-cellular plants and animals appear.

560 mya
Beginning of Cambrian period of geological timescale, during which animals evolve eyes and jointed legs.

400 mya
The first land plants and animals appear.

220 mya
A massive extinction event wipes out 90% of species.

65 mya
An extinction event, probably caused by an asteroid impact, kills the land-living dinosaurs.

c.5 mya
Australopithicenes appear in s Africa.

c.2 mya
The most recent ice age starts; *Homo habilis* appears in SE Africa.

c.1.7 mya
Homo erectus appears in E Africa.

c.250,000 BC
Archaic *Homo sapiens* appears in E Africa.

c.200,000 BC
Homo neandethalensis appears in Europe and Asia.

c.150,000 BC
Modern *Homo sapiens* appears in E Africa.

c.55,000 BC
Modern *Homo sapiens* moves into Europe and Australia.

c.35,000 BC
Neanderthals become extinct in Europe.

ASIA AND AUSTRALASIA

15,000 BC

*c.*15,000 BC End of the coldest period of the most recent ice age.

*c.*10,000 BC Emergence of Natufian culture in the Middle East to the W of the River Euphrates, based on the intensive gathering of wild cereals.

*c.*10,000 BC Earliest firm evidence of domesticated dogs (from a grave in Palestine).

*c.*9000 BC Earliest-known permanent human settlements established by Natufian peoples; they build villages with circular houses in parts of the Middle East and Asia Minor.

*c.*9000 BC Sheep and goats are domesticated in the Middle East.

*c.*8500 BC Earliest-known rectangular houses are built in Mesopotamia.

*c.*8500 BC Wheat (einkorn and emmer) and barley are domesticated in the Middle East.

*c.*8500 BC End of the Palaeolithic period (Old Stone Age) in the Middle East.

*c.*8000 BC First pottery is made in China.

*c.*8000 BC Village of Jericho (on the West Bank of the River Jordan) has a population of *c.*1000, and is surrounded by a stone wall with a fortified tower.

*c.*7000 BC Cattle and pigs are domesticated in the Middle East.

*c.*7000 BC Pigs are domesticated in China.

*c.*7000 BC Tropical horticulture begins in the highlands of New Guinea.

c. 6500 BC Farming starts in the NE of the Indian subcontinent.

*c.*6000 BC Domestication of millet and broomcorn in N China and rice in S China; start of Yangshao culture.

*c.*5400 BC Start of the Early Ubaid period in Mesopotamia; beginnings of urbanization.

5000 BC

*c.*5000 BC First permanent settlement is established at Eridu (by tradition the first city) in Mesopotamia.

*c.*5000 BC Longshan culture emerges around the Shandong peninsula in N China.

*c.*4500 BC Zebu cattle are domesticated in Pakistan.

c. 4500 BC Permanent settlement is established at Ur in S Mesopotamia.

*c.*4300 BC Start of the Late Ubaid period in Mesopotamia; many cities are established and temples and ziggurats are built.

*c.*4200 BC Copper mining starts in Oman in SE Arabia.

*c.*4200 BC Elamites establish the city of Susa in present-day W Iran.

4000 BC

*c.*3500 BC Floodplain of the River Indus in present-day Pakistan is settled by farmers who use some copper tools; start of the Early Indus period (*c.*3500–*c.*2800 BC).

*c.*3500 BC Start of the Uruk period in S Mesopotamia; development of urban civilization.

*c.*3300 BC Sumerians (who probably originated in central Asia) settle in S Mesopotamia.

*c.*3300 BC City-states develop in Syria and Palestine.

*c.*3200 BC Bronze comes into widespread use for tools in Mesopotamia; start of the Bronze Age in the Middle East.

*c.*3100 BC End of the Uruk period in S Mesopotamia; start of the Jamdat Nasr period.

3000 BC

*c.*3000 BC Agriculture starts at oases in SE Arabia.

*c.*2900 BC First sizeable town is established on the site of Troy, NW Asia Minor.

*c.*2900 BC Start of the Early Dynastic period in Sumerian Mesopotamia; the first conflicts between rival city-states occur.

*c.*2800 BC Akkadians establish a kingdom to the N of Sumeria.

*c.*2800 BC Indus valley civilization emerges in present-day Pakistan.

*c.*2700 BC Reign of Gilgamesh, the legendary Sumerian king of Uruk.

*c.*2600 BC Domestication of breadfruit in SE Asia.

*c.*2600 BC Walled towns are built in N China.

AFRICA

*c.*15,000 BC End of the coldest period of the most recent ice age.

*c.*7500 BC Earliest-known African pottery is produced in S Sahara region.

*c.*6000 BC Wheat, barley, sheep and goats are introduced to Egypt from the N.

*c.*6000 BC Onset of dryer climatic conditions begins the desertification of the Sahara.

*c.*5500 BC Bullrush millet is domesticated in the Sahara.

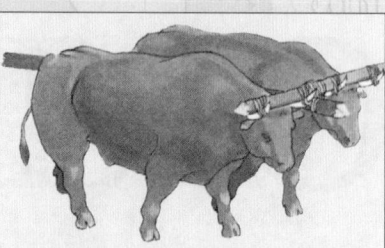

ox-drawn plough *The application of animal power to farming implements was a great advance in agricultural history. Primitive ploughs were drawn by a pair of oxen. The plough bar was tied to the centre of a bar of wood which was lashed to the horns of the animals.*

*c.*5000 BC Badarian culture emerges in central Egypt.

*c.*4500 BC Start of cattle herding in the Sahara; either with locally domesticated stock or with animals introduced via Egypt.

*c.*4250 BC Local sorghum and rice are domesticated in Sudan.

*c.*4000 BC Nagada culture emerges along the River Nile in Egypt.

*c.*4000 BC Donkeys are domesticated in Egypt.

*c.*3500 BC First fortified towns are built in Egypt; two distinct centres of urbanization emerge in Upper (S) and Lower (N) Egypt.

*c.*3100 BC Egypt is unified by King Menes (also known as Narmer) of Upper Egypt, who establishes a capital city at Memphis; start of the Early Dynastic period.

*c.*2800 BC Egyptian expeditions make first contact with Nubian cultures to the S.

2686 BC Early Dynastic period ends in Egypt; start of the Old Kingdom period (2686–2181 BC).

*c.*2550–*c.*2525 BC Great Pyramid is built for the Egyptian pharaoh Cheops (Khufu) at Giza.

◄ **The ancient Egyptians** worshipped a pantheon of anthropomorphic deities. These deities included (from left to right): Hathor, the mother-goddess; Bast, a god of fertility; and Thoth, the scribe.

EUROPE

*c.*15,000 BC End of the coldest period of the most recent ice age.

*c.*9500 BC Ice sheets start to melt in Europe and North America.

*c.*8500 BC End of Palaeolithic period in Europe; start of Mesolithic period (Middle Stone Age); bows and arrows come into widespread use.

*c.*6500 BC Farming (wheat, barley, goats and sheep) starts in Greece and the Balkans.

*c.*6400 BC Emergence of Karanovo culture in present-day S Bulgaria.

*c.*5400 BC Start of Vinca culture in present-day Bosnia.

*c.*5400 BC Farming spreads across the Hungarian Plain to central Europe.

*c.*5200 BC Farming starts in Spain.

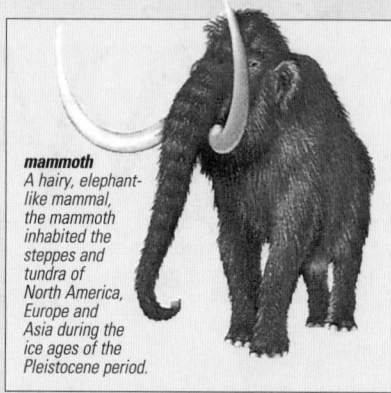

mammoth
A hairy, elephant-like mammal, the mammoth inhabited the steppes and tundra of North America, Europe and Asia during the ice ages of the Pleistocene period.

*c.*4500 BC Earliest megaliths are built in NW Europe to accommodate collective burials.

*c.*4500 BC Spread of farming reaches the Netherlands.

*c.*4400–4100 BC Extensive forest clearance takes place in Britain.

*c.*4400 BC Start of Gumelnita culture in present-day N Bulgaria and S Romania.

*c.*4250 BC Plough is first used in the Balkans.

*c.*4200 BC Horses are domesticated (for food) in Ukraine.

*c.*4000 BC Olives, figs, almonds and pomegranates are domesticated in the E Mediterranean region.

*c.*3800 BC Rise of TRB (*Trichterbecher*) farming culture in Denmark and N Germany and Poland.

*c.*3500 BC Copper mining starts near present-day Granada in S Spain.

*c.*3400 BC Earliest evidence of wheeled vehicles in Europe (from a grave in Poland).

*c.*3300 BC Megalithic temple is built at Tarxien, Malta.

*c.*3200 BC Farming spreads to S Sweden.

*c.*3200 BC The 'Man in the Ice', equipped with a cast copper axe, dies in a blizzard while crossing the Alps near the present-day Italian–Austrian border.

*c.*3100 BC First ritual earthworks are constructed at Stonehenge, England.

*c.*2500 BC Horses are introduced to Ireland.

*c.*2400 BC People of the Beaker culture begin migration from Spain to France, Germany and Britain.

*c.*2300 BC Start of Bronze Age in central Europe.

*c.*2100 BC Circle of bluestones at Stonehenge, England, is erected.

THE AMERICAS

*c.***15,000 BC** End of the coldest period of the most recent ice age.

*c.***9500 BC** Ice sheets start to melt in Europe and North America.

*c.***9200–***c.***8900 BC** Clovis period hunters are active in North America.

*c.***8500 BC** Disappearance of the ice-bridge across the Bering Strait ends first period of human migration into the Americas.

*c.***8900–8400 BC** Fulsom period hunters are active in North America.

*c.***8000 BC** Large mammals (including the mammoth and the horse) become extinct in North America.

*c.***7000 BC** Beans and squash are first cultivated in Peru.

7000 BC Start of the Archaic Period in Mesoamerican history.

*c.***5200 BC** Onset of drier climatic conditions on the Great Plains of North America forces people and animals to migrate E.

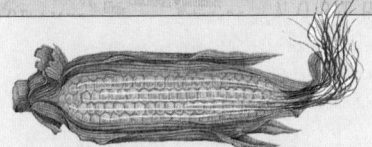

maize *Also known as corn or sweetcorn, maize was first cultivated in Central America, where it became central to the diet of most people. Because of its importance, it acquired a symbolic and religious significance.*

*c.***5000 BC** Guinea pigs are domesticated in Colombia.

*c.***4800 BC** Peoples from the Central American mainland become the first inhabitants of the Caribbean islands.

c. **4300 BC** A variety of cotton is domesticated in Mexico.

*c.***4000 BC** Llamas and alpacas are domesticated in Peru.

*c.***4000 BC** Maize is domesticated in Mexico.

*c.***3600 BC** First American pottery is produced in Guyana on N coast of South America.

c. **3500 BC** A variety of cotton is domesticated in lowland Peru.

*c.***3000 BC** Start of Old Copper Culture on S shore of Lake Superior; jewellery and other artifacts are produced from hammered native copper.

*c.***3000 BC** Chillis, avocados, groundnuts and sweet potatoes are domesticated in the coastal region of Peru.

*c.***2800 BC** Several varieties of potato are domesticated in highland Peru.

*c.***2600 BC** First temple mounds are constructed in Peru.

*c.***2400 BC** First Mesoamerican pottery is made.

*c.***2300 BC** Stone temple and ritual centre is built at La Galada in lowland Peru.

*c.***2200 BC** People in present-day SW USA first make pottery.

*c.***2200 BC** Domestication in present-day E USA of sunflowers, sumpweed, goosegrass and a variety of squash.

SCIENCE AND THE ARTS

*c.***15,000 BC** Bow and arrow (the bow consisting of a single piece of wood) is invented towards the end of the Palaeolithic period (Old Stone Age).

*c.***15,000–12,000 BC** Main period of European cave painting, including the sites of Lascaux in France and Altamira in Spain, although the earliest sites date from *c.*30–25,000 BC.

*c.***11,000 BC** World's earliest-known fired-clay vessels (bag-shaped pots) are made by hunter-gatherers in Japan.

*c.***10,000 BC** Jomon cord-marked pottery is first produced in Japan.

*c.***8500 BC** Earliest-known mudbricks are used to build houses in Mesopotamia.

*c.***7500 BC** Peoples living in Mesopotamia use fermentation to produce the earliest-known beer.

*c.***7000 BC** Shrine at Çatal Hüyük in central Asia Minor is decorated with sculpted bull's heads and goddess figures.

c. **7000 BC** Copper (lumps of naturally occurring native copper hammered and cut into shape with stone tools) is first used for jewellery in parts of the Middle East.

*c.***7000 BC** Pottery comes into general use in many parts of the Middle East.

*c.***6500 BC** Earliest-known textile (linen) is woven at Çatal Hüyük.

*c.***5400 BC** Farmers in N central Europe produce distinctive pottery vessels.

*c.***5500 BC** Copper smelting (the extraction of metal from ore) starts in Asia Minor and present-day W Iran. Start of the Chalcolithic (or Copper) Age in the Middle East.

*c.***5300 BC** Earliest-known complex buildings are constructed in Mesopotamia, with upper storeys and numerous internal rooms.

▶ **Sumeria** *This Sumerian vessel dates from c..3,500 BC. It was made of clay, one of the few materials available. The quality of their glazes and decorations was very advanced.*

*c.***5000 BC** Earliest-known canals are dug in Mesopotamia. They are used to irrigate crops and to drain marshy ground for settlement and cultivation.

*c.***5000 BC** *Thinker* (also known as the *Sorrowing God*) statue is carved at Cernavoda in present-day E Romania.

*c.***4800 BC** Stamp seals are first used to identify property and goods in Mesopotamia and SE Europe.

*c.***4500 BC** Ox-drawn plough is invented in Mesopotamia; crop farming is extended to soils too difficult to be worked with hand-held sticks.

*c.***4500 BC** Small clay tokens in different shapes are first used for accounting purposes in Mesopotamia.

*c.***4300 BC** Turntable (tournette or slow wheel) for pottery making is invented in N Mesopotamia.

*c.***4200 BC** First deliberate production of bronze (copper alloyed with arsenic or tin) occurs in present-day W Iran.

*c.***4000 BC** A burial at Varna in Bulgaria contains the earliest-known large deposit of gold objects (weighing more than 1.5kg/3.3lb).

*c.***4000 BC** By using the Nilometer (which measures the height of the River Nile's annual flood), the Egyptians calculate that the year is 365 days long.

*c.***4000 BC** First copper axes are produced in present-day W Iran and SE Europe.

*c.***3800 BC** Earliest-known metal tools with an integrally cast shaft-hole are made at Sialk, present-day NW Iran.

*c.***3800 BC** Wheel is invented in Mesopotamia; the first ox-drawn carts are used to transport agricultural produce.

*c.***3500 BC** Start of the Secondary Products Revolution in agriculture; widespread use of animal power, use of wool for textiles, and introduction of dairying.

*c.***3500 BC** First systematic use of pictographs for writing occurs in Sumeria (S Mesopotamia).

*c.***3400 BC** Potter's wheel (fast wheel) is invented in Mesopotamia.

c. **3400 BC** Cylinder seal is developed in Mesopotamia.

*c.***3200 BC** Walls of the so-called Stone Mosaic temple at Uruk are decorated with thousands of small, multicoloured, baked clay cones.

*c.***3200 BC** Food rations for workers in the city of Uruk are distributed in pottery bowls mass-produced in moulds.

*c.***3200 BC** Lost-wax technique (*cire perdue*) for casting metals is developed in Mesopotamia.

*c.***3000 BC** Hieroglyphic writing is first used in Egypt.

*c.***2850 BC** First Cycladic statues are produced on Mediterranean islands to the E of Greece.

*c.***2800 BC** Silkworms and mulberry trees are domesticated in China.

*c.***2700 BC** Earliest examples of Egyptian literature,containing spells, prophesies and moralistic tales, are written down on papyrus using a brush and ink.

*c.***2700 BC** Cuneiform writing (wedge-shaped marks made by pressing the end of a reed into clay tablets) is developed in Mesopotamia.

*c.***2650 BC** Egyptian architect Imhotep designs the world's earliest-known pyramid (the so-called stepped pyramid) for the pharaoh Zoser

*c.***2600 BC** Earliest-known glass is made for jewellery beads in Mesopotamia.

*c.***2600 BC** Earliest-known large-scale use of fired bricks occurs with the construction of the Indus valley cities of Harappa and Mohenjo Daro.

*c.***2500 BC** Earliest-known examples of Sumerian literature are written down at Abu Salabikh in Mesopotamia.

*c.***2500 BC** Reflex bow made from a composite of wood and horn is invented in N Mesopotamia.

*c.***2500 BC** Royal burials at Ur contain lavishly decorated musical instruments.

ASIA AND AUSTRALASIA

2500 BC

*c.*2500 BC Potters wheel is first used in China.

*c.*2500 BC One-humped dromedary camel in Arabia and two-humped Bactrian camel in central Asia are domesticated.

*c.*2400 BC City of Ebla in N Syria becomes a major trading and commercial centre.

2334 BC Akkadians under Sargon establish an empire in Mesopotamia.

*c.*2300 BC Indus valley civilization starts trade with Mesopotamia and the Arabian Gulf region via the port of Lothal.

2190 BC Akkadian empire collapses under attack from the nomadic Guti people.

2119 BC Utuhegal, king of Uruk, defeats the Gutians in battle and re-establishes Sumerian control.

2112 BC King Urnammu takes control of Mesopotamia and founds the Third Dynasty of Ur.

*c.*2100 BC Amorite nomads move into Mesopotamia from the E.

2004 BC Ur is destroyed by Elamites from present-day SW Iran.

2000 BC

*c.*2000 BC Start of the Bronze Age in China and SE Asia.

*c.*1994–1523 BC Xia dynasty establishes central control over city-states in N China.

*c.*1900 BC Start of the decline of the Indus valley civilization; collapse of international trade; port of Lothal is abandoned.

1830 BC Having taken over several Mesopotamian cities, Amorite king Sumuabum founds a new dynasty in Babylonia.

1792–1750 BC King Hammurabi of Babylonia extends Amorite control over all Mesopotamia.

*c.*1650 BC Hittites settle in Asia Minor and establish a capital at Hattusas.

*c.*1600 BC Chariots are introduced to China from central Asia.

*c.*1600 BC Start of Polynesian expansion by boat E from NE New Guinea.

*c.*1600 BC Aryan peoples begin migrating into the Indus valley region.

1595 BC Hittites sack Babylonia and establish temporary control in Mesopotamia.

*c.*1550 BC Hurrians in N Syria unite to create the kingdom of Mitanni.

1530 BC Kassites from present-day NW Iran invade Mesopotamia and take over Hammurabi's empire.

1523 BC Beginning of the Shang dynasty in China.

1500 BC

*c.*1500 BC Sabaeans establish a state in present-day Yemen, SW Arabia.

*c.*1400 BC Kassites from present-day NW Iran overthrow the Amorites and establish control in Mesopotamia.

*c.*1350 BC Hittites conquer the kingdom of Mitanni; the Hittite empire reaches its greatest extent under King Suppiluliumas (*c.*1380–*c.*1346 BC).

*c.*1300 BC Emergence of the first Assyrian empire in present-day S Syria.

1275 BC Battle of Kadesh in present-day Syria between the Egyptians and Hittites establishes the frontier between their empires.

*c.*1220–1190 BC East Mediterranean is raided by Sea Peoples, who weaken the Hittite empire.

*c.*1200 BC Hittite empire collapses under attacks from the Sea Peoples and the Assyrians.

1154 BC Kassites are conquered by the Assyrians, who extend their empire into S Mesopotamia.

*c.*1100 BC Rise of Phoenician city-states in present-day Lebanon, Palestine and Israel.

*c.*1100 BC Jews establish the kingdom of Israel in Palestine.

1076 BC First Assyrian empire reaches its greatest extent under King Tiglath-Pileser I (r.1114–1076 BC).

1030 BC End of the Shang dynasty in China; start of the Zhou dynasty.

1000 BC

*c.*1000 BC Polynesian expansion across the Pacific Ocean reaches Samoa and Tonga.

962 BC Solomon (r.962–922 BC) succeeds David (r.1000–962 BC) as king of Israel.

935 BC Second Assyrian empire is established by King Assurdan II.

*c.*900 BC Kingdom of Urartu is founded in present-day Armenia.

771 BC Western capital of the Chinese Zhou emperors is sacked by warrior nomads.

AFRICA

*c.*2500 BC Egyptians establish a trading post in Nubia, at Buhen near the second cataract of the River Nile

2181 BC End of Old Kingdom in Egypt; collapse of central control; start of the First Intermediate period.

2040 BC Pharaoh Menuhotep re-establishes central control in Egypt; end of the First Intermediate period; start of Middle Kingdom period (2040–1640 BC).

▶ **Bell beakers** *were a distinctive type of pottery introduced into England as the so-called Beaker Culture spread throughout Europe in the late 3rd millennium BC. They were buried as prestige objects with chieftains.*

*c.*2000 BC Egyptians conquer N Nubia.

*c.*1900 BC Egyptians establish a series of fortresses around the second cataract of the Nile to protect against raids by Nubians from Kush (present-day Sudan).

*c.*1700 BC Hyksos peoples from Palestine introduce horses into Egypt.

1640 BC Hyksos peoples establish control of the Nile delta region; end of the Middle Kingdom period; start of Second Intermediate period.

*c.*1550 BC Pharaoh Ahmose unites Egyptians and expels the Hyksos; end of the Second Intermediate period; start of the New Kingdom period.

*c.*1500 BC Egypt regains control of N Nubia.

*c.*1490 BC Queen Hatshepsut of Egypt (r.1494–1482 BC) sends expeditions to Punt (present-day Somalia).

*c.*1480 BC Following victory at the battle of Megiddo, Egypt conquers the city-states of present-day Lebanon and Israel; beginning of the Egyptian empire.

*c.*1450 BC Egyptians establish the fortified town of Napata in central Nubia, near the fourth cataract of the River Nile.

*c.*1360 BC Pharaoh Akhnaten (r.*c.*1379–1362 BC) unsuccessfully tries to replace traditional Egyptian religion with sun-worship.

*c.*1190 BC Sea Peoples attack Egypt, but are defeated by pharaoh Ramses III (r.*c.*1194–1163 BC).

1085 BC End of the New Kingdom period in Egypt; end of the Egyptian empire; start of the Late Period.

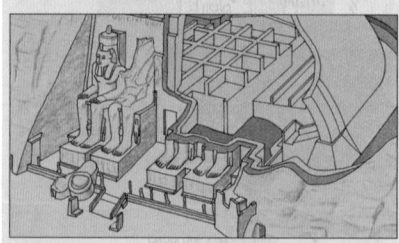

*c.*1000 BC Horses are introduced into sub-Saharan Africa via Egypt.

*c.*920 BC Nubian peoples establish Kush (capital Napata) as an independent state in present-day Sudan.

814 BC Traditional date for the founding of the city of Carthage, near present-day Tunis, by Phoenicians from the city of Tyre.

727 BC King Piankhi of Kush completes his conquest of Egypt and establishes the Kushite dynasty.

EUROPE

*c.*2300 BC Start of Bronze Age in central Europe.

*c.*2100 BC Circle of stones at Stonehenge, England, is erected.

*c.*2000 BC Farming cultures of SE Europe collapse, perhaps because of population movements.

*c.*2000 BC Rise of Urnfield culture in E central Europe.

*c.*2000 BC Greek-speakers migrate into Greece from the N.

*c.*2000 BC Start of Old Palace period of Minoan civilization in Crete.

*c.*1900 BC Large sarsen stones are added to Stonehenge in England.

*c.*1650 BC Mycenaean warlords establish control of Greek mainland and engage in long-distance trade with central and N Europe.

*c.*1620 BC Massive eruption of the Thíra volcano buries the city of Acrotiri on the island of Thíra.

*c.*1600 BC Cretan palaces are destroyed then rebuilt; start of the New Palace period of Minoan civilization.

◀ **camel** *There are two species of camel – the Arabian single-humped dromedary (left) and the two-humped Bactrian (far left)) of central Asia. Camels are well adapted to their desert environment: they are able to walk for eight days without drinking or eating by using up fat stored in their humps.*

*c.*1500–*c.*1200 BC Spread of Urnfield culture to Germany and Italy.

*c.*1450–1375 bc Mycenaeans conquer Crete; Minoan palaces are sacked.

*c.*1225 BC Legendary Trojan War ends with the capture of Troy by Greeks.

*c.*1200 BC Citadel at Mycenae is sacked; end of the Mycenaean civilization.

*c.*1100 BC Iron is first used in SE Europe and Italy.

*c.*1100 BC Etruscan peoples migrate into N Italy.

*c.*1050 BC Start of first period of Greek migration to Aegean islands and W coast of Asia Minor.

◀ **Abu Simbel** *is the location of two rock-cut sandstone temples built by Ramses II. In front of the façade of the Great Temple are four seated colossi of Ramses, two of which are shown here, each over 19m (62ft) high. Between 1963 and 1966, the temples and statuary were cut into some 1,000 blocks and reassembled on higher ground in order to prevent their disappearance under the waters of Lake Nasser, created by the construction of the Aswan High Dam.*

*c.*1000 BC Start of the Iron Age in S and central Europe.

*c.*900 BC Etruscan civilization emerges in N Italy.

*c.*800 BC Establishment of a town near salt and iron ore mines at Halstatt, Austria.

776 BC Traditional date for the founding of the Olympic Games.

753 BC Traditional date for the founding of Rome by Romulus and Remus.

*c.*750 BC Rise of city-states in mainland Greece.

THE AMERICAS

*c.*2400 BC First Mesoamerican pottery is made.

*c.*2300 BC Stone temple and ritual centre is built at La Galada in lowland Peru.

*c.*2200 BC People in present-day SW USA first make pottery.

*c.*2200 BC Domestication in present-day E USA of sunflowers, sumpweed, goosegrass and a variety of squash.

*c.*2000 BC Establishment of irrigated farming villages in coastal Peru, with terracing on mountainsides; start of Initial Period of South American history.

*c.*2000 BC People in present-day E USA first make pottery.

*c.*1800 BC People in Peru first make pottery.

*c.*1700 BC Ritual centre is established at Poverty Point, Louisiana (in present-day USA).

1500 BC Start of the Formative period in Mesoamerican history; beginnings of Olmec civilization on Mexico's Gulf coast.

*c.*1200 BC End of the Initial period in South American history; start of Early Horizon period; beginnings of Chavín culture in Andes region.

*c.*1150 BC Town of San Lorenzo becomes the Olmec political and ritual centre.

*c.*1000 BC Beginning of Adena culture in Ohio valley, present-day USA; it is also known as Early Woodland culture.

*c.*1000 BC Cultivation of maize is introduced to present-day SW USA from Mexico.

*c.*900 BC Olmec capital San Lorenzo, on Gulf coast of Mexico, is destroyed by warfare; the town of La Venta becomes the new political centre of the region.

*c.*850 BC Emergence of Zapotec civilization around the town of San Jose Mogote in the Oaxaca valley region of Mexico.

SCIENCE AND THE ARTS

*c.*2450 BC Vultures Steele is carved to commemorate the victories of the Sumerian king Eannatum of Lagash in Mesopotamia.

2350 BC Earliest-known law code is compiled for Urukagina, the Sumerian king of Lagash in S Mesopotamia.

*c.*2300 BC First houses with mains drainage are built in Indus valley cities.

*c.*2300 BC An as-yet-undeciphered script is developed in the Indus valley.

*c.*2225 BC Stone victory stela is carved to commemorate the military success of of the Akkadian king Naramsin.

*c.*2130 BC Stone statues of King Gudea of Lagash mark a brief revival of Sumerian art.

*c.*2100 BC Mathematicians in Mesopotamia divide a circle into 360 degrees in accordance with their 60-based number system.

*c.*2000 BC Egyptian scribes develop their cursive hieratic script.

*c.*2000 BC Minoans in Crete develop a pictographic writing system.

*c.*2000 BC Carved statue menhirs are erected in S France and N Italy.

*c.*1900 BC Earliest-known copy of the Epic of Gilgamesh is written down in Babylon, Mesopotamia.

*c.*1800 BC Horse-drawn, two-wheeled war chariot is invented on the SW fringes of the Eurasian steppes.

*c.*1780 BC Law code of King Hammurabi of Babylon is written down and publicized throughout his empire.

*c.*1700 BC Earliest-known Chinese script is used to pose questions on oracle bones thrown into a fire.

*c.*1600 BC Minoans in Crete begin to use the as-yet-undeciphered Linear A script.

*c.*1600 BC Hittites in Asia Minor develop the first iron-making techniques; the invention remains a Hittite 'secret weapon' for several centuries.

*c.*1500 BC Earliest-known alphabet is devised in the city of Ugarit in present-day Syria.

*c.*1500 BC Mycenaeans build beehive tombs in Greece.

*c.*1500 BC Earliest-known glass vessels are buried in an Egyptian pharaoh's tomb.

◄ *Minoan civilization* This period was noted for decorative pottery, frescos and costumes. The woman's costume shown here comprises a sleeved bodice, joined under bare breasts; the hip corselet and bell-shaped flounced skirt are tightly belted. The narrow-waisted effect is echoed in the man's costume – a simple loin cloth worn tightly belted. Bright materials, bracelets and fillets are worn by both.

*c.*1400 BC Mycenaeans in Crete begin to use Linear B script to write the Greek language.

1323 BC Pharaoh Tutankhamun (b.1341 BC) is buried in the Valley of the Kings near Luxor in Egypt.

*c.*1250 BC Rock-cut temple at Abu Simbel is constructed on the orders of pharaoh Ramses II (r.1290–1224 BC).

*c.*1200 BC Egyptian capital Memphis is the world's largest city with a population of up to one million.

*c.*1200 BC The *Vedas*, ancient and most sacred writings of Hinduism, are composed by the Aryan invaders of India.

*c.*1200 BC Start of the Iron Age in the Middle East – the breakup of the Hittite empire ends their monopoly on iron production.

*c.*1100 BC An alphabet is developed by Phoenicians in present-day Lebanon.

◄ *Minoan art* The prosperity of Minoan Crete provided the resources for monumental building and creative artistic achievement. The introduction of the potter's wheel allowed the Minoans to craft more elegant, symmetrical pottery. Designs tended to depict naturalistic scenes.

*c.*1000 BC Developments in Egyptian writing produce demotic script.

*c.*900 BC First Geometric-style pottery is produced in Athens.

*c.*900 BC Peoples of the Eurasian steppes invent the saddle and develop horse-archer cavalry.

*c.*900 BC *Brahmanas* and *Aranyakas*, ancient writings of Hinduism, are composed in India.

*c.*800 BC Latest date for the introduction of the Phoenician alphabet to Greece.

*c.*750 BC *Illiad* and *Odyssey* are written down in their final form, supposedly by the poet Homer.

*c.*750 BC City of Argos in Greece develops an army of hoplites – armoured citizen soldiers.

ASIA AND AUSTRALASIA

c.750 BC Start of the Iron Age in China and SE Asia.

722 BC Collapse of central control in China; Zhou emperors rule in name only; start of the Spring and Autumn period; rival states emerge.

c. 650 BC Scythian peoples from the steppes begin raiding the Middle East.

627 BC Under Chaldean rulers, the Neo-Babylonian kingdom breaks away from the Assyrian empire.

605 BC Medes and Neo-Babylonians under King Nebuchadnezzar II (d.562 BC) defeat the Assyrians at the battle of Carchemish; end of the Assyrian empire.

586 BC Neo-Babylonian empire conquers Jerusalem and destroys the Temple.

550 BC Cyrus the Great (600–529 BC) of Persia establishes the Persian Achaemenid dynasty.

550 BC Zoroastrianism, based on the teachings of Zoroaster (Zarathustra), becomes the state religion of the Persian empire.

546 BC Persians conquer the Greek cities in Asia Minor.

545 BC King Bimbisara of Magadha in the Ganges valley of India initiates a policy of expansion.

538 BC Persians capture Babylonia.

499–494 BC Greek-speaking cities in W Asia Minor revolt against Persian overlordship; Athens and Sparta lend assistance but the revolt is crushed.

c.460 BC State of Qin in W China is partitioned; end of the Spring and Autumn period.

449 BC Peace treaty signed between Athens and Persia.

c.420 BC Nabataeans establish a kingdom with its capital at Petra in present-day Jordan.

c.403 BC Start of Warring States period in China as rival states battle for overall control.

Persian soldiers *Roughly corresponding with modern-day Iran, Persia was ruled by a succession of strong military commanders, including Cyrus the Great (c.590–529 BC) and Alexander the Great (356–323 BC).*

c.400 BC The S Indian kingdoms of the Cholas and the Pandyas are established.

334 BC Alexander the Great (Alexander of Macedon, 356–323 BC) invades Persian Empire, defeats King Darius III (380–330 BC) at the River Granicus, and gains control of Asia Minor.

333 BC Alexander cuts the legendary Gordian knot, and defeats the Persians at the battle of Issus on the N border of Syria.

331 BC Victory over the Persians at the battle of Gaugamela gives Alexander control of Mesopotamia.

330 BC Alexander's troops burn the Persian royal palace at Persepolis; Darius is murdered by his bodyguard; end of the Persian empire.

c. 330 BC Chinese philosopher Mencius (Mengzi) (c.372–289 BC) expands and develops the ideas of Confucius.

AFRICA

671 BC Kushite dynasty overthrown by Assyrian conquest of Egypt.

664 BC King Psamtek I establishes a Saite dynasty in N Egypt under Assyrian overlordship.

c.620 BC Greek traders establish the port of Naucratis in the Nile delta.

c.600 BC Beginnings of Nok culture in the River Niger valley.

c.600 BC Phoenician seafarers circumnavigate Africa.

591 BC Saite dynasty sacks Napata; the capital of Kush moves to Meroë.

c.580 BC First African production of iron takes place in Meroë.

c.550 BC Kushite kingdom is extended S to present-day Khartoum.

525 BC Persians conquer Egypt.

c.500 BC Peoples from SW Arabia settle in Ethiopia.

c.500 BC Iron-working techniques reach W Africa.

480 BC Carthaginians under Hamilcar invade Sicily in support of Phoenician colonies on the island; they are defeated by Greek forces led by Gelon of Syracuse.

c.470 BC Carthaginians under Hanno explore W African coast.

460–454 BC Athens sends an expedition to support an Egyptian revolt against the Persians; the Greek troops are defeated in battle and wiped out.

Celtic soldier *Warfare was an essential part of Celtic life. Celtic soldiers, such as the one shown here, were armed with highly efficient iron weapons. They swept through central Europe in the fourth and third centuries BC.*

c.400 BC Start of migration E and S by iron-working Bantu farmers from W Africa.

331 BC Alexander the Great (Alexander of Macedon) invades Egypt, visits the oracle of Ammon at Siwa. and founds the city of Alexandria.

304 BC Ptolemy I (d.283 BC) establishes control over Egypt; start of Ptolemaic period.

EUROPE

734 BC Greek settlers found the city of Syracuse in Sicily.

730–710 BC City-state of Sparta in Greece conquers neighbouring Messenia.

669 BC Defeat by rival city-state Argos and revolt of subjugated Messenians (helots) causes militarization of Spartan society.

c.650 BC Greek colonies are established by the Black Sea.

621 BC Draco introduces a strict (hence draconian) law code in the Greek city-state of Athens.

c.600 BC Rome is conquered by the Etruscans.

600 BC Greek traders establish a colony at Massilia, S France.

594 BC Solon (c.639–c.559 BC) begins reforms in Athens.

c.580 BC Phoenicians establish colonies in W Sicily.

540 BC A Greek fleet is defeated by an alliance of Etruscans and Carthaginians near Corsica.

512 BC Persian armies invade Europe and occupy NE Greece.

509 BC Tarquin Superbus, last of the Etruscan kings of Rome, is expelled; start of Roman Republic.

507 BC Reforms of Cleisthenes mark beginnings of Athenian democracy.

499 BC Rome defeats neighbouring Latin cities at battle of Lake Regillus.

490 BC Persians under Darius I (r.521–486 BC) invade Greece, but are defeated by Athens and Sparta at the battle of Marathon.

480 BC Persians under Xerxes (r.486–465 BC) invade Greece and sack Athens after the battle of Thermopylae; they are defeated by a Greek fleet at the battle of Salamis.

479 BC Persians are defeated at the battle of Plataea and driven from Greece.

477 BC Foundation of Delian League; start of Athenian empire under Cimon's leadership.

464 BC Earthquake in Sparta followed by a helot revolt.

461 BC Pericles (490–429 BC) leads democratic revolution in Athens.

461–451 BC First Peloponnesian War is fought between Athens and Sparta.

445 BC Athens and Sparta sign the Thirty Year Peace agreement.

431 BC Start of the Second, or Great, Peloponnesian War between Athens and Sparta.

425–424 BC Sparta and its ally Thebes win a series of victories against Athens.

421 BC Peace of Nicias between Athens and Sparta fails to end hostilities.

415–413 BC Athenian naval expedition to capture Sicily ends in defeat and disaster.

411 BC Sparta makes an alliance with Persia against Athens.

411 BC Council of Four Hundred takes control in Athens.

405 BC Persia destroys the Athenian fleet at battle of Aegospotami.

404 BC Athens surrenders to Sparta; end of Second Peloponnesian War.

396 BC Start of the Corinthian War, in which Sparta fights against Athens and Corinth allied with Persia.

396 BC Romans capture the Etruscan city of Veii.

390 BC Rome is sacked during a Celtic raid into central Italy.

386 BC King's Peace ends the Corinthian War; Persia regains control of the Greek cities in Asia Minor.

371 BC Thebes allied with Athens defeats Sparta at battle of Leuctra; end of Spartan power; Thebes becomes the dominant city-state in Greece.

359 BC Philip II (382–336 BC) becomes king of Macedon.

355 BC Athenian orator Demosthenes (383–322 BC) denounces the growing power of Philip II of Macedon.

343 BC Rome fights the First Samnite War.

THE AMERICAS

*c.*850 BC Temple centre at Chavín de Huántar is established in Peru.

*c.*700 BC Abandonment of the ritual centre at Poverty Point, Louisiana, marks the end of the Archaic period in North American history.

*c.*600 BC Mayan people start the construction of the city of Tikal in present-day Guatemala.

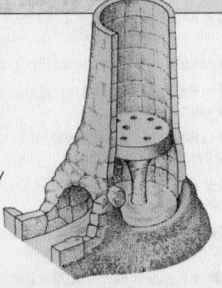

Etruscan kiln
The wealth of the Etruscan civilization was based on their iron-working skills. This Etruscan iron-smelting kiln dates from the 7th century BC. It probably provided iron for the grave goods found in their elaborate tombs.

*c.*500 BC Emergence of Paracas culture in s Peru.

*c.*500 BC Zapotecs build a new ritual and political centre at Monte Albán.

Acropolis, Athens
The Archaic Acropolis was sacked by the Persians in 480 BC. All the buildings shown here date from the rebuilding project of Pericles in the 5th century BC. Construction was interrupted by the Peloponnesian War.

*c.*400 BC Start of Nazca culture in coastal s Peru.

*c.*400 BC Sack of the Olmec capital La Venta and collapse of Olmec power; start of Late Formative period in Mesoamerican history.

SCIENCE AND THE ARTS

*c.*750 BC Start of the Halstatt period of Celtic art.

*c.*730–*c.*680 BC Orientalizing period of Greek art.

*c.*720 BC First black-figure pottery is produced in Athens.

*c.*700 BC Greek author Hesiod writes *Theogeny* and *Works and Days*.

*c.*700 BC Coinage is invented in Greek colonies in SW Asia Minor.

*c.*700 BC Etruscans adopt the Greek alphabet.

*c.*690 BC Sabaeans complete the Marib dam in present-day Yemen.

*c.*600 BC Development in present-day Mexico of Zapotec pictograph writing.

*c.*600 BC *Upanishads*, texts of Hinduism, are compiled in India.

585 BC Thales of Miletus (636–546 BC) predicts an eclipse of the Sun; this traditionally marks the beginning of Greek philosophy.

*c.*575 BC Etruscan engineers dig the Cloaca Maxima sewer in Rome.

*c.*570 BC Death of the Greek poet Sappho.

*c.*563 BC Birth of Siddhartha Gautama (d.483 BC) – the Buddha.

*c.*560 BC Death of Aesop (b.*c.*620 BC), reputed author of animal fables.

*c.*557 BC Indian teacher Mahavira (*c.*599–527 BC) develops the philosophy of Jainism.

551 BC Birth of the philosopher Confucius (d.479 BC) in China

*c.*550 BC Method for mass-producing cast iron is invented in China.

*c.*534 BC First Greek tragedy is written by Thespis.

531 BC Death of the Chinese philosopher Lao Tzu (b.604 BC), the founder of Taoism.

*c.*530 BC Red-figure pottery replaces black-figure pottery at Athens.

*c.*530 BC Greek philosopher Pythagoras (*c.*580–500 BC) moves from the island of Samos to Croton in Italy.

SCIENCE AND TECHNOLOGY

*c.*500 BC First Chinese coins are manufactured, in the shapes of miniature tools.

*c.*430 BC Earliest-known woven wool carpet is buried with a Scythian chief in s Siberia.

*c.*425 BC Greek philosopher Democritus (460–370 BC) theorizes that all matter is made of very small atoms.

423 BC Greek astronomer Meton proposes inserting extra months into a 19-year cycle to align the calendar.

*c.*400 BC Horse-collar is invented in China.

*c.*400 BC Crossbow is invented in China.

335 BC Greek scientist and philosopher Aristotle (384–322 BC) founds the Lyceum in Athens.

*c.*325 BC Indian mathematicians add a symbol for zero to their numerals 1–9 to create a decimal positional number system.

*c.*325–300 BC Influenced by Alexandria, many Greek cities are built (or existing ones rebuilt) on a grid pattern.

*c.*310 BC First Roman aqueduct, the Aqua Appia, is completed.

ARTS AND HUMANITIES

*c.*490 BC Multicoloured enamelled bricks are used to decorate the palace of Darius I at Susa.

*c.*490 BC Start of the Classical period of Greek art.

487 BC Comedies are entered for the first time in literary competition in Athens.

476 BC Greek poet Pindar (522–438 BC) visits Sicily at the invitation of the tyrant Hiero I of Syracuse.

*c.*475 BC Bronze statue of a *Charioteer* (from Delphi) is cast in Greece.

*c.*458 BC Greek dramatist Aeschylus (525–456 BC) completes the *Oresteia*.

450 BC Greek philosopher Xeno publishes his logical paradoxes.

*c.*445–438 BC Parthenon in Athens is rebuilt under the direction of the sculptor Phidias (490–430 BC).

430 BC Greek dramatist Sophocles (496–406 BC) writes *Oedipus Rex*.

425 BC Greek historian Herodotus (b. *c.*485 BC) dies at Thurii in s Italy.

415 BC Greek dramatist Euripides (480–406 BC) writes *Trojan Women*.

405 BC Greek dramatist Aristophanes (448–380 BC) writes the comedy *Frogs*.

500 BC

399 BC Greek philosopher Socrates (b.469 BC) is condemned to commit suicide by drinking hemlock having been found guilty of corrupting Athenian youth.

395 BC Greek historian Thucydides (460–400 BC) publishes *History of the Peloponnesian War*.

387 BC Greek philosopher Plato (427–347 BC) founds his Academy at Athens.

377 BC Death of Hippocrates of Cos (b.460 BC), who is considered to be the father of western medicine.

*c.*350 BC Greek theatre at Epidaurus is built.

*c.*330 BC Start of the Hellenistic period in European and w Asian art.

*c.*320 BC Nabataeans construct the first of the monumental rock-cut tombs at Petra.

400 BC

ASIA AND AUSTRALASIA

329 BC Alexander invades Bactria and Sogdiana; he founds cities and attempts to establish control over local rulers.

327 BC Alexander crosses Hindu Kush mountains, invades NW India and defeats King Poros at battle of Hydaspes.

325 BC Alexander leads his army back to Persia.

323 BC Alexander dies in Babylon.

321 BC Chandragupta (d.297 bc) takes over kingdom of Magadha in N India; start of Mauryan Empire.

312 BC Seleucus I (d.281 bc) establishes control of Asia Minor, Persia and Alexander's e conquests; start of Seleucid Empire.

303 BC Seleucus loses control of Indus valley region and present-day s Afghanistan to Mauryan empire.

c.300 BC Settlers from Korea introduce agriculture into Japan.

BCEc.280 BC King Bindusara (r.298–c.270 BC) extends the Mauryan empire into central India.

c.260 BC King Eumenes (r.263–241 BC) establishes Pergamum in s Asia Minor as an independent kingdom.

256 BC Sickened by the excesses of warfare, King Ashoka (r.264–238 bc) declares Buddhism to be the state religion of the Mauryan empire.

256 BC Qin dynasty begins the overthrow of the Zhou dynasty in China.

c.250 BC Diodotus, ruler of Bactria, breaks away from the Seleucid empire.

c.250 BC Emergence of Theravada (Hinayana) Buddhism in s India.

248 BC Parthian leader Arsaces I revolts against Seleucid rule in NE Persia; beginnings of the Parthian empire.

238 BC King Attalus I of Pergamum defeats the Galatian Celts in Asia Minor.

221 BC Qin king, Qin Shihuangdi (259–210 BC), completes the conquest of other Chinese states and declares himself emperor of China.

210 BC Death of Chinese emperor leads to collapse of central power and civil wars.

c.210 BC Seleucids make unsuccessful attempt to regain control of Bactria and N India.

c.210 BC Emergence of Mahayana Buddhism in N India.

c.209 BC Nomadic Hun tribes (known to the Chinese as Xiongnu) form a confederation to the N and W of China.

202 BC Liu Bang declares himself emperor of China; start of the Han dynasty.

190 BC Artaxiad I establishes the independent Kingdom of Armenia.

187 BC Collapse of the Mauryan empire in India; in the River Ganges valley region the Sunga dynasty seizes control.

171 BC Revolt by Eucratides in Bactria establishes rival Indo-Greek kingdoms in NW India.

171 BC Parthian king Mithridates I (r.171–138 BC) establishes complete independence from the Seleucid empire.

170 BC Nomadic warriors Xiongnu (Huns) drive the Yueh-chi confederation from the steppe N of China.

167 BC Led by Judas Maccabaeus (d.161 BC), the Jews revolt against Seleucid rule.

160 BC Wu Ti (d.86 BC) becomes emperor of China and begins a series of campaigns against the Huns.

c.150 BC Nomadic Sakas (related to the Scythians) begin settling in parts of present-day Afghanistan.

141 BC Parthians capture the Seleucid capital; end of Seleucid control of Persia and Mesopotamia.

136 BC Confucianism is adopted as the state ideology in China, largely as a result of the work of the philosopher and scholar Dong Zongshu (179–104 BC).

133 BC Kingdom of Pergamum is bequeathed to the Romans by its last king, Attalus III (r.138–133 BC).

115 BC Chinese envoy Zhang Qian travels to Parthia to trade silk for horses.

111 BC Chinese emperor establishes control over sw China and Annam (present-day N Vietnam).

102 BC China achieves temporary control of the oases of the Tarim Basin in central Asia.

92 BC First official contact between the Parthian and Roman empires takes place in Mesopotamia.

AFRICA

295 BC Independent kingdom of Meroë is established in present-day Sudan.

274–217 BC Four wars are fought between Ptolemaic Egypt and Seleucid Persia for control of Palestine.

256 BC Romans invade North Africa and march on Carthage.

255 BC Spartan-trained Carthaginian troops crush the Roman invaders.

c.250 BC Dromedaries (one-humped camels) are introduced into Egypt.

204 BC Roman general Scipio Africanus Major (236–183 BC) invades Africa.

202 BC Scipio defeats the Carthaginians at the battle of Zama s of Carthage; end of the Second Punic War.

168 BC Seleucid king Antiochus IV (r.175–164 BC) invades Egypt, but retreats after being intimidated by a Roman envoy.

150 BC A Carthaginian army is wiped out in battle against the forces of King Masinissa (238–149 BC) of neighbouring Numidia.

149 BC Romans lay siege to Carthage; start of the Third Punic War.

146 BC Carthage falls to the Romans; the city is razed to the ground; end of the Third Punic war.

112 BC War breaks out between Rome and Numidia.

106 BC Roman troops commanded by General Gaius Marius defeat the Numidians led by King Jugurtha (156–106 BC).

c.100 BC Aksumite state established in present-day Ethiopia and Eritrea.

EUROPE

340 BC Athenians declare war on Philip.

338 BC Victory against Athens at the battle of Chaeronea establishes Philip II of Macedon as sole ruler of Greece; end of independent Greek city-states.

336 BC Philip dies during an attempted invasion of Persia; he is succeeded by his son Alexander III (also known as Alexander the Great or Alexander of Macedon).

327–304 BC During the Second Samnite War, Roman control expands into central Italy.

323 BC Start of power struggle between various contending successors (the Diadochi) to Alexander the Great.

295 BC Romans defeat an Etruscan/Samnite confederation at the battle of Sentinum.

280 BC King Pyrrhus of Epirus (c.319–272 BC) sends troops to Italy to help the Greek-speaking cities resist Roman expansion.

279 BC Celts pillage the sacred Greek shrine at Delphi.

275 BC Pyrrhus withdraws his support, and s Italy falls under Roman control.

264 BC First Punic War (between Rome and Carthage) breaks out over Roman intervention in Sicily.

260 BC First Roman naval battle (against the Carthaginians at Mylae) results in victory.

241 BC Roman naval victory off the Aegates Islands ends the First Punic War; Rome gains Sicily.

c.238 BC Hamilcar Barca (d.228 BC) revives Carthaginian power in E Spain.

237 BC Rome conquers Sardinia and Corsica from the Carthaginians.

225 BC Romans defeat the Celts at battle of Telamon in N Italy.

219 BC Romans gain control of E coastline of the Adriatic Sea.

218 BC Carthaginians from Spain under Hannibal (247–183 BC) invade Italy by crossing the Alps; start of the Second Punic War.

217 BC Hannibal defeats the Romans at battle of Lake Trasimene.

216 BC Massive victory over the Romans at the battle of Cannae gives Hannibal control of s Italy.

211 BC Hannibal makes unsuccessful attempt to capture the city of Rome.

211–206 BC Roman victories bring much of Spain under Roman control.

202 BC Rome gains Spain at the end of the Second Punic War.

197 BC Roman victory at the battle of Cynoscephalae ends the Second Macedonian War (200–197 BC).

196 BC Seleucid king Antiochus III (r.223–187 BC) occupies NW Greece.

191 BC Roman victory at the battle of Thermopylae drives the Seleucids from Europe.

190 BC Roman victory at Magnesia reduces Seleucid power in Asia Minor.

190–180 BC Roman troops force the Celts out of N Italy.

168 BC Roman victory at the battle of Pydna ends the Third Macedonian War (171–168 BC).

151 BC While suppressing a revolt in Spain, the Romans massacre 20,000 men in the city of Cauca.

148 BC Macedonia becomes a Roman province.

146 BC Cities in Greece rise against Roman rule; after they are defeated, the city of Corinth is sacked and razed to the ground as punishment.

133 BC Tiberius Gracchus (c.163–133 BC) attempts land reforms in Rome.

122 BC Gaius Gracchus (c.153–121 BC, brother of Tiberius) makes further attempts at land reform.

121 BC Southern Gaul (France) is incorporated into the Roman empire.

102–101 BC General Gaius Marius (157–86 BC) defeats the Cimbri and Teutones – Germanic tribes that had invaded s Gaul.

88 BC Mithridates VI of Pontus invades N Greece and liberates Athens from Roman control.

300 BC

200 BC

100 BC

THE AMERICAS

*c.*300 BC Domestication in present-day E USA of knotweed, maygrass and little barley.

*c.*300 BC Maya build cities in the lowland region of Peten in Guatemala.

The Romans *The toga was the principal form of civil attire for both men and women during the Roman empire (500 BC–AD 400). Later on, tunics were worn.*

*c.*200 BC Start of Hopewell culture in the Ohio valley region of present-day USA; it is also known as Middle Woodland culture.

*c.*200 BC Emergence of the Zapotec state in present-day Mexico.

*c.*200 BC Decline of the ritual centre at Chavín de Huántar.

SCIENCE AND TECHNOLOGY

*c.*300 BC Museum and Great Library are founded at Alexandria, Egypt.

*c.*290 BC Greek mathematician Euclid (*c.*330–260 BC) publishes *The Elements*, which codifies the mathematical knowledge that the Greeks had inherited from the Babylonians and Egyptians.

*c.*280 BC King Ptolemy II (r.284–246 BC) of Egypt completes a canal between the Mediterranean Sea and the Red Sea and builds a lighthouse at Alexandria.

*c.*275 BC Greek astronomer Aristarchus (*c.*310–230 BC) of Samos proposes that the Earth orbits the Sun.

*c.*260 BC Roman naval architects invent the *corvus* – a weighted gangplank for boarding enemy ships in battle.

*c.*240 BC Greek astronomer Eratosthenes (*c.*276–194 BC) of Cyrene calculates the tilt of the Earth's axis.

238 BC Ptolemy II orders the length of the year in the Egyptian calendar revised from 365 days to 365.25 days.

*c.*214 BC Chinese emperor Qin Shihuangdi orders existing scattered fortifications to be joined together to make the Great Wall.

212 BC Greek mathematician and engineer Archimedes (b. 287 BC) is killed during the Roman attack on Syracuse in Sicily.

193 BC Newly invented concrete is used to build the Porticus Aemilia in Rome.

*c.*130 BC Greek astronomer Hipparchus (d.127 BC) discovers the precession of the equinoxes.

119 BC Iron-making and salt production become state monopolies in China.

86 BC Crop rotation introduced in China.

ARTS AND HUMANITIES

*c.*315–*c.*305 BC Menander (342–292 BC) writes plays in the New Comedy style in Athens.

307 BC Epicurus (341–270 BC) founds a school of philosophy in Athens.

300 BC Zeno of Citium (*c.*334–*c.*262 BC) founds the Stoic school of philosophy, which meets under a stoa (portico) in Athens.

*c.*250 BC Development in present-day Mexico of Mayan hieroglyphs.

241 BC First play in Latin (translated from a Greek original) is performed in Rome.

*c.*240 BC Ashoka builds the Great Stupa at Sanchi, India.

*c.*220 BC Roman dramatist Plautus (*c.*254–184 BC) completes his first comedy.

*c.*220 BC Work starts on the construction of the 7,000-strong terracotta army that is to be buried alongside the Qin emperor of China, Qin Shihuangdi.

204 BC Poet Ennius (239–169 BC), author of the *Annals*, is brought to Rome by Cato the Elder (234–149 BC).

202 BC Fabius Pictor publishes the first history of Rome (in Greek).

*c.*200 BC Greek influence produces the Gandaharan art style in NW India.

*c.*200 BC Earliest of the Dead Sea Scrolls is written.

196 BC Tri-lingual Rosetta Stone is inscribed in Egypt to record the gratitude of the priests of Memphis to King Ptolemy V.

*c.*190 BC *Victory of Samothrace* statue is carved in Greece.

*c.*165 BC Plays of Terence (190–159 BC) become popular in Rome.

124 BC Confucian university is established in China to prepare students for work in the civil service.

*c.*120 BC *Venus de Milo* statue is carved in Greece.

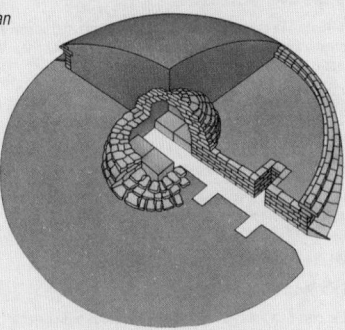

Etruscan tomb *The Etruscan cult of the dead led to the construction of elaborate tombs, usually a vault of overlapping stones covered with a mound of earth. Inside, the walls and ceilings were brightly painted with figures from religion or Greek literature, or depictions of the banqueting and dancing that accompanied a funeral. The corpses were placed in sarcophagi and accompanied by funerary urns and offerings.*

55 BC Publication in Rome of *On the Nature of Things* by the poet and philosopher Lucretius (*c.*95–55 BC).

ASIA AND AUSTRALASIA

91 BC Huns inflict a crushing defeat on a Chinese army in central Asia.

90 BC Sakas under Maues capture Taxilla in present-day Pakistan and occupy parts of the Indus valley.

89 BC King Mithridates VI (r.120–63 BC) of Pontus in Asia Minor forms an anti-Roman coalition.

73 BC Fall of Sunga dynasty in India. Kanva dynasty takes control of Magadha, the last remnant of the Mauryan empire.

66–63 BC Roman general Pompey (106–48 BC) conquers the remnants of the Seleucid empire in Asia Minor and Syria.

58 BC Azes I becomes Saka ruler in N India; start of the Vikram era.

57 BC Kingdom of Silla is established in S Korea during a period of decreased Chinese influence.

c.50 BC Romans begin trade with India for spices and Chinese silk.

c.50 BC Kushans under Kujula Kadphises emerge as the leaders of the Yueh-chi confederation and begin the takeover of Saka India; start of the Kushan empire.

43 BC Huns make peace with the Chinese empire.

37 BC Herod the Great (7–04 BC) is made King of Judaea by the Romans.

c.10 BC Last of the Indo-Greek kingdoms is overthrown by the Sakas.

c.10 BC Satavahana dynasty replaces the Kanvas in India's Magadha kingdom.

c.4 BC Birth of Jesus Christ in Bethlehem.

AD 1

AD 8 Regent Wang Mang (33 BC–AD 23) appoints himself emperor of China and begins radical reforms; end of the Former Han dynasty.

23 Rebels kill Wang Mang; a Han emperor is restored in China; start of Later Han dynasty.

30 Jesus Christ is crucified outside Jerusalem.

53 Tiridates I (d.75) becomes king of Armenia and founds the Arsacid dynasty.

53–63 Roman general Corbulo (d.67) campaigns unsuccessfully against the Parthians over control of Armenia.

70 Roman legions under General Titus (39–81) sack Jerusalem and destroy the temple while crushing a Jewish revolt.

78 Accession of King Kaniska (d.103) marks the highpoint of the Kushan empire in N India and S central Asia.

90 Chinese troops under General Ban Chao curtail Kushan expansion in central Asia.

c.95 Nahapana, the Kushan-appointed Saka satrap (governor) of W India forms an independent state.

97 Chinese military expedition attempts to establish control over the Silk Road to the Middle East; an advance party reaches the Black Sea.

c.100 Buddhism spreads to China via central Asia.

100

106 Romans annex the Nabataean kingdom – the Roman province of Arabia is created.

114–16 Roman emperor Trajan invades Parthia and occupies Armenia and Mesopotamia – the Roman empire reaches its greatest extent.

117 Hadrian abandons Armenia and Mesopotamia.

c.130 Saka state in W India establishes control over the city of Ujain in central India.

132–35 Second Jewish revolt against the Romans.

138 Independent kingdoms of Palmyra in Syria and Elymais in SW Persia attempt a trade alliance to circumvent the Parthian empire.

c.150 Huns drive the Chinese out of Central Asia.

166 Roman merchants visit China for the first time.

162 Lucius Septimius Severus (146–211) leads a Roman campaign against the Parthians.

168 Romans capture from the Parthians the trade centre of Dura Europos near the end of the Silk Road in Mesopotamia.

184 Yellow Turbans rebellion breaks out in China.

AFRICA

c.100 BC Camels are introduced into the Sahara desert.

46 BC Romans found a new city of Carthage on the site of the Phoenician city.

30 BC Following the suicides of Antony and Cleopatra, Egypt becomes a province under Roman control.

c.25 BC Kushites from Meroë invade S Egypt; a Roman reprisal raid sacks Napata.

> "I sing of arms and of the hero who first came from the shore of Troy, exiled by Fate, to Italy and its Lavinian shore."
>
> Virgil (Aeneid)

AD c.15 Death of King Natakamani of Meroë (ruled from c.15 BC), who built the Lion Temple at Naqa.

40 Roman emperor Gaius (Caligula) annexes Mauretania (present day Algeria and Morocco).

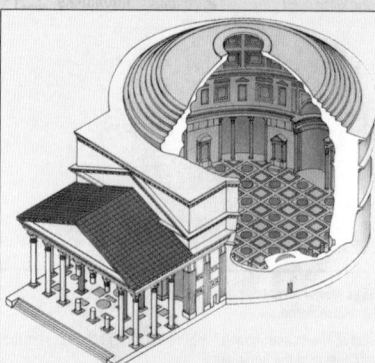

Pantheon *One of the most influential buildings in the history of architecture, the Pantheon was the largest domed structure until modern times. The dome, a perfect hemisphere, is remarkable not only for its size but also for its apparent lightness, an illusion skilfully created by the use of coffering, once stuccoed and gilded, and a single central light source.*

c.150 Kingdom of Meroë goes into decline because of trade competition from Aksum.

EUROPE

87 BC Gaius Marius (157–86 BC) declares himself dictator in Rome; he dies the following year.

85 BC Roman general Lucius Cornelius Sulla (138–78 BC) makes peace with Mithridates.

82 BC Sulla declares himself dictator.

79 BC Sulla retires from Roman politics.

73–71 BC Slave uprising in Italy led by Spartacus (d.71 BC).

60 BC Establishment of First Triumvirate – Pompey (106–48 BC), Julius Caesar (100–44 BC) and Crassus (115–53 BC) – to rule Rome.

58–52 BC Roman legions under Julius Caesar conquer Gaul (present-day France).

55 BC Romans invade Britain, but leave the following year.

53 BC Crassus killed at battle of Carrhae against the Parthians.

49–47 BC Civil war between Pompey and Caesar results in Pompey's death; Caesar becomes dictator of Rome.

44 BC Caesar is assasinated in Rome.

43 BC Second Triumvirate – Mark Antony (82–30 BC), Lepidus (d. c.13 BC) and Octavian (63 BC–14 AD) – established to rule Rome and avenge Caesar's death.

42 BC Caesar's assassins are defeated at battle of Philippi in Greece.

31 BC Antony and Cleopatra are defeated by Octavian at the sea-battle of Actium; Octavian becomes sole ruler of Rome.

27 BC Octavian takes the name Augustus. This date marks the end of the Roman republic and the beginning of the Principiate (Roman empire).

AD 9 Germanic tribes led by Arminius (d.19) ambush and destroy three Roman legions in the Tutoberg Forest, present-day NW Germany.

14 Roman emperor Augustus dies. His will names his son-in-law Tiberius (42 BC–AD 37) as the next emperor; this establishes the principle of succession for Roman emperors.

37–41 Short reign of Roman emperor Gaius (better known as Caligula, b.12) is marked by extravagance and decadence.

41 Claudius (10–54) becomes Roman emperor.

43 Romans occupy S Britain.

59 Emperor Nero (r.54–68) murders his mother Agrippina (b.15).

60 Boadicea (Boudicca, d.62), queen of the Iceni, leads a short-lived revolt against the Romans in Britain.

64 Great Fire of Rome is blamed on Christians and leads to their first persecution.

68–69 Death of Nero leads to civil war in the Roman empire. There are four self-proclaimed emperors; Vespasian (9–79) emerges as the victor and founds the Flavian dynasty.

79 Eruption of Mount Vesuvius in S Italy buries the towns of Pompeii and Herculaneum.

79 Titus succeeds his father Vespasian as Roman emperor.

81 Domitian (51–96) succeeds his brother Titus as emperor.

82–86 Eastern border of the Roman empire is established along the rivers Rhine and Danube.

83 Roman control in Britain is extended to S Scotland.

96 Domitian is assassinated and Nerva (30–98) is appointed.

98 Trajan (53–117) becomes emperor when Nerva dies.

101 Emperor Trajan (53–117) invades Dacia.

106 Trajan defeats the Dacian king Decebalus; Dacia becomes part of the Roman empire.

117 Trajan dies and is succeeded as Roman emperor by Hadrian (76–138).

121 Hadrian's Wall is built across Britain as the N border of the Roman empire.

138 Hadrian is succeeded as emperor by Antoninus Pius (86–161), whose reign is regarded as the Golden age of the Roman empire.

161 Marcus Aurelius (121–80) succeeds Antoninus Pius as Roman emperor.

161 Outbreak of plague devastates the city of Rome.

168 Germanic tribes invade the Roman empire across the River Danube.

175 Germanic tribes are defeated and expelled from the empire.

180 Commodus (161–92) becomes emperor on the death of his father Marcus Aurelius.

THE AMERICAS

Pont du Gard *A magnificent example of Roman engineering, the Pont du Gard aqueduct, Nîmes, was constructed to bring water from Uzes. Nearly 274m (900ft) long, it is built in three tiers of arches and spans the valley 47m (154ft) above the Gard.*

AD *c*.1 Basketmaker culture emerges in present-day SW USA; villages of circular houses are built.

***c*.25** Mochica (Moche) state is established in river valleys along the N coast of Peru.

***c*.50** City of Teotihuacán establishes control of the valley of Mexico; work starts on the construction of the Pyramid of the Sun.

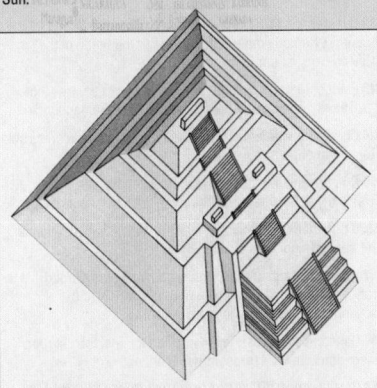

Teotihuacán *This city was the centre of a considerable empire and, at its greatest, housed c.100,000 people. It was built on a cruciform shape, with the Pyramid of the Moon, shown here, in the N, and the great Pyramid of the Sun in the E.*

***c*.100** Adena culture in the Ohio valley becomes absorbed into the geographically more extensive Hopewell culture.

***c*.150** End of the Formative period in Mesoamerican history; start of the Classic period.

SCIENCE AND TECHNOLOGY

***c*.50 BC** Roman craftworkers perfect the technique of glass-blowing.

46 BC In Rome, Caesar introduces the Julian calendar, which has 365 days and an extra day every fourth year.

***c*.23 BC** Roman engineer Vitruvius completes *On Architecture*, which later becomes a standard work on construction.

AD *c*.10 Greek geographer Strabo (*c*.63 BC–AD *c*.24) produces a reasonably accurate map of the Roman world.

***c*.39** A wooden ship 71m (233ft) long and 24m (80ft) wide is built on Lake Nemi near Rome for the entertainment of the emperor Gaius (Caligula).

***c*.50** Rome is the world's largest city, with a population of about one million.

***c*.60** Greek engineer Hero of Alexandria (b. *c*.20) experiments with hydraulic machinery and invents a simple steam engine.

***c*.67** Emperor Nero completes the construction of his palace in Rome – the Golden House – on the ruins of the Great Fire.

79 Roman encyclopedist Pliny the Elder (b.23), author of *The Natural History*, dies in the eruption of Mount Vesuvius.

80 Construction of the Colosseum begins in Rome.

***c*.100** Single-wheeled cart or wheelbarrow is invented in China.

***c*.100** Knowledge of the monsoon wind systems of the Indian Ocean becomes widespread, leading to an increase in trade between India and the Arabian Gulf.

105 Invention of paper is announced to the Chinese court.

***c*.110** Greek mathematician Menelaus writes *Sphaerica*, a treatise on trigonometry.

***c*.118** Pantheon is built in Rome with a 43-m (140-ft) concrete dome.

***c*.150** Roman doctor Galen (129–99) uses dissection and experimentation to establish the function of bodily organs.

***c*.160** Greek astronomer Ptolemy (90–168) publishes *The Mathematical Collection* (later known as *The Almagest*).

ARTS AND HUMANITIES

***c*.50 BC** Great Stupa at Sanchi, India, is enlarged and refurbished by the Sunga dynasty.

43 BC Roman writer and politician Cicero (b.106 BC), author of *On the Republic*, is murdered.

24 BC Roman poet Horace (65–08 BC) publishes the first of his *Odes*.

***c*.25 BC** Pont du Gard aqueduct built at Nîmes, S France.

19 BC Death of the Roman poet Virgil (b.70 BC); his *Aeneid* is published posthumously by Emperor Augustus.

AD *c*.3 Roman poet Ovid (43 BC–AD 18) publishes *Metamorphoses*.

17 Death of the Roman historian Livy (b.59 BC), author of a 142-volume history of Rome entitled *From the Beginning of the City*.

***c*.50** Under Kushan patronage, the Mathura art style develops in N India.

65 Seneca (b.4), the orator, philosopher and tutor of Nero, commits suicide in Rome after being condemned for undue political influence.

66–70 Dead Sea Scrolls are concealed in a cave during the Jewish revolt.

***c*.105** Roman historian Suetonius (*c*.69–140) writes *The Lives of the Caesars*.

***c*.110** Roman historian Tacitus (55–120) writes *Annals* and *Histories*.

110 Roman writer Juvenal (55–140) publishes the first of his *Satires*.

112 Trajan's Column is erected in Rome.

114 Death of the historian Ban Zhou (b.45), the leading woman intellectual in China.

120 Death of the Greek writer Plutarch (b.46), author of *The Parallel Lives*.

***c*.150** Earliest-known inscription in Sanskrit is carved in W India.

***c*.165** Roman novelist Apuleius (*c*.125–*c*.170) writes the *The Golden Ass*.

172–80 Emperor Marcus Aurelius composes *Meditations*.

AD 1

100

ASIA AND AUSTRALASIA

190 Chinese Han emperor is murdered and civil wars ensue.

197–99 Severus invades Parthia and temporarily adds Mesopotamia to the Roman empire.

200

220 Civil wars bring the Han dynasty in China to an end; start of the Three Kingdoms (Wei, Wu and Shu) period.

224 King Ardashir (r.224–41) of Persis, S Persia, takes over the Parthian empire; start of the Sassanian empire.

c.235 Sassanians defeat the Kushans near the River Oxus, central Asia.

c.240 Kushan empire in India breaks up, with local rulers coming to power.

244 Sassanians under Shapur I (r.244–72) conquer Armenia.

238 Sassanians conquer Mesopotamia from the Romans.

c.250 Chief of the Yamato clan establishes control over central Japan.

253 Sassanians sack the Roman city of Antioch, present-day Syria.

260 Roman emperor Valerian (r.253–60) is captured while campaigning against the Sassanians under Shapur I.

260 King Odaenath (d.267) of Palmyra declares his independence from Rome.

267 Zenobia makes herself queen of Palmyra and establishes control over Egypt and much of Asia Minor.

271 Zenobia declares her son to be Roman emperor.

273 Roman legions under Aurelian (c.215–75) crush the Palmyrans; Zenobia is taken to Rome in chains.

280 China is reunified under the Western Jin dynasty.

297 Roman legions under Galerius (d.311) defeat the Sassanians. A peace treaty gives the Sassanians a monopoly over the silk trade with Rome.

300

311 Huns and other nomad peoples sack the Chinese city of Luoyang.

316 Western Jin emperor is captured by the Huns who occupy N China.

320 Accession of King Chandragupta I at Palipatura (present-day Patna) in India marks the beginning of the Gupta dynasty.

325 Council of Nicaea (in present-day NW Turkey) establishes the basis of Christian belief and denounces the heresy of Arius (c.250–336).

c.360 King Samudragupta (r.335–76) conquers N and NE India and expands the Gupta empire.

363 Roman emperor Julian is killed in battle against the Sassanians.

369 Japanese empress Jing orders the invasion of Korea.

374 Huns attack the Alans (nomads living on the W bank of the River Volga), who are driven W and in turn attack and defeat the Visigoths.

383 Chinese victory at the battle of River Fei repulses a Hun invasion of S China.

c.395 King Chandragupta II (r. c.380–414) conquers W India; the Gupta empire reaches its greatest extent.

400

420 Fall of the Eastern Jin dynasty in central China; it is replaced by the Former Song dynasty.

c.450 Ruan-ruan nomads replace the Huns as the dominant force on the steppes of central Asia.

c.450 Steppe nomads the Hepthalites (White Huns) invade N India and occupy the Punjab; they are fought to a standstill by Gupta king Skandagupta.

479 Former Song dynasty in China is replaced by the Southern Qi dynasty.

484 Hepthalites attack the Sassanian empire, kill King Peroz and occupy parts of E Persia.

c.495 Hepthalites invade central India and conquer some Gupta territory.

AFRICA

c.200 Bantu peoples reach the E coast of Africa.

249 Bishop Cyprian of Carthage (d.258) leads the Christians during the persecution initiated by the Roman emperor Decius (200–51).

c.285 King Aphilas of Aksum invades SW Arabia.

> "For in all adversity of fortune the worst sort of misery is to have been happy."
>
> *Boethius (Consolation of Philosophy)*

c.305 Anthony the Hermit (c.250–c.355) establishes the tradition of Christian monasticism in Egypt.

343 King Ezana of Aksum is converted to Christianity by missionaries from Egypt.

c.350 King Ezana conquers the kingdom of Meroë and sacks the capital city.

Gothic soldiers *The Goths were Eastern Germanic warrior people who invaded parts of the Roman Empire from the 3rd to the 5th century. Their principle weapon was the spear. They were adept at coping with harsh winter conditions and wore cloaks of fur into battle.*

c.400 Seafaring peoples from Indonesia begin settling on the island of Madagascar off the E coast of Africa.

429 Vandals under Gaeseric cross from Spain to N Africa.

439 Vandals capture the city of Carthage and establish a kingdom.

451 Council of Chalcedon results in the Coptic Christians in Egypt splitting away from the influence of Rome and Constantinople.

468 Combined forces of the E and W Roman empire make disastrous attempt to invade Vandal kingdom.

EUROPE

192 Assassination of Commodus precipitates civil wars between rival emperors for control of the empire.

197 Lucius Septimius Severus (146–211) emerges as sole emperor and founds the Severan dynasty.

211 Severus dies and his sons, Caracalla and Geta, succeed as joint emperors. Caracalla has Geta murdered.

212 Caracalla (118–217) extends Roman citizenship to all free subjects of the empire.

218–22 Emperor Elagabalus (204–22) introduces sun-worship to Rome, which leads to his assassination.

235 Death of emperor Severus Alexander (b.208) marks the end of the Several dynasty. During the next fifty years there are 36 Roman emperors.

248 Emperor Philip I (r.244–49) holds games to celebrate Rome's 1000th anniversary.

260 Roman emperor Gallienus (r.253–68) defeats the invading Germanic tribe, the Alemanni, near present-day Milan, N Italy.

260–74 Gallic empire (parts of present-day France and Germany) under Postumus and his successors breaks away from Rome.

c.260 Goths migrate from Scandinavia to the shores of the Black Sea.

267 A 500-ship fleet of Goths and other Germanic tribes raids the coast of Greece and sacks the city of Athens.

274 Emperor Aurelian re-establishes Roman control over the Gallic empire.

284 Roman general Diocletian (245–313) makes himself emperor.

293 Diocletian introduces the Tetrarchy, under which the Roman empire is ruler by two joint emperors (*Augustii*) each assisted by a deputy (*Caesar*).

305 Diocletian's retirement begins a 20-year period of rivalry for control of the Roman empire.

312 Constantine I (285–337) converts to Christianity and becomes Roman emperor in the W after the battle of the Milvian Bridge near Rome.

313 Edict of Mediolanum (present-day Milan) declares that Christianity is to be tolerated throughout the Roman empire.

324 Constantine defeats Licinius (c.270–325) and becomes sole Roman emperor.

330 Constantine founds Constantinople, on the site of the Greek city of Byzantium, as the E capital of the Roman empire.

c.330 Christianity is proclaimed as the only official religion of the Roman empire.

337 After the death of Constantine, the empire is divided between his sons Constans (emperor in the W) and Constantius II (emperor in the E).

350 Constans (b.c.323) is killed in battle against the usurper Magnentius in Gaul (present-day France).

353 Constantius II (317–61) re-establishes sole control of the Roman empire.

360 Julian (331–63) becomes Roman emperor and briefly reintroduces pagan worship.

364 Valentinian I (321–75) and Valens (328–78) become Roman emperors in W and E respectively.

378 Visigoths invade SE Europe and defeat the Romans, led by the emperor Valens, at the battle of Adrianople.

392 Theodosius (347–95) becomes sole Roman emperor.

395 On the death of Theodosius the Roman empire is formally split into W and E parts ruled respectively by his sons Honorius and Arcadius (c.377–408).

407 Burgundians establish a kingdom in present-day central and SE France.

409 Vandals and Suevi move into Spain.

410 Goths under Alaric (370–410) sack Rome.

418 Visigoths establish a kingdom in S France.

c.420 Angles, Saxons and Jutes begin settling in Britain.

c.430 Franks begin settling in N France.

c.430 Visigoths take over most of Spain.

434 Attila (406–53) is declared leader of the Huns.

441–48 Huns plunder the Balkans until bribed by E Roman emperor to turn W.

451 Huns are defeated at the battle of Chalons in France.

THE AMERICAS

*c.*200 Warfare breaks out between rival Mayan city-states in the Yucatán region of Mexico.

*c.*200 City of Teotihuacán establishes an empire than controls most of highland Mexico.

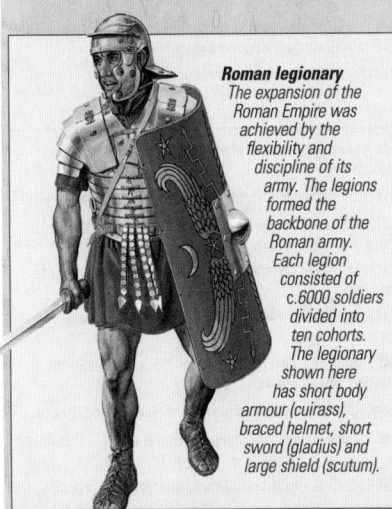

Roman legionary *The expansion of the Roman Empire was achieved by the flexibility and discipline of its army. The legions formed the backbone of the Roman army. Each legion consisted of c.6000 soldiers divided into ten cohorts. The legionary shown here has short body armour (cuirass), braced helmet, short sword (gladius) and large shield (scutum).*

c. 300 City of Teotihuacán establishes control over the highland Mayan cities in present-day Gautemala.

*c.*300 Lowland Mayan city-state of Tikal conquers neighbouring El Mirador.

*c.*350 City of Teotihuacán extends its influence over the lowland Mayan cities in the Yucatán region of Mexico.

401–50 Hopewell culture declines and collapses.

*c.*425 Teotihuacán completes its subjugation of the lowland Mayan cities of Tikal, Uaxactun and Becan.

SCIENCE AND TECHNOLOGY

*c.*216 Baths of Caracalla in Rome are completed.

*c.*250 Diophantus of Alexandria establishes algebra as a branch of mathematics and introduces the use of symbols in equations.

*c.*260 Sassanian royal palace Taq-i-Kisra, containing a 22-m (75-ft) wide arch, is built at Ctesiphon near present-day Baghdad, Iraq.

*c.*265 Rock-cut reliefs at Bishapur, Persia, celebrate the Sassanian's humiliation of the Roman emperor Valerian.

321 Constantine I introduces the seven-day week into the calendar used throughout the Roman empire.

*c.*340 Greek mathematician Pappus of Alexandria explores the geometry of curved surfaces.

*c.*375 Stirrups are invented in w China, from where they spread to Europe with the AVARS.

*c.*400 Supposedly rustproof pillar of pure iron is erected in Delhi, India.

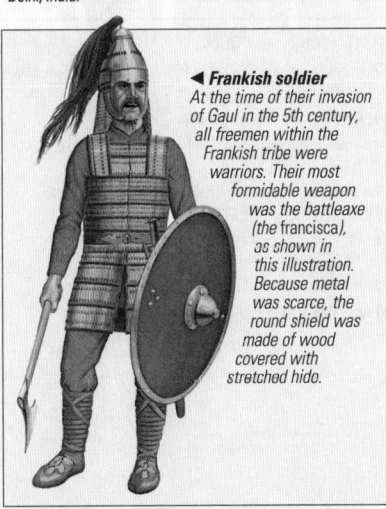

◄ Frankish soldier *At the time of their invasion of Gaul in the 5th century, all freemen within the Frankish tribe were warriors. Their most formidable weapon was the battleaxe (the francisca), as shown in this illustration. Because metal was scarce, the round shield was made of wood covered with stretched hide.*

415 Philosopher and mathematician Hypatia (b.370) is killed in Alexandria by a Christian mob, who equate her learning with paganism.

*c.*485 Chinese mathematician Tsu Chung Chi calculates the value of *pi* to an accuracy that is not bettered for a thousand years.

*c.*499 Indian mathematician Aryabhata (476–550) publishes *Aryabhatiya*, a compendium of scientific knowledge.

ARTS AND HUMANITIES

*c.*244 Philosopher Plotinus (205–70) opens a school in Rome where he teaches the ideas of Neoplatonism.

*c.*250 Prophet Mani (216–76) preaches his new philosophy of Manichaeism in Persia.

Saxon soldier *During the 5th century, Angles, Saxons and Jutes began settling in England. Saxons, such as the soldier shown here, came to England as a result of Frankish expansion in Europe, which had put pressure on their homelands. The word Saxon survives in the names Sussex (South Saxon) and Essex (East Saxon).*

341 Ulfilas devises the Gothic alphabet for his translation of the Bible into Gothic.

365 Birth of the Chinese writer and landscape poet Tao Qian (d.427), author of the short story *Peach Tree Spring*.

375 Wall painting in caves at Ajanta, India, mark the flowering of Gupta-period art.

*c.*380 Ambrose (339–97), bishop of Milan, introduces plainsong into Christian services.

*c.*385 Jerome (347–420) starts translating the Bible from Greek into Latin (the Vulgate Bible).

*c.*397 Christian philosopher Augustine of Hippo (354–430) writes *Confessions*.

*c.*405 Indian poet and dramatist Kalidasa writes *Sakuntala Recognized* at the Gupta court.

413 Traveller monk Faxian returns to China with large numbers of Buddhist texts.

*c.*425 Galla Placidia (388–450) adorns her mausoleum in Ravenna, Italy, with mosaics.

438 Law code of Theodosius II (r.408–50) published throughout the Roman empire; the code is later adopted by many Germanic rulers.

480 Birth of the Italian scholar Boethius (d.524), who translates the works of Aristotle into Latin.

200

300

400

ASIA AND AUSTRALASIA

495 Northern Wei dynasty in N China moves its capital from Datong to Luoyang.

c.500 Polynesians settle on Easter Island.

527 Accession of Justinian (482–565) marks the end of the Roman empire in the E, and the start of the Byzantine empire.

535 Hepthalites invade the remaining Gupta territories in India; end of the Gupta dynasty.

540 Sassanians under King Khoshru I (r.531–79) sack the city of Antioch on the Mediterranean coast in Syria.

c.550 Buddhism spreads to Japan.

552 Nomadic Turks under Bumin (r.546–53) win a decisive victory over the Ruan-ruan, and establish control across central Asia.

561 Silkworms are smuggled to the Byzantine court from China.

562 Sassanians and Turks in alliance crush the Hepthalites, who cease to be an effective force.

c.575 Sassanians expel the Aksumites and occupy present-day Yemen.

580 Marib dam in Yemen collapses, causing economic decline.

581 Sui Yang Jian (d.604) becomes emperor in China; start of the Sui dynasty.

589 Through military conquest, the Sui dynasty achieves the reunification of China under a single ruler.

591 Khoshru II (d.628) becomes Sassanian king with Byzantine military assistance.

c.600 Polynesians settle in Hawaii.

604 Prince Shotoku Taishi (573–621) establishes formal principles of government in Japan.

612–15 Sassanians under King Khoshru II (d.628) conquer Asia Minor, Syria and Palestine.

618 Tang dynasty is founded by the Sui official Li Yuan.

c.620 Ganges valley king Harsha (r.606–47) conquers and temporarily unites N India.

622 Muhammad (c.570–632) and his followers flee from Mecca to Medina (the Hejira); start of the Islamic calendar.

c.625 Srong-brtsan (r.608–50) unifies the Tibetan peoples.

627 Byzantine army sacks the Sassanian capital of Ctesiphon.

630 Chinese establish control over much of central Asia.

630 Muhammad's army marches on Mecca, which surrenders.

632 Death of the prophet Muhammad marks the beginning of the Arab empire.

636–37 Arab armies under the caliph Omar (r.634–44) conquer Syria and Palestine.

642 Arabs defeat the Sassanians at the battle of Nihawand and overrun Persia; end of the Sassanian empire.

645 Taika reforms establish central government over all Japan.

656–61 Civil wars are waged for control of the Arab empire during the caliphate of Ali (c.600–61); the Umayyad family emerges as the ruling dynasty.

668 Kingdom of Silla unifies most of Korea under its rule.

690 Wu (d.705), the only woman emperor of China, becomes sole ruler.

705 Arab armies carry Islam into Turkistan, central Asia.

710 City of Nara is established as the capital of Japan.

713 Arab expansion to the E reaches the upper Indus valley.

c.710 Rise of the city of Srivijaya in Sumatra as an important trade centre.

AFRICA

533 Byzantine armies under General Belisarius (505–65) recapture N Africa from the Vandals.

536 Byzantine authorities close the temple at Philae in Egypt; this marks the end of traditional Egyptian religion.

c.550 Kingdom of Ghana is established in W Africa.

570 Aksumite armies make an unsuccessful attempt to conquer the city of Mecca in W Arabia.

Hagia Sophia Built for Emperor Justinian, Hagia Sophia is a masterpiece of Byzantine architecture. This illustration shows acanthus leaf decoration from an arch within it. The elaborate internal ornamentation of much Byzantine architecture contrasts with the simple exteriors.

616 Sassanians conquer Egypt.

628 Byzantine emperor Heraclius (575–641) restores Byzantine control over Egypt.

639–42 Arab armies conquer Egypt.

648 Byzantine forces temporarily halt Arab expansion in N Africa.

c.650 Traders from Arabia establish the first Islamic settlements on the E coast of Africa.

652 Arab rulers of Egypt agree to respect the existing borders of the Nubian kingdoms.

670 Arab forces move into present-day Tunisia.

697 Arab forces destroy the Byzantine city of Carthage.

702 Aksumites attack the port of Jiddah in present-day Saudi Arabia.

702–11 Arab conquests are extended W along the N African coastline to the Atlantic ocean.

739 Port of Zanzibar on the E coast of Africa is founded by Islamic traders from S Arabia.

EUROPE

452 Huns plunder N Italy.

453 Death of Attila.

455 Vandals sack Rome.

458 Sicily is captured by the Vandals.

476 Overthrow of Emperor Romulus Augustulus (r.475–76) by Odoacer (433–93) marks end of W Roman empire.

481 Clovis I (465–511) establishes a Frankish kingdom in France; start of Merovingian dynasty.

491–99 Fiscal and administrative reforms of the emperor Anastasius I (d.518) revive the E Roman empire.

493 Theodoric (454–526) assassinates Odoacer and establishes an Ostrogoth kingdom in Italy.

498 Clovis I is converted to Christianity.

502 Franks defeat the Alemanni and conquer present-day S Germany.

511 Ostrogoths under Theodoric (454–526) annex Spain.

527 Justinian becomes Roman emperor in Constantinople; start of the Byzantine empire.

532 Nika riots in Constantinople cause extensive damage to buildings.

534 Franks under Theudebert I conquer the Burgundian kingdom.

541 Europe's first encounter with smallpox devastates the Mediterranean region.

c.540–50 Slav peoples migrate into the Balkans and Greece.

548 Frankish kingdom disintegrates on the death of Theudebert I.

552 Byzantine armies conquer S Spain from the Ostrogoths.

557 Avar nomads invade and settle in Hungary.

558 Clotaire I (497–561) reunites the Frankish kingdom.

568 Lombards invade N Italy and establish a kingdom in the Po valley.

582 Combined force of Avars and Slavs attacks Athens, Sparta and Corinth.

583 King Leovigild (r.569–86) defeats the Suevi in NW Spain and reunites N and central Spain under Visigoth control.

599 Visigoth king Reccared (r.586–601) converts to Christianity.

626 Combined force of Avars and Sassanians besiege Constantinople.

629 Visigoths drive the Byzantines from S spain.

663 Byzantine emperor Constans II (630–68) leads an army against the Lombards, but retreats to Sicily.

673–78 Arab armies besiege Constantinople by land and sea.

673 Visigoth king Wamba (r.672–81) defeats an Arab fleet near the Straits of Gibraltar.

681 Onogur Huns establish the kingdom of Bulgaria.

687 Victory over dynastic rivals at the battle of Tertry in N France extends the power of the Frankish king Pepin II (d.714).

Byzantine soldiers The Byzantine empire was at its height in the 6th century. The soldier on the right wears lamellar armour, a complicated form of chain-mail.

711–18 Arab and Berber armies invade and conquer Visigoth Spain.

717–18 Arab armies besiege Constantinople.

732 Frankish armies led by Charles Martel (688–741) defeat the Arabs at the battle of Tours and confine them S of the Pyrenees mountains.

THE AMERICAS

Anasazi *Various examples of Anasazi pottery have been found in present-day sw USA. The pottery was generally painted with black-on-white designs, though other colours were sometimes used.*

c.500 Settlement is established at Mesa Verde in SE Colorado, present-day USA.

c.500 Mochica state reaches its greatest extent along the lowland coast of Peru.

c.500 Cities of Tiahuanaco and Huari rise to prominence in the Andes highlands of central Peru.

c.600 Mochica state in Peru is absorbed by the city-state of Huari.

c.650 City of Teotihuacán is destroyed by warfare: collapse of the Teotihuacán empire.

682 King Ah-Cacaw becomes ruler of the Mayan city of Tikal.

▶ **Dome of the Rock** *Dating from the 7th century ad, the Dome of the Rock was the first domed mosque. By tradition, it encloses the rock where Muhammad ascended to Heaven. It is also a sacred site for Jews. It is he only extant piece of the Temple of Solomon and stands within the Haram esh-Sharif which is bordered on one side by the Western (Wailing) Wall.*

c.750 Start of the decline of classic Mayan civilization.

c.750 Decline of Huari control in highland Peru.

SCIENCE AND TECHNOLOGY

▶ **Darius I** *The so-called Fire Temple of Naqsh-i Rustam, near Persepolis (now Takht-e-Jamshid), sw Iran, stands in front of a cliff in which the tomb of Darius I is carved.*

525 Mathematician Dionysius Exiguus (500–50) begins the practice of dating years using the birth of Jesus Christ as a starting point; beginning of the Christian, Common, or Current Era.

531–37 Church of Hagia Sophia is constructed in Constantinople.

c.600 Earliest-known windmills are used to grind flour in Persia.

c.628 Indian mathematician Brahmagupta (598–665) publishes *The Opening of the Universe*.

c.650 Chinese scholars develop a technique for printing texts from engraved wooden blocks.

c.650 Chinese capital Changan (Xian) is the world's largest city, with a population of about one million.

c.675 Byzantine defenders of Constantinople deploy a new weapon, Greek fire – a type of flamethrower.

685–92 Dome of the Rock mosque (Qubbat al-Sakhrah) is built in Jerusalem.

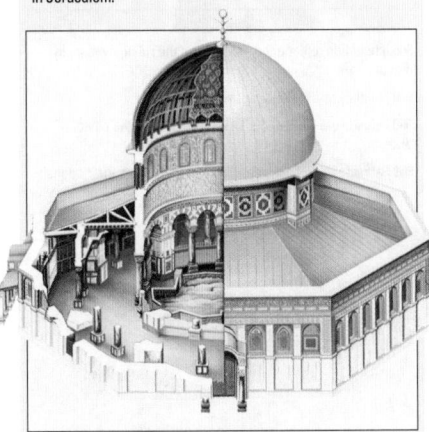

715 Great Mosque at Damascus is built.

780 Birth of the Islamic mathematician Al-Khwarizmi, who wrote *Calculation with Hindu Numerals* (825), which adopted the Indian 10-digit number system and positional notation.

c.784 First Arab paper factory opens in Baghdad using skills learned from Chinese prisoners taken at the battle of Talas.

ARTS AND HUMANITIES

534 Emperor Justinian publishes a Law Code; it forms the basis for medieval law in w Europe.

c.550 Byzantine historian Procopius publishes *Secret History*.

c.550 Italian scholar Cassiodorus (490–585) collects and preserves the work of Greek and Latin writers and establishes the practice of monks copying manuscripts.

c.570 Birth of the prophet Muhammad.

c.590 Gregory of Tours (538–94) completes *History of the Franks*.

c.590 Isidore (c.560–636), bishop of Seville, begins work on his 20-volume *Etymologies*.

c.600 Pope Gregory (540–604) reforms the use of plainsong in Christian services and is thought to have introduced Gregorian chant.

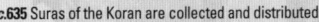

c.635 Suras of the Koran are collected and distributed.

641 Great Library at Alexandria is destroyed by fire during an Arab attack.

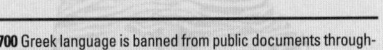

700 Greek language is banned from public documents throughout the Arab empire.

726 Iconoclasm movement starts in the Byzantine empire when emperor Leo III (c.750–816) bans the use of figurative images in Christian art.

500

600

700

ASIA AND AUSTRALASIA

744 Revolt by the Abbasid family in present-day Iran leads to civil war in the Arab empire.

745 Uighurs establish themselves as the ruling dynasty of the Turks.

747 Rajputs (the descendants of Hepthalites and other central Asian invaders in NW India) formally join the Hindu warrior caste.

750 Abbasids defeat the Umayyads at the battle of Zab and take over as the ruling Islamic dynasty in the Middle East.

c.750 Pala dynasty establishes control over present-day Bangladesh.

751 Combined armies of the Arabs and Turks defeat the Chinese at the battle of Talas; Tang dynasty control of central Asia is lost.

753 Rashtrakuta dynasty establishes control over W central India.

755–63 Revolt of General An Lushan (703–57) seriously weakens Tang dynasty control of China for the next half century.

762 Abbasids found the city of Baghdad as their new capital.

763 Tibetan power in central Asia reaches its height with the sacking of the Chinese capital of Changan.

794 Capital of Japan moves to Kyōto, start of the Heian period.

c.800 Polynesians reach New Zealand.

802 Jayavarman II (c.770–850) establishes the kingdom of Angkor in present-day Cambodia.

818 Tang dynasty re-establishes strong central control in China.

823 Arabs conquer Sicily from the Byzantine empire.

845 Buddhism is banned in China and Confucianism is restored as the state ideology.

849 City-state of Pagan is founded in Burma.

857 Yoshifusa (804–72) establishes the Fujiwara family as the power behind the emperor in Japan.

c.880 Tibetan unity dissolves into local rivalries.

> "If many people follow your enthusiastic endeavours, perhaps a new Athens might be created in the land of the Franks, or rather a much better one."
>
> *Alcuin (letter to Charlemagne)*

907 Rebellion in China leads to the end of the Tang dynasty; disunity and civil wars ensue – the period of the Five Dynasties.

c.925 Chola kingdom in S India annexes the neighbouring Pallava kingdom.

945 Buyid dynasty from present-day N Iran captures Baghdad from the Abbasid dynasty.

960 General Zhao Kuang-yin reunifies N China and establishes the Song dynasty.

971 Fatimids conquer Syria and Palestine from the Abbasids.

974 Byzantines establish control over N Syria and N Palestine.

985 Cholas invade the island of Sri Lanka.

998 Warlord Mahmud (971–1030) seizes control in Afghanistan and E Persia and expands the Ghaznavid dynasty.

AFRICA

c.740 Berber peoples in the N Sahara region revolt against Umayyad rule and form independent Islamic kingdoms.

753 Arab expedition crosses the Sahara desert and makes contact with the kingdom of Ghana.

789 Idrisid dynasty establishes Morocco as an independent Islamic kingdom.

800 Aghlabids establish an independent Islamic dynasty in present-day Tunisia.

c.800 Kingdom of Kanem is established around the W shore of Lake Chad.

808 City of Fez becomes the capital of the kingdom of Morocco.

868 Independent Tulunid dynasty is established in Egypt.

Carolingian nobility *Under Charlemagne (742–814), the nobility enjoyed significant political influence. Their affluence was reflected in their colourful dress and the quality of detail, such as the jewelled cloak pin above.*

905 Ikhshidids replace the Tulunids as the ruling dynasty in Egypt.

909 Fatimid dynasty seizes power in W Tunisia.

960 Falasha warriors under Queen Gudit sack the city of Aksum.

969 Fatimids invade Egypt and establish Cairo as their capital.

EUROPE

750 Palace coup makes Pepin III (the short, 714–68) king of the Franks; end of the Merovingian dynasty.

756 Pepin gives territories in central Italy to the pope; these become the Papal States.

756 Umayyads retain power in Islamic Spain and establish the independent Emirate of Córdoba.

772 New Frankish king Charlemagne (742–814) campaigns against the Saxons in present-day N Germany.

774 Charlemagne defeats the Lombards and annexes N and central Italy.

781 Charlemagne establishes his capital at Aachen.

793 Danish raiders (Vikings) pillage the island monastery of Lindisfarne off NE England.

795 Charlemagne extends Frankish territory to S of the Pyrenees.

796 Frankish armies defeat and conquer the Avars in present-day Hungary.

800 Charlemagne (742–814) is crowned Holy Roman emperor in Aachen by Pope Leo III (c.750–816); start of the Holy Roman Empire.

804 Charlemagne completes the conquest of present-day N Germany.

812 Byzantines recognize Charlemagne as emperor in the W in return for Venice and present-day N Yugoslavia.

825 Islamic fleet captures the island of Crete.

c.830 King Egbert of Wessex (d.839) establishes control over the Anglo-Saxon states in England.

843 Treaty of Verdun divides the Carolingian empire into three kingdoms.

846 Arab army raids Italy and sacks Rome.

c.850 Magyars migrate into Hungary, replacing the Avars, and begin raiding W Europe.

858 Swedes establish the state of Kiev in Ukraine.

859–62 Danes raid along the coast of present-day S France.

c.865 Bulgarians are converted to Christianity.

866 Danes invade SE England.

867 Basil I (c.813–86) becomes Byzantine emperor and founds the Macedonian dynasty.

869 Swedish warrior Rurik (d.879) founds the town of Novgorod, NW Russia.

874 Norwegians begin to settle in Iceland.

878–85 King Alfred of Wessex (Alfred the Great, 849–99) defeats the Danes and confines them to E England (Danelaw).

882 Unification of Novgorod and Kiev under King Oleg creates the first Russian state.

911 Danish warleader Rollo (c.860–931) establishes an independent dukedom of Normandy in NW France.

919 Henry I (the Fowler) (c.876–936) is elected the first king of Germany.

927 Anglo-Saxon king Ethelstan (d.939) expels the Danes from England.

944 Russians from Kiev attack Constantinople.

952 King Otto I of Germany (912–73) declares himself king of the Franks.

955 Magyars are decisively defeated by Otto I at the battle of Lechfeld (near present-day Augsburg) in Germany.

961 Byzantines recapture Crete from the Arabs.

962 Otto I is crowned Holy Roman emperor in Rome.

c.969 Miezko I (d.992) establishes the Christian kingdom of Poland.

973 Christian kingdom of Bohemia is established in present-day Czech Republic.

986 Emirate of Córdoba conquers the remaining Christian kingdoms in N Spain.

987 Hugh Capet (938–96) becomes king of France; start of the Capetian dynasty.

988 Russian king Vladimir I (956–1015) converts to Christianity.

996 Byzantines recapture Greece from the Bulgarians.

THE AMERICAS

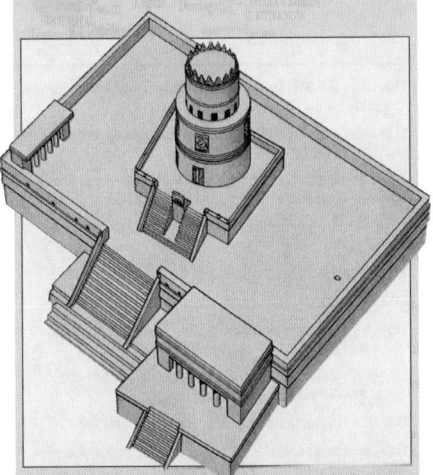

c.800 Metalworking is introduced into Mesoamerica from the S.

c.800 Cultivation of beans and maize is introduced to present-day E USA.

c.800 Huari abandon their capital city in highland Peru.

c.850 Toltecs establish military supremacy in central Mexico.

900 End of the Classic period of Mesoamerican history; start of the Early Postclassic period

c.900 Chimú people establish the city-state of Chan Chan in N Peru.

o.900 Maya abandon their cities in Guatemala and retreat to the Yucatán region of Mexico.

c.900 Anasazi peoples establish towns around Chaco Canyon in New Mexico, with a ritual centre at Pueblo Bonito.

c.900 Hohokam people establish a town and ritual centre at Snaketown in s Arizona.

c.950 Toltecs build a capital city at Tula in central Mexico.

982–86 Norwegian explorers discover Greenland and establish a colony.

c.987 Toltecs seize control of the Mayan city of Chichén Itzá.

SCIENCE AND TECHNOLOGY

◀ **Carolingian architecture** *The monastery church of St Riquier at Centula near Abbeville, France, was a celebrated example of a Carolingian double-ended church. Built in the decade after 790, it was largely financed by Charlemagne. The church no longer exists; this reconstruction uses details of its exterior and layout found in the present church and in contemporary illustrations.*

c.825 Abbasid caliph Al-Mamun (786–833) establishes the House of Wisdom, a library and translation academy at Baghdad.

839 Birth of the Islamic historian Al-Tabri (d.923), who wrote a world history detailing the conquests of the Arabs.

c.850 Gunpowder is invented in China.

c.850 First European windmills are built in Islamic Spain.

870 Birth of the Islamic philosopher Al-Farab (d.950), who studied the works of Plato and Aristotle, and wrote *Views of the Perfect Citizen of the Perfect State*.

◀ **Chichén Itzá** *A conjectural reconstruction of the astronomical observatory at Chichén Itzá, the chief city and shrine of the Mayan and Toltec peoples. There were two distinct cities; the earlier Mayan city was abandoned c.900 and the new Toltec city was built c.1.5km (1mi) away. The style of the vaulting and lintels on the observatory is Mayan and the general design of the tower is Toltec.*

925 Death of the Islamic doctor Al-Razi (b.865), author of *Al-Hawi* – a comprehensive survey of Greek, Arab and Indian medical knowledge.

929 Death of the Islamic mathematician Al-Battani (Albategnius) (b.850), author of *On the Motion of Stars*.

953 Arab mathematician Al-Uqlidsi produces the first decimal fractions.

973 Birth of the Islamic scientist Al-Biruni (d.1048), who compiled an analysis of Indian mathematics.

976 Arabic (Indian) numerals are first used in Europe (in N Spain).

▶ **Byzantine art and architecture** *St Mark's Cathedral, Venice, was built between 829 and 1071. Like many of the buildings in Venice, its design shows a strong Byzantine influence, demonstrated by the five vaulted domes which form the shape of a Greek cross formed by the nave, transepts and choir.*

ARTS AND HUMANITIES

731 English monk and scholar Bede (673–735) publishes his *Ecclesiastical History of the English People*.

c.750 *Book of Kells* illuminated manuscript is produced in Ireland.

c.750 Anglo-Saxon poem *Beowulf* is written down.

c.750 Poets Li Po (701–62) and Tu Fu (712–70) become popular in China.

780 Birth of Sankara (d.820), the Indian philosopher who founded the Advaita Vedanta branch of Hinduism.

800

804 Death of the Anglo-Saxon monk Alcuin (b.c.732), who instigated civil service training and a revival of classical learning at Charlemagne's court.

c.820 Reign of the Abbasid caliph Harun al-Rashid (r.786–809) inspires the writing of the *Thousand and One Nights*.

824 Death in China of Han Yu (b.768), the leading exponent of Neo-Confucianism.

843 End of iconoclasm in the Byzantine empire; images (icons) are once again permitted in Christian art.

c.860 Cyril (c.827–69) and Methodius (c.825–84) devise the Cyrillic alphabet to assist their conversion of the Slavs.

868 Earliest-known printed book, the *Diamond Sutra*, is produced in China.

869 Death of the Islamic philosopher and essayist Al-Jahiz (b.776).

900

965 Death of the Arab poet Al-Mutanabbi (b.915), who worked at the Ikhshidid court in Egypt.

978 Birth of the Japanese woman novelist Murasaki Shikibu (d.1014), author of *The Tale of Genji*.

ASIA AND AUSTRALASIA

1000 Ghaznavid armies begin raiding and pillaging cities in N India.

1022 Chola king Rajendra I (r.1016–44) conquers the E coast of India.

1026 Cholas invade Sumatra and Malaya.

1040 Seljuk Turks defeat the Ghaznavids and invade Persia.

1055 Seljuk Turks under Tughril Bey (c.990–1063) capture Baghdad.

1064 Armenia is incorporated into the Byzantine empire.

1060–67 King Anawrahta (r.1044–77) of Pagan unifies Burma under his rule.

1071 Seljuks led by Alp Arslan (1029–72) defeat the Byzantines at the battle of Manzikert and occupy most of Asia Minor.

1075–78 Turks occupy Syria and Palestine.

1096 People's Crusade is massacred by Turks in NW Asia Minor.

1099 First Crusade, under Godfrey of Bouillon (1060–1100), captures Jerusalem; independent Christian kingdoms are established along the E coast of the Mediterranean.

Knights Templar
The military religious order of the Knights Templar had its headquarters in the Temple of Solomon, Jerusalem. The Templars protected routes to Jerusalem for Christians during the Crusades.

1100 Baldwin (1058–1118) becomes king of Jerusalem.

1118 Order of the Knights Templar is established in Jerusalem.

1127 Jurchen nomads overrun N China; the Song dynasty retreats to S China; start of the Southern Song dynasty.

1149 Second Crusade ends after unsuccessful campaigns against the Turks in Palestine.

1156 Civil war between rival clans breaks out in Japan; end of the Heian period.

1173 Muhammad of Ghur overthrows the Ghaznavid dynasty in Afghanistan.

1187 Victory over Christian forces at the battle of Hattin allows the Islamic general Saladin to recapture Jerusalem.

1191 Third Crusade captures the island of Cyprus and the town of Acre but fails to recapture Jerusalem.

1192 Yoritomo Minamoto (d.1199) institutes the shōgunate in Japan.

1192 Muhammad of Ghur's victory over the Rajputs at the battle of Thanesar leads to the Islamic conquest of N India.

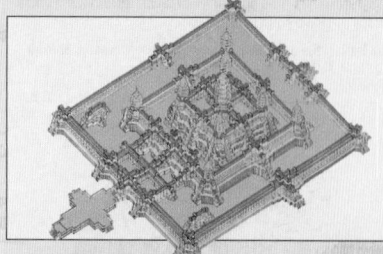

1204 Empires of Nicaea (NW Asia Minor) and Trebizond (NE Asia Minor) are created out of remnants of the Byzantine empire.

1206 Islamic Delhi Sultanate is established in N India.

1206 Mongol warrior Temüjin (c.1162–1227) establishes control over the nomads of the Eurasian steppes and adopts the title Genghis Khan (Emperor of the World).

1211 Mongol warriors invade Jurchen-controlled N China.

1215 Mongol advance in China reaches the Yellow River.

1218–25 Mongols conquer E Persia.

1219 Last shogun of the Minamoto family killed in Japan; after the brief Shokyu War, the Hojo family takes control.

AFRICA

1054 Berber chieftain Abu Bakr (d.1087) launches an empire-building campaign in N Africa and establishes the Almoravid dynasty.

1070 Abu Bakr founds the city of Marrakesh in S Morocco.

1075–77 Almoravids conquer N Morocco and W Algeria.

1076 City of Kumbi, capital of Ghana, is sacked by an Almoravid army.

Romanesque architecture *The west façade of the Cathedral of San Maggiori, Pisa, Italy, is a fine example of Romanesque architecture. Construction of the cathedral, designed by Buscheto, started in 1063, was interrupted in 1095 and resumed in 1099.*

1117 City of Lalibela becomes the capital of Christian Ethiopia.

1143–47 Berber Almohad dynasty overthrows the Almoravids in NW Africa.

1171 Turkish general Saladin (1138–93) overthrows the Fatimid dynasty in Egypt and establishes the Ayyubid dynasty.

◄ ***Angkor Wat*** *Created by Suryavarman II, Angkor Wat was the ritual centre of his kingdom. The outer cloister enclosed a complex of buildings, the main group arranged as a square of four at the corners and one in the centre. All were covered in exquisite low relief with divine dancers, plants, birds and animals.*

c.1200 Kingdom of Mwenemutapa is established in Zimbabwe.

1203 Samanguru establishes himself as ruler of the remnants of the kingdom of Ghana.

1212 Thousands of children who joined the Children's Crusade are sold into slavery in Alexandria, Egypt.

1219 Fifth Crusade captures the Egyptian port of Damietta, but fails to take Cairo.

EUROPE

997 Following their conversion to Christianity, the Magyars establish a kingdom in Hungary under Stephen I (977–1038).

1003 War between Pisa and Florence is the first recorded war between Italian city-states.

1008–28 Civil wars fragment the Emirate of Córdoba; Christian kingdoms re-emerge in N Spain; end of the Umayyad dynasty.

1013 Danes conquer England.

1014 Emperor Basil II (c.958–1025) completes the Byzantine reconquest of Bulgaria and the Balkan region.

1016 Danish prince Canute (c.994–1035) is elected king of England.

1028 Danes under King Canute conquer Norway.

1033 German emperor Conrad II (990–1039) adds Burgundy to the Holy Roman Empire.

1037 Christian kingdoms of León and Navarre in N Spain form an alliance and attack the Islamic S.

1040–52 Normans establish control over Byzantine S Italy.

1054 Great Schism divides the Catholic and Orthodox churches.

1054 Following the death of King Yaroslav (b.980), the Russian state breaks up.

1061–72 Normans under Roger I conquer Sicily from the Arabs.

1066 William of Normandy (1027–87) invades England, wins the battle of Hastings, and becomes King William I (the Conqueror).

1085 Christian forces capture the city of Toledo in central Spain.

1086 Berber Almoravids under Yusuf (d.1106) are invited to intervene against the Christians in Spain.

1095 Following the Council of Clermont in France, pope Urban II (c.1035–99) proclaims a Crusade to free Palestine from Islamic rule.

1096 First Crusade departs.

1108 Louis VI (1081–1137) becomes king of France and extends the power of the Capetian dynasty.

1138 Conrad III (1093–1152) becomes Holy Roman emperor and establishes the Hohenstaufen dynasty.

1147 Second Crusade departs under the leadership of German emperor Conrad III and King Louis VII (c.1120–80) of France.

c.1150 Almohad dynasty establishes control over Islamic Spain.

1151 Independent Serbian kingdom is established.

1153 Frederick I (1123–90) becomes Holy Roman emperor.

1154 Dynastic disputes in the Holy Roman empire erupt into open warfare in Italy.

1154 Henry II (1133–89) becomes king of England and establishes the Plantagenet dynasty.

1158 German merchants found the Baltic port of Lübeck.

1159 Contested papal elections result in both a pope and an antipope being recognized by the warring factions in Italy.

1167 Lombard League is formed against Frederick I in N Italy.

1171–73 Henry II of England establishes formal control over Ireland, Wales and Scotland.

1177 Peace treaty of Venice re-establishes a single papacy.

1186 Independent Bulgarian kingdom is re-established.

1189 Third Crusade departs under the leadership of Frederick I.

1198 Otto IV (1174–1218), a member of the Guelph family, becomes Holy Roman emperor; civil war breaks out in Germany.

1199 John (1167–1216) becomes king of England on the death of his brother Richard I (b.1157).

1201 German Crusaders establish the town of Riga in present-day Latvia.

1203 Fourth Crusade captures the Byzantine port of Zara (in present-day Yugoslavia) for Venice.

1204 Danes under King Waldemar II (d.1241) conquer Norway.

1204 At the behest of Venice, the Fourth Crusade captures and sacks Constantinople; the Latin empire is created on former Byzantine territory in Greece and the Balkans; Venice gains key ports and Crete.

1209 At the request of Pope Innocent III (1161–1216), an English-led Crusader army invades S France to suppress the Albigensian heretics (Cathars); the town of Beziers is burned.

THE AMERICAS

c.1000 Norwegian explorers discover North America and establish temporary settlements on the E coast of Canada.

Normans *Norman knights fought on horseback with spears and swords. They wore heavy chain-mail and conical helmets and carried brightly coloured shields.*

1156 Last Toltec king, Heumac, flees the destruction of Tula.

1187 Mayan leader Hunac Ceel leads a rebellion that evicts the Toltecs from Chichén Itzá and establishes a new Mayan capital at Mayapan.

c.1190 Aztecs establish a small state on the shore of Lake Texcoco in Mexico.

> "To no one will we sell, or deny, or delay, right or justice."
>
> *Magna Carta (clause 40)*

c.1200 Manco Capac establishes the Inca ruling dynasty with its capital at Cuzco, Peru.

c.1200 Monks Mound constructed at Cahokia, Illinois, present-day USA.

SCIENCE AND TECHNOLOGY

1003 Death of the scholar Gerbert of Aurillac (b.946), who translated Arabic texts on the abacus and astrolabe into Latin.

1010 Arab mathematician Ibn al-Haytham (*c*.965–1039), known in Europe as Alhazen, describes the properties of glass lenses.

1037 Death of the Islamic doctor and philosopher Ibn Sina (b.979), known in Europe as Avicenna, who wrote *Canon of Medicine.*

1050 Technique for printing using moveable ceramic type is invented in China.

1054 Chinese astronomers observe the supernova explosion that creates the Crab nebula.

1055–65 Westminster Abbey built in London, England.

1104 Construction of the Arsenal begins in Venice, Italy.

1120 Robert of Chester visits Spain and translates Al-Khwarizmi's *Calculation with Hindu Numerals* into Latin.

c.1140 Adelard of Bath (*c*.1075–1160) translates Euclid into Latin using both Greek and Arabic texts.

1150 A university is established in Paris, France.

1163 External flying buttresses are used for the first time, in the construction of Notre Dame in Paris.

1167 A university is established in Oxford, England.

1170 Roger of Salerno writes the first European surgery textbook, *Practica chirurgiae.*

1174 Construction work begins on the unintentionally leaning tower in Pisa, Italy.

1187 Death of the Italian scholar Gerard of Cremona (*c*.1114–87), who translated the works of Galen (129–99) from Arabic texts captured at Toledo.

c.1200 Sternpost rudders (invented in China) are first used on European ships.

1202 Italian mathematician Leonardo Fibonacci of Pisa (*c*.1170–*c*.1240) publishes his *Book of the Abacus* – the first European book to explain Indian numerals.

1215 Syllabus of the university of Paris is revised, with logic replacing Latin literature.

ARTS AND HUMANITIES

1000

1020 Death of the Persian Islamic poet Firdausi (b.935) author of the historical epic *Shah-nameh.*

1033 Birth of the philosopher Anselm of Canterbury (d.1109), who proposed a logical proof for the existence of God.

1048 Birth of the Islamic scientist and poet Omar Khayyám (d.1131).

c.1070–80 Bayeux tapestry is woven to commemorate William of Normandy's invasion of Britain.

1078 Death of the historian Michael Psellus (b.1018), author of *Chronographia*, a history of the reigns of 14 Byzantine emperors.

1088 First officially sanctioned university in Europe is established in Bologna, Italy.

Franciscan *The friars belonging to the religious order of the Franciscans travelled Europe preaching, possessing neither property nor money and relying on begging for a livelihood. Originally called Greyfriars, Franciscans now wear brown robes.*

1100

1111 Death of the Islamic philosopher Al-Ghazali (b.1058), who wrote *The Revival of the Religious Sciences* to counter the Greek-influenced philosophies of Avicenna and Averroës.

c.1120 Scholar Pierre Abélard (1079–1142) revives the teaching of Aristotle in Paris, France.

c.1130 Construction of the temples at Angkor Wat in Cambodia begins.

1139 Scholar Geoffrey of Monmouth (1100–54) composes *History of the Kings of Britain.*

1140 Birth of the Japanese philosopher Eisa (d.1215) whose teachings founded Zen Buddhism.

1153 Death of the Byzantine scholar Anna Comnena (b.1083), author of *The Alexiad*, a biography of her father the emperor Alexius (1048–1118).

c.1180 Chinese philosopher Zhu Xi (1130–1200) compiles the Confucian Canon.

1198 Death of the Islamic philosopher Ibn Rushd (b.1126), known in Europe as Averroës, who wrote an extended commentary on Aristotelian thought.

1200

c.1200 Churches, such as that of St George, carved out of solid rock at Lalibela in Ethiopia.

1200 Birth of the Japanese Zen master Dogen (d.1253).

1209 Franciscans, the first order of mendicant friars, are founded by Francis of Assisi (1182–1226).

c.1210 German minnesinger Wolfram von Eschenbach (1170–1220) writes the romance *Parzival.*

1210 German poet Gottfried von Strassburg writes his version of *Tristan and Isolde.*

1212 Order of the Poor Clares founded.

ASIA AND AUSTRALASIA

1220

1222 Mongols conquer Afghanistan and invade N India.

1227 Mongols conquer the Xi-Xai kingdom in NW China. Genghis Khan (b.c.1162) dies and the Mongol empire is divided between his three sons and a grandson.

1228–29 Sixth Crusade, led by Frederick II of Germany, obtains Jerusalem, Bethlehem and Nazareth by treaty.

1229 Shan people establish the kingdom of Assam in E India.

1229 Genghis Khan's son Ogedei (1186–1241) is elected chief khan of the Mongol empire.

1231 Mongols invade Korea.

1234 Islamic Delhi Sultanate sacks the Hindu city of Ujjain in central India.

1234 Mongols complete their conquest of N China.

1240

1242 Mongols capture the city of Lahore in present-day Pakistan.

1244 Jerusalem is captured by Islamic armies.

c.1250 Turks begin settling in Asia Minor.

1253 Mongols under Hulegu (1217–65) invade W Persia and establish the Ilkhanid dynasty.

1253 Mongols capture the N Burma region; Thai peoples migrate S.

1253 Rivalry between Venetian and Genoese merchants at Acre, Palestine, leads to war between the two Italian city-states.

1255 Mongol khan Mongke (1208–59) bans Taoist books in China.

1256 Mongols exterminate the Assassins in Syria.

1257 Mongol armies conquer present-day N Vietnam.

1258 Mongols launch attacks against the Southern Song dynasty in S China.

1258 Baghdad is destroyed by Mongol armies.

1259 Following the death of Mongke, the division of the Mongol empire into four khanates becomes permanent.

1260

1260 Mongols are defeated by the Mamluks at the battle of Ain Jalut in Palestine.

1260 Mongol khan Kublai (1215–94) becomes Emperor of N China.

1267 Kublai establishes as his capital the city of Khanbalik, which later becomes Beijing.

1268 Mamluks sack the city of Antioch in Syria.

AFRICA

Church at Lalibela, Ethiopia The 13th-century church at Lalibela was one of several hewn out of solid rock. The Middle Ages was a time of great church building and of revival and expansion in the ancient Christian empire of Ethiopia.

1228 Hafsid dynasty takes over from the Almohads in Tunisia.

1230 Sundiata I (d.1255) becomes king of the city-state of Mali.

1239 Ziyanid dynasty overthrows the Almohads in Algeria.

Teutonic Knight
The military religious order of the Teutonic Knights was founded (1190–91) during the Third Crusade. Its members, of aristocratic class, took monastic vows of poverty and chastity. They waged war on non-Christian peoples.

1240 Sundiata, king of Mali, defeats Samanguru, king of Ghana, and establishes the empire of Mali.

1249 Seventh Crusade, led by Louis IX (1214–70) of France, invades Egypt and captures the port of Damietta.

1250 Louis IX is defeated by the Egyptians and is taken prisoner.

1250 Mamluks (Turkish slave bodyguards), led by Baybars, seize power in Egypt; end of the Fatimid dynasty; start of the Bahri Mameluke dynasty.

1269 Marinid dynasty takes over from the Almohads in Morocco.

1270 Warlord Yekuno Amlak (r.1270–85) seizes control of Ethiopia and establishes the Solomonid dynasty.

1270 Louis IX of France leads the Eighth Crusade to Tunis, where he dies of fever.

EUROPE

1212 Civil wars in Germany end with Frederick II (1194–1250) becoming the German king.

1212 Christian victory at the battle of Las Navas de Toloso leads to the downfall of the Islamic Almohad dynasty in Spain.

1214 French king Philip II (1165–1223), supported by Frederick II, defeats the English, supported by Otto IV (1174–1218), at the battle of Bouvines; he conquers the English-controlled territory N of the River Loire.

1215 King John (1167–1216) signs the Magna Carta at Runnymede, England.

c.1218 Rivalry between Guelphs (supporters of papal authority) and Ghibellines (supporters of the German emperor) becomes a major factor in Italian politics.

1220 Frederick II (1194–1250) becomes Holy Roman emperor. and king of S Italy.

1226 Teutonic Knights settle in Riga and NE Poland.

1226 Louis IX (1214–70) becomes king of France, with his mother, Blanche of Castile, as regent.

1227 Della Torre family (Guelphs) gains control of the city-state of Milan in Italy.

1228 Italian city-state of Florence adopts a democratic constitution.

1228 Mercenaries are used for the first time in Europe in wars between Italian city-states.

1229 At the end of the wars against the Albigensians, the French crown acquires territory in S France.

1231 Constitutions of Melfi establish a modern administrative state in Sicily.

1231 Teutonic Knights begin the conquest of Prussia.

1232 Frederick II's son, Henry, leads the N Italian cities in a revolt against German control.

1232 Emirate of Granada is established by the Islamic Nasrid dynasty in S Spain.

1235 Kingdom of Aragón, N Spain, captures the Balearic Islands from Islamic rule.

1236 Ferdinand III (1199–1252) of Castile captures Córdoba and conquers most of S Spain.

1236 Mongols invade Europe.

1237 Armies of Frederick II defeat the N Italian cities at the battle of Cortenuova.

1237 Mongol khanate of the Golden Horde is established in S Russia.

1240 Mongols destroy Kiev.

1240 Prince of Novgorod, Alexander Nevski (1220–63), defeats a Swedish invasion on the River Neva.

1241 Mongols defeat an army of Polish and German knights at the battle of Liegnitz.

1241 Mongols defeat the Hungarians at the battle of Sajo.

1241 Conflicts between Frederick II (1194–1250) and the pope lead to German troops pillaging central Italy.

1242 Teutonic Knights attack Novgorod, but are defeated by Alexander Nevski at the battle of Lake Peipus.

1242 Mongols withdraw from Europe after the death of Khan Ogodei (1185–1241).

1242 English under King Henry III (1207–72) invade France.

1250 Frederick II dies and is succeeded by his son Conrad IV (1228–54).

1253 Kingdom of Portugal conquers the Algarve region from Islamic rule.

1254 Death of Conrad IV marks the end of the Hohenstaufen dynasty in Germany and the beginning of an interregnum.

1258 English barons rebel against King Henry III.

1259 English are forced to cede territory to the French king, Louis IX, at the Peace of Paris.

1259 German port cities of Lübeck, Hamburg and Rostock form a *Hansa* (union).

1260 City of Siena defeats the ruling Guelph faction of Florence at the battle of Montaperti.

1261 King Ottokar II (d.1278) of Bohemia captures Austria from Hungary; this marks the highpoint of Bohemian power.

1261 Greeks, with Genoese help, seize Constantinople and re-establish the Byzantine empire; end of the Latin empire.

1264 Venice regains control of Constantinople after defeating Genoa at the battle of Trepani.

THE AMERICAS	SCIENCE AND TECHNOLOGY	ARTS AND HUMANITIES

1213 French historian Geoffrey de Villehardouin (1150–1213) writes an account of the Fourth Crusade, *Conquest of Constantinople*.

*c.***1230** Explosive bombs and rockets are first used by the defenders of Chinese cities against the Mongols.

*c.***1220** In s China the landscape artists Ma Yuan (1190–1224) and Xia Gui (1180–1230) emphasize mist and clouds. — **1220**

1220 Building of Amiens cathedral marks the beginning of the Rayonnant Gothic style of architecture, characterized by large circular windows.

1222 Icelandic poet Snorri Sturluson (1179–1241) writes the epic *Prose Edda*.

1225 Qutb Minar tower is built in Delhi, India.

1225 Francis of Assisi (1182–1226) writes *Canticle of Brother Sun*.

*c.***1230** French poet Guillaume de Lorris (1210–37) writes the first part of *Roman de la Rose*.

13th-century fashion *These examples from England show the fashion among both men and women for long dress-like garments. Although hidden by the cloak, the woman's garment was likely to have had long trailing sleeves.*

*c.***1250** Gunpowder is first mentioned in European manuscripts; the secret of its manufacture was learned either from Arabs in Spain or from Mongol prisoners.

1248 Construction starts on the Alhambra fortress and palace in Granada, s Spain. — **1240**

1248 Building of Cologne cathedral marks the spread of Gothic architecture across N Europe.

*c.***1250** 'Black Pagoda' Temple of the Sun at Konarak in India built by King Narasimhadeva (r.1238–64).

1259 Death of the English historian and biographer Matthew Paris, author of *Great Chronicle*.

▶ **Gothic art and architecture** *Chartres Cathedral, NW France, was one of the earliest examples of High Gothic architecture and established the basic principles of Gothic design. The gallery, which had been a feature of Romanesque churches, was omitted to make room for a three-tier elevation. Built between 1194 and 1220, it was the first cathedral to use ribbed vaults and flying buttresses, which provided better structural support and allowed for greater height and more windows. Chartres Cathedral has c.150 stained-glass windows, including a front-facing rose window depicting scenes from the Old Testament. The Cathedral has more than 2000 sculpted figures, many of which reflect the more naturalistic style of sculpture that emerged during the 13th century.*

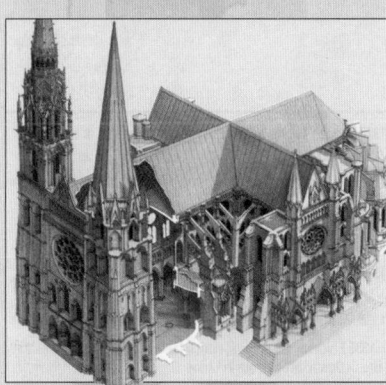

1262 Death of the Islamic astronomer Ibn Omar al-Marrakashi, who wrote *Of Beginnings and Ends*.

1264 French scholar Vincent of Beauvais (1190–1264) publishes his *Great Mirror*, a combination of encyclopedia and universal history.

1266 English scholar and mathematician Roger Bacon (1220–92) completes *Longer Work*, which advocates the use of scientific experiment.

1260 Italian artist Nicola Pisano (1225–84) sculpts a pulpit for the Baptistry in Pisa. — **1260**

1262 Death of the philosopher and reformer Shinran (b.1173), who established True Pure Land Buddhism in Japan.

1273 Italian scholar and philosopher Thomas Aquinas (1225–74) completes *Theological Digest*.

1275–80 Tibetan scholar Phags-pa devises a script for writing Mongolian.

ASIA AND AUSTRALASIA

1268 Mongols invade s China.

1271 Mamluks capture the Christian fortress of Krak des Chevaliers in Syria.

1274 Mongols make an unsuccessful attempt to invade Japan.

1277 Mongol forces capture the city of Guangzhou (Canton) in s China.

1277 Mamluks invade Asia Minor and defeat the Mongols, but later withdraw.

1279 Pandya dynasty completes its conquest of s India; end of the Chola dynasty.

1279 Mongols complete their conquest of s China; end of the Southern Song dynasty, start of the Yuan dynasty.

1280

1281 Mongols attempt to invade Japan but are repulsed by samurai; the Mongol fleet is destroyed by a storm – the *kamikaze* (divine wind).

1282–88 Mongols make repeated attempts to subdue the kingdom of Champa in present-day s Vietnam.

1287 Mongols conquer and destroy the kingdom of Pagan in Burma.

1291 Mamluks capture the city of Acre, Palestine, the last remnant of the Crusader kingdoms.

1292–93 Mongols attempt a seaborne invasion of Java.

1294 Death of the Mongol Chinese emperor Kublai (b.1215).

1297 Delhi Sultanate conquers the Hindu kingdom of Gujarat in w India.

1299 Mongol Chaghati khanate of central Asia invades N India.

1300

1300 Turkish general Osman I (1258–1326) proclaims himself sultan of the Turks in Asia Minor; start of the Ottoman empire.

1300 Thai peoples under King Rama Kamheng establish a kingdom around the city of Sukhothai in present-day Thailand.

1303 Delhi Sultanate conquers the Rajput fortress of Chitor, the last Hindu stronghold in N India.

1306 Chaghati Mongols are expelled from India by the Delhi Sultanate.

1311 Delhi Sultanate annexes the Pandya kingdom in s India.

1313 Delhi Sultanate conquers central India.

1320

1320 Turkish Tughluk dynasty takes over control of the Delhi Sultanate.

1323 Delhi Sultanate conquers the Hindu kingdom of Telingana in India.

1330 Hindu kingdom of Madjapahit in Java begins extending its control over nearby islands.

1333 Emperor Go-daigo tries to re-establish imperial power in Japan.

1335 Mongol Ilkhanid dynasty in Persia is overthrown.

***c*.1335** Epidemic of plague, which later becomes known as the Black Death, breaks out in China.

1336 Revolt establishes the Hindu kingdom of Vijayanagar in s India; start of the Sangama dynasty.

1336 Civil wars break out in Japan, which is split between rival imperial courts.

1337 Ottoman Turks capture Nicaea, the last remaining Byzantine territory in Asia Minor.

1338 Bengal breaks away from the Delhi Sultanate to become an independent Islamic state.

AFRICA

> "The whole city is arrayed in squares just like a chess-board, and disposed in a manner so perfect and masterly that it is impossible to give a description that should do it justice."
>
> Marco Polo, referring to Kublai Khan's capital Khanbalik
> *(The Book of Marco Polo)*

***c*.1300** Kingdom of Benin is established on the w coast of Africa.

1316 Military expedition from Egypt establishes an Islamic ruler in Nubia.

1320 King Amda Seyon (r.1314–44) extends Christian control to s Ethiopia.

Mosque, Timbuktu *The great mosque at Timbuktu was designed in the 14th century by As Saheli, one of the Egyptians brought back to Mali by Mansa Musa after his pilgrimage to Mecca. Timbuktu grew to be an important centre of commerce, religion and learning.*

1324 Pilgrimage of Mansa Musa (r.1312–37) to Mecca marks the highpoint of the Empire of Mali.

1332 War breaks out between Christian Ethiopia and neighbouring Islamic kingdoms.

EUROPE

1266 French invade s Italy; Charles (1226–85), brother of French king Louis IX (1214–70), becomes king of Sicily.

1265 Rebellious English barons are defeated by Prince Edward (later Edward I) at the battle of Evesham.

1271 Marco Polo (1254–1324) departs for China.

1277 Visconti family (Ghibellines) gains control of Milan.

1277 Genoese merchants establish the first regular Atlantic sea-route between the Mediterranean Sea and N Europe.

1278 After victory over Ottokar II of Bohemia at the battle of Marchfeld, Rudolph of Habsburg gains control of Austria.

1278–84 Edward I (1239–1307) of England invades and conquers Wales.

1282 French soldiers in Palermo are massacred during the 'Sicilian Vespers'; the Sicilians invite Pedro of Aragón to be their king.

1283 Teutonic Knights complete the conquest of Prussia.

1284 Italian city-state of Genoa defeats Pisa at the battle of Meliora.

1285 Bulgarian kingdom disintegrates under Mongol overlordship.

1291 Three Swiss cantons revolt against Habsburg rule and form a confederation.

1291 Knights of St John move to Cyprus.

1297 William Wallace (1270–1305) leads a rising against English rule in Scotland.

1297 English king Edward I (1239–1307) invades France in support of Flanders.

1297 French king Philip IV (1268–1314) occupies Flanders (NE France and Belgium).

1299 Genoa defeats Venice at a naval battle near the island of Curzola in the Adriatic Sea.

1302 Citizens of Flanders defeat the French at the battle of the Spurs at Courtrai.

1305 Flanders submits to French rule.

1305 English execute the Scottish rebel William Wallace (b.1270).

1307 Knights Templar are disbanded in Paris.

1309 French king Philip IV (1268–1314) compels the pope, Clement V, to move to Avignon in s France; start of the 'Babylonian Captivity'.

1309 Teutonic Knights make Marienburg their capital.

1309 A Bourse (stock exchange) is founded at Bruges, present-day Belgium.

1309 Knights of St John move to the island of Rhodes.

1310 City-state of Venice establishes its Council of Ten.

1314 Scots, led by Robert the Bruce (1274–1329), defeat the English at the battle of Bannockburn and establish Scottish independence.

1314 First Venetian merchant ships visit N Europe.

1315 Swiss defeat the Austrian army at the battle of Morgarten.

1319 Sweden and Norway are united under the rule of Magnus VII (1316–74).

1325 Ivan I becomes ruler of the Grand Duchy of Moscow under the overlordship of the khanate of the Golden Horde.

1328 Seat of the Russian Church is moved from Vladimir to Moscow.

1328 Death of the French king Charles IV (b.1294) ends the Capetian dynasty; start of the Valois dynasty.

1329 Byzantines capture the island of Chios from Genoa.

1330 After defeating the Greeks and Bulgarians at the battle of Velbuzdhe, Serbia becomes the dominant power in the Balkans

1331 Cities in s Germany, including Ulm and Augsburg, establish the Swabian League.

1332 Gerhard of Holstein, supported by the Hanseatic League, seizes the Danish crown.

1332 Lucerne is the first city to join the Swiss Confederation.

1337 Edward III (1312–77) of England lays claim to the French throne; beginning of the Hundred Years' War (to 1453).

1339 City of Genoa in Italy adopts a republican constitution.

1339 Island city of Venice conquers the town of Treviso on the Italian mainland.

THE AMERICAS

English military *In the 14th century, the nature of warfare was dramatically changed by the adoption of the longbow. The longbow made England a formidable power.*

c.1300 Chimú state in Peru expands to rival that of the Incas.

c.1300 Mesa Verde and other Anasazi centres in present-day sw USA are abandoned.

> "All abandon hope,
> ye who enter here."
>
> *Dante (Divine Comedy, "Inferno")*

c.1325 Aztecs establish the city of Tenochtitlán on an island in Lake Texcoco, Mexico.

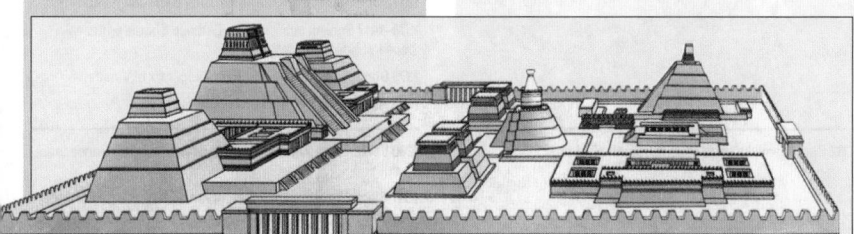

▲ **Tenochtitlán** *The ancient Aztec capital Tenochtitlán in Mexico housed between 150,000 and 300,000 inhabitants. The sacred centre, illustrated here, housed many temples, including the great pyramid, seen on the left, dedicated to Huitzilopochtli, the God of the Sun and war.*

SCIENCE AND TECHNOLOGY

c.1270 Firearms and cannon (made of reinforced bamboo) are first used in battles between the Mongols and the Chinese.

c.1270 Double-entry book-keeping is developed in the Italian city of Florence.

1275 German scholar and scientist Theodoric of Freiburg describes how a rainbow is formed by reflections within raindrops.

c.1280 Belt-driven spinning wheel is introduced to Europe from India.

1280s Establishment of the Mongol empire across Asia re-opens overland trade routes, such as the Silk Road, between Europe and the Far East.

1291 Venetians move their glass factories to the island of Murano for fire safety.

c.1300 Earliest-known European spectacles are manufactured in Italy.

1311 Pietro Vesaconte makes the earliest-known portolan sea-chart (navigational chart) of the Mediterranean.

1316 Italian doctor Modinus publishes *Anatomy*, a textbook of human anatomy.

c.1320 Cannon are first used on a European battlefield.

1324 Earliest-known European cannon are manufactured in France.

ARTS AND HUMANITIES

1282 Death of the philosopher Nichiren (b.1222), who established Lotus Sutra Buddhism in Japan.

1283 Italian artist Giovanni Cimabue (*c.*1240–*c.*1302) paints his *Sta Croce* crucifix.

1283 Catalan scholar and author Raimon Lull (1235–1315) writes his utopian novel *Blanquerna*.

1285 Italian artist Duccio di Buoninsegna (*c.*1265–1319) paints the *Rucellai Madonna*, which revolutionizes the Byzantine style of Sienese painting.

c.1300 Polynesian settlers on Easter Island begin a period of intensive statue carving.

1304–09 Italian artist Giotto di Bondone (1266–1337) begins painting his frescos in the Arena chapel, Padua.

1309 French knight Jean, Sire de Joinville (1224–1319) publishes *Life of St Louis* (the French king Louis IX).

1314 Persian statesman Rashid al-Din (1247–1318) publishes his illustrated world history, *Collection of Histories*.

1314 Italian poet Dante Alighieri (1265–1321) begins writing *Divine Comedy*.

1315 Italian historian and dramatist Albertino Massato writes his play *Ecerimis* about the political struggles in Padua.

1317 Italian artist Simone Martini (1284–1344) paints *St Louis*.

1324 Italian politician Marciglio of Padua (*c.*1275–1342) writes *Defensor Pacis*, an essay on relations between Church and State.

c.1325 Beginning of the Renaissance in Italian art is accompanied by a revival of interest in ancient Greece and Rome, and the development of secular thought – humanism.

1332 Birth of the Islamic philosopher Ibn Khaldun (d.1406), author of an *Introduction to History*.

1334 Giotto di Bondone (1266–1337) designs the bell tower of Florence cathedral.

1335 Italian artist Andrea Pisano (d.1348) casts the bronze s doors of the baptistry in Florence.

1335 Mosque of Al-Nasir in Cairo is completed.

1337 Italian artist Ambrogio Lorenzetti paints frescos of *Good and Bad Government* in the town hall in Siena.

1337 Death of the Chinese dramatist Wang Shifu (b.1250), author of *The Romance of the Western Chamber*.

1338 Italian artist Taddeo Gaddi (*c.*1300–*c.*1366) paints frescos in the Church of Santa Croce, Florence.

1280

1300

1320

ASIA AND AUSTRALASIA

1340

1341–43 Epidemic of plague – the Black Death – sweeps across China.

1344 Flooding of the Yellow River devastates E China.

1346 Independent Islamic dynasty is founded in Kashmir, N India.

1347 Thai capital is moved to the city of Ayutthaya.

1350 Unrest begins in China among workers repairing the Grand Canal. They are followers of the Buddhist White Lotus cult and wear red turbans.

1353 Kingdom of Laos is established in SE Asia.

1355 Red Turbans, led by former monk Hong-wu (1328–98), foment a popular revolt against Mongol rule in China.

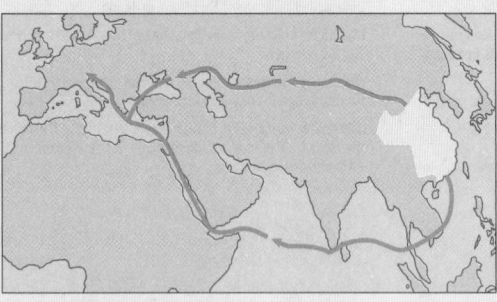

Black Death *Originating in China c.1335, the Black Death spread w across Asia and Europe, via trade and pilgrimage routes, reaching the Crimea in 1347, as illustrated in the larger map. From the Crimea, the plague spread throughout*

1360

1367 Victory in battle by the Delhi Sultanate over the Hindu kingdom of Vijayanagar leads to the massacre of 400,000 civilians.

1368 Red Turbans expel the Mongols from China and Hong-wu (1328–98) becomes emperor; start of the Ming dynasty.

1369 Thais sack the Khmer capital of Angkor.

1369 Tamerlane (1336–1405), or Timur, a Turkish soldier, rebels against the Chaghati Mongols and captures their capital, Samarkand.

1377 Islamic empire of Java conquers Hindu Sumatra.

1380

1381–87 Tamerlane (Timur, 1336–1405) invades and conquers Persia.

1382 All districts of China are reunited under Ming control.

1389 Islamic empire of Java collapses after the death of king Rajasanagara (b.1334).

1392 Yoshimitsu (1358–1408) becomes ruler of Japan and establishes the Muromachi shōgunate.

1392 General Yi Song-gye establishes the Yi (Choson) dynasty in Korea.

1393–94 Tamerlane invades and conquers Mesopotamia.

1394 Islamic kingdom of Jaunpur in N India is established.

AFRICA

1340 Portuguese sailors discover the Canary Islands.

1344 Canary Islands are allocated to Castile by the pope.

1348 Black Death devastates Egypt.

1349 Moroccan traveller Ibn Battutah (1304–68) returns home after a 25-year journey to India and China.

Europe. The red lines on the smaller map indicate the approximate extent of plague in Europe at six monthly intervals from 31 December 1347 to 30 June 1350. The region spared partly or wholly from the plague is in white.

1365 Crusade led by the king of Cyprus sacks the city of Alexandria in Egypt.

1375 Kingdom of Songhai breaks away from the empire of Mali.

> "Entities should not be multiplied unnecessarily. No more things should be presumed to exist than are absolutely necessary."
>
> *William of Occam's statement of the rule of economy that has come to be known as Occam's razor*

1382 Burji Mamluks seize control from the Bahris in Egypt.

EUROPE

1340 English defeat the French at a naval battle near the port of Sluys (in present-day Belgium).

1340 Spanish king of Castile, Alfonso XI (1311–50), decisively repels an Islamic attack at the battle of Rio Salado.

1341–47 Civil war further disrupts the Byzantine empire.

1344 Hungarian king Louis I (1326–82) expels the Mongols from Transylvania.

1346 Black Death sweeps through S Russia.

1346 Teutonic Knights gain control of Estonia.

1346 English defeat the French at the battle of Crécy, the first major battle of the Hundred Years War.

1347 English capture the French port of Calais.

1347 Black Death reaches Constantinople, Italy and S France; in 1348 it reaches Spain. N France and Britain; in 1349 Germany and Scandinavia. This initial outbreak kills c.25% of Europe's population.

1348 Danish king Waldemar IV (1320–75) recaptures Jutland from German control.

1351 War breaks out in Italy between Florence and Milan.

1352 Ottoman Turks establish a foothold in Europe at Gallipoli.

1354 Genoese destroy the Venetian fleet at the sea battle of Sapieanza.

1356 English, led by Edward the Black Prince (1330–76), defeat the French at Maupertuis and capture the French king.

1356 Hanseatic League (a commercial union of c.160 German, Dutch and Flemish towns) is formally established.

1358 Rising in Paris, led by Étienne Marcel (c.1316–58), and peasant revolts in the countryside weaken France.

1360 By the Peace of Bretigny, Edward III (1312–77) of England gives up his claim to the French throne in return for sovereignty over SW France.

1361 Ottoman Turks capture the city of Adrianople; the Byzantine empire is reduced to the city of Constantinople..

1361–63 Second outbreak of the Black Death devastates parts of Europe.

1361–70 Wars between the Hanseatic League and Denmark leave the League dominant in the Baltic region.

1367 Civil war breaks out between the Swabian League and the German emperor.

1369 French king Charles V (1337–80) attacks English possessions in France.

1370 Teutonic Knights defeat the Lithuanians at the battle of Rudau.

1370 Bastille fortress is built in Paris.

1371 Robert II (1316–90) becomes king of Scotland; start of the Stuart dynasty.

1372 Swabian League is defeated.

1372 Spanish, allied with the French, defeat the English at the sea battle of La Rochelle.

1375–78 War of the Eight Saints is fought between Florence and the papacy.

1376 Swabian League is revived by the city of Ulm.

1377 Pope returns to Rome; end of the 'Babylonian Captivity'.

1378–1417 Schism occurs in the Catholic Church with rival popes at Rome and Avignon.

1378 Genoa captures the town of Chioggia, S of Venice.

1378 Flanders revolts against French rule.

1380 Venice recaptures Chioggia and destroys the Genoese fleet.

1381 *Ciompi* (low-paid workers) revolt against the rule of the Guelphs in Florence.

1381 Peasants' Revolt in England ends with the death of its leader, Wat Tyler.

1382 Flanders revolt is crushed at the battle of Roosebeke by Philip the Bold (1342–1404), who becomes overlord of the region.

1383 Venice captures Corfu.

1385 Victory at the battle of Aljubarrota establishes Portuguese independence from Spain.

THE AMERICAS

*c.***1350** King Mayta Capa begins expanding Inca control in Peru.

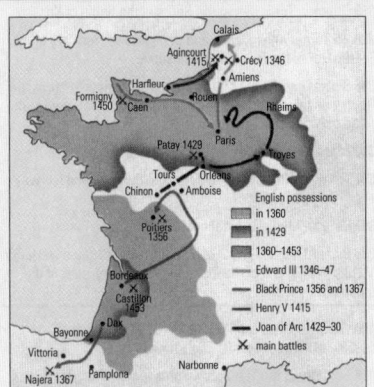

Hundred Years' War *The conflict between the Plantagenet and the Valois dynasties was marked by short campaigns, longer truces and periods of stalemate. English campaigns consisted of plundering raids on W and N France. Except for a few captured strongholds, from which expeditions could be launched, there was little attempt to conquer French territory until Henry V invaded Normandy in 1417. Various campaigns and possessions are illustrated on the map.*

*c.***1370** Acamapitchtli becomes king of the Aztecs.

*c.***1370** Chimú complete their conquest of coastal N Peru.

14th-century fashion *After the bubonic plague (c.1350) Europe experienced a period of economic prosperity, reflected in the swiftly changing fashions of the time. The man wears extravagently pointed shoes and the woman has adapted the surcote worn by the crusaders.*

SCIENCE AND TECHNOLOGY

1340 First European factory for making paper opens in Fabriano, Italy.

1340s Wind-driven pumps are used to drain marshes in Holland.

1343 English philosopher and scholar William of Occam (1285–1349) publishes *Dialogus*, which contains his 'razor' of logic.

1363 French doctor Guy de Chauliac (d.1368) completes his textbook of surgery, *Great surgery*.

1364 A university is established in Kraków, Poland.

1370 French king Charles V establishes standard time according to a weight-driven mechanical clock in the royal palace in Paris.

*c.***1377** French scholar William of Oresme (1320–82) writes his essay on monetary policy, *On money*.

1377 Single arch bridge with a span of 72m (236ft) is completed at Trezzo, N Italy.

1379 Rockets are first used on a European battlefield by the army of Padua in Italy.

1385 Heidelberg university is established.

1392 Moveable metal type is first used for printing in Korea.

ARTS AND HUMANITIES

1341 Italian poet Francesco Petrarch (1304–74) publishes *Poems*, a collection of love poems

1348 Death from plague of Italian historian Giovanni Villani (b.1276) brings to an end his chronicle of Florentine history.

1352 Palace of the popes at Avignon, France, completed.

1357 Italian artist Andrea Orcagna (1308–68) creates the altarpiece for the Strozzi family chapel in Florence.

1357 Death of the Italian lawyer Bartolus of Sassoferrato (b.1314), who advocated republican government in his *On the government of cities*.

1357 Italian scholar Zanobi da Strada discovers a forgotten manuscript copy of Tacitus' *Annals* in a monastery library.

1358 Italian poet and author Giovanni Boccaccio (1313–75) completes his *Decameron* of tales told during the Black Death.

> "This world nis but a thurghfare ful of wo, / And we ben pilgrimes, passinge to and fro; / Dethe is an ende of every worldly sore."
>
> *Chaucer (Canterbury Tales)*

1360 Italian lawyer Giovanni di Legnano writes his *Treatise on War*.

1360 Construction of the Alcázar palace in Seville begins.

*c.***1362** English priest William Langland (1331–99) writes the poem *Piers Plowman*.

*c.***1365** Flemish painters establish the Bruges school of painting.

*c.***1370** Japanese dramatist Kanami Motokiyo (1333–84) establishes the classic form of No drama.

1372 Egyptian scholar and zoologist Al-Damiri (1344–1405) writes *Lives of animals*.

1378 Nun and philosopher Catherine of Siena (1347–80) writes *Dialogo*.

1380 English religious reformer John Wycliffe (1330–84) translates the Bible into English

*c.***1380** English poet Geoffrey Chaucer (1346–1400) begins writing the first of the *Canterbury Tales*.

1386 Construction of Milan cathedral begins.

1391 Byzantine scholar Manuel Chrysolaurus arrives in Italy and begins popularizing the Classical Greek philosophers.

1396 Italian humanist philosopher Coluccio Salutati (1331–1406) publishes *On destiny and fortune*.

1397 Chinese law code *Laws of the Great Ming* published.

ASIA AND AUSTRALASIA

1398–99 Tamerlane invades N India and sacks Delhi.

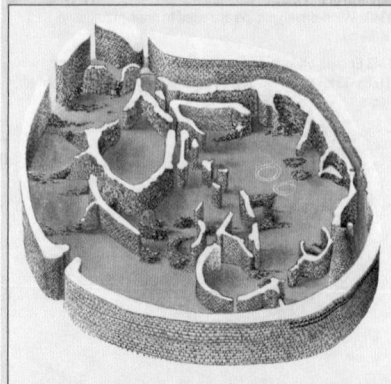

▶ *Great Zimbabwe* The walled enclosure was built mainly in the 14th and 15th centuries on a site used for ritual purposes since c.1000. The Mwenemutapa kingdom, of which Great Zimbabwe was the capital, traded gold with Arabs on the E African coast.

1400

1400 Tamerlane (Timur, 1336–1405) invades and conquers Syria.

1402 Tamerlane defeats the Ottoman Turks at the battle of Ankara; collapse of the Ottoman empire in Asia.

1403 Islamic warlord establishes the city of Malacca in Malaya.

1404–07 Chinese admiral Cheng Ho (1371–1433) subdues Sumatra.

1405 Tamerlane dies and his empire collapses; a Timurid dynasty continues to rule in Persia and Turkistan.

1408–11 Cheng Ho defeats the Ceylonese.

1409 Chinese invade Vietnam.

1413 Sultan Muhammad I (1389–1421) re-establishes Ottoman control over Asia Minor.

1416–19 Chinese fleet sails to Yemen.

1418 Vietnamese leader Le Loi organizes resistance against the Chinese.

1419 Sejong (1397–1450) becomes king of Korea.

1420

1420 Beijing replaces Nanjing as the capital of China.

c.1420 Coffee, introduced from Ethiopia via Yemen, is domesticated near Mecca, Arabia.

1429 City of Bidur becomes the capital of the much-reduced Delhi Sultanate.

1428 Le Loi declares himself ruler of Annam (N Vietnam).

1431 Annam wins independence from China.

1433 Chinese emperor Xuan-zong prohibits any further long-distance sea voyages.

1440

1448 Trailok (r.1448–88) becomes king of Thailand.

1449 Chinese emperor captured by a Mongol raiding party.

AFRICA

1415 Portuguese under King John I (1357–1433) capture the town of Ceuta on the Mediterranean coast of Morocco.

1416 Portuguese explorers reach Cape Bojador on the W coast of Africa.

15th-century fashion In Europe, both men and women wore formal gowns, often with long, trailing sleeves. Men wore a turban-like hat, called a chaperon. Women wore impractical headdresses.

1420 Portuguese occupy the island of Madeira.

1421 Ships from Ming China establish direct contact with the Islamic towns of E Africa.

1424 Chinese ships again visit E Africa.

1425 Portuguese fail to conquer the Canary Islands from Castile.

1430 Portuguese discover the Azores.

1433 Chinese ships make a final visit to E Africa.

1433 Desert nomads capture the city of Timbuktu in the SW Sahara desert.

1434 Zara Yaqob (d.1468) becomes king of Ethiopia.

1437 Portuguese make a disastrous attempt to capture Tangier, Morocco.

1440 Walled enclosure and tower are built at Great Zimbabwe, capital of the Mwenemutapa kingdom.

1445 Portuguese explorers reach Cape Verde, W Africa.

EUROPE

1386–88 Milan conquers the Italian cities of Verona, Vicenza and Padua.

1386 King Jagiello (1351–1434) of Poland forms a union with the Grand Duchy of Lithuania.

1387 Danish regent Margaret (1363–1412) becomes queen of Sweden and Norway.

1389 Ottoman Turks defeat the Serbs at the battle of Kosovo.

1388–95 Tamerlane invades and conquers the territory of the Golden Horde but fails to take Moscow.

1396 Sigismund (1368–1437) of Hungary attempts to break the Turkish encirclement of Constantinople but is defeated at the battle of Nicopolis.

1396 Bulgaria becomes part of the Ottoman empire.

1397 Treaty of Kalmar unites Denmark, Sweden and Norway under Danish control.

1397 Bank of Medici is established in Florence.

1399 Richard II (1367–1400) of England is overthrown by Henry IV (1367–1413); end of the Plantagenet dynasty, start of the Lancaster dynasty.

1400 Welsh led by Owain Glyn Dŵr (Owen Glendower, c.1359–1416) rebel against English rule.

1404 Territory of the Teutonic Knights reaches its greatest extent after acquisition of Brandenburg.

1405 Venetians attack and occupy the city of Padua in NE Italy, initiating their conquest of the *Terrafirma*.

1406 Italian city of Florence gains access to the sea through control of neighbouring Pisa.

1408 Khanate of the Golden Horde unsuccessfully besieges Moscow, but re-establishes its overlordship

1410 Polish-Lithuanian armies defeat the Teutonic Knights at the battle of Tannenberg.

1413 Henry V (1387–1422) becomes king of England and renews claims against France.

1414 Attempted rising by Lollards (followers of the religious reformer John Wycliffe) in England is suppressed.

1415 Czech religious reformer Jan Hus (b.1369) is executed.

1415 Henry V of England invades France, wins the battle of Agincourt, and occupies Paris.

1416 Venetians defeat the Ottoman Turks in a sea battle.

1417 Council of Constance restores a single papacy, ending the Great Schism.

1419 Predominantly Czech supporters of Hus rise against German rule in Bohemia (the defenestration of Prague); start of the Hussite Wars.

1420–22 Supporters of Jan Hus (1369–1415) in Bohemia defeat a Crusade against them led by Sigismund (1368–1437) of Hungary.

1425 Cities of Florence and Venice ally against Milan.

1427 War breaks out between Denmark and the Hanseatic League.

1427 Venetians conquer the city of Bergamo in NE Italy, and complete their *Terrafirma*.

1429 Joan of Arc (1412–31) leads French forces to relieve the English siege of Orléans; she escorts Charles VII (1403–61) of France to his coronation at Reims.

1429 Florence attacks the nearby city of Lucca.

1430 Ottoman Turks capture the city of Thessaloníki from the Venetians.

1431 Joan of Arc is executed by the English.

1433 Hungarian king Sigismund, also king of Germany and Bohemia, is crowned Holy Roman emperor.

1434 Defeat by the Holy Roman emperor at the battle of Lipany leads to civil war between moderate and radical Hussites; it ends in the defeat of the radicals.

1434 Cosimo de' Medici (1389–1464) becomes the effective ruler of Florence.

1435 Spanish ruler of Sicily, Alfonso V, unites his kingdom with that of Naples.

1436 French recapture Paris from the English.

1438 Albert of Habsburg (1397–1439) becomes German emperor and king of Hungary and Bohemia as Albert II.

1440 Alliance between Florence and Venice defeats Milan at the battle of Anghiari.

1444 Ottoman sultan Murad II (1403–51) defeats a Christian army at the battle of Varna in Bulgaria.

THE AMERICAS

*c.*1400 Start of the Middle Period of Mississippi mound-building.

Hundred Years' War 1337–1453
- Plantagenet territory *c.*1300
- Plantagenet territory recognized by the Treaty of Brétigny 1360
- Area recognizing Plantagenet kingship 1420–28
- ✕ Major battle with date

1426 Itzcoatl (d.1440) becomes Aztec king and begins a policy of military expansion.

1437 While the Lord Inca is campaigning elsewhere, Cuzco is besieged by the neighbouring Chanca people.

1438 Incas led by Pachacuti conquer the Chancas.

1440 Montezuma I (r.1440–69) becomes the Aztec king.

1441 Aztecs conquer Mayapan.

1450 Incas under Pachacuti conquer the Lake Titicaca region.

SCIENCE AND TECHNOLOGY

1410 Flagship of the Chinese admiral Cheng Ho is 130m (426ft) long and has five masts and 12 decks; it is the biggest wooden sailing ship ever built.

1419 Portuguese prince Henry (known as Henry the Navigator, 1394–1460) establishes a school of navigation at Sagres.

◄ **Hundred Years' War** *The outcome of the Hundred Years' War brought an end to English claims to French territory and established the two countries as distinct nations.*

1420 Italian architect Filippo Brunelleschi (1377–1446) begins designing the dome of Florence cathedral.

1424 Persian mathematician al-Kashi (d.1429) publishes a value for pi (π) that is correct to 16 decimal places.

*c.*1430 Hussite leader Jan Zizka (*c.*1376–1424) invents the cannon-equipped armoured fighting vehicle.

1435 Italian architect Leon Alberti (1404–72) outlines the mathematical laws of perspective in painting in *On painting*.

1437 Islamic astronomers in Samarkand publish the *Tables of Ulugh Beg*, named after the Mongol ruler who established their observatory.

*c.*1445 German goldsmith Johann Gutenberg (1400–68) develops moveable metal type for printing.

1443 Phonetic alphabet is developed in Korea.

ARTS AND HUMANITIES

*c.*1399 Greek artist Theophanes (*c.*1330–1405) paints the icon *The Deeds of the Archangel Michael* for the Kremlin cathedral in Moscow.

1400 French scholar Jean Froissart (*c.*1337–1410) completes his *Chronicles*, describing events in the Hundred Years War.

1402 Italian humanist Pietro Paulo Vergerio (1370–1444) writes *Conduct worthy of free men*.

1406 Construction work starts on the Forbidden Palace in Beijing.

1410 French artists the Limbourg brothers produce the illustrated *Les tres riches heures du Duc de Berry*.

1413 Czech philosopher and religious reformer Jan Hus (1369–1415) writes *Exposition of Belief*.

1413 University of St Andrews is founded in Scotland.

1415 French poet Christine de Pisan (1364–1430) writes *The Rights of Women*.

1416 *Hsing Li Ta Ch'uan*, the 120-volume compilation of moral philosophy, is published in China.

1419 Italian sculptor Jacopo della Quercia (1374–1438) creates the *Gaia* fountain in Siena.

1423 Italian artist Gentile da Fabriano (*c.*1370–1427) paints *Adoration of the Magi*.

1424 French poet Alain Chartier (1385–1440) writes *La Belle Dame Sans Merci*, an attack on courtly love.

1425 Italian sculptor Lorenzo Ghiberti (1378–1455) begins work on the bronze N doors of the Baptistry in Florence.

1426 Italian artist Masaccio (1401–28) paints polyptych panels for the Carmelite Church, Pisa.

1429 Italian humanist Guarino da Verona (1374–1460) becomes professor of classics at Ferrara University.

1434 Flemish artist Jan van Eyck (*c.*1390–1441) paints the *Arnolfini Wedding*.

1434 Italian sculptor Donatello (1386–1466) casts his bronze statue of *David* in Florence.

1436 Italian artist Paolo Uccello (1397–1475) paints a frescoed portrait for the tomb of the English condottieri (mercenary) John Hawkwood (d.1394).

1439 Cosimo de' Medici founds the Florentine Academy.

1439 Byzantine scholar Gemistus Pletho (1355–1452) publishes his treatise on the differences between the Platonic and Aristotelian philosophies.

*c.*1440 Italian artist Pisanello (*c.*1395–1455) turns the making of bronze portrait medals into an art form.

ASIA AND AUSTRALASIA

Istanbul *The Topkapi Sarayi (Old Palace) was built by Muhammad II, the conqueror (1453) of Constantinople, on the site of the old Acropolis. One of the earliest Ottoman buildings in the new capital, it was the sultan's official residence and also housed the harem. It was conceived on a grand scale.*

▶ **Spanish soldiers** *During the 16th century Spain was the leading imperialist power and gained the whole of Central and South America, with the exception of Brazil. The halberd (pictured) was used alongside more modern weaponry, such as gunpowder.*

1461 Trebizond, the last remnant of the Byzantine empire, is conquered by the Ottomans.

1467 Onin war starts in Japan between rival feudal warlords.

1469 Last Timurid ruler of Persia is overthrown by Uzun Huzan (*c.*1420–78), leader of the White Sheep Turkmens.

1471 Annam (N Vietnam) conquers Champa (S Vietnam).

1477 At the end of the Onin war in Japan, power lies in the hands of new *daimyo* (territorial rulers).

1479 Vietnam conquers the kingdom of Laos.

1487 Portuguese explorers sailing from the Red Sea visit India.

1498 Portuguese explorer Vasco da Gama (1469–1524) reaches the port of Calicut in India.

> "Of the two lights of Christendom, one has been extinguished."
>
> *Aeneas Silvius, Bishop of Trieste, on hearing of the fall of Constantinople to the Turks*

1501 Persian leader Ismail (1486–1524) defeats Turkish tribes at the battle of Shurur and gains control of Persia.

1502 Portuguese ships commanded by Vasco da Gama (1469–1524) destroy the Indian port of Calicut.

1502 Ismail is proclaimed shah of Persia; start of the Safavid dynasty in Persia.

AFRICA

1448 Portuguese establish a settlement on Arguim Island off the coast of Mauritania.

1455 Portuguese explorers discover the Cape Verde islands.

1463 Portuguese capture Casablanca in Morocco.

1464 King of Songhai, Sonni Ali (d.1492), begins campaigns to overthrow Mali; start of Songhai empire.

1468 Songhai empire conquers Timbuktu.

1469 Portuguese explorers cross the Equator.

1471 Portuguese establish a trading post at El Mina on the coast of present-day Ghana.

1471 Portuguese capture the city of Tangier on the N coast of Morocco.

1478 Portuguese ships defeat a fleet sent from Spain and establish supremacy along the W African coast.

1480 Under the treaty of Toledo, Portugal gets exclusive trading rights in Africa in return for agreeing to Spanish control of the Canary Islands.

1482 Portuguese build the fort of São Jorge to protect El Mina in Ghana.

1483 Portuguese explorers make contact with the W African kingdom of Kongo.

1487 Portuguese explorer Bartholomeu Diaz (*c.*1450–1500) sails around the S tip of Africa into the Indian Ocean.

1489 Portuguese explorers sailing from the Red Sea visit E Africa.

1490 Nzinga Nkuwu (d.*c.*1506), king of Kongo, converts to Christianity.

1493 Muhammad Askia becomes emperor of Songhai, with the city of Gao as his capital.

1496 Spanish capture the town of Melilla on the N coast of Morocco.

1498 Sailing from Portugal, Vasco da Gama calls at the E African port of Mombasa en route to India.

1501 Portuguese attempt to close the Red Sea to Islamic shipping.

1504 Christian kingdom of Soba in Nubia is conquered by Islamic forces.

1505 Portuguese under Francisco de Almeida (1450–1510) sack the Islamic ports of Kilwa and Mombasa in E Africa.

EUROPE

1445 African slaves are auctioned for the first time in Portugal.

1449 Milan defeats Venice and conquers the Lombardy region of N Italy.

1449 French invade the English territory in W France.

1450 Denmark and Norway are united under Danish king Christian I (1426–81).

1450 Sforza family gains control of Milan

1452 Frederick III (1415–93) becomes the first Habsburg Holy Roman emperor.

1453 Ottoman Turks besiege and capture Constantinople, which is henceforth known as Istanbul.

1453 French victory over the English at the battle of Castillon near Bordeaux marks the end of the Hundred Years War.

1454 Peace of Lodi brings to an end the wars in Italy between Milan, Venice and Florence.

1455 Wars of the Roses break out in England between the rival dynasties of Lancaster and York.

1456 Turks capture Athens.

1457 Poland captures Marienberg from the Teutonic Knights who move their capital to Königsberg.

1459 Turks conquer Serbia.

1462 Ivan III (1440–1505) becomes the first ruler of Moscow not to pay tribute to the Golden Horde; end of the 'Tartar Yoke'.

1466 Teutonic Knights accept Polish overlordship.

1468 Charles the Bold (1433–77), duke of Burgundy (NE France, Belgium and Holland), allies with England against the French.

1469 Lorenzo 'il Magnifico' Medici (1449–92) becomes ruler of Florence.

1470 Louis XI (1423–83) of France allies with the Swiss against Burgundy.

1471 Right to feud is formally abolished in Germany in an attempt to stem rising lawlessness.

1475 Ottoman Turks conquer the Crimean peninsula on the N coast of the Black Sea

1477 Inquisition is revived in Spain.

1477 Charles the Bold is killed at the battle of Nancy. France occupies parts of Burgundy; the Low Countries come under Habsburg control by marriage.

1478 Albania is conquered by the Ottomans.

1479 Habsburg heir, Maximilian (1459–1519), defeats French attempts to gain control of the Low Countries.

1479 Ferdinand V (1452–1516) becomes Spanish king, uniting Castile and Aragón.

1483 Tomás Torquemada (1420–98) becomes head of the Spanish Inquisition.

1485 Battle of Bosworth ends the Wars of the Roses in England. Henry VII (1457–1509) becomes king; start of the Tudor dynasty.

1486 Habsburg Maximilian I (1459–1519) is elected king of Germany.

1488 Great Swabian League of princes, knights and cities is formed in S Germany.

1492 Spanish, under Ferdinand V (1452–1516) and Isabella I (1451–1504), conquer the Islamic emirate of Granada; the whole of Spain is united under Christian rule

1493 Maximilian I becomes Holy Roman emperor.

1493 Ottoman Turks invade Croatia.

1493 By the treaty of Senlis, France cedes the rest of Burgundy to Habsburg control.

1494–95 French under Charles VIII (1470–98) invade Italy, capture Florence and Naples, but are then forced to retreat.

1497 Denmark enforces union on Sweden.

1499 French under Louis XII (1462–1515), allied with Venice, invade Italy and capture Milan.

1499 Switzerland wins political independence from the Habsburg empire in the Swabian War.

1499 Cesare Borgia (1475–1507), son of Pope Alexander IV, begins the conquest of central Italy.

1501 French invade Italy and conquer Naples.

1501 Portuguese establish a direct sea-route to import pepper and spices from India into Europe.

1504 Spain regains control of Naples.

1509 French-led coalition attacks and captures Venetian-controlled towns in N Italy.

THE AMERICAS

*c.*1460 Manchancaman becomes Chimú king and attacks the Incas.

1463 Pachacutec becomes the Inca king.

1470 Incas defeat and annex the Chimú kingdom.

1471 Tupac Yupanqui becomes the Inca king.

*c.*1490 Incas expand their empire into parts of Bolivia and Colombia.

1492 Christopher Columbus (1451–1506), a Genoese in the service of Spain, reaches an island he names San Salvador in the Bahamas; he founds the first European settlement, Navidad, on the island of Hispaniola.

1493 On his second voyage, Columbus plants the first sugar cane cuttings in the Caribbean.

1494 Treaty of Tordesillas between Spain and Portugal grants most of the New World to Spain.

1496 Town of Santo Domingo is established on Hispaniola as the Spanish centre of government in the Americas.

1497 John Cabot (*c.*1450–*c.*1498), a Genoese sailing from England, discovers the coast of Newfoundland.

1498 Columbus reaches the American mainland at the mouth of the River Orinoco.

1499 Italian explorer Amerigo Vespucci (1454–1512) discovers the mouth of the River Amazon.

1500 Portuguese explorer Pedro Cabral (1467–1520) lands in Brazil and establishes Vera Cruz.

1501 First African slaves are landed in the West Indies.

1502 Montezuma II (r.1502–20) becomes the Aztec king.

SCIENCE AND TECHNOLOGY

1449 Italian artist and inventor Mariano di Jacopo Taccola (1381–1453) completes 10 books of civil and military machines.

1453 Hungarian armourers cast a 7.3m (26ft), 50-tonne cannon to be used by the Ottoman Turks in the siege of Constantinople.

1455 Construction of the Grand Bazaar begins in Istanbul.

1456 German astronomer Johannes Regiomontanus (1436–76) introduces the mathematical symbols for plus and minus in an unpublished manuscript.

◀ *Florence* The Baptistry of San Giovanni, built between the 11th and 15th centuries, is noted for its Romanesque green and white marble-facing and gilded bronze doors.

*c.*1460 Italian glassmaker Anzolo Barovier perfects the technique of making completely colourless glass by adding manganese.

1462 Pope declares his monopoly over the supply of alum (used in the dyeing industry) to Europe.

1469 Pliny the Elder's *Natural History* is printed for the first time.

1474 Government of Venice issues the world's first patents to protect inventors' rights.

*c.*1475 Italian astronomer and mathematician Paolo Toscanelli (1397–1482) proposes voyaging to China by sailing w across the Atlantic ocean.

▶ *Renaissance* Prominent figures in the Florentine Renaissance often worked in a variety of cultural and political fields. Illustrated here are, from left to right: Macchiavelli, statesman and political theorist; Leonardo da Vinci, painter, sculptor, architect, engineer and scientist; Verrocchio, sculptor and painter; and Michelangelo, sculptor, painter, architect and poet.

1480 Italian artist and inventor Leonardo da Vinci (1452–1519) designs a parachute.

1494 Italian mathematician Luca Pacioli (*c.*1445–1517) introduces algebra to Europe in *Summa de arithmetica, geometrica, proportione et proportionalita.*

1500 Leonardo da Vinci (1452–1519) designs an impractical, but correctly principled, helicopter.

1502 Italian mineralogist Leonardus Camillus publishes his *Speculum Lapidum*, which catalogues over 250 minerals.

*c.*1505 Pocket watch is invented by German clockmaker Peter Henlein (1480–1542).

ARTS AND HUMANITIES

1444 Italian architect Michelozzi di Bartolommeo (1396–1472) designs the Medici Palace in Florence.

1445 Italian sculptor Bernado Rossellino (1409–64) carves a marble tomb in Florence for the humanist Leonardo Bruni.

1446 Flemish artist Rogier van der Weyden (1400–64) paints *The Last Judgement.*

1449–52 *Gideon Tapestries* are woven in Tournais, present-day Belgium, for Philip the Good (1396–1467), Duke of Burgundy.

1452 Italian artist Fra Filippo Lippi (1406–69) paints his frescos for Prato cathedral.

1455 *Gutenberg Bible* is printed.

1456 French poet François Villon (1430–63) completes *Le petit testament.*

1457 Italian artist Antonio Pollaiuolo (1432–98) completes a silver reliquary of St Giovanni in Florence.

1465 Italian artist Andrea del Verrocchio (1435–88) starts work on his bronze statues of *Christ and St Thomas* in Florence.

1469 Birth of Nanak (d.1539) the Indian philosopher and founder of Sikhism.

1470 Italian artist Piero della Francesca (1415–92) paints portraits of the Duke and Duchess of Urbino.

*c.*1472 Italian artist Giovanni Bellini (*c.*1430–1516) paints his Pesaro altarpiece in Venice.

*c.*1478 Italian artist Sandro Botticelli (1444–1510) paints his *Primavera.*

1481 Death of the French artist Jean Fouquet (b.1420), who painted miniature portraits and illustrated manuscripts.

*c.*1482 Italian architect Giuliano da Sangallo (1445–1516) designs the villa Poggio a Caiano in Florence.

1485 William Caxton (1422–91) prints *Le Morte D'Arthur* by Sir Thomas Malory.

1486 Italian humanist Giovanni Pico della Mirandola (1463–94) writes *Oration on the Dignity of Man.*

1486 Italian artist Andrea Mantegna (1431–1506) paints *Triumphs of Caesar* in Mantua.

1489 German inquisitors publish the *Hammer of Witchcraft.*

1489 German sculptor Viet Stoss (1440–1533) completes his carved limewood altar for the church of St Mary's in Kraków, Poland.

1494 German humanist poet Sebastian Brandt (1458–1521) writes *Ship of Fools.*

1495 Flemish painter Hieronymus Bosch (*c.*1450–1516) paints *The Garden of Earthly Delights.*

1496 Japanese artist-priest Sesshū Toyo (1420–1506) paints *Winter Landscape.*

1498 German artist Albrecht Dürer (1471–1528) publishes his album of woodcuts *The Apocalypse.*

1498 Ottavanio Petrucci (1466–1539) obtains a licence in Venice to become the first commercial music printer.

1502 Italian architect Donato Bramante (1444–1514) reintroduces the Doric order in his tempietto at San Pietro in Montorio, Rome.

1503 Leonardo da Vinci paints the *Mona Lisa.*

1504 Italian artist Michelangelo Buonarotti (1475–1564) carves his marble sculpture of *David* in Florence.

1460

1480

1500

ASIA AND AUSTRALASIA

1504 Warlord Babur (1483–1530) captures Kabul, Afghanistan.

1506 Portuguese build a fort at Cochin in India.

1507 Portuguese sack the port of Muscat near the mouth of the Arabian Gulf.

1508 Turkish fleet destroys some Portuguese ships at the Indian port of Chaul.

1509 Portuguese destroy a combined Turkish-Indian fleet near the island of Diu.

1510 Portuguese conquer Goa and make it their capital in India.

1511 Portuguese, led by Afonso d'Albuquerque (1453–1515), capture Malacca in Malaya.

1512 Portuguese reach the Spice Islands (the Moluccas).

1514 Ottoman Turks invade Persia and defeat the Safavids at the battle of Chaldiran.

1515 Ottoman Turks conquer Kurdistan.

1515 Portuguese capture and fortify Hormuz in Yemen.

1516 Ottoman Turks defeat the Egyptian Mamluks and the Persian Safavids at the battle of Marj Dabik in Syria.

1516 Portuguese establish a trading post at Guangzhou (Canton) in s China.

1517 Portuguese establish a trading post at Columbo in Ceylon.

1520

1521 Ferdinand Magellan (1480–1521) discovers and claims the Philippine Islands for Spain.

1521 Portuguese establish a settlement on Amboina, one of the Spice Islands.

1522 Portuguese traders are expelled from China.

1523 Afghan warlord Babur (1483–1530) invades India and captures the city of Lahore.

1526 Babur conquers the w half of the Delhi Sultanate after the battle of Panipat and establishes the Mogul empire.

1526 Portuguese explorers reach New Guinea.

1529 Victory at the battle of the River Gogra completes the Mogul conquest of N India.

1534 Ottomans conquer Mesopotamia.

1537 Portuguese obtain trading concessions at Macao on the coast of s China.

1538 Alliance of Ottoman Turks and Gujaratis fails to evict the Portuguese from Diu in India.

1538 Turkish naval expedition conquers the w coast of Arabia.

1539 Mogul dynasty in India is overthrown by the Afghan warlord Sher Shah (d.1545).

1540

1543 Portuguese first make contact with Japan.

1546 With Portuguese assistance, Tabin Shwehti (r.1531–50) makes himself king of Burma.

1555 Burmese invade N Thailand.

1555 Peace treaty is signed between the Ottoman Turks and Safavid Persia.

1556 Emperor Akbar I (1542–1605) restores Mogul rule in India and defeats Hindu forces at the second battle of Panipat.

1557 Portuguese establish a colony at Macao in China.

AFRICA

1506 Portuguese build a fort at Sofala on the E coast of Africa.

1509 Spanish capture the town of Oran on the coast of Algeria.

1510 Spanish capture the town of Tripoli in Libya.

1517 Ottomans under Sultan Selim I (1467–1520) conquer Egypt; end of the Mameluke dynasty.

1517 Hausa states defeat the Songhai Empire in w Africa.

Spanish fashion, 1500 Both men and women wore rigid, high-necked clothing. Corsets became fashionable.

1527 Islamic Somalis invade Ethiopia.

1529 Ottoman Turks invade and conquer Algeria.

1535 Charles V campaigns against the Turkish pirate Khayr ad-Din (Barbarossa, 1466–1546) and captures the city of Tunis.

▶ **Palladio** The Villa Rotunda was begun c.1550 in Vicenza. Designed by Italian architect Palladio, it is exceptional among villas for its perfect symmetry, designed to take advantage of the view from the hilltop site.

1541 Expedition of Charles V (1500–58) against the Ottoman Turks at Algiers fails.

1543 Ethiopian forces, assisted by Portuguese troops, expel Islamic invaders.

Château de Chambord Built for French king Francis I, the château was probably designed by Italian architect Domenica da Cortona.

EUROPE

1511 Henry VIII (1491–1547) of England joins the Holy League against France in Italy.

1512 Hanseatic League permits Dutch ships to trade in the Baltic Sea.

1513 French are defeated at the battle of Novara in Italy.

1513 English destroy the Scottish army at the battle of Flodden.

1515 A marriage alliance gives the Habsburgs control over Spain.

1515 German emperor obtains Bohemia and Hungary from Poland in exchange for Prussia.

1515 After defeat by the French at the battle of Marignano, Switzerland adopts a policy of neutrality.

1517 Pope Leo X (1475–1521) revives the sale of indulgences to pay for the rebuilding of St Peter's cathedral in Rome.

1517 German priest and reformer Martin Luther (1483–1546) writes his 95 theses against Church corruption; start of the Reformation in Europe.

1518 Swiss religious reformer Ulrich Zwingli (1484–1531) begins preaching in Zurich.

1519 Charles V (1500–58), Habsburg king of Spain and Burgundy, wins election as German emperor over Francis I (1494–1547) of France.

1521 At the diet of Worms, Emperor Charles V (1500–58) condemns Martin Luther's ideas.

1521 Ottoman Turks capture Belgrade and raid s central Europe.

1521–26 First war for control of Italy is fought between France and Spain.

1522 Knights of St John surrender the island of Rhodes to the Turks after a siege.

1523 Gustavus I (1496–1560) establishes the Swedish state; start of the Vasa dynasty.

1524–25 Violent peasant uprisings sweep across Germany.

1525 Spain defeats France at the battle of Pavia in Italy and captures Francis I (1494–1547).

1526 King Louis II (b.1506) of Hungary is killed in the battle of Mohács against the Ottoman Turks; the Hungarian crown passes to the Habsburgs.

1527 During his second Italian war (1526–29), Spanish king and Habsburg emperor Charles V sacks Rome.

1528 Genoese admiral Andrea Doria (1466–1560) frees Genoa from French rule.

1529 Ottoman Turks unsuccessfully besiege Vienna.

1529 German emperor Charles V ends toleration of Lutheran reforms. Some German princes protest, becoming Protestants.

1531 War breaks out between Protestant and Catholic cantons in Switzerland.

1531 Hungary is partitioned between the Habsburgs and the Ottomans.

1531 Protestant rulers in Germany form the Schmalkaldic League.

1534 Act of Supremacy is passed in England, making Henry VIII (1491–1547) head of the English Church.

1541 French religious reformer John Calvin (1509–64) establishes religious rule in Geneva.

1541 Ottoman Turks capture Budapest and conquer Hungary.

1545 Council of Trent meets to reform the Catholic Church.

1546–47 Charles V defeats the Protestants in the Schmalkaldic War in s and central Germany.

1547 Protestant reformer John Knox (1514–72) is arrested by French soldiers in Scotland.

1547 Ivan IV (the Terrible, 1530–84) of Moscow is crowned first tsar of Russia.

1552 Emperor Charles V invades E France.

1553 Following the death of Henry VIII in 1547, and his only son, Edward VI, in 1553, his daughter Mary (1516–58) becomes queen as Mary I. She marries the future Philip II (1527–98) of Spain and restores Catholic worship in England; Protestants are persecuted.

1555 Religious peace of Augsburg establishes freedom of worship in Germany.

1556 Charles V abdicates; his empire is split between Ferdinand I (Austria and Germany) and Philip II (Spain, Low Countries, parts of Italy, and America).

THE AMERICAS

1507 German mapmaker Martin Waldseemüller (c.1470–c.1518) proposes that the New World be named America.

1508–15 Spanish conquer Puerto Rico and Cuba.

1509 Spanish establish a colony on the isthmus of Panama.

1512 Spanish governor of Puerto Rico, Juan Ponce de León (1460–1521), discovers Florida.

1513 Spanish explorer Vasco Núñez de Balboa (1475–1519) crosses the Ithsmus of Panama and discovers and names the Pacific Ocean.

1516 Bananas are introduced into the Caribbean from the Canary Islands.

1517 Spanish explorer Francisco de Córdoba discovers the Yucatán peninsula in Mexico.

1517 First asiento (agreement) for the supply of African slaves to the American colonies is issued to a Flemish merchant by the Spanish government.

1518 Spanish conquistador Hernán Cortés (1485–1547) lands in Mexico and conquers the Tlaxcalans.

1519 Cortés enters the Aztec capital Tenochtitlan, captures Montezuma II and establishes Spanish control.

1520 Montezuma II dies and the Aztecs force the Spanish from Tenochtitlan.

c.1520 Inca king Huayna Capac conquers parts of Ecuador.

1521 Spanish attack and destroy Tenochtitlan.

1522 Viceroyalty of New Spain is created and Mexico City is founded on the ruins of Tenochtitlan.

1521 Sailing in the pay of Spain, the Portuguese navigator Ferdinand Magellan sails around Cape Horn at the S tip of South America.

1522 Spanish expedition from Panama reaches Peru.

1525 Death of Inca king Huayna Capac leads to dispute over throne between sons Huascar (d.1532) and Atahualpa.

1529 Welser family (German bankers) establish a colony in Venezuela.

1530 Portuguese begin the colonization of Brazil.

1531 Inca king Atahualpa invites Spanish soldiers, led by Francisco Pizarro (1471–1541), to join his side in the Inca civil war.

1532 Pizarro captures Atahualpa and holds him to ransom.

1533 Atahualpa is killed by the Spanish, who occupy Cuzco and conquer the Inca empire.

1535 Pizarro founds the city of Lima in Peru.

1537 Spanish establish colonies at Buenos Aires, at the mouth of the River Plate, and Asunción, on the River Paraguay.

1538 Spanish conquistador Gonzalo de Quesada founds the city of Bogotá.

1539 Spanish begin the conquest of the Mayan cities in the Yucatán region of Mexico.

1540–42 Spanish expedition led by Francisco de Coronado (1510–54) discovers the Grand Canyon.

1541 Spanish explorer Hernando De Soto (1500–42) discovers the River Mississippi.

1541 Spanish explorer Francisco de Orellana (c.1490–c.1546) completes his journey down the River Amazon from the Andes to the Atlantic Ocean.

1541 French explorer Jacques Cartier (1491–1557) makes an unsuccessful attempt to establish a colony at Quebec in Canada.

1541 Spanish found the city of Santiago in Chile.

1542 Spanish create the viceroyalty of Peru.

1545 Spanish begin mining silver at Potosi in Peru.

1546 Revolt by the Maya against Spanish rule in Mexico is crushed.

1548 Spanish open silver mines at Zaatecar in Mexico.

1548 Spanish viceroyalty of New Galicia is created in NW Mexico with Guadalajara as its capital.

1549 Spanish viceroyalty of New Granada created, comprising South America E of the Andes and N of the River Amazon.

SCIENCE AND TECHNOLOGY

c.1510 Polish astronomer and mathematician Nicolas Copernicus (1473–1543) formulates his theory that the Earth orbits the Sun.

c.1515 Wheel lock for igniting firearms is invented in Italy.

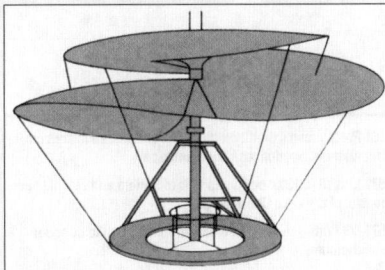

helicopter Leonardo da Vinci sketched this design for a rotating-wing aircraft in c.1500. The spiral wing would have lifted the machine in much the same way as the rotor of a helicopter. It is certain, however, that this machine never flew because there was no engine in existence that was capable of powering the device.

c.1520 Rifling for firearms is invented in central Europe.

1522 Spanish ships returning from Ferdinand Magellan's voyage complete the first circumnavigation of the world.

1525 German mathematician Christoff Rudolff introduces the square root symbol in Die Coss.

1533 German surveyor Gemma Frisius (1508–55) discovers the principles of triangulation.

1537 Italian mathematician Niccoló Tartaglia (1449–1557) discusses the trajectory of projectiles in Nova scientia.

1540 Italian gunsmith Vannoccio Biringuccio's Pirotechnia, a handbook of metal smelting and casting techniques, is published.

▲ **Copernicus'** study of planetary motions led him to develop a Sun-centred theory of the Universe known as the Copernican system.

1542 French scholar Konrad Gesner (1516–65) publishes Historia Plantarum, the first modern work of botany.

1543 Copernicus' heliocentric theory is published in his De revolutionibus orbium coelestium.

1543 Belgian doctor Andreas Vesalius (1514–64) publishes On the Structure of the Human Body, an illustrated handbook of human anatomy based on dissection.

1545 Italian scientist Giramolo Cardano (1501–76) introduces negative numbers to European mathematics in his book Ars magna.

1551 English mathematician Leonard Digges (c.1520–59) invents the theodolite.

1551 German mathematician Georg Rhaeticus (1514–74) publishes the six basic trigonometrical functions in Canon doctrinae triangulorum.

1556 German mineralogist Georg Bauer (1494–1555), also known as Agricola, publishes De re metallica, a systematic study of mining and assaying techniques.

1557 English mathematician Robert Recorde (c.1510–58) introduces the symbol for equality in his algebra textbook The Whetstone of Whit.

ARTS AND HUMANITIES

c.1504 Flemish composer Josquin Desprez (1445–1521) writes the mass Hercules Dux Ferrariae.

c.1505 Italian artist Giorgione (c.1478–1510) paints his Tempest.

1506 Ancient Roman sculpture known as the Laocoön is rediscovered in Rome.

1511 Dutch humanist Desiderius Erasmus (1466–1536) publishes In Praise of Folly.

1512 Michelangelo finishes painting the ceiling of the Sistine Chapel in Rome.

1512 Italian artist Raphael Santi (1483–1520) paints a portrait of Pope Julius II.

1513 Italian politician Niccolò Machiavelli (1469–1527) writes The Prince.

1515 German artist Mathias Grünewald (1470–1528) paints The Crucifixion for the Isenheim altarpiece, Alsace.

1516 English scholar Thomas More (1478–1535) publishes Utopia.

1516 Italian poet Lodovico Ariosto (1474–1533) publishes the epic Orlando Furioso.

1520 German Christian reformer Martin Luther (1483–1546) writes The Freedom of a Christian Man, which proclaims salvation through faith.

1524 German artist Lucas Cranach (1472–1553) paints Judgement of Paris.

1525 Luther writes Against the Murderous Thieving Hordes of Peasants.

1525 English religious reformer William Tyndale (c.1494–1536) starts printing English versions of the New Testament in Cologne, Germany.

1528 Italian courtier Baldassare Castiglione (1478–1529) publishes Libro del Cortegiano.

c.1528 German artist Albrecht Altdorfer (1480–1538) paints unpopulated landscapes.

1530 German religious reformer Philip Melanchthon (1497–1560) writes the Confessions of Augsburg, a statement of Protestant beliefs.

1530 Italian artist Correggio (c.1490–1534) paints Adoration of the Shepherds.

1533 German artist Hans Holbein the Younger (1497–1543) paints The Ambassadors.

1534 Luther completes his translation of the Bible into German.

1534 French humanist François Rabelais (1494–1553) writes his satire Gargantua.

1534 Society of Jesus (Jesuits) is founded by Ignatius Loyola (1491–1556) and Francis Xavier (1506–52).

c.1535 Italian artist Parmigiano (1503–40) paints Madonna with the Long Neck.

1538 Italian artist Titian (1485–1576) paints Venus of Urbino.

1540 Holy Carpet of Ardebil, with an area of 61sq m (72sq yd), is woven in N Persia.

1541 Spanish priest and protector of Native Americans Bartolomé de Las Casas (1474–1566) writes his Very Brief Account of the Destruction of the Indies.

1541 Death of the Swiss doctor known as Paracelsus (b.1493).

1545 Indian architect Aliwal Khan designs the octagonal tomb of the Afghan warlord Sher Shah at Sasaram, India.

1545 Italian goldsmith and sculptor Benvenuto Cellini (1500–71) casts his bronze statue of Perseus in Florence.

1548 Italian artist Tintoretto (1518–94) paints The Miracle of the Slave in Venice.

1549 French poet Joachim du Bellay (1522–60) writes Defense et Illustration de la Langue Francaise.

1549 English priest Thomas Cranmer (1489–1556) publishes his Book of Common Prayer.

1555 Italian architect Andrea Palladio (1508–80) publishes a guidebook to Roman antiquities.

1559 Index of Forbidden Books published by the Roman Catholic Church.

ASIA AND AUSTRALASIA

1561 Moguls under Emperor Akbar I (1542–1605) conquer Malwa in central India.

1563 Chinese destroy Japanese pirates who have been raiding coastal cities.

1565 Muslim Deccan sultanates conquer the Hindu kingdom of Vijayanagar in s India after the Battle of Talikota.

1568 Oda Nobunaga (1534–82) seizes power in central Japan; start of the Azuchi-Momoyama period.

1570 Port of Nagasaki in Japan is opened to foreign traders.

1571 Spanish found the city of Manila in the Philippines.

1573 Moguls under Akbar I conquer Gujarat in w India

1576 Moguls conquer Bengal in E India.

▶ **Globe Theatre** Built in 1599 but destroyed by fire in 1613, the Globe Theatre was rebuilt (1614) in the form shown above. It was a tiled and brick-built, three-storey structure, surrounding an uncovered yard, where poorer patrons could stand. It was a small building, with a diameter of only 25m (83ft), but with its galleries it could hold 2000. It was closed down by the Puritans in 1642, demolished in 1644 and finally rebuilt and reopened in 1995.

1581 The Cossack chieftain Yermak Timofeyevich (d.1584) begins the Russian conquest of Siberia.

1581 Akbar I conquers Afghanistan.

1581 Turkish ships sack the Portuguese fortress at Muscat.

1583 Mogul Emperor Akbar I proclaims toleration of all religions in India.

1584 General Toyotomi Hideyoshi (1536–98) establishes himself as ruler of central Japan.

1586 Abbas I (1571–1629) becomes Shah of Safavid Persia.

1590 Ottoman Turks wrest control of Georgia and Azerbaijan from Persia.

1590 Hideyoshi conquers E and N Japan, reuniting the country under his rule.

1592 Akbar conquers Sind in s Pakistan.

1592 Japanese invade Korea, but are forced out by the Chinese.

1597 Japanese again invade Korea, then withdraw.

1597 Persians defeat the nomadic Uzbeks and expel them from w Afghanistan.

1598 Tokugawa Ieyasu (1543–1616) seizes power in Japan on the death of Hideyoshi.

1600 Victory at the Battle of Sekigahara leaves Tokugawa Ieyasu as sole ruler of Japan; start of the Tokugawa (or Edo) period.

1600 English East India Company formed.

1602 Dutch East India Company formed.

1603 Persians under Abbas I capture Baghdad from the Ottomans.

1605 Dutch seize the spice island of Amboina from the Portuguese.

1606 Spanish explorer Luis de Torres sights the York peninsula on the N coast of Australia.

AFRICA

1561 Portuguese expedition up the River Zambezi makes contact with the kingdom of Mwenemutapa.

1571 Idris III (d.1603) becomes king of Kanem and establishes control of the Lake Chad region.

1571–73 Portuguese make a disastrous attempt to conquer Mwenemutapa.

1572 Spanish capture Tunis from the Ottoman Turks.

1574 Portuguese found the city of Luanda in Angola.

1574 Ottoman Turks recapture Tunis.

1578 Portuguese attempt to conquer the interior of Morocco is defeated at the battle of Alcázar-Kabir.

1581 Morocco begins expanding s into the w Sahara and captures the town of Tuat.

1589 Portuguese defeat the Ottoman Turks at Mombasa, E Africa.

1591 Invading Moroccans crush Songhai forces at the Battle of Tondibi and destroy the city of Gao; end of the Songhai Empire.

1595 Dutch establish a trading post in Guinea on the w coast of Africa.

1598 Dutch establish a small colony on the island of Mauritius.

1612 City-state of Timbuktu becomes independent of Morocco.

EUROPE

1557 Russia invades Livonia, the former territory of the Teutonic Knights.

1558 English, allied to Spain, lose the port of Calais to the French.

1558 Ivan IV orders the colonization of Siberia.

1558 Elizabeth I (1533–1603) becomes Queen of England.

1559 Philip II (1527–98) of Spain defeats France; the Peace of Cateau-Cambrésis restores Naples and the Low Countries to Spanish control.

1560 Scottish Parliament establishes Presbyterianism as the state religion.

1560 Charles IX (1550–74) becomes boy-king of France with his mother Catherine de Medici (1519–89) as regent.

1562 Massacre of Huguenots (French Protestants) at Vassy in France starts a series of religious civil wars.

1563 Start of the Catholic Counter Reformation in s Germany.

1564 Boyars (Russian aristocrats) revolt against Ivan IV (1530–84).

1566 Dutch nobles form an anti-Spanish alliance.

1567 Duke of Alba enforces Spanish control in the Low Countries.

1569 Poland and Lithuania unite under Polish control.

1569–71 Revolt by former Muslims crushed in Spain.

1570 Novgorod destroyed by armies from Moscow.

1570 Turks attack Cyprus.

1571 Stock Exchange established in London, England.

1571 Venetian and Spanish fleets defeat the Ottoman Turks at the Battle of Lepanto in the Mediterranean Sea.

1572 Thousands of Huguenots (French Protestants) massacred on St Bartholomew's Day.

1573 Venetians abandon Cyprus to the Turks.

1574 Dutch under William I (the Silent), Prince of Orange, open dykes to relieve the Spanish siege of Leyden.

1576 Following the Spanish sack of Antwerp, the Dutch provinces unite under William I (the Silent).

1579 Dutch republic formed; Belgium remains under Spanish control.

1580 King Philip II of Spain succeeds to the throne of Portugal and the two countries unite under Habsburg rule.

1581 Spain agrees a peace treaty with the Ottoman Turks.

1584 Dutch leader William I of Orange (b.1533) murdered and succeeded by Maurice of Nassau (1567–1625).

1585 Queen Elizabeth I of England refuses the Dutch throne but takes the Netherlands under her protection by the Treaty of Nonsuch.

1585–89 War of the Three Henrys fought for the French throne.

1588 Spanish invasion fleet (the Armada) sent against England is defeated at the naval Battle of Gravelines.

1589 Russian Church becomes independent of the Greek Orthodox Church.

1589 Victorious Henry III (b.1551) of France assassinated; Henry IV (1553–1610) accedes to the throne; start of the Bourbon dynasty.

1593 War breaks out in Transylvania between Austria and the Ottoman Turks.

1595 After intervening in the Livonian wars, Sweden acquires Estonia by the Treaty of Teusina.

1598 Boris Godunov (1551–1605) becomes Tsar of Russia.

1598 Edict of Nantes grants limited freedom of worship and legal equality for Huguenots (Protestants) in France.

1603 James VI (1566–1625) of Scotland inherits the English throne as James I on the death of Elizabeth I; end of the Tudor dynasty, start of the Stuart dynasty.

1604 Protestant Charles IX (1550–1611) becomes Kng of Sweden.

1605 Gunpowder Plot fails to blow up the English Parliament; Guy Fawkes (b.1570) executed for treason the following year.

1608 Protestant Union of German rulers formed.

1609 Catholic League of German rulers formed.

1609 Truce ends the fighting in the Netherlands between Philip III (1578–1621) of Spain and the Dutch rebels.

THE AMERICAS

1549 Portuguese establish the port of Bahia in Brazil. **1554** Portuguese establish the city of São Paulo in Brazil.

1555 Dutch, English and French sailors form the Guild of Merchant Adventurers to raid Spanish shipping routes from America.

1555 French establish a colony at the bay of Rio de Janeiro on the coast of Brazil.

1561 Following the failure of a settlement at Pensacola, South Carolina, present-day USA, the Spanish king abandons attempts to colonize the E coast of North America.

1561 Spanish treasure fleets are forced to adopt a convoy system as a defence against 'pirate' attacks.

1564 French establish a colony at Fort Caroline in Florida, present-day USA.

1565 Spanish destroy Fort Caroline and found the town of St Augustine in Florida.

1567 Portuguese destroy the French colony in Brazil and found the city of Rio de Janeiro.

1568 Spanish destroy the fleet of the English slave-trader John Hawkins (1532–95) at Vera Cruz.

1578 English explorer Francis Drake (1540–96) sails along the W coast of present-day USA and lays claim to California.

1585 Expedition organized by Walter Raleigh (1552–1618) establishes a colony (which immediately fails) on Roanoke Island off the coast of Virginia, present-day USA.

1587 Second, unsuccessful attempt is made to found an English colony on Roanoke Island.

Spanish Armada
A Spanish pikeman of the Armada era. The Armada was intended to convey an army of some 17,000 men from the Spanish-controlled Netherlands to invade Britain.

1606 London Company and Plymouth Company established in England.

1607 London Company establishes a colony at Jamestown, Virginia, under the leadership of John Smith (1580–1631).

1608 French explorer Samuel de Champlain (1567–1635) founds Québec as the capital of the colony of New France.

1609 English explorer Henry Hudson (d.1611) discovers and sails up the Hudson River.

1610 Sailing in search of a Northwest Passage to the Far East, Hudson discovers Hudson Bay.

1612 English establish a settlement on the island of Bermuda.

SCIENCE AND TECHNOLOGY

1569 Flanders mapmaker Gerardus Mercator (1512–94) publishes a world navigation chart that has meridians and parallels at right-angles

1572 Italian mathematician Raffaele Bombelli (1526–72) introduces imaginary numbers in his *Algebra*.

1576 Danish astronomer Tycho Brahe (1546–1601) builds a royal observatory for King Frederick II (1534–88).

▲ **Galileo Galilei** *is well known for his discovery that a pendulum could be used for timekeeping. His support for the Copernican view of the Universe, with the Earth moving round the Sun, brought him into conflict with the Church.*

1582 Pope Gregory XIII (1502–85) introduces the New Style (Gregorian) calendar to Catholic countries.

1583 Danish mathematician Thomas Finke (1561–1656) publishes the law of tangents in *Geometriae rotundi*.

1586 Dutch mathematician Simon Stevin (1548–1620) demonstrates that objects fall at an equal rate in a vacuum, irrespective of their weights.

1589 Stocking-frame knitting machine is invented by William Lee (c.1550–c.1610) in Cambridge, England.

1591 French mathematician François Viete (1540–1603) introduces literal notation to algebra, with the systematic use of letters to represent unknowns and coefficients.

1593 German astronomer Christopher Clavius (1537–1612) invents and uses the decimal point in a table of mathematical sines.

1593 Death of doctor Li Shizen (b.1518) who compiled *The Comprehensive Pharmacopoeia* of traditional Chinese medicine.

1600 English scientist William Gilbert (1544–1603) publishes *Concerning Magnetism*, which discusses the Earth's magnetism.

1602 Italian astronomer and scientist Galileo Galilei (1564–1642) discovers the constancy of a swinging pendulum.

1606 Belgian scholar Justus Lipsius (1547–1606) completes the final revisions and corrections to his edition of Tacitus' *Annals*.

1608 Dutch optician Hans Lippershey (1570–1619) invents a refracting telescope.

1614 Scottish mathematician John Napier (1550–1617) invents logarithms.

ARTS AND HUMANITIES

1560

1562 Italian artist Paolo Veronese (1528–88) paints *The marriage of Cana*.

1563 Dutch artist Pieter Bruegel the Elder (1525–69) paints his *The Tower of Babel*.

1563 English historian John Foxe (1516–87) publishes the book known as *Foxe's Book of Protestant Martyrs*.

1563 Building work starts on the monastery and palace of Escorial near Madrid, Spain, designed by Juan de Herrera (c.1530–97).

1568 Italian art critic Giorgio Vasari (1511–74) publishes a revised edition of *Lives of the most excellent Painters, Sculptors and Architects*.

1572 Portuguese poet Luíz vaz de Camões (1524–80) publishes his epic *The Lusiads*.

1575 Italian architect Giacomo della Porta (1537–1602) designs the church of Il Gesù in Rome; this marks the beginning of the Baroque period of European art.

1576 French political philosopher Jean Bodin (1530–96) publishes *Of the Republic*.

1580

1580 French scholar and author Michel Montaigne (1533–92) publishes the first of his *Essays*.

1580 Flemish sculptor Jean de Boulogne (1529–1608) cast his bronze statue of *Mercury*.

1582 Death of the Spanish religious philosopher Teresa of Avila (b.1515).

1586 Greek-born Spanish artist El Greco (1541–1614) paints *Burial of Count Orgasz* in Toledo, Spain.

1589 English poet and dramatist William Shakespeare (1564–1616) writes his first play *Henry VI (part I)*.

1590 English dramatist Christopher Marlowe (1564–93) writes his play *Tamburlaine the Great*.

1595 William Shakespeare writes the play *Romeo and Juliet*.

1596 English poet (1552–99) Edmund Spenser completes *The Faerie Queen*.

1597 Italian composer Giovanni Gabrieli (c.1553–1612) writes *Sonata Pian'e Forte*.

1598 Italian artist Caravaggio (1571–1610) paints *Supper at Emmaus*.

1599 Globe Theatre is built in London.

1600

1600 Italian artist Annibale Carracci (1560–1609) paints his *The Virgin mourning Christ*.

1600 William Shakespeare writes *Hamlet*.

1602 Italian philosopher Tommaso Campanella (1568–1639) publishes *City of Sun*.

1604 Confucian Tung-lin Academy is founded in China.

1605 Spanish author Miguel de Cervantes (1547–1616) publishes the first volume of *Don Quixote of the Mancha*.

1605 English dramatist Ben Jonson (1572–1637) writes *Volpone*.

1605 English philosopher Francis Bacon (1561–1626) publishes *Advancement of Learning*.

ASIA AND AUSTRALASIA

1606 Turkey makes peace with Austria.

1609 Dutch conquer Ceylon (present-day Sri Lanka) from the Portuguese.

1609 Dutch establish a trading post at Hirado, w Japan.

1609 Persians defeat the Turks at the battle of Urmia and recapture Baghdad.

1610 Russian expansion into Siberia reaches the River Yenisei.

1612 England gains trading rights at Surat in India after defeating the Portuguese in a naval battle.

1615 Nomad tribes of Manchuria form a military coalition under their leader Nurhachi (1559–1626).

1615 Japanese ruler Tokugawa Ieyasu (1543–1616) destroys Osaka castle after a siege.

1619 Dutch establish the fortified port of Batavia (present-day Jakarta) on the island of Java.

1620

1620 English defeat the Portuguese at the sea battle of Jask off the w coast of India.

1622 English, allied with the Persians, capture Hormuz from the Portuguese.

1623 Dutch massacre English merchants on the island of Amboina.

1624 Spanish traders are expelled from Japan.

1624 Dutch establish a trading post on the island of Formosa.

1625 Janissaries (slave soldiers) revolt against Ottoman rule in Turkey.

1635–37 Manchurian confederation conquers s Mongolia and Korea.

1637 Christian-led Shimabara rebellion is suppressed in Japan.

1638 Japan is closed to foreigners.

1638 Ottoman Turks under Murad IV (1607–1640) recapture Baghdad.

1639 Treaty of Kasr-i-Shirim establishes a permanent border between Turkey and Persia.

1639 English acquire a site for a colony at Madras in India.

▶ *Augsburg Town Hall in s Germany was designed in the Palladian style (1615–29) by Elias Holl. The building's three storey Golden Hall was destroyed in World War 2.*

1640

1641 Dutch capture the Malaysian port of Malacca from the Portuguese.

1641 Dutch traders are permitted to operate from an island in Nagasaki harbour in Japan.

1643 Dutch explorer Abel Tasman (1603–59) discovers New Zealand and Tasmania.

1644 Manchurians enter Beijing at the invitation of the last Ming emperor; end of the Ming dynasty in China; start of the Qing dynasty.

1645 Russian explorers in Siberia reach the Sea of Okhotsk.

1648 Janissaries revolt in Turkey and depose Sultan Ibrahim I (1615–48).

1652 Russian colonists found the city of Irkutsk in Siberia.

1656 Ottoman Turks are defeated by the Venetians at a sea battle near the Dardanelles.

1656 Muhammad Köprülü (c.1586–1661) becomes Ottoman vizier (chief minister) and stabilizes the Ottoman empire.

▶ *Royalist captain of infantry (left) and cuirassier (right) The Royalist cavalry was superior in number to the Parliamentarian forces at the start of the War, but the formation of the New Model Army tipped the balance.*

AFRICA

1621 Dutch capture the w African island slave ports of Arguin and Goree from the Portuguese.

1626 French establish the colony of St Louis at the mouth of the River Senegal.

1626 French settlers and traders establish a colony on the island of Madagascar.

1637 Dutch capture the fortified port of El Mina from the Portuguese.

1650 Ali Bey establishes himself as hereditary ruler of Tunis.

1652 Dutch settlers found the colony of Capetown in South Africa.

1654 French occupy the island of Réunion.

EUROPE

1610 Henry IV (b.1553) of France assassinated; Louis XIII (1601–43) becomes king, with his mother Marie de' Medici (1573–1642) as regent.

1610 Poland invades Russia and occupies Moscow in an attempt to gain control of the Russian throne.

1613 Following the expulsion of the Poles, Michael Romanov (d.1645) becomes Tsar of Russia; start of Romanov dynasty.

1617 Under the Peace of Stolbovo with Sweden, Russia loses access to the Baltic Sea.

1618 Protestant revolt in Prague (the second defenestration) begins the Bohemian War; it marks the start of the Thirty Years' War.

◀ *Harvey was one of England's most prestigious physicians, being successively physician to James I and Charles I.*

1620 Catholic victory at the Battle of the White Mountain leads to the dissolution of the Protestant Union in Germany.

1621 Gustavus II (1594–1632) of Sweden creates the first modern army and conquers Livonia from Poland.

1621 Warfare between the Dutch and Spanish renews.

1625 Huguenots rebel in NW France.

1625 Charles I (1600–49) becomes King of England, Scotland, and Ireland.

1625 Christian IV (1577–1648) of Denmark intervenes as leader of the Protestants in Germany; start of the Danish phase of the Thirty Years' War.

1628 French forces under chief minister Cardinal Armand Richelieu capture the Huguenot stronghold of La Rochelle.

1629 After defeat by Catholic armies, Denmark withdraws from German politics under the Peace of Lübeck.

1630 Gustavus II of Sweden lands in N Germany in support of the Protestants; start of the Swedish phase of the Thirty Years' War.

1631 Swedes defeat the German Catholics at the battle of Breitenfeld and invade s Germany.

1632 Gustavus II dies following his victory at the Battle of Lützen.

1635 Catholic victory at the Battle of Nordlingen forces the Swedes out of s Germany; France enters the Thirty Years' War as Sweden's ally.

1640 Portugal and Catalonia revolt against Spanish rule.

1640 Frederick William (1620–88) becomes Great Elector of Prussia.

1642 Civil War breaks out in England between Royalists and Parliamentarians.

1646 French and Swedes invade Bavaria in s Germany.

1648 Spain recognizes Dutch independence.

1648–53 Fronde rebellions erupt in France.

1648 Treaty of Westphalia ends the Thirty Years' War.

1649 Charles I (b.1600) of England executed; the monarchy abolished and a Commonwealth established.

1652 Spain reunited when Catalonia submits to Spanish rule.

1652–54 England wins a naval war against the Dutch over shipping rights.

1653 Oliver Cromwell (1599–1658) becomes Lord Protector of England.

1654 Cossacks in the Ukraine defect from Poland to Russia, starting a war.

1656 War breaks out between Protestant and Catholic cantons in Switzerland.

1656 English ships capture a Spanish treasure fleet near the port of Cádiz.

1656 Swedes invade Poland and capture Warsaw.

1658 English, allied with the French, capture the Spanish-held port of Dunkirk after the Battle of the Dunes.

1659 Peace of the Pyrenees ends recent warfare between France and Spain.

THE AMERICAS

1612 Tobacco is first cultivated by English settlers in Virginia.

1612 French establish a colony on the island of Maranhão at the mouth of the River Amazon.

1613 Dutch set up a trading post on Manhattan Island.

1614 Expedition organized by the Plymouth Company makes an unsuccessful attempt to establish a colony in New England.

1614 Dutch New Netherland Company is established.

1616 Portuguese conquer the French colony at the mouth of the Amazon and found the city of Belém.

1616 Dutch establish the colony of New Netherland on the site of present-day New York, USA.

1616 English explorer William Baffin (1584–1622) discovers Baffin Bay.

1619 First African slaves arrive in Virginia, and the first representative assembly is held.

1620 English Protestant settlers cross the Atlantic in the *Mayflower* and establish a colony in Massachusetts, present-day USA.

1623 English Council for New England establishes colonies at Dover and Plymouth in New Hampshire.

1624 English settlement in Virginia becomes a royal colony.

1624–25 Dutch capture and briefly hold the port of Bahía in Brazil.

1625 English settlers establish a colony on the island of Barbados.

1626 Dutch administrator Peter Minuit (1580–1638) purchases Manhattan Island and establishes the city of New Amsterdam.

1627 French minister Armand Richelieu (1585–1642) organizes the Company of 100 Associates to colonize New France.

1628 John Endicott (*c.*1588–1665) establishes an English colony at Salem.

1630 Dutch capture the port of Recife in Brazil from the Portuguese.

1630 Twelve-year period of intensive migration from England to Massachusetts begins.

1632 English colony of Maryland is established by George Calvert (1580–1632).

1635 French establish colonies of the islands of Martinique and Guadeloupe.

1636 Dutch capture the island of Curaçao from the Spanish.

1636 English colonist Roger Williams (1603–83) settles in Providence, Rhode Island.

1638 English colony is established at New Haven on Long Island.

1638 Swedes establish the colony of New Sweden in Delaware.

1641 Body of Liberties law code is established in Massachusetts.

1643 French establish the city of Montreal in Canada.

1643 English colonies form the New England Confederation.

1645 Portuguese settlers revolt against Dutch rule in N Brazil.

1654 Portuguese expel the Dutch from Brazil.

1655 French capture the island of Haiti from Spain.

1656 English ships capture Jamaica from Spain, provoking a war.

1655 Under Dutch governor Peter Stuyvesant (1610–72), New Netherland occupies New Sweden.

SCIENCE AND TECHNOLOGY

1615 Dutch mathematician Ludolp van Ceulen (1540–1610) publishes a value for pi (π) that is correct to 32 decimal places in his posthumous *Arithmetische en Geometishe fondamenten.*

1618 Dutch scientist Snellius (1591–1626) discovers his law of the diffraction of light.

1619 German astronomer Johannes Kepler (1571–1630) outlines the third of his three laws of planetary motion in *Harmonies of the World.*

1628 English doctor William Harvey (1578–1657) explains the circulation of blood pumped around the body by the heart.

1631 English mathematician William Oughtred (1575–1660) introduces the symbol for multiplication in his *The Keys to Mathematics.*

1635 Italian mathematician Bonaventura Cavalieri (1598–1647) publishes the first textbook on integration, *Geometry of Continuous Indivisibles*

1637 French philosopher and mathematician René Descartes (1596–1650) introduces analytical geometry in his *Geometry.*

1639 French mathematician Girard Desargues (1591–1661) introduces projective geometry in his *Brouillon project.*

1641 French scientist Blaise Pascal (1623–62) invents a mechanical adding machine.

1643 Italian scientist Evangelista Torricelli (1608–47) invents the mercury barometer.

1644 French mathematician Marin Mersenne (1558–1648) studies prime numbers.

1647 German astronomer Johannes Hevelius (1611–87) draws a map of the Moon's surface.

1650 German scientist Otto von Guericke (1602–86) invents a vacuum pump.

1650 German scientist Athanasius Kircher (1601–80) discovers that sound will not travel in a vacuum.

1654 German engraver Ludwig von Siegen (*c.*1609–80) reveals his methods of producing mezzotints.

1655 English mathematician John Wallis (1616–1703) introduces the symbol for infinity in *The Arithmetic of Infinitesimals.*

1657 Academia del Cimento, the first scientific research institute, is established in Florence, Italy.

1657 Dutch scientist Christiaan Huygens (1629–95) constructs a pendulum clock.

1659 Swiss mathematician Johann Rahn (1622–76) introduces the symbol for division in *Teutsche Algebra.*

1659 French mathematician Pierre de Fermat (1601–65), in correspondence with Pascal, develops the theory of probability.

◀ **Puritan clothing 1650** *In comparison with the rich and flamboyant fashions of the European upper classes, Puritan clothing was unadorned and sober.*

ARTS AND HUMANITIES

1611 Flemish artist Peter Paul Rubens (1577–1640) paints *Raising of the Cross.*

1612 English poet John Donne (1572–1631) writes *Of the Progress of the Soul.*

c.1613 Spanish poet and dramatist Felix Lope de Vega Carpio (1562–1635) writes his *All Citizens are Soldiers.*

1615 *Bukeshohatto* book of warriors' wisdom is published in Japan.

1619 English architect Inigo Jones (1573–1652) designs the Banqueting House in London.

1623 Death of the Indian poet Tulsi Das (b.1532), author of the Hindu classic *Tulsi-krit Ramayan.*

1624 Dutch artist Frans Hals (*c.*1580–1666) paints *Laughing Cavalier.*

1625 Dutch lawyer Hugo Grotius (1583–1645) publishes *On the laws of war and peace.*

1632 Dutch artist Rembrandt Harmenszoon van Rijn (1606–69) paints *Anatomy Lesson of Dr Tulp.*

1632 Flemish artist Anthony Van Dyck (1599–1641) becomes court painter to English king Charles I.

1633 Italian architect and sculptor Gianlorenzo Bernini (1598–1680) designs the canopy over the altar at St Peter's in Rome.

1634 Taj Mahal is built in Agra, India, as a tomb for Mumtaz Mahal the wife of Mogul emperor Shah Jahan (1592–1666).

1634 Passion play is inaugurated at Oberammagau, s Germany

1635 Académie Française is established.

1637 French dramatist Pierre Corneille (1606–84) writes his play *Le Cid.*

1638 Italian architect Francesco Borromini (1599–1667) designs the church of San Carlo alle Quattro Fontane in Rome.

1638 Spanish dramatist Pedro Calderón de la Barca (1600-81) writes his play *Life is a Dream.*

c.1637 French artist Nicolas Poussin (1594–1665) paints *The Rape of the Sabine Women.*

1642 Italian composer Claudio Monteverdi (1567–1643) completes his opera *The Coronation of Poppea.*

1646 Spanish artist Bartolomé Murillo (1617–82) completes his paintings of the lives of Franciscan saints.

1651 English political philosopher Thomas Hobbes (1588–1679) publishes *Leviathan.*

c.1652 English religious reformer George Fox (1624–91) founds the Society of Friends, whose adherents become known as Quakers.

1654 Dutch poet and dramatist Joost van den Vondel (1587–1679) writes his play *Lucifer.*

1656 Spanish artist Diego Velázquez (1599–1660) paints his *The Maids of Honour.*

1656 Dutch artist Rembrandt Harmenszoon van Rijn (1606–69) paints his *Jacob Blessing the Sons of Joseph.*

1620

1640

Cromwell
An outstanding parliamentary commander, Cromwell rose to prominence in the English Civil War. Guided by his Calvinist faith, he attributed the victory of his New Model Army to God's providence.

ASIA AND AUSTRALASIA

1660

1662 Chinese pirate warlord Jeng Cheng-gong (Koxinga, 1624–62) expels the Dutch from Formosa.

1662 Kang-Xi (1654–1722) becomes emperor of China.

1664 Hindu raiders sack the Mogul port of Surat in India.

1664 Russian cossacks raid N Persia.

1669 Hindu religion is prohibited throughout the Mogul empire in India and Hindu temples are destroyed.

1674 French establish a colony at Pondicherry in E India.

1674 Hindu raider Sivaji (1630–80) becomes independent ruler of Maharashtra in India.

1674 Regional rulers rebel against central control in China.

1675–78 Sikhs rebel against their Mogul overlords in India.

1680

1681 Manchu Qing dynasty re-establishes central control in China.

1683 Qing dynasty conquers the island of Formosa, which comes under direct rule from the Chinese mainland for the first time.

1685 Mogul emperor Aurangzeb (1619–1707) attempts to expel English merchants from Surat.

1689 Russian settlers are forced to withdraw from NW China; the treaty of Nerchinsk establishes the Russian–Chinese border in the Amur region.

1690 English establish a colony at Calcutta, N India.

1691 Mogul empire in India reaches its greatest extent.

1696 Chinese establish a protectorate in N Mongolia.

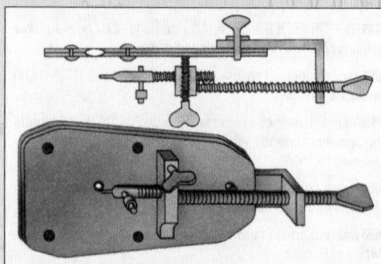

1700

1700 Charles Eyre reorganizes the administration of the British East India Company.

1703 The 'Forty-seven *ronin*' avenge the execution of their lord in Japan, and are ordered to commit suicide.

1705 Chinese attempt to impose their candidate for Dalai Lama provokes risings and unrest in Tibet.

1707 Death of Emperor Aurangzeb leads to the rapid disintegration of the Mughal empire in India.

1708 Sikhs establish independent control of the Punjab region of N India.

1709 Mir Vais, Afghan chieftain of Kandahar, rebels against Persian rule and proclaims independence.

AFRICA

1662 Portugal cedes the city of Tangier in Morocco to England.

1662 English build a fort at the mouth of the River Gambia, W Africa.

1677 French expel the Dutch from Senegal in W Africa.

Armies In the 18th century armies consisted of long-service volunteers or conscripts. Harsh discipline, low pay and bad conditions attracted only the poor and criminals into the ranks. Officers, from the nobility, used influence to gain commissions. Distinctive uniforms were chosen because long-range weapons were inaccurate. Illustrated below are, from left to right, a British Grenadier, an Austrian infantryman and a soldier of the Spanish Imperial Army.

1683 Prussians build a fort on the coast of Guinea in W Africa.

1684 England gives Tangier back to Morocco.

1684 French mount naval expeditions to suppress the Islamic pirates at Algiers.

1686 French formally annex Madagascar.

1688 Huguenot refugees from France arrive in S Africa.

1697 French complete the conquest of Senegal.

1698 Portuguese are expelled from most E African ports by Omanis from SE Arabia.

◀ *Leeuwenhoek's microscope With the powerful, single-lens microscopes that he designed, such as the one shown right, Leeuwenhoek was able to study blood and spermatozoa as well as microscopic life forms. It was with one of these microscopes that he discovered bacteria in 1680.*

1704 British capture Gibraltar from Spain.

1705 Husseinid dynasty takes control in Tunis and establishes independence from the Turks.

1708 Spanish are expelled from Oran in Algeria.

1709 Dutch cattle farmers in South Africa trek E across the Hottentot Holland Mountains.

EUROPE

1660 Monarchy is re-established in England with the accession of Charles II (1630–85).

1660 By the peace of Olivia, Sweden gains territory from Poland.

1661 On the death of cardinal Mazarin (b.1602), Louis XIV (1638–1715) becomes sole ruler of France.

1662–63 Spanish invade Portugal in an attempt to re-establish control, but are defeated.

1664 Austria defeats the Ottoman Turks at the battle of St Gotthard.

1665 War breaks out between the Dutch, supported by France, and England.

1667 By the treaty of Andrussovo, Russia acquires E Ukraine from Poland.

1667 France occupies Spanish towns in Flanders.

1668 Spain recognizes Portuguese independence.

1669 Ottoman Turks capture Crete from Venice.

1670 Peasants and cossacks revolt in S Russia.

1672 France invades the Netherlands; William III of Orange (1650–1702) becomes Dutch head of state and opens the sluices to save Amsterdam.

1674 German emperor enters the wars against France.

1675 Prussian army defeats France's ally Sweden at the battle of Fehrbellin.

1678 French capture the towns of Ypres and Ghent in Belgium from Spain.

1678 Treaties of Nijmegen end the wars between France and the Dutch, Germans and Spanish; France gains territory from Spain.

1683 Ottoman Turks under Vizier Kara Mustafa (1634–83) besiege Vienna and are defeated by a German-Polish army at the battle of the Kahlenberg.

1683 French under Louis XIV (1638–1715) invade Belgium and occupy Luxembourg and Lorraine.

1684 Venice, Austria and Poland form a Holy Alliance against the Turks.

1685 Louis XIV revokes the Edict of Nantes in France (1598).

1686 German rulers form the League of Augsburg against France.

1688 France invades the Rhineland region of Germany.

1688 Austrian armies liberate Belgrade from the Turks.

1688 Glorious Revolution in England deposes Catholic king James II (1633–1701); the Dutch Protestant ruler William of Orange (1650–1702) becomes William III of England.

1689 Peter I (1672–1725) becomes sole ruler of Russia.

1689 England and the Netherlands join the League of Augsburg against France.

1690 William III of England defeats French troops under former king James II at the battle of the Boyne in Ireland.

1692 English and Dutch ships defeat a French fleet at Cap La Hogue.

1696 Russians capture Azov from the Turks.

1697 Austrians defeat the Turks at the battle of Zenta.

1697 Peace of Ryswick ends the War of the League of Augsburg against France.

1699 Turks lose territory to the Holy Alliance under the peace of Kalowitz.

1700 Sweden is attacked by Poland, allied to Denmark and Russia; start of the Great Northern War. Swedes, under Charles XII (1682–1718), defeat the Russians under Peter I (1672–1725) at the battle of Navara.

1700 Charles II (b.1661) of Spain dies childless; the French duke of Anjou is proclaimed King Philip V (1683–1746); end of the Habsburg dynasty in Spain; start of the Bourbon dynasty.

1701 Frederick III (1657–1713) of Brandenburg is crowned Frederick I king of Prussia at Königsburg.

1701 England, Holland and Austria form the Grand Alliance against France.

1701 Grand Alliance declares war on France and Spain; the War of the Spanish Succession begins.

1702 William III's daughter Anne (1665–1714) becomes queen of England.

THE AMERICAS

1663 English colony of Carolina is established.

1664 Colonies of New Haven and Connecticut unite.

1664 New Amsterdam surrenders to the English; the city becomes known as New York.

1667 Bahamas are added to the colony of Carolina

1667 Under the treaty of Breda, English occupation of New Netherland is exchanged for the Dutch occupation of Surinam.

1669 English philosopher John Locke (1632–1704) writes the Fundamental Constitutions for Carolina.

1673 French priests Jacques Marquette (1637–75) and Louis Joliet (1646–1700) explore the upper reaches of the River Mississippi.

1673 Dutch briefly recapture New York.

1674 English establish the Hudson's Bay trading post.

1675–76 English colonists fight King Philip's war against Massoit Native Americans.

1676 Nathaniel Bacon (1647–76) leads a rebellion in Virginia.

> "A thing well said will be wit in all languages."
>
> Dryden (Of Dramatick Poesie)

1680 Colony of New Hampshire is separated from Massachusetts.

1680 Portuguese establish the colony of Sacramento in w Brazil.

1680 Revolt by Pueblo Native Americans drives the Spanish from New Mexico.

1682 French explorer Robert de La Salle (1643–87) reaches the mouth of the Mississippi and claims the Louisiana Territory for France.

1683 Portuguese establish the colony of Colonia on the River Plate in Argentina.

1682 English Quaker William Penn (1644–1718) establishes the colony of Pennsylvania.

1684 Charter of Massachusetts is annulled.

1686 English colonies are organized into the Dominion of New England.

1689–97 King William's War, the first of the French and Indian Wars, is fought between English and French colonists and their native allies.

1691 King William III issues a new charter for Massachusetts.

1692 Witchcraft trials are held in Salem, Massachusetts.

1693 College of William and Mary is established in Virginia.

1696 Spanish reconquer New Mexico.

1699 French establish a colony at Biluxi in Louisiana.

▶ **seed drill** Jethro Tull's famous horse-drawn seed drill, first used in 1701, is regarded as having initiated the mechanization of agriculture. Before this invention, seed was laboriously broadcast by hand.

1701 French explorer Antoine de Cadillac (1658–1730) founds the town of Detroit between lakes Erie and Huron.

1701 Yale College is founded in Connecticut, present-day USA.

1702 French acquire the asiento to supply African slaves to the Spanish colonies in America.

1702 English attack and burn St Augustine in Florida at the start of Queen Anne's War (the American phase of the War of the Spanish Succession).

1703 English colony of Delaware separates from Pennsylvania.

1704 Native Americans allied to the French massacre English settlers at Deerfield in Connecticut.

1706 Spanish establish the town Albuquerque in New Mexico.

1707 British troops from New England march into Canada and besiege French settlers at Port Royal, Nova Scotia.

SCIENCE AND TECHNOLOGY

1662 Royal Society of London established.

1662 Irish scientist Robert Boyle (1627–91) formulates his law of gas expansion.

c.1665 English scientist Isaac Newton (1642–1727) formulates the law of gravity.

1666 Italian astronomer Giovanni Cassini (1625–1712) discovers polar ice caps on Mars.

1666 French minister Jean Colbert (1619–83) orders the construction of the Canal du Midi.

1667 French king Louis XIV founds the Observatoire de Paris.

1668 English mathematician John Wallis (1616–1703) discovers the principle of conservation of momentum.

1669 Isaac Newton creates the first system of calculus.

1672 French astronomer N. Cassegrain invents an improved reflecting telescope.

1673 German scientist Gottfried von Leibniz (1646–1716) invents a calculating machine.

1673 French military engineer Sebastien de Vauban (1633–1707) introduces his system for attacking fortresses at the siege of Maastricht.

1675 Isaac Newton proposes the particle theory of light.

1675 Royal Observatory at Greenwich, near London, is established.

1676 Danish astronomer Ole Romer (1644–1710) discovers that light travels at a finite speed.

1678 Dutch scientist Christiaan Huygens (1629–95) proposes the wave theory of light.

1679 French scientist Denis Papin (1647–c.1712) invents the pressure cooker.

1680 Dutch scientist Anton van Leeuwenhoek (1632–1723) discovers bacteria.

1681 Dodo becomes extinct on the island of Mauritius in the Indian Ocean.

1682 English astronomer Edmond Halley (1656–1742) establishes the periodicity of Halley's Comet.

1684 Gottfried von Leibniz publishes his differential calculus and introduces the integral symbol.

1687 Isaac Newton publishes Mathematical Principles of Natural Philosophy.

1694 Bank of England is established in London.

1696 French Mathematician Guillaume de L'Hopital (1661–1704) publishes Analyse des infiniment petits, the first textbook of infinitesimal calculus.

1698 Swiss mathematician Jakob Bernoulli (1654–1705) studies the properties of the logarithmic spiral.

1698 English engineer Thomas Savery (c.1650–1715) invents a practical steam-driven water pump.

1700 German Protestants adopt the Gregorian calendar.

1701 English farmer Jethro Tull (1674–1741) invents the seed drill.

1701 Academy of Sciences is established in Berlin.

1705 English engineer Thomas Newcomen (1663–1729) invents the atmospheric steam engine, which uses a vacuum to drive a piston.

1706 English mathematician William Jones (1675–1749) introduces the symbol for pi (π) in Synopsis palmariorum matheseos.

1709 British ironworker Abraham Darby (c.1677–1717) perfects a technique for producing iron in a coke-fired blast furnace.

ARTS AND HUMANITIES

1662 French landscape gardener André Le Nôtre (1613–1700) designs the grounds of the palace of Versailles in France.

c.1663 French artist Claude Lorrain (1600–82) paints Landscape with sacrifice to Apollo.

1664 French dramatist Jean Baptiste Racine (1639–99) writes La Thebaïde.

1667 French dramatist Molière (1622–73) writes his comedy The Misanthrope.

1667 English poet John Milton (1608–74) publishes his epic Paradise Lost.

1668 Dutch artist Jan Vermeer (1632–75) paints Astronomer.

1668 English poet and dramatist John Dryden (1631–1700) writes his essay Of Dramatick Poesie.

1669 German author Hans von Grimmelshausen (1621–76) writes his novel Simplicissimus.

1669 English government official Samuel Pepys (1633–1703) completes his 10-year diary of life in London.

1670 English architect Christopher Wren (1632–1723) begins rebuilding 50 London churches destroyed by the Fire of London (1666).

1673 French composer Jean-Baptiste Lully (1632–87) writes his opera Cadmus and Hermione.

1677 Dutch philosopher Baruch Spinoza (1632–77) publishes Ethics.

1678 English preacher John Bunyan (1628–88) writes The Pilgrim's Progress.

1678 French architect Jules Hardouin-Mansart (1646–1708) designs the Hall of Mirrors for the palace of Versailles.

1678 French poet Jean de La Fontaine (1621–95) publishes his second book of Fables.

1681 Italian composer Arcangelo Corelli (1653–1713) writes his sonate da chiesa.

1689 English composer Henry Purcell (1659–95) writes his opera Dido and Aeneas.

1689 English philosopher John Locke (1632–1704) publishes his Two Treatise on Government.

1694 Death of the Japanese haiku poet Matsuo Bashō (b.1644).

1696 German architect Fischer von Erlach (1656–1723) introduces Italian baroque to central Europe with his collegiate church in Salzburg, Austria.

1697 French scholar Pierre Bayle (1647–1706) sets the trend for the Enlightenment with his Historical and Critical Dictionary.

1690 Italian musical instrument maker Antonio Stradivari (1644–1737) introduces his 'long' pattern with his 'Tuscan' violin.

◀ **Newton** developed theories of mechanics and of gravitation that survived unchallenged until the 20th century.

1700 English dramatist William Congreve (1670–1729) writes his comedy The Way of the World.

1700 Samuel Sewell (1652–1730) publishes his anti-slavery tract, The Selling of Joseph, in Boston, Massachusetts, present-day USA.

1702 World's first daily newspaper, the Daily Courant, is published in London.

1705 French writer Bernard de Mandeville (1670–1733) argues that self-interest leads to the general good in his book The Grumbling Hive.

1705 German-born English composer George Frideric Handel (1685–1759) writes his opera Almira.

1708 Death of Gobind Singh (b.1666), the tenth and last guru of Sikhism, who promoted the warrior ethic.

ASIA AND AUSTRALASIA

1710

1711 Mir Vais, Afghan chieftain of Kandahar, defeats an invading Persian army.

1712 War of succession in India between the sons of the Mughal emperor Bahadur divides India.

1717 Abdali dynasty of Herat establishes another independent Afghan state.

1717 Mongol army seizes control of Lhasa, the Tibetan capital.

1717 British East India Company obtains trading concessions from the Mughal emperor.

1718 Chinese army sent to Tibet is destroyed by Mongol warriors.

▶ *Habsburg expansion The accession of Philip of Anjou to the Spanish throne risked upsetting the balance of power in Europe. Britain and the Netherlands in particular feared the resurrection of the Spanish Habsburg Empire which had existed under Charles V of Austria, stretching from Spain to the Netherlands and Austria. As a result of the War of the Spanish Succession, the Austrian Habsburgs gained territory in the Netherlands and Italy, beginning a process of expansion that continued throughout the 18th century.*

1720

1720 Japanese shōgun Yoshimune (d.1751) permits the importation of non-religious European books.

1722 Dutch explorer Jacob Roggeveen discovers Easter Island and Samoa.

1722 Afghan ruler of Kandahar, Mir Mahmud (d.1725), invades Persia and makes himself shah.

1723 Russians capture Baku on the Caspian Sea from Persia.

1724 Chinese establish a protectorate over Tibet.

1724 Russia and Turkey agree to divide Persia between them.

1724 Persian shah Mahmud goes insane and orders the massacre of the Persian aristocracy.

1726 Ashraf (d.1730), the Afghan shah of Persia, defeats an invading Turkish army.

1727 Kiakhta treaty fixes the borders between Russia and China.

1728 Dutch explorer Vitus Bering (1680–1741), sailing for Russia, discovers the Bering Strait, between Siberia and Alaska.

1730

1730 Persian chieftain Nadir Kuli (1688–1747) drives the Afghans from Persia and restores the Safavid dynasty.

1731 Trade rivalries in India between Britain and Austria are settled in Britain's favour by the treaty of Vienna.

AFRICA

1710 French take the island of Mauritius from the Dutch.

1714 Ahmed Bey establishes the Karamanlid dynasty as independent rulers in Tripoli, Libya.

1717 Dutch begin importing slaves to Cape Colony, South Africa.

1723 British Africa Company claims the Gambia region of W Africa.

1728–29 Portuguese briefly re-occupy the E African port of Mombasa.

1730 Dutch northward expansion in South Africa reaches the River Olifants.

1732 Spanish recapture Oran in Algeria.

EUROPE

1702 Swedes invade Poland and capture Warsaw and Kraków.

1703 Peter I establishes the city of St Petersburg at the mouth of the River Neva.

1704 English army led by John Churchill (1650–1722), 1st Duke of Marlborough, defeats the French at the battle of Blenheim.

1706 Following their defeat at Turin, the French are expelled from Italy.

1706 English defeat the French at the battle of Ramilles and conquer Belgium.

1707 England and Scotland are united as Great Britain.

1709 British defeat the French at the battle of Malplaquet.

1709 Swedes in alliance with Ukrainian cossacks invade Russia but are defeated at the battle of Poltava.

1710 South Sea Company is set up in London.

1711 Turks regain Azov from Russia under the treaty of Pruth.

1711 Following an uprising, Austria grants Hungary self-administration under the peace of Sathmar.

1711 Charles XII (1682–1718) of Sweden persuades the Turks to attack Russia.

1713 Treaty of Utrecht between Britain and France ends the War of the Spanish Succession; Britain gains overseas colonies in the Mediterranean and America.

1713 Frederick William I (1688–1740) becomes king of Prussia.

1713 Austrian emperor Charles VI (1685–1740) issues the Pragmatic Sanction, which allows a female to inherit the Habsburg throne.

1714 Russia captures Finland from Sweden after victory at the battle of Storkyro.

1714 Austria makes a separate peace with France and gains territory in Italy and Belgium.

1714 George, Elector of Hanover, becomes King George I (1660–1727) of Britain on the death of Queen Anne (b.1665).

1715 Louis XV (1710–74) becomes king of France with Philip of Orléans as regent.

1715 First Jacobite rebellion in Scotland is defeated by British troops.

1717 Spain conquers Sardinia.

1717 Austria liberates Belgrade from the Turks.

1718 Spain conquers Sicily; Britain, Austria, France and Holland form the Quadruple Alliance and defeat Spain at the sea battle of Cape Passaro.

1719 Russia invades Sweden.

1720 Defeat in the Great Northern War ends Swedish dominance in the Baltic region; Russia gains Livonia and Estonia under the treaty of Nystad.

1720 Savoy gains Sardinia in return for Austrian control of Sicily.

1720 Collapse of John Law's Mississippi Company leads to widespread bankruptcies in France.

1720 South Seas Company fails and creates financial panic in London.

1721 Robert Walpole (1676–1745) becomes Britain's first prime minister.

1722 Peter I (1672–1725) makes administrative reforms in Russia and limits the traditional privileges of the aristocracy.

1723 Frederick William I (1688–1740) establishes the General Directory for the centralized administration of Prussia.

1725 French king Louis XV (1710–74) breaks his engagement to a Spanish princess and marries the daughter of the ex-king of Poland; as a result the Spanish make an alliance with Austria.

1725 Following the death of Peter I, his wife Catherine I (1684–1727) becomes the first of a series of weak Russian rulers.

1726 Cardinal Andre Hercule de Fleury (1653–1743) becomes chief minister in France.

1727 George II (1683–1760) accedes to the British throne.

1727 War breaks out between Spain and Britain allied with France.

1729 Treaty of Seville ends the war between Britain and Spain.

1729 Corsica revolts against Genoese rule.

1732 Genoa suppresses the Corsican revolt.

1732 Military conscription is introduced in Prussia.

1733–35 Russia invades Poland after the death of King Augustus II (1670–1733); France allied to Spain fights the War of the Polish Succession against Austria allied to Russia.

THE AMERICAS

1708–09 Portuguese destroy the power of the Paulistas (slave-raiders) in s Brazil in the War of the Emboabas.

1709 Large numbers of Germans from the Palatinate region begin migrating to the English colonies in North America, especially Pennsylvania.

1710–11 Portuguese defeat Brazilian natives in the War of the Mascates.

1711–12 Tuscarora Native Americans massacre British colonists in North Carolina and are subsequently defeated.

1711 French capture and ransom Rio de Janeiro in Brazil.

1713 By the treaty of Utrecht, Britain gains Newfoundland and Nova Scotia from the French, and acquires a monopoly on the asiento slave trade with Spanish colonies.

1715 British colonists defeat the Yamasee Native Americans in South Carolina.

1715 Scots-Irish immigrants begin the settlement of the Appalachian foothills.

1716 Governor Alexander Spotswood (1676–1740) of Virginia leads an expedition into the Shenandoah valley.

1717 Mississippi Company, promoted by Scottish economist John Law (1671–1729), is given a monopoly on trade with the French colony of Louisiana.

1717 Portuguese build a fort at Montevideo on the River Plate in Uruguay.

1718 French found the port of New Orleans in Louisiana.

1718 Spanish establish the settlement of Pensacola in Florida.

1718 Warfare breaks out between France and Spain in Florida and Texas.

1720 Spain occupies Texas after hostilities with France.

1720 British establish the colony of Honduras in Central America.

1721 Jose de Antequerra leads the revolt of the communeros against the Spanish in Paraguay.

1726 Spanish capture Montevideo in Uruguay from the Portuguese.

1728 British colonists from New York make a treaty with the Native American Iroquois League against the French

1729 Natchez Native Americans massacre French settlers at Fort Rosalie in Louisiana.

1729 British colonies of North and South Carolina are brought under royal control.

> "I told him... that we ate when we were not hungry, and drank without the provocation of thirst."
>
> Jonathan Swift
> *(Gulliver's Travels)*

1730 Cherokee Native Americans acknowledge British supremacy.

1731 Paraguayan revolutionary Jose de Antequerra is defeated and executed.

SCIENCE AND TECHNOLOGY

1711 Italian naturalist Luigi Marsigli (1658–1730) shows that corals are animals not plants.

1712 British clockmaker John Rowley constructs the first clockwork orrery.

1714 German scientist Gabriel Fahrenheit (1686–1736) invents the mercury thermometer.

East Indiaman ship *During the 18th century, Europe's trading empire expanded worldwide. Such expansion was made possible by the development of fast and reliable sailing ships such as the Dutch East Indiaman illustrated below. Heavily armed and extremely robust, these merchant ships could also be used as warships.*

1721 First smallpox inoculations are carried out in Boston.

1725 Academy of Sciences is established at St Petersburg, Russia.

1725 Italian philosophical historian Giambattista Vico (1668–1744) emphasizes the importance of social and cultural history in his *New Science*.

1727 British biologist Stephen Hales (1677–1761) publishes *Vegetable Staticks*, which establishes the science of plant physiology.

1728 British astronomer James Bradley (1693–1762) discovers the aberration of light.

1730 British navigator John Hadley (1682–1744) invents the reflecting quadrant.

1730 British politician and farmer Charles Townshend (1674–1738) introduces four-course crop rotation with turnips and clover.

ARTS AND HUMANITIES

1709 Italian instrument-maker Bartolommeo Cristofori (1655–1731) invents the piano by substituting hammer action for the plucking action of the harpsichord.

1710 English bishop George Berkeley (1685–1753) introduces empiricist philosophy in his *Treatise concerning the Principles of Human Knowledge*.

1710 Puritan minister Cotton Mather (1663–1728) publishes his *Essays to do Good*.

1712 British poet Alexander Pope (1688–1744) publishes *Rape of the Lock*.

1714 German philosopher Gottfried Leibniz (1646–1716) outlines his philosophy in *Monadologie*.

1713 School of dance is established at the Paris Opéra.

1715 Italian composer Alessandro Scarlatti (1660–1725) writes his opera *Il Tigrane*.

1715 French novelist Alain le Sage (1688–1747) publishes *Gil Blas*.

***c*.1715** Japanese dramatist Chikamatsu Mozaemon (1652–1725) writes *Love Suicides*.

1716 French artist Jean Antoine Watteau (1684–1721) paints his *The Lesson of Love*.

1717 German-born English composer George Frideric Handel (1685–1759) composes *Water Music*.

1719 British author Daniel Defoe (1660–1731) publishes his novel *Robinson Crusoe*.

1721 German composer Johann Sebastian Bach (1685–1750) completes his *Brandenburg Concertos*.

1721 French philosopher Charles de Montesquieu (1689–1755) publishes his *Persian Letters* – the first major work of the Enlightenment.

1725 Italian artist Canaletto (1697–1768) paints his *Four Views of Venice*.

1725 Italian composer Antonio Vivaldi (1675–1741) publishes *The Four Seasons*.

1726 British author Jonathan Swift (1667–1745) publishes his satirical *Gulliver's Travels*.

1726 Chinese Academy of Letters publishes its *c.*5000-volume *T'u Shu Chi Ch'eng* encyclopedia.

1728 British poet John Gay (1685–1732) writes *The Beggar's Opera*.

1731 French author Antoine Prévost (1697–1763) publishes his novel *Manon Lescaut*.

1732 Italian sculptor Niccolo Salvi (1697–1751) begins his work on the Trevi fountain in Rome.

1710

1720

1730

ASIA AND AUSTRALASIA

1733 Turks defeat the Persians at the battle of Kirkuk.

1735 Russia allies with Persia against the Turks, who are defeated at the battle of Baghavand.

1736 Nadir becomes shah of Persia on the death of Abbas III; end of the Safavid dynasty.

1737 Persians invade Afghanistan.

1739 Persians invade India, defeat a Mughal army at the battle of Karnal, and capture Delhi.

1740

1742 Marathas raid Bengal in India.

1744 Al-Saud family of central Arabia allies with the new Wahhabi Islamic sect.

1745 Persians under Nadir Shah (1688–1747) defeat the Turks at the battle of Kars.

1746 French capture Madras from the British.

1747 Nadir Shah is assassinated, leading to a period of anarchy in Persia.

1747 Ahmad Shah (1722–73) establishes the Afghan national state ruled by the Durrani dynasty.

1748 British besiege the French port of Pondicherry in E India.

1748 Madras is returned to the British.

▶ *French fashion, 1750* In the 18th century, Paris was at the forefront of fashion. Although colours and styles varied, the outfits shown here were typical of the period. Women wore hooped skirts of various widths with a fitted overcoat called a contouche. Both men and women powdered their hair grey or white.

1750

1750 Tibetans rebel against Chinese overlordship.

1750 French colonial administrator Joseph Dupleix (1697–1763) wins the battle of Tanjore and gains control of the Carnatic region of S India.

1750 Karim Khan (1705–79) establishes himself as shah of Persia and founds the Zand dynasty.

1751 China invades Tibet.

1751 British colonial administrator Robert Clive (1725–74) captures Arcot and ends French control of the Carnatic.

1752 British troops under Robert Clive capture Trichinopoly in S India from the French.

1752 Afghans capture the city of Lahore in N India from the Mughals.

1753–55 King Alaungpaya (1711–60) reunites Burma, with British assistance, and founds a new capital city at Rangoon.

1755 Afghans conquer the Punjab region of N India and plunder Delhi.

1756 Indian ruler of Bengal captures Calcutta from the British and imprisons British soldiers in the 'Black Hole'.

1757 Robert Clive recaptures Calcutta and defeats the native ruler of Bengal at the battle of Plassey.

1758 Marathas occupy the Punjab region of N India.

1758 China occupies E Turkistan.

AFRICA

▲ *Hume's* Treatise of Human Nature *was initially a literary failure. He achieved greater success with his* History of England *and various essays and philosophical "inquiries".*

1744 Mazrui the Omani governor of Mombasa declares his independence from the sultan of Oman.

1745 Ashanti warriors armed with muskets defeat Dagomba armoured cavalry in W Africa.

1750 French establish a settlement on the island of Sainte Marie off Madagascar.

1752 Portuguese settlements in SE Africa are placed under a separate government from that of Goa in India.

1755 Death of Emperor Jesus II marks the end of strong government in Ethiopia, which becomes divided between rival claimants to the throne.

1756 City of Tunis is captured by the Algerians.

1757 Muhammad XVI (d.1790) becomes ruler of Morocco and starts economic and military reforms.

1758 British capture Senegal from the French.

EUROPE

1733 Treaty (the first Family Compact) between France and Spain declares the indivisibility of the two branches of the Bourbon dynasty.

1734 Russians capture Danzig in Poland.

1734 Spanish troops conquer Sicily and Naples from Austria.

1735 Charles III (1716–88), son of Philip V (1683–1746) of Spain, becomes king of Sicily and Naples.

1735 French troops occupy Lorraine.

1736–39 War between Austria allied to Russia and the Turks results in Russia regaining Azov and Austria losing Serbia.

1738 Treaty of Vienna settles the War of the Polish Succession; Spain gains Naples and Sicily on condition they are never united with Spain; France gains the promise of Lorraine.

1738 Corvée system of forced labour for road repairs is introduced in France.

1739 War of Jenkin's Ear breaks out between Britain and Spain.

1740 Frederick William I (b.1688) of Prussia dies and is succeeded by Frederick II (the Great, 1712–86).

1740 Austrian emperor Charles VI (b.1685) dies; under the Pragmatic Sanction his daughter Maria Theresa (1717–80) becomes empress.

1740 War of the Austrian Succession begins when Frederick II (the Great) invades Austrian-controlled Silesia in the first Silesian War.

1741–43 Sweden attacks Russia, but is defeated and forced to cede parts of Finland.

1741 France, Spain and Prussia ally against Austria.

1742 Austrians make a separate peace with Prussia, ceding Silesia under the treaty of Breslau and Berlin.

1743 Holland allies with Britain and Austria against France.

1743 France and Spain strengthen their alliance, with the second Family Compact.

1743 British-led Pragmatic Army defeats the French at the battle of Dettingen.

1744 Prussians invade Bohemia in the second Silesian War.

1745 French defeat the Pragmatic Army at the battle of Fontenoy.

1745 Second Jacobite rebellion breaks out in Scotland.

1746 British troops defeat the Jacobite Scots at the battle of Culloden and the rebellion ends.

1746 French conquer Austrian-controlled Belgium.

1747 Orangists restore the monarchy in Holland.

1748 Treaty of Aix-la-Chapelle ends the War of the Austrian Succession; Prussia emerges as a major European power.

1750 Joseph I (1714–77) becomes king of Portugal, although the real ruler is his chief minister the future marquês de Pombal (1699–1782).

1753 Wenzel von Kaunitz (1711–94) becomes chancellor of Austria. His negotiations, through the marquise de Pompadour (1721–64), the mistress of Louis XV, persuade France to ally with Austria.

1755 Portuguese capital, Lisbon, is destroyed by an earthquake.

1756 French capture the island of Minorca from the British.

1756 Russia and Sweden join the Franco-Austrian alliance against Prussia.

1756 Prussia allies with Britain, invades Saxony, and starts the Seven Years War.

1757 Prussia invades Bohemia and defeats the French and Austrians at the battle of Rossbach in Bohemia.

1757 William Pitt the Elder (1707–78) becomes prime minister of Britain.

1758 Prussians fight the Russians to a standstill at the battle of Zorndorf in S Germany.

1759 Combined Austrian-Russian army defeats the Prussians at the battle of Kunersdorf.

1759 British defeat the French at the naval battle of Quiberon Bay.

THE AMERICAS

1733 British colony of Georgia is established by James Oglethorpe (1696–1785).

1733 Molasses Act places prohibitive duties on non-British sugar products imported into British North America

1735 Spanish authorities finally suppress the revolt of the comuneros in Paraguay.

1735 Trial in New York of newspaperman John Zenger (1697–1746) establishes the freedom of the press in the British colonies.

1737 William Byrd (1674–1744) founds Richmond, Virginia.

1739 British capture the Spanish settlement of Porto Bello in Panama.

1739 African slaves revolt and kill white settlers at Stono River, South Carolina.

1742 Spanish attack Georgia from Florida.

1743 Hostilities between Britain and Spain become absorbed into King George's War, the American phase of the War of the Austrian Succession.

1746 Princeton University is founded in New Jersey.

1748 British fleet captures Port Louis in Haiti from the French.

1748 Treaty of Aix-la-Chapelle ends King George's War.

1749 British colonists form the Ohio Company to extend British territory w.

1750 By the treaty of Madrid, Spain recognizes Portuguese claims in s and w Brazil.

1752 French capture a British trading-post in the Ohio valley.

1753 French build Fort Duquesne (present-day Pittsburgh) on the River Ohio.

1754 French troops attack the British Fort Necessity in the Ohio valley.

1754 At the Albany Congress, Benjamin Franklin proposes limited union of the British colonies to combat French aggression.

1754 Start of the French and Indian War between French and British settlers, which becomes the American phase of the Seven Years War.

1755 British expedition against Fort Duquesne is defeated at the battle of the Wilderness.

1756 Leading Quakers resign from the Pennsylvania Assembly in protest against participation in hostilities.

1756 French under the marquis de Montcalm (1712–59) drive the British from the Great Lakes region.

1757 French capture Fort William Henry; the British garrison is massacred by Native Americans.

1758 British forces capture forts Frontenac and Duquesne.

1759 City of Quebec in Canada is captured after British general James Wolfe (1727–59) wins the battle of the Plains of Abraham.

SCIENCE AND TECHNOLOGY

1730 French scientist René Réaumur (1683–1757) invents an alcohol thermometer.

1732 English farmer Jethro Tull (1674–1741) publishes *Horse Hoeing Husbandry*.

1732 French engineer Henri de Pitot (1695–1771) invents a tube for measuring the speed of fluid flow.

1732 Dutch scientist and physician Hermann Boerhaave (1668–1738) publishes his chemistry textbook *Chemical Elements*.

1733 French scientist Charles du Fray (1698–1739) identifies positive and negative static electricity.

1733 British clothworker John Kay (1704–64) invents the flying shuttle.

1735 Explorer Charles Condamine (1701–74) discovers rubber trees in South America.

1735 Swedish scientist Carolus Linnaeus (1707–78) publishes *Systema naturae*, which classifies all living organisms according to a binomial nomenclature.

1736 Swiss mathematician Leonhard Euler (1707–83) publishes his textbook of mechanics *Mechanica sive mortus analytice exposita*.

1738 Swiss mathematician Daniel Bernoulli (1700–82) demonstrates the relationship between pressure and velocity of fluid flow in his *Hydrodynamics*.

***c.*1740** British ironworker Benjamin Huntsman perfects the crucible process for casting steel.

1742 Swedish astronomer Anders Celsius (1701–44) invents the Celsius, or centigrade, temperature scale.

1742 French scientist Paul Malouin invents a process for galvanizing steel.

1743 American Philosophical Society is founded in Philadelphia.

***c.*1745** Leyden jar electrical capacitor is invented in Holland.

1745 French astronomer Pierre Maupertuis (1698–1759) publishes *Venus physique*.

1746 British chemist John Roebuck (1718–94) develops a process for manufacturing sulphuric acid.

1747 German scientist Andreas Marggraf (1709–82) invents a process for extracting sugar from sugar beet.

1749 French naturalist Georges Buffon (1707–88) publishes the first volumes of *Natural History*.

◀ **rococo** *This style of art, architecture and decoration developed in early 18th-century France and soon spread to Germany, Austria, Italy and Britain. The style was particularly suited to interiors, as illustrated right. Doors and windows alternated with decorative panels. Square ceiling structures and corners were softened by curved and moulded panelling, minimizing the transition from wall to ceiling. Ground plans followed the serpentine curves of the interiors.*

1750 British astronomer Thomas Wright (1711–1786) suggests that the Milky Way is a huge disc of stars.

1752 Gregorian calendar is adopted in Britain.

1752 American writer, scientist and politician Benjamin Franklin (1706–90) publishes *Experiments and Observations in Electricity*.

1757 British optician John Dollond (1706–61) produces the first achromatic lenses.

1758 French economist François Quesnay (1694–1774) sums up his physiocratic system of political economy in *Tableau economique*.

1758 British optical instrument maker John Bird (1709–76) invents an improved sextant.

1758 British wheelwright Jebediah Strutt (1726–97) invents a ribbing machine for making hosiery.

1759 British clockmaker John Harrison (1693–1776) constructs the first marine chronometer.

ARTS AND HUMANITIES

1732 American writer, scientist and politician Benjamin Franklin (1706–90) publishes the first issue of *Poor Richard's Almanac*.

1734 Johann Sebastian Bach (1685–1750) composes his *Christmas Oratorio*.

1735 French composer Jean Rameau (1683–1764) writes his ballet *Les Indes Galantes*.

1735 British artist William Hogarth (1697–1764) publishes his engravings of *A Rake's Progress*.

1734 French philosopher and author Voltaire (1694–1778) publishes *English or Philosophical Letters*.

1738 John Wesley (1703–91) experiences a religious conversion and lays the foundations of Methodism.

1738 Archaeological excavation starts of the Roman town of Herculaneum in Italy.

1738 Russian Imperial Ballet School is founded in St Petersburg.

1739 Scottish philosopher David Hume (1711–76) publishes *Treatise on Human Nature*.

1739 Prince Frederick of Prussia, later Frederick II (the Great), publishes his political theories in *Anti-Machiavelli*.

1740 British author Samuel Richardson (1689–1761) publishes his novel *Pamela*.

1741 Italian architect Bartolomeo Rastrelli designs the Summer Palace in St Petersburg.

1741 German-born English composer George Frideric Handel's oratorio *Messiah* is first performed in Dublin.

1742 French artist François Boucher (1703–70) paints his *Bath of Diana*.

1745 Italian dramatist Carlo Goldoni (1707–93) publishes his comedy *The Servant of Two Masters*.

1746 French philosopher Denis Diderot (1713–84) publishes his *Philosophic Thoughts*.

1746 French philosopher Étienne Condillac (1715–1780) publishes his *Essay on the Origin of Human Knowledge*.

1747 French philosopher Julien La Mettrie (1709–51) publishes his aetheist views in his book *Man, A Machine*.

1748 French philosopher Charles de Montesquieu (1689–1755) publishes *The Spirit of Laws*.

1749 British novelist Henry Fielding (1707–54) publishes *Tom Jones*.

> "All is for the best in the best of all possible worlds."
>
> *Voltaire (Candide)*

1751 First volume of the French *Encyclopedia, or Classified Dictionary of Sciences, Arts and Trades* is published.

1752 Death of the German preacher Johann Bengel (b.1687), who established the evangelical movement Pietism.

1753 Italian artist Giovanni Tiepolo (1696–1770) completes his frescos decorates the Kaisersaal in Wurzburg, Germany.

1754 British furniture-maker Thomas Chippendale (1718–79) publishes *The Gentleman and Cabinetmaker's Directory*.

1755 Austrian composer Franz Haydn (1732–1809) writes his first string quartet.

1755 British writer Samuel Johnson (1709–84) publishes his *Dictionary of the English Language*.

1755 French philosopher Jean Jacques Rousseau (1712–78) writes his essay *A Discourse upon the Origin of Inequality*.

1755 German archaeologist Johann Winckelmann (1717–68) publishes *Thoughts on the Imitation of Greek Painting and Sculpture*.

1756 Italian artist Giambattista Piranesi (1720–78) publishes his book of engravings *The Roman Antiquities*.

1757 Scottish philosopher David Hume (1711–86) publishes *Natural History of Religion*.

1740

1750

ASIA AND AUSTRALASIA	AFRICA	EUROPE

ASIA AND AUSTRALASIA

1759 British defeat a Dutch naval expedition and capture Chinsura.

1760 British defeat the French at the battle of Wandiwash in S India.

1760 Chinese emperor declares that all foreign trade shall pass through the port of Canton (Guangzhou).

1761 British capture Pondicherry from the French.

1761 Hyder Ali (1722–82) makes himself ruler of Mysore in S India.

1761 Afghans invade N India and defeat the Marathas at the battle of Panipat.

1762 Afghans defeat the Sikhs at Lahore.

1762 British bombard Manila and capture the Philippines from Spain.

1763 British establish a trading-post at Bushire in SW Persia.

1764 British return the Philippines to Spain.

1764 British defeat a native coalition at the battle of Baskar and gain control of the whole of Bengal.

1765–69 Chinese invade Burma and establish overlordship.

1767 Burma invades and conquers Thailand.

1767–69 War between British troops and the Indian state of Mysore ends in a truce.

1768 French explorer Louis de Bougainville (1729–1811) claims Tahiti for France.

▶ ***North America*** *The pattern of settlement in America between 1700 and 1774. In the 17th century the English and the French went to the West Indies and North America. After 1700 free migration, as distinct from the importation of African slaves, was nearly all into the English colonies of the E seaboard.*

1770 British establish a trading-post at Basra, S Iraq.

1770 British explorer James Cook (1728–79) lands at Botany Bay and claims SE Australia for Britain.

1773 British merchants obtain a monopoly over opium production in Bengal.

1774 British appoint Warren Hastings (1732–1818) as Governor General of India; he begins a series of economic and administrative reforms.

1774 White Lotus Society foments a rebellion in NE China.

1775 War breaks out between the British and the Marathas in India.

1775 Persians attack and briefly capture Basra from the British.

1778 British forces attack and capture Pondicherry, S India, from the French.

1778 James Cook discovers Hawaii.

1779 British force defeats the Marathas at Surat.

▶ ***American Revolution*** *Illustrated right are an American soldier, left, and a British soldier, right. British "redcoats" were professional soldiers who were generally superior in conventional battles to the imperfectly trained American volunteers. Commander in chief George Washington kept the American army in existence despite repeated disappointments and used the American skill in guerrilla tactics to wear down the British until they could be outmanoeuvred.*

AFRICA

1760 Dutch farmers moving N cross the Orange River in South Africa.

1763 Kayambugu (d.1780) becomes king of Buganda in E Africa.

1763 Treaty of Paris confirms British control of Senegal.

1766 Ali Bey (1728–73) establishes himself as ruler of Egypt and declares independence from the Turks.

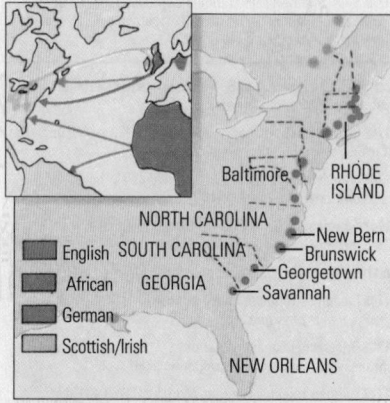

Baltimore · RHODE ISLAND

NORTH CAROLINA
New Bern
SOUTH CAROLINA — Brunswick
■ English
■ African — Georgetown
GEORGIA — Savannah
■ German
□ Scottish/Irish

NEW ORLEANS

1774 Abiodun (d.1789) becomes king of Oyo in present-day S Nigeria.

1775 Maritius Benyowski establishes the town of Louisbourg on the coast of Madagascar for the French, who later refuse to support him.

1778 French recapture Senegal.

1778 Dutch settlers moving E cross the Great Fish River in South Africa.

1779 First Suurveld War starts in South Africa when native Khoisan and Xhosa peoples try to stop the E expansion of Dutch Boers (farmers).

EUROPE

1759 Prussians defeat the French at the battle of Minden.

1759 Jesuits are expelled from Portugal.

1759 Charles III (1716–88) becomes king of Spain and hands the throne of Sicily and Naples to his son Ferdinand (1751–1825).

1760 George III (1738–1820) becomes king of Britain.

1760 Russian army sacks Berlin.

1761 Third Family Compact strengthens the alliance between France and Spain.

1762 Catherine II (1729–96) seizes power in Russia and restores strong government.

1762 Spain invades Portugal but is repulsed.

1763 Austria makes the peace of Hubertsburg with Prussia, ending the European phase of the Seven Years War.

1763 'Whiteboys' revolt against British rule in Ireland.

1764 Russia and Prussia form an alliance to control Poland.

1764 Jesuits are expelled from France.

1765 Joseph II (1741–90) is elected Holy Roman emperor and becomes co-ruler, with his mother Maria Theresa (1717–80), of the Austrian empire.

1766 Lorraine formally becomes a part of France.

1767 Jesuits are expelled from Spain.

1767 Catherine II of Russia appoints a commission for the modernization of the Russian state.

1768 Anti-Russian confederation is formed in Poland; its formation leads to a civil war in which Russia intervenes.

1768 Turkey declares war on Russia in defence of Poland.

1768 Genoa cedes Corsica to France.

1770 Louis (1754–93), later Louis XVI, marries Marie Antoinette (1755–93), daughter of Maria Theresa.

1770 Russian fleet defeats the Turks at the battle of Chesme.

1770 John Struensee (1737–72) attempts radical reforms in Denmark.

1771 Russians conquer the Crimea from the Turks.

1771 Louis XV (1710–74) abolishes the French *parlements*.

1772 John Struensee is executed in Denmark after an aristocratic coup.

1772 Gustavus III (1746–92) restores the power of the monarchy in Sweden.

1772 Following Russian victories against the Turks, Austria and Prussia enforce the first Partition of Poland. Russia, Austria and Prussia annex about 30% of Polish territory.

1773–75 Emelyan Pugachev (1726–75) leads a revolt of cossacks and peasants in SE Russia.

1774 Louis XVI becomes king of France and restores the *parlements*.

1774 Treaty of Kuchuk Kainarji ends the war between Russia and Turkey; Russia gains Crimean ports.

1777 Marquês de Pombal (1699–1782) is dismissed in Portugal and exiled.

1777 French financier Jacques Necker (1732–1804) is appointed finance minister in an attempt to solve the debt crisis.

1778 France declares war on Britain.

1778–79 War of the Bavarian Succession between Prussia and Austria is settled by the treaty of Teschen.

1779 Spain declares war on Britain and besieges Gibraltar.

THE AMERICAS

1759 British capture the island of Guadaloupe from the French.

1760 British capture Montreal from the French.

1761 British capture Cuba from the Spanish.

1761 James Otis (1725–83) argues against British writs of assistance in a Massachusetts court.

1763 Peace of Paris ends the French and Indian War; Britain gains Canada, Tobago and Grenada from France and Florida from Spain; France cedes Louisiana to Spain.

1763 King George III of Britain issues a proclamation prohibiting N and W expansion from British colonies in North America.

1763 Surveyors Charles Mason and Jeremiah Dixon establish the boundary between Pennsylvania and Maryland.

1763–66 Pontiac (1720–69), chief of the Ottawa Native Americans, wages an unsuccessful war against the British.

1765 Stamp Act places a tax on books and documents in British North America; rioting breaks out in Boston and other cities.

1765 In New York, the Stamp Act Congress adopts a declaration of rights and liberties.

1765 British establish a colony on the Falkland Islands.

1766 Stamp Act is repealed.

1767 New York Assembly is suspended by the British.

1767 Townshend Acts place duties on many goods imported to British North America.

1768 Boston lawyer Samuel Adams (1722–1803) calls for united action against Britain.

1769 American explorer Daniel Boone (1734–1820) opens a route into Kentucky.

1769 Spanish establish a settlement at San Diego in California.

1770 British troops shoot several Massachusetts citizens in what becomes known as the 'Boston Massacre'.

1772 American protesters burn the British customs ship *Gaspee* off Rhode Island.

1773 'Boston Tea Party' occurs when protesters dressed as Native Americans board British ships and dump tea into Boston harbour.

1773–74 Committees of Correspondence are set up throughout the British colonies.

1774 British pass the so-called Coercive Acts restricting American colonial rights.

1774 British fight and win Lord Dunmore's War against the Shawnee Native Americans.

1774 First Continental Congress meets at Philadelphia and draws up a Declaration of Rights and Grievances to be presented to Britain.

1774 Ann Lee (1736–84) establishes the first Shaker colony.

1775 American Revolution (American War of Independence) starts with the battles of Lexington and Concord, after which the British retreat to Boston.

1775 American general Ethan Allen (1738–89) captures Fort Ticonderoga from the British.

1775 Second Continental Congress meets at Philadelphia.

1775 Continental Army is formed outside Boston with George Washington (1732–99) as commander-in-chief.

1775 British win the battle of Bunker Hill; the Americans besiege Boston.

1775 American troops capture Montreal, but fail to take Quebec.

1776 British evacuate Boston.

1776 Congress adopts the Declaration of Independence written by American Statesman Thomas Jefferson (1743–1826).

1776 British win the battle of Long Island and occupy New York City.

1776 British defeat George Washington at the battle of White Plains and force an American retreat.

1776 Washington crosses the River Delaware and defeats the British at the battle of Trenton.

SCIENCE AND TECHNOLOGY

1763 First exhibition of industrial arts is held in Paris.

1763 Scottish scientist Joseph Black (1728–99) discovers latent heat.

1764 British engineer James Hargreaves (1722–78) invents the Spinning Jenny.

1765 Scottish engineer James Watt (1736–1819) improves the steam engine by adding a separate condenser.

1766 American writer, scientist and politician Benjamin Franklin (1706–90) invents bifocal spectacles.

1766 British chemist Henry Cavendish (1731–1810) discovers hydrogen.

1769 British engineer Richard Arkwright (1732–92) invents a water-powered spinning frame.

1770 Grand Trunk Canal is completed in Britain.

> "Stand your ground. Don't fire unless fired upon, but if they mean to
> have a war, let it
> begin here!"
>
> US general John Parker
> *(command given at the start of
> the Battle of Lexington)*

1771 French astronomer Charles Messier (1730–1817) publishes the first volume of his star catalogue.

1771 Italian scientist Luigi Galvani (1737–98) conducts experiments that demonstrate a connection between muscular contractions and electricity.

1772 Imperial library in China begins compiling the *Complete Works of the Four Treasuries*, which contains more than 3000 works of literature.

1774 British chemist Joseph Priestley (1733–1804) discovers oxygen.

1774 British astronomer Nevil Maskelyne (1732–1811) discovers the value of the gravitational constant.

1774 British engineer John Wilkinson (1728–1808) invents a boring machine for making steam-engine cylinders and cannon.

1774 French chemist Antoine Lavoisier (1743–94) demonstrates the conservation of mass in chemical reactions.

1775 Austrian physician Franz Mesmer (1734–1815) claims to be able to heal using 'animal magnetism'

1779 British engineer Samuel Crompton (1753–1827) invents the spinning mule.

1779 Cast-iron bridge is completed at Coalbrookdale in Britain.

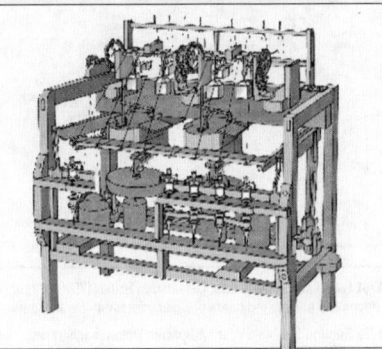

ARTS AND HUMANITIES

1758 French philosopher Claude Helvetius (1715–71) publishes his atheistic book *On the Mind*, which is condemned and burned.

1758 Swedish scientist Emanuel Swedenborg (1688–1772) publishes his religious treatise *The New Jerusalem*.

1759 French philosopher and author Voltaire (1694–1778) publishes his satirical novel *Candide*.

1760

1760 English novelist Laurence Sterne (1713–68) publishes the first volumes of *Tristram Shandy*.

1760 British artist Joshua Reynolds (1723–92) paints portrait of *Georgiana, Countess Spencer*.

1762 British artist George Stubbs (1724–1806) paints *Mares and Foals*.

1762 French philosopher Jean Jacques Rousseau (1712–78) publishes *The Social Contract*.

1762 Scottish poet James Macpherson (1736–96) –'Ossian' – publishes *Fingal*.

1762 German composer Christoph Gluck (1714–87) writes his opera *Orfeo and Euridice*.

1762 Building work starts on the Petit Trianon at Versailles in France.

1764 British author Horace Walpole (1717–97) publishes his Gothic horror novel *Castle of Otranto*.

1766 Irish novelist Oliver Goldsmith (1730–74) publishes *The Vicar of Wakefield*.

1766 German philosopher and critic Gotthold Lessing (1729–81) publishes *Laocoön*.

1766 First purpose-built American theatre opens in Philadelphia.

1766 German poet Heinrich Gerstenberg (1737–1823) publishes the first of his *Letters on the Curiosities of Literature*; this work establishes the *Sturm und Drang* literary movement.

1770

1770 British artist Thomas Gainsborough (1727–88) paints *Blue Boy*.

1770 French philosopher Paul Holbach (1723–89) expounds materialism and determinism in *System of Nature*.

1770 American artist Benjamin West (1738–1820) paints *The Death of General Wolfe*.

1771 Encyclopedia Britannica is first published.

1772 French *L'Encyclopédie* is completed with the publication of the *Supplement to Bougainville's Voyage* by French philosopher and writer Denis Diderot (1713–84).

1773 Scottish architects Robert (1728–92) and James Adams publish their *Works of Architecture*.

1774 German poet and author Johann Goethe (1749–1832) publishes his novel *The Sorrows of Young Werther*.

1775 German historian Johann Herder (1744–1803) publishes his *Philosophy of History and Culture*.

1776 British historian Edward Gibbon (1737–94) publishes the first volume of *The History of the Decline and Fall of the Roman Empire*.

1776 British economist Adam Smith (1723–90) publishes *An Inquiry into the Nature and Causes of the Wealth of Nations*.

1777 British dramatist Richard Sheridan (1751–1816) writes *School for Scandal*.

1778 La Scala in Milan hosts its first opera.

1779 Italian sculptor Antonio Canova (1757–1822) carves *Daedalus and Icarus*.

◀ ***spinning frame*** *Shown here is Arkwright's spinning frame of 1769, which introduced powered machinery to the textile industry. The machine produced an unusually firm thread, which made it possible for the first time to produce a fabric consisting wholly of cotton. Arkwright called his invention a water frame, as it was powered by a water wheel. Spinning frames of this kind were made and used by Arkwright at Cromford, Derbyshire, from 1775.*

ASIA AND AUSTRALASIA

18th-century samurai swords In feudal Japan, the samurai were part of a warrior ruling class. Although they fought with a number of weapons, their most famous weapon was the samurai sword. The samurai declined in importance in the 17th to 19th centuries and became bureaucrats and scholars.

1780

1781 Assisted by the French, Hyder Ali (1722–82), sultan of Mysore, attacks the British and is defeated at the battle of Porto Novo.

1781 British conquer the Dutch settlements in Sumatra.

1782 Ruler of Mysore, Hyder Ali, dies during a campaign against the British; his son Tipu Sultan (1747–99) continues the war.

1782 New Thai king Rama I (1737–1809) expels the Burmese and establishes a new capital at Bangkok.

1782 Treaty of Salbai ends the war between the British and the Marathas in India.

1784 India Act places the British colonies in India under government control.

1784 Tipu Sultan is defeated by the British when the French fail to send aid; he signs the treaty of Mangalore.

1784 US merchants start trading with China.

1784 Dutch cede the settlement of Negapatam in SE India to the British.

1786 British establish a settlement at Rangoon in Burma.

1787 Chinese suppress a rebellion in Formosa (present-day Taiwan).

1787 Matsudaira Sadanobu (1759–1829) becomes chief minister to the infant Japanese shōgun Ienari (d.1838) and introduces a series of administrative reforms.

1788 Britain transports the first shipment of convicts to Australia.

1789 Crew of the British ship *Bounty* mutiny and cast captain William Bligh (1754–1817) adrift in an open boat.

AFRICA

▶ *Marquis de Lafayette* became a popular hero when he led the French volunteers who helped the American colonists break free from Britain. He joined the French National Assembly in 1789, presenting a declaration of rights and organizing the National Guard. A moderate reformer, he became trapped between Jacobin extremists and the court and fled in 1792.

1781 First Suurveld War in E South Africa ends with Boer victory.

1783 Portuguese build a fort at Cabinda in Angola, SW Africa.

1786 United States pays a bribe to Morocco to purchase immunity from pirate attacks.

1786 French expedition attacks Louisbourg in Madagascar and kills Maritius Benyowski.

1787 British establish the colony of Sierra Leone in W Africa.

1789 On the death of Abiodun, Awole becomes king of Oyo in present-day S Nigeria.

1789 Second Suurveld War breaks out when the Xhosa attempt to regain their traditional lands.

▼ *Military* conflicts within Europe in this period were caused largely by the territorial ambitions of the French, the Russians and the Prussians. Smaller conflicts arose as Belgium, Greece, Hungary, Italy and, at the very end of the period, the Balkan states, fought off colonial rule and established their independence.

MAJOR EUROPEAN CONFLICTS 1770–1913
— Boundary in 1913
⊗ Campaign within Napoleonic Wars 1796–1815
War of:
× territorial expansion ⚙ civil strife
🏛 independence

EUROPE

1780 Russia forms the League of Armed Neutrality against British interference with shipping.

1780 Britain declares war on Holland.

1780 Anti-Catholic Gordon Riots occur in London.

1781 French financier Jacques Necker (1732–1804) is dismissed as French finance minister.

1781 Russia and Austria form an anti-Turkish treaty for control of the Balkans.

1781 Joseph II (1741–90) of Austria abolishes serfdom and establishes freedom of worship.

1782 Spanish capture Minorca from the British.

1783 Treaty of Paris ends the war against Britain by France, Spain and the USA.

1783 Russia annexes the Crimea.

1783 William Pitt the Younger (1759–1806) becomes British prime minister.

1784 Treaty of Versailles ends the war between Holland and Britain.

1785 Catherine II (1729–96) issues charters recognizing the rights of the Russian aristocracy and towns.

1785 Prussia forms the League of German princes against Austria.

1786 Frederick William II (1744–97) becomes King of Prussia.

1787 Dutch ruler William V (1748–1806) calls in Prussian troops to suppress the pro-French Patriot Party.

1787 Charles III (1716–88) of Spain establishes the *junta* (council of ministers).

1787 French king Louis XVI (1754–93) dismisses an assembly of notables and banishes, then recalls, the Paris *parlement*.

1787 Russia allied to Austria attacks the Turks.

1787 Britain, Holland and Prussia form an alliance against France.

1787 Austria incorporates Belgium as a royal province.

1788 Paris *parlement* presents a list of grievances to Louis XVI, who recalls Jacques Necker and summons the States General.

1788 Sweden invades Russian-controlled Finland.

1789 Austrians capture Belgrade from the Turks; the Russian advance reaches the River Danube.

1789 States General meets at Versailles; the third estate declares themselves the National (Constituent) Assembly and takes the 'tennis court oath' to establish a constitution.

1789 Louis XVI dismisses Jacques Necker again; the Paris mob storms the Bastille and establishes a Commune as a provisional government; French general the marquis de Lafayette (1757–1834) becomes commander of the new National Guard; peasant risings and urban rioting create the 'Great Fear'; the National Assembly abolishes the feudal system and issues the Declaration of the Rights of Man.

1789 Parisian women march to Versailles and escort Louis XVI to Paris; National Assembly moves to Paris and debates a constitution; church property is confiscated by the state.

1789 Belgians rise against Austrian rule and defeat an Austrian army at the battle of Turnhout.

1790

1790 Tipu Sultan (1747–99) attacks the pro-British S Indian state of Travancore.

1792 Tipu Sultan defeated by the British.

1791 Fulani scholar and poet Usman dan Fodio (1754–1817) is appointed tutor to the rulers of Gobir in present-day N Nigeria.

1793 Second Suurveld War ends when Dutch magistrates compel the Boers to concede territory to the Xhosa.

1790 French revolutionary leader Maximilien Robespierre (1758–94) is elected leader of the Jacobin political club in Paris.

1790 Swedes defeat Russians at the naval battle of Svenksund.

THE AMERICAS

1777 Washington defeats the British at the battle of Princeton.

1777 Following defeat at the battle of Saratoga, British general John Burgoyne (1722–92) surrenders to the Americans.

1777 British win the battle of Brandywine and occupy Philadelphia.

1777 British defeat Washington at the battle of Germanstown.

1777 Congress approves the Articles of Confederation that create the United States.

1777–78 Continental army spends the winter at Valley Forge.

1778 France makes an alliance with the United States and sends a fleet.

1778 British evacuate Philadelphia.

1778 Washington wins the battle of Monmouth.

1778 British capture Savannah.

1779 American privateer John Paul Jones (1747–92) captures the British ship *Serapis*.

1779 Britain captures St Lucia from the French.

1780 British capture Charleston.

1780 British defeat the Americans at the battle of Camden.

1780 Treacherous American general Benedict Arnold (1741–1801) flees to the British.

1780 American troops drive the Iroquois Native Americans from the state of New York.

1780 British defeat the Americans at the battle of King's Mountain.

1780 Tupac Amaru (c.1742–81), a descendant of the Inca rulers, leads a short-lived rebellion against the Spanish in Peru.

1780 French general the marquis de Lafayette (1757–1834) persuades French king Louis XVI (1754–93) to send troops to reinforce the Americans.

1781 Americans win the battle of the Cowpens.

1781 Combined American and French force besieges the British at Yorktown.

1781 British under General Charles Cornwallis (1738–1805) surrender to the Americans at Yorktown.

1781 Communeros revolt against the Spanish breaks out in Colombia.

1782 British fleet under admiral George Rodney (1718–92) defeats the French at the battle of the Saints in the Caribbean.

1783 Britain recognizes US independence and cedes Tobago to France and Florida to Spain.

1784 Russia establishes a colony on Kodiak Island, Alaska.

1786 Shays' rebellion is suppressed in Massachusetts.

1787 Northwest Ordinance regulates the creation of new states in the USA.

1787 Constitutional Convention meets in Philadelphia and signs the US constitution.

1788 US constitution comes into effect when New Hampshire becomes the ninth state to ratify it.

1788 New York becomes the capital of the USA.

1789 George Washington (1732–99) is elected the first president of the United States.

1789 Attempted revolution in s Brazil is led by army officer Joaquim de Silva.

1789 US Congress adopts the Bill of Rights, 10 amendments to the constitution.

1789 Spanish challenge British claims to the Nookta Sound region of w Canada.

▶ **Hot-air balloon** *Man's first balloon flight took place on November 21, 1783, when a balloon designed by the Montgolfier brothers flew c.8km (5mi) across Paris. The balloon was made of paper-lined linen and was coated with alum to reduce the fire risk.*

1790 Spain withdraws its claims to Nookta Sound.

1790 Washington D.C. is designated the US capital.

1791 US Bill of Rights is ratified.

SCIENCE AND TECHNOLOGY

> "A bill of rights is what the people are entitled to against every government on earth... and what no just government should refuse to rest on inference."
>
> Thomas Jefferson
> *(letter to James Madison)*

1781 German-born English astronomer William Herschel (1738–1822) discovers the planet Uranus.

1782 Scottish engineer James Watt (1736–1819) perfects the double-acting steam engine producing rotary motion.

1783 Hot-air balloon built by the French Montgolfier brothers, Joseph (1740–1810) and Jacques (1745–99), makes the first crewed flight.

1783 French physicist Jacques Charles (1746–1823) makes the first hydrogen balloon flight.

1783 Swiss scientist Horace de Saussure (1740–99) invents an improved hair hygrometer.

1783 French engineer Claude de Jouffroy d'Abbans (1751–1832) builds a full-sized, paddle-wheel steamboat.

1784 British chemist Henry Cavendish (1731–1810) establishes the chemical composition of water.

1784 British ironworker Henry Cort (1740–1800) devises the puddling process to produce wrought iron.

1785 British clergyman Edmund Cartwright (1743–1823) invents the power loom.

1785 French physicist Charles Coulomb (1736–1806) publishes his law of electrical attraction in his *Memoirs on Electricity and Magnetism*.

1785 French chemist Claude Berthollet (1748–1822) invents chlorine bleach.

1785 Steam engine produced by James Watt and Matthew Boulton (1728–1809) is installed in a British factory.

1787 French mathematician Joseph Lagrange (1736–1813) publishes *Analytical Mechanics*.

1788 Scottish engineer Andrew Meikle (1719–1811) patents a threshing machine.

1789 French chemist Antoine Lavoisier (1743–94) expounds his theory of combustion in his *Elementary Treatise on Chemistry*.

1790 British engineer Matthew Boulton (1728–1809) patents the steam-powered coining press.

1790 French adopt decimal system of weights and measures.

ARTS AND HUMANITIES

1781 German philosopher Immanuel Kant (1724–1804) publishes *Critique of Pure Reason*. — 1780

1782 British artist Henry Fuseli (1741–1825) paints *The Nightmare*.

1783 Death of the French philosopher and mathematician Jean d'Alembert (b.1717) who jointly edited *L'Encyclopédie* with French philosopher and writer Denis Diderot (1713–84).

1783 American publisher Noah Webster (1758–1843) produces *The American Spelling Book*.

1785 French artist Jacques David (1748–1825) paints *Oath of the Horatii*.

1786 Austrian composer Wolfgang Amadeus Mozart (1756–91) writes his opera *Marriage of Figaro*.

1786 Scottish poet Robert Burns (1759–96) publishes *Poems, Chiefly in the Scottish Dialect*.

1787 Freed African slave Ottobah Cugoana publishes his book *Thoughts and Sentiments on Slavery*.

1788 Kant publishes *Critique of Practical Reason*.

1788 *Times* newspaper is founded in London.

1789 English social philosopher Jeremy Bentham (1748–1832) expounds his theory of utilitarianism in *Introduction to the Principles of Morals and Legislation*.

1789 British poet William Blake (1757–1827) publishes *Songs of Innocence*.

1789 French revolutionary Camille Desmoulins (1760–94) publishes his republican manifesto *Free France*.

1789 French politician Emmanuel Joseph Sieyes (1748–1836) publishes his pamphlet *What is the Third Estate?*

Louis XVI *During the 17th and 18th centuries, furniture making flourished in parts of Europe, particularly in France. Louis XVI's reign was characterized by the neoclassical style as applied to this elegant writing table.*

1790 British author Edmund Burke (1729–97) criticizes liberalism in *Reflections on the Revolution in France*. — 1790

1791 British biographer James Boswell (1740–95) publishes his *Life of Samuel Johnson*.

ASIA AND AUSTRALASIA

1792 Ranjit Singh (1780–1839) becomes king of the Sikhs.

1793 Burma under King Bodawpaya (d.1819) acquires coastal territory Thailand.

1793 French royalists surrender Pondicherry to the British.

1793 Shōgun Ienari (d.1838) takes personal control of the Japanese government.

1793 Chinese emperor refuses to lift restrictions on the import of British goods.

1793 First free settlers arrive in Australia.

1794 Last Persian shah of the Zand dynasty is killed and Aga Muhammad (d.1797) founds the Kajar dynasty.

1794 British capture the Seychelles from the French.

1795 British take Dutch Malacca to deny it to the French.

1796 Britain conquers Ceylon (present-day Sri Lanka) from the Dutch.

1796 Jia Qing (d.1820) becomes Chinese emperor and begins campaigns to suppress the White Lotus society.

1798 Persians under Shah Fath Ali (1771–1834) attack Afghanistan.

1799 Tipu Sultan is killed fighting against British forces led by Arthur Wellesley (1769–1852).

1799 French invade Syria and capture Jaffa but withdraw after an outbreak of plague.

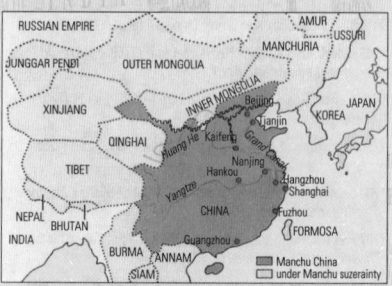

▲ **Qing dynasty** This Manchurian dynasty of China reached its greatest extent at the end of the 18th century. Its authority spread to Mongolia, Tibet and Turkistan and to Burma, Nepal and Annam (present-day Vietnam). As the empire grew in size and wealth, European expansion in search of trade threatened its security and stability.

AFRICA

1795 British capture Cape Colony in South Africa from the Dutch.

1797 US government agrees to pay bribes to Algiers and Tripoli to further safeguard US shipping from pirate attacks.

1798 Napoléon Bonaparte lands an army at Alexandria, invades Egypt, and defeats the Mamluks at the battle of the Pyramids.

1798 British admiral Horatio Nelson (1758–1805) destroys the French fleet at the naval battle of Aboukir.

1798 French settlers on the island of Mauritius overthrow the colonial government.

1799 Bonaparte defeats a Turkish attempt to recapture Egypt at the land battle of Aboukir.

▼ **slave trade** The triangular route taken by slave ships from European ports such as Liverpool, Bristol and Bordeaux took them to Africa to collect slaves, across the Atlantic Ocean to sell them and back again with cargos bartered in exchange. By the end of the 18th century, the major share of the slave traffic was carried on by Great Britain, supplying slaves to plantations in the West Indies and the Americas.

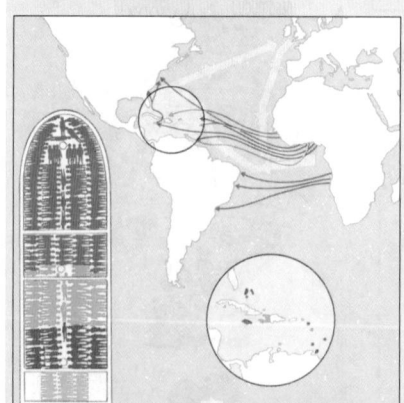

EUROPE

1791 Irish lawyer Wolfe Tone (1763–98) founds the society of United Irishmen.

1791 Louis XVI (1754–93) attempts to flee France but is escorted back to Paris; a constitution is proclaimed and elections held for the new Legislative Assembly.

1791 Polish Diet proclaims the May Constitution, which is opposed by Russia.

1792 Turks cede the N coast of the Black Sea to the Russians by the treaty of Jassy.

1792 Paris mob storms the Tuileries palace and imprisons the royal family; revolutionary Georges Danton (1759–94) takes control of a provisional government; National Convention is elected; France is proclaimed a republic; Louis XVI is put on trial.

1792 Austria and Prussia form an alliance against France; France declares war on Austria; the Prussian commander issues a manifesto calling for the freeing of Louis XVI.

1792 Austria and Prussia invade France; the French defeat the Prussians at the battle of Valmy and the Austrians at the battle of Jemappes; they conquer Belgium and annex Savoy.

1793 Poland loses 60% of its territory to Russia and Prussia in the second partition of Poland.

1793 Louis XVI is guillotined; Jacobins take control of the national convention, revolutionary Jean Marat (b.1743) is murdered by Charlotte Corday; a revolutionary tribunal is set up to judge 'enemies of the state'; start of the Reign of Terror; General Lazare Carnot (1753–1823) reorganizes the French army; Corsican artillery officer Napoléon Bonaparte (1769–1821) is promoted to general.

1793 Britain, Holland and Spain declare war on France; Austria defeats the French at the battle of Neerwinden and recaptures Belgium; Britain attempts to invade S France.

1794 French royalists in the Vendée region are exterminated; churches are closed; Robespierre and his followers are condemned by the National Convention and executed; the revolutionary tribunal and political clubs are abolished; end of the Reign of Terror.

1794 French reconquer Belgium and invade Spain; the British capture Corsica.

1794 Thadeus Kósciuszko (1746–1817) leads a popular rising in Poland; it is suppressed by Russian and Prussian troops.

1795 Some French aristocrats return and begin a White Terror in S France; new constitution establishes the Directory in Paris.

1795 France invades Holland and establishes the Batavian Republic; Prussia makes the separate peace of Basle with France.

1795 Polish state is dissolved by the third Partition of Poland between Russia, Austria and Prussia.

1796 France invades S Germany but is repelled; Bonaparte defeats the Austrians at Lodi and captures Milan; Spain makes the treaty of San Ildefonso with France and declares war on Britain; the Spanish fleet is destroyed by the British at Cape St Vincent.

1797 French conquer Venice and N Italy; the peace of Campo Formio ends hostilities with Austria; end of first war of the Coalition against France.

1797 Frederick William III (1770–1840) becomes King of Prussia.

1798 French occupy Rome, establish a republic, and imprison the pope; French invade Switzerland and annex Geneva; French capture the island of Malta; a second Coalition against France is formed; French conquer S Italy; Russians capture Corfu and the Ionian Islands

1798 British troops defeat the United Irishmen at the battle of Vinegar Hill; an invading French force surrenders.

1799 Austrians and Russians defeat the French at the battles of Zurich, the Trebbia and Novi; they regain control of Italy and drive the French from Switzerland; a British invasion of Holland is unsuccessful; Russia withdraws from the Coalition.

1799 Bonaparte returns to Paris, seizes power and abolishes the Directory; he establishes the Consulate with himself as First Consul.

1799 Balkan state of Montenegro becomes independent of the Ottoman empire.

1800 Chinese emperor bans the smoking of opium.

1801 Britain annexes the Carnatic region of S India.

1802 Vietnamese emperor Nguyen Anh (1762–1820) reunites Annam under his control.

1802 British return Malacca to the Dutch.

1800 French defeat the Turks and Egyptians outside Cairo.

1801 Yusef Karamanli of Tripoli demands an increased pirate-protection bribe from the USA and declares war; the USA blockades Tripoli; start of the Tripolitanian War.

1801 British defeat the French at Alexandria.

1802 French withdraw from Egypt.

1800 Napoléon Bonaparte (1769–1821) defeats the Austrians at the battle of Marengo; a French army captures Munich and defeats the Austrians at the battle of Hohenlinden; French begin the invasion of Austria.

1801 Alexander I (1777–1825) becomes tsar of Russia.

1801 Act of Union joins Ireland to Britain.

1800

THE AMERICAS

1791 Alexander Hamilton (1755–1804) founds the Bank of the United States.

1791 Remaining British possessions in North America are organized into French-speaking Lower Canada and English-speaking Upper Canada.

1791 Slave revolt breaks out on the French island of Haiti in the Caribbean.

1791 Vermont becomes a state of the USA.

1792 New York Stock Exchange is established.

1792 George Washington (1732–99) is re-elected US president.

1792 Kentucky becomes a state of the USA.

1793 Slave rising causes extensive damage in Albany, New York.

1794 Slavery is abolished in French colonies.

1794 Whiskey Insurrection in Pennsylvania is suppressed.

1794 USA signs Jay's treaty regularizing trade with Britain and borders with Canada.

1794 US general Anthony Wayne (1745–96) defeats the Ohio Native Americans at the battle of the Fallen Timbers.

1795 USA signs Pinckney's treaty with Spain establishing the border with Florida.

1796 Tennessee becomes a state of the USA.

1796 US settlers found Cleveland in Ohio.

1796 John Adams (1735–1826) is elected US president.

1797 XYZ Affair leads to a naval war between the USA and France.

1798 Slave leader Toussaint L'Ouverture (1744–1803) drives the French from Haiti.

1799 Russian governor of Alaska founds the city of Sitka.

SCIENCE AND TECHNOLOGY

1791 French military engineer Claude Chappe (1763–1805) invents the semaphore tower for long-distance communication.

1792 French revolutionaries adopt a new calendar starting at Year 1.

1792 Scottish engineer William Murdock (1754–1839) produces coal gas.

1793 US engineer Eli Whitney (1765–1825) invents the cotton gin.

1794 French revolutionary calendar is modified to have three 10-day weeks per month.

1795 Scottish geologist James Hutton (1726–97) publishes his *Theory of the Earth*.

1797 French scientist André Garnerin (1769–1823) demonstrates his parachute by jumping from a hot-air balloon.

1798 US engineer Robert Fulton (1765–1815) demonstrates his submarine *Nautilus* to the French navy.

1798 British physician Edward Jenner (1749–1823) inoculates patients against smallpox using cowpox vaccine.

1798 US scientist Benjamin Rumford (1753–1814) publishes *Inquiry Concerning the Heat which is Caused by Friction*, outlining the kinetic theory of heat.

1799 German mathematician Karl Gauss (1777–1855) establishes the fundamental algebraic proof.

1799 French historians in Egypt discover the tri-lingual Rosetta stone.

ARTS AND HUMANITIES

1791 French revolutionary Louis de Saint-Just (1767–94) publishes *The Spirit of the Revolution*.

1791 French author Marquis de Sade (1740–1814) publishes *Justine*.

1791 Austrian composer Wolfgang Amadeus Mozart (1756–91) writes his opera *The Magic Flute*.

1792 US writer Thomas Paine (1737–1809) publishes *The Rights of Man*.

1792 British feminist Mary Wollstonecraft (1759–97) publishes *Vindication of the Rights of Women*.

1792 French revolutionary soldier Claude de l'Isle composes the *Marseillaise*.

1794 British poet William Blake (1757–1827) publishes *Songs of Experience*.

1795 Spanish artist Francisco Goya (1746–1828) paints his portrait of *The Duchess of Alba*.

1796 US artist Gilbert Stuart (1755–1828) paints his unfinished portrait of George Washington.

1797 German philosopher Friedrich von Schelling (1775–1854) publishes his *Philosophy of Nature*.

1798 British poets William Wordsworth (1770–1850) and Samuel Taylor Coleridge (1772–1834) publish their *Lyrical Ballads*.

1798 British economist Thomas Malthus (1766–1834) publishes the first edition of his *Essay on the Principle of Population*.

1799 German author and dramatist Friedrich von Schiller (1759–1805) completes his *Wallenstein* trilogy.

▲ **Paine** emigrated to Philadelphia from England in 1774 and soon became one of America's most influential revolutionaries. His pamphlet Common Sense and his Crisis papers profoundly stirred popular sentiment, with their impassioned pleas for liberty, condemnation of tyranny and powerful arguments favouring American Independence.

◄ **In 1800** the majority of Latin America was under Spanish control, administered by viceroys and captains-general. The Portuguese were still in control of Brazil and the British ruled in Guiana, where they had temporarily expanded to take over the adjacent Dutch territory (now Surinam). The French had taken control of Santo Domingo from the Spanish but were to lose it in 1809. They had already lost the colony of Saint Domingue in 1804, when it became independent Haiti. The Spanish territory was rich in minerals and included Potosí, the silver-mining capital of the world, although its resources were by now on the verge of being exhausted.

Map: LATIN AMERICA AND THE CARIBBEAN 1800

UNITED STATES

New Orleans
Rio Grande
San Antonio
VICEROYALTY
OF NEW SPAIN
Gulf of Mexico
Havana
CUBA
Mexico City
SAINT DOMINGUE
SANTO DOMINGO
Atlantic Ocean
BELIZE
JAMAICA
Caribbean Sea
Guatemala
San José
CAPTAINCY-GENERAL
OF GUATEMALA
Panama
Caracas
VICEROYALTY
Bogotá
OF NEW GRANADA
GUIANA
Quito
Amazon
Belém
São Luís
Pacific Ocean
BRAZIL
Recife
VICEROYALTY
OF PERU
Lima
La Paz
PRESIDENCY
OF CHARCAS
"UPPER PERU"
Rio de Janeiro
VICEROYALTY OF
RÍO DE LA PLATA
CAPTAINCY-GENERAL
of CHILE
Santiago
Montevideo
Buenos Aires
Atlantic Ocean
PATAGONIA

Colonial power:
- Spain
- Britain
- Portugal
- France

1800 France acquires Louisiana from Spain.

1800 Leaders of an intended slave revolt are hanged in Virginia.

1800 Thomas Jefferson (1743–1826) is elected US president.

1803 Ohio becomes a state of the USA.

1803 USA purchases New Orleans and Louisiana from France.

1800 Italian scientist Alessandro Volta (1745–1827) invents the galvanic cell electrical battery.

1800 Joseph Finlay builds an iron chain suspension bridge in Pennsylvania.

1800 German-born English astronomer William Herschel (1738–1822) discovers infrared light.

1800 German philosopher Johann Fichte (1762–1814) publishes *The Destiny of Man*.

1800 German poet Friedrich von Hardenberg (1772–1801) – Novalis – publishes *Hymns of the Night*.

1802 German composer Ludwig van Beethoven (1770–1827) writes *Moonlight* sonata.

ASIA AND AUSTRALASIA

1802 Ranjit Singh (1780–1839) leads the Sikhs into Amritsar.

1802 British gain control of central India by the treaty of Bassein.

1803 British navigator Matthew Flinders (1774–1814) circumnavigates Australia.

1804 Founding of Hobart marks the beginning of the colonization of Tasmania.

1803 Second Maratha War begins; the British capture Delhi; Arthur Wellesley (1769–1852) wins the battle of Assaye in S India.

1804 British annex Calcutta.

1804 Chinese emperor finally suppresses the White Lotus society.

1807 Ottoman Janisseries revolt and replace sultan Selim III (1761–1808) with Mustafa IV (1779–1808).

1808 Colonial officers in Australia stage the Rum Rebellion against governor William Bligh (1754–1817).

1808 Dutch conquer the independent state of Bantam in Indonesia.

1808 Mahmud II (1785–1839) becomes Ottoman sultan.

1809 Treaty of Amritsar fixes the boundary between British territory in India and the Sikh kingdom.

1809 British make a defence treaty with the Afghans.

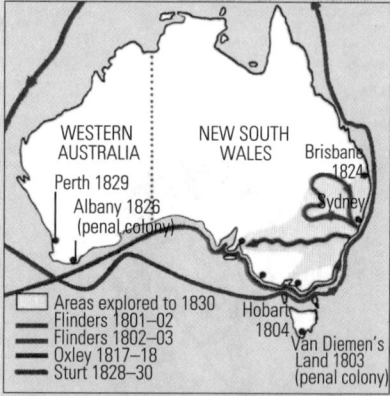

WESTERN AUSTRALIA

NEW SOUTH WALES

Perth 1829
Albany 1826
(penal colony)

Brisbane 1824
Sydney

☐ Areas explored to 1830
── Flinders 1801–02
── Flinders 1802–03
── Oxley 1817–18
── Sturt 1828–30

Hobart 1804
Van Diemen's Land 1803
(penal colony)

1810

1811 British recapture Malacca and invade Dutch Java and Sumatra.

1812 Russia defeats the Persians at the battle of Aslanduz.

1813 Persia cedes Baku and Caucasus territories to Russia under the treaty of Gulistan.

1813 British government abolishes the East India Company's monopoly on trade with India.

1814 Persia signs a defence treaty with Britain.

1814 Border dispute provokes a war between the British and the Gurkhas in Nepal.

1816 Persians invade Afghanistan but are forced to withdraw.

1816 Nepal becomes an independent British protectorate.

1816 Britain returns Java and Sumatra to the Dutch.

1816–18 Egyptian army under General Ibrahim Pasha (1789–1848) suppresses the Wahhabi state in W Arabia.

1817–18 During the third Maratha War Britain gains control of the Rajput states of W central India.

1818 Britain returns Malacca to the Dutch.

1818 Afghanistan disintegrates into small states after a tribal revolt.

1819 Bagyidaw (d.1837) becomes king of Burma and continues the policy of expansion.

1819 Sikhs under Ranjit Singh (1780–1839) conquer Kashmir.

1819 British colonial administrator Stamford Raffles (1781–1826) founds Singapore.

▶ **Napoleonic soldiers** The uniforms worn during the French invasion of Russia (1812) proved inadequate in the harsh Russian climate and many soldiers died of hypothermia.

AFRICA

1802 British return Cape Colony to the Dutch.

1803 Tripolitanians capture the US ship *Philadelphia*.

1804 US forces capture the port of Derna near Tripoli.

1804 Usman dan Fodio (1754–1817) leads the Fulani people against the Hausa states in Nigeria and establishes the Sokoto caliphate.

1805 Ottoman governor Muhammad Ali (1769–1849) seizes power in Egypt.

1805 Tripolitanian War ends when the bey of Tunis renounces the right to levy pirate-protection bribes on the USA.

1806 British recapture Cape Colony in South Africa.

1807 Slave trade is abolished throughout the British empire; a W African naval patrol is established to enforce the ban.

1807 British, allied to Russia, occupy Alexandria but withdraw after Turkish opposition.

1809 British capture Senegal from the French.

◀ **Australia** *Explorers during the early 19th century sailed around uncharted coasts of Australia and probed the interior from settled areas in the southeast. They journeyed up the great rivers and across mountains and deserts in search of fertile land and an inland sea which they believed to exist. The map shows areas explored between 1800 and 1830.*

1810 British capture Mauritius and Réunion from the French.

1810 Radama I (1791–1828) becomes king of the Hovas in Madagascar and encourages British influence.

1811 Muhammad Ali secures his position in Egypt by massacring Mameluke generals in Cairo.

1815 US navy threatens to bombard Algiers unless piracy against American shipping ends.

1815 France abolishes the slave trade.

1815 Revolt by Boers is suppressed by British troops in South Africa.

1817 Senegal is returned to French control.

1819 Zulu people under King Shaka (1787–1828) establish control of the Natal region of South Africa.

EUROPE

1801 Concordat joins church and state in France.

1801 Austria makes the peace of Luneville with France.

1801 Russia makes peace with France and joins the neutral Northern Coalition.

1802 Britain makes the peace of Amiens with France; peace is established throughout Europe.

1802 Bonaparte (1769–1821) becomes consul for life and president of the Italian republic; France annexes Piedmont.

1803 Switzerland regains its independence.

1803 Russia annexes Georgia.

1803 France occupies Hanover and prepares to invade Britain.

1804 Bonaparte is crowned Napoleon I emperor of France by the pope; the Code Napoléon law code is issued.

1804 Kara George (1766–1827) leads a Serbian insurrection against the Turks.

1805 Britain forms a third Coalition with Russia, Sweden and Austria to make war on France; an Austrian army surrenders at Ulm; British under Horatio Nelson (1758–1805) win the naval battle of Trafalgar; French occupy Vienna; Napoleon defeats the Russians and Austrians at the battle of Austerlitz; Austrians sign the treaty of Pressburg; Napoleon becomes king of Italy.

1806 Turks, allied to France, attack the Russians.

1806 Napoleon organizes German states into a pro-French Confederation of the Rhine; his brother Joseph Bonaparte (1768–1844) becomes king of Naples; the Holy Roman Empire is dissolved; Prussia attacks the French and is defeated at the battles of Jena and Auerstadt; Napoleon occupies Berlin and proclaims a blockade of Britain (the Continental System).

1807 French defeat the Prussians, capture Danzig and defeat the Russians at the battle of Friedland; peace of Tilsit ends fighting between France and Russia allied to Prussia; grand duchy of Warsaw is created in Poland; British destroy the Danish fleet; French marshal Andache Junot (1771–1813) conquers Portugal.

1808 Russia conquers Finland from Sweden.

1808 French troops invade Spain; Charles IV (1748–1819) abdicates and Joseph Bonaparte becomes king, marshal Joachim Murat (1767–1815) takes the throne of Naples; British troops under Arthur Wellesley (1769–1852) land in Portugal and force a French evacuation; a Spanish revolt is suppressed by Napoleon.

1809 French win the battle of Coruña, force the British out of Spain, and invade Portugal; an Austrian uprising is defeated by Napoleon at the battle of Wagram; Austria signs the peace of Schönbrunn.

1810 Napoleon marries Marie Louise (1791–1847), daughter of Austrian emperor Francis I (1768–1835); France annexes Holland; in Spain Arthur Wellesley (1769–1852) captures Ciudad Rodrigo and Badajoz from the French and defeats them at the battle of Salamanca.

1811–12 Machine-breaking Luddite riots occur in Britain.

1812 Turks cede Bessarabia (part of present-day Romania) to Russia.

1812 Napoleon invades Russia, wins the battles of Smolensk and Borodino, and occupies Moscow; the Russians burn Moscow and the French withdraw; most of the retreating French army dies.

1812 Liberal constitution is adopted by the Cortes of Spain.

1812 Russia gains control of Poland.

1813 Prussia declares war on France and is joined by Britain, Sweden and Austria; Napoleon is defeated at the battle of the Nations at Leipzig; Holland and Italy are freed from French rule; Wellesley wins the battle of Vittoria and drives the French from Spain; Swedes under French general Jean Bernadotte (1763–1844) invade pro-French Denmark.

1814 Sweden and Norway are united under the Swedish king.

1814 Ferdinand VII (1784–1833) is restored as king of Spain; Prussians under Gebhard Blücher (1742–1819) invade N France; British capture Bordeaux and Paris is occupied; a provisional government under Charles Talleyrand (1754–1838) exiles Napoleon to Elba; Louis XVIII (1755–1824) becomes king of France and issues a liberal constitution; peace of Paris restores the borders of Europe to the status quo of 1792; Austrian foreign minister Klemens Metternich (1773–1859) organizes the congress of Vienna; Wellesley becomes duke of Wellington.

1815 Napoleon (1769–1821) lands in S France, assembles an army, and marches to Paris; Louis XVIII (1755–1824) flees to Belgium; Austrians defeat Joachim Murat (1767–1815) at the battle of Tolentino; Ferdinand I (1751–1825) is restored as the king of the Two Sicilies.

THE AMERICAS

1803 Russians occupy E Alaska.

1804 Haiti declares independence from France under Emperor Jacques Dessalines (1748–1806).

1804 US vice president Aaron Burr (1756–1836) kills Alexander Hamilton (b.1755) in a duel.

1804 Meriwether Lewis (1774–1809) and William Clark (1770–1838) lead a US expedition across Louisiana.

1806 British occupy Buenos Aires but are evicted by a colonial militia.

1806 Francisco de Miranda (1754–1816) leads an unsuccessful rebellion against the Spanish in Venezuela.

1807 British fleet captures Montevideo but local opposition forces it to leave.

1807 Portuguese royal family flee to Brazil after the French invasion.

1808 Eastern part of Haiti returns to Spanish control.

1808 USA prohibits the importation of slaves.

1808 James Madison (1751–1836) is elected US president.

1809 Shawnee Native American chief Tecumseh (1768–1813) starts a campaign against US westward expansion.

French fashion, 1800 The fashion at the start of the 19th century was for less flamboyant clothes with thinner lines. The empire-line style of dress (right) was named for Napoleon's First Empire.

1810 Provisional junta takes power in Buenos Aires.

1810 USA annexes W Florida.

1810 Mexican priest Miguel Hidalgo (1753–1811) leads a popular revolt against the Spanish.

1811 Paraguay declares independence from Spain.

1811 Venezuelan leader Francisco de Miranda (1750–1816) declares independence from Spain.

1811 US settlers defeat the Shawnee Native Americans at the battle of Tippecanoe.

1812 Louisiana becomes a state of the USA.

1812 USA declares war on Britain; British capture Detroit.

1813 Americans recapture Detroit but fail to take Montreal.

1813 Mexican revolutionary Jose Morelos (1765–1815) declares Mexican independence.

1813 Simón Bolívar (1783–1830) takes command of Venezuelan independence forces.

1814 Americans defeat the British at a naval battle on Lake Champlain; British capture and burn Washington, D.C.; treaty of Ghent ends the war between Britain and the USA.

1814 Spanish regain control of Venezuela.

1814 José de Francia (c.1766–1840) is declared dictator of Paraguay.

1815 US troops under General Andrew Jackson (1767–1845) defeat the British at the battle of New Orleans.

1816 Argentines led by José de San Martín (1778–1850) declare their independence from Spain.

1816 Spanish regain control of Mexico.

1816 James Monroe (1758–1831) is elected US president.

1816 Indiana becomes a state of the USA.

1817 Argentina annexes Uruguay.

SCIENCE AND TECHNOLOGY

1801 German mathematician Karl Gauss (1777–1855) publishes *Arithmetical Investigations*.

1801 Italian astronomer Giuseppe Piazzi (1746–1826) discovers the asteroid Ceres.

1801 French clothworker Joseph Jacquard (1752–1834) invents a loom to make figured fabric.

1801 German scientist Johann Ritter (1776–1810) discovers ultraviolet light.

1802 British engineer Richard Trevithick (1771–1833) invents a high-pressure steam engine.

1802 French physicist Jacques Charles (1746–1823) formulates his law of gas expansion.

1803 British chemist William Henry (1774–1836) discovers his law of the volume of dissolved gases.

1804 Swiss scientist Nicholas de Saussure (1767–1845) discovers that carbon dioxide and nitrogen are essential for plant growth.

1806 British admiral Francis Beaufort (1774–1857) devises a practical scale for measuring wind speed.

1806 British chemist Humphry Davy (1778–1829) discovers sodium and potassium.

1807 US engineer Robert Fulton (1765–1815) opens the first commercial steamboat service in New York.

1807 British physicist Thomas Young (1773–1829) discovers the modulus of elasticity.

1808 British chemist John Dalton (1766–1844) outlines atomic theory in his *New System of Chemical Philosophy*.

1808 French physicist Étienne Malus (1775–1812) announces his discovery of the polarization of light.

1808 French chemist Joseph Gay-Lussac (1778–1850) announces his law of combining gas volumes.

1809 Gas street lighting is installed in Pall Mall, London.

1809 French biologist Jean Baptiste Lamarck (1744–1829) publishes *Zoological Philosophy*.

1810 French chef Nicholas Appert (c.1750–1840) publishes his method for preserving food in tin cans.

1811 German printer Friedrich König (1774–1833) invents the power-driven, flat-bed, cylinder press.

1811 Italian physicist Amedo Avogadro (1776–1856) discovers that equal volumes of gases have an equal number of molecules.

1812 French zoologist Georges Cuvier (1769–1832) publishes his *Researches into the Fossil Bones of Quadrupeds*.

1812 French mathematician Pierre Laplace (1749–1827) refines probability theory in *Analytical Theory*.

1812 British scientist William Wollaston (1766–1828) invents the camera lucida.

1812 German mineralogist Friedrich Mohs (1773–1839) classifies the hardness of materials.

1814 British engineer George Stephenson (1781–1848) builds a steam locomotive, the *Blucher*.

1814 Swedish scientist Jöns Berzelius (1779–1848) introduces modern chemical symbols.

1815 German scientist Joseph von Fraunhofer (1787–1826) discovers black lines in the solar spectrum.

1816 Scottish scientist Robert Stirling (1790–1878) invents a closed-cycle external combustion engine.

1816 French hobbyist Nicéphore Niepce (1765–1833) begins experimenting with photography using a silver chloride solution.

1819 French physician René Laennec (1781–1826) invents the stethoscope.

ARTS AND HUMANITIES

1805 British artist Joseph Turner (1775–1851) paints *Shipwreck*.

1806 German bookseller Johann Palm publishes a pamphlet entitled *Germany in its Deepest Humiliation* and is executed by the French.

1806 French sculptor Claude Clodion (1738–1814) designs the Arc de Triomphe in Paris.

1807 British poet William Wordsworth (1770–1850) publishes his *Ode on Intimations of Immortality*.

1808 French artist Jean Ingres (1780–1867) paints *Bather of Valpinçon*.

1808 French social reformer Charles Fourier (1772–1837) proposes a system of co-operative farms in his *Theory of the Four Movements*.

1808 German poet and author Johann Goethe (1749–1832) publishes the first part of his drama *Faust*.

1808 German composer Ludwig van Beethoven (1770–1827) writes his Symphony No.5 in C minor.

> "Whither is fled the visionary gleam? / Where is it now, the glory and the dream? / Our birth is but a sleep and a forgetting."
>
> *William Wordsworth (Ode on Intimations of Immortality)*

1810 Scottish poet Walter Scott (1771–1832) publishes *The Lady of the Lake*.

1810 Spanish artist Francisco Goya (1746–1828) begins his series of engravings *The Disasters of War*.

1810 British architect John Nash (1752–1835) begins designing the Royal Pavilion in Brighton, England.

1811 Swedish poet Esaias Tegner (1782–1846) publishes *Svea*.

1812 British poet George Byron (1788–1824) publishes the first cantos of *Childe Harold's Pilgrimage*.

1812 German language scholars Jakob (1785–1863) and Wilhelm (1786–1859) Grimm publish a collection of folktales and fairy stories.

1813 British novelist Jane Austen (1775–1817) publishes *Pride and Prejudice*.

1813 French novelist Madame de Staël (1766–1817) publishes *On Germany*.

1813 British industrialist Robert Owen (1771–1858) publishes *A New View of Society*.

1814 Kurozumi Munetada (1780–1850) revives popular Shintoism in Japan.

1816 Italian composer Gioacchino Rossini (1792–1868) writes his opera *The Barber of Seville*.

1816 German philosopher Georg Hegel (1770–1831) introduces his dialectical system in *The Science of Logic*.

1817 British artist John Constable (1776–1831) paints *View on the Stour*.

1817 British economist David Ricardo (1772–1823) publishes his *Principles of Political Economy and Taxation*.

1818 British novelist Mary Shelley (1797–1851) publishes *Frankenstein*.

1819 German philosopher Arthur Schopenhauer (1788–1860) publishes his pessimistic *The World as Will and Idea*.

1810

ASIA AND AUSTRALASIA

▶ *Europe* The 1815 Congress of Vienna was convened to restore order in Europe after the Napoleonic Wars. The fear was that France might cause another European war so three buffer states were created to hinder her expansion eastwards. The Kingdom of Piedmont was strengthened. Belgium was joined with Holland in the Kingdom of the Netherlands. The Holy Roman Empire became the German Confederation.

GREAT BRITAIN AND IRELAND

KINGDOM OF NORWAY AND SWEDEN

—— Boundary of German Confederation 1815
▢ Kingdom of Poland united with Russia 1815

RUSSIAN EMPIRE

PRUSSIA • Warsaw

UNITED NETHERLANDS

FRANCE

SWITZERLAND

PIEDMONT

BAVARIA

AUSTRO-HUNGARIAN EMPIRE

PORTUGAL

SPAIN

PAPAL STATES

OTTOMAN EMPIRE

THE TWO SICILIES

SARDINIA

1820

1822 Burmese annex Assam.

1824 British declare war on Burma and capture Rangoon.

1824 Dutch cede Malacca to Britain in return for territory in Sumatra.

1825 Persia attempts to recapture Georgia from Russia.

1826 Anti-Sikh jihad is organized by Muslims in N India.

1826 Russians defeat Persians at the battle of Ganja and gain part of Armenia.

1826 Afghan chieftain Dost Muhammad (1789–1863) captures Kabul.

1826 King Rama III (d.1851) of Thailand signs a trade agreement with Britain.

1826 After defeating the Burmese, Britain gains Assam and part of the Malay peninsula by the treaty of Yandabu.

1826 British unite Penang, Singapore and Malacca into the Straits Settlements.

1826 Sultan Mahmud II (1785–1839) massacres the Janisseries in Turkey.

1826 Dipo Negoro (c.1785–1855) leads a Javanese revolt against the Dutch.

1828 Russian forces capture Tehran; Persia cedes territory to Russia by the treaty of Turkmanchai.

1828 Dutch annex W New Guinea.

1829 British claim the whole of Australia.

AFRICA

1820 Egypt invades Sudan.

1820 Several thousand British settlers are sent to South Africa.

1820 Mfecane Wars start in S Africa when Zulu expansion displaces other African peoples; Ngoni raiding parties invade Mozambique.

1821 Sierra Leone, the Gold Coast (present-day Ghana) and Gambia are joined into British West Africa.

1822 Liberia, on the coast of West Africa, is established as a colony for freed American slaves.

1822 Mfecane Wars spread to South Africa.

1823 Egyptians found Khartoum as the capital of Sudan.

1824 British interference in West African affairs angers the Ashanti people, who destroy a British force; start of the first Ashanti War.

1824 Omani governor of Mombasa dies and the British occupy the port.

1825 King Radama I (1791–1828) evicts the French from Madagascar.

1826 Boundary of Cape Colony is extended N to the Orange River.

1827 British defeat an Ashanti invasion of the Gold Coast; end of the first Ashanti War.

1828 British evacuate Mombasa.

1828 Ranavalona I (1800–61) becomes Hova queen in Madagascar.

1828 Zulu leader Shaka (1787–1828) is assassinated by his brothers.

> "Nothing except a battle lost can be half so melancholy as a battle won."
>
> *Arthur Wellesley, Duke of Wellington (despatch from the Battle of Waterloo)*

EUROPE

1815 Napoleon invades Belgium and defeats Gebhard Blücher (1742–1819) at Ligny, but is defeated by the British and Prussians under the Duke of Wellington (1769–1852) at the Battle of Waterloo; Napoleon is exiled to St Helena; a second White Terror occurs.

1815 Congress of Vienna establishes the balance of power in Europe. Poland is united with Russia; Holland and Belgium are united as the Kingdom of the Netherlands; German Confederation is formed; perpetual neutrality of Switzerland is declared.

1815 Russia, Austria and Prussia form the anti-liberal Holy Alliance.

1815 British parliament passes a protectionist Corn Law that restricts the importation of foreign grains.

1817 Liberal German students protest in Wartburg.

1818 Miloš Obrenović (1780–1860) leads a Serbian uprising against the Turks and establishes a degree of self-government.

1818 France joins the Holy Alliance by the treaty of Aix-la-Chapelle.

1818 Jean Bernadotte (1763–1844) becomes Charles XIV of Sweden.

1819 Carlsbad decrees impose strict censorship and control over university admissions throughout the German Confederation.

1819 Anti-Corn Law protesters are killed by troops at the Peterloo massacre in Britain.

1820 Soldiers join a liberal revolution in S Spain and force Ferdinand VII (1784–1833) to restore the constitution.

1820 Carbonari secret societies foment a liberal revolt in Naples which forces Ferdinand I (1751–1825) to issue a constitution.

1820 Liberal revolution starts in Oporto, Portugal.

1820 George IV (1762–1830) becomes king of Britain.

1821 Liberal unrest spreads to N Italy; the king of Piedmont-Sardinia abdicates; the Congress of Laibach authorizes the Austrians to restore monarchical power in Italy.

1821 Greeks led by Alexander Ypsilante (1792–1828) revolt against Turkish rule and seize Bucharest.

1822 Congress of Verona authorizes the French to intervene in Spain to restore the monarchy.

1822 Greeks declare independence; Turks invade and massacre the inhabitants of Chios, but fail to subdue the rebels.

1822 Egyptians occupy Crete.

1822 Portugal adopts a liberal constitution under King John VI (1767–1826).

1823 John VI withdraws the Portuguese constitution; reactionaries led by his son start a civil war.

1823 French occupy Madrid, defeat the revolutionaries at the battle of the Trocadero, and restore Ferdinand VII.

1824 Greek rebels are divided by civil war.

1824 Charles X (1757–1836), becomes king of France and attempts to restore the power of the monarchy.

1825 Egyptian army invades S Greece.

1825 Alexander I (b.1777) of Russia dies; an attempted military coup (the Decembrists) fails; Nicholas I (1796–1855) becomes tsar.

1826 Infant Maria II (1819–53) becomes queen of Portugal.

1826 Turks capture the Greek stronghold of Missolongi.

1827 Turks capture the Acropolis in Athens.

1828 Force of British, French and Russian ships destroys the Egyptian fleet at the battle of Navarino; Egyptians evacuate Greece.

1828 Russians declare war on Turkey.

1828 British Corn Law is reformed.

1828 Portuguese regent Dom Miguel (1802–66) proclaims himself king.

1829 South German state of Bavaria signs a trade tariff treaty with Prussia.

1829 London protocol establishes Greek independence under a monarchy.

1829 Russia gains the E coast of the Black Sea from the Turks under the treaty of Adrianople.

1829 Catholic Emancipation Act is passed in Britain.

1829 Ultra-conservative Prince de Polignac (1780–1847) becomes prime minister in France.

THE AMERICAS

1817 San Martín invades and liberates Chile.

1817 Mississippi becomes a state of the USA.

1818 Simón Bolívar (1783–1830) leads a revolutionary army into Venezuela.

1818 USA and Britain agree on the 49th parallel as the Canadian boundary, with joint occupation of Oregon.

1818 Illinois becomes a state of the USA.

1818 Revolutionary leader Bernardo O'Higgins (1778–1842) becomes Supreme Director of Chile.

1818 Steamship service opens on the Great Lakes, central North America.

1819 USA purchases Florida from Spain.

1819 Bolívar defeats the Spanish and becomes president of Gran Colombia (present-day Venezuela, Ecuador and Colombia).

1819 Alabama becomes a state of the USA.

1820 Missouri compromise prohibits slavery in the N part of the Louisiana Purchase territory.

1820 Maine becomes a state of the USA.

1821 Aristocratic revolutionaries declare Mexican independence from Spain.

1821 Brazil incorporates Uruguay.

1821 US farmers begin to settle in Texas.

1821 José de San Martín (1778–1850) and Simón Bolívar (1783–1830) liberate Peru.

1821 Missouri becomes a state of the USA.

1822 Mexican general Agustín de Iturbide (1783–1824) is crowned Emperor Agustín I; Central American states become part of the Mexican empire.

1822 Brazil under Emperor Pedro I (1798–1834) declares its independence from Portugal.

1823 Revolution overthrows the Mexican emperor.

1823 Guatemala, San Salvador, Nicaragua, Honduras and Costa Rica establish independence from Mexico and form the United Provinces of Central America.

1823 US president James Monroe (1758–1831) issues the Monroe doctrine forbidding European colonialism in the Americas.

1824 Mexico becomes a republic under President Guadalupe Vittoria (1768–1843).

1825 US House of Representatives elects John Quincy Adams (1767–1848) president.

1825 Erie canal is completed, linking New York City with the Great Lakes.

1825 Portugal recognizes the independence of Brazil.

1825 Bolivia under President Antonio de Sucre (1795–1830) gains independence from Peru.

1825 Argentina sends troops to aid Uruguay against Brazil.

1827 Argentines defeat the Brazilians at the battle of Ituzaingo.

1828 Uruguay obtains independence from Brazil.

1828 General Andrew Jackson (1767–1845) is elected US president.

1829 First US public railway opens.

1829 Peru and Bolivia form a confederation.

1829 Mexican general Antonio de Santa Anna (1794–1876) defeats an attempted Spanish invasion.

1829 Workingmen's party formed in the USA.

SCIENCE AND TECHNOLOGY

▲ **Faraday** is considered to be one of the world's greatest experimental scientists. He made fundamental contributions in electricity, magnetism and chemistry.

1820 French physicians Pierre Pelletier (1788–1842) and Joseph Caventou (1795–1877) discover the anti-malarial drug quinine.

1820 French physicist André Ampère (1775–1836) establishes the science of electromagnetism.

1821 French physicist Augustin Fresnel (1788–1827) finalizes his transverse wave theory of light.

1821 German physicist Thomas Seebeck (1770–1831) invents the thermocouple.

1821 British physicist Michael Faraday (1791–1867) discovers electromagnetic rotation.

1822 French scientist and mathematician Jean Fourier (1768–1830) publishes his theory of heat conduction.

1822 French scholar Jean Champollion (1790–1832) translates Egyptian hieroglyphics.

1823 British mathematician Charles Babbage (1791–1871) begins building a working model of his difference engine calculating machine.

1824 British builder Joseph Aspidin (1779–1855) invents Portland cement.

1824 Scottish chemist Charles Macintosh (1766–1843) devises a method of bonding rubber to fabric for waterproof clothing.

1824 French engineer Sadi Carnot (1796–1832) lays the foundations of thermodynamics in *On the Motive Power of Fire*.

1825 George Stephenson (1781–1848) builds the first public railway between Stockton and Darlington.

1825 Danish physicist Hans Uersted (1777–1851) discovers how to produce aluminium metal.

1825 French engineer Marc Seguin (1786–1875) builds the first wire suspension bridge.

1827 German scientist Georg Ohm (1787–1854) publishes his law of electrical voltage and current.

1827 Scottish scientist Robert Brown (1773–1858) observes the random movements of minute particles (Brownian motion).

1827 British chemist John Walker (c.1781–1859) invents friction matches.

1828 German chemist Friedrich Wöhler (1800–82) synthesizes urea.

1829 British chemist Thomas Graham (1805–69) formulates his law of gas diffusion.

1829 French mathematician Gaspard de Coriolis (1792–1843) explains the effect that causes objects moving in the atmosphere to be deflected.

ARTS AND HUMANITIES

1819 Austrian composer Franz Schubert (1797–1828) writes his *Trout* quinte

1819 Walter Scott publishes his novel *Ivanhoe*.

1819 French artist Theodore Géricault (1791–1824) paints *Raft of the Medusa*.

1820 Venus de Milo sculpture is discovered.

1820 French poet Alphonse Lamartine (1790–1869) publishes *Poetic Meditations*.

1820 British poet John Keats (1795–1821) publishes *Ode to a Nightingale*.

1820 British poet Percy Shelley (1792–1822) publishes *Prometheus Unbound*.

1821 French social reformer Claude de Saint-Simon (1760–1825) publishes *Of the Industrial System*.

1822 German composer Carl von Weber (1786–1826) writes his opera *Der Freischütz*.

1822 British writer Thomas De Quincey (1785–1859) publishes *Confessions of an English Opium Eater*.

1822 Hungarian composer Franz Liszt (1811–86) makes his debut as a pianist.

1824 French artist Eugène Delacroix (1798–1863) paints *Massacre at Chios*.

1825 Russian poet Alexander Pushkin (1799–1837) publishes *Boris Godunov*.

1826 US novelist James Fenimore Cooper (1789–1851) publishes *The Last of the Mohicans*.

1826 French poet and author Alfred de Vigny (1797–1863) publishes his novel *Cinq-Mars*.

1827 German poet Heinrich Heine (1797–1856) publishes *The Book of Songs*.

1827 Italian poet and author Alessandro Manzoni (1785–1873) publishes his novel *The Betrothed*.

1828 American publisher Noah Webster (1758–1843) publishes the *American Dictionary of the English Language*.

1828 *Memoirs* of Giovanni Casanova (1725–98) are published.

1828 Italian violinist Niccolò Paganini (1782–1840) arrives in Vienna.

1829 French novelist Honore de Balzac (1788–1850) publishes *The Chouans* and begins *The Human Comedy*.

1829 Scottish philosopher James Mill (1773–1836) publishes *An Analysis of the Phenomena of the Human Mind*.

ASIA AND AUSTRALASIA

1830

1830 Dutch suppress the Javanese revolt.

1831 Muslims defeat the Sikhs at the battle of Balakot in NW India.

1832 Ottoman governor Muhammad Ali (1769–1849) invades Syria and Asia Minor and defeats the Turks at the battle of Konya.

1833 Russia sends ships to assist the Turks; France and Britain protest against Russian interference; Muhammad Ali gains control of Syria.

1834 Sikhs capture the Muslim city of Peshawar in present-day Pakistan.

1834 Muhammad Shah becomes ruler of Persia after the death of Fath Ali (b.1771).

1835 Dost Muhammad (1789–1863) becomes ruler of all Afghanistan and establishes the Barakzai dynasty.

1838 Ismaili leader Aga Khan I (1800–81) flees to India after his rebellion against the shah of Persia is defeated.

1839 British occupy the port of Aden in Yemen.

1839 Turks invade Syria and are defeated by the Egyptians at the battle of Nesib.

1839 British invade Afghanistan and overthrow Dost Muhammad.

1839 Chinese officials burn British opium in the port of Canton (Guangzhou).

Darwin sailed from Plymouth, England, on HMS Beagle on 17 December 1831. For five years, he explored parts of South America and the Pacific Islands. Darwin is renowned for his theory of evolution based on natural selection. As well as The Origin of Species *(1859), Darwin published other books discussing evolution, including* The Descent of Man *(1871).*

1840

1840 British colonists land in New Zealand; Maori chiefs cede sovereignty to Britain by the treaty of Waitangi.

1840 British occupy Chinese forts in Canton (Guangzhou).

1841 During the first Opium War, the British navy seizes ports along the Chinese coast.

1841 Afghans rebel against British occupation.

1841 Sultan of Brunei cedes Sarawak to a British merchant.

1841 European powers persuade Egypt to withdraw from Syria.

1842 British are forced to withdraw from Afghanistan; Dost Muhammad (1789–1863) regains power.

1842 Peace of Nanjing ends the first Opium War; Britain obtains Hong Kong.

1842 Tahiti becomes a French protectorate.

1843 British conquer Sind in present-day SW Pakistan.

1843 First Maori War breaks out over a land dispute.

1843 Chinese port of Shanghai is opened to foreign trade.

1843 Chinese emperor repeats his ban on opium smoking.

1844 Cambodia comes under the control of Thailand.

1844 Sayyid Ali Muhammad (c.1820–50) proclaims himself Bab and founds Babism in Persia.

AFRICA

1830 French invade Algeria and occupy the cities of Algiers and Oran.

1831 Britain signs a peace treaty with the Ashanti.

1831 Mfecane Wars spread N to Zimbabwe.

1831 French foreign legion is founded in Algeria.

1832 Abd al-Kadir (1808–83) becomes leader of the Algerian resistance.

1834 Slavery is abolished throughout the British empire.

1835 Mfecane Wars spread further N to Zambia and Malawi.

1835 Turks overthrow the Karamanli dynasty in Tripoli and impose direct rule.

1835 Boers in South Africa begin the Great Trek to escape British repression.

1836 Abd al-Kadir (1808–83) occupies the inland Algerian city of Mascara.

1837 Boers establish the republic of Natal to the NE of the British Cape Colony.

1838 Boers in Natal inflict a heavy defeat on the Zulus.

1840 Sultan of Oman, Sayyid Said (1791–1856), makes Zanzibar his capital.

1841 Algerian leader Abd al-Kadir is driven into Morocco by the French.

1842 French sign trade treaties with chieftains of the Ivory Coast in W Africa.

1843 British conquer Natal from the Boers.

1843 Basutoland in S Africa comes under British protection.

1843 The Gambia is made a separate British colony.

1844 French acquire Gabon in W central Africa.

1844 French bombard Tangier in Morocco and defeat al-Kadir and his Moroccan allies at the battle of Isly.

▶ *Neoclassicism A movement of the late 18th and early 19th centuries, neoclassicism was inspired by the forms of Greek and Roman art. In architecture, the trend culminated with the Greek revival buildings of Karl Schinkel, such as the Old Museum (1822–30) in Berlin, built to house the art collection of the Prussian state.*

EUROPE

1830 William IV (1765–1827) becomes king of Britain.

1830 Revolution in Paris overthrows Charles X (1757–1836); Louis Philippe I (1773–1850) becomes king of France with a more liberal constitution.

1830 Revolutionaries in Brussels declare Belgian independence from the Netherlands.

1830 Rising in Warsaw led by Adam Jerzy Czartoryski (1770–1861) establishes a Polish national government.

1830 German revolutionaries force the rulers of Saxony and Brunswick to abdicate.

1831 Russian troops crush the Polish rebels.

1831 Leopold I (1790–1865) becomes king of Belgium with a liberal constitution.

1831 Nationalist risings in the Italian cities of Parma and Modena are suppressed by the Austrians.

1832 Italian nationalist Giuseppe Mazzini (1805–72) founds the Young Italy movement.

1832 Poland is made a province of Russia.

1832 British parliament is reformed.

1833 German revolutionaries force the ruler of Hanover to issue a constitution.

1833 Maria II (1819–53) is restored to the Portuguese throne.

1833 Infant Isabella II (1830–1904) becomes queen of Spain.

1834 German *Zollverein* (customs union) is formed under Prussian leadership.

1834 Isabella's brother Don Carlos (1788–1845) claims the Spanish throne; start of the Carlist War.

1834 Republican revolts in French cities are repressed.

1835 Ferdinand I (1793–1875) becomes Austrian emperor.

1836 Louis Napoleon (1808–73) attempts to seize power in France and is exiled to America.

1836 Rebellion in Spain forces the regent Maria Christina (1806–78) to grant a new constitution.

1837 Victoria (1819–1901) becomes queen of Britain; Hanover is separated from Britain.

1837 Under Austrian influence, the constitution of Hanover is withdrawn.

1838 British advocates of free trade John Bright (1811–89) and Richard Cobden (1805–65) found the Anti-Corn Law league.

1838 Protestant cantons in Switzerland adopt more liberal constitutions.

1839 First Carlist War in Spain ends when Don Carlos (1788–1845) leaves the country.

1839 Radical Chartists cause riots in Britain.

1839 The Netherlands recognizes the independence of Belgium and the grand duchy of Luxembourg by the treaty of London.

1840 Frederick William VI (1795–1861) becomes king of Prussia.

1840 Louis Napoleon (1808–73) attempts another coup in France and is imprisoned.

1840 General Baldomero Espartero (1793–1879) makes himself dictator in Spain.

1840 Britain, France and Russia agree to aid Turkey and send troops to Palestine.

1841 Straits Convention closes the Dardanelles (the entrance to the Black Sea) to non-Turkish warships.

1842 Rising in Barcelona, Spain, declares a republic, which is crushed by Espartero.

1843 Coup overthrows Espartero in Spain; Queen Isabella II (1830–1904) is declared of age.

1843 Revolution forces King Otto I (1815–67) of Greece to grant a constitution.

1844 Anti-industrial rebellion by Prussian weavers is suppressed by troops.

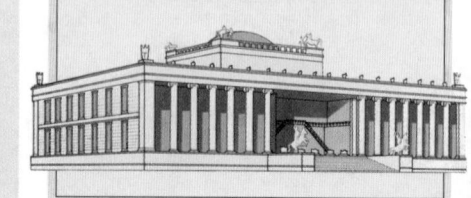

THE AMERICAS

1830 Ecuador under President Juan Flores (1800–64) gains independence from Colombia.

1830 US Indian Removal Act organizes the removal of Native Americans to w of the River Mississippi.

1830 First American settlers arrive in California having crossed the Rocky Mountains.

1831 Nat Turner (b.1800) is executed after leading a slave revolt in Virginia.

1831 Pedro II (1825–91) becomes emperor of Brazil.

1833 Antonio de Santa Anna (1794–1876) is elected president of Mexico.

1833 Britain claims sovereignty over the Falkland Islands.

1835 American settlers declare the independent republic of Texas.

1836 US congressman Davy Crockett (b.1786) and colonel Jim Bowie (b.1796) are killed when Mexican troops defeat Texan rebels at the Alamo mission house; the Mexicans are decisively defeated at the battle of San Jacinto by Texans under General Sam Houston (1793–1863).

1836 Martin Van Buren (1782–1862) is elected US president.

1836 Arkansas becomes a state of the USA.

1836 Settlers in California declare independence from Mexico.

1837 French-speakers in Lower Canada rebel against British administration; a similar revolt occurs in Upper Canada.

1837 Michigan becomes a state of the USA.

1838 British restore order in Canada.

1838 Underground Railroad is organized in the USA to smuggle slaves from the s states.

1838 Britain and France blockade the Argentine coast in a dispute over the Falkland Islands.

1839 Former slave-owners rebel against British rule in Jamaica.

1839 Chilean troops overthrow the Peru–Bolivia confederation.

> "The history of the world is but the biography of great men."
>
> *Thomas Carlyle (On Heroes and Hero-worship)*

Colt revolver The Colt Navy revolver is probably the most famous percussion revolving pistol. As with most of Colt's revolvers, it was open-framed, having no strap over the top of the frame. It had a six-chambered cylinder and was of 0.36in calibre. Each chamber was normally loaded from the muzzle with powder and a ball or conical bullet.

1840 Confederation of Central American States breaks up.

1840 William Harrison (1773–1841) is elected US president.

1840 Upper and Lower Canada are united and the country is granted self-governing status by the British.

1841 John Tyler (1790–1862) becomes US president.

1841 Peruvian attempt to annex Bolivia is defeated at the battle of Ingavi.

1842 Treaty between the USA and Britain settles the E stretch of the US–Canadian border.

1844 James Polk (1795–1849) is elected US president.

1844 Dominican Republic becomes independent of Haiti.

SCIENCE AND TECHNOLOGY

1830 British geologist Charles Lyell (1797–1875) publishes the first volume of his *Principles of Geology*.

1830 British engineer Joseph Whitworth (1803–87) introduces standardized screw threads.

1830 British physicist Michael Faraday (1791–1867) discovers electromagnetic induction.

1831 British explorer James Ross (1800–62) reaches the N magnetic pole.

1831 British naturalist Charles Darwin (1809–82) embarks on his round-the-world expedition on HMS *Beagle*.

1831 US physicist Joseph Henry (1797–1878) publishes a description of his electric motor

1832 French instrument maker Hippolyte Pixii (1808–35) constructs a practical, heteropolar, electrical generator.

1833 Steamship *Royal William* becomes the first to cross the Atlantic Ocean entirely by steam power.

1834 French teacher Louis Braille (1809–52) perfects his system of embossed dots that enable blind people to read.

1834 US farmer Cyrus McCormick (1809–84) invents the horse-drawn reaper-harvester.

1835 US inventor Samuel Colt (1814–62) patents his revolver handgun.

1836 British electrical engineer William Sturgeon (1783–1850) invents the moving-coil galvanometer.

1836 Belgian scientist Joseph Plateau (1801–83) invents the stroboscope.

1837 British educator Isaac Pitman (1813–97) invents his system of shorthand writing.

1837 US metalworker John Deere (1804–86) invents the steel plough.

1837 British physicists Charles Wheatstone (1802–75) and William Cooke (1806–79) jointly invent an electric telegraph.

1837 US inventor Samuel Morse (1791–1872) devises an electric telegraph and a simple dot-dash message code.

1838 German astronomer Friedrich Bessel (1784–1846) discovers stellar parallax.

1839 German biologist Theodor Schwann (1810–82) publishes his cell theory.

1839 French artist Louis Daguerre (1789–1851) announces his invention of a photographic process for producing images on copper plates.

1839 British scientist William Talbot (1800–77) invents a process for making photographic negatives.

1839 US manufacturer Charles Goodyear (1800–60) discovers the process for vulcanizing rubber.

1839 Scottish engineer James Nasmyth (1808–90) invents the steam hammer.

1839 French physicist Anton Becquerel (1788–1878) invents a photoelectric cell.

1840 German chemist Christian Schönbein (1799–1868) discovers ozone.

1840 Scottish engineer Alexander Bain (1810–77) invents an electric clock.

1840 Swiss geologist Louis Agassiz (1807–73) proposes his ice ages theory of global glaciation.

1840 'Needle-fire' breech-loading rifle, designed by German locksmith Nikolaus von Dreyse (1787–1867), is introduced into the Prussian army.

1841 German chemist Robert Bunsen (1811–99) invents a zinc-carbon battery.

1841 US engineer John Roebling (1806–69) invents a machine for making wire rope.

1841 British palaeontologist Richard Owen (1804–92) introduces the term 'dinosaur'.

1841 British astronomer John Couch Adams (1819–92) and French astronomer Urbain Leverrier (1811–77) independently predict the existence and position of the planet Neptune.

1842 Austrian physicist Christian Doppler (1805–53) discovers the change in frequency of sound waves from a moving source.

1842 US physician Crawford Long (1815–78) first uses ether as a surgical anaesthetic.

1843 British physicist James Joule (1818–89) establishes the first law of thermodynamics.

1844 US dentist Horace Wells (1815–48) first uses nitrous oxide as an anaesthetic for tooth extraction.

ARTS AND HUMANITIES

1830

1830 US religious leader Joseph Smith (1805–44) publishes *The Book of Mormon*.

1830 French composer Hector Berlioz (1803–69) writes *Symphonie fantastique*.

1830 French novelist Stendhal (Henry Beyle, 1783–1842) publishes *Scarlet and Black*.

1830 French-born Polish composer Frédéric Chopin (1810–49) writes his first piano concerto.

1831 French Barbizon school of landscape painters exhibits at the Paris Salon.

1832 French novelist George Sand (1804–76) publishes *Indiana*.

1832 US artist George Catlin (1796–1872) completes his portfolio of paintings of Native Americans.

1832 Military theories of Prussian general Carl von Clausewitz (1780–1831) are published posthumously as *On War*.

1833 Russian novelist and dramatist Nikolai Gogol (1809–52) publishes his play *The Government Inspector*.

1833 Japanese artist Ando Hiroshige (1797–1858) publishes his woodcuts of the *Fifty-three Stages of the Tokaido*.

1835 French historian Alexis de Tocqueville (1805–1859) publishes *Of Democracy in America*.

1836 German composer Felix Mendelssohn (1809–47) writes his *St Paul* oratorio.

1837 British novelist Charles Dickens (1812–70) publishes *Oliver Twist*.

1835 Italian composer Gaetano Donizetti (1797–1848) writes his opera *Lucy of Lammermoor*.

1835 Danish writer Hans Christian Andersen (1805–75) publishes *Tales Told for Children*.

1836 US writer Oliver Wendell Holmes (1809–94) publishes *Poems*.

1836 German theologian David Strauss (1808–74) treats the gospels as myth in his *Life of Jesus*.

1836 US philosopher Ralph Waldo Emerson (1803–82) introduces Transcendentalism in his collection of essays *Nature*.

1838 US artist John Audubon (1785–1851) publishes the fourth and final volume of illustrations for his *Birds of America*.

1839 French socialist Louis Blanc (1811–82) publishes *The Organization of Labour*.

1839 US poet Henry Longfellow (1807–82) publishes *Voices of the Night*.

1840

1840 French anarchist philosopher Pierre Proudhon (1809–65) publishes *What is Property?*

1840 German composer Robert Schumann (1810–56) publishes his *Women's Love and Life* song-cycle.

1841 German educator Friedrich Froebel (1782–1852) opens the first kindergarten.

1841 German economist Friedrich List (1789–1846) publishes *The National System of Political Economy*.

1841 Scottish historian Thomas Carlyle (1795–1881) publishes *On Heroes and Hero-worship*.

1843 Italian nationalist Vincenzo Gioberti (1801–52) publishes *On the Moral and Civil Primacy of the Italians*.

1844 French writer Alexandre Dumas (1802–70) publishes his novel *The Three Musketeers*.

1844 Danish philosopher Søren Kierkegaard (1813–55) publishes *The Concept of Dread*.

1844 Italian composer Giuseppe Verdi (1813–1901) writes his opera *Ernani*.

1844 Turner paints *Rain, Steam and Speed*.

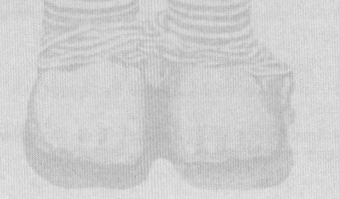

ASIA AND AUSTRALASIA

1848 Nasir al-Din (1829–96) becomes Shah of Persia.

1845 Sikhs invade British territory in N India; start of the Anglo-Sikh War.

1846 British conquer Kashmir from the Sikhs and sell it to a Hindu ruler.

1848 Babists in Persia rebel and declare an independent state.

1849 British annex the Sikh kingdom in the Punjab region of India.

1850 Babist rebellion in Persia crushed and the self-proclaimed 'Bab', Sayyid Ali Muhammad (b.c.1820), executed.

1850 Quasi-Christian Taiping rebellion breaks out in SW China led by Hong Xiuquan.

1850 Britain's Australian colonies are granted self-government.

1851 Colonists discover gold in Victoria, Australia.

1852 During the second Burmese War Britain annexes Pegu (S Burma); Mindon Min (1814–78) becomes king of N Burma.

1853 French annex the islands of New Caledonia in the S Pacific.

1853 Taiping rebels conquer the Chinese city of Nanjing and make it their capital.

1853 Heaven and Earth secret society captures the port of Shanghai in China.

1854 US naval officer Matthew Perry (1794–1858) forces Japan to open to limited foreign trade.

1855 Chinese troops prevent the Taiping rebels from capturing Beijing; imperial troops also recapture Shanghai with French assistance.

1856 Ottoman sultan Abdul Medjid I (1823–61) approves the Hatt-i Humayun reforms, giving religious freedom to Christians.

1856 Britain annexes the Indian state of Oudh.

1856 Persians capture the Afghan city of Herat; Britain declares war on Persia.

1856 Chinese authorities arrest the British crew of the *Arrow* for smuggling; start of the second Opium War.

1857 British and French troops capture Canton (Guangzhou), China.

1857 British forces occupy Bushire in Persia.

1857 French occupy Saigon in S Vietnam.

1857 Mandalay becomes the new capital of Burma.

1857 Sepoys (local troops) in India mutiny and massacre British civilians in many cities; British forces recapture Delhi.

1858 Indian Mutiny is completely suppressed; the British East India company is dissolved and India comes under the control of the British crown.

1858 Treaty of Tianjin opens more Chinese ports to foreign ships and legalizes the opium trade.

1858 China cedes N bank of Amur river to Russia by the treaty of Aigun.

1859 Portuguese and Dutch agree to divide Timor.

1859 US ships assist the British and the French against the Chinese.

1859 Dispute over land sparks the second Maori War in New Zealand.

AFRICA

1846 British defeat an incursion by the Xhosa people in South Africa.

1847 Liberia becomes an independent republic.

1847 Abd al-Kadir surrenders to the French in Algeria.

1848 Algeria becomes a part of France.

1849 French acquire territory in Guinea, W Africa.

1849 French establish Libreville in Gabon as a refuge for escaped slaves.

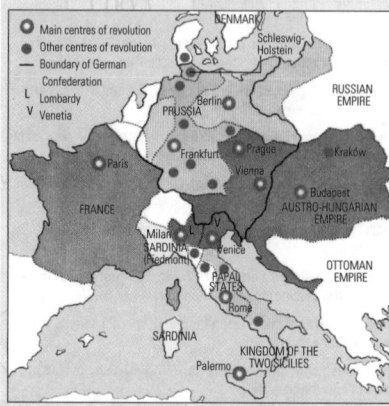

▶ **Revolutions of 1848** *Urban uprisings occurred in most European countries. They were caused by frustration with governing authorities and economic depression.*

1850 Denmark sells its trading posts in W Africa to Britain

1852 Fulani leader Al-Hadj Umar (c.1797–1864) launches a war of expansion against W African states.

1853 Boers establish the independent republic of Transvaal.

1853 Ethiopian chieftain Ras Kasa (c.1818–68) reunifies the country and proclaims himself Emperor Tewodros II.

1854 British agree to the Boers establishing an Orange Free State.

1856 Transvaal becomes the South African Republic, with Pretoria as its capital.

1856 David Livingstone (1813–73) completes the first E–W crossing of Africa by a European, having 'discovered' and named the Victoria Falls.

1857 Fulani led by Al-Hadj Umar (c.1797–1864) besiege the French fort of Medine in Senegal.

1857 French found Dakar in Senegal.

1857 French forces conquer the Berbers in S Algeria.

1859 Construction of the Suez canal begins under the direction of French engineer Ferdinand de Lesseps (1805–94).

1859 Spanish troops invade Morocco in a dispute over the enclaves of Ceuta and Melila.

EUROPE

1845–46 Potato blight causes famine in Ireland.

1846 British corn laws are repealed.

1846 Polish rising in Kraków is suppressed by Austria.

1847 Protestant Swiss cantons defeat the Catholic Sonderbund.

1847 Unrest in N Italy is suppressed by Austria.

1848 Revolution in France overthrows Louis Philippe I (1773–1850) and forms a provisional government; Paris workers stage a second rising; Louis Napoleon (1808–73) is elected president of the second French republic.

1848 Central and S Italian states receive constitutions; rebels drive Austrians from Milan; Venice declares a republic; Piedmont declares war on Austria.

1848 Switzerland adopts a new federal constitution.

1848 Rising in Berlin leads to a German national assembly meeting in Frankfurt.

1848 Denmark and Prussia go to war over Schleswig-Holstein.

1848 Rising in Vienna causes Klemens Metternich (1773–1859) to flee Austria; a constituent assembly meets; Franz Joseph I (1830–1916) becomes Austrian emperor; Hungarians establish a national government.

1849 Louis Kossuth (1802–94) is elected Hungarian leader; the Russians crush the Hungarian rising.

1849 Ferdinand II (1810–59) restores control in S Italy; Roman republic is suppressed by the French despite resistance of Giuseppe Garibaldi (1807–82); Austrians defeat Piedmontese at the battle of Novara and crush the Venetian republic.

1849 German national assembly collapses.

1850 German Confederation restored under Austrian leadership.

1850 British gunboats blockade the Greek port of Piraeus.

1851 Austrian emperor withdraws the constitution.

1851 Louis Napoleon overthrows the French constitution.

1852 Louis Napoleon (1808–73) is declared Emperor Napoleon III.

1852 Camillo di Cavour (1810–61) becomes prime minister of Piedmont-Sardinia.

1852 Schleswig-Holstein comes under Danish protection.

1853 Central and N German states renew the Zollverein agreement from which Austria is excluded.

1853 Russia invades Turkish-occupied Romania.

1854 Britain and France support Turkey against Russia in the Crimean War; British and French forces besiege the Russians at Sebastopol and win the battle of Balaclava; Florence Nightingale (1820–1910) nurses the British wounded.

1854 British and French ships occupy Piraeus to prevent Greece joining the war against Turkey.

1854 General Leopoldo O'Donnell (1809–67) leads a liberal revolution in Spain.

1855 Alexander II (1818–81) becomes tsar of Russia; Sebastopol falls to British and French troops.

1855 Lord Palmerston (1784–1865) becomes prime minister of Britain.

1856 Peace of Paris ends the Crimean War; Russia loses the Danube delta region; the Black Sea is declared neutral; Britain and France guarantee the Ottoman empire against further disintegration.

1858 William I (1797–1888) becomes regent of Prussia

1858 At a secret meeting at Plombiers, Napoleon III (1808–73) and Camillo di Cavour (1810–61) plan the unification of Italy.

1859 During the Italian war of unification, Piedmontese armies defeat the Austrians at the battles of Magenta and Solferino; France captures Lombardy from Austria and cedes it to Piedmont in return for Savoy and Nice.

◀ **Victorian fashion** *Fashion changed rapidly in Europe during the reign (1837–1901) of Queen Victoria. Formal wear for men became more simple, while women's skirts c.1850 were constructed of hoops of flexible steel wire.*

THE AMERICAS

1845 British and French ships blockade the River Plate during further disputes with Argentina.

1845 Florida becomes a state of the USA.

1845 Texas annexed and becomes a state of the USA.

1846 Britain cedes Oregon to the USA; the 49th parallel becomes the w stretch of the US–Canadian border.

1846 USA declares war on Mexico.

1846 Iowa becomes a state of the USA.

1847 US forces make an amphibious landing and capture Vera Cruz in Mexico.

1847 Brigham Young (1801–77) founds Salt Lake City.

1848 Zachary Taylor (1785–1850) elected US president

1848 Wisconsin becomes a state of the USA.

1848 California Gold Rush starts.

1848 US troops enter Mexico City; by the Peace of Guadaloupe-Hidalgo, Mexico cedes all territory N of Rio Grande to the USA.

1850 Millard Fillmore (1800–74) becomes US president.

1850 Clay Compromise abolishes the right of the US government to impose anti-slavery polices on new states.

1850 California becomes a state of the USA.

1851 Spanish defeat a nationalist invasion of Cuba.

1852 Franklin Pierce (1804–69) elected US president.

1852 Argentine dictator Juan de Rosas (1793–1877) overthrown after his defeat at the Battle of Caseros.

1854 US Kansas-Nebraska Act abolishes the Missouri Compromise; the 'War for Bleeding Kansas' starts between pro- and anti-slavery factions.

1855 President Antonio de Santa Anna (1794–1876) overthrown in Mexico.

1856 US adventurer William Walker (1824–60) seizes power in Nicaragua.

1856 James Buchanan (1791–1868) elected US president.

1857 Dredd-Scott decision reinforces the rights of US slave-owners.

1858 Minnesota becomes a state of the USA.

1858 Benito Juárez (1806–72) elected president of Mexico.

1858 Civil war breaks out in Mexico.

1859 Oregon becomes a state of the USA.

Crystal Palace Built to house the Great Exhibition (1851), the Crystal Palace, London, contained exhibits from all over the world. The first world trade fair, the Exhibition's aim was to promote Britain's imperial strength.

SCIENCE AND TECHNOLOGY

1844 French scientist Lucien Vidi (1805–66) invents the aneroid barometer.

1845 William McNaught builds the first compound (high-pressure/low-pressure) steam engine.

1846 US engineer Elias Howe (1819–67) invents the lockstitch sewing machine.

1846 Italian scientist Ascanio Sobrero (1812–88) invents nitroglycerine.

1846 German astronomer Johann Galle (1812–1910) makes the first sighting of the planet Neptune.

1846 Smithsonian Institution is founded in Washington, D.C.

1847 Scottish physician James Simpson (1811–70) first uses chloroform as an anaesthetic for childbirth.

1847 US engineer Richard Hoe (1812–86) invents the rotary printing press.

1848 British mathematician George Boole (1815–64) introduces symbolic logic in *The Mathematical Analysis of Logic*.

1848 British physicist William Kelvin (1824–1907) devises the absolute temperature scale.

1848 French physicist Armand Fizeau (1819–96) applies the Doppler effect to light waves.

1848 French chemist Louis Pasteur (1822–95) introduces the study of stereochemistry.

1849 French engineer Joseph Monier (1823–1906) invents reinforced concrete.

1849 US inventor Walter Hunt (1796–1859) patents safety pin.

1849 French army officer and engineer Claude Minié (1814–79) invents a rifle that fires expanding lead bullets.

1850 US scientist Charles Page (1812–68) builds an electric locomotive.

1850 British physician Alfred Higginson (1808–84) introduces the use of the hypodermic syringe.

1850 German physicist Rudolph Clausius (1822–88) formulates the second law of thermodynamics.

1850 First submarine telegraph cable laid (between Britain and France).

1851 US manufacturer Isaac Singer (1811–75) invents the single-thread domestic sewing machine.

1851 German mathematician Bernhard Riemann (1826–66) proposes a general function theory.

1851 Great Exhibition, organized largely by Prince Albert (1819–61), opens in the specially built Crystal Palace in London, England.

1852 British chemist Edward Frankland (1825–99) proposes the theory of valency.

1852 French scientist Henri Regnault (1810–78) discovers a method for determining the density of a gas.

1852 French physicist Jean Foucault (1819–68) invents the gyroscope.

1853 British engineer Josiah Clark (1822–98) invents the pneumatic message tube.

1853 Swedish physicist Anders Ångström (1814–74) explains the formation of emission and absorption spectra.

1854 Canadian geologist Abraham Gesner (1797–1864) starts to manufacture paraffin.

1854 Dutch physician Anthonius Mathijsen (1805–78) introduces the use of plaster of Paris for bone-setting.

1855 British chemist Alexander Parkes (1813–90) accidentally discovers celluloid.

1856 German engineer Werner von Siemens (1816–92) designs an improved armature for electrical generators.

1856 Fossil human bones found in the Neander Tal (Neander Valley) in NW Germany.

1856 British engineer Henry Bessemer (1813–98) perfects his air-blast method of converting iron to steel.

1856 German anatomist Hermann Helmholtz (1821–94) publishes his *Handbook of Physiological Optics*.

1856 Swiss food technologist Henri Nestlé (1814–90) invents condensed milk.

1856 US inventor Elisha Otis (1811–61) installs the first passenger safety elevator.

1856 British chemist William Perkins (1838–1907) produces aniline mauve, the first synthetic dye.

1857 German physicist Gustav Kirchhoff (1824–87) discovers emission spectroscopy.

1858 First transatlantic telegraph cable goes into service.

ARTS AND HUMANITIES

1845 British politician and author Benjamin Disraeli (1804–81) publishes his novel *Sybil*.

1845 German socialist Friedrich Engels (1820–95) publishes *The Condition of the Working Classes in England*.

1845 US writer Edgar Allan Poe (1809–49) publishes *The Raven and Other Poems*.

1846 Belgian musical instrument maker Adolphe Sax (1814–94) patents the saxophone.

1847 British novelist Charlotte Brontë (1816–55) publishes *Jane Eyre*.

1847 British novelist Emily Brontë (1818–48) publishes *Wuthering Heights*.

1848 British novelist William Thackeray (1811–63) publishes *Vanity Fair*.

1848 British artists form the Pre-Raphaelite Brotherhood.

1848 German socialists Karl Marx (1818–83) and Friedrich Engels issue their *Communist Manifesto*.

> "I am as content to die on the scaffold for God's eternal truth as in any other way."
>
> *John Brown*

1850 US novelist Nathaniel Hawthorne (1804–64) publishes *The Scarlet Letter*.

1850 German composer Richard Wagner (1813–83) writes his opera *Lohengrin*.

1850 French artist Gustave Courbet (1819–77) paints *The Stone-Breakers*.

1851 US novelist Herman Melville (1819–91) publishes *Moby Dick*.

1852 British artist William Holman Hunt (1827–1910) paints *The Light of the World*.

1852 French philosopher Auguste Comte (1798–1857) publishes his *System of Positive Polity*

1852 US author Harriet Beecher Stowe (1811–96) publishes *Uncle Tom's Cabin*.

1853 French financier and administrator Georges Haussmann (1809–91) begins the rebuilding of Paris.

1853 Heinrich Steinway (1797–1871) opens a piano factory in New York.

1854 British poet Alfred Tennyson (1809–92) publishes *The Charge of the Light Brigade*.

1854 French anthropologist Joseph de Gobineau (1816–82) publishes his racist *Essay on the Inequality of the Human Races*.

1855 British poet Robert Browning (1812–89) publishes *Men and Women*.

1855 US poet Walt Whitman (1819–92) publishes *Leaves of Grass*.

1856 French novelist Gustave Flaubert (1821–80) publishes *Madame Bovary*.

1857 French artist Jean-François Millet (1814–75) paints *The Gleaners*.

1857 French poet Charles Baudelaire (1821–67) publishes *Les fleurs du mal*.

1857 British novelist Anthony Trollope (1815–82) publishes *Barchester Towers*.

1857 British poet (1806–61) Elizabeth Barrett Browning publishes *Aurora Leigh*.

1859 French composer Jacques Offenbach (1819–80) writes his opera *Orpheus in the Underworld*.

1859 British philosopher John Stuart Mill (1806–73) publishes his essay *On Liberty*.

1859 French artist Édouard Manet (1832–83) paints *The Absinthe Drinker*.

1859 French artist Jean-Baptiste Corot (1796–1875) paints *Dante and Virgil*.

ASIA AND AUSTRALASIA

1860 Irish explorer Robert Burke (1820–61) and English explorer William Wills (1834–61) lead the first expedition to cross Australia S-N.

1860 In S China, British and French troops defeat the Taiping rebels; in N China they capture the Dagu forts from the emperor; occupy Beijing and burn the summer palace; the treaty of Beijing ends the second Opium War.

1860 Russia founds the port of Vladivostok.

1860 French troops land at Beirut (present-day Lebanon) to restore order.

1860 Japanese nationalists murder foreign sailors and officials.

1862 Tongzhi (1856–75) becomes emperor of China, with dowager empress Cixi (1835–1908) as regent.

1862 France annexes SE Vietnam.

1862 Russia annexes parts of Turkistan.

1863 Japanese forts fire at US, French and Dutch merchant ships.

1863 King Norodom (1838–1904) places Cambodia under French protection.

1863 Mercenary Ever-Victorious Army, led by British officer Charles Gordon (1833–85), liberates the city of Suzhou from the Taiping rebels.

1864 Joint French, Dutch, British and US expedition destroys Japanese coastal forts.

1864 Imperial Chinese troops recapture Nanjing: end of the Taiping Rebellion.

1865 Muslim rebels set up an independent state in Chinese Turkistan.

1865 Russians occupy Tashkent in central Asia.

1865 Wellington is established as the capital of New Zealand.

1866 Korean troops defeat a French military expedition marching on Seoul.

1867 Last Japanese shōgun abdicates; Emperor Meiji (1852–1912) takes personal control in the Meiji Restoration (1868); Tokyo becomes the new capital.

1867 Turkish radicals form the Young Turks secret society.

1867 Last shipment of British convicts lands in Australia.

1868 Muslim state in Chinese Turkistan is suppressed.

1870 Chinese mob massacres a French consul and missionaries in Tianjin.

1871 US military expedition tries to force Korea to accept foreign trade, but is defeated.

1873 French annex Hanoi and the Red River delta area of Vietnam.

AFRICA

1860 German traders establish a settlement in Cameroon, W Africa.

1861 Zanzibar becomes independent of Oman.

1861 Britain acquires the Lagos coast of Nigeria.

1861 Fulani, under Al-Hadj Umar (c.1797–1864), conquer the kingdom of Segu.

1862 France purchases the port of Obock on the coast of Somalia, NE Africa.

1863 Ismail Pasha (1830–95) becomes ruler of Egypt.

1863 French establish a protectorate over Dahomey, W Africa.

1863 Madagascan chiefs overthrow pro-European king Radama II.

1864 Tewodros II (c.1818–68) of Ethiopia imprisons a British consul and merchants.

1865 Boers from a new Orange Free State defeat Basuto chief Moshoeshoe I (c.1786–1870), who cedes territory.

1868 British expedition to Ethiopia defeats Tewodros II at the battle of Arogee and frees British prisoners.

1868 British annex Basutoland (Lesotho) in South Africa.

1869 Suez canal opens, linking the Mediterranean with the Red Sea and the Indian Ocean..

Union infantryman
The Union was able to muster many more troops than the Confederacy, and suffered a smaller proportion of casualties. Overall, 20% of soldiers in the Civil War died – the majority of them as a result of disease.

1870 Arab slave trader Tippu Tip (1837–1905) establishes himself as ruler in present-day Democratic Republic of Congo.

1871 Dutch cede their Gold Coast (present-day Ghana) forts and trading posts to Britain

1871 US journalist Henry Stanley (1841–1904) finds British explorer David Livingstone (1813–73).

EUROPE

1860 France and Britain sign a free trade treaty.

1860 Giuseppe Garibaldi (1807–82) and his red shirts liberate Naples.

1861 Victor Emmanuel II (1820–78) of Piedmont becomes king of a united Italy, with its capital at Turin.

1861 William I (1797–1888) becomes king of Prussia.

1861 Serfdom is abolished in Russia.

1862 Otto von Bismarck (1815–98) becomes prime minister of Prussia.

1862 Garibaldi marches on Rome but is defeated by Italian troops.

1863 Polish uprising torn by internal disputes is savagely repressed by Russian and Prussian troops.

1863 Christian IX (1818–1906) becomes king of Denmark.

1863 Prince William of Denmark becomes King George I (1845–1913) of Greece.

1864 Prussia makes war on Denmark and gains control of Schleswig-Holstein.

1864 Red Cross is established by the Geneva convention.

1864 Regional elected assemblies (*zemstvos*) are established in Russia.

1864 Britain cedes the Ionian Islands to Greece.

1864 Karl Marx (1818–83) organizes the First International Workingmen's Association in London.

1865 Otto von Bismarck (1815–98) and Napoleon III (1808–73) meet at Biarritz and agree mutual neutrality in the event of war with Austria.

1865 Leopold II (1835–1909) becomes king of Belgium.

1866 Prussia and Italy declare war on Austria; the Austrians defeat the Italians at the battle of Custozza, but are defeated by the Prussians at the battle of Sadowa near Königgratz.

1866 Venice joins the kingdom of Italy.

1866 Cretans rise in revolt against the Turks.

1867 North German Confederation is formed under Prussian control.

1867 The Netherlands agrees to sell Luxembourg to France; the treaty of London establishes the independence and neutrality of Luxembourg.

1867 Turkish troops withdraw from Serbia.

1867 Garibaldi again marches on Rome and is defeated by French troops at the battle of Mentana.

1867 Austria and Hungary become a joint monarchy.

1867 Cretan revolt is crushed.

1868 William Gladstone (1809–98) becomes prime minister of Britain.

1868 Revolution deposes Queen Isabella II (1830–1904) in Spain.

1869 Spanish parliament offers the throne to a German prince, provoking French hostility.

1870 An Italian duke becomes King Amadeo I (1845–90) of Spain.

1870 France declares war on Prussia and is disastrously defeated at the battle of Sedan; Napoleon III (1808–73) is overthrown and the third republic is declared; the Prussians besiege Paris.

1860

1870

THE AMERICAS

◄ *Lincoln, US president during the civil war, believed the country could not survive "half slave, half free". He led the northern states (the Union) with firmness and urged fairness and charity after the southern states (the Confederacy) were defeated.*

1860 Abraham Lincoln (1809–65) elected US president; South Carolina secedes from the Union.

1861 Kansas becomes a state of the USA.

1861 French, British and Spanish troops land in Mexico in a dispute over loan repayments.

1861 Confederate States of America formed with Jefferson Davis (1808–89) as president; Confederate forces capture Fort Sumter and under Thomas 'Stonewall' Jackson (1824–63) defeat a Federal army at the First Battle of Bull Run in Virginia.

1862 Nashville in Tennessee falls to Federal troops under Ulysses S. Grant (1822–85); the Confederates, under commander-in-chief Robert E. Lee (1807–70), invade Maryland, fight the inconclusive Battle of Antietam, and win the Battle of Fredericksburg; Federal troops win the Battle of Shiloh, and take Memphis in Tennessee; US President Lincoln proclaims the emancipation of slaves.

1862 Slavery abolished in Dutch West Indies.

1863 West Virginia becomes a state of the USA; the Confederates win the Battle of Chancellorsville in Virginia; Federal troops win the Battle of Gettysburg in Pennsylvania; Grant captures Vicksburg in Mississippi.

1863 French troops enter Mexico City; Maximilian (1832–67) is declared Emperor.

1863 US government decides upon the forcible removal of Native Americans from Kansas.

1864 Nevada becomes a US state; Federal troops under William Sherman (1820–91) invade Georgia, destroy Atlanta, and capture Savannah; Lincoln re-elected US president.

1864 Cheyenne Native Americans defeated by US troops in Colorado.

1865 Federal army destroys Richmond, Virginia; Robert E. Lee (1807–70) surrenders at Appomattox Court House, ending the Civil War; the 13th Amendment to the Constitution of the United States prohibits slavery

1865 Abraham Lincoln (b.1809) assassinated; Andrew Johnson (1808–75) becomes US president.

1865 Paraguay invaded by the forces of Brazil, Argentina, and Uruguay.

1865 Spain fights a naval war against Peru and other South American states.

1865 Klu Klux Klan founded in Tennessee.

1866 Civil Rights Bill adopted by the 14th Amendment to the Constitution of the United States.

1866 France withdraws support for Emperor Maximilian (1832–67) in Mexico.

1866 Fenians from the US attack a British fort on the Canadian border.

1867 Emperor Maximilian of Mexico overthrown and executed.

1867 Canada becomes an independent Dominion of the British Empire.

1867 Basic Reconstruction Act sets conditions for the readmission of Confederate States to the USA.

1867 USA purchases Alaska from Russia.

1867 Nebraska becomes a state of the USA.

1868 Paraguayan capital Asunción captured.

1868 Ulysses S. Grant (1822–85) elected US president.

1869 First American transcontinental railway completed.

1869 Red River Rebellion in central Canada establishes a short-lived provisional government.

1870 Paraguay loses much territory after defeat by Brazil and Argentina.

1871 British Columbia becomes a part of Canada.

1871 Treaty of Washington settles outstanding differences with Britain over borders, fishing rights and war damage.

SCIENCE AND TECHNOLOGY

1858 German chemist Friedrich Kekulé (1829–96) discovers that carbon atoms form chain molecules.

1858 British engineer Isambard Kingdom Brunel (1806–59) builds the *Great Eastern* steamship.

1859 British naturalist Charles Darwin (1809–82) publishes *The Origin of Species by means of Natural Selection,* which proposes his theory of evolution.

1859 British naturalist Alfred Wallace (1823–1913), independently of Darwin, develops a theory of evolution.

1859 First oil-well drilled in Pennsylvania, USA.

1860 German metalworker Reinhard Mannesmann (1856–1922) invents a process for making seamless steel tubes.

1861 French anatomist Pierre Broca (1824–80) discovers the speech-centre of the human brain.

1861 Belgian industrialist Ernest Solvay (1938–1922) invents a process for manufacturing soda ash.

1862 US engineer Richard Gatling (1818–1903) invents a rapid-fire, multi-barrelled, machine gun.

1862 US engineer Joseph Brown (1810–76) builds a universal milling machine.

1862 First engagement between iron-clad ships takes place when the Confederate *Merrimac* and the Federal *Monitor* exchange shots in the US Civil War.

1862 US industrialist John Rockefeller (1839–1937) builds an oil refinery in Cleveland, Ohio.

1863 French engineer Pierre Martin (1824–1915) develops the open-hearth method of steel manufacture in France.

1863 London Underground railway opens.

1864 Scottish mathematician James Maxwell (1831–79) announces his equations that link light and electricity.

1864 French chemist Louis Pasteur (1822–95) proves the existence of airborne micro-organisms.

1865 German botanist Julius von Sachs (1833–97) discovers chloroplasts in plant cells.

1865 Austrian monk Gregor Mendel (1822–84) describes his experiments cross-breeding plants; the results suggest rules of heredity.

1865 US inventor Thaddeus Lowe (1832–1913) builds a compression ice machine.

1866 French scientist Georges Leclanché (1839–82) invents a zinc-carbon dry cell.

1867 French engineer Pierre Michaux manufactures the velocipede pedalled bicycle.

1867 Swedish industrialist Alfred Nobel (1833–96) invents dynamite.

1867 British physician Joseph Lister (1827–1912) introduces antiseptic surgery when he sprays phenol in an operating theatre.

1867 US engineer Christopher Sholes (1819–90) invents a typewriter with a QWERTY keyboard.

1868 US engineer George Westinghouse (1846–1914) invents the air-brake.

1868 French palaeontologist Édouard Lartet (1801–71) discovers the fossil bones of Cro-Magnon man.

1868 British astronomer William Huggins (1824–1910) measures the radial velocity of a star.

1869 Russian scientist Dmitri Mendeleyev (1834–1907) publishes the periodic table of elements in *Principles of Chemistry.*

1869 French scientist Hippolyte Mege-Mouries invents a process for making margarine.

1869 Irish physicist John Tyndall (1820–93) discovers that the scattering of light by atmospheric particles makes the sky blue.

1870 US inventor Rufus Gilbert (1832–85) patents an elevated railway system.

1870 German mathematician Georg Cantor (1845–1918) founds set theory.

1871 British naturalist Charles Darwin (1809–82) publishes *The Descent of Man.*

ARTS AND HUMANITIES

1860 British novelist George Eliot (1819–80) publishes her *The Mill on the Floss.*

1861 French artist Gustave Doré (1832–83) publishes his illustrations for Dante's *Inferno.*

1862 Russian author and dramatist Ivan Turgenev (1818–83) publishes his novel *Fathers and Sons.*

1862 British artist Edward Burne-Jones (1833–98) paints *King Cophetua and the Beggar Maid.*

1862 French author and poet Victor Hugo (1802–85) publishes his novel *Les Miserables.*

1864 British theologian John Newman (1801–90) explains his conversion to catholicism in *Apologia pro vita sua.*

1864 Austrian composer Anton Bruckner (1824–96) writes his Mass No.1 in D minor.

1865 English mathematician Charles Dodgson (pen-name Lewis Carroll, 1832–98) publishes *Alice in Wonderland.*

1866 Russian novelist Fyodor Dostoevsky (1821–81) publishes *Crime and Punishment.*

1867 French artist Edgar Degas (1834–1917) paints his *Mlle Fiocre in the Ballet "La Source".*

1867 Norwegian dramatist Henrik Ibsen (1828–1906) writes his play *Peer Gynt.*

1869 Russian novelist Leo Tolstoy (1828–1910) publishes *War and Peace.*

1867 Karl Marx (1818–83) publishes the first volume of *Das Kapital.*

1867 Austrian composer Johann Strauss (1825–99) writes *The Blue Danube* waltz.

1868 German composer Johannnes Brahms (1833–97) writes *German Requiem.*

1868 Norwegian composer Edward Grieg (1843–1907) writes his piano concerto in A minor.

1868 US writer Louisa May Alcott (1832–88) publishes *Little Women.*

1869 French poet Paul Verlaine (1844–96) publishes *Fêtes Galantes.*

1869 French author Jules Verne (1828–1905) publishes *20,000 Leagues under the Sea.*

1869 British poet and social commentator Matthew Arnold (1822–88) publishes *Culture and Anarchy.*

▲ *Mendel laid the foundations of the modern science of genetics. The experiments that led to his discovery of heredity were begun in his monastery garden in 1856.*

1871 Premiere of Verdi's opera *Aïda* at La Scala, Milan.

1871 US artist James Whistler (1834–1903) paints *Arrangement in Gray and Black – the Artist's Mother.*

1871 British artist John Millais (1829–96) paints *The Boyhood of Raleigh.*

ASIA AND AUSTRALASIA

1874 Turkish Ottoman empire begins to disintegrate rapidly under economic pressure.

1873 Russia annexes Khiva in Uzbekistan.

1874 British annex Fiji in the s Pacific.

1874 Japanese expedition briefly captures Formosa (present-day Taiwan).

1874 Russia conquers Kashgaria in Turkistan.

1875 Infant Zai Tian (1871–1908) becomes Emperor Guangxu of China with the dowager empress Cixi (1835–1908) as regent.

1875 Russia cedes the Kuril Islands to Japan in return for part of Sakhalin Island.

1876 Japan occupies the Ryukyu Islands.

1876 Turkish chief minister Midhat Pasha (1822–84) replaces sultan Murad V (1840–1904) with Abdul Hamid II (1842–1918) and issues a constitution

1877 Turkish constitution is set aside by Sultan Abdul Hamid II.

1877 Saigo Takamori (1828–77) leads a samurai uprising (the Satsuma rebellion) against modernization in Japan.

1878 During the second Afghan War, the British invade and overthrow Sher Ali (1825–79).

1878 Chinese reconquer part of Turkistan from Islamic rebels.

1879 Abd Al-Rahman (c.1830–1901) becomes ruler of Afghanistan; the British gain control of the Khyber pass.

▶ **Franco-Prussian War** (1870–71)
Württemberg infantryman (left) and Prussian infantryman (right). French troops were greatly outnumbered by these Prussian forces, who were also more highly trained and organized.

1880

1880 France annexes Tahiti.

1880 Outlaw Ned Kelly (b.1855) is executed in Australia.

1881 China regains territory in Turkistan from Russia by the treaty of St Petersburg.

1881 Russia annexes the entire Transcaucus region.

1882 Korean nationalists attack Japanese officials in Seoul.

1883 Treaty of Hué establishes a French protectorate over Annam (N Vietnam).

1883 Volcano on the island of Krakatoa erupts violently, causing great destruction.

1884 France and China go to war over control of the Gulf of Tonkin region.

1884 Russians conquer the city of Merv in central Asia.

1884 Chinese Turkistan becomes a province of China.

1884 Germany acquires Kaiser Wilhelmland in New Guinea; Britain annexes the SE part of island.

1884 Dowager empress Cixi (1835–1908) becomes the sole ruler of China.

1884 Chinese troops defeat a pro-Japanese coup in Korea.

AFRICA

1871 British annex the diamond-producing area of the Orange Free State.

1872 John IV (1831–89) becomes emperor of Ethiopia.

1873 Second Ashanti War begins.

1873 Slave markets in Zanzibar are closed.

1874 British forces destroy the Ashanti capital of Kumasi.

1874 British West Africa is broken up into separate colonies.

1874 British officer Charles Gordon (1833–85) becomes governor of the Egyptian Sudan.

1875 Britain buys Egypt's shares in the Suez canal.

1875 Egypt invades Ethiopia and occupies the coastal region.

1876 Leopold II (1835–1909) of Belgium founds the International Association for the Exploration and Civilization of Africa.

1876 Ethiopian army defeats the Egyptians at the battles of Gura and forces them to withdraw.

1877 British annex the Boer South African republic.

1877 British annex Walvis Bay on the sw coast of Africa.

1879 Ismail Pasha (1830–95) is deposed as Egyptian ruler by the Ottoman sultan and replaced by Tewfik (1852–92).

1879 Zulus under Cetewayo (1825–84) attack the British in South Africa; they win the battle of Isandhlwana but are defeated at the battle of Ulundi.

1879 Algeria comes under French civil government.

1880 French found Brazzaville in the Congo region of central Africa.

1880 Boers in Transvaal, South Africa, revolt against British rule and declare a republic.

1881 Henry Stanley (1841–1904) founds Leopoldville in the Congo for Leopold II (1835–1909) of Belgium.

1881 French invade Tunisia and declare a protectorate.

1881 Nationalist army officers stage a rising in Egypt.

1881 British grant limited independence to the Boer South African republic.

1882 British bombard Alexandria, defeat the Egyptian army at the battle of Tel-el-Kebir, and occupy Cairo.

1882 Muhammad Ahmed (1840–85) declares himself Mahdi and starts an uprising in Sudan.

1882 Italy acquires the port of Assab in Eritrea.

1883 Britain declares a protectorate over Egypt.

1883 British are defeated by the Mahdists at the battle of El Obeid.

1883 Paul Kruger (1825–1904) becomes president of the South African republic.

1883 French expand inland from the coast of Dahomey, w Africa.

EUROPE

1870 International treaty establishes the neutrality of Belgium.

1870 Vatican Council proclaims papal infallibility.

1870 Italian troops occupy the papal states.

1871 Paris surrenders to Prussians; France cedes Alsace-Lorraine to Germany by the peace of Frankfurt; Paris Commune is declared and crushed; Louis Thiers (1797–1877) becomes president of France.

1871 Germany is united into an empire under William I (1797–1888) of Prussia.

1871 Rome becomes the capital of Italy; the Vatican state is established.

1871 Otto von Bismarck (1815–98) begins the *Kulturkamf* struggle with the Roman Catholic church.

1872 Austria, Prussia and Russian form the league of three emperors against France.

1872 Civil war breaks out in Spain.

1873 Amadeo I abdicates; a Spanish republic is established.

1874 Benjamin Disraeli (1804–81) becomes prime minister of Britain.

1874 Group of Spanish generals declare Alfonso XII (1857–85) king.

1874 Universal postal union is formed in Berne, Switzerland.

1875 Socialist congress at Gotha in Germany founds the Socialist Workingmen's Party.

1875 French third Republic is officially proclaimed with Marshal Patrice McMahon (1808–93) as president.

1875 Kálmán Tisza (1830–92) becomes prime minister of Hungary and begins a programme of Magyarization.

1875 Anti-Turkish revolts break out in Bosnia and Herzegovina; Serbia and Russia support the rebels.

1876 Risings against the Turks in Bulgaria are brutally suppressed; Serbs declare war on Turkey and are defeated at the battle of Alexinatz.

1876 Mikhail Bakunin (1814–76) organizes the Land and Liberty secret society in Russia.

1877 Russia declares war and invades Turkey; Russian troops reach the walls of Istanbul.

1877 Queen Victoria (1819–1901) of Britain formally becomes Empress of India.

1877 President MacMahon's monarchist policies create a political crisis in France.

1878 Umberto I (1844–1900) becomes king of Italy.

1878 Romania, Serbia and Montenegro become independent states by the treaty of San Stefano between Turkey and Russia.

1878 At the Congress of Berlin, Austria gains control of Bosnia and Herzegovina, Russia gains control of Bulgaria and Britain gains control of Cyprus.

1878 Anti-socialist laws are passed in Germany.

1879 Germany and Austria sign an alliance against Russia.

1879 Terrorist Will of the People secret society is founded by Russian radicals.

1880 Otto von Bismarck ends his *Kulturkampf* policy in Germany.

1881 Tsar Alexander II (b.1818) is assassinated; Alexander III (1845–94) becomes ruler of Russia; the *Okhrana* political police are founded.

1881 Serbia places itself under Austrian protection by a secret treaty.

1881 Turks cede Thessaly to Greece but keep Macedonia.

1882 Irish nationalists murder senior British officials in Phoenix Park, Dublin.

1882 Milan Obrenović (1854–1901) declares himself king of Serbia.

1882 Italy, Germany and Austria sign the anti-French Triple Alliance.

1883 Romania signs a secret anti-Russian treaty with Austria.

1883 Georgy Plekhanov (1857–1918) introduces Marxism to Russia.

1884 Carl Peters (1856–1918) founds the society for German colonization.

1884 International conference in Berlin decides the future of Africa; Belgian king Leopold II's Congo state is recognized, and the principle of ownership through occupation of coastline is established; start of the 'scramble for Africa'.

THE AMERICAS

1871 US Indian Appropriations Bill abolishes the collective rights of Native American peoples.

1875 Fighting breaks out between Sioux Native Americans and US prospectors in Dakota.

1876 Colorado becomes a state of the USA.

1876 US troops commanded by George Custer (1839–76) are massacred by Sioux and other Native American tribes led by chief Sitting Bull (1831–90) at the Battle of Little Big Horn in Dakota.

1876 US presidential election produces a disputed result.

1877 Sioux Native American chief Crazy Horse (1842–77) surrenders to US troops.

1877 Electoral commission decides that Rutherford Hayes (1822–93) becomes US president.

1877 Porfirio Díaz (1830–1915) becomes President of Mexico after leading a coup.

1878 Concession to construct a canal across Panama granted to a French company.

1879 Chile wages war on Peru and Bolivia for control of the nitrate deposits in the Atacama region.

Victorian fashion Late Victorian European fashion was very different to that of the early period. Full skirts had been replaced with a hard shelf-like bustle at the back of the skirt. Pinstripes were now acceptable for men.

1880 After a brief civil war in Argentina, Buenos Aires becomes the federal capital.

1880 James Garfield (1831–81) elected US president

1881 US outlaw William Bonney 'Billy the Kid' (b.1859) shot dead in New Mexico.

1881 US marshal Wyatt Earp (1848–1929) wins a gunfight at the OK Corral in Tombstone, Arizona.

1881 Chester Arthur (1830–86) becomes US president.

1882 Chinese Exclusion Act prohibits Chinese immigration into the USA.

1882 US outlaw Jesse James (b.1847) shot dead in Missouri.

1883 Northern Pacific Railroad completed.

1883 Slavery abolished in the remaining Spanish colonies.

1884 Peru and Bolivia cede nitrate-rich territory to Chile; Bolivia becomes landlocked.

1884 Grover Cleveland (1837–1908) elected US president.

SCIENCE AND TECHNOLOGY

1872 US inventor Thomas Edison (1847–1931) patents an electric typewriter.

1873 Dutch physicist Johannes van der Waals (1837–1923) calculates intermolecular forces.

1873 US engineer Joseph Glidden (1813–1906) invents a machine for making barbed wire.

1874 US librarian Melvil Dewey (1851–1931) invents a decimal system for cataloguing books.

1876 British research ship HMS *Challenger* completes a three-year voyage that lays the foundations of oceanography.

1876 German engineer Nikolaus Otto (1832–91) builds a practical internal combustion gas engine.

1876 Scottish engineer Alexander Graham Bell (1847–1922) invents the telephone in the USA.

1876 German engineer Carl von Linde (1842–1934) patents the ammonia compression refrigerator.

1877 First telephone exchange installed in New Haven, USA.

1877 Thomas Edison invents the phonograph.

1877 Austrian physicist Ludwig Boltzmann (1844–1906) formulates equations linking kinetic energy and temperature.

1877 Italian astronomer Giovanni Schiaparelli (1835–1910) announces his observation of 'canals' on the surface of Mars.

1878 British scientist Joseph Swan (1828–1914) makes a carbon filament electric light.

1878 German chemist Adolf von Bayer synthesizes indigo dye.

1879 Russian psychologist Ivan Pavlov (1849–1936) discovers how to produce a conditioned reflex in dogs.

1879 Edison patents an incandescent electric light bulb.

▲ **Edison** patented his first invention – a mechanical vote recorder – at the age of 21. In 1876 he set up an 'invention factory', where new inventions were patented at a prodigious rate.

▶ **Twain** was the first US author of world rank to write authentically colloquial novels employing a genuine American idiom. His work, which began as pure humour and developed to bitter satire, was marked by an egalitarian attitude and a strong desire for social justice.

1880 French chemist Louis Pasteur (1822–95) discovers streptococcus bacteria.

1880 British engineer John Milne (1850–1913) invents an accurate seismograph.

1881 German scientist Karl Eberth (1835–1926) discovers the typhoid bacillus.

1881 First commercial electricity generating station is opened in New York, USA.

1882 German bacteriologist Robert Koch (1843–1910) discovers the tuberculosis bacillus.

1882 St Gotthard railway tunnel through the Alps opened.

1882 German scientist Walther Flemming (1843–1905) observes and describes cell division.

1883 First steel-frame skyscraper is built in Chicago.

1883 US engineer Hiram Maxim (1840–1916) invents the recoil-operated machine gun.

1884 US industrialist George Eastman (1854–1932) invents a roll film for cameras.

1884 British engineer Charles Parsons (1854–1931) patents a steam turbine.

ARTS AND HUMANITIES

1872 British author Samuel Butler (1835–1902) publishes his novel *Erewhon*.

1872 German philosopher Friedrich Nietzsche (1844–1900) publishes *The Death of Tragedy*.

1873 French poet Arthur Rimbaud (1854–91) publishes *A Season in Hell*.

1874 British novelist Thomas Hardy (1840–1928) publishes *Far from the Madding Crowd*.

1874 First exhibition of Impressionist paintings held in Paris.

1874 Russian composer Modest Mussorgsky (1839–81) writes *Pictures at an Exhibition*.

1875 French composer Georges Bizet (1838–75) writes his opera *Carmen*.

1875 US founder of the Christian Science movement Mary Baker Eddy (1821–1910) publishes *Science and Health with Key to the Scriptures*.

1875 US author Mark Twain (1835–1910) publishes *The Adventures of Tom Sawyer*.

1876 *The Ring of the Nibelungen* by German composer Richard Wagner (1813–83) receives its first complete performance at the inaugural Bayreuth festival.

1876 French artist Auguste Renoir (1841–1919) paints *Le Moulin de la Galette*.

1876 French symbolist poet Stephane Mallarmé (1842–98) publishes his *The Afternoon of a Faun*.

1877 Russian composer Alexander Borodin (1833–87) writes his Symphony No.2 in B minor.

1878 British social reformer William Booth (1829–1912) founds the Salvation Army in London.

*c.*1878 French artist Paul Cezanne (1839–1906) paints *Still Life with a Fruit Dish*.

1878 British composers Arthur Sullivan (1842–1900) and William Gilbert (1836–1911) write their comic operetta *HMS Pinafore*.

1878 Russian composer Peter Tchaikovsky (1840–93) composes his ballet *Swan Lake*.

1879 German socialist Albert Bebel (1840–1913) publishes *Women and Socialism*.

1880 US artist John Singer Sargent (1856–1925) paints his portrait of *Mrs Charles Gifford Dyer*.

1880 French artist Auguste Rodin (1840–1917) sculpts his statue *The Thinker*.

1880 French novelist Emile Zola (1840–1902) publishes *Nana*.

1880 Swiss author Johanna Spyri (1827–1901) publishes her children's novel *Heidi*.

1881 French author known as Anatole France (1844–1924) publishes his novel *The Crime of Sylvester Bonnard*.

1881 US author Henry James (1843–1916) publishes the novel *The Portrait of a Lady*.

1882 Indian author Bankim Chandra Chatterji (1838–94) publishes his novel *Anandamath*.

1883 Scottish author Robert Stevenson (1850–94) publishes the children's adventure *Treasure Island*.

1883 German philosopher Friedrich Nietzsche (1844–1900) publishes *Thus Spake Zarathustra*.

1883 Spanish architect Antonio Gaudí (1852–1926) begins work on the Church of the Holy Family in Barcelona, Spain.

1884 French artist Georges Seurat (1859–91) paints *Bathers at Asnières*.

1884 French composer Jules Massenet (1842–1912) writes the opera *Manon*.

ASIA AND AUSTRALASIA

1885 Dispute over the borders of Afghanistan takes Britain and Russia to the brink of war.

1885 Indian National congress is founded.

1885–86 Britain annexes the whole of Burma after the third Burmese War.

1887 French organize their colonies in Vietnam and Cambodia into the Union of Indo-China.

1887 Britain annexes Baluchistan in w Pakistan.

1887 USA gains the use of Pearl Harbor in Hawaii as a naval base.

1888 Britain establishes protectorates over Sarawak and N Borneo.

1888 First railway in China is opened.

1889 Constitution guaranteeing the rights of the emperor is issued in Japan.

▲ **Sun Yat-sen** formed the Revive China Society in 1894 and, the following year, attempted to organize an uprising in Guangzhou (Canton). The uprising failed, and Sun Yat-sen was forced into exile for 16 years. On his return to China, he was part of the revolution that overthrew the Qing dynasty. He served as provisional president of the Chinese Republic from 1911 to 1912.

1890

1891 Work starts on the trans-Siberian railway.

1893 Revolution overthrows Queen Lydia Liliuokalani (1838–1917) in Hawaii.

1893 King Chulalongkorn (1853–1910) of Thailand recognizes a French protectorate over Laos by the treaty of Bangkok.

1894 Republic of Hawaii is declared.

1894 Japan defeats China in a war for control of Korea.

1894 Turks massacre thousands of Armenians near the town of Sassun.

1894 Sun Yat-sen (1866–1925) organizes a secret revolutionary society in Guangzhou (Canton), China.

1895 China acknowledges Korean independence under Japanese influence by the treaty of Shimonseki; Japan also gains Formosa (present-day Taiwan) and other islands.

1896 Malay states form a federation under British control.

1896 Japan extends its control of Korea after the murder of Queen Min (b.1851).

1896 Turks again murder thousands of Armenians.

AFRICA

1883 French go to war with the Hovas of Madagascar.

1884 Germany establishes colonies in Cameroon and Togo in w Africa and in sw Africa.

1884 Britain withdraws from Sudan.

1884 Britain establishes a protectorate over part of the Somali coast; French expand inland from Obock and establish French Somaliland.

1885 Mahdists besiege and take Khartoum in Sudan and kill governor Charles Gordon (b.1833).

1885 British colonialist Cecil Rhodes (1853–1902) gains control of Bechuanaland, s Africa.

1885 Spanish establish a protectorate over part of Guinea, w Africa.

1885 Congo Free State is established under the personal control of Leopold II (1835–1909) of Belgium.

1885 French declare a protectorate over parts of the Congo region.

1885 Germans establish a colony in Tanganyika (present-day Tanzania), E Africa.

1885 Italy occupies the port of Massawa and expands into Eritrea.

1886 Gold is discovered in the Transvaal; the city of Johannesburg is established.

1886 Britain acquires Kenya, E Africa.

1887 Henry Stanley (1841–1904) leads an expedition to rescue Emin Pasha (1840–92), an Egyptian governor of the Sudan, from the Mahdists.

1887 Ethiopians attack the Italians and defeat them at the battle of Dogali.

1887 Britain establishes a protectorate over Nigeria.

1887 French expand into Djibouti.

1887 Britain annexes Zululand.

1889 With Italian support Menelik II (1844–1913) overthrows John IV (1831–89) and becomes emperor of Ethiopia; Italy annexes part of Somalia.

1889 French declare a protectorate over the Ivory Coast.

1889 British grant Rhodes control of a large area of SE Africa.

1890 Britain establishes a protectorate over Zanzibar.

1890 British force the Portuguese to abandon attempts to acquire territory linking Angola to Mozambique.

1891 Italians defeat the Mahdists in Ethiopia.

1891 Belgium conquers the Katanga region of Congo.

1892 French defeat the Fulani in w Africa.

1892 Belgium defeats Arab slave-owners in the Congo.

1893 France captures Timbuktu from the Tuaregs.

1893 French establish a colony in Guinea, w Africa.

1894 After victory in the third Ashanti War, Britain establishes a protectorate over Ghana.

1894 Britain establishes a protectorate over Uganda.

1894 British colonialist Leander Starr Jameson (1853–1917) occupies Matabeleland, s Africa.

1894 Italians invade Ethiopia.

1895 British organize and name Rhodesia in SE Africa.

1895 British colonialist Leander Starr Jameson (1853–1917) leads a British raid on the Boer republic in South Africa.

1895 French conquer Madagascar.

EUROPE

1885 King Alfonso XII (b.1857) of Spain dies; his wife Maria Christina becomes regent for her unborn child, the future Alfonso XIII (1886–1941).

1885 Bulgaria annexes E Roumelia; Serbia declares war on Bulgaria; the Serbs are defeated at the battle of Slivnitza; Austria intervenes to prevent the invasion of Serbia.

1886 King Ludwig II (1845–86) of Bavaria is declared insane and deposed.

1886 French minister of war General Georges Boulanger (1837–91) becomes a national hero for his anti-German views.

1886 Influenced by Irish politician Charles Parnell (1846–91), the British government attempts to introduce Home Rule in Ireland, but the bill is rejected by Parliament.

1887 Francesco Crispi (1819–1901) becomes Italian prime minister and pursues a policy of colonial expansion.

1888 William II (1859–1941) becomes Emperor of Germany.

1889 Having failed to seize power, General Boulanger flees France.

1889 French Panama canal company collapses causing a financial scandal.

1889 International convention declares the Suez canal to be neutral and open to all ships in both peace and war.

1889 Heir to the Austrian throne Archduke Rudolf (b.1858) commits suicide at Mayerling.

1890 Otto von Bismarck (1815–98) is dismissed by the German emperor.

1890 Britain cedes the island of Heligoland to Germany in return for Zanzibar.

1890 Anti-socialist laws are repealed in Germany.

1890 Socialists in Europe initiate May Day celebrations.

1890 Luxembourg becomes independent of the Netherlands.

1890 Wilhelmina (1880–1962) becomes Queen of the Netherlands, with her mother, Emma (1858–1934), as regent.

1890 International convention in Brussels agrees on the suppression of the African slave trade.

1891 France and Russia sign a defensive entente.

1891 German Social Democratic party adopts Marxist policies under Karl Kautsky (1854–1938).

1892 Ferdinand De Lesseps (1805–94) goes on trial for his part in the Panama canal company scandal.

1892 German general Alfred von Schlieffen (1833–1913) devises a plan for the eventuality of war on two fronts against France and Russia.

1893 Corinth canal opens.

1893 Irish Home Rule bill is passed by the lower house of the British parliament, but is rejected by the upper house.

1894 French president Sadi Carnot (b.1837) is stabbed to death by an Italian anarchist.

1894 French army officer Alfred Dreyfus (1859–1935) is court-martialled for treason and is sent to Devil's Island in French Guiana.

1894 Nicholas II (1868–1918) becomes Tsar of Russia.

1895 Kiel Canal opens, linking the North and Baltic seas.

1895 French trades unionists form the *Confederation Generale du Travail*.

1896 Olympic Games revived in Greece.

1896 Cretans revolt against Turkish rule.

THE AMERICAS

1885 Northwest Rebellion suppressed by Canadian troops; leader Louis Riel (b.1844) executed.

1885 President Justo Barrios (b.1835) of Guatemala leads an invasion of El Salvador but is defeated and killed at the Battle of Chalchuapa.

1886 Colombia adopts a centralized constitution.

1886 American Federation of Labor formed under the leadership of Samuel Gompers (1850–1924).

1886 'Statue of Liberty' erected at the entrance to New York harbour.

1886 Apache Native American leader Geronimo (1829–1908) surrenders to US troops.

1887 Canadian Pacific Railroad opened.

1888 Slavery abolished in Brazil.

1888 US Allotment Act allows for the dividing up of Native American reservations.

1888 Benjamin Harrison (1833–1901) elected US president.

1889 Revolution establishes a republic in Brazil.

1889 North Dakota, South Dakota, Washington and Montana become states of the USA.

1889 US Oklahoma territory opened for settlement by a 'land race'.

1889 First Pan-American conference held in Washington, D.C.

1890 Wyoming and Idaho become states of the USA.

1890 US troops massacre Native Americans at the Battle of Wounded Knee.

1891 United States of Brazil established.

1891 Civil war establishes parliamentary government in Chile.

1892 US reformer Susan Anthony (1820–1906) becomes president of the National American Women's Suffrage Association.

1892 Immigration facilities opened at Ellis Island in New York harbour.

1892 Grover Cleveland re-elected US president.

1893 US anarchist Emma Goldman (1869–1940) arrested in Philadelphia.

1893 Serious rebellions suppressed in s Brazil.

1895 Nicaragua, El Salvador, and Honduras form the Greater Republic of Central America.

1895 Anti-saloon League starts a nationwide anti-alcohol campaign in the USA.

1895 Britain clashes with Venezuela about the borders of British Guiana.

1895 Nationalist revolution occurs in Cuba.

1896 Gold discovered in the Yukon region of Canada.

1896 Utah becomes a state of the USA.

1896 William McKinley (1843–1901) elected US president.

SCIENCE AND TECHNOLOGY

1885 German engineer Gottleib Daimler (1834–1900) patents the internal combustion petrol engine and builds the first motorcycle.

1885 German engineer Karl Benz (1844–1929) builds a prototype car with a four-stroke internal combustion engine.

1889 French engineer Gustave Eiffel (1832–1923) designs and builds a steel tower in Paris.

1886 US scientist Charles Hall (1863–1914) develops a process for obtaining aluminium from bauxite by electrolysis.

1886 Construction starts on a hydroelectric power station at Niagara Falls.

1887 German physicist Heinrich Hertz (1857–94) discovers the propagation of electromagnetic waves produced by electrical discharges.

1888 US engineer Nikola Tesla (1856–1943) invents an electric motor that runs on alternating current.

1888 US engineer William Burroughs (1857–98) patents a recording adding machine.

1888 Scottish inventor John Dunlop (1840–1921) develops the pneumatic tyre.

1888 US industrialist George Eastman (1854–1932) perfects a hand-held (Kodak) camera.

> "Science is nothing but trained and organized common sense."
>
> *Thomas Huxley*
>
> *(Collected Essays)*

1890 US engineer Emile Berliner (1851–1929) introduces the use of discs for sound recording.

1890 German bacteriologist Emil von Behring (1854–1917) discovers the viruses that cause diphtheria and tetanus.

1890 Electric chair introduced as a method of capital punishment in New York.

1890 British mathematician John Venn (1834–1923) devises an overlapping diagram for depicting the relationships between sets.

1892 German engineer Rudolf Diesel (1858–1913) patents his design for an engine that uses compression to ignite fuel oil.

1892 British scientist Charles Cross (1855–1935) invents the viscose method of making artificial fibres.

1892 Scottish chemist James Dewar (1842–1943) invents the silvered vacuum flask.

1892 French chemist Henri Moissan (1852–1907) invents the acetylene lamp.

1892 German engineer Leon Arons (1860–1919) invents the mercury vapour lamp.

1892 French engineer François Hennebique (1842–1921) invents pre-stressed concrete.

1893 British biologist Thomas Huxley (1825–95) publishes *Evolution and Ethics*.

1893 US scientist Theobald Smith (1859–1934) shows that parasites such as ticks can spread disease.

1894 British scientists Lord Rayleigh (1842–1919) and William Ramsay (1852–1916) discover the inert gas argon.

1895 Wilhelm Röntgen (1845–1923) publishes *A New Kind of Radiation*, in which he announces the discovery of X-rays.

1895 French inventors Louis (1864–1948) and Auguste (1862–1954) Lumière give the first public cinema presentation in Paris.

1895 French mathematician Henri Poincaré (1854–1912) founds algebraic topology.

1895 Italian physicist Guglielmo Marconi (1874–1937) invents the wireless telegraph.

1895 US industrialist King Gillette (1855–1932) invents the safety razor with disposable blades.

ARTS AND HUMANITIES

1885 French writer Guy de Maupassant (1850–93) publishes *Bel Ami*.

1885 British explorer and scholar Richard Burton (1821–90) publishes the first volume of his translation of *The Arabian Nights*.

1885 French composer César Franck (1822–1890) writes *Symphonic Variations*.

1885 US artist Winslow Homer (1836–1910) paints *The Herring Net*.

1886 French composer Camille Saint-Saëns (1835–1921) writes *Carnival of the Animals*.

1887 French poet Stephane Mallarmé (1842–98) publishes *Poésies*.

1888 Dutch artist Vincent Van Gogh (1853–90) paints *Sunflowers*.

1888 Russian composer Nikolai Rimsky-Korsakov (1844–1908) writes *Sheherazade*.

1888 Swedish dramatist August Strindberg (1849–1912) writes *Miss Julie*.

1889 Irish dramatist and critic George Bernard Shaw (1856–1950) edits a collection of *Fabian Essays*.

1889 French composer Gabriel Fauré (1845–1924) writes his song *Clair de lune*.

1889 French philosopher Henri Bergson (1859–1941) publishes *Time and Free Will: an Essay on the Immediate Data of Conscience*.

1889 Italian poet Gabriel D'Annunzio (1863–1938) publishes the first volume of his *Romances of the Rose*.

1890 British scholar James Frazer (1854–1951) publishes *The Golden Bough; A Study in Magic and Religion*.

1890 Verse of US poet Emily Dickinson (1830–86) published posthumously.

1890 US historian Alfred Mahan (1840–1914) publishes *The Influence of Sea Power on History*.

1890 Italian composer Pietro Mascagni (1863–1945) writes his opera *Cavalleria Rusticana*.

1891 French artist Paul Gaugin (1848–1903) arrives in Tahiti.

1891 British writer Arthur Conan Doyle (1859–1930) publishes the first of his *Adventures of Sherlock Holmes*.

1891 Irish dramatist and poet Oscar Wilde (1854–1900) publishes his novel *The Picture of Dorian Gray*.

1891 French artist Henri Rousseau (1844–1910) paints *Surprised! (Tropical Storm with Tiger)*.

1892 French artist Henri Toulouse-Lautrec (1864–1901) produces his poster advertising: *The Ambassadors: Aristide Bruant*.

1893 Antonín Dvořák (1841–1904) writes his Symphony No.9 in E minor, known as "From the New World".

1893 Norwegian artist Edvard Munch (1863–1944) paints *The Scream*.

1894 French composer Claude Debussy (1862–1918) writes *Prelude to the Afternoon of a Faun*.

1894 British poet and author Rudyard Kipling (1865–1936) publishes his children's stories *The Jungle Book*.

1895 Austrian composer Gustav Mahler (1860–1911) writes his Symphony No.2.

1895 US author Stephen Crane (1871–1900) publishes his novel *The Red Badge of Courage*.

1896 French dramatist Alfred Jarry (1873–1907) writes the play *Ubu Roi*.

1896 Italian composer Giacomo Puccini (1858–1924) writes his opera *La Bohème*.

1896 Hungarian Zionist Theodor Herzl (1860–1904) publishes *The Jewish State*.

1896 Nicaraguan poet Rubén Darío (1867–1916) publishes *Profane Hymns*.

ASIA AND AUSTRALASIA

1897 Germans occupy Qingdao, N China.

1898 Russia obtains a lease on Port Arthur on the coast of N China.

1898 France obtains a lease on Leizhou Bandao in China; Britain gains Kowloon.

1898 USA captures Manila from the Spanish and gains the Philippines and Guam.

1898 USA formally annexes Hawaii.

1898 Influenced by reformer Kang Youwei (1858–1927), the Chinese Emperor Guangxu (1871–1908) begins the '100-days' reforms, which are quickly withdrawn by Dowager Empress Cixi (1835–1908) and the Emperor imprisoned.

1899 British administrator George Curzon (1859–1925) becomes Viceroy of India.

1899 Huk insurrection against the USA breaks out in the Philippines.

1899 British sign a treaty with the Sheikh of Kuwait.

1899 Concession to build the Berlin to Baghdad railway is granted to a Germany company.

1899 Chinese court begins giving aid to the anti-foreigner Society of Harmonious Fists ('the Boxers').

1899 USA and Germany partition Samoa.

1900 Foreign legations in Beijing are besieged by the Society of Harmonious Fists in the 'Boxer Rebellion'; Empress Cixi flees; the Russians annex Manchuria; an international military force restores order.

1900 Turks begin the construction of the Hejaz railway to the holy places of Medina and Mecca in Arabia.

1901 Boxer protocol imposes a huge fine on China.

1901 Britain grants dominion status to the Commonwealth of Australia .

1902 Chinese court returns to Beijing and begins reforms to strengthen the armed forces.

1902 Japan signs an alliance with Britain.

1902 Japanese raid the Russian base at Port Arthur in protest over the continuing occupation of Manchuria.

1903 Trans-Siberian railway is completed.

1903 British declare the Arabian Gulf to be within their sphere of control.

1904 Japanese attack on Port Arthur starts the Russo-Japanese War; the Japanese win the battles of Yalu River and Liaoyang.

1904 British expedition occupies Lhasa, the capital of Tibet.

1905 Japanese capture Port Arthur, defeat the Russians at the battle of Mukden and annihilate the Russian fleet at the battle of Tsushima Straits; the treaty of Portsmouth, New Hampshire, ends the Russo–Japanese War.

1905 Britain partitions the Indian province of Bengal.

1905 Papua New Guinea is joined to Australia.

1906 Revolution in Persia (Iran) compels the shah to adopt a new constitution.

1906 All-India Muslim league formed.

1906 China acknowledges British control of Tibet.

1907 Britain and Russia divide Persia into spheres of influence by the treaty of St Petersburg

1907 Britain grants New Zealand dominion status.

1907 Dutch finally subdue the native revolt in Sumatra.

1907 Japan acquires a protectorate over Korea and disbands the Korean army, provoking rebellion.

1908 Dutch take control of Bali.

1908 Henry Pu Yi (1906–67) becomes child Emperor of China after the death of the Dowager Empress Cixi (b.1835). He grants a draft constitution.

1908 Shah Muhammad Ali of Iran withdraws the constitution and closes the national assembly; popular opposition causes Russian troops to invade N Iran in support of the Shah.

1908 Rising by the 'Young Turks', supported by the military, restores the Turkish constitution.

1908 Oil discovered in Iran.

1909 Muhammad V (1844–1918) becomes Turkish sultan; a new constitution removes almost all his powers.

AFRICA

1896 British General Horatio Kitchener (1850–1916) captures the Mahdist city of Dongola.

1896 Ethiopia routs the Italians at the Battle of Adowa; the treaty of Addis Ababa secures Ethiopian independence.

1896 British bombard Zanzibar.

1897 Slavery abolished in Zanzibar.

1898 British decisively defeat the Mahdists at the Battle of Omdurman; British and French troops confront each other at Fashoda; the French are forced to withdraw from Sudan.

1898 Menelik II brings all of upland Ethiopia under his control.

1898 British and French agree the division of Nigeria.

1899 British and French reach agreement over joint control of the Sudan.

1899 British lose the early battles of the South African War (Boer War); Boer forces besiege Ladysmith and Mafeking.

1899 Germany takes control of Rwanda, E Africa.

1900 British forces in South Africa under General Frederick Roberts (1832–1914) relieve Ladysmith and Mafeking, invade and annex the Orange Free State and Transvaal, and capture Johannesburg and Pretoria; the Boers adopt guerrilla warfare tactics.

1900 British suppress an Ashanti uprising.

1900 France and Italy make a secret agreement giving France control of Morocco and Italy control of Libya.

1900 French defeat the African leader Rabeh Zobeir in the Lake Chad region.

1900 French capture the main Saharan oases S of Morocco and Algeria.

1901 British introduce concentration camps in South Africa for captured Boer civilians.

1901 Britain annexes the Ashanti kingdom.

1902 Portuguese suppress a native rising in Angola.

1902 Peace of Vereeniging ends the South African War (Boer War) and hopes of Boer independence.

1902 Completion of the Aswan Dam across the River Nile.

1903 Britain captures the cities of Kano and Sokoto, completing the conquest of N Nigeria.

1904 Spain and Morocco sign a treaty agreeing the division of Morocco.

1904 Herero people begin an insurrection in German Southwest Africa.

1905 German Emperor William II (1859–1941) visits Tangier and provokes a crisis about French interests in Morocco.

1906 Egypt gains the Sinai peninsula from Turkey.

1906 Conference at Algerciras confirms Moroccan independence with an open door policy.

1906 Lagos joined to the British colony of S Nigeria.

1906 Britain, France, and Italy agree to respect the independence of Ethiopia.

1907 Proclamation of Mulay Hafid as Sultan of Morocco leads to unrest; French bombard Casablanca and occupy the Atlantic coast region.

1907 Indian lawyer Mohandas Gandhi (1869–1948) leads a campaign of passive resistance against South African immigration policies.

1907 Nairobi becomes the capital of Kenya.

1908 Belgium annexes Congo Free State.

1908 Herero rebellion in German Southwest Africa finally suppressed, with genocidal ferocity.

1909 French complete the conquest of Mauritania.

1909 Spanish enclave of Melilla attacked by Moroccans from the Rif mountains.

▶ *Fashion, 1900* Women's fashion at the start of the century still involved manipulation of the figure, this time into an s-shape. By the 1920s, curves were considered unfashionable.

EUROPE

1897 Greece declares war on Turkey and is heavily defeated.

1897 Rosa Luxemburg (1871–1919), leader of the Social Democratic Party of Congress in Poland, flees to Germany.

1898 Bread riots occur in Milan and other Italian cities.

1898 French nationalists found the *Action Française* movement.

1898 German naval law passed authorizing a larger navy as envisaged by Admiral Alfred von Tirpitz (1849–1930).

1898 Turks forced to evacuate Crete, later occupied by British, French, Italian, and Russian troops.

1898 Empress Elizabeth of Austria (b.1837) assassinated in Switzerland by an Italian anarchist.

1898 Social Democratic party founded in Russia.

1899 First Hague peace conference outlaws the use of poison gas and dum-dum bullets in warfare.

1899 French president pardons Alfred Dreyfus (1859–1935).

1900 Bernhard von Bülow (1849–1929) becomes Chancellor of Germany.

1900 Victor Emmanuel III (1869–1947) becomes King of Italy.

1901 Edward VII (1841–1910) crowned King of Britain.

1902 Alfonso XIII (1886–1941) becomes King of Spain.

1903 Serbian army officers murder King Alexander Obrenović (b.1876) and set up King Peter I (1844–1921) as a puppet ruler.

1903 Russian Social Democratic party splits into minority Mensheviks and majority Bolsheviks under Vladimir Ilyich Lenin (1870–1924).

1903 Emmeline Pankhurst (1858–1928) founds the Women's Social and Political Union to campaign for female suffrage in Britain.

1905 Norway under King Haakon VII (1872–1957) becomes independent of Denmark.

1905 Dissent turns to revolution in Russia; the crew of the battleship *Potemkin* mutiny; Tsar Nicholas II (1868–1918) issues his October manifesto granting a constitution; the suppression of the St Petersburg *soviet* leads to a workers' rising in Moscow.

1906 British Labour party established under the leadership of Ramsay MacDonald (1866–1937).

1906 Georges Clemenceau (1841–1929) becomes Prime Minister of France.

1906 First Russian *Duma* (parliament) meets.

1907 Severe famine devastates Russia.

1907 Sinn Féin league formed in Ireland.

1908 Crete proclaims union with Greece.

1908 Ferdinand I (1861–1948) declares himself Tsar of an independent Bulgaria; Austria annexes Bosnia and Herzegovina; Serbia, backed by Russia, threatens war against Austria.

1909 Serbia backs down; Italy and Russia sign the secret Treaty of Raconnigi to maintain the status quo in the Balkans.

1900

THE AMERICAS

1898 USS *Maine* blown up in Havana harbour, Cuba; USA declares war on Spain, wins the battles of San Juan Hill and Santiago, and invades Puerto Rico.

1898 Under the Peace of Paris, Spain evacuates Cuba and the USA gains Puerto Rico.

1899 US Secretary of State John Hay (1838–1905) proposes that the European powers adopt an 'open door' policy, allowing equal treatment of all foreign goods through treaty ports in China.

1901 Theodore Roosevelt (1858–1919) becomes US president, following the assassination of William McKinley (b.1843).

1901 New constitution in Cuba makes the country virtually a US protectorate.

1902 Argentina obtains the greater part of Patagonia by agreement with Chile.

1902 European powers blockade Venezuela in a dispute over loan repayments.

1903 After a US-inspired coup, Panama separates from Colombia.

1903 USA obtains perpetual rights to a canal zone across Panama.

1903 Alaska-Canada border fixed.

1904 Theodore Roosevelt re-elected President of the USA.

1904 Roosevelt warns European powers against further intervention in America.

1906 US troops occupy Cuba after political unrest; William Taft (1857–1930) declares himself governor.

1906 Massive earthquake and fire devastates San Francisco, sw USA.

1907 Nicaragua invades Honduras, installs a puppet ruler, and prepares to invade El Salvador; US pressure forces Nicaragua to withdraw.

1907 US Army starts work on the construction of the Panama Canal.

1907 Oklahoma becomes a state of the USA.

1908 William Taft elected President of the United States.

1909 Nationalist revolt in Honduras leads to civil war.

1909 US troops withdraw from Cuba; José Gómez (1858–1921) becomes president.

Ford *The introduction of the Model T (1908) brought motoring to the general public. It was affordable and easy to maintain and could reach a top speed of 72km/h (45mph).*

SCIENCE AND TECHNOLOGY

1896 Alfred Nobel (1833–96) endows prizes for achievements in various branches of science.

1896 German pioneer of non-powered flight Otto Lilienthal (b.1848) killed in a glider crash.

1896 French physicist Henri Becquerel (1852–1908) discovers radioactivity in uranium compounds.

1897 British bacteriologist Ronald Ross (1857–1932) discovers the malaria parasite in mosquitos.

1897 British physicist Joseph Thomson (1856–1940) discovers the electron.

1897 German physicist Ferdinand Braun (1850–1918) invents the cathode-ray tube.

1897 German scientist Felix Hoffman discovers a method of producing pure aspirin.

1898 Danish engineer Valdemar Poulsen (1869–1942) invents magnetic sound recording on steel wire.

1898 Scientists Marie (1867–1934) and Pierre Curie (1859–1906) discover the radioactive elements radium and polonium.

1899 Aspirin goes on sale in Europe.

◄ ***Freud*** *was the founder of the psychoanalytic movement. His new methods of treating mental disorder, using free association and dream interpretation, were summarized in* The Interpretation of Dreams.

1900 German inventor Ferdinand von Zeppelin (1838–1917) builds a rigid airship.

1900 German physicist Max Planck (1858–1947) proposes that energy radiates in discontinuous quanta, the beginning of quantum theory.

1900 French physicist Paul Villard (1860–1934) discovers gamma rays.

1900 Austrian phsyician Karl Landsteiner (1868–1943) discovers the A, B, and O blood groups.

1901 Italian physicist Guglielmo Marconi (1874–1937) transmits a Morse code message across the Atlantic.

1901 Wilhelm Conrad Röntgen (1845–1923) receives the first Nobel Prize in physics "in recognition of the extraordinary services he has rendered by the discovery of the remarkable rays subsequently named after him."

1901 Emil Adolf von Behring (1854–1917) receives the Nobel Prize in physiology or medicine "for his work on serum therapy, especially its application against diphtheria."

1902 British scientist Oliver Heaviside (1850–1925) predicts the existence of an atmospheric layer that will reflect radio waves.

1903 US inventors Orville (1971–1948) and Wilbur (1867–1912) Wright make the first powered aircraft flight at Kitty Hawk in North Carolina, USA.

1903 Russian engineer Konstantin Tsiolkovsky (1857–1935) proposes multi-stage rockets for the exploration of space.

1904 British engineer John Fleming (1849–1945) invents the diode thermionic valve.

1905 French psychologist Alfred Binet (1857–1911) devises a practical intelligence test.

1905 German-born US physicist Albert Einstein (1879–1955) publishes his special theory of relativity and introduces the concept of photons to quantum theory.

1905 German chemist Hermann Nernst (1864–1941) formulates the third law of thermodynamics.

1906 US scientist Lee de Forest (1873–1961) invents the amplifying audion triode valve.

1906 British Navy launch HMS *Dreadnought*, the first big-gun battleship.

1906 US engineer Richard Fessenden (1866–1932) introduces music and speech on AM radio.

1907 German chemist Emil Fischer (1852–1919) discovers that proteins are made up of amino acids.

1908 US industrialist Henry Ford (1863–1947) announces the production of the Model T.

1908 German chemist Fritz Haber (1868–1934) invents a process for synthesizing ammonia.

1909 French aviator Louis Blériot (1872–1936) flies a monoplane across the English Channel.

1909 Belgian-born US chemist Leo Baekeland (1863–1944) invents Bakelite, a thermosetting plastic polymer.

ARTS AND HUMANITIES

1896 British poet A.E. Housman (1859–1936) publishes *A Shropshire Lad*.

1896 German composer Richard Strauss (1864–1949) writes *Thus Spake Zarathustra*.

1897 Russian dramatist Anton Chekov (1960–1904) writes his play *Uncle Vanya*.

1897 French sociologist Emile Durkheim (1858–1917) publishes *Suicide*, outlining his theory of alienation.

1897 French author André Gide (1869–1951) writes his novel *The Fruits of the Earth*.

1897 French poet Edmond Rostand (1868–1918) writes his verse play *Cyrano de Bergerac*.

1898 Spanish novelist Vicente Blasco Ibáñez (1867–1928) publishes *The Cabin*.

1898 French novelist Emile Zola (1840–1902) writes an open letter about the Dreyfus affair that begins "*J'accuse…*".

1898 British author H.G. Wells (1856–1946) publishes his novel *The War of the Worlds*.

1899 Finnish composer Jean Sibelius (1865–1957) writes *Finlandia*.

1899 British composer Edward Elgar (1857–1934) writes *Enigma Variations*.

1900 Austrian phsyician Sigmund Freud (1856–1939) publishes *The Interpretation of Dreams*, the founding text of psychoanalysis.

1900 British archaeologist Arthur Evans (1851–1941) discovers the ruins of Minoan civilization in Crete.

1900 French author Colette (1873–1954) publishes the first of her *Claudine* novels.

1900 British novelist Joseph Conrad (1857–1924) writes *Lord Jim*.

1901 Russian composer Sergei Rachmaninov (1873–1943) writes his Piano Concerto No.2.

1902 Russian anarchist Peter Kropotkin (1842–1921) publishes *Mutual Aid*.

1902 French artist Camille Pissaro (1830–1903) paints *Louvre from Pont Neuf*.

1902 US psychologist William James (1842–1910) publishes *Varieties of Religious Experience*.

1902 US ragtime composer Scott Joplin (1868–1917) writes "The Entertainer".

1902 Russian author Maxim Gorky (1868–1936) writes his play *The Lower Depths*.

1903 US author Jack London (1876–1916) publishes his novel *Call of the Wild*.

1904 German sociologist Max Weber (1864–1920) publishes *The Protestant Ethic and the Spirit of Capitalism*.

1904 Italian philosopher Benedetto Croce (1866–1952) founds the review *La Critica*.

1904 Scottish artist and architect Charles Rennie Mackintosh (1868–1928) designs the Willow Tea Rooms in Glasgow.

1904 Scottish author James Barrie (1860–1937) writes his play *Peter Pan*.

1905 German artist Ernst Kirchner (1880–1938) founds *Die Brücke* ('The Bridge') group of expressionist artists.

1905 Spanish artist Pablo Picasso (1881–1973) paints *Acrobat and Young Harlequin*.

1905 French composer Claude Debussy (1862–1918) writes *La Mer*.

1905 Austrian composer Franz Lehár (1870–1948) writes his operetta *The Merry Widow*.

1906 British novelist John Galsworthy (1867–1933) publishes *The Man of Property*, the first volume of *The Forsyte Saga*.

1907 British ex-army officer Robert Baden-Powell (1857–1941) founds the Boy Scout youth movement.

1907 British writer Hilaire Belloc (1870–1953) publishes *Cautionary Tales* for children.

1907 Irish dramatist J.M. Synge writes *The Playboy of the Western World*.

1908 Russian artist Marc Chagall (1887–1985) paints *Nu Rouge*.

1908 US writer and educator Helen Keller (1880–1968) publishes *The World I Live In*.

ASIA AND AUSTRALASIA

1910 Chinese invade Tibet.

1910 Anti-Turkish revolt in Albania brutally suppressed.

1910 National assembly meets in China and abolishes slavery.

1910 Japan annexes Korea, which is renamed Chosen.

1911 Military revolution breaks out in s China; the national assembly signs a truce and forms a provisional government.

1911 Russians invade and occupy Iran.

1911 British reverse the partition of Bengal in India.

1911 Outer Mongolia becomes a Russian protectorate.

1911 Tibet declares independence from China.

1912 Chinese Emperor Pu Yi (1906–67) abdicates, signalling the end of the Qing dynasty.

1912 Albanian leader Essad Pasha (1864–1920) proclaims independence from Turkey.

1913 Yuan Shikai (1859–1916) elected president of China and purges the nationalist Kuomintang party, led by Sun Yat-sen (1866–1925), from government.

1913 Young Turks, led by Enver Pasha (1881–1922), seize power in Turkey and suppress opposition.

1914 Japan declares war on Germany.

1914 Britain, France, and Russia declare war on Turkey.

1914 British occupy Basra in present-day Iraq.

1914 New Zealand troops occupy German Samoa.

1914 Australian troops occupy German New Guinea.

1915 China accepts 21 demands made by Japan that undermine Chinese sovereignty.

1915 British and Australian troops land at Gallipoli, Turkey, in an attempt to seize control of the Dardanelles; further landings are made at Suvla.

1915 British capture Kut-el-Amra in Mesopotamia from the Turks; and occupy Bushehr in Iran.

AFRICA

1910 France takes control of the port of Agadir, Morocco.

1910 British grant the Union of South Africa dominion status; Louis Botha (1862–1919) becomes prime minister.

1910 French Congo renamed French Equatorial Africa.

1911 French troops occupy Fez; the Germans send the gunboat *Panther* to Agadir; France cedes parts of Congo to Germany in return for freedom of action in Morocco.

1911 Italy invades and annexes Tripoli in Libya, despite fierce Turkish resistance; a naval war develops between Italy and Turkey.

1911 British colony of Northern Rhodesia created.

1912 Sultan of Morocco forced to accept a French protectorate.

1912 Italy bombards ports on the Dardanelles and conquers Rhodes and other Turkish islands; the Treaty of Lausanne ends hostilities; Italy gains Libya.

1912 Spain and France sign a treaty dividing Morocco between them.

1913 Italians subdue the inland regions of Libya.

1914 British proclaim a protectorate over Egypt.

1914 Arab revolt against the Italians breaks out in Libya.

1914 Indian lawyer Mohandas Gandhi (1869–1948) leaves South Africa for India.

1914 British unite N and s Nigeria.

1914 British and French forces invade and occupy Cameroon and Togoland.

1914 British bombard Dar es Salaam, Tanganyika; the Germans defeat a landing by British Indian troops at the Battle of Tanga.

1915 South African forces under Louis Botha (1862–1919) defeat the Germans in Southwest Africa.

1915 Turkish forces attempt to seize the Suez Canal.

EUROPE

German aircraft
Gotha IIIs were used for armed reconnaissance over the battlefields as well as for bombing. They were developed to take over the Zeppelin's role in bombing English cities.

1910 George V (1865–1936) becomes King of Britain.

1910 Portuguese king Manuel II (1889–1932) flees after a revolution in Lisbon; a republic is proclaimed.

1911 Serbian army officers form the 'Union or Death' (Black Hand) secret society to promote Serbian expansion.

1912 Italian socialist leader Benito Mussolini (1883–1945) becomes editor of the newspaper *Avanti*.

1912 Balkan crisis provoked by Albanian independence; Serbia and Bulgaria form the Balkan League with Russian support and are joined by Greece and Montenegro; the League declares war on Turkey and wins the Battles of Kumanovo and Lule Burgas; Italy and Austria oppose Serbian expansion in Albania.

1913 Treaty of London ends the first Balkan War; Bulgaria attacks Serbia, which is supported by Greece, Romania and Turkey; Austria threatens to intervene to aid Bulgaria; the Peace of Bucharest ends the second Balkan War; Bulgaria loses most of Macedonia to Greece and Serbia.

1914 Heir to the Austrian throne Archduke Franz Ferdinand (b.1863) assassinated in Sarajevo by an agent of the Black Hand; Serbia rejects an Austrian ultimatum and gains Russian support; Austria declares war and Russia mobilizes; Germany declares war on Russia and France and invades Belgium; Britain issues Germany an ultimatum over Belgian neutrality and goes to war; Serbia declares war on Germany; Romania declares its neutrality.

1914 Germany signs an alliance with Turkey.

1914 German troops invade Luxembourg and Belgium and capture Brussels; British troops first encounter the Germans at the Battle of Mons; British and French forces, under the command of French General Joseph Joffre (1852–1931), halt the German advance on Paris at the Battle of the Marne; Germans capture Ostend, Belgium, but defeat in the first Battle of Ypres prevents them from capturing further ports on the English Channel; the positions of the opposing armies become fixed with the Germans occupying c.10% of French territory; beginning of trench warfare.

1914 German aircraft attack Paris.

1914 St Petersburg renamed Petrograd.

1914 Britain sinks German ships in a raid on Heligoland Bight; German submarines sink British warships in the North Sea.

1914 Russian armies invade N and central Poland; in N Poland the Germans, under General Paul von Hindenburg (1847–1934), win the Battles of Tannenberg and the Masurian Lakes but fail to take Warsaw; an Austrian advance into central Poland fails to dislodge the Russians but prevents their capture of Kraków; two Austrian invasions of Serbia are repulsed; the Germans capture Łódź.

1914 Britain annexes Cyprus.

1915 After signing the secret Treaty of London, Italy quits the Triple Alliance, attacks Austria and fights a series of inconclusive battles along the Isonzo front.

1915 Bulgaria allies with Germany; German and Austrian forces invade Serbia and Montenegro.

1915 German Zeppelin airships make bombing raids on London.

1915 French and British attacks at Champagne and Neuve Chapelle achieve little; the second Battle of Ypres results in slight German gains; French advance slightly at the second Battle of Artois but achieve little at the second Battle of Champagne; Britain fails to exploit its successes at the third Battle of Artois and the Battle of Loos; General Douglas Haig (1861–1928) becomes British commander in chief.

1915 Germany orders a submarine blockade of Britain; the liner *Lusitania* with US citizens aboard is sunk off the coast of Ireland.

1915 Russian advance into Hungary defeated; Germans capture Memel and advance into Lithuania; Austro-German offensive drives the Russians from central Poland and captures Warsaw, Vilna and Brest-Litovsk; Tsar Nicholas II (1868–1918) takes personal control of the Russian army.

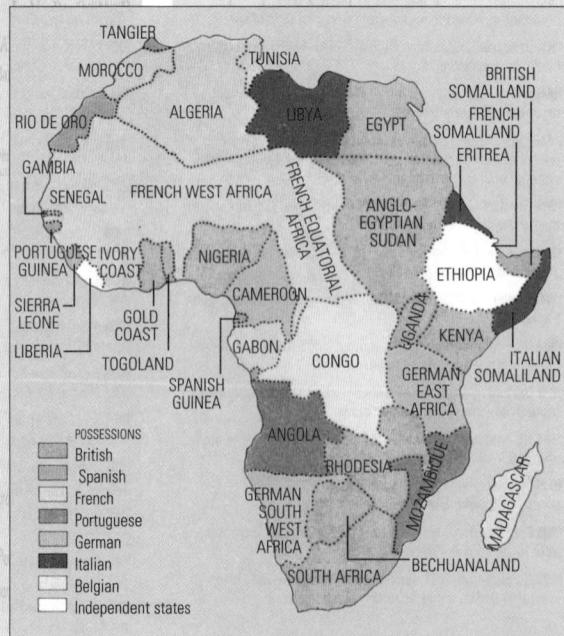

▶ **Africa** This map of Africa in 1914 shows how it had been partitioned among seven European countries. This partition had taken place rapidly in the last 20 years of the 19th century. Only Liberia and Ethiopia remained independent of European rule. Although some territories were termed protectorates (such as Uganda and Morocco) rather than colonies, Europeans were still firmly in control. The Union of South Africa had been formed in 1910, but it remained a British dominion. Colonial boundaries drawn up by Europeans were often merely straight lines on the map. These artificial boundaries have been the cause of many problems since African countries regained their independence.

TANGIER
MOROCCO
TUNISIA
RIO DE ORO
ALGERIA
LIBYA
EGYPT
BRITISH SOMALILAND
FRENCH SOMALILAND
ERITREA
GAMBIA
SENEGAL
FRENCH WEST AFRICA
FRENCH EQUATORIAL AFRICA
ANGLO-EGYPTIAN SUDAN
PORTUGUESE GUINEA
IVORY COAST
NIGERIA
ETHIOPIA
SIERRA LEONE
GOLD COAST
CAMEROON
UGANDA
KENYA
LIBERIA
GABON
TOGOLAND
CONGO
GERMAN EAST AFRICA
ITALIAN SOMALILAND
SPANISH GUINEA
ANGOLA
RHODESIA
MOZAMBIQUE
MADAGASCAR
GERMAN SOUTH WEST AFRICA
SOUTH AFRICA
BECHUANALAND

POSSESSIONS
British
Spanish
French
Portuguese
German
Italian
Belgian
Independent states

THE AMERICAS

1911 National Association for the Advancement of Colored People founded in the USA.

1911 President Porfirio Díaz (1830–1915) overthrown by a revolution in Mexico.

1912 Woodrow Wilson (1856–1924) elected US president.

1912 New Mexico and Arizona become states of the USA.

1912 *Titanic*, a liner, sinks off the coast of Newfoundland.

1913 Victoriano Huerta (1854–1916) seizes power in Mexico.

1914 Huerta ousted by Venustiano Carranza (1859–1920); civil war breaks out in Mexico.

1914 British warships win the naval battle of the Falklands.

1914 Panama canal opens.

1914 US marines seize Vera Cruz, Mexico.

1915 Klu Klux Klan revived in the USA.

1915 American nations recognize Venustiano Carranza (1859–1920) as President of Mexico.

1915 US troops land in Haiti to restore order after political and financial instability.

▼ *Japanese territory* The expansion of Japanese territory at the end of the 19th and the beginning of the 20th century was the result of war and of treaties. In 1875 the Kurile Islands were acquired from Russia by treaty, Formosa (present-day Taiwan) was won in the Sino–Japanese War; South Sakhalin, the lease of Port Arthur and rights in south Manchuria were won in the Russo–Japanese war. Korea was annexed in 1910.

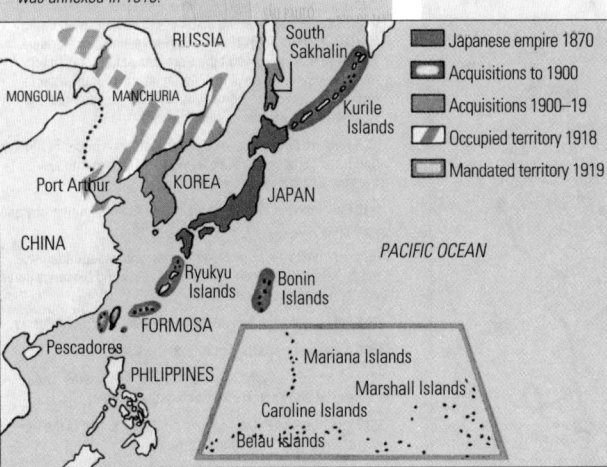

SCIENCE AND TECHNOLOGY

1910 French scientist Georges Claude (1870–1960) invents neon lighting.

1910 US astronomer George Hale (1877–1945) invents the spectroheliograph.

1911 Polish biochemist Casimir Funk (1884–1967) discovers vitamins.

1911 Scottish physicist Charles Wilson (1869–1959) invents the cloud chamber.

1912 German physicist Max von Laue (1879–1960) uses X-ray diffraction to study crystal structure.

1912 Austrian engineer Viktor Kaplan (1876–1934) invents a low-pressure water turbine.

1913 Danish physicist Niels Bohr (1885–1962) proposes a new model of atomic structure.

1913 British chemist Frederick Soddy (1877–1956) discovers isotopes.

1913 US astronomer Henry Russell (1877–1957) devises a diagram of the magnitude and temperature of stars; the diagram was independently conceived by Ejnar Hertzsprung (1873–1967).

1913 British mathematicians Bertrand Russell (1872–1970) and Alfred Whitehead (1861–1947) publish their *Principia Mathematica*.

1914 US industrialist Henry Ford (1863–1947) introduces conveyor-belt production lines in his car factory.

1915 German-born US physicist Albert Einstein (1879–1955) publishes his general theory of relativity.

1915 German Fokker aircraft revolutionize aerial warfare with a machine gun synchronized to fire through the propeller.

1915 Poison gas (chlorine) is first used in warfare by the Germans, during the first battle of Ypres.

1915 German geologist Alfred Wegener (1880–1930) proposes his theory of continental drift.

ARTS AND HUMANITIES

1908 French philosopher Georges Sorel (1847–1922) publishes *Reflections on Violence*.

1908 Hungarian composer Béla Bartók (1881–1945) writes his String Quartet No.1.

1908 British author E M Forster (1879–1970) publishes the novel *A Room with a View*.

1909 US architect Frank Lloyd Wright (1869–1959) designs the Robie House in Chicago, Illinois.

1909 Indian poet Rabindranath Tagore (1861–1941) publishes his *Gitanjali*.

1909 Italian poet Filippo Marinetti (1876–1944) publishes *First Futurist Manifesto*.

1910 British author Arnold Bennett (1867–1931) publishes his novel *Clayhanger*.

1910 French artist Henri Matisse (1869–1954) paints *Dance II*.

1910 British composer Ralph Vaughan Williams (1872–1958) writes *A Sea Symphony*.

1911 US composer Irving Berlin (1888–1989) writes his song "Alexander's Ragtime Band".

1911 Russian impresario Serge Diaghilev (1872–1929) forms the *Ballets Russes* in Paris.

1912 Swiss psychiatrist Carl Jung (1875–1964) publishes *The Psychology of the Unconscious*.

1912 US author Edgar Rice Burroughs (1875–1950) publishes the novel *Tarzan of the Apes*.

1912 British composer Frederick Delius (1862–1934) writes *On Hearing the First Cuckoo in Spring*.

1912 French artist Marcel Duchamp (1887–1968) paints *Nude Descending A Staircase, II*.

1912 Russian dancer Vaslav Nijinsky (1880–1950) creates his ballet *Afternoon of a Faun*.

1912 German author Thomas Mann (1875–1955) publishes his novella *Death in Venice*.

1913 Russian composer Igor Stravinsky (1882–1971) writes his ballet *The Rite of Spring*.

1913 French author Marcel Proust (1871–1922) publishes his novel *Swann's War*, the first volume of *Remembrance of Things Past*.

1913 French writer Henri Alain-Fournier (1886–1914) publishes his novel *Le Grand Meaulnes*.

1913 French artist Maurice Utrillo (1883–1955) paints *Rue Saint-Vincent*.

1913 British architect Edwin Lutyens (1869–1944) designs the Viceroy's House in New Delhi, India.

1913 French poet and dramatist Guillame Apollinaire (1880–1918) attempts to define Cubism in his essay *Cubist Painters*.

1913 Italian artist Umberto Boccioni (1882–1916) creates the sculpture *Unique Forms of Continuity in Space*.

1913 British writer D.H. Lawrence (1885–1930) publishes his novel *Sons and Lovers*.

1914 British composer Gustav Holst (1872–1934) writes his orchestral suite *The Planets*.

1914 Scottish author Saki (Hector Munro, 1870–1916) publishes his collection of stories *Beasts and Superbeasts*.

1914 US poet Robert Frost (1874–1963) publishes *North of Boston*.

1914 Irish poet and dramatist William Butler Yeats (1865–1939) publishes his collection of poems *Responsibilities*.

1914 US musician W.C. Handy (1873–1958) writes "St Louis Blues", the first published blues tune.

1915 British poet Rupert Brooke (1887–1915) publishes *1914 and Other Poems*.

1915 US poet Ezra Pound (1885–1968) publishes *Cathay*.

1915 British writer John Buchan (1875–1940) publishes his novel *The Thirty-Nine Steps*.

1915 US film director D.W. Griffith's (1875–1948) *Birth of a Nation* released.

1915 Romanian artist Tristan Tzara (1896–1963) and Alsatian sculptor Jean Arp (1887–1966) found the Dada movement in Zurich.

1915 British author W. Somerset Maugham (1874–1965) publishes his novel *Of Human Bondage*.

ASIA AND AUSTRALASIA

1916 British troops evacuated from the Turkish coast.

1916 Indian Hindus and Muslims sign the Pact of Lucknow, calling for independence from Britain.

1916 Russian forces invade Armenia.

1916 Civil wars break out in N China as rival warlords, with foreign support, battle for control of Beijing.

1916 Hussein (1856–1931), Sharif of Mecca, declared king of the Arabs; a general Arab revolt against the Turks begins.

1916 British troops surrender to the Turks at Kut el-Amra.

1916 British and French reach the Sykes-Picot Agreement over the future partition of the Ottoman Empire.

1917 Arab forces, led by T.E. Lawrence (1888–1935), capture Aqaba.

1917 British forces capture Baghdad and Jerusalem.

1917 Kuomintang forms a S Chinese government in Guangzhou (Canton) and appoints Sun Yat-sen (1866–1925) commander in chief.

1917 China declares war on Germany.

1917 British foreign minister Arthur Balfour (1848–1930) declares his support for the settlement of Jews in Palestine.

1918 British troops capture Damascus; French forces take Beirut.

1918 Britain occupies Iran after Russian troops are withdrawn.

1918 Armenia becomes an independent state.

1919 Britain recognizes the independence of Afghanistan.

1919 Japan acquires from Germany Qingdao in China and the Marshall, Mariana, and Caroline islands in the Pacific.

1919 British troops kill hundreds of Indian protestors at Amritsar.

► **East Africa campaign** Fighting in East Africa during World War 1 was protracted due to the military genius of the German commander, Paul von Lettow-Vorbeck. After the capture of the Tanganyika Central Railway in 1916 by General Smuts, commander of the British forces in East Africa, Lettow-Vorbeck moved his troops south. Despite drastically outnumbered forces, he invaded Portuguese East Africa and N Rhodesia. He fought on until the Armistice, finally surrendering at Abercorn (present-day Mbala, Zambia) on 25 November 1918.

AFRICA

1916 Boer forces under Jan Smuts (1870–1950) win control of Tanganyika (present-day Tanzania).

1916 Zauditu becomes Empress of Ethiopia with Ras Tafari Makonnen (1892–1975) as regent.

1916 South African and Portuguese troops capture Dar es Salaam, Tanganyika.

1917 Germans invade Portuguese East Africa.

1918 Germans invade Rhodesia.

1919 Belgium acquires Rwanda and Burundi from Germany.

1919 Britain gains Tanganyika from Germany and also shares Cameroon and Togo with France.

1919 South Africa gains a mandate over German Southwest Africa.

1919 International agreement limits the sale of alcohol and arms in Africa.

1919 French create the colony of Upper Volta (present-day Burkina Faso).

EUROPE

1916 Romania declares war on Austria; German and Austrian forces invade and occupy Bucharest.

1916 Germany and Austria proclaim an independent Poland.

1916 Russian mystic Rasputin (b.1872) murdered.

1916 Easter Rising by Irish nationalists in Dublin crushed by British troops.

1916 Austrian Emperor dies and martial law is declared.

1916 David Lloyd George (1863–1945) becomes Prime Mnister of Britain.

1916 Germans capture some of the French fortresses protecting Verdun; British offensive at the Battle of the Somme gains little ground at appalling cost; French recapture the Verdun forts; General Paul von Hindenburg (1847–1934) takes overall control of German forces.

1916 British and German fleets fight the inconclusive Battle of Jutland in the North Sea.

1916 German aircraft bomb London.

1916 Russian Brusilov offensives gain little territory in central Poland and huge casualties severely affect morale.

1917 Germans withdraw to the Hindenburg Line; Canadian troops take Vimy Ridge during the Battle of Arras; French capture the Chemin des Dames in the third Battle of Champagne; British take Messines Ridge but fail to make progress in the third Battle of Ypres (Passchendale); US troops under General John Pershing (1860–1948) arrive in France; Austrians and Germans defeat the Italians at the Battles of the Caporetto.

1917 Germans capture Riga, Lithuania.

1917 Italy declares a protectorate over Albania.

1917 Germans declare unlimited submarine warfare.

1917 February Revolution forces Russian Tsar Nicholas II to abdicate; a provisional government shares power with the Petrograd Soviet of Workers and Soldiers; Germans allow Vladimir Ilyich Lenin (1870–1924) to return from Switzerland in a sealed train; Alexander Kerensky (1881–1970) becomes prime minister and declares a republic; Bolsheviks establish a politburo which includes Lenin, Leon Trotsky (1879–1940), and Joseph Stalin (1879–1953); Bolsheviks overthrow Kerensky in the October Revolution; Congress of Soviets establishes a ruling Council of People's Commissars, takes Russia out of World War 1, and confiscates the estates of large landowners; a constituent assembly is elected.

1917 Ukraine, Estonia, and Moldavia declare independence from Russia.

1917 Finns under General Carl von Mannerheim (1867–1951) begin a war of independence against Russia.

1918 Ukraine makes a separate peace with Austria and Germany.

1918 By the Treaty of Brest-Litovsk, Russia recognizes Finland, Latvia, Lithuania, Estonia, and Ukraine as independent states.

1918 'White' Russia declares independence and civil war breaks out; British, French and US troops land at Russian ports in support of the Whites.

1918 Bolsheviks order the Red Army to dissolve the constituent assembly; communist Central Committee given supreme power; Russian Socialist Federative Soviet Republic formed; Moscow becomes the capital; Tsar Nicholas II and his family executed.

1918 Women get the vote in Britain.

1918 German offensive breaks through British and French lines at the second Battle of the Somme and advances on Paris; Ferdinand Foch (1851–1929) becomes French commander; French and US troops halt the Germans at Chateau Thierry and the second Battle of the Marne; allied counter-attacks force the Germans to retreat into Belgium; Italians rout the Austrians at the Battle of Vittorio Veneto.

1918 German fleet at Kiel mutinies; revolutions occur in Munich and Berlin; Emperor William II (1859–1941) goes into exile; a German republic is proclaimed.

1918 Revolution in Vienna dissolves the Austrian monarchy and dismantles the Austro-Hungarian Empire.

1918 Czechoslovakia and Hungary proclaim independence; independent Kingdom of the Serbs, Croats and Slovenes (later named Yugoslavia) established.

1918 Latvia and Lithuania declare independence from Russia.

1918 Armistice stops the fighting on the Western Front.

1919 Allied troops withdraw from Russia; Red armies, under minister of war Leon Trotsky, defeat the Whites.

1919 Independent Polish republic declared, linked to the free city of Danzig by a corridor of territory.

THE AMERICAS

1916 Denmark sells the Virgin Islands to the USA.

1916 Mexican revolutionary Francisco ('Pancho') Villa (1877–1923) raids New Mexico; the USA sends a punitive expedition.

1916 US troops land in Cuba to suppress a liberal revolution.

1916 USA occupies the Dominican Republic and takes over the government.

1917 USA declares war on Germany and Austria.

1918 US President Woodrow Wilson (1856–1924) proposes 14 points for a peace agreement.

1919 Volstead Act passed in the USA, prohibiting the sale and distribution of alcohol.

1919 Murder of Mexican peasant revolutionary Emiliano Zapata (b.1880).

"The Tsar is not treacherous but he is weak. Weakness is not treachery, but it fulfils all its functions."

German emperor William II, referring to Tsar Nicholas II

SCIENCE AND TECHNOLOGY

1916 The British Army use the newly invented tank at the Battle of the Somme.

1916 German scientists develop mustard gas as a weapon.

1917 French scientist Felix d'Herelle (1873–1949) discovers bacteriophages.

1918 US astronomer Harlow Shapley (1885–1972) estimates the size and shape of our galaxy.

1919 British physicist Ernest Rutherford (1871–1937) transmutes one element into another.

1919 British physicist Arthur Eddington (1882–1944) observes the gravitational bending of light predicted by Einstein's theories.

1919 Austrian zoologist Karl von Frisch (1886–1982) discovers the communication dance of honeybees.

1919 British aviators John Alcock (1892–1919) and Arthur Brown (1886–1948) fly non-stop across the Atlantic Ocean from Newfoundland to Ireland

The Mark IV tank *was first used by the British in World War 1. Its shape was largely dictated by conflicting requirements: it had to cross wide trenches and also be transported to the front on narrow railway wagons. Mark IV tanks were first used in the Battle of Cambrai, France (20 November 1917), to break through German defences.*

ARTS AND HUMANITIES

1916 British poet Edith Sitwell (1887–1964) publishes her experimental anthology *Wheels*.

1916 Mexican artist José Orozco (1883–1949) completes his wash drawings *Mexico in Revolution*.

1916 French artist Claude Monet (1840–1926) paints *Water Lilies* murals at the specially constructed Musée d'orangerie in Paris.

1916 US artist Naum Gabo (1890–1977) creates his sculpture *Head No. 2*.

1916 Spanish dramatist Jacinto Benavente y Martínez (1866–1954) writes his play *La cuidad alegre y confiada*.

1917 French poet Paul Valéry (1871–1945) publishes *The Young Fate*.

1917 US novelist Upton Sinclair (1878–1968) publishes *King Coal*.

1917 British author P.G. Wodehouse (1881–1975) publishes the first of his stories about Jeeves and Wooster.

1918 British writer Lytton Strachey (1880–1932) publishes his biographies of *Eminent Victorians*.

1918 British artist Paul Nash (1889–1946) paints *We are Making a New World*.

1918 Swiss artist Paul Klee (1879–1940) paints *Zoological Garden*.

1918 Italian dramatist Luigi Pirandello (1867–1936) writes his play *Six Characters in Search of an Author*.

1918 Russian composer Sergei Prokofiev (1891–1953) writes his Symphony No.1 in D major, known as the "Classical".

1918 US poet Carl Sandberg (1878–1967) publishes *Cornhuskers*.

1918 German historian Oswald Spengler (1880–1936) publishes volume 1 of *The Decline of the West*.

1918 Collected works of British poet Gerard Manley Hopkins (1844–89) are published posthumously.

1919 Swiss theologian Karl Barth (1886–1968) publishes *The Epistle to the Romans*.

1919 German architect and designer Walter Gropius (1883–1969) founds the Bauhaus school of design, building and crafts in Weimar, Germany.

1919 US poet Amy Lowell (1872–1925) publishes *Pictures of the Floating World*.

1919 US author Sherwood Anderson (1876–1941) publishes his collection of stories *Winesburg, Ohio*.

KEY
- Russian empire 1914
- Germany 1914
- Austro-Hungarian empire 1914
- Ottoman empire 1914
- boundaries 1920
- French mandate 1920
- British mandate 1920
- Emirate under British suzerainty 1923
- Serb-Croat-Slovene kingdom created 1918

Peace of Paris *At the Paris Peace Conference of 1919, the five leading victorious powers of World War 1 drew up a peace plan and established new national boundaries. New East European states emerged from the wreckage of the German, Austro-Hungarian and Russian empires. Although these states were founded on the basis of national self-determination, they also included alien minorities, such as the Germans in Czechoslovakia. Britain and France divided the former Ottoman Middle East between them. Both faced rising Arab nationalism and, in Britain's case, increasing Arab-Zionist conflict in Palestine. In the Ottoman empire nationalists formally established the Republic of Turkey in 1923.*

ASIA AND AUSTRALASIA

▲ **Mao Zedong** was a founder of the Chinese Communist Party in 1921. He soon became one of the foremost leaders in the world communist movement. Mao believed that the path to power lay through the mobilization of the peasantry.

1920

1920 France acquires a mandate over Syria and Lebanon.

1920 Britain acquires a mandate over Palestine and Mesopotamia, renaming the latter Iraq.

1921 Faisal I (1885–1933) proclaimed King of Iraq.

1921 Sun Yat-sen (1866–1925) elected President of China.

1921 Cossack officer Reza Pahlavi (1878–1944) stages a coup in Iran and becomes minister of war.

1922 Sultanate abolished in Turkey.

1922 Kurds in Iraq begin an armed campaign for independence.

1922 Mohandas Gandhi (1869–1948) arrested in India for civil disobedience.

1923 Treaty of Lausanne confirms the dismemberment of the Ottoman Empire and provides for compulsory population exchanges between Greece and Turkey.

1923 Mustafa Kemal (1881–1938) elected President of Turkey; Ankara becomes the capital.

1923 Earthquake devastates Yokohama and Tokyo, Japan.

1923 Transjordan separated from Palestine.

1924 Chinese communists admitted to the Kuomintang.

1924 Abdul Aziz ibn Saud (1880–1953) captures Mecca and Medina from Hussein (1856–1931), Sharif of Mecca.

1924 Mongol People's Republic declared a satellite of the Soviet Union.

1925 Chiang Kai-shek (1887–1975) becomes head of the Kuomintang nationalist government in China.

1925 Reza Pahlavi (1878–1944) becomes Shah of Iran.

1925–27 Druze rebel against French control in Lebanon and Syria.

1926 Nationalists begin military campaigns to regain control of central and N China.

1926 Abdul Aziz ibn Saud (1880–1953) proclaimed King of Hejaz and Nejd in Arabia.

1926 Communist-inspired revolt breaks out in the Dutch East Indies.

1926 Lebanon established as an independent republic.

1927 Communists liquidated from the Kuomintang, which establishes a new government in Nanjing.

1927 Britain recognizes the independence of Iraq.

1928 Transjordan becomes self-governing under Emir Abdullah ibn Hussein (1882–1951).

1928 Chiang Kai-shek captures Beijing and reunites China under nationalist rule.

1928 Mao Zedong (1893–1976) creates the Chinese communist Red Army in Hunan province.

1928 Hirohito (1901–89) crowned Emperor of Japan.

1929 Fighting breaks out between the Chinese and the Russians along the Manchurian border.

1929 Arabs attack Jewish settlements near Jerusalem.

AFRICA

1920 Britain annexes Kenya.

1921 Spanish defeated by the peoples of the Rif at the Battle of Anual in Morocco.

1921 Mauritania and Niger become French colonies.

1922 Egypt becomes a self-governing monarchy, the Sultan becomes King Fuad I (1868–1936).

1922 Italy starts the conquest of S Libya.

1923 Southern Rhodesia becomes a British colony.

1924 Slavery abolished in Ethiopia.

1924 Rif uprising revived against Spanish expansion in N Morocco.

1926 International convention gives the League of Nations responsibility for the suppression of slavery.

1926 French and Spanish troops defeat the rebels in N Morocco.

1928 Ethiopian regent Ras Tafari Makonnen (1892–1975) assumes the title 'Negus'.

> "Fascism is a religion; the 20th century will be known in history as the century of Fascism."
>
> *Benito Mussolini*

EUROPE

1919 Warfare breaks out in Ireland between nationalists and British forces.

1919 Radical Spartacists revolt in Berlin and Rosa Luxemburg (b.1871) shot and killed; republics declared in Bavaria and Rhineland; Weimar constitution adopted; German national assembly elects Friedrich Ebert (1871–1925) as President.

1919 Peace conference in Paris limits the future size of European armies and establishes the League of Nations.

1919 Under the Treaty of Versailles, Germany agrees to cede territory overseas and in Europe, accept war guilt, and pay huge financial reparations.

1919 Benito Mussolini (1883–1945) forms fascist street-fighting gangs in Milan.

1919 Italian nationalist poet Gabriel D'Annunzio (1863–1938) seizes Fiume in Yugoslavia.

1920 Defeated White Russians withdraw from Crimea; end of the Russian civil war.

1920 League of Nations comes into existence.

1920 Poland, in alliance with Ukraine, invades S Russia and defeats a Russian counter-attack outside Warsaw.

1920 Greece declares war on Turkey.

1921 Vladimir Ilyich Lenin (1870–1924) introduces the New Economic Policy in Russia.

1921 Peace of Riga fixes the Polish-Russian border.

1921 Adolf Hitler (1889–1945) becomes chairman of the National Socialist German Workers (Nazi) party.

1922 Ireland partitioned; an independent Irish Free State is proclaimed; civil war breaks out.

1922 Italian fascists march on Rome; Benito Mussolini asked to form a government.

1921 Hyperinflation begins in Germany.

1922 Union of Soviet Socialist Republics (USSR or Soviet Union) formally established, joining Russia and Ukraine.

1923 French and Belgian troops occupy Germany's Ruhr region.

1923 Nationalist and socialist risings take place in Germany, including Hitler's attempted putsch in Munich; martial law declared and the currency stabilized.

1923 General Primo de Rivera (1870–1930) becomes dictator in Spain.

1923 Alexander Zankoff seizes power in Bulgaria following a military coup.

1924 Joseph Stalin (1879–1953) takes control of the Soviet Union on Lenin's death.

1924 Albania and Greece become republics.

1925 At a conference in Locarno, France, Belgium and Germany sign treaties guaranteeing their mutual borders; France also signs treaties with Poland and Czechoslovakia.

1925 Paul von Hindenburg (1847–1934) elected President of Germany.

1925 President Ahmed Zogu (1895–1961) of Albania declares himself King Zog.

1925 Joseph Stalin removes Leon Trotsky from power in Russia.

1926 Josef Pilsudski (1867–1935) seizes power in Poland.

1926 Military coup overthrows the Portuguese government.

1926 Antanas Smetona (1874–1944) seizes power and makes himself dictator in Lithuania.

1926 General strike afflicts British industry.

1926 Italy establishes a virtual protectorate over Albania.

1928 Kellogg-Briand Pact outlaws war and proposes international arbitration in cases of dispute.

1928 Stalin ends the New Economic Policy in Russia and introduces the first five-year plan.

1929 Lateran treaties between Italy and the papacy normalize relations and create Vatican City as an independent state.

1929 Alexander I (1888–1934) declares his royal dictatorship over the country he officially renames Yugoslavia.

1929 Trotsky forced into exile from Russia.

THE AMERICAS

1920 Transcontinental air-mail service begins in the USA.

1920 Women get the right to vote in the USA.

1920 US government refuses to join the League of Nations.

1920 Warren Harding (1865–1923) elected US president.

1921 Washington conference limits the size of Pacific fleets and affirms the independence of China.

1921–22 Costa Rica, Guatemala, Honduras and El Salvador form the short-lived Federation of Central America.

1922 USA restores self-government to the Dominican Republic.

1923 Calvin Coolidge (1872–1933) becomes President of the United States on the death of Warren Harding.

1924 US politician Charles Dawes (1865–1961) chairs a committee that devises a plan to collect German reparations.

1924 Coolidge elected President of the United States.

1925 US aviator Charles Lindbergh (1902–74) flies solo non-stop from New York to Paris.

1925 Scopes trial confirms the ban on the teaching of evolution in some US schools.

1928 US secretary of state Frank Kellogg (1856–1937) proposes the international renunciation of war.

1928 Herbert Hoover (1874–1964) elected President of the United States.

1929 New York Stock Exchange slumps in the Wall Street Crash and causes financial collapse and economic depression around the world.

1929 US troops occupy Haiti to restore order after political unrest.

SCIENCE AND TECHNOLOGY

▶ **art deco** *A fashionable style of design and interior decoration in the 1920s and 1930s, art deco is characterized by sleek forms, simplified lines and geometric patterns.*

1920 US astronomer Edwin Hubble (1889–1953) discovers that the universe is expanding.

1920 Radio broadcasting begins in Pittsburgh, USA.

1920 US engineer John Thompson (1860–1940) designs a sub-machine gun.

1921 US scientist Albert Hull (1880–1966) invents the magnetron microwave-generating valve.

1921 US engineer Thomas Midgley (1889–1944) discovers the anti-knock properties of tetraethyl lead.

1921 Canadian phsyician Frederick Banting (1891–1941) isolates the hormone insulin.

1922 German engineer Herbert Kalmus invents Technicolour movie film.

1923 Spanish engineer Juan de le Cierva (1896–1936) invents the autogyro.

1924 French physicist Louis Victor de Broglie (1892–1987) proposes that electrons should sometimes behave as waves.

1924 South African anthropologist Raymond Dart (1893–1988) discovers the fossil remains of *Australopithecus.*

1924 US industrialist Clarence Birdseye (1886–1956) puts quick-frozen fish on sale.

1925 US physicist Wolfgang Pauli (1900–1958) formulates his exclusion principle.

1925 Austrian physicist Edwin Schrödinger (1887–1961) establishes the study of quantum wave mechanics.

1925 British physicist Paul Dirac (1902–84) independently formulates wave mechanics.

1926 Scottish engineer John Logie Baird (1888–1946) demonstrates television in London.

1926 US engineer Robert Goddard (1882–1945) launches the first liquid-fuelled rocket.

1926 US aviator Richard Byrd (1888–1957) flies across the North Polo.

1927 French astrophysicist Georges Lemaître (1894–1966) formulates the Big Bang theory of the origin of the universe.

1927 German physicist Werner Heisenberg (1901–76) formulates his 'uncertainty principle'.

1927 German geneticist Hermann Muller (1890–1967) induces mutations in fruit flies with X-rays.

1927 Release of the first talking motion picture, *The Jazz Singer.*

1928 US engineer Vladimir Zworykin (1889–1982) patents a colour television system.

1928 German physicist Hans Geiger (1882–1945) produces an improved version of his radiation counter.

1928 Scottish bacteriologist Alexander Fleming (1881–1955) discovers the antibiotic properties of the penicillin mould.

ARTS AND HUMANITIES

1920 US author Sinclair Lewis (1885–1951) publishes his novel *Main Street.*

1921 German artist Max Ernst (1891–1976) paints *The Elephant Celebes.*

1921 French artist Georges Braque (1882–1963) paints *Still Life with Guitar.*

1921 US novelist John Dos Passos (1896–1970) publishes *Three Soldiers.*

1922 German poet Rainer Maria Rilke (1875–1926) publishes his *Sonnets to Orpheus.*

1922 German philosopher Ludwig Wittgenstein (1889–1951) publishes *Tractatus Logico-Philosophicus.*

1922 US photographer Man Ray (1890–1976) publishes *Delightful Fields,* an album of Rayographs.

1922 British archaeologist Howard Carter (1874–1939) discovers the tomb of Tutankhamun.

1922 British poet and critic T.S. Eliot (1888–1965) publishes his poem *The Waste Land.*

1922 Irish author James Joyce (1882–1941) publishes the novel *Ulysses.*

1923 Spanish artist Jean Miró (1893–1983) paints *Catalan Landscape.*

1923 British writer Walter De la Mare (1873–1956) publishes his poetry anthology *Come Hither.*

1924 US composer George Gershwin (1898–1937) writes *Rhapsody in Blue.*

1924 French poet André Breton (1896–1966) writes the *Manifesto of Surrealism.*

1924 German artist Otto Dix (1891–1969) publishes his satirical etchings *The War.*

1924 Mexican artist Diego Rivera (1886–1957) paints murals for the Ministry of Education in Mexico City.

1925 Austrian composer Alban Berg (1885–1935) writes his opera *Wozzeck.*

1925 Adolf Hitler (1889–1945) publishes the first volume of *Mein Kampf.*

1925 Russian film director Sergei Eisenstein (1898–1948) releases *Bronenosets Potyomkin* (*Battleship Potemkin*).

1925 US author F. Scott Fitzgerald (1886–1940) publishes his novel *The Great Gatsby.*

1925 *Exposition des Arts Décoratifs* in Paris popularizes the Art Deco style.

1925 US author Theodore Dreiser (1871–1945) publishes his novel *An American Tragedy.*

1925 *The Trial* by German novelist Franz Kafka (1883–1924) published posthumously.

1925 Russian composer Dmitri Shostakovich (1906–75) writes his Symphony No.1 in F minor.

1926 Irish dramatist Sean O'Casey (1880–1964) writes *The Plough and the Stars.*

1927 German philosopher Martin Heidegger (1889–1976) publishes *Being and Time.*

1927 British writer Virginia Woolf (1882–1841) publishes *To The Lighthouse.*

1928 French composer Maurice Ravel (1875–1937) writes *Bolero.*

1928 British writer Siegfried Sassoon (1886–1967) publishes his novel *Memoirs of a Fox-hunting Man.*

ASIA AND AUSTRALASIA

1930

1930 Kurdish rising erupts on the Turkey-Iran border.

1930 Mohandas Gandhi (1869–1948) organizes and leads the salt march in India and is arrested and imprisoned.

1930 Three-way civil war breaks out in China.

1930 Vietnamese reformer Ho Chi Minh (1880–1969) founds the Indochinese communist party.

1931 Japanese invade Manchuria.

1932 Military coup introduces representative government in Thailand.

1932 Sydney Harbour Bridge opens.

1932 Indian National Congress banned by the British.

1932 Kingdom of Saudi Arabia formally established.

1932 Japanese declare Manchuria the independent state of Manchukuo.

1934 Saudi capture of Hodeida ends border war with Yemen.

1934 Turkish President Mustafa Kemal (1881–1938) introduces the use of surnames and himself adopts the surname Atatürk, meaning 'father of the Turks'.

1934 Chinese communist Red Army begins the Long March to evade nationalist forces.

1934 Former Emperor of China, Henry Pu Yi (1906–67), becomes Japanese puppet Emperor of Manchukuo.

1935 New constitution establishes the Philippine Commonwealth as a semi-independent state.

1935 Britain separates Burma and Aden from India and introduces a central legislature in Delhi.

1936 Jawaharlal Nehru (1889–1964) elected leader of the Indian National Congress.

1936 Britain sends reinforcements to Palestine to impose order on warring Jews and Arabs.

1937 Japanese forces invade NE China and capture Beijing, Shanghai, and Nanjing; nationalist and communist Chinese leaders agree on joint defence.

1939 Baron Kiichura Hiranuma (1887–1952) becomes Prime Minister of Japan.

1939 Faisal II (1935–58) crowned King of Iraq, at age four.

1939 Soviet and Mongolian troops defeat the Japanese at the Battle of Nomonhan.

1939 Turkey allies with France and Britain.

AFRICA

1930 Ras Tafari Makonnen (1892–1975) proclaims himself Emperor Haile Selassie of Ethiopia.

1932 French complete their conquest of S Morocco.

1934 Italian and Ethiopian troops clash near Ethiopia's border with Italian Somaliland.

1935 Benito Mussolini (1883–1945) formally creates the Italian colony of Libya.

1935 Italy invades Ethiopia and captures the regional capital of Makale.

1936 Egypt gains independence from Britain under King Farouk I (1920–65).

1936 Italians capture Addis Ababa and annex Ethiopia.

1937 French suppress a nationalist uprising in Morocco.

> "I have found it impossible to carry the heavy burden of responsibility and to discharge my duties as King as I would wish to do without the help and support of the woman I love."
>
> *Edward VIII*
> *(abdication speech)*

coelacanth The coelacanth was thought to have become extinct 60 million years ago until its discovery in deep waters off the African coast in 1938. Its scales and bony plates are unlike those of modern fish.

EUROPE

1930 London naval treaty limits the size of fleets.

1930 King Carol II (1893–1953) returns to Romania and resumes the throne.

1930 Joseph Stalin (1879–1953) introduces the forced collectivization of farms in Russia.

1930 France starts to build the Maginot line of defences against Germany.

1931 British Commonwealth of Nations established.

1931 King Alfonso XIII (1886–1941) flees Spain; a republic is declared.

1931 Bank failure in Austria starts a financial collapse in central Europe.

1932 Eamon De Valera (1882–1975) becomes prime minister of the Irish Free State.

1932 António Salazar (1889–1970) becomes Prime Minister of Portugal and introduces a new fascist-style constitution.

1932 Catalonia receives a degree of autonomy from Spain.

1933 Adolf Hitler (1889–1945) elected Chancellor of Germany; after the Reichstag fire, he assumes emergency powers and declares the Third Reich.

1933 Austrian Chancellor Engelbert Dollfuss (1892–1934) makes himself dictator.

1933 Nazis establish a concentration camp at Dachau.

1934 Dictatorships established in Estonia and Latvia.

1934 Hitler purges the Nazi party in the 'Night of the Long Knives' and declares himself Führer of Germany.

1934 Dollfuss murdered during an attempted Nazi coup.

1934 Fascist coup takes power in Bulgaria.

1935 Greek monarchy restored under King George II (1890–1947).

1935 Saarland region returned to Germany after a plebiscite.

1935 New constitution ends democratic government in Poland.

1935 Anti-Jewish Nuremberg laws passed in Germany.

1935 Germany denounces the disarmament clauses of the Versailles treaty.

1936 Popular Front under Leon Blum (1872–1950) forms a government in France.

1936 General Joannis Metaxas (1871–1941) becomes dictator in Greece.

1936 German troops occupy the demilitarized Rhineland.

1936 General Franciso Franco (1892–1975) leads a nationalist uprising in Spanish Morocco; he invades Spain and is proclaimed head of state; start of the Spanish Civil War.

1936 Germany and Italy form the Rome-Berlin Axis alliance.

1936 Edward VIII (1894–1972) becomes King of Britain. He is forced to abdicate and George VI (1895–1952) becomes king.

1937 Italian troops and German aircraft provide military aid to the nationalists in Spain.

1937 Joseph Stalin begins to purge the Soviet armed forces; many officers are executed.

1937 Irish Free State formally becomes Eire.

1938 German troops occupy Austria; Adolf Hitler announces the Anschluss (union) of the two countries.

1938 British Prime Minister Neville Chamberlain (1869–1940) meets with Hitler to discuss German demands on Czechoslovakia.

1938 Conference of European leaders at Munich decides to appease German ambitions and to permit the annexation of the Sudetenland region of Czechoslovakia; Poland and Hungary also gain areas of Czech territory.

1938 Jewish shops and businesses are smashed during *Kristallnacht* in Germany.

1939 Nazi-Soviet Pact secretly agrees to partition Poland.

1939 Germany occupies the remainder of Czechoslovakia, annexes Memel in Lithuania and demands Danzig from Poland.

1939 Italy invades Albania.

THE AMERICAS

1930 Rafael Trujillo (1891–1961) makes himself President of the Dominican Republic

1930 Army coup brings Getulio Vargas (1883–1954) to power as President of Brazil.

1931 US gangster Al Capone (1899–1947) jailed for tax evasion.

1932 Bolivia and Paraguay go to war over control of the Chaco region.

1932 Franklin Roosevelt (1884–1945) elected US president.

1933 US government introduces New Deal legislation to promote recovery from economic depression; Federal Emergency Relief Act establishes the Public Works Administration; National Industrial Recovery Act establishes the National Recovery Administration; Tennessee Valley Authority is formed.

1933 Fulgencio Batista (1901–73) leads a military coup in Cuba.

1934 Drought and bad farming techniques combine to form the 'Dust Bowl' in the US Midwest.

1934 US troops withdraw from Haiti.

1935 Chaco War ends with Paraguay gaining most of the disputed territory; Bolivia gains access to the sea.

1936 Fascist seize power in coup in Paraguay.

1936 Anastasio Somoza (1896–1956) makes himself dictator in Nicaragua

1938 Mexico nationalizes US and British oil companies.

1939 German warship *Graf Spee* scuttled after the Battle of the River Plate.

> "I pledge you – I pledge myself – to a new deal for the American people."
>
> *Franklin D. Roosevelt*

Spanish Civil War 1936–39

Nationalist gains by:
- September 1936
- March 1937
- October 1937
- July 1938
- February 1939

- Republican-controlled area February 1939
- ■ Nationalist stronghold
- ■ Republican stronghold
- ✛ Nationalist airfield
- ✛ Republican airfield
- — Front April 1937

SCIENCE AND TECHNOLOGY

1930 US astronomer Clyde Tombaugh (1906–97) discovers the planet Pluto.

1930 Invention of acrylic plastics Perspex and Lucite.

1930 US engineer Eugene Houdry (1892–1962) invents the catalytic process of cracking crude oil.

1931 US physicist Ernest Lawrence (1901-58) invents the cyclotron particle accelerator.

1931 US physicist Robert Van de Graaff (1901–67) invents a high-voltage electrostatic generator.

1931 US mathematician Kurt Gödel (1906–78) publishes his proof that any system based on the laws of arithmetic must contain inaccuracies.

1931 Empire State Building opens in New York.

1932 Swiss physicist Auguste Piccard (1884–1962) and an assistant ascend into the stratosphere in a balloon.

1932 US physicist Carl Anderson (1905–91) discovers positrons.

1932 US engineer Karl Jansky (1905–50) detects cosmic radio waves.

1932 US physicist Edwin Land (1909–91) invents polarized glass.

1932 German chemist Gerhard Domagk (1895–1964) discovers the first of the sulpha drugs

1932 British physicist James Chadwick (1891–1974) discovers the neutron.

1932 Dutch complete the drainage of the Zuider Zee.

1933 US engineer Edwin Armstrong (1890–1954) invents FM radio transmission.

1935 British engineer Robert Watson-Watt (1892–1973) builds a radar system to detect aircraft.

1935 Development of fluorescent lighting and sodium vapour lamps.

1935 US geologist Charles Richter (1900–85) devises a scale to measure the intensity of earthquakes.

1936 British mathematician Alan Turing (1912–54) develops the mathematical theory of computing.

1937 British engineer Frank Whittle (1907–96) builds a prototype jet engine.

1937 Nylon, invented by US chemist Wallace Carothers (1896–1937), is patented.

1938 Hungarian engineer Ladislao Biró (1899–1985) invents a ballpoint pen.

1938 US physicist Chester Carlson (1906–68) invents a process for photocopying documents.

1938 Coelacanth 'living fossil' fish caught in the Indian Ocean.

1939 German chemist Otto Hahn (1879–1968) discovers atomic fission.

1939 Helicopter designed by US engineer Igor Sikorsky (1889–1972) goes into production.

1939 Swiss scientist Paul Müller (1899–1965) synthesizes DDT as an insecticide.

1939 British engineers John Randall (1905–84) and Henry Boot (1917–83) invent the cavity magnetron.

◀ *Spanish Civil War* By November 1936, Franco's forces had laid siege to Madrid. In 1937 they took the Basque n provinces, and by the end of 1938 Republican forces were confined to Catalonia and Madrid.

ARTS AND HUMANITIES

1929 US author Ernest Hemingway (1898–1961) publishes *A Farewell to Arms*.

1929 Spanish philosopher José Ortega y Gasset (1883–1955) publishes *The Revolt of the Masses*.

1929 French artist and writer Jean Cocteau (1892–) publishes his novel *Les Enfants terribles*.

1929 German novelist Erich Remarque (1898–11970) publishes *All Quiet on the Western Front*.

1930 Belgian artist René Magritte (1898–1967) paints *The Key of Dreams*.

1930 British dramatist and composer Noel Coward (1899–1973) writes his play *Private Lives*.

1930 *All Quiet on the Western Front* wins best picture Oscar.

1930 US poet Hart Crane (1899–1932) publishes *The Bridge*.

1931 French novelist Antoine de Saint-Exupéry (1900–44) publishes *Night Flight*.

1931 US dramatist Eugene O'Neill (1888–1953) writes *Mourning Becomes Electra*.

1931 British composer William Walton (1902–83) writes his oratorio *Belshazzar's Feast*.

1931 Spanish artist Salvador Dali (1904–89) paints *The Persistence of Memory*.

1931 French artist Raoul Dufy (1877–1953) paints *Riders in the Wood*.

1932 British novelist Aldous Huxley (1894–1963) publishes *Brave New World*.

1933 French novelist André Malraux (1901–76) writes *La condition humaine*.

1933 Spanish poet and dramatist Federico García Lorca (1898–1936) writes his play *Blood Wedding*.

1933 US author Gertrude Stein (1874–1946) publishes *The Autobiography of Alice B. Toklas*.

1934 US composer Cole Porter (1891–1964) writes his musical *Anything Goes*.

1934 British poet and author Robert Graves (1895–1985) publishes the novel *I, Claudius*.

1934 US writer Henry Miller (1891–1980) publishes the novel *Tropic of Cancer*.

1934 Russian novelist Mikhail Sholokhov (1905–84) publishes *And Quiet Flows the Don*.

1935 T.S. Eliot writes his play *Murder in the Cathedral*.

1935 British artist Ben Nicholson (1894–1982) paints *White Relief*.

1936 British economist John Keynes (1883–1946) publishes his *General Theory of Employment, Interest and Money*.

1936 Dutch artist Piet Mondrian (1872–1944) paints his *Composition in Red and Blue*.

1936 US novelist William Faulkner (1897–1962) publishes *Absalom, Absalom!*.

1937 US sociologist Talcott Parsons (1902–79) publishes *The Structure of Social Action*.

1937 Spanish artist Pablo Picasso (1881–1973) paints *Guernica* in protest at the German air-raid on the town in N Spain.

1938 British author Graham Greene (1904–91) publishes the novel *Brighton Rock*.

1938 US actor Orson Welles (1915–85) panics radio audiences with his performance of *War of the Worlds*.

1939 US author John Steinbeck (1902–68) publishes his novel *The Grapes of Wrath*.

1939 Irish author James Joyce (1882–1941) publishes his novel *Finnegan's Wake*.

1939 US novelist Raymond Chandler (1888–1959) writes *The Big Sleep*.

1939 British author Christopher Isherwood (1904–86) publishes his short story *Goodbye to Berlin*.

1939 French philosopher and author Jean-Paul Sartre (1905–80) publishes his novel *Nausea*.

1939 US dramatist and author Lillian Hellman (1907–84) writes her play *Little Foxes*.

1939 *Gone with the Wind* wins ten Academy Awards, including best picture.

ASIA AND AUSTRALASIA

1940 Japan invades French Indochina and captures Saigon.

1941 British troops capture Damascus from Vichy French forces.

1941 British and Soviet troops occupy Tehran; Muhammad Reza Pahlavi (1919–80) succeeds his father as Shah of Iran.

1941 General Hideki Tojo (1885–1948) becomes Prime Minister of Japan.

1941 Japanese aircraft make a surprise attack on US ships in Pearl Harbor, Hawaii; Japanese troops capture Wake Island and Guam.

1941 Thailand allies with Japan and declares war on Britain and the USA.

1941 Japanese forces invade the Philippines.

1941 Hong Kong surrenders to the Japanese.

1942 Japanese take Kuala Lumpar in Malaya and invade Burma and Java; Singapore surrenders; British force the Japanese to retreat from NE India into Burma.

1942 US forces surrender at Bataan and Corregidor Fort in the Philippines; the Japanese take Manila.

1942 Allied victory in the naval Battle of the Coral Sea prevents the Japanese invasion of Australia.

1942 US fleet defeats the Japanese at the Battle of Midway Island.

1942 US aircraft make a bombing raid on Tokyo.

1942 US troops capture the Henderson Field airstrip on Guadalcanal Island.

1942 Japanese defeated by the nationalist Chinese at the Battle of Changsha.

1943 At a conference in Tehran, Britain and the USA agree with Russia to open a second front against Germany by invading W Europe.

1943 Syria and Lebanon gain independence from France.

1944 USA starts a large-scale bombing campaign against Japanese cities.

1944 US forces take the Marshall Islands, Guam and Saipan in the Marianas; landings at Leyte begin the recapture of the Philippines under General Douglas MacArthur (1880–1964).

1944 General Tojo resigns as prime minister of Japan.

AFRICA

1940 British troops repel an Italian invasion of Egypt and advance into Libya.

1940 Italians capture British Somaliland.

1940 British warships destroy part of the French fleet at the Algerian port of Oran.

1940 British and Free French forces attempt to capture Dakar in Senegal.

1941 British capture Torbruk and Benghazi, Libya, from the Italians; German General Erwin Rommel (1891–1944) takes command; German Afrika Korps besieges the British at Torbruk.

1941 Ethiopian troops capture the Italian stronghold of Burye.

1941 British forces capture Mogadishu, in Italian Somaliland, and occupy Addis Ababa, Ethiopia.

1942 German forces capture Torbruk; the British under General Bernard Montgomery (1887–1976) halt the German advance on Cairo at the Battle of El Alamein.

1942 US and British troops land in Morocco and Algeria.

1943 US troops retake the Kasserine Pass and join up with British troops in Tunisia; the German army in North Africa surrenders.

1944 France promises its African colonies independence after the war.

▼ **World War 2** By August 1942 Japan had seized a vast oceanic and continental empire, as illustrated on the map. It was not until early in 1944 that Allied sea power reversed these successes. While the Chinese nationalists and communists tied down large numbers of Japanese troops in a war of attrition and Allied supply lines were restored in Burma, American amphibious offensives in the Philippines and Gilbert Islands established bases from which air power could be brought to bear on Japan itself. In 1945, after atomic bombs had destroyed Hiroshima and Nagasaki, Japan agreed to an unconditional surrender.

EUROPE

1939 Nationalist forces capture Barcelona and Madrid, signalling the end of the Spanish Civil War.

1939 Hitler and Mussolini sign the 'pact of steel'.

1939 Germany invades Poland; Britain and France declare war; Russia invades Poland; the Poles surrender; Poland is partitioned; British troops are sent to France.

1939 German submarine sinks the British battleship *Royal Oak* in a Scottish harbour.

1939 Russian troops invade Finland and encounter strong resistance.

1940 Russians capture the Karelian isthmus; a treaty ends the Russo-Finnish War.

1940 German troops occupy Denmark and invade Norway; British and French troops land in Norway but then withdraw.

1940 Winston Churchill (1874–1965) becomes Prime Minister of Britain.

1940 Italy declares war on France and Britain.

1940 Germany conquers the Netherlands, Belgium and Luxembourg, and invades France; British troops evacuate from Dunkirk; the Germans take Paris; Marshal Henri Pétain (1856–1951) surrenders; France divided into occupied and unoccupied (Vichy) zones; Alsace and Lorraine become part of Germany; free Polish and French governments formed in exile in London.

1940 Germany commences a massive bombing campaign that leads to the Battle of Britain; the 'Blitz' against London begins.

1940 Ion Antonescu (1882–1946) becomes dictator in Romania.

1940 Estonia, Lithuania, and Latvia become part of the Soviet Union.

1940 British occupy Iceland.

1940 German submarines commence attacks on neutral shipping in British waters.

1940 Italy invades Greece but suffers defeat at the Battle of Koritza.

1941 Germans invade Yugoslavia and Greece; German paratroops take Crete and British forces are evacuated.

1941 In 'Operation Barbarossa', German troops invade the Soviet Union, capture Kiev, occupy Ukraine, besiege Leningrad, but fail to capture Moscow.

1941 German minister Rudolf Hess (1894–1987) lands in Scotland on a peace mission.

1941 Germany and Italy declare war on the USA.

1942 Nazi Wannsee conference decides upon the 'final solution'; Polish, Russian and French Jews are sent to death camps such as those at Bergen-Belsen, Auschwitz, and Treblinka.

1942 Vidkun Quisling (1887–1945) heads a collaborationist government in Norway.

1942 Nazi official Reinhard Heydrich (b.1904) assassinated by the Czech resistance; the village of Lidice is destroyed in reprisal.

1942 Germans take Sebastopol and surround Stalingrad.

1942 British and Canadian troops raid the French port of Dieppe.

1942 Josip Tito (1892–1980) organizes the Yugoslavian resistance and captures Bihacs.

1942 Germans occupy Vichy France; the French navy is scuttled at Toulon.

1943 Russian troops break the Siege of Leningrad; German General Friedrich von Paulus (1890–1957) surrenders at Stalingrad; the Russians win a tank battle at Kursk, retake Kiev, and occupy Romania and Bulgaria.

1943 Jews in the Warsaw ghetto attempt an uprising against the Germans.

1943 British bombers fly the 'dambusters' mission.

1943 US and British troops land in Sicily and occupy Messina; Benito Mussolini (1883–1945) is overthrown; Allied troops land at Salerno and take Naples; Italy surrenders; German troops occupy Rome; the German Gustav line halts the Allied advance in Italy.

1944 Allied troops land at Anzio, break through at Monte Cassino, and enter Rome.

1944 In 'Operation Overlord', Allied forces under General Dwight Eisenhower (1890–1969) invade Normandy, capture Cherbourg, and break through German lines near St Lo; Allied troops land in s France; Free French troops enter Paris; General Charles De Gaulle (1890–1970) heads a provisional government; British troops liberate Brussels.

1940

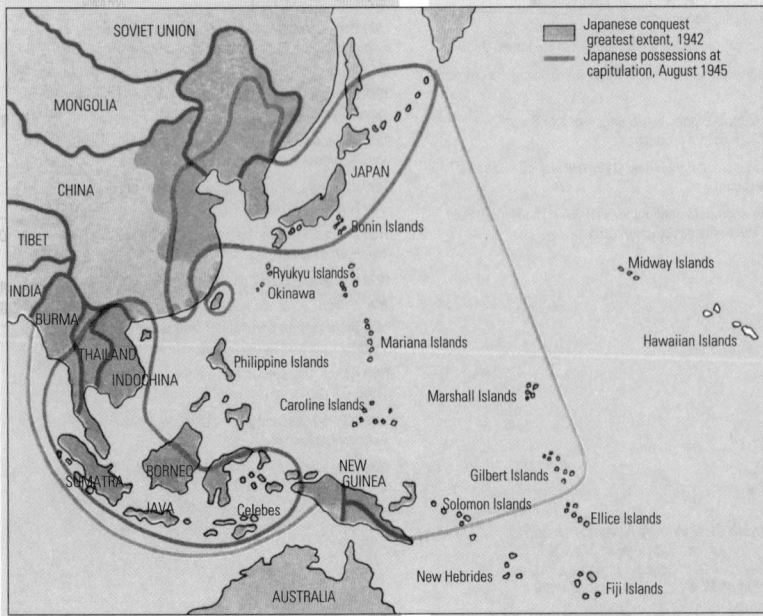

SOVIET UNION

MONGOLIA

CHINA

TIBET

INDIA

BURMA

THAILAND

INDOCHINA

SUMATRA

BORNEO

JAVA

Celebes

JAPAN

Bonin Islands

Ryukyu Islands

Okinawa

Philippine Islands

Caroline Islands

NEW GUINEA

AUSTRALIA

New Hebrides

Midway Islands

Mariana Islands

Hawaiian Islands

Marshall Islands

Gilbert Islands

Solomon Islands

Ellice Islands

Fiji Islands

> ☐ Japanese conquest greatest extent, 1942
> Japanese possessions at capitulation, August 1945

THE AMERICAS

1940 Leon Trotsky (b.1879) assassinated in Mexico City.

1940 Pan-American Conference adopts joint trusteeship of European colonies in the Western Hemisphere.

1941 US government passes the Lend-Lease Act enabling the supply of equipment to Britain.

1941 Franklin Roosevelt (1884–1945) and Winston Churchill (1874–1965) issue the Atlantic Charter setting out joint war aims.

1941 USA declares war on Japan after the attack on Pearl Harbor, Hawaii.

1941 Manhattan Project to build an atomic weapon starts in the USA.

1942 Inter-American conference at Rio de Janeiro agrees a joint position against Germany and Japan.

1942 Japan captures several of the Aleutian Islands.

1942 Japanese-Americans relocated away from the w coast of the USA.

1944 Conference at Bretton Woods, New Hampshire, agrees the postwar establishment of a World Bank and an International Monetary Fund (IMF).

1944 Conference at Dumbarton Oaks agrees the post-war foundation of the United Nations (UN) to replace the League of Nations.

1944 Roosevelt elected for a fourth term as US president.

German armed forces *Shown here, from left: a lance sergeant, senior private, and regimented sergeant major. World War 2 involved more than three quarters of the world's population, from a total of 61 countries, and was the most deadly conflict in human history. Technological developments led to a new kind of warfare. The battlefield consisted of entire countries, rather than specific areas, making the distinction between civilian and soldier less clear.*

SCIENCE AND TECHNOLOGY

1940 British scientist Hans Krebs (1900–81) discovers the citric-acid cycle.

1940 Canadian scientist James Hillier (1915–) invents an electron microscope.

1942 French divers Emile Gagnan and Jacques Cousteau (1910–97) devise the scuba aqualung.

1942 German Me-262 flies in combat as the first jet fighter.

1942 US physicist Enrico Fermi (1901–54) builds a nuclear reactor, based on a controlled chain reaction, in Chicago.

1942 Team led by German engineer Werner von Braun (1912–77) designs the A4 (V2) rocket.

1943 German scientist Albert Hoffman discovers the hallucinogenic drug LSD.

1943 Codebreakers at Bletchley Park, England, construct a programmable electronic computer.

1944 US scientist Oswald Avery (1877–1955) discovers that DNA is the agent of inheritance.

1944 US astronomer Walter Baade (1893–1960) classifies stars into young Population I and old Population II.

▲ **Fermi** *produced the first controlled, self-sustaining nuclear fission reaction – the key to a new and virtually inexhaustible source of energy. In 1942 he built the world's first nuclear reactor.*

ARTS AND HUMANITIES

1940 Russian artist Wassily Kandinsky (1866–1944) paints *Sky Blue*.

1940 US author Ernest Hemingway (1898–1961) publishes his novel *For Whom the Bell Tolls*.

1940 Japanese artist Yasuo Kuniyoshi (1893–1953) paints *Upside Down Table and Mask*.

1940 British author Graham Greene (1904–91) publishes his novel *The Power and the Glory*.

1941 Illinois Institute of Technology, designed by German architect Ludwig Mies van der Rohe (1886–1969), is completed.

1941 German poet and dramatist Berthold Brecht (1898–1956) writes his play *Mother Courage and Her Children*.

1941 US film director Orson Welles (1915–85) releases *Citizen Kane*.

1942 French writer Albert Camus (1913–60) publishes his novel *The Outsider*.

1942 French philosopher Maurice Merleau-Ponty (1908–61) publishes *The Structure of Behaviour*.

1942 US artist Edward Hopper (1882–1967) paints *Nighthawks*.

1942 French dramatist Jean Anouilh (1910–87) writes his play *Antigone*.

1943 British artist Barbara Hepworth (1903–75) creates the sculpture *Wave*.

1943 *Casablanca* wins the Academy Award for best picture.

1943 US composers Richard Rodgers (1902–79) and Oscar Hammerstein (1895–1963) write their musical *Oklahoma*.

1944 US dramatist Tennessee Williams (1911–83) writes his play *The Glass Menagerie*.

1944 US swing musician Glenn Miller (b.1904) is killed in an aircraft accident.

ASIA AND AUSTRALASIA

1945 Burma liberated from the Japanese.

1945 US forces capture the islands of Iwo Jima and Okinawa.

1945 USA drops atomic bombs on Hiroshima and Nagasaki; Japan surrenders; US occupation forces land and establish a military government.

1945 Ho Chi Minh (1880–1969) declares the independent republic of Vietnam.

1945 Cambodia declares its independence.

1945 Truce between nationalists and communists in China breaks down with fighting for control of Manchuria.

1945 Independent republics of Syria and Lebanon are established.

1945 Arab League founded.

1946 War crimes tribunal set up in Tokyo.

1946 Jewish *Irgun* terrorists blow up the King David Hotel in Jerusalem.

1946 Jordan becomes an independent kingdom.

1946 French bombard the port of Haiphong while suppressing Vietnamese rebels.

1946 The Philippines becomes an independent republic.

1946 USA tests atomic weapons at Bikini Atoll.

1947 Britain grants the status of independent dominions to India and Pakistan (E and W); millions die in factional fighting and there are massive population exchanges.

1947 New constitution proclaimed in Japan.

1948 Burma gaind independence from Britain.

1948 Ceylon (now Sri Lanka) becomes a self governing British Dominion.

1948 State of Israel established and attacked by the Egyptians and the Jordanian Arab Legion.

1949 Chiang Kai-shek (1887–1975) resigns as Chinese president following communist victories .

1949 Chinese nationalists evacuate to Formosa (now Taiwan); Mao Zedong (1893–1976) declares the People's Republic of China.

1949 Independent republics of North Korea, under President Kim II Sung (1912–94), and South Korea, under President Syngman Rhee (1875–1965), established.

1949 Indonesia gains independence under President Achmad Sukarno (1901–70).

1949 France grants independence to Vietnam but does not recognize Ho Chi Minh's regime.

1949 Warfare between India and Pakistan over disputed territory in Kashmir ended by a UN ceasefire.

1949 Israel and Egypt agree an armistice.

1949 Cambodia becomes independent under King Norodom Sihanouk (1922–).

1950

1950 India becomes a federal republic with Jawaharlal Nehru (1889–1964) as prime minister.

1950 Jordan annexes the West Bank and E Jerusalem.

1950 Soviet Union and China sign a treaty of alliance and co-operation.

1950 North Korean forces invade South Korea, marking the start of the Korean War; UN troops land at Inchon, liberate Seoul and invade North Korea; China sends troops to aid North Korea.

AFRICA

1947 Britain grants Nigeria limited self-government.

1947 Algerians granted French citizenship.

1949 South Africa passes legislation enforcing a policy of 'apartheid', separate development of races.

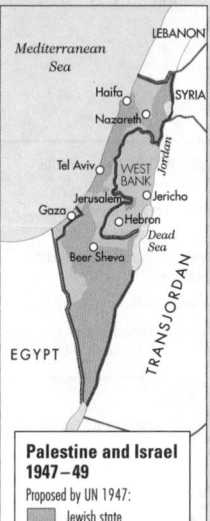

Palestine and Israel 1947–49
Proposed by UN 1947:
- Jewish state
- Arab state
- International zone
- Boundary of Israel 1949

◄ *Palestine The United Nations' (UN) proposed (1947) partition of Palestine into Jewish and Arab states with Jerusalem under international control was rejected by the majority Arab population. The Zionist forces won the ensuing civil war and the state of Israel was proclaimed on 14 May 1948. The new state immediately faced attack from the Arab Legion of Transjordan (now Jordan), led by John Bagot Glubb, and forces from Egypt, Iraq, Lebanon and Syria. Israel defeated the Arab armies, and in the armistices (January–July 1949) gained Galilee, the Negev Desert, the entire Palestinian coast except a smaller Gaza Strip (occupied by Egypt), and land between West Jerusalem and the Mediterranean. Jordan received the rest of Jerusalem.*

▼ *Palestine Migration to Palestine began in the late 19th century as groups of Jews sought freedom from persecution. After the foundation of the World Zionist Organization (1897) more Jews arrived, buying land for collectives. Up to 1948 most arrivals were from Europe. After 1948, many Jews living in Arab countries migrated or fled to Israel. The Palestinians fled their homes in two waves, the majority (more than half a million) in 1948 and a second group of between 200,00 and 400,000 during the 1967 war.*

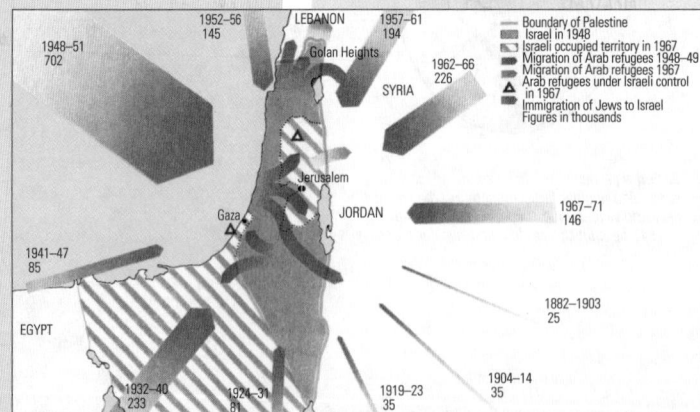

1951 Libya gains full independence under King Idris I (1890–1983).

1951 British troops occupy the Suez Canal zone.

1952 Mau Mau secret society starts a campaign of terrorism against British settlers in Kenya.

1952 King Farouk (1920–65) overthrown in Egypt; the infant King Fuad II (1952–) becomes a figurehead leader as Prime Minister Muhammad Naguib (1901–84) assumes power.

1952 Eritrea becomes a part of Ethiopia.

EUROPE

1944 Germans launch V1 and V2 rockets against British and other European cities.

1944 British paratroop assault fails to capture a bridge at Arnhem; Allied troops invade Germany; a German counter-attack is defeated in the Battle of the Bulge.

1944 Soviet troops capture Crimea, Minsk, and Brest-Litovsk; Polish resistance attempts a rising in Warsaw; Soviet troops invade Czechoslovakia and Hungary.

1944 Failed attempt by German army officers to assassinate Adolf Hitler (1889–1945).

1944 Iceland becomes an independent republic.

1944 Greece liberated from the Germans; civil war starts between monarchists and communists.

1944 Yugoslav resistance forces and Russian troops jointly capture Belgrade.

1945 Warsaw and Kraków liberated by Polish and Soviet troops.

1945 At a conference at Yalta in the Crimea, the USA and Britain tacitly agree to Soviet occupation of postwar Europe.

1945 Benito Mussolini (b.1883) shot dead by Italian resistance fighters; the German army in Italy surrenders.

1945 British air raid creates a firestorm in the city of Dresden.

1945 Soviet armies take Vienna; US and Soviet forces meet at the River Elbe; Russians under General Georgi Zhukov (1896–1974) take Berlin; Hitler commits suicide; Admiral Doenitz (1891–1980) surrenders; Germany and Austria are occupied in zones; the Potsdam Conference agrees stringent controls on postwar Germany.

1945 Clement Attlee (1883–1967) elected Prime Minister of Britain.

1945 Republic of Austria established under Karl Renner (1870–1950).

1945 Josip Tito (1892–1980) declares the People's Republic of Yugoslavia.

1945 War crimes tribunal set up at Nuremberg.

1946 Charles de Gaulle (1890–1970) resigns as President of France in protest against socialists.

1946 Communists win Czech elections.

1946 Albania becomes an independent republic under prime minister Enver Hoxha (1908–85).

1946 Italy becomes a republic.

1946 British government nationalizes coal mines and lays the foundations of a welfare state.

1947 Belgium, Netherlands, and Luxembourg form a customs union.

1947 Italy, Romania and Hungary lose small areas of territory under the Paris peace treaties.

1947 Communist coups seize power in Czechoslovakia, Hungary and Romania.

1948 Brussels Treaty, agreeing European military and economic co-operation, signed by Britain, France, Belgium, Netherlands, and Luxembourg.

1948 Juliana (1909–2004) becomes Queen of the Netherlands.

1948 Russians blockade Berlin; the Western powers organize an airlift ito keep the city supplied.

1949 Republic of Ireland declared.

1949 Soviet Union breaks off close relations with Yugoslavia.

1949 Council of Europe and the European Court of Human Rights established.

1949 Federal Republic of (West) Germany, with its capital in Bonn, and the (East) German Democratic Republic established.

1949 Greek civil war ends with a monarchist victory.

1949 Soviet Union tests an atomic bomb.

1949 Soviet Union and the communist-controlled countries of Eastern Europe form the Comecon organization for economic co-operation.

1950 French foreign minister Robert Schuman (1886–1963) proposes a plan for the integration of the French and German coal and steel industries, forerunner of the European Union.

1950 Gustav VI (1882–1973) becomes King of Sweden.

1951 West Germany admitted to the Council of Europe.

1951 Leopold III (1901–83) of Belgium abdicates in favour of his son Baudouin (1930–93).

1951 Marshall Plan economic aid to Europe ends.

THE AMERICAS

1945 Harry S. Truman (1884–1972) becomes President of the United States on Roosevelt's death.

1945 Founding United Nations' conference held in San Francisco; Spain and Portugal are among the countries excluded from membership.

1946 Juan Perón (1895–1974) elected President of Argentina.

1947 US President Truman pledges a doctrine of support for regimes threatened by communism.

1947 US Secretary of State George Marshall (1880–1959) proposes a plan for European economic recovery.

1948 US government pledges massive financial aid to Europe for the implementation of the Marshall Plan.

1948 Truman re-elected President of the United States.

1948 UN issues a declaration of human rights.

1948 Organization of American States (OAS) established.

1949 North Atlantic Treaty Organization (NATO) formed for mutual defence by the USA, Canada, and w European states.

1949 Newfoundland becomes part of Canada.

> "We are advocates of the abolition of war, we do not want war; but war can only be abolished through war, and in order to get rid of the gun it is necessary to take up the gun."
>
> *Mao Zedong*
> *(Quotations from Chairman Mao Zedong)*

SCIENCE AND TECHNOLOGY

1945 US scientists and engineers working at Los Alamos, New Mexico, under Robert Oppenheimer (1904–67) design and test an atomic bomb.

1945 US engineer Percy Spencer (1894–1970) patents the microwave oven.

1946 US paediatrician Benjamin Spock (1903–98) writes *The Common Sense Book of Baby and Child Care*.

1946 US chemist Willard Libby (1908–80) devises a method of radiocarbon dating.

1946 British engineer Maurice Wilkes (1913–) devises assembler computer-programming language.

1947 Atomic power station opens at Harwell, England.

1947 US aviator Chuck Yeager (1923–) breaks the sound barrier in the Bell X1 rocket-powered aircraft.

1947 US engineers John Bardeen (1908–91), Walter Brattain (1902–87) and William Shockley (1910–89) invent the transistor.

1947 US engineer Buckminster Fuller (1895–1983) designs his geodesic dome.

1948 British physicist Dennis Gabor (1900–79) invents holography.

1948 US physicists Richard Feynman (1918–88) and Julian Schwinger (1918–94) formulate quantum electrodynamics.

ARTS AND HUMANITIES

1945 British artist Francis Bacon (1909–92) paints his *Three Studies for Figures at the Base of a Crucifixion*.

1945 British philosopher Karl Popper (1902–94) publishes *The Open Society and Its Enemies*.

1945 Italian author Carlo Levi (1902–75) publishes his novel *Christ Stopped at Eboli*.

1945 British novelist Evelyn Waugh (1903–66) publishes his novel *Brideshead Revisited*.

1945 British author J.B. Priestley (1894–1984) writes his play *An Inspector Calls*.

1945 British writer George Orwell (1903–50) publishes his novel *Animal Farm*.

1946 French philosopher and author Jean-Paul Sartre (1905–80) publishes *Existentialism and Humanism*.

1947 Italian writer Primo Levi (1919–87) publishes *If This is a Man*.

1947 Italian artist Marino Marini (1901–80) creates his sculpture *Horseman*.

1947 British poet W.H. Auden (1907–73) publishes *The Age of Anxiety*.

1948 US novelist Norman Mailer (1923–) publishes *The Naked and the Dead*.

1948 US artist Jackson Pollock (1912–56) paints *Composition No.1*.

1949 US dramatist Arthur Miller (1915–2005) writes his play *Death of a Salesman*.

1949 French anthropologist Claude Lévi-Strauss (1908–90) publishes *The Elementary Structures of Kinship*.

1949 French feminist and novelist Simone de Beauvoir (1908–86) publishes *The Second Sex*.

1949 French author and dramatist Jean Genet (1910–86) publishes his novel *Diary of a Thief*.

The expansion of the British Commonwealth (the Commonwealth of Nations) in 1947 to include India and Pakistan enabled the organization to evolve into a multi-ethnic grouping, which nearly all Britain's former colonies decided to join. South Africa left the Commonwealth in the face of condemnation of its policy of apartheid, but rejoined in 1994. Pakistan left in 1972 in protest at the admission of Bangladesh to the Commonwealth, but rejoined in 1989. In 1997 the first countries not previously British colonies – Cameroon and Mozambique – were admitted.

COMMONWEALTH OF NATIONS

— British dependencies

▨ Commonwealth members 1998

1994 Period of membership of Commonwealth (if not continuous)

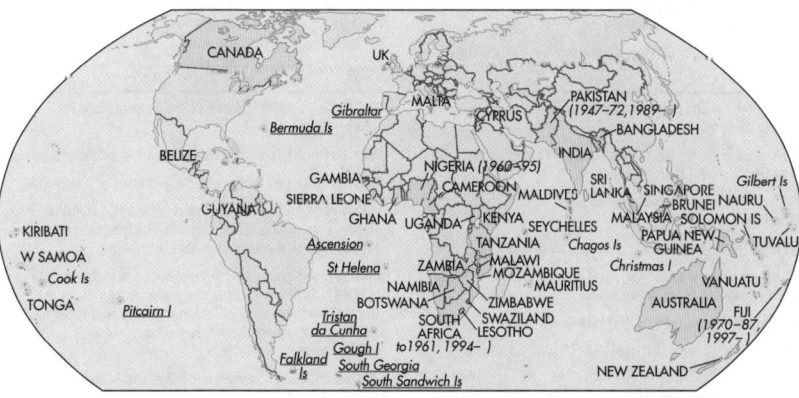

1951 Twenty-second amendment to the US constitution limits presidents to two terms of office.

1952 Dwight Eisenhower (1890–1969) elected US president.

1952 Fulgencio Batista (1901–73) appoints himself President of Cuba.

1952 Eva 'Evita' Perón (b.1919), second wife of Argentine president Juan Perón, dies.

1951 US engineers John Eckert (1919–1995) and John Mauchly (1907–80) build UNIVAC I, the first commercial computer.

1952 United States explode a hydrogen bomb.

1952 British explode an atom bomb.

1952 US researcher Jonas Salk (1914–95) develops a vaccine against poliomyelitis.

1952 British Comet aircraft makes the first jet passenger flight.

1953 US physicist Charles Townes (1915–) invents the maser.

1950 Chilean poet Pablo Neruda (1904–73) publishes his epic *General Song*.

1950 British novelist Doris Lessing (1919–) publishes *The Grass is Singing*.

1951 US novelist J.D. Salinger (1919–) publishes his *Catcher in the Rye*.

1951 US writer Herman Wouk (1915–) publishes his novel *The Caine Mutiny*.

1951 British composer Benjamin Britten (1913–76) writes his opera *Billy Budd*.

ASIA AND AUSTRALASIA

1950 Viet Minh forces under Ho Chi Minh (1880–1969) defeat the French at the battle of Kaobang in Vietnam.

1950 China invades Tibet.

1951 North Korean and Chinese forces take Seoul; UN forces recapture the city and halt a communist offensive at the battle of Imjin River.

1951 Iran, guided by Prime Minister Muhammad Mossadegh (1880–1967), nationalizes the oil industry and occupies the port of Abadan.

1951 Colombo Plan starts to distribute US aid to s Asian nations.

1953 Hussein I (1935–99) becomes King of Jordan.

1953 Laos gains full independence from France.

1953 Shah of Iran dismisses Mossadegh.

1953 Armistice signed at Panmunjom ends the Korean War.

1954 French forces in Vietnam surrender after defeat by the Viet Minh at the battle of Dien Bien Phu; the Geneva peace treaty splits Vietnam at the 17th parallel.

1954 Manila treaty establishes the South East Asian Treaty Organization (SEATO).

1955 After a civil war, South Vietnam becomes a republic under President Ngo Dinh Diem (1901–63).

1955 Turkey and Iraq sign the Baghdad Pact defence treaty.

1955 Portuguese police kill Indian demonstrators in Goa.

1955 Twenty-nine non-aligned nations meet at Bandung in Indonesia.

1956 Islamic Republic of Pakistan declared.

1956 Solomon Bandaranaike (1899–1959) elected prime minister of Ceylon (now Sri Lanka).

1956 France cedes its colonies on the subcontinent to India.

1957 Malayan Federation gains independence.

1957 Israel evacuates the Gaza strip.

1957 Norodom Sihanouk (1922–) again becomes head of state in Cambodia.

1957 Anti-British revolt breaks out in Aden.

1958 Egypt and Syria form the United Arab Republic (UAR).

1958 Iraq and Jordan form a short-lived Arab Federation; the federation ends after a military coup in Iraq, which then becomes a republic.

1958 Chinese bombard the Quemoy Islands off Formosa (now Taiwan).

1958 US troops intervene during elections in Beirut, Lebanon.

1958 After a military coup in Pakistan, Muhammad Ayub Khan (1907–74) becomes president

1959 Singapore becomes an independent state.

1959 Antarctica safeguarded by international treaty.

1959 Iraq leaves the Baghdad Pact, which becomes the Central Treaty Organization (CENTO).

1959 Chinese troops suppress a rising in Tibet, and the Dalai Lama (1935–) flees.

1960

1960 Ideological and political differences split the Soviet-Chinese alliance.

1960 Mrs Sirimavo Bandaranaike (1916–2000) elected Prime Minister of Ceylon (now Sri Lanka).

1960 Achmad Sukarno (1901–70) assumes dictatorial powers in Indonesia.

1961 India conquers the Portuguese colony of Goa.

1961 German Nazi war criminal Adolf Eichmann (1906–62) tried and sentenced to death in Israel.

1961 Coup in Syria breaks up the United Arab Republic.

1961 Burmese diplomat U Thant (1909–74) elected Secretary-General of the United Nations (UN).

1962 Western Samoa gains independence from New Zealand.

1962 Army seize power in a coup in Thailand.

1962 Chinese troops invade N India, then withdraw to the disputed border in Kashmir.

1963 Malaya, Northern Borneo, Sarawak, and Singapore form the Federation of Malaysia.

1963 Military coup overthrows Ngo Dinh Diem (1901–63) in South Vietnam.

1963 Arrest of Islamic reformer Ruhollah Khomeini (1900–89) sparks riots in Tehran.

1964 Indonesian troops invade Malaysia.

AFRICA

1953 Britain establishes the Federation of Rhodesia (Northern and Southern) and Nyasaland.

1953 Berber rising overthrows the pro-French sultan.

1953 Kenyan politician Jomo Kenyatta (1893–1978) jailed by the British for involvement with the Mau Mau.

1954 Nigeria becomes a self-governing federation.

1954 Gamal Nasser (1918–70) becomes prime minister of Egypt.

1954 National Liberation Front (FLN) organizes an anti-French revolt in Algeria.

1956 Sudan and Morocco gain independence.

1956 Nasser becomes President of Egypt and nationalizes the Suez Canal; Israel invades Egypt; Britain and France send troops but withdraw under international pressure.

1957 British colonies of the Gold Coast and Togoland joined to form Ghana, the first British colony in Africa to gain independence. Kwame Nkrumah (1909–72) becomes Prime Minister.

1957 Habib Bourguiba (1903–2000) becomes President of the Republic of Tunisia.

1957 Morocco becomes a kingdom under Muhammad V (1909–61).

1958 Niger, Upper Volta, Ivory Coast, Dahomey, Senegal, Mauritania, Congo, and Gabon gain limited independence from France.

1958 Guinea becomes an independent republic.

1958 Mali and Senegal form the Federation of Mali.

1958 FLN rebels declare a provisional government in Algeria.

1959 Pro-independence riots occur in Nyasaland.

1959 Rioting breaks out in Stanleyville in the Belgian Congo.

1959 Hutu people organize an uprising against the Tutsi in Rwanda.

1959 Ceasefire agreed in the Algerian revolt.

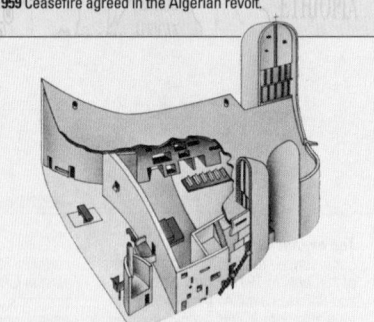

Le Corbusier *The chapel of Notre-Dame-du-Haut, Ronchamp, France, was built by Le Corbusier in 1955. The flowing, highly sculptural concrete structure deliberately resembles a nun's headdress. Set among hills, its design also echoes the forms of the surrounding landscape.*

1960 French settlers in Algeria rebel against plans for independence.

1960 Nkrumah becomes president of the Republic of Ghana.

1960 South African troops kill demonstrators at Sharpeville.

1960 Nigeria, Upper Volta, Chad, Ivory Coast, Cameroon, Togo, Gabon, Congo, Mauritania, Somalia and the Malagassy republic gain full independence.

1960 Belgian Congo gains independence with Patrice Lumumba (1925–61) as prime minister; the Congo army mutinies; Belgian troops arrive; the province of Katanga declares independence; UN troops replace Belgian forces; Joseph Mobutu (1930–97) seizes power.

1961 South Africa becomes a republic and leaves the British Commonwealth.

1962 Algeria becomes independent; the French nationalist OAS organizes a revolt.

1962 Uganda becomes independent.

1963 Organization of African Unity (OAU) formed in Addis Ababa.

1963 Katanga surrenders to the Congo government.

1964 Tanganyika and Zanzibar unite to form Tanzania with Julius Nyerere (1922–99) as president.

1964 ANC leader Nelson Mandela (1918–) sentenced to life imprisonment in South Africa.

EUROPE

1951 Conservative leader Winston Churchill (1874–1965) elected prime minister of Britain.

1952 Swedish diplomat Dag Hammarskjöld (1905–61) elected Secretary General of the United Nations (UN).

1952 European Coal and Steel community formed.

1952 Elizabeth II (1926–) becomes Queen of Britain.

1952 Greece and Turkey join NATO.

1953 Tito formally appointed President of the Federal People's republic of Yugoslavia.

1953 Konrad Adenauer (1876–1967) re-elected Chancellor of West Germany.

1953 Nikita Khrushchev (1894–1971) becomes First Secretary of the Communist Party in the Soviet Union after the death of Joseph Stalin (b.1879).

1954 Greek nationalist EOKA movement carries out attacks on British troops in Cyprus.

1954 Italy and Yugoslavia reach agreement over the ownership of Trieste.

1955 Allied occupation troops withdraw from West Germany, which joins the North Atlantic Treaty Organization (NATO).

1955 Communist countries of Eastern Europe form the Warsaw Pact with the Soviet Union.

1955 Austria, Spain, Italy, Portugal, Ireland, Bulgaria, and Hungary admitted to the United Nations (UN).

1955 First summit conference of world leaders takes place in Geneva, Switzerland.

1956 British deport Archbishop Makarios (1913–77) from Cyprus.

1956 Hungarian Prime Minister Imre Nagy (1896–1958) takes charge of an anti-communist uprising that is quickly crushed by Soviet troops.

1957 Conservative leader Harold Macmillan (1894–1986) becomes prime minister of Britain.

1957 Saar region returned to West Germany.

1957 Olaf V (1903–91) becomes King of Norway.

1957 France, Belgium, Netherlands, Luxembourg, Italy and West Germany sign the Treaty of Rome, establishing the European Economic Community (EEC) or Common Market.

1959 Belgium, Netherlands, and Luxembourg become a single economic unit – Benelux.

1958 New constitution establishes the Fifth Republic in France; Charles De Gaulle (1890–1970) elected president.

1958 Khrushchev replaces Nikolai Bulganin (1895–1975) as Soviet premier.

1959 Eamon De Valera (1882–1975) elected president of Ireland.

1960 Soviets shoot down a US U2 spyplane and capture pilot Gary Powers (1929–77).

1960 Non-Common Market countries form the European Free Trade Association (EFTA).

1960 Army seize power in a coup in Turkey.

1960 Cyprus gains independence under President Makarios (1913–77).

1960 USA and Canada join w European nations to form the Organization for Economic Co-operation and Development (OECD).

1961 Soviet authorities build a concrete wall across the divided city of Berlin.

1961 Twenty-five countries attend a conference of non-aligned nations in Belgrade.

1962 Disarmament conference starts in Geneva.

1963 France vetoes the British application to join the Common Market.

1963 Britain, the Soviet Union, and the USA sign a nuclear-test treaty banning all but underground explosions.

1964 UN peace-keeping troops are sent to Cyprus, to prevent fighting between Greeks and Turks.

1964 Labour leader Harold Wilson (1916–95) elected prime minister of Britain.

1964 Malta gains independence from Britain.

THE AMERICAS

1954 Anti-communist crusade of Senator Joseph McCarthy (1908–57) reaches a climax with televised hearings of his investigation committee.

1955 US Supreme Court rules that racial segregation in public schools must be halted.

1955 Juan Perón (1895–1974) forced into exile from Argentina.

1955 General Alfredo Stroessner (1912–2006) becomes dictator of Paraguay after a coup.

1955 US civil rights activist Rosa Parks (1913–2005) sits in a whites-only seat on a bus in Montgomery, Alabama.

1956 Revolutionary Fidel Castro (1926–) lands in Cuba.

1957 Jamaica becomes self-governing.

1957 François 'Papa Doc' Duvalier (1907–71) becomes President of Haiti.

1957 President Eisenhower (1890–1969) states his doctrine to oppose communism in the Middle East.

1957 US Civil Rights Act appoints a commission to examine African-American voting rights.

1958 British form the Federation of the West Indies.

1958 Military coup overthrows Venezuelan President Pérez Jiménez (1914–2001).

1958 US National Aeronautics and Space Administration (NASA) is established.

1959 Cuban revolutionaries capture Havana; Batista flees; Castro becomes prime minister.

1959 Alaska and Hawaii become states of the USA.

1959 St Lawrence Seaway opens.

Cuban Missile Crisis 1962
- US-backed invasion force April 1961
- Soviet ships
- US naval blockade
- US naval base
- Soviet missile base
- US military build-up

1960 New city of Brasília becomes the capital of Brazil.

1960 US civil rights activist Martin Luther King (1929–68) organizes a sit-in demonstration in Greesboro, North Carolina.

1960 USA embargos exports to Cuba and cuts Cuban sugar quotas by 95%.

1960 Israeli agents kidnap Nazi war criminal Adolf Eichmann (1906–62) in Argentina.

1960 John F. Kennedy (1917–63) elected President of the United States.

1961 President Kennedy announces the formation of the Peace Corps.

1961 Cuban exiles in the USA attempt invasion of Cuba at the Bay of Pigs.

1961 US civil rights activists organize 'freedom rides' on segregated buses.

1962 Jamaica and Trinidad and Tobago gain independence.

1962 Soviet Union attempts to install nuclear missiles in Cuba; the USA imposes a naval blockade.

1963 Hotline is installed between the White House and the Kremlin.

1963 Martin Luther King leads a civil rights march to Washington, D.C.

1963 Kennedy assassinated in Dallas, Texas; Lyndon B. Johnson (1908–73) becomes President of the United States.

SCIENCE AND TECHNOLOGY

1953 German chemist Karl Ziegler (1898–1973) invents a process for making high-density polyethene.

1953 British biophysicist Francis Crick (1916–2004) and US bio physicist James Watson (1928–) discover the helical structure of DNA.

1953 US engineer An Wang (1920–90) invents magnetic core computer memory.

1954 Swiss psychologist Jean Piaget (1896–1980) publishes *The Origin of Intelligence in Children*.

1954 Chinese scientist Min-Chueh Chang (1909–91) and US biologists Gregory Pincus (1903–67) and Frank Colton (1923–2003) invent the contraceptive pill.

1955 British engineer Christopher Cockerell (1910–99) invents the hovercraft.

1955 US physicists Clyde Cowan (1919–1974) and Frederick Reines (1918–98) discover the neutrino.

1956 US engineer Alexander Poniatoff (1892–80) invents a video tape recorder.

1956 Implantable heart pacemaker is invented.

1956 US engineer Jack Backus leads a team that devises the FORTRAN computer programming language.

1957 Soviet Union launches an artificial satellite – *Sputnik I*.

1957 Soviet satellite *Sputnik II* carries the dog Laika into orbit.

1957 UN forms the International Atomic Energy Commission.

1957 Scottish virologist Alick Isaacs (1921–67) discovers interferon.

1957 International Geophysical Year promotes earth sciences.

1958 Nuclear-powered submarine USS *Nautilus* passes beneath the North Pole.

1958 British industrialist Alistair Pilkington (1920–95) invents the float-glass process for making plate glass.

1958 US satellite *Explorer I* discovers the Van Allen radiation belts around the Earth.

1958 Stereophonic music records go on sale in the USA.

1959 Soviet spaceprobe *Lunik 3* photographs the far side of the Moon.

◀ **Cuban Missile Crisis** In 1962, US reconnaissance flights detected evidence that the Soviet Union was building nuclear missile bases on Cuba within range of the US mainland. A US naval blockade and the threat of nuclear war eventually forced Nikita Khrushchev to dismantle the bases.

1960 France explode an atom bomb.

1960 US chemist Robert Woodward (1917–79) synthesizes chlorophyll.

1960 US physicist Theodore Maiman (1927–) invents the laser.

1961 Soviet cosmonaut Yuri Gagarin (1934–68) orbits the Earth.

1961 US astronaut Alan Shepard (1923–98) makes a sub-orbital flight.

1962 US astronaut John Glenn (1921–) orbits the Earth.

1962 US telecommunications satellite *Telstar* is launched.

1963 Soviet cosmonaut Valentina Tereshkova (1937–) orbits the Earth.

1963 US astronomer Maarten Schmidt (1929–) discovers quasars.

1964 US physicist Murray Gell-Mann (1929–) proposes the existence of quarks.

1964 Japanese railways run high-speed 'bullet' trains.

1964 US engineer Robert Moog (1934–) invents an electronic music synthesizer.

ARTS AND HUMANITIES

1951 French artist Fernand Léger (1881–1955) designs stained glass windows for the Church of Sacre Coeur at Audicourt in France.

1952 British artist Henry Moore (1898–1986) creates his sculpture *King and Queen*.

1952 Alsatian humanitarian Albert Schweitzer (1987–1965) wins the Nobel Peace Prize.

1952 US composer John Cage (1912–92) conceives *4'33"*.

1952 *Unité d'Habitation*, designed by Swiss architect Le Corbusier (1887–1965), opens in Marseilles, France.

1953 British scholar Michael Ventris (1922–56) deciphers Linear B as the Greek script of the Mycenaeans.

1953 US artist Willem de Kooning (1904–97) paints *Women*.

1954 British author and poet Dylan Thomas (1914–53) writes the verse play *Under Milk Wood*.

1954 British novelist William Golding (1911–93) publishes *Lord of the Flies*.

1954 Japanese film director Akira Kurosawa (1910–98) releases *Shichinin no samurai* (*The Seven Samurai*).

1954 French author Françoise Sagan (1935–) publishes *Bonjour Tristesse*.

1954 British novelist J.R.R. Tolkien (1892–1973) publishes the first volume of his *Lord of the Rings*.

1955 Irish dramatist and novelist Samuel Beckett (1906–89) writes the play *Waiting for Godot*.

1955 French novelist Alain Robbe-Grillet (1922–) publishes *nouveau roman Le Voyeur*.

1955 US novelist Vladimir Nabokov (1899–1977) publishes *Lolita*.

1956 British dramatist John Osborne (1929–95) writes the play *Look Back in Anger*.

1956 US singer Elvis Presley (1935–77) releases the single "Heartbreak Hotel".

1956 British philosopher A.J. Ayer (1910–89) publishes *The Problem of Knowledge*.

1956 US singer Frank Sinatra (1915–98) releases the album *Songs for Swinging Lovers*.

1957 US sculptor Alexander Calder (1898–1976) creates his *Mobile* for New York airport.

1957 US poet and novelist Jack Kerouac (1922–69) publishes *On the Road*.

1957 Australian novelist Patrick White (1912–90) publishes *Voss*.

1958 US economist J.K. Galbraith (1908–2006) publishes *The Affluent Society*.

1958 Russian poet and author Boris Pasternak (1890–1960) publishes his novel *Dr Zhivago*.

1959 US novelist William S. Burroughs (1914–97) publishes *The Naked Lunch*.

1959 *Ben Hur* receives 11 Academy Awards.

1959 German poet and author Günter Grass (1927–) publishes his novel *The Tin Drum*.

1959 Irish author Brendan Behan (1923–64) writes his play *The Hostage*.

1960 Guggenheim Museum, designed by US architect Frank Lloyd Wright (1869–1959), opens in New York.

1960 US author John Updike (1932–) publishes the novel *Rabbit Run*.

1960 French dramatist Eugène Ionesco (1912–94) writes his absurdist play *The Rhinoceros*.

1960 British author Elias Canetti (1905–94) publishes *Crowds and Power*.

1961 British pop group The Beatles play their first gig at the Cavern Club, Liverpool.

1961 US novelist Joseph Heller (1923–99) publishes *Catch-22*.

1961 US singer-songwriter Bob Dylan (1941–) makes his debut performance in Greenwich Village, New York.

1961 Soviet dancer Rudolf Nureyev (1938–93) defects to the USA.

1962 US economist Milton Friedman (1912–2006) publishes *Capitalism and Freedom*.

1962 British artist Graham Sutherland (1903–80) creates his *Christ in Glory* tapestry for the rebuilt Coventry Cathedral.

1962 Soviet novelist Alexander Solzhenitsyn (1918–) publishes *One Day in the Life of Ivan Denisovich*.

1963 US artist Roy Lichtenstein (1923–97) paints *Whaam!*.

1963 US environmentalist Rachel Carson (1907–64) publishes *Silent Spring*.

ASIA AND AUSTRALASIA

1965 USA begins a bombing campaign ('Rolling Thunder') against North Vietnam.

1965 Singapore becomes an independent republic.

1965 War breaks out between India and Pakistan.

1966 Mao Zedong (1893–1976) launches the Cultural Revolution in China; the Red Guards are formed.

1966 Indonesian-Malay conflict ends.

1967 Israeli defeats its Arab neighbours in the Six-Day War; it recaptures the West Bank and E Jerusalem and occupies the Golan Heights.

1968 North Vietnam launches the Tet offensive; the US bombing campaign halts; US troops massacre villagers at My Lai.

1968 Ba'athist officers seize power in Iraq.

1969 US troops begin withdrawing from Vietnam.

1969 Soviet and Chinese troops clash along their border.

1969 Dhofar rebellion starts in S Oman.

1970 Norodom Sihanouk (1922–) overthrown; communist guerrillas threaten Phnom Penh; Cambodia becomes the Khmer Republic.

1970 USA resumes bombing North Vietnam.

1970 Jordanian forces loyal to King Hussein evict the PLO in a brief civil war.

1970 Hafez al-Assad (1928–2000) seizes power and becomes president of Syria.

1971 East Pakistan declares independence; West Pakistan declares war; India intervenes in the fighting; East Pakistan gains independence as the Republic of Bangladesh.

1971 Bahrain and Qatar gain independence as does the newly formed United Arab Emirates (UAE).

1971 China admitted to the UN; nationalist Taiwan expelled.

1972 Ceylon becomes the independent republic of Sri Lanka.

1973 Last US combat troops leave Vietnam.

1973 President Zulfikar Ali Bhutto (1929–79) issues a new constitution in Pakistan.

1973 Arab countries attack Israel; Egyptian forces invade across the Suez Canal but Israel forces them to retreat.

1973 Afghanistan becomes a republic after a coup.

1973 Arab states cut oil production and cause a worldwide energy crisis.

1974 India explodes an atom bomb.

1975 Clashes in Beirut between Palestinians and Christian Falangists start the Lebanese civil war.

1975 Cambodian Khmer Rouge guerrillas under Pol Pot (1928–98) capture Phnom Penh; 'year zero' marks the systematic extermination of educated city-dwellers.

1975 Saigon occupied by North Vietnam; end of the Vietnam War; Vietnam becomes one country with Hanoi as its capital.

1975 Indonesia annexes East Timor.

1975 Papua New Guinea gains independence from Australia.

1975 Communists take control in Laos.

1976 Deaths of Mao Zedong (b.1893) and Prime Minister Zhou Enlai (b.1898) cause a leadership crisis in China.

1977 Menachem Begin (1913–92) elected Prime Minister of Israel.

1977 General Zia al-Huq (1924–88) seizes power in Pakistan.

1977 Chinese GANG OF FOUR expelled from power; Deng Xiaoping (1904–97) becomes Chinese premier.

1978 Revolution overthrows the Republic in Afghanistan.

1978 Vietnam invades Cambodia.

1979 Vietnamese troops expel Pol Pot from Phnom Penh.

1979 Shah Muhammad Reza Pahlavi (1919–80) flees revolution in Iran; Ayatollah Khomeini (1900–89) arrives from Paris; students storm US Embassy in Tehran, taking staff hostage.

1979 Soviet Union invades Afghanistan.

1979 Chinese and Vietnamese troops involved in heavy border clashes.

1979 Saddam Hussein (1937–2006) seizes power in Iraq.

1980 Syrian government forces ruthlessly crush opposition groups in the cities of Homs and Aleppo.

AFRICA

1964 Zambia gains independence under President Kenneth Kaunda (1924–).

1964 Kenya becomes independent under President Jomo Kenyatta (1893–1978).

1965 Gambia gains independence.

1965 White settlers opposed to black majority rule unilaterally declare independence (UDI) in Southern Rhodesia.

1966 Milton Obote (1924–2005) becomes President of Uganda.

1966 Bechuanaland gains independence as Botswana; Basutoland becomes independent as Lesotho.

1967 State of Biafra declares independence and secedes from Nigeria; civil war erupts.

1967 Britain evacuates Aden and the People's Democratic Republic of Yemen is established.

1968 Swaziland becomes an independent kingdom.

1968 Equatorial Guinea gains independence from Spain.

1970 Biafran War ends with victory for Nigeria's federal government forces.

1970 Anwar Sadat (1918–81) becomes president of Egypt.

1970 Rhodesia declares itself a republic.

1971 Former Belgian Congo renamed Zaïre.

1971 Army sergeant Idi Amin (1925–2003) seizes power and becomes President of Uganda.

1972 Amin expels Asians from Uganda.

1974 Ethiopian Emperor Haile Selassie (1892–1975) deposed and a republic declared.

1975 Mozambique and Angola gain independence from Portugal.

1975 South Africa establishes Transkei as an 'independent' black homeland.

1976 South African security forces kill school children demonstrating in Soweto township.

1976 Israeli commandos raid Entebbe airport in Uganda to free hijacked passengers.

1976 Seychelles gains independence.

1977 South African political activist Steve Biko (b.1956) murdered in police custody.

1977 Cuban troops assist Ethiopian forces against rebels in Eritrea.

1977 Jean Bokassa (1921–96) proclaims himself Emperor of a Central African Empire.

1978 French and Belgian paratroops try to restore order in Kolwezi after a secessionist rebellion in Zaïre.

1979 Tanzanian troops invade Uganda and oust Idi Amin.

1979 Conference in London ends the civil war in Rhodesia between guerrillas and the white minority government.

▲ **Sadat** led Egypt into war with Israel in 1973, demanding the return of land occupied by Israel in 1967. Five years later, Sadat worked out peace terms with the Israeli premier Menachem Begin. They shared the 1978 Nobel Peace Prize.

EUROPE

1964 Nikita Khrushchev (1894–1971) deposed in the Soviet Union; Leonid Brezhnev (1906–82) becomes First Secretary and Aleksei Kosygin (1904–80) becomes Prime Minister.

1964 Constantine II (1940–) becomes King of Greece.

1966 France withdraws from NATO.

1967 Greek colonels seize power in Greece; King Constantine flees after a failed counter-coup.

1967 Nicolae Ceauşescu (1918–89) becomes head of state in Romania.

1967 EEC becomes the European Community (EC).

1968 Students and workers build barricades in Paris; student leader Rudi Dutschke (1940–79) shot in West Germany.

1968 Czech politician Alexander Dubček (1921–92) introduces reforms; a Soviet invasion ends the 'Prague Spring'.

1968 Albania withdraws from the Warsaw Pact.

1969 Violence flares between Catholics and Protestants in Ulster.

1970 Strategic Arms Limitation Treaty (SALT) talks begin in Helsinki.

1970 Portuguese dictator António Salazar (b.1889) dies.

1971 Angry Brigade terrorists send letter bombs to British politicians.

1972 Britain, Denmark, and Ireland join the EC.

1972 British impose direct rule in Ulster.

1972 Palestinian terrorists kidnap and kill Israeli athletes at the Munich Olympics.

1973 'Cod war' breaks out between Iceland and Britain over fishing rights.

1973 British Prime Minister Edward Heath (1916–2005) declares a state of emergency and a three-day working week because of strikes.

1974 Left-wingers seize power in a bloodless revolution in Portugal.

1974 Valéry Giscard d'Estaing (1926–) becomes President of France.

1974 Greek nationalists stage a coup in Cyprus and declare union with Greece; Turkish troops invade and conquer half the island.

1974 Junta of Greek colonels abdicates power.

1974 Irish Republican Army (IRA) intensifies its bombing campaign against British targets.

1975 Franco dies (b.1892); Juan Carlos (1938–) becomes King of Spain.

1975 Helsinki Accords on peace and human rights mark a major step in the process of détente between NATO and the Warsaw Pact.

1975 Britain becomes an oil-producing nation.

1975 Turkish Federated State of North Cyprus established; UN forces maintain the border with the Greek sector of the island.

1975 Terrorists led by 'Carlos the Jackal' take hostage members of the Organization of Petroleum Exporting Countries (OPEC) in Vienna, Austria.

1977 Czech political reformers form the Charter 77 organization.

1977 Dutch marines rescue hostages on a train hijacked by South Moluccan terrorists.

1977 Adolfo Suarez (1932–) elected Prime Minister of Spain.

1978 Italian Red Brigade terrorists kidnap and murder politician Alberto Moro (b.1916).

1978 Group of Seven (G7) industrialized nations meet to discuss economic policy.

1979 Conservative leader Margaret Thatcher (1925–) elected Prime Minister of Britain.

1980 Following the death of President Tito (b.1892), Yugoslavia comes under collective leadership.

1970

THE AMERICAS

1964 US government passes the Gulf of Tonkin resolution authorizing military action in Southeast Asia.

1965 African-American activist Malcolm X (b.1925) assassinated in New York.

1965 Race riots erupt in the Watts district of Los Angeles.

1965 Military coup leads to widespread fighting in the Dominican Republic; US marines land and are then replaced by OAS forces.

1966 British Guyana and Barbados gain independence.

1967 US Court of Appeals orders the desegregation of Southern schools

1967 Revolutionary Che Guevara (b.1928) killed by Bolivian troops.

1968 Martin Luther King (b.1929) assassinated in Memphis, Tennessee.

1968 Senator Robert Kennedy (b.1925) assassinated in Los Angeles, California.

1969 War breaks out between Honduras and El Salvador.

1970 US National Guard soldiers kill four protesting students at Kent State University in Ohio.

1970 Salvador Allende (1908–73) elected President of Chile.

1971 US army officer William Calley found guilty of the My Lai massacre in Vietnam.

1972 Burglars arrested in the Democratic Party election head-quarters at the Watergate Hotel in Washington, D.C.

1973 Juan Perón (1895–1974) returns to Argentina and becomes president.

1973 British Honduras renamed Belize.

1973 General Augusto Pinochet (1915–2006) leads a military coup that seizes power in Chile.

1974 Isabel Perón (1931–) assumes the presidency of Argentina on her husband's death.

1974 US President Richard Nixon resigns over the Watergate scandal; Gerald Ford (1913–2006) becomes president.

1975 Dutch Guiana becomes the independent state of Surinam.

1976 Coup overthrows Isabel Perón (1931–) in Argentina.

1976 Jimmy Carter (1924–) elected President of the United States.

1977 USA and Panama sign a treaty for the return of the canal zone to Panama.

1978 Egyptian President Anwar Sadat (1918–81) and Israeli Prime Minister Menachem Begin (1913–92) meet at Camp David, Maryland.

1978 Dominica gains independence from Britain.

1978 Mass suicide of 912 members of the US People's Temple cult, led by Jim Jones (1931–78), at Jonestown, Guyana.

1979 Israel and Egypt sign a peace treaty in Washington, D.C.

1979 Sandinista guerrillas capture Managua; President Anastasio Somoza (1925–80) flees Nicaragua; Daniel Ortega (1945–) forms a revolutionary government.

1979 Nuclear accident occurs at Three Mile Island power station in Pennsylvania.

SCIENCE AND TECHNOLOGY

1965 Soviet cosmonaut Alexei Leonov (1934–) takes a 'space walk' while in orbit.

1965 US physicists Arno Penzias (1933–) and Robert Wilson (1936–) discover microwave cosmic background radiation.

1966 Soviet spaceprobe *Luna 9* lands on the Moon.

1966 British engineers Charles Kao (1933–) and George Hockham invent fibre-optic telephone cable.

1967 South African surgeon Christiaan Barnard (1922–2001) performs a heart transplant.

1967 British astronomer Jocelyn Bell (1943–) discovers pulsars.

1968 US astronauts orbit the Moon in the *Apollo 8* spacecraft.

1969 Anglo-French Concorde supersonic passenger aircraft makes its first flight.

1969 US spacecraft *Apollo 11* lands on the Moon; astronaut Neil Armstrong (1930–) takes the first steps.

1970 China launches an artificial satellite.

1970 Soviet space probe *Venera VII* soft-lands on Venus and sends information from the surface.

1970 Boeing 747 'Jumbo jet' enters service.

1971 US engineer Ted Hoff (1937–) invents the computer microprocessor ('chip').

1971 Electronic pocket calculator invented.

1971 Soviet Union launches the *Salyut* space station into orbit.

1971 US palaeontologist Stephen Jay Gould (1941–2002) proposes his theory of punctuated equilibrium in evolution.

1972 Launch of US space probe *Pioneer 10*.

1973 US engineer Nolan Bushnell (1943–) invents the video game Pong.

1973 USA launches the *Skylab* space station.

1973 US biochemists Stanley Cohen (1935–) and Herbert Boyer (1936–) invent recombinant DNA genetic engineering when they use restriction enzymes to 'cut and splice' DNA.

1974 US palaeontologist Donald Johanson (1942–) discovers 'Lucy' – a partial skeleton of *Australopithecus afarensis* – in Ethiopia.

1975 *Apollo* and *Soyuz* spacecraft link up while in orbit.

1975 Personal computer (PC) in kit form goes on sale in the United States.

1976 Legionnaire's disease identified in the USA.

1976 US *Viking* probes send back pictures from the surface of Mars.

1977 British biochemist Frederick Sanger (1918–) dicovers the full sequence of bases in DNA.

1977 US engineer Paul MacCready (1925–) designs a human-powered aircraft.

1977 Apple II personal computer introduced.

1978 World Health Organization (WHO) announces that, apart from some laboratory samples, smallpox has been eradicated.

1978 First in-vitro fertilization (IVF) baby born in Britain.

1978 British palaeontologist Mary Leakey (1913–96) discovers 3.5-million-year-old human footprints in Tanzania.

1979 US *Voyager* spaceprobes transmit close-up pictures of Jupiter and its moons.

1979 British scientist James Lovelock (1919–) proposes his 'Gaia hypothesis' of the co-evolution of Earth and its life-forms.

1979 Liquid crystal display (LCD) television developed in Japan.

ARTS AND HUMANITIES

1964 US novelist Saul Bellow (1915–) publishes *Herzog*.

1965 US author Truman Capote (1924–84) publishes his 'non-fictional' novel *In Cold Blood*.

1966 Japanese author Yukio Mishima (1925–70) publishes his novel *The Sailor Who fell from Grace with the Sea*.

1966 *Ariel* by US poet Syvia Plath (1932–63) is published posthumously.

1967 Colombian novelist Gabriel García Márquez (1928–) publishes *One Hundred Years of Solitude*.

1968 Film director Stanley Kubrick (1928–99) releases *2001: A Space Odyssey*.

1969 US novelist Philip Roth (1933–) publishes *Portnoy's Complaint*.

1969 US novelist Kurt Vonnegut Jr (1922–2007) publishes *Slaughterhouse Five*.

1969 US director Dennis Hopper (1936–) releases *Easy Rider*.

1970 Australian feminist Germaine Greer (1939–) publishes *The Female Eunuch*.

1970 Complete *New English Bible* is published.

1970 British poet Ted Hughes (1930–98) publishes *Crow*.

1970 US musician Jimi Hendrix (b.1942) dies of a drug overdose.

1970 The Beatles split up to pursue separate careers.

1970 Italian dramatist Dario Fo (1926–) writes *Accidental Death of an Anarchist*.

1971 Death of the US jazz musician Louis Armstrong (b.1900).

1972 British novelist (1917–93) Anthony Burgess writes *A Clockwork Orange*.

1972 US film director Francis Ford Coppola's (1939–) *The Godfather* wins the Academy Award for best picture.

1973 Sydney Opera House, designed by Danish architect Jorn Utzon (1918–), opens.

1974 US poet and author Erica Jong (1942–) publishes her novel *Fear of Flying*.

1974 US author Robert Pirsig (1928–) publishes *Zen and the Art of Motorcycle Maintenance*.

1974 US journalists Bob Woodward and Carl Bernstein publish *All the President's Men*, on the Watergate Affair.

1975 Mexican novelist Carlos Fuentes (1928–) publishes *Terra Nostra*.

1975 Czech film director Milos Forman's (1932–) *One Flew Over the Cuckoo's Nest* receives the Oscar for best picture.

1976 US linguist Noam Chomsky (1928–) publishes *Reflections on Language*.

1976 US author Alex Haley (1921–92) publishes *Roots: The Saga of an American Family*.

1977 Pompidou Centre designed by Richard Rogers (1933–) and Italian architect Renzo Piano (1937–), opens in Paris.

1977 British novelist Paul Scott (1930–78) publishes *Staying On*.

1978 US novelist John Irving (1942–) publishes *The World According to Garp*.

1978 British novelist A.S. Byatt (1936–) publishes *The Virgin in the Garden*.

1978 US author Susan Sontag (1933–) publishes *Illness as Metaphor*.

1978 US film director Michael Cimino's (1943–) *The Deer Hunter* receives the Academy Award for best picture.

1978 French philosopher Jacques Derrida (1930–2004) publishes *Truth in Painting*.

1978 US author Armistead Maupin (1944–) publishes *Tales of the City*.

1979 Czech novelist Milan Kundera (1929–) publishes *The Book of Laughter and Forgetting*.

◄ **Brezhnev** (left, with Alexander Dubček) ordered the Soviet invasion (1968) of Czechoslovakia that crushed the Dubček-inspired 'Prague Spring' of liberal reforms. Brezhnev renewed the authority of the vast Soviet bureaucracy that had declined under Nikita Khrushchev. The powers of the KGB increased and the Soviet propaganda machine continued to control the flow of information.

ASIA AND AUSTRALASIA

1980 Attempt by US special forces to rescue hostages held in Tehran ends in disastrous failure.

1980 Iraq invades Iran in order to gain control of the Shatt al-Arab waterway.

1981 Chinese 'Gang of Four' convicted of treason.

1981 Israeli aircraft destroy an Iraqi nuclear reactor in a secret bombing raid.

1982 Israel invades Lebanon and forces the PLO to evacuate to Tunisia and Cyprus; S Lebanon comes under Israeli occupation; an international peacekeeping force arrives in Beirut.

1984 Brunei becomes an independent sultanate.

1984 Indian troops storm Sikh protestors at the Golden Temple in Amritsar; Indira Gandhi (b.1917) is assassinated.

1985 French secret agents blow up the Greenpeace ship *Rainbow Warrior* in New Zealand.

1986 Ferdinand Marcos (1917–89) flees the Philippines; Corazon Aquino (1933–) becomes president.

1987 Iran and Iraq use missiles to bombard each other's cities.

1987 Indian troops impose a ceasefire in the conflict between the Tamil Tiger guerrillas and Sri Lankan government forces.

1987 Syrian troops enter Beirut to keep the peace.

1988 Soviet republics of Azerbaijan and Armenia clash over the enclave of Nagorno-Karabakh.

1988 Iran-Iraq War ends in stalemate.

1988 General Zia (b.1924) assassinated; Benazir Bhutto (1953–) becomes prime minister of Pakistan.

1988 Soviet Union begins withdrawing troops from Afghanistan.

1989 Chinese troops kill pro-democracy protestors in Tiananmen Square in Beijing.

1989 Ayatollah Khomeini (b.1900) dies; Hashemi Rafsanjani (1934–) becomes President of Iran.

1990 North and South Yemen unite to form a single state.

1990 Iran and Iraq restore diplomatic relations.

1990 Iraq invades and annexes Kuwait; the USA, EU countries, and Arab nations form an opposing coalition.

1991 A massive US-lead land invasion liberates Kuwait.

1991 Risings against Saddam Hussein (1937–2006) in N and S Iraq fail; UN 'safe havens' created for the Kurds in the N.

1991 Rajiv Gandhi (b.1944) assassinated during an election campaign in India.

1992 Afghan Islamic rebels capture Kabul and overthrow the communist government.

1995 Israeli Prime Minister Yitzhak Rabin (b.1922) killed by a Jewish extremist.

1996 Yasir Arafat (1929–2004) elected President of the Palestinian National Authority.

1996 Iraqi aircraft attack Kurds in a 'safe haven'; the USA launches cruise missiles against Iraq.

1996 Taliban capture Kabul, Afghanistan, and form a militant Islamic government.

1996 Israel attacks Hezbollah bases in S Lebanon.

1997 China regains Hong Kong.

1997 Hun Sen stages coup and replaces Cambodian Prime Minister Prince Norodom Ranariddh.

1997 Israeli troops withdraw from Hebron on the West Bank.

1997 Financial crisis in Japan leads to economic crisis throughout Southeast Asia.

1997 Pol Pot (1928–97) sentenced to life imprisonment by the Khmer Rouge in Cambodia.

1998 Iraq refuses access to UN arms inspectors, the US attacks Iraqi military targets.

1998 Bangladesh devastated by worst floods of the century.

1998 India carries out nuclear tests which are soon followed by Pakistani nuclear tests.

1998 Earthquake kills an estimated 5000 people in Afghanistan.

1999 Ehud Barak (1942–) defeats Netanyahu in Israeli elections.

1999 Pakistani prime minister Nawaz Sharif (1949–) ousted in a military coup led by General Pervez Musharraf (1943–).

1999 More than 15,000 die in earthquake in Turkey.

1999 East Timor votes for independence from Indonesia; anti-independence militia kill thousands in a campaign of terror.

AFRICA

1980 Rhodesia gains independence as Zimbabwe; Robert Mugabe (1925–) elected prime minister.

1980 Libya invades and occupies N Chad.

1981 Anwar Sadat (1918–81) assassinated; Hosni Mubarak (1928–) becomes President of Egypt.

1982 Israel returns the Sinai peninsula to Egypt.

1984 South African president P.W. Botha (1916–2006) grants limited political rights to Asians and 'coloureds'.

1985 USA and the EU impose economic sanctions against South Africa.

1985 Famine in Ethiopia partially alleviated by funds raised by the international Live Aid pop concert.

1986 US war planes bomb Libya.

1987 Chadian forces, assisted by the French Foreign Legion, expel the Libyans from N Chad.

1989 Cuban troops withdraw from Angola; a ceasefire is declared in the civil war.

1989 F.W. de Klerk (1936–) becomes President of South Africa.

Thatcher was the only British prime minister to win three consecutive general elections in the 20th century. Her single-minded determination to transform British society earned her the epithet the 'Iron Lady'.

1990 Nelson Mandela (1918–) released after 27 years in prison in South Africa.

1990 UN imposes sanctions on Libya for sheltering terrorists responsible for bombing of the Pan-Am flight 107 over Lockerbie, Scotland.

1990 Namibia becomes an independent republic.

1990 Robert Mugabe (1925–) elected President of Zimbabwe.

1993 Eritrea gains independence.

1994 Angolan government and the National Union for the Total Independence of Angola (UNITA) sign the Lusaka Protocol peace accord.

1994 Libya returns the Aozou strip to Chad.

1994 US troops withdraw from Somalia.

1994 African National Congress (ANC) wins the South African elections; Nelson Mandela becomes president.

1994 Genocide of the minority Tutsis by extremist Hutus begins in Rwanda.

1995 All Palestinians deported from Libya in protest against the Israeli-Palestinian Accord (1993).

1995 Ken Saro-Wiwa (b.1941) and eight other members of the Movement for Survival of the Ogoni People executed in Nigeria.

1996 Renewed violence between Hutus and Tutsis in Rwanda.

1996 Idriss Déby (1952–) wins the presidency in the first multi-party elections in Chad.

1997 Massacre of 58 tourists at the Temple of Hatshepsut near Luxor, Egypt.

1997 Zaïre renamed the Democratic Republic of Congo (DRC).

1998 Border dispute between Eritrea and Ethiopia flares into full-scale war.

EUROPE

1980 Polish shipyard workers led by Lech Walesa (1943–) form the Solidarity trades union.

1980 Greece joins the EC.

1981 Solidarity protests result in martial law being declared in Poland under General Wojciech Jaruzelski (1923–).

1983 Green party wins its first parliamentary seats in West German elections.

1983 Martial law ends in Poland.

1983 Turkish Northern Cyprus declares its independence under President Rauf Denktas.

1985 Palestinian terrorists hijack the cruise ship *Achille Lauro* and attack Israeli airline desks at Rome and Vienna airports.

1986 Spain and Portugal join the EC.

1986 Accident at the Chernobyl nuclear reactor in Ukraine releases a radioactive cloud over central and N Europe.

1986 Swedish Prime Minister Olaf Palme (b.1927) is murdered.

1987 Gorbachev adopts policies of *glasnost* (openness) and *perestroika* (restructuring) in the Soviet Union.

1988 US passenger jet blown up by a terrorist bomb over Lockerbie in Scotland.

1989 Solidarity candidates win a majority in Polish elections.

1989 Hungary adopts a new constitution and opens its borders; popular protests in East Germany lead to the dismantling of the Berlin Wall.

1989 Popular revolution overthrows Nicolae Ceauşescu (1918–89) in Romania.

1989 Vaclav Havel (1936–) forms a democratic government in Czechoslovakia.

1989 US and Soviet presidents officially declare the end of the Cold War.

1990 Lithuania, Latvia, and Estonia, Uzbekistan, and Ukraine declare independence from the Soviet Union.

1990 Polish communist party disbanded; Lech Walesa (1943–) elected president of Poland.

1990 East and West Germany reunited.

1990 Margaret Thatcher (1925–) resigns.

1991 Warsaw Pact dissolved as a military alliance.

1991 Croatia and Slovenia declare independence from Yugoslavia; the Serb-dominated Yugoslav army invades Croatia and captures Vukovar.

1992 Maastricht Treaty on European Union (EU) signed by the leaders of 12 nations.

1992 Bosnia-Herzegovina declares independence from Yugoslavia; the Serbs attack Sarajevo.

1993 Czech and Slovak republics established as separate states.

1993 Yeltsin orders tanks to attack rebels in the Moscow parliament building.

1993 UN declares 'safe' areas in Yugoslavia including Goradze and Srebrenica.

1993 Bovine spongiform encephalopathy (BSE), popularly known as 'mad cow disease', devastates British beef industry.

1994 Chechenia declares independence from Russia.

1995 Austria, Finland, and Sweden join the European Union (EU).

1995 Russian troops capture Grozny, capital of Chechenia, but fail to defeat rebels.

1995 Bosnian Serb forces attack the 'safe haven' of Srebrenica; Muslims and Croats join forces and attack, forcing Bosnian Serbs to negotiate; the Dayton Accord ends the war in Bosnia.

1996 Russian troops withdraw from Chechenia.

1997 Referenda on devolution sees Scotland and Wales gain their own legislative assemblies.

1998 Albanian separatists rebel against Serb rule in Kosovo.

1998 Nationalists (led by John Hume, 1937–), Republicans (led by Gerry Adams, 1948–), Unionists (led by David Trimble, 1944–), and the British and Irish governments, sign the Good Friday Agreement in Northern Ireland.

1999 Birth of single European currency (the euro).

1999 Reports of atrocities by Serb forces in Kosovo prompts NATO air strikes against targets in Kosovo and Serbia; tens of thousands of ethnic Albanians flee Kosovo; Serb forces withdraw after 11 weeks of NATO bombing.

THE AMERICAS

1980 Mount St Helens erupts in Washington state.

1980 Ronald Reagan (1911–2004) elected US president.

1980 Ex-Nicaraguan President Somoza assassinated in Paraguay.

1981 Belize, Antigua, and Barbuda gain independence from Britain.

1981 Peruvian diplomat Pérez de Cuéllar (1920–) becomes Secretary General of the United Nations (UN).

1982 Argentine troops invade the Falkland Islands (Malvinas); British forces invade and recapture the islands.

1983 US President Ronald Reagan announces the development of a Strategic Defence Initiative (SDI) or 'Star Wars' defence system; he also announces support for the Nicaraguan Contras.

1983 US marines invade Grenada and overthrow the revolutionary government.

1984 US troops withdraw from Lebanon.

1984 Daniel Ortega (1945–) elected president of Nicaragua.

1985 Earthquake devastates Mexico City.

1986 Space shuttle *Challenger* explodes shortly after launch.

1986 Jean Claude 'Baby Doc' Duvalier (1951–) flees Haiti to exile in France.

1987 New York stock market crashes, triggering a worldwide financial crisis; computerized dealing blamed for the severity of the collapse.

1988 George Bush (1924–) elected US president.

1988 Sandinistas and Contras agree an armistice in Nicaragua.

1989 General Manuel Noriega (1934–) proclaims himself President of Panama; US troops invade.

1989 San Francisco suffers a major earthquake.

1990 Argentina restores full diplomatic relations with the United Kingdom.

1991 Strategic Arms Reduction Talks (START) limit the size of US and Russian nuclear arsenals.

1991 Peace agreement ends 11-year civil war in El Salvador.

1992 Canada, the USA, and Mexico form the North American Free Trade Association (NAFTA).

1992 Noriega found guilty of drug trafficking offences and sentenced to 40 years' imprisonment by a US court.

1992 Abimael Guzman (1934–), leader of the Shining Path guerrillas, arrested in Peru.

1993 World Trade Center, New York City, damaged by a terrorist bomb; six people killed and c.1000 injured.

1993 US government agents storm the headquarters of the Branch Davidian cult in Waco, Texas; 80 cult members and four federal agents die in the confrontation.

1994 Zapatista National Liberation Army leads a revolt in Chiapas state, Mexico.

1994 US troops invade Haiti.

1995 168 people die in a bomb attack on a government office in Oklahoma City, Oklahoma, USA.

1995 World Trade Organisation (WTO) succeeds GATT.

1995 Louis Farrakhan (1933–) leads up to 400,000 men on a march in Washington, D.C, calling for African-American unity.

1996 Agreement ends 36 years of civil war in Guatemala; the war claimed more than 200,000 lives.

1997 Massacre of 45 Indian peasants by paramilitary gunmen in a village in Chiapas, Mexico.

1997 Jean Chrétien (1934–) re-elected Premier of Canada.

1998 General Augusto Pinochet (1915–2006), former president of Chile, arrested in Britain for genocide.

1999 President Clinton acquitted in Senate impeachment trial.

1999 Inuit land of Nunavut created in Northwest Territories, Canada.

1999 Panama gains full jurisdiction of the Panama Canal after almost 100 years of control by the USA.

▶ *Milošević was indicted for war crimes by the United Nations (UN) in May 1999, for trying to 'ethnically cleanse' the Albanian population in the Serbian province of Kosovo and for his involvement in the war in Bosnia.*

SCIENCE AND TECHNOLOGY

1981 US space shuttle makes its first orbital flight.

1981 IBM launch a PC using the Microsoft MS-DOS operating system.

1981 Acquired Immune Deficiency Syndrome (AIDS) disease identified.

1982 Compact music discs (CDs) introduced.

1982 Genetically engineered insulin produced for human use.

1983 French physician Luc Montagnier (1932–) identifies the human immunodeficiency virus (HIV) as the infective agent that causes AIDS.

1983 *Pioneer 10* leaves our solar system.

1984 Cellphone network launched in Chicago, USA.

1984 British geneticist Alec Jeffreys (1950–) devises a technique for genetic fingerprinting.

1984 Apple company launches the Macintosh computer, featuring windows, icons, a mouse, and pull-down menus.

1986 European space probe *Giotto* intercepts Halley's comet.

1986 *Voyager II* transmits pictures of Uranus.

1986 US aviators Jeana Yeager (1952–)and Dick Rutan (1938–) fly *Voyager* non-stop around the world without refuelling.

1987 International agreement reached to limit the amounts of chloroflurocarbons (CFCs) released into the atmosphere.

1987 Work starts on a tunnel between Britain and France.

1987 Supernova SN1987A visible to the unaided eye.

1988 US scientists start project to map the human genome.

1989 Convention on the International Trade in Endangered Species (CITES) imposes a worldwide ban on the sale of elephant ivory.

1989 *Voyager II* transmits pictures of Neptune.

1990 US Hubble space telescope carried into orbit by the space shuttle.

1992 US COBE satellite discovers ripples in the microwave background that confirm the 'Big Bang' origin of the universe.

1993 Genetically engineered tomato devised by the US Calgene Company.

1993 Bovine spongiform encephalopathy (BSE) epidemic peaks among beef cattle in Britain.

1994 Fragments of comet Shoemaker-Levi impact on Jupiter.

1994 Rail tunnel opens between Britain and France.

1994 Technique of DNA recombination devised to produce new 'synthetic' genes from different parent genes.

1994 World Wide Web (www) created.

1996 US government bans the use of CFCs (chlorofluoro-carbons).

1996 Physicists at CERN, Geneva, Switzerland create anti-atoms – nine anti-hydrogen atoms.

1997 The Roslin Institute, Edinburgh, clone an adult sheep named 'Dolly'. In 2003 she dies prematurely.

1997 Digital video discs (DVD) available in the USA.

1997 'Deep Blue' computer defeats world chess champion Gary Kasparov (1963–).

1998 Lunar Prospector discovers water-ice near the Moon's poles.

1999 Breitling Orbiter 3 completes the first non-stop flight around the world in a balloon.

ARTS AND HUMANITIES

1980 Former-Beatle John Lennon (b.1940) shot and killed outside his apartment in Manhattan, New York.

1981 Italian author Umberto Eco (1932–) publishes his novel *The Name of the Rose*.

1981 Death of Jamaican reggae musician Bob Marley (b.1945).

1982 US architect Maya Lin (1959–) designs the Vietnam Veterans' Memorial in Washington, D.C.

1982 British director Ridley Scott (1937–) releases *Blade Runner*.

1983 US poet and novelist Alice Walker (1944–) publishes her novel *The Color Purple*.

1984 Scottish novelist Iain Banks (1954–) publishes *The Wasp Factory*.

1984 British novelist J.G. Ballard (1930–) publishes *Empire of the Sun*.

1986 Japanese novelist Kazuo Ishiguro (1954–) publishes *An Artist of the Floating World*.

1986 British composer Andrew Lloyd Webber (1948–) writes the musical *Phantom of the Opera*.

1987 US author Tom Wolfe (1931–) publishes his novel *Bonfire of the Vanities*.

1987 Danish film director Gabriel Axel (1918–) releases *Babettes gaestebud* (*Babette's Feast*), which wins the Oscar for best foreign language film.

1988 German composer Karlheinz Stockhausen (1928–) writes *Montag aus Licht*.

1988 British author Salman Rushdie (1947–) publishes *Satanic Verses*.

1988 Australian novelist Peter Carey (1943–) publishes *Oscar and Lucinda*.

1990 US artist Jeff Koons (1955–) creates the sculpture *Jeff and Ilona (Made in Heaven)*.

1990 British novelist Ian McEwan (1948–) publishes *The Innocent*.

1990 Poet and essayist Octavio Paz (1914–98) receives the Nobel Prize in literature.

1991 British composer Harrison Birtwistle (1934–) writes the opera *Sir Gawain and the Green Knight*.

1991 British novelist Martin Amis (1949–) publishes *Time's Arrow*.

1991 Director/producer team Joel (1954–) and Ethan (1957–) Coen win the Palme d'Or at the Cannes Film Festival for their film *Barton Fink*.

1992 British artist Damien Hirst (1965–) creates his sculpture *The Physical Impossibility of Death in the Mind of Someone Living*.

1992 Chinese novelist Jung Chang (1952–) publishes her *Wild Swans*.

1992 Sri Lankan-born Canadian novelist Michael Ondaatje (1943–) publishes *The English Patient*.

1993 US film director Steven Spielberg's (1946–) *Schindler's List* receives the Academy Award for best picture.

1993 Indian novelist Vikram Seth (1952–) publishes the epic *A Suitable Boy*.

1993 Nick Park's (1958–) *The Wrong Trousers* wins the Academy Award for best animated short film.

1994 Quentin Tarantino's (1963–) *Pulp Fiction* wins the Palme d'Or at the Cannes Film Festival.

1995 Irish poet Seamus Heaney (1939–) receives the Nobel Prize in literature.

1995 *The Stone Diaries* by US writer Carol Shields (1935–2003) wins the Pulitzer Prize in fiction.

1996 Polish poet Wislawa Szymborska (1923–) receives the Nobel Prize in literature.

1996 Restored Globe Theatre opens in London.

1997 Italian playwright Dario Fo (1926–) receives the Nobel Prize in literature.

1997 *The God of Small Things* by Arundhati Roy (1961–) wins the Booker Prize.

1997 British novelist J.K. Rowling (1966–) publishes *Harry Potter and the Philosopher's Stone*.

1997 Guggenheim Museum opens in Bilbao, Spain, designed by Canadian Frank Gehry (1929–).

1980

1990

WORLD EVENTS

2000 **2000** Augusto Pinochet (1915–2006, ex-President of Chile, ruled too ill to face British trial for genocide, is returned to Chile.

2000 Fighting intensifies between government and rebels in Sierra Leone; British troops stay to train the army, and monitor the cease-fire and disarmament process.

2000 Russian troops renew war against Chechen separatists.

2000 Explosion aboard the *Kursk*, a Russian nuclear submarine, kills the entire crew of 118.

2000 Vojislav Kostunica (1944–) defeats Slobodan Milošević (1941–2006) in Yugoslav elections; Milošević reluctantly resigns after a general strike.

2001 Slobodan Milošević extradited to The Hague, to face charges of crimes against humanity.

2001 Earthquake in Gujarat, W India, kills 30,000 people.

2001 Ariel Sharon (1928–) elected Prime Minister of Israel after the renewal of the Palestinian Intifada.

2001, September 11 Terrorists pilot two passenger aircraft into the twin towers of the World Trade Center, New York City; millions watch on television as the towers collapse; a third plane destroys part of the Pentagon, Arlington, Virginia; a fourth crashes near Shanksville, Pennsylvania; more than 3000 people die in the attacks; Osama bin Laden (1957–), head of al-Qaeda and based in Afghanistan, held responsible.

2001 US and Britain launch air strikes in Afghanistan; Taliban regime overthrown by Afghan opposition and US special forces; Hamid Karzai (1957–) becomes interim leader.

2001 President Fernando de la Rua (1941–) of Argentina resigns after riots over government austerity measures kill 25.

2002 Euro notes and coins adopted in 12 European countries.

2002 Zimbabwe's President Robert Mugabe (1924–) wins a fifth term; the Commonwealth suspends Zimbabwe after allegations of vote-rigging and voter intimidation.

2002 British Queen Mother Elizabeth dies at the age of 101.

2003 US and British troops invade Iraq. After 26 days of fighting, the Allies seize Saddam Hussein's home town of Tikrit and the Iraqi dictatorship collapses. In December, Saddam Hussein is captured by US forces and placed under arrest.

2003 President Charles Taylor of Liberia goes into exile and Nigerian peacekeepers enter the country.

2003 Europe experiences its hottest summer on record. In France *c*.15,000 people die from heat-related causes.

2003 In SE Iran, an earthquake strikes the town of Bam killing over 30,000 people.

2004 Terrorist bombs on commuter trains in Madrid kill *c*.200.

2004 Ten more countries join the European Union.

2004 US returns sovereignty to Iraqis on June 28.

2004 More than 300 people, more than half children, die when Chechen rebels take hostages at a school in Beslan, Russia.

2004 Hamid Karzai wins first Afghan presidential elections.

2004 Disputed Ukrainian presidential elections won by Viktor Yushchenko after mass street demonstrations.

2004 Massive Tsunami on December 26 hits countries around the Indian Ocean causing massive death and destruction, particularly in Indonesia, killing more than 200,000.

2005 Elections are held in Iraq. Long negotiations are required to choose a president and agree a constitution. The constitution is approved by the electorate.

2005 Israel withdraws from the Gaza Strip, forcibly removing Israeli settlers.

2006 After months of negotiations, a coalition government is formed in Iraq, but it fails to prevent the country destabilising into civil war.

2006 Palestinian Hamas forces kidnap two Israeli soldiers and begin rocket bombardment of Israel. The Israeli army responds with an invasion and air raids but withdraws after fighting to a costly stalemate.

2006 North Korea tests a nuclear weapon

2007 In Somalia, the Islamic Courts Union is defeated by transitional government and Ethiopian forces.

2007 Saddam Hussein is executed by the Iraqi government.

2007 Ban Ki-Moon becomes UN Secretary General.

2007 Fear of bad debt in the international banking system causes a global financial crisis.

2008 Kosovo, under UN administration since 1999, unilaterally declares its independence from Serbia to mixed response.

2008 Cyclone in Burma causes tens of thousands of fatalities; Burmese government blocks international aid workers, greatly worsening the aftermath of the crisis.

SCIENCE AND TECHNOLOGY

2000 Scientists publish the rough draft of the sequence of the human genetic code.

2000 Zhores I. Alferov (1930–), Herbert Kroemer (1928–) receive the Nobel Prize in physics "for developing semiconductor heterostructures used in high-speed- and opto-electronics." Jack S. Kilby (1923–2005) receives the Nobel Prize in physics "for his part in the invention of the integrated circuit."

2000 Alan J. Heeger (1936–), Alan G. MacDiarmid (1927–2007) and Hideki Shirakawa (1936–) receive the Nobel Prize in chemistry "for the discovery and development of conductive polymers."

2000 Launch of the International Space Station (ISS).

2000 'Love Bug' virus paralyses many computer systems.

2000 The NEAR space probe enters orbit around Eros, a deep space asteroid.

2000 Arvid Carlsson (1923–), Paul Greengard (1925–) and Eric R. Kandel (1929–) receive the Nobel Prize in physiology or medicine "for their discoveries concerning signal transduction in the nervous system."

2000 Concorde, the world's first supersonic passenger aircraft, crashes in France, killing 113 people.

2000 Investments in new Internet businesses create overnight 'dot.com' millionaires. Many businesses rapidly collapse in the 'dot.gone' crash.

2000 Øresund bridge opens, linking Sweden and Denmark.

2000 Microsoft, the giant computer software company, is found guilty of violating US anti-trust laws.

2001 Mir space station drops out of orbit and burns up in the Earth's atmosphere.

2001 Eric A. Cornell (1961–), Wolfgang Ketterle (1957–) and Carl E. Wieman (1951–) receive the Nobel Prize in physics "for the achievement of Bose-Einstein condensation... and for early fundamental studies of the properties of the condensates."

2001 William S. Knowles (1917–) and Ryoji Noyori (1938–) receive the Nobel Prize in chemistry "for their work on chirally catalysed hydrogenation reactions"; K. Barry Sharples (1941–) receives the Nobel Prize in chemistry "for his work on chirally catalyzed oxidation reactions."

2001 Leland H.Hartwell (1939–), R. Timothy Hunt (1943–), and Sir Paul M. Nurse (1949–) receive the Nobel Prize in physiology or medicine "for their discoveries of key regulators of the cell cycle".

2001 Dennis Tito (1940–) pays US$20 million to become the first space tourist.

2002 Bonn Conference saves the Kyoto Protocol (1995) on climate change, without US participation.

2002 Mars *Odyssey* mission discovers vast reservoirs of ice beneath the surface of the polar regions of Mars.

2002 Cern particle accelerator in Geneva, Switzerland, produces more than 50,000 atoms of antihydrogen antimatter.

2002 Raymond Davis Jr. (1914–2006), Masatoshi Koshiba (1926–), and Riccardo Giacconi (1931–) receive the Nobel Prize in physics for "pioneering contributions to astrophysics, in particular for the detection of cosmic neutrinos."

2002 Sydney Brenner (1927–), H. Robert Horvitz (1947–), and John E. Sulston (1942–) receive the Nobel Prize in physiology or medicine "for their discoveries concerning genetic regulation of organ development and programmed cell death".

2003 US space shuttle *Columbia* breaks up soon after re-entering Earth's atmosphere, killing all seven crew members.

2003 World Health Organization issue a global alert on the potentially fatal virus known as Sars (Severe Acute Respiratory Syndrome).

2003 The *Galileo* space probe finishes its 14 year mission by plunging into Jupiter's atmosphere.

2003 China joins the space age by sending its first astronaut into space on *Shenzou 5*, becoming the third nation to develop manned space capabilities.

2004 SpaceShipOne is first private manned craft to fly to the edge of space twice in one week, winning the Ansari XPrize.

2004 NASA Mars probe sends back pictures and finds evidence that water once lay on the surface.

2005 The Huygens probe, launched from Cassini orbiting Saturn, lands on Titan.

2005 Kyoto Protocol comes into effect – without support from the United States.

2006 The rise of the deadly H5N1 strain of avian influenza causes fears of a devastating pandemic. The virus does not appear to be able to spread between humans, and deaths are few.

2007 Planets of Earthlike size and temperature are discovered around other stars.

ARTS AND HUMANITIES

2000 Tate Modern art gallery, designed by Swiss architects Herzog and de Meuron, opens in London, UK, in the former Bankside power station.

2000 Gao Xiangjian (1940–) becomes the first Chinese writer to receive the Nobel Prize in literature.

2000 Kim Dae-jung (1924–), president of South Korea, receives the Nobel Peace Prize "for his work for democracy and human rights in South Korea and in East Asia in general, and for peace and reconciliation with North Korea in particular."

2000 *The Blind Assassin* by Canadian novelist Margaret Atwood (1939–) wins the Booker Prize.

2000 *American Beauty*, starring Kevin Spacey (1959–), gains Academy Awards for best picture and best actor.

2000 *English Passengers* by English writer Matthew Kneale (1960–) wins the Whitbread book of the year award.

2001 Archaeologists discover drawings more than 28,000 years old in a cave in Dordogne, SW France.

2001 English film director Ridley Scott's (1937–) *Gladiator*, starring Russell Crowe (1964–), receives Oscars for best picture and best actor.

2001 Ellen MacArthur (1977–) becomes the fastest woman to sail single-handedly around the world.

2001 Australian writer Peter Carey (1943–) receives the Booker Prize for *The True History of the Kelly Gang*.

2001 US writer Michael Chabon's (1964–) *The Amazing Adventures of Kavalier and Clay* receives the Pulitzer Prize for fiction.

2001 British writer V.S. Naipaul (1932–) receives the Nobel Prize in literature.

2002 *The Amber Spyglass* by English writer Philip Pullman (1946–) becomes the first children's book to win the Whitbread Prize.

2002 Halle Berry (1968–) in *Monster's Ball* becomes the first black actress to receive an Academy Award for best actress. *A Beautiful Mind*, directed by Ron Howard (1954–), gains Oscars for best picture and best director.

2002 US writer Suzan-Lori Parks (1964–) becomes the first black woman to recieve the Pulitzer Prize for drama for her play *Topdog/Underdog*.

2002 Canadian writer Yann Martel (1963–) gains the Booker Prize for the surreal allegory *Life of Pi*.

2002 Brazil defeat Germany 2-0 in the final of football's World Cup. Co-hosts South Korea reach the semi-final.

2002 Peter-Paul Rubens' (1577–1640) painting *The Massacre of the Innocents* fetches £49.5 million at auction.

2003 US writer Jeffrey Eugenides' (1960–) *Middlesex*, a novel about a hermaphrodite, wins the Pulitzer Prize for fiction.

2003 Australian-born author DBC Pierre (1962–) gains the Booker Prize for *Vernon God Little*.

2004 Mark Haddon (1962–)gains the Whitbread book of the year award for *The Curious Incident of the Dog in the Night-Time*.

2004 *The Lord of the Rings: The Return of the King* wins 11 Oscars, including best picture and best director for Peter Jackson (1961–).

2004 Author John Banville wins Man Booker Prize for his novel *The Sea*.

2005 Playwright Harold Pinter (1930–) awarded Nobel Prize for literature.

2006 *Crash* wins three Oscars including best picture.

2007 Doris Lessing (1919–) awarded Nobel Prize for literature.

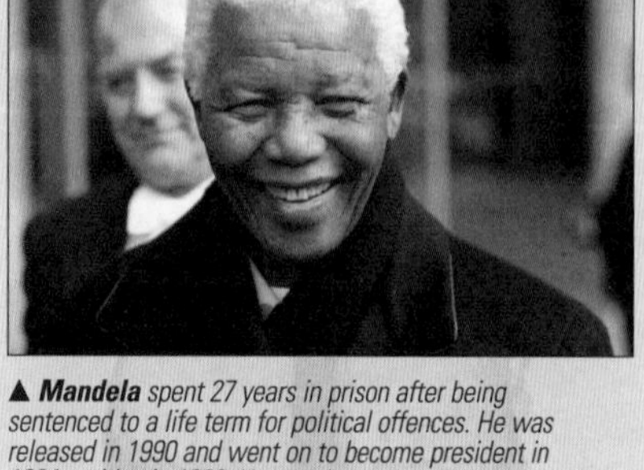

▲ ***Mandela*** *spent 27 years in prison after being sentenced to a life term for political offences. He was released in 1990 and went on to become president in 1994, retiring in 1999. He remains an important statesman on the world stage.*

REGIONS in the NEWS

SUDAN

Scale: 0 250 500 km

AREA: 2,505,810 sq km (967,000 sq miles).
POPULATION: 40,187,486 (Black 52%, Arab 39%, Beja 6% Other 3%)
RELIGION: Sunni Muslim 70% (mostly north), Indigenous beliefs 25%, Christian 5% (mostly south)

Sudan has more internally displaced people (6 million in 2005) than any other country and there are 225,000 Sudanese refugees in neighbouring Chad. 400,000 people are estimated to have been killed since conflict began in the Darfur region in early 2003.

Legend:
- Refugee sites
- IDP sites (Internally Displaced Persons)
- Area of damaged/ destroyed villages
- Regional boundaries
- Capital cities
- Main towns

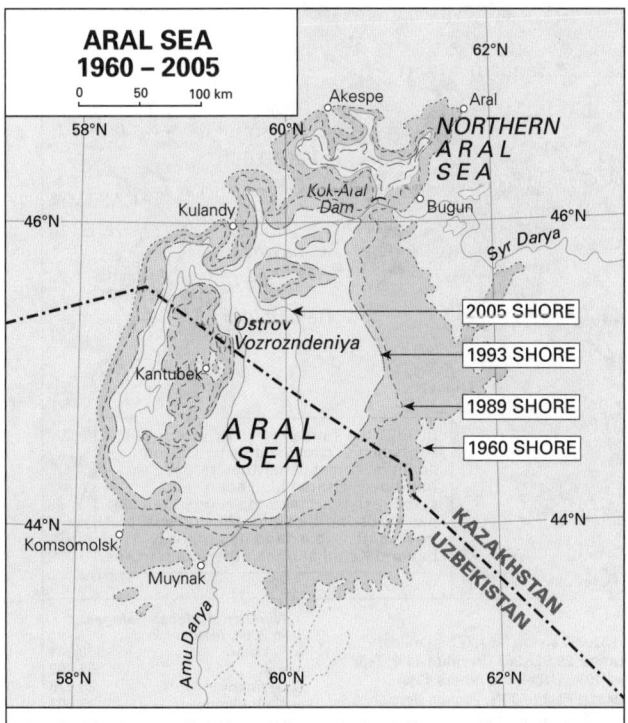

ARAL SEA 1960 – 2005

Scale: 0 50 100 km

- 2005 SHORE
- 1993 SHORE
- 1989 SHORE
- 1960 SHORE

The Aral Sea has been shrinking rapidly over the last half century. The principal cause is water taken from the sea's feeder rivers for irrigation of crops such as cotton. The effects on the local economy and environment have been disastrous.

THE NEAR EAST

Scale: 0 25 50 km

- –·–·– 1949 Armistice Line
- –··–··– 1950 Armistice Line
- – – – – 1974 Cease–fire Line
- Palestinian control
- Joint Israeli/ Palestinian control
- *Efrata* Main Jewish settlements
- Halhul Main Palestinian Arab towns
- Israeli security fence (April 2006)
- Israeli security fence subject to further ministerial examination

ISRAEL
POPULATION: 6,277,000 (inc. Israeli settlers in West Bank, and Golan Heights)
INFANT MORTALITY: 7.2 deaths per 1000 births
RELIGION: Jewish 80.1%, Muslim 14.6%, Christian 2.1%
GDP PER CAPITA: US$ 22,200 (2005)

West Bank
POPULATION: 2,386,000 (Muslim 75%, Jewish 17%)
INFANT MORTALITY: 20.2 deaths per 1,000 births
GDP PER CAPITA: US$ 1,100 (2003)

Gaza Strip
POPULATION: 1,376,000 (Muslim 98.7% Christian 0.7%, Jewish 0.6%)
INFANT MORTALITY: 23.5 deaths per 1,000 births
GDP PER CAPITA: US$ 600 (2003)

JORDAN
POPULATION: 5,760,000 (50% Palestinian Arab)

LEBANON
POPULATION: 3,826,000 (11% Palestinian Arab)

KOSOVO

Scale: 0 20 40 km

- Capital city
- Other towns
- International boundaries

Kosovo is a province of Serbia, but its status has been in question since the majority Albanian population rebelled in 1988. Kosovo is now effectively an international protectorate. Plans for its independence, opposed by Serbia, are being considered.

IRAQ

0   100   200 km

—·—·— International boundaries

— — — Province boundaries

Arbīl Underlined towns give their name to the administrative area in which they stand

⬭ Oilfields

〰 Oil pipelines

▨ Kurdish area

▥ Shi'ite area

■ Capital cities

● Main towns

∴ Archaeological sites

— Roads

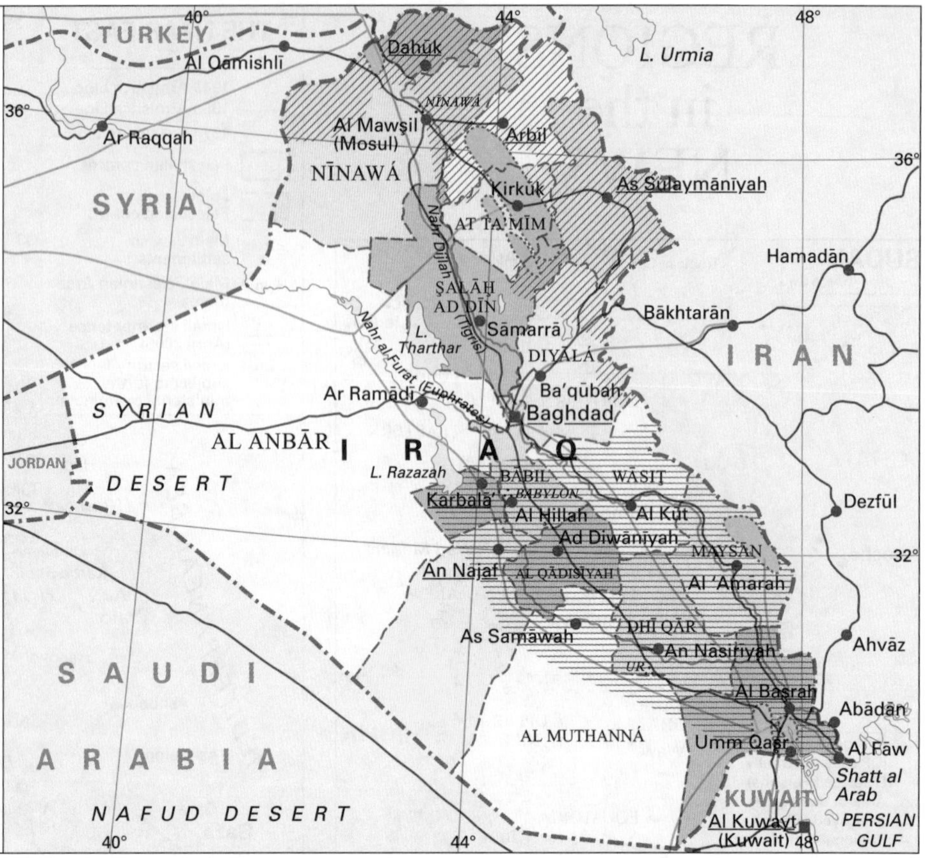

AREA: 438,317 sq km [169,234 sq miles]

POPULATION: 26,074,906 (Arab 77%, Kurdish 19%, Assyrian and others 4%)

RELIGIONS: Islam 97% (Shi'ite Muslim 60%, Sunni Muslim 37%, others 3%

OIL RESERVES: Between 112 and 186 billion barrels (second in the world after Saudi Arabia)

CONFLICTS: Iran 1980–88, Kuwait invasion (Gulf War) 1990–91, US-led Coalition 2003

GDP PER CAPITA: US $3,400 (2005)

TURKEY

L. Urmia

Al Qāmishlī

Dahūk

Ar Raqqah

Al Mawşil (Mosul)

Arbīl

NINAWĀ

NĪNAWĀ

Kirkūk

As Sulaymānīyah

AT TA'MĪM

Hamadān

SYRIA

ŞALĀḤ AD DĪN

Nahr Dijlah (Tigris)

Sāmarrā

Bākhtarān

L. Tharthar

DIYĀLĀ

Ba'qūbah

IRAN

SYRIAN

Nahr al Furāt (Euphrates)

Ar Ramādī

Baghdad

JORDAN

AL ANBĀR

I R A Q

L. Razazah

BĀBIL

WĀSIŢ

Karbalā'

BABYLON

Al Kūt

DESERT

Al Hillah

Dezfūl

An Najaf

Ad Dīwānīyah

MAYSĀN

AL QĀDISĪYAH

Al 'Amārah

S A U D I

As Samāwah

DHĪ QĀR

An Nāsirīyah

Ahvāz

A R A B I A

UR

Al Başrah

Abādān

AL MUTHANNĀ

Umm Qaşr

Al Fāw

KUWAIT

Shatt al Arab

NAFUD DESERT

Al Kuwayt (Kuwait)

PERSIAN GULF

AFGHANISTAN

0   100   200 km

—·—·— International boundaries

— — — Province boundaries

■ Capital cities

● Main towns

⊢⊣ Roads and road tunnel

▨ Land over 3,000 m

⅄ Mountain passes

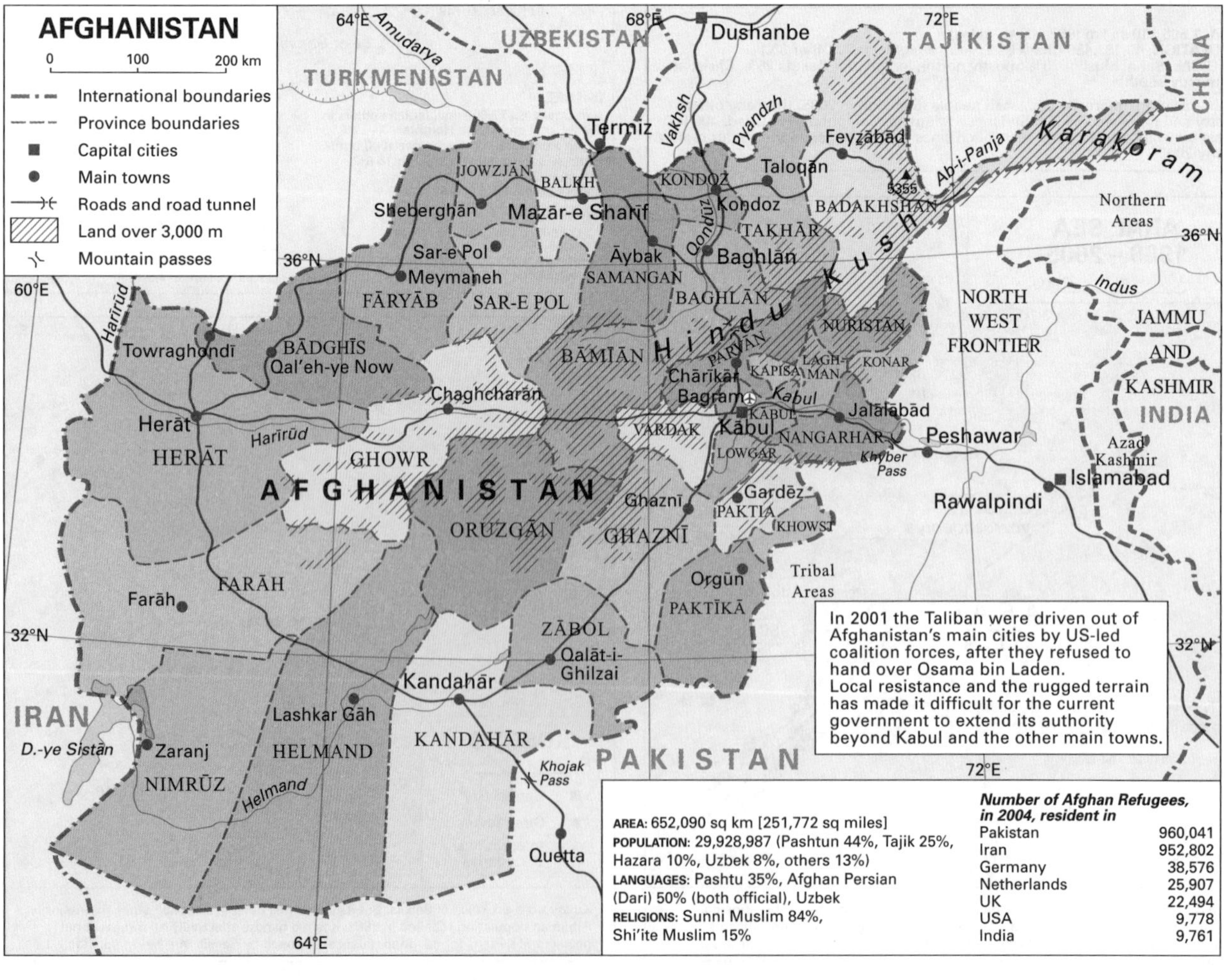

AREA: 652,090 sq km [251,772 sq miles]

POPULATION: 29,928,987 (Pashtun 44%, Tajik 25%, Hazara 10%, Uzbek 8%, others 13%)

LANGUAGES: Pashtu 35%, Afghan Persian (Dari) 50% (both official), Uzbek

RELIGIONS: Sunni Muslim 84%, Shi'ite Muslim 15%

UZBEKISTAN

Amudarya

Dushanbe

TAJIKISTAN

TURKMENISTAN

CHINA

Termiz

Vakhsh

Pyandzh

Feyzābād

Karakoram

JOWZJĀN

BALKH

KONDOZ

Taloqan

Ab-i-Panja

Sheberghān

Mazār-e Sharīf

Kondoz

BADAKHSHĀN

Qonduz

5355

Northern Areas

Sar-e Pol

Āybak

TAKHĀR

Indus

36°N

Meymaneh

SAMANGAN

Baghlān

FĀRYĀB

SAR-E POL

BAGHLĀN

Hindu Kush

NORTH WEST FRONTIER

JAMMU

Towraghondī

BĀDGHĪS

BĀMIĀN

PARVĀN

NURISTĀN

AND

Qal'eh-ye Now

Charīkār

KAPISA

LAGH-MAN

KONAR

KASHMIR

Herāt

Harīrūd

Bagrām

Kābul

Jalālābād

Peshawar

INDIA

HERĀT

Chaghcharān

VARDAK

KABUL

NANGARHĀR

Azad Kashmir

GHOWR

A F G H A N I S T A N

LOWGAR

Khyber Pass

Islāmābād

IRAN

FARĀH

ORUZGĀN

Ghaznī

PAKTIĀ

Gardēz

KHOWST

Tribal Areas

Rawalpindi

Farāh

GHAZNĪ

ZĀBOL

Orgūn

PAKTĪKĀ

D.-ye Sīstān

Zaranj

Kandahār

Qalāt-i-Ghilzai

NIMRŪZ

HELMAND

Lashkar Gāh

Helmand

KANDAHĀR

Khojak Pass

PAKISTAN

Quetta

In 2001 the Taliban were driven out of Afghanistan's main cities by US-led coalition forces, after they refused to hand over Osama bin Laden. Local resistance and the rugged terrain has made it difficult for the current government to extend its authority beyond Kabul and the other main towns.

Number of Afghan Refugees, in 2004, resident in	
Pakistan	960,041
Iran	952,802
Germany	38,576
Netherlands	25,907
UK	22,494
USA	9,778
India	9,761

READY REFERENCE

PLANET EARTH

Mean distance from the Sun	149.6 million km (93 million mi)
Average speed around the Sun	108,000km/h (66,600mph)
Age	c.4600 million years
Mass	5.9×10^{21} tonnes
Density (water = 1)	5.52
Volume	$1,083,230 \times 10^6$cu km ($260,000 \times 10^6$cu mi)
Area	510 million sq km (197 million sq mi)
Land surface	149 million sq km (58 million sq mi) = 29.2% of total area
Water surface	361 million sq km (139 million sq mi) = 70.7% of total area
Equatorial circumference	40,077km (24,904mi)
Polar circumference	40,009km (24,862mi)
Equatorial diameter	12,757km (7927mi)
Polar diameter	12,714km (7900mi)

INSIDE THE EARTH

	Density	Temperature		State	Thickness	
Continental crust	2.8	<500°C	(930°F)	Solid	c.40km	(c.25mi)
Oceanic crust	2.9	<1100°C	(2010°F)	Solid	c.7km	(c.4mi)
Upper mantle	4.3	<1400°C	(2550°F)	Molten	c.900km	(c.560mi)
Lower mantle	5.5	<1700°C	(3090°F)	Solid	c.1900km	(c.1180mi)
Outer core	10.0	<2300°C	(4170°F)	Molten	c.2200km	(c.1370mi)
Inner core	13.5	<5500°C	(9930°F)	Solid	c.1300km	(c.810mi)

SELECTED EARTH RECORDS

Greatest tide	Bay of Fundy, Nova Scotia, Canada, 16.3m (53.5ft)
Deepest gorge	River Colca, Peru, 4360m (14,300ft)
Longest gorge	Grand Canyon, Arizona, USA, 350km (217mi)
Deepest lake	Lake Baikal, Siberia, Russia, 1742m (5714ft)
Highest navigable lake	Lake Titicaca, Peru/Bolivia, c.3810m (c.12,500ft)
Deepest cave	Réseau Jean Bernard, Haute-Savoie, France, 1602m (5256ft)
Longest cave system	Mammoth Cave, Kentucky, USA, c.560km (c.350mi)
Deepest valley	Kali Gandaki, Nepal, c.4400m (c.14,400ft)
Longest glacier	Lambert-Fisher Ice Passage, Antarctica, 515km (320mi)
Deepest depression	Dead Sea, Israel/Jordan, −403m (−1322ft)

CLIMATE RECORDS

Temperature

Highest recorded temperature: Al Aziziyah, Libya, 58°C (136.4°F), September 13, 1922
Highest mean annual temperature: Dallol, Ethiopia, 34.4°C (94°F), 1960-66
Longest heatwave: Marble Bar, W Australia, 162 days over 38°C (100°F), October 23, 1923 to April 7, 1924
Lowest recorded temperature (outside poles): Verkhoyansk, Siberia, −68°C (−90°F), February 6, 1933*
Lowest mean annual temperature: Polus Nedostupnosti (Pole of Cold) Antarctica, −57.8°C (−72°F)

Precipitation

Driest place: Arica, N Chile, 0.8mm (0.03in) per year (60-year average)
Longest drought: Calama, N Chile. No recorded rainfall in 400 years to 1971
Wettest place (average): Tututendo, Colombia. Mean annual rainfall 11,770mm (463.4in)
Wettest place (12 months): Cherrapunji, Meghalaya, NE India, 26,470mm (1040in), August 1860 to August 1861†
Wettest place (24-hour period): Cilaos, Réunion, Indian Ocean, 1870mm (73.6in), March 15-16, 1952
Heaviest hailstones: Gopalganj, Bangladesh, up to 1.02kg (2.25lb), 14 April 1986‡
Heaviest snowfall (continuous): Bessans, Savoie France, 1730mm (68in) in 19 hours, April 5-6, 1969
Heaviest snowfall (season/year): Paradise Ranger Station, Mt Rainier, Washington, USA, 31,102mm (1224.5in), February 19, 1971 to February 18, 1972

Pressure and winds

Highest barometric pressure: Agata, Siberia, 1083.8mb (32in) at altitude 262m (862 ft), December 31, 1968
Lowest barometric pressure: Typhoon Tip, 480km (300mi) W of Guam, Pacific Ocean, 870mb (25.69in), October 12, 1979
Highest recorded wind speed: Mt Washington, New Hampshire, USA, 371km/h (231mph), April 12, 1934§
Windiest place: Commonwealth Bay, George V Coast, Antarctica, where gales regularly exceed 320km/h (200mph)

* Verkhoyansk also registered the greatest annual range of temperature: −70°C to 37°C (−94°F to 98°F)
† Cherrapunji also holds the record for rainfall in one month: 930mm (37in) fell in July 1861
‡ Killed 92 people
§ Three times as strong as hurricane force on the Beaufort Scale

LARGEST ISLANDS

	sq km	sq mi
Europe		
Great Britain [8]	229,900	88,700
Iceland	103,000	39,800
Ireland	84,400	32,600
Novaya Zemlya (N)	48,200	18,600
Sicily	25,700	9900
Sardinia	24,090	9300
Asia		
Borneo [3]	743,000	287,400
Sumatra [6]	425,000	164,000
Honshu [7]	230,800	89,100
Sulawesi	189,200	73,000
Java	126,500	48,800
Luzon	104,700	40,400
Mindanao	95,000	36,600
Hokkaido	83,500	32,200
Sakhalin	76,400	29,500
Sri Lanka	65,600	25,300
Africa		
Madagascar [4]	587,000	226,700
Socotra	3100	1200
Réunion	2,510	969
North America		
Greenland [1]	2,175,000	840,000
Baffin Island [5]	507,500	195,900
Victoria Island [9]	212,200	81,900
Ellesmere Island [10]	196,200	75,800
Cuba	110,860	42,800
Newfoundland	96,000	37,100
Hispaniola	76,500	29,500
Jamaica	11,000	4200
Puerto Rico	8,900	3400
South America		
Tierra del Fuego	47,000	18,100
Falkland Island (E)	6800	2600
Oceania*		
New Guinea [2]	885,800	342,000
New Zealand (S)	150,500	58,100
New Zealand (N)	114,700	44,300
Tasmania	68,300	26,400
Hawaii	10,450	4000

* Geographers consider Australia to be a continental landmass

LARGEST INLAND LAKES AND SEAS

	Location	sq km	sq mi
Europe			
Lake Ladoga	Russia	17,700	6800
Lake Onega	Russia	9600	3700
Saimaa system	Finland	8000	3100
Vänern	Sweden	6500	2100
Asia			
Caspian Sea [1]	W. Central Asia	371,000	143,000
Aral Sea* [6]	Kazakstan/ Uzbekistan	33,640	13,000
Lake Baikal [9]	Russia	31,500	12,200
Tonlé Sap	Cambodia	20,000	7700
Lake Balkhash	Kazakstan	18,400	7100
Africa			
Victoria Nyanza [3]	East Africa	68,000	26,000
Lake Tanganyika [7]	Central Africa	33,000	12,700
Lake Malawi [10]	East Africa	29,600	11,400
Lake Chad	Central Africa	26,000	10,000
Lake Turkana	Ethiopia/Kenya	8500	3300
Lake Volta†	Ghana	8480	3250
North America			
Lake Superior [2]	Canada/USA	82,400	31,800
Lake Huron [4]	Canada/USA	59,600	23,010
Lake Michigan [5]	USA	58,000	22,300
Great Bear Lake [8]	Canada	31,800	12,280
Great Slave Lake	Canada	28,400	11,000
Lake Erie	Canada/USA	25,700	9900
Lake Winnipeg	Canada	24,500	9500
Lake Ontario	Canada/USA	19,700	7600
Lake Nicaragua	Nicaragua	8000	3100
South America			
Lake Titicaca‡	Bolivia/Peru	8300	3200
Lake Poopó	Peru	2800	1100
Australia			
Lake Eyre§	Australia	9300	3600
Lake Torrens§	Australia	5800	2200
Lake Gairdner§	Australia	4800	1900

* Shrinking in area due to environmental factors; until the 1980s it was the world's 4th largest
† Artificial lake created by Akosombo Dam (1966)
‡ Lake Maracaibo, in Venezuela, is far larger at 13,260 sq km (5,120 sq mi), but is linked to the Caribbean by a narrow channel and therefore not an 'inland' lake
§ Salt lakes that vary in size with rainfall

BEAUFORT SCALE

Named after the 19th-century British naval officer who devised it, the Beaufort Scale assesses wind speed according to its effects. Originally designed in 1806 as an aid for sailors, it has since been adapted for use on land and was internationally recognised in 1874.

Scale	Wind speed		Name
	km/h	mph	
0	0–1	0–1	Calm
1	1–5	1–3	Light air
2	6–11	4–7	Light breeze
3	12–19	8–12	Gentle breeze
4	20–28	13–18	Moderate
5	29–38	19–24	Fresh
6	39–49	25–31	Strong
7	50–61	32–38	Near gale
8	62–74	39–46	Gale
9	75–88	47–54	Strong gale
10	89–102	55–63	Storm
11	103–117	64–72	Violent storm
12–17	118+	73+	Hurricane

WIND-CHILL FACTORS

A combination of cold and wind makes the human body feel cooler than the actual air temperature. The charts below give approximate equivalents for combinations of wind speed and temperature. In sub-zero temperatures, even moderate winds will significantly reduce effective temperatures: if human skin was exposed to winds of 48km/h (30mph) in a temperature of −34°C (−30°F) it would freeze solid in 30 seconds.

Temp. °C	Wind speed (km/h)				Temp. °F	Wind speed (mph)			
	16	32	48	64*		10	20	30	40*
15	11	9	8	6	30	16	4	−2	−5
10	6	3	2	−1	20	3	−10	−18	−21
5	1	4	−5	−8	10	−9	−24	−33	−37
0	−8	−14	−17	−19	0	−2	−39	−44	−53
−5	−14	−21	−25	−27	−10	−34	−53	−6	−69
−10	−20	−28	−33	−35	−20	−46	−67	−79	−84
−15	−26	−36	−40	−43	−30	−58	−81	−93	−100
−20	−32	−42	−48	−51	−40	−71	−95	−109	−115

*Wind speeds of more than c.64km/h (40mph) have only a marginally greater cooling effect

CONTINENTS

Continent	Area			Highest point above sea level		m	ft	Lowest point below sea level		m	ft
	sq km	sq mi	%								
Asia	44,391,000	17,139,000	29.8	Mt Everest (China/Nepal)		8848	29,029	Dead Sea, Israel/Jordan		−403	−1322
Africa	30,000,000	11,700,000	20.3	Mt Kilimanjaro, Tanzania		5895	19,340	Lake Assal, Djibouti		−153	−502
North America	24,454,000	9,442,000	16.2	Mt McKinley, Alaska		6194	20,321	Death Valley, California, USA		−86	−282
South America	17,793,000	6,868,000	11.9	Mt Aconcagua, Argentina		6960	22,834	Peninsular Valdés, Argentina		−40	−131
Antarctica	14,200,000	5,500,000	9.4	Vinson Massif		4897	16,066	*Bentley Trench, West Antarctica		−2540	−8333
Europe	10,360,000	4,000,000	6.7	Mt Elbrus, Russia		5633	18,481	Caspian Sea, W. Central Asia		−28	−92
Oceania	8,945,000	3,454,000	5.7	Puncak Jaya (Ngga Pulu), Indonesia		5029	16,499	Lake Eyre (N), South Australia		−15	−50

The Bentley trench is englacial and therefore not a surface point

OCEANS

Ocean	Area			Average depth		Greatest known depth		m	ft
	sq km	sq mi	%	m	ft				
Pacific	166,000,000	69,356,000	49.9	4300	14,100	Mariana Trench		11,033	36,198
Atlantic	82,000,000	32,000,000	25.7	3700	12,100	Puerto Rico Trench*		8650	28,370
Indian	73,600,000	28,400,000	20.5	4000	13,000	Java Trench		7725	25,344
Arctic	13,986,000	5,400,000	3.9	1330	4300	Molloy Deep		5,608	18,399

7th deepest trench in the world; 8 of the deepest 10, including 1-6, are in the Pacific Ocean

HIGHEST MOUNTAINS

	Location	m	ft		Location	m	ft
Europe				Ruwenzori	Uganda/Zaïre	5109	16,763
Elbrus*	Russia	5633	18,481				
Mont Blanc†‡	France/Italy	4810	15,781	**North America**			
Monte Rosa‡	Italy/Switzerland	4634	15,203	Mt McKinley (Denali)‡	USA (Alaska)	6194	20,321
also				Mt Logan	Canada	6050	19,849
Matterhorn (Cervino)‡	Italy/Switzerland	4478	14,691	Citlaltépetl (Orizaba)	Mexico	5700	18,701
Jungfrau	Switzerland	4158	13,642	Mt St Elias	USA/Canada	5489	18,008
Grossglockner	Austria	3797	12,457	Popocatépetl	Mexico	5452	17,887
Mulhacen	Spain	3478	11,411	*also*			
Etna	Italy (Sicily)	3340	10,958	Mt Whitney	USA	4418	14,495
Zugspitze	Germany	2962	9718	Tajumulco	Guatemala	4220	13,845
Olympus	Greece	2917	9570	Chirripo Grande	Costa Rica	3837	12,589
Galdhopiggen	Norway	2468	8100	Pico Duarte	Dominican Rep.	3175	10,417
Ben Nevis	UK (Scotland)	1343	4406				
				South America			
Asia§				Aconcagua#	Argentina	6960	22,834
Everest	China/Nepal	8850	29,035	Ojos del Salado	Argentina/Chile	6863	22,516
K2 (Godwin Austen)	China/Kashmir	8611	28,251	Pissis	Argentina	6779	22,241
Kanchenjunga‡	India/Nepal	8586	28,169	Mercedario	Argentina/Chile	6770	22,211
Lhotse‡	China/Nepal	8516	27,939	Huascarán‡	Peru	6768	22,204
Makalu‡	China/Nepal	8481	27,824				
Cho Oyu	China/Nepal	8201	26,906	**Oceania**			
Dhaulagiri‡	Nepal	8172	26,811	Puncak Jaya	Indonesia (W Irian)	5029	16,499
Manaslu (Kutang)‡	Nepal	8156	26,758	Puncak Trikora	Indonesia (W Irian)	4750	15,584
Nanga Parbat	Kashmir	8126	26,660	Puncak Mandala	Indonesia (W Irian)	4702	15,427
Annapurna‡	Nepal	8078	26,502	Mt Wilhelm	Papua New Guinea	4508	14,790
also				*also*			
Kommunizma Pik	Tajikistan	7495	24,590	Mauna Kea	USA (Hawaii)	4205	13 796
Ararat	Turkey	5165	16,945	Mauna Loa	USA (Hawaii)	4169	13,678
Gunong Kinabalu	Malaysia (Borneo)	4101	13,455	Mt Cook (Aorangi)	New Zealand	3764	12,349
Fujiyama (Fuji-san)	Japan	3776	12,388	Mt Kosciusko	Australia	2228	7310
Africa				**Antarctica**			
Kilimanjaro	Tanzania	5895	19,340	Vinson Massif	—	4897	16,066
Mt Kenya	Kenya	5200	17,058	Mt Kirkpatrick	—	4528	14,855

* Caucasus Mountains include 14 other peaks higher than Mont Blanc, the highest point in non-Russian Europe
† Highest point is in France; the highest point wholly in Italian territory is 4760m (15,616ft)
‡ Many mountains, especially in Asia, have two or more significant peaks; only the highest ones are listed here
§ The ranges of Central Asia have more than 100 peaks over 7315m (24,000ft); thus the first 10 listed here constitute the world's 10 highest mountains
# Highest mountain outside Asia

LONGEST RIVERS

	Outflow	km	mi
Europe			
Volga	Caspian Sea	3750	2330
Danube	Black Sea	2859	1770
Ural*	Caspian Sea	2535	1575
Asia			
Yangtze [3]	Pacific Ocean	6300	3900
Yenisey-Angara [5]	Arctic Ocean	5550	3445
Huang He [6]	Pacific Ocean	5500	3400
Ob-Irtysh [7]	Arctic Ocean	5410	3360
Amur [10]	Pacific Ocean	4400	2730
Mekong [9]	Pacific Ocean	4180	2600
Africa			
Nile [1]	Mediterranean	6700	4160
Congo (Zaïre) [8]	Atlantic Ocean	4670	2900
Niger	Atlantic Ocean	4180	2600
Zambezi	Indian Ocean	2740	1700
North America			
Mississippi-Missouri[4]	Gulf of Mexico	6050	3760
Mackenzie	Arctic Ocean	4240	2630
Missouri	Mississippi	4120	2560
Mississippi	Gulf of Mexico	3780	2350
Yukon	Pacific Ocean	3185	1980
Rio Grande	Gulf of Mexico	3030	1880
Arkansas	Mississippi	2335	1450
Colorado	Pacific Ocean	2333	1450
South America			
Amazon [2]	Atlantic Ocean	6430	3990
Paraná-Plata	Atlantic Ocean	4000	2400
Purus	Amazon	3350	2080
Madeira	Amazon	3200	1990
Sao Francisco	Atlantic Ocean	2900	1800
Australia			
Murray-Darling	Southern Ocean	3750	2830
Darling	Murray	3070	1905
Murray	Southern Ocean	2575	1600
Murrumbidgee	Murray	1690	1050

* Flows through Europe and Asia

MAJOR EARTHQUAKES SINCE 1900

Year	Location	Magnitude†	Deaths
1920	Gansu, China	8.6	180,000
1923	Yokohama, Japan	8.3	143,000
1927	Nan Xian, China	8.3	200,000
1932	Gansu, China	7.6	70,000
1933	Honshu Japan	8.9	2990
1935	Quetta, India (now Pakistan)	7.5	60,000
1939	Chillan, Chile	8.3	28,000
1939	Erzincan, Turkey	7.9	30,000
1960	Valdivia, Chile	9.5‡	6000
1970	N Peru	7.7	86,794
1976	Guatemala	7.5	22,778
1976	Tangshan, China	8.2	252,000
1978	Tabas, Iran	7.7	25,000
1980	El Asnam, Algeria	7.3	20,000
1985	Mexico City, Mexico	8.1	4200
1988	NW Armenia	6.8	55,000
1990	N Iran	7.7	36,000
1993	Maharastra, India	6.4	30,000
1995	Kobe, Japan	7.2	5000
1995	Sakhalin Island, Russia	7.5	2000
1999	Izmit, Turkey	7.4	15,000
2001	Gujarat, India	7.7	20,085
2003	Bam, Iraq	6.6	26,000
2004	Indian Ocean	9.1-9.3	230,000
2005	Kashmir, Pakistan	7.6	87,000
2008	Sichuan, China	8.0	80,000

† On the Richter scale ‡ Highest ever recorded

HIGHEST WATERFALLS

Name	Total height		Location	River	Highest fall	
	m	ft			m	ft
Angel	980	3212	La Gran Sabrana, Venezuela	Caroni	807	2648
Tugela	947	3110	Natal, South Africa	Tugela	410	1350
Utigård	800	2625	Nesdale, Norway	Jostedal Glacier	600	1970
Mongefoseen	774	2540	Mongebekk, Norway	Monge	—	—
Yosemite	739	2425	California, USA	Yosemite Creek	739	2425
Østre Mardøla Foss	656	2154	Eikisdal, Norway	Mardals	296	974
Tyssestrengane	646	2120	Hardanger, Norway	Tysso	289	948
Cuquenán	610	2000	Venezuela	Arabopó	—	—
Sutherland	580	1904	Otago, New Zealand	Arthur	248	815
Takkakaw	502	1650	British Columbia, Canada	Daly Glacie	365	1200
Ribbon	491	1612	California, USA	Ribbon Fall Stream	491	1612

The greatest falls by volume are the Boyoma (formerly Stanley) Falls on the River Congo (Zaïre), with a mean annual flow of 17,000 cu m/sec (600,000 cu ft/sec). The Niagara Falls and the Victoria Falls (*Mosi oa Tunya*, "the smoke that thunders") are 4th and 9th respectively, in terms of volume; though both are relatively modest in height.

WORLD POPULATION

Date	Millions	Date	Millions	Date	Millions
2000BC	100	1800	900	1970	3,700
1000BC	120	1850	1,250	1980	4,450
1	180	1900	1,620	1990	5,245
1000	275	1920	1,860	1995	5,735
1250	375	1930	2,070	2000	6,080
1500	420	1940	2,300	2005	6,465
1650	500	1950	2,500	2010*	6,824
1700	615	1960	3,050	2050*	9,104

* United Nations 'medium' estimates

MOST POPULOUS COUNTRIES

Country	Population thousands	Density per sq km	Density per sq mile
China	1,321,852	138	357
India	1,129,866	344	890
USA	301,140	31	81
Indonesia	234,694	123	319
Brazil	190,011	22	58
Pakistan	164,742	207	536
Bangladesh	150,448	1045	2706
Russia	141,378	8	21
Nigeria	135,031	146	379
Japan	127,433	337	874
Mexico	108,700	56	144
Philippines	91,077	304	786
Vietnam	85,262	257	666
Germany	82,400	231	598
Egypt	80,335	80	208
Ethiopia	76,512	69	179
Turkey	71,159	92	238
Congo (Dem. Rep.)	65,752	28	73
Iran	65,398	40	103
Thailand	65,068	127	328
France	60,876	110	286
United Kingdom	60,776	251	651
Italy	58,148	193	500
Korea, South	49,054	494	1280
Burma (Myanmar)	47,374	70	181
Ukraine	46,300	77	199
Colombia	44,380	39	101

LEAST POPULOUS COUNTRIES

Country	Population thousands	Density per sq km	Density per sq mile
Vatican City	1	2,273	5,882
Tuvalu	12	394	1,181
Nauru	13	664	1,661
Palau	21	45	114
San Marino	29	488	1,463
Monaco	33	32,543	81,358
Liechtenstein	34	212	566
St Kitts & Nevis	39	150	391
Marshall Islands	60	336	863
Dominica	69	92	238

Only independent sovereign states are listed

MAJOR ESTABLISHED RELIGIONS

The figures are estimates, based primarily on UN reports and statistics released by most of the religious bodies. The table does not include the various folk and tribal religions of Africa and Asia, which could total as many as 300 million adherents, including more than 10 million Shamanists.

Religion	Millions	Religion	Millions
Christianity	1,669	Hinduism	720
Roman Catholic	952	Confucianism*	350
Protestant	337	Buddhism *†	320
Orthodox	162	Taoism*	25
Anglican	70	Sikhism	19
Other	148	Judaism	18
Islam	1,050	Baha'ism	5.9
Sunni	960	Jainism	3.8
Shia (Shiite)	90	Shintoism†	3.5

* The number of practising Confucians, Buddhists and Taoists in China cannot be accurately estimated; there are c.6 million Confucians outside China
† Many people in the Far East, notably in Japan, claim to adhere to more than one religion and figures are therefore only approximate at best

LARGEST COUNTRIES

No.	Country	Area sq km	Area sq mi
1	Russia*	17,075,400	6,592,812
2	Canada†	9,970,610	3,849,653
3	USA	9,629,091	3,717,792
4	China‡	9,596,961	3,705,387
5	Brazil§	8,514,215	3,287,3386
6	Australia#	7,741,220	2,988,885
7	India¶	3,287,263	1,269,212
8	Argentina	2,780,400	1,073,512
9	Kazakhstan	2,724,900	1,052,084
10	Sudan**	2,505,813	967,494
11	Algeria	2,381,741	919,590
12	Dem. Rep. Congo	2,344,858	905,350
13	Saudi Arabia	2,149,690	829,995
14	Mexico	1,958,201	756,061
15	Indonesia	1,904,569	735,354
16	Libya	1,759,540	679,358
17	Iran	1,648,195	636,368
18	Mongolia	1,566,500	604,826
19	Peru	1,285,216	496,222
20	Chad	1,284,000	495,752

* Largest country in Asia and in Europe † Largest in North America ‡ Excluding Taiwan § Largest in South America # Largest in Oceania ¶ Excluding parts of Jammu and Kashmir occupied by Pakistan and China ** Largest country in Africa

SMALLEST COUNTRIES

Country	Area sq km	Area sq mi
Vatican City	0.44	0.17
Monaco	1	0.39
Nauru	21	8.1
Tuvalu	26	10.0
San Marino	61	23.6
Liechtenstein	160	61.8
Marshall Islands	181	69.9
Saint Kitts & Nevis	261	101
Maldives	298	115
Malta	316	122

LARGEST CITIES

UN estimates for 'urban agglomerations', which take no account of administrative boundaries.

City	Country	Population (thousands)
Mexico City	Mexico	19,013
Mumbai (Bombay)	India	18,336
São Paulo	Brazil	18,333
New York	USA	17,800
Delhi	India	15,334
Kolkata (Calcutta)	India	14,299
Buenos Aires	Argentina	13,349
Jakarta	Indonesia	13,194
Shanghai	China	12,665
Dhaka	Nigeria	12,560
Tokyo	Japan	12,064
Karachi	Pakistan	11,819

MAJOR LANGUAGES

There are more than 5,000 languages in the world, 845 of them in India alone. The tables below give the approximate numbers of native speakers (their 'mother tongue') and the populations of countries where the language has official status.

Language	Millions	Language	Millions
Native speakers		Punjabi	84
Chinese	1,070	Korean	71
Mandarin	864		
English	443	**Official populations**	
Hindi	352	English	1,420
Spanish	341	Chinese	1,070
Russian	293	Hindi	800
Arabic	197	Spanish	290
Bengali	184	Russian	275
Portuguese	173	French	220
Malay-Indonesian	142	Arabic	190
Japanese	125	Portuguese	185
French	121	Bengali	177
German	118	Malay	165
Urdu	92	Japanese	140

LARGEST ECONOMIES

Country	GDP*
USA	12,370
China	8,158
Japan	3,867
India	3,678
Germany	2,446
United Kingdom	1,867
France	1,816
Italy	1,645
Brazil	1,580
Russia	1,535
Canada	1,077
Mexico	1,066
Spain	1,014
Korea, South	983
Indonesia	899
Australia	643
Taiwan	611
Iran	552
Turkey	552
Thailand	546

* Gross Domestic Product US$ billions

RICHEST COUNTRIES

Country	GDP*
Luxembourg	62,700
Norway	42,400
USA	41,800
Switzerland	35,000
Iceland	34,600
San Marino	34,600
Ireland	34,100
Denmark	33,500
Austria	32,900
Canada	32,800
Australia	32,000
Belgium	31,800
United Kingdom	30,900
Netherlands	30,500
Japan	30,400
Finland	30,300
France	29,900
Germany	29,700
Singapore	29,700
Sweden	29,600

* GDP per capita in US$

ENERGY SOURCES BY NATION

Percentages of power sources in selected countries

Country	Fossil fuels	Hydroelectric power	Nuclear power
Saudi Arabia	100	—	—
Denmark	97.8	0.1	—
Australia	89.7	10.3	—
Netherlands	95.3	0.2	4.5
China	81.5	18.5	—
Italy	78.0	20.5	—
India	76.4	21.8	1.8
UK	76.2	1.9	21.9
Russia	73.7	15.4	10.9
USA	70.1	9.4	19.9
Germany	67.9	3.7	28.4
Japan	63.9	11.9	24.0
Spain	46.1	18.2	35.3
Belgium	39.1	1.3	59.6
Canada	22.5	60.7	16.8
France	13.5	13.6	72.9
Brazil	6.5	92.9	0.6
Sweden	4.7	43.1	52.2
Iceland	0.2	93.5	—

WORLD TOURISM

Country	Arrivals from abroad millions (2000)	Receipts US$ billions (2000)
France	75.5	29.9
USA	50.9	85.2
Spain	48.2	31.0
Italy	41.2	27.4
China	31.2	16.2
UK	25.2	19.5
Russia	21.2	7.5
Mexico	20.6	8.3
Canada	20.4	10.8
Germany	19	17.8
Austria	18	11.4
Poland	17.4	6.1

TRANSPORT NETWORKS

Road and rail networks for the leading countries of the world (1995), given in thousands

Total road network			Total rail network		
Country	km	mi	Country	km	mi
USA	6277.9	3,901	USA	239.7	148.9
India	2,962.5	1,840.9	Russia	87.5	54.4
Brazil	1,824.4	1,133.7	India	62.5	38.8
Japan	1,130.9	702.7	China	54	33.6
China	1,041.1	646.9	Germany	40.4	25.1
Russia	884	549.3	Australia	35.8	22.2
Canada	849.4	527.8	Argentina	34.2	21.3
France	811.6	504.3	France	32.6	20.3
Australia	810.3	503.5	Mexico	26.5	16.5
Germany	636.3	395.4	Poland	24.9	15.8
Romania	461.9	287	S. Africa	23.6	14.7

ABUNDANCE OF ELEMENTS

Universe: It is estimated that up to 99% of the known universe is made up of hydrogen and helium, with hydrogen in a ratio of 20:1 to helium and some 10,000:1 of other elements. The next, in order, are oxygen, carbon, nitrogen, silicon, magnesium, neon, sulphur and iron.

Earth's crust*	%	Living things	%	Sea water†	%
Oxygen	46.6	Oxygen	62.0	Oxygen	85.7
Silicon	27.7	Carbon	20.0	Hydrogen	10.7
Aluminium	8.1	Hydrogen	10.0	Chlorine	1.9
Iron	5.0	Nitrogen	3.0	Sodium	1.1
Calcium	3.6	Calcium	2.5	Magnesium	0.1
Sodium	2.8	Phosphorous	1.14		
Potassium	2.6	Chlorine	0.16		
Magnesium	2.1	Sulphur	0.14		
Titanium	0.44	Potassium	0.11		
Hydrogen	0.14				

* Igneous rocks in the lithosphere † Average ocean concentration

SI UNITS

The *Systéme International d'Unités* is the worldwide standard system of units used by scientists. Originally proposed in 1960, it is based on seven basic units.

Measurement	Unit	Symbol
Basic units		
Length	metre	m
Mass	kilogram	kg
Time	second	s
Electric current	ampere	A
Thermodynamic temperature	kelvin	K
Amount of substance	mole	mol
Luminous intensity	candela	cd
Supplementary units		
Plane angle	radian	rad
Solid angle	steradian	sr
Derived units		
Frequency	hertz	Hz
Force	newton	N
Pressure, stress	pascal	Pa
Work (energy, heat)	joule	J
Power	watt	W
Electric charge	coulomb	C
Electromotive force	volt	V
Electric resistance	ohm	Ω
Electric conductance	siemens	S
Electric capacitance	farad	F
Inductance	henry	H
Magnetic flux	weber	Wb
Magnetic flux density	tesla	T
Illuminance	lux	lx
Luminous flux	lumen	lm
Radiation exposure	röntgen	r
Radiation activity	becquerel	Bq
Radiation absorbed dose	gray	Gy
Radiation dose equivalent	sievert	Sv
Celsius temperature	°Celsius	°C

ROMAN NUMERALS

Arabic	Roman
1	I
2	II
3	III
4	IV
5	V
6	VI
7	VII
8	VIII
9	IX
10	X
11	XI
12	XII
13	XIII
14	XIV
15	XV
16	XVI
17	XVII
18	XVIII
19	XIX
20	XX
30	XXX
40	XL
50	L
60	LX
70	LXX
80	LXXX
90	XC
100	C
200	CC
300	CCC
400	CD
500	D
1000	M
5000	$\bar{V}$
10,000	$\bar{X}$
100,000	$\bar{C}$

SI DERIVED UNITS

Measurement	Unit	Symbol
Area	square metre	m^2
Volume	cubic metre	m^3
Velocity	metre per second	$m\ s^{-1}$
Acceleration	metre per second squared	$m\ s^{-2}$
Angular velocity	radian per second	$rad\ s^{-1}$
Angular acceleration	radian per second squared	$rad\ s^{-2}$
Density	kilogram per cubic metre	$kg\ m^{-3}$
Momentum	kilogram metre per second	$kg\ m\ s^{-1}$
Angular momentum	kilogram metre squared per second	$kg\ m^2\ s^{-1}$
Mass rate of flow	kilogram per second	$kg\ s^{-1}$
Volume rate of flow	cubic metre per second	$m^3\ s^{-1}$
Torque	newton metre	$N\ m$
Surface tension	newton per metre	$N\ m^{-1}$
Dynamic viscosity	newton second per metre squared	$N\ s\ m^{-2}$
Kinematic viscosity	metre squared per second	$m^2\ s^{-1}$
Thermal coefficient	per °Celsius, or per kelvin	$°C^{-1}$, or K^{-1}
Thermal conductivity	watt per metre °C	$W\ m^{-1}\ °C^{-1}$
Heat capacity	joule per kelvin	$J\ K^{-1}$
Specific latent heat	joule per kilogram	$J\ kg^{-1}$
Specific heat capacity	joule per kilogram kelvin	$J\ kg^{-1}\ K^{-1}$
Velocity of light	metre per second	$m\ s^{-1}$
Permeability	henry per metre	$H\ m^{-1}$
Permittivity	farad per metre	$F\ m^{-1}$
Electric force	volt per metre	$v\ m^{-1}$
Electric flux density	coulomb per metre squared	$C\ m^{-2}$

ALLOYS

Name	Composition of metals	Common uses
Aluminium bronze	90% copper, 10% aluminium	Marine engineering
Manganese bronze	95% copper, 5% manganese	Marine engineering
Gun metal bronze	90% copper, 10% tin	'Copper' coins
Silicon bronze	Copper with silicon and small amounts of iron, nickel, manganese	Telegraph wires
Bell metal	Copper with 15% or more tin	Casting bells
Red brass	85% copper, 14% zinc, 1% tin	Plumbing
Yellow brass	67% copper, 33% zinc	Door handles
Nickel silver (cupronickel)	55% copper, 27% zinc, 18% nickel	'Silver' coins
Steel	99% iron, 1% carbon	
Stainless steel	Iron with 0.1-2.0% carbon, up to 27% chromium or 20% tungsten or 15% nickel and lesser amounts of other elements	Cutlery, kettles, pans, etc
18-carat gold	75% gold, 25% gold and copper	Jewellery
Palladium (white gold)	90% gold, 10% palladium	Jewellery
Sterling silver	92.5% silver, 7.5% copper	Jewellery
US silver	90% silver, 10% copper	Jewellery
Dentist's amalgam	70% mercury, 30% copper	Filling teeth
Type metal	82% lead, 15% antimony, 3% tin	Printing
Pewter	91% tin, 7.5% antimony, 1.5% copper	Tankards
Solder	Lead, tin	Joining metals

GEMSTONES

Diamond, emerald, ruby and sapphire were formerly classified as 'precious' stones, with others termed 'semi-precious'. This division is usually no longer made.

Mineral	Colour	Mohs' no.	Birthstone
Agate	Striped grey-white, blue	6.5-7.0	May
Amber*	Yellow, honey	2.0-2.5	
Amethyst	Purple	7.0	February
Aquamarine†	Pale blue-green	7.5	March
Beryl	Green, blue, pink	7.5	
Bloodstone	Dark green with red spots	7.0	March
Carnelian§	Green and yellow shades	8.5	August
Chrysoberyl‡	Green and yellow	8.5	June
Coral*	Varies, often red	Soft	
Diamond	Clear (pure), various colour tints	10.0	April
Emerald#	Green	7.5-8.0	May
Garnet	Red and other various colours	6.5-7.0	January
Jade	Green	6.5-7.0	
Lapis lazuli	Azure blue	6.5-7.0	September
Moonstone	Whitish blue	6.0-6.5	June
Onyx	Various, black and white stripes	6.5-7.0	July
Opal	Milky white, black, rainbow streaks	5.5-6.5	October
Pearl*	White, pearl grey	Soft	June
Quartz	Clear	7.0	April
Rose quartz	Pink	7.0	October
Ruby	Red	9.0	July
Sapphire	Blue	9.0	September
Smoky quartz	Smoky brown, red, yellow	7.0	
Topaz	Blue, yellow, greenish, pink, clear	8.0	November
Tourmaline	Black, blue-black, red, green	7.0-7.5	October
Turquoise	Sky blue, greenish blue-grey	6.0-7.0	December

* Amber (fossilized plant resin), coral (skeletal remains of microscopic warm water creatures) and pearl (secretions in molluscs, notably mussels and oysters) are organic gems † Blue-green beryl ‡ Alexandrite – also called cat's eye when brownish § Also called cornelian # Green beryl

PHYSICAL CONSTANTS

Universal constant	Symbol	Value	Unit
speed of light in vacuum	c	299,792,458	ms^{-1}
permeability of vacuum	μ_0	12.566370614	$10^{-7}NA^{-2}$
permittivity of vacuum	ϵ_0	8.854187817	$10^{-12}\ Fm^{-1}$
Newtonian constant of gravitation	G	6.67259	$10^{-11}m^3kg^{-1}s^{-2}$
Planck constant	h	6.6260755	$10^{-34}Js$
Electromagnetic constants			
elementary charge	e	1.60217733	$10^{-19}C$
Electron			
electron mass	m_e	9.1093897	$10^{-31}kg$
electron specific charge	$-e/m_e$	-1.75881962	$10^{11}Ckg^{-1}$
Muon, proton and neutron			
muon mass	m_μ	1.8825327	$10^{-28}kg$
proton mass	m_p	1.6726231	$10^{-27}kg$
neutron mass	m_n	1.6749286	$10^{-27}kg$
Physico-chemical constants			
Avogadro constant	N_A,L	6.0221367	$10^{23}mol^{-1}$
atomic mass constant	m_u	1.6605402	$10^{-27}kg$
Faraday constant	F	96,485.309	$Cmol^{-1}$
molar gas constant	R	8.314510	$Jmol^{-1}K^{-1}$
Boltzmann constant	k	1.380658	$10^{-23}JK^{-1}$

CHEMICAL ELEMENTS

Name	Symbol	Atomic number	Relative atomic mass*	Valency	Melting point °C	Boiling point °C	Date of discovery
Actinium	Ac	89	(227)	—	1230	3200	1899
Aluminium	Al	13	26.98154	3	660.2	2350	1827
Americium	Am	95	(243)	3, 4 ,5, 6	995	2600	1944
Antimony	Sb	51	121.75	3.5	630.5	1750	c.1000BC
Argon	Ar	18	39.948	0	−189.4	−185.9	1894
Arsenic	As	33	74.9216	3.5	613	—	1250
Astatine	At	85	(210)	1, 3 ,5, 7	302	377	1940
Barium	Ba	56	137.34	2	725	1640	1808
Berkelium	Bk	97	(247)	3, 4	986	—	1949
Beryllium	Be	4	9.01218	2	1285	2470	1798
Bismuth	Bi	83	208.9804	3, 5	271.3	1560	1753
Boron	B	5	10.81	3	2079	3700	1808
Bromine	Br	35	79.904	1, 3, 5, 7	−7.2	58.8	1826
Cadmium	Cd	48	112.40	2	320.9	765	1817
Caesium	Cs	55	132.9054	1	28 4	678	1860
Calcium	Ca	20	40.08	2	839	1484	1808
Californium	Cf	98	(251)	—	—	—	1950
Carbon	C	6	12.011	2.4	3550	4200	—
Cerium	Ce	58	140.12	3, 4	798	3257	1803
Chlorine	Cl	17	35.453	1, 3, 5, 7	−101	−34.6	1774
Chromium	Cr	24	51.996	2, 3, 6	1890	2672	1797
Cobalt	Co	27	58.9332	2, 3	1495	2870	1735
Copper	Cu	29	63.546	1, 2	1083	2567	c.8000BC
Curium	Cm	96	(247)	3	1340	—	1944
Dubnium‡	Db	104	(261)	—	—	—	1969
Dysprosium	Dy	66	162.50	3	1409	2335	1896
Einsteinium	Es	99	(254)	—	—	—	1952
Erbium	Er	68	167.26	3	1522	2863	1843
Europium	Eu	63	151.96	2, 3	822	1597	1896
Fermium	Fm	100	(257)	—	—	—	1952
Fluorine	F	9	18.9984	1	−219.6	−188.1	1886
Francium	Fr	87	(223)	1	30	650	1939
Gadolinium	Gd	64	157.25	3	1311	3233	1880
Gallium	Ga	31	69.72	2, 3	29.78	2403	1875
Germanium	Ge	32	72.59	4	937.4	2830	1886
Gold	Au	79	196.9665	1, 3	1063	2800	—
Hafnium	Hf	72	178.49	4	2227	4602	1923
Helium	He	2	4.0026	0	−272	268.9	1895
Holmium	Ho	67	164.9304	3	1470	2300	1878
Hydrogen	H	1	1.0079	1	−259.1	−252.9	1766
Indium	In	49	114.82	3	156.6	2080	1863
Iodine	I	53	126.9045	1, 3, 5, 7	113.5	184.4	1811
Iridium	Ir	77	192.22	3, 4	2410	4130	1804
Iron	Fe	26	55.847	2, 3	1540	2760	c.4000BC
Krypton	Kr	36	83.80	0	−156.6	−152.3	1898
Lanthanum	La	57	138.9055	3	920	3454	1839
Lawrencium	Lr	103	(256)	—	—	—	1961
Lead	Pb	82	207.2	2, 4	327.5	1740	—
Lithium	Li	3	6.941	1	180.5	1347	1817
Lutetium	Lu	71	174.97	3	1656	3315	1907
Magnesium	Mg	12	24.305	2	648.8	1090	1808
Manganese	Mn	25	54.9380	2, 3, 4, 6, 7	1244	1962	1774
Mendelevium	Md	101	(258)	—	—	—	1955
Mercury	Hg	80	200.59	1, 2	−38.9	356.6	c.1500BC
Molybdenum	Mo	42	95.94	3, 4, 6	2610	5560	1778
Neodymium	Nd	60	144.24	3	1010	3068	1885
Neon	Ne	10	20.179	0	−248.7	−246.1	1898
Neptunium	Np	93	237.0482	4, 5, 6	640	3902	1940
Nickel	Ni	28	58.70	2, 3	1453	2732	1751
Niobium	Nb	41	92.9064	3, 5	2468	4742	1801
Nitrogen	N	7	14.0067	3, 5	−210	−195.8	1772
Nobelium	No	102	(255)	—	—	—	1958
Osmium	Os	76	190.2	2, 3, 4, 8	3045	5027	1903
Oxygen	O	8	15.9994	2	−218.4	−183	1774
Palladium	Pd	46	106.4	2, 4, 6	1552	3140	1803
Phosphorus	P	15	30.97376	3, 5	44.1	280	1669
Platinum	Pt	78	195.09	2, 4	1772	3800	1735
Plutonium	Pu	94	(244)	3, 4, 5, 6	641	3232	1940
Polonium	Po	84	(209)	—	254	962	1898
Potassium	K	19	39.098	1	63.2	777	1807
Praseodymium	Pr	59	140.9077	3	931	3512	1885
Promethium	Pm	61	(145)	3	1080	2460	1941
Protactinium	Pa	91	231.0359	—	1200	4000	1913
Radium	Ra	88	226.0254	2	700	1140	1898
Radon	Rn	86	(222)	0	−71	−61.8	1899
Rhenium	Re	75	186.207	—	3180	5627	1925
Rhodium	Rh	45	102.9055	3	1966	3727	1803
Rubidium	Rb	37	85.4678	1	38.8	688	1861
Ruthenium	Ru	44	101.07	3, 4, 6, 8	2310	3900	1827
Samarium	Sm	62	150.35	2, 3	1072	1791	1879
Scandium	Sc	21	44.9559	3	1539	2832	1879
Selenium	Se	34	78.96	2, 4, 6	217	684.9	1817
Silicon	Si	14	28.086	4	1410	2355	1823
Silver	Ag	47	107.868	1	961.9	2212	c.4000BC
Sodium	Na	11	22.98977	1	97.8	882	1807
Strontium	Sr	38	87.62	2	769	1384	1808
Sulphur	S	16	32.06	2, 4, 6	112.8	444.7	—
Tantalum	Ta	73	180.9479	5	2996	5425	1802
Technetium	Tc	43	(97)	6, 7	2172	4877	1937
Tellurium	Te	52	127.60	2, 4, 6	449.5	989.8	1782
Terbium	Tb	65	158.9254	3	1360	3041	1843
Thallium	Tl	81	204.37	1, 3	303.5	1457	1861
Thorium	Th	90	232.0381	4	1750	4790	1828
Thulium	Tm	69	168.9342	3	1545	1947	1879
Tin	Sn	50	118.69	2, 4	232	2270	c.3500BC
Titanium	Ti	22	47.90	3, 4	1660	3287	1791
Tungsten§	W	74	183.85	6	3410	5660	1783
Unnilpentium†	Unp	105	(262)	—	—	—	1970
Uranium	U	92	238.029	4, 6	1132	3818	1789
Vanadium	V	23	50.9414	3, 5	1890	3380	1801
Xenon	Xe	54	131.30	0	−111.9	−107.1	1898
Ytterbium	Yb	70	173.04	2, 3	824	1193	1907
Yttrium	Y	39	88.9059	3	1510	3300	1828
Zinc	Zn	30	65.38	2	419.6	907	1800
Zirconium	Zr	40	91.22	4	1852	4377	1789

* Relative atomic mass: values given in parentheses are for radioactive elements whose relative atomic mass cannot be given precisely without knowledge of origin, and is the atomic mass number of the isotope of longest known half-life † Also called hahnium, nielsbohrium, rutherfordium, or element 105 ‡ Also called unnilquadium (Unq) or element 104 § Also called wolfram

GEOMETRIC SHAPES (PLANE FIGURES)

TYPES OF TRIANGLE

Equilateral	All the sides are the same length and all the angles are equal.
Isosceles	Two sides are of the same length and two angles are of equal size.
Scalene	All sides are different lengths and all the angles are of different sizes.
Acute angle	A triangle with three acute angles, each less than 90°.
Right angle	A triangle containing one right angle (90°).
Obtuse angle	A triangle containing one obtuse angle (over 90°).

TYPES OF QUADRILATERAL

Square	All the sides are the same length and all the angles are right angles.
Rectangle	Opposite sides are the same length and all angles are right angles.
Rhombus	All the sides are the same length but none of the angles are right angles.
Parallelogram	Opposite sides are parallel to each other and of the same length.
Trapezium	One pair of the opposite sides is parallel.
Kite	Adjacent sides are equal length and the diagonals intersect at right angles.

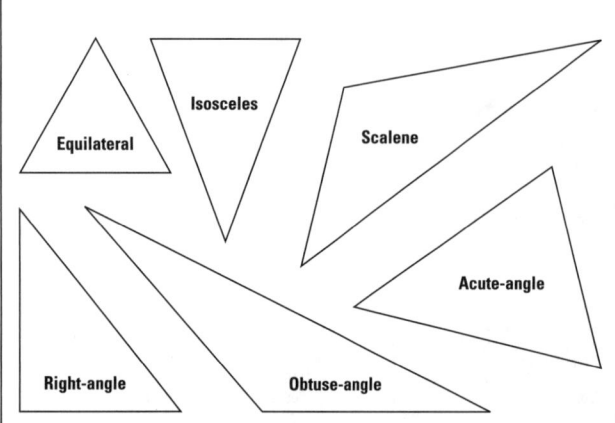

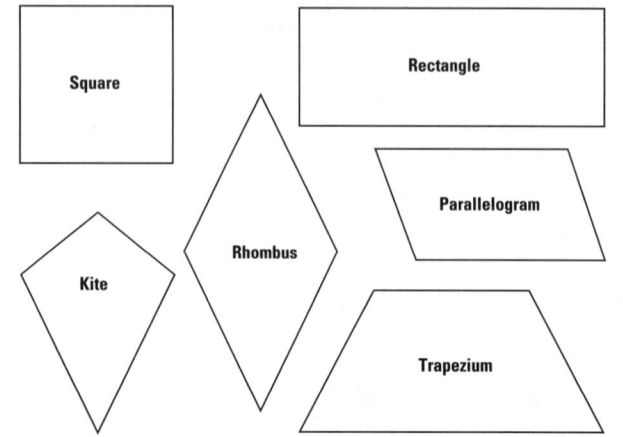

MOHS' SCALE OF HARDNESS

The scale is not regular. Diamond, the hardest known natural substance, is 90 times harder than corundum.

Mineral	Hardness	Simple hardness test
Talc	1.0	Crushed by fingernail
Gypsum	2.0	Scratched by fingernail
Calcite	3.0	Scratched by copper coin
Fluorspar	4.0	Scratched by glass
Apatite	5.0	Scratched by knife blade
Feldspar	6.0	Scratched by quartz
Quartz	7.0	Scratched by steel file
Topaz	8.0	Scratched by corundum
Corundum	9.0	Scratched by diamond
Diamond	10.0	—

SELECTED RELATIVE DENSITIES

Relative density (or specific gravity) is the density (at 20°C/68°F) of a solid or liquid relative to (divided by) the maximum density of water (at 4°C/39.2°F). The relative density of a gas is its density divided by the density of hydrogen at the same pressure and temperature.

Substance	R.D.	Substance	R.D.
Alcohol	0.8	Perspex	1.2
Aluminium	2.7	Petroleum	0.8
Balsa wood	0.2	Pitch	1.1
Benzene	0.7	Plaster of Paris	1.8
Butter	0.9	Platinum	21.9
Charcoal	0.4	Polystyrene	1.06
Copper	8.9	Polythene	0.93
Cork	0.25	PVC	1.4
Diamond	3.5	Sand	1.6
Gold	19.3	Sea water	1.03
Granite	2.7	Silver	10.5
Ice (at 0°C/32°F)	0.92	Stainless steel	7.8
Lead	11.3	Talc	2.8
Limestone	2.6	Tar	1.0
Marble	2.7	Teak	0.9
Milk	1.03	Tin	7.3
Nylon	1.14	Tungsten	19.3
Olive oil	0.9	Turpentine	0.85
Osmium*	22.57	Uranium	19.0
Paraffin	0.8	Water	1.0

* Most dense of all measurable elements

POWER OF NUMBERS

Factor	Number	Name
10^2	100	Hundred
10^3	1000	Thousand
10^6	1,000,000	Million
10^9	1,000,000,000	Billion
10^{12}	1,000,000,000,000	Trillion
10^{15}	1,000,000,000,000,000	Quadrillion
10^{18}	1,000,000,000,000,000,000	Quintillion
10^{100}	1 with 100 zeroes	Googol

In Britain, one billion was traditionally used for a million million (US trillion), while in the USA the billion repesented a thousand million. From 1 January 1975, the UK has employed the US system in its finances, with a billion standing for £1,000 million. Since then, the American system has been adopted throughout the English-speaking world.

SI PREFIXES

Prefix	Symbol	Power	Multiple in full
Exa-	E	10^{18}	1,000,000,000,000,000,000
Peta-	P	10^{15}	1,000,000,000,000,000
Tera-	T	10^{12}	1,000,000,000,000
Giga-	G	10^9	1,000,000,000
Mega-	M	10^6	1,000,000
Kilo-	k	10^3	1,000
Hecto-	h	10^2	100
Deca-	da	10^1	10
Deci-	d	10^{-1}	0.1
Centi-	c	10^{-2}	0.01
Milli-	m	10^{-3}	0.001
Micro-	μ	10^{-6}	0.000001
Nano-	n	10^{-9}	0.000000001
Pico-	p	10^{-12}	0.000000000001
Femto-	f	10^{-15}	0.000000000000001
Atto-	a	10^{-18}	0.000000000000000001

GEOMETRIC FORMULAE

Shape	Circumference	Area
circle	$2\pi r$	πr^2
parallelogram		lh
(l = length, h = perpendicular distance to side parallel to l)		
rectangle		lw
(l = length, w = width)		
triangle		$1/2lh$

Shape	Volume	Surface area
cone	$1/3\pi r^2 h$	$\pi r^2 + \pi rl$
(h = perpendicular height)		
cylinder	$\pi r^2 h$	$\pi r^2 + 2\pi rh$
pyramid	$1/3Bh$	
(B = area of base)		
sphere	$4/3\pi r^3$	$4\pi r^2$

Pythagoras' theorem: $a^2 = b^2 + c^2$

$\pi = 3.1415926$ (to seven decimal places)

r = radius

PRIME NUMBERS

These are whole numbers that have only two factors – the number itself and the number one. The only even prime number is two: all other prime numbers are odd. These are the prime numbers below 100.

2 3 5 7 11 13 17 19 23 29 31 37 41
43 47 53 59 61 67 71 73 79 83 89 97

SQUARES, CUBES AND ROOTS

No.	Square	Cube	Square root	Cube root
1	1	1	1	1
2	4	8	1.414	1.260
3	9	27	1.732	1.442
4	16	64	2	1.587
5	25	125	2.236	1.710
6	36	216	2.449	1.817
7	49	343	2.646	1.913
8	64	512	2.828	2
9	81	729	3	2.080
10	100	1000	3.162	2.154
11	121	1331	3.317	2.224
12	144	1728	3.464	2.289
13	169	2197	3.606	2.351
14	196	2744	3.742	2.410
15	225	3375	3.873	2.466
16	256	4096	4	2.520
17	289	4913	4.123	2.571
18	324	5832	4.243	2.621
19	361	6859	4.359	2.668
20	400	8000	4.472	2.714
25	625	15,625	5	2.924
30	900	27,000	5.477	3.107
40	1600	64,000	6.325	3.420
50	2500	125,000	7.071	3.684

PERFECT NUMBERS

Numbers that are equal to the sum of all their factors, excluding themselves. The lowest is 6 (1+2+3) and next come 28 (1+2+4+7+14); then 496; then 8128; then 33,550,336.

POLYGONS

Name	Number of sides	Each internal angle	Sum of internal angles
Triangle	3	60°	180°
Square	4	90°	360°
Pentagon	5	108°	540°
Hexagon	6	120°	720°
Heptagon	7	128.6°	900°
Octagon	8	135°	1080°
Nonagon	9	140°	1260°
Decagon	10	144°	1440°
Undecagon	11	147.3°	1620°
Dodecagon	12	150°	1800°

CONVERSIONS

Length
1 inch (in)	= 2.54 centimetres (cm)
	= 25.4 millimetres (mm)
1 foot (ft)	= 0.3048 metre (m)
1 yard (yd)	= 0.9144 metre
1 mile (mi)	= 1.6093 kilometres (km)
1 centimetre	= 0.3937 inch
1 metre	= 3.2808 feet = 1.0936 yards
1 kilometre	= 0.6214 mile

Area
1 square inch	= 6.4516 square centimetres
1 square foot	= 0.0929 square metre
1 acre	= 0.4047 hectare
1 sq mile	= 2.5899 square kilometres
1 square centimetre	= 0.155 square inch
1 square metre	= 10.7639 square feet
1 hectare	= 2.471 acres
1 square kilometre	= 0.3861 square mile

Volume
1 cubic inch	= 16.3871 cubic centimetres
1 cubic foot	= 0.0283 cubic metre
1 cubic yard	= 0.7646 cubic metre
1 cubic centimetre	= 0.061 cubic inch
1 cubic metre	= 35.3147 cubic feet
1 cubic metre	= 1.3030 cubic yards

Capacity
1 UK fluid ounce (fl oz)	= 0.02841 litre (l)
1 US fluid ounce	= 0.02961 litre
1 UK pint (pt)	= 0.56821 litre
1 US pint	= 0.47321 litre
1 UK gallon	= 4.546 litres
1 US gallon	= 3.7854 litres
1 litre	= 35.1961 fluid ounces (UK)
	= 33.814 fluid ounces (US)
	= 1.7598 pints (UK)
	= 2.1134 pints (US)
	= 0.22 gallon (UK)
	= 0.2642 gallon (US)
1 US cup	= 8 fluid ounces
1 UK pint	= 1.2 US pints
1 UK gallon	= 1.2009 US gallons
1 US pint	= 0.83 UK pint
1 US gallon	= 0.8327 UK gallon

Weight*
1 ounce (oz)	= 28.3495 grams (g)
1 pound (lb)	= 0.454 kilogram (kg)
1 UK ton	= 1.016 tonnes
1 US ton	= 0.9072 tonne
1 gram	= 0.0353 ounce
1 kilogram	= 2.205 pounds
1 tonne	= 0.9842 UK ton
	= 1.1023 US tons
1 UK ton	= 1.1199 US tons
1 US ton	= 0.8929 UK ton

Temperature
°Celsius to °Fahrenheit: ×9, ÷5, +32
°Fahrenheit to °Celsius: −32, ×5, ÷9

Energy†
1000 British thermal units (Btu)	= 0.293 kilowatt hour
100,000 British thermal units	= 1 therm
1 UK horsepower	= 550 ft-lb per second
	= 745.7 watts
1 US horsepower	= 746 watts

Nautical length and speed
UK nautical mile	= 6080 feet
International nautical mile	= 6076.1 feet
	= 0.9994 UK nautical mile
1 knot = 1 UK nautical mile per hour = 1.15 mph	

Petroleum
1 barrel = 34.97 UK gallons = 42 US gallons
= 0.159 cubic metres

Precious stones
1 troy ounce	= 480 grains
1 metric carat	= 200 milligrams

Type sizes
72 1/4 points	= 1 inch
1 didot point	= 0.376 mm
1 pica em	= 12 points

*Avoirdupois † Work, heat

US PRESIDENTS

No.	President	Years	Party	Age*
1.	George Washington	1789-97	Federalist	57
2.	John Adams	1797-1801	Federalist	61
3.	Thomas Jefferson	1801-09	Dem-Rep	57
4.	James Madison	1809-17	Dem-Rep	57
5.	James Monroe	1817-25	Dem-Rep	58
6.	John Quincy Adams	1825-29	Dem-Rep	57
7.	Andrew Jackson	1829-37	Democrat	61
8.	Martin Van Buren	1837-41	Democrat	54
9.	William H. Harrison†	1841	Whig	68
10.	John Tyler	1841-45	Whig	51
11.	James K. Polk	1845-49	Democrat	49
12.	Zachary Taylor†	1849-50	Whig	64
13.	Millard Fillmore	1850-53	Whig	50
14.	Franklin Pierce	1853-57	Democrat	48
15.	James Buchanan	1857-61	Democrat	65
16.	Abraham Lincoln‡	1861-65	Republican	52
17.	Andrew Johnson§	1865-69	Nat. Union	56
18.	Ulysses S. Grant#	1869-77	Republican	46
19.	Rutherford B. Hayes‡	1877-81	Republican	54
20.	James A. Garfield‡	1881	Republican	49
21.	Chester A. Arthur	1881-85	Republican	51
22.	Grover Cleveland	1885-89	Democrat	47
23.	Benjamin Harrison	1889-93	Republican	55
24.	Grover Cleveland	1893-97	Democrat	55
25.	William McKinley‡	1897-1901	Republican	54
26.	Theodore Roosevelt	1901-09	Republican	43
27.	William H. Taft	1909-13	Republican	51
28.	Woodrow Wilson	1913-21	Democrat	56
29.	Warren Harding†	1921-23	Republican	55
30.	Calvin Coolidge	1923-29	Republican	51
31.	Herbert Hoover	1929-33	Republican	54
32.	Franklin D. Roosevelt†	1933-45	Democrat	51
33.	Harry S. Truman	1945-53	Democrat	60
34.	Dwight D. Eisenhower	1953-61	Republican	62
35.	John Kennedy‡	1961-63	Democrat	43
36.	Lyndon Johnson	1963-69	Democrat	55
37.	Richard Nixon¶	1969-74	Republican	56
38.	Gerald Ford**	1974-77	Republican	61
39.	Jimmy Carter	1977-81	Democrat	52
40.	Ronald Reagan	1981-89	Republican	69
41.	George Bush	1989-93	Republican	64
42.	Bill Clinton	1993-2001	Democrat	46
43.	George W. Bush	2001-2009	Republican	54

*At inauguration; Kennedy was the youngest, Reagan the oldest † Died in office and succeeded by the vice president ‡ Assassinated in office and succeeded by the vice president § A Democrat, Johnson was nominated vice president by Republicans and elected with Lincoln on a National Union ticket # Born Hiram Grant ¶ Resigned in face of impeachment proceedings following the Watergate scandal ** Born Leslie Lynch King

CANADIAN PRIME MINISTERS

Years	Prime Minister	Party
1917-20	Sir Robert Borden	Unionist†
1920-21	Arthur Meighen	Conservative
1921-26	William Lyon Mackenzie King	Liberal
1926	Arthur Meighen	Conservative
1926-30	William Lyon Mackenzie King	Liberal
1930-35	Richard Bennett	Conservative
1935-48	William Lyon Mackenzie King	Liberal
1948-57	Louis St Laurent	Liberal
1957-63	John Diefenbaker	Conservative
1963-68	Lester Pearson	Liberal
1968-79	Pierre Trudeau	Liberal
1979-80	Joe Clark	Conservative
1980-84	Pierre Trudeau	Liberal
1984	John Turner	Liberal
1984-93	Brian Mulroney	Conservative
1993	Kim Campbell	Conservative
1993-2003	Jean Chrétien	Liberal
2003-06	Paul Martin	Liberal
2006-	Stephen Harper	Conservative

† National Liberal and Conservative

UN SECRETARIES-GENERAL

Secretary-General	Country	Tenure
Trygve Lie	Norway	1946-53
Dag Hammarskjöld	Sweden	1953-61
U Thant	Burma	1962-71
Kurt Waldheim	Austria	1971-81
Javier Pérez de Cuéllar	Peru	1982-92
Boutros Boutros Ghali	Egypt	1992-96
Kofi Annan	Ghana	1997-

UK PRIME MINISTERS

Years	Prime Minister	Party
1721-42	Sir Robert Walpole	Whig
1742-43	Earl of Wilmington	Whig
1743-54	Henry Pelham	Whig
1754-56	Duke of Newcastle	Whig
1756-57	Duke of Devonshire	Whig
1757-62	Duke of Newcastle	Whig
1762-63	Earl of Bute	Tory
1763-65	George Grenville	Whig
1765-66	Marquis of Rockingham	Whig
1766-67	Earl of Chatham*	Whig
1767-70	Duke of Grafton	Whig
1770-82	Lord North	Tory
1782	Marquis of Rockingham	Whig
1782-83	Earl of Shelbourne	Whig
1783	Duke of Portland	Coalition
1783-1801	William Pitt†	Tory
1801-04	Henry Addington	Tory
1804-06	William Pitt†	Tory
1806-07	Lord Grenville	Whig
1807-09	Duke of Portland	Coalition
1809-12	Spencer Perceval	Tory
1812-27	Earl of Liverpool	Tory
1827	George Canning	Tory
1827-28	Viscount Goderich	Tory
1828-30	Duke of Wellington	Tory
1830-34	Earl Grey	Whig
1834	Viscount Melbourne	Whig
1834-35	Sir Robert Peel	Tory
1835-41	Viscount Melbourne	Whig
1841-46	Sir Robert Peel	Conservative
1846-52	Lord John Russell‡	Whig
1852	Earl of Derby	Conservative
1852-55	Earl of Aberdeen	Peelite
1855-58	Viscount Palmerston	Liberal
1858-59	Earl of Derby	Conservative
1859-65	Viscount Palmerston	Liberal
1865-66	Earl Russell‡	Liberal
1866-68	Earl of Derby	Conservative
1868	Benjamin Disraeli	Conservative
1868-74	William Gladstone	Liberal
1874-80	Benjamin Disraeli	Conservative
1880-85	William Gladstone	Liberal
1885-86	Marquis of Salisbury	Conservative
1886	William Gladstone	Liberal
1886-92	Marquis of Salisbury	Conservative
1892-94	William Gladstone	Liberal
1894-95	Earl of Rosebery	Liberal
1895-1902	Marquis of Salisbury	Conservative
1902-05	Arthur Balfour	Conservative
1905-08	Henry Campbell-Bannerman	Liberal
1908-15	Herbert Asquith	Liberal
1915-16	Herbert Asquith	Coalition§
1916-22	David Lloyd George	Coalition§
1922-23	Andrew Bonar Law	Conservative
1923-24	Stanley Baldwin	Conservative
1924	Ramsay MacDonald	Labour
1924-29	Stanley Baldwin	Conservative
1929-31	Ramsay MacDonald	Labour
1931-35	Ramsay MacDonald	National#
1935-37	Stanley Baldwin	National#
1937-40	Neville Chamberlain	National#
1940-45	Winston Churchill	Coalition
1945-51	Clement Attlee	Labour
1951-55	Winston Churchill	Conservative
1955-57	Anthony Eden	Conservative
1957-63	Harold Macmillan	Conservative
1963-64	Alec Douglas-Home	Conservative
1964-70	Harold Wilson	Labour
1970-74	Edward Heath	Conservative
1974-76	Harold Wilson	Labour
1976-79	James Callaghan	Labour
1979-90	Margaret Thatcher	Conservative
1990-97	John Major	Conservative
1997-2007	Tony Blair	Labour
2007-	Gordon Brown	Labour

*William Pitt the Elder † William Pitt the Younger ‡ Lord John Russell later became 1st Earl Russell
§ Coalition governments; Lloyd-George was Liberal # National Coalition governments; Chamberlain was a Conservative

GERMAN CHANCELLORS

Years	Chancellor	Party
German Empire		
1871-90	Prince Otto von Bismarck-Schönhausen	
1890-94	Count Leo von Caprivi	
1894-00	Prince Chlodwig von Hoh.-Schillingsfirst	
1900-09	Prince Bernhard von Bülow	
1909-17	Theobald von Bethmann-Hollweg	
1917	George Michaelis	
1917-18	Count George von Hertling	
1918	Prince Maximilian of Baden	
1918	Friedrich Ebert	
Weimar Republic		
1919	Philipp Scheidemann	SPD
1919-20	Gustav Bauer	SPD
1920	Hermann Müller	SPD
1920-21	Konstantin Fehrenbach	Centre-Catholic
1921-22	Joseph Wirth	Centre
1922-23	Wilhelm Cuno	—
1923	Gustav Stresemannn	D. Volk
1923-25	Wilhelm Marx	Centre
1925-26	Hans Luther	—
1926-28	Wilhelm Marx	Centre
1928-30	Hermann Müller	SPD
1930-32	Heinrich Brüning	Centre
1932	Franz von Papen	National
1932-33	Curt von Schleider	—
1933-45	Adolf Hitler*	Nazi
Federal German Republic		
1949-63	Konrad Adenauer	CDU
1963-66	Ludwig Erhard	CDU
1966-69	Kurt Georg Kiesinger	CDU
1969-74	Willy Brandt†	SPD
1974-82	Helmut Schmidt	SPD
1982-90	Helmut Kohl	CDU
Reunified Germany		
1990-98	Helmut Kohl	CDU
1998-2005	Gerhard Schröder	SPD
2005-	Angela Merkel	CDU

D. Volk = German People's Party, SPD = Social Democratic Party, CDU = Christian Democratic Union, FDP = Free Democratic Party

*Führer from 1934 to 1945 † Born Karl Herbert Frahm

FRENCH LEADERS

Years	President	Party
President of the Fifth Republic		
1958-69	Charles de Gaulle	Gaullist
1969-74	Georges Pompidou	Gaullist
1974-81	Valéry Giscard d'Estaing	UDF
1981-95	François Mitterrand	PS
1995-2007	Jacques Chirac	RPR
2007-	Nicolas Sarkozy	UMP
Prime Minister of the Fifth Republic		
1962-68	Georges Pompidou	Gaullist
1968-69	Maurice Couve de Murville	Gaullist
1969-72	Jacques Chaban-Delmas	Gaullist
1972-74	Pierre Mesmer	Gaullist
1974-76	Jacques Chirac	Gaullist
1976-81	Raymond Barre	—
1981-84	Pierre Mauroy	PS
1984-86	Laurent Fabius	PS
1986-88	Jacques Chirac	Gaullist
1988-91	Michel Rocard	PS
1991-92	Edith Cresson	PS
1992-93	Pierre Bérégovoy	PS
1993-95	Edouard Balladur	RPR
1995-97	Alain Juppé	RPR
1997-2002	Lionel Jospin	PS
2002-05	Jean-Pierre Raffarin	DL
2005-07	Dominique Villepin	UMP
2007-	François Fillon	UMP

UDF = French Democratic Union, PS = Socialist Party, RPR = Rally For The Republic, DL = Liberal Democracy Party, UMP = Union pour un Mouvement Populaire

SPANISH PRIME MINISTERS

Years	Prime Minister	Party
1939-73	Francisco Franco	Falange
1973-76	Carlos Navarro	—
1976-81	Adolfo Suárez	UCD
1981-82	Leopoldo Sotelo	UCD
1982-96	Felipe González	PSOE
1996-2004	José María Aznar	Popular
2004-	José Zapatero	PSOE

UCD = Centre Democrat
PSOE = Socialist Workers' Party

RUSSIAN AND SOVIET LEADERS

General Secretary of the Communist Party

1922-53	Joseph Stalin (b. Dzhugashvili)
1953	Georgi Malenkov
1953-64	Nikita Khrushchev
1964-82	Leonid Brezhnev
1982-84	Yuri Andropov
1984-85	Konstantin Chernenko
1985-91	Mikhail Gorbachev

President of the Union of Soviet Socialist Republics

1919-46	Mikhail Kalinin
1946-53	Nikolai Shvernik
1953-60	Kliment Voroshilov
1960-64	Leonid Brezhnev
1964-65	Anastas Mikoyan
1965-77	Nikolai Podgorny
1977-82	Leonid Brezhnev
1982-83	Vassili Kuznetsov
1983-84	Yuri Andropov
1984	Vassili Kuznetsov
1984-85	Konstantin Chernenko
1985	Vassili Kuznetsov
1985-88	Andrei Gromyko
1988-91	Mikhail Gorbachev†

Chairman of the Council of Ministers‡

1917-24§	Vladimir Ilyich Lenin (b. Ulyanov)
1924-30§	Aleksei Rykov
1930-31§	Genrikh Yagoda
1931-41§	Vyacheslav Molotov
1941-53§	Joseph Stalin (b. Dzhugashvili)
1953-55	Georgi Malenkov
1955-58	Nikolai Bulganin
1958-64	Nikita Khrushchev
1964-80	Alexei Kosygin
1980-85	Nikolai Tikhonov
1985-90	Nikolai Ryzhkov
1990-91	Yuri Maslyukov
1991	Valentin Pavlov

Russian President

1991-99	Boris Yeltsin
2000-07	Vladimir Putin
2007-	Dmitry Medvedev

Russian Prime Minister

1991-98	Viktor Chernomyrdin
1998	Sergei Kiriyenko
1998-99	Yevgeni Primakov
1999-2000	Vladimir Putin
2000-04	Mikhail Kasianov
2004-07	Mikhail Fradkov
2007-	Vladimir Putin

‡ *Equivalent of Prime Minister* § *Council of Ministers replaced by Council of People's Commissars 1917-1953.*

CHINESE LEADERS

Chairman of the Communist Party

1935-76	Mao Zedong (Mao Tse-tung)
1976-81	Hua Guofeng (Huo Kuo-feng)
1981-82	Hu Yaobang (Hu Yao-pang)

General Secretary of the Communist Party

1982-87	Hu Yaobang
1987-89	Zhao Ziyang (Chao Tzu-yang)
1989-	Jiang Zemin (Chiang Tse-min)

President

1949-59	Mao Zedong
1959-68	Liu Shaoqi (Liu Shao-ch'i)
1968-75	Dong Biwu (Tung Pi-wu)
1975-76	Zhu De (Chu Te)
1976-78	Song Qingling (Sung Ch'ing-ling)
1978-83	Ye Jianying (Yeh Chien-ying)
1983-88	Li Xiannian (Li Hsien-nien)
1988-93	Yang Shangkun (Yang Shang-k'un)
1993-2003	Jiang Zemin
2003-	Hu Jintao

Prime Minister

1949-76	Zhou Enlai (Chou En-lai)
1976-80	Hua Guofeng
1980-87	Zhao Ziyang
1987-98	Li Peng (Li P'eng)
1998-2003	Zhu Rongji
2003-	Wen Jiabao

1978-1997, China was controlled by Deng Xiaoping (Teng Hsiao-ping), State Vice-Premier and Chief of Staff.

AUSTRALIAN PRIME MINISTERS

Years	Prime Minister	Party
1900-03	Edmund Barton	Protectionist
1903-04	Alfred Deakin	Protectionist
1904	John Watson	Labor
1904-05	George Reid	Free Trade
1905-08	Alfred Deakin	Protectionist
1908-09	Andrew Fisher	Labor
1909-10	Alfred Deakin	Fusion
1910-13	Andrew Fisher	Labor
1913-14	Joseph Cook	Liberal
1914-15	Andrew Fisher	Labor
1915-17	William Hughes	National Labor
1917-23	William Hughes	Nationalist
1923-29	Stanley Bruce	Nationalist
1929-32	James Scullin	Labor
1932-39	Joseph Lyons	United Australia†
1939	Earle Page	Country
1939-41	Robert Menzies	United Australia†
1941	Arthur Fadden	Country
1941-45	John Curtin	Labor
1945	Francis Forde	Labor
1945-49	Joseph Chifley	Labor
1949-66	Robert Menzies	Liberal
1966-67	Harold Holt	Liberal
1967-68	John McEwen	Country
1968-71	John Gorton	Liberal
1971-72	William McMahon	Liberal
1972-75	Gough Whitlam	Labor
1975-83	Malcolm Fraser	Liberal
1983-91	Bob Hawke	Labor
1991-96	Paul Keating	Labor
1996-2007	John Howard	Liberal-National‡
2007-	Kevin Rudd	Labor

† *Became the Liberal Party in 1944* ‡ *Coalition*

INDIAN PRIME MINISTERS

Years	Prime Minister	Government
1947-64	Jawaharlal Nehru	Congress
1964	Gulzari Lal Nanda	Congress
1964-66	Lal Shastri	Congress
1966	Gulzari Lal Nanda	Congress
1966-77	Indira Gandhi	Congress
1977-79	Morarji Desai	Janata
1979-80	Charan Singh	Coalition
1980-84	Indira Gandhi	Congress (I)
1984-89	Rajiv Gandhi	Congress (I)
1989-90	V.P. Singh	Coalition
1990-91	Chandra Shekhar	Janata
1991-96	P.V. Narasimha Rao	Congress (I)
1996-97	H.D. Deve Gowda	Coalition
1997-98	Inder Kumar Gujral	Coalition
1998-2004	Atal Bihari Vajpayee	Coalition
2004-	Manmohan Singh	Congress (I)

NEW ZEALAND PRIME MINISTERS

Years	Prime Minister	Party
1949-57	Sidney Holland	National†
1957	Keith Holyoake	National
1957-60	Walter Nash	Labour
1960-72	Keith Holyoake	National
1972	John Marshall	National
1972-74	Norman Kirk	Labour
1974	Hugh Watt‡	Labour
1974-75	Wallace Rowling	Labour
1975-84	Robert Muldoon	National
1984-89	David Lange	Labour
1989-90	Geoffrey Palmer	Labour
1990	Michael Moore	Labour
1990-96	Jim Bolger	National
1997-99	Jenny Shipley	National
1999-	Helen Clark	Labour

† *Formed from merger of Reform Party and United Party in 1936* ‡ *Acting Prime Minister*

JAPANESE EMPERORS

Years	Emperor	Era
1867-1912	Mutsuhito	Meiji
1912-26	Yoshihito	Taisho
1926-89	Hirohito	Showa
1989-	Akihito	Heisei

SOUTH AFRICAN LEADERS

Until the Republic of South Africa left the Commonwealth in 1961 the Governor-General performed the role of President, and until 1984, when the prime ministership was abolished, the presidential function remained largely non-political.

Years	Prime Minister	Party
1910-19	Louis Botha	South Africa Party
1919-24	Jan Christiaan Smuts	South Africa Party
1924-39	James Hertzog	National
1939-48	Jan Christiaan Smuts	United
1949-54	Daniel Malan	National
1954-58	Johannes Strijdom	National
1958-66	Hendrik Verwoerd	National
1966-78	Johannes Vorster	National
1978-84	Pieter Botha	National

Years	President	
1989-94	F.W. de Klerk	National
1994-99	Nelson Mandela	ANC
1999-	Thabo Mbeki	ANC

POPES SINCE AD 1000

Years	Pope	Years	Pope	Years	Pope	Years	Pope
999-1003	Sylvester II	1181-85	Lucius III	1389-1404	Boniface IX	1623-44	Urban VIII
1003	John XVII	1185-87	Urban III	1404-06	Innocent VII	1644-55	Innocent X
1004-09	John XVIII	1187	Gregory VIII	1406-15	Gregory XII	1655-67	Alexander VII
1009-12	Sergius IV	1187-91	Clement III	1417-31	Martin V	1667-69	Clement IX
1012-24	Benedict VIII	1191-98	Celestine III	1431-47	Eugenius IV	1670-76	Clement X
1024-32	John XIX	1198-1216	Innocent III	1447-55	Nicholas V	1676-89	Innocent XI
1032-44	Benedict IX	1216-27	Honorius III	1455-58	Callixtus III	1689-91	Alexander VIII
1045	Sylvester III	1227-41	Gregory IX	1458-64	Pius II	1691-1700	Innocent XII
1045	Benedict IX	1241	Celestine IV	1464-71	Paul II	1700-21	Clement XI
1045-46	Gregory VI	1243-54	Innocent IV	1471-84	Sixtus IV	1721-24	Innocent XIII
1046-47	Clement II	1254-61	Alexander IV	1484-92	Innocent VIII	1724-30	Benedict XIII
1047-48	Benedict IX	1261-64	Urban IV	1492-1503	Alexander VI	1730-40	Clement XII
1048	Damasus II	1265-68	Clement IV	1503	Pius III	1740-58	Benedict XIV
1048-54	Leo IX	1271-76	Gregory X	1503-13	Julius II	1758-69	Clement XIII
1055-57	Victor II	1276	Innocent V	1513-21	Leo X	1769-74	Clement XIV
1057-58	Stephen IX	1276	Adrian V	1522-23	Adrian VI§	1775-99	Pius VI
1059-61	Nicholas II	1276-77	John XXI‡	1523-34	Clement VII	1800-23	Pius VII
1061-73	Alexander II	1277-80	Nicholas III	1534-49	Paul III	1823-29	Leo XII
1073-85	Gregory VII	1281-85	Martin IV	1550-55	Julius III	1829-30	Pius VIII
1086-87	Victor III	1285-87	Honorius IV	1555	Marcellus II	1831-46	Gregory XVI
1088-99	Urban II	1288-92	Nicholas IV	1555-59	Paul IV	1846-78	Pius IX
1099-1118	Paschal II	1294	Celestine V	1559-65	Pius IV	1878-1903	Leo XIII
1118-19	Gelasius II	1294-1303	Boniface VIII	1566-72	Pius V	1903-14	Pius X
1119-24	Callixtus II	1303-04	Benedict XI	1572-85	Gregory XIII	1914-22	Benedict XV
1124-30	Honorius II	1305-14	Clement V	1585-90	Sixtus V	1922-39	Pius XI
1130-43	Innocent II	1316-34	John XXII	1590	Urban VII	1939-58	Pius XII
1143-44	Celestine II	1334-42	Benedict XII	1590-91	Gregory XIV	1958-63	John XXIII
1144-45	Lucius II	1342-52	Clement VI	1591	Innocent IX	1963-78	Paul VI
1145-53	Eugenius III	1352-62	Innocent VI	1592-1605	Clement VIII	1978	John Paul I
1153-54	Anastasius IV	1362-70	Urban V	1605	Leo XI	1978-2005	John Paul II
1154-59	Adrian IV	1370-78	Gregory XI	1605-21	Paul V	2005-	Benedict XVI
1159-81	Alexander III	1378-89	Urban VI	1621-23	Gregory XV		

‡ *John XX non-existent pope, mistake in numbering system* § *Only English pope*

KINGS AND QUEENS OF ENGLAND AND BRITAIN

Years	Monarch	Age*	Reign†
KINGS AND QUEENS OF ENGLAND			
West Saxon Kings (House of Cerdic)			
802-839	Egbert‡	—	37
839-858	Ethelwulf	—	19
858-860	Ethelbald	—	2
860-866	Ethelbert	—	6
866-871	Ethelred I	—	5
871-899	Alfred (the Great)	52	28
899-924	Edward (the Elder)	55	25
924-939	Athelstan (the Glorious)	45	15
939-946	Edmund I	25	6
946-955	Edred	32	9
955-959	Edwy (the Fair)	18	3
959-975	Edgar (the Peaceful)	32	16
975-978	Edward I (the Martyr)	17	3
978-1016	Ethelred II (the Unready)	47	38
1016	Edmund II (Ironside)	2	7m
Danish Kings (House of Denmark)			
1016-35	Canute (Cnut)‡	40	19
1035-40	Harold I (Harefoot)	23	4
1040-42	Hardecanute (Harthacnut)	24	2
West Saxon Kings (restored)			
1042-66	Edward II (the Confessor)	61	23
1066	Harold II (Godwinesson)	45	10m
House of Normandy			
1066-87	William I (the Conqueror)‡	60	20
1087-1100	William II (Rufus)	41	12
1100-35	Henry I (Beauclerc)	67	35
1135-54	Stephen§	53	18
House of Anjou (Plantagenets)			
1154-89	Henry II (Curtmantle)	56	34
1189-99	Richard I (the Lionheart)	42	9
1199-1216	John (Lackland)	48	17
1216-72	Henry III	65	56
1272-1307	Edward I (Longshanks)	68	34
1307-27	Edward II	43	19
1327-77	Edward III	64	50
1377-99	Richard II	33	22
House of Lancaster			
1399-1413	Henry IV	47	13

Years	Monarch	Age*	Reign†
1413-22	Henry V	34	9
1422-61	Henry VI#	49	39
House of York			
1461-83	Edward IV¶	40	21
1483	Edward V	12	2m
1483-85	Richard III	32	2
House of Tudor			
1485-1509	Henry VII	52	23
1509-47	Henry VIII	55	37
1547-53	Edward VI	15	6
1553	Jane (Lady Jane Grey)**	16	9d
1553-58	Mary I (Mary Tudor)	42	5
1558-1603	Elizabeth I	69	44
KINGS AND QUEENS OF BRITAIN			
House of Stuart			
1603-25	James I (VI of Scotland)	58	22
1625-49	Charles I	48	23
1649-60	Commonwealth††		
1660-85	Charles II	54	24
1685-88	James II	67	3
Interregnum December 11, 1688 to February 12, 1689			
1689-1702	William III	51	13
[and to 1694	Mary II	32	5]
1702-14	Anne	49	12
House of Hanover			
1714-27	George I (Elector of Hanover)	67	13
1727-60	George II	76	33
1760-1820	George III	81	59
1820-30	George IV	67	10
1830-37	William IV	71	7
1837-1901	Victoria	81	63
House of Saxe-Coburg and Gotha			
1901-1910	Edward VII	68	9
House of Windsor‡‡			
1910-36	George V	70	25
1936	Edward VIII§§	77	10m
1936-52	George VI	56	15
1952-	Elizabeth II	—	—

* On death † Duration of reign in years (m = months, d=days) ‡ Became ruler by conquest § Son of William's daughter Adele and Stephen, Count of Blois; sometimes given as the monarch of the House of Blois # Deposed March 1461, restored October 1470, deposed April 1471, and killed in Tower of London May 1471 ¶ Acceded March 1461, deposed October 1470, restored April 1471 ** Edward was forced to name Lady Jane as his successor and a Council of State proclaimed her Queen; Mary, proclaimed Queen by the Council, had Jane beheaded in 1554 †† 1649-53 Council of State; 1653-58 Oliver Cromwell, Lord Protector; 1658-60 Richard Cromwell (son), Lord Protector ‡‡ Name changed from the German Saxe-Coburg and Gotha on July 17, 1917 (during World War 1) §§ Abdicated at the age of 42

KINGS OF FRANCE

Dates	King	Relationship
House of Valois*		
1328-50	Philip VI	Grandson of Philip III
1350-64	John II	Son of Philip VI
1364-80	Charles V	Son of John II
1380-1422	Charles VI	Son of Charles V
1422-61	Charles VII	Son of Charles VI
1461-83	Louis XI	Son of Charles VII
1483-98	Charles VIII	Son of Louis XI
1498-1515	Louis XII	Great-grandson of Charles V
1515-47	Francis I	Cousin of Louis XII
1547-59	Henry II	Son of Francis I
1559-60	Francis II	Son of Henry II
1560-74	Charles IX	Brother of Francis II
1574-89	Henry III	Brother of Charles IX
House of Bourbon		
1589-1610	Henry IV	Son of Queen of Navarre
1610-43	Louis XIII	Son of Henri IV
1643-1715	Louis XIV	Son of Louis XIII
1715-74	Louis XV	Great-grandson of Louis XIV
1774-93†	Louis XVI	Grandson of Louis XV
Restoration		
1814-24	Louis XVIII	Brother of Louis XVI
1824-30‡	Charles X	Brother of Louis XVIII
1830-48	Louis Philippe	Son of Duke or Orléans§

* The Carolingians ruled from 741 to 986, the Capets from 987 to 1322
† Louis XVII, son of Louis XVI, was nominally king while in prison 1793-95
‡ Louis XIX and Henry V were nominally kings in 1830, for one day and eight days respectively
§ 'The Citizen King', he fled to England

TSARS OF RUSSIA

Years	Tsar
House of Rurik	
1547-84	Ivan IV (the Terrible)
1584-98	Theodore I
1598	Irina
House of Godunov	
1598-1605	Boris Godunov
1605	Theodore II
Usurpers*	
1605-06	Dimitri III
1606-10	Basil IV
House of Romanov	
1613-45	Michael Romanov
1645-76	Alexei
1676-82	Theodore III
1682-96	Peter I and Ivan V (brothers)
1696-1725	Peter I (the Great)
1725-27	Catherine I
1727-30	Peter II
1730-40	Anna Ivanovna
1740-41	Ivan VI
1741-62	Elizabeth
1762	Peter III
1762-96	Catherine II (the Great)
1796-1801	Paul I
1801-25	Alexander I
1825-55	Nicholas I
1855-81	Alexander II
1881-94	Alexander III
1894-1917	Nicholas II

* Interregnum (no tsar) from 1610 to 1613

SEVEN WONDERS OF THE ANCIENT WORLD

Designated in the 2nd century BC by the Greek poet, Antipatus of Sidon.

Name	Date built
Egyptian Pyramids	From c.2700 BC
Hanging Gardens of Babylon	6th century BC
Temple of Artemis (Diana) at Ephesus, Asia Minor	6th century BC
Statue of Zeus at Olympia, Greece	c.430 BC
Mausoleum at Halicarnassus (now, Bodrum) Asia Minor	4th century BC
Colossus of Rhodes	c.292-280 BC
Pharos of Alexandria, Egypt	c.280 BC

GREEK GODS AND GODDESSES

Aeolus: God of the winds
Aphrodite: Goddess of love, beauty and procreation
Apollo: God of beauty, poetry and music
Ares: God of war
Artemis: Goddess of the Moon, hunting and fertility
Athene: Goddess of wisdom; protectress of Athens
Boreas: God of the north wind
Cronus: God of harvests
Cybele: Goddess of fertility and the mountains
Demeter: Goddess of fruit, crops and vegetation
Dionysus: God of wine
Eos: Goddess of the dawn
Eros: God of love
Gaia: Goddess of the earth
Hades (Dis): God of the Underworld
Hebe: Goddess of youth
Hecate: Goddess of magic, ghosts and witchcraft
Helios: God of the Sun
Hephaestus: God of fire and metalcraft
Hera: Goddess of women, marriage; queen of heaven
Hermes: God of science, commerce and physicians; messenger of the gods
Hestia: Goddess of the hearth
Iris: Goddess of the rainbow; messenger of the gods
Morpheus: God of dreams
Nemesis: Goddess of vengeance and retribution
Nike: Goddess of victory
Oceanus: God of the waters
Pan: God of pastures, forests, flocks, and herds
Persephone: Goddess of the underworld
Poseidon: God of the sea
Rhea: Mother of the gods
Uranus: God of the sky
Zeus: Overlord of the Olympian gods and goddesses; lord of heaven

ROMAN GODS AND GODDESSES

Apollo: God of the Sun
Aurora: Goddess of the dawn
Bacchus: God of wine
Bellona: Goddess of war
Ceres: Goddess of agriculture
Cupid: God of love
Diana: Goddess of fertility, hunting, and the Moon
Faunus: God of prophecy
Flora: Goddess of flowers
Janus: God of gates and doors
Juno: Goddess of marriage and women
Jupiter: Supreme god and god of the sky
Lares: Gods of the household and descendants
Libitina: Goddess of funerals
Maia: Goddess of growth and increase
Mars: God of war
Mercury: Messenger god; god of commerce
Minerva: Goddess of wisdom, the arts, and trades
Mithras: God of the Sun, light and regeneration
Neptune: God of the sea
Ops: Goddess of fertility
Pales: Goddess of flocks and shepherds
Pluto: God of the Underworld
Pomona: Goddess of fruit trees and fruit
Proserpine: Goddess of the Underworld
Saturn: God of seed time and harvest
Venus: Goddess of beauty and love
Vertumnus: God of the seasons
Vesta: Goddess of the hearth
Vulcan: God of fire

BASIC TIME PERIODS

Year	Time taken by the Earth to revolve around the Sun, or 365.24 days
Leap Year	Calendar year of 366 days, 29 February being the additional day. It offsets the difference between the calendar year (365 days) and the solar year
Month	Approximate time taken by the Moon to revolve around the Earth. The 12 months of the year in fact vary from 28 days (29 in a Leap Year) to 31 days
Week	Artificial period of 7 days, not based on astronomical time
Day	Time taken by the Earth to complete one rotation on its axis; 1 day = 24 hours = 1440 minutes = 86,400 seconds
Hour	24 hours make one day. Usually the day divides into hours AM (ante meridiem, or before noon) and PM (post meridiem, or after noon), although most timetables now use the 24-hour system
Minute	1/60 of an hour = 60 seconds
Second	1/60 of a minute

Recurring intervals

Annual	Yearly
Perennial	Year after year
Bi-annual	Twice a year
Bi-ennial	Every two years
Bi-monthly	Every two months; twice a month
Bi-weekly	Every 2 weeks; twice a week
Diurnal	Daily (especially with temperature)

MONTHS OF THE YEAR

Month	Derivation
January	From the Roman month Januarius and named after Janus – god of doors, gates and new beginnings [31 days]
February	From the Roman month Februarius and named after Februa, festival of purification on the 15th [28 days, and 29 in Leap Years]
March	From the Roman month of Martius and named after Mars, god of war [31 days]
April	From the Roman month Aprilis – possibly derived from the Latin aperire in reference to the blossoming of spring [30 days]
May	From the Roman month Maius, after Maia, goddess of growth [31 days]
June	From the Roman month Junius and named after Juno, goddess of marriage [30 days]
July	From the Roman month Julius and named after the Emperor Julius Caesar in 44 BC [31 days]
August	From the Roman month Augustus and named after the Emperor Augustus in 8 BC [31 days]
September	7th month of the early Roman calendar, from the Latin septem (seven) [30 days]
October	8th month of the early Roman calendar, from the Latin octo (eight) [31 days]
November	9th month of the early Roman calendar, from the Latin novem (nine) [30 days]
December	10th month of the early Roman calendar, from the Latin decem (ten) [31 days]

DAYS OF THE WEEK

Day	Derivation
Sunday	Named after the Sun
Monday	Named after the Moon
Tuesday	Named after Tiw or Tiu, Anglo-Saxon equivalent of the Norse god of battle Tyr, son of Odin
Wednesday	Named after Woden, the Anglo-Saxon equivalent of Odin, chief of Norse gods
Thursday	Named after Thor, Norse god of thunder and sky, eldest son of Odin
Friday	Named after Frigg, Norse goddess of love and fertility, wife of Odin
Saturday	Named after Saturn, the Roman god of agriculture and fertility

EASTER 2008–2016

Year	Ash Wednesday	Easter Sunday
2008	6 February	23 March
2009	25 February	12 April
2010	17 February	4 April
2011	9 March	24 April
2012	22 February	8 April
2013	13 February	31 March
2014	5 March	20 April
2015	18 February	5 April
2016	10 February	27 March

CHINESE CALENDAR

Animal	Years (1913–2020)								
Buffalo or Cow	1913	1925	1937	1949	1961	1973	1985	1997	2009
Tiger	1914	1926	1938	1950	1962	1974	1986	1998	2010
Rabbit	1915	1927	1939	1951	1963	1975	1987	1999	2011
Dragon	1916	1928	1940	1952	1964	1976	1988	2000	2012
Snake	1917	1929	1941	1953	1965	1977	1989	2001	2013
Horse	1918	1930	1942	1954	1966	1978	1990	2002	2014
Goat	1919	1931	1943	1955	1967	1979	1991	2003	2015
Monkey	1920	1932	1944	1956	1968	1980	1992	2004	2016
Rooster or Chicken	1921	1933	1945	1957	1969	1981	1993	2005	2017
Dog	1922	1934	1946	1958	1970	1982	1994	2006	2018
Pig	1923	1935	1947	1959	1971	1983	1995	2007	2019
Rat	1924	1936	1948	1960	1972	1984	1996	2008	2020

Although officially banned in 1930 the ancient Chinese calendar is still widely used in China, and the New Year (the second new moon after the beginning of winter) is a national holiday. It also remains in use in Tibet, Malaysia and other parts of Southeast Asia. Based on the lunar year, it comprises 12 months of 29 or 30 days, each starting with a new moon. A month is repeated seven times during each 19-year cycle.

MOVABLE CHRISTIAN FEASTS

Ash Wednesday (first day in Lent) falls between 4 February and 10 March
Mothering Sunday (4th Sunday in Lent) falls between 29 February and 4 April
Palm (Passion) Sunday is the Sunday before Easter
Good Friday is the Friday before Easter
Easter Day falls between 22 March and 25 April
Ascension Day (40 days after Easter) falls between 30 April and 3 June
Pentecost (Whit Sunday, 7 weeks after Easter) falls between 10 May and 13 June
Trinity Sunday is the Sunday after Pentecost
Corpus Christi is the Thursday after Trinity Sunday
Advent Sunday (first Sunday of Advent) is the Sunday nearest to 30 November

YEAR SPANS

10	Decade
50	Half-century
100	Century
1000	Millennium
100	Centenary
200	Bicentenary
300	Tricentenary
400	Quadricentenary
500	Quincentenary

MAJOR FIXED CHRISTIAN FEASTS

Saints' Days vary between different branches of Christianity and calendars and are not included here.

January 1	Solemenity of Mary, Mother of God
January 6	Epiphany
January 11	Baptism of Jesus
January 25	Conversion of the Apostle Paul
February 2	Presentation of Jesus (Candlemas Day)
February 22	The Chair of the Apostle Peter
March 25	Annunciation of the Virgin Mary
June 24	Birth of John the Baptist
August 6	Transfiguration
August 15	Assumption of the Virgin Mary
August 22	Queenship of Mary
September 8	Birthday of the Virgin Mary
September 14	Exaltation of the Holy Cross
October 2	Guardian Angels
November 1	All Saints
November 2	All Souls
November 9	Dedication of the Lateran Basilica
November 21	Presentation of the Virgin Mary
December 8	Immaculate Conception
December 25	Christmas Day
December 28	Holy Innocents

NOTABLE NATIONAL DAYS

Country	Date	Name	Anniversary
Australia	Jan 26	Australia Day	Birth of the Commonwealth of Australia (1901)
Brazil	Sep 7	Independence Day	Decl. of independence from Portugal (1822)
Canada	Jul 1	Canada Day	Birth of the Confederation of Canada (1867)
China	Oct 1-2	National Days	Proclamation of the People's Republic (1949)
France	Jul 14	National Day	Storming of the Bastille prison (1789)
Germany	Oct 3	Unity Day	Unification of West and East Germany (1990)
Italy	Jun 2	National Day	Foundation of the Republic (1946)
Japan	Dec 17	Emperor's Birthday	Birthday of Akihito (1933)
Russia	Jun 12	Independence Day	Decl. of Russian Federation's sovereignty (1991)
USA	Jul 4	Independence Day	Declaration of independence from Britain (1776)

ARISTOCRATIC RANKS (UK)

1	King/ Queen
2	Prince (royal duke)
3	Duke
4	Marquess
5	Earl
6	Viscount
7	Baron

NOBEL PEACE PRIZE

Year	Winner(s)
1984	Archbishop Desmond Tutu (South Africa)
1985	International Physicians for the Prevention of Nuclear War*
1986	Elie Wiesel (US)
1987	Oscar Arias Sánchez (Costa Rica)
1988	United Nations peacekeeping forces*
1989	Dalai Lama (Tibet)
1990	Mikhail Gorbachev (Soviet Union)
1991	Aung San Suu Kyi (Burma)
1992	Rigoberta Menchú (Guatemala)
1993	Frederik W. de Klerk and Nelson Mandela (South Africa)
1994	Yasser Arafat (Palestine), Shimon Peres & Yitzhak Rabin (Israel)
1995	Joseph Rotblat (UK)
1996	Bishop Belo & José Ramos Horta (East Timor)
1997	International Campaign to Ban Landmines & Jody Williams (USA)
1998	John Hume and David Trimble (UK)§
1999	Médecins Sans Frontières*
2000	Kim Dae Jung (South Korea)
2001	United Nations and Kofi Annan
2002	Jimmy Carter (US)
2003	Shirin Ebadi (Iran)
2004	Wangari Maathai (Kenya)
2005	International Atomic Energy Agency (IAEA) and Mohamed ElBaradei
2006	Muhammad Yunus and Grameen Bank
2007	Intergovernmental Panel on Climate Change and Al Gore

Prize awarded to organization rather than to individual(s)   ‡ Le Duc Tho (Vietnam) declined   § Northern Ireland

12 SIGNS OF THE ZODIAC

The dates when the Sun is in each astrological sign are approximate.

Sign	Element	Symbol	Dates
Aries	Fire	Ram	Mar 21-Apr 19
Taurus	Earth	Bull	Apr 20-May 20
Gemini	Air	Twins	May 21-Jun 21
Cancer	Water	Crab	Jun 22-Jul 22
Leo	Fire	Lion	Jul 23-Aug 22
Virgo	Earth	Virgin	Aug 23-Sep 22
Libra	Air	Scales	Sep 23-Oct 23
Scorpio	Water	Scorpion	Oct 24-Nov 21
Sagittarius	Fire	Archer	Nov 22-Dec 21
Capricorn	Earth	Goat	Dec 22-Jan 19
Aquarius	Air	Water-carrier	Jan 20-Feb 18
Pisces	Water	Fishes	Feb 19-Mar 20

ACADEMY AWARDS ('OSCARS') – BEST FILM

Year	Film	Year	Film
1987	The Last Emperor	1998	Shakespeare in Love
1988	Rain Man	1999	American Beauty
1989	Driving Miss Daisy	2000	Gladiator
1990	Dances With Wolves	2001	A Beautiful Mind
1991	The Silence of the Lambs	2002	Chicago
1992	Unforgiven	2003	The Lord of the Rings: The Return of the King
1993	Schindler's List		
1994	Forrest Gump	2004	Million Dollar Baby
1995	Braveheart	2005	Crash
1996	The English Patient	2006	The Departed
1997	Titanic	2007	No Country for Old Men

POETS LAUREATE

1668	John Dryden*	1843	William Wordsworth
1689	Thomas Shadwell	1850	Alfred, Lord Tennyson‡
1692	Nahum Tate	1896	Alfred Austin
1715	Nicholas Rowe	1913	Robert Bridges
1718	Laurence Eusden	1930	John Masefield
1730	Colley Cibber	1968	Cecil Day Lewis
1757	William Whitehead†	1972	Sir John Betjeman
1785	Thomas Warton	1984	Ted Hughes
1790	Henry Pye	1999	Andrew Motion
1813	Robert Southey		

*post not officially established until 1668; the previous laureates had included Ben Jonson
† Appointed after Thomas Gray declined ‡ Appointed after Samuel Rogers declined

ARCHBISHOPS OF CANTERBURY

Years	Name
1896–1902	Frederick Temple
1903–28	Randall Thomas Davidson
1928–42	Cosmo Gordon Lang
1942–44	William Temple†
1945–61	Geoffrey Francis Fisher
1961–74	Arthur Michael Ramsey
1974–80	Frederick Donald Coggan
1980–91	Robert Alexander Kennedy Runcie
1991–2002	George Leonard Carey
2002–	Rowan Douglas Williams

CHESS WORLD CHAMPIONS

Reign	Player	Country
1866–1894	Wilhelm Steinitz*	Austria
1894–1921	Emanuel Lasker	Germany
1921–27	José Capablanca	Cuba
1927–35	Alexander Alekhine	France
1935–37	Max Euwe	Netherlands
1937–46†	Alexander Alekhine	France
1948–57	Mikhail Botvinnik	Soviet Union
1957–58	Vassili Smyslov	Soviet Union
1958–60	Mikhail Botvinnik	Soviet Union
1960–61	Mikhail Tal	Soviet Union
1961–63	Mikhail Botvinnik	Soviet Union
1963–69	Tigran Petrosian	Soviet Union
1969–72	Boris Spassky	Soviet Union
1972–75	Bobby Fischer†	USA
1975–85	Anatoli Karpov	Soviet Union
1985–2000§	Gary Kasparov	Russia
2000–2007	Vladimir Kramnik	Russia
2007–	Viswanathan Anand	India

* Official world championship dates from 1888
† Alekhine's death and the reorganization of the sport meant there was no champion 1946–48
‡ Defaulted title after refusing to accept ICC rules
§ From 1993 to 2006 there was also a FIDE champion

PLAYS OF WILLIAM SHAKESPEARE

Title (in order of composition)	Principal Characters
Henry VI Part 1	Henry, Talbot
Henry VI Part 2	Henry, Margaret
Henry VI Part 3	Henry, Margaret
Titus Andronicus	Titus, Aaron
Richard III	Richard, Clarence
The Comedy of Errors	Antipholus, Dromio
Love's Labour's Lost	Ferdinand, Berowne
The Two Gentlemen of Verona	Valentine, Proteus
The Taming of the Shrew	Petruchio, Katherine
Richard II	Richard, Bolingbroke
Romeo and Juliet	Romeo, Juliet
A Midsummer Night's Dream	Oberon, Titania
King John	John, Arthur
The Merchant of Venice	Antonio, Shylock
Henry IV Part 1	Henry, Hal, Hotspur
Henry IV Part 2	Henry. Falstaff, Hal
Much Ado About Nothing	Beatrice, Benedick
Henry V	Henry, Pistol
Julius Caesar	Brutus, Antony
As You Like It	Rosalind, Orlando
Twelfth Night	Orsino, Viola, Olivia
Hamlet, Prince of Denmark	Hamlet, Ophelia
The Merry Wives of Windsor	Falstaff, Ford
Troilus and Cressida	Troilus, Cressida
All's Well That Ends Well	Bertram, Helena
Measure for Measure	Vincentio, Angelo
Othello	Othello, Iago, Desdemona
King Lear	Lear, Cordelia, Regan, Gloucester, Goneril
Macbeth	Macbeth, Lady Macbeth, Banquo
Antony and Cleopatra	Antony, Cleopatra
Coriolanus	Coriolanus, Volumnia
Timon of Athens	Timon, Apemantus
Pericles, Prince of Tyre	Pericles, Marina
Cymbeline	Imogen, Iachimo
The Winter's Tale	Leontes, Perdita
The Tempest	Prospero, Miranda
Henry VIII	Henry, Catherine

MAN BOOKER PRIZE

Year	Writer and title
1992	Michael Ondaatje The English Patient; Barry Unsworth Sacred Hunger
1993	Roddy Doyle Paddy Clarke Ha Ha Ha
1994	James Kelman How Late It Was, How Late
1995	Pat Barker The Ghost Road
1996	Graham Swift Last Orders
1997	Arundhati Roy The God of Small Things
1998	Ian McEwan Amsterdam
1999	J.M. Coetzee Disgrace
2000	Margaret Atwood The Blind Assassin
2001	Peter Carey The True History of the Kelly Gang
2002	Yann Martel Life of Pi
2003	DBC Pierre Vernon God Little
2004	Alan Hollinghurst The Line of Beauty
2005	John Banville The Sea
2006	Kiran Desai The Inheritance of Loss
2007	Anne Enright The Gathering

PULITZER PRIZE FOR FICTION

Year	Writer and title
1994	E. Annie Proulx, The Shipping News
1995	Carol Shields The Stone Diaries
1996	Richard Ford Independence Day
1997	Steven Millhauser Martin Dressler: The Tale of an American Dreamer
1998	Philip Roth American Pastoral
1999	Michael Cunningham The Hours
2000	Jhumpa Lahiri Interpreter of Maladies
2001	Michael Chabon The Amazing Adventures of Kavalier & Clay
2002	Richard Russo Empire Falls
2003	Jeffrey Eugenides Middlesex
2004	Edward P. Jones The Known World
2005	Marilynne Robinson Gilead
2006	Geraldine Brooks March
2007	Cormac McCarthy The Road
2008	Junot Díaz The Brief Wondrous Life of Oscar Wao

EUROPEAN UNION MEMBERS

	Area ('000) Sq km	Area ('000) Sq mi	Pop'n ('000)	Per capita GDP (US$)	Date of joining	Seats in Parliament
Austria	83.9	32.4	8,200	32,900	1995	18
Belgium	30.5	11.8	10,392	31,800	1957	24
Bulgaria	111	42.8	7,323	9,000	2007	18
Cyprus	9.3	3.6	788	21,600	2004	6
Czech Republic*	78.9	30.5	10,229	18,100	2004	24
Denmark*†	43.1	16.6	5,468	33,500	1973	14
Estonia*	45.1	17.4	1,316	16,400	2004	6
Finland	338	131	5,238	30,300	1995	14
France	552	213	60,876	29,900	1957	78
Germany	357	138	82,401	29,700	1957	99
Greece	132	50.9	10,706	22,800	1981	24
Hungary*	93	35.9	9,956	15,900	2004	24
Ireland	70.3	27.1	4,109	34,100	1973	13
Italy	301	116	58,148	28,300	1957	78
Latvia*	64.6	24.9	2,260	12,800	2004	9
Lithuania*	65.2	25.2	3,575	13,700	2004	13
Luxembourg	2.6	1	480	62,700	1957	6
Malta	0.32	0.12	402	18,800	2004	5
Netherlands	41.5	16	16,571	30,500	1957	27
Poland*	323	125	38,518	12,700	2004	54
Portugal	88.8	34.3	10,643	18,400	1986	24
Romania	238	92	22,276	8,300	2007	35
Slovak Republic*	49	18.9	5,448	15,700	2004	14
Slovenia	20.3	7.8	2,009	20,900	2004	7
Spain	498	192	40,448	25,100	1986	54
Sweden*	450	174	9,031	29,600	1995	19
United Kingdom*	242	93.4	60,776	30,900	1973	78

* Outside the euro zone † Greenland seceded from the Community in 1985

LONGEST RAIL AND ROAD TUNNELS

Name	Location	Length km	Length mi	Date
Rail				
Seikan	Honshu-Hokkaido, Japan	53.9	33.86	1988
Eurotunnel	England-France	49.94	31.03	1996
Dai-shimuzu	Honshu, Japan	22.17	13.78	1982
Simplon I & II	Alps, Switzerland-Italy	19.92	12.56	1906, 1922
Road				
St Gotthard	Swiss Alps	16.32	10.25	1980
Rogers Pass	British Columbia, Canada	14.66	9.1	1989
Arlberg	Austrian Alps	14	8.12	1978
Fréjus	France-Italy	13	8.1	1980
Mont Blanc	France-Italy	11.59	7.35	1965

MAJOR INTERNATIONAL AIRPORTS

Name	City	Passengers*	Movements†
Hartsfield Atlanta International	Atlanta, USA	80,162	915.5
O'Hare International	Chicago, USA	72,144	908.9
Los Angeles International	Los Angeles, USA	66,425	783.4
Heathrow	London, UK	64,607	466.8
Dallas/Fort Worth International	Dallas, USA	60,687	837.8
Haneda	Tokyo, Japan	56,402	211.0‡
Frankfurt/Main	Frankfurt, Germany	49,360	458.7
Charles de Gaulle	Paris, France	48,246	517.7
San Francisco International	San Francisco, USA	41,041	429.2
Amsterdam Schiphol	Amsterdam, Holland	39,607	432.5

* Thousands, 2000 † Total aircraft, in thousands, 2000, ‡ 1995 figure

MUSICAL SYMBOLS

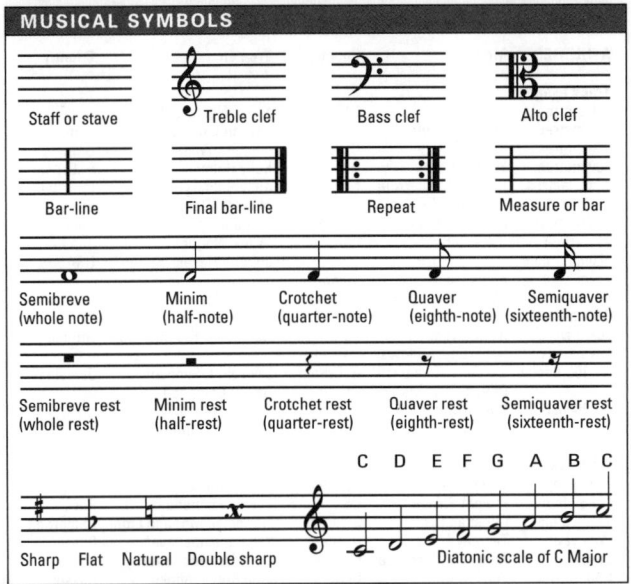

Staff or stave	Treble clef	Bass clef	Alto clef
Bar-line	Final bar-line	Repeat	Measure or bar

Semibreve (whole note)	Minim (half-note)	Crotchet (quarter-note)	Quaver (eighth-note)	Semiquaver (sixteenth-note)
Semibreve rest (whole rest)	Minim rest (half-rest)	Crotchet rest (quarter-rest)	Quaver rest (eighth-rest)	Semiquaver rest (sixteenth-rest)

C D E F G A B C

Sharp Flat Natural Double sharp — Diatonic scale of C Major

GREEK ALPHABET

α	A	alpha
β	B	beta
γ	Γ	gamma
δ	Δ	delta
ε	E	epsilon
ζ	Z	zeta
η	H	eta
θ	Θ	theta
ι	I	iota
κ	K	kappa
λ	Λ	lambda
μ	M	mu
ν	N	nu
ξ	Ξ	xi
ο	O	omicron
π	Π	pi
ρ	P	rho
σ, ς	Σ	sigma
τ	T	tau
υ	Υ	upsilon
φ	Φ	phi
χ	X	chi
ψ	Ψ	psi
ω	Ω	omega

In mathematics, π (pi) equals 3.14159

CODES AND ALPHABETS

Letter	Morse code	Braille	Semaphore
A	• —		
B	— • • •		
C	— • — •		
D	— • •		
E	•		
F	• • — •		
G	— — •		
H	• • • •		
I	• •		
J	• — — —		
K	— • —		
L	• — • •		
M	— —		
N	— •		
O	— — —		
P	• — — •		
Q	— — • —		
R	• — •		
S	• • •		
T	—		
U	• • —		
V	• • • —		
W	• — —		
X	— • • —		
Y	— • — —		
Z	— — • •		

CHESS – OPENING POSITION

QR P	QN P	QB P	Q P	K P	KB P	KN P	KR P

P QR	P QN	P QB	P Q	P K	P KB	P KN	P KR

Abbreviations

B	Bishop	**P**	Pawn
K	King	**Q**	Queen
KB	King's bishop	**QB**	Queen's bishop
KN	King's knight	**QN**	Queen's knight
KR	King's rook	**QR**	Queen's rook
N	Knight	**R**	Rook (Castle)

BASIC MATHEMATICAL SYMBOLS

+	plus; positive
−	minus; negative
±	plus or minus; positive or negative; degree of accuracy
×	multiplied by ('times') (3×2)
÷	divided by (6 ÷ 2)
/	divided by; ratio of (2:1)
!	factorial (4! = 4×3×2×1)
=	equal to
≠	not equal to
≡	identical with
≢	not identical with
≘	corresponds to
:	ratio of (2:1)
::	proportionately equals (2:3 :: 4:6)
≈	approximately equal to; equivalent to; similar to
>	greater than
≫	much greater than
≯	not greater than
<	less than
≪	much less than
≮	not less than
≥	greater than or equal to
≤	less than or equal to
∝	directly proportional to
( )	parentheses
[ ]	brackets
{ }	braces
∞	infinity
→	approaches the limit
√	square root
$\sqrt[3]{}$ / $\sqrt[4]{}$	cube root, fourth root, etc
%	per cent
′	prime; minute(s) of arc; foot/feet
″	double prime; second(s) of arc; inch(es)
⌒	arc of circle
°	degree of arc
≙	equiangular
⊥	perpendicular
∥	parallel
∴	therefore
∵	because
Δ	increment
Σ	summation
Π	product
∫	integral sign

SYMBOLS IN COMMON USE

&	ampersand (and)		corrosive
@	at; per (in costs)		explosive
©	copyright	✕	irritant
®	registered		high voltage
"	ditto		highly flammable
TM	trademark		oxidizing/ supports fire
♀	female		radiation (laser)
♂	male		radiation (non-ionising)
	disabled		radioactive
	first aid		toxic
i	information		
	recycling		

ACCENTS

Name	Example	Name	Example
Acute	é	Diaeresis	ï
Breve	ă	Grave	è
Caron	ˇo	Macron	ā
Cedilla	ç	Tilde	ñ
Circumflex	ô	Umlaut	ü

ENGLISH PHONETIC ALPHABET

Letter	Code name	Letter	Code name
A	Alpha	N	November
B	Bravo	O	Oscar
C	Charlie	P	Papa
D	Delta	Q	Quebec
E	Echo	R	Romeo
F	Foxtrot	S	Sierra
G	Golf	T	Tango
H	Hotel	U	Uniform
I	India	V	Victor
J	Juliet	W	Whisk(e)y
K	Kilo	X	X-ray
L	Lima	Y	Yankee
M	Mike	Z	Zulu

SUMMER OLYMPIC GAMES

The VIth Olympiad of 1916 was scheduled for Berlin. The XIIth of 1940 was scheduled for Tokyo, later changed to Helsinki, and the XIIIth 1944 was scheduled for London.

Games	Year	Venue	Competitors	Sports	Events	Leading medal-winning nation
I	1896	Athens, Greece	200	9	43	Greece (47)*
II	1900	Paris, France	1225	24	166	France (102)
III	1904	St Louis, USA	687	16	104	USA (238)
IV	1908	London, UK	2035	21	110	Great Britain (145)
V	1912	Stockholm, Sweden	2537	13	102	Sweden (65)
VII§	1920	Antwerp, Belgium	2668	21	154	USA (94)
VIII	1924	Paris, France	3092	17	126	USA (99)
IX	1928	Amsterdam, Netherlands	3014	14	109	USA (56)
X	1932	Los Angeles, USA	1408	14	117	USA (103)
XI	1936	Berlin, Germany	4066	19	129	Germany (89)
XIV	1948	London, UK	4099	17	136	USA (84)
XV	1952	Helsinki, Finland	4925	17	149	USA (76)
XVI	1956	Melbourne, Australia	3184	17	151	Soviet Union (98)
XVII	1960	Rome, Italy	5346	17	150	Soviet Union (99)
XVIII	1964	Tokyo, Japan	5140	19	163	Soviet Union (96)†
XIX	1968	Mexico City, Mexico	5530	18	172	Soviet Union (107)
XX	1972	Munich, West Germany	7123	21	195	Soviet Union (99)
XXI	1976	Montréal, Canada	6028	21	198	Soviet Union (125)
XXII	1980	Moscow, Soviet Union	5217	21	204	Soviet Union (195)
XXIII	1984	Los Angeles, USA	6797	21	221	Soviet Union (174)
XXIV	1988	Seoul, South Korea	8465	23	237	Soviet Union (132)
XXV	1992	Barcelona, Spain	9364	24	257	Unified Team (111)‡
XXVI	1996	Atlanta, USA	10,744	29	271	USA (101)
XXVII	2000	Sydney, Australia	10,651	28	300	USA (97)
XXVII	2004	Athens, Greece	11,099	28	296	USA (103)

*USA won 11 gold medals, but only 19 in total †USA won 36 gold medals to Soviet Union's 30, but only 92 in all ‡Former Soviet republics §The Olympics were also held in 1916.

WINTER OLYMPIC GAMES

Games	Year	Venue	Competitors	Sports	Events	Leading nation
I	1924	Chamonix, France	258	5	14	Norway (17)
II	1928	St Moritz, Switzerland	464	6	14	Norway (15)
III	1932	Lake Placid, USA	252	5	14	USA (12)
IV	1936	Garmisch, Germany	668	6	17	Norway (15)
V	1948	St Moritz, Switzerland	669	7	22	Norway/Sweden (10)
VI	1952	Oslo, Norway	694	6	22	Norway (16)
VII	1956	Cortina d'Ampezzo, Italy	820	6	24	Soviet Union (14)
VIII	1960	Squaw Valley, USA	665	6	27	Soviet Union (21)
IX	1964	Innsbruck, Austria	1091	8	34	Soviet Union (25)
X	1968	Grenoble, France	1158	8	35	Norway (14)
XI	1972	Sapporo, Japan	1006	8	35	Soviet Union (16)
XII	1976	Innsbruck, Austria	1123	8	37	Soviet Union (27)
XIII	1980	Lake Placid, USA	1072	8	38	East Germany (23)†
XIV	1984	Sarajevo, Yugoslavia	1274	8	39	Soviet Union (25)‡
XV	1988	Calgary, Canada	1423	8	46	Soviet Union (29)
XVI	1992	Albertville, France	1801	10	57	Germany (26)
XVII	1994	Lillehammer, Norway	1737	10	61	Norway (26)§
XVIII	1998	Nagano, Japan	2302	13	68	Germany (29)
XIX	2002	Salt Lake City, USA	2399	15	78	Germany (35)
XX	2006	Turin, Italy	2508	15	84	Germany (35)

†Soviet Union won 10 gold medals to East Germany's 9, but only 22 in total
‡East Germany won 9 gold medals to the USSR's 6, but only 24 in total
§Russia won 11 gold medals to Norway's 10, but only 23 in total

SKIING WORLD CUP

Year	Overall winner
Men	
2001	H. Maier (A)
2002	S. Eberharter (A)
2003	S. Eberharter (A)
2004	H. Maier (A)
2005	B. Miller (USA)
2006	B. Raich (A)
2007	A. L. Svindal (N)
2008	B. Miller (USA)
Women	
2001	J. Kostelic (Cro)
2002	M. Dorfmeister (A)
2003	J. Kostelic (Cro)
2004	A. Pärson (Swe)
2005	A. Pärson (Swe)
2006	J. Kostelic (Cro)
2007	N. Hosp (A)
2008	L. Vonn (USA)

N = Norway
A = Austria
Swe = Sweden
Cro = Croatia

2004 SUMMER OLYMPIC GAMES – LEADING MEDAL-WINNERS

Country	Gold	Silver	Bronze	Total
United States	35	39	29	103
China	32	17	14	63
Russia	27	27	38	92
Australia	17	16	16	49
Japan	16	9	12	37
Germany	14	16	18	48
France	11	9	13	33
Italy	10	11	11	32
South Korea	9	12	9	30
Great Britain	9	9	12	30
Cuba	9	7	11	27
Ukraine	9	5	9	23
Hungary	8	6	3	17
Romania	8	5	6	19
Greece	6	6	4	16
Norway	5	0	1	6
Netherlands	4	9	9	22
Brazil	4	3	3	10
Sweden	4	1	2	7
Spain	3	11	5	19
Canada	3	6	3	12

Countries are listed in order of the number of gold medals won.

2004 SUMMER OLYMPIC GAMES GOLD MEDALLISTS

ATHLETICS	Men	Country	Women	Country
Track events				
100 metres	Justin Gatlin	USA	Yuliya Nesterenko	Belarus
200 metres	Shawn Crawford	USA	Veronica Campbell	Jamaica
400 metres	Jeremy Wariner	USA	Tonique Williams-Darling	Bahamas
800 metres	Yuriy Borzakovskiy	Russia	Kelly Holmes	G. Britain
1,500 metres	Hicham El Guerrouj	Morocco	Kelly Holmes	G. Britain
5,000 metres	Hicham El Guerrouj	Morocco	Meseret Defar	Ethiopia
10,000 metres	Kenenisa Bekele	Ethiopia	Huina Xing	China
Marathon	Stefano Baldini	Italy	Mizuki Noguchi	Japan
100m hurdles	–	–	Joanna Hayes	USA
110m hurdles	Xiang Liu	China	–	
400m hurdles	Felix Sanchez	Dominica	Fani Halkia	Greece
3,000m steeple	Ezekiel Kemboi	Kenya	–	
20km walk	Ivano Brugnetti	Italy	Athanasia Tsoumeleka	Greece
50km walk	Robert Korzeniowski	Poland	–	
4 x 100m relay	Gardener/Campbell/ Devonish/Lewis-Francis	G. Britain	Lawrence/Simpson/ Bailey/Campbell	Jamaica
4 x 400m relay	Harris/Brew/ Wariner/Williamson	USA	Trotter/Henderson/ Richards/Hennagan	USA
Field events				
High jump	Stefan Holm	Sweden	Yelena Slesarenko	Russia
Long jump	Dwight Phillips	USA	Tatyana Lebedeva	Russia
Triple jump	Christian Olsson	Sweden	Francoise Mbango Etone	Cameroon
Pole vault	Timothy Mack	USA	Yelena Isinbayeva*	Russia
Javelin	Andreas Thorkildsen	Norway	Osleidys Menendez	Cuba
Shot put	Yuriy Bilonog	Ukraine	Irina Korzhanenko	Russia
Discus	Virgilijus Alekna	Lithuania	Natalya Sadova	Russia
Hammer	Koji Murofushi	Japan	Olga Kuzenkova	Russia
Multi-discipline				
Heptathlon	–	–	Carolina Kluft	Sweden
Decathlon	Roman Sebrle	Czech Rep.	–	–

SWIMMING	Men	Country	Women	Country
50m freestyle	Gary Hall	USA	Inge de Bruijn	Netherlands
100m freestyle	P. Hoogenband	Neths.	Jodie Henry	Australia
200m freestyle	Ian Thorpe	Australia	Camelia Potec	Romania
400m freestyle	Ian Thorpe	Australia	Laure Manaudou	France
800m freestyle	–		Ai Shibata	Japan
1500m freestyle	Grant Hackett	Australia	–	
100m breaststroke	Kosuke Kitajima	Japan	Xuejuan Luo	China
200m breaststroke	Kosuke Kitajima	Japan	Amanda Beard	USA
100m backstroke	Aaron Peirsol	USA	Natalie Coughlin	USA
200m backstroke	Aaron Peirsol	USA	Kirsty Coventry	Zimbabwe
100m butterfly	Michael Phelps	USA	Petria Thomas	Australia
200m butterfly	Michael Phelps	USA	Otylia Jedrzejczak	Poland
200m medley	Michael Phelps	USA	Yana Klochkova	Ukraine
400m medley	Michael Phelps	USA	Yana Klochkova	Ukraine
4x100m freestyle relay	Schoeman/Ferns/ Townsend/Neethling*	S. Africa	Mills/Lenton/ Thomas/Henry*	Australia
4x200m freestyle relay	Phelps/Lochte/ Vanderkaay/Keller	Australia	Coughlin/Piper/ Vollmer/Sandeno*	USA
4x100m medley relay	Peirsol/Hansen/ Crocker/Lezak*	USA	Rooney/Jones/ Thomas/Henry*	Australia

DIVING	Men	Country	Women	Country
3m springboard	Bo Peng	China	Jingjing Guo	China
10m platform	Jia Hu	China	Chantelle Newbery	Australia
3m synchronized	Nikolaos Siranidis, Thomas Bimis	Greece	Minxia Wu, Jingjing Guo	China
10m synchronized	Liang Tian, Jinghui Yang	China	Lishi Lao, Ting Li	China

GYMNASTICS	Men	Country	Women	Country
All-round	Paul Hamm	USA	Carly Patterson	USA
Floor exercise	Kyle Shewfelt	Canada	Catalina Ponor	Romania
Balance beam	–		Catalina Ponor	Romania
Assymetrical bars	–		Emilie Lepennec	France
Rings	Dimosthenis Tampakos	Greece	–	–
Parallel bars	Valeri Goncharov	Ukraine	–	–
Horizontal bar	Igor Cassina	Italy	–	–
Pommel horse	Marius Daniel Urzica	Romania	–	
Vault	Gervasio Deferr	Spain	Monica Rosu	Romania
Team event	Kashima/Mizutori/ Nakano/Tomita/ Tsukahara/Yoneda	Japan	Ban/Eremia/ Ponor/Rosu/ Sofronie/Stroescu	Romania

*New world record

WORLD ATHLETICS CHAMPIONSHIP VENUES

Year	Venue	Year	Venue	Year	Venue
1997	Athens, Greece	2001	Edmonton, Canada	2005	Helsinki, Finland
1999	Seville, Spain	2003	Paris, France	2007	Osaka, Japan

FORMULA 1 MOTOR RACING CHAMPIONS

Year	Driver	Country	Car	Constructors' Cup
1980	Alan Jones	Australia	Williams-Ford	Williams-Ford
1981	Nelson Piquet	Brazil	Brabham-Ford	Williams-Ford
1982	Keke Rosberg	Finland	Williams-Ford	Ferrari
1983	Nelson Piquet	Brazil	Brabham-BMW	Ferrari
1984	Niki Lauda	Austria	McLaren-Porsche	McLaren-Porsche
1985	Alain Prost	France	McLaren-Porsche	McLaren-Porsche
1986	Alain Prost	France	McLaren-Porsche	Williams-Honda
1987	Nelson Piquet	Brazil	Williams-Honda	Williams-Honda
1988	Ayrton Senna	Brazil	McLaren-Honda	McLaren-Honda
1989	Alain Prost	France	McLaren-Honda	McLaren-Honda
1990	Ayrton Senna	Brazil	McLaren-Honda	McLaren-Honda
1991	Ayrton Senna	Brazil	McLaren-Honda	McLaren-Honda
1992	Nigel Mansell	England	Williams-Renault	Williams-Renault
1993	Alain Prost	France	Williams-Renault	Williams-Renault
1994	Michael Schumacher	Germany	Benetton-Ford	Williams-Renault
1995	Michael Schumacher	Germany	Benetton-Renault	Benetton-Renault
1996	Damon Hill	England	Williams-Renault	Williams-Renault
1997	Jacques Villeneuve	Canada	Williams-Renault	Williams-Renault
1998	Mika Haakinen	Finland	McLaren-Mercedes	McLaren-Mercedes
1999	Mika Haakinen	Finland	McLaren-Mercedes	Ferrari
2000	Michael Schumacher	Germany	Ferrari	Ferrari
2001	Michael Schumacher	Germany	Ferrari	Ferrari
2002	Michael Schumacher	Germany	Ferrari	Ferrari
2003	Michael Schumacher	Germany	Ferrari	Ferrari
2004	Michael Schumacher	Germany	Ferrari	Ferrari
2005	Fernando Alonso	Spain	Renault	Renault
2006	Fernando Alonso	Spain	Renault	Renault
2007	Kimi Räikkönen	Finland	Ferrari	Ferrari

FIFA WORLD CUP FOOTBALL FINALS

Year	Venue	Attendance	Winners		Runners-up	
1930	Montevideo	90,000	Uruguay*	4	Argentina	2
1934	Rome	50,000	Italy*	2[†]	Czechoslovakia	1
1938	Paris	45,000	Italy	4	Hungary	2
1950	Rio de Janeiro	199,854	Uruguay	2	Brazil	1
1954	Bern	60,000	West Germany	3	Hungary	2
1958	Stockholm	49,737	Brazil	5	Sweden*	2
1962	Santiago	68,679	Brazil	3	Czechoslovakia	1
1966	London	93,802	England*	4[†]	West Germany	2
1970	Mexico City	107,412	Brazil	4	Italy	1
1974	Munich	77,833	West Germany*	2	Netherlands	1
1978	Buenos Aires	77,000	Argentina*	3	Netherlands	1
1982	Madrid	90,080	Italy	3	West Germany	1
1986	Mexico City	114,580	Argentina	3	West Germany	2
1990	Rome	73,603	West Germany	1	Argentina	0
1994	Los Angeles	94,194	Brazil	0[‡]	Italy	0
1998	Paris	75,000	France*	3	Brazil	0
2002	Yokohama	69,029	Brazil	2	Germany	0
2006	Berlin	69,000	Italy	1[‡]	Germany	1

Host nation † After extra time ‡ Won on penalties after extra time

ICE SKATING WORLD CHAMPIONS

Year	Men	Country	Women	Country
2002	Alexei Yagudin	Russia	Irina Slutskaya	Russia
2003	Evgeni Plushenko	Russia	Michelle Kwan	USA
2004	Evgeni Plushenko	Russia	Shizuka Arakawa	Japan
2005	Stephane Lambiel	Switzerland	Irina Slutskaya	Russia
2006	Stephane Lambiel	Switzerland	Kimmie Meissner	USA
2007	Brian Joubert	France	Miki Ando	Japan
2008	Jeffrey Buttle	Canada	Mao Asada	Japan

US MAJORS GOLF CHAMPIONS

Year	US Open	US Masters	US PGA
1998	Lee Janzen	Mark O'Meara	Vijay Singh[2]
1999	Payne Stewart	José-Maria Olazábal[5]	Tiger Woods
2000	Tiger Woods	Vijay Singh[2]	Tiger Woods
2001	Retief Goosen[4]	Tiger Woods	David Toms
2002	Tiger Woods	Tiger Woods	Rich Beem
2003	Jim Furyk	Mike Weir[1]	Shaun Micheel
2004	Retief Goosen[4]	Phil Mickelson	Vijay Singh[2]
2005	Michael Campbell[7]	Tiger Woods	Phil Mickelson
2006	Geoff Ogilvy[8]	Phil Mickelson	Tiger Woods
2007	Ángel Gabrera[6]	Zach Johnson	Tiger Woods
2008	Tiger Woods	Trevor Immelman[4]	Pádraig Harrington[3]

*All players US except: 1 Canada 2 Fiji 3 Ireland 4 South Africa
5 Spain 6 Argentina 7 New Zealand 8 Australia*

GYMNASTICS WORLD CHAMPIONSHIPS

Year	Men*	Country	Team	Women*	Country	Team
1999	Nikolai Krukov	Russia	China	Maria Olaru	Romania	Romania
2001	Jing Feng	China	Belarus	Svetlana Khorkina	Russia	Romania
2002	Li Xiaopeng	China	†	Ashley Postell	USA	†
2003	Paul Hamm	USA	China	Svetlana Khorkina	Russia	USA
2005	Paul Hamm	USA	China	Svetlana Khorkina	Russia	USA
2006	Yang Wei	China	China	Vanessa Ferrari	Italy	China
2007	Yang Wei	China	China	Shawn Johnson	USA	USA

Combined exercises (all-round champion) † No team championships were held

US OPEN TENNIS CHAMPIONS

Year	Men	Women
1995	Pete Sampras (US)	Steffi Graf (Ger)
1996	Pete Sampras (US)	Steffi Graf (Ger)
1997	Patrick Rafter (Aus)	Martina Hingis (Swi)
1998	Patrick Rafter (Aus)	Lindsay Davenport (US)
1999	Andre Agassi (US)	Serena Williams (US)
2000	Marat Safin (Rus)	Venus Williams (US)
2001	Lleyton Hewitt (Aus)	Venus Williams (US)
2002	Pete Sampras (US)	Serena Williams (US)
2003	Andy Roddick (US)	Justine Henin-Hardenne (Bel)
2004	Roger Federer (Swi)	Svetlana Kuznetsova (Rus)
2005	Roger Federer (Swi)	Kim Clijsters (Swi)
2006	Roger Federer (Swi)	Maria Sharapova (Rus)
2007	Roger Federer (Swi)	Justine Henin (Bel)

RYDER CUP

Year	USA	Europe
1985	11½	16½[†]
1987	13[†]	15
1989	14	14[†]
1991	15[†]	13
1993	15	13[†]
1995	13½[†]	14½
1997	13½	14½[†]
1999	14½[†]	13½
2002	12½	15½[†]
2004	9½[†]	18½
2006	9½	18½[†]

† Home team

TOUR DE FRANCE

Year	Winner	Country
1996	Bjarne Riis	Denmark
1997	Jan Ullrich	Germany
1998	Marco Pantini	Italy
1999	Lance Armstrong	USA
2000	Lance Armstrong	USA
2001	Lance Armstrong	USA
2002	Lance Armstrong	USA
2003	Lance Armstrong	USA
2004	Lance Armstrong	USA
2005	Lance Armstrong	USA
2006	Oscar Pereiro	Spain
2007	Alberto Contador	Spain
2008	Carlos Sastre	Spain

DAVIS CUP

Year	Winner
1995	USA
1996	France
1997	Sweden
1998	Sweden
1999	Australia
2000	Spain
2001	France
2002	Russia
2003	Australia
2004	Spain
2005	Croatia
2006	Russia
2007	USA

BRITISH OPEN GOLF CHAMPIONS

Year	Winner	Country	Venue	Score
1991	Ian Baker-Finch	Australia	Royal Birkdale	272
1992	Nick Faldo	England	Muirfield	272
1993	Greg Norman	Australia	Sandwich	267
1994	Nick Price	Zimbabwe	Turnberry	268
1995	John Daly	USA	St Andrews	282
1996	Tom Lehman	USA	Royal Lytham	271
1997	Justin Leonard	USA	Royal Troon	272
1998	Mark O'Meara*	USA	Royal Birkdale	280
1999	Paul Lawrie*	Scotland	Carnoustie	290
2000	Tiger Woods	USA	St Andrews	269
2001	David Duval	USA	Royal Lytham	274
2002	Ernie Els*	South Africa	Muirfield	278
2003	Ben Curtis	USA	Royal St George's	283
2004	Todd Hamilton	USA	Royal Troon	274
2005	Tiger Woods	USA	St Andrews	274
2006	Tiger Woods	USA	Royal Liverpool	270
2007	Pádraig Harrington	Ireland	Carnoustie	277
2008	Pádraig Harrington	Ireland	Royal Birkdale	283

Won title after a play-off

WIMBLEDON SINGLES CHAMPIONS

Year	Men	Country	Women	Country
1989	Boris Becker	W. Germany	Steffi Graf	W. Germany
1990	Stefan Edberg	Sweden	Martina Navratilova	USA
1991	Michael Stich	Germany	Steffi Graf	Germany
1992	Andre Agassi	USA	Steffi Graf	Germany
1993	Pete Sampras	USA	Steffi Graf	Germany
1994	Pete Sampras	USA	Conchita Martinez	Spain
1995	Pete Sampras	USA	Steffi Graf	Germany
1996	Richard Krajicek	Netherlands	Steffi Graf	Germany
1997	Pete Sampras	USA	Martina Hingis	Switz
1998	Pete Sampras	USA	Jana Novotna	Czech
1999	Pete Sampras	USA	Lindsay Davenport	USA
2000	Pete Sampras	USA	Venus Williams	USA
2001	Goran Ivanisevic	Croatia	Venus Williams	USA
2002	Lleyton Hewitt	Australia	Serena Williams	USA
2003	Roger Federer	Switzerland	Serena Williams	USA
2004	Roger Federer	Switzerland	Maria Sharapova	Russia
2005	Roger Federer	Switzerland	Venus Williams	USA
2006	Roger Federer	Switzerland	Amelie Mauresmo	France
2007	Roger Federer	Switzerland	Venus Williams	USA
2008	Rafael Nadal	Spain	Venus Williams	USA

UEFA EUROPEAN CHAMPIONSHIP

Year	Winners	Year	Winners
1964	Spain*	1988	Netherlands
1968	Italy*	1992	Denmark
1972	West Germany	1996	Germany
1976	Czechoslovakia	2000	France
1980	West Germany	2004	Greece
1984	France*	2008	Spain

Host nation

UEFA CHAMPIONS LEAGUE

Year	Winners	Year	Winners
1981	Liverpool	1995	Ajax Amsterdam
1982	Aston Villa	1996	Juventus†
1983	SV Hamburg	1997	Bor. Dortmund
1984	Liverpool†	1998	Real Madrid
1985	Juventus	1999	Manchester U.
1986	Steaua Bucharest†	2000	Real Madrid
1987	FC Porto	2001	Bayern Munich†
1988	PSV Eindhoven†	2002	Real Madrid
1989	AC Milan	2003	AC Milan
1990	AC Milan	2004	Porto
1991	R. Star Belgrade†	2005	Liverpool
1992	Barcelona	2006	Barcelona
1993	AC Milan‡	2007	AC Milan
1994	AC Milan	2008	Manchester U.

† Won on penalties ‡ Olympique Marseilles won the final but were stripped of the title by UEFA for financial irregularities

UEFA CUP

Year	Winners	Year	Winners
1981	Ipswich Town	1995	Parma
1982	AFK Gothenburg	1996	Bayern Munich
1983	Anderlecht	1997	Schalke†
1984	Tottenham H.†	1998	Internazionale
1985	Real Madrid	1999	Parma
1986	Real Madrid	2000	Galatasaray†
1987	AFK Gothenburg	2001	Liverpool
1988	Bayer Leverkusen†	2002	Feyenoord
1989	Napoli	2003	FC Porto
1990	Juventus	2004	Valencia
1991	Internazionale	2005	CSKA Moscow
1992	Ajax Amsterdam*	2006	Sevilla
1993	Juventus	2007	Sevilla
1994	Internazionale	2008	Zenit St. Petersburg

* Won on away goals rule † Won on penalties

FOOTBALL LEAGUE CHAMPIONS

Season	Winners	Season	Winners
1980–81	Aston Villa	1994–95	Blackburn R.
1981–82	Liverpool	1995–96	Manchester U.
1982–83	Liverpool	1996–97	Manchester U.
1983–84	Liverpool	1997–98	Arsenal
1984–85	Everton	1998–99	Manchester U.
1985–86	Liverpool	1999–2000	Manchester U.
1986–87	Everton	2000–01	Manchester U.
1987–88	Liverpool	2001–02	Arsenal
1988–89	Arsenal	2002–03	Manchester U.
1989–90	Liverpool	2003–04	Arsenal
1990–91	Arsenal	2004–05	Chelsea
1991–92	Leeds United	2005–06	Chelsea
1992–93	Manchester U.	2006–07	Manchester U.
1993–94	Manchester U.	2007–08	Manchester U.

NBA CHAMPIONSHIP

Year	Winners	Year	Winners
1987	L.A. Lakers	1998	Chicago Bulls
1988	L.A. Lakers	1999	San Antonio Spurs
1989	Detroit Pistons	2000	L.A. Lakers
1990	Detroit Pistons	2001	L.A. Lakers
1991	Chicago Bulls	2002	L.A. Lakers
1992	Chicago Bulls	2003	San Antonio Spurs
1993	Chicago Bulls	2004	Detroit Pistons
1994	Houston Rockets	2005	San Antonio Spurs
1995	Houston Rockets	2006	Miami Heat
1996	Chicago Bulls	2007	San Antonio Spurs
1997	Chicago Bulls	2008	Boston Celtics

RUGBY UNION WORLD CUP

Year	Venue	Winners	Runners-up	Score
1999	Cardiff	Australia	France	35–12
2003	Sydney	England	Australia	20–17
2007	France	S. Africa	England	15–6

RUGBY UNION SIX NATIONS CHAMPIONSHIP

Year	Winners	Year	Winners
1991	England†	2000	England
1992	England†	2001	England
1993	France	2002	France†
1994	Wales	2003	England†
1995	England†	2004	France†
1996	England	2005	Wales†
1997	France†	2006	France
1998	France†	2007	France
1999	Scotland	2008	Wales

† Grand Slam

CRICKET WORLD CUP FINALS

Year	Venue	Winners	Runners-up	Margin
1992	Melbourne	Pakistan	England	22 runs
1996	Lahore	Sri Lanka	Australia	7 wickets
1999	Lord's	Australia	Pakistan	8 wickets
2003	Jo'burg	Australia	India	125 runs
2007	Bridgetown	Australia	Sri Lanka	53 runs

CRICKET UK COUNTY CHAMPIONS

Year	Winners	Year	Winners
1990	Middlesex	1999	Surrey
1991	Essex	2000	Surrey
1992	Essex	2001	Yorkshire
1993	Middlesex	2002	Surrey
1994	Warwickshire	2003	Sussex
1995	Warwickshire	2004	Warwickshire
1996	Leicestershire	2005	Nottinghamshire
1997	Glamorgan	2006	Sussex
1998	Leicestershire	2007	Sussex

FA CUP WINNERS

Year	Winners	Year	Winners
1981	Tottenham H.*	1995	Everton
1982	Tottenham H.*	1996	Manchester U.
1983	Manchester U.*	1997	Chelsea
1984	Everton	1998	Arsenal
1985	Manchester U.	1999	Manchester U.
1986	Liverpool	2000	Chelsea
1987	Coventry City	2001	Liverpool
1988	Wimbledon	2002	Arsenal
1989	Liverpool	2003	Arsenal
1990	Manchester U.*	2004	Manchester U.
1991	Tottenham H.	2005	Arsenal
1992	Liverpool	2006	Liverpool
1993	Arsenal*	2007	Chelsea
1994	Manchester U.	2008	Portsmouth

*Won replay after first final was drawn

HOCKEY WORLD CHAMPIONS

Year	Winners	Year	Winners
Men		**Women**	
1994	Pakistan	1994	Australia
1998	Netherlands	1998	Australia
2002	Germany	2002	Argentina
2006	Germany	2006	Netherlands

NBA LEADING SCORERS

Year	Name	Team	Points
2001–02	Allen Iverson	Philadelphia 76ers	1883
2002–03	Tracy McGrady	Orlando Magic	2407
2003–04	Tracy McGrady	Orlando Magic	1878
2004–05	Allen Iverson	Philadelphia 76ers	2302
2005–06	Kobe Bryant	L.A. Lakers	2832
2006–07	Kobe Bryant	L.A. Lakers	2430

SNOOKER WORLD CHAMPIONS

Year	Winner	Country
1992	Stephen Hendry	Scotland
1993	Stephen Hendry	Scotland
1994	Stephen Hendry	Scotland
1995	Stephen Hendry	Scotland
1996	Stephen Hendry	Scotland
1997	Ken Doherty	Ireland
1998	John Higgins	Scotland
1999	Stephen Hendry	Scotland
2000	Mark Williams	Wales
2001	Ronnie O'Sullivan	England
2002	Peter Ebdon	England
2003	Mark Williams	Wales
2004	Ronnie O'Sullivan	England
2005	Shaun Murphy	England
2006	Graeme Dott	Scotland
2007	John Higgins	Scotland
2008	Ronnie O'Sullivan	England

COMMONWEALTH GAMES VENUES

The first Inter-Empire Sports meeting was held at Crystal Palace, London in 1911.

Games	Year	Venue
II*	1934	London, England
III*	1938	Sydney, Australia
IV*	1950	Auckland, New Zealand
V†	1954	Vancouver, Canada
VI†	1958	Cardiff, Wales
VII†	1962	Perth, Australia
VIII†	1966	Kingston, Jamaica
IX‡	1970	Edinburgh, Scotland
X‡	1974	Christchurch, New Zealand
XI§	1978	Edmonton, Canada
XII§	1982	Brisbane, Australia
XIII§	1986	Edinburgh, Scotland
XIV§	1990	Auckland, New Zealand
XV§	1994	Victoria, Canada
XVI§	1998	Kuala Lumpur, Malaysia
XVII§	2002	Manchester, England
XVIII§	2006	Melbourne, Australia

*British Empire Games † British Empire and Commonwealth Games ‡ British Commonwealth Games § Commonwealth Games

ENGLISH GRAND NATIONAL

Year	Horse	Jockey
1992	Party Politics	Carl Llewellyn
1993	Race void owing to false start	
1994	Minnehoma	Richard Dunwoody
1995	Royal Athlete	Jason Titley
1996	Rough Quest	Mick Fitzgerald
1997	Lord Gyllene	Tony Dobbin
1998	Earth Summit	Carl Llewellyn
1999	BobbyJo	Paul Carberry
2000	Papillon	Ruby Walsh
2001	Red Marauder	Richard Guest
2002	Bindaree	Jim Culloty
2003	Monty's Pass	Barry Geraghty
2004	Amberleigh House	Graham Lee
2005	Hedgehunter	Ruby Walsh
2006	Numbersixvalverde	Niall Madden
2007	Silver Birch	Robbie Power
2008	Comply Or Die	Timmy Murphy

EPSOM DERBY

Year	Horse	Jockey
1992	Dr Devious	John Reid
1993	Commander-in-Chief	Michael Kinane
1994	Erhaab	Willie Carson
1995	Lammtarra	Walter Swinburn
1996	Shaamit	Michael Hills
1997	Benny the Dip	Willie Ryan
1998	High-Rise	Olivier Peslier
1999	Oath	Kieren Fallon
2000	Sinndar	Johnny Murtagh
2001	Galileo	Michael Kinane
2002	High Chaparral	Johnny Murtagh
2003	Kris Kin	Kieren Fallon
2004	North Light	Kieren Fallon
2005	Motivator	Johnny Murtagh
2006	Sir Percy	Martin Dwyer
2007	Authorized	Frankie Dettori
2008	New Approach	Kevin Manning

WORLD ATLAS

SETTLEMENTS

■ PARIS   ■ Berne   ◉ Livorno   ◉ Brugge   ◉ Algeciras   ○ Frejus   ○ Oberammergau   ○ Thira

Settlement symbols and type styles vary according to the scale of each map and indicate the importance of towns on the map rather than specific population figures. Capital cities have red infills.

ADMINISTRATION

——————— International boundaries   – – – International boundaries (undefined or disputed)   ·········· Internal boundaries

International boundaries show the *de facto* situation where there are rival claims to territory

COMMUNICATIONS

╾╌╾ Principal roads   ～～ Principal railways   ⊣·⊢ Railway tunnels

⊣···⊢ Road tunnels   ––~– Railways under construction   ·········· Principal canals

≍ Passes   ⊕ Airfields

PHYSICAL FEATURES

～～ Perennial streams   Intermittent lakes   ▲ 8848 Elevations in metres

– – – Intermittent streams   Swamps and marshes   ▼ 8500 Sea depths in metres

Perennial lakes   Permanent ice and glaciers   *1134* Height of lake surface above sea level in metres

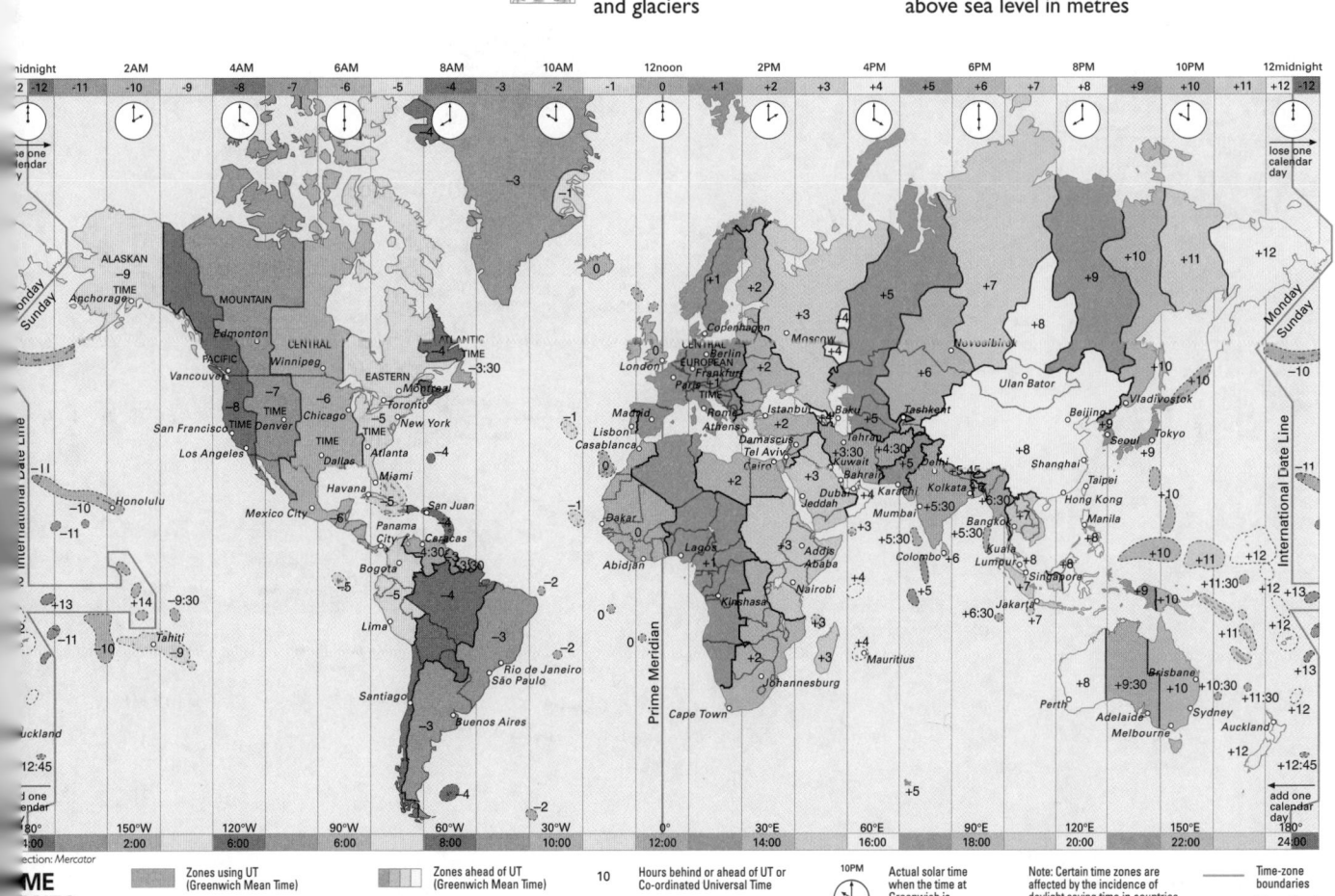

| | Zones using UT (Greenwich Mean Time) | | Zones ahead of UT (Greenwich Mean Time) | 10 | Hours behind or ahead of UT or Co-ordinated Universal Time | 10PM | Actual solar time when the time at Greenwich is 12:00 (noon) | Note: Certain time zones are affected by the incidence of daylight saving time in countries where it is adopted. | Time-zone boundaries |
| | Zones behind UT (Greenwich Mean Time) | | Half-hour zones | - - - - | International boundaries | | | | International Date Line |

A

B

C

D

E

F

G

H

Beaufort
Sea

GREENLAND
(Denmark)

ALASKA
(U.S.A.)

North

C A N A D A

Aleutian Is. (U.S.A.)

ICELAND

UNITED
KINGDO

IRELAN

UNITED STATES

America

OF AMERICA

NORTH

ATLANTIC

OCEAN

PORTUGAL
Lisbon

Azores
(Port.)

MOROC

Tropic of Cancer

Hawaiian Is.
(U.S.A.)

Honolulu

Hawaii

WESTERN
SAHARA

El Aaiún

Canary Is.
(Sp.)

MEXICO

Gulf of
Mexico

CUBA

Bahamas

Havana

MAURITAN

León

MÉXICO

HAITI
Port-au-Prince
JAMAICA
Kingston

DOMINICAN REP.

Santo
Domingo

Virgin Is. (U.S.A.) & (U.K.)

ANTIGUA & BARBUDA
ST. KITTS & NEVIS

DOMINICA

ST. LUCIA

GRENADA

TRINIDAD &
TOBAGO

CAPE VERDE
IS.

SENEGA

Dakar

GAMBI

GUINEA-BISSAU

Bissau

Conakry

Freetown

SIERRA
LEONE

GUINEA

Yamoussoukro

Monrovia

Central

America

Belmopan

BELIZE

GUATEMALA

Guatemala

San Salvador

EL SALVADOR

HONDURAS

Tegucigalpa

NICARAGUA

Managua

COSTA RICA

San José

Panamá

PANAMÁ

Barranquilla

Caracas

VENEZUELA

Georgetown

Paramaribo

Cayenne

GUYANA

SURINAME

FRENCH
GUIANA

P A C I F I C

Medellín

Cali

BOGOTÁ

COLOMBIA

Palmyra Is.
(U.S.A.)

Equator

Galápagos
(Ecuador)

Quito
ECUADOR

Guayaquil

Iquitos

Manaus

South

B R A Z I L

America

São Paulo
(Brazil)

Belém

Fortaleza

Natal

Recife

Fernando de Noronha
(Brazil)

KIRIBATI

Malden Is.

Phoenix Is.

Starbuck I.

Tokelau Is.
(N.Z.)

Marquesas Is.

PERU

LIMA

Callao

Arequipa

Lago Titicaca

La Paz

BOLIVIA

Sucre

Brasília

Belo Horizonte

Salvador

SAMOA

AMERICAN
SAMOA

O C E A N

FIJI

TONGA

Niue
(N.Z.)

Cook Is.
(N.Z.)

Society Is.

Tahiti

Tuamotu
Is.

F R E N C H

P O L Y N E S I A

Tubuai Is.

Antofagasta

PARAGUAY

Asunción

SÃO PAULO

RIO DE JANEIRO

Santos

Curitiba

Pôrto Alegre

SOUTH

ATLANTI

OCEAN

Tropic of Capricorn

Tucumán

Córdoba

Rosario

Valparaíso

SANTIAGO

Talcahuano

BUENOS AIRES

ARGENTINA

URUGUAY

Montevideo

Bahía Blanca

Rio Grande

Juan Fernández
(Chile)

Falkland Is.
(U.K.)

South Georgia
(U.K.)

Tierra del Fuego

Punta Arenas

C. Horn

Scotia Sea

South Sandwich Is.
(U.K.)

Drake Passage

South Orkney Is.

Antarctic Circle

Bellingshausen Sea

Weddell
Sea

Amundsen Sea

Antarctica

Projection: *Hammer Equal Area*

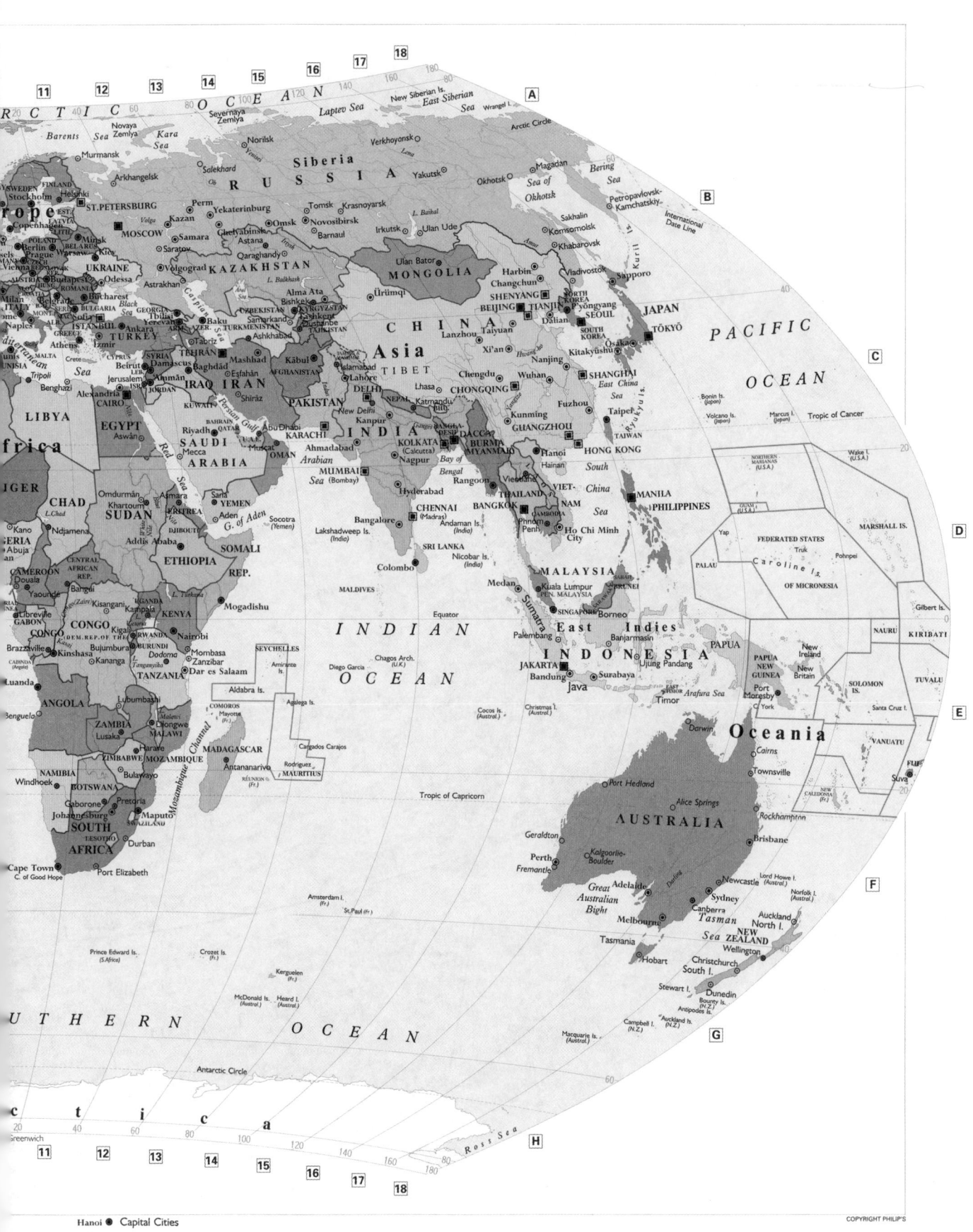

Hanoi ● Capital Cities

COPYRIGHT PHILIP'S

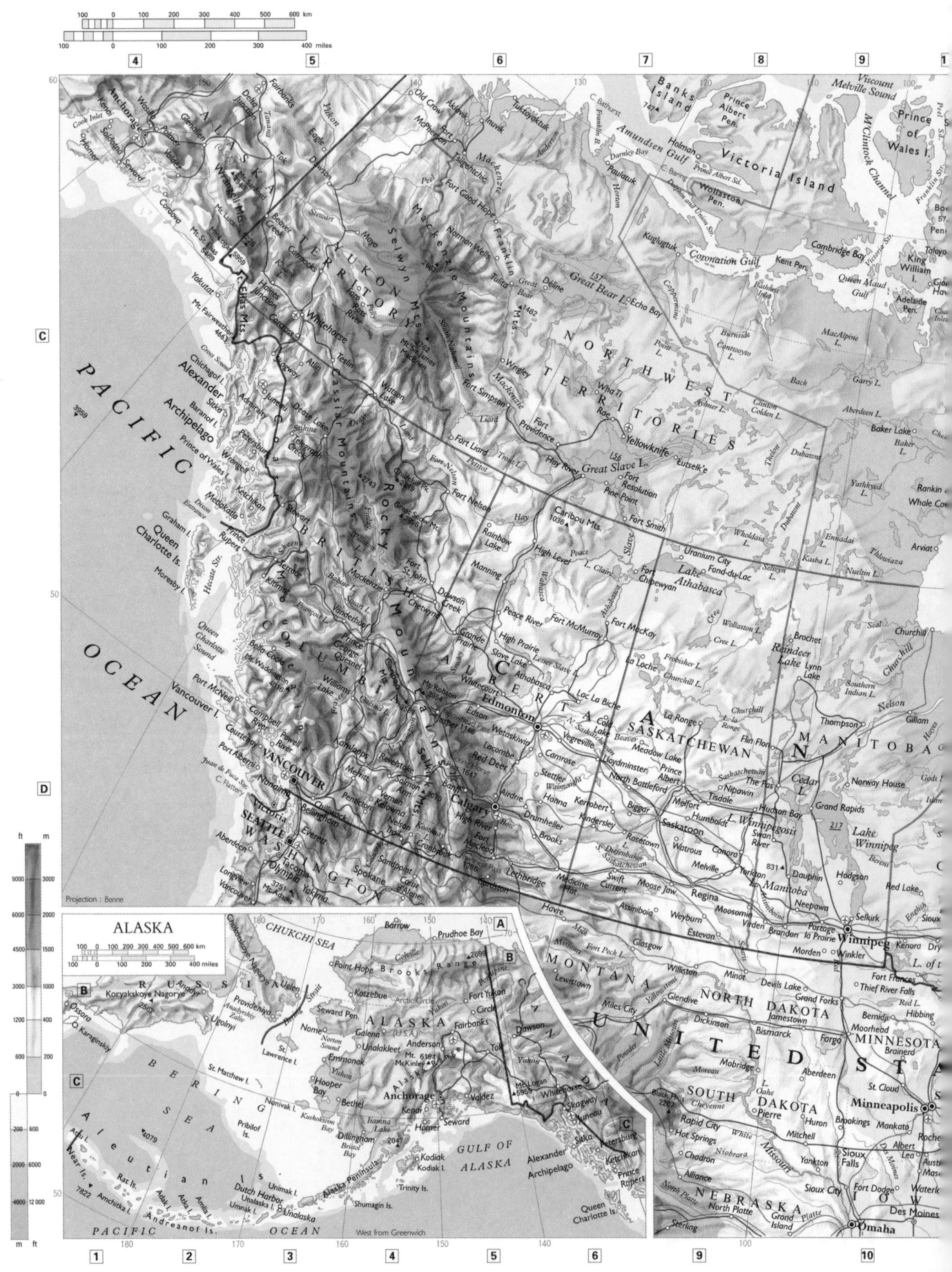

ALASKA

PACIFIC OCEAN

Devon I.
Lancaster Sound
Arctic Bay
Nanisivik
Borden
Pen.
Melville
Peninsula
Fury and Hecla Str.
Igloolik
Hall Beach
Committee B.
Isthmus
Repulse
Bay
Roes Welcome Sound
Southampton I.
Coral
Harbour
Bell
Pen.
Nottingham I.
Coats
I.
Mansel
I.

Bylot I.
Eclipse
Pond Inlet
C. Adair
Clyde River
C. Raper
Home B.
Cumberland
Peninsula
Pangnirtung
Hoare B.
C. Mercy
Cumberland Sd.
Resolution I.

Baffin Bay
Nunavut

Davis Strait

GREENLAND
(KALAALLIT NUNAAT)
(Denmark)
Kong Frederik VI's Kyst
Ammassalik

Baffin Island

Foxe
Basin

NUNAVUT
C. Dorchester
Foxe
Pen.
Cape Dorset
Meta
Incognita
Peninsula
Kimmirut
Frobisher Bay
Iqaluit
Hall
Peninsula
C. Dyer

Qeqertarsuaq
Qeqertarsuaq
Sisimiut
Nuuk
Arsuk
Qeqertarsuatsiaat
Paamiut
Qaqortoq
Nanortalik
Nunap Isua

Hudson Strait

ATLANTIC

Foxe Channel

Salisbury I.

Quaqtaq
Akpatok I.
C. Chidley

Labrador
Sea

Ivujivik
Kangiqsujuaq
Salluit
Kangirsuk

Péninsule
d'Ungava
Puvirnituq
L. Payne
Arnaud
Ungava Bay
Kangiqsualujjuaq
Hebron
Nain

Inukjuak
Feuilles
Kuujjuaq
Baleine
Hopedale

Hudson

Ottawa Is.
257

Bay

Sleeper Is.
King George Is.
Baker's
Dozen
Sanikiluaq
Is.
Belcher Is.

Kuujjuarapik
Grande Baleine
C. Henrietta
Maria
Pte. Louis
XIV
Chisasibi
La Grande

James Bay
Peawanuck
Winisk

Akimiski I.
Wemindji
Eastmain
Waskaganish

NEWFOUNDLAND &
LABRADOR
C. Harrison
Rigolet
Cartwright
Port Hope Simpson
Belle Isle
Smallwood
Res.
North West River
Happy Valley-
Goose Bay
Churchill
Falls
Churchill
Labrador
Labrador
City
Fermont
Ashuanipi
Gagnon
Havre-
St-Pierre
I. d'Anticosti

St-Augustin
Natashquan
C. Bauld
St. Anthony
Deer
Lake
Grand Falls-
Windsor
Gander
Bonavista
Carbonear
St. John's
Corner Brook
Stephenville
Channel-Port
aux Basques
Marystown
Placentia
C. Race
Newfoundland

ATTAWAPISKAT
Attawapiskat
Fort Albany
Moosonee
Albany
Nakina
Kenogami
Greenstone
Marathon
Oba
Hearst
Kapuskasing
Cochrane
Timmins
Kirkland
Lake
Rouyn-
Noranda
Val-d'Or
Amos
Matagami

Charlton
I.
Eastmain
Rupert
L.
Albanel
L.
Mistassini
Chibougamau
Baie-Comeau
Sept-Îles
Port-Cartier
Matane
Gaspé
Pén. de la
Gaspésie
Îs. de la Madeleine
Cape Breton I.
Glace Bay
Sydney
Port Hawkesbury
Antigonish
New Glasgow

QUEBEC
1135
Rés.
Manicouagan
St. Lawrence
Dolbeau-
Mistassini
St-Jean
Chicoutimi
Rimouski
Rivière-du-Loup
Edmundston
Campbellton
Bathurst
Chatham
PR. EDWARD I.
Summerside
Charlottetown
Cumberland Str.
Amherst
Truro
Dartmouth
Halifax
Bridgewater
Liverpool

Chapleau
Wawa
New
Liskeard
Mont-
Laurier
La Tuque
Shawinigan
Trois-Rivières
Québec
Lévis
Thetford
Mines
Grand Falls
Woodstock
Fredericton
Moncton
NEW
BRUNSWICK
Saint
John
B. of Fundy
Yarmouth
C. Sable
NOVA
SCOTIA
Sable I.
(Nova Scotia)

Thunder Bay
Superior
Houghton
Marquette
Manistique
Escanaba
Menominee
Green
Bay
Milwaukee
Racine
Kenosha
CHICAGO
Gary
South Bend
INDIANA

Sault Ste.
Marie
Elliot
Lake
Sudbury
North
Bay
Pembroke
Ottawa
Hull
MONTRÉAL
Granby
Sherbrooke
MAINE
Bangor
Augusta
Lewiston
Portland

Lake
Huron
Manitoulin
Georgian
Bay
Parry
Sound
Huntsville
Barrie
Peterborough
Belleville
Kingston
Cornwall
VERMONT
Montpelier
NEW
HAMPSHIRE
Concord
Manchester
Boston
C. Cod
Providence
R.I.

Petoskey
Traverse City
Cadillac
Saginaw
Flint
London
Sarnia
Windsor
TORONTO
Kitchener
Hamilton
Niagara
Falls
Buffalo
Rochester
Syracuse
Albany
MASS.
Springfield
Hartford
CONN.
New Haven
Bridgeport
NEW YORK
Lansing
DETROIT
Toledo
OHIO
CLEVELAND
Erie
Jamestown
Elmira
Binghamton
Scranton
PENNSYLVANIA
Newark
N.J.
Allentown
Trenton
NEW YORK
Lake
Michigan
Lake
Ontario

West from Greenwich

COPYRIGHT PHILIP'S

917

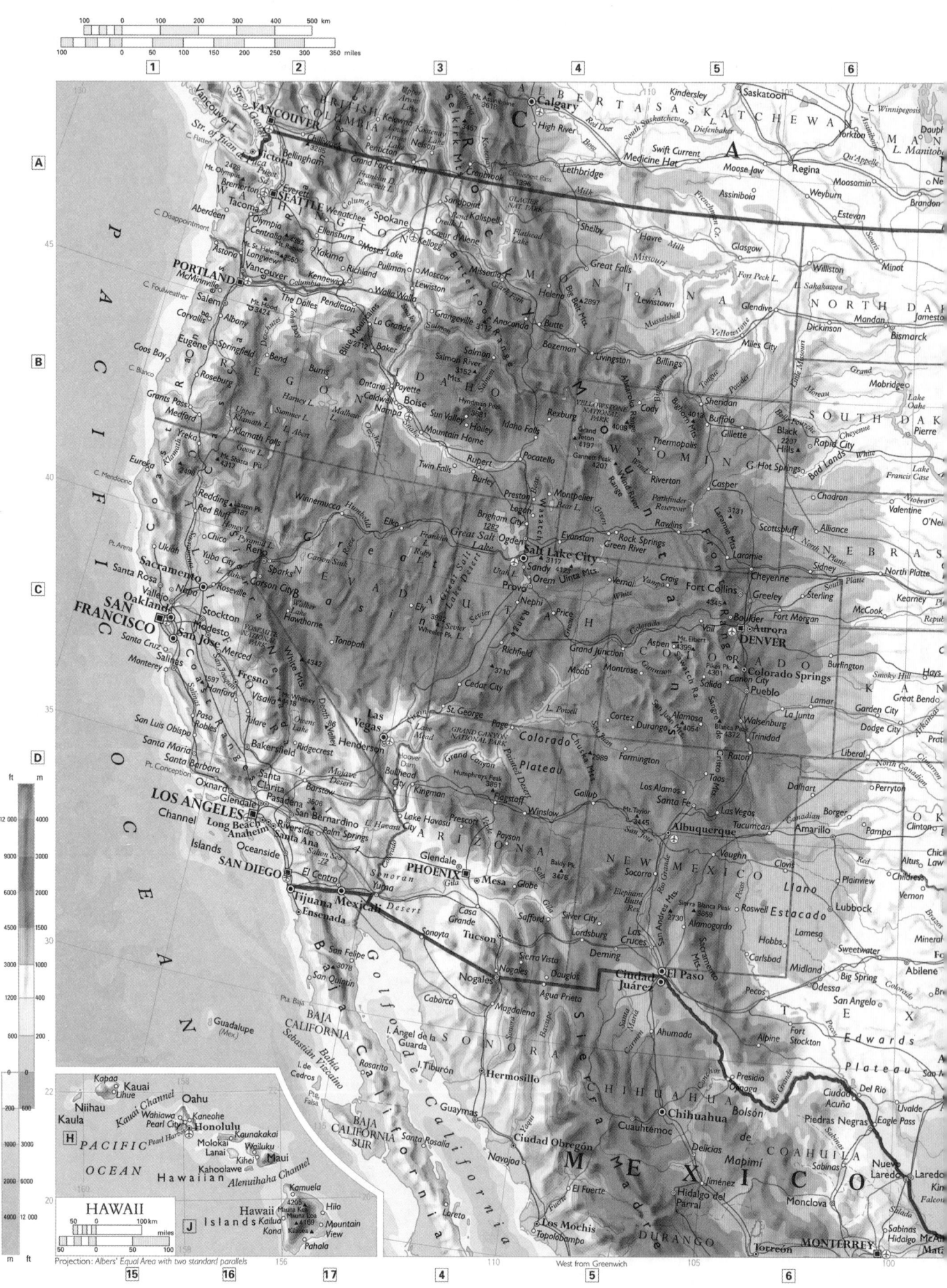

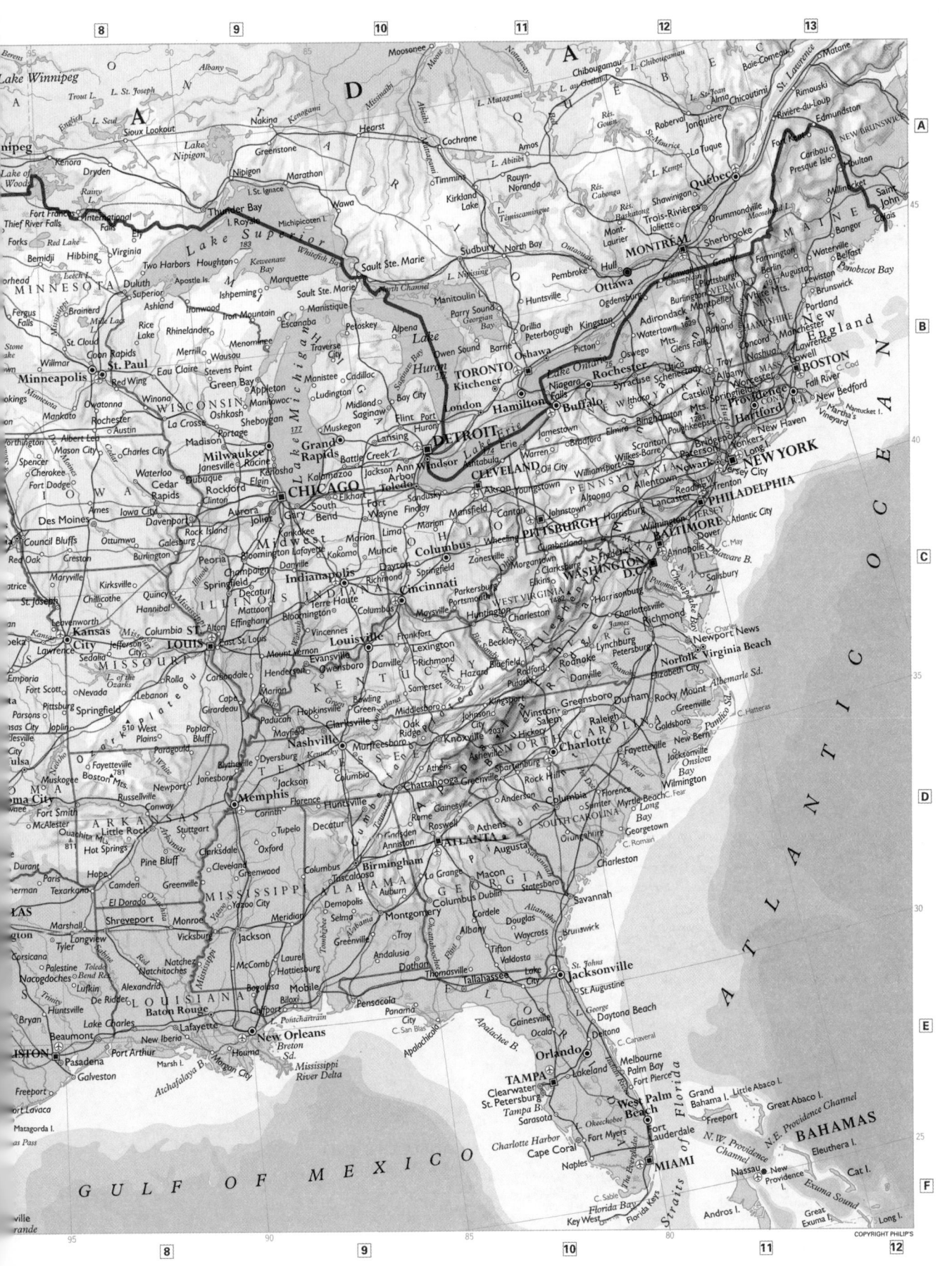

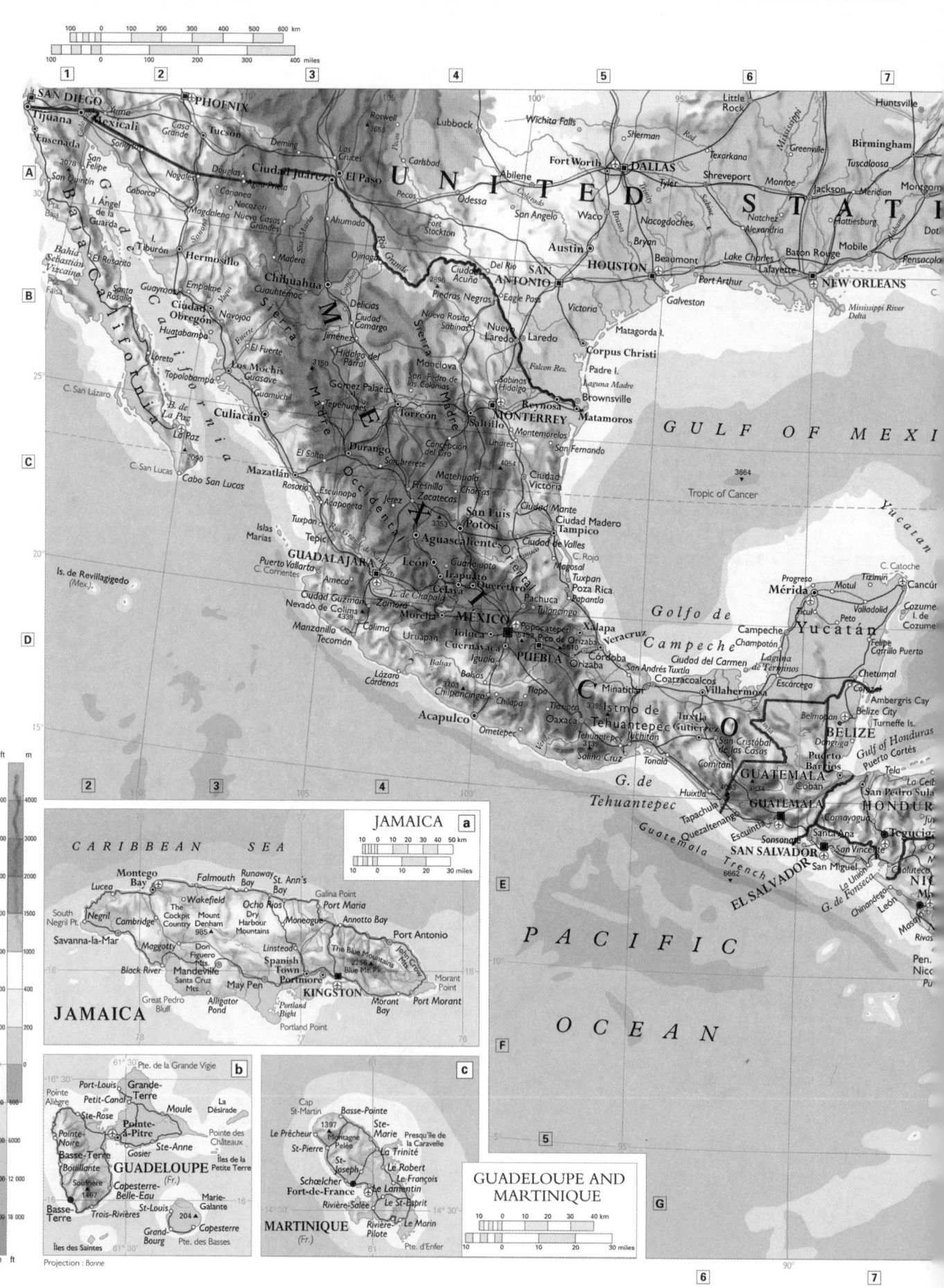

JAMAICA **a**

10 0 10 20 30 40 50 km
10 0 10 20 30 miles

CARIBBEAN   SEA

Montego
Bay   Falmouth Runaway St. Ann's
Lucea   Bay   Bay
                  Ocho Rios   Galina Point
Negril   Wakefield Dry   Port Maria
South   The   Harbour   Annotto Bay
Negril Pt.   Cockpit   Mountains   Moneague
         Cambridge Country Mount   Port Antonio
              Denham 985▲
Savanna-la-Mar   The Blue Mountains
        Maggotty Don   2256▲
Black River   Figuero   Blue Mtn Pk.   John Crow
         Santa Cruz Mts. Linstead Spanish   Mts.
              Mandeville   Town   Morant
Great Pedro   May Pen   Portmore   Point
Bluff   Alligator   KINGSTON Morant
            Pond   Portland   Bay Port Morant
JAMAICA   Bight
            Portland Point

b

Pte. de la Grande Vigie
61°30'
16°30'   Port-Louis Grande-
Pointe   Petit-Canal Terre
Allègre   Ste-Rose   La
Pointe-   Ste-   Pointe-   Désirade
Noire   à-Pitre   Moule
          Gosier   Ste-Anne   Pointe des
Basse-Terre   Châteaux
Bouillante   Îles de la
Soufrière   Capesterre- Petite Terre
1467▲   **GUADELOUPE** Belle-Eau
16°   (Fr.)
              Capesterre   Marie-
Basse-   Trois-Rivières St-Louis Galante
Terre   204▲   Capesterre
    Îles des Saintes   Grand-
61°30'   Bourg Pte. des Basses

c

61°30'
Cap
St-Martin Basse-Pointe
Le Prêcheur 1397   Ste-
       Montagne Marie
St-Pierre   Pelée   La Trinité Presqu'île de
       St-   Le Robert la Caravelle
       Joseph Le François
Schœlcher   Le Lamentin
Fort-de-France   Le St-Esprit
       Rivière-Salée   Le Marin
MARTINIQUE   Rivière- 14°30'
    (Fr.)   Pilote Le Marin
              Pte. d'Enfer

GUADELOUPE AND MARTINIQUE

10 0 10 20 30 40 km
10 0 10 20 30 miles

Projection : Bonne

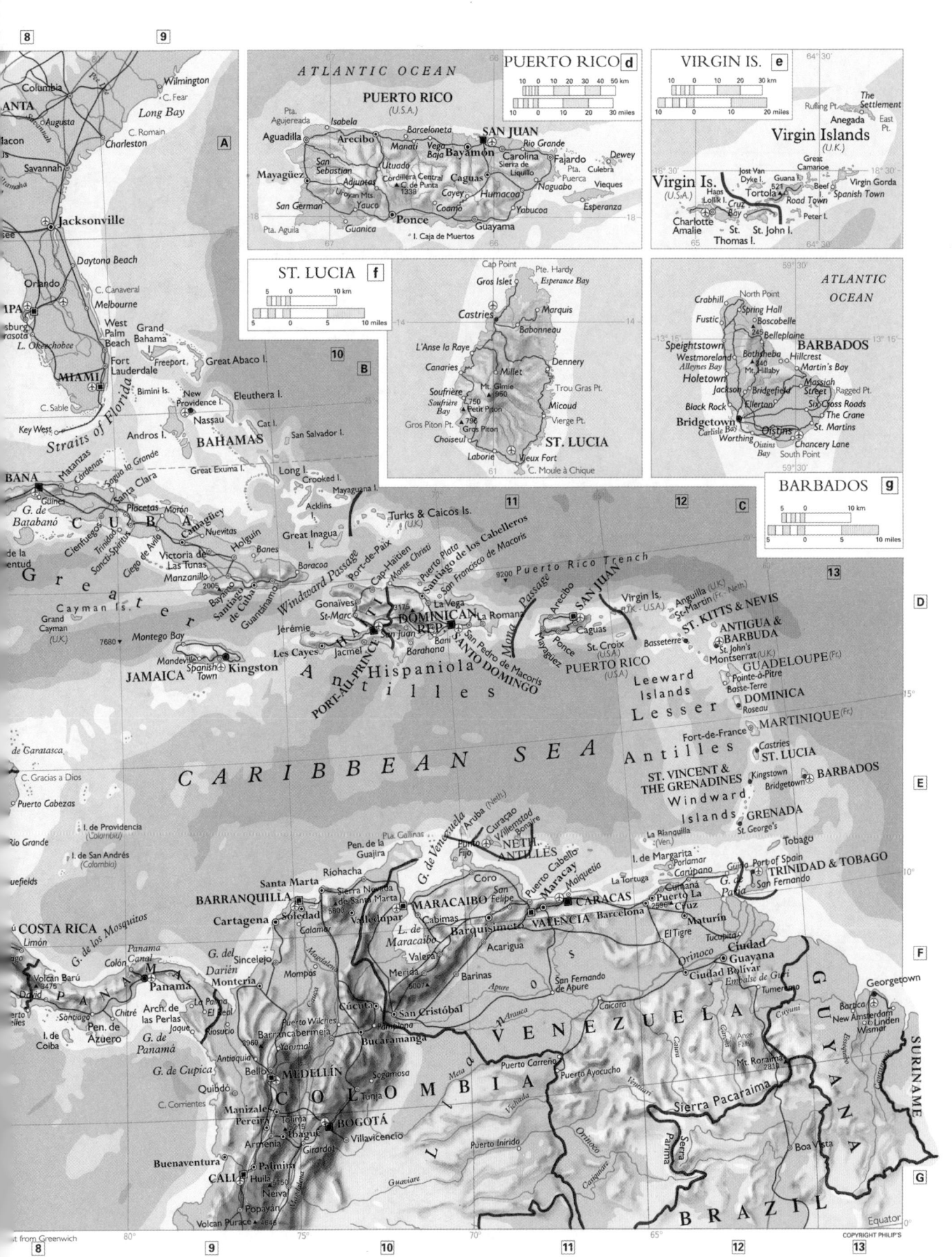

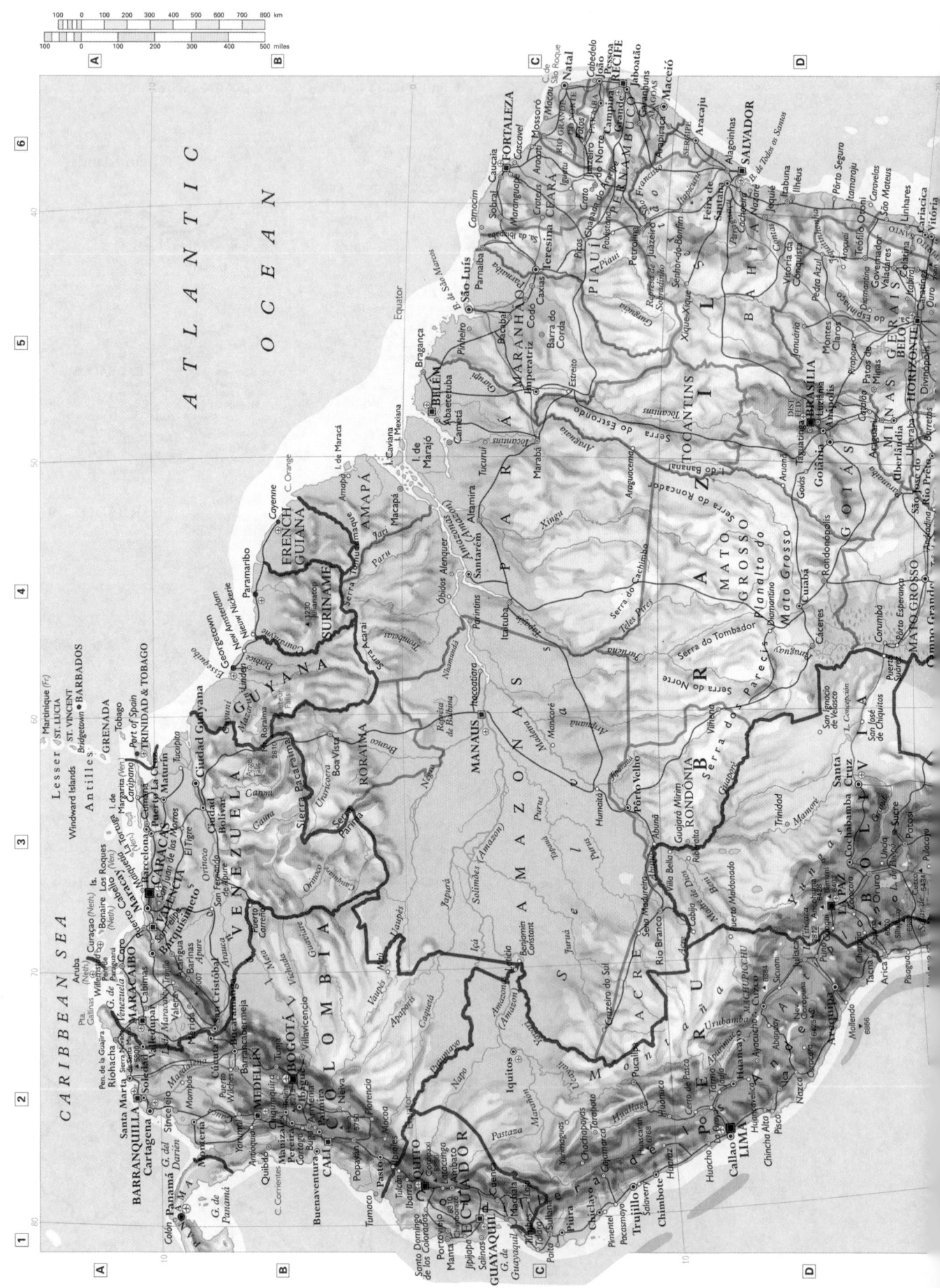

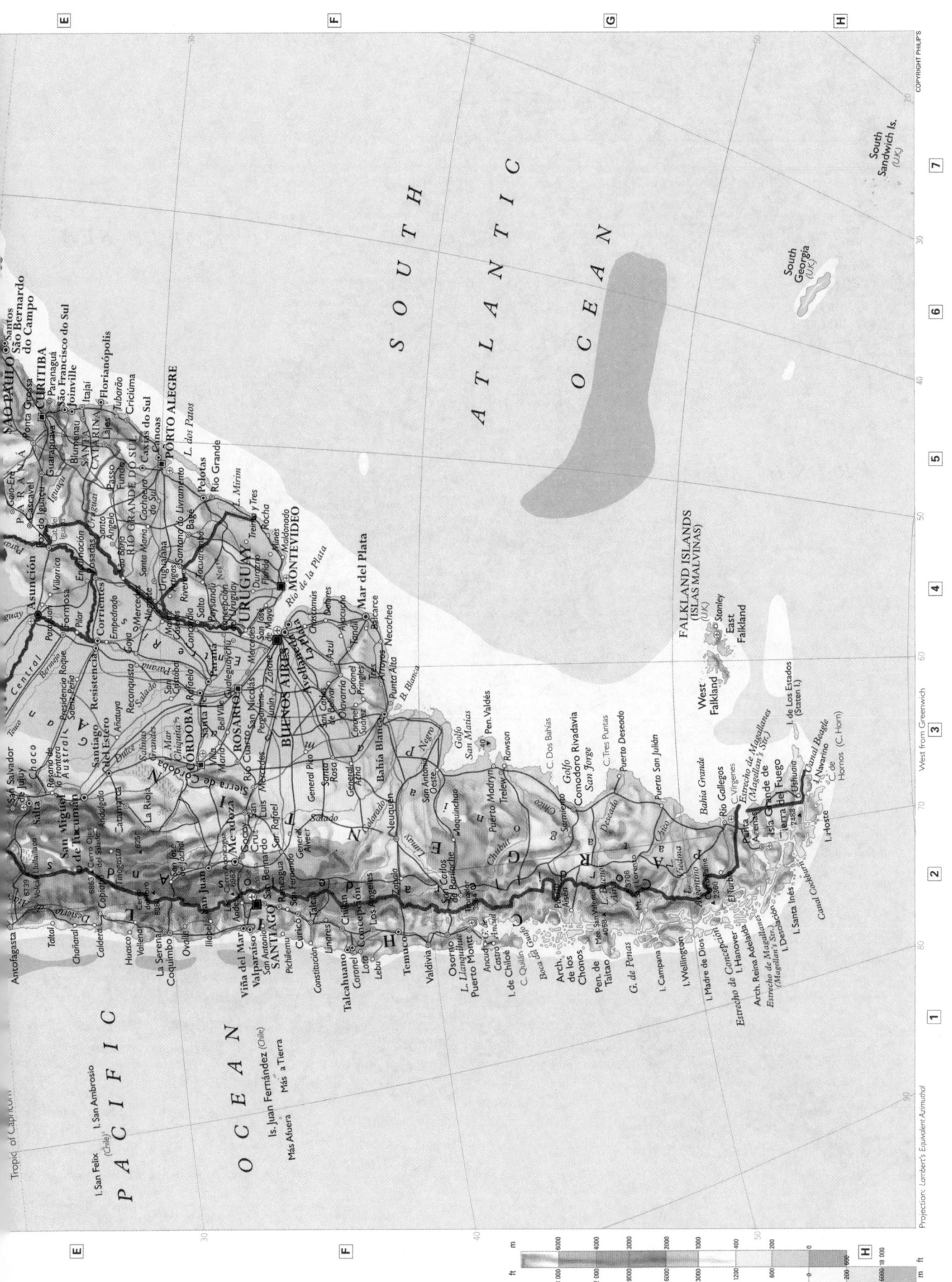

Tropic of Capricorn

I. San Felix (Chile)   I. San Ambrosio (Chile)

Is. Juan Fernández (Chile)   Más a Tierra
Más Afuera

P A C I F I C

O C E A N

S O U T H

A T L A N T I C

O C E A N

SÃO PAULO
Santos
São Bernardo
do Campo
Ponta Grossa
CURITIBA
Paranaguá
São Francisco do Sul
Joinville
Itajaí
Florianópolis
Tubarão
Criciúma
PARANÁ
SANTA
CATARINA
Blumenau
Lajes
Passo
Fundo
PÔRTO ALEGRE
Caxias do Sul
Canoas
RIO GRANDE DO SUL
L. dos Patos
Pelotas
Rio Grande
L. Mirim
Treinta y Tres
Rocha
Maldonado
MONTEVIDEO
URUGUAY
Mar del Plata

São Sandwich Is. (UK)

South Georgia (UK)

FALKLAND ISLANDS
(ISLAS MALVINAS)
(UK)
West
Falkland
East
Falkland
Stanley

I. de Los Estados (Staten I.)
C. de Hornos (C. Horn)
Canal Beagle
Navarino
I. Hoste

Asunción
PARAGUAY
Formosa
Resistencia
Corrientes
Santa Fe
CÓRDOBA
ROSARIO
BUENOS AIRES
La Plata
Río de la Plata

Antofagasta
Taltal
Chañaral
Caldera
Copiapó
Huasco
Vallenar
La Serena
Coquimbo
Ovalle
Illapel
Viña del Mar
Valparaíso
SANTIAGO
San Antonio
Rancagua
Talca
Linares
Chillán
Concepción
Coronel
Lota
Lebu
Temuco
Valdivia
Osorno
Puerto Montt
I. de Chiloé
Castro
Arch. de los Chonos
Pen. de Taitao
G. de Penas
I. Wellington
I. Campana
I. Madre de Dios
Estrecho de Magallanes (Magellan's Str.)
Punta Arenas
Tierra del Fuego
Ushuaia

Salta
San Miguel de Tucumán
Santiago del Estero
La Rioja
San Juan
Mendoza
San Rafael
San Luis
Bahía Blanca
Neuquén
San Carlos de Bariloche
Puerto Madryn
Trelew
Rawson
Comodoro Rivadavia
Puerto Deseado
Puerto San Julián
Río Gallegos

Projection: Lambert's Equivalent Azimuthal   West from Greenwich

COPYRIGHT PHILIP'S

m   ft

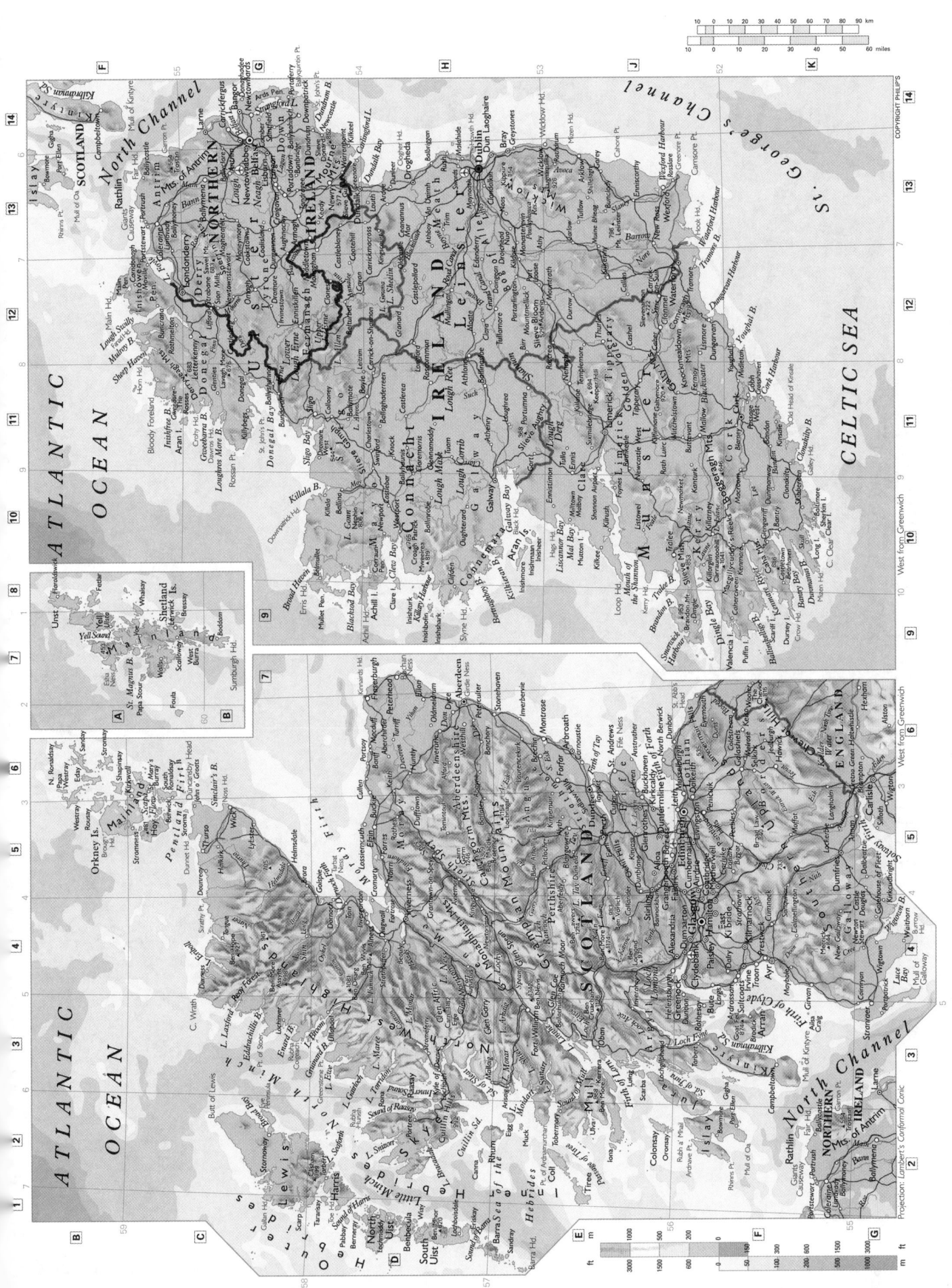

Projection: Lambert's Conformal Conic

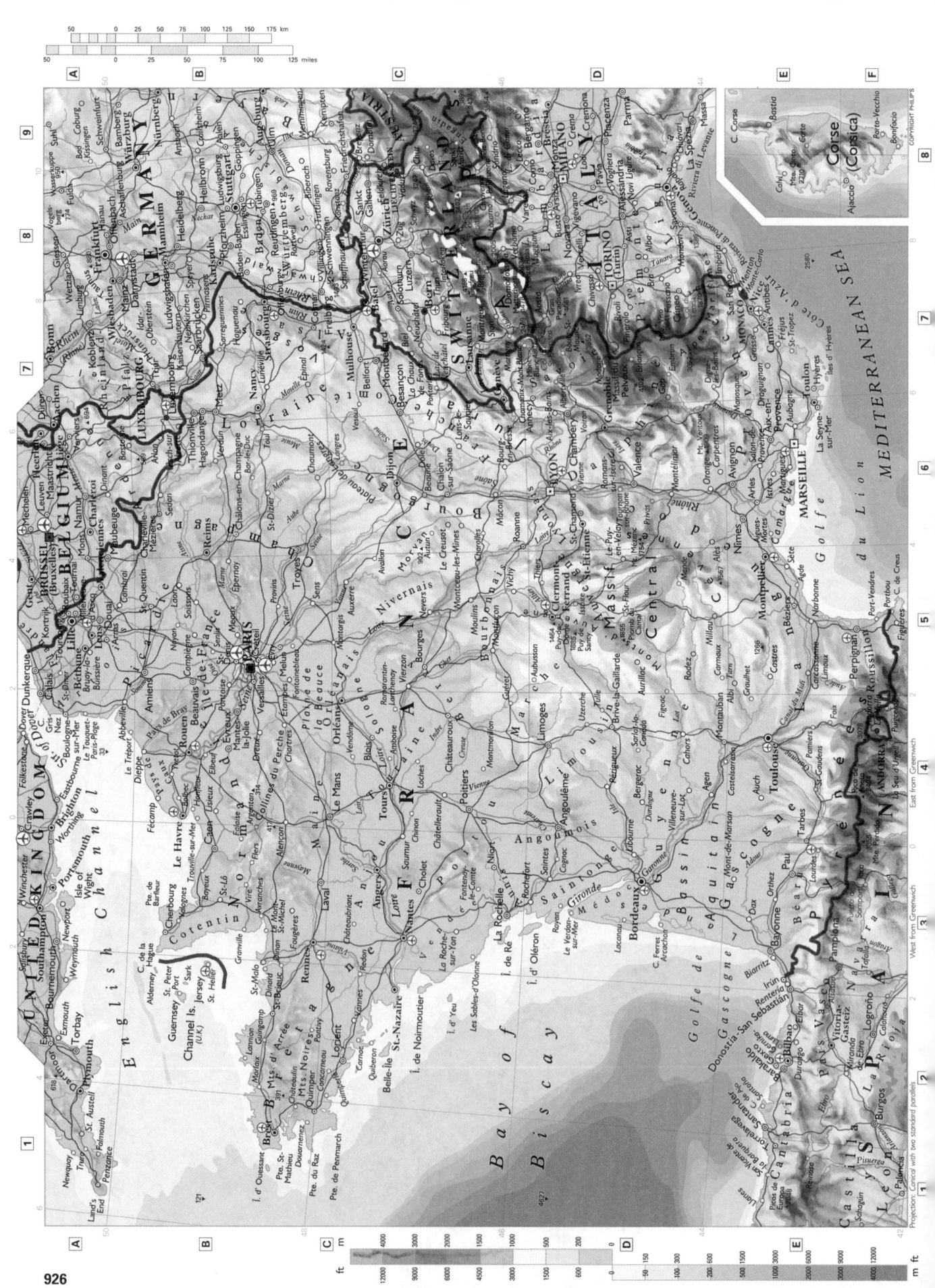

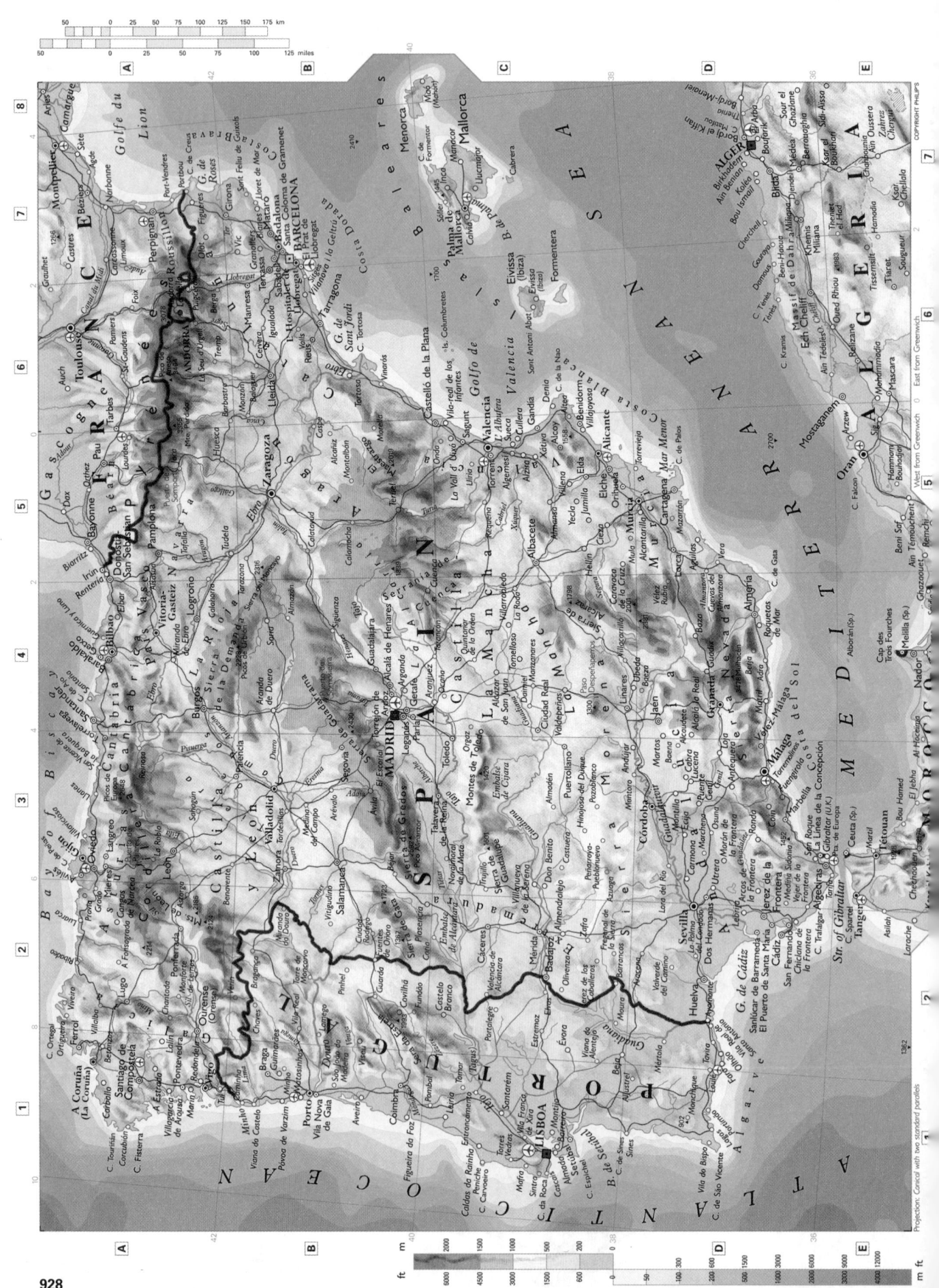

Projection: Conical with two standard parallels

COPYRIGHT PHILIP'S

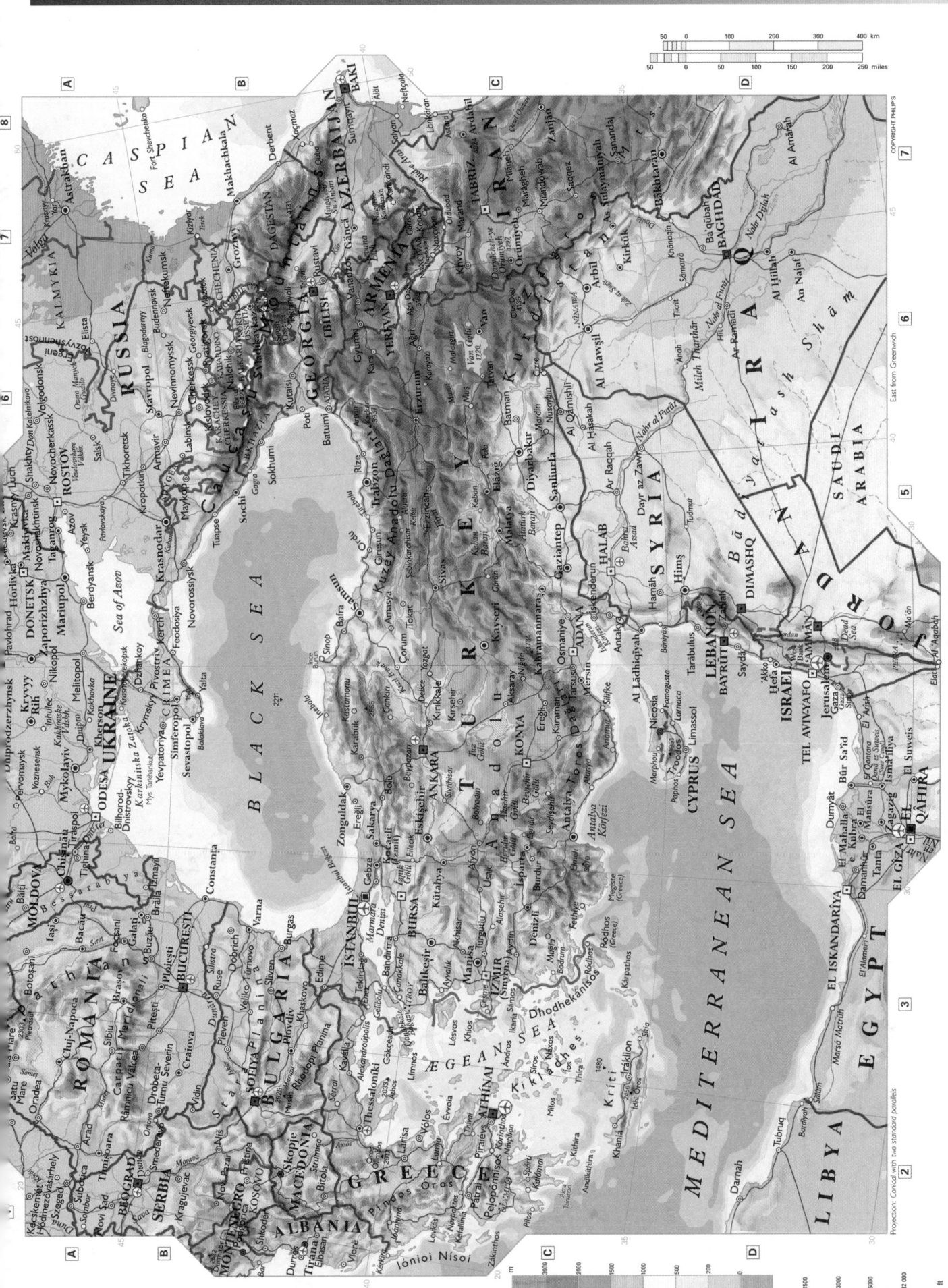

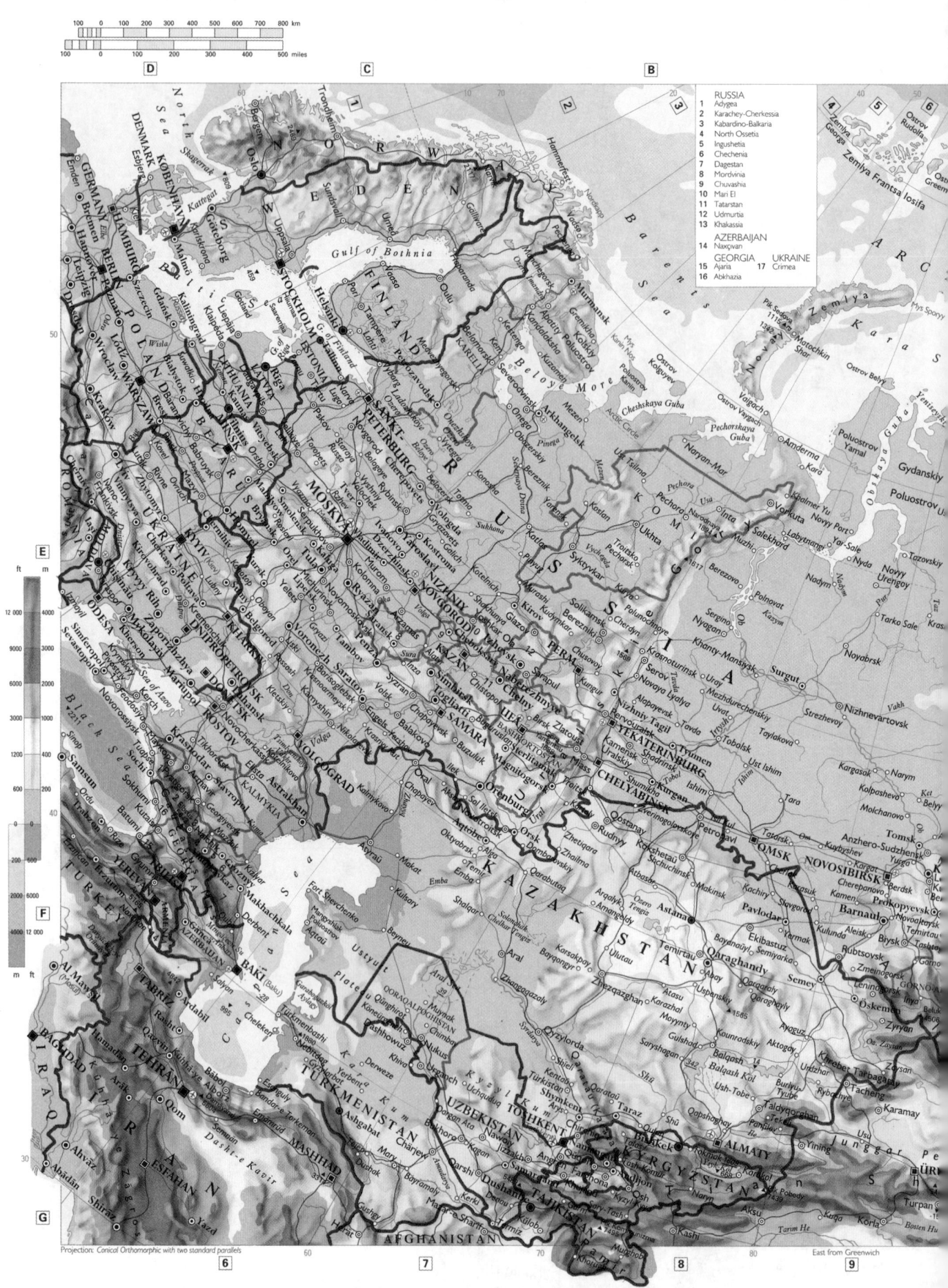

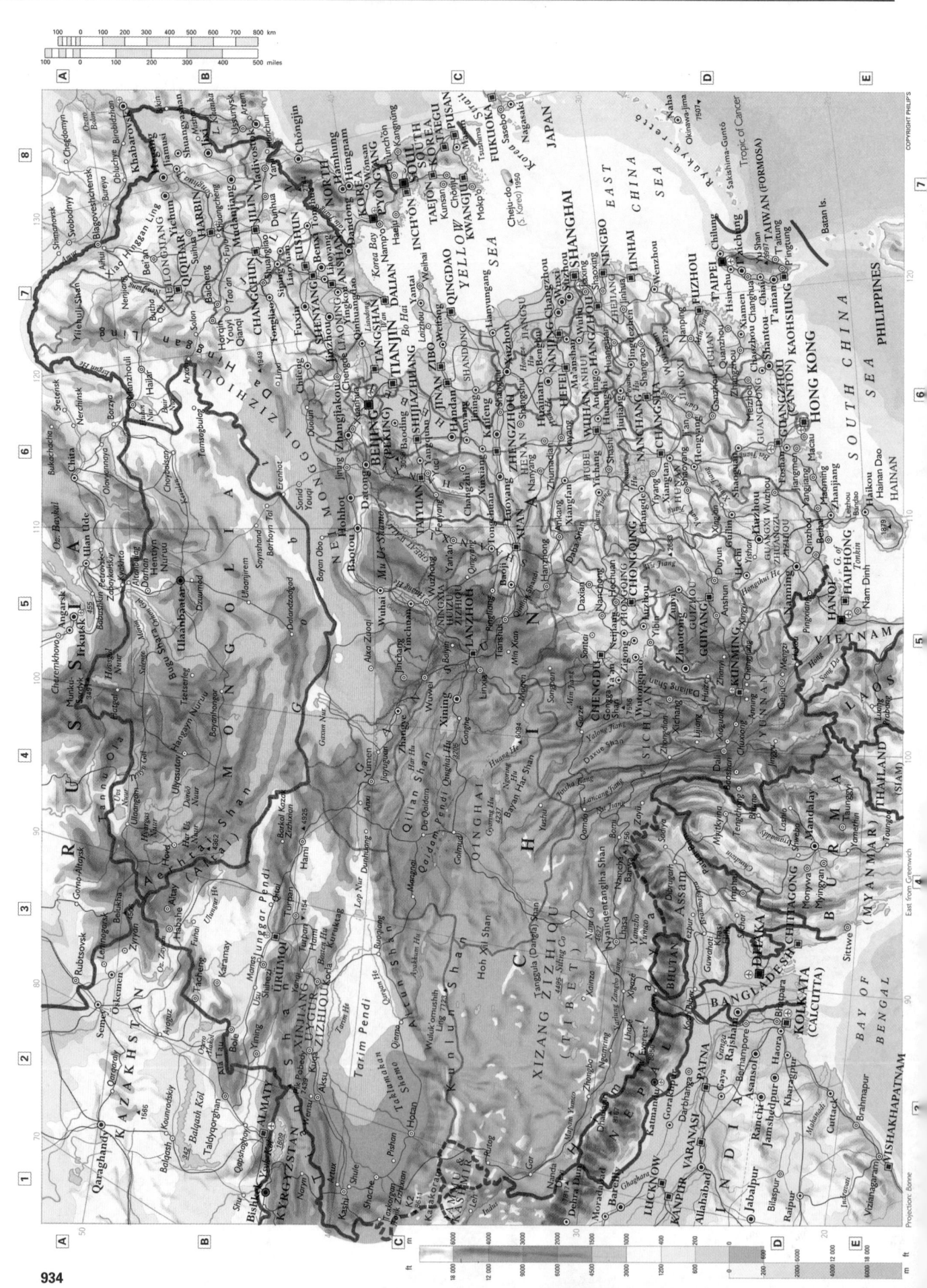

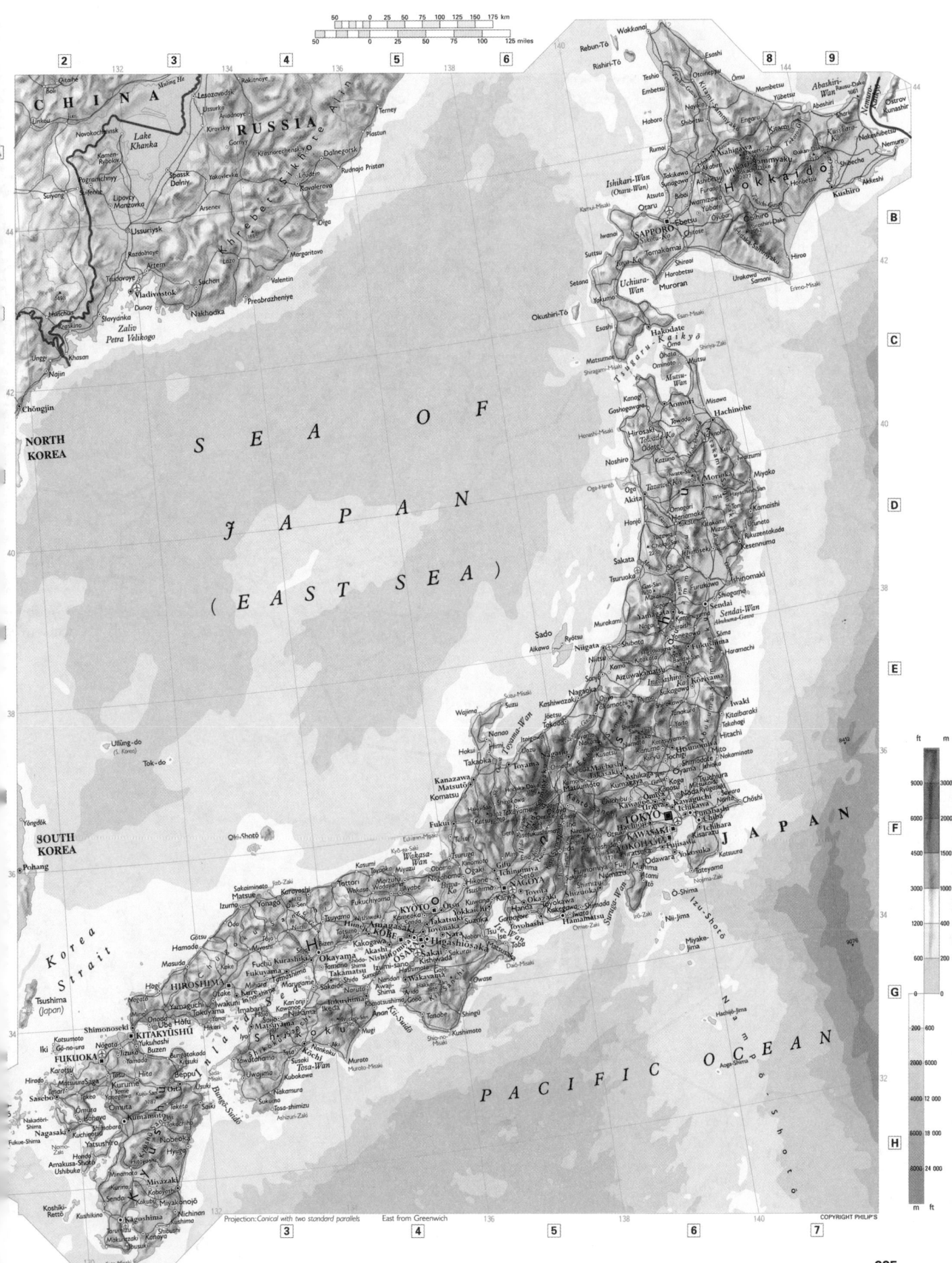

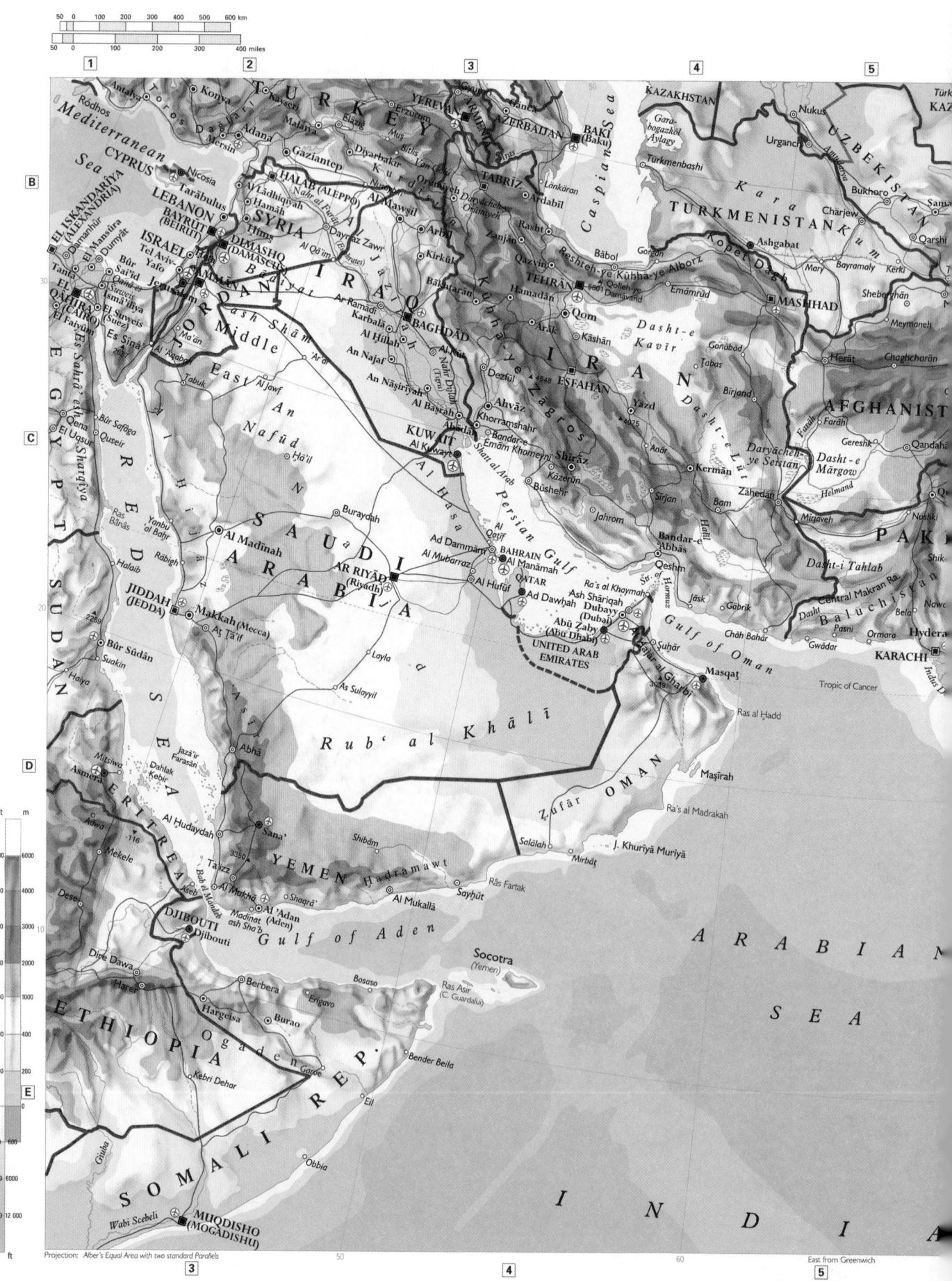

50 0   100   200   300   400   500   600 km
50 0   100   200   300   400 miles

1   **2**   **3**   **4**   **5**

Ródhos
Antalya
Toros Dağları
Konya
Kayseri
Malatya
Erzurum
YEREVAN
ARMENIA
AZERBAIJAN
BAKI (Baku)
KAZAKHSTAN
Nukus
Türk
KAZ

Mediterranean
Sea
Nicosia
CYPRUS
Tarābulus
Adana
Mersin
Gaziantep
Diyarbakır
Van Gölü
Bitlis
Muş
Elazığ
Orūmīyeh
Daryācheh-ye
Ōrūmīyeh
TABRĪZ
Ardabīl
Lenkoran
Caspian
Sea
Garabogazköl
Aylagy
TURKMENBASHI
Urganch
UZBEKISTAN
Bukhoro
Sama

EL ISKANDARĪYA
(ALEXANDRIA)
Damanhūr
Tanta
El Mansūra
Būr Sa'īd
Ismâ'iliya
HALAB (ALEPPO)
Al Lādhiqīyah
Hamāh
Nahr al Furāt
Al Mawşil
Arbīl
Rasht
Resht
Qazvīn
Kūhha-ye Alborz
Bābol
Gorgan
Emāmrūd
Ashgabat
Kopet Dagh
Kara
Kum
Chärjew
Qarshi
TURKMENISTAN

BAYRŪT
(BEIRUT)
LEBANON
SYRIA
DIMASHQ
(DAMASCUS)
Hims
Dayr az Zawr
Al Jazīra
Kirkūk
Zanjān
TEHRĀN
Sadd-e
Qolleh-ye Damāvand
MASHHAD
Meymaneh
Sheberghān
ISRAEL
Tel Aviv-Yafo
Jerusalem
AMMAN
JORDAN
Bādiyat
Ar Ramādī
An Najaf
BAGHDĀD
Karbalā
Al Hillah
Bākhtarān
Hamadān
Qom
Arāk
Kāshān
Dasht-e Kavīr
Birjand
Gonābād
Tabas
Chaghcharān
HERĀT
AFGHANIST

El Qāhira
(CAIRO)
El Faiyūm
JORDAN
Ma'ān
Middle
East
An
Nafūd
Tabūk
Al Jawf
Dezfūl
Ahvāz
Khorramshahr
ESFAHĀN
IRAN
Yazd
Kūhha-ye Zagros
Anār
Dasht-e Lūt
Farāh
Gereshk
Dasht-e Mārgow
QANDAHĀR

EGYPT
Es Sahrâ esh Sharqîya
Qena
El Uqsur
RED
SEA
Būr Safāga
Quseir
Ra's
Bānas
SAUDI
Burāydah
Hā'il
Al Hasā
Al Basrah
KUWAIT
Al Kuwayt
Shatt al Arab
Ābādān
Bandar-e Emām Khomeynī
Shīrāz
Kāzerūn
Jahrom
Kermān
Bam
Zāhedān
Sīrjān
Mirjāveh
Nushki
Kerman
Qena

Yanbū' al Bahr
Rābigh
Al Madīnah
ARABIA
Ad Dammām
Al Mubarraz
Al Qatif
BAHRAIN
Al Manāmah
QATAR
Ad Dawhah
Būshehr
Persian Gulf
Bandar-e Abbās
Qeshm
Ra's al Khaymah
Ash Shāriqah
Dubayy (Dubai)
Abū Zaby (Abu Dhabi)
Gulf of Oman
Jāsk
Gabrik
Chāh Bahār
Central Makran Ra
Baluchistan
Gwādar
Pasni
Ormara
Hydera
KARACHI

JIDDAH (JEDDA)
Makkah (Mecca)
At Tā'if
AR RIYĀD
(Riyadh)
Al Hufūf
UNITED ARAB
EMIRATES
Suhār
Sur
Str. of Hormuz
Masqat

Būr Sūdân
Suakin
SUDAN
Layla
As Sulayyil
Rub' al Khālī
OMAN
Maşīrah
Ra's al Hadd
Tropic of Cancer
Indus D

Haiya
Mitsiwa
Asmera
ERITREA
Dahlak Kebir
Jazā'ir Farasan
Abha
Zufār
Salālah
Ra's al Madrakah
J. Khurīyā Murīyā
Mirbāt
ARABIAN
SEA

Adwa
Mekele
Dese
Al Hudaydah
Sana'
Shibām
YEMEN
Hadramawt
Sayhūt
Al Mukallā
Rās Fartak
Socotra
(Yemen)
Ras Asir
(C. Guardafui)

ft   m
18 000   6000
12 000   4000
9000   3000
6000   2000
3000   1000
1200   400
600   200
0   0
200   600
2000   6000
4000   12 000
m   ft

ETHIOPIA
Dire Dawa
Harer
Taizz
Ta'izz
Al Makhā
Bāb al Mandab
Aseb
Shaqrā
DJIBOUTI
Madinat ash Sha'b
Al 'Adan (Aden)
Gulf of Aden
Bosaso
Berbera
Erigavo
Burao
Bender Beila

SOMALI
REP.
Kebri Dehar
Ogaden
Gazoe
Eil
Obbia

ETHIOPIA
Wabi Scebeli
Giuba
MUQDISHO
(MOGADISHU)
I N D I A

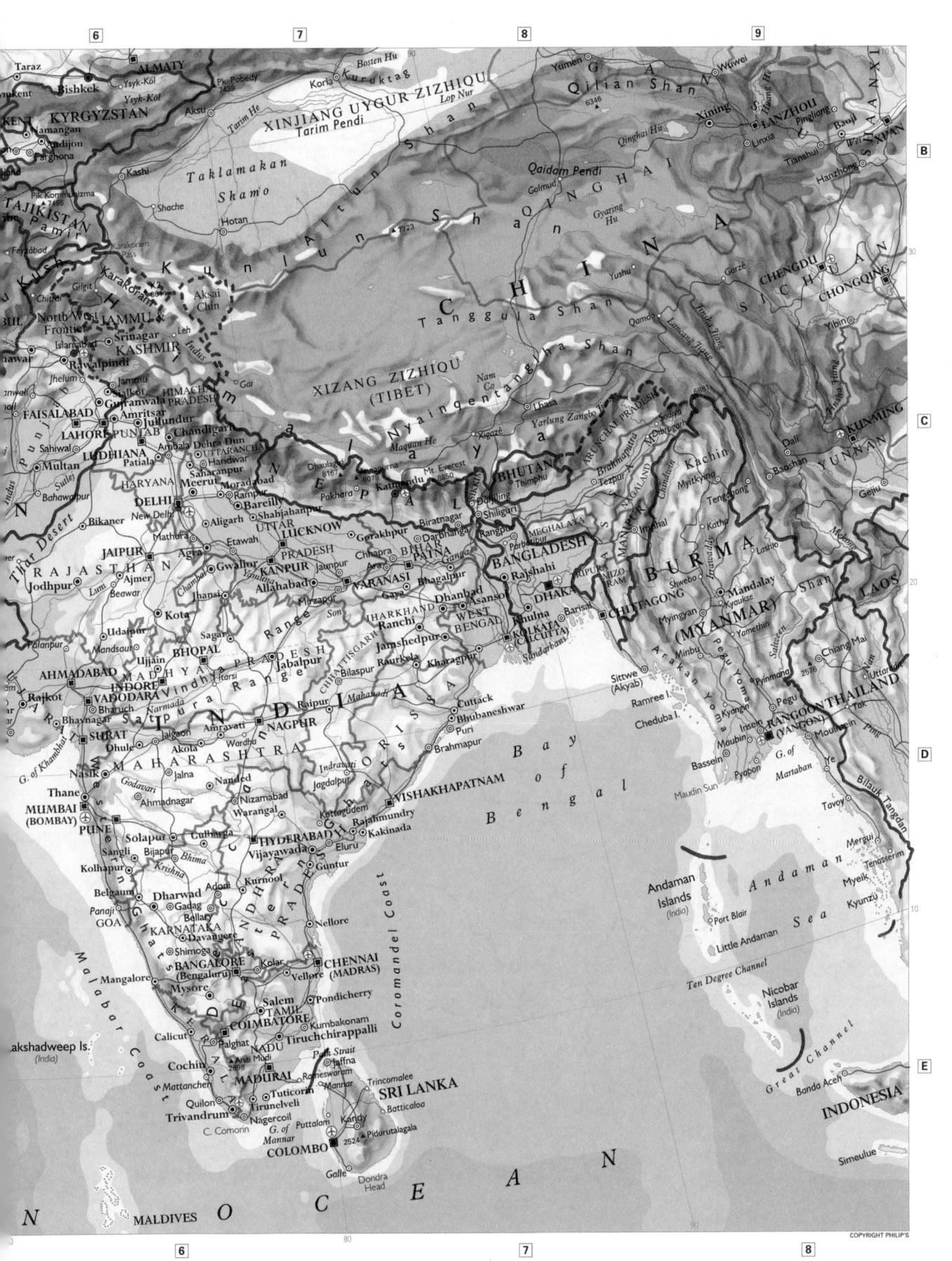

COPYRIGHT PHILIP'S

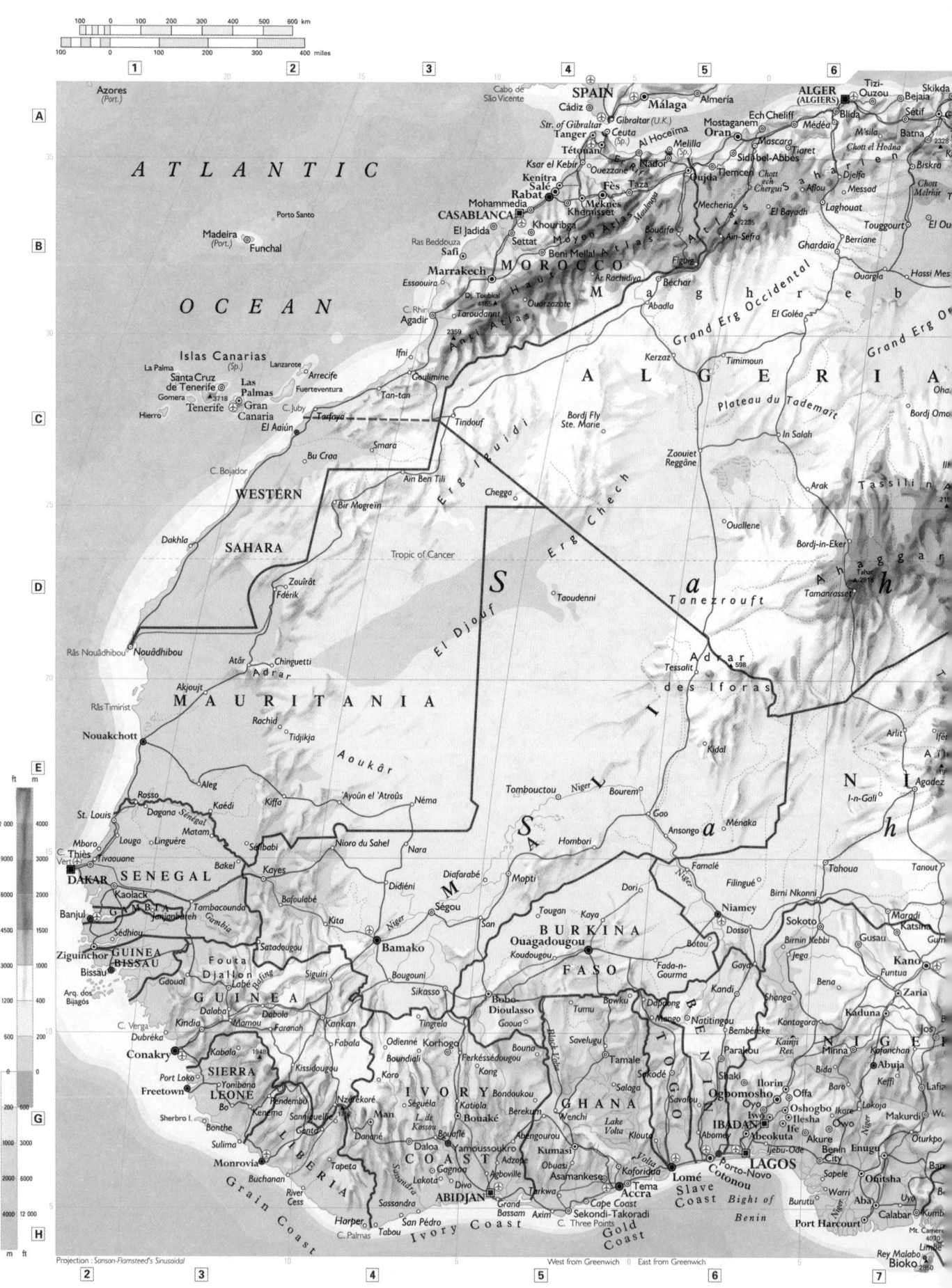

A

B

C

D

E

F

G

H

8 9 10 11 12 13 14

TUNIS
Nabeul
Sousse
Mahdia
Sfax
Golfe de Gabès
Île de Djerba
Zarzis
Bizerte
CARTHAGE
Sicilia
MALTA
Valletta

GREECE
Iráklion
Kríti
Ródhos

TURKEY
Antalya
Antakya
ADANA
HALAB
Nahr al Furāt
SYRIA
CYPRUS
Nicosia
Al Lādhiqiyah
Tarābulus
Hims
LEBANON
BAYRŪT
(BEIRUT)
DIMASHQ
(DAMASCUS)
Jabal ad Durūz
IRAQ
Ar Rutbah
Bādiyat
ash Shām
ISRAEL
Tel Aviv-Yafo
Ashdod
Dumyât
Jerusalem
WEST BANK
AMMĀN
JORDAN

MEDITERRANEAN SEA

Zuwārah Tarābulus (Tripoli)
Al Khums
As Zāwiyah Misrātah
Gharyān
Mizdāh
Daraj
Tripolitania
Zāwiyat al Baydâ Darnah
Banghāzī Al Marj
Tubruq
Sulūq
Ajdābiya
Bardiyah
Salūm
EL ISKANDARIYA
(ALEXANDRIA)
El Mahalla el Kubra
Damanhûr
Marsâ Matrûh
El Alamein
Tanta
El Faiyûm
EL GÎZA
Helwân
El Mansûra
Bûr Sa'îd
El Suweis (Suez)
EL QÂHIRA
(CAIRO)
Beni Suef
Es Sînâ'
Al 'Aqabah
SAUDI
ARABIA
Tabūk

Khalīj Surt
Surt
Cyrenaica
Hūn
Awjilah
Munkhafed el Qattâra
Siwa
Al Jaghbūb
Sahrâ' Lîbîya
EGYPT
Es Sahrâ Esh Sharqîya
Beni Suef
Maghâgha
El Minyâ
Mallawi
Manfalût
Asyût
Sohâg
Girga Qena
THEBES KARNAK
El Uqsur
Hurghada
Bûr Safâga
Al Wajh
RED SEA
Hijaz

Idehan Awbārī
Brach
Sabhah
Awbārī
Marzūq
Fezzan
Al Qaṭrūn
Waw al Kabīr
Sahrâ' Rebiana
Al Jawf
Al Kufrah
El Wâhât el-Dakhla
Mût
Qasr Farâfra
Tahta
El Wâhât el-Khârga
El Khârga
Idfû
Kom Ombo
Aswân
Sadd el Aali
Ras Bânâs
Yanbu' al Bahr
Rābigh

a r a Bukhairat en Naser
Bîr Shalatein
Ras Hadarba

Toummo
Madama
Chirfa
Aozou
Bardaï
Pic Toussidé Tarso Emissi
Zouar
Emi Koussi 3415
Tibesti
Aozou Strip
Ma'tan as Sarra
J. Uweinât 1893
El Wâhât el Selima
Wadi Halfa
Muhammad Qol
Halaib
ABU SIMBEL
Kosha
Delgo
Es Sahrâ en Nûbîya
Bûr Sûdân
Suakin
Trinkitat
Haiya
Karora
Nkfa

Bilma
Grand Erg du Bilma
Borkou
Faya-Largeau
Ouniango Sérir
Dépression du Mourdi
Fada Ennedi
Zagaoua
Oum Chalouba
3rd Cataract
Dongola
Kareima
Ed Debba
Abu Hamed
4th Cataract
Berber
5th Cataract
Atbara
Adarama
ERITREA
Akordat

Nguigmi
Bosso
Geidam
Maiduguri
Kousseri
Bama
N'djamena
Lac Tchad
Mao Bahr el Ghazal
Moussoro
Massakory
Ati
Bokoro
Abéché
Oum Hadjer
Mongo
Goz Beïda
Al Junaynah
Zalingei
Djebel Marra 3088
Nyâlâ
Kutum
El Fâsher
Darfur
Umm Keddada
En Nahud
El Odaiya
Kordofân
Abu Zabad
Er Rahad
El Obeid
Umm Ruwaba
Sodiri
Ed Dueim
Kôstî
Omdurmân El Khartûm (Khartoum)
El Gezira
Wâd Medani
Gedaref
Kashm el Girba
Kassalâ
El Wuz
6th Cataract
Wâd Hamid
Shendi
Nahr 'Atbara
CHAD

Geidam
Biu
Garoua
Ngaoundéré
Bongor
Kélo
Laï
Sarh
Koumra
Doba
Ndélé
Am-Timan
Birao
Songo
Said
Bahr el Ghazâl
Raga
Bahr el Arab
Malakâl
Bahr el Jebel
Kâdugli
Ed Damazin
Nil el Abyad (White Nile)
Nil el Azraq (Blue Nile)
L. Tana
Bahir Dar
Debre Markos
ETHIOPIA
Nekemte

CENTRAL AFRICAN REPUBLIC
Bossangoa
Bozoum
Bouar
Yalinga
Ippy
Bambari
Bakouma
Bangassou
Obo
El Istiwa'îya
Bahr el Ghazâl
Gogrial
Wâw
Tonj
Rumbêk
Bôr
Toinya
Amâdi
Tali Post
Mongalla
Juba
Kapoeta
Yambio
Yei
Dungu
Faradje
Torit
Lokichokio
L. Turkana
Metu
Gore
Jimma
Arba Minch
Gondar
Demdidala

Bangui
Zongo
Mbaïki
Libenge
Bosobolo
Mobaye
Bondo
Uele
Yaoundé

COPYRIGHT PHILIPS

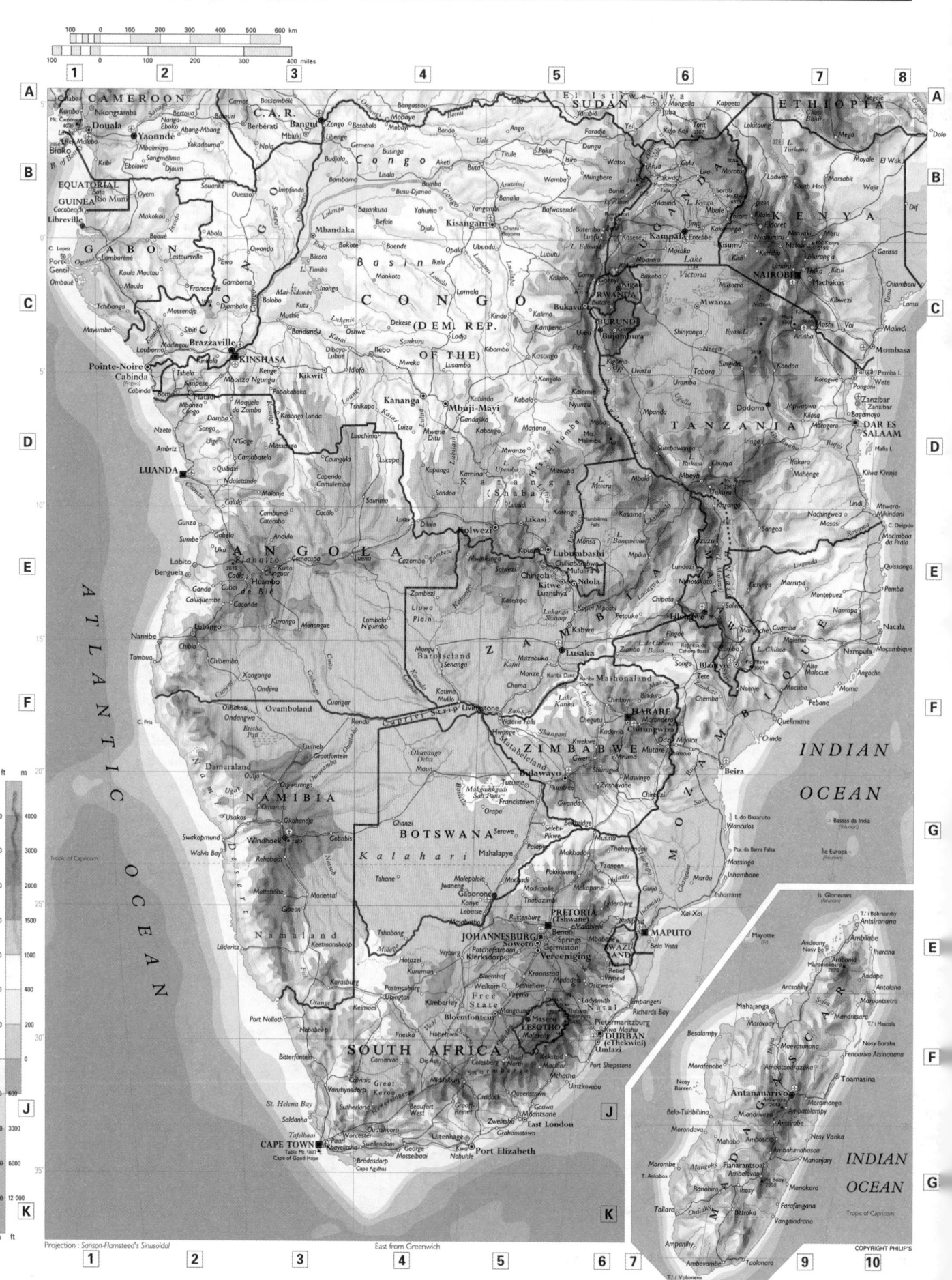

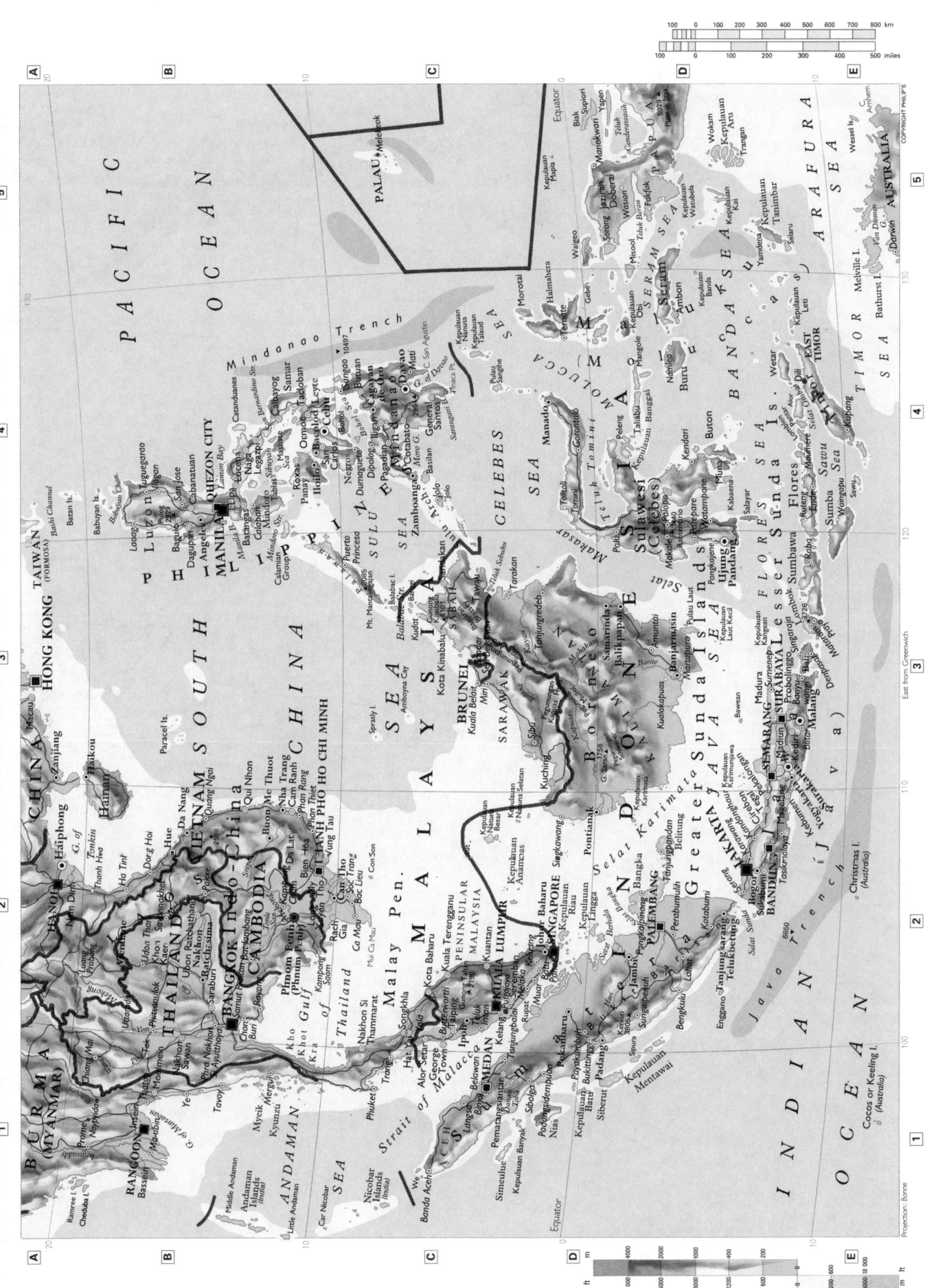

100   0   100   200   300   400   500   600   700   800 km

100   0   100   200   300   400   500 miles

COPYRIGHT PHILIP'S

A

PACIFIC

OCEAN

CHINA

Macau
Zhanjiang
HONG KONG

Haikou

TAIWAN
(FORMOSA)

Hainan

BURMA
(MYANMAR)

RANGOON

Bassein

Ramree I.
Cheduba I.

Andaman Islands
(India)

Middle Andaman
Little Andaman

Nicobar Islands
(India)
Car Nicobar

B

HANOI
Nam Dinh
G. of
Tonkin
Ha Tinh

Thanh Hoa

Luang Prabang

THAILAND

Chiang Mai

Nakhon
Sawan

BANGKOK
INDO-China
CAMBODIA

Phnom Penh
(Phnum Penh)

Malay Pen.
MALAYSIA

PENINSULAR
MALAYSIA

VIETNAM

Da Nang
Quang Ngai
Qui Nhon
Buon Me Thuot

Nha Trang
Cam Ranh
Phan Rang
Phan Thiet

THANH PHO HO CHI MINH

Vung Tau

Con Son

C

Mindanao Trench

Luzon

MANILA
QUEZON CITY

PHILIPPINES

SOUTH

CHINA

SEA

Paracel Is.

Spratly I.

SABAH

SARAWAK

BRUNEI

Kuching

MALAYSIA

KUALA LUMPUR

SINGAPORE

Johor Baharu

Pontianak

D

Equator

PALAU

CELEBES
SEA

SULU
SEA

Davao

Mindanao

Manado

SULAWESI
(Celebes)

Ujung
Pandang

BORNEO

INDONESIA

Banjarmasin

Balikpapan
Samarinda

Java Sea

JAKARTA
BANDUNG
Bogor

SEMARANG
SURABAYA

Greater Sunda Islands

Java

E

PAPUA

SERAM SEA

AUSTRALIA

Darwin

TIMOR
SEA

ARAFURA

SEA

BANDA SEA

FLORES SEA

Lesser Sunda Islands

Sumbawa
Flores
Sumba

Timor

EAST
TIMOR

INDIAN

OCEAN

Christmas I.
(Australia)

Cocos or Keeling I.
(Australia)

Projection: Bonne

East from Greenwich

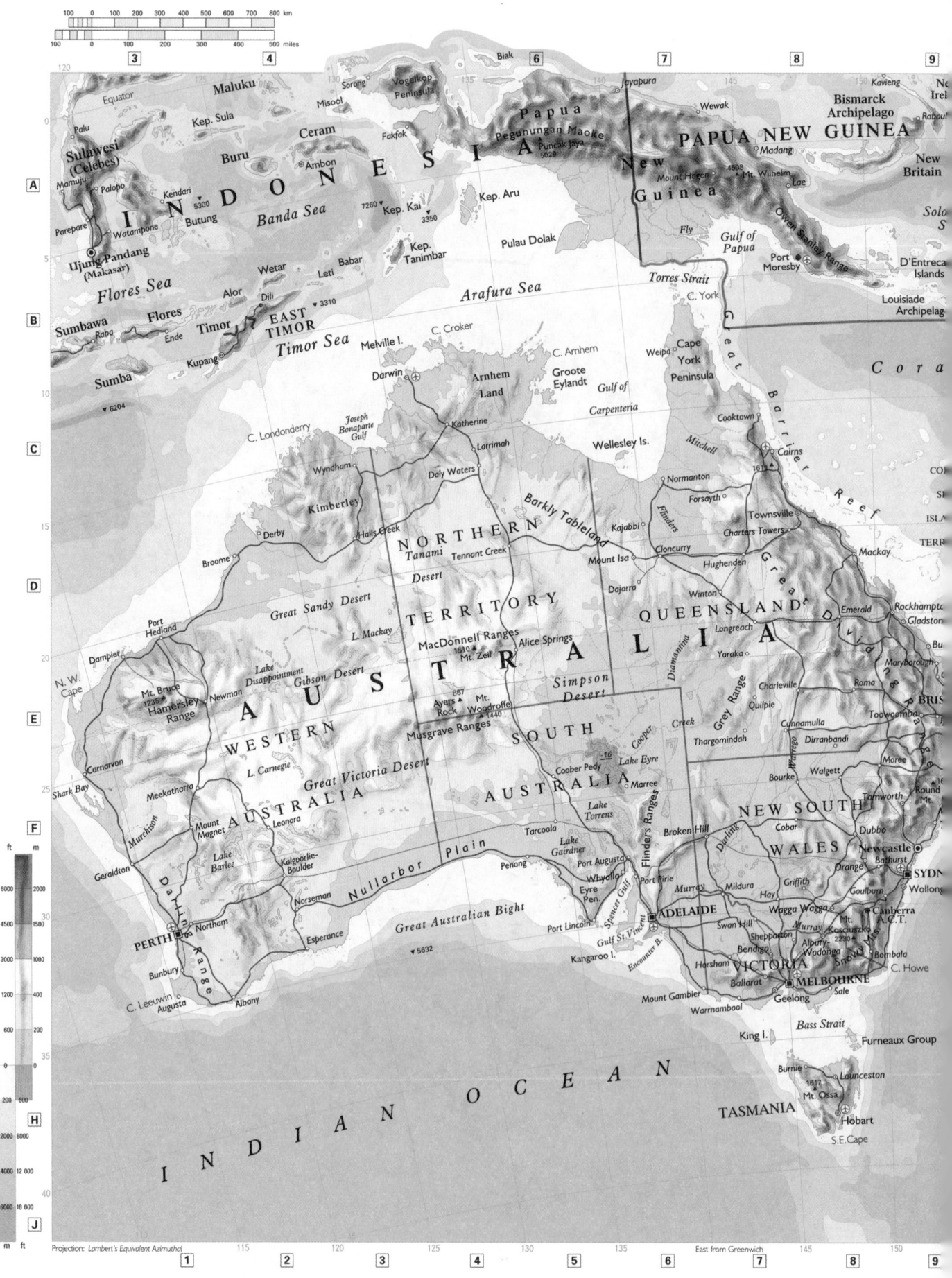

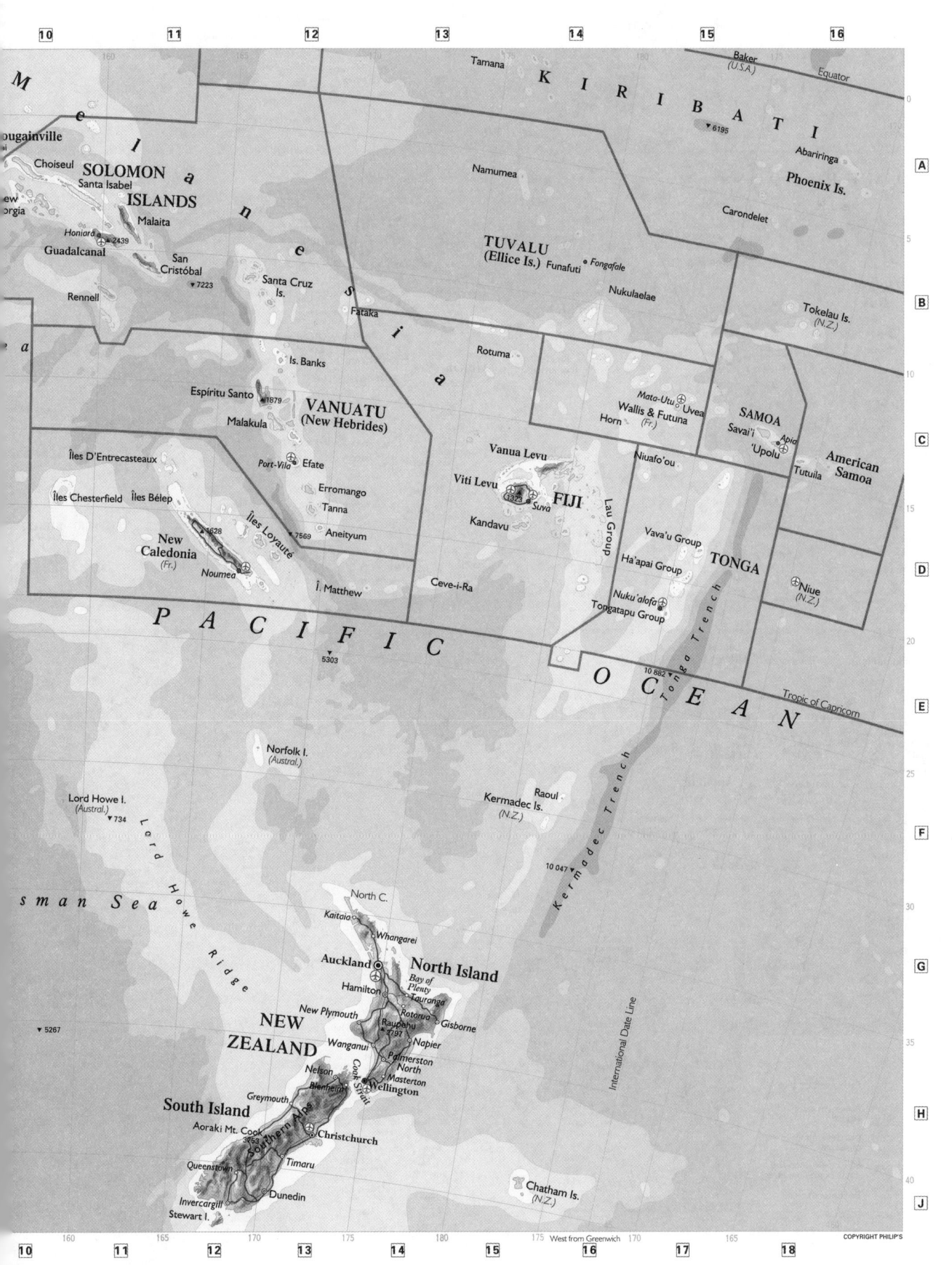

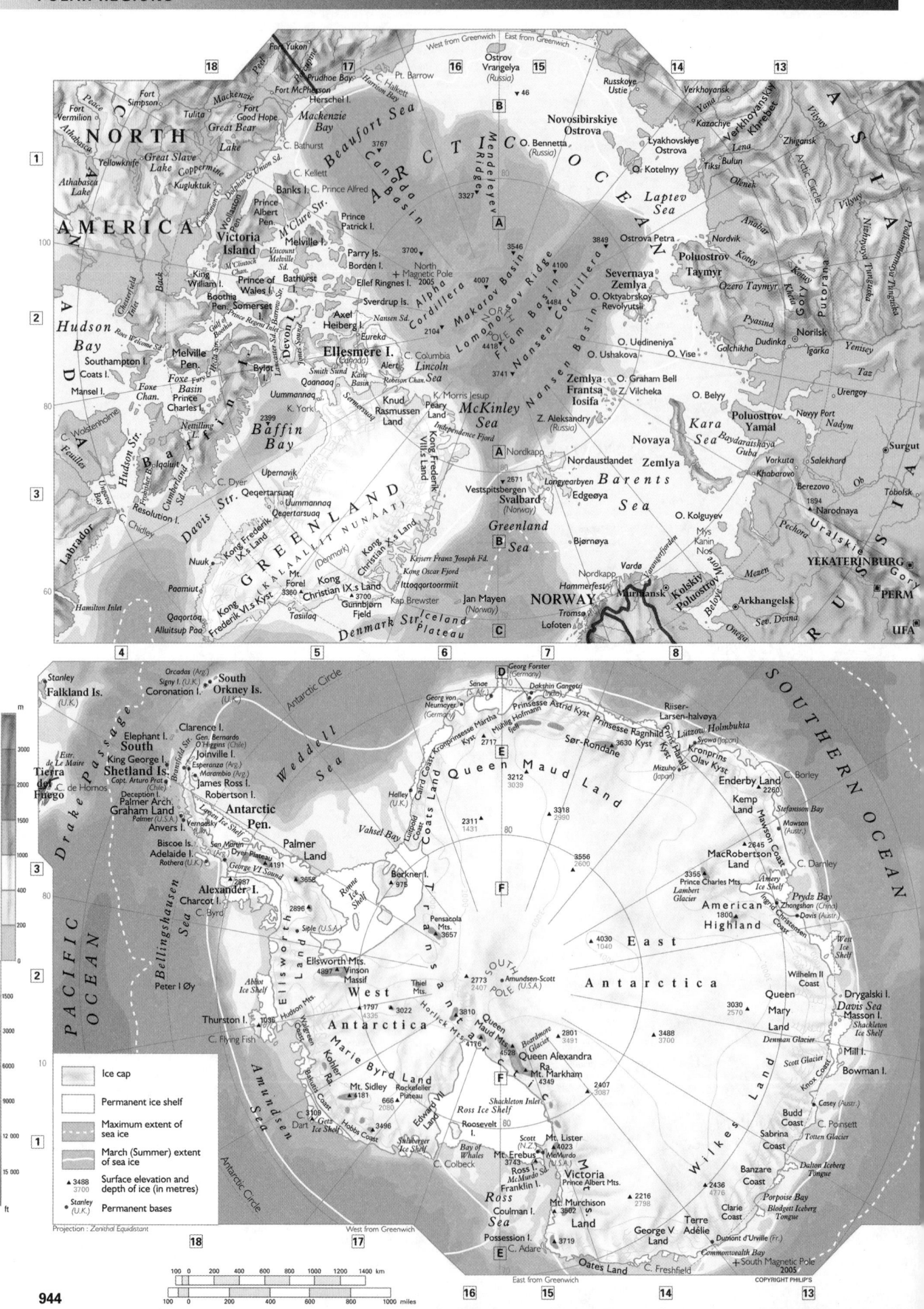

POLAR REGIONS

North map:

West from Greenwich   East from Greenwich

18   17   16   Ostrov Vrangelya (Russia)   15   14   13

B   ▼ 46

NORTH   Fort Yukon   Pt. Barrow   O. Bennetta (Russia)   Novosibirskiye Ostrova   Verkhoyansk   Yana   Kazachye
Fort Simpson   Peace   Prudhoe Bay   Flaxx   Herschel I.   Lyakhovskiye Ostrova   Lena   Zhigansk
Fort Vermilion   Tulita   Fort McPherson   O. Kotelnyy   Tiksi   Bulun   A S I A
Athabasca   Great Bear   Mackenzie   Harrison Bay   Anabar   Olenek   Vilyuy
1   Yellowknife   Lake   Mackenzie   3767   Tiksi   Laptev   Olenek   Nizhnyaya Tunguska
Great Slave   Coppermine   Bay   C. Bathurst   80   Sea   Nordvik   Kotuy   Putorana
Lake   Kugluktuk   Banks I.   C. Prince Alfred   3327   Ostrova Petra   Kotuy   Norilsk
Coppermine   Prince   3546   4100   Poluostrov   Dudinka   Igarka   Yenisey
C A N A D A   Albert   Pen.   3849   Taymyr   Ozero Taymyr   Kha   Golchikha
A M E R I C A   McClintock   Viscount   Melville I.   A   4007   Severnaya   Oktyabrskoy   Pyasina
Victoria   Chan.   Melville Sd.   3700   NORTH   Zemlya   Revolyutsii   Gory
Island   Prince   Parry Is.   North   POLE   4484   Urengoy
King   of Wales   Borden I.   Magnetic Pole   4418   O. Uedineniya   O. Vise
William I.   Bathurst I.   Ellef Ringnes I.   2005   Fram   O. Ushakova   Kara   Novyy Port
2   Boothia   Somerset I.   Alpha   Basin   Zemlya   O. Graham Bell   Sea   Nadym
Pen.   Sverdrup Is.   Cordillera   2104   4418   Frantsa   Poluostrov
Hudson   Prince Regent Inlet   Axel   Nansen Sd.   Lomonosov   Iosifa   Yamal
Bay   Gulf of Boothia   Heiberg I.   Ridge   Z. Vilcheka   Baydaratskaya
Southampton I.   Melville   Eureka   Nansen   O. Belyy   Guba   Vorkuta   Salekhard
Coats I.   Pen.   Devon I.   C. Columbia   Cordillera   Novaya   Khabarovo
Mansel I.   Foxe   Ellesmere I.   Alert   Lincoln   Z. Aleksandry   O. Vise   Zemlya   Berezovo   Narodnaya
Basin   Prince   (Canada)   Sea   (Russia)   3741   Zemlya   1894
Charles I.   Smith Sund   McKinley   Frantsa   O. Kolguyev
3   Foxe   Kane   Qaanaaq   Knud   Sea   Iosifa   Uralskie
Chan.   Basin   Rasmussen   Nordaustlandet   Barents   Vorkuta
Baffin   Robeson Chan.   Land   Nordkapp   Sea
Bay   K. Morris Jesup   Svalbard   Novaya   YEKATERINBURG
C. Dyer   Upernavik   Peary   Independence Fjord   2571   Longyearbyen   (Norway)   O. Kolguyev   PERM
Qeqertarsuaq   Land   Vestspitsbergen   Zemlya   UFA
Qeqertarsuaq   Kong Frederik   Svalbard   Edgeøya
Resolution I.   Uummannaq   VIII.s Land   (Norway)   Mys Kanin Nos
C. Chidley   GREENLAND   Nordkapp   Barents
Labrador   (KALAALLIT NUNAAT)   Greenland   Varde   Sea   Mezen
Nuuk   (Denmark)   Kong   Sea   Hammerfest   Nordkapp   Arkhangelsk   R U S S I A
Kong   Christian   Kong   Bjørnøya   Murmansk
Frederik   Xs Land   Oscar Fjord   Tromsø   Kolskiy   Sev. Dvina
IX.s Kyst   Kejser Franz Joseph Fd.   Jan Mayen   NORWAY   Poluostrov   Pechora
Paamiut   Mt.   Kong   Ittoqqortoormiit   (Norway)   Beloye   Onega
Forel   Christian IX.s Land   Kap Brewster   Lofoten
Qaqortoq   Gunnbjørn   Iceland   Omo
Alluitsup Paa   Fjeld   Plateau
Hamilton Inlet   Tasiilaq   Denmark Str.   60   C

4   5   6   7   8

Scale bar (left side):

ft   m
9000   3000
6000   2000
4500   1500
3000   1000
1200   400
600   200
0   0
500   1500
1000   3000
2000   6000
3000   9000
4000   12 000
5000   15 000
m   ft

South map (Antarctica):

SOUTHERN OCEAN

D   Georg Forster (Germany)   Dakshin Gangotri (India)
Sanae (S. Afr.)   Riiser-
Georg von Neumayer   Prinsesse Astrid Kyst   Larsen-halvøya
(Germany)   Prinsesse Ragnhild Kyst   Syowa (Japan)
Stanley   Orcadas (Arg.)   Kronprins   Lützow-Holmbukta   Kronprins
Falkland Is.   Signy I. (U.K.)   South   Prinsesse Martha   Mühlig Hofmann   Olav Kyst
(U.K.)   Coronation I.   Orkney Is.   Kyst   Sør-Rondane   3630
Antarctic Circle   (U.K.)   2717   Mizuho   Enderby Land   C. Borley
Clarence I.   Coats   Queen Maud Land   (Japan)   2260
South   Elephant I.   Land   3212   Kemp   Stefansson Bay
King George I.   Gen. Bernardo   3039   Land   Mawson (Austr.)
Shetland Is.   O'Higgins (Chile)   3318   2645   Mawson Coast
Joinville I.   Weddell   Halley   2990   MacRobertson
Esperanza (Arg.)   (U.K.)   2311   3556   3355   Land   C. Darnley
Palmer Arch.   Marambio (Arg.)   Sea   1431   2600   Prince Charles Mts.   Prydz Bay
Graham Land   James Ross I.   Vahsel Bay   3658   Amery   Zhongshan (China)
Palmer (U.S.A.)   Robertson I.   Berkner I.   975   Ice Shelf   Lambert   Davis (Austr.)
Anvers I.   Vernadsky   Ronne   Glacier   American   1800
Biscoe Is.   San Martin (Arg.)   Palmer   Ice Shelf   Highland   Christensen Coast
Adelaide I.   Dyer Plateau   Land   Pensacola   4030   East   Coast
Rothera (U.K.)   2987   George VI Sound   Mts.   1040   Wilhelm II   West
Alexander I.   C. Byrd   Siple (U.S.A.)   3657   Antarctica   Coast   Ice Shelf
Charcot I.   2896   Ellsworth Mts.   2773   Queen   Drygalski I.
4335   4897   Vinson   2407   SOUTH POLE   Mary   Davis Sea
Peter I Øy   Massif   Amundsen-Scott   Land   Masson I.
Thiel   (U.S.A.)   3030   Shackleton Ice Shelf
PACIFIC OCEAN   Thurston I.   1797   3022   Mts.   2570   Mill I.
1035   West   3810   Queen   3488   Bowman I.
Bellingshausen Sea   Antarctica   Horlick Mts.   4776   Maud Mts.   3700   Scott Glacier
Marie Byrd Land   4528   Queen Alexandra   Budd   Knox
Kohler Ra.   Mt. Sidley   Ra.   2801   Coast   Coast
4181   Rockefeller   Mt. Markham   3491   Casey (Austr.)
666   Plateau   4349   2407   Sabrina   C. Poinsett
2080   Shackleton Inlet   3087   Coast   Totten Glacier
Amundsen Sea   3109   Getz   3496   Ross Ice Shelf   Victoria   Banzare   Dalton Iceberg
Dart   Ice Shelf   Hobbs Coast   Roosevelt I.   80   Land   Coast   Tongue
Bakutis Coast   Sulzberger   Edward VII   Scott (N.Z.)   Mt. Lister   Clarie   Porpoise Bay
C. Flying Fish   Ice Shelf   Pen.   Bay of   Mt. Erebus   4023   Prince Albert Mts.   2436   Coast   Blodgett Iceberg
Antarctic Circle   Whales   Ross   3743   McMurdo (U.S.A.)   4776   Terre   Tongue
C. Colbeck   Sd.   McMurdo Sd.   Victoria   Adélie   Commonwealth Bay
Franklin I.   Land   2216   George V   South Magnetic
Coulman I.   Mt. Murchison   2798   Land   Pole 2005
3502   Possession I.   Dumont d'Urville (Fr.)
3719   Oates Land   C. Freshfield
C. Adare

West from Greenwich
18   17   East from Greenwich
16   15   14   13

Legend:

- Ice cap
- Permanent ice shelf
- Maximum extent of sea ice
- March (Summer) extent of sea ice
- ▲3488 / 3700   Surface elevation and depth of ice (in metres)
- • Stanley (U.K.)   Permanent bases

Projection : Zenithal Equidistant

Scale:
100 0   200   400   600   800   1000   1200   1400 km
100 0   200   400   600   800   1000 miles

COPYRIGHT PHILIP'S

MAP INDEX

The index contains the names of all the principal places and features shown on the maps. Names in bold type denote encyclopaedia entries. The alphabetical order of names composed of two or more words is governed primarily by the first word and then by the second. This is an example of the rule:

New South Wales □, *Australia* . **942 G8**
New York □, *U.S.A.* **919 B11**
New Zealand ■, *Oceania* **943 J14**
Newark, *N.J., U.S.A.* **919 B12**
Newark, *Ohio, U.S.A.* **919 B10**

Physical features composed of a proper name (Erie) and a description (Lake) are positioned alphabetically by the proper name. The description is positioned after the proper name and is usually abbreviated:

Erie, L., *N. Amer.* **919 B10**
Everest, Mt., *Nepal* **937 C7**

Where a description forms part of a settlement name or administrative name, however, it is always written in full and put in its true alphabetical position:

Lake Charles, *U.S.A.* **919 D8**
Mount Isa, *Australia* **942 E6**

The number in bold type which follows each name in the index refers to the number of the map page where that place or feature will be found. This is usually the largest scale at which the place or feature appears.

The letter and figure which are immediately after the page number give the grid square on the map page, within which the feature is situated. The letter represents the latitude and the figure the longitude. In some cases the feature itself may fall within the specified square, while the name is outside.

Rivers are indexed to their mouths or confluences, and carry the symbol → after their names.

The following symbols are also used in the index: ■ country, ☒ overseas territory or dependency, □ first order administrative area, △ national park, ✈ (LHR) principal airport (and location identifier).

A

A Coruña, *Spain* 928 A1
Aachen, *Germany* 927 C3
Aalborg = Ålborg, *Denmark* 930 F5
Aarau, *Switz.* 926 C8
Aare →, *Switz.* 926 C8
Aarhus = Århus, *Denmark* 930 F6
Aba, *Nigeria* 938 G7
Ābādān, *Iran* 936 B3
Abakan, *Russia* 933 D10
Abancay, *Peru* 922 D2
Abariringa, *Kiribati* 943 A16
Ābay = Nîl el Azraq →, *Sudan* 939 E12
Abbay = Nîl el Azraq →, *Sudan* 939 E12
Abbeville, *France* 926 A4
Abéché, *Chad* 939 F10
Abeokuta, *Nigeria* 938 G6
Aberaeron, *U.K.* 924 D3
Aberayron = Aberaeron, *U.K.* 924 D3
Aberchirder, *U.K.* 925 D6
Abercorn = Mbala, *Zambia* 940 D6
Aberdare, *U.K.* 924 E4
Aberdeen, *U.K.* 925 D6
Aberdeen, *S. Dak., U.S.A.* 918 A7
Aberdeen, *Wash., U.S.A.* 918 A2
Aberdeenshire □, *U.K.* 925 D6
Aberdovey = Aberdyfi, *U.K.* 924 D3
Aberdyfi, *U.K.* 924 D3
Aberfeldy, *U.K.* 925 E5
Abergavenny, *U.K.* 924 E4
Abergele, *U.K.* 924 C4
Abert, L., *U.S.A.* 918 B2
Aberystwyth, *U.K.* 924 D3
Abhā, *Si. Arabia* 936 D3
Abidjan, *Ivory C.* 938 G5
Abilene, *U.S.A.* 918 D7
Abingdon, *U.K.* 924 E6
Abitibi, L., *Canada* 917 D12
Abkhaz Republic = Abkhazia □, *Georgia* 931 B6
Abkhazia □, *Georgia* 931 B6
Åbo = Turku, *Finland* 930 E8
Abomey, *Benin* 938 G6
Aboyne, *U.K.* 925 D6
Absaroka Range, *U.S.A.* 918 B5
Abu Dhabi = Abū Ẓāby, *U.A.E.* 936 C4
Abu Hamed, *Sudan* 939 E12
Abū Ẓāby, *U.A.E.* 936 C4
Abuja, *Nigeria* 938 G7
Abunã, *Brazil* 922 C3
Abunã →, *Brazil* 922 C3
Acaponeta, *Mexico* 920 C3
Acapulco, *Mexico* 920 D5
Acarai, Serra, *Brazil* 922 B4
Accra, *Ghana* 938 G5
Aceh □, *Indonesia* 941 C1
Achill Hd., *Ireland* 925 H9
Achill I., *Ireland* 925 H8
Acklins I., *Bahamas* 921 C10
Aconcagua, Cerro, *Argentina* 923 F3
Açores, Is. dos, *Atl. Oc.* 938 A1
Acre = 'Akko, *Israel* 931 D5
Acre □, *Brazil* 922 C2
Acre →, *Brazil* 922 C3
Ad Dammām, *Si. Arabia* 936 C4
Ad Dawḥah, *Qatar* 936 C4
Adair, C., *Canada* 917 A12
Adak I., *U.S.A.* 916 C2
Adamaoua, Massif de l', *Cameroon* 939 G7
Adamawa Highlands = Adamaoua, Massif de l', *Cameroon* 939 G7
Adana, *Turkey* 931 C5
Adapazarı = Sakarya, *Turkey* 931 B4
Adare, C., *Antarctica* 944 E15
Addis Ababa = Addis Abeba, *Ethiopia* 915 D11
Addis Abeba, *Ethiopia* 915 D11
Adelaide, *Australia* 942 G6
Adelaide I., *Antarctica* 944 D3
Adelaide Pen., *Canada* 916 B10
Adélie, Terre, *Antarctica* 944 D14
Adélie Land = Adélie, Terre, *Antarctica* 944 D14
Aden = Al 'Adan, *Yemen* 936 D3
Aden, G. of, *Asia* 936 D3
Adirondack Mts., *U.S.A.* 919 B12
Adjuntas, *Puerto Rico* 921 d
Adour →, *France* 926 E3
Adrar, *Mauritania* 938 D3
Adrar des Iforas, *Algeria* 938 C5
Adriatic Sea, *Medit. S.* 929 C5
Adygea □, *Russia* 931 B6
Adzhar Republic = Ajaria □, *Georgia* 931 B6
Ægean Sea, *Medit. S.* 931 C3
Aerhtai Shan, *Mongolia* 934 B4
Afghanistan ■, *Asia* 936 B5
Africa 915 D11
Afyon, *Turkey* 931 C4
Afyonkarahisar = Afyon, *Turkey* 931 C4
Agadès = Agadez, *Niger* 938 E7
Agadez, *Niger* 938 E7
Agadir, *Morocco* 938 B4
Agen, *France* 926 D4
Agra, *India* 937 C6
Ağri, *Turkey* 931 C6
Ağrı Dağı, *Turkey* 931 C6
Ağri Karakose = Ağri, *Turkey* 931 C6
Agrigento, *Italy* 929 F4
Agua Prieta, *Mexico* 920 A3
Aguadilla, *Puerto Rico* 921 d
Aguascalientes, *Mexico* 920 C4
Aguila, Punta, *Puerto Rico* 921 d
Agujereada, Pta., *Puerto Rico* 921 d
Agulhas, C., *S. Africa* 940 J4
Ahaggar, *Algeria* 938 D7
Ahmadabad, *India* 937 C6
Ahmadnagar, *India* 937 D6
Ahmedabad = Ahmadabad, *India* 937 C6
Ahmednagar = Ahmadnagar, *India* 937 D6
Ahvāz, *Iran* 936 B3
Ahvenanmaa = Åland, *Finland* 930 E8
Aihui, *China* 934 A7
Ailsa Craig, *U.K.* 925 F3
Aïr, *Niger* 938 E7
Air Force I., *Canada* 917 B12
Airdrie, *Canada* 916 C8
Airdrie, *U.K.* 925 F5
Aire →, *U.K.* 924 C7
Aisne →, *France* 926 B5
Aix-en-Provence, *France* 926 E6
Aix-la-Chapelle = Aachen, *Germany* 927 C3
Aix-les-Bains, *France* 926 D6
Aizuwakamatsu, *Japan* 935 E6
Ajaccio, *France* 926 F8
Ajari Rep. = Ajaria □, *Georgia* 931 B6
Ajaria □, *Georgia* 931 B6
Ajdābiyā, *Libya* 939 B10
Ajmer, *India* 937 C6
Akhisar, *Turkey* 931 C3
Akimiski I., *Canada* 917 C11
Akita, *Japan* 935 D7
'Akko, *Israel* 931 D5
Aklavik, *Canada* 916 B6
Akmolinsk = Astana, *Kazakhstan* 932 D8
Akola, *India* 937 C6
Akpatok I., *Canada* 917 B13
Akranes, *Iceland* 930 B1
Akron, *U.S.A.* 919 B10
Aksai Chin, *China* 937 B6
Aksaray, *Turkey* 931 C4
Akşehir Gölü, *Turkey* 931 C4
Aksu, *China* 934 B3
Aktyubinsk = Aqtöbe, *Kazakhstan* 932 D6
Akure, *Nigeria* 938 G7
Akureyri, *Iceland* 930 A2
Akyab = Sittwe, *Burma* 937 C8
Al 'Adan, *Yemen* 936 D3
Al Aḥsā = Hasa □, *Si. Arabia* 936 C3
Al 'Aqabah, *Jordan* 936 C2
Al Baḥral Mayyit = Dead Sea, *Asia* 931 D5
Al Baṣrah, *Iraq* 936 B3
Al Bayḍā, *Libya* 939 B10
Al Ḥillah, *Iraq* 936 B3
Al Hoceïma, *Morocco* 938 A5
Al Ḥudaydah, *Yemen* 936 D3
Al Hufūf, *Si. Arabia* 936 C3
Al Jawf, *Libya* 939 D10
Al Jawf, *Si. Arabia* 936 C2
Al Jazirah, *Iraq* 936 B3
Al Khums, *Libya* 939 B8
Al Kufrah, *Libya* 939 D10
Al Kūt, *Iraq* 936 B3
Al Kuwayt, *Kuwait* 936 C3
Al Lādhiqīyah, *Syria* 936 B2
Al Madīnah, *Si. Arabia* 936 C2
Al Manāmah, *Bahrain* 936 C4
Al Mawṣil, *Iraq* 936 B3
Al Mubarraz, *Si. Arabia* 936 C3
Al Mukallā, *Yemen* 936 D3
Al Qaṭīf, *Si. Arabia* 936 C4
Al Quds = Jerusalem, *Israel* 931 D5
Alabama □, *U.S.A.* 919 D9
Alabama →, *U.S.A.* 919 D9
Alagoas □, *Brazil* 922 C6
Alagoinhas, *Brazil* 922 D6
Alamogordo, *U.S.A.* 918 D5
Alamosa, *U.S.A.* 918 C5
Åland, *Finland* 930 E8
Alania = North Ossetia □, *Russia* 931 B6
Alanya, *Turkey* 931 C4
Alaşehir, *Turkey* 931 C3
Alaska □, *U.S.A.* 916 B5
Alaska, G. of, *Pac. Oc.* 916 C5
Alaska Peninsula, *U.S.A.* 916 C4
Alaska Range, *U.S.A.* 916 B4
Albacete, *Spain* 928 C5
Albanel, L., *Canada* 917 C12
Albania ■, *Europe* 931 B2
Albany, *Australia* 942 H2
Albany, *Ga., U.S.A.* 919 D10
Albany, *N.Y., U.S.A.* 919 B12
Albany, *Oreg., U.S.A.* 918 B2
Albany →, *Canada* 917 C11
Albemarle Sd., *U.S.A.* 919 C11
Albert, L., *Africa* 940 B6
Albert Lea, *U.S.A.* 919 B8
Albert Nile →, *Uganda* 940 B6
Alberta □, *Canada* 916 C8
Albertville = Kalemie, *Dem. Rep. of the Congo* 940 D5
Albertville, *France* 926 D7
Albi, *France* 926 E5
Ålborg, *Denmark* 930 F5
Alborz, Reshteh-ye Kūhhā-ye, *Iran* 936 B4
Albuquerque, *U.S.A.* 918 C5
Albury = Albury-Wodonga, *Australia* 942 H8
Albury-Wodonga, *Australia* 942 H8
Alcalá de Henares, *Spain* 928 B4
Alchevsk, *Ukraine* 931 A5
Aldabra Is., *Seychelles* 915 E12
Aldan →, *Russia* 933 C13
Aldeburgh, *U.K.* 924 D9
Alegrete, *Brazil* 923 E4
Alençon, *France* 926 B4
Alenuihaha Channel, *U.S.A.* 918 H17
Aleppo = Ḥalab, *Syria* 936 B2
Alès, *France* 926 D6
Alessándria, *Italy* 926 D8
Ålesund, *Norway* 930 E5
Aleutian Is., *Pac. Oc.* 916 C2
Alexander Arch., *U.S.A.* 916 C6
Alexander I., *Antarctica* 944 D3
Alexandria = El Iskandarîya, *Egypt* 939 B11
Alexandria, *U.K.* 925 F4
Alexandria, *U.S.A.* 919 D8
Alford, *U.K.* 925 D6
Alfreton, *U.K.* 924 C6
Algarve, *Portugal* 928 D1
Algeciras, *Spain* 928 D3
Alger, *Algeria* 938 A6
Algeria ■, *Africa* 938 C6
Algiers = Alger, *Algeria* 938 A6
Alhucemas = Al Hoceïma, *Morocco* 938 A5
Alicante, *Spain* 928 C5
Alice Springs, *Australia* 942 E5
Aligarh, *India* 937 C6
Alkmaar, *Neths.* 927 B2
Allahabad, *India* 937 C7
Allegheny Mts., *U.S.A.* 919 C11
Allègre, Pte., *Guadeloupe* 920 b
Allen, Bog of, *Ireland* 925 H13
Allen, L., *Ireland* 925 G11
Allentown, *U.S.A.* 919 B11
Alleynes B., *Barbados* 921 g
Alliance, *U.S.A.* 918 B6
Allier →, *France* 926 C5
Alligator Pond, *Jamaica* 920 a
Alloa, *U.K.* 925 E5
Alluitsup Paa, *Greenland* 917 B15
Alma Ata = Almaty, *Kazakhstan* 932 E8
Almaty, *Kazakhstan* 932 E8
Almelo, *Neths.* 927 B3
Almería, *Spain* 928 D4
Alness, *U.K.* 925 D4
Alnmouth, *U.K.* 924 A6
Alnwick, *U.K.* 924 A6
Alor, *Indonesia* 941 D4
Alor Setar, *Malaysia* 941 C2
Alpine, *U.S.A.* 918 D6
Alps, *Europe* 926 C8
Alsace, *France* 926 B7
Alsask, *Canada* 916 C9
Alston, *U.K.* 924 B5
Altai = Aerhtai Shan, *Mongolia* 934 B4
Altanbulag, *Mongolia* 934 A5
Altay, *China* 934 B3
Alton, *U.K.* 924 E7
Alton, *U.S.A.* 919 C8
Altoona, *U.S.A.* 919 B11
Altun Shan, *China* 934 C3
Altus, *U.S.A.* 918 D7
Alucra, *Turkey* 931 B5
Alxa Zuoqi, *China* 934 C5
Alyth, *U.K.* 925 E5
Amadjuak L., *Canada* 917 B12
Amagasaki, *Japan* 935 F4
Amapá, *Brazil* 922 B4
Amapá □, *Brazil* 922 B4
Amarillo, *U.S.A.* 918 C6
Amazon = Amazonas →, *S. Amer.* 922 C4
Amazonas □, *Brazil* 922 C3
Amazonas →, *S. Amer.* 922 C4
Ambala, *India* 937 B6
Ambato, *Ecuador* 922 C2
Ambergris Cay, *Belize* 920 D7
Ambilobé, *Madag.* 940 E9
Amble, *U.K.* 924 A6
Ambleside, *U.K.* 924 B5
Ambon, *Indonesia* 941 D4
Amchitka I., *U.S.A.* 916 C1
Ameca, *Mexico* 920 C4
American Highland, *Antarctica* 944 E10
American Samoa ☒, *Pac. Oc.* 943 C16
Ames, *U.S.A.* 919 B8
Amherst, *Canada* 917 D13
Amiens, *France* 926 B5
Amirante Is., *Seychelles* 915 E12
Amlia I., *U.S.A.* 916 C2
Amlwch, *U.K.* 924 C3
'Ammān, *Jordan* 936 B2
Ammanford, *U.K.* 924 E4
Ammochostos = Famagusta, *Cyprus* 931 C4
Amos, *Canada* 917 D12
Amoy = Xiamen, *China* 934 D6
Amravati, *India* 937 C6
Amritsar, *India* 937 B6
Amsterdam, *Neths.* 927 B2
Amsterdam, I. = Nouvelle-Amsterdam, I., *Ind. Oc.* 915 F13
Amudarya →, *Uzbekistan* 932 E6
Amundsen Gulf, *Canada* 916 A7
Amundsen Sea, *Antarctica* 944 E1
Amur →, *Russia* 933 D15
Amyderya = Amudarya →, *Uzbekistan* 932 E6
An Nafūd, *Si. Arabia* 936 C3
An Najaf, *Iraq* 936 B3
An Nāṣirīyah, *Iraq* 936 B3
An Uaimh, *Ireland* 925 H13
Anaconda, *U.S.A.* 918 A4
Anadolu, *Turkey* 931 C4
Anadyr, *Russia* 933 C18
Anadyrskiy Zaliv, *Russia* 933 C19
Anaheim, *U.S.A.* 918 D3
Anambas, Kepulauan, *Indonesia* 941 C2
Anambas Is. = Anambas, Kepulauan, *Indonesia* 941 C2
Anamur, *Turkey* 931 C4
Anār, *Iran* 936 B4
Anatolia = Anadolu, *Turkey* 931 C4
Añatuya, *Argentina* 923 E3
Anchorage, *U.S.A.* 916 B5
Ancohuma, Nevado, *Bolivia* 922 D3
Ancona, *Italy* 929 C4
Ancud, *Chile* 923 G2
Ancud, G. de, *Chile* 923 G2
Andalgalá, *Argentina* 923 E3
Andalucía □, *Spain* 928 D3
Andalusia = Andalucía □, *Spain* 928 D3
Andalusia, *U.S.A.* 919 D9
Andaman Is., *Ind. Oc.* 941 B1
Andaman Sea, *Ind. Oc.* 937 D8
Anderson, *Alaska, U.S.A.* 916 B5
Anderson, *S.C., U.S.A.* 919 D10
Anderson →, *Canada* 916 B7
Andes, Cord. de los, *S. Amer.* 923 E3
Andhra Pradesh □, *India* 937 D6
Andijon, *Uzbekistan* 932 E8
Andizhan = Andijon, *Uzbekistan* 932 E8
Andorra ■, *Europe* 926 E4
Andorra La Vella, *Andorra* 926 E4
Andover, *U.K.* 924 E6
Andradina, *Brazil* 922 E4
Andreanof Is., *U.S.A.* 916 C2
Ándria, *Italy* 929 D6
Andropov = Rybinsk, *Russia* 932 D4
Andros I., *Bahamas* 921 C9
Anegada I., *Br. Virgin Is.* 921 e
Aneityum, *Vanuatu* 943 E12
Angara →, *Russia* 933 D10
Angarsk, *Russia* 933 D11
Ånge, *Sweden* 930 E7
Ángel, Salto = Angel Falls, *Venezuela* 922 B3
Angel Falls, *Venezuela* 922 B3
Angeles, *Phil.* 941 B4
Ångermanälven →, *Sweden* 930 E7
Angers, *France* 926 C3
Angoche, *Mozam.* 940 F7
Angola ■, *Africa* 940 E3
Angoulême, *France* 926 D4
Angoumois, *France* 926 D3
Angren, *Uzbekistan* 932 E8
Anguilla ☒, *W. Indies* 921 D12
Angus □, *U.K.* 925 E6
Anhui □, *China* 934 C6
Anhwei = Anhui □, *China* 934 C6
Anjou, *France* 926 C3
Ankang, *China* 934 C5
Ankara, *Turkey* 931 C4
Ann Arbor, *U.S.A.* 919 B10
Annaba, *Algeria* 938 A7
Annalee →, *Ireland* 925 G12
Annan, *U.K.* 925 G5
Annan →, *U.K.* 925 G5
Annapolis, *U.S.A.* 919 C11
Annapurna, *Nepal* 937 C7
Annecy, *France* 926 D7
Anning, *China* 934 D5
Anniston, *U.S.A.* 919 D9
Annotto Bay, *Jamaica* 920 a
Anqing, *China* 934 C6
Anshan, *China* 934 B7
Anshun, *China* 934 D5
Anstruther, *U.K.* 925 E6
Antakya, *Turkey* 931 C5
Antalya, *Turkey* 931 C4
Antananarivo, *Madag.* 940 F9
Antarctic Pen., *Antarctica* 944 D4
Antarctica 944 F7
Anti Atlas, *Morocco* 938 C4
Antibes, *France* 926 E7
Anticosti, Î. d', *Canada* 917 D13
Antigonish, *Canada* 917 D13
Antigua & Barbuda ■, *W. Indies* 921 D12
Antilles = West Indies, *Cent. Amer.* 921 E12
Antioquia, *Colombia* 922 B2
Antofagasta, *Chile* 923 E2
Antrim, *U.K.* 925 G13
Antrim □, *U.K.* 925 G13
Antrim, Mts. of, *U.K.* 925 F13
Antsirabe, *Madag.* 940 F9
Antsiranana, *Madag.* 940 E9
Antwerp = Antwerpen, *Belgium* 927 C2
Antwerpen, *Belgium* 927 C2
Anvers = Antwerpen, *Belgium* 927 C2
Anxi, *China* 934 B4
Anyang, *China* 934 C6
Aomen = Macau, *China* 934 D6
Aomori, *Japan* 935 C7
Aoraki Mount Cook, *N.Z.* 943 J13
Aosta, *Italy* 926 D7
Aotearoa = New Zealand ■, *Oceania* 943 J14
Aozou Strip, *Chad* 939 D9
Apalachee B., *U.S.A.* 919 E10
Apaporis →, *Colombia* 922 C3
Apatity, *Russia* 932 C4
Apeldoorn, *Neths.* 927 B2
Apennines = Appennini, *Italy* 929 B3
Apia, *Samoa* 943 C16
Apostle Is., *U.S.A.* 919 A8
Appalachian Mts., *U.S.A.* 919 C11
Appennini, *Italy* 929 B3
Appleby-in-Westmorland, *U.K.* 924 B5
Apure →, *Venezuela* 922 B3
Apurimac →, *Peru* 922 D2
Aqaba = Al 'Aqabah, *Jordan* 936 C2
Aqmola = Astana, *Kazakhstan* 932 D8
Aqtöbe, *Kazakhstan* 932 D6
Ar Rachidiya = Er Rachidia, *Morocco* 938 B5
Ar Ramādī, *Iraq* 936 B3
Ar Riyāḍ, *Si. Arabia* 936 C3
Ara, *India* 937 C7
Arabian Desert = Es Sahrâ' Esh Sharqîya, *Egypt* 939 C12
Arabian Gulf = Persian Gulf, *Asia* 936 C4
Arabian Sea, *Ind. Oc.* 936 D5
Aracaju, *Brazil* 922 D6
Aracati, *Brazil* 922 C6
Araçatuba, *Brazil* 922 E4
Araçuaí, *Brazil* 922 D5
Arad, *Romania* 931 A2
Arafura Sea, *E. Indies* 941 D5
Aragón □, *Spain* 928 B5
Araguacema, *Brazil* 922 C5
Araguaia →, *Brazil* 922 C5
Araguari, *Brazil* 922 D5
Arāk, *Iran* 936 B3
Arakan Yoma, *Burma* 937 D8
Aral, *Kazakhstan* 932 E7
Aral Sea, *Asia* 932 E7
Aral Tengizi = Aral Sea, *Asia* 932 E7
Aralsk = Aral, *Kazakhstan* 932 E7
Aralskoye More = Aral Sea, *Asia* 932 E7
Aran I., *Ireland* 925 F11
Aransas Pass, *U.S.A.* 919 E7
Arapiraca, *Brazil* 922 C6
Araraquara, *Brazil* 922 E5
Ararat, Mt. = Ağrı Dağı, *Turkey* 931 C6
Araripe, Chapada do, *Brazil* 922 C5
Arauca →, *Venezuela* 922 B3
Arbīl, *Iraq* 936 B3
Arbroath, *U.K.* 925 E6
Arcachon, *France* 926 D3
Archangel = Arkhangelsk, *Russia* 932 C5
Arctic Bay, *Canada* 917 A11
Arctic Ocean, *Arctic* 944 B17
Arctic Red River = Tsiigehtchic, *Canada* 916 B6
Ardabīl, *Iran* 936 B3
Ardee, *Ireland* 925 H13
Ardenne, *Belgium* 927 D2
Ardennes = Ardenne, *Belgium* 927 D2
Arderin, *Ireland* 925 H12
Ardmore, *U.S.A.* 919 D7
Ardnamurchan, Pt. of, *U.K.* 925 E2
Ardrossan, *U.K.* 925 F4
Ards Pen., *U.K.* 925 G14
Arecibo, *Puerto Rico* 921 d
Arena, Pt., *U.S.A.* 918 C2
Arendal, *Norway* 930 F5
Arequipa, *Peru* 922 D2
Argentan, *France* 926 B3
Argentina ■, *S. Amer.* 923 F3
Argentino, L., *Argentina* 923 H2
Århus, *Denmark* 930 F6
Arica, *Chile* 922 D2
Aripuanã →, *Brazil* 922 C3
Arisaig, *U.K.* 925 E3
Arizona □, *U.S.A.* 918 D4
Arkaig, L., *U.K.* 925 E3
Arkansas □, *U.S.A.* 919 D8
Arkansas →, *U.S.A.* 919 D8
Arkansas City, *U.S.A.* 919 C7
Arkhangelsk, *Russia* 932 C5
Arklow, *Ireland* 925 J13
Arles, *France* 926 E6
Arlon, *Belgium* 927 D2
Armagh, *U.K.* 925 G13
Armavir, *Russia* 931 A6
Armenia ■, *Asia* 932 E5
Arnaud →, *Canada* 917 B12

Châttagâm

Blida, *Algeria* 938 A6
Bloemfontein, *S. Africa* 940 H5
Blois, *France* 926 C4
Bloody Foreland, *Ireland* 925 F11
Bloomington, *Ill., U.S.A.* 919 B9
Bloomington, *Ind., U.S.A.* 919 C9
Blue Mountain Pk., *Jamaica* 920 a
Blue Mts., *Jamaica* 920 a
Blue Mts., *U.S.A.* 918 A3
Blue Nile = Nîl el Azraq →, *Sudan* 939 E12
Blue Ridge Mts., *U.S.A.* 919 C10
Bluefield, *U.S.A.* 919 C10
Bluefields, *Nic.* 921 E8
Blumenau, *Brazil* 923 E5
Blyth, *U.K.* 924 A6
Bo Hai, *China* 934 C6
Boa Vista, *Brazil* 922 B3
Bobo-Dioulasso, *Burkina Faso* 938 F5
Bóbr →, *Poland* 927 B7
Bobruysk = Babruysk, *Belarus* 932 D3
Bochum, *Germany* 927 C3
Boddam, *U.K.* 925 B7
Boden, *Sweden* 930 D8
Bodensee, *Europe* 926 C8
Bodmin, *U.K.* 924 F3
Bodmin Moor, *U.K.* 924 F3
Bodø, *Norway* 930 D6
Bodrum, *Turkey* 931 C3
Bogalusa, *U.S.A.* 919 D9
Boggeragh Mts., *Ireland* 925 J11
Bognor Regis, *U.K.* 924 F7
Bogor, *Indonesia* 941 D2
Bogotá, *Colombia* 922 B2
Bohemian Forest = Böhmerwald, *Germany* 927 D6
Böhmerwald, *Germany* 927 D6
Bohol Sea, *Phil.* 941 C4
Boise, *U.S.A.* 918 B3
Bole, *China* 934 B3
Bolivia ■, *S. Amer.* 922 D3
Bologna, *Italy* 929 B3
Bologoye, *Russia* 932 D4
Bolshoy Kavkas = Caucasus Mountains, *Eurasia* 932 E5
Bolton, *U.K.* 924 C5
Bolu, *Turkey* 931 B4
Bolvadin, *Turkey* 931 C4
Bolzano, *Italy* 929 A3
Boma, *Dem. Rep. of the Congo* 940 D2
Bombala, *Australia* 942 H8
Bombay = Mumbai, *India* 937 D6
Bonaire, *Neth. Ant.* 921 E11
Bonavista, *Canada* 917 D14
Bo'ness, *U.K.* 925 E5
Bongor, *Chad* 939 F9
Bonifacio, *France* 926 F8
Bonn, *Germany* 927 C3
Boosaaso = Bosaso, *Somali Rep.* 936 D3
Boothia, Gulf of, *Canada* 917 A11
Boothia Pen., *Canada* 916 A10
Bootle, *U.K.* 924 C4
Borås, *Sweden* 930 F6
Bordeaux, *France* 926 D3
Borden Pen., *Canada* 917 A11
Borders = Scottish Borders □, *U.K.* 925 F6
Borger, *U.S.A.* 918 C6
Borhoyn Tal, *Mongolia* 934 B6
Borisoglebsk, *Russia* 932 D5
Borisov = Barysaw, *Belarus* 930 C9
Borkou, *Chad* 939 E9
Borneo, *E. Indies* 941 C3
Bornholm, *Denmark* 930 F7
Borth, *U.K.* 924 D3
Bosaso, *Somali Rep.* 936 D3
Boscastle, *U.K.* 924 F3
Boscobelle, *Barbados* 921 g
Bosna i Hercegovina = Bosnia-Herzegovina ■, *Europe* 929 B7
Bosnia-Herzegovina ■, *Europe* 929 B7
Bosporus = İstanbul Boğazı, *Turkey* 931 B3
Bosten Hu, *China* 934 B3
Boston, *U.K.* 924 D7
Boston, *U.S.A.* 919 B12
Bothnia, G. of, *Europe* 930 E8
Botletle →, *Botswana* 940 G4
Botoşani, *Romania* 931 A3
Botswana ■, *Africa* 940 G4
Bouaké, *Ivory C.* 938 G4
Bouârfa, *Morocco* 938 B5
Bougainville I., *Papua N. G.* 943 B10
Bougie = Bejaïa, *Algeria* 938 A7
Bouillante, *Guadeloupe* 920 b
Boulder, *U.S.A.* 918 B5
Boulder Dam = Hoover Dam, *U.S.A.* 918 C4
Boulogne-sur-Mer, *France* 926 A4
Bourbonnais, *France* 926 C5
Bourg-en-Bresse, *France* 926 C6
Bourges, *France* 926 C5
Bourgogne, *France* 926 C6
Bourke, *Australia* 942 G8
Bourne, *U.K.* 924 D7
Bournemouth, *U.K.* 924 F6
Bouvet I. = Bouvetøya, *Antarctica* 915 G10
Bouvetøya, *Antarctica* 915 G10
Bow →, *Canada* 916 C8
Bowland, Forest of, *U.K.* 924 C5
Bowling Green, *U.S.A.* 919 C9
Bowmore, *U.K.* 925 F2
Boyle, *Ireland* 925 H11
Boyne →, *Ireland* 925 H13
Bozeman, *U.S.A.* 918 A4
Bozen = Bolzano, *Italy* 929 A3
Bracadale, L., *U.K.* 925 D2
Bräcke, *Sweden* 930 E7
Bradenton, *U.S.A.* 919 E10
Bradford, *U.K.* 924 C6
Braga, *Portugal* 928 B1
Bragança, *Brazil* 922 C5
Brahmapur, *India* 937 D7
Brahmaputra →, *Asia* 937 C7
Braich-y-pwll, *U.K.* 924 D3
Brăila, *Romania* 931 A3
Brainerd, *U.S.A.* 919 A8
Braintree, *U.K.* 924 E8
Brampton, *U.K.* 924 B5
Branco →, *Brazil* 922 C3
Brandenburg, *Germany* 927 B6
Brandenburg □, *Germany* 927 B6
Brandon, *Canada* 916 D10
Brandon B., *Ireland* 925 J9
Brandon Mt., *Ireland* 925 J9
Brasília, *Brazil* 922 D5
Braşov, *Romania* 931 A3
Bratislava, *Slovak Rep.* 927 D8
Bratsk, *Russia* 933 D11
Braunschweig, *Germany* 927 B5
Braunton, *U.K.* 924 E3
Bravo del Norte, Rio = Grande, Rio →, *U.S.A.* 919 E7
Bray, *Ireland* 925 H13
Brazil ■, *S. Amer.* 922 D4
Brazos →, *U.S.A.* 919 E7
Brazzaville, *Congo* 940 C3
Brechin, *U.K.* 925 E6
Brecon, *U.K.* 924 E4
Brecon Beacons, *U.K.* 924 E4
Breda, *Neths.* 927 C2
Bregenz, *Austria* 927 E4
Breiðafjörður, *Iceland* 930 A1
Bremen, *Germany* 927 B4
Bremerhaven, *Germany* 927 B4
Bremerton, *U.S.A.* 918 A2
Brennerpass, *Austria* 927 E5
Brentwood, *U.K.* 924 E8
Bréscia, *Italy* 926 D9
Breslau = Wrocław, *Poland* 927 C8
Bressay, *U.K.* 925 A7
Brest, *Belarus* 932 D3
Brest, *France* 926 B1
Brest-Litovsk = Brest, *Belarus* 932 D3
Bretagne, *France* 926 B2
Breton Sd., *U.S.A.* 919 E9
Brezhnev = Naberezhnyye Chelny, *Russia* 932 D6
Briançon, *France* 926 D7
Bridgefield, *Barbados* 921 g
Bridgend, *U.K.* 924 E4
Bridgeport, *U.S.A.* 919 B12
Bridgetown, *Barbados* 921 g
Bridgewater, *Canada* 917 D13
Bridgwater, *U.K.* 924 E5
Bridgwater B., *U.K.* 924 E4
Bridlington, *U.K.* 924 B7
Bridlington B., *U.K.* 924 B7
Brigham City, *U.S.A.* 918 B4
Brighton, *U.K.* 924 F7
Bríndisi, *Italy* 929 D6
Brisbane, *Australia* 942 F9
Bristol, *U.K.* 924 E5
Bristol B., *U.S.A.* 916 C4
Bristol Channel, *U.K.* 924 E3
British Columbia □, *Canada* 916 C7
British Virgin Is. ⊠, *W. Indies* 921 e
Brittany = Bretagne, *France* 926 B2
Brive-la-Gaillarde, *France* 926 D4
Brixham, *U.K.* 924 F4
Brno, *Czech Rep.* 927 D8
Broach = Bharuch, *India* 937 C6
Broad B., *U.K.* 925 C2
Broad Haven, *Ireland* 925 G10
Broad Law, *U.K.* 925 F5
Brochet, *Canada* 916 C9
Brocken, *Germany* 927 C5
Brodeur Pen., *Canada* 917 A11
Brodick, *U.K.* 925 F3
Broken Hill = Kabwe, *Zambia* 940 E5
Broken Hill, *Australia* 942 G7
Bromsgrove, *U.K.* 924 D5
Brookhaven, *U.S.A.* 919 D8
Brookings, *U.S.A.* 919 B7
Brooks, *Canada* 916 C8
Brooks Range, *U.S.A.* 916 B5
Broom, L., *U.K.* 925 D3
Broome, *Australia* 942 D3
Brora, *U.K.* 925 C5
Brora →, *U.K.* 925 C5
Brosna →, *Ireland* 925 H12
Brough, *U.K.* 924 B5
Brough Hd., *U.K.* 925 B5
Broughton Island = Qikiqtarjuaq, *Canada* 917 B13
Brownsville, *U.S.A.* 919 E7
Brownwood, *U.S.A.* 918 D7
Bruay-la-Buissière, *France* 926 A5
Bruce, Mt., *Australia* 942 E2
Bruges = Brugge, *Belgium* 927 C1
Brugge, *Belgium* 927 C1
Brunei = Bandar Seri Begawan, *Brunei* 941 C3
Brunei ■, *Asia* 941 C3
Brunswick = Braunschweig, *Germany* 927 B5
Brunswick, *U.S.A.* 919 D10
Brussel, *Belgium* 927 C2
Brussels = Brussel, *Belgium* 927 C2
Bruxelles = Brussel, *Belgium* 927 C2
Bryan, *U.S.A.* 919 D7
Bryansk, *Russia* 932 D4
Bucaramanga, *Colombia* 922 B2
Buchan Ness, *U.K.* 925 D7
Bucharest = Bucureşti, *Romania* 931 B3
Buckhaven, *U.K.* 925 E5
Buckie, *U.K.* 925 D6
Buckingham, *U.K.* 924 E7
Bucureşti, *Romania* 931 B3
Budapest, *Hungary* 927 E9
Bude, *U.K.* 924 F3
Buenaventura, *Colombia* 922 B2
Buenos Aires, *Argentina* 923 F4
Buenos Aires, L., *Chile* 923 G2
Buffalo, *N.Y., U.S.A.* 919 B11
Buffalo, *Wyo., U.S.A.* 918 B5
Bug = Buh →, *Ukraine* 931 A4
Bug →, *Poland* 930 G8
Bugun Shara, *Mongolia* 934 B5
Buguruslan, *Russia* 932 D6
Buh →, *Ukraine* 931 A4
Builth Wells, *U.K.* 924 D4
Buir Nur, *Mongolia* 934 B6
Bujumbura, *Burundi* 940 C5
Bukavu, *Dem. Rep. of the Congo* 940 C5
Bukhara = Bukhoro, *Uzbekistan* 932 F7
Bukhoro, *Uzbekistan* 932 F7
Bukittinggi, *Indonesia* 941 D2
Bulawayo, *Zimbabwe* 940 G5
Bulgaria ■, *Europe* 931 B3
Bullhead City, *U.S.A.* 918 C4
Bunbury, *Australia* 942 G2
Bunclody, *Ireland* 925 J13
Buncrana, *Ireland* 925 F12
Bundaberg, *Australia* 942 E9
Bundoran, *Ireland* 925 G11
Buon Ma Thuot, *Vietnam* 941 B2
Bûr Safâga, *Egypt* 939 C12
Bûr Sa'îd, *Egypt* 939 B12
Bûr Sûdân, *Sudan* 939 E13
Burao, *Somali Rep.* 936 E3
Buraydah, *Si. Arabia* 936 C3
Burdur, *Turkey* 931 C4
Bure →, *U.K.* 924 D9
Burgas, *Bulgaria* 931 B3
Burgos, *Spain* 928 A4
Burgundy = Bourgogne, *France* 926 C6
Burkina Faso ■, *Africa* 938 F5
Burley, *U.S.A.* 918 B4
Burlington, *Colo., U.S.A.* 918 C6
Burlington, *Iowa, U.S.A.* 919 B8
Burlington, *Vt., U.S.A.* 919 B12
Burma ■, *Asia* 937 C8
Burnham-on-Sea, *U.K.* 924 E5
Burnie, *Australia* 942 J8
Burnley, *U.K.* 924 C5
Burns, *U.S.A.* 918 B3
Burnside →, *Canada* 916 B9
Burray, *U.K.* 925 C6
Burrow Hd., *U.K.* 925 G4
Bursa, *Turkey* 931 B3
Burton upon Trent, *U.K.* 924 D6
Buru, *Indonesia* 941 D4
Burundi ■, *Africa* 940 C6
Burwick, *U.K.* 925 C6
Bury, *U.K.* 924 C5
Bury St. Edmunds, *U.K.* 924 D8
Buryatia □, *Russia* 933 D11
Busan = Pusan, *S. Korea* 934 C7
Büshehr, *Iran* 936 C4
Bushire = Büshehr, *Iran* 936 C4
Bute, *U.K.* 925 F3
Butha Qi, *China* 934 B7
Buton, *Indonesia* 941 D4
Butte, *U.S.A.* 918 A4
Butterworth, *Malaysia* 941 C2
Butuan, *Phil.* 941 C4
Butung = Buton, *Indonesia* 941 D4
Buxton, *U.K.* 924 C6
Buzău, *Romania* 931 A3
Buzuluk, *Russia* 932 D6
Bydgoszcz, *Poland* 927 B9
Byelarus = Belarus ■, *Europe* 932 D3
Byelorussia = Belarus ■, *Europe* 932 D3
Bylot I., *Canada* 917 A12
Bytom, *Poland* 927 C9

C

Ca Mau, *Vietnam* 941 C2
Cabanatuan, *Phil.* 941 B4
Cabedelo, *Brazil* 922 C6
Cabimas, *Venezuela* 922 A2
Cabinda □, *Angola* 940 D2
Cabonga, Réservoir, *Canada* 917 D12
Cabora Bassa Dam = Cahora Bassa, Reprêsa de, *Mozam.* 940 F6
Cabot Str., *Canada* 917 D14
Cáceres, *Spain* 928 C2
Cachimbo, Serra do, *Brazil* 922 C4
Cachoeira do Sul, *Brazil* 923 F4
Cachoeiro de Itapemirim, *Brazil* 922 E5
Cader Idris, *U.K.* 924 D4
Cádiz, *Spain* 928 D2
Caen, *France* 926 B3
Caernarfon, *U.K.* 924 C3
Caernarfon B., *U.K.* 924 C3
Caernarvon = Caernarfon, *U.K.* 924 C3
Caerphilly, *U.K.* 924 E4
Cagayan de Oro, *Phil.* 941 C4
Cágliari, *Italy* 929 E2
Caguas, *Puerto Rico* 921 d
Caha Mts., *Ireland* 925 K10
Caher, *Ireland* 925 J12
Caherciveen, *Ireland* 925 K9
Cahora Bassa, Reprêsa de, *Mozam.* 940 F6
Cahore Pt., *Ireland* 925 J13
Cahors, *France* 926 D4
Cairn Gorm, *U.K.* 925 D5
Cairngorm Mts., *U.K.* 925 D5
Cairnryan, *U.K.* 925 G3
Cairns, *Australia* 942 D8
Cairo = El Qâhira, *Egypt* 939 B12
Caja de Muertos, I., *Puerto Rico* 921 d
Cajamarca, *Peru* 922 C2
Calabar, *Nigeria* 938 H7
Calábria □, *Italy* 929 E6
Calais, *France* 926 A4
Calama, *Chile* 923 E3
Calamar, *Colombia* 922 A2
Calamian Group, *Phil.* 941 B3
Calapan, *Phil.* 941 B4
Calbayog, *Phil.* 941 B4
Calcutta = Kolkata, *India* 937 C7
Caldera, *Chile* 923 E2
Caldwell, *U.S.A.* 918 B3
Calf of Man, *U.K.* 924 B3
Calgary, *Canada* 916 C8
Cali, *Colombia* 922 B2
Calicut, *India* 937 D6
California □, *U.S.A.* 918 C2
California, G. de, *Mexico* 920 B2
Callan, *Ireland* 925 J12
Callander, *U.K.* 925 E4
Callao, *Peru* 922 D2
Caltanissetta, *Italy* 929 F5
Calvi, *France* 926 E8
Calvinia, *S. Africa* 940 J3
Cam →, *U.K.* 924 D8
Cam Ranh, *Vietnam* 941 B2
Camagüey, *Cuba* 921 C9
Cambay, G. of = Khambhat, G. of, *India* 937 C6
Cambodia ■, *Asia* 941 B2
Camborne, *U.K.* 924 F2
Cambrai, *France* 926 A5
Cambrian Mts., *U.K.* 924 D4
Cambridge, *Jamaica* 920 a
Cambridge, *U.K.* 924 D8
Cambridge Bay = Ikaluktutiak, *Canada* 916 B9
Camden, *U.S.A.* 919 D8
Cameroon ■, *Africa* 939 G7
Cameroun, Mt., *Cameroon* 940 B1
Camocim, *Brazil* 922 C5
Campana, I., *Chile* 923 G2
Campánia □, *Italy* 929 D5
Campbell River, *Canada* 916 C7
Campbellton, *Canada* 917 D13
Campbeltown, *U.K.* 925 F3
Campeche, *Mexico* 920 D6
Campeche, Golfo de, *Mexico* 920 D6
Campina Grande, *Brazil* 922 C6
Campinas, *Brazil* 923 E5
Campo Grande, *Brazil* 922 E4
Campos, *Brazil* 922 E5
Camrose, *Canada* 916 C8
Can Tho, *Vietnam* 941 B2
Canada ■, *N. Amer.* 916 C10
Canadian →, *U.S.A.* 919 C7
Çanakkale, *Turkey* 931 B3
Çanakkale Boğazı, *Turkey* 931 B3
Cananea, *Mexico* 920 A2
Canarias, Is., *Atl. Oc.* 938 C2
Canaries, *St. Lucia* 921 f
Canary Is. = Canarias, Is., *Atl. Oc.* 938 C2
Canaveral, C., *U.S.A.* 919 E10
Canberra, *Australia* 942 H8
Cancún, *Mexico* 920 C7
Candia = Iráklion, *Greece* 931 C3
Caniapiscau →, *Canada* 917 C13
Caniapiscau, L. de, *Canada* 917 C13
Çankırı, *Turkey* 931 B4
Canna, *U.K.* 925 D2
Cannes, *France* 926 E7
Cannock, *U.K.* 924 D5
Canoas, *Brazil* 923 E4
Canon City, *U.S.A.* 918 C5
Canora, *Canada* 916 C9
Cantabria □, *Spain* 928 A4
Cantabrian Mts. = Cantábrica, Cordillera, *Spain* 928 A3
Cantábrica, Cordillera, *Spain* 928 A3
Canterbury, *U.K.* 924 E9
Canton = Guangzhou, *China* 934 D6
Canton, *U.S.A.* 919 B10
Cap-Haïtien, *Haiti* 921 D10
Cap Pt., *St. Lucia* 921 f
Cape Breton I., *Canada* 917 D13
Cape Coast, *Ghana* 938 G5
Cape Dorset, *Canada* 917 B12
Cape Fear →, *U.S.A.* 919 D11
Cape May Point, *U.S.A.* 919 C12
Cape Town, *S. Africa* 940 J3
Cape Verde Is. ■, *Atl. Oc.* 914 D8
Cape York Peninsula, *Australia* 942 C7
Capesterre, *Guadeloupe* 920 b
Capesterre-Belle-Eau, *Guadeloupe* 920 b
Capri, *Italy* 929 D5
Caprivi Strip, *Namibia* 940 F4
Caquetá →, *Colombia* 922 C3
Caracas, *Venezuela* 922 A3
Caratasca, L., *Honduras* 921 D8
Caratinga, *Brazil* 922 D5
Caravelas, *Brazil* 922 D6
Caravelle, Presqu'île de la, *Martinique* 920 c
Carbonear, *Canada* 917 D14
Carcassonne, *France* 926 E5
Carcross, *Canada* 916 B6
Cárdenas, *Cuba* 921 C8
Cardiff, *U.K.* 924 E4
Cardigan, *U.K.* 924 D3
Cardigan B., *U.K.* 924 D3
Cardston, *Canada* 916 D8
Cariacica, *Brazil* 922 E5
Caribbean Sea, *W. Indies* 921 E10
Cariboo Mts., *Canada* 916 C7
Caribou, *U.S.A.* 919 A13
Caribou Mts., *Canada* 916 C8
Carinthia = Kärnten □, *Austria* 927 E6
Carlingford L., *U.K.* 925 G13
Carlisle, *U.K.* 924 B5
Carlisle B., *Barbados* 921 g
Carlow, *Ireland* 925 J13
Carlsbad, *U.S.A.* 918 D6
Carluke, *U.K.* 925 F5
Carmacks, *Canada* 916 B6
Carmarthen, *U.K.* 924 E3
Carmarthen B., *U.K.* 924 E3
Carmaux, *France* 926 D5
Carn Eige, *U.K.* 925 D3
Carnac, *France* 926 C2
Carnarvon, *Australia* 942 E1
Carnarvon, *S. Africa* 940 J4
Carndonagh, *Ireland* 925 F12
Carnegie, L., *Australia* 942 F3
Carnoustie, *U.K.* 925 E6
Carnsore Pt., *Ireland* 925 J13
Carolina, *Puerto Rico* 921 d
Caroline Is., *Micronesia* 915 D17
Carondelet, *Kiribati* 943 B16
Caroni →, *Venezuela* 922 B3
Carpathians, *Europe* 931 A2
Carpaţii Meridionali, *Romania* 931 A3
Carpentaria, G. of, *Australia* 942 C6
Carpentras, *France* 926 D6
Carrauntoohill, *Ireland* 925 J10
Carrick-on-Shannon, *Ireland* 925 H11
Carrick-on-Suir, *Ireland* 925 J12
Carrickfergus, *U.K.* 925 G14
Carrickmacross, *Ireland* 925 H13
Carron →, *U.K.* 925 D4
Carson City, *U.S.A.* 918 C3
Carson Sink, *U.S.A.* 918 C3
Cartagena, *Colombia* 922 A2
Cartagena, *Spain* 928 D5
Cartago, *Colombia* 922 B2
Carthage, *Tunisia* 939 A8
Carthage, *U.S.A.* 919 C8
Cartwright, *Canada* 917 C14
Carúpano, *Venezuela* 922 A3
Casa Grande, *U.S.A.* 918 D4
Casablanca, *Morocco* 938 B4
Cascade Ra., *U.S.A.* 918 A2
Cascavel, *Brazil* 923 E4
Caseyr, Raas = Asir, Ras, *Somali Rep.* 936 D4
Cashel, *Ireland* 925 J12
Casiquiare →, *Venezuela* 922 B3
Casper, *U.S.A.* 918 B5
Caspian Sea, *Eurasia* 932 E6
Cassiar Mts., *Canada* 916 C6
Castelló de la Plana, *Spain* 928 C5
Castelsarrasin, *France* 926 E4
Castilla-La Mancha □, *Spain* 928 C4
Castilla y Leon □, *Spain* 928 B3
Castle Douglas, *U.K.* 925 G5
Castlebar, *Ireland* 925 H10
Castleblaney, *Ireland* 925 G13
Castlederg, *U.K.* 925 G12
Castleford, *U.K.* 924 C6
Castlepollard, *Ireland* 925 H12
Castlerea, *Ireland* 925 H11
Castletown, *U.K.* 924 B3
Castletown Bearhaven, *Ireland* 925 K10
Castres, *France* 926 E5
Castries, *St. Lucia* 921 f
Castro, *Chile* 923 G2
Cat I., *Bahamas* 921 C9
Catalão, *Brazil* 922 D5
Catalonia = Cataluña □, *Spain* 928 B6
Cataluña □, *Spain* 928 B6
Catamarca, *Argentina* 923 E3
Catanduanes □, *Phil.* 941 B4
Catánia, *Italy* 929 F5
Catanzaro, *Italy* 929 E6
Catoche, C., *Mexico* 920 C7
Catskill Mts., *U.S.A.* 919 B12
Caucasus Mountains, *Eurasia* 932 E5
Caura →, *Venezuela* 922 B3
Cavan, *Ireland* 925 F12
Caviana, I., *Brazil* 922 B4
Cawnpore = Kanpur, *India* 937 C7
Caxias, *Brazil* 922 C5
Caxias do Sul, *Brazil* 923 E4
Cayenne, *Fr. Guiana* 922 B4
Cayey, *Puerto Rico* 921 d
Cayman Is. ⊠, *W. Indies* 921 D8
Ceanannus Mor, *Ireland* 925 H13
Ceará = Fortaleza, *Brazil* 922 C6
Ceará □, *Brazil* 922 C6
Cebu, *Phil.* 941 B4
Cedar City, *U.S.A.* 918 C4
Cedar L., *Canada* 916 C10
Cedar Rapids, *U.S.A.* 919 B8
Cegléd, *Hungary* 927 E9
Celaya, *Mexico* 920 C4
Celebes = Sulawesi □, *Indonesia* 941 D4
Celebes Sea, *Indonesia* 941 C4
Central, Cordillera, *Puerto Rico* 921 d
Central African Rep. ■, *Africa* 939 G9
Central America, *America* 914 D5
Central Makran Range, *Pakistan* 936 C5
Centralia, *U.S.A.* 918 A2
Ceram = Seram, *Indonesia* 941 D4
Ceram Sea = Seram Sea, *Indonesia* 941 D4
Ceredigion □, *U.K.* 924 D3
Cerignola, *Italy* 929 D5
České Budějovice, *Czech Rep.* 927 D7
Çeşme, *Turkey* 931 C3
Ceuta, *N. Afr.* 928 E3
Ceve-i-Ra, *Fiji* 943 E13
Cévennes, *France* 926 D5
Ceylon = Sri Lanka ■, *Asia* 937 E7
Chachapoyas, *Peru* 922 C2
Chaco Austral, *S. Amer.* 923 E3
Chaco Boreal, *S. Amer.* 923 E4
Chaco Central, *S. Amer.* 923 E3
Chad ■, *Africa* 939 F8
Chad, L. = Tchad, L., *Chad* 939 F8
Chadron, *U.S.A.* 918 B6
Chalon-sur-Saône, *France* 926 C6
Châlons-en-Champagne, *France* 926 B6
Chambal →, *India* 937 C6
Chambéry, *France* 926 D6
Chamonix-Mont Blanc, *France* 926 D7
Champagne, *France* 926 B6
Champaign, *U.S.A.* 919 B9
Champlain, L., *U.S.A.* 919 B12
Chañaral, *Chile* 923 E2
Chancery Lane, *Barbados* 921 g
Chandigarh, *India* 937 B6
Ch'ang Chiang = Chang Jiang →, *China* 934 C7
Chang Jiang →, *China* 934 C7
Changchiak'ou = Zhangjiakou, *China* 934 B6
Ch'angchou = Changzhou, *China* 934 C6
Changchun, *China* 934 B7
Changde, *China* 934 D6
Changhai = Shanghai, *China* 934 C7
Changhua, *Taiwan* 934 D7
Changsha, *China* 934 D6
Changzhi, *China* 934 C6
Changzhou, *China* 934 C6
Channel Is., *U.K.* 926 B2
Channel Is., *U.S.A.* 918 D2
Channel-Port aux Basques, *Canada* 917 D14
Chantrey Inlet, *Canada* 916 B10
Chaozhou, *China* 934 D6
Chapala, L. de, *Mexico* 920 C4
Chapayevsk, *Russia* 932 D5
Chapleau, *Canada* 917 D11
Chapra = Chhapra, *India* 937 C7
Charaña, *Bolivia* 922 D3
Chard, *U.K.* 924 F5
Chardzhou = Chärjew, *Turkmenistan* 932 F7
Chari →, *Chad* 939 F8
Chärjew, *Turkmenistan* 932 F7
Charleroi, *Belgium* 927 C2
Charles, C., *U.S.A.* 919 C11
Charles City, *U.S.A.* 919 B8
Charleston, *S.C., U.S.A.* 919 D11
Charleston, *W. Va., U.S.A.* 919 C10
Charlestown, *Ireland* 925 H11
Charleville = Rath Luirc, *Ireland* 925 J11
Charleville, *Australia* 942 F8
Charleville-Mézières, *France* 926 B6
Charlotte, *U.S.A.* 919 C10
Charlotte Amalie, *U.S. Virgin Is.* 921 e
Charlotte Harbor, *U.S.A.* 919 E10
Charlottesville, *U.S.A.* 919 C11
Charlottetown, *Canada* 917 D13
Charlton I., *Canada* 917 C12
Charolles, *France* 926 C6
Charters Towers, *Australia* 942 E8
Chartres, *France* 926 B4
Chascomús, *Argentina* 923 F4
Châteaubriant, *France* 926 C3
Châteaulin, *France* 926 B1
Châteauroux, *France* 926 C4
Châteaux, Pte. des, *Guadeloupe* 920 b
Châtellerault, *France* 926 C4
Chatham = Miramichi, *Canada* 917 D13
Chatham, *U.K.* 924 E8
Chatham Is., *Pac. Oc.* 943 J15
Châttagâm = Chittagong, *Bangla.* 937 C8

Fort Nelson

Detroit, U.S.A. 919 B10
Deutsche Bucht, Germany 927 A4
Deventer, Neths. 927 B3
Deveron →, U.K. 925 D6
Devils Lake, U.S.A. 918 A7
Devizes, U.K. 924 E6
Devon □, U.K. 924 F4
Devon I., Canada 944 B2
Dewey, Puerto Rico 921 d
Dezfūl, Iran 936 B3
Dezhneva, Mys, Russia 933 C19
Dhaka, Bangla. 937 C8
Dhanbad, India 937 C7
Dharwad, India 937 D6
Dhaulagiri, Nepal 937 C7
Dhodhekánisos, Greece 931 C3
Dhule, India 937 C6
Diamantina, Brazil 922 D5
Diamantina →, Australia 942 F6
Diamantino, Brazil 922 D4
Dibrugarh, India 937 C8
Dickinson, U.S.A. 918 A6
Diefenbaker, L., Canada 916 C9
Diego Garcia, Ind. Oc. 915 E13
Dieppe, France 926 B4
Digby, Canada 917 D13
Digne-les-Bains, France 926 D7
Dihang = Brahmaputra →, Asia 937 C7
Dijlah, Nahr →, Asia 936 B3
Dijon, France 926 C6
Dili, E. Timor 941 D4
Dilli = Delhi, India 937 C6
Dillingham, U.S.A. 916 C4
Dimashq, Syria 936 B2
Dinan, France 926 B2
Dinant, Belgium 927 C2
Dinara Planina, Croatia 929 C6
Dinaric Alps = Dinara Planina, Croatia 929 C6
Dingle, Ireland 925 J9
Dingle B., Ireland 925 J9
Dingwall, U.K. 925 D4
Dire Dawa, Ethiopia 936 E3
Dirranbandi, Australia 942 F8
Disappointment, C., U.S.A. 918 A2
Disappointment, L., Australia 942 E3
Disko = Qeqertarsuaq, Greenland 917 B5
Diss, U.K. 924 D9
Distrito Federal □, Brazil 922 D5
Dixon Entrance, U.S.A. 916 C6
Diyarbakır, Turkey 931 C6
Djakarta = Jakarta, Indonesia 941 D2
Djawa = Jawa, Indonesia 941 D3
Djerba, I. de, Tunisia 939 B8
Djerid, Chott, Tunisia 938 B7
Djibouti, Djibouti 936 D3
Djibouti ■, Africa 936 D3
Dnepr = Dnipro →, Ukraine 931 A4
Dneprodzerzhinsk = Dniprodzerzhynsk, Ukraine 931 A4
Dnepropetrovsk = Dnipropetrovsk, Ukraine 931 A5
Dnestr = Dnister →, Europe 932 E4
Dnestrovski = Belgorod, Russia 932 D4
Dnieper = Dnipro →, Ukraine 931 A4
Dniester = Dnister →, Europe 932 E4
Dnipro →, Ukraine 931 A4
Dniprodzerzhynsk, Ukraine 931 A4
Dnipropetrovsk, Ukraine 931 A5
Dnister →, Europe 932 E4
Dnyapro = Dnipro →, Ukraine 931 A4
Doba, Chad 939 G9
Doberai, Jazirah, Indonesia 941 D5
Dodecanese = Dhodhekánisos, Greece 931 C3
Dodge City, U.S.A. 918 C6
Dodoma, Tanzania 940 D7
Doha = Ad Dawḥah, Qatar 936 C4
Dolbeau-Mistassini, Canada 917 D12
Dole, France 926 C6
Dolgellau, U.K. 924 D4
Dolgelley = Dolgellau, U.K. 924 D4
Dolomites = Dolomiti, Italy 929 A3
Dolomiti, Italy 929 A3
Dolores, Argentina 923 F4
Dolphin and Union Str., Canada 916 B8
Dominica ■, W. Indies 921 D12
Dominican Rep. ■, W. Indies 921 D10
Don →, Russia 932 E4
Don →, Aberds., U.K. 925 D6
Don →, S. Yorks., U.K. 924 C7
Don Figuero Mts., Jamaica 920 a
Donaghadee, U.K. 925 G14
Donau = Dunărea →, Europe 931 A3
Doncaster, U.K. 924 C6
Dondra Head, Sri Lanka 937 E7
Donegal, Ireland 925 G11
Donegal □, Ireland 925 G12
Donegal B., Ireland 925 G11
Donetsk, Ukraine 931 A5
Dong Hoi, Vietnam 941 B2
Dongbei, China 933 E13
Dongola, Sudan 939 E12
Dongting Hu, China 934 D6
Donostia = Donostia-San Sebastián, Spain 928 A5
Donostia-San Sebastián, Spain 928 A5
Doon →, U.K. 925 F4
Dorchester, U.K. 924 F5
Dorchester, C., Canada 917 B12
Dordogne →, France 926 D3
Dordrecht, Neths. 927 C2
Dornie, U.K. 925 D3
Dornoch, U.K. 925 D4
Dornoch Firth, U.K. 925 D4
Döröö Nuur, Mongolia 934 B4
Dorset □, U.K. 924 F5
Dortmund, Germany 927 C3
Dos Bahías, C., Argentina 923 G3
Dothan, U.S.A. 919 D9
Douai, France 926 A5
Douala, Cameroon 940 B1
Doubs →, France 926 C6
Douglas, U.K. 924 B3
Douglas, U.S.A. 918 D5
Dounreay, U.K. 925 C5
Dourados, Brazil 922 E4
Douro →, Europe 928 B1
Dove →, U.K. 924 D6
Dover, U.K. 924 E9
Dover, Str. of, Europe 924 F9
Dovey = Dyfi →, U.K. 924 D3
Dovrefjell, Norway 930 E5
Down □, U.K. 925 G13
Downpatrick, U.K. 925 G14
Downpatrick Hd., Ireland 925 G10
Draguignan, France 926 E7
Drake Passage, S. Ocean 944 B
Drakensberg, S. Africa 940 J5
Drammen, Norway 930 F6
Drau = Drava →, Croatia 929 B7
Drava →, Croatia 929 B7
Dresden, Germany 927 C6
Dreux, France 926 B4
Driffield, U.K. 924 B7
Drobeta-Turnu Severin, Romania 931 B2
Drogheda, Ireland 925 H13
Droichead Atha = Drogheda, Ireland 925 H13
Droichead Nua, Ireland 925 H13
Droitwich, U.K. 924 D5
Dromore, U.K. 925 G12
Dromore West, Ireland 925 G11
Dronning Maud Land, Antarctica 944 E7
Drumheller, Canada 916 C8
Dry Harbour Mts., Jamaica 920 a
Dryden, Canada 916 D10
Drygalski I., Antarctica 944 D11
Dubai = Dubayy, U.A.E. 936 C4
Dubawnt →, Canada 916 B9
Dubawnt L., Canada 916 B9
Dubayy, U.A.E. 936 C4
Dubbo, Australia 942 G8
Dublin, Ireland 925 H13
Dublin, U.S.A. 919 D10
Dubrovnik, Croatia 929 C7
Dubuque, U.S.A. 919 B8
Dudinka, Russia 933 C9
Dudley, U.K. 924 D5
Duero = Douro →, Europe 928 B1
Dufftown, U.K. 925 D5
Duisburg, Germany 927 C3
Dulce →, Argentina 923 F3
Duluth, U.S.A. 919 A8
Dumbarton, U.K. 925 F4
Dumfries, U.K. 925 F5
Dumyât, Egypt 939 B12
Dún Dealgan = Dundalk, Ireland 925 G13
Dún Laoghaire, Ireland 925 H13
Duna = Dunărea →, Europe 931 A3
Dunaj = Dunărea →, Europe 931 A3
Dunărea →, Europe 931 A3
Dunav = Dunărea →, Europe 931 A3
Dunbar, U.K. 925 E6
Dunblane, U.K. 925 E5
Duncan, U.S.A. 918 D7
Duncansby Head, U.K. 925 C5
Dundalk, Ireland 925 G13
Dundalk Bay, Ireland 925 H13
Dundee, U.K. 925 E6
Dundrum, U.K. 925 G14
Dundrum B., U.K. 925 G14
Dunedin, N.Z. 943 K13
Dunfermline, U.K. 925 E5
Dungannon, U.K. 925 G13
Dungarvan, Ireland 925 J12
Dungarvan Harbour, Ireland 925 J12
Dungeness, U.K. 924 F8
Dunhuang, China 934 B4
Dunkeld, U.K. 925 E5
Dunkerque, France 926 A5
Dunkirk = Dunkerque, France 926 A5
Dúnleary = Dún Laoghaire, Ireland 925 H13
Dunleer, Ireland 925 H13
Dunmanus B., Ireland 925 K10
Dunmanway, Ireland 925 K10
Dunnet Hd., U.K. 925 C5
Dunoon, U.K. 925 F4
Duns, U.K. 925 F6
Dunstable, U.K. 924 E7
Durance →, France 926 E6
Durango, Mexico 920 C4
Durango, U.S.A. 918 C5
Durant, U.S.A. 919 D7
Durazno, Uruguay 923 F4
Durazzo = Durrës, Albania 929 D7
Durban, S. Africa 940 H6
Düren, Germany 927 C3
Durham, U.K. 924 B6
Durham, U.S.A. 919 C11
Durness, U.K. 925 C4
Durrës, Albania 929 D7
Durrow, Ireland 925 J12
Dursey I., Ireland 925 K9
Dushanbe, Tajikistan 932 F7
Düsseldorf, Germany 927 C3
Dutch Harbor, U.S.A. 916 C3
Duyun, China 934 D5
Duzdab = Zāhedān, Iran 936 C5
Dvina, Severnaya →, Russia 932 C5
Dvinsk = Daugavpils, Latvia 932 D3
Dyce, U.K. 925 D6
Dyer, C., Canada 917 B13
Dyersburg, U.S.A. 919 C9
Dyfi →, U.K. 924 D3
Dzamin Üüd = Borhoyn Tal, Mongolia 934 B6
Dzerzhinsk, Russia 932 D5
Dzhambul = Taraz, Kazakhstan 932 E8
Dzhankoy, Ukraine 931 A4
Dzhezkazgan = Zhezqazghan, Kazakhstan 932 E7
Dzhizak = Jizzakh, Uzbekistan 932 E7
Dzhugdzur, Khrebet, Russia 933 D14
Dzungaria = Junggar Pendi, China 934 B3
Dzuumod, Mongolia 934 B5

E

Eagle, U.S.A. 916 B5
Eagle Pass, U.S.A. 918 E6
Earn →, U.K. 925 E5
Earn, L., U.K. 925 E4
East China Sea, Asia 934 C7
East Dereham = Dereham, U.K. 924 D8
East Falkland, Falk. Is. 923 H4
East Indies, Asia 915 E16
East Kilbride, U.K. 925 F4
East London, S. Africa 940 J5
East Main = Eastmain, Canada 917 C12
East Pt., Br. Virgin Is. 921 e
East Retford = Retford, U.K. 924 C7
East Sea = Japan, Sea of, Asia 935 D4
East Siberian Sea, Russia 933 B17
East Timor ■, Asia 941 D4
Eastbourne, U.K. 924 F8
Easter I. = Pascua, I. de, Chile 914 F4
Eastern Ghats, India 937 D6
Eastern Group = Lau Group, Fiji 943 D15
Eastleigh, U.K. 924 F6
Eastmain, Canada 917 C12
Eastmain →, Canada 917 C12
Eau Claire, U.S.A. 919 B8
Eau Claire, L. à l', Canada 917 C12
Ebbw Vale, U.K. 924 E4
Ebetsu, Japan 935 B7
Ebro →, Spain 928 B6
Ech Chéliff, Algeria 938 A6
Echo Bay, Canada 916 B8
Eclipse Sd., Canada 917 A11
Ecuador ■, S. Amer. 922 C2
Ed Damazin, Sudan 939 F12
Ed Dar el Beida = Casablanca, Morocco 938 B4
Eday, U.K. 925 B6
Eddrachillis B., U.K. 925 C3
Eden →, U.K. 924 B4
Edenderry, Ireland 925 H12
Edinburgh, U.K. 925 F5
Edirne, Turkey 931 B3
Edmonton, Canada 916 C8
Edmundston, Canada 917 D13
Edson, Canada 916 C8
Edward, L., Africa 940 C5
Edward VII Land, Antarctica 944 F17
Edwards Plateau, U.S.A. 918 D6
Efate, I., Vanuatu 943 D12
Eger = Cheb, Czech Rep. 927 C6
Eğridir, Turkey 931 C4
Eğridir Gölü, Turkey 931 C4
Egypt ■, Africa 939 C12
Eifel, Germany 927 C3
Eigg, U.K. 925 E2
Eindhoven, Neths. 927 C2
Eire ■, Europe 925 H12
Eivissa, Spain 928 C6
El Aaiún, W. Sahara 938 C3
El 'Alamein, Egypt 939 B11
El Asnam = Ech Chéliff, Algeria 938 A6
El Centro, U.S.A. 918 D3
El Dorado, U.S.A. 919 D8
El Faiyûm, Egypt 939 C12
El Fâsher, Sudan 939 F11
El Ferrol = Ferrol, Spain 928 A1
El Fuerte, Mexico 920 B3
El Giza, Egypt 939 C12
El Iskandarîya, Egypt 939 B11
El Istiwa'iya, Sudan 939 G11
El Jadida, Morocco 938 B4
El Khârga, Egypt 939 C12
El Khartûm, Sudan 939 E12
El Mahalla el Kubra, Egypt 939 B12
El Mansûra, Egypt 939 B12
El Minyâ, Egypt 939 C12
El Obeid, Sudan 939 F12
El Oued, Algeria 938 B7
El Paso, U.S.A. 918 D5
El Qâhira, Egypt 939 B12
El Reno, U.S.A. 918 C7
El Salvador ■, Cent. Amer. 920 E7
El Suweis, Egypt 939 C12
El Tigre, Venezuela 922 B3
El Uqsur, Egypt 939 C12
Elat, Israel 931 E4
Elâzığ, Turkey 931 C5
Elba, Italy 929 C3
Elbe →, Europe 927 B4
Elbert, Mt., U.S.A. 918 C5
Elbeuf, France 926 B4
Elbing = Elbląg, Poland 927 A9
Elbląg, Poland 927 A9
Elbrus, Asia 932 E5
Elburz Mts. = Alborz, Reshteh-ye Kūhhā-ye, Iran 936 B4
Elche, Spain 928 C5
Eldoret, Kenya 940 B7
Elefantes →, Africa 940 G6
Elephant Butte Reservoir, U.S.A. 918 D5
Elephant I., Antarctica 944 D4
Eleuthera, Bahamas 921 C9
Elgin, U.K. 925 D5
Elgin, U.S.A. 919 B9
Elgon, Mt., Africa 940 B6
Elista, Russia 931 A6
Elizabeth City, U.S.A. 919 C11
Elkhart, U.S.A. 919 B9
Elkins, U.S.A. 919 C11
Elko, U.S.A. 918 B3
Ellensburg, U.S.A. 918 A2
Ellerton, Barbados 921 g
Ellesmere I., Canada 944 B3
Ellesmere Port, U.K. 924 C5
Ellice Is. = Tuvalu ■, Pac. Oc. 943 B14
Elliot Lake, Canada 917 D11
Ellon, U.K. 925 D6
Ellore = Eluru, India 937 D7
Ellsworth Land, Antarctica 944 E2
Elmalı, Turkey 931 C3
Elmira, U.S.A. 919 B11
Eluru, India 937 D7
Elx = Elche, Spain 928 C5
Ely, U.K. 924 D8
Ely, U.S.A. 918 C4
eMalahleni, S. Africa 940 H5
Emāmrūd, Iran 936 B4
Embarcación, Argentina 923 E3
Emden, Germany 927 B3
Emerald, Australia 942 E8
Emmen, Neths. 927 B3
Emmonak, U.S.A. 916 B3
Empalme, Mexico 920 B2
Empangeni, S. Africa 940 H6
Empedrado, Argentina 923 E4
Emporia, U.S.A. 919 C7
Empty Quarter = Rub' al Khālī, Si. Arabia 936 D3
Ems →, Germany 927 B3
Enard B., U.K. 925 C3
Enare = Inarijärvi, Finland 930 D9
Encarnación, Paraguay 923 E4
Encounter B., Australia 942 H6
Ende, Indonesia 941 D4
Enderby Land, Antarctica 944 D9
Enez, Turkey 931 B3
Enfer, Pte. d', Martinique 920 c
Engadin, Switz. 926 C9
Engels, Russia 932 D5
Enggano, Indonesia 941 D2
England □, U.K. 924 D6
English →, Canada 916 C10
English Channel, Europe 924 F6
Enid, U.S.A. 918 C7
Ennadai L., Canada 916 B9
Ennedi, Chad 939 E10
Ennis, Ireland 925 J11
Enniscorthy, Ireland 925 J13
Enniskillen, U.K. 925 G12
Ennistimon, Ireland 925 J10
Enns →, Austria 927 D7
Enschede, Neths. 927 B3
Ensenada, Mexico 920 A1
Entebbe, Uganda 940 B6
Enugu, Nigeria 938 G7
Épernay, France 926 B5
Épinal, France 926 B7
Epsom, U.K. 924 E7
Equatorial Guinea ■, Africa 940 B1
Er Rachidia, Morocco 938 B5
Erāwadī Myit = Irrawaddy →, Burma 937 D8
Erbil = Arbīl, Iraq 936 B3
Erebus, Mt., Antarctica 944 E15
Ereğli, Konya, Turkey 931 C4
Ereğli, Zonguldak, Turkey 931 B4
Erfurt, Germany 927 C5
Eriboll, L., U.K. 925 C4
Erie, U.S.A. 919 B10
Erie, L., N. Amer. 919 B10
Eriskay, U.K. 925 D1
Eritrea ■, Africa 936 D2
Erlangen, Germany 927 D5
Erne →, Ireland 925 G11
Erne, Lower L., U.K. 925 G12
Erne, Upper L., U.K. 925 G12
Erris Hd., Ireland 925 G9
Erromango, Vanuatu 943 D12
Ertis = Irtysh →, Russia 932 C7
Erzgebirge, Germany 927 C6
Erzincan, Turkey 931 C5
Erzurum, Turkey 931 C6
Es Sahrâ' Esh Sharqîya, Egypt 939 C12
Es Sînâ', Egypt 939 C12
Esbjerg, Denmark 930 F5
Escanaba, U.S.A. 919 A9
Esch-sur-Alzette, Lux. 926 B6
Escuinapa, Mexico 920 C3
Escuintla, Guatemala 920 E6
Eşfahān, Iran 936 B4
Esh Sham = Dimashq, Syria 936 B2
Esha Ness, U.K. 925 A7
Esk →, Cumb., U.K. 925 G5
Esk →, N. Yorks., U.K. 924 B7
Esker, Canada 917 C13
Eskilstuna, Sweden 930 F7
Eskimo Point = Arviat, Canada 916 B10
Eskişehir, Turkey 931 C4
Esperance, Australia 942 G3
Esperance B., St. Lucia 921 f
Esperanza, Puerto Rico 921 d
Espinazo, Sierra del = Espinhaço, Serra do, Brazil 922 D5
Espinhaço, Serra do, Brazil 922 D5
Espírito Santo □, Brazil 922 E5
Espíritu Santo, Vanuatu 943 D12
Espoo, Finland 930 E8
Essaouira, Morocco 938 B4
Essen, Germany 927 C3
Essequibo →, Guyana 922 B4
Essex □, U.K. 924 E8
Estados, I. de Los, Argentina 923 H3
Estevan, Canada 916 D9
Estonia ■, Europe 932 D3
Estrela, Serra da, Portugal 928 B2
Estrondo, Serra do, Brazil 922 C5
Etawah, India 937 C6
eThekwini = Durban, S. Africa 940 H6
Ethiopia ■, Africa 940 A8
Etive, L., U.K. 925 E3
Etna, Italy 929 F5
Etosha Pan, Namibia 940 F3
Ettrick Water →, U.K. 925 F6
Euboea = Évvoia, Greece 931 C2
Eugene, U.S.A. 918 B2
Euphrates = Furāt, Nahr al →, Asia 936 B3
Eureka, U.S.A. 918 B2
Europa, Île, Ind. Oc. 940 G8
Europa, Picos de, Spain 928 A3
Europe 915 B11
Evanston, Ill., U.S.A. 919 B9
Evanston, Wyo., U.S.A. 918 B4
Evansville, U.S.A. 919 C9
Everest, Mt., Nepal 937 C7
Everett, U.S.A. 918 A2
Everglades, The, U.S.A. 919 E10
Evesham, U.K. 924 D6
Évora, Portugal 928 C2
Évreux, France 926 B4
Évvoia, Greece 931 C2
Ewe, L., U.K. 925 D3
Exe →, U.K. 924 F4
Exeter, U.K. 924 F4
Exmoor, U.K. 924 E4
Exmouth, U.K. 924 F4
Extremadura □, Spain 928 C2
Eyasi, L., Tanzania 940 C7
Eye Pen., U.K. 925 C2
Eyemouth, U.K. 925 F6
Eyre, L., Australia 942 F6
Eyre Pen., Australia 942 G6

F

Færoe Is. = Føroyar, Atl. Oc. 914 A9
Fair Hd., U.K. 925 F13
Fairbanks, U.S.A. 916 B5
Fairweather, Mt., U.S.A. 916 C6
Faisalabad, Pakistan 937 B6
Fajardo, Puerto Rico 921 d
Fakenham, U.K. 924 D8
Falcon Reservoir, U.S.A. 918 E7
Falkirk, U.K. 925 F5
Falkland Is. ⊠, Atl. Oc. 923 H4
Fall River, U.S.A. 919 B12
Falmouth, Jamaica 920 a
Falmouth, U.K. 924 F2
Falun, Sweden 930 E7
Famagusta, Cyprus 931 C4
Fanad Hd., Ireland 925 F12
Fannich, L., U.K. 925 D4
Farāh, Afghan. 936 B5
Farasān, Jazā'ir, Si. Arabia 936 D3
Farasan Is. = Farasān, Jazā'ir, Si. Arabia 936 D3
Farewell C. = Nunap Isua, Greenland 917 C15
Fargo, U.S.A. 919 A7
Farmington, U.S.A. 918 C5
Faro, Canada 916 B6
Farvel, Kap = Nunap Isua, Greenland 917 C15
Fataka, Solomon Is. 943 C12
Fayetteville, Ark., U.S.A. 919 C8
Fayetteville, N.C., U.S.A. 919 D11
Fdérik, Mauritania 938 D3
Feale →, Ireland 925 J10
Fear, C., U.S.A. 919 D11
Fécamp, France 926 B4
Fedala = Mohammedia, Morocco 938 B4
Feira de Santana, Brazil 922 D6
Felipe Carrillo Puerto, Mexico 920 D7
Felixstowe, U.K. 924 E9
Fens, The, U.K. 924 D7
Fenyang, China 934 C6
Feodosiya, Ukraine 931 A5
Fergus Falls, U.S.A. 919 A7
Ferkéssédougou, Ivory C. 938 G4
Fermanagh □, U.K. 925 G12
Fermont, Canada 917 C13
Fermoy, Ireland 925 J11
Fernando Póo = Bioko, Eq. Guin. 940 B1
Ferrara, Italy 929 B3
Ferret, C., France 926 D3
Ferrol, Spain 928 A1
Fès, Morocco 938 B5
Fethiye, Turkey 931 C3
Fetlar, U.K. 925 A8
Feuilles →, Canada 917 C12
Feyẕābād, Afghan. 937 B6
Fez = Fès, Morocco 938 B5
Fezzan, Libya 939 C8
Fianarantsoa, Madag. 940 G9
Fife □, U.K. 925 E5
Fife Ness, U.K. 925 E6
Figeac, France 926 D5
Fiji ■, Pac. Oc. 943 D14
Filey, U.K. 924 B7
Filey B., U.K. 924 B7
Findhorn →, U.K. 925 D5
Findlay, U.S.A. 919 B10
Finisterre, C. = Fisterra, C., Spain 928 A1
Finland ■, Europe 930 E9
Finland, G. of, Europe 930 F9
Finlay →, Canada 916 C7
Finn →, Ireland 925 G12
Firat = Furāt, Nahr al →, Asia 936 B3
Firenze, Italy 929 C3
Fish →, Namibia 940 H3
Fishguard, U.K. 924 D3
Fisterra, C., Spain 928 A1
Fiume = Rijeka, Croatia 929 B5
Flagstaff, U.S.A. 918 C4
Flamborough Hd., U.K. 924 B7
Flanders = Flandre, Europe 926 A5
Flandre, Europe 926 A5
Flathead L., U.S.A. 918 A4
Flattery, C., U.S.A. 918 A2
Fleetwood, U.K. 924 C4
Flensburg, Germany 927 A4
Flers, France 926 B3
Flin Flon, Canada 916 C9
Flinders →, Australia 942 D7
Flinders Ranges, Australia 942 G6
Flint, U.K. 924 C4
Flint, U.S.A. 919 B10
Flint →, U.S.A. 919 D10
Flodden, U.K. 924 A5
Florence = Firenze, Italy 929 C3
Florence, U.S.A. 919 D11
Florencia, Colombia 922 B2
Flores, Indonesia 941 D4
Flores Sea, Indonesia 941 D4
Florianópolis, Brazil 923 E5
Florida, Uruguay 923 F4
Florida □, U.S.A. 919 E10
Florida, Straits of, U.S.A. 921 C9
Florida Keys, U.S.A. 919 F10
Florø, Norway 930 E5
Flushing = Vlissingen, Neths. 927 C1
Fly →, Papua N. G. 942 B7
Focşani, Romania 931 A3
Fóggia, Italy 929 D5
Foix, France 926 E4
Folkestone, U.K. 924 E9
Fond-du-Lac, Canada 916 C9
Fongafale, Tuvalu 943 B14
Fontainebleau, France 926 B5
Fontenay-le-Comte, France 926 C3
Foochow = Fuzhou, China 934 D6
Forel, Mt., Greenland 944 C5
Forfar, U.K. 925 E6
Forlì, Italy 929 B4
Formby Pt., U.K. 924 C4
Formosa = Taiwan ■, Asia 934 D7
Formosa, Argentina 923 E4
Føroyar, Atl. Oc. 914 A9
Forres, U.K. 925 D5
Forsayth, Australia 942 D7
Fort Albany, Canada 917 C11
Fort Augustus, U.K. 925 D4
Fort Chipewyan, Canada 916 C8
Fort Collins, U.S.A. 918 B5
Fort-de-France, Martinique 920 c
Fort Dodge, U.S.A. 919 B8
Fort Franklin = Déline, Canada 916 B7
Fort George = Chisasibi, Canada 917 C12
Fort Good Hope, Canada 916 B7
Fort Lauderdale, U.S.A. 919 E10
Fort Liard, Canada 916 B7
Fort MacKay, Canada 916 C8
Fort Macleod, Canada 916 D8
Fort McMurray, Canada 916 C8
Fort McPherson, Canada 916 B6
Fort Morgan, U.S.A. 918 B6
Fort Myers, U.S.A. 919 E10
Fort Nelson, Canada 916 C7
Fort Nelson →, Canada 916 C7

Fort Norman

Fort Norman = Tulita, Canada 916 B7
Fort Peck L., U.S.A. 918 A5
Fort Providence, Canada 916 B8
Fort Resolution, Canada 916 B8
Fort Rupert = Waskaganish, Canada 917 C12
Fort St. John, Canada 916 C7
Fort Scott, U.S.A. 919 C8
Fort Shevchenko, Kazakhstan 932 E6
Fort Simpson, Canada 916 B7
Fort Smith, Canada 916 B8
Fort Smith, U.S.A. 919 C8
Fort Stockton, U.S.A. 918 D6
Fort Wayne, U.S.A. 919 B9
Fort William, U.K. 925 E3
Fort Worth, U.S.A. 919 D7
Fort Yukon, U.S.A. 916 B5
Fortaleza, Brazil 922 C6
Forth →, U.K. 925 E5
Forth, Firth of, U.K. 925 E6
Fortrose, U.K. 925 D4
Foshan, China 934 D6
Fougères, France 926 B3
Foula, U.K. 925 A6
Foulness I., U.K. 924 E8
Foulweather, C., U.S.A. 918 B2
Fouta Djallon, Guinea 938 F3
Fowey, U.K. 924 F3
Foxe Basin, Canada 917 B12
Foxe Chan., Canada 917 B11
Foxe Pen., Canada 917 B12
Foyle, Lough, U.K. 925 F12
Foynes, Ireland 925 J10
Foz do Iguaçu, Brazil 923 E4
Franca, Brazil 922 E5
France ■, Europe 926 C5
Franceville, Gabon 940 C2
Franche-Comté, France 926 C6
Francis Case, L., U.S.A. 918 B7
Francistown, Botswana 940 G5
François L., Canada 916 C7
Frankfort, U.S.A. 919 C10
Frankfurt, Brandenburg, Germany 927 B7
Frankfurt, Hessen, Germany 927 C4
Franklin B., Canada 916 B7
Franklin D. Roosevelt L., U.S.A. 918 A3
Franklin L., U.S.A. 918 B3
Franklin Mts., Canada 916 B7
Franklin Str., Canada 916 A10
Frantsa Iosifa, Zemlya, Russia 932 A6
Franz Josef Land = Frantsa Iosifa, Zemlya, Russia 932 A6
Fraser →, Canada 916 D7
Fraserburgh, U.K. 925 D6
Fredericton, Canada 917 D13
Frederikshåb = Paamiut, Greenland 917 B15
Frederikshavn, Denmark 930 F6
Fredrikstad, Norway 930 F6
Free State □, S. Africa 940 H5
Freeport, Bahamas 921 B9
Freeport, U.S.A. 919 E7
Freetown, S. Leone 938 G3
Freiburg, Germany 927 E3
French Guiana ☒, S. Amer. 922 B4
French Polynesia ☒, Pac. Oc. 915
Frenchman Cr. →, N. Amer. 918 A5
Fresnillo, Mexico 920 C4
Fresno, U.S.A. 918 C3
Fria, C., Namibia 940 F2
Friendly Is. = Tonga ■, Pac. Oc. 943 D16
Frobisher B., Canada 917 B13
Frobisher Bay = Iqaluit, Canada 917 B13
Frobisher L., Canada 916 C9
Front Range, U.S.A. 918 C5
Frunze = Bishkek, Kyrgyzstan 932 E8
Frýdek-Místek, Czech Rep. 927 D9
Fuchou = Fuzhou, China 934 D6
Fuchū, Japan 935 F3
Fuerte →, Mexico 920 B3
Fuerteventura, Canary Is. 938 C3
Fuhai, China 934 B3
Fuji, Japan 935 F6
Fuji-San, Japan 935 F6
Fujian □, China 934 D6
Fujiyama, Mt. = Fuji-San, Japan 935 F6
Fukien = Fujian □, China 934 D6
Fukui, Japan 935 E5
Fukuoka, Japan 935 G2
Fukushima, Japan 935 E7
Fukuyama, Japan 935 F3
Fulda, Germany 927 C4
Fulda →, Germany 927 C4
Funabashi, Japan 935 F7
Funafuti = Fongafale, Tuvalu 943 B14
Funchal, Madeira 938 B2
Fundy, B. of, Canada 917 D13
Furāt, Nahr al →, Asia 936 B3
Furneaux Group, Australia 942 J8
Fürth, Germany 927 D5
Fury and Hecla Str., Canada 917 B11
Fushun, China 934 B7
Fustic, Barbados 921 g
Fuxin, China 934 B7
Fuzhou, China 934 D6
Fyn, Denmark 930 F6
Fyne, L., U.K. 925 F3

G

Gabès, Tunisia 939 B8
Gabès, G. de, Tunisia 939 B8
Gabon ■, Africa 940 C2
Gaborone, Botswana 940 G5
Gadsden, U.S.A. 919 D9
Gafsa, Tunisia 938 B7
Gagnoa, Ivory C. 938 G4
Gagnon, Canada 917 C13
Gaillimh = Galway, Ireland 925 H10
Gainesville, Fla., U.S.A. 919 E10
Gainesville, Ga., U.S.A. 919 D10
Gainsborough, U.K. 924 C7
Gairdner, L., Australia 942 G6
Gairloch, L., U.K. 925 D3
Galápagos = Colón, Arch. de, Ecuador 914 E5
Galashiels, U.K. 925 F6
Galaţi, Romania 931 A3
Galdhøpiggen, Norway 930 E5
Galena, U.S.A. 916 B4
Galesburg, U.S.A. 919 B8
Galicia □, Spain 928 A2
Galina Pt., Jamaica 920 a
Gallan Hd., U.K. 925 C1
Galle, Sri Lanka 937 E7
Galley Hd., Ireland 925 K11
Gallinas, Pta., Colombia 922 A2
Gallipoli = Gelibolu, Turkey 931 B3
Gällivare, Sweden 930 D8
Galloway, U.K. 925 F4
Galloway, Mull of, U.K. 925 G4
Gallup, U.S.A. 918 C5
Galty Mts., Ireland 925 J11
Galtymore, Ireland 925 J11
Galveston, U.S.A. 919 E8
Galway, Ireland 925 H10
Galway □, Ireland 925 H10
Galway B., Ireland 925 H10
Gambia ■, W. Afr. 938 F2
Gambia →, W. Afr. 938 F2
Gamlakarleby = Kokkola, Finland 930 E8
Gan Jiang →, China 934 D6
Gäncä, Azerbaijan 931 B7
Gand = Gent, Belgium 927 C1
Gander, Canada 917 D14
Ganga →, India 937 C8
Ganges = Ganga →, India 937 C8
Gannett Peak, U.S.A. 918 B5
Gansu □, China 934 C5
Ganzhou, China 934 D6
Gao, Mali 938 E5
Gaoxiong = Kaohsiung, Taiwan 934 D7
Gap, France 926 D7
Gar, China 934 C2
Garabogazköl Aylagy, Turkmenistan 932 E6
Garanhuns, Brazil 922 C6
Garda, L. di, Italy 929 B3
Garden City, U.S.A. 918 C6
Garissa, Kenya 940 C7
Garmo, Qullai = Kommunizma, Pik, Tajikistan 932 F8
Garoe, Somali Rep. 936 E3
Garonne →, France 926 D3
Garoowe = Garoe, Somali Rep. 936 E3
Garoua, Cameroon 939 G8
Garrison Res. = Sakakawea, L., U.S.A. 918 A6
Garron Pt., U.K. 925 F14
Garry →, U.K. 925 E5
Garry, L., Canada 916 B9
Garwa = Garoua, Cameroon 939 G8
Gary, U.S.A. 919 B9
Garzê, China 934 C5
Gascogne, France 926 E4
Gascogne, G. de, Europe 926 D2
Gascony = Gascogne, France 926 E4
Gaspé, Canada 917 D13
Gaspé Pen. = Gaspésie, Pén. de la, Canada 917 D13
Gaspésie, Pén. de la, Canada 917 D13
Gasteiz = Vitoria-Gasteiz, Spain 928 A4
Gatehouse of Fleet, U.K. 925 G4
Gateshead, U.K. 924 B6
Gatwick, London ✈ (LGW), U.K. 924 E7
Gävle, Sweden 930 E7
Gaxun Nur, China 934 B5
Gaya, India 937 C7
Gaza, Gaza Strip 931 D4
Gaza Strip ☒, Asia 931 D4
Gaziantep, Turkey 931 C5
Gazimağosa = Famagusta, Cyprus 931 C4
Gdańsk, Poland 927 A9
Gdynia, Poland 927 A9
Gebze, Turkey 931 B3
Gedaref, Sudan 939 F13
Gedser, Denmark 930 G6
Geelong, Australia 942 H7
Gejiu, China 934 D5
Gelibolu, Turkey 931 B3
Gelsenkirchen, Germany 927 C3
General Acha, Argentina 923 F3
General Alvear, Argentina 923 F3
General Pico, Argentina 923 F3
General Santos, Phil. 941 C4
Geneva = Genève, Switz. 926 C7
Geneva, L. = Léman, L., Europe 926 C7
Genève, Switz. 926 C7
Gennargentu, Mti. del, Italy 929 D2
Genoa = Génova, Italy 926 D8
Génova, Italy 926 D8
Gent, Belgium 927 C1
George, S. Africa 940 J4
George →, Canada 917 C13
George, L., U.S.A. 919 E10
George River = Kangiqsualujjuaq, Canada 917 C13
George Town, Malaysia 941 C2
George V Land, Antarctica 944 D14
Georgetown, Guyana 922 B4
Georgetown, U.S.A. 919 D11
Georgia □, U.S.A. 919 D10
Georgia ■, Asia 932 E5
Georgian B., Canada 917 D11
Georgiu-Dezh = Liski, Russia 932 D4
Georgiyevsk, Russia 931 B6
Gera, Germany 927 C6
Geraldton, Australia 942 F1
Germany ■, Europe 927 C5
Germiston, S. Africa 940 H5
Gerona = Girona, Spain 928 B7
Getafe, Spain 928 B4
Ghana ■, W. Afr. 938 G5
Ghardaïa, Algeria 938 B6
Gharyān, Libya 939 B8
Ghats, Eastern, India 937 D6
Ghats, Western, India 937 D6
Ghawdex = Gozo, Malta 929 F5
Ghazal, Bahr el →, Chad 939 F9
Ghazâl, Bahr el →, Sudan 939 G12
Ghaznī, Afghan. 936 B5
Ghent = Gent, Belgium 927 C1
Giants Causeway, U.K. 925 F13
Gibraltar ☒, Europe 928 D3
Gibraltar, Str. of, Medit. S. 928 E3
Gibson Desert, Australia 942 E4
Giebnegáisi = Kebnekaise, Sweden 930 D7
Gifu, Japan 935 F5
Gigha, U.K. 925 F3
Gijón, Spain 928 A3
Gila →, U.S.A. 918 D4
Gilbert Is., Kiribati 914
Gilgit, India 937 B6
Gillam, Canada 916 C10
Gillette, U.S.A. 918 B5
Gillingham, U.K. 924 E8
Gimie, Mt, St. Lucia 921 f
Girdle Ness, U.K. 925 D6
Giresun, Turkey 931 B5
Girona, Spain 928 B7
Gironde →, France 926 D3
Gisborne, N.Z. 943 H14
Gitega, Burundi 940 C5
Giuba →, Somali Rep. 936 E3
Giza = El Gîza, Egypt 939 C12
Gizhiga, Russia 933 C17
Gjoa Haven, Canada 916 B10
Glace Bay, Canada 917 D14
Glacier △, U.S.A. 918 A4
Gladstone, Australia 942 E9
Glåma = Glomma →, Norway 930 F6
Glasgow, U.K. 925 F4
Glasgow, U.S.A. 918 A5
Glastonbury, U.K. 924 E5
Glazov, Russia 932 D6
Gleiwitz = Gliwice, Poland 927 C9
Glen Affric, U.K. 925 D3
Glen Coe, U.K. 925 E3
Glen Garry, U.K. 925 D3
Glen Mor, U.K. 925 D4
Glen Moriston, U.K. 925 D4
Glen Spean, U.K. 925 E4
Glendale, Ariz., U.S.A. 918 D4
Glendale, Calif., U.S.A. 918 D3
Glendive, U.S.A. 918 A6
Glengarriff, Ireland 925 K10
Glennallen, U.S.A. 916 B5
Glennamaddy, Ireland 925 H11
Glenrothes, U.K. 925 E5
Glens Falls, U.S.A. 919 B12
Glenties, Ireland 925 G11
Gliwice, Poland 927 C9
Globe, U.S.A. 918 D4
Głogów, Poland 927 C8
Glomma →, Norway 930 F6
Gloucester, U.K. 924 E5
Gniezno, Poland 927 B8
Goa □, India 937 D6
Goat Fell, U.K. 925 F3
Gobi, Asia 934 B6
Godavari →, India 937 D7
Godhavn = Qeqertarsuaq, Greenland 917 B14
Gods →, Canada 916 C10
Gods L., Canada 916 C10
Godthåb = Nuuk, Greenland 917 B14
Godwin Austen = K2, Pakistan 937 B6
Goeie Hoop, Kaap die = Good Hope, C. of, S. Africa 940 J3
Goiânia, Brazil 922 D5
Goiás, Brazil 922 D4
Goiás □, Brazil 922 D5
Goio-Erê, Brazil 923 E4
Gold Coast, Australia 942 F9
Gold Coast, W. Afr. 938 H5
Golden Vale, Ireland 925 J11
Goldsboro, U.S.A. 919 C11
Golspie, U.K. 925 D5
Goma, Dem. Rep. of the Congo 940 C5
Gomel = Homyel, Belarus 932 D4
Gomera, Canary Is. 938 C2
Gómez Palacio, Mexico 920 B4
Gonābād, Iran 936 B4
Gonaïves, Haiti 921 D10
Gonghe, China 934 C5
Good Hope, C. of, S. Africa 940 J3
Goole, U.K. 924 C7
Goose L., U.S.A. 918 B2
Gorakhpur, India 937 C7
Gorey, Ireland 925 J13
Gorgān, Iran 936 B4
Gorkiy = Nizhniy Novgorod, Russia 932 D5
Görlitz, Germany 927 C7
Gorlovka = Horlivka, Ukraine 931 A5
Gorno-Altay □, Russia 932 D9
Gorontalo, Indonesia 941 C4
Gort, Ireland 925 H11
Gorzów Wielkopolski, Poland 927 B7
Gosier, Guadeloupe 920 b
Gosport, U.K. 924 F6
Göta kanal, Sweden 930 F7
Göteborg, Sweden 930 F6
Gotha, Germany 927 C5
Gothenburg = Göteborg, Sweden 930 F6
Gotland, Sweden 930 F7
Gotō-Rettō, Japan 935 G1
Göttingen, Germany 927 C4
Gottwaldov = Zlín, Czech Rep. 927 D8
Gouda, Neths. 927 B2
Gough I., Atl. Oc. 914 G9
Gouin, Rés., Canada 917 D12
Goulburn, Australia 942 G8
Goulimine, Morocco 938 C3
Governador Valadares, Brazil 922 D5
Gower, U.K. 924 E3
Gowna, L., Ireland 925 H12
Goya, Argentina 923 E4
Gozo, Malta 929 F5
Graaff-Reinet, S. Africa 940 J4
Gracias a Dios, C., Honduras 921 E8
Grafham Water, U.K. 924 D7
Grafton, Australia 942 F9
Grafton, U.S.A. 919 A7
Graham Land, Antarctica 944 D3
Grahamstown, S. Africa 940 J5
Grain Coast, W. Afr. 938 H3
Grampian Highlands = Grampian Mts., U.K. 925 E5
Grampian Mts., U.K. 925 E5
Gran Canaria, Canary Is. 938 C2
Gran Chaco, S. Amer. 923 E3
Gran Sasso d'Itália, Italy 929 C4
Granada, Nic. 920 E7
Granada, Spain 928 D4
Granard, Ireland 925 H12
Granby, Canada 917 D12
Grand →, U.S.A. 918 A6
Grand Bahama, Bahamas 921 B9
Grand-Bourg, Guadeloupe 920 b
Grand Canyon, U.S.A. 918 C4
Grand Canyon △, U.S.A. 918 C4
Grand Cayman, Cayman Is. 921 D8
Grand Falls, Canada 917 D13
Grand Falls-Windsor, Canada 917 D14
Grand Forks, U.S.A. 919 A7
Grand Island, U.S.A. 918 B7
Grand Junction, U.S.A. 918 C5
Grand Rapids, Canada 916 C10
Grand Rapids, U.S.A. 919 B9
Grand St-Bernard, Col du, Europe 926 D7
Grand Teton, U.S.A. 918 B4
Grand Union Canal, U.K. 924 D7
Grand-Vigie, Pte. de la, Guadeloupe 920 b
Grande →, Bolivia 922 D3
Grande, B., Argentina 923 H3
Grande, Rio →, U.S.A. 919 E7
Grande Baleine, R. de la →, Canada 917 C12
Grande Prairie, Canada 916 C8
Grande-Terre, I., Guadeloupe 920 b
Grangemouth, U.K. 925 E5
Grangeville, U.S.A. 918 A3
Grantham, U.K. 924 D7
Grantown-on-Spey, U.K. 925 D5
Grants Pass, U.S.A. 918 B2
Grasse, France 926 E7
Graulhet, France 926 E4
's-Gravenhage, Neths. 927 B2
Gravesend, U.K. 924 E8
Graz, Austria 927 E7
Great Abaco I., Bahamas 921 B9
Great Australian Bight, Australia 942 G5
Great Barrier Reef, Australia 942 D8
Great Basin, U.S.A. 918 B3
Great Bear →, Canada 916 B7
Great Bear L., Canada 916 B7
Great Belt = Store Bælt, Denmark 930 F6
Great Bend, U.S.A. 918 C7
Great Camanoe, Br. Virgin Is. 921 e
Great Dividing Ra., Australia 942 E8
Great Driffield = Driffield, U.K. 924 B7
Great Exuma I., Bahamas 921 C9
Great Falls, U.S.A. 918 A4
Great Inagua I., Bahamas 921 C10
Great Indian Desert = Thar Desert, India 937 C6
Great Karoo, S. Africa 940 J4
Great Malvern, U.K. 924 D5
Great Ormes Head, U.K. 924 C4
Great Ouse →, U.K. 924 D8
Great Pedro Bluff, Jamaica 920 a
Great Plains, N. Amer. 918 A6
Great Saint Bernard Pass = Grand St-Bernard, Col du, Europe 926 D7
Great Salt L., U.S.A. 918 B4
Great Salt Lake Desert, U.S.A. 918 B4
Great Sandy Desert, Australia 942 E3
Great Sangi = Sangihe, Pulau, Indonesia 941 C4
Great Slave L., Canada 916 B8
Great Snow Mt., Canada 916 C7
Great Victoria Desert, Australia 942 F4
Great Wall, China 934 C5
Great Whernside, U.K. 924 B6
Great Yarmouth, U.K. 924 D9
Greater Antilles, W. Indies 921 D10
Greater Sudbury = Sudbury, Canada 917 D11
Greater Sunda Is., Indonesia 941 D3
Greece ■, Europe 931 C2
Greeley, U.S.A. 918 B6
Green →, Ky., U.S.A. 919 C9
Green →, Utah, U.S.A. 918 C5
Green Bay, U.S.A. 919 B9
Green River, U.S.A. 918 B5
Greenland ☒, N. Amer. 944 C4
Greenland Sea, Arctic 944 B6
Greenock, U.K. 925 F4
Greenore, Ireland 925 G13
Greenore Pt., Ireland 925 J13
Greensboro, U.S.A. 919 C11
Greenstone Pt., U.K. 925 D3
Greenville, Ala., U.S.A. 919 D9
Greenville, Miss., U.S.A. 919 D8
Greenville, S.C., U.S.A. 919 D10
Greenwood, U.S.A. 919 D8
Gremikha, Russia 932 C4
Grenada ■, W. Indies 921 E12
Grenoble, France 926 D6
Grey Ra., Australia 942 F7
Greymouth, N.Z. 943 J13
Greystones, Ireland 925 H13
Griffith, Australia 942 G8
Grimsby, U.K. 924 C7
Gris-Nez, C., France 926 A4
Grodno = Hrodna, Belarus 932 D3
Groningen, Neths. 927 B3
Groote Eylandt, Australia 942 C6
Gros Islet, St. Lucia 921 f
Gros Piton, St. Lucia 921 f
Gros Piton Pt., St. Lucia 921 f
Grossglockner, Austria 927 E6
Groznyy, Russia 931 B7
Grudziądz, Poland 927 B9
Gruinard B., U.K. 925 D3
Guadalajara, Mexico 920 C4
Guadalajara, Spain 928 B4
Guadalcanal, Solomon Is. 943 B11
Guadalete →, Spain 928 D2
Guadalquivir →, Spain 928 D2
Guadalupe = Guadeloupe ☒, W. Indies 920 b
Guadarrama, Sierra de, Spain 928 B4
Guadeloupe ☒, W. Indies 920 b
Guadiana →, Portugal 928 D2
Guadix, Spain 928 D4
Guafo, Boca del, Chile 923 G2
Guajará-Mirim, Brazil 922 D3
Guajira, Pen. de la, Colombia 922 A2
Gualeguaychú, Argentina 923 F4
Guam ☒, Pac. Oc. 915 D17
Guamúchil, Mexico 920 B3
Guana I., Br. Virgin Is. 921 e
Guanahani = San Salvador I., Bahamas 921 C10
Guanajuato, Mexico 920 C4
Guane, Cuba 921 C8
Guangdong □, China 934 D6
Guangxi Zhuangzu Zizhiqu □, China 934 D5
Guangzhou, China 934 D6
Guanica, Puerto Rico 921 d
Guantánamo, Cuba 921 C9
Guaporé →, Brazil 922 D3
Guaqui, Bolivia 922 D3
Guarapuava, Brazil 923 E4
Guardafui, C. = Asir, Ras, Somali Rep. 936 D4
Guatemala, Guatemala 920 E6
Guatemala ■, Cent. Amer. 920 D6
Guaviare →, Colombia 922 B3
Guayama, Puerto Rico 921 d
Guayaquil, Ecuador 922 C2
Guayaquil, G. de, Ecuador 922 C1
Guaymas, Mexico 920 B2
Guelmine = Goulimine, Morocco 938 C3
Guéret, France 926 C4
Guernsey, U.K. 926 B2
Guildford, U.K. 924 E7
Guilin, China 934 D6
Guinea ■, W. Afr. 938 F3
Guinea, Gulf of, Atl. Oc. 915 D10
Guinea-Bissau ■, Africa 938 F3
Güines, Cuba 921 C8
Guingamp, France 926 B2
Guiyang, China 934 D5
Guizhou □, China 934 D5
Gujarat □, India 937 C6
Gulbarga, India 937 D6
Gulf, The = Persian Gulf, Asia 936 C4
Gulfport, U.S.A. 919 D9
Gunnison →, U.S.A. 918 C5
Guntur, India 937 D7
Gurgueia →, Brazil 922 C5
Gürün, Turkey 931 C5
Gurupi →, Brazil 922 C5
Guryev = Atyraū, Kazakhstan 932 E6
Gusau, Nigeria 938 F7
Gushgy, Turkmenistan 932 F7
Guyana ■, S. Amer. 922 B4
Guyane française = French Guiana ☒, S. Amer. 922 B4
Guyenne, France 926 D4
Güzelyurt = Morphou, Cyprus 931 C4
Gwādar, Pakistan 936 C5
Gwalior, India 937 C6
Gwanda, Zimbabwe 940 G5
Gweebarra B., Ireland 925 G11
Gweedore, Ireland 925 F11
Gweru, Zimbabwe 940 F5
Gyandzha = Gäncä, Azerbaijan 931 B7
Gyaring Hu, China 934 C4
Gympie, Australia 942 F9
Győr, Hungary 927 E8
Gyumri, Armenia 931 B6
Gyzylarbat, Turkmenistan 932 F6

H

Ha Tinh, Vietnam 941 B2
Ha'apai Group, Tonga 943 D16
Haarlem, Neths. 927 B2
Hachinohe, Japan 935 C7
Ḥadd, Ra's al, Oman 936 C4
Hadhramaut = Ḥaḍramawt, Yemen 936 D3
Ḥaḍramawt, Yemen 936 D3
Haeju, N. Korea 934 C7
Haerhpin = Harbin, China 934 B7
Hagen, Germany 927 C3
Hags Hd., Ireland 925 J10
Hague, C. de la, France 926 B3
Hague, The = 's-Gravenhage, Neths. 927 B2
Haguenau, France 926 B7
Haidarâbâd = Hyderabad, India 937 D6
Haifa = Ḥefa, Israel 931 D5
Haikou, China 934 D6
Ḥā'il, Si. Arabia 936 C3
Hailar, China 934 B6
Hailey, U.S.A. 918 B4
Hainan □, China 934 E5
Haines Junction, Canada 916 B6
Haiphong, Vietnam 934 D5
Haiti ■, W. Indies 921 D10
Hakodate, Japan 935 C7
Ḥalab, Syria 936 B2
Halberstadt, Germany 927 C5
Halden, Norway 930 F6
Halifax, Canada 917 D13
Halifax, U.K. 924 C6
Halkirk, U.K. 925 C5
Hall Beach = Sanirajak, Canada 917 B11
Hall Pen., Canada 917 B13
Halle, Germany 927 C5
Halls Creek, Australia 942 D4
Halmahera, Indonesia 941 C4
Halmstad, Sweden 930 F6
Hälsingborg = Helsingborg, Sweden 930 F6
Halstead, U.K. 924 E8
Haltwhistle, U.K. 924 B5
Hamadān, Iran 936 B3
Ḥamāh, Syria 936 B2
Hamamatsu, Japan 935 F5
Hamar, Norway 930 E6
Hamburg, Germany 927 B4
Hämeenlinna, Finland 930 E8
Hameln, Germany 927 B4
Hamersley Ra., Australia 942 E2
Hamhung, N. Korea 934 B7
Hami, China 934 B4
Hamilton, Canada 917 D12
Hamilton, N.Z. 943 H14
Hamilton, U.K. 925 F4
Hamlin = Hameln, Germany 927 B4
Hamm, Germany 927 C3
Hammerfest, Norway 930 C8
Hampshire □, U.K. 924 E6
Handan, China 934 C6
Hanford, U.S.A. 918 C3
Hangayn Nuruu, Mongolia 934 B4
Hangchou = Hangzhou, China 934 C7
Hangzhou, China 934 C7
Hangzhou Wan, China 934 C7

Kahoolawe

Hanna, Canada 916 C8
Hannibal, U.S.A. 919 C8
Hannover, Germany 927 B4
Hanoi, Vietnam 934 D5
Hanover = Hannover, Germany 927 B4
Hanover, I., Chile 923 H2
Hans Lollik I., U.S. Virgin Is. 921 e
Hanzhong, China 934 C5
Haparanda, Sweden 930 D8
Happy Valley-Goose Bay, Canada 917 C13
Har Hu, China 934 C4
Har Us Nuur, Mongolia 934 B4
Harare, Zimbabwe 940 F6
Harbin, China 934 B7
Hardangerfjorden, Norway 930 E5
Hardwar = Haridwar, India 937 C6
Hardy, Pte., St. Lucia 921 f
Harer, Ethiopia 936 E3
Hargeisa, Somali Rep. 936 E3
Haridwar, India 937 C6
Harlech, U.K. 924 D3
Harlingen, U.S.A. 918 E7
Harlow, U.K. 924 E8
Harney L., U.S.A. 918 B3
Härnösand, Sweden 930 E7
Haroldswick, U.K. 925 A8
Harricana →, Canada 917 C12
Harris, U.K. 925 D2
Harris, Sd. of, U.K. 925 D1
Harrisburg, U.S.A. 919 B11
Harrison, C., Canada 917 C14
Harrisonburg, U.S.A. 919 C11
Harrogate, U.K. 924 B6
Hartford, U.S.A. 919 B12
Hartland Pt., U.K. 924 E3
Hartlepool, U.K. 924 B6
Harwich, U.K. 924 E9
Haryana □, India 937 C6
Harz, Germany 927 C5
Hasa □, Si. Arabia 936 C3
Hastings, U.K. 924 F8
Hastings, U.S.A. 918 B7
Hat Yai, Thailand 941 C2
Hatay = Antalya, Turkey 931 C4
Hatgal, Mongolia 934 A5
Hatteras, C., U.S.A. 919 C11
Hattiesburg, U.S.A. 919 D9
Haugesund, Norway 930 F5
Haut Atlas, Morocco 938 B4
Havana = La Habana, Cuba 921 C8
Havant, U.K. 924 F7
Havasu, L., U.S.A. 918 D4
Havel →, Germany 927 B6
Haverfordwest, U.K. 924 E3
Havre, U.S.A. 918 A5
Havre-St.-Pierre, Canada 917 C13
Hawaii □, U.S.A. 918 H16
Hawaii I., Pac. Oc. 918 J17
Hawaiian Is., Pac. Oc. 918 H17
Hawick, U.K. 925 F6
Hay →, Australia 942 G8
Hay →, Canada 916 B8
Hay River, Canada 916 B8
Hayes →, Canada 916 C10
Hays, U.S.A. 918 C7
Haywards Heath, U.K. 924 F7
Heard I., Ind. Oc. 915 G13
Hearst, Canada 917 D11
Heathrow, London ✕ (LHR), U.K. 924 E7
Hebei □, China 934 C6
Hebron, Canada 917 C13
Hecate Str., Canada 916 C6
Hechi, China 934 D5
Hechuan, China 934 C5
Heerlen, Neths. 926 A6
Ḥefa, Israel 931 D5
Hefei, China 934 C6
Hegang, China 934 B8
Heidelberg, Germany 927 D4
Heilbronn, Germany 927 D4
Heilongjiang □, China 934 B7
Heilunkiang = Heilongjiang □, China 934 B7
Heimaey, Iceland 930 B1
Hejaz = Ḥijāz □, Si. Arabia 936 C3
Hekou, China 934 D5
Helena, U.S.A. 918 A4
Helensburgh, U.K. 925 E4
Helgoland, Germany 927 A3
Heligoland = Helgoland, Germany 927 A3
Heligoland B. = Deutsche Bucht, Germany 927 A4
Hellespont = Çanakkale Boğazı, Turkey 931 B3
Helmand →, Afghan. 936 B5
Helmsdale, U.K. 925 C5
Helmsdale →, U.K. 925 C5
Helsingborg, Sweden 930 F6
Helsingfors = Helsinki, Finland 930 E9
Helsinki, Finland 930 E9
Helston, U.K. 924 F2
Helvellyn, U.K. 924 B4
Helwân, Egypt 939 C12
Hemel Hempstead, U.K. 924 E7
Henan □, China 934 C6
Henderson, Ky., U.S.A. 919 C9
Henderson, Nev., U.S.A. 918 C3
Hengyang, China 934 D6
Henrietta Maria, C., Canada 917 C11
Hentiyn Nuruu, Mongolia 934 B5
Heraklion = Iráklion, Greece 931 C3
Herāt, Afghan. 936 B5
Hereford, U.K. 924 D5
Herford, Germany 927 B4
Hermosillo, Mexico 920 B2
Herne Bay, U.K. 924 E9
Heroica Nogales = Nogales, Mexico 920 A2
Hertford, U.K. 924 E7
's-Hertogenbosch, Neths. 927 C2
Hesse = Hessen □, Germany 927 C4
Hessen □, Germany 927 C4
Hexham, U.K. 924 B5
Heysham, U.K. 924 B5
Hibbing, U.S.A. 919 A8
Hidalgo del Parral, Mexico 920 B3
Hierro, Canary Is. 938 C2
Higashiōsaka, Japan 935 F4
High Level, Canada 916 C8
High Prairie, Canada 916 C8
High River, Canada 916 C8
High Tatra = Tatry, Slovak Rep. 927 D10
High Wycombe, U.K. 924 E7
Ḥijāz □, Si. Arabia 936 C3
Hildesheim, Germany 927 B4
Hillaby, Mt., Barbados 921 g
Hillcrest, Barbados 921 g
Hilo, U.S.A. 918 J17
Hilversum, Neths. 927 B2
Himachal Pradesh □, India 937 B6
Himalaya, Asia 937 C7
Himeji, Japan 935 F4
Ḥimş, Syria 936 B2
Hindu Kush, Asia 937 B6
Hirosaki, Japan 935 C7
Hiroshima, Japan 935 F3
Hispaniola, W. Indies 921 D10
Hitachi, Japan 935 E7
Hitchin, U.K. 924 E7
Hjälmaren, Sweden 930 F7
Ho Chi Minh City = Thanh Pho Ho Chi Minh, Vietnam 941 B2
Hoare B., Canada 917 B13
Hobart, Australia 942 J8
Hobbs, U.S.A. 918 D6
Hodeida = Al Ḥudaydah, Yemen 936 D3
Hodgson, Canada 916 C10
Hōfu, Japan 935 F2
Hoggar = Ahaggar, Algeria 938 D7
Hoher Rhön = Rhön, Germany 927 C4
Hohhot, China 934 B6
Hokkaidō □, Japan 935 B8
Holetown, Barbados 921 g
Holguín, Cuba 921 C9
Holman, Canada 916 A8
Holsworthy, U.K. 924 F3
Holy I., Angl., U.K. 924 C3
Holy I., Northumb., U.K. 924 A6
Holyhead, U.K. 924 C3
Home B., Canada 917 B13
Homer, U.S.A. 916 C4
Homs = Ḥimş, Syria 936 B2
Homyel, Belarus 932 D4
Honan = Henan □, China 934 C6
Honduras ■, Cent. Amer. 920 E7
Honduras, G. de, Caribbean 920 D7
Honey L., U.S.A. 918 B2
Hong Kong □, China 934 D6
Hongjiang, China 934 D5
Hongshui He →, China 934 D5
Hongze Hu, China 934 C6
Honiara, Solomon Is. 943 B10
Honiton, U.K. 924 F4
Honolulu, U.S.A. 918 H16
Honshū, Japan 935 F6
Hood, Mt., U.S.A. 918 A2
Hook Hd., Ireland 925 J13
Hooper Bay, U.S.A. 916 B3
Hoorn, Neths. 927 B2
Hoover Dam, U.S.A. 918 C4
Hope, U.S.A. 919 D8
Hopedale, Canada 917 C13
Hopei = Hebei □, China 934 C6
Hopetown, S. Africa 940 H4
Hopkinsville, U.S.A. 919 C9
Horlivka, Ukraine 931 A5
Hormuz, Str. of, The Gulf 936 C4
Horn, Cape = Hornos, C. de, Chile 923 H3
Horn, Is., Wall. & F. Is. 943 C15
Horn Head, Ireland 925 F11
Hornavan, Sweden 930 D7
Hornos, C. de, Chile 923 H3
Hornsea, U.K. 924 C7
Horqin Youyi Qianqi, China 934 B7
Horsham, Australia 942 H7
Horsham, U.K. 924 E7
Horton →, Canada 916 B7
Hoste, I., Chile 923 H3
Hot Springs, Ark., U.S.A. 919 D8
Hot Springs, S. Dak., U.S.A. 918 B6
Hotan, China 934 C2
Houma, U.S.A. 919 E8
Houston, U.S.A. 919 E7
Hovd, Mongolia 934 B4
Hove, U.K. 924 F7
Hövsgöl Nuur, Mongolia 934 A5
Howe, C., Australia 942 H9
Howth Hd., Ireland 925 H13
Hoy, U.K. 925 C5
Høyanger, Norway 930 E5
Hradec Králové, Czech Rep. 927 C7
Hrodna, Belarus 932 D3
Hron →, Slovak Rep. 927 E9
Hrvatska = Croatia ■, Europe 929 B6
Hsiamen = Xiamen, China 934 D6
Hsian = Xi'an, China 934 C5
Hsinchu, Taiwan 934 D7
Hsinhailien = Lianyungang, China 934 C6
Hsüchou = Xuzhou, China 934 C6
Huacho, Peru 922 D2
Huai He →, China 934 C6
Huainan, China 934 C6
Huallaga →, Peru 922 C2
Huambo, Angola 940 E3
Huancavelica, Peru 922 D2
Huancayo, Peru 922 D2
Huang Hai = Yellow Sea, China 934 C7
Huang He →, China 934 C6
Huangshan, China 934 D6
Huangshi, China 934 C6
Huánuco, Peru 922 C2
Huaraz, Peru 922 C2
Huascarán, Peru 922 C2
Huasco, Chile 923 E2
Huatabampo, Mexico 920 B3
Hubei □, China 934 C6
Hucknall, U.K. 924 C6
Huddersfield, U.K. 924 C6
Hudiksvall, Sweden 930 E7
Hudson →, U.S.A. 919 B12
Hudson Bay, Canada 917 C11
Hudson Str., Canada 917 B13
Hue, Vietnam 941 B2
Huelva, Spain 928 D2
Huesca, Spain 928 A5
Hughenden, Australia 942 E7
Huila, Nevado del, Colombia 922 B2
Huize, China 934 D5
Huld = Ulaanjirem, Mongolia 934 B5
Hull = Kingston upon Hull, U.K. 924 C7
Hull, Canada 917 D12
Hull →, U.K. 924 C7
Hulun Nur, China 934 B6
Humacao, Puerto Rico 921 d
Humaitá, Brazil 922 C3
Humber →, U.K. 924 C7
Humboldt, Canada 916 C9
Humboldt →, U.S.A. 918 B3
Humphreys Peak, U.S.A. 918 C4
Hunan □, China 934 D6
Hungary ■, Europe 927 E9
Hüngnam, N. Korea 934 C7
Hunsrück, Germany 927 D3
Hunstanton, U.K. 924 D8
Huntingdon, U.K. 924 D7
Huntington, U.S.A. 919 C10
Huntly, U.K. 925 D6
Huntsville, Canada 917 D12
Huntsville, Ala., U.S.A. 919 D9
Huntsville, Tex., U.S.A. 919 D7
Hupeh = Hubei □, China 934 C6
Huron, U.S.A. 918 B7
Huron, L., U.S.A. 919 B10
Húsavik, Iceland 930 A2
Hutchinson, U.S.A. 918 C7
Hwang Ho = Huang He →, China 934 C6
Hwange, Zimbabwe 940 F5
Hyargas Nuur, Mongolia 934 B4
Hyderabad, India 937 D6
Hyderabad, Pakistan 936 C5
Hyères, France 926 E7
Hyères, Îs. d', France 926 E7
Hyndman Peak, U.S.A. 918 B4

I

Iaşi, Romania 931 A3
Ibadan, Nigeria 938 G6
Ibagué, Colombia 922 B2
Ibarra, Ecuador 922 B2
Ibiapaba, Sa. da, Brazil 922 C5
Ibiza = Eivissa, Spain 928 C6
Ica, Peru 922 D2
Iça →, Brazil 922 C3
Içel = Mersin, Turkey 931 C4
Iceland ■, Europe 930 B2
Ich'ang = Yichang, China 934 C6
Ichihara, Japan 935 F7
Ichinomiya, Japan 935 F5
Idaho □, U.S.A. 918 B4
Idaho Falls, U.S.A. 918 B4
Idar-Oberstein, Germany 927 D3
Ife, Nigeria 938 G6
Iglésias, Italy 929 E2
Igloolik, Canada 917 B11
Igluligaarjuk = Chesterfield Inlet, Canada 916 B10
Iglulik = Igloolik, Canada 917 B11
Iguaçu →, Brazil 923 E4
Iguaçu, Cat. del, Brazil 923 E4
Iguaçu Falls = Iguaçu, Cat. del, Brazil 923 E4
Iguala, Mexico 920 D5
Iguassu = Iguaçu →, Brazil 923 E4
Iguatu, Brazil 922 C6
Iisalmi, Finland 930 E9
IJsselmeer, Neths. 927 B2
Ikaluktutiak, Canada 916 B9
Ikeda, Japan 935 F3
Ikparjuk = Arctic Bay, Canada 917 A11
Ilagan, Phil. 941 B4
Ile →, Kazakhstan 932 E8
Île-de-France □, France 926 B5
Ilebo, Dem. Rep. of the Congo 940 C4
Ilesha, Nigeria 938 G6
Ilfracombe, U.K. 924 E3
Ilhéus, Brazil 922 D6
Ili = Ile →, Kazakhstan 932 E8
Iliamna L., U.S.A. 916 C4
Iligan, Phil. 941 C4
Ilkeston, U.K. 924 D6
Ilkley, U.K. 924 C6
Illampu = Ancohuma, Nevado, Bolivia 922 D3
Illapel, Chile 923 F2
Iller →, Germany 927 D4
Illimani, Nevado, Bolivia 922 D3
Illinois □, U.S.A. 919 B9
Illinois →, U.S.A. 919 C8
Illium = Troy, Turkey 931 C3
Iloilo, Phil. 941 B4
Ilorin, Nigeria 938 G6
Imabari, Japan 935 F3
Imandra, Ozero, Russia 932 C4
Immingham, U.K. 924 C7
Imperatriz, Brazil 922 C5
Imphal, India 937 C8
In Salah, Algeria 938 C6
Inari, Finland 930 D9
Inarijärvi, Finland 930 D9
İnce Burun, Turkey 931 B4
Inch'ŏn, S. Korea 934 C7
Incomáti →, Mozam. 940 H6
Indalsälven →, Sweden 930 E7
India ■, Asia 937 C6
Indian Ocean 915 E13
Indiana □, U.S.A. 919 C9
Indianapolis, U.S.A. 919 C9
Indigirka →, Russia 933 B15
Indo-China, Asia 941 B2
Indonesia ■, Asia 941 D3
Indore, India 937 C6
Indre →, France 926 C4
Indus →, Pakistan 936 C5
İnebolu, Turkey 931 B4
Ingleborough, U.K. 924 B5
Ingolstadt, Germany 927 D5
Ingushetia □, Russia 931 B6
Ining = Yining, China 932 E9
Inishbofin, Ireland 925 H9
Inisheer, Ireland 925 H10
Inishfree B., Ireland 925 F11
Inishmaan, Ireland 925 H10
Inishmore, Ireland 925 H10
Inishowen Pen., Ireland 925 F12
Inishshark, Ireland 925 H9
Inishturk, Ireland 925 H9
Inland Sea = Setonaikai, Japan 935 F3
Inn →, Austria 927 D6
Inner Hebrides, U.K. 925 E2
Inner Mongolia = Nei Monggol Zizhiqu □, China 934 B6
Inner Sound, U.K. 925 D3
Innsbruck, Austria 927 E5
Inny →, Ireland 925 H12
Inoucdjouac = Inukjuak, Canada 917 C12
Inowrocław, Poland 927 B9
Insein, Burma 937 D8
Inta, Russia 932 C6
Interlaken, Switz. 926 C7
Inukjuak, Canada 917 C12
Inuvik, Canada 916 B6
Inveraray, U.K. 925 E3
Inverbervie, U.K. 925 E6
Invercargill, N.Z. 943 K12
Invergordon, U.K. 925 D4
Inverness, U.K. 925 D4
Inverurie, U.K. 925 D6
Iona, U.K. 925 E2
Ionian Is. = Iónioi Nísoi, Greece 931 C2
Ionian Sea, Medit. S. 929 F6
Iónioi Nísoi, Greece 931 C2
Iowa □, U.S.A. 919 B8
Iowa City, U.S.A. 919 B8
Ipin = Yibin, China 934 D5
Ipoh, Malaysia 941 C2
Ipswich, Australia 942 F9
Ipswich, U.K. 924 D9
Iqaluit, Canada 917 B13
Iquique, Chile 922 E2
Iquitos, Peru 922 C2
Iráklion, Greece 931 C3
Iran ■, Asia 936 B4
Irapuato, Mexico 920 C4
Iraq ■, Asia 936 B3
Ireland ■, Europe 925 H12
Ireland, Northern = Northern Ireland □, U.K. 925 G13
Irian Jaya = Papua □, Indonesia 941 D5
Iringa, Tanzania 940 D7
Irish Republic ■, Europe 925 H12
Irish Sea, U.K. 924 C3
Irkutsk, Russia 933 D11
Iron Mountain, U.S.A. 919 A9
Ironwood, U.S.A. 919 A8
Irrawaddy →, Burma 937 D8
Irtysh →, Russia 932 C7
Irunea = Pamplona, Spain 928 A5
Irvine, U.K. 925 F4
Irvinestown, U.K. 925 G12
Isabela, Puerto Rico 921 d
Ísafjörður, Iceland 930 A1
Isar →, Germany 927 D6
Isère →, France 926 D6
Isfahan = Eşfahān, Iran 936 B4
Ishinomaki, Japan 935 D7
Ishpeming, U.S.A. 919 A9
İskenderun, Turkey 931 C5
Isla →, U.K. 925 E5
Islamabad, Pakistan 937 B6
Island L., Canada 916 C10
Islay, U.K. 925 F2
Ismail = Izmayil, Ukraine 931 A3
Ismâ'ilîya, Egypt 939 B12
Isparta, Turkey 931 C4
Israel ■, Asia 931 D4
Issoire, France 926 D5
Issyk-Kul, Ozero = Ysyk-Köl, Kyrgyzstan 932 E8
İstanbul, Turkey 931 B3
İstanbul Boğazı, Turkey 931 B3
Istra, Croatia 929 B5
Istres, France 926 E6
Istria = Istra, Croatia 929 B5
Itabira, Brazil 922 D5
Itabuna, Brazil 922 D6
Itacoatiara, Brazil 922 C4
Itajaí, Brazil 923 E5
Italy ■, Europe 929 C4
Itapicuru →, Brazil 922 D6
Ithaca, U.S.A. 919 B11
Ivano-Frankivsk, Ukraine 932 E3
Ivano-Frankovsk = Ivano-Frankivsk, Ukraine 932 E3
Ivanovo, Russia 932 D5
Ivory Coast ■, Africa 938 G4
Ivujivik, Canada 917 B12
Ivybridge, U.K. 924 F4
Iwaki, Japan 935 E7
Iwakuni, Japan 935 F3
Iwo, Nigeria 938 G6
Izhevsk, Russia 932 D6
Izmayil, Ukraine 931 A3
İzmir, Turkey 931 C3
İzmit = Kocaeli, Turkey 931 B3
İznik Gölü, Turkey 931 B3
Izumi-Sano, Japan 935 F4

J

Jabalpur, India 937 C6
Jaboatão, Brazil 922 C6
Jackson, Barbados 921 g
Jackson, Mich., U.S.A. 919 B10
Jackson, Miss., U.S.A. 919 D8
Jackson, Tenn., U.S.A. 919 C9
Jacksonville, U.S.A. 919 D10
Jacmel, Haiti 921 D10
Jadotville = Likasi, Dem. Rep. of the Congo 940 E5
Jaén, Spain 928 D4
Jaffa = Tel Aviv-Yafo, Israel 931 D4
Jaffna, Sri Lanka 937 E7
Jahrom, Iran 936 C4
Jaipur, India 937 C6
Jakarta, Indonesia 941 D2
Jalapa Enríquez = Xalapa, Mexico 920 D5
Jalna, India 937 D6
Jamaica ■, W. Indies 920 a
Jambi, Indonesia 941 D2
James →, U.S.A. 919 B7
James B., Canada 917 C11
Jamestown, N. Dak., U.S.A. 918 A7
Jamestown, N.Y., U.S.A. 919 B11
Jammu, India 937 B6
Jammu & Kashmir □, India 937 B6
Jamnagar, India 937 C6
Jamshedpur, India 937 C7
Jan Mayen, Arctic 944 B6
Janesville, U.S.A. 919 B9
Januária, Brazil 922 D5
Japan ■, Asia 935 F5
Japan, Sea of, Asia 935 D4
Japen = Yapen, Indonesia 941 D5
Japurá →, Brazil 922 C3
Jargalant = Hovd, Mongolia 934 B4
Jari →, Brazil 922 C4
Jäsk, Iran 936 C4
Jasper, Canada 916 C8
Jauja, Peru 922 D2
Jaunpur, India 937 C7
Java = Jawa, Indonesia 941 D3
Java Sea, Indonesia 941 D2
Java Trench, Ind. Oc. 941 D2
Jawa, Indonesia 941 D3
Jaya, Puncak, Indonesia 941 D5
Jebel, Bahr el →, Sudan 939 G12
Jedburgh, U.K. 925 F6
Jedda = Jiddah, Si. Arabia 936 C2
Jefferson City, U.S.A. 919 C8
Jeju = Cheju do, S. Korea 934 C7
Jelenia Góra, Poland 927 C7
Jena, Germany 927 C5
Jequié, Brazil 922 D5
Jequitinhonha →, Brazil 922 D6
Jérémie, Haiti 921 D10
Jerez de la Frontera, Spain 928 D2
Jerid, Chott el = Djerid, Chott, Tunisia 938 B7
Jersey, U.K. 926 B2
Jersey City, U.S.A. 919 B12
Jerusalem, Israel 931 D5
Jesselton = Kota Kinabalu, Malaysia 941 C3
Jhaarkand = Jharkhand □, India 937 C7
Jhansi, India 937 C6
Jharkhand □, India 937 C7
Jhelum →, Pakistan 937 B6
Jiamusi, China 934 B8
Ji'an, China 934 D6
Jiangmen, China 934 D6
Jiangsu □, China 934 C7
Jiangxi □, China 934 D6
Jiaxing, China 934 C7
Jiayi = Chiai, Taiwan 934 D7
Jibuti = Djibouti ■, Africa 936 D3
Jiddah, Si. Arabia 936 C2
Jihlava →, Czech Rep. 927 D8
Jilin, China 934 B7
Jilong = Chilung, Taiwan 934 D7
Jiménez, Mexico 920 B4
Jinan, China 934 C6
Jinchang, China 934 C5
Jingdezhen, China 934 D6
Jinggu, China 934 D5
Jinhua, China 934 D6
Jining, Nei Monggol Zizhiqu, China 934 B6
Jining, Shandong, China 934 C6
Jinja, Uganda 940 B6
Jinzhou, China 934 B7
Jiujiang, China 934 D6
Jixi, China 934 B8
Jizzakh, Uzbekistan 932 E7
João Pessoa, Brazil 922 C6
Jodhpur, India 937 C6
Jogjakarta = Yogyakarta, Indonesia 941 D3
Johannesburg, S. Africa 940 H5
John Crow Mts., Jamaica 920 a
John Day →, U.S.A. 918 A2
John o' Groats, U.K. 925 C5
Johnson City, U.S.A. 919 C10
Johnstown, U.S.A. 919 B11
Johor Baharu, Malaysia 941 C2
Joinville, Brazil 923 E5
Joliet, U.S.A. 919 B9
Joliette, Canada 917 D12
Jolo, Phil. 941 C4
Jonesboro, U.S.A. 919 C8
Jönköping, Sweden 930 F6
Jonquière, Canada 917 D12
Joplin, U.S.A. 919 C8
Jordan ■, Asia 936 B2
Jordan →, Asia 931 D5
Jos, Nigeria 938 G7
Joseph Bonaparte G., Australia 942 C4
Jost Van Dyke, Br. Virgin Is. 921 e
Jotunheimen, Norway 930 E5
Juan de Fuca Str., Canada 918 A2
Juan Fernández, Arch. de, Pac. Oc. 914 F6
Juàzeiro, Brazil 922 C5
Juàzeiro do Norte, Brazil 922 C6
Juba = Giuba →, Somali Rep. 936 E3
Juba, Sudan 939 H12
Jubbulpore = Jabalpur, India 937 C6
Juchitán, Mexico 920 D5
Jugoslavia = Serbia ■, Europe 931 B2
Juiz de Fora, Brazil 922 E5
Juliaca, Peru 922 D2
Julianatop, Suriname 922 B4
Julianehåb = Qaqortoq, Greenland 917 B6
Jullundur, India 937 B6
Jumna = Yamuna →, India 937 C7
Junagadh, India 937 C6
Jundiaí, Brazil 923 E5
Juneau, U.S.A. 916 C6
Junggar Pendi, China 934 B3
Junín, Argentina 923 F3
Jura = Jura, Mts. du, Europe 926 C7
Jura = Schwäbische Alb, Germany 927 D4
Jura, U.K. 925 F3
Jura, Mts. du, Europe 926 C7
Jura, Sd. of, U.K. 925 F3
Juruá →, Brazil 922 C3
Juruena →, Brazil 922 C4
Jutland = Jylland, Denmark 930 F5
Juventud, I. de la, Cuba 921 C8
Jylland, Denmark 930 F5
Jyväskylä, Finland 930 E9

K

K2, Pakistan 937 B6
Kaapstad = Cape Town, S. Africa 940 J3
Kabardino-Balkar Republic = Kabardino-Balkaria □, Russia 931 B6
Kabardino-Balkaria □, Russia 931 B6
Kābul, Afghan. 937 B5
Kabwe, Zambia 940 E5
Kachchh, Gulf of, India 937 C5
Kachin □, Burma 937 C8
Kaçkar, Turkey 931 B6
Kadavu, Fiji 943 E14
Kadiyevka = Stakhanov, Ukraine 931 A5
Kadoma, Zimbabwe 940 F5
Kaduna, Nigeria 938 F7
Kaesŏng, N. Korea 934 C7
Kafue →, Zambia 940 F5
Kagoshima, Japan 935 H2
Kahoolawe, U.S.A. 918 H16

Marbella

Lamesa, U.S.A. 918 D6
Lammermuir Hills, U.K. 925 F6
Lamon B., Phil. 941 B4
Lampeter, U.K. 924 D3
Lanark, U.K. 925 F5
Lancashire □, U.K. 924 C5
Lancaster, U.K. 924 B5
Lancaster, Calif., U.S.A. 918 D3
Lancaster, Pa., U.S.A. 919 B11
Lancaster Sd., Canada 917 A11
Lanchow = Lanzhou, China 934 C5
Landes, France 926 D3
Land's End, U.K. 924 F2
Langholm, U.K. 925 F5
Langres, France 926 C6
Langres, Plateau de, France 926 C6
Langsa, Indonesia 941 C1
Languedoc, France 926 E5
Lannion, France 926 B2
L'Anse la Raye, St. Lucia 921 f
Lansing, U.S.A. 919 B10
Lanzarote, Canary Is. 938 C3
Lanzhou, China 934 C5
Laoag, Phil. 941 B4
Laon, France 926 B5
Laos ■, Asia 941 B2
Lapland = Lappland, Europe 930 D8
Lappland, Europe 930 D8
Laptev Sea, Russia 933 B13
Laramie, U.S.A. 918 B5
Laramie Mts., U.S.A. 918 B5
Laredo, U.S.A. 918 E7
Largs, U.K. 925 F4
Larnaca, Cyprus 931 D4
Larne, U.K. 925 G14
Larrimah, Australia 942 D5
Larsen Ice Shelf, Antarctica 944 D3
Larvik, Norway 930 F6
Las Cruces, U.S.A. 918 D5
Las Palmas, Canary Is. 938 C2
Las Vegas, N. Mex., U.S.A. 918 C5
Las Vegas, Nev., U.S.A. 918 C3
Lashio, Burma 937 C8
Lassen Pk., U.S.A. 918 B2
Lastoursville, Gabon 940 C2
Latacunga, Ecuador 922 C2
Latakia = Al Lādhiqīyah, Syria 936 B2
Latina, Italy 929 D4
Latium = Lazio □, Italy 929 C4
Latvia ■, Europe 932 D3
Lau Group, Fiji 943 D15
Launceston, Australia 942 J8
Launceston, U.K. 924 F3
Laune →, Ireland 925 J10
Laurel, U.S.A. 919 D9
Laurencekirk, U.K. 925 E6
Lausanne, Switz. 926 C7
Lavagh More, Ireland 925 G11
Laval, France 926 B3
Lawrence, Kans., U.S.A. 919 C7
Lawrence, Mass., U.S.A. 919 B12
Lawton, U.S.A. 918 D7
Lazio □, Italy 929 C4
Le Creusot, France 926 C6
Le François, Martinique 920 c
Le Havre, France 926 B4
Le Lamentin, Martinique 920 c
Le Mans, France 926 C4
Le Marin, Martinique 920 c
Le Mont-St-Michel, France 926 B3
Le Prêcheur, Martinique 920 c
Le Puy-en-Velay, France 926 D5
Le Robert, Martinique 920 c
Le St-Esprit, Martinique 920 c
Le Touquet-Paris-Plage, France 926 A4
Lea →, U.K. 924 E8
Leamington Spa = Royal Leamington Spa, U.K. 924 D6
Leane, L., Ireland 925 J10
Leavenworth, U.S.A. 919 C8
Lebanon, U.S.A. 919 C8
Lebanon ■, Asia 931 D5
Lebu, Chile 923 F2
Lecce, Italy 929 D7
Lee →, Ireland 925 K11
Leech L., U.S.A. 919 A8
Leeds, U.K. 924 C6
Leek, U.K. 924 C5
Leeuwarden, Neths. 927 B2
Leeuwin, C., Australia 942 G2
Leeward Is., Atl. Oc. 921 D12
Leganés, Spain 928 B4
Legazpi, Phil. 941 B4
Leghorn = Livorno, Italy 929 C3
Legnica, Poland 927 C8
Leicester, U.K. 924 D6
Leiden, Neths. 927 B2
Leine →, Germany 927 B4
Leinster □, Ireland 925 H12
Leinster, Mt., Ireland 925 J13
Leipzig, Germany 927 C6
Leith, U.K. 925 F5
Leitrim, Ireland 925 G11
Leizhou Bandao, China 934 D6
Léman, L., Europe 926 C7
Lena →, Russia 933 B13
Leninabad = Khŭjand, Tajikistan 932 E7
Leninakan = Gyumri, Armenia 931 B6
Leningrad = Sankt-Peterburg, Russia 932 D4
Lens, France 926 A5
Leodhas = Lewis, U.K. 925 C2
Leominster, U.K. 924 D5
León, Mexico 920 C4
León, Nic. 920 E7
León, Spain 928 A3
Leonora, Australia 942 F3
Lérida = Lleida, Spain 928 B6
Lerwick, U.K. 925 A7
Les Cayes, Haiti 921 D10
Les Sables-d'Olonne, France 926 C3
Lesbos = Lésvos, Greece 931 C3
Lesotho ■, Africa 940 H5
Lesser Antilles, W. Indies 921 E12
Lesser Slave L., Canada 916 C8
Lesser Sunda Is., Indonesia 941 D4
Lésvos, Greece 931 C3
Leszno, Poland 927 C8
Letchworth, U.K. 924 E7
Lethbridge, Canada 916 D8
Leti, Kepulauan, Indonesia 941 D4
Leti Is. = Leti, Kepulauan, Indonesia 941 D4
Leticia, Colombia 922 C2
Letterkenny, Ireland 925 G12
Leuven, Belgium 927 C2
Levelland, U.S.A. 918 D6
Leven, U.K. 925 E6
Leven, L., U.K. 925 E5
Lévis, Canada 917 D12
Levkôsia = Nicosia, Cyprus 931 C4
Lewes, U.K. 924 F8
Lewis, U.K. 925 C2
Lewis, Butt of, U.K. 925 C2
Lewisporte, Canada 917 D14
Lewiston, U.S.A. 918 A3
Lewistown, U.S.A. 918 A5
Lexington, U.S.A. 919 C10
Leyte □, Phil. 941 B4
Lhasa, China 934 D4
Lhazê, China 934 D3
L'Hospitalet de Llobregat, Spain 928 B7
Lianyungang, China 934 C6
Liaoning □, China 934 B7
Liaoyuan, China 934 B7
Liard →, Canada 916 B7
Libau = Liepāja, Latvia 932 D3
Liberal, U.S.A. 918 C6
Liberec, Czech Rep. 927 C7
Liberia ■, W. Afr. 938 G4
Lîbîya, Sahrâ', Africa 939 C10
Libourne, France 926 D3
Libreville, Gabon 940 B1
Libya ■, N. Afr. 939 C9
Libyan Desert = Lîbîya, Sahrâ', Africa 939 C10
Lichfield, U.K. 924 D6
Liechtenstein ■, Europe 926 C8
Liège, Belgium 927 C2
Liegnitz = Legnica, Poland 927 C8
Lienyünchiangshih = Lianyungang, China 934 C6
Liepāja, Latvia 932 D3
Liffey →, Ireland 925 H13
Lifford, Ireland 925 G12
Liguria □, Italy 926 D8
Ligurian Sea, Medit. S. 929 C2
Lihue, U.S.A. 918 H15
Lijiang, China 934 D5
Likasi, Dem. Rep. of the Congo 940 E5
Lille, France 926 A5
Lillehammer, Norway 930 E6
Lilongwe, Malawi 940 E6
Lima, Peru 922 D2
Lima, U.S.A. 919 B10
Limassol, Cyprus 931 D4
Limavady, U.K. 925 F13
Limay →, Argentina 923 F3
Limbe, Cameroon 940 B1
Limerick, Ireland 925 J11
Limerick □, Ireland 925 J11
Limfjorden, Denmark 930 F5
Limoges, France 926 D4
Limón, Costa Rica 921 F8
Limousin, France 926 D4
Limoux, France 926 E5
Limpopo →, Africa 940 H6
Linares, Chile 923 F2
Linares, Mexico 920 C5
Linares, Spain 928 C4
Lincoln, U.K. 924 C7
Lincoln, U.S.A. 919 B7
Lincoln Hav = Lincoln Sea, Arctic 944 A4
Lincoln Sea, Arctic 944 A4
Lincolnshire Wolds, U.K. 924 C7
Lindesnes, Norway 930 F5
Lingga, Kepulauan, Indonesia 941 D2
Lingga Arch. = Lingga, Kepulauan, Indonesia 941 D2
Linhai, China 934 D7
Linhares, Brazil 922 D6
Linköping, Sweden 930 F7
Linnhe, L., U.K. 925 E3
Linstead, Jamaica 920 a
Linxia, China 934 C5
Linz, Austria 927 D7
Lion, G. du, France 926 E6
Lions, G. of = Lion, G. du, France 926 E6
Lipa, Phil. 941 B4
Lipetsk, Russia 932 D4
Lippe →, Germany 927 C3
Liquillo, Sierra de, Puerto Rico 921 d
Lisboa, Portugal 928 C1
Lisbon = Lisboa, Portugal 928 C1
Lisburn, U.K. 925 G13
Liscannor B., Ireland 925 J10
Lisichansk = Lysychansk, Ukraine 931 A5
Lisieux, France 926 B4
Liski, Russia 932 D4
Lismore, Australia 942 F9
Lismore, Ireland 925 J12
Listowel, Ireland 925 J10
Lithuania ■, Europe 932 D3
Little Minch, U.K. 925 D2
Little Missouri →, U.S.A. 918 A6
Little Rock, U.S.A. 919 D8
Littlehampton, U.K. 924 F7
Liuwa Plain, Zambia 940 E4
Liuzhou, China 934 D5
Liverpool, Canada 917 D13
Liverpool, U.K. 924 C4
Liverpool Bay, U.K. 924 C4
Livingston, U.K. 925 F5
Livingston, U.S.A. 918 A4
Livingstone, Zambia 940 F5
Livorno, Italy 929 C3
Lizard Pt., U.K. 924 G2
Ljubljana, Slovenia 929 A5
Llandeilo, U.K. 924 E4
Llandovery, U.K. 924 E4
Llandrindod Wells, U.K. 924 D4
Llandudno, U.K. 924 C4
Llanelli, U.K. 924 E3
Llangollen, U.K. 924 D4
Llano Estacado, U.S.A. 918 D6
Llanos, S. Amer. 922 B2
Llanquihue, L., Chile 923 G2
Llanwrtyd Wells, U.K. 924 D4
Lleida, Spain 928 B6
Lleyn Peninsula, U.K. 924 D3
Lloret de Mar, Spain 928 B7
Lloydminster, Canada 916 C9
Llullaillaco, Volcán, S. Amer. 923 E3
Lobatse, Botswana 940 H5
Lobito, Angola 940 E2
Loch Baghasdail = Lochboisdale, U.K. 925 D1
Loch Garman = Wexford, Ireland 925 J13
Loch Nam Madadh = Lochmaddy, U.K. 925 D1
Lochboisdale, U.K. 925 D1
Loches, France 926 C4
Lochgilphead, U.K. 925 E3
Lochinver, U.K. 925 C3
Lochmaddy, U.K. 925 D1
Lochnagar, U.K. 925 E5
Lochy, L., U.K. 925 E4
Lockerbie, U.K. 925 F5
Łódź, Poland 927 C9
Lofoten, Norway 930 D6
Logan, U.S.A. 918 B4
Logan, Mt., Canada 916 B5
Logroño, Spain 928 A4
Loir →, France 926 C3
Loire →, France 926 C2
Loja, Ecuador 922 C2
Lombárdia □, Italy 926 D8
Lombardy = Lombárdia □, Italy 926 D8
Lomblen, Indonesia 941 D4
Lombok, Indonesia 941 D3
Lomé, Togo 938 G6
Lomond, L., U.K. 925 E4
London, Canada 917 D11
London, U.K. 924 E7
London Gatwick ✈ (LGW), U.K. 924 E7
London Heathrow ✈ (LHR), U.K. 924 E7
Londonderry, U.K. 925 G12
Londonderry □, U.K. 925 G12
Londonderry, C., Australia 942 C4
Londrina, Brazil 923 E4
Long Beach, U.S.A. 918 D3
Long Eaton, U.K. 924 D6
Long I., Bahamas 921 C9
Long I., Ireland 925 K10
Long I., U.S.A. 919 B12
Long Xuyen, Vietnam 941 B2
Longford, Ireland 925 H12
Longreach, Australia 942 E7
Longview, Tex., U.S.A. 919 D8
Longview, Wash., U.S.A. 918 A2
Lons-le-Saunier, France 926 C6
Looe, U.K. 924 F3
Loop Hd., Ireland 925 J10
Lop Nor = Lop Nur, China 934 B4
Lop Nur, China 934 B4
Lopez, C., Gabon 940 C1
Lorca, Spain 928 D5
Lord Howe I., Pac. Oc. 943 G10
Lord Howe Ridge, Pac. Oc. 943 H12
Lordsburg, U.S.A. 918 D5
Lorient, France 926 C2
Lorn, Firth of, U.K. 925 E3
Lorraine □, France 926 B7
Los Alamos, U.S.A. 918 C5
Los Andes, Chile 923 F2
Los Angeles, Chile 923 F2
Los Angeles, U.S.A. 918 D3
Los Mochis, Mexico 920 B3
Los Roques Is., Venezuela 922 A3
Lossiemouth, U.K. 925 D5
Lostwithiel, U.K. 924 F3
Lot →, France 926 D4
Lota, Chile 923 F2
Loughborough, U.K. 924 D6
Loughrea, Ireland 925 H11
Loughros More B., Ireland 925 G11
Louis XIV, Pte., Canada 917 C12
Louisiade Arch., Papua N. G. 942 C9
Louisiana □, U.S.A. 919 D8
Louisville, U.S.A. 919 C9
Lourdes, France 926 E3
Louth, Ireland 925 H13
Louth, U.K. 924 C7
Louvain = Leuven, Belgium 927 C2
Lowell, U.S.A. 919 B12
Lower California = Baja California, Mexico 920 A1
Lower Saxony = Niedersachsen □, Germany 927 B4
Lower Tunguska = Tunguska, Nizhnyaya →, Russia 933 C9
Lowestoft, U.K. 924 D9
Loyalty Is. = Loyauté, Îs., N. Cal. 943 E12
Loyang = Luoyang, China 934 C6
Loyauté, Îs., N. Cal. 943 E12
Lualaba →, Dem. Rep. of the Congo 940 B5
Luanda, Angola 940 D2
Luang Prabang, Laos 941 B2
Luangwa →, Zambia 940 E6
Luanshya, Zambia 940 E5
Luapula →, Africa 940 D5
Lubango, Angola 940 E2
Lubbock, U.S.A. 918 D6
Lübeck, Germany 927 B5
Lubero = Luofu, Dem. Rep. of the Congo 940 C5
Lublin, Poland 930 G8
Lubumbashi, Dem. Rep. of the Congo 940 E5
Lucania, Mt., Canada 916 B5
Luce Bay, U.K. 925 G4
Lucea, Jamaica 920 a
Lucena, Phil. 941 B4
Lucerne = Luzern, Switz. 926 C8
Lucknow, India 937 C7
Lüda = Dalian, China 934 C7
Lüderitz, Namibia 940 H3
Ludhiana, India 937 B6
Ludington, U.S.A. 919 B9
Ludlow, U.K. 924 D5
Ludwigshafen, Germany 927 D4
Lufkin, U.S.A. 919 D8
Luga, Russia 932 D3
Lugano, Switz. 926 C8
Lugansk = Luhansk, Ukraine 931 A5
Lugnaquillia, Ireland 925 J13
Lugo, Spain 928 A2
Luhansk, Ukraine 931 A5
Luimneach = Limerick, Ireland 925 J11
Luing, U.K. 925 E3
Lule älv →, Sweden 930 D8
Luleå, Sweden 930 D8
Lundy, U.K. 924 E3
Lune →, U.K. 924 B5
Lüneburg Heath = Lüneburger Heide, Germany 927 B5
Lüneburger Heide, Germany 927 B5
Lunéville, France 926 B7
Luni →, India 937 C6
Luofu, Dem. Rep. of the Congo 940 C5
Luoyang, China 934 C6
Lurgan, U.K. 925 G13
Lusaka, Zambia 940 F5
Lūt, Dasht-e, Iran 936 B4
Luta = Dalian, China 934 C7
Luton, U.K. 924 E7
Łutsel'ke, Canada 916 B8
Lutsk, Ukraine 932 D3
Luxembourg, Lux. 926 B7
Luxembourg ■, Europe 926 B7
Luxor = El Uqsur, Egypt 939 C12
Luzern, Switz. 926 C8
Luzhou, China 934 D5
Luzon, Phil. 941 B4
Lviv, Ukraine 932 E3
Lvov = Lviv, Ukraine 932 E3
Lyakhovskiye, Ostrova, Russia 933 B15
Lyallpur = Faisalabad, Pakistan 937 B6
Lybster, U.K. 925 C5
Lyme B., U.K. 924 F5
Lyme Regis, U.K. 924 F5
Lynchburg, U.S.A. 919 C11
Lynn Lake, Canada 916 C9
Lyon, France 926 D6
Lyonnais, France 926 D6
Lyons = Lyon, France 926 D6
Lysychansk, Ukraine 931 A5
Lytham St. Anne's, U.K. 924 C4

M

Ma'ān, Jordan 936 B2
Ma'anshan, China 934 C6
Maas →, Neths. 927 C2
Maastricht, Neths. 926 A6
Mablethorpe, U.K. 924 C8
McAlester, U.S.A. 919 D7
McAllen, U.S.A. 918 E7
MacAlpine L., Canada 916 B9
Macao = Macau, China 934 D6
Macapá, Brazil 922 B4
Macau, Brazil 922 C6
Macau, China 934 D6
Macclesfield, U.K. 924 C5
M'Clintock Chan., Canada 916 A9
M'Clure Str., Canada 944 B1
McComb, U.S.A. 919 D8
McCook, U.S.A. 918 B6
McDonald Is., Ind. Oc. 915 G13
MacDonnell Ranges, Australia 942 E5
Macduff, U.K. 925 D6
Maceió, Brazil 922 C6
Macgillycuddy's Reeks, Ireland 925 K10
Machakos, Kenya 940 C7
Machala, Ecuador 922 C2
Machynlleth, U.K. 924 D4
Mackay, Australia 942 E8
Mackay, L., Australia 942 E4
Mackenzie, Canada 916 C7
Mackenzie →, Canada 916 B6
Mackenzie Mts., Canada 916 B6
McKinley, Mt., U.S.A. 916 B4
McKinley Sea, Arctic 944 A6
McMinnville, U.S.A. 918 A2
McMurdo Sd., Antarctica 944 E15
McMurray = Fort McMurray, Canada 916 C8
Mâcon, France 926 C6
Macon, U.S.A. 919 D10
McPherson, U.S.A. 918 C7
Macroom, Ireland 925 K11
Madagascar ■, Africa 940 G9
Madang, Papua N. G. 942 B8
Madeira, Atl. Oc. 938 B2
Madeira →, Brazil 922 C4
Madeleine, Îs. de la, Canada 917 D13
Madhya Pradesh □, India 937 C6
Madison, S. Dak., U.S.A. 919 B7
Madison, Wis., U.S.A. 919 B9
Madiun, Indonesia 941 D3
Madras = Chennai, India 937 D7
Madras = Tamil Nadu □, India 937 D6
Madre de Dios →, Bolivia 922 D3
Madre de Dios, I., Chile 923 H2
Madre Occidental, Sierra, Mexico 920 B3
Madre Oriental, Sierra, Mexico 920 C5
Madrid, Spain 928 B4
Madura, Indonesia 941 D3
Madurai, India 937 E6
Maebashi, Japan 935 E6
Mafia I., Tanzania 940 D7
Magadan, Russia 933 D16
Magallanes, Estrecho de, Chile 923 H2
Magangué, Colombia 922 B2
Magdalen Is. = Madeleine, Îs. de la, Canada 917 D13
Magdalena →, Colombia 922 A2
Magdeburg, Germany 927 B5
Magelang, Indonesia 941 D3
Magellan's Str. = Magallanes, Estrecho de, Chile 923 H2
Maggiore, Lago, Italy 926 D8
Maggotty, Jamaica 920 a
Magherafelt, U.K. 925 G13
Maghreb, N. Afr. 938 B5
Magnetic Pole (North), Canada 944 B1
Magnetic Pole (South), Antarctica 944 D13
Magnitogorsk, Russia 932 D6
Magosa = Famagusta, Cyprus 931 C4
Maġusa = Famagusta, Cyprus 931 C4
Mahajanga, Madag. 940 F9
Mahakam →, Indonesia 941 D3
Mahalapye, Botswana 940 G5
Mahanadi →, India 937 C7
Maharashtra □, India 937 C6
Mahdia, Tunisia 939 A8
Mahilyow, Belarus 932 D4
Mai-Ndombe, L., Dem. Rep. of the Congo 940 C3
Maidenhead, U.K. 924 E7
Maidstone, U.K. 924 E8
Maiduguri, Nigeria 939 F8
Main →, Germany 927 D4
Main →, U.K. 925 G13
Maine, France 926 C3
Maine □, U.S.A. 919 A13
Maine →, Ireland 925 J10
Mainland, Orkney, U.K. 925 C5
Mainland, Shet., U.K. 925 A7
Mainz, Germany 927 C4
Maiquetía, Venezuela 922 A3
Majorca = Mallorca, Spain 928 C7
Makale, Indonesia 941 D3
Makarikari = Makgadikgadi Salt Pans, Botswana 940 G5
Makasar = Ujung Pandang, Indonesia 941 D3
Makasar, Selat, Indonesia 941 D3
Makasar, Str. of = Makasar, Selat, Indonesia 941 D3
Makgadikgadi Salt Pans, Botswana 940 G5
Makhachkala, Russia 931 B7
Makhado, S. Africa 940 G5
Makkah, Si. Arabia 936 C2
Makurdi, Nigeria 938 G7
Mal B., Ireland 925 J10
Malabar Coast, India 937 D6
Malabo = Rey Malabo, Eq. Guin. 940 B1
Malacca, Str. of, Indonesia 941 C2
Málaga, Spain 928 D3
Malagasy Rep. = Madagascar ■, Africa 940 G9
Malahide, Ireland 925 H13
Malaita, Solomon Is. 943 B11
Malakâl, Sudan 939 G12
Malakula, Vanuatu 943 D12
Malang, Indonesia 941 D3
Malanje, Angola 940 D3
Mälaren, Sweden 930 F7
Malatya, Turkey 931 C5
Malawi ■, Africa 940 E6
Malawi, L. = Nyasa, L., Africa 940 E6
Malay Pen., Asia 941 C2
Malaysia ■, Asia 941 C3
Maldives ■, Ind. Oc. 937 E6
Maldonado, Uruguay 923 F4
Malheur L., U.S.A. 918 B3
Mali ■, Africa 938 E5
Malin Hd., Ireland 925 F12
Malin Pen., Ireland 925 F12
Malindi, Kenya 940 C8
Malines = Mechelen, Belgium 927 C2
Mallaig, U.K. 925 D3
Mallicolo = Malakula, Vanuatu 943 D12
Mallorca, Spain 928 C7
Mallow, Ireland 925 J11
Malmö, Sweden 930 F6
Malta ■, Europe 929 G5
Malton, U.K. 924 B7
Maluku, Indonesia 941 D4
Maluku Sea = Molucca Sea, Indonesia 941 D4
Malvern Hills, U.K. 924 D5
Malvinas, Is. = Falkland Is. ☑, Atl. Oc. 923 H4
Mamoré →, Bolivia 922 D3
Man, Ivory C. 938 G4
Man, I. of, U.K. 924 B3
Manaar, G. of = Mannar, G. of, Asia 937 E6
Manado, Indonesia 941 C4
Managua, Nic. 920 E7
Manama = Al Manāmah, Bahrain 936 C4
Manaos = Manaus, Brazil 922 C3
Manas, China 934 B3
Manatí, Puerto Rico 921 d
Manaus, Brazil 922 C3
Manchester, U.K. 924 C5
Manchester, U.S.A. 919 B12
Manchuria = Dongbei, China 933 E13
Mandal, Norway 930 F5
Mandalay, Burma 937 C8
Mandale = Mandalay, Burma 937 C8
Mandan, U.S.A. 918 A6
Mandeville, Jamaica 920 a
Mandsaur, India 937 C6
Mangalore, India 937 D6
Mangnai, China 934 C4
Mangole, Indonesia 941 D4
Manhattan, U.S.A. 919 C7
Manica, Mozam. 940 F6
Manicoré, Brazil 922 C3
Manicouagan →, Canada 917 D13
Manicouagan, Rés., Canada 917 C13
Manila, Phil. 941 B4
Manipur □, India 937 C8
Manisa, Turkey 931 C3
Manistee, U.S.A. 919 B9
Manistique, U.S.A. 919 A9
Manitoba □, Canada 916 C10
Manitoba, L., Canada 916 C10
Manitoulin I., Canada 917 D11
Manitowoc, U.S.A. 919 B9
Manizales, Colombia 922 B2
Mankato, U.S.A. 919 B8
Mannar, Sri Lanka 937 E6
Mannar, G. of, Asia 937 E6
Mannheim, Germany 927 D4
Manning, Canada 916 C8
Manokwari, Indonesia 941 D5
Manosque, France 926 E6
Mansel I., Canada 917 B11
Mansfield, U.K. 924 C6
Mansfield, U.S.A. 919 B10
Manta, Ecuador 922 C1
Mantes-la-Jolie, France 926 B4
Mántova, Italy 929 B3
Mantua = Mántova, Italy 929 B3
Manzanillo, Cuba 921 C9
Manzanillo, Mexico 920 D4
Manzhouli, China 934 B6
Maoming, China 934 D6
Mapam Yumco, China 934 C3
Maputo, Mozam. 940 H6
Maquan He = Brahmaputra →, Asia 937 C7
Maquinchao, Argentina 923 G3
Mar Chiquita, L., Argentina 923 F3
Mar del Plata, Argentina 923 F4
Marabá, Brazil 922 C5
Maracá, I. de, Brazil 922 B4
Maracaibo, Venezuela 922 A2
Maracaibo, L. de, Venezuela 922 B2
Maracay, Venezuela 922 A3
Maradi, Niger 938 F7
Marajó, I. de, Brazil 922 C5
Maranhão = São Luís, Brazil 922 C5
Maranhão □, Brazil 922 C5
Marañón →, Peru 922 C2
Maraş = Kahramanmaraş, Turkey 931 C5
Marbella, Spain 928 D3

O

P

Serbia

Rhodopi Planina, Bulgaria 931 B2
Rhön, Germany 927 C4
Rhondda, U.K. 924 E4
Rhône →, France 926 E6
Rhum, U.K. 925 E2
Rhyl, U.K. 924 C4
Riau, Kepulauan, Indonesia 941 C2
Riau Arch. = Riau, Kepulauan, Indonesia 941 C2
Ribble →, U.K. 924 C5
Ribeirão Prêto, Brazil 922 E5
Riberalta, Bolivia 922 D3
Richards Bay, S. Africa 940 H6
Richfield, U.S.A. 918 C4
Richland, U.S.A. 918 A3
Richmond, U.K. 924 B6
Richmond, Ind., U.S.A. 919 C10
Richmond, Ky., U.S.A. 919 C10
Richmond, Va., U.S.A. 919 C11
Ridgecrest, U.S.A. 918 C3
Rīga, Latvia 932 D3
Rigolet, Canada 917 C14
Rijeka, Croatia 929 B5
Rímini, Italy 929 B4
Rimouski, Canada 917 D13
Rio Branco, Brazil 922 C3
Rio Claro, Brazil 923 E5
Río Cuarto, Argentina 923 F3
Rio de Janeiro, Brazil 923 E5
Rio de Janeiro □, Brazil 922 E5
Río Gallegos, Argentina 923 H3
Rio Grande, Brazil 923 F4
Río Grande, Nic. 921 E8
Río Grande, Puerto Rico 921 d
Rio Grande, U.S.A. 919 E7
Río Grande de Santiago →, Mexico 920 C3
Rio Grande do Norte □, Brazil 922 C6
Rio Grande do Sul □, Brazil 923 E4
Río Muni □, Eq. Guin. 940 B2
Ríobamba, Ecuador 922 C2
Ríohacha, Colombia 922 A2
Ripon, U.K. 924 B6
Rivera, Uruguay 923 F4
Riverside, U.S.A. 918 D3
Riverton, U.S.A. 918 B5
Rivière-du-Loup, Canada 917 D13
Rivière-Pilote, Martinique 920 c
Rivière-Salée, Martinique 920 c
Rivne, Ukraine 932 D3
Riyadh = Ar Riyāḍ, Si. Arabia 936 C3
Rize, Turkey 931 B6
Road Town, Br. Virgin Is. 921 e
Roanne, France 926 C6
Roanoke, U.S.A. 919 C11
Roanoke →, U.S.A. 919 C11
Roberval, Canada 917 D12
Robson, Mt., Canada 916 C8
Roca, C. da, Portugal 928 C1
Rocha, Uruguay 923 F4
Rochdale, U.K. 924 C5
Rochefort, France 926 D3
Rochester, U.K. 924 E8
Rochester, Minn., U.S.A. 919 B8
Rochester, N.Y., U.S.A. 919 B11
Rock Hill, U.S.A. 919 D10
Rock Island, U.S.A. 919 B8
Rock Springs, U.S.A. 918 B5
Rockford, U.S.A. 919 B9
Rockhampton, Australia 942 E9
Rocky Mount, U.S.A. 919 C11
Rocky Mts., N. Amer. 916 C7
Rodez, France 926 D5
Ródhos, Greece 931 C3
Rodriguez, Ind. Oc. 915 E13
Roe →, U.K. 925 F13
Roes Welcome Sd., Canada 917 B11
Rojo, C., Mexico 920 C5
Rolla, U.S.A. 919 C8
Roma, Australia 942 F8
Roma, Italy 929 D4
Romaine →, Canada 917 C13
Romania ■, Europe 931 A3
Romans-sur-Isère, France 926 D6
Rome = Roma, Italy 929 D4
Rome, U.S.A. 919 D9
Romorantin-Lanthenay, France 926 C4
Romsey, U.K. 924 F6
Rona, U.K. 925 D3
Roncador, Serra do, Brazil 922 D4
Rondônia □, Brazil 922 D3
Ronge, L. la, Canada 916 C9
Ronne Ice Shelf, Antarctica 944 E4
Roosevelt I., Antarctica 944 E16
Roraima □, Brazil 922 B3
Roraima, Mt., Venezuela 922 B3
Rosario, Argentina 923 F3
Rosario, Mexico 920 C3
Rosario de la Frontera, Argentina 923 E3
Roscommon, Ireland 925 H11
Roscrea, Ireland 925 J12
Roseau, Domin. 921 D12
Roseburg, U.S.A. 918 B2
Rosenheim, Germany 927 E6
Rosetown, Canada 916 C9
Roseville, U.S.A. 918 C2
Roslavl, Russia 932 D4
Ross Ice Shelf, Antarctica 944 F16
Ross-on-Wye, U.K. 924 E5
Ross River, Canada 916 B6
Ross Sea, Antarctica 944 E15
Rossall Pt., U.K. 924 C4
Rossan Pt., Ireland 925 G11
Rosses, The, Ireland 925 F11
Rosslare, Ireland 925 J13
Rossosh, Russia 932 D4
Rostock, Germany 927 A6
Rostov, Russia 931 A5
Roswell, U.S.A. 918 D6
Rotherham, U.K. 924 C6
Rothes, U.K. 925 D5
Rotorua, N.Z. 943 H14
Rotterdam, Neths. 927 C2
Rotuma, Fiji 943 C14
Roubaix, France 926 A5
Rouen, France 926 B4
Round Mt., Australia 942 G9
Rousay, U.K. 925 B5
Roussillon, France 926 E5
Rouyn-Noranda, Canada 917 D12
Rovaniemi, Finland 930 D9
Rovno = Rivne, Ukraine 932 D3
Rovuma = Ruvuma →, Tanzania 940 E8
Roxas, Phil. 941 B4
Royal Canal, Ireland 925 H12
Royal Leamington Spa, U.K. 924 D6
Royal Tunbridge Wells, U.K. 924 E8
Royale, Isle, U.S.A. 919 A9
Royan, France 926 D3
Royston, U.K. 924 D7
Rub' al Khālī, Si. Arabia 936 D3
Rubh a' Mhail, U.K. 925 F2
Rubha Hunish, U.K. 925 D2
Rubha Robhanais = Lewis, Butt of, U.K. 925 C2
Ruby L., U.S.A. 918 B3
Rufiji →, Tanzania 940 D7
Rufling Pt., Br. Virgin Is. 921 e
Rugby, U.K. 924 D6
Ruhr →, Germany 927 C3
Rum = Rhum, U.K. 925 E2
Rumania = Romania ■, Europe 931 A3
Runaway Bay, Jamaica 920 a
Runcorn, U.K. 924 C5
Rundu, Namibia 940 F3
Ruoqiang, China 934 C3
Rupert, U.S.A. 918 B4
Rupert →, Canada 917 C12
Rupert House = Waskaganish, Canada 917 C12
Rush, Ireland 925 H13
Russellville, U.S.A. 919 C8
Russia ■, Eurasia 933 C11
Rustavi, Georgia 931 B7
Rustenburg, S. Africa 940 H5
Rutland Water, U.K. 924 D7
Ruvuma →, Tanzania 940 E8
Ruwenzori, Africa 940 B5
Rwanda ■, Africa 940 C6
Ryazan, Russia 932 D4
Rybinsk, Russia 932 D4
Ryde, U.K. 924 F6
Rye, U.K. 924 F8
Rye →, U.K. 924 B7
Rye Bay, U.K. 924 F8
Ryūkyū Is. = Ryūkyū-rettō, Japan 934 D7
Ryūkyū-rettō, Japan 934 D7
Rzeszów, Poland 930 G8
Rzhev, Russia 932 D4

S

Saale →, Germany 927 C5
Saar →, Europe 926 B7
Saarbrücken, Germany 927 D3
Saaremaa, Estonia 932 D3
Sabadell, Spain 928 B7
Sabah □, Malaysia 941 C3
Sabhah, Libya 939 C8
Sabinas, Mexico 920 B4
Sabinas Hidalgo, Mexico 920 B4
Sabine →, U.S.A. 919 E8
Sable, C., Canada 917 D13
Sable, C., U.S.A. 919 E10
Sable I., Canada 917 D14
Sachsen □, Germany 927 C6
Sachsen-Anhalt □, Germany 927 C6
Sacramento, U.S.A. 918 C2
Sacramento →, U.S.A. 918 C2
Sacramento Mts., U.S.A. 918 D5
Sadd el Aali, Egypt 939 D12
Sado, Japan 935 E6
Safford, U.S.A. 918 D5
Saffron Walden, U.K. 924 D8
Safi, Morocco 938 B4
Saga, Japan 935 G2
Sagarmatha = Everest, Mt., Nepal 937 C7
Sagar, India 937 C6
Saglouc = Salluit, Canada 917 B12
Sagua la Grande, Cuba 921 C8
Sahara, Africa 938 D6
Saharan Atlas = Saharien, Atlas, Algeria 938 B6
Saharanpur, India 937 C6
Saharien, Atlas, Algeria 938 B6
Sahel, Africa 938 E5
Sahiwal, Pakistan 937 B6
Sahrawi = Western Sahara ■, Africa 938 D3
Sa'īdābād = Sīrjān, Iran 936 C4
Saigon = Thanh Pho Ho Chi Minh, Vietnam 941 B2
St. Abb's Head, U.K. 925 F6
St. Albans, U.K. 924 E7
St. Alban's Head, U.K. 924 F5
St. Andrews, U.K. 925 E6
St. Ann's Bay, Jamaica 920 a
St. Anthony, Canada 917 C14
St-Augustin, Canada 917 C14
St. Augustine, U.S.A. 919 E10
St. Austell, U.K. 924 F3
St. Bees Hd., U.K. 924 B4
St. Brides B., U.K. 924 E2
St-Brieuc, France 926 B2
St. Christopher-Nevis = St. Kitts & Nevis ■, W. Indies 921 D12
St. Cloud, U.S.A. 919 A8
St. Croix, U.S. Virgin Is. 921 D12
St. David's, U.K. 924 E2
St. David's Head, U.K. 924 E2
St-Dizier, France 926 B6
St. Elias, Mt., U.S.A. 916 B5
St. Elias Mts., N. Amer. 916 C6
St-Étienne, France 926 D6
St-Flour, France 926 D5
St. Gallen = Sankt Gallen, Switz. 926 C8
St-Gaudens, France 926 E4
St. George, U.S.A. 918 C4
St. George's, Grenada 921 E12
St. George's Channel, Europe 925 K14
St. Gotthard P. = San Gottardo, P. del, Switz. 926 C8
St. Helena, Atl. Oc. 914 E9
St. Helens, U.K. 924 C5
St. Helens, Mt., U.S.A. 918 A2
St-Hyacinthe, Canada 917 D12
St. Ives, U.K. 924 F2
St-Jean, L., Canada 917 D12
St. John, Canada 917 D13
St. John I., U.S. Virgin Is. 921 e
St. John's, Antigua 921 D12
St. John's, Canada 917 D14
St. Johns →, U.S.A. 919 D10
St. John's Pt., Ireland 925 G11
St-Joseph, Martinique 920 c
St. Joseph, U.S.A. 919 C8
St. Joseph, L., Canada 917 C10
St. Kitts & Nevis ■, W. Indies 921 D12
St. Lawrence →, Canada 917 D13
St. Lawrence, Gulf of, Canada 917 D13
St. Lawrence I., U.S.A. 916 B3
St-Lô, France 926 B3
St-Louis, Guadeloupe 920 b
St. Louis, Senegal 938 E2
St. Louis, U.S.A. 919 C8
St. Lucia ■, W. Indies 921 f
St. Magnus B., U.K. 925 A7
St-Malo, France 926 B2
St-Marc, Haiti 921 D10
St-Martin, W. Indies 921 D12
St-Martin, C., Martinique 920 c
St. Martins, Barbados 921 g
St. Mary's, U.K. 925 C6
St. Matthew I., U.S.A. 916 B2
St-Nazaire, France 926 C2
St. Neots, U.K. 924 D7
St-Omer, France 926 A5
St. Paul, U.S.A. 919 B8
St. Paul, I., Ind. Oc. 915 F13
St. Petersburg = Sankt-Peterburg, Russia 932 D4
St. Petersburg, U.S.A. 919 E10
St-Pierre, Martinique 920 c
St-Pierre et Miquelon □, N. Amer. 917 D14
St-Quentin, France 926 B5
St. Thomas I., U.S. Virgin Is. 921 e
St-Tropez, France 926 E7
St. Vincent, G., Australia 942 G6
St. Vincent & the Grenadines ■, W. Indies 921 E12
Ste-Anne, Guadeloupe 920 b
Ste-Marie, Martinique 920 c
Ste-Rose, Guadeloupe 920 b
Saintes, France 926 D3
Saintes, I. des, Guadeloupe 920 b
Saintfield, U.K. 925 G14
Saintonge, France 926 D3
Sajama, Bolivia 922 D3
Sakakawea, L., U.S.A. 918 A6
Sakarya, Turkey 931 B4
Sakata, Japan 935 D6
Sakhalin, Russia 933 D15
Sala, Sweden 930 F7
Salado →, La Pampa, Argentina 923 F3
Salado →, Santa Fe, Argentina 923 F3
Salālah, Oman 936 D4
Salamanca, Spain 928 B3
Salar de Uyuni, Bolivia 922 E3
Salaverry, Peru 922 C2
Salayar, Indonesia 941 D4
Salcombe, U.K. 924 F4
Saldanha, S. Africa 940 J3
Sale, Australia 942 H8
Salé, Morocco 938 B4
Salekhard, Russia 932 C7
Salem, India 937 D6
Salem, U.S.A. 918 B2
Salerno, Italy 929 D5
Salford, U.K. 924 C5
Salida, U.S.A. 918 C5
Salina, U.S.A. 918 C7
Salina Cruz, Mexico 920 D5
Salinas, U.S.A. 918 C2
Salinas →, U.S.A. 918 C2
Salinas Grandes, Argentina 923 E3
Salisbury = Harare, Zimbabwe 940 F6
Salisbury, U.K. 924 E6
Salisbury, U.S.A. 919 C11
Salisbury I., Canada 917 B12
Salisbury Plain, U.K. 924 E6
Salliq = Coral Harbour, Canada 917 B11
Salluit, Canada 917 B12
Salmon, U.S.A. 918 A4
Salmon →, U.S.A. 918 A3
Salmon Arm, Canada 916 C8
Salmon River Mts., U.S.A. 918 B4
Salon-de-Provence, France 926 E6
Salonica = Thessaloníki, Greece 931 B2
Salsk, Russia 931 A6
Salt →, U.S.A. 918 D4
Salt Lake City, U.S.A. 918 B4
Salta, Argentina 923 E3
Saltash, U.K. 924 F3
Saltburn by the Sea, U.K. 924 B7
Saltcoats, U.K. 925 F4
Saltillo, Mexico 920 B4
Salton Sea, U.S.A. 918 D3
Salvador, Brazil 922 D6
Salvador, El ■, Cent. Amer. 920 E7
Salween →, Burma 937 D8
Salyan, Azerbaijan 931 C7
Salzburg, Austria 927 E6
Salzgitter, Germany 927 B5
Samar, Phil. 941 B4
Samara, Russia 932 D6
Samarinda, Indonesia 941 D3
Samarkand = Samarqand, Uzbekistan 932 F7
Samarqand, Uzbekistan 932 F7
Samoa ■, Pac. Oc. 943 C16
Samsun, Turkey 931 B5
San Andrés, I. de, Caribbean 921 E8
San Andres Mts., U.S.A. 918 D5
San Andrés Tuxtla, Mexico 920 D5
San Angelo, U.S.A. 918 D6
San Antonio, Chile 923 F2
San Antonio, U.S.A. 918 E7
San Antonio →, U.S.A. 919 E7
San Antonio Oeste, Argentina 923 G3
San Bernardino, U.S.A. 918 D3
San Bernardino Str., Phil. 941 B4
San Bernardo, Chile 923 F2
San Blas, C., U.S.A. 919 E9
San Carlos, Phil. 941 B4
San Carlos de Bariloche, Argentina 923 G2
San Carlos de Bolívar, Argentina 923 F3
San Cristóbal, Argentina 923 F3
San Cristóbal, Solomon Is. 943 C11
San Cristóbal, Venezuela 922 B2
San Cristóbal de la Casas, Mexico 920 D6
San Diego, U.S.A. 918 D3
San Felipe, Venezuela 922 A3
San Fernando, Chile 923 F2
San Fernando de Apure, Venezuela 922 B3
San Francisco, U.S.A. 918 C2
San Francisco de Macorís, Dom. Rep. 921 D10
San German, Puerto Rico 921 d
San Gottardo, P. del, Switz. 926 C8
San Ignacio, Bolivia 922 D3
San Joaquin →, U.S.A. 918 C2
San Jorge, G., Argentina 923 G3
San José, Costa Rica 921 F8
San Jose, Phil. 941 B4
San Jose, U.S.A. 918 C2
San Jose →, U.S.A. 918 D5
San José de Chiquitos, Bolivia 922 D3
San José de Jáchal, Argentina 923 F3
San José de Mayo, Uruguay 923 F4
San Juan, Argentina 923 F3
San Juan, Dom. Rep. 921 D10
San Juan, Puerto Rico 921 d
San Juan →, Nic. 921 E8
San Juan →, U.S.A. 918 C5
San Juan de los Morros, Venezuela 922 B3
San Juan Mts., U.S.A. 918 C5
San Lorenzo, Mte., Argentina 923 G2
San Lucas, C., Mexico 920 C3
San Luis, Argentina 923 F3
San Luis Obispo, U.S.A. 918 C2
San Luis Potosí, Mexico 920 C4
San Marcos, U.S.A. 918 E7
San Marino ■, Europe 929 C4
San Matías, G., Argentina 923 G3
San Miguel, El Salv. 920 E7
San Miguel de Tucumán, Argentina 923 E3
San Nicolás de los Arroyas, Argentina 923 F3
San Pedro de las Colonias, Mexico 920 B4
San Pedro de Macorís, Dom. Rep. 921 D11
San Pedro Sula, Honduras 920 D7
San Rafael, Argentina 923 F3
San Remo, Italy 926 E7
San Salvador, El Salv. 920 E7
San Salvador de Jujuy, Argentina 923 E3
San Salvador I., Bahamas 921 C10
San Sebastián = Donostia-San Sebastián, Spain 928 A5
San Sebastian, Puerto Rico 921 d
San Valentin, Mte., Chile 923 G2
Sana', Yemen 936 D3
Sancti Spíritus, Cuba 921 C9
Sancy, Puy de, France 926 D5
Sandakan, Malaysia 941 C3
Sanday, U.K. 925 B6
Sandpoint, U.S.A. 918 A3
Sandray, U.K. 925 E1
Sandusky, U.S.A. 919 B10
Sandy, U.S.A. 918 B4
Sandy L., Canada 916 C10
Sanford, U.S.A. 919 E10
Sanford, Mt., U.S.A. 916 B5
Sangihe, Pulau, Indonesia 941 C4
Sangli, India 937 D6
Sangre de Cristo Mts., U.S.A. 918 C5
Sanikiluaq, Canada 917 C12
Sanirajak, Canada 917 B11
Sankt Gallen, Switz. 926 C8
Sankt Moritz, Switz. 926 C8
Sankt-Peterburg, Russia 932 D4
Sankuru →, Dem. Rep. of the Congo 940 C4
Sanliurfa, Turkey 931 C5
Sanmenxia, China 934 C6
Sanquhar, U.K. 925 F5
Santa Ana, El Salv. 920 E7
Santa Ana, U.S.A. 918 D3
Santa Barbara, U.S.A. 918 D3
Santa Catarina □, Brazil 923 E5
Santa Clara, Cuba 921 C9
Santa Cruz, Bolivia 922 D3
Santa Cruz, U.S.A. 918 C2
Santa Cruz de Tenerife, Canary Is. 938 C2
Santa Cruz Is., Solomon Is. 943 C12
Santa Cruz Mts., Jamaica 920 a
Santa Fe, Argentina 923 F3
Santa Fe, U.S.A. 918 C5
Santa Inés, I., Chile 923 H2
Santa Isabel = Rey Malabo, Eq. Guin. 940 B1
Santa Isabel, Solomon Is. 943 B10
Santa Maria, Brazil 923 E4
Santa Maria, U.S.A. 918 D2
Santa María →, Mexico 920 A3
Santa Marta, Colombia 922 A2
Santa Rosa, Argentina 923 F3
Santa Rosa, U.S.A. 918 C2
Santai, China 934 C5
Santana do Livramento, Brazil 923 F4
Santander, Spain 928 A4
Santarém, Brazil 922 C4
Santarém, Portugal 928 C1
Santiago, Chile 923 F2
Santiago de Compostela, Spain 928 A1
Santiago de Cuba, Cuba 921 D9
Santiago de los Cabelleros, Dom. Rep. 921 D10
Santiago del Estero, Argentina 923 E3
Santo Domingo, Dom. Rep. 921 D11
Santo Tomé de Guayana = Ciudad Guayana, Venezuela 922 B3
Santos, Brazil 923 E5
São Bernardo do Campo, Brazil 923 E5
São Borja, Brazil 923 E4
São Francisco →, Brazil 922 D6
São José do Rio Prêto, Brazil 922 E5
São Luís, Brazil 922 C5
São Marcos, B. de, Brazil 922 C5
São Paulo, Brazil 923 E5
São Paulo □, Brazil 922 E5
São Paulo I., Atl. Oc. 914 D8
São Roque, C. de, Brazil 922 C6
São Tomé & Príncipe ■, Africa 915 D10
Saône →, France 926 D6
Sapporo, Japan 935 B7
Sara Buri = Saraburi, Thailand 941 B2
Saraburi, Thailand 941 B2
Saragossa = Zaragoza, Spain 928 B5
Sarajevo, Bos.-H. 929 C7
Saransk, Russia 932 D5
Sarapul, Russia 932 D6
Sarasota, U.S.A. 919 E10
Saratov, Russia 932 D5
Sarawak □, Malaysia 941 C3
Sardegna □, Italy 929 D2
Sardinia = Sardegna □, Italy 929 D2
Sarh, Chad 939 G9
Sark, U.K. 926 B2
Sarlat-la-Canéda, France 926 D4
Sarmiento, Argentina 923 G3
Sarnia, Canada 917 D11
Sarre = Saar →, Europe 926 B7
Sarreguemines, France 926 B7
Sarthe →, France 926 C3
Sasebo, Japan 935 G1
Saskatchewan □, Canada 916 C9
Saskatchewan →, Canada 916 C9
Saskatoon, Canada 916 C9
Sássari, Italy 929 D2
Sassnitz, Germany 927 A6
Satpura Ra., India 937 C6
Satu Mare, Romania 931 A2
Saudi Arabia ■, Asia 936 C3
Sault Ste. Marie, Canada 917 D11
Sault Ste. Marie, U.S.A. 917 D11
Saumur, France 926 C3
Sava →, Serbia 931 B2
Savage I. = Niue, Cook Is. 943 D17
Savai'i, Samoa 943 C16
Savanna-la-Mar, Jamaica 920 a
Savannah, U.S.A. 919 D10
Savannah →, U.S.A. 919 D10
Savannakhet, Laos 941 B2
Savoie □, France 926 D7
Savona, Italy 926 D8
Savoy = Savoie □, France 926 D7
Sawatch Range, U.S.A. 918 C5
Sawel Mt., U.K. 925 G12
Sawu, Indonesia 941 E4
Sawu Sea, Indonesia 941 D4
Saxmundham, U.K. 924 D9
Saxony = Sachsen □, Germany 927 C6
Saxony, Lower = Niedersachsen □, Germany 927 B4
Sayan, Vostochnyy, Russia 933 D10
Saydā, Lebanon 931 D5
Saynshand, Mongolia 934 B6
Sázava →, Czech Rep. 927 D7
Scafell Pike, U.K. 924 B4
Scalloway, U.K. 925 A7
Scandinavia, Europe 930 E6
Scapa Flow, U.K. 925 C5
Scarba, U.K. 925 E3
Scarborough, U.K. 924 B7
Scariff I., Ireland 925 K9
Scarp, U.K. 925 C1
Scebeli, Wabi →, Somali Rep. 936 E3
Schaffhausen, Switz. 926 C8
Schefferville, Canada 917 C13
Schelde →, Belgium 927 C2
Schenectady, U.S.A. 919 B12
Schleswig, Germany 927 A4
Schleswig-Holstein □, Germany 927 A4
Schœlcher, Martinique 920 c
Schwäbische Alb, Germany 927 D4
Schwarzwald, Germany 927 D4
Schwerin, Germany 927 B5
Schwyz, Switz. 926 C8
Scotland □, U.K. 925 E5
Scottish Borders □, U.K. 925 F6
Scottsbluff, U.S.A. 918 B6
Scranton, U.S.A. 919 B11
Scunthorpe, U.K. 924 C7
Scutari = Shkodër, Albania 929 C7
Seaford, U.K. 924 F8
Seaforth, L., U.K. 925 D2
Seaham, U.K. 924 B6
Seal →, Canada 916 C10
Seascale, U.K. 924 B4
Seattle, U.S.A. 918 A2
Sebastián Vizcaíno, B., Mexico 920 B2
Sebastopol = Sevastopol, Ukraine 931 B4
Sebha = Sabhah, Libya 939 C8
Şebinkarahisar, Turkey 931 B5
Sebta = Ceuta, N. Afr. 928 E3
Sedalia, U.S.A. 919 C8
Sedan, France 926 B6
Ségou, Mali 938 F4
Segovia = Coco →, Cent. Amer. 921 E8
Segovia, Spain 928 B3
Seine →, France 926 B4
Sekondi-Takoradi, Ghana 938 H5
Selby, U.K. 924 C6
Selebi-Pikwe, Botswana 940 G5
Selenga = Selenge Mörön →, Asia 934 A5
Selenge Mörön →, Asia 934 A5
Selkirk, Canada 916 C10
Selkirk, U.K. 925 F6
Selkirk Mts., Canada 916 C8
Selma, U.S.A. 919 D9
Selsey Bill, U.K. 924 F7
Selvas, Brazil 922 C3
Selwyn L., Canada 916 B9
Selwyn Mts., Canada 916 B6
Semarang, Indonesia 941 D3
Semey, Kazakhstan 932 D9
Semipalatinsk = Semey, Kazakhstan 932 D9
Sena Madureira, Brazil 922 C3
Sendai, Kagoshima, Japan 935 H2
Sendai, Miyagi, Japan 935 D7
Senegal ■, W. Afr. 938 F3
Sénégal →, W. Afr. 938 E2
Senge Khambab = Indus →, Pakistan 936 C5
Senhor-do-Bonfim, Brazil 922 D5
Senja, Norway 930 D7
Senlis, France 926 B5
Sens, France 926 B5
Seoul = Sŏul, S. Korea 934 C7
Sept-Îles, Canada 917 C13
Seram, Indonesia 941 D4
Seram Sea, Indonesia 941 D4
Serang, Indonesia 941 D2
Serbia ■, Europe 931 B2

Seremban

Seremban, Malaysia .. 941 C2
Sergipe □, Brazil 922 D6
Serov, Russia 932 D7
Serpukhov, Russia ... 932 D4
Sète, France 926 E5
Sétif, Algeria 938 A7
Setonaikai, Japan 935 F3
Settat, Morocco 938 B4
Settle, U.K. 924 B5
Setúbal, Portugal 928 C1
Seul, Lac, Canada 916 C10
Sevan, Ozero = Sevana Lich, Armenia 931 B7
Sevana Lich, Armenia 931 B7
Sevastopol, Ukraine .. 931 B4
Severn →, Canada ... 917 C11
Severn →, U.K. 924 E5
Severnaya Zemlya, Russia 933 B10
Severodvinsk, Russia . 932 C4
Sevier →, U.S.A. 918 C4
Sevier L., U.S.A. 918 C4
Sevilla, Spain 928 D2
Seville = Sevilla, Spain 928 D2
Seward, U.S.A. 916 B5
Seward Peninsula, U.S.A. 916 B3
Seychelles ■, Ind. Oc. 915 E12
Seyðisfjörður, Iceland 930 A3
Seydişehir, Turkey ... 931 C4
Sfax, Tunisia 939 B8
Shaanxi □, China 934 C5
Shaba = Katanga □, Dem. Rep. of the Congo 940 D5
Shaballe = Scebeli, Wabi →, Somali Rep. 936 E3
Shache, China 934 C2
Shaftesbury, U.K. 924 E5
Shahjahanpur, India .. 937 C6
Shakhty, Russia 931 A6
Shaki, Nigeria 938 G6
Shām, Bādiyat ash, Asia 936 B3
Shamo = Gobi, Asia .. 934 B6
Shan □, Burma 937 C8
Shandong □, China .. 934 C6
Shanghai, China 934 C7
Shangqiu, China 934 C6
Shangrao, China 934 D6
Shangshui, China 934 C6
Shannon →, Ireland .. 925 J10
Shannon, Mouth of the, Ireland 925 J10
Shannon Airport, Ireland 925 J11
Shansi = Shanxi □, China 934 C6
Shantou, China 934 D6
Shantung = Shandong □, China . 934 C6
Shanxi □, China 934 C6
Shaoguan, China 934 D6
Shaoxing, China 934 C7
Shaoyang, China 934 D6
Shap, U.K. 924 B5
Shapinsay, U.K. 925 B6
Shaqrā', Yemen 936 D3
Sharjah = Ash Shāriqah, U.A.E. ... 936 C4
Shark B., Australia ... 942 F1
Shashi, China 934 C6
Shasta, Mt., U.S.A. ... 918 B2
Shawinigan, Canada .. 917 D12
Shawnee, U.S.A. 919 C7
Shcherbakov = Rybinsk, Russia 932 D4
Shebele = Scebeli, Wabi →, Somali Rep. 936 E3
Sheboygan, U.S.A. ... 919 B9
Sheelin, L., Ireland .. 925 H12
Sheep Haven, Ireland . 925 F12
Sheerness, U.K. 924 E8
Sheffield, U.K. 924 C6
Shelby, U.S.A. 918 A4
Shelikhova, Zaliv, Russia 933 D16
Shensi = Shaanxi □, China 934 C5
Shenyang, China 934 B7
Shepparton, Australia 942 H8
Shepton Mallet, U.K. . 924 E5
Sherborne, U.K. 924 F5
Sherbrooke, Canada .. 917 D12
Sheridan, U.S.A. 918 B5
Sherkin I., Ireland ... 925 K10
Sherman, U.S.A. 919 D7
Sherwood Forest, U.K. 924 C6
Sheyenne →, U.S.A. .. 919 A7
Shibām, Yemen 936 D3
Shiel, L., U.K. 925 E3
Shihchiachuangi = Shijiazhuang, China 934 C6
Shihezi, China 934 B3
Shijiazhuang, China .. 934 C6
Shikarpur, Pakistan ... 936 C5
Shikoku □, Japan 935 G3
Shiliguri, India 937 C7
Shillelagh, Ireland ... 925 J13
Shimoga, India 937 D6
Shimonoseki, Japan .. 935 G2
Shin, L., U.K. 925 C4
Shinyanga, Tanzania . 940 C6
Shiquan He = Indus →, Pakistan 936 C5
Shīrāz, Iran 936 C4
Shire →, Africa 940 F7
Shirwa, L. = Chilwa, L., Malawi 940 F7
Shizuoka, Japan 935 F6
Shkodër, Albania 929 C7
Sholapur = Solapur, India 937 D6
Shreveport, U.S.A. ... 919 D8
Shrewsbury, U.K. 924 D5
Shropshire □, U.K. .. 924 D5
Shuangyashan, China 934 B8
Shule, China 934 C2
Shumagin Is., U.S.A. . 916 C4
Shwebo, Burma 937 C8
Shymkent, Kazakhstan 932 E7
Si Kiang = Xi Jiang →, China 934 D6
Si-ngan = Xi'an, China 934 C5
Sialkot, Pakistan 937 B6
Siam = Thailand ■, Asia 941 B2
Sian = Xi'an, China ... 934 C5
Šiauliai, Lithuania 930 F8
Siberia, Russia 915 B15
Siberut, Indonesia ... 941 D1
Sibi, Pakistan 936 C5
Sibiu, Romania 931 A2
Sibolga, Indonesia ... 941 C1
Sibu, Malaysia 941 C3
Sibuyan Sea, Phil. 941 B4
Sichuan □, China 934 C5
Sicilia, Italy 929 F5
Sicily = Sicilia, Italy .. 929 F5
Sicuani, Peru 922 D2
Sidi-bel-Abbès, Algeria 938 A5
Sidlaw Hills, U.K. 925 E5
Sidmouth, U.K. 924 F4
Sidney, Mont., U.S.A. . 918 A6
Sidney, Nebr., U.S.A. . 918 B6
Sidon = Saydā, Lebanon 931 D5
Sidra, G. of = Surt, Khalīj, Libya 939 B9
Siegen, Germany 927 C4
Siena, Italy 929 C3
Sierra Blanca Peak, U.S.A. 918 D5
Sierra Leone ■, W. Afr. 938 G3
Sierra Nevada, Spain . 928 D4
Sierra Nevada, U.S.A. . 918 C2
Sierra Vista, U.S.A. ... 918 D4
Sihanoukville = Kampong Saom, Cambodia 941 B2
Sikhote Alin, Khrebet, Russia 933 E14
Sikhote Alin Ra. = Sikhote Alin, Khrebet, Russia 933 E14
Sikkim □, India 937 C7
Silesia = Śląsk, Poland 927 C8
Silifke, Turkey 931 C4
Siliguri = Shiliguri, India 937 C7
Siling Co, China 934 C3
Silloth, U.K. 924 B4
Silver City, U.S.A. 918 D5
Simbirsk, Russia 932 D5
Simeulue, Indonesia .. 941 C1
Simferopol, Ukraine .. 931 B4
Simplonpass, Switz. .. 926 C8
Simpson Desert, Australia 942 F6
Simpson Pen., Canada 917 B11
Sinai = Es Sînâ', Egypt 939 C12
Sinai, Mt. = Mûsa, Gebel, Egypt 939 C12
Sind □, Pakistan 937 C5
Sindh = Sind □, Pakistan 937 C5
Singapore ■, Asia ... 941 C2
Singaraja, Indonesia .. 941 D3
Singkawang, Indonesia 941 C2
Singora = Songkhla, Thailand 941 C2
Sinkiang Uighur = Xinjiang Uygur Zizhiqu □, China .. 934 B3
Sinop, Turkey 931 B5
Sion, Switz. 926 C7
Sion Mills, U.K. 925 G12
Sioux City, U.S.A. 919 B7
Sioux Falls, U.S.A. ... 919 B7
Sioux Lookout, Canada 916 C10
Siping, China 934 B7
Sir James MacBrien, Mt., Canada 916 B7
Siracusa, Italy 929 F5
Sirdaryo = Syrdarya →, Kazakhstan 932 E7
Sīrjān, Iran 936 C4
Sitka, U.S.A. 916 C6
Sittwe, Burma 937 C8
Sivas, Turkey 931 C5
Sivrihisar, Turkey 931 C4
Sîwa, Egypt 939 C11
Six Cross Roads, Barbados .... 921 g
Sixmilebridge, Ireland 925 J11
Sjælland, Denmark ... 930 F6
Skagerrak, Denmark . 930 F5
Skagway, U.S.A. 916 C6
Skeena →, Canada .. 916 C6
Skegness, U.K. 924 C8
Skellefte älv →, Sweden 930 E8
Skellefteå, Sweden ... 930 E8
Skerries, The, U.K. ... 924 C3
Skibbereen, Ireland .. 925 K10
Skiddaw, U.K. 924 B4
Skien, Norway 930 F5
Skikda, Algeria 938 A7
Skipton, U.K. 924 C5
Skopje, Macedonia ... 931 B2
Skovorodino, Russia .. 933 D13
Skull, Ireland 925 K10
Skye, U.K. 925 D2
Slaney →, Ireland ... 925 J13
Śląsk, Poland 927 C8
Slave →, Canada 916 B8
Slave Coast, W. Afr. .. 938 G6
Slave Lake, Canada .. 916 C8
Slavyansk = Slovyansk, Ukraine 931 A5
Sleaford, U.K. 924 C7
Sleat, Sd. of, U.K. ... 925 D3
Sleeper Is., Canada .. 917 C11
Slieve Aughty, Ireland 925 H11
Slieve Bloom, Ireland . 925 H12
Slieve Donard, U.K. .. 925 G14
Slieve Gamph, Ireland 925 G11
Slieve Gullion, U.K. .. 925 G13
Slieve Mish, Ireland .. 925 J10
Slievenamon, Ireland . 925 J12
Sligeach = Sligo, Ireland 925 G11
Sligo, Ireland 925 G11
Sligo □, Ireland 925 G11
Sligo B., Ireland 925 G11
Slough, U.K. 924 E7
Slovak Rep. ■, Europe 927 D9
Slovakia = Slovak Rep. ■, Europe 927 D9
Slovenia ■, Europe ... 929 B5
Slovenija = Slovenia ■, Europe 929 B5
Slovyansk, Ukraine ... 931 A5
Slyne Hd., Ireland ... 925 H9
Smallwood Res., Canada 917 C13
Smerwick Harbour, Ireland 925 J9
Smith Sd., N. Amer. .. 944 B3
Smoky →, Canada ... 916 C8
Smoky Hill →, U.S.A. . 919 C7
Smolensk, Russia ... 932 D4
Smyrna = İzmir, Turkey 931 C3
Snaefell, U.K. 924 B3
Snake →, U.S.A. 918 A3
Snizort, L., U.K. 925 D2
Snøhetta, Norway 930 E5
Snowdon, U.K. 924 C3
Snowdrift = Łutselk'e, Canada 916 B8
Snowy Mts., Australia 942 H8
Sobral, Brazil 922 C5
Soc Trang, Vietnam .. 941 C2
Soch'e = Shache, China 934 C2
Sochi, Russia 931 B5
Société, Is. de la, Pac. Oc. 914 E2
Society Is. = Société, Is. de la, Pac. Oc. 914 E2
Socorro, U.S.A. 918 D5
Socotra, Yemen 936 D4
Söderhamn, Sweden . 930 E7
Sofia = Sofiya, Bulgaria 931 B2
Sofiya, Bulgaria 931 B2
Sognefjorden, Norway 930 E5
Sohâg, Egypt 939 C12
Soissons, France 926 B5
Sokhumi, Georgia 931 B6
Sokodé, Togo 938 G6
Sokoto, Nigeria 938 F7
Solapur, India 937 D6
Soldotna, U.S.A. 916 B4
Solent, The, U.K. 924 F6
Solihull, U.K. 924 D6
Solikamsk, Russia ... 932 D6
Solimões = Amazonas →, S. Amer. 922 C4
Solingen, Germany ... 927 C3
Solomon Is. ■, Pac. Oc. 943 B10
Solomon Sea, Papua N. G. 942 B9
Solon, China 934 B7
Solothurn, Switz. 926 C7
Solway Firth, U.K. ... 924 B4
Somali Rep. ■, Africa . 936 E3
Somalia = Somali Rep. ■, Africa 936 E3
Sombrerete, Mexico .. 920 C4
Somerset, U.S.A. 919 C10
Somerset □, U.K. ... 924 E5
Somerset I., Canada . 916 A10
Somme →, France ... 926 A4
Songhua Jiang →, China 934 B8
Songkhla, Thailand .. 941 C2
Songpan, China 934 C5
Sonora →, Mexico ... 920 B2
Sonoran Desert, U.S.A. 918 D4
Sonoyta, Mexico 920 A2
Sonsonate, El Salv. .. 920 E7
Soochow = Suzhou, China 934 C7
Sopot, Poland 927 A9
Soria, Spain 928 B4
Sorocaba, Brazil 923 E5
Sørøya, Norway 930 C8
Sosnowiec, Poland .. 927 C9
Soufrière, Guadeloupe 920 b
Soufrière, St. Lucia .. 921 f
Soufrière Bay, St. Lucia 921 f
Sŏul, S. Korea 934 C7
Sound, The, U.K. 924 F3
Souris →, Canada ... 916 D9
Sousse, Tunisia 939 A8
South Africa ■, Africa 940 J4
South America 914 E7
South Australia □, Australia 942 G6
South Bend, U.S.A. ... 919 B9
South Carolina □, U.S.A. 919 D10
South China Sea, Asia 941 C3
South Dakota □, U.S.A. 918 B7
South Downs, U.K. ... 924 F7
South East C., Australia 942 J8
South Esk →, U.K. ... 925 E6
South Georgia, Antarctica 914 G8
South I., N.Z. 943 J13
South Korea ■, Asia .. 934 C7
South Magnetic Pole, Antarctica 944 D13
South Molton, U.K. ... 924 E4
South Nahanni →, Canada 916 B7
South Negril Pt., Jamaica .... 920 a
South Orkney Is., Antarctica 944 D4
South Ossetia □, Georgia 931 B6
South Platte →, U.S.A. 918 B6
South Pole, Antarctica 944 F
South Pt., Barbados .. 921 g
South Ronaldsay, U.K. 925 C6
South Sandwich Is., Antarctica 914 G8
South Saskatchewan →, Canada 916 C9
South Shetland Is., Antarctica 944 D4
South Shields, U.K. ... 924 B6
South Tyne →, U.K. .. 924 B5
South Uist, U.K. 925 D1
South West Africa = Namibia ■, Africa .. 940 G3
Southampton, U.K. .. 924 F6
Southampton I., Canada 917 B11
Southend-on-Sea, U.K. 924 E8
Southern Alps, N.Z. .. 943 J13
Southern Indian L., Canada 916 C10
Southern Ocean, Antarctica 944 D10
Southern Uplands, U.K. 925 F5
Southport, U.K. 924 C4
Southwold, U.K. 924 D9
Sovetskaya Gavan = Vanino, Russia 933 E15
Soweto, S. Africa 940 H5
Spain ■, Europe 928 B4
Spalding, U.K. 924 D7
Spanish Town, Br. Virgin Is. .... 921 e
Spanish Town, Jamaica 920 a
Sparks, U.S.A. 918 C3
Spartanburg, U.S.A. .. 919 D10
Spartivento, C., Italy . 929 F6
Spean →, U.K. 925 E4
Speightstown, Barbados .... 921 g
Spence Bay = Taloyoak, Canada 916 B10
Spencer, U.S.A. 919 B7
Spencer G., Australia . 942 G6
Sperrin Mts., U.K. ... 925 G13
Spey →, U.K. 925 D5
Spithead, U.K. 924 F6
Spitzbergen = Svalbard, Arctic 944 B7
Split, Croatia 929 C6
Spokane, U.S.A. 918 A3
Spratly Is., S. China Sea 941 C3
Spree →, Germany ... 927 B6
Spring Hall, Barbados 921 g
Springfield, Ill., U.S.A. 919 C9
Springfield, Mass., U.S.A. 919 B12
Springfield, Mo., U.S.A. 919 C8
Springfield, Ohio, U.S.A. 919 C10
Springfield, Oreg., U.S.A. 918 B2
Springs, S. Africa 940 H5
Spurn Hd., U.K. 924 C8
Sredinny Ra. = Sredinnyy Khrebet, Russia 933 D16
Sredinnyy Khrebet, Russia 933 D16
Sri Lanka ■, Asia ... 937 E7
Srinagar, India 937 B6
Stafford, U.K. 924 D5
Staines, U.K. 924 E7
Stakhanov, Ukraine .. 931 A5
Stalingrad = Volgograd, Russia 932 E5
Staliniri = Tskhinvali, Georgia 931 B6
Stalino = Donetsk, Ukraine 931 A5
Stalinogorsk = Novomoskovsk, Russia 932 D4
Stalybridge, U.K. 924 C5
Stamford, U.K. 924 D7
Stanislav = Ivano-Frankivsk, Ukraine .. 932 E3
Stanley, Falk. Is. ... 923 H4
Stanovoy Khrebet, Russia 933 D13
Stanovoy Ra. = Stanovoy Khrebet, Russia 933 D13
Stara Planina, Bulgaria 931 B2
Staraya Russa, Russia 932 D4
Start Pt., U.K. 924 F4
Staten, I. = Estados, I. de Los, Argentina .. 923 H3
Stavanger, Norway ... 930 F5
Stavropol, Russia 931 A6
Steiermark □, Austria . 927 E7
Steinkjer, Norway ... 930 E6
Steornabhaigh = Stornoway, U.K. 925 C2
Stepanakert = Xankändi, Azerbaijan 931 C7
Stephenville, Canada . 917 D14
Stepnoi = Elista, Russia 931 A6
Sterling, U.S.A. 918 B6
Sterlitamak, Russia ... 932 D6
Stettin = Szczecin, Poland 927 B7
Stettler, Canada 916 C8
Stevenage, U.K. 924 E7
Stevens Point, U.S.A. . 919 B9
Stewart, Canada 916 C7
Stewart →, Canada .. 916 B6
Stewart I., N.Z. 943 K12
Steyr, Austria 927 D7
Stikine →, Canada .. 916 C6
Stillwater, Minn., U.S.A. 919 A8
Stillwater, Okla., U.S.A. 919 C7
Stirling, U.K. 925 E5
Stockholm, Sweden .. 930 F7
Stockport, U.K. 924 C5
Stockton, U.S.A. 918 C2
Stockton-on-Tees, U.K. 924 B6
Stoer, Pt. of, U.K. ... 925 C3
Stoke-on-Trent, U.K. . 924 C5
Stone, U.K. 924 D5
Stonehaven, U.K. ... 925 E6
Stora Lulevatten, Sweden 930 D7
Storavan, Sweden ... 930 D7
Store Bælt, Denmark . 930 F6
Stornoway, U.K. 925 C2
Storsjön, Sweden 930 E6
Storuman, Sweden ... 930 D7
Stour →, U.K. 924 F6
Stourbridge, U.K. 924 D5
Stowmarket, U.K. ... 924 D9
Strabane, U.K. 925 G12
Stralsund, Germany .. 927 A6
Strangford L., U.K. ... 925 G14
Stranraer, U.K. 925 G3
Strasbourg, France .. 926 B7
Stratford-upon-Avon, U.K. 924 D6
Strath Spey, U.K. 925 D5
Strathaven, U.K. 925 F4
Strathmore, U.K. 925 E5
Strathpeffer, U.K. ... 925 D4
Strathy Pt., U.K. 925 C4
Stroma, U.K. 925 C5
Strómboli, Italy 929 E5
Stromeferry, U.K. ... 925 D3
Stromness, U.K. 925 C5
Stronsay, U.K. 925 B6
Stroud, U.K. 924 E5
Stuart L., Canada ... 916 C7
Stuttgart, Germany .. 927 D4
Stuttgart, U.S.A. 919 D8
Styria = Steiermark □, Austria 927 E7
Suakin, Sudan 939 E13
Subotica, Serbia 931 A1
Suchou = Suzhou, China 934 C7
Süchow = Xuzhou, China 934 C6
Suck →, Ireland 925 H11
Sucre, Bolivia 922 D3
Sudan ■, Africa 939 E11
Sudbury, Canada 917 D11
Sudbury, U.K. 924 D8
Sûdd, Sudan 939 G12
Sudeten Mts. = Sudety, Europe 927 C8
Sudety, Europe 927 C8
Suez = El Suweis, Egypt 939 C12
Suez, G. of = Suweis, Khalîg el, Egypt ... 939 C12
Suez Canal = Suweis, Qanâ es, Egypt 939 B12
Suffolk □, U.K. 924 D9
Sugluk = Salluit, Canada 917 B12
Şuḩār, Oman 936 C4
Suihua, China 934 B7
Suir →, Ireland 925 J12
Sukabumi, Indonesia . 941 D2
Sukhona →, Russia .. 932 D4
Sukhumi = Sokhumi, Georgia 931 B6
Sukkur, Pakistan 937 C5
Sulaiman Range, Pakistan 937 B5
Sulawesi □, Indonesia 941 D4
Sulawesi Sea = Celebes Sea, Indonesia 941 C4
Sullana, Peru 922 C1
Sulu Arch., Phil. 941 C4
Sulu Sea, E. Indies ... 941 C4
Sumatera □, Indonesia 941 C2
Sumatra = Sumatera □, Indonesia 941 C2
Sumba, Indonesia ... 941 D3
Sumbawa, Indonesia . 941 D3
Sumburgh Hd., U.K. .. 925 B7
Sumenep, Indonesia .. 941 D3
Sumgait = Sumqayıt, Azerbaijan 931 B7
Summer L., U.S.A. ... 918 B2
Summerside, Canada . 917 D13
Sumqayıt, Azerbaijan . 931 B7
Sumter, U.S.A. 919 D10
Sumy, Ukraine 932 D4
Sun Valley, U.S.A. ... 918 B4
Sunart, L., U.K. 925 E3
Sunda, Selat, Indonesia 941 D2
Sunda Str. = Sunda, Selat, Indonesia 941 D2
Sundarbans, Asia 937 C7
Sunderland, U.K. ... 924 B6
Sundsvall, Sweden ... 930 E7
Sungaipenuh, Indonesia 941 D2
Sungari = Songhua Jiang →, China 934 B8
Sunghua Chiang = Songhua Jiang →, China 934 B8
Superior, U.S.A. 919 A8
Superior, L., N. Amer. . 917 D11
Suqutra = Socotra, Yemen 936 D4
Sura →, Russia 932 D5
Surabaja = Surabaya, Indonesia 941 D3
Surabaya, Indonesia .. 941 D3
Surakarta, Indonesia . 941 D3
Surat, India 937 C6
Surgut, Russia 932 C8
Surigao, Phil. 941 C4
Surinam = Suriname ■, S. Amer. 922 B4
Suriname ■, S. Amer. 922 B4
Surrey □, U.K. 924 E7
Surt, Libya 939 B9
Surt, Khalīj, Libya ... 939 B9
Surtsey, Iceland 930 B1
Sutlej →, Pakistan ... 937 C6
Sutton Coldfield, U.K. . 924 D6
Suva, Fiji 943 D14
Suweis, Khalîg el, Egypt 939 C12
Suweis, Qanâ es, Egypt 939 B12
Suzhou, China 934 C7
Svalbard, Arctic 944 B7
Svealand □, Sweden . 930 E7
Sverdlovsk = Yekaterinburg, Russia 932 D7
Sverdrup Is., Canada . 944 B2
Swabian Alps = Schwäbische Alb, Germany 927 D4
Swakopmund, Namibia 940 G2
Swale →, U.K. 924 B6
Swan Hill, Australia .. 942 H7
Swan River, Canada .. 916 C9
Swanage, U.K. 924 F6
Swansea, U.K. 924 E4
Swatow = Shantou, China 934 D6
Swaziland ■, Africa .. 940 H6
Sweden ■, Europe ... 930 F7
Sweetwater, U.S.A. .. 918 D6
Swellendam, S. Africa 940 J4
Swift Current, Canada 916 C9
Swilly, L., Ireland 925 F12
Swindon, U.K. 924 E6
Swinford, Ireland ... 925 H11
Switzerland ■, Europe 926 C8
Swords, Ireland 925 H13
Sydney, Australia ... 942 G9
Sydney, Canada 917 D13
Sydprøven = Alluitsup Paa, Greenland 917 B15
Sydra, G. of = Surt, Khalīj, Libya 939 B9
Syktyvkar, Russia ... 932 C6
Syracuse, U.S.A. 919 B11
Syrdarya →, Kazakhstan 932 E7
Syria ■, Asia 936 B2
Syrian Desert = Shām, Bādiyat ash, Asia ... 936 B3
Syzran, Russia 932 D5
Szczecin, Poland ... 927 B7
Szechwan = Sichuan □, China 934 C5
Szeged, Hungary 927 E10
Székesfehérvár, Hungary 927 E9
Szekszárd, Hungary .. 927 E9
Szolnok, Hungary ... 927 E10
Szombathely, Hungary 927 E8

T

Ţabas, Iran 936 B4
Tablas I., Phil. 941 B4
Table B., S. Africa ... 940 J3
Table Mt., S. Africa ... 940 J3
Tabora, Tanzania ... 940 D6
Tabrīz, Iran 936 B3
Tacheng, China 934 B3
Tacloban, Phil. 941 B4
Tacna, Peru 922 D2
Tacoma, U.S.A. 918 A2
Tacuarembó, Uruguay 923 F4
Tadzhikistan = Tajikistan ■, Asia ... 932 F8
Taegu, S. Korea 934 C7
Taejŏn, S. Korea 934 C7
Tafelbaai = Table B., S. Africa 940 J3
Taganrog, Russia ... 931 A5
Tagus = Tejo →, Europe 928 C1
Tahiti, Pac. Oc. 914 E2
Tahoe, L., U.S.A. 918 C2
Tahoua, Niger 938 F7
Taibei = T'aipei, Taiwan 934 D7
T'aichung, Taiwan ... 934 D7
Taimyr Peninsula = Taymyr, Poluostrov, Russia 933 B11
Tain, U.K. 925 D4
T'ainan, Taiwan 934 D7
T'aipei, Taiwan 934 D7
Taiping, Malaysia ... 941 C2
Tairbeart = Tarbert, U.K. 925 D2
Taitao, Pen. de, Chile . 923 G2
T'aitung, Taiwan 934 D7
Taiwan ■, Asia 934 D7
Taiyuan, China 934 C6
Taizhong = T'aichung, Taiwan 934 D7
Ta'izz, Yemen 936 D3
Tajikistan ■, Asia ... 932 F8
Tajo = Tejo →, Europe 928 C1
Tak, Thailand 941 B1
Takamatsu, Japan ... 935 F4
Takaoka, Japan 935 E5
Takasaki, Japan 935 E6
Takla Makan = Taklamakan Shamo, China 934 C3
Taklamakan Shamo, China 934 C3
Talara, Peru 922 C1
Talaud, Kepulauan, Indonesia 941 C4
Talaud Is. = Talaud, Kepulauan, Indonesia 941 C4
Talca, Chile 923 F2
Talcahuano, Chile ... 923 F2
Taldy Kurgan = Taldyqorghan, Kazakhstan 932 E8
Taldyqorghan, Kazakhstan 932 E8
Taliabu, Indonesia ... 941 D4
Tallahassee, U.S.A. .. 919 D10
Tallinn, Estonia 932 D3
Taloyoak, Canada ... 916 B10
Taltal, Chile 923 E2
Tamale, Ghana 938 G5
Tamana, Kiribati 943 A13
Tamanrasset, Algeria . 938 D7
Tamar →, U.K. 924 F3
Tambov, Russia 932 D5
Tamil Nadu □, India .. 937 D6
Tammerfors = Tampere, Finland .. 930 E8
Tampa, U.S.A. 919 E10
Tampa B., U.S.A. ... 919 E10
Tampere, Finland ... 930 E8

Queen Elizabeth Is.
Ellesmere I.
North Magnetic Pole
Greenland
Alaska
Victoria I.
Baffin Island
Iceland
Bering Sea
Bering Str.
Yukon
Gr. Bear L.
Davis Str.
Arc
Mt. McKinley 6194 (Denali)
Gr. Slave L.
Hudson Str.
Brit Isl
Gulf of Alaska
Mackenzie
North America
Hudson Bay
Labrador
Aleutian Is.
Coast Mts.
L. Winnipeg
C. Farewell
Vancouver I.
Great Lakes
St. Lawrence
Newfoundland
Cascade
Rocky Mountains
Great Plains
Missouri
Ohio
C. Race
Azores
Str. of Gibr
Mt. Whitney 4418
Sierra Nevada
Mt. Elbert 4399
Arkansas
Mt. Mitchell 2037
Appalachian Mts.
C. Hatteras
Bermuda
NORTH
J. Tou 4168
Death Valley -86
Colorado
Mississippi
Canary Is.
C. Verde
Lower California
Rio Grande
Gulf of Mexico
Florida Str.
Bahamas
West
ATLANTIC
Tropic
Sierra Madre
Popocatepetl 5452
Citlaltepetl 5700
Yucatan
Cuba
Greater
Hispaniola
Milwaukee Deep 9220
Indies
C. Verde Is.
C.Verde
A
Jamaica
Antilles
Hawaiian Is.
Mauna Kea 4205
Caribbean Sea
Lesser Antilles
OCEAN
PACIFIC
Isthmus of Panama
Llanos
Orinoco
Guiana Highlands
C. Palm
Palmyra Is
Mt. Roraima 2810
Galapagos Is.
Chimborazo 6267
Negro
South
Equa
Kiritimati
Andes
Amazon
Selvas
C. de São Roque
Phoenix Is.
OCEAN
Madeira
Ascension
Tokelau Is.
Marquesas Is.
Plateau of Mato Grosso
Brazilian Highlands
SOUTH
Samoa Is.
America
St. He
Society Is.
Tuamotu Is.
L. Titicaca
C. Frio
Tropic of Ca
Tahiti
Gran Chaco
Paraguay
Cook Is.
Atacama Desert
Paraná
ATLAN
Tonga Is.
Tubuai Is
Pitcairn I.
Cerro Ojos del Salado 6863
Pampas
R. de la Plata
Andes
Tristai
Kermadec Is.
Easter I.
Cerro Aconcagua 6960
Negro
OCE
Chatham Is.
Patagonia
Falkland Is.
40
Tierra del Fuego
Scotia Sea
S. Georgia
Magellan's Str.
C. Horn
Drake Passage
Antarctic Peninsula
Weddell Sea
Palmer Land
Caird C
Ross Sea
Byrd Land
Ellsworth Land
Antar
Coats